2009 Standard Catalog of®

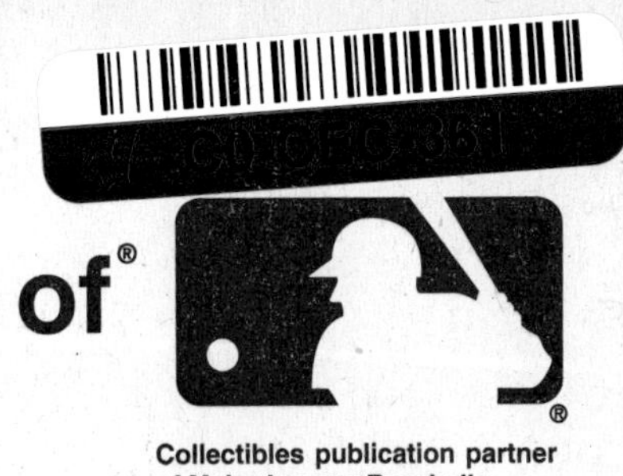

Collectibles publication partner
of Major League Baseball

BASEBALL CARDS

18th Edition

Edited by

Don Fluckinger

and the editors of Sports Collectors Digest® /Tuff Stuff®

"The way a team plays as a whole determines its success. You may have the greatest bunch of individual stars in the world, but if they don't play together, the club won't be worth a dime."

—Babe Ruth

Published by

700 East State Street • Iola, WI 54990-0001
715-445-2214 • 888-457-2873
www.krausebooks.com

Our toll-free number to place an order or obtain
a free catalog is (800) 258-0929.

ISSN 1935-0546
ISBN-13: 978-0-89689-648-2
ISBN-10: 0-89689-648-X

Designed by: Stacy Bloch

Edited by: Justin Moen

Printed in the United States of America

FOREWORD

Editor's Note: *Larry Fritsch, a longtime Wisconsin collector, dealer and hobby stalwart, passed away Dec. 8, 2007, We asked Bob Lemke to write about his hobby legacy.*

It is fitting that the editors of the *SCBC* have chosen to dedicate this edition to the late Larry Fritsch. Few readers know the extent to which Larry's contributions over the span of more than two decades enhanced this book and, by extension, the collective knowledge of the card-collecting hobby.

While he was among the hobby's earliest and largest card dealers, Larry was first and foremost a collector; no one has ever assembled a more comprehensive collection of vintage baseball cards. His lifelong association with baseball cards and the scope of his daily professional handling of them gave him an insider's knowledge that he could have easily hoarded to the exclusive benefit of his business interests, yet, each year as the "big book's" deadline approached, Larry would make the short drive from his headquarters to ours carrying a much-annotated and dog-eared copy of the Standard Catalog into which he had penciled a year's worth of checklist additions, corrections, set discoveries and other enhancements that he wanted to share with the hobby through these pages.

Other than the earnestness of his pursuit of expanded hobby knowledge, what most impressed me about these contributions was that "book value" was never mentioned. Larry simply did not care what this book (or any other price guide) proffered as a card's catalog value. His lifetime of collecting and dealing him made his intrinsic internal calculator of card value more accurate than any citation in ink on paper or pixels on an Internet website.

Larry Fritsch knew that card values fluctuated from year to year as player popularity and hobby demand waxed and waned, so he directed his efforts towards building a single source from which collectors could draw information and entertainment for all time. I was honored that he chose the Standard Catalog of Baseball Cards to be that depository of his passion.

— Bob Lemke
Editor, Standard Catalog of Baseball Cards,
1985-2006

ACKNOWLEDGMENTS

Hundreds of individuals have made countless valuable contributions that have been incorporated into the *Standard Catalog of Baseball Cards*. While all cannot be acknowledged, special appreciation is extended to the following principal contributors who have exhibited a special dedication by creating, revising or verifying listings and technical data, reviewing market valuations or providing cards to be illustrated.

Rob Adesso • Ken Agona • Gary Agostino • Lisa Albano • Dan Albaugh • Will Allison • Mark Anker • Ellis Anmuth • Steve Applebaum • Bill Atkinson

Rand Bailey • Bill Ballew • Andy Baran • Gary Bartolett • Judy Bartolett • Bob Bartosz • John Beisiegel • Karen Bell • Dr. Charles E. Belles • Dave Berman • Cathy Black • Jerry A. Blum • Ralph Blunt Jr. • Mike Bodner • Bill Bossert • Bob Bostoff • Brian Boston • Jim Boushley • Mark Bowers • Mike Boyd • Roland Bracken • John Brigandi • Scott Brockelman • Lou Brown • Dan Bruner • Greg Bussineau

Billy Caldwell • Len Caprisecca • Tony Carrafiell • Brian Cataquet • Lee Champion • Dwight Chapin • Lou Chericoni • Ryan Christoff • Jim Clarke • Shane Cohen • Rich Cole • Paul Conan Jr. • Charles Conlon • Eric Cooper • Bill Cornell • Bryan Couling • Bob Crabill • Clyde Cripe • Al Cristafulli • Jim Cumpton • Robert Curtiss

Pete D'Luhosch • Tom Daniels • Stuart Dansinger • James Davis • Dick DeCourcy • Ken Degnan • Dan DeKing • Mike Del Gado • Bill Diebold • Larry Dluhy • Brett Domue • John Dorsey

Curtis Earl • Eric Eichelkraut • Mark Elliott • Jeff Emerson • Brian Engles • Shirley Eross • John B. Esch • Joe Esposito • Dan Even • Doak Ewing

Julian Fernandez • David Festberg • Robert Fisk • Jay Finglass • Nick Flaviano • Rick Fleury • Jeff Fritsch • Larry Fritsch

Gary Gagen • Richard Galasso • Tom Galic • Richard R. Gallagher • Chris Gallutia • Tony Galovich • Phillip Garrou • Gary Gatanis • Frank Giffune • Richard Gilkeson • Gerald J. Glasser • Philip Glazer • Keith David Goldfarb • Jack Goodman • Bill Goodwin • Dick Goddard • Howard Gordon • Mike Gordon • Sean Gottlieb • Bob Gray • Wayne Grove • Gerry Guenther • Don Guilbert • Tom Guilfoile

David Hall • Joel Hall • Walter Hall • Gary Hamilton • Tom Harbin • Michael Harrington • Don Harrison • Rich Hawksley • Herbert Hecht • Bill Henderson • Mike Henderson • Kathy Henry • Pete Henrici • Steve Hershkowitz • Bob Hicks • Gregg Hitesman • John Hoffman • Dennis Hollenbeck • Jack Horkan • Jim Horne • Brent Horton • Ron Hosmer • Marvin Huck • Brad Hudecek

Bob Ivanjack

Robert Jacobsen • David Jenkins • Donn Jennings • Scott Jensen • Andrew Jerome • Jim Johnston • Stewart Jones • Larry Jordan

Judy Kay • Allan Kaye • Michael Keedy • Frank Keetz • Mark Kemmerle • Rick Keplinger • John King • John Kitleson • Terry Knouse • Bob Koehler • David Kohler • A.F. Kokol • Dan Kravitz

Steve Lacasse • Jason Lange • Mark K. Larson • Lee Lasseigne • William Lawrence • Scott Lawson • Richard Leech • Morley Leeking • Tom Leon • Don Lepore • Rod Lethbridge • Scott Letts • David Levin • Stuart Leviton • Howie Levy • Hal Lewis • Rob Lifson • Lew Lipset • Jeff Litteral • Dick Lloyd • Chuck Lobenthal • Leon Luckey

Mark Macrae • Paul Marchant • Robert Marek • Bob Marotto • Art Martineau • Bob Marquette • Richard Masson • Bill Mastro • Ralph Maya • Dan McKee • Fred McKie • Tony McLaughlin • Don McPherson • Doug McWilliams • John Mehlin • Bill Mendel • H. Dexter • Joe Merkel • Blake Meyer • Louis Middleton • Bob Miller • Jay Miller • Keith Mitchell • J.A. Monaco • Robert Montgomery • Joe Moreno • Brian Morris • Mike Mosier • Scott Mosley • Mike Mowrey • Peter Mudavin • Mark Murphy • David Musser

Frank Nagy • Steve Neimand • Roger Neufeldt • Tim Newcomb • Joe Newman • Bill Nicolls • Chuck Nobriga • Mark Nochta • Wayne Nochta

Bud Obermeyer • Jeff Obermeyer • Keith Olbermann

D.J. Panaia • Joe Pasternack • Marty Perry • Tom Pfirrman • Dan Piepenbrok • Stan Pietruska • Paul Pollard • Harvey Poris • Don "Barefoot" Post

Pat Quinn

Ed Ranson • Fred Rapaport • Jim Resseque • Steve Rice • Mike Rich • Bob Richardson • Al Richter • Gavin Riley • Mark Rios • Ron Ritzler • Tom Reid • Bob Robles • Mike Rodell • Scott Roemer • Mike Rogers • Chris Ronan • Rocky Rosato • Alan Rosen • John Rumierz • Bob Rund • Moe Ryan

Len Samworth • Jon Sands • Kevin Savage • Stephen Schauer • Allan Schoenberger • Dave Schwartz • Robert Scott • Larry Serota • 707 Sports Cards • Jim Sexton • Corey Shanus • Max Silberman • Al Simeone • Paul Sjolin • Barry Sloate • Joe Smith • Mark Soltan • John Spalding • Kevin Spears • Gene Speranza • Nigel Spill • Jerry Spillman • David Spivack • Dana Sprague • Don Steinbach • Paul Stewart • Dan Stickney • Larry Stone • Ken Stough • Al Strumpf • Doug Stultz • Jim Suckow • Rich Suen • Joe Szeremet

J.J. Teaparty • Erik Teller • Lee Temanson • K.J. Terplak • Mark Theotikos • Dick Tinsley • Gary Tkac • Bud Tompkins • Joseph Tonely • Scott Torrey • Dan Tripper

Rich Unruh • Jack Urban • Glen Van Aken • Frank Van Damme • Brian Van Horn

Geno Wager • Frank Wakefield • Pete Waldman • Eric Waller • Tony Walls • Gary Walter • Frank Ward • Adam Warshaw • Dave Weber • Ken Weimer • Jeff Weiss • Richard Weiss • Dale Weselowski • E.C. Wharton-Tigar • Charles Williamson • Jay Wolt • Frank Wozny • Bill Wright

Rhys Yeakley • Kit Young

Ted Zanidakis

2009 Standard Catalog of Baseball Cards

HOW TO USE THIS CATALOG

This catalog has been uniquely designed to serve the needs of collectors and dealers at all levels from beginning to advanced. It provides a comprehensive guide to more than 140 years of baseball card issues, arranged so that even the most novice hobbyist can consult it with confidence and ease.

The following explanations summarize the general practices used in preparing this catalog's listings. However, because of specialized requirements which may vary from card set to card set, these must not be considered ironclad. Where these standards have been set aside, appropriate notations are usually incorporated.

ARRANGEMENT

The most important feature in identifying and pricing a baseball card is its set of origin. Therefore the main body of this catalog, covering cards issued from 1863-date, has been alphabetically arranged within specific eras of issue according to the name by which the set is most popularly known to collectors, or by which it can be most easily identified by a person examining a card.

Previous editions of this catalog relied heavily upon card set identification numbers originated in Jefferson Burdick's pioneering "American Card Catalog." However, since that work was last updated over 40 years ago its numbering system has become arcane and is little used by the present generation of hobbyists. Where practical, sets which were listed in previous editions by their ACC designations have been reclassified alphabetically by a more readily identifiable signpost, such as manufacturer's name. Most of those sets however continue to bear the ACC catalog number in the set heading.

Among card issuers that produced sets for more than a single year, their sets are then listed chronologically, from earliest to most recent, again within specific eras.

Within each set, the cards are listed by their designated card number, or in the absence of card numbers, alphabetically according to the last name of the player pictured. Listing numbers found in parentheses indicate the number does not appear on the card. Certain cards which fall outside the parameters of the normal card numbering for a specific set may be found at the beginning or end of the listings for that set.

Listings are generally arranged in two major sections – major league and minor league issues.

MAJOR LEAGUE ISSUES

The main body of the book details major league baseball card issues from 1863 through the first half of 2008, divided into two sections: Vintage (1863-1980) and Modern (1981-date). In general, prior to about 1990, this will include issues that picture one or more baseball players, usually contemporary with their playing days, printed on paper or cardboard in a variety of shapes and sizes and given away as a premium with the purchase of another product or service. After 1990 or so the definition is broadened to remove the restriction of the card as an ancillary product and to include those printed on plastic, wood, metal, etc.

Included within each era's listings are related non-card collectibles featuring baseball players which do not fit under the definition previously given for baseball cards. These include many items on which players are depicted on materials other than paper or cardboard, such as pins, coins, silks, leathers, patches, felts, pennants, metallic ingots, statues, figurines, limited-edition artworks and others.

Also presented herein are foreign issues, one of the growth areas of the baseball card hobby in recent years. These encompass the various issues from countries outside of North America, particularly Latin America. Since the 1920s a variety of baseball cards, stamps and stickers have emanated from the Caribbean, South America and elsewhere chronicling the various winter baseball leagues that have flourished there, often stocked with former and future major league stars and, in the early years, providing the only contemporary cards of many U.S. and Latin Negro Leagues players.

Incorporated into the listings are some modern collectors' issues. There exists within the hobby a great body of cards known as "collectors' issues" (sometimes generically known as "broders") by virtue of their nature of having been produced solely for the hobby card market. These cards and sets are distinguished from "legitimate" issues in not having been created as a sales promotional item for another product or service – bubble gum, soda, snack cakes, dog food, cigarettes, gasoline, etc. This distinction, however, is no longer so easy to make since the early 1990s, when many baseball card issues by even the major national companies began to be sold without an accompanying product.

By their nature, and principally because the person issuing them was always free to print and distribute more of the same if they should ever attain any real value, collectors' issues were generally regarded by the hobby as having little or no premium value. Since the leagues and players' union began to enforce licensing restrictions in the early 1990s, the nature of collector's issues changed dramatically. The sets that were the work of an individual catering to the hobby market with an issue of relatively limited numbers and basic technology have given way to more sophisticated productions, often marketed to the general public, as well as the hobby.

The distinction between "collectors" and "legitimate" cards may be barely perceptible but is noted whenever possible. Generally, those collectors' emissions share some or all of these characteristics: 1) Prior to around 1990 they were not licensed by the players depicted, nor by their teams or leagues. 2) They were sold as complete sets rather than by pack or as singles. 3) The issue was marketed almost exclusively to the card collecting hobby audience through advertising in trade papers and public sporting press, and within the hobby's dealer network. 4) The cards were sold on a stand-alone basis, that is, not as a premium or adjunct to the sale of another product or service.

MINOR LEAGUE ISSUES (1867-1969)

Prior to 1970 virtually all minor league baseball cards were issued as single cards rather than as complete sets. Like contemporary major league cards they were usually intended as premiums given away with the purchase of goods and services.

The listings which follow offer individual card prices in three grades of preservation to allow accurate valuations of superstar and other special interest cards, along with cards that were short-printed or otherwise are scarce.

IDENTIFICATION

While most modern baseball cards are well identified on front, back or both, as to date and issue, such has not always been the case. In general, the back of the card is more useful in identifying the set of origin than the front. The issuer or sponsor's name will usually appear on the back since, after all, baseball cards were first produced as a promotional item to stimulate sales of other products. As often as not, that issuer's name is the name by which the set is known to collectors and under which it will be found listed in this catalog.

In some difficult cases, identifying a baseball card's general age, if not specific year of issue, can usually be accomplished by studying the biological or statistical information on the back of the card. The last year mentioned in either the biography or stats is usually the year which preceded the year of issue.

Over the years there have been many cards issued that bear no identification features at all with which to pinpoint the issuer. In such cases, they are cataloged by the names under which they are best known in the hobby. Many of the strip-card issues of the 1920s, for example, remain listed under the "W" catalog number where they were originally enumerated in the "American Card Catalog."

It is the ultimate goal, through the use of cross listings and more detailed indexes, to allow a person holding a card in his hand to find the catalog listing for that card with the greatest ease.

PHOTOGRAPHS

Wherever possible a photograph of the front and (prior to 1981) back of at least one representative card from most of the sets listed in this catalog has been incorporated into the listings to assist identification. (Persons who can provide sample cards for photography purposes for those sets which are missing photos in this volume are encouraged to contact the editor.)

Photographs have been printed in reduced size. The actual size of cards in each set is usually given in the introductory text preceding its listing, unless the card is the current standard size (2.5" by 3.5").

DATING

The dating of baseball cards by year of issue on the front or back of the card itself is a relatively new phenomenon. In most cases, to accurately determine a date of issue for an unidentified card, it must be studied for clues. As mentioned, the biography, career summary or statistics on the back of the card are the best way to pinpoint a year of issue. In most cases, the year of issue will be the year after the last season mentioned on the card.

Luckily for today's collector, earlier generations have done much of the research in determining year of issue for those cards that bear no clues. The painstaking task of matching the players' listed and/or pictured team against their career records often allowed an issue date to be determined.

In some cases, particular card sets were issued over a period of more than one calendar year, but since they are collected together as a single set, their specific year of issue is not important. Such sets will be listed with their complete known range of issue years.

There remain some early issues for which an exact year of issue cannot be reliably pinpointed. In those cases a "best guess" date or one in the middle of the possible range has been used to identify the issue; such cases are usually noted in the introductory text.

NUMBERING

While many baseball card issues as far back as the 1880s have featured card numbers assigned by the issuer to facilitate the collecting of a complete set, the practice has by no means been universal. Even today, not every set bears card numbers.

Logically, those baseball cards that were numbered by their manufacturer are presented in that numerical order within the listings of this catalog whenever possible. In a few cases, complete player checklists were obtained from earlier published sources that did not note card numbers, and so numbers have been arbitrarily assigned. Many other unnumbered issues have been assigned catalog numbers to facilitate their universal identification within the hobby, especially when buying and selling by mail. Among some issues for which the complete checklist remains unknown and for which new discoveries are still being reported, gaps have been left in the assigned numbering to facilitate future additions.

In all cases, numbers that have been assigned, or which otherwise do not appear on the card through error or by design, are shown in this catalog within parentheses. In virtually all cases, unless a more natural system suggested itself by the unique matter of a particular set, the assignment of numbers by the cataloging staff has been done by alphabetical arrangement of the players' last names or the card's principal title.

Significant collectible variations for any particular card are noted within the listings by the application of a suffix letter. In instances of variations, the suffix "a" is assigned to the variation which was created first, when it can be so identified.

NAMES

The identification of a player by full name on the front of his baseball card has been a common practice only since the 1920s. Prior to that, the player's last name and team were the usual information found on the card front.

As a general – though not universally applied – practice, the listings in this volume present the player's name exactly as it appears on the front of the card. If the player's full name only appears on the back, rather than on the front of the card, the listing may correspond to that designation.

A player's name checklisted in ***bold italic*** type indicates a rookie card as defined later in this introduction.

Cards that contain misspelled first or last names, or even wrong initials, will usually have included in their listings the incorrect information, with a correction accompanying in parentheses. This extends also to cases where the name on the card does not correspond to the player actually pictured.

In some cases, to facilitate efficient presentations, to maintain ease of use for the reader, or to allow for proper computer sorting of data, a player's name or card title may be listed other than as it actually appears on the card.

GRADING

It is necessary that some sort of card grading standard be used so that buyer and seller (especially when dealing through the Internet or by mail) may reach an informed agreement on the value of a card.

Pre-1981 cards are generally priced in the three grades of preservation in which those cards are most commonly encountered in the daily buying and selling in the hobby marketplace. They are listed in grades of Near Mint (NR MT), Excellent (EX) and Very Good (VG), reflecting the basic fact that few cards were able to survive for 25, 50 or even 100 years in close semblance to the condition of their issue.

The pricing of cards in these three conditions will allow readers to accurately price cards which fall in intermediate grades, such as EX-MT, or VG-EX.

Although grades below Very Good are not generally priced in this volume, close approximations of low-grade card values may be figured on the following formula: Good condition cards are valued at about 50 percent of VG price, with Fair cards about 50 percent of Good.

Cards in Poor condition have little or no market value except in the cases of the rarest and most expensive cards. In such cases, value has to be negotiated individually.

Modern (1981-date) issues, which have been preserved in top condition in considerable numbers, are listed only in the grade of Near Mint-to-Mint (NM/M). Earlier editions of this book priced such cards under the heading of Mint condition. However, the rise of independent grading services in the past decade and their use of the NM/M designation to describe the vast majority of new card specimens has influenced the marketplace to the extent that only a small percentage of cards, even fresh from the pack, can meet the strict standards for a true Mint example. The switch to a NM/M designation is part of the catalog's commitment to accurately reflect the current conditions of the card market.

As with older cards, values for lower-grade cards from 1981-date may be generally figured by using a figure of 75 percent of the

NM/M price for Near Mint specimens, and 40 percent of the Mint price for Excellent cards.

For the benefit of the reader, we present herewith the grading guide which was originally formulated in 1981 by *Baseball Cards* magazine and *Sports Collectors Digest*, and has been continually refined since that time.

These grading definitions have been used in the pricing of cards in this book, but they are by no means a universally-accepted grading standard.

The potential buyer of a baseball card should keep that in mind when encountering cards of nominally the same grade, but at a price which differs widely from that quoted in this book.

Ultimately, the collector must formulate his/her own personal grading standards in deciding whether cards available for purchase meet the needs of their collection.

No collector is required to adhere to the grading standards presented herewith – nor to any other published grading standards.

Mint (MT): A perfect card. Well-centered, with parallel borders that appear equal to the naked eye. Four sharp, square corners. No creases, edge dents, surface scratches, paper flaws, loss of luster, yellowing or fading, regardless of age. No imperfectly printed card – out of register, badly cut or ink flawed – or card stained by contact with gum, wax or other substances can be considered truly Mint, even if new out of the pack. Generally, to be considered in Mint condition, a card's borders must exist in a ratio of no greater than 60/40 side to side and top to bottom.

Near Mint/Mint (NM/M): A nearly perfect card. Well-centered, with at least three sharp, square corners. No creases, edge dents, surface scratches, paper flaws, loss of luster, yellowing or fading, regardless of age. No imperfectly printed card – out of register, badly cut or ink flawed – or card stained by contact with gum, wax or other substances can be considered Near Mint/ Mint, even if new out of the pack. Generally, to be considered in NM/M condition, a card's borders must exist in a ratio of no greater than 65/35 side to side and top to bottom.

Near Mint (NR MT): At first glance, a Near Mint card appears perfect; upon closer examination, however, a minor flaw will be discovered. On well-centered cards, at least two of the four corners must be perfectly sharp; the others showing a minor imperfection upon close inspection. A slightly off-center card with one or more borders being noticeably unequal – no worse than in a ratio of 70/30 S/S or T/B – would also fit this grade.

Excellent (EX): Corners are still fairly sharp with only moderate wear. Card borders may be off-center as much as 80/20. No creases. May have very minor gum, wax or product stains, front or back. Surfaces may show slight loss of luster from rubbing across other cards.

Very Good (VG): Show obvious handling. Corners rounded and/or perhaps showing minor creases. Other minor creases may be visible. Surfaces may exhibit loss of luster, but all printing is intact. May show major gum, wax or other packaging stains. No major creases, tape marks or extraneous markings or writing. All four borders visible, though the ratio may be as poor as 95/5. Exhibits honest wear.

Good (G): A well-worn card, but exhibits no intentional damage or abuse. May have major or multiple creases and/or corners rounded well beyond the border. A Good card will generally sell for about 50 percent the value of a card in Very Good condition.

Fair (F or Fr.): Shows excessive wear, along with damage or abuse. Will show all the wear characteristics of a Good card, along with such damage as thumb tack holes in or near margins, evidence of having been taped or pasted, perhaps small tears around the edges, or creases so heavy as to break the cardboard. Backs may show minor added pen or pencil writing, or be missing small bits of paper. Still, basically a complete card. A Fair card will generally sell for 50 percent the value of a Good specimen.

Poor (P): A card that has been tortured to death. Corners or other areas may be torn off. Card may have been trimmed, show holes from a paper punch or have been used for BB gun practice. Front may have extraneous pen or pencil writing, or other defacement. Major portions of front or back design may be missing. Not a pretty sight.

In addition to these terms, collectors may encounter intermediate grades, such as VG-EX or EX-MT. These cards usually have characteristics of both the lower and higher grades, and are generally priced midway between those two values.

With the rise in popularity of third-party authentication/grading services since the mid-1990s, it must be stressed that the grades and corresponding values presented in this book are for "raw" cards – cards which have not been independently graded. Depending on the reputation of the certification firm, cards that have been graded and encased in plastic slabs may sell for a significant premium over the values found here. This is especially true of high-grade specimens of vintage cards that in certified grades of Near Mint/Mint, Mint or Gem Mint may bring multiples of "catalog" value. Even collector-grade vintage cards can command a premium when authenticated, graded and slabbed because potential buyers may feel more secure in such cards' authenticity and freedom from tampering.

ROOKIE CARDS

While the status (and automatic premium value) that a player's rookie card carries has fluctuated in recent years, and though the hobby still has not reached a universal definition of a rookie card, many significant vintage-era rookie cards are noted in this catalog's listings by the use of ***bold italic*** type. Conversely, many significant modern-era rookie cards are noted in this catalog's listings by the use of **RC** or **(RC)**. Beginning with products issued in 2006, cards with an **(RC)** logo indicate the featured player has a rookie card issued prior to that year. For purposes of this catalog, a player's rookie card is considered to be any card in a nationally distributed, licensed Major League base (non-insert) set from a major manufacturer in the first year in which that player appears on a card, regardless of whether that player has yet appeared in a Major League game or is technically a rookie according to MLB definition.

VALUATIONS

Values quoted in this book represent the current retail market at the time of compilation (Summer, 2008). The quoted values are the result of a unique system of evaluation and verification created by the catalog's editors. Utilizing specialized computer analysis and drawing upon recommendations provided through their daily involvement in the publication of the hobby's leading sports collectors' periodicals, as well as the input of consultants, dealers and collectors, each listing is, in the final analysis, the interpretation of that data by one or more of the editors.

It should be stressed, however, that this book is intended to serve only as an aid in evaluating cards; actual market conditions are constantly changing. This is especially true of the cards of current players, whose on-field performance during the course of a season can greatly affect the value of their cards – upwards or downwards. Because of the extremely volatile nature of new card prices, especially high-end issues, we have chosen not to include the very latest releases from the major companies, feeling it is better to have no listings at all for those cards than to have inaccurate values in print. For the same reasons, many 21st century cards and sets are presented here without pricing. Extremely limited-production (or even unique) cards, often autographs and game-used equipment cards, may not be seen in the hobby market with enough frequency to establish realistic "book" values.

Because this volume is intended to reflect the national market, users will find regional price variances caused by demand differences. Cards of Astros slugger Jeff Bagwell will, for instance, often sell at prices greater than quoted herein at shops and shows in the Houston area. Conversely, his cards may be acquired at a discount from those valuations when purchased on the East or West Coast.

Publication of this book is not intended as a solicitation to buy or sell the listed cards by the editors, publisher or contributors.

Again, the values here are retail prices – what a collector can expect to pay when buying a card from a dealer. The wholesale price, that which a collector can expect to receive from a dealer when selling cards, will be significantly lower.

Many dealers operate on a 100 percent mark-up, generally paying about 50 percent of a card's retail value for cards that they are purchasing for inventory. On some high-demand cards, dealers will pay 100 percent or more of retail value, anticipating continued price increases. Conversely, for many low-demand cards, such as common (non-star) players' cards, dealers may pay as little as 10 percent or even less of retail with many base-brand cards of recent years having no resale value at all.

SET PRICES

Collectors may note that the complete set prices for newer issues quoted in these listings are usually significantly lower than the total of the value of the individual cards that comprise the set. This reflects two factors in the baseball card market. First, a seller is often willing to take a lower composite price for a complete set as a "volume discount" and to avoid carrying in inventory a large number of common-player or other lower-demand cards.

Second, to a degree, the value of common cards can be said to be inflated as a result of having a built-in overhead charge to justify the dealer's time in sorting cards, carrying them in stock and filling orders. This accounts for the fact that even brand new base-brand baseball cards, which cost the dealer around two cents each when bought in bulk, carry individual price tags of five cents or higher.

Some set prices shown, especially for vintage cards in top condition, are merely theoretical in that it is unlikely that a complete set exists in that condition. In general among older cards the range of conditions found in even the most painstakingly assembled complete set make the set values quoted useful only as a starting point for price negotiations.

ERRORS/VARIATIONS

It is often hard for the beginning collector to understand that an error on a baseball card, in and of itself, does not necessarily add premium value to that card. It is usually only when the correcting of an error in a subsequent printing creates a variation that premium value attaches to an error.

Minor errors, such as wrong stats or personal data, misspellings, inconsistencies, etc. – usually affecting the back of the card – are very common, especially in recent years. Unless a corrected variation was also printed, these errors are not noted in the listings of this book because they are not generally perceived by collectors to have premium value.

On the other hand, major effort has been expended to include the most complete listings ever for collectible variation cards. Many scarce and valuable variations are included in these listings because they are widely collected and often have significant premium value.

In the boom years of the early 1990s, some card companies produced their basic sets at more than one printing facility. This frequently resulted in numerous minor variations in photo cropping and back data presentation. Combined with a general decline in quality control from the mid-1980s through the early 1990s, which allowed unprecedented numbers of uncorrected error cards to be released, this caused a general softening of collector interest in errors and variations. Despite the fact most of these modern variations have no premium value, they are listed here as a matter of record.

COUNTERFEITS/REPRINTS

As the value of baseball cards has risen in the past 25+ years, certain cards and sets have become too expensive for the average collector to obtain. This, along with changes in the technology of color printing, has given rise to increasing numbers of counterfeit and reprint cards.

While both terms describe essentially the same thing – a modern-day copy that attempts to duplicate as closely as possible an original baseball card – there are differences that are important to the collector.

Generally a counterfeit is made with the intention of deceiving somebody into believing it is genuine, and thus paying large amounts of money for it. The counterfeiter takes every pain to try to make their fakes look as authentic as possible.

A reprint, on the other hand, while it may have been made to look as close as possible to an original card, is made with the intention of allowing collectors to buy them as substitutes for cards they may never be otherwise able to afford. The big difference is that a reprint is generally marked as such, usually on the back of the card.

In other cases, like the Topps 1952 reprint set and later Archives issues, the replicas are printed in a size markedly different from the originals, or utilizing current technology that differs from that available in the past. Collectors should be aware, however, that unscrupulous persons will sometimes cut off or otherwise obliterate the distinguishing word – "Reprint," "Copy," – or modern copyright date on the back of a reprint card in an attempt to pass it as genuine.

A collector's best defense against reprints and counterfeits is to acquire a knowledge of the look and feel of genuine baseball cards of various eras and issues.

UNLISTED CARDS

Persons encountering cards which are not listed in this reference should not immediately infer that they have something rare and/or valuable. With hundreds of thousands of baseball cards issued over the past century and thousands more being issued each year, this catalog's comprehensiveness will always remain relative. This is especially true in the area of modern cards and sets released regionally, and the vast universe of foreign and collectors' issues for which coverage has only recently begun. Readers who have cards or sets that are not covered in this edition are invited to correspond with the editor for purposes of adding to the compilation work now in progress. A photocopy or scan of the card's front and back will assist in determining its status. **For questions relating to modern-era cards, contact: Joe Clemens, *Standard Catalog of Baseball Cards*, 700 E. State St., Iola, Wis. 54990; e-mail Joseph.Clemens@fwpubs.com. For questions relating to vintage era cards, contact: Don Fluckinger, *Prospect Hill Publishing*, 32 Montgomery Ave., Nashua, NH 03060-5008; email tuffstuff@prospecthillpub.com.** Major contributions will be acknowledged in future editions.

NEW ISSUES

Because new baseball cards are being issued all the time, the cataloging of them remains an on-going challenge. The editors will attempt to keep abreast of new issues so that they may be added to future editions of this book. Readers are invited to submit news of new issues, especially limited-edition or regionally issued cards, to the editor at the address above.

Abbreviation Key

IS: Interleague Showdown
OPS: Overprinted "Promotional Sample"
ED: Expansion Draft
AS: All-Star
HL: Hit List
RC: Rookie Class
RC or (RC): Rookie Card
UPT: Unlimited Potential/Talent
SF: Star Factor
SP: Short Print
DT: Double Team
GLS: Gold Leaf Stars
CC: Curtain Calls
GLR: Gold Leaf Rookies
TP: Top Performers
FF: Future Foundation
DK: Diamond King
RR: Rated Rookie
DP: Double Print
IA: In Action
PC: Promo Card
SR: Star Rookie

HOW TO USE THE DVD

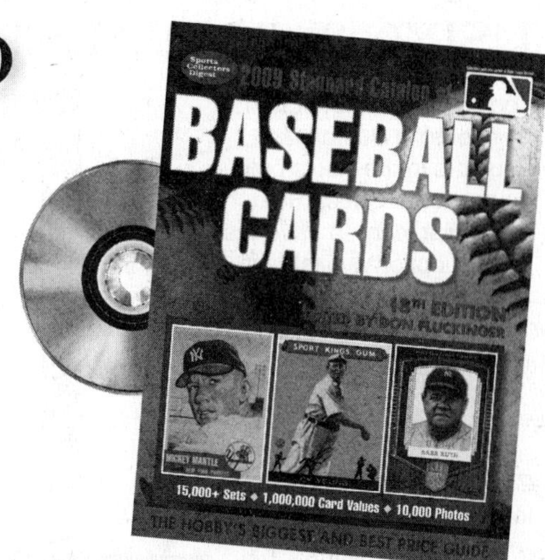

This DVD is PC and Macintosh® compatible when used with Adobe Acrobat Reader® version 6.0 or later. A step-by-step free download of Adobe Acrobat Reader® 8 is available at www.adobe.com. Adobe Reader® 8 was used in creating the instructions that follow.

To help you successfully navigate through the PDF document, several types of searches are available.

USING BOOKMARKS

Click on the Bookmarks icon to open the Bookmarks window. Use these links to go to specific points of interest. To scroll through pages in each section, use the arrows at the top of the screen (see next page for instructions to find page navigators).

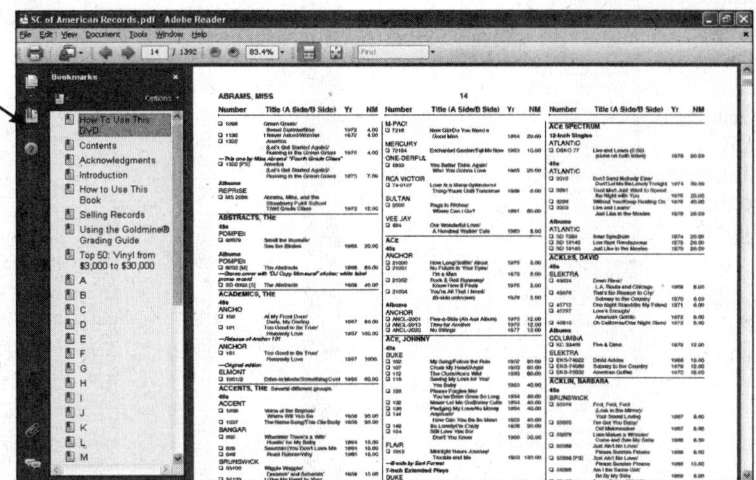

USING THE FIND BOX

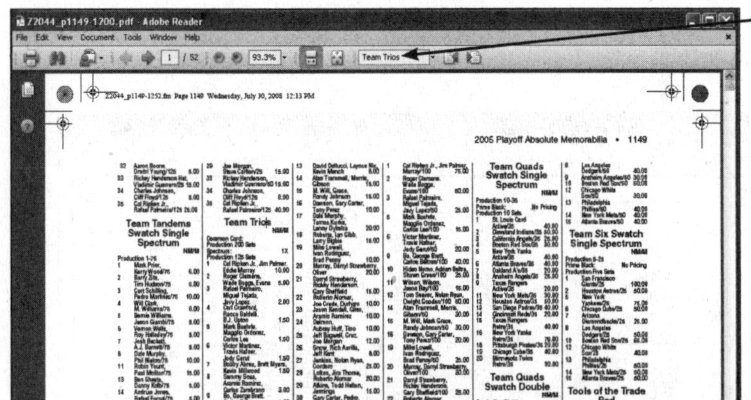

Locate the find box in the tool bar and enter the word(s) you are searching for.

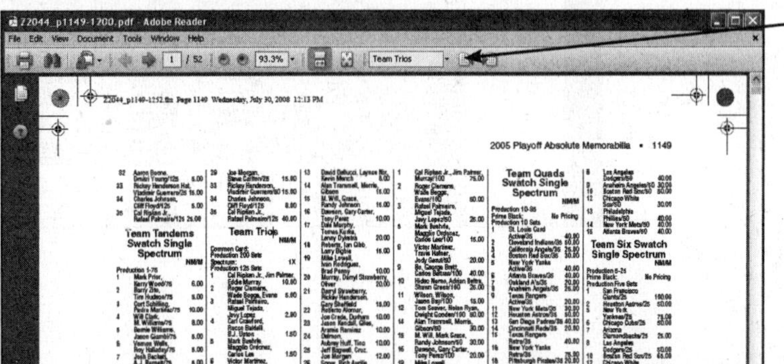

To navigate through the results of your search, use the Find Next icon.

USING THE SEARCH OPTION

Locate the Search button by choosing Customize Toolbars in the Tools pull-down menu. Check Search (binocular icon) to have the Search option available in the toolbar.

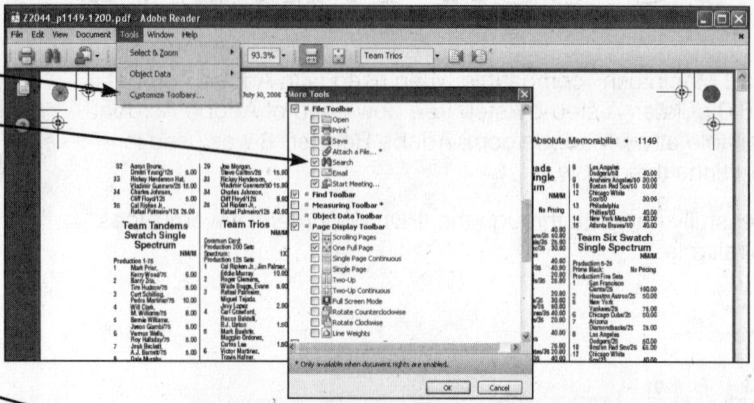

Click on the Search icon to open the Search dialog box.

In the Search dialog box, enter the word(s) you are searching for and click on the Search button.

The list of results will appear in the dialog box. Click on the listings to view each page that contains your searched word(s).

To begin a new word search, click on the New Search button.

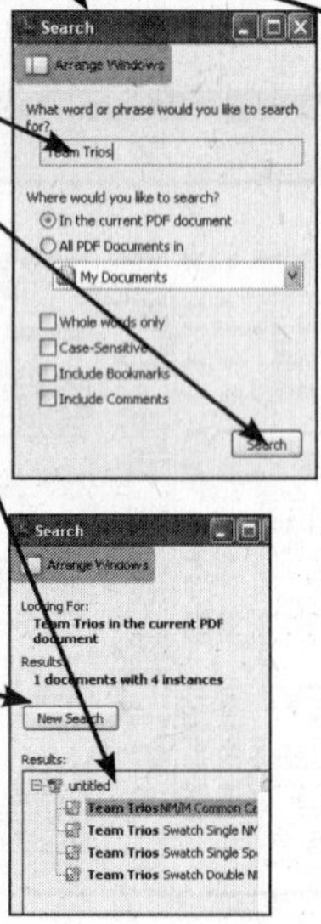

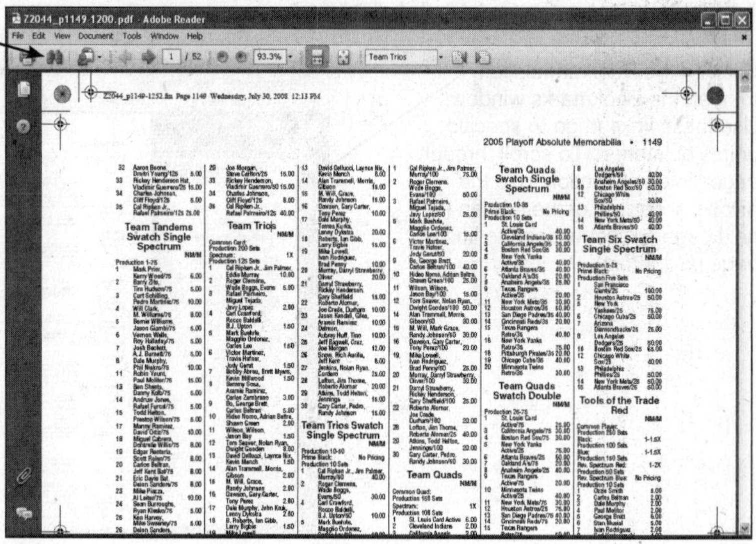

USING PAGE NAVIGATORS

Activate the Page Navigator Toolbar by choosing Customize Toolbars in the Tools pull-down menu. Check each tool as shown at right. You are now able to page through the PDF document by using the arrows at the top of the screen or by entering a page number you wish to view.

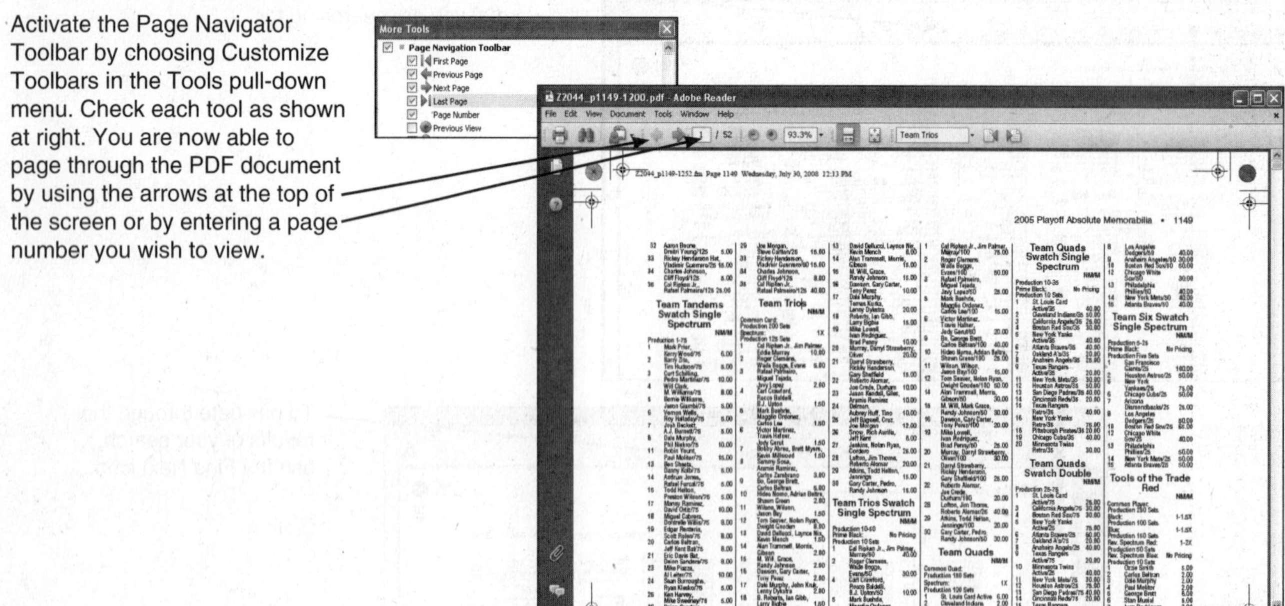

VINTAGE MAJOR LEAGUE CARDS (1869-1980)

The vast majority of cards and collectibles listed in this section were issued between 1869 and 1980 and feature major league players only. The term "card" is used rather loosely as in this context it is construed to include virtually any cardboard or paper product, of whatever size and/or shape, depicting baseball players and issued to stimulate the sales of another product or service.

1976 A & P Brewers

The Aaron and Yount cards from this regional issue support the set price. The set was issued by the A & P grocery chain. Oversize - 5-7/8" x 9" - cards (actually printed on semi-gloss paper) were given out at the stores in 1976 in series of four with the purchase of select weekly grocery specials. Players are pictured in tight capless portraits. Each photo has a black facsimile autograph; backs are blank. The unnumbered cards are checklisted here in alphabetical order.

	NM	EX	VG
Complete Set (16):	35.00	17.50	10.50
Common Player:	3.00	1.50	.90
(1) Henry Aaron	20.00	10.00	6.00
(2) Pete Broberg	3.00	1.50	.90
(3) Jim Colborn	3.00	1.50	.90
(4) Mike Hegan	3.00	1.50	.90
(5) Tim Johnson	3.00	1.50	.90
(6) Von Joshua	3.00	1.50	.90
(7) Sixto Lezcano	3.00	1.50	.90
(8) Don Money	3.00	1.50	.90
(9) Charlie Moore	3.00	1.50	.90
(10) Darrell Porter	3.00	1.50	.90
(11) George Scott	3.00	1.50	.90
(12) Bill Sharp	3.00	1.50	.90
(13) Jim Slaton	3.00	1.50	.90
(14) Bill Travers	3.00	1.50	.90
(15) Robin Yount	10.00	5.00	3.00
(16) County Stadium	3.00	1.50	.90

1976 A & P Royals

Identical in format to the Brewers' set issued around Milwaukee, these 5-7/8" x 9" photos picture players without their caps in posed portraits. The cards were given away four per week with the purchase of selected grocery item specials. Cards have a Players Association logo in the upper-left corner, and a black facsimile autograph on front. Backs are blank. The unnumbered cards are checklisted here alphabetically.

	NM	EX	VG
Complete Set (16):	40.00	20.00	12.00
Common Player:	3.00	1.50	.90
(1) Doug Bird	3.00	1.50	.90
(2) George Brett	20.00	10.00	6.00
(3) Steve Busby	3.00	1.50	.90
(4) Al Cowens	3.00	1.50	.90
(5) Al Fitzmorris	3.00	1.50	.90
(6) Dennis Leonard	3.00	1.50	.90
(7) Buck Martinez	3.00	1.50	.90
(8) John Mayberry	3.00	1.50	.90
(9) Hal McRae	4.50	2.25	1.25
(10) Amos Otis	4.50	2.25	1.25
(11) Fred Patek	3.00	1.50	.90
(12) Tom Poquette	3.00	1.50	.90
(13) Mel Rojas	3.00	1.50	.90
(14) Tony Solaita	3.00	1.50	.90
(15) Paul Splittorff	3.00	1.50	.90
(16) Jim Wohlford	3.00	1.50	.90

1968 Aamco Roger Maris Postcard

"It's a real pennant winner!"

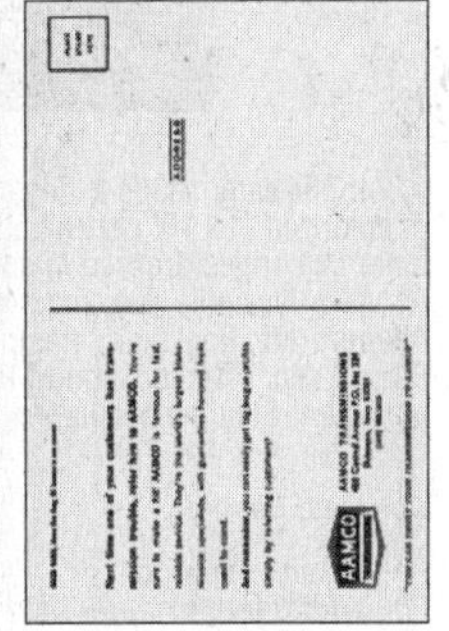

The cited date is approximate on this large-format (about 6" x 9") postcard. The borderless front has a color pose of the reigning home run king with the legend, "It's a real pennant winner!" The postcard format back is directed at auto service professionals, encouraging them to refer transmission problems to a local Aamco facility. A color Aamco logo is at bottom-left.

	NM	EX	VG
Roger Maris	150.00	75.00	45.00

1954 ABC Freight Postcard

So far only one player is known in this black-and-white glossy postcard issue. The front has a posed photo with facsimile autograph. The wide white border at bottom was likely to accomodate an authentic signature. The divided back carries in its upper-left corner the two-line message "You can't miss by playing ball with / ABC Freight Forwarding Corp." However, on the sole known specimen, that message has been obliterated by being overprinted with a decorative black design. Format is 3-1/2" x 5-7/16".

	NM	EX	VG
(1) Ted Kluszewski/Btg	150.00	75.00	45.00
(2) Ted Kluszewski/Fldg	150.00	75.00	45.00

1932 Abdulla Tobacco

Babe Ruth, Amerika

Along with several other contemporary card issues from Germany, Babe Ruth is the lone representative from American baseball in this series of 200 cards. Cards are 1-11/16" x 2-1/2" and feature sepia-tone photos on front, with the celebrity's name and nation printed in the white border at bottom. Backs are in German and include a card number.

	NM	EX	VG
196 Babe Ruth	1,750	875.00	525.00

1949-1950 Acebo y Cia

These small (about 1-1/2" x 1-3/4") Cuban cards were issued in matchboxes, probably over more than one season, as some players are known in photo variations. Fronts have a black-and-white or duotone photo, bordered, with the player name in plain type. Backs have player information presented in one of several different styles, or are blank-backed. It is likely this checklist, which includes a significant contingent of American players, is not complete.

	NM	EX	VG
Common Player:	100.00	50.00	30.00
(1) Bob Addis	100.00	50.00	30.00
(2) Luis Aloma	100.00	50.00	30.00
(3) Ferrel (Ferrell) Anderson	100.00	50.00	30.00
(4) Bill Antonello	100.00	50.00	30.00
(5) Mario Arencibia	100.00	50.00	30.00
(6) Maurice Atwright	100.00	50.00	30.00
(7) Wesley Bailey	100.00	50.00	30.00
(8) Vic Barnhart	100.00	50.00	30.00
(9) Carlos Blanco	100.00	50.00	30.00
(10) Herberto Blanco	100.00	50.00	30.00
(11) Adolfo Cabrera	100.00	50.00	30.00
(12) Emilio Cabrera	100.00	50.00	30.00
(13) Lorenzo "Chiquitin" Cabrera	100.00	50.00	30.00
(14) Rafael Villa Cabrera	100.00	50.00	30.00
(15) Samuel Calderone	100.00	50.00	30.00
(16) Avelino Canizares	100.00	50.00	30.00
(17) Clemente "Sungo" Carreras	100.00	50.00	30.00
(18) Jack Cassini	100.00	50.00	30.00
(19) Aristonico Cocorreoso	100.00	50.00	30.00
(20) Carlos Colas	100.00	50.00	30.00
(21) Kevin (Chuck) Connors	450.00	225.00	135.00
(22) Sandalio "Potrellilo" Consuegra	125.00	62.00	37.00
(23) Agustin Cordeiro	100.00	50.00	30.00
(24) Reinaldo Cordeiro	100.00	50.00	30.00
(25) Reinaldo Cordeiro	100.00	50.00	30.00
(26) Alejandro Crespo	100.00	50.00	30.00
(27) Raymond "Talua" Dandridge	500.00	250.00	150.00

(28)	Jose "Pipo" de la Noval	100.00	50.00	30.00
(29)	Carlos "Yiqui" De Souza	100.00	50.00	30.00
(30)	Mario Diaz	100.00	50.00	30.00
(31)	Lino Donoso	100.00	50.00	30.00
(32)	Claro Duany	100.00	50.00	30.00
(33)	Gumersindo Elba	100.00	50.00	30.00
(34)	Paul (Al) Epperly	100.00	50.00	30.00
(35)	Roberto "Tarzan" Estalella	125.00	65.00	35.00
(36)	Jose Ma. Fernandez	100.00	50.00	30.00
(37)	Jose Ma. Fernandez Jr.	100.00	50.00	30.00
(38)	Rodolfo Fernandez	100.00	50.00	30.00
(39)	Thomas Fine	100.00	50.00	30.00
(40)	Andres Fleitas	100.00	50.00	30.00
(41)	Pedro Formental	100.00	50.00	30.00
(42)	"Sojito" Gallardo	100.00	50.00	30.00
(43)	Chicuelo Garcia	100.00	50.00	30.00
(44)	Manuel "Cocaina" Garcia	150.00	75.00	45.00
(45)	Pablo Garcia	100.00	50.00	30.00
(46)	Silvio Garcia	100.00	50.00	30.00
(47)	Lloyd Gearhart (Reverse image.)	100.00	50.00	30.00
(48)	Lloyd Gearhart (Corrected)	100.00	50.00	30.00
(49)	(Al) Gerheauser	100.00	50.00	30.00
(50)	Albert Gionfrido (Gionfriddo)	125.00	65.00	35.00
(51)	Leonardo Goicochea	100.00	50.00	30.00
(52)	Enrique Gonzalez	100.00	50.00	30.00
(53)	Hiram Gonzalez	100.00	50.00	30.00
(54)	Miguel Angel Gonzalez	125.00	65.00	35.00
(55)	Fermin Guerra	100.00	50.00	30.00
(56)	Wes Hamner	100.00	50.00	30.00
(57)	Eugene Handley	100.00	50.00	30.00
(58)	Rollie Hemsley	100.00	50.00	30.00
(59)	Salvador Hernandez	100.00	50.00	30.00
(60)	Clarence Hicks	100.00	50.00	30.00
(61)	Manuel "Chino" Hidalgo	100.00	50.00	30.00
(62)	Bob Hooper	100.00	50.00	30.00
(63)	Amado Ibanez	100.00	50.00	30.00
(64)	Don Lenhardt	100.00	50.00	30.00
(65)	Vicente Lopez	100.00	50.00	30.00
(66)	Raul Lopez	100.00	50.00	30.00
(67)	"Tony" Lorenzo	100.00	50.00	30.00
(68)	Adolfo Luque	150.00	75.00	45.00
(69)	John Bill Maldovan	100.00	50.00	30.00
(70)	Max Manning	250.00	125.00	75.00
(71)	Conrado Marrero	125.00	65.00	35.00
(72)	Rogelio "Limonar" Martinez/ Pitching	100.00	50.00	30.00
(73)	Rogelio "Limonar" Martinez/ Portrait	100.00	50.00	30.00
(74)	Agapito Mayor	100.00	50.00	30.00
(75)	Lester McCrabb	100.00	50.00	30.00
(76)	Guillermo "Willy" Miranda	125.00	65.00	35.00
(77)	Rene Monteagudo	100.00	50.00	30.00
(78)	Julio "Jiqui" Moreno	100.00	50.00	30.00
(79)	Ernesto Morrilla	100.00	50.00	30.00
(80)	Howie Moss	100.00	50.00	30.00
(81)	Rafael Sam Noble	100.00	50.00	30.00
(82)	Regino Otero	100.00	50.00	30.00
(83)	Oliverio Ortiz	100.00	50.00	30.00
(84)	Roberto Ortiz/Btg	100.00	50.00	30.00
(85)	Roberto Ortiz/Portrait	100.00	50.00	30.00
(86)	Pedro Pages	100.00	50.00	30.00
(87)	Leonard Pearson	250.00	125.00	75.00
(88)	Eddie Pellagrin (Pellagrini)	100.00	50.00	30.00
(89)	Conrado Perez	100.00	50.00	30.00
(90)	Damon Phillips	100.00	50.00	30.00
(91)	Jose "Pototo" Piloto	100.00	50.00	30.00
(92)	William Powell	100.00	50.00	30.00
(93)	Al Prendergast	100.00	50.00	30.00
(94)	Napoleon Reyes (Holding bat.)	100.00	50.00	30.00
(95)	Napoleon Reyes (No bat.)	100.00	50.00	30.00
(96)	Donald Richmond	100.00	50.00	30.00
(97)	Hector Rodriguez	100.00	50.00	30.00
(98)	Oscar Rodriguez	100.00	50.00	30.00
(99)	Julio Rojo	100.00	50.00	30.00
(100)	Octavio Rubert	100.00	50.00	30.00
(101)	Arturo Seijas	100.00	50.00	30.00
(102)	Raymond Shore (Arms crossed.)	100.00	50.00	30.00
(103)	Raymond Shore (Pose unrecorded.)	100.00	50.00	30.00
(104)	Ford Smith	100.00	50.00	30.00
(105)	Rene Solis	100.00	50.00	30.00
(106)	Roberto Fernandez Tapanes	100.00	50.00	30.00
(107)	Don Thompson	100.00	50.00	30.00
(108)	Gilberto Torres	100.00	50.00	30.00
(109)	Quincy Trouppe	150.00	75.00	45.00
(110)	Christian Van Cuyk	100.00	50.00	30.00
(111)	John Van Cuyk	100.00	50.00	30.00
(112)	Ben Wade	100.00	50.00	30.00
(113)	Archie Wilson	100.00	50.00	30.00
(114)	Edward Wright	100.00	50.00	30.00
(115)	Adrian Zabala	100.00	50.00	30.00

1970 Action Cartridge

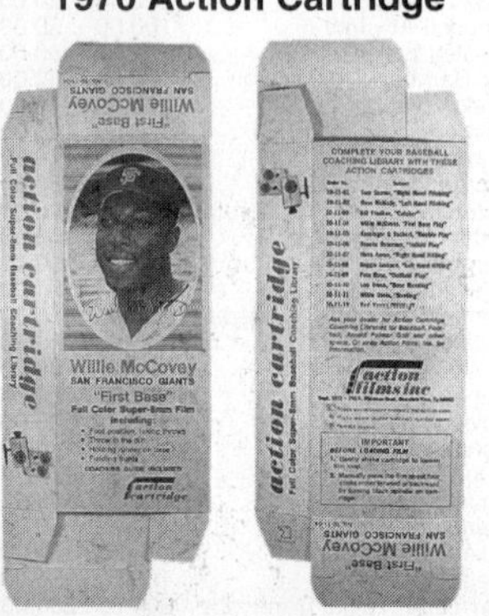

This set of boxes with baseball players' pictures on them was issued by Action Films Inc. of Mountain View, Calif., in 1970-71. The boxes, measuring 2-5/8" x 6" x 1" deep, contained 8mm film cartridges of various professional athletes demonstrating playing tips. The movie series include 12 baseball players. (Other sports represented were football, golf, tennis, hockey and skiing, a total of 40, in all). Boxes feature color player portraits inside an oval and include a facsimile autograph. The values listed are for complete boxes or player panels, without the movie cartridge.

		NM	EX	VG
Complete Set (12):		275.00	135.00	85.00
Common Player:		7.50	3.75	2.25
Box w/Cartridge: 2X				
Viewer:		60.00	30.00	20.00
1	Tom Seaver	40.00	20.00	12.00
2	Dave McNally	7.50	3.75	2.25
3	Bill Freehan	7.50	3.75	2.25
4	Willie McCovey	25.00	12.50	7.50
5	Glenn Beckert, Don Kessinger	7.50	3.75	2.25
6	Brooks Robinson	30.00	15.00	9.00
7	Hank Aaron	60.00	30.00	18.00
8	Reggie Jackson	45.00	22.50	13.50
9	Pete Rose	50.00	25.00	15.00
10	Lou Brock	25.00	12.50	7.50
11	Willie Davis	7.50	3.75	2.25
12	Rod Carew	25.00	12.50	7.50

1933-1934 Adams Hat Stores

In the early 1930s a men's haberdasher issued a series of colorized 8" x 10" portrait photos of baseball players and other celebrities dressed in suit-and-tie and wearing a hat. Above a facsimile autograph on front is a testimonial for Adams Hats. Backs are stamped, "Property of Adams Hat Stores, Inc." The location of the issuing store or stores in unknown. Only the ballplayers are listed here.

		NM	EX	VG
Complete Set (3):		1,750	875.00	525.00
Common Player:		600.00	300.00	180.00
(1)	Carl Hubbell	600.00	300.00	180.00
(2)	Lefty Gomez	600.00	300.00	180.00
(3)	John McGraw	600.00	300.00	180.00

1910 A Fan For A Fan

These cardboard novelties were produced by the American Tobacco Co. About 7-1/4" in diameter, the bursting baseball and portrait are printed in color with a facsimile autograph. The handle is about 5" long. The back is blank. The known fans are listed here alphabetically; the checklist is likely incomplete.

		NM	EX	VG
Complete Set (5):		30,000	16,000	9,750
Common Player:		2,400	1,200	725.00
(1)	Frank Baker	4,500	2,250	1,350
(2)	Hal Chase	3,600	1,800	1,100
(3)	Ty Cobb	15,000	7,500	4,500
(4)	Larry Doyle	2,400	1,200	725.00
(5)	Christy Mathewson	5,500	2,750	1,650

1939 African Tobacco

The unlikely venue of the "other" U.S.A. (Union of South Africa) is the provenance of this rare Babe Ruth card. The African Tobacco Co. issued a set of 100 cards in a series titled "The World of Sport." The cards were issued in both a large (2-1/4" x 3-1/4") and small (1-3/4" x 2-1/2") format. Fronts

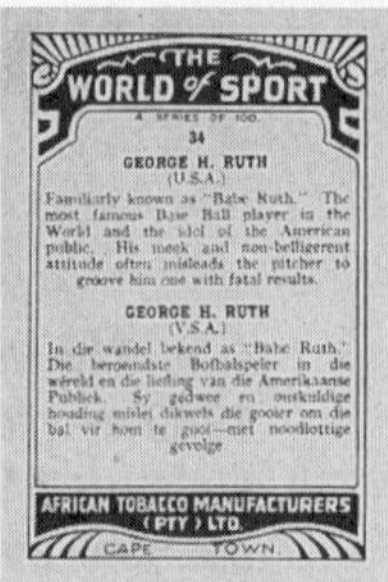

have a black-and-white photo of Ruth, with a white border all around. Backs are printed in both English and Afrikaner.

		NM	EX	VG
34	Babe Ruth (Large)	1,250	625.00	375.00
34	Babe Ruth (Small)	1,250	625.00	375.00

1924-1925 Aguilitas Segundas

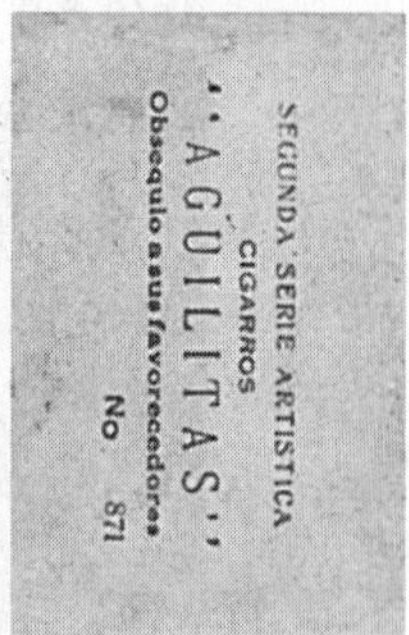

This set is known to collectors as Aguilitas Segundas for the top line of the ad on back. In reality, this second series cigarette card issue was issued several years before the Aguilitas first series counterpart. About 1-1/2" x 2-3/8", the cards have round black-and-white player portrait photos in a debossed rectangular area on glossy stock. Beneath the photo is a player name or nickname, with "BASE BALL" below. The ballplayers are a subset of a 900-card issue which included movie and stage stars, soccer players, boxers and other subjects. All baseball players are known within the numerical range of 841 through 899, though only four cards are known above #880, and none between #880-895. The known ballplayers comprise 44, many of whom were stars of the Negro Leagues, including several Hall of Famers and some who appear on no other career-contemporary cards. Cards are checklisted with the name as shown on the card, further identification, where necessary, is listed parenthetically. Many surviving specimens show evidence of having been glued into an album which largely accounts for their survival in the area's hot, humid climate. Examples are rarely seen in condition approaching Excellent.

		NM	EX	VG
Common Player:		220.00	120.00	65.00
841	(Pablo "Champion") Mesa	220.00	120.00	65.00
842	A. (Armando) Marsans	250.00	125.00	75.00
843	C. (Cristobal) Torriente	7,500	2,250	1,350
844	Merito Acosta	220.00	120.00	65.00
845	Cheo Ramos	220.00	120.00	65.00
846	Joe (John Henry "Pop" Lloyd)	10,000	2,750	1,650
847	(Herman Matias) Rios	220.00	120.00	65.00
848	(Lucas) Boada	220.00	120.00	65.00
849	(Jose) Mendez	6,000	1,750	1,000
850	(Valentin) Dreke	350.00	175.00	100.00
851	(Eugenio) Morin	220.00	120.00	65.00
852	Mayari (Esteban "Mayari" Montalvo)	250.00	125.00	75.00
853	(Valentin) Dreke	350.00	175.00	105.00
854	(Julio) Rojo	220.00	120.00	65.00
855	(Rafael) Almeida	250.00	125.00	75.00
856	(Emilio) Palmero	220.00	120.00	65.00
857	(Adolfo) Luque	800.00	250.00	150.00
858	(Isidro) Fabre	250.00	125.00	75.00
859	(Manuel) Cueto	220.00	120.00	65.00
860	Dibu (Pedro Dibut)	220.00	120.00	65.00
861	Cheo Ramos	220.00	120.00	65.00
862	(Jesse) Hubbard	750.00	375.00	225.00
863	Kakin (Gonzalez)	220.00	120.00	65.00
864	(Jose Maria) Fernandez	220.00	120.00	65.00
865	(Snake) Henry	450.00	225.00	135.00
866	Cruje (Ernie Krueger)	450.00	225.00	135.00
867	(Manuel) Parrado	220.00	120.00	65.00
868	(Chuck) Dressen	250.00	125.00	75.00
869	(Oscar) Charleston	10,000	3,500	2,150
870	Sam (John Henry "Pop") Lloyd	10,000	2,750	1,650
871	Mc. Key (Raleigh "Biz" Mackey)	6,000	2,250	1,350
872	P. (Eusebio "Papo") Gonzalez	220.00	120.00	65.00
873	(Clint) Thomas	600.00	300.00	180.00
874	(Dobie) Moore	600.00	300.00	180.00
875	(Frank) Duncan	600.00	300.00	180.00
876	O. (Oscar) Rodriguez	220.00	120.00	65.00
877	Lopito (Jose "Lopito" Lopez)	200.00	100.00	60.00
878	E. (Eustaquio "Bombin") Pedroso	1,000	500.00	300.00

		NM	EX	VG
879	(Dick) Lundy	6,000	1,375	825.00
880	Sirike (Valentin "Sirique" Gonzalez)	220.00	120.00	65.00
895	(Oscar) Tuero	220.00	120.00	65.00
897	(Alejandro) Oms	1,200	600.00	360.00
898	Peter (Jesse Petty)	250.00	125.00	75.00
899	(Danny) Clark	220.00	120.00	65.00

1926-1927 Aguilitas

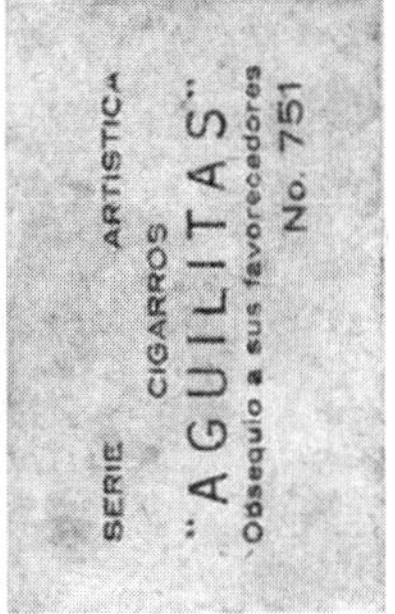

Uniforms worn by some of the players indicate this set was produced after the related series known as "Segundas," or Second Series. The baseball players - all Cuban nationals - are among 100 athletes (including soccer players and boxers) in a 900-card multi-subject set issued in packs of Aguilitas cigarettes. The cards are printed in black-and-white on glossy stock. On front is a large square portrait or action pose. In the bottom border is "BASE-BALL" with the player name and position below. Names as shown on the cards are presneted in this checklist, with further identification as necessary provided parenthetically. Several of the cards are duplicated in the series with different card numbers. Like most contemporary Latin American issues, surviving examples are seldom found in high-grade and often with evidence of having been mounted in an album.

		NM	EX	VG
	Common Player:	165.00	85.00	50.00
751	Cheo Hernandez	165.00	85.00	50.00
752	(Jose Maria) Fernandez	200.00	100.00	60.00
756	R. (Ricardo) Torres	165.00	85.00	50.00
759	Jacinto Calvo	165.00	85.00	50.00
761	E. (Emilio) Palmero	165.00	85.00	50.00
763	Champion (Pablo) Mesa	250.00	125.00	75.00
769	C. (Carlos) Zarza	165.00	85.00	50.00
771	Fernando Rios	165.00	85.00	50.00
772	J. (Joseito) Rodriguez	165.00	85.00	50.00
774	(Juanelo) Mirabal (Same as #824.)	250.00	125.00	75.00
776	L. (Lalo) Rodriguez	165.00	85.00	50.00
777	A. (Adolfo) Luque	350.00	175.00	100.00
778	Alejandro Oms	3,500	1,250	750.00
779	(Armando) Marsans (Same as #829.)	375.00	185.00	110.00
782a	A. (Alfredo) Cabrera	165.00	85.00	50.00
782b	Daniel Blanco (Same as #832.)	165.00	85.00	50.00
787	B. (Bartolo) Portuando	250.00	125.00	75.00
791	A. (Agustin) Navarro	165.00	85.00	50.00
796	R. (Raphael "Busta") Quintana	165.00	85.00	50.00
797	(Roberto) Puig (Same as #847.)	165.00	85.00	50.00
817	(Oscar) Levis	165.00	85.00	50.00
819	Raul Atan	165.00	85.00	50.00
821	(Jose) Pepin Perez	165.00	85.00	50.00
822	(Isidro) Fabre	200.00	100.00	60.00
823	(Bienvenido "Hooks") Jimenez	250.00	125.00	75.00
824	(Juanelo) Mirabal (Same as #774.)	250.00	125.00	75.00
825	Tomas Calvo	165.00	85.00	50.00
826	(Pelayo) Chacon	250.00	125.00	75.00
829	(Armando) Marsans (Same as #779.)	375.00	185.00	110.00
832	Daniel Blanco (Same as #782.)	165.00	85.00	50.00
836	(Valentin) Dreke	250.00	125.00	75.00
838	(Jose) Echarri	165.00	85.00	50.00
839	Miguel Angel (Gonzalez)	300.00	150.00	90.00
841	(Oscar) Estrada	300.00	150.00	90.00
846	Acostica (Jose Acosta)	300.00	150.00	90.00
847	(Roberto) Puig (Same as #797.)	165.00	85.00	50.00
849	(Cesar) Alvarez	165.00	85.00	50.00

1954 Alaga Syrup Willie Mays Postcard

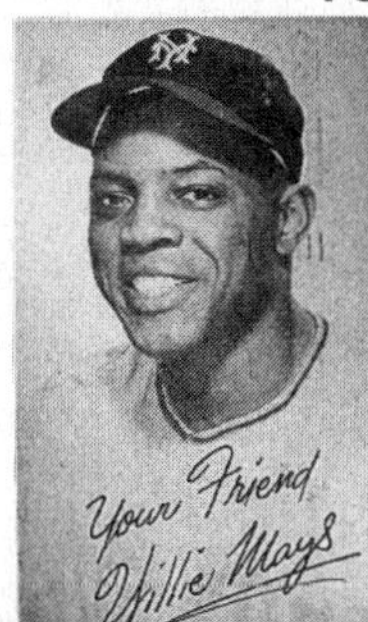

The year of issue on this one-card set is approximate. In 3-1/4" x 5-1/2" format the black-and-white card has a borderless portrait on front with a facsimile autograph. Back has an ad for Alaga Syrup, along with standard postcard elements.

		NM	EX	VG
(1)	Willie Mays	300.00	150.00	90.00

1944-45 Albertype Hall of Fame Plaque Postcards - Type 1

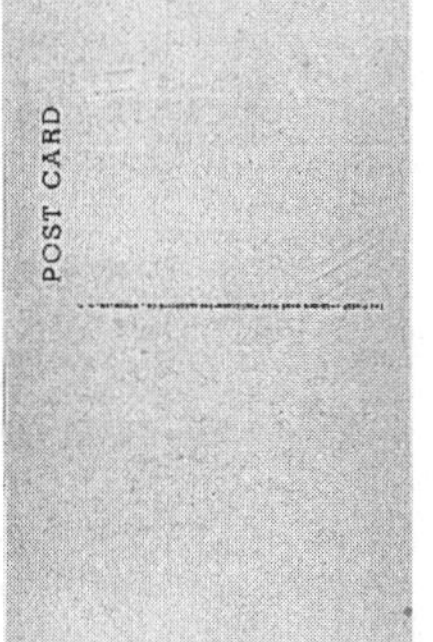

From 1944-1952, Albertype was the official producer of the Baseball Hall of Fame's postcards available for public sale. The 3-1/2" x 5-1/2" black-and-white cards depict the bronze plaque of each inductee. Fronts have a white border. Postcard-style backs have a bit of player data and identification of the specific producer. In the first type of Albertype plaque postcards, issued 1944-45, the line of type beneath the plaque photo has an abbreviation for New York. Later Albertypes spelled out the state name. The unnumbered cards are checklisted here alphabetically.

		NM	EX	VG
	Complete Set (38):	800.00	400.00	240.00
	Common Player:	20.00	10.00	6.00
(1)	G.C. Alexander	25.00	12.50	7.50
(2)	Adrian Anson	20.00	10.00	6.00
(3)	Roger Bresnahan	20.00	10.00	6.00
(4)	Dan Brouthers	20.00	10.00	6.00
(5)	Morgan Bulkeley	20.00	10.00	6.00
(6)	Alexander Cartwright	20.00	10.00	6.00
(7)	Henry Chadwick	20.00	10.00	6.00
(8)	Fred Clarke	20.00	10.00	6.00
(9)	Ty Cobb	40.00	20.00	12.00
(10)	Eddie Collins	20.00	10.00	6.00
(11)	Jimmy Collins	20.00	10.00	6.00
(12)	Charles A. Comiskey	20.00	10.00	6.00
(13)	Candy Cummings	20.00	10.00	6.00
(14)	Ed Delahanty	20.00	10.00	6.00
(15)	Hugh Duffy	20.00	10.00	6.00
(16)	Buck Ewing	20.00	10.00	6.00
(17)	Lou Gehrig	50.00	25.00	15.00
(18)	Rogers Hornsby	20.00	10.00	6.00
(19)	Hughie Jennings	20.00	10.00	6.00
(20)	Ban Johnson	20.00	10.00	6.00
(21)	Walter Johnson	30.00	15.00	9.00
(22)	Willie Keeler	20.00	10.00	6.00
(23)	King Kelly	20.00	10.00	6.00
(24)	Nap Lajoie	20.00	10.00	6.00
(25)	Kenesaw Landis	20.00	10.00	6.00
(26)	Connie Mack	20.00	10.00	6.00
(27)	Christy Mathewson	30.00	15.00	9.00
(28)	John McGraw	20.00	10.00	6.00
(29)	Jim O'Rourke	20.00	10.00	6.00
(30)	Chas. Radbourn	20.00	10.00	6.00
(31)	Wilbert Robinson	20.00	10.00	6.00
(32)	Babe Ruth	65.00	32.00	19.50
(33)	George Sisler	20.00	10.00	6.00
(34)	Al Spalding	20.00	10.00	6.00
(35)	Tris Speaker	20.00	10.00	6.00
(36)	Honus Wagner	30.00	15.00	9.00
(37)	George Wright	20.00	10.00	6.00
(38)	Cy Young	30.00	15.00	9.00

1946-52 Albertype Hall of Fame Plaque Postcards - Type 2

From 1944-1952, Albertype was the official producer of the Baseball Hall of Fame's postcards available for public sale. The 3-1/2" x 5-1/2" black-and-white cards depict the bronze plaque of each inductee. Fronts have a white border. Postcard-style backs have a bit of biographical data and identification of the specific issuer. In the second series of Albertype plaque postcards, issued 1946-52, the line of type beneath the plaque photo spells out the New York state name. The unnumbered cards are checklisted here alphabetically. Those cards found only in this series are noted with an asterisk. Because the Foxx and Ott cards were first issued in 1951, and the Paul Waner, Heilmann and 1864 Knickerboker Nine in 1952, they are scarcer than those issued earlier.

		NM	EX	VG
	Complete Set (63):	1,325	675.00	425.00
	Common Player:	20.00	10.00	6.00
(1)	G.C. Alexander	25.00	12.50	7.50
(2)	Adrian Anson	20.00	10.00	6.00
(3)	Roger Bresnahan	20.00	10.00	6.00
(4)	Dan Brouthers	20.00	10.00	6.00
(5)	Mordecai Brown (*)	25.00	12.50	7.50
(6)	Morgan Bulkeley	20.00	10.00	6.00
(7)	Jesse Burkett (*)	25.00	12.50	7.50
(8)	Alexander Cartwright	20.00	10.00	6.00
(9)	Henry Chadwick	20.00	10.00	6.00
(10)	Frank Chance (*)	25.00	12.50	7.50
(11)	Jack Chesbro (*)	25.00	12.50	7.50
(12)	Fred Clarke	20.00	10.00	6.00
(13)	Ty Cobb	40.00	20.00	12.00
(14)	Mickey Cochrane (*)	25.00	12.50	7.50
(15)	Eddie Collins	20.00	10.00	6.00
(16)	Jimmy Collins	20.00	10.00	6.00
(17)	Charles A. Comiskey	20.00	10.00	6.00
(18)	Candy Cummings	20.00	10.00	6.00
(19)	Ed Delahanty	20.00	10.00	6.00
(20)	Hugh Duffy	20.00	10.00	6.00
(21)	Johnny Evers (*)	25.00	12.50	7.50
(22)	Buck Ewing	20.00	10.00	6.00
(23)	James E. (Jimmy) Foxx (*)	45.00	22.00	13.50
(24)	Frankie Frisch (*)	25.00	12.50	7.50
(25)	Lou Gehrig	50.00	25.00	15.00
(26)	Charlie Gehringer (*)	25.00	12.50	7.50
(27)	Clark Griffith (*)	25.00	12.50	7.50
(28)	Lefty Grove (*)	25.00	12.50	7.50
(29)	Harry Heilmann (*)	40.00	20.00	12.00
(30)	Rogers Hornsby	20.00	10.00	6.00
(31)	Carl Hubbell (*)	25.00	12.50	7.50
(32)	Hughie Jennings	20.00	10.00	6.00
(33)	Ban Johnson	20.00	10.00	6.00
(34)	Walter Johnson	30.00	15.00	9.00
(35)	Willie Keeler	20.00	10.00	6.00
(36)	King Kelly	20.00	10.00	6.00
(37)	Nap Lajoie	20.00	10.00	6.00
(38)	Kenesaw Landis	20.00	10.00	6.00
(39)	Connie Mack	20.00	10.00	6.00
(40)	Christy Mathewson	30.00	15.00	9.00
(41)	Tommy McCarthy (*)	25.00	12.50	7.50
(62)	Joe McGinnity (*)	25.00	12.50	7.50
(43)	John McGraw	20.00	10.00	6.00
(44)	Kid Nichols (*)	25.00	12.50	7.50
(45)	Jim O'Rourke	20.00	10.00	6.00
(46)	Mel Ott (*)	35.00	17.50	10.50
(47)	Herb Pennock (*)	25.00	12.50	7.50
(48)	Ed Plank (*)	25.00	12.50	7.50
(49)	Chas. Radbourn	20.00	10.00	6.00
(50)	Wilbert Robinson	20.00	10.00	6.00
(51)	Babe Ruth	65.00	32.00	19.50
(52)	George Sisler	20.00	10.00	6.00
(53)	Al Spalding	20.00	10.00	6.00
(54)	Tris Speaker	20.00	10.00	6.00
(55)	Joe Tinker (*)	25.00	12.50	7.50
(56)	Pie Traynor (*)	25.00	12.50	7.50
(57)	Rube Waddell (*)	25.00	12.50	7.50
(58)	Honus Wagner	30.00	15.00	9.00
(59)	Ed Walsh (*)	25.00	12.50	7.50
(60)	Paul Waner (*)	35.00	17.50	10.50
(61)	George Wright	20.00	10.00	6.00
(62)	Cy Young	30.00	15.00	9.00
(63)	Knickerbocker Nine 1864	35.00	17.50	10.50

1970 Carl Aldana Orioles

Little is known about the distribution or origin of this 12-card regional set, which was available in 1970 in the Baltimore area. Measuring 3-1/4" x 2-1/8", the unnumbered cards picture members of the Baltimore Orioles and include two poses of Brooks Robinson. The cards feature line drawings of the players surrounded by a plain border. The player's last name appears below the portrait sketch. The set was named after Carl Aldana, who supplied the artwork for the cards.

		NM	EX	VG
Complete Set (12):		125.00	65.00	40.00
Common Player:		12.00	6.00	3.50
(1)	Mark Belanger	12.00	6.00	3.50
(2)	Paul Blair	12.00	6.00	3.50
(3)	Mike Cuellar	12.00	6.00	3.50
(4)	Ellie Hendricks	12.00	6.00	3.50
(5)	Dave Johnson	12.00	6.00	3.50
(6)	Dave McNally	12.00	6.00	3.50
(7)	Jim Palmer	45.00	22.50	13.50
(8)	Boog Powell	25.00	12.50	7.50
(9)	Brooks Robinson (Diving - face showing.)	40.00	20.00	12.00
(10)	Brooks Robinson (Diving - back showing.)	40.00	20.00	12.00
(11)	Frank Robinson	60.00	30.00	18.00
(12)	Earl Weaver	15.00	7.50	4.50

1971 Carl Aldana

Devoid of any indication of when produced or by whom, this set of obscure players of the 1940s and 1950s was a collectors' issue from Carl Aldana circa 1971. The cards are blank-backed, about 2-1/8" x 2-3/4". Fronts have a red background with an artwork player portrait in blue. The player's last name and card number are in dark blue, his first name in white. For a few of the players, this is their only known baseball card.

		NM	EX	VG
Complete Set (16):		125.00	60.00	37.50
Common Player:		10.00	5.00	3.00
1	Wally Hood	10.00	5.00	3.00
2	Jim Westlake	10.00	5.00	3.00
3	Stan McWilliams	10.00	5.00	3.00
4	Les Fleming	10.00	5.00	3.00
5	John Ritchey	10.00	5.00	3.00
6	Steve Nagy	10.00	5.00	3.00
7	Ken Gables	10.00	5.00	3.00
8	Maurice Fisher	10.00	5.00	3.00
9	Don Lang	10.00	5.00	3.00
10	Harry Malmburg (Malmberg)	10.00	5.00	3.00
11	Jack Conway	10.00	5.00	3.00
12	Don White	10.00	5.00	3.00
13	Dick Lajeskie	10.00	5.00	3.00
14	Walt Judnich	10.00	5.00	3.00
15	Joe Kirrene	10.00	5.00	3.00
16	Ed Sauer	10.00	5.00	3.00

1940s Alerta Antonio Alcalde Premium Pictures

There are still gaps in the hobby's knowledge of this late-1940s/early-1950s Cuban issue. Evidently a premium used in a contest conducted by a newspaper or sports periodical, these pictures are printed on semi-gloss paper in an 8" x 11" format. Featured on front are black-and-white posed action or portrait photos. The team name and symbol are above and a portrait, presumably of Antonio, is at bottom. Pictures are highlighted by color graphics: blue for Almendares, green for Cienfuegos, red for Havana and orange for Marianao. Backs are blank, but are sometimes seen with a round rubber-stamped "Alerta" logo or red boxed "ANTONIO, ALCALDE." The unnumbered pictures are listed here alphabetically within team. The pictures include many American players and those who spent time in the major leagues.

		NM	EX	VG
Complete Set (70):		2,000	1,000	400.00
Common Player:		30.00	15.00	6.00
	ALMENDARES SCORPIONS			
(1)	Bill Antonello	35.00	17.50	7.00
(2)	Francisco Campos	35.00	17.50	7.00
(3)	Avelino Canizares	30.00	15.00	6.00
(4)	Yiqui De Souza	30.00	15.00	6.00
(5)	Rodolfo Fernandez	30.00	15.00	6.00
(6)	Andres Fleitas	30.00	15.00	6.00
(7)	Al Gionfriddo	35.00	17.50	7.00
(8)	Fermin Guerra	35.00	17.50	7.00
(9)	Bob Hooper	35.00	17.50	7.00
(10)	Vincente Lopez	30.00	15.00	6.00
(11)	Conrado Marrero	35.00	17.50	7.00
(12)	Agapito Mayor	30.00	15.00	6.00
(13)	Willy Miranda	35.00	17.50	7.00
(14)	Rene Monteagudo	35.00	17.50	7.00
(15)	Roberto Ortiz	35.00	17.50	7.00
(16)	Hector Rodriguez	35.00	17.50	7.00
(17)	Octavio Rubert	30.00	15.00	6.00
(18)	Rene Solis	30.00	15.00	6.00
	CIENFUEGOS ELEPHANTS			
(1)	Bob Addis	35.00	17.50	7.00
(2)	Sam Calderone	35.00	17.50	7.00
(3)	Jack Cassini	35.00	17.50	7.00
(4)	Alejandro Crespo	35.00	17.50	7.00
(5)	Paul (Al) Epperly	35.00	17.50	7.00
(6)	Thomas Fine	35.00	17.50	7.00
(7)	Pedro Formental (Formenthal)	30.00	15.00	6.00
(8)	Francisco Gallardo	30.00	15.00	6.00
(9)	Lloyd Gearhart	35.00	17.50	7.00
(10)	Leonardo Goicochea	30.00	15.00	6.00
(11)	Salvador Hernandez	35.00	17.50	7.00
(12)	Clarence (Buddy) Hicks	35.00	17.50	7.00
(13)	Max Manning	45.00	22.00	9.00
(14)	San (Ray) Noble	35.00	17.50	7.00
(15)	Regino Otero	35.00	17.50	7.00
(16)	Pedro Pages	30.00	15.00	6.00
(17)	Napoleon Reyes	35.00	17.50	7.00
(18)	Ernie Shore	35.00	17.50	7.00
(19)	Adrian Zabala	35.00	17.50	7.00
	HAVANA LIONS			
(1)	Ferrell Anderson	35.00	17.50	7.00
(2)	Wess Bailey	30.00	15.00	6.00
(3)	Vic Barnhart	35.00	17.50	7.00
(4)	Herberto Blanco	30.00	15.00	6.00
(5)	Emilio Cabrera	30.00	15.00	6.00
(6)	Pedro Formental (Formenthal)	30.00	15.00	6.00
(7)	Al Gerheauser	35.00	17.50	7.00
(8)	Miguel Angel Gonzalez	60.00	30.00	12.00
(9)	Chino Hidalgo	30.00	15.00	6.00
(10)	Jimmy Lenhart	30.00	15.00	6.00
(11)	Adolfo Luque	60.00	30.00	12.00
(12)	Max Manning	45.00	22.50	9.00
(13)	Julio Moreno	35.00	17.50	7.00
(14)	Lenox Pearson	45.00	22.50	9.00
(15)	Don Richmond	35.00	17.50	7.00
(16)	John Ford Smith	30.00	15.00	6.00
(17)	Don Thompson	35.00	17.50	7.00
(18)	Gilberto Torres	35.00	17.50	7.00
	MARIANAO TIGERS			
(1)	Mario Arencibia	30.00	15.00	6.00
(2)	Carlos Blanco	30.00	15.00	6.00
(3)	Chiquitin Cabbera	30.00	15.00	6.00
(4)	Sandalio Consuegra	35.00	17.50	7.00
(5)	Reinaldo Cordeiro	30.00	15.00	6.00
(6)	Talua (Ray) Dandridge	350.00	175.00	75.00
(7)	Mario Diaz	30.00	15.00	6.00
(8)	Claro Duany	35.00	17.50	7.00
(9)	Roberto Estalella	35.00	17.50	7.00
(10)	Chicuelo Garcia	30.00	15.00	6.00
(11)	Wesley Hamner	35.00	17.50	7.00
(12)	Rollie Hemsley	35.00	17.50	7.00
(13)	Amado Ibanez	30.00	15.00	6.00
(14)	Limonar (Rogelio) Martinez	35.00	17.50	7.00
(15)	Don Phillips	30.00	15.00	6.00
(16)	Bartholomew (Jim) Prendergast	35.00	17.50	7.00
(17)	John Trouppe	35.00	17.50	7.00

1904 Allegheny Card Co.

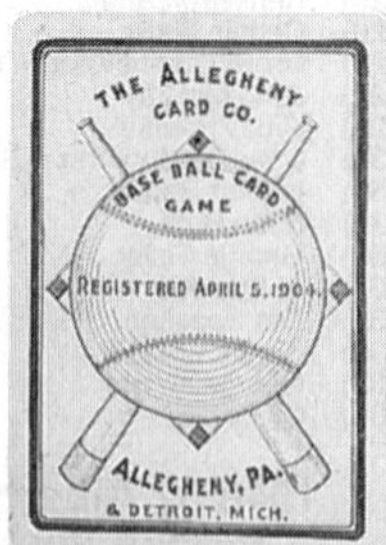

By definition the rarest card issue of the early 20th Century is this baseball game set featuring only National League players. It is thought that the sole known boxed set was produced as a prototype and never actually reached distribution. The issue contains 104 player cards and a "Ball Counter" card for each team. Cards are in playing-card format, about 2-1/2" x 3-1/2" with rounded corners. Backs are printed in red with baseball equipment pictured. Fronts are printed in blue with a circular player portrait at center. Team name is at top, with player's last name (occasionally with initials and occasionally misspelled) beneath. The unique boxed set was discovered in the late 1980s. It was sold at auction in 1991 for $26,400, and again in 1995 for $11,000, after which it was broken up for individual card sales. The checklist is presented here in alphabetical order. All cards appear to have been hand-cut.

		NM	EX	VG
Common Player:		1,500	750.00	450.00
(1)	Ed Abbaticchio	1,500	750.00	450.00
(2)	Harry Aubrey	1,500	750.00	450.00
(3)	Charlie Babb	1,500	750.00	450.00
(4)	George Barclay	1,500	750.00	450.00
(5)	Shad Barry	1,500	750.00	450.00
(6)	Bill Beagen (Bergen)	1,500	750.00	450.00
(7)	Ginger Beaumont	1,500	750.00	450.00
(8)	Jake Beckley	2,500	875.00	525.00
(9)	Frank Bowerman	1,500	750.00	450.00
(10)	Dave Brain	1,500	750.00	450.00
(11)	Kitty Bransfield	1,500	750.00	450.00
(12)	Roger Bresnahan	2,500	875.00	525.00
(13)	Mordecai Brown	2,500	875.00	525.00
(14)	George Browne	1,500	750.00	450.00
(15)	Al Buckenberger	1,500	750.00	450.00
(16)	Jimmy Burke	1,500	750.00	450.00
(17)	Fred Carisch	1,500	750.00	450.00
(18)	Pat Carney	1,500	750.00	450.00
(19)	Doc Casey	1,500	750.00	450.00
(20)	Frank Chance	3,000	875.00	525.00
(21)	Fred Clarke	2,500	875.00	525.00
(22)	Dick Cooley	1,500	750.00	450.00
(23)	Bill Dahlen	1,750	750.00	450.00
(24)	Tom Daly	1,500	750.00	450.00
(25)	Charlie Dexter	1,500	750.00	450.00
(26)	Johnny Dobbs	1,500	750.00	450.00
(27)	Mike Donlin	1,500	750.00	450.00
(28)	Patsy Donovan	1,500	750.00	450.00
(29)	Red Dooin	1,500	750.00	450.00
(30)	Klondike Douglas (Douglass)	1,500	750.00	450.00
(31)	Jack Doyle	1,500	750.00	450.00
(32)	Bill Duggleby	1,500	750.00	450.00
(33)	Jack Dunn	1,500	750.00	270.00
(34)	Johnny Evers	3,000	875.00	525.00
(35)	John Farrel (Farrell)	1,500	750.00	450.00
(36)	Tim Flood	1,500	750.00	450.00
(37)	Chick Fraser	1,500	750.00	450.00
(38)	Ned Garver	1,500	750.00	450.00
(39)	Doc Gessler	1,500	750.00	450.00
(40)	Billy Gilbert	1,500	750.00	450.00
(41)	Kid Gleason	2,500	750.00	450.00
(42)	Ed Greminger (Gremminger)	1,500	750.00	450.00
(43)	Jim Hackett	1,500	750.00	450.00
(44)	Noodles Hahn	1,500	750.00	450.00
(45)	Ed. Hanlon	2,500	875.00	525.00
(46)	Jack Harper	1,500	750.00	450.00
(47)	Rudy Hulswitt	1,500	750.00	450.00
(48)	Fred Jacklitsch	1,500	750.00	450.00
(49)	Davy Jones	1,500	750.00	450.00
(50)	Oscar Jones	1,500	750.00	450.00
(51)	Bill Keister	1,500	750.00	450.00
(52)	Joe Kelley	2,500	875.00	525.00
(53)	Brickyard Kennedy	1,500	750.00	450.00
(54)	Johnny Kling	1,500	750.00	450.00
(55)	Otto Kruger (Krueger)	1,500	750.00	450.00
(56)	Tommy Leach	1,500	750.00	450.00
(57)	Sam Leever	1,500	750.00	450.00
(58)	Bobby Lowe	1,750	875.00	525.00
(59)	Carl Lundgren	1,500	750.00	450.00
(60)	Christy Mathewson	8,000	2,000	1,200
(61)	Tom McCreery	1,500	750.00	450.00
(62)	Chappie McFarland	1,500	750.00	450.00
(63)	Dan McGann	1,500	750.00	450.00
(64)	Iron Man McGinnity	2,500	875.00	525.00
(65)	John McGraw	2,500	875.00	525.00
(66)	Jock Menefee	1,500	750.00	450.00
(67)	Sam Mertes	1,500	750.00	450.00
(68)	Fred Mitchell	1,500	750.00	450.00
(69)	Pat Moran	1,500	750.00	450.00
(70)	Ed Murphy	1,500	750.00	450.00
(71)	Jack O'Neill	1,500	750.00	450.00
(72)	Mike O'Neill	1,500	750.00	450.00
(73)	Heinie Peitz	1,500	750.00	450.00
(74)	Ed Phelps	1,500	750.00	450.00
(75)	Deacon Phillippe	1,500	750.00	450.00
(76)	Togie Pittinger	1,500	750.00	450.00
(77)	Ed Poole	1,500	750.00	450.00
(78)	Tommy Raub	1,500	750.00	450.00
(79)	Bill Reidy	1,500	750.00	450.00
(80)	Claude Ritchie	1,500	750.00	450.00
(81)	Lew Ritter	1,500	750.00	450.00
(82)	Frank Roth	1,500	750.00	450.00
(83)	Jack Ryan	1,500	750.00	450.00
(84)	Jimmy Scheckard (Sheckard)	1,500	750.00	450.00
(85)	Jimmy Sebring	1,500	750.00	450.00
(86)	Frank Selee	7,500	2,000	1,200
(87)	Cy Seymour	1,500	750.00	450.00
(88)	Harry Smith	1,500	750.00	450.00
(89)	Homer Smoot	1,500	750.00	450.00
(90)	Tully Sparks	1,500	750.00	450.00
(91)	Joe Stanley	1,500	750.00	450.00
(92)	Harry Steinfeldt	1,500	750.00	450.00
(93)	Sammy Strang	1,500	750.00	450.00
(94)	Jack Suthoff (Sutthoff)	1,500	750.00	450.00
(95)	Jack Taylor	1,500	750.00	450.00
(96)	Luther Taylor	1,750	875.00	525.00
(97)	Roy Thomas	1,500	750.00	450.00
(98)	Joe Tinker	1,750	875.00	525.00
(99)	Fred Tinney (Tenney)	1,500	750.00	450.00
(100)	Honus Wagner	10,000	2,000	1,200
(101)	Jack Warner	1,500	750.00	450.00
(102)	Jake Weimer	1,500	750.00	450.00
(103)	Vic Willis	1,750	875.00	525.00
(104)	Harry Wolverton	1,500	750.00	450.00
(105)	Boston Ball Counter	165.00	80.00	50.00
(106)	Brooklyn Ball Counter	165.00	80.00	50.00
(107)	Chicago Ball Counter	165.00	80.00	50.00
(108)	Cincinnati Ball Counter	165.00	80.00	50.00
(109)	New York Ball Counter	165.00	80.00	50.00
(110)	Philadelphia Ball Counter	165.00	80.00	50.00
(111)	Pittsburgh Ball Counter	165.00	80.00	50.00
(112)	St. Louis Ball Counter	165.00	80.00	50.00

1888 Allen & Ginter World's Champions (N28)

This 50-card set was titled "The World Champions" and includes 10 baseball players and 40 other sports personalities such as John L. Sullivan and Buffalo Bill Cody. The approximately 1-1/2" x 2-3/4" cards were inserted in boxes of

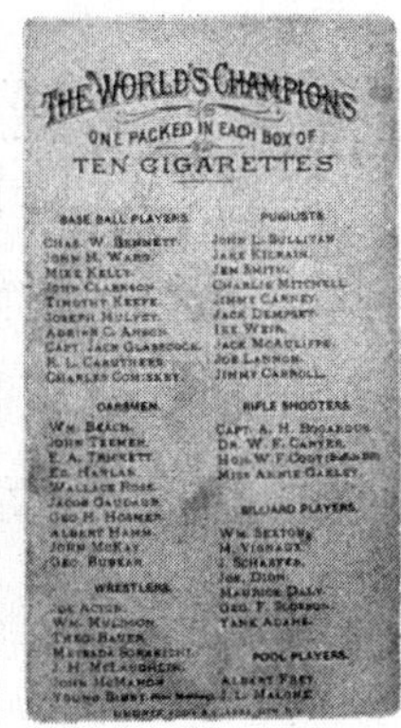

Allen & Ginter cigarettes. The card fronts are color lithographs on white card stock, and are considered among the most attractive cards ever produced. All card backs have a complete checklist for this unnumbered set, which includes six eventual Hall of Famers.

	NM	EX	VG
Complete Set (10):	16,750	8,250	5,500
Common Player:	850.00	425.00	250.00
(1) Adrian C. Anson	6,000	2,500	1,500
(2) Chas. W. Bennett	1,000	425.00	250.00
(3) R.L. Caruthers	1,000	425.00	250.00
(4) John Clarkson	2,500	925.00	550.00
(5) Charles Comiskey	3,000	1,300	760.00
(6) Capt. John Glasscock	1,000	425.00	250.00
(7) Timothy Keefe	2,500	875.00	500.00
(8) Mike Kelly	4,000	1,500	900.00
(9) Joseph Mulvey	1,000	425.00	250.00
(10) John Ward	2,500	875.00	500.00

1888 Allen & Ginter World's Champions Album (A16)

By redeeming 50 of the coupons found in boxes of A&G cigarettes, a lithographed album could be obtained in which to house the 50 cards of The World's Champions, Series 1 (N28). About 6" x 8", the album features an ornately decorated cover reproducing the cards of the day's top atlhletes, John L. Sullivan and Monte Ward. The back cover is blank. Inside, secured by means of string ties at three places, are 12 dual-sided color pages on which to glue the cards in the series. The album had its own designation in the American Card Catalog, A16.

	NM	EX	VG
World's Champions Album (A16)	4,500	2,500	1,250

1888 Allen & Ginter World's Champions (N29)

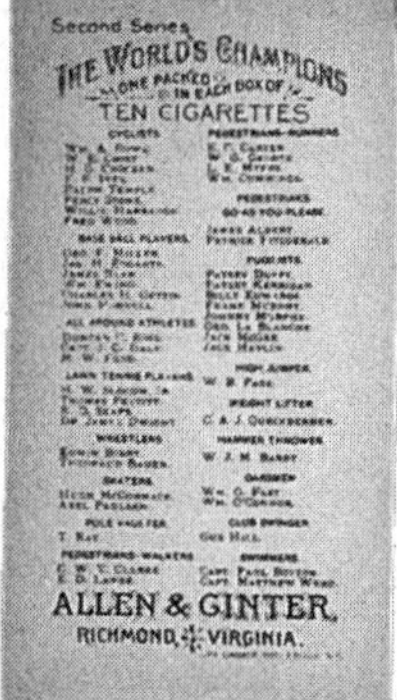

Building on the success of its first series of tobacco cards, Allen & Ginter issued a second series of "World Champions" in 1888. Once again, 50 of these approximately 1-1/2" x 2-3/4" color cards were produced, in virtually the same format. Only six baseball players are included in this set. The most obvious difference from the first series cards is the absence of the Allen & Ginter name on the card fronts.

	NM	EX	VG
Complete Set (6):	9,350	4,675	2,750
Common Player:	1,050	400.00	300.00
(1) Wm. Ewing	3,000	1,100	850.00
(2) Jas. H. Fogarty (Middle initial actually G.)	1,050	400.00	300.00
(3) Charles H. Getzin (Getzien)	1,050	400.00	300.00
(4) Geo. F. Miller	1,050	400.00	300.00
(5) John Morrell (Morrill)	1,150	450.00	325.00
(6) James Ryan	1,050	400.00	300.00

1888 Allen & Ginter World's Champions Album (A17)

By redeeming 50 of the coupons found in boxes of A&G cigarettes, a lithographed album could be obtained in which to house the 50 cards of The World's Champions, Series 2 (N29). About 6" x 8", the album features a handsomely decorated cover of a trumpeteer. The back cover is also in color with A&G's pipe-smoking man logo. Inside, secured by means of string ties at three places, are 12 dual-sided color pages on which to glue the cards in the series. The album had its own designation in the American Card Catalog, A16.

	NM	EX	VG
World's Champions Album (A17)	4,000	2,000	1,000

1888 Allen & Ginter World's Champions (N43)

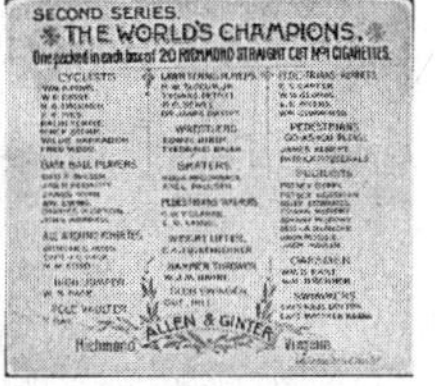

Presumably issued in a larger-than-standard cigarette package, the 50 cards designated N43 in the "American Card Catalog" are enhanced versions of the Allen & Ginter World's Champions (N29) series of 1888. As with the N29 set, six of the athletes in N43 are baseball players. The larger cards measure about 3-1/4" x 2-7/8" compared to the 1-1/2" x 2-3/4" size of the N29s. The larger format allows for the use of baseball-related color lithography to the right and left of the central player portrait. Like the N29 cards, backs of the N43 A&Gs present the entire "Series Two" checklist along with advertising of the Richmond tobacco company. Only the baseball players are cataloged here.

	NM	EX	VG
Complete Set (6):	26,400	14,000	7,700
Common Player:	3,850	1,500	1,000
(1) Wm. Ewing	7,150	3,000	2,500
(2) Jas. H. Fogarty (Middle initial actually G.)	3,850	1,500	1,000
(3) Charles H. Getzin (Getzien)	3,850	1,500	1,000
(4) Geo. F. Miller	3,850	1,500	1,000
(5) John Morrell (Morrill)	3,850	1,700	1,100
(6) James Ryan	3,850	1,500	1,000

1888 Allen & Ginter Girl Baseball Players (N48, N508)

At least three different brands of cigarette advertising can be found on the several different styles of photographic cards depicting women in baseball uniforms. About 1-1/2" x 2-5/8", the cards picture models, rather than real ballplayers. The sepia-toned full-length photos are usually captioned with a position and a number and have a small square or other device advertising a particular brand. Some Dixie- and Virginia Brights-brand cards are known with advertising on back but most cards are blank-backed. As many as 36 different photos are thought to exist.

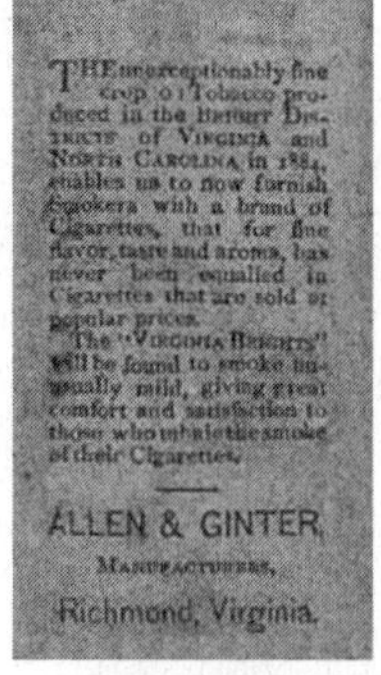

	NM	EX	VG
Ad Backs: 2X			
Common Player	650.00	325.00	200.00

1946-1947 Almanaque Deportivo

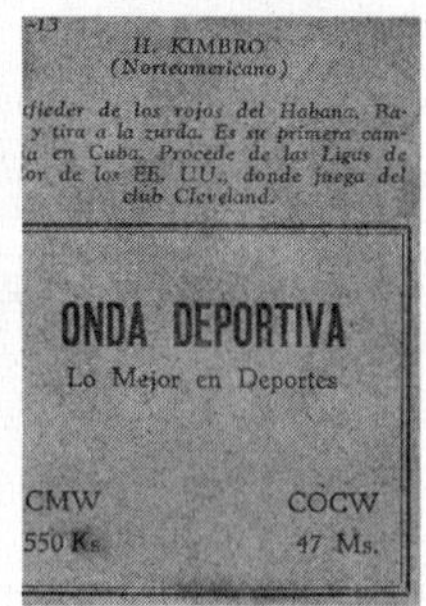

Former and future Major Leaguers mix with Negro Leaguers and Caribbean stars in this issue. Apparently sold in sheets of four, well-cut examples of these cards measure a nominal 1-7/8" x 2-1/2" and are printed in color on thin paper. Player identification is on the back of the card, usually with career notes and a large advertisement from one of many different sponsors. A colorful album was issued to house the set. Like all Cuban cards of the era, specimens surviving in grades of VG or better are scarce.

	NM	EX	VG
Complete Set (160):	6,000	3,000	1,800
Common Player:	35.00	17.50	10.00
Album:	400.00	200.00	120.00
A-1 Adolfo Luque	60.00	30.00	20.00
A-2 Tomas de la Cruz	35.00	17.50	10.00
A-3 Roberto Ortiz	45.00	22.50	13.50
A-4 Evelio Martinez	35.00	17.50	10.00
A-5 Jess Jessup	90.00	45.00	27.50
A-6 Santos Amaro	35.00	17.50	10.00
A-7 Rene Gonzalez	35.00	17.50	10.00
A-8 Buck O'Neil	625.00	310.00	185.00
A-9 J. (Lefty) Gaines	90.00	45.00	27.50
A-10 Max Lanier	45.00	22.50	13.50
A-11 George Hausmann	35.00	17.50	10.00
A-12 Avelino Canizares	35.00	17.50	10.00
A-13 Calampio Leon	35.00	17.50	10.00
A-14 Conrado Marrero	50.00	25.00	15.00
A-15 Alberto Leal	35.00	17.50	10.00
A-16 Lloyd Davenport	90.00	45.00	27.50
A-17 Teodoro Oxamendi	35.00	17.50	10.00
A-18 Santiago Ulrich	35.00	17.50	10.00
A-19 Lazaro Salazar	100.00	50.00	30.00
A-20 Cheo Ramos	35.00	17.50	10.00
A-21 Jorge Comellas	35.00	17.50	10.00
A-22 Agapito Mayor	35.00	17.50	10.00
A-23 Hector Rodriguez	45.00	22.50	13.50
A-24 Joe Williams	35.00	17.50	10.00
A-25 Andres Fleitas	35.00	17.50	10.00
C-1 Martin Dihigo	500.00	250.00	150.00
C-2 Alejandro Carrasquel	35.00	17.50	10.00
C-3 Adrian Zabala	35.00	17.50	10.00
C-4 Jimmy Roy	35.00	17.50	10.00
C-5 Napoleon Reyes	80.00	40.00	25.00
C-6 Stanislas Bread	35.00	17.50	10.00
C-7 Roland Gladu	35.00	17.50	10.00
C-8 Roy Zimmerman	35.00	17.50	10.00
C-9 Max Manning	125.00	62.50	37.50
C-10 Myron Hayworth	35.00	17.50	10.00
C-11 Pedro Miro	35.00	17.50	10.00
C-12 Jose Luis Colas	35.00	17.50	10.00
C-13 Conrado Perez	35.00	17.50	10.00
C-14 Luis Tiant Sr.	45.00	22.50	13.50
C-15 Ramon Heredia	35.00	17.50	10.00
C-16 Vinicio Garcia	35.00	17.50	10.00
C-17 (Walt) Nothe	35.00	17.50	10.00
C-18 Danny Gardella	35.00	17.50	10.00
C-19 Alejandro Crespo	60.00	30.00	20.00
C-20 Ray Noble	35.00	17.50	10.00
C-21 Pedro Pages	35.00	17.50	10.00
F-1 Napoleon y C. Blanco/Action	35.00	17.50	10.00
F-2 Chanquilon y H. Rodriguez/Action	35.00	17.50	10.00
F-3 Estalella y Fleitas/Action	35.00	17.50	10.00
F-4 Castano y Kimbro/Action	35.00	17.50	10.00
H-1 Miguel Angel Gonzalez	55.00	27.50	16.50
H-2 Pedro (Natilla) Jimenez	35.00	17.50	10.00
H-3 Fred Martin	35.00	17.50	10.00

H-4	James Lamarque	80.00	40.00	25.00
H-5	Salvador Hernandez	35.00	17.50	10.00
H-6	S. (Hank) Thompson	50.00	25.00	15.00
H-7	Antonio Ordenana	35.00	17.50	10.00
H-8	Manuel Garcia	35.00	17.50	10.00
H-9	Alberto Hernandez	35.00	17.50	10.00
H-10	Terry McDuffie	45.00	22.50	13.50
H-11	Louis Frank Klein	35.00	17.50	10.00
H-12	Herberto Blanco	35.00	17.50	10.00
H-13	H.(Henry) Kimbro	150.00	75.00	45.00
H-14	Rene Monteagudo	35.00	17.50	10.00
H-15	Lennox Pearson	100.00	50.00	30.00
H-16	Carlos Blanco	35.00	17.50	10.00
H-17	Pedro Formental	55.00	27.50	16.50
H-18	William Bell	35.00	17.50	10.00
H-19	Raul Navarro	35.00	17.50	10.00
H-20	Lazaro Medina	35.00	17.50	10.00
L-1	Julio Moreno	35.00	17.50	10.00
L-2	Daniel Parra	35.00	17.50	10.00
L-3	Rogelio Martinez	35.00	17.50	10.00
L-4	J. Antonio Zardon	35.00	17.50	10.00
L-5	Julian Acosta	35.00	17.50	10.00
L-6	Orlando Suarez	35.00	17.50	10.00
L-7	Manuel Hidalgo	35.00	17.50	10.00
L-8	Fermin Guerra	35.00	17.50	10.00
L-9	Regino Otero	35.00	17.50	10.00
L-10	Jorge Juan Torres	35.00	17.50	10.00
L-11	Valeriano Fano	35.00	17.50	10.00
L-12	Amado Ibanez	35.00	17.50	10.00
L-13	"Atares" Garcia	35.00	17.50	10.00
L-14	Armando Gallart	35.00	17.50	10.00
L-15	Perdo Dunabeitia	35.00	17.50	10.00
L-16	Oscar del Calvo	35.00	17.50	10.00
L-17	Johnny Davis	100.00	50.00	30.00
L-18	Emilio Cabrera	35.00	17.50	10.00
L-19	Lee Holleman	35.00	17.50	10.00
L-20	Antonio Napoles	35.00	17.50	10.00
L-21	Pedro Diaz	35.00	17.50	10.00
L-22	Lazaro Bernal	35.00	17.50	10.00
L-23	Hector Arago	35.00	17.50	10.00
L-24	Oscar Garmendia	35.00	17.50	10.00
L-25	Barney Serrell	90.00	45.00	27.50
L-26	Armando Marsans	55.00	27.50	16.50
L-27	Mario Diaz	35.00	17.50	10.00
L-28	Raymond Dandridge	350.00	175.00	105.00
L-29	Leon Tredway	35.00	17.50	10.00
L-30	Orestes Perera	35.00	17.50	10.00
L-31	Armando Vazquez	35.00	17.50	10.00
L-32	Cleveland Clark	50.00	25.00	15.00
L-33	Johnny Williams	90.00	45.00	27.50
L-34	Clarence Iott	35.00	17.50	10.00
L-35	Gilberto Torres	35.00	17.50	10.00
L-36	George Brown	35.00	17.50	10.00
L-37	Wayne Johnson	35.00	17.50	10.00
L-38	Miguel Angel Carmona	35.00	17.50	10.00
L-39	Leovigildo Xiques	35.00	17.50	10.00
L-40	Rafael Rivas	35.00	17.50	10.00
L-41	Joaquin Gutierrez	35.00	17.50	10.00
L-42	Miguel Lastra	35.00	17.50	10.00
L-43	Francisco Quicutis	35.00	17.50	10.00
L-44	Silvio Garcia	90.00	45.00	27.50
L-45	Angel Fleitas	35.00	17.50	10.00
L-46	Eddy Chandler	35.00	17.50	10.00
L-47	Gilberto Castillo	35.00	17.50	10.00
L-48	Isidoro Leon	35.00	17.50	10.00
L-49	Antonio Rodriguez	35.00	17.50	10.00
L-50	Laniel Hooker	90.00	45.00	27.50
L-51	Charles Perez	35.00	17.50	10.00
L-52	Ruben Garcia	35.00	17.50	10.00
L-53	Raquel Antunez	35.00	17.50	10.00
L-54	Claro Duany	45.00	22.50	13.50
L-55	Bucker (Booker) McDaniels	90.00	45.00	27.50
L-56	Francisco Jimenez	35.00	17.50	10.00
L-57	Luis Minsal	35.00	17.50	10.00
L-58	Rogelio Linares	35.00	17.50	10.00
L-59	Isasio Gonzalez	35.00	17.50	10.00
L-60	Manolo Parrado	35.00	17.50	10.00
L-61	Jose Maria Fernandez	35.00	17.50	10.00
L-62	Rogelio Valdes	35.00	17.50	10.00
L-63	R. Franco	35.00	17.50	10.00
L-64	J. Cedan	35.00	17.50	10.00
L-65	Jacinto Roque	35.00	17.50	10.00
L-66	Pablo Garcia	35.00	17.50	10.00
M-1	Pipo de la Noval	35.00	17.50	10.00
M-2	J. Valenzuela	35.00	17.50	10.00
M-3	Oliverio Ortiz	35.00	17.50	10.00
M-4	Antonio Castanos	35.00	17.50	10.00
M-5	Sandalio Consuegra	45.00	22.50	13.50
M-6	(Jim) Lindsey	35.00	17.50	10.00
M-7	Roberto Estalella	35.00	17.50	10.00
M-8	Lino Donoso	35.00	17.50	10.00
M-9	Paul Calvert	35.00	17.50	10.00
M-10	Gilberto Valdivia	35.00	17.50	10.00
M-11	Orestes Minoso	125.00	65.00	37.50
M-12	J. Cabrera	35.00	17.50	10.00
M-13	Manuel Godinez	35.00	17.50	10.00
M-14	Frank Casanovas	35.00	17.50	10.00
M-15	Roberto Avila	60.00	30.00	20.00
M-16	Pedro Orta	35.00	17.50	10.00
M-17	Feliciano Castro	35.00	17.50	10.00
M-18	Mario Arencibia	35.00	17.50	10.00
M-19	Antonio Diaz	35.00	17.50	10.00
M-20	Aristonico Correoso	35.00	17.50	10.00
M-21	Angel Gonzalez	35.00	17.50	10.00
M-22	Murray Franklin	35.00	17.50	10.00
M-23	Francisco Campos	35.00	17.50	10.00
M-24	Angel Castro	35.00	17.50	10.00

1910 All Star Base-Ball

This rare set was issued circa 1910 by candy maker J.H. Dockman & Son. The cards, measuring approximately 1-7/8" x 3-3/8", were printed on the front and back of boxes of candy sold as "All Star Base-Ball Package." There are two players on each box; one on front (with a thumbnail notch at top), the other on back. The cards consist of drawings that bear no resemblance to the player named. In fact, the artwork on

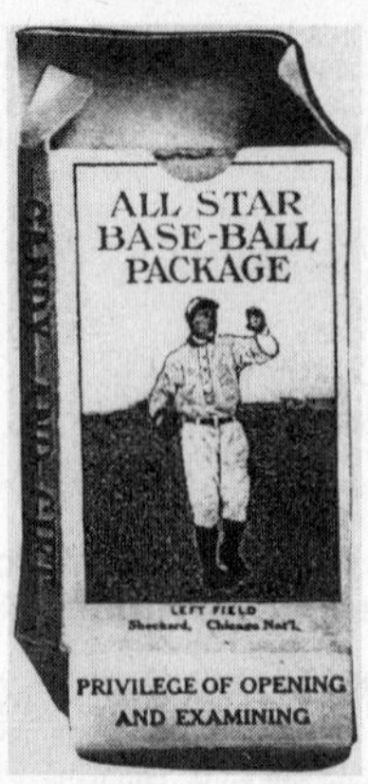

these cards crudely reproduces the images from the T3 Turkey Red cabinet series, giving a different player's name to each of the borrowed images. Many are found which were cut from the box immediately below the "PACKAGE" line, while others were cut to the full size of the panel. Values shown here presume the latter format.

		NM	EX	VG
Complete Set (24):		50,000	25,000	12,500
Common Player:		1,800	900.00	500.00
(1)	Johnny Bates	1,800	900.00	500.00
(2)	Heinie Beckendorf	1,800	900.00	500.00
(3)	Joe Birmingham	1,800	900.00	500.00
(4)	Roger Bresnahan	2,400	1,200	800.00
(5)	Al Burch	1,800	900.00	500.00
(6)	Donie Bush	1,800	900.00	500.00
(7)	Frank Chance	2,400	1,200	800.00
(8)	Ty Cobb	4,000	2,000	1,200
(9)	Wid Conroy	1,800	900.00	500.00
(10)	Jack Coombs	1,800	900.00	500.00
(11)	George Gibson	1,800	900.00	500.00
(12)	Dick Hoblitzel	1,800	900.00	500.00
(13)	Johnny Kling	1,800	900.00	500.00
(14)	Frank LaPorte	1,800	900.00	500.00
(15)	Ed Lennox	1,800	900.00	500.00
(16)	Connie Mack	2,400	1,200	800.00
(17)	Christy Mathewson	4,500	2,250	1,375
(18)	Matty McIntyre	1,800	900.00	500.00
(19)	Al Schweitzer	1,800	900.00	500.00
(20)	Jimmy Sheckard	1,800	900.00	500.00
(21)	Bill Sweeney	1,800	900.00	500.00
(22)	Terry Turner	1,800	900.00	500.00
(23)	Hans Wagner	3,600	1,800	1,100
(24)	Harry Wolter	1,800	900.00	500.00

1950 All-Star Baseball "Pin-Ups"

This set of 10 7" diameter black-and-white player photos was issued in the form of a booklet, with the individual pictures perforated to be punched out. Each picture has a hole at the top for hanging. The front and back cover of the book are identical and picture Ted Williams, along with a list of the players inside. Backs of each player picture have how-to tips for playing a specific position, hitting, base stealing, etc. Published by Garden City Publishing Co., Inc., the book carried a cover price of 50 cents. The unnumbered pictures are checklisted here alphabetically.

		NM	EX	VG
Complete Book:		1,250	625.00	375.00
Complete Set, Singles (10):		800.00	400.00	240.00
Common Player:		25.00	12.50	7.50
(1)	Joe DiMaggio	200.00	100.00	60.00
(2)	Jim Hegan	25.00	12.50	7.50
(3)	Gil Hodges	75.00	37.50	22.50
(4)	George Kell	35.00	17.50	10.00
(5)	Ralph Kiner	45.00	22.50	13.50
(6)	Stan Musial	100.00	50.00	30.00
(7)	Mel Parnell	25.00	12.50	7.50
(8)	Phil Rizzuto	75.00	37.50	22.50
(9)	Jackie Robinson	150.00	75.00	45.00
(10)	Ted Williams	150.00	75.00	45.00

1954 All-Star Photo Pack

The complete checklist for this series of 6" x 8-3/4" blank-back, black-and-white player photos is unknown. The method of distribution is also speculative, though it is most likely they were sold in photo packs at concession stands. Photos,

mostly posed action shots, are bordered in white and have the player name in a white strip near the bottom.

		NM	EX	VG
Complete Set (24):		400.00	200.00	120.00
Common Player:		10.00	5.00	3.00
(1)	Bobby Avila	10.00	5.00	3.00
(2)	Ernie Banks	25.00	12.50	7.50
(3)	Larry "Yogi" Berra	25.00	12.50	7.50
(4)	Ray Boone	10.00	5.00	3.00
(5)	Roy Campanella	25.00	12.50	7.50
(6)	Alvin Dark	10.00	5.00	3.00
(7)	Mike Garcia	10.00	5.00	3.00
(8)	Al Kaline	20.00	10.00	6.00
(9)	Ralph Kiner	15.00	7.50	4.50
(10)	Ted Kluszewski	15.00	7.50	4.50
(11)	Harvey Kuenn	10.00	5.00	3.00
(12)	Mickey Mantle	90.00	45.00	27.50
(13)	Ed Mathews	20.00	10.00	6.00
(14)	Willie Mays	50.00	25.00	15.00
(15)	Orestes Minoso	12.50	6.25	3.75
(16)	Stan Musial	35.00	17.50	10.00
(17)	Don Newcombe	12.50	6.25	3.75
(18)	Allie Reynolds	12.50	6.25	3.75
(19)	Robin Roberts	15.00	7.50	4.50
(20)	Eddie Robinson	10.00	5.00	3.00
(21)	Jackie Robinson	45.00	22.50	13.50
(22)	Al Schoendienst	15.00	7.50	4.50
(23)	Duke Snider	20.00	10.00	6.00
(24)	Ted Williams	80.00	40.00	24.00

1949 All Stars Photo Pack

This set of "American and National League All Stars" player pictures is comprised of 6-1/4" x 9" black-and-white photos bordered in white with a simulated signature printed on front. Backs are blank. The set came in a red, black and white paper envelope with several of the pictures shown on front and red stars for decoration. The unnumbered pictures are listed here alphabetically.

		NM	EX	VG
Complete Set (20):		375.00	185.00	110.00
Common Player:		12.50	6.00	4.00
(1)	Luke Appling	17.50	9.00	5.00
(2)	Lou Boudreau	17.50	9.00	5.00
(3)	Dom DiMaggio	15.00	7.50	4.50
(4)	Joe DiMaggio	60.00	30.00	18.00
(5)	Bobby Doerr	17.50	9.00	5.00
(6)	Bob Feller	25.00	12.50	7.50
(7)	Joe Gordon	12.50	6.00	4.00
(8)	Tommy Henrich	12.50	6.00	4.00
(9)	George Kell	17.50	9.00	5.00
(10)	Ralph Kiner	17.50	9.00	5.00
(11)	Bob Lemon	17.50	9.00	5.00
(12)	Marty Marion	12.50	6.00	4.00
(13)	Stan Musial	35.00	17.50	10.00
(14)	Don Newcomb (Newcombe)	17.50	9.00	5.00
(15)	Pee Wee Reese	25.00	12.50	7.50
(16)	Phil Rizzuto	25.00	12.50	7.50
(17)	Jackie Robinson	45.00	22.50	13.50
(18)	Enos Slaughter	17.50	9.00	5.00
(19)	Vern Stephens	12.50	6.00	4.00
(20)	Ted Williams	45.00	22.50	13.50

1971 Allstate Insurance

This four-card series was distributed as part of an internal sales promotion for Allstate Insurance. Graphic artist Ray Lending, an Allstate employee, created the 2-1/2" x 3-1/4" cards in duo-tone black and green on white. Card fronts show

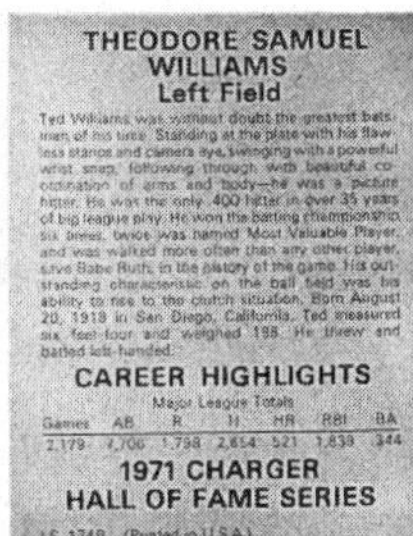

the players in batting stance, with the player name in one of the upper corners and the "Hall of Fame Series" logo printed across the bottom of the card. The card backs carry the player's full name and position, followed by a brief career summary, biography, and Career Highlights chart listing major league totals. "1971 Charger" and "Hall of Fame Series" are printed at the bottom of the card back. 8,000 sets were distributed.

	NM	EX	VG
Complete Set (4):	400.00	200.00	120.00
Common Player:	50.00	25.00	15.00
(1) Ty Cobb	50.00	25.00	15.00
(2) Stan Musial	50.00	25.00	15.00
(3) Babe Ruth	200.00	100.00	60.00
(4) Ted Williams	150.00	75.00	45.00

1894 Alpha Photo-Engraving Baltimore Orioles

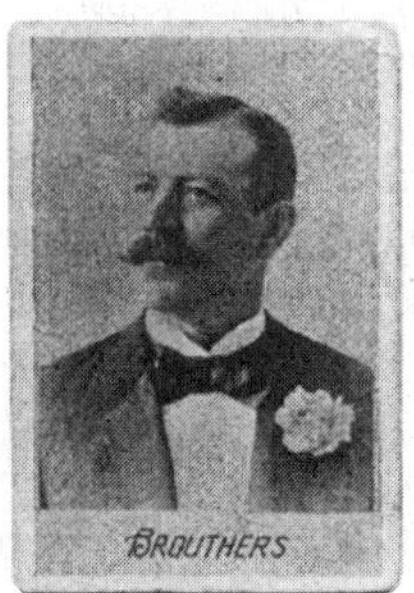

The rarest baseball card set of the 1890s (each card is known in only a single example) is the Baltimore Orioles team set issued by The Alpha Photo-Engraving Co. of that city. The round-corner 2-3/8" x 3-7/16" cards feature black-and-white photos of the National League champions in formalwear. Last-name identification is in a strip below the photo and a white border surrounds both. On the red-and-white backs a large ad for the producer is at center, while small baseball batter figures are in each corner surrounded by a leafy background. The unnumbered cards are checklisted here alphabetically, though the list may not be complete; one glaring omission is Hall of Fame outfielder Willie Keeler. In early 2006 the set was sold and broken up. Each card was authenticated and graded by SGC, with grades ranging from Fair to Very Good.

	NM	EX	VG
Common Player:			7,500
(1) Frank Bonner			7,500
(2) Steve Brodie			7,500
(3) Dan Brouthers			37,500
(4) Duke Esper			7,500
(5) Kid Gleason			7,500
(6) Ned Hanlon			32,500
(7) Bill Hawke			7,500
(8) George Hemming			7,500
(9) Hughie Jennings			32,500
(10) Joe Kelley			62,500
(11) John McGraw			62,500
(12) Sadie McMahon			7,500
(13) Heinie Reitz			7,500
(14) Wilbert Robinson			32,500

1916 Altoona Tribune

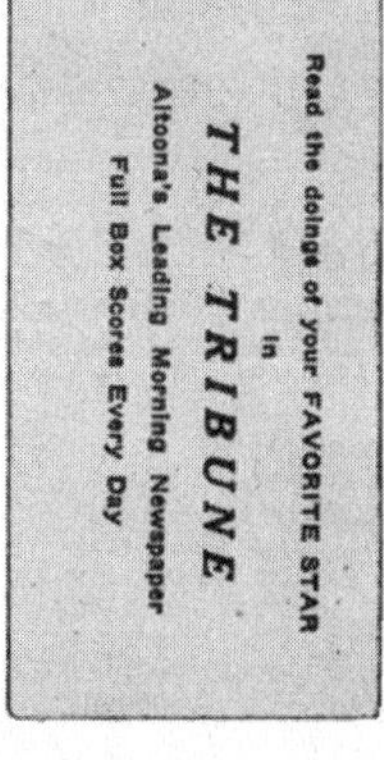

This Pennsylvania daily newspaper was one of several regional advertisers to use this black-and-white, 1-5/8" x 3" 200-card set for promotional purposes. The Altoona issue shares the checklist of the 1916 M101-4 Blank Backs. Type card and superstar collectors will pay a significant premium for a Tribune version of a specific card.

PREMIUM:
Common Player: 4-6X
Hall of Famer: 2-4X
(See 1916 M101-4 Blank Backs for checklist and base card values.)

1948 American Association Babe Ruth

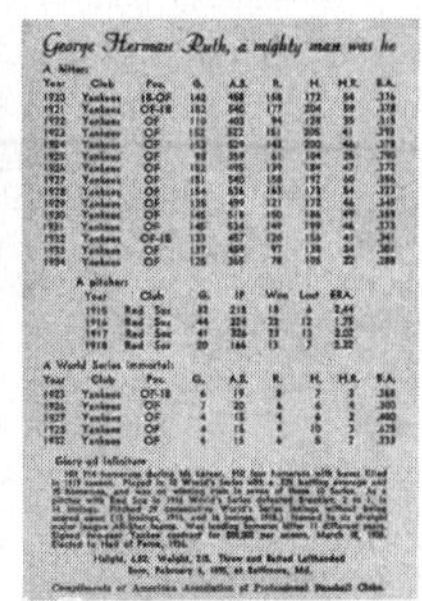

According to the credit line at bottom back (a version of the card is known without the credit line), this card was produced by the Midwestern AAA minor league known as the American Association. Recent discoveries also indicate that this card was probably both produced and issued by Pacific Coast Publishing Co. about a month after Ruth's death. The black and white card measures 4" x 5-11/16".

	NM	EX	VG
Babe Ruth	200.00	100.00	60.00

1909-11 American Beauty Cigarettes

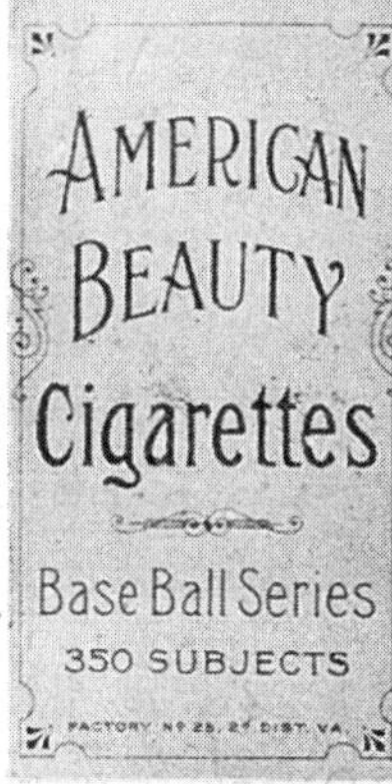

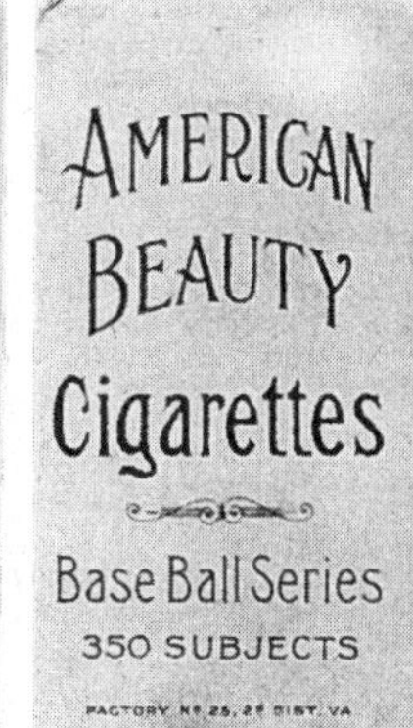

Two versions of the American Beauty Cigarettes advertising on the backs of T206 can be found; with and without a decorative border surrounding the typography, which is printed in green. All "350 Subjects" American Beauty cards originated from Factory No. 25 in Virginia. Because of the size of the original cigarette packaging in which they were a premium insert, American Beauty T206s may be a bit narrower than the standard 1-7/16". While the "350 Subjects" series is designated here as a 1910 issue, it is possible some cards were actually issued in 1909 or 1911. Among T205, AB backs may be found printed in either black or green, the latter somewhat scarcer.

PREMIUM:
T205: 2X
T206 350 Series: 1.5-2X
T206 460 Series: 2-2.5X
(See T205, T206 for checklists and base card values.
Note: Cards with American Beauty backs may be somewhat narrower than standard 1-7/16" due to smaller original cigarette packaging.)

1908 American Caramel (E91, Set A)

Issued by Philadelphia's American Caramel Co., 1908-1910, the E91 set of Base Ball Caramels has limited popularity with collectors because many of the color drawings show "generic" players rather than the named major leaguers; the same artwork was used to depict two or three different players. The player's name, position and team appear in the white border at bottom. The cards measure approximately 1-1/2" x 2-3/4" and were issued in three separate series. They can be differentiated by their backs, which checklist the cards. Set A lists the Athletics in the upper-left, the Giants at upper-right and the Cubs below. Set B lists the Cubs and Athletics on top with the Giants below, and Set C list Pittsburg and Washington on top with Boston below. A line indicating the cards were "Manufactured Only by the American Caramel Co." appears at the bottom.

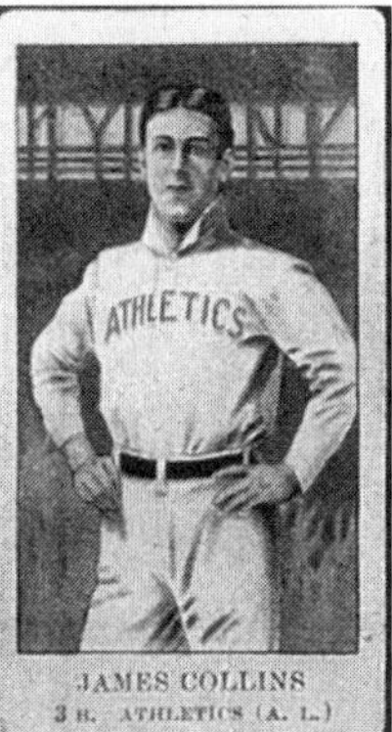

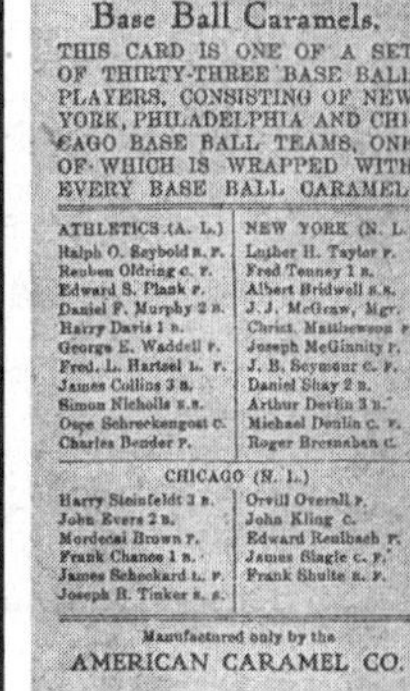

	NM	EX	VG
Complete Set (33):	10,000	4,000	2,500
Common Player:	200.00	75.00	40.00
(1) Charles Bender	425.00	175.00	100.00
(2) Roger Bresnahan	425.00	175.00	100.00
(3) Albert Bridwell	200.00	75.00	45.00
(4) Mordecai Brown	425.00	175.00	100.00
(5) Frank Chance	425.00	175.00	100.00
(6) James Collins	425.00	175.00	100.00
(7) Harry Davis	200.00	75.00	40.00
(8) Arthur Devlin	200.00	75.00	40.00
(9) Michael Donlin	200.00	75.00	40.00
(10) John Evers	425.00	175.00	100.00
(11) Frederick L. Hartsel	200.00	75.00	40.00
(12) John Kling	200.00	75.00	40.00
(13) Christopher Matthewson (Mathewson)	1,750	785.00	435.00
(14) Joseph McGinnity	425.00	175.00	100.00
(15) John J. McGraw	425.00	175.00	100.00
(16) Daniel F. Murphy	200.00	75.00	40.00
(17) Simon Nicholls	200.00	75.00	40.00
(18) Reuben Oldring	200.00	75.00	40.00
(19) Orvill Overall (Orval)	200.00	75.00	40.00
(20) Edward S. Plank	750.00	325.00	185.00
(21) Edward Reulbach	200.00	75.00	40.00
(22) James Scheckard (Sheckard)	200.00	75.00	40.00
(23) Osee Schreckengost (Ossee)	200.00	75.00	40.00
(24) Ralph O. Seybold	200.00	75.00	40.00
(25) J. Bentley Seymour	200.00	75.00	40.00
(26) Daniel Shay	200.00	75.00	40.00
(27) Frank Shulte (Schulte)	200.00	75.00	40.00
(28) James Slagle	200.00	75.00	40.00
(29) Harry Steinfeldt	200.00	75.00	40.00
(30) Luther H. Taylor	400.00	160.00	100.00
(31) Fred Tenney	200.00	75.00	40.00
(32) Joseph B. Tinker	425.00	175.00	100.00
(33) George Edward Waddell	425.00	175.00	100.00

1909 American Caramel (E91, Set B)

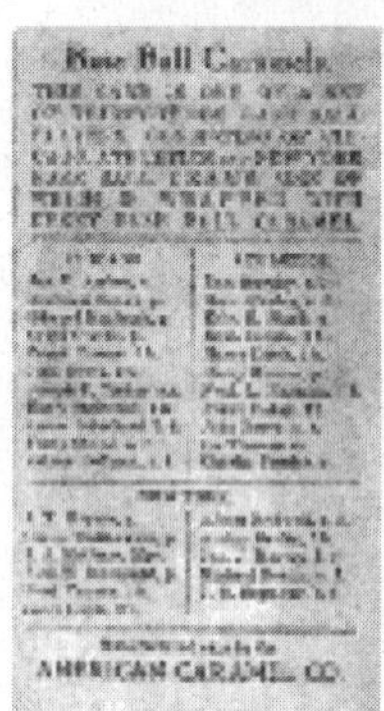

	NM	EX	VG
Complete Set (33):	9,500	4,000	2,400
Common Player:	200.00	75.00	40.00
(1) James Archer	200.00	75.00	40.00
(2) Frank Baker	425.00	175.00	100.00
(3) John Barry	200.00	75.00	40.00
(4) Charles Bender	425.00	175.00	100.00
(5) Albert Bridwell	200.00	75.00	40.00
(6) Mordecai Brown	425.00	175.00	100.00
(7) Frank Chance	425.00	175.00	100.00
(8) Edw. Collins	425.00	175.00	100.00
(9) Harry Davis	200.00	75.00	40.00
(10) Arthur Devlin	200.00	75.00	40.00
(11) Michael Donlin	200.00	75.00	40.00
(12) Larry Doyle	200.00	75.00	40.00
(13) John Evers	425.00	175.00	100.00
(14) Robt. Ganley	200.00	75.00	40.00
(15) Frederick L. Hartsel	200.00	75.00	40.00
(16) Arthur Hoffman (Hofman)	200.00	75.00	40.00
(17) Harry Krause	200.00	75.00	40.00
(18) Rich. W. Marquard	425.00	175.00	100.00
(19) Christopher Matthewson (Mathewson)	1,100	450.00	275.00
(20) John J. McGraw	425.00	175.00	100.00
(21) J.T. Meyers	200.00	75.00	40.00
(22) Dan Murphy	200.00	75.00	40.00
(23) Jno. J. Murray	200.00	75.00	40.00
(24) Orvill Overall (Orval)	200.00	75.00	40.00

		NM	EX	VG
(25)	Edward S. Plank	750.00	325.00	185.00
(26)	Edward Reulbach	200.00	75.00	40.00
(27)	James Scheckard (Sheckard)	200.00	75.00	40.00
(28)	J. Bentley Seymour	200.00	75.00	40.00
(29)	Harry Steinfeldt	200.00	75.00	40.00
(30)	Frank Shulte (Schulte)	200.00	75.00	40.00
(31)	Fred Tenney	200.00	75.00	40.00
(32)	Joseph B Tinker	425.00	175.00	100.00
(33)	Ira Thomas	200.00	75.00	40.00

1910 American Caramel (E91, Set C)

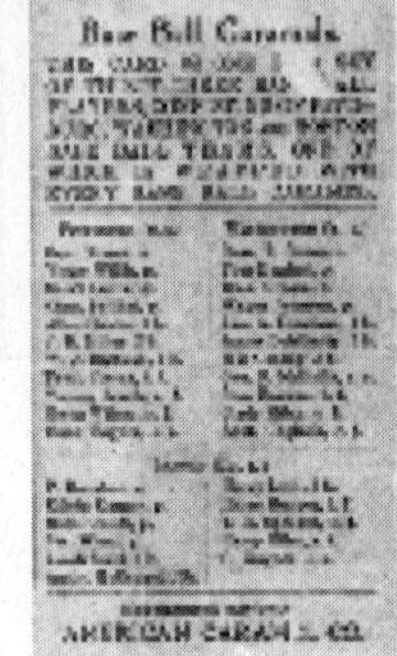

		NM	EX	VG
Complete Set (33):		11,000	4,400	2,850
Common Player:		200.00	75.00	40.00
(1)	W.J. Barbeau	200.00	75.00	40.00
(2)	Geo. Browne	200.00	75.00	40.00
(3)	Robt. Chech (Charles)	200.00	75.00	40.00
(4)	Fred Clarke	425.00	175.00	100.00
(5)	Wid Conroy	200.00	75.00	40.00
(6)	James Delehanty (Delahanty)	200.00	75.00	40.00
(7)	Jon A. Donohue (Donahue)	200.00	75.00	40.00
(8)	P. Donahue	200.00	75.00	40.00
(9)	Geo. Gibson	200.00	75.00	40.00
(10)	Robt. Groom	200.00	75.00	40.00
(11)	Harry Hooper	425.00	175.00	100.00
(12)	Tom Hughes	200.00	75.00	40.00
(13)	Walter Johnson	1,000	400.00	250.00
(14)	Edwin Karger	200.00	75.00	40.00
(15)	Tommy Leach	200.00	75.00	40.00
(16)	Sam'l Leever	200.00	75.00	40.00
(17)	Harry Lord	200.00	75.00	40.00
(18)	Geo. F. McBride	200.00	75.00	40.00
(19)	Ambr. McConnell	200.00	75.00	40.00
(20)	Clyde Milan	200.00	75.00	40.00
(21)	J.B. Miller	200.00	75.00	40.00
(22)	Harry Niles	200.00	75.00	40.00
(23)	Chas. Phillipi (Phillippe)	200.00	75.00	40.00
(24)	T.H. Speaker	650.00	275.00	125.00
(25)	Jacob Stahl	200.00	75.00	40.00
(26)	Chas. E. Street	200.00	75.00	40.00
(27)	Allen Storke	200.00	75.00	40.00
(28)	Robt. Unglaub	200.00	75.00	40.00
(29)	C. Wagner	200.00	75.00	40.00
(30)	Hans Wagner	2,900	1,250	575.00
(31)	Victor Willis	425.00	175.00	100.00
(32)	Owen Wilson	200.00	75.00	40.00
(33)	Jos. Wood	300.00	125.00	75.00

1909-11 American Caramel (E90-1)

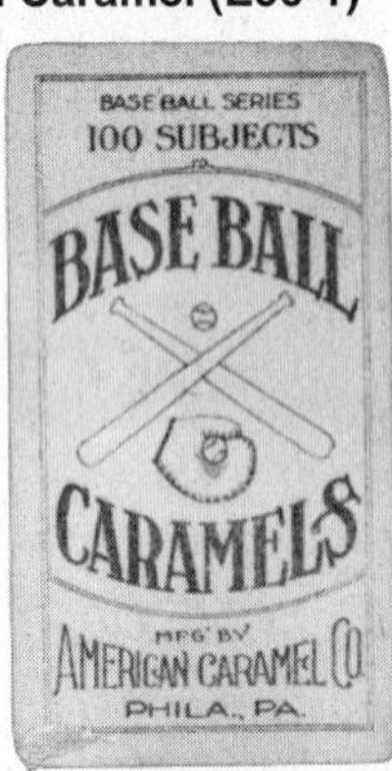

The E90-1 set was issued by the American Caramel Co. from 1909 through 1911, with the bulk of the set being produced in the first year. The cards, which nominally measure 1-1/2" x 2-3/4" (with the usual tolerances for original cutting variations), were issued with sticks of caramel candy. They are color renderings of photographs. Backs state that 100 subjects are included in the set though more actually do exist. There are several levels of scarcity in the set, those levels being mostly determined by the year the cards were issued. For the reader's convenience, the players' first names have been added in the checklist that follows. The complete set price includes all variations.

		NM	EX	VG
Complete Set (120):		150,000	75,000	40,000
Common Player:		250.00	115.00	65.00
(1)	Bill Bailey	250.00	115.00	65.00
(2)	Home Run Baker	925.00	425.00	240.00
(3)	Jack Barry	400.00	185.00	100.00
(4)	George Bell	250.00	115.00	65.00
(5)	Harry Bemis	1,200	550.00	310.00
(6)	Chief Bender	750.00	345.00	200.00
(7)	Bob Bescher	250.00	115.00	65.00
(8)	Cliff Blankenship	325.00	150.00	85.00
(9)	John Bliss	280.00	130.00	75.00
(10)	Bill Bradley	300.00	140.00	80.00
(11)	Kitty Bransfield ("P" on shirt.)	325.00	150.00	85.00
(12)	Kitty Bransfield (No "P.")	450.00	200.00	115.00
(13)	Roger Bresnahan	550.00	255.00	145.00
(14)	Al Bridwell	400.00	185.00	100.00
(15)	Buster Brown (Boston)	1,000	460.00	260.00
(16)	Mordecai Brown (Chicago)	685.00	315.00	180.00
(17)	Donie Bush	250.00	115.00	65.00
(18)	John Butler	350.00	160.00	90.00
(19)	Howie Camnitz	800.00	375.00	210.00
(20)	Frank Chance	925.00	425.00	240.00
(21)	Hal Chase	525.00	240.00	135.00
(22)	Fred Clarke (Philadelphia)	525.00	240.00	135.00
(23)	Fred Clarke (Pittsburgh)	2,625	1,200	675.00
(24)	Wally Clement	280.00	130.00	75.00
(25)	"Ty" Cobb	6,500	3,000	1,700
(26)	Eddie Collins	600.00	275.00	155.00
(27)	Sam Crawford	800.00	375.00	210.00
(28)	Frank Corridon	375.00	175.00	100.00
(29)	Lou Criger	425.00	200.00	110.00
(30)	George Davis	1,800	825.00	475.00
(31)	Harry Davis	250.00	115.00	65.00
(32)	Ray Demmitt	750.00	350.00	200.00
(33)	Mike Donlin	935.00	430.00	245.00
(34)	Wild Bill Donovan	250.00	115.00	65.00
(35)	Red Dooin	325.00	150.00	85.00
(36)	Patsy Dougherty	400.00	185.00	100.00
(37)	Hugh Duffy	4,000	1,850	1,000
(38)	Jimmy Dygert	325.00	150.00	85.00
(39)	Rube Ellis	250.00	115.00	65.00
(40)	Clyde Engle	425.00	200.00	110.00
(41)	Art Fromme	400.00	185.00	100.00
(42)	George Gibson (Back view.)	725.00	335.00	190.00
(43)	George Gibson (Front view.)	525.00	240.00	135.00
(44)	Peaches Graham	3,000	925.00	525.00
(45)	Eddie Grant	600.00	275.00	155.00
(46)	Dolly Gray	250.00	115.00	65.00
(47)	Bob Groom	375.00	175.00	100.00
(48)	Charley Hall	900.00	415.00	235.00
(49)	Roy Hartzell/Fldg	450.00	200.00	115.00
(50)	Roy Hartzell/Btg	750.00	345.00	200.00
(51)	Heinie Heitmuller	280.00	130.00	75.00
(52)	Harry Howell (Follow-through.)	650.00	300.00	175.00
(53)	Harry Howell (Wind-up.)	350.00	160.00	90.00
(54)	Tex Irwin (Erwin)	800.00	375.00	210.00
(55)	Frank Isbell	250.00	115.00	65.00
(56)	Joe Jackson	30,000	13,750	7,750
(57)	Hughie Jennings	575.00	265.00	150.00
(58)	Buck Jordon (Jordan)	250.00	115.00	65.00
(59)	Addie Joss/Portrait	750.00	350.00	200.00
(60)	Addie Joss/Pitching	2,500	700.00	400.00
(61)	Ed Karger	1,200	550.00	310.00
(62)	Willie Keeler/Portrait (Pink background.)	950.00	435.00	245.00
(63)	Willie Keeler/Portrait (Red background.)	1,900	875.00	500.00
(64)	Willie Keeler/Throwing	3,000	825.00	475.00
(65)	John Knight	500.00	230.00	130.00
(66)	Harry Krause	350.00	160.00	90.00
(67)	Nap Lajoie	1,500	700.00	400.00
(68)	Tommy Leach/Throwing	250.00	115.00	65.00
(69)	Tommy Leach/Btg	300.00	140.00	80.00
(70)	Sam Leever	250.00	115.00	65.00
(71)	Hans Lobert	1,250	575.00	325.00
(72)	Harry Lumley	325.00	150.00	85.00
(73)	Rube Marquard	875.00	400.00	225.00
(74)	Christy Matthewson (Mathewson)	3,750	1,725	975.00
(75)	Stuffy McInnes (McInnis)	250.00	115.00	65.00
(76)	Harry McIntyre	250.00	115.00	65.00
(77)	Larry McLean	5,000	1,600	910.00
(78)	George McQuillan	250.00	115.00	65.00
(79)	Dots Miller	400.00	185.00	100.00
(80)	Fred Mitchell (New York)	250.00	115.00	65.00
(81)	Mike Mitchell (Cincinnati)	12,000	5,525	3,125
(82)	George Mullin	300.00	140.00	80.00
(83)	Rebel Oakes	250.00	115.00	65.00
(84)	Paddy O'Connor	500.00	230.00	130.00
(85)	Charley O'Leary	280.00	130.00	75.00
(86)	Orval Overall	1,000	460.00	260.00
(87)	Jim Pastorius	500.00	230.00	130.00
(88)	Ed Phelps	450.00	200.00	115.00
(89)	Eddie Plank	1,700	780.00	440.00
(90)	Lew Richie	1,200	550.00	310.00
(91)	Germany Schaefer	250.00	115.00	65.00
(92)	Biff Schlitzer	430.00	200.00	110.00
(93)	Johnny Seigle (Siegle)	285.00	130.00	75.00
(94)	Dave Shean	3,500	1,600	910.00
(95)	Jimmy Sheckard	280.00	130.00	75.00
(96)	Tris Speaker	3,500	1,275	715.00
(97)	Jake Stahl	2,600	1,200	675.00
(98)	Oscar Stanage	325.00	150.00	85.00
(99)	George Stone (No hands visible.)	250.00	115.00	65.00
(100)	George Stone (Left hand visible.)	400.00	185.00	100.00
(101)	George Stovall	500.00	230.00	130.00
(102)	Ed Summers	400.00	185.00	100.00
(103)	Bill Sweeney (Boston)	4,000	1,600	900.00
(104)	Jeff Sweeney (New York)	500.00	230.00	130.00
(105)	Jesse Tannehill (Chicago A.L.)	250.00	115.00	65.00
(106)	Lee Tannehill (Chicago N.L.)	250.00	115.00	65.00
(107)	Fred Tenney	750.00	345.00	200.00
(108)	Ira Thomas (Philadelphia)	250.00	115.00	65.00
(109)	Roy Thomas (Boston)	375.00	175.00	95.00
(110)	Joe Tinker	650.00	300.00	175.00
(111)	Bob Unglaub	250.00	115.00	65.00
(112)	Jerry Upp	3,500	1,600	910.00
(113)	Honus Wagner/Btg	4,250	1,950	1,100
(114)	Honus Wagner/Throwing	4,250	1,950	1,100
(115)	Bobby Wallace	575.00	265.00	150.00
(116)	Ed Walsh	6,000	2,300	1,300
(117)	Vic Willis	800.00	375.00	210.00
(118)	Hooks Wiltse	280.00	130.00	75.00
(119)	Cy Young (Cleveland)	2,750	1,275	725.00
(120)	Cy Young (Boston)	4,000	1,850	1,000

1910 American Caramel Pirates (E90-2)

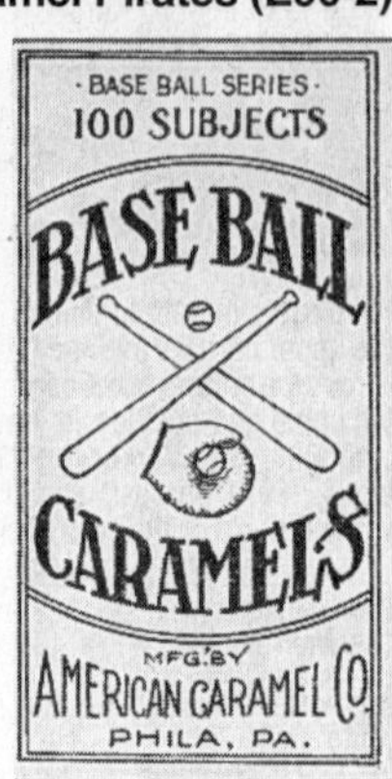

Closely related to the E90-1 American Caramel set, the E90-2 set consists of 11 cards featuring members of the 1909 champion Pittsburgh Pirates. The cards measure a nominal 1-1/2" x 2-5/8", though tolerances must be allowed for original cutting variations common to the era. They display a color lithograph on front set upon a solid color background of either red, green blue or pink. The player's name and "Pittsburg" appear in blue capital letters in the border beneath the portrait. The backs are identical to those in the E90-1 set, depicting a drawing of a ball, glove and crossed bats with the words "Base Ball Caramels" and a reference to "100 Subjects." The set includes Hall of Famers Honus Wagner and Fred Clarke.

		NM	EX	VG
Complete Set (11):		30,000	13,500	7,000
Common Player:		1,200	550.00	300.00
(1)	Babe Adams	1,200	550.00	300.00
(2)	Fred Clarke	2,000	900.00	500.00
(3)	George Gibson	1,200	550.00	300.00
(4)	Ham Hyatt	1,200	550.00	300.00
(5)	Tommy Leach	1,200	550.00	300.00
(6)	Sam Leever	1,200	550.00	300.00
(7)	Nick Maddox	1,200	550.00	300.00
(8)	Dots Miller	1,200	550.00	300.00
(9)	Deacon Phillippe	1,200	550.00	300.00
(10)	Honus Wagner	17,500	7,875	4,375
(11)	Owen Wilson	1,200	550.00	300.00

1910 American Caramel White Sox/ Cubs (E90-3)

Similar in size (nominally 1-1/2" x 2-3/4", but with the usual tolerances for cutting variations on cards of the era) and style to the more popular E90-1 set, the E90-3 set was issued by the American Caramel Co. in 1910. The 20-card, color lithograph set includes 11 Chicago Cubs and nine White Sox. The fronts of the cards have a similar design to the E90-1 set, although different pictures were used. The backs can be differentiated by two major changes: The bottom of the card indicates the American Caramel Co. of "Chicago," rather than Philadelphia, and the top of the card contains the phrase "All The Star Players," rather than "100 Subjects."

		NM	EX	VG
Complete Set (20):		30,000	13,500	6,750
Common Player:		1,700	850.00	425.00
(1)	Jimmy Archer	1,700	850.00	425.00
(2)	Lena Blackburne	1,700	850.00	425.00
(3)	Mordecai Brown	3,000	1,500	750.00
(4)	Frank Chance	3,000	1,500	750.00
(5)	King Cole	1,700	850.00	425.00
(6)	Patsy Dougherty	1,700	850.00	425.00

(7)	Johnny Evers	3,000	1,500	750.00
(8)	Chick Gandil	4,500	2,250	1,125
(9)	Ed Hahn	1,700	850.00	425.00
(10a)	Solly Hofman	1,700	850.00	425.00
(10b)	Solly Hofman (Broken "m" in last name gives appearance of "Hofnlan." Discovery specimen graded SGC Good auctioned for $3,190 in 2006.)			
(11)	Orval Overall	1,700	850.00	425.00
(12)	Fred Payne	1,700	850.00	425.00
(13)	Billy Purtell	1,700	850.00	425.00
(14)	Wildfire Schulte	1,700	850.00	425.00
(15)	Jimmy Sheckard	1,700	850.00	425.00
(16)	Frank Smith	1,700	850.00	425.00
(17)	Harry Steinfeldt	1,700	850.00	425.00
(18a)	Joe Tinker (Blue background.)	3,000	1,500	750.00
(18b)	Joe Tinker (Green background.)	3,000	1,500	750.00
(19)	Ed Walsh	3,000	1,500	750.00
(20)	Rollie Zeider	1,700	850.00	425.00

1910 American Caramel Die-cuts (E125)

Issued circa 1910 by the American Caramel Co., this set of die-cut cards is so rare that it wasn't even known to exist until the late 1960s. Apparently inserted in boxes of caramels, these cards, which are die-cut figures of baseball players, vary in size but are all relatively large - some measuring 7" high and 4" wide. Players from the Athletics, Red Sox, Giants and Pirates are known with a team checklist appearing on the back.

		NM	EX	VG
	Common Player:	3,000	1,375	905.00
(1)	Babe Adams (Arms at sides.)	3,000	1,375	905.00
(2)	Red Ames/Throwing	3,000	1,375	905.00
(3)	Home Run Baker	5,000	2,250	1,500
(4)	Jack Barry/Fldg	3,000	1,375	905.00
(5)	Chief Bender	5,625	2,530	1,690
(6)	Al Bridwell/Fldg	3,000	1,375	905.00
(7)	Bobby Byrne/Throwing	3,000	1,375	905.00
(8)	Bill Carrigan/Catching	3,000	1,375	905.00
(9)	Ed Cicotte/Throwing	3,000	1,375	905.00
(10)	Fred Clark/Fldg (Clarke)	5,000	2,250	1,500
(11)	Eddie Collins	5,000	2,250	1,500
(12)	Harry Davis/Fldg	3,000	1,375	905.00
(13)	Art Devlin/Fldg	3,000	1,375	905.00
(14)	Josh Devore	3,000	1,375	905.00
(15)	Larry Doyle/Throwing	3,000	1,375	905.00
(16)	John Flynn/Running	3,000	1,375	905.00
(17)	George Gibson (Hands in glove.)	3,000	1,375	905.00
(18)	Topsy Hartzell/Fldg (Hartsel)	3,000	1,375	905.00
(19)	Harry Hooper/Throwing	5,000	2,250	1,500
(20)	Harry Krause	3,000	1,375	905.00
(21)	Tommy Leach/Fldg	3,000	1,375	905.00
(22)	Harry Lord/Throwing	3,000	1,375	905.00
(23)	Christy Mathewson (Wind-up.)	18,750	8,440	5,625
(24)	Amby McConnell/Fldg	3,000	1,375	905.00
(25)	Fred Merkle	3,000	1,375	905.00
(26)	Dots Miller/Throwing	3,000	1,375	905.00
(27)	Danny Murphy	3,000	1,375	905.00
(28)	Red Murray/Fldg	3,000	1,375	905.00
(29)	Harry Niles/Fldg	3,000	1,375	905.00
(30)	Rube Oldring	3,000	1,375	905.00
(31)	Eddie Plank/Throwing	18,750	8,440	5,625
(32)	Cy Seymour/Fldg	3,000	1,375	905.00
(33)	Tris Speaker/Btg	11,250	5,065	3,375
(34)	Tris Speaker/Fldg	11,250	5,065	3,375
(35)	Jake Stahl/Fldg	3,000	1,375	905.00
(36)	Ira Thomas	3,000	1,375	905.00
(37)	Heinie Wagner/Throwing	3,000	1,375	905.00
(38)	Honus Wagner/Btg	25,000	11,250	7,500
(39)	Honus Wagner/Throwing	25,000	11,250	7,500
(40)	Art Wilson	3,000	1,375	905.00
(41)	Owen Wilson/Throwing	3,000	1,375	905.00
(42)	Hooks Wiltse/Throwing	3,000	1,375	905.00

1915 American Caramel (E106)

This 48-card set, designated E106 by the American Card Catalog, was produced by the American Caramel Co., of York, Pa., in 1915 and includes players from the National, American and Federal Leagues. Cards measure 1-1/2" x 2-3/4". The set is related to the E90-1 and E92 sets, from which the artwork is taken, but this issue has a glossy coating on front, which makes the cards very susceptible to cracking.

This card is one of a set of forty-eight leading Baseball Players in the National, American and Federal Leagues. One card is given with every piece of Baseball Caramel manufactured by the

AMERICAN CARAMEL CO.
YORK, PA.
UNDER THE FAMOUS BRAND OF THE
P. C. W.

		NM	EX	VG
	Complete Set (48):	40,000	20,000	12,500
	Common Player:	700.00	350.00	200.00
(1)	Jack Barry	700.00	350.00	200.00
(2)	Chief Bender (White hat.)	1,300	650.00	400.00
(3)	Chief Bender (Striped hat.)	1,300	650.00	400.00
(4)	Bob Bescher	700.00	350.00	200.00
(5)	Roger Bresnahan	1,300	650.00	400.00
(6)	Al Bridwell	700.00	350.00	200.00
(7)	Donie Bush	700.00	350.00	200.00
(8)	Hal Chase/Portrait	700.00	350.00	200.00
(9)	Hal Chase/Catching	700.00	350.00	200.00
(10)	Ty Cobb (W/bat, facing front.)	9,000	4,500	2,700
(11)	Ty Cobb/Btg (Facing to side.)	8,500	4,250	2,250
(12)	Eddie Collins	1,300	650.00	400.00
(13)	Sam Crawford	1,300	650.00	400.00
(14)	Ray Demmitt	700.00	350.00	200.00
(15)	Wild Bill Donovan	700.00	350.00	200.00
(16)	Red Dooin	700.00	350.00	200.00
(17)	Mickey Doolan	700.00	350.00	200.00
(18)	Larry Doyle	700.00	350.00	200.00
(19)	Clyde Engle	700.00	350.00	200.00
(20)	Johnny Evers	1,300	650.00	400.00
(21)	Art Fromme	700.00	350.00	200.00
(22)	George Gibson/Catching (Back view.)	700.00	350.00	200.00
(23)	George Gibson/Catching (Front view.)	700.00	350.00	200.00
(24)	Roy Hartzell	700.00	350.00	200.00
(25)	Fred Jacklitsch	700.00	350.00	200.00
(26)	Hugh Jennings	1,300	650.00	400.00
(27)	Otto Knabe	700.00	350.00	200.00
(28)	Nap Lajoie	1,300	650.00	400.00
(29)	Hans Lobert	700.00	350.00	200.00
(30)	Rube Marquard	1,300	650.00	400.00
(31)	Christy Matthewson (Mathewson)	4,450	2,200	1,330
(32)	John McGraw	1,300	650.00	400.00
(33)	George McQuillan	700.00	350.00	200.00
(34)	Dots Miller	700.00	350.00	200.00
(35)	Danny Murphy	700.00	350.00	200.00
(36)	Rebel Oakes	700.00	350.00	200.00
(37)	Eddie Plank	1,500	750.00	450.00
(38)	Germany Schaefer	700.00	350.00	200.00
(39)	Tris Speaker	1,800	900.00	550.00
(40)	Oscar Stanage	700.00	350.00	200.00
(41)	George Stovall	700.00	350.00	200.00
(42)	Jeff Sweeney	700.00	350.00	200.00
(43)	Joe Tinker/Portrait	1,300	650.00	400.00
(44)	Joe Tinker/Btg	1,300	650.00	400.00
(45)	Honus Wagner/Btg	13,040	6,250	3,750
(46)	Honus Wagner/Throwing	13,040	6,250	3,750
(47)	Hooks Wiltse	700.00	350.00	200.00
(48)	Heinie Zimmerman	700.00	350.00	200.00

1921 American Caramel Series of 80 (E121)

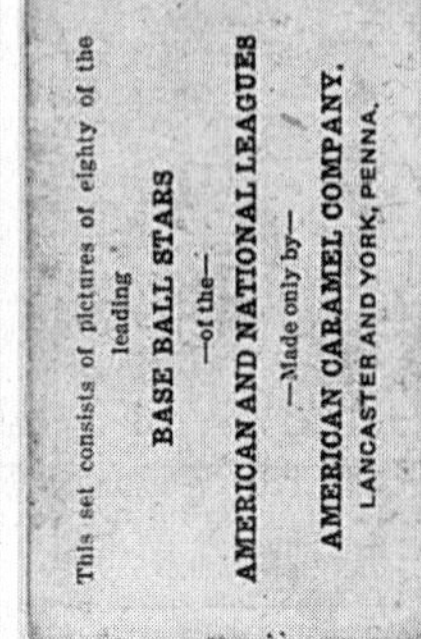

Issued circa 1921, the E121 Series of 80 is designated as such because of the card reverses which indicate the player pictured is just one of 80 baseball stars in the set. The figure of 80 supplied by the American Caramel Co. is incorrect as over 100 different pictures do exist. The unnumbered cards, which measure about 2" x 3-1/4", feature black and white photos. Two different backs exist for the Series of 80. The common back variation has the first line ending with the word "the," while the scarcer version ends with the word "eighty." The complete set price does not include the variations.

		NM	EX	VG
	Complete Set (121):	52,500	21,500	10,000
	Common Player:	150.00	60.00	30.00
(1)	G.C. Alexander (Arms above head.)	750.00	300.00	150.00
(2)	Grover Alexander (Right arm forward.)	1,500	600.00	300.00
(3)	Jim Bagby	150.00	60.00	30.00
(4a)	J. Franklin Baker	400.00	160.00	80.00
(4b)	Frank Baker	400.00	160.00	80.00
(5)	Dave Bancroft/Btg	400.00	160.00	80.00
(6)	Dave Bancroft/Leaping	400.00	160.00	80.00
(7)	Ping Bodie	150.00	60.00	30.00
(8)	George Burns	150.00	60.00	30.00
(9)	Geo. J. Burns	150.00	60.00	30.00
(10)	Owen Bush	150.00	60.00	30.00
(11)	Max Carey/Btg	400.00	160.00	80.00
(12)	Max Carey (Hands at hips.)	400.00	160.00	80.00
(13)	Cecil Causey	150.00	60.00	30.00
(14)	Ty Cobb/Throwing (Looking front.)	1,800	725.00	360.00
(15a)	Ty Cobb/Throwing (Looking right, Mgr. on front.)	1,800	725.00	360.00
(15b)	Ty Cobb/Throwing (Looking right, Manager on front.)	1,800	725.00	360.00
(16)	Eddie Collins	400.00	160.00	80.00
(17)	"Rip" Collins	150.00	60.00	30.00
(18)	Jake Daubert	150.00	60.00	30.00
(19)	George Dauss	150.00	60.00	30.00
(20)	Charles Deal (Dark uniform.)	150.00	60.00	30.00
(21)	Charles Deal (White uniform.)	150.00	60.00	30.00
(22)	William Doak	150.00	60.00	30.00
(23)	Bill Donovan	150.00	60.00	30.00
(24)	"Phil" Douglas	150.00	60.00	30.00
(25a)	Johnny Evers (Manager)	400.00	160.00	80.00
(25b)	Johnny Evers (Mgr.)	400.00	160.00	80.00
(26)	Urban Faber (Dark uniform.)	400.00	160.00	80.00
(27)	Urban Faber (White uniform.)	400.00	160.00	80.00
(28)	William Fewster (First name actually Wilson.)	150.00	60.00	30.00
(29)	Eddie Foster	150.00	60.00	30.00
(30)	Frank Frisch	400.00	160.00	80.00
(31)	W.L. Gardner	150.00	60.00	30.00
(32a)	Alexander Gaston (No position on front.)	150.00	60.00	30.00
(32b)	Alexander Gaston (Position on front.)	150.00	60.00	30.00
(33)	"Kid" Gleason	150.00	60.00	30.00
(34)	"Mike" Gonzalez	150.00	60.00	30.00
(35)	Hank Gowdy	150.00	60.00	30.00
(36)	John Graney	150.00	60.00	30.00
(37)	Tom Griffith	150.00	60.00	30.00
(38)	Heinie Groh	150.00	60.00	30.00
(39)	Harry Harper	150.00	60.00	30.00
(40)	Harry Heilman (Heilmann)	400.00	160.00	80.00
(41)	Walter Holke/Portrait	150.00	60.00	30.00
(42)	Walter Holke/Throwing	150.00	60.00	30.00
(43)	Charles Hollacher (Hollocher)	150.00	60.00	30.00
(44)	Harry Hooper	400.00	160.00	80.00
(45)	Rogers Hornsby	1,100	450.00	225.00
(46)	Waite Hoyt	400.00	160.00	80.00
(47)	Miller Huggins	400.00	160.00	80.00
(48)	Wm. C. Jacobson	150.00	60.00	30.00
(49)	Hugh Jennings	400.00	160.00	80.00
(50)	Walter Johnson/Throwing	1,350	550.00	275.00
(51)	Walter Johnson (Hands at chest.)	1,425	575.00	285.00
(52)	James Johnston	150.00	60.00	30.00
(53)	Joe Judge	150.00	60.00	30.00
(54)	George Kelly	400.00	160.00	80.00
(55)	Dick Kerr	150.00	60.00	30.00
(56)	P.J. Kilduff	150.00	60.00	30.00
(57a)	Bill Killifer (Incorrect name.)	150.00	60.00	30.00
(57b)	Bill Killefer (Correct name.)	150.00	60.00	30.00
(58)	John Lavan	150.00	60.00	30.00
(59)	"Nemo" Leibold	150.00	60.00	30.00
(60)	Duffy Lewis	150.00	60.00	30.00
(61)	Al. Mamaux	150.00	60.00	30.00
(62)	"Rabbit" Maranville	400.00	160.00	80.00
(63a)	Carl May (Mays)	200.00	80.00	40.00
(63b)	Carl Mays (Correct name.)	200.00	80.00	40.00
(64)	John McGraw	400.00	160.00	80.00
(65)	Jack McInnis	150.00	60.00	30.00
(66)	M.J. McNally	150.00	60.00	30.00
(67)	Emil Muesel (Photo is Lou DeVormer.)	150.00	60.00	30.00
(68)	R. Meusel	150.00	60.00	30.00
(69)	Clyde Milan	150.00	60.00	30.00
(70)	Elmer Miller	150.00	60.00	30.00
(71)	Otto Miller	150.00	60.00	30.00
(72)	Guy Morton	150.00	60.00	30.00
(73)	Eddie Murphy	150.00	60.00	30.00
(74)	"Hy" Myers	150.00	60.00	30.00
(75)	Arthur Nehf	150.00	60.00	30.00
(76)	Steve O'Neill	150.00	60.00	30.00
(77a)	Roger Peckinbaugh (Incorrect name.)	150.00	60.00	30.00
(77b)	Roger Peckinpaugh (Correct name.)	150.00	60.00	30.00
(78a)	Jeff Pfeffer (Brooklyn)	150.00	60.00	30.00
(78b)	Jeff Pfeffer (St. Louis)	150.00	60.00	30.00
(79)	Walter Pipp	250.00	100.00	50.00
(80)	Jack Quinn	150.00	60.00	30.00
(81)	John Rawlings	150.00	60.00	30.00
(82)	E.C. Rice	400.00	160.00	80.00
(83)	Eppa Rixey, Jr.	400.00	160.00	80.00
(84)	Robert Roth	150.00	60.00	30.00
(85a)	Ed. Roush (C.F.)	400.00	160.00	80.00
(85b)	Ed. Roush (L.F.)	400.00	160.00	80.00
(86a)	Babe Ruth	17,500	7,000	3,500
(86b)	"Babe" Ruth	17,500	7,000	3,500
(86c)	George Ruth	19,000	7,600	3,800
(87)	"Bill" Ryan	150.00	60.00	30.00
(88)	"Slim" Sallee (Glove showing.)	150.00	60.00	30.00
(89)	"Slim" Sallee (No glove showing.)	150.00	60.00	30.00

(90)	Ray Schalk	400.00	160.00	80.00
(91)	Walter Schang	150.00	60.00	30.00
(92a)	Fred Schupp (Name incorrect.)	150.00	60.00	30.00
(92b)	Ferd Schupp (Name correct.)	150.00	60.00	30.00
(93)	Everett Scott	150.00	60.00	30.00
(94)	Hank Severeid	150.00	60.00	30.00
(95)	Robert Shawkey	150.00	60.00	30.00
(96a)	Pat Shea	150.00	60.00	30.00
(96b)	"Pat" Shea	150.00	60.00	30.00
(97)	George Sisler/Btg	400.00	160.00	80.00
(98)	George Sisler/Throwing	400.00	160.00	80.00
(99)	Earl Smith	150.00	60.00	30.00
(100)	Frank Snyder	150.00	60.00	30.00
(101a)	Tris Speaker (Mgr.)	800.00	325.00	160.00
(101b)	Tris Speaker (Manager - large projection.)	800.00	325.00	160.00
(101c)	Tris Speaker (Manager - small projection.)	800.00	325.00	160.00
(102)	Milton Stock	150.00	60.00	30.00
(103)	Amos Strunk	150.00	60.00	30.00
(104)	Zeb Terry	150.00	60.00	30.00
(105)	Chester Thomas	150.00	60.00	30.00
(106)	Fred Toney (Trees in background.)	150.00	60.00	30.00
(107)	Fred Toney (No trees.)	150.00	60.00	30.00
(108)	George Tyler	150.00	60.00	30.00
(109)	Jim Vaughn (Dark hat.)	150.00	60.00	30.00
(110)	Jim Vaughn (White hat.)	150.00	60.00	30.00
(111)	Bob Veach (Glove in air.)	150.00	60.00	30.00
(112)	Bob Veach (Arms crossed.)	150.00	60.00	30.00
(113)	Oscar Vitt	150.00	60.00	30.00
(114)	W. Wambsganss (Photo actually Fred Coumbe.)	150.00	60.00	30.00
(115)	Aaron Ward	150.00	60.00	30.00
(116)	Zach Wheat	400.00	160.00	80.00
(117)	George Whitted	150.00	60.00	30.00
(118)	Fred Williams	150.00	60.00	30.00
(119)	Ivy B. Wingo	150.00	60.00	30.00
(120)	Joe Wood	300.00	125.00	60.00
(121)	"Pep" Young	150.00	60.00	30.00

1922 American Caramel Series of 120 (E121)

ELMER SMITH
O. F.—Boston Americans

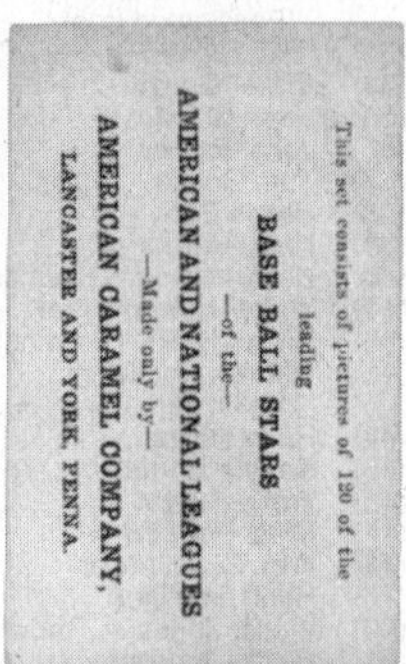
This set consists of pictures of 120 of the leading
BASE BALL STARS
—of the—
AMERICAN AND NATIONAL LEAGUES
—Made only by—
AMERICAN CARAMEL COMPANY,
LANCASTER AND YORK, PENNA.

Produced by American Caramel Co. the E121 Series of 120 has back advertising that claims that the set contained 120 subjects. Identical in design to the E121 Series of 80 set except for the card backs, the black-and-white cards measure about 2" x 3-1/4". Numerous variations are found in the set, most involving a change in the player's name, team or position. The complete set price does not include variations.

		NM	EX	VG
Complete Set (127):		60,000	24,000	12,000
Common Player:		100.00	40.00	25.00
(1)	Chas. "Babe" Adams	150.00	60.00	30.00
(2)	G.C. Alexander	750.00	300.00	150.00
(3)	Jim Bagby	150.00	60.00	30.00
(4)	Dave Bancroft	400.00	160.00	80.00
(5)	Turner Barber	150.00	60.00	30.00
(6a)	Carlson Bigbee (Correct name Carson L. Bigbee.)	150.00	60.00	30.00
(6b)	Carlson L. Bigbee	150.00	60.00	30.00
(6c)	Corson L. Bigbee	150.00	60.00	30.00
(6d)	L. Bigbee	150.00	60.00	30.00
(7)	"Bullet Joe" Bush	150.00	60.00	30.00
(8)	Max Carey	400.00	160.00	80.00
(9)	Cecil Causey	150.00	60.00	30.00
(10)	Ty Cobb/Btg	2,500	1,000	500.00
(11)	Ty Cobb/Throwing	2,250	900.00	450.00
(12)	Eddie Collins	400.00	160.00	80.00
(13)	A. Wilbur Cooper	150.00	60.00	30.00
(14)	Stanley Coveleskie (Coveleski)	400.00	160.00	80.00
(15)	Dave Danforth	150.00	60.00	30.00
(16)	Jake Daubert	150.00	60.00	30.00
(17)	George Dauss	150.00	60.00	30.00
(18)	Dixie Davis	150.00	60.00	30.00
(19)	Chas. A. Deal	150.00	60.00	30.00
(20)	Lou DeVormer (Photo actually Irish Meusel.)	150.00	60.00	30.00
(21)	William Doak	150.00	60.00	30.00
(22)	Phil Douglas	150.00	60.00	30.00
(23)	Urban Faber	400.00	160.00	80.00
(24)	Bib Falk (Bibb)	150.00	60.00	30.00
(25)	Wm. Fewster (First name actually Wilson.)	150.00	60.00	30.00
(26)	Max Flack	150.00	60.00	30.00
(27)	Ira Falgstead (Flagstead)	150.00	60.00	30.00
(28)	Frank Frisch	400.00	160.00	80.00
(29)	W.L. Gardner	150.00	60.00	30.00
(30)	Alexander Gaston	150.00	60.00	30.00
(31)	E.P. Gharrity	150.00	60.00	30.00
(32)	George Gibson	150.00	60.00	30.00
(33)	Chas. "Whitey" Glazner	150.00	60.00	30.00
(34)	"Kid" Gleason	150.00	60.00	30.00
(35)	Hank Gowdy	150.00	60.00	30.00
(36)	John Graney	150.00	60.00	30.00
(37)	Tom Griffith	150.00	60.00	30.00
(38)	Chas. Grimm	150.00	60.00	30.00
(39)	Heine Groh	150.00	60.00	30.00
(40)	Jess Haines	400.00	160.00	80.00
(41)	Harry Harper	150.00	60.00	30.00
(42)	Harry Heilman/Fldg (Name incorrect.)	450.00	180.00	90.00
(43)	Harry Heilmann/Btg (Name correct.)	600.00	240.00	120.00
(44)	Clarence Hodge	150.00	60.00	30.00
(45)	Walter Holke/Portrait	150.00	60.00	30.00
(46)	Walter Holke/Throwing	150.00	60.00	30.00
(47)	Charles Hollocher	150.00	60.00	30.00
(48)	Harry Hooper	400.00	160.00	80.00
(49a)	Rogers Hornsby (2B.)	1,100	450.00	225.00
(49b)	Rogers Hornsby (O.F.)	1,100	450.00	225.00
(50)	Waite Hoyt	400.00	160.00	80.00
(51)	Miller Huggins	400.00	160.00	80.00
(52)	Walter Johnson	1,350	550.00	275.00
(53)	Joe Judge	150.00	60.00	30.00
(54)	George Kelly	400.00	160.00	80.00
(55)	Dick Kerr	150.00	60.00	30.00
(56)	P.J. Kilduff	150.00	60.00	30.00
(57)	Bill Killifer/Btg (Killefer)	150.00	60.00	30.00
(58)	Bill Killifer/Throwing (Killefer)	150.00	60.00	30.00
(59)	John Lavan	150.00	60.00	30.00
(60)	Walter Mails	150.00	60.00	30.00
(61)	"Rabbit" Maranville	400.00	160.00	80.00
(62)	Elwood Martin	150.00	60.00	30.00
(63)	Carl Mays	200.00	80.00	40.00
(64)	John J. McGraw	400.00	160.00	80.00
(65)	Jack McInnis	150.00	60.00	30.00
(66)	M.J. McNally	150.00	60.00	30.00
(67)	Emil Meusel (Photo actually Lou DeVormer.)	150.00	60.00	30.00
(68)	R. Meusel	150.00	60.00	30.00
(69)	Clyde Milan	150.00	60.00	30.00
(70)	Elmer Miller	150.00	60.00	30.00
(71)	Otto Miller	150.00	60.00	30.00
(72)	Johnny Mostil	150.00	60.00	30.00
(73)	Eddie Mulligan	150.00	60.00	30.00
(74a)	Hy Myers	150.00	60.00	30.00
(74b)	"Hy" Myers	150.00	60.00	30.00
(75)	Earl Neale	300.00	120.00	60.00
(76)	Arthur Nehf	150.00	60.00	30.00
(77)	Leslie Nunamaker	150.00	60.00	30.00
(78)	Joe Oeschger	150.00	60.00	30.00
(79)	Chas. O'Leary	150.00	60.00	30.00
(80)	Steve O'Neill	150.00	60.00	30.00
(81)	D.B. Pratt	150.00	60.00	30.00
(82a)	John Rawlings (2B.)	150.00	60.00	30.00
(82b)	John Rawlings (Utl.)	150.00	60.00	30.00
(83)	E.S. Rice (Initials actually E.C.)	400.00	160.00	80.00
(84)	Eppa J. Rixey	400.00	160.00	80.00
(85)	Eppa Rixey, Jr.	400.00	160.00	80.00
(86)	Wilbert Robinson	400.00	160.00	80.00
(87)	Tom Rogers	150.00	60.00	30.00
(88a)	Ed Rounnel (Rommel)	150.00	60.00	30.00
(88b)	Ed. Rommel	150.00	60.00	30.00
(89)	Ed Roush	400.00	160.00	80.00
(90)	"Muddy" Ruel	150.00	60.00	30.00
(91)	Walter Ruether	150.00	60.00	30.00
(92a)	Babe Ruth (Photo montage.)	10,000	4,000	2,000
(92b)	"Babe" Ruth (Photo montage.)	10,000	4,000	2,000
(93a)	Babe Ruth (Holding bird.)	10,000	4,000	2,000
(93b)	"Babe" Ruth (Holding bird.)	10,000	4,000	2,000
(94)	"Babe" Ruth (Holding ball.)	10,000	4,000	2,000
(95)	Bill Ryan	150.00	60.00	30.00
(96)	Ray Schalk/Catching	400.00	160.00	80.00
(97)	Ray Schalk/Btg	400.00	160.00	80.00
(98)	Wally Schang	150.00	60.00	30.00
(99)	Ferd Schupp	150.00	60.00	30.00
(100)	Everett Scott	150.00	60.00	30.00
(101)	Joe Sewell	400.00	160.00	80.00
(102)	Robert Shawkey	150.00	60.00	30.00
(103)	Pat Shea	150.00	60.00	30.00
(104)	Earl Sheely	150.00	60.00	30.00
(105)	Urban Schocker	150.00	60.00	30.00
(106)	George Sisler/Btg	400.00	160.00	80.00
(107)	George Sisler/Throwing	400.00	160.00	80.00
(108)	Earl Smith	150.00	60.00	30.00
(109)	Elmer Smith	150.00	60.00	30.00
(110)	Frank Snyder	150.00	60.00	30.00
(111)	Bill Southworth	150.00	60.00	30.00
(112a)	Tris Speaker (Large projection.)	600.00	240.00	120.00
(112b)	Tris Speaker (Small projection.)	600.00	240.00	120.00
(113a)	Milton Stock	150.00	60.00	30.00
(113b)	Milton J. Stock	150.00	60.00	30.00
(114)	Amos Strunk	150.00	60.00	30.00
(115)	Zeb Terry	150.00	60.00	30.00
(116)	Fred Toney	150.00	60.00	30.00
(117)	George Topocer (Toporcer)	150.00	60.00	30.00
(118)	Bob Veach	150.00	60.00	30.00
(119)	Oscar Vitt	150.00	60.00	30.00
(120)	Curtis Walker	150.00	60.00	30.00
(121)	W. Wambsganss (Photo actually Fred Coumbe.)	150.00	60.00	30.00
(122)	Aaron Ward	150.00	60.00	30.00
(123)	Zach Wheat	400.00	160.00	80.00
(124a)	George Whitted (Pittsburgh)	150.00	60.00	30.00
(124b)	George Whitted (Brooklyn)	150.00	60.00	30.00
(125)	Fred Williams	150.00	60.00	30.00
(126)	Ivy B. Wingo	150.00	60.00	30.00
(127)	Ross Young (Youngs)	400.00	160.00	80.00

1922 American Caramel Series of 80 (E122)

CLAUDE HENDRIX
P.-Chicago Cubs

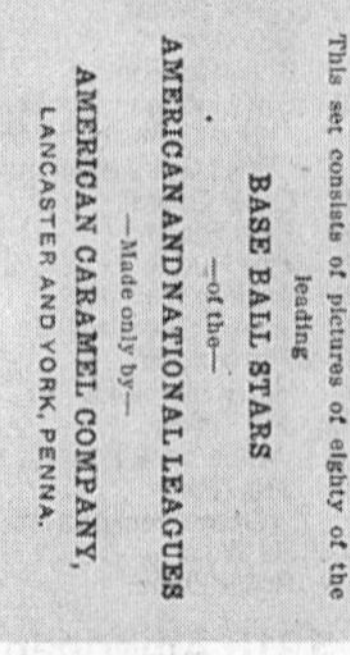
This set consists of pictures of eighty of the leading
BASE BALL STARS
—of the—
AMERICAN AND NATIONAL LEAGUES
—Made only by—
AMERICAN CARAMEL COMPANY,
LANCASTER AND YORK, PENNA.

Known as E122 in the American Card Catalog, this set is actually a parallel of the E121 American Caramel set. The cards are nearly identical to E121's "Series of 80," except the player's name, position and team are printed inside a gray rectangle at the bottom of the card, and the photos have a more coarse appearance. At 2" x 3-1/4", the E122s are slightly shorter than E121s.

		NM	EX	VG
Complete Set (81):		30,000	12,000	6,000
Common Player:		100.00	40.00	25.00
(1)	Grover Alexander	750.00	300.00	150.00
(2)	Jim Bagby	150.00	60.00	30.00
(3)	J. Franklin Baker	400.00	160.00	80.00
(4)	Dave Bancroft	400.00	160.00	80.00
(5)	Ping Bodie	150.00	60.00	30.00
(6)	George Burns	150.00	60.00	30.00
(7)	Geo. J. Burns	150.00	60.00	30.00
(8)	Owen Bush	150.00	60.00	30.00
(9)	Max Carey	400.00	160.00	80.00
(10)	Cecil Causey	150.00	60.00	30.00
(11)	Ty Cobb	1,900	760.00	380.00
(12)	Eddie Collins	400.00	160.00	80.00
(13)	Jake Daubert	150.00	60.00	30.00
(14)	George Dauss	150.00	60.00	30.00
(15)	Charles Deal	150.00	60.00	30.00
(16)	William Doak	150.00	60.00	30.00
(17)	Bill Donovan	150.00	60.00	30.00
(18)	Johnny Evers	400.00	160.00	80.00
(19)	Urban Faber	400.00	160.00	80.00
(20)	Eddie Foster	150.00	60.00	30.00
(21)	W.L. Gardner	150.00	60.00	30.00
(22)	"Kid" Gleason	150.00	60.00	30.00
(23)	Hank Gowdy	150.00	60.00	30.00
(24)	John Graney	150.00	60.00	30.00
(25)	Tom Griffith	150.00	60.00	30.00
(26)	Sam Harris (Stan "Bucky")	400.00	160.00	80.00
(27)	Harry Heilman (Heilmann)	400.00	160.00	80.00
(28)	Walter Holke	150.00	60.00	30.00
(29)	Charles Hollacher (Hollocher)	150.00	60.00	30.00
(30)	Harry Hooper	400.00	160.00	80.00
(31)	Rogers Hornsby	600.00	240.00	120.00
(32)	Wm. C. Jacobson	150.00	60.00	30.00
(33)	Walter Johnson	1,100	450.00	225.00
(34)	James Johnston	150.00	60.00	30.00
(35)	Joe Judge	150.00	60.00	30.00
(36)	George Kelly	400.00	160.00	80.00
(37)	Dick Kerr	150.00	60.00	30.00
(38)	P.J. Kilduff	150.00	60.00	30.00
(39)	Bill Killefer	150.00	60.00	30.00
(40)	John Lavan	150.00	60.00	30.00
(41)	Duffy Lewis	150.00	60.00	30.00
(42)	Perry Lipe	150.00	60.00	30.00
(43)	Al. Mamaux	150.00	60.00	30.00
(44)	"Rabbit" Maranville	400.00	160.00	80.00
(45)	Carl May (Mays)	200.00	80.00	40.00
(46)	John McGraw	400.00	160.00	80.00
(47)	Jack McInnis	150.00	60.00	30.00
(48)	Clyde Milan	150.00	60.00	30.00
(49)	Otto Miller	150.00	60.00	30.00
(50)	Guy Morton	150.00	60.00	30.00
(51)	Eddie Murphy	150.00	60.00	30.00
(52)	"Hy" Myers	150.00	60.00	30.00
(53)	Steve O'Neill	150.00	60.00	30.00
(54)	Roger Peckinbaugh (Peckinpaugh)	150.00	60.00	30.00
(55)	Jeff Pfeffer	150.00	60.00	30.00
(56)	Walter Pipp	175.00	70.00	35.00
(57)	E.C. Rice	400.00	160.00	80.00
(58)	Eppa Rixey, Jr.	400.00	160.00	80.00
(59)	Babe Ruth	9,000	3,600	1,800
(60)	"Slim" Sallee	150.00	60.00	30.00
(61)	Ray Schalk	400.00	160.00	80.00
(62)	Walter Schang	150.00	60.00	30.00
(63a)	Fred Schupp (Name incorrect.)	150.00	60.00	30.00
(63b)	Ferd Schupp (Name correct.)	150.00	60.00	30.00
(64)	Everett Scott	150.00	60.00	30.00
(65)	Hank Severeid	150.00	60.00	30.00
(66)	George Sisler/Btg	400.00	160.00	80.00
(67)	George Sisler/Throwing	400.00	160.00	80.00
(68)	Tris Speaker	750.00	300.00	150.00
(69)	Milton Stock	150.00	60.00	30.00
(70)	Amos Strunk	150.00	60.00	30.00
(71)	Chester Thomas	150.00	60.00	30.00
(72)	George Tyler	150.00	60.00	30.00
(73)	Jim Vaughn	150.00	60.00	30.00
(74)	Bob Veach	150.00	60.00	30.00
(75)	Oscar Vitt	150.00	60.00	30.00
(76)	W. Wambsganss	150.00	60.00	30.00
(77)	Zach Wheat	400.00	160.00	80.00
(78)	Fred Williams	150.00	60.00	30.00
(79)	Ivy B. Wingo	150.00	60.00	30.00
(80)	Joe Wood	150.00	60.00	30.00
(81)	Pep Young	150.00	60.00	30.00

1922 American Caramel Series of 240 (E120)

WASHINGTON AMERICANS
"SENATORS"
MANAGER--CLYDE MILAN

WALTER JOHNSON	PITCHER
TOM PHILLIPS	PITCHER
GEORGE MOGRIDGE	PITCHER
HARRY COURTNEY	PITCHER
J. T. ZACHARY	PITCHER
ED GHARRITY	CATCHER
VAL PICINICH	CATCHER
JOE JUDGE	FIRST BASE
STANLEY HARRIS	SECOND BASE
ROGER PECKINPAUGH	SHORT STOP
HOWARD SHANKS	THIRD BASE
LEON GOSLIN	OUTFIELD
SAM RICE	OUTFIELD
CLYDE MILAN	OUTFIELD
EARL SMITH	OUTFIELD

THIS PICTURE IS ONE OF A SERIES OF 240 PICTURES OF BASEBALL STARS—15 PLAYERS IN EACH OF THE 16 MAJOR LEAGUE TEAMS. WE SUPPLY HANDSOME BLANK ALBUMS TO HOLD 120 PICTURES—ONE FOR AMERICAN LEAGUE, ONE FOR NATIONAL LEAGUE—FOR 15 CENTS EACH POSTPAID.

AMERICAN CARAMEL CO.
LANCASTER, PA. YORK, PA.

One of the most popular sets of the 1920s candy cards, the 1922 E120s were produced by the American Caramel Co. and distributed with sticks of caramel candy. The unnumbered cards measure 2" x 3-1/2". Cards depicting players from the American League are printed in brown ink on thin cream cardboard; National Leaguers are printed in green on blue-green stock. Backs carry team checklists. Many of the E120 photos were used in other sets of the era. A pair of 11-1/2" x 10-1/2" albums, holding 120 each and stamped American or National League were also issued.

	NM	EX	VG
Complete Set (240):	70,000	27,500	14,500
Common Player:	110.00	50.00	30.00
Album:	300.00	150.00	90.00
(1) Charles (Babe) Adams	175.00	70.00	35.00
(2) Eddie Ainsmith	175.00	70.00	35.00
(3) Vic Aldridge	175.00	70.00	35.00
(4) Grover C. Alexander	900.00	360.00	180.00
(5) Jim Bagby	175.00	70.00	35.00
(6) Frank (Home Run) Baker	500.00	200.00	100.00
(7) Dave (Beauty) Bancroft	500.00	200.00	100.00
(8) Walt Barbare	175.00	70.00	35.00
(9) Turner Barber	175.00	70.00	35.00
(10) Jess Barnes	175.00	70.00	35.00
(11) Clyde Barnhart	175.00	70.00	35.00
(12) John Bassler	175.00	70.00	35.00
(13) Will Bayne	175.00	70.00	35.00
(14) Walter (Huck) Betts	175.00	70.00	35.00
(15) Carson Bigbee	175.00	70.00	35.00
(16) Lu Blue	175.00	70.00	35.00
(17) Norman Boeckel	175.00	70.00	35.00
(18) Sammy Bohne	400.00	160.00	80.00
(19) George Burns	175.00	70.00	35.00
(20) George Burns	175.00	70.00	35.00
(21) "Bullet Joe" Bush	175.00	70.00	35.00
(22) Leon Cadore	175.00	70.00	35.00
(23) Marty Callaghan	175.00	70.00	35.00
(24) Frank Calloway (Callaway)	175.00	70.00	35.00
(25) Max Carey	500.00	200.00	100.00
(26) Jimmy Caveney	175.00	70.00	35.00
(27) Virgil Cheeves	175.00	70.00	35.00
(28) Vern Clemons	175.00	70.00	35.00
(29) Ty Cob (Cobb)	3,500	1,400	700.00
(30) Bert Cole	175.00	70.00	35.00
(31) Eddie Collins	500.00	200.00	100.00
(32) John (Shano) Collins	175.00	70.00	35.00
(33) T.P. (Pat) Collins	175.00	70.00	35.00
(34) Wilbur Cooper	175.00	70.00	35.00
(35) Harry Courtney	175.00	70.00	35.00
(36) Stanley Coveleskie (Coveleski)	500.00	200.00	100.00
(37) Elmer Cox	175.00	70.00	35.00
(38) Sam Crane	175.00	70.00	35.00
(39) Walton Cruise	175.00	70.00	35.00
(40) Bill Cunningham	175.00	70.00	35.00
(41) George Cutshaw	175.00	70.00	35.00
(42) Dave Danforth	175.00	70.00	35.00
(43) Jake Daubert	175.00	70.00	35.00
(44) George Dauss	175.00	70.00	35.00
(45) Frank (Dixie) Davis	175.00	70.00	35.00
(46) Hank DeBerry	175.00	70.00	35.00
(47) Albert Devormer (Lou DeVormer)	175.00	70.00	35.00
(48) Bill Doak	175.00	70.00	35.00
(49) Pete Donohue	175.00	70.00	35.00
(50) "Shufflin" Phil Douglas	175.00	70.00	35.00
(51) Joe Dugan	175.00	70.00	35.00
(52) Louis (Pat) Duncan	175.00	70.00	35.00
(53) Jimmy Dykes	175.00	70.00	35.00
(54) Howard Ehmke	175.00	70.00	35.00
(55) Frank Ellerbe	175.00	70.00	35.00
(56) Urban (Red) Faber	500.00	200.00	100.00
(57) Bib Falk (Bibb)	175.00	70.00	35.00
(58) Dana Fillingim	175.00	70.00	35.00
(59) Max Flack	175.00	70.00	35.00
(60) Ira Flagstead	175.00	70.00	35.00
(61) Art Fletcher	175.00	70.00	35.00
(62) Horace Ford	175.00	70.00	35.00
(63) Jack Fournier	175.00	70.00	35.00
(64) Frank Frisch	500.00	200.00	100.00
(65) Ollie Fuhrman	175.00	70.00	35.00
(66) Clarance Galloway	175.00	70.00	35.00
(67) Larry Gardner	175.00	70.00	35.00
(68) Walter Gerber	175.00	70.00	35.00
(69) Ed Gharrity	175.00	70.00	35.00
(70) John Gillespie	175.00	70.00	35.00
(71) Chas. (Whitey) Glazner	175.00	70.00	35.00
(72) Johnny Gooch	175.00	70.00	35.00
(73) Leon Goslin	500.00	200.00	100.00
(74) Hank Gowdy	175.00	70.00	35.00
(75) John Graney	175.00	70.00	35.00
(76) Tom Griffith	175.00	70.00	35.00
(77) Burleigh Grimes	500.00	200.00	100.00
(78) Oscar Ray Grimes	175.00	70.00	35.00
(79) Charlie Grimm	175.00	70.00	35.00
(80) Heinie Groh	175.00	70.00	35.00
(81) Jesse Haines	500.00	200.00	100.00
(82) Earl Hamilton	175.00	70.00	35.00
(83) Gene (Bubbles) Hargrave	175.00	70.00	35.00
(84) Bryan Harris (Harriss)	175.00	70.00	35.00
(85) Joe Harris	175.00	70.00	35.00
(86) Stanley Harris	500.00	200.00	100.00
(87) Chas. (Dowdy) Hartnett	500.00	200.00	100.00
(88) Bob Hasty	175.00	70.00	35.00
(89) Joe Hauser	225.00	90.00	45.00
(90) Clif Heathcote	175.00	70.00	35.00
(91) Harry Heilmann	500.00	200.00	100.00
(92) Walter (Butch) Henline	175.00	70.00	35.00
(93) Clarence (Shovel) Hodge	175.00	70.00	35.00
(94) Walter Holke	175.00	70.00	35.00
(95) Charles Hollocher	175.00	70.00	35.00
(96) Harry Hooper	500.00	200.00	100.00
(97) Rogers Hornsby	900.00	360.00	180.00
(98) Waite Hoyt	500.00	200.00	100.00
(99) Wilbur Hubbell (Wilbert)	175.00	70.00	35.00
(100) Bernard (Bud) Hungling	175.00	70.00	35.00
(101) Will Jacobson	175.00	70.00	35.00
(102) Charlie Jamieson	175.00	70.00	35.00
(103) Ernie Johnson	175.00	70.00	35.00
(104) Sylvester Johnson	175.00	70.00	35.00
(105) Walter Johnson	1,600	650.00	325.00
(106) Jimmy Johnston	175.00	70.00	35.00
(107) W.R. (Doc) Johnston	175.00	70.00	35.00
(108) "Deacon" Sam Jones	175.00	70.00	35.00
(109) Bob Jones	175.00	70.00	35.00
(110) Percy Jones	175.00	70.00	35.00
(111) Joe Judge	175.00	70.00	35.00
(112) Ben Karr	175.00	70.00	35.00
(113) Johnny Kelleher	175.00	70.00	35.00
(114) George Kelly	500.00	200.00	100.00
(115) Lee King	175.00	70.00	35.00
(116) Wm (Larry) Kopff (Kopf)	175.00	70.00	35.00
(117) Marty Krug	175.00	70.00	35.00
(118) Johnny Lavan	175.00	70.00	35.00
(119) Nemo Leibold	175.00	70.00	35.00
(120) Roy Leslie	175.00	70.00	35.00
(121) George Leverette (Leverett)	175.00	70.00	35.00
(122) Adolfo Luque	175.00	70.00	35.00
(123) Walter Mails	175.00	70.00	35.00
(124) Al Mamaux	175.00	70.00	35.00
(125) "Rabbit" Maranville	500.00	200.00	100.00
(126) Cliff Markle	175.00	70.00	35.00
(127) Richard (Rube) Marquard	500.00	200.00	100.00
(128) Carl Mays	200.00	80.00	40.00
(129) Hervey McClellan (Harvey)	175.00	70.00	35.00
(130) Austin McHenry	175.00	70.00	35.00
(131) "Stuffy" McInnis	175.00	70.00	35.00
(132) Martin McManus	175.00	70.00	35.00
(133) Mike McNally	175.00	70.00	35.00
(134) Hugh McQuillan	175.00	70.00	35.00
(135) Lee Meadows	175.00	70.00	35.00
(136) Mike Menosky	175.00	70.00	35.00
(137) Bob (Dutch) Meusel	175.00	70.00	35.00
(138) Emil (Irish) Meusel	175.00	70.00	35.00
(139) Clyde Milan	175.00	70.00	35.00
(140) Edmund (Bing) Miller	175.00	70.00	35.00
(141) Elmer Miller	175.00	70.00	35.00
(142) Lawrence (Hack) Miller	175.00	70.00	35.00
(143) Clarence Mitchell	175.00	70.00	35.00
(144) George Mogridge	175.00	70.00	35.00
(145) Roy Moore	175.00	70.00	35.00
(146) John L. Mokan	175.00	70.00	35.00
(147) John Morrison	175.00	70.00	35.00
(148) Johnny Mostil	175.00	70.00	35.00
(149) Elmer Myers	175.00	70.00	35.00
(150) Hy Myers	175.00	70.00	35.00
(151) Roliene Naylor (Roleine)	175.00	70.00	35.00
(152) Earl "Greasy" Neale	175.00	70.00	35.00
(153) Art Nehf	175.00	70.00	35.00
(154) Les Nunamaker	175.00	70.00	35.00
(155) Joe Oeschger	175.00	70.00	35.00
(156) Bob O'Farrell	175.00	70.00	35.00
(157) Ivan Olson	175.00	70.00	35.00
(158) George O'Neil	175.00	70.00	35.00
(159) Steve O'Neill	175.00	70.00	35.00
(160) Frank Parkinson	175.00	70.00	35.00
(161) Roger Peckinpaugh	175.00	70.00	35.00
(162) Herb Pennock	500.00	200.00	100.00
(163) Ralph (Cy) Perkins	175.00	70.00	35.00
(164) Will Pertica	175.00	70.00	35.00
(165) Jack Peters	175.00	70.00	35.00
(166) Tom Phillips	175.00	70.00	35.00
(167) Val Picinich	175.00	70.00	35.00
(168) Herman Pillette	175.00	70.00	35.00
(169) Ralph Pinelli	175.00	70.00	35.00
(170) Wallie Pipp	175.00	70.00	35.00
(171) Clark Pittenger (Clarke)	175.00	70.00	35.00
(172) Raymond Powell	175.00	70.00	35.00
(173) Derrill Pratt	175.00	70.00	35.00
(174) Jack Quinn	175.00	70.00	35.00
(175) Joe (Goldie) Rapp	175.00	70.00	35.00
(176) John Rawlings	175.00	70.00	35.00
(177) Walter (Dutch) Reuther (Ruether)	175.00	70.00	35.00
(178) Sam Rice	500.00	200.00	100.00
(179) Emory Rigney	175.00	70.00	35.00
(180) Jimmy Ring	175.00	70.00	35.00
(181) Eppa Rixey	500.00	200.00	100.00
(182) Charles Robertson	175.00	70.00	35.00
(183) Ed Rommel	175.00	70.00	35.00
(184) Eddie Roush	500.00	200.00	100.00
(185) Harold (Muddy) Ruel (Herold)	175.00	70.00	35.00
(186) Babe Ruth	15,000	6,000	3,000
(187) Ray Schalk	500.00	200.00	100.00
(188) Wallie Schang	175.00	70.00	35.00
(189) Ray Schmandt	175.00	70.00	35.00
(190) Walter Schmidt	175.00	70.00	35.00
(191) Joe Schultz	175.00	70.00	35.00
(192) Everett Scott	175.00	70.00	35.00
(193) Henry Severeid	175.00	70.00	35.00
(194) Joe Sewell	500.00	200.00	100.00
(195) Howard Shanks	175.00	70.00	35.00
(196) Bob Shawkey	175.00	70.00	35.00
(197) Earl Sheely	175.00	70.00	35.00
(198) Will Sherdel	175.00	70.00	35.00
(199) Ralph Shinners	175.00	70.00	35.00
(200) Urban Shocker	175.00	70.00	35.00
(201) Charles (Chick) Shorten	175.00	70.00	35.00
(202) George Sisler	500.00	200.00	100.00
(203) Earl Smith (N.Y. Giants)	175.00	70.00	35.00
(204) Earl Smith (Washington)	175.00	70.00	35.00
(205) Elmer Smith	175.00	70.00	35.00
(206) Jack Smith	175.00	70.00	35.00
(207) Sherrod Smith	175.00	70.00	35.00
(208) Colonel Snover	175.00	70.00	35.00
(209) Frank Snyder	175.00	70.00	35.00
(210) Al Sothoron	175.00	70.00	35.00
(211) Bill Southworth	175.00	70.00	35.00
(212) Tris Speaker	900.00	360.00	180.00
(213) Arnold Statz	175.00	70.00	35.00
(214) Milton Stock	175.00	70.00	35.00
(215) Amos Strunk	175.00	70.00	35.00
(216) Jim Tierney	175.00	70.00	35.00
(217) John Tobin	175.00	70.00	35.00
(218) Fred Toney	175.00	70.00	35.00
(219) George Toporcer	175.00	70.00	35.00
(220) Harold (Pie) Traynor	500.00	200.00	100.00
(221) George Uhle	175.00	70.00	35.00
(222) Elam Vangilder	175.00	70.00	35.00
(223) Bob Veach	175.00	70.00	35.00
(224) Clarence (Tillie) Walker	175.00	70.00	35.00
(225) Curtis Walker	175.00	70.00	35.00
(226) Al Walters	175.00	70.00	35.00
(227) Bill Wambsganss	175.00	70.00	35.00
(228) Aaron Ward	175.00	70.00	35.00
(229) John Watson	175.00	70.00	35.00
(230) Frank Welch	175.00	70.00	35.00
(231) Zach Wheat	500.00	200.00	100.00
(232) Fred (Cy) Williams	175.00	70.00	35.00
(233) Kenneth Williams	175.00	70.00	35.00
(234) Ivy Wingo	175.00	70.00	35.00
(235) Joe Wood	400.00	160.00	80.00
(236) Lawrence Woodall	175.00	70.00	35.00
(237) Russell Wrightstone	175.00	70.00	35.00
(238) Everett Yaryan	175.00	70.00	35.00
(239) Ross Young (Youngs)	500.00	200.00	100.00
(240) J.T. Zachary	175.00	70.00	35.00

1927 American Caramel Series of 60 (E126)

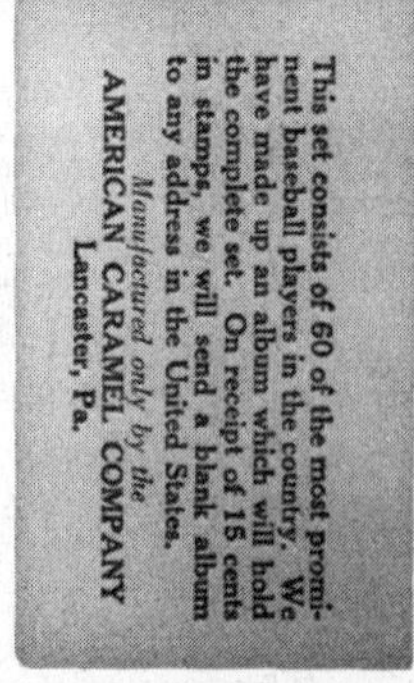

Issued in 1927 by the American Caramel Co., of Lancaster, Pa., this obscure 60-card set was one of the last of the caramel card issues. Measuring 2" x 3-1/4", the cards differ from most sets of the period because they are numbered. The back of each card includes an offer for an album to house the set which includes players from all 16 major league teams. The set has the American Card Catalog designation E126.

	NM	EX	VG
Complete Set (60):	36,500	14,500	7,250
Common Player:	125.00	55.00	30.00
1 John Gooch	200.00	80.00	40.00
2 Clyde L. Barnhart	200.00	80.00	40.00
3 Joe Busch (Bush)	200.00	80.00	40.00
4 Lee Meadows	200.00	80.00	40.00
5 E.T. Cox	200.00	80.00	40.00
6 "Red" Faber	600.00	240.00	120.00
7 Aaron Ward	200.00	80.00	40.00
8 Ray Schalk	600.00	240.00	120.00
9 "Specks" Toporcer ("Specs")	200.00	80.00	40.00
10 Bill Southworth	200.00	80.00	40.00
11 Allen Sothoron	200.00	80.00	40.00
12 Will Sherdel	200.00	80.00	40.00
13 Grover Alexander	1,000	400.00	200.00
14 Jack Quinn	200.00	80.00	40.00
15 C. Galloway	200.00	80.00	40.00
16 "Eddie" Collins	600.00	240.00	120.00
17 "Ty" Cobb	3,800	1,550	775.00
18 Percy Jones	200.00	80.00	40.00
19 Chas. Grimm	200.00	80.00	40.00
20 "Bennie" Karr	200.00	80.00	40.00
21 Charlie Jamieson	200.00	80.00	40.00
22 Sherrod Smith	200.00	80.00	40.00
23 Virgil Cheeves	200.00	80.00	40.00
24 James Ring	200.00	80.00	40.00
25 "Muddy" Ruel	200.00	80.00	40.00
26 Joe Judge	200.00	80.00	40.00
27 Tris Speaker	1,000	400.00	200.00
28 Walter Johnson	2,000	800.00	400.00
29 E.C. "Sam" Rice	600.00	240.00	120.00

30	Hank DeBerry	200.00	80.00	40.00
31	Walter Henline	200.00	80.00	40.00
32	Max Carey	600.00	240.00	120.00
33	Arnold J. Statz	200.00	80.00	40.00
34	Emil Meusel	200.00	80.00	40.00
35	T.P. "Pat" Collins	200.00	80.00	40.00
36	Urban Shocker	200.00	80.00	40.00
37	Bob Shawkey	200.00	80.00	40.00
38	"Babe" Ruth	15,000	6,000	3,000
39	Bob Meusel	200.00	80.00	40.00
40	Alex Ferguson	200.00	80.00	40.00
41	"Stuffy" McInnis	200.00	80.00	40.00
42	"Cy" Williams	200.00	80.00	40.00
43	Russel Wrightstone (Russell)	200.00	80.00	40.00
44	John Tobin	200.00	80.00	40.00
45	Wm. C. Jacobson	200.00	80.00	40.00
46	Bryan "Slim" Harriss	200.00	80.00	40.00
47	Elam Vangilder	200.00	80.00	40.00
48	Ken Williams	200.00	80.00	40.00
49	Geo. R. Sisler	800.00	325.00	160.00
50	Ed Brown	200.00	80.00	40.00
51	Jack Smith	200.00	80.00	40.00
52	Dave Bancroft	600.00	240.00	120.00
53	Larry Woodall	200.00	80.00	40.00
54	Lu Blue	200.00	80.00	40.00
55	Johnny Bassler	200.00	80.00	40.00
56	"Jakie" May	200.00	80.00	40.00
57	Horace Ford	200.00	80.00	40.00
58	"Curt" Walker	200.00	80.00	40.00
59	"Artie" Nehf	200.00	80.00	40.00
60	Geo. Kelly	600.00	240.00	120.00

1908 American League Pub. Co. Postcards

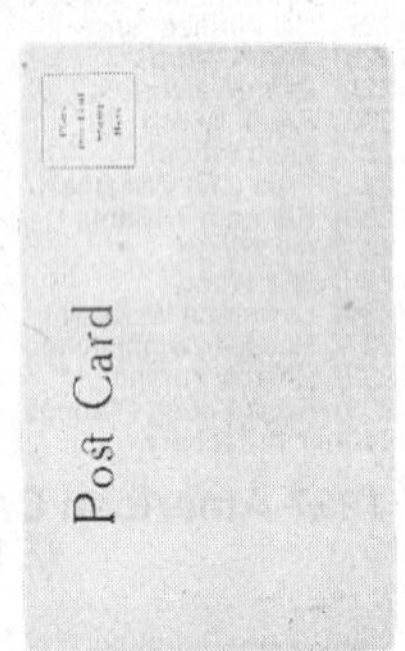

This set of black-and-white postcards was produced by the American League Publishing Co., Cleveland. The 3-1/2" x 5" cards have a large player posed-action photo against a white background and a smaller oval portrait photo in one of the top corners. A box at bottom contains some biographical data. The otherwise blank back has postcard indicia printed in black. The set carries an American Card Catalog designation of PC770. As might be expected, all but two of the players in the known checklist were contemporary members of the Cleveland ballclub.

		NM	EX	VG
Complete Set (16):		10,000	5,000	3,000
Common Player:		350.00	175.00	100.00
(1)	Harry Bay	350.00	175.00	100.00
(2)	Harry Bemis	350.00	175.00	100.00
(3)	Charles Berger	350.00	175.00	100.00
(4)	Joseph Birmingham	350.00	175.00	100.00
(5)	W. Bradley	350.00	175.00	100.00
(6)	Tyrus R. Cobb	2,500	1,250	750.00
(7)	Walter Clarkson	350.00	175.00	100.00
(8)	Elmer Flick	600.00	300.00	180.00
(9)	C.T. Hickman	350.00	175.00	100.00
(10)	William Hinchman	350.00	175.00	100.00
(11)	Addie Joss	750.00	375.00	225.00
(12)	Glen Liebhardt (Glenn)	350.00	175.00	100.00
(13)	Nap Lajoie	750.00	375.00	225.00
(14)	George Nill	350.00	175.00	100.00
(15)	George Perring	350.00	175.00	100.00
(16)	Honus Wagner	1,800	900.00	540.00

1950 American Nut & Chocolate Pennants (F150)

Although there is nothing on these small (1-7/8" x 4") felt pennants to identify the issuer, surviving ads show that the American Nut & Chocolate Co. of Boston sold them as a set of 22 for 50 cents. The pennants of American League players are printed in blue on white, while National Leaguers are printed in red on white. The pennants feature crude line-art drawings of the players at left, along with a facsimile autograph. A 10% variation in the size of the printing on the Elliott and Sain pennants has been noted, and may exist on others, as well. An approximately 17" x 7" version of the Ted Williams pennant is known and was available as a mail-in premium. Other players may also exist in that format. The checklist here is arranged alphabetically.

		NM	EX	VG
Complete Set (22):		1,800	900.00	550.00
Common Player:		65.00	32.50	20.00
(1)	Ewell Blackwell	65.00	32.50	20.00
(2)	Harry Brecheen	65.00	32.50	20.00
(3)	Phil Cavarretta	65.00	32.50	20.00
(4)	Bobby Doerr	100.00	50.00	30.00
(5)	Bob Elliott	65.00	32.50	20.00
(6)	Boo Ferriss	65.00	32.50	20.00
(7)	Joe Gordon	65.00	32.50	20.00
(8)	Tommy Holmes	65.00	32.50	20.00
(9)	Charles Keller	65.00	32.50	20.00
(10)	Ken Keltner	65.00	32.50	20.00
(11)	Ralph Kiner	100.00	50.00	30.00
(12)	Whitey Kurowski	65.00	32.50	20.00
(13)	Johnny Pesky	65.00	32.50	20.00
(14)	Pee Wee Reese	130.00	65.00	40.00
(15)	Phil Rizzuto	130.00	65.00	40.00
(16)	Johnny Sain	65.00	32.50	20.00
(17)	Enos Slaughter	100.00	50.00	30.00
(18)	Warren Spahn	100.00	50.00	30.00
(19)	Vern Stephens	65.00	32.50	20.00
(20)	Earl Torgeson	65.00	32.50	20.00
(21)	Dizzy Trout	65.00	32.50	20.00
(22)	Ted Williams	260.00	130.00	80.00
(22)	Ted Williams (17" x 7")	900.00	450.00	275.00

1968 American Oil Sweepstakes

Babe Ruth won fame as the greatest slugger in baseball history. He set many records including his 714 regular-season home runs which made him one of baseball's biggest attractions.
BABE RUTH
$1.00 ONE DOLLAR
Right side

One of several contemporary sweepstakes run by gas stations, this game required matching right- and left-side game pieces of the same athletic figure (or sporty auto) to win the stated prize. Naturally one side or the other was distributed in extremely limited quantities to avoid paying out too many prizes. Cards were given away in perforated pairs with a qualifying gasoline purchase. Uncut pairs carry a small premium over single cards. Data on which card halves were the rare part needed for redemption is incomplete and would have an effect on the collector value of surviving specimens. Individual game pieces measure 2-9/16" x 2-1/8" and are printed in color. Only the baseball players in the set are listed here.

		NM	EX	VG
(1a)	Mickey Mantle/Action (Left side, $10.)	40.00	20.00	12.00
(1b)	Mickey Mantle/Portrait (Right side, $10.)	30.00	15.00	9.00
(2a)	Willie Mays/Action (Left side, $10.)	40.00	20.00	12.00
(2b)	Willie Mays/Portrait (Right side, $10.)	25.00	12.50	7.50
(3a)	Babe Ruth/Action (Left side, $1.)	40.00	20.00	12.00
(3b)	Babe Ruth/Portrait (Right side, $1.)	25.00	12.50	7.50

1910 American Sports Candy and Jewelry

(See 1910 Orange Borders.)

1962 American Tract Society

These full-color cards, which carry religious messages on the back, were issued in 1962 by the American Tract Society, an interdenominational, non-sectarian publisher of Christian literature in the United States since 1825. Known as "Tracards," the cards measure 2-3/4" x 3-1/2" and feature color photographs on the fronts. The set includes religious scenes along with photos of various celebrities and sports stars, including baseball players Felipe Alou, Bobby Richardson, Jerry Kindall and Al Worthington. (There are two poses each of Alou and Kindall.) The backs carry rather lengthy, first-person religious testimonials from the players. The cards are numbered on the back in the lower right corner.

		NM	EX	VG
Complete Set (6):		70.00	35.00	20.00
Common Player:		10.00	5.00	3.00
43	Bobby Richardson	25.00	12.50	7.50
51a	Jerry Kindall (Cleveland)	10.00	5.00	3.00
51b	Jerry Kindall (Minnesota)	10.00	5.00	3.00
52a	Felipe Alou/Kneeling	15.00	7.50	4.50
52b	Felipe Alou/Btg	15.00	7.50	4.50
66	Al Worthington	10.00	5.00	3.00

1973 John B. Anderson Former Greats

This set of postcard-sized black-and-white cards features the artwork of John B. Anderson, a New York collector. Each card includes a facsimile autograph on front; backs are blank. The unnumbered cards are checklisted here in alphabetical order.

		NM	EX	VG
Complete Set (12):		30.00	15.00	9.00
Common Player:		4.00	2.00	1.25
(1)	Ty Cobb	6.00	3.00	1.75
(2)	Mickey Cochrane	4.00	2.00	1.25
(3)	Roberto Clemente	10.00	5.00	3.00
(4)	Lou Gehrig	10.00	5.00	3.00
(5)	Frank Frisch	4.00	2.00	1.25
(6)	Gil Hodges	6.00	3.00	1.75
(7)	Rogers Hornsby	4.00	2.00	1.25
(8)	Connie Mack	4.00	2.00	1.25
(9)	Christy Mathewson	6.00	3.00	1.75
(10)	Jackie Robinson	10.00	5.00	3.00
(11)	Babe Ruth	10.00	5.00	3.00
(12)	Pie Traynor	4.00	2.00	1.25

1977 John B. Anderson Aaron-Mays

This set of postcard size, black-and-white drawings is a collectors issue. Cards are blank-backed.

		NM	EX	VG
Complete Set (4):		5.00	2.50	1.50
Common Card:		2.00	1.00	.60
(1)	Hank Aaron (Arm in air.)	2.00	1.00	.60
(2)	Hank Aaron/Portrait	2.00	1.00	.60
(3)	Willie Mays (Giants)	2.00	1.00	.60
(4)	Willie Mays (Mets)	2.00	1.00	.60

1977 John B. Anderson New York Teams

Stars and local favorites of the three New York teams of the 1940s and 1950s are featured in this set of collectors cards. The 3-1/2" x 5-1/2" blank-back, black-and-white cards feature artwork by John B. Anderson. The unnumbered cards are checklisted here in alphabetical order.

		NM	EX	VG
Complete Set (24):		45.00	27.50	13.50
Common Player:		4.00	2.00	1.25
(1)	Yogi Berra	6.00	3.00	1.75
(2)	Ralph Branca	4.00	2.00	1.25
(3)	Dolf Camilli	4.00	2.00	1.25
(4)	Roy Campanella	6.00	3.00	1.75
(5)	Jerry Coleman	4.00	2.00	1.25
(6)	Frank Crosetti	4.00	2.00	1.25
(7)	Bill Dickey	4.00	2.00	1.25
(8)	Joe DiMaggio	15.00	7.50	4.50
(9)	Sid Gordon	4.00	2.00	1.25
(10)	Babe Herman	4.00	2.00	1.25
(11)	Carl Hubbell	4.00	2.00	1.25
(12)	Billy Johnson	4.00	2.00	1.25
(13)	Ernie Lombardi	4.00	2.00	1.25
(14)	Willard Marshall	4.00	2.00	1.25
(15)	Willie Mays	10.00	5.00	3.00
(16)	Joe McCarthy	4.00	2.00	1.25
(17)	Joe Medwick	4.00	2.00	1.25
(18)	Joe Moore	4.00	2.00	1.25
(19)	Andy Pafko	4.00	2.00	1.25
(20)	Jackie Robinson	10.00	5.00	3.00
(21)	Red Ruffing	4.00	2.00	1.25
(22)	Bill Terry	4.00	2.00	1.25
(23)	Hoyt Wilhelm	4.00	2.00	1.25
(24)	Gene Woodling	4.00	2.00	1.25

1904 Anonymous Studio Cabinets

The origins of this series of cabinet photos are unknown, as is the full entent of the issue. It is known that the portraits are the uncredited work of Boston photographer Carl Horner. Sixteen pieces were sold in the 1991 Copeland Auction, though only the players listed here have been reliably checklisted. The cabinets measure about 5-3/8" x 6-7/8" and have black or dark gray borders. Some pieces are reported to have slate-blue blank backs. The player's last name is presented in the lower-left corner in black or white outline scrip. The unnumbered cards are checklisted here in alphabetical order.

		NM	EX	VG
Common Player:		750.00	375.00	225.00
(1)	Jake Beckley	750.00	375.00	225.00
(2)	Roger Bresnahan	750.00	375.00	225.00
(3)	Jimmy Collins	750.00	375.00	225.00
(4)	Lave Cross	600.00	300.00	180.00
(5)	Hugh Duffy	600.00	300.00	180.00
(6)	Clark Griffith	750.00	375.00	225.00
(7)	Danny Hoffman	600.00	300.00	180.00
(8)	Connie Mack	750.00	375.00	225.00
(9)	Iron Man McGinity (McGinnity)	750.00	375.00	225.00
(10)	John McGraw	750.00	375.00	225.00
(11)	Matty McIntyre	600.00	300.00	180.00

1912 Anonymous T207

While most T207s are found with one of five different cigarette brands advertised on back, there is a less commonly encountered type with no such ad. They are known as Anonymous backs. Two types are known, one originating from Factory 3 in Louisiana and one from Virginia's Factory 25. The latter is much scarcer though commands little additional premium.

(See 1912 T207 for checklist and price guide.)

1925 Anonymous Postcards

The date attributed is speculative based on the limited number of known subjects. These 3-1/4" x 5-1/2" cards have a square portrait photo at center in black-and-white. With the exception of Babe Ruth, all known subjects were managers in 1925. The subject is identified by name (in either all-caps or upper- and lower-case, team, and, sometimes, title "Mgr." At least two styles of undivided backs have been found, with an ornate "POST CARD" device at top and a stamp box. The cards are printed on low-grade cardboard. Collector uncertainty as to the origins of the cards and the potential supply has kept market prices down.

	NM	EX	VG
Common Player:	300.00	150.00	90.00
Tyrus Cobb	400.00	200.00	120.00
Mgr. Tyrus Cobb	400.00	200.00	120.00
Stanley Harris	200.00	100.00	60.00
Walter Johnson	300.00	150.00	90.00
John McGraw	200.00	100.00	60.00
"Bill" McKechnie	200.00	100.00	60.00
Wilbert Robinson	200.00	100.00	60.00
Babe Ruth	600.00	300.00	180.00

1940s-50s Anonymous Premium Photos

There is no indication on these 8" x 10" black-and-white photos as to who produced them or for what purpose. The blank-backed, white-bordered pictures have the player iden-

tified with a sometimes-misspelled script signature. It is not known if this checklist is complete.

		NM	EX	VG
Complete Set (12):		300.00	150.00	90.00
Common Player:		20.00	10.00	6.00
(1)	Ty Cobb	40.00	20.00	12.00
(2)	Dizzy Dean	25.00	12.50	7.50
(3)	Bob Feller	25.00	12.50	7.50
(4)	Lou Gehrig	40.00	20.00	12.00
(5)	Harry Heilman (Heilmann)	20.00	10.00	6.00
(6)	Roger (Rogers) Hornsby	25.00	12.50	7.50
(7)	Walter Johnson	25.00	12.50	7.50
(8)	Christy Mathewson	30.00	15.00	9.00
(9)	Bob Meusel	20.00	10.00	6.00
(10)	Irish Emil Meusel	20.00	10.00	6.00
(11)	Babe Ruth	50.00	25.00	15.00
(12)	Zack Wheat	20.00	10.00	6.00

1949-1950 Ansco Almendares Scorpions

This set of the Cuban Professional League champions of the 1949-50 season was sponsored by Ansco Cameras and Film, whose logo appears on front. Some cards have on back a rubber-stamp with the name of an Havana photo studio, which may have distributed the cards. The cards are actual black-and-white photos on glossy photo paper, measuring about 3" x 3-7/8". The Scorpions had many former and future major leaguers on their roster. Cards are listed alphabetically here.

		NM	EX	VG
Complete Set (20):		3,250	1,625	975.00
Common Player:		150.00	60.00	40.00
(1)	Bill Antonello	175.00	70.00	45.00
(2)	Zungo Cabrera	150.00	60.00	40.00
(3)	Tony Castanos	150.00	60.00	40.00
(4)	Avelino Canizares	150.00	60.00	40.00
(5)	Kevin (Chuck) Connors	450.00	180.00	110.00
(6)	Andres Fleitas	150.00	60.00	40.00
(7)	Al Gionfriddo	175.00	70.00	45.00
(8)	Fermin Guerra	150.00	60.00	40.00
(9)	Gene Handley	150.00	60.00	40.00
(10)	Bob Hooper	150.00	60.00	40.00
(11)	Vincente Lopez	150.00	60.00	40.00
(12)	Conrado Marrero	175.00	70.00	45.00
(13)	Agapito Mayor	150.00	60.00	40.00
(14)	Willie Miranda	175.00	70.00	45.00
(15)	Rene Monteagudo	150.00	60.00	40.00
(16)	Roberto Ortiz	150.00	60.00	40.00
(17)	Hector Rodriguez	150.00	60.00	40.00
(18)	Octavio Rubert	150.00	60.00	40.00
(19)	Rene Solis	150.00	60.00	40.00
(20)	Ed Wright	150.00	60.00	40.00

1961-62 Apple Fresh Milk Minnesota Twins

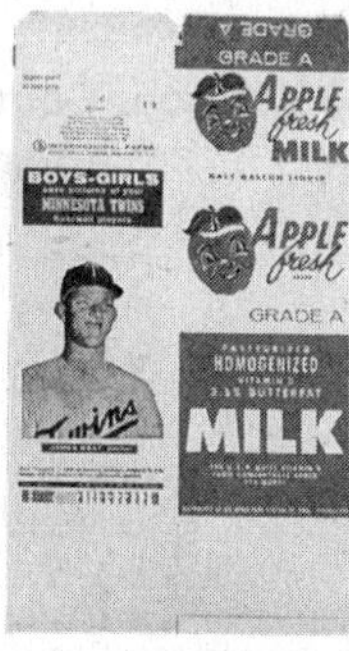

(See 1961, 1962 Cloverleaf Dairy Minnesota Twins.)

1971 Arco

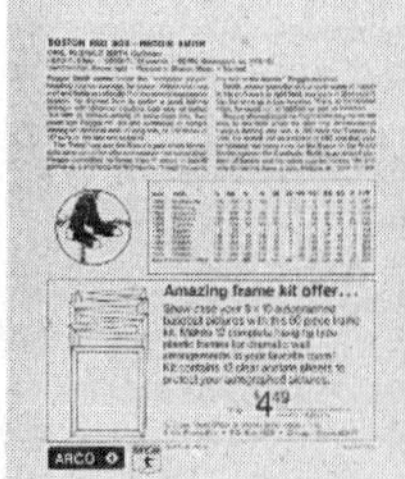

In 1971, players from four major league teams in the east were featured in a set of facsimile autographed color photos in a gas station giveaway program. Following the promotion, leftover pictures were sold directly to collectors in the pages of the existing hobby media. The photos share an 8" x 10" format, with virtually all of the players being pictured without caps. Red, white and blue stars flank the player name in the bottom border. Black-and-white backs have career summary and stats, personal data, team sponsor and union logos and an ad for frames for the pictures. The unnumbered photos are listed here alphabetically within team.

		NM	EX	VG
Complete Set (49):		175.00	90.00	50.00
Common Player:		3.00	1.50	.90
	RED SOX TEAM SET:	60.00	30.00	18.00
(1)	Luis Aparicio	10.00	5.00	3.00
(2)	Ken Brett	4.00	2.00	1.25
(3)	Billy Conigliaro	4.00	2.00	1.25
(4)	Ray Culp	4.00	2.00	1.25
(5)	Doug Griffin	4.00	2.00	1.25
(6)	Bob Montgomery	4.00	2.00	1.25
(7)	Gary Peters	4.00	2.00	1.25
(8)	George Scott	5.00	2.50	1.50
(9)	Sonny Siebert	4.00	2.00	1.25
(10)	Reggie Smith	5.00	2.50	1.50
(11)	Ken Tatum	4.00	2.00	1.25
(12)	Carl Yastrzemski	15.00	7.50	4.50
	YANKEES TEAM SET:	65.00	32.50	20.00
(1)	Jack Aker	6.00	3.00	1.75
(2)	Stan Bahnsen	6.00	3.00	1.75
(3)	Frank Baker	6.00	3.00	1.75
(4)	Danny Cater	6.00	3.00	1.75
(5)	Horace Clarke	6.00	3.00	1.75
(6)	John Ellis	6.00	3.00	1.75
(7)	Gene Michael	6.00	3.00	1.75
(8)	Thurman Munson	12.00	6.00	3.50
(9)	Bobby Murcer	7.50	3.75	2.25
(10)	Fritz Peterson	6.00	3.00	1.75
(11)	Mel Stottlemyre	6.00	3.00	1.75
(12)	Roy White	7.50	3.75	2.25
	PHILLIES TEAM SET:	40.00	20.00	12.00
(1)	Larry Bowa	3.00	1.50	.90
(2)	Jim Bunning	10.00	5.00	3.00
(3)	Roger Freed	3.00	1.50	.90
(4)	Terry Harmon	3.00	1.50	.90
(5)	Larry Hisle	3.00	1.50	.90
(6)	Joe Hoerner	3.00	1.50	.90
(7)	Deron Johnson	3.00	1.50	.90
(8)	Tim McCarver	5.00	2.50	1.50
(9)	Don Money	3.00	1.50	.90
(10)	Dick Selma	3.00	1.50	.90
(11)	Chris Short	3.00	1.50	.90
(12)	Tony Taylor	3.00	1.50	.90
(13)	Rick Wise	3.00	1.50	.90
	PIRATES TEAM SET:	65.00	32.50	20.00
(1)	Gene Alley	3.00	1.50	.90
(2)	Steve Blass	3.00	1.50	.90
(3)	Roberto Clemente	30.00	15.00	9.00
(4)	Dave Giusti	3.00	1.50	.90
(5)	Richie Hebner	3.00	1.50	.90
(6)	Bill Mazeroski	7.50	3.75	2.25
(7)	Bob Moose	3.00	1.50	.90
(8)	Al Oliver	4.50	2.25	1.25
(9)	Bob Robertson	3.00	1.50	.90
(10)	Manny Sanguillen	3.00	1.50	.90
(11)	Willie Stargell	7.50	3.75	2.25
(12)	Luke Walker	3.00	1.50	.90

1980-81 Argus Publishing Reggie Jackson

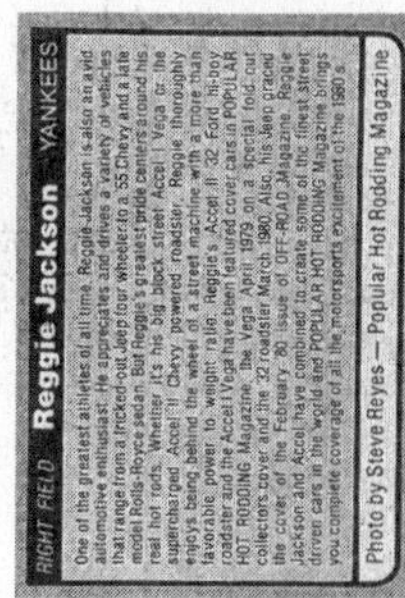

Some of the cars from Reggie Jackson's collection of hot rods and vintage vehicles were featured on a series of promotional cards issued by the publisher of Hot Rodding and Super Chevy magazines. The standard-size color cards have photos of Jackson with his cars on front, along with magazine and other logos. Backs have information on Jackson's cars. It was reported 10,000 of each were produced for distribution at automotive trade shows and a California drag strip.

		NM	EX	VG
Complete Set (3):		40.00	20.00	12.00
(1)	1980 SEMA Show (Reggie Jackson) (1932 Ford highboy)	20.00	10.00	6.00
2	1981 SEMA (Reggie Jackson) (1932 Ford 5-window)	10.00	5.00	3.00
3	1981 Super Chevy Sunday (Reggie Jackson) (1955 Chevrolet)	10.00	5.00	3.00

1955 Armour Coins

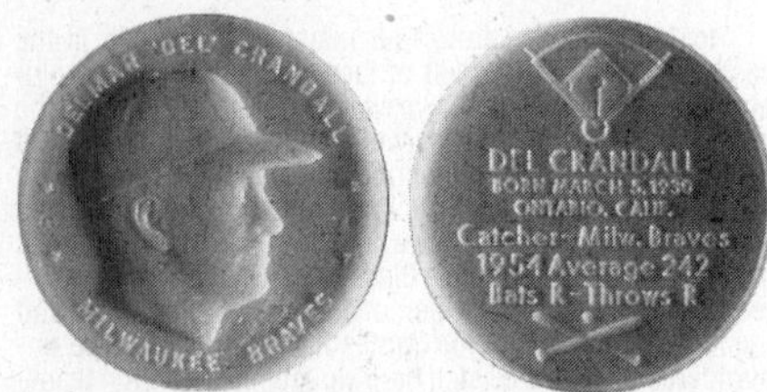

In 1955, Armour inserted a plastic "coin" into packages of hot dogs. A raised profile of a ballplayer is on front along with the player's name and team. On back, between a diamond diagram and crossed bats are name, team, position, birthplace and date, batting and throwing preference, and 1954 hitting or pitching record. The coins measure 1-1/2" in diameter and are unnumbered. They can be found in a variety of colors, some of which are much scarcer than others and elicit higher prices from Armour specialists who have studied their relative scarcities. Values shown are for coins in the most common colors (aqua, blue, green, orange and red). Each 1955 coin can be found in two different "bust tilts" in which the tip of the cap and back point of the bust point to distinctly different areas of the rim. These variations are too arcane for the average collector. The complete set price includes only the most common variations.

		NM	EX	VG
Complete Set (24):		700.00	350.00	210.00
Common Player:		15.00	6.00	3.75
(1a)	John "Johnny" Antonelli ("New York Giants" on back.)	80.00	40.00	25.00
(1b)	John "Johnny" Antonelli ("N.Y. Giants" on back.)	15.00	7.50	4.50
(2)	Larry "Yogi" Berra	25.00	12.50	7.50
(3)	Delmar "Del" Crandall	15.00	7.50	4.50
(4)	Lawrence "Larry" Doby	25.00	12.50	7.50
(5)	James "Jim" Finigan	15.00	7.50	4.50
(6)	Edward "Whitey" Ford	40.00	20.00	12.00
(7a)	James "Junior" Gilliam ("bats L or R,")	60.00	30.00	18.00
(7b)	James "Junior" Gilliam ("bats L - R," thick lips, wide gap between "BROOKLYN" and "DODGERS")	35.00	17.50	10.00
(7c)	James "Junior" Gilliam ("bats L - R," thin lips, narrow gap between "BROOKLYN" and "DODGERS")	45.00	22.50	13.50
(8)	Harvey "Kitten" Haddix	15.00	7.50	4.50
(9a)	Ranson "Randy" Jackson (Ransom)("nfielder" on back)	30.00	15.00	9.00
(9b)	Ranson "Randy" Jackson (Ransom) ("Infielder" on back.)	50.00	25.00	15.00
(10a)	Jack "Jackie" Jensen ("Boston Reb Sox")	60.00	30.00	18.00
(10b)	Jack "Jackie" Jensen ("Boston Red Sox")	20.00	10.00	6.00
(11)	Theodore "Ted" Kluszewski	20.00	10.00	6.00
(12a)	Harvey E. Kuenn (Widely spaced letters in name; last line on back is bats/throws.)	30.00	15.00	9.00
(12b)	Harvey E. Kuenn (Widely spaced letters in name; last line on back is 1954 average.)	100.00	50.00	30.00
(12c)	Harvey E. Kuenn (Condensed letters in name; last line on back is 1954 average.)	70.00	35.00	20.00
(13a)	Charles "Mickey" Mantel (Incorrect spelling.)	115.00	55.00	35.00
(13b)	Charles "Mickey" Mantle (Corrected)("bats L or R")	400.00	200.00	120.00
(13c)	Charles "Mickey" Mantle (Corrected)("bats L - R")	400.00	200.00	120.00
(14)	Donald "Don" Mueller/SP	30.00	15.00	9.00
(15)	Harold "Pee Wee" Reese	25.00	12.50	7.50
(16)	Allie P. Reynolds	15.00	7.50	4.50
(17)	Albert "Flip" Rosen	20.00	10.00	6.00
(18)	Curtis "Curt" Simmons	20.00	10.00	6.00
(19)	Edwin "Duke" Snider	100.00	50.00	30.00
(20)	Warren Spahn	40.00	20.00	12.00
(21)	Frank Thomas/SP	25.00	12.50	7.50
(22a)	Virgil "Fire" Trucks (WHITESOX)	25.00	12.50	7.50
(22b)	Virgil "Fire" Trucks (WHITE SOX)	50.00	25.00	15.00
(23)	Robert "Bob" Turley	25.00	12.50	7.50
(24)	James "Mickey" Vernon	15.00	7.50	4.50

1958 Armour S.F. Giants Tabs

In the Giants' first season on the West Coast, packages of Armour hot dogs in the Bay Area could be found with a small (about 2" x 1-5/8") lithographed tin player "tab" enclosed. In team colors of black, white and orange the tabs have black-and-white portraits at center, around which is a round, square or diamond shaped device bearing the team name and other graphic touches. At the sides are wings with baseballs or caps printed thereon. A 1/2" tab is at top with a slotted panel at bottom. The tab of one piece could be inserted into the slot of another to create a chain of these pieces, or the top tab could be folded over a shirt pocket to wear the item as a badge. The unnumbered pieces are checklisted here alphabetically. NM values quoted are for unbent pieces only.

		NM	EX	VG
Complete Set (10):		2,700	1,350	825.00
Common Player:		250.00	125.00	75.00
(1)	Johnny Antonelli	250.00	125.00	75.00
(2)	Curt Barclay	250.00	125.00	75.00
(3)	Ray Crone	250.00	125.00	75.00
(4)	Whitey Lockman	250.00	125.00	75.00
(5a)	Willie Mays (Portrait in circle.)	450.00	225.00	135.00
(5b)	Willie Mays (Portrait in diamond.)	450.00	225.00	135.00
(6)	Don Mueller	250.00	125.00	75.00
(7)	Danny O'Connell	250.00	125.00	75.00
(8)	Hank Sauer	250.00	125.00	75.00
(9)	Daryl Spencer	250.00	125.00	75.00
(10)	Bobby Thomson	250.00	125.00	75.00

1959 Armour Bacon K.C. Athletics

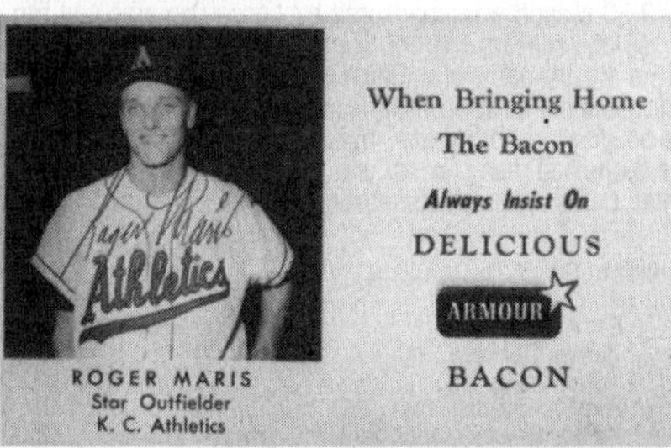

Not so much a baseball card set as a handful of related single-card issues used at player promotional appearances, a total of four cards are currently known of this issue. Measuring either 5-1/2" x 3-1/4" or 5-1/2" x 4", the horizontal-format cards are printed in black-and-white on paper stock and are blank-backed. A posed player photo appears at left, with an ad for Armour bacon at right. Cards were given out at player appearances at local supermarkets. To date, all known specimens have been found autographed and are priced as such.

		NM	EX	VG
Complete Set (4):		900.00	450.00	275.00
Common Player:		75.00	37.00	22.00
(1)	Harry Chiti	75.00	37.50	22.50
(2)	Whitey Herzog	90.00	45.00	27.50
(3)	Roger Maris (Photo to waist.)	600.00	300.00	180.00
(4)	Roger Maris (Hands on knees.)	600.00	300.00	180.00

1959 Armour Coins

After a three-year layoff, Armour again inserted plastic "coins" into its hot dog packages. The coins retained their 1-1/2" size but did not include as much detailed information as in 1955. Missing from the coins' backs is information such as birthplace and date, team, and batting and throwing preference. The fronts contain the player's name and, unlike 1955, only the team nickname is given. The set consists of 20 coins which come in a myriad of colors. Common colors are navy blue, royal blue, medium green, orange and red. Many other colors are known, many of them scarce and of extra value to Armour specialists. In 1959 Armour had a mail-in offer of 10 coins for $1, which accounts for half of the coins in the set being much more plentiful than the others.

		NM	EX	VG
Complete Set (20):		400.00	200.00	120.00
Common Player:		15.00	7.50	4.50
(1)	Hank Aaron	30.00	15.00	9.00
(2)	John Antonelli	15.00	7.50	4.50
(3)	Richie Ashburn	30.00	15.00	9.00
(4)	Ernie Banks	30.00	15.00	9.00
(5)	Don Blasingame	15.00	7.50	4.50
(6)	Bob Cerv	15.00	7.50	4.50
(7)	Del Crandall	15.00	7.50	4.50
(8)	Whitey Ford	25.00	12.50	7.50
(9)	Nellie Fox	20.00	10.00	6.00
(10)	Jackie Jensen	20.00	10.00	6.00
(11)	Harvey Kuenn	30.00	15.00	9.00
(12)	Frank Malzone	20.00	10.00	6.00
(13)	Johnny Podres	30.00	15.00	9.00
(14)	Frank Robinson	30.00	15.00	9.00
(15)	Roy Sievers	15.00	7.50	4.50
(16)	Bob Skinner	15.00	7.50	4.50
(17)	Frank Thomas	15.00	7.50	4.50
(18)	Gus Triandos	15.00	7.50	4.50
(19)	Bob Turley	20.00	10.00	6.00
(20)	Mickey Vernon	15.00	7.50	4.50

1960 Armour Coins

The 1960 Armour coin issue is identical in number and style to the 1959 set. The unnumbered coins, 1-1/2" in diameter, once again came in a variety of colors. Common colors for 1960 are pale blue, royal blue, red, red-orange, light green, dark green and yellow. Values shown are for common-colored pieces. Scarcer colors exist and may be of premium value to specialists. The Bud Daley coin is very scarce, although it is not known why. Theories for the scarcity center on broken molding equipment, contract disputes, or that the coin was only inserted in a test product that quickly proved to be unsuccessful. As in 1959, a mail-in offer for 10 free coins was made available by Armour. The complete set price includes only the most common variations. Many 1960 Armour coins are found with only partial rims on back (Mantle is particularly susceptible to this condition). Coins without full back rims can grade no higher than VG.

		NM	EX	VG
Complete Set (20):		1,100	550.00	325.00
Common Player:		12.50	6.25	3.75
(1a)	Hank Aaron (Braves)	25.00	12.50	7.50
(1b)	Hank Aaron (Milwaukee Braves)	40.00	20.00	12.00
(2)	Bob Allison	20.00	10.00	6.00
(3)	Ernie Banks	30.00	15.00	9.00
(4)	Ken Boyer	12.50	6.25	3.75
(5)	Rocky Colavito	35.00	17.50	10.50
(6)	Gene Conley	12.50	6.25	3.75
(7)	Del Crandall	12.50	6.25	3.75
(8)	Bud Daley	750.00	375.00	225.00
(9a)	Don Drysdale (L.A condensed.)	35.00	17.50	10.50
(9b)	Don Drysdale (Space between L. and A.)	25.00	12.50	7.50
(10)	Whitey Ford	20.00	10.00	6.00
(11)	Nellie Fox	15.00	7.50	4.50
(12)	Al Kaline	20.00	10.00	6.00
(13a)	Frank Malzone (Red Sox)	12.50	6.25	3.75
(13b)	Frank Malzone (Boston Red Sox)	20.00	10.00	6.00
(14)	Mickey Mantle	75.00	37.50	22.50
(15)	Ed Mathews	20.00	10.00	6.00
(16)	Willie Mays	50.00	25.00	15.00
(17)	Vada Pinson	12.50	6.25	3.75
(18)	Dick Stuart	12.50	6.25	3.75
(19)	Gus Triandos	12.50	6.25	3.75
(20)	Early Wynn	12.50	6.25	3.75

1908 Art Post Card Co. Our Home Team

This set of team post cards presents players from five Midwestern teams in a foldout format. The cover of the accordian-fold novelty is in orange and green. A 3-1/2" x 5-1/2" postcard depicts a ballfield and various pieces of baseball equipment. Printed on a large baseball is "Our Home Team." Folded inside are a number of 2" x 2-1/4" panels with one or two player photos printed on each side. Each player is identified, though misspelled names are common.

		NM	EX	VG
Complete Set (5):		5,500	2,750	1,650
Common Team Card:		800.00	400.00	250.00
(1)	Chicago Cubs (Three Finger Brown, Frank Chance, Johnny Evers, Chick Fraser, Solly Hofman, Johnny Kling, Carl Lundgren, Pat Moran, Jake Pfeister, Ed Reulbach, Wildfire Schulte, Jimmy Sheckard, Jimmy Slagle, Harry Steinfeldt, Joe Tinker, Heinie Zimmerman)	1,200	600.00	360.00
(2)	Chicago White Sox (Nick Altrock, John Anderson, Jake Atz, George Davis, Jiggs Donohue (Donahue), Patsy Dougherty, Eddie Hahn, Frank Isbell, Fielder Jones, Frank Owen, George Rohe, Billy Sullivan, Lee Tannehill, Ed Walsh, Doc White)	1,850	925.00	550.00
(3)	Detroit Tigers (William Caughlin (Coughlin), Ty Cobb, Sam Crawford, Wild Bill Donovan, Red Downs, Hughie Jennings, Davy Jones, Red Killefer, Ed Killian, Matty McIntyre, George Mullin, Charley O'Leary, Fred Payne, Claude Rossman, Germany Schaefer, Boss Schmidt, George Suggs, Ed Summers, Ira Thomas, George Winter, Ed Willett)	2,000	1,000	600.00
(4)	St. Louis Browns (Bob Bailey, Bert Blue, Dode Criss, Bill Dinneen, Hobe Ferris, Bill Graham, Roy Hartzell, Danny Hoffman, Harry Howell, Charlie Jones, Tom Jones, Jimmy McAleer, Jack O'Connor, Barney Pelty, Jack Powell, Al Schweitzer, Tubby Spencer, George Stone, Rube Waddell, Bobby Wallace, Jimmy Williams, Joe Yeager)	950.00	475.00	285.00
(5)	St. Louis Cardinals	800.00	400.00	240.00

1953-55 Artvue Hall of Fame Plaque Postcards - Type 1

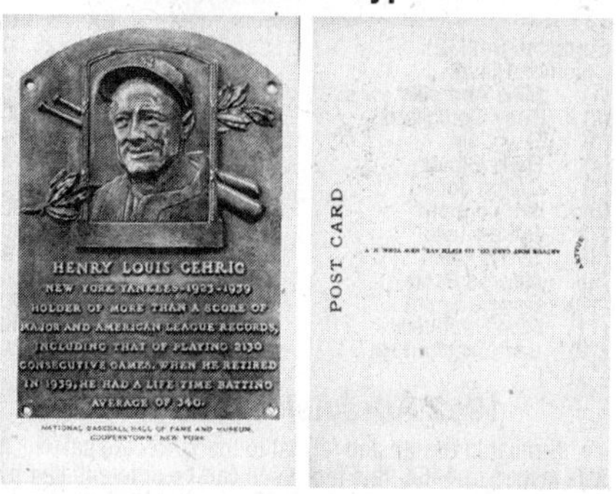

From 1953-1963, Artvue was the official producer of the Baseball Hall of Fame's postcards available for public sale. The 3-1/2" x 5-1/2" black-and-white cards depict the bronze plaque of each inductee. Fronts have a white border. Postcard-style backs have a bit of player data and identification of the specific producer. On Type 1 Artvue cards, issued 1953-55, the bolt holes in the four corners of the plaque are open. The Type 2 Artvues have baseball bolts in each corner of the plaque. The unnumbered cards are checklisted here alphabetically.

		NM	EX	VG
Complete Set (79):		2,000	1,000	600.00
Common Player:		30.00	15.00	9.00
(1)	G.C. Alexander	30.00	15.00	9.00
(2)	Adrian Anson	30.00	15.00	9.00
(3)	Frank Baker	30.00	15.00	9.00
(4)	Ed Barrow	30.00	15.00	9.00
(5)	Chief Bender	30.00	15.00	9.00
(6)	Roger Bresnahan	30.00	15.00	9.00
(7)	Dan Brouthers	30.00	15.00	9.00
(8)	Mordecai Brown	30.00	15.00	9.00
(9)	Morgan Bulkeley	30.00	15.00	9.00
(10)	Jesse Burkett	30.00	15.00	9.00
(11)	Alexander Cartwright	30.00	15.00	9.00
(12)	Henry Chadwick	30.00	15.00	9.00
(13)	Frank Chance	30.00	15.00	9.00
(14)	Jack Chesbro	30.00	15.00	9.00
(15)	Fred Clarke	30.00	15.00	9.00
(16)	Ty Cobb	80.00	40.00	24.00
(17)	Mickey Cochrane	30.00	15.00	9.00
(18)	Eddie Collins	30.00	15.00	9.00
(19)	Jimmy Collins	30.00	15.00	9.00
(20)	Charles Comiskey	30.00	15.00	9.00
(21)	Tom Connolly	30.00	15.00	9.00
(22)	Candy Cummings	30.00	15.00	9.00
(23)	Dizzy Dean	30.00	15.00	9.00
(24)	Ed Delahanty	30.00	15.00	9.00
(25)	Bill Dickey	30.00	15.00	9.00
(26)	Joe DiMaggio	80.00	40.00	24.00
(27)	Hugh Duffy	30.00	15.00	9.00
(28)	Johnny Evers	30.00	15.00	9.00
(29)	Buck Ewing	30.00	15.00	9.00
(30)	Jimmie Foxx	30.00	15.00	9.00
(31)	Frankie Frisch	30.00	15.00	9.00
(32)	Lou Gehrig	90.00	45.00	27.50
(33)	Charlie Gehringer	30.00	15.00	9.00
(34)	Clark Griffith	30.00	15.00	9.00
(35)	Lefty Grove	30.00	15.00	9.00
(36)	Gabby Hartnett	30.00	15.00	9.00
(37)	Harry Heilmann	30.00	15.00	9.00
(38)	Rogers Hornsby	30.00	15.00	9.00
(39)	Carl Hubbell	30.00	15.00	9.00
(40)	Hughie Jennings	30.00	15.00	9.00
(41)	Ban Johnson	30.00	15.00	9.00
(42)	Walter Johnson	60.00	30.00	18.00
(43)	Willie Keeler	30.00	15.00	9.00
(44)	King Kelly	30.00	15.00	9.00
(45)	Bill Klem	30.00	15.00	9.00
(46)	Nap Lajoie	30.00	15.00	9.00
(47)	Kenesaw Landis	30.00	15.00	9.00
(48)	Ted Lyons	30.00	15.00	9.00
(49)	Connie Mack	30.00	15.00	9.00
(50)	Rabbit Maranville	30.00	15.00	9.00
(51)	Christy Mathewson	60.00	30.00	18.00
(52)	Tommy McCarthy	30.00	15.00	9.00
(53)	Joe McGinnity	30.00	15.00	9.00
(54)	John McGraw	30.00	15.00	9.00
(55)	Kid Nichols	30.00	15.00	9.00
(56)	Jim O'Rourke	30.00	15.00	9.00
(57)	Mel Ott	30.00	15.00	9.00
(58)	Herb Pennock	30.00	15.00	9.00
(59)	Ed Plank	30.00	15.00	9.00
(60)	Chas. Radbourn	30.00	15.00	9.00
(61)	Wilbert Robinson	30.00	15.00	9.00
(62)	Babe Ruth	120.00	60.00	35.00
(63)	Ray Schalk	30.00	15.00	9.00
(64)	Al Simmons	30.00	15.00	9.00
(65)	George Sisler	30.00	15.00	9.00
(66)	Al Spalding	30.00	15.00	9.00
(67)	Tris Speaker	30.00	15.00	9.00
(68)	Bill Terry	30.00	15.00	9.00
(69)	Joe Tinker	30.00	15.00	9.00
(70)	Pie Traynor	30.00	15.00	9.00
(71)	Dazzy Vance	30.00	15.00	9.00
(72)	Rube Waddell	30.00	15.00	9.00
(73)	Honus Wagner	60.00	30.00	18.00
(74)	Bobby Wallace	30.00	15.00	9.00
(75)	Ed Walsh	30.00	15.00	9.00
(76)	Paul Waner	30.00	15.00	9.00
(77)	George Wright	30.00	15.00	9.00
(78)	Harry Wright	30.00	15.00	9.00
(79)	Cy Young	60.00	30.00	18.00

1956-63 Artvue Hall of Fame Plaque Postcards - Type 2

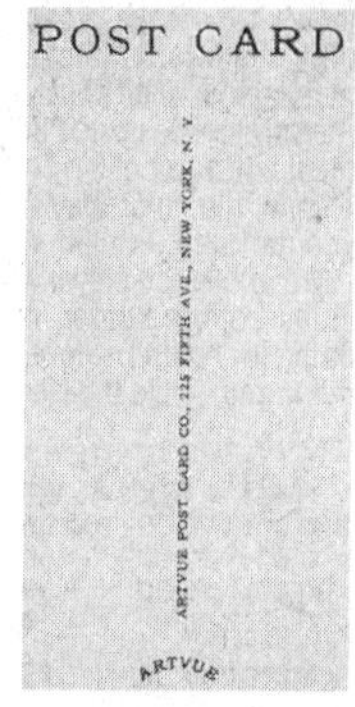

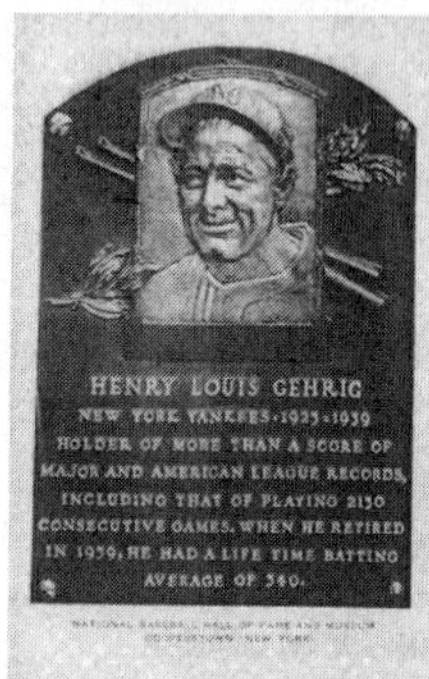

From 1953-1963, Artvue was the official producer of the Baseball Hall of Fame's postcards available for public sale. The 3-1/2" x 5-1/2" black-and-white cards depict the bronze plaque of each inductee. Fronts have a white border. Postcard-style backs have a bit of player data and identification of the specific producer. On Type 2 Artvue cards, issued 1956-63, there are baseball bolts in each corner of the plaque. The unnumbered cards are checklisted here alphabetically. Players unique to Type 2 are noted with an asterisk.

		NM	EX	VG
Complete Set (94):		2,000	1,000	600.00
Common Player:		25.00	12.50	7.50
(1)	G.C. Alexander	25.00	12.50	7.50
(2)	Adrian Anson	25.00	12.50	7.50
(3)	Frank Baker	25.00	12.50	7.50
(4)	Ed Barrow	25.00	12.50	7.50
(5)	Chief Bender	25.00	12.50	7.50
(6)	Roger Bresnahan	25.00	12.50	7.50
(7)	Dan Brouthers	25.00	12.50	7.50
(8)	Mordecai Brown	25.00	12.50	7.50
(9)	Morgan Bulkeley	25.00	12.50	7.50
(10)	Jesse Burkett	25.00	12.50	7.50
(11)	Max Carey (*)	25.00	12.50	7.50
(12)	Alexander Cartwright	25.00	12.50	7.50
(13)	Henry Chadwick	25.00	12.50	7.50
(14)	Frank Chance	25.00	12.50	7.50
(15)	Jack Chesbro	25.00	12.50	7.50
(16)	Fred Clarke	25.00	12.50	7.50
(17)	John Clarkson (*)	25.00	12.50	7.50
(18)	Ty Cobb	60.00	30.00	18.00
(19)	Mickey Cochrane	25.00	12.50	7.50
(20)	Eddie Collins	25.00	12.50	7.50
(21)	Jimmy Collins	25.00	12.50	7.50
(22)	Charles Comiskey	25.00	12.50	7.50
(23)	Tom Connolly	25.00	12.50	7.50
(24)	Sam Crawford (*)	25.00	12.50	7.50
(25)	Joe Cronin (*)	25.00	12.50	7.50
(26)	Candy Cummings	25.00	12.50	7.50
(27)	Dizzy Dean	25.00	12.50	7.50
(28)	Ed Delahanty	25.00	12.50	7.50
(29)	Bill Dickey	25.00	12.50	7.50
(30)	Joe DiMaggio	80.00	40.00	24.00
(31)	Hugh Duffy	25.00	12.50	7.50
(32)	Johnny Evers	25.00	12.50	7.50
(33)	Buck Ewing	25.00	12.50	7.50
(34)	Bob Feller (*)	25.00	12.50	7.50
(35)	Elmer Flick (*)	25.00	12.50	7.50
(36)	Jimmie Foxx	25.00	12.50	7.50
(37)	Frank Frisch	25.00	12.50	7.50
(38)	Lou Gehrig	80.00	40.00	24.00
(39)	Charlie Gehringer	25.00	12.50	7.50
(40)	Hank Greenberg (*)	25.00	12.50	7.50
(41)	Clark Griffith	25.00	12.50	7.50
(42)	Lefty Grove	25.00	12.50	7.50
(43)	Billy Hamilton (*)	25.00	12.50	7.50
(44)	Gabby Hartnett	25.00	12.50	7.50
(45)	Harry Heilmann	25.00	12.50	7.50
(46)	Rogers Hornsby	25.00	12.50	7.50
(47)	Carl Hubbell	25.00	12.50	7.50
(48)	Hughie Jennings	25.00	12.50	7.50
(49)	Ban Johnson	25.00	12.50	7.50
(50)	Walter Johnson	40.00	20.00	12.00
(51)	Willie Keeler	25.00	12.50	7.50
(52)	King Kelly	25.00	12.50	7.50
(53)	Bill Klem	25.00	12.50	7.50
(54)	Nap Lajoie	25.00	12.50	7.50
(55)	Kenesaw Landis	25.00	12.50	7.50
(56)	Ted Lyons	25.00	12.50	7.50
(57)	Connie Mack	25.00	12.50	7.50
(58)	Rabbit Maranville	25.00	12.50	7.50
(59)	Christy Mathewson	40.00	20.00	12.00
(60)	Joe McCarthy (*)	25.00	12.50	7.50
(61)	Tommy McCarthy	25.00	12.50	7.50
(62)	Joe McGinnity	25.00	12.50	7.50
(63)	John McGraw	25.00	12.50	7.50
(64)	Bill McKechnie (*)	25.00	12.50	7.50
(65)	Kid Nichols	25.00	12.50	7.50
(66)	Jim O'Rourke	25.00	12.50	7.50
(67)	Mel Ott	25.00	12.50	7.50
(68)	Herb Pennock	25.00	12.50	7.50
(69)	Ed Plank	25.00	12.50	7.50
(70)	Charles Radbourn	25.00	12.50	7.50
(71)	Sam Rice (*)	25.00	12.50	7.50
(72)	Eppa Rixey (*)	25.00	12.50	7.50
(73)	Jackie Robinson (*)	40.00	20.00	12.00
(74)	Wilbert Robinson	25.00	12.50	7.50
(75)	Edd Roush (*)	25.00	12.50	7.50
(76)	Babe Ruth	120.00	60.00	35.00
(77)	Ray Schalk	25.00	12.50	7.50
(78)	Al Simmons	25.00	12.50	7.50
(79)	George Sisler	25.00	12.50	7.50
(80)	Albert Spalding	25.00	12.50	7.50
(81)	Tris Speaker	25.00	12.50	7.50
(82)	Bill Terry	25.00	12.50	7.50
(83)	Joe Tinker	25.00	12.50	7.50
(84)	Pie Traynor	25.00	12.50	7.50
(85)	Dazzy Vance	25.00	12.50	7.50
(86)	Rube Waddell	25.00	12.50	7.50
(87)	Honus Wagner	40.00	20.00	12.00
(88)	Bobby Wallace	25.00	12.50	7.50
(89)	Ed Walsh	25.00	12.50	7.50
(90)	Paul Waner	25.00	12.50	7.50
(91)	Zack Wheat (*)	25.00	12.50	7.50
(92)	George Wright	25.00	12.50	7.50
(93)	Harry Wright	25.00	12.50	7.50
(94)	Cy Young	40.00	20.00	12.00

1967 Ashland Oil Grand Slam Baseball

These baseball player folders were issued in conjunction with a sweepstakes conducted at Ashland gas stations. The cards were originally issued in the form of a sealed tri-fold. When opened to 7-1/2" x 2", a black-and-white player photo is pictured

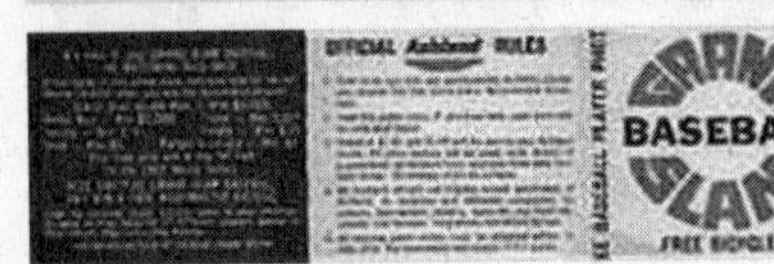

at center. Back of the panel offers contest rules. The unnumbered panels are listed here in alphabetical order. Note: the existence of the (6) Jim Maloney card is now in question.

	NM	EX	VG
Complete Set (12):	375.00	185.00	110.00
Common Player:	20.00	10.00	6.00
(1) Jim Bunning	30.00	15.00	9.00
(2) Elston Howard	25.00	12.50	7.50
(3) Al Kaline	50.00	25.00	15.00
(4) Harmon Killebrew	30.00	15.00	9.00
(5) Ed Kranepool	20.00	10.00	6.00
(6) Jim Maloney/SP (Existence now in question.)	75.00	37.00	22.00
(7) Bill Mazeroski	30.00	15.00	9.00
(8) Frank Robinson	40.00	20.00	12.00
(9) Ron Santo	25.00	12.50	7.50
(10) Joe Torre	25.00	12.50	7.50
(11) Leon Wagner	20.00	10.00	6.00
(12) Pete Ward	20.00	10.00	6.00

1895 Ashman Studio Cabinets

The date attributed is speculative and about at the mid-point of the sole known subject's tenure with the Baltimore Orioles of the National League. In typical cabinet format, about 4-1/2" x 6-1/2", the card features a sepia-toned portrait photo attached to a blank-back, cream-colored thick cardboard mount bearing the advertising at bottom of the Baltimore photographer's studio. It is unknown whether cabinets of any of McGraw's teammates or adversaries were also produced.

	NM	EX	VG
John McGraw	10,000	5,000	3,000

1933 Astra Margarine

One of several "foreign" Babe Ruth cards issued during his prime was included in a 112-card set produced as premiums for Astra Margarine in Germany. Ruth is the only major league ballplayer in the issue. Cards are in full color, measuring 2-3/4" x 4-1/8". Backs of the unnumbered cards are printed in German. Three types of backs can be found on the Ruth card. Type 1, has the Astra name nearly centered. The Type 2 back has the brand name printed closer to the bottom of the card, with only four lines of type under it. Type 3 is a variation of Type 2 on which the appropriate page number (83) of the accompanying album is mentioned on the line immediately above "Handbuch des Sports" near the top. One card was given with the purchase of each 1/2 pound of margarine and the album could be ordered by mail. See also Sanella Margarine.

	NM	EX	VG
Type 1 Babe Ruth (Astra centered.)	1,500	750.00	450.00
Type 2 Babe Ruth (Astra at bottom.)	1,750	875.00	525.00
Type 3 Babe Ruth (Astra at bottom w/83.)	3,500	1,750	1,000

1978 Atlanta Nobis Center

In conjunction with a May 1978 card show to benefit the training/rehabilitation center supported by Hall of Fame linebacker Tommy Nobis, this collectors' set was issued. Most of the players on the 2-1/2" x 3-1/2" cards are former stars of the Boston, Milwaukee or Atlanta Braves, though players from a few other teams and footballer Nobis are also included; several of the players appeared at the show as autograph guests. The cards are in the style of 1959 Topps, with black-and-white player photos in a circle at center and a light green background. The career summary on back is in black-and-white. The unnumbered cards are checklisted here in alphabetical order.

	NM	EX	VG
Complete Set (24):	25.00	12.50	7.50
Common Player:	1.50	.70	.45
(1) Hank Aaron	6.00	3.00	1.75
(2) Joe Adcock	1.50	.70	.45
(3) Felipe Alou	1.50	.70	.45
(4) Frank Bolling	1.50	.70	.45
(5) Orlando Cepeda	2.00	1.00	.60
(6) Ty Cline	1.50	.70	.45
(7) Tony Cloninger	1.50	.70	.45
(8) Del Crandall	1.50	.70	.45
(9) Fred Haney	1.50	.70	.45
(10) Pat Jarvis	1.50	.70	.45
(11) Ernie Johnson	1.50	.70	.45
(12) Ken Johnson	1.50	.70	.45
(13) Denny Lemaster	1.50	.70	.45
(14) Eddie Mathews	2.00	1.00	.60
(15) Lee Maye	1.50	.70	.45
(16) Denis Menke	1.50	.70	.45
(17) Felix Millan	1.50	.70	.45
(18) Johnny Mize	2.00	1.00	.60
(19) Tommy Nobis	1.50	.70	.45
(20) Gene Oliver	1.50	.70	.45
(21) Johnny Sain	1.75	.90	.50
(22) Warren Spahn	2.00	1.00	.60
(23) Joe Torre	2.00	1.00	.60
(24) Bob Turley	1.75	.90	.50

1968 Atlantic Oil Play Ball Game Cards

Because some of the cards were redeemable either alone or in combination for cash awards, and thus were issued in lesser quantities, completion of this game issue was difficult from Day 1. Fifty different players are known in the issue, along with a number of variations. The majority of the cards can be found with card backs either explaining the game rules or picturing a pitcher throwing to a batter. The cards were issued in two-card panels, designed to be separated into a pair of 2-1/2" x 3-1/2" cards. For lack of an MLB license, the color player photos at center have the uniform logos removed. Printed at top is the face value of the particular card, while the player's name, team and league are printed in the bottom border. A large player number is printed in a white circle at bottom-right. American Leaguers' cards are bordered in red, while the National League cards have blue borders.

	NM	EX	VG
Complete Set (Non-winners.) (40):	350.00	175.00	100.00
Common Player:	6.00	3.00	1.50
Instant Winner Card:	30.00	15.00	9.00
AMERICAN LEAGUE			
1a Tony Oliva	6.00	3.00	1.75
1b Brooks Robinson	15.00	7.50	4.50
1c Pete Ward	6.00	3.00	1.75
2a Max Alvis	6.00	3.00	1.75
2b Campy Campaneris	6.00	3.00	1.75
2c Jim Fregosi	6.00	3.00	1.75
2d Al Kaline	20.00	10.00	6.00
2e Tom Tresh	6.00	3.00	1.75
3 Bill Freehan ($2,500 winner)	300.00	150.00	90.00
4 Tommy Davis ($100 winner)	100.00	50.00	30.00
5a Norm Cash	7.50	3.75	2.25
5b Frank Robinson	15.00	7.50	4.50
5c Carl Yastrzemski	25.00	12.50	7.50
6a Joe Pepitone	7.50	3.75	2.25
6b Boog Powell	10.00	5.00	3.00
6c George Scott	6.00	3.00	1.75
6d Fred Valentine	6.00	3.00	1.75
7 Tom McCraw ($10 winner)	75.00	37.00	22.00
8 Andy Etchebarren ($5 winner)	50.00	25.00	15.00
9a Dean Chance	6.00	3.00	1.75
9b Joel Horlen	6.00	3.00	1.75
9c Jim Lonborg	6.00	3.00	1.75
9d Sam McDowell	6.00	3.00	1.75
10 Earl Wilson ($1 winner)	35.00	17.50	10.50
11 Jose Santiago	6.00	3.00	1.75
NATIONAL LEAGUE			
1a Bob Aspromonte	6.00	3.00	1.75
1b Lou Brock	12.00	6.00	3.50
1c Johnny Callison	6.00	3.00	1.75
1d Pete Rose	25.00	12.50	7.50
1e Maury Wills	7.50	3.75	2.25
2 Tommie Agee ($2,500 winner)	300.00	150.00	90.00
3a Felipe Alou	7.50	3.75	2.25
3b Jim Hart	6.00	3.00	1.75
3c Vada Pinson	7.50	3.75	2.25
4a Hank Aaron	25.00	12.50	7.50
4b Orlando Cepeda	10.00	5.00	3.00
4c Willie McCovey	12.00	6.00	3.50
4d Ron Santo	9.00	4.50	2.75
5 Ernie Banks ($100 winner)	450.00	225.00	135.00
6 Ron Fairly ($10 winner)	75.00	37.50	22.50
7a Roberto Clemente	75.00	37.50	22.50
7b Roger Maris	25.00	12.50	7.50
7c a Ron Swoboda (Collect w/ N.L. #6, win $10.)	6.00	3.00	1.75
7c b Ron Swoboda (Collect w/ N.L. #8, win $5.)	45.00	22.00	13.50
8 Billy Williams ($5 winner)	95.00	47.00	28.00
9a Jim Bunning	9.00	4.50	2.75
9b Bob Gibson	12.00	6.00	3.50
9c Jim Maloney	6.00	3.00	1.75
9d Mike McCormick	6.00	3.00	1.75
10 Milt Pappas	6.00	3.00	1.75
11 Claude Osteen ($1 winner)	35.00	17.50	10.00

1969 Atlantic-Richfield Boston Red Sox

One of many larger-format (8" x 10") baseball premiums sponsored as gas station giveaways in the late 1960s and early 1970s was this set of Boston Red Sox player pictures by celebrity artist John Wheeldon sponsored by the Atlantic-Richfield Oil Co. Done in pastel colors, the pictures feature large portraits and smaller action pictures of the player against a bright background. A facsimile autograph is pencilled in beneath the pictures, and the player's name is printed in the white bottom border. Backs are printed in black-and-white and inculde biographical and career data, full major and minor legaue stats, a self-portrait and biography of the artist and the logos of the team, players' association and sponsor. The unnumbered pictures are checklisted here alphabetically.

	NM	EX	VG
Complete Set (12):	75.00	35.00	25.00
Common Player:	6.00	3.00	1.75
(1) Mike Andrews	6.00	3.00	1.75
(2) Tony Conigliaro	10.00	5.00	3.00
(3) Ray Culp	6.00	3.00	1.75
(4) Russ Gibson	6.00	3.00	1.75
(5) Dalton Jones	6.00	3.00	1.75
(6) Jim Lonborg	8.00	4.00	2.50
(7) Sparky Lyle	8.00	4.00	2.50
(8) Syd O'Brien	6.00	3.00	1.75
(9) George Scott	8.00	4.00	2.50
(10) Reggie Smith	8.00	4.00	2.50
(11) Rico Petrocelli	8.00	4.00	2.50
(12) Carl Yastrzemski	25.00	12.50	7.50

1962 Auravision Records

Similar in design and format to the 16-record set which was issued in 1964, this test issue can be differentiated by the stats on the back. On the 1962 record, Mantle is shown in a right-handed batting pose, as compared to a follow-through on the 1964 record. Where Gentile and Colavito are

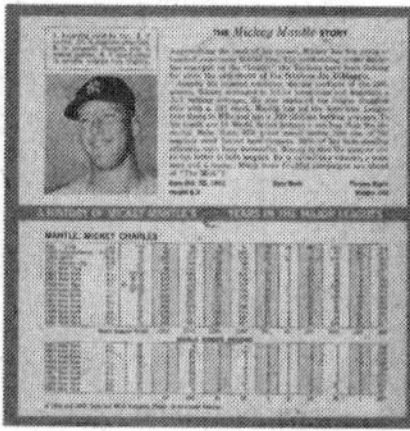

shown in the uniform of K.C. A's on the 1964 records, they are shown as a Tiger (Colavito) and Oriole (Gentile) on the earlier version. The set is checklisted here alphabetically.

	NM	EX	VG
Complete Set (8):	300.00	150.00	90.00
Common Player:	15.00	7.50	4.50
(1) Ernie Banks	30.00	15.00	9.00
(2) Rocky Colavito	25.00	12.50	7.50
(3) Whitey Ford	30.00	15.00	9.00
(4) Jim Gentile	15.00	7.50	4.50
(5) Mickey Mantle	100.00	50.00	30.00
(6) Roger Maris	35.00	17.50	10.50
(7) Willie Mays	50.00	25.00	15.00
(8) Warren Spahn	30.00	15.00	9.00

1964 Auravision Records

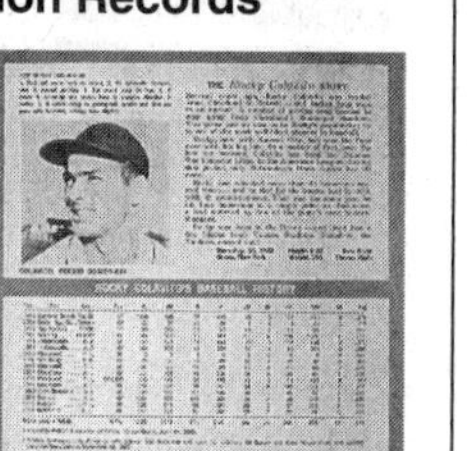

Never a candidate for the Billboard "Hot 100," this series of baseball picture records is popular with collectors due to the high-quality photos on front and back. On the grooved front side of the 6-3/4" x 6-3/4" plastic-laminated cardboard record is a color player photo with facsimile autograph, Sports Record trophy logo and 33-1/3 RPM notation. A color border surrounds the photo and is carried over to the unrecorded back side. There is another photo on back, along with a career summary and complete major and minor league stats and instructions for playing the record. In the bottom border is a copyright notice by Sports Champions Inc., and a notice that the Auravision Record is a product of Columbia Records. A hole at center of the record could be punched out for playing and the records featured a five-minute interview with the player by sportscaster Marty Glickman. The records were originally a mail-in premium available through an offer on Milk Dud candy boxes. Large quantities of the records made their way into the hobby as remainders. For early-1960s baseball items they remain reasonably priced today. The unnumbered records are checklisted here alphabetically. The Mays record is unaccountably much scarcer than the others.

	NM	EX	VG
Complete Set (16):	150.00	75.00	45.00
Common Player:	6.00	3.00	1.75
(1) Bob Allison	6.00	3.00	1.75
(2) Ernie Banks	9.00	4.50	2.75
(3) Ken Boyer	6.00	3.00	1.75
(4) Rocky Colavito	7.50	3.75	2.25
(5) Don Drysdale	9.00	4.50	2.75
(6) Whitey Ford	10.00	5.00	3.00
(7) Jim Gentile	6.00	3.00	1.75
(8) Al Kaline	10.00	5.00	3.00
(9) Sandy Koufax	20.00	10.00	6.00
(10) Mickey Mantle	25.00	12.50	7.50
(11) Roger Maris	12.50	6.25	3.75
(12) Willie Mays	75.00	37.50	22.50
(13) Bill Mazeroski	9.00	4.50	2.75
(14) Frank Robinson	9.00	4.50	2.75
(15) Warren Spahn	9.00	4.50	2.75
(16) Pete Ward	6.00	3.00	1.75

1945 Autographs Game

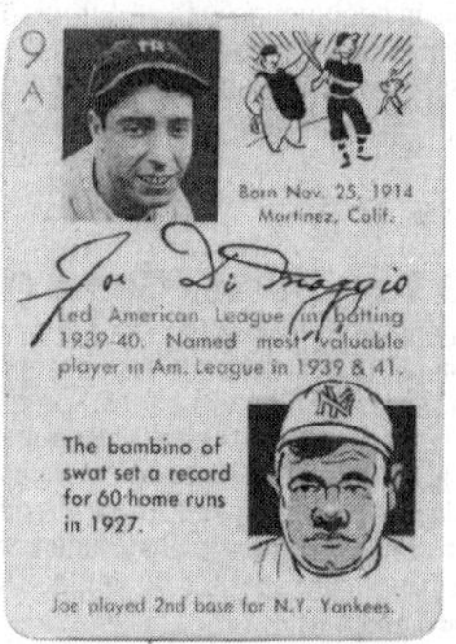

Politicians, movie stars and athletes are among the celebrities featured in this game from Leister Game Co. The 2-1/2" x 3-1/2" cards are printed in red and black on white and were found in pairs. The celebrity whose signature was reproduced on the card was seen in a photograph and top, while his paired partner was shown at bottom in an artist's depiction. Only two baseball players are included in the set.

	NM	EX	VG
Complete Boxed Set (55):	650.00	325.00	195.00
9A Joe DiMaggio, Babe Ruth (DiMaggio signature.)	75.00	37.50	22.50
9A Babe Ruth, Joe DiMaggio (Ruth signature.)	125.00	62.50	37.50

B

1949 Baas Cheri-Cola

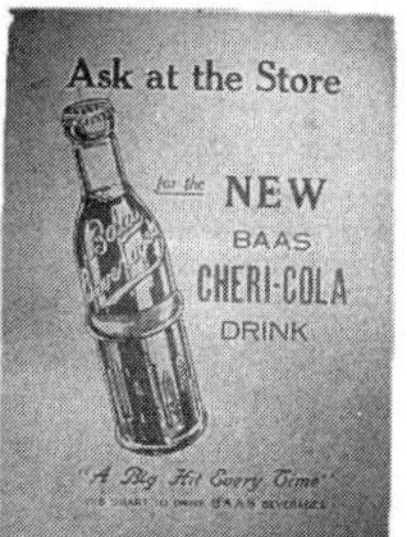

Only five of these premium issues have ever been cataloged so it's unknown how many comprise a set. The 7-5/8" x 9-1/2" pictures feature black-and-white player photos on front, with the player's name printed in white script. On back, printed in red, is an ad for Baas Cheri-Cola Drink. The unnumbered pictures are checklisted in alphabetical order.

	NM	EX	VG
Common Player:	125.00	65.00	40.00
(1) Bobby Doerr	150.00	75.00	45.00
(2) Bob Feller	250.00	125.00	75.00
(3) Ken Keltner	125.00	65.00	40.00
(4) John Sain	125.00	65.00	40.00
(5) Ted Williams	600.00	300.00	180.00

1930 Baguer Chocolate

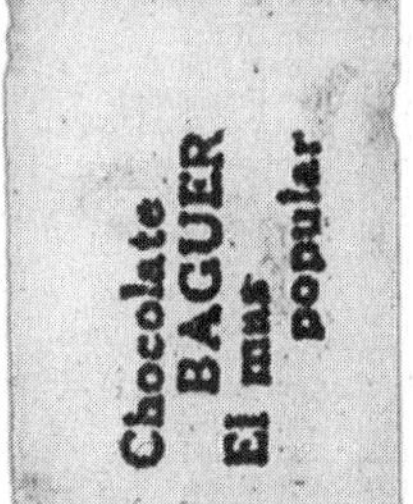

This rare Cuban issue was apparently current between the start of the 1930 season and the redemption expiration date of Jan. 31, 1931. The set consists of 90 black-and-white player photos, about 5/8" x 7/8". The pictures have white borders and a white strip at the bottom of photo with some form of the player's name. Backs are printed in red, "Chocolate BAGUER El mas popular." An album was issued to collect the pictures and when full it could be exchanged for baseball equipment, toys or candy. The unnumbered cards are checklisted here in alphabetical order.

	NM	EX	VG
Complete Set (90):	5,500	3,750	2,200
Common Player:	30.00	20.00	12.00
Album:	75.00	52.00	30.00
(1) George Bancroft (Dave)	65.00	45.00	25.00
(2) Clyde Beck	30.00	20.00	12.00
(3) Larry Benton	30.00	20.00	12.00
(4) Max Bishop	30.00	20.00	12.00
(5) Clarence Blair	30.00	20.00	12.00
(6) Fred Blake	30.00	20.00	12.00
(7) Mitchell Blake/SP	80.00	55.00	30.00
(8) Joe Boley	30.00	20.00	12.00
(9) Jim Bottomley	65.00	45.00	25.00
(10) George Burns	30.00	20.00	12.00
(11) Guy Bush	30.00	20.00	12.00
(12) Mickey Cochrane	75.00	50.00	30.00
(13) Eddie Collins	75.00	50.00	30.00
(14) Kiki Cuyler	65.00	45.00	25.00
(15) Jimmy Dikes (Dykes)	30.00	20.00	12.00
(16) Leo Dixon	30.00	20.00	12.00
(17) Pete Donohue	30.00	20.00	12.00
(18) Taylor Douthit	30.00	20.00	12.00
(19) George Earnshaw	30.00	20.00	12.00
(20) R. Elliot (Jumbo Elliott)	30.00	20.00	12.00
(21) Joe (Woody) English	30.00	20.00	12.00
(22) Urban Faber	65.00	45.00	25.00
(23) Lewis Fonseca	30.00	20.00	12.00
(24) Jimmy Foxx	275.00	190.00	110.00
(25) Walter French	30.00	20.00	12.00
(26) Frankie Frisch	75.00	50.00	30.00
(27) Lou Gehrig	600.00	420.00	240.00
(28) Walter Gerber	30.00	20.00	12.00
(29) Miguel A. Gonzalez	65.00	45.00	25.00
(30) Goose Goslin	65.00	45.00	25.00
(31) W. Grampp (Henry)	30.00	20.00	12.00
(32) Burleigh Grimes	65.00	45.00	25.00
(33) Charlie Grimm	30.00	20.00	12.00
(34) Lefty Grove	75.00	50.00	30.00
(35) Geo. Haas	30.00	20.00	12.00
(36) (Bill) Hallahan	30.00	20.00	12.00
(37) Stanley Harris	65.00	45.00	25.00
(38) Geo. (Charles "Gabby) Hartnett	65.00	45.00	25.00
(39) Cliff Heathcote	30.00	20.00	12.00
(40) Babe Herman	30.00	20.00	12.00
(41) Andy High	30.00	20.00	12.00
(42) Rogers Hornsby	100.00	70.00	40.00
(43) Dan Howley	30.00	20.00	12.00
(44) Travis Jackson	65.00	45.00	25.00
(45) Walter Johnson	250.00	175.00	100.00
(46) Fred Lindstrom	65.00	45.00	25.00
(47) Alfonso Lopez	75.00	50.00	30.00
(48) Red Lucas	30.00	20.00	12.00
(49) (Dolf) Luque	65.00	45.00	25.00
(50) Pat Malone	30.00	20.00	12.00
(51) Harry (Heinie) Manush	65.00	45.00	25.00
(52) Fred Marberry	30.00	20.00	12.00
(53) Joe McCarthy	65.00	45.00	25.00
(54) J.J. McGraw	65.00	45.00	25.00
(55) G. Mc. Millan (Norman McMillan)	30.00	20.00	12.00
(56) Bing Miller	30.00	20.00	12.00
(57) J. (Johnny) Moore	30.00	20.00	12.00
(58) Buddy Myers (Myer)	30.00	20.00	12.00
(59) Bob O'Farrell	30.00	20.00	12.00
(60) Melvin Ott	75.00	50.00	30.00
(61) Herb Pennock	65.00	45.00	25.00
(62) Cy Perkins	30.00	20.00	12.00
(63) Jack Quinn	30.00	20.00	12.00
(64) Chas. Rhen (Rhem)	30.00	20.00	12.00
(65) Harry Rice	30.00	20.00	12.00
(66) Sam Rice	65.00	45.00	35.00
(67) Lance Richbourg	30.00	20.00	12.00
(68) W. (Wilbert) Robinson	65.00	45.00	25.00
(69) Eddie Rommell (Rommel)	30.00	20.00	12.00
(70) Charles Root	30.00	20.00	12.00
(71) Muddy Ruel	30.00	20.00	12.00
(72) Babe Ruth	900.00	630.00	360.00
(73) Wally Schang	30.00	20.00	12.00
(74) Bill Shores	30.00	20.00	12.00
(75) Al Simmons	65.00	45.00	25.00
(76) Geo. Sisler	75.00	50.00	30.00
(77) Earl Smith	30.00	20.00	12.00
(78) Riggs Stephenson	30.00	20.00	12.00
(79) Joe (Walter "Lefty") Stewart	30.00	20.00	12.00
(80) H. Summa	30.00	20.00	12.00
(81) Bill Terry	65.00	45.00	25.00
(82) Fresco Thompson	30.00	20.00	12.00
(83) Charley Tolson	30.00	20.00	12.00
(84) 'Pie' Traynor	65.00	45.00	25.00
(85) Dazzy Vance	65.00	45.00	25.00
(86) Rube Walberg	30.00	20.00	12.00
(87) 'Hack' Wilson	65.00	45.00	25.00
(88) Jimmy Wilson	30.00	20.00	12.00
(89) Glenn Wright	30.00	20.00	12.00
(90) Tom Zachary	30.00	20.00	12.00

1950s-70s Mel Bailey Player Postcards

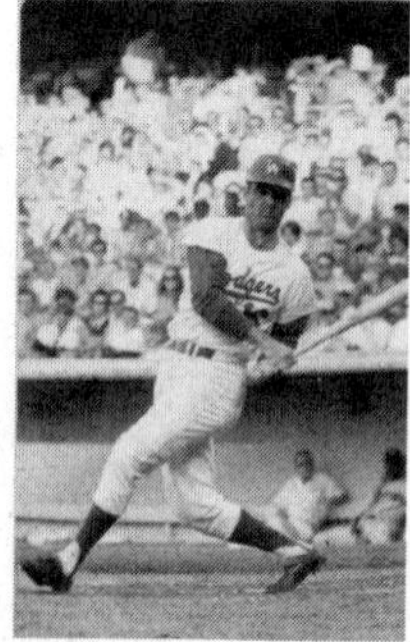
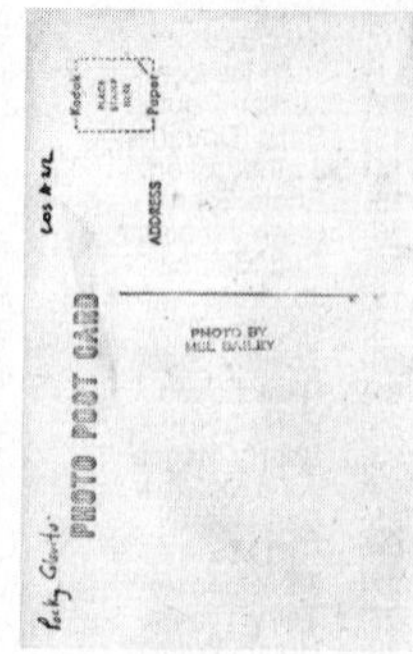

Photographer and hobbyist Mel Bailey was a prolific baseball photographer who produced many player postcards for their use in responding to fan requests for pictures and autographs. Several different formats of back design may be found. No checklist has been promulgated.

(Typical players $3-5; stars and Hall of Famers $10-30.)

1941 Ballantine Coasters

National League pitcher-catcher pairs are featured on this set of drink coasters issued by Ballentine Ale & Beer. The 4-1/2" diameter composition coasters are printed in black with orange, blue or red highlights. Fronts have line drawings of the batterymates and a few words about the previous or coming season. Backs have a Ballentine's ad. It is unknown whether there are more than these three coasters in the series.

		NM	EX	VG
	Common Coaster:	35.00	17.50	10.00
(1)	Bob Klinger, Virgil Davis (Pirates)	35.00	17.50	10.00
(2a)	Lon Warneke, Gus Mancuso (Cardinals) ("AT THE GAME IT'S . . ." above portraits.)	35.00	17.50	10.00
(2b)	Lon Warneke, Gus Mancuso (Cardinals)("At the Game it's" below portraits.)	35.00	17.50	10.00
(3)	Whit Wyatt, Mickey Owen (Dodgers)	35.00	17.50	10.00

1911 Baltimore News Newsboys Series

The Baltimore News Newsboys Series
Prize of $1.00 to First 35 Boys Getting Full Set of the Following:
MOORE, Philadelphia National
GRANT, Cincinnati National
MURRAY, New York National
BYRNE, Pittsburg National
CRAWFORD, Detroit American
AUSTIN, New York American
"JOE" LAKE, St. Louis National
LOBERT, Philadelphia National
MAGEE, Philadelphia National
"HUGH" JENNINGS, Det. American
DOOLAN, Philadelphia National
"OLD" CY YOUNG, Cleveland Amer.
"HARRY" DAVIS, Phila. American
McGRAW, New York National
"TY" COBB, Detroit American
"TOMMY" LEACH, Pittsburg Natl.
LORD, Chicago American
DOUGHERTY, New York American
LAJOIE, Cleveland American
DEVORE, New York National
CHANCE, Chicago National
CICOTTE, Boston American
BATES, Philadelphia National
"HANS" WAGNER, Pittsburg Nat.
SPEAKER, Boston American
KLEINOW, New York American
BESCHER, Cincinnati National
TURNER, Cleveland American
EVERS, Chicago National
DEVLIN, New York National

This scarce version of E94 carries on its back the notation, "Baltimore News Newsboy Series" and offers $1 to the first 35 boys completing the full set. Unlike the Close Candy Co. cards, the newspaper version is found only with the light blue background on front. The issue was designated M131 in the American Card Catalog.

		NM	EX	VG
	Complete Set (30):	85,000	42,500	25,000
	Common Player:	3,000	1,500	1,000
(1)	Jimmy Austin	3,000	1,500	1,000
(2)	Johnny Bates	3,000	1,500	1,000
(3)	Bob Bescher	3,000	1,500	1,000
(4)	Bobby Byrne	3,000	1,500	1,000
(5)	Frank Chance	7,500	3,750	2,250
(6)	Ed Cicotte	6,000	3,000	1,800
(7)	Ty Cobb	75,000	37,500	22,500
(8)	Sam Crawford	7,500	3,750	2,250
(9)	Harry Davis	3,000	1,500	1,000
(10)	Art Devlin	3,000	1,500	1,000
(11)	Josh Devore	3,000	1,500	1,000
(12)	Mickey Doolan	3,000	1,500	1,000
(13)	Patsy Dougherty	3,000	1,500	1,000
(14)	Johnny Evers	7,500	3,750	2,250
(15)	Eddie Grant	3,000	1,500	1,000
(16)	Hugh Jennings	7,500	3,750	2,250
(17)	Red Kleinow	3,000	1,500	1,000
(18)	Joe Lake	3,000	1,500	1,000
(19)	Nap Lajoie	9,000	4,500	2,700
(20)	Tommy Leach	3,000	1,500	1,000
(21)	Hans Lobert	3,000	1,500	1,000
(22)	Harry Lord	3,000	1,500	1,000
(23)	Sherry Magee	3,000	1,500	1,000
(24)	John McGraw	11,250	5,625	3,375
(25)	Earl Moore	3,000	1,500	1,000
(26)	Red Murray	3,000	1,500	1,000
(27)	Tris Speaker	13,500	6,750	4,050
(28)	Terry Turner	3,000	1,500	1,000
(29)	Honus Wagner	55,500	27,750	16,650
(30)	"Old" Cy. Young	22,500	11,250	6,750

1914 Baltimore News Terrapins

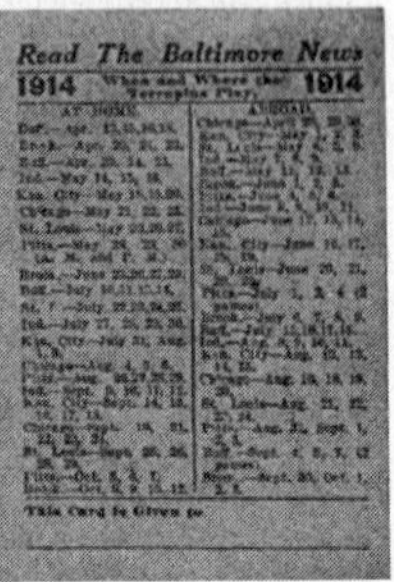

Players from both of Baltimore's professional baseball teams are included in this set of schedule cards from the local newspaper. That season fans could support the Orioles of the International League or the Terrapins of the Federal League. The newspaper's cards are 2-5/8" x 3-5/8", monochrome printed in either red or blue with a wide border. Players are pictured in full-length posed action photos with the backgrounds erased in favor of a few artificial shadows. The player name, position and league are shown on front. Backs have a schedule "AT HOME" and "ABROAD" of the appropriate team with an ad for the paper at top and a curious line at bottom which reads, "This Card is Given to," with space for a signature. The unnumbered cards are checklisted here in alphabetical order, though it is presumed the checklist is incomplete. Only the Federal Leaguers' cards are listed here; the Orioles will be found in the minor league section of this catalog. This scarce version of E94 carries on its back the notation, "Baltimore Newsboy Series." Unlike the Close Candy Co. cards, the newspaper version is found only with the light blue background on front.

		NM	EX	VG
	Common Player:	8,800	4,400	2,640
(1)	Neal Ball	8,800	4,400	2,640
(2)	Mike Doolan	8,800	4,400	2,640
(3)	Happy Finneran	8,800	4,400	2,640
(4)	Fred Jacklitch (Jacklitsch)	8,800	4,400	2,640
(5)	Otto Knabe	8,800	4,400	2,640
(6)	Benny Meyers (Meyer)	8,800	4,400	2,640
(7)	Jack Quinn	8,800	4,400	2,640
(8)	Hack Simmons	8,800	4,400	2,640
(9)	Frank Smith	8,800	4,400	2,640
(10)	George Suggs	8,800	4,400	2,640
(11)	Harry (Swats) Swacina	8,800	4,400	2,640
(12)	Ducky Yount	8,800	4,400	2,640
(13)	Guy Zinn	8,800	4,400	2,640

1954 Baltimore Orioles Picture Pack

This appears to be a team-issued photo pack in the O's first season after moving from St. Louis. The black-and-white poses are 6" x 8" in format, bordered in white and blank-backed. Pictures have a facsimile autograph on front. At least three versions of the photo pack were issued over the course of the season to reflect roster changes. It is unknown whether this checklist is complete.

		NM	EX	VG
	Complete Set (33):	600.00	300.00	180.00
	Common Player:	20.00	10.00	6.00
(1)	Cal Abrams	20.00	10.00	6.00
(2)	Neil Berry	20.00	10.00	6.00
(3)	Vern Bickford	20.00	10.00	6.00
(4)	Jim Brideweser	20.00	10.00	6.00
(5)	Bob Chakales	20.00	10.00	6.00
(6)	Gil Coan	20.00	10.00	6.00
(7)	Joe Coleman	20.00	10.00	6.00
(8)	Clint Courtney	20.00	10.00	6.00
(9)	Chuck Diering	20.00	10.00	6.00
(10)	Jim Dyck	20.00	10.00	6.00
(11)	Howie Fox	20.00	10.00	6.00
(12)	Jim Fridley/Btg	20.00	10.00	6.00
(13)	Jim Fridley/Portrait	20.00	10.00	6.00
(14)	Jehosie Heard	25.00	12.50	7.50
(15)	Bill Hunter	20.00	10.00	6.00
(16)	Darrell Johnson	20.00	10.00	6.00
(17)	Dick Kokos	20.00	10.00	6.00
(18)	Lou Kretlow	20.00	10.00	6.00
(19)	Dick Kryhoski	20.00	10.00	6.00
(20)	Don Larsen	40.00	20.00	12.00
(21)	Don Lenhardt	20.00	10.00	6.00
(22)	Dick Littlefield	20.00	10.00	6.00
(23)	Sam Mele	20.00	10.00	6.00
(24)	Les Moss	20.00	10.00	6.00
(25)	Ray Murray	20.00	10.00	6.00
(26)	Billy O'Dell	20.00	10.00	6.00
(27)	Duane Pillette	20.00	10.00	6.00
(28)	Vern Stephens	20.00	10.00	6.00
(29)	Marlin Stuart	20.00	10.00	6.00
(30)	Bob Turley	40.00	20.00	12.00
(31)	Eddie Waitkus	20.00	10.00	6.00
(32)	Vic Wertz	25.00	12.50	7.50
(33)	Bob Young	20.00	10.00	6.00

1958 Baltimore Orioles team issue

These blank-backed, black-and-white cards are approximately postcard size at 3-1/4" x 5-1/2" and feature posed portraits of the players printed on semi-gloss cardboard. The unnumbered cards are checklisted here alphabetically.

		NM	EX	VG
	Complete Set (16):	165.00	82.00	49.00
	Common Player:	12.00	6.00	3.50
(1)	Bob Boyd	12.00	6.00	3.50
(2)	Harry Brecheen	12.00	6.00	3.50
(3)	Hal Brown	12.00	6.00	3.50
(4)	Jim Busby	12.00	6.00	3.50
(5)	Foster Castleman	12.00	6.00	3.50
(6)	Billy Gardner	12.00	6.00	3.50
(7)	Connie Johnson	12.00	6.00	3.50
(8)	Ken Lehman	12.00	6.00	3.50
(9)	Willie Miranda	12.00	6.00	3.50
(10)	Bob Nieman	12.00	6.00	3.50
(11)	Paul Richards	12.00	6.00	3.50
(12)	Brooks Robinson	36.00	18.00	11.00
(13)	Gus Triandos	12.00	6.00	3.50
(14)	Dick Williams	12.00	6.00	3.50
(15)	Gene Woodling	18.00	9.00	5.50
(16)	George Zuverink	12.00	6.00	3.50

1970 Baltimore Orioles Traffic Safety

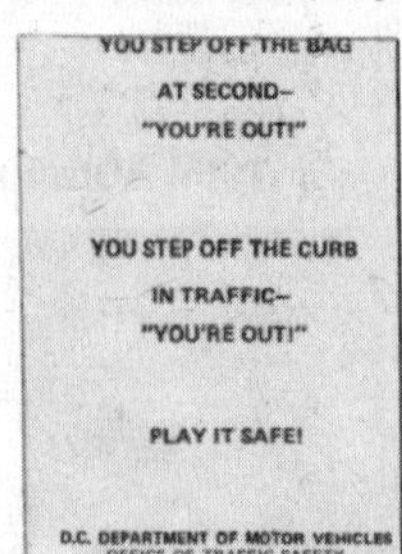

Similar in concept and design to the much more common Washington Senators safety issue of the same year, the Orioles cards are printed on yellow paper in 2-1/2" x 3-7/8" format. Fronts have player photo, name, team and position; backs have a safety message and notice of sponsorship by the D.C. Department of Motor Vehicles Office of Traffic Safety.

		NM	EX	VG
	Complete Set (10):	25.00	12.50	7.50
	Common Player:	2.50	1.25	.75
(1)	Mark Bellanger (Belanger)	2.50	1.25	.75
(2)	Paul Blair	2.50	1.25	.75
(3)	Don Buford	2.50	1.25	.75
(4)	Mike Cuellar (Back in Spanish.)	4.00	2.00	1.25
(5)	Dave Johnson	2.50	1.25	.75
(6)	Dave McNally	2.50	1.25	.75
(7)	Boog Powell	5.00	2.50	1.50
(8)	Merv Rettenmund	2.50	1.25	.75
(9)	Brooks Robinson	10.00	5.00	3.00
(10)	Earl Weaver	3.50	1.75	1.00

1971 Bank of Montreal Rusty Staub

This 4" x 6" color card was issued by the Bank of Montreal, probably in conjunction with an autograph appearance by the popular Expos slugger. The front has a photo of the player working on his war club. The team and sponsor's logo are at top-right. On back are the player's stats.

	NM	EX	VG
Rusty Staub	32.50	16.00	10.00

1913 Tom Barker Game (WG6)

Nearly identical in format to "The National Game" card set, this issue features a different back design of a red-and-white line art representation of a batter. Fronts of the round-cornered, 2-1/2" x 3-1/2" cards have a black-and-white player pose, or game action photo, along with two game scenarios used when playing the card game. There are nine action photos in the set. Player cards are checklisted here alphabetically. The set originally sold for 50 cents. The set was reprinted in the 1980s.

		NM	EX	VG
Complete Set (54):		6,155	2,760	1,530
Common Player:		48.00	24.00	15.00
Game Box:		78.00	36.00	18.00
(1)	Grover Alexander	360.00	162.00	90.00
(2)	Frank Baker	120.00	54.00	30.00
(3)	Chief Bender	120.00	54.00	30.00
(4)	Bob Bescher	48.00	24.00	15.00
(5)	Joe Birmingham	48.00	24.00	15.00
(6)	Roger Bresnahan	120.00	54.00	30.00
(7)	Nixey Callahan	48.00	24.00	15.00
(8)	Bill Carrigan	48.00	24.00	15.00
(9)	Frank Chance	120.00	54.00	30.00
(10)	Hal Chase	78.00	36.00	19.00
(11)	Fred Clarke	120.00	54.00	30.00
(12)	Ty Cobb	810.00	360.00	210.00
(13)	Sam Crawford	120.00	54.00	30.00
(14)	Jake Daubert	48.00	24.00	15.00
(15)	Red Dooin	48.00	24.00	15.00
(16)	Johnny Evers	120.00	54.00	30.00
(17)	Vean Gregg	48.00	24.00	15.00
(18)	Clark Griffith	120.00	54.00	30.00
(19)	Dick Hoblitzel	48.00	24.00	15.00
(20)	Miller Huggins	120.00	54.00	30.00
(21)	Joe Jackson	1,920	870.00	480.00
(22)	Hughie Jennings	120.00	54.00	30.00
(23)	Walter Johnson	420.00	180.00	110.00
(24)	Ed Konetchy	48.00	24.00	15.00
(25)	Nap Lajoie	120.00	54.00	30.00
(26)	Connie Mack	120.00	54.00	30.00
(27)	Rube Marquard	120.00	54.00	30.00
(28)	Christy Mathewson	420.00	180.00	110.00
(29)	John McGraw	120.00	54.00	30.00
(30)	Chief Meyers	48.00	24.00	15.00
(31)	Clyde Milan	48.00	24.00	15.00
(32)	Marty O'Toole	48.00	24.00	15.00
(33)	Nap Rucker	48.00	24.00	15.00
(34)	Tris Speaker	160.00	75.00	40.00
(35)	George Stallings	48.00	24.00	15.00
(36)	Bill Sweeney	48.00	24.00	15.00
(37)	Joe Tinker	120.00	54.00	30.00
(38)	Honus Wagner	720.00	330.00	180.00
(39)	Ed Walsh	120.00	54.00	30.00
(40)	Zach Wheat	120.00	54.00	30.00
(41)	Ivy Wingo	48.00	24.00	15.00
(42)	Joe Wood	72.00	33.00	18.00
(43)	Cy Young	420.00	180.00	100.00
(---)	Rules Card	48.00	24.00	15.00
(---)	Score Card	48.00	24.00	15.00
	ACTION PHOTO CARDS			
(A1)	Batter swinging, looking forward.	18.00	8.10	4.50
(A2)	Batter swinging, looking back.	18.00	8.10	4.50
(A3)	Runner sliding, fielder at bag.	18.00	8.10	4.50
(A4)	Runner sliding, umpire behind.	48.00	24.00	15.00
(A5)	Runner sliding, hugging base.	18.00	8.10	4.50
(A6)	Sliding play at plate, umpire at left.	18.00	8.10	4.50
(A7)	Sliding play at plate, umpire at right.	18.00	8.10	4.50
(A8)	Play at plate, runner standing.	18.00	8.10	4.50
(A9)	Runner looking backwards.	18.00	8.10	4.50

1974-80 Bob Bartosz Postcards

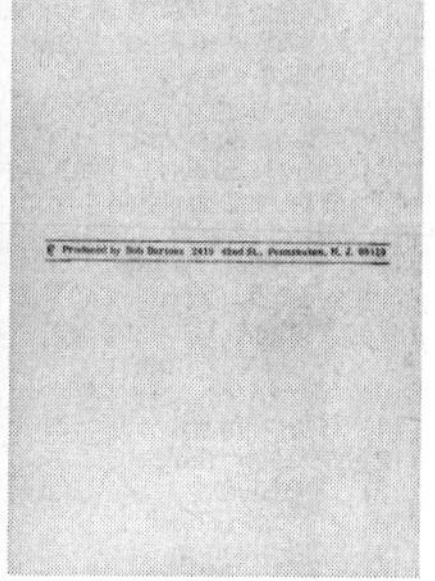

Through the last half of the 1970s, Bob Bartosz, who was a photographer covering the Phillies for a New Jersey daily newspaper, produced a series of player postcards. Most cards were produced at the request of the players for use in handling fan requests. Generally, no more than 500 cards of each player were ever produced. Most of the cards are in black-and-white with player name in a white stripe. Three cards were done in color. Size varies, but averages about 3-5/8" x 5-1/2". Back designs also vary, with most simply having Bartosz' credit line vertically at center. The unnumbered cards are checklisted here in alphabetical order.

		NM	EX	VG
Complete Set (32):				
Common Player:		3.00	1.50	.90
	BLACK-AND-WHITE POSTCARDS			
(1)	Hank Aaron (16th career grand slam)	7.50	3.75	2.25
(2)	Richie Ashburn (5th Delaware Valley Show)	3.00	1.50	.90
(3)	James Cool Papa Bell	3.00	1.50	.90
(4)	Bob Boone	4.00	2.00	1.25
(5)	Jimmie Crutchfield	3.00	1.50	.90
(6)	Barry Foote	3.00	1.50	.90
(7)	Steve Garvey	4.00	2.00	1.25
(8)	Tommy Hutton (Phillies)	3.00	1.50	.90
(9)	Tommy Hutton (Blue Jays)	3.00	1.50	.90
(10)	Dane Iorg	3.00	1.50	.90
(11)	Davey Johnson	3.00	1.50	.90
(12)	Jay Johnstone	3.00	1.50	.90
(13)	Dave Kingman (Stadium background.)	3.00	1.50	.90
(14)	Dave Kingman (Black background.)	3.00	1.50	.90
(15)	Greg Luzinski (Both feet show.)	3.00	1.50	.90
(16)	Greg Luzinski (Only left foot shows.)	3.00	1.50	.90
(17)	Jerry Martin (Phillies)	3.00	1.50	.90
(18)	Jerry Martin (Cubs)	3.00	1.50	.90
(19)	Tim McCarver	4.00	2.00	1.25
(20)	John Montefusco	3.00	1.50	.90
(21)	Jerry Mumphrey	3.00	1.50	.90
(22)	Phil Niekro	4.00	2.00	1.25
(23)	Robin Roberts (Hall of Fame induction.)	3.00	1.50	.90
(24)	Robin Roberts (4th Delaware Valley Show)	3.00	1.50	.90
(25)	Steve Swisher	3.00	1.50	.90
(26)	Tony Taylor (Uniform number visible.)	3.00	1.50	.90
(27)	Tony Taylor (Number is covered.)	3.00	1.50	.90
(28)	Tom Underwood	3.00	1.50	.90
(29)	Billy Williams (N.L. umpire.)	3.00	1.50	.90
(30)	1974 National League All-Stars	4.00	2.00	1.25
	COLOR POSTCARDS			
(1)	Greg Luzinski	7.50	3.75	2.25
(2)	Bill Madlock	7.50	3.75	2.25
(3)	Jason Thompson	6.00	3.00	1.75

1978 Bob Bartosz Baseball Postcards

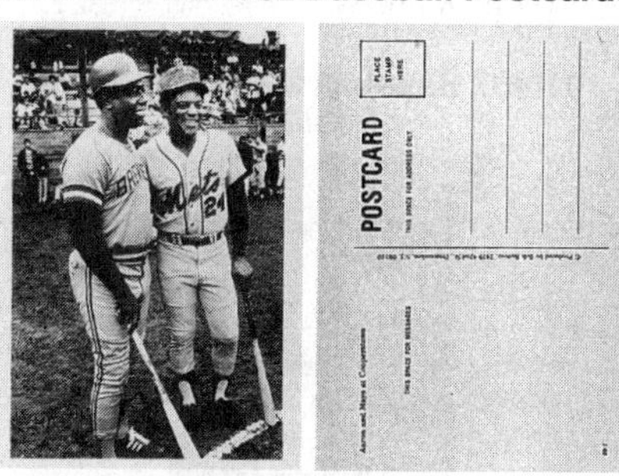

Newspaper photographer Bob Bartosz produced a book of postcards in 1978 combining player poses, action shots and stadium photos. Two dozen cards are printed in 4" x 5-1/2" black-and-white format and perforated on pages of four in the 8-1/2" x 11" book. Backs have standard postcard indicia and are numbered with a "BB" prefix and titled, all printing in black.

		NM	EX	VG
Complete Book (24):		30.00	15.00	9.00
Common Player:		1.50	.70	.45
1	25th anniversary of the 1950 Phillies (Group photo at old-timers game.)	1.50	.70	.45
2	Aaron and Mays at Cooperstown (Hank Aaron, Willie Mays)	4.00	2.00	1.25
3	Willie Mays	7.50	3.75	2.25
4	Aaron signing autographs (Hank Aaron)	3.00	1.50	.90
5	Dizzy Dean (Old-timers action sequence.)	2.50	1.25	.70
6	Jack Russell Stadium, Clearwater, Fla.	1.50	.70	.45
7	Paddy Livingston	1.50	.70	.45
8	Bob Feller (Old-timers game.)	2.50	1.25	.70
9	Hall of Fame Game at Doubleday Field	1.50	.70	.45
10	Doubleday Field at Cooperstown, N.Y.	1.50	.70	.45
11	Three Rivers Stadium, Pittsburgh	1.50	.70	.45
12	Hall of Fame Game at Doubleday Field	1.50	.70	.45
13	Shibe Park from the air	1.50	.70	.45
14	Olympic Stadium, Montreal	1.50	.70	.45
15	A tree grows at home plate (Shibe Park - 1974)	1.50	.70	.45
16	The Bleachers, Wrigley Field	1.50	.70	.45
17	Another Home Run (Hank Aaron)	2.50	1.25	.70
18	Home Run King (Hank Aaron)	2.25	1.25	.70
19	Autograph Time - 1950 (Phillies signing balls.)	1.50	.70	.45
20	The Champs (1976 Phillies)	1.50	.70	.45
21	Last Day - Shibe Park, 1977	1.50	.70	.45
22	Connie Mack Stadium, Philadelphia	1.50	.70	.45
23	Shibe Park	1.50	.70	.45
24	Shibe Park	1.50	.70	.45

1911 Baseball Bats

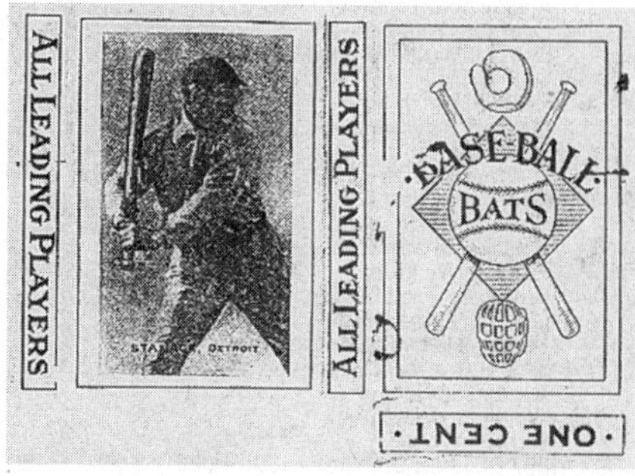

Issued circa 1911, cards in this rare 47-card issue were printed on the back panel of "Baseball Bats" penny candy. The cards themselves measure approximately 1-3/8" x 2-3/8" and feature a black-and-white player photo surrounded by an orange or white border. Player's name and team are printed in small, black capital letters near the bottom of the photo. Cards are blank-backed.

		NM	EX	VG
Complete Set (50):		40,000	20,000	12,000
Common Player:		550.00	275.00	165.00
(1)	Red Ames	550.00	275.00	165.00
(2)	Home Run Baker	1,100	550.00	330.00
(3)	Jack Barry	550.00	275.00	165.00
(4)	Ginger Beaumont	550.00	275.00	165.00
(5)	Chief Bender	1,100	550.00	330.00
(6)	Al Bridwell	550.00	275.00	165.00
(7)	Mordecai Brown	1,100	550.00	330.00
(8)	Bill Corrigan (Carrigan)	550.00	275.00	165.00
(9)	Frank Chance	1,100	550.00	330.00
(10)	Hal Chase	850.00	425.00	250.00
(11)	Ed Cicotte	925.00	460.00	275.00
(12)	Fred Clark (Clarke)	1,100	550.00	330.00
(13)	Ty Cobb	6,000	4,000	2,000
(14)	King Cole	550.00	275.00	165.00
(15)	Eddie Collins	1,100	550.00	330.00
(16)	Sam Crawford	1,100	550.00	330.00
(17)	Lou Criger	550.00	275.00	165.00
(18)	Harry Davis	550.00	275.00	165.00
(19)	Jim Delehanty	550.00	275.00	165.00
(20)	Art Devlin	550.00	275.00	165.00
(21)	Josh Devore	550.00	275.00	165.00
(22)	Wild Bill Donovan	550.00	275.00	165.00
(23)	Larry Doyle	550.00	275.00	165.00
(24)	Johnny Evers	1,100	550.00	330.00
(25)	John Flynn	550.00	275.00	165.00
(26)	George Gibson	550.00	275.00	165.00
(27)	Solly Hoffman (Hofman)	550.00	275.00	165.00
(28)	Walter Johnson	2,200	1,100	660.00
(29)	Johnny Kling	550.00	275.00	165.00
(30)	Nap Lajoie	1,100	550.00	330.00
(31)	Christy Mathewson	3,000	2,000	1,000
(32)	Matty McIntyre	550.00	275.00	165.00
(33)	Fred Merkle	550.00	275.00	165.00
(34)	Danny Murphy	550.00	275.00	165.00
(35)	Tom Needham	550.00	275.00	165.00
(36)	Harry Niles	550.00	275.00	165.00
(37)	Rube Oldring	550.00	275.00	165.00
(38)	Wildfire Schulte	550.00	275.00	165.00
(39)	Cy Seymour	550.00	275.00	165.00
(40)	Jimmy Sheckard	550.00	275.00	165.00
(41)	Tris Speaker	2,400	1,600	800.00
(42)	Oscar Stanage/Btg (Front view.)	550.00	275.00	165.00
(43)	Oscar Stanage/Btg (Side view.)	550.00	275.00	165.00
(44)	Ira Thomas	550.00	275.00	165.00
(45)	Joe Tinker	1,100	550.00	330.00
(46)	Heinie Wagner	550.00	275.00	165.00
(47)	Honus Wagner	4,500	2,250	1,350
(48)	Ed Walsh	1,100	550.00	330.00
(49)	Art Wilson	550.00	275.00	165.00
(50)	Owen Wilson	550.00	275.00	165.00

1887-1893 Baseball Currency

Because of their similarity in size (about 7-3/4" x 3-3/8"), design and color to then-circulating U.S. paper money, this form of advertising flyer was thought to catch the attention of the general public. The notes were printed in black-and-green (some 1889 Chicago notes are printed in black-and-red) on white. Fronts have at left a large oval portrait of the team's president or manager. At right on the Chicago and Detroit notes is a full-figure rendering of an unnamed Cap Anson. On the St. Louis notes, there is a picture of the Wilman Trophy indicative of the team's 1886 World's Championship. On the 1893 note, National League President N.E. Young is pictured at left, with a grouping of baseball equipment at right. In the center is a large ornate date with either "National Base Ball League" or "National / Base Ball Association" at top in gothic typography. Backs have black-and-white woodcuts of the team's players on a decorative green (or red) background. The notes were originally printed with large open spaces on front and back so that advertising messages could be overprinted by local merchants. The value of the notes can be affected by the location of a specific advertiser and/or the content of his message. Sports collectors compete with numismatists for examples of these advertising pieces.

	NM	EX	VG
1887 Chicago White Stockings (Front: Pres. A.G. Spalding. Back: Cap Anson, Mark Baldwin, John Clarkson, Tom Daily (Daly), Dell Darling, Silver Flint, Lou Hardie, Fred Pfeffer, Jimmy Ryan, Marty Sullivan, Billy Sunday, Ed Williamson.)	2,300	1,150	750.00
1887 Detroit Wolverines (Front: Manager Bill Watkins. Back: Lady Baldwin, Charlie Bennett, Fatty Briody, Dan Brouthers, Fred Dunlap, Charlie Ganzel, Ned Hanlon, Hardy Richardson, Jack Rowe, Sam Thompson, Stump Weidman (Wiedman), Deacon White.)	2,600	1,300	775.00
1887 St. Louis Browns (Front: Pres. Chris Von Der Ahe. Back: Jack Boyle, Doc Bushong, Bob Caruthers, Charlie Comiskey, Dave Foutz, Bill Gleason, Arlie Latham, Tip O'Neil (O'Neill), Yank Robinson, Curt Welch.)	4,000	2,000	1,200
1888 Chicago White Stockings (Front: Pres. A.G. Spalding. Back: Cap Anson, Mark Baldwin, John Clarkson, Tom Daily (Daly), Dell Darling, Silver Flint, Lou Hardie, Fred Pfeffer, Jimmy Ryan, Marty Sullivan, Billy Sunday, Ed Williamson.)	2,600	1,300	750.00
1888 Detroit Wolverines (Front: Manager Bill Watkins. Back: Lady Baldwin, Charlie Bennett, Fatty Briody, Dan Brouthers, Fred Dunlap, Charlie Ganzel, Ned Hanlon, Hardy Richardson, Jack Rowe, Sam Thompson, Stump Weidman (Wiedman), Deacon White.)	2,600	1,300	775.00
1889 Chicago White Stockings (Front: Pres. A.G. Spalding. Back: Cap Anson, Mark Baldwin, Tom Burns, Tom Daily (Daly), Dell Darling, Silver Flint, Bob Pettit, Fred Pfeffer, Jimmy Ryan, Marty Sullivan, George Van Haltren, Ed Williamson.)	2,600	1,300	750.00
1893 National League All-Stars (Front: Pres. N.E. Young. Back: Bob Allen, Cap Anson, Mark Baldwin, John Clarkson, Charles Comiskey, Dave Foutz, King Kelly, Billy Nash, Jim O'Rourke, Fred Pfeffer, George Van Haltren, John Ward.)(VALUE UNDETERMINED)			

1979 Baseball Favorites "1953 Bowman"

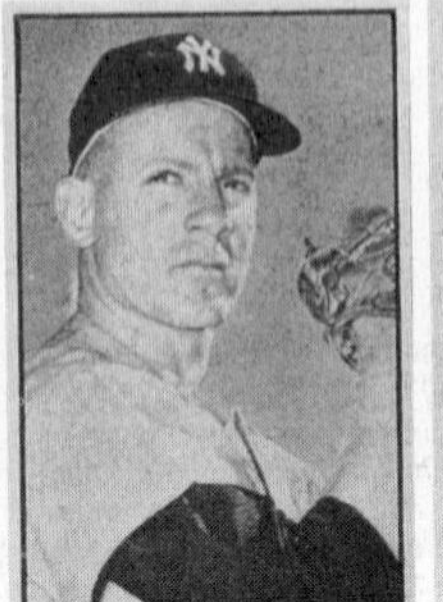

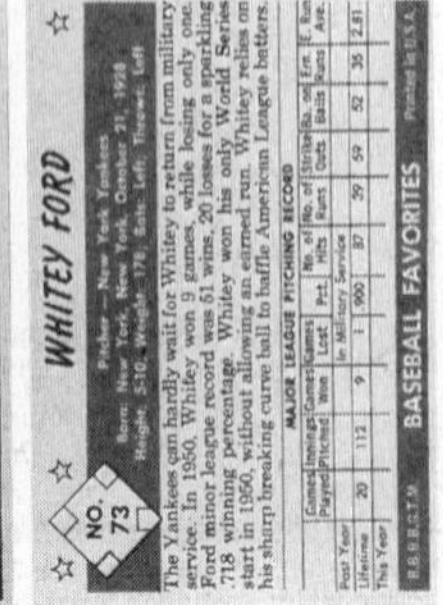

This collectors' series was designed to represent an extension of the 64-card 1953 Bowman black-and-white card issue. This series uses the same design on its 2-1/2" x 3-3/4" format. Fronts have a black-and-white player photo with no extraneous graphics. Backs are printed in red and black and offer career highlights, stats and biographical data, written as if in 1953. Many of the players in this collectors' edition originally appeared in Bowman's 1953 color series. Issue price was about $7.

		NM	EX	VG
Complete Set (16):		25.00	12.50	7.50
Common Player:		.75	.40	.25
65	Monte Irvin	.75	.40	.25
66	Early Wynn	.75	.40	.25
67	Robin Roberts	.75	.40	.25
68	Stan Musial	3.00	1.50	.90
69	Ernie Banks	1.50	.75	.45
70	Willie Mays	4.50	2.25	1.25
71	Yogi Berra	2.25	1.25	.70
72	Mickey Mantle	9.00	4.50	2.75
73	Whitey Ford	1.25	.60	.40
74	Bob Feller	.75	.40	.25
75	Ted Williams	4.50	2.25	1.25
76	Satchel Paige	3.00	1.50	.90
77	Jackie Robinson	3.00	1.50	.90
78	Ed Mathews	.75	.40	.25
79	Warren Spahn	.75	.40	.25
80	Ralph Kiner	.75	.40	.25

1964 Baseball Greats Postcard

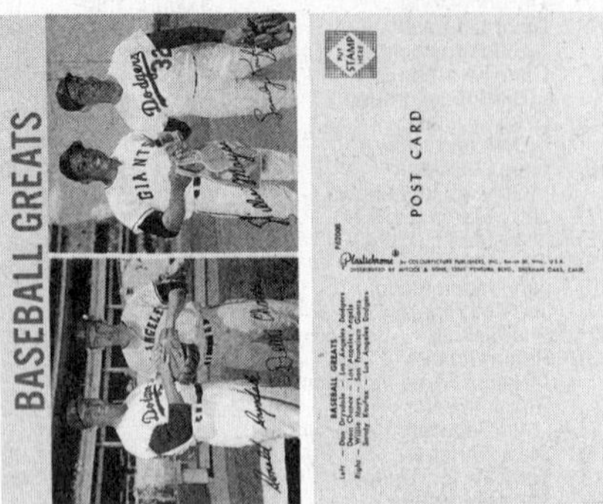

Four of California's star players are pictured on this standard-format (5-1/2" x 3-1/2") color postcard in a pair of two-player poses. Each player's facsimile autograph appears on front. Back is in typical postcard format with player identification, a stamp box and vertical center divider with publisher and distributor information. (See also Baseball Stars - Present and Future.)

	NM	EX	VG
Don Drysdale, Dean Chance, Willie Mays, Sandy Koufax	40.00	20.00	12.00

1910-57 Baseball Magazine Player Posters

Beginning shortly after its 1908 debut, Baseball Magazine produced a lengthy series of player posters which it offered as premiums to readers. Ranging in size from 9" x 12-1/4" to 9" x 20" (and a series of super-size 1957s), the posters feature poses of top players in sepia tones bordered in white. In the bottom border over the years appeared various formats of player identification, copyright information and promotion for the magazine. The unnumbered posters are listed here alphabetically by year. Some posters were reprinted over the years and there may exist pose variations as well as posters which have escaped this list. Names shown here may not coincide with the form in which they actually appear on the posters. Inaccuracies in, or incompleteness of, the checklist is the likely result of its having been compiled from ads appearing in the magazine.

		NM	EX	VG
	1910			
(1)	Ty Cobb	350.00	175.00	105.00
(2)	Johnny Evers	150.00	75.00	45.00
(3)	Hughie Jennings	100.00	50.00	30.00
(4)	Honus Wagner	300.00	150.00	90.00
	1912			
(1)	Babe Adams	60.00	30.00	18.00
(2)	Howie Camnitz	60.00	30.00	18.00
(3)	Frank Chance	125.00	62.00	37.00
(4)	Claude Hendrix	60.00	30.00	18.00
(5)	Marty O'Toole	60.00	30.00	18.00
(6)	Boston Red Sox Team	250.00	125.00	75.00
(7)	New York Giants Team	250.00	125.00	75.00
	1913			
(1)	Jimmy Archer	60.00	30.00	18.00
(2)	Jack Barry	60.00	30.00	18.00
(3)	Joe Bush	60.00	30.00	18.00
(4)	Sam Crawford	100.00	50.00	30.00
(5)	Eddie Collins	125.00	62.00	37.00
(6)	Jake Daubert	60.00	30.00	18.00
(7)	Larry Doyle	60.00	30.00	18.00
(8)	Art Fletcher	60.00	30.00	18.00
(9)	Joe Jackson	1,000	500.00	300.00
(10)	Walter Johnson	250.00	125.00	75.00
(11)	Nap Lajoie	200.00	100.00	60.00
(12)	Connie Mack	100.00	50.00	30.00
(13)	Fritz Maisel	60.00	30.00	18.00
(14)	Rube Marquard	100.00	50.00	30.00
(15)	Christy Mathewson	250.00	125.00	75.00
(16)	John McGraw	125.00	62.00	37.00
(17)	Stuffy McInnis	60.00	30.00	18.00
(18)	"Chief" Meyers	60.00	30.00	18.00
(19)	Red Murray	60.00	30.00	18.00
(20)	Eddie Plank	125.00	62.00	37.00
(21)	"Nap" Rucker	60.00	30.00	18.00
(22)	Reb Russell	60.00	30.00	18.00
(23)	Tris Speaker	125.00	62.00	37.00
(24)	Ed Walsh	100.00	50.00	30.00
(25)	Smokey Joe Wood	75.00	37.00	22.00
(26)	Boston Braves Team	250.00	125.00	75.00
(27)	Philadelphia Athletics Team	250.00	125.00	75.00
	1914			
(1)	Home Run Baker	100.00	50.00	30.00
(2)	Larry Cheney	60.00	30.00	18.00
(3)	Joe Connolly	60.00	30.00	18.00
(4)	Hank Gowdy	60.00	30.00	18.00
(5)	Bill James	60.00	30.00	18.00
(6)	Jimmy Lavender	60.00	30.00	18.00
(7)	Rabbit Maranville	100.00	50.00	30.00
(8)	Dick Rudolph	60.00	30.00	18.00
(9)	Wally Schang	60.00	30.00	18.00
(10)	Bob Shawkey	60.00	30.00	18.00
(11)	Jimmy Sheckard	60.00	30.00	18.00
(12)	Charles Schmidt	60.00	30.00	18.00
(13)	Wildfire Schulte	60.00	30.00	18.00
(14)	Lefty Tyler	60.00	30.00	18.00
(15)	Boston Braves Team	200.00	100.00	60.00
(16)	Chicago Cubs Team	200.00	100.00	60.00
(17)	Chicago Whales Team	250.00	125.00	75.00
(18)	Cincinnati Reds Team	200.00	100.00	60.00
(19)	Cleveland Indians Team	200.00	100.00	60.00
(20)	Detroit Tigers Team	200.00	100.00	60.00
(21)	New York Yankees Team	200.00	100.00	60.00
(22)	St. Louis Browns Team	200.00	100.00	60.00
(23)	Washington Senators Team	200.00	100.00	60.00
	1915			
(1)	Grover Alexander	125.00	62.00	37.00
(2)	Chief Bender	100.00	50.00	30.00
(3)	Harry Hooper	100.00	50.00	30.00
(4)	Duffy Lewis	60.00	30.00	18.00
(5)	Tris Speaker	100.00	50.00	30.00
(6)	Boston Red Sox Team	200.00	100.00	60.00
(7)	Chicago White Sox Team	200.00	100.00	60.00
(8)	Philadelphia Athletics Team	200.00	100.00	60.00
(9)	Philadelphia Phillies Team	200.00	100.00	60.00
(10)	St. Louis Cardinals Team	200.00	100.00	60.00
	1916			
(1)	Larry Gardner	50.00	25.00	15.00
(2)	Buck Herzog	50.00	25.00	15.00
(3)	Rogers Hornsby	75.00	37.00	22.00
(4)	Walter Johnson	160.00	80.00	48.00
(5)	Fielder Jones	50.00	25.00	15.00
(6)	Benny Kauff	50.00	25.00	15.00
(7)	Dave Robertson	50.00	25.00	15.00
(8)	Babe Ruth/Pitching	300.00	150.00	90.00
(9)	George Sisler	75.00	37.00	22.00
(10)	Zack Wheat	75.00	37.00	22.00
(11)	Boston Red Sox Team	150.00	75.00	45.00
(12)	Brooklyn Dodgers Team	100.00	50.00	30.00
(13)	Philadelphia Phillies Team	100.00	50.00	30.00
	1917			
(1)	George Burns	50.00	25.00	15.00
(2)	Ed Cicotte	150.00	75.00	45.00
(3)	Art Fletcher	50.00	25.00	15.00
(4)	Red Faber	50.00	25.00	15.00
(5)	Happy Felsch	150.00	75.00	45.00
(6)	Ferd Schupp	50.00	25.00	15.00
(7)	Ray Schalk	50.00	25.00	15.00
(8)	Buck Weaver	150.00	75.00	45.00
(9)	Boston Red Sox Team	150.00	75.00	45.00
(10)	New York Giants Team	150.00	75.00	45.00
	1918			
(1)	Home Run Baker	75.00	37.00	22.00
	1919			
(1)	Ed Cicotte	75.00	37.00	22.00
(2)	Chicago White Sox Team	400.00	200.00	120.00
(3)	Cincinnati Reds Team	125.00	62.00	37.00
	1920			
(1)	Jim Bagby	30.00	15.00	9.00
(2)	Dave Bancroft	45.00	22.00	13.50
(3)	Max Carey	45.00	22.00	13.50
(4)	Harry Coveleski	45.00	22.00	13.50
(5)	Hod Eller	30.00	15.00	9.00
(6)	Burleigh Grimes	45.00	22.00	13.50
(7)	Heinie Groh	30.00	15.00	9.00
(8)	Rogers Hornsby	45.00	22.00	13.50
(9)	Walter Johnson	75.00	37.00	22.00
(10)	Dick Kerr	30.00	15.00	9.00
(11)	Pat Moran	30.00	15.00	9.00
(12)	Duster Mails	30.00	15.00	9.00
(13)	Hy Myers	30.00	15.00	9.00
(14)	Steve O'Neill	30.00	15.00	9.00
(15)	Edd Roush	45.00	22.00	13.50
(16)	Dutch Ruether	30.00	15.00	9.00
(17)	Babe Ruth/Btg (No stands in background.)	700.00	350.00	210.00
(18)	Ray Schalk	45.00	22.00	13.50
(19)	Earl Smith	30.00	15.00	9.00
(20)	Sherrod Smith	30.00	15.00	9.00
(21)	Tris Speaker	45.00	22.00	13.50
(22)	Hippo Vaughn	30.00	15.00	9.00
(23)	Bobby Veach	30.00	15.00	9.00
(24)	Bill Wambsganss	30.00	15.00	9.00
(25)	Brooklyn Dodgers Team	125.00	62.00	37.00

(26) Cleveland Indians Team 125.00 62.00 37.00

1921

(1) Dave Bancroft 45.00 22.00 13.50
(2) Wilbur Cooper 30.00 15.00 9.00
(3) Phil Douglas 30.00 15.00 9.00
(4) Frank Frisch 50.00 25.00 15.00
(5) Harry Heilmann 45.00 22.00 13.50
(6) Waite Hoyt 45.00 22.00 13.50
(7) George Kelly 45.00 22.00 13.50
(8) Carl Mays 45.00 22.00 13.50
(9) Mike McNally 30.00 15.00 9.00
(10) Irish Meusel 30.00 15.00 9.00
(11) Bob Meusel 30.00 15.00 9.00
(12) Art Nehf 30.00 15.00 9.00
(13) Wally Schang 30.00 15.00 9.00
(14) Walter Schmidt 30.00 15.00 9.00
(15) Frank Snyder 30.00 15.00 9.00
(16) Aaron Ward 30.00 15.00 9.00
(17) Ross Youngs 45.00 22.00 13.50
(18) New York Giants Team 100.00 50.00 30.00
(19) New York Yankees Team 300.00 150.00 90.00
(20) Pittsburgh Pirates Team 100.00 50.00 30.00

1922 - NONE

1923

(1) New York Giants Team 90.00 45.00 27.00
(2) New York Yankees Team 200.00 100.00 60.00

1924

(1) Johnny Bassler 30.00 15.00 9.00
(2) Jim Bottomley 45.00 22.00 13.50
(3) Kiki Cuyler 45.00 22.00 13.50
(4) Joe Dugan 30.00 15.00 9.00
(5) Bibb Falk 30.00 15.00 9.00
(6) Jack Fournier 30.00 15.00 9.00
(7) Goose Goslin 45.00 22.00 13.50
(8) Sam Harris 30.00 15.00 9.00
(9) Gabby Hartnett 45.00 22.00 13.50
(10) Travis Jackson 45.00 22.00 13.50
(11) Baby Doll Jacobson 30.00 15.00 9.00
(12) Charlie Jamieson 30.00 15.00 9.00
(13) Herb Pennock 45.00 22.00 13.50
(14) Sam Rice 45.00 22.00 13.50
(15) Eppa Rixey 45.00 22.00 13.50
(16) Muddy Ruel 30.00 15.00 9.00
(17) Hollis Thurston 30.00 15.00 9.00
(18) Pie Traynor 45.00 22.00 13.50
(19) Dazzy Vance 45.00 22.00 13.50
(20) Kenny Williams 30.00 15.00 9.00
(21) New York Giants Team 90.00 45.00 27.00
(22) Washington Senators Team 90.00 45.00 27.00

1925

(1) Vic Aldridge 30.00 15.00 9.00
(2) Mickey Cochrane 45.00 22.00 13.50
(3) Ted Lyons 45.00 22.00 13.50
(4) Eddie Rommel 30.00 15.00 9.00
(5) Al Simmons 45.00 22.00 13.50
(6) Glenn Wright 30.00 15.00 9.00
(7) Pittsburgh Pirates Team 90.00 45.00 27.00
(8) Washington Senators Team 90.00 45.00 27.00

1926

(1) Les Bell 30.00 15.00 9.00
(2) George H. Burns 30.00 15.00 9.00
(3) Hughie Critz 30.00 15.00 9.00
(4) Henry (Lou) Gehrig/Portrait 250.00 125.00 75.00
(5) Ray Kremer 30.00 15.00 9.00
(6) Bob O'Farrell 30.00 15.00 9.00
(7) Tommy Thevenow 30.00 15.00 9.00
(8) George Uhle 30.00 15.00 9.00
(9) Hack Wilson 45.00 22.00 13.50
(10) New York Yankees Team 250.00 125.00 75.00
(11) St. Louis Cardinals Team 90.00 45.00 27.00

1927

(1) Carmen Hill 30.00 15.00 9.00
(2) Tony Lazzeri 45.00 22.00 13.50
(3) Fred Lindstrom 45.00 22.00 13.50
(4) Charlie Root 30.00 15.00 9.00
(5) Lloyd Waner 45.00 22.00 13.50
(6) Paul Waner 45.00 22.00 13.50
(7) New York Yankees Team 200.00 100.00 60.00
(8) Pittsburgh Pirates Team 90.00 45.00 27.00

1928

(1) Jimmie Foxx 60.00 30.00 18.00

1929

(1) Guy Bush 30.00 15.00 9.00
(2) Lefty Grove 45.00 22.00 13.50
(3) Chicago Cubs Team 125.00 62.00 37.00
(4) Philadelphia Athletics Team 90.00 45.00 27.00

1930

(1) George Earnshaw 30.00 15.00 9.00
(2) Wes Ferrell 30.00 15.00 9.00
(3) Charley Gelbert 30.00 15.00 9.00
(4) Babe Herman 30.00 15.00 9.00
(5) Chuck Klein 45.00 22.00 13.50
(6) Philadelphia Athletics Team 90.00 45.00 27.00
(7) St. Louis Cardinals Team 90.00 45.00 27.00

1931

(1) Earl Averill 45.00 22.00 13.50
(2) Ed Brandt 30.00 15.00 9.00
(3) Ben Chapman 30.00 15.00 9.00
(4) Joe Cronin 45.00 22.00 13.50
(5) Bill Hallahan 30.00 15.00 9.00
(6) Pepper Martin 40.00 20.00 12.00

1932 - NONE

1933

(1) Dizzy Dean 75.00 37.00 22.00
(2) Lou Gehrig/Btg 225.00 110.00 67.00
(3) Carl Hubbell 60.00 30.00 18.00
(4) Heinie Manush 45.00 22.00 13.50
(5) Mel Ott 45.00 22.00 13.50
(6) Babe Ruth/Btg 250.00 125.00 75.00
(Stands in background.)
(7) Hal Schumacher 30.00 15.00 9.00
(8) Lon Warneke 30.00 15.00 9.00
(9) New York Giants Team 90.00 45.00 27.00
(10) Washington Senators Team 90.00 45.00 27.00

1934

(1) Dick Bartell 30.00 15.00 9.00
(2) Paul Dean 45.00 22.00 13.50
(3) Lefty Gomez 45.00 22.00 13.50
(4) Rogers Hornsby 45.00 22.00 13.50
(5) Ducky Medwick 45.00 22.00 13.50
(6) Van Lingle Mungo 30.00 15.00 9.00
(7) Schoolboy Rowe 30.00 15.00 9.00
(8) Arky Vaughan 45.00 22.00 13.50
(9) Lloyd Waner 45.00 22.00 13.50
(10) Paul Waner 45.00 22.00 13.50
(11) Detroit Tigers Team 100.00 50.00 30.00

1935

(1) Wally Berger 30.00 15.00 9.00
(2) Ripper Collins 30.00 15.00 9.00
(3) Charley Gehringer 45.00 22.00 13.50
(4) Hank Greenberg 60.00 30.00 18.00
(5) Mel Harder 30.00 15.00 9.00
(6) Billy Herman 45.00 22.00 13.50
(7) Buddy Myer 30.00 15.00 9.00
(8) Al Simmons 45.00 22.00 13.50
(9) Bill Terry 45.00 22.00 13.50
(10) Joe Vosmik 30.00 15.00 9.00
(11) Chicago Cubs Team 100.00 50.00 30.00
(12) Detroit Tigers Team 90.00 45.00 27.00

1936

(1) Luke Appling 45.00 22.00 13.50
(2) Frank Demaree 30.00 15.00 9.00
(3) Paul Derringer 30.00 15.00 9.00
(4) Joe DiMaggio 80.00 40.00 24.00
(5) Vern Kennedy 30.00 15.00 9.00
(6) Ernie Lombardi 45.00 22.00 13.50
(7) Joe Moore 30.00 15.00 9.00
(8) Terry Moore 30.00 15.00 9.00
(9) Moose Solters 30.00 15.00 9.00
(10) Hal Trosky 30.00 15.00 9.00
(11) Bill Werber 30.00 15.00 9.00
(12) New York Giants Team 100.00 50.00 30.00
(13) New York Yankees Team 200.00 100.00 60.00

1937

(1) Cy Blanton 30.00 15.00 9.00
(2) Dolph Camilli 30.00 15.00 9.00
(3) Joe Cronin 45.00 22.00 13.50
(4) Bill Dickey 50.00 25.00 15.00
(5) Bob Feller 50.00 25.00 15.00
(6) Stan Hack 30.00 15.00 9.00
(7) Buddy Hassett 30.00 15.00 9.00
(8) Bill Lee 30.00 15.00 9.00
(9) Buddy Lewis 30.00 15.00 9.00
(10) Johnny Mize 45.00 22.00 13.50
(11) Jimmy Ripple 30.00 15.00 9.00
(12) Charles Ruffing 45.00 22.00 13.50
(13) Cecil Travis 30.00 15.00 9.00
(14) Gee Walker 30.00 15.00 9.00

1938

(1) Ethan Allen 30.00 15.00 9.00
(2) Clay Bryant 30.00 15.00 9.00
(3) Harlond Clift 30.00 15.00 9.00
(4) Frank Crosetti 35.00 17.50 10.50
(5) Harry Danning 30.00 15.00 9.00
(6) Bobby Doerr 45.00 22.00 13.50
(7) Augie Galan 30.00 15.00 9.00
(8) Ival Goodman 30.00 15.00 9.00
(9) Joe Gordon 30.00 15.00 9.00
(10) Tommy Henrich 35.00 17.50 10.50
(11) Mike Kreevich 30.00 15.00 9.00
(12) Frank McCormick 30.00 15.00 9.00
(13) Babe Phelps 30.00 15.00 9.00
(14) Johnny Rizzo 30.00 15.00 9.00
(15) Red Rolfe 30.00 15.00 9.00
(16) Johnny Vander Meer 35.00 17.50 10.50
(17) Rudy York 30.00 15.00 9.00

1939

(1) Morrie Arnovich 30.00 15.00 9.00
(2) Jimmie Foxx 45.00 22.00 13.50
(3) Luke Hamlin 30.00 15.00 9.00
(4) Bob Johnson 35.00 17.50 10.50
(5) Charlie Keller 35.00 17.50 10.50
(6) Ken Keltner 35.00 17.50 10.50
(7) Emil "Dutch" Leonard 30.00 15.00 9.00
(8) Bobo Newsom 30.00 15.00 9.00
(9) Don Padgett 30.00 15.00 9.00
(10) Bucky Walters 30.00 15.00 9.00
(11) Ted Williams 120.00 60.00 36.00

1940 (9-1/2" x 12")

(1) George Case 20.00 10.00 6.00
(2) Babe Dahlgren 20.00 10.00 6.00
(3) Elbie Fletcher 20.00 10.00 6.00
(4) Cookie Lavagetto 20.00 10.00 6.00
(5) Barney McCosky 20.00 10.00 6.00
(6) Bill McGee 20.00 10.00 6.00
(7) Ducky Medwick 40.00 20.00 12.00
(8) Eddie Miller 20.00 10.00 6.00
(9) Hugh Mulcahy 20.00 10.00 6.00
(10) Claude Passeau 20.00 10.00 6.00
(11) Rip Radcliff 20.00 10.00 6.00
(12) Jim Tabor 20.00 10.00 6.00
(13) Eugene "Junior" Thompson 20.00 10.00 6.00
(14) Mike Tresh 20.00 10.00 6.00
(15) Roy Weatherly 20.00 10.00 6.00
(16) Norm "Babe" Young 20.00 10.00 6.00

1941 (9-1/2" x 12")

(1) Sam Chapman 20.00 10.00 6.00
(2) Ty Cobb 60.00 30.00 18.00
(3) Mort Cooper 20.00 10.00 6.00
(4) Dom DiMaggio 40.00 20.00 12.00
(5) Jeff Heath 20.00 10.00 6.00
(6) Thornton Lee 20.00 10.00 6.00
(7) Danny Litwhiler 20.00 10.00 6.00
(8) Al Lopez 40.00 20.00 12.00
(9) Christy Mathewson 60.00 30.00 18.00
(10) Joe McCarthy 40.00 20.00 12.00
(11) Bill Nicholson 20.00 10.00 6.00
(12) Pete Reiser 20.00 10.00 6.00
(13) Elmer Riddle 20.00 10.00 6.00
(14) Phil Rizzuto 60.00 30.00 18.00
(15) Johnny Rucker 20.00 10.00 6.00
(16) Hans Wagner 60.00 30.00 18.00

1942 (9-1/2" x 12")

(1) Jim Bagby 20.00 10.00 6.00
(2) Ernie Bonham 20.00 10.00 6.00
(3) Lou Boudreau 40.00 20.00 12.00
(4) Tommy Bridges 20.00 10.00 6.00
(5) Jimmy Brown 20.00 10.00 6.00
(6) Dolph Camilli 20.00 10.00 6.00
(7) Walker Cooper 20.00 10.00 6.00
(8) Bob Elliott 20.00 10.00 6.00
(9) Lou Gehrig/Btg 100.00 50.00 30.00
(10) Tex Hughson 20.00 10.00 6.00
(11) Eddie Joost 20.00 10.00 6.00
(12) Don Kolloway 20.00 10.00 6.00
(13) Phil Marchildon 20.00 10.00 6.00
(14) Clyde McCullough 20.00 10.00 6.00
(15) George McQuinn 20.00 10.00 6.00
(16) Cliff Melton 20.00 10.00 6.00
(17) Lou Novikoff 20.00 10.00 6.00
(18) Mickey Owen 20.00 10.00 6.00
(19) Pee Wee Reese 50.00 25.00 15.00
(20) Stan Spence 20.00 10.00 6.00
(21) Vern Stephens 20.00 10.00 6.00
(22) Virgil Trucks 20.00 10.00 6.00
(23) Fred "Dixie" Walker 20.00 10.00 6.00
(24) Max West 20.00 10.00 6.00

1943 (9-1/2" x 12")

(1) Hiram Bithorn 20.00 10.00 6.00
(2) Spud Chandler 20.00 10.00 6.00
(3) Al Javery 20.00 10.00 6.00
(4) Bill Johnson 20.00 10.00 6.00
(5) Kenesaw Landis 40.00 20.00 12.00
(6) Tony Lupien 20.00 10.00 6.00
(7) Marty Marion 25.00 12.50 7.50
(8) Stan Musial 60.00 30.00 18.00
(9) Bobo Newsom 20.00 10.00 6.00
(10) Babe Ruth (Portrait) 80.00 40.00 24.00
(11) Rip Sewell 20.00 10.00 6.00
(12) Joe Schultz 20.00 10.00 6.00
(13) Dizzy Trout 20.00 10.00 6.00
(14) Mickey Vernon 20.00 10.00 6.00
(15) Dick Wakefield 20.00 10.00 6.00
(16) Mickey Witek 20.00 10.00 6.00
(17) Early Wynn 40.00 20.00 12.00
(18) New York Yankees Team 90.00 45.00 27.00
(19) St. Louis Cardinals Team 90.00 45.00 27.00

1944 (9-1/2" x 12")

(1) Augie Galan 20.00 10.00 6.00
(2) Johnny Hopp 20.00 10.00 6.00
(3) Jack Kramer 20.00 10.00 6.00
(4) Johnny Lindell 20.00 10.00 6.00
(5) Ray Mueller 20.00 10.00 6.00
(6) Hal Newhouser 40.00 20.00 12.00
(7) Nelson Potter 20.00 10.00 6.00
(8) Ray Sanders 20.00 10.00 6.00
(9) "Snuffy" Stirnweiss 20.00 10.00 6.00
(10) Jim Tobin 20.00 10.00 6.00
(11) Thurman Tucker 20.00 10.00 6.00
(12) Bill Voiselle 20.00 10.00 6.00
(13) Ted Wilks 20.00 10.00 6.00
(14) Detroit Tigers Team 90.00 45.00 27.00
(15) St. Louis Browns Team 90.00 45.00 27.00
(16) St. Louis Cardinals Team 90.00 45.00 27.00

1945 (9-1/2" x 12")

(1) Phil Cavarretta 20.00 10.00 6.00
(2) Russ Christopher 20.00 10.00 6.00
(3) Tony Cuccinello 20.00 10.00 6.00
(4) Boo Ferriss 20.00 10.00 6.00
(5) Hal Gregg 20.00 10.00 6.00
(6) Steve Gromek 20.00 10.00 6.00
(7) Ducky Medwick 40.00 20.00 12.00
(8) George Myatt 20.00 10.00 6.00
(9) Frank Overmire 20.00 10.00 6.00
(10) Andy Pafko 25.00 12.50 7.50
(11) Red Schoendienst 40.00 20.00 12.00
(12) Chicago Cubs Team 90.00 45.00 27.00
(13) Detroit Tigers Team 75.00 37.00 22.00

1946

(1) Joe Beggs 20.00 10.00 6.00
(2) Johnny Berardino 25.00 12.50 7.50
(3) Bill Bevens 20.00 10.00 6.00
(4) Harry Brecheen 20.00 10.00 6.00
(5) Mickey Harris 20.00 10.00 6.00
(6) Kirby Higbe 20.00 10.00 6.00
(7) Dave Koslo 20.00 10.00 6.00
(8) Whitey Kurowski 20.00 10.00 6.00
(9) Vic Lombardi 20.00 10.00 6.00
(10) Phil Masi 20.00 10.00 6.00
(11) Mike McCormick 20.00 10.00 6.00
(12) Johnny Mize 40.00 20.00 12.00
(13) Hal Newhouser 40.00 20.00 12.00
(14) Johnny Pesky 20.00 10.00 6.00
(15) Howie Pollett 20.00 10.00 6.00
(16) Jerry Priddy 20.00 10.00 6.00
(17) Aaron Robinson 20.00 10.00 6.00
(18) Enos Slaughter 40.00 20.00 12.00
(19) Eddie Stanky 20.00 10.00 6.00
(20) Hal Wagner 20.00 10.00 6.00
(21) Rudy York 20.00 10.00 6.00
(22) Boston Red Sox Team 75.00 37.00 22.00
(23) St. Louis Cardinals Team 75.00 37.00 22.00

1947

(1) Ewell Blackwell 20.00 10.00 6.00
(2) Ralph Branca 20.00 10.00 6.00
(3) Billy Cox 20.00 10.00 6.00
(4) Bob Dillinger 20.00 10.00 6.00
(5) Joe Dobson 20.00 10.00 6.00
(6) Joe Gordon 20.00 10.00 6.00
(7) Hank Greenberg 45.00 22.00 13.50
(8) Clint Hartung 20.00 10.00 6.00
(9) Jim Hegan 20.00 10.00 6.00
(10) Larry Jansen 20.00 10.00 6.00
(11) George Kell 40.00 20.00 12.00
(12) Ken Keltner 20.00 10.00 6.00
(13) Ralph Kiner 40.00 20.00 12.00
(14) Willard Marshall 20.00 10.00 6.00
(15) Walt Masterson 20.00 10.00 6.00
(16) "Red" Munger 20.00 10.00 6.00
(17) Don Newcombe 25.00 12.50 7.50
(18) Hal Newhouser 40.00 20.00 12.00
(19) Joe Page 20.00 10.00 6.00
(20) Babe Ruth/Portrait 100.00 50.00 30.00
(21) Warren Spahn 40.00 20.00 12.00

(22)	Harry Taylor	20.00	10.00	6.00
(23)	Harry "The Hat" Walker	20.00	10.00	6.00
(24)	Brooklyn Dodgers Team	100.00	50.00	30.00
(25)	New York Yankees Team	150.00	75.00	45.00
	1948			
(1)	Richie Ashburn	40.00	20.00	12.00
(2)	Rex Barney	20.00	10.00	6.00
(3)	Gene Bearden	20.00	10.00	6.00
(4)	Lou Brissie	20.00	10.00	6.00
(5)	Alvin Dark	20.00	10.00	6.00
(6)	Larry Doby	40.00	20.00	12.00
(7)	Carl Furillo	25.00	12.50	7.50
(8)	Frank Gustine	20.00	10.00	6.00
(9)	Fred Hutchinson	20.00	10.00	6.00
(10)	Sheldon Jones	20.00	10.00	6.00
(11)	Bob Lemon	40.00	20.00	12.00
(12)	Hank Majeski	20.00	10.00	6.00
(13)	Barney McCosky	20.00	10.00	6.00
(14)	Mel Parnell	20.00	10.00	6.00
(15)	Carl Scheib	20.00	10.00	6.00
(16)	Al Zarilla	20.00	10.00	6.00
(17)	Boston Braves Team	75.00	37.00	22.00
(18)	Cleveland Indians Team	75.00	37.00	22.00
	1949			
(1)	Hoot Evers	20.00	10.00	6.00
(2)	Bob Feller	40.00	20.00	12.00
(3)	Billy Goodman	20.00	10.00	6.00
(4)	Sid Gordon	20.00	10.00	6.00
(5)	Gil Hodges	40.00	20.00	12.00
(6)	Art Houtteman	20.00	10.00	6.00
(7)	Dale Mitchell	20.00	10.00	6.00
(8)	Vic Raschi	20.00	10.00	6.00
(9)	Robin Roberts	40.00	20.00	12.00
(10)	Ray Scarborough	20.00	10.00	6.00
(11)	Duke Snider	50.00	25.00	15.00
(12)	Vic Wertz	20.00	10.00	6.00
(13)	Ted Williams	75.00	37.00	22.00
(14)	Brooklyn Dodgers Team	90.00	45.00	27.00
(15)	New York Yankees Team	90.00	45.00	27.00
	1950			
(1)	Hank Bauer	15.00	7.50	4.50
(2)	Yogi Berra	30.00	15.00	9.00
(3)	Walt Dropo	12.00	6.00	3.50
(4)	Del Ennis	12.00	6.00	3.50
(5)	Johnny Groth	12.00	6.00	3.50
(6)	Granny Hamner	12.00	6.00	3.50
(7)	Ted Kluszewski	15.00	7.50	4.50
(8)	Johnny Lipon	12.00	6.00	3.50
(9)	Hank Sauer	12.00	6.00	3.50
(10)	Earl Torgeson	12.00	6.00	3.50
(11)	New York Yankees Team	50.00	25.00	15.00
(12)	Philadelphia Phillies Team	35.00	17.50	10.50
	1951			
(1)	Grover Alexander	15.00	7.50	4.50
(2)	Chico Carrasquel	15.00	7.50	4.50
(3)	Bubba Church	12.00	6.00	3.50
(4)	Alvin Dark	12.00	6.00	3.50
(5)	Luke Easter	12.00	6.00	3.50
(6)	Carl Erskine	15.00	7.50	4.50
(7)	Ned Garver	12.00	6.00	3.50
(8)	Rogers Hornsby	15.00	7.50	4.50
(9)	Walter Johnson	25.00	12.50	7.50
(10)	Tony Lazzeri	15.00	7.50	4.50
(11)	Whitey Lockman	12.00	6.00	3.50
(12)	Ed Lopat	15.00	7.50	4.50
(13)	Sal Maglie	12.00	6.00	3.50
(14)	Willie Mays	150.00	75.00	45.00
(15)	Gil McDougald	20.00	10.00	6.00
(16)	Irv Noren	12.00	6.00	3.50
(17)	Eddie Robinson	12.00	6.00	3.50
(18)	Jackie Robinson	125.00	62.00	37.00
(19)	Red Rolfe	12.00	6.00	3.50
(20)	Tris Speaker	20.00	10.00	6.00
(21)	Eddie Stanky	12.00	6.00	3.50
(22)	Clyde Vollmer	12.00	6.00	3.50
(23)	Wes Westrum	12.00	6.00	3.50
(24)	Cy Young	25.00	12.50	7.50
(25)	New York Giants Team	40.00	20.00	12.00
(26)	New York Yankees Team	60.00	30.00	18.00
	1952			
(1)	Bobby Avila	12.00	6.00	3.50
(2)	Lou Boudreau	20.00	10.00	6.00
(3)	Jim Busby	12.00	6.00	3.50
(4)	Roy Campanella	30.00	15.00	9.00
(5)	Gil Coan	12.00	6.00	3.50
(6)	Walker Cooper	12.00	6.00	3.50
(7)	Al Corwin	12.00	6.00	3.50
(8)	Murry Dickson	12.00	6.00	3.50
(9)	Leo Durocher	20.00	10.00	6.00
(10)	Bob Elliott	12.00	6.00	3.50
(11)	Ferris Fain	12.00	6.00	3.50
(12)	Jimmie Foxx	20.00	10.00	6.00
(13)	Mike Garcia	12.00	6.00	3.50
(14)	Hank Greenberg	25.00	12.50	7.50
(15)	Solly Hemus	12.00	6.00	3.50
(16)	Monte Irvin	20.00	10.00	6.00
(17)	Sam Jethroe	12.00	6.00	3.50
(18)	Ellis Kinder	12.00	6.00	3.50
(19)	Dick Kryhoski	12.00	6.00	3.50
(20)	Clem Labine	15.00	7.50	4.50
(21)	Mickey Mantle	200.00	100.00	60.00
(22)	Connie Marrero	12.00	6.00	3.50
(23)	Cass Michaels	12.00	6.00	3.50
(24)	Minnie Minoso	15.00	7.50	4.50
(25)	Don Mueller	12.00	6.00	3.50
(26)	Mel Parnell	12.00	6.00	3.50
(27)	Allie Reynolds	15.00	7.50	4.50
(28)	"Preacher" Roe	15.00	7.50	4.50
(29)	Saul Rogovin	12.00	6.00	3.50
(30)	Al Rosen	15.00	7.50	4.50
(31)	Red Schoendienst	20.00	10.00	6.00
(32)	Andy Seminick	12.00	6.00	3.50
(33)	Bobby Shantz	12.00	6.00	3.50
(34)	Duke Snider	25.00	12.50	7.50
(35)	Gerry Staley	12.00	6.00	3.50
(36)	Gene Stephens	12.00	6.00	3.50
(37)	Max Surkont	12.00	6.00	3.50
(38)	Bobby Thomson	12.00	6.00	3.50
(39)	Elmer Valo	12.00	6.00	3.50
(40)	Eddie Waitkus	12.00	6.00	3.50
(41)	Gene Woodling	15.00	7.50	4.50
(42)	Eddie Yost	12.00	6.00	3.50
(43)	Gus Zernial	12.00	6.00	3.50
(44)	Brooklyn Dodgers Team	50.00	25.00	15.00
(45)	New York Yankees Team	75.00	37.00	22.00
	1953			
(1)	Joe Black	15.00	7.50	4.50
(2)	Billy Cox	12.00	6.00	3.50
(3)	Billy Loes	12.00	6.00	3.50
(4)	Billy Martin	15.00	7.50	4.50
(5)	Eddie Mathews	25.00	12.50	7.50
(6)	George Shuba	12.00	6.00	3.50
(7)	Hoyt Wilhelm	20.00	10.00	6.00
	1954			
(1)	Joe Adcock	12.00	6.00	3.50
(2)	Johnny Antonelli	12.00	6.00	3.50
(3)	Gus Bell	12.00	6.00	3.50
(4)	Jim Greengrass	12.00	6.00	3.50
(5)	Bob Grim	12.00	6.00	3.50
(6)	Frank House	12.00	6.00	3.50
(7)	Jackie Jensen	12.00	6.00	3.50
(8)	Al Kaline	25.00	12.50	7.50
(9)	Harvey Kuenn	15.00	7.50	4.50
(10)	Willie Miranda	12.00	6.00	3.50
(11)	Wally Moon	12.00	6.00	3.50
(12)	Ray Moore	12.00	6.00	3.50
(13)	Don Mossi	12.00	6.00	3.50
(14)	Stan Musial	30.00	15.00	9.00
(15)	Hal Naragon	12.00	6.00	3.50
(16)	Chet Nichols	12.00	6.00	3.50
(17)	Billy Pierce	12.00	6.00	3.50
(18)	Arnie Portocarrero	12.00	6.00	3.50
(19)	James "Dusty" Rhodes	12.00	6.00	3.50
(20)	Babe Ruth	50.00	25.00	15.00
(21)	Dean Stone	12.00	6.00	3.50
(22)	Bob Turley	15.00	7.50	4.50
(23)	Jim Wilson	12.00	6.00	3.50
(24)	New York Giants Team	50.00	25.00	15.00
	1955			
(1)	Gene Conley	12.00	6.00	3.50
(2)	Elston Howard	15.00	7.50	4.50
(3)	Hank Sauer	12.00	6.00	3.50
	1956			
(1)	Hank Bauer	15.00	7.50	4.50
(2)	Yogi Berra	25.00	12.50	7.50
(3)	Ray Boone	12.00	6.00	3.50
(4)	Ken Boyer	15.00	7.50	4.50
(5)	Tom Brewer	12.00	6.00	3.50
(6)	Bob Buhl	12.00	6.00	3.50
(7)	Nellie Fox	20.00	10.00	6.00
(8)	Bob Keegan	12.00	6.00	3.50
(9)	Don Larsen	15.00	7.50	4.50
(10)	Jim Lemon	12.00	6.00	3.50
(11)	Danny O'Connoll	12.00	6.00	3.50
(12)	Jim Pendleton	12.00	6.00	3.50
(13)	Bob Rush	12.00	6.00	3.50
(14)	Roy Sievers	12.00	6.00	3.50
(15)	Gus Zernial	12.00	6.00	3.50
	1957			
(1)	Hank Aaron	30.00	15.00	9.00
(2)	Joe Adcock	12.00	6.00	3.50
(3)	Luis Arroyo	12.00	6.00	3.50
(4)	Ed Bailey	12.00	6.00	3.50
(5)	Ernie Banks	25.00	12.50	7.50
(6)	Roy Campanella	20.00	10.00	6.00
(7)	Billy Cox	12.00	6.00	3.50
(8)	Del Crandall	12.00	6.00	3.50
(9)	Whitey Ford	25.00	12.50	7.50
(10)	Bob Friend	12.00	6.00	3.50
(11)	Carl Furillo	15.00	7.50	4.50
(12)	Granny Hamner	12.00	6.00	3.50
(13)	Gil Hodges	15.00	7.50	4.50
(14)	Billy Hoeft	12.00	6.00	3.50
(15)	Walter Johnson	25.00	12.50	7.50
(16)	George Kell	20.00	10.00	6.00
(17)	Ted Kluszewski	20.00	10.00	6.00
(18)	Johnny Kucks	12.00	6.00	3.50
(19)	Harvey Kuenn	12.00	6.00	3.50
(20)	Clem Labine	12.00	6.00	3.50
(21)	Vern Law	12.00	6.00	3.50
(22)	Brooks Lawrence	12.00	6.00	3.50
(23)	Bob Lemon	20.00	10.00	6.00
(24)	Sherman Lollar	12.00	6.00	3.50
(25)	Billy Martin	15.00	7.50	4.50
(25)	Eddie Mathews	20.00	10.00	6.00
(26)	Charlie Maxwell	12.00	6.00	3.50
(27)	Willie Mays	60.00	30.00	18.00
(28)	Gil McDougald	15.00	7.50	4.50
(29)	Willie Miranda	12.00	6.00	3.50
(30)	Jimmy Piersall	12.00	6.00	3.50
(31)	Pee Wee Reese	25.00	12.50	7.50
(32)	"Rip" Repulski	12.00	6.00	3.50
(33)	Robin Roberts	20.00	10.00	6.00
(34)	Frank Robinson	30.00	15.00	9.00
(35)	Al Rosen	12.00	6.00	3.50
(36)	Babe Ruth	60.00	30.00	18.00
(37)	Herb Score	15.00	7.50	4.50
(38)	Enos Slaughter	20.00	10.00	6.00
(39)	Warren Spahn	20.00	10.00	6.00
(40)	Johnny Temple	12.00	6.00	3.50
(41)	Mickey Vernon	12.00	6.00	3.50
	1957 (17-1/2" x 20")			
(1)	Johnny Antonelli	30.00	15.00	9.00
(2)	Hank Bauer	45.00	22.00	13.50
(3)	Frank House	30.00	15.00	9.00
(4)	Jackie Jensen	35.00	17.50	10.00
(5)	Al Kaline	45.00	22.00	13.50
(6)	Bob Lemon	35.00	17.50	10.00
(7)	Chet Nichols	30.00	15.00	9.00
(8)	Al Rosen	30.00	15.00	9.00
(9)	Dean Stone	30.00	15.00	9.00
(10)	Bob Turley	35.00	17.50	10.00
(11)	Mickey Vernon	30.00	15.00	9.00

1915 Baseball Magazine Premium

A special "Park Edition" of the April "Baseball Magazine," produced for sale at major league ballparks, was published in 1915. The cover features a J.F. Kernan portrait of Walter Johnson. Bound inside was a Kernan portrait of Christy Mathewson, printed on heavy, slick paper designed to be removed for display.

	NM	EX	VG
Complete Magazine:	3,500	2,500	1,500
Christy Mathewson (Premium)	2,000	1,000	600.00

1913 Baseball Managers Scorecard/Fan

This novelty souvenir item was presumable made for sale or as a giveaway promotion which could be customized with sponsors' advertising on the back. The body of the fan is a heavy cardboard ovoid about 9-1/2" x 9". At center is a scorecard. Printed in color around the scoring section are colorful caricatures of each National and American League manager either in a costume representing the team nickname or holding a mascot, etc. The piece is stapled to a 6" wooden stick. Local advertising may or may not appear on the back.

	NM	EX	VG
Joe Birmingham, Nixey Callahan, Frank, Chance, Fred Clarke, Bill Dahlen, Red, Dooin, Jonny Evers, Clark Griffith,, Miller Huggins, Hughie Jennings, Connie, Mack, John McGraw, Jake Stahl, George, Stallings, George Stovall, Joe Tinker	1,150	575.00	345.00

1950 Baseball Player Charms

The date of issue for this novelty item is conjectural, based on known player selection. Packaged in plastic bubbles for sale in vending machines, these charms are found in several different shapes - rectangle, octagon, etc. - and colors of plastic. A black-and-white photo appears at center with a loop at top for hanging. Size also varies but is about 3/4" x 1-1/4". Players are not identified on the charm and there is no number. The checklist here is in alphabetical order, and likely not complete.

	NM	EX	VG
Common Player:	20.00	10.00	6.00
(1) Yogi Berra	45.00	22.00	13.50
(2) Ewell Blackwell	20.00	10.00	6.00
(3) Roy Campanella	45.00	22.00	13.50
(4) Joe DiMaggio	75.00	37.00	22.00
(5) Carl Erskine	20.00	10.00	6.00
(6) Bob Feller	25.00	12.50	7.50
(7) Carl Furillo	22.50	11.00	6.75
(8) Lou Gehrig	65.00	32.00	19.50
(9) Ralph Kiner	20.00	10.00	6.00
(10) Stan Musial	55.00	27.00	16.50
(11) Andy Pafko	20.00	10.00	6.00
(12) Pee Wee Reese	35.00	17.50	10.50
(13) Phil Rizzuto	30.00	15.00	9.00
(14) Jackie Robinson	65.00	32.00	19.50
(15) Babe Ruth	95.00	47.00	28.00
(16) Duke Snider	35.00	17.50	10.50
(17) Wally Westlake	20.00	10.00	6.00
(18) Ted Williams	60.00	30.00	18.00

1952 Baseball Player Doubleheader Charms

These vending machine prizes were probably issued in the early 1950s, though pinning down a date via player selection is imprecise. About 7/8" in diameter, these novelties have black-and-white player photos on front and back, with the player's name in script beneath his portrait. A clear plastic dome covers the photos and is wrapped with a looped band for hanging. The unnumbered charms are listed here in alphabetical order.

	NM	EX	VG
Complete Set (31):	550.00	275.00	175.00
Common Player:	25.00	12.50	7.50
(1) Richie Ashburn, Phil Masi	30.00	15.00	9.00
(2) Hank Bauer, Johnny Pesky	25.00	12.50	7.50
(3) Yogi Berra, Duke Snider	45.00	22.00	13.50
(4) Ewell Blackwell, "Big" Jim Konstanty	25.00	12.50	7.50
(5) Lou Boudreau, Allie Reynolds	27.50	13.50	8.25
(6) Leland Brissie, Albert Schoendienst	27.50	13.50	8.25
(7) Roy Campanella, Bob Elliott	30.00	15.00	9.00
(8) Phil Cavarretta, Virgil Stallcup	25.00	12.50	7.50
(9) Sam Chapman, Larry Jansen	25.00	12.50	7.50
(10) Jerry Coleman, George Kell	27.50	13.50	8.25
(11) Billy Cox, Junior Thompson	25.00	12.50	7.50
(12) Walt Dropo, Myron McCormick	25.00	12.50	7.50
(13) Al Evans, Wes Westrum	25.00	12.50	7.50
(14) Walter Evers, Cliff Mapes	25.00	12.50	7.50
(15) Bob Feller, Phil Rizzuto	35.00	17.50	10.50
(16) Gordon Goldsberry, Stan Musial	30.00	15.00	9.00
(17) Clint Hartung, Don Kolloway	25.00	12.50	7.50
(18) Grady Hatton, Tommy Holmes	25.00	12.50	7.50
(19) Tommy Henrich, Ted Kluszewski	27.50	13.50	8.25
(20) Gene Hermanski, Hal Newhouser	25.00	12.50	7.50
(21) Art Houtteman, Jackie Robinson	45.00	22.00	13.50
(22) Sid Hudson, Andy Pafko	25.00	12.50	7.50
(23) Ed Kazak, Bob Lemon	27.50	13.50	8.25
(24) Ellis Kinder, Gus Zernial	25.00	12.50	7.50
(25) Ralph Kiner, Joe Page	27.50	13.50	8.25
(26) Ed Lopat, Paul Trout	25.00	12.50	7.50
(27) Don Newcombe, Vic Wertz	25.00	12.50	7.50
(28) Dave Philley, Aaron Robinson	25.00	12.50	7.50
(29) Vic Raschi, Enos Slaughter	27.50	13.50	8.25
(30) Pee Wee Reese, Gene Woodling	30.00	15.00	9.00
(31) George Tebbetts, Eddie Yost	25.00	12.50	7.50

1961 Baseball Player Key Chains

The maker of these postage-stamp size (1-1/8" x 1-1/2") black-and-white, blank-back "cards" is unknown. From the inclusion of numerous journeyman Pirates players in the set, it probably has a Pittsburgh origin. Possibly intended for sale at stadium souvenir counters, they were made to be inserted into clear plastic key chain novelties, and have a semi-gloss front surface. Unnumbered, they are checklisted here alphabetically.

	NM	EX	VG
Complete Set (69):	400.00	200.00	120.00
Common Player:	5.00	2.50	1.50
(1) Hank Aaron	15.00	7.50	4.50
(2) Bob Allison	5.00	2.50	1.50
(3) George Altman	5.00	2.50	1.50
(4) Luis Aparicio	7.50	3.75	2.25
(5) Richie Ashburn	7.50	3.75	2.25
(6) Ernie Banks	10.00	5.00	3.00
(7) Earl Battey	5.00	2.50	1.50
(8) Hank Bauer	6.00	3.00	1.75
(9) Gus Bell	5.00	2.50	1.50
(10) Yogi Berra	10.00	5.00	3.00
(11) Ken Boyer	6.00	3.00	1.75
(12) Lew Burdette	5.00	2.50	1.50
(13) Smoky Burgess	5.00	2.50	1.50
(14) Orlando Cepeda	7.50	3.75	2.25
(15) Gino Cimoli	5.00	2.50	1.50
(16) Roberto Clemente	20.00	10.00	6.00
(17) Del Crandall	5.00	2.50	1.50
(18) Dizzy Dean	9.00	4.50	2.75
(19) Don Drysdale	7.50	3.75	2.25
(20) Sam Esposito	5.00	2.50	1.50
(21) Roy Face	5.00	2.50	1.50
(22) Nelson Fox	7.50	3.75	2.25
(23) Bob Friend	5.00	2.50	1.50
(24) Lou Gehrig	12.50	6.25	3.75
(25) Joe Gibbon	5.00	2.50	1.50
(26) Jim Gilliam	6.00	3.00	1.75
(27) Fred Green	5.00	2.50	1.50
(28) Pumpsie Green	5.00	2.50	1.50
(29) Dick Groat	6.00	3.00	1.75
(30) Harvey Haddix	5.00	2.50	1.50
(31) Don Hoak	5.00	2.50	1.50
(32) Glen Hobbie	5.00	2.50	1.50
(33) Frank Howard	6.00	3.00	1.75
(34) Jackie Jensen	5.00	2.50	1.50
(35) Sam Jones	5.00	2.50	1.50
(36) Al Kaline	9.00	4.50	2.75
(37) Harmon Killebrew	7.50	3.75	2.25
(38) Harvey Kuenn	5.00	2.50	1.50
(39) Norm Larker	5.00	2.50	1.50
(40) Vernon Law	5.00	2.50	1.50
(41) Mickey Mantle	30.00	15.00	9.00
(42) Roger Maris	12.00	6.00	3.50
(43) Eddie Mathews	7.50	3.75	2.25
(44) Willie Mays	12.00	6.00	3.50
(45) Bill Mazeroski	7.50	3.75	2.25
(46) Willie McCovey	7.50	3.75	2.25
(47) Lindy McDaniel	5.00	2.50	1.50
(48) Roy McMillan	5.00	2.50	1.50
(49) Minnie Minoso	6.00	3.00	1.75
(50) Danny Murtaugh	5.00	2.50	1.50
(51) Stan Musial	12.00	6.00	3.50
(52) Rocky Nelson	5.00	2.50	1.50
(53) Bob Oldis	5.00	2.50	1.50
(54) Vada Pinson	6.00	3.00	1.75
(55) Vic Power	5.00	2.50	1.50
(56) Robin Roberts	7.50	3.75	2.25
(57) Pete Runnels	5.00	2.50	1.50
(58) Babe Ruth	20.00	10.00	6.00
(59) Ron Santo	6.00	3.00	1.75
(60) Dick Schofield	5.00	2.50	1.50
(61) Bob Skinner	5.00	2.50	1.50
(62) Hal Smith	5.00	2.50	1.50
(63) Duke Snider	9.00	4.50	2.75
(64) Warren Spahn	7.50	3.75	2.25
(65) Dick Stuart	5.00	2.50	1.50
(66) Willie Tasby	5.00	2.50	1.50
(67) Tony Taylor	5.00	2.50	1.50
(68) Bill Virdon	5.00	2.50	1.50
(69) Ted Williams	17.50	9.00	5.00

1978 Baseball Player Patches

These card-size (about 2-1/2" x 3-1/4") cloth patches feature embroidered player portraits on a white background with a color border. Uniform logos are not present. The patches originally sold for $2.50 apiece from the Penn Emblem Co., Philadelphia, though the company's name is not found on the patches. The unnumbered patches are listed here in alphabetical order.

	NM	EX	VG
Complete Set (103):	350.00	175.00	100.00
Common Player:	3.00	1.50	.90
(1) Buddy Bell	3.00	1.50	.90
(2) Johnny Bench	10.00	5.00	3.00
(3) Vida Blue	3.00	1.50	.90
(4) Bobby Bonds	3.00	1.50	.90
(5) Bob Boone	3.00	1.50	.90
(6) Larry Bowa	3.00	1.50	.90
(7) George Brett	12.00	6.00	3.50
(8) Lou Brock	9.00	4.50	2.75
(9) Rick Burleson	3.00	1.50	.90
(10) Jeff Burroughs	3.00	1.50	.90
(11) Bert Campaneris	3.00	1.50	.90
(12) John Candelaria	3.00	1.50	.90
(13) Rod Carew	9.00	4.50	2.75
(14) Steve Carlton	9.00	4.50	2.75
(15) Gary Carter	7.50	3.75	2.25
(16) Dave Cash	3.00	1.50	.90
(17) Cesar Cedeno	3.00	1.50	.90
(18) Ron Cey	3.00	1.50	.90
(19) Chris Chambliss	3.00	1.50	.90
(20) Jack Clark	3.00	1.50	.90
(21) Dave Concepcion	3.00	1.50	.90
(22) Cecil Cooper	3.00	1.50	.90
(23) Jose Cruz	3.00	1.50	.90
(24) Andre Dawson	3.00	1.50	.90
(25) Dan Driessen	3.00	1.50	.90
(26) Rawly Eastwick	3.00	1.50	.90
(27) Dwight Evans	3.00	1.50	.90
(28) Mark Fidrych	4.50	2.25	1.25
(29) Rollie Fingers	7.50	3.75	2.25
(30) Carlton Fisk	9.00	4.50	2.75
(31) George Foster	3.00	1.50	.90
(32) Steve Garvey	6.00	3.00	1.75
(33) Rich Gossage	3.00	1.50	.90
(34) Bobby Grich	3.00	1.50	.90
(35) Ross Grimsley	3.00	1.50	.90
(36) Ron Guidry	3.00	1.50	.90
(37) Mike Hargrove	3.00	1.50	.90
(38) Keith Hernandez	3.00	1.50	.90
(39) Larry Hisle	3.00	1.50	.90
(40) Bob Horner	3.00	1.50	.90
(41) Roy Howell	3.00	1.50	.90
(42) "Catfish" Hunter	7.50	3.75	2.25
(43) Reggie Jackson	12.00	6.00	3.50
(44) Tommy John	4.00	2.00	1.25
(45) Jim Kern	3.00	1.50	.90
(46) Chet Lemon	3.00	1.50	.90
(47) Davey Lopes	3.00	1.50	.90
(48) Greg Luzinski	3.00	1.50	.90
(49) Fred Lynn	3.00	1.50	.90
(50) Garry Maddox	3.00	1.50	.90
(51) Bill Madlock	3.00	1.50	.90
(52) Jon Matlack	3.00	1.50	.90
(53) John Mayberry	3.00	1.50	.90
(54) Lee Mazzilli	3.00	1.50	.90
(55) Rick Monday	3.00	1.50	.90
(56) Don Money	3.00	1.50	.90
(57) Willie Montanez	3.00	1.50	.90
(58) John Montefusco	3.00	1.50	.90
(59) Joe Morgan	9.00	4.50	2.75
(60) Thurman Munson	7.50	3.75	2.25
(61) Bobby Murcer	3.00	1.50	.90
(62) Graig Nettles	3.00	1.50	.90
(63) Phil Niekro	7.50	3.75	2.25
(64) Al Oliver	3.00	1.50	.90
(65) Amos Otis	3.00	1.50	.90
(66) Jim Palmer	9.00	4.50	2.75
(67) Dave Parker	3.00	1.50	.90
(68) Fred Patek	3.00	1.50	.90
(69) Tony Perez	7.50	3.75	2.25
(70) Lou Piniella	4.00	2.00	1.25
(71) Biff Pocoroba	3.00	1.50	.90
(72) Darrell Porter	3.00	1.50	.90
(73) Rick Reuschel	3.00	1.50	.90
(74) Jim Rice	6.00	3.00	1.75
(75a) Pete Rose (Red border.)	12.00	6.00	3.50
(75b) Pete Rose (Blue border.)	12.00	6.00	3.50
(76) Joe Rudi	3.00	1.50	.90
(77) Rick Reuschel	3.00	1.50	.90
(78) Nolan Ryan	15.00	7.50	4.50
(79) Manny Sanguillen	3.00	1.50	.90
(80) Mike Schmidt	12.00	6.00	3.50
(81) George Scott	3.00	1.50	.90
(82) Tom Seaver	9.00	4.50	2.75
(83) Ted Simmons	3.00	1.50	.90
(84) Reggie Smith	3.00	1.50	.90
(85) Willie Stargell	9.00	4.50	2.75
(86) Rennie Stennett	3.00	1.50	.90
(87) Jim Sundberg	3.00	1.50	.90
(88) Bruce Sutter	7.50	3.75	2.25
(89) Frank Tanana	3.00	1.50	.90
(90) Garry Templeton	3.00	1.50	.90
(91) Gene Tenace	3.00	1.50	.90
(92) Jason Thompson	3.00	1.50	.90
(93) Luis Tiant	3.00	1.50	.90
(94) Joe Torre	4.50	2.25	1.25
(95) Ellis Valentine	3.00	1.50	.90
(96) Bob Watson	3.00	1.50	.90
(97) Frank White	3.00	1.50	.90
(98) Lou Whitaker	3.00	1.50	.90
(99) Bump Wills	3.00	1.50	.90
(100) Dave Winfield	9.00	4.50	2.75
(101) Butch Wynegar	3.00	1.50	.90
(102) Carl Yastrzemski	12.00	6.00	3.50
(103) Richie Zisk	3.00	1.50	.90

Fantasy Baseball Player Pencil Clips

This series of modern (circa late 1990s) pencil clips features old-time baseball stars. The pieces feature enameled round buttons in various sizes attached to a steel frame designed to be slipped over a pencil, ostensibly for use with a scorecard during a ball game. These are often sold on eBay and at flea markets by persons purporting them to be old.

NO COLLECTIBLE VALUE
- Ty Cobb
- Christy Mathewson
- Satchel Paige (St. Louis Browns
- Babe Ruth (Champions)
- Honus Wagner
- 1959 World Series White Sox

1913 Baseball Player Stamps

The extent of this issue and the exact date and manner of its issue are not known. The large-format (about 1-13/16" x 2-1/2") stamps have color artwork of the players on a baseball diamond background. A solid colored frame with art deco detailing separates the picture from the white border. Backs are, of course, blank.

	NM	EX	VG
Chief Bender	200.00	100.00	60.00
Ty Cobb	1,750	875.00	525.00
Joe Jackson	2,250	1,125	675.00
Christy Mathewson	475.00	235.00	140.00
Tris Speaker	200.00	100.00	60.00

1892 Base Ball Scenes (N360)

The N360 American Card Catalog designation covers the several tobacco manufacturers who issued this type of card to advertise various brands. Obviously, the cards do not picture actual ballplayers, but rather have on their fronts color lithographs of attractive women in baseball uniforms and in game action. Approximately 2-3/16" x 3-15/16" most cards have a tiny line of type at bottom carrying a Donaldson Bros., N.Y., copyright. Those cards issued to promote the Little Rhody Cut Plus brand have a script ad message on front and a monthly schedule of the 12-team National League on back. Advertising for the various brands of tobacco companies may be printed directly on the card back, on a paper label pasted over another ad or overprinted on a previously printed ad. Cards are known with these manufacturers and brands. S.W. Venable: Cockade, Gay Head, Helmet, Ideal and Pluck; G.F. Young & Bro.: Little Rhody, and M.T. Coffey. Nine different poses are known for the card fronts.

	NM	EX	VG
Common Card:	600.00	300.00	180.00

1913 Base Ball Series Notebooks

The issue date cited is conjectural, based on writing found in a survivng specimen of this child's notebook. The 8" x 10" notebook has on its cover a baseball diamond and bleachers drawing in white on a beige background. Printed above and below the artwork are full-color reproductions of five baseball cards from the Philadelphia Caramel issues of 1909 (E95) and 1910 (E96). The cover is printed on thinner stock the original cards and has no printing on the reverse side. This has led to cut copies of these cards being misidentified as proofs. Because similar blank-back, thin stock cards are known of other players, it is possible other notebook covers may exist.

	NM	EX	VG
Complete Notebook:			
Fred Clark (Clarke)(E96), Nap Lajoie (E96), Jake Pfeister (E96), Honus Wagner (E95), Ed Willetts (Willett)(E95)	750.00	375.00	225.00
OBSERVED SINGLES			
Harry Krause (E95)	100.00	40.00	20.00

1911 Baseball Scorecard Fan

This unusual player collectible is a combination fan and scorecard published circa 1911. The cardboard scorecard is about 10-1/2" x 9" and stapled to an approximately 11" long wooden handle. Printed in black-and-white, there are 16 player portraits at top, separated by a baseball. At center is the portrait of young lady and at bottom is a ball-in-mitt photo. The fans can be found with various local advertising overprinted on front or back: Barton's Barber Shop, Ira P. File Ice Cream and Confectionery, Maine's Bliss School of Business, Poole Pianos, Kemper pharmacy, etc. The players are identified by last name and for lack of uniform details, specific identification of a few of them is speculative.

	NM	EX	VG
Germany Schaeffer (Schaefer), Bobby Wallace, Billy Sullivan, Hal Chase, George Moriarty, Harry Lord, Harry Davis, Nap Lajoie, Mickey Doolan, Clark Griffith, Bill Dahlen, Jeff Sweeney, Frank Chance, Art Devlin, Fred Clark (Clarke), Roger Bresnahan	1,500	750.00	400.00

1964 Baseball Stars - Present and Future Photocard

This large-format (11" x 8-1/2") color card features three group photos of top stars of the day. In addition to the photos, there are facsimile autographs of each player on the bright yellow background. Back is blank. (See also Baseball Greats Postcard.)

	NM	EX	VG
Sheet:	25.00	12.50	7.50

Dean Chance, Don Drysdale, Dick Farrell, Jim Fregosi, Sandy Koufax, Willie Mays, Joe Pepitone, Dick Radatz

1912 Base Ball Stars Series

This set of blank-backed, black-and-white 6" x 9" pictures features the contestants of the 1912 World Series - the Red Sox and Giants. It is possible these pictures were sold at the ballparks during the Series. The checklist here is probably incomplete. The unnumbered pictures have been listed alphabetically within team.

		NM	EX	VG
	Common Player:	450.00	225.00	135.00
	BOSTON RED SOX			
(1)	Hugh Bedient	450.00	225.00	135.00
(2)	Joe Wood	480.00	240.00	145.00
	N.Y. GIANTS			
(1)	Rube Marquard	525.00	260.00	150.00
(2)	Christy Mathewson	1,050	525.00	315.00
(3)	Jeff Tesreau	450.00	225.00	135.00

1938 Baseball Tabs

The issuer and manner of distribution for these baseball tabs is unknown. About 3/4" diameter, with bendable wings at each side, the points of which could be stuck through fabric and thus attached to a cap or jacket, the tabs have black-and-white player portraits on a baseball-style background in one of several colors. Most of the player first names have parentheses around them. The team tabs have a large nickname at center and the city and league at bottom. The inclusion of American Association teams argues for distribution in the upper Midwest. The unnumbered tabs are listed here in alphabetical order.

		NM	EX	VG
	Complete Set (53):	3,000	1,500	900.00
	Common Player:	50.00	25.00	15.50
	Common Team:	50.00	25.00	15.00
(1)	Luke Appling	75.00	37.00	22.00
(2)	Earl Averill	75.00	37.00	22.00
(3)	Phil Cavarretta	50.00	25.00	15.00
(4)	Dizzy Dean	100.00	50.00	30.00
(5)	Paul Derringer	50.00	25.00	15.00
(6)	Bill Dickey	90.00	45.00	27.00
(7)	Joe DiMaggio	450.00	225.00	135.00
(8)	Bob Feller	75.00	37.00	22.00
(9)	Lou Fette	50.00	25.00	15.00
(10)	Jimmie Foxx	100.00	50.00	30.00
(11)	Lou Gehrig	375.00	185.00	110.00
(12)	Charley Gehringer	75.00	37.00	22.00
(13)	Lefty Gomez	75.00	37.00	22.00
(14)	Hank Greenberg	90.00	45.00	27.00
(15)	Lefty Grove	75.00	37.00	22.00
(16)	Mule Haas	50.00	25.00	15.00
(17)	Gabby Hartnett	75.00	37.00	22.00
(18)	Rollie Hemsley	50.00	25.00	15.00
(19)	Carl Hubbell	75.00	37.00	22.00
(20)	Chuck Klein	75.00	37.00	22.00
(21)	Red Kress	50.00	25.00	15.00
(22)	Push-Em-Up-Tony Lazzeri	75.00	37.00	22.00
(23)	Ted Lyons	75.00	37.00	22.00
(24)	Joe Medwick	75.00	37.00	22.00
(25)	Van Lingle Mungo	50.00	25.00	15.00
(26)	Rip Radcliff	50.00	25.00	15.00
(27)	Schoolboy Rowe	50.00	25.00	15.00
(28)	Al Simmons	75.00	37.00	22.00
(29)	Little Poison Waner	75.00	37.00	22.00
(30)	Athletics (Philadelphia)	50.00	25.00	15.00
(31)	Bees (Boston)	50.00	25.00	15.00
(32)	Blues (Kansas City)	50.00	25.00	15.00

		NM	EX	VG
(33)	Brewers (Milwaukee)	50.00	25.00	15.00
(34)	Browns (St. Louis)	50.00	25.00	15.00
(35)	Cardinals (St. Louis)	50.00	25.00	15.00
(36)	Colonels (Louisville)	50.00	25.00	15.00
(37)	Cubs (Chicago)	50.00	25.00	15.00
(38)	Dodgers (Brooklyn)	50.00	25.00	15.00
(39)	Giants (New York)	50.00	25.00	15.00
(40)	Indians (Cleveland)	50.00	25.00	15.00
(41)	Indians (Indianapolis)	50.00	25.00	15.00
(42)	Millers (Minneapolis)	50.00	25.00	15.00
(43)	Mud-Hens (Toledo)	50.00	25.00	15.00
(44)	Nationals (Washington)	50.00	25.00	15.00
(45)	Phillies (Philadelphia)	50.00	25.00	15.00
(46)	Pirates (Pittsburgh)	50.00	25.00	15.00
(47)	Red Birds (Columbus)	50.00	25.00	15.00
(48)	Reds (Cincinnati)	50.00	25.00	15.00
(49)	Red Sox (Boston)	50.00	25.00	15.00
(50)	Saints (St. Paul)	50.00	25.00	15.00
(51)	Tigers (Detroit)	50.00	25.00	15.00
(52)	White Sox (Chicago)	50.00	25.00	15.00
(53)	Yankees (New York)	65.00	32.00	19.50

1934-36 Batter-Up (R318)

National Chicle's 192-card "Batter-Up" set was issued over a three-year period. The blank-backed cards are die-cut, enabling collectors of the era to fold the top of the card over so that it could stand upright on its own support. The cards can be found in black-and-white or a variety of color tints. Card numbers 1-80 measure 2-3/8" x 3-1/4" in size, while the high-numbered cards (#81-192) measure 2-3/8" x 3" (1/4" smaller in height). The high-numbered cards are significantly more difficult to find than the lower numbers. The set's ACC designation is R318.

		NM	EX	VG
Complete Set (192):		25,000	10,000	5,000
Common Player (1-80):		95.00	40.00	20.00
Common Player (81-192):		175.00	70.00	35.00
1	Wally Berger	175.00	60.00	30.00
2	Ed Brandt	95.00	40.00	20.00
3	Al Lopez	300.00	120.00	60.00
4	Dick Bartell	95.00	40.00	20.00
5	Carl Hubbell	300.00	120.00	60.00
6	Bill Terry	300.00	120.00	60.00
7	Pepper Martin	95.00	40.00	20.00
8	Jim Bottomley	300.00	120.00	60.00
9	Tommy Bridges	95.00	40.00	20.00
10	Rick Ferrell	300.00	120.00	60.00
11	Ray Benge	95.00	40.00	20.00
12	Wes Ferrell	95.00	40.00	20.00
13	Bill Cissell	95.00	40.00	20.00
14	Pie Traynor	300.00	120.00	60.00
15	Roy Mahaffey	95.00	40.00	20.00
16	Chick Hafey	300.00	120.00	60.00
17	Lloyd Waner	300.00	120.00	60.00
18	Jack Burns	95.00	40.00	20.00
19	Buddy Myer	95.00	40.00	20.00
20	Bob Johnson	95.00	40.00	20.00
21	Arky Vaughn (Vaughan)	300.00	120.00	60.00
22	Red Rolfe	95.00	40.00	20.00
23	Lefty Gomez	300.00	120.00	60.00
24	Earl Averill	300.00	120.00	60.00
25	Mickey Cochrane	300.00	120.00	60.00
26	Van Mungo	95.00	40.00	20.00
27	Mel Ott	425.00	175.00	85.00
28	Jimmie Foxx	550.00	225.00	110.00
29	Jimmy Dykes	95.00	40.00	20.00
30	Bill Dickey	300.00	120.00	60.00
31	Lefty Grove	300.00	120.00	60.00
32	Joe Cronin	300.00	120.00	60.00
33	Frankie Frisch	300.00	120.00	60.00
34	Al Simmons	300.00	120.00	60.00
35	Rogers Hornsby	475.00	190.00	95.00
36	Ted Lyons	300.00	120.00	60.00
37	Rabbit Maranville	300.00	120.00	60.00
38	Jimmie Wilson	95.00	40.00	20.00
39	Willie Kamm	95.00	40.00	20.00
40	Bill Hallahan	95.00	40.00	20.00
41	Gus Suhr	95.00	40.00	20.00
42	Charlie Gehringer	300.00	120.00	60.00
43	Joe Heving	95.00	40.00	20.00
44	Adam Comorosky	95.00	40.00	20.00
45	Tony Lazzeri	300.00	120.00	60.00
46	Sam Leslie	95.00	40.00	20.00
47	Bob Smith	95.00	40.00	20.00
48	Willis Hudlin	95.00	40.00	20.00
49	Carl Reynolds	95.00	40.00	20.00
50	Fred Schulte	95.00	40.00	20.00
51	Cookie Lavagetto	95.00	40.00	20.00
52	Hal Schumacher	95.00	40.00	20.00
53	Doc Cramer	95.00	40.00	20.00
54	Si Johnson	95.00	40.00	20.00
55	Ollie Bejma	95.00	40.00	20.00
56	Sammy Byrd	95.00	40.00	20.00
57	Hank Greenberg	425.00	175.00	85.00
58	Bill Knickerbocker	95.00	40.00	20.00
59	Billy Urbanski	95.00	40.00	20.00
60	Ed Morgan	95.00	40.00	20.00
61	Eric McNair	95.00	40.00	20.00
62	Ben Chapman	95.00	40.00	20.00
63	Roy Johnson	95.00	40.00	20.00
64	"Dizzy" Dean	625.00	250.00	125.00
65	Zeke Bonura	95.00	40.00	20.00
66	Firpo Marberry	95.00	40.00	20.00
67	Gus Mancuso	95.00	40.00	20.00
68	Joe Vosmik	95.00	40.00	20.00
69	Earl Grace	95.00	40.00	20.00
70	Tony Piet	95.00	40.00	20.00
71	Rollie Hemsley	95.00	40.00	20.00
72	Fred Fitzsimmons	95.00	40.00	20.00
73	Hack Wilson	300.00	120.00	60.00
74	Chick Fullis	95.00	40.00	20.00
75	Fred Frankhouse	95.00	40.00	20.00
76	Ethan Allen	95.00	40.00	20.00
77	Heinie Manush	300.00	120.00	60.00
78	Rip Collins	95.00	40.00	20.00
79	Tony Cuccinello	95.00	40.00	20.00
80	Joe Kuhel	125.00	50.00	25.00
81	Thomas Bridges	175.00	70.00	35.00
82	Clinton Brown	175.00	70.00	35.00
83	Albert Blanche	175.00	70.00	35.00
84	"Boze" Berger	175.00	70.00	35.00
85	Goose Goslin	425.00	175.00	85.00
86	Vernon Gomez	475.00	190.00	95.00
87	Joe Glen (Glenn)	175.00	70.00	35.00
88	Cy Blanton	175.00	70.00	35.00
89	Tom Carey	175.00	70.00	35.00
90	Ralph Birkhofer	175.00	70.00	35.00
91	Frank Gabler	175.00	70.00	35.00
92	Dick Coffman	175.00	70.00	35.00
93	Ollie Bejma	175.00	70.00	35.00
94	Leroy Earl Parmalee	175.00	70.00	35.00
95	Carl Reynolds	175.00	70.00	35.00
96	Ben Cantwell	175.00	70.00	35.00
97	Curtis Davis	175.00	70.00	35.00
98	Wallace Moses, Billy Webb	400.00	160.00	80.00
99	Ray Benge	175.00	70.00	35.00
100	"Pie" Traynor	425.00	175.00	85.00
101	Phil. Cavarretta	175.00	70.00	35.00
102	"Pep" Young	175.00	70.00	35.00
103	Willis Hudlin	175.00	70.00	35.00
104	Mickey Haslin	175.00	70.00	35.00
105	Oswald Bluege	175.00	70.00	35.00
106	Paul Andrews	175.00	70.00	35.00
107	Edward A. Brandt	175.00	70.00	35.00
108	Dan Taylor	175.00	70.00	35.00
109	Thornton T. Lee	175.00	70.00	35.00
110	Hal Schumacher	175.00	70.00	35.00
111	Minter Hayes, Ted Lyons	450.00	180.00	90.00
112	Odell Hale	175.00	70.00	35.00
113	Earl Averill	425.00	175.00	85.00
114	Italo Chelini	175.00	70.00	35.00
115	Ivy Andrews, Jim Bottomley	550.00	225.00	110.00
116	Bill Walker	175.00	70.00	35.00
117	Bill Dickey	600.00	250.00	125.00
118	Gerald Walker	175.00	70.00	35.00
119	Ted Lyons	425.00	175.00	85.00
120	Elden Auker (Eldon)	175.00	70.00	35.00
121	Wild Bill Hallahan	175.00	70.00	35.00
122	Freddy Lindstrom	425.00	175.00	85.00
123	Oral C. Hildebrand	175.00	70.00	35.00
124	Luke Appling	425.00	175.00	85.00
125	"Pepper" Martin	300.00	120.00	60.00
126	Rick Ferrell	425.00	175.00	85.00
127	Ival Goodman	175.00	70.00	35.00
128	Joe Kuhel	175.00	70.00	35.00
129	Ernest Lombardi	425.00	175.00	85.00
130	Charles Gehringer	425.00	175.00	85.00
131	Van L. Mungo	200.00	80.00	40.00
132	Larry French	175.00	70.00	35.00
133	"Buddy" Myer	175.00	70.00	35.00
134	Mel Harder	175.00	70.00	35.00
135	Augie Galan	175.00	70.00	35.00
136	"Gabby" Hartnett	425.00	175.00	85.00
137	Stan Hack	175.00	70.00	35.00
138	Billy Herman	425.00	175.00	85.00
139	Bill Jurges	175.00	70.00	35.00
140	Bill Lee	175.00	70.00	35.00
141	"Zeke" Bonura	175.00	70.00	35.00
142	Tony Piet	175.00	70.00	35.00
143	Paul Dean	275.00	110.00	55.00
144	Jimmy Foxx	725.00	300.00	150.00
145	Joe Medwick	425.00	175.00	85.00
146	Rip Collins	175.00	70.00	35.00
147	Melo Almada	175.00	70.00	35.00
148	Allan Cooke	175.00	70.00	35.00
149	Moe Berg	525.00	225.00	110.00
150	Adolph Camilli	175.00	70.00	35.00
151	Oscar Melillo	175.00	70.00	35.00
152	Bruce Campbell	175.00	70.00	35.00
153	Lefty Grove	525.00	225.00	110.00
154	John Murphy	175.00	70.00	35.00
155	Luke Sewell	175.00	70.00	35.00
156	Leo Durocher	425.00	175.00	85.00
157	Lloyd Waner	425.00	175.00	85.00
158	Guy Bush	175.00	70.00	35.00
159	Jimmy Dykes	175.00	70.00	35.00
160	Steve O'Neill	175.00	70.00	35.00
161	Gen. Crowder	175.00	70.00	35.00
162	Joe Cascarella	175.00	70.00	35.00
163	"Bud" Hafey	175.00	70.00	35.00
164	"Gilly" Campbell	175.00	70.00	35.00
165	Ray Hayworth	175.00	70.00	35.00
166	Frank Demaree	175.00	70.00	35.00
167	John Babich	175.00	70.00	35.00
168	Marvin Owen	175.00	70.00	35.00
169	Ralph Kress	175.00	70.00	35.00
170	"Mule" Haas	175.00	70.00	35.00
171	Frank Higgins	175.00	70.00	35.00
172	Walter Berger	175.00	70.00	35.00
173	Frank Frisch	425.00	175.00	85.00
174	Wess Ferrell (Wes)	175.00	70.00	35.00
175	Pete Fox	175.00	70.00	35.00
176	John Vergez	175.00	70.00	35.00
177	William Rogell	175.00	70.00	35.00
178	"Don" Brennan	175.00	70.00	35.00
179	James Bottomley	425.00	175.00	85.00
180	Travis Jackson	425.00	175.00	85.00
181	Robert Rolfe	175.00	70.00	35.00
182	Frank Crosetti	250.00	100.00	50.00
183	Joe Cronin	425.00	175.00	85.00
184	"Schoolboy" Rowe	200.00	80.00	40.00
185	"Chuck" Klein	425.00	175.00	85.00
186	Lon Warneke	175.00	70.00	35.00
187	Gus Suhr	175.00	70.00	35.00
188	Ben Chapman	175.00	70.00	35.00
189	Clint. Brown	200.00	80.00	40.00
190	Paul Derringer	200.00	80.00	40.00
191	John Burns	200.00	80.00	40.00
192	John Broaca	375.00	100.00	50.00

1958 Bazooka "My Favorite Team" Patches

These screen-printed felt patches were available via a mail-in offer found in Topps baseball cards. Approximately 5" in diameter, they were intended to be sewn on jackets, caps, etc.

		NM	EX	VG
Complete Set (16):		450.00	225.00	135.00
Common Patch:		30.00	15.00	9.00
(1)	Baltimore Orioles	30.00	15.00	9.00
(2)	Boston Red Sox	35.00	17.50	10.50
(3)	Chicago Cubs	45.00	22.00	13.50
(4)	Chicago White Sox	30.00	15.00	9.00
(5)	Cincinnati Reds	30.00	15.00	9.00
(6)	Cleveland Indians	30.00	15.00	9.00
(7)	Detroit Tigers	30.00	15.00	9.00
(8)	Kansas City A's	30.00	15.00	9.00
(9)	Los Angeles Dodgers	40.00	20.00	12.00
(10)	Milwaukee Braves	35.00	17.50	10.50
(11)	New York Yankees	50.00	25.00	15.00
(12)	Philadelphia Phillies	30.00	15.00	9.00
(13)	Pittsburgh Pirates	30.00	15.00	9.00
(14)	San Francisco Giants	40.00	20.00	12.00
(15)	St. Louis Cardinals	30.00	15.00	9.00
(16)	Washington Senators	35.00	17.50	10.50

1959 Bazooka

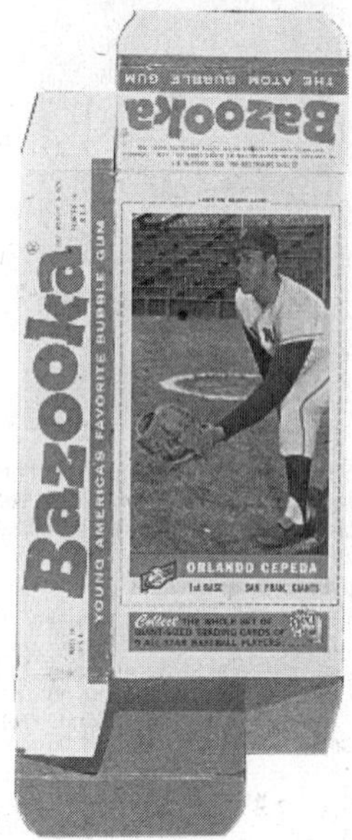

The 1959 Bazooka set, consisting of 23 full-color, unnumbered cards, was printed on boxes of one-cent Topps bubble gum. The blank-backed cards measure 2-13/16" x 4-15/16", when properly cut. Nine cards were first issued, with 14 being added to the set later. The nine more plentiful cards are #'s 1, 5, 8, 9, 14, 15, 16, 17 and 22. Complete boxes would command double the price shown.

	NM	EX	VG
Complete Set (23):	8,500	4,250	2,500
Common Player:	100.00	50.00	30.00
(1a) Hank Aaron (Name in white.)	500.00	250.00	150.00
(1b) Hank Aaron (Name in yellow.)	485.00	240.00	145.00
(2) Richie Ashburn/SP	450.00	225.00	135.00
(3) Ernie Banks/SP	500.00	250.00	150.00
(4) Ken Boyer/SP	250.00	125.00	75.00
(5) Orlando Cepeda	200.00	100.00	60.00
(6) Bob Cerv/SP	250.00	125.00	75.00
(7) Rocky Colavito/SP	450.00	225.00	135.00
(8) Del Crandall	100.00	50.00	30.00
(9) Jim Davenport	100.00	50.00	30.00
(10) Don Drysdale/SP	485.00	240.00	145.00
(11) Nellie Fox/SP	450.00	225.00	135.00
(12) Jackie Jensen/SP	250.00	125.00	75.00
(13) Harvey Kuenn/SP	250.00	125.00	75.00
(14) Mickey Mantle	1,750	875.00	525.00
(15) Willie Mays	500.00	250.00	150.00
(16) Bill Mazeroski	225.00	110.00	65.00
(17) Roy McMillan	100.00	50.00	30.00
(18) Billy Pierce/SP	250.00	125.00	75.00
(19) Roy Sievers/SP	250.00	125.00	75.00
(20) Duke Snider/SP	750.00	375.00	225.00
(21) Gus Triandos/SP	250.00	125.00	75.00
(22) Bob Turley	200.00	100.00	60.00
(23) Vic Wertz/SP	250.00	125.00	75.00

1959 Bazooka Pennants

These screen-printed felt pennants were available via a mail-in offer found in Topps baseball cards. Approximately 15" long and 5" wide, they have a "COPYRIGHT BAZOOKA" bar near the wide end.

	NM	EX	VG
Complete Set (16):	600.00	300.00	180.00
Common Team:	40.00	20.00	12.00
(1) Baltimore Orioles	40.00	20.00	12.00
(2) Boston Red Sox	40.00	20.00	12.00
(3) Chicago Cubs	40.00	20.00	12.00
(4) Chicago White Sox	45.00	22.50	13.50
(5) Cincinnati Redlegs	40.00	20.00	12.00
(6) Cleveland Indians	40.00	20.00	12.00
(7) Detroit Tigers	40.00	20.00	12.00
(8) Kansas City A's	40.00	20.00	12.00
(9) Los Angeles Dodgers	45.00	22.50	13.50
(10) Milwaukee Braves	40.00	20.00	12.00
(11) New York Yankees	50.00	25.00	15.00
(12) Philadelphia Phillies	40.00	20.00	12.00
(13) Pittsburgh Pirates	40.00	20.00	12.00
(14) San Francisco Giants	40.00	20.00	12.00
(15) St. Louis Cardinals	40.00	20.00	12.00
(16) Washington Senators	40.00	20.00	12.00

1960 Bazooka

ROCKY COLAVITO
CLEVELAND INDIANS outfield
NO. 30 OF 36 CARDS

Three-card panels were printed on the bottoms of Bazooka bubble gum boxes in 1960. The blank- backed set is comprised of 36 cards with the card number located at the bottom of each full-color card. Individual cards measure 1-13/16" x 2-3/4"; the panels measure 2-3/4" x 5-1/2".

	NM	EX	VG
Complete Panel Set (12):	2,200	1,100	650.00
Complete Singles Set (36):	2,000	1,000	600.00
Common Player:	15.00	7.50	4.50
Panel (1)	125.00	62.00	37.00
1 Ernie Banks	90.00	45.00	27.00
2 Bud Daley	15.00	7.50	4.50
3 Wally Moon	15.00	7.50	4.50
Panel (2)	200.00	100.00	60.00
4 Hank Aaron	150.00	75.00	45.00
5 Milt Pappas	15.00	7.50	4.50
6 Dick Stuart	15.00	7.50	4.50
Panel (3)	325.00	160.00	97.00
7 Roberto Clemente	200.00	100.00	60.00
8 Yogi Berra	90.00	45.00	27.00
9 Ken Boyer	25.00	12.50	7.50
Panel (4)	100.00	50.00	30.00
10 Orlando Cepeda	50.00	25.00	15.00
11 Gus Triandos	15.00	7.50	4.50
12 Frank Malzone	15.00	7.50	4.50
Panel (5)	200.00	100.00	60.00
13 Willie Mays	150.00	75.00	45.00
14 Camilo Pascual	15.00	7.50	4.50
15 Bob Cerv	15.00	7.50	4.50
Panel (6)	125.00	62.00	37.00
16 Vic Power	15.00	7.50	4.50
17 Larry Sherry	15.00	7.50	4.50
18 Al Kaline	75.00	37.00	22.00
Panel (7)	200.00	100.00	60.00
19 Warren Spahn	75.00	37.00	22.00
20 Harmon Killebrew	75.00	37.00	22.00
21 Jackie Jensen	25.00	12.50	7.50
Panel (8)	175.00	87.00	52.00
22 Luis Aparicio	50.00	25.00	15.00
23 Gil Hodges	50.00	25.00	15.00
24 Richie Ashburn	50.00	25.00	15.00
Panel (9)	125.00	62.00	37.00
25 Nellie Fox	50.00	25.00	15.00
26 Robin Roberts	50.00	25.00	15.00
27 Joe Cunningham	15.00	7.50	4.50
Panel (10)	200.00	100.00	60.00
28 Early Wynn	50.00	25.00	15.00
29 Frank Robinson	75.00	37.00	22.00
30 Rocky Colavito	50.00	25.00	15.00
Panel (11)	750.00	375.00	225.00
31 Mickey Mantle	500.00	250.00	150.00
32 Glen Hobbie	15.00	7.50	4.50
33 Roy McMillan	15.00	7.50	4.50
Panel (12)	60.00	30.00	18.00
34 Harvey Kuenn	15.00	7.50	4.50
35 Johnny Antonelli	15.00	7.50	4.50
36 Del Crandall	15.00	7.50	4.50

1960 Bazooka Hot Iron Transfers

Team logo transfers were available via a mail-in offer found on cards inserted into packs of 1960 Topps. Varying in size and shape, but generally about 5" square, the transfers were packaged in a colorful envelope which provided instructions for ironing the logo to a t-shirt or other cloth surface. Unlike earlier Bazooka mail-in premiums, the gum is not named on the transfers. Values shown are for transfers without the envelope. Envelopes, which carried the name and logo of the team inside, are valued about the same as the transfer itself.

	NM	EX	VG
Complete Set (16):	300.00	150.00	90.00
Common Team:	20.00	10.00	6.00
Envelope: 1X			
(1) Baltimore Orioles	20.00	10.00	6.00
(2) Boston Red Sox	20.00	10.00	6.00
(3) Chicago Cubs	20.00	10.00	6.00
(4) Chicago White Sox	20.00	10.00	6.00
(5) Cincinnati Redlegs	20.00	10.00	6.00
(6) Cleveland Indians	20.00	10.00	6.00
(7) Detroit Tigers	20.00	10.00	6.00
(8) Kansas City A's	20.00	10.00	6.00
(9) Los Angeles Dodgers	22.50	11.00	6.75
(10) Milwaukee Braves	20.00	10.00	6.00
(11) New York Yankees	25.00	12.50	7.50
(12) Philadelphia Phillies	20.00	10.00	6.00
(13) Pittsburgh Pirates	22.50	11.00	6.75
(14) San Francisco Giants	20.00	10.00	6.00
(15) St. Louis Cardinals	20.00	10.00	6.00
(16) Washington Senators	20.00	10.00	6.00

1961 Bazooka

Similar in design to the 1960 Bazooka set, the 1961 edition consists of 36 cards printed in panels of three on the bottom of Bazooka bubble gum boxes. The full-color cards, which measure 1-13/16" x 2-3/4" individually and 2-3/4" x 5-1/2" as panels, are numbered 1 through 36. The backs are blank.

	NM	EX	VG
Complete Set, Panels (12):	1,500	750.00	450.00
Complete Set, Singles (36):	1,200	600.00	350.00
Common Player:	12.00	6.00	3.50
Panel (1)	750.00	375.00	225.00
1 Art Mahaffey	12.00	6.00	3.50
2 Mickey Mantle	650.00	325.00	200.00
3 Ron Santo	25.00	12.50	7.50
Panel (2)	225.00	110.00	65.00
4 Bud Daley	12.00	6.00	3.50
5 Roger Maris	100.00	50.00	30.00
6 Eddie Yost	12.00	6.00	3.50
Panel (3)	75.00	37.50	22.50
7 Minnie Minoso	15.00	7.50	4.50
8 Dick Groat	13.50	7.00	4.00
9 Frank Malzone	12.00	6.00	3.50
Panel (4)	100.00	50.00	30.00
10 Dick Donovan	12.00	6.00	3.50
11 Ed Mathews	45.00	22.50	13.50
12 Jim Lemon	12.00	6.00	3.50
Panel (5)	75.00	37.50	22.50
13 Chuck Estrada	12.00	6.00	3.50
14 Ken Boyer	15.00	7.50	4.50
15 Harvey Kuenn	12.00	6.00	3.50
Panel (6)	100.00	50.00	30.00
16 Ernie Broglio	12.00	6.00	3.50
17 Rocky Colavito	25.00	12.50	7.50
18 Ted Kluszewski	25.00	12.50	7.50
Panel (7)	250.00	125.00	75.00
19 Ernie Banks	100.00	50.00	30.00
20 Al Kaline	45.00	22.50	13.50
21 Ed Bailey	12.00	6.00	3.50
Panel (8)	250.00	125.00	75.00
22 Jim Perry	12.00	6.00	3.50
23 Willie Mays	100.00	50.00	30.00
24 Bill Mazeroski	40.00	20.00	12.00
Panel (9)	100.00	50.00	30.00
25 Gus Triandos	12.00	6.00	3.50
26 Don Drysdale	45.00	22.50	13.50
27 Frank Herrera	12.00	6.00	3.50
Panel (10)	100.00	50.00	30.00
28 Earl Battey	12.00	6.00	3.50
29 Warren Spahn	45.00	22.50	13.50
30 Gene Woodling	12.00	6.00	3.50
Panel (11)	100.00	50.00	30.00
31 Frank Robinson	45.00	22.50	13.50
32 Pete Runnels	12.00	6.00	3.50
33 Woodie Held	12.00	6.00	3.50
Panel (12)	100.00	50.00	30.00
34 Norm Larker	12.00	6.00	3.50
35 Luis Aparicio	35.00	17.50	10.00
36 Bill Tuttle	12.00	6.00	3.50

1962 Bazooka

In 1962, Bazooka increased the size of its set to 45 full-color cards. The set is unnumbered and was printed in panels of three on the bottoms of bubble gum boxes. Individual cards measure 1-13/16" x 2-3/4" in size, with panels at 2-3/4" x 5-1/2". In the checklist that follows the cards have been numbered alphabetically, using the name of the player who appears on the left end of the panel. Panels (1), (11) and (15) were issued in much shorter supply and command a higher price.

	NM	EX	VG
Complete Set, Panels (15):	4,000	2,000	1,200
Complete Set, Singles (45)	3,750	1,850	1,100
Common Player:	12.50	6.25	3.75
Panel (1)	850.00	425.00	255.00
(1) Bob Allison	160.00	80.00	45.00
(2) Ed Mathews	400.00	200.00	120.00
(3) Vada Pinson	200.00	100.00	60.00
Panel (2)	100.00	50.00	30.00
(4) Earl Battey	12.50	6.25	3.75
(5) Warren Spahn	45.00	22.50	13.50
(6) Lee Thomas	12.50	6.25	3.75
Panel (3)	75.00	40.00	25.00
(7) Orlando Cepeda	30.00	15.00	9.00
(8) Woodie Held	12.50	6.25	3.75
(9) Bob Aspromonte	12.50	6.25	3.75
Panel (4)	200.00	100.00	60.00
(10) Dick Howser	12.50	6.25	3.75
(11) Roberto Clemente	125.00	65.00	35.00
(12) Al Kaline	45.00	22.50	13.50
Panel (5)	125.00	65.00	35.00
(13) Joey Jay	12.50	6.25	3.75
(14) Roger Maris	85.00	42.50	25.00
(15) Frank Howard	15.00	7.50	4.50
Panel (6)	175.00	90.00	50.00
(16) Sandy Koufax	125.00	65.00	35.00
(17) Jim Gentile	12.50	6.25	3.75
(18) Johnny Callison	12.50	6.25	3.75

		NM	EX	VG
	Panel (7)	50.00	25.00	15.00
(19)	Jim Landis	12.50	6.25	3.75
(20)	Ken Boyer	13.00	6.50	4.00
(21)	Chuck Schilling	12.50	6.25	3.75
	Panel (8)	575.00	285.00	175.00
(22)	Art Mahaffey	12.50	6.25	3.75
(23)	Mickey Mantle	500.00	250.00	150.00
(24)	Dick Stuart	13.50	6.75	4.00
	Panel (9)	100.00	50.00	30.00
(25)	Ken McBride	12.50	6.25	3.75
(26)	Frank Robinson	45.00	22.50	13.50
(27)	Gil Hodges	30.00	15.00	9.00
	Panel (10)	175.00	85.00	50.00
(28)	Milt Pappas	12.50	6.25	3.75
(29)	Hank Aaron	125.00	65.00	35.00
(30)	Luis Aparicio	30.00	15.00	9.00
	Panel (11)	900.00	450.00	275.00
(31)	Johnny Romano	160.00	80.00	50.00
(32)	Ernie Banks	500.00	250.00	150.00
(33)	Norm Siebern	160.00	80.00	50.00
	Panel (12)	75.00	35.00	25.00
(34)	Ron Santo	20.00	10.00	6.00
(35)	Norm Cash	15.00	7.50	4.50
(36)	Jimmy Piersall	15.00	7.50	4.50
	Panel (13)	175.00	85.00	50.00
(37)	Don Schwall	12.50	6.25	3.75
(38)	Willie Mays	125.00	65.00	35.00
(39)	Norm Larker	12.50	6.25	3.75
	Panel (14)	110.00	55.00	35.00
(40)	Bill White	12.50	6.25	3.75
(41)	Whitey Ford	50.00	25.00	15.00
(42)	Rocky Colavito	30.00	15.00	9.00
	Panel (15)	750.00	375.00	225.00
(43)	Don Zimmer	200.00	100.00	60.00
(44)	Harmon Killebrew	350.00	175.00	100.00
(45)	Gene Woodling	160.00	80.00	50.00

1963 Bazooka

The 1963 Bazooka issue reverted to a 12-panel, 36-card set, but saw a change in the size of the cards. Individual cards measure 1-9/16" x 2-1/2", while panels are 2-1/2" x 4-11/16". The card design was altered also, with the player's name, team and position situated in a white oval at the bottom of the card. The full-color, blank-backed set is numbered 1-36. The complete set was counterfeited circa 2002, with many cards sold in "FGA" certified slabs, depressing the value of cards not graded by a major certification company.

		NM	EX	VG
	Complete Set, Panels (12):	1,750	875.00	525.00
	Complete Set, Singles (36):	1,200	600.00	350.00
	Common Player:	10.00	5.00	3.00
	Panel (1)	450.00	225.00	135.00
1	Mickey Mantle (Batting righty.)	325.00	160.00	100.00
2	Bob Rodgers	10.00	5.00	3.00
3	Ernie Banks	60.00	30.00	18.00
	Panel (2)	95.00	50.00	30.00
4	Norm Siebern	10.00	5.00	3.00
5	Warren Spahn/Portrait	35.00	17.50	10.00
6	Bill Mazeroski	25.00	12.50	7.50
	Panel (3)	175.00	90.00	50.00
7	Harmon Killebrew/Btg	50.00	25.00	15.00
8	Dick Farrell/Portrait	10.00	5.00	3.00
9	Hank Aaron (Glove in front.)	90.00	45.00	27.50
	Panel (4)	150.00	75.00	45.00
10	Dick Donovan	10.00	5.00	3.00
11	Jim Gentile/Btg	10.00	5.00	3.00
12	Willie Mays (Bat in front.)	100.00	50.00	30.00
	Panel (5)	125.00	65.00	35.00
13	Camilo Pascual (Hands at waist.)	10.00	5.00	3.00
14	Roberto Clemente/Portrait	100.00	50.00	30.00
15	Johnny Callison (Pinstriped uniform.)	10.00	5.00	3.00
	Panel (6)	150.00	75.00	45.00
16	Carl Yastrzemski/Kneeling	60.00	30.00	18.00
17	Don Drysdale	35.00	17.50	10.00
18	Johnny Romano/Portrait	10.00	5.00	3.00
	Panel (7)	45.00	22.50	13.50
19	Al Jackson	10.00	5.00	3.00
20	Ralph Terry	10.00	5.00	3.00
21	Bill Monbouquette	10.00	5.00	3.00
	Panel (8)	150.00	75.00	45.00
22	Orlando Cepeda	35.00	17.50	10.00
23	Stan Musial	75.00	40.00	25.00
24	Floyd Robinson (No pinstripes.)	10.00	5.00	3.00
	Panel (9)	45.00	22.50	13.50
25	Chuck Hinton/Btg	10.00	5.00	3.00
26	Bob Purkey	10.00	5.00	3.00
27	Ken Hubbs	12.50	6.25	3.75
	Panel (10)	75.00	40.00	25.00
28	Bill White	10.00	5.00	3.00
29	Ray Herbert	10.00	5.00	3.00
30	Brooks Robinson (Glove in front.)	40.00	20.00	12.00
	Panel (11)	100.00	50.00	30.00
31	Frank Robinson/Btg	40.00	20.00	12.00
32	Lee Thomas	10.00	5.00	3.00
33	Rocky Colavito (Detroit)	30.00	15.00	9.00
	Panel (12)	90.00	45.00	27.50
34	Al Kaline/Kneeling	45.00	22.50	13.50
35	Art Mahaffey	10.00	5.00	3.00
36	Tommy Davis (Follow-through.)	10.00	5.00	3.00

1963 Bazooka All-Time Greats

Consisting of 41 cards, the Bazooka All-Time Greats set was issued as inserts (five per box) in boxes of Bazooka bubble gum. A black-and-white portrait photo of the player is placed inside a gold plaque within a white border. Card backs contain a brief biography of the player. The numbered cards measure 1-9/16" x 2-1/2". Cards can be found with silver fronts instead of gold; the silver are worth double the values listed.

		NM	EX	VG
	Complete Set (41):	675.00	335.00	200.00
	Common Player:	13.50	6.75	4.00
	Silver: 2.5X			
1	Joe Tinker	13.50	6.75	4.00
2	Harry Heilmann	13.50	6.75	4.00
3	Jack Chesbro	13.50	6.75	4.00
4	Christy Mathewson	30.00	15.00	9.00
5	Herb Pennock	13.50	6.75	4.00
6	Cy Young	30.00	15.00	9.00
7	Ed Walsh	13.50	6.75	4.00
8	Nap Lajoie	13.50	6.75	4.00
9	Eddie Plank	13.50	6.75	4.00
10	Honus Wagner	35.00	17.50	10.00
11	Chief Bender	13.50	6.75	4.00
12	Walter Johnson	30.00	15.00	9.00
13	Three-Fingered Brown	13.50	6.75	4.00
14	Rabbit Maranville	13.50	6.75	4.00
15	Lou Gehrig	60.00	30.00	18.00
16	Ban Johnson	13.50	6.75	4.00
17	Babe Ruth	65.00	32.50	20.00
18	Connie Mack	13.50	6.75	4.00
19	Hank Greenberg	20.00	10.00	6.00
20	John McGraw	13.50	6.75	4.00
21	Johnny Evers	13.50	6.75	4.00
22	Al Simmons	13.50	6.75	4.00
23	Jimmy Collins	13.50	6.75	4.00
24	Tris Speaker	13.50	6.75	4.00
25	Frank Chance	13.50	6.75	4.00
26	Fred Clarke	13.50	6.75	4.00
27	Wilbert Robinson	13.50	6.75	4.00
28	Dazzy Vance	13.50	6.75	4.00
29	Grover Alexander	16.00	8.00	4.75
30	Kenesaw Landis	13.50	6.75	4.00
31	Willie Keeler	13.50	6.75	4.00
32	Rogers Hornsby	16.00	8.00	4.75
33	Hugh Duffy	13.50	6.75	4.00
34	Mickey Cochrane	13.50	6.75	4.00
35	Ty Cobb	60.00	30.00	18.00
36	Mel Ott	13.50	6.75	4.00
37	Clark Griffith	13.50	6.75	4.00
38	Ted Lyons	13.50	6.75	4.00
39	Cap Anson	13.50	6.75	4.00
40	Bill Dickey	13.50	6.75	4.00
41	Eddie Collins	13.50	6.75	4.00

1964 Bazooka

The 1964 Bazooka set is identical in design and size to the previous year's effort. However, different photographs were used from year to year. The 1964 set consists of 36 full-color, blank-backed cards numbered 1 through 36. Individual cards measure 1-9/16" x 2-1/2"; three-card panels measure 2-1/2" x 4-11/16". Sheets of 10 full-color baseball stamps were inserted in each box of bubble gum.

		NM	EX	VG
	Complete Set, Panels (12):	1,400	700.00	425.00
	Complete Set, Singles (36):	950.00	475.00	275.00
	Common Player:	10.00	5.00	3.00
	Panel (1)	225.00	110.00	70.00
1	Mickey Mantle (Bat on shoulder.)	200.00	100.00	60.00
2	Dick Groat	10.00	5.00	3.00
3	Steve Barber	10.00	5.00	3.00
	Panel (2)	75.00	37.00	22.00
4	Ken McBride	10.00	5.00	3.00
5	Warren Spahn (Cap to waist.)	35.00	17.50	10.50
6	Bob Friend	10.00	5.00	3.00
	Panel (3)	150.00	75.00	45.00
7	Harmon Killebrew/Portrait	35.00	17.50	10.50
8	Dick Farrell (Hands above head.)	10.00	5.00	3.00
9	Hank Aaron (Glove to left.)	75.00	37.50	22.50
	Panel (4)	150.00	75.00	45.00
10	Rich Rollins	10.00	5.00	3.00
11	Jim Gentile/Portrait	10.00	5.00	3.00
12	Willie Mays (Looking to left.)	75.00	37.50	22.50
	Panel (5)	150.00	75.00	45.00
13	Camilo Pascual (Follow-through.)	10.00	5.00	3.00
14	Roberto Clemente/Throwing	75.00	37.50	22.50
15	Johnny Callison/Btg (Screen showing.)	10.00	5.00	3.00
	Panel (6)	125.00	62.00	37.00
16	Carl Yastrzemski/Btg	40.00	20.00	12.00
17	Billy Williams/Kneeling	30.00	15.00	9.00
18	Johnny Romano/Btg	10.00	5.00	3.00
	Panel (7)	65.00	32.50	20.00
19	Jim Maloney	10.00	5.00	3.00
20	Norm Cash	12.50	6.25	3.75
21	Willie McCovey	30.00	15.00	9.00
	Panel (8)	40.00	20.00	12.00
22	Jim Fregosi/Btg	10.00	5.00	3.00
23	George Altman	10.00	5.00	3.00
24	Floyd Robinson (Pinstriped uniform.)	10.00	5.00	3.00
	Panel (9)	40.00	20.00	12.00
25	Chuck Hinton/Portrait	10.00	5.00	3.00
26	Ron Hunt/Btg	10.00	5.00	3.00
27	Gary Peters/Pitching	10.00	5.00	3.00
	Panel (10)	90.00	45.00	27.00
28	Dick Ellsworth	10.00	5.00	3.00
29	Elston Howard (W/ bat.)	20.00	10.00	6.00
30	Brooks Robinson (Kneeling w/ glove.)	35.00	17.50	10.50
	Panel (11)	175.00	87.00	52.00
31	Frank Robinson (Uniform number shows.)	35.00	17.50	10.50
32	Sandy Koufax (Glove in front.)	75.00	37.50	22.50
33	Rocky Colavito (Kansas City)	25.00	12.50	7.50
	Panel (12)	90.00	45.00	27.00
34	Al Kaline (Holding two bats.)	40.00	20.00	12.00
35	Ken Boyer (Cap to waist.)	10.00	5.00	3.00
36	Tommy Davis/Btg	10.00	5.00	3.00

1964 Bazooka Stamps

Occasionally mislabeled "Topps Stamps," the 1964 Bazooka stamps were produced by Topps, but found only in boxes of Bazooka bubble gum. Issued in sheets of 10, 100 color stamps make up the set. Each stamp measures 1" x 1-1/2" in size. While the stamps are not individually numbered, the sheets are numbered one through 10. The stamps are commonly found as complete sheets of 10 and are priced in that fashion in the checklist that follows.

		NM	EX	VG
	Complete Sheet Set (10x10):	750.00	375.00	225.00
	Common Sheet:	35.00	17.50	10.00
	Common Stamp:	4.00	2.00	1.25
1	Max Alvis, Ed Charles, Dick Ellsworth, Jimmie Hall, Frank Malzone, Milt Pappas, Vada Pinson, Tony Taylor, Pete Ward, Bill White	35.00	17.50	10.50
2	Bob Aspromonte, Larry Jackson, Willie Mays, Al McBean, Bill Monbouquette, Bobby Richardson, Floyd Robinson, Frank Robinson, Norm Siebern, Don Zimmer	80.00	40.00	25.00

3	Ernie Banks, Roberto Clemente, Curt Flood, Jesse Gonder, Woody Held, Don Lock, Dave Nicholson, Joe Pepitone, Brooks Robinson, Carl Yastrzemski	120.00	60.00	35.00
4	Hank Aguirre, Jim Grant, Harmon Killebrew, Jim Maloney, Juan Marichal, Bill Mazeroski, Juan Pizarro, Boog Powell, Ed Roebuck, Ron Santo	85.00	45.00	25.00
5	Jim Bouton, Norm Cash, Orlando Cepeda, Tommy Harper, Chuck Hinton, Albie Pearson, Ron Perranoski, Dick Radatz, Johnny Romano, Carl Willey	45.00	25.00	15.00
6	Steve Barber, Jim Fregosi, Tony Gonzalez, Mickey Mantle, Jim O'Toole, Gary Peters, Rich Rollins, Warren Spahn, Dick Stuart, Joe Torre	165.00	80.00	50.00
7	Felipe Alou, George Altman, Ken Boyer, Rocky Colavito, Jim Davenport, Tommy Davis, Bill Freehan, Bob Friend, Ken Johnson, Billy Moran	40.00	20.00	12.00
8	Earl Battey, Ernie Broglio, Johnny Callison, Donn Clendenon, Don Drysdale, Jim Gentile, Elston Howard, Claude Osteen, Billy Williams, Hal Woodeshick	55.00	27.50	16.50
9	Hank Aaron, Jack Baldschun, Wayne Causey, Moe Drabowsky, Dick Groat, Frank Howard, Al Jackson, Jerry Lumpe, Ken McBride, Rusty Staub	65.00	32.50	19.50
10	Vic Davalillo, Dick Farrell, Ron Hunt, Al Kaline, Sandy Koufax, Eddie Mathews, Willie McCovey, Camilo Pascual, Lee Thomas	85.00	45.00	25.00

1965 Bazooka

The 1965 Bazooka set is identical to the 1963 and 1964 sets. Different players were added each year and different photographs were used for those players being included again. Individual cards cut from the boxes measure 1-9/16" x 2-1/2". Complete three-card panels measure 2-1/2" x 4-11/16". Cards are again blank-backed.

		NM	EX	VG
	Complete Set, Panels (12):	1,300	650.00	400.00
	Complete Set, Singles (36):	900.00	450.00	275.00
	Common Player:	10.00	5.00	3.00
	Panel (1)	275.00	135.00	85.00
1	Mickey Mantle (Batting lefty.)	200.00	100.00	60.00
2	Larry Jackson	10.00	5.00	3.00
3	Chuck Hinton	10.00	5.00	3.00
	Panel (2)	40.00	20.00	12.00
4	Tony Oliva	12.50	6.25	3.75
5	Dean Chance	10.00	5.00	3.00
6	Jim O'Toole	10.00	5.00	3.00
	Panel (3)	125.00	65.00	35.00
7	Harmon Killebrew (Bat on shoulder.)	35.00	17.50	10.50
8	Pete Ward	10.00	5.00	3.00
9	Hank Aaron/Btg	75.00	37.50	22.50
	Panel (4)	125.00	62.00	37.00
10	Dick Radatz	10.00	5.00	3.00
11	Boog Powell	12.50	6.25	3.75
12	Willie Mays (Looking down.)	75.00	37.50	22.50
	Panel (5)	250.00	125.00	75.00
13	Bob Veale	10.00	5.00	3.00
14	Roberto Clemente/Btg	100.00	50.00	30.00
15	Johnny Callison/Btg (No screen in background.)	10.00	5.00	3.00
	Panel (6)	60.00	30.00	18.00
16	Joe Torre	15.00	7.50	4.50
17	Billy Williams/Btg	25.00	12.50	7.50
18	Bob Chance	10.00	5.00	3.00
	Panel (7)	50.00	25.00	15.00
19	Bob Aspromonte	10.00	5.00	3.00
20	Joe Christopher	10.00	5.00	3.00
21	Jim Bunning	25.00	12.50	7.50
	Panel (8)	75.00	37.50	22.50
22	Jim Fregosi	10.00	5.00	3.00
23	Bob Gibson	30.00	15.00	9.00
24	Juan Marichal	25.00	12.50	7.50
	Panel (9)	40.00	20.00	12.00
25	Dave Wickersham	10.00	5.00	3.00
26	Ron Hunt /Throwing	10.00	5.00	3.00
27	Gary Peters/Portrait	10.00	5.00	3.00
	Panel (10)	85.00	42.50	25.00
28	Ron Santo	15.00	7.50	4.50
29	Elston Howard (W/ glove.)	12.50	6.25	3.75
30	Brooks Robinson/Portrait	35.00	17.50	10.50
	Panel (11)	200.00	100.00	60.00
31	Frank Robinson/Portrait	35.00	17.50	10.50
32	Sandy Koufax (Hands over head.)	100.00	50.00	30.00
33	Rocky Colavito (Cleveland)	20.00	10.00	6.00
	Panel (12)	75.00	37.00	22.00
34	Al Kaline/Portrait	35.00	17.50	10.50
35	Ken Boyer/Portrait	10.00	5.00	3.00
36	Tommy Davis/Fldg	10.00	5.00	3.00

1966 Bazooka

The 1966 Bazooka set was increased to 48 cards. Printed in panels of three on the bottoms of boxes of bubble gum, the full-color cards are blank-backed and numbered. Individual cards measure 1-9/16" x 2-1/2"; panels measure 2-1/2" x 4-11/16". Most of those 1966 Bazooka cards which have the same player/number combination as 1967 share the same photo and are indistinguishable as singles or panels; year of issue for complete boxes can be distinguished by the small photo on front of Koufax (1966) or Mantle (1967).

		NM	EX	VG
	Complete Set, Panels (16):	2,200	1,100	650.00
	Complete Set, Singles (48):	1,500	750.00	450.00
	Common Player:	10.00	5.00	3.00
	Panel (1)	175.00	85.00	50.00
1	Sandy Koufax	100.00	50.00	30.00
2	Willie Horton	13.50	6.75	4.00
3	Frank Howard	13.50	6.75	4.00
	Panel (2)	60.00	30.00	18.00
4	Richie Allen	16.50	8.25	5.00
5	Mel Stottlemyre	10.00	5.00	3.00
6	Tony Conigliaro	20.00	10.00	6.00
	Panel (3)	400.00	200.00	120.00
7	Mickey Mantle	300.00	150.00	90.00
8	Leon Wagner	10.00	5.00	3.00
9	Ed Kranepool	10.00	5.00	3.00
	Panel (4)	120.00	60.00	36.00
10	Juan Marichal	35.00	17.50	10.00
11	Harmon Killebrew	50.00	25.00	15.00
12	Johnny Callison	10.00	5.00	3.00
	Panel (5)	100.00	50.00	30.00
13	Roy McMillan	10.00	5.00	3.00
14	Willie McCovey	40.00	20.00	12.00
15	Rocky Colavito	30.00	15.00	9.00
	Panel (6)	150.00	75.00	45.00
16	Willie Mays	80.00	40.00	24.00
17	Sam McDowell	10.00	5.00	3.00
18	Vern Law	10.00	5.00	3.00
	Panel (7)	80.00	40.00	24.00
19	Jim Fregosi	10.00	5.00	3.00
20	Ron Fairly	10.00	5.00	3.00
21	Bob Gibson	40.00	20.00	12.00
	Panel (8)	110.00	55.00	35.00
22	Carl Yastrzemski	60.00	30.00	18.00
23	Bill White	10.00	5.00	3.00
24	Bob Aspromonte	10.00	5.00	3.00
	Panel (9)	150.00	75.00	45.00
25	Dean Chance (California)	10.00	5.00	3.00
26	Roberto Clemente	100.00	50.00	30.00
27	Tony Cloninger	10.00	5.00	3.00
	Panel (10)	135.00	65.00	40.00
28	Curt Blefary	10.00	5.00	3.00
29	Milt Pappas	10.00	5.00	3.00
30	Hank Aaron	80.00	40.00	24.00
	Panel (11)	130.00	65.00	40.00
31	Jim Bunning	40.00	20.00	12.00
32	Frank Robinson/Portrait	50.00	25.00	15.00
33	Bill Skowron	13.50	6.75	4.00
	Panel (12)	100.00	50.00	30.00
34	Brooks Robinson	50.00	25.00	15.00
35	Jim Wynn	10.00	5.00	3.00
36	Joe Torre	17.50	8.75	5.25
	Panel (13)	225.00	110.00	65.00
37	Jim Grant	10.00	5.00	3.00
38	Pete Rose	135.00	65.00	40.00
39	Ron Santo	20.00	10.00	6.00
	Panel (14)	90.00	45.00	27.50
40	Tom Tresh	13.50	6.75	4.00
41	Tony Oliva	13.50	6.75	4.00
42	Don Drysdale	40.00	20.00	12.00
	Panel (15)	40.00	20.00	12.00
43	Pete Richert	10.00	5.00	3.00
44	Bert Campaneris	10.00	5.00	3.00
45	Jim Maloney	10.00	5.00	3.00
	Panel (16)	130.00	65.00	40.00
46	Al Kaline	50.00	25.00	15.00
47	Eddie Fisher	10.00	5.00	3.00
48	Billy Williams	40.00	20.00	12.00

1967 Bazooka

The 1967 Bazooka set is identical in design to the sets of 1964-1966. Printed in panels of three on the bottoms of bubble gum boxes, the set is made up of 48 full-color, blank-backed, numbered cards. Individual cards measure 1-9/16" x 2-1/2"; complete panels measure 2-1/2" x 4-11/16". Most of those 1967 Bazooka cards which have the same player/number combination as 1966 share the same photo and are indistinguishable as singles or panels; complete boxes can be distinguished by the small photo on front of Koufax (1966) or Mantle (1967).

		NM	EX	VG
	Complete Set, Panels (18):	2,400	1,200	700.00
	Complete Set, Singles (48):	1,500	750.00	450.00
	Common Player:	10.00	5.00	3.00
	Panel (1)	40.00	20.00	12.00
1	Rick Reichardt	10.00	5.00	3.00
2	Tommie Agee	10.00	5.00	3.00
3	Frank Howard	12.50	6.25	3.75
	Panel (2)	55.00	27.50	16.50
4	Richie Allen	17.50	8.75	5.25
5	Mel Stottlemyre	12.50	6.25	3.75
6	Tony Conigliaro	12.50	6.25	3.75
	Panel (3)	600.00	300.00	180.00
7	Mickey Mantle	400.00	200.00	120.00
8	Leon Wagner	10.00	5.00	3.00
9	Gary Peters	10.00	5.00	3.00
	Panel (4)	150.00	75.00	45.00
10	Juan Marichal	50.00	25.00	15.00
11	Harmon Killebrew	60.00	30.00	18.00
12	Johnny Callison	10.00	5.00	3.00
	Panel (5)	135.00	65.00	40.00
13	Denny McLain	20.00	10.00	6.00
14	Willie McCovey	50.00	25.00	15.00
15	Rocky Colavito	30.00	15.00	9.00
	Panel (6)	150.00	75.00	45.00
16	Willie Mays	90.00	45.00	27.00
17	Sam McDowell	10.00	5.00	3.00
18	Jim Kaat	13.50	6.75	4.00
	Panel (7)	100.00	50.00	30.00
19	Jim Fregosi	10.00	5.00	3.00
20	Ron Fairly	10.00	5.00	3.00
21	Bob Gibson	50.00	25.00	15.00
	Panel (8)	120.00	60.00	36.00
22	Carl Yastrzemski	65.00	32.50	20.00
23	Bill White	10.00	5.00	3.00
24	Bob Aspromonte	10.00	5.00	3.00
	Panel (9)	175.00	85.00	50.00
25	Dean Chance (Minnesota)	10.00	5.00	3.00
26	Roberto Clemente	100.00	50.00	30.00
27	Tony Cloninger	10.00	5.00	3.00
	Panel (10)	150.00	75.00	45.00
28	Curt Blefary	10.00	5.00	3.00
29	Phil Regan	10.00	5.00	3.00
30	Hank Aaron	90.00	45.00	27.00
	Panel (11)	175.00	85.00	50.00
31	Jim Bunning	50.00	25.00	15.00
32	Frank Robinson/Btg	60.00	30.00	18.00
33	Ken Boyer	10.00	5.00	3.00
	Panel (12)	120.00	60.00	36.00
34	Brooks Robinson	60.00	30.00	18.00
35	Jim Wynn	10.00	5.00	3.00
36	Joe Torre	17.50	8.75	5.25
	Panel (13)	275.00	135.00	80.00
37	Tommy Davis	10.00	5.00	3.00
38	Pete Rose	150.00	75.00	45.00
39	Ron Santo	20.00	10.00	6.00
	Panel (14)	100.00	50.00	30.00
40	Tom Tresh	12.00	6.00	3.50
41	Tony Oliva	12.50	6.25	3.75
42	Don Drysdale	50.00	25.00	15.00
	Panel (15)	40.00	20.00	12.00
43	Pete Richert	10.00	5.00	3.00
44	Bert Campaneris	10.00	5.00	3.00
45	Jim Maloney	10.00	5.00	3.00
	Panel (16)	175.00	85.00	50.00
46	Al Kaline	60.00	30.00	18.00
47	Matty Alou	10.00	5.00	3.00
48	Billy Williams	50.00	25.00	15.00

1968 Bazooka

The design of the 1968 Bazooka set is radically different from previous years. The player cards are situated on the sides of the boxes with the box back containing "Tipps From The Topps." Four unnumbered player cards, measuring 1-1/4" x

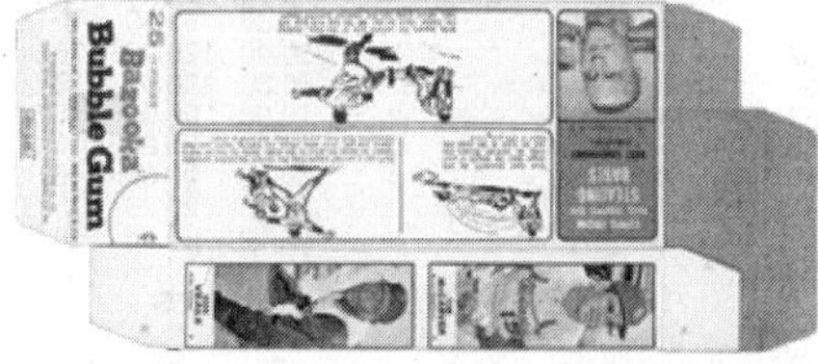

3-1/8", are featured on each box. The box back includes a small player photo plus illustrated tips on various aspects of the game of baseball. Boxes are numbered 1-15 on the top panels. There are 56 different player cards in the set, with four of the cards (Agee, Drysdale, Rose, Santo) being used twice to round out the set of 15 boxes.

		NM	EX	VG
	Complete Box Set (15):	4,250	2,125	1,250
	Complete Singles Set (60):	3,000	1,500	900.00
	Common Player:	10.00	5.00	3.00
	Box 1 - Bunting	275.00	135.00	80.00
1	Maury Wills	15.00	7.50	4.50
(1)	Clete Boyer	15.00	7.50	4.50
(2)	Paul Casanova	10.00	5.00	3.00
(3)	Al Kaline	65.00	32.50	20.00
(4)	Tom Seaver	80.00	40.00	25.00
	Box 2 - Batting	250.00	125.00	75.00
2	Carl Yastrzemski	80.00	40.00	25.00
(5)	Matty Alou	10.00	5.00	3.00
(6)	Bill Freehan	10.00	5.00	3.00
(7)	Jim Hunter	45.00	22.50	13.50
(8)	Jim Lefebvre	10.00	5.00	3.00
	Box 3 - Stealing Bases	175.00	85.00	50.00
3	Bert Campaneris	10.00	5.00	3.00
(9)	Bobby Knoop	10.00	5.00	3.00
(10)	Tim McCarver	15.00	7.50	4.50
(11)	Frank Robinson	65.00	32.50	20.00
(12)	Bob Veale	10.00	5.00	3.00
	Box 4 - Sliding	100.00	50.00	30.00
4	Maury Wills	15.00	7.50	4.50
(13)	Joe Azcue	10.00	5.00	3.00
(14)	Tony Conigliaro	15.00	7.50	4.50
(15)	Ken Holtzman	10.00	5.00	3.00
(16)	Bill White	10.00	5.00	3.00
	Box 5 - The Double Play	315.00	155.00	95.00
5	Julian Javier	10.00	5.00	3.00
(17)	Hank Aaron	175.00	87.00	52.00
(18)	Juan Marichal	45.00	22.50	13.50
(19)	Joe Pepitone	17.50	9.00	5.00
(20)	Rico Petrocelli	15.00	7.50	4.50
	Box 6 - Playing 1st Base	375.00	185.00	110.00
6	Orlando Cepeda	50.00	25.00	15.00
(21)	Tommie Agee	10.00	5.00	3.00
(22a)	Don Drysdale (No period after "A" in team name.)	40.00	20.00	12.00
(22b)	Don Drysdale (Period after "A.")	40.00	20.00	12.00
(23)	Pete Rose	175.00	87.00	52.00
(24)	Ron Santo	17.50	9.00	5.00
	Box 7 - Playing 2nd Base	225.00	110.00	65.00
7	Bill Mazeroski	50.00	25.00	15.00
(25)	Jim Bunning	45.00	22.50	13.50
(26)	Frank Howard	15.00	7.50	4.50
(27)	John Roseboro	10.00	5.00	3.00
(28)	George Scott	10.00	5.00	3.00
	Box 8 - Playing 3rd Base	275.00	135.00	80.00
8	Brooks Robinson	65.00	32.50	20.00
(29)	Tony Gonzalez	10.00	5.00	3.00
(30)	Willie Horton	15.00	7.50	4.50
(31)	Harmon Killebrew	65.00	32.50	20.00
(32)	Jim McGlothlin	10.00	5.00	3.00
	Box 9 - Playing Shortstop	150.00	75.00	45.00
9	Jim Fregosi	10.00	5.00	3.00
(33)	Max Alvis	10.00	5.00	3.00
(34)	Bob Gibson	45.00	22.50	13.50
(35)	Tony Oliva	15.00	7.50	4.50
(36)	Vada Pinson	15.00	7.50	4.50
	Box 10 - Catching	160.00	80.00	45.00
10	Joe Torre	17.50	9.00	5.00
(37)	Dean Chance	10.00	5.00	3.00
(38)	Tommy Davis	10.00	5.00	3.00
(39)	Ferguson Jenkins	45.00	22.00	13.50
(40)	Rick Monday	10.00	5.00	3.00
	Box 11 - Pitching	850.00	425.00	255.00
11	Jim Lonborg	15.00	7.50	4.50
(41)	Curt Flood	15.00	7.50	4.50
(42)	Joel Horlen	10.00	5.00	3.00
(43)	Mickey Mantle	650.00	325.00	195.00
(44)	Jim Wynn	10.00	5.00	3.00
	Box 12 - Fielding the Pitcher's Position	375.00	185.00	110.00
12	Mike McCormick	10.00	5.00	3.00
(45)	Roberto Clemente	200.00	100.00	60.00
(46)	Al Downing	10.00	5.00	3.00
(47)	Don Mincher	10.00	5.00	3.00
(48)	Tony Perez	45.00	22.00	13.50
	Box 13 - Coaching	225.00	110.00	65.00
13	Frank Crosetti	15.00	7.50	4.50
(49)	Rod Carew	55.00	27.50	16.50
(50)	Willie McCovey	55.00	27.50	16.50
(51)	Ron Swoboda	10.00	5.00	3.00
(52)	Earl Wilson	10.00	5.00	3.00
	Box 14 - Playing the Outfield	250.00	125.00	75.00
14	Willie Mays	175.00	87.00	52.00
(53)	Richie Allen	15.00	7.50	4.50
(54)	Gary Peters	10.00	5.00	3.00
(55)	Rusty Staub	17.50	9.00	5.00
(56)	Billy Williams	50.00	25.00	15.00
	Box 15 - Base Running	375.00	185.00	110.00
15	Lou Brock	55.00	27.50	16.50
(57)	Tommie Agee	10.00	5.00	3.00
(58)	Don Drysdale	40.00	20.00	12.00
(59)	Pete Rose	175.00	87.00	52.00
(60)	Ron Santo	17.50	9.00	5.00

1969-70 Bazooka

Issued over a two-year span, the 1969-70 Bazooka set utilized the box bottom and sides. The bottom, entitled "Baseball Extra," features an historic event in baseball; the 3" x 6-1/4" panels are numbered 1-12. Two "All-Time Great" cards were located on each side of the box. These cards are not numbered and have no distinct borders; individual cards measure 1-1/4" x 3-1/8". The prices in the checklist that follows are for complete boxes only. Cards/panels cut from the boxes have a greatly reduced value - 25 percent of the complete box prices for all cut pieces.

		NM	EX	VG
	Complete Set (12):	325.00	160.00	100.00
	Common Box:	20.00	10.00	6.00
1	No-Hit Duel By Toney & Vaughn (Mordecai Brown, Ty Cobb, Willie Keeler, Eddie Plank)	30.00	15.00	9.00
2	Alexander Conquers Yanks (Rogers Hornsby, Ban Johnson, Walter Johnson, Al Simmons)	20.00	10.00	6.00
3	Yanks' Lazzeri Sets AL Record (Grover Alexander, Chief Bender, Christy Mathewson, Cy Young)	25.00	12.50	7.50
4	HR Almost Hit Out Of Stadium (Hugh Duffy, Lou Gehrig, Tris Speaker, Joe Tinker)	20.00	10.00	6.00
5	4 Consecutive Homers By Lou (Frank Chance, Mickey Cochrane, John McGraw, Babe Ruth)	35.00	17.50	10.00
6	No-Hit Game By Walter Johnson (Johnny Evers, Walter Johnson, John McGraw, Cy Young)	20.00	10.00	6.00
7	Twelve RBIs By Bottomley (Ty Cobb, Eddie Collins, Johnny Evers, Lou Gehrig)	35.00	17.50	10.00
8	Ty Ties Record (Mickey Cochrane, Eddie Collins, Mel Ott, Honus Wagner)	20.00	10.00	6.00
9	Babe Ruth Hits 3 HRs In Game (Cap Anson, Jack Chesbro, Al Simmons, Tris Speaker)	35.00	17.50	10.00
10	Calls Shot In Series Game (Nap Lajoie, Connie Mack, Rabbit Maranville, Ed Walsh)	35.00	17.50	10.00
11	Ruth's 60th HR Sets New Record (Frank Chance, Nap Lajoie, Mel Ott, Joe Tinker)	35.00	17.50	10.00
12	Double Shutout By Ed Reulbach (Rogers Hornsby, Rabbit Maranville, Christy Mathewson, Honus Wagner)	20.00	10.00	6.00

1971 Bazooka Numbered Set

The 1971 Bazooka numbered set is a proof set produced by the company after the unnumbered set was released. The set is comprised of 48 cards as opposed to the 36 cards which make up the unnumbered set. Issued in panels of three, the 12 cards not found in the unnumbered set are #1-3, 13-15, 34-36 and 43-45. All other cards are identical to those found in the unnumbered set. The cards, which measure 2" x 2-5/8", contain full-color photos and are blank-backed.

		NM	EX	VG
	Complete Panel Set (16):	1,300	655.00	400.00
	Complete Singles Set (48):	950.00	475.00	275.00
	Common Player:	7.50	3.75	2.25
	Panel (1)	100.00	50.00	30.00
1	Tim McCarver	12.50	6.25	3.75
2	Frank Robinson	35.00	17.50	10.00
3	Bill Mazeroski	30.00	15.00	9.00
	Panel (2)	100.00	50.00	30.00
4	Willie McCovey	30.00	15.00	9.00
5	Carl Yastrzemski	40.00	20.00	12.00
6	Clyde Wright	7.50	3.75	2.25
	Panel (3)	60.00	30.00	18.00
7	Jim Merritt	7.50	3.75	2.25
8	Luis Aparicio	25.00	12.50	7.50
9	Bobby Murcer	12.50	6.25	3.75
	Panel (4)	30.00	15.00	9.00
10	Rico Petrocelli	7.50	3.75	2.25
11	Sam McDowell	7.50	3.75	2.25
12	Cito Gaston	7.50	3.75	2.25
	Panel (5)	85.00	42.50	25.00
13	Ferguson Jenkins	25.00	12.50	7.50
14	Al Kaline	35.00	17.50	10.00
15	Ken Harrelson	7.50	3.75	2.25
	Panel (6)	115.00	55.00	35.00
16	Tommie Agee	7.50	3.75	2.25
17	Harmon Killebrew	35.00	17.50	10.00
18	Reggie Jackson	45.00	22.50	13.50
	Panel (7)	60.00	30.00	18.00
19	Juan Marichal	25.00	12.50	7.50
20	Frank Howard	10.00	5.00	3.00
21	Bill Melton	7.50	3.75	2.25
	Panel (8)	125.00	65.00	35.00
22	Brooks Robinson	35.00	17.50	10.00
23	Hank Aaron	60.00	30.00	18.00
24	Larry Dierker	7.50	3.75	2.25
	Panel (9)	60.00	30.00	18.00
25	Jim Fregosi	7.50	3.75	2.25
26	Billy Williams	30.00	15.00	9.00
27	Dave McNally	7.50	3.75	2.25
	Panel (10)	65.00	32.50	20.00
28	Rico Carty	7.50	3.75	2.25
29	Johnny Bench	35.00	17.50	10.00
30	Tommy Harper	7.50	3.75	2.25
	Panel (11)	110.00	55.00	30.00
31	Bert Campaneris	7.50	3.75	2.25
32	Pete Rose	50.00	25.00	15.00
33	Orlando Cepeda	25.00	12.50	7.50
	Panel (12)	65.00	32.50	20.00
34	Maury Wills	7.50	3.75	2.25
35	Tom Seaver	35.00	17.50	10.00
36	Tony Oliva	10.00	5.00	3.00
	Panel (13)	120.00	60.00	35.00
37	Bill Freehan	7.50	3.75	2.25
38	Roberto Clemente	75.00	37.50	22.50
39	Claude Osteen	7.50	3.75	2.25
	Panel (14)	65.00	32.50	20.00
40	Rusty Staub	12.50	6.25	3.75
41	Bob Gibson	30.00	15.00	9.00
42	Amos Otis	7.50	3.75	2.25
	Panel (15)	55.00	27.50	16.50
43	Jim Wynn	7.50	3.75	2.25
44	Richie Allen	20.00	10.00	6.00
45	Tony Conigliaro	15.00	7.50	4.50
	Panel (16)	110.00	55.00	35.00
46	Randy Hundley	7.50	3.75	2.25
47	Willie Mays	60.00	30.00	18.00
48	Jim Hunter	25.00	12.50	7.50

1971 Bazooka Unnumbered Set

This Bazooka set was issued in 1971, consisting of 36 full-color, blank-backed, unnumbered cards. Printed in panels of three on the bottoms of bubble gum boxes, individual cards measure 2" x 2-5/8"; complete panels measure 2-5/8" x 5-5/16". In the checklist that follows, the cards have been numbered by panel using the name of the player who appears on the left end of the panel.

		NM	EX	VG
	Complete Panel Set (12):	700.00	350.00	210.00
	Complete Singles Set (36):	600.00	300.00	180.00
	Common Player:	5.00	2.50	1.50
	Panel (1)	110.00	55.00	30.00
(1)	Tommie Agee	5.00	2.50	1.50

		NM	EX	VG
(2)	Harmon Killebrew	35.00	17.50	10.00
(3)	Reggie Jackson	45.00	22.50	13.50
	Panel (2)	110.00	55.00	30.00
(4)	Bert Campaneris	5.00	2.50	1.50
(5)	Pete Rose	50.00	25.00	15.00
(6)	Orlando Cepeda	25.00	12.50	7.50
	Panel (3)	65.00	32.50	20.00
(7)	Rico Carty	5.00	2.50	1.50
(8)	Johnny Bench	40.00	20.00	12.00
(9)	Tommy Harper	5.00	2.50	1.50
	Panel (4)	90.00	45.00	27.50
(10)	Bill Freehan	5.00	2.50	1.50
(11)	Roberto Clemente	60.00	30.00	18.00
(12)	Claude Osteen	5.00	2.50	1.50
	Panel (5)	55.00	27.50	16.50
(13)	Jim Fregosi	5.00	2.50	1.50
(14)	Billy Williams	30.00	15.00	9.00
(15)	Dave McNally	5.00	2.50	1.50
	Panel (6)	110.00	55.00	30.00
(16)	Randy Hundley	5.00	2.50	1.50
(17)	Willie Mays	50.00	25.00	15.00
(18)	Jim Hunter	25.00	12.50	7.50
	Panel (7)	55.00	27.50	16.50
(19)	Juan Marichal	25.00	12.50	7.50
(20)	Frank Howard	7.50	3.75	2.25
(21)	Bill Melton	5.00	2.50	1.50
	Panel (8)	100.00	50.00	30.00
(22)	Willie McCovey	30.00	15.00	9.00
(23)	Carl Yastrzemski	40.00	20.00	12.00
(24)	Clyde Wright	5.00	2.50	1.50
	Panel (9)	55.00	27.50	16.50
(25)	Jim Merritt	5.00	2.50	1.50
(26)	Luis Aparicio	25.00	12.50	7.50
(27)	Bobby Murcer	9.00	4.50	2.75
	Panel (10)	25.00	12.50	7.50
(28)	Rico Petrocelli	5.00	2.50	1.50
(29)	Sam McDowell	5.00	2.50	1.50
(30)	Cito Gaston	5.00	2.50	1.50
	Panel (11)	115.00	55.00	35.00
(31)	Brooks Robinson	35.00	17.50	10.50
(32)	Hank Aaron	50.00	25.00	15.00
(33)	Larry Dierker	5.00	2.50	1.50
	Panel (12)	60.00	30.00	18.00
(34)	Rusty Staub	7.50	3.75	2.25
(35)	Bob Gibson	30.00	15.00	9.00
(36)	Amos Otis	7.50	3.75	2.25

1930 Becker Bros. Theatre

Only recently brought to light, the issue date attributed here is uncertain and may be clarified if and when additions to the checklist are made. About postcard size, the cards have sepia portraits of Philadelphia A's players on front, identified in the white border at bottom. Backs have advertisng for the theatre, including a list of upcoming features.

		NM	EX	VG
	Common Player:	150.00	75.00	45.00
(1)	Max Bishop	150.00	75.00	45.00
(2)	Mickey Cochrane	250.00	125.00	75.00
(3)	Sammy Hale	150.00	75.00	45.00
(4)	Jimmie Foxx	300.00	150.00	90.00
(5)	Al Simmons	250.00	125.00	75.00

1958 Bell Brand Dodgers

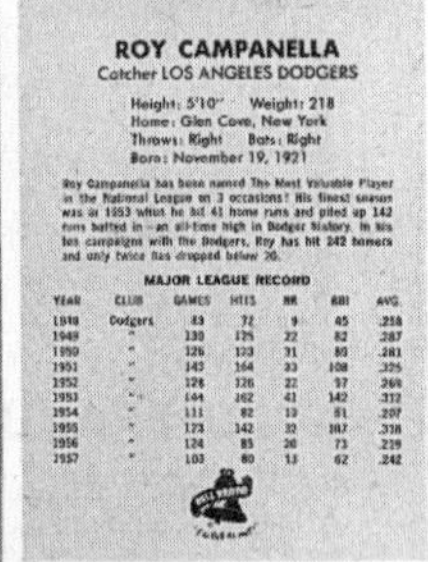

Celebrating the Dodgers first year of play in Los Angeles, Bell Brand inserted 10 different unnum- bered cards in their bags of potato chips and corn chips. The cards, which measure 3" x 4", have a sepia-colored photo inside a 1/4" green woodgrain border. The card backs feature statistical and biographical information and include the Bell Brand logo. Roy Campanella is included in the set despite a career-ending car wreck that prevented him from ever playing in Los Angeles.

		NM	EX	VG
	Complete Set (10):	5,500	2,750	1,650
	Common Player:	125.00	65.00	35.00
1	Roy Campanella	400.00	200.00	120.00
2	Gino Cimoli/SP	1,200	600.00	360.00
3	Don Drysdale	350.00	175.00	100.00
4	Junior Gilliam	125.00	65.00	35.00
5	Gil Hodges	350.00	175.00	105.00
6	Sandy Koufax	1,350	675.00	410.00
7	Johnny Podres/SP	600.00	300.00	180.00
8	Pee Wee Reese	400.00	200.00	120.00
9	Duke Snider	900.00	450.00	270.00
10	Don Zimmer	135.00	65.00	40.00

1958 Bell Brand Dodgers Ad Poster

Evidently a point-of-purchase in-store display to draw attention to its premiere offering of baseball cards, this 22" x 36" blank-back poster is, like the cards themselves, printed in green and sepia on white. The top pictures a super-size picture of Don Drysdale's card from the set.

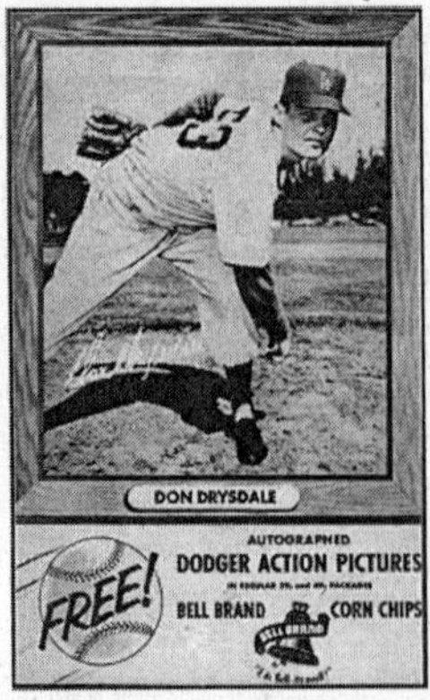

	NM	EX	VG
Bell Brand Dodgers Ad Poster (Don Drysdale)	4,250	2,100	1,250

1960 Bell Brand Dodgers

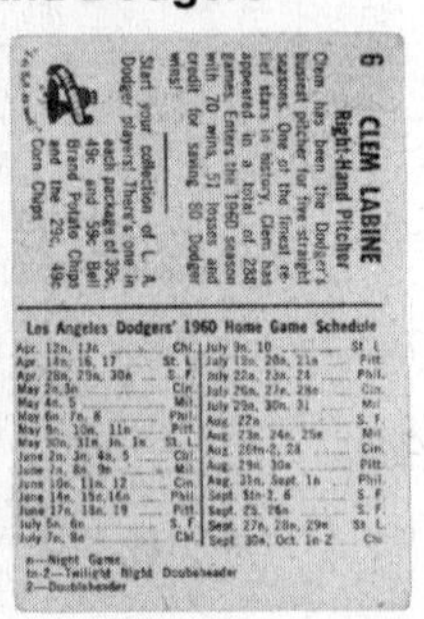

Bell Brand returned with a baseball card set in 1960 that was entirely different in style to their previous effort. The cards, which measure 2-1/2" x 3-1/2", feature beautiful, full-color photos. The backs carry a short player biography, the 1960 Dodgers home schedule, and the Bell Brand logo. Twenty different numbered cards were inserted in various size bags of potato chips and corn chips. Although sealed in cellophane, the cards were still subject to grease stains. Cards #'s 6, 12 and 18 are the scarcest in the set.

		NM	EX	VG
	Complete Set (20):	1,500	750.00	450.00
	Common Player:	45.00	22.50	13.50
1	Norm Larker	45.00	22.50	13.50
2	Duke Snider	150.00	75.00	45.00
3	Danny McDevitt	45.00	22.50	13.50
4	Jim Gilliam	50.00	25.00	15.00
5	Rip Repulski	45.00	22.50	13.50
6	Clem Labine/SP	90.00	45.00	27.50
7	John Roseboro	45.00	22.50	13.50
8	Carl Furillo	60.00	30.00	18.00
9	Sandy Koufax	300.00	150.00	90.00
10	Joe Pignatano	45.00	22.50	13.50
11	Chuck Essegian	45.00	22.50	13.50
12	John Klippstein/SP	150.00	75.00	45.00
13	Ed Roebuck	45.00	22.50	13.50
14	Don Demeter	45.00	22.50	13.50
15	Roger Craig	45.00	22.50	13.50
16	Stan Williams	45.00	22.50	13.50
17	Don Zimmer	60.00	30.00	18.00
18	Walter Alston/SP	100.00	50.00	30.00
19	Johnny Podres	60.00	30.00	18.00
20	Maury Wills	75.00	37.50	22.50

1961 Bell Brand Dodgers

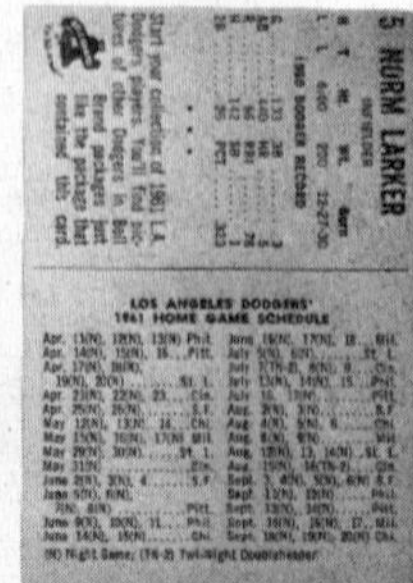

The 1961 Bell Brand set is identical in format to the previous year, although printed on thinner stock. Cards can be distinguished from the 1960 set by the 1961 schedule on the backs. The cards, which measure 2-7/16" x 3-1/2", are numbered by the player's uniform number. Twenty different cards were inserted into various size potato chip and corn chip packages, each card being sealed in a cellophane wrapper.

		NM	EX	VG
	Complete Set (20):	1,500	750.00	450.00
	Common Player:	50.00	25.00	15.00
3	Willie Davis	60.00	30.00	18.00
4	Duke Snider	175.00	85.00	50.00
5	Norm Larker	50.00	25.00	15.00
8	John Roseboro	50.00	25.00	15.00
9	Wally Moon	50.00	25.00	15.00
11	Bob Lillis	50.00	25.00	15.00
12	Tom Davis	60.00	30.00	18.00
14	Gil Hodges	150.00	75.00	45.00
16	Don Demeter	50.00	25.00	15.00
19	Jim Gilliam	60.00	30.00	18.00
22	John Podres	60.00	30.00	18.00
24	Walter Alston	75.00	37.50	22.50
30	Maury Wills	110.00	55.00	30.00
32	Sandy Koufax	250.00	125.00	75.00
34	Norm Sherry	60.00	30.00	18.00
37	Ed Roebuck	50.00	25.00	15.00
38	Roger Craig	50.00	25.00	15.00
40	Stan Williams	50.00	25.00	15.00
43	Charlie Neal	50.00	25.00	15.00
51	Larry Sherry	60.00	30.00	18.00

1962 Bell Brand Dodgers

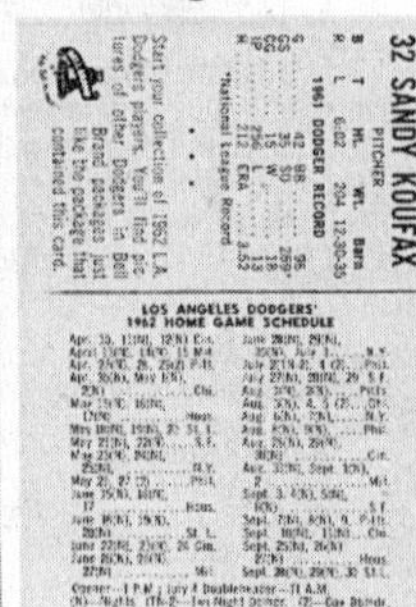

The 1962 Bell Brand set is identical in style to the previous two years and cards can be distinguished by the 1962 Dodgers schedule on the back. Each card measures 2-7/16" x 3-1/2" and is numbered by the player's uniform number. Printed on glossy stock, the 1962 set was less susceptible to grease stains.

		NM	EX	VG
	Complete Set (20):	1,700	850.00	500.00
	Common Player:	50.00	25.00	15.00
3	Willie Davis	50.00	25.00	15.00
4	Duke Snider	200.00	100.00	60.00
6	Ron Fairly	50.00	25.00	15.00
8	John Roseboro	50.00	25.00	15.00
9	Wally Moon	50.00	25.00	15.00
12	Tom Davis	50.00	25.00	15.00
16	Ron Perranoski	50.00	25.00	15.00
19	Jim Gilliam	55.00	27.50	16.50
20	Daryl Spencer	50.00	25.00	15.00
22	John Podres	55.00	27.50	16.50
24	Walter Alston	75.00	37.50	22.50
25	Frank Howard	55.00	27.50	16.50
30	Maury Wills	90.00	45.00	27.50
32	Sandy Koufax	250.00	125.00	75.00
34	Norm Sherry	60.00	30.00	18.00
37	Ed Roebuck	50.00	25.00	15.00
40	Stan Williams	50.00	25.00	15.00
51	Larry Sherry	60.00	30.00	18.00
53	Don Drysdale	125.00	65.00	35.00
56	Lee Walls	50.00	25.00	15.00

1962 Bell Brand Dodgers Ad Poster

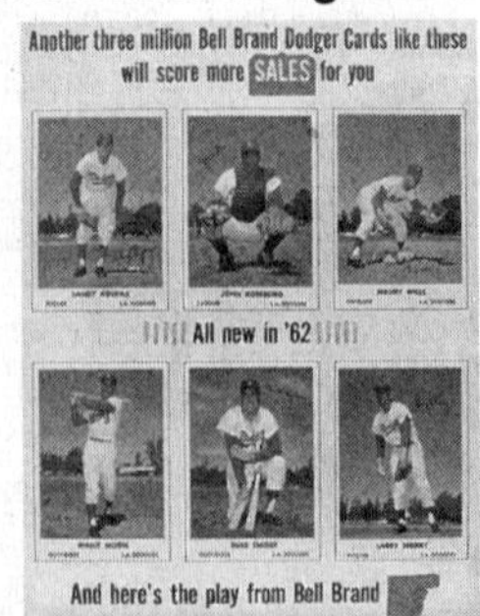

This 8-1/2" x 11-1/2" color poster was distributed to retailers to solicit sales of Bell Brand items. The sheet has actual size pictures of six of the cards from the set. On back is retailer information.

	NM	EX	VG
1962 Bell Brand Ad Poster (Koufax, Roseboro, Wills, Moon, Snider, Sherry)	900.00	450.00	275.00

1951 Berk Ross

Entitled "Hit Parade of Champions," the 1951 Berk Ross set features 72 stars of various sports. The cards, which measure 2-1/16" x 2-1/2" and have tinted color photographs, were issued in four boxes containing two-card panels. The issue is divided into four subsets with the first ten players of each series being baseball players. Only the baseball players are listed in the checklist that follows. Complete panels are valued 50 percent higher than the sum of the individual cards.

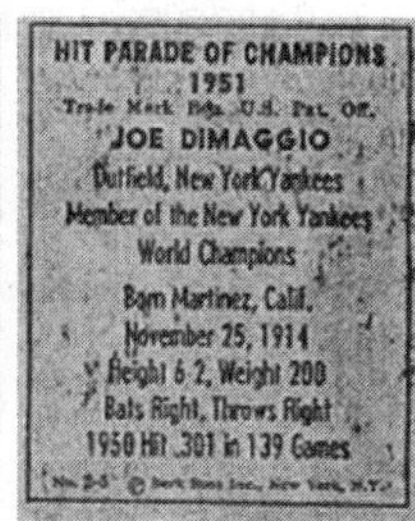

	NM	EX	VG
Complete Boxed Set (72):	2,100	1,100	650.00
Complete Baseball Set (40):	1,325	660.00	395.00
Common Player:	13.50	6.75	4.00
1-1 Al Rosen	16.00	8.00	5.00
1-2 Bob Lemon	20.00	10.00	6.00
1-3 Phil Rizzuto	50.00	25.00	15.00
1-4 Hank Bauer	16.00	8.00	5.00
1-5 Billy Johnson	13.50	6.75	4.00
1-6 Jerry Coleman	13.50	6.75	4.00
1-7 Johnny Mize	25.00	12.50	7.50
1-8 Dom DiMaggio	20.00	10.00	6.00
1-9 Richie Ashburn	30.00	15.00	9.00
1-10 Del Ennis	13.50	6.75	4.00
2-1 Stan Musial	150.00	75.00	45.00
2-2 Warren Spahn	25.00	12.50	7.50
2-3 Tommy Henrich	16.00	8.00	5.00
2-4 Larry "Yogi" Berra	100.00	50.00	30.00
2-5 Joe DiMaggio	300.00	150.00	90.00
2-6 Bobby Brown	13.50	6.75	4.00
2-7 Granville Hamner	13.50	6.75	4.00
2-8 Willie Jones	13.50	6.75	4.00
2-9 Stanley Lopata	13.50	6.75	4.00
2-10 Mike Goliat	13.50	6.75	4.00
3-1 Ralph Kiner	20.00	10.00	6.00
3-2 Billy Goodman	13.50	6.75	4.00
3-3 Allie Reynolds	16.00	8.00	5.00
3-4 Vic Raschi	16.00	8.00	5.00
3-5 Joe Page	13.50	6.75	4.00
3-6 Eddie Lopat	13.50	6.75	4.00
3-7 Andy Seminick	13.50	6.75	4.00
3-8 Dick Sisler	13.50	6.75	4.00
3-9 Eddie Waitkus	13.50	6.75	4.00
3-10 Ken Heintzelman	13.50	6.75	4.00
4-1 Gene Woodling	16.00	8.00	5.00
4-2 Cliff Mapes	13.50	6.75	4.00
4-3 Fred Sanford	13.50	6.75	4.00
4-4 Tommy Bryne	13.50	6.75	4.00
4-5 Eddie (Whitey) Ford	180.00	90.00	55.00
4-6 Jim Konstanty	13.50	6.75	4.00
4-7 Russ Meyer	13.50	6.75	4.00
4-8 Robin Roberts	20.00	10.00	6.00
4-9 Curt Simmons	13.50	6.75	4.00
4-10 Sam Jethroe	13.50	6.75	4.00

1952 Berk Ross

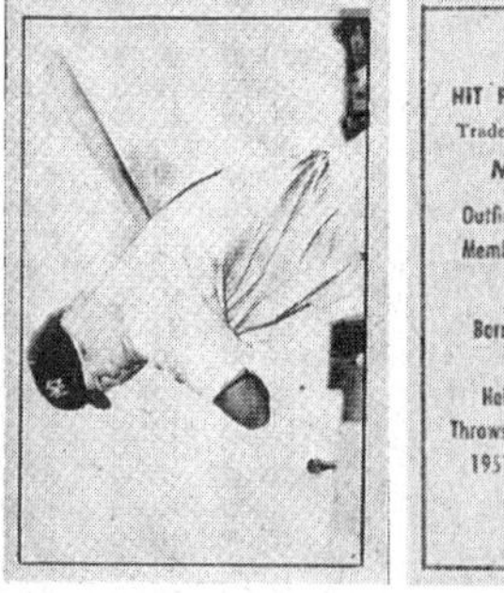
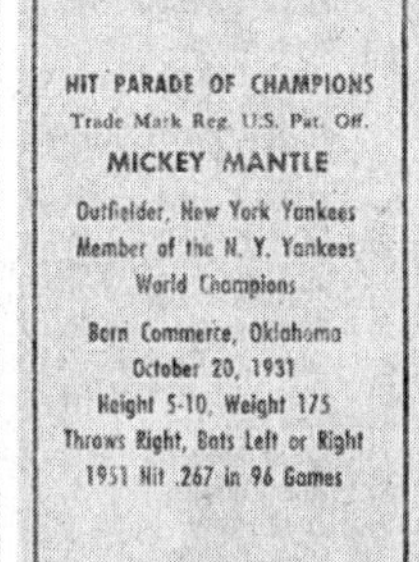

Although the card size is different (2" x 3"), the style of the fronts and backs of the 1952 Berk Ross set is similar to the previous year's effort. Seventy-two unnumbered cards make up the set. Rizzuto is included twice in the set and the Blackwell and Fox cards have transposed backs. The cards were issued individually rather than as two-card panels like in 1951.

	NM	EX	VG
Complete Set (72):	5,000	2,500	1,500
Common Player:	25.00	12.50	7.50
(1) Richie Ashburn	50.00	25.00	15.00
(2) Hank Bauer	30.00	15.00	9.00
(3) Larry "Yogi" Berra	175.00	85.00	50.00
(4) Ewell Blackwell (Photo actually Nelson Fox.)	75.00	37.50	22.50
(5) Bobby Brown	25.00	12.50	7.50
(6) Jim Busby	25.00	12.50	7.50
(7) Roy Campanella	140.00	70.00	40.00
(8) Chico Carrasquel	25.00	12.50	7.50
(9) Jerry Coleman	25.00	12.50	7.50
(10) Joe Collins	25.00	12.50	7.50
(11) Alvin Dark	25.00	12.50	7.50
(12) Dom DiMaggio	35.00	17.50	10.00
(13) Joe DiMaggio	400.00	200.00	120.00
(14) Larry Doby	40.00	20.00	12.00
(15) Bobby Doerr	40.00	20.00	12.00
(16) Bob Elliot (Elliott)	25.00	12.50	7.50
(17) Del Ennis	25.00	12.50	7.50
(18) Ferris Fain	25.00	12.50	7.50
(19) Bob Feller	100.00	50.00	30.00
(20) Nelson Fox (Photo actually Ewell Blackwell.)	125.00	60.00	35.00
(21) Ned Garver	25.00	12.50	7.50
(22) Clint Hartung	25.00	12.50	7.50
(23) Jim Hearn	25.00	12.50	7.50
(24) Gil Hodges	75.00	37.50	22.50
(25) Monte Irvin	40.00	20.00	12.00
(26) Larry Jansen	25.00	12.50	7.50
(27) George Kell	40.00	20.00	12.00
(28) Sheldon Jones	25.00	12.50	7.50
(29) Monte Kennedy	25.00	12.50	7.50
(30) Ralph Kiner	40.00	20.00	12.00
(31) Dave Koslo	25.00	12.50	7.50
(32) Bob Kuzava	25.00	12.50	7.50
(33) Bob Lemon	40.00	20.00	12.00
(34) Whitey Lockman	25.00	12.50	7.50
(35) Eddie Lopat	25.00	12.50	7.50
(36) Sal Maglie	25.00	12.50	7.50
(37) Mickey Mantle	2,100	1,050	650.00
(38) Billy Martin	90.00	45.00	27.50
(39) Willie Mays	500.00	250.00	150.00
(40) Gil McDougal (McDougald)	30.00	15.00	9.00
(41) Orestes Minoso	30.00	15.00	9.00
(42) Johnny Mize	50.00	25.00	15.00
(43) Tom Morgan	25.00	12.50	7.50
(44) Don Mueller	25.00	12.50	7.50
(45) Stan Musial	250.00	125.00	75.00
(46) Don Newcombe	35.00	17.50	10.00
(47) Ray Noble	25.00	12.50	7.50
(48) Joe Ostrowski	25.00	12.50	7.50
(49) Mel Parnell	25.00	12.50	7.50
(50) Vic Raschi	25.00	12.50	7.50
(51) Pee Wee Reese	125.00	65.00	35.00
(52) Allie Reynolds	30.00	15.00	9.00
(53) Bill Rigney	25.00	12.50	7.50
(54) Phil Rizzuto/Bunting	90.00	45.00	27.00
(55) Phil Rizzuto/Swinging	200.00	100.00	60.00
(56) Robin Roberts	40.00	20.00	12.00
(57) Eddie Robinson	25.00	12.50	7.50
(58) Jackie Robinson	325.00	160.00	100.00
(59) Elwin "Preacher" Roe	25.00	12.50	7.50
(60) Johnny Sain	30.00	15.00	9.00
(61) Albert "Red" Schoendienst	40.00	20.00	12.00
(62) Duke Snider	140.00	70.00	40.00
(63) George Spencer	25.00	12.50	7.50
(64) Eddie Stanky	25.00	12.50	7.50
(65) Henry Thompson	25.00	12.50	7.50
(66) Bobby Thomson	30.00	15.00	9.00
(67) Vic Wertz	25.00	12.50	7.50
(68) Waldon Westlake	25.00	12.50	7.50
(69) Wes Westrum	25.00	12.50	7.50
(70) Ted Williams	450.00	225.00	135.00
(71) Gene Woodling	30.00	15.00	9.00
(72) Gus Zernial	25.00	12.50	7.50

1956 Big League Stars Statues

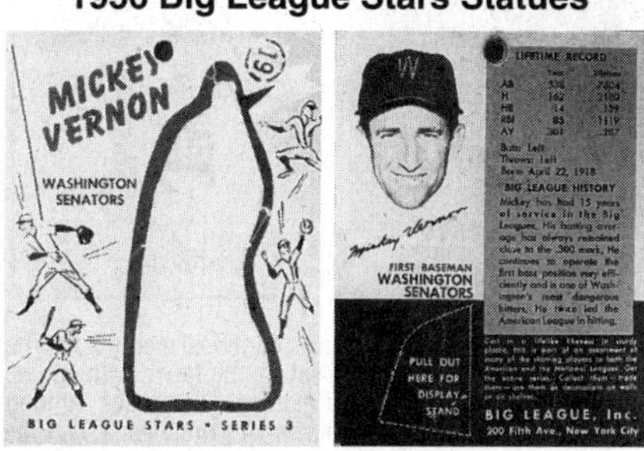

While the plastic statues in this set are virtually identical to the set issued in 1955 by Dairy Queen, the packaging of the Big League Stars statues on a card with all the usual elements of a baseball card makes them more collectible. The DQ versions of the statues are white, while the Big League versions are bronze colored. The statues measure about 3" tall and were sold in a 4" x 5" cardboard and plastic blister pack for about 19 cents. Complete league sets were also sold in a large package. The singles package features the player's name in a large banner near the top with his team printed below and line drawings of ballplayers in action around the statue. Backs have a player portrait photo with facsimile autograph, position, team, previous year and career stats and a career summary. A perforated tab at bottom can be pulled out to make a stand for the display. Most packages are found with the hole at top punched out to allow for hanging on a hook. Besides singles, larger packages of nine National or American league statues were also sold in a window-box. The set is checklisted alphabetically.

	NM	EX	VG
Complete Set (18):	4,000	2,000	1,200
Common Player:	60.00	30.00	18.00
UNOPENED PACKAGED STATUES			
(1) John Antonelli	125.00	65.00	35.00
(2) Bob Avila	125.00	65.00	35.00
(3) Yogi Berra	400.00	200.00	120.00
(4) Roy Campanella	400.00	200.00	120.00
(5) Larry Doby	175.00	85.00	50.00
(6) Del Ennis	125.00	65.00	35.00
(7) Jim Gilliam	150.00	75.00	45.00
(8) Gil Hodges	400.00	200.00	120.00
(9) Harvey Kuenn	125.00	65.00	35.00
(10) Bob Lemon	150.00	75.00	45.00
(11) Mickey Mantle	2,000	1,000	600.00
(12) Ed Mathews	300.00	150.00	90.00
(13) Minnie Minoso	125.00	65.00	35.00
(14) Stan Musial	600.00	300.00	180.00
(15) Pee Wee Reese	400.00	200.00	120.00
(16) Al Rosen	125.00	65.00	35.00
(17) Duke Snider	400.00	200.00	120.00
(18) Mickey Vernon	125.00	65.00	35.00
STATUES			
(1) John Antonelli	40.00	20.00	12.00
(2) Bob Avila	40.00	20.00	12.00
(3) Yogi Berra	150.00	75.00	45.00
(4) Roy Campanella	150.00	75.00	45.00
(5) Larry Doby	60.00	30.00	18.00
(6) Del Ennis	40.00	20.00	12.00
(7) Jim Gilliam	50.00	25.00	15.00
(8) Gil Hodges	125.00	62.00	37.00
(9) Harvey Kuenn	40.00	20.00	12.00
(10) Bob Lemon	60.00	30.00	18.00
(11) Mickey Mantle	300.00	150.00	90.00
(12) Ed Mathews	100.00	50.00	30.00
(13) Minnie Minoso	50.00	25.00	15.00
(14) Stan Musial	200.00	100.00	60.00
(15) Pee Wee Reese	150.00	75.00	45.00
(16) Al Rosen	45.00	22.00	13.50
(17) Duke Snider	150.00	75.00	45.00
(18) Mickey Vernon	40.00	20.00	12.00
PACKAGE/CARD ONLY			
(1) John Antonelli	50.00	25.00	15.00
(2) Bob Avila	50.00	25.00	15.00
(3) Yogi Berra	150.00	75.00	45.00
(4) Roy Campanella	150.00	75.00	45.00
(5) Larry Doby	75.00	37.50	22.00
(6) Del Ennis	50.00	25.00	15.00
(7) Jim Gilliam	65.00	32.50	20.00
(8) Gil Hodges	100.00	50.00	30.00
(9) Harvey Kuenn	50.00	25.00	15.00
(10) Bob Lemon	75.00	37.50	22.00
(11) Mickey Mantle	1,200	600.00	360.00
(12) Ed Mathews	125.00	62.50	37.50
(13) Minnie Minoso	75.00	37.50	22.00
(14) Stan Musial	175.00	85.00	50.00
(15) Pee Wee Reese	150.00	75.00	45.00
(16) Al Rosen	50.00	25.00	15.00
(17) Duke Snider	150.00	75.00	45.00
(18) Mickey Vernon	50.00	25.00	15.00

1978 Big T/Tastee Freeze discs

One player from each major league team was selected for inclusion in this discs set distributed by Big T family restaurants and Tastee Freeze stands in North Carolina, and possibly other parts of the country. The 3-3/8" diameter discs have a sepia-toned player portrait photo at center within a white diamond and surrounded by a brightly colored border with four colored stars at top. Licensed by the Players Association through Michael Schecter Associates, the photos have had uniform logos removed. Backs are printed in red, white and blue and have the sponsor's logos and a line of 1977 stats, along with a card number.

	NM	EX	VG
Complete Set (26):	30.00	15.00	9.00
Common Player:	2.00	1.00	.60
1 Buddy Bell	2.00	1.00	.60
2 Jim Palmer	8.00	4.00	2.50
3 Steve Garvey	5.00	2.50	1.50
4 Jeff Burroughs	2.00	1.00	.60
5 Greg Luzinski	2.00	1.00	.60
6 Lou Brock	8.00	4.00	2.50
7 Thurman Munson	5.00	2.50	1.50
8 Rod Carew	8.00	4.00	2.50
9 George Brett	20.00	10.00	6.00
10 Tom Seaver	15.00	7.50	4.50
11 Willie Stargell	8.00	4.00	2.50
12 Jerry Koosman	2.00	1.00	.60
13 Bill North	2.00	1.00	.60
14 Richie Zisk	2.00	1.00	.60
15 Bill Madlock	2.00	1.00	.60
16 Carl Yastrzemski	15.00	7.50	4.50
17 Dave Cash	2.00	1.00	.60
18 Bob Watson	2.00	1.00	.60
19 Dave Kingman	2.00	1.00	.60
20 Gene Tenace	2.00	1.00	.60
21 Ralph Garr	2.00	1.00	.60
22 Mark Fidrych	4.00	2.00	1.25
23 Frank Tanana	2.00	1.00	.60
24 Larry Hisle	2.00	1.00	.60
25 Bruce Bochte	2.00	1.00	.60
26 Bob Bailor	2.00	1.00	.60

1955-60 Bill and Bob Braves Postcards

One of the most popular and scarce of the 1950s color postcard series is the run of Milwaukee Braves known as "Bill and Bobs." While some of the cards do carry a photo credit acknowledging the pair, and a few add a Bradenton, Fla., (spring training home of the Braves) address, little else is known about the issuer. The cards themselves appear to have been purchased by the players to honor photo and autograph requests. Several of the cards carry facsimile autographs preprinted on the front. The cards feature crisp full-color photos on their borderless fronts. Postcard backs have a variety of printing including card numbers, photo credits, a Kodachrome logo and player name. Some cards are found with some of those elements, some with none. There is some question

whether Frank Torre's card is actually a Bill and Bob product, because it is 1/16" narrower than the standard 3-1/2" x 5-1/2" format of the other cards, features the player with a Pepsi bottle in his hand and is rubber-stamped on back with a Pepsi bottler's address. The Torre card is usually collected along with the rest of the set.

		NM	EX	VG
Complete Set (20):		4,600	2,300	1,350
Common Player:		100.00	50.00	30.00
(1)	Hank Aaron	1,200	600.00	360.00
(2)	Joe Adcock/Fldg	185.00	90.00	55.00
(3)	Joe Adcock (Bat on shoulder.)	185.00	90.00	55.00
(4)	Joe Adcock (Kneeling with two bats.)	145.00	75.00	45.00
(5)	Billy Bruton/Kneeling	185.00	90.00	55.00
(6)	Billy Bruton/Throwing	250.00	125.00	75.00
(7)	Bob Buhl	100.00	50.00	30.00
(8)	Lou Burdette	100.00	50.00	30.00
(9)	Gene Conley	100.00	50.00	30.00
(10)	Wes Covington/Kneeling (One bat.)	145.00	75.00	45.00
(11)	Wes Covington/Kneeling (Seven bats.)	145.00	75.00	45.00
(12)	Del Crandall/Kneeling (One bat.)	135.00	65.00	40.00
(13)	Del Crandall/Kneeling (Two bats.)	135.00	65.00	40.00
(14)	Chuck Dressen	145.00	75.00	45.00
(15)	Charlie Grimm	245.00	120.00	75.00
(16)	Fred Haney	235.00	115.00	70.00
(17)	Bob Keely	185.00	90.00	55.00
(18)	Eddie Mathews	400.00	200.00	120.00
(19)	Warren Spahn	500.00	250.00	150.00
(20)	Frank Torre	245.00	120.00	75.00

1923-24 Billiken

Colección
"BILLIKEN"
Cigarros Ovalados
Esta hermosa colección de fotografías consta de todos los Sports Nacionales.
Villaamil, Santalla y Ca.

Apparently issued as a premium with its Billiken brand cigars, these cards were issued by Villaamil, Santalla y Ca. About 2" x 2-5/8", the cards have black-and-white posed photos surrounded with a white border. Below the picture the player's last name and team are presented in typewriter style. Among the scarcest and most popular of the pre-war Cuban issues, the set features many players from the Negro Leagues. Counterfeits are known.

		NM	EX	VG
Common Player:		800.00	325.00	160.00
	ALMENDARES			
(1)	Bernardo Baro	1,200	480.00	240.00
(2)	Manuel Cueto	900.00	360.00	180.00
(3)	Valentin Dreke	1,200	480.00	240.00
(4)	Isidro Fabre	900.00	360.00	180.00
(5)	Jose Maria Fernandez	900.00	360.00	180.00
(6)	Oscar Fuhr	800.00	325.00	160.00
(7)	Bienvenido "Hooks" Gimenez (Jimenez)	1,200	480.00	240.00
(8)	"Snake" Henrry (Henry)	1,000	400.00	200.00
(9)	Ramon "Mike" Herrera	800.00	325.00	160.00
(10)	Jesse Hubbard	1,500	600.00	300.00
(11)	Armando Marsans	1,800	720.00	360.00
(12)	Jackie May (Jakie)	900.00	360.00	180.00
(13)	Eugenio Morin	800.00	325.00	160.00
(14)	Joseito Rodriguez	800.00	325.00	160.00
(15)	Nip Winters	2,000	800.00	400.00
	HABANA			
(16)	Eufemio Abreu	900.00	360.00	180.00
(17)	John Bischoff	800.00	325.00	160.00
(18)	Clark	800.00	325.00	160.00
(19)	Andy Cooper	5,000	2,000	1,000
(20)	Mack Eglefton (Eggleston)	1,300	520.00	260.00
(21)	Bienvenido "Hooks" Gimenez (Jimenez)	1,200	480.00	240.00
(22)	Marcelino Guerra	800.00	325.00	160.00
(23)	Oscar Levis	900.00	360.00	180.00
(24)	John Henry "Pop" Lloid (Lloyd)	15,000	6,000	3,000
(25)	Juanelo Mirabal	900.00	360.00	180.00
(26)	Bartolo Portuando (Portuondo)	1,200	480.00	240.00
(27)	Raphael "Busta" Quintana	800.00	325.00	160.00
(28)	Buster Ross	800.00	325.00	160.00
(29)	Clint Thomas	1,500	600.00	300.00
(30)	Edgar Westley (Wesley)	1,500	600.00	300.00
	MARIANAO			
(31)	Merito Acosta	800.00	325.00	160.00
(32)	Jose Acostica	800.00	325.00	160.00
(33)	D. Brown	800.00	325.00	160.00
(34)	E. Brown	800.00	325.00	160.00
(35)	Rogelio Crespo	800.00	325.00	160.00
(36)	Harry Deberry	800.00	325.00	160.00
(37)	Charlie Dressen	900.00	360.00	180.00
(38)	Freddie Fitzsmann (Fitzsimmons)	800.00	325.00	160.00
(39)	Griffin	800.00	325.00	160.00
(40)	Ernie Krueger	800.00	325.00	160.00
(41)	Slim Love	800.00	325.00	160.00
(42)	Jose "Pepin" Perez	800.00	325.00	160.00
(43)	Rgal (Rigal)	800.00	325.00	160.00
(44)	Hank Sceiber (Schreiber)	800.00	325.00	160.00
(45)	Cristobal Torriente	15,000	6,000	3,000
	SANTA CLARA			
(46)	Oscar Charleston	15,000	6,000	3,000
(47)	Rube Currie	1,500	600.00	300.00
(48)	Pedro Dibut	900.00	360.00	180.00
(49)	Eddie Douglas (Douglass)	1,500	600.00	300.00
(50)	Frank Duncan	1,500	600.00	300.00
(51)	Oliver Marcell (Marcelle)	5,000	2,000	1,000
(52)	Mayari (Esteban Montalvo)	900.00	360.00	180.00
(53)	Jose Mendez	6,000	2,400	1,200
(54)	Augustin "Tinti" Molina	800.00	325.00	160.00
(55)	Dobie Moore	1,500	600.00	300.00
(56)	Alejandro Oms	2,000	800.00	400.00
(57)	Herman Rios	900.00	360.00	180.00
(58)	Julio Rojo	900.00	360.00	180.00
(59)	Red Ryan	1,200	480.00	240.00
(60)	Frank Wardfield (Warfield)	1,500	600.00	300.00

1916 Block and Kuhl Co.

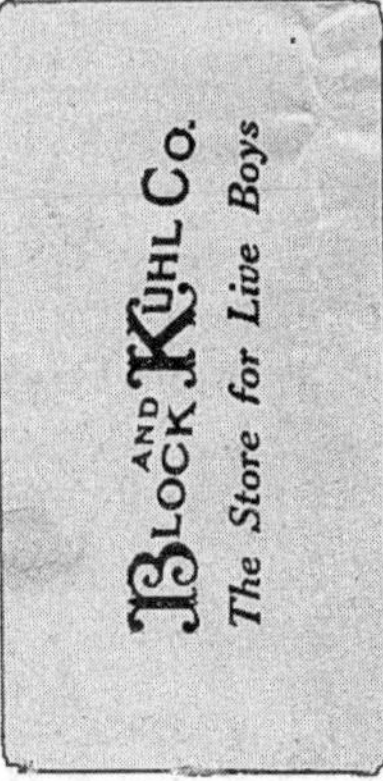

Best known for its use as a promotional medium for The Sporting News, this 200-card set can be found with ads on the back for several local and regional businesses. Among them is the Block and Kuhl department store, Peoria, Ill. Type card and superstar collectors can expect to pay a significant premium for individual cards with Block and Kuhl's advertising. The checklist is believed to generally parallel the 1916 M101-4 Blank Backs. Cards measure 1-5/8" x 3" and are printed in black-and-white.

(See 1916 M101-4 Blank Backs for checklist.)

1911 Blome's Chocolates (E94)

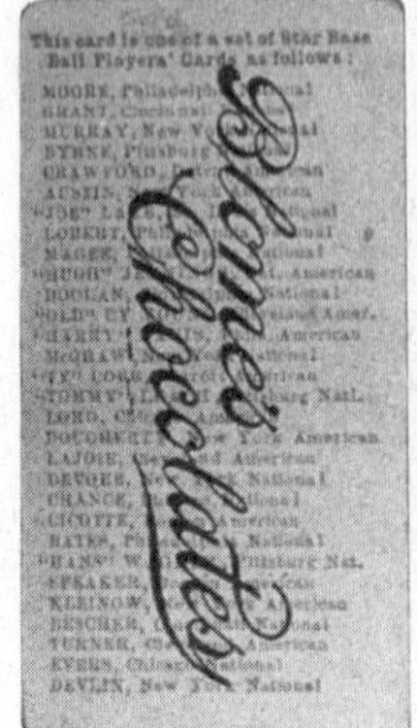

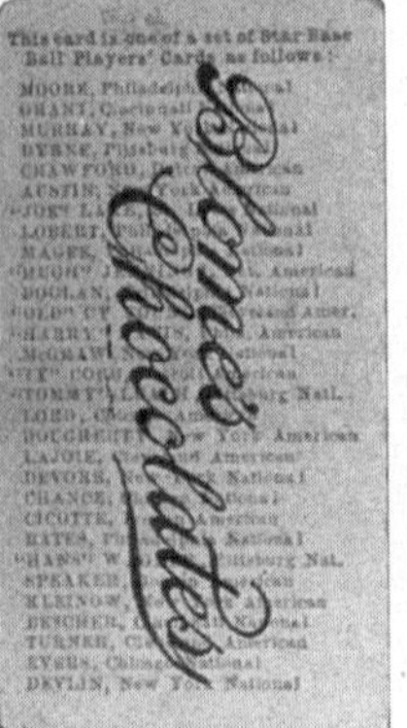

Advertising for Blome's Chocolates overprinted in purple on the back of these cards is one of several brands produced by George Close Candy Co. Type collectors will pay a premium of up to 5-7X for a Blome's version as opposed to the generic Close Candy version of the same player.

(See 1911 George Close Candy Co. for checklist and base card values.)

1933 Blue Bird Babe Ruth

A small hoard of the (a) cards appeared in the market in early 1994 making available a card which had previously been virtually unknown. Printed in black-and-white on thin card stock, the piece measures 3-7/8" x 5-7/8". The photo on front was used in modified form on several other early-1930s issues. The back offers balls and gloves available for redemption with soft drink bottle caps and cash. The discovery of the (b) version came in 1999.

		NM	EX	VG
(1a)	Babe Ruth (Batting follow-through, front view.)	2,000	1,000	600.00
(1b)	Babe Ruth (Batting follow-through, side view.)	3,500	1,750	1,000

1930 Blue Ribbon Malt Chicago Cubs

These player pictures were originally printed as part of a 40" x 12" advertising piece by Blue Ribbon Malt. However, if cut from the piece, there is no identification of the issuer. Individual black-and-white pictures have facsimile autographs on front and measure 3-1/2" high by 1-7/16" to 3" wide. The backs are blank. The unnumbered pictures are checklisted here in alphabetical order, with names as they appear on the photos.

		NM	EX	VG
Complete Uncut Sheet:		500.00	250.00	150.00
Complete Set, Singles (28):		335.00	165.00	100.00
Common Player:		20.00	10.00	6.00
(1)	Clyde Beck	20.00	10.00	6.00
(2)	Lester Bell	20.00	10.00	6.00
(3)	Clarence Blair	20.00	10.00	6.00
(4)	Fred Blake	20.00	10.00	6.00
(5)	Jimmie Burke	20.00	10.00	6.00
(6)	Guy Bush	20.00	10.00	6.00
(7)	Hazen "Kiki" Cuyler	40.00	20.00	12.00
(8)	Woody English	20.00	10.00	6.00
(9)	Eddie Farrell	20.00	10.00	6.00
(10)	Charlie Grimm	20.00	10.00	6.00
(11)	Leo "Gabby" Hartnett	40.00	20.00	12.00
(12)	Clift Heathcote	20.00	10.00	6.00
(13)	Rogers Hornsby	65.00	32.00	19.50
(14)	George L. Kelly	40.00	20.00	12.00
(15)	Pierce "Pat" Malone	20.00	10.00	6.00
(16)	Joe McCarthy	20.00	10.00	6.00
(17)	Lynn Nelson	20.00	10.00	6.00
(18)	Bob Osborn	20.00	10.00	6.00
(19)	Jess Petty	20.00	10.00	6.00
(20)	Charlie Root	20.00	10.00	6.00
(21)	Ray Schalk	40.00	20.00	12.00
(22)	John Schulte	20.00	10.00	6.00
(23)	Al Shealy	20.00	10.00	6.00
(24)	Riggs Stephenson	20.00	10.00	6.00
(25)	Dan Taylor	20.00	10.00	6.00
(26)	Zack Taylor	20.00	10.00	6.00
(27)	Bud Teachout	20.00	10.00	6.00
(28)	Lewis "Hack" Wilson	60.00	30.00	18.00

1930 Blue Ribbon Malt Chicago White Sox

These player pictures were originally printed as part of a 40" x 12" advertising piece by Blue Ribbon Malt. However, if cut from the piece, there is no identification of the issuer. Individual black-and-white pictures have facsimile autographs on front and measure 3-1/2" high by 1-7/16" to 2-7/8" wide. The backs are blank. The unnumbered pictures are checklisted here in alphabetical order, with names as they appear on the photos.

	NM	EX	VG
Complete Uncut Sheet:	1,000	500.00	300.00
Complete Set (27):	400.00	200.00	120.00
Common Player:	20.00	10.00	6.00

		NM	EX	VG
(1)	"Chick" Autry	20.00	10.00	6.00
(2)	"Red" Barnes	20.00	10.00	6.00
(3)	Moe Berg	60.00	30.00	18.00
(4)	Garland Braxton	20.00	10.00	6.00
(5)	Donie Bush	20.00	10.00	6.00
(6)	Pat Caraway	20.00	10.00	6.00
(7)	Bill Cissell	20.00	10.00	6.00
(8)	"Bud" Clancy	20.00	10.00	6.00
(9)	Clyde Crouse	20.00	10.00	6.00
(10)	U.C. Faber	50.00	25.00	15.00
(11)	Bob Fothergill	20.00	10.00	6.00
(12)	Frank J. "Dutch" Henry	20.00	10.00	6.00
(13)	Smead Jolley	20.00	10.00	6.00
(14)	Bill "Willie" Kamm	20.00	10.00	6.00
(15)	Bernard "Mike" Kelly	20.00	10.00	6.00
(16)	Johnny Kerr	20.00	10.00	6.00
(17)	Ted Lyons	50.00	25.00	15.00
(18)	Harold McKain	20.00	10.00	6.00
(19)	"Jim" Moore	20.00	10.00	6.00
(20)	"Greg" Mulleavy	20.00	10.00	6.00
(21)	Carl N. Reynolds	20.00	10.00	6.00
(22)	Blondy Ryan	20.00	10.00	6.00
(23)	"Benny" Tate	20.00	10.00	6.00
(24)	Tommy Thomas	20.00	10.00	6.00
(25)	Ed Walsh, Jr.	20.00	10.00	6.00
(26)	Johnny Watwood	20.00	10.00	6.00
(27)	Bob Weiland	20.00	10.00	6.00

1930 Blue Ribbon Malt Premiums

The manner of distribution for this series is unknown. And, while the name of the sponsor does not appear, the similarity to other Blue Ribbon Malt issues pinpoints their source. The premiums are a 5" x 7" black-and-white photo (sometimes, but not always, mounted on a heavy gray cardboard 6-1/4" x 8-3/4" backing). A facsimile autograph is on the photo. This incomplete checklist is presented alphabetically by team.

		NM	EX	VG
Common Player:		225.00	110.00	65.00
	CHICAGO CUBS			
(1)	Clyde Beck	225.00	110.00	65.00
(2)	Lester Bell	225.00	110.00	65.00
(3)	Clarence Blair	225.00	110.00	65.00
(4)	Fred Blake	225.00	110.00	65.00
(5)	Jimmy Burke	225.00	110.00	65.00
(6)	Guy Bush	225.00	110.00	65.00
(7)	Hal Carlson	225.00	110.00	65.00
(8)	Hazen "Kiki" Cuyler	300.00	150.00	90.00
(9)	Woody English	225.00	110.00	65.00
(10)	Charlie Grimm	225.00	110.00	65.00
(11)	Leo "Gabby" Hartnett	300.00	150.00	90.00
(12)	Cliff Heathcote	225.00	110.00	65.00
(13)	Rogers Hornsby	400.00	200.00	120.00
(14)	Perce "Pat" Malone	225.00	110.00	65.00
(15)	Joe McCarthy	275.00	135.00	80.00
(16)	Malcolm Moss	225.00	110.00	65.00
(17)	Lynn Nelson	225.00	110.00	65.00
(18)	Bob Osborn	225.00	110.00	65.00
(19)	Charles Root	225.00	110.00	65.00
(20)	Ray Schalk	275.00	135.00	80.00
(21)	John Schulte	225.00	110.00	65.00
(22)	Al Shealy	225.00	110.00	65.00
(23)	Riggs Stephenson	225.00	110.00	65.00
(24)	Dan Taylor	225.00	110.00	65.00
(25)	Zack Taylor	225.00	110.00	65.00
(26)	Chas. J. Tolson	225.00	110.00	65.00
(27)	Hal Totten (Announcer)	225.00	110.00	65.00
(28)	Lewis "Hack" Wilson	350.00	175.00	105.00
	CHICAGO WHITE SOX			
(1)	Donie Bush	225.00	110.00	65.00
(2)	Bill Cissell	225.00	110.00	65.00
(4)	Red Faber	275.00	135.00	85.00
(5)	Smead Jolley	225.00	110.00	65.00
(7)	Willie Kamm	225.00	110.00	65.00
(9)	Ted Lyons	275.00	135.00	85.00
(11)	Carl Reynolds	225.00	110.00	65.00
(13)	Art Shires	225.00	110.00	65.00
(15)	Tommy Thomas	225.00	110.00	65.00
(16)	Johnny Watwood	225.00	110.00	65.00

1931 Blue Ribbon Malt

Players of the Chicago Cubs and White Sox are featured in this series of 4-7/8" x 6-7/8" black-and-white photos. Each blank-backed photo is bordered in white with "Compliments of BLUE RIBBON MALT-America's Biggest Seller" printed in the bottom border and a facsimile autograph across the photo. It is likely players other than those listed here were also issued.

		NM	EX	VG
Common Player:		90.00	45.00	27.00
(1)	Lu Blue	90.00	45.00	27.00
(2)	Lew Fonseca	90.00	45.00	27.00
(3)	Vic Frazier	90.00	45.00	27.00
(4)	John Kerr	90.00	45.00	27.00
(5)	Bob Smith	90.00	45.00	27.00
(6)	Billy Sullivan	90.00	45.00	27.00
(7)	Lewis "Hack" Wilson	125.00	62.00	37.00

1933 Blum's Baseball Bulletin Premiums

The year of issue presented is speculative, based on biographical information on the relatively few examples studied. This series of 9-1/2" x 13-5/8" (Small) or 11-1/2" x 13-3/4" (Large) black-and-white blank-back pictures was, according to a credit line beneath the bottom frame of baseballs, "Compiled by Fred J. Blum, Publisher, Blum's Baseball Bulletin." The checklist here is incomplete.

		NM	EX	VG
Common Player:		200.00	100.00	60.00
(1)	Edward T. Collins/S	300.00	150.00	90.00
(2)	Jacob E. Daubert/S	200.00	100.00	60.00
(3)	William E. Donovan/L	200.00	100.00	60.00
(4)	John J. Evers/S	300.00	150.00	90.00
(5)	Lou Gehrig/L	350.00	175.00	105.00
(6)	Henry K. Groh/L	200.00	100.00	60.00
(7)	Lefty Grove/L	400.00	200.00	120.00
(8)	Walter Johnson/S	500.00	250.00	150.00
(9)	Napoleon Lajoie/S	350.00	175.00	105.00
(10)	Walter J.V. Maranville/S	300.00	150.00	90.00
(11)	James (Wicky) McAvoy/L	200.00	100.00	60.00
(12)	Rochester 1911/L (Team composite.)	200.00	100.00	60.00
(13)	Billy Southworth/L	200.00	100.00	60.00
(14)	Tristam Speaker/S	400.00	200.00	120.00
(15)	George Toporcer/L	200.00	100.00	60.00

1961-1963 Bobbin' Head Dolls

Some of the top stars of the day were caricatured in the first generation of bobbin' head dolls. Additionally, Mantle and Maris were depicted in a pair of color 5" x 7" advertising photos depicting the home run heroes of 1961 holding their dolls. The players are pictured in belt-to-cap photos wearing road uniforms and posed in a stadium setting. Backs are blank.

	NM	EX	VG
Roberto Clemente (6-1/2" doll)	4,500	2,250	1,350
Roberto Clemente (Picture box.)	1,000	500.00	300.00
Mickey Mantle (Ad photo.)	325.00	160.00	95.00
Mickey Mantle (6-1/2" doll, round or square base)	1,100	550.00	330.00
Mickey Mantle (Mini (4-1/2") doll.)	1,500	750.00	450.00
Mickey Mantle (Large or small picture box.)	750.00	375.00	225.00
Roger Maris (Ad photo.)	175.00	87.00	52.00
Roger Maris (6-1/2" doll)	450.00	225.00	135.00
Roger Maris (Mini (5-1/2") doll.)	650.00	325.00	195.00
Roger Maris (Large or small picture box.)	900.00	450.00	275.00
Willie Mays (White base, dark face, 6-1/2" doll.)	750.00	375.00	225.00
Willie Mays (White base, light face, 6-1/2" doll.)	475.00	235.00	140.00
Willie Mays (Gold base, 6-1/2" doll.)	2,250	1,125	675.00

1947 Bond Bread

Issued by "Homogenized" Bond Bread in 1947, this set consists of 48 unnumbered black-and-white cards, each measuring about 2-1/4" x 3-1/2" with rounded or square corners. Of the 48 cards, 44 are baseball players; four picture boxers. Borderless fronts have either portraits or posed action photos and the player's facsimile autograph or name in script. In the 1980s a large quantity of half the cards in the set (all with square corners) was uncovered in a New York warehouse. Sometime after 2000, the square-cornered cards were illegally reprinted, often sold in high-graded slabs from unknown grading companies. Those cards that were not known to be affected by the find/reprinting are indicated in the checklist here with an "SP." The issue was designated in the American Card Catalog as W571 / D305.

		NM	EX	VG
Complete Set (48):		1,600	800.00	475.00
Common Player:		15.00	7.50	4.50
(1)	Rex Barney/SP	20.00	10.00	6.00
(2)	Yogi Berra/SP	75.00	37.50	22.50
(3)	Ewell Blackwell	15.00	7.50	4.50
(4)	Lou Boudreau	20.00	10.00	6.00
(5)	Ralph Branca/SP	20.00	10.00	6.00
(6)	Harry Brecheen	15.00	7.50	4.50
(7)	Dom DiMaggio/SP	50.00	25.00	15.00
(8)	Joe DiMaggio/SP	275.00	135.00	85.00
(9)	Bobbie Doerr (Bobby)	20.00	10.00	6.00
(10)	Bruce Edwards/SP	20.00	10.00	6.00
(11)	Bob Elliott	15.00	7.50	4.50
(12)	Del Ennis	15.00	7.50	4.50
(13)	Bob Feller	25.00	12.50	7.50
(14)	Carl Furillo/SP	35.00	17.50	10.00
(15)	Cid Gordon (Sid)/SP	20.00	10.00	6.00
(16)	Joe Gordon	15.00	7.50	4.50
(17)	Joe Hatten/SP	20.00	10.00	6.00
(18)	Gil Hodges/SP	75.00	37.50	22.50
(19)	Tommy Holmes	15.00	7.50	4.50
(20)	Larry Janson (Jansen)/SP	20.00	10.00	6.00
(21)	Sheldon Jones/SP	20.00	10.00	6.00
(22)	Edwin Joost/SP	20.00	10.00	6.00
(23)	Charlie Keller/SP	20.00	10.00	6.00
(24)	Ken Keltner	15.00	7.50	4.50
(25)	Buddy Kerr/SP	20.00	10.00	6.00
(26)	Ralph Kiner	20.00	10.00	6.00
(27)	John Lindell/SP	20.00	10.00	6.00
(28)	Whitey Lockman/SP	20.00	10.00	6.00
(29)	Willard Marshall/SP	20.00	10.00	6.00
(30)	Johnny Mize	20.00	10.00	6.00
(31)	Stan Musial	60.00	30.00	18.00
(32)	Andy Pafko	15.00	7.50	4.50
(33)	Johnny Pesky	15.00	7.50	4.50
(34)	Pee Wee Reese/SP	125.00	65.00	35.00
(35)	Phil Rizzuto	30.00	15.00	9.00
(36)	Aaron Robinson	15.00	7.50	4.50
(37)	Jackie Robinson	90.00	45.00	27.50
(38)	John Sain	15.00	7.50	4.50
(39)	Enos Slaughter	20.00	10.00	6.00
(40)	Vern Stephens	15.00	7.50	4.50
(41)	George Tebbetts/SP	20.00	10.00	6.00
(42)	Bob Thomson/SP	25.00	12.50	7.50

		NM	EX	VG
(43)	Johnny Vandermeer/SP (VanderMeer)	20.00	10.00	6.00
(44)	Ted Williams	90.00	45.00	27.00
	BOXERS			
(45)	Primo Carnera	15.00	7.50	4.50
(46)	Marcel Cerdan/SP	40.00	20.00	12.00
(47)	Jake LaMotta/SP	60.00	30.00	18.00
(48)	Joe Louis	30.00	15.00	9.00

1947 Bond Bread Exhibits

The manner of distribution of these variants of the "Bond Bread" (W571 / D305) baseball cards is believed to have been via penny arcade dispensers. About the same size as contemporary Exhibit Supply Co. cards (3-3/8" x 5-3/8"), these are printed in black-and-white and blank-backed. Over 75 percent of the baseball players known in the base Bond Bread set have been reported in this format, plus one player, Walker Cooper, not in the base set. The four W571/D305 boxers have not yet been reported in this format.

		NM	EX	VG
	Complete Set (33):	1,250	625.00	375.00
	Common Player:	25.00	12.50	7.50
(1)	Rex Barney			
(2)	Yogi Berra			
(3)	Ewell Blackwell	25.00	12.50	7.50
(4)	Lou Boudreau	30.00	15.00	9.00
(5)	Ralph Branca			
(6)	Harry Brecheen	25.00	12.50	7.50
(--)	Walker Cooper	50.00	25.00	15.00
(7)	Dom DiMaggio	30.00	15.00	9.00
(8)	Joe DiMaggio	200.00	100.00	60.00
(9)	Bobbie Doerr (Bobby)	35.00	17.50	10.00
(10)	Bruce Edwards			
(11)	Bob Elliott	25.00	12.50	7.50
(12)	Del Ennis	25.00	12.50	7.50
(13)	Bob Feller	40.00	20.00	12.00
(14)	Carl Furillo	100.00	50.00	30.00
(15)	Cid Gordon (Sid)			
(16)	Joe Gordon	25.00	12.50	7.50
(17)	Joe Hatten			
(18)	Gil Hodges	90.00	45.00	27.50
(19)	Tommy Holmes	25.00	12.50	7.50
(20)	Larry Janson (Jansen)	25.00	12.50	7.50
(21)	Sheldon Jones	25.00	12.50	7.50
(22)	Edwin Joost	25.00	12.50	7.50
(23)	Charlie Keller			
(24)	Ken Keltner	25.00	12.50	7.50
(25)	Buddy Kerr	25.00	12.50	7.50
(26)	Ralph Kiner	30.00	15.00	9.00
(27)	John Lindell	25.00	12.50	7.50
(28)	Whitey Lockman	25.00	12.50	7.50
(29)	Willard Marshall			
(30)	Johnny Mize	30.00	15.00	9.00
(31)	Stan Musial	75.00	37.50	22.50
(32)	Andy Pafko	25.00	12.50	7.50
(33)	Johnny Pesky	25.00	12.50	7.50
(34)	Pee Wee Reese	100.00	50.00	30.00
(35)	Phil Rizzuto	50.00	25.00	15.00
(36)	Aaron Robinson	25.00	12.50	7.50
(37)	Jackie Robinson	175.00	90.00	55.00
(38)	John Sain	25.00	12.50	7.50
(39)	Enos Slaughter	30.00	15.00	9.00
(40)	Vern Stephens	25.00	12.50	7.50
(41)	George Tebbetts	25.00	12.50	7.50
(42)	Bob Thomson			
(43)	Johnny Vandermeer (VanderMeer)	25.00	12.50	7.50
(44)	Ted Williams	175.00	85.00	55.00

1947 Bond Bread Premiums

While there is no empirical evidence, it is believed these 6-5/8" x 9" black-and-white, blank-back player pictures are associated with the Bond Bread card issue, since they share the same photos and script names, right down to the misspellings. They were likely made available to bread buyers as some sort of premium. The checklist presented here is the same as that of the card issue. Though not all of the premium pictures have been confirmed, it is reasonable to presume their existence.

		NM	EX	VG
	Common Player:	40.00	20.00	12.00
(1)	Rex Barney	40.00	20.00	12.00
(2)	Yogi Berra	150.00	75.00	45.00
(3)	Ewell Blackwell	40.00	20.00	12.00
(4)	Lou Boudreau	75.00	37.50	22.50
(5)	Ralph Branca	60.00	30.00	18.00
(6)	Harry Brecheen	40.00	20.00	12.00
(7)	Dom DiMaggio	60.00	30.00	18.00
(8)	Joe DiMaggio	600.00	300.00	180.00
(9)	Bobbie Doerr (Bobby)	60.00	30.00	18.00
(10)	Bruce Edwards	40.00	20.00	12.00
(11)	Bob Elliott	40.00	20.00	12.00
(12)	Del Ennis	50.00	25.00	15.00
(13)	Bob Feller	150.00	75.00	45.00
(14)	Carl Furillo	60.00	30.00	18.00
(15)	Cid Gordon (Sid)	40.00	20.00	12.00
(16)	Joe Gordon	40.00	20.00	12.00
(17)	Joe Hatten	40.00	20.00	12.00
(18)	Gil Hodges	100.00	50.00	30.00
(19)	Tommy Holmes	40.00	20.00	12.00
(20)	Larry Janson (Jansen)	40.00	20.00	12.00
(21)	Sheldon Jones	40.00	20.00	12.00
(22)	Edwin Joost	40.00	20.00	12.00
(23)	Charlie Keller	45.00	22.50	13.50
(24)	Ken Keltner	40.00	20.00	12.00
(25)	Buddy Kerr	40.00	20.00	12.00
(26)	Ralph Kiner	75.00	37.50	22.50
(27)	John Lindell	40.00	20.00	12.00
(28)	Whitey Lockman	40.00	20.00	12.00
(29)	Willard Marshall	40.00	20.00	12.00
(30)	Johnny Mize	75.00	37.50	22.50
(31)	Stan Musial	300.00	150.00	90.00
(32)	Andy Pafko	40.00	20.00	12.00
(33)	Johnny Pesky	40.00	20.00	12.00
(34)	Pee Wee Reese	150.00	75.00	45.00
(35)	Phil Rizzuto	150.00	75.00	45.00
(36)	Aaron Robinson	40.00	20.00	12.00
(37)	Jackie Robinson	1,000	500.00	300.00
(38)	John Sain	50.00	25.00	15.00
(39)	Enos Slaughter	75.00	37.50	22.50
(40)	Vern Stephens	40.00	20.00	12.00
(41)	George Tebbetts	40.00	20.00	12.00
(42)	Bob Thomson	60.00	30.00	18.00
(43)	Johnny Van Der Meer (VanderMeer)	40.00	20.00	12.00
(44)	Ted Williams	350.00	175.00	100.00
	BOXERS			
(45)	Primo Carnera	45.00	22.50	13.50
(46)	Marcel Cerdan	40.00	20.00	12.00
(47)	Jake LaMotta	60.00	30.00	18.00
(48)	Joe Louis	75.00	37.50	22.50

1947 Bond Bread Perforated, Dual-Sided

The manner of distribtion for this variant of the "Bond Bread" (W571/D305) cards is unknown, although anecdotal evidence suggests a connection with Bar Nunn show stores. About the size of the commonly seen blank-backed baseball cards (2-1/4" x 3-1/2"), these differ in that they have two, three or four sides perforated, indicating they were issued in sheet form. Also, this group has, instead of a blank back, another picture. All but one of the pictures seen thus far are of Western movie stars. None are named on the cards, but they include John Wayne, Hopalong Cassidy, Gene Autry and Noah Berry. The only non-Western back seen is Michigan quarterback Bob Chappius, paired with Tommy Holmes. Thus far, none of the short-printed Bond Bread cards have been seen in this format. Assigned numbers correspond to the Bond Bread set.

		NM	EX	VG
	Complete Set (24):	550.00	275.00	165.00
	Common Card:			
(3)	Ewell Blackwell	15.00	7.50	4.50
(4)	Lou Boudreau	22.50	11.00	6.75
(6)	Harry Brecheen	15.00	7.50	4.50
(9)	Bobbie Doerr (Bobby)	22.50	11.00	6.75
(11)	Bob Elliott	15.00	7.50	4.50
(12)	Del Ennis	15.00	7.50	4.50
(13)	Bob Feller	25.00	12.50	7.50
(16)	Joe Gordon	15.00	7.50	4.50
(19)	Tommy Holmes	15.00	7.50	4.50
(24)	Ken Keltner	15.00	7.50	4.50
(26)	Ralph Kiner	22.50	11.00	6.75
(30)	Johnny Mize	22.50	11.00	6.75
(31)	Stan Musial	60.00	30.00	18.00
(32)	Andy Pafko	15.00	7.50	4.50
(33)	Johnny Pesky	15.00	7.50	4.50
(35)	Phil Rizzuto	30.00	15.00	9.00
(36)	Aaron Robinson	15.00	7.50	4.50
(37)	Jackie Robinson	110.00	55.00	35.00
(38)	John Sain	15.00	7.50	4.50
(39)	Enos Slaughter	22.50	11.00	6.75
(40)	Vern Stephens	15.00	7.50	4.50
(44)	Ted Williams	110.00	55.00	35.00
	BOXERS			
(45)	Primo Carnera	15.00	7.50	4.50
(48)	Joe Louis	30.00	15.00	9.00

1947 Bond Bread Jackie Robinson

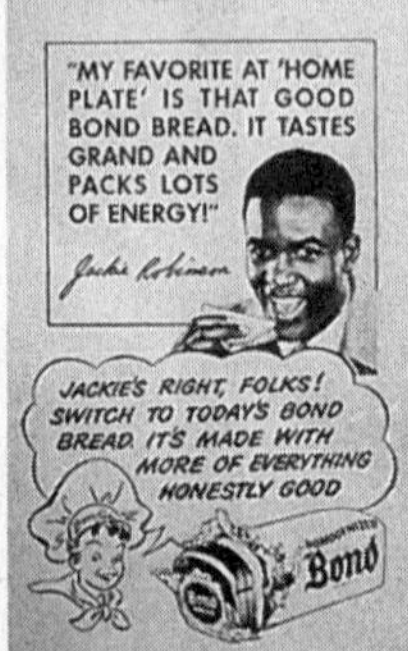

The modern major leagues' first black player is featured in this set issued by Bond Bread in 1947. The cards, measuring 2-1/4" x 3-1/2", are black-and-white photos of Robinson in various action and portrait poses. The unnumbered cards bear three different backs advertising Bond Bread. Four cards use a horizontal format. Card #6 was issued in greater quantities and perhaps was a promotional card; its back is the only one containing a short biography of Robinson.

		NM	EX	VG
	Complete Set (13):	9,500	4,750	2,850
	Common Card:	750.00	375.00	225.00
(1)	Jackie Robinson (Awaiting pitch.)	750.00	375.00	225.00
(2)	Jackie Robinson/Btg (White shirt sleeves.)	750.00	375.00	225.00
(3)	Jackie Robinson/Btg (No shirt sleeves.)	750.00	375.00	225.00
(4)	Jackie Robinson/Leaping (Scoreboard in background.)	750.00	375.00	225.00
(5)	Jackie Robinson/Leaping (No scoreboard.)	750.00	375.00	225.00
(6)	Jackie Robinson/Portrait (Facsimile autograph.)	750.00	375.00	225.00
(7)	Jackie Robinson/Portrait (Holding glove in air.)	750.00	375.00	225.00
(8)	Jackie Robinson (Running down baseline.)	750.00	375.00	225.00
(9)	Jackie Robinson (Running to catch ball.)	750.00	375.00	225.00
(10)	Jackie Robinson/Sliding	750.00	375.00	225.00
(11)	Jackie Robinson (Stretching for throw, ball in glove.)	750.00	375.00	225.00
(12)	Jackie Robinson (Stretching for throw, no ball visible.)	750.00	375.00	225.00
(13)	Jackie Robinson/Throwing	750.00	375.00	225.00

1912 Boston American Series Red Sox Postcards

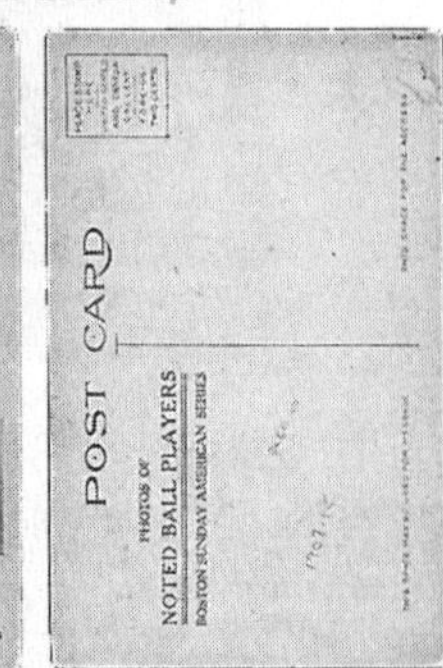

Star players from the World Champion Red Sox are featured in two sets of postcards issued by one of the city's daily newspapers. This set carries the notation "Boston American Series" at bottom right and is approximately 3-1/2" x 5-1/2". The cards are printed in sepia tones with a cream border. At bottom is the player name and position on two lines. Backs have typical postcard markings and a three-line notation, "PHOTOS OF / NOTED BALL PLAYERS / BOSTON SUNDAY AMERICAN SERIES."

		NM	EX	VG
	Complete Set (6):	2,400	1,200	725.00
	Common Player:	400.00	200.00	120.00
(1)	Forrest Cady	400.00	200.00	120.00
(2)	Hub Perdue	400.00	200.00	120.00
(3)	Tris Speaker	550.00	275.00	165.00
(4)	Jake Stahl	400.00	200.00	120.00
(5)	Heinie Wagner	400.00	200.00	120.00
(6)	Joe Wood	400.00	200.00	120.00

1936 Boston American Sport Stamps

Similar to several contemporary issues, the Sport Stamps were printed on the pages of the daily newspaper over the course of the season. About 2" x 3-1/2", depending on the length of the biography and how well they were cut off the paper, they are printed in black-and-white. A tightly cropped player portrait is centered on a 2" x 2-5/8" stamp design with the paper's name above and the player's name, position and team below. This checklist may not be complete. Two of the players (Castleman, R. Johnson) have the paper at top listed as "SUNDAY ADVERTISER." Many of the stamps were issued in pairs, and at least a couple of football players are known, as well as the listed baseball players.

		NM	EX	VG
Common Player:		12.00	6.00	3.50
(1)	J. (John) Allen	12.00	6.00	3.50
(2)	I. (Ivy) Andrews	12.00	6.00	3.50
(3)	E. (Elden)(Eldon) Auker	12.00	6.00	3.50
(4)	E. (Earl) Averill	20.00	10.00	6.00
(5)	R. (Richard) Bartell	12.00	6.00	3.50
(6)	R. (Roy) Bell	12.00	6.00	3.50
(7)	R. (Raymond) Benge	12.00	6.00	3.50
(8)	M. (Morris) Berg	30.00	15.00	9.00
(9)	Walter Berger	12.00	6.00	3.50
(10)	C. (Charles) Berry	12.00	6.00	3.50
(11)	(George) Blaeholder	12.00	6.00	3.50
(12)	A. (Albert) Blanche	12.00	6.00	3.50
(13)	D. (Darrell) Blanton	12.00	6.00	3.50
(14)	O. (Oswald) Bleuge (Bluege)	12.00	6.00	3.50
(15)	W. (William) Bolton	12.00	6.00	3.50
(16)	H. (Henry) Bonura	12.00	6.00	3.50
(17)	J. (James) Bottomley	20.00	10.00	6.00
(18)	J. (Joseph) Bowman	12.00	6.00	3.50
(19)	E. (Edward) Brandt	12.00	6.00	3.50
(20)	C. (Clinton) Brown	12.00	6.00	3.50
(21)	J. (John) Burnett	12.00	6.00	3.50
(22)	G. (Guy) Bush	12.00	6.00	3.50
(23)	A. (Albert) Butcher	12.00	6.00	3.50
(24)	E. (Earl) Caldwell	12.00	6.00	3.50
(25)	D. (Dolph) Camilli	12.00	6.00	3.50
(26)	B. (Bruce) Campbell	12.00	6.00	3.50
(27)	J. (Joseph) Cascarella	12.00	6.00	3.50
(28)	C. (Clyde) Castleman	12.00	6.00	3.50
(29)	P. (Philip) Cavarretta	12.00	6.00	3.50
(30)	W. (William) Chapman	12.00	6.00	3.50
(31)	L. (Louis) Chiozza	12.00	6.00	3.50
(32)	H. (Harland)(Harlond) Clift	12.00	6.00	3.50
(33)	G. (Gordon) Cochrane	25.00	12.50	7.50
(34)	J. (James) Collins	12.00	6.00	3.50
(35)	A. (Allen) Cooke	12.00	6.00	3.50
(36)	J. (Joseph) Coscarart	12.00	6.00	3.50
(37)	Roger Cramer	12.00	6.00	3.50
(38)	J. (Joseph) Cronin	20.00	10.00	6.00
(39)	F. (Frank) Crosetti	15.00	7.50	4.50
(40)	A. (Alvin) Crowder	12.00	6.00	3.50
(41)	A. (Anthony) Cuccinello	12.00	6.00	3.50
(42)	H. (Hazen) Cuyler	20.00	10.00	6.00
(43)	H. (Harry) Danning	12.00	6.00	3.50
(44)	V. (Virgil) Davis	12.00	6.00	3.50
(45)	J. (Jerome) Dean	35.00	17.50	10.50
(46)	P. (Paul) Dean	16.00	8.00	4.75
(47)	J. (Joseph) Demaree	12.00	6.00	3.50
(48)	Paul Derringer	12.00	6.00	3.50
(49)	G. (George) Dickey	12.00	6.00	3.50
(50)	W. (William) Dickey	25.00	12.50	7.50
(51)	L. (Leo) Durocher	20.00	10.00	6.00
(52)	J. (James) Dykes	12.00	6.00	3.50
(53)	G. (George) Earnshaw	12.00	6.00	3.50
(54)	E. (Elmwood)(Elwood) English	12.00	6.00	3.50
(55)	R. (Robert) Feller	25.00	12.50	7.50
(56)	R. (Richard) Ferrell	20.00	10.00	6.00
(57)	Wes Ferrell	12.00	6.00	3.50
(58)	(Louis) Finney	12.00	6.00	3.50
(59)	F. (Fred) Fitzsimmons	12.00	6.00	3.50
(60)	Jimmy Foxx	30.00	15.00	9.00
(61)	(Fred) Frankhouse	12.00	6.00	3.50
(62)	L. (Lawrence) French	12.00	6.00	3.50
(63)	(Frank) Frisch	20.00	10.00	6.00
(64)	A. (August) Galan	12.00	6.00	3.50
(65)	H. (Heny)(Henry) Gehrig	60.00	30.00	18.00
(66)	C. (Charles) Gehringer	20.00	10.00	6.00
(67)	(Charles) Gelbert	12.00	6.00	3.50
(68)	A. (Angelo) Giuliani	12.00	6.00	3.50
(69)	V. (Vernon) Gomez	20.00	10.00	6.00
(70)	L. (Leon) Goslin	20.00	10.00	6.00
(71)	R. (Robert) Grace	12.00	6.00	3.50
(72)	C. (Charles) Grimm	12.00	6.00	3.50
(73)	Robert Grove	25.00	12.50	7.50
(74)	G. (George) Haas	12.00	6.00	3.50
(75)	I. (Irving) Hadley	12.00	6.00	3.50
(76)	M. (Melvin) Harder	12.00	6.00	3.50
(77)	C. (Charles) Hartnett	20.00	10.00	6.00
(78)	M. (Minter) Hayes	12.00	6.00	3.50
(79)	R. (Ralston) Hemsley	12.00	6.00	3.50
(80)	F. (Floyd) Herman	12.00	6.00	3.50
(81)	(Michael) Higgins	12.00	6.00	3.50
(82)	M. (Myril) Hoag	12.00	6.00	3.50
(83)	E. (Elon) Hogsett	12.00	6.00	3.50
(84)	R. (Rogers) Hornsby	25.00	12.50	7.50
(85)	W. (Waite) Hoyt	20.00	10.00	6.00
(86)	W. (Willis) Hudlin	12.00	6.00	3.50
(87)	T. (Travis) Jackson	20.00	10.00	6.00
(88)	R. (Robert) Johnson	12.00	6.00	3.50
(89)	R. (Roy) Johnson	12.00	6.00	3.50
(90)	B. (Baxter) Jordan	12.00	6.00	3.50
(91)	W. (William) Jurgess (Jurges)	12.00	6.00	3.50
(92)	(Lloyd) Kennedy	12.00	6.00	3.50
(93)	C. (Charles) Klein	20.00	10.00	6.00
(94)	(William) Knickerbocker	12.00	6.00	3.50
(95)	J. (John) Knott	12.00	6.00	3.50
(96)	M. (Mark) Koenig	12.00	6.00	3.50
(97)	J. (Joseph) Kuhel	12.00	6.00	3.50
(98)	L. (Lynford) Lary	12.00	6.00	3.50
(99)	H. (Harry) Lavagetto	12.00	6.00	3.50
(100)	A. (Anthony) Lazzeri	20.00	10.00	6.00
(101)	W. (William) Lee	12.00	6.00	3.50
(102)	H. (Henry) Leiber	12.00	6.00	3.50
(103)	Wm. (William) Lewis	12.00	6.00	3.50
(104)	E. (Edward) Linke	12.00	6.00	3.50
(105)	E. (Ernest) Lombardi	20.00	10.00	6.00
(106)	Al Lopez	20.00	10.00	6.00
(107)	C. (Charles) Lucas	12.00	6.00	3.50
(108)	T. (Theodore) Lyons	20.00	10.00	6.00
(109)	Dan MacFayden	12.00	6.00	3.50
(110)	P. (Percy)(Perce) Malone	12.00	6.00	3.50
(111)	A. (Augustus) Mancuso	12.00	6.00	3.50
(112)	(John) Martin	15.00	7.50	4.50
(113)	J. (Joseph) Medwick	12.00	6.00	3.50
(114)	E. (Edmund) Miller	12.00	6.00	3.50
(115)	J. (John) Mize	20.00	10.00	6.00
(116)	Gene Moore	12.00	6.00	3.50
(117)	R. (Randolph) Moore	12.00	6.00	3.50
(118)	V. (Van Lingle) Mungo	12.00	6.00	3.50
(119)	C. (Charles) Myer	12.00	6.00	3.50
(120)	A. (Alfred) Niemiec	12.00	6.00	3.50
(121)	(Fred) Ostermueller	12.00	6.00	3.50
(122)	M. (Melvin) Ott	25.00	12.50	7.50
(123)	L. (LeRoy) Parmelee	12.00	6.00	3.50
(124)	A. (Anthony) Piet	12.00	6.00	3.50
(125)	A. (Alvin) Powell	12.00	6.00	3.50
(126)	F. (Frank) Pytlak	12.00	6.00	3.50
(127)	R. (Ray) Radcliff	12.00	6.00	3.50
(128)	R. (Robert) Reis	12.00	6.00	3.50
(129)	(Carl) Reynolds	12.00	6.00	3.50
(130)	J. (John) Rhodes	12.00	6.00	3.50
(131)	R. (Robert) Rolfe	12.00	6.00	3.50
(132)	C. (Charles) Root	12.00	6.00	3.50
(133)	L. (Lynwood) Rowe	12.00	6.00	3.50
(134)	C. (Charles) Ruffing	20.00	10.00	6.00
(135)	F. (Fred) Schulte	12.00	6.00	3.50
(136)	H. (Harold) Schumacher	12.00	6.00	3.50
(137)	J. (James) Sewell	12.00	6.00	3.50
(138)	A. (Aloysius) Simmons	20.00	10.00	6.00
(139)	J. (Julius) Soulters (Solters)	12.00	6.00	3.50
(140)	G. (George) Stainback	12.00	6.00	3.50
(141)	J. (Johnathan)(John) Stone	12.00	6.00	3.50
(142)	J. (Joseph) Stripp	12.00	6.00	3.50
(143)	W. (William) Terry	20.00	10.00	6.00
(144)	T. (Thomas) Thevenow	12.00	6.00	3.50
(145)	A. (Alphonse) Thomas	12.00	6.00	3.50
(146)	C. (Cecil) Travis	12.00	6.00	3.50
(147)	H. (Harold) Traynor	20.00	10.00	6.00
(148)	H. (Harold) Trosky	12.00	6.00	3.50
(149)	R. (Russell) Van Atta	12.00	6.00	3.50
(150)	F. (Floyd) Vaughan	20.00	10.00	6.00
(151)	J. (Joseph) Vosmik	12.00	6.00	3.50
(152)	G. (Gerald) Walker	12.00	6.00	3.50
(153)	W. (William) Walter	12.00	6.00	3.50
(154)	L. (Lloyd) Waner	20.00	10.00	6.00
(155)	P. (Paul) Waner	20.00	10.00	6.00
(156)	L. (Lonnie) Warneke	12.00	6.00	3.50
(157)	G. (George) Watkins	12.00	6.00	3.50
(158)	J. (Joyner) White	12.00	6.00	3.50
(159)	(Burgess) Whitehead	12.00	6.00	3.50
(160)	(Earl) Whitehill	12.00	6.00	3.50
(161)	A. (Arthur) Whitney	12.00	6.00	3.50
(162)	J. (Jack) Wilson	12.00	6.00	3.50
(163)	J. (James) Wilson	12.00	6.00	3.50

1912 Boston Daily American Souvenir Postcards

A second style of postcard issued by a local newspaper to honor the World Champions is labeled at bottom-left "Boston American Souvenir." The 3-1/2" x 5-1/2" cards are printed in black on a cream-colored stock. The player name and position are printed inside the photo frame. In the bottom-right border is a union logo and the number "96." The back has standard postcard markings.

		NM	EX	VG
Common Player:		450.00	225.00	135.00
(1)	Forrest Cady	450.00	225.00	135.00
(2)	Ray Collins	450.00	225.00	135.00
(3)	Rabbit Maranville	600.00	300.00	180.00
(4)	Heinie Wagner	450.00	225.00	135.00
(5)	Joe Wood	500.00	250.00	150.00

1912 Boston Garter

If it weren't for the checklist printed on the back of the few known specimens, the extent of this extremely rare issue would be unknown. Many of the cards mentioned on the back have yet to be seen. Issued by the George Frost Co. of Boston, and packed one card per box of a dozen garters, the approximately 4" x 8-1/4" cards are printed in color lithography on the front, and black-and-white on the back. Fronts have a picture of the player standing near his locker or sitting in a chair, dressing in his uniform. The issuer's Boston-brand garter is prominently shown below the player's boxer shorts. A window in the background displays a cityscape or ballpark scene. There was a card issued for one player on each of the

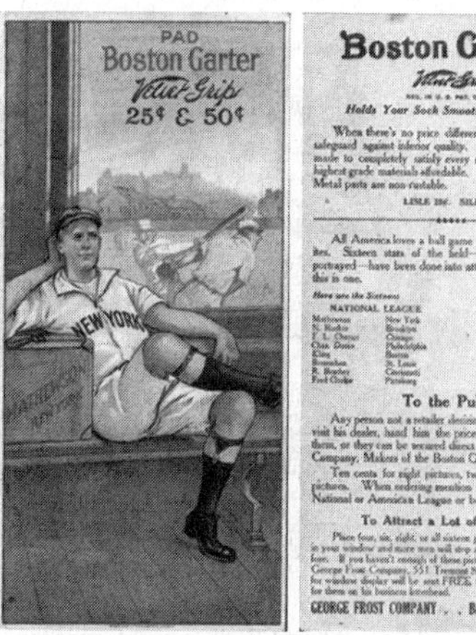

16 major league teams of the day. Large-format (21-1/2" x 11-1/4") cardboard window display posters which reproduce pairs of the cards are sometimes seen in the hobby.

		NM	EX	VG
Common Player:		30,000	12,000	7,250
(1)	Bob Bescher	30,000	12,000	7,250
(2)	Roger Bresnahan	40,000	13,750	8,250
(3)	Frank Chance	40,000	15,000	9,000
(4)	Hal Chase	30,000	12,500	7,500
(5)	Fred Clarke	40,000	13,750	8,250
(6)	Eddie Collins	40,000	13,750	8,250
(7)	Charles Dooin	30,000	12,000	7,250
(8)	Hugh Jennings	40,000	13,750	8,250
(9)	Walter Johnson	60,000	17,500	10,500
(10)	Johnny Kling	30,000	12,000	7,250
(11)	Larry Lajoie	45,000	15,000	9,000
(12)	Frank LaPorte	30,000	12,000	7,250
(13)	Christy Mathewson	75,000	37,500	22,500
(14)	Nap Rucker	30,000	12,000	7,250
(15)	Tris Speaker	45,000	15,000	9,000
(16)	Ed Walsh	40,000	13,750	8,250

1914 Boston Garter - Color

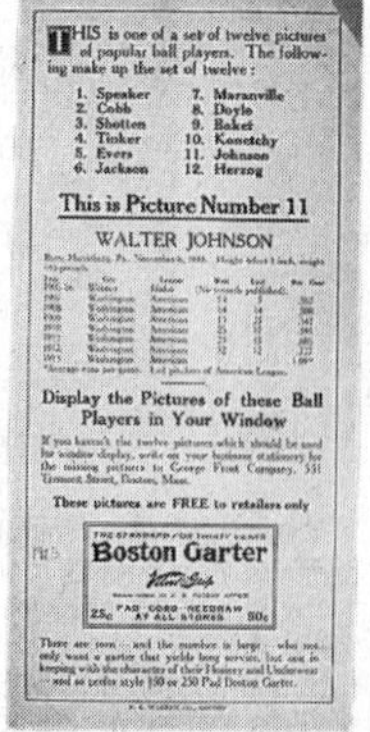

The second of what are presumed to have been three annual issue by the George Frost Co., Boston, contains 12 cards. The colorful lithograph fronts have a player picture in front of a ballpark diagram. A large Boston-brand garter appears at the bottom. Baseballs with the Boston Garter name appear in each upper corner. Black-and-white backs have a checklist for the set, career statistics for the player pictured and details on the cards' availability. Retailers received one card per box of dozen garters and could write to the company to complete the set. About 4" x 8-1/4", they were intended to be displayed in shop windows.

		NM	EX	VG
Common Player:		7,500	3,000	1,800
1	Tris Speaker	30,000	10,000	6,000
2	Ty Cobb	60,000	17,500	10,500
3	Burt Shotten (Shotton)	7,500	3,000	1,800
4	Joe Tinker	15,000	6,250	3,750
5	Johnny Evers	15,500	6,250	3,750
6	Joe Jackson	100,000	30,000	18,000
7	Rabbit Maranville	15,000	6,250	3,750
8	Larry Doyle	7,500	3,000	1,800
9	Frank Baker	15,000	6,250	3,750
10	Ed Konetchy	7,500	3,000	1,800
11	Walter Johnson	35,000	10,000	6,000
12	Buck Herzog	7,500	3,000	1,800

1914 Boston Garter - Sepia

The 1914 date attributed to this 10-card set may or may not be accurate. Since the company's other two known issues can be reliably dated and were produced using the color lithographic process, it is presumed that the use of photographs would have come later. Fronts of the approximately 3-3/4" x 6-1/4" cards feature a green duo-tone photo of the player. His last name appears in white script at the bottom, along with a baseball with the Boston Garter name. Backs

have a checklist of the set and information on how retail store owners can send for additional cards to supplement those which were packaged one per box of a dozen garters.

		NM	EX	VG
Complete Set (10):		140,000	70,000	42,500
Common Player:		15,000	7,500	4,500
1	Christy Mathewson	35,000	20,000	12,500
2	Red Murray	7,500	3,750	2,250
3	Eddie Collins	15,000	7,500	4,500
4	Hugh Jennings	15,000	7,500	4,500
5	Hal Chase	12,000	6,000	3,600
6	Bob Bescher	7,500	3,750	2,250
7	Red Dooin	7,500	3,750	2,250
8	Larry Lajoie	15,000	7,500	4,500
9	Tris Speaker	20,000	10,000	6,000
10	Heinie Zimmerman	7,500	3,750	2,250

1909 Boston Herald Supplements

Members of the Red Sox and Braves were featured in this series of supplements in the Boston Sunday Herald. About 7-1/4" x 9-3/4", the blank-back, posed-action pictures are sepia toned. A black box at bottom has player identification, an issue date and a note to "See Story on Sporting Page." While the pictures themselves are numbered, this checklist, almost certainly incomplete, is arranged alphabetically. Some of the pictures show cross-town rivals on the same piece.

		NM	EX	VG
	BOSTON BRAVES			
(1)	Chick Autry	200.00	100.00	60.00
(2)	Johnny Bates	200.00	100.00	60.00
(3)	Ginger Beaumont	200.00	100.00	60.00
(4)	Beals Becker	200.00	100.00	60.00
(5)	Frank Bowerman	200.00	100.00	60.00
(6)	Jack Coffey	200.00	100.00	60.00
(7)	Peaches Graham	200.00	100.00	60.00
(8)	Al Mattern	200.00	100.00	60.00
(9)	Harry Smith	200.00	100.00	60.00
(10)	Bill Sweeney	200.00	100.00	60.00
(11)	("Tom") Thomas H. Tuckey	200.00	100.00	60.00
	BOSTON RED SOX			
(1)	Charlie Chech	200.00	100.00	60.00
(2)	Bill Carrigan	200.00	100.00	60.00
(3)	Pat Donahue	200.00	100.00	60.00
(4)	"Doc" (Harry H.) Gessler	200.00	100.00	60.00
(5)	Harry Hooper	300.00	150.00	90.00
(5)	Harry Lord	200.00	100.00	60.00
(6)	Amby McConnell	200.00	100.00	60.00
(7)	Harry Niles	200.00	100.00	60.00
(8)	Tris Speaker	400.00	200.00	120.00
	BOSTON BRAVES/RED SOX			
(1)	Johnny Bates, Harry Hooper	150.00	75.00	45.00
(2)	Ginger Beaumont, Tris Speaker	150.00	75.00	45.00
(3)	Ed Cicotte, Tommy Tuckey	250.00	125.00	75.00
(4)	Bill Dahlen, Heinie Wagner	150.00	75.00	45.00
(5)	Doc Gessler, Frank Bowerman	150.00	75.00	45.00
(6)	Harry Lord, Unknown Brave	150.00	75.00	45.00
(7)	Amby McConnell, Jack Coffey	150.00	75.00	45.00
(8)	Harry Smith, Pat Donahue	150.00	75.00	45.00
(9)	Jake Stahl, Chick Autrey (Autry)	150.00	75.00	45.00

1908 Boston Oyster House Chicago Cubs

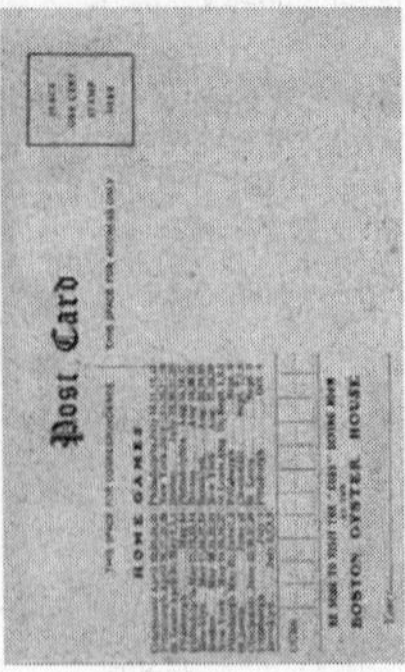

Located in Chicago, not Boston, this restaurant featured, according to its advertising, "The 'Cubs' Dining Room." In keeping with that theme, the business adopted as a promotion the set of Cubs/Teddy Bear postcards issued the previous year by Grignon, a local publisher. The restaurant version has on its back a 1908 Cubs home schedule and rudimentary scorecard, along with standard postcard markings.

	NM	EX	VG
Common Player:	500.00	250.00	150.00
Stars: 1X			

(See 1907 Grignon Chicago Cubs postcards for checklist and base values.)

1908 Boston Red Sox Foldout Postcard

At first glance this standard-size (about 5-1/2" x 3-1/2") postcard reveals on its front only portrait photos of the the owners and grounds of the Boston Red Sox, with a cotter-pinned baseball at left printed in red. Hidden behind the ball, however, is an accordian-folded strip of black-and-white player photos, printed front-to-back, in a size of about 1-1/8" x 1-3/4".

	NM	EX	VG
1908 Boston Red Sox	4,500	2,250	1,350

1910 Boston Red Sox Cabinets

Details are lacking on this high-quality photographic issue depicting the 1910 Red Sox. The sepia photos picture the players in full-length poses and are glued to cardboard mattes. There is no identification on the pieces, nor on the decorative paper folders in which they were apparently originally sold.

		NM	EX	VG
Common Player:		350.00	175.00	100.00
(1)	Hugh Bradley	350.00	175.00	100.00
(2)	Bill Carrigan	350.00	175.00	100.00
(3)	Ed Cicotte	1,000	500.00	300.00
(4)	Ray Collins	350.00	175.00	100.00
(5)	Clyde Engle	350.00	175.00	100.00
(6)	Larry Gardner	350.00	175.00	100.00
(7)	Charley Hall	350.00	175.00	100.00
(8)	Harry Hooper	750.00	375.00	225.00
(9)	Ben Hunt	350.00	175.00	100.00
(10)	Duffy Lewis	500.00	250.00	150.00
(11)	Tom Madden	350.00	175.00	100.00
(12)	Doc Moskiman	350.00	175.00	100.00
(13)	Harry Smith	350.00	175.00	100.00
(14)	Tris Speaker	1,000	500.00	300.00
(15)	Jake Stahl	350.00	175.00	100.00
(16)	Heinie Wagner	350.00	175.00	100.00

1912 Boston Red Sox Tattoos

This set of tattoos is similar to a number of other issues of the era, most of which were made in Germany. This issue features members of the World Champion Boston Red Sox. Approximately 1-3/8" x 1-3/4", the tattoos are printed in mirror-image in bright colors. Images are crude line art with no resemblance to the actual players. Players are identified at bottom by at least a last name. A position is designated in the background of the picture. These items were issued on a perforated sheet. "Collins" may represent retired Red Sox Jimmy Collins or 1912 pitcher Ray Collins. The unnumbered tattoos are listed here alphabetically, though the listing may not be complete.

		NM	EX	VG
Complete Set (13):		475.00	235.00	140.00
Common Player:		35.00	17.50	10.00
(1)	Hugh Bedient	35.00	17.50	10.00
(2)	Hick Cady	35.00	17.50	10.00
(3)	Collins	35.00	17.50	10.00
(4)	Clyde Engle	35.00	17.50	10.00
(5)	Charley Hall	35.00	17.50	10.00
(6)	Martin Krug	35.00	17.50	10.00
(7)	Jerry McCarthy (Mascot)	35.00	17.50	10.00
(8)	Les Nunamaker	35.00	17.50	10.00
(9)	Larry Pape	35.00	17.50	10.00
(10)	Tris Speaker	125.00	65.00	35.00
(11)	Jake Stahl	35.00	17.50	10.00
(12)	Heinie Wagner	35.00	17.50	10.00
(13)	Joe Wood	50.00	25.00	15.00

1940 Boston Red Sox Photo Pack

Approximately 6" x 9", these blank-back, black-and-white pictures depict the BoSox in (usually) neck-to-cap poses. The pictures are bordered in white and there is a facsimile autograph on each photo.

		NM	EX	VG
Complete Set (25):		300.00	150.00	75.00
Common Player:		8.00	4.00	2.50
(1)	Jim Bagby	8.00	4.00	2.50
(2)	Bill Butland	8.00	4.00	2.50
(3)	Tom Carey	8.00	4.00	2.50
(4)	Doc Cramer	8.00	4.00	2.50
(5)	Joe Cronin	15.00	7.50	4.50
(6)	Gene Desautels	8.00	4.00	2.50
(7)	Emerson Dickman	8.00	4.00	2.50
(8)	Dom DiMaggio	15.00	7.50	4.50
(9)	Bobby Doerr	15.00	7.50	4.50
(10)	Lou Finney	8.00	4.00	2.50
(11)	Jimmie Foxx	35.00	17.50	10.00
(12)	Denny Galehouse	8.00	4.00	2.50
(13)	Joe Glenn	8.00	4.00	2.50
(14)	Lefty Grove	30.00	15.00	9.00
(15)	Mickey Harris	8.00	4.00	2.50
(16)	Herbie Hash	8.00	4.00	2.50
(17)	Joe Heving	8.00	4.00	2.50
(18)	Leo Nonnenkamp	8.00	4.00	2.50
(19)	Fritz Ostermueller	8.00	4.00	2.50
(20)	Mickey Owen	8.00	4.00	2.50
(21)	John Peacock	8.00	4.00	2.50
(22)	Jim Tabor	8.00	4.00	2.50
(23)	Charles Wagner	8.00	4.00	2.50
(24)	Ted Williams	60.00	30.00	18.00
(25)	Jack Wilson	8.00	4.00	2.50

1941 Boston Red Sox Photo Pack

Approximately 6" x 9", these blank-back, black-and-white pictures depict the BoSox in informal poses, most leaning on the dugout top step. The pictures are bordered in white and there is a facsimile autograph on each photo. It is possible this checklist (arranged alphabetically) is incomplete as other players may have been added to or deleted from the set to conform to roster changes during the season.

		NM	EX	VG
Complete Set (25):		200.00	100.00	60.00
Common Player:		8.00	4.00	2.50
(1)	Paul Campbell	8.00	4.00	2.50
(2)	Tom Carey	8.00	4.00	2.50
(3)	Joe Cronin	20.00	10.00	6.00
(4)	Emerson Dickman	8.00	4.00	2.50
(5)	Dom DiMaggio	15.00	7.50	4.50
(6)	Joe Dobson	8.00	4.00	2.50
(7)	Bobby Doerr	12.00	6.00	3.50
(8)	Lou Finney	8.00	4.00	2.50
(9)	Bill Fleming	8.00	4.00	2.50
(10)	Pete Fox	8.00	4.00	2.50
(11)	Jimmie Foxx	30.00	15.00	9.00
(12)	Lefty Grove	25.00	12.50	7.50
(13)	Mickey Harris	8.00	4.00	2.50
(14)	Tex Hughson	8.00	4.00	2.50
(15)	Earl Johnson	8.00	4.00	2.50
(16)	Lefty Judd	8.00	4.00	2.50
(17)	Dick Newsome	8.00	4.00	2.50
(18)	Skeeter Newsome	8.00	4.00	2.50
(19)	John Peacock	8.00	4.00	2.50
(20)	Frank Pytlak	8.00	4.00	2.50
(21)	Mike Ryba	8.00	4.00	2.50
(22)	Stan Spence	8.00	4.00	2.50
(23)	Jim Tabor	8.00	4.00	2.50
(24)	Charlie Wagner	8.00	4.00	2.50
(25)	Ted Williams	50.00	25.00	15.00
(26)	Jack Wilson	8.00	4.00	2.50

1942 Boston Red Sox Photo Pack

In a format of approximately 6-1/2" x 9", these team-issued player portraits are blank-backed, black-and-white with a white border. Most photos are chest-to-cap presentations and all have a facsimile autograph. Some of the players in the issue can be seen wearing the "HEALTH" patch which MLB adopted during World War II. This checklist may not be complete as it is possible some players were added or deleted from the set to reflect mid-season roster moves.

		NM	EX	VG
Complete Set (25):		275.00	135.00	85.00
Common Player:		10.00	5.00	3.00
(1)	Mace Brown	10.00	5.00	3.00
(2)	Bill Butland	10.00	5.00	3.00
(3)	Paul Campbell	10.00	5.00	3.00
(4)	Tom Carey	10.00	5.00	3.00
(5)	Ken Chase	10.00	5.00	3.00
(6)	Bill Conroy	10.00	5.00	3.00
(7)	Joe Cronin	20.00	10.00	6.00
(8)	Dom DiMaggio	20.00	10.00	6.00
(9)	Joe Dobson	10.00	5.00	3.00
(10)	Bobby Doerr	20.00	10.00	6.00
(11)	Lou Finney	10.00	5.00	3.00
(12)	Pete Fox	10.00	5.00	3.00
(13)	Jimmie Foxx	40.00	20.00	12.00
(14)	Tex Hughson	10.00	5.00	3.00
(15)	Oscar Judd	10.00	5.00	3.00
(16)	Tony Lupien	10.00	5.00	3.00
(17)	Dick Newsome	10.00	5.00	3.00
(18)	Skeeter Newsome	10.00	5.00	3.00
(19)	John Peacock	10.00	5.00	3.00
(20)	Johnny Pesky	10.00	5.00	3.00
(21)	Mike Ryba	10.00	5.00	3.00
(22)	Jim Tabor	10.00	5.00	3.00
(23)	Yank Terry	10.00	5.00	3.00
(24)	Charlie Wagner	10.00	5.00	3.00
(25)	Ted Williams	60.00	30.00	18.00

1943 Boston Red Sox Photo Pack

In a format of approximately 6-1/2" x 9", these team-issued player portraits are blank-backed, black-and-white with a white border. Most photos are chest-to-cap presentations and all have a facsimile autograph. Some of the players in the issue can be seen wearing the "HEALTH" patch which MLB adopted during World War II. This checklist may not be complete as it is possible some players were added or deleted from the set to reflect mid-season roster moves.

		NM	EX	VG
Complete Set (24):		125.00	65.00	40.00
Common Player:		8.00	4.00	2.50
(1)	Mace Brown	8.00	4.00	2.50
(2)	Ken Chase	8.00	4.00	2.50
(3)	Bill Conroy	8.00	4.00	2.50
(4)	Joe Cronin	15.00	7.50	4.50
(5)	Joe Dobson	8.00	4.00	2.50
(6)	Bobby Doerr	15.00	7.50	4.50
(7)	Pete Fox	8.00	4.00	2.50
(8)	Ford Garrison	8.00	4.00	2.50
(9)	Tex Hughson	8.00	4.00	2.50
(10)	Oscar Judd	8.00	4.00	2.50
(11)	Andy Karl	8.00	4.00	2.50
(12)	Eddie Lake	8.00	4.00	2.50
(13)	John Lazor	8.00	4.00	2.50
(14)	Lou Lucier	10.00	5.00	3.00
(15)	Tony Lupien	8.00	4.00	2.50
(16)	Dee Miles	8.00	4.00	2.50
(17)	Dick Newsome	8.00	4.00	2.50
(18)	Skeeter Newsome	8.00	4.00	2.50
(19)	Roy Partee	8.00	4.00	2.50
(20)	John Peacock	8.00	4.00	2.50
(21)	Mike Ryba	8.00	4.00	2.50
(22)	Al Simmons	15.00	7.50	4.50
(23)	Jim Tabor	8.00	4.00	2.50
(24)	Yank Terry	8.00	4.00	2.50

1946 Boston Red Sox Photo Pack

The American League champion Red Sox are featured in this team-issue photo pack. The player portraits are printed in black-and-white on heavy paper in 6-1/2" x 9" format. The photos have a white border and a facsimile autograph on front. Backs are blank. The unnumbered pictures are listed here in alphabetical order.

		NM	EX	VG
Complete Set (25):		225.00	110.00	65.00
Common Player:		6.00	3.00	1.75
(1)	Ernie Andres	6.00	3.00	1.75
(2)	Jim Bagby	6.00	3.00	1.75
(3)	Mace Brown	6.00	3.00	1.75
(4)	Joe Cronin	12.00	6.00	3.50
(5)	Leon Culberstson	6.00	3.00	1.75
(6)	Mel Deutsch	6.00	3.00	1.75
(7)	Dom DiMaggio	10.00	5.00	3.00
(8)	Joe Dobson	6.00	3.00	1.75
(9)	Bobby Doerr	12.00	6.00	3.50
(10)	Boo Ferriss	6.00	3.00	1.75
(11)	Mickey Harris	6.00	3.00	1.75
(12)	Randy Heflin	6.00	3.00	1.75
(13)	Tex Hughson	6.00	3.00	1.75
(14)	Earl Johnson	6.00	3.00	1.75
(15)	Ed McGah	6.00	3.00	1.75
(16)	George Metkovich	6.00	3.00	1.75
(17)	Roy Partee	6.00	3.00	1.75
(18)	Eddie Pellagrini	6.00	3.00	1.75
(19)	Johnny Pesky	7.50	3.75	2.25
(20)	Rip Russell	6.00	3.00	1.75
(21)	Mike Ryba	6.00	3.00	1.75
(22)	Charlie Wagner	6.00	3.00	1.75
(23)	Hal Wagner	6.00	3.00	1.75
(24)	Ted Williams	60.00	30.00	18.00
(25)	Rudy York	6.00	3.00	1.75

1947 Boston Red Sox Photo Pack

In the same 6-1/2" x 9" format which the team had used for its photo packs since 1942, this set of black-and-white, blank-back pictures features (usually) chest-to-cap portraits with white borders, a dark background and a facsimile autograph within the picture. Some of the photos were re-used from previous years' issues, or were re-issued in subsequent years. The unnumbered pictures are checklisted here in alphabetical order. This list may or may not be complete; it is possible other players' photos were added or deleted to reflect seasonal roster changes.

		NM	EX	VG
Complete Set (25):		200.00	100.00	60.00
Common Player:		6.00	3.00	1.75
(1)	Joe Cronin	15.00	7.50	4.50
(2)	Leon Culberson	6.00	3.00	1.75
(3)	Dom DiMaggio	12.50	6.25	3.75
(4)	Joseph Dobson	6.00	3.00	1.75
(5)	Bobby Doerr	15.00	7.50	4.50
(6)	Harry Dorish	6.00	3.00	1.75
(7)	Dave "Boo" Ferriss	6.00	3.00	1.75
(8)	Tommy Fine	6.00	3.00	1.75
(9)	Don Gutteridge	6.00	3.00	1.75
(10)	Mickey Harris	6.00	3.00	1.75
(11)	Tex Hughson	6.00	3.00	1.75
(12)	Earl Johnson	6.00	3.00	1.75
(13)	Bob Klinger	6.00	3.00	1.75
(14)	Sam Mele	6.00	3.00	1.75
(15)	Wally Moses	6.00	3.00	1.75
(16)	Johnny Murphy	6.00	3.00	1.75
(17)	Mel Parnell	6.00	3.00	1.75
(18)	Roy Partee	6.00	3.00	1.75
(19)	Eddie Pellagrini	6.00	3.00	1.75
(20)	Johnny Pesky	7.50	3.75	2.25
(21)	Rip Russell	6.00	3.00	1.75
(22)	Birdie Tebbetts	6.00	3.00	1.75
(23)	Ted Williams	60.00	30.00	18.00
(24)	Rudy York	6.00	3.00	1.75
(25)	Bill Zuber	6.00	3.00	1.75

1948 Boston Red Sox Photo Pack

In the same 6-1/2" x 9" format which the team had used for its photo packs since 1942, this set of black-and-white, blank-back pictures features (usually) chest-to-cap portraits with white borders, a dark background and a facsimile autograph within the picture. Some of the photos were re-used from previous years' issues, or were re-issued in subsequent years. The unnumbered pictures are checklisted here in alphabetical order. This list may or may not be complete; it is possible other players' photos were added or deleted to reflect seasonal roster changes.

		NM	EX	VG
Complete Set (25):		200.00	100.00	60.00
Common Player:		6.00	3.00	1.75
(1)	Matt Batts	6.00	3.00	1.75
(2)	Dom DiMaggio	15.00	7.50	4.50
(3)	Joseph Dobson	6.00	3.00	1.75
(4)	Bobby Doerr	15.00	7.50	4.50
(5)	Harry Dorish	6.00	3.00	1.75
(6)	Dave "Boo" Ferriss	6.00	3.00	1.75
(7)	Dennis Galehouse	6.00	3.00	1.75
(8)	Billy Goodman	6.00	3.00	1.75
(9)	Mickey Harris	6.00	3.00	1.75
(10)	Bill Hitchcock	6.00	3.00	1.75
(11)	Earl Johnson	6.00	3.00	1.75
(12)	Jake Jones	6.00	3.00	1.75
(13)	Ellis Kinder	6.00	3.00	1.75
(14)	Jack Kramer	6.00	3.00	1.75
(15)	Joe McCarthy	15.00	7.50	4.50
(16)	Maurice McDermott	6.00	3.00	1.75
(17)	Sam Mele	6.00	3.00	1.75
(18)	Wally Moses	6.00	3.00	1.75
(19)	Mel Parnell	6.00	3.00	1.75
(20)	Johnny Pesky	7.50	3.75	2.25
(21)	Stan Spence	6.00	3.00	1.75
(22)	Vern Stephens	6.00	3.00	1.75
(23)	Chuck Stobbs	6.00	3.00	1.75
(24)	Birdie Tebbetts	6.00	3.00	1.75
(25)	Ted Williams	60.00	30.00	18.00

1949 Boston Red Sox Photo Pack

In the same 6-1/2" x 9" format the team used for its photo packs since 1942, this set of black-and-white, blank-back pictures features (usually) chest-to-cap portraits with white borders, a dark background and a facsimile autograph within the picture. Some of the photos were re-used from previous years' issues, or were re-issued in subsequent years. The unnumbered pictures are checklisted here in alphabetical order.

		NM	EX	VG
Complete Set (25):		200.00	100.00	60.00
Common Player:		6.00	3.00	1.80
(1)	Matt Batts	6.00	3.00	1.80
(2)	Merrill Combs	6.00	3.00	1.80
(3)	Dom DiMaggio	15.00	7.50	4.50
(4)	Joe Dobson	6.00	3.00	1.80

(5)	Bobby Doerr	15.00	7.50	4.50
(6)	David "Boo" Ferris	6.00	3.00	1.80
(7)	Bill Goodman	6.00	3.00	1.80
(8)	Mickey Harris	6.00	3.00	1.80
(9)	Billy Hitchcock	6.00	3.00	1.80
(10)	Tex Hughson	6.00	3.00	1.80
(11)	Earl Johnson	6.00	3.00	1.80
(12)	Ellis Kinder	6.00	3.00	1.80
(13)	Jack Kramer	6.00	3.00	1.80
(14)	Joe McCarthy	15.00	7.50	4.50
(15)	Sam Mele	6.00	3.00	1.80
(16)	Tommy O'Brien	6.00	3.00	1.80
(17)	Mel Parnell	6.00	3.00	1.80
(18)	Johnny Pesky	6.00	3.00	1.80
(19)	Frank Quinn	6.00	3.00	1.80
(20)	Vern Stephens	6.00	3.00	1.80
(21)	Chuck Stobbs	6.00	3.00	1.80
(22)	Lou Stringer	6.00	3.00	1.80
(23)	Birdie Tebbetts	6.00	3.00	1.80
(24)	Ted Williams	60.00	30.00	18.00
(25)	Al Zarilla	6.00	3.00	1.80

1950 Boston Red Sox Photo Pack

In the same approximately 6-1/2" x 9" format which the team had used for its photo packs since the 1940s, this set of black-and-white, blank-back pictures features (usually) chest-to-cap portraits with white borders, a dark background and a facsimile autograph within the photo. Some of the photos were re-used from previous years' issues. The unnumbered pictures are checklisted here in alphabetical order. This list may or may not be complete; it is possible other players' photos were added or deleted to reflect seasonal roster changes.

		NM	EX	VG
Complete Set (25):		150.00	75.00	40.00
Common Player:		4.00	2.00	1.25
(1)	Matt Batts	4.00	2.00	1.25
(2)	Earle Combs	7.50	3.75	2.25
(3)	Dom DiMaggio	9.00	4.50	2.75
(4)	Joe Dobson	4.00	2.00	1.25
(5)	Bobby Doerr	9.00	4.50	2.75
(6)	Walt Dropo	12.00	6.00	3.50
(7)	Bill Goodman	4.00	2.00	1.25
(8)	Earl Johnson	4.00	2.00	1.25
(9)	Ken Keltner	4.00	2.00	1.25
(10)	Ellis Kinder	4.00	2.00	1.25
(11)	Walt Masterson	4.00	2.00	1.25
(12)	Joe McCarthy	9.00	4.50	2.75
(13)	Maurice McDermott	4.00	2.00	1.25
(14)	Al Papai	4.00	2.00	1.25
(15)	Mel Parnell	4.00	2.00	1.25
(16)	Johnny Pesky	4.00	2.00	1.25
(17)	Buddy Rosar	4.00	2.00	1.25
(18)	Charley Schanz	4.00	2.00	1.25
(19)	Vern Stephens	4.00	2.00	1.25
(20)	Chuck Stobbs	4.00	2.00	1.25
(21)	Lou Stringer	4.00	2.00	1.25
(22)	Birdie Tebbetts	4.00	2.00	1.25
(23)	Ted Williams	30.00	15.00	9.00
(24)	Tom Wright	4.00	2.00	1.25
(25)	Al Zarilla	4.00	2.00	1.25

1953 Boston Red Sox Photo Pack

In the same approximately 6-1/2" x 9" format which the team had used for its photo packs since the 1940s, this set of black-and-white, blank-back pictures features (usually) chest-to-cap portraits with white borders and a facsimile autograph within the photo. Some of the photos were re-used from previous years' issues. The unnumbered pictures are checklisted here in alphabetical order. This list may or may not be complete; it is possible other players' photos were added or deleted to reflect seasonal roster changes.

		NM	EX	VG
Complete Set (30):		120.00	60.00	35.00
Common Player:		4.00	2.00	1.25
(1)	Milt Bolling	4.00	2.00	1.25
(2)	Lou Boudreau	9.00	4.50	2.75
(3)	Harold Brown	4.00	2.00	1.25
(4)	Bill Consolo	4.00	2.00	1.25
(5)	Dom DiMaggio	15.00	7.50	4.50
(6)	Hoot Evers	4.00	2.00	1.25
(7)	Ben Flowers	4.00	2.00	1.25
(8)	Hershell Freeman	4.00	2.00	1.25
(9)	Dick Gernert	4.00	2.00	1.25
(10)	Bill Goodman	4.00	2.00	1.25
(11)	Marv Grissom	4.00	2.00	1.25
(12)	Ken Holcombe	4.00	2.00	1.25
(13)	Sid Hudson	4.00	2.00	1.25
(14)	George Kell	9.00	4.50	2.75
(15)	Bill Kennedy	4.00	2.00	1.25
(16)	Ellis Kinder	4.00	2.00	1.25
(17)	Ted Lepcio	4.00	2.00	1.25
(18)	Johnny Lipon	4.00	2.00	1.25
(19)	Maurice McDermott	4.00	2.00	1.25
(20)	John Merson	4.00	2.00	1.25
(21)	Gus Niarhos	4.00	2.00	1.25
(22)	Willard Nixon	4.00	2.00	1.25
(23)	Mel Parnell	4.00	2.00	1.25
(24)	Jim Piersall	6.00	3.00	1.75
(25)	Gene Stephens	4.00	2.00	1.25
(26)	Tommy Umphlett	4.00	2.00	1.25
(27)	Bill Werle	4.00	2.00	1.25
(28)	Sam White	4.00	2.00	1.25
(29)	Del Wilber	4.00	2.00	1.25
(30)	Al Zarilla	4.00	2.00	1.25

1954 Boston Red Sox Photo Pack

In the same approximately 6-1/2" x 9" format which the team had used for its photo packs since the 1940s, this set of black-and-white, blank-back pictures features (usually) chest-to-cap portraits with white borders and a facsimile autograph within the photo. Some of the photos were re-used from previous years' issues. The unnumbered pictures are checklisted here in alphabetical order. This list may or may not be complete; it is possible other players' photos were added or deleted to reflect seasonal roster changes. The set was sold in a red and white paper envelope.

		NM	EX	VG
Complete Set (30):		125.00	62.50	37.50
Common Player:		4.00	2.00	1.25
(1)	Harry Agganis	15.00	7.50	4.50
(2)	Milt Bolling	4.00	2.00	1.25
(3)	Lou Boudreau	9.00	4.50	2.75
(4)	Tom Brewer	4.00	2.00	1.25
(5)	Harold Brown	4.00	2.00	1.25
(6)	Truman Clevenger	4.00	2.00	1.25
(7)	Bill Consolo	4.00	2.00	1.25
(8)	Joe Dobson	4.00	2.00	1.25
(9)	Hoot Evers	4.00	2.00	1.25
(10)	Dick Gernert	4.00	2.00	1.25
(11)	Bill Goodman	4.00	2.00	1.25
(12)	Bill Henry	4.00	2.00	1.25
(13)	Tom Herrin	4.00	2.00	1.25
(14)	Sid Hudson	4.00	2.00	1.25
(15)	Jackie Jensen	6.00	3.00	1.75
(16)	George Kell	9.00	4.50	2.75
(17)	Leo Kiely	4.00	2.00	1.25
(18)	Ellis Kinder	4.00	2.00	1.25
(19)	Ted Lepcio	4.00	2.00	1.25
(20)	Charlie Maxwell	4.00	2.00	1.25
(21)	Willard Nixon	4.00	2.00	1.25
(22)	Karl Olsen	4.00	2.00	1.25
(23)	Mickey Owen	4.00	2.00	1.25
(24)	Mel Parnell	4.00	2.00	1.25
(25)	Jim Piersall	6.00	3.00	1.75
(26)	Frank Sullivan	4.00	2.00	1.25
(27)	Bill Werle	4.00	2.00	1.25
(28)	Sammy White	4.00	2.00	1.25
(29)	Ted Williams	30.00	15.00	9.00
(30)	Del Wilber	4.00	2.00	1.25

1957 Boston Red Sox Photo Pack

JIMMY PIERSALL

In approximately the same 5" x 7" black-and-white, blank-back format as the later Jay Publishing issues, this team issue is distinguished by the lack of a team name in the bottom border. Some of the photos were re-used in the following year's issue. Sets were originally sold in a manila envelope for 25 cents.

		NM	EX	VG
Complete Set (12):		45.00	22.00	13.50
Common Player:		3.00	1.50	.90
(1)	Tom Brewer	3.00	1.50	.90
(2)	Dick Gernert	3.00	1.50	.90
(3)	Mike Higgins	3.00	1.50	.90
(4)	Jackie Jensen	4.50	2.25	1.25
(5)	Frank Malzone	3.00	1.50	.90
(6)	Gene Mauch	4.50	2.25	1.25
(7)	Jimmy Piersall	4.50	2.25	1.25
(8)	Dave Sisler	3.00	1.50	.90
(9)	Frank Sullivan	3.00	1.50	.90
(10)	Mickey Vernon	3.00	1.50	.90
(11)	Sammy White	3.00	1.50	.90
(12)	Ted Williams	20.00	10.00	6.00

1958 Boston Red Sox Photo Pack

In approximately the same 5" x 7" black-and-white, blank-back format as the contemporary Jay Publishing issues, this team issue is distinguished by the lack of a team name in the bottom border. Some of the photos were re-used from the previous year's issue. Sets were originally sold in a manila envelope for 25 cents.

		NM	EX	VG
Complete Set (12):		45.00	22.00	13.50
Common Player:		3.00	1.50	.90
(1)	Ken Aspromonte	3.00	1.50	.90
(2)	Tom Brewer	3.00	1.50	.90
(3)	Mike Higgins	3.00	1.50	.90
(4)	Jack Jensen	4.50	2.25	1.25
(5)	Frank Malzone	3.00	1.50	.90
(6)	Will Nixon	3.00	1.50	.90
(7)	Jim Piersall	4.50	2.25	1.25
(8)	Pete Runnels	3.00	1.50	.90
(9)	Gene Stephens	3.00	1.50	.90
(10)	Frank Sullivan	3.00	1.50	.90
(11)	Sam White	3.00	1.50	.90
(12)	Ted Williams	20.00	10.00	6.00

1959 Boston Red Sox Photo Pack

In approximately the same 5" x 7" black-and-white, blank-back format as the contemporary Jay Publishing issues, this team issue is distinguished by the lack of a team name in the bottom border. Some of the photos were re-used from the previous years' issues. Sets were originally sold in a manila envelope for 25 cents.

		NM	EX	VG
Complete Set (12):		45.00	22.00	13.50
Common Player:		3.00	1.50	.90
(1)	Tom Brewer	3.00	1.50	.90
(2)	Don Buddin	3.00	1.50	.90
(3)	Dick Gernert	3.00	1.50	.90
(4)	Mike Higgins	3.00	1.50	.90
(5)	Jack Jensen	4.50	2.25	1.25
(6)	Frank Malzone	3.00	1.50	.90
(7)	Jim Piersall	4.50	2.25	1.25
(8)	Pete Runnels	3.00	1.50	.90
(9)	Gene Stephens	3.00	1.50	.90
(10)	Frank Sullivan	3.00	1.50	.90
(11)	Sam White	3.00	1.50	.90
(12)	Ted Williams	20.00	10.00	6.00

1960 Boston Red Sox Photo Pack

In approximately the same 5" x 7" black-and-white, blank-back format as the contemporary Jay Publishing issues, this team issue is distinguished by the lack of a team name in the bottom border. Some of the photos were re-used from the previous years' issues. Sets were originally sold in a manila envelope for 25 cents. The fact that more than 12 players are known indicates there were some changes in specific contents over the course of the season to reflect roster changes.

		NM	EX	VG
Complete Set (14):		50.00	25.00	15.00
Common Player:		3.00	1.50	.90
(1)	Tom Brewer	3.00	1.50	.90
(2)	Don Buddin	3.00	1.50	.90
(3)	Jerry Casale	3.00	1.50	.90

(4)	Ike Delock	3.00	1.50	.90
(5)	Pumpsie Green	3.00	1.50	.90
(6)	Bill Jurges	3.00	1.50	.90
(7)	Frank Malzone	3.00	1.50	.90
(8)	Pete Runnels	3.00	1.50	.90
(9)	Ed Sadowski	3.00	1.50	.90
(10)	Gene Stephens	3.00	1.50	.90
(11)	Willie Tasby	3.00	1.50	.90
(12)	Bobby Thomson	3.00	1.50	.90
(13)	Vic Wertz	3.00	1.50	.90
(14)	Ted Williams	20.00	10.00	6.00

1968 Boston Red Sox Team Issue

About 5-1/2" x 7-1/2", these black-and-white player pictures have posed photos, bordered in white, with a facsimile autograph. Backs are blank. The alphabetized checklist here is likely incomplete.

		NM	EX	VG
Complete Set (8):		15.00	7.50	4.50
Common Player:		2.00	1.00	.60
(1a)	Mike Andrews ("B" on cap.)	2.00	1.00	.60
(1b)	Mike Andrews (No "B.")	2.00	1.00	.60
(2)	Darrell Brandon	2.00	1.00	.60
(3)	Bobby Doerr	3.00	1.50	.90
(4)	Ken Harrelson	2.50	1.25	.70
(5)	Jim Lonborg	2.50	1.25	.70
(6)	Rico Petrocelli	3.00	1.50	.90
(7)	Reggie Smith	2.50	1.25	.70
(8)	Dick Williams	2.00	1.00	.60

1969 Boston Red Sox Team Issue

This team-issue photo pack features black-and-white portrait photos on a 4-1/4" x 7" blank-back format, similar to the team's 1971 issue. The player's name and team nickname are designated in the white border at top. The unnumbered cards are checklisted here in alphabetical order.

		NM	EX	VG
Complete Set (12):		60.00	30.00	15.00
Common Player:		4.00	2.00	1.25
(1)	Mike Andrews	4.00	2.00	1.25
(2)	Tony Conigliaro	9.00	4.50	2.75
(3)	Russ Gibson	4.00	2.00	1.25
(4)	Dalton Jones	4.00	2.00	1.25
(5)	Bill Landis	4.00	2.00	1.25
(6)	Jim Lonborg	5.00	2.50	1.50
(7)	Sparky Lyle	4.00	2.00	1.25
(8)	Rico Petrocelli	5.00	2.50	1.50
(9)	George Scott	5.00	2.50	1.50
(10)	Reggie Smith	4.00	2.00	1.25
(11)	Dick Williams	4.00	2.00	1.25
(12)	Carl Yastrzemski	15.00	7.50	4.50

1978 Boston Red Sox of the 1950s-1960s

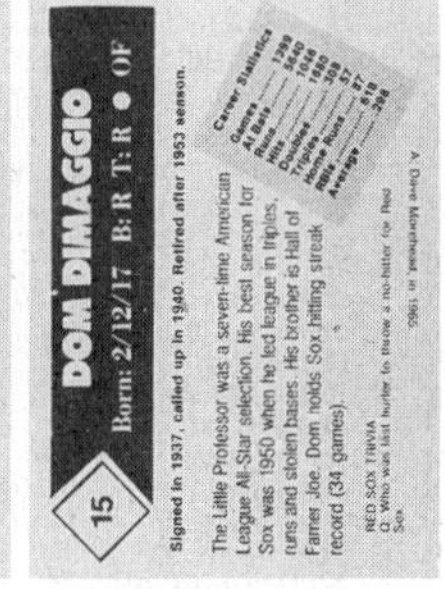

The date of actual issue, the name of the issuer and even the "official" title of this collectors' edition card set is currently unknown. The 2-1/2" x 3-1/2" cards are printed in black-and-white on front and backs. Fronts have the style of the 1953 Bowmans, with only a player photo and a white border. Backs are reminiscent of the 1955 Bowman, with player identification, career highlights, stats and a Red Sox trivia question. Cards #1-64 concentrate on the 1950s, cards #65-128 feature 1960s players.

		NM	EX	VG
Complete Set (128):		100.00	50.00	30.00
Common Player:		4.00	2.00	1.25
1	Harry Agganis	12.00	6.00	3.50
2	Ken Aspromonte	4.00	2.00	1.25
3	Bobby Avila	4.00	2.00	1.25
4	Frank Baumann	4.00	2.00	1.25
5	Lou Berberet	4.00	2.00	1.25
6	Milt Bolling	4.00	2.00	1.25
7	Lou Boudreau	6.00	3.00	1.75
8	Ted Bowsfield	4.00	2.00	1.25
9	Tom Brewer	4.00	2.00	1.25
10	Don Buddin	4.00	2.00	1.25
11	Jerry Casale	4.00	2.00	1.25
12	Billy Consolo	4.00	2.00	1.25
13	Pete Daley	4.00	2.00	1.25
14	Ike Delock	4.00	2.00	1.25
15	Dom DiMaggio	9.00	4.50	2.75
16	Bobby Doerr	6.00	3.00	1.75
17	Walt Dropo	5.00	2.50	1.50
18	Arnie Earley	4.00	2.00	1.25
19	Hoot Evers	4.00	2.00	1.25
20	Mike Fornieles	4.00	2.00	1.25
21	Gary Geiger	4.00	2.00	1.25
22	Don Gile	4.00	2.00	1.25
23	Joe Ginsberg	4.00	2.00	1.25
24	Billy Goodman	4.00	2.00	1.25
25	Pumpsie Green	4.00	2.00	1.25
26	Grady Hatton	4.00	2.00	1.25
27	Billy Herman	5.00	2.50	1.50
28	Jackie Jensen	5.00	2.50	1.50
29	George Kell	6.00	3.00	1.75
30	Marty Keough	4.00	2.00	1.25
31	Leo Kiely	4.00	2.00	1.25
32	Ellis Kinder	4.00	2.00	1.25
33	Billy Klaus	4.00	2.00	1.25
34	Don Lenhardt	4.00	2.00	1.25
35	Ted Lepcio	4.00	2.00	1.25
36	Frank Malzone	4.00	2.00	1.25
37	Gene Mauch	4.00	2.00	1.25
38	Maury McDermott	4.00	2.00	1.25
39	Bill Monbouquette	4.00	2.00	1.25
40	Chet Nichols	4.00	2.00	1.25
41	Willard Nixon	4.00	2.00	1.25
42	Jim Pagliaroni	4.00	2.00	1.25
43	Mel Parnell	4.00	2.00	1.25
44	Johnny Pesky	4.00	2.00	1.25
45	Jimmy Piersall	5.00	2.50	1.50
46	Bob Porterfield	4.00	2.00	1.25
47	Pete Runnels	4.00	2.00	1.25
48	Dave Sisler	4.00	2.00	1.25
49	Riverboat Smith	4.00	2.00	1.25
50	Gene Stephens	4.00	2.00	1.25
51	Vern Stephens	4.00	2.00	1.25
52	Chuck Stobbs	4.00	2.00	1.25
53	Dean Stone	4.00	2.00	1.25
54	Frank Sullivan	4.00	2.00	1.25
55	Haywood Sullivan	4.00	2.00	1.25
56	Birdie Tebbetts	4.00	2.00	1.25
57	Mickey Vernon	4.00	2.00	1.25
58	Vic Wertz	4.00	2.00	1.25
59	Sammy White	4.00	2.00	1.25
60	Ted Williams	20.00	10.00	6.00
61	Ted Wills	4.00	2.00	1.25
62	Earl Wilson	4.00	2.00	1.25
63	Al Zarilla	4.00	2.00	1.25
64	Norm Zauchin	4.00	2.00	1.25
65	Ted Williams, Carl Yastrzemski	12.00	6.00	3.50
66	Dick Williams, Carl Yastrzemski, Jim Lonborg, George Scott	10.00	5.00	3.00
67	Tony Conigliaro, Billy Conigliaro	9.00	4.50	2.75
68	Jerry Adair	4.00	2.00	1.25
69	Mike Andrews	4.00	2.00	1.25
70	Gary Bell	4.00	2.00	1.25
71	Dennis Bennett	4.00	2.00	1.25
72	Ed Bressoud	4.00	2.00	1.25
73	Ken Brett	4.00	2.00	1.25
74	Lu Clinton	4.00	2.00	1.25
75	Billy Conigliaro	5.00	2.50	1.50
76	Tony Conigliaro	6.00	3.00	1.75
77	Gene Conley	4.00	2.00	1.25
78	Ray Culp	4.00	2.00	1.25
79	Dick Ellsworth	4.00	2.00	1.25
80	Joe Foy	4.00	2.00	1.25
81	Russ Gibson	4.00	2.00	1.25
82	Jim Gosger	4.00	2.00	1.25
83	Lennie Green	4.00	2.00	1.25
84	Ken Harrelson	4.00	2.00	1.25
85	Tony Horton	4.00	2.00	1.25
86	Elston Howard	5.00	2.50	1.50
87	Dalton Jones	4.00	2.00	1.25
88	Eddie Kasko	4.00	2.00	1.25
89	Joe Lahoud	4.00	2.00	1.25
90	Jack Lamabe	4.00	2.00	1.25
91	Jim Lonborg	5.00	2.50	1.50
92	Sparky Lyle	5.00	2.50	1.50
93	Felix Mantilla	4.00	2.00	1.25
94	Roman Mejias	4.00	2.00	1.25
95	Don McMahon	4.00	2.00	1.25
96	Dave Morehead	4.00	2.00	1.25
97	Gerry Moses	4.00	2.00	1.25
98	Mike Nagy	4.00	2.00	1.25
99	Russ Nixon	4.00	2.00	1.25
100	Gene Oliver	4.00	2.00	1.25
101	Dan Osinski	4.00	2.00	1.25
102	Rico Petrocelli	5.00	2.50	1.50
103	Juan Pizarro	4.00	2.00	1.25
104	Dick Radatz	4.00	2.00	1.25
105	Vicente Romo	4.00	2.00	1.25
106	Mike Ryan	4.00	2.00	1.25
107	Jose Santiago	4.00	2.00	1.25
108	Chuck Schilling	4.00	2.00	1.25
109	Dick Schofield	4.00	2.00	1.25
110	Don Schwall	4.00	2.00	1.25
111	George Scott	4.00	2.00	1.25
112	Norm Siebern	4.00	2.00	1.25
113	Sonny Seibert	4.00	2.00	1.25
114	Reggie Smith	4.00	2.00	1.25
115	Bill Spanswick	4.00	2.00	1.25
116	Tracy Stallard	4.00	2.00	1.25
117	Lee Stange	4.00	2.00	1.25
118	Jerry Stephenson	4.00	2.00	1.25
119	Dick Stuart	4.00	2.00	1.25
120	Tom Sturdivant	4.00	2.00	1.25
121	Jose Tartabull	4.00	2.00	1.25
122	George Thomas	4.00	2.00	1.25
123	Lee Thomas	4.00	2.00	1.25
124	Bob Tillman	4.00	2.00	1.25
125	Gary Waslewski	4.00	2.00	1.25
126	Dick Williams	4.00	2.00	1.25
127	John Wyatt	4.00	2.00	1.25
128	Carl Yastrzemski	12.00	6.00	3.50

1979 Boston Red Sox Team Issue

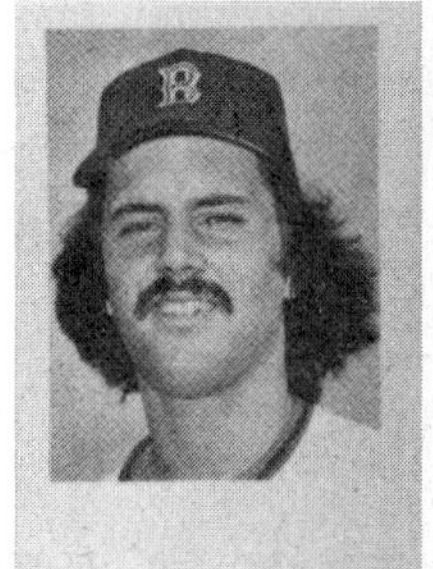

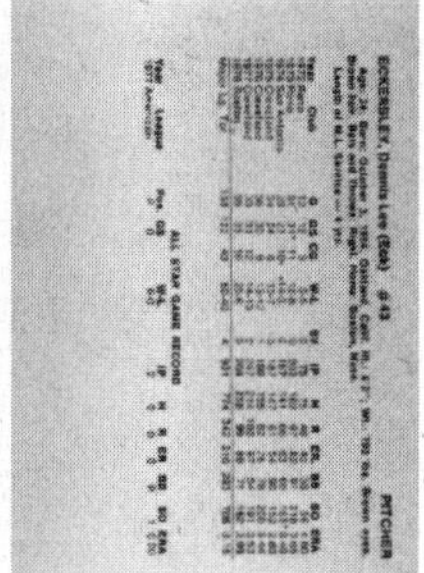

The origins of this Boston Red Sox card set are unclear. It may have been a team issue. The wide white bottom border beneath the black-and-white photo on the 2-1/2" x 3-1/2" cards may have been intended for autographing. Backs have player personal data and complete major and minor league stats. The checklist here, listed alphabetically, may not be complete.

		NM	EX	VG
Complete Set (24):		50.00	25.00	15.00
Common Player:		3.00	1.50	.90
(1)	Gary Allenson	3.00	1.50	.90
(2)	Jack Brohamer	3.00	1.50	.90
(3)	Tom Burgmeier	3.00	1.50	.90
(4)	Rick Burleson	3.00	1.50	.90
(5)	Bill Campbell	3.00	1.50	.90
(6)	Dick Drago	3.00	1.50	.90
(7)	Dennis Eckersley	12.00	6.00	3.50
(8)	Dwight Evans	4.50	2.25	1.25
(9)	Carlton Fisk	15.00	7.50	4.50
(10)	Andy Hassler	3.00	1.50	.90
(11)	Butch Hobson	3.00	1.50	.90
(12)	Fred Lynn	7.50	3.75	2.25
(13)	Bob Montgomery	3.00	1.50	.90
(14)	Mike O'Berry	3.00	1.50	.90
(15)	Jerry Remy	3.00	1.50	.90
(16)	Steve Renko	3.00	1.50	.90
(17)	Jim Rice	7.50	3.75	2.25
(18)	George Scott	4.50	2.25	1.25
(19)	Bob Stanley	3.00	1.50	.90
(20)	Mike Torrez	3.00	1.50	.90
(21)	Larry Wolfe	3.00	1.50	.90
(22)	Jim Wright	3.00	1.50	.90
(23)	Carl Yastrzemski	20.00	10.00	6.00
(24)	Gary Hancock, Stan Papi (Two-sided.)	3.00	1.50	.90

1917 Boston Store

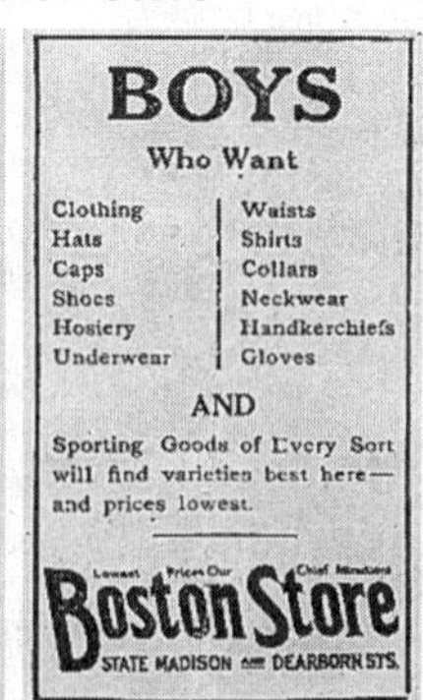

One of several regional advertisers to use this 200-card set as a promotional medium was this Chicago department store. While variations are known of cards #76, 90, 121, 146, and 190 in the Collins-McCarthy ad-back version of this set, it is unclear whether those variations also exist in the Boston Store issue. The American Card Catalog listed these 2" x 3-1/4" black-and-white cards as H801-8.

		NM	EX	VG
Complete Set (200):		80,000	40,000	24,000
Common Player:		150.00	75.00	45.00
1	Sam Agnew	150.00	75.00	45.00
2	Grover Alexander	800.00	400.00	240.00
3	W.S. Alexander (W.E.)	150.00	75.00	45.00
4	Leon Ames	150.00	75.00	45.00
5	Fred Anderson	150.00	75.00	45.00
6	Ed Appleton	150.00	75.00	45.00
7	Jimmy Archer	150.00	75.00	45.00
8	Jimmy Austin	150.00	75.00	45.00

9	Jim Bagby	150.00	75.00	45.00
10	H.D. Baird	150.00	75.00	45.00
11	J. Franklin Baker	500.00	250.00	150.00
12	Dave Bancroft	500.00	250.00	150.00
13	Jack Barry	150.00	75.00	45.00
14	Joe Benz	150.00	75.00	45.00
15	Al Betzel	150.00	75.00	45.00
16	Ping Bodie	150.00	75.00	45.00
17	Joe Boehling	150.00	75.00	45.00
18	Eddie Burns	150.00	75.00	45.00
19	George Burns	150.00	75.00	45.00
20	Geo. J. Burns	150.00	75.00	45.00
21	Joe Bush	150.00	75.00	45.00
22	Owen Bush	150.00	75.00	45.00
23	Bobby Byrne	150.00	75.00	45.00
24	Forrest Cady	150.00	75.00	45.00
25	Max Carey	500.00	250.00	150.00
26	Ray Chapman	200.00	100.00	60.00
27	Larry Cheney	150.00	75.00	45.00
28	Eddie Cicotte	900.00	450.00	275.00
29	Tom Clarke	150.00	75.00	45.00
30	Ty Cobb	4,250	2,125	1,275
31	Eddie Collins	500.00	250.00	150.00
32	"Shauno" Collins (Shano)	150.00	75.00	45.00
33	Fred Coumbe	150.00	75.00	45.00
34	Harry Coveleskie (Coveleski)	150.00	75.00	45.00
35	Gavvy Cravath	150.00	75.00	45.00
36	Sam Crawford	500.00	250.00	150.00
37	Geo. Cutshaw	150.00	75.00	45.00
38	Jake Daubert	150.00	75.00	45.00
39	Geo. Dauss	150.00	75.00	45.00
40	Charles Deal	150.00	75.00	45.00
41	"Wheezer" Dell	150.00	75.00	45.00
42	William Doak	150.00	75.00	45.00
43	Bill Donovan	150.00	75.00	45.00
44	Larry Doyle	150.00	75.00	45.00
45	Johnny Evers	500.00	250.00	150.00
46	Urban Faber	500.00	250.00	150.00
47	"Hap" Felsch	1,500	750.00	450.00
48	Bill Fischer	150.00	75.00	45.00
49	Ray Fisher	150.00	75.00	45.00
50	Art Fletcher	150.00	75.00	45.00
51	Eddie Foster	150.00	75.00	45.00
52	Jacques Fournier	150.00	75.00	45.00
53	Del Gainer (Gainor)	150.00	75.00	45.00
54	Bert Gallia	150.00	75.00	45.00
55	"Chic" Gandil (Chick)	450.00	225.00	135.00
56	Larry Gardner	150.00	75.00	45.00
57	Joe Gedeon	150.00	75.00	45.00
58	Gus Getz	150.00	75.00	45.00
59	Frank Gilhooley	150.00	75.00	45.00
60	Wm. Gleason	150.00	75.00	45.00
61	M.A. Gonzales (Gonzalez)	200.00	100.00	60.00
62	Hank Gowdy	150.00	75.00	45.00
63	John Graney	150.00	75.00	45.00
64	Tom Griffith	150.00	75.00	45.00
65	Heinie Groh	150.00	75.00	45.00
66	Bob Groom	150.00	75.00	45.00
67	Louis Guisto	150.00	75.00	45.00
68	Earl Hamilton	150.00	75.00	45.00
69	Harry Harper	150.00	75.00	45.00
70	Grover Hartley	150.00	75.00	45.00
71	Harry Heilmann	500.00	250.00	150.00
72	Claude Hendrix	150.00	75.00	45.00
73	Olaf Henriksen	150.00	75.00	45.00
74	John Henry	150.00	75.00	45.00
75	"Buck" Herzog	150.00	75.00	45.00
76a	Hugh High (White stockings, photo actually Claude Williams.)	400.00	200.00	120.00
76b	Hugh High (Black stockings, correct photo.)	200.00	100.00	60.00
77	Dick Hoblitzell	150.00	75.00	45.00
78	Walter Holke	150.00	75.00	45.00
79	Harry Hooper	500.00	250.00	150.00
80	Rogers Hornsby	750.00	375.00	225.00
81	Ivan Howard	150.00	75.00	45.00
82	Joe Jackson	12,500	6,250	3,750
83	Harold Janvrin	150.00	75.00	45.00
84	William James	150.00	75.00	45.00
85	C. Jamieson	150.00	75.00	45.00
86	Hugh Jennings	500.00	250.00	150.00
87	Walter Johnson	1,100	550.00	330.00
88	James Johnston	150.00	75.00	45.00
89	Fielder Jones	150.00	75.00	45.00
90a	Joe Judge (Bat on right shoulder, photo actually Ray Morgan.)	400.00	200.00	120.00
90b	Joe Judge (Bat on left shoulder, correct photo.)	200.00	100.00	60.00
91	Hans Lobert	150.00	75.00	45.00
92	Benny Kauff	150.00	75.00	45.00
93	Wm. Killefer Jr.	150.00	75.00	45.00
94	Ed. Konetchy	150.00	75.00	45.00
95	John Lavan	150.00	75.00	45.00
96	Jimmy Lavender	150.00	75.00	45.00
97	"Nemo" Leibold	150.00	75.00	45.00
98	H.B. Leonard	150.00	75.00	45.00
99	Duffy Lewis	150.00	75.00	45.00
100	Tom Long	150.00	75.00	45.00
101	Wm. Louden	150.00	75.00	45.00
102	Fred Luderus	150.00	75.00	45.00
103	Lee Magee	150.00	75.00	45.00
104	Sherwood Magee	150.00	75.00	45.00
105	Al Mamaux	150.00	75.00	45.00
106	Leslie Mann	150.00	75.00	45.00
107	"Rabbit" Maranville	500.00	250.00	150.00
108	Rube Marquard	500.00	250.00	150.00
109	Armando Marsans	240.00	120.00	72.00
110	J. Erskine Mayer	150.00	75.00	45.00
111	George McBride	150.00	75.00	45.00
112	Lew McCarty	150.00	75.00	45.00
113	John J. McGraw	500.00	250.00	150.00
114	Jack McInnis	150.00	75.00	45.00
115	Lee Meadows	150.00	75.00	45.00
116	Fred Merkle	150.00	75.00	45.00
117	"Chief" Meyers	150.00	75.00	45.00
118	Clyde Milan	150.00	75.00	45.00
119	Otto Miller	150.00	75.00	45.00
120	Clarence Mitchell	150.00	75.00	45.00
121a	Ray Morgan (Bat on left shoulder, photo actually Joe Judge.)	400.00	200.00	120.00
121b	Ray Morgan (Bat on right shoulder, correct photo.)	200.00	100.00	60.00
122	Guy Morton	150.00	75.00	45.00
123	"Mike" Mowrey	150.00	75.00	45.00
124	Elmer Myers	150.00	75.00	45.00
125	"Hy" Myers	150.00	75.00	45.00
126	A.E. Neale	300.00	150.00	90.00
127	Arthur Nehf	150.00	75.00	45.00
128	J.A. Niehoff	150.00	75.00	45.00
129	Steve O'Neill	150.00	75.00	45.00
130	"Dode" Paskert	150.00	75.00	45.00
131	Roger Peckinpaugh	200.00	100.00	60.00
132	"Pol" Perritt	150.00	75.00	45.00
133	"Jeff" Pfeffer	150.00	75.00	45.00
134	Walter Pipp	150.00	75.00	45.00
135	Derril Pratt (Derrill)	150.00	75.00	45.00
136	Bill Rariden	150.00	75.00	45.00
137	E.C. Rice	500.00	250.00	150.00
138	Wm. A. Ritter (Wm. H.)	150.00	75.00	45.00
139	Eppa Rixey	500.00	250.00	150.00
140	Davey Robertson	150.00	75.00	45.00
141	"Bob" Roth	150.00	75.00	45.00
142	Ed. Roush	500.00	250.00	150.00
143	Clarence Rowland	150.00	75.00	45.00
144	Dick Rudolph	150.00	75.00	45.00
145	William Rumler	150.00	75.00	45.00
146a	Reb Russell (Pitching follow-thru, photo actually Mellie Wolfgang.)	400.00	200.00	120.00
146b	Reb Russell (Hands at side, correct photo.)	200.00	100.00	60.00
147	"Babe" Ruth	25,000	12,500	7,500
148	Vic Saier	150.00	75.00	45.00
149	"Slim" Sallee	150.00	75.00	45.00
150	Ray Schalk	500.00	250.00	150.00
151	Walter Schang	150.00	75.00	45.00
152	Frank Schulte	150.00	75.00	45.00
153	Ferd Schupp	150.00	75.00	45.00
154	Everett Scott	150.00	75.00	45.00
155	Hank Severeid	150.00	75.00	45.00
156	Howard Shanks	150.00	75.00	45.00
157	Bob Shawkey	150.00	75.00	45.00
158	Jas. Sheckard	150.00	75.00	45.00
159	Ernie Shore	150.00	75.00	45.00
160	C.H. Shorten	150.00	75.00	45.00
161	Burt Shotton	150.00	75.00	45.00
162	Geo. Sisler	800.00	400.00	240.00
163	Elmer Smith	150.00	75.00	45.00
164	J. Carlisle Smith	150.00	75.00	45.00
165	Fred Snodgrass	150.00	75.00	45.00
166	Tris Speaker	750.00	375.00	225.00
167	Oscar Stanage	150.00	75.00	45.00
168	Charles Stengel	500.00	250.00	150.00
169	Milton Stock	150.00	75.00	45.00
170	Amos Strunk	150.00	75.00	45.00
171	"Zeb" Terry	150.00	75.00	45.00
172	"Jeff" Tesreau	150.00	75.00	45.00
173	Chester Thomas	150.00	75.00	45.00
174	Fred Toney	150.00	75.00	45.00
175	Terry Turner	150.00	75.00	45.00
176	George Tyler	150.00	75.00	45.00
177	Jim Vaughn	150.00	75.00	45.00
178	Bob Veach	150.00	75.00	45.00
179	Oscar Vitt	150.00	75.00	45.00
180	Hans Wagner	3,000	1,500	900.00
181	Clarence Walker	150.00	75.00	45.00
182	Jim Walsh	150.00	75.00	45.00
183	Al Walters	150.00	75.00	45.00
184	W. Wambsganss	150.00	75.00	45.00
185	Buck Weaver	1,200	600.00	350.00
186	Carl Weilman	150.00	75.00	45.00
187	Zack Wheat	500.00	250.00	150.00
188	Geo. Whitted	150.00	75.00	45.00
189	Joe Wilhoit	150.00	75.00	45.00
190a	Claude Williams (Black stockings, photo actually Hugh High.)	800.00	400.00	240.00
190b	Claude Williams (White stockings, correct photo.)	1,500	750.00	450.00
191	Fred Williams	150.00	75.00	45.00
192	Art Wilson	150.00	75.00	45.00
193	Lawton Witt	150.00	75.00	45.00
194	Joe Wood	200.00	100.00	60.00
195	William Wortman	150.00	75.00	45.00
196	Steve Yerkes	150.00	75.00	45.00
197	Earl Yingling	150.00	75.00	45.00
198	"Pep" Young (Photo actually Ralph Young.)	150.00	75.00	45.00
199	Rollie Zeider	150.00	75.00	45.00
200	Henry Zimmerman	150.00	75.00	45.00

1909 Boston Sunday Post Red Sox Stars

Members of the Boston American League team are presented in this series of Sunday supplements from one of the city's daily newspapers. Measuring about 8" x 10", and possibly having been issued in two-page spreads, the blank-back pieces combine artist's renderings of action photos with circular portraits about 2-3/8" in diameter, printed in sepia tones. At bottom is printed the player name, team, position and a caption for the picture, along with the newspaper's credit line. It is possible this checklist is incomplete since a few of the team's stars have yet to be reported.

		NM	EX	VG
Common Player:		150.00	75.00	45.00
(1)	Frank Arellanes	150.00	75.00	45.00
(2)	William Carrigan	150.00	75.00	45.00
(3)	Charles Chech	150.00	75.00	45.00
(4)	Edward Cicotte	250.00	125.00	75.00
(5)	Harry Hooper	250.00	125.00	75.00
(6)	Harry Lord	150.00	75.00	45.00
(7)	Ambrose McConnell	150.00	75.00	45.00
(8)	Harry Niles	150.00	75.00	45.00
(9)	Tris Speaker	300.00	150.00	90.00
(10)	Edward Spencer	150.00	75.00	45.00
(11)	Garland Stahl	150.00	75.00	45.00
(12)	Harry Wolter	150.00	75.00	45.00

1972 Bowery Bank Joe DiMaggio

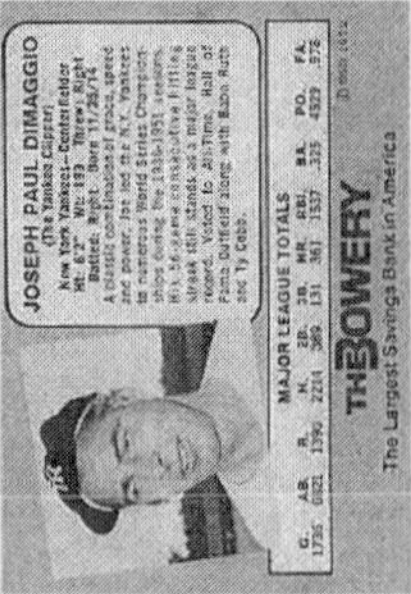

These cards were issued to promote the New York City bank's relationship with spokesman Joe DiMaggio. The 2-1/2" x 3-1/2" cards have a posed color photo on front. The back has a black-and-white portrait, biographical data, career highlights and stats on a pink background.

	NM	EX	VG
Joe DiMaggio	17.50	9.00	5.00

1948 Bowman

36 — STAN MUSIAL
In- Outfielder—St. Louis Cardinals
Born: Donora, Pa. Nov. 21, 1920
Bats: Left Throws: Left
Height: 6:00 Weight: 175
Started his baseball career as a pitcher. Shoulder injury cut that short but he developed into an outstanding fielder. His stance at bat is something to see. Winding up like a windmill, he has made season averages of .347 and .357. In 1943 he won the Most Valuable Player award and again won the coveted award in 1946 with a batting average of .365. Three times an All Star.
ASK FOR BLONY BUBBLE GUM
The Bubble Gum with the three different flavors
BOWMAN GUM, INC. Copyright 1948

Bowman Gum Co.'s premiere set of 1948 was one of the first major issues of the post-war period. Forty-eight black-and-white cards comprise the set, with each card measuring 2-1/16" x 2-1/2". The card backs, printed in black ink on gray stock, include the card number and the player's name, team, position, and a short biography. Twelve cards (marked with an "SP") were printed in short supply when they were removed from the 36-card printing sheet to make room for the set's high numbers (#37-48).

		NM	EX	VG
Complete Set (48):		5,000	2,500	1,500
Common Player (1-36):		60.00	30.00	18.00
Common Player (37-48):		60.00	30.00	18.00
1	***Bob Elliott***	150.00	60.00	18.00
2	***Ewell Blackwell***	140.00	70.00	40.00
3	***Ralph Kiner***	300.00	150.00	90.00
4	Johnny Mize	170.00	84.50	50.00
5	Bob Feller	450.00	220.00	130.00
6	***Yogi Berra***	980.00	510.00	250.00
7	Pete Reiser/SP	300.00	150.00	90.00
8	***Phil Rizzuto***/SP	550.00	270.00	160.00
9	Walker Cooper	60.00	30.00	18.00
10	Buddy Rosar	60.00	30.00	18.00
11	Johnny Lindell	60.00	30.00	18.00
12	***Johnny Sain***	140.00	70.00	40.00
13	***Willard Marshall*** /SP	120.00	60.00	36.00
14	***Allie Reynolds***	130.00	64.50	40.00
15	Eddie Joost	60.00	30.00	18.00
16	Jack Lohrke/SP	120.00	60.00	36.00
17	Enos Slaughter	210.00	100.00	60.00
18	***Warren Spahn***	800.00	400.00	240.00
19	Tommy Henrich	120.00	60.00	36.00
20	Buddy Kerr/SP	120.00	60.00	36.00
21	***Ferris Fain***	80.00	40.00	24.00
22	Floyd (Bill) Bevens/SP	120.00	60.00	36.00
23	Larry Jansen	60.00	30.00	18.00
24	Emil (Dutch) Leonard/SP	120.00	60.00	36.00

		NM	EX	VG
25	Barney McCoskey (McCosky)	60.00	30.00	18.00
26	Frank Shea/SP	120.00	60.00	36.00
27	Sid Gordon	60.00	30.00	18.00
28	Emil Verban/SP	120.00	60.00	36.00
29	***Joe Page***/SP	250.00	130.00	70.00
30	***Whitey Lockman***/SP	150.00	75.00	45.00
31	Bill McCahan	60.00	30.00	18.00
32	***Bill Rigney***	60.00	30.00	18.00
33	Billy Johnson	60.00	30.00	18.00
34	Sheldon Jones/SP	120.00	60.00	36.00
35	Snuffy Stirnweiss	60.00	30.00	18.00
36	***Stan Musial***	1,500	750.00	450.00
37	Clint Hartung	120.00	60.00	36.00
38	***Red Schoendienst***	600.00	250.00	150.00
39	Augie Galan	120.00	60.00	36.00
40	***Marty Marion***	200.00	100.00	60.00
41	Rex Barney	170.00	85.00	50.00
42	Ray Poat	120.00	60.00	36.00
43	Bruce Edwards	160.00	80.00	48.00
44	Johnny Wyrostek	120.00	60.00	36.00
45	Hank Sauer	120.00	60.00	36.00
46	Herman Wehmeier	120.00	60.00	36.00
47	***Bobby Thomson***	280.00	140.00	80.00
48	Dave Koslo	320.00	80.00	45.00

1949 Bowman

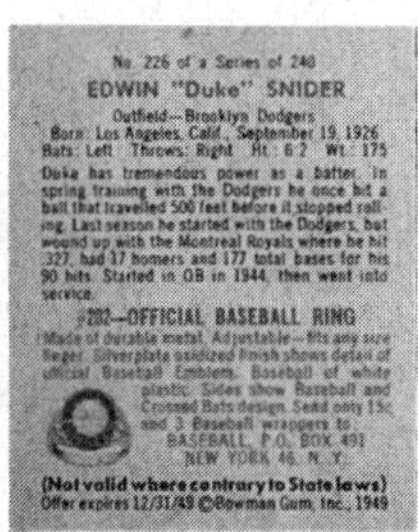

In 1949, Bowman increased the size of its issue to 240 numbered cards. The 2-1/16" x 2-1/2" cards are black-and-white photos overprinted with team uniform colors on a background of various solid pastel colors. Beginning with card #109 in the set, Bowman added the players' names on the card fronts. Twelve cards (#4, 78, 83, 85, 88, 98, 109, 124, 127, 132 and 143), which were produced in the first four series of printings, were reprinted in the seventh series with either a card front or back modification. These variations are noted in the checklist. Cards #1-3 and 5-73 can be found with either white or gray backs. The complete set value shown here does not include the higher priced variation cards.

		NM	EX	VG
Complete Set (240):		15,000	7,500	4,500
Common Player (1-144):		20.00	10.00	6.00
Common Player (145-240):		50.00	25.00	15.00
1	Vernon Bickford	200.00	15.00	9.00
2	"Whitey" Lockman	20.00	10.00	6.00
3	Bob Porterfield	20.00	10.00	6.00
4a	Jerry Priddy	20.00	10.00	6.00
	(No name on front.)			
4b	Jerry Priddy (Name on front.)	60.00	30.00	18.00
5	Hank Sauer	20.00	10.00	6.00
6	Phil Cavarretta	20.00	10.00	6.00
7	Joe Dobson	20.00	10.00	6.00
8	Murry Dickson	20.00	10.00	6.00
9	Ferris Fain	20.00	10.00	6.00
10	Ted Gray	20.00	10.00	6.00
11	Lou Boudreau	60.00	30.00	18.00
12	Cass Michaels	20.00	10.00	6.00
13	Bob Chesnes	20.00	10.00	6.00
14	***Curt Simmons***	50.00	25.00	15.00
15	***Ned Garver***	30.00	15.00	9.00
16	Al Kozar	20.00	10.00	6.00
17	Earl Torgeson	20.00	10.00	6.00
18	Bobby Thomson	65.00	32.50	20.00
19	***Bobby Brown***	75.00	37.50	22.50
20	Gene Hermanski	20.00	10.00	6.00
21	Frank Baumholtz	20.00	10.00	6.00
22	Harry "P-Nuts" Lowrey	20.00	10.00	6.00
23	Bobby Doerr	60.00	30.00	18.00
24	Stan Musial	425.00	180.00	100.00
25	Carl Scheib	20.00	10.00	6.00
26	George Kell	65.00	32.50	20.00
27	Bob Feller	225.00	110.00	60.00
28	Don Kolloway	20.00	10.00	6.00
29	Ralph Kiner	95.00	47.50	27.50
30	Andy Seminick	20.00	10.00	6.00
31	Dick Kokos	20.00	10.00	6.00
32	Eddie Yost	20.00	10.00	6.00
33	Warren Spahn	135.00	65.00	40.00
34	Dave Koslo	20.00	10.00	6.00
35	***Vic Raschi***	100.00	50.00	30.00
36	Pee Wee Reese	165.00	85.00	50.00
37	John Wyrostek	20.00	10.00	6.00
38	Emil Verban	20.00	10.00	6.00
39	Bill Goodman	20.00	10.00	6.00
40	"Red" Munger	20.00	10.00	6.00
41	Lou Brissie	20.00	10.00	6.00
42	"Hoot" Evers	20.00	10.00	6.00
43	Dale Mitchell	20.00	10.00	6.00
44	Dave Philley	20.00	10.00	6.00
45	Wally Westlake	20.00	10.00	6.00
46	***Robin Roberts***	200.00	100.00	60.00
47	Johnny Sain	50.00	25.00	15.00
48	Willard Marshall	20.00	10.00	6.00
49	Frank Shea	30.00	15.00	9.00
50	***Jackie Robinson***	950.00	475.00	230.00
51	Herman Wehmeier	20.00	10.00	6.00
52	Johnny Schmitz	20.00	10.00	6.00
53	Jack Kramer	20.00	10.00	6.00
54	Marty Marion	35.00	17.50	10.00
55	Eddie Joost	20.00	10.00	6.00
56	Pat Mullin	20.00	10.00	6.00
57	Gene Bearden	20.00	10.00	6.00
58	Bob Elliott	20.00	10.00	6.00
59	Jack Lohrke	20.00	10.00	6.00
60	Yogi Berra	275.00	135.00	80.00
61	Rex Barney	25.00	12.50	7.50
62	Grady Hatton	20.00	10.00	6.00
63	Andy Pafko	20.00	10.00	6.00
64	Dom DiMaggio	75.00	37.50	22.50
65	Enos Slaughter	80.00	40.00	24.00
66	Elmer Valo	20.00	10.00	6.00
67	***Alvin Dark***	50.00	25.00	15.00
68	Sheldon Jones	20.00	10.00	6.00
69	Tommy Henrich	55.00	27.50	16.50
70	***Carl Furillo***	135.00	65.00	40.00
71	Vern Stephens	20.00	10.00	6.00
72	Tommy Holmes	20.00	10.00	6.00
73	Billy Cox	45.00	22.50	13.50
74	Tom McBride	20.00	10.00	6.00
75	Eddie Mayo	20.00	10.00	6.00
76	Bill Nicholson	20.00	10.00	6.00
77	Ernie Bonham	20.00	10.00	6.00
78a	Sam Zoldak	20.00	10.00	6.00
	(No name on front.)			
78b	Sam Zoldak	60.00	30.00	18.00
	(Name on front.)			
79	Ron Northey	20.00	10.00	6.00
80	Bill McCahan	20.00	10.00	6.00
81	Virgil "Red" Stallcup	20.00	10.00	6.00
82	Joe Page	35.00	17.50	10.00
83a	Bob Scheffing	20.00	10.00	6.00
	(No name on front.)			
83b	Bob Scheffing	60.00	30.00	18.00
	(Name on front.)			
84	***Roy Campanella***	625.00	310.00	185.00
85a	Johnny Mize	85.00	42.50	25.00
	(No name on front.)			
85b	Johnny Mize	120.00	60.00	36.00
	(Name on front.)			
86	Johnny Pesky	20.00	10.00	6.00
87	Randy Gumpert	20.00	10.00	6.00
88a	Bill Salkeld	20.00	10.00	6.00
	(No name on front.)			
88b	Bill Salkeld	60.00	30.00	18.00
	(Name on front.)			
89	Mizell Platt	20.00	10.00	6.00
90	Gil Coan	20.00	10.00	6.00
91	Dick Wakefield	20.00	10.00	6.00
92	Willie Jones	20.00	10.00	6.00
93	Ed Stevens	20.00	10.00	6.00
94	***Mickey Vernon***	30.00	15.00	9.00
95	Howie Pollett	20.00	10.00	6.00
96	Taft Wright	20.00	10.00	6.00
97	Danny Litwhiler	20.00	10.00	6.00
98a	Phil Rizzuto	150.00	75.00	45.00
	(No name on front.)			
98b	Phil Rizzuto	275.00	135.00	85.00
	(Name on front.)			
99	Frank Gustine	20.00	10.00	6.00
100	***Gil Hodges***	215.00	100.00	60.00
101	Sid Gordon	25.00	12.50	7.50
102	Stan Spence	20.00	10.00	6.00
103	Joe Tipton	20.00	10.00	6.00
104	***Ed Stanky***	35.00	17.50	10.00
105	Bill Kennedy	20.00	10.00	6.00
106	Jake Early	20.00	10.00	6.00
107	Eddie Lake	20.00	10.00	6.00
108	Ken Heintzelman	20.00	10.00	6.00
109a	Ed Fitz Gerald	20.00	10.00	6.00
	(Script name on back.)			
109b	Ed Fitz Gerald	60.00	30.00	18.00
	(Printed name on back.)			
110	***Early Wynn***	165.00	80.00	45.00
111	Red Schoendienst	80.00	40.00	24.00
112	Sam Chapman	20.00	10.00	6.00
113	Ray Lamanno	20.00	10.00	6.00
114	Allie Reynolds	65.00	32.50	20.00
115	Emil "Dutch" Leonard	20.00	10.00	6.00
116	Joe Hatten	20.00	10.00	6.00
117	Walker Cooper	20.00	10.00	6.00
118	Sam Mele	20.00	10.00	6.00
119	Floyd Baker	20.00	10.00	6.00
120	Cliff Fannin	20.00	10.00	6.00
121	Mark Christman	20.00	10.00	6.00
122	George Vico	20.00	10.00	6.00
123	Johnny Blatnick	20.00	10.00	6.00
124a	Danny Murtaugh	20.00	10.00	6.00
	(Script name on back.)			
124b	Danny Murtaugh	60.00	30.00	18.00
	(Printed name on back.)			
125	Ken Keltner	20.00	10.00	6.00
126a	Al Brazle	20.00	10.00	6.00
	(Script name on back.)			
126b	Al Brazle	60.00	30.00	18.00
	(Printed name on back.)			
127a	Henry Majeski	20.00	10.00	6.00
	(Script name on back.)			
127b	Henry Majeski	60.00	30.00	18.00
	(Printed name on back.)			
128	Johnny Vander Meer	35.00	17.50	10.00
129	Billy Johnson	30.00	15.00	9.00
130	Harry "The Hat" Walker	25.00	12.50	7.50
131	Paul Lehner	20.00	10.00	6.00
132a	Al Evans	20.00	10.00	6.00
	(Script name on back.)			
132b	Al Evans	60.00	30.00	18.00
	(Printed name on back.)			
133	Aaron Robinson	20.00	10.00	6.00
134	Hank Borowy	20.00	10.00	6.00
135	Stan Rojek	20.00	10.00	6.00
136	Hank Edwards	20.00	10.00	6.00
137	Ted Wilks	20.00	10.00	6.00
138	"Buddy" Rosar	20.00	10.00	6.00
139	Hank "Bow-Wow" Arft	20.00	10.00	6.00
140	Ray Scarborough	20.00	10.00	6.00
141	"Tony Lupien	20.00	10.00	6.00
142	Eddie Waitkus	20.00	10.00	6.00
143a	Bob Dillinger	20.00	10.00	6.00
	(Script name on back.)			
143b	Bob Dillinger	60.00	30.00	18.00
	(Printed name on back.)			
144	Mickey Haefner	20.00	10.00	6.00
145	"Blix" Donnelly	50.00	25.00	15.00
146	Mike McCormick	55.00	27.50	16.50
147	Elmer Singleton	50.00	25.00	15.00
148	Bob Swift	50.00	25.00	15.00
149	Roy Partee	60.00	30.00	18.00
150	Allie Clark	50.00	25.00	15.00
151	Mickey Harris	50.00	25.00	15.00
152	Clarence Maddern	50.00	25.00	15.00
153	Phil Masi	50.00	25.00	15.00
154	Clint Hartung	50.00	25.00	15.00
155	Mickey Guerra	50.00	25.00	15.00
156	Al Zarilla	50.00	25.00	15.00
157	Walt Masterson	50.00	25.00	15.00
158	Harry Brecheen	50.00	25.00	15.00
159	Glen Moulder	50.00	25.00	15.00
160	Jim Blackburn	50.00	25.00	15.00
161	"Jocko" Thompson	50.00	25.00	15.00
162	***Preacher Roe***	200.00	100.00	60.00
163	Clyde McCullough	50.00	25.00	15.00
164	***Vic Wertz***	70.00	35.00	20.00
165	"Snuffy" Stirnweiss	60.00	30.00	18.00
166	Mike Tresh	50.00	25.00	15.00
167	Boris "Babe" Martin	50.00	25.00	15.00
168	Doyle Lade	50.00	25.00	15.00
169	Jeff Heath	50.00	25.00	15.00
170	Bill Rigney	50.00	25.00	15.00
171	Dick Fowler	50.00	25.00	15.00
172	Eddie Pellagrini	50.00	25.00	15.00
173	Eddie Stewart	50.00	25.00	15.00
174	***Terry Moore***	125.00	65.00	35.00
175	Luke Appling	175.00	85.00	50.00
176	Ken Raffensberger	50.00	25.00	15.00
177	Stan Lopata	50.00	25.00	15.00
178	Tommy Brown	55.00	27.50	16.50
179	Hugh Casey	55.00	27.50	16.50
180	Connie Berry	50.00	25.00	15.00
181	Gus Niarhos	50.00	25.00	15.00
182	Hal Peck	50.00	25.00	15.00
183	Lou Stringer	50.00	25.00	15.00
184	Bob Chipman	50.00	25.00	15.00
185	Pete Reiser	70.00	35.00	20.00
186	"Buddy" Kerr	50.00	25.00	15.00
187	Phil Marchildon	50.00	25.00	15.00
188	Karl Drews	50.00	25.00	15.00
189	Earl Wooten	50.00	25.00	15.00
190	***Jim Hearn***	60.00	30.00	18.00
191	Joe Haynes	50.00	25.00	15.00
192	Harry Gumbert	50.00	25.00	15.00
193	Ken Trinkle	50.00	25.00	15.00
194	Ralph Branca	95.00	47.50	27.50
195	Eddie Bockman	50.00	25.00	15.00
196	Fred Hutchinson	50.00	25.00	15.00
197	Johnny Lindell	60.00	30.00	18.00
198	Steve Gromek	50.00	25.00	15.00
199	"Tex" Hughson	50.00	25.00	15.00
200	Jess Dobernic	50.00	25.00	15.00
201	Sibby Sisti	50.00	25.00	15.00
202	Larry Jansen	50.00	25.00	15.00
203	Barney McCosky	50.00	25.00	15.00
204	Bob Savage	50.00	25.00	15.00
205	Dick Sisler	50.00	25.00	15.00
206	Bruce Edwards	55.00	27.50	16.50
207	Johnny Hopp	50.00	25.00	15.00
208	"Dizzy" Trout	50.00	25.00	15.00
209	Charlie Keller	85.00	42.50	25.00
210	Joe Gordon	50.00	25.00	15.00
211	Dave "Boo" Ferris	50.00	25.00	15.00
212	Ralph Hamner	50.00	25.00	15.00
213	Charles "Red" Barrett	50.00	25.00	15.00
214	***Richie Ashburn***	555.00	290.00	175.00
215	Kirby Higbe	50.00	25.00	15.00
216	"Schoolboy" Rowe	50.00	25.00	15.00
217	Marino Pieretti	50.00	25.00	15.00
218	Dick Kryhoski	50.00	25.00	15.00
219	***Virgil "Fire" Trucks***	60.00	30.00	18.00
220	Johnny McCarthy	50.00	25.00	15.00
221	Bob Muncrief	50.00	25.00	15.00
222	Alex Kellner	50.00	25.00	15.00
223	Bob Hofman	50.00	25.00	15.00
224	***Satchel Paige***	1,250	850.00	525.00
225	***Gerry Coleman***	100.00	50.00	30.00
226	***Duke Snider***	900.00	475.00	300.00
227	Fritz Ostermueller	50.00	25.00	15.00
228	Jackie Mayo	50.00	25.00	15.00
229	***Ed Lopat***	100.00	50.00	30.00
230	Augie Galan	50.00	25.00	15.00
231	Earl Johnson	50.00	25.00	15.00
232	George McQuinn	50.00	25.00	15.00
233	***Larry Doby***	375.00	185.00	110.00
234	"Rip" Sewell	50.00	25.00	15.00
235	Jim Russell	50.00	25.00	15.00
236	Fred Sanford	60.00	30.00	18.00
237	Monte Kennedy	50.00	25.00	15.00
238	***Bob Lemon***	265.00	130.00	80.00
239	Frank McCormick	50.00	25.00	15.00
240	Norm "Babe" Young	125.00	30.00	15.00
	(Photo actually Bobby Young.)			

1950 Bowman

The quality of the 1950 Bowman issue showed a marked improvement over the company's previous efforts. The cards are color art reproductions of actual photographs and measure 2-1/16" x 2-1/2". Backs include the same type of information found in the previous year's issue but are designed in a horizontal format. Cards found in the first two series (#1-72) are the scarcer of the issue. The backs of the final 72 cards (#181-252) can be found with or without the copyright line at the bottom of the card, the "without" version being the less common.

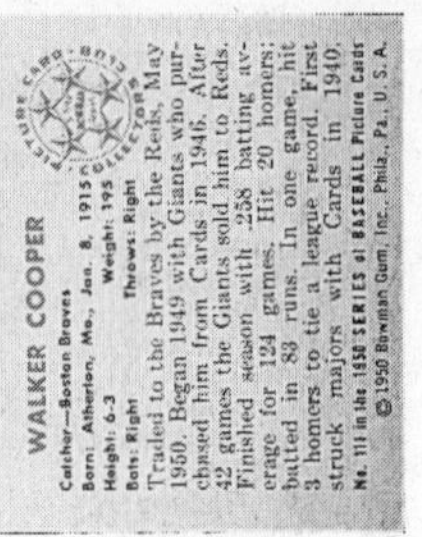

		NM	EX	VG
Complete Set (252):		12,500	6,000	3,500
Common Player (1-72):		50.00	25.00	15.00
Common Player (73-252):		20.00	10.00	6.00
1	Mel Parnell	550.00	35.00	15.00
2	Vern Stephens	50.00	25.00	15.00
3	Dom DiMaggio	130.00	65.00	40.00
4	***Gus Zernial***	90.00	45.00	27.50
5	Bob Kuzava	50.00	25.00	15.00
6	Bob Feller	300.00	150.00	90.00
7	Jim Hegan	50.00	25.00	15.00
8	George Kell	125.00	65.00	35.00
9	Vic Wertz	50.00	25.00	15.00
10	Tommy Henrich	75.00	37.50	22.50
11	Phil Rizzuto	265.00	130.00	80.00
12	Joe Page	65.00	32.50	20.00
13	Ferris Fain	50.00	25.00	15.00
14	Alex Kellner	50.00	25.00	15.00
15	Al Kozar	50.00	25.00	15.00
16	***Roy Sievers***	90.00	45.00	27.50
17	Sid Hudson	50.00	25.00	15.00
18	Eddie Robinson	50.00	25.00	15.00
19	Warren Spahn	365.00	175.00	100.00
20	Bob Elliott	50.00	25.00	15.00
21	Pee Wee Reese	275.00	125.00	80.00
22	Jackie Robinson	900.00	400.00	225.00
23	***Don Newcombe***	175.00	85.00	50.00
24	Johnny Schmitz	50.00	25.00	15.00
25	Hank Sauer	50.00	25.00	15.00
26	Grady Hatton	50.00	25.00	15.00
27	Herman Wehmeier	50.00	25.00	15.00
28	Bobby Thomson	100.00	50.00	30.00
29	Ed Stanky	60.00	30.00	18.00
30	Eddie Waitkus	50.00	25.00	15.00
31	***Del Ennis***	80.00	40.00	24.00
32	Robin Roberts	225.00	110.00	65.00
33	Ralph Kiner	125.00	60.00	35.00
34	Murry Dickson	50.00	25.00	15.00
35	Enos Slaughter	125.00	60.00	35.00
36	Eddie Kazak	50.00	25.00	15.00
37	Luke Appling	100.00	50.00	30.00
38	Bill Wight	50.00	25.00	15.00
39	Larry Doby	175.00	85.00	50.00
40	Bob Lemon	125.00	60.00	35.00
41	"Hoot" Evers	50.00	25.00	15.00
42	Art Houtteman	50.00	25.00	15.00
43	Bobby Doerr	100.00	50.00	30.00
44	Joe Dobson	50.00	25.00	15.00
45	Al Zarilla	50.00	25.00	15.00
46	Yogi Berra	425.00	210.00	125.00
47	Jerry Coleman	60.00	30.00	18.00
48	Lou Brissie	50.00	25.00	15.00
49	Elmer Valo	50.00	25.00	15.00
50	Dick Kokos	50.00	25.00	15.00
51	Ned Garver	50.00	25.00	15.00
52	Sam Mele	50.00	25.00	15.00
53	Clyde Vollmer	50.00	25.00	15.00
54	Gil Coan	50.00	25.00	15.00
55	"Buddy" Kerr	50.00	25.00	15.00
56	***Del Crandell*** (Crandall)	55.00	27.50	16.50
57	Vernon Bickford	50.00	25.00	15.00
58	Carl Furillo	65.00	32.50	20.00
59	Ralph Branca	60.00	30.00	18.00
60	Andy Pafko	50.00	25.00	15.00
61	Bob Rush	50.00	25.00	15.00
62	Ted Kluszewski	150.00	75.00	45.00
63	Ewell Blackwell	50.00	25.00	15.00
64	Alvin Dark	50.00	25.00	15.00
65	Dave Koslo	50.00	25.00	15.00
66	Larry Jansen	50.00	25.00	15.00
67	Willie Jones	50.00	25.00	15.00
68	Curt Simmons	50.00	25.00	15.00
69	Wally Westlake	50.00	25.00	15.00
70	Bob Chesnes	50.00	25.00	15.00
71	Red Schoendienst	85.00	42.50	25.00
72	Howie Pollet	50.00	25.00	15.00
73	Willard Marshall	20.00	10.00	6.00
74	***Johnny Antonelli***	40.00	20.00	12.00
75	Roy Campanella	200.00	100.00	60.00
76	Rex Barney	25.00	12.50	7.50
77	Duke Snider	200.00	100.00	60.00
78	Mickey Owen	20.00	10.00	6.00
79	Johnny Vander Meer	25.00	12.50	7.50
80	Howard Fox	20.00	10.00	6.00
81	Ron Northey	20.00	10.00	6.00
82	"Whitey" Lockman	20.00	10.00	6.00
83	Sheldon Jones	20.00	10.00	6.00
84	Richie Ashburn	190.00	95.00	55.00
85	Ken Heintzelman	20.00	10.00	6.00
86	Stan Rojek	20.00	10.00	6.00
87	Bill Werle	20.00	10.00	6.00
88	Marty Marion	30.00	15.00	9.00
89	George Munger	20.00	10.00	6.00
90	Harry Brecheen	20.00	10.00	6.00
91	Cass Michaels	20.00	10.00	6.00
92	Hank Majeski	20.00	10.00	6.00
93	Gene Bearden	20.00	10.00	6.00
94	Lou Boudreau	70.00	35.00	20.00
95	Aaron Robinson	20.00	10.00	6.00
96	Virgil "Fire" Trucks	20.00	10.00	6.00
97	Maurice McDermott	20.00	10.00	6.00
98	Ted Williams	800.00	350.00	210.00
99	Billy Goodman	20.00	10.00	6.00
100	Vic Raschi	50.00	25.00	15.00
101	Bobby Brown	55.00	27.50	16.50
102	Billy Johnson	30.00	15.00	9.00
103	Eddie Joost	20.00	10.00	6.00
104	Sam Chapman	20.00	10.00	6.00
105	Bob Dillinger	20.00	10.00	6.00
106	Cliff Fannin	20.00	10.00	6.00
107	Sam Dente	20.00	10.00	6.00
108	Ray Scarborough	20.00	10.00	6.00
109	Sid Gordon	20.00	10.00	6.00
110	Tommy Holmes	20.00	10.00	6.00
111	Walker Cooper	20.00	10.00	6.00
112	Gil Hodges	125.00	60.00	35.00
113	Gene Hermanski	20.00	10.00	6.00
114	***Wayne Terwilliger***	25.00	12.50	7.50
115	Roy Smalley	20.00	10.00	6.00
116	Virgil "Red" Stallcup	20.00	10.00	6.00
117	Bill Rigney	20.00	10.00	6.00
118	Clint Hartung	20.00	10.00	6.00
119	Dick Sisler	20.00	10.00	6.00
120	Jocko Thompson	20.00	10.00	6.00
121	Andy Seminick	20.00	10.00	6.00
122	Johnny Hopp	20.00	10.00	6.00
123	Dino Restelli	20.00	10.00	6.00
124	Clyde McCullough	20.00	10.00	6.00
125	Del Rice	20.00	10.00	6.00
126	Al Brazle	20.00	10.00	6.00
127	Dave Philley	20.00	10.00	6.00
128	Phil Masi	20.00	10.00	6.00
129	Joe Gordon	20.00	10.00	6.00
130	Dale Mitchell	20.00	10.00	6.00
131	Steve Gromek	20.00	10.00	6.00
132	Mickey Vernon	20.00	10.00	6.00
133	Don Kolloway	20.00	10.00	6.00
134	"Dizzy" Trout	20.00	10.00	6.00
135	Pat Mullin	20.00	10.00	6.00
136	"Buddy" Rosar	20.00	10.00	6.00
137	Johnny Pesky	20.00	10.00	6.00
138	Allie Reynolds	60.00	30.00	18.00
139	Johnny Mize	65.00	32.50	20.00
140	Pete Suder	20.00	10.00	6.00
141	Joe Coleman	20.00	10.00	6.00
142	***Sherman Lollar***	25.00	12.50	7.50
143	Eddie Stewart	20.00	10.00	6.00
144	Al Evans	20.00	10.00	6.00
145	Jack Graham	20.00	10.00	6.00
146	Floyd Baker	20.00	10.00	6.00
147	***Mike Garcia***	30.00	15.00	9.00
148	Early Wynn	70.00	35.00	20.00
149	Bob Swift	20.00	10.00	6.00
150	George Vico	20.00	10.00	6.00
151	Fred Hutchinson	20.00	10.00	6.00
152	Ellis Kinder	20.00	10.00	6.00
153	Walt Masterson	20.00	10.00	6.00
154	Gus Niarhos	30.00	15.00	9.00
155	Frank "Spec" Shea	30.00	15.00	9.00
156	Fred Sanford	30.00	15.00	9.00
157	Mike Guerra	20.00	10.00	6.00
158	Paul Lehner	20.00	10.00	6.00
159	Joe Tipton	20.00	10.00	6.00
160	Mickey Harris	20.00	10.00	6.00
161	Sherry Robertson	20.00	10.00	6.00
162	Eddie Yost	20.00	10.00	6.00
163	Earl Torgeson	20.00	10.00	6.00
164	Sibby Sisti	20.00	10.00	6.00
165	Bruce Edwards	25.00	12.50	7.50
166	Joe Hatten	25.00	12.50	7.50
167	Preacher Roe	50.00	25.00	15.00
168	Bob Scheffing	20.00	10.00	6.00
169	Hank Edwards	20.00	10.00	6.00
170	Emil Leonard	20.00	10.00	6.00
171	Harry Gumbert	20.00	10.00	6.00
172	Harry Lowrey	20.00	10.00	6.00
173	Lloyd Merriman	20.00	10.00	6.00
174	***Henry Thompson***	30.00	15.00	9.00
175	Monte Kennedy	20.00	10.00	6.00
176	"Blix" Donnelly	20.00	10.00	6.00
177	Hank Borowy	20.00	10.00	6.00
178	Eddy Fitz Gerald	20.00	10.00	6.00
179	Charles Diering	20.00	10.00	6.00
180	Harry "The Hat" Walker	20.00	10.00	6.00
181	Marino Pieretti	20.00	10.00	6.00
182	Sam Zoldak	20.00	10.00	6.00
183	Mickey Haefner	20.00	10.00	6.00
184	Randy Gumpert	20.00	10.00	6.00
185	Howie Judson	20.00	10.00	6.00
186	Ken Keltner	20.00	10.00	6.00
187	Lou Stringer	20.00	10.00	6.00
188	Earl Johnson	20.00	10.00	6.00
189	Owen Friend	20.00	10.00	6.00
190	Ken Wood	20.00	10.00	6.00
191	Dick Starr	20.00	10.00	6.00
192	Bob Chipman	20.00	10.00	6.00
193	Pete Reiser	30.00	15.00	9.00
194	Billy Cox	35.00	17.50	10.00
195	Phil Cavarretta	20.00	10.00	6.00
196	Doyle Lade	20.00	10.00	6.00
197	Johnny Wyrostek	20.00	10.00	6.00
198	Danny Litwhiler	20.00	10.00	6.00
199	Jack Kramer	20.00	10.00	6.00
200	Kirby Higbe	20.00	10.00	6.00
201	Pete Castiglione	20.00	10.00	6.00
202	Cliff Chambers	20.00	10.00	6.00
203	Danny Murtaugh	20.00	10.00	6.00
204	Granny Hamner	20.00	10.00	6.00
205	Mike Goliat	20.00	10.00	6.00
206	Stan Lopata	20.00	10.00	6.00
207	Max Lanier	20.00	10.00	6.00
208	Jim Hearn	20.00	10.00	6.00
209	Johnny Lindell	20.00	10.00	6.00
210	Ted Gray	20.00	10.00	6.00
211	Charlie Keller	30.00	15.00	9.00
212	Gerry Priddy	20.00	10.00	6.00
213	Carl Scheib	20.00	10.00	6.00
214	Dick Fowler	20.00	10.00	6.00
215	Ed Lopat	50.00	25.00	15.00
216	Bob Porterfield	30.00	15.00	9.00
217	Casey Stengel	70.00	35.00	20.00
218	Cliff Mapes	30.00	15.00	9.00
219	***Hank Bauer***	70.00	35.00	20.00
220	Leo Durocher	60.00	30.00	18.00
221	Don Mueller	20.00	10.00	6.00
222	Bobby Morgan	25.00	12.50	7.50
223	Jimmy Russell	25.00	12.50	7.50
224	Jack Banta	25.00	12.50	7.50
225	Eddie Sawyer	20.00	10.00	6.00
226	***Jim Konstanty***	30.00	15.00	9.00
227	Bob Miller	20.00	10.00	6.00
228	Bill Nicholson	20.00	10.00	6.00
229	Frank Frisch	40.00	20.00	12.00
230	Bill Serena	20.00	10.00	6.00
231	Preston Ward	20.00	10.00	6.00
232	***Al Rosen***	55.00	27.50	16.50
233	Allie Clark	20.00	10.00	6.00
234	***Bobby Shantz***	45.00	22.50	13.50
235	Harold Gilbert	20.00	10.00	6.00
236	Bob Cain	20.00	10.00	6.00
237	Bill Salkeld	20.00	10.00	6.00
238	Nippy Jones	20.00	10.00	6.00
239	Bill Howerton	20.00	10.00	6.00
240	Eddie Lake	20.00	10.00	6.00
241	Neil Berry	20.00	10.00	6.00
242	Dick Kryhoski	20.00	10.00	6.00
243	Johnny Groth	20.00	10.00	6.00
244	Dale Coogan	20.00	10.00	6.00
245	Al Papai	20.00	10.00	6.00
246	***Walt Dropo***	35.00	17.50	10.00
247	***Irv Noren***	30.00	15.00	9.00
248	***Sam Jethroe***	40.00	20.00	12.00
249	"Snuffy" Stirnweiss	20.00	10.00	6.00
250	Ray Coleman	20.00	10.00	6.00
251	Les Moss	20.00	10.00	6.00
252	Billy DeMars	65.00	20.00	7.50

1951 Bowman

MICKEY VERNON
JAMES VERNON
First Base—Washington Senators
Born: Marcus Hook, Pa., April 22, 1918
Height: 6-2 Weight: 180
Bats: Left Throws: Left
James "Mickey" Vernon batted .281 in 118 games in 1950. Drove in 75 runs. Tied for top fielding percentage in the League with a .991 mark. Began the season with Cleveland, but after 28 games was switched back to Washington where all of major-league career has been spent except 1949 which was with Cleveland. First full season in the majors: 1941. Top AL batter, 1946. In service 2 years.
No. 65 in the 1951 SERIES
BASEBALL
PICTURE CARDS
©1951 Bowman Gum, Inc., Phila., Pa., U.S.A.

In 1951, Bowman increased the number of cards in its set for the third consecutive year when it issued 324 cards. The cards are, like 1950, color art reproductions of actual photographs but now measure 2-1/16" x 3-1/8" in size. The player's name is in a black strip on front. Several of the pictures are enlargements of the 1950 version. The high-numbered series (#253-324), which includes the rookie cards of Mantle and Mays, are the scarcest of the issue.

		NM	EX	VG
Complete Set (324):		20,000	9,500	5,500
Common Player (1-252):		17.50	9.00	5.00
Common Player (253-324):		40.00	20.00	12.00
1	***Whitey Ford***	1,200	460.00	200.00
2	Yogi Berra	375.00	125.00	75.00
3	Robin Roberts	75.00	37.50	22.50
4	Del Ennis	17.50	9.00	5.00
5	Dale Mitchell	17.50	9.00	5.00
6	Don Newcombe	75.00	37.50	22.50
7	Gil Hodges	80.00	40.00	25.00
8	Paul Lehner	17.50	9.00	5.00
9	Sam Chapman	17.50	9.00	5.00
10	Red Schoendienst	75.00	37.50	22.50
11	"Red" Munger	17.50	9.00	5.00
12	Hank Majeski	17.50	9.00	5.00
13	Ed Stanky	20.00	10.00	6.00
14	Alvin Dark	17.50	9.00	5.00
15	Johnny Pesky	17.50	9.00	5.00
16	Maurice McDermott	17.50	9.00	5.00
17	Pete Castiglione	17.50	9.00	5.00
18	Gil Coan	17.50	9.00	5.00
19	Sid Gordon	17.50	9.00	5.00
20	Del Crandall	17.50	9.00	5.00
21	"Snuffy" Stirnweiss	17.50	9.00	5.00
22	Hank Sauer	17.50	9.00	5.00
23	"Hoot" Evers	17.50	9.00	5.00
24	Ewell Blackwell	17.50	9.00	5.00
25	Vic Raschi	40.00	20.00	12.00
26	Phil Rizzuto	145.00	70.00	40.00
27	Jim Konstanty	17.50	9.00	5.00
28	Eddie Waitkus	17.50	9.00	5.00
29	Allie Clark	17.50	9.00	5.00
30	Bob Feller	120.00	60.00	35.00
31	Roy Campanella	190.00	95.00	55.00
32	Duke Snider	200.00	100.00	60.00
33	Bob Hooper	17.50	9.00	5.00
34	Marty Marion	25.00	12.50	7.50
35	Al Zarilla	17.50	9.00	5.00
36	Joe Dobson	17.50	9.00	5.00
37	Whitey Lockman	17.50	9.00	5.00
38	Al Evans	17.50	9.00	5.00
39	Ray Scarborough	17.50	9.00	5.00
40	***Gus Bell***	30.00	15.00	9.00
41	Eddie Yost	17.50	9.00	5.00
42	Vern Bickford	17.50	9.00	5.00

43	Billy DeMars	17.50	9.00	5.00
44	Roy Smalley	17.50	9.00	5.00
45	Art Houtteman	17.50	9.00	5.00
46	George Kell	50.00	25.00	15.00
47	Grady Hatton	17.50	9.00	5.00
48	Ken Raffensberger	17.50	9.00	5.00
49	Jerry Coleman	20.00	10.00	6.00
50	Johnny Mize	50.00	25.00	15.00
51	Andy Seminick	17.50	9.00	5.00
52	Dick Sisler	17.50	9.00	5.00
53	Bob Lemon	50.00	25.00	15.00
54	***Ray Boone***	35.00	17.50	10.00
55	Gene Hermanski	20.00	10.00	6.00
56	Ralph Branca	50.00	25.00	15.00
57	Alex Kellner	17.50	9.00	5.00
58	Enos Slaughter	50.00	25.00	15.00
59	Randy Gumpert	17.50	9.00	5.00
60	"Chico" Carrasquel	20.00	10.00	6.00
61	Jim Hearn	17.50	9.00	5.00
62	Lou Boudreau	45.00	22.50	13.50
63	Bob Dillinger	17.50	9.00	5.00
64	Bill Werle	17.50	9.00	5.00
65	Mickey Vernon	17.50	9.00	5.00
66	Bob Elliott	17.50	9.00	5.00
67	Roy Sievers	17.50	9.00	5.00
68	Dick Kokos	17.50	9.00	5.00
69	Johnny Schmitz	17.50	9.00	5.00
70	Ron Northey	17.50	9.00	5.00
71	Jerry Priddy	17.50	9.00	5.00
72	Lloyd Merriman	17.50	9.00	5.00
73	Tommy Byrne	20.00	10.00	6.00
74	Billy Johnson	20.00	10.00	6.00
75	Russ Meyer	17.50	9.00	5.00
76	Stan Lopata	17.50	9.00	5.00
77	Mike Goliat	17.50	9.00	5.00
78	Early Wynn	60.00	30.00	18.00
79	Jim Hegan	17.50	9.00	5.00
80	Pee Wee Reese	125.00	65.00	35.00
81	Carl Furillo	55.00	27.50	16.50
82	Joe Tipton	17.50	9.00	5.00
83	Carl Scheib	17.50	9.00	5.00
84	Barney McCosky	17.50	9.00	5.00
85	Eddie Kazak	17.50	9.00	5.00
86	Harry Brecheen	17.50	9.00	5.00
87	Floyd Baker	17.50	9.00	5.00
88	Eddie Robinson	17.50	9.00	5.00
89	Henry Thompson	17.50	9.00	5.00
90	Dave Koslo	17.50	9.00	5.00
91	Clyde Vollmer	17.50	9.00	5.00
92	Vern Stephens	17.50	9.00	5.00
93	Danny O'Connell	17.50	9.00	5.00
94	Clyde McCullough	17.50	9.00	5.00
95	Sherry Robertson	17.50	9.00	5.00
96	Sandy Consuegra	17.50	9.00	5.00
97	Bob Kuzava	17.50	9.00	5.00
98	Willard Marshall	17.50	9.00	5.00
99	Earl Torgeson	17.50	9.00	5.00
100	Sherman Lollar	17.50	9.00	5.00
101	Owen Friend	17.50	9.00	5.00
102	Emil "Dutch" Leonard	17.50	9.00	5.00
103	Andy Pafko	17.50	9.00	5.00
104	Virgil "Fire" Trucks	17.50	9.00	5.00
105	Don Kolloway	17.50	9.00	5.00
106	Pat Mullin	17.50	9.00	5.00
107	Johnny Wyrostek	17.50	9.00	5.00
108	Virgil Stallcup	17.50	9.00	5.00
109	Allie Reynolds	45.00	22.50	13.50
110	Bobby Brown	30.00	15.00	9.00
111	Curt Simmons	17.50	9.00	5.00
112	Willie Jones	17.50	9.00	5.00
113	Bill "Swish" Nicholson	17.50	9.00	5.00
114	Sam Zoldak	17.50	9.00	5.00
115	Steve Gromek	17.50	9.00	5.00
116	Bruce Edwards	20.00	10.00	6.00
117	Eddie Miksis	20.00	10.00	6.00
118	Preacher Roe	60.00	30.00	18.00
119	Eddie Joost	17.50	9.00	5.00
120	Joe Coleman	17.50	9.00	5.00
121	Gerry Staley	17.50	9.00	5.00
122	***Joe Garagiola***	75.00	37.50	22.50
123	Howie Judson	17.50	9.00	5.00
124	Gus Niarhos	17.50	9.00	5.00
125	Bill Rigney	17.50	9.00	5.00
126	Bobby Thomson	50.00	25.00	15.00
127	***Sal Maglie***	75.00	37.50	22.50
128	Ellis Kinder	17.50	9.00	5.00
129	Matt Batts	17.50	9.00	5.00
130	Tom Saffell	17.50	9.00	5.00
131	Cliff Chambers	17.50	9.00	5.00
132	Cass Michaels	17.50	9.00	5.00
133	Sam Dente	17.50	9.00	5.00
134	Warren Spahn	135.00	65.00	40.00
135	Walker Cooper	17.50	9.00	5.00
136	Ray Coleman	17.50	9.00	5.00
137	Dick Starr	17.50	9.00	5.00
138	Phil Cavarretta	17.50	9.00	5.00
139	Doyle Lade	17.50	9.00	5.00
140	Eddie Lake	17.50	9.00	5.00
141	Fred Hutchinson	17.50	9.00	5.00
142	Aaron Robinson	17.50	9.00	5.00
143	Ted Kluszewski	60.00	30.00	18.00
144	Herman Wehmeier	17.50	9.00	5.00
145	Fred Sanford	17.50	9.00	5.00
146	Johnny Hopp	17.50	9.00	5.00
147	Ken Heintzelman	17.50	9.00	5.00
148	Granny Hamner	17.50	9.00	5.00
149	"Bubba" Church	17.50	9.00	5.00
150	Mike Garcia	17.50	9.00	5.00
151	Larry Doby	70.00	35.00	20.00
152	Cal Abrams	20.00	10.00	6.00
153	Rex Barney	20.00	10.00	6.00
154	Pete Suder	17.50	9.00	5.00
155	Lou Brissie	17.50	9.00	5.00
156	Del Rice	17.50	9.00	5.00
157	Al Brazle	17.50	9.00	5.00
158	Chuck Diering	17.50	9.00	5.00
159	Eddie Stewart	17.50	9.00	5.00
160	Phil Masi	17.50	9.00	5.00
161	Wes Westrum	17.50	9.00	5.00
162	Larry Jansen	17.50	9.00	5.00
163	Monte Kennedy	17.50	9.00	5.00
164	Bill Wight	17.50	9.00	5.00
165	Ted Williams	625.00	240.00	155.00
166	Stan Rojek	17.50	9.00	5.00
167	Murry Dickson	17.50	9.00	5.00
168	Sam Mele	17.50	9.00	5.00
169	Sid Hudson	17.50	9.00	5.00
170	Sibby Sisti	17.50	9.00	5.00
171	Buddy Kerr	17.50	9.00	5.00
172	Ned Garver	17.50	9.00	5.00
173	Hank Arft	17.50	9.00	5.00
174	Mickey Owen	17.50	9.00	5.00
175	Wayne Terwilliger	17.50	9.00	5.00
176	Vic Wertz	17.50	9.00	5.00
177	Charlie Keller	17.50	9.00	5.00
178	Ted Gray	17.50	9.00	5.00
179	Danny Litwhiler	17.50	9.00	5.00
180	Howie Fox	17.50	9.00	5.00
181	Casey Stengel	75.00	37.50	22.50
182	Tom Ferrick	20.00	10.00	6.00
183	Hank Bauer	35.00	17.50	10.00
184	Eddie Sawyer	17.50	9.00	5.00
185	Jimmy Bloodworth	17.50	9.00	5.00
186	Richie Ashburn	100.00	50.00	30.00
187	Al Rosen	35.00	17.50	10.00
188	***Roberto Avila***	25.00	12.50	7.50
189	Erv Palica	20.00	10.00	6.00
190	Joe Hatten	20.00	10.00	6.00
191	Billy Hitchcock	17.50	9.00	5.00
192	Hank Wyse	17.50	9.00	5.00
193	Ted Wilks	17.50	9.00	5.00
194	Harry "Peanuts" Lowrey	17.50	9.00	5.00
195	Paul Richards	20.00	10.00	6.00
196	***Bill Pierce***	32.50	16.00	10.00
197	Bob Cain	17.50	9.00	5.00
198	***Monte Irvin***	110.00	55.00	35.00
199	Sheldon Jones	17.50	9.00	5.00
200	Jack Kramer	17.50	9.00	5.00
201	Steve O'Neill	17.50	9.00	5.00
202	Mike Guerra	17.50	9.00	5.00
203	***Vernon Law***	40.00	20.00	12.00
204	Vic Lombardi	17.50	9.00	5.00
205	Mickey Grasso	17.50	9.00	5.00
206	Connie Marrero	17.50	9.00	5.00
207	Billy Southworth	17.50	9.00	5.00
208	"Blix" Donnelly	17.50	9.00	5.00
209	Ken Wood	17.50	9.00	5.00
210	Les Moss	17.50	9.00	5.00
211	Hal Jeffcoat	17.50	9.00	5.00
212	Bob Rush	17.50	9.00	5.00
213	Neil Berry	17.50	9.00	5.00
214	Bob Swift	17.50	9.00	5.00
215	Kent Peterson	17.50	9.00	5.00
216	Connie Ryan	17.50	9.00	5.00
217	Joe Page	27.50	13.50	8.00
218	Ed Lopat	32.50	16.00	10.00
219	***Gene Woodling***	40.00	20.00	12.00
220	Bob Miller	17.50	9.00	5.00
221	Dick Whitman	17.50	9.00	5.00
222	Thurman Tucker	17.50	9.00	5.00
223	Johnny Vander Meer	25.00	12.50	7.50
224	Billy Cox	27.50	13.50	8.00
225	***Dan Bankhead***	30.00	15.00	9.00
226	Jimmy Dykes	17.50	9.00	5.00
227	Bobby Shantz	20.00	10.00	6.00
228	***Cloyd Boyer***	17.50	9.00	5.00
229	Bill Howerton	17.50	9.00	5.00
230	Max Lanier	17.50	9.00	5.00
231	Luis Aloma	17.50	9.00	5.00
232	***Nellie Fox***	145.00	70.00	40.00
233	Leo Durocher	40.00	20.00	12.00
234	Clint Hartung	17.50	9.00	5.00
235	Jack Lohrke	17.50	9.00	5.00
236	"Buddy" Rosar	17.50	9.00	5.00
237	Billy Goodman	17.50	9.00	5.00
238	Pete Reiser	20.00	10.00	6.00
239	Bill MacDonald	17.50	9.00	5.00
240	Joe Haynes	17.50	9.00	5.00
241	Irv Noren	17.50	9.00	5.00
242	Sam Jethroe	17.50	9.00	5.00
243	Johnny Antonelli	17.50	9.00	5.00
244	Cliff Fannin	17.50	9.00	5.00
245	John Berardino	25.00	12.50	7.50
246	Bill Serena	17.50	9.00	5.00
247	Bob Ramazotti	17.50	9.00	5.00
248	***Johnny Klippstein***	17.50	9.00	5.00
249	Johnny Groth	17.50	9.00	5.00
250	Hank Borowy	17.50	9.00	5.00
251	Willard Ramsdell	17.50	9.00	5.00
252	"Dixie" Howell	17.50	9.00	5.00
253	***Mickey Mantle***	7,000	3,500	2,100
254	***Jackie Jensen***	85.00	40.00	25.00
255	Milo Candini	40.00	20.00	12.00
256	Ken Silvestri	40.00	20.00	12.00
257	Birdie Tebbetts	40.00	20.00	12.00
258	***Luke Easter***	45.00	22.50	13.50
259	Charlie Dressen	40.00	20.00	12.00
260	***Carl Erskine***	75.00	37.50	22.00
261	Wally Moses	40.00	20.00	12.00
262	Gus Zernial	40.00	20.00	12.00
263	Howie Pollet	40.00	20.00	12.00
264	Don Richmond	40.00	20.00	12.00
265	***Steve Bilko***	40.00	20.00	12.00
266	Harry Dorish	40.00	20.00	12.00
267	Ken Holcombe	40.00	20.00	12.00
268	Don Mueller	40.00	20.00	12.00
269	Ray Noble	40.00	20.00	12.00
270	Willard Nixon	40.00	20.00	12.00
271	Tommy Wright	40.00	20.00	12.00
272	Billy Meyer	40.00	20.00	12.00
273	Danny Murtaugh	40.00	20.00	12.00
274	George Metkovich	40.00	20.00	12.00
275	Bucky Harris	50.00	25.00	15.00
276	Frank Quinn	40.00	20.00	12.00
277	Roy Hartsfield	40.00	20.00	12.00
278	Norman Roy	40.00	20.00	12.00
279	Jim Delsing	40.00	20.00	12.00
280	Frank Overmire	40.00	20.00	12.00
281	Al Widmar	40.00	20.00	12.00
282	Frank Frisch	55.00	27.50	16.50
283	Walt Dubiel	40.00	20.00	12.00
284	Gene Bearden	40.00	20.00	12.00
285	Johnny Lipon	40.00	20.00	12.00
286	Bob Usher	40.00	20.00	12.00
287	Jim Blackburn	40.00	20.00	12.00
288	Bobby Adams	40.00	20.00	12.00
289	Cliff Mapes	50.00	25.00	15.00
290	Bill Dickey	85.00	42.50	25.00
291	Tommy Henrich	55.00	27.50	16.50
292	Eddie Pellagrini	40.00	20.00	12.00
293	Ken Johnson	40.00	20.00	12.00
294	Jocko Thompson	40.00	20.00	12.00
295	Al Lopez	70.00	35.00	20.00
296	Bob Kennedy	40.00	20.00	12.00
297	Dave Philley	40.00	20.00	12.00
298	Joe Astroth	40.00	20.00	12.00
299	Clyde King	50.00	25.00	15.00
300	Hal Rice	40.00	20.00	12.00
301	Tommy Glaviano	40.00	20.00	12.00
302	Jim Busby	40.00	20.00	12.00
303	Marv Rotblatt	40.00	20.00	12.00
304	Allen Gettel	40.00	20.00	12.00
305	***Willie Mays***	2,400	900.00	480.00
306	***Jim Piersall***	90.00	45.00	27.50
307	Walt Masterson	40.00	20.00	12.00
308	Ted Beard	40.00	20.00	12.00
309	Mel Queen	40.00	20.00	12.00
310	Erv Dusak	40.00	20.00	12.00
311	Mickey Harris	40.00	20.00	12.00
312	***Gene Mauch***	50.00	25.00	15.00
313	Ray Mueller	40.00	20.00	12.00
314	Johnny Sain	45.00	22.50	13.50
315	Zack Taylor	40.00	20.00	12.00
316	Duane Pillette	40.00	20.00	12.00
317	***Smoky Burgess***	60.00	30.00	18.00
318	Warren Hacker	40.00	20.00	12.00
319	Red Rolfe	40.00	20.00	12.00
320	Hal White	40.00	20.00	12.00
321	Earl Johnson	40.00	20.00	12.00
322	Luke Sewell	40.00	20.00	12.00
323	***Joe Adcock***	80.00	35.00	20.00
324	Johnny Pramesa	100.00	22.50	12.00

1952 Bowman

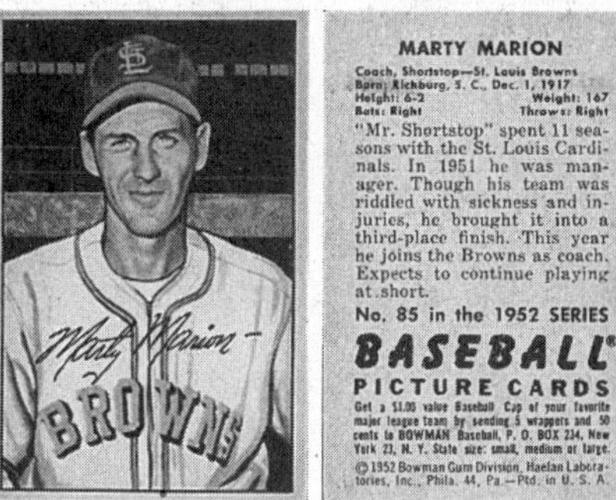

Bowman reverted to a 252-card set in 1952, but retained the card size (2-1/16" x 3-1/8") employed the preceding year. The cards, which are color art reproductions of actual photographs, feature a facsimile autograph on front.

		NM	EX	VG
Complete Set (252):		10,000	5,000	3,000
Common Player (1-216):		20.00	10.00	6.00
Common Player (217-252):		40.00	20.00	12.00
1	Yogi Berra	525.00	160.00	65.00
2	Bobby Thomson	70.00	35.00	20.00
3	Fred Hutchinson	20.00	10.00	6.00
4	Robin Roberts	100.00	50.00	30.00
5	***Minnie Minoso***	90.00	45.00	27.50
6	Virgil "Red" Stallcup	20.00	10.00	6.00
7	Mike Garcia	20.00	10.00	6.00
8	Pee Wee Reese	95.00	47.50	27.50
9	Vern Stephens	20.00	10.00	6.00
10	Bob Hooper	20.00	10.00	6.00
11	Ralph Kiner	60.00	30.00	18.00
12	Max Surkont	20.00	10.00	6.00
13	Cliff Mapes	20.00	10.00	6.00
14	Cliff Chambers	20.00	10.00	6.00
15	Sam Mele	20.00	10.00	6.00
16	Omar Lown	20.00	10.00	6.00
17	Ed Lopat	55.00	27.50	16.50
18	Don Mueller	20.00	10.00	6.00
19	Bob Cain	20.00	10.00	6.00
20	Willie Jones	20.00	10.00	6.00
21	Nellie Fox	65.00	32.50	20.00
22	Willard Ramsdell	20.00	10.00	6.00
23	Bob Lemon	60.00	30.00	18.00
24	Carl Furillo	50.00	25.00	15.00
25	Maurice McDermott	20.00	10.00	6.00
26	Eddie Joost	20.00	10.00	6.00
27	Joe Garagiola	30.00	15.00	9.00
28	Roy Hartsfield	20.00	10.00	6.00
29	Ned Garver	20.00	10.00	6.00
30	Red Schoendienst	45.00	22.50	13.50
31	Eddie Yost	20.00	10.00	6.00
32	Eddie Miksis	20.00	10.00	6.00
33	***Gil McDougald***	60.00	30.00	18.00
34	Al Dark	20.00	10.00	6.00
35	Granny Hamner	20.00	10.00	6.00
36	Cass Michaels	20.00	10.00	6.00
37	Vic Raschi	30.00	15.00	9.00
38	Whitey Lockman	20.00	10.00	6.00

39 Vic Wertz 20.00 10.00 6.00
40 "Bubba" Church 20.00 10.00 6.00
41 "Chico" Carrasquel 20.00 10.00 6.00
42 Johnny Wyrostek 20.00 10.00 6.00
43 Bob Feller 120.00 60.00 35.00
44 Roy Campanella 160.00 80.00 50.00
45 Johnny Pesky 20.00 10.00 6.00
46 Carl Scheib 20.00 10.00 6.00
47 Pete Castiglione 20.00 10.00 6.00
48 Vernon Bickford 20.00 10.00 6.00
49 Jim Hearn 20.00 10.00 6.00
50 Gerry Staley 20.00 10.00 6.00
51 Gil Coan 20.00 10.00 6.00
52 Phil Rizzuto 125.00 65.00 35.00
53 Richie Ashburn 90.00 45.00 27.50
54 Billy Pierce 25.00 12.50 7.50
55 Ken Raffensberger 20.00 10.00 6.00
56 Clyde King 25.00 12.50 7.50
57 Clyde Vollmer 20.00 10.00 6.00
58 Hank Majeski 20.00 10.00 6.00
59 Murry Dickson 20.00 10.00 6.00
60 Sid Gordon 20.00 10.00 6.00
61 Tommy Byrne 20.00 10.00 6.00
62 Joe Presko 20.00 10.00 6.00
63 Irv Noren 20.00 10.00 6.00
64 Roy Smalley 20.00 10.00 6.00
65 Hank Bauer 50.00 25.00 15.00
66 Sal Maglie 25.00 12.50 7.50
67 Johnny Groth 20.00 10.00 6.00
68 Jim Busby 20.00 10.00 6.00
69 Joe Adcock 20.00 10.00 6.00
70 Carl Erskine 40.00 20.00 12.00
71 Vernon Law 20.00 10.00 6.00
72 Earl Torgeson 20.00 10.00 6.00
73 Jerry Coleman 30.00 15.00 9.00
74 Wes Westrum 20.00 10.00 6.00
75 George Kell 45.00 22.50 13.50
76 Del Ennis 20.00 10.00 6.00
77 Eddie Robinson 20.00 10.00 6.00
78 Lloyd Merriman 20.00 10.00 6.00
79 Lou Brissie 20.00 10.00 6.00
80 Gil Hodges 100.00 50.00 30.00
81 Billy Goodman 20.00 10.00 6.00
82 Gus Zernial 20.00 10.00 6.00
83 Howie Pollet 20.00 10.00 6.00
84 Sam Jethroe 20.00 10.00 6.00
85 Marty Marion 25.00 12.50 7.50
86 Cal Abrams 25.00 12.50 7.50
87 Mickey Vernon 20.00 10.00 6.00
88 Bruce Edwards 20.00 10.00 6.00
89 Billy Hitchcock 20.00 10.00 6.00
90 Larry Jansen 20.00 10.00 6.00
91 Don Kolloway 20.00 10.00 6.00
92 Eddie Waitkus 20.00 10.00 6.00
93 Paul Richards 20.00 10.00 6.00
94 Luke Sewell 20.00 10.00 6.00
95 Luke Easter 20.00 10.00 6.00
96 Ralph Branca 40.00 20.00 12.00
97 Willard Marshall 20.00 10.00 6.00
98 Jimmy Dykes 20.00 10.00 6.00
99 Clyde McCullough 20.00 10.00 6.00
100 Sibby Sisti 20.00 10.00 6.00
101 Mickey Mantle 1,450 650.00 365.00
102 Peanuts Lowrey 20.00 10.00 6.00
103 Joe Haynes 20.00 10.00 6.00
104 Hal Jeffcoat 20.00 10.00 6.00
105 Bobby Brown 35.00 17.50 10.00
106 Randy Gumpert 20.00 10.00 6.00
107 Del Rice 20.00 10.00 6.00
108 George Metkovich 20.00 10.00 6.00
109 Tom Morgan 30.00 15.00 9.00
110 Max Lanier 20.00 10.00 6.00
111 "Hoot" Evers 20.00 10.00 6.00
112 "Smoky" Burgess 20.00 10.00 6.00
113 Al Zarilla 20.00 10.00 6.00
114 Frank Hiller 20.00 10.00 6.00
115 Larry Doby 60.00 30.00 18.00
116 Duke Snider 200.00 100.00 60.00
117 Bill Wight 20.00 10.00 6.00
118 Ray Murray 20.00 10.00 6.00
119 Bill Howerton 20.00 10.00 6.00
120 Chet Nichols 20.00 10.00 6.00
121 Al Corwin 20.00 10.00 6.00
122 Billy Johnson 20.00 10.00 6.00
123 Sid Hudson 20.00 10.00 6.00
124 Birdie Tebbetts 20.00 10.00 6.00
125 Howie Fox 20.00 10.00 6.00
126 Phil Cavarretta 20.00 10.00 6.00
127 Dick Sisler 20.00 10.00 6.00
128 Don Newcombe 45.00 22.50 13.50
129 Gus Niarhos 20.00 10.00 6.00
130 Allie Clark 20.00 10.00 6.00
131 Bob Swift 20.00 10.00 6.00
132 Dave Cole 20.00 10.00 6.00
133 Dick Kryhoski 20.00 10.00 6.00
134 Al Brazle 20.00 10.00 6.00
135 Mickey Harris 20.00 10.00 6.00
136 Gene Hermanski 20.00 10.00 6.00
137 Stan Rojek 20.00 10.00 6.00
138 Ted Wilks 20.00 10.00 6.00
139 Jerry Priddy 20.00 10.00 6.00
140 Ray Scarborough 20.00 10.00 6.00
141 Hank Edwards 20.00 10.00 6.00
142 Early Wynn 45.00 22.50 13.50
143 Sandy Consuegra 20.00 10.00 6.00
144 Joe Hatten 20.00 10.00 6.00
145 Johnny Mize 80.00 40.00 24.00
146 Leo Durocher 45.00 22.50 13.50
147 Marlin Stuart 20.00 10.00 6.00
148 Ken Heintzelman 20.00 10.00 6.00
149 Howie Judson 20.00 10.00 6.00
150 Herman Wehmeier 20.00 10.00 6.00
151 Al Rosen 30.00 15.00 9.00
152 Billy Cox 40.00 20.00 12.00
153 Fred Hatfield 20.00 10.00 6.00
154 Ferris Fain 20.00 10.00 6.00
155 Billy Meyer 20.00 10.00 6.00
156 Warren Spahn 90.00 45.00 27.50
157 Jim Delsing 20.00 10.00 6.00
158 Bucky Harris 30.00 15.00 9.00
159 Dutch Leonard 20.00 10.00 6.00
160 Eddie Stanky 20.00 10.00 6.00
161 Jackie Jensen 45.00 22.50 13.50
162 Monte Irvin 55.00 27.50 16.50
163 Johnny Lipon 20.00 10.00 6.00
164 Connie Ryan 20.00 10.00 6.00
165 Saul Rogovin 20.00 10.00 6.00
166 Bobby Adams 20.00 10.00 6.00
167 Bob Avila 20.00 10.00 6.00
168 Preacher Roe 35.00 17.50 10.00
169 Walt Dropo 20.00 10.00 6.00
170 Joe Astroth 20.00 10.00 6.00
171 Mel Queen 20.00 10.00 6.00
172 Ebba St. Claire 20.00 10.00 6.00
173 Gene Bearden 20.00 10.00 6.00
174 Mickey Grasso 20.00 10.00 6.00
175 Ransom Jackson 20.00 10.00 6.00
176 Harry Brecheen 20.00 10.00 6.00
177 Gene Woodling 35.00 17.50 10.00
178 Dave Williams 20.00 10.00 6.00
179 Pete Suder 20.00 10.00 6.00
180 Eddie Fitz Gerald 20.00 10.00 6.00
181 Joe Collins 30.00 15.00 9.00
182 Dave Koslo 20.00 10.00 6.00
183 Pat Mullin 20.00 10.00 6.00
184 Curt Simmons 20.00 10.00 6.00
185 Eddie Stewart 20.00 10.00 6.00
186 Frank Smith 20.00 10.00 6.00
187 Jim Hegan 20.00 10.00 6.00
188 Charlie Dressen 30.00 15.00 9.00
189 Jim Piersall 30.00 15.00 9.00
190 Dick Fowler 20.00 10.00 6.00
191 ***Bob Friend*** 25.00 12.50 7.50
192 John Cusick 20.00 10.00 6.00
193 Bobby Young 20.00 10.00 6.00
194 Bob Porterfield 20.00 10.00 6.00
195 Frank Baumholtz 20.00 10.00 6.00
196 Stan Musial 335.00 160.00 85.00
197 ***Charlie Silvera*** 35.00 17.50 10.00
198 Chuck Diering 20.00 10.00 6.00
199 Ted Gray 20.00 10.00 6.00
200 Ken Silvestri 20.00 10.00 6.00
201 Ray Coleman 20.00 10.00 6.00
202 Harry Perkowski 20.00 10.00 6.00
203 Steve Gromek 20.00 10.00 6.00
204 Andy Pafko 20.00 10.00 6.00
205 Walt Masterson 20.00 10.00 6.00
206 Elmer Valo 20.00 10.00 6.00
207 George Strickland 20.00 10.00 6.00
208 Walker Cooper 20.00 10.00 6.00
209 Dick Littlefield 20.00 10.00 6.00
210 Archie Wilson 20.00 10.00 6.00
211 Paul Minner 20.00 10.00 6.00
212 Solly Hemus 20.00 10.00 6.00
213 Monte Kennedy 20.00 10.00 6.00
214 Ray Boone 20.00 10.00 6.00
215 Sheldon Jones 20.00 10.00 6.00
216 Matt Batts 20.00 10.00 6.00
217 Casey Stengel 125.00 60.00 35.00
218 Willie Mays 925.00 400.00 175.00
219 Neil Berry 40.00 20.00 12.00
220 Russ Meyer 40.00 20.00 12.00
221 Lou Kretlow 40.00 20.00 12.00
222 "Dixie" Howell 40.00 20.00 12.00
223 ***Harry Simpson*** 45.00 22.50 13.50
224 Johnny Schmitz 40.00 20.00 12.00
225 Del Wilber 40.00 20.00 12.00
226 Alex Kellner 40.00 20.00 12.00
227 Clyde Sukeforth 40.00 20.00 12.00
228 Bob Chipman 40.00 20.00 12.00
229 Hank Arft 40.00 20.00 12.00
230 Frank Shea 40.00 20.00 12.00
231 ***Dee Fondy*** 40.00 20.00 12.00
232 Enos Slaughter 95.00 47.50 27.50
233 Bob Kuzava 50.00 25.00 15.00
234 Fred Fitzsimmons 40.00 20.00 12.00
235 Steve Souchock 40.00 20.00 12.00
236 Tommy Brown 40.00 20.00 12.00
237 Sherman Lollar 40.00 20.00 12.00
238 ***Roy McMillan*** 40.00 20.00 12.00
239 Dale Mitchell 40.00 20.00 12.00
240 ***Billy Loes*** 45.00 22.50 13.50
241 Mel Parnell 40.00 20.00 12.00
242 Everett Kell 40.00 20.00 12.00
243 "Red" Munger 40.00 20.00 12.00
244 ***Lew Burdette*** 60.00 30.00 18.00
245 George Schmees 40.00 20.00 12.00
246 Jerry Snyder 40.00 20.00 12.00
247 John Pramesa 40.00 20.00 12.00
248a Bill Werle (. after G and most of W missing) 40.00 20.00 12.00
248b Bill Werle (Full signature.) 40.00 20.00 12.00
249 Henry Thompson 40.00 20.00 12.00
250 Ike Delock 40.00 20.00 12.00
251 Jack Lohrke 40.00 20.00 12.00
252 Frank Crosetti 180.00 30.00 15.00

1952 Bowman Proofs

Coincident to Topps issue of its "Giant Size" baseball cards in 1952, Bowman began experimenting with up-sizing its card issues from the then-current 2-1/16" x 3-1/8". A group of proof cards was produced using 12 players from the '52 Bowman set. The proofs are 2-1/2" x 3-3/4", overall about 45% larger than the issued '52s. Each proof is found in two types, black-and-white and color. Both have blank-backs except for hand-written notes with the player's name, team and card number in the '52 set. Many of the proofs feature slight differences from the issued versions, such as uniform changes, elimination of background elements or picture cropping. The color proofs include a facsimile autograph. A small group of these proof cards entered the hobby

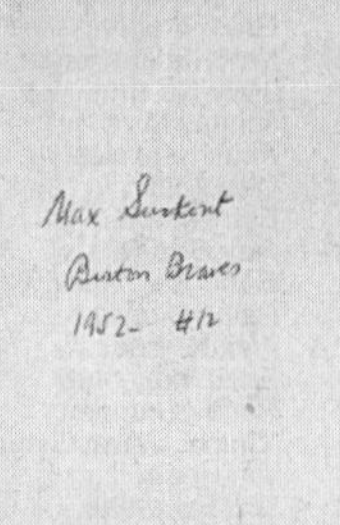

early in the 1980s when a former Bowman executive disposed of his hobby card files. The proofs are numbered according to their number within the 1952 Bowman set.

		NM	EX	VG
Common Player, B/W:		300.00	150.00	90.00
Common Player, Color:		450.00	225.00	135.00
1	Yogi Berra (B/W)	1,000	500.00	300.00
1	Yogi Berra (Color)	1,600	800.00	480.00
2	Bobby Thomson (B/W)	600.00	300.00	180.00
2	Bobby Thomson (Color)	1,000	500.00	300.00
3	Fred Hutchinson (B/W)	400.00	200.00	120.00
3	Fred Hutchinson (Color)	450.00	225.00	135.00
4	Robin Roberts (B/W)	725.00	360.00	215.00
4	Robin Roberts (Color)	1,200	600.00	360.00
10	Bob Hooper (B/W)	400.00	200.00	120.00
10	Bob Hooper (Color)	450.00	225.00	135.00
11	Ralph Kiner (B/W)	725.00	360.00	215.00
11	Ralph Kiner (Color)	1,200	600.00	360.00
12	Max Surkont (B/W)	400.00	200.00	120.00
12	Max Surkont (Color)	450.00	225.00	135.00
13	Cliff Mapes (B/W)	400.00	200.00	120.00
13	Cliff Mapes (Color)	450.00	225.00	135.00
14	Cliff Chambers (B/W)	400.00	200.00	120.00
14	Cliff Chambers (Color)	450.00	225.00	135.00
34	Alvin Dark (B/W)	400.00	200.00	120.00
34	Alvin Dark (Color)	450.00	225.00	135.00
39	Vic Wertz (B/W)	400.00	200.00	120.00
39	Vic Wertz (Color)	450.00	225.00	135.00
142	Early Wynn (B/W)	650.00	325.00	195.00
142	Early Wynn (Color)	1,200	600.00	360.00
176	Harry Brecheen (B/W)	400.00	200.00	120.00
176	Harry Brecheen (Color)	450.00	225.00	135.00

1953 Bowman

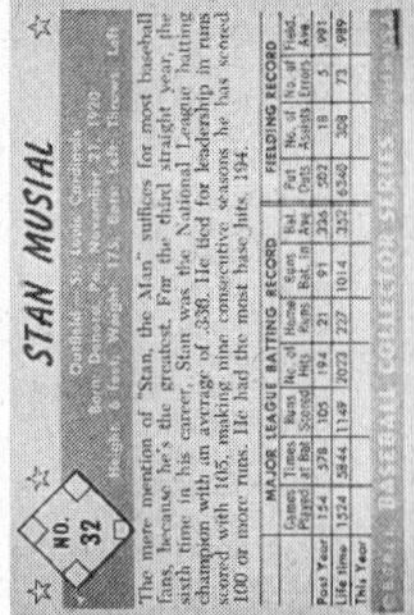

The first set of contemporary major league players featuring actual color photographs, the 160-card 1953 Bowman color set remains one of the most popular issues of the postwar era. The set is greatly appreciated for its uncluttered look; card fronts that contain no names, teams or facsimile autographs. Bowman increased the size of the cards to 2-1/2" x 3-3/4" to better compete with Topps' larger format. Bowman copied an idea from the 1952 Topps set and developed card backs that gave player career and previous-year statistics. The high-numbered cards (#113-160) are the scarcest of the set, with #113-128 being especially scarce.

		NM	EX	VG
Complete Set (160):		16,000	7,500	4,250
Common Player (1-112):		35.00	17.50	10.00
Common Player (113-160):		90.00	45.00	25.00
1	Davey Williams	300.00	45.00	13.50
2	Vic Wertz	45.00	17.50	10.00
3	Sam Jethroe	35.00	17.50	10.00
4	Art Houtteman	35.00	17.50	10.00
5	Sid Gordon	35.00	17.50	10.00
6	Joe Ginsberg	35.00	17.50	10.00
7	Harry Chiti	35.00	17.50	10.00
8	Al Rosen	55.00	27.50	16.50
9	Phil Rizzuto	210.00	105.00	60.00
10	Richie Ashburn	110.00	55.00	35.00
11	Bobby Shantz	35.00	17.50	10.00
12	Carl Erskine	50.00	25.00	15.00
13	Gus Zernial	35.00	17.50	10.00
14	Billy Loes	55.00	27.50	16.50
15	Jim Busby	35.00	17.50	10.00
16	Bob Friend	35.00	17.50	10.00
17	Gerry Staley	35.00	17.50	10.00
18	Nellie Fox	90.00	45.00	25.00
19	Al Dark	35.00	17.50	10.00
20	Don Lenhardt	35.00	17.50	10.00
21	Joe Garagiola	50.00	25.00	15.00

22	Bob Porterfield	35.00	17.50	10.00
23	Herman Wehmeier	35.00	17.50	10.00
24	Jackie Jensen	45.00	22.50	13.50
25	"Hoot" Evers	35.00	17.50	10.00
26	Roy McMillan	35.00	17.50	10.00
27	Vic Raschi	70.00	35.00	20.00
28	"Smoky" Burgess	45.00	22.50	13.50
29	Roberto Avila	35.00	17.50	10.00
30	Phil Cavarretta	35.00	17.50	10.00
31	Jimmy Dykes	35.00	17.50	10.00
32	Stan Musial	465.00	160.00	90.00
33	Pee Wee Reese	550.00	275.00	165.00
34	Gil Coan	35.00	17.50	10.00
35	Maury McDermott	35.00	17.50	10.00
36	Minnie Minoso	85.00	42.50	25.00
37	Jim Wilson	35.00	17.50	10.00
38	Harry Byrd	35.00	17.50	10.00
39	Paul Richards	35.00	17.50	10.00
40	Larry Doby	145.00	75.00	45.00
41	Sammy White	35.00	17.50	10.00
42	Tommy Brown	35.00	17.50	10.00
43	Mike Garcia	35.00	17.50	10.00
44	Hank Bauer, Yogi Berra, Mickey Mantle	675.00	230.00	125.00
45	Walt Dropo	35.00	17.50	10.00
46	Roy Campanella	215.00	105.00	65.00
47	Ned Garver	35.00	17.50	10.00
48	Hank Sauer	35.00	17.50	10.00
49	Eddie Stanky	35.00	17.50	10.00
50	Lou Kretlow	35.00	17.50	10.00
51	Monte Irvin	55.00	27.50	16.50
52	Marty Marion	45.00	22.50	13.50
53	Del Rice	35.00	17.50	10.00
54	"Chico" Carrasquel	35.00	17.50	10.00
55	Leo Durocher	70.00	35.00	20.00
56	Bob Cain	35.00	17.50	10.00
57	Lou Boudreau	75.00	37.50	22.50
58	Willard Marshall	35.00	17.50	10.00
59	Mickey Mantle	1,200	525.00	290.00
60	Granny Hamner	35.00	17.50	10.00
61	George Kell	60.00	30.00	18.00
62	Ted Kluszewski	90.00	45.00	27.50
63	Gil McDougald	85.00	42.50	25.00
64	Curt Simmons	35.00	17.50	10.50
65	Robin Roberts	110.00	55.00	35.00
66	Mel Parnell	35.00	17.50	10.00
67	Mel Clark	35.00	17.50	10.00
68	Allie Reynolds	85.00	42.50	25.00
69	Charlie Grimm	35.00	17.50	10.00
70	Clint Courtney	35.00	17.50	10.00
71	Paul Minner	35.00	17.50	10.00
72	Ted Gray	35.00	17.50	10.00
73	Billy Pierce	40.00	20.00	12.00
74	Don Mueller	35.00	17.50	10.00
75	Saul Rogovin	35.00	17.50	10.00
76	Jim Hearn	35.00	17.50	10.00
77	Mickey Grasso	35.00	17.50	10.00
78	Carl Furillo	80.00	40.00	25.00
79	Ray Boone	35.00	17.50	10.00
80	Ralph Kiner	115.00	55.00	35.00
81	Enos Slaughter	145.00	70.00	45.00
82	Joe Astroth	35.00	17.50	10.00
83	Jack Daniels	35.00	17.50	10.00
84	Hank Bauer	80.00	40.00	25.00
85	Solly Hemus	35.00	17.50	10.00
86	Harry Simpson	35.00	17.50	10.00
87	Harry Perkowski	35.00	17.50	10.00
88	Joe Dobson	35.00	17.50	10.00
89	Sandalio Consuegra	35.00	17.50	10.00
90	Joe Nuxhall	35.00	17.50	10.00
91	Steve Souchock	35.00	17.50	10.00
92	Gil Hodges	190.00	95.00	55.00
93	Billy Martin, Phil Rizzuto	235.00	115.00	70.00
94	Bob Addis	35.00	17.50	10.00
95	Wally Moses	35.00	17.50	10.00
96	Sal Maglie	65.00	32.50	20.00
97	Eddie Mathews	275.00	135.00	80.00
98	Hector Rodriquez	35.00	17.50	10.00
99	Warren Spahn	280.00	140.00	85.00
100	Bill Wight	35.00	17.50	10.00
101	Red Schoendienst	95.00	47.50	27.50
102	Jim Hegan	35.00	17.50	10.00
103	Del Ennis	35.00	17.50	10.00
104	Luke Easter	35.00	17.50	10.00
105	Eddie Joost	35.00	17.50	10.00
106	Ken Raffensberger	35.00	17.50	10.00
107	Alex Kellner	35.00	17.50	10.00
108	Bobby Adams	35.00	17.50	10.00
109	Ken Wood	35.00	17.50	10.00
110	Bob Rush	35.00	17.50	10.00
111	Jim Dyck	35.00	17.50	10.00
112	Toby Atwell	35.00	17.50	10.00
113	Karl Drews	90.00	45.00	25.00
114	Bob Feller	525.00	230.00	125.00
115	Cloyd Boyer	90.00	45.00	25.00
116	Eddie Yost	90.00	45.00	25.00
117	Duke Snider	625.00	265.00	145.00
118	Billy Martin	425.00	210.00	125.00
119	Dale Mitchell	90.00	45.00	25.00
120	Marlin Stuart	90.00	45.00	25.00
121	Yogi Berra	600.00	300.00	180.00
122	Bill Serena	90.00	45.00	25.00
123	Johnny Lipon	90.00	45.00	25.00
124	Charlie Dressen	110.00	55.00	35.00
125	Fred Hatfield	90.00	45.00	25.00
126	Al Corwin	90.00	45.00	25.00
127	Dick Kryhoski	90.00	45.00	25.00
128	"Whitey" Lockman	90.00	45.00	25.00
129	Russ Meyer	95.00	47.50	27.50
130	Cass Michaels	90.00	45.00	25.00
131	Connie Ryan	90.00	45.00	25.00
132	Fred Hutchinson	90.00	45.00	25.00
133	Willie Jones	90.00	45.00	25.00
134	Johnny Pesky	90.00	45.00	25.00
135	Bobby Morgan	95.00	47.50	27.50
136	Jim Brideweser	100.00	50.00	30.00
137	Sam Dente	90.00	45.00	25.00
138	"Bubba" Church	90.00	45.00	25.00
139	Pete Runnels	90.00	45.00	25.00
140	Alpha Brazle	90.00	45.00	25.00
141	Frank "Spec" Shea	90.00	45.00	25.00
142	Larry Miggins	90.00	45.00	25.00
143	Al Lopez	115.00	55.00	35.00
144	Warren Hacker	90.00	45.00	25.00
145	George Shuba	125.00	60.00	35.00
146	Early Wynn	210.00	105.00	60.00
147	Clem Koshorek	90.00	45.00	25.00
148	Billy Goodman	90.00	45.00	25.00
149	Al Corwin	90.00	45.00	25.00
150	Carl Scheib	90.00	45.00	25.00
151	Joe Adcock	90.00	45.00	25.00
152	Clyde Vollmer	90.00	45.00	25.00
153	Whitey Ford	700.00	350.00	210.00
154	Omar "Turk" Lown	90.00	45.00	25.00
155	Allie Clark	90.00	45.00	25.00
156	Max Surkont	90.00	45.00	25.00
157	Sherman Lollar	90.00	45.00	25.00
158	Howard Fox	90.00	45.00	25.00
159	Mickey Vernon (Photo actually Floyd Baker.)	95.00	47.50	27.50
160	Cal Abrams	425.00	50.00	27.50

1953 Bowman Black & White

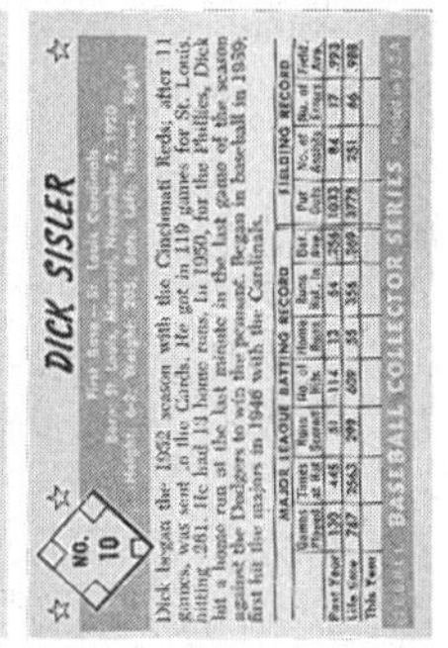

The 1953 Bowman black-and-white set is similar in all respects to the 1953 Bowman color cards, except that it lacks color. Sixty-four cards, which measure 2-1/2" x 3-3/4", comprise the set.

		NM	EX	VG
Complete Set (64):		4,500	2,125	1,275
Common Player:		55.00	25.00	15.00
1	Gus Bell	215.00	35.00	20.00
2	Willard Nixon	65.00	30.00	15.00
3	Bill Rigney	55.00	25.00	15.00
4	Pat Mullin	55.00	25.00	15.00
5	Dee Fondy	55.00	25.00	15.00
6	Ray Murray	55.00	25.00	15.00
7	Andy Seminick	55.00	25.00	15.00
8	Pete Suder	55.00	25.00	15.00
9	Walt Masterson	55.00	25.00	15.00
10	Dick Sisler	55.00	25.00	15.00
11	Dick Gernert	55.00	25.00	15.00
12	Randy Jackson	55.00	25.00	15.00
13	Joe Tipton	55.00	25.00	15.00
14	Bill Nicholson	55.00	25.00	15.00
15	Johnny Mize	100.00	50.00	30.00
16	Stu Miller	55.00	25.00	15.00
17	Virgil Trucks	55.00	25.00	15.00
18	Billy Hoeft	55.00	25.00	15.00
19	Paul LaPalme	55.00	25.00	15.00
20	Eddie Robinson	55.00	25.00	15.00
21	Clarence "Bud" Podbielan	55.00	25.00	15.00
22	Matt Batts	55.00	25.00	15.00
23	Wilmer Mizell	55.00	25.00	15.00
24	Del Wilber	55.00	25.00	15.00
25	Johnny Sain	100.00	50.00	30.00
26	Preacher Roe	90.00	45.00	25.00
27	Bob Lemon	130.00	65.00	35.00
28	Hoyt Wilhelm	140.00	70.00	40.00
29	Sid Hudson	55.00	25.00	15.00
30	Walker Cooper	55.00	25.00	15.00
31	Gene Woodling	100.00	50.00	30.00
32	Rocky Bridges	55.00	25.00	15.00
33	Bob Kuzava	55.00	25.00	15.00
34	Ebba St. Clair (St. Claire)	55.00	25.00	15.00
35	Johnny Wyrostek	55.00	25.00	15.00
36	Jim Piersall	90.00	45.00	25.00
37	Hal Jeffcoat	55.00	25.00	15.00
38	Dave Cole	55.00	25.00	15.00
39	Casey Stengel	600.00	225.00	115.00
40	Larry Jansen	55.00	25.00	15.00
41	Bob Ramazotti	55.00	25.00	15.00
42	Howie Judson	55.00	25.00	15.00
43a	Hal Bevan (Birth year 1950.)	55.00	25.00	15.00
43b	Hal Bevan (Birth year 1930.)	120.00	60.00	35.00
44	Jim Delsing	55.00	25.00	15.00
45	Irv Noren	100.00	50.00	30.00
46	Bucky Harris	100.00	50.00	35.00
47	Jack Lohrke	55.00	25.00	15.00
48	Steve Ridzik	55.00	25.00	15.00
49	Floyd Baker	55.00	25.00	15.00
50	Emil "Dutch" Leonard	55.00	25.00	15.00
51	Lew Burdette	75.00	35.00	20.00
52	Ralph Branca	100.00	50.00	30.00
53	Morris Martin	55.00	25.00	15.00
54	Bill Miller	55.00	25.00	15.00
55	Don Johnson	55.00	25.00	15.00
56	Roy Smalley	55.00	25.00	15.00
57	Andy Pafko	55.00	25.00	15.00
58	Jim Konstanty	55.00	25.00	15.00
59	Duane Pillette	55.00	25.00	15.00
60	Billy Cox	100.00	50.00	30.00
61	Tom Gorman	80.00	40.00	25.00
62	Keith Thomas	55.00	25.00	15.00
63	Steve Gromek	55.00	25.00	15.00
64	Andy Hansen	75.00	25.00	15.00

1953 Bowman Color Proofs

Four subjects are known to have survived in proof form created prior to the production of Bowman's landmark 1953 color card set. In the same 2-1/2" x 3-3/4" size as the issued cards, the proofs are blank-backed and lack the black frame line separating the picture from the white border. The Enos Slaughter card is otherwise identical to the issued version. The Spahn was changed to a different, more close-up picture for the issued card. The "Dodgers In Action" card was never issued, nor was the Ferris Fain card, probably due to Fain's trade from the A's to the White Sox prior to the 1953 season.

		NM	EX	VG
Complete Set (4):		4,800	2,400	1,450
Common Player:		750.00	375.00	225.00
(1)	Dodgers In Action	2,200	1,100	660.00
(2)	Ferris Fain	1,650	825.00	495.00
(3)	Enos Slaughter	750.00	375.00	225.00
(4)	Warren Spahn	1,800	900.00	540.00

1954 Bowman

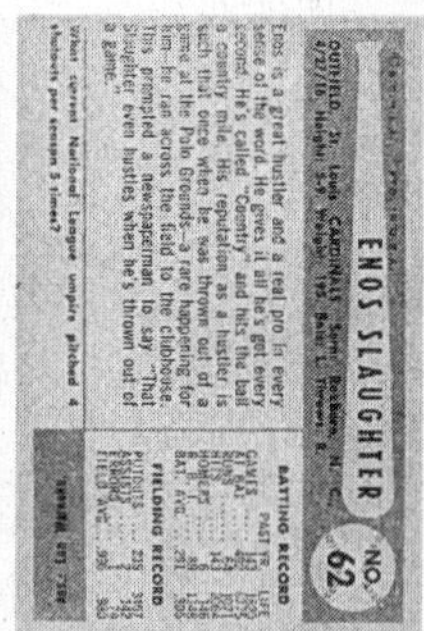

Bowman's 1954 set consists of 224 full-color cards that measure 2-1/2" x 3-3/4". It is believed that contractual problems caused the withdrawal of card #66 (Ted Williams) from the set, creating one of the most sought-after scarcities of the postwar era. The Williams card was replaced by Jim Piersall (who is also #210) in subsequent print runs. The set contains over 40 variations, most involving statistical errors on the card backs that were corrected. On most cards neither variation carries a premium value as both varieties appear to have been printed in equal amounts. The complete set price that follows does not include all variations or #66 Williams.

		NM	EX	VG
Complete Set (224):		5,000	2,400	1,400
Common Player (1-128):		10.00	5.00	3.00
Common Player (129-224):		12.00	6.00	3.50
1	Phil Rizzuto	100.00	35.00	20.00
2	Jack Jensen	25.00	7.50	4.50
3	Marion Fricano	10.00	5.00	3.00
4	Bob Hooper	10.00	5.00	3.00
5	Billy Hunter	10.00	5.00	3.00
6	Nellie Fox	45.00	22.50	13.50
7	Walter Dropo	10.00	5.00	3.00
8	Jim Busby	10.00	5.00	3.00
9	Dave Williams	10.00	5.00	3.00
10	Carl Erskine	25.00	12.50	7.50
11	Sid Gordon	10.00	5.00	3.00
12a	Roy McMillan (551/1290 At Bat)	12.00	6.00	3.50
12b	Roy McMillan (557/1296 At Bat)	15.00	7.50	4.50
13	Paul Minner	10.00	5.00	3.00
14	Gerald Staley	10.00	5.00	3.00
15	Richie Ashburn	55.00	27.50	16.50
16	Jim Wilson	10.00	5.00	3.00
17	Tom Gorman	12.50	6.25	3.75
18	"Hoot" Evers	10.00	5.00	3.00
19	Bobby Shantz	10.00	5.00	3.00
20	Artie Houtteman	10.00	5.00	3.00
21	Vic Wertz	10.00	5.00	3.00
22a	Sam Mele (213/1661 Putouts)	12.00	6.00	3.50
22b	Sam Mele (217/1665 Putouts)	15.00	7.50	4.50
23	***Harvey Kuenn***	20.00	10.00	6.00

24	Bob Porterfield	10.00	5.00	3.00
25a	Wes Westrum	12.00	6.00	3.50
	(1.000/.987 Field Avg.)			
25b	Wes Westrum	15.00	7.50	4.50
	(.982/.986 Field Avg.)			
26a	Billy Cox	15.00	7.50	4.50
	(1.000/.960 Field Avg.)			
26b	Billy Cox	20.00	10.00	6.00
	(.972/.960 Field Avg.)			
27	Dick Cole	10.00	5.00	3.00
28a	Jim Greengrass	20.00	10.00	6.00
	(Birthplace Addison, N.J.)			
28b	Jim Greengrass	12.00	6.00	3.50
	(Birthplace Addison, N.Y.)			
29	Johnny Klippstein	10.00	5.00	3.00
30	Del Rice	10.00	5.00	3.00
31	"Smoky" Burgess	10.00	5.00	3.00
32	Del Crandall	10.00	5.00	3.00
33a	Vic Raschi	27.50	13.50	8.25
	(No trade line.)			
33b	Vic Raschi (Traded line.)	50.00	25.00	15.00
34	Sammy White	10.00	5.00	3.00
35a	Eddie Joost	12.00	6.00	3.50
	(Quiz answer is 8.)			
35b	Eddie Joost	15.00	7.50	4.50
	(Quiz answer is 33.)			
36	George Strickland	10.00	5.00	3.00
37	Dick Kokos	10.00	5.00	3.00
38a	Minnie Minoso	25.00	12.50	7.50
	(.895/.961 Field Avg.)			
38b	Minnie Minoso	30.00	15.00	9.00
	(.963/.963 Field Avg.)			
39	Ned Garver	10.00	5.00	3.00
40	Gil Coan	10.00	5.00	3.00
41a	Alvin Dark	12.00	6.00	3.50
	(.986/.960 Field Avg.)			
41b	Alvin Dark	15.00	7.50	4.50
	(.968/.960 Field Avg.)			
42	Billy Loes	15.00	7.50	4.50
43a	Bob Friend (20 shutouts in quiz question)	12.00	6.00	3.50
43b	Bob Friend (16 shutouts in quiz question)	15.00	7.50	4.50
44	Harry Perkowski	10.00	5.00	3.00
45	Ralph Kiner	35.00	17.50	10.00
46	"Rip" Repulski	10.00	5.00	3.00
47a	Granny Hamner	12.00	6.00	3.50
	(.970/.953 Field Avg.)			
47b	Granny Hamner	15.00	7.50	4.50
	(.953/.951 Field Avg.)			
48	Jack Dittmer	10.00	5.00	3.00
49	Harry Byrd	12.50	6.25	3.75
50	George Kell	30.00	15.00	9.00
51	Alex Kellner	10.00	5.00	3.00
52	Joe Ginsberg	10.00	5.00	3.00
53a	Don Lenhardt	12.00	6.00	3.50
	(.969/.984 Field Avg.)			
53b	Don Lenhardt	15.00	7.50	4.50
	(.966/.983 Field Avg.)			
54	"Chico" Carrasquel	10.00	5.00	3.00
55	Jim Delsing	10.00	5.00	3.00
56	Maurice McDermott	10.00	5.00	3.00
57	Hoyt Wilhelm	27.50	13.50	8.25
58	Pee Wee Reese	70.00	35.00	20.00
59	Bob Schultz	10.00	5.00	3.00
60	Fred Baczewski	10.00	5.00	3.00
61a	Eddie Miksis	12.00	6.00	3.50
	(.954/.962 Field Avg.)			
61b	Eddie Miksis	15.00	7.50	4.50
	(.954/.961 Field Avg.)			
62	Enos Slaughter	35.00	17.50	10.00
63	Earl Torgeson	10.00	5.00	3.00
64	Eddie Mathews	65.00	32.50	20.00
65	Mickey Mantle	900.00	350.00	215.00
66a	Ted Williams	2,100	975.00	500.00
66b	Jimmy Piersall	60.00	30.00	18.00
67a	Carl Scheib (.306 Pct. with two lines under bio)	25.00	12.50	7.50
67b	Carl Scheib (.306 Pct. with one line under bio)	12.00	6.00	3.50
67c	Carl Scheib (.300 Pct.)	15.00	7.50	4.50
68	Bob Avila	10.00	5.00	3.00
69	Clinton Courtney	10.00	5.00	3.00
70	Willard Marshall	10.00	5.00	3.00
71	Ted Gray	10.00	5.00	3.00
72	Ed Yost	10.00	5.00	3.00
73	Don Mueller	10.00	5.00	3.00
74	Jim Gilliam	35.00	17.50	10.00
75	Max Surkont	10.00	5.00	3.00
76	Joe Nuxhall	10.00	5.00	3.00
77	Bob Rush	10.00	5.00	3.00
78	Sal Yvars	10.00	5.00	3.00
79	Curt Simmons	10.00	5.00	3.00
80a	Johnny Logan (106 Runs)	12.00	6.00	3.50
80b	Johnny Logan (100 Runs)	15.00	7.50	4.50
81a	Jerry Coleman	15.00	7.50	4.50
	(1.000/.975 Field Avg.)			
81b	Jerry Coleman	20.00	10.00	6.00
	(.952/.975 Field Avg.)			
82a	Bill Goodman	12.00	6.00	3.50
	(.965/.986 Field Avg.)			
82b	Bill Goodman	15.00	7.50	4.50
	(.972/.985 Field Avg.)			
83	Ray Murray	10.00	5.00	3.00
84	Larry Doby	45.00	22.50	13.50
85a	Jim Dyck	12.00	6.00	3.50
	(.926/.956 Field Avg.)			
85b	Jim Dyck	15.00	7.50	4.50
	(.947/.960 Field Avg.)			
86	Harry Dorish	10.00	5.00	3.00
87	Don Lund	10.00	5.00	3.00
88	Tommy Umphlett	10.00	5.00	3.00
89	Willie Mays	390.00	125.00	75.00
90	Roy Campanella	105.00	50.00	30.00
91	Cal Abrams	10.00	5.00	3.00
92	Ken Raffensberger	10.00	5.00	3.00
93a	Bill Serena	12.00	6.00	3.50
	(.983/.966 Field Avg.)			
93b	Bill Serena	15.00	7.50	4.50
	(.977/.966 Field Avg.)			
94a	Solly Hemus	12.00	6.00	3.50
	(476/1343 Assists)			
94b	Solly Hemus	15.00	7.50	4.50
	(477/1343 Assists)			
95	Robin Roberts	40.00	20.00	12.00
96	Joe Adcock	10.00	5.00	3.00
97	Gil McDougald	20.00	10.00	6.00
98	Ellis Kinder	10.00	5.00	3.00
99a	Peter Suder	12.00	6.00	3.50
	(.985/.974 Field Avg.)			
99b	Peter Suder	15.00	7.50	4.50
	(.978/.974 Field Avg.)			
100	Mike Garcia	10.00	5.00	3.00
101	***Don Larsen***	40.00	20.00	12.00
102	Bill Pierce	10.00	5.00	3.00
103a	Stephen Souchock	12.00	6.00	3.50
	(144/1192 Putouts)			
103b	Stephen Souchock	15.00	7.50	4.50
	(147/1195 Putouts)			
104	Frank Spec Shea	10.00	5.00	3.00
105a	Sal Maglie	20.00	10.00	6.00
	(Quiz answer is 8.)			
105b	Sal Maglie	30.00	15.00	9.00
	(Quiz answer is 1904.)			
106	Clem Labine	20.00	10.00	6.00
107	Paul LaPalme	10.00	5.00	3.00
108	Bobby Adams	10.00	5.00	3.00
109	Roy Smalley	10.00	5.00	3.00
110	Red Schoendienst	30.00	15.00	9.00
111	Murry Dickson	10.00	5.00	3.00
112	Andy Pafko	10.00	5.00	3.00
113	Allie Reynolds	20.00	10.00	6.00
114	Willard Nixon	10.00	5.00	3.00
115	Don Bollweg	10.00	5.00	3.00
116	Luke Easter	10.00	5.00	3.00
117	Dick Kryhoski	10.00	5.00	3.00
118	Bob Boyd	10.00	5.00	3.00
119	Fred Hatfield	10.00	5.00	3.00
120	Mel Hoderlein	10.00	5.00	3.00
121	Ray Katt	10.00	5.00	3.00
122	Carl Furillo	30.00	15.00	9.00
123	Toby Atwell	10.00	5.00	3.00
124a	Gus Bell (15/27 Errors)	12.00	6.00	3.50
124b	Gus Bell (11/26 Errors)	15.00	7.50	4.50
125	Warren Hacker	10.00	5.00	3.00
126	Cliff Chambers	10.00	5.00	3.00
127	Del Ennis	10.00	5.00	3.00
128	Ebba St. Claire	10.00	5.00	3.00
129	Hank Bauer	35.00	17.50	10.00
130	Milt Bolling	12.00	6.00	3.50
131	Joe Astroth	12.00	6.00	3.50
132	Bob Feller	80.00	40.00	25.00
133	Duane Pillette	12.00	6.00	3.50
134	Luis Aloma	12.00	6.00	3.50
135	Johnny Pesky	12.00	6.00	3.50
136	Clyde Vollmer	12.00	6.00	3.50
137	Al Corwin	12.00	6.00	3.50
138a	Gil Hodges	70.00	35.00	20.00
	(.993/.991 Field Avg.)			
138b	Gil Hodges	100.00	50.00	30.00
	(.992/.991 Field Avg.)			
139a	Preston Ward	15.00	7.50	4.50
	(.961/.992 Field Avg.)			
139b	Preston Ward	17.50	8.75	5.25
	(.990/.992 Field Avg.)			
140a	Saul Rogovin (7-12 Won/Lost with 2 Strikeouts)	15.00	7.50	4.50
140b	Saul Rogovin (7-12 Won/Lost with 62 Strikeouts)	17.50	8.75	5.25
140c	Saul Rogovin (8-12 Won/Lost)	40.00	20.00	12.00
141	Joe Garagiola	30.00	15.00	9.00
142	Al Brazle	12.00	6.00	3.50
143	Willie Jones	12.00	6.00	3.50
144	***Ernie Johnson***	30.00	15.00	9.00
145a	Billy Martin	60.00	30.00	18.00
	(.985/.983 Field Avg.)			
145b	Billy Martin	70.00	35.00	20.00
	(.983/.982 Field Avg.)			
146	Dick Gernert	12.00	6.00	3.50
147	Joe DeMaestri	12.00	6.00	3.50
148	Dale Mitchell	12.00	6.00	3.50
149	Bob Young	12.00	6.00	3.50
150	Cass Michaels	12.00	6.00	3.50
151	Pat Mullin	12.00	6.00	3.50
152	Mickey Vernon	12.00	6.00	3.50
153a	"Whitey" Lockman	15.00	7.50	4.50
	(100/331 Assists)			
153b	"Whitey" Lockman	17.50	8.75	5.25
	(102/333 Assists)			
154	Don Newcombe	60.00	30.00	18.00
155	***Frank Thomas***	25.00	12.50	7.50
156a	Rocky Bridges	15.00	7.50	4.50
	(320/467 Assists)			
156b	Rocky Bridges	17.50	8.75	5.25
	(328/475 Assists)			
157	Omar Lown	12.00	6.00	3.50
158	Stu Miller	12.00	6.00	3.50
159	John Lindell	12.00	6.00	3.50
160	Danny O'Connell	12.00	6.00	3.50
161	Yogi Berra	110.00	55.00	35.00
162	Ted Lepcio	12.00	6.00	3.50
163a	Dave Philley	50.00	25.00	15.00
	(152 Games, no traded line)			
163b	Dave Philley	22.50	11.00	6.75
	(152 Games, traded line)			
163c	Dave Philley	27.50	13.50	8.25
	(157 Games, traded line)			
164	Early Wynn	45.00	22.50	13.50
165	Johnny Groth	12.00	6.00	3.50
166	Sandy Consuegra	12.00	6.00	3.50
167	Bill Hoeft	12.00	6.00	3.50
168	Edward Fitz Gerald	12.00	6.00	3.50
169	Larry Jansen	12.00	6.00	3.50
170	Duke Snider	125.00	60.00	35.00
171	Carlos Bernier	12.00	6.00	3.50
172	Andy Seminick	12.00	6.00	3.50
173	Dee Fondy	12.00	6.00	3.50
174a	Pete Castiglione	15.00	7.50	4.50
	(.966/.959 Field Avg.)			
174b	Pete Castiglione	17.50	8.75	5.25
	(.970/.959 Field Avg.)			
175	Mel Clark	12.00	6.00	3.50
176	Vernon Bickford	12.00	6.00	3.50
177	Whitey Ford	100.00	50.00	30.00
178	Del Wilber	12.00	6.00	3.50
179a	Morris Martin (44 ERA)	15.00	7.50	4.50
179b	Morris Martin (4.44 ERA)	17.50	8.75	5.25
180	Joe Tipton	12.00	6.00	3.50
181	Les Moss	12.00	6.00	3.50
182	Sherman Lollar	12.00	6.00	3.50
183	Matt Batts	12.00	6.00	3.50
184	Mickey Grasso	12.00	6.00	3.50
185a	***Daryl Spencer***	15.00	7.50	4.50
	(.941/.944 Field Avg.)			
185b	***Daryl Spencer***	17.50	8.75	5.25
	(.933/.936 Field Avg.)			
186	Russ Meyer	15.00	7.50	4.50
187	Vern Law	12.00	6.00	3.50
188	Frank Smith	12.00	6.00	3.50
189	Ransom Jackson	12.00	6.00	3.50
190	Joe Presko	12.00	6.00	3.50
191	Karl Drews	12.00	6.00	3.50
192	Lew Burdette	12.00	6.00	3.50
193	Eddie Robinson	15.00	7.50	4.50
194	Sid Hudson	12.00	6.00	3.50
195	Bob Cain	12.00	6.00	3.50
196	Bob Lemon	30.00	15.00	9.00
197	Lou Kretlow	12.00	6.00	3.50
198	Virgil Trucks	12.00	6.00	3.50
199	Steve Gromek	12.00	6.00	3.50
200	Connie Marrero	12.00	6.00	3.50
201	Bob Thomson	20.00	10.00	6.00
202	George Shuba	15.00	7.50	4.50
203	Vic Janowicz	25.00	12.50	7.50
204	Jack Collum	12.00	6.00	3.50
205	Hal Jeffcoat	12.00	6.00	3.50
206	Steve Bilko	12.00	6.00	3.50
207	Stan Lopata	12.00	6.00	3.50
208	Johnny Antonelli	12.00	6.00	3.50
209	Gene Woodling	35.00	17.50	10.00
	(Photo reversed.)			
210	Jimmy Piersall	35.00	17.50	10.00
211	Jim Robertson	12.00	6.00	3.50
212a	Owen Friend	15.00	7.50	4.50
	(.964/.957 Field Avg.)			
212b	Owen Friend	17.50	8.75	5.25
	(.967/.958 Field Avg.)			
213	Dick Littlefield	12.00	6.00	3.50
214	Ferris Fain	12.00	6.00	3.50
215	Johnny Bucha	12.00	6.00	3.50
216a	Jerry Snyder	15.00	7.50	4.50
	(.988/.988 Field Avg.)			
216b	Jerry Snyder	17.50	8.75	5.25
	(.968/.968 Field Avg.)			
217a	Henry Thompson	15.00	7.50	4.50
	(.956/.951 Field Avg.)			
217b	Henry Thompson	17.50	8.75	5.25
	(.958/.952 Field Avg.)			
218	Preacher Roe	35.00	17.50	10.00
219	Hal Rice	12.00	6.00	3.50
220	Hobie Landrith	12.00	6.00	3.50
221	Frank Baumholtz	12.00	6.00	3.50
222	Memo Luna	15.00	7.50	4.50
223	Steve Ridzik	12.00	6.00	3.50
224	Billy Bruton	45.00	12.00	5.00

1955 Bowman

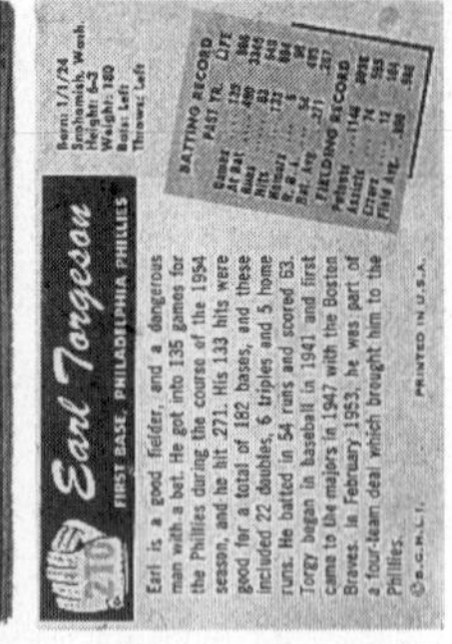

Bowman produced its final baseball card set as an independent card maker in 1955, a popular issue that has color player photographs placed inside a television set design. The set consists of 320 cards measuring 2-1/2" x 3-3/4". High-numbered cards (#225-320) appear to have replaced certain low-numbered cards on the press sheets and are scarcer. The high series includes 31 umpire cards.

		NM	EX	VG
Complete Set (320):		7,000	3,500	2,000
Common Player (1-224):		12.50	6.25	3.75
Common Player (225-320):		25.00	12.50	7.50
1	Hoyt Wilhelm	65.00	30.00	18.00
2	Al Dark	15.00	7.50	4.50
3	Joe Coleman	12.50	6.25	3.75
4	Eddie Waitkus	12.50	6.25	3.75
5	Jim Robertson	12.50	6.25	3.75
6	Pete Suder	12.50	6.25	3.75
7	Gene Baker	12.50	6.25	3.75
8	Warren Hacker	12.50	6.25	3.75
9	Gil McDougald	25.00	12.50	7.50
10	Phil Rizzuto	60.00	30.00	18.00
11	Billy Bruton	12.50	6.25	3.75
12	Andy Pafko	12.50	6.25	3.75

13	Clyde Vollmer	12.50	6.25	3.75
14	Gus Keriazakos	12.50	6.25	3.75
15	***Frank Sullivan***	12.50	6.25	3.75
16	Jim Piersall	12.50	6.25	3.75
17	Del Ennis	12.50	6.25	3.75
18	Stan Lopata	12.50	6.25	3.75
19	Bobby Avila	12.50	6.25	3.75
20	Al Smith	12.50	6.25	3.75
21	Don Hoak	15.00	7.50	4.50
22	Roy Campanella	75.00	37.50	22.50
23	Al Kaline	80.00	40.00	24.00
24	Al Aber	12.50	6.25	3.75
25	Minnie Minoso	30.00	15.00	9.00
26	Virgil Trucks	12.50	6.25	3.75
27	Preston Ward	12.50	6.25	3.75
28	Dick Cole	12.50	6.25	3.75
29	Red Schoendienst	25.00	12.50	7.50
30	Bill Sarni	12.50	6.25	3.75
31	Johnny Temple	12.50	6.25	3.75
32	Wally Post	12.50	6.25	3.75
33	Nellie Fox	35.00	17.50	10.00
34	Clint Courtney	12.50	6.25	3.75
35	Bill Tuttle	12.50	6.25	3.75
36	Wayne Belardi	12.50	6.25	3.75
37	Pee Wee Reese	50.00	25.00	15.00
38	Early Wynn	25.00	12.50	7.50
39	Bob Darnell	15.00	7.50	4.50
40	Vic Wertz	12.50	6.25	3.75
41	Mel Clark	12.50	6.25	3.75
42	Bob Greenwood	12.50	6.25	3.75
43	Bob Buhl	12.50	6.25	3.75
44	Danny O'Connell	12.50	6.25	3.75
45	Tom Umphlett	12.50	6.25	3.75
46	Mickey Vernon	12.50	6.25	3.75
47	Sammy White	12.50	6.25	3.75
48a	Milt Bolling (Frank Bolling back.)	20.00	10.00	6.00
48b	Milt Bolling (Milt Bolling back.)	20.00	10.00	6.00
49	Jim Greengrass	12.50	6.25	3.75
50	Hobie Landrith	12.50	6.25	3.75
51	Elvin Tappe	12.50	6.25	3.75
52	Hal Rice	12.50	6.25	3.75
53	Alex Kellner	12.50	6.25	3.75
54	Don Bollweg	12.50	6.25	3.75
55	Cal Abrams	12.50	6.25	3.75
56	Billy Cox	12.50	6.25	3.75
57	Bob Friend	12.50	6.25	3.75
58	Frank Thomas	12.50	6.25	3.75
59	Whitey Ford	70.00	35.00	20.00
60	Enos Slaughter	30.00	15.00	9.00
61	Paul LaPalme	12.50	6.25	3.75
62	Royce Lint	12.50	6.25	3.75
63	Irv Noren	15.00	7.50	4.50
64	Curt Simmons	12.50	6.25	3.75
65	***Don Zimmer***	30.00	15.00	9.00
66	George Shuba	15.00	7.50	4.50
67	Don Larsen	30.00	15.00	9.00
68	***Elston Howard***	80.00	40.00	24.00
69	Bill Hunter	15.00	7.50	4.50
70	Lew Burdette	12.50	6.25	3.75
71	Dave Jolly	12.50	6.25	3.75
72	Chet Nichols	12.50	6.25	3.75
73	Eddie Yost	12.50	6.25	3.75
74	Jerry Snyder	12.50	6.25	3.75
75	Brooks Lawrence	12.50	6.25	3.75
76	Tom Poholsky	12.50	6.25	3.75
77	Jim McDonald	12.50	6.25	3.75
78	Gil Coan	12.50	6.25	3.75
79	Willie Miranda	12.50	6.25	3.75
80	Lou Limmer	12.50	6.25	3.75
81	Bob Morgan	12.50	6.25	3.75
82	Lee Walls	12.50	6.25	3.75
83	Max Surkont	12.50	6.25	3.75
84	George Freese	12.50	6.25	3.75
85	Cass Michaels	12.50	6.25	3.75
86	Ted Gray	12.50	6.25	3.75
87	Randy Jackson	12.50	6.25	3.75
88	Steve Bilko	12.50	6.25	3.75
89	Lou Boudreau	25.00	12.50	7.50
90	Art Ditmar	12.50	6.25	3.75
91	Dick Marlowe	12.50	6.25	3.75
92	George Zuverink	12.50	6.25	3.75
93	Andy Seminick	12.50	6.25	3.75
94	Hank Thompson	12.50	6.25	3.75
95	Sal Maglie	12.50	6.25	3.75
96	Ray Narleski	12.50	6.25	3.75
97	John Podres	30.00	15.00	9.00
98	Jim Gilliam	27.50	13.50	8.25
99	Jerry Coleman	15.00	7.50	4.50
100	Tom Morgan	15.00	7.50	4.50
101a	Don Johnson (Ernie Johnson (Braves) on front.)	60.00	30.00	18.00
101b	Don Johnson (Don Johnson (Orioles) on front.)	27.50	13.50	8.25
102	Bobby Thomson	17.50	8.75	5.25
103	Eddie Mathews	55.00	27.50	16.50
104	Bob Porterfield	12.50	6.25	3.75
105	Johnny Schmitz	12.50	6.25	3.75
106	Del Rice	12.50	6.25	3.75
107	Solly Hemus	12.50	6.25	3.75
108	Lou Kretlow	12.50	6.25	3.75
109	Vern Stephens	12.50	6.25	3.75
110	Bob Miller	12.50	6.25	3.75
111	Steve Ridzik	12.50	6.25	3.75
112	Granny Hamner	12.50	6.25	3.75
113	Bob Hall	12.50	6.25	3.75
114	Vic Janowicz	12.50	6.25	3.75
115	Roger Bowman	12.50	6.25	3.75
116	Sandy Consuegra	12.50	6.25	3.75
117	Johnny Groth	12.50	6.25	3.75
118	Bobby Adams	12.50	6.25	3.75
119	Joe Astroth	12.50	6.25	3.75
120	Ed Burtschy	12.50	6.25	3.75
121	Rufus Crawford	12.50	6.25	3.75
122	Al Corwin	12.50	6.25	3.75
123	Marv Grissom	12.50	6.25	3.75
124	Johnny Antonelli	12.50	6.25	3.75
125	Paul Giel	12.50	6.25	3.75
126	Billy Goodman	12.50	6.25	3.75
127	Hank Majeski	12.50	6.25	3.75
128	Mike Garcia	12.50	6.25	3.75
129	Hal Naragon	12.50	6.25	3.75
130	Richie Ashburn	50.00	25.00	15.00
131	Willard Marshall	12.50	6.25	3.75
132a	Harvey Kueen (Misspelled last name.)	25.00	12.50	7.50
132b	Harvey Kuenn (Corrected)	35.00	17.50	10.00
133	Charles King	12.50	6.25	3.75
134	Bob Feller	60.00	30.00	18.00
135	Lloyd Merriman	12.50	6.25	3.75
136	Rocky Bridges	12.50	6.25	3.75
137	Bob Talbot	12.50	6.25	3.75
138	Davey Williams	12.50	6.25	3.75
139	Billy & Bobby Shantz	15.00	7.50	4.50
140	Bobby Shantz	12.50	6.25	3.75
141	Wes Westrum	12.50	6.25	3.75
142	Rudy Regalado	12.50	6.25	3.75
143	Don Newcombe	25.00	12.50	7.50
144	Art Houtteman	12.50	6.25	3.75
145	Bob Nieman	12.50	6.25	3.75
146	Don Liddle	12.50	6.25	3.75
147	Sam Mele	12.50	6.25	3.75
148	Bob Chakales	12.50	6.25	3.75
149	Cloyd Boyer	12.50	6.25	3.75
150	Bill Klaus	12.50	6.25	3.75
151	Jim Brideweser	12.50	6.25	3.75
152	Johnny Klippstein	12.50	6.25	3.75
153	Eddie Robinson	15.00	7.50	4.50
154	***Frank Lary***	12.50	6.25	3.75
155	Gerry Staley	12.50	6.25	3.75
156	Jim Hughes	15.00	7.50	4.50
157a	Ernie Johnson (Don Johnson (Orioles) picture on front.)	15.00	7.50	4.50
157b	Ernie Johnson (Ernie Johnson (Braves) picture on front.)	30.00	15.00	9.00
158	Gil Hodges	40.00	20.00	12.00
159	Harry Byrd	12.50	6.25	3.75
160	Bill Skowron	40.00	20.00	12.00
161	Matt Batts	12.50	6.25	3.75
162	Charlie Maxwell	12.50	6.25	3.75
163	Sid Gordon	12.50	6.25	3.75
164	Toby Atwell	12.50	6.25	3.75
165	Maurice McDermott	12.50	6.25	3.75
166	Jim Busby	12.50	6.25	3.75
167	Bob Grim	15.00	7.50	4.50
168	Yogi Berra	100.00	50.00	30.00
169	Carl Furillo	27.50	13.50	8.25
170	Carl Erskine	25.00	12.50	7.50
171	Robin Roberts	32.50	16.00	10.00
172	Willie Jones	12.50	6.25	3.75
173	"Chico" Carrasquel	12.50	6.25	3.75
174	Sherman Lollar	12.50	6.25	3.75
175	Wilmer Shantz	12.50	6.25	3.75
176	Joe DeMaestri	12.50	6.25	3.75
177	Willard Nixon	12.50	6.25	3.75
178	Tom Brewer	12.50	6.25	3.75
179	Hank Aaron	200.00	70.00	40.00
180	Johnny Logan	12.50	6.25	3.75
181	Eddie Miksis	12.50	6.25	3.75
182	Bob Rush	12.50	6.25	3.75
183	Ray Katt	12.50	6.25	3.75
184	Willie Mays	180.00	85.00	45.00
185	Vic Raschi	12.50	6.25	3.75
186	Alex Grammas	12.50	6.25	3.75
187	Fred Hatfield	12.50	6.25	3.75
188	Ned Garver	12.50	6.25	3.75
189	Jack Collum	12.50	6.25	3.75
190	Fred Baczewski	12.50	6.25	3.75
191	Bob Lemon	30.00	15.00	9.00
192	George Strickland	12.50	6.25	3.75
193	Howie Judson	12.50	6.25	3.75
194	Joe Nuxhall	12.50	6.25	3.75
195a	Erv Palica (No traded line.)	30.00	15.00	9.00
195b	Erv Palica (Traded line.)	125.00	60.00	35.00
196	Russ Meyer	15.00	7.50	4.50
197	Ralph Kiner	35.00	17.50	10.00
198	Dave Pope	12.50	6.25	3.75
199	Vernon Law	12.50	6.25	3.75
200	Dick Littlefield	12.50	6.25	3.75
201	Allie Reynolds	25.00	12.50	7.50
202	Mickey Mantle	525.00	250.00	125.00
203	Steve Gromek	12.50	6.25	3.75
204a	Frank Bolling (Milt Bolling back.)	45.00	22.50	13.50
204b	Frank Bolling (Frank Bolling back.)	30.00	15.00	9.00
205	"Rip" Repulski	12.50	6.25	3.75
206	Ralph Beard	12.50	6.25	3.75
207	Frank Shea	12.50	6.25	3.75
208	Ed Fitz Gerald	12.50	6.25	3.75
209	"Smoky" Burgess	12.50	6.25	3.75
210	Earl Torgeson	12.50	6.25	3.75
211	John "Sonny" Dixon	12.50	6.25	3.75
212	Jack Dittmer	12.50	6.25	3.75
213	George Kell	30.00	15.00	9.00
214	Billy Pierce	12.50	6.25	3.75
215	Bob Kuzava	12.50	6.25	3.75
216	Preacher Roe	15.00	7.50	4.50
217	Del Crandall	12.50	6.25	3.75
218	Joe Adcock	12.50	6.25	3.75
219	"Whitey" Lockman	12.50	6.25	3.75
220	Jim Hearn	12.50	6.25	3.75
221	Hector "Skinny" Brown	12.50	6.25	3.75
222	Russ Kemmerer	12.50	6.25	3.75
223	Hal Jeffcoat	12.50	6.25	3.75
224	Dee Fondy	12.50	6.25	3.75
225	Paul Richards	25.00	12.50	7.50
226	W.F. McKinley (Umpire)	30.00	15.00	9.00
227	Frank Baumholtz	25.00	12.50	7.50
228	John M. Phillips	25.00	12.50	7.50
229	Jim Brosnan	25.00	12.50	7.50
230	Al Brazle	25.00	12.50	7.50
231	Jim Konstanty	25.00	12.50	7.50
232	Birdie Tebbetts	25.00	12.50	7.50
233	Bill Serena	25.00	12.50	7.50
234	Dick Bartell	25.00	12.50	7.50
235	J.A. Paparella/Umpire	30.00	15.00	9.00
236	Murry Dickson	25.00	12.50	7.50
237	Johnny Wyrostek	25.00	12.50	7.50
238	Eddie Stanky	25.00	12.50	7.50
239	Edwin A. Rommel/Umpire	30.00	15.00	9.00
240	Billy Loes	25.00	12.50	7.50
241	John Pesky	25.00	12.50	7.50
242	Ernie Banks	240.00	100.00	70.00
243	Gus Bell	25.00	12.50	7.50
244	Duane Pillette	25.00	12.50	7.50
245	Bill Miller	25.00	12.50	7.50
246	Hank Bauer	45.00	22.50	13.50
247	Dutch Leonard	25.00	12.50	7.50
248	Harry Dorish	25.00	12.50	7.50
249	Billy Gardner	25.00	12.50	7.50
250	Larry Napp/Umpire	30.00	15.00	9.00
251	Stan Jok	25.00	12.50	7.50
252	Roy Smalley	25.00	12.50	7.50
253	Jim Wilson	25.00	12.50	7.50
254	Bennett Flowers	25.00	12.50	7.50
255	Pete Runnels	25.00	12.50	7.50
256	Owen Friend	25.00	12.50	7.50
257	Tom Alston	25.00	12.50	7.50
258	John W. Stevens/Umpire	30.00	15.00	9.00
259	***Don Mossi***	35.00	17.50	10.00
260	Edwin H. Hurley/Umpire	30.00	15.00	9.00
261	Walt Moryn	25.00	12.50	7.50
262	Jim Lemon	25.00	12.50	7.50
263	Eddie Joost	25.00	12.50	7.50
264	Bill Henry	25.00	12.50	7.50
265	Al Barlick/Umpire	75.00	37.50	22.50
266	Mike Fornieles	25.00	12.50	7.50
267	George Honochick/Umpire	50.00	25.00	15.00
268	Roy Lee Hawes	25.00	12.50	7.50
269	Joe Amalfitano	25.00	12.50	7.50
270	Chico Fernandez	25.00	12.50	7.50
271	Bob Hooper	25.00	12.50	7.50
272	John Flaherty/Umpire	30.00	15.00	9.00
273	"Bubba" Church	25.00	12.50	7.50
274	Jim Delsing	25.00	12.50	7.50
275	William T. Grieve/Umpire	30.00	15.00	9.00
276	Ike Delock	25.00	12.50	7.50
277	Ed Runge/Umpire	30.00	15.00	9.00
278	***Charles Neal***	35.00	17.50	10.00
279	Hank Soar/Umpire	30.00	15.00	9.00
280	Clyde McCullough	25.00	12.50	7.50
281	Charles Berry/Umpire	30.00	15.00	9.00
282	Phil Cavarretta	25.00	12.50	7.50
283	Nestor Chylak/Umpire	65.00	32.50	20.00
284	William A. Jackowski/Umpire	30.00	15.00	9.00
285	Walt Dropo	25.00	12.50	7.50
286	Frank Secory/Umpire	30.00	15.00	9.00
287	Ron Mrozinski	25.00	12.50	7.50
288	Dick Smith	25.00	12.50	7.50
289	Art Gore/Umpire	30.00	15.00	9.00
290	Hershell Freeman	25.00	12.50	7.50
291	Frank Dascoli/Umpire	30.00	15.00	9.00
292	Marv Blaylock	25.00	12.50	7.50
293	Thomas D. Gorman/Umpire	30.00	15.00	9.00
294	Wally Moses	25.00	12.50	7.50
295	Lee Ballanfant/Umpire	30.00	15.00	9.00
296	***Bill Virdon***	30.00	15.00	9.00
297	"Dusty" Boggess/Umpire	30.00	15.00	9.00
298	Charlie Grimm	25.00	12.50	7.50
299	Lonnie Warneke/Umpire	30.00	15.00	9.00
300	Tommy Byrne	30.00	15.00	9.00
301	William Engeln/Umpire	30.00	15.00	9.00
302	***Frank Malzone***	30.00	15.00	9.00
303	Jocko Conlan/Umpire	65.00	32.50	20.00
304	Harry Chiti	25.00	12.50	7.50
305	Frank Umont/Umpire	30.00	15.00	9.00
306	Bob Cerv	30.00	15.00	9.00
307	"Babe" Pinelli/Umpire	25.00	12.50	7.50
308	Al Lopez	35.00	17.50	10.00
309	Hal Dixon/Umpire	30.00	15.00	9.00
310	Ken Lehman	30.00	15.00	9.00
311	Larry Goetz/Umpire	30.00	15.00	9.00
312	Bill Wight	25.00	12.50	7.50
313	Augie Donatelli/Umpire	30.00	15.00	9.00
314	Dale Mitchell	25.00	12.50	7.50
315	Cal Hubbard/Umpire	60.00	30.00	18.00
316	Marion Fricano	25.00	12.50	7.50
317	Bill Summers/Umpire	30.00	15.00	9.00
318	Sid Hudson	25.00	12.50	7.50
319	Al Schroll	25.00	12.50	7.50
320	George Susce, Jr.	50.00	15.00	7.00

1956 Bowman Prototypes

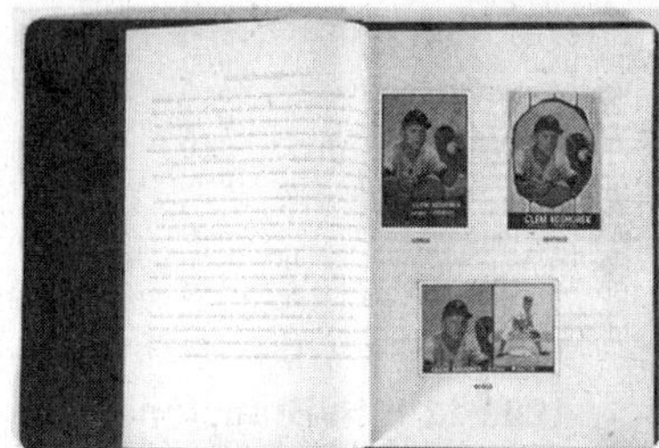

To gauge consumer demand for a 1956 baseball card set that it never issued, Bowman produced a "Baseball Card Preference Study" report. The report survives today in the form of a 24-page notebook that includes samples of the three designs apparently preferred by the pre-teen boys surveyed. All three cards are glued to one page of the report and all feature the photo of Pirates catcher Clem Koshorek used in the 1953 Bowman set. It is believed only two of the reports survive.

(Sold for $10,440 in 5/05 auction.)

1963 George Brace All Time Chicago Cubs

The year of issue attributed here is only theoretical. The set consists of a window envelope which contains 18 5-1/4" x 7" black-and-white photos of former Cubs greats by famed Chicago baseball photographer George Brace. The blank-backed unnumbered pictures have player identification in the white border at bottom. They are checklisted here alphabetically.

		NM	EX	VG
Complete Set (18):		50.00	25.00	15.00
Common Player:		7.50	3.75	2.25
(1)	Grover Cleveland Alexander	10.00	5.00	3.00
(2)	Cap Anson	10.00	5.00	3.00
(3)	Three Finger Brown	9.00	4.50	2.75
(4)	Frank Chance	9.00	4.50	2.75
(5)	Johnny Evers	9.00	4.50	2.75
(6)	Charlie Grimm	7.50	3.75	2.25
(7)	Stan Hack	7.50	3.75	2.25
(8)	Gabby Hartnett	7.50	3.75	2.25
(9)	Billy Herman	7.50	3.75	2.25
(10)	Charlie Hollocher	7.50	3.75	2.25
(11)	Billy Jurges	7.50	3.75	2.25
(12)	Johnny Kling	7.50	3.75	2.25
(13)	Joe McCarthy	7.50	3.75	2.25
(14)	Ed Reulbach	7.50	3.75	2.25
(15)	Albert Spalding	7.50	3.75	2.25
(16)	Joe Tinker	9.00	4.50	2.75
(17)	Hippo Vaughn	7.50	3.75	2.25
(18)	Hack Wilson	9.00	4.50	2.75

1974 Bramac 1933 National League All-Stars

This early collectors issue features black-and-white photos of the premiere N.L. All-Star team in their distinctive game uniforms. Cards are in a 2-1/2" x 3-1/4" format.

		NM	EX	VG
Complete Set (18):		30.00	15.00	9.00
Common Player:		6.00	3.00	1.75
1	Paul Waner	6.00	3.00	1.75
2	Woody English	6.00	3.00	1.75
3	Dick Bartell	6.00	3.00	1.75
4	Chuck Klein	6.00	3.00	1.75
5	Tony Cuccinello	6.00	3.00	1.75
6	Lefty O'Doul	6.00	3.00	1.75
7	Gabby Hartnett	6.00	3.00	1.75
8	Lon Warneke	6.00	3.00	1.75
9	Wally Berger	6.00	3.00	1.75
10	Chick Hafey	6.00	3.00	1.75
11	Frank Frisch	6.00	3.00	1.75
12	Carl Hubbell	6.00	3.00	1.75
13	Bill Hallahan	6.00	3.00	1.75
14	Hal Schumacher	6.00	3.00	1.75
15	Pie Traynor	6.00	3.00	1.75
16	Bill Terry	6.00	3.00	1.75
17	Pepper Martin	6.00	3.00	1.75
18	Jimmy Wilson	6.00	3.00	1.75

1908-11 H.H. Bregstone Browns/Cardinals Post Cards (PC743)

Among the rarest of the early 20th Century baseball player postcards are those of the St. Louis Browns and Cardinals from H.H. Bregstone, also of St. Louis. The 3-1/2" x 5-1/2" cards feature sepia player photos that are borderless at top and sides. At bottom is a box with the player's name, team, position, league and the issuer's address. Backs are standard postcard format. The unnumbered cards are checklisted here alphabetically within team. With a single exception (Gregory), all of the Browns players are from 1909, while the range of Cardinals spans the era 1908-1911.

WADDELL, p
St. Louis "BROWNS" American B. B. League.

		NM	EX	VG
Complete Set, Browns (22):		9,500	4,750	2,750
Complete Set, Cardinals (34):		18,000	9,000	5,500
Common Player:		500.00	250.00	150.00
	ST. LOUIS BROWNS			
(1)	Bill Bailey	500.00	250.00	150.00
(2)	Lou Criger	500.00	250.00	150.00
(3)	Dode Criss	500.00	250.00	150.00
(4)	Bill Dineen	500.00	250.00	150.00
(5)	Hobe Ferris	500.00	250.00	150.00
(6)	Bill Graham	500.00	250.00	150.00
(7)	B Gregory	500.00	250.00	150.00
(8)	Art Griggs	500.00	250.00	150.00
(9)	Roy Hartzell	500.00	250.00	150.00
(10)	Danny Hoffman	500.00	250.00	150.00
(11)	Harry Howell	500.00	250.00	150.00
(12)	Tom Jones	500.00	250.00	150.00
(13)	Jimmy McAleer	500.00	250.00	150.00
(14)	Ham Patterson	500.00	250.00	150.00
(15)	Barney Pelty	500.00	250.00	150.00
(16)	Al Schweitzer	500.00	250.00	150.00
(17)	Wib Smith	500.00	250.00	150.00
(18)	Jim Stephens	500.00	250.00	150.00
(19)	George Stone	500.00	250.00	150.00
(20)	Rube Waddell	750.00	375.00	225.00
(21)	Bobby Wallace	750.00	375.00	225.00
(22)	Jimmy Williams	500.00	250.00	150.00
	ST. LOUIS CARDINALS			
(1)	Jap Barbeau	500.00	250.00	150.00
(2)	Shad Barry	500.00	250.00	150.00
(3)	Fred Beebe	500.00	250.00	150.00
(4)	Frank Betcher	500.00	250.00	150.00
(5)	Jack Bliss	500.00	250.00	150.00
(6)	Roger Bresnahan	800.00	400.00	240.00
(7)	Bobby Byrne	500.00	250.00	150.00
(8)	Chappie Charles	500.00	250.00	150.00
(9)	Frank Corridon	500.00	250.00	150.00
(10)	Joe Delahanty	700.00	350.00	210.00
(11)	Rube Ellis	500.00	250.00	150.00
(12)	Steve Evans	500.00	250.00	150.00
(13)	Art Fromme	500.00	250.00	150.00
(14)	Rube Geyer	500.00	250.00	150.00
(15)	Billy Gilbert	500.00	250.00	150.00
(16)	Bob Harmon	500.00	250.00	150.00
(17)	Irv Higginbotham	500.00	250.00	150.00
(18)	Tom Higgins	500.00	250.00	150.00
(19)	Art Hoelskoetter	500.00	250.00	150.00
(20)	Miller Huggins	750.00	375.00	225.00
(21)	Rudy Hulswitt	500.00	250.00	150.00
(22)	Adam Johnson	500.00	250.00	150.00
(23)	Ed Konetchy	500.00	250.00	150.00
(24)	Johnny Lush	500.00	250.00	150.00
(25)	Lee Magee	500.00	250.00	150.00
(26)	Stoney McGlynn	500.00	250.00	150.00
(27)	Rebel Oakes	500.00	250.00	150.00
(28)	Bill O'Hara	500.00	250.00	150.00
(29)	Patsy O'Rourke	500.00	250.00	150.00
(30)	Ed Phelps	500.00	250.00	150.00
(31)	Charlie Rhodes	500.00	250.00	150.00
(32)	Elmer Rieger	500.00	250.00	150.00
(33)	Slim Sallee	500.00	250.00	150.00
(34)	Vic Willis	750.00	375.00	225.00

1903-1904 Breisch-Williams

Many veteran collectors now believe that Breisch Williams Confectionary Co. of Oxford, Pa., was just one of several firms that used the black-and-white card issue cataloged as E107 as a premium. A relatively small percentage of E107s are found with a purple rubber-stamped "THE BREISCH-WILLIAMS CO" message diagonally on back. It is speculated the stamp may have been used to "cancel" cards there were returned in a prize redemption program. The overprinted cards currently carry a premium of 2-3X the value of blank-backed or "One of a ..." E107s. With only a single known exception, all Breisch-Williams stamped cards are of Type 1.

(See E107 Type 1 and Type 2 for checklist and base value information.)

1909-10 C.A. Briggs Co. (E97)

Measuring approximately 1-1/2" x 2-3/4", this set is nearly identical to several other candy issues of the same period. Designated as E97 in the American Card Catalog, the set was issued in 1909-1910 by "C.A. Briggs Co., Lozenge Makers of Boston, Mass." The front of the card shows a tinted player photo, with the player's last name, position and team printed below. Backs are printed in brown and checklist the 30 players in the set alphabetically. The C.A. Briggs Co. name appears at the bottom. Black-and-white examples of this set have also been found on a thin paper stock with blank backs and are believed to be "proof cards." They are valued about 2-3X the figures shown here. Five variations are also found in the set. The more expensive variations are not included in the complete set price.

CY. YOUNG. BOSTON, NAT'L

This card is one of a set of
30 BALL PLAYERS
Cards, as follows:
AUSTIN, New York American
BRADLEY, Cleveland American
BIRMINGHAM, Cleveland American
BRANSFIELD, Philadelphia National
CARRIGAN, Boston American
CAMNITZ, Pittsburg National
DURHAM, New York National
DYGERT, Philadelphia American
DOOLAN, Philadelphia National
DEVORE, New York National
DAVIS, Philadelphia American
HEMPHILL, New York American
HEINCHMAN, Cleveland American
HARTSEL, Philadelphia American
KROH, Chicago National
KLEINOW, New York American
KELLY, Boston National
KEELER, New York National
McINTYRE, Detroit American
McCONNELL, Boston American
MOORE, Philadelphia National
MULLIN, Detroit American
MURRAY, New York National
MEYERS, New York National
NICHOLS, Cleveland American
ROSSMAN, Detroit American
SULLIVAN, Chicago American
STEINFELDT, Chicago National
SCHLEI, New York National
CY. YOUNG, Cleveland American
C.A. BRIGGS CO., Lozenge Makers
Boston, Mass.

		NM	EX	VG
Complete Set (30):		60,000	24,000	12,000
Common Player:		2,500	1,000	500.00
Proofs: 2-3X				
(1)	Jimmy Austin	2,500	1,000	500.00
(2)	Joe Birmingham	2,500	1,000	500.00
(3)	Bill Bradley	2,500	1,000	500.00
(4)	Kitty Bransfield	2,500	1,000	500.00
(5)	Howie Camnitz	2,500	1,000	500.00
(6)	Bill Carrigan	2,500	1,000	500.00
(7)	Harry Davis	2,500	1,000	500.00
(8)	Josh Devore	2,500	1,000	500.00
(9a)	Mickey Dolan (Doolan)	2,500	1,000	500.00
(9b)	Mickey Doolan	2,500	1,000	500.00
(10)	Bull Durham	2,500	1,000	500.00
(11)	Jimmy Dygert	2,500	1,000	500.00
(12a)	Topsy Hartsell (Hartsel)	4,000	1,500	750.00
(12b)	Topsy Hartsel	2,500	1,000	500.00
(13)	Bill Heinchman (Hinchman)	2,500	1,000	500.00
(14)	Charlie Hemphill	2,500	1,000	500.00
(15)	Wee Willie Keeler	8,000	3,200	1,600
(16)	Joe Kelly (Kelley)	8,000	3,200	1,600
(17)	Red Kleinow	2,500	1,000	500.00
(18)	Rube Kroh	2,500	1,000	500.00
(19)	Matty McIntyre	2,500	1,000	500.00
(20)	Amby McConnell	2,500	1,000	500.00
(21)	Chief Meyers	2,500	1,000	500.00
(22)	Earl Moore	2,500	1,000	500.00
(23)	George Mullin	2,500	1,000	500.00
(24)	Red Murray	2,500	1,000	500.00
(25a)	Simon Nichols (Nicholls) (Philadelphia)	8,000	3,200	1,600
(25b)	Simon Nichols (Nicholls) (Cleveland)	4,000	1,500	750.00
(26)	Claude Rossman	4,000	1,500	750.00
(27)	Admiral Schlei	2,500	1,000	500.00
(28a)	Harry Steinfeld (Name incorrect.)	4,400	1,800	900.00
(28b)	Harry Steinfeldt (Name correct.)	4,400	1,800	900.00
(29a)	Dennis Sullivan (Chicago)	2,500	1,000	500.00
(29b)	Dennis Sullivan (Boston)	20,000	12,000	6,000
(30a)	Cy. Young (Cleveland) (Picture actually Irv Young.)	15,000	6,000	3,000
(30b)	Cy. Young (Boston) (Picture actually Irv Young.)	20,000	12,000	6,000

1933 C.A. Briggs Co. Babe Ruth

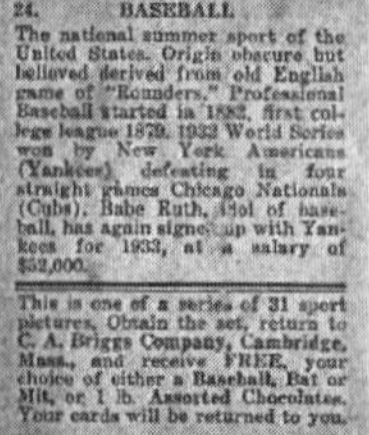
24. BASEBALL
The national summer sport of the United States. Origin obscure but believed derived from old English game of "Rounders." Professional Baseball started in 1882, first college league 1879. 1932 World Series won by New York Americans (Yankees) defeating in four straight games Chicago Nationals (Cubs). Babe Ruth, idol of baseball, has again signed up with Yankees for 1933, at a salary of $52,000.

This is one of a series of 31 sport pictures. Obtain the set, return to C. A. Briggs Company, Cambridge, Mass., and receive FREE, your choice of either a Baseball, Bat or Mit, or 1 lb. Assorted Chocolates. Your cards will be returned to you.

Stars in a variety of sports are featured in this series of candy issues. Card #24 has a drawing on front against a red background. The player bears more than a passing resemblance to Babe Ruth and on the back of the 2-3/8" x 2-7/8" card, along with a short history of baseball, Babe Ruth and his $52,000 contract for 1933 are mentioned. At bottom are details for redeeming a set of the 31 cards for baseball equipment or a pound of chocolates.

		NM	EX	VG
24	Baseball (Babe Ruth)	1,000	500.00	300.00

1953-54 Briggs Meats

The Briggs Meat set was issued over a two-year span (1953-54) and features 28 players from the Washington Senators and 12 from the New York teams. The set was issued

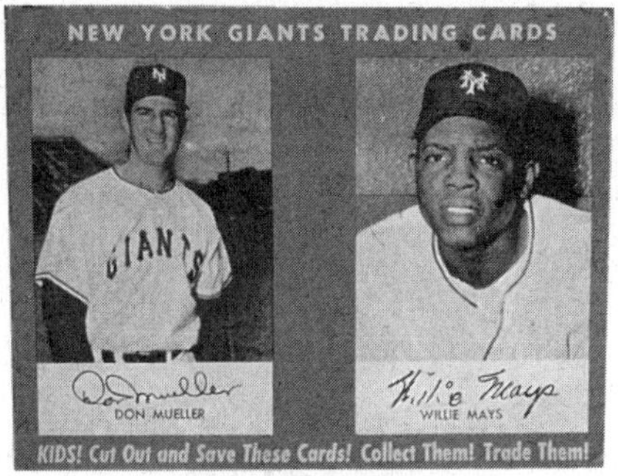

in two-card panels on hot dog packages sold in the Washington, D.C. vicinity. The color cards, which are blank-backed and measure 2-1/4" x 3-1/2", are printed on waxed cardboard. Pictures of the New York players can also be found on cards in the 1954 Dan-Dee Potato Chips and 1953-1955 Stahl-Meyer Franks sets. There is a slight difference in style between the Senators cards and those of the New York players. The white panel beneath the photo of the Washington players includes a facsimile autograph plus a few biographical details about the player. The New York players' cards have only the player's name and facsimile signature in that panel. Several of the Senators cards command a premium for scarcity.

		NM	EX	VG
Complete Set (40):		35,000	17,500	7,000
Common Player:		900.00	450.00	180.00
(1)	Hank Bauer	1,000	500.00	200.00
(2)	James Busby	900.00	450.00	180.00
(3)	Tommy Byrne	900.00	450.00	180.00
(4)	Gil Coan	900.00	450.00	180.00
(5)	John Dixon	900.00	450.00	180.00
(6)	Carl Erskine	1,000	500.00	200.00
(7)	Edward Fitzgerald (Fitz Gerald)	900.00	450.00	180.00
(8)	Newton Grasso	900.00	450.00	180.00
(9)	Melvin Hoderlein	900.00	450.00	180.00
(10)	Gil Hodges	1,500	750.00	300.00
(11)	Monte Irvin	1,000	500.00	200.00
(12)	Jackie Jensen	950.00	475.00	190.00
(13)	Whitey Lockman	900.00	450.00	180.00
(14)	Mickey Mantle	7,500	3,750	1,500
(15)	Conrado Marrero	900.00	450.00	180.00
(16)	Walter Masterson	900.00	450.00	180.00
(17)	Carmen Mauro	900.00	450.00	180.00
(18)	Willie Mays	4,500	2,250	900.00
(19)	Mickey McDermott	900.00	450.00	180.00
(20)	Gil McDougald	1,000	500.00	200.00
(21)	Julio Moreno	900.00	450.00	180.00
(22)	Don Mueller	900.00	450.00	180.00
(23)	Don Newcombe	1,000	500.00	200.00
(24)	Robert Oldis	900.00	450.00	180.00
(25)	Erwin Porterfield	900.00	450.00	180.00
(26)	Phil Rizzuto	1,200	600.00	240.00
(27)	James Runnels	900.00	450.00	180.00
(28)	John Schmitz	900.00	450.00	180.00
(29)	Angel Scull	900.00	450.00	180.00
(30)	Frank Shea	900.00	450.00	180.00
(31)	Albert Sima	900.00	450.00	180.00
(32)	Duke Snider	1,800	900.00	360.00
(33)	Charles Stobbs	900.00	450.00	180.00
(34)	Willard Terwilliger	900.00	450.00	180.00
(35)	Joe Tipton	900.00	450.00	180.00
(36)	Thomas Umphlett	900.00	450.00	180.00
(37)	Gene Verble	900.00	450.00	180.00
(38)	James Vernon	900.00	450.00	180.00
(39)	Clyde Vollmer	900.00	450.00	180.00
(40)	Edward Yost	900.00	450.00	180.00

1947 Brillantina Sol de Oro Managers

The approximately 6" x 8" black-and-white pictures were issued in conjunction with a contest run by an Havana shampoo company. Fronts have photos of the managers of Cuba's four professional teams, bordered in white, with a facsimile autograph and message. A sponsor's credit line is in the bottom border. Backs have further promotional copy for the shampoo and rules of the contest.

		NM	EX	VG
Complete Set (4):		600.00	300.00	180.00
Common Player:		150.00	75.00	45.00
(1)	Salvador Hernandez	150.00	75.00	45.00
(2)	Adolfo Luque	250.00	125.00	75.00
(3)	Napoleon Reyes	200.00	100.00	60.00
(4)	Lazaro Salazar	150.00	75.00	45.00

1909-12 Broad Leaf Cigarettes

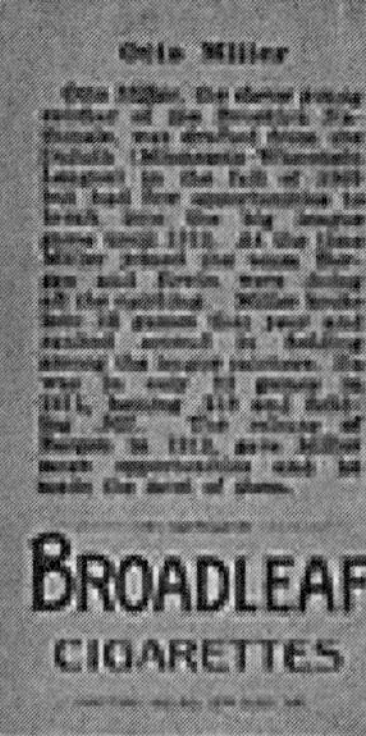

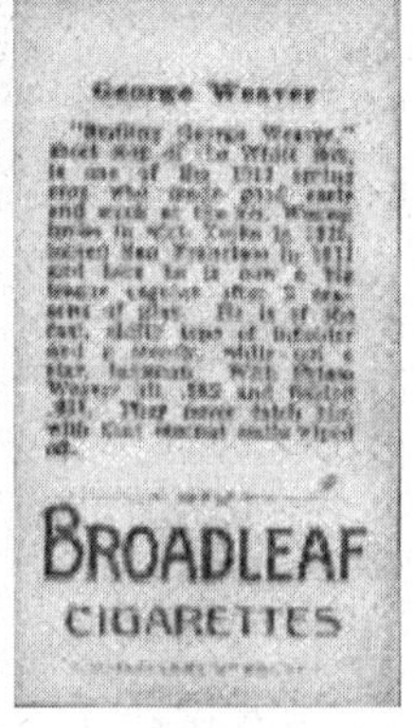

Cards with the Broad Leaf brand advertising on back can be found among the three most popular cigarette card issues circa 1910: T205 Gold Border, T206 White Border and T207 Brown Background. Two types are seen in T206, one that mentions "350 Subjects" and another, much rarer, that mentions "460 Subjects." Because some of the scarcer cards in T207 are often found with Broadleaf (as it was then spelled) backs, it is not practical to quote a value multipler; premiums for such cards have already been factored into the prices under T207. In T205, Broad Leaf backs can be found printed in either black or brown-olive green.

PREMIUMS:
T205: 6X
T206 350 Subjects: 6-8X
T206 460 Subjects, Common: 50-60X
T206 460 Subjects, HoF: 15-25X
(See T205, T206, T207 for checklists.)

1974 Broder N.Y. Mets Tour of Japan

Veteran collector Ed Broder who was stationed with the U.S. Army in Japan, produced this collectors' issue chronicling the goodwill tour undertaken by the National League Champion N.Y. Mets. Nominally measuring about 1-7/8" x 3", cards have borderless black-and-white photos on front with no player identification or other graphics. Backs have player name, team and "1974 New York Mets Tour of Japan" in typewriter font along with a team logo. The unnumbered cards are checklisted here alphabetically.

		NM	EX	VG
Complete Set (20):		60.00	30.00	18.00
Common Player:		4.00	2.00	1.25
(1)	Yogi Berra	20.00	10.00	6.00
(2)	Wayne Garrett	8.00	4.00	2.50
(3)	Ron Hodges	8.00	4.00	2.50
(4)	Tsuneo Horiuchi	8.00	4.00	2.50
(5)	Kazumasa Kono	4.00	2.00	1.25
(6)	Jerry Koosman	8.00	4.00	2.50
(7)	Ed Kranepool, John Milner, unidentified Japanese player, Joe Torre	4.00	2.00	1.25
(8)	Jon Matlack	8.00	4.00	2.50
(9)	Felix Millan	8.00	4.00	2.50
(10)	John Milner	8.00	4.00	2.50
(11)	Shigeo Nagashima	10.00	5.00	3.00
(12)	Sadaharu Oh	15.00	7.50	4.50
(13)	Tom Seaver	40.00	20.00	12.00
(14)	Yososhi Sekimoto	4.00	2.00	1.25
(15)	Tamio Suetsugu	4.00	2.00	1.25
(16)	Kazumi Takahashi	4.00	2.00	1.25
(17)	Yoshima Takahashi	4.00	2.00	1.25
(18)	George Theodore	8.00	4.00	2.50
(19)	Joe Torre, Kazuyoshi Yamamoto	15.00	7.50	4.50
(20)	Kazuyoshi Yamamoto, Tetsuhara Kawakami	10.00	5.00	3.00

1975 Broder All-Time N.Y. Mets

Veteran collector Ed Broder produced this collectors' issue. Nominally measuring about 1-7/8" x 3-1/8", cards have borderless black-and-white photos on front. Some cards have the dates of their tenure with the team on front. The unnumbered cards are checklisted here alphabetically.

		NM	EX	VG
Complete Set (12):		45.00	22.50	13.50
Common Player:		4.00	2.00	1.25
(1)	Yogi Berra	7.50	3.75	2.25
(2)	Bud Harrelson	4.00	2.00	1.25
(3)	Jim Hickman	4.00	2.00	1.25
(4)	Al Jackson	4.00	2.00	1.25
(5)	Cleon Jones	4.00	2.00	1.25
(6)	Jerry Koosman	4.00	2.00	1.25
(7)	Ed Kranepool	4.00	2.00	1.25
(8)	Tug McGraw	4.00	2.00	1.25
(9)	Nolan Ryan	15.00	7.50	4.50
(10)	Tom Seaver	9.00	4.50	2.75
(11)	Warren Spahn	6.00	3.00	1.75
(12)	Casey Stengal (Stengel)	6.00	3.00	1.75

1975 Broder 1962 "Original" N.Y. Mets

Veteran collector Ed Broder produced this collectors' issue. Nominally measuring about 2" x 3", cards have borderless black-and-white photos on front with only the player name for identification. Backs are blank. The unnumbered cards are checklisted here alphabetically.

		NM	EX	VG
Complete Set (15):		50.00	25.00	15.00
Common Player:		5.00	2.50	1.50
(1)	Richie Ashburn	10.00	5.00	3.00
(2)	Gus Bell	5.00	2.50	1.50
(3)	Roger Craig	5.00	2.50	1.50
(4)	Gil Hodges	10.00	5.00	3.00
(5)	Rogers Hornsby	7.50	3.75	2.25
(6)	Sherman Jones	5.00	2.50	1.50
(7)	Rod Kanehl	5.00	2.50	1.50
(8)	Clem Labine	5.00	2.50	1.50
(9)	Hobie Landrith	5.00	2.50	1.50
(10)	R.G. Miller	5.00	2.50	1.50
(11)	Wilmer Mizell	5.00	2.50	1.50
(12)	Charley Neal	5.00	2.50	1.50
(13)	Casey Stengal (Stengel)	7.50	3.75	2.25
(14)	Frank Thomas	5.00	2.50	1.50
(15)	Marv Throneberry	5.00	2.50	1.50

1975 Broder Major Leagues - The 1950's

Veteran collector Ed Broder produced this collectors' issue. Nominally measuring about 2" x 3", cards have borderless black-and-white photos on front with only the player name for identification. Backs are blank. The unnumbered cards are checklisted here alphabetically. The set is notable in that a number of familiar players are pictured with teams not seen on their Topps and Bowman cards. The set sold originally for $2.20.

		NM	EX	VG
Complete Set (28):		100.00	50.00	30.00
Common Player:		4.00	2.00	1.25
(1)	Bobby Adams	4.00	2.00	1.25
(2)	Richie Ashburn	6.50	3.25	2.00
(3)	Ken Aspromonte	4.00	2.00	1.25
(4)	Ray Boone	5.00	2.50	1.50
(5)	Lou Boudreau	6.50	3.25	2.00
(6)	Smoky Burgess	4.00	2.00	1.25
(7)	Phil Cavaretta (Cavarretta)	4.00	2.00	1.25
(8)	Gene Conley	4.00	2.00	1.25
(9)	Del Crandell (Crandall)	4.00	2.00	1.25

		NM	EX	VG
(10)	Bob Friend	4.00	2.00	1.25
(11)	Harvey Haddix	4.00	2.00	1.25
(12)	Fred Haney	4.00	2.00	1.25
(13)	Ted Kluszewski	5.00	2.50	1.50
(14)	Jim Konstanty	4.00	2.00	1.25
(15)	Sandy Koufax	7.50	3.75	2.25
(16)	Harvey Kuenn	4.00	2.00	1.25
(17)	Bob Lemon	6.00	3.00	1.75
(18)	Marty Marion	4.00	2.00	1.25
(19)	Minnie Minoso	5.00	2.50	1.50
(20)	Stan Musial	7.00	3.50	2.00
(21)	Albie Pearson	4.00	2.00	1.25
(22)	Paul Richards	4.00	2.00	1.25
(23)	Hank Sauer	4.00	2.00	1.25
(24)	Herb Score	4.00	2.00	1.25
(25)	Bob Skinner	4.00	2.00	1.25
(26)	Enos Slaughter	6.00	3.00	1.75
(27)	Gus Triandos	4.00	2.00	1.25
(28)	Gus Zernial	4.00	2.00	1.25

1975 Broder Major League Postcards

This series of 3-1/8" x 5-1/8", borderless, blank-back pictures was advertised as the first in a proposed series designed to accommodate player autographs. Only California Angels and Montreal Expos players are included. The cards are printed on thin cardboard and feature close-up portraits with the player name in black type.

		NM	EX	VG
Complete Set (9):		25.00	12.50	7.50
Common Player:		3.00	1.50	.90
(1)	Tim Foli	3.00	1.50	.90
(2)	Barry Foote	3.00	1.50	.90
(3)	Mike Jorgensen	3.00	1.50	.90
(4)	Larry Lintz	3.00	1.50	.90
(5)	Dave McNally	3.00	1.50	.90
(6)	Steve Rodgers (Rogers)	3.00	1.50	.90
(7)	Nolan Ryan	10.00	5.00	3.00
(8)	Bill Singer	3.00	1.50	.90
(9)	Dick Williams	3.00	1.50	.90

1978 Broder Photocards

This collectors' issue features late 1970s photos of some of the game's stars from the 1920s-1960s. Cards are printed in 3-1/2" x 5-1/2", blank-back, black-and-white format on thick grayback card stock. Cards were printed four to a sheet and often found on uncut sheets.

		NM	EX	VG
Complete Set (20):		40.00	20.00	12.00
Common Player:		3.00	1.50	.90
(1)	Walt Alston	3.00	1.50	.90
(2)	Luke Appling	3.00	1.50	.90
(3)	Ernie Banks	4.50	2.25	1.25
(4)	Yogi Berra	4.50	2.25	1.25
(5)	Bill Dickey	4.00	2.00	1.25
(6)	Bob Feller/Pitching	4.00	2.00	1.25
(7)	Bob Feller/Portrait	4.00	2.00	1.25
(8)	Billy Herman	3.00	1.50	.90
(9)	Bob Lemon	3.00	1.50	.90
(10)	Mickey Mantle	6.00	3.00	1.75
(11)	Willie Mays/Btg	5.00	2.50	1.50
(12)	Willie Mays/Portrait	5.00	2.50	1.50
(13)	Johnny Mize	3.00	1.50	.90
(14)	Pee Wee Reese	4.00	2.00	1.25
(15)	Allie Reynolds	3.00	1.50	.90
(16)	Brooks Robinson	4.00	2.00	1.25
(17)	Enos Slaughter	3.00	1.50	.90
(18)	Warren Spahn	3.00	1.50	.90
(19)	Lloyd Waner	3.00	1.50	.90
(20)	Ted Williams	5.00	2.50	1.50

1940 Brooklyn Dodgers Picture Pack

Rookie Pee Wee Reese appears in this team-issued set of black-and-white pictures. The 6" x 9" pictures have player portraits surrounded by a white border. A facsimile autograph appears on front. Backs are blank. The unnumbered pictures are checklisted here in alphabetical order. Because of roster changes, it is possible the specific makeup of the packs may have changed once or more over the course of the season. Some of the pictures were reused in subsequent years' offerings.

		NM	EX	VG
Complete Set (25):		150.00	75.00	45.00
Common Player:		8.00	4.00	2.50
(1)	Dolf Camilli	8.00	4.00	2.50
(2)	Tex Carleton	8.00	4.00	2.50
(3)	Hugh Casey	8.00	4.00	2.50
(4)	Pete Coscarart	8.00	4.00	2.50
(5)	Curt Davis	8.00	4.00	2.50
(6)	Leo Durocher	12.00	6.00	3.50
(7)	Fred Fitzsimmons	8.00	4.00	2.50
(8)	Herman Franks	8.00	4.00	2.50
(9)	Joe Gallagher	8.00	4.00	2.50
(10)	Charlie Gilbert	8.00	4.00	2.50
(11)	Luke Hamlin	8.00	4.00	2.50
(12)	Johnny Hudson	8.00	4.00	2.50
(13)	Newt Kimball	8.00	4.00	2.50
(14)	Cookie Lavagetto	8.00	4.00	2.50
(15)	Gus Mancuso	8.00	4.00	2.50
(16)	Joe Medwick	12.00	6.00	3.50
(17)	Van Lingle Mungo	10.00	5.00	3.00
(18)	Babe Phelps	8.00	4.00	2.50
(19)	Tot Pressnell	8.00	4.00	2.50
(20)	Pee Wee Reese	24.00	12.00	7.25
(21)	Vito Tamulis	8.00	4.00	2.50
(22)	Joe Vosmik	8.00	4.00	2.50
(23)	Dixie Walker	8.00	4.00	2.50
(24)	Jimmy Wasdell	8.00	4.00	2.50
(25)	Whitlow Wyatt	8.00	4.00	2.50

1941 Brooklyn Dodgers Picture Pack

This team-issued set of 6" x 9" black-and-white pictures has player portraits surrounded by a white border. A facsimile autograph appears on front. Backs are blank. The unnumbered pictures are checklisted here in alphabetical order. Because of roster changes, it is possible the specific makeup of the packs may have changed once or more over the course of the season and that there may have been players issued other than those listed here. Some of the pictures were reused the 1940 offering. Team-issued pictures of 1940-41 can be differentiated from later years by their ballpark backgrounds.

		NM	EX	VG
Complete Set (25):		185.00	95.00	55.00
Common Player:		10.00	5.00	3.00
(1)	Mace Brown	10.00	5.00	3.00
(2)	Dolph Camilli	10.00	5.00	3.00
(3)	Hugh Casey	10.00	5.00	3.00
(4)	Pete Coscarart	10.00	5.00	3.00
(5)	Curt Davis	10.00	5.00	3.00
(6)	Leo Durocher	15.00	7.50	4.50
(7)	Fred Fitzsimmons	10.00	5.00	3.00
(8)	Luke Hamlin	10.00	5.00	3.00
(9)	Billy Herman	15.00	7.50	4.50
(10)	Kirby Higbe	10.00	5.00	3.00
(11)	Newt Kimball	10.00	5.00	3.00
(12)	Harry "Cookie" Lavagetto	10.00	5.00	3.00
(13)	Joe Medwick	15.00	7.50	4.50
(14)	Mickey Owen	10.00	5.00	3.00
(15)	Babe Phelps	10.00	5.00	3.00
(16)	Pee Wee Reese	25.00	12.50	7.50
(17)	Pete Reiser	10.00	5.00	3.00
(18)	Lew Riggs	10.00	5.00	3.00
(19)	Bill Swift	10.00	5.00	3.00
(20)	Vito Tamulis	10.00	5.00	3.00
(21)	Joe Vosmik	10.00	5.00	3.00
(22)	Dixie Walker	10.00	5.00	3.00
(23)	Jimmy Wasdell	10.00	5.00	3.00
(24)	Kemp Wicker	10.00	5.00	3.00
(25)	Whit Wyatt	10.00	5.00	3.00

1942 Brooklyn Dodgers Picture Pack

This set of 6" x 9" black-and-white team-issued pictures features player portrait photos in a studio setting. The pictures have a white border all around, and there is a facsimile autograph on front. Backs are blank. The unnumbered pictures are checklisted here alphabetically. Pictures from the 1942 and 1943 photo packs are indistinguishable except for player selection.

		NM	EX	VG
Complete Set (25):		150.00	75.00	45.00
Common Player:		8.00	4.00	2.50
(1)	Johnny Allen	8.00	4.00	2.50
(2)	Frenchy Bordagaray	8.00	4.00	2.50
(3)	Dolf Camilli	8.00	4.00	2.50
(4)	Hugh Casey	8.00	4.00	2.50
(5)	Curt Davis	8.00	4.00	2.50
(6)	Leo Durocher	12.00	6.00	3.50
(7)	Larry French	8.00	4.00	2.50
(8)	Augie Galan	8.00	4.00	2.50
(9)	Ed Head	8.00	4.00	2.50
(10)	Billy Herman	12.00	6.00	3.50
(11)	Kirby Higbe	8.00	4.00	2.50
(12)	Alex Kampouris	8.00	4.00	2.50
(13)	Newt Kimball	8.00	4.00	2.50
(14)	Joe Medwick	12.00	6.00	3.50
(15)	Mickey Owen	8.00	4.00	2.50
(16)	Pee Wee Reese	16.00	8.00	4.75
(17)	Pete Reiser	10.00	5.00	3.00
(18)	Lew Riggs	8.00	4.00	2.50
(19)	Johnny Rizzo	8.00	4.00	2.50
(20)	Schoolboy Rowe	10.00	5.00	3.00
(21)	Billy Sullivan	8.00	4.00	2.50
(22)	Arky Vaughan	12.00	6.00	3.50
(23)	Dixie Walker	8.00	4.00	2.50
(24)	Les Webber	8.00	4.00	2.50
(25)	Whitlow Wyatt	8.00	4.00	2.50

1943 Brooklyn Dodgers Picture Pack

This set of 6" x 9" black-and-white team-issued pictures features player portrait photos in a studio setting. The pictures have a white border all around, and there is a facsimile autograph on front. Backs are blank. The unnumbered pictures are checklisted here alphabetically. Pictures from the 1942 and 1943 photo packs are indistinguishable except for player selection.

		NM	EX	VG
Complete Set (25):		150.00	75.00	45.00
Common Player:		8.00	4.00	2.50
(1)	Johnny Allen	8.00	4.00	2.50
(2)	Frenchy Bordagaray	8.00	4.00	2.50
(3)	Bob Bragan	10.00	5.00	3.00
(4)	Dolf Camilli	8.00	4.00	2.50
(5)	Johnny Cooney	8.00	4.00	2.50
(6)	John Corriden	8.00	4.00	2.50
(7)	Curt Davis	8.00	4.00	2.50
(8)	Leo Durocher	12.00	6.00	3.50
(9)	Fred Fitzsimmons	8.00	4.00	2.50
(10)	Augie Galan	8.00	4.00	2.50
(11)	Al Glossop	8.00	4.00	2.50
(12)	Ed Head	8.00	4.00	2.50
(13)	Billy Herman	12.00	6.00	3.50
(14)	Kirby Higbe	8.00	4.00	2.50
(15)	Max Macon	8.00	4.00	2.50
(16)	Joe Medwick	12.00	6.00	3.50
(17)	Rube Melton	8.00	4.00	2.50
(18)	Dee Moore	8.00	4.00	2.50
(19)	"Buck" Newsom	10.00	5.00	3.00
(20)	Mickey Owen	8.00	4.00	2.50
(21)	Arky Vaughan	12.00	6.00	3.50
(22)	Dixie Walker	8.00	4.00	2.50
(23)	Paul Waner	12.00	6.00	3.50
(24)	Les Webber	8.00	4.00	2.50
(25)	Whitlow Wyatt	8.00	4.00	2.50

1946 Brooklyn Dodgers Picture Pack

This team-issued set of player portrait pictures is in a blank-back 6-1/2" x 9" format. A facsimile autograph appears on front. Like many souvenir-stand photo packs of the era,

it is possible the specific contents of this product may have changed during the course of the season as players joined and left the team.

	NM	EX	VG
Complete Set (25):	125.00	65.00	40.00
Common Player:	6.00	3.00	1.80
(1) Andy Anderson	6.00	3.00	1.80
(2) Henry Behrman	6.00	3.00	1.80
(3) Ralph Branca	6.00	3.00	1.80
(4) Hugh Casey	6.00	3.00	1.80
(5) Leo Durocher	9.00	4.50	2.75
(6) Carl Furillo	12.00	6.00	3.50
(7) Augie Galan	6.00	3.00	1.80
(8) Hal Gregg	6.00	3.00	1.80
(9) Joe Hatten	6.00	3.00	1.80
(10) Al Head	6.00	3.00	1.80
(11) Art Herring	6.00	3.00	1.80
(12) Billy Herman	9.00	4.50	2.75
(13) Gene Hermanski	6.00	3.00	1.80
(14) Kirby Higbe	6.00	3.00	1.80
(15) Harry "Cookie" Lavagetto	6.00	3.00	1.80
(16) Vic Lombardi	6.00	3.00	1.80
(17) Pee Wee Reese	12.00	6.00	3.50
(18) Pete Reiser	6.00	3.00	1.80
(19) Stan Rojek	6.00	3.00	1.80
(20) Mike Sandlock	6.00	3.00	1.80
(21) Eddie Stanky	7.50	3.75	2.25
(22) Ed Stevens	6.00	3.00	1.80
(23) Dixie Walker	6.00	3.00	1.80
(24) Les Webber	6.00	3.00	1.80
(25) Dick Whitman	6.00	3.00	1.80

1947 Brooklyn Dodgers Picture Pack

This team-issued set of player portrait pictures is in a blank-back 6-1/2" x 9" format. A facsimile autograph appears on front. Like many souvenir-stand photo packs of the era, it is possible the specific contents of this product may have changed during the course of the season as players joined and left the team.

	NM	EX	VG
Complete Set (25):	350.00	175.00	105.00
Common Player:	9.00	4.50	2.75
(1) Ray Blades	9.00	4.50	2.75
(2) Bobby Bragan	9.00	4.50	2.75
(3) Ralph Branca	9.00	4.50	2.75
(4) Tommy Brown	9.00	4.50	2.75
(5) Hugh Casey	9.00	4.50	2.75
(6) Ed Chandler	9.00	4.50	2.75
(7) Carl Furillo	20.00	10.00	6.00
(8) Hal Gregg	9.00	4.50	2.75
(9) Joe Hatten	9.00	4.50	2.75
(10) Gene Hermanski	9.00	4.50	2.75
(11) Gil Hodges	40.00	20.00	12.00
(12) Spider Jorgensen	9.00	4.50	2.75
(13) Clyde King	9.00	4.50	2.75
(14) Vic Lombardi	9.00	4.50	2.75
(15) Rube Melton	9.00	4.50	2.75
(16) Eddie Miksis	9.00	4.50	2.75
(17) Pee Wee Reese	30.00	15.00	9.00
(18) Pete Reiser	9.00	4.50	2.75
(19) Jackie Robinson	80.00	40.00	24.00
(20) Stan Rojek	9.00	4.50	2.75
(21) Burt Shotton	9.00	4.50	2.75
(22) Duke Snider	40.00	20.00	12.00
(23) Eddie Stanky	12.50	6.25	3.75
(24) Harry Taylor	9.00	4.50	2.75
(25) Dixie Walker	9.00	4.50	2.75

1948 Brooklyn Dodgers Picture Pack

This team-issued set of player portrait pictures is in a blank-back 6-1/2" x 9" format. A facsimile autograph appears on front. Like many souvenir-stand photo packs of the era, it is possible the specific contents of this product may have changed during the course of the season as players joined and left the team, and that pictures were re-used from year-to-year.

	NM	EX	VG
Complete Set (26):	300.00	150.00	95.00
Common Player:	8.00	4.00	2.50
(1) Rex Barney	8.00	4.00	2.50
(2) Ray Blades	8.00	4.00	2.50
(3) Bobby Bragan	8.00	4.00	2.50
(4) Ralph Branca	8.00	4.00	2.50
(5) Tommy Brown	8.00	4.00	2.50
(6) Hugh Casey	8.00	4.00	2.50
(7) Billy Cox	8.00	4.00	2.50
(8) Leo Durocher	15.00	7.50	4.50
(9) Bruce Edwards	8.00	4.00	2.50
(10) Carl Furillo	20.00	10.00	6.00
(11) Joe Hatten	8.00	4.00	2.50
(12) Gene Hermanski	8.00	4.00	2.50
(13) Gil Hodges	30.00	15.00	9.00
(14) Spider Jorgensen	8.00	4.00	2.50
(15) Don Lund	8.00	4.00	2.50
(16) Eddie Miksis	8.00	4.00	2.50
(17) Jake Pitler	8.00	4.00	2.50
(18) Pee Wee Reese	25.00	12.50	7.50
(19) Pete Reiser	8.00	4.00	2.50
(20) Jackie Robinson	65.00	32.00	19.50
(21) Preacher Roe	12.00	6.00	3.50
(22) Burt Shotton	8.00	4.00	2.50
(23) Clyde Sukeforth	8.00	4.00	2.50
(24) Harry Taylor	8.00	4.00	2.50
(25) Arky Vaughan	15.00	7.50	4.50
(26) Preston Ward	8.00	4.00	2.50

1949 Brooklyn Dodgers Picture Pack

This team-issued set of player portrait pictures is in a blank-back 6-1/2" x 9" format. A facsimile autograph appears on front. Like many souvenir-stand photo packs of the era, it is possible the specific contents of this product may have changed during the course of the season as players joined and left the team, and that pictures were re-used from year-to-year.

	NM	EX	VG
Complete Set (25):	575.00	300.00	160.00
Common Player:	8.00	5.00	3.00
(1) Jack Banta	8.00	5.00	3.00
(2) Rex Barney	8.00	5.00	3.00
(3) Ralph Branca	12.50	6.25	3.75
(4) Tommy Brown	8.00	5.00	3.00
(5) Roy Campanella	200.00	100.00	60.00
(6) Billy Cox	8.00	5.00	3.00
(7) Bruce Edwards	8.00	5.00	3.00
(8) Carl Furillo	20.00	10.00	6.00
(9) Joe Hatten	8.00	5.00	3.00
(10) Gene Hermanski	8.00	5.00	3.00
(11) Gil Hodges	40.00	20.00	12.00
(12) Johnny Hopp	8.00	5.00	3.00
(13) Spider Jorgensen	8.00	5.00	3.00
(14) Mike McCormick	8.00	5.00	3.00
(15) Eddie Miksis	8.00	5.00	3.00
(16) Don Newcombe	100.00	50.00	30.00
(17) Erv Palica	8.00	5.00	3.00
(18) Jake Pitler	8.00	5.00	3.00
(19) Pee Wee Reese	50.00	25.00	15.00
(20) Jackie Robinson	75.00	37.00	22.00
(21) Preacher Roe	12.50	6.25	3.75
(22) Burt Shotton	8.00	5.00	3.00
(23) Duke Snider	50.00	25.00	15.00
(24) Milt Stock	8.00	5.00	3.00
(25) Clyde Sukeforth	8.00	5.00	3.00

1952 Brooklyn Dodgers Schedule Cards

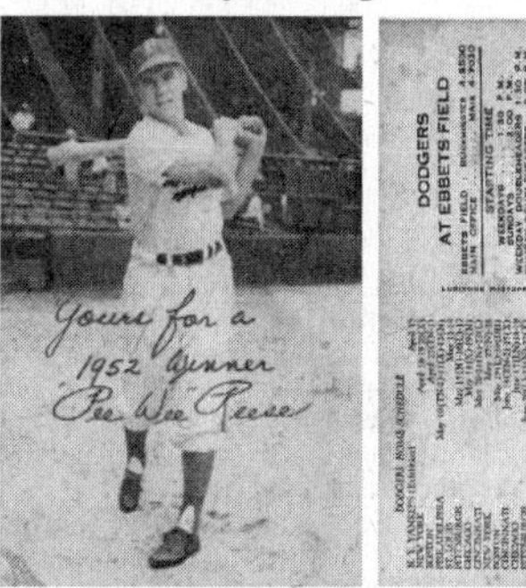

These postcard-size black-and-white cards have popular Dodgers players on front and the 1952 season's schedule printed on back. Some cards have a postcard-style back on which the right side has space for an address. Others cards have ticket price information in that space. How many different cards were issued is not known. Credit on the back is given to Lumitone Photoprint of New York.

	NM	EX	VG
Common Card:	400.00	200.00	120.00
Gil Hodges	400.00	200.00	120.00
Pee Wee Reese	400.00	200.00	120.00
Jackie Robinson	600.00	300.00	180.00
Duke Snider	400.00	200.00	120.00

1955 Brooklyn Dodgers Picture Pack

This set of approximately 5" x 7" blank-back, black-and-white pictures was a souvenir stand item at Ebbets Field. Player photos are chest-to-cap portraits surrounded by a white border with the player name at bottom in all-caps, followed by the team nickname in upper- and lower-case type. The unnumbered pictures are listed here alphabetically. The set was sold for 25 cents in a white paper envelope with "WORLD CHAMPION Dodgers" printed in blue.

	NM	EX	VG
Complete Set (12):	100.00	50.00	30.00
Common Player:	8.00	4.00	2.50
(1) Walter Alston	8.00	4.00	2.50
(2) Roy Campanella	20.00	10.00	6.00
(3) Carl Erskine	8.00	4.00	2.50
(4) Carl Furillo	10.00	5.00	3.00
(5) Gil Hodges	16.00	8.00	4.75
(6) Randy Jackson	8.00	4.00	2.50
(7) Clem Labine	8.00	4.00	2.50
(8) Don Newcombe	8.00	4.00	2.50
(9) Johnny Podres	8.00	4.00	2.50
(10) Peewee Reese	13.50	6.75	4.00
(11) Jackie Robinson	24.00	12.00	7.25
(12) Duke Snider	16.00	8.00	4.75

1956 Brooklyn Dodgers Picture Pack

DON DRYSDALE, Dodgers

This set of 5" x 7" blank-back, black-and-white pictures was a souvenir stand item at Ebbets Field. Player photos are surrounded by a white border with the player name at bottom in all-caps, followed by the team nickname in upper- and lower-case type. The unnumbered pictures are listed here alphabetically. The same photos were offered in a 50-piece Yankees-Dodgers "World Series Picture Portfolio."

	NM	EX	VG
Complete Set (25):	250.00	125.00	75.00
Common Player:	10.00	5.00	3.00
(1) Walter Alston	12.50	6.25	3.75
(2) Sandy Amoros	12.50	6.25	3.75
(3) Joe Becker	10.00	5.00	3.00
(4) Don Bessent	10.00	5.00	3.00
(5) Roy Campanella	30.00	15.00	9.00
(6) Roger Craig	10.00	5.00	3.00

(7)	Don Drysdale	25.00	12.50	7.50
(8)	Carl Erskine	12.50	6.25	3.75
(9)	Chico Fernandez	10.00	5.00	3.00
(10)	Carl Furillo	15.00	7.50	4.50
(11)	Jim Gilliam	15.00	7.50	4.50
(12)	Billy Herman	12.50	6.25	3.75
(13)	Gil Hodges	25.00	12.50	7.50
(14)	Randy Jackson	10.00	5.00	3.00
(15)	Sandy Koufax	35.00	17.50	10.50
(16)	Clem Labine	12.50	6.25	3.75
(17)	Sal Maglie	10.00	5.00	3.00
(18)	Charlie Neal	10.00	5.00	3.00
(19)	Don Newcombe	12.50	6.25	3.75
(20)	Jake Pitler	10.00	5.00	3.00
(21)	Peewee Reese	20.00	10.00	6.00
(22)	Jackie Robinson	35.00	17.50	10.50
(23)	Ed Roebuck	10.00	5.00	3.00
(24)	Duke Snider	25.00	12.50	7.50
(25)	Al Walker	10.00	5.00	3.00

1957 Brooklyn Dodgers Picture Pack

In their final year in Brooklyn, the Dodgers issued this souvenir-stand picture pack, offered for 25 cents. The pictures are 5" x 7", blank-back, black-and-white. Player portraits are surrounded by a white border with the player name at bottom in all-caps and "Dodgers" in upper- and lower-case type. The unnumbered pictures are listed here alphabetically.

		NM	EX	VG
Complete Set (12):		125.00	65.00	40.00
Common Player:		10.00	5.00	3.00
(1)	Walter Alston	15.00	7.50	4.50
(2)	Roy Campanella	25.00	12.50	7.50
(3)	Carl Furillo	15.00	7.50	4.50
(4)	Jim Gilliam	15.00	7.50	4.50
(5)	Gil Hodges	20.00	10.00	6.00
(6)	Randy Jackson	10.00	5.00	3.00
(7)	Clem Labine	10.00	5.00	3.00
(8)	Sal Maglie	10.00	5.00	3.00
(9)	Don Newcombe	12.50	6.25	3.75
(10)	Johnny Podres	15.00	7.50	4.50
(11)	Peewee Reese	20.00	10.00	6.00
(12)	Duke Snider	20.00	10.00	6.00

1953-55 Brown & Bigelow

Some of baseball's biggest stars, either as they appeared in the mid-1950s or as spirit images, instruct All-American boys in the skills of baseball on this series of cards. Produced by the St. Paul firm of Brown & Bigelow, the 2-1/4" x 3-1/2", round-cornered cards can be found either as playing cards or with schedules printed on the back. The cards could be customized by local sponsors in a panel at the bottom of the artwork. The Medcalf artwork is also seen on contemporary wall and desk calendars and other printed items.

		NM	EX	VG
	UNOPENED DECKS			
(1)	Ty Cobb	45.00	22.50	13.50
(2)	Lou Gehrig	50.00	25.00	15.00
(3)	Connie Mack	30.00	15.00	9.00
(4)	John McGraw	30.00	15.00	9.00
(5)	Babe Ruth	65.00	32.50	20.00
(6)	Honus Wagner	40.00	20.00	12.00
	SINGLE CARDS			
(1)	Ty Cobb	6.00	3.00	1.75
(2)	Lou Gehrig	8.00	4.00	2.50
(3)	Connie Mack	4.00	2.00	1.25
(4)	John McGraw	4.00	2.00	1.25
(5)	Babe Ruth	10.00	5.00	3.00
(6)	Honus Wagner	5.00	2.50	1.50

1911-14 Brunners Bread (D304)

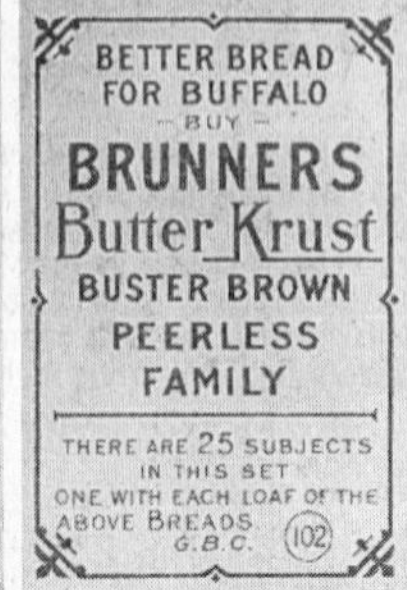

(See 1911-1914 General Baking Co. for checklist and values.)

1908-1910 Brush Detroit Tigers Postcards

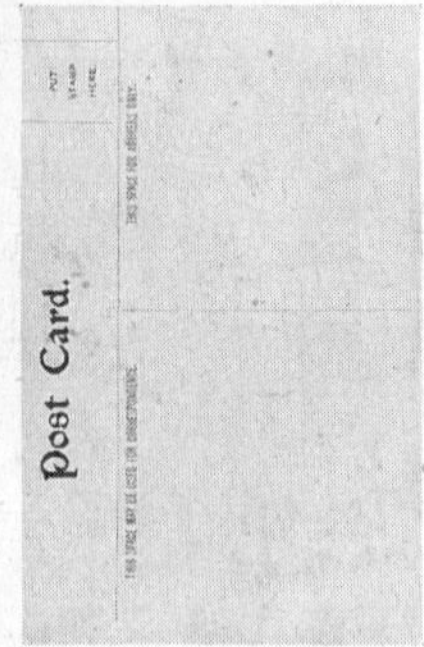

The makers of this short-lived (1907-11) automobile evidently engaged members of the hometown team to endorse their product. The 3-1/2" x 5-3/8" black-and-white postcards have a bordered photo on front showing a Tigers player (in uniform or suit) with the auto. A few lines of petry about the player complete the design. Backs have typical postcard format. It is likely the checklist here is incomplete.

		NM	EX	VG
(1)	Ty Cobb	4,000	2,000	1,200
(2)	William Coughlin	750.00	375.00	225.00
(3)	Bill Donovan	750.00	375.00	225.00
			750.00	
(4)	Hughie Jennings (Hands on steering wheel.)	1,500	750.00	450.00
(5)	Hughie Jennings (Hands in air.)	1,500	750.00	450.00
(6)	Matty McIntyre	750.00	375.00	225.00
(7)	George Mullin	750.00	375.00	225.00
(8)	Germany Schaefer, Charley O'Leary	750.00	375.00	225.00
(9)	Charlie Schmidt	750.00	375.00	225.00
(10)	Ira Thomas	750.00	375.00	225.00

1979 Bubble Yum Toronto Blue Jays

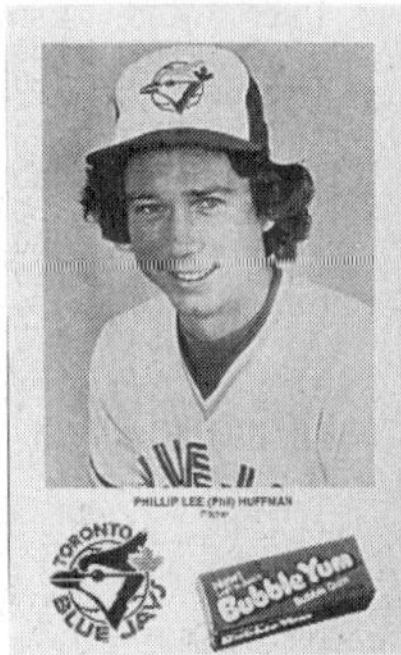

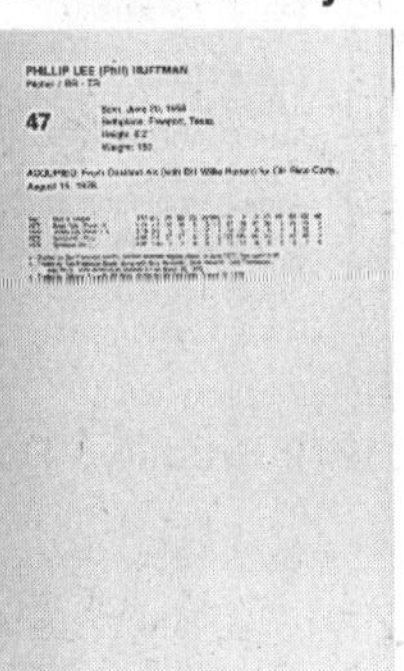

Members of the Toronto Blue Jays in the team's third season are featured in this set of 5-1/2" x 8-1/2" black-and-white player pictures. Fronts feature player portraits identified by their full name and position. In the wide bottom border are team and sponsor logos. Backs have player biographical data, major and minor league stats, acquisition information and career highlights. Cards are numbered by uniform number.

		NM	EX	VG
Complete Set (20):		65.00	32.50	20.00
Common Player:		4.00	2.00	1.25
1	Bob Bailor	4.00	2.00	1.25
4	Alfredo Griffin	4.00	2.00	1.25
7	Roy Hartsfield	4.00	2.00	1.25
9	Rick Cerone	4.00	2.00	1.25
10	John Mayberry	4.00	2.00	1.25
11	Luis Gomez	4.00	2.00	1.25
13	Roy Howell	4.00	2.00	1.25
18	Jim Clancy	4.00	2.00	1.25
19	Otto Velez	4.00	2.00	1.25
20	Al Woods	4.00	2.00	1.25
21	Rico Carty	4.00	2.00	1.25
22	Rick Bosetti	4.00	2.00	1.25
23	Dave Lemanczyk	4.00	2.00	1.25
24	Tom Underwood	4.00	2.00	1.25
31	Bobby Doerr	6.00	3.00	1.75
34	Jesse Jefferson	4.00	2.00	1.25
38	Balor Moore	4.00	2.00	1.25
44	Tom Buskey	4.00	2.00	1.25
46	Dave Freisleben	4.00	2.00	1.25
47	Phil Huffman	4.00	2.00	1.25

1976 Buckmans Discs

One of several regional sponsors of player disc sets in 1976 was Buckmans Ice Cream Village in Rochester, N.Y. The discs are 3-3/8" diameter with a black-and-white player portrait photo in the center of the baseball design. A line of red stars is above, while the left and right panels feature one of several bright colors. Produced by Michael Schecter Associates under license from the Major League Baseball Players Association,

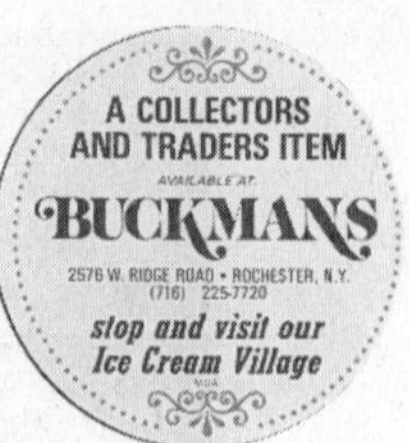

the player photos have had uniform and cap logos removed. Backs are printed in red and purple. The unnumbered checklist here is presented in alphabetical order.

		NM	EX	VG
Complete Set (70):		60.00	30.00	18.00
Common Player:		.75	.40	.25
(1)	Henry Aaron	6.00	3.00	1.75
(2)	Johnny Bench	3.50	1.75	1.00
(3)	Vida Blue	.75	.40	.25
(4)	Larry Bowa	.75	.40	.25
(5)	Lou Brock	2.50	1.25	.70
(6)	Jeff Burroughs	.75	.40	.25
(7)	John Candelaria	.75	.40	.25
(8)	Jose Cardenal	.75	.40	.25
(9)	Rod Carew	2.50	1.25	.70
(10)	Steve Carlton	2.50	1.25	.70
(11)	Dave Cash	.75	.40	.25
(12)	Cesar Cedeno	.75	.40	.25
(13)	Ron Cey	.75	.40	.25
(14)	Carlton Fisk	2.50	1.25	.70
(15)	Tito Fuentes	.75	.40	.25
(16)	Steve Garvey	2.00	1.00	.60
(17)	Ken Griffey	.75	.40	.25
(18)	Don Gullett	.75	.40	.25
(19)	Willie Horton	.75	.40	.25
(20)	Al Hrabosky	.75	.40	.25
(21)	Catfish Hunter	2.50	1.25	.70
(22)	Reggie Jackson (A's)	5.00	2.50	1.50
(23)	Randy Jones	.75	.40	.25
(24)	Jim Kaat	.75	.40	.25
(25)	Don Kessinger	.75	.40	.25
(26)	Dave Kingman	.75	.40	.25
(27)	Jerry Koosman	.75	.40	.25
(28)	Mickey Lolich	.75	.40	.25
(29)	Greg Luzinski	.75	.40	.25
(30)	Fred Lynn	.75	.40	.25
(31)	Bill Madlock	.75	.40	.25
(32)	Carlos May (White Sox)	.75	.40	.25
(33)	John Mayberry	.75	.40	.25
(34)	Bake McBride	.75	.40	.25
(35)	Doc Medich	.75	.40	.25
(36)	Andy Messersmith (Dodgers)	.75	.40	.25
(37)	Rick Monday	.75	.40	.25
(38)	John Montefusco	.75	.40	.25
(39)	Jerry Morales	.75	.40	.25
(40)	Joe Morgan	2.50	1.25	.70
(41)	Thurman Munson	2.50	1.25	.70
(42)	Bobby Murcer	.75	.40	.25
(43)	Al Oliver	.75	.40	.25
(44)	Jim Palmer	2.50	1.25	.70
(45)	Dave Parker	.75	.40	.25
(46)	Tony Perez	2.50	1.25	.70
(47)	Jerry Reuss	.75	.40	.25
(48)	Brooks Robinson	3.00	1.50	.90
(49)	Frank Robinson	3.00	1.50	.90
(50)	Steve Rogers	.75	.40	.25
(51)	Pete Rose	6.00	3.00	1.75
(52)	Nolan Ryan	20.00	10.00	6.00
(53)	Manny Sanguillen	.75	.40	.25
(54)	Mike Schmidt	5.00	2.50	1.50
(55)	Tom Seaver	3.00	1.50	.90
(56)	Ted Simmons	.75	.40	.25
(57)	Reggie Smith	.75	.40	.25
(58)	Willie Stargell	2.50	1.25	.70
(59)	Rusty Staub	.75	.40	.25
(60)	Rennie Stennett	.75	.40	.25
(61)	Don Sutton	2.50	1.25	.70
(62)	Andy Thornton (Cubs)	.75	.40	.25
(63)	Luis Tiant	.75	.40	.25
(64)	Joe Torre	1.50	.70	.45
(65)	Mike Tyson	.75	.40	.25
(66)	Bob Watson	.75	.40	.25
(67)	Wilbur Wood	.75	.40	.25
(68)	Jimmy Wynn	.75	.40	.25
(69)	Carl Yastrzemski	3.50	1.75	1.00
(70)	Richie Zisk	.75	.40	.25

1916 Bucyrus Brewing Co. (M101-4)

One of a dozen or so firms that utilized Felix Mendelsohn's baseball card issue as an advertising medium was this Ohio brewery. Unlike the other companies, however,

Bucyrus did not issue individual cards, but only a 42" x 28" uncut sheet containing all 200 cards and labeled "1916 - BASEBALL'S HALL OF FAME - 1916." If cut from the sheet, the single cards would be indistinguishable from the blank-back version of M101-4.

	NM	EX	VG
Complete Uncut Sheet:	35,000	25,000	15,000

(See 1916 M101-4 Blank Backs for checklist.)

1950 Buitoni Macaroni Joe DiMaggio Pins

At least two styles of 1-1/2" diameter pinback buttons are known from the Yankee Clipper's association with a New York pasta company. One style has a black-and-white portrait photo at the center of a red-stiched baseball design. Printed in red at top is "JOE DiMAGGIO / TV CLUB." At bottom is the program sponsor's name. Another style has a photo of the player with a bat over his shoulder on a yellow background. "JOE DiMAGGIO CLUB" is at top, "BUITONI/FOODS CORP." at bottom, both in red. Each style was reproduced in 2-1/4" size early in the 21st Century; those replicas have no collectible value.

	NM	EX	VG
Joe DiMaggio/Portrait	500.00	250.00	150.00
Joe DiMaggio (W/ bat.)	1,200	600.00	360.00

1932 Bulgaria Sport Tobacco

Bulgaria Sport-Photos
* Bild Nr. 256 *

Schmeling und Babe Ruth

Das bei uns unbekannte Baseball ist jenseits des Ozeans Volkssport. „Babe" Ruth, der Baseball-König, erfreut sich mit jährlich 100 000 Dollar eines größeren Einkommens als der Präsident der Vereinigten Staaten. Max Schmeling hat Babe Ruth bei einem Baseball-Match in Ohio bewundert; selbstverständlich haben die Photographen dies „historische" Ereignis festgehalten.

Bulgaria Sport
3 1/3 Pfg. - Zigarette
Album RM. 1.- beim Zigarettenhändler od. in Briefmarken direkt durch Bulgaria Zigarettenfabrik, Dresden A. 21

Despite the name of the sponsoring issuer, this set of cards is a product of Germany. Only a single major league ballplayer is pictured among the 272 cards in the set: Babe Ruth, who shares a card with boxing great Max Schmeling in a photo taken in the U.S. The black-and-white cards in the set measure 1-5/8" x 2-3/8" and have backs printed in German, including a card number.

		NM	EX	VG
256	Babe Ruth, Max Schmeling	300.00	150.00	90.00

1952-1953 Burger Beer Cincinnati Reds

Whether or not they were a promotional issue of Burger Beer (they are not marked as to issuer), advanced collectors of 1950s Reds memorabilia ascribe these 8" x 10-1/2" black-and-white photos to the long-time Reds sponsor because of their similarity to later Burger editions. The blank-back photos have portraits or posed action shots surrounded with white borders. In the wide bottom border is a C Reds logo, with the player name and (usually) position at right in all-capitals. The Clyde King picture, which can be reliably dated to 1953, his only season with the Reds, is a portrait drawing, rather than a photo, and has no position listed. The unnumbered pictures are listed here alphabetically and the checklist presented is likely incomplete.

		NM	EX	VG
	Common Player:	30.00	15.00	9.00
(1)	Joe Adcock/Fldg	40.00	20.00	12.00
(2)	Bob Borkowski (Batting follow-through.)	30.00	15.00	9.00
(3)	Jim Greengrass	30.00	15.00	9.00
(4)	Grady Hatton/Portrait	30.00	15.00	9.00
(5)	Niles Jordan/Portrait	30.00	15.00	9.00
(6)	Clyde King (Portrait art.)	30.00	15.00	9.00
(7)	Willard Marshall (Batting follow-through.)	30.00	15.00	9.00
(8)	Ed Pellagrini/Portrait	30.00	15.00	9.00
(9)	Bud Podbielan/Portrait	30.00	15.00	9.00
(10)	Frank Smith	30.00	15.00	9.00
(11)	John Temple (Batting follow-through.)	30.00	15.00	9.00
(12)	Herm Wehmeier	30.00	15.00	9.00

1955 Burger Beer Cincinnati Reds

The evidence attributing these 8-1/2" x 11" black-and-white player pictures to one of the team's radio sponsors, Burger Beer, is apocryphal, based largely on the format, which is similar to the company's 1956-64 promotional issues. This series has player portraits or poses bordered in white. In the bottom border, flanked by team logos are three lines of capital-letter typography with the player's name, position and team. Backs are blank. This checklist is likely not complete.

		NM	EX	VG
	Common Player:	30.00	15.00	9.00
(1)	Gus Bell	30.00	15.00	9.00
(2)	Rocky Bridges	30.00	15.00	9.00
(3)	Jackie Collum	30.00	15.00	9.00
(4)	Art Fowler	30.00	15.00	9.00
(5)	Ray Jablonski	30.00	15.00	9.00
(6)	Johnny Klippstein	30.00	15.00	9.00
(7)	Ted Kluszewski	45.00	22.00	13.50
(8)	Roy McMillan	30.00	15.00	9.00
(9)	Rudy Minarcin	30.00	15.00	9.00
(10)	Joe Nuxhall	45.00	22.00	13.50
(11)	Wally Post	30.00	15.00	9.00
(12)	Gerry Staley	30.00	15.00	9.00
(13)	Birdie Tebbetts	30.00	15.00	9.00

1956-1957 Burger Beer Cincinnati Reds

The 1956 and 1957 series of 8-1/2" x 11" black-and-white player photos from one of the Reds' broadcast sponsors can be distinguished from later issues by the presence of an advertising slogan at the bottom of the otherwise blank black, "COURTESY OF BURGER - A FINER BEER YEAR AFTER YEAR." Players are identified on the bottom front border in large capital letters. Because at least one player is known in both portrait and posed action photos, poses other than portraits are indicated in parentheses.

		NM	EX	VG
	Common Player:	30.00	15.00	9.00
(1)	Ed Bailey (Portrait to top button.)	30.00	15.00	9.00
(2)	Ed Bailey (Portrait to chest showing number.)	30.00	15.00	9.00
(3)	Gus Bell (Portrait to chest showing number.)	30.00	15.00	9.00
(4)	Joe Black	30.00	15.00	9.00
(5)	Smoky Burgess/Btg	35.00	17.50	10.50
(6)	George Crowe/Btg	30.00	15.00	9.00
(7)	Don Hoak	30.00	15.00	9.00
(8)	Waite Hoyt (Broadcaster)	30.00	15.00	9.00
(9)	Ray Jablonski/Throwing	30.00	15.00	9.00
(10)	Hal Jeffcoat (Follow-through.)	30.00	15.00	9.00
(11)	Ted Kluszewski/Btg	50.00	25.00	15.00
(12)	Ted Kluszewski (Portrait to top button.)	50.00	25.00	15.00
(13)	Brooks Lawrence (Follow-through.)	30.00	15.00	9.00
(14)	Roy McMillan/Btg	30.00	15.00	9.00
(15)	Roy McMillan/Fldg	30.00	15.00	9.00
(16)	Roy McMillan (Portrait to second button.)	30.00	15.00	9.00
(17)	Jackie Moran (Broadcaster)	30.00	15.00	9.00
(18)	Joe Nuxhall	30.00	15.00	9.00
(19)	Wally Post	30.00	15.00	9.00
(20)	Frank Robinson/Fldg	150.00	75.00	45.00
(21)	Frank Robinson/Portrait (White cap.)	125.00	62.00	37.00
(22)	Birdie Tebbetts	30.00	15.00	9.00
(23)	Johnny Temple (Portrait to second button.)	30.00	15.00	9.00
(24)	Johnny Temple (Portrait to chest showing number.)	30.00	15.00	9.00
(25)	Johnny Temple (Ready to throw.)	30.00	15.00	9.00
(26)	Bob Thurman/Btg	30.00	15.00	9.00

1958-1959 Burger Beer Cincinnati Reds

The 1958-1959 series of 8-1/2" x 11" black-and-white player photos can be distinguished by the presence of an advertising slogan at the bottom of the otherwise blank black, "COURTESY OF SPARKLE * BREWED BURGER BEER / HAVE FUN - HAVE A BURGER." Players are identified by first and last name, or by last name only on the bottom front border in large capital letters. The team name may or may not appear, as well.

		NM	EX	VG
	Common Player:	30.00	15.00	9.00
(1)	Ed. Bailey/Portrait	30.00	15.00	9.00
(2)	Gus Bell/Portrait (Dark cap.)	30.00	15.00	9.00
(4)	Waite Hoyt (At microphone.)	30.00	15.00	9.00
(6)	Jerry Lynch/Portrait	30.00	15.00	9.00
(7)	Roy McMillan/Portrait	30.00	15.00	9.00
(8)	(Don) Newcombe/Portrait	30.00	15.00	9.00
(9)	Joe Nuxhall (Follow-through.)	30.00	15.00	9.00
(11)	Vada Pinson/Portrait	45.00	22.00	13.50
(12)	Bob Purkey/Portrait	30.00	15.00	9.00
(13)	Frank Robinson/Btg (Dark cap.)	125.00	62.00	37.00
(14)	Frank Robinson/Fldg	125.00	62.00	37.00
(15)	Frank Robinson/Portrait (White cap.)	125.00	62.00	37.00
(16)	Manager Mayo Smith (Adjusting cap.)	30.00	15.00	9.00
(17)	John Temple/Portrait	30.00	15.00	9.00
(18)	Frank Thomas/Btg	30.00	15.00	9.00
(19)	(Frank) Thomas/Portrait	30.00	15.00	9.00

1960-64 Burger Beer Cincinnati Reds

The sponsor is not identified (except on 1959 issues which are marked on back, "COURTESY OF SPARKLE * BREWED BURGER BEER / HAVE FUN - HAVE A BURGER)," nor the year of issue published on these 8-1/2" x 11" player photos. Uniform and cap styles can give some idea of when the photos were taken. Photos are black-and-white portraits or action poses surrounded by white borders with the player and team names at bottom. Backs are blank. The unnumbered photos are listed here in alphabetical order. Some photos were re-issued year after year with only minor changes in cropping; these are not listed separately. This checklist will likely remain incomplete for some time. Gaps have been in the assigned numbering to accommodate future additions.

		NM	EX	VG
	Common Player:	15.00	7.50	4.50
(1)	Ed Bailey/Portrait	15.00	7.50	4.50
(2)	Ed. Bailey/Portrait	15.00	7.50	4.50
(3)	Don Blasingame/Fldg	15.00	7.50	4.50
(4)	Gus Bell/Bat	15.00	7.50	4.50
(5)	Gus Bell (Fielding fly ball.)	15.00	7.50	4.50
(6)	Gus Bell/Portrait	15.00	7.50	4.50
(7)	Gordon Coleman (Bat behind cap.)	15.00	7.50	4.50
(8)	Gordon Coleman (Bat behind shoulder.)	15.00	7.50	4.50
(9)	Gordon Coleman/Fldg	15.00	7.50	4.50
(11)	John Edwards/Portrait (Light tower in background.)	15.00	7.50	4.50
(12)	John Edwards/Portrait (No tower.)	15.00	7.50	4.50

(13)	Gene Freese/Fldg	15.00	7.50	4.50
(14)	Jay Hook (Follow-through.)	15.00	7.50	4.50
(15)	Waite Hoyt (Portrait at microphone.) (Announcer)	15.00	7.50	4.50
(16)	Waite Hoyt (Portrait w/ folder.) (Announcer)	15.00	7.50	4.50
(17)	Fred Hutchinson/Portrait (C on vest.)	15.00	7.50	4.50
(18)	Fred Hutchinson/Portrait (Half of "1" and "C.")	15.00	7.50	4.50
(19)	Fred Hutchinson/Portrait (C Reds on vest.)	15.00	7.50	4.50
(20)	Fred. Hutchinson (Only top of chest emblem shows.)	15.00	7.50	4.50
(22)	Joey Jay (Follow-through.)	15.00	7.50	4.50
(23)	Joey Jay/Portrait	15.00	7.50	4.50
(24)	Eddie Kasko/Btg	15.00	7.50	4.50
(25)	Eddie Kasko/Fldg	15.00	7.50	4.50
(26)	Gene Kelly/Announcer	15.00	7.50	4.50
(27)	Jerry Lynch/Btg	15.00	7.50	4.50
(28)	Jim Maloney/Portrait	15.00	7.50	4.50
(29)	Roy McMillan/Fldg	15.00	7.50	4.50
(31)	Don Newcombe (Wind-up.)	20.00	10.00	6.00
(32)	Joe Nuxhall (Follow-through, long-sleeve undershirt.)	15.00	7.50	4.50
(33)	Joe Nuxhall (Follow-through, short-sleeve undershirt.)	15.00	7.50	4.50
(34)	Jim O'Toole/Portrait	15.00	7.50	4.50
(35)	Jim O'Toole (Wind-up.)	15.00	7.50	4.50
(36)	Jim O'Toole (Follow-through.)	15.00	7.50	4.50
(37)	Don Pavletich/Portrait	15.00	7.50	4.50
(38)	Vada Pinson/Btg (No players in background.)	20.00	10.00	6.00
(39)	Vada Pinson/Btg (Players in background.)	20.00	10.00	6.00
(40)	Vada Pinson (Catching fly ball.)	20.00	10.00	6.00
(41)	Vada Pinson (Hands on knees.)	20.00	10.00	6.00
(43)	Wally Post/Btg	15.00	7.50	4.50
(44)	Wally Post/Portrait	15.00	7.50	4.50
(45)	Bob Purkey/Pitching (Right foot visible.)	15.00	7.50	4.50
(46)	Bob Purkey/Pitching (Right foot not visible.)	15.00	7.50	4.50
(47)	Bob Purkey/Portrait (Teeth don't show.)	15.00	7.50	4.50
(48)	Bob Purkey/Portrait (Teeth show.)	15.00	7.50	4.50
(50)	Frank Robinson/Btg (Dark cap.)	45.00	22.00	13.50
(51)	Frank Robinson/Btg (White cap.)	45.00	22.00	13.50
(52)	Frank Robinson (Fielding fly ball.)	45.00	22.00	13.50
(53)	Frank Robinson/Portrait (Pinstripes, black background.)	45.00	22.00	13.50
(54)	Frank Robinson/Portrait (Pinstripes, natural sky background.)	45.00	22.00	13.50
(55)	Frankie Robinson (Head turned back to camera.)	45.00	22.00	13.50
(56)	Pete Rose (Portrait to chest.)	200.00	100.00	60.00

1977 Burger Chef Funmeal Discs

The largest of the disc sets produced by Michael Schechter Associates is the 216-piece issue for the Burger Chef fast food restaurant chain. The discs were issued nine-per-team on a cardboard tray accompanying a 69-cent Funmeal for kids. The 2-3/8" discs could be punched out of the tray. They share the basic design of other MSA discs of the era. A black-and-white player photo is in the center of a baseball design. Because the discs were licensed only by the Players Association, the player photos have had cap logos air-brushed away. The left and right side panels are in one of several bright colors. Backs feature a Burger Chef cartoon character in color. The individual discs are unnumbered.

		NM	EX	VG
Complete Set, Trays (24):		100.00	50.00	30.00
Complete Set, Singles (216):		90.00	45.00	27.00
Common Player:		.75	.35	.20
1A	Cincinnati Reds (Full tray.)	20.00	10.00	6.00
(1A1)	Johnny Bench	4.50	2.25	1.25
(1A2)	Dave Concepcion	.75	.35	.20
(1A3)	Dan Driessen	.75	.35	.20
(1A4)	George Foster	.75	.35	.20
(1A5)	Cesar Geronimo	.75	.35	.20
(1A6)	Ken Griffey	1.25	.60	.40
(1A7)	Joe Morgan	3.50	1.75	1.00
(1A8)	Gary Nolan	.75	.35	.20
(1A9)	Pete Rose	7.50	3.75	2.25
2A	St. Louis Cardinals (Full tray.)	10.00	5.00	3.00
(2A1)	Lou Brock	3.50	1.75	1.00
(2A2)	John Denny	.75	.35	.20
(2A3)	Pete Falcone	.75	.35	.20
(2A4)	Keith Hernandez	.75	.40	.25
(2A5)	Al Hrabosky	.75	.35	.20
(2A6)	Bake McBride	.75	.35	.20
(2A7)	Ken Reitz	.75	.35	.20
(2A8)	Ted Simmons	.75	.35	.20
(2A9)	Mike Tyson	.75	.35	.20
3A	Detroit Tigers (Full tray.)	8.00	4.00	2.50
(3A1)	Mark Fidrych	1.50	.70	.45
(3A2)	Bill Freehan	.75	.35	.20
(3A3)	John Hiller	.75	.35	.20
(3A4)	Willie Horton	.75	.35	.20
(3A5)	Ron LeFlore	.75	.35	.20
(3A6)	Ben Oglivie	.75	.35	.20
(3A7)	Aurelio Rodriguez	.75	.35	.20
(3A8)	Rusty Staub	1.25	.60	.40
(3A9)	Jason Thompson	.75	.35	.20
4A	Cleveland Indians (Full tray.)	8.00	4.00	2.50
(4A1)	Buddy Bell	.75	.35	.20
(4A2)	Frank Duffy	.75	.35	.20
(4A3)	Dennis Eckersley	2.75	1.50	.80
(4A4)	Ray Fosse	.75	.35	.20
(4A5)	Wayne Garland	.75	.35	.20
(4A6)	Duane Kuiper	.75	.35	.20
(4A7)	Dave LaRoche	.75	.35	.20
(4A8)	Rick Manning	.75	.35	.20
(4A9)	Rick Waits	.75	.35	.20
5A	Chicago White Sox (Full tray.)	8.00	4.00	2.50
(5A1)	Jack Brohamer	.75	.35	.20
(5A2)	Bucky Dent	1.00	.50	.30
(5A3)	Ralph Garr	.75	.35	.20
(5A4)	Bart Johnson	.75	.35	.20
(5A5)	Lamar Johnson	.75	.35	.20
(5A6)	Chet Lemon	.75	.35	.20
(5A7)	Jorge Orta	.75	.35	.20
(5A8)	Jim Spencer	.75	.35	.20
(5A9)	Richie Zisk	.75	.35	.20
6A	Chicago Cubs (Full tray.)	8.00	4.00	2.50
(6A1)	Bill Bonham	.75	.35	.20
(6A2)	Bill Buckner	1.25	.60	.40
(6A3)	Ray Burris	.75	.35	.20
(6A4)	Jose Cardenal	.75	.35	.20
(6A5)	Bill Madlock	.75	.35	.20
(6A6)	Jerry Morales	.75	.35	.20
(6A7)	Rick Reuschel	.75	.35	.20
(6A8)	Manny Trillo	.75	.35	.20
(6A9)	Joe Wallis	.75	.35	.20
7A	Minnesota Twins (Full tray.)	10.00	5.00	3.00
(7A1)	Lyman Bostock	.75	.35	.20
(7A2)	Rod Carew	3.50	1.75	1.00
(7A3)	Mike Cubbage	.75	.35	.20
(7A4)	Dan Ford	.75	.35	.20
(7A5)	Dave Goltz	.75	.35	.20
(7A6)	Larry Hisle	.75	.35	.20
(7A7)	Tom Johnson	.75	.35	.20
(7A8)	Bobby Randall	.75	.35	.20
(7A9)	Butch Wynegar	.75	.35	.20
8A	Houston Astros (Full tray.)	8.00	4.00	2.50
(8A1)	Enos Cabell	.75	.35	.20
(8A2)	Cesar Cedeno	.75	.35	.20
(8A3)	Jose Cruz	.75	.35	.20
(8A4)	Joe Ferguson	.75	.35	.20
(8A5)	Ken Forsch	.75	.35	.20
(8A6)	Roger Metzger	.75	.35	.20
(8A7)	J.R. Richard	.75	.35	.20
(8A8)	Leon Roberts	.75	.35	.20
(8A9)	Bob Watson	.75	.35	.20
1B	Baltimore Orioles (Full tray.)	15.00	7.50	4.50
(1B1)	Mark Belanger	.75	.35	.20
(1B2)	Paul Blair	.75	.35	.20
(1B3)	Al Bumbry	.75	.35	.20
(1B4)	Doug DeCinces	.75	.35	.20
(1B5)	Ross Grimsley	.75	.35	.20
(1B6)	Lee May	.75	.35	.20
(1B7)	Jim Palmer	3.50	1.75	1.00
(1B8)	Brooks Robinson	4.50	2.25	1.25
(1B9)	Ken Singleton	.75	.35	.20
2B	Boston Red Sox (Full tray.)	15.00	7.50	4.50
(2B1)	Rick Burleson	.75	.35	.20
(2B2)	Dwight Evans	.75	.40	.25
(2B3)	Carlton Fisk	3.50	1.75	1.00
(2B4)	Fergie Jenkins	2.75	1.50	.80
(2B5)	Bill Lee	.75	.35	.20
(2B6)	Fred Lynn	.75	.40	.25
(2B7)	Jim Rice	1.50	.70	.45
(2B8)	Luis Tiant	.75	.35	.20
(2B9)	Carl Yastrzemski	4.50	2.25	1.25
3B	Kansas City Royals (Full tray.)	13.50	6.75	4.00
(3B1)	Doug Bird	.75	.35	.20
(3B2)	George Brett	6.00	3.00	1.75
(3B3)	Dennis Leonard	.75	.35	.20
(3B4)	John Mayberry	.75	.35	.20
(3B5)	Hal McRae	.75	.35	.20
(3B6)	Amos Otis	.75	.35	.20
(3B7)	Fred Patek	.75	.35	.20
(3B8)	Tom Poquette	.75	.35	.20
(3B9)	Paul Splittorff	.75	.35	.20
4B	Milwaukee Brewers (Full tray.)	10.00	5.00	3.00
(4B1)	Jerry Augustine	.75	.35	.20
(4B2)	Sal Bando	.75	.35	.20
(4B3)	Von Joshua	.75	.35	.20
(4B4)	Sixto Lezcano	.75	.35	.20
(4B5)	Charlie Moore	.75	.35	.20
(4B6)	Ed Rodriguez	.75	.35	.20
(4B7)	Jim Slaton	.75	.35	.20
(4B8)	Bill Travers	.75	.35	.20
(4B9)	Robin Yount	3.50	1.75	1.00
5B	Texas Rangers (Full tray.)	10.00	5.00	3.00
(5B1)	Juan Beniquez	.75	.35	.20
(5B2)	Bert Blyleven	.75	.35	.20
(5B3)	Bert Campaneris	.75	.35	.20
(5B4)	Tom Grieve	.75	.35	.20
(5B5)	Mike Hargrove	.75	.35	.20
(5B6)	Toby Harrah	.75	.35	.20
(5B7)	Gaylord Perry	2.75	1.50	.80
(5B8)	Lenny Randle	.75	.35	.20
(5B9)	Jim Sundberg	.75	.35	.20
6B	Atlanta Braves (Full tray.)	8.00	4.00	2.50
(6B1)	Jeff Burroughs	.75	.35	.20
(6B2)	Darrel Chaney	.75	.35	.20
(6B3)	Gary Matthews	.75	.35	.20
(6B4)	Andy Messersmith	.75	.35	.20
(6B5)	Willie Montanez	.75	.35	.20
(6B6)	Phil Niekro	2.75	1.50	.80
(6B7)	Tom Paciorek	.75	.35	.20
(6B8)	Jerry Royster	.75	.35	.20
(6B9)	Dick Ruthven	.75	.35	.20
7B	Pittsburgh Pirates (Full tray.)	10.00	5.00	3.00
(7B1)	John Candelaria	.75	.35	.20
(7B2)	Duffy Dyer	.75	.35	.20
(7B3)	Al Oliver	1.25	.60	.40
(7B4)	Dave Parker	.75	.40	.25
(7B5)	Jerry Reuss	.75	.35	.20
(7B6)	Bill Robinson	.75	.35	.20
(7B7)	Willie Stargell	3.50	1.75	1.00
(7B8)	Rennie Stennett	.75	.35	.20
(7B9)	Frank Taveras	.75	.35	.20
8B	New York Yankees (Full tray.)	20.00	10.00	6.00
(8B1)	Chris Chambliss	.75	.35	.20
(8B2)	Don Gullett	.75	.35	.20
(8B3)	Catfish Hunter	2.75	1.50	.80
(8B4)	Reggie Jackson	5.00	2.50	1.50
(8B5)	Thurman Munson	4.50	2.25	1.25
(8B6)	Graig Nettles	.75	.35	.20
(8B7)	Willie Randolph	.75	.35	.20
(8B8)	Mickey Rivers	.75	.35	.20
(8B9)	Roy White	.75	.35	.20
1C	California Angels (Full tray.)	25.00	12.50	7.50
(1C1)	Bobby Bonds	.75	.35	.20
(1C2)	Dave Chalk	.75	.35	.20
(1C3)	Bobby Grich	.75	.35	.20
(1C4)	Paul Hartzell	.75	.35	.20
(1C5)	Ron Jackson	.75	.35	.20
(1C6)	Jerry Remy	.75	.35	.20
(1C7)	Joe Rudi	.75	.35	.20
(1C8)	Nolan Ryan	16.00	8.00	4.75
(1C9)	Frank Tanana	.75	.35	.20
2C	Oakland A's (Full tray.)	8.00	4.00	2.50
(2C1)	Stan Bahnsen	.75	.35	.20
(2C2)	Vida Blue	.75	.35	.20
(2C3)	Phil Garner	.75	.35	.20
(2C4)	Paul Lindblad	.75	.35	.20
(2C5)	Mike Norris	.75	.35	.20
(2C6)	Bill North	.75	.35	.20
(2C7)	Manny Sanguillen	.75	.35	.20
(2C8)	Mike Torrez	.75	.35	.20
(2C9)	Claudell Washington	.75	.35	.20
3C	Los Angeles Dodgers (Full tray.)	10.00	5.00	3.00
(3C1)	Ron Cey	.75	.35	.20
(3C2)	Steve Garvey	2.00	1.00	.60
(3C3)	Davey Lopes	.75	.35	.20
(3C4)	Rick Monday	.75	.35	.20
(3C5)	Doug Rau	.75	.35	.20
(3C6)	Rick Rhoden	.75	.35	.20
(3C7)	Reggie Smith	.75	.35	.20
(3C8)	Don Sutton	2.75	1.50	.80
(3C9)	Steve Yeager	.75	.35	.20
4C	Montreal Expos (Full tray.)	10.00	5.00	3.00
(4C1)	Gary Carter	3.00	1.50	.90
(4C2)	Dave Cash	.75	.35	.20
(4C3)	Tim Foli	.75	.35	.20
(4C4)	Barry Foote	.75	.35	.20
(4C5)	Larry Parrish	.75	.35	.20
(4C6)	Tony Perez	3.00	1.50	.90
(4C7)	Steve Rogers	.75	.35	.20
(4C8)	Del Unser	.75	.35	.20
(4C9)	Ellis Valentine	.75	.35	.20
5C	New York Mets (Full tray.)	13.50	6.75	4.00
(5C1)	Bud Harrelson	.75	.35	.20
(5C2)	Dave Kingman	1.00	.50	.30
(5C3)	Jerry Koosman	.75	.35	.20
(5C4)	Ed Kranepool	.75	.35	.20
(5C5)	Skip Lockwood	.75	.35	.20
(5C6)	Jon Matlack	.75	.35	.20
(5C7)	Felix Millan	.75	.35	.20
(5C8)	Tom Seaver	4.50	2.25	1.25
(5C9)	John Stearns	.75	.35	.20
6C	Philadelphia Phillies (Full tray.)	15.00	7.50	4.50
(6C1)	Bob Boone	1.00	.50	.30
(6C2)	Larry Bowa	.75	.35	.20
(6C3)	Steve Carlton	3.50	1.75	1.00
(6C4)	Jay Johnstone	.75	.35	.20
(6C5)	Jim Kaat	1.25	.60	.40
(6C6)	Greg Luzinski	.75	.40	.25
(6C7)	Garry Maddox	.75	.35	.20
(6C8)	Tug McGraw	1.25	.60	.40
(6C9)	Mike Schmidt	6.00	3.00	1.75
7C	San Diego Padres (Full tray.)	10.00	5.00	3.00
(7C1)	Rollie Fingers	2.75	1.50	.80
(7C2)	George Hendrick	.75	.35	.20
(7C3)	Enzo Hernandez	.75	.35	.20
(7C4)	Mike Ivie	.75	.35	.20
(7C5)	Randy Jones	.75	.35	.20
(7C6)	Butch Metzger	.75	.35	.20
(7C7)	Dave Rader	.75	.35	.20
(7C8)	Gene Tenace	.75	.35	.20
(7C9)	Dave Winfield	3.50	1.75	1.00
8C	San Francisco Giants (Full tray.)	8.00	4.00	2.50
(8C1)	Jim Barr	.75	.35	.20
(8C2)	Willie Crawford	.75	.35	.20
(8C3)	Larry Herndon	.75	.35	.20
(8C4)	Randy Moffitt	.75	.35	.20
(8C5)	John Montefusco	.75	.35	.20
(8C6)	Bobby Murcer	.75	.35	.20
(8C7)	Marty Perez	.75	.35	.20
(8C8)	Chris Speier	.75	.35	.20
(8C9)	Gary Thomasson	.75	.35	.20

1977 Burger King Tigers

This series of color 8" x 10" player portraits was given away one per week at Detroit area Burger Kings. Backs are blank and there is no player identification on the front. The photos are checklisted here alphabetically.

		NM	EX	VG
	Complete Set (4):	40.00	20.00	12.00
	Common Player:	10.00	5.00	3.00
(1)	Mark Fidrych (Holding glove.)	15.00	7.50	4.50
(2)	Ron LeFlore (Black guy w/bat.)	10.00	5.00	3.00
(3)	Dave Rozema (Winding up.)	10.00	5.00	3.00
(4)	Mickey Stanley (White guy w/bat.)	10.00	5.00	3.00

1977 Burger King Yankees

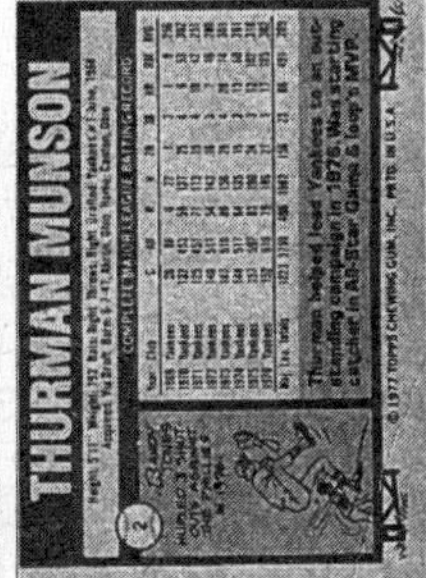

The first Topps-produced set for Burger King restaurants was issued in the New York area, featuring the A.L. champion Yankees. Twenty-two players plus an unnumbered checklist were issued at the beginning of the promotion with card #23 (Lou Piniella) being added to the set later. The "New York Post" reported production of the first 22 player cards at about 170,000 of each. The Piniella card was issued in limited quantities. Cards are 2-1/2" x 3-1/2" and have fronts identical to the regular 1977 Topps set except for numbers 2, 6, 7, 13, 14, 15, 17, 20 and 21. These cards feature different poses or major picture-cropping variations. It should be noted that very minor cropping variations between the regular Topps sets and the Burger King issues exist throughout the years the sets were produced.

		NM	EX	VG
	Complete Set w/Piniella (24):	20.00	10.00	6.00
	Complete Set no Piniella (23):	13.50	6.75	4.00
	Common Player:	.25	.13	.08
1	Yankees Team (Billy Martin)	.75	.40	.25
2	Thurman Munson	5.00	2.50	1.50
3	Fran Healy	.25	.13	.08
4	Catfish Hunter	1.50	.70	.45
5	Ed Figueroa	.25	.13	.08
6	Don Gullett	.25	.13	.08
7	Mike Torrez	.25	.13	.08
8	Ken Holtzman	.25	.13	.08
9	Dick Tidrow	.25	.13	.08
10	Sparky Lyle	.40	.20	.12
11	Ron Guidry	.45	.25	.14
12	Chris Chambliss	.25	.13	.08
13	Willie Randolph	.45	.25	.14
14	Bucky Dent	.45	.25	.14
15	Graig Nettles	.60	.30	.20
16	Fred Stanley	.25	.13	.08
17	Reggie Jackson	5.00	2.50	1.50
18	Mickey Rivers	.25	.13	.08
19	Roy White	.40	.20	.12
20	Jim Wynn	.40	.20	.12
21	Paul Blair	.25	.13	.08
22	Carlos May	.25	.13	.08
23	Lou Piniella	15.00	7.50	4.50
---	Checklist	.05	.03	.02

1978 Burger King Astros

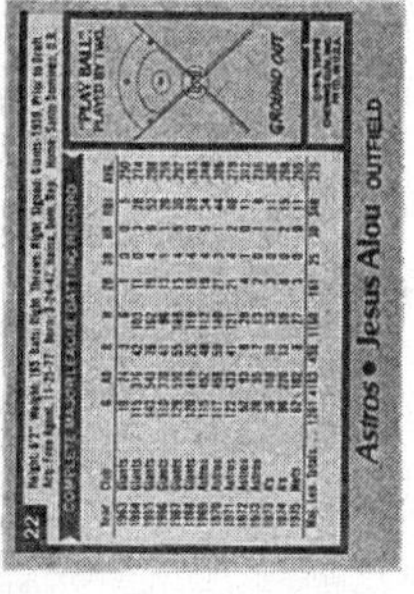

Burger King restaurants in the Houston area distributed a Topps-produced set showcasing the Astros. Cards are standard 2-1/2" x 3-1/2" and are numbered 1-22, plus and unnumbered checklist. Fronts are identical to the regular 1978 Topps set with the exception of card numbers 21, Dave Bergman, who appeared on a Rookie Outfielders cards in the '78 Topps set; and 22, Jesus Alou, who did not have a card in the regular issue. Although not noted in the following checklist, it should be remembered that very minor picture-cropping variations between the regular Topps issues and the 1977-1980 Burger King sets do exist.

		NM	EX	VG
	Complete Set (23):	15.00	7.50	4.50
	Common Player:	.75	.40	.25
1	Bill Virdon	.90	.45	.25
2	Joe Ferguson	.75	.40	.25
3	Ed Herrmann	.75	.40	.25
4	J.R. Richard	1.50	.70	.45
5	Joe Niekro	1.25	.60	.40
6	Floyd Bannister	.75	.40	.25
7	Joaquin Andujar	.75	.40	.25
8	Ken Forsch	.75	.40	.25
9	Mark Lemongello	.75	.40	.25
10	Joe Sambito	.75	.40	.25
11	Gene Pentz	.75	.40	.25
12	Bob Watson	.90	.45	.25
13	Julio Gonzalez	.75	.40	.25
14	Enos Cabell	.75	.40	.25
15	Roger Metzger	.75	.40	.25
16	Art Howe	.90	.45	.25
17	Jose Cruz	1.00	.50	.30
18	Cesar Cedeno	1.00	.50	.30
19	Terry Puhl	.75	.40	.25
20	Wilbur Howard	.75	.40	.25
21	Dave Bergman	.75	.40	.25
22	Jesus Alou	1.00	.50	.30
---	Checklist	.10	.05	.03

1978 Burger King Rangers

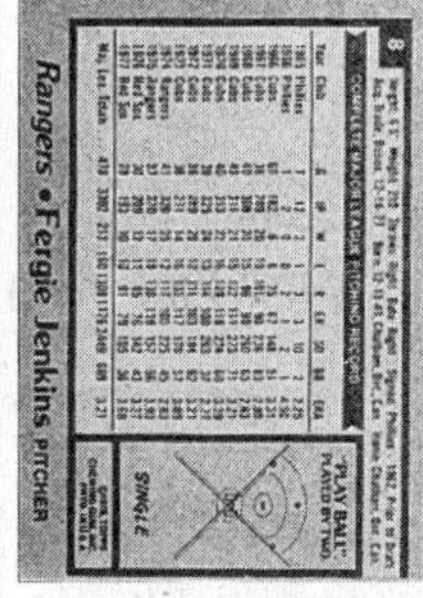

Issued by Burger King restaurants in the Dallas-Fort Worth area, this Topps-produced set features the Texas Rangers. Cards are standard 2-1/2" x 3-1/2" and identical in style to the regular 1978 Topps set with the following exceptions: #'s 5, 8, 10, 12, 17, 21 and 22. An unnumbered checklist card was included with the set.

		NM	EX	VG
	Complete Set (23):	15.00	7.50	4.50
	Common Player:	.75	.40	.25
1	Billy Hunter	.75	.40	.25
2	Jim Sundberg	.75	.40	.25
3	John Ellis	.75	.40	.25
4	Doyle Alexander	.75	.40	.25
5	Jon Matlack	.75	.40	.25
6	Dock Ellis	.75	.40	.25
7	George Medich	.75	.40	.25
8	Fergie Jenkins	6.00	3.00	1.75
9	Len Barker	.75	.40	.25
10	Reggie Cleveland	.75	.40	.25
11	Mike Hargrove	1.00	.50	.30
12	Bump Wills	1.00	.50	.30
13	Toby Harrah	1.00	.50	.30
14	Bert Campaneris	1.00	.50	.30
15	Sandy Alomar	1.00	.50	.30
16	Kurt Bevacqua	.75	.40	.25
17	Al Oliver	1.50	.70	.45
18	Juan Beniquez	.75	.40	.25
19	Claudell Washington	.75	.40	.25
20	Richie Zisk	.75	.40	.25
21	John Lowenstein	.75	.40	.25
22	Bobby Thompson	.75	.40	.25
---	Checklist	.10	.05	.03

1978 Burger King Tigers

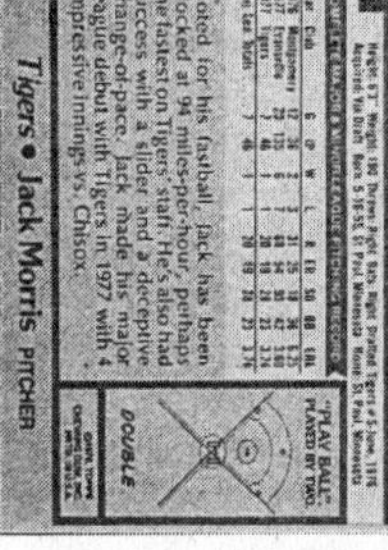

Rookie cards of Morris, Trammell and Whitaker make the Topps-produced 1978 Burger King Detroit Tigers issue the most popular of the BK sets. Twenty-two player cards and an unnumbered checklist make up the set which was issued in the Detroit area. Cards measure 2-1/2" x 3-1/2", and are identical to the regular 1978 Topps issue with the following exceptions: #'s 6, 7, 8, 13, 15 and 16. Numerous minor picture-cropping variations between the regular Topps issues and the Burger King sets appear from 1977-1980; these minor variations are not noted in the following checklist.

		NM	EX	VG
	Complete Set (23):	25.00	12.50	7.50
	Common Player:	.75	.40	.25
1	Ralph Houk	.90	.45	.25
2	Milt May	.75	.40	.25
3	John Wockenfuss	.75	.40	.25
4	Mark Fidrych	2.50	1.25	.70
5	Dave Rozema	.75	.40	.25
6	Jack Billingham	.75	.40	.25
7	Jim Slaton	.75	.40	.25
8	Jack Morris	3.00	1.50	.90
9	John Hiller	.75	.40	.25
10	Steve Foucault	.75	.40	.25
11	Milt Wilcox	.75	.40	.25
12	Jason Thompson	.75	.40	.25
13	Lou Whitaker	6.00	3.00	1.75
14	Aurelio Rodriguez	.75	.40	.25
15	Alan Trammell	10.00	5.00	3.00
16	Steve Dillard	.75	.40	.25
17	Phil Mankowski	.75	.40	.25
18	Steve Kemp	.75	.40	.25
19	Ron LeFlore	.90	.45	.25
20	Tim Corcoran	.75	.40	.25
21	Mickey Stanley	.75	.40	.25
22	Rusty Staub	.90	.45	.25
---	Checklist	.10	.05	.03

1978 Burger King Yankees

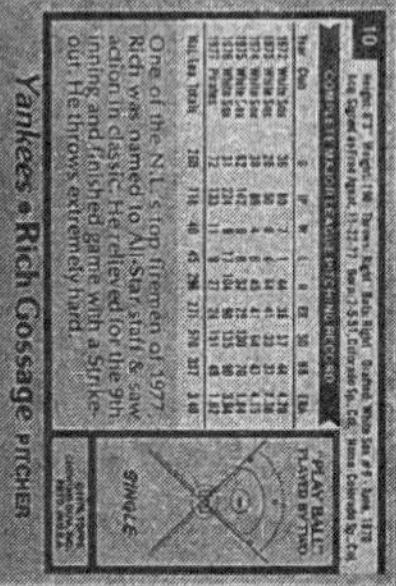

Produced by Topps for Burger King outlets in the New York area for the second year in a row, the 1978 Yankees set contains 22 cards plus an unnumbered checklist. The cards are numbered 1 through 22 and are the standard size of 2-1/2" x 3-1/2". The cards feature the same pictures found in the regular 1978 Topps set except for numbers 10, 11 and 16. Only those variations containing different poses or major picture-cropping differences are noted. Numerous minor picture-cropping variations, that are very insignificant in nature, exist between the regular Topps sets and the Burger King issues of 1977-1980.

		NM	EX	VG
	Complete Set (23):	15.00	7.50	4.50
	Common Player:	.50	.25	.15
1	Billy Martin	1.50	.70	.45
2	Thurman Munson	5.00	2.50	1.50
3	Cliff Johnson	.50	.25	.15
4	Ron Guidry	1.00	.50	.30
5	Ed Figueroa	.50	.25	.15
6	Dick Tidrow	.50	.25	.15
7	Catfish Hunter	2.00	1.00	.60
8	Don Gullett	.50	.25	.15
9	Sparky Lyle	1.00	.50	.30
10	Rich Gossage	1.50	.70	.45
11	Rawly Eastwick	.50	.25	.15
12	Chris Chambliss	.50	.25	.15
13	Willie Randolph	1.00	.50	.30
14	Graig Nettles	1.00	.50	.30
15	Bucky Dent	1.00	.50	.30
16	Jim Spencer	.50	.25	.15
17	Fred Stanley	.50	.25	.15
18	Lou Piniella	1.25	.60	.40
19	Roy White	1.00	.50	.30
20	Mickey Rivers	.50	.25	.15
21	Reggie Jackson	6.00	3.00	1.75
22	Paul Blair	.50	.25	.15
---	Checklist	.10	.05	.03

1979 Burger King Phillies

Twenty-two Phillies players are featured in the 1979 Burger King issue given out in the Philadelphia area. The Topps-produced set, measuring 2-1/2" x 3-1/2", also includes an unnumbered checklist. Cards are identical to the regular 1979 Topps set except #1, 11, 12, 13, 14, 17 and 22, which have different poses. Very minor picture-cropping variations between the regular Topps issues and the Burger King sets can be found throughout the four years the cards were produced, but only those variations featuring major changes are noted in the checklists.

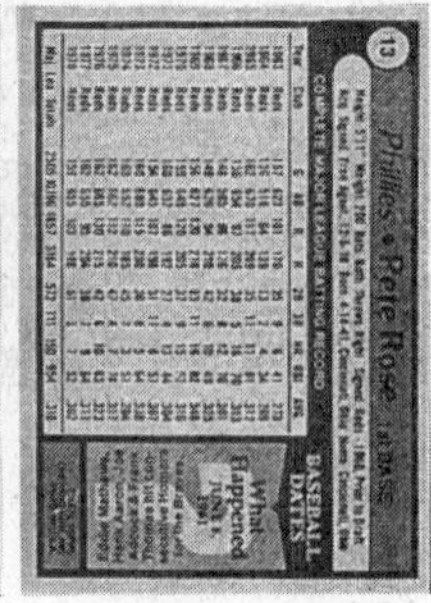

		NM	EX	VG
Complete Set (23):		7.50	3.75	2.25
Common Player:		.25	.13	.08
1	Danny Ozark	.25	.13	.08
2	Bob Boone	.45	.25	.14
3	Tim McCarver	.50	.25	.15
4	Steve Carlton	1.50	.70	.45
5	Larry Christenson	.25	.13	.08
6	Dick Ruthven	.25	.13	.08
7	Ron Reed	.25	.13	.08
8	Randy Lerch	.25	.13	.08
9	Warren Brusstar	.25	.13	.08
10	Tug McGraw	.40	.20	.12
11	Nino Espinosa	.25	.13	.08
12	Doug Bird	.25	.13	.08
13	Pete Rose	3.00	1.50	.90
14	Manny Trillo	.25	.13	.08
15	Larry Bowa	.40	.20	.12
16	Mike Schmidt	3.00	1.50	.90
17	Pete Mackanin	.25	.13	.08
18	Jose Cardenal	.25	.13	.08
19	Greg Luzinski	.25	.13	.08
20	Garry Maddox	.25	.13	.08
21	Bake McBride	.25	.13	.08
22	Greg Gross	.25	.13	.08
---	Checklist	.08	.04	.02

1979 Burger King Yankees

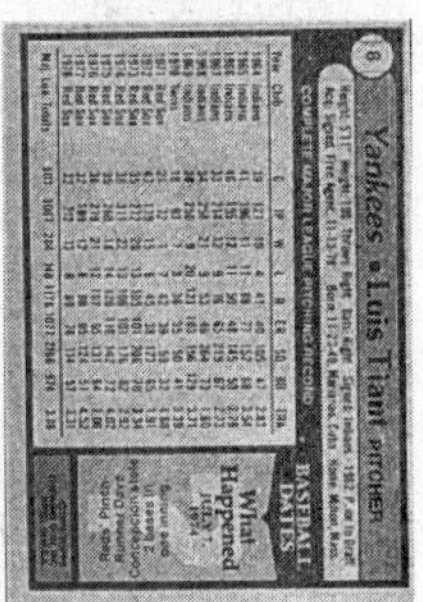

The New York Yankees were featured in a Topps-produced Burger King set for the third consecutive year in 1979. Once again, 22 numbered player cards and an unnumbered checklist made up the set. Cards measure 2-1/2" x 3-1/2", and are identical to the 1979 Topps regular set except for #4, 8, 9 and 22 which included new poses. Numerous minor picture cropping variations between the regular Topps issue and the Burger King sets of 1977-1980 exist.

		NM	EX	VG
Complete Set (23):		7.50	3.75	2.25
Common Player:		.25	.13	.08
1	Yankees Team (Bob Lemon)	.75	.40	.25
2	Thurman Munson	2.50	1.25	.70
3	Cliff Johnson	.25	.13	.08
4	Ron Guidry	.60	.30	.20
5	Jay Johnstone	.40	.20	.12
6	Catfish Hunter	1.25	.60	.40
7	Jim Beattie	.25	.13	.08
8	Luis Tiant	.40	.20	.12
9	Tommy John	.75	.40	.25
10	Rich Gossage	.60	.30	.20
11	Ed Figueroa	.25	.13	.08
12	Chris Chambliss	.25	.13	.08
13	Willie Randolph	.40	.20	.12
14	Bucky Dent	.40	.20	.12
15	Graig Nettles	.40	.20	.12
16	Fred Stanley	.25	.13	.08
17	Jim Spencer	.25	.13	.08
18	Lou Piniella	.60	.30	.20
19	Roy White	.40	.20	.12
20	Mickey Rivers	.25	.13	.08
21	Reggie Jackson	4.00	2.00	1.25
22	Juan Beniquez	.25	.13	.08
---	Checklist	.06	.03	.02

1980 Burger King Phillies

Philadelphia-area Burger King outlets issued a 23-card set featuring the Phillies for the second in a row in 1980. The Topps-produced set, measuring 2-1/2" x 3-1/2", contains 22 player cards and an unnumbered checklist. Fronts are identical in design to the regular 1980 Topps sets with the following exceptions: #1, 3, 8, 14 and 22 feature new poses. Very minor picture-cropping variations between the regular Topps issues and the Burger King sets exist in all years.

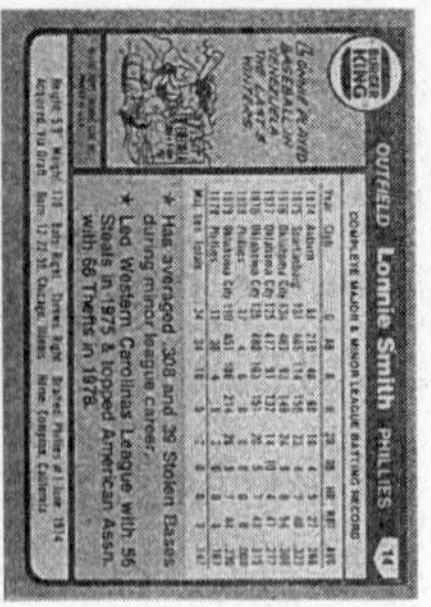

Those minor differences are not noted in the checklists. The 1980 Burger King sets were the first to include the Burger King logo on the card backs.

		NM	EX	VG
Complete Set (23):		6.00	3.00	1.75
Common Player:		.10	.05	.03
1	Dallas Green	.15	.08	.05
2	Bob Boone	.50	.25	.15
3	Keith Moreland	.25	.13	.08
4	Pete Rose	2.50	1.25	.70
5	Manny Trillo	.10	.05	.03
6	Mike Schmidt	2.50	1.25	.70
7	Larry Bowa	.20	.10	.06
8	John Vukovich	.10	.05	.03
9	Bake McBride	.10	.05	.03
10	Garry Maddox	.10	.05	.03
11	Greg Luzinski	.25	.13	.08
12	Greg Gross	.10	.05	.03
13	Del Unser	.10	.05	.03
14	Lonnie Smith	.40	.20	.12
15	Steve Carlton	1.00	.50	.30
16	Larry Christenson	.10	.05	.03
17	Nino Espinosa	.10	.05	.03
18	Randy Lerch	.10	.05	.03
19	Dick Ruthven	.10	.05	.03
20	Tug McGraw	.15	.08	.05
21	Ron Reed	.10	.05	.03
22	Kevin Saucier	.10	.05	.03
---	Checklist	.05	.03	.02

1980 Burger King Pitch, Hit & Run

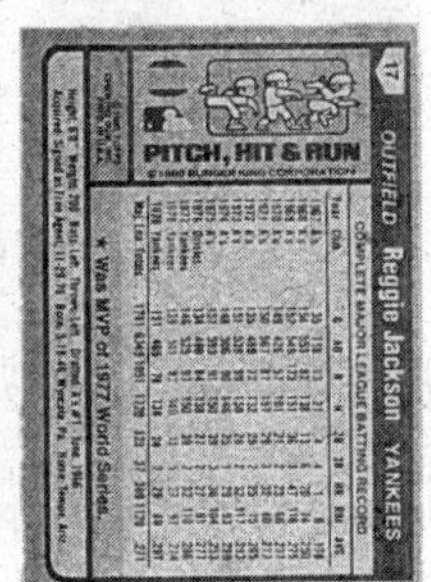

In 1980, Burger King issued, in conjunction with its "Pitch, Hit & Run" promotion, a Topps-produced set featuring pitchers (card #s 1-11), hitters (#s 12-22), and base stealers (#s 23-33). Fronts, which carry the Burger King logo, are identical in design to the regular 1980 Topps set except for numbers 1, 4, 5, 7, 9, 10, 16, 17, 18, 22, 23, 27, 28, 29 and 30, which feature different poses. Cards measure 2-1/2" x 3-1/2" in size. An unnumbered checklist was included with the set.

		NM	EX	VG
Complete Set (34):		10.00	5.00	3.00
Common Player:		.10	.05	.03
1	Vida Blue	.10	.05	.03
2	Steve Carlton	1.00	.50	.30
3	Rollie Fingers	.65	.35	.20
4	Ron Guidry	.25	.13	.08
5	Jerry Koosman	.10	.05	.03
6	Phil Niekro	.65	.35	.20
7	Jim Palmer	1.00	.50	.30
8	J.R. Richard	.10	.05	.03
9	Nolan Ryan	4.00	2.00	1.25
10	Tom Seaver	1.00	.50	.30
11	Bruce Sutter	1.00	.50	.30
12	Don Baylor	.10	.05	.03
13	George Brett	2.00	1.00	.60
14	Rod Carew	1.00	.50	.30
15	George Foster	.10	.05	.03
16	Keith Hernandez	.10	.05	.03
17	Reggie Jackson	1.50	.70	.45
18	Fred Lynn	.10	.05	.03
19	Dave Parker	.10	.05	.03
20	Jim Rice	.30	.15	.09
21	Pete Rose	3.00	1.50	.90
22	Dave Winfield	1.00	.50	.30
23	Bobby Bonds	.10	.05	.03
24	Enos Cabell	.10	.05	.03
25	Cesar Cedeno	.10	.05	.03
26	Julio Cruz	.10	.05	.03
27	Ron LeFlore	.10	.05	.03
28	Dave Lopes	.10	.05	.03
29	Omar Moreno	.10	.05	.03
30	Joe Morgan	1.00	.50	.30
31	Bill North	.10	.05	.03
32	Frank Taveras	.10	.05	.03
33	Willie Wilson	.10	.05	.03
---	Checklist	.05	.03	.02

1916 Burgess-Nash Clothiers

Burgess-Nash Co.
BOY'S CLOTHING

This 200-card set can be found with ads on the back for several local and regional businesses. Among them is Burgess-Nash clothiers, from Omaha, Neb. Type card and superstar collectors can expect to pay a significant premium for cards with the Burgess-Nash advertising, compared to the generic M101-4 Blank Backs values. Cards measure about 1-5/8" x 3" and are printed in black-and-white.

PREMIUM: 2-3X

(See 1916 M101-4 Blank Backs for checklist.)

1935 George Burke Detroit Tigers Photo Stamps

This team set of black-and-white, 1-1/16" x 1-1/4" photo stamps was produced by baseball photographer George Burke. The set was printed on two sheets of 12 players each. Each stamp has the player's name, position abbreviation and city in black or white typography. The blank-backed ungummed stamps of the 1935 World's Champs are checklisted here in alphabetical order.

		NM	EX	VG
Complete Set (24):		325.00	160.00	95.00
Common Player:		10.00	5.00	3.00
(1)	Elden Auker	10.00	5.00	3.00
(2)	Del Baker	10.00	5.00	3.00
(3)	Tom Bridges	10.00	5.00	3.00
(4)	Herman Clifton	10.00	5.00	3.00
(5)	Mickey Cochrane	30.00	15.00	9.00
(6)	Alvin Crowder	10.00	5.00	3.00
(7)	Ervin Fox	10.00	5.00	3.00
(8)	Charles Gehringer	30.00	15.00	9.00
(9)	Leon Goslin	30.00	15.00	9.00
(10)	Henry Greenberg	45.00	22.50	13.50
(11)	Raymond Hayworth	10.00	5.00	3.00
(12)	Elon Hogsett	10.00	5.00	3.00
(13)	Roxie Lawson	10.00	5.00	3.00
(14)	Marvin Owen	10.00	5.00	3.00
(15)	Ralph Perkins	10.00	5.00	3.00
(16)	Frank Reiber	10.00	5.00	3.00
(17)	Wm. Rogell	10.00	5.00	3.00
(18)	Lynwood Rowe	12.50	6.25	3.75
(19)	Henry Schuble	10.00	5.00	3.00
(20)	Hugh Shelley	10.00	5.00	3.00
(21)	Victor Sorrell	10.00	5.00	3.00
(22)	Joseph Sullivan	10.00	5.00	3.00
(23)	Gerald Walker	10.00	5.00	3.00
(24)	Joyner White	10.00	5.00	3.00

1935-37 George Burke Postage Stamp Photos

These small (3/4" x 1") black-and-white stamps were produced by Chicago baseball portraitist George Burke for sale to individual players for use in answering fan mail. The stamps were not a big seller, though the checklist presented alphabetically here is surely incomplete. The unnumbered stamps, which are blank-backed, were not self-adhesive and were printed in sheets of at least six of the same player. Some of the photo-stamps have facsimile autographs, others do not.

	NM	EX	VG
Common Player:	10.00	5.00	3.00
Luke Appling	20.00	10.00	6.00
Jimmy Austin	10.00	5.00	3.00
Dick Bartell	10.00	5.00	3.00
Huck Betts	10.00	5.00	3.00
George Blaeholder	10.00	5.00	3.00
Jim Bottomley	20.00	10.00	6.00
Earl Browne	10.00	5.00	3.00
Irving Burns	10.00	5.00	3.00
Sam Byrd	10.00	5.00	3.00
Gilly Campbell	10.00	5.00	3.00
James (Tex) Carleton	10.00	5.00	3.00
Hugh Casey	10.00	5.00	3.00
James "Rip" Collins	10.00	5.00	3.00
Earle Combs	20.00	10.00	6.00
Adam Comorosky	10.00	5.00	3.00
Jocko Conlan	20.00	10.00	6.00
Kiki Cuyler	20.00	10.00	6.00
Paul Derringer	10.00	5.00	3.00
Jim DeShong	10.00	5.00	3.00
Bill Dickey	20.00	10.00	6.00
Bill Dietrich	10.00	5.00	3.00
Carl Doyle	10.00	5.00	3.00
Chuck Dressen	10.00	5.00	3.00
Jimmy Dykes	10.00	5.00	3.00
Hank Erickson	10.00	5.00	3.00
Wes Ferrell	10.00	5.00	3.00
Arthur Fletcher	10.00	5.00	3.00
Jimmie Foxx (Facsimile autograph.)	40.00	20.00	12.00
Jimmie Foxx (No autograph.)	40.00	20.00	12.00
Larry French	10.00	5.00	3.00
Benny Frey	10.00	5.00	3.00
Tony Freitas	10.00	5.00	3.00
Frankie Frisch	20.00	10.00	6.00
Ed Gharrity	10.00	5.00	3.00
Lefty Gomez	20.00	10.00	6.00
Charlie Grimm	10.00	5.00	3.00
Stan Hack	10.00	5.00	3.00
Chick Hafey	20.00	10.00	6.00
Mel Harder	10.00	5.00	3.00
Bucky Harris	20.00	10.00	6.00
Gabby Hartnett	20.00	10.00	6.00
Roy Henshaw	10.00	5.00	3.00
Babe Herman	15.00	7.50	4.50
Billy Herman	20.00	10.00	6.00
Leroy Herrmann	10.00	5.00	3.00
Myril Hoag	10.00	5.00	3.00
Al Hollingsworth	10.00	5.00	3.00
Carl Hubbell	30.00	15.00	9.00
Bob Johnson	10.00	5.00	3.00
Douglas Johnson	10.00	5.00	3.00
Si Johnson	10.00	5.00	3.00
George L. Kelly	20.00	10.00	6.00
Chuck Klein	20.00	10.00	6.00
Mark Koenig	10.00	5.00	3.00
Tony Lazzeri	30.00	15.00	9.00
Bill Lee	10.00	5.00	3.00
Dutch Leonard	10.00	5.00	3.00
Ernie Lombardi	20.00	10.00	6.00
Al Lopez	20.00	10.00	6.00
Adolfo Luque	15.00	7.50	4.50
Earle Mack	10.00	5.00	3.00
Roy Mahaffey	10.00	5.00	3.00
Gus Mancuso	10.00	5.00	3.00
Rabbit Maranville	20.00	10.00	6.00
Johnny Marcum	10.00	5.00	3.00
Joe McCarthy	20.00	10.00	6.00
Eric McNair	10.00	5.00	3.00
Van Lingle Mungo	10.00	5.00	3.00
Skeeter Newsome	10.00	5.00	3.00
Mel Ott	40.00	20.00	12.00
Claude Passeau	10.00	5.00	3.00
Monte Pearson	10.00	5.00	3.00
Raymond Pepper	10.00	5.00	3.00
Charlie Root	10.00	6.00	3.00
Red Ruffing	20.00	10.00	6.00
George Selkirk	10.00	5.00	3.00
Joe Sewell	20.00	10.00	6.00
Luke Sewell	10.00	5.00	3.00
Al Simmons	20.00	10.00	6.00
Casey Stengel	20.00	10.00	6.00
Riggs Stephenson	10.00	5.00	3.00
Alan Strange	10.00	5.00	3.00
Gus Suhr	10.00	5.00	3.00
Billy Sullivan	10.00	5.00	3.00
Dan Taylor	10.00	5.00	3.00
Fay Thomas	10.00	5.00	3.00
Hal Trosky	10.00	5.00	3.00
Honus Wagner	40.00	20.00	12.00
Rube Walberg	10.00	5.00	3.00
Paul Waner	20.00	10.00	6.00
Lon Warneke	10.00	5.00	3.00
Harold Warstler	10.00	5.00	3.00
Billy Webb	10.00	5.00	3.00
Whitlow Wyatt	10.00	5.00	3.00

1933 Butter Cream (R306)

The 1933 Butter Cream set consists of unnumbered, black-and-white cards which measure 1-1/4" x 3-1/2". Backs feature a contest in which the collector was to estimate players' statistics by a specific date. Two different backs are known: 1) Estimate through Sept. 1 and no company address, and 2) Estimate through Oct. 1 with the Butter Cream address. The ACC designation for the set is R306.

Net Weight ¾ oz.   Center Field, N. L.   1932 Bat. Aver. .348
CHARLES KLEIN
Your Estimate of This Year to Oct. 1 (..........)
BUTTER CREAM CONFECTIONERY CORP.
123-33 THIRTY-THIRD ST., UNION CITY, N. J.
Name ....
Address ....

		NM	EX	VG
Complete Set (30):		30,000	15,000	7,500
Common Player:		750.00	375.00	165.00
(1)	Earl Averill	1,000	500.00	225.00
(2)	Ed. Brandt	750.00	375.00	165.00
(3)	Guy T. Bush	750.00	375.00	165.00
(4)	Gordon Cochrane	1,000	500.00	225.00
(5)	Joe Cronin	1,000	500.00	225.00
(6)	George Earnshaw	750.00	375.00	165.00
(7)	Wesley Ferrell	750.00	375.00	165.00
(8)	"Jimmy" E. Foxx	2,000	1,000	440.00
(9)	Frank C. Frisch	1,000	500.00	225.00
(10)	Charles M. Gelbert	750.00	375.00	165.00
(11)	"Lefty" Robert M. Grove	1,200	600.00	265.00
(12)	Leo Charles Hartnett	1,000	500.00	225.00
(13)	"Babe" Herman	750.00	375.00	165.00
(14)	Charles Klein	1,000	500.00	220.00
(15)	Ray Kremer	750.00	375.00	165.00
(16)	Fred C. Linstrom (Lindstrom)	1,000	500.00	225.00
(17)	Ted A. Lyons	1,000	500.00	225.00
(18)	"Pepper" John L. Martin	900.00	450.00	200.00
(19)	Robert O'Farrell	750.00	375.00	165.00
(20)	Ed. A. Rommel	750.00	375.00	165.00
(21)	Charles Root	750.00	375.00	165.00
(22)	Harold "Muddy" Ruel (Herold)	750.00	375.00	165.00
(23)	Babe Ruth	8,000	4,000	1,750
(24)	"Al" Simmons	1,000	500.00	225.00
(25)	"Bill" Terry	1,000	500.00	225.00
(26)	George E. Uhle	750.00	375.00	165.00
(27)	Lloyd J. Waner	1,000	500.00	225.00
(28)	Paul G. Waner	1,000	500.00	225.00
(29)	Hack Wilson	1,000	500.00	225.00
(30)	Glen. Wright	750.00	375.00	165.00

1934 Butterfinger (R310)

Cards in this set were available as a premium with Butterfinger and other candy products. The unnumbered cards measure approximately 7-3/4" x 9-1/2" and can be found printed either on paper or heavy cardboard. The cardboard variety carry red advertising for Butterfinger and are valued about 4X the paper version. The black-and-white cards feature a player photo with facsimile autograph. Similar cards in a 6-1/2" x 8-1/2" format are a companion Canadian issue.

		NM	EX	VG
Complete Set (65):		6,500	3,250	2,000
Common Player:		60.00	30.00	18.00
Cardboard Ad Variety: 4X				
(1)	Earl Averill	110.00	55.00	35.00
(2)	Richard Bartell	60.00	30.00	18.00
(3)	Larry Benton	60.00	30.00	18.00
(4)	Walter Berger	60.00	30.00	18.00
(5)	Jim Bottomly (Bottomley)	110.00	55.00	35.00
(6)	Ralph Boyle	60.00	30.00	18.00
(7)	Tex Carleton	60.00	30.00	18.00
(8)	Owen T. Carroll	60.00	30.00	18.00
(9)	Ben Chapman	60.00	30.00	18.00
(10)	Gordon (Mickey) Cochrane	110.00	55.00	35.00
(11)	James Collins	60.00	30.00	18.00
(12)	Joe Cronin	110.00	55.00	35.00
(13)	Alvin Crowder	60.00	30.00	18.00
(14)	"Dizzy" Dean	240.00	120.00	75.00
(15)	Paul Derringer	60.00	30.00	18.00
(16)	William Dickey	125.00	62.00	37.00
(17)	Leo Durocher	110.00	55.00	35.00
(18)	George Earnshaw	60.00	30.00	18.00
(19)	Richard Ferrell	110.00	55.00	35.00
(20)	Lew Fonseca	60.00	30.00	18.00
(21a)	Jimmy Fox (Name incorrect.)	225.00	110.00	70.00
(21b)	Jimmy Foxx (Name correct.)	185.00	95.00	55.00
(22)	Benny Frey	60.00	30.00	18.00
(23)	Frankie Frisch	110.00	55.00	35.00
(24)	Lou Gehrig	750.00	375.00	225.00
(25)	Charles Gehringer	110.00	55.00	35.00
(26)	Vernon Gomez	110.00	55.00	35.00
(27)	Ray Grabowski	60.00	30.00	18.00
(28)	Robert (Lefty) Grove	150.00	75.00	45.00
(29)	George (Mule) Haas	60.00	30.00	18.00
(30)	"Chick" Hafey	110.00	55.00	35.00
(31)	Stanley Harris	110.00	55.00	35.00
(32)	J. Francis Hogan	60.00	30.00	18.00
(33)	Ed Holley	60.00	30.00	18.00
(34)	Rogers Hornsby	150.00	75.00	45.00
(35)	Waite Hoyt	110.00	55.00	35.00
(36)	Walter Johnson	250.00	125.00	75.00
(37)	Jim Jordan	60.00	30.00	18.00
(38)	Joe Kuhel	60.00	30.00	18.00
(39)	Hal Lee	60.00	30.00	18.00
(40)	Gus Mancuso	60.00	30.00	18.00
(41)	Henry Manush	110.00	55.00	35.00
(42)	Fred Marberry	60.00	30.00	18.00
(43)	Pepper Martin	85.00	45.00	25.00
(44)	Oscar Melillo	60.00	30.00	18.00
(45)	Johnny Moore	60.00	30.00	18.00
(46)	Joe Morrissey	60.00	30.00	18.00
(47)	Joe Mowrey	60.00	30.00	18.00
(48)	Bob O'Farrell	60.00	30.00	18.00
(49)	Melvin Ott	125.00	65.00	35.00
(50)	Monte Pearson	60.00	30.00	18.00
(51)	Carl Reynolds	60.00	30.00	18.00
(52)	Charles Ruffing	110.00	55.00	35.00
(53)	Babe Ruth	750.00	375.00	225.00
(54)	John "Blondy" Ryan	60.00	30.00	18.00
(55)	Al Simmons	110.00	55.00	35.00
(56)	Al Spohrer	60.00	30.00	18.00
(57)	Gus Suhr	60.00	30.00	18.00
(58)	Steve Swetonic	60.00	30.00	18.00
(59)	Dazzy Vance	110.00	55.00	35.00
(60)	Joe Vosmik	60.00	30.00	18.00
(61)	Lloyd Waner	110.00	55.00	35.00
(62)	Paul Waner	110.00	55.00	35.00
(63)	Sam West	60.00	30.00	18.00
(64)	Earl Whitehill	60.00	30.00	18.00
(65)	Jimmy Wilson	60.00	30.00	18.00

1934 Butterfinger - Canadian (V94)

Similar to the U.S. issue, though smaller in size at 6-1/2" x 8-1/2", these black-and-white paper cards include a number of players not found in the U.S. issue. Like the "regular" Butterfinger cards, each of the Canadian pieces includes a facsimile autograph on the front; backs are blank.

		NM	EX	VG
Complete Set (58):		4,500	2,250	1,350
Common Player:		50.00	25.00	15.00
(1)	Earl Averill	100.00	50.00	30.00
(2)	Larry Benton	50.00	25.00	15.00
(3)	Jim Bottomly (Bottomley)	100.00	50.00	30.00
(4)	Tom Bridges	50.00	25.00	15.00
(5)	Bob Brown	50.00	25.00	15.00
(6)	Owen T. Carroll	50.00	25.00	15.00
(7)	Gordon (Mickey) Cochrane	100.00	50.00	30.00
(8)	Roger Cramer	50.00	25.00	15.00
(9)	Joe Cronin	100.00	50.00	30.00
(10)	Alvin Crowder	50.00	25.00	15.00
(11)	"Dizzy" Dean	185.00	95.00	55.00
(12)	Edward Delker	50.00	25.00	15.00
(13)	William Dickey	125.00	62.00	37.00
(14)	Richard Ferrell	100.00	50.00	30.00
(15)	Lew Fonseca	50.00	25.00	15.00
(16a)	Jimmy Fox (Name incorrect.)	145.00	75.00	45.00
(16b)	Jimmy Foxx (Name correct.)	145.00	75.00	45.00
(17)	Chick Fullis	50.00	25.00	15.00
(18)	Lou Gehrig	600.00	300.00	180.00
(19)	Charles Gehringer	100.00	50.00	30.00
(20)	Vernon Gomez	100.00	50.00	30.00
(21)	Robert (Lefty) Grove	125.00	62.00	37.00
(22)	George (Mule) Haas	50.00	25.00	15.00
(23)	"Chick" Hafey	100.00	50.00	30.00
(24)	Stanley Harris	100.00	50.00	30.00
(25)	Frank Higgins	50.00	25.00	15.00
(26)	J. Francis Hogan	50.00	25.00	15.00
(27)	Ed Holley	50.00	25.00	15.00
(28)	Waite Hoyt	100.00	50.00	30.00
(29)	Jim Jordan	50.00	25.00	15.00
(30)	Hal Lee	50.00	25.00	15.00
(31)	Gus Mancuso	50.00	25.00	15.00
(32)	Oscar Melillo	50.00	25.00	15.00
(33)	Austin Moore	50.00	25.00	15.00
(34)	Randy Moore	50.00	25.00	15.00
(35)	Joe Morrissey	50.00	25.00	15.00
(36)	Joe Mowrey	50.00	25.00	15.00
(37)	Bobo Newsom	50.00	25.00	15.00
(38)	Ernie Orsatti	50.00	25.00	15.00
(39)	Carl Reynolds	50.00	25.00	15.00
(40)	Walter Roettger	50.00	25.00	15.00
(41)	Babe Ruth	650.00	325.00	200.00
(42)	John "Blondy" Ryan	50.00	25.00	15.00
(43)	John Salveson	50.00	25.00	15.00
(44)	Al Simmons	100.00	50.00	30.00
(45)	Al Smith	50.00	25.00	15.00
(46)	Harold Smith	50.00	25.00	15.00
(47)	Allyn Stout	50.00	25.00	15.00
(48)	Fresco Thompson	50.00	25.00	15.00
(49)	Art Veltman	50.00	25.00	15.00
(50)	Johnny Vergez	50.00	25.00	15.00
(51)	Gerald Walker	50.00	25.00	15.00
(52)	Paul Waner	100.00	50.00	30.00
(53)	Burgess Whitehead	50.00	25.00	15.00
(54)	Earl Whitehill	50.00	25.00	15.00
(55)	Robert Weiland	50.00	25.00	15.00
(56)	Jimmy Wilson	50.00	25.00	15.00
(57)	Bob Worthington	50.00	25.00	15.00
(58)	Tom Zachary	50.00	25.00	15.00

1911-14 Butter Krust Bread (D304)

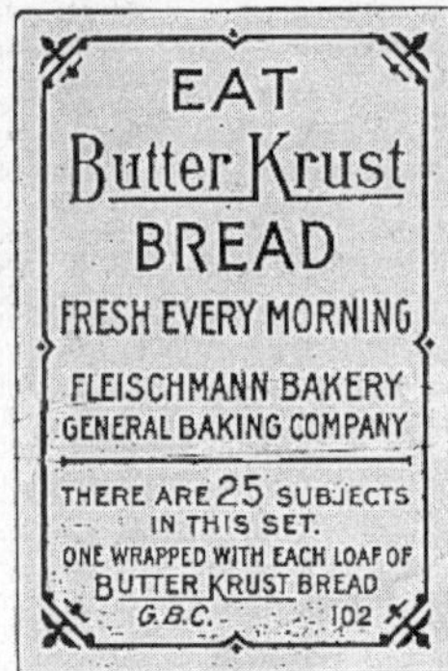

EAT
Butter Krust
BREAD
FRESH EVERY MORNING
FLEISCHMANN BAKERY
GENERAL BAKING COMPANY
THERE ARE 25 SUBJECTS IN THIS SET.
ONE WRAPPED WITH EACH LOAF OF BUTTER KRUST BREAD
G.B.C. 102

(See 1911-14 General Baking Co. for checklist and values.)

1933 Button Gum

(See 1933 Cracker Jack.)

1914 B18 Blankets

These 5-1/4"-square flannels were issued in 1914 wrapped around several popular brands of tobacco. The flannels, whose American Card Catalog designation is B18, picked up the nickname blankets because many of them were sewn together to form bed covers or throws. Different color combinations on the flannels exist for all 10 teams included in the set. The complete set price includes only the lowest-priced variation for each of the 90 players.

		NM	EX	VG
Complete Set (90):		7,000	3,500	2,000
Complete Set W/Variations (202):		55,000	27,500	16,500
Common Player:		40.00	20.00	12.00
(1a)	Babe Adams (Purple pennants.)	80.00	40.00	25.00
(1b)	Babe Adams (Red pennants.)	130.00	65.00	40.00
(2a)	Sam Agnew (Purple basepaths.)	80.00	40.00	25.00
(2b)	Sam Agnew (Red basepaths.)	125.00	65.00	35.00
(3a)	Eddie Ainsmith (Green pennants.)	40.00	20.00	12.00
(3b)	Eddie Ainsmith (Brown pennants.)	40.00	20.00	12.00
(4a)	Jimmy Austin (Purple basepaths.)	80.00	40.00	25.00
(4b)	Jimmy Austin (Red basepaths.)	90.00	45.00	27.00
(5a)	Del Baker (White infield.)	40.00	20.00	12.00
(5b)	Del Baker (Brown infield.)	150.00	75.00	45.00
(5c)	Del Baker (Red infield.)	1,650	825.00	495.00
(6a)	Johnny Bassler (Purple pennants.)	90.00	45.00	27.00
(6b)	Johnny Bassler (Yellow pennants.)	125.00	65.00	35.00
(7a)	Paddy Bauman (Baumann) (White infield.)	40.00	20.00	12.00
(7b)	Paddy Bauman (Baumann) (Brown infield.)	150.00	75.00	45.00
(7c)	Paddy Bauman (Baumann) (Red infield.)	1,650	825.00	495.00
(8a)	Luke Boone (Blue infield.)	40.00	20.00	12.00
(8b)	Luke Boone (Green infield.)	40.00	20.00	12.00
(9a)	George Burns (Brown basepaths.)	40.00	20.00	12.00
(9b)	George Burns (Green basepaths.)	40.00	20.00	12.00
(10a)	Tioga George Burns (White infield.)	40.00	20.00	12.00
(10b)	Tioga George Burns (Brown infield.)	150.00	75.00	45.00
(10c)	Tioga George Burns (Red infield.)	1,650	825.00	495.00
(11a)	Max Carey (Purple pennants.)	150.00	75.00	45.00
(11b)	Max Carey (Red pennants.)	175.00	85.00	55.00
(12a)	Marty Cavanaugh (Kavanagh) (White infield.)	40.00	20.00	12.00
(12b)	Marty Cavanaugh (Kavanagh) (Brown infield.)	150.00	75.00	45.00
(12c)	Marty Cavanaugh (Kavanagh) (Red infield.)	1,650	825.00	495.00
(12d)	Marty Kavanaugh (Kavanagh)	200.00	100.00	60.00
(13a)	Frank Chance (Green infield.)	100.00	50.00	30.00
(13b)	Frank Chance (Brown pennants, blue infield.)	100.00	50.00	30.00
(13c)	Frank Chance (Yellow pennants, blue infield.)	450.00	225.00	135.00
(14a)	Ray Chapman (Purple pennants.)	125.00	65.00	35.00
(14b)	Ray Chapman (Yellow pennants.)	200.00	100.00	60.00
(15a)	Ty Cobb (White infield.)	500.00	250.00	150.00
(15b)	Ty Cobb (Brown infield.)	700.00	350.00	210.00
(15c)	Ty Cobb (Red infield.)	15,000	7,500	4,500
(16a)	King Cole (Blue infield.)	40.00	20.00	12.00
(16b)	King Cole (Green infield.)	40.00	20.00	12.00
(17a)	Joe Connolly (White infield.)	40.00	20.00	12.00
(17b)	Joe Connolly (Brown infield.)	150.00	75.00	45.00
(17c)	Joe Connolly (Red infield.)	1,650	825.00	495.00
(18a)	Harry Coveleski (White infield.)	40.00	20.00	12.00
(18b)	Harry Coveleski (Brown infield.)	150.00	75.00	45.00
(18c)	Harry Coveleski (Red infield.)	1,650	825.00	495.00
(19a)	George Cutshaw (Blue infield.)	40.00	20.00	12.00
(19b)	George Cutshaw (Green infield.)	40.00	20.00	12.00
(20a)	Jake Daubert (Blue infield.)	45.00	22.50	13.50
(20b)	Jake Daubert (Green infield.)	45.00	22.50	13.50
(21a)	Ray Demmitt (White infield.)	40.00	20.00	12.00
(21b)	Ray Demmitt (Brown infield.)	150.00	75.00	45.00
(21c)	Ray Demmitt (Red infield.)	1,650	825.00	495.00
(22a)	Bill Doak (Purple pennants.)	80.00	40.00	24.00
(22b)	Bill Doak (Yellow pennants.)	125.00	65.00	35.00
(23a)	Cozy Dolan (Purple pennants.)	80.00	40.00	25.00
(23b)	Cozy Dolan (Yellow pennants.)	150.00	75.00	45.00
(24a)	Larry Doyle (Brown basepaths.)	45.00	22.50	13.50
(24b)	Larry Doyle (Green basepaths.)	45.00	22.50	13.50
(25a)	Art Fletcher (Brown basepaths.)	40.00	20.00	12.00
(25b)	Art Fletcher (Green basepaths.)	40.00	20.00	12.00
(26a)	Eddie Foster (Brown pennants.)	40.00	20.00	12.00
(26b)	Eddie Foster (Green pennants.)	40.00	20.00	12.00
(27a)	Del Gainor (White infield.)	50.00	25.00	15.00
(27b)	Del Gainor (Brown infield.)	150.00	75.00	45.00
(28a)	Chick Gandil (Brown pennants.)	100.00	50.00	30.00
(28b)	Chick Gandil (Green pennants.)	125.00	65.00	35.00
(29a)	George Gibson (Purple pennants.)	80.00	40.00	25.00
(29b)	George Gibson (Red pennants.)	90.00	45.00	27.00
(30a)	Hank Gowdy (White infield.)	40.00	20.00	12.00
(30b)	Hank Gowdy (Brown infield.)	150.00	75.00	45.00
(30c)	Hank Gowdy (Red infield.)	1,650	825.00	495.00
(31a)	Jack Graney (Purple pennants.)	90.00	45.00	27.00
(31b)	Jack Graney (Yellow pennants.)	125.00	65.00	35.00
(32a)	Eddie Grant (Brown basepaths.)	40.00	20.00	12.00
(32b)	Eddie Grant (Green basepaths.)	40.00	20.00	12.00
(33a)	Tommy Griffith (White infield, green pennants.)	40.00	20.00	12.00
(33b)	Tommy Griffith (White infield, red pennants.)	1,500	750.00	450.00
(33c)	Tommy Griffith (Brown infield.)	125.00	65.00	35.00
(33d)	Tommy Griffith (Red infield.)	1,650	825.00	495.00
(34a)	Earl Hamilton (Purple basepaths.)	80.00	40.00	25.00
(34b)	Earl Hamilton (Red basepaths.)	90.00	45.00	27.00
(35a)	Roy Hartzell (Blue infield.)	40.00	20.00	12.00
(35b)	Roy Hartzell (Green infield.)	40.00	20.00	12.00
(36a)	Miller Huggins (Purple pennants.)	160.00	80.00	45.00
(36b)	Miller Huggins (Yellow pennants.)	245.00	120.00	75.00
(37a)	John Hummel (Blue infield.)	40.00	20.00	12.00
(37b)	John Hummel (Green infield.)	40.00	20.00	12.00
(38a)	Ham Hyatt (Purple pennants.)	80.00	40.00	24.00
(38b)	Ham Hyatt (Red pennants.)	90.00	45.00	27.00
(39a)	Joe Jackson (Purple pennants.)	1,350	675.00	400.00
(39b)	Joe Jackson (Yellow pennants.)	1,100	550.00	330.00
(40a)	Bill James (White infield.)	40.00	20.00	12.00
(40b)	Bill James (Brown infield.)	160.00	80.00	50.00
(40c)	Bill James (Red infield.)	1,650	825.00	495.00
(41a)	Walter Johnson (Brown pennants.)	300.00	150.00	90.00
(41b)	Walter Johnson (Green pennants.)	275.00	135.00	80.00
(42a)	Ray Keating (Blue infield.)	40.00	20.00	12.00
(42b)	Ray Keating (Green infield.)	40.00	20.00	12.00
(43a)	Joe Kelley (Kelly) (Purple pennants.)	90.00	45.00	27.00
(43b)	Joe Kelley (Kelly) (Red pennants.)	90.00	45.00	27.00
(44a)	Ed Konetchy (Purple pennants.)	60.00	30.00	18.00
(44b)	Ed Konetchy (Red pennants.)	90.00	45.00	27.00
(45a)	Nemo Leibold (Purple pennants.)	75.00	37.50	22.00
(45b)	Nemo Leibold (Yellow pennants.)	150.00	75.00	45.00
(46a)	Fritz Maisel (Blue infield.)	40.00	20.00	12.00
(46b)	Fritz Maisel (Green infield.)	40.00	20.00	12.00
(47a)	Les Mann (White infield.)	40.00	20.00	12.00
(47b)	Les Mann (Brown infield.)	150.00	75.00	45.00
(47c)	Les Mann (Red infield.)	1,650	825.00	495.00
(48a)	Rabbit Maranville (White infield.)	130.00	65.00	39.00
(48b)	Rabbit Maranville (Brown infield.)	250.00	125.00	75.00
(48c)	Rabbit Maranville (Red infield.)	3,000	1,500	900.00
(49a)	Bill McAllister (McAllester) (Purple basepaths.)	80.00	40.00	25.00
(49b)	Bill McAllister (McAllester) (Red basepaths.)	100.00	50.00	30.00
(50a)	George McBride (Brown pennants.)	40.00	20.00	12.00
(50b)	George McBride (Green pennants.)	40.00	20.00	12.00
(51a)	Chief Meyers (Brown basepaths.)	40.00	20.00	12.00
(51b)	Chief Meyers (Green basepaths.)	40.00	20.00	12.00
(52a)	Clyde Milan (Brown pennants.)	40.00	20.00	12.00
(52b)	Clyde Milan (Green pennants.)	40.00	20.00	12.00
(53a)	J. Miller (Purple pennants.)	80.00	40.00	25.00
(53b)	J. Miller (Yellow pennants.)	125.00	65.00	35.00
(54a)	Otto Miller (Blue infield.)	40.00	20.00	12.00
(54b)	Otto Miller (Green infield.)	40.00	20.00	12.00
(55a)	Willie Mitchell (Purple pennants.)	80.00	40.00	25.00
(55b)	Willie Mitchell (Yellow pennants.)	150.00	75.00	45.00
(56a)	Danny Moeller (Brown pennants.)	40.00	20.00	12.00
(56b)	Danny Moeller (Green pennants.)	40.00	20.00	12.00
(57a)	Ray Morgan (Brown pennants.)	40.00	20.00	12.00
(57b)	Ray Morgan (Green pennants.)	40.00	20.00	12.00
(58a)	George Moriarty (White infield.)	40.00	20.00	12.00
(58b)	George Moriarty (Brown infield.)	150.00	75.00	45.00
(58c)	George Moriarty (Red infield.)	1,650	825.00	495.00
(59a)	Mike Mowrey (Purple pennants.)	80.00	40.00	25.00
(59b)	Mike Mowrey (Red pennants.)	90.00	45.00	27.00
(60a)	Red Murray (Brown basepaths.)	40.00	20.00	12.00
(60b)	Red Murray (Green basepaths.)	40.00	20.00	12.00
(61a)	Ivy Olson (Purple pennants.)	80.00	40.00	25.00
(61b)	Ivy Olson (Yellow pennants.)	160.00	80.00	50.00
(62a)	Steve O'Neill (Purple pennants.)	75.00	37.50	22.00
(62b)	Steve O'Neill (Red pennants.)	150.00	75.00	45.00
(62c)	Steve O'Neill (Yellow pennants.)	150.00	75.00	45.00
(63a)	Marty O'Toole (Purple pennants.)	80.00	40.00	25.00
(63b)	Marty O'Toole (Red pennants.)	90.00	45.00	27.00
(64a)	Roger Peckinpaugh (Blue infield.)	45.00	22.50	13.50
(64b)	Roger Peckinpaugh (Green infield.)	45.00	22.50	13.50
(65a)	Hub Perdue (White infield.)	40.00	20.00	12.00
(65b)	Hub Perdue (Brown infield.)	150.00	75.00	45.00
(65c)	Hub Purdue (Red infield.)	1,650	825.00	495.00
(66a)	Del Pratt (Purple basepaths.)	80.00	40.00	25.00
(66b)	Del Pratt (Red basepaths.)	90.00	45.00	27.00
(67a)	Hank Robinson (Purple pennants.)	80.00	40.00	25.00
(67b)	Hank Robinson (Yellow pennants.)	130.00	65.00	40.00
(68a)	Nap Rucker (Blue infield.)	40.00	20.00	12.00
(68b)	Nap Rucker (Green infield.)	40.00	20.00	12.00
(69a)	Slim Sallee (Purple pennants.)	100.00	50.00	30.00
(69b)	Slim Sallee (Yellow pennants.)	150.00	75.00	45.00
(70a)	Howard Shanks (Brown pennants.)	40.00	20.00	12.00
(70b)	Howard Shanks (Green pennants.)	40.00	20.00	12.00
(70c)	Howard Shanks (White infield.)	40.00	20.00	12.00
(71a)	Burt Shotton (Purple basepaths.)	80.00	40.00	25.00
(71b)	Burt Shotton (Red basepaths.)	75.00	37.50	22.00
(72a)	Red Smith (Blue infield.)	40.00	20.00	12.00
(72b)	Red Smith (Green infield.)	40.00	20.00	12.00
(73a)	Fred Snodgrass (Brown basepaths.)	40.00	20.00	12.00
(73b)	Fred Snodgrass (Green basepaths.)	40.00	20.00	12.00
(74a)	Bill Steele (Purple pennants.)	80.00	40.00	24.00
(74b)	Bill Steele (Yellow pennants.)	150.00	75.00	45.00
(75a)	Casey Stengel (Blue infield.)	100.00	50.00	30.00
(75b)	Casey Stengel (Green infield.)	100.00	50.00	30.00
(76a)	Jeff Sweeney (Blue infield.)	40.00	20.00	12.00
(76b)	Jeff Sweeney (Green infield.)	40.00	20.00	12.00
(77a)	Jeff Tesreau (Brown basepaths.)	40.00	20.00	12.00
(77b)	Jeff Tesreau (Green basepaths.)	40.00	20.00	12.00
(78a)	Terry Turner (Purple pennants.)	80.00	40.00	25.00
(78b)	Terry Turner (Yellow pennants.)	150.00	75.00	45.00
(79a)	Lefty Tyler (White infield.)	40.00	20.00	12.00
(79b)	Lefty Tyler (Brown infield.)	150.00	75.00	45.00
(79c)	Lefty Tyler (Red infield.)	1,650	825.00	495.00
(80a)	Jim Viox (Purple pennants.)	80.00	40.00	25.00

(80b)	Jim Viox (Red pennants.)	90.00	45.00	27.00
(81a)	Bull Wagner (Blue infield.)	40.00	20.00	12.00
(81b)	Bull Wagner (Green infield.)	40.00	20.00	12.00
(82a)	Bobby Wallace (Purple basepaths.)	150.00	75.00	45.00
(82b)	Bobby Wallace (Red basepaths.)	150.00	75.00	45.00
(83a)	Dee Walsh (Purple basepaths.)	80.00	40.00	25.00
(83b)	Dee Walsh (Red basepaths.)	90.00	45.00	27.00
(84a)	Jimmy Walsh (Blue infield.)	40.00	20.00	12.00
(84b)	Jimmy Walsh (Green infield.)	40.00	20.00	12.00
(85a)	Bert Whaling (White infield.)	40.00	20.00	12.00
(85b)	Bert Whaling (Brown infield.)	150.00	75.00	45.00
(85c)	Bert Whaling (Red infield.)	1,650	825.00	495.00
(86a)	Zach Wheat (Blue infield.)	125.00	65.00	35.00
(86b)	Zach Wheat (Green infield.)	100.00	50.00	30.00
(87a)	Possum Whitted (Purple pennants.)	80.00	40.00	25.00
(87b)	Possum Whitted (Yellow pennants.)	125.00	65.00	35.00
(88a)	Gus Williams (Purple basepaths.)	80.00	40.00	25.00
(88b)	Gus Williams (Red basepaths.)	90.00	45.00	27.00
(89a)	Owen Wilson (Purple pennants.)	80.00	40.00	25.00
(89b)	Owen Wilson (Yellow pennants.)	150.00	75.00	45.00
(90a)	Hooks Wiltse (Brown basepaths.)	40.00	20.00	12.00
(90b)	Hooks Wiltse (Green basepaths.)	40.00	20.00	12.00

1937 BF-UNC Felt Pennants

Based on the known player-team combinations in this probably incomplete checklist, 1937 seems the most likely date of issue. The pennants measure about 2-1/4" across the top and taper to a point at the end of their 5" length. About halfway down is a blue-and-white trapezoid with a player photo within a circle on a pinstriped background. The team name is printed in two lines at top. It is believed each player can be found with more than one base pennant color and team-name printing.

		NM	EX	VG
	Common Player:	150.00	75.00	45.00
(1)	Dizzy Dean	650.00	325.00	195.00
(2)	Bobby Feller	500.00	250.00	150.00
(3)	Hank Greenberg	500.00	250.00	150.00
(4)	Lefty Grove	450.00	225.00	135.00
(5)	Joe Moore	150.00	75.00	45.00
(6)	Wallace Moses	150.00	75.00	45.00
(7)	Lynwood Rowe	150.00	75.00	45.00
(7)	Joe Stripp	150.00	75.00	45.00
(8)	Floyd Vaughan	400.00	200.00	120.00

1916 BF2 Felt Pennants

Issued circa 1916, this unnumbered set consists of 97 felt pennants with a small black-and-white player photo glued to each. The triangular pennants measure approximately 2-7/8" across the top and taper to a length of about 5-3/4" long, while the photos are 1-3/4" x 1-1/4" and appear to be identical to photos used for M101-4/M101-5 issues of the same period. The pennants list the player's name and team. The pennants were given away as premiums with the purchase of five-cent loaves of Ferguson Bakery bread in the Roxbury, Mass., area.

(See 1916 Ferguson Bakery Felt Pennants for checklist and values.)

1936-37 BF3 Felt Player/Team Pennants

The checklists for these series of felt pennants issued circa 1936-1938 are not complete, and new examples are still being reported. The pennants do not carry any manufacturer's name although packages found with various pieces attribute the issues to Red Ball Sales, a gum company in Chicago, and Grandpa Brands Co., Cincinnati, another gum company. One pennant was given away with the purchase of a stick of gum, and at least one wrapper indicates large format (28" x 12") versions of the Red Ball pennants could be had in a redemption program. The pennants vary in size slightly but generally measure approximately 2-1/2" x 4-1/2" and were issued in various styles and colors. Most of the printing is white, although some pennants have been found with other colors of printing, and the same pennant is often found in more than one color combination. The pennants feature both individual players and teams, including some minor league clubs. The pennants were grouped together in the American Card Catalog under the designation of BF3. Advanced collectors have categorized the pennants into a number of basic design types, depending on what elements are included on the pennant. The unnumbered felts are listed alphabetically within type. Gaps have been left in the assigned numbers to accommodate future discoveries.

	NM	EX	VG
Common Pennant:	25.00	12.50	7.50

1936-37 Type 1 - Player Name and Silhouette

Generic silhouette figures in action poses are featured at the left end of this series of pennants. Player names at right can be found in a number of different typographic styles. Gaps have been left in the assigned numbering for future additions.

		NM	EX	VG
	Common Pennant:	60.00	30.00	18.00
(1)	Luke Appling/Btg	80.00	40.00	25.00
(2)	Earl Averill/Btg	80.00	40.00	25.00
(3)	Wally Berger/Fldg	60.00	30.00	18.00
(4)	Zeke Bonura/Fldg	60.00	30.00	18.00
(5)	Dolph Camilli/Fldg	60.00	30.00	18.00
(6)	Ben Chapman/Btg	60.00	30.00	18.00
(7)	Mickey Cochrane/Catching	90.00	45.00	27.00
(8)	Rip Collins/Btg	60.00	30.00	18.00
(9)	Joe Cronin/Btg	80.00	40.00	25.00
(10)	Kiki Cuyler/Running	80.00	40.00	25.00
(11)	Dizzy Dean/Pitching	135.00	65.00	40.00
(12)	Frank Demaree/Btg	60.00	30.00	18.00
(13)	Paul Derringer/Pitching	60.00	30.00	18.00
(14)	Bill Dickey/Catching	90.00	45.00	27.00
(15)	Jimmy Dykes/Fldg	60.00	30.00	18.00
(16)	Bob Feller/Pitching	110.00	55.00	35.00
(17)	Wes Ferrell/Btg	60.00	30.00	18.00
(19)	Jimmy Foxx	100.00	50.00	30.00
(20)	Larry French/Btg	60.00	30.00	18.00
(21)	Franky Frisch/Running	90.00	45.00	27.00
(23)	Lou Gehrig/Throwing	300.00	150.00	90.00
(24)	Charlie Gehringer/Running	90.00	45.00	27.00
(25)	Lefty Gomez/Pitching	80.00	40.00	25.00
(26)	Goose Goslin/Btg	80.00	40.00	25.00
(30)	Hank Greenberg/Fldg	110.00	55.00	35.00
(31)	Charley Grimm/Fldg	60.00	30.00	18.00
(33)	Lefty Grove/Pitching	90.00	45.00	27.00
(34)	Gabby Hartnett/Catching	80.00	40.00	25.00
(35)	Rollie Hemsley/Catching	60.00	30.00	18.00
(36)	Billy Herman/Fldg	80.00	40.00	25.00
(37)	Frank Higgins/Fldg	60.00	30.00	18.00
(38)	Rogers Hornsby/Btg	100.00	50.00	30.00
(39)	Carl Hubbell/Pitching	90.00	45.00	27.00
(40)	Chuck Klein/Throwing	80.00	40.00	25.00
(41)	Tony Lazzeri/Btg	80.00	40.00	25.00
(42)	Hank Leiber/Fldg	60.00	30.00	18.00
(43)	Ernie Lombardi/Catching	80.00	40.00	25.00
(44)	Al Lopez/Throwing	80.00	40.00	25.00
(45)	Gus Mancuso/Running	60.00	30.00	18.00
(46)	Heinie Manush/Btg	80.00	40.00	25.00
(47)	Pepper Martin/Btg	70.00	35.00	20.00
(48)	Joe McCarthy/Kneeling	80.00	40.00	25.00
(49)	Wally Moses/Running	60.00	30.00	18.00
(50)	Van Mungo/Standing	60.00	30.00	18.00
(52)	Mel Ott/Throwing	90.00	45.00	27.00
(53)	Schoolboy Rowe/Pitching	60.00	30.00	18.00
(54)	Babe Ruth/Btg	450.00	225.00	135.00
(55)	George Selkirk/Btg	60.00	30.00	18.00
(56)	Luke Sewell/Sliding	60.00	30.00	18.00
(57)	Joe Stripp/Btg	60.00	30.00	18.00
(58)	Pie Traynor/Btg	80.00	40.00	25.00
(59)	Hal Trosky/Fldg	60.00	30.00	18.00
(60)	Floyd Vaughan/Running (Script name.)	80.00	40.00	25.00
(61)	Floyd Vaughan/Running (Block name.)	80.00	40.00	25.00
(62)	Joe Vosmik/Running	60.00	30.00	18.00
(64)	Paul Waner/Btg	80.00	40.00	25.00
(65)	Lon Warneke/Pitching	60.00	30.00	18.00
(66)	Jimmy Wilson/Fldg	60.00	30.00	18.00

1936-37 Type 2 - Player's Name, Team Nickname, Figure

Team nicknames have been added at the spine of this style of pennant. As with Type 1, some players can be found in more than one pose and/or typography. Gaps have been left in the assigned numbering to accomodate future additions.

		NM	EX	VG
	Common Pennant:	60.00	30.00	18.00
(1)	Luke Appling/Btg (Block name.)	80.00	40.00	25.00
(2)	Luke Appling/Btg (Script name.)	80.00	40.00	25.00
(3)	Earl Averill/Fldg	80.00	40.00	25.00
(4)	Earl Averill/Running	80.00	40.00	24.00
(5)	Wally Berger/Throwing	60.00	30.00	18.00
(6)	Zeke Bonura/Btg	60.00	30.00	18.00
(7)	Dolph Camilli/Btg	60.00	30.00	18.00
(8)	Ben Chapman/Throwing	60.00	30.00	18.00
(9)	Mickey Cochrane/Throwing	90.00	45.00	27.00
(10)	Rip Collins/Btg	60.00	30.00	18.00
(11)	Joe Cronin/Throwing	80.00	40.00	25.00
(12)	Kiki Cuyler/Throwing	80.00	40.00	25.00
(13)	Dizzy Dean/Btg	110.00	55.00	35.00
(14)	Dizzy Dean/Throwing	110.00	55.00	35.00
(15)	Frank Demaree/Btg	60.00	30.00	18.00
(16)	Paul Derringer/Throwing	60.00	30.00	18.00
(17)	Bill Dickey/Throwing	110.00	55.00	35.00
(18)	Joe DiMaggio (Block letters through figure.)	260.00	130.00	80.00
(19)	Joe DiMaggio (Script)	260.00	130.00	80.00
(20)	Jimmy Dykes/Throwing	60.00	30.00	18.00
(21)	Bob Feller (Block letters.)	110.00	55.00	35.00
(22)	Bob Feller (Script)	110.00	55.00	35.00
(23)	Wes Ferrell/Throwing	60.00	30.00	18.00
(24)	Larry French/Btg	60.00	30.00	18.00
(25)	Frank Frisch/Fldg	90.00	45.00	27.00
(27)	Lou Gehrig/Btg (Block letters.)	300.00	150.00	90.00
(28)	Lou Gehrig/Btg (Script.)	300.00	150.00	90.00
(29)	Lou Gehrig/Fldg	300.00	150.00	90.00
(31)	Lefty Gomez/Pitching	90.00	45.00	27.00
(32)	Goose Goslin/Throwing	90.00	45.00	27.00
(33)	Hank Greenberg/Btg	110.00	55.00	35.00
(34)	Hank Greenberg/Throwing	110.00	55.00	35.00
(35)	Charlie Grimm/Fldg	60.00	30.00	18.00
(36)	Lefty Grove/Btg	90.00	45.00	27.00
(37)	Lefty Grove/Pitching	90.00	45.00	27.00
(38)	Gabby Hartnett/Btg	80.00	40.00	25.00
(39)	Gabby Hartnett/Catching	80.00	40.00	25.00
(40)	Billy Herman/Btg (Facing right, name over figure.)	80.00	40.00	25.00
(41)	Billy Herman/Btg (Facing right, name through body.)	80.00	40.00	25.00
(42)	Billy Herman/Btg (Facing left.)	80.00	40.00	25.00
(44)	Roger (Rogers) Hornsby/Btg	100.00	50.00	30.00
(45)	Carl Hubbell/Pitching	90.00	45.00	27.00
(49)	Tony Lazzeri/Throwing	80.00	40.00	25.00
(50)	Hank Leiber/Btg	60.00	30.00	18.00
(52)	Ernie Lombardi/Btg	80.00	40.00	25.00
(54)	Gus Mancuso/Btg	60.00	30.00	18.00
(55)	Heinie Manush/Btg	80.00	40.00	25.00
(56)	Pepper Martin/Btg	75.00	37.50	22.00
(57)	Joe McCarthy/Btg	80.00	40.00	25.00
(58)	Joe Medwick/Btg	80.00	40.00	25.00
(59)	Van Lingle Mungo/Btg	60.00	30.00	18.00
(60)	Van Lingo Mungo (Lingle)/Btg	60.00	30.00	18.00
(64)	Schoolboy Rowe/Btg	60.00	30.00	18.00
(65)	Babe Ruth/Btg	450.00	225.00	135.00
(67)	George Selkirk/Btg	60.00	30.00	18.00
(68)	Luke Sewell/Btg	60.00	30.00	18.00
(69)	Joe Stripp/Btg	60.00	30.00	18.00
(70)	Bill Terry/Btg	80.00	40.00	25.00
(71)	Bill Terry/Fldg	80.00	40.00	25.00
(73)	Pie Traynor/Throwing	80.00	40.00	25.00
(74)	Hal Trosky/Btg	60.00	30.00	18.00
(75)	Floyd Vaughan/Btg	80.00	40.00	25.00
(76)	Joe Vosmik/Throwing	60.00	30.00	18.00
(77)	Paul Waner/Btg	80.00	40.00	25.00
(80)	Lon Warneke/Btg	60.00	30.00	18.00
(81)	Lon Warneke (Wind-up.)	60.00	30.00	18.00
(83)	Jimmy Wilson/Pitching	60.00	30.00	18.00

1936-37 Type 3 - Player's Name, Team Nickname

No player silhouettes are found on this series of pennants. The player name is at right, with his team's nickname at the spine. Despite the fact he left the team in 1934, Babe Ruth's pennant shows him with the Yankees. Gaps have been left in the assigned numbering to accomodate future additions.

No.	Pennant	NM	EX	VG
	Common Pennant:	60.00	30.00	18.00
(1)	Luke Appling (Block letters.)	80.00	40.00	25.00
(2)	Luke Appling (Script)	80.00	40.00	25.00
(4)	Wally Berger	60.00	30.00	18.00
(6)	Zeke Bonura	60.00	30.00	18.00
(7)	Dolph Camilli	60.00	30.00	18.00
(9)	Ben Chapman	60.00	30.00	18.00
(10)	Mickey Cochrane	80.00	40.00	25.00
(11)	Rip Collins	60.00	30.00	18.00
(12)	Joe Cronin	80.00	40.00	25.00
(13)	Kiki Cuyler	80.00	40.00	25.00
(14)	Dizzy Dean	135.00	65.00	40.00
(15)	Frank Demaree	60.00	30.00	18.00
(16)	Paul Derringer	60.00	30.00	18.00
(17)	Bill Dickey	110.00	55.00	35.00
(18)	Joe DiMaggio (Script name.)	300.00	150.00	90.00
(19)	Jimmy Dykes	60.00	30.00	18.00
(20)	Bob Feller (Script name.)	110.00	55.00	35.00
(21)	Wes Ferrell	60.00	30.00	18.00
(22)	Jimmie Foxx	90.00	45.00	27.00
(23)	Larry French	60.00	30.00	18.00
(24)	Franky Frisch	80.00	40.00	25.00
(25)	Lou Gehrig (Script name.)	300.00	150.00	90.00
(26)	Charlie Gehringer	80.00	40.00	25.00
(28)	Lefty Gomez	80.00	40.00	25.00
(29)	Goose Goslin	80.00	40.00	24.00
(30)	Hank Greenberg	90.00	45.00	27.00
(31)	Charley Grimm	60.00	30.00	18.00
(32)	Lefty Grove	90.00	45.00	27.00
(33)	Gabby Hartnett	80.00	40.00	25.00
(35)	Rollie Hemsley	60.00	30.00	18.00
(36)	Billy Herman (Block letters.)	80.00	40.00	25.00
(37)	Billy Herman (Script)	80.00	40.00	25.00
(38)	Frank Higgins	60.00	30.00	18.00
(39)	Roger Hornsby (Rogers)	90.00	45.00	27.00
(40)	Carl Hubbell	80.00	40.00	25.00
(42)	Chuck Klein	80.00	40.00	25.00
(43)	Tony Lazzeri	80.00	40.00	25.00
(44)	Hank Leiber	60.00	30.00	18.00
(45)	Ernie Lombardi	80.00	40.00	25.00
(46)	Al Lopez	80.00	40.00	25.00
(48)	Gus Mancuso	60.00	30.00	18.00
(49)	Heinie Manush	80.00	40.00	25.00
(50)	Pepper Martin	70.00	35.00	20.00
(51)	Joe McCarthy	80.00	40.00	25.00
(52)	Joe Medwick	80.00	40.00	25.00
(53)	Wally Moses	60.00	30.00	18.00
(54)	Van Mungo	60.00	30.00	18.00
(55)	Mel Ott	80.00	40.00	25.00
(56)	Schoolboy Rowe	60.00	30.00	18.00
(57)	Babe Ruth	400.00	200.00	120.00
(58)	George Selkirk	60.00	30.00	18.00
(59)	Luke Sewell	60.00	30.00	18.00
(60)	Al Simmons	80.00	40.00	25.00
(61)	Joe Stripp	60.00	30.00	18.00
(62)	Bill Terry	80.00	40.00	25.00
(63)	Pie Traynor	80.00	40.00	25.00
(64)	Hal Trosky	60.00	30.00	18.00
(65)	Joe Vosmik	60.00	30.00	18.00
(66)	Floyd Vaughan	80.00	40.00	25.00
(67)	Paul Waner	80.00	40.00	25.00
(68)	Lon Warneke	60.00	30.00	18.00
(71)	Jimmy Wilson	60.00	30.00	18.00

1936-37 Type 4 - Team Nickname and Silhouette Player

One of two closely related series of these collectible pennants, this type has a team nickname in combination with a silhouette figure of one or more baseball figures. Collectors should be aware that similar pennants, perhaps even sharing the same designs, were issued circa 1950 in boxes of candy from American Nut & Chocolate of Boston. The AN&C pennants should be distinguishable by their smaller size of approximately 4" x 1-7/8". Gaps in the assigned numbering have been left to accomodate future additions.

No.	Pennant	NM	EX	VG
	Common Pennant:	40.00	20.00	12.00
(1)	Athletics/Fielder	40.00	20.00	12.00
(2)	Browns/Catcher	40.00	20.00	12.00
(3)	Cubs/Batter	40.00	20.00	12.00
(4)	Dodgers/Batter	40.00	20.00	12.00
(5)	Dodgers/Fielder	40.00	20.00	12.00
(7)	Giants (Sliding into base.)	40.00	20.00	12.00
(8)	Giants (Standing at base.)	40.00	20.00	12.00
(9)	Giants (Two players.)	40.00	20.00	12.00
(10)	Phillies/Pitcher	40.00	20.00	12.00
(12)	Reds/Batter	40.00	20.00	12.00
(13)	Reds/Catcher	40.00	20.00	12.00
(14)	Reds/Pitcher	40.00	20.00	12.00
(15)	Red Sox (Batter and catcher.)	40.00	20.00	12.00
(16)	White Sox (Batter left of team name.)	40.00	20.00	12.00
(17)	White Sox (Batter inside "W.")	40.00	20.00	12.00
(18)	White Sox/Catcher	40.00	20.00	12.00
(19)	White Sox (Profile)	40.00	20.00	12.00
(20)	White Sox/Pitcher	40.00	20.00	12.00
(21)	Yankees/Batter	40.00	20.00	12.00
(22)	Yankees/Fielder	40.00	20.00	12.00

1936-37 Type 5 - Team Nickname with Emblem

Closely related to the Type 4 style, these pennants combine a team nickname with a symbolic figure or depictions of baseball equipment. Collectors should be aware that similar pennants, perhaps even sharing the same designs, were issued circa 1950 in boxes of candy from American Nut & Chocolate of Boston. The AN&C pennants should be distinguishable by their smaller size of approximately 4" x 1-7/8". Gaps have been left in the numbering to accomodate future additions.

No.	Pennant	NM	EX	VG
	Common Pennant:	40.00	20.00	12.00
(1)	Athletics (Elephant, no tusks.)	40.00	20.00	12.00
(2)	Athletics (Elephant, w/tusks.)	40.00	20.00	12.00
(3)	Athletics (Gothic script, w/bat, ball.)	40.00	20.00	12.00
(5)	Bees (Bee is crossbar of "B.")	40.00	20.00	12.00
(6)	Bees (Bee is loops of "B.")	40.00	20.00	12.00
(7)	Brooklyn (Crossed bats over "B.")	40.00	20.00	12.00
(9)	Browns/Ball	40.00	20.00	12.00
(10)	Browns/Bat	40.00	20.00	12.00
(11)	Browns (Bat is spine of "B," balls in loops.	40.00	20.00	12.00
(12)	Cardinals (Bat)	40.00	20.00	12.00
(13)	Cardinals (Cardinal inside "C," profile.)	40.00	20.00	12.00
(14)	Cardinals (Cardinal inside "C" front view.)	40.00	20.00	12.00
(15)	Cardinals (Four birds on "C.")	40.00	20.00	12.00
(16)	Cubs (Cub w/bat.)	40.00	20.00	12.00
(17)	Cubs (Cub's head.)	40.00	20.00	12.00
(18)	Cubs (Cub sitting in "C.")	40.00	20.00	12.00
19	Cubs (Full-body profile.)	40.00	20.00	12.00
(20)	Dodgers/Ball	40.00	20.00	12.00
(21)	Dodgers/Ball (Bat and glove.)	40.00	20.00	12.00
(22)	Dodgers (Trolley car.)	40.00	20.00	12.00
(23)	Giants (Crossed bats and ball.)	40.00	20.00	12.00
(25)	Indians (Indians)	40.00	20.00	12.00
(26)	Indians (Indian profile, nine feathers.)	40.00	20.00	12.00
(27)	Indians (Indian profile, headdress.)	40.00	20.00	12.00
(30)	Phillies (Liberty Bell)	40.00	20.00	12.00
(32)	Pirates (Pirate, no knife.)	40.00	20.00	12.00
(33)	Pirates (Pirate w/knife.)	40.00	20.00	12.00
(34)	Pirates (Peg-legged pirate w/sword.)	40.00	20.00	12.00
(35)	Pirates (Skull and crossed bones.)	40.00	20.00	12.00
(36)	Reds (Man with stein.)	40.00	20.00	12.00
(37)	Reds (W/ball.)	40.00	20.00	12.00
(39)	Red Sox/Ball	40.00	20.00	12.00
(40)	Red Sox/Bat	40.00	20.00	12.00
(41)	Red Sox (Ball and bat.)	40.00	20.00	12.00
(42)	Red Sox (Stocking)	40.00	20.00	12.00
(44)	Senators/Bat	40.00	20.00	12.00
(45)	Senators/Cap (Cap. Dome, "S" superimposed.)	40.00	20.00	12.00
(46)	Senators (Capital Dome, "S" to right.)	40.00	20.00	12.00
(47)	Senators (Man's profile in top hat.)	40.00	20.00	12.00
(48)	Sox (W/bat and ball.)	40.00	20.00	12.00
(49)	Tigers (Bat left, ball right.)	40.00	20.00	12.00
(50)	Tigers/Cap	40.00	20.00	12.00
(51)	Tigers (Prowling tiger.)	40.00	20.00	12.00
(52)	Tigers (Tiger head in circle.)	40.00	20.00	12.00
(53)	Tigers (Tiger head, no circle.)	40.00	20.00	12.00

1936-37 Type 6 - Team Name Only

No.	Pennant	NM	EX	VG
	Common Pennant:	40.00	20.00	12.00
(1)	ATHLETICS	40.00	20.00	12.00
(2)	ATHLETICS (PHILA. on spine.)	40.00	20.00	12.00
(3)	BEES	40.00	20.00	12.00
(4)	BEES (BOSTON on spine.)	40.00	20.00	12.00
(5)	CARDINALS	40.00	20.00	12.00
(6)	CUBS	40.00	20.00	12.00
(7)	CUBS (CHICAGO on spine.)	40.00	20.00	12.00
(8)	DODGERS	40.00	20.00	12.00
(9)	DODGERS (BROOKLYN on spine.)	40.00	20.00	12.00
(10)	GIANTS	40.00	20.00	12.00
(11)	GIANTS (NEW YORK on spine.)	40.00	20.00	12.00
(12)	INDIANS	40.00	20.00	12.00
(13)	PHILLIES	40.00	20.00	12.00
(14)	PHILLIES (PHILLIES on spine.)	40.00	20.00	12.00
(15)	PIRATES	40.00	20.00	12.00
(16)	PIRATES (PITTSBURGH on spine.)	40.00	20.00	12.00
(17)	REDS	40.00	20.00	12.00
(18)	REDS (CINCINNATI on spine.)	40.00	20.00	12.00
(19)	SENATORS	40.00	20.00	12.00
(20)	WASH. SENATORS	40.00	20.00	12.00
(21)	SOX	40.00	20.00	12.00
(22)	TIGERS	40.00	20.00	12.00
(23)	WHITE SOX	40.00	20.00	12.00
(24)	YANKEES	40.00	20.00	12.00
(25)	YANKEES (NEW YORK on spine.)	40.00	20.00	12.00

1936 Type 7 - Player, Team w/Pennant, Cap, Ball, Etc.

This group of pennants is slightly longer, at about 5-1/4", than the majority of BF 3 pennants. It is believed that two players from each team will eventually be accounted for.

No.	Pennant	NM	EX	VG
	Common Pennant:	40.00	20.00	12.00
(1)	Luke Appling	55.00	27.00	16.50
(2)	Wally Berger	40.00	20.00	12.00
(3)	Dolph Camilli	40.00	20.00	12.00
(4)	Dizzy Dean	90.00	45.00	27.00
(5)	Frank Demaree	40.00	20.00	12.00
(6)	Joe DiMaggio	200.00	100.00	60.00
(7)	Jimmie Foxx	75.00	37.00	22.00
(8)	Lou Gehrig	200.00	100.00	60.00
(9)	Earl Grace	40.00	20.00	12.00
(10)	Hank Greenberg	75.00	37.00	22.00
(11)	Gabby Hartnett	55.00	27.00	16.50
(12)	Rollie Hemsley	40.00	20.00	12.00
(13)	Carl Hubbell	55.00	27.00	16.50
(14)	Bob Johnson	40.00	20.00	12.00
(15)	Ernie Lombardi	55.00	27.00	16.50
(16)	Al Lopez	55.00	27.00	16.50
(17)	Joe Medwick	55.00	27.00	16.50
(18)	Van Lingle Mungo	45.00	22.00	13.50
(19)	Billy Myers	40.00	20.00	12.00
(20)	Mel Ott	55.00	27.00	16.50
(21)	Frank Pytlak	40.00	20.00	12.00
(23)	Schoolboy Rowe	40.00	20.00	12.00
(25)	Hal Trosky	40.00	20.00	12.00
(28)	Arky Vaughan	55.00	27.00	16.50
(29)	Paul Waner	55.00	27.00	16.50
(30)	Earl Whitehill	40.00	20.00	12.00

1936-37 Type 8 - Misc. Designs

Pennants in this series are generally unique in their style and do not fit into any of the other categories.

		NM	EX	VG
Common Pennant:		60.00	30.00	18.00
(1)	Wes Ferrell ("RED SOX" reversed out of bat on spine.)	60.00	30.00	18.00
(2)	Larry French (Name, team, year on ball.)	60.00	30.00	18.00
(3)	Goose Goslin (Name above and below bat, "TIGERS" on bat.)	75.00	37.50	22.00
(4)	Charley Root (Name above and below bat, "CUBS" on bat.)	60.00	30.00	18.00
(5)	Billy Sullivan ("INDIANS" reversed out of bat on spine.)	60.00	30.00	18.00
(6)	CHAMPIONS/YANKEES/ 1936 (Team name in red triangle at center.)	100.00	50.00	30.00

1937 Type 9 - Player Name, 1937 On Ball, Team Name

Players from only four teams - Bees, Cardinals, Cubs and White Sox - are known in this style. The pennants have a large baseball at left with three panels containing the player's first name, last name and "1937." At right is the team nickname.

		NM	EX	VG
Common Pennant:		60.00	30.00	18.00
(1)	Luke Appling	80.00	40.00	25.00
(2)	Wally Berger	60.00	30.00	18.00
(3)	Zeke Bonura	60.00	30.00	18.00
(4)	Frenchy Bordagaray	60.00	30.00	18.00
(5)	Clint Brown	60.00	30.00	18.00
(6)	Clay Bryant	60.00	30.00	18.00
(7)	Guy Bush	60.00	30.00	18.00
(8)	Sugar Cain	60.00	30.00	18.00
(9)	Tex Carleton	60.00	30.00	18.00
(10)	Phil Cavaretta (Cavarretta)	60.00	30.00	18.00
(11)	Phil Cavarretta	60.00	30.00	18.00
(12)	Irving Cherry	60.00	30.00	18.00
(13)	Ripper Collins	60.00	30.00	18.00
(14)	Tony Cuccinello	60.00	30.00	18.00
(15)	Curt Davis	60.00	30.00	18.00
(16)	Dizzy Dean	135.00	65.00	40.00
(17)	Paul Dean	75.00	37.50	22.00
(18)	Frank Demaree	60.00	30.00	18.00
(19)	Bill Dietrich	60.00	30.00	18.00
(21)	Vinc DiMaggio (Vince)	75.00	37.50	22.00
(22)	Leo Durocher	80.00	40.00	25.00
(23)	Jimmy Dykes	60.00	30.00	18.00
(24)	Burt Fletcher	60.00	30.00	18.00
(25)	Wes Flowers	60.00	30.00	18.00
(26)	Vic Frasier	60.00	30.00	18.00
(27)	Larry French	60.00	30.00	18.00
(28)	Linus Frey	60.00	30.00	18.00
(29)	Frank Frisch	80.00	40.00	25.00
(30)	Augie Galan	60.00	30.00	18.00
(31)	Charlie Grimm	60.00	30.00	18.00
(32)	Geo. Haas	60.00	30.00	18.00
(33)	Stan Hack	70.00	35.00	21.00
(34)	Jessie Haines	80.00	40.00	25.00
(35)	Gabby Hartnett	80.00	40.00	25.00
(36)	Minter Hayes	60.00	30.00	18.00
(37)	Billy Herman	80.00	40.00	25.00
(38)	Walter Highbee (Kirby Higbe)	60.00	30.00	18.00
(39)	Roy Johnson	60.00	30.00	18.00
(41)	Baxter Jordan	60.00	30.00	18.00
(42)	Billy Jurges	60.00	30.00	18.00
(43)	Vernon Kennedy	60.00	30.00	18.00
(44)	Mike Kreevich	60.00	30.00	18.00
(45)	Bill Lee	60.00	30.00	18.00
(46)	Thorn Lee	60.00	30.00	18.00
(47)	Al Lopez	80.00	40.00	25.00
(48)	Andy Lotshaw	60.00	30.00	18.00
(49)	Ted Lyons	80.00	40.00	25.00
(50)	Dan MacFayden	60.00	30.00	18.00
(51)	Henry Majeski	60.00	30.00	18.00
(52)	Pepper Martin	70.00	35.00	20.00
(53)	Stuart Martin	60.00	30.00	18.00
(54)	Joe Marty	60.00	30.00	18.00
(55)	Tommy McBride	60.00	30.00	18.00
(56)	Bill McKechnie	80.00	40.00	25.00
(57)	Joe Medwick	80.00	40.00	25.00
(58)	Steve Mesner	60.00	30.00	18.00
(59)	Hank Meyer	60.00	30.00	18.00
(61)	Johnny Mize	80.00	40.00	25.00
(62)	Gene Moore	60.00	30.00	18.00
(63)	Terry Moore	60.00	30.00	18.00
(64)	Ken O'Dea	60.00	30.00	18.00
(65)	Brusie Ogrodowski	60.00	30.00	18.00
(66)	Tony Piet	60.00	30.00	18.00
(67)	Ray Radcliff	60.00	30.00	18.00
(68)	Bob Reis	60.00	30.00	18.00
(69)	Dunc Rigney	60.00	30.00	18.00
(70)	Les Rock	60.00	30.00	18.00
(71)	Chas. Root	60.00	30.00	18.00
(72)	Larry Rosenthal	60.00	30.00	18.00
(73)	Luke Sewell	60.00	30.00	18.00
(74)	Merv Shea	60.00	30.00	18.00
(75)	Tuck Stainback	60.00	30.00	18.00
(76)	Hank Steinbacher	60.00	30.00	18.00
(77)	Monty Stratton	70.00	35.00	20.00
(78)	Ken Sylvestri	60.00	30.00	18.00
(79)	Billie Urbanski	60.00	30.00	18.00
(81)	Fred Walker	60.00	30.00	18.00
(82)	Lon Warneke	60.00	30.00	18.00
(83)	Johnnie Whitehead	60.00	30.00	18.00

1938 Type 10 - Player Name, 1938 On Ball, Team Name

Identical in format to the 1937 version, these pennants feature only members of the Detroit Tigers. The player's first name, last name and "1938" are stacked on the panels of a large baseball design at left, while "TIGERS" is at right.

		NM	EX	VG
Common Pennant:		60.00	30.00	18.00
(1)	Harry Eisenstat	60.00	30.00	18.00
(2)	Pete Fox	60.00	30.00	18.00
(3)	Vern Kennedy	60.00	30.00	18.00
(4)	Roxie Lawson	60.00	30.00	18.00
(5)	Tony Piet	60.00	30.00	18.00
(6)	Rudy York	60.00	30.00	18.00

1936-37 Type 11 - Minor League and Team

Minor league team nicknames and a league designation are combined with a player figure or symbol in this series. The checklist is believed complete with eight teams each from the Southern Association, International League and American Association.

		NM	EX	VG
Complete Set (24):		950.00	475.00	275.00
Common Pennant:		40.00	20.00	12.00
(1)	Barons - Southern	40.00	20.00	12.00
(2)	Bears - International	40.00	20.00	12.00
(3)	Bisons - International	40.00	20.00	12.00
(4)	Blues - Amer. Assn.	40.00	20.00	12.00
(5)	Brewers - Amer. Assn.	40.00	20.00	12.00
(6)	Chicks - Southern	40.00	20.00	12.00
(7)	Chiefs - International	40.00	20.00	12.00
(8)	Colonels - Amer. Assn.	40.00	20.00	12.00
(9)	Crackers - Sou'n. Ass'n.	40.00	20.00	12.00
(10)	Giants - International	40.00	20.00	12.00
(11)	Indians - Amer. Assn.	40.00	20.00	12.00
(12)	Lookouts - Sou'n. Ass'n.	40.00	20.00	12.00
(13)	Maple Leafs - International	40.00	20.00	12.00
(14)	Millers - Amer. Assn.	40.00	20.00	12.00
(15)	Mud Hens - Amer. Assn.	40.00	20.00	12.00
(16)	Orioles - International	40.00	20.00	12.00
(17)	Pelicans - Sou'n. Ass'n.	40.00	20.00	12.00
(18)	Red Birds - Amer. Assn.	40.00	20.00	12.00
(19)	Red Wings - Int'l	40.00	20.00	12.00
(20)	Royals - Int'l	40.00	20.00	12.00
(21)	Saints - Amer. Assn.	40.00	20.00	12.00
(22)	Smokies - Southern	40.00	20.00	12.00
(23)	Travelers - Sou'n. Ass'n.	40.00	20.00	12.00
(24)	Vols - Sou'n Ass'n.	40.00	20.00	12.00

1936-37 Type 12 - Jumbo Teams

According to advertising on the Red Ball Gum packaging with which most types of the Bf3 felt pennants were sold, jumbo size - about 28-1/2" x 11" - versions of 16 team pennants could be had by redeeming 25 wrappers and 15 cents for each desired pennant. The large-format pennants are identical in design to some of the smaller pieces from Types 4, 5 and 8.

		NM	EX	VG
Complete Set (16):				
Common Pennant:		300.00	150.00	90.00
(1)	Boston Bees	300.00	150.00	90.00
(2)	Boston Red Sox	300.00	150.00	90.00
(3)	Brooklyn Dodgers	300.00	150.00	90.00
(4)	Chicago Cubs	300.00	150.00	90.00
(5)	Chicago White Sox	300.00	150.00	90.00
(6)	Cincinnati Reds	300.00	150.00	90.00
(7)	Cleveland Indians	300.00	150.00	90.00
(8)	Detroit Tigers	300.00	150.00	90.00
(9)	New York Giants	300.00	150.00	90.00
(10)	New York Yankees	400.00	200.00	120.00
(11)	Philadelphia Athletics	300.00	150.00	90.00
(12)	Philadelphia Phillies	300.00	150.00	90.00
(13)	Pittsburgh Pirates	300.00	150.00	90.00
(14)	St. Louis Browns	300.00	150.00	90.00
(15)	St. Louis Cardinals	300.00	150.00	90.00
(16)	Washington Senators	300.00	150.00	90.00

1937 BF104 Blankets

A throwback to the 1914 B18 blankets, little is known about these 3-1/2"-square felts. They were designated as BF104 in the American Card Catalog. The issuer and manner of distribution remain a mystery. Subjects are depicted in either portrait or action artwork. This checklist likely is not complete.

		NM	EX	VG
Common Player:		300.00	150.00	90.00
(1)	Moe Berg	500.00	250.00	150.00
(2)	Cy Blanton	300.00	150.00	90.00
(3)	Earle Brucker	300.00	150.00	90.00
(4)	Mickey Cochrane	600.00	300.00	180.00
(5)	Joe Cronin	600.00	300.00	180.00
(6)	Tony Cuccinello	300.00	150.00	90.00
(7)	Dizzy Dean	1,200	600.00	360.00
(8)	Frank Demaree	300.00	150.00	90.00
(9)	Jimmie Foxx	900.00	450.00	275.00
(10)	Larry French	300.00	150.00	90.00
(11)	Frankie Frisch	600.00	300.00	180.00
(12)	Hank Greenberg	1,000	500.00	300.00
(13)	Gabby Hartnett	600.00	300.00	180.00
(14)	Billy Herman	600.00	300.00	180.00
(15)	Woody Jensen	300.00	150.00	90.00
(16)	Billy Jurges	300.00	150.00	90.00
(17)	Harry Kelly (Kelley)	300.00	150.00	90.00
(18)	Thornton Lee	300.00	150.00	90.00
(19)	Danny MacFayden	300.00	150.00	90.00
(20)	Connie Mack	600.00	300.00	180.00
(21)	Stu Martin	300.00	150.00	90.00
(22)	Joe Medwick	600.00	300.00	180.00
(23)	Ray Mueller	300.00	150.00	90.00
(24)	L. Newsome	300.00	150.00	90.00
(25)	Monty Stratton	405.00	200.00	120.00
(26)	Pie Traynor	600.00	300.00	180.00
(27)	Jim Turner	300.00	150.00	90.00
(28)	Bill Werber	300.00	150.00	90.00
(29)	Jack Wilson	300.00	150.00	90.00
(30)	Rudy York	300.00	150.00	90.00

C

1909 Cabanas

In conjunction with a post-season visit by the A.L. Champion Detroit Tigers (who without Hall of Famer Ty Cobb and Sam Crawford won only four of 12 games from the locals), Cabanas brand cigarettes issued this set. About 1-1/2" x 2-1/4" the cards feature black-and-white portrait photos. Players from the Almendares team have a blue frame and some colorized blue details on their uniforms, Havana players are in red, the Tigers are in gray. Printed on backs of the cards

CABAÑAS
LA MEJOR MANERA DE FORMAR UNA PRECIOSA COLECCION DE LOS JUGADORES DE BASE BALL DE LOS CLUBS CUBANOS Y EXTRANJEROS, QUE NOS VISITEN, ES FUMANDO LOS AFAMADOS CIGARROS DE
CABAÑAS

is (roughly translated) "The best way to form a valuable collection of baseball players of the Cuban clubs and the foreign visitors is to smoke Cabanas." It is unknown whether the checklists presented here alphabetically are complete.

		NM	EX	VG
Common Cuban Player:		600.00	300.00	175.00
Common Tigers Player:		900.00	450.00	275.00
	ALMENDARES B.B.C.			
(1)	Rafael Almeida	700.00	350.00	210.00
(2)	Armando Cabanas	700.00	350.00	210.00
(3)	Alfredo Cabrera	600.00	300.00	175.00
(4)	Regino "Mamelo" Garcia	1,150	575.00	345.00
(5a)	Heliodoro Hidalgo (C.F.)	1,150	575.00	345.00
(5b)	Heliodoro Hidalgo (C.F. Jabuco)	1,150	575.00	345.00
(6)	Armando Marsans	700.00	350.00	210.00
(7)	Esteban Prats	600.00	300.00	175.00
(8)	Carlos "Bebe" Royer	700.00	350.00	210.00
	HABANA B.B.C.			
(1)	Luis Bustamante	2,250	1,125	675.00
(2)	Luis "Chico" Gonzalez	600.00	300.00	175.00
(3)	Valentin "Sirique" Gonzalez	600.00	300.00	175.00
(4)	Ricardo Hernandez	600.00	300.00	175.00
(5)	Preston "Pete" Hill (Value Undetermined)			
(6)	Angel D. Mesa	600.00	300.00	175.00
(7)	Augustin "Tinti" Molina	700.00	350.00	210.00
(8)	Carlos "Chino" Moran	600.00	300.00	175.00
(9)	Luis "Mulo" Padron	3,500	1,750	1,050
(10)	Elilio Palomino	600.00	300.00	175.00
(11)	Pastor H. Pareda	600.00	300.00	180.00
(12)	Agustin Parpetti	2,000	1,000	600.00
(13)	Inocencio Perez	600.00	300.00	175.00
(14)	Bruce Petway	7,500	3,750	2,250
(15)	Gonzalo Sanchez	600.00	300.00	175.00
	DETROIT TIGERS			
(1)	C. Beckendorff (Beckendorf)	900.00	450.00	275.00
(2)	Owen (Donie) Bush	900.00	450.00	275.00
(3)	Hopke	900.00	450.00	275.00
(4)	David Jones	900.00	450.00	275.00
(5)	William Lelivelt	900.00	450.00	275.00
(6)	Matty Mc. Intyre	900.00	450.00	275.00
(7)	George Moriarty	900.00	450.00	275.00
(8)	George Mullin	900.00	450.00	275.00
(9)	Frank O'Laughlin/Umpire (O'Loughlin)	1,200	600.00	360.00
(10)	Charles O'Leary	900.00	450.00	275.00
(11)	Charles Schmidt	900.00	450.00	275.00
(12)	Edgar Willetts (Willett)	900.00	450.00	275.00

1955 Cain's Jimmy Piersall

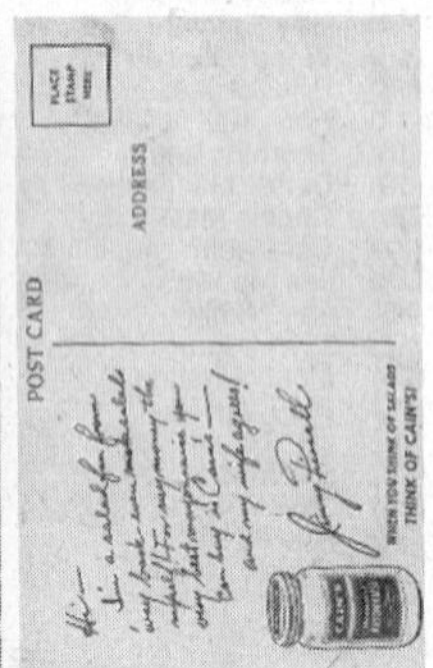

The date of issue is speculative for these promotional postcards. The borderless black-and-white photo on the front of the 3-1/2" x 5-1/2" cards shows the popular BoSox star in a fielding pose. A blue facsimile autograph is printed at top. The postcard-format back has a drawing of the product beneath an advertising message bearing Piersall's signature. Similar cards advertising Colonial Meats are also known.

	NM	EX	VG
Autographed:	125.00	65.00	35.00
Jimmy Piersall (Mayonnaise)	80.00	40.00	24.00
Jimmy Piersall (Potato chips.)	80.00	40.00	24.00
Jimmy Piersall (Riviera dressing.)	80.00	40.00	24.00

1965 California Angels Matchbook Covers

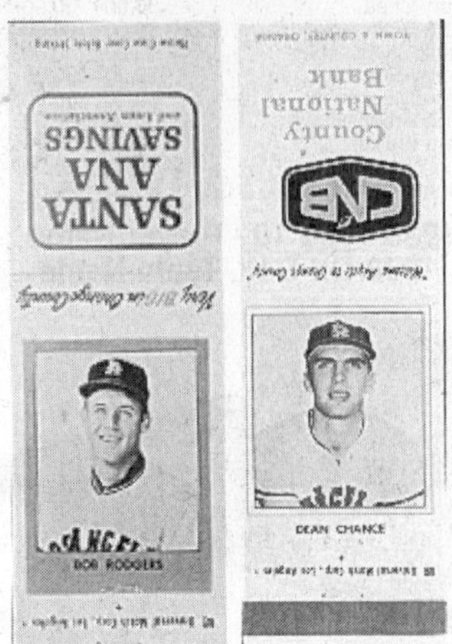

These 1-1/2" x 4-1/2" matchbooks can be found with the advertising of two different banks printed on them; both are products of the local Universal Match Corp., and are printed in black and gold on white on front, with the inside surface in black-and-white. The County National Bank version has the player portrait photo within a plain black frame. Inside, the CNB matchbooks have player identification and personal data and 1964 stats. There is also an offer to redeem 15 different players' matchbooks for two free game tickets. The Santa Ana Savings matchbooks have the same player information and ads for the bank and the Angels' radio station. The player photos on front of the Santa Ana matchbooks have a gold frame. Values shown are for complete but empty covers, with the striker surface intact. Complete matchbooks with matches bring about 2X the values quoted.

		NM	EX	VG
Complete Set (15):		120.00	60.00	35.00
Common Player:		10.00	5.00	3.00
(1)	Dean Chance	12.50	6.25	3.75
(2)	Lu Clinton	10.00	5.00	3.00
(3)	Jim Fregosi	10.00	5.00	3.00
(4)	Ed Kirkpatrick	10.00	5.00	3.00
(5)	Bobby Knoop	10.00	5.00	3.00
(6)	Barry Latman	10.00	5.00	3.00
(7)	Bob Lee	10.00	5.00	3.00
(8)	Ken McBride	10.00	5.00	3.00
(9)	Fred Newman	10.00	5.00	3.00
(10)	Jimmy Piersall	20.00	10.00	6.00
(11)	Rick Reichardt	10.00	5.00	3.00
(12)	Bill Rigney	10.00	5.00	3.00
(13)	Bob Rodgers	10.00	5.00	3.00
(14)	Tom Satriano	10.00	5.00	3.00
(15)	Willie Smith	10.00	5.00	3.00

1976 California Pacific Bank

Whether these are a legitimate promotional issue or a made-for-collectors set is unknown. The cards may have been created for use at autograph appearances at a Fullerton, Calif., bank. About 3-5/8" x 5", though the size varies, the black-and-white blank-back cards have player photos on front (some of which are reproductions of team-issued photos) and a promotional message describing the bank's "Big League Service." Two poses of Steve Carlton are known.

		NM	EX	VG
Complete Set (7):		60.00	30.00	18.00
Common Player:		5.00	2.50	1.50
(1)	Steve Busby	5.00	2.50	1.50
(2)	Steve Carlton	15.00	7.50	4.50
(3)	Steve Carlton	15.00	7.50	4.50
(4)	Bill Russell	5.00	2.50	1.50
(5)	Mike Schmidt	20.00	10.00	6.00
(6)	Ted Simmons	5.00	2.50	1.50
(7)	Don Sutton	10.00	5.00	3.00

1950 Callahan Hall of Fame

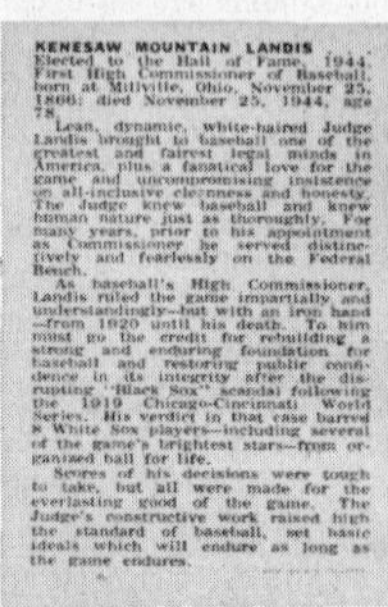

KENESAW MOUNTAIN LANDIS
Elected to the Hall of Fame, 1944. First High Commissioner of Baseball, born at Millville, Ohio, November 20, 1866; died November 25, 1944, age 78.

Lean, dynamic, white-haired Judge Landis brought to baseball one of the greatest and fairest legal minds in America, plus a fanatical love for the game and uncompromising insistence on all-inclusive cleanness and honesty. The Judge knew baseball and knew human nature just as thoroughly. For many years, prior to his appointment as Commissioner he served distinctively and fearlessly on the Federal Bench.

As baseball's High Commissioner, Landis ruled the game impartially and understandingly—but with an iron hand—from 1920 until his death. To him must go the credit for rebuilding a strong and enduring foundation for baseball and restoring public confidence in its integrity after the disrupting "Black Sox" scandal following the 1919 Chicago-Cincinnati World Series. His verdict in that case barred 8 White Sox players—including several of the game's brightest stars—from organized ball for life.

Scores of his decisions were tough to take, but all were made for the everlasting good of the game. The Judge's constructive work raised high the standard of baseball, set basic ideals which will endure as long as the game endures.

These cards, which feature artist Mario DeMarco's drawings of Hall of Famers, were produced from 1950 through 1956 and sold by the Baseball Hall of Fame in Cooperstown and at major league ballparks. The cards measure 1-3/4" x 2-1/2" and include a detailed player biography on the back. When introduced in 1950 the set included all members of the Hall of Fame up to that time, and then new cards were added each year as more players were elected. Therefore, cards of players appearing in all previous editions are more common than those players who appeared in just one or two years. When the set was discontinued in 1956 it consisted of 82 cards, which is now considered a complete set. The cards are not numbered and are listed here alphabetically. B.E. Callahan of Chicago, the publisher of "Who's Who in Baseball," produced the card set.

		NM	EX	VG
Original 1950 Boxed Set (62):		500.00	250.00	150.00
Complete Set (82):		1,900	950.00	575.00
Common Player:		6.00	3.00	1.75
(1)	Grover Alexander	25.00	12.50	7.50
(2)	"Cap" Anson	15.00	7.50	4.50
(3)	J. Franklin "Home Run" Baker	150.00	75.00	45.00
(4)	Edward G. Barrow	35.00	17.50	10.00
(5a)	Charles "Chief" Bender (Bio ends ". . . immortal name for him.")	25.00	12.50	7.50
(5b)	Charles "Chief" Bender (Bio ends ". . . died in 1954.")	35.00	17.50	10.00
(6)	Roger Bresnahan	10.00	5.00	3.00
(7)	Dan Brouthers	15.00	7.50	4.50
(8)	Mordecai Brown	10.00	5.00	3.00
(9)	Morgan G. Bulkeley	10.00	5.00	3.00
(10)	Jesse Burkett	16.00	8.00	4.75
(11)	Alexander Cartwright	12.50	6.25	3.75
(12)	Henry Chadwick	12.00	6.00	3.50
(13)	Frank Chance	16.00	8.00	4.75
(14)	Albert B. Chandler	350.00	175.00	100.00
(15)	Jack Chesbro	7.50	3.75	2.25
(16)	Fred Clarke	10.00	5.00	3.00
(17)	Ty Cobb	50.00	25.00	15.00
(18a)	Mickey Cochran (Name incorrect.)	10.00	5.00	3.00
(18b)	Mickey Cochrane (Name correct.)	12.00	6.00	3.50
(19a)	Eddie Collins (Second paragraph of bio begins "Eddie had every . . . ")	9.00	4.50	2.75
(19b)	Eddie Collins (Second paragraph of bio begins "He was brilliant . . . ")	13.50	6.75	4.00
(20)	Jimmie Collins	12.50	6.25	3.75
(21)	Charles A. Comiskey	12.50	6.25	3.75
(22)	Tom Connolly	50.00	25.00	15.00
(23)	Candy Cummings	9.00	4.50	2.75
(24)	Dizzy Dean	45.00	22.50	13.50
(25)	Ed Delahanty	6.00	3.00	1.75
(26a)	Bill Dickey (First paragraph of bio ends ". . . He was right-handed all the way.")	30.00	15.00	9.00
(26b)	Bill Dickey (First paragraph of bio ends ". . . during his final year.")	35.00	17.50	10.50
(27)	Joe DiMaggio	180.00	90.00	54.00
(28)	Hugh Duffy	7.50	3.75	2.25
(29)	Johnny Evers	13.50	6.75	4.00
(30)	Buck Ewing	10.00	5.00	3.00
(31)	Jimmie Foxx	20.00	10.00	6.00
(32)	Frank Frisch	6.00	3.00	1.75
(33)	Lou Gehrig	85.00	42.50	25.00
(34a)	Charles Gehringer (White cap.)	9.00	4.50	2.75
(34b)	Charlie Gehringer (Dark cap.)	11.00	5.50	3.25
(35)	Clark Griffith	6.00	3.00	1.75
(36)	Lefty Grove	10.00	5.00	3.00
(37)	Leo "Gabby" Hartnett	40.00	20.00	12.00
(38)	Harry Heilmann	25.00	12.50	7.50
(39)	Rogers Hornsby	16.00	8.00	4.75
(40)	Carl Hubbell	12.00	6.00	3.50
(41)	Hughey Jennings	6.00	3.00	1.75
(42)	Ban Johnson	7.50	3.75	2.25
(43)	Walter Johnson	10.00	5.00	3.00
(44)	Willie Keeler	7.50	3.75	2.25
(45)	Mike Kelly	10.00	5.00	3.00
(46)	Bill Klem	65.00	32.50	20.00
(47)	Napoleon Lajoie	11.00	5.50	3.25
(48)	Kenesaw M. Landis	6.00	3.00	1.75
(49)	Ted Lyons	100.00	50.00	30.00
(50)	Connie Mack	12.00	6.00	3.50
(51)	Walter Maranville	20.00	10.00	6.00
(52)	Christy Mathewson	10.00	5.00	3.00
(53)	Tommy McCarthy	12.50	6.25	3.75

#	Player	NM	EX	VG
(54)	Joe McGinnity	6.00	3.00	1.75
(55)	John McGraw	10.00	5.00	3.00
(56)	Charles Nichols	16.00	8.00	4.75
(57)	Jim O'Rourke	9.00	4.50	2.75
(58)	Mel Ott	16.00	8.00	4.75
(59)	Herb Pennock	9.00	4.50	2.75
(60)	Eddie Plank	10.00	5.00	3.00
(61)	Charles Radbourne	10.00	5.00	3.00
(62)	Wilbert Robinson	6.00	3.00	1.75
(63)	Babe Ruth	90.00	45.00	27.50
(64)	Ray "Cracker" Schalk	30.00	15.00	9.00
(65)	Al Simmons	60.00	30.00	18.00
(66a)	George Sisler (Bio ends "Sisler today is . . .")	13.50	6.75	4.00
(66b)	George Sisler (Bio ends "Sisler was chosen as . . .")	9.00	4.50	2.75
(67)	A. G. Spalding	10.00	5.00	3.00
(68)	Tris Speaker	16.00	8.00	4.75
(69)	Bill Terry	30.00	15.00	9.00
(70)	Joe Tinker	10.00	5.00	3.00
(71)	"Pie" Traynor	10.00	5.00	3.00
(72)	Clarence A. "Dazzy" Vance	30.00	15.00	9.00
(73)	Rube Waddell	9.00	4.50	2.75
(74)	Hans Wagner	30.00	15.00	9.00
(75)	Bobby Wallace	13.50	6.75	4.00
(76)	Ed Walsh	10.00	5.00	3.00
(77a)	Paul Waner (Complete black frame line around picture.)	9.00	4.50	2.75
(77b)	Paul Waner (Bottom missing on black frame line around picture.)	40.00	20.00	12.00
(78)	George Wright	7.50	3.75	2.25
(79)	Harry Wright	20.00	10.00	6.00
(80)	Cy Young	12.50	6.25	3.75
(---)	Museum Exterior View (No date at top of list on back.)	35.00	17.50	10.00
(---)	Museum Exterior View (Date "1954" on top of list on back.)	60.00	30.00	18.00
(---)	Museum Interior View (Back copy ends, ". . . to all baseball men.")	30.00	15.00	9.00
(---)	Museum Interior View (Back copy ends ". . . playing days are concluded.")	13.50	6.75	4.00

1898 Cameo Pepsin Gum Pins

The first large set of baseball player pins is this issue from Whitehead & Hoag, advertising Cameo Pepsin Gum. The 1-1/4" pins have a sepia player portrait photo at center, with name and team at top left and right. It is very difficult to find pins with clear pictures as they tend to darken or fade with time. Pins were issued with a paper inset in back advertising the gum, but are often found with the paper missing. It is likely that there will be future additions to this checklist. The unnumbered pins are presented here in alphabetical order.

#	Player	NM	EX	VG
	Common Player:	1,050	525.00	325.00
(1)	John Anderson	1,050	525.00	325.00
(2)	Cap Anson	3,300	1,300	800.00
(3)	Jimmy Bannon	1,050	525.00	325.00
(4)	Billy Barnie	1,050	525.00	325.00
(5)	Marty Bergen	1,050	525.00	325.00
(6)	Beville (Indianapolis)	1,050	525.00	325.00
(7)	Louis Bierbauer	1,050	525.00	325.00
(8)	Frank Bowerman	1,050	525.00	325.00
(9)	Ted Breitenstein	1,050	525.00	325.00
(10)	Herbert Briggs	1,050	525.00	325.00
(11)	Richard Brown	1,050	525.00	325.00
(12)	Eddie Burk (Burke)	1,050	525.00	325.00
(13)	Jesse Burkett	3,300	1,300	800.00
(14)	Frank "Buster" Burrell	1,050	525.00	325.00
(15)	Jimmy Canavan	1,050	525.00	325.00
(16)	William Clark (Clarke)	1,050	525.00	325.00
(17)	Jack Clements	1,050	525.00	325.00
(18)	Jimmy Collins	2,850	1,300	800.00
(19)	Tommy Corcoran	1,050	525.00	325.00
(20)	Corkman (Indianapolis)	1,050	525.00	325.00
(21)	Lave Cross	1,050	525.00	325.00
(22)	Nig Cuppy	1,050	525.00	325.00
(23)	Bill Dahlen	1,050	525.00	325.00
(24)	Bill Dammon (Dammann)	1,050	525.00	325.00
(25)	Dan Daub	1,050	525.00	325.00
(26)	George Decker	1,050	525.00	325.00
(27)	Ed Delahanty	3,300	1,300	800.00
(28)	Cozy Dolan	1,050	525.00	325.00
(29)	Tim Donahue	1,050	525.00	325.00
(30)	Patsy Donovan	1,050	525.00	325.00
(31)	Donnelly (Cedar Rapids)	1,050	525.00	325.00
(32)	Hugh Duffy	2,850	1,300	800.00
(33)	Jack Dunn	1,050	525.00	325.00
(34)	Frank Dwyer	1,050	525.00	325.00
(35)	Bones Ely	1,050	525.00	325.00
(36)	Everett	1,050	525.00	325.00
(37)	Buck Ewing	3,300	1,650	1,000
(38)	Fields (Buffalo)	1,050	525.00	325.00
(39)	Tim Flood	1,050	525.00	325.00
(40)	Foreman (Indianapolis)	1,050	525.00	325.00
(41)	Charlie Ganzel	1,050	525.00	325.00
(42)	Jot Goar (Pittsburgh)	1,050	525.00	325.00
(43)	Jot Goar (Indianapolis)	1,050	525.00	325.00
(44)	Gray (Indianapolis)	1,050	525.00	325.00
(45)	Mike Griffin	1,050	525.00	325.00
(46)	Clark Griffith	2,650	1,300	800.00
(47)	John Grim	1,050	525.00	325.00
(48)	Billy Hamilton	2,750	1,375	825.00
(49)	Bill Hart	1,050	525.00	325.00
(50)	Charles Hastings	1,050	525.00	325.00
(51)	Pink Hawley	1,050	525.00	325.00
(52)	B. Hill (Cedar Rapids)	1,050	525.00	325.00
(53)	Bill Hoffer	1,050	525.00	325.00
(54)	George Hogriever (Indianapolis)	1,050	525.00	325.00
(55)	Bug Holliday	1,050	525.00	325.00
(56)	Horton (Baltimore)	1,050	525.00	325.00
(57)	Dummy Hoy	2,450	1,550	900.00
(58)	Jim Hughey	1,050	525.00	325.00
(59)	Charlie Irwin	1,050	525.00	325.00
(60)	Hughie Jennings	2,650	1,300	800.00
(61)	Willie Keeler	2,650	1,300	800.00
(62)	Kennedy (Cedar Rapids)	1,050	525.00	325.00
(63)	Frank Killen	1,050	525.00	325.00
(64)	Malachi Kittredge	1,050	525.00	325.00
(65)	Candy LaChance	1,050	525.00	325.00
(66)	Bill Lange	1,050	525.00	325.00
(67)	Herman Long	1,050	525.00	325.00
(68)	Bobby Lowe	1,050	525.00	325.00
(69)	Denny Lyons	1,050	525.00	325.00
(70)	Connie Mack	3,300	1,300	800.00
(71)	Willard Mains	1,050	525.00	325.00
(72)	Barry McCormick	1,050	525.00	325.00
(73)	Chippy McGarr	1,050	525.00	325.00
(74)	John McGraw	1,750	1,100	650.00
(75)	Sadie McMann (McMahon)	1,050	525.00	325.00
(76)	Bid McPhee	4,200	2,450	1,100
(77)	Bill Merritt	1,050	525.00	325.00
(78)	Dusty Miller	1,050	525.00	325.00
(79)	Motz (Indianapolis)	1,050	525.00	325.00
(80)	Kid Nichols	2,750	1,375	825.00
(81)	Jack O'Connor	1,050	525.00	325.00
(82)	John Pappaulan (Pappalau) (Pitcher, not R.F.)	1,050	525.00	325.00
(83)	Harley Payne	1,050	525.00	325.00
(84)	Heinie Peitz	1,050	525.00	325.00
(85)	Phillips (Indianapolis)	1,050	525.00	325.00
(86)	Arlie Pond	1,050	525.00	325.00
(87)	Jack Powell	1,050	525.00	325.00
(88)	Bill Reidy	1,050	525.00	325.00
(89)	Heinie Reitz	1,050	525.00	325.00
(90)	Billy Rhines	1,050	525.00	325.00
(91)	Claude Richie (Ritchey)	1,050	525.00	325.00
(92)	Rowe (Buffalo)	1,050	525.00	325.00
(93)	John Ryan	1,050	525.00	325.00
(94)	Pop Schreiver (Schriver)	1,050	525.00	325.00
(95)	Bill Shindle	1,050	525.00	325.00
(96)	Broadway Aleck Smith	1,050	525.00	325.00
(97)	Elmer Smith (Pittsburg)	1,050	525.00	325.00
(98)	Germany Smith	1,050	525.00	325.00
(99)	Louis Sockalexis	2,000	1,300	650.00
(100)	Speer (Milwaukee)	1,050	525.00	325.00
(101)	Jake Stenzel	1,050	525.00	325.00
(102)	Joe Sugden	1,050	525.00	325.00
(103)	Jim Sullivan	1,050	525.00	325.00
(104)	Patsy Tebeau	1,050	525.00	325.00
(105)	Fred Tenney	1,050	525.00	325.00
(106)	Adonis Terry	1,050	525.00	325.00
(107)	Tucker (Boston)	1,050	525.00	325.00
(108)	Urquhart (Buffalo)	1,050	525.00	325.00
(109)	Farmer Vaughn	1,050	525.00	325.00
(110)	Bobby Wallace	2,650	1,300	800.00
(111)	Watkins (Indianapolis)	1,050	525.00	325.00
(112)	Weaver (Milwaukee)	1,050	525.00	325.00
(113)	Wood (Indianapolis)	1,050	525.00	325.00
(114)	Cy Young	4,400	2,200	1,300
(115)	Chief Zimmer	1,300	625.00	400.00
(116)	1897 Brooklyn Team	1,400	700.00	400.00
(117)	1897 Buffalo Team	1,400	700.00	400.00
(118)	1897 Indianapolis Team	1,400	700.00	400.00
(119)	1897 Pittsburgh Team	1,400	700.00	400.00
(120)	1897 Toronto Team	1,400	700.00	400.00

1958 Roy Campanella Career Summary Card

This card was probably produced to allow Campy to respond to fan mail following his career-ending auto wreck in 1957. The 3-1/8" x 5" card is printed in black-and-white on thin semi-gloss cardboard. Front has a portrait photo and facsimile autograph, with a white stripe at top and bottom. The back has a career statistical summary, apparently taken from a contemporary Baseball Register.

	NM	EX	VG
Roy Campanella	20.00	10.00	6.00

1974 Capital Publishing Co.

This ambitious collectors issue offered more than 100 cards of "old-timers" in an attractive 4-1/8" x 5-1/4" format. Card fronts have black-and-white photos with white borders all-around. Backs have player identification, biographical data and major league stats.

#	Player	NM	EX	VG
	Complete Set (104):	200.00	100.00	60.00
	Common Player:	6.00	3.00	1.75
1	Babe Ruth	15.00	7.50	4.50
2	Lou Gehrig	10.00	5.00	3.00
3	Ty Cobb	9.00	4.50	2.75
4	Jackie Robinson	7.50	3.75	2.25
5	Roger Connor	6.00	3.00	1.75
6	Harry Heilmann	6.00	3.00	1.75
7	Clark Griffith	6.00	3.00	1.75
8	Ed Walsh	6.00	3.00	1.75
9	Hugh Duffy	6.00	3.00	1.75
10	Russ Christopher	6.00	3.00	1.75
11	Snuffy Stirnweiss	6.00	3.00	1.75
12	Willie Keeler	6.00	3.00	1.75
13	Buck Ewing	6.00	3.00	1.75
14	Tony Lazzeri	6.00	3.00	1.75
15	King Kelly	6.00	3.00	1.75
16	Jimmy McAleer	6.00	3.00	1.75
17	Frank Chance	6.00	3.00	1.75
18	Sam Zoldak	6.00	3.00	1.75
19	Christy Mathewson	7.50	3.75	2.25
20	Eddie Collins	6.00	3.00	1.75
21	Cap Anson	6.00	3.00	1.75
22	Steve Evans	6.00	3.00	1.75
23	Mordecai Brown	6.00	3.00	1.75
24	Don Black	6.00	3.00	1.75
25	Home Run Baker	6.00	3.00	1.75
26	Jack Chesbro	6.00	3.00	1.75
27	Gil Hodges	6.00	3.00	1.75
28	Dan Brouthers	6.00	3.00	1.75
29	Don Hoak	6.00	3.00	1.75
30	Herb Pennock	6.00	3.00	1.75
31	Vern Stephens	6.00	3.00	1.75
32	Cy Young	7.50	3.75	2.25
33	Ed Cicotte	7.50	3.75	2.25
34	Sam Jones	6.00	3.00	1.75
35	Ed Waitkus	6.00	3.00	1.75
36	Roger Bresnahan	6.00	3.00	1.75
37	Fred Merkle	6.00	3.00	1.75
38	Ed Delehanty (Delahanty)	6.00	3.00	1.75
39	Tris Speaker	6.00	3.00	1.75
40	Fred Clarke	6.00	3.00	1.75
41	Johnny Evers	6.00	3.00	1.75
42	Mickey Cochrane	6.00	3.00	1.75
43	Nap Lajoie	6.00	3.00	1.75
44	Charles Comiskey	6.00	3.00	1.75
45	Sam Crawford	6.00	3.00	1.75
46	Ban Johnson	6.00	3.00	1.75
47	Ray Schalk	6.00	3.00	1.75
48	Pat Moran	6.00	3.00	1.75
49	Walt Judnich	6.00	3.00	1.75
50	Bill Killefer	6.00	3.00	1.75
51	Jimmie Foxx	6.00	3.00	1.75
52	Red Rolfe	6.00	3.00	1.75
53	Howie Pollett	6.00	3.00	1.75
54	Wally Pipp	6.00	3.00	1.75
55	Chief Bender	6.00	3.00	1.75
56	Connie Mack	6.00	3.00	1.75
57	Bump Hadley	6.00	3.00	1.75
58	Al Simmons	6.00	3.00	1.75
59	Hughie Jennings	6.00	3.00	1.75
60	Johnny Allen	6.00	3.00	1.75
61	Fred Snodgrass	6.00	3.00	1.75
62	Heinie Manush	6.00	3.00	1.75
63	Dazzy Vance	6.00	3.00	1.75
64	George Sisler	6.00	3.00	1.75
65	Jim Bottomley	6.00	3.00	1.75
66	Ray Chapman	6.00	3.00	1.75
67	Hal Chase	6.00	3.00	1.75
68	Jack Barry	6.00	3.00	1.75
69	George Burns	6.00	3.00	1.75
70	Jim Barrett	6.00	3.00	1.75
71	Grover Alexander	6.00	3.00	1.75
72	Elmer Flick	6.00	3.00	1.75
73	Jake Flowers	6.00	3.00	1.75
74	Al Orth	6.00	3.00	1.75
75	Cliff Aberson	6.00	3.00	1.75
76	Moe Berg	7.50	3.75	2.25
77	Bill Bradley	6.00	3.00	1.75
78	Max Bishop	6.00	3.00	1.75
79	Jimmy Austin	6.00	3.00	1.75
80	Beals Becker	6.00	3.00	1.75
81	Jack Clements	6.00	3.00	1.75
82	Cy Blanton	6.00	3.00	1.75
83	Garland Braxton	6.00	3.00	1.75
84	Red Ames	6.00	3.00	1.75
85	Hippo Vaughn	6.00	3.00	1.75
86	Ray Caldwell	6.00	3.00	1.75
87	Clint Brown	6.00	3.00	1.75
88	Joe Jackson	15.00	7.50	4.50

#	Player			
89	Pete Appleton	6.00	3.00	1.75
90	Ed Brandt	6.00	3.00	1.75
91	Walter Johnson	7.50	3.75	2.25
92	Dizzy Dean	6.00	3.00	1.75
93	Nick Altrock	6.00	3.00	1.75
94	Buck Weaver	7.50	3.75	2.25
95	George Blaeholder	6.00	3.00	1.75
96	Jim Bagby	6.00	3.00	1.75
97	Ted Blankenship	6.00	3.00	1.75
98	Babe Adams	6.00	3.00	1.75
99	Lefty Williams	7.50	3.75	2.25
100	Tommy Bridges	6.00	3.00	1.75
101	Rube Benton	6.00	3.00	1.75
102	Unknown	6.00	3.00	1.75
103	Max Butcher	6.00	3.00	1.75
104	Chick Gandil	7.50	3.75	2.25

1945-46 Caramelo Deportivo Cuban League

One of the better-known of Cuba's baseball card issues is the 100-card set issued by Caramelo Deportivo (Sporting Caramels) covering the 1945-46 Cuban winter league season. Printed in black-and-white on very thin 1-7/8" x 2-5/8" paper, the cards were intended to be pasted into an album issued for the purpose. Fronts have a card number, but no player identification; backs have the player's name, a few biographical and career details and an ad for the issuer, in as many as three different configurations. Many former and future Major Leaguers and stars of the U.S. Negro Leagues will be found on this checklist; sometimes providing the only cards issued contemporary with their playing careers.

		NM	EX	VG
Complete Set, No Reyes (99):		6,500	3,250	1,950
Common Player:		25.00	12.50	7.50
Album:		200.00	100.00	60.00
1	Caramelo Deportivo Title Card	7.50	3.75	2.25
2	Action Scene	12.50	6.25	3.75
3	Amado Maestri/Umpire	25.00	12.50	7.50
4	Bernardino Rodriguez/Umpire	25.00	12.50	7.50
5	Quico Magrinat/Umpire	25.00	12.50	7.50
6	Cuco Conder (Announcer)	25.00	12.50	7.50
7	Marianao Team Banner	10.00	5.00	3.00
8	Armando Marsans	75.00	37.50	22.00
9	Jose Fernandez	25.00	12.50	7.50
10	Jose Luis Colas	25.00	12.50	7.50
11	"Charlotio" Orta (Charolito)	25.00	12.50	7.50
12	Barney Serrell	50.00	25.00	15.00
13	Claro Duany	30.00	15.00	9.00
14	Antonio Castanos	25.00	12.50	7.50
15	Virgilio Arteaga	25.00	12.50	7.50
16	Gilberto Valdivia	25.00	12.50	7.50
17	Jugo Cabrera	25.00	12.50	7.50
18	Lazaro Salazar	75.00	37.50	22.00
19	Julio Moreno	25.00	12.50	7.50
20	Oliverio Ortiz	25.00	12.50	7.50
21	Lou Knerr	25.00	12.50	7.50
22	Francisco Campos	25.00	12.50	7.50
23	Red Adams	25.00	12.50	7.50
24	Sandalio Consuegra	25.00	12.50	7.50
25	Ray Dandridge	800.00	400.00	240.00
26	Booker McDaniels	40.00	20.00	12.00
27	Orestes Minoso	675.00	335.00	200.00
28	Daniel Parra	25.00	12.50	7.50
29	Roberto Estalella	25.00	12.50	7.50
30	Raymond Brown	2,150	1,100	650.00
31	Havana Team Banner	10.00	5.00	3.00
32	Miguel Gonzalez	40.00	20.00	12.00
33	Julio Rojo	25.00	12.50	7.50
34	Herberto Blanco	25.00	12.50	7.50
35	Pedro Formenthal	30.00	15.00	9.00
36	Rene Monteagudo	25.00	12.50	7.50
37	Carlos Blanco	25.00	12.50	7.50
38	Salvandor Hernandez	25.00	12.50	7.50
39	Rogelio Linares	25.00	12.50	7.50
40	Antionio Ordenana	25.00	12.50	7.50
41	Pedro Jiminez	25.00	12.50	7.50
42	Charley Kaiser	25.00	12.50	7.50
43	Manuel "Cocaina" Garcia	80.00	40.00	24.00
44	Sagua Hernandez	25.00	12.50	7.50
45	Lou Klein	25.00	12.50	7.50
46	Manuel Hidalgo	25.00	12.50	7.50
47	Dick Sisler	35.00	17.50	10.00
48	Jim Rebel	25.00	12.50	7.50
49	Raul Navarro	25.00	12.50	7.50
50	Pedero Medina	25.00	12.50	7.50
51	Charlie (Terries) McDuffie	75.00	37.50	22.00
52	Fred Martin	25.00	12.50	7.50
53	Julian Acosta	25.00	12.50	7.50
54	Cienfuegos Team Banner	10.00	5.00	3.00
55	Adolfo Luque	125.00	62.00	37.00
56	Jose Ramos	25.00	12.50	7.50
57	Conrado Perez	25.00	12.50	7.50
58	Antonio Rodriguez	25.00	12.50	7.50
59	Alejandro Crespo	30.00	15.00	9.00
60	Roland Gladu	25.00	12.50	7.50
61	Pedro Pages	25.00	12.50	7.50
62	Silvio Garcia	80.00	40.00	24.00
63	Carlos Colas	25.00	12.50	7.50
64	Salvatore Maglie	125.00	60.00	35.00
65	Martin Dihigo	1,250	625.00	375.00
66	Luis Tiant Sr.	185.00	90.00	55.00
67	Jim Roy	25.00	12.50	7.50
68	Ramon Roger	25.00	12.50	7.50
69	Adrian Zabala	25.00	12.50	7.50
70	Armando Gallart	25.00	12.50	7.50
71	Jose Zardon	25.00	12.50	7.50
72	Ray Berres	25.00	12.50	7.50
73	Napoleon Reyes/SP	1,500	750.00	450.00
74	Jose Gomez	25.00	12.50	7.50
75	Loevigildo Xiques	25.00	12.50	7.50
76	Almendares Team Banner	10.00	5.00	3.00
77	Reinaldo Coreiro	25.00	12.50	7.50
78	Bartalo Portaundo (Bartolo Portuondo)	25.00	12.50	7.50
79	Jacinto Roque	25.00	12.50	7.50
80	Hector Arago	25.00	12.50	7.50
81	Gilberto Torres	30.00	15.00	9.00
82	Roberto Ortiz	30.00	15.00	9.00
83	Hector Rodriguez	25.00	12.50	7.50
84	Chifian Clark	40.00	20.00	12.00
85	Fermin Guerra	30.00	15.00	9.00
86	Jorge Comellas	25.00	12.50	7.50
87	Regino Otero	25.00	12.50	7.50
88	Tomas de la Cruz	30.00	15.00	9.00
89	Mario Diaz	25.00	12.50	7.50
90	Luis Aloma	25.00	12.50	7.50
91	Lloyd Davenport	40.00	20.00	12.00
92	Agapito Mayor	25.00	12.50	7.50
93	Ramon Bragana	100.00	50.00	30.00
94	Avelino Canizares	25.00	12.50	7.50
95	Santiago Ulrich	25.00	12.50	7.50
96	Beto Avila	50.00	25.00	15.00
97	Santos Amaro	30.00	15.00	9.00
98	Andres Fleitas	25.00	12.50	7.50
99	Limonar Martinez	25.00	12.50	7.50
100	Juan Montero	25.00	12.50	7.50

1946-47 Caramelo Deportivo Cuban League

43—LLOYD PEARSON
Primera base del Habana.
Pertenece al Club Aguilas de Newark.
OBSEQUIO DEL CARAMELO
DEPORTIVO
Fabricado y distribuido por
"F E L I C E S"
A. Seco 270, Telf. U-2233
Para articulos de Sport
"CASA VASSALLO"
La casa de los Deportes

Following its 100-card issue of the previous Cuban winter league season, this candy company issued a 185-card set for 1946-47. Besides more players, extra cards included banners, stadiums, managers, umpires and sportscasters. Printed on paper stock and intended to be pasted into an accompanying album, the cards measure about 1-7/8" x 2-1/2", though inconsistent cutting creates both over- and under-sized cards. Fronts have black-and-white player photos and a circle with a card number. Photos are often fuzzy or dark, indicative of their having been picked up from another source, such as a newspaper. Backs repeat the card number and have the player name at top, along with his Cuban League and, frequently, U.S. professional affiliation. Some 60 of the players in the set played in the segregated Negro Leagues of the era. A large ad for the candy and its sellers appear at bottom of the back. Because of the thin stock and placement in albums, these cards are usually found creased and/or with back damage.

		NM	EX	VG
Complete Set (185):		12,000	6,000	3,600
Common Player:		50.00	25.00	15.00
Album:		250.00	125.00	75.00
1	Introduction Card	25.00	12.50	7.50
2	New El Cerro Stadium	25.00	12.50	7.50
3	Stadium La Tropical	25.00	12.50	7.50
4	Maestri, Bernardino and Magrinat (El Cerro umpires.)	50.00	25.00	15.00
5	La Tropical umpires (Atan, Lopez, Vidal and Morales)	50.00	25.00	15.00
6	Cuco Conde (Announcer)	25.00	12.50	7.50
7	Cienfuegos Team Banner	25.00	12.50	7.50
8	Martin Dihigo	750.00	375.00	225.00
9a	Napoleon Reyes	60.00	30.00	18.00
9b	Napoleon Reyes	60.00	30.00	18.00
10	Adrian Zabala	50.00	25.00	15.00
11	Roland Gladu	50.00	25.00	15.00
12	Alejandro Crespo	100.00	50.00	30.00
13	Alejandro Carrasquel	50.00	25.00	15.00
14	Napoleon Heredia	50.00	25.00	15.00
15	Andres Mesa	50.00	25.00	15.00
16	Pedro Pages	50.00	25.00	15.00
17	Danny Gardella	50.00	25.00	15.00
18	Conrado Perez	50.00	25.00	15.00
19	Myron Hayworth	50.00	25.00	15.00
20	Pedro Miro	50.00	25.00	15.00
21	Guillermo Vargas	50.00	25.00	15.00
22	Hoot Gibson	50.00	25.00	15.00
23	Rafael Noble	55.00	27.50	16.50
24	Ramon Roger	50.00	25.00	15.00
25	Luis Arango	50.00	25.00	15.00
26	Roy Zimmerman	50.00	25.00	15.00
27	Luis Tiant Sr.	125.00	65.00	35.00
28	Jean Roy	55.00	27.50	16.50
29	Stanislov Bread	50.00	25.00	15.00
30	Walter Nothe	50.00	25.00	15.00
31	Vinicio Garcia	50.00	25.00	15.00
32	Dan (Max) Manning	200.00	100.00	60.00
33	Habana Lions Team Banner	25.00	12.50	7.50
34	Miguel A. Gonzalez	80.00	40.00	24.00
35	Pedro Formental	100.00	50.00	30.00
36	Ray Navarro	50.00	25.00	15.00
37	Pedro Jiminez	50.00	25.00	15.00
38	Rene Monteagudo	50.00	25.00	15.00
39	Salvador Hernandez	50.00	25.00	15.00
40	Hugh (Terris) Mc. Duffie	70.00	35.00	20.00
41	Herberto Blanco	50.00	25.00	15.00
42	Harry (Henry) Kimbro	130.00	65.00	40.00
43	Lloyd (Lennie) Pearson	180.00	90.00	55.00
44	W. Bell	55.00	27.50	16.50
45	Carlos Blanco	50.00	25.00	15.00
46	Hank Thompson	70.00	35.00	20.00
47	Manuel ("Cocaina") Garcia	150.00	75.00	45.00
48	Alberto Hernandez	50.00	25.00	15.00
49	Tony Ordenana	50.00	25.00	15.00
50	Lazaro Medina	50.00	25.00	15.00
51	Fred Martin	50.00	25.00	15.00
52	Eddie (Jim) Lamarque	150.00	75.00	45.00
53	Juan Montero	50.00	25.00	15.00
54	Lou Klein	50.00	25.00	15.00
55	Pablo Garcia	50.00	25.00	15.00
56	Julio Rojo	50.00	25.00	15.00
57	Almendares Team Banner	25.00	12.50	7.50
58	Adolfo Luque	90.00	45.00	27.50
59	Cheo Ramos	50.00	25.00	15.00
60	Avelino Canizares	50.00	25.00	15.00
61	George Hausmann	50.00	25.00	15.00
62	Homero Ariosa	50.00	25.00	15.00
63	Santos Amaro	50.00	25.00	15.00
64	Hank Robinson	60.00	30.00	18.00
65	Lazaro Salazar	200.00	100.00	60.00
66	Andres Fleitas	50.00	25.00	15.00
67	Hector Rodriguez	80.00	40.00	24.00
68	Jorge Comellas	50.00	25.00	15.00
69	Lloyd Davenport	130.00	65.00	40.00
70	Tomas de la Cruz	50.00	25.00	15.00
71a	Roberto Ortiz	80.00	40.00	24.00
71b	Roberto Ortiz	50.00	25.00	15.00
72	Jess (Gentry) Jessup	130.00	65.00	40.00
73	Agapito Mayor	50.00	25.00	15.00
74	William	50.00	25.00	15.00
75	Santiago Ullrich	50.00	25.00	15.00
76	Coty Leal	50.00	25.00	15.00
77	Max Lanier	55.00	27.50	16.50
78	Buck O'Neill	800.00	400.00	240.00
79	Mario Ariosa	50.00	25.00	15.00
80	Lefty Gaines	130.00	65.00	40.00
81	Marianao Team Banner	25.00	12.50	7.50
82	Armando Marsans	80.00	40.00	24.00
83	Antonio Castanos	50.00	25.00	15.00
84	Orestes Minoso	200.00	100.00	60.00
85	Murray Franklin	50.00	25.00	15.00
86	Roberto Estalella	50.00	25.00	15.00
87	A. Castro	50.00	25.00	15.00
88	Gilberto Valdivia	50.00	25.00	15.00
89	Baffeth (Lloyd "Pepper" Bassett)	130.00	65.00	40.00
90	Oliverio Ortiz	50.00	25.00	15.00
91	Francisco Campos	50.00	25.00	15.00
92	Sandalio Consuegra	65.00	32.50	20.00
93	Lorenzo Cabrera	50.00	25.00	15.00
94	Roberto Avila	80.00	40.00	24.00
95	Chanquilon Diaz	50.00	25.00	15.00
96	Pedro Orta	50.00	25.00	15.00
97	Cochihuila Valenzuela	50.00	25.00	15.00
98	Ramon Carneado	50.00	25.00	15.00
99	Aristonico Correoso	50.00	25.00	15.00
100	Daniel Doy	50.00	25.00	15.00
101	Joe Lindsay	50.00	25.00	15.00
102	Habana Reds Team Banner	25.00	12.50	7.50
103	Gilberto Torres	50.00	25.00	15.00
104	Oscar Rodriguez	50.00	25.00	15.00
105	Isidoro Leon	50.00	25.00	15.00
106	Julio Moreno	50.00	25.00	15.00
107	Chulungo del Monte	50.00	25.00	15.00
108	Len Hooker	100.00	50.00	30.00
109	Antonio Napoles	50.00	25.00	15.00
110	Orlando Suarez	50.00	25.00	15.00
111	Guillermo Monje	50.00	25.00	15.00
112	Isasio Gonzalez	50.00	25.00	15.00
113	Regino Otero	50.00	25.00	15.00
114	Angel Fleitas	50.00	25.00	15.00
115	Jorge Torres	50.00	25.00	15.00
116	Claro Duany	100.00	50.00	30.00
117	Charles Perez	50.00	25.00	15.00
118	Francisco Quicutis	50.00	25.00	15.00
119	Lazaro Bernal	50.00	25.00	15.00
120	Tommy Warren	50.00	25.00	15.00
121	Clarence Iott	55.00	27.00	16.50
122	P. Newcomb (Don Newcombe)	600.00	300.00	180.00
123	Gilberto Castillo	50.00	25.00	15.00
124	Matanzas Team Banner	25.00	12.50	7.50
125	Silvio Garcia	200.00	100.00	60.00
126	Bartolo Portuondo	50.00	25.00	15.00
127	Pedro Arango	50.00	25.00	15.00
128	Yuyo Acosta	50.00	25.00	15.00
129	Jose Cendan	50.00	25.00	15.00
130	Eddie Chandler	50.00	25.00	15.00
131	Rogelio Martinez	50.00	25.00	15.00
132	Atares Garcia	50.00	25.00	15.00
133	Manuel Godinez	50.00	25.00	15.00
134	John Williams	130.00	65.00	40.00
135	Emilio Cabrera	50.00	25.00	15.00
136	Barney Serrell	130.00	65.00	40.00
137	Armando Gallart	50.00	25.00	15.00
138	Ruben Garcia	50.00	25.00	15.00
139	Loevigildo Xiques	50.00	25.00	15.00
140	Chifian (Chiflan) Clark	130.00	65.00	40.00

141	Jacinto Roque	50.00	25.00	15.00
142	John (Johnny) Davis	150.00	75.00	45.00
143	Norman Wilson	50.00	25.00	15.00
144	Camaguey Team Banner	25.00	12.50	7.50
145	Antonio Rodriguez	50.00	25.00	15.00
146	Manuel Parrado	50.00	25.00	15.00
147	Leon Treadway	50.00	25.00	15.00
148	Amado Ibanez	50.00	25.00	15.00
149	Teodoro Oxamendi	50.00	25.00	15.00
150	Adolfo Cabrera	50.00	25.00	15.00
151	Oscar Garmendia	50.00	25.00	15.00
152	Hector Arago	50.00	25.00	15.00
153	Evelio Martinez	50.00	25.00	15.00
154	Raquel Antunez	50.00	25.00	15.00
155	Lino Donoso	50.00	25.00	15.00
156	Eliecer Alvarez	50.00	25.00	15.00
157	George Brown	50.00	25.00	15.00
158	Roberto Johnson	50.00	25.00	15.00
159	Rafael Franco	50.00	25.00	15.00
160	Miguel A. Carmona	50.00	25.00	15.00
161	Lilo Fano	50.00	25.00	15.00
162	Orestes Pereda	50.00	25.00	15.00
163	Pedro Diaz	50.00	25.00	15.00
164	Oriente Team Banner	25.00	12.50	7.50
165	Fermin Guerra	50.00	25.00	15.00
166	Jose M. Fernandez	50.00	25.00	15.00
167	Cando Lopez	50.00	25.00	15.00
168	Conrado Marrero	60.00	30.00	18.00
169	Oscar del Calvo	50.00	25.00	15.00
170	Booker McDaniels	150.00	75.00	45.00
171	Rafael Rivas	50.00	25.00	15.00
172	Daniel Parra	50.00	25.00	15.00
173	L. Holleman	50.00	25.00	15.00
174	Rogelio Valdes	50.00	25.00	15.00
175	Raymond Dandridge	950.00	475.00	285.00
176	Manuel Hidalgo	50.00	25.00	15.00
177	Miguel Lastra	50.00	25.00	15.00
178	Luis Minsal	50.00	25.00	15.00
179	Andres Vazquez	50.00	25.00	15.00
180	Jose A. Zardon	50.00	25.00	15.00
181	Jose Luis Colas	50.00	25.00	15.00
182	Rogelio Linares	50.00	25.00	15.00
183	Mario Diaz	50.00	25.00	15.00
184	R. Verdes	50.00	25.00	15.00
185	Indio Jiminez	50.00	25.00	15.00

1948-1949 Caramelos El Indio

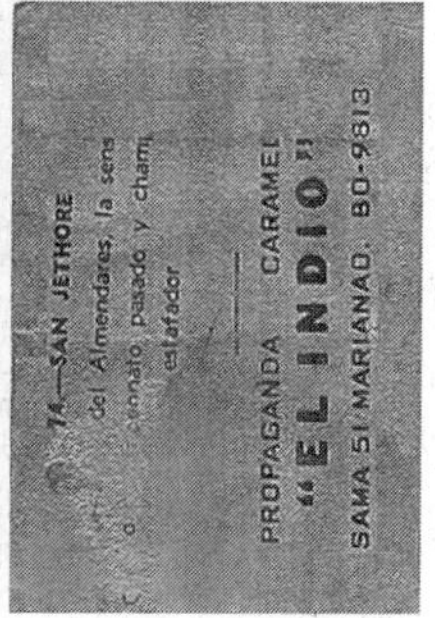

Perhaps the rarest of the late-1940s Cuban caramel cards is this issue picturing members of the island's four-team professional winter league. Measuring 1-5/8" x 2-7/16", the cards are printed in black-and-white on thick paper stock. Front photos are bordered in black with no player identification. On back at top is a card number and player name, along with a few words about the player. At bottom is an ad for the sponsor. Many American players, including Negro Leaguers, are included in the issue. The set is arranged alphabetically by team. An album was available in which to mount the cards. As with most contemporary Cuban issues, low-grade survivors are the norm, with Good condition being about the best seen, making the pricing here somewhat hypothetical.

		NM	EX	VG
Common Player:		200.00	100.00	60.00
Album:		300.00	150.00	90.00
1	Fermin Guerra	275.00	135.00	80.00
2	Rodolfo Fernandez	200.00	100.00	60.00
3	Reinaldo Cordeiro	200.00	100.00	60.00
4	Andres Fleitas	200.00	100.00	60.00
5	Tango Suarez	200.00	100.00	60.00
6	Ken Connors (Kevin "Chuck")	600.00	300.00	180.00
7	Rene Gonzalez	200.00	100.00	60.00
8	Jinny Bloodwrth (Jimmy Bloodworth)	275.00	135.00	80.00
9	Sojito Gallardo	200.00	100.00	60.00
10	Hector Rodriguez	275.00	135.00	80.00
11	Avelino Canizares	200.00	100.00	60.00
12	Gilberto Torres	200.00	100.00	60.00
13	Monte Yrving (Monte Irvin)	1,600	800.00	475.00
14	San Jethore (Sam Jethroe)	325.00	160.00	100.00
15	Al Gionfrido (Gionfriddo)	275.00	135.00	80.00
16	Santos Amaro	275.00	135.00	80.00
17	Hiram Gonzalez	200.00	100.00	60.00
18	Conrado Marrero	275.00	135.00	80.00
19	Jorge Comellas	200.00	100.00	60.00
20	Agapito Mayor	200.00	100.00	60.00
21	Octavio Rubert	200.00	100.00	60.00
22	Tata Solis	200.00	100.00	60.00
23	Morris Martin	275.00	135.00	80.00
24	Cyde (Clyde) King	275.00	135.00	80.00
25	Miguel Angel Gonzalez	325.00	160.00	100.00
26	Joseito Rodriguez	200.00	100.00	60.00
27	Sungo Carreras	200.00	100.00	60.00
28	Hank Anderson	275.00	135.00	80.00
29	Emilio Cabrera	200.00	100.00	60.00
30	Lennox Pearson	325.00	160.00	100.00
31	Herberto Blanco	200.00	100.00	60.00
32	Pablo Garcia	200.00	100.00	60.00
33	Chino Hidalgo	200.00	100.00	60.00
34	Amado Ibanez	200.00	100.00	60.00
35	Carlos Blanco	200.00	100.00	60.00
36	Henry Thompson	275.00	135.00	80.00
37	Henry Kimbro	275.00	135.00	80.00
38	Pedro Formental	275.00	135.00	80.00
39	Saguita Hernandez	200.00	100.00	60.00
40	Francisco Quicutis	200.00	100.00	60.00
41	George Stancer (Stanceu)	275.00	135.00	80.00
42	Jim Yockin (Yochim)	275.00	135.00	80.00
43	Tony Lorenzo	200.00	100.00	60.00
44	Rafael Rivas	200.00	100.00	60.00
45	Jose Cerdan	200.00	100.00	60.00
46	Cocaina Garcia	325.00	160.00	100.00
47	Bill Schuster	275.00	135.00	80.00
48	Oliverio Ortiz	200.00	100.00	60.00
49	Salvador Hernandez	200.00	100.00	60.00
50	Oscar Rodriguez	200.00	100.00	60.00
51	Julio Rojo	200.00	100.00	60.00
52	Ray Noble	250.00	125.00	75.00
53	Regino Otero	200.00	100.00	60.00
54	Peter Coscarat (Coscarart)	275.00	135.00	80.00
55	Jimmy Redmond	275.00	135.00	80.00
56	Mc. Quillan (Glenn McQuillen)	275.00	135.00	80.00
57	Stan Bread	275.00	135.00	80.00
58	Armando Gallart	200.00	100.00	60.00
59	Angel Fleitas	200.00	100.00	60.00
60	Pedro Pages	200.00	100.00	60.00
61	Alejandro Crespo	275.00	135.00	80.00
62	Jose Luis Colas	200.00	100.00	60.00
63	Conrado Perez	200.00	100.00	60.00
64	Coaker Triplet (Triplett)	275.00	135.00	80.00
65	Pedro Dunabeitia	200.00	100.00	60.00
66	Maik Sukont (Max Surkont)	275.00	135.00	80.00
67	Max Mamming (Manning)	525.00	260.00	150.00
68	Jom Mikan	275.00	135.00	80.00
69	Herman Bess (Besse)	275.00	135.00	80.00
70	Wito (Luis) Aloma	275.00	135.00	80.00
71	Raul Lopez	200.00	100.00	60.00
72	Silvio Garcia	300.00	150.00	90.00
73	Gilberto Torres	200.00	100.00	60.00
74	Pipo de la Noval	200.00	100.00	60.00
75	Jose Maria Fernandez	200.00	100.00	60.00
76	Vitico Munoz	200.00	100.00	60.00
77	Luis Suarez	200.00	100.00	60.00
78	Wilfredo Salas	200.00	100.00	60.00
79	Julio Moreno	200.00	100.00	60.00
80	Bill Harrington	275.00	135.00	80.00
81	Oreste (Minnie) Minoso	525.00	260.00	150.00
82	Clarence Hicks	275.00	135.00	80.00
83	Pedro Ballester	200.00	100.00	60.00
84	Jose Hawerton	200.00	100.00	60.00
85	Ramon Roger	200.00	100.00	60.00
86	M Arenciba	200.00	100.00	60.00
87	Louis Kahn	275.00	135.00	80.00
88	Mario Diaz	200.00	100.00	60.00
89	Chiquitin Cabrera	200.00	100.00	60.00
90	Beto Avila	200.00	100.00	60.00
91	Cisco Campos	200.00	100.00	60.00
92	Johnny Simmons	275.00	135.00	80.00
93	Claro Duany	275.00	135.00	80.00
94	Clyde (Dave) Barnhill	800.00	400.00	240.00
95	Clarence Beer	275.00	135.00	80.00
96	Joaquin Gutierrez	200.00	100.00	60.00

1955 Carling Beer Cleveland Indians

Apparently the first of a line of premium photos which extended into the early 1960s. Measuring 8-1/2" x 12" and printed in black-and-white on semi-gloss thin card stock, these photocards are blank-backed. The 1955 Carling photos are identifiable from the 1956 issue, with which they share a "DBL" prefix to the card number in the lower-right corner, by the phrase "Great Champions" appearing just under the player photo.

		NM	EX	VG
Complete Set (11):		750.00	375.00	225.00
Common Player:		60.00	30.00	18.00
96A	Ralph Kiner	110.00	55.00	35.00
96Ba	Larry Doby	100.00	50.00	30.00
96Bb	Herb Score	75.00	37.50	22.50
96C	Al Rosen	75.00	37.50	22.50
96D	Mike Garcia	60.00	30.00	18.00
96E	Early Wynn	90.00	45.00	27.50
96F	Bob Feller	150.00	75.00	45.00
96G	Jim Hegan	60.00	30.00	18.00
96H	George Strickland	60.00	30.00	18.00
96K	Bob Lemon	90.00	45.00	27.50
96L	Art Houtteman	60.00	30.00	18.00

1956 Carling Beer Cleveland Indians

This set was sponsored by Carling Black Label Beer. The oversized (8-1/2" x 12") cards feature black-and-white posed photos with the player's name in a white strip and a Carling ad at the bottom of the card front. Backs are blank. Like the cards issued in 1955, the 1956 set carries a DBL 96 series indication in the lower-right corner and lists brewery locations as Cleveland, St. Louis and Belleville, Ill. Unlike the '55 photocards, however, the first line under the player photo on the 1956 issue is "Premium Quality." Cards numbered DBL 96I and DBL 96J are unknown.

		NM	EX	VG
Complete Set (10):		900.00	450.00	275.00
Common Player:		60.00	30.00	18.00
96A	Al Smith	60.00	30.00	18.00
96B	Herb Score	120.00	60.00	35.00
96C	Al Rosen	90.00	45.00	27.50
96D	Mike Garcia	60.00	30.00	18.00
96E	Early Wynn	120.00	60.00	35.00
96F	Bob Feller	200.00	100.00	60.00
96G	Jim Hegan	60.00	30.00	18.00
96H	George Strickland	60.00	30.00	18.00
96K	Bob Lemon	120.00	60.00	35.00
96L	Art Houtteman	60.00	30.00	18.00

1957 Carling Beer Cleveland Indians

The fact that Kerby Farrell managed the Indians only in 1957 pinpoints the year of issue for those Carling Beer photocards which carry a DBL 179 series number in the lower-right corner. Following the black-and-white, blank-backed 8-1/2" x 12" format of earlier issues, the 1957 Carlings list on the bottom line breweries at Cleveland; Frankenmuth, Mich.; Natick, Mass., and, Belleville, Ill. Cards numbered DBL 179I and DBL 179J are currently unknown.

		NM	EX	VG
Complete Set (10):		900.00	450.00	275.00
Common Player:		60.00	30.00	18.00
179A	Vic Wertz	60.00	30.00	18.00
179B	Early Wynn	100.00	50.00	30.00
179C	Herb Score	90.00	45.00	27.50
179D	Bob Lemon	100.00	50.00	30.00
179E	Ray Narleski	60.00	30.00	18.00
179F	Jim Hegan	60.00	30.00	18.00
179G	Bob Avila	60.00	30.00	18.00
179H	Al Smith	60.00	30.00	18.00
179K	Kerby Farrell	60.00	30.00	18.00
179L	Rocky Colavito	300.00	150.00	90.00

1958 Carling Beer Cleveland Indians

Identical in format to earlier issues, the 1958 premium photos can be distinguished by the card number printed in the lower-right corner. Cards in the 1958 series have numbers which begin with a DBL 2 or DBL 217 prefix.

		NM	EX	VG
Complete Set (10):		725.00	360.00	215.00
Common Player:		60.00	30.00	18.00
2	Vic Wertz	60.00	30.00	18.00
217	Minnie Minoso	100.00	50.00	30.00
217B	Gene Woodling	60.00	30.00	18.00
217C	Russ Nixon	60.00	30.00	18.00
217D	Bob Lemon	120.00	60.00	35.00
217E	Bobby Bragan	60.00	30.00	18.00
217F	Cal McLish	60.00	30.00	18.00
217G	Rocky Colavito	150.00	75.00	45.00
217H	Herb Score	100.00	50.00	30.00
217J	Chico Carrasquel	60.00	30.00	18.00

1959 Carling Beer Cleveland Indians

The appearance of Billy Martin among Carling photocards labeled with a DBL 266 prefix fixes the year of issue to 1959, the fiery second baseman's only year with the Tribe. Once again the 8-1/2" x 12" black-and-white, blank-backed cards follow the format of previous issues. Breweries listed on the bottom of the 1959 Carlings are Cleveland; Atlanta; Frankenmuth, Mich.; Natick, Mass.; Belleville, Ill., and, Tacoma, Wash.

	NM	EX	VG
Complete Set (6):	600.00	300.00	180.00
Common Player:	75.00	37.50	22.50
266A Vic Power	75.00	37.50	22.50
266B Minnie Minoso	100.00	50.00	30.00
266C Herb Score	100.00	50.00	30.00
266D Rocky Colavito	150.00	75.00	45.00
266E Jimmy Piersall	100.00	50.00	30.00
266F Billy Martin	150.00	75.00	45.00

1961 Carling Beer Cleveland Indians

Totally different player selection and the use of an LB prefix to the number in the lower-right corner define the 1961 issue from Carling Beer. Otherwise the photocards share the same 8-1/2" x 12" black-and-white format with earlier issues. The blank-backed cards of the 1961 issue list only a single brewery, Cleveland, at the bottom of the ad portion of the issues. The checklist here is arranged alphabetically. Cards numbered LB 420I and LB420J are unknown.

	NM	EX	VG
Complete Set (10):	600.00	300.00	180.00
Common Player:	60.00	30.00	18.00
420A Jimmy Piersall	100.00	50.00	30.00
420B Willie Kirkland	60.00	30.00	18.00
420C Johnny Antonelli	60.00	30.00	18.00
420D John Romano	60.00	30.00	18.00
420E Woodie Held	60.00	30.00	18.00
420F Tito Francona	60.00	30.00	18.00
420G Jim Perry	90.00	45.00	27.50
420H Bubba Phillips	60.00	30.00	18.00
420K John Temple	60.00	30.00	18.00
420L Vic Power	60.00	30.00	18.00

1909-11 Carolina Brights

Among the last of the T206 cards printed, those with Carolina Brights advertising on back are scarce and command a significant premium. The advertising on back is printed in black.

PREMIUMS:
Common Player: 5-6X
Typical Hall of Famer: 3-4X
(See T206 for checklist and base card values.)

1976 Carousel Discs

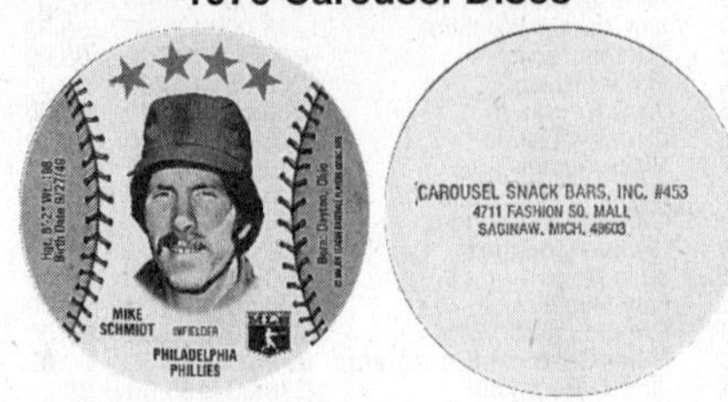

One of several regional sponsors of player disc sets in 1976 was the Michigan snack bar chain, Carousel. The sponsor's discs are unique in that they do not have pre-printed backs, but rather have a black rubber-stamp on the otherwise blank back. To date more than 20 such stamps have been seen, reportedly from New Jersey to Alaska. The discs are 3-3/8" diameter with a black-and-white player portrait photo in the center of the baseball design. A line of red stars is above, while the left and right panels feature one of several bright colors. Produced by Michael Schecter Associates under license from the Major League Baseball Players Association, the player photos have had uniform and cap logos removed. The unnumbered checklist here is presented in alphabetical order.

		NM	EX	VG
Complete Set (70):		35.00	17.50	10.00
Common Player:		2.00	1.00	.60
(1)	Henry Aaron	12.50	6.25	3.75
(2)	Johnny Bench	7.50	3.75	2.25
(3)	Vida Blue	2.00	1.00	.60
(4)	Larry Bowa	2.00	1.00	.60
(5)	Lou Brock	5.00	2.50	1.50
(6)	Jeff Burroughs	2.00	1.00	.60
(7)	John Candelaria	2.00	1.00	.60
(8)	Jose Cardenal	2.00	1.00	.60
(9)	Rod Carew	5.00	2.50	1.50
(10)	Steve Carlton	5.00	2.50	1.50
(11)	Dave Cash	2.00	1.00	.60
(12)	Cesar Cedeno	2.00	1.00	.60
(13)	Ron Cey	2.00	1.00	.60
(14)	Carlton Fisk	5.00	2.50	1.50
(15)	Tito Fuentes	2.00	1.00	.60
(16)	Steve Garvey	3.50	1.75	1.00
(17)	Ken Griffey	2.00	1.00	.60
(18)	Don Gullett	2.00	1.00	.60
(19)	Willie Horton	2.00	1.00	.60
(20)	Al Hrabosky	2.00	1.00	.60
(21)	Catfish Hunter	5.00	2.50	1.50
(22a)	Reggie Jackson (A's)	7.50	3.75	2.25
(22b)	Reggie Jackson (Orioles)	10.00	5.00	3.00
(23)	Randy Jones	2.00	1.00	.60
(24)	Jim Kaat	2.00	1.00	.60
(25)	Don Kessinger	2.00	1.00	.60
(26)	Dave Kingman	1.75	.90	.50
(27)	Jerry Koosman	2.00	1.00	.60
(28)	Mickey Lolich	2.00	1.00	.60
(29)	Greg Luzinski	2.00	1.00	.60
(30)	Fred Lynn	2.00	1.00	.60
(31)	Bill Madlock	2.00	1.00	.60
(32a)	Carlos May (White Sox)	3.00	1.50	.90
(32b)	Carlos May (Yankees)	2.00	1.00	.60
(33)	John Mayberry	2.00	1.00	.60
(34)	Bake McBride	2.00	1.00	.60
(35)	Doc Medich	2.00	1.00	.60
(36a)	Andy Messersmith (Dodgers)	3.00	1.50	.90
(36b)	Andy Messersmith (Braves)	2.00	1.00	.60
(37)	Rick Monday	2.00	1.00	.60
(38)	John Montefusco	2.00	1.00	.60
(39)	Jerry Morales	2.00	1.00	.60
(40)	Joe Morgan	5.00	2.50	1.50
(41)	Thurman Munson	4.50	2.25	1.25
(42)	Bobby Murcer	2.00	1.00	.60
(43)	Al Oliver	2.00	1.00	.60
(44)	Jim Palmer	5.00	2.50	1.50
(45)	Dave Parker	2.00	1.00	.60
(46)	Tony Perez	5.00	2.50	1.50
(47)	Jerry Reuss	2.00	1.00	.60
(48)	Brooks Robinson	6.00	3.00	1.75
(49)	Frank Robinson	6.00	3.00	1.75
(50)	Steve Rogers	2.00	1.00	.60
(51)	Pete Rose	12.50	6.25	3.75
(52)	Nolan Ryan	15.00	7.50	4.50
(53)	Manny Sanguillen	2.00	1.00	.60
(54)	Mike Schmidt	12.00	6.00	3.50
(55)	Tom Seaver	5.00	2.50	1.50
(56)	Ted Simmons	2.00	1.00	.60
(57)	Reggie Smith	2.00	1.00	.60
(58)	Willie Stargell	5.00	2.50	1.50
(59)	Rusty Staub	1.75	.90	.50
(60)	Rennie Stennett	2.00	1.00	.60
(61)	Don Sutton	5.00	2.50	1.50
(62a)	Andy Thornton (Cubs)	3.00	1.50	.90
(62b)	Andy Thornton (Expos)	2.00	1.00	.60
(63)	Luis Tiant	2.00	1.00	.60
(64)	Joe Torre	3.00	1.50	.90
(65)	Mike Tyson	2.00	1.00	.60
(66)	Bob Watson	2.00	1.00	.60
(67)	Wilbur Wood	2.00	1.00	.60
(68)	Jimmy Wynn	2.00	1.00	.60
(69)	Carl Yastrzemski	6.00	3.00	1.75
(70)	Richie Zisk	2.00	1.00	.60

1973 Norm Cash Day Card

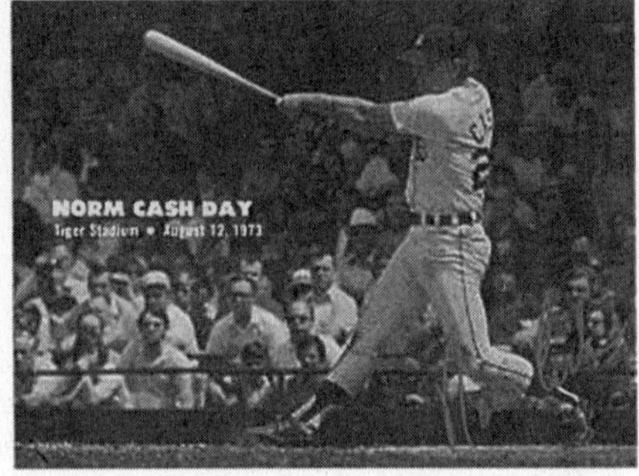

As part of the Tiger Stadium festivities on August 12, this 7" x 5" color card was given to fans. Besides an action photo of the feared slugger, his facsimile autograph appears.

	NM	EX	VG
Norm Cash	12.50	6.25	3.75

1939 Centennial of Baseball Stamps

Part of the pagentry surrounding the 1939 centennial of the fabled beginnings of baseball was this set of player and history stamps and an accompanying 36-page album. The single stamps measure about 1-5/8" x 2-1/8" and are blank-backed. Stamps #1-13 deal with the game's history; most feature artwork by famed baseball artist and former major league pitcher Al Demaree. Stamps #14-25 feature photos of the game's greats in tombstone frames surrounded by colorful borders.

		NM	EX	VG
Complete Set, w/Album (25):		1,000	500.00	300.00
Common Player:		50.00	25.00	15.00
Common Historical:		20.00	10.00	6.00
Uncut Stamp Sheet (25):		1,000	500.00	300.00
Album:		80.00	40.00	25.00
1	Abner Doubleday	50.00	25.00	15.00
2	1849 Knickerbockers	50.00	25.00	15.00
3	Ball/bat Standards	20.00	10.00	6.00
4	1858 Brooklyn vs. New York Series	50.00	25.00	15.00
5	1859 Amherst vs. Williams Series	20.00	10.00	6.00
6	Curve Ball (Arthur Cummings)	50.00	25.00	15.00
7	First Admission Fee	20.00	10.00	6.00
8	First Professional Players	50.00	25.00	15.00
9	First No-Hitter (George Bradley)	50.00	25.00	15.00
10	Morgan G. Bulkeley	50.00	25.00	15.00
11	First World's Champions	50.00	25.00	15.00
12	Byron Bancroft (Ban) Johnson	50.00	25.00	15.00
13	First Night Game	20.00	10.00	6.00
14	Grover Cleveland Alexander	60.00	30.00	18.00
15	Tyrus Raymond Cobb	150.00	75.00	45.00
16	Eddie Collins	50.00	25.00	15.00
17	Wee Willie Keeler	50.00	25.00	15.00
18	Walter Perry Johnson	75.00	37.50	22.50
19	Napoleon (Larry) Lajoie	50.00	25.00	15.00
20	Christy Mathewson	75.00	37.50	22.50
21	George Herman (Babe) Ruth	300.00	150.00	90.00
22	George Sisler	50.00	25.00	15.00
23	Tristam E. (Tris) Speaker	60.00	30.00	18.00
24	Honus Wagner	100.00	50.00	30.00
25	Denton T. (Cy) Young	75.00	37.50	22.50

1952 Central National Bank of Cleveland

The scope of this issue is undetermined. It is possible a player card was given as a premium for deposits in the bank's "Baseball Savings Club." The cards are about 6-3/4" x 4-3/4", printed in dark blue on cream-colored stock with a blank back. Titled "OFFICIAL "PLAYER-HISTORY" CARD," it features an action pose, facsimile signature, personal data, career summary and complete stats.

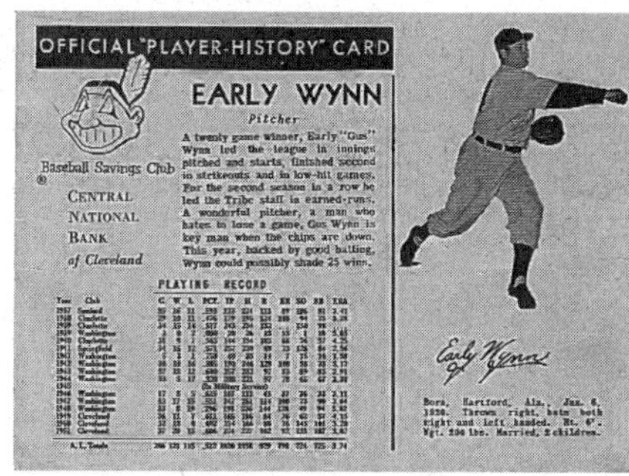

	NM	EX	VG
Common Player:	100.00	50.00	30.00
Early Wynn	200.00	100.00	60.00

1929 Certified's Ice Cream Pins

Unless or until further players are seen in this series, the date of issue will have to remain uncertain. Apparently given away by Wrigley Field's ice cream concessionaire, these 1" diameter pin-backs feature player portraits and typography in sepia tones lithographed on a white background.

	NM	EX	VG
Complete Set (5):	2,600	1,300	775.00
Common Player:	450.00	225.00	135.00
(1) Joe Bush	450.00	225.00	135.00
(2) Kiki Cuyler	600.00	300.00	180.00
(3) Rogers Hornsby	725.00	360.00	215.00
(4) Riggs Stephenson	450.00	225.00	135.00
(5) Hack Wilson	600.00	300.00	180.00

1964 Challenge the Yankees Game

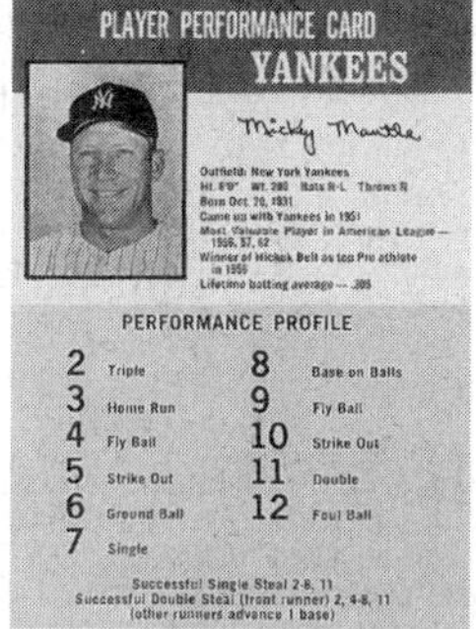

The 50 player cards in this set were part of a boxed dice baseball game produced by Hassenfeld Bros. of Pawtucket, R.I. Cards are approximately 4" x 5-1/2" and blank-backed, featuring a small black-and-white photo, a facsimile autograph and a few biographical details and stats. Player selection is virtually the same for the games issued in 1964 and 1965, and the only way to distinguish cards from each year is to study the stats. Cards are unnumbered and are checklisted below in alphabetical order.

	NM	EX	VG
Complete Boxed Set:	1,200	600.00	350.00
Complete Card Set (50):	850.00	425.00	250.00
Common Player:	9.00	4.50	2.75
(1) Hank Aaron	150.00	75.00	45.00
(2) Yogi Berra	45.00	22.50	13.50
(3) Johnny Blanchard	9.00	4.50	2.75
(4) Jim Bouton	20.00	10.00	6.00
(5) Clete Boyer	15.00	7.50	4.50
(6) Marshall Bridges	9.00	4.50	2.75
(7) Harry Bright	9.00	4.50	2.75
(8) Tom Cheney	9.00	4.50	2.75
(9) Del Crandall	9.00	4.50	2.75
(10) Al Downing	9.00	4.50	2.75
(11) Whitey Ford	40.00	20.00	12.00
(12) Tito Francona	9.00	4.50	2.75
(13) Jake Gibbs	9.00	4.50	2.75
(14) Pedro Gonzalez	9.00	4.50	2.75
(15) Dick Groat	9.00	4.50	2.75
(16) Steve Hamilton	9.00	4.50	2.75
(17) Elston Howard	20.00	10.00	6.00
(18) Al Kaline	45.00	22.50	13.50
(19) Tony Kubek	30.00	15.00	9.00
(20) Phil Linz	9.00	4.50	2.75
(21) Hector Lopez	9.00	4.50	2.75
(22) Art Mahaffey	9.00	4.50	2.75
(23) Frank Malzone	9.00	4.50	2.75
(24) Mickey Mantle	250.00	125.00	75.00
(25) Juan Marichal	30.00	15.00	9.00
(26) Roger Maris	75.00	37.50	22.50
(27) Eddie Mathews	30.00	15.00	9.00
(28) Bill Mazeroski	30.00	15.00	9.00
(29) Ken McBride	9.00	4.50	2.75
(30) Willie McCovey	30.00	15.00	9.00
(31) Tom Metcalf	9.00	4.50	2.75
(32) Jim O'Toole	9.00	4.50	2.75
(33) Milt Pappas	9.00	4.50	2.75
(34) Joe Pepitone	15.00	7.50	4.50
(35) Ron Perranoski	9.00	4.50	2.75
(36) Johnny Podres	9.00	4.50	2.75
(37) Dick Radatz	9.00	4.50	2.75
(38) Hal Reniff	9.00	4.50	2.75
(39) Bobby Richardson	30.00	15.00	9.00
(40) Rich Rollins	9.00	4.50	2.75
(41) Ron Santo	20.00	10.00	6.00
(42) Moose Skowron	20.00	10.00	6.00
(43) Duke Snider	30.00	15.00	9.00
(44) Bill Stafford	9.00	4.50	2.75
(45) Ralph Terry	9.00	4.50	2.75
(46) Tom Tresh	15.00	7.50	4.50
(47) Pete Ward	9.00	4.50	2.75
(48) Carl Warwick	9.00	4.50	2.75
(49) Stan Williams	9.00	4.50	2.75
(50) Carl Yastrzemski	75.00	37.50	22.50

1965 Challenge the Yankees Game

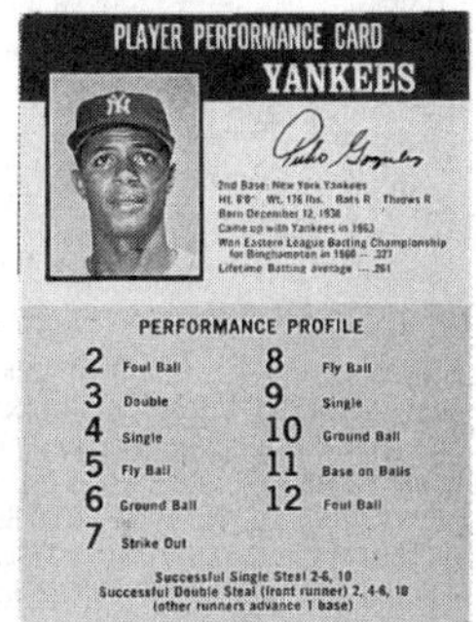

The player cards in this set were part of a boxed dice baseball game produced by Hassenfeld Bros. of Pawtucket, R.I. Cards are approximately 4" x 5-1/2" and blank-backed, featuring a small black-and-white photo, a facsimile autograph and a few biographical details and stats. Player selection is virtually the same for the games issued in 1964 and 1965, and the only way to distinguish cards from each year is to study the stats. Cards are unnumbered and are checklisted below in alphabetical order. The card of Yankee pitcher Rollie Sheldon was apparently withdrawn following his May 3 trade to Kansas City and is scarcer than the rest of the set.

	NM	EX	VG
Complete Boxed Set:	1,500	750.00	450.00
Complete Card Set (50):	1,000	500.00	300.00
Common Player:	10.00	5.00	3.00
(1) Henry Aaron	125.00	62.00	37.00
(2) Johnny Blanchard	10.00	5.00	3.00
(3) Jim Bouton	12.50	6.25	3.75
(4) Clete Boyer	12.50	6.25	3.75
(5) Leon Carmel	10.00	5.00	3.00
(6) Joe Christopher	10.00	5.00	3.00
(7) Vic Davalillo	10.00	5.00	3.00
(8) Al Downing	10.00	5.00	3.00
(9) Whitey Ford	50.00	25.00	15.00
(10) Bill Freehan	10.00	5.00	3.00
(11) Jim Gentile	10.00	5.00	3.00
(12) Jake Gibbs	10.00	5.00	3.00
(13) Pedro Gonzalez	10.00	5.00	3.00
(14) Dick Groat	10.00	5.00	3.00
(15) Steve Hamilton	10.00	5.00	3.00
(16) Elston Howard	20.00	10.00	6.00
(17) Al Kaline	50.00	25.00	15.00
(18) Tony Kubek	25.00	12.50	7.50
(19) Phil Linz	10.00	5.00	3.00
(20) Don Lock	10.00	5.00	3.00
(21) Hector Lopez	10.00	5.00	3.00
(22) Art Mahaffey	10.00	5.00	3.00
(23) Frank Malzone	10.00	5.00	3.00
(24) Mickey Mantle	350.00	175.00	100.00
(25) Juan Marichal	40.00	20.00	12.00
(26) Roger Maris	90.00	45.00	27.00
(27) Eddie Mathews	50.00	25.00	15.00
(28) Bill Mazeroski	40.00	20.00	12.00
(29) Ken McBride	10.00	5.00	3.00
(30) Tim McCarver	15.00	7.50	4.50
(31) Willie McCovey	40.00	20.00	12.00
(32) Tom Metcalf	10.00	5.00	3.00
(33) Pete Mikkelsen	10.00	5.00	3.00
(34) Jim O'Toole	10.00	5.00	3.00
(35) Milt Pappas	10.00	5.00	3.00
(36) Joe Pepitone	12.50	6.25	3.75
(37) Ron Perranoski	10.00	5.00	3.00
(38) Johnny Podres	12.50	6.25	3.75
(39) Dick Radatz	10.00	5.00	3.00
(40) Pedro Ramos	10.00	5.00	3.00
(41) Hal Reniff	10.00	5.00	3.00
(42) Bobby Richardson	25.00	12.50	7.50
(43) Rich Rollins	10.00	5.00	3.00
(44) Ron Santo	20.00	10.00	6.00
(45) Rollie Sheldon/SP	75.00	37.00	22.00
(46) Bill Stafford	10.00	5.00	3.00
(47) Mel Stottlemyre	12.50	6.25	3.75
(48) Tom Tresh	12.50	6.25	3.75
(49) Pete Ward	10.00	5.00	3.00
(50) Carl Yaztrzemski	75.00	37.00	22.00

1947 Champ Hats Premiums

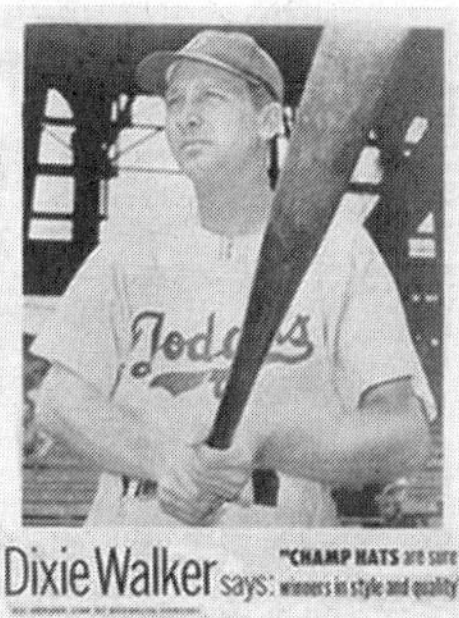

Dixie Walker says:
"CHAMP HATS are sure winners in style and quality"

The attributed date is speculative, based on the limited known player selection. These 8" x 10" sepia photo cards have player pictures in uniform. In the wide bottom border is: "(Player Name) says:" and an ad message. Backs are blank.

	NM	EX	VG
Common Player:	250.00	125.00	75.00
(1) Mickey Vernon	250.00	125.00	75.00
(2) Dixie Walker	250.00	125.00	75.00

1957-1962 Charcoal Steak House Ted Kluszewski

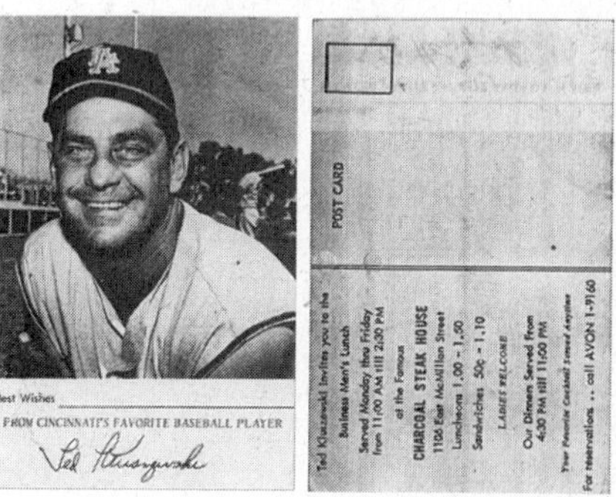

The true scope of this issue combined with the related Ted Kluszewski Steak House cards (see also) is not known. Based on cards showing Klu in Reds and Angels uniforms, it is possible examples may yet be seen in Pirates and White Sox uniforms. About 4" x 6", the black-and-white cards have a facsimile signature of Kluszewski on front. The back is in postcard style and advertises the Cincinnati restaurant he operated with Jack Stayin.

	NM	EX	VG
Ted Kluszewski (Angels)	75.00	40.00	25.00

1961 Chemstrand Iron-On Patches

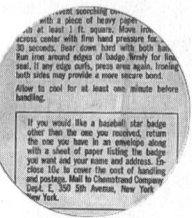

These colorful 2-1/2" diameter cloth patches were included with the purchase of a boy's sport shirt for a short period in 1961. The patches were issued in a cello package with instructions for ironing it onto the shirt. The package also offered the opportunity to trade the player patch for a different star.

	NM	EX	VG
Complete Set (9):	550.00	275.00	165.00
Common Player:	40.00	20.00	12.00
(1) Ernie Banks	75.00	37.50	22.00
(2) Yogi Berra	75.00	37.50	22.00
(3) Nellie Fox	60.00	30.00	18.00
(4) Dick Groat	40.00	20.00	12.00
(5) Al Kaline	60.00	30.00	18.00
(6) Harmon Killebrew	60.00	30.00	18.00
(7) Frank Malzone	40.00	20.00	12.00
(8) Willie Mays	115.00	55.00	35.00
(9) Warren Spahn	60.00	30.00	18.00

1976 Chevrolet Baseball Centennial Prints

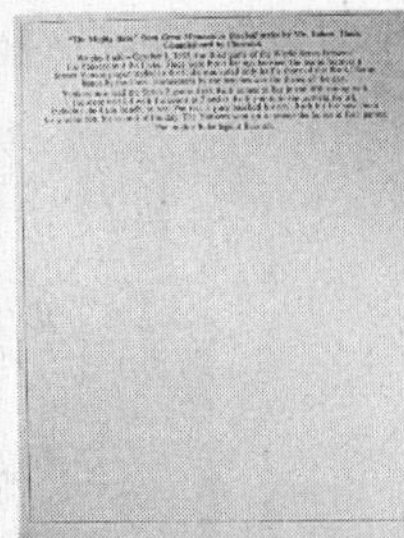

In conjunction with the centennial of organized baseball, Chevrolet commissioned a set of paintings by artist Robert Thom which were reproduced in an 8-1/2" x 11" format and distributed by local auto dealers. Fronts carry the picture's title in the white border at bottom. Backs have a description of the picture on front.

	NM	EX	VG
Complete Set (4):	40.00	20.00	12.00
Common Print:	8.00	4.00	2.50
(1) The First Game (1876)	8.00	4.00	2.50
(2) The Gashouse Gang (Pepper Martin, Bill Werber)	8.00	4.00	2.50
(3) The Mighty Babe (Babe Ruth)	15.00	7.50	4.50
(4) The Record Breaker (Hank Aaron)	12.50	6.25	3.75

1908 Chicago Cubs/White Sox Postcards

The issuer of this postcard set is unknown. The only identification on the card is a dollar sign within a shield which apears near the center on back, along with standard postcard indicia. Fronts of the 3-7/16" x 5-3/8" cards have black-and-white player photos on a gray background. A plain strip at bottom has the player's name on a top line; his position and team on a second line. The checklist presented here is probably not complete.

	NM	EX	VG
Complete Set, Cubs (11):	3,000	1,500	900.00
Complete Set, White Sox (9):	3,500	1,750	1,000
Common Player:	200.00	100.00	60.00
CUBS			
(1) Mordecai Brown	400.00	200.00	120.00
(2) Frank Chance	400.00	200.00	120.00
(3) Johnny Evers	400.00	200.00	120.00
(4) Solly Hoffman (Hofman)	200.00	100.00	60.00
(5) John Kling	200.00	100.00	60.00
(6) "Jack" Pfiester	200.00	100.00	60.00
(7) Edw. Reulbach	200.00	100.00	60.00
(8) James Sheckard	200.00	100.00	60.00
(9) Harry Steinfeldt	200.00	100.00	60.00
(10) Joe Tinker	400.00	200.00	120.00
(11) Chicago National League, Cubs. (Team photo.)	500.00	250.00	150.00
WHITE SOX			
(1) "Nic" Altrock	400.00	200.00	120.00
(2) "Jakey" Atz	500.00	250.00	150.00
(3) Geo. Davis	600.00	300.00	180.00
(4) "Jiggs" Donahue	300.00	150.00	90.00
(5) "Pat" Dougherty	300.00	150.00	90.00
(6) "Eddie" Hahn	300.00	150.00	90.00
(7) Frank Isbell	300.00	150.00	90.00
(8) Fielder Jones	300.00	150.00	90.00
(9) "Ed" Walsh	650.00	325.00	195.00

1972 Chicago Cubs & Chicago White Sox Color Caricatures

Produced by Chi-Foursome, Inc., these color caricatures were intended for sale at gas stations and supermarkets, but were never released at these locations. Apparently, only a small quantity was sold at Wrigley Field, and it is believed only about 3,000 of each player was produced. The caricatures were produced on 11" x 14" textured cardboard stock, with a facsimile autograph next to each player on front. Backs are blank.

	NM	EX	VG
CUBS	10.00	5.00	3.00
Complete Set (15):	100.00	50.00	30.00
Common Player:	10.00	5.00	3.00
Ernie Banks	20.00	10.00	6.00
Glenn Beckert	10.00	5.00	3.00
Fergie Jenkins	14.00	7.00	4.50
Don Kessinger	10.00	5.00	3.00
Milt Pappas	10.00	5.00	3.00
Joe Pepitone	10.00	5.00	3.00
Ron Santo	20.00	10.00	6.00
Billy Williams	10.00	5.00	3.00
WHITE SOX	10.00	5.00	3.00
Mike Andrews	10.00	5.00	3.00
Ed Herrmann	10.00	5.00	3.00
Pat Kelly	10.00	5.00	3.00
Carlos May	10.00	5.00	3.00
Bill Melton	14.00	7.00	4.50
Chuck Tanner	10.00	5.00	3.00
Wilbur Wood	14.00	7.00	4.50

1931 Chicago Cubs Picture Pack

In the second-year of team-issued photo packs during the 1930s-1940s was this set of 1931 Cubs. The 6-1/8" x 9-1/2" sepia-toned pictures have facsimile autographs across the front and a white border around. Backs are blank. Like all the team's other photo packs, it is possible the specific make-up of the 30 pictures in each set changed as personnel came and went during the season. A number of non-playing team personnel are also in the set.

	NM	EX	VG
Complete Set (35):	450.00	225.00	135.00
Common Player:	12.50	6.25	3.75
(1) Ed Baecht	12.50	6.25	3.75
(2) Clyde Beck	12.50	6.25	3.75
(3) Les Bell	12.50	6.25	3.75
(4) Clarence Blair	12.50	6.25	3.75
(5) John F. Blake	12.50	6.25	3.75
(6) Guy Bush	12.50	6.25	3.75
(7) Kiki Cuyler	30.00	15.00	9.00
(8) Woody English	12.50	6.25	3.75
(9) Earl Grace	12.50	6.25	3.75
(10) Charlie Grimm	15.00	7.50	4.50
(11) Gabby Hartnett	30.00	15.00	9.00
(12) Rollie Hemsley	12.50	6.25	3.75
(13) Rogers Hornsby	60.00	30.00	18.00
(14) Bill Jurges	12.50	6.25	3.75
(15) Pat Malone	12.50	6.25	3.75
(16) Jakie May	12.50	6.25	3.75
(17) John Moore	12.50	6.25	3.75
(18) Charley O'Leary	12.50	6.25	3.75
(19) Charlie Root	15.00	7.50	4.50
(20) Ray Schalk	30.00	15.00	9.00
(21) Bob Smith	12.50	6.25	3.75
(22) Riggs Stephenson	15.00	7.50	4.50
(23) Les Sweetland	12.50	6.25	3.75
(24) Dan Taylor	12.50	6.25	3.75
(25) Zack Taylor	12.50	6.25	3.75
(26) Bud Teachout	12.50	6.25	3.75
(27) Lon Warneke	12.50	6.25	3.75
(28) Hack Wilson	45.00	22.00	13.50
Non-Playing Personnel			
(29) Margaret Donahue	12.50	6.25	3.75
(30) Bob Lewis (Traveling secretary.)	12.50	6.25	3.75
(31) Andy Lotshaw (Trainer)	12.50	6.25	3.75
(32) John Seys	12.50	6.25	3.75
(33) William Veeck (President)	45.00	22.00	13.50
(34) W.M. Walker (VP)	12.50	6.25	3.75
(35) P.K. Wrigley	12.50	6.25	3.75
(36) William Wrigley (Owner)	17.50	8.75	5.25

1932 Chicago Cubs Picture Pack

This is one of many Cubs team issues of player pictures in the 1930s-1940s. The large format (6-1/8" x 9-1/4"), set features action poses of the players in black-and-white on a black background. A bit of the ground at the players' feet is also included in the photo portion. A white facsimile autograph in the black background identifies the player. Backs are blank. The unnumbered pictures are checklisted here in alphabetical order. Some pictures of non-playing personnel were also issued.

	NM	EX	VG
Complete Set (35):	325.00	165.00	100.00
Common Player:	12.50	6.25	3.75
(1) Guy Bush	12.50	6.25	3.75
(2) Gilly Campbell	12.50	6.25	3.75
(3) Red Corriden	12.50	6.25	3.75
(4) Kiki Cuyler	25.00	12.50	7.50
(5) Frank Demaree	12.50	6.25	3.75
(6) Woody English	12.50	6.25	3.75
(7) Burleigh Grimes	25.00	12.50	7.50
(8) Charlie Grimm	12.50	6.25	3.75
(9) Marv Gudat	12.50	6.25	3.75
(10) Stan Hack	15.00	7.50	4.50
(11) Gabby Hartnett	25.00	12.50	7.50
(12) Rollie Hemsley	12.50	6.25	3.75
(13) Billy Herman	25.00	12.50	7.50
(14) LeRoy Herrmann	12.50	6.25	3.75
(15) Billy Jurges	12.50	6.25	3.75
(16) Mark Koenig	12.50	6.25	3.75
(17) Pat Malone	12.50	6.25	3.75
(18) Jake May	12.50	6.25	3.75
(19) Johnny Moore	12.50	6.25	3.75
(20) Charley O'Leary	12.50	6.25	3.75
(21) Lance Richbourg	12.50	6.25	3.75
(22) Charlie Root	15.00	7.50	4.50
(23) Bob Smith	12.50	6.25	3.75
(24) Riggs Stephenson	15.00	7.50	4.50
(25) Harry Taylor	12.50	6.25	3.75
(26) Zack Taylor	12.50	6.25	3.75
(27) Bud Tinning	12.50	6.25	3.75
(28) Lon Warneke	12.50	6.25	3.75
Non-playing Personnel			
(29) Marge Donahue	12.50	6.25	3.75
(30) Bob Lewis (Traveling secretary.)	12.50	6.25	3.75
(31) John Seys	12.50	6.25	3.75
(32) Bill Veeck (President)	25.00	12.50	7.50
(33) W.M. Walker	12.50	6.25	3.75
(34) Phil Wrigley	12.50	6.25	3.75
(35) William Wrigley	12.50	6.25	3.75

1932 Chicago Cubs Team Issue

Because of its similarity in format to the team's picture pack issue of 1932, it is presumed this card set was also a team production. The blank-back cards are about 2-1/4" x 2-1/2" with player poses and a bit of ground underfoot set against a white background which has a facsimile autograph. This checklist is incomplete and arranged alphabetically.

	NM	EX	VG
Common Player:	300.00	150.00	90.00
Charlie Grimm	300.00	150.00	90.00
Marv Gudat	300.00	150.00	90.00
Stanley C. Hack	350.00	175.00	100.00
Rolly Hemsley	300.00	150.00	90.00
Jakie May	300.00	150.00	90.00
Bud Tinning	300.00	150.00	90.00

1933 Chicago Cubs Picture Pack

Likely a concession stand souvenir item, this large format (5-7/8" x 8-7/8"), set features action poses of the players in black-and-white on a black background. A bit of the ground at the players' feet is also included in the photo portion. A white facsimile autograph in the black background identifies the player. Backs are blank. The unnumbered pictures are checklisted here in alphabetical order. Some pictures of non-playing personnel were included.

	NM	EX	VG
Complete Set (30):	275.00	135.00	85.00
Common Player:	12.50	6.25	3.75
(1) Guy Bush	12.50	6.25	3.75
(2) Gilly Campbell	12.50	6.25	3.75
(3) John M. Corriden	12.50	6.25	3.75
(4) Kiki Cuyler	25.00	12.50	7.50
(5) J. Frank Demaree	12.50	6.25	3.75
(6) Woody English	12.50	6.25	3.75
(7) Burleigh A. Grimes	25.00	12.50	7.50
(8) Charlie Grimm	12.50	6.25	3.75
(9) Leo "Gabby" Hartnett	25.00	12.50	7.50
(10) Harvey Hendrick	12.50	6.25	3.75
(11) Roy Henshaw	12.50	6.25	3.75
(12) Babe Herman	15.00	7.50	4.50
(13) William Herman	25.00	12.50	7.50
(14) William Jurges	12.50	6.25	3.75
(15) Mark Koenig	12.50	6.25	3.75
(16) Perce "Pat" Malone	12.50	6.25	3.75
(17) Lynn Nelson	12.50	6.25	3.75
(18) Charlie Root	15.00	7.50	4.50
(19) John Schulte	12.50	6.25	3.75
(20) Riggs Stephenson	15.00	7.50	4.50
(21) Zack Taylor	12.50	6.25	3.75
(22) Bud Tinning	12.50	6.25	3.75
(23) L. Warneke	12.50	6.25	3.75
Non-playing Personnel			
(24) Margaret Donahue	12.50	6.25	3.75
(25) Robert C. Lewis (Traveling secretary.)	12.50	6.25	3.75
(26) John O. Seys	12.50	6.25	3.75
(27) William L. Veeck (President)	25.00	12.50	7.50
(28) W.M. Walker	12.50	6.25	3.75
(29) Philip K. Wrigley	12.50	6.25	3.75
(30) Wm. Wrigley	12.50	6.25	3.75

1936 Chicago Cubs Picture Pack

Nearly identical in format to the 1933 issue, these 5-7/8" x 8-7/8" pictures are printed in black-and-white on a black background with (usually) a white facsimile autograph. Backs are blank. The specific make-up of photo packs sold at Wrigley Field may have changed over the course of the season as players came and went. The unnumbered pictures are checklisted here in alphabetical order.

	NM	EX	VG
Complete Set (34):	240.00	120.00	72.00
Common Player:	9.00	4.50	2.75
(1) Ethan Allen	9.00	4.50	2.75
(2) Clay Bryant	9.00	4.50	2.75
(3) Tex Carleton	9.00	4.50	2.75
(4) Phil Cavarretta	12.00	6.00	3.50
(5) John Corriden	9.00	4.50	2.75
(6) Frank Demaree	9.00	4.50	2.75
(7) Curt Davis	9.00	4.50	2.75
(8) Woody English	9.00	4.50	2.75
(9) Larry French	9.00	4.50	2.75
(10) Augie Galan	9.00	4.50	2.75
(11) Johnny Gill	9.00	4.50	2.75
(12) Charlie Grimm	12.00	6.00	3.50
(13) Stan Hack	12.00	6.00	3.50
(14) Gabby Hartnett	18.00	9.00	5.50
(15) Roy Henshaw	9.00	4.50	2.75
(16) Billy Herman	18.00	9.00	5.50
(17) Roy Johnson	9.00	4.50	2.75
(18) Bill Jurges	9.00	4.50	2.75
(19) Chuck Klein	18.00	9.00	5.50
(20) Fabian Kowalik	9.00	4.50	2.75
(21) Bill Lee	9.00	4.50	2.75
(22) Gene Lillard	9.00	4.50	2.75
(23) Ken O'Dea	9.00	4.50	2.75
(24) Charlie Root	12.00	6.00	3.50
(25) Clyde Shoun	9.00	4.50	2.75
(26) Tuck Stainback	9.00	4.50	2.75
(27) Walter Stephenson	9.00	4.50	2.75
(28) Lon Warneke	9.00	4.50	2.75
Non-playing personnel			
(29) Margaret Donahue	9.00	4.50	2.75
(30) Bob Lewis (Traveling secretary.)	9.00	4.50	2.75
(31) Andy Lotshaw (Trainer)	9.00	4.50	2.75
(32) John O. Seys	9.00	4.50	2.75
(33) Charles Weber	9.00	4.50	2.75
(34) Wrigley Field	18.00	9.00	5.50

1939 Chicago Cubs Picture Pack

The use of a textured paper stock for these 6-1/2" x 9" pictures helps identify the 1939 team issue. The pictures once again feature sepia portrait photos with a white border. A facsimile autograph is at bottom. Backs are blank. The specific make-up of photo packs sold at Wrigley Field may have changed over the course of the season as players came and went. The unnumbered pictures are checklisted here in alphabetical order.

	NM	EX	VG
Complete Set (25):	225.00	115.00	65.00
Common Player:	9.00	4.50	2.75
(1) Dick Bartell	9.00	4.50	2.75
(2) Clay Bryant	9.00	4.50	2.75
(3) Phil Cavarretta	12.00	6.00	3.50
(4) John Corriden	9.00	4.50	2.75
(5) Dizzy Dean	40.00	20.00	12.00
(6) Larry French	9.00	4.50	2.75
(7) Augie Galan	9.00	4.50	2.75
(8) Bob Garbark	9.00	4.50	2.75
(9) Jim Gleeson	9.00	4.50	2.75
(10) Stan Hack	12.00	6.00	3.50
(11) Gabby Hartnett	20.00	10.00	6.00
(12) Billy Herman	20.00	10.00	6.00
(13) Roy Johnson	9.00	4.50	2.75
(14) Bill Lee	9.00	4.50	2.75
(15) Hank Leiber	9.00	4.50	2.75
(16) Gene Lillard	9.00	4.50	2.75
(17) Gus Mancuso	9.00	4.50	2.75
(18) Bobby Mattick	9.00	4.50	2.75
(19) Vance Page	9.00	4.50	2.75
(20) Claude Passeau	9.00	4.50	2.75
(21) Carl Reynolds	9.00	4.50	2.75
(22) Charlie Root	12.00	6.00	3.50
(23) Glenn "Rip" Russell	9.00	4.50	2.75
(24) Jack Russell	9.00	4.50	2.75
(25) Earl Whitehill	9.00	4.50	2.75

1940 Chicago Cubs Picture Pack

The 1940 team-issue is identical in format to the 1939s: 6-1/2" x 9", printed on rough-surfaced paper stock with black-and-white portraits surrounded by a wide border and a facsimile autograph on front. Study of the uniforms, however, may help differentiate the issue from 1939, as the 1940 uniforms have no stripe on the shoulders. It is possible that 1939 pictures continued to be issued in the 1940 photo packs and that specific make-up of the packs changed with the team's roster. The blank-back pictures are unnumbered and checklisted here in alphabetical order.

	NM	EX	VG
Complete Set (25):	80.00	40.00	24.00
Common Player:	9.00	4.50	2.75
(1) Dick Bartell	9.00	4.50	2.75
(2) Clay Bryant	9.00	4.50	2.75
(3) Phil Cavarretta	12.00	6.00	3.50
(4) John Corriden	9.00	4.50	2.75
(5) Bob Collins	9.00	4.50	2.75
(6) "Del" Dallessandro	9.00	4.50	2.75
(7) Larry French	9.00	4.50	2.75
(8) Augie Galan	9.00	4.50	2.75
(9) Jim Gleeson	9.00	4.50	2.75
(10) Stan Hack	12.00	6.00	3.50
(11) Gabby Hartnett	20.00	10.00	6.00
(12) Billy Herman	20.00	10.00	6.00
(13) Roy Johnson	9.00	4.50	2.75
(14) Bill Lee	9.00	4.50	2.75
(15) Hank Leiber	9.00	4.50	2.75
(16) Bobby Mattick	9.00	4.50	2.75
(17) Jake Mooty	9.00	4.50	2.75
(18) Bill Nicholson	9.00	4.50	2.75
(19) Vance Page	9.00	4.50	2.75
(20) Claude Passeau	9.00	4.50	2.75
(21) Ken Raffensberger	9.00	4.50	2.75
(22) Bill Rogell	9.00	4.50	2.75
(23) Charlie Root	9.00	4.50	2.75
(24) Rip Russell	9.00	4.50	2.75
(25) Al Todd	9.00	4.50	2.75

1941 Chicago Cubs Picture Pack

A change of paper stock to a smooth finish helps differentiate the 1941 team-issue from previous years' offerings. Size remains at 6-1/2" x 9" with sepia player portraits surrounded by a white border and overprinted with a facsimile autograph. Backs are blank on these unnumbered photos. The pictures are listed here in alphabetical order.

	NM	EX	VG
Complete Set (25):	190.00	95.00	57.00
Common Player:	9.00	4.50	2.75
(1) Phil Cavarretta	12.00	6.00	3.50
(2) Dom Dallessandro	9.00	4.50	2.75
(3) Paul Erickson	9.00	4.50	2.75
(4) Larry French	9.00	4.50	2.75
(5) Augie Galan	9.00	4.50	2.75
(6) Greek George	9.00	4.50	2.75
(7) Charlie Gilbert	9.00	4.50	2.75
(8) Stan Hack	12.00	6.00	3.50
(9) Johnny Hudson	9.00	4.50	2.75
(10) Bill Lee	9.00	4.50	2.75
(11) Hank Leiber	9.00	4.50	2.75
(12) Clyde McCullough	9.00	4.50	2.75
(13) Jake Mooty	9.00	4.50	2.75
(14) Bill Myers	9.00	4.50	2.75
(15) Bill Nicholson	9.00	4.50	2.75
(16) Lou Novikoff	9.00	4.50	2.75
(17) Vern Olsen	9.00	4.50	2.75
(18) Vance Page	9.00	4.50	2.75
(19) Claude Passeau	9.00	4.50	2.75
(20) Tot Pressnell	9.00	4.50	2.75
(21) Charlie Root	12.00	6.00	3.50
(22) Bob Scheffing	9.00	4.50	2.75
(23) Lou Stringer	9.00	4.50	2.75
(24) Bob Sturgeon	9.00	4.50	2.75
(25) Cubs Staff (Dizzy Dean, Charlie Grimm, Dick Spalding, Jimmie Wilson)	12.00	6.00	3.50

1942 Chicago Cubs Picture Pack

The relatively small number of photos in this team-issued set indicates it may have been issued as a supplement to update earlier photo packs with players who were new to the Cubs. In the same 6-1/2" x 9" format as previous issues, the 1942s are printed in sepia on a smooth-surfaced paper. A facsimile autograph graces the front and the portrait photo is surrounded by a border. Backs are blank and the pictures are not numbered. The checklist here is in alphabetical order.

	NM	EX	VG
Complete Set (26):	175.00	90.00	55.00
Common Player:	9.00	4.50	2.75
(1) Hiram Bithorn	12.00	6.00	3.50
(2) Phil Cavarretta	9.00	4.50	2.75
(3) "Del" Dallasandro	9.00	4.50	2.75
(4) Paul Erickson	9.00	4.50	2.75
(5) Bill Fleming	9.00	4.50	2.75
(6) Charlie Gilbert	9.00	4.50	2.75
(7) Stan Hack	15.00	7.50	4.50
(8) Ed Hanyzewski	9.00	4.50	2.75
(9) Chico Hernandez	9.00	4.50	2.75
(10) Bill Lee	9.00	4.50	2.75
(11) Harry Lowrey	9.00	4.50	2.75
(12) Clyde McCullough	9.00	4.50	2.75
(13) Lennie Merullo	9.00	4.50	2.75
(14) Jake Mooty	9.00	4.50	2.75
(15) Bill Nicholson	9.00	4.50	2.75
(16) Lou Novikoff	9.00	4.50	2.75
(17) Vern Olsen	9.00	4.50	2.75
(18) Claude Passeau	9.00	4.50	2.75
(19) Tot Pressnell	9.00	4.50	2.75
(20) Glen "Rip" Russell	9.00	4.50	2.75
(21) Bob Scheffing	9.00	4.50	2.75
(22) Johnny Schmitz	9.00	4.50	2.75
(23) Lou Stringer	9.00	4.50	2.75
(24) Bob Sturgeon	9.00	4.50	2.75
(25) Kiki Cuyler, Dick Spalding, Jimmie Wilson	9.00	4.50	2.75
(26) Jimmie Wilson, Dick Spalding, Charlie Grimm, Dizzy Dean	15.00	7.50	4.50

1943 Chicago Cubs Picture Pack

It is impossible to differentiate pictures from the 1943 issue from those of early years and of 1944, since many pictures were reused and the format is identical: 6-1/2" x 9", black-and-white portrait photos with facsimile autograph and white borders. Backs are blank and the photos are not numbered. They are checklisted here alphabetically.

		NM	EX	VG
Complete Set (25):		215.00	105.00	65.00
Common Player:		9.00	4.50	2.75
(1)	Dick Barrett	9.00	4.50	2.75
(2)	Heinz Becker	9.00	4.50	2.75
(3)	Hiram Bithorn	12.00	6.00	3.50
(4)	Phil Cavarretta	9.00	4.50	2.75
(5)	"Del" Dallasandro	9.00	4.50	2.75
(6)	Paul Derringer	9.00	4.50	2.75
(7)	Paul Erickson	9.00	4.50	2.75
(8)	Bill Fleming	9.00	4.50	2.75
(9)	Stan Hack	12.00	6.00	3.50
(10)	Ed Hanyzewski	9.00	4.50	2.75
(11)	Chico Hernandez	9.00	4.50	2.75
(12)	Bill Lee	9.00	4.50	2.75
(13)	Peanuts Lowrey	9.00	4.50	2.75
(14)	Stu Martin	9.00	4.50	2.75
(15)	Clyde McCullough	9.00	4.50	2.75
(16)	Len Merullo	9.00	4.50	2.75
(17)	Bill Nicholson	9.00	4.50	2.75
(18)	Lou Novikoff	9.00	4.50	2.75
(19)	Claude Passeau	9.00	4.50	2.75
(20)	Ray Prim	9.00	4.50	2.75
(21)	Eddie Stanky	12.00	6.00	3.50
(22)	Al Todd	9.00	4.50	2.75
(23)	Lon Warneke	9.00	4.50	2.75
(24)	Hank Wyse	9.00	4.50	2.75
(25)	Cubs Coaches (Kiki Cuyler, Dick Spalding, Jimmie Wilson)	9.00	4.50	2.75

1944 Chicago Cubs Picture Pack

A slight size reduction, to 6" x 8-1/2", helps identify the team's 1944 photo pack. The pictures feature black-and-white portrait photos with a white border. A facsimile autograph is at bottom. Backs are blank. The specific make-up of photo packs sold at Wrigley Field may have changed over the course of the season as players came and went. The unnumbered pictures are checklisted here in alphabetical order.

		NM	EX	VG
Complete Set (25):		215.00	105.00	65.00
Common Player:		9.00	4.50	2.75
(1)	Heinz Becker	9.00	4.50	2.75
(2)	John Burrows	9.00	4.50	2.75
(3)	Phil Cavarretta	12.00	6.00	3.50
(4)	"Del" Dallessandro	9.00	4.50	2.75
(5)	Paul Derringer	9.00	4.50	2.75
(6)	Roy Easterwood	9.00	4.50	2.75
(7)	Paul Erickson	9.00	4.50	2.75
(8)	Bill Fleming	9.00	4.50	2.75
(9)	Jimmie Foxx	30.00	15.00	9.00
(10)	Ival Goodman	9.00	4.50	2.75
(11)	Ed Hanyzewski	9.00	4.50	2.75
(12)	Billy Holm	9.00	4.50	2.75
(13)	Don Johnson	9.00	4.50	2.75
(14)	Garth Mann	9.00	4.50	2.75
(15)	Len Merullo	9.00	4.50	2.75
(16)	John Miklos	9.00	4.50	2.75
(17)	Bill Nicholson	9.00	4.50	2.75
(18)	Lou Novikoff	9.00	4.50	2.75
(19)	Andy Pafko	12.00	6.00	3.50
(20)	Ed Sauer	9.00	4.50	2.75
(21)	Bill Schuster	9.00	4.50	2.75
(22)	Eddie Stanky	12.00	6.00	3.50
(23)	Hy Vandenberg	9.00	4.50	2.75
(24)	Hank Wyse	9.00	4.50	2.75
(25)	Tony York	9.00	4.50	2.75

1924 Chicago Evening American Cubs/White Sox Pins

These 1-3/8" diameter pins were issued by the Chicago Evening American newspaper to promote its peach-colored sports section. Rather crude blue-and-white line drawings of the players are at center, within an orange peach with the player's name at bottom. Borders are either white or dark blue. The pins were produced by Greenduck Metal Stamping of Chicago.

		NM	EX	VG
Complete Set (12):		3,500	1,750	1,000
Common Player:		200.00	100.00	65.00
(1)	Grover Alexander	750.00	375.00	225.00
(2)	Eddie Collins	450.00	225.00	135.00
(3)	"Red" Faber	350.00	175.00	105.00
(4)	Ray Grimes	200.00	100.00	65.00
(5)	Charlie Hollocher	200.00	100.00	65.00
(6)	Harry Hooper	350.00	175.00	105.00
(7)	Willie Kamm	200.00	100.00	65.00
(8)	Bill Killefer	200.00	100.00	65.00
(9)	Bob O'Farrell	200.00	100.00	65.00
(10)	Charlie Robertson	200.00	100.00	65.00
(11)	Ray Schalk	350.00	175.00	100.00
(12)	Jigger Statz	200.00	100.00	65.00

1930 Chicago Evening American Pins

Members of the Cubs and White Sox are featured on this series of pins issued by one of the local daily newspapers. Player portraits are featured in black-and-white on a white background on these 1-1/4" celluloid pins. Above the picture are the player's position, last name and team; below is the sponsor's name. The unnumbered pins are listed here in alphabetical order within team.

		NM	EX	VG
Complete Set (20):		6,500	3,250	1,950
Common Player:		250.00	125.00	75.00
	Chicago Cubs Team Set (11):	3,500	1,750	1,000
(1)	Les Bell	250.00	125.00	75.00
(2)	Guy Bush	250.00	125.00	75.00
(3)	Kiki Cuyler	350.00	175.00	100.00
(4)	Woody English	250.00	125.00	75.00
(5)	Charlie Grimm	250.00	125.00	75.00
(6)	Gabby Hartnett	350.00	175.00	100.00
(7)	Rogers Hornsby	750.00	375.00	225.00
(8)	Joe McCarthy	350.00	175.00	100.00
(9)	Charlie Root	250.00	125.00	75.00
(10)	Riggs Stephenson	250.00	125.00	75.00
(11)	Hack Wilson	400.00	200.00	120.00
	Chicago White Sox Team Set (9):	3,000	1,500	900.00
(1)	Moe Berg	1,000	500.00	300.00
(2)	Bill Cissel (Cissell)	250.00	125.00	75.00
(3)	Red Faber	350.00	175.00	105.00
(4)	Bill Hunnefield	250.00	125.00	75.00
(5)	Smead Jolley	250.00	125.00	75.00
(6)	Willie Kamm	250.00	125.00	75.00
(7)	Jimmy Moore	250.00	125.00	75.00
(8)	Carl Reynolds	250.00	125.00	75.00
(9)	Art Shires	250.00	125.00	75.00

1930 Chicago Herald and Examiner Babe Ruth Premium

This premium picture with a black-and-white batting pose of Ruth was issued by a Chicago newspaper. Two sizes are known, approximately 8-1/2" x 11-1/2" and 5" x 7". The pictures are blank-back. The year attributed is speculative.

	NM	EX	VG
Babe Ruth (Large)	1,350	625.00	400.00
Babe Ruth (Small)	1,350	625.00	400.00

1976 Chicagoland Collectors Association Chicago Greats

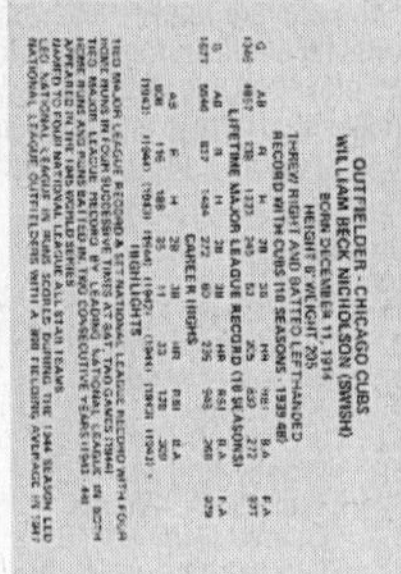

Former stars of the Cubs and White Sox are featured in this collectors issue produced in conjunction with an early sports card and memorabilia show in Chicago. The 2-1/2" x 3-1/2" cards feature black-and-white action photos at center of most cards, with a portrait photo inset at top. Graphics around the front are in red. Backs have detailed career summaries. A starting team, manager and president for each of the Chicago teams is represented in the issue. Complete sets were originally sold for about $2 with uncut sheets sold for $6.

		NM	EX	VG
Complete Set (25):		15.00	7.50	4.50
Common Player:		2.00	1.00	.60
(1)	Luke Appling	2.00	1.00	.60
(2)	Ernie Banks	6.00	3.00	1.75
(3)	Zeke Bonura	2.00	1.00	.60
(4)	Phil Cavarretta	2.00	1.00	.60
(5)	Jimmy Dykes	2.00	1.00	.60
(6)	Red Faber, Ted Lyons	2.00	1.00	.60
(7)	Nellie Fox	4.00	2.00	1.25
(8)	Larry French	2.00	1.00	.60
(9)	Charlie Grimm	2.00	1.00	.60
(10)	Gabby Hartnett	2.00	1.00	.60
(11)	Billy Herman	2.00	1.00	.60
(12)	Mike Kreevich	2.00	1.00	.60
(13)	Sherman Lollar	2.00	1.00	.60
(14)	Al Lopez	2.00	1.00	.60
(15)	Minnie Minoso	3.00	1.50	.90
(16)	Wally Moses	2.00	1.00	.60
(17)	Bill Nicholson	2.00	1.00	.60
(18)	Claude Passeau	2.00	1.00	.60
(19)	Billy Pierce	2.00	1.00	.60
(20)	Ron Santo	2.00	1.00	.60
(21)	Hank Sauer	2.00	1.00	.60
(22)	Riggs Stephenson	2.00	1.00	.60
(23)	Bill Veeck	2.00	1.00	.60
(24)	P.K. Wrigley	2.00	1.00	.60
(25)	Checklist	2.00	1.00	.60

1915 Chicago Tribune Supplements

As the 1915 baseball season opened, the Chicago Sunday Tribune ran supplements in its April 4 and April 11 editions featuring pictures of Chicago players. The black-and-white pictures are 8" x 11". Saier is pictured in uniform, the others are in street clothes. Printed in the white border beneath each photo is "Supplement to The Chicago Sunday Tribune, April 4 (or) 11, 1915." Each picture bears a facsimile autograph of the player and is blank-backed.

		NM	EX	VG
Complete Set (4):		400.00	200.00	120.00
Common Player:		50.00	25.00	15.00
(1)	Roger Bresnahan (April 11)	100.00	50.00	30.00
(2)	Eddie Collins (April 11)	100.00	50.00	30.00
(3)	Vic Saier (April 11)	50.00	25.00	15.00
(4)	Joe Tinker (April 4)	150.00	75.00	45.00

1917 Chicago White Sox Team Issue

This set of the World Champion White Sox (including several of the notorious Black Sox) was produced by Davis Printing Works in Chicago and apparently sold as a complete boxed set by the team. Individual cards measure about 1-11/16" x 2-3/4". Fronts feature full-length black-and-white photos of the players on a light background with a white border. Player name and position are in black beneath the picture. Backs are blank. To date, only one set is known to exist. It sold at auction in 1991 for $45,100, again in 1997 for $46,000 and in 2001 for $50,330. The unnumbered cards are checklisted here alphabetically.

Complete Set (25):
Value undetermined.

(1)	Joe Benz
(2)	Eddie Cicotte
(3)	Eddie Collins
(4)	Shano Collins
(5)	Charles Comiskey
(6)	Dave Danforth
(7)	Red Faber
(8)	Happy Felsch
(9)	Chick Gandil
(10)	Kid Gleason
(11)	Joe Jackson
(12)	Joe Jenkins
(13)	Ted Jourdan
(14)	Nemo Leibold
(15)	Byrd Lynn
(16)	Fred McMullin
(17)	Eddie Murphy
(18)	Swede Risberg
(19)	Pants Rowland
(20)	Reb Russell
(21)	Ray Schalk
(22)	James Scott
(23)	Buck Weaver
(24)	Lefty Williams
(25)	Mellie Wolfgang

1940 Chicago White Sox Photo Pack

This set of souvenir photos was produced by Andy Lotshaw, who was a Cubs trainer. The 5-1/2" x 6-3/4" pictures have a sepia pose bordered in white, with a facsimile autograph. Backs are blank. The unnumbered pictures are checklisted here in alphabetical order.

		NM	EX	VG
Complete Set (25):		300.00	150.00	90.00
Common Player:		15.00	7.50	4.50
(1)	Pete Appleton	15.00	7.50	4.50
(2)	Luke Appling	30.00	15.00	9.00
(3)	Clint Brown	15.00	7.50	4.50
(4)	Bill Dietrich	15.00	7.50	4.50
(5)	Jimmy Dykes	15.00	7.50	4.50
(6)	Mule Haas	15.00	7.50	4.50
(7)	Jack Hayes	15.00	7.50	4.50
(8)	Bob Kennedy	15.00	7.50	4.50
(9)	Jack Knott	15.00	7.50	4.50
(10)	Mike Kreevich	15.00	7.50	4.50
(11)	Joe Kuhel	15.00	7.50	4.50
(12)	Thornton Lee	15.00	7.50	4.50
(13)	Ted Lyons	25.00	12.50	7.50
(14)	Eric McNair	15.00	7.50	4.50
(15)	John Rigney	15.00	7.50	4.50
(16)	Larry Rosenthal	15.00	7.50	4.50
(17)	Ken Silvestri	15.00	7.50	4.50
(18)	Eddie Smith	15.00	7.50	4.50
(19)	J. Solters	15.00	7.50	4.50
(20)	Monty Stratton	20.00	10.00	6.00
(21)	Mike Tresh	15.00	7.50	4.50
(22)	Tom Turner	15.00	7.50	4.50
(23)	Skeeter Webb	20.00	10.00	6.00
(24)	Ed Weiland	15.00	7.50	4.50
(25)	Taft Wright	15.00	7.50	4.50

1948 Chicago White Sox Photo Pack

The last-place White Sox of 1948 are immortalized in this team-issued set of player photos. Individual players are pictured in a 6-1/2" x 9" portrait photo with a thin white border around. A facsimile autograph also appears on front. Backs are blank. A team photo was also included in the set. The photo pack was sold in a large white envelope with a red and blue team logo. The unnumbered pictures are checklisted here in alphabetical order.

		NM	EX	VG
Complete Set (30):		180.00	90.00	54.00
Common Player:		7.50	3.75	2.25
(1)	Luke Appling	18.00	9.00	5.50
(2)	Floyd Baker	7.50	3.75	2.25
(3)	Fred Bradley	7.50	3.75	2.25
(4)	Earl Caldwell	7.50	3.75	2.25
(5)	Red Faber	15.00	7.50	4.50
(6)	Bob Gillespie	7.50	3.75	2.25
(7)	Jim Goodwin	12.00	6.00	3.50
(8)	Orval Grove	7.50	3.75	2.25
(9)	Earl Harrist	7.50	3.75	2.25
(10)	Joe Haynes	7.50	3.75	2.25
(11)	Ralph Hodgin	7.50	3.75	2.25
(12)	Howie Judson	7.50	3.75	2.25
(13)	Bob Kennedy	7.50	3.75	2.25
(14)	Don Kolloway	7.50	3.75	2.25
(15)	Tony Lupien	7.50	3.75	2.25
(16)	Ted Lyons	15.00	7.50	4.50
(17)	Cass Michaels	7.50	3.75	2.25
(18)	Bing Miller	7.50	3.75	2.25
(19)	Buster Mills	7.50	3.75	2.25
(20)	Glen Moulder	7.50	3.75	2.25
(21)	Frank Papish	7.50	3.75	2.25
(22)	Ike Pearson	7.50	3.75	2.25
(23)	Dave Philley	7.50	3.75	2.25
(24)	Aaron Robinson	7.50	3.75	2.25
(25)	Mike Tresh	7.50	3.75	2.25
(26)	Jack Wallaesa	7.50	3.75	2.25
(27)	Ralph Weigel	7.50	3.75	2.25
(28)	Bill Wight	7.50	3.75	2.25
(29)	Taft Wright	7.50	3.75	2.25
(30)	Team picture	18.00	9.00	5.50

1960-64 Chicago White Sox Ticket Stubs

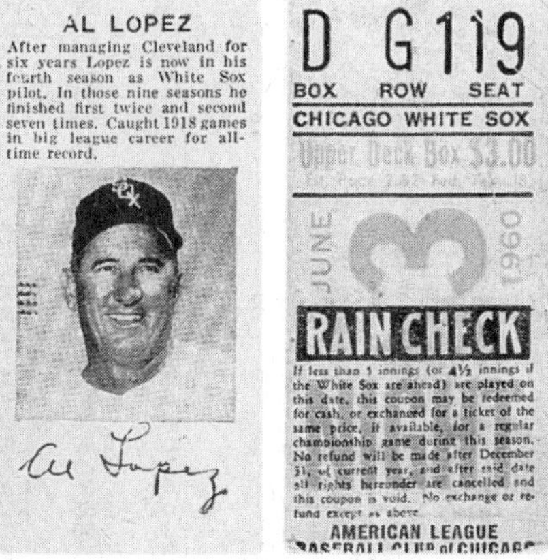

From 1960-64 tickets to White Sox home games at Comiskey Park were issued bearing player photos. Along with the photos on the backs of the 1-5/16" x 2-5/8" ticket stubs are career information and facsimile autographs. Photos were generally re-used from year to year and color variations, depending on the type of ticket, are known. Players from each year are listed here alphabetically.

		NM	EX	VG
Complete Set (113):		2,250	1,125	675.00
Common Player:		30.00	15.00	9.00
60-1	Luis Aparicio	75.00	37.00	22.00
60-2	Earl Battey	30.00	15.00	9.00
60-3	Frank Baumann	30.00	15.00	9.00
60-4	Dick Donovan	30.00	15.00	9.00
60-5	Nelson Fox	75.00	37.00	22.00
60-6	Gene Freese	30.00	15.00	9.00
60-7	Ted Kluszewski	60.00	30.00	18.00
60-8	Jim Landis	30.00	15.00	9.00
60-9	Barry Latman	30.00	15.00	9.00
60-10	Sherm Lollar	30.00	15.00	9.00
60-11	Al Lopez	45.00	22.00	13.50
60-12	Turk Lown	30.00	15.00	9.00
60-13	Orestes Minoso	50.00	25.00	15.00
60-14	Bill Pierce	30.00	15.00	9.00
60-15	Jim Rivera	30.00	15.00	9.00
60-16	Bob Shaw	30.00	15.00	9.00
60-17	Roy Sievers	30.00	15.00	9.00
60-18	Al Smith	30.00	15.00	9.00
60-19	Gerry Staley	30.00	15.00	9.00
60-20	Early Wynn	45.00	22.00	13.50
61-1	Luis Aparicio	75.00	37.00	22.00
61-2	Frank Baumann	30.00	15.00	9.00
61-3	Camilo Carreon	30.00	15.00	9.00
61-4	Sam Esposito	30.00	15.00	9.00
61-5	Nelson Fox	75.00	37.00	22.00
61-6	Billy Goodman	30.00	15.00	9.00
61-7	Jim Landis	30.00	15.00	9.00
61-8	Sherman Lollar	30.00	15.00	9.00
61-9	Al Lopez	45.00	22.00	13.50
61-10	J.C. Martin	30.00	15.00	9.00
61-11	Cal McLish	30.00	15.00	9.00
61-12	Orestes Minoso	50.00	25.00	15.00
61-13	Bill Pierce	30.00	15.00	9.00
61-14	Juan Pizarro	30.00	15.00	9.00
61-15	Bob Roselli	30.00	15.00	9.00
61-16	Herb Score	35.00	17.50	10.50
61-17	Bob Shaw	30.00	15.00	9.00
61-18	Roy Sievers	30.00	15.00	9.00
61-19	Al Smith	30.00	15.00	9.00
61-20	Gerry Staley	30.00	15.00	9.00
61-21	Early Wynn	45.00	22.00	13.50
62-1	Luis Aparicio	75.00	37.00	22.00
62-2	Frank Baumann	30.00	15.00	9.00
62-3	John Buzhardt	30.00	15.00	9.00
62-4	Camilo Carreon	30.00	15.00	9.00
62-5	Joe Cunningham	30.00	15.00	9.00
62-6	Bob Farley	30.00	15.00	9.00
62-7	Eddie Fisher	30.00	15.00	9.00
62-8	Nelson Fox	75.00	37.00	22.00
62-9	Jim Landis	30.00	15.00	9.00
62-10	Sherm Lollar	30.00	15.00	9.00
62-11	Al Lopez	45.00	22.00	13.50
62-12	Turk Lown	30.00	15.00	9.00
62-13	J.C. Martin	30.00	15.00	9.00
62-14	Cal McLish	30.00	15.00	9.00
62-15	Gary Peters	30.00	15.00	9.00
62-16	Juan Pizarro	30.00	15.00	9.00
62-17	Floyd Robinson	30.00	15.00	9.00
62-18	Bob Roselli	30.00	15.00	9.00
62-19	Herb Score	35.00	17.50	10.50
62-20	Al Smith	30.00	15.00	9.00
62-21	Charles Smith	30.00	15.00	9.00
62-22	Early Wynn	45.00	22.00	13.50
63-1	Frank Baumann	30.00	15.00	9.00
63-2	John Buzhardt	30.00	15.00	9.00
63-3	Camilo Carreon	30.00	15.00	9.00
63-4	Joe Cunningham	30.00	15.00	9.00
63-5	Dave DeBusschere	40.00	20.00	12.00
63-6	Eddie Fisher	30.00	15.00	9.00
63-7	Nelson Fox	75.00	37.00	22.00
63-8	Ron Hansen	30.00	15.00	9.00
63-9	Ray Herbert	30.00	15.00	9.00
63-10	Mike Hershberger	30.00	15.00	9.00
63-11	Joe Horlen	30.00	15.00	9.00
63-12	Grover Jones	30.00	15.00	9.00
63-13	Mike Joyce	30.00	15.00	9.00
63-14	Frank Kreutzer	30.00	15.00	9.00
63-15	Jim Landis	30.00	15.00	9.00
63-16	Sherman Lollar	30.00	15.00	9.00
63-17	Al Lopez	45.00	22.00	13.50
63-18	J.C. Martin	30.00	15.00	9.00
63-19	Charlie Maxwell	30.00	15.00	9.00
63-20	Dave Nicholson	30.00	15.00	9.00
63-21	Juan Pizarro	30.00	15.00	9.00
63-22	Floyd Robinson	30.00	15.00	9.00
63-23	Charley Smith	30.00	15.00	9.00
63-24	Pete Ward	30.00	15.00	9.00
63-25	Al Weis	30.00	15.00	9.00
63-26	Hoyt Wilhelm	45.00	22.00	13.50
63-27	Dom Zanni	30.00	15.00	9.00
64-1	Fritz Ackley	30.00	15.00	9.00
64-2	Frank Baumann	30.00	15.00	9.00
64-3	Don Buford	30.00	15.00	9.00
64-4	John Buzhardt	30.00	15.00	9.00
64-5	Camilo Carreon	30.00	15.00	9.00
64-6	Joe Cunningham	30.00	15.00	9.00
64-7	Dave DeBusschere	40.00	20.00	12.00
64-8	Eddie Fisher	30.00	15.00	9.00
64-9	Jim Golden	30.00	15.00	9.00
64-10	Ron Hansen	30.00	15.00	9.00
64-11	Ray Herbert	30.00	15.00	9.00
64-12	Mike Hershberger	30.00	15.00	9.00
64-13	Joe Horlen	30.00	15.00	9.00
64-14	Jim Landis	30.00	15.00	9.00
64-15	Al Lopez	45.00	22.00	13.50
64-16	J.C. Martin	30.00	15.00	9.00
64-17	Dave Nicholson	30.00	15.00	9.00
64-18	Gary Peters	30.00	15.00	9.00
64-19	Juan Pizarro	30.00	15.00	9.00
64-20	Floyd Robinson	30.00	15.00	9.00
64-21	Gene Stephens	30.00	15.00	9.00
64-22	Pete Ward	30.00	15.00	9.00
64-23	Al Weis	30.00	15.00	9.00
64-24	Hoyt Wilhelm	45.00	22.00	13.50

1899 Chickering Studio Boston Beaneaters Cabinets

These oversize (8-7/8" x 9-7/8") cabinet cards feature virtually every regular on the 1899 National League runners-up and this checklist may not be complete. The cards feature chest-up, capless sepia portraits of the players, glued to either black or gray cardboard mounts with the advertising of Boston's Elmer Chickering Studio in silver or gold leaf at bottom. Players are identified by first and last name in fancy black script at the bottom of the photo. Backs are blank.

		NM	EX	VG
Common Player:		3,000	650.00	425.00
(1)	Harvey Bailey	3,000	650.00	425.00

(2)	Martin Bergen	3,000	650.00	425.00
(3)	William Clarke	3,000	650.00	425.00
(4)	Jimmy Collins	7,500	2,700	1,725
(5)	Hugh Duffy	9,000	3,200	1,900
(6)	Billy Hamilton	7,500	3,000	1,800
(7)	Frank Killen	3,000	650.00	425.00
(8)	Ted Lewis	3,000	650.00	425.00
(9)	Herman Long	7,500	2,425	1,450
(10)	Bobby Lowe	3,000	1,125	675.00
(11)	Jouett Meekin	7,500	1,500	900.00
(12)	Charles Nichols	9,000	3,200	1,875
(13)	Fred Tenney	3,000	650.00	425.00

1956-1957 Chicle Peloteros

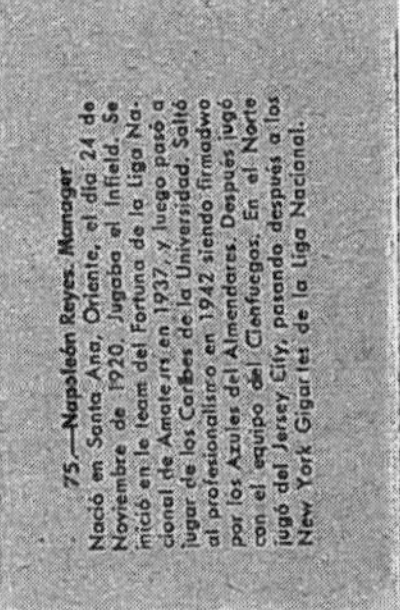

One of the few gumcard issues from Cuba, this set took a cue from American companies by skip-numbering the set to keep youngsters buying gum in search of cards that did not exist. The cards measure about 2" x 3". Fronts have color portrait photos bordered in white with the player name and card number in a colored strip below. Backs are in black-and-white with a few biographical notes and career highlights. The cards are printed on thick gray stock. A colorful album to house the cards was also produced.

		NM	EX	VG
Complete Set (40):		2,750	1,375	850.00
Common Player:		60.00	30.00	18.00
Album:		100.00	50.00	30.00
2	Emilio Cabrera	60.00	30.00	18.00
4	Conrado Marrero	100.00	50.00	30.00
5	Silvio Garcia	250.00	125.00	75.00
6	Russel (Russell) Nixon	75.00	37.50	22.50
7	Enrique Izquierdo	60.00	30.00	18.00
8	Lou Skinner	60.00	30.00	18.00
9	Robert Mc Kee	60.00	30.00	18.00
10	Gonzalo Naranjo	60.00	30.00	18.00
11	Trompoloco Rodriguez	60.00	30.00	18.00
12	Evelio Hernandez	60.00	30.00	18.00
26	Oscar Rodriguez	60.00	30.00	18.00
27	Jose (Cheo) Ramos	60.00	30.00	18.00
28	Napoleon Heredia	60.00	30.00	18.00
29	Camilo Pascual	150.00	75.00	45.00
30	Pedro Ramos	90.00	45.00	27.50
31	Rene Gutierrez	60.00	30.00	18.00
32	Julio (Jiqui) Moreno	65.00	32.50	20.00
33	Bud Daley	65.00	32.50	20.00
34	Dick Tomaneck (Tomanek)	60.00	30.00	18.00
35	Rafael Noble	65.00	32.50	20.00
50	Gilberto Torres	60.00	30.00	18.00
51	Salvador Hernandez	60.00	30.00	18.00
52	Pipo de la Noval	60.00	30.00	18.00
53	Juan Soler	60.00	30.00	18.00
54	Oscar Sierra	60.00	30.00	18.00
55	Billy Muffet (Muffett)	60.00	30.00	18.00
56	Robert Bluaylock (Blaylock)	60.00	30.00	18.00
57	Edwin Mayers	60.00	30.00	18.00
58	Vicente Amor	60.00	30.00	18.00
59	Raul Sanchez	60.00	30.00	18.00
75	Napoleon Reyes	90.00	45.00	27.50
76	Jose Maria Fernandez	90.00	45.00	27.50
77	Juan Izaguirre	60.00	30.00	18.00
79	Rene Friol	60.00	30.00	18.00
80	Asdrubal Baro	60.00	30.00	18.00
82	Juan Delis	60.00	30.00	18.00
83	Julio Becquer	60.00	30.00	18.00
84	Rodolfo Arias	60.00	30.00	18.00
86	Patricio Quintana	60.00	30.00	18.00
87	Aldo Salvent	60.00	30.00	18.00

1900 Chickering Studio Cabinets

The extent of this issue of standard-format (about 4-1/4" x 6-1/2") cabinets is unknown. Fronts have a studio pose with a decorative studio logo in the bottom border. Backs have a large ad for the renowned Boston photographer.

		NM	EX	VG
Common Player:				
(1)	Win Mercer	1,500	750.00	450.00
(2)	Kid Nichols	9,000	4,500	2,750

1977 Chilly Willee Discs

Virtually identical in format to the several locally sponsored disc sets of the previous year, these 3-3/8" diameter player discs were given away at participating frozen drink stands. Discs once again feature black-and-white player portrait photos in the center of a baseball design. The left and right panels are in one of several bright colors. Licensed by the Players Association through Mike Schechter Associates, the player photos carry no uniform logos. Backs are printed in blue and red. The unnumbered discs are checklisted here alphabetically.

		NM	EX	VG
Complete Set (70):		65.00	32.50	20.00
Common Player:		1.00	.50	.30
(1)	Sal Bando	1.00	.50	.30
(2)	Buddy Bell	1.00	.50	.30
(3)	Johnny Bench	5.00	2.50	1.50
(4)	Larry Dowa	1.00	.50	.30
(5)	Steve Braun	1.00	.50	.30
(6)	George Brett	12.00	6.00	3.50
(7)	Lou Brock	5.00	2.50	1.50
(8)	Jeff Burroughs	1.00	.50	.30
(9)	Bert Campaneris	1.00	.50	.30
(10)	John Candelaria	1.00	.50	.30
(11)	Jose Cardenal	1.00	.50	.30
(12)	Rod Carew	5.00	2.50	1.50
(13)	Steve Carlton	5.00	2.50	1.50
(14)	Dave Cash	1.00	.50	.30
(15)	Cesar Cedeno	1.00	.50	.30
(16)	Ron Cey	1.00	.50	.30
(17)	Dave Concepcion	1.00	.50	.30
(18)	Dennis Eckersley	5.00	2.50	1.50
(19)	Mark Fidrych	2.50	1.25	.70
(20)	Rollie Fingers	4.00	2.00	1.25
(21)	Carlton Fisk	5.00	2.50	1.50
(22)	George Foster	1.00	.50	.30
(23)	Wayne Garland	1.00	.50	.30
(24)	Ralph Garr	1.00	.50	.30
(25)	Steve Garvey	2.00	1.00	.60
(26)	Cesar Geronimo	1.00	.50	.30
(27)	Bobby Grich	1.00	.50	.30
(28)	Ken Griffey Sr.	1.00	.50	.30
(29)	Don Gullett	1.00	.50	.30
(30)	Mike Hargrove	1.00	.50	.30
(31)	Al Hrabosky	1.00	.50	.30
(32)	Catfish Hunter	4.00	2.00	1.25
(33)	Reggie Jackson	10.00	5.00	3.00
(34)	Randy Jones	1.00	.50	.30
(35)	Dave Kingman	1.00	.50	.30
(36)	Jerry Koosman	1.00	.50	.30
(37)	Dave LaRoche	1.00	.50	.30
(38)	Greg Luzinski	1.00	.50	.30
(39)	Fred Lynn	1.00	.50	.30
(40)	Bill Madlock	1.00	.50	.30
(41)	Rick Manning	1.00	.50	.30
(42)	Jon Matlock	1.00	.50	.30
(43)	John Mayberry	1.00	.50	.30
(44)	Hal McRae	1.00	.50	.30
(45)	Andy Messersmith	1.00	.50	.30
(46)	Rick Monday	1.00	.50	.30
(47)	John Montefusco	1.00	.50	.30
(48)	Joe Morgan	5.00	2.50	1.50
(49)	Thurman Munson	4.00	2.00	1.25
(50)	Bobby Murcer	1.00	.50	.30
(51)	Bill North	1.00	.50	.30
(52)	Jim Palmer	5.00	2.50	1.50
(53)	Tony Perez	5.00	2.50	1.50
(54)	Jerry Reuss	1.00	.50	.30
(55)	Brooks Robinson	5.00	2.50	1.50
(56)	Pete Rose	10.00	5.00	3.00
(57)	Joe Rudi	1.00	.50	.30
(58)	Nolan Ryan	20.00	10.00	6.00
(59)	Manny Sanguillen	1.00	.50	.30
(60)	Mike Schmidt	12.00	6.00	3.50
(61)	Tom Seaver	5.00	2.50	1.50
(62)	Bill Singer	1.00	.50	.30
(63)	Willie Stargell	5.00	2.50	1.50
(64)	Rusty Staub	1.50	.70	.45
(65)	Luis Tiant	1.00	.50	.30
(66)	Bob Watson	1.00	.50	.30
(67)	Butch Wynegar	1.00	.50	.30
(68)	Carl Yastrzemski	5.00	2.50	1.50
(69)	Robin Yount	5.00	2.50	1.50
(70)	Richie Zisk	1.00	.50	.30

1929 Churchman's Cigarettes

Though he is identified nowhere on this English cigarette card, the home run swing of Babe Ruth on the front is unmistakable. The last of a set of 25 "Sports & Games in Many Lands" series, the approximately 2-5/8" x 1-3/8" cards have color artwork on the front and green-and-white backs. The back of the baseball card provides a short history of "The great national sport of the U.S.A."

		NM	EX	VG
25	Baseball, U.S.A. (Babe Ruth)	350.00	175.00	100.00

1963 Cincinnati Enquirer Reds' Scrapbook

One of the city's newspapers carried this series that could be out of the newspaper and saved. The black-and-white clippings feature a player photo, stats, career notes and biographical data.

		NM	EX	VG
Complete Set (33):		150.00	75.00	45.00
Common Player:		3.00	1.50	.90
(1)	Don Blasingame	3.00	1.50	.90
(2)	Harry Bright	3.00	1.50	.90
(3)	Jim Brosnan	3.00	1.50	.90
(4)	Leo Cardenas	3.00	1.50	.90
(5)	Gerry Coleman	3.00	1.50	.90
(6)	John Edwards	3.00	1.50	.90
(7)	Sam Ellis	3.00	1.50	.90
(8)	Hank Foiles	3.00	1.50	.90
(9)	Gene Freese	3.00	1.50	.90
(10)	Jesse Gonder	3.00	1.50	.90
(11)	Tommy Harper	3.00	1.50	.90
(12)	Bill Henry	3.00	1.50	.90
(13)	Ken Hunt	3.00	1.50	.90
(14)	Fred Hutchinson	3.00	1.50	.90
(15)	Joey Jay	3.00	1.50	.90
(16)	Eddie Kasko	3.00	1.50	.90
(17)	Marty Keough	3.00	1.50	.90
(18)	Johnny Klippstein	3.00	1.50	.90
(19)	Jerry Lynch	3.00	1.50	.90
(20)	Jim Maloney	3.00	1.50	.90
(21)	Joe Nuxhall	4.50	2.25	1.25
(22)	Jim O'Toole	3.00	1.50	.90
(23)	Jim Owens	3.00	1.50	.90
(24)	Don Pavletich	3.00	1.50	.90
(25)	Vada Pinson	6.00	3.00	1.75
(26)	Wally Post	3.00	1.50	.90
(27)	Bob Purkey	3.00	1.50	.90
(28)	Frank Robinson	20.00	10.00	6.00
(29)	Pete Rose	90.00	45.00	27.00
(30)	Dave Sisler	3.00	1.50	.90
(31)	John Tsitouris	3.00	1.50	.90
(32)	Ken Walters	3.00	1.50	.90
(33)	Al Worthington	3.00	1.50	.90

1980 Cincinnati Enquirer Cincinnati Reds

This set of paper "cards" was printed within the pages of the Cincinnati Enquirer newspaper. The 2-1/4" x 3" cards are printed in black-and-white (both front and back) on newsprint. Dotted lines show where the cards were to be cut. Fronts have a player photo and a drawing of Riverfront Stadium. The team logo is in an upper corner and player identification in a black

SHELDON JOHN BURNSIDE, relief pitcher. Born Dec. 22, 1954 in South Bend, Ind. Lives in Toronto suburb of Etobicoke. Bats right, throws left. Height: 6-5. Weight: 200. Acquired from Detroit for Champ Summers on Oct. 24, 1979.

BURNSIDE'S RECORD

Burnside grew up around Toronto, where no high school baseball was played, and grew to love tennis. The southpaw served right-handed and whizzed through local competition "until some 14-year-old kid beat me." Then baseball took over as Burnside's No. 1 interest. He was brought up in May when Bill Bonham went on the diasabled list.

THE CINCINNATI ENQUIRER

band towards the bottom. Backs have biographical and career details along with stats. Cards are checklisted here according to the uniform numbers printed on front.

		NM	EX	VG
Complete Set (32):		100.00	50.00	30.00
Common Player:		3.00	1.50	.90
2	Russ Nixon	3.00	1.50	.90
3	John McNamara	3.00	1.50	.90
4	Harry Dunlop	3.00	1.50	.90
5	Johnny Bench	9.00	4.50	2.75
6	Bill Fischer	3.00	1.50	.90
7	Hector Cruz	3.00	1.50	.90
9	Vic Correll	3.00	1.50	.90
11	Ron Plaza	3.00	1.50	.90
12	Harry Spilman	3.00	1.50	.90
13	Dave Concepcion	3.00	1.50	.90
15	George Foster	3.00	1.50	.90
16	Ron Oester	3.00	1.50	.90
19	Don Werner	3.00	1.50	.90
20	Cesar Geronimo	3.00	1.50	.90
22	Dan Driessen	3.00	1.50	.90
23	Rick Auerbach	3.00	1.50	.90
25	Ray Knight	3.00	1.50	.90
26	Junior Kennedy	3.00	1.50	.90
28	Sam Mejias	3.00	1.50	.90
29	Dave Collins	3.00	1.50	.90
30	Ken Griffey	3.00	1.50	.90
31	Paul Moskau	3.00	1.50	.90
34	Sheldon Burnside	3.00	1.50	.90
35	Frank Pastore	3.00	1.50	.90
36	Mario Soto	3.00	1.50	.90
37	Dave Tomlin	3.00	1.50	.90
40	Doug Bair	3.00	1.50	.90
41	Tom Seaver	7.50	3.75	2.25
42	Bill Bonham	3.00	1.50	.90
44	Charlie Leibrandt	3.00	1.50	.90
47	Tom Hume	3.00	1.50	.90
51	Mike LaCoss	3.00	1.50	.90

1938 Cincinnati Post Reds

Over the course of several weeks during the summer of 1938, daily editions of the Cincinnati Post sports section carried a set of player portraits designed to be cut out and saved. The pieces measure 6" x 11" and feature a large photo with facsimile autograph, topped by a headline and carrying a short biography below. Everything is in black-and-white. The unnumbered series is checklisted here in alphabetical order.

		NM	EX	VG
Complete Set (25):		450.00	225.00	135.00
Common Player:		20.00	10.00	6.00
(1)	Wally Berger	30.00	15.00	9.00
(2)	Joe Cascarella	20.00	10.00	6.00
(3)	Harry Craft	20.00	10.00	6.00
(4)	Dusty Cooke	20.00	10.00	6.00
(5)	Peaches Davis	20.00	10.00	6.00
(6)	Paul Derringer	25.00	12.50	7.50
(7)	Linus (Junior) Frey	20.00	10.00	6.00
(8)	Lee Gamble	20.00	10.00	6.00
(9)	Ival Goodman	20.00	10.00	6.00
(10)	Hank Gowdy	20.00	10.00	6.00
(11)	Lee Grissom	20.00	10.00	6.00
(12)	Willard Hershberger	25.00	12.50	7.50
(13)	Don Lang	20.00	10.00	6.00
(14)	Ernie Lombardi	35.00	17.50	10.50
(15)	Buck McCormick	20.00	10.00	6.00
(16)	Bill McKechnie	35.00	17.50	10.50
(17)	Whitey Moore	20.00	10.00	6.00
(18)	Billy Myers	20.00	10.00	6.00
(19)	Clifford Richardson	20.00	10.00	6.00
(20)	Lewis Riggs	20.00	10.00	6.00
(21)	Edd Roush	35.00	17.50	10.50
(22)	Gene Schott	20.00	10.00	6.00
(23)	Johnny Vander Meer	30.00	15.00	9.00
(24)	Bucky Walter	20.00	10.00	6.00
(25)	James Weaver	20.00	10.00	6.00

1919-20 Cincinnati Reds Postcards

Two versions of each of the cards in this issue are known. Picturing members of the 1919 World Champions, the foils of the Black Sox scandal, these 3-1/2" x 5-1/2" cards have black-and-white player poses on front. In the white border at bottom (or occasionally, at top) are two lines of type. The top line has the player name and position. The second line can be found in two versions. One reads, "Cincinnati 'Reds' - Champions of National League 1919," the other, presumably a second printing following the World Series, reads, "Cincinnati 'Reds' World's Champions 1919." Backs are printed with standard postcard indicia. Some cards have been found with the advertising of Mt. Union Dairy on the back. The unnumbered cards are checklisted here in alphabetical order.

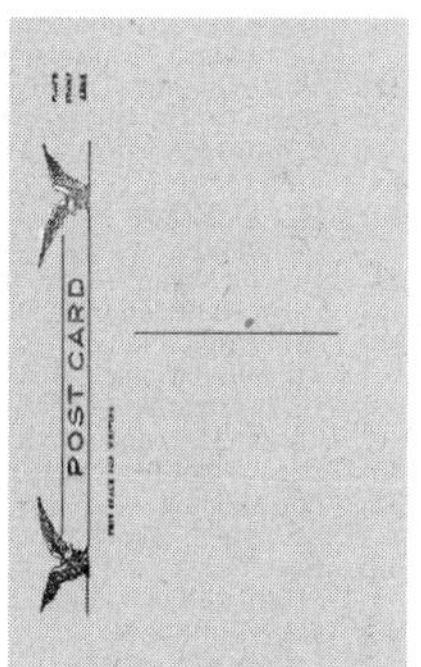

		NM	EX	VG
Complete Set (24):		3,000	1,500	900.00
Common Player:		150.00	75.00	45.00
(1)	Nick Allen	150.00	75.00	45.00
(2)	Rube Bressler	150.00	75.00	45.00
(3)	Jake Daubert	150.00	75.00	45.00
(4)	Pat Duncan	150.00	75.00	45.00
(5)	Hod Eller	150.00	75.00	45.00
(6)	Ray Fisher	150.00	75.00	45.00
(7)	Eddie Gerner	150.00	75.00	45.00
(8)	Heinie Groh	150.00	75.00	45.00
(9)	Larry Kopf	150.00	75.00	45.00
(10)	Adolfo Luque	175.00	85.00	50.00
(11)	Sherwood Magee	150.00	75.00	45.00
(12)	Roy Mitchell	150.00	75.00	45.00
(13)	Pat Moran	150.00	75.00	45.00
(14)	Greasy Neale	200.00	100.00	60.00
(15)	Bill Rariden	150.00	75.00	45.00
(16)	Morris Rath	150.00	75.00	45.00
(17)	Walter Reuther (Ruether)	150.00	75.00	45.00
(18)	Jimmy Ring	150.00	75.00	45.00
(19)	Eddie Roush	400.00	200.00	120.00
(20)	Harry Sallee	150.00	75.00	45.00
(21)	Hank Schreiber	150.00	75.00	45.00
(22)	Charles See	150.00	75.00	45.00
(23)	Jimmy Smith	150.00	75.00	45.00
(24)	Ivy Wingo	150.00	75.00	45.00

1938 Cincinnati Reds Team Issue

This set of 2" x 3" cards were sold as a boxed set at the ballpark. Fronts feature a black-and-white photo of the player with his name and position in a red strip beneath the picture. Backs have the player's name, position and a generally flattering description of the player's talents. The cards are not numbered. In the American Card Catalog, this issue was designated W711-1.

		NM	EX	VG
Complete Set (23):		1,000	500.00	300.00
Common Player:		40.00	20.00	12.00
(1)	Wally Berger ("... in a trade with the Giants in June.")	40.00	20.00	12.00
(2)	Joe Cascarella	40.00	20.00	12.00
(3)	Allen "Dusty" Cooke	40.00	20.00	12.00
(4)	Harry Craft	40.00	20.00	12.00
(5)	Ray "Peaches" Davis	40.00	20.00	12.00
(6)	Paul Derringer ("Won 22 games...this season.")	40.00	20.00	12.00
(7)	Linus Frey ("... only 25 now.")	40.00	20.00	12.00
(8)	Lee Gamble ("... Syracuse last year.")	40.00	20.00	12.00
(9)	Ival Goodman (No mention of 30 homers.)	40.00	20.00	12.00
(10)	Harry "Hank" Gowdy	40.00	20.00	12.00
(11)	Lee Grissom (No mention of 1938.)	40.00	20.00	12.00
(12)	Willard Hershberger	100.00	50.00	30.00
(13)	Ernie Lombardi (No mention of 1938 MVP.)	225.00	110.00	67.00
(14)	Frank McCormick	40.00	20.00	12.00
(15)	Bill McKechnie ("Last year he led ...")	200.00	100.00	60.00
(16)	Lloyd "Whitey" Moore ("... last year with Syracuse.")	40.00	20.00	12.00
(17)	Billy Myers ("... in his fourth year.")	40.00	20.00	12.00
(18)	Lee Riggs ("... in his fourth season ...")	40.00	20.00	12.00
(19)	Eddie Roush	200.00	100.00	60.00
(20)	Gene Schott	40.00	20.00	12.00
(21)	Johnny Vander Meer/Portrait	75.00	37.00	22.00
(22)	Wm. "Bucky" Walter ("... won 14 games ...")	40.00	20.00	12.00
(23)	Jim Weaver	40.00	20.00	12.00

1939 Cincinnati Reds Team Issue

PAUL DERRINGER
Pitcher

This big Kentuckian has been one of the National League's greatest hurlers since he came up with the St. Louis Cardinals in 1931. He was the league's leading hurler as a rookie and started the first game of the 1931 World Series. Came to the Reds in 1933. Won 22 games for the Reds in 1935 and 21 last year.

An updating by one season of the team-issued 1938 W711-1 set, most of the players and poses on the 2" x 3" cards remained the same. A close study of the career summary on the card's back is necessary to determine which year of issue is at hand. The Livengood card is believed to have been withdrawn from distribution early and is scarce.

		NM	EX	VG
Complete Set (27):		1,250	625.00	375.00
Common Player:		40.00	20.00	12.00
(1)	Wally Berger ("... in a trade with the Giants in June, 1938.")	40.00	20.00	12.00
(2)	Nino Bongiovanni	40.00	20.00	12.00
(3)	Stanley "Frenchy" Bordagaray	40.00	20.00	12.00
(4)	Harry Craft	40.00	20.00	12.00
(5)	Ray "Peaches" Davis	40.00	20.00	12.00
(6)	Paul Derringer ("Won 21 games ... last year.")	45.00	22.00	13.50
(7)	Linus Frey ("... only 26 now.")	40.00	20.00	12.00
(8)	Lee Gamble ("... Syracuse in 1937.")	40.00	20.00	12.00
(9)	Ival Goodman (Mentions hitting 30 homers.)	40.00	20.00	12.00
(10)	Harry "Hank" Gowdy	40.00	20.00	12.00
(11)	Lee Grissom (Mentions 1938.)	40.00	20.00	12.00
(12)	Willard Hershberger	100.00	50.00	30.00
(13)	Eddie Joost	40.00	20.00	12.00
(14)	Wes Livengood	250.00	125.00	75.00
(15)	Ernie Lombardi (Mentions MVP of 1938.)	225.00	110.00	67.00
(16)	Frank McCormick	40.00	20.00	12.00
(17)	Bill McKechnie ("In 1937 he led ...")	200.00	100.00	60.00
(18)	Lloyd "Whitey" Moore ("... in 1937 with Syracuse.")	40.00	20.00	12.00
(19)	Billy Myers ("... in his fifth year ...")	40.00	20.00	12.00
(20)	Lee Riggs ("... in his fifth season...")	40.00	20.00	12.00
(21)	Les Scarsella	40.00	20.00	12.00
(22)	Eugene "Junior" Thompson	40.00	20.00	12.00
(23)	Johnny Vander Meer/Pitching	50.00	25.00	15.00
(24)	Wm. "Bucky" Walters ("Won 15 games ...")	40.00	20.00	12.00
(25)	Jim Weaver	40.00	20.00	12.00
(26)	Bill Werber	40.00	20.00	12.00
(27)	Jimmy Wilson	40.00	20.00	12.00

1940 Cincinnati Reds Team Issue

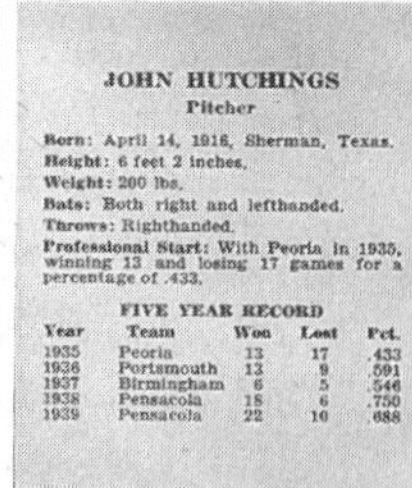

JOHN HUTCHINGS
Pitcher

Born: April 14, 1916, Sherman, Texas.
Height: 6 feet 2 inches.
Weight: 200 lbs.
Bats: Both right and lefthanded.
Throws: Righthanded.
Professional Start: With Peoria in 1935, winning 13 and losing 17 games for a percentage of .433.

FIVE YEAR RECORD

Year	Team	Won	Lost	Pct.
1935	Peoria	13	17	.433
1936	Portsmouth	13	9	.591
1937	Birmingham	6	5	.546
1938	Pensacola	18	6	.750
1939	Pensacola	22	10	.688

Another early Reds team issue, this set of black-and-white 2-1/8" x 2-5/8" cards is unnumbered and features player portrait photos on the front. Name, position, biographical information and five years' worth of stats are on the back. The Reds were World Champions in 1940 (defeating Detroit), and the set features several special World Series cards, making it one of the first to feature events as well as individuals. The set was listed in the American Card Catalog as W711-2.

		NM	EX	VG
Complete Set (35):		900.00	450.00	275.00
Common Player:		25.00	12.50	7.50
(1)	Morris Arnovich	25.00	12.50	7.50
(2)	William (Bill) Baker	25.00	12.50	7.50
(3)	Joseph Beggs	25.00	12.50	7.50
(4)	Harry Craft	25.00	12.50	7.50
(5)	Paul Derringer	25.00	12.50	7.50
(6)	Linus Frey	25.00	12.50	7.50
(7)	Ival Goodman	25.00	12.50	7.50
(8)	Harry (Hank) Gowdy	25.00	12.50	7.50
(9)	Witt Guise	25.00	12.50	7.50
(10)	Harry (Socko) Hartman	25.00	12.50	7.50
(11)	Willard Hershberger	35.00	17.50	10.50
(12)	John Hutchings	25.00	12.50	7.50
(13)	Edwin Joost	25.00	12.50	7.50
(14)	Ernie Lombardi	60.00	30.00	18.00
(15)	Frank McCormick	25.00	12.50	7.50
(16)	Myron McCormick	25.00	12.50	7.50
(17)	William Boyd McKechnie	60.00	30.00	18.00
(18)	Lloyd (Whitey) Moore	25.00	12.50	7.50
(19)	William (Bill) Myers	25.00	12.50	7.50
(20)	Lewis Riggs	25.00	12.50	7.50
(21)	Elmer Riddle	25.00	12.50	7.50
(22)	James A. Ripple	25.00	12.50	7.50
(23)	Milburn Shoffner	25.00	12.50	7.50
(24)	Eugene Thompson	25.00	12.50	7.50
(25)	James Turner	25.00	12.50	7.50
(26)	John Vander Meer	30.00	15.00	9.00
(27)	Wm. (Bucky) Walters	25.00	12.50	7.50
(28)	William (Bill) Werber	25.00	12.50	7.50
(29)	James Wilson	25.00	12.50	7.50
(30)	The Cincinnati Reds	25.00	12.50	7.50
(31)	The Cincinnati Reds World Champions	25.00	12.50	7.50
(32)	Tell the World About the Cincinnati Reds	25.00	12.50	7.50

(33)	Tell the World About the Cincinnati Reds Champions	25.00	12.50	7.50
(34)	Results 1940 World's Series	25.00	12.50	7.50
(35)	Debt. of Gratitude to Wm. Koeh Co.	25.00	12.50	7.50

1954-1955 Cincinnati Reds Postcards

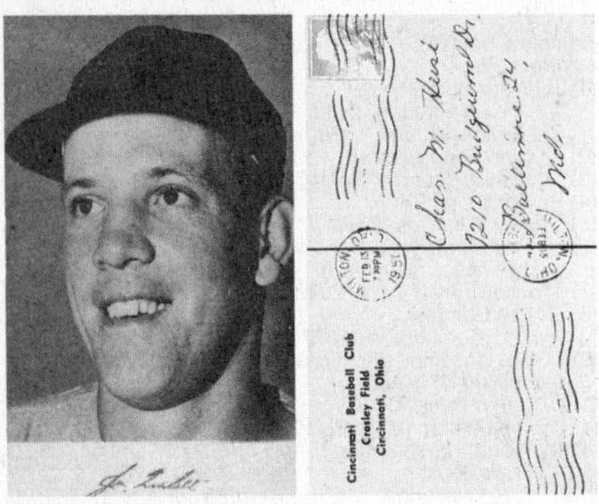

The first team-issued Redlegs postcards of the modern era were produced during the 1954 and 1955 seasons for use by players in answering fan requests for pictures and autographs. The cards are 3-1/2" x 5-5/8", printed in black-and-white on non-glossy cardboard stock. Fronts have poses which are borderless at top and sides. At bottom is a 3/4" white strip which is either blank or which has the player and team name printed. Many cards are found with stamped facsimile autographs, and/or authentically signed. Backs have a vertical line at center. At top-left is: "Cincinnati Baseball Club / Crosley Field / Cincinnati, Ohio." While there is no stamp box on the back, many of the cards have been postally used. The issue was listed in the "American Card Catalog" as PC746.

		NM	EX	VG
Common Player:		15.00	7.50	4.50
(1)	Bobby Adams/Fldg	15.00	7.50	4.50
(2)	Bobby Adams (Portrait to neck.)	15.00	7.50	4.50
(3)	Dr. Wayne Anderson (Trainer)(Chest-up.))	30.00	15.00	9.00
(4)	Fred Baczewski (Ready to pitch.)	15.00	7.50	4.50
(5)	Ed Bailey (Batting to waist.)	15.00	7.50	4.50
(6)	Dick Bartell (Portrait to neck.)	15.00	7.50	4.50
(7)	Dick Bartell (Portrait to shoulders.)	15.00	7.50	4.50
(8)	Matt Batts (Batting follow-through.)	15.00	7.50	4.50
(9)	Gus Bell (Portrait to neck.)	15.00	7.50	4.50
(10)	Gus Bell (Waist up, ready to hit.)	15.00	7.50	4.50
(11)	Joe Black (Standing in dugout.)	15.00	7.50	4.50
(12)	Bob Borkowski (Batting follow-through.)	15.00	7.50	4.50
(13)	Buzz Boyle (Scout) (Chest-up in suit.))	40.00	20.00	12.00
(14)	Rocky Bridges (Portrait to neck.)	15.00	7.50	4.50
(15)	Smoky Burgess (Portrait to neck.)	15.00	7.50	4.50
(16)	Jackie Collum (Pitching follow-through.)	15.00	7.50	4.50
(17)	Jackie Collum (Portrait to neck.)	15.00	7.50	4.50
(18)	Powell Crosley, Jr./Portrait (President)	15.00	7.50	4.50
(19)	Jimmy Dykes (Standing in dugout.)	15.00	7.50	4.50
(20)	Nino Escalera (Portrait to neck.)	15.00	7.50	4.50
(21)	Tom Ferrick (Portrait to neck.)	15.00	7.50	4.50
(22)	Art Fowler (Hands over head.)	15.00	7.50	4.50
(23)	Art Fowler (Portrait to neck.)	15.00	7.50	4.50
(24)	Hershell Freeman (Portrait to shoulders.)	15.00	7.50	4.50
(26)	Jim Greengrass/Btg (Waist-up.)	15.00	7.50	4.50
(27)	Don Gross (Portrait to neck.)	15.00	7.50	4.50
(28)	Charley Harmon (Batting to belt.)	15.00	7.50	4.50
(29)	Ray Jablonski (Batting to belt.)	15.00	7.50	4.50
(30)	Howie Judson (Portrait to neck.)	15.00	7.50	4.50
(31)	Johnny Klippstein (Pitching follow-through.)	15.00	7.50	4.50
(32)	Ted Kluszewski/Btg (Cut out sleeves.)	30.00	15.00	9.00
(33)	Ted Kluszewski (Batting to belt.)	30.00	15.00	9.00
(34)	Ted Kluszewski (Batting follow-through, full length.)	30.00	15.00	9.00
(35)	Ted Kluszewski (Batting follow-through to waist.)	30.00	15.00	9.00
(36)	Ted Kluszewski (Batting follow-through, #18 on back.)	30.00	15.00	9.00
(37)	Ted Kluszewski (Stretching at 1B.)	30.00	15.00	9.00
(38)	Ted Kluszewski (Standing w/ four bats.)	30.00	15.00	9.00
(39)	Ted Kluszewski (Portrait to neck, looking right.)	30.00	15.00	9.00
(40)	Ted Kluszewski (Portrait to shoulders, leaning right.)	30.00	15.00	9.00
(41)	Hobie Landrith/Catching	15.00	7.50	4.50
(42)	Hobie Landrith (Pose to neck.)	15.00	7.50	4.50
(43)	William McKechnie, Jr./Portrait (Farm club supervisor.)	15.00	7.50	4.50
(44)	Roy McMillan (Portrait to neck.)	15.00	7.50	4.50
(45)	Roy McMillan (Ready to hit.)	15.00	7.50	4.50
(46)	Lloyd Merriman (Ready to hit.)	15.00	7.50	4.50
(47)	Rudy Minarcin (Portrait to neck.)	15.00	7.50	4.50
(48)	Rudy Minarcin (Portrait to shoulders, chain.)	15.00	7.50	4.50
(49)	Joe Nuxhall (Portrait to neck.)	15.00	7.50	4.50
(51)	Joe Nuxhall (Pitching follow-through.)	15.00	7.50	4.50
(52)	Stan Palys (Batting follow-through.)	15.00	7.50	4.50
(53)	Harry Perkowski (Portrait to neck.)	15.00	7.50	4.50
(54)	Bud Podbielan (Ready to pitch, belt visible.)	15.00	7.50	4.50
(55)	Bud Podbielan (Ready to pitch, no belt.)	15.00	7.50	4.50
(56)	Wally Post (Ready to hit to belt, fans in back.)	22.50	11.00	6.75
(57)	Wally Post (Ready to hit to hips.)	22.50	11.00	6.75
(58)	Wally Post (Batting follow-through, pole on left.)	22.50	11.00	6.75
(59)	Wally Post (Batting follow-through, no pole.)	22.50	11.00	6.75
(60)	Wally Post (Portrait to neck.)	22.50	11.00	6.75
(61)	Ken Raffensberger (Pitching wind-up.)	15.00	7.50	4.50
(62)	Steve Ridzik (Portrait to neck.)	15.00	7.50	4.50
(63)	Connie Ryan (Portrait to neck.)	15.00	7.50	4.50
(64)	Moe Savransky (Portrait to neck.)	15.00	7.50	4.50
(65)	Andy Seminick (Batting follow-through.)	15.00	7.50	4.50
(66)	Al Silvera (Portrait to shoulders.)	15.00	7.50	4.50
(67)	Frank Smith (Ready to pitch.)	15.00	7.50	4.50
(68)	Milt Smith (Portrait to shoulders.)	15.00	7.50	4.50
(69)	Gerry Staley (Ready to pitch.)	15.00	7.50	4.50
(70)	Birdie Tebbetts (Portrait to neck.)	15.00	7.50	4.50
(71)	Birdie Tebbetts (Portrait to shoulders.)	15.00	7.50	4.50
(72)	Johnny Temple (Portrait to neck, mouth closed.)	15.00	7.50	4.50
(73)	Johnny Temple (Portrait to neck, mouth open.)	15.00	7.50	4.50
(74)	Bob Thurman (Batting follow-through.)	15.00	7.50	4.50
(76)	Corky Valentine (Pitching follow-through.)	15.00	7.50	4.50
(77)	Herm Wehmeier (Portrait to neck.)	15.00	7.50	4.50
(78)	George Zuverink (Portrait to neck.)	15.00	7.50	4.50
(79)	Crosley Field	15.00	7.50	4.50

1956 Cincinnati Reds Postcards

After a number of years issuing printed postcards for players to answer fan mail, the team began a three-year run of glossy black-and-white photographic card sets in 1956. About 3-1/2" x 5-3/4", the cards usually feature portrait photos, though some action poses are also seen. The pictures are bordered in white with a 1" or so border at bottom with the player and team names. Differentiating the 1956s from similarly formatted issues in 1957-1958 is best done on back. The 1956 cards are divided-back with "Post Card" at top. At right, in the stamp box, is "Place Postage Stamp Here" and, at bottom, "This space for address." Cards are numbered here alphabetically, with gaps left in the assigned numbering for future additions.

		NM	EX	VG
Complete Set (31):		350.00	175.00	105.00
Common Player:		10.00	5.00	3.00
(1)	Tom Acker	10.00	5.00	3.00
(2)	Ed Bailey	10.00	5.00	3.00
(3)	Gus Bell	10.00	5.00	3.00
(4)	Joe Black	10.00	5.00	3.00
(5)	"Rocky" Bridges	10.00	5.00	3.00
(6)	"Smoky" Burgess	12.50	6.25	3.75
(7)	George Crowe	10.00	5.00	3.00
(8)	Jim Dyck	10.00	5.00	3.00
(9)	Jimmy Dykes	10.00	5.00	3.00
(11)	Bruce Edwards (Non-'56 back.)	10.00	5.00	3.00
(12)	Tom Ferrick	10.00	5.00	3.00
(13)	Joe Frazier	10.00	5.00	3.00
(14)	Hersh Freeman	10.00	5.00	3.00
(15)	Alex Grammas	10.00	5.00	3.00
(16)	Don Gross	10.00	5.00	3.00
(17)	Ray Jablonski	10.00	5.00	3.00
(18)	Larry Jansen	10.00	5.00	3.00
(19)	Hal Jeffcoat	10.00	5.00	3.00
(21)	Johnny Klippstein	10.00	5.00	3.00
(22)	Ted Kluszewski	20.00	10.00	6.00
(23)	Brooks Lawrence	10.00	5.00	3.00
(24)	Frank McCormick	10.00	5.00	3.00
(25)	Roy McMillan	10.00	5.00	3.00
(26)	Joe Nuxhall	12.50	6.25	3.75
(27)	Stan Palys ('56 back)	10.00	5.00	3.00
(28)	Stan Palys (Non-'56 back.)	10.00	5.00	3.00
(29)	Wally Post	10.00	5.00	3.00
(31)	Frank Robinson	75.00	37.00	22.00
(32)	"Birdie" Tebbetts	10.00	5.00	3.00
(33)	Johnny Temple	10.00	5.00	3.00
(34)	Bob Thurman	10.00	5.00	3.00

1957 Cincinnati Reds Picture Pack

Similar in format to the Jay Publishing photo packs, this appears to be a team-issued souvenir item, with many of the pictures having been seen in other team-related contexts. The black-and-white, blank-backed pictures measure 5" x 7". They can be differentiated from contemporary Jay photos by the fact that only the team nickname, "Redlegs," appears, rather than city and team. Player names are in all-caps.

		NM	EX	VG
Complete Set (12):		45.00	22.50	13.50
Common Player:		4.00	2.00	1.25
(1)	Ed Bailey	4.00	2.00	1.25
(2)	Gus Bell	4.00	2.00	1.25
(3)	Smoky Burgess	4.00	2.00	1.25
(4)	Hersh Freeman	4.00	2.00	1.25
(5)	Ted Kluszewski	7.50	3.75	2.25
(6)	Brooks Lawrence	4.00	2.00	1.25
(7)	Roy McMillan	4.00	2.00	1.25
(8)	Joe Nuxhall	4.00	2.00	1.25
(9)	Wally Post	4.00	2.00	1.25
(10)	Frank Robinson	15.00	7.50	4.50
(11)	Birdie Tebbetts	4.00	2.00	1.25
(12)	Johnny Temple	4.00	2.00	1.25

1957 Cincinnati Reds Postcards

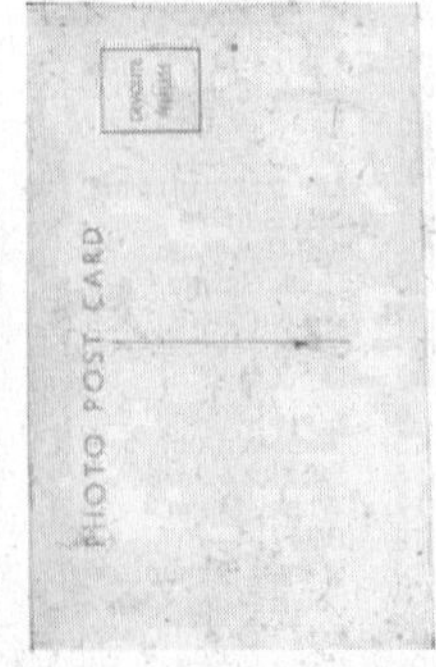

The second in a long run of glossy-front, black-and-white annual postcard issues, the 1957 can often be distinguished from the 1956 and 1958 cards by the appearance of players in sleeveless uniforms with dark undershirts. Even more distinguishing is that the 1957s, on back, have "PHOTO POST CARD" across the top, and lack the notice "This Space for Address" which appeared on the 1956 cards. The '57s can also be identified by "Divolite Peerless" which appears in the postage-stamp box. The 3-1/2" x 5-3/4" cards have white borders. At bottom is 1" white space with the player name and "Cincinnati Redlegs" and space for an autograph. The unnumbered cards are checklisted here in alphabetical order.

		NM	EX	VG
Complete Set (34):		300.00	150.00	90.00
Common Player:		9.00	4.50	2.75
(1)	Tom Acker	9.00	4.50	2.75
(2)	Ed Bailey	9.00	4.50	2.75
(3)	Gus Bell	9.00	4.50	2.75
(4)	"Rocky" Bridges	9.00	4.50	2.75

(5)	"Smoky" Burgess	11.00	5.50	3.25
(6)	George Crowe	9.00	4.50	2.75
(7)	Bobby Durnbaugh	9.00	4.50	2.75
(8)	Jimmy Dykes	9.00	4.50	2.75
(9)	Tom Ferrick	9.00	4.50	2.75
(10)	Art Fowler	9.00	4.50	2.75
(11)	Hersh Freeman	9.00	4.50	2.75
(12)	Alex Grammas	9.00	4.50	2.75
(13)	Don Gross	9.00	4.50	2.75
(14)	Warren Hacker	9.00	4.50	2.75
(15)	Bobby Henrich	9.00	4.50	2.75
(16)	Don Hoak	11.00	5.50	3.25
(17)	Hal Jeffcoat	9.00	4.50	2.75
(18)	Johnny Klippstein	9.00	4.50	2.75
(19)	Ted Kluszewski/Btg	18.00	9.00	5.50
(20)	Ted Kluszewski/Portrait	18.00	9.00	5.50
(21)	Brooks Lawrence	9.00	4.50	2.75
(22)	Jerry Lynch	9.00	4.50	2.75
(23)	Frank McCormick	9.00	4.50	2.75
(24)	Roy McMillan	9.00	4.50	2.75
(25)	Joe Nuxhall	9.00	4.50	2.75
(26)	Wally Post	9.00	4.50	2.75
(27)	Frank Robinson	45.00	22.00	13.50
(28)	Raul Sanchez	9.00	4.50	2.75
(29)	Art Schult	9.00	4.50	2.75
(30)	"Birdie" Tebbetts	9.00	4.50	2.75
(31)	Johnny Temple	9.00	4.50	2.75
(32)	Bob Thurman	9.00	4.50	2.75
(33)	Pete Whisenant/Btg	9.00	4.50	2.75
(34)	Pete Whisenant/Portrait	9.00	4.50	2.75

1958 Cincinnati Reds Postcards

Cards from the third of a long run of glossy-front, black-and-white annual postcard issues can be most often distinguished from similarly formatted 1956-57 cards by the appearance of players in white uniforms with white caps. Two back styles are known. One, like the 1957 issue, has a postage box with "Divolite Peerless" inside and one without the box, but with "Post Card" and "Actual Photograph." Both have a vertical dividing line. The 3-1/2" x 5-3/4" cards have white borders. At bottom is 1" white space with the player name and "Cincinnati Redlegs" and space for an autograph. The unnumbered cards are checklisted here in alphabetical order, though this list may not be complete as several stars are unknown in this style.

		NM	EX	VG
Complete Set (30):		300.00	150.00	90.00
Common Player:		9.00	4.50	2.75
(1)	Tom Acker	9.00	4.50	2.75
(2)	Dr. Wayne Anderson (Trainer)	9.00	4.50	2.75
(3)	Ed Bailey	9.00	4.50	2.75
(4)	Steve Bilko	9.00	4.50	2.75
(5)	"Smoky" Burgess	11.00	5.50	3.25
(6)	George Crowe	9.00	4.50	2.75
(7)	Walt Dropo	9.00	4.50	2.75
(8)	Jimmie Dykes	9.00	4.50	2.75
(9)	Tom Ferrick	9.00	4.50	2.75
(10)	Dee Fondy	9.00	4.50	2.75
(11)	Alex Grammas	9.00	4.50	2.75
(12)	Harvey Haddix	9.00	4.50	2.75
(13)	Hal Jeffcoat	9.00	4.50	2.75
(14)	Alex Kellner	9.00	4.50	2.75
(15)	Johnny Klippstein	9.00	4.50	2.75
(16)	Turk Lown	9.00	4.50	2.75
(17)	Jerry Lynch	9.00	4.50	2.75
(18)	Roy McMillan	9.00	4.50	2.75
(19)	Ed Miksis (Pinstripes)	9.00	4.50	2.75
(20)	Joe Nuxhall	10.00	5.00	3.00
(21)	Vada Pinson	15.00	7.50	4.50
(22)	Bob Purkey	9.00	4.50	2.75
(23)	Charley Rabe	9.00	4.50	2.75
(24)	John Riddle	9.00	4.50	2.75
(25)	Willard Schmidt	9.00	4.50	2.75
(26)	Manager "Birdie" Tebbetts (Portrait to neck.)	9.00	4.50	2.75
(27)	Manager "Birdie" Tebbetts/ Portrait (White background, #1 shows.)	9.00	4.50	2.75
(28)	Johnny Temple	9.00	4.50	2.75
(29)	Bob Thurman	9.00	4.50	2.75
(30)	Pete Whisenant	9.00	4.50	2.75

1969 Citgo Coins

This 20-player set of small (about 1" in diameter) metal coins was issued by Citgo in 1969 to commemorate professional baseball's 100th anniversary. The brass-coated coins, susceptible to oxidation, display the player in a crude portrait with his name across the top. The backs honor the 100th anniversary of pro ball. The coins are unnumbered but are

generally checklisted according to numbers that appear on a red, white and blue paper display folder that was available from Citgo by mail.

		NM	EX	VG
Complete Set (20):		80.00	40.00	25.00
Common Player:		2.00	1.00	.60
Cardboard Display Folder:		30.00	15.00	9.00
Unopened Pack:		12.00		
1	Denny McLain	2.50	1.25	.70
2	Dave McNally	2.00	1.00	.60
3	Jim Lonborg	2.00	1.00	.60
4	Harmon Killebrew	6.50	3.25	2.00
5	Mel Stottlemyre	2.00	1.00	.60
6	Willie Horton	2.00	1.00	.60
7	Jim Fregosi	2.00	1.00	.60
8	Rico Petrocelli	2.00	1.00	.60
9	Stan Bahnsen	2.00	1.00	.60
10	Frank Howard	2.50	1.25	.70
11	Joe Torre	2.50	1.25	.70
12	Jerry Koosman	2.00	1.00	.60
13	Ron Santo	3.50	1.75	1.00
14	Pete Rose	20.00	10.00	6.00
15	Rusty Staub	2.00	1.00	.60
16	Henry Aaron	20.00	10.00	6.00
17	Richie Allen	3.50	1.75	1.00
18	Ron Swoboda	2.00	1.00	.60
19	Willie McCovey	6.50	3.25	2.00
20	Jim Bunning	5.00	2.50	1.50

1969 Citgo New York Mets

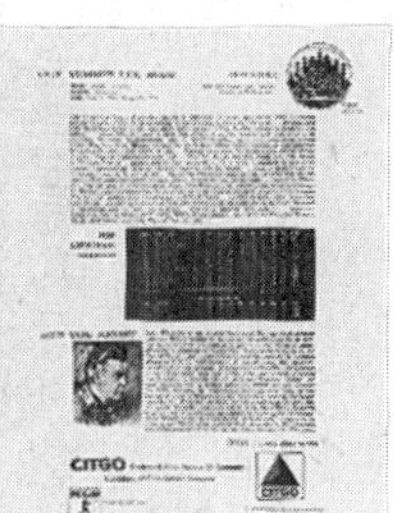

One of several regional issues in the Mets World Championship season of 1969, this set of 8" x 10" player portraits was sponsored by Citgo, whose gas stations distributed the pictures with fuel purchases. Fronts feature large portraits and smaller action pictures of the player, done in pastels, set against a bright pastel background. The paintings are the work of noted celebrity artist John Wheeldon. Beneath the pictures is a facsimile autograph. The player's name is printed in the bottom border. Backs are printed in black-and-white and include biography and career details, full major and minor league stats and a self-portrait and biography of the artist. Logos of the Mets, the Players Association and the sponsor complete the back design. The unnumbered player pictures are checklisted here in alphabetical order.

		NM	EX	VG
Complete Set (8):		65.00	32.00	19.50
Common Player:		6.50	3.25	2.00
(1)	Tommie Agee	8.00	4.00	2.50
(2)	Ken Boswell	6.50	3.25	2.00
(3)	Gary Gentry	6.50	3.25	2.00
(4)	Jerry Grote	6.50	3.25	2.00
(5)	Cleon Jones	6.50	3.25	2.00
(6)	Jerry Koosman	8.00	4.00	2.50
(7)	Ed Kranepool	6.50	3.25	2.00
(8)	Tom Seaver	25.00	12.50	7.50

1975 Clark & Sons Baseball Favorites

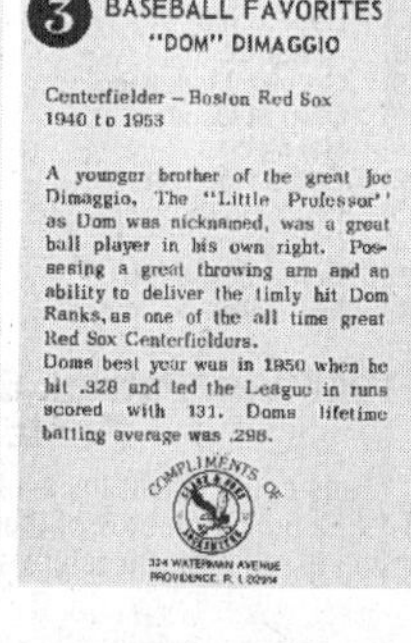
3 BASEBALL FAVORITES
"DOM" DIMAGGIO

Centerfielder – Boston Red Sox
1940 to 1953

A younger brother of the great Joe Dimaggio, The "Little Professor" as Dom was nicknamed, was a great ball player in his own right. Possesing a great throwing arm and an ability to deliver the timly hit Dom Ranks, as one of the all time great Red Sox Centerfielders.
Doms best year was in 1950 when he hit .328 and led the League in runs scored with 131. Doms lifetime batting average was .298.

COMPLIMENTS OF
324 WATERMAN AVENUE
PROVIDENCE, R.I. 02904

To commemorate the firm's 10 years in business and the Boston Red Sox first pennant since 1967, Clark & Sons Locksmiths of Rhode Island issued this set of Red Sox greats. Two versions were issued. The first has a "324 Waterman Avenue, Providence" address on back. A second printing corrected the errors to "324A Waterman Avenue, East Providence" and added a wavy line around the photo and name on front. Cards measure 2-1/2" x 3-5/8" and are printed in black-and-white.

		NM	EX	VG
Complete Set (4):		12.50	6.25	3.75
Common Player:		1.25	.60	.40
1	Bobby Doerr	2.00	1.00	.60
2	Ted Williams	10.00	5.00	3.00
3	Dom DiMaggio	2.50	1.25	.70
4	Johnny Pesky	1.25	.60	.40

1921 Clark's Bread

It is not known to what extent this set's checklist of base cards and possible variations parallels the contemporary blank-back 1921-1922 W575-1 strip cards. The cards measure about 2" x 3-1/4" and are printed in black-and-white. It is unknown into which region the bread cards might have been issued. Collectors have been known to pay a premium of 10X for this version.

	NM	EX	VG
Common Player:	600.00	300.00	180.00

(See 1921 American Caramel Series of 80 or 1922 W575-1 for checklists and base card values.)

1972 Classic Cards

The set depicts players from 1900-1909 in sepiatone photos printed on thin, cream-colored card stock by the Flint, MI company not related to the 1990s card maker of the same name. The first series features sequentially numbered cards, the remainder marked only with a series number. Card size is 2-3/4" x 4-1/2" for the first series and 2-3/4" x 4-1/4" for the last three 30-card series.

		NM	EX	VG
Complete Set (120):		50.00	25.00	10.00
Common Player:		2.00	1.00	.60
1	Griffith, Cincinnati	2.00	1.00	.60
2	Johnson, Washington	2.00	1.00	.60
3	Ganley, Washington	2.00	1.00	.60
4	Tinker, Chicago	2.00	1.00	.60
5	Chance, Chicago	2.00	1.00	.60
6	Conroy, Washington	2.00	1.00	.60
7	Bresnahan, N.Y.	2.00	1.00	.60
8	Powell, Pittsburgh	2.00	1.00	.60
9	Pfeister, Chicago	2.00	1.00	.60
10	McCarthy, Boston	2.00	1.00	.60
11	McConnell, Boston	2.00	1.00	.60
12	Jennings, Detroit	2.00	1.00	.60
13	Lennox, Brooklyn	2.00	1.00	.60
14	McCormick, N.Y.	2.00	1.00	.60
15	Merkle, N.Y.	2.00	1.00	.60
16	Hoblitzell, Cincinnati	2.00	1.00	.60
17	Dahlen, Boston	2.00	1.00	.60
18	Chance, Chicago	2.00	1.00	.60
19	Ferguson, Boston	2.00	1.00	.60
20	Camnitz, Pittsburgh	2.00	1.00	.60
21	N.Y. (Neal Ball)	2.00	1.00	.60
22	Hemphill, N.Y.	2.00	1.00	.60
23	Baker, Philadelphia	2.00	1.00	.60
24	Mathewson, N.Y.	5.00	2.50	1.50
25	Burch, Brooklyn	2.00	1.00	.60
26	Grant, Philadelphia	2.00	1.00	.60
27	Ames, N.Y.	2.00	1.00	.60
28	Newton, N.Y.	2.00	1.00	.60
29	Moran, Chicago	2.00	1.00	.60
30	Lajoie, Cleveland	2.00	1.00	.60
(31)	Abstein, Pittsburgh	2.00	1.00	.60
(32)	Brown, Chicago	2.00	1.00	.60
(33)	Campbell, Cincinnati	2.00	1.00	.60
(34)	Cobb, Detroit	5.00	2.50	1.50
(35)	Crawford, Detroit	2.00	1.00	.60
(36)	Devlin, N.Y.	2.00	1.00	.60
(37)	Dooin, Philadelphia	2.00	1.00	.60
(38)	Dougherty, Chicago	2.00	1.00	.60
(39)	Downey, Cincinnati	2.00	1.00	.60
(40)	Doyle, New York	2.00	1.00	.60
(41)	Dunn, Brooklyn	2.00	1.00	.60
(42)	Durham, N.Y.	2.00	1.00	.60
(43)	Gibson, Pittsburgh	2.00	1.00	.60
(44)	Hartzel, Philadelphia	2.00	1.00	.60
(45)	Higginbotham, Chicago	2.00	1.00	.60
(46)	Hinchman	2.00	1.00	.60

(47) Lajoie	2.00	1.00	.60
(48) Mowery, Cincinnati	2.00	1.00	.60
(49) Mullin, Detroit	2.00	1.00	.60
(50) O'Hara, New York	2.00	1.00	.60
(51) Overall, Chicago	2.00	1.00	.60
(52) Perring, Cleveland	2.00	1.00	.60
(53) Rossman, Detroit	2.00	1.00	.60
(54) Schmidt, Detroit	2.00	1.00	.60
(55) Steinfeldt, Chicago	2.00	1.00	.60
(56) Stone, St. Louis	2.00	1.00	.60
(57) Titus, Philadelphia	2.00	1.00	.60
(58) Wagner, Pittsburgh	2.00	1.00	.60
(59) Wamhow, N.Y.	2.00	1.00	.60
(60) Wiltse, New York	2.00	1.00	.60
(61) Barger, Brooklyn	2.00	1.00	.60
(62) Bergen, Brooklyn	2.00	1.00	.60
(63) Bowerman, Boston	2.00	1.00	.60
(64) Bransfeld, Philadelphia	2.00	1.00	.60
(65) Bresnahan, St. Louis	2.00	1.00	.60
(66) Coakley, Chicago	2.00	1.00	.60
(67) Donovan, Detroit	2.00	1.00	.60
(68) Elberfeld, New York	2.00	1.00	.60
(69) Evers, Chicago	2.00	1.00	.60
(70) Fromme, Cincinnati	2.00	1.00	.60
(71) Herzog, N.Y.	2.00	1.00	.60
(72) Hummell, Cincinnati	2.00	1.00	.60
(73) Jordan, Brooklyn	2.00	1.00	.60
(74) Keeler, New York	2.00	1.00	.60
(75) Lumley, Brooklyn	2.00	1.00	.60
(76) Maddox, Pittsburgh	2.00	1.00	.60
(77) McGinnity, New York	2.00	1.00	.60
(78) McGraw, New York	2.00	1.00	.60
(79) McIntyre, Brooklyn	2.00	1.00	.60
(80) Moriarity, New York	2.00	1.00	.60
(81) Pastorius, Brooklyn	2.00	1.00	.60
(82) Purtell, Chicago	2.00	1.00	.60
(83) Schulte, Chicago	2.00	1.00	.60
(84) Sebring, Brooklyn	2.00	1.00	.60
(85) Smith, Washington	2.00	1.00	.60
(86) Speaker, Boston	5.00	2.50	1.50
(87) Spencer, Boston	2.00	1.00	.60
(88) Tuckey, Boston	2.00	1.00	.60
(89) Vaughn, New York	2.00	1.00	.60
(90) Wheat, Brooklyn	2.00	1.00	.60
(91) Altzier, Chicago	2.00	1.00	.60
(92) Bender, Philadelphia	2.00	1.00	.60
(93) Cincinnati (Bob Ewing)	2.00	1.00	.60
(94) Bresnahan, St. Louis	2.00	1.00	.60
(95) Chappelle, Boston	2.00	1.00	.60
(96) Chase, New York	2.00	1.00	.60
(97) Daley, Cincinnati	2.00	1.00	.60
(98) Davis, Chicago	2.00	1.00	.60
(99) Delahanty, St. Louis	2.00	1.00	.60
(100) Donohue, Washington	2.00	1.00	.60
(101) Doyle, New York	2.00	1.00	.60
(102) Ellis, St. Louis	2.00	1.00	.60
(103) Graham, St. Louis	2.00	1.00	.60
(104) Herzog, New York	2.00	1.00	.60
(105) Hyatt, Pittsburgh	2.00	1.00	.60
(106) Konetchy, St. Louis	2.00	1.00	.60
(107) Lake, New York	2.00	1.00	.60
(108) Lord, Boston	2.00	1.00	.60
(109) New York (Luther Taylor)	2.00	1.00	.60
(110) McLean, Cincinnati	2.00	1.00	.60
(111) Needham, Chicago	2.00	1.00	.60
(112) Pearce, Cincinnati	2.00	1.00	.60
(113) Powell, Pittsburgh	2.00	1.00	.60
(114) Purtell, Chicago	2.00	1.00	.60
(115) Schreck, Philadelphia	2.00	1.00	.60
(116) Storke, Pittsburgh	2.00	1.00	.60
(117) Strunk, Philadelphia	2.00	1.00	.60
(118) Summers, Detroit	2.00	1.00	.60
(119) Thomas, Philadelphia	2.00	1.00	.60
(120) Wagner, Boston	2.00	1.00	.60

1973 Roberto Clemente Memorial Postcard

This collectors' issue postcard was isused as a memorial. In standard 3-1/2" x 5-1/2" format with a postcard-style back, the black-and-white card has printed in the wide bottom border, the player's name, dates of his birth and death and, "In Memory OF A COURAGEOUS HUMAN BEING." On back is a credit line to Allied Printing.

	NM	EX	VG
Roberto Clemente	25.00	12.50	7.50

1913 Cleveland Indians Schedule Postcards

The extent to which the team may have used this type of postcard to announce forthcoming home series is unknown. It can be assumed other cards with other players featured were used during the course of the season. About 7" x 3-1/2", the card has a portrait photo on the left end of its black-and-white front. On back, in red and black, are details of upcoming series and ticket outlet information.

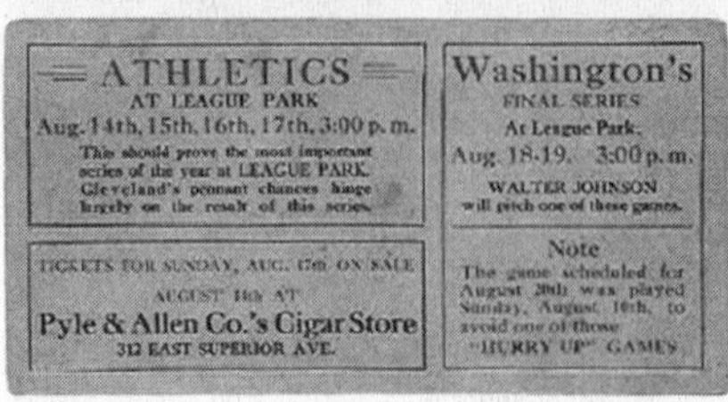

ATHLETICS
AT LEAGUE PARK
Aug. 14th, 15th, 16th, 17th, 3:00 p.m.
This should prove the most important series of the year at LEAGUE PARK. Cleveland's pennant chances hinge largely on the result of this series.

TICKETS FOR SUNDAY, AUG. 17th ON SALE AUGUST 11th AT
Pyle & Allen Co.'s Cigar Store
312 EAST SUPERIOR AVE.

Washington's
FINAL SERIES
At League Park
Aug. 18-19, 3:00 p.m.
WALTER JOHNSON will pitch one of these games.

Note
The game scheduled for August 20th was played Sunday, August 10th, to avoid one of those "HURRY UP" GAMES.

	NM	EX	VG
Joe Birmingham	900.00	450.00	275.00
Ray Chapman	1,350	675.00	400.00
Jack Graney	900.00	450.00	275.00
Joe Jackson, Fred Clarke (Pirates exhibition game.)	2,500	1,250	750.00
Doc Johnston	900.00	450.00	275.00
Willie Mitchell	900.00	450.00	275.00

1947 Cleveland Indians Picture Pack

The first of several annual issues of player photo packs, the 1947 version offered "autographed photos" of all players on the team's roster as of July 1. All players were presented in studio quality portraits in 6" x 8-1/2" format, lithographed on heavy paper with a facsimile autograph. A thin white border surrounds the photo. Backs are blank. The photos were sold in sets for 50 cents. The unnumbered pictures are checklisted here alphabetically.

	NM	EX	VG
Complete Set (25):	100.00	50.00	30.00
Common Player:	3.00	1.50	.90
(1) Don Black	4.00	2.00	1.25
(2) Eddie Bockman	3.00	1.50	.90
(3) Lou Boudreau	9.00	4.50	2.75
(4) Jack Conway	3.00	1.50	.90
(5) Larry Doby	25.00	12.50	7.50
(6) Hank Edwards	3.00	1.50	.90
(7) "Red" Embree	3.00	1.50	.90
(8) Bob Feller	25.00	12.50	7.50
(9) Les Fleming	3.00	1.50	.90
(10) Allen Gettel	3.00	1.50	.90
(11) Joe Gordon	3.00	1.50	.90
(12) Steve Gromek	3.00	1.50	.90
(13) Mel Harder	4.50	2.25	1.25
(14) Jim Hegan	3.00	1.50	.90
(15) Ken Keltner	4.50	2.25	1.25
(16) Ed Klieman	3.00	1.50	.90
(17) Bob Lemon	9.00	4.50	2.75
(18) Al Lopez	9.00	4.50	2.75
(19) George Metkovich	3.00	1.50	.90
(20) Dale Mitchell	4.00	2.00	1.25
(21) Hal Peck	3.00	1.50	.90
(22) Eddie Robinson	3.00	1.50	.90
(23) Hank Ruszkowski	3.00	1.50	.90
(24) Pat Seerey	3.00	1.50	.90
(25) Bryan Stephens	3.00	1.50	.90
(26) Les Willis	3.00	1.50	.90

1947 Van Patrick Cleveland Indians Postcards

Fans could obtain these black-and-white postcard-size (3-1/2" x 5-1/2") photos of their favorite Indians players by writing to radio broadcaster Van Patrick. Backs do not have postcard markings, and carry a message from Patrick. The unnumbered cards are checklisted here alphabetically, though the listing may not be complete.

	NM	EX	VG
Common Player:	100.00	50.00	30.00
(1) Don Black	100.00	50.00	30.00
(2) Eddie Bockman	100.00	50.00	30.00
(3) Lou Boudreau	200.00	100.00	60.00
(4) Jack Conway	100.00	50.00	30.00
(5) Hank Edwards	100.00	50.00	30.00
(6) Red Embree	100.00	50.00	30.00
(7) Bob Feller/Pitching	300.00	150.00	90.00
(8) Bob Feller/Pitching (Leg in air)	300.00	150.00	90.00
(9) Les Fleming	100.00	50.00	30.00
(10) Allen Gettel	100.00	50.00	30.00
(11) Joe Gordon	125.00	62.00	37.00
(12) Steve Gromek	100.00	50.00	30.00
(13) Mel Harder	125.00	62.00	37.00
(14) Jim Hegan	110.00	55.00	33.00
(15) Ken Keltner	110.00	55.00	33.00
(16) Ed Klieman	100.00	50.00	30.00
(17) Bob Lemon	200.00	100.00	60.00
(18) Al Lopez	200.00	100.00	60.00
(19) George Metkovich	100.00	50.00	30.00
(20) Dale Mitchell	100.00	50.00	30.00
(21) Hal Peck	100.00	50.00	30.00
(22) Eddie Robinson	100.00	50.00	30.00
(23) Hank Ruszkowski	100.00	50.00	30.00
(24) Pat Seerey	100.00	50.00	30.00
(25) Bryan Stephens	100.00	50.00	30.00
(26) Les Willis	100.00	50.00	30.00

1948-52 Cleveland Indians Pencil Clips

These celluloid and steel pencil clips were sold at the ballpark to be used on pencils given away with scorecards, The round button portion of the clip is about 3/4" in diameter, while the clip itself is a little over 1-1/2". Black-and-white player portraits are centered in a colored border with the team name at top and player name at bottom. While many of the same players and photos were used year after year, issue date of the clips can be determined by the border color. In 1951-1952, when blue borders were used, the year is distinguished by the presence (1951) or absence (1952) of a white union logo on back.

	NM	EX	VG
Common Player:	35.00	17.50	10.50
1948 (Black)			
(1) Gene Bearden	35.00	17.50	10.50
(2) John Berardino	40.00	20.00	12.00
(3) Don Black	35.00	17.50	10.50
(4) Lou Boudreau	45.00	22.00	13.50
(5) Russ Christopher	35.00	17.50	10.50
(6) Allie Clark	35.00	17.50	10.50
(7) Larry Doby	60.00	30.00	18.00
(8) Hank Edwards	35.00	17.50	10.50
(9) Bob Feller	50.00	25.00	15.00
(10) Al Gettel	35.00	17.50	10.50
(11) Joe Gordon	35.00	17.50	10.50
(12) Walt Judnich	35.00	17.50	10.50
(13) Ken Keltner	35.00	17.50	10.50
(14) Bob Lemon	45.00	22.00	13.50
(15) Dale Mitchell	35.00	17.50	10.50
(16) Bob Muncrief	35.00	17.50	10.50
(17) Eddie Robinson	35.00	17.50	10.50
(18) Pat Seerey	35.00	17.50	10.50
(19) Joe Tipton	35.00	17.50	10.50
(20) Thurman Tucker	35.00	17.50	10.50

	1949 (Brown)			
(1)	Gene Bearden	35.00	17.50	10.50
(2)	Ray Boone	35.00	17.50	10.50
(3)	Lou Boudreau	45.00	22.00	13.50
(4)	Allie Clark	35.00	17.50	10.50
(5)	Larry Doby	55.00	27.00	16.50
(6)	Bob Feller	50.00	25.00	15.00
(7)	Mike Garcia	35.00	17.50	10.50
(8)	Joe Gordon	35.00	17.50	10.50
(9)	Steve Gromek	35.00	17.50	10.50
(10)	Jim Hegan	35.00	17.50	10.50
(11)	Ken Keltner	35.00	17.50	10.50
(12)	Bob Kennedy	35.00	17.50	10.50
(13)	Bob Lemon	45.00	22.00	13.50
(14)	Dale Mitchell	35.00	17.50	10.50
(15)	Satchel Paige	125.00	62.00	37.00
(16)	Mike Tresh	35.00	17.50	10.50
(17)	Bill Veeck	45.00	22.00	13.50
(18)	Mickey Vernon	35.00	17.50	10.50
(19)	Early Wynn	45.00	22.00	13.50
(20)	Sam Zoldak	35.00	17.50	10.50
	1950 (White)			
(1)	Bobby Avila	35.00	17.50	10.50
(2)	Al Benton	35.00	17.50	10.50
(3)	Ray Boone	35.00	17.50	10.50
(4)	Lou Boudreau	45.00	22.00	13.50
(5)	Larry Doby	55.00	27.00	16.50
(6)	Luke Easter	40.00	20.00	12.00
(7)	Bob Feller	50.00	25.00	15.00
(8)	Mike Garcia	40.00	20.00	12.00
(9)	Steve Gromek	35.00	17.50	10.50
(10)	Jim Hegan	35.00	17.50	10.50
(11)	Bob Kennedy	35.00	17.50	10.50
(12)	Bob Lemon	45.00	22.00	13.50
(13)	Dale Mitchell	35.00	17.50	10.50
(14)	Ray Murray	35.00	17.50	10.50
(15)	Al Rosen	40.00	20.00	12.00
(16)	Thurman Tucker	35.00	17.50	10.50
(17)	Dick Weik	35.00	17.50	10.50
(18)	Early Wynn	45.00	22.00	13.50
	1950 (Blue w/union logo.)			
(1)	Bobby Avila	35.00	17.50	10.50
(2)	Ray Boone	35.00	17.50	10.50
(3)	Larry Doby	55.00	27.00	16.50
(4)	Luke Easter	40.00	20.00	12.00
(5)	Bob Feller	50.00	25.00	15.00
(6)	Jim Hegan	35.00	17.50	10.50
(7)	Bob Kennedy	35.00	17.50	10.50
(8)	Bob Lemon	45.00	22.00	13.50
(9)	Al Lopez	45.00	22.00	13.50
(10)	Dale Mitchell	35.00	17.50	10.50
(11)	Al Rosen	40.00	20.00	12.00
(12)	Early Wynn	45.00	22.00	13.50
	1952 (Blue, no logo.)			
(1)	Bobby Avila	35.00	17.50	10.50
(2)	Lou Brissie	35.00	17.50	10.50
(3)	Bob Chakales	35.00	17.50	10.50
(4)	Merrill Combs	35.00	17.50	10.50
(5)	Larry Doby	55.00	27.00	16.50
(6)	Luke Easter	40.00	20.00	12.00
(7)	Bob Feller	50.00	25.00	15.00
(8)	Mike Garcia	40.00	20.00	12.00
(9)	Steve Gromek	35.00	17.50	10.50
(10)	Jim Hegan	35.00	17.50	10.50
(11)	Sam Jones	35.00	17.50	10.50
(12)	Bob Lemon	45.00	22.00	13.50
(13)	Barney McCosky	35.00	17.50	10.50
(14)	Dale Mitchell	35.00	17.50	10.50
(15)	Pete Reiser	35.00	17.50	10.50
(16)	Al Rosen	45.00	22.50	13.50
(17)	Harry Simpson	35.00	17.50	10.50
(18)	Birdie Tebbetts	35.00	17.50	10.50
(19)	Early Wynn	45.00	22.00	13.50

1948 Cleveland Indians Picture Pack

For its second year of production as a souvenir sales item, the Indians picture pack utilized the basic format of the previous year: black-and-white photos with a white border and facsimile autograph. Backs were again blank. The 1948 set can be differentiated from the 1947 issue by its size; at 6-1/2" x 9", the '48s are larger by a half-inch horizontally and vertically. The unnumbered pictures are checklisted here in alphabetical order. The specific content of the packs may have changed over the course of the season with roster moves.

		NM	EX	VG
Complete Set (33):		300.00	150.00	90.00
Common Player:		6.00	3.00	1.75
(1)	Gene Bearden	6.00	3.00	1.75
(2)	Johnny Berardino	12.00	6.00	3.50
(3)	Don Black	7.50	3.75	2.25
(4)	Lou Boudreau	20.00	10.00	6.00
(5)	Russ Christopher	6.00	3.00	1.75
(6)	Allie Clark	6.00	3.00	1.75
(7)	Larry Doby	25.00	12.50	7.50
(8)	Hank Edwards	6.00	3.00	1.75
(9)	Bob Feller	25.00	12.50	7.50
(10)	Joe Gordon	6.00	3.00	1.75
(11)	Hank Greenberg (GM, in uniform.)	40.00	20.00	12.00
(12)	Hank Greenberg (GM, in civies.)	20.00	10.00	6.00
(13)	Steve Gromek	6.00	3.00	1.75
(14)	Mel Harder	6.00	3.00	1.75
(15)	Jim Hegan	6.00	3.00	1.75
(16)	Walt Judnich	6.00	3.00	1.75
(17)	Ken Keltner	6.00	3.00	1.75
(18)	Bob Kennedy	6.00	3.00	1.75
(19)	Ed Klieman	6.00	3.00	1.75
(20)	Bob Lemon	20.00	10.00	6.00
(21)	Al Lopez	20.00	10.00	6.00
(22)	Bill McKechnie	20.00	10.00	6.00
(23)	Dale Mitchell	6.00	3.00	1.75
(24)	Bob Muncrief	6.00	3.00	1.75
(25)	Satchel Paige	60.00	30.00	18.00
(26)	Hal Peck	6.00	3.00	1.75
(27)	Eddie Robinson	6.00	3.00	1.75
(28)	Muddy Ruel	6.00	3.00	1.75
(29)	Joe Tipton	6.00	3.00	1.75
(30)	Thurman Tucker	6.00	3.00	1.75
(31)	Bill Veeck (owner)	20.00	10.00	6.00
(32)	Sam Zoldak	6.00	3.00	1.75
(33)	Cleveland Municipal Stadium	9.00	4.50	2.75

1949 Cleveland Indians Display Photos

Members of the Tribe are pictured (in the same poses found on their photo-pack issues) on these large-format (11" x 14") display photos, said to have been used for in-stadium promotions. It is possible there are others besides those checklisted here.

		NM	EX	VG
Complete Set (11):		650.00	325.00	200.00
Common Player:		40.00	20.00	12.00
(1)	Ray Boone	45.00	22.00	13.50
(2)	Larry Doby	100.00	50.00	30.00
(3)	Luke Easter	50.00	25.00	15.00
(4)	Bob Feller	125.00	62.00	37.00
(5)	Jim Hegan	40.00	20.00	12.00
(6)	Bob Kennedy	40.00	20.00	12.00
(7)	Bob Lemon	75.00	37.00	22.00
(8)	Al Lopez	75.00	37.00	22.00
(9)	Dale Mitchell	40.00	20.00	12.00
(10)	Al Rosen	50.00	25.00	15.00
(11)	Early Wynn	75.00	37.00	22.00

1949 Cleveland Indians Picture Pack - Action

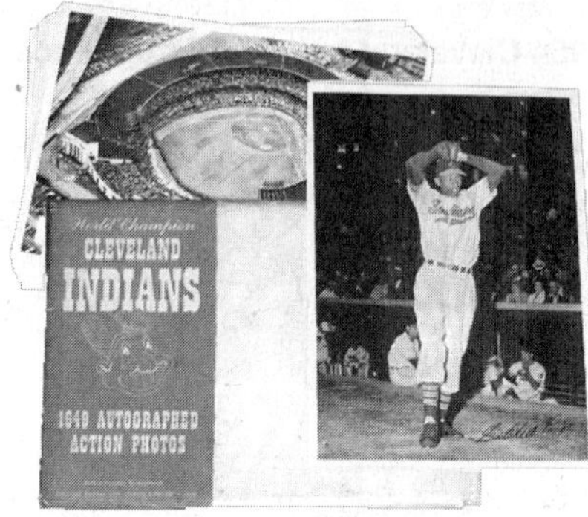

Posed action photos are the focus of this team-issued picture pack. The black-and-white 6-1/2" x 9" photos feature white borders all around and a facsimile autograph on front. Backs are blank. The set was sold in a red and white paper envelope labeled "World Champion Cleveland Indians Autographed Action Photos." Backs are blank. The unnumbered pictures are checklisted here alphabetically. Unmarked reprints of this team-issue, complete with mailing envelope, were made in the late 1980s.

		NM	EX	VG
Complete Set (30):		175.00	90.00	55.00
Common Player:		4.00	2.00	1.25
(1)	Bob Avila	6.00	3.00	1.75
(2)	Gene Bearden	4.00	2.00	1.25
(3)	Al Benton	4.00	2.00	1.25
(4)	John Berardino	12.00	6.00	3.50
(5)	Ray Boone	6.00	3.00	1.75
(6)	Lou Boudreau	16.00	8.00	4.75
(7)	Allie Clark	4.00	2.00	1.25
(8)	Larry Doby	17.50	8.75	5.25
(9)	Bob Feller	20.00	10.00	6.00
(10)	Mike Garcia	6.00	3.00	1.75
(11)	Joe Gordon	4.00	2.00	1.25
(12)	Hank Greenberg (GM)	12.00	6.00	3.50
(13)	Steve Gromek	4.00	2.00	1.25
(14)	Jim Hegan	4.00	2.00	1.25
(15)	Ken Keltner	4.00	2.00	1.25
(16)	Bob Kennedy	4.00	2.00	1.25
(17)	Bob Lemon	12.00	6.00	3.50
(18)	Dale Mitchell	4.00	2.00	1.25
(19)	Satchel Paige	40.00	20.00	12.00
(20)	Frank Papish	4.00	2.00	1.25
(21)	Hal Peck	4.00	2.00	1.25
(22)	Al Rosen	8.00	4.00	2.50
(23)	Mike Tresh	4.00	2.00	1.25
(24)	Thurman Tucker	4.00	2.00	1.25
(25)	Bill Veeck (Owner)	12.00	6.00	3.50
(26)	Mickey Vernon	6.00	3.00	1.75
(27)	Early Wynn	12.00	6.00	3.50
(28)	Sam Zoldak	4.00	2.00	1.25
(29)	Indians coaches (Mel Harder, Steve O'Neill, Bill McKechnie, Muddy Ruel, George Susce)	4.00	2.00	1.25
(30)	Municipal Stadium	6.00	3.00	1.75

1949 Cleveland Indians Picture Pack - Portraits

This set of player photos was produced by Big League Novelty Co., Cleveland, as credited on the paper envelope in which they were sold. The envelope has a crowned, big-nosed Indian caricature and mini-pictures of three of the players. The pictures are in a 6-1/2" x 9" blank-back format. They are black-and-white and virtually all depict the players in chest-to-cap portraits (many the same as previous and later years' issues) with a facsimile autograph. The unnumbered pictures are checklisted here alphabetically.

		NM	EX	VG
Complete Set (20):		75.00	40.00	25.00
Common Player:		3.00	1.50	.90
(1)	Bob Avila	4.50	2.25	1.25
(2)	Gene Bearden	3.00	1.50	.90
(3)	John Berardino	4.50	2.25	1.25
(4)	Lou Boudreau	7.50	3.75	2.25
(5)	Larry Doby	10.00	5.00	3.00
(6)	Bob Feller	12.50	6.25	3.75
(7)	Mike Garcia	4.50	2.25	1.25
(8)	Joe Gordon	3.00	1.50	.90
(9)	Steve Gromek	3.00	1.50	.90
(10)	Jim Hegan	3.00	1.50	.90
(11)	Ken Keltner	3.00	1.50	.90
(12)	Bob Kennedy	3.00	1.50	.90
(13)	Bob Lemon	5.00	2.50	1.50
(14)	Dale Mitchell	3.00	1.50	.90
(15)	Satchel Paige	30.00	15.00	9.00
(16)	Hal Peck	3.00	1.50	.90
(17)	Thurman Tucker	3.00	1.50	.90
(18)	Mickey Vernon	4.00	2.00	1.25
(19)	Early Wynn	5.00	2.50	1.50
(20)	Sam Zoldak	3.00	1.50	.90

1949 Cleveland Indians Sun Picture Camera

These novelty cards are self-developing photoprints sold by the team in packages of four that included negatives and pieces of photo-sensative paper which were used to make the 1-7/8" x 2" black-and-white blank-back pictures. Because existing negatives could be used to make many new prints, values for the prints themselves are low. Prices quoted here are for negative/print combinations.

	NM	EX	VG
Complete Set Negatives/Prints (20):	3,000	1,500	900.00
Common Negative/Print:	125.00	65.00	35.00
(1) Gene Bearden	125.00	65.00	35.00
(2) Al Benton	125.00	65.00	35.00
(3) Ray Boone	125.00	65.00	35.00
(4) Lou Boudreau	200.00	100.00	60.00
(5) Allie Clark	125.00	65.00	35.50
(6) Larry Doby	250.00	125.00	75.00
(7) Bob Feller	250.00	125.00	75.00
(8) Mike Garcia	135.00	70.00	40.00
(9) Joe Gordon	125.00	65.00	35.00
(10) Steve Gromek	125.00	65.00	35.00
(11) Jim Hegan	125.00	65.00	35.00
(12) Ken Keltner	135.00	70.00	40.00
(13) Bob Kennedy	125.00	65.00	35.00
(14) Bob Lemon	200.00	100.00	60.00
(15) Dale Mitchell	125.00	65.00	35.00
(16) Hal Peck	125.00	65.00	35.00
(17) Satchel Paige	400.00	200.00	120.00
(18) Thurman Tucker	125.00	65.00	35.00
(19) Mickey Vernon	125.00	65.00	35.00
(20) Early Wynn	200.00	100.00	60.00

1950 Cleveland Indians Picture Pack

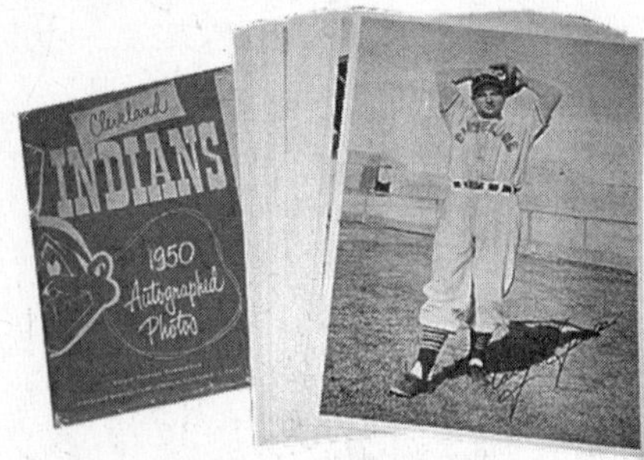

Similar in format to previous years' issues, these 6-1/2" x 9" black-and-white player poses have a white border and facsimile autograph on front. Backs are blank. The unnumbered photos are checklisted here alphabetically. It is possible the contents of specific picture packs changed over the course of the season to reflect roster moves.

	NM	EX	VG
Complete Set (27):	160.00	80.00	50.00
Common Player:	4.00	2.00	1.20
(1) Bobby Avila	5.00	2.50	1.50
(2) Gene Bearden	4.00	2.00	1.20
(3) Al Benton	4.00	2.00	1.20
(4) Ray Boone	5.00	2.50	1.50
(5) Lou Boudreau	12.00	6.00	3.50
(6) Allie Clark	4.00	2.00	1.20
(7) Larry Doby	17.50	8.75	5.25
(8) Luke Easter	6.00	3.00	1.75
(9) Bob Feller	20.00	10.00	6.00
(10) Jess Flores	4.00	2.00	1.20
(11) Mike Garcia	5.00	2.50	1.50
(12) Joe Gordon	4.00	2.00	1.20
(13) Hank Greenberg (GM)	12.00	6.00	3.50
(14) Steve Gromek	4.00	2.00	1.20
(15) Jim Hegan	4.00	2.00	1.20
(16) Bob Kennedy	4.00	2.00	1.20
(17) Bob Lemon	12.00	6.00	3.50
(18) Dale Mitchell	4.00	2.00	1.20
(19) Ray Murray	4.00	2.00	1.20
(20) Chick Pieretti	4.00	2.00	1.20
(21) Al Rosen	6.00	3.00	1.75
(22) Dick Rozek	4.00	2.00	1.20
(23) Ellis Ryan (Owner)	4.00	2.00	1.20
(24) Thurman Tucker	4.00	2.00	1.20
(25) Early Wynn	12.00	6.00	3.50
(26) Sam Zoldak	4.00	2.00	1.20
(27) Cleveland Municipal Stadium	8.00	4.00	2.50

1951 Cleveland Indians Picture Pack

While this set of Indians pictures shares the 6-1/2" x 9" format of the Tribe's other team issues of the era, it is unique in its use of a much glossier front surface. Pictures are, with the exception of the manager, game-action or posed-action in black-and-white, bordered in white and with a facsimile autograph. Backs are blank. It is unknown whether this checklist is complete or whether players were added or removed to reflect in-season roster changes.

	NM	EX	VG
Complete Set (26):	150.00	75.00	45.00
Common Player:	4.00	2.00	1.25
(1) Bob Avila	4.00	2.00	1.25
(2) Gene Bearden	4.00	2.00	1.25
(3) Ray Boone	6.00	3.00	1.75
(4) Lou Brissie	4.00	2.00	1.25
(5) Bob Chakales	4.00	2.00	1.25
(6) Sam Chapman	4.00	2.00	1.25
(7) Merrill Combs	4.00	2.00	1.25
(8) Larry Doby	15.00	7.50	4.50
(9) Luke Easter	6.00	3.00	1.75
(10) Red Fahr	4.00	2.00	1.25
(11) Bob Feller	20.00	10.00	6.00
(12) Mike Garcia	6.00	3.00	1.75
(13) Steve Gromek	4.00	2.00	1.25
(14) Jim Hegan	4.00	2.00	1.25
(15) Bob Kennedy	4.00	2.00	1.25
(16) Bob Lemon	12.50	6.25	3.75
(17) Al Lopez	12.50	6.25	3.75
(18) Milt Neilsen	4.00	2.00	1.25
(19) Al Rosen	8.00	4.00	2.50
(20) Dick Rozek	4.00	2.00	1.25
(21) Harry Simpson	4.00	2.00	1.25
(22) Snuffy Stirnweiss	4.00	2.00	1.25
(23) Birdie Tebbetts	4.00	2.00	1.25
(24) Johnny Vander Meer	6.00	3.00	1.75
(25) Early Wynn	12.50	6.25	3.75
(26) George Zuverink	4.00	2.00	1.25

1952 Cleveland Indians Picture Pack

Like the 1951 Picture Pack, these pictures contain action poses, but are slightly smaller at 6" x 8-3/4". Unnumbered prints here are checklisted alphabetically.

	NM	EX	VG
Complete Set (25):	150.00	75.00	45.00
Common Player:	6.00	3.00	2.00
(1) Bobby Avila	6.00	3.00	2.00
(2) Johnny Bernardino	6.00	3.00	2.00
(3) Ray Boone	6.00	3.00	2.00
(4) Lou Brissie	6.00	3.00	2.00
(5) Merrill Combs	6.00	3.00	2.00
(6) Larry Doby	12.00	6.00	4.00
(7) Luke Easter	6.00	3.00	2.00
(8) Bob Feller	20.00	10.00	6.00
(9) Jim Fridley	6.00	3.00	2.00
(10) Mike Garcia	6.00	3.00	2.00
(11) Steve Gromek	6.00	3.00	2.00
(12) Mickey Harris	6.00	3.00	2.00
(13) Jim Hegan	6.00	3.00	2.00
(14) Sam Jones	6.00	3.00	2.00
(15) Bob Lemon	12.00	6.00	4.00
(16) Al Lopez	12.00	6.00	4.00
(17) Dale Mitchell	6.00	3.00	2.00
(18) Barney McCosky	6.00	3.00	2.00
(19) Pete Reiser	6.00	3.00	2.00
(20) Al Rosen	6.00	3.00	2.00
(21) Dick Rozek	6.00	3.00	2.00
(22) Harry Simpson	6.00	3.00	2.00
(23) Birdie Tebbetts	6.00	3.00	2.00
(24) Joe Tipton	6.00	3.00	2.00
(25) Early Wynn	12.00	6.00	4.00

1954 Cleveland Indians Picture Pack

Because many of the pictures found in the championship season picture pack are the same poses found in earlier issues, size can be used to differentiate the years of issue. For 1954, the pictures were down-sized slightly in height, to a 6" x 8-3/4" format, and printed on heavier paper than in previous years. Each of the portraits, poses and action photos are bordered in white and include a facsimile autograph. The unnumbered pictures are checklisted here alphabetically.

	NM	EX	VG
Complete Set (27):	125.00	65.00	40.00
Common Player:	4.00	2.00	1.25
(1) Bobby Avila	4.00	2.00	1.25
(2) Sam Dente	4.00	2.00	1.25
(3) Larry Doby	10.00	5.00	3.00
(4) Bob Feller	15.00	7.50	4.50
(5) Mike Garcia	4.00	2.00	1.25
(6) Bill Glynn	4.00	2.00	1.25
(7) Mike Hegan	4.00	2.00	1.25
(8) Bob Hooper	4.00	2.00	1.25
(9) Dave Hoskins	4.00	2.00	1.25
(10) Art Houtteman	4.00	2.00	1.25
(11) Bob Lemon	7.50	3.75	2.25
(12) Al Lopez	7.50	3.75	2.25
(13) Hank Majeski	4.00	2.00	1.25
(14) Dale Mitchell	4.00	2.00	1.25
(15) Don Mossi	6.00	3.00	1.75
(16) Hal Naragon	4.00	2.00	1.25
(17) Ray Narleski	4.00	2.00	1.25
(18) Hal Newhouser	7.50	3.75	2.25
(19) Dave Philley	4.00	2.00	1.25
(20) Dave Pope	4.00	2.00	1.25
(21) Rudy Regaldo	4.00	2.00	1.25
(22) Al Rosen	6.00	3.00	1.75
(23) Al Smith	4.00	2.00	1.25
(24) George Strickland	4.00	2.00	1.25
(25) Vic Wertz	4.00	2.00	1.25
(26) Wally Westlake	4.00	2.00	1.25
(27) Early Wynn	7.50	3.75	2.25

1955 Cleveland Indians Postcards

These team-issued black-and-white player postcards can be distinguished from earlier and later issues by the uniformity of the photos. All pictures are head-and-shoulder portraits against a white background. Players are wearing caps with Chief Wahoo inside a "C." Some cards are found with a notation on back, "Pub. by Ed Wood, Forestville, Calif." Cards were sent out to fans by the team and/or player and are usually found with an autograph on front.

	NM	EX	VG
Complete Set (29):	400.00	200.00	120.00
Common Player:	12.00	6.00	3.50
(1) Bob Avila	15.00	7.50	4.50
(2) Tony Cuccinello	12.00	6.00	3.50
(3) Bud Daley	12.00	6.00	3.50
(4) Sam Dente	12.00	6.00	3.50
(5) Larry Doby	18.00	9.00	5.50
(6) Bob Feller	30.00	15.00	9.00
(7) Hank Foiles	12.00	6.00	3.50
(8) Mike Garcia	12.00	6.00	3.50
(9) Mel Harder	12.00	6.00	3.50
(10) Jim Hegan	12.00	6.00	3.50
(11) Art Houtteman	12.00	6.00	3.50
(12) Ralph Kiner	20.00	10.00	6.00
(13) Red Kress	12.00	6.00	3.50
(14) Ken Kuhn	12.00	6.00	3.50
(15) Bob Lemon	18.00	9.00	5.50
(16) Bill Lobe	12.00	6.00	3.50
(17) Dale Mitchell	12.00	6.00	3.50
(18) Don Mossi	12.00	6.00	3.50
(19) Hal Naragon	12.00	6.00	3.50
(20) Ray Narleski	12.00	6.00	3.50
(21) Dave Philley	12.00	6.00	3.50
(22) Al Rosen	15.00	7.50	4.50
(23) Herb Score	24.00	12.00	7.25
(24) Al Smith	12.00	6.00	3.50
(25) George Strickland	12.00	6.00	3.50
(26) Vic Wertz	12.00	6.00	3.50
(27) Wally Westlake	12.00	6.00	3.50
(28) Bill Wright	12.00	6.00	3.50
(29) Early Wynn	18.00	9.00	5.50

1956 Cleveland Indians Picture Pack

The Indians used a mix of styles in its souvenir picture pack for 1956. About 6-1/8" x 8-7/8", with white borders and blank backs, the pictures have a mix of portraits and posed action photos. Some pictures have a facsimile autograph while others have the players name in a white strip.

	NM	EX	VG
Complete Set (22):	90.00	45.00	27.50
Common Player:	4.00	2.00	1.25
(1) Earl Averill	4.00	2.00	1.25
(2) Bob Avila	4.00	2.00	1.25
(3) Jim Busby	4.00	2.00	1.25
(4) Chico Carrasquel	4.00	2.00	1.25
(5) Rocky Colavito	20.00	10.00	6.00
(6) Bob Feller	15.00	7.50	4.50
(7) Mike Garcia	4.00	2.00	1.25
(8) Jim Hegan	4.00	2.00	1.25
(9) Art Houtteman	4.00	2.00	1.25
(10) Bob Lemon	7.50	3.75	2.25
(11) Al Lopez	7.50	3.75	2.25
(12) Sam Mele	4.00	2.00	1.25
(13) Dale Mitchell	4.00	2.00	1.25
(14) Don Mossi	4.00	2.00	1.25
(15) Hal Naragon	4.00	2.00	1.25
(16) Ray Narleski	4.00	2.00	1.25
(17) Al Rosen	5.00	2.50	1.50
(18) Herb Score	7.50	3.75	2.25
(19) Al Smith	4.00	2.00	1.25
(20) George Strickland	4.00	2.00	1.25
(21) Gene Woodling	4.00	2.00	1.25
(22) Early Wynn	7.50	3.75	2.25

1884 Climax Poster

"Representatives of Professional Baseball in America" is the title of this sepia-toned lithograph produced by Lorillard tobacco as a premium for its Climax Red Tin Tag Plug chew. About 26" x 20", the poster depicts 16 top stars, managers and executives in street-clothed portraits on a background of ballplayers, equipment and ballparks.

	NM	EX	VG
1884 Climax Representatives of Baseball	25,000	12,500	7,500

1911 George Close Candy Co. (E94)

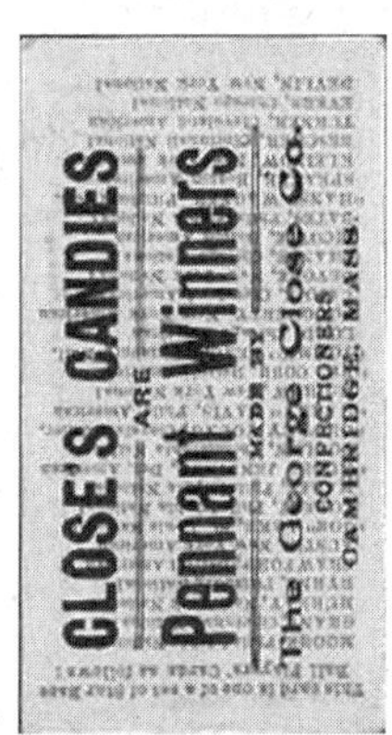

This 1911 issue is nearly identical to several contemporary candy and caramel sets. Issued by The George Close Co. of Cambridge, Mass., the approximately 1-1/2" x 2-3/4" cards feature color-tinted black-and-white player photos. Each card can be found with any of seven different background colors (blue, gold, green, olive, red, violet and yellow). Backs carry a set checklist. Eleven different back variations are known to exist. One variation contains just the checklist without any advertising, while 10 other variations include overprinted backs advertising various candy products manufactured by Close. The set carries the ACC designation E94.

	NM	EX	VG
Complete Set (30):	103,500	52,000	31,000
Common Player:	1,800	900.00	475.00
Advertising Backs: 4-6X			
(1) Jimmy Austin	1,800	900.00	475.00
(2) Johnny Bates	1,800	900.00	475.00
(3) Bob Bescher	1,800	900.00	475.00
(4) Bobby Byrne	1,800	900.00	475.00
(5) Frank Chance	2,500	1,250	700.00
(6) Ed Cicotte	3,000	1,500	900.00
(7) Ty Cobb	20,000	10,000	5,000
(8) Sam Crawford	2,100	1,050	630.00
(9) Harry Davis	1,800	900.00	475.00
(10) Art Devlin	1,800	900.00	475.00
(11) Josh Devore	1,800	900.00	475.00
(12) Mickey Doolan	1,800	900.00	475.00
(13) Patsy Dougherty	1,800	900.00	475.00
(14) Johnny Evers	2,500	1,250	700.00
(15) Eddie Grant	1,800	900.00	475.00
(16) Hugh Jennings	2,500	1,250	700.00
(17) Red Kleinow	1,800	900.00	475.00
(18) Joe Lake	1,800	900.00	475.00
(19) Nap Lajoie	3,000	1,500	900.00
(20) Tommy Leach	1,800	900.00	475.00
(21) Hans Lobert	1,800	900.00	475.00
(22) Harry Lord	1,800	900.00	475.00
(23) Sherry Magee	1,800	900.00	475.00
(24) John McGraw	2,500	1,250	700.00
(25) Earl Moore	1,800	900.00	475.00
(26) Red Murray	1,800	900.00	475.00
(27) Tris Speaker	4,000	2,000	1,250
(28) Terry Turner	1,800	900.00	475.00
(29) Honus Wagner	20,000	10,000	5,000
(30) "Old" Cy. Young	15,000	7,500	4,500

1961 Cloverleaf Dairy Minnesota Twins

These unnumbered cards picture members of the debut Minnesota Twins team. Measuring approximately 3-3/4" x 7-3/4", the cards were actually side panels from Cloverleaf (and Apple Fresh brand) Milk cartons. Complete cartons are valued at about twice the prices listed. The card includes a black-and-white player photo with name, position, personal data and year-by-year statistics appearing below. Green graphics highlight the panels. Some pictures were reissued in 1962 but can be differentiated from the 1961 set by the stats at bottom.

	NM	EX	VG
Complete Set (17):	1,125	550.00	335.00
Common Player:	75.00	37.00	22.00
(1) Earl Battey	75.00	37.00	22.00
(2) Reno Bertoia	75.00	37.00	22.00
(3) Billy Gardner	75.00	37.00	22.00
(4) Paul Giel	75.00	37.00	22.00
(5) Lenny Green	75.00	37.00	22.00
(6) Jim Kaat	80.00	40.00	24.00
(7) Jack Kralick	75.00	37.00	22.00
(8) Don Lee	75.00	37.00	22.00
(9) Jim Lemon	75.00	37.00	22.00
(10) Billy Martin	90.00	45.00	27.00
(11) Don Mincher	75.00	37.00	22.00
(12) Camilo Pascual	80.00	40.00	24.00
(13) Pedro Ramos	75.00	37.00	22.00
(14) Chuck Stobbs	75.00	37.00	22.00
(15) Bill Tuttle	75.00	37.00	22.00
(16) Jose Valdivielso	75.00	37.00	22.00
(17) Zoilo Versalles	80.00	40.00	24.00

1962 Cloverleaf Dairy Minnesota Twins

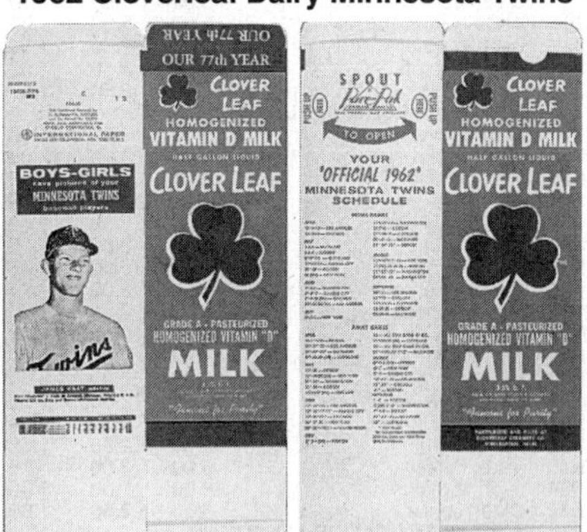

These unnumbered cards picture members of the Minnesota Twins. Measuring approximately 3-3/4" x 7-3/4", the cards were actually side panels from Cloverleaf (and Apple Fresh brand) Milk cartons. Complete cartons are valued at about twice the prices listed. The card includes a black-and-white player photo with name, position, personal data and year-by-year statistics appearing below. Green graphics highlight the panels. Some pictures were reissued in 1962 but can be differentiated from the 1961 set by the stats at bottom.

	NM	EX	VG
Complete Set (24):	1,400	700.00	425.00
Common Player:	75.00	37.00	22.00
(1) Bernie Allen	75.00	37.00	22.00
(2) George Banks	75.00	37.00	22.00
(3) Earl Battey	75.00	37.00	22.00
(4) Joe Bonikowski	75.00	37.00	22.00
(5) John Goryl	75.00	37.00	22.00
(6) Lenny Green	75.00	37.00	22.00
(7) Jim Kaat	80.00	40.00	24.00
(8) Jack Kralick	75.00	37.00	22.00
(9) Jim Lemon	75.00	37.00	22.00
(10) Georges Maranda	75.00	37.00	22.00
(11) Orlando Martinez	75.00	37.00	22.00
(12) Don Mincher	75.00	37.00	22.00
(13) Ray Moore	75.00	37.00	22.00
(14) Hal Naragon	75.00	37.00	22.00
(15) Camilo Pascual	80.00	40.00	24.00
(16) Vic Power	80.00	40.00	24.00
(17) Rich Rollins	75.00	37.00	22.00
(18) Theodore Sadowski	75.00	37.00	22.00
(19) Albert Stange	75.00	37.00	22.00
(20) Dick Stigman	75.00	37.00	22.00
(21) Bill Tuttle	75.00	37.00	22.00
(22) Zoilo Versalles	80.00	40.00	24.00
(23) Gerald Zimmerman	75.00	37.00	22.00
(24) Manager and Coaches (Floyd Baker, Edward Fitz Gerald, Gordon Maltzberger, Sam Mele, George Strickland)	75.00	37.00	22.00

1912 Ty Cobb Postcard

There is no indication of a publisher on this card, nor that it is part of a multi-player series. In standard postcard format of 5-1/2" x 3-1/2", the card has a black-and-white photograph of a smiling Cobb and a caption in the bottom border, "TY COBB WORLDS'S GREATEST BALL PLAYER AND HIS FAVORITE BAT." The divided back has standard postcard markings.

	NM	EX	VG
Ty Cobb	3,500	1,750	1,000

1947 Coca-Cola All Time Sports Favorite

In 1947 Coke produced a series of 10 All Time Sports Favorite cardboard signs. On heavy cardboard with a framed look, the 13" x 15" signs have color artwork at center. In the bottom border are a few words about the athlete, along with a Coke bottle and round red logo. Only one baseball player appears in the series.

	NM	EX	VG
Ty Cobb	2,000	1,000	600.00

1952 Coca-Cola Playing Tips Test Cards

Apparently a regional issue to test the concept of baseball playing tips cards inserted into cartons of soda bottles, these test cards have a number of differences to the version which was more widely issued. The test cards feature a colorful drawing of the player with a bottle of Coke, along with his name in script and his team. Backs are printed in red on gray cardboard. Rizzuto's card has been seen with three different playing tips. Mays' card has a biography instead of a playing tip. The cards are irregularly shaped, measuring about 3-1/2" at their widest point, and about 7-1/2" in length.

	NM	EX	VG
Complete Set (4):	9,000	4,500	2,700
(1) Willie Mays	5,000	2,500	1,500
(2) Phil Rizzuto (Bunting tips.)	2,500	1,250	750.00
(3) Phil Rizzuto (Pitching tips.)	2,500	1,250	750.00
(4) Phil Rizzuto (SS fielding tips.)	2,500	1,250	750.00

1952 Coca-Cola Playing Tips

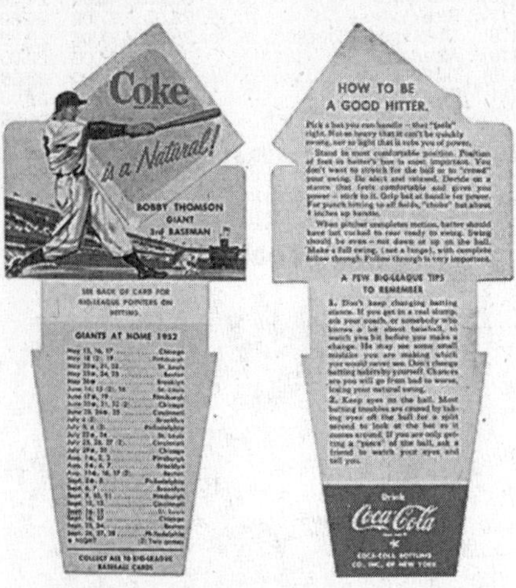

While more widely distributed than the three test cards, the 10-card set of playing tips cards is still scarce today. Issued in the metropolitan New York region, the cards include only players from the Yankees, Giants and Dodgers. Fronts feature color paintings of players in action, though the artwork bears little actual resemblance to the players named. The phrase "Coke is a natural" is in the background on pennants, panels, etc. The player's name, team and position are included in the picture. In the portion of the card meant to be inserted into the soda-bottle carton, the home schedule of the player's team for 1952 is presented. Printed in red on back are tips for playing the position of the pictured player. Cards are irregularly shaped, measuring about 3-1/2" at their widest point, and 7-1/2" in length. The unnumbered cards are checklisted here in alphabetical order.

		NM	EX	VG
Complete Set (10):		2,100	1,050	625.00
Common Player:		160.00	80.00	50.00
(1)	Hank Bauer	275.00	135.00	82.00
(2)	Carl Furillo	350.00	175.00	105.00
(3)	Gil Hodges	450.00	225.00	135.00
(4)	Ed Lopat	190.00	95.00	57.00
(5)	Gil McDougald	250.00	125.00	75.00
(6)	Don Mueller	150.00	75.00	45.00
(7)	Pee Wee Reese	450.00	225.00	135.00
(8)	Bobby Thomson (3B)	250.00	125.00	75.00
(9)	Bobby Thomson/Hitting	350.00	175.00	105.00
(10)	Wes Westrum	150.00	75.00	45.00

1953 Coca-Cola Signs

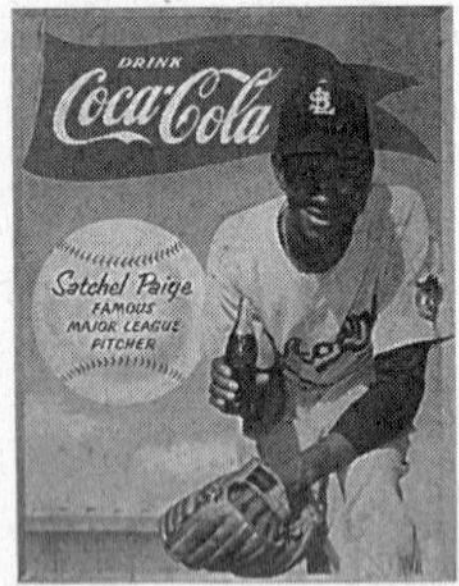

The attributed date is approximate, based on the uniforms in which the players are pictured. It is possible the series was issued over more than one year. The signs vary in size from about 10" x 12" to 12" x 15" and are made of cardboard. Some are die-cut to produce an irregular shape. Players are pictured in color artwork holding a bottle of Coke with one of several styles of Coca-Cola logo in the background.

		NM	EX	VG
Common Player:		750.00	375.00	225.00
(1)	Bill Bruton	800.00	400.00	240.00
(2)	Roy Campanella	2,500	1,250	750.00
(3)	Larry Doby	1,500	750.00	450.00
(4)	Monte Irvin	1,500	750.00	450.00
(5)	Satchel Paige	4,000	2,000	1,200
(6)	Phil Rizzuto	1,500	750.00	450.00

1967-68 Coca-Cola Bottle Caps

Over two seasons, bottles of Coke products (Coca-Cola, Fresca, Tab and Fanta) were sealed with caps bearing the pictures of major league ballplayers. The 1" diameter caps have a small baseball symbol on the top of the cap. Inside, protected by a clear plastic liner, is a black-and-white portrait photo of a player. (Most photos have cap insignia blacked out.) His team nickname is printed at top, his name at bottom and his position at right. To the left of the picture is an identification number, usually with a letter prefix. In areas with major league baseball teams, regional issues of the caps featured local players with a letter prefix to the number. Also released in those areas were American League or National League All-Star sets, with cap number preceded by an "A" or "N." In areas not served by major league teams, a 35-cap All-Star series with no prefix letter was issued. While most caps were identical in both years of issue, some player team changes, etc., were reflected in updated caps in 1968. Severe bending by bottle openers and rust are specific detriments to condition often found on these caps. Collectors usually save these caps without regard to which specific brand of soda appears on top, though obviously the Coca-Cola pieces are much more common. Cap-saver sheets were available which, when filled, could be exchanged for a team set of photocards (see 1967 Dexter Press Premiums) or other prizes.

		NM	EX	VG
Complete Set (580):		4,000	2,000	1,200
Common Player:		5.00	2.50	1.50
Playing Tips (16):		3.00	1.50	.90
Sprite, Fresca, Tab + 10 Percent				
	MAJOR LEAGUE ALL-STARS			
1	Richie Allen	7.50	3.75	2.25
2	Pete Rose	32.50	16.00	9.75
3	Brooks Robinson	25.00	12.50	7.50
4	Marcelino Lopez	5.00	2.50	1.50
5	Rusty Staub	5.00	2.50	1.50
6	Ron Santo	7.50	3.75	2.25
7	Jim Nash	5.00	2.50	1.50
8	Jim Fregosi	5.00	2.50	1.50
9	Paul Casanova	5.00	2.50	1.50
10	Willie Mays	45.00	22.50	13.50
11	Willie Stargell	15.00	7.50	4.50
12	Tony Oliva	7.50	3.75	2.25
13	Joe Pepitone	7.50	3.75	2.25
14	Juan Marichal	12.00	6.00	3.50
15	Jim Bunning	12.00	6.00	3.50
16	Claude Osteen	5.00	2.50	1.50
17	Carl Yastrzemski	25.00	12.50	7.50
18	Harmon Killebrew	25.00	12.50	7.50
19	Hank Aaron	45.00	22.50	13.50
20	Joe Torre	7.50	3.75	2.25
21	Ernie Banks	25.00	12.50	7.50
22	Al Kaline	25.00	12.50	7.50
23	Frank Robinson	25.00	12.50	7.50
24	Max Alvis	5.00	2.50	1.50
25	Elston Howard	7.50	3.75	2.25
26	Gaylord Perry	12.00	6.00	3.50
27	Bill Mazeroski	12.00	6.00	3.50
28	Ron Swoboda	5.00	2.50	1.50
29	Vada Pinson	7.50	3.75	2.25
30	Joe Morgan	25.00	12.50	7.50
31	Cleon Jones	5.00	2.50	1.50
32	Willie Horton	5.00	2.50	1.50
33	Leon Wagner	5.00	2.50	1.50
34	George Scott	5.00	2.50	1.50
35	Ed Charles	5.00	2.50	1.50
	NATIONAL LEAGUE ALL-STARS			
N7	Tom Seaver	15.00	7.00	4.50
N19	Hank Aaron	40.00	20.00	12.00
N20	Jim Bunning	10.00	5.00	3.00
N21	Joe Torre	6.00	3.00	1.75
N22	Claude Osteen	5.00	2.50	1.50
N23	Ron Santo	6.00	3.00	1.75
N24	Joe Morgan	20.00	10.00	6.00
N25	Richie Allen	6.00	3.00	1.75
N26	Ron Swoboda	5.00	2.50	1.50
N27	Ernie Banks	20.00	10.00	6.00
N28	Bill Mazeroski	12.00	6.00	3.50
N29	Willie Stargell	12.00	6.00	3.50
N30	Pete Rose	25.00	12.50	7.50
N31	Gaylord Perry	10.00	5.00	3.00
N32	Rusty Staub	5.00	2.50	1.50
N33	Vada Pinson	6.00	3.00	1.75
N34	Juan Marichal	10.00	5.00	3.00
N35	Cleon Jones	5.00	2.50	1.50
	AMERICAN LEAGUE ALL-STARS			
A19	Al Kaline	20.00	10.00	6.00
A20	Frank Howard	5.00	2.50	1.50
A21	Brooks Robinson	20.00	10.00	6.00
A22	George Scott	5.00	2.50	1.50
A23	Willie Horton	5.00	2.50	1.50
A24	Jim Fregosi	5.00	2.50	1.50
A25	Ed Charles	5.00	2.50	1.50
A26	Harmon Killebrew	20.00	10.00	6.00
A27	Tony Oliva	6.00	3.00	1.75
A28	Joe Pepitone	6.00	3.00	1.75
A29	Elston Howard	6.00	3.00	1.75
A30	Jim Nash	5.00	2.50	1.50
A31	Marcelino Lopez	5.00	2.50	1.50
A32	Frank Robinson	20.00	10.00	6.00
A33	Leon Wagner	5.00	2.50	1.50
A34	Max Alvis	5.00	2.50	1.50
A35	Paul Casanova	5.00	2.50	1.50
	PLAYING TIPS			
19	SS fields ball . . .	3.00	1.50	.90
20	2b relays . . .	3.00	1.50	.90
21	1b completes DP	3.00	1.50	.90
22	Pitcher fields bunt . . .	3.00	1.50	.90
23	2b relays . . .	3.00	1.50	.90
24	1b complete DP	3.00	1.50	.90
25	CF makes catch . . .	3.00	1.50	.90
26	Catcher tags runner	3.00	1.50	.90
	1967 ATLANTA BRAVES			
B1	Gary Geiger	5.00	2.50	1.50
B2	Ty Cline	5.00	2.50	1.50
B3	Hank Aaron	45.00	22.50	13.50
B4	Gene Oliver	5.00	2.50	1.50
B5	Tony Cloninger	5.00	2.50	1.50
B6	Denis Menke	5.00	2.50	1.50
B7	Denny Lemaster	5.00	2.50	1.50
B8	Woody Woodward	5.00	2.50	1.50
B9	Joe Torre	7.50	3.75	2.25
B10	Ken Johnson	5.00	2.50	1.50
B11	Bob Bruce	5.00	2.50	1.50
B12	Felipe Alou	7.50	3.75	2.25
B13	Clete Boyer	5.00	2.50	1.50
B14	Wade Blasingame	5.00	2.50	1.50
B15	Don Schwall	5.00	2.50	1.50
B16	Dick Kelley	5.00	2.50	1.50
B17	Rico Carty	6.00	3.00	1.75
B18	Mack Jones	5.00	2.50	1.50
	1968 ATLANTA BRAVES			
B1	Cecil Upshaw	5.00	2.50	1.50
B2	Tito Francona	5.00	2.50	1.50
B3	Hank Aaron	40.00	20.00	12.00
B4	Pat Jarvis	5.00	2.50	1.50
B5	Tony Cloninger	5.00	2.50	1.50
B6	Phil Niekro	15.00	7.50	4.50
B7	Felix Millan	5.00	2.50	1.50
B8	Woody Woodward	5.00	2.50	1.50
B9	Joe Torre	7.50	3.75	2.25
B10	Ken Johnson	5.00	2.50	1.50
B11	Marty Martinez	5.00	2.50	1.50
B12	Felipe Alou	7.50	3.75	2.25
B13	Clete Boyer	5.00	2.50	1.50
B14	Sonny Jackson	5.00	2.50	1.50
B15	Deron Johnson	5.00	2.50	1.50
B16	Claude Raymond	5.00	2.50	1.50
B17	Rico Carty	6.00	3.00	1.75
B18	Mack Jones	5.00	2.50	1.50
	1967 BALTIMORE ORIOLES			
O1	Dave McNally	5.00	2.50	1.50
O2	Luis Aparicio	20.00	10.00	6.00
O3	Paul Blair	5.00	2.50	1.50
O4	Frank Robinson	25.00	12.50	7.50
O5	Jim Palmer	30.00	15.00	9.00
O6	Russ Snyder	5.00	2.50	1.50
O7	Stu Miller	5.00	2.50	1.50
O8	Dave Johnson	5.00	2.50	1.50
O9	Andy Etchebarren	5.00	2.50	1.50
O10	Brooks Robinson	25.00	12.50	7.50
O11	John Powell	12.00	6.00	3.50
O12	Sam Bowens	5.00	2.50	1.50
O13	Curt Blefary	5.00	2.50	1.50
O14	Ed Fisher	5.00	2.50	1.50
O15	Wally Bunker	5.00	2.50	1.50
O16	Moe Drabowsky	5.00	2.50	1.50
O17	Larry Haney	5.00	2.50	1.50
O18	Tom Phoebus	5.00	2.50	1.50
	1968 BALTIMORE ORIOLES			
O1	Dave McNally	5.00	2.50	1.50
O2	Jim Hardin	5.00	2.50	1.50
O3	Paul Blair	5.00	2.50	1.50
O4	Frank Robinson	25.00	12.50	7.50
O5	Bruce Howard	5.00	2.50	1.50
O6	John O'Donoghue	5.00	2.50	1.50
O7	Dave May	5.00	2.50	1.50
O8	Dave Johnson	5.00	2.50	1.50
O9	Andy Etchebarren	5.00	2.50	1.50
O10	Brooks Robinson	25.00	12.50	7.50
O11	John Powell	8.00	4.00	2.50
O12	Pete Richert	5.00	2.50	1.50
O13	Curt Blefary	5.00	2.50	1.50
O14	Mark Belanger	6.00	3.00	1.75
O15	Wally Bunker	5.00	2.50	1.50
O16	Don Buford	5.00	2.50	1.50
O17	Larry Haney	5.00	2.50	1.50
O18	Tom Phoebus	5.00	2.50	1.50
	1967 BOSTON RED SOX			
R1	Lee Stange	5.00	2.50	1.50
R2	Carl Yastrzemski	30.00	15.00	9.00
R3	Don Demeter	5.00	2.50	1.50
R4	Jose Santiago	5.00	2.50	1.50
R5	Darrell Brandon	5.00	2.50	1.50
R6	Joe Foy	5.00	2.50	1.50
R7	Don McMahon	5.00	2.50	1.50
R8	Dalton Jones	5.00	2.50	1.50
R9	Mike Ryan	5.00	2.50	1.50
R10	Bob Tillman	5.00	2.50	1.50
R11	Rico Petrocelli	6.00	3.00	1.75
R12	George Scott	5.00	2.50	1.50
R13	George Smith	5.00	2.50	1.50
R14	Dennis Bennett	5.00	2.50	1.50
R15	Hank Fischer	5.00	2.50	1.50
R16	Jim Lonborg	6.00	3.00	1.75
R17	Jose Tartabull	5.00	2.50	1.50
R18	George Thomas	5.00	2.50	1.50
	1968 BOSTON RED SOX			
R1	Lee Stange	5.00	2.50	1.50
R2	Gary Waslewski	5.00	2.50	1.50
R3	Gary Bell	5.00	2.50	1.50
R4	John Wyatt	5.00	2.50	1.50
R5	Darrell Brandon	5.00	2.50	1.50
R6	Joe Foy	5.00	2.50	1.50
R7	Ray Culp	5.00	2.50	1.50
R8	Dalton Jones	5.00	2.50	1.50
R9	Gene Oliver	5.00	2.50	1.50
R10	Jose Santiago	5.00	2.50	1.50
R11	Rico Petrocelli	6.00	3.00	1.75
R12	George Scott	5.00	2.50	1.50
R13	Mike Andrews	5.00	2.50	1.50
R14	Dick Ellsworth	5.00	2.50	1.50
R15	Norm Siebern	5.00	2.50	1.50
R16	Jim Lonborg	6.00	3.00	1.75
R17	Jerry Adair	5.00	2.50	1.50
R18	Elston Howard	5.00	2.50	1.50
	1967 CALIFORNIA ANGELS			
L19	Len Gabrielson	5.00	2.50	1.50
L20	Jackie Hernandez	5.00	2.50	1.50
L21	Paul Schaal	5.00	2.50	1.50
L22	Lew Burdette	5.00	2.50	1.50
L23	Jimmie Hall	5.00	2.50	1.50
L24	Fred Newman	5.00	2.50	1.50

L25	Don Mincher	5.00	2.50	1.50
L26	Bob Rodgers	5.00	2.50	1.50
L27	Jack Sanford	5.00	2.50	1.50
L28	Bobby Knoop	5.00	2.50	1.50
L29	Jose Cardenal	5.00	2.50	1.50
L30	Jim Fregosi	5.00	2.50	1.50
L31	George Brunet	5.00	2.50	1.50
L32	Marcelino Lopez	5.00	2.50	1.50
L33	Minnie Rojas	5.00	2.50	1.50
L34	Jay Johnstone	5.00	2.50	1.50
L35	Ed Kirkpatrick	5.00	2.50	1.50
	1967 CHICAGO CUBS			
C1	Ferguson Jenkins	15.00	7.50	4.50
C2	Ernie Banks	30.00	15.00	9.00
C3	Glenn Beckert	5.00	2.50	1.50
C4	Bob Hendley	5.00	2.50	1.50
C5	John Boccabella	5.00	2.50	1.50
C6	Ron Campbell	5.00	2.50	1.50
C7	Ray Culp	5.00	2.50	1.50
C8	Adolfo Phillips	5.00	2.50	1.50
C9	Don Bryant	5.00	2.50	1.50
C10	Randy Hundley	5.00	2.50	1.50
C11	Ron Santo	6.00	3.00	1.75
C12	Lee Thomas	5.00	2.50	1.50
C13	Billy Williams	25.00	12.50	7.50
C14	Ken Holtzman	5.00	2.50	1.50
C15	Cal Koonce	5.00	2.50	1.50
C16	Curt Simmons	5.00	2.50	1.50
C17	George Altman	5.00	2.50	1.50
C18	Bryon Browne	5.00	2.50	1.50
	CHICAGO WHITE SOX			
L1	Gary Peters	5.00	2.50	1.50
L2	Jerry Adair	5.00	2.50	1.50
L3	Al Weis	5.00	2.50	1.50
L4	Pete Ward	5.00	2.50	1.50
L5	Hoyt Wilhelm	15.00	7.50	4.50
L6	Don Buford	5.00	2.50	1.50
L7	John Buzhardt	5.00	2.50	1.50
L8	Wayne Causey	5.00	2.50	1.50
L9	Jerry McNertney	5.00	2.50	1.50
L10	Ron Hansen	5.00	2.50	1.50
L11	Tom McCraw	5.00	2.50	1.50
L12	Jim O'Toole	5.00	2.50	1.50
L13	Bill Skowron	6.00	3.00	1.75
L14	Joel Horlen	5.00	2.50	1.50
L15	Tommy John	12.00	6.00	3.50
L16	Bob Locker	5.00	2.50	1.50
L17	Ken Berry	5.00	2.50	1.50
L18	Tommie Agee	5.00	2.50	1.50
	1967 CINCINNATI REDS			
F1	Floyd Robinson	5.00	2.50	1.50
F2	Leo Cardenas	5.00	2.50	1.50
F3	Gordy Coleman	5.00	2.50	1.50
F4	Tommy Harper	5.00	2.50	1.50
F5	Tommy Helms	5.00	2.50	1.50
F6	Deron Johnson	5.00	2.50	1.50
F7	Jim Maloney	5.00	2.50	1.50
F8	Tony Perez	25.00	12.50	7.50
F9	Don Pavletich	5.00	2.50	1.50
F10	John Edwards	5.00	2.50	1.50
F11	Vada Pinson	7.50	3.75	2.25
F12	Chico Ruiz	5.00	2.50	1.50
F13	Pete Rose	40.00	20.00	12.00
F14	Bill McCool	5.00	2.50	1.50
F15	Joe Nuxhall	5.00	2.50	1.50
F16	Milt Pappas	5.00	2.50	1.50
F17	Art Shamsky	5.00	2.50	1.50
F18	Dick Simpson	5.00	2.50	1.50
	1967 CLEVELAND INDIANS			
I1	Luis Tiant	6.00	3.00	1.75
I2	Max Alvis	5.00	2.50	1.50
I3	Larry Brown	5.00	2.50	1.50
I4	Rocky Colavito	10.00	5.00	3.00
I5	John O'Donoghue	5.00	2.50	1.50
I6	Pedro Gonzalez	5.00	2.50	1.50
I7	Gary Bell	5.00	2.50	1.50
I8	Sonny Siebert	5.00	2.50	1.50
I9	Joe Azcue	5.00	2.50	1.50
I10	Lee Maye	5.00	2.50	1.50
I11	Chico Salmon	5.00	2.50	1.50
I12	Leon Wagner	5.00	2.50	1.50
I13	Fred Whitfield	5.00	2.50	1.50
I14	Jack Kralick	5.00	2.50	1.50
I15	Sam McDowell	6.00	3.00	1.75
I16	Dick Radatz	5.00	2.50	1.50
I17	Vic Davalillo	5.00	2.50	1.50
I18	Chuck Hinton	5.00	2.50	1.50
	1968 CLEVELAND INDIANS			
I1	Luis Tiant	6.00	3.00	1.75
I2	Max Alvis	5.00	2.50	1.50
I3	Larry Brown	5.00	2.50	1.50
I4	Tommy Harper	5.00	2.50	1.50
I5	Vern Fuller	5.00	2.50	1.50
I6	Jose Cardenal	5.00	2.50	1.50
I7	Dave Nelson	5.00	2.50	1.50
I8	Sonny Siebert	5.00	2.50	1.50
I9	Joe Azcue	5.00	2.50	1.50
I10	Lee Maye	5.00	2.50	1.50
I11	Chico Salmon	5.00	2.50	1.50
I12	Leon Wagner	5.00	2.50	1.50
I13	Eddie Fisher	5.00	2.50	1.50
I14	Stan Williams	5.00	2.50	1.50
I15	Sam McDowell	6.00	3.00	1.75
I16	Steve Hargan	5.00	2.50	1.50
I17	Vic Davalillo	5.00	2.50	1.50
I18	Duke Sims	5.00	2.50	1.50
	1967 DETROIT TIGERS			
T1	Larry Sherry	5.00	2.50	1.50
T2	Norm Cash	7.50	3.75	2.25
T3	Jerry Lumpe	5.00	2.50	1.50
T4	Dave Wickersham	5.00	2.50	1.50
T5	Joe Sparma	5.00	2.50	1.50
T6	Dick McAuliffe	5.00	2.50	1.50
T7	Fred Gladding	5.00	2.50	1.50
T8	Jim Northrup	5.00	2.50	1.50
T9	Bill Freehan	5.00	2.50	1.50
T10	Earl Wilson	5.00	2.50	1.50
T11	Dick Tracewski	5.00	2.50	1.50
T12	Don Wert	5.00	2.50	1.50
T13	Jake Wood	5.00	2.50	1.50
T14	Mickey Lolich	6.00	3.00	1.75
T15	Johnny Podres	5.00	2.50	1.50
T16	Bill Monbouquette	5.00	2.50	1.50
T17	Al Kaline	30.00	15.00	9.00
T18	Willie Horton	5.00	2.50	1.50
	1968 DETROIT TIGERS			
T1	Ray Oyler	5.00	2.50	1.50
T2	Norm Cash	7.50	3.75	2.25
T3	Mike Marshall	5.00	2.50	1.50
T4	Mickey Stanley	5.00	2.50	1.50
T5	Joe Sparma	5.00	2.50	1.50
T6	Dick McAuliffe	5.00	2.50	1.50
T7	Gates Brown	5.00	2.50	1.50
T8	Jim Northrup	5.00	2.50	1.50
T9	Bill Freehan	5.00	2.50	1.50
T10	Earl Wilson	5.00	2.50	1.50
T11	Dick Tracewski	5.00	2.50	1.50
T12	Don Wert	5.00	2.50	1.50
T13	Dennis Ribant	5.00	2.50	1.50
T14	Mickey Lolich	6.00	3.00	1.75
T15	Denny McLain	12.00	6.00	3.50
T16	Ed Mathews	25.00	12.50	7.50
T17	Al Kaline	30.00	15.00	9.00
T18	Willie Horton	5.00	2.50	1.50
	1967 HOUSTON ASTROS			
H1	Dave Giusti	5.00	2.50	1.50
H2	Bob Aspromonte	5.00	2.50	1.50
H3	Ron Davis	5.00	2.50	1.50
H4	Claude Raymond	5.00	2.50	1.50
H5	Barry Latman	5.00	2.50	1.50
H6	Chuck Harrison	5.00	2.50	1.50
H7	Bill Heath	5.00	2.50	1.50
H8	Sonny Jackson	5.00	2.50	1.50
H9	John Bateman	5.00	2.50	1.50
H10	Ron Brand	5.00	2.50	1.50
H11	Aaron Pointer	5.00	2.50	1.50
H12	Joe Morgan	25.00	12.50	7.50
H13	Rusty Staub	6.00	3.00	1.75
H14	Mike Cuellar	5.00	2.50	1.50
H15	Larry Dierker	5.00	2.50	1.50
H16	Dick Farrell	5.00	2.50	1.50
H17	Jim Landis	5.00	2.50	1.50
H18	Ed Mathews	25.00	12.50	7.50
	1968 HOUSTON ASTROS			
H1	Dave Giusti	5.00	2.50	1.50
H2	Bob Aspromonte	5.00	2.50	1.50
H3	Ron Davis	5.00	2.50	1.50
H4	Julio Gotay	5.00	2.50	1.50
H5	Fred Gladding	5.00	2.50	1.50
H6	Lee Thomas	5.00	2.50	1.50
H7	Wade Blasingame	5.00	2.50	1.50
H8	Denis Menke	5.00	2.50	1.50
H9	John Bateman	5.00	2.50	1.50
H10	Ron Brand	5.00	2.50	1.50
H11	Doug Rader	5.00	2.50	1.50
H12	Joe Morgan	25.00	12.50	7.50
H13	Rusty Staub	6.00	3.00	1.75
H14	Mike Cuellar	5.00	2.50	1.50
H15	Larry Dierker	5.00	2.50	1.50
H16	Denny Lemaster	5.00	2.50	1.50
H17	Jim Wynn	5.00	2.50	1.50
H18	Don Wilson	5.00	2.50	1.50
	1967 KANSAS CTIY ATHLETICS			
K1	Jim Nash	5.00	2.50	1.50
K2	Bert Campaneris	5.00	2.50	1.50
K3	Ed Charles	5.00	2.50	1.50
K4	Wes Stock	5.00	2.50	1.50
K5	John Odom	5.00	2.50	1.50
K6	Ossie Chavarria	5.00	2.50	1.50
K7	Jack Aker	5.00	2.50	1.50
K8	Dick Green	5.00	2.50	1.50
K9	Phil Roof	5.00	2.50	1.50
K10	Rene Lacheman	5.00	2.50	1.50
K11	Mike Hershberger	5.00	2.50	1.50
K12	Joe Nossek	5.00	2.50	1.50
K13	Roger Repoz	5.00	2.50	1.50
K14	Chuck Dobson	5.00	2.50	1.50
K15	Jim Hunter	15.00	7.50	4.50
K16	Lew Krausse	5.00	2.50	1.50
K17	Danny Cater	5.00	2.50	1.50
K18	Jim Gosger	5.00	2.50	1.50
	1967 LOS ANGELES DODGERS			
L1	Phil Regan	5.00	2.50	1.50
L2	Bob Bailey	5.00	2.50	1.50
L3	Ron Fairly	5.00	2.50	1.50
L4	Joe Moeller	5.00	2.50	1.50
L5	Don Sutton	15.00	7.50	4.50
L6	Ron Hunt	5.00	2.50	1.50
L7	Jim Brewer	5.00	2.50	1.50
L8	Lou Johnson	5.00	2.50	1.50
L9	John Roseboro	5.00	2.50	1.50
L10	Jeff Torborg	5.00	2.50	1.50
L11	John Kennedy	5.00	2.50	1.50
L12	Jim Lefebvre	5.00	2.50	1.50
L13	Wes Parker	5.00	2.50	1.50
L14	Bob Miller	5.00	2.50	1.50
L15	Claude Osteen	5.00	2.50	1.50
L16	Ron Perranoski	5.00	2.50	1.50
L17	Willie Davis	5.00	2.50	1.50
L18	Al Ferrera	5.00	2.50	1.50
	1968 LOS ANGELES DODGERS			
L1	Phil Regan	5.00	2.50	1.50
L2	Bob Bailey	5.00	2.50	1.50
L3	Ron Fairly	5.00	2.50	1.50
L4	Jim Brewer	5.00	2.50	1.50
L5	Don Sutton	15.00	7.50	4.50
L6	Tom Haller	5.00	2.50	1.50
L7	Rocky Colavito	12.00	6.00	3.50
L8	Jim Grant	5.00	2.50	1.50
L9	Jim Campanis	5.00	2.50	1.50
L10	Jeff Torborg	5.00	2.50	1.50
L11	Zoilo Versalles	6.00	3.00	1.75
L12	Jim Lefebvre	5.00	2.50	1.50
L13	Wes Parker	5.00	2.50	1.50
L14	Bill Singer	5.00	2.50	1.50
L15	Claude Osteen	5.00	2.50	1.50
L16	Len Gabrielson	5.00	2.50	1.50
L17	Willie Davis	5.00	2.50	1.50
L18	Al Ferrera	5.00	2.50	1.50
	1967 MINNESOTA TWINS			
M1	Ron Kline	5.00	2.50	1.50
M2	Bob Allison	6.00	3.00	1.75
M3	Earl Battey	5.00	2.50	1.50
M4	Jim Merritt	5.00	2.50	1.50
M5	Jim Perry	6.00	3.00	1.75
M6	Harmon Killebrew	25.00	12.50	7.50
M7	Dave Boswell	5.00	2.50	1.50
M8	Rich Rollins	5.00	2.50	1.50
M9	Jerry Zimmerman	5.00	2.50	1.50
M10	Al Worthington	5.00	2.50	1.50
M11	Cesar Tovar	5.00	2.50	1.50
M12	Sandy Valdespino	5.00	2.50	1.50
M13	Zoilo Versalles	6.00	3.00	1.75
M14	Dean Chance	6.00	3.00	1.75
M15	Jim Grant	5.00	2.50	1.50
M16	Jim Kaat	9.00	4.50	2.75
M17	Tony Oliva	10.00	5.00	3.00
M18	Andy Kosco	5.00	2.50	1.50
	1968 MINNESOTA TWINS			
M1	Rich Reese	5.00	2.50	1.50
M2	Bob Allison	6.00	3.00	1.75
M3	Ron Perranoski	5.00	2.50	1.50
M4	John Roseboro	5.00	2.50	1.50
M5	Jim Perry	6.00	3.00	1.75
M6	Harmon Killebrew	25.00	12.50	7.50
M7	Dave Boswell	5.00	2.50	1.50
M8	Rich Rollins	5.00	2.50	1.50
M9	Jerry Zimmerman	5.00	2.50	1.50
M10	Al Worthington	5.00	2.50	1.50
M11	Cesar Tovar	5.00	2.50	1.50
M12	Jim Merritt	5.00	2.50	1.50
M13	Bob Miller	5.00	2.50	1.50
M14	Dean Chance	6.00	3.00	1.75
M15	Ted Uhlaender	5.00	2.50	1.50
M16	Jim Kaat	9.00	4.50	2.75
M17	Tony Oliva	10.00	5.00	3.00
M18	Rod Carew	40.00	20.00	12.00
	1967 NEW YORK METS			
V19	Chuck Hiller	5.00	2.50	1.50
V20	Johnny Lewis	5.00	2.50	1.50
V21	Ed Kranepool	5.00	2.50	1.50
V22	Al Luplow	5.00	2.50	1.50
V23	Don Cardwell	5.00	2.50	1.50
V24	Cleon Jones	5.00	2.50	1.50
V25	Bob Shaw	5.00	2.50	1.50
V26	John Stephenson	5.00	2.50	1.50
V27	Ron Swoboda	5.00	2.50	1.50
V28	Ken Boyer	6.00	3.00	1.75
V29	Ed Bressoud	5.00	2.50	1.50
V30	Tommy Davis	5.00	2.50	1.50
V31	Roy McMillan	5.00	2.50	1.50
V32	Jack Fisher	5.00	2.50	1.50
V33	Tug McGraw	6.00	3.00	1.75
V34	Jerry Grote	5.00	2.50	1.50
V35	Jack Hamilton	5.00	2.50	1.50
	1967 NEW YORK YANKEES			
V1	Mel Stottlemyre	5.00	2.50	1.50
V2	Ruben Amaro	5.00	2.50	1.50
V3	Jake Gibbs	5.00	2.50	1.50
V4	Dooley Womack	5.00	2.50	1.50
V5	Fred Talbot	5.00	2.50	1.50
V6	Horace Clarke	5.00	2.50	1.50
V7	Jim Bouton	6.00	3.00	1.75
V8	Mickey Mantle	125.00	60.00	35.00
V9	Elston Howard	7.50	3.75	2.25
V10	Hal Reniff	5.00	2.50	1.50
V11	Charley Smith	5.00	2.50	1.50
V12	Bobby Murcer	6.00	3.00	1.75
V13	Joe Pepitone	6.00	3.00	1.75
V14	Al Downing	5.00	2.50	1.50
V15	Steve Hamilton	5.00	2.50	1.50
V16	Fritz Peterson	5.00	2.50	1.50
V17	Tom Tresh	6.00	3.00	1.75
V18	Roy White	6.00	3.00	1.75
	1967 PHILADELPHIA PHILLIES			
P1	Richie Allen	7.50	3.75	2.25
P2	Bob Wine	5.00	2.50	1.50
P3	Johnny Briggs	5.00	2.50	1.50
P4	John Callison	5.00	2.50	1.50
P5	Doug Clemens	5.00	2.50	1.50
P6	Dick Groat	5.00	2.50	1.50
P7	Dick Ellsworth	5.00	2.50	1.50
P8	Phil Linz	5.00	2.50	1.50
P9	Clay Dalrymple	5.00	2.50	1.50
P10	Bob Uecker	10.00	5.00	3.00
P11	Cookie Rojas	5.00	2.50	1.50
P12	Tony Taylor	5.00	2.50	1.50
P13	Bill White	5.00	2.50	1.50
P14	Larry Jackson	5.00	2.50	1.50
P15	Chris Short	5.00	2.50	1.50
P16	Jim Bunning	15.00	7.50	4.50
P17	Tony Gonzalez	5.00	2.50	1.50
P18	Don Lock	5.00	2.50	1.50
	1967 PITTSBURGH PIRATES			
E1	Al McBean	5.00	2.50	1.50
E2	Gene Alley	5.00	2.50	1.50
E3	Donn Clendenon	5.00	2.50	1.50
E4	Bob Veale	5.00	2.50	1.50
E5	Pete Mikkelsen	5.00	2.50	1.50
E6	Bill Mazeroski	20.00	10.00	6.00
E7	Steve Blass	5.00	2.50	1.50
E8	Manny Mota	5.00	2.50	1.50
E9	Jim Pagliaroni	5.00	2.50	1.50
E10	Jesse Gonder	5.00	2.50	1.50
E11	Jose Pagan	5.00	2.50	1.50
E12	Willie Stargell	25.00	12.50	7.50
E13	Maury Wills	9.00	4.50	2.75
E14	Elroy Face	5.00	2.50	1.50
E15	Woodie Fryman	5.00	2.50	1.50
E16	Vern Law	5.00	2.50	1.50
E17	Matty Alou	5.00	2.50	1.50
E18	Roberto Clemente	60.00	30.00	18.00
	1967 SAN FRANCISCO GIANTS			
G1	Bob Bolin	5.00	2.50	1.50

G2	Ollie Brown	5.00	2.50	1.50
G3	Jim Davenport	5.00	2.50	1.50
G4	Tito Fuentes	5.00	2.50	1.50
G5	Norm Siebern	5.00	2.50	1.50
G6	Jim Hart	5.00	2.50	1.50
G7	Juan Marichal	15.00	7.50	4.50
G8	Hal Lanier	5.00	2.50	1.50
G9	Tom Haller	5.00	2.50	1.50
G10	Bob Barton	5.00	2.50	1.50
G11	Willie McCovey	20.00	10.00	6.00
G12	Mike McCormick	5.00	2.50	1.50
G13	Frank Linzy	5.00	2.50	1.50
G14	Ray Sadecki	5.00	2.50	1.50
G15	Gaylord Perry	15.00	7.50	4.50
G16	Lindy McDaniel	5.00	2.50	1.50
G17	Willie Mays	60.00	30.00	18.00
G18	Jesus Alou	5.00	2.50	1.50
	1968 SAN FRANCISCO GIANTS			
G1	Bob Bolin	5.00	2.50	1.50
G2	Ollie Brown	5.00	2.50	1.50
G3	Jim Davenport	5.00	2.50	1.50
G4	Bob Barton	5.00	2.50	1.50
G5	Jack Hiatt	5.00	2.50	1.50
G6	Jim Hart	5.00	2.50	1.50
G7	Juan Marichal	15.00	7.50	4.50
G8	Hal Lanier	5.00	2.50	1.50
G9	Ron Hunt	5.00	2.50	1.50
G10	Ron Herbel	5.00	2.50	1.50
G11	Willie McCovey	20.00	10.00	6.00
G12	Mike McCormick	5.00	2.50	1.50
G13	Frank Linzy	5.00	2.50	1.50
G14	Ray Sadecki	5.00	2.50	1.50
G15	Gaylord Perry	15.00	7.50	4.50
G16	Lindy McDaniel	5.00	2.50	1.50
G17	Willie Mays	60.00	30.00	18.00
G18	Jesus Alou	5.00	2.50	1.50
	1967 WASHINGTON SENATORS			
S1	Bob Humphreys	5.00	2.50	1.50
S2	Bernie Allen	5.00	2.50	1.50
S3	Ed Brinkman	5.00	2.50	1.50
S4	Pete Richert	5.00	2.50	1.50
S5	Camilo Pascual	5.00	2.50	1.50
S6	Frank Howard	7.50	3.75	2.25
S7	Casey Cox	5.00	2.50	1.50
S8	Jim King	5.00	2.50	1.50
S9	Paul Casanova	5.00	2.50	1.50
S10	Dick Lines	5.00	2.50	1.50
S11	Dick Nen	5.00	2.50	1.50
S12	Ken McMullen	5.00	2.50	1.50
S13	Bob Saverine	5.00	2.50	1.50
S14	Jim Hannan	5.00	2.50	1.50
S15	Darold Knowles	5.00	2.50	1.50
S16	Phil Ortega	5.00	2.50	1.50
S17	Ken Harrelson	5.00	2.50	1.50
S18	Fred Valentine	5.00	2.50	1.50

1971 Coca-Cola Houston Astros

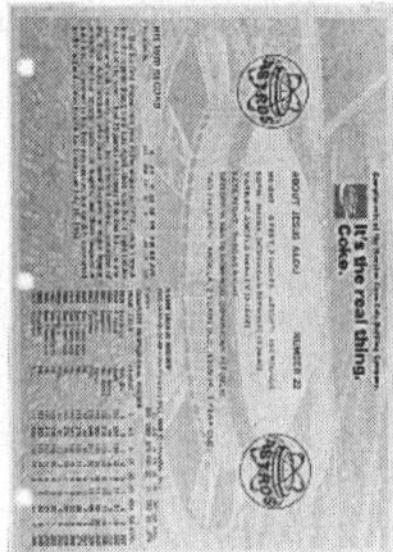

The constitution and distribution of these Coke premium pictures is unknown. Players are pictured in pastel drawings on the semi-gloss fronts of these 8" x 11" sheets. (The punch holes on the photographed card are not original.) A black facsimile autograph appears in the lower portion of the drawing and the player's name is printed in black in the white bottom border. Backs are printed in blue and red with a background photo of the Astrodome. Data on back includes biographical information, complete pro record and career summary. The unnumbered cards are checklisted here in alphabetical order; but this list is probably not complete.

		NM	EX	VG
Complete Set (12):		50.00	25.00	15.00
Common Player:		5.00	2.50	1.50
(1)	Jesus Alou	5.00	2.50	1.50
(2)	Wade Blasingame/SP	9.00	4.50	2.75
(3)	Cesar Cedeno	7.50	3.75	2.25
(4)	Larry Dierker	7.50	3.75	2.25
(5)	John Edwards	5.00	2.50	1.50
(6)	Denis Menke	5.00	2.50	1.50
(7)	Roger Metzger	5.00	2.50	1.50
(8)	Joe Morgan	15.00	7.50	4.50
(9)	Doug Rader	5.00	2.50	1.50
(10)	Bob Watson	5.00	2.50	1.50
(11)	Don Wilson	5.00	2.50	1.50
(12)	Jim Wynn/SP	12.00	6.00	3.50

1978 Coca-Cola/ WPLO Atlanta Braves

Co-sponsored by Coke and a local radio station, this set of Braves cards is rendered in blue-and-white line art portraits in a 3" x 4-1/4" format. A soda discount coupon was distributed with the set.

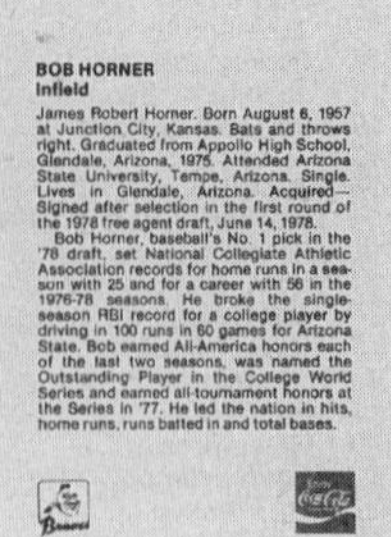
BOB HORNER
Infield

James Robert Horner. Born August 6, 1957 at Junction City, Kansas. Bats and throws right. Graduated from Appollo High School, Glendale, Arizona, 1975. Attended Arizona State University, Tempe, Arizona. Single. Lives in Glendale, Arizona. Acquired—Signed after selection in the first round of the 1978 free agent draft, June 14, 1978.

Bob Horner, baseball's No. 1 pick in the '78 draft, set National Collegiate Athletic Association records for home runs in a season with 25 and for a career with 56 in the 1976-78 seasons. He broke the single-season RBI record for a college player by driving in 100 runs in 60 games for Arizona State. Bob earned All-America honors each of the last two seasons, was named the Outstanding Player in the College World Series and earned all-tournament honors at the Series in '77. He led the nation in hits, home runs, runs batted in and total bases.

		NM	EX	VG
Complete Set (14):		30.00	15.00	9.00
Common Player:		3.00	1.50	.90
(1)	Barry Bonnell	3.00	1.50	.90
(2)	Jeff Burroughs	3.00	1.50	.90
(3)	Rick Camp	3.00	1.50	.90
(4)	Gene Garber	3.00	1.50	.90
(5)	Rod Gilbreath	3.00	1.50	.90
(6)	Bob Horner	4.50	2.25	1.25
(7)	Glenn Hubbard	3.00	1.50	.90
(8)	Gary Matthews	3.00	1.50	.90
(9)	Larry McWilliams	3.00	1.50	.90
(10)	Dale Murphy	9.00	4.50	2.75
(11)	Phil Niekro	5.00	2.50	1.50
(12)	Rowland Office	3.00	1.50	.90
(13)	Biff Pocoroba	3.00	1.50	.90
(14)	Jerry Royster	3.00	1.50	.90

1979 Coca-Cola/7-Eleven MVPs

The co-MVPs of the National League for 1979 are pictured on this 5" x 7" blank-back photo card. A red band at top identifies the player and the award. At bottom are Coke and 7-Eleven logos.

	NM	EX	VG
Keith Hernandez, Willie Stargell	6.00	3.00	1.80

1955 Coffee-Time Syrup Jimmy Piersall

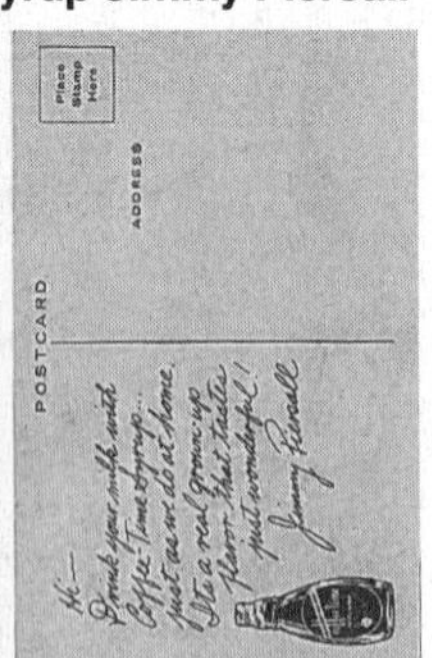

The date of issue is speculative for this promotional postcard. The borderless black-and-white photo on the front on this 3-1/2" x 5-1/2" card shows the popular BoSox star in a relaxed pose with right arm on knee. A blue facsimile autograph is printed at center. The postcard-format back has at left a product picture and an advertising message bearing Piersall's signature. Similar cards advertising Colonial Meats, Cain's and other products are also known, valued similarly.

	NM	EX	VG
Autographed: 2-3X	125.00	65.00	35.00
Jimmy Piersall	80.00	40.00	24.00

1909-1911 Colgan's Chips Stars of the Diamond (E254)

This unusual set of 1-7/16"-diameter round cards was issued over a three-year period by the Colgan Gum Co., Louisville, Ky. The cards were inserted in five-cent tins of Colgan's Mint Chips and Violet Chips

brands of gum. The borderless cards feature a black-and-white player portrait on the front along with the player's last name, team and league. On more than a dozen cards, variations are known in the size of the photo and/or lettering on front. Since they cannot be identified without another card to compare with, they are noted here only with an asterisk. The card back identifies the set as "Stars of the Diamond" and carries advertising for Colgan's Gum. Some backs are seen with a line of type at the bottom stating, "208 IN PRESENT SERIES." Over 225 different players were pictured over the three-year period, but because of team changes and other notable variations, at least 289 different cards exist. This issue was catalogued as E254 in the American Card Catalog. A number of cards and variations which had been listed in earlier editions of this catalog have been eliminated for lack of proof of their existence. Gaps have been left in the assigned numbering to accommodate future additions. Persons with "Stars of the Diamond" players or variations that do no appear on this list should contact the editor.

		NM	EX	VG
Common Player:		75.00	35.00	20.00
Round Tin Package:		30.00	15.00	9.00
(1)	Ed Abbaticchio	75.00	35.00	20.00
(2)	Fred Abbott	75.00	35.00	20.00
(3a)	Bill Abstein (Pittsburg)	75.00	35.00	20.00
(3b)	Bill Abstein (Jersey City)	75.00	35.00	20.00
(4)	Babe Adams	75.00	35.00	20.00
(5)	Doc Adkins	75.00	35.00	20.00
(6a)	Dave Altizer (Cincinnati)	75.00	35.00	20.00
(6b)	Dave Altizer (Minneapolis)	75.00	35.00	20.00
(7)	Nick Altrock	95.00	50.00	30.00
(8)	Red Ames	75.00	35.00	20.00
(9a)	Jimmy Austin (New York)	75.00	35.00	20.00
(9b)	Jimmy Austin (St. Louis)	75.00	35.00	20.00
(10a)	Charlie Babb (Memphis)	75.00	35.00	20.00
(10b)	Charlie Babb (Norfolk)	75.00	35.00	20.00
(11)	Baerwald	75.00	35.00	20.00
(12)	Bill Bailey	75.00	35.00	20.00
(13)	Home Run Baker (*)	215.00	110.00	65.00
(14)	Jack Barry (*)	75.00	35.00	20.00
(15a)	Bill Bartley (Curved letters.)	75.00	35.00	20.00
(15b)	Bill Bartley (Horizontal letters.)	75.00	35.00	20.00
(16a)	Johnny Bates (Cincinnati)	75.00	35.00	20.00
(16b)	Johnny Bates (Philadelphia, black letters.)	75.00	35.00	20.00
(16c)	Johnny Bates (Philadelphia, white letters.)	75.00	35.00	20.00
(17)	Dick Bayless	75.00	35.00	20.00
(18a)	Ginger Beaumont (Boston)	75.00	35.00	20.00
(18b)	Ginger Beaumont (Chicago)	75.00	35.00	20.00
(18c)	Ginger Beaumont (St. Paul)	75.00	35.00	20.00
(19)	Beals Becker	75.00	35.00	20.00
(20)	George Bell	75.00	35.00	20.00
(21a)	Harry Bemis (Cleveland)	75.00	35.00	20.00
(21b)	Harry Bemis (Columbus)	75.00	35.00	20.00
(22a)	Heinie Berger (Cleveland)	75.00	35.00	20.00
(22b)	Heinie Berger (Columbus)	75.00	35.00	20.00
(23)	Beumiller	75.00	35.00	20.00
(24)	Joe Birmingham	75.00	35.00	20.00
(25)	Kitty Bransfield	75.00	35.00	20.00
(26)	Roger Bresnahan	215.00	110.00	65.00
(27)	Al Bridwell	75.00	35.00	20.00
(28)	Lew Brockett	75.00	35.00	20.00
(29)	Al Burch (*)	75.00	35.00	20.00
(30)	Burke	75.00	35.00	20.00
(31)	Donie Bush	75.00	35.00	20.00
(32)	Bill Byers	75.00	35.00	20.00
(33)	Howie Cammitz (Camnitz)	75.00	35.00	20.00
(34a)	Charlie Carr (Indianapolis)	75.00	35.00	20.00
(34b)	Charlie Carr (Utica)	75.00	35.00	20.00
(35)	Frank Chance	215.00	110.00	65.00
(36)	Hal Chase	150.00	80.00	40.00
(37)	Bill Clancy (Clancey)	75.00	35.00	20.00
(38a)	Fred Clarke (Pittsburg)	215.00	110.00	65.00
(38b)	Fred Clarke (Pittsburgh)	215.00	110.00	65.00
(39)	Tommy Clarke (Cincinnati)	75.00	35.00	20.00
(40)	Bill Clymer	75.00	35.00	20.00
(41)	Ty Cobb (*)	1,140	570.00	340.00
(42)	Eddie Collins	215.00	110.00	65.00
(43)	Bunk Congalton	75.00	35.00	20.00
(44)	Wid Conroy	75.00	35.00	20.00
(45)	Ernie Courtney	75.00	35.00	20.00
(46a)	Harry Coveleski (Cincinnati)	75.00	35.00	20.00
(46b)	Harry Coveleski (Chattanooga)	75.00	35.00	20.00
(47)	Doc Crandall	75.00	35.00	20.00
(48)	Gavvy Cravath	75.00	35.00	20.00
(49)	Dode Criss	75.00	35.00	20.00
(50a)	Jake Daubert (Memphis)	75.00	35.00	20.00
(50b)	Jake Daubert (Brooklyn)	75.00	35.00	20.00
(51)	Harry Davis (Philadelphia)	75.00	35.00	20.00
(52)	Davis (St. Paul)	75.00	35.00	20.00
(53)	Frank Delahanty	75.00	35.00	20.00
(54a)	Ray Demmett (Demmitt) (New York)	75.00	35.00	20.00

No.	Player	NM	EX	VG
(54b)	Ray Demmett (Demmitt) (Montreal)	75.00	35.00	20.00
(55)	Art Devlin	75.00	35.00	20.00
(56)	Wild Bill Donovan	75.00	35.00	20.00
(57)	Mickey Doolin (Doolan)	75.00	35.00	20.00
(58)	Patsy Dougherty	75.00	35.00	20.00
(59)	Tom Downey	75.00	35.00	20.00
(60)	Larry Doyle	75.00	35.00	20.00
(61)	Jack Dunn	95.00	50.00	30.00
(62)	Dick Eagan (Egan)	75.00	35.00	20.00
(63a)	Kid Elberfield (Elberfeld) (Washington)	75.00	35.00	20.00
(63b)	Kid Elberfield (Elberfeld) (New York)	75.00	35.00	20.00
(64)	Rube Ellis	75.00	35.00	20.00
(65)	Clyde Engle (Boston)	75.00	35.00	20.00
(66)	Steve Evans (Horizontal letters.)	75.00	35.00	20.00
(67)	Johnny Evers	215.00	110.00	65.00
(68)	Cecil Ferguson	75.00	35.00	20.00
(69)	Hobe Ferris	75.00	35.00	20.00
(70)	Field (*)	75.00	35.00	20.00
(71)	Fitzgerald	75.00	35.00	20.00
(72a)	Patsy Flaherty (Kansas City)	75.00	35.00	20.00
(72b)	Patsy Flaherty (Atlanta)	75.00	35.00	20.00
(73)	Jack Flater	75.00	35.00	20.00
(74a)	Elmer Flick (Cleveland)	215.00	110.00	65.00
(74b)	Elmer Flick (Toledo)	215.00	110.00	65.00
(75a)	James Freck (Frick, Baltimore)	90.00	45.00	30.00
(75b)	James Freck (Frick, Toronto)	75.00	35.00	20.00
(76)	Jerry Freeman (Photo actually Buck Freeman.)	75.00	35.00	20.00
(77)	Art Fromme (*)	75.00	35.00	20.00
(78a)	Larry Gardner (Boston)	75.00	35.00	20.00
(78b)	Larry Gardner (New York)	75.00	35.00	20.00
(79)	Harry Gaspar	75.00	35.00	20.00
(80a)	Gus Getz (Boston)	75.00	35.00	20.00
(80b)	Gus Getz (Indianapolis)	75.00	35.00	20.00
(81)	George Gibson	75.00	35.00	20.00
(82a)	Moose Grimshaw (Toronto)	75.00	35.00	20.00
(82b)	Moose Grimshaw (Louisville)	75.00	35.00	20.00
(83)	Ed Hahn	75.00	35.00	20.00
(84)	John Halla (*)	75.00	35.00	20.00
(85)	Ed Hally (Holly)	75.00	35.00	20.00
(86)	Charlie Hanford	75.00	35.00	20.00
(87)	Topsy Hartsel	75.00	35.00	20.00
(88a)	Roy Hartzell (St. Louis)	75.00	35.00	20.00
(88b)	Roy Hartzell (New York)	75.00	35.00	20.00
(89)	Weldon Henley	75.00	35.00	20.00
(91)	Harry Hinchman	75.00	35.00	20.00
(92)	Solly Hofman	75.00	35.00	20.00
(93a)	Harry Hooper (Boston Na'l)	215.00	110.00	65.00
(93b)	Harry Hooper (Boston Am. L.)	240.00	120.00	75.00
(94)	Howard (*)	75.00	35.00	20.00
(95a)	Hughes (No name in uniform.)	75.00	35.00	20.00
(95b)	Hughes (Name and team name in uniform.)	75.00	35.00	20.00
(96b)	Rudy Hulswitt (St. Louis)	75.00	35.00	20.00
(96c)	Rudy Hulswitt (Chattanooga)	75.00	35.00	20.00
(97)	John Hummel	75.00	35.00	20.00
(98)	George Hunter	75.00	35.00	20.00
(99)	Hugh Jennings	215.00	110.00	65.00
(100)	Davy Jones	75.00	35.00	20.00
(101)	Tom Jones	75.00	35.00	20.00
(102a)	Tim Jordon (Jordan, Brooklyn)	75.00	35.00	20.00
(102b)	Tim Jordon (Jordan, Atlanta)	75.00	35.00	20.00
(102c)	Tim Jordon (Jordan, Louisville)	75.00	35.00	20.00
(103)	Addie Joss	240.00	120.00	75.00
(104)	Al Kaiser	75.00	35.00	20.00
(105)	Joe Kelly (Kelley)	215.00	110.00	65.00
(106)	Bill Killefer (*)	75.00	35.00	20.00
(107a)	Ed Killian (Detroit)	75.00	35.00	20.00
(107b)	Ed Killian (Toronto)	75.00	35.00	20.00
(108)	Otto Knabe	75.00	35.00	20.00
(109)	Jack Knight	75.00	35.00	20.00
(111)	Ed Konetchy	75.00	35.00	20.00
(112)	Rube Kroh	75.00	35.00	20.00
(113)	James Lafitte	75.00	35.00	20.00
(114)	Lakoff	75.00	35.00	20.00
(115)	Frank Lange	75.00	35.00	20.00
(116a)	Frank LaPorte (St. Louis)	75.00	35.00	20.00
(116b)	Frank LaPorte (New York)	75.00	35.00	20.00
(117)	Tommy Leach	75.00	35.00	20.00
(118)	Bill Lelivelt	75.00	35.00	20.00
(119a)	Jack Lewis (Milwaukee)	75.00	35.00	20.00
(119b)	Jack Lewis (Indianapolis)	75.00	35.00	20.00
(120a)	Vive Lindaman (Boston)	75.00	35.00	20.00
(120b)	Vive Lindaman (Louisville)	75.00	35.00	20.00
(120c)	Vive Lindaman (Indianapolis)	75.00	35.00	20.00
(121)	Bris Lord	75.00	35.00	20.00
(122a)	Harry Lord (Boston)	75.00	35.00	20.00
(122b)	Harry Lord (Chicago)	75.00	35.00	20.00
(123)	Bill Ludwig (Milwaukee)	75.00	35.00	20.00
(124)	Nick Maddox	75.00	35.00	20.00
(125a)	Manser (Jersey City)	75.00	35.00	20.00
(125b)	Manser (Rochester)	75.00	35.00	20.00
(126)	Al Mattern	75.00	35.00	20.00
(127)	Bill Matthews	75.00	35.00	20.00
(128)	George McBride	75.00	35.00	20.00
(129)	Joe McCarthy (Toledo)	215.00	110.00	65.00
(130)	McConnell	75.00	35.00	20.00
(131)	Moose McCormick	75.00	35.00	20.00
(132)	Dan McGann	75.00	35.00	20.00
(133)	Jim McGinley	75.00	35.00	20.00
(134)	Iron Man McGinnity	215.00	110.00	65.00
(135a)	Matty McIntyre (Detroit)	75.00	35.00	20.00
(135b)	Matty McIntyre (Chicago)	75.00	35.00	20.00
(136)	Larry McLean (*)(Three photo size variations known.)	75.00	35.00	20.00
(137)	Fred Merkle	75.00	35.00	20.00
(138a)	Merritt (Buffalo)	75.00	35.00	20.00
(138b)	Merritt (Jersey City)	75.00	35.00	20.00
(139)	Meyer (Newark)	75.00	35.00	20.00
(140)	Chief Meyers (New York)	75.00	35.00	20.00
(141)	Clyde Milan	75.00	35.00	20.00
(142)	Dots Miller	75.00	35.00	20.00
(143)	Mike Mitchell	75.00	35.00	20.00
(144)	Moran	75.00	35.00	20.00
(145a)	Bill Moriarty (Louisville)	75.00	35.00	20.00
(145b)	Bill Moriarty (Omaha)	75.00	35.00	20.00
(146)	George Moriarty	75.00	35.00	20.00
(147a)	George Mullen (Name incorrect.)	75.00	35.00	20.00
(147b)	George Mullin (Name correct.)	75.00	35.00	20.00
(148a)	Simmy Murch (Chattanooga)	75.00	35.00	20.00
(148b)	Simmy Murch (Indianapolis)	75.00	35.00	20.00
(149)	Danny Murphy	75.00	35.00	20.00
(150a)	Red Murray (New York, white letters.)	75.00	35.00	12.00
(150b)	Red Murray (St. Paul)	75.00	35.00	20.00
(151)	Billy Nattress (*)	75.00	35.00	20.00
(152a)	Red Nelson (St. Louis)	75.00	35.00	20.00
(152b)	Red Nelson (Toledo)	75.00	35.00	20.00
(153)	Rebel Oakes	75.00	35.00	20.00
(154)	Fred Odwell	75.00	35.00	20.00
(155a)	Al Orth (New York)	75.00	35.00	20.00
(155b)	Al Orth (Indianapolis)	75.00	35.00	20.00
(156)	Fred Osborn	75.00	35.00	20.00
(157)	Orval Overall	75.00	35.00	20.00
(158)	Owens	75.00	35.00	20.00
(159)	Fred Parent	75.00	35.00	20.00
(161a)	Dode Paskert (Cincinnati)	75.00	35.00	20.00
(161b)	Dode Paskert (Philadelphia)	75.00	35.00	20.00
(162)	Heinie Peitz	75.00	35.00	20.00
(163)	Bob Peterson	75.00	35.00	20.00
(164)	Jake Pfeister	75.00	35.00	20.00
(165)	Deacon Phillipe (Phillippe)	75.00	35.00	20.00
(166a)	Ollie Pickering (Louisville)	75.00	35.00	20.00
(166b)	Ollie Pickering (Minneapolis)	75.00	35.00	20.00
(166c)	Ollie Pickering (Omaha)	75.00	35.00	20.00
(167a)	Billy Purtell (Chicago)	75.00	35.00	20.00
(167b)	Billy Purtell (Boston)	75.00	35.00	20.00
(168)	Bugs Raymond	75.00	35.00	20.00
(169)	Pat Regan (Ragan)	75.00	35.00	20.00
(170)	Barney Reilly	75.00	35.00	20.00
(171)	Duke Reilly (Reilley)	75.00	35.00	20.00
(172)	Ed Reulbach	75.00	35.00	20.00
(173)	Claude Ritchey	75.00	35.00	20.00
(174)	Lou Ritter	75.00	35.00	20.00
(175)	William "Rabbit" Robinson (Louisville)	75.00	35.00	20.00
(176)	Rock	75.00	35.00	20.00
(177a)	Jack Rowan (Cincinnati)	75.00	35.00	20.00
(177b)	Jack Rowan (Philadelphia)	75.00	35.00	20.00
(178)	Nap Rucker	75.00	35.00	20.00
(179a)	Dick Rudolph (New York)	75.00	35.00	20.00
(179b)	Dick Rudolph (Toronto)	75.00	35.00	20.00
(180)	Jack Ryan ((St. Paul)(Photo actually Jimmy Ryan.)	75.00	35.00	20.00
(181)	Slim Sallee	75.00	35.00	20.00
(182a)	Bill Schardt (Birmingham)	75.00	35.00	20.00
(182b)	Bill Schardt (Milwaukee)	75.00	35.00	20.00
(183)	Jimmy Scheckard (Sheckard)	75.00	35.00	20.00
(184a)	George Schirm (Birmingham)	75.00	35.00	20.00
(184b)	George Schirm (Buffalo)	75.00	35.00	20.00
(185)	Larry Schlafly	75.00	35.00	20.00
(186)	Wildfire Schulte	75.00	35.00	20.00
(187a)	James Seabaugh (Looking to left, photo actually Julius Weisman.)	75.00	35.00	20.00
(187b)	James Seabaugh (Looking straight ahead, correct photo.)	75.00	35.00	20.00
(188)	Selby (*)	75.00	35.00	20.00
(189a)	Cy Seymour (New York)	75.00	35.00	20.00
(189b)	Cy Seymour (Baltimore)	75.00	35.00	20.00
(190)	Hosea Siner	75.00	35.00	20.00
(191)	G. Smith	75.00	35.00	20.00
(192a)	Sid Smith (Atlanta)	75.00	35.00	20.00
(192b)	Sid Smith (Buffalo)	75.00	35.00	20.00
(193)	Fred Snodgrass	75.00	35.00	20.00
(194a)	Bob Spade (Cincinnati)	75.00	35.00	20.00
(194b)	Bob Spade (Newark)	75.00	35.00	20.00
(195a)	Tully Sparks (Philadelphia)	75.00	35.00	20.00
(195b)	Tully Sparks (Richmond)	75.00	35.00	20.00
(196)	Tris Speaker (Boston Am.)	260.00	120.00	80.00
(197)	Tubby Spencer	75.00	35.00	20.00
(198)	Jake Stahl	75.00	35.00	20.00
(199)	John Stansberry (Stansbury)	75.00	35.00	20.00
(200)	Harry Steinfeldt (*)	75.00	35.00	20.00
(201)	George Stone	75.00	35.00	20.00
(202)	George Stovall	75.00	35.00	20.00
(203)	Gabby Street	75.00	35.00	20.00
(204a)	Sullivan (Louisville)	75.00	35.00	20.00
(204b)	Sullivan (Omaha)	75.00	35.00	20.00
(205a)	Ed Summers (No white in uniform.)	75.00	35.00	20.00
(205b)	Ed Summers (White in uniform.)	75.00	35.00	20.00
(206)	Suter	75.00	35.00	20.00
(207)	Lee Tannehill	75.00	35.00	20.00
(208)	Taylor	75.00	35.00	20.00
(209)	Joe Tinker	215.00	110.00	65.00
(210)	John Titus	75.00	35.00	20.00
(211)	Terry Turner	75.00	35.00	20.00
(212a)	Bob Unglaub (Washington)	75.00	35.00	20.00
(212b)	Bob Unglaub (Lincoln)	75.00	35.00	20.00
(213a)	Rube Waddell (St. Louis)	215.00	110.00	65.00
(213b)	Rube Waddell (Minneapolis)	215.00	110.00	65.00
(213c)	Rube Waddell (Newark)	215.00	110.00	65.00
(214)	Honus Wagner (*)	1,140	570.00	340.00
(215)	Walker	75.00	35.00	20.00
(216)	Waller	75.00	35.00	20.00
(217)	Clarence Wauner (Wanner)	75.00	35.00	20.00
(218)	Julius Weisman (Name correct.)	75.00	35.00	20.00
(219)	Jack White (Buffalo)	75.00	35.00	20.00
(220)	Kirby White (Boston)	75.00	35.00	20.00
(221)	Julius Wiesman (Weisman)	75.00	35.00	20.00
(222)	Ed Willett	75.00	35.00	20.00
(223)	Otto Williams	75.00	35.00	20.00
(224)	Owen Wilson	75.00	35.00	20.00
(225)	Hooks Wiltse	75.00	35.00	20.00
(226a)	Orville Woodruff (Indianapolis)	75.00	35.00	20.00
(226b)	Orville Woodruff (Louisville)	75.00	35.00	20.00
(227)	Woods	75.00	35.00	20.00
(228)	Cy Young	570.00	280.00	170.00
(229)	Bill Zimmerman	75.00	35.00	20.00
(230)	Heinie Zimmerman	75.00	35.00	20.00

1912 Colgan's Chips Red Borders (E270)

This set, issued in 1912 by Colgan Gum Co., Louisville, Ky., is very similar to the 1909-11 Colgan's release. Measuring about 1-3/8" in diameter, the black-and-white player pictures were inserted in tins of Colgan's Mint and Violet Chips gum. They are differentiated from the earlier issues by their distinctive red borders and by the back of the cards, which advises collectors to "Send 25 Box Tops" for a photo of the "World's Pennant Winning Team." The issue is designated as the E270 Red Border set in the American Card Catalog. A Red Border card of Gavvy Cravath previous cataloged is now believed not to exist.

No.	Player	NM	EX	VG
	Complete Set (181):	50,000	25,000	14,400
	Common Player:	250.00	125.00	75.00
(1)	Ed Abbaticchio	250.00	125.00	75.00
(2)	Fred Abbott	250.00	125.00	75.00
(3)	Babe Adams	250.00	125.00	75.00
(4)	Doc Adkins	250.00	125.00	75.00
(5)	Red Ames	250.00	125.00	75.00
(6)	Charlie Babb	250.00	125.00	75.00
(7)	Bill Bailey	250.00	125.00	75.00
(8)	Home Run Baker	400.00	250.00	150.00
(9)	Jack Barry	250.00	125.00	75.00
(10)	Johnny Bates	250.00	125.00	75.00
(11)	Dick Bayless	250.00	125.00	75.00
(12)	Ginger Beaumont	250.00	125.00	75.00
(13)	Beals Becker	250.00	125.00	75.00
(14)	George Bell	250.00	125.00	75.00
(15)	Harry Bemis	250.00	125.00	75.00
(16)	Heinie Berger	250.00	125.00	75.00
(17)	Beumiller	250.00	125.00	75.00
(18)	Joe Birmingham	250.00	125.00	75.00
(19)	Kitty Bransfield	250.00	125.00	75.00
(20)	Roger Bresnahan	500.00	250.00	150.00
(21)	Lew Brockett	250.00	125.00	75.00
(22)	Al Burch	250.00	125.00	75.00
(23)	Donie Bush	250.00	125.00	75.00
(24)	Bill Byers	250.00	125.00	75.00
(25)	Howie Cammitz (Camnitz)	250.00	125.00	75.00
(26)	Charlie Carr	250.00	125.00	75.00
(27)	Frank Chance	500.00	250.00	150.00
(28)	Hal Chase	305.00	150.00	91.00
(29)	Fred Clarke (Pittsburg)	500.00	250.00	150.00
(30)	Tommy Clarke (Cincinnati)	250.00	125.00	75.00
(31)	Bill Clymer	250.00	125.00	75.00
(32)	Ty Cobb	3,750	1,875	1,125
(33)	Eddie Collins	500.00	250.00	150.00
(34)	Wid Conroy	250.00	125.00	75.00
(35)	Harry Coveleski	250.00	125.00	75.00
(37)	Dode Criss	250.00	125.00	75.00
(38)	Jake Daubert	250.00	125.00	75.00
(39)	Harry Davis (Philadelphia)	250.00	125.00	75.00
(40)	Davis (St. Paul)	250.00	125.00	75.00
(41)	Frank Delahanty	250.00	125.00	75.00
(42)	Ray Demmett (Demmitt)	250.00	125.00	75.00
(43)	Art Devlin	250.00	125.00	75.00
(44)	Wild Bill Donovan	250.00	125.00	75.00
(45)	Mickey Doolin (Doolan)	250.00	125.00	75.00
(46)	Patsy Dougherty	250.00	125.00	75.00
(47)	Tom Downey	250.00	125.00	75.00
(48)	Larry Doyle	250.00	125.00	75.00
(49)	Jack Dunn	250.00	125.00	75.00
(50)	Dick Eagan (Egan)	250.00	125.00	75.00
(51)	Kid Elberfield (Elberfeld)	250.00	125.00	75.00
(52)	Rube Ellis	250.00	125.00	75.00
(53)	Steve Evans	250.00	125.00	75.00
(54)	Johnny Evers	500.00	250.00	150.00
(55)	Cecil Ferguson	250.00	125.00	75.00
(56)	Hobe Ferris	250.00	125.00	75.00
(57)	Fisher	250.00	125.00	75.00
(58)	Fitzgerald	250.00	125.00	75.00
(59)	Elmer Flick	500.00	250.00	150.00
(60)	James Freck (Frick)	250.00	125.00	75.00
(61)	Art Fromme	250.00	125.00	75.00
(62)	Harry Gaspar	250.00	125.00	75.00
(63)	George Gibson	250.00	125.00	75.00
(64)	Moose Grimshaw	250.00	125.00	75.00
(65)	John Halla	250.00	125.00	75.00
(66)	Ed Hally (Holly)	250.00	125.00	75.00
(67)	Charlie Hanford	250.00	125.00	75.00
(68)	Topsy Hartsel	250.00	125.00	75.00
(69)	Roy Hartzell	250.00	125.00	75.00
(70)	Weldon Henley (Two sizes photo variations noted.)	250.00	125.00	75.00
(71)	Harry Hinchman	250.00	125.00	75.00
(72)	Solly Hofman	250.00	125.00	75.00
(73)	Harry Hooper	500.00	250.00	150.00
(74)	Howard	250.00	125.00	75.00
(75)	Hughes	250.00	125.00	75.00
(76)	Rudy Hulswitt	250.00	125.00	75.00

(77)	John Hummel	250.00	125.00	75.00
(78)	George Hunter	250.00	125.00	75.00
(79)	Hugh Jennings	500.00	250.00	150.00
(80)	Davy Jones	250.00	125.00	75.00
(81)	Tom Jones	250.00	125.00	75.00
(82)	Tim Jordon (Jordan)	250.00	125.00	75.00
(83)	Joe Kelly (Kelley)	500.00	250.00	150.00
(84)	Bill Killefer	250.00	125.00	75.00
(85)	Ed Killian	250.00	125.00	75.00
(86)	Otto Knabe	250.00	125.00	75.00
(87)	Jack Knight	250.00	125.00	75.00
(88)	Ed Konetchy	250.00	125.00	75.00
(89)	Rube Kroh	250.00	125.00	75.00
(90)	LaCrosse	250.00	125.00	75.00
	(Photo actually Bill Schardt.)			
(91)	Frank LaPorte	250.00	125.00	75.00
(92)	Tommy Leach	250.00	125.00	75.00
(93)	Jack Lelivelt	250.00	125.00	75.00
(94)	Jack Lewis	250.00	125.00	75.00
(95)	Vive Lindaman	250.00	125.00	75.00
(96)	Bris Lord	250.00	125.00	75.00
(97)	Harry Lord	250.00	125.00	75.00
(98)	Bill Ludwig	250.00	125.00	75.00
(99)	Nick Maddox	250.00	125.00	75.00
(100)	Manser	250.00	125.00	75.00
(101)	Al Mattern	250.00	125.00	75.00
(102)	George McBride	250.00	125.00	75.00
(103)	Joe McCarthy (Toledo)	500.00	250.00	150.00
(104)	McConnell	250.00	125.00	75.00
(105)	Moose McCormick	250.00	125.00	75.00
(106)	Dan McGann	250.00	125.00	75.00
(107)	Jim McGinley	250.00	125.00	75.00
(108)	Iron Man McGinnity	500.00	250.00	150.00
(109)	Matty McIntyre	250.00	125.00	75.00
(110)	Larry McLean	250.00	125.00	75.00
(111)	Fred Merkle	250.00	125.00	75.00
(112)	Merritt	250.00	125.00	75.00
(113)	Meyer (Newark)	250.00	125.00	75.00
(114)	Chief Meyers	250.00	125.00	75.00
(115)	Clyde Milan	250.00	125.00	75.00
(116)	Dots Miller	250.00	125.00	75.00
(117)	Mike Mitchell	250.00	125.00	75.00
(118)	Bill Moriarty (Omaha)	250.00	125.00	75.00
(119)	George Moriarty (Detroit)	250.00	125.00	75.00
(120)	George Mullen (Mullin)	250.00	125.00	75.00
(121)	Simmy Murch (Chattanooga)	250.00	125.00	75.00
(122)	Simmy Murch (Indianapolis)	250.00	125.00	75.00
(123)	Danny Murphy	250.00	125.00	75.00
(124)	Red Murray	250.00	125.00	75.00
(125)	Red Nelson	250.00	125.00	75.00
(126)	Rebel Oakes	250.00	125.00	75.00
(127)	Orval Overall	250.00	125.00	75.00
(128)	Owens	250.00	125.00	75.00
(129)	Fred Parent	250.00	125.00	75.00
(130)	Dode Paskert	250.00	125.00	75.00
(131)	Bob Peterson	250.00	125.00	75.00
(132)	Jake Pfeister (Pfiester)	250.00	125.00	75.00
(133)	Deacon Phillipe (Phillippe)	250.00	125.00	75.00
(134)	Ollie Pickering	250.00	125.00	75.00
(135)	Heinie Pietz (Peitz)	250.00	125.00	75.00
(136)	Bugs Raymond	250.00	125.00	75.00
(137)	Pat Regan (Ragan)	250.00	125.00	75.00
(138)	Ed Reulbach	250.00	125.00	75.00
(139)	Robinson	250.00	125.00	75.00
(140)	Rock	250.00	125.00	75.00
(141)	Jack Rowan	250.00	125.00	75.00
(142)	Nap Rucker	250.00	125.00	75.00
(143)	Dick Rudolph	250.00	125.00	75.00
(144)	Slim Sallee	250.00	125.00	75.00
(145)	Jimmy Scheckard (Sheckard)	250.00	125.00	75.00
(146)	George Schirm	250.00	125.00	75.00
(147)	Wildfire Schulte	250.00	125.00	75.00
(148)	James Seabaugh	250.00	125.00	75.00
(149)	Selby	250.00	125.00	75.00
(150)	Cy Seymour	250.00	125.00	75.00
(151)	Hosea Siner	250.00	125.00	75.00
(152)	Sid Smith	250.00	125.00	75.00
(153)	Fred Snodgrass	250.00	125.00	75.00
(154)	Bob Spade	250.00	125.00	75.00
(155)	Tully Sparks	250.00	125.00	75.00
(156)	Tris Speaker	750.00	375.00	225.00
(157)	Tubby Spencer	250.00	125.00	75.00
(158)	John Stausberry (Stansbury)	250.00	125.00	75.00
(159)	Harry Steinfeldt	250.00	125.00	75.00
(160)	George Stone	250.00	125.00	75.00
(161)	George Stovall	250.00	125.00	75.00
(162)	Gabby Street	250.00	125.00	75.00
(163)	Sullivan (Omaha)	250.00	125.00	75.00
(164)	John Sullivan (Louisville)	250.00	125.00	75.00
(165)	Ed Summers	250.00	125.00	75.00
(166)	Joe Tinker	500.00	250.00	150.00
(167)	John Titus	250.00	125.00	75.00
(168)	Terry Turner	250.00	125.00	75.00
(169)	Bob Unglaub	250.00	125.00	75.00
(170)	Rube Waddell	500.00	250.00	150.00
(171)	Walker	250.00	125.00	75.00
(172)	Waller	250.00	125.00	75.00
(173)	Kirby White (Boston)	250.00	125.00	75.00
(174)	Jack White (Buffalo)	250.00	125.00	75.00
(175)	Julius Wiesman (Weisman)	250.00	125.00	75.00
(176)	Otto Williams	250.00	125.00	75.00
(177)	Hooks Wiltse	250.00	125.00	75.00
(178)	Orville Woodruff	250.00	125.00	75.00
(179)	Woods	250.00	125.00	75.00
(180)	Cy Young	1,560	780.00	470.00
(181)	Bill Zimmerman	250.00	125.00	75.00
(182)	Heinie Zimmerman	250.00	125.00	75.00

1913 Colgan's Chips Tin Tops

Except for the backs, these round black-and-white cards (about 1-7/16" in diameter) are identical to the 1909-11 Colgan's Chips issue, and were inserted in tin cannisters of Colgan's Mint Chips and Violet Chips. The front features a portrait photo along with the player's last name, team and, where necessary, league. The back advises collectors to "Send 25 Tin Tops" and a two-cent stamp to receive a photo of the "World's Pennant Winning Team." The set carries the designation E270 in the American Card Catalog.

		NM	EX	VG
	Complete Set (222):	60,000	30,000	18,000
	Common Player:	180.00	90.00	54.00
(1)	Ed Abbaticchio	180.00	90.00	54.00
(2)	Doc Adkins	180.00	90.00	54.00
(3)	Joe Agler	180.00	90.00	54.00
(4)	Eddie Ainsmith	180.00	90.00	54.00
(5)	Whitey Alperman	180.00	90.00	54.00
(6)	Red Ames (New York)	180.00	90.00	54.00
(7)	Red Ames (Cincinnati)	180.00	90.00	54.00
(8)	Jimmy Archer	180.00	90.00	54.00
(9)	Tommy Atkins (Atlanta)	180.00	90.00	54.00
(10)	Tommy Atkins (Ft. Wayne)	180.00	90.00	54.00
(11)	Jake Atz (New Orleans)	180.00	90.00	54.00
(12)	Jake Atz (Providence)	180.00	90.00	54.00
(13)	Jimmy Austin	180.00	90.00	54.00
(14)	Home Run Baker	360.00	180.00	110.00
(15)	Johnny Bates	180.00	90.00	54.00
(16)	Beck (Buffalo)	180.00	90.00	54.00
(17)	Beebe	180.00	90.00	54.00
(18)	Harry Bemis	180.00	90.00	54.00
(19)	Bob Bescher	180.00	90.00	54.00
(20)	Beumiller (Louisville)	180.00	90.00	54.00
(21)	Joe Birmingham	180.00	90.00	54.00
(22)	Bliss	180.00	90.00	54.00
(23)	Roger Bresnahan	360.00	180.00	110.00
(24)	Al Bridwell	180.00	90.00	54.00
(25)	George Brown (Browne)	180.00	90.00	54.00
(26)	Al Burch	180.00	90.00	54.00
(27)	Burns	180.00	90.00	54.00
(28)	Donie Bush	180.00	90.00	54.00
(29)	Bobby Byrne	180.00	90.00	54.00
(30)	Nixey Callahan	180.00	90.00	54.00
(31)	Howie Camnitz	180.00	90.00	54.00
(32)	Billy Campbell	180.00	90.00	54.00
(33)	Charlie Carr	180.00	90.00	54.00
(34)	Jay Cashion	180.00	90.00	54.00
(35)	Frank Chance	360.00	180.00	110.00
(36)	Hal Chase	220.00	110.00	65.00
(37)	Ed Cicotte	270.00	135.00	80.00
(38)	Clarke (Indianapolis)	180.00	90.00	54.00
(39)	Fred Clarke (Pittsburg)	360.00	180.00	110.00
(40)	Tommy Clarke (Cincinnati)	180.00	90.00	54.00
(41)	Clemons	180.00	90.00	54.00
(42)	Bill Clymer	180.00	90.00	54.00
(43)	Ty Cobb	2,400	1,200	720.00
(44)	Eddie Collins	360.00	180.00	110.00
(45)	Bunk Congalton (Omaha)	180.00	90.00	54.00
(46)	Bunk Congalton (Toledo)	180.00	90.00	54.00
(47)	Cook	180.00	90.00	54.00
(48)	Jack Coombs	180.00	90.00	54.00
(49)	Corcoran	180.00	90.00	54.00
(50)	Gavvy Cravath	180.00	90.00	54.00
(51)	Sam Crawford	360.00	180.00	110.00
(52)	Bill Dahlen	180.00	90.00	54.00
(53)	Bert Daniels	180.00	90.00	54.00
(54a)	Jake Daubert	180.00	90.00	54.00
(54b)	Jake Daubert ((White cap.))	180.00	90.00	54.00
(55)	Josh Devore (Cincinnati)	180.00	90.00	54.00
(56)	Josh Devore (New York)	180.00	90.00	54.00
(57)	Mike Donlin	180.00	90.00	54.00
(58)	Wild Bill Donovan	180.00	90.00	54.00
(59)	Red Dooin	180.00	90.00	54.00
(60)	Mickey Doolan	180.00	90.00	54.00
(61)	Larry Doyle	180.00	90.00	54.00
(62)	Delos Drake	180.00	90.00	54.00
(63)	Dick Egan	180.00	90.00	54.00
(64)	Kid Elberfield (Elberfeld)	180.00	90.00	54.00
(65)	Roy Ellam	180.00	90.00	54.00
(66)	Elliott	180.00	90.00	54.00
(67)	Rube Ellis	180.00	90.00	54.00
(68)	Elwert	180.00	90.00	54.00
(69)	Clyde Engle	180.00	90.00	54.00
(70)	Jimmy Esmond	180.00	90.00	54.00
(71)	Steve Evans	180.00	90.00	54.00
(72)	Johnny Evers	360.00	180.00	110.00
(73)	Hobe Ferris	180.00	90.00	54.00
(74)	Russ Ford	180.00	90.00	54.00
(75)	Ed Foster	180.00	90.00	54.00
(76)	Friel	180.00	90.00	54.00
(77)	John Frill	180.00	90.00	54.00
(78)	Art Fromme	180.00	90.00	54.00
(79)	Gus Getz (Newark)	180.00	90.00	54.00
(80)	George Gibson	180.00	90.00	54.00
(81)	Graham	180.00	90.00	54.00
(82)	Eddie Grant (Cincinnati)	180.00	90.00	54.00
(83)	Eddie Grant (New York)	180.00	90.00	54.00
(84)	Gravath	180.00	90.00	54.00
(85)	Grief	180.00	90.00	54.00
(86)	Bob Groom	180.00	90.00	54.00
(87)	Topsy Hartsel	180.00	90.00	54.00
(88)	Roy Hartzell	180.00	90.00	54.00
(89)	Harry Hinchman	180.00	90.00	54.00
(90)	Dick Hoblitzell	180.00	90.00	54.00
(91)	Happy Hogan (St. Louis)	180.00	90.00	54.00
(92)	Happy Hogan (San Francisco)	180.00	90.00	54.00
(93)	Harry Hooper	360.00	180.00	110.00
(94)	Miller Huggins	360.00	180.00	110.00
(95)	Hughes (Milwaukee)	180.00	90.00	54.00
(96)	Hughes (Rochester)	180.00	90.00	54.00
(97)	Rudy Hulswitt	180.00	90.00	54.00
(98)	John Hummel	180.00	90.00	54.00
(99)	George Hunter	180.00	90.00	54.00
(100)	Shoeless Joe Jackson	20,000	4,800	2,880
(101)	Jameson (Buffalo)	180.00	90.00	54.00
(102)	Hugh Jennings	360.00	180.00	110.00
(103)	Pete Johns	180.00	90.00	54.00
(104)	Walter Johnson	780.00	390.00	235.00
(105)	Davy Jones (Toledo)	180.00	90.00	54.00
(106)	Tim Jordan	180.00	90.00	54.00
(107)	Bob Keefe	180.00	90.00	54.00
(108)	Wee Willie Keeler	360.00	180.00	110.00
(109)	Joe Kelly (Kelley)	360.00	180.00	110.00
(110)	Ed Killian	180.00	90.00	54.00
(111)	Bill Killifer (Killefer)	180.00	90.00	54.00
(112)	Johnny Kling (Boston)	180.00	90.00	54.00
(113)	Klipfer	180.00	90.00	54.00
(114)	Otto Knabe	180.00	90.00	54.00
(115)	Jack Knight	180.00	90.00	54.00
(116)	Ed Konetchy	180.00	90.00	54.00
(117)	Paul Krichell	180.00	90.00	54.00
(118)	James Lafitte	180.00	90.00	54.00
(119)	Nap Lajoie	360.00	180.00	110.00
(120)	Frank Lange	180.00	90.00	54.00
(121)	Lee	180.00	90.00	54.00
(122)	Jack Lewis	180.00	90.00	54.00
(123)	Harry Lord	180.00	90.00	54.00
(124)	Johnny Lush	180.00	90.00	54.00
(125)	Madden	180.00	90.00	54.00
(126)	Nick Maddox	180.00	90.00	54.00
(127)	Sherry Magee	180.00	90.00	54.00
(128)	Manser	180.00	90.00	54.00
(129)	Frank Manusch (Manush) (New Orleans)	180.00	90.00	54.00
(130)	Frank Manush (Toledo)	180.00	90.00	54.00
(131)	Rube Marquard	360.00	180.00	110.00
(132)	McAllister	180.00	90.00	54.00
(133)	George McBride	180.00	90.00	54.00
(134)	McCarthy (Newark)	180.00	90.00	54.00
(135)	Joe McCarthy (Toledo)	360.00	180.00	110.00
(136)	McConnell	180.00	90.00	54.00
(137)	Moose McCormick	180.00	90.00	54.00
(138)	Larry McLean	180.00	90.00	54.00
(139)	Fred Merkle	180.00	90.00	54.00
(140)	Chief Meyers	180.00	90.00	54.00
(141)	Clyde Milan	180.00	90.00	54.00
(142)	Miller (Columbus)	180.00	90.00	54.00
(143)	Dots Miller (Pittsburg)	180.00	90.00	54.00
(144)	Clarence Mitchell	180.00	90.00	54.00
(145)	Mike Mitchell	180.00	90.00	54.00
(146)	Roy Mitchell	180.00	90.00	54.00
(147)	Carlton Molesworth	180.00	90.00	54.00
(148)	Herbie Moran	180.00	90.00	54.00
(149)	George Moriarty	180.00	90.00	54.00
(150)	George Mullen (Mullin)	180.00	90.00	54.00
(151)	Danny Murphy	180.00	90.00	54.00
(152)	Murray (Buffalo)	180.00	90.00	54.00
(153)	Jim Murray	180.00	90.00	54.00
(154)	Niles ((Indianapolis))	180.00	90.00	54.00
(155)	Jake Northrop	180.00	90.00	54.00
(156)	Rebel Oakes	180.00	90.00	54.00
(157)	Rube Oldring	180.00	90.00	54.00
(158)	Steve O'Neil (O'Neill)	180.00	90.00	54.00
(159)	O'Rourke	180.00	90.00	54.00
(160)	Owens (Minneapolis)	180.00	90.00	54.00
(161)	Larry Pape	180.00	90.00	54.00
(162)	Fred Parent	180.00	90.00	54.00
(163)	Dode Paskert	180.00	90.00	54.00
(164)	Heinie Peitz	180.00	90.00	54.00
(165)	Perry	180.00	90.00	54.00
(166)	Billy Purtell	180.00	90.00	54.00
(167)	Bill Rariden	180.00	90.00	54.00
(168)	Morrie Rath	180.00	90.00	54.00
(169)	Bugs Raymond	180.00	90.00	54.00
(170)	Ed Reulbach	180.00	90.00	54.00
(171)	Nap Rucker	180.00	90.00	54.00
(172)	Dick Rudolph	180.00	90.00	54.00
(173)	Bud Ryan	180.00	90.00	54.00
(174)	Slim Sallee	180.00	90.00	54.00
(176)	Ray Schalk	180.00	90.00	54.00
(177)	Schardt ((Indianapolis))	180.00	90.00	54.00
(178)	Jimmy Scheckard (Sheckard)	180.00	90.00	54.00
(179)	Wildfire Schulte	180.00	90.00	54.00
(180)	Bob Shawkey	180.00	90.00	54.00
(181)	Skeeter Shelton	180.00	90.00	54.00
(182)	Burt Shotten (Shotton)	180.00	90.00	54.00
(183)	Sisson ((Atlanta))	180.00	90.00	54.00
(184)	Smith (Montreal)	180.00	90.00	54.00
(185)	Sid Smith (Atlanta)	180.00	90.00	54.00
(186)	Sid Smith (Newark)	180.00	90.00	54.00
(187)	Fred Snodgrass	180.00	90.00	54.00
(188)	Tris Speaker	540.00	270.00	160.00
(189)	Jake Stahl	180.00	90.00	54.00
(190)	John Stansberry (Stansbury)	180.00	90.00	54.00
(191)	Amos Strunk	180.00	90.00	54.00
(192)	Sullivan	180.00	90.00	54.00
(193)	Suter	180.00	90.00	54.00
(194)	Harry Swacina	180.00	90.00	54.00
(195)	Bill Sweeney	180.00	90.00	54.00
(196)	Jeff Sweeney	180.00	90.00	54.00
(197)	Lee Tannehill	180.00	90.00	54.00
(198)	Dummy Taylor (Topeka)	300.00	150.00	90.00
(199)	Jim Thorpe	12,000	3,900	2,340
(200)	Joe Tinker	360.00	180.00	110.00
(201)	John Titus (Boston)	180.00	90.00	54.00
(202)	John Titus (Philadelphia)	180.00	90.00	54.00
(203)	Terry Turner	180.00	90.00	54.00
(204)	Bob Unglaub	180.00	90.00	54.00
(205)	Viebahn	180.00	90.00	54.00
(206)	Rube Waddell	360.00	180.00	110.00
(207)	Honus Wagner	2,500	750.00	450.00
(208)	Bobby Wallace	360.00	180.00	110.00
(209)	Ed Walsh	360.00	180.00	110.00
(210)	Jack Warhop	180.00	90.00	54.00
(211)	Harry Welchouce (Welchonce)	180.00	90.00	54.00

(212) Zach Wheat	360.00	180.00	110.00
(213) Kirb. White	180.00	90.00	54.00
(214) Kaiser Wilhelm	180.00	90.00	54.00
(215a) Ed Willett	180.00	90.00	54.00
(215b) Ed Willett ((White cap.))	180.00	90.00	54.00
(216) Otto Williams	180.00	90.00	54.00
(217) Owen Wilson	180.00	90.00	54.00
(218) Hooks Wiltse	180.00	90.00	54.00
(219) Joe Wood	180.00	90.00	54.00
(220) Orville Woodruff	180.00	90.00	54.00
(221) Joe Yeager	180.00	90.00	54.00
(222) Bill Zimmerman	180.00	90.00	54.00
(223) Heinie Zimmerman	180.00	90.00	54.00

1909 "Colgan's Chips" Square Proofs

COLLINS
Phila. Am. L.

Though widely identified as being connected to the Colgan's Chips disc issues of 1909-1912, there is nothing to tie these square cards to the gum company except for the shared use of player photos. The squares measure about 1-3/8" x 1-3/4" and are blank-backed. Black-and-white player portrait photos have a last name and team identification beneath. Many, but not all, of the surviving specimens have paper and/or glue residue on back, leading to speculation they may have been part of an advertising piece. The extent of the checklist is unknown, with verified examples listed here.

	NM	EX	VG
Common Player:	250.00	120.00	80.00
(9) Red Ames	250.00	120.00	80.00
(12) Charlie Babb (Memphis)	250.00	120.00	80.00
(13) Baerwald (Memphis)	250.00	124.00	74.00
(15) Home Run Baker	600.00	300.00	180.00
(18) Johnny Bates	250.00	120.00	80.00
(20) Ginger Beaumont (Boston)	250.00	120.00	80.00
(21) Beals Becker	250.00	120.00	80.00
(29) Roger Bresnahan	600.00	300.00	180.00
(30) Al Bridwell	250.00	120.00	80.00
(31) Lew Brockett	250.00	124.00	74.00
(32) Al Burch	250.00	120.00	80.00
(34) Donie Bush	250.00	120.00	80.00
(36) Howie Camnitz	250.00	120.00	80.00
(38) Frank Chance	600.00	300.00	180.00
(41) Fred Clarke (Pittsburg)	600.00	300.00	180.00
(44) Ty Cobb	4,000	2,000	1,200
(45) Eddie Collins	600.00	300.00	180.00
(52) Dode Criss	250.00	120.00	80.00
(54) Jake Daubert (Memphis)	250.00	120.00	80.00
(55) Harry Davis (Philadelphia)	250.00	120.00	80.00
(58) Ray Demmett (Demmitt) (New York)	250.00	120.00	80.00
(69) Clyde Engle (New York)	250.00	120.00	80.00
(70) Steve Evans	250.00	120.00	80.00
(71) Johnny Evers	600.00	300.00	180.00
(83) Harry Gaspar	250.00	120.00	80.00
(84) Gus Getz (Boston)	250.00	120.00	80.00
(85) George Gibson	250.00	120.00	80.00
(96) Harry Hooper (Boston A.L.)	600.00	300.00	180.00
(103) Hugh Jennings	600.00	300.00	180.00
(107) Addie Joss	600.00	300.00	180.00
(114) Otto Knabe	250.00	120.00	80.00
(118) James Lafitte	250.00	120.00	80.00
(124) Bill Lelivelt	250.00	120.00	80.00
(129) Bill Ludwig (Milwaukee)	250.00	120.00	80.00
(131) Nick Maddox	250.00	120.00	80.00
(150) Dots Miller	250.00	120.00	80.00
(151) Mike Mitchell	250.00	120.00	80.00
(157) Danny Murphy	250.00	120.00	80.00
(170) Heinie Peitz	250.00	120.00	80.00
(190) Bill Schardt (Milwaukee)	250.00	120.00	80.00
(197) Cy Seymour (New York)	250.00	124.00	74.00
(201) Fred Snodgrass	250.00	120.00	80.00
(209) Bob Spade (Cincinnati)	250.00	120.00	80.00
(215) Bob Unglaub	250.00	120.00	80.00
(220) Rube Waddell (St. Louis)	600.00	300.00	180.00
(221) Honus Wagner (Pittsburg)	1,500	750.00	450.00
(231) Owen Wilson	250.00	120.00	80.00
(232) Hooks Wiltse	250.00	120.00	80.00
(234) Woods (Buffalo)	250.00	120.00	80.00

1917 Collins-McCarthy (E135)

Produced by the Collins-McCarthy Candy Co. of San Francisco, the 200-card, black-and-white set represents the company's only venture into issuing non-Pacific Coast League players. The cards, numbered alphabetically, measure 2" x 3-1/4" and are printed on thin stock. Though the set is entitled "Baseball's Hall of Fame," many nondescript players appear in the issue. The complete set price does not include the more expensive variations. The same cards can be found with the advertising of other regional issuers on back, or blank-backed.

CLAUDE HENDRIX
P.—Chicago Cubs
72

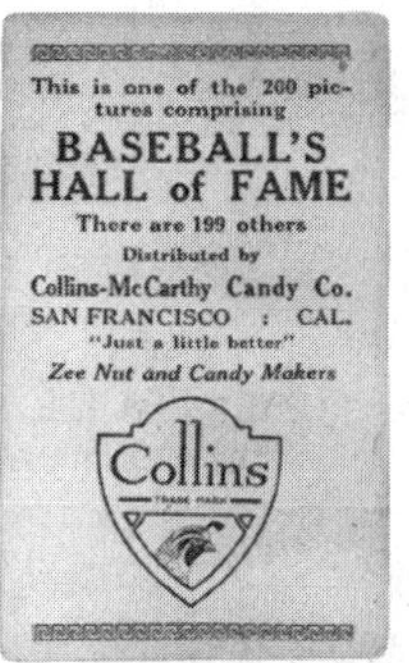
This is one of the 200 pictures comprising
BASEBALL'S HALL of FAME
There are 199 others
Distributed by
Collins-McCarthy Candy Co.
SAN FRANCISCO : CAL.
"Just a little better"
Zee Nut and Candy Makers
Collins

		NM	EX	VG
	Complete Set (200):	70,000	35,000	21,000
	Common Player:	150.00	75.00	45.00
1	Sam Agnew	150.00	75.00	45.00
2	Grover Alexander	600.00	300.00	180.00
3	W.S. Alexander (W.E.)	150.00	75.00	45.00
4	Leon Ames	150.00	75.00	45.00
5	Fred Anderson	150.00	75.00	45.00
6	Ed Appleton	150.00	75.00	45.00
7	Jimmy Archer	150.00	75.00	45.00
8	Jimmy Austin	150.00	75.00	45.00
9	Jim Bagby	150.00	75.00	45.00
10	H.D. Baird	150.00	75.00	45.00
11	J. Franklin Baker	350.00	175.00	100.00
12	Dave Bancroft	350.00	175.00	100.00
13	Jack Barry	150.00	75.00	45.00
14	Joe Benz	150.00	75.00	45.00
15	Al Betzel	150.00	75.00	45.00
16	Ping Bodie	150.00	75.00	45.00
17	Joe Boehling	150.00	75.00	45.00
18	Eddie Burns	150.00	75.00	45.00
19	George Burns	150.00	75.00	45.00
20	Geo. J. Burns	150.00	75.00	45.00
21	Joe Bush	150.00	75.00	45.00
22	Owen Bush	150.00	75.00	45.00
23	Bobby Byrne	150.00	75.00	45.00
24	Forrest Cady	150.00	75.00	45.00
25	Max Carey	350.00	175.00	100.00
26	Ray Chapman	175.00	85.00	50.00
27	Larry Cheney	150.00	75.00	45.00
28	Eddie Cicotte	450.00	225.00	135.00
29	Tom Clarke	150.00	75.00	45.00
30	Ty Cobb	4,500	2,250	1,350
31	Eddie Collins	350.00	175.00	100.00
32	"Shauno" Collins (Shano)	150.00	75.00	45.00
33	Fred Coumbe	150.00	75.00	45.00
34	Harry Coveleskie (Coveleski)	150.00	75.00	45.00
35	Gavvy Cravath	150.00	75.00	45.00
36	Sam Crawford	350.00	175.00	100.00
37	Geo. Cutshaw	150.00	75.00	45.00
38	Jake Daubert	150.00	75.00	45.00
39	Geo. Dauss	150.00	75.00	45.00
40	Charles Deal	150.00	75.00	45.00
41	"Wheezer" Dell	150.00	75.00	45.00
42	William Doak	150.00	75.00	45.00
43	Bill Donovan	150.00	75.00	45.00
44	Larry Doyle	150.00	75.00	45.00
45	Johnny Evers	350.00	175.00	100.00
46	Urban Faber	350.00	175.00	100.00
47	"Hap" Felsch	750.00	375.00	225.00
48	Bill Fischer	150.00	75.00	45.00
49	Ray Fisher	150.00	75.00	45.00
50	Art Fletcher	150.00	75.00	45.00
51	Eddie Foster	150.00	75.00	45.00
52	Jacques Fournier	150.00	75.00	45.00
53	Del Gainer (Gainor)	150.00	75.00	45.00
54	Bert Gallia	150.00	75.00	45.00
55	"Chic" Gandil (Chick)	450.00	225.00	135.00
56	Larry Gardner	150.00	75.00	45.00
57	Joe Gedeon	150.00	75.00	45.00
58	Gus Getz	150.00	75.00	45.00
59	Frank Gilhooley	150.00	75.00	45.00
60	Wm. Gleason	150.00	75.00	45.00
61	M.A. Gonzales (Gonzalez)	165.00	80.00	50.00
62	Hank Gowdy	150.00	75.00	45.00
63	John Graney	150.00	75.00	45.00
64	Tom Griffith	150.00	75.00	45.00
65	Heinie Groh	150.00	75.00	45.00
66	Bob Groom	150.00	75.00	45.00
67	Louis Guisto	150.00	75.00	45.00
68	Earl Hamilton	150.00	75.00	45.00
69	Harry Harper	150.00	75.00	45.00
70	Grover Hartley	150.00	75.00	45.00
71	Harry Heilmann	350.00	175.00	100.00
72	Claude Hendrix	150.00	75.00	45.00
73	Olaf Henriksen	150.00	75.00	45.00
74	John Henry	150.00	75.00	45.00
75	"Buck" Herzog	150.00	75.00	45.00
76a	Hugh High (White stockings, photo actually Claude Williams.)	200.00	100.00	60.00
76b	Hugh High (Black stockings, correct photo.)	175.00	85.00	50.00
77	Dick Hoblitzell	150.00	75.00	45.00
78	Walter Holke	150.00	75.00	45.00
79	Harry Hooper	350.00	175.00	100.00
80	Rogers Hornsby	650.00	325.00	195.00
81	Ivan Howard	150.00	75.00	45.00
82	Joe Jackson	16,500	8,500	5,000
83	Harold Janvrin	150.00	75.00	45.00
84	William James	150.00	75.00	45.00
85	C. Jamieson	150.00	75.00	45.00
86	Hugh Jennings	350.00	175.00	100.00
87	Walter Johnson	750.00	375.00	225.00
88	James Johnston	150.00	75.00	45.00
89	Fielder Jones	150.00	75.00	45.00
90a	Joe Judge (Bat on right shoulder, photo actually Ray Morgan.)	200.00	100.00	60.00
90b	Joe Judge (Bat on left shoulder, correct photo.)	175.00	85.00	50.00
91	Hans Lobert	150.00	75.00	45.00
92	Benny Kauff	150.00	75.00	45.00
93	Wm. Killefer Jr.	150.00	75.00	45.00
94	Ed. Konetchy	150.00	75.00	45.00
95	John Lavan	150.00	75.00	45.00
96	Jimmy Lavender	150.00	75.00	45.00
97	"Nemo" Leibold	150.00	75.00	45.00
98	H.B. Leonard	150.00	75.00	45.00
99	Duffy Lewis	150.00	75.00	45.00
100	Tom Long	150.00	75.00	45.00
101	Wm. Louden	150.00	75.00	45.00
102	Fred Luderus	150.00	75.00	45.00
103	Lee Magee	150.00	75.00	45.00
104	Sherwood Magee	150.00	75.00	45.00
105	Al Mamaux	150.00	75.00	45.00
106	Leslie Mann	150.00	75.00	45.00
107	"Rabbit" Maranville	350.00	175.00	100.00
108	Rube Marquard	350.00	175.00	100.00
109	Armando Marsans	165.00	80.00	50.00
110	J. Erskine Mayer	150.00	75.00	45.00
111	George McBride	150.00	75.00	45.00
112	Lew McCarty	150.00	75.00	45.00
113	John J. McGraw	350.00	175.00	100.00
114	Jack McInnis	150.00	75.00	45.00
115	Lee Meadows	150.00	75.00	45.00
116	Fred Merkle	150.00	75.00	45.00
117	"Chief" Meyers	150.00	75.00	45.00
118	Clyde Milan	150.00	75.00	45.00
119	Otto Miller	150.00	75.00	45.00
120	Clarence Mitchell	150.00	75.00	45.00
121a	Ray Morgan (Bat on left shoulder, photo actually Joe Judge.)	200.00	100.00	60.00
121b	Ray Morgan (Bat on right shoulder, correct photo.)	175.00	85.00	50.00
122	Guy Morton	150.00	75.00	45.00
123	"Mike" Mowrey	150.00	75.00	45.00
124	Elmer Myers	150.00	75.00	45.00
125	"Hy" Myers	150.00	75.00	45.00
126	A.E. Neale	165.00	80.00	50.00
127	Arthur Nehf	150.00	75.00	45.00
128	J.A. Niehoff	150.00	75.00	45.00
129	Steve O'Neill	150.00	75.00	45.00
130	"Dode" Paskert	150.00	75.00	45.00
131	Roger Peckinpaugh	150.00	75.00	45.00
132	"Pol" Perritt	150.00	75.00	45.00
133	"Jeff" Pfeffer	150.00	75.00	45.00
134	Walter Pipp	150.00	75.00	45.00
135	Derril Pratt (Derrill)	150.00	75.00	45.00
136	Bill Rariden	150.00	75.00	45.00
137	E.C. Rice	350.00	175.00	100.00
138	Wm. A. Ritter (Wm. H.)	150.00	75.00	45.00
139	Eppa Rixey	350.00	175.00	100.00
140	Davey Robertson	150.00	75.00	45.00
141	"Bob" Roth	150.00	75.00	45.00
142	Ed. Roush	350.00	175.00	100.00
143	Clarence Rowland	150.00	75.00	45.00
144	Dick Rudolph	150.00	75.00	45.00
145	William Rumler	150.00	75.00	45.00
146a	Reb Russell (Pitching follow-thru, photo actually Mellie Wolfgang.)	200.00	100.00	60.00
146b	Reb Russell (Hands at side, correct photo.)	175.00	85.00	50.00
147	"Babe" Ruth	12,500	6,250	3,750
148	Vic Saier	150.00	75.00	45.00
149	"Slim" Sallee	150.00	75.00	45.00
150	Ray Schalk	350.00	175.00	100.00
151	Walter Schang	150.00	75.00	45.00
152	Frank Schulte	150.00	75.00	45.00
153	Ferd Schupp	150.00	75.00	45.00
154	Everett Scott	150.00	75.00	45.00
155	Hank Severeid	150.00	75.00	45.00
156	Howard Shanks	150.00	75.00	45.00
157	Bob Shawkey	150.00	75.00	45.00
158	Jas. Sheckard	150.00	75.00	45.00
159	Ernie Shore	150.00	75.00	45.00
160	C.H. Shorten	150.00	75.00	45.00
161	Burt Shotton	150.00	75.00	45.00
162	Geo. Sisler	350.00	175.00	100.00
163	Elmer Smith	150.00	75.00	45.00
164	J. Carlisle Smith	150.00	75.00	45.00
165	Fred Snodgrass	150.00	75.00	45.00
166	Tris Speaker	650.00	325.00	195.00
167	Oscar Stanage	150.00	75.00	45.00
168	Charles Stengel	350.00	175.00	100.00
169	Milton Stock	150.00	75.00	45.00
170	Amos Strunk	150.00	75.00	45.00
171	"Zeb" Terry	150.00	75.00	45.00
172	"Jeff" Tesreau	150.00	75.00	45.00
173	Chester Thomas	150.00	75.00	45.00
174	Fred Toney	150.00	75.00	45.00
175	Terry Turner	150.00	75.00	45.00
176	George Tyler	150.00	75.00	45.00
177	Jim Vaughn	150.00	75.00	45.00
178	Bob Veach	150.00	75.00	45.00
179	Oscar Vitt	150.00	75.00	45.00
180	Hans Wagner	3,500	1,750	1,000
181	Clarence Walker	150.00	75.00	45.00
182	Jim Walsh	150.00	75.00	45.00
183	Al Walters	150.00	75.00	45.00
184	W. Wambsganss	150.00	75.00	45.00
185	Buck Weaver	1,000	500.00	300.00
186	Carl Weilman	150.00	75.00	45.00
187	Zack Wheat	350.00	175.00	100.00
188	Geo. Whitted	150.00	75.00	45.00
189	Joe Wilhoit	150.00	75.00	45.00
190a	Claude Williams (Black stockings, photo actually Hugh High.)	600.00	300.00	180.00

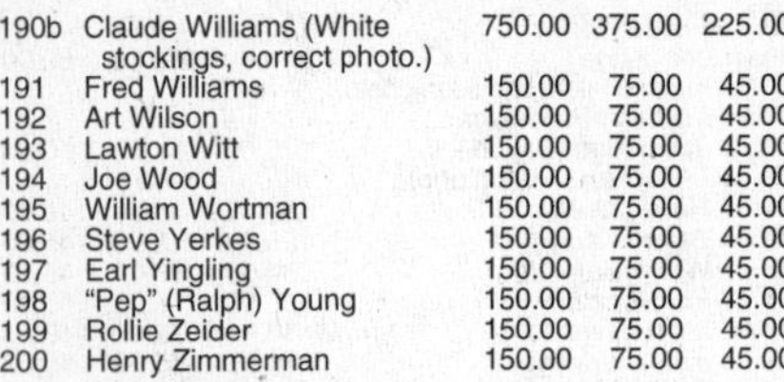

190b	Claude Williams (White stockings, correct photo.)	750.00	375.00	225.00
191	Fred Williams	150.00	75.00	45.00
192	Art Wilson	150.00	75.00	45.00
193	Lawton Witt	150.00	75.00	45.00
194	Joe Wood	150.00	75.00	45.00
195	William Wortman	150.00	75.00	45.00
196	Steve Yerkes	150.00	75.00	45.00
197	Earl Yingling	150.00	75.00	45.00
198	"Pep" (Ralph) Young	150.00	75.00	45.00
199	Rollie Zeider	150.00	75.00	45.00
200	Henry Zimmerman	150.00	75.00	45.00

1954 Colonial Meats Jimmy Piersall

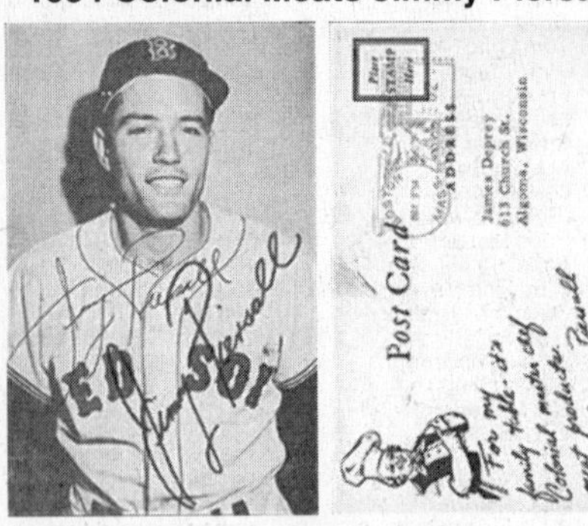

These promotional postcards are known in at least two varieties. Each of the 3-1/2" x 5-1/2" cards shows the popular BoSox star in a portrait pose with facsimile autograph. The postcard-format back has at left a cartoon butcher and an advertising message bearing Piersall's signature. Similar cards advertising Cain's grocery products are also known.

		NM	EX	VG
	Autographed: 2-3X	125.00	65.00	35.00
(1)	Jimmy Piersall (Chest-to-cap, back printed in black.)	80.00	40.00	24.00
(2)	Jimmy Piersall (Waist-to-cap, back printed in black and blue.)	80.00	40.00	24.00

1888 Conly Cabinets

Contemporary, but much less numerous than, the Old Judge cabinet cards is this issue from a Boston photo studio. Carrying an April, 1888, copyright date, the 4-1/4" x 6-1/2" have sepia photos of the players in action poses. Backs have decorative advertising for the studio. The extent of the checklist is unknown.

	NM	EX	VG
John Clarkson (Ball in hands at chest.)	3,000	1,200	725.00
John Clarkson (Ball in hands at chest.)	3,000	1,200	725.00
John Clarkson (Right arm at back.)	3,000	1,200	725.00
John Clarkson (Right arm extended.)	3,000	1,200	725.00

1891 Conly Studio Cabinets

The extent of this issue from a Boston photo studio is unknown. The checklist begins here with three players from the Boston Reds American Associations champions. The 4-1/4" x 6-1/2" cards have a sepia portrait photo of the player in street clothes. Back has decorative advertising for the studio.

		NM	EX	VG
	Common Player:	1,000	500.00	300.00
(1)	Duke Farrell	1,200	500.00	300.00
(2)	George Haddock	1,200	500.00	300.00
(3)	Cub Stricker	1,200	500.00	300.00

1950s-70s L.L. Cook Milwaukee Braves/Brewers Postcards

From a period of (roughly) 1956 through 1972 the L.L. Cook Co. of Milwaukee undertook the production of black-and-white photo postcards for various members of the local teams. Apparently printed to order to allow players and staff to respond to fan requests for pictures and autographs, the 3-1/2" x 5-1/2" cards have (usually) borderless poses on front. Postcard-style divided backs may or may not have a credit line vertically at center, and various versions of the standard postcard markings are seen. This checklist is likely incomplete.

		NM	EX	VG
	Common Player:	30.00	15.00	9.00
(1)	Hank Aaron	150.00	75.00	45.00
(2)	Tommie Aaron	30.00	15.00	9.00
(3)	Joe Adcock	40.00	20.00	12.00
(4)	Ed Bailey	30.00	15.00	9.00
(5)	Frank Bolling	30.00	15.00	9.00
(6)	Bobby Bragan	30.00	15.00	9.00
(7)	Ty Cline	30.00	15.00	9.00
(8)	Wes Covington	30.00	15.00	9.00
(9)	Ray Crone (White name on front.)	30.00	15.00	9.00
(10)	Ray Crone (No name.)	30.00	15.00	9.00
(11)	Fred Haney	30.00	15.00	9.00
(12)	Ernie Johnson	30.00	15.00	9.00
(13)	Ernie Johnson (Part of light tower shows.)	30.00	15.00	9.00
(14)	Charlie Lau	30.00	15.00	9.00
(15)	Mike Krsnich	30.00	15.00	9.00
(16)	Roy McMillan	30.00	15.00	9.00
(17)	Jerry McNertney (Brewers)	30.00	15.00	9.00
(18)	Don Nottebart	30.00	15.00	9.00
(19)	Phil Paine	30.00	15.00	9.00
(20)	Ron Piche	30.00	15.00	9.00
(21)	Juan Pizarro	30.00	15.00	9.00
(22)	Bob Sadowski	30.00	15.00	9.00
(13)	Red Schoendienst	50.00	25.00	15.00
(14)	George Scott (Brewers)	30.00	15.00	9.00
(15)	Bob Shaw	30.00	15.00	9.00
(16)	Warren Spahn (Artwork portrait, white background.)	40.00	20.00	12.00
(17)	Warren Spahn (Artwork portrait, yellow in background.)	40.00	20.00	12.00
(18)	Warren Spahn (Eating with son.)	30.00	15.00	9.00
(19)	Warren Spahn (Showing son new car.)	30.00	15.00	9.00
(20)	Warren Spahn (In car, waving to family.)	30.00	15.00	9.00
(21)	Al Spangler	30.00	15.00	9.00
(22)	Frank Torre (Holding Pepsi.)	30.00	15.00	9.00
(23)	Frank Torre (Holding Pepsi, facsimile autograph.)	30.00	15.00	9.00
(24)	Frank Torre (Holding Pepsi, Brave patch shows.)	30.00	15.00	9.00
(25)	Joe Torre/Kneeling	40.00	20.00	12.00
(26)	Joe Torre/Portrait	40.00	20.00	12.00

1910 Coupon Cigarettes Type 1 (T213)

Though they feature the same pictures used in the contemporary T206 tobacco issue, Coupon Cigarette cards make up three distinct sets, produced between 1910 and 1919. Type 1 Coupon cards feature a mix of players from the National and American Leagues, and the Southern League. Nominally the traditional 1-7/16" x 2-1/8" cigarette-card size, fronts of the Coupons are identical to the more popular T206 series. Backs, however, clearly identify the cards as being a product of Coupon Cigarettes and allow the collector to easily differentiate among the three types. Type 1 cards, produced in 1910, carry a general advertisement for Coupon "Mild" Cigarettes, with no mention of price. Distribution of the Coupons was limited to the Louisiana area, making the set very difficult to checklist and even moreso to collect. Numerous variations further complicate the situation. It is quite possible

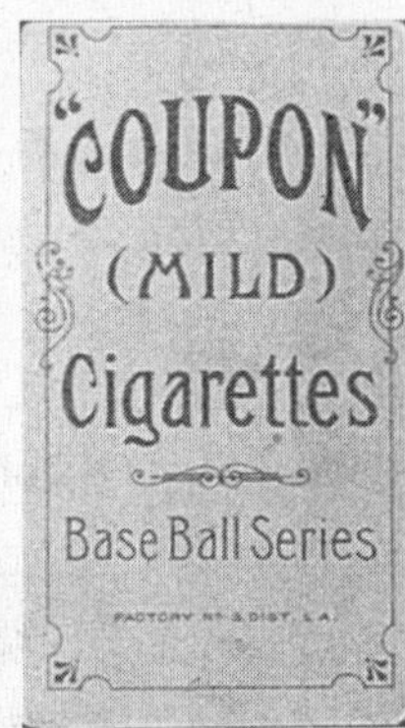

the checklists here are incomplete and additions will surface in the future. Type 1 cards are considered the rarest of the Coupon issues, and, because they were printed on a thinner stock, they are especially difficult to find in top condition.

		NM	EX	VG
	Complete Set (68):	30,000	15,000	8,500
	Common Player:	450.00	170.00	85.00
(1)	Harry Bay	450.00	170.00	85.00
(2)	Beals Becker	450.00	170.00	85.00
(3)	Chief Bender	1,275	500.00	250.00
(4)	Bernhard	450.00	170.00	85.00
(5)	Ted Breitenstein	450.00	170.00	85.00
(6)	Bobby Byrne	450.00	170.00	85.00
(7)	Billy Campbell	450.00	170.00	85.00
(8)	Scoops Carey	1,275	500.00	250.00
(9)	Frank Chance	1,275	500.00	250.00
(10)	Chappy Charles	450.00	170.00	85.00
(11)	Hal Chase/Portrait	625.00	250.00	125.00
(12)	Hal Chase/Throwiing	625.00	250.00	125.00
(13)	Ty Cobb	11,625	4,650	2,325
(14)	Bill Cranston	450.00	170.00	85.00
(15)	Birdie Cree	450.00	170.00	85.00
(16)	Wild Bill Donovan	450.00	170.00	85.00
(17)	Mickey Doolan	450.00	170.00	85.00
(18)	Jean Dubuc	450.00	170.00	85.00
(19)	Joe Dunn	450.00	170.00	85.00
(20)	Roy Ellam	450.00	170.00	85.00
(21)	Clyde Engle	450.00	170.00	85.00
(22)	Johnny Evers	1,275	500.00	250.00
(23)	Art Fletcher	450.00	170.00	85.00
(24)	Charlie Fritz	450.00	170.00	85.00
(25)	Ed Greminger	450.00	170.00	85.00
(26)	Bill Hart (Little Rock)	450.00	170.00	85.00
(27)	Jimmy Hart (Montgomery)	450.00	170.00	85.00
(28)	Topsy Hartsel	450.00	170.00	85.00
(29)	Gordon Hickman	450.00	170.00	85.00
(30)	Danny Hoffman	450.00	170.00	85.00
(31)	Harry Howell	450.00	170.00	85.00
(32)	Miller Huggins (Hands at mouth.)	1,275	500.00	250.00
(33)	Miller Huggins/Portrait	1,275	500.00	250.00
(34)	George Hunter	450.00	170.00	85.00
(35)	A.O. "Dutch" Jordan	450.00	170.00	85.00
(36)	Ed Killian	450.00	170.00	85.00
(37)	Otto Knabe	450.00	170.00	85.00
(38)	Frank LaPorte	450.00	170.00	85.00
(39)	Ed Lennox	450.00	170.00	85.00
(40)	Harry Lentz (Sentz)	450.00	170.00	85.00
(41)	Rube Marquard	1,275	500.00	250.00
(42)	Doc Marshall	450.00	170.00	85.00
(43)	Christy Mathewson	3,225	1,300	650.00
(44)	George McBride	450.00	170.00	85.00
(45)	Pryor McElveen	450.00	170.00	85.00
(46)	Matty McIntyre	450.00	170.00	85.00
(47)	Mike Mitchell	450.00	170.00	85.00
(48)	Carlton Molesworth	450.00	170.00	85.00
(49)	Mike Mowrey	450.00	170.00	85.00
(50)	Chief Myers (Meyers)/Btg	450.00	170.00	85.00
(51)	Chief Myers (Meyers)/Fldg	450.00	170.00	85.00
(52)	Dode Paskert	450.00	170.00	85.00
(53)	Hub Perdue	450.00	170.00	85.00
(54)	Arch Persons	450.00	170.00	85.00
(55)	Ed Reagan	450.00	170.00	85.00
(56)	Bob Rhoades (Rhoads)	450.00	170.00	85.00
(57)	Ike Rockenfeld	450.00	170.00	85.00
(58)	Claude Rossman	450.00	170.00	85.00
(59)	Boss Schmidt	450.00	170.00	85.00
(60)	Sid Smith	450.00	170.00	85.00
(61)	Charlie Starr	450.00	170.00	85.00
(62)	Gabby Street	450.00	170.00	85.00
(63)	Ed Summers	450.00	170.00	85.00
(64)	Jeff Sweeney	450.00	170.00	85.00
(65)	Ira Thomas	450.00	170.00	85.00
(66)	Woodie Thornton	450.00	170.00	85.00
(67)	Ed Willett	450.00	170.00	85.00
(68)	Owen Wilson	450.00	170.00	85.00

1914-16 Coupon Cigarettes Type 2 (T213)

Though they feature the same photos used in the contemporary T206 tobacco issue, Coupon Cigarette cards make up three distinct sets, produced between 1910 and 1919. Type 2 Coupons feature a mix of players from the three major leagues (National, American and Federal), and several minor leagues. The 1-7/16" x 2-5/8" Coupon fronts are virtually identical, except for the use of blue typography, to the more popular T206 series. Backs, however, clearly identify the cards as being a product of Coupon Cigarettes and allow the

collector to easily differentiate among the three types. Type 2 cards, issued from 1914 to 1916, contain the words "MILD and SWEET" and "20 for 5 cents." Distribution of the Coupon cards was limited to the Louisiana area, making the set difficult to checklist and even moreso to collect. Numerous variations further complicate the situation. It is quite possible the checklists here are incomplete and additions will surface in the future. Although Type 2 cards are the most common, they were printed with a "glossy" coating, making them susceptible to cracking and creasing.

		NM	EX	VG
Complete Set (188):		80,000	36,000	17,500
Common Player:		275.00	125.00	60.00
(1)	Red Ames (Cincinnati)	275.00	125.00	60.00
(2)	Red Ames (St. Louis)	275.00	125.00	60.00
(3)	Home Run Baker (Phila. Amer.)	550.00	245.00	120.00
(4)	Home Run Baker (Philadelphia Amer.)	600.00	275.00	130.00
(5)	Home Run Baker (New York)	550.00	245.00	120.00
(6)	Cy Barger	275.00	125.00	60.00
(7)	Chief Bender (Trees in background, Philadelphia Amer.)	550.00	245.00	120.00
(8)	Chief Bender (Trees in background, Baltimore.)	550.00	245.00	120.00
(9)	Chief Bender (Trees in background, Philadelphia Nat.)	550.00	245.00	120.00
(10)	Chief Bender (No trees, Philadelphia Amer.)	550.00	245.00	120.00
(11)	Chief Bender (No trees, Baltimore.)	550.00	245.00	120.00
(12)	Chief Bender (No trees, Philadelphia Natl.)	550.00	240.00	120.00
(13)	Bill Bradley	275.00	125.00	60.00
(14)	Roger Bresnahan (Chicago)	550.00	245.00	120.00
(15)	Roger Bresnahan (Toledo)	550.00	245.00	120.00
(16)	Al Bridwell (St. Louis)	275.00	125.00	60.00
(17)	Al Bridwell (Nashville)	275.00	125.00	60.00
(18)	Mordecai Brown (Chicago)	550.00	245.00	120.00
(19)	Mordecai Brown (St. Louis)	550.00	245.00	120.00
(20)	Bobby Byrne	275.00	125.00	60.00
(21)	Howie Camnitz (Arm at side.)	275.00	125.00	60.00
(22)	Howie Camnitz (Pittsburgh, hands above head.)	275.00	125.00	60.00
(23)	Howie Camnitz (Savannah, hands above head.)	275.00	125.00	60.00
(24)	Billy Campbell	275.00	125.00	60.00
(25)	Frank Chance/Btg (New York.)	550.00	245.00	120.00
(26)	Frank Chance/Btg (Los Angeles)	600.00	270.00	130.00
(27)	Frank Chance/Portrait (New York)	550.00	245.00	120.00
(28)	Frank Chance/Portrait (Los Angeles)	600.00	270.00	130.00
(29)	Bill Chapelle (Brooklyn, "R" on shirt.)	275.00	125.00	60.00
(30)	Larry Chapelle (Chappel) (Cleveland, no "R" on shirt, photo actually Bill Chapelle.)	275.00	125.00	60.00
(31)	Hal Chase (Chicago, holding trophy.)	365.00	165.00	80.00
(32)	Hal Chase (Buffalo, holding trophy.)	365.00	165.00	80.00
(33)	Hal Chase/Portrait (Chicago, blue background.)	365.00	165.00	80.00
(34)	Hal Chase/Portrait (Buffalo, blue background.)	365.00	165.00	80.00
(35)	Hal Chase/Throwing (Chicago)	365.00	165.00	80.00
(36)	Hal Chase/Throwing (Buffalo)	365.00	165.00	80.00
(37)	Ty Cobb/Portrait	7,250	3,250	1,600
(38)	Ty Cobb (Bat off shoulder.)	6,000	2,700	1,325
(39)	Eddie Collins (Philadelphia, "A" on shirt.)	600.00	270.00	130.00
(40)	Eddie Collins (Chicago, "A" on shirt.)	600.00	270.00	130.00
(41)	Eddie Collins (Chicago, no "A" on shirt.)	600.00	270.00	130.00
(42)	Doc Crandall (St. Louis Fed.)	275.00	125.00	60.00
(43)	Doc Crandall (St. Louis Amer.)	275.00	125.00	60.00
(44)	Sam Crawford	550.00	245.00	120.00
(45)	Birdie Cree	275.00	125.00	60.00
(46)	Harry Davis (Phila. Amer.)	275.00	125.00	60.00
(47)	Harry Davis (Philadelphia Amer.)	275.00	125.00	60.00
(48)	Ray Demmitt (Chicago Amer. (New York uniform.))	275.00	125.00	60.00
(49)	Ray Demmitt (Chicago Amer. (St. Louis uniform.))	275.00	125.00	60.00
(50)	Josh Devore (Philadelphia)	275.00	125.00	60.00
(51)	Josh Devore (Chillicothe)	275.00	125.00	60.00
(52)	Mike Donlin (New York)	275.00	125.00	60.00
(53)	Mike Donlin (.300 batter 7 years)	275.00	125.00	60.00
(54)	Wild Bill Donovan	275.00	125.00	60.00
(55)	Mickey Doolan/Btg (Baltimore)	275.00	125.00	60.00
(56)	Mickey Doolan/Btg (Chicago)	275.00	125.00	60.00
(57)	Mickey Doolan/Fldg (Baltimore)	275.00	125.00	60.00
(58)	Mickey Doolan/Fldg (Chicago)	275.00	125.00	60.00
(59)	Tom Downey	275.00	125.00	60.00
(60)	Larry Doyle/Btg	275.00	125.00	60.00
(61)	Larry Doyle/Portrait	275.00	125.00	60.00
(62)	Jean Dubuc	275.00	125.00	60.00
(63)	Jack Dunn (Picture is Joe Dunn.)	275.00	125.00	60.00
(64)	Kid Elberfield (Elberfeld) (Brooklyn)	275.00	125.00	60.00
(65)	Kid Elberfield (Elberfeld) (Chatanooga)	275.00	125.00	60.00
(66)	Steve Evans	275.00	125.00	60.00
(67)	Johnny Evers	550.00	245.00	120.00
(68)	Russ Ford	275.00	125.00	60.00
(69)	Art Fromme	275.00	125.00	60.00
(70)	Chick Gandil (Washington)	1,000	450.00	220.00
(71)	Chick Gandil (Cleveland)	550.00	245.00	120.00
(72)	Rube Geyer	275.00	125.00	60.00
(73)	Clark Griffith	550.00	245.00	120.00
(74)	Bob Groom	275.00	125.00	60.00
(75)	Buck Herzog ("B" on shirt.)	300.00	135.00	66.00
(76)	Buck Herzog (No "B" on shirt.)	400.00	180.00	88.00
(77)	Dick Hoblitzell (Cincinnati)	275.00	125.00	60.00
(78)	Dick Hoblitzell (Boston Nat.)	275.00	125.00	60.00
(79)	Dick Hoblitzell (Boston Amer.)	275.00	125.00	60.00
(80)	Solly Hofman	275.00	125.00	60.00
(81)	Solly Hofmann (Hofman)	275.00	125.00	60.00
(82)	Miller Huggins (Hands at mouth.)	550.00	245.00	120.00
(83)	Miller Huggins/Portrait	550.00	245.00	120.00
(84)	John Hummel (Brooklyn Nat.)	275.00	125.00	60.00
(85)	John Hummel (Brooklyn)	275.00	125.00	60.00
(86)	Hughie Jennings (Both hands showing.)	550.00	245.00	120.00
(87)	Hughie Jennings (One hand showing.)	550.00	245.00	120.00
(88)	Walter Johnson	2,500	1,125	550.00
(89)	Tim Jordan (Toronto)	275.00	125.00	60.00
(90)	Tim Jordan (Ft. Worth)	275.00	125.00	60.00
(91)	Joe Kelley (New York)	550.00	245.00	120.00
(92)	Joe Kelley (Toronto)	550.00	245.00	120.00
(93)	Otto Knabe	275.00	125.00	60.00
(94)	Ed Konetchy (Pittsburgh Nat.)	275.00	125.00	60.00
(95)	Ed Konetchy (Pittsburgh Fed.)	275.00	125.00	60.00
(96)	Ed Konetchy (Boston)	275.00	125.00	60.00
(97)	Harry Krause	275.00	125.00	60.00
(98)	Nap Lajoie (Phila. Amer.)	550.00	245.00	120.00
(99)	Nap Lajoie (Philadelphia Amer.)	550.00	245.00	120.00
(100)	Nap Lajoie (Cleveland)	550.00	245.00	120.00
(101)	Tommy Leach (Chicago)	275.00	125.00	60.00
(102)	Tommy Leach (Cincinnati)	275.00	125.00	60.00
(103)	Tommy Leach (Rochester)	275.00	125.00	60.00
(104)	Ed Lennox	275.00	125.00	60.00
(105)	Sherry Magee (Phila. Nat.)	275.00	125.00	60.00
(106)	Sherry Magee (Philadelphia Nat.)	275.00	125.00	60.00
(107)	Sherry Magee (Boston)	275.00	125.00	60.00
(108)	Rube Marquard (New York, pitching, "NY" on shirt.)	600.00	270.00	130.00
(109)	Rube Marquard (Brooklyn, pitching, no "NY" on shirt.)	550.00	245.00	120.00
(110)	Rube Marquard/Portrait (New York, "NY" on shirt.)	550.00	245.00	120.00
(111)	Rube Marquard/Portrait (Brooklyn, no "NY" on shirt.)	550.00	245.00	120.00
(112)	Christy Mathewson	3,000	1,350	660.00
(113)	John McGraw (Glove at side.)	550.00	245.00	120.00
(114)	John McGraw/Portrait	550.00	245.00	120.00
(115)	Larry McLean	275.00	125.00	60.00
(116)	George McQuillan (Pittsburgh)	275.00	125.00	60.00
(117)	George McQuillan (Phila. Nat.)	275.00	125.00	60.00
(118)	George McQuillan (Philadelphia Nat.)	275.00	125.00	60.00
(119)	Fred Merkle	275.00	125.00	60.00
(120)	Chief Meyers/Fldg (New York)	275.00	125.00	60.00
(121)	Chief Meyers/Fldg (Brooklyn)	275.00	125.00	60.00
(122)	Chief Meyers/Portrait (New York)	275.00	125.00	60.00
(123)	Chief Meyers/Portrait (Brooklyn)	275.00	125.00	60.00
(124)	Dots Miller	275.00	125.00	60.00
(125)	Mike Mitchell	275.00	125.00	60.00
(126)	Mike Mowrey (Pittsburgh Nat.)	275.00	125.00	60.00
(127)	Mike Mowrey (Pittsburgh Fed.)	275.00	125.00	60.00
(128)	Mike Mowrey (Brooklyn)	275.00	125.00	60.00
(129)	George Mullin (Indianapolis)	275.00	125.00	60.00
(130)	George Mullin (Newark)	275.00	125.00	60.00
(131)	Danny Murphy	275.00	125.00	60.00
(132)	Red Murray (New York)	275.00	125.00	60.00
(133)	Red Murray (Chicago)	275.00	125.00	60.00
(134)	Red Murray (Kansas City)	275.00	125.00	60.00
(135)	Tom Needham	275.00	125.00	60.00
(136)	Rebel Oakes	275.00	125.00	60.00
(137)	Rube Oldring (Phila. Amer.)	275.00	125.00	60.00
(138)	Rube Oldring (Philadelphia Amer.)	275.00	125.00	60.00
(139)	Dode Paskert (Phila. Nat.)	275.00	125.00	60.00
(140)	Dode Paskert (Philadelphia Nat.)	275.00	125.00	60.00
(141)	Billy Purtell	275.00	125.00	60.00
(142)	Jack Quinn (Baltimore)	275.00	125.00	60.00
(143)	Jack Quinn (Vernon)	275.00	125.00	60.00
(144)	Ed Reulbach (Brooklyn Nat.)	275.00	125.00	60.00
(145)	Ed Reulbach (Brooklyn Fed.)	275.00	125.00	60.00
(146)	Ed Reulbach (Pittsburgh)	275.00	125.00	60.00
(147)	Nap Rucker (Brooklyn)	275.00	125.00	60.00
(148)	Nap Rucker (Brooklyn Nat.)	275.00	125.00	60.00
(149)	Dick Rudolph	275.00	125.00	60.00
(150)	Germany Schaefer (Washington, "W" on shirt.)	275.00	125.00	60.00
(151)	Germany Schaefer (K.C. Fed., "W" on shirt.)	275.00	125.00	60.00
(152)	Germany Schaefer (New York, no "W" on shirt.)	275.00	125.00	60.00
(153)	Admiral Schlei/Btg	275.00	125.00	60.00
(154)	Admiral Schlei/Portrait	275.00	125.00	60.00
(155)	Boss Schmidt	275.00	125.00	60.00
(156)	Wildfire Schulte	275.00	125.00	60.00
(157)	Frank Smith	275.00	125.00	60.00
(158)	Tris Speaker	1,200	540.00	265.00
(159)	George Stovall	275.00	125.00	60.00
(160)	Gabby Street/Catching	275.00	125.00	60.00
(161)	Gabby Street/Portrait	275.00	125.00	60.00
(162)	Ed Summers	275.00	125.00	60.00
(163)	Bill Sweeney (Boston)	275.00	125.00	60.00
(164)	Bill Sweeney (Chicago)	275.00	125.00	60.00
(165)	Jeff Sweeney (New York)	275.00	125.00	60.00
(166)	Jeff Sweeney (Richmond)	275.00	125.00	60.00
(167)	Ira Thomas (Phila. Amer.)	275.00	125.00	60.00
(168)	Ira Thomas (Philadelphia Amer.)	275.00	125.00	60.00
(169)	Joe Tinker (Chicago Fed., bat off shoulder.)	550.00	245.00	120.00
(170)	Joe Tinker (Chicago Nat., bat off shoulder.)	550.00	245.00	120.00
(171)	Joe Tinker (Chicago Fed., bat off shoulder.)	550.00	245.00	120.00
(172)	Joe Tinker (Chicago Nat., bat off shoulder.)	550.00	245.00	120.00
(173)	Heinie Wagner	275.00	125.00	60.00
(174)	Jack Warhop (New York, "NY" on shirt.)	275.00	125.00	60.00
(175)	Jack Warhop (St. Louis, no "NY" on shirt.)	275.00	125.00	60.00
(176)	Zach Wheat (Brooklyn)	550.00	245.00	120.00
(177)	Zach Wheat (Brooklyn Nat.)	550.00	245.00	120.00
(178)	Kaiser Wilhelm	275.00	125.00	60.00
(179)	Ed Willett (St. Louis)	275.00	125.00	60.00
(180)	Ed Willett (Memphis)	275.00	125.00	60.00
(181)	Owen Wilson	275.00	125.00	60.00
(182)	Hooks Wiltse/Pitching (New York)	275.00	125.00	60.00
(183)	Hooks Wiltse/Pitching (Brooklyn)	275.00	125.00	60.00
(184)	Hooks Wiltse/Pitching (Jersey City)	275.00	125.00	60.00
(185)	Hooks Wiltse/Portrait (New York)	275.00	125.00	60.00
(186)	Hooks Wiltse/Portrait (Brooklyn)	275.00	125.00	60.00
(187)	Hooks Wiltse/Portrait (Jersey City)	275.00	125.00	60.00
(188)	Heinie Zimmerman	275.00	125.00	60.00

1919 Coupon Cigarettes Type 3 (T213)

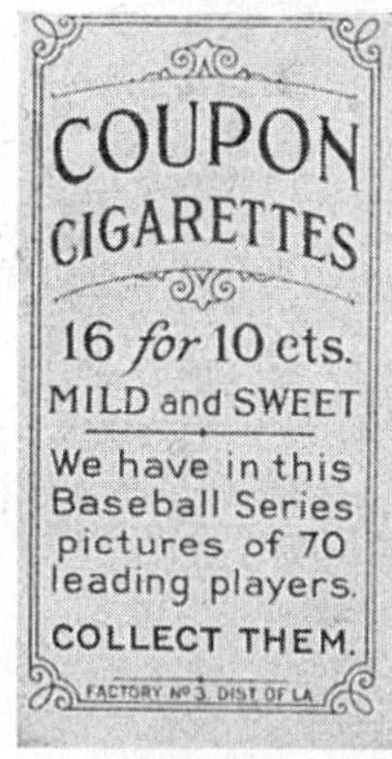

COUPON
CIGARETTES
16 for 10 cts.
MILD and SWEET
We have in this
Baseball Series
pictures of 70
leading players.
COLLECT THEM.
FACTORY No 3. DIST OF LA.

Though using the same photos seen in the contemporary T206 tobacco issue, Coupon Cigarette cards comprise three distinct sets produced between 1910 and 1919. Coupon cards feature a mix of players from the National and American Leagues, and several minor leagues. Slightly smaller than the usual cigarette-card format, Type 3 Coupons nominally measure 1-3/8" x 2-9/16", but are more prone to original size deviations than Type 1 or Type 2 Coupons. Except for the blue ink used in the player identification line, the fronts of the Coupon cards are virtually identical to the more popular T206 series. Backs, however, clearly identify the cards as being a product of Coupon Cigarettes and allow the collector to easily differentiate among the three types. Type 3 cards, issued in 1919, advertise "16 for 10 cts." and mention "70 leading players." Distribution of the Coupon cards was limited to the Louisiana area, making the set difficult to checklist and even more difficult to collect. Numerous variations further complicate the situation. It is quite possible the checklists here are incomplete and additions will surface in the future. While most Type 3 Coupons mention on their backs, "FACTORY No. 3, DIST OF LA," some have been seen with that designation blacked out and an overprint applied citing "FACTORY No. 8, DIST OF LA."

		NM	EX	VG
Complete Set (70):		30,000	13,500	6,750
Common Player:		300.00	135.00	65.00
(1)	Red Ames	300.00	135.00	65.00

(2)	Home Run Baker	600.00	275.00	130.00
(3)	Chief Bender (No trees in background.)	600.00	275.00	130.00
(4)	Chief Bender (Trees in background.)	600.00	275.00	130.00
(5)	Roger Bresnahan	600.00	275.00	130.00
(6)	Al Bridwell	300.00	135.00	65.00
(7)	Miner Brown	600.00	275.00	130.00
(8)	Bobby Byrne	300.00	135.00	65.00
(9)	Frank Chance/Btg	600.00	275.00	130.00
(10)	Frank Chance/Portrait	600.00	275.00	130.00
(11)	Hal Chase (Holding trophy.)	450.00	200.00	100.00
(12)	Hal Chase/Portrait	450.00	200.00	100.00
(13)	Hal Chase/Throwing	450.00	200.00	100.00
(14)	Ty Cobb/Btg	3,750	1,675	825.00
(15)	Ty Cobb/Portrait	3,750	1,675	825.00
(16)	Eddie Collins	600.00	275.00	130.00
(17)	Sam Crawford	600.00	275.00	130.00
(18)	Harry Davis	300.00	135.00	65.00
(19)	Mike Donlin	300.00	135.00	65.00
(20)	Wild Bill Donovan	300.00	135.00	65.00
(21)	Mickey Doolan/Btg	300.00	135.00	65.00
(22)	Mickey Doolan/Fldg	300.00	135.00	65.00
(23)	Larry Doyle/Btg	300.00	135.00	65.00
(24)	Larry Doyle/Portrait	300.00	135.00	65.00
(25)	Jean Dubuc	300.00	135.00	65.00
(26)	Jack Dunn	300.00	135.00	65.00
(27)	Kid Elberfeld	300.00	135.00	65.00
(28)	Johnny Evers	600.00	275.00	130.00
(29)	Chick Gandil	550.00	250.00	125.00
(30)	Clark Griffith	600.00	275.00	130.00
(31)	Buck Herzog	300.00	135.00	65.00
(32)	Dick Hoblitzell	300.00	135.00	65.00
(33)	Miller Huggins (Hands at mouth.)	600.00	275.00	130.00
(34)	Miller Huggins/Portrait	600.00	275.00	130.00
(35)	John Hummel	300.00	135.00	65.00
(36)	Hughie Jennings (Both hands showing.)	600.00	275.00	130.00
(37)	Hughie Jennings (One hand showing.)	600.00	275.00	130.00
(38)	Walter Johnson	900.00	400.00	200.00
(39)	Tim Jordan	300.00	135.00	65.00
(40)	Joe Kelley	600.00	275.00	130.00
(41)	Ed Konetchy	300.00	135.00	65.00
(42)	Larry Lajoie	600.00	275.00	130.00
(43)	Sherry Magee	300.00	135.00	65.00
(44)	Rube Marquard	600.00	275.00	130.00
(45)	Christy Mathewson	1,200	540.00	265.00
(47)	John McGraw (Glove at side.)	600.00	275.00	130.00
(48)	John McGraw/Portrait	600.00	275.00	130.00
(49)	George McQuillan	300.00	135.00	65.00
(50)	Fred Merkle	300.00	135.00	65.00
(51)	Dots Miller	300.00	135.00	65.00
(52)	Mike Mowrey	300.00	135.00	65.00
(53)	Chief Myers (Meyers) (Brooklyn)	300.00	135.00	65.00
(54)	Chief Myers (Meyers) (New Haven)	300.00	135.00	65.00
(55)	Dode Paskert	300.00	135.00	65.00
(56)	Jack Quinn	300.00	135.00	65.00
(57)	Ed Reulbach	300.00	135.00	65.00
(58)	Nap Rucker	300.00	135.00	65.00
(59)	Dick Rudolph	300.00	135.00	65.00
(60)	Herman Schaeffer (Schaefer)	300.00	135.00	65.00
(61)	Wildfire Schulte	300.00	135.00	65.00
(62)	Tris Speaker	750.00	335.00	165.00
(63)	Gabby Street/Catching	300.00	135.00	65.00
(64)	Gabby Street/Portrait	300.00	135.00	65.00
(65)	Jeff Sweeney	300.00	135.00	65.00
(66)	Ira Thomas	300.00	135.00	65.00
(67)	Joe Tinker	600.00	275.00	130.00
(68)	Zach Wheat	600.00	275.00	130.00
(69)	Geo. Wiltse	300.00	135.00	65.00
(70)	Heinie Zimmerman	300.00	135.00	65.00

1919 Coupon Cigarettes Type 3, Factory 8 Overprint

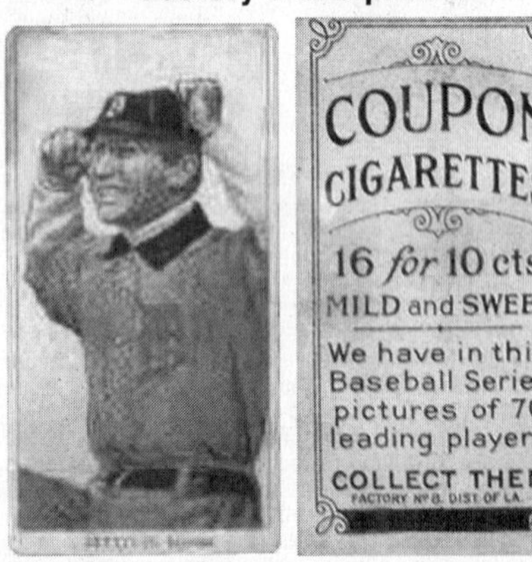

Of interest to specialty collectors is a variation of Type 3 Coupon cards on which the normal "FACTORY No. 3 . . ." line at bottom back has been blacked out and a "FACTORY No. 8 . . ." designation overprinted. The extent of the overprint checklist is unknown and at least one card (Cobb, bat off shoulder) is found as a Factory 8, but not yet verified to exist as a Factory 3 version.

	NM	EX	VG
Common Player:	600.00	300.00	180.00
Hall of Famers: 4-6X			

Chief Bender (No trees.)
Ty Cobb (Bat off shoulder.)
Eddie Collins
Jean Dubuc
Hughie Jennings (Both hands showing.)
Rube Marquard
John McGraw/Portrait

1914 Cracker Jack (E145)

The 1914 Cracker Jack set, whose ACC designation is E145-1, is one of the most popular of the "E" card sets and features baseball stars from the American, National and Federal leagues. The 2-1/4" x 3" cards, are printed on thin stock and were inserted in boxes of Cracker Jack. The 1914 issue consists of 144 cards with tinted color photographs on a red background. Numbered backs feature a short biography plus an advertisement. The advertising on the low-numbered cards in the set indicates that 10 million cards were issued, while the high-numbered cards boast that 15 million were printed.

		NM	EX	VG
Complete Set (144):		375,000	115,000	45,000
Common Player:		850.00	260.00	100.00
1	Otto Knabe	2,000	325.00	125.00
2	Home Run Baker	2,350	775.00	350.00
3	Joe Tinker	2,350	775.00	350.00
4	Larry Doyle	850.00	260.00	100.00
5	Ward Miller	850.00	260.00	100.00
6	Eddie Plank	2,500	825.00	375.00
7	Eddie Collins	2,300	760.00	345.00
8	Rube Oldring	850.00	260.00	100.00
9	Artie Hoffman (Hofman)	850.00	260.00	100.00
10	Stuffy McInnis	850.00	260.00	100.00
11	George Stovall	850.00	260.00	100.00
12	Connie Mack	3,600	1,200	540.00
13	Art Wilson	850.00	260.00	100.00
14	Sam Crawford	2,300	760.00	345.00
15	Reb Russell	850.00	260.00	100.00
16	Howie Camnitz	850.00	260.00	100.00
17a	Roger Bresnahan (No number on back.)	27,500	9,100	4,125
17b	Roger Bresnahan (Number on back.)	2,300	760.00	345.00
18	Johnny Evers	2,300	760.00	345.00
19	Chief Bender	2,300	760.00	345.00
20	Cy Falkenberg	850.00	260.00	100.00
21	Heinie Zimmerman	850.00	260.00	100.00
22	Smokey Joe Wood	1,500	495.00	225.00
23	Charles Comiskey	2,300	760.00	345.00
24	George Mullen (Mullin)	850.00	260.00	100.00
25	Mike Simon	850.00	260.00	100.00
26	Jim Scott	850.00	260.00	100.00
27	Bill Carrigan	850.00	260.00	100.00
28	Jack Barry	850.00	260.00	100.00
29	Vean Gregg	850.00	260.00	100.00
30	Ty Cobb	30,000	10,000	4,500
31	Heinie Wagner	850.00	260.00	100.00
32	Mordecai Brown	2,300	760.00	345.00
33	Amos Strunk	850.00	260.00	100.00
34	Ira Thomas	850.00	260.00	100.00
35	Harry Hooper	2,300	760.00	345.00
36	Ed Walsh	2,300	760.00	345.00
37	Grover C. Alexander	9,000	2,975	1,350
38	Red Dooin	850.00	260.00	100.00
39	Chick Gandil	1,625	535.00	245.00
40	Jimmy Austin	850.00	260.00	100.00
41	Tommy Leach	850.00	260.00	100.00
42	Al Bridwell	850.00	260.00	100.00
43	Rube Marquard	3,900	1,300	585.00
44	Jeff Tesreau	850.00	260.00	100.00
45	Fred Luderus	850.00	260.00	100.00
46	Bob Groom	850.00	260.00	100.00
47	Josh Devore	850.00	260.00	100.00
48	Harry Lord	850.00	260.00	100.00
49	Dots Miller	850.00	260.00	100.00
50	John Hummell (Hummel)	850.00	260.00	100.00
51	Nap Rucker	850.00	260.00	100.00
52	Zach Wheat	2,300	760.00	345.00
53	Otto Miller	850.00	260.00	100.00
54	Marty O'Toole	850.00	260.00	100.00
55	Dick Hoblitzel (Hoblitzell)	850.00	260.00	100.00
56	Clyde Milan	850.00	260.00	100.00
57	Walter Johnson	8,500	2,800	1,275
58	Wally Schang	850.00	260.00	100.00
59	Doc Gessler	850.00	260.00	100.00
60	Rollie Zeider	850.00	260.00	100.00
61	Ray Schalk	2,300	760.00	345.00
62	Jay Cashion	850.00	260.00	100.00
63	Babe Adams	850.00	260.00	100.00
64	Jimmy Archer	850.00	260.00	100.00
65	Tris Speaker	7,200	2,400	1,080
66	Nap Lajoie	7,200	2,400	1,080
67	Doc Crandall	850.00	260.00	100.00
68	Honus Wagner	13,500	4,450	2,000
69	John McGraw	2,300	760.00	345.00
70	Fred Clarke	2,300	760.00	345.00
71	Chief Meyers	850.00	260.00	100.00
72	Joe Boehling	850.00	260.00	100.00
73	Max Carey	2,300	760.00	345.00
74	Frank Owens	850.00	260.00	100.00
75	Miller Huggins	2,300	760.00	345.00
76	Claude Hendrix	850.00	260.00	100.00
77	Hughie Jennings	2,300	760.00	345.00
78	Fred Merkle	850.00	260.00	100.00
79	Ping Bodie	850.00	260.00	100.00
80	Ed Reulbach	850.00	260.00	100.00
81	Jim Delehanty (Delahanty)	850.00	260.00	100.00
82	Gavvy Cravath	850.00	260.00	100.00
83	Russ Ford	850.00	260.00	100.00
84	Elmer Knetzer	850.00	260.00	100.00
85	Buck Herzog	850.00	260.00	100.00
86	Burt Shotten	850.00	260.00	100.00
87	Hick Cady	850.00	260.00	100.00
88	Christy Mathewson	120,000	40,000	18,000
89	Larry Cheney	850.00	260.00	100.00
90	Frank Smith	850.00	260.00	100.00
91	Roger Peckinpaugh	900.00	295.00	135.00
92	Al Demaree	850.00	260.00	100.00
93	Del Pratt	850.00	260.00	100.00
94	Eddie Cicotte	2,200	725.00	330.00
95	Ray Keating	850.00	260.00	100.00
96	Beals Becker	850.00	260.00	100.00
97	Rube Benton	850.00	260.00	100.00
98	Frank Laporte (LaPorte)	850.00	260.00	100.00
99	Frank Chance	9,000	3,000	1,350
100	Tom Seaton	850.00	260.00	100.00
101	Wildfire Schulte	850.00	260.00	100.00
102	Ray Fisher	850.00	260.00	100.00
103	Joe Jackson	45,000	15,000	7,500
104	Vic Saier	850.00	260.00	100.00
105	Jimmy Lavender	850.00	260.00	100.00
106	Joe Birmingham	850.00	260.00	100.00
107	Tom Downey	850.00	260.00	100.00
108	Sherry Magee	850.00	260.00	100.00
109	Fred Blanding	850.00	260.00	100.00
110	Bob Bescher	850.00	260.00	100.00
111	Nixey Callahan	850.00	260.00	100.00
112	Jeff Sweeney	850.00	260.00	100.00
113	George Suggs	850.00	260.00	100.00
114	George Moriarity (Moriarty)	850.00	260.00	100.00
115	Ad Brennan	850.00	260.00	100.00
116	Rollie Zeider	850.00	260.00	100.00
117	Ted Easterly	850.00	260.00	100.00
118	Ed Konetchy	850.00	260.00	100.00
119	George Perring	850.00	260.00	100.00
120	Mickey Doolan	850.00	260.00	100.00
121	Hub Perdue	850.00	260.00	100.00
122	Donie Bush	850.00	260.00	100.00
123	Slim Sallee	850.00	260.00	100.00
124	Earle Moore (Earl)	850.00	260.00	100.00
125	Bert Niehoff	850.00	260.00	100.00
126	Walter Blair	850.00	260.00	100.00
127	Butch Schmidt	850.00	260.00	100.00
128	Steve Evans	850.00	260.00	100.00
129	Ray Caldwell	850.00	260.00	100.00
130	Ivy Wingo	850.00	260.00	100.00
131	George Baumgardner	850.00	260.00	100.00
132	Les Nunamaker	850.00	260.00	100.00
133	Branch Rickey	2,300	760.00	345.00
134	Armando Marsans	900.00	295.00	135.00
135	Bill Killifer (Killefer)	850.00	260.00	100.00
136	Rabbit Maranville	2,750	900.00	410.00
137	Bill Rariden	850.00	260.00	100.00
138	Hank Gowdy	850.00	260.00	100.00
139	Rebel Oakes	850.00	260.00	100.00
140	Danny Murphy	850.00	260.00	100.00
141	Cy Barger	850.00	260.00	100.00
142	Gene Packard	850.00	260.00	100.00
143	Jake Daubert	850.00	260.00	100.00
144	Jimmy Walsh	2,000	350.00	110.00

1915 Cracker Jack (E145)

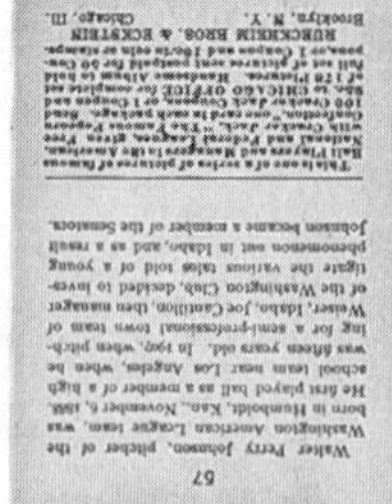

The 1915 Cracker Jack set (E145-2) is a reissue of the 1914 edition with some card additions and deletions, team designation changes, and new poses. A total of 176 cards comprise the set. Cards can be distinguished as either 1914 or 1915 by the advertising on the backs. The 1914 cards call the set complete at 144 pictures; the 1915 version notes 176 pictures. Backs of 1915 Cracker Jack cards are printed upside-down in relation to the front. A complete set and an album were available from the company.

		NM	EX	VG
Complete Set (176):		130,000	50,000	25,000
Common Player (1-144):		300.00	110.00	65.00
Common Player (145-176):		325.00	130.00	65.00
Album:		750.00	375.00	225.00
1	Otto Knabe	1,400	475.00	125.00
2	Home Run Baker	1,100	450.00	225.00
3	Joe Tinker	1,100	450.00	225.00
4	Larry Doyle	300.00	110.00	65.00
5	Ward Miller	300.00	110.00	65.00
6	Eddie Plank	1,350	550.00	275.00
7	Eddie Collins	1,200	480.00	240.00
8	Rube Oldring	300.00	110.00	65.00

#	Player	NM	EX	VG
9	Artie Hoffman (Hofman)	300.00	110.00	65.00
10	Stuffy McInnis	300.00	110.00	65.00
11	George Stovall	300.00	110.00	65.00
12	Connie Mack	1,100	450.00	225.00
13	Art Wilson	300.00	110.00	65.00
14	Sam Crawford	1,100	450.00	225.00
15	Reb Russell	300.00	110.00	65.00
16	Howie Camnitz	300.00	110.00	65.00
17	Roger Bresnahan	1,100	450.00	225.00
18	Johnny Evers	1,100	450.00	225.00
19	Chief Bender	1,100	450.00	225.00
20	Cy Falkenberg	300.00	110.00	65.00
21	Heinie Zimmerman	300.00	110.00	65.00
22	Smokey Joe Wood	800.00	325.00	160.00
23	Charles Comiskey	1,100	450.00	225.00
24	George Mullen (Mullin)	300.00	110.00	65.00
25	Mike Simon	300.00	110.00	65.00
26	Jim Scott	300.00	110.00	65.00
27	Bill Carrigan	300.00	110.00	65.00
28	Jack Barry	300.00	110.00	65.00
29	Vean Gregg	300.00	110.00	65.00
30	Ty Cobb	11,500	4,600	2,300
31	Heinie Wagner	300.00	110.00	65.00
32	Mordecai Brown	1,250	500.00	250.00
33	Amos Strunk	300.00	110.00	65.00
34	Ira Thomas	300.00	110.00	65.00
35	Harry Hooper	1,100	450.00	225.00
36	Ed Walsh	1,100	450.00	225.00
37	Grover C. Alexander	3,250	1,300	650.00
38	Red Dooin	300.00	110.00	65.00
39	Chick Gandil	800.00	325.00	160.00
40	Jimmy Austin	300.00	110.00	65.00
41	Tommy Leach	300.00	110.00	65.00
42	Al Bridwell	300.00	110.00	65.00
43	Rube Marquard	1,100	450.00	225.00
44	Jeff Tesreau	300.00	110.00	65.00
45	Fred Luderus	300.00	110.00	65.00
46	Bob Groom	300.00	110.00	65.00
47	Josh Devore	300.00	110.00	65.00
48	Steve O'Neill	300.00	110.00	65.00
49	Dots Miller	300.00	110.00	65.00
50	John Hummell (Hummel)	300.00	110.00	65.00
51	Nap Rucker	300.00	110.00	65.00
52	Zach Wheat	1,100	450.00	225.00
53	Otto Miller	300.00	110.00	65.00
54	Marty O'Toole	300.00	110.00	65.00
55	Dick Hoblitzel (Hoblitzell)	300.00	110.00	65.00
56	Clyde Milan	300.00	110.00	65.00
57	Walter Johnson	5,000	2,000	1,000
58	Wally Schang	300.00	110.00	65.00
59	Doc Gessler	300.00	110.00	65.00
60	Oscar Dugey	300.00	110.00	65.00
61	Ray Schalk	1,100	450.00	225.00
62	Willie Mitchell	300.00	110.00	65.00
63	Babe Adams	300.00	110.00	65.00
64	Jimmy Archer	300.00	110.00	65.00
65	Tris Speaker	1,700	680.00	340.00
66	Nap Lajoie	1,550	625.00	310.00
67	Doc Crandall	300.00	110.00	65.00
68	Honus Wagner	9,000	3,600	1,800
69	John McGraw	1,100	450.00	225.00
70	Fred Clarke	1,100	450.00	225.00
71	Chief Meyers	300.00	110.00	65.00
72	Joe Boehling	300.00	110.00	65.00
73	Max Carey	1,100	450.00	225.00
74	Frank Owens	300.00	110.00	65.00
75	Miller Huggins	1,100	450.00	225.00
76	Claude Hendrix	300.00	110.00	65.00
77	Hughie Jennings	1,100	450.00	225.00
78	Fred Merkle	300.00	110.00	65.00
79	Ping Bodie	300.00	110.00	65.00
80	Ed Reulbach	300.00	110.00	65.00
81	Jim Delehanty (Delahanty)	300.00	110.00	65.00
82	Gavvy Cravath	300.00	110.00	65.00
83	Russ Ford	300.00	110.00	65.00
84	Elmer Knetzer	300.00	110.00	65.00
85	Buck Herzog	300.00	110.00	65.00
86	Burt Shotten	300.00	110.00	65.00
87	Hick Cady	300.00	110.00	65.00
88	Christy Mathewson	6,000	2,400	1,200
89	Larry Cheney	300.00	110.00	65.00
90	Frank Smith	300.00	110.00	65.00
91	Roger Peckinpaugh	350.00	140.00	70.00
92	Al Demaree	300.00	110.00	65.00
93	Del Pratt	300.00	110.00	65.00
94	Eddie Cicotte	1,000	400.00	200.00
95	Ray Keating	300.00	110.00	65.00
96	Beals Becker	300.00	110.00	65.00
97	Rube Benton	300.00	110.00	65.00
98	Frank Laporte (LaPorte)	300.00	110.00	65.00
99	Hal Chase	600.00	240.00	120.00
100	Tom Seaton	300.00	110.00	65.00
101	Wildfire Schulte	300.00	110.00	65.00
102	Ray Fisher	300.00	110.00	65.00
103	Joe Jackson	17,500	7,000	3,500
104	Vic Saier	300.00	110.00	65.00
105	Jimmy Lavender	300.00	110.00	65.00
106	Joe Birmingham	300.00	110.00	65.00
107	Tom Downey	300.00	110.00	65.00
108	Sherry Magee	300.00	110.00	65.00
109	Fred Blanding	300.00	110.00	65.00
110	Bob Bescher	300.00	110.00	65.00
111	Herbie Moran	300.00	110.00	65.00
112	Ed Sweeney	300.00	110.00	65.00
113	George Suggs	300.00	110.00	65.00
114	George Moriarity (Moriarty)	300.00	110.00	65.00
115	Ad Brennan	300.00	110.00	65.00
116	Rollie Zeider	300.00	110.00	65.00
117	Ted Easterly	300.00	110.00	65.00
118	Ed Konetchy	300.00	110.00	65.00
119	George Perring	300.00	110.00	65.00
120	Mickey Doolan	300.00	110.00	65.00
121	Hub Perdue	300.00	110.00	65.00
122	Donie Bush	300.00	110.00	65.00
123	Slim Sallee	300.00	110.00	65.00
124	Earle Moore (Earl)	300.00	110.00	65.00
125	Bert Niehoff	300.00	110.00	65.00
126	Walter Blair	300.00	110.00	65.00
127	Butch Schmidt	300.00	110.00	65.00
128	Steve Evans	300.00	110.00	65.00
129	Ray Caldwell	300.00	110.00	65.00
130	Ivy Wingo	300.00	110.00	65.00
131	George Baumgardner	300.00	110.00	65.00
132	Les Nunamaker	300.00	110.00	65.00
133	Branch Rickey	1,100	450.00	225.00
134	Armando Marsans	425.00	175.00	85.00
135	Bill Killifer (Killefer)	300.00	110.00	65.00
136	Rabbit Maranville	1,100	450.00	225.00
137	Bill Rariden	300.00	110.00	65.00
138	Hank Gowdy	300.00	110.00	65.00
139	Rebel Oakes	300.00	110.00	65.00
140	Danny Murphy	300.00	110.00	65.00
141	Cy Barger	300.00	110.00	65.00
142	Gene Packard	300.00	110.00	65.00
143	Jake Daubert	300.00	110.00	65.00
144	Jimmy Walsh	300.00	110.00	65.00
145	Ted Cather	325.00	130.00	65.00
146	Lefty Tyler	325.00	130.00	65.00
147	Lee Magee	325.00	130.00	65.00
148	Owen Wilson	325.00	130.00	65.00
149	Hal Janvrin	325.00	130.00	65.00
150	Doc Johnston	325.00	130.00	65.00
151	Possum Whitted	325.00	130.00	65.00
152	George McQuillen (McQuillan)	325.00	130.00	65.00
153	Bill James	325.00	130.00	65.00
154	Dick Rudolph	325.00	130.00	65.00
155	Joe Connolly	325.00	130.00	65.00
156	Jean Dubuc	325.00	130.00	65.00
157	George Kaiserling	325.00	130.00	65.00
158	Fritz Maisel	325.00	130.00	65.00
159	Heinie Groh	325.00	130.00	65.00
160	Benny Kauff	325.00	130.00	65.00
161	Edd Rousch (Roush)	1,250	500.00	250.00
162	George Stallings	325.00	130.00	65.00
163	Bert Whaling	325.00	130.00	65.00
164	Bob Shawkey	325.00	130.00	65.00
165	Eddie Murphy	325.00	130.00	65.00
166	Bullet Joe Bush	325.00	130.00	65.00
167	Clark Griffith	1,250	500.00	250.00
168	Vin Campbell	325.00	130.00	65.00
169	Ray Collins	325.00	130.00	65.00
170	Hans Lobert	325.00	130.00	65.00
171	Earl Hamilton	325.00	130.00	65.00
172	Erskine Mayer	450.00	180.00	90.00
173	Tilly Walker	325.00	130.00	65.00
174	Bobby Veach	325.00	130.00	65.00
175	Joe Benz	325.00	130.00	65.00
176	Hippo Vaughn	1,300	200.00	75.00

1933 Cracker Jack Pins (PR4)

Although no manufacturer is indicated on the pins themselves, the manufacturer has been identified as Button Gum, but there is still some indication that Cracker Jack inserted this 25-player set in their products circa 1933. Each pin measures 13/16" in diameter and features a line drawing of a player portrait. The unnumbered pins are printed in blue and gray with backgrounds found in either yellow or gray.

		NM	EX	VG
Complete Set (25):		1,600	800.00	475.00
Common Player:		35.00	17.50	10.00
(1)	Charles Berry	35.00	17.50	10.00
(2)	Bill Cissell	35.00	17.50	10.00
(3)	KiKi Cuyler	60.00	30.00	18.00
(4)	Dizzy Dean	100.00	50.00	30.00
(5)	Wesley Ferrell	35.00	17.50	10.00
(6)	Frank Frisch	60.00	30.00	18.00
(7)	Lou Gehrig	250.00	125.00	75.00
(8)	Vernon Gomez	60.00	30.00	18.00
(9)	Goose Goslin	60.00	30.00	18.00
(10)	George Grantham	35.00	17.50	10.00
(11)	Charley Grimm	35.00	17.50	10.00
(12)	Lefty Grove	75.00	37.00	22.00
(13)	Gabby Hartnett	60.00	30.00	18.00
(14)	Travis Jackson	60.00	30.00	18.00
(15)	Tony Lazzeri	60.00	30.00	18.00
(16)	Ted Lyons	60.00	30.00	18.00
(17)	Rabbit Maranville	60.00	30.00	18.00
(18)	Carl Reynolds	35.00	17.50	10.00
(19)	Charles Ruffing	60.00	30.00	18.00
(20)	Al Simmons	60.00	30.00	18.00
(21)	Gus Suhr	35.00	17.50	10.00
(22)	Bill Terry	60.00	30.00	18.00
(23)	Dazzy Vance	60.00	30.00	18.00
(24)	Paul Waner	60.00	30.00	18.00
(25)	Lon Warneke	35.00	17.50	10.00

1979 Larry Crain Prints

"Baseball's Greatest Team," as voted during baseball's centennial, was featured on a set of 8-1/2" x 11" black-and-white prints by artist Larry Crain. Each print is signed and numbered by the artist. The set of 11 was originally sold for $25.

		NM	EX	VG
Complete Set (11):		25.00	12.50	7.50
Common Player:		3.00	1.50	.90
(1)	Yogi Berra	3.00	1.50	.90
(2)	Joe DiMaggio	5.00	2.50	1.50
(3)	Lou Gehrig	4.00	2.00	1.25
(4)	Rogers Hornsby	3.00	1.50	.90
(5)	Walter Johnson	3.00	1.50	.90
(6)	Willie Mays	4.00	2.00	1.25
(7)	Brooks Robinson	3.00	1.50	.90
(8)	Babe Ruth	5.00	2.50	1.50
(9)	Warren Spahn	3.00	1.50	.90
(10)	Casey Stengel	3.00	1.50	.90
(11)	Honus Wagner	3.00	1.50	.90

1976 Crane Potato Chips Discs

This unnumbered 70-card set of player discs was issued with Crane Potato Chips in 1976. The front of the discs are designed to look like a baseball with the player's black-and-white portrait in the center and vital data in side panels containing one of several bright colors. Discs measure 3-3/8" in diameter. This is the most common among several regionally issued sets sharing the same card fronts with different ads on back. The discs were produced by Michael Schechter Associates under license from the players' union. All uniform and cap logos have been deleted from the discs' photos. The unnumbered discs are checklisted here in alphabetical order. Several of the discs have team variations reflecting player moves. These are known only among the Crane discs and have not been verified in the issues of other advertisers.

		NM	EX	VG
Complete Set (70):		25.00	12.50	7.50
Common Player:		1.00	.50	.30
(1)	Henry Aaron	9.00	4.50	2.75
(2)	Johnny Bench	4.00	2.00	1.25
(3)	Vida Blue	1.00	.50	.30
(4)	Larry Bowa	1.00	.50	.30
(5)	Lou Brock	3.00	1.50	.90
(6)	Jeff Burroughs	1.00	.50	.30
(7)	John Candelaria	1.00	.50	.30
(8)	Jose Cardenal	1.00	.50	.30
(9)	Rod Carew	3.00	1.50	.90
(10)	Steve Carlton	3.00	1.50	.90
(11)	Dave Cash	1.00	.50	.30
(12)	Cesar Cedeno	1.00	.50	.30
(13)	Ron Cey	1.00	.50	.30
(14)	Carlton Fisk	3.00	1.50	.90
(15)	Tito Fuentes	1.00	.50	.30
(16)	Steve Garvey	2.00	1.00	.60
(17)	Ken Griffey	1.00	.50	.30
(18)	Don Gullett	1.00	.50	.30
(19)	Willie Horton	1.00	.50	.30
(20)	Al Hrabosky	1.00	.50	.30
(21)	Catfish Hunter	3.00	1.50	.90
(22a)	Reggie Jackson (A's)	6.00	3.00	1.75
(22b)	Reggie Jackson (Orioles)	15.00	7.50	4.50
(23)	Randy Jones	1.00	.50	.30
(24)	Jim Kaat	1.00	.50	.30
(25)	Don Kessinger	1.00	.50	.30
(26)	Dave Kingman	1.00	.50	.30
(27)	Jerry Koosman	1.00	.50	.30
(28)	Mickey Lolich	1.00	.50	.30
(29)	Greg Luzinski	1.00	.50	.30
(30)	Fred Lynn	1.00	.50	.30
(31)	Bill Madlock	1.00	.50	.30
(32a)	Carlos May (White Sox)	1.00	.50	.30
(32b)	Carlos May (Yankees)	1.00	.50	.30
(33)	John Mayberry	1.00	.50	.30
(34)	Bake McBride	1.00	.50	.30
(35)	Doc Medich	1.00	.50	.30
(36a)	Andy Messersmith (Dodgers)	1.00	.50	.30
(36b)	Andy Messersmith (Braves)	1.00	.50	.30
(37)	Rick Monday	1.00	.50	.30
(38)	John Montefusco	1.00	.50	.30
(39)	Jerry Morales	1.00	.50	.30
(40)	Joe Morgan	3.00	1.50	.90
(41)	Thurman Munson	3.00	1.50	.90
(42)	Bobby Murcer	1.00	.50	.30
(43)	Al Oliver	1.00	.50	.30
(44)	Jim Palmer	3.00	1.50	.90
(45)	Dave Parker	1.00	.50	.30
(46)	Tony Perez	3.00	1.50	.90
(47)	Jerry Reuss	1.00	.50	.30
(48)	Brooks Robinson	3.50	1.75	1.00
(49)	Frank Robinson	3.50	1.75	1.00
(50)	Steve Rogers	1.00	.50	.30
(51)	Pete Rose	8.00	4.00	2.50
(52)	Nolan Ryan	15.00	7.50	4.50
(53)	Manny Sanguillen	1.00	.50	.30
(54)	Mike Schmidt	6.00	3.00	1.75
(55)	Tom Seaver	4.00	2.00	1.25
(56)	Ted Simmons	1.00	.50	.30
(57)	Reggie Smith	1.00	.50	.30
(58)	Willie Stargell	3.00	1.50	.90
(59)	Rusty Staub	1.00	.50	.30
(60)	Rennie Stennett	1.00	.50	.30
(61)	Don Sutton	3.00	1.50	.90
(62a)	Andy Thornton (Cubs)	1.00	.50	.30
(62b)	Andy Thornton (Expos)	1.00	.50	.30
(63)	Luis Tiant	1.00	.50	.30
(64)	Joe Torre	2.00	1.00	.60

(65)	Mike Tyson	1.00	.50	.30
(66)	Bob Watson	1.00	.50	.30
(67)	Wilbur Wood	1.00	.50	.30
(68)	Jimmy Wynn	1.00	.50	.30
(69)	Carl Yastrzemski	4.00	2.00	1.25
(70)	Richie Zisk	1.00	.50	.30

1913 Cravats Felt Pennants

Little is known about this felt pennant issue, including the complete checklist. The name "Cravats" in the baseball above the player picture may represent the issuer, or describe the issue; the word "cravat" is an arcane term for a triangular piece of cloth. The pennants measure 4-1/8" across the top and are 9" long. Background colors are dark, with all printing in white. At center is a line art represntation of the player, with his name horizontally beneath and his team nickname vertically at bottom. At top is a bat and ball logo with the "Cravats" name. Most specimens are seen with a metal ring reinforcing the hole punched at top center. The known checklist points to 1913 as the most probable year of issue.

		NM	EX	VG
	Common Player:	250.00	125.00	75.00
(1)	Eddie Ainsmith	250.00	125.00	75.00
(2)	"Home Run" Baker	450.00	225.00	135.00
(3)	Hugh Bedient	250.00	125.00	75.00
(4)	Ray Caldwell	250.00	125.00	75.00
(5)	Jack Coombs	250.00	125.00	75.00
(6)	C.S. Dooin	250.00	125.00	75.00
(7)	Lawrence Doyle	250.00	125.00	75.00
(8)	Ed Konethy (Konetchy)	250.00	125.00	75.00
(9)	James Lavender	250.00	125.00	75.00
(10)	John J. McGraw	450.00	225.00	135.00
(11)	Stuffy McInnes (McInnis)	250.00	125.00	75.00
(12)	Christy Mathewson	1,150	575.00	345.00
(13)	J.T. (Chief) Meyer (Meyers)	250.00	125.00	75.00
(14)	Nap Rucker	250.00	125.00	75.00
(15)	Tris Speaker	600.00	300.00	180.00
(16)	Ed Sweeney	250.00	125.00	75.00
(17)	Jeff Tesreau	250.00	125.00	75.00
(18)	Ira Thomas	250.00	125.00	75.00
(19)	Joe Tinker	450.00	225.00	135.00
(20)	Ed Walsh	450.00	225.00	135.00

1922 Cream Nut/Goodie Bread

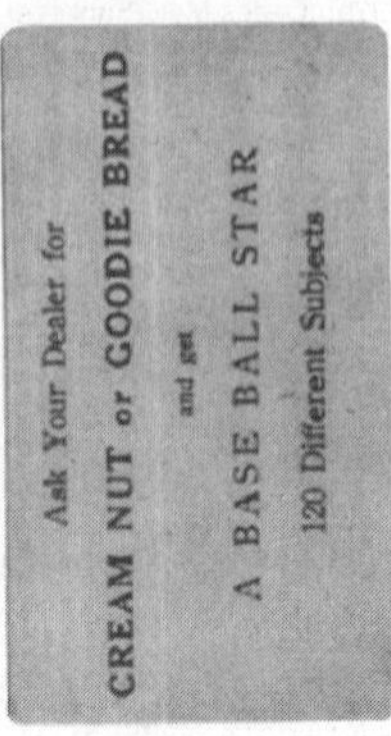

According to the advertising on back this set should comprise half of the known players from the generic W573 strip card issue. The black-and-white cards, about 2-1/16" x 3-3/8", share their format and player selection not only with W573, but also E120 American Caramel. Printed horizontally on the backs is: "Ask Your Dealer for / CREAM NUT or GOODIE BREAD / and get / A BASE BALL STAR / 120 Different Subjects." The location of the issuing entity, the specific manner of distribution and the checklist are unknown as only a handful of this particular ad-back series have survived. Collectors will pay a premium for this version above the normal W573 blank-back.

(See 1922 W573.)

1909 Croft's Candy (E92)

Wagner, s.s. Pittsburg Nat'l

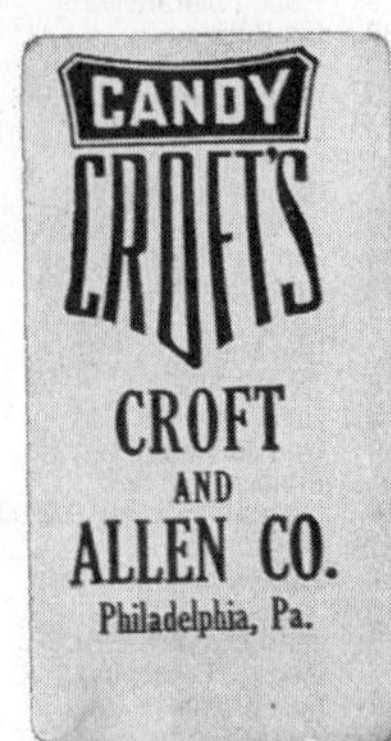

Because they share the format and pictures with several related issues (Croft's Cocoa, Dockman Gum, Nadja Caramels, etc.) this set shared the E92 designation in the American Card Catalog. It is more logical to present these sets as separate issues, based on the advertising which appears on back. Fronts of the 1-1/2" x 2-3/4" cards feature a color lithograph of the player. His last name, position and team are printed in black in the border below. Backs have a shield-shaped logo for Croft's Candy, a product of Croft & Allen Co., Philadelphia. Backs can be found printed in black, in blue (scarcer) or in red (extremely rare). Cards are unnumbered and the checklist is presented here alphabetically.

		NM	EX	VG
	Complete Set (50):	125,000	50,000	25,000
	Common Player:	1,065	425.00	220.00
	Blue Back: 2-3X			
	Red Back: Value Undeterminted			
(1)	Jack Barry	1,565	625.00	315.00
(2)	Harry Bemis	1,065	425.00	220.00
(3)	Chief Bender (Striped cap.)	4,065	1,625	815.00
(4)	Chief Bender (White cap.)	3,440	1,375	690.00
(5)	Bill Bergen	1,065	425.00	220.00
(6)	Bob Bescher	1,065	425.00	220.00
(7)	Al Bridwell	1,065	425.00	220.00
(8)	Doc Casey	1,065	425.00	220.00
(9)	Frank Chance	3,440	1,375	690.00
(10)	Hal Chase	2,000	815.00	405.00
(11)	Ty Cobb	18,750	7,500	3,750
(12)	Eddie Collins	3,750	1,500	750.00
(13)	Sam Crawford	2,815	1,125	565.00
(14)	Harry Davis	1,065	425.00	220.00
(15)	Art Devlin	1,065	425.00	220.00
(16)	Wild Bill Donovan	1,065	425.00	220.00
(17)	Red Dooin	1,500	600.00	300.00
(18)	Mickey Doolan	1,065	425.00	220.00
(19)	Patsy Dougherty	1,065	425.00	220.00
(20)	Larry Doyle/Throwing	1,065	425.00	220.00
(21)	Larry Doyle (With bat.)	1,065	425.00	220.00
(22)	Johnny Evers	3,440	1,375	690.00
(23)	George Gibson	1,065	425.00	220.00
(24)	Topsy Hartsel	1,065	425.00	220.00
(25)	Fred Jacklitsch	1,500	600.00	300.00
(26)	Hugh Jennings	2,815	1,125	565.00
(27)	Red Kleinow	1,065	425.00	220.00
(28)	Otto Knabe	1,250	500.00	250.00
(29)	Jack Knight	1,500	600.00	300.00
(30)	Nap Lajoie	4,065	1,625	815.00
(31)	Hans Lobert	1,065	425.00	220.00
(32)	Sherry Magee	1,065	425.00	220.00
(33)	Christy Matthewson (Mathewson)	9,690	3,875	1,940
(34)	John McGraw	2,815	1,125	565.00
(35)	Larry McLean	1,065	425.00	220.00
(36)	Dots Miller/Btg	1,065	425.00	220.00
(37)	Dots Miller/Fldg	1,500	600.00	300.00
(38)	Danny Murphy	1,065	425.00	220.00
(39)	Bill O'Hara	4,065	425.00	220.00
(40)	Germany Schaefer	1,065	425.00	220.00
(41)	Admiral Schlei	1,065	425.00	220.00
(42)	Boss Schmidt	1,065	425.00	220.00
(43)	Johnny Seigle (Siegle)	1,065	425.00	220.00
(44)	Dave Shean	1,065	425.00	220.00
(45)	Boss Smith (Schmidt)	1,065	425.00	220.00
(46)	Joe Tinker	2,815	1,125	565.00
(47)	Honus Wagner/Btg	15,000	6,000	3,000
(48)	Honus Wagner/Throwing	15,000	6,000	3,000
(49)	Cy Young	8,125	3,250	1,625
(50)	Heinie Zimmerman	1,065	425.00	220.00

1909 Croft's Cocoa (E92)

Like related issues once cataloged together as E92 (Croft's Candy, Dockman Gum, Nadja Caramels, etc.), these 1-1/2" x 2-3/4" cards feature a color player lithograph on front, which his name, position and team printed in the white border below. Backs have an ad for Crofts Swiss Milk Cocoa of Philadelphia. The checklist, presented here alphabetically, is identical to that of Croft's Candy.

Bender, p. Phila. Am.

		NM	EX	VG
	Complete Set (50):	97,500	37,500	18,750
	Common Player:	790.00	315.00	150.00
(1)	Jack Barry	1,200	490.00	240.00
(2)	Harry Bemis	790.00	315.00	150.00
(3)	Chief Bender (Striped hat.)	3,000	1,200	600.00
(4)	Chief Bender (White hat.)	1,800	720.00	360.00
(5)	Bill Bergen	790.00	315.00	150.00
(6)	Bob Bescher	790.00	315.00	150.00
(7)	Al Bridwell	790.00	315.00	150.00
(8)	Doc Casey	790.00	315.00	150.00
(9)	Frank Chance	1,650	660.00	330.00
(10)	Hal Chase	1,240	495.00	250.00
(11)	Ty Cobb	22,500	9,000	4,500
(12)	Eddie Collins	1,650	675.00	340.00
(13)	Sam Crawford	1,650	675.00	340.00
(14)	Harry Davis	790.00	315.00	150.00
(15)	Art Devlin	790.00	315.00	150.00
(16)	Wild Bill Donovan	790.00	315.00	150.00
(17)	Red Dooin	1,240	495.00	250.00
(18)	Mickey Doolan	790.00	315.00	150.00
(19)	Patsy Dougherty	790.00	315.00	150.00
(20)	Larry Doyle/Throwing	790.00	315.00	150.00
(21)	Larry Doyle (With bat.)	790.00	315.00	150.00
(22)	Johnny Evers	3,150	1,260	640.00
(23)	George Gibson	790.00	315.00	150.00
(24)	Topsy Hartsel	790.00	315.00	150.00
(25)	Fred Jacklitsch	1,240	495.00	250.00
(26)	Hugh Jennings	1,650	675.00	340.00
(27)	Red Kleinow	790.00	315.00	150.00
(28)	Otto Knabe	1,240	495.00	250.00
(29)	Jack Knight	1,240	495.00	250.00
(30)	Nap Lajoie	2,025	825.00	415.00
(31)	Hans Lobert	790.00	315.00	150.00
(32)	Sherry Magee	790.00	315.00	150.00
(33)	Christy Matthewson (Mathewson)	10,125	4,050	2,025
(34)	John McGraw	1,650	675.00	340.00
(35)	Larry McLean	790.00	315.00	150.00
(36)	Dots Miller/Btg	790.00	315.00	150.00
(37)	Dots Miller/Fldg	1,240	495.00	250.00
(38)	Danny Murphy	790.00	315.00	150.00
(39)	Bill O'Hara	790.00	315.00	150.00
(40)	Germany Schaefer	790.00	315.00	150.00
(41)	Admiral Schlei	790.00	315.00	150.00
(42)	Boss Schmidt	790.00	315.00	150.00
(43)	Johnny Seigle (Siegle)	1,015	405.00	205.00
(44)	Dave Shean	790.00	315.00	150.00
(45)	Boss Smith (Schmidt)	790.00	315.00	150.00
(46)	Joe Tinker	1,650	675.00	340.00
(47)	Honus Wagner/Btg	5,625	2,250	1,125
(48)	Honus Wagner/Throwing	5,625	2,250	1,125
(49)	Cy Young	5,250	2,100	1,050
(50)	Heinie Zimmerman	790.00	315.00	150.00

1969 Crown Brooks Robinson

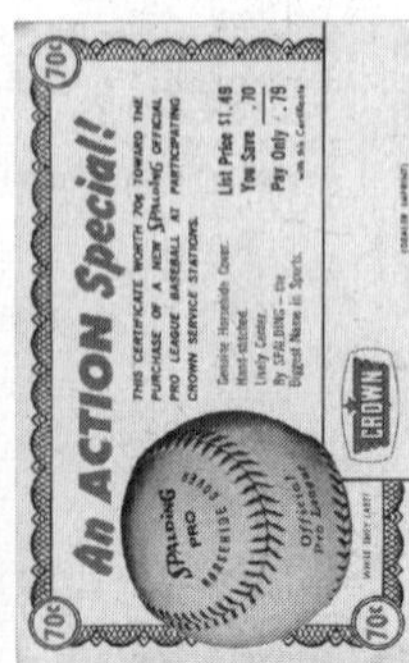

The attributed date is speculative. This 3-9/16" x 5-11/16" card feaures a black-and-white portrait photo on front with the player name in blue scrip. A blue panel at bottom has the gas company's logo and an ad slogan. On back is a black, red and white coupon offering a discount on a baseball. A blank panel at bottom was intended for use by individual service stations to print their name and address.

	NM	EX	VG
Brooks Robinson	150.00	75.00	45.00

1977-78 Cubic Corp. Sports Deck Playing Cards

Playing cards featuring pencil drawings of stars in various sports were produced on a limited basis in the late 1970s by Cubic Corp. of San Diego. The cards are standard bridge size (2-1/4" x 3-1/2") with rounded corners and feature the artwork of Al Landsman along with a facsimile autograph within a colored frame. Each deck has the same athlete on the back and sold for $1.60. There is no indication of the manufacturer on individual cards, it is only found on the box. It is believed most of the decks were only produced in limited sample quantities. Similar cards were produced for Pepsi and are listed thereunder. Only the baseball players are checklisted here, in alphabetical order.

		NM	EX	VG
(1)	Johnny Bench (Boxed deck.)	17.50	8.75	5.25
(1)	Johnny Bench (Single card.)	.50	.25	.15
(2)	Lou Gehrig (Boxed deck.)	25.00	12.50	7.50
(2)	Lou Gehrig (Single card.)	1.50	.70	.45
(3)	Catfish Hunter (Boxed deck.)	15.00	7.50	4.50
(3)	Catfish Hunter (Single card.)	.50	.25	.15
(4)	Randy Jones (Boxed deck.)	10.00	5.00	3.00
(4)	Randy Jones (Single card.)	.50	.25	.15
(5)	Mickey Mantle (Boxed deck.)	40.00	20.00	12.00
(5)	Mickey Mantle (Single card.)	4.00	2.00	1.25
(6)	Butch Metzger (Boxed deck.)	10.00	5.00	3.00
(6)	Butch Metzger (Single card.)	.50	.25	.15
(7)	Joe Morgan (Boxed deck.)	12.50	6.25	3.75
(7)	Joe Morgan (Single card.)	.50	.25	.15
(8)	Stan Musial (Boxed deck.)	25.00	12.50	7.50
(8)	Stan Musial (Single card.)	1.50	.70	.45
(9)	Jackie Robinson (Boxed deck.)	25.00	12.50	7.50
(9)	Jackie Robinson (Single card.)	1.50	.70	.45
(10)	Pete Rose (Boxed deck.)	35.00	17.50	10.00
(10)	Pete Rose (Single card.)	1.00	.50	.30
(11)	Babe Ruth (Boxed deck.)	30.00	15.00	9.00
(11)	Babe Ruth (Single card.)	3.00	1.50	.90
(12)	Tom Seaver (Boxed deck.)	30.00	15.00	9.00
(12)	Tom Seaver (Single card.)	1.00	.50	.30
(13)	Frank Tanana (Boxed deck.)	10.00	5.00	3.00
(13)	Frank Tanana (Single card.)	.50	.25	.15
(14)	Phillies logo/Auto. (Boxed deck.)	10.00	5.00	3.00
(14)	Phillies logo/Auto. (Single card.)	1.00	.50	.30

1911 Cullivan's Fireside Philadelphia A's (T208)

The 1911 T208 Firesides, an 18-card Philadelphia Athletics set issued by the Thomas Cullivan Tobacco Company of Syracuse, N.Y., is among the rarest of all 20th Century tobacco issues. Cullivan issued the set to commemorate the Athletics' 1910 Championship season, and, except for pitcher Jack Coombs, the checklist includes nearly all key members of the club, including manager Connie Mack. The cards are the standard size for tobacco issues, about 1-1/2" x 2-5/8". The front of each card features a player portrait set against a colored background. The player's name and the word "Athletics" appear at the bottom, while "World's Champions 1910" is printed along the top. Backs advertise the set as the "Athletics Series" and advise that one card is included in each package of "Cullivan's Fireside Plain Scrap" tobacco. The same checklist was used for a similar Athletics set issued by Rochester Baking/Williams Baking (D359). Blank-backed versions are also known to exist.

		NM	EX	VG
	Common Player:	11,250	5,625	3,375
(1)	Home Run Baker	25,000	12,500	7,500
(2)	Jack Barry	11,250	5,625	3,375
(3)	Chief Bender	25,000	12,500	7,500
(4)	Eddie Collins	25,000	12,500	7,500
(5)	Harry Davis	11,250	5,625	3,375
(6)	Jimmy Dygert	11,250	5,625	3,375
(7)	Topsy Hartsel	11,250	5,625	3,375
(8)	Harry Krause	11,250	5,625	3,375
(9)	Jack Lapp	11,250	5,625	3,375
(10)	Paddy Livingston	11,250	5,625	3,375
(11)	Bris Lord	11,250	5,625	3,375
(12)	Connie Mack	25,000	12,500	7,500
(13)	Cy Morgan	11,250	5,625	3,375
(14)	Danny Murphy	11,250	5,625	3,375
(15)	Rube Oldring	12,500	5,625	3,375
(16)	Eddie Plank	28,125	14,065	8,440
(17)	Amos Strunk	11,250	5,625	3,375
(18)	Ira Thomas	11,250	5,625	3,375

1964+ Curteichcolor Hall of Fame Plaque Postcards

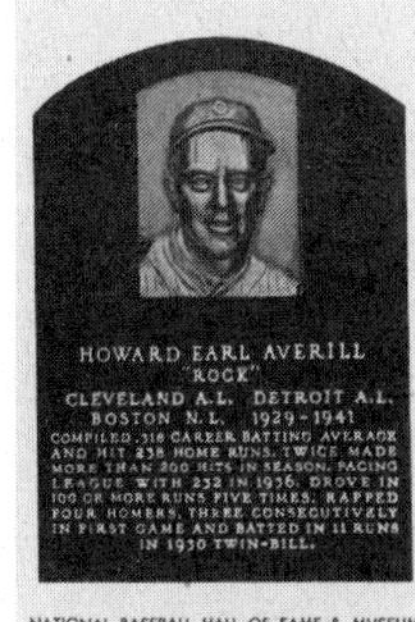

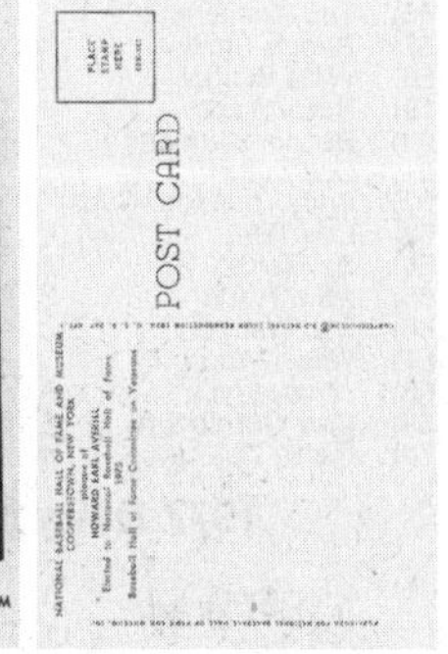

(See Hall of Fame Yellow Plaque Postcards for checklist, price data.)

1909-12 Cycle Cigarettes

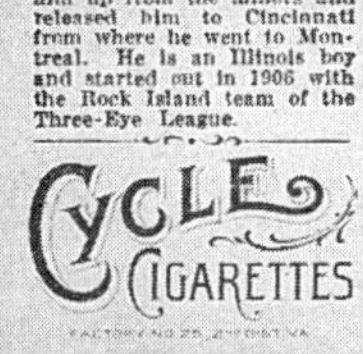

Cycle brand advertising found on the backs of T205, T206 and T207 cards generally indicates a slightly greater degree of scarcity than the most common back variations from those sets. While a value multiplier can generate a ballpark approximation of value for most cards from T205 and T206, it is not practical for T207s because all Cycle cards from that set are scarce and much of that scarcity has already been factored into the individual player prices quoted in the base T207 listings.

PREMIUMS:
T205: 1-1.5X
T206 350 Series: 1-1.5X
T206 460 Series: 2-3X
(See T205, T206, T207 for checklists and base card values.)

D

1959 Dad's Cookies Exhibits

A Vancouver bakery that issued several type of hockey cards in later years created this set of baseball cards by overprinting the usually blank backs of the 64 cards in Exhibit Supply Co.'s 1959 issue. Cards measure 3-3/8" x 5-3/8" and are printed in reddish-gray-brown. The back indicates an album was available to house the set.

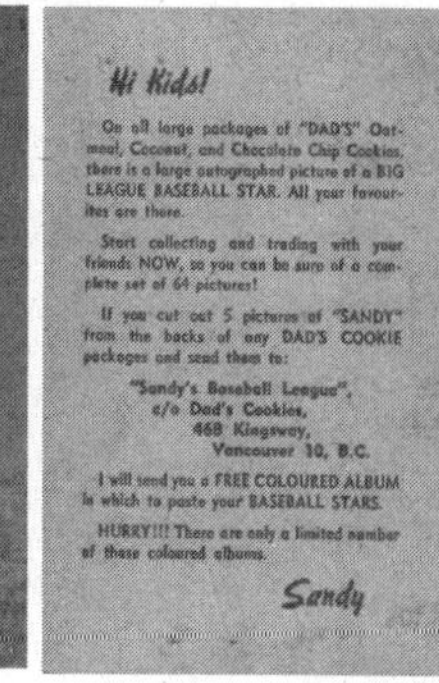

		NM	EX	VG
	Complete Set (64):	3,000	1,500	900.00
	Common Player:	35.00	17.50	10.00
(1)	Hank Aaron	200.00	100.00	60.00
(2)	Joe Adcock (Script name.)	35.00	17.50	10.00
(3)	Johnny Antonelli (Giants)	35.00	17.50	10.00
(4)	Luis Aparicio/Portrait	80.00	40.00	24.00
(5)	Richie Ashburn (Phillies)	100.00	50.00	30.00
(6)	Ed Bailey (With cap.)	35.00	17.50	10.00
(7)	Ernie Banks (Bat on shoulder, script name.)	150.00	75.00	45.00
(8)	Hank Bauer (N.Y. cap.)	50.00	25.00	15.00
(9)	Yogi Berra	150.00	75.00	45.00
(10)	Don Blasingame	35.00	17.50	10.00
(11)	Bill Bruton	35.00	17.50	10.00
(12)	Lew Burdette/Pitching (Side view.)	35.00	17.50	10.00
(13)	Chico Carrasquel/Portrait	35.00	17.50	10.00
(14)	Orlando Cepeda (To chest.)	80.00	40.00	24.00
(15)	Bob Cerv (A's cap.)	35.00	17.50	10.00
(16)	Delmar Crandall	35.00	17.50	10.00
(17)	Alvin Dark (Cubs)	35.00	17.50	10.00
(18)	Larry Doby	80.00	40.00	24.00
(19)	Dick Donovan (Sox cap.)	35.00	17.50	10.00
(20)	Don Drysdale/Portrait	90.00	45.00	27.00
(21)	Del Ennis	35.00	17.50	10.00
(22)	Whitey Ford/Pitching	125.00	62.00	37.00
(23)	Nelson Fox	80.00	40.00	24.00
(24)	Bob Friend	35.00	17.50	10.00
(25)	Billy Goodman/Btg	35.00	17.50	10.00
(26)	Whitey Herzog	35.00	17.50	10.00
(27)	Gil Hodges (LA on cap.)	75.00	37.50	22.00
(28)	Elston Howard	50.00	25.00	15.00
(29)	Jackie Jensen	50.00	25.00	15.00
(30)	Al Kaline (Portrait w/ two bats.)	100.00	50.00	30.00
(31)	Harmon Killebrew/Btg	100.00	50.00	30.00
(32)	Billy Klaus	35.00	17.50	10.00
(33)	Ted Kluzewski (Kluszewski) (Pirates uniform.)	60.00	30.00	18.00
(34)	Tony Kubek (Light background.)	60.00	30.00	18.00
(35)	Harvey Kuenn (D on cap.)	35.00	17.50	10.00
(36)	Don Larsen	35.00	17.50	10.00
(37)	Johnny Logan	35.00	17.50	10.00
(38)	Dale Long (C on cap.)	35.00	17.50	10.00
(39)	Mickey Mantle/Btg (No pinstripes, "c k" of "Mickey" separated.)	350.00	175.00	100.00
(40)	Eddie Mathews	100.00	50.00	30.00
(41)	Willie Mays/Portrait	200.00	100.00	60.00
(42)	Bill Mazeroski/Portrait	80.00	40.00	24.00
(43)	Lindy McDaniel	35.00	17.50	10.00
(44)	Gil McDougald	45.00	22.50	13.50
(45)	Orestes Minoso (C on cap.)	45.00	22.50	13.50
(46)	Stan Musial	175.00	87.00	52.00
(47)	Don Newcombe (Plain jacket.)	45.00	22.50	13.50
(48)	Andy Pafko (Yours truly.) (Plain uniform.)	35.00	17.50	10.00
(49)	Billy Pierce	35.00	17.50	10.00
(50)	Robin Roberts (Script name.)	80.00	40.00	24.00
(51)	Carl Sawatski (P on cap.)	35.00	17.50	10.00
(52)	Herb Score (C on cap.)	35.00	17.50	10.00
(53)	Roy Sievers/Portrait (W on cap, light background.)	35.00	17.50	10.00
(54)	Curt Simmons	35.00	17.50	10.00
(55)	Bill Skowron	50.00	25.00	15.00
(56)	Duke Snider (LA on cap.)	100.00	50.00	30.00
(57)	Warren Spahn (M on cap.)	100.00	50.00	30.00
(58)	Frankie Thomas (Photo actually Bob Skinner.)	50.00	25.00	15.00
(59)	Earl Torgeson (Plain uniform.)	35.00	17.50	10.00
(60)	Gus Triandos	35.00	17.50	10.00
(61)	Vic Wertz/Portrait	35.00	17.50	10.00
(62)	Ted Williams (Sincerely yours.) (#9 not showing)	200.00	100.00	60.00
(63)	Gene Woodling (Script name.)	35.00	17.50	10.00
(64)	Gus Zernial (Script name.)	35.00	17.50	10.00

1972 Daily Juice Co.

This one-card "set" was regionally issued to Roberto Clemente Fan Club members. Large numbers of the cards found their way into the hobby, including in uncut sheet form. The cards feature a full-color front black-and-white back. The card measures the standard 2-1/2" in width but is somewhat longer, at 3-3/4". This unnumbered card remains about the least expensive baseball card that was issued during Clemente's lifetime.

MEMBERSHIP CARD

ROBERTO CLEMENTE FAN CLUB

Name

Send for latest FREE 8 x 10 Full Color Picture of Roberto Clemente suitable for framing. Send to Roberto Clemente Fan Club, P.O. Box 2100, Pittsburgh, Pa. 15230. Enclose 25c for postage and handling.

Sponsored by DAILY JUICE CO., Oakmont, Pa.

	NM	EX	VG
Uncut Sheet (30):	200.00	100.00	60.00
1 Roberto Clemente	15.00	7.50	4.50

1950s Dairy Council Curt Simmons Postcard

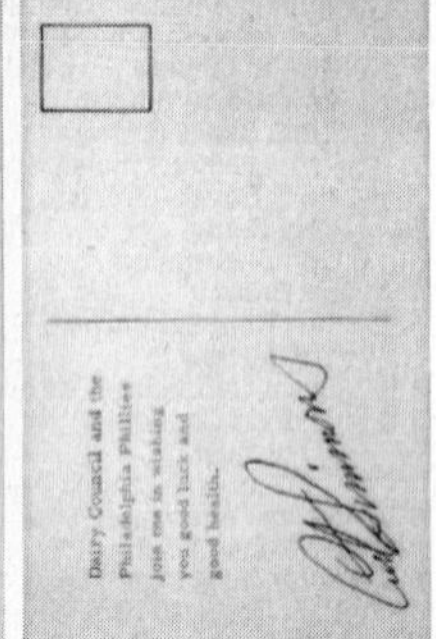

Issued by "The Dairy Council," probably locally, this black-and-white postcard features an action-pose photo of the star Phillies pitcher. There is a white facsimile autograph on front. Back of the 3-3/4" x 5-3/4" card has another facsimile autograph and the legend, "Dairy Council and the Philadelphia Phillies join me in wishing you good luck and good health."

	NM	EX	VG
Curt Simmons	60.00	30.00	18.00

1976 Dairy Isle Discs

One of several regional sponsors of player disc sets in 1976 was the upstate New York area chain, Dairy Isle. The discs are 3-3/8" diameter with a black-and-white player portrait photo in the center of the baseball design. A line of red stars is above, while the left and right panels feature one of several bright colors. Produced by Michael Schecter Associates under license from the Major League Baseball Players Association, the player photos have had uniform and cap logos removed. Backs are printed in red and purple. The unnumbered checklist here is presented in alphabetical order.

	NM	EX	VG
Complete Set (70):	45.00	22.50	13.50
Common Player:	1.00	.50	.30
(1) Henry Aaron	10.00	5.00	3.00
(2) Johnny Bench	4.50	2.25	1.25
(3) Vida Blue	1.00	.50	.30
(4) Larry Bowa	1.00	.50	.30
(5) Lou Brock	4.00	2.00	1.25
(6) Jeff Burroughs	1.00	.50	.30
(7) John Candelaria	1.00	.50	.30
(8) Jose Cardenal	1.00	.50	.30
(9) Rod Carew	4.00	2.00	1.25
(10) Steve Carlton	4.00	2.00	1.25
(11) Dave Cash	1.00	.50	.30
(12) Cesar Cedeno	1.00	.50	.30
(13) Ron Cey	1.00	.50	.30
(14) Carlton Fisk	4.00	2.00	1.25
(15) Tito Fuentes	1.00	.50	.30
(16) Steve Garvey	3.00	1.50	.90
(17) Ken Griffey	1.00	.50	.30
(18) Don Gullett	1.00	.50	.30
(19) Willie Horton	1.00	.50	.30
(20) Al Hrabosky	1.00	.50	.30
(21) Catfish Hunter	4.00	2.00	1.25
(22) Reggie Jackson (A's)	6.00	3.00	1.75
(23) Randy Jones	1.00	.50	.30
(24) Jim Kaat	1.00	.50	.30
(25) Don Kessinger	1.00	.50	.30
(26) Dave Kingman	1.00	.50	.30
(27) Jerry Koosman	1.00	.50	.30
(28) Mickey Lolich	1.00	.50	.30
(29) Greg Luzinski	1.00	.50	.30
(30) Fred Lynn	1.00	.50	.30
(31) Bill Madlock	1.00	.50	.30
(32) Carlos May (White Sox)	1.00	.50	.30
(33) John Mayberry	1.00	.50	.30
(34) Bake McBride	1.00	.50	.30
(35) Doc Medich	1.00	.50	.30
(36) Andy Messersmith	1.00	.50	.30
(37) Rick Monday	1.00	.50	.30
(38) John Montefusco	1.00	.50	.30
(39) Jerry Morales	1.00	.50	.30
(40) Joe Morgan	4.00	2.00	1.25
(41) Thurman Munson	3.00	1.50	.90
(42) Bobby Murcer	1.00	.50	.30
(43) Al Oliver	1.00	.50	.30
(44) Jim Palmer	4.00	2.00	1.25
(45) Dave Parker	1.00	.50	.30
(46) Tony Perez	4.00	2.00	1.25
(47) Jerry Reuss	1.00	.50	.30
(48) Brooks Robinson	4.50	2.25	1.25
(49) Frank Robinson	4.50	2.25	1.25
(50) Steve Rogers	1.00	.50	.30
(51) Pete Rose	10.00	5.00	3.00
(52) Nolan Ryan	20.00	10.00	6.00
(53) Manny Sanguillen	1.00	.50	.30
(54) Mike Schmidt	6.00	3.00	1.75
(55) Tom Seaver	4.50	2.25	1.25
(56) Ted Simmons	1.00	.50	.30
(57) Reggie Smith	1.00	.50	.30
(58) Willie Stargell	4.00	2.00	1.25
(59) Rusty Staub	1.25	.60	.40
(60) Rennie Stennett	1.00	.50	.30
(61) Don Sutton	4.00	2.00	1.25
(62) Andy Thornton (Cubs)	1.00	.50	.30
(63) Luis Tiant	1.00	.50	.30
(64) Joe Torre	3.00	1.50	.90
(65) Mike Tyson	1.00	.50	.30
(66) Bob Watson	1.00	.50	.30
(67) Wilbur Wood	1.00	.50	.30
(68) Jimmy Wynn	1.00	.50	.30
(69) Carl Yastrzemski	4.50	2.25	1.25
(70) Richie Zisk	1.00	.50	.30

1977 Dairy Isle Discs

Virtually identical in format to the 1976 issue (substituting red and blue for the back ad in 1977, instead of the previous year's red and purple), these 3-3/8" diameter player discs were given away at Dairy Isle outlets. Discs once again feature black-and-white player portrait photos in the center of a baseball design. The left and right panels are in one of several bright colors. Licensed by the players' association through Mike Schechter Associates, the player photos carry no uniform logos. The unnumbered discs are checklisted here alphabetically.

	NM	EX	VG
Complete Set (70):	30.00	15.00	9.00
Common Player:	1.00	.50	.30
(1) Sal Bando	1.00	.50	.30
(2) Buddy Bell	1.00	.50	.30
(3) Johnny Bench	4.50	2.25	1.25
(4) Larry Bowa	1.00	.50	.30
(5) Steve Braun	1.00	.50	.30
(6) George Brett	10.00	5.00	3.00
(7) Lou Brock	3.50	1.75	1.00
(8) Jeff Burroughs	1.00	.50	.30
(9) Bert Campaneris	1.00	.50	.30
(10) John Candelaria	1.00	.50	.30
(11) Jose Cardenal	1.00	.50	.30
(12) Rod Carew	3.50	1.75	1.00
(13) Steve Carlton	3.50	1.75	1.00
(14) Dave Cash	1.00	.50	.30
(15) Cesar Cedeno	1.00	.50	.30
(16) Ron Cey	1.00	.50	.30
(17) Dave Concepcion	1.00	.50	.30
(18) Dennis Eckersley	3.50	1.75	1.00
(19) Mark Fidrych	2.00	1.00	.60
(20) Rollie Fingers	3.50	1.75	1.00
(21) Carlton Fisk	3.50	1.75	1.00
(22) George Foster	1.00	.50	.30
(23) Wayne Garland	1.00	.50	.30
(24) Ralph Garr	1.00	.50	.30
(25) Steve Garvey	3.50	1.75	1.00
(26) Cesar Geronimo	1.00	.50	.30
(27) Bobby Grich	1.00	.50	.30
(28) Ken Griffey	1.00	.50	.30
(29) Don Gullett	1.00	.50	.30
(30) Mike Hargrove	1.00	.50	.30
(31) Al Hrabosky	1.00	.50	.30
(32) Jim Hunter	3.50	1.75	1.00
(33) Reggie Jackson	6.00	3.00	1.75
(34) Randy Jones	1.00	.50	.30
(35) Dave Kingman	1.00	.50	.30
(36) Jerry Koosman	1.00	.50	.30
(37) Dave LaRoche	1.00	.50	.30
(38) Greg Luzinski	1.00	.50	.30
(39) Fred Lynn	1.00	.50	.30
(40) Bill Madlock	1.00	.50	.30
(41) Rick Manning	1.00	.50	.30
(42) Jon Matlack	1.00	.50	.30
(43) John Mayberry	1.00	.50	.30
(44) Hal McRae	1.00	.50	.30
(45) Andy Messersmith	1.00	.50	.30
(46) Rick Monday	1.00	.50	.30
(47) John Montefusco	1.00	.50	.30
(48) Joe Morgan	3.50	1.75	1.00
(49) Thurman Munson	2.50	1.25	.70
(50) Bobby Murcer	1.00	.50	.30
(51) Bill North	1.00	.50	.30
(52) Jim Palmer	3.50	1.75	1.00
(53) Tony Perez	3.50	1.75	1.00
(54) Jerry Reuss	1.00	.50	.30
(55) Brooks Robinson	4.50	2.25	1.25
(56) Pete Rose	10.00	5.00	3.00
(57) Joe Rudi	1.00	.50	.30
(58) Nolan Ryan	15.00	7.50	4.50
(59) Manny Sanguillen	1.00	.50	.30
(60) Mike Schmidt	6.00	3.00	1.75
(61) Tom Seaver	4.50	2.25	1.25
(62) Bill Singer	1.00	.50	.30
(63) Willie Stargell	3.50	1.75	1.00
(64) Rusty Staub	1.25	.60	.40
(65) Luis Tiant	1.00	.50	.30
(66) Bob Watson	1.00	.50	.30
(67) Butch Wynegar	1.00	.50	.30
(68) Carl Yastrzemski	4.50	2.25	1.25
(69) Robin Yount	3.50	1.75	1.00
(70) Richie Zisk	1.00	.50	.30

1956 Dairy Queen Stars Statues

This set is identical in composition and manufacture to the carded figures sold as Big League Stars (see listing). The DQ versions of the statues are white, while the Big League versions are bronze colored. The statues measure about 3" tall and were evidently sold or given away with a purchase at the chain of ice cream shops.

	NM	EX	VG
Complete Set (18):	1,100	550.00	350.00
Common Player:	40.00	20.00	12.00
(1) John Antonelli	40.00	20.00	12.00
(2) Bob Avila	40.00	20.00	12.00
(3) Yogi Berra	100.00	50.00	30.00
(4) Roy Campanella	100.00	50.00	30.00
(5) Larry Doby	65.00	32.50	20.00
(6) Del Ennis	40.00	20.00	12.00
(7) Jim Gilliam	40.00	20.00	12.00
(8) Gil Hodges	75.00	37.50	22.50
(9) Harvey Kuenn	40.00	20.00	12.00
(10) Bob Lemon	50.00	25.00	15.00
(11) Mickey Mantle	325.00	160.00	100.00
(12) Ed Mathews	75.00	37.50	22.50
(13) Minnie Minoso	40.00	20.00	12.00
(14) Stan Musial	160.00	80.00	50.00
(15) Pee Wee Reese	100.00	50.00	30.00
(16) Al Rosen	40.00	20.00	12.00
(17) Duke Snider	100.00	50.00	30.00
(18) Mickey Vernon	40.00	20.00	12.00

1954 Dan-Dee Potato Chips

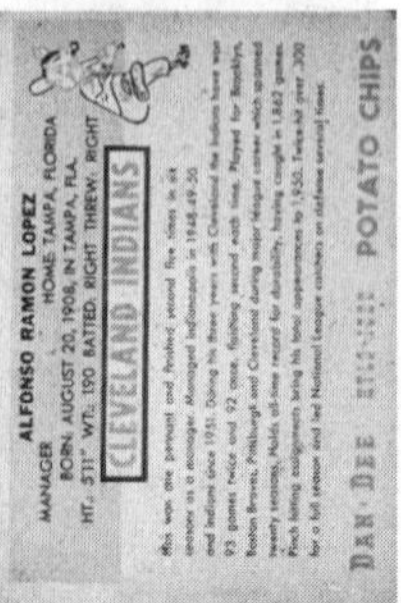

Issued in bags of potato chips, the cards in this 29-card set are commonly found with grease stains despite their waxed surface. The unnumbered cards, which measure 2-1/2" x 3-5/8", feature color pictures. Backs have player statistical and biographical information. The set consists mostly of players from the Indians and Pirates. Photos of the Yankees players were also used for the Briggs Meats and Stahl-Meyer Franks sets.

	NM	EX	VG
Complete Set (29):	7,000	2,750	1,350
Common Player:	110.00	45.00	20.00
(1) Bob Avila	110.00	45.00	20.00

(2)	Hank Bauer	135.00	55.00	25.00
(3)	Walker Cooper/SP	375.00	150.00	75.00
(4)	Larry Doby	140.00	55.00	25.00
(5)	Luke Easter	125.00	50.00	25.00
(6)	Bob Feller	350.00	140.00	70.00
(7)	Bob Friend	110.00	45.00	20.00
(8)	Mike Garcia	110.00	45.00	20.00
(9)	Sid Gordon	110.00	45.00	20.00
(10)	Jim Hegan	110.00	45.00	20.00
(11)	Gil Hodges	450.00	180.00	90.00
(12)	Art Houtteman	110.00	45.00	20.00
(13)	Monte Irvin	140.00	55.00	25.00
(14)	Paul LaPalm (LaPalme)	110.00	45.00	20.00
(15)	Bob Lemon	140.00	55.00	25.00
(16)	Al Lopez	140.00	55.00	25.00
(17)	Mickey Mantle	2,400	960.00	460.00
(18)	Dale Mitchell	110.00	45.00	20.00
(19)	Phil Rizzuto	250.00	100.00	50.00
(20)	Curtis Roberts	110.00	45.00	20.00
(21)	Al Rosen	125.00	50.00	25.00
(22)	Red Schoendienst	140.00	55.00	25.00
(23)	Paul Smith/SP	390.00	150.00	75.00
(24)	Duke Snider	300.00	120.00	60.00
(25)	George Strickland	110.00	45.00	20.00
(26)	Max Surkont	110.00	45.00	20.00
(27)	Frank Thomas/SP	200.00	80.00	40.00
(28)	Wally Westlake	110.00	45.00	20.00
(29)	Early Wynn	140.00	55.00	25.00

1977 Tom Daniels Burleigh Grimes

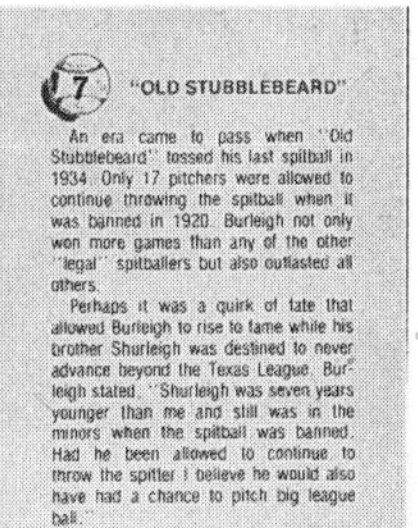

7
"OLD STUBBLEBEARD"
An era came to pass when "Old Stubblebeard" tossed his last spitball in 1934. Only 17 pitchers were allowed to continue throwing the spitball when it was banned in 1920. Burleigh not only won more games than any of the other "legal" spitballers but also outlasted all others.
Perhaps it was a quirk of fate that allowed Burleigh to rise to fame while his brother Shurleigh was destined to never advance beyond the Texas League. Burleigh stated, "Shurleigh was seven years younger than me and still was in the minors when the spitball was banned. Had he been allowed to continue to throw the spitter I believe he would also have had a chance to pitch big league ball."
Copyright 1977, Tom Daniels and Burleigh Grimes

The career of Hall of Fame spitballer Burleigh Grimes is traced in this collectors' issue. The 2-1/2" x 3-1/2" cards have black-and-white photos from Grimes' collection, bordered in bright blue. A card title is in black in the bottom border. Backs are printed in black and blue on white and have a description of the front photo. One card in each set is authentically autographed by Grimes. Price at issue was $3.50; uncut sheets were also available.

		NM	EX	VG
Complete Set (16):		10.00	5.00	3.00
Common Card:		1.00	.50	.30
1	Dodger Manager 1937-38	1.00	.50	.30
2	"Lord Burleigh"	1.00	.50	.30
3	Last Spitballers	1.00	.50	.30
4	Grimes, Hornsby, McGraw, Roush	1.00	.50	.30
5	Winning Combination	1.00	.50	.30
6	World Champion	1.00	.50	.30
7	"Old Stubblebeard"	1.00	.50	.30
8	Grimes Meets McCarthy	1.00	.50	.30
9	Dodger Greats	1.00	.50	.30
10	"The Babe"	2.00	1.00	.60
11	Dodger Strategists	1.00	.50	.30
12	Bender and Grimes	1.00	.50	.30
13	Number '270'	1.00	.50	.30
14	The Origin	1.00	.50	.30
15	1964 HoF Inductees	1.00	.50	.30
16	"Lord Burleigh" 1977	1.00	.50	.30

1910 Darby Chocolates (E271)

The 1910 Darby Chocolates cards are among the rarest of all candy cards. The cards were printed on boxes of "Pennant" Chocolates, two players per box - one each on front and back. The cards feature black-and-white player action photos outlined with a thick dark shadow. The boxes are accented with orange or green graphics. Most of the known examples of this set were not found until 1982 when a group in fire-damaged condition was inadvisedly subjected to restoration. Values shown here are for cards in untampered-with state of preservation. Values for restored cards must be adjusted significantly downward. This checklist may or may not be complete.

		NM	EX	VG
Common Player:		12,000	6,000	3,500
(1)	Jimmy Archer	12,000	6,000	3,600
(2)	Chief Bender	16,000	8,000	4,800
(3)	Bob Bescher	12,000	6,000	3,600
(4)	Roger Bresnahan	16,000	8,000	4,800
(5)	Al Bridwell	12,000	6,000	3,600
(6)	Mordicai Brown (Mordecai)	16,000	8,000	4,800
(7)	"Eddie" Cicotte	13,500	6,750	4,000
(8)	Fred Clark (Clarke)	12,000	6,000	3,600
(9)	Ty. Cobb/Btg	30,000	15,000	9,000
(10)	"Ty" Cobb/Fldg	30,000	15,000	9,000
(11)	King Cole	12,000	6,000	3,600
(12)	E. Collins	16,000	8,000	4,800
(13)	Wid Conroy	12,000	6,000	3,600
(14)	"Sam" Crawford	16,000	8,000	4,800
(15)	Bill Dahlin (Dahlen)	12,000	6,000	3,600
(16)	Bill Donovan	12,000	6,000	3,600
(17)	"Pat" Dougherty	12,000	6,000	3,600
(18)	Kid Elberfeld	12,000	6,000	3,600
(19)	"Johnny" Evers	16,000	8,000	4,800
(20)	Charlie Herzog	12,000	6,000	3,600
(21)	Hughie Jennings	16,000	8,000	4,800
(22)	Walter Johnson	20,000	10,000	6,000
(23)	Ed Konetchy	12,000	6,000	3,600
(24)	Tommy Leach	12,000	6,000	3,600
(25)	Fred Luderous (Luderus)	12,000	6,000	3,600
(26)	"Mugsy" McGraw	16,000	8,000	4,800
(27)	"Mike" Mowery (Mowrey)	12,000	6,000	3,600
(28)	Jack Powell	12,000	6,000	3,600
(29)	Slim Sallee	12,000	6,000	3,600
(30)	James Scheckard (Sheckard)	12,000	6,000	3,600
(31)	Walter Snodgrass	12,000	6,000	3,600
(32)	"Tris" Speaker	17,500	8,750	5,250
(33)	Charlie Suggs	12,000	6,000	3,600
(34)	Fred Tenney	12,000	6,000	3,600
(35)	"Jim" Vaughn	12,000	6,000	3,600
(36)	"Hans" Wagner	40,000	13,750	8,250

1911 Harry Davis Day Postcard

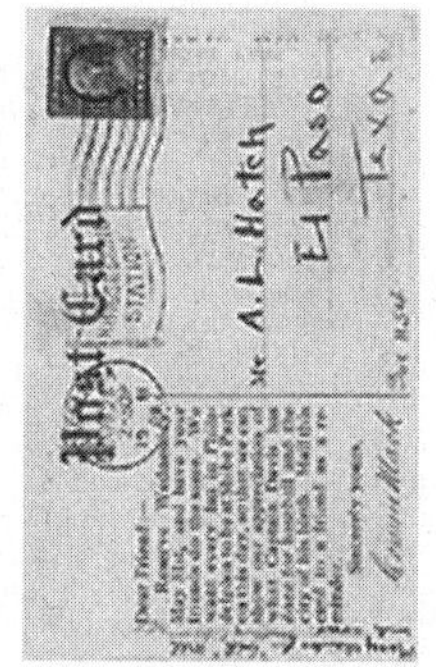

In his final season with the Philadelphia Athletics, the star first baseman of the famed $100,000 Infield was honored with a "day" at Shibe Park. This standard-size black-and-white postcard was created to remind fans to attend the event. A pre-printed message on back over the facsimile signature of Connie Mack urges fans to "show our appreciation of what Captain Davis has done for baseball and the city of his birth."

	NM	EX	VG
Harry Davis	750.00	375.00	225.00

1970 Dayton Daily News Bubble-Gumless Cards

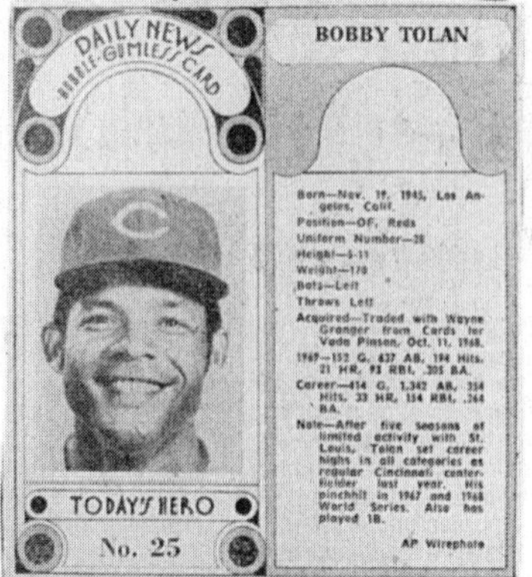

These "cards" are actually newspaper clippings which were issued on a daily basis during the baseball season by the Ohio newspaper. Labeled "Today's Hero," the clippings measure approximately 3-1/2" x 4" and are printed in black-and-white. At left is a portrait photo of the player, at right are personal data, stats and career highlights.

		NM	EX	VG
Complete Set (160):		2,000	1,000	600.00
Common Player:		9.00	4.50	2.75
1	Pete Rose	40.00	20.00	12.00
2	Johnny Bench	20.00	10.00	6.00
3	Maury Wills	12.00	6.00	3.50
4	Harmon Killebrew	20.00	10.00	6.00
5	Frank Robinson	20.00	10.00	6.00
6	Willie Mays	60.00	30.00	18.00
7	Hank Aaron	60.00	30.00	18.00
8	Tom Seaver	20.00	10.00	6.00
9	Sam McDowell	9.00	4.50	2.75
10	Rico Petrocelli	9.00	4.50	2.75
11a	Tony Perez (Dark cap.)	20.00	10.00	6.00
11b	Tony Perez (Light cap.)	20.00	10.00	6.00
12	Hoyt Wilhelm	15.00	7.50	4.50
13	Alex Johnson	9.00	4.50	2.75
14	Gary Nolan	9.00	4.50	2.75
15	Al Kaline	25.00	12.50	7.50
16	Bob Gibson	15.00	7.50	4.50
17	Larry Dierker	9.00	4.50	2.75
18	Ernie Banks	30.00	15.00	9.00
19	Lee May	9.00	4.50	2.75
20	Claude Osteen	9.00	4.50	2.75
21	Tony Horton	9.00	4.50	2.75
22	Mack Jones	9.00	4.50	2.75
23	Wally Bunker	9.00	4.50	2.75
24	Bill Hands	9.00	4.50	2.75
25	Bobby Tolan	9.00	4.50	2.75
26	Jim Wynn	9.00	4.50	2.75
27	Tom Haller	9.00	4.50	2.75
28	Carl Yastrzemski	25.00	12.50	7.50
29	Jim Merritt	9.00	4.50	2.75
30	Tony Oliva	12.00	6.00	3.50
31	Reggie Jackson	40.00	20.00	12.00
32	Bob Clemente	90.00	45.00	27.00
33	Tommy Helms	9.00	4.50	2.75
34	Boog Powell	12.00	6.00	3.50
35	Mickey Lolich	9.00	4.50	2.75
36	Frank Howard	12.00	6.00	3.50
37	Jim McGlothlin	9.00	4.50	2.75
38	Rusty Staub	12.00	6.00	3.50
39	Mel Stottlemyre	9.00	4.50	2.75
40	Rico Carty	9.00	4.50	2.75
41	Nate Colbert	9.00	4.50	2.75
42	Wayne Granger	9.00	4.50	2.75
43	Mike Hegan	9.00	4.50	2.75
44	Jerry Koosman	9.00	4.50	2.75
45	Jim Perry	9.00	4.50	2.75
46	Pat Corrales	9.00	4.50	2.75
47	Dick Bosman	9.00	4.50	2.75
48	Bert Campaneris	9.00	4.50	2.75
49	Larry Hisle	9.00	4.50	2.75
50	Bernie Carbo	9.00	4.50	2.75
51	Wilbur Wood	9.00	4.50	2.75
52	Dave McNally	9.00	4.50	2.75
53	Andy Messersmith	9.00	4.50	2.75
54	Jimmy Stewart	9.00	4.50	2.75
55	Luis Aparicio	15.00	7.50	4.50
56	Mike Cuellar	9.00	4.50	2.75
57	Bill Grabarkewitz	9.00	4.50	2.75
58	Dick Dietz	9.00	4.50	2.75
59	Dave Concepcion	9.00	4.50	2.75
60	Gary Gentry	9.00	4.50	2.75
61	Don Money	9.00	4.50	2.75
62	Rod Carew	20.00	10.00	6.00
63	Denis Menke	9.00	4.50	2.75
64	Hal McRae	9.00	4.50	2.75
65	Felipe Alou	9.00	4.50	2.75
66	Richie Hebner	9.00	4.50	2.75
67	Don Sutton	15.00	7.50	4.50
68	Wayne Simpson	9.00	4.50	2.75
69	Art Shamsky	9.00	4.50	2.75
70	Luis Tiant	9.00	4.50	2.75
71	Clay Carroll	9.00	4.50	2.75
72	Jim Hickman	9.00	4.50	2.75
73	Clarence Gaston	9.00	4.50	2.75
74	Angel Bravo	9.00	4.50	2.75
75	Jim Hunter	15.00	7.50	4.50
76	Lou Piniella	10.00	5.00	3.00
77	Jim Bunning	15.00	7.50	4.50
78	Don Gullett	9.00	4.50	2.75
79	Dan Cater	9.00	4.50	2.75
80	Richie Allen	13.50	6.75	4.00
81	Jim Bouton	10.00	5.00	3.00
82	Jim Palmer	15.00	7.50	4.50
83	Woody Woodward	9.00	4.50	2.75
84	Tom Agee	9.00	4.50	2.75
85	Carlos May	9.00	4.50	2.75
86	Ray Washburn	9.00	4.50	2.75
87	Denny McLain	10.00	5.00	3.00
88	Lou Brock	15.00	7.50	4.50
89	Ken Henderson	9.00	4.50	2.75
90	Roy White	9.00	4.50	2.75
91	Chris Cannizzaro	9.00	4.50	2.75
92	Willie Horton	9.00	4.50	2.75
93	Jose Cardenal	9.00	4.50	2.75
94	Jim Fregosi	9.00	4.50	2.75
95	Richie Hebner	9.00	4.50	2.75
96	Tony Conigliaro	10.00	5.00	3.00
97	Tony Cloninger	9.00	4.50	2.75
98	Mike Epstein	9.00	4.50	2.75
99	Ty Cline	9.00	4.50	2.75
100	Tommy Harper	9.00	4.50	2.75
101	Jose Azcue	9.00	4.50	2.75
102a	Glenn Beckert	9.00	4.50	2.75
102b	Ray Fosse	9.00	4.50	2.75
103	NOT ISSUED			
104	Gerry Moses	9.00	4.50	2.75
105	Bud Harrelson	9.00	4.50	2.75
106	Joe Torre	13.50	6.75	4.00
107	Dave Johnson	9.00	4.50	2.75
108	Don Kessinger	9.00	4.50	2.75
109	Bill Freehan	9.00	4.50	2.75
110	Sandy Alomar	9.00	4.50	2.75
111	Matty Alou	9.00	4.50	2.75
112	Joe Morgan	15.00	7.50	4.50

113	John Odom	9.00	4.50	2.75
114	Amos Otis	9.00	4.50	2.75
115	Jay Johnstone	9.00	4.50	2.75
116	Ron Perranoski	9.00	4.50	2.75
117	Manny Mota	9.00	4.50	2.75
118	Billy Conigliaro	9.00	4.50	2.75
119	Leo Cardenas	9.00	4.50	2.75
120	Rich Reese	9.00	4.50	2.75
121	Ron Santo	12.00	6.00	3.50
122	Gene Michael	9.00	4.50	2.75
123	Milt Pappas	9.00	4.50	2.75
124	Joe Pepitone	10.00	5.00	3.00
125	Jose Cardenal	9.00	4.50	2.75
126	Jim Northrup	9.00	4.50	2.75
127	Wes Parker	9.00	4.50	2.75
128	Fritz Peterson	9.00	4.50	2.75
129	Phil Regan	9.00	4.50	2.75
130	John Callison	9.00	4.50	2.75
131	Cookie Rojas	9.00	4.50	2.75
132	Claude Raymond	9.00	4.50	2.75
133	Darrel Chaney	9.00	4.50	2.75
134	Gary Peters	9.00	4.50	2.75
135	Del Unser	9.00	4.50	2.75
136	Joey Foy	9.00	4.50	2.75
137	Luke Walker	9.00	4.50	2.75
138	Bill Mazeroski	15.00	7.50	4.50
139	Tony Taylor	9.00	4.50	2.75
140	Leron Lee	9.00	4.50	2.75
141	Jesus Alou	9.00	4.50	2.75
142	Donn Clendenon	9.00	4.50	2.75
143	Merv Rettenmund	9.00	4.50	2.75
144	Bob Moose	9.00	4.50	2.75
145	Jim Kaat	10.00	5.00	3.00
146	Randy Hundley	9.00	4.50	2.75
147	Jim McAndrew	9.00	4.50	2.75
148	Manny Sanguillen	9.00	4.50	2.75
149	Bob Allison	9.00	4.50	2.75
150	Jim Maloney	9.00	4.50	2.75
151	Don Buford	9.00	4.50	2.75
152	Gene Alley	9.00	4.50	2.75
153	Cesar Tovar	9.00	4.50	2.75
154	Brooks Robinson	20.00	10.00	6.00
155	Milt Wilcox	9.00	4.50	2.75
156	Willie Stargell	20.00	10.00	6.00
157	Paul Blair	9.00	4.50	2.75
158	Andy Etchebarren	9.00	4.50	2.75
159	Mark Belanger	9.00	4.50	2.75
160	Elrod Hendricks	9.00	4.50	2.75

1973 Dean's Photo Service San Diego Padres

A true rookie-year issue for Dave Winfield is included in this set of 5-1/2" x 8-1/2" black-and-white, blank-backed player photos sponsored by Dean's Photo Service and given away by the team in five six-card series at various home games. Pictures have posed player portraits surrounded by a white border. Beneath are the name and position, with team and sponsor logos at bottom. The set is checklisted here alphabetically.

		NM	EX	VG
Complete Set (31):		80.00	40.00	24.00
Common Player:		4.00	2.00	1.25
(1)	Steve Arlin	4.00	2.00	1.25
(2)	Mike Caldwell	4.00	2.00	1.25
(3)	Dave Campbell	4.00	2.00	1.25
(4)	Nate Colbert	4.00	2.00	1.25
(5)	Mike Corkins	4.00	2.00	1.25
(6)	Pat Corrales	4.00	2.00	1.25
(7)	Jim Davenport	4.00	2.00	1.25
(8)	Dave Garcia	4.00	2.00	1.25
(9)	Clarence Gaston	4.00	2.00	1.25
(10)	Bill Greif	4.00	2.00	1.25
(11)	John Grubb	4.00	2.00	1.25
(12)	Enzo Hernandez	4.00	2.00	1.25
(13)	Randy Jones	4.00	2.00	1.25
(14)	Fred Kendall	4.00	2.00	1.25
(15)	Clay Kirby	4.00	2.00	1.25
(16)	Leron Lee	4.00	2.00	1.25
(17)	Dave Marshall	4.00	2.00	1.25
(18)	Don Mason	4.00	2.00	1.25
(19)	Jerry Morales	4.00	2.00	1.25
(20)	Ivan Murrell	4.00	2.00	1.25
(21)	Fred Norman	4.00	2.00	1.25
(22)	Johnny Podres	4.00	2.00	1.25
(23)	Dave Roberts	4.00	2.00	1.25
(24)	Vicente Romo	4.00	2.00	1.25
(25)	Gary Ross	4.00	2.00	1.25
(26)	Bob Skinner	4.00	2.00	1.25
(27)	Derrel Thomas	4.00	2.00	1.25
(28)	Rich Troedson	4.00	2.00	1.25
(29)	Whitey Wietelmann	4.00	2.00	1.25
(30)	Dave Winfield	25.00	12.50	7.50
(31)	Don Zimmer	5.00	2.50	1.50

1974 Dean's Photo Service San Diego Padres

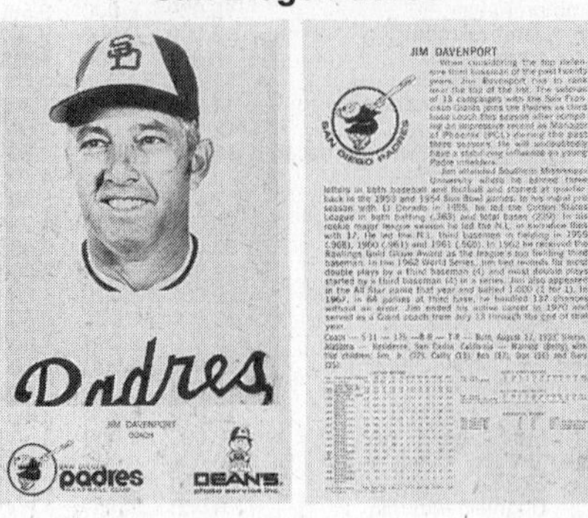

This issue shares the same basic format as the years which preceded it and succeeded it. Fronts of the 5-1/2" x 8-1/2" cards have a large player portrait or pose at top, with the player's name and position below. In the wide white border at bottom are the team and sponsor's logos. Backs, for the first time, have a lengthy career summary, personal data and full professional stats. All printing is in black-and-white. The unnumbered cards are checklisted here alphabetically.

		NM	EX	VG
Complete Set (30):		70.00	35.00	21.00
Common Player:		4.00	2.00	1.25
(1)	Matty Alou	4.00	2.00	1.25
(2)	Bob Barton	4.00	2.00	1.25
(3)	Glenn Beckert	4.00	2.00	1.25
(4)	Jack Bloomfield	4.00	2.00	1.25
(5)	Nate Colbert	4.00	2.00	1.25
(6)	Mike Corkins	4.00	2.00	1.25
(7)	Jim Davenport	4.00	2.00	1.25
(8)	Dave Freisleben	4.00	2.00	1.25
(9)	Cito Gaston	4.00	2.00	1.25
(10)	Bill Greif	4.00	2.00	1.25
(11)	Johnny Grubb	4.00	2.00	1.25
(12)	Larry Hardy	4.00	2.00	1.25
(13)	Enzo Hernandez	4.00	2.00	1.25
(14)	Dave Hilton	4.00	2.00	1.25
(15)	Randy Jones	4.00	2.00	1.25
(16)	Fred Kendall	4.00	2.00	1.25
(17)	Gene Locklear	4.00	2.00	1.25
(18)	Willie McCovey	10.00	5.00	3.00
(19)	John McNamara	4.00	2.00	1.25
(20)	Rich Morales	4.00	2.00	1.25
(21)	Bill Posedel	4.00	2.00	1.25
(22)	Dave Roberts	4.00	2.00	1.25
(23)	Vicente Romo	4.00	2.00	1.25
(24)	Dan Spillner	4.00	2.00	1.25
(25)	Bob Tolan	4.00	2.00	1.25
(26)	Derrel Thomas	4.00	2.00	1.25
(27)	Rich Troedson	4.00	2.00	1.25
(28)	Whitey Wietelmann	4.00	2.00	1.25
(29)	Bernie Williams	4.00	2.00	1.25
(30)	Dave Winfield	15.00	7.50	4.50

1975 Dean's Photo Service San Diego Padres

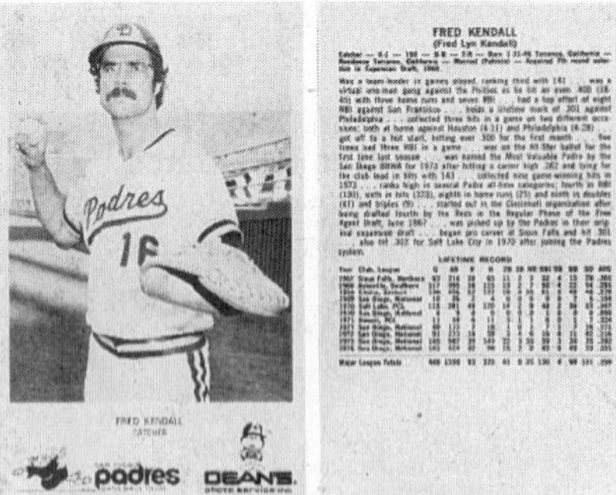

Player biographical data and stats continued on the backs of the cards in the 1975 series sponsored by Dean's. Once again the black-and-white pictures were in 5-1/2" x 8-1/2" format. Fronts have the player photo at top, with his name and position beneath. At bottom are the team and sponsor logos. The Padres logo consists of a cartoon character robed monk in various baseball poses. The pictures were given away at autograph nights during the season. The unnumbered photos are checklisted here in alphabetical order.

		NM	EX	VG
Complete Set (30):		60.00	30.00	18.00
Common Player:		4.00	2.00	1.25
(1)	Jim Davenport	4.00	2.00	1.25
(2)	Bob Davis	4.00	2.00	1.25
(3)	Rich Folkers	4.00	2.00	1.25
(4)	Alan Foster	4.00	2.00	1.25
(5)	Dave Freisleben	4.00	2.00	1.25
(6)	Danny Frisella	4.00	2.00	1.25
(7)	Tito Fuentes	4.00	2.00	1.25
(8)	Bill Greif	4.00	2.00	1.25
(9)	Johnny Grubb	4.00	2.00	1.25
(10)	Enzo Hernandez	4.00	2.00	1.25
(11)	Randy Hundley (Blank back.)	4.00	2.00	1.25
(12)	Mike Ivie	4.00	2.00	1.25
(13)	Jerry Johnson	4.00	2.00	1.25
(14)	Randy Jones	4.00	2.00	1.25
(15)	Fred Kendall	4.00	2.00	1.25
(16)	Ted Kubiak	4.00	2.00	1.25
(17)	Gene Locklear	4.00	2.00	1.25
(18)	Willie McCovey	10.00	5.00	3.00
(19)	Joe McIntosh	4.00	2.00	1.25
(20)	John McNamara	4.00	2.00	1.25
(21)	Tom Morgan	4.00	2.00	1.25
(22)	Dick Sharon	4.00	2.00	1.25
(23)	Dick Sisler	4.00	2.00	1.25
(24)	Dan Spillner	4.00	2.00	1.25
(25)	Brent Strom	4.00	2.00	1.25
(26)	Bobby Tolan	4.00	2.00	1.25
(27)	Dave Tomlin	4.00	2.00	1.25
(28)	Hector Torres (Blank back.)	4.00	2.00	1.25
(29)	Whitey Wietelmann	4.00	2.00	1.25
(30)	Dave Winfield	15.00	7.50	4.50

1976 Dean's Photo Service San Diego Padres

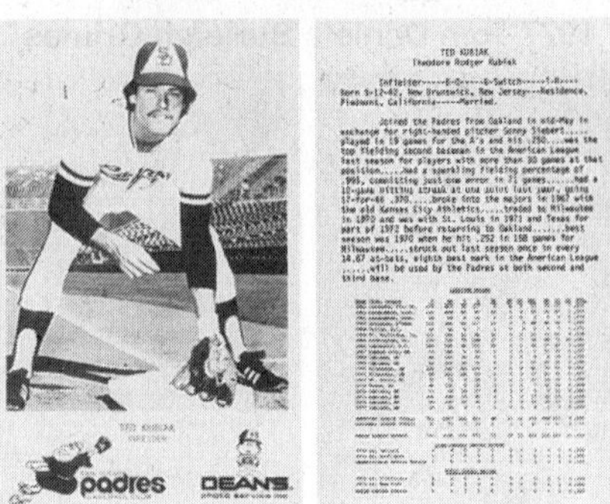

The last of four black-and-white team sets which were sponsored by Dean's was issued in 1976. The format was little different than previous years. Cards are 5-1/2" x 8-1/2" black-and-white. Fronts have a player portrait or pose surrounded by a white border. At bottom front are team and sponsor logos. Backs have personal data, a career summary and complete professional stats. The unnumbered cards are checklisted here in alphabetical order.

		NM	EX	VG
Complete Set (30):		60.00	30.00	18.00
Common Player:		4.00	2.00	1.25
(1)	Joe Amalfitano	4.00	2.00	1.25
(2)	Roger Craig	4.00	2.00	1.25
(3)	Bob Davis	4.00	2.00	1.25
(4)	Willie Davis	4.00	2.00	1.25
(5)	Rich Folkers	4.00	2.00	1.25
(6)	Alan Foster	4.00	2.00	1.25
(7)	Dave Freisleben	4.00	2.00	1.25
(8)	Tito Fuentes	4.00	2.00	1.25
(9)	John Grubb	4.00	2.00	1.25
(10)	Enzo Hernandez	4.00	2.00	1.25
(11)	Mike Ivie	4.00	2.00	1.25
(12)	Jerry Johnson	4.00	2.00	1.25
(13)	Randy Jones	4.00	2.00	1.25
(14)	Fred Kendall	4.00	2.00	1.25
(15)	Ted Kubiak	4.00	2.00	1.25
(16)	Willie McCovey	10.00	5.00	3.00
(17)	John McNamara	4.00	2.00	1.25
(18)	Luis Melendez	4.00	2.00	1.25
(19)	Butch Metzger	4.00	2.00	1.25
(20)	Doug Rader	4.00	2.00	1.25
(21)	Merv Rettenmund	4.00	2.00	1.25
(22)	Ken Reynolds	4.00	2.00	1.25
(23)	Dick Sisler	4.00	2.00	1.25
(24)	Dan Spillner	4.00	2.00	1.25
(25)	Brent Strom	4.00	2.00	1.25
(26)	Dave Tomlin	4.00	2.00	1.25
(27)	Hector Torres	4.00	2.00	1.25
(28)	Jerry Turner	4.00	2.00	1.25
(29)	Whitey Wietelmann	4.00	2.00	1.25
(30)	Dave Winfield	15.00	7.50	4.50

1938 Dizzy Dean's Service Station

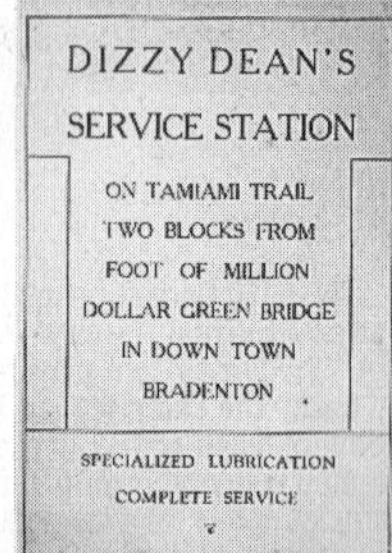
DIZZY DEAN'S
SERVICE STATION
ON TAMIAMI TRAIL
TWO BLOCKS FROM
FOOT OF MILLION
DOLLAR GREEN BRIDGE
IN DOWN TOWN
BRADENTON
SPECIALIZED LUBRICATION
COMPLETE SERVICE
STANDARD OIL PRODUCTS

The date of issue of this one-card set is only a guess. The 4" x 6" black-and-white card advertises Dean's service station in Florida.

	NM	EX	VG
Dizzy Dean	350.00	175.00	100.00

1978 Dearborn Show

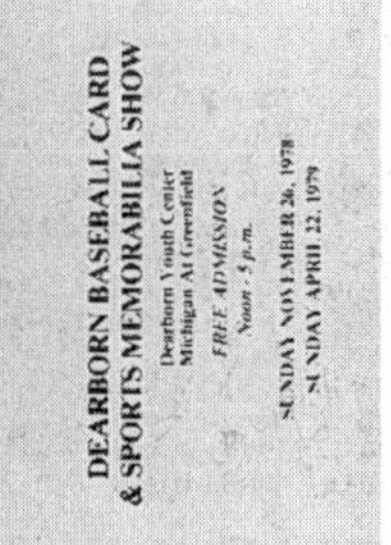

Former members of the Detroit Tigers, some of whom were scheduled to appear as autograph guests, are featured in this collectors' issue produced in conjunction with the 1978 Dearborn Baseball Card & Sports Memorabilia Show. The 2-5/8" x 3-5/8" cards have black-and-white player photos on front with the player name and card number in the white border at bottom. Backs, also in black-and-white, advertise the fall, 1978, and spring, 1979 shows.

		NM	EX	VG
Complete Set (18):		60.00	30.00	18.00
Common Player:		4.00	2.00	1.25
1	Rocky Colavito	15.00	7.50	4.50
2	Ervin Fox	4.00	2.00	1.25
3	Lynwood Rowe	4.00	2.00	1.25
4	Gerald Walker	4.00	2.00	1.25
5	Leon Goslin	4.00	2.00	1.25
6	Harvey Kuenn	6.00	3.00	1.75
7	Frank Howard	6.00	3.00	1.75
8	Woodie Fryman	4.00	2.00	1.25
9	Don Wert	4.00	2.00	1.25
10	Jim Perry	4.00	2.00	1.25
11	Mayo Smith	4.00	2.00	1.25
12	Al Kaline	20.00	10.00	6.00
13	Norm Cash	12.00	6.00	3.50
14	Mickey Cochrane	9.00	4.50	2.75
15	Fred Marberry	4.00	2.00	1.25
16	Bill Freehan	6.00	3.00	1.75
17	Charlie Gehringer	9.00	4.50	2.75
18	Jim Northrup	4.00	2.00	1.25

1980 Delacorte Press

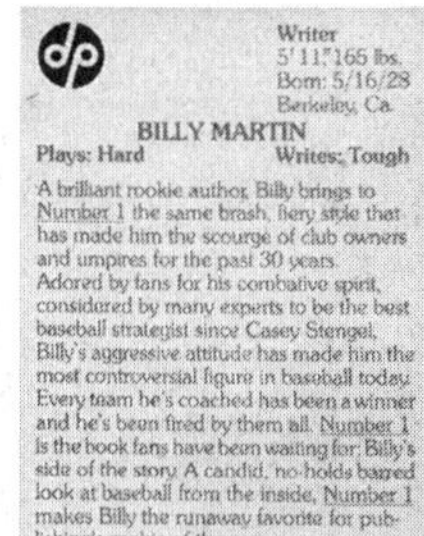

As a promotion for its book, "Number 1," written by Billy Martin, Delacorte Press issued this card picturing Martin somewhat in the style of a 1978 Topps manager card. The 3-1/2" x 2-1/2" card has a black-and-white photo of Martin as a Yankees manager, and a color photo as the A's manager. The front is bordered in red. Backs are printed in black, white and red with biographical details and promotional copy for the book.

		NM	EX	VG
1	Billy Martin	6.00	3.00	1.75

1971 Dell Today's Team Stamps

JACK
DILAURO
Pitcher – Bats right and left, throws right. Born 1943. Height 6-2. Weight 185. Relieved 42 times in 1970. Has good breaking ball and control. Good fielding pitcher who demonstrated ability to win three straight years in Triple-A ball. Originally signed by Tigers.

This issue was produced as a series of individual team (plus one All-Star) albums. The 8-1/2" x 10-7/8" booklets offer team and league histories and stats, photos of all-time team stars and two pages of 12 player stamps each. Each stamp is 1-7/8" x 2-15/16" and has a posed color photo and black facsimile autograph on front. Backs have the player name, biographical details and a few career highlights, along with an underprint of the team logo. The stamps are perforated for easy seperation, though there are no spaces in the 12-page album for their housing once removed from the sheet. The team albums were sold individually (39 cents) as well as in six-team divisional sets ($2). The checklist is arranged alphabetically by team within league; individual stamps are unnumbered.

		NM	EX	VG
Complete Set, Albums (25):		225.00	110.00	65.00
Complete Set, Stamps (600):		175.00	90.00	50.00
Common Player:		1.00	.50	.30
	Complete All-Star Album:	20.00	10.00	6.00
(1)	Hank Aaron	7.50	3.75	2.25
(2)	Luis Aparicio	2.50	1.25	.70
(3)	Ernie Banks	5.00	2.50	1.50
(4)	Johnny Bench	3.00	1.50	.90
(5)	Rico Carty	1.00	.50	.30
(6)	Roberto Clemente	10.00	5.00	3.00
(7)	Bob Gibson	2.50	1.25	.70
(8)	Willie Horton	1.00	.50	.30
(9)	Frank Howard	1.50	.70	.45
(10)	Reggie Jackson	6.00	3.00	1.75
(11)	Fergie Jenkins	1.50	.70	.45
(12)	Alex Johnson	1.00	.50	.30
(13)	Al Kaline	3.00	1.50	.90
(14)	Harmon Killebrew	3.00	1.50	.90
(15)	Willie Mays	7.50	3.75	2.25
(16)	Sam McDowell	1.00	.50	.30
(17)	Denny McLain	1.50	.70	.45
(18)	Boog Powell	1.50	.70	.45
(19)	Brooks Robinson	3.00	1.50	.90
(20)	Frank Robinson	3.00	1.50	.90
(21)	Pete Rose	7.50	3.75	2.25
(22)	Tom Seaver	3.00	1.50	.90
(23)	Rusty Staub	1.50	.70	.45
(24)	Carl Yastrzemski	3.00	1.50	.90
	Complete Atlanta Braves Album:	15.00	7.50	4.50
(1)	Hank Aaron	7.50	3.75	2.25
(2)	Tommie Aaron	1.00	.50	.30
(3)	Hank Allen	1.00	.50	.30
(4)	Clete Boyer	1.50	.70	.45
(5)	Oscar Brown	1.00	.50	.30
(6)	Rico Carty	1.00	.50	.30
(7)	Orlando Cepeda	2.50	1.25	.70
(8)	Bob Didier	1.00	.50	.30
(9)	Ralph Garr	1.00	.50	.30
(10)	Gil Garrido	1.00	.50	.30
(11)	Ron Herbel	1.00	.50	.30
(12)	Sonny Jackson	1.00	.50	.30
(13)	Pat Jarvis	1.00	.50	.30
(14)	Larry Jaster	1.00	.50	.30
(15)	Hal King	1.00	.50	.30
(16)	Mike Lum	1.00	.50	.30
(17)	Felix Millan	1.00	.50	.30
(18)	Jim Nash	1.00	.50	.30
(19)	Phil Niekro	2.00	1.00	.60
(20)	Bob Priddy	1.00	.50	.30
(21)	Ron Reed	1.00	.50	.30
(22)	George Stone	1.00	.50	.30
(23)	Cecil Upshaw	1.00	.50	.30
(24)	Hoyt Wilhelm	2.00	1.00	.60
	Complete Chicago Cubs Album:	15.00	7.50	4.50
(1)	Ernie Banks	5.00	2.50	1.50
(2)	Glenn Beckert	1.00	.50	.30
(3)	Danny Breeden	1.00	.50	.30
(4)	Johnny Callison	1.00	.50	.30
(5)	Jim Colborn	1.00	.50	.30
(6)	Joe Decker	1.00	.50	.30
(7)	Bill Hands	1.00	.50	.30
(8)	Jim Hickman	1.00	.50	.30
(9)	Ken Holtzman	1.00	.50	.30
(10)	Randy Hundley	1.00	.50	.30
(11)	Fergie Jenkins	2.00	1.00	.60
(12)	Don Kessinger	1.00	.50	.30
(13)	J.C. Martin	1.00	.50	.30
(14)	Bob Miller	1.00	.50	.30
(15)	Milt Pappas	1.00	.50	.30
(16)	Joe Pepitone	1.00	.50	.30
(17)	Juan Pizarro	1.00	.50	.30
(18)	Paul Popovich	1.00	.50	.30
(19)	Phil Regan	1.00	.50	.30
(20)	Roberto Rodriguez	1.00	.50	.30
(21)	Ken Rudolph	1.00	.50	.30
(22)	Ron Santo	1.50	.70	.45
(23)	Hector Torres	1.00	.50	.30
(24)	Billy Williams	2.50	1.25	.70
	Complete Cincinnati Reds Album:	20.00	10.00	6.00
(1)	Johnny Bench	3.00	1.50	.90
(2)	Angel Bravo	1.00	.50	.30
(3)	Bernie Carbo	1.00	.50	.30
(4)	Clay Carroll	1.00	.50	.30
(5)	Darrel Chaney	1.00	.50	.30
(6)	Ty Cline	1.00	.50	.30
(7)	Tony Cloninger	1.00	.50	.30
(8)	Dave Concepcion	1.00	.50	.30
(9)	Pat Corrales	1.00	.50	.30
(10)	Greg Garrett	1.00	.50	.30
(11)	Wayne Granger	1.00	.50	.30
(12)	Don Gullett	1.00	.50	.30
(13)	Tommy Helms	1.00	.50	.30
(14)	Lee May	1.00	.50	.30
(15)	Jim McGlothlin	1.00	.50	.30
(16)	Hal McRae	1.00	.50	.30
(17)	Jim Merritt	1.00	.50	.30
(18)	Gary Nolan	1.00	.50	.30
(19)	Tony Perez	2.50	1.25	.70
(20)	Pete Rose	7.50	3.75	2.25
(21)	Wayne Simpson	1.00	.50	.30
(22)	Jimmy Stewart	1.00	.50	.30
(23)	Bobby Tolan	1.00	.50	.30
(24)	Woody Woodward	1.00	.50	.30
	Complete Houston Astros Album:	10.00	5.00	3.00
(1)	Jesus Alou	1.00	.50	.30
(2)	Jack Billingham	1.00	.50	.30
(3)	Ron Cook	1.00	.50	.30
(4)	George Culver	1.00	.50	.30
(5)	Larry Dierker	1.00	.50	.30
(6)	Jack DiLauro	1.00	.50	.30
(7)	Johnny Edwards	1.00	.50	.30
(8)	Fred Gladding	1.00	.50	.30
(9)	Tom Griffin	1.00	.50	.30
(10)	Skip Guinn	1.00	.50	.30
(11)	Jack Hiatt	1.00	.50	.30
(12)	Denny Lemaster	1.00	.50	.30
(13)	Marty Martinez	1.00	.50	.30
(14)	John Mayberry	1.00	.50	.30
(15)	Denis Menke	1.00	.50	.30
(16)	Norm Miller	1.00	.50	.30
(17)	Joe Morgan	2.50	1.25	.70
(18)	Doug Rader	1.00	.50	.30
(19)	Jim Ray	1.00	.50	.30
(20)	Scipio Spinks	1.00	.50	.30
(21)	Bob Watkins	1.00	.50	.30
(22)	Bob Watson	1.00	.50	.30
(23)	Don Wilson	1.00	.50	.30
(24)	Jim Wynn	1.00	.50	.30
	Complete Los Angeles Dodgers Album:	12.50	6.25	3.75
(1)	Rich Allen	1.50	.70	.45
(2)	Jim Brewer	1.00	.50	.30
(3)	Bill Buckner	1.00	.50	.30
(4)	Willie Crawford	1.00	.50	.30
(5)	Willie Davis	1.00	.50	.30
(6)	Al Downing	1.00	.50	.30
(7)	Steve Garvey	6.00	3.00	1.75
(8)	Billy Grabarkewitz	1.00	.50	.30
(9)	Tom Haller	1.00	.50	.30
(10)	Jim Lefebvre	1.00	.50	.30
(11)	Pete Mikkelsen	1.00	.50	.30
(12)	Joe Moeller	1.00	.50	.30
(13)	Manny Mota	1.00	.50	.30
(14)	Claude Osteen	1.00	.50	.30
(15)	Wes Parker	1.00	.50	.30
(16)	Jose Pena	1.00	.50	.30
(17)	Bill Russell	1.00	.50	.30
(18)	Duke Sims	1.00	.50	.30
(19)	Bill Singer	1.00	.50	.30
(20)	Mike Strahler	1.00	.50	.30
(21)	Bill Sudakis	1.00	.50	.30
(22)	Don Sutton	2.00	1.00	.60
(23)	Jeff Torborg	1.00	.50	.30
(24)	Maury Wills	1.00	.50	.30
	Complete Montreal Expos Album:	10.00	5.00	3.00
(1)	Bob Bailey	1.00	.50	.30
(2)	John Bateman	1.00	.50	.30
(3)	John Boccabella	1.00	.50	.30
(4)	Ron Brand	1.00	.50	.30
(5)	Boots Day	1.00	.50	.30
(6)	Jim Fairey	1.00	.50	.30
(7)	Ron Fairly	1.00	.50	.30
(8)	Jim Gosger	1.00	.50	.30
(9)	Don Hahn	1.00	.50	.30
(10)	Ron Hunt	1.00	.50	.30
(11)	Mack Jones	1.00	.50	.30
(12)	Jose Laboy	1.00	.50	.30
(13)	Mike Marshall	1.00	.50	.30
(14)	Dan McGinn	1.00	.50	.30
(15)	Carl Morton	1.00	.50	.30
(16)	John O'Donoghue	1.00	.50	.30
(17)	Adolfo Phillips	1.00	.50	.30
(18)	Claude Raymond	1.00	.50	.30
(19)	Steve Renko	1.00	.50	.30
(20)	Marv Staehle	1.00	.50	.30
(21)	Rusty Staub	1.25	.60	.40
(22)	Bill Stoneman	1.00	.50	.30
(23)	Gary Sutherland	1.00	.50	.30
(24)	Bobby Wine	1.00	.50	.30
	Complete New York Mets Album:	25.00	12.50	7.50
(1)	Tommie Agee	1.00	.50	.30
(2)	Bob Aspromonte	1.00	.50	.30
(3)	Ken Boswell	1.00	.50	.30
(4)	Dean Chance	1.00	.50	.30
(5)	Donn Clendenon	1.00	.50	.30
(6)	Duffy Dyer	1.00	.50	.30
(7)	Dan Frisella	1.00	.50	.30
(8)	Wayne Garrett	1.00	.50	.30
(9)	Gary Gentry	1.00	.50	.30
(10)	Jerry Grote	1.00	.50	.30
(11)	Bud Harrelson	1.00	.50	.30
(12)	Cleon Jones	1.00	.50	.30
(13)	Jerry Koosman	1.00	.50	.30
(14)	Ed Kranepool	1.00	.50	.30
(15)	Dave Marshall	1.00	.50	.30
(16)	Jim McAndrew	1.00	.50	.30
(17)	Tug McGraw	1.00	.50	.30
(18)	Nolan Ryan	20.00	10.00	6.00
(19)	Ray Sadecki	1.00	.50	.30
(20)	Tom Seaver	3.00	1.50	.90
(21)	Art Shamsky	1.00	.50	.30
(22)	Ron Swoboda	1.00	.50	.30
(23)	Ron Taylor	1.00	.50	.30
(24)	Al Weis	1.00	.50	.30
	Complete Philadelphia Phillies Album:	10.00	5.00	3.00
(1)	Larry Bowa	1.00	.50	.30
(2)	Johnny Briggs	1.00	.50	.30
(3)	Bryon Browne	1.00	.50	.30
(4)	Jim Bunning	2.00	1.00	.60
(5)	Billy Champion	1.00	.50	.30

(6)	Mike Compton	1.00	.50	.30
(7)	Denny Doyle	1.00	.50	.30
(8)	Roger Freed	1.00	.50	.30
(9)	Woody Fryman	1.00	.50	.30
(10)	Oscar Gamble	1.00	.50	.30
(11)	Terry Harmon	1.00	.50	.30
(12)	Larry Hisle	1.00	.50	.30
(13)	Joe Hoerner	1.00	.50	.30
(14)	Deron Johnson	1.00	.50	.30
(15)	Barry Lersch	1.00	.50	.30
(16)	Tim McCarver	1.50	.70	.45
(17)	Don Money	1.00	.50	.30
(18)	Mike Ryan	1.00	.50	.30
(19)	Dick Selma	1.00	.50	.30
(20)	Chris Short	1.00	.50	.30
(21)	Ron Stone	1.00	.50	.30
(22)	Tony Taylor	1.00	.50	.30
(23)	Rick Wise	1.00	.50	.30
(24)	Billy Wilson	1.00	.50	.30
	Complete Pittsburgh Pirates Album:	30.00	15.00	9.00
(1)	Gene Alley	1.00	.50	.30
(2)	Steve Blass	1.00	.50	.30
(3)	Nelson Briles	1.00	.50	.30
(4)	Jim Campanis	1.00	.50	.30
(5)	Dave Cash	1.00	.50	.30
(6)	Roberto Clemente	10.00	5.00	3.00
(7)	Vic Davalillo	1.00	.50	.30
(8)	Dock Ellis	1.00	.50	.30
(9)	Jim Grant	1.00	.50	.30
(10)	Dave Giusti	1.00	.50	.30
(11)	Richie Hebner	1.00	.50	.30
(12)	Jackie Hernandez	1.00	.50	.30
(13)	Johnny Jeter	1.00	.50	.30
(14)	Lou Marone	1.00	.50	.30
(15)	Jose Martinez	1.00	.50	.30
(16)	Bill Mazeroski	2.50	1.25	.70
(17)	Bob Moose	1.00	.50	.30
(18)	Al Oliver	1.25	.60	.40
(19)	Jose Pagan	1.00	.50	.30
(20)	Bob Robertson	1.00	.50	.30
(21)	Manny Sanguillen	1.00	.50	.30
(22)	Willie Stargell	2.50	1.25	.70
(23)	Bob Veale	1.00	.50	.30
(24)	Luke Walker	1.00	.50	.30
	Complete San Diego Padres Album:	10.00	5.00	3.00
(1)	Jose Arcia	1.00	.50	.30
(2)	Bob Barton	1.00	.50	.30
(3)	Fred Beene	1.00	.50	.30
(4)	Ollie Brown	1.00	.50	.30
(5)	Dave Campbell	1.00	.50	.30
(6)	Chris Cannizzaro	1.00	.50	.30
(7)	Nate Colbert	1.00	.50	.30
(8)	Mike Corkins	1.00	.50	.30
(9)	Tommy Dean	1.00	.50	.30
(10)	Al Ferrara	1.00	.50	.30
(11)	Rod Gaspar	1.00	.50	.30
(12)	Cito Gaston	1.00	.50	.30
(13)	Enzo Hernandez	1.00	.50	.30
(14)	Clay Kirby	1.00	.50	.30
(15)	Don Mason	1.00	.50	.30
(16)	Ivan Murrell	1.00	.50	.30
(17)	Gerry Nyman	1.00	.50	.30
(18)	Tom Phoebus	1.00	.50	.30
(19)	Dave Roberts	1.00	.50	.30
(20)	Gary Ross	1.00	.50	.30
(21)	Al Santorini	1.00	.50	.30
(22)	Al Severinsen	1.00	.50	.30
(23)	Ron Slocum	1.00	.50	.30
(24)	Ed Spiezio	1.00	.50	.30
	Complete San Francisco Giants Album:	12.50	6.25	3.75
(1)	Bobby Bonds	1.25	.60	.40
(2)	Ron Bryant	1.00	.50	.30
(3)	Don Carrithers	1.00	.50	.30
(4)	John Cumberland	1.00	.50	.30
(5)	Mike Davison	1.00	.50	.30
(6)	Dick Dietz	1.00	.50	.30
(7)	Tito Fuentes	1.00	.50	.30
(8)	Russ Gibson	1.00	.50	.30
(9)	Jim Ray Hart	1.00	.50	.30
(10)	Bob Heise	1.00	.50	.30
(11)	Ken Henderson	1.00	.50	.30
(12)	Steve Huntz	1.00	.50	.30
(13)	Frank Johnson	1.00	.50	.30
(14)	Jerry Johnson	1.00	.50	.30
(15)	Hal Lanier	1.00	.50	.30
(16)	Juan Marichal	2.00	1.00	.60
(17)	Willie Mays	7.50	3.75	2.25
(18)	Willie McCovey	2.50	1.25	.70
(19)	Don McMahon	1.00	.50	.30
(20)	Jim Moyer	1.00	.50	.30
(21)	Gaylord Perry	2.00	1.00	.60
(22)	Frank Reberger	1.00	.50	.30
(23)	Rich Robertson	1.00	.50	.30
(24)	Bernie Williams	1.00	.50	.30
	Complete St. Louis Cardinals Album:	10.00	5.00	3.00
(1)	Matty Alou	1.00	.50	.30
(2)	Jim Beauchamp	1.00	.50	.30
(3)	Frank Bertaina	1.00	.50	.30
(4)	Lou Brock	2.50	1.25	.70
(5)	George Brunet	1.00	.50	.30
(6)	Jose Cardenal	1.00	.50	.30
(7)	Steve Carlton	2.50	1.25	.70
(8)	Moe Drabowsky	1.00	.50	.30
(9)	Bob Gibson	2.50	1.25	.70
(10)	Joe Hague	1.00	.50	.30
(11)	Julian Javier	1.00	.50	.30
(12)	Leron Lee	1.00	.50	.30
(13)	Frank Linzy	1.00	.50	.30
(14)	Dal Maxvill	1.00	.50	.30
(15)	Jerry McNertney	1.00	.50	.30
(16)	Fred Norman	1.00	.50	.30
(17)	Milt Ramirez	1.00	.50	.30
(18)	Dick Schofield	1.00	.50	.30
(19)	Mike Shannon	1.00	.50	.30
(20)	Ted Sizemore	1.00	.50	.30
(21)	Bob Stinson	1.00	.50	.30
(22)	Carl Taylor	1.00	.50	.30
(23)	Joe Torre	1.50	.70	.45
(24)	Mike Torrez	1.00	.50	.30
	Complete Baltimore Orioles Album:	15.00	7.50	4.50
(1)	Mark Belanger	1.00	.50	.30
(2)	Paul Blair	1.00	.50	.30
(3)	Don Buford	1.00	.50	.30
(4)	Terry Crowley	1.00	.50	.30
(5)	Mike Cuellar	1.00	.50	.30
(6)	Clay Dalrymple	1.00	.50	.30
(7)	Pat Dobson	1.00	.50	.30
(8)	Andy Etchebarren	1.00	.50	.30
(9)	Dick Hall	1.00	.50	.30
(10)	Jim Hardin	1.00	.50	.30
(11)	Elrod Hendricks	1.00	.50	.30
(12)	Grant Jackson	1.00	.50	.30
(13)	Dave Johnson	1.00	.50	.30
(14)	Dave Leonhard	1.00	.50	.30
(15)	Marcelino Lopez	1.00	.50	.30
(16)	Dave McNally	1.00	.50	.30
(17)	Curt Motton	1.00	.50	.30
(18)	Jim Palmer	2.00	1.00	.60
(19)	Boog Powell	1.00	.50	.30
(20)	Merv Rettenmund	1.00	.50	.30
(21)	Brooks Robinson	3.00	1.50	.90
(22)	Frank Robinson	3.00	1.50	.90
(23)	Pete Richert	1.00	.50	.30
(24)	Chico Salmon	1.00	.50	.30
	Complete Boston Red Sox Album:	15.00	7.50	4.50
(1)	Luis Aparicio	2.50	1.25	.70
(2)	Bobby Bolin	1.00	.50	.30
(3)	Ken Brett	1.00	.50	.30
(4)	Billy Conigliaro	1.00	.50	.30
(5)	Ray Culp	1.00	.50	.30
(6)	Mike Flore	1.00	.50	.30
(7)	John Kennedy	1.00	.50	.30
(8)	Cal Koonce	1.00	.50	.30
(9)	Joe Lahoud	1.00	.50	.30
(10)	Bill Lee	1.00	.50	.30
(11)	Jim Lonborg	1.00	.50	.30
(12)	Sparky Lyle	1.00	.50	.30
(13)	Mike Nagy	1.00	.50	.30
(14)	Don Pavletich	1.00	.50	.30
(15)	Gary Peters	1.00	.50	.30
(16)	Rico Petrocelli	1.00	.50	.30
(17)	Vicente Romo	1.00	.50	.30
(18)	Tom Satriano	1.00	.50	.30
(19)	George Scott	1.00	.50	.30
(20)	Sonny Siebert	1.00	.50	.30
(21)	Reggie Smith	1.00	.50	.30
(22)	Jarvis Tatum	1.00	.50	.30
(23)	Ken Tatum	1.00	.50	.30
(24)	Carl Yastrzemski	3.00	1.50	.90
	Complete California Angels Album:	10.00	5.00	3.00
(1)	Sandy Alomar	1.00	.50	.30
(2)	Joe Azcue	1.00	.50	.30
(3)	Ken Berry	1.00	.50	.30
(4)	Gene Brabender	1.00	.50	.30
(5)	Billy Cowan	1.00	.50	.30
(6)	Tony Conigliaro	1.50	.70	.45
(7)	Eddie Fisher	1.00	.50	.30
(8)	Jim Fregosi	1.00	.50	.30
(9)	Tony Gonzales (Gonzalez)	1.00	.50	.30
(10)	Alex Johnson	1.00	.50	.30
(11)	Fred Lasher	1.00	.50	.30
(12)	Jim Maloney	1.00	.50	.30
(13)	Rudy May	1.00	.50	.30
(14)	Ken McMullen	1.00	.50	.30
(15)	Andy Messersmith	1.00	.50	.30
(16)	Gerry Moses	1.00	.50	.30
(17)	Syd O'Brien	1.00	.50	.30
(18)	Mel Queen	1.00	.50	.30
(19)	Roger Repoz	1.00	.50	.30
(20)	Archie Reynolds	1.00	.50	.30
(21)	Chico Ruiz	1.00	.50	.30
(22)	Jim Spencer	1.00	.50	.30
(23)	Clyde Wright	1.00	.50	.30
(24)	Billy Wynne	1.00	.50	.30
	Complete Chicago White Sox Album:	10.00	5.00	3.00
(1)	Luis Alvarado	1.00	.50	.30
(2)	Mike Andrews	1.00	.50	.30
(3)	Tom Egan	1.00	.50	.30
(4)	Steve Hamilton	1.00	.50	.30
(5)	Ed Hermann	1.00	.50	.30
(6)	Joel Horlen	1.00	.50	.30
(7)	Tommy John	1.25	.60	.40
(8)	Bart Johnson	1.00	.50	.30
(9)	Jay Johnstone	1.00	.50	.30
(10)	Duane Josephson	1.00	.50	.30
(11)	Pat Kelly	1.00	.50	.30
(12)	Bobby Knoop	1.00	.50	.30
(13)	Carlos May	1.00	.50	.30
(14)	Lee Maye	1.00	.50	.30
(15)	Tom McGraw	1.00	.50	.30
(16)	Bill Melton	1.00	.50	.30
(17)	Rich Morales	1.00	.50	.30
(18)	Tom Murphy	1.00	.50	.30
(19)	Don O'Riley	1.00	.50	.30
(20)	Rick Reichardt	1.00	.50	.30
(21)	Bill Robinson	1.00	.50	.30
(22)	Bob Spence	1.00	.50	.30
(23)	Walt Williams	1.00	.50	.30
(24)	Wilbur Wood	1.00	.50	.30
	Complete Cleveland Indians Album:	10.00	5.00	3.00
(1)	Rick Austin	1.00	.50	.30
(2)	Buddy Bradford	1.00	.50	.30
(3)	Larry Brown	1.00	.50	.30
(4)	Lou Camilli	1.00	.50	.30
(5)	Vince Colbert	1.00	.50	.30
(6)	Ray Fosse	1.00	.50	.30
(7)	Alan Foster	1.00	.50	.30
(8)	Roy Foster	1.00	.50	.30
(9)	Rich Hand	1.00	.50	.30
(10)	Steve Hargan	1.00	.50	.30
(11)	Ken Harrelson	1.00	.50	.30
(12)	Jack Heidemann	1.00	.50	.30
(13)	Phil Hennigan	1.00	.50	.30
(14)	Dennis Higgins	1.00	.50	.30
(15)	Chuck Hinton	1.00	.50	.30
(16)	Tony Horton	1.00	.50	.30
(17)	Ray Lamb	1.00	.50	.30
(18)	Eddie Leon	1.00	.50	.30
(19)	Sam McDowell	1.00	.50	.30
(20)	Graig Nettles	1.25	.60	.40
(21)	Mike Paul	1.00	.50	.30
(22)	Vada Pinson	1.25	.60	.40
(23)	Ken Suarez	1.00	.50	.30
(24)	Ted Uhlaender	1.00	.50	.30
	Complete Detroit Tigers Album:	10.00	5.00	3.00
(1)	Ed Brinkman	1.00	.50	.30
(2)	Gates Brown	1.00	.50	.30
(3)	Ike Brown	1.00	.50	.30
(4)	Les Cain	1.00	.50	.30
(5)	Norm Cash	1.50	.70	.45
(6)	Joe Coleman	1.00	.50	.30
(7)	Bill Freehan	1.00	.50	.30
(8)	Cesar Gutierrez	1.00	.50	.30
(9)	John Hiller	1.00	.50	.30
(10)	Willie Horton	1.00	.50	.30
(11)	Dalton Jones	1.00	.50	.30
(12)	Al Kaline	3.00	1.50	.90
(13)	Mike Kilkenny	1.00	.50	.30
(14)	Mickey Lolich	1.00	.50	.30
(15)	Dick McAuliffe	1.00	.50	.30
(16)	Joe Niekro	1.00	.50	.30
(17)	Jim Northrup	1.00	.50	.30
(18)	Daryl Patterson	1.00	.50	.30
(19)	Jimmie Price	1.00	.50	.30
(20)	Bob Reed	1.00	.50	.30
(21)	Aurelio Rodriguez	1.00	.50	.30
(22)	Fred Scherman	1.00	.50	.30
(23)	Mickey Stanley	1.00	.50	.30
(24)	Tom Timmermann	1.00	.50	.30
	Complete Kansas City Royals Album:	10.00	5.00	3.00
(1)	Ted Abernathy	1.00	.50	.30
(2)	Wally Bunker	1.00	.50	.30
(3)	Tom Burgmeier	1.00	.50	.30
(4)	Bill Butler	1.00	.50	.30
(5)	Bruce Dal Canton	1.00	.50	.30
(6)	Dick Drago	1.00	.50	.30
(7)	Bobby Floyd	1.00	.50	.30
(8)	Gail Hopkins	1.00	.50	.30
(9)	Joe Keough	1.00	.50	.30
(10)	Ed Kirkpatrick	1.00	.50	.30
(11)	Tom Matchick	1.00	.50	.30
(12)	Jerry May	1.00	.50	.30
(13)	Aurelio Monteagudo	1.00	.50	.30
(14)	Dave Morehead	1.00	.50	.30
(15)	Bob Oliver	1.00	.50	.30
(16)	Amos Otis	1.00	.50	.30
(17)	Fred Patek	1.00	.50	.30
(18)	Lou Piniella	1.25	.60	.40
(19)	Cookie Rojas	1.00	.50	.30
(20)	Jim Rooker	1.00	.50	.30
(21)	Paul Schaal	1.00	.50	.30
(22)	Rich Severson	1.00	.50	.30
(23)	George Spriggs	1.00	.50	.30
(24)	Carl Taylor	1.00	.50	.30
	Complete Milwaukee Brewers Album:	10.00	5.00	3.00
(1)	Dave Baldwin	1.00	.50	.30
(2)	Dick Ellsworth	1.00	.50	.30
(3)	John Gelnar	1.00	.50	.30
(4)	Tommy Harper	1.00	.50	.30
(5)	Mike Hegan	1.00	.50	.30
(6)	Bob Humphreys	1.00	.50	.30
(7)	Andy Kosco	1.00	.50	.30
(8)	Lew Krausse	1.00	.50	.30
(9)	Ted Kubiak	1.00	.50	.30
(10)	Skip Lockwood	1.00	.50	.30
(11)	Dave May	1.00	.50	.30
(12)	Bob Meyer	1.00	.50	.30
(13)	John Morris	1.00	.50	.30
(14)	Marty Pattin	1.00	.50	.30
(15)	Roberto Pena	1.00	.50	.30
(16)	Eduardo Rodriguez	1.00	.50	.30
(17)	Phil Roof	1.00	.50	.30
(18)	Ken Sanders	1.00	.50	.30
(19)	Ted Savage	1.00	.50	.30
(20)	Russ Snyder	1.00	.50	.30
(21)	Bob Tillman	1.00	.50	.30
(22)	Bill Voss	1.00	.50	.30
(23)	Danny Walton	1.00	.50	.30
(24)	Floyd Wicker	1.00	.50	.30
	Complete Minnesota Twins Album:	15.00	7.50	4.50
(1)	Brant Alyea	1.00	.50	.30
(2)	Bert Blyleven	1.00	.50	.30
(3)	Dave Boswell	1.00	.50	.30
(4)	Leo Cardenas	1.00	.50	.30
(5)	Rod Carew	2.50	1.25	.70
(6)	Tom Hall	1.00	.50	.30
(7)	Jim Holt	1.00	.50	.30
(8)	Jim Kaat	1.00	.50	.30
(9)	Harmon Killebrew	2.50	1.25	.70
(10)	Charlie Manuel	1.00	.50	.30
(11)	George Mitterwald	1.00	.50	.30
(12)	Tony Oliva	1.25	.60	.40
(13)	Ron Perranoski	1.00	.50	.30
(14)	Jim Perry	1.00	.50	.30
(15)	Frank Quilici	1.00	.50	.30
(16)	Rich Reese	1.00	.50	.30
(17)	Rick Renick	1.00	.50	.30
(18)	Danny Thompson	1.00	.50	.30
(19)	Luis Tiant	1.00	.50	.30
(20)	Tom Tischinski	1.00	.50	.30
(21)	Cesar Tovar	1.00	.50	.30

(22)	Stan Williams	1.00	.50	.30
(23)	Dick Woodson	1.00	.50	.30
(24)	Bill Zepp	1.00	.50	.30
	Complete New York Yankees Album:	15.00	7.50	4.50
(1)	Jack Aker	1.00	.50	.30
(2)	Stan Bahnsen	1.00	.50	.30
(3)	Curt Blefary	1.00	.50	.30
(4)	Bill Burbach	1.00	.50	.30
(5)	Danny Cater	1.00	.50	.30
(6)	Horace Clarke	1.00	.50	.30
(7)	John Ellis	1.00	.50	.30
(8)	Jake Gibbs	1.00	.50	.30
(9)	Ron Hansen	1.00	.50	.30
(10)	Mike Kekich	1.00	.50	.30
(11)	Jerry Kenney	1.00	.50	.30
(12)	Ron Klimkowski	1.00	.50	.30
(13)	Steve Kline	1.00	.50	.30
(14)	Mike McCormick	1.00	.50	.30
(15)	Lindy McDaniel	1.00	.50	.30
(16)	Gene Michael	1.00	.50	.30
(17)	Thurman Munson	1.50	.70	.45
(18)	Bobby Murcer	1.25	.60	.40
(19)	Fritz Peterson	1.00	.50	.30
(20)	Mel Stottlemyre	1.00	.50	.30
(21)	Pete Ward	1.00	.50	.30
(22)	Gary Waslewski	1.00	.50	.30
(23)	Roy White	1.00	.50	.30
(24)	Ron Woods	1.00	.50	.30
	Complete Oakland A's Album:	15.00	7.50	4.50
(1)	Felipe Alou	1.00	.50	.30
(2)	Sal Bando	1.00	.50	.30
(3)	Vida Blue	1.00	.50	.30
(4)	Bert Campaneris	1.00	.50	.30
(5)	Ron Clark	1.00	.50	.30
(6)	Chuck Dobson	1.00	.50	.30
(7)	Dave Duncan	1.00	.50	.30
(8)	Frank Fernandez	1.00	.50	.30
(9)	Rollie Fingers	2.00	1.00	.60
(10)	Dick Green	1.00	.50	.30
(11)	Steve Hovley	1.00	.50	.30
(12)	Catfish Hunter	2.00	1.00	.60
(13)	Reggie Jackson	6.00	3.00	1.75
(14)	Marcel Lacheman	1.00	.50	.30
(15)	Paul Lindblad	1.00	.50	.30
(16)	Bob Locker	1.00	.50	.30
(17)	Don Mincher	1.00	.50	.30
(18)	Rick Monday	1.00	.50	.30
(19)	John Odom	1.00	.50	.30
(20)	Jim Roland	1.00	.50	.30
(21)	Joe Rudi	1.00	.50	.30
(22)	Diego Segui	1.00	.50	.30
(23)	Bob Stickels	1.00	.50	.30
(24)	Gene Tenace	1.00	.50	.30
	Complete Washington Senators Album:	12.50	6.25	3.75
(1)	Bernie Allen	1.00	.50	.30
(2)	Dick Bosman	1.00	.50	.30
(3)	Jackie Brown	1.00	.50	.30
(4)	Paul Casanova	1.00	.50	.30
(5)	Casey Cox	1.00	.50	.30
(6)	Tim Cullen	1.00	.50	.30
(7)	Mike Epstein	1.00	.50	.30
(8)	Curt Flood	1.25	.60	.40
(9)	Joe Foy	1.00	.50	.30
(10)	Jim French	1.00	.50	.30
(11)	Bill Gogolewski	1.00	.50	.30
(12)	Tom Grieve	1.00	.50	.30
(13)	Joe Grzenda	1.00	.50	.30
(14)	Frank Howard	1.25	.60	.40
(15)	Joe Janeski	1.00	.50	.30
(16)	Darold Knowles	1.00	.50	.30
(17)	Elliott Maddox	1.00	.50	.30
(18)	Denny McLain	1.25	.60	.40
(19)	Dave Nelson	1.00	.50	.30
(20)	Horacio Pina	1.00	.50	.30
(21)	Jim Shellenback	1.00	.50	.30
(22)	Ed Stroud	1.00	.50	.30
(23)	Del Unser	1.00	.50	.30
(24)	Don Wert	1.00	.50	.30

1933 DeLong (R333)

The DeLong Co. of Boston was among the first to sell baseball cards with gum, issuing a set of 24 cards in 1933. DeLong cards measure about 1-15/16" x 2-15/16", with black-and-white player photos on a color background. The photos show the players in various action poses and positions them in the middle of a miniature stadium setting so that they appear to be giants. Most of the cards are vertically designed, but a few are horizontal. Backs were by Austen Lake, editor of the Boston Transcript, and contain tips to help youngsters become better ballplayers. The ACC designation for this set is R333.

		NM	EX	VG
	Complete Set (24):	30,000	8,000	4,000
	Common Player:	700.00	280.00	140.00
1	"Marty" McManus	1,260	280.00	140.00
2	Al Simmons	945.00	385.00	190.00
3	Oscar Melillo	700.00	280.00	140.00
4	William (Bill) Terry	945.00	385.00	190.00
5	Charlie Gehringer	945.00	385.00	190.00
6	Gordon (Mickey) Cochrane	945.00	385.00	190.00
7	Lou Gehrig	7,700	3,080	1,260
8	Hazen S. (Kiki) Cuyler	945.00	385.00	190.00
9	Bill Urbanski	700.00	280.00	140.00
10	Frank J. (Lefty) O'Doul	980.00	395.00	195.00
11	Freddie Lindstrom	945.00	385.00	190.00
12	Harold (Pie) Traynor	945.00	385.00	190.00
13	"Rabbit" Maranville	945.00	385.00	190.00
14	Vernon "Lefty" Gomez	945.00	385.00	190.00
15	Riggs Stephenson	700.00	280.00	140.00
16	Lon Warneke	700.00	280.00	140.00
17	Pepper Martin	700.00	280.00	140.00
18	Jimmy Dykes	700.00	280.00	140.00
19	Chick Hafey	945.00	385.00	190.00
20	Joe Vosmik	700.00	280.00	140.00
21	Jimmy Foxx (Jimmie)	1,260	505.00	250.00
22	Charles (Chuck) Klein	945.00	385.00	190.00
23	Robert (Lefty) Grove	1,540	595.00	300.00
24	"Goose" Goslin	945.00	385.00	190.00

1934 Al Demaree Die-cuts (R304)

Among the rarest 1930s gum cards are those issued by Dietz Gum Co., a Chicago confectioner, in packages of "Ball Players in Action Chewing Gum." The cards are so rare that the complete checklist may never be known. The set was cataloged as R304 in the American Card Catalog. The cards feature photographic portraits of players set upon cartoon bodies drawn by former major league pitcher Demaree. The photo and artwork are generally in black-and-white, while the players on some teams have blue or red uniform details printed on. The cards can be folded to create a stand-up figure, but did not have a background to be cut or torn away, as is common with most die-cut baseball cards. Unfolded, the cards measure 6-1/2" long and from 1-5/8" to 1-3/4" wide, depending on pose.

		NM	EX	VG
	Common Player:	500.00	250.00	150.00
3	Earle Combs	825.00	410.00	245.00
4	Babe Ruth	12,500	6,250	3,750
5	Sam Byrd	600.00	300.00	180.00
6	Tony Lazzeri	825.00	410.00	245.00
7	Frank Crosetti	750.00	375.00	225.00
9	Lou Gehrig	12,000	6,000	3,600
10	Lefty Gomez	825.00	410.00	245.00
11	Mule Haas	500.00	250.00	150.00
12	Evar Swenson	500.00	250.00	150.00
13	Marv Shea	500.00	250.00	150.00
14	Al Simmons/Throwing	825.00	410.00	245.00
15	Jack Hayes	500.00	250.00	150.00
16	Al Simmons/Btg	825.00	410.00	245.00
17	Jimmy Dykes	500.00	250.00	150.00
18	Luke Appling	825.00	410.00	245.00
19	Ted Lyons	825.00	410.00	245.00
20	Red Kress	500.00	250.00	150.00
21	Gee Walker	500.00	250.00	150.00
22	Charlie Gehringer	825.00	410.00	245.00
23	Mickey Cochrane/Catching	825.00	410.00	245.00
24	Mickey Cochrane/Btg	825.00	410.00	245.00
25	Pete Fox	500.00	250.00	150.00
26	Firpo Marberry	500.00	250.00	150.00
28	Mickey Owen	500.00	250.00	150.00
35	Joe Vosmik	500.00	250.00	150.00
38	Harley Boss	500.00	250.00	150.00
41	Jack Burns	500.00	250.00	150.00
45	Ray Pepper	500.00	250.00	150.00
46	Bruce Campbell	500.00	250.00	150.00
48	Art Scharein	500.00	250.00	150.00
49	George Blaeholder	500.00	250.00	150.00
50	Rogers Hornsby	1,100	550.00	330.00
51	Eric McNair	500.00	250.00	150.00
54	Jimmie Foxx	1,250	625.00	375.00
56	Dib Williams	500.00	250.00	150.00
57	Lou Finney	500.00	250.00	150.00
61	Ossie Bluege	500.00	250.00	150.00
63	John Stone	500.00	250.00	150.00
64	Joe Cronin	825.00	410.00	245.00
66	Buddy Myer	500.00	250.00	150.00
67	Earl Whitehill	500.00	250.00	150.00
68	Fred Schulte	500.00	250.00	150.00
71	Ed Morgan	500.00	250.00	150.00
74	Carl Reynolds	500.00	250.00	150.00
76	Bill Cissell	500.00	250.00	150.00
77	Johnny Hodapp	500.00	250.00	150.00
78	Dusty Cooke	500.00	250.00	150.00
79	Lefty Grove	825.00	410.00	245.00
80	Max Bishop	500.00	250.00	150.00
81	Hughie Critz	500.00	250.00	150.00
82	Gus Mancuso	500.00	250.00	150.00
83	Kiddo Davis	500.00	250.00	150.00
84	Blondy Ryan	500.00	250.00	150.00
86	Travis Jackson	825.00	410.00	245.00
87	Mel Ott	1,100	550.00	330.00
89	Bill Terry	825.00	410.00	245.00
90	Carl Hubbell	1,100	550.00	330.00
91	Tony Cuccinello	500.00	250.00	150.00
92	Al Lopez	825.00	410.00	245.00
94	Johnny Frederick	500.00	250.00	150.00
96	Hack Wilson	850.00	425.00	255.00
97	Danny Taylor	500.00	250.00	150.00
98	Van Mungo	500.00	250.00	150.00
99	John Frederick	500.00	250.00	150.00
100	Sam Leslie	500.00	250.00	150.00
101	Sparky Adams	500.00	250.00	150.00
102a	Mark Koenig	500.00	250.00	150.00
102b	Ernie Lombardi	825.00	410.00	245.00
107	Syl Johnson	500.00	250.00	150.00
108	Jim Bottomley	825.00	410.00	245.00
110	Adam Comorosky	500.00	250.00	150.00
111	Dick Bartell	500.00	250.00	150.00
112	Harvey Hendrick	500.00	250.00	150.00
115	Don Hurst/Btg	500.00	250.00	150.00
117	Prince Oana	900.00	450.00	270.00
118	Ed Holley	500.00	250.00	150.00
120	Don Hurst/Throwing	500.00	250.00	150.00
121	Spud Davis	500.00	250.00	150.00
122	George Watkins	500.00	250.00	150.00
123	Frankie Frisch	825.00	410.00	245.00
124	Pepper Martin/Btg	500.00	250.00	150.00
125	Ripper Collins	500.00	250.00	150.00
126	Dizzy Dean	1,250	625.00	375.00
127	Pepper Martin/Fldg	500.00	250.00	150.00
128	Joe Medwick	825.00	410.00	245.00
129	Leo Durocher	825.00	410.00	245.00
130	Ernie Orsatti	500.00	250.00	150.00
132	Shanty Hogan	500.00	250.00	150.00
133a	Wes Shulmerich (Schulmerich)	500.00	250.00	150.00
133b	Randy Moore	500.00	250.00	150.00
135	Wally Berger	500.00	250.00	150.00
136	Pinky Whitney	500.00	250.00	150.00
137	Wally Berger	500.00	250.00	150.00
139	Rabbit Maranville	825.00	410.00	245.00
140	Ben Cantwell	500.00	250.00	150.00
141	Gus Suhr	500.00	250.00	150.00
142	Earl Grace	500.00	250.00	150.00
144	Arky Vaughan	825.00	410.00	245.00
145	Pie Traynor/Htg	825.00	410.00	245.00
146	Tommy Thevenow	500.00	250.00	150.00
147	Lloyd Waner	825.00	410.00	245.00
148	Paul Waner	825.00	410.00	245.00
149	Pie Traynor/Throwing	825.00	410.00	245.00
151	Kiki Cuyler	825.00	410.00	245.00
152	Gabby Hartnett	825.00	410.00	245.00
153	Chuck Klein/Throwing	825.00	410.00	245.00
154	Chuck Klein	825.00	410.00	245.00
155	Bill Jurges	500.00	250.00	150.00
156	Woody English	500.00	250.00	150.00
158	Billy Herman	825.00	410.00	245.00
160	Charlie Grimm	500.00	250.00	150.00
161	Cy Rigler/Umpire	900.00	450.00	275.00
162	Bill Klem/Umpire	1,250	625.00	375.00
167	George Hildebrand/Umpire	500.00	250.00	150.00
	(Observed specimens of cards below have had the tabs removed making it impossible to identify card numbers.)			
----	Willie Kamm	500.00	250.00	150.00
----	Pinky Higgins	500.00	250.00	150.00
----	Bob Johnson	500.00	250.00	150.00
----	Roy Mahaffey	500.00	250.00	150.00
----	Buck Jordan	500.00	250.00	150.00

1950-51 Denia Puerto Rican League

This issue was produced in conjunction with the 1950-51 Puerto Rican League winter season. Measurements vary slightly from a norm of about 1-3/4" x 2-1/8". Cards have colorized portrait photos with blank backs, probably intended to be glued into an album. Cards are unnumbered. This checklist is alphabetized, with gaps left for what is believed to be 57 uncataloged cards. Some of the players are veterans of the Negro Leagues and American major and minor leagues. Black-and-white reprints of the cards are known. A few cards have been found with a prize-redemption stamp on back.

		NM	EX	VG
Common Player:		125.00	65.00	40.00
(1)	Alberto Alberdeston	125.00	65.00	40.00
(2)	Jaime Almendro	125.00	65.00	40.00
(3)	Yiyo Alonso	125.00	65.00	40.00
(4)	Luis (Tite) Arroyo	150.00	75.00	45.00
(5)	Pedro J. Arroyo	125.00	65.00	40.00
(6)	Joe Atkins	150.00	75.00	45.00
(7)	Eugene Baker	200.00	100.00	60.00
(8)	Dan Bankhead	200.00	100.00	60.00
(9)	Sammy Bankhead	1,200	600.00	360.00
(10)	Ramon Bayron	125.00	65.00	40.00
(11)	Hiram Bithorn	200.00	100.00	60.00
(12)	Rafael Blasini	125.00	65.00	40.00
(13)	Bob Boyd	150.00	75.00	45.00
(14)	Roger Breard	125.00	65.00	40.00
(15)	Stan Breard	125.00	65.00	40.00
(16)	Barney Brown	1,000	500.00	300.00
(17)	Raymond Brown	2,000	1,000	600.00
(18)	Willard Brown	2,000	1,000	600.00
(19)	Jose A. Burgos	125.00	65.00	40.00
(20)	Joe Buzas	125.00	65.00	40.00
(21)	Luis R. Cabrera	125.00	65.00	40.00
(22)	Rafael Casanovas	125.00	65.00	40.00
(23)	N. Zurdo Castro	125.00	65.00	40.00
(24)	Perucho Cepeda	800.00	400.00	240.00
(25)	T. Gomez Checo	125.00	65.00	40.00
(26)	Al Cihoki (Cihocki)	125.00	65.00	40.00
(27)	Buster Clarkson	250.00	125.00	75.00
(28)	Francisco Coimbre	800.00	400.00	240.00
(29)	Eugene Collins	350.00	175.00	105.00
(30)	Monchile Concepcion	150.00	75.00	45.00
(31)	Charlie Corin	125.00	65.00	40.00
(32)	Herminio Cortfu	125.00	65.00	40.00
(33)	Johnny Cox	125.00	65.00	40.00
(34)	George Crowe	200.00	100.00	60.00
(35)	Jim Davis	125.00	65.00	40.00
(36)	Johnny Davis	450.00	225.00	135.00
(37)	Piper Davis	450.00	225.00	135.00
(38)	Leon Day	6,000	3,000	1,800
(39)	Ellis "Cot" Deal	150.00	75.00	45.00
(40)	Jack Dittmer	125.00	65.00	40.00
(41)	Verdes Drake	150.00	75.00	45.00
(42)	Saturnino Escalera	125.00	65.00	40.00
(43)	C. Guillaro Estrella	125.00	65.00	40.00
(44)	S. Federico	125.00	65.00	40.00
(45)	Dumbo Fernandez	125.00	65.00	40.00
(46)	Elias Frias	125.00	65.00	40.00
(47)	Les Fusselmann (Fusselman)	125.00	65.00	40.00
(48)	Felipe Garcia	125.00	65.00	40.00
(49)	(Carden) Gillenwater	125.00	65.00	40.00
(50)	Jim Gilliam	250.00	125.00	75.00
(51)	Ruben Gomez	200.00	100.00	60.00
(52)	Faelo Gonzalez	125.00	65.00	40.00
(53)	Gely Goyco	125.00	65.00	40.00
(54)	Jack Harshmann (Harshman)	125.00	65.00	40.00
(55)	Rudy Hernandez	125.00	65.00	40.00
(56)	Roy Hughes	125.00	65.00	40.00
(57)	Pachy Irizarry	125.00	65.00	40.00
(58)	Indian (Indio) Jiminez	125.00	65.00	40.00
(59)	Sam Jones	125.00	65.00	40.00
(60)	Walt Judnich	125.00	65.00	40.00
(61)	Russ Kearns	125.00	65.00	40.00
(62)	Billy Klaus	150.00	75.00	45.00
(63)	Jim Lamarque	350.00	175.00	105.00
(64)	Red Lynn	125.00	65.00	40.00
(65)	Bob Malloy	125.00	65.00	40.00
(66)	Clifford Mapes	125.00	65.00	40.00
(67)	Canena Marquez	450.00	225.00	135.00
(68)	Achin Matos	125.00	65.00	40.00
(69)	Benny Meyers	125.00	65.00	40.00
(70)	Henry Miller	150.00	75.00	45.00
(71)	Oscar Mir Flores	125.00	65.00	40.00
(72)	Jose E. Montalvo	125.00	65.00	40.00
(73)	Willie Morales	125.00	65.00	40.00
(74)	Gallego Munoz	125.00	65.00	40.00
(75)	Earl Naylor	125.00	65.00	40.00
(76)	Ernest Nevel	125.00	65.00	40.00
(77)	Don Nicholas	125.00	65.00	40.00
(78)	John O'Donnell	125.00	65.00	40.00
(79)	Guayuvin Olivo	150.00	75.00	45.00
(80)	Miguel Payano	125.00	65.00	40.00
(81)	Les Peden	125.00	65.00	40.00
(82)	Juan Perez	125.00	65.00	40.00
(83)	Palomo Perez	125.00	65.00	40.00
(84)	German Pizarro	125.00	65.00	40.00
(85)	Dave Pope	150.00	75.00	45.00
(86)	Milton Ralat	125.00	65.00	40.00
(87)	Enrique Reinoso	125.00	65.00	40.00
(88)	Roberto Rivera	125.00	65.00	40.00
(89)	Julio Rodriguez	125.00	65.00	40.00
(90)	Pedro Rodriguez	125.00	65.00	40.00
(91)	Domingo Rosello	125.00	65.00	40.00
(92)	Joe Rossi	125.00	65.00	40.00
(93)	Miguel Rueda	125.00	65.00	40.00
(94)	Ramon Salgado	125.00	65.00	40.00
(95)	Juan Sanchez	125.00	65.00	40.00
(96)	Carlos M. Santiago	125.00	65.00	40.00
(97)	Jose G. Santiago	125.00	65.00	40.00
(98)	V. Scarpatte	125.00	65.00	40.00
(99)	Jose Seda	125.00	65.00	40.00
(100)	Barney Serrell	350.00	175.00	105.00
(101)	Al Smith	200.00	100.00	60.00
(102)	Jose St. Clair	125.00	65.00	40.00
(103)	Tetelo Sterling	125.00	65.00	40.00
(104)	Russ Sullivan	125.00	65.00	40.00
(105)	Lonnie Summers	150.00	75.00	45.00
(106)	Jim Tabor	125.00	65.00	40.00
(107)	Bert Thiel	125.00	65.00	40.00
(108)	Valmy Thomas	125.00	65.00	40.00
(109)	Bob Thurman	350.00	175.00	105.00
(110)	Tiant Tineo	125.00	65.00	40.00
(111)	Gilberto Torres	125.00	65.00	40.00
(112)	Manuel Traboux	125.00	65.00	40.00
(113)	Joe Tuminelli	125.00	65.00	40.00
(114)	Jose L. Velazquez	125.00	65.00	40.00
(115)	Ben Wade	150.00	75.00	45.00
(116)	Johnny Williams	250.00	125.00	75.00
(117)	Marvin Williams	150.00	75.00	45.00
(118)	Artie Wilson	450.00	225.00	135.00
(119)	Pedrin Zorrilla	125.00	65.00	40.00
(120)	Pito entrevista a Hornsby	300.00	150.00	90.00
(121)	El galardon del triunfo	125.00	65.00	40.00
(122)	Fanaticos de alta posicion	125.00	65.00	40.00
(123)	VOLO LA VERJA	125.00	65.00	40.00

1950-51 Denia Puerto Rican League - Action

115- Gilliam dió out a Casanovas

These 2-1/2" x 3-1/2" cards are part of a set of about 150 covering many different sports. The pictures are colorized photographs and the cards are blank-backed, intended to be glued into an album. The number of baseball subjects is not known. Confirmed subjects are listed here, with identified players listed parenthetically.

		NM	EX	VG
Common Card:		50.00	25.00	15.00
1	Tetelo tambien joronea. (Tetelo Vargas)	85.00	40.00	25.00
2	Taborn saca en home. (Earl Taborn)	50.00	25.00	15.00
3	Se la aguo la blanqueada.	50.00	25.00	15.00
4	R. Blasini se lesiona. (Rafael Blasini)	50.00	25.00	15.00
5	Atkins mofa, Polaco safe. (Joe Atkins)	50.00	25.00	15.00
6	CERCADO-	50.00	25.00	15.00
7	Pitcher se desliza - safe.	50.00	25.00	15.00
8	Fdo. Ramos tras homer (Fernando Ramos)	50.00	25.00	15.00
9	Wilson safe en terecera. (Artie Wilson)	65.00	30.00	20.00
10	Tiro malo - SAFE.	50.00	25.00	15.00
11	VILLODAS LO ESPERA - OUT. (Luis Villodas)	50.00	25.00	15.00
12	Perry da out a Gilliam - (Alonso Perry, Jim Gilliam)	85.00	40.00	25.00
13	Safe en primera -	50.00	25.00	15.00
14	Medina obsequia a Brown. (Medina Chapman, Willard Brown)	200.00	100.00	60.00
15	Tiro malo, Almendaro anota. (Jaime Almendro)	50.00	25.00	15.00
16	Ramos toco primero - OUT. (Fernando Ramos)	50.00	25.00	15.00
17	Brazo contra brazo -	50.00	25.00	15.00
18	Pedroso felicitado tras homer - (Fernando Pedroso)	50.00	25.00	15.00
19	QUE PASA, CEFO? (Cefo Conde)	50.00	25.00	15.00
20	Canena estafa home - (Canena Marquez)	65.00	30.00	20.00
21	Buen slide - SAFE.	50.00	25.00	15.00
22	Mucha vista, Powell. (Bill Powell)	50.00	25.00	15.00
23	OUT FORZADO.	50.00	25.00	15.00
24	Alomar out en home. (Guinea Alomar)	50.00	25.00	15.00
25	Regreso a base - SAFE.	50.00	25.00	15.00
26	Pitcher trata sorprender - SAFE.	50.00	25.00	15.00
27	LOS RECUERDA USTED?	50.00	25.00	15.00
28	Leo Thomas sale de juego. (Leo Thomas)	50.00	25.00	15.00
29	Atkins es felicitado por tribu. (Joe Atkins)	50.00	25.00	15.00
30	Trio campeonil cagueno (Manuel Hernandez, Quincy Trouppe, Chet Brewer)	135.00	65.00	40.00
31	Llegando y llegando -	50.00	25.00	15.00
32	El fotografoen accion -	50.00	25.00	15.00
33	El fotografo en accion	50.00	25.00	15.00
34	No me toques Arroyito - OUT. (Luis "Tite" Arroyo)	50.00	25.00	15.00
35	Taborn propina out. (Earl Taborn)	50.00	25.00	15.00
36	El Mucaro conecta homer - (Bob Thurman)	65.00	30.00	20.00
37	PANTALONES Y FALDAS. (Jose G. Santiago)	50.00	25.00	15.00
38	Buzas en la derrota. (Joe Buzas)	50.00	25.00	15.00
39	El Gran Jurado se reune. (Raymond Brown)	135.00	65.00	40.00
40	Canena se desliza - (Canena Marquez)	65.00	30.00	20.00
41	Que dijo el umpire?	50.00	25.00	15.00
42	Bernier sabe escurrirse - (Carlos Bernier)	50.00	25.00	15.00
43	Se la escapo, la bola - SAFE.	50.00	25.00	15.00
44	Squeeze play perfecto.	50.00	25.00	15.00
45	Cuidado, que la lleva!	50.00	25.00	15.00
46	Que el umpire diga -	50.00	25.00	15.00
47	Pepe Lucas boto la bola. (Pepe Lucas)	50.00	25.00	15.00
48	Gachito se apunta hit.	50.00	25.00	15.00
49	Peloteros o Luchadores?	50.00	25.00	15.00
50	Otoniel lo toca - OUT. (Otoniel Ortiz)	50.00	25.00	15.00
51	Premian a Jorge Rosas. (Jorge Rosas)	50.00	25.00	15.00
52	Markland dio homerun - (Jim Markland)	50.00	25.00	15.00
53	Blasini safe en primera. (Rafael Blasini)	50.00	25.00	15.00
54	Graham conecto homer - (Jack Graham)	50.00	25.00	15.00
55	Penalver se prepara - SAFE.	50.00	25.00	15.00
56	No quiere riesgos	50.00	25.00	15.00
57	Bin Torres esquiva - SAFE. (Bin Torres)	50.00	25.00	15.00
58	Mutua embestida- SAFE.	50.00	25.00	15.00
59	Lo sacaron a media base.	50.00	25.00	15.00
60	Llego transqueando.	50.00	25.00	15.00
61	Quedate quieto - dice el coach.	50.00	25.00	15.00
62	Buscando en vano su presa -	50.00	25.00	15.00
63	Besando la base?	50.00	25.00	15.00
64	Pescaron al Jueyito. (Jueyito Andrade)	50.00	25.00	15.00
65	Greco da tremendo toletazo.	50.00	25.00	15.00
66	Thomas catcher, Wallaesa al bate. (Valmy Thomas, Jack Wallaesa)	50.00	25.00	15.00
67	Trofeos de TRIPLE CAMPEON.	50.00	25.00	15.00
74	H. Reyes lanza, Sanchez Batea. (Herminio Reyes, Juan Sanchez)	50.00	25.00	15.00
77	Wilson apacigua a Bernier . . . (Artie Wilson, Carlos Bernier)	85.00	40.00	25.00
78	Cogida de cuatro estrellas . . .	50.00	25.00	15.00
80	Davis out de Gachito - Wallaesa . . . (Johnny Davis, Jack Wallaesa)	50.00	25.00	15.00
81	Arroyo busca double-play. (Pedro J. Arroyo)	50.00	25.00	15.00
82	Ruben sale por lesion. (Ruben Gomez)	50.00	25.00	15.00
83	SAFE EN EL PLATO.	50.00	25.00	15.00
84	Buen esfuerzo, pero en vano . . .	50.00	25.00	15.00
85	ESTAS TRISTE, JONES? (Sam Jones)	50.00	25.00	15.00
87	Equipo ESTRELLAS NATIVAS	50.00	25.00	15.00
88	Arroyo batea, Scarpatte recibe (Pedro J. Arroyo, V. Scarpatte)	50.00	25.00	15.00
93	Cihoki recoge . . . out (Al Cihocki)	50.00	25.00	15.00
95	El arbitro pensativo . . . out.	50.00	25.00	15.00
97	Buena atrapada . . . del fotografo.	50.00	25.00	15.00
103	Villodas da hit. . . (Luis Villodas)	50.00	25.00	15.00
106	HIT EL BATAZO . . .	50.00	25.00	15.00
110	LO COGIERON LLEGANDO . . .	50.00	25.00	15.00
115	Gilliam dio out a Casanovas (Jim Gilliam, Rafael Casanovas)	85.00	40.00	25.00
124	Canena pone fuera a Bernier . . . (Canena Marquez, Carlos Bernier)	50.00	25.00	15.00
137	Terminado el swing . . .	50.00	25.00	15.00

1932 Charles Denby Cigars Cubs

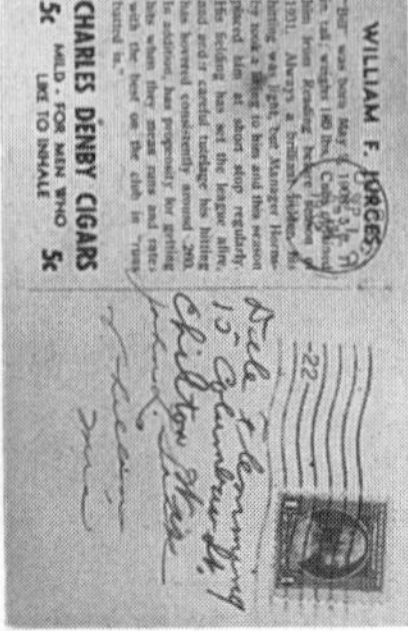

This series of Chicago Cubs postcards was issued by the Fendrich Cigar Co., Evansville, Ind., to promote its Charles Denby brand in 1932. It is the last major tobacco-card issue produced before World War II. The cards are a standard postcard size (5-1/4" x 3-3/8") and feature a glossy black-and-white player photo with a facsimile autograph. In typical postcard style, the back of the card is divided in half, with a printed player profile on the left and room for the mailing address on the right. The back also includes an advertisement for Charles Denby Cigars, the mild five-cent cigar "for men who like to inhale." Eight players are known but more may exist.

	NM	EX	VG
Complete Set (8):	3,750	1,850	1,100
Common Player:	500.00	200.00	100.00
(1) Hazen Cuyler	625.00	250.00	125.00
(2) Elwood English	500.00	200.00	100.00
(3) Charles J. Grimm	500.00	200.00	100.00
(4) William Herman	750.00	300.00	150.00
(5) Rogers Hornsby	1,000	400.00	200.00
(6) William F. Jurges	500.00	200.00	100.00
(7) Riggs Stephenson	500.00	200.00	100.00
(8) Lonnie Warneke	500.00	200.00	100.00

1909 Derby Cigars N.Y. Giants

Although there is no advertising on these cards to indicate their origin, it is believed that this set was issued by Derby Cigars, a product of American Tobacco Co. A dozen different subjects, all New York Giants, have been found. The cards, many of which appear to be hand-cut measure about 1-3/4" x 2-3/4". The cards feature an oval black-and-white player portrait on a red background. The player's name and position are in a white strip at bottom.

	NM	EX	VG
Complete Set (12):	40,000	16,000	8,000
Common Player:	3,250	1,300	650.00
(1) Josh Devore	3,250	1,300	650.00
(2) Larry Doyle	3,250	1,300	650.00
(3) Art Fletcher	3,250	1,300	650.00
(4) Buck Herzog	3,250	1,300	650.00
(5) Rube Marquard	3,750	1,500	750.00
(6) Christy Mathewson	7,500	3,000	1,500
(7) Fred Merkle	3,250	1,300	650.00
(8) Chief Meyers	3,250	1,300	650.00
(9) Red Murray	3,250	1,300	650.00
(10) John McGraw	3,500	1,400	700.00
(11) Fred Snodgrass	3,250	1,300	650.00
(12) Hooks Wiltse	3,250	1,300	650.00

1977 Detroit Caesars Discs

Virtually identical in format to the several locally sponsored disc sets of the previous year, these 3-3/8" diameter player discs were sponsored by a professional slow-pitch softball team. Discs once again feature black-and-white player portrait photos in the center of a baseball design. The left and right panels are in one of several bright colors. Licensed by the Players Association through Mike Schechter Associates, the player photos carry no uniform logos. Backs are printed in green. The unnumbered discs are checklisted here alphabetically.

	NM	EX	VG
Complete Set (70):	125.00	65.00	35.00
Common Player:	2.50	1.25	.75
(1) Sal Bando	2.50	1.25	.75
(2) Buddy Bell	2.50	1.25	.75
(3) Johnny Bench	6.00	3.00	1.75
(4) Larry Bowa	2.50	1.25	.75
(5) Steve Braun	2.50	1.25	.75
(6) George Brett	15.00	7.50	4.50
(7) Lou Brock	6.00	3.00	1.75
(8) Jeff Burroughs	2.50	1.25	.75
(9) Bert Campaneris	2.50	1.25	.75
(10) John Candelaria	2.50	1.25	.75
(11) Jose Cardenal	2.50	1.25	.75
(12) Rod Carew	4.50	2.25	1.25
(13) Steve Carlton	4.50	2.25	1.25
(14) Dave Cash	2.50	1.25	.75
(15) Cesar Cedeno	2.50	1.25	.75
(16) Ron Cey	2.50	1.25	.75
(17) Dave Concepcion	2.50	1.25	.75
(18) Dennis Eckersley	3.00	1.50	.90
(19) Mark Fidrych	5.00	2.50	1.50
(20) Rollie Fingers	5.00	2.50	1.50
(21) Carlton Fisk	6.00	3.00	1.75
(22) George Foster	2.50	1.25	.75
(23) Wayne Garland	2.50	1.25	.75
(24) Ralph Garr	2.50	1.25	.75
(25) Steve Garvey	4.00	2.00	1.25
(26) Cesar Geronimo	2.50	1.25	.75
(27) Bobby Grich	2.50	1.25	.75
(28) Ken Griffey Sr.	2.50	1.25	.75
(29) Don Gullett	2.50	1.25	.75
(30) Mike Hargrove	2.50	1.25	.75
(31) Al Hrabosky	2.50	1.25	.75
(32) Jim Hunter	5.00	2.50	1.50
(33) Reggie Jackson	9.00	4.50	2.75
(34) Randy Jones	2.50	1.25	.75
(35) Dave Kingman	3.50	1.75	1.00
(36) Jerry Koosman	2.50	1.25	.75
(37) Dave LaRoche	2.50	1.25	.75
(38) Greg Luzinski	2.50	1.25	.75
(39) Fred Lynn	2.50	1.25	.75
(40) Bill Madlock	2.50	1.25	.75
(41) Rick Manning	2.50	1.25	.75
(42) Jon Matlock	2.50	1.25	.75
(43) John Mayberry	2.50	1.25	.75
(44) Hal McRae	2.50	1.25	.75
(45) Andy Messersmith	2.50	1.25	.75
(46) Rick Monday	2.50	1.25	.75
(47) John Montefusco	2.50	1.25	.75
(48) Joe Morgan	6.00	3.00	1.75
(49) Thurman Munson	5.00	2.50	1.50
(50) Bobby Murcer	2.50	1.25	.75
(51) Bill North	2.50	1.25	.75
(52) Jim Palmer	6.00	3.00	1.75
(53) Tony Perez	5.00	2.50	1.50
(54) Jerry Reuss	2.50	1.25	.75
(55) Brooks Robinson	5.00	2.50	1.50
(56) Pete Rose	15.00	7.50	4.50
(57) Joe Rudi	2.50	1.25	.75
(58) Nolan Ryan	30.00	15.00	9.00
(59) Manny Sanguillen	2.50	1.25	.75
(60) Mike Schmidt	15.00	7.50	4.50
(61) Tom Seaver	7.50	3.75	2.25
(62) Bill Singer	2.50	1.25	.75
(63) Willie Stargell	6.00	3.00	1.75
(64) Rusty Staub	3.50	1.75	1.00
(65) Luis Tiant	2.50	1.25	.75
(66) Bob Watson	2.50	1.25	.75
(67) Butch Wynegar	2.50	1.25	.75
(68) Carl Yastrzemski	7.50	3.75	2.25
(69) Robin Yount	6.00	3.00	1.75
(70) Richie Zisk	2.50	1.25	.75

1908 Detroit Free Press Tigers Postcards

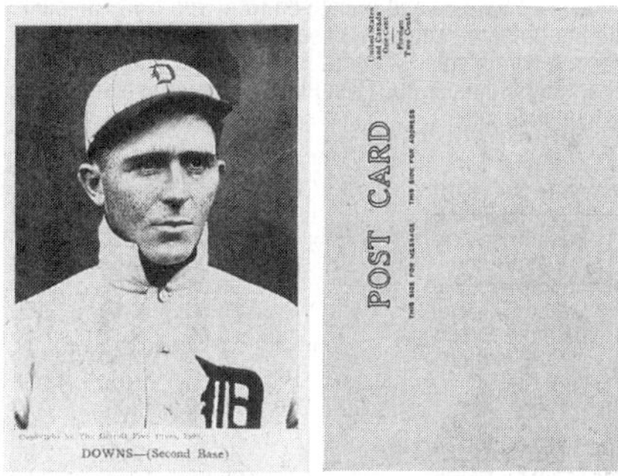

Most of the stars of the 1907-09 American League Champion Detroit Tigers are found in this set of postcards issued by a local newspaper and reportedly sold at the stadium for $1 a set. The cards are 3-1/2" x 5-1/4", printed in black-and-white. Fronts have a border around the photo with the line, "Copyright by the Detroit Free Press, 1908" beneath the photo. At bottom is the player's last name in capital letters with his position in parentheses. Backs have standard postcard indicia. The unnumbered cards are checklisted here alphabetically. It is possible this list is not complete.

	NM	EX	VG
Complete Set (11):	4,000	2,000	1,200
Common Player:	400.00	200.00	120.00
(1) Ty Cobb	950.00	475.00	285.00
(2) Sam Crawford	400.00	200.00	120.00
(3) Wild Bill Donovan	400.00	200.00	120.00
(4) Hughie Jennings	400.00	200.00	120.00
(5) Ed Killian	400.00	200.00	120.00
(6) Matty McIntyre	400.00	200.00	120.00
(7) George Mullen (Mullin)	400.00	200.00	120.00
(8) Charley O'Leary	400.00	200.00	120.00
(9) Boss Schmidt	400.00	200.00	120.00
(10) Ed Summer (Summers)	400.00	200.00	120.00
(11) Ed Willett	400.00	200.00	120.00

1934 Detroit Tigers Team Issue

This set of blank-back, postcard-sized black-and-white player photo cards is presumed to have been a team issue. A recently-discovered poster associates them with Detroit retailer Newton Annis Furs. Photos have white borders with the wider top border having three stipes. Player name and position are printed within the picture. The unnumbered cards are checklisted here alphabetically.

	NM	EX	VG
Complete Set (23):	1,200	600.00	350.00
Common Player:	60.00	30.00	18.00
(1) Eldon Auker	60.00	30.00	18.00
(2) Del Baker	60.00	30.00	18.00
(3) Tommy Bridges	60.00	30.00	18.00
(4) Mickey Cochrane	150.00	75.00	45.00
(5) General Crowder	60.00	30.00	18.00
(6) Frank Doljack	60.00	30.00	18.00
(7) Carl Fischer	60.00	30.00	18.00
(8) Pete Fox	60.00	30.00	18.00
(9) Charlie Gehringer	150.00	75.00	45.00
(10) Goose Goslin	150.00	75.00	45.00
(11) "Hank" Greenberg	250.00	125.00	75.00
(12) Luke Hamlin	60.00	30.00	18.00
(13) Ray Hayworth	60.00	30.00	18.00
(14) Elon Hogsett	60.00	30.00	18.00
(15) Firpo Marberry	60.00	30.00	18.00
(16) Marvin Owen	60.00	30.00	18.00
(17) Cy Perkins	60.00	30.00	18.00
(18) Billy Rogell	60.00	30.00	18.00
(19) Schoolboy Rowe	60.00	30.00	18.00
(20) Heinie Schuble	60.00	30.00	18.00
(21) Vic Sorrell	60.00	30.00	18.00
(22) Gee Walker	60.00	30.00	18.00
(23) Jo-Jo White	60.00	30.00	18.00

1935 Detroit Free Press Tigers

Henry Greenberg

Colorized photos with brightly colored backgrounds and borders are featured in this series of newspaper pictures featuring the World Champion Detroit Tigers. About 9" x 11", the pictures are blank-backed. It is unclear whether these pictures were included with newspaper purchases or were sold as sets. The unnumbered pictures are checklisted here in alphabetical order. In the American Card Catalog, the set carried the designation M120.

	NM	EX	VG
Complete Set (26):	1,000	500.00	300.00
Common Player:	40.00	20.00	12.00
(1) Eldon Auker	40.00	20.00	12.00
(2) Del Baker	40.00	20.00	12.00
(3) Tommy Bridges	40.00	20.00	12.00
(4) Flea Clifton	40.00	20.00	12.00
(5) Gordon Stanley (Mickey) Cochrane	100.00	50.00	30.00
(6) Alvin Crowder	40.00	20.00	12.00
(7) Frank Doljack	40.00	20.00	12.00
(8) Carl Fischer	40.00	20.00	12.00
(9) Pete Fox	40.00	20.00	12.00
(10) Charles Gehringer	75.00	37.50	22.50
(11) Goose Goslin	75.00	37.50	22.50
(12) Henry Greenberg	125.00	65.00	35.00
(13) Luke Hamlin	40.00	20.00	12.00
(14) Ray Hayworth	40.00	20.00	12.00
(15) Elon Hogsett	40.00	20.00	12.00
(16) Joe Louis (boxer)	100.00	50.00	30.00
(17) Firpo Marberry	40.00	20.00	12.00
(18) Marvin Owen	40.00	20.00	12.00
(19) Cy Perkins	40.00	20.00	12.00
(20) Billy Rogell	40.00	20.00	12.00
(21) Lynwood (Schoolboy) Rowe	45.00	22.50	13.50
(22) Heinie Schuble	40.00	20.00	12.00
(23) Vic Sorrell	40.00	20.00	12.00
(24) Joe Sullivan	40.00	20.00	12.00
(25) Jerry Walker	40.00	20.00	12.00
(26) Jo-Jo White	40.00	20.00	12.00

1968 Detroit Free Press Bubblegumless Tiger Cards

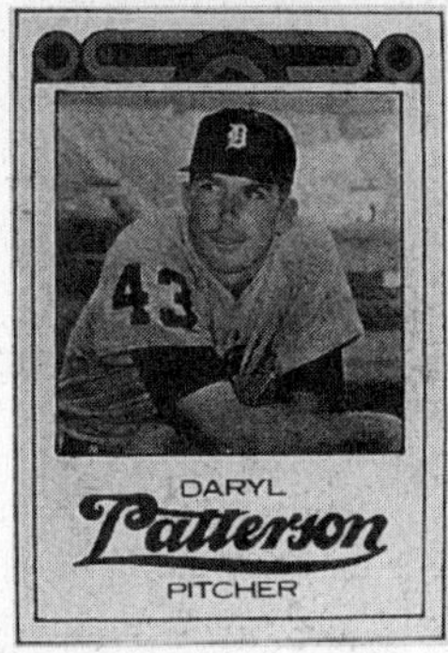

The World Champion Tigers are featured in this series of newspaper inserts published in August, 1968, by the "Detroit Magazine" rotogravure section of the Sunday "Detroit Free Press." The full-color fronts and the backs were printed on separate pages to allow them to be cut out and pasted on cardboard to make a baseball card. Backs are horizontally formatted and include a drawing of the player at left; biographical data and recent stats at right. Card elements measure 2-1/2" x 3-1/2". Values quoted are for front/back pairs. Unmatched fronts are priced at 45 percent of the prices shown; backs should be priced at 30 percent.

	NM	EX	VG
Complete Set, Uncut Pages:	250.00	125.00	75.00
Complete Set, Singles (28):	200.00	100.00	60.00
Common Player:	10.00	5.00	3.00
(1) Gates Brown	10.00	5.00	3.00
(2) Norm Cash	15.00	7.50	4.50
(3) Tony Cuccinello	10.00	5.00	3.00
(4) Pat Dobson	10.00	5.00	3.00
(5) Bill Freehan	12.50	6.25	3.75
(6) John Hiller	10.00	5.00	3.00
(7) Willie Horton	10.00	5.00	3.00
(8) Al Kaline	35.00	17.50	10.50
(9) Fred Lasher	10.00	5.00	3.00
(10) Mickey Lolich	15.00	7.50	4.50
(11) Tom Matchick	10.00	5.00	3.00
(12) Dick McAuliffe	10.00	5.00	3.00
(13) Denny McLain	12.50	6.25	3.75
(14) Don McMahon	10.00	5.00	3.00
(15) Wally Moses	10.00	5.00	3.00
(16) Jim Northrup	10.00	5.00	3.00
(17) Ray Oyler	10.00	5.00	3.00
(18) Daryl Patterson	10.00	5.00	3.00
(19) Jim Price	10.00	5.00	3.00
(20) Johnny Sain	10.00	5.00	3.00
(21) Mayo Smith	10.00	5.00	3.00
(22) Joe Sparma	10.00	5.00	3.00
(23) Mickey Stanley	10.00	5.00	3.00
(24) Dick Tracewski	10.00	5.00	3.00
(25) Jon Warden	10.00	5.00	3.00
(26) Don Wert	10.00	5.00	3.00
(27) Earl Wilson	10.00	5.00	3.00
(28) Jon Wyatt (John)	10.00	5.00	3.00

1978 Detroit Free Press Tigers

In its Sunday color magazine of April 16, 1978, the newspaper printed presumably authorized reproductions of all 1978 Topps cards which featured members of the Detroit Tigers. The magazine has a cover photo of Mark Fidrych. In the centerspread, reproduced in color, are pictures of the fronts of 20 Tigers cards. Two pages later the cards of three departed Tigers, five multi-player rookie cards and the team card are printed, also in full color. Three more pages have the backs of the cards, printed in black-and-white, rather than the orange-and-blue of genuine Topps cards. Instructions with the article invited readers to cut out the fronts and backs and paste them onto pieces of cardboard to make their own cards. Values shown are for complete front/back pairs.

	NM	EX	VG
Complete Magazine:	60.00	30.00	20.00
Complete Set, Singles (28):	30.00	15.00	9.00
Common Player:	3.00	1.50	.90
21 Steve Kemp	3.00	1.50	.90
45 Mark Fidrych	6.00	3.00	1.75
68 Steve Foucault	3.00	1.50	.90
94 Chuck Scrivener	3.00	1.50	.90
124 Dave Rozema	3.00	1.50	.90
151 Milt Wilcox	3.00	1.50	.90
176 Milt May	3.00	1.50	.90
232 Mickey Stanley	3.00	1.50	.90
258 John Hiller	3.00	1.50	.90
286 Ben Oglivie	3.00	1.50	.90
342 Aurelio Rodriguez	3.00	1.50	.90
370 Rusty Staub	6.00	3.00	1.75
385 Tito Fuentes	3.00	1.50	.90
404 Tigers team card (Color checklist back.)	6.00	3.00	1.75
456 Vern Ruhle	3.00	1.50	.90
480 Ron LeFlore	3.50	1.75	1.00
515 Tim Corcoran	3.00	1.50	.90
536 Roric Harrison	3.00	1.50	.90
559 Phil Mankowski	3.00	1.50	.90
607 Fernando Arroyo	3.00	1.50	.90
633 Tom Veryzer	3.00	1.50	.90
660 Jason Thompson	3.00	1.50	.90
684 Ralph Houk	3.50	1.75	1.00
701 Tom Hume, Larry Landreth, Steve McCatty, Bruce Taylor (Rookie Pitchers)	3.00	1.50	.90
703 Larry Andersen, Tim Jones, Mickey Mahler, Jack Morris (Rookie Pitchers)	7.50	3.75	2.25
704 Garth Iorg, Dave Oliver, Sam Perlozzo, Lou Whitaker (Rookie 2nd Basemen)	9.00	4.50	2.75
707 Mickey Klutts, Paul Molitor, Alan Trammell, U.L. Washington (Rookie Shortstops)	20.00	10.00	6.00
708 Bo Diaz, Dale Murphy, Lance Parrish, Ernie Whitt (Rookie Catchers)	10.00	5.00	3.00
723 Johnny Wockenfuss	3.00	1.50	.90

1964 Detroit Tigers Milk Bottle Caps

VISIT TIGER STADIUM
Frank Lary
SEE THE TIGERS MORE IN '64

These small (1-5/16" diameter) cardboard milk bottle caps feature line drawings of the 1964 Tigers. The caps are printed in dark blue and orange on front and blank on back. The unnumbered caps are checklisted here in alphabetical order. A wire staple is found in most caps. The caps were reportedly produced for Twin Pines Dairy for use on bottles of chocolate milk.

	NM	EX	VG
Complete Set (14):	400.00	200.00	120.00
Common Player:	25.00	12.50	7.50
(1) Hank Aguirre	25.00	12.50	7.50
(2) Billy Bruton	25.00	12.50	7.50
(3) Norman Cash	50.00	25.00	15.00
(4) Don Demeter	25.00	12.50	7.50
(5) Chuck Dressen	25.00	12.50	7.50
(6) Bill Freehan	35.00	17.50	10.50
(7) Al Kaline	150.00	75.00	45.00
(8) Frank Lary	25.00	12.50	7.50
(9) Jerry Lumpe	25.00	12.50	7.50
(10) Dick McAuliffe	25.00	12.50	7.50
(11) Bubba Phillips	25.00	12.50	7.50
(12) Ed Rakow	25.00	12.50	7.50
(13) Phil Regan	25.00	12.50	7.50
(14) Dave Wickersham	25.00	12.50	7.50

1936 Detroit Times Sports Stamps

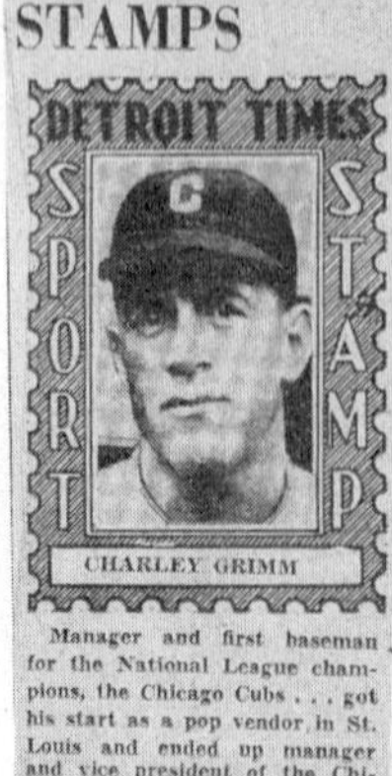

STAMPS

DETROIT TIMES

SPORT STAMP

CHARLEY GRIMM

Manager and first baseman for the National League champions, the Chicago Cubs . . . got his start as a pop vendor in St. Louis and ended up manager and vice president of the Chicago Cubs . . . Born St. Louis, Aug. 28, 1899 . . . followed Hornsby as manager and nine days after taking charge had the team in first place.

The date of issue listed is approximate and the actual period of issue may have spanned more than one year. Printed as part of the regular newspaper page, these feature items have a stamp-design photo element of about 2" x 2-1/2" atop a biographical and career summary.

	NM	EX	VG
Common Player:	15.00	7.50	4.50
(1) Eldon Auker	15.00	7.50	4.50
(2) Del Baker	15.00	7.50	4.50
(3) Tommy Bridges	15.00	7.50	4.50
(4) Jack Burns	15.00	7.50	4.50
(5) Ty Cobb	40.00	20.00	12.00
(6) Mickey Cochrane (Dark cap.)	20.00	10.00	6.00
(7) Mickey Cochrane (White cap.)	20.00	10.00	6.00
(8) Joe Cronin	20.00	10.00	6.00
(9) Alvin Crowder	15.00	7.50	4.50
(10a) Dizzy Dean (Bio first line "Star pitcher of.")	30.00	15.00	9.00
(10b) Dizzy Dean (Bio "of" on second line.)	30.00	15.00	9.00
(11) Paul Dean	15.00	7.50	4.50
(12) Wes Ferrell	15.00	7.50	4.50
(13) Pete Fox	15.00	7.50	4.50
(14) Jimmy Foxx	30.00	15.00	9.00
(15) Frank Frisch	20.00	10.00	6.00
(16a) Lou Gehrig (Bio first line "...slugging first.")	40.00	20.00	12.00
(16b) Lou Gehrig (Bio first line "slugging.")	40.00	20.00	12.00
(17) Charles Gehringer	20.00	10.00	6.00
(18) Chas. Gehringer	20.00	10.00	6.00
(19) Lefty Gomez	20.00	10.00	6.00
(20a) Goose Goslin (White cap.)	20.00	10.00	6.00
(20b) Goose Goslin (Dark cap.)	20.00	10.00	6.00
(21) Hank Greenberg	20.00	10.00	6.00
(22) Charley Grimm	15.00	7.50	4.50
(23) Ray Hayworth	15.00	7.50	4.50
(24) Elon Hogsett	15.00	7.50	4.50
(25) Walter Johnson	30.00	15.00	9.00
(26) Chuck Klein	20.00	10.00	6.00
(27) Connie Mack	20.00	10.00	6.00
(28) Heinie Manush	20.00	10.00	6.00
(29) Van Lingle Mungo	15.00	7.50	4.50
(30) Glenn Myatt	15.00	7.50	4.50
(31) Steve O'Neill	15.00	7.50	4.50
(32) Billy Rogell	15.00	7.50	4.50
(33a) Schoolboy Rowe (White cap.)	15.00	7.50	4.50
(33b) Schoolboy Rowe (Dark cap.)	15.00	7.50	4.50
(34) Babe Ruth	40.00	20.00	12.00
(35) Al Simmons	30.00	15.00	9.00
(36) Vic Sorrell	15.00	7.50	4.50
(37) Tris Speaker	30.00	15.00	9.00
(38) Casey Stengel	20.00	10.00	6.00
(39) Joe Sullivan	15.00	7.50	4.50
(40) Bill Terry	15.00	7.50	4.50
(41) Joe Vosmik	15.00	7.50	4.50
(42) Gerry Walker	15.00	7.50	4.50
(43) Lon Warneke	15.00	7.50	4.50
(44) Jo Jo White	15.00	7.50	4.50
(45) Earl Whitehill	15.00	7.50	4.50
(46) Jimmy Wilson	15.00	7.50	4.50

1966 Dexter Press California Angels

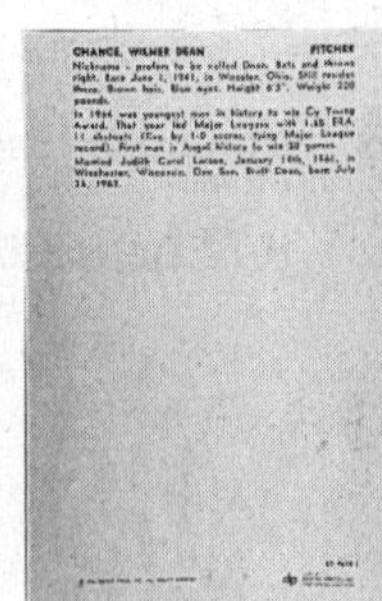

Less well-known than the New York firm's premium issues for Coca-Cola are Dexter Press' team issues. Sold for 50 cents in a cellophane bag with a colorful cardboard header the team issues are in the same basic design as the premium cards of 1967, but measure only 4" x 5-7/8". Though they were sold in sets of eight, more individual cards exist for the known teams, so it is evident there was some exchange of cards within the sets over the course of the sales period. Cards have color player poses with a black facsimile autograph at top and with or wihout a white border around. Backs are printed in blue with personal data and career highlights at top and copyright information at bottom. The cards are checklisted here alphabetically.

	NM	EX	VG
Complete Set (17):	100.00	50.00	30.00
Common Player:	10.00	5.00	3.00
(1) Jose Cardenal	10.00	5.00	3.00
(2) George Brunet	10.00	5.00	3.00
(3) Dean Chance	12.00	6.00	3.50
(4) Jim Fregosi	10.00	5.00	3.00
(5) Ed Kirkpatrick	10.00	5.00	3.00
(6) Bob Knoop	10.00	5.00	3.00
(7) Bob Lee	10.00	5.00	3.00
(8) Marcelino Lopez	10.00	5.00	3.00
(9) Fred Newman	10.00	5.00	3.00
(10) Albie Pearson	10.00	5.00	3.00
(11) Jim Piersall	13.50	6.75	4.00
(12) Rick Reichardt	10.00	5.00	3.00
(13) Bob Rodgers	10.00	5.00	3.00
(14) Paul Schaal	10.00	5.00	3.00
(15) Norm Siebern	10.00	5.00	3.00
(16) Willie Smith	10.00	5.00	3.00
(17) Anaheim Stadium	10.00	5.00	3.00

1966 Dexter Press California Angels 8x10

The extent to which this larger format premium parallels the smaller set is currently unknown.

	NM	EX	VG
Common Player:	10.00	5.00	3.00
(1) Dean Chance	15.00	7.50	4.50
(2) Willie Smith	10.00	5.00	3.00

1966 Dexter Press California Angels Booklet

This souvenir-stand bound booklet offered pictures of the 1966 California Angels in two different sizes. Each 8-1/8" x 3-1/2" page features a pair of identical color photo cards. A postcard-size (3-1/2" x 5-1/2") portrait has a facsimile autograph of the player at top, attached by perforations to a 2-1/4" x 3-1/2" card, which in turn is perforated into the bound end of the book. Booklets originally sold for 50 cents. The unnumbered cards are checklisted here in alphabetical order.

	NM	EX	VG
Complete Booket:	150.00	75.00	45.00
Complete Set, Large (10):	60.00	30.00	18.00
Complete Set, Small (10):	40.00	20.00	12.00
Common Player, Large:	8.00	4.00	2.40
Common Player, Small:	6.00	3.00	1.80
Large Format (3-1/2" x 5-1/2")			
(1) Jose Cardenal	8.00	4.00	2.50
(2) Dean Chance	8.00	4.00	2.50
(3) Jim Fregosi	8.00	4.00	2.50
(4) Bob Knoop	8.00	4.00	2.50
(5) Albie Pearson	8.00	4.00	2.50
(6) Rick Reichardt	8.00	4.00	2.50
(7) Bob Rodgers	8.00	4.00	2.50
(8) Paul Schaal	8.00	4.00	2.50
(9) Willie Smith	8.00	4.00	2.50
(10) Anaheim Stadium	8.00	4.00	2.50
Small Format (2-1/4" x 3-1/2")			
(1) Jose Cardenal	6.00	3.00	1.80
(2) Dean Chance	6.00	3.00	1.80
(3) Jim Fregosi	6.00	3.00	1.80
(4) Bob Knoop	6.00	3.00	1.80
(5) Albie Pearson	6.00	3.00	1.80
(6) Rick Reichardt	6.00	3.00	1.80
(7) Bob Rodgers	6.00	3.00	1.80
(8) Paul Schaal	6.00	3.00	1.80
(9) Willie Smith	6.00	3.00	1.80
(10) Anaheim Stadium	6.00	3.00	1.80

1966-67 Dexter Press N.Y. Yankees

Less commonly encountered than the later Dexter Press/Coca-Cola premium issues are the team-set photo-cards produced by the New York firm. Cards were sold in bagged sets with a colorful cardboard header. Virtually identical in design to the 5-1/2" x 7" premium cards of 1967, the team-set pictures measure 4" x 5-7/8" with a white border around, and a black facsimile autograph at the top of, color player poses. Backs are printed in blue with a few biographical details at top and copyright information at bottom. The unnumbered cards are checklisted here in alphabetical order.

	NM	EX	VG
Complete Set (12):	200.00	100.00	60.00
Common Player:	15.00	7.50	4.50
(1) Jim Bouton	17.50	8.75	5.25
(2) Horace Clarke	15.00	7.50	4.50
(3) Al Downing	15.00	7.50	4.50
(4) Whitey Ford	20.00	10.00	6.00
(5) Steve Hamilton	15.00	7.50	4.50
(6) Elston Howard	17.50	8.75	5.25
(7) Mickey Mantle	60.00	30.00	18.00
(8) Joe Pepitone	17.50	8.75	5.25
(9) Bill Robinson	15.00	7.50	4.50
(10) Mel Stottlemyre	15.00	7.50	4.50
(11) Tom Tresh	17.50	8.75	5.25
(12) Steve Whitaker	15.00	7.50	4.50

1967 Dexter Press Premiums

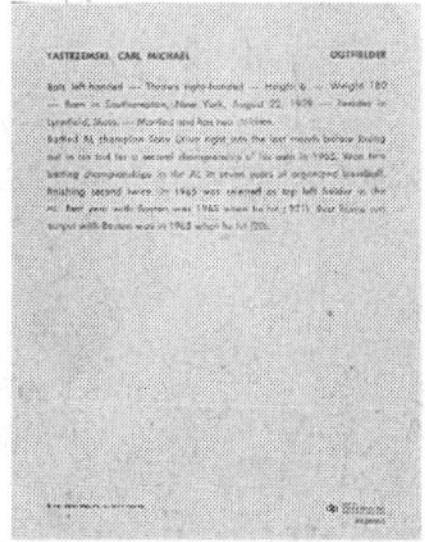

Among the most attractive baseball collectibles issued during the 1960s were the cards produced by Dexter Press and issued in team sets as a premium by Coca-Cola. Eighteen of the 20 Major League teams participated in the promotion (only one California Angels player and no St. Louis Cardinals). The cards are in 5-1/2" x 7" glossy format. All of the color photos are waist-to-cap poses shot during spring training, and all cards feature a black facsimile autograph at the top of the photo. The cards have a 1/4" white border around the picture. Backs are printed in blue on white and include a few biographical details and career highlights. Nine of the 12 players in the All-Star issue can be differentiated from the same players' cards in the team sets by the lengthier biographies on back. The bios on the cards of Bunning, Mays and Santo are the same in both versions. While each of the cards has a number printed on back in the lower-right, they are checklisted here alphabetically within team. Sixteen of the Dexter Press premiums were issued in a smaller, borderless sticker set in 1983; it is an unauthorized collector issue.

	NM	EX	VG
Complete Set (229):	1,500	750.00	450.00
Common Player:	5.00	2.50	1.50
ALL-STARS			
(1) Jim Bunning	7.50	3.75	2.25
(2) Roberto Clemente	15.00	7.50	4.50
(3) Willie Davis	5.00	2.50	1.50
(4) Al Kaline	10.00	5.00	3.00
(5) Harmon Killebrew	10.00	5.00	3.00
(6) Willie Mays	12.50	6.25	3.75
(7) Joe Pepitone	6.00	3.00	1.75
(8) Brooks Robinson	10.00	5.00	3.00
(9) Frank Robinson	10.00	5.00	3.00
(10) Ron Santo	6.00	3.00	1.75
(11) Joe Torre	6.00	3.00	1.75
(12) Carl Yastrzemski	12.00	6.00	3.50
CALIFORNIA ANGELS			
(13) Paul Schall	125.00	62.00	37.00
HOUSTON ASTROS			
(14) Bob Aspromonte	5.00	2.50	1.50
(15) John Bateman	5.00	2.50	1.50
(16) Ron Davis	5.00	2.50	1.50
(17) Larry Dierker	5.00	2.50	1.50
(18) Dick Farrell	5.00	2.50	1.50
(19) Dave Giusti	5.00	2.50	1.50
(20) Chuck Harrison	5.00	2.50	1.50
(21) Sonny Jackson	5.00	2.50	1.50
(22) Jim Landis	5.00	2.50	1.50
(23) Eddie Mathews	10.00	5.00	3.00
(24) Joe Morgan	12.00	6.00	3.50
(25) Rusty Staub	7.50	3.75	2.25
KANSAS CITY ATHLETICS			
(26) Jack Aker	5.00	2.50	1.50
(27) Campy Campaneris	5.00	2.50	1.50
(28) Danny Cater	5.00	2.50	1.50
(29) Ed Charles	5.00	2.50	1.50
(30) Ossie Chavarria	5.00	2.50	1.50
(31) Dick Green	5.00	2.50	1.50
(32) Mike Hershberger	5.00	2.50	1.50
(33) Lew Krausse	5.00	2.50	1.50
(34) Jim Nash	5.00	2.50	1.50
(35) Joe Nossek	5.00	2.50	1.50
(36) Roger Repoz	5.00	2.50	1.50
(37) Phil Roof	5.00	2.50	1.50
ATLANTA BRAVES			
(38) Hank Aaron	25.00	12.50	7.50
(39) Felipe Alou	6.00	3.00	1.75
(40) Wade Blasingame	5.00	2.50	1.50
(41) Clete Boyer	5.00	2.50	1.50
(42) Bob Bruce	5.00	2.50	1.50
(43) Ty Cline	5.00	2.50	1.50
(44) Tony Cloninger	5.00	2.50	1.50
(45) Ken Johnson	5.00	2.50	1.50
(46) Dennis Menke	5.00	2.50	1.50
(47) Gene Oliver	5.00	2.50	1.50
(48) Joe Torre	7.50	3.75	2.25
(49) Woody Woodward	5.00	2.50	1.50
CHICAGO CUBS			
(50) George Altman	5.00	2.50	1.50
(51) Ernie Banks	18.00	9.00	5.50
(52) Glen Beckert (Glenn)	5.00	2.50	1.50
(53) John Boccabella	5.00	2.50	1.50
(54) Ray Culp	5.00	2.50	1.50
(55) Ken Holtzman	5.00	2.50	1.50
(56) Randy Hundley	5.00	2.50	1.50
(57) Cal Koonce	5.00	2.50	1.50
(58) Adolfo Phillips	5.00	2.50	1.50
(59) Ron Santo	6.00	3.00	1.75
(60) Lee Thomas	5.00	2.50	1.50
(61) Billy Williams	10.00	5.00	3.00
LOS ANGELES DODGERS			
(62) Bob Bailey	5.00	2.50	1.50
(63) Willie Davis	5.00	2.50	1.50
(64) Ron Fairly	5.00	2.50	1.50
(65) Ron Hunt	5.00	2.50	1.50
(66) Lou Johnson	5.00	2.50	1.50
(67) John Kennedy	5.00	2.50	1.50
(68) Jim Lefebvre	5.00	2.50	1.50
(69) Claude Osteen	5.00	2.50	1.50
(70) Wes Parker	5.00	2.50	1.50
(71) Ron Perranoski	5.00	2.50	1.50
(72) Phil Regan	5.00	2.50	1.50
(73) Don Sutton	7.50	3.75	2.25
SAN FRANCISCO GIANTS			
(74) Jesus Alou	5.00	2.50	1.50
(75) Ollie Brown	5.00	2.50	1.50
(76) Jim Davenport	5.00	2.50	1.50
(77) Tito Fuentes	5.00	2.50	1.50
(78) Tom Haller	5.00	2.50	1.50
(79) Jim Hart	5.00	2.50	1.50
(80) Hal Lanier	5.00	2.50	1.50
(81) Willie Mays	15.00	7.50	4.50
(82) Mike McCormick	5.00	2.50	1.50
(83) Willie McCovey	12.00	6.00	3.50
(84) Gaylord Perry	8.00	4.00	2.50
(85) Norman Siebern	5.00	2.50	1.50
CLEVELAND INDIANS			
(86) Max Alvis	5.00	2.50	1.50
(87) Joe Azcue	5.00	2.50	1.50
(88) Gary Bell	5.00	2.50	1.50
(89) Larry Brown	5.00	2.50	1.50
(90) Rocky Colavito	7.50	3.75	2.25
(91) Vic Davalillo	5.00	2.50	1.50
(92) Pedro Gonzalez	5.00	2.50	1.50
(93) Chuck Hinton	5.00	2.50	1.50
(94) Sam McDowell	6.00	3.00	1.75
(95) Luis Tiant	6.00	3.00	1.75
(96) Leon Wagner	5.00	2.50	1.50
(97) Fred Whitfield	5.00	2.50	1.50
NEW YORK METS			
(98) Ed Bressoud	5.00	2.50	1.50
(99) Ken Boyer	7.00	3.50	2.00
(100) Tommy Davis	6.00	3.00	1.75
(101) Jack Fisher	5.00	2.50	1.50
(102) Jerry Grote	5.00	2.50	1.50
(103) Jack Hamilton	5.00	2.50	1.50
(104) Cleon Jones	6.00	3.00	1.75
(105) Ed Kranepool	5.00	2.50	1.50
(106) Johnny Lewis	5.00	2.50	1.50
(107) Bob Shaw	5.00	2.50	1.50
(108) John Stephenson	5.00	2.50	1.50
(109) Ron Swoboda	5.00	2.50	1.50
BALTIMORE ORIOLES			
(110) Luis Aparicio	10.00	5.00	3.00
(111) Curt Blefary	5.00	2.50	1.50
(112) Wally Bunker	5.00	2.50	1.50
(113) Andy Etchebarren	5.00	2.50	1.50
(114) Eddie Fisher	5.00	2.50	1.50
(115) Dave Johnson	5.00	2.50	1.50
(116) Dave McNally	5.00	2.50	1.50
(117) Jim Palmer	10.00	5.00	3.00
(118) John "Boog" Powell	8.00	4.00	2.50
(119) Brooks Robinson	15.00	7.50	4.50
(120) Frank Robinson	15.00	7.50	4.50
(121) Russ Snyder	5.00	2.50	1.50
PHILADELPHIA PHILLIES			
(122) Rich Allen	7.50	3.75	2.25
(123) John Briggs	5.00	2.50	1.50
(124) Jim Bunning	7.50	3.75	2.25
(125) Johnny Callison	5.00	2.50	1.50
(126) Clay Dalrymple	5.00	2.50	1.50
(127) Dick Groat	5.00	2.50	1.50
(128) Larry Jackson	5.00	2.50	1.50
(129) Don Lock	5.00	2.50	1.50
(130) Cookie Rojas	5.00	2.50	1.50
(131) Chris Short	5.00	2.50	1.50
(132) Tony Taylor	5.00	2.50	1.50
(133) Bill White	5.00	2.50	1.50
PITTSBURGH PIRATES			
(134) Gene Alley	5.00	2.50	1.50
(135) Matty Alou	5.00	2.50	1.50
(136) Roberto Clemente	45.00	22.00	13.50
(137) Donn Clendenon	5.00	2.50	1.50
(138) Woodie Fryman	5.00	2.50	1.50
(139) Vern Law	5.00	2.50	1.50
(140) Bill Mazeroski	10.00	5.00	3.00
(141) Manny Mota	5.00	2.50	1.50
(142) Jim Pagliaroni	5.00	2.50	1.50
(143) Wilver Stargell	12.00	6.00	3.50
(144) Bob Veale	5.00	2.50	1.50
(145) Maury Wills	6.00	3.00	1.75
CINCINNATI REDS			
(146) Leo Cardenas	5.00	2.50	1.50
(147) Gordy Coleman	5.00	2.50	1.50
(148) Johnny Edwards	5.00	2.50	1.50
(149) Tommy Harper	5.00	2.50	1.50
(150) Tommy Helms	5.00	2.50	1.50
(151) Deron Johnson	5.00	2.50	1.50
(152) Jim Maloney	5.00	2.50	1.50
(153) Bill McCool	5.00	2.50	1.50
(154) Milt Pappas	5.00	2.50	1.50
(155) Vada Pinson	6.00	3.00	1.75
(156) Pete Rose	30.00	15.00	9.00
(157) Art Shamsky	5.00	2.50	1.50
BOSTON RED SOX			
(158) Don Demeter	5.00	2.50	1.50
(159) Bill Fischer	5.00	2.50	1.50
(160) Joe Foy	5.00	2.50	1.50
(161) Dalton Jones	5.00	2.50	1.50
(162) Jim Lonborg	5.00	2.50	1.50
(163) Rico Petrocelli	5.00	2.50	1.50
(164) Jose Santiago	5.00	2.50	1.50
(165) George Scott	5.00	2.50	1.50
(166) George Smith	5.00	2.50	1.50
(167) Jose Tartabull	5.00	2.50	1.50
(168) Bob Tillman	5.00	2.50	1.50

	NM	EX	VG
(169) Carl Yastrzemski	15.00	7.50	4.50
WASHINGTON SENATORS			
(170) Bernie Allen	5.00	2.50	1.50
(171) Ed Brinkman	5.00	2.50	1.50
(172) Paul Casanova	5.00	2.50	1.50
(173) Ken Harrelson	5.00	2.50	1.50
(174) Frank Howard	6.00	3.00	1.75
(175) Jim King	5.00	2.50	1.50
(176) Ken McMullen	5.00	2.50	1.50
(177) Dick Nen	5.00	2.50	1.50
(178) Phil Ortega	5.00	2.50	1.50
(179) Pete Richert	5.00	2.50	1.50
(180) Bob Saverine	5.00	2.50	1.50
(181) Fred Valentine	5.00	2.50	1.50
DETROIT TIGERS			
(182) Norm Cash	6.00	3.00	1.75
(183) Bill Freehan	5.00	2.50	1.50
(184) Willie Horton	5.00	2.50	1.50
(185) Al Kaline	12.00	6.00	3.50
(186) Mickey Lolich	5.00	2.50	1.50
(187) Jerry Lumpe	5.00	2.50	1.50
(188) Dick McAuliffe	5.00	2.50	1.50
(189) Johnny Podres	5.00	2.50	1.50
(190) Joe Sparma	5.00	2.50	1.50
(191) Dave Wickersham	5.00	2.50	1.50
(192) Earl Wilson	5.00	2.50	1.50
(193) Don Wert	5.00	2.50	1.50
MINNESOTA TWINS			
(194) Bob Allison	5.00	2.50	1.50
(195) Earl Battey	5.00	2.50	1.50
(196) Dave Boswell	5.00	2.50	1.50
(197) Dean Chance	5.00	2.50	1.50
(198) Mudcat Grant	5.00	2.50	1.50
(199) Harmon Killebrew	12.00	6.00	3.50
(200) Jim Merritt	5.00	2.50	1.50
(201) Tony Oliva	8.00	4.00	2.50
(202) Rich Rollins	5.00	2.50	1.50
(203) Ted Uhlaender	5.00	2.50	1.50
(204) Sandy Valdespino	5.00	2.50	1.50
(205) Zoilo Versalles	5.00	2.50	1.50
CHICAGO WHITE SOX			
(206) Tommie Agee	5.00	2.50	1.50
(207) Ken Berry	5.00	2.50	1.50
(208) Don Buford	5.00	2.50	1.50
(209) Ron Hansen	5.00	2.50	1.50
(210) Joel Horlen	5.00	2.50	1.50
(211) Tommy John	6.00	3.00	1.75
(212) Bob Locker	5.00	2.50	1.50
(213) Tommy McCraw	5.00	2.50	1.50
(214) Jerry McNertney	5.00	2.50	1.50
(215) Jim O'Toole	5.00	2.50	1.50
(216) Bill "Moose" Skowron	7.00	3.50	2.00
(217) Pete Ward	5.00	2.50	1.50
NEW YORK YANKEES			
(218) Jim Bouton	6.00	3.00	1.75
(219) Horace Clarke	5.00	2.50	1.50
(220) Al Downing	5.00	2.50	1.50
(221) Steve Hamilton	5.00	2.50	1.50
(222) Elston Howard	7.50	3.75	2.25
(223) Mickey Mantle	40.00	20.00	12.00
(224) Joe Pepitone	6.00	3.00	1.75
(225) Fritz Peterson	5.00	2.50	1.50
(226) Charley Smith	5.00	2.50	1.50
(227) Mel Stottlemyre	6.00	3.00	1.75
(228) Tom Tresh	6.00	3.00	1.75
(229) Roy White	6.00	3.00	1.75

1967 Dexter Press Team Posters

These 17" x 11" color posters reproduce the 12 cards (or on the Cubs sheet, three additional players) found in the 1967 Dexter Press premium team sets, in images about 2" x 3". The cards are pictured on a solid color background with color team logos. Printed on back are player identification and biographical information. Dexter Press copyright and credit lines are at bottom. It is not known whether other teams involved in the premium program can also be found in poster format.

	NM	EX	VG
California Angels	135.00	65.00	40.00
Chicago Cubs	180.00	90.00	55.00
Chicago White Sox	135.00	65.00	40.00
N.Y. Mets	180.00	90.00	55.00
N.Y. Yankees	300.00	150.00	90.00
Washington Senators	180.00	90.00	55.00

1968 Dexter Press Postcards

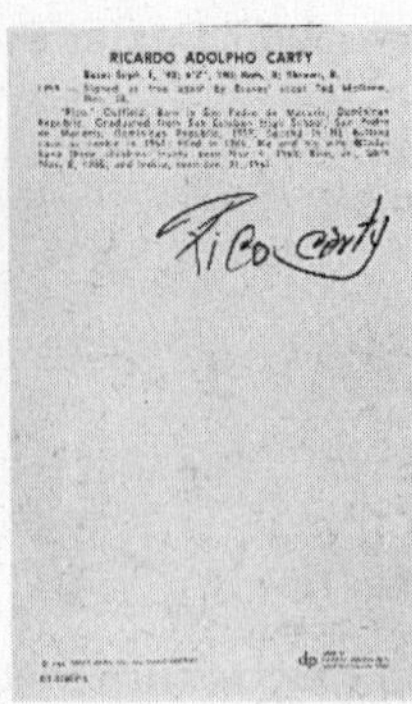

In its second year of printing premium cards for Coca-Cola, Dexter Press changed format and greatly reduced the number of participating teams and players. Only six teams were represented by 12-card sets, while an additional four teams had one or two players included. For 1968, Dexter Press produced its premiums in postcard (3-1/2" x 5-1/2") size. The cards featured borderless color player poses on front. Backs were printed in blue on white and included a facsimile autograph, biographical details and career highlights. Cards carry a Dexter Press serial number on back, but are checklisted here alphabetically within team.

	NM	EX	VG
Complete Set (77):	400.00	200.00	120.00
Common Player:	4.00	2.00	1.25
CALIFORNIA ANGELS			
(1) Jim Fregosi	6.00	3.00	1.75
HOUSTON ASTROS			
(2) Bob Aspromonte	4.00	2.00	1.25
(3) John Bateman	4.00	2.00	1.25
(4) Ron Brand	4.00	2.00	1.25
(5) Mike Cuellar	4.00	2.00	1.25
(6) Ron Davis	4.00	2.00	1.25
(7) Dave Giusti	4.00	2.00	1.25
(8) Julio Gotay	4.00	2.00	1.25
(9) Denny Lemaster	4.00	2.00	1.25
(10) Denis Menke	4.00	2.00	1.25
(11) Joe Morgan	10.00	5.00	3.00
(12) Rusty Staub	5.00	2.50	1.50
(13) Jim Wynn	4.00	2.00	1.25
ATLANTA BRAVES			
(14) Hank Aaron	15.00	7.50	4.50
(15) Felipe Alou	5.00	2.50	1.50
(16) Clete Boyer	4.00	2.00	1.25
(17) Clay Carroll	4.00	2.00	1.25
(18) Rico Carty	4.00	2.00	1.25
(19) Tony Cloninger	4.00	2.00	1.25
(20) Sonny Jackson	4.00	2.00	1.25
(21) Ray Jarvis	4.00	2.00	1.25
(22) Ken Johnson	4.00	2.00	1.25
(23) Phil Niekro	8.00	4.00	2.50
(24) Joe Torre	7.50	3.75	2.25
(25) Woody Woodward	4.00	2.00	1.25
SAN FRANCISCO GIANTS			
(26) Jesus Alou	4.00	2.00	1.25
(27) Bob Bolin	4.00	2.00	1.25
(28) Jim Davenport	4.00	2.00	1.25
(29) Jim Hart	4.00	2.00	1.25
(30) Jack Hiatt	4.00	2.00	1.25
(31) Ron Hunt	4.00	2.00	1.25
(32) Frank Linzy	4.00	2.00	1.25
(33) Juan Marichal	9.00	4.50	2.75
(34) Willie Mays	15.00	7.50	4.50
(35) Mike McCormick	4.00	2.00	1.25
(36) Gaylord Perry	8.00	4.00	2.50
(37) Ray Sadecki	4.00	2.00	1.25
BALTIMORE ORIOLES			
(38) Mark Belanger	4.00	2.00	1.25
(39) Paul Blair	4.00	2.00	1.25
(40) Curt Blefary	4.00	2.00	1.25
(41) Don Buford	4.00	2.00	1.25
(42) Moe Drabowsky	4.00	2.00	1.25
(43) Andy Etchebarren	4.00	2.00	1.25
(44) Dave Johnson	4.00	2.00	1.25
(45) Dave McNally	4.00	2.00	1.25
(46) Tom Phoebus	4.00	2.00	1.25
(47) Boog Powell	5.00	2.50	1.50
(48) Brooks Robinson	12.00	6.00	3.50
(49) Frank Robinson	12.00	6.00	3.50
PHILADELPHIA PHILLIES			
(50) Dick Allen	9.00	4.50	2.75
PITTSBURGH PIRATES			
(51) Roberto Clemente	25.00	12.50	7.50
(52) Bill Mazeroski	10.00	5.00	3.00
BOSTON RED SOX			
(53) Jerry Adair	4.00	2.00	1.25
(54) Mike Andrews	4.00	2.00	1.25
(55) Gary Bell	4.00	2.00	1.25
(56) Darrell Brandon	4.00	2.00	1.25
(57) Dick Ellsworth	4.00	2.00	1.25
(58) Joe Foy	4.00	2.00	1.25
(59) Dalton Jones	4.00	2.00	1.25
(60) Jim Lonborg	5.00	2.50	1.50
(61) Dave Morehead	4.00	2.00	1.25
(62) Rico Petrocelli	4.00	2.00	1.25
(63) George Scott	4.00	2.00	1.25
(64) John Wyatt	4.00	2.00	1.25
DETROIT TIGERS			
(65) Bill Freehan	6.00	3.00	1.75
MINNESOTA TWINS			
(66) Bob Allison	4.00	2.00	1.25
(67) Dave Boswell	4.00	2.00	1.25
(68) Rod Carew	10.00	5.00	3.00
(69) Dean Chance	4.00	2.00	1.25
(70) Jim Kaat	4.00	2.00	1.25
(71) Harmon Killebrew	10.00	5.00	3.00
(72) Russ Nixon	4.00	2.00	1.25
(73) Tony Oliva	6.00	3.00	1.75
(74) Rich Rollins	4.00	2.00	1.25
(75) John Roseboro	4.00	2.00	1.25
(76) Cesar Tovar	4.00	2.00	1.25
(77) Ted Uhlaender	4.00	2.00	1.25

1979 Dexter Press Hall of Fame Plaque Postcards

(See Hall of Fame (Dexter Press) for checklist, value data.)

1960 Diamond Associates Postcards

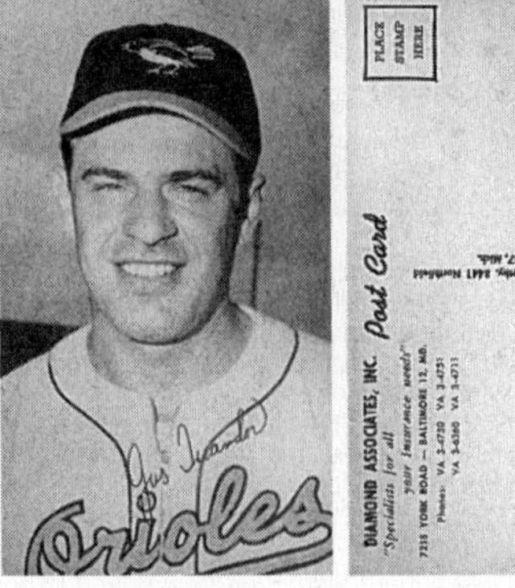

Based on the uniform style depicted on front, the actual year of issue for this card could be anywhere between 1958-1962. Produced by photographer J.D. McCarthy, apparently for the star catcher's off-season business, the 3-1/4" x 5-1/2" black-and-white card has a facsimile autograph on front. The postcard-style back has the address and phone numbers of the insurance company.

	NM	EX	VG
Gus Triandos	30.00	15.00	9.00

1940 Diamond Dust Punchboard Cards

These paper cards are the consolation prizes from a popular gambling device of the Depression era, the punchboard. For five cents a customer could choose one of 624 holes on the punchboard and push a wood or metal punch through the paper on front, driving out the back a 1" x about 1-3/4" picture of a baseball player. Fifteen of the players were $1 winners and were produced in much shorter supply than the others; any which were redeemed would probably have been destroyed. The pictures are printed on ribbed paper to assist in fitting them into the board. They are pictures taken from the photos on contemporary "Salutation" Exhibit cards, though without uniform logos. They are printed in bright colors with the player name in a color bar at bottom. Backs are blank. The unnumbered cards are listed here in alphabetical order, with an asterisk indicating winners. The punchboard itself is highly collectible, with colorful baseball graphics and player pictures and names. Earlier and later versions of Diamond Dust punchboards are also known, but have not been checklisted.

	NM	EX	VG
Complete Set (33):	850.00	425.00	250.00
Common Player:	15.00	7.50	4.50
Complete Unused Punchboard:	1,200	600.00	350.00
(1) Luke Appling (*)	45.00	22.00	13.50
(2) Earl Averill (*)	45.00	22.00	13.50
(3) Adolf Camilli	15.00	7.50	4.50
(4) Harland Clift (Harlond)	15.00	7.50	4.50
(5) Joe Cronin (*)(Unconfirmed)	45.00	22.00	13.50
(6) Tony Cuccinello	15.00	7.50	4.50
(7) Dizzy Dean	35.00	17.50	10.50
(8) Bill Dickey (*)	50.00	25.00	15.00
(9) Joe DiMaggio (*)	125.00	62.00	37.00
(10) Bob Feller	30.00	15.00	9.00

(11)	Jimmie Foxx (*)	45.00	22.00	13.50
(12)	Charlie Gehringer (*)	45.00	22.00	13.50
(13)	Lefty Gomez	25.00	12.50	7.50
(14)	Hank Greenberg	30.00	15.00	9.00
(15)	Lefty Grove	25.00	12.50	7.50
(16)	Gabby Hartnett	15.00	7.50	4.50
(17)	Carl Hubbell	25.00	12.50	7.50
(18)	Bob Johnson	15.00	7.50	4.50
(19)	Chuck Klein	25.00	12.50	7.50
(20)	Bill Lee	15.00	7.50	4.50
(21)	Ernie Lombardi (*)	45.00	22.00	13.50
(22)	Frank McCormick (*)	25.00	12.50	7.50
(23)	Joe Medwick	25.00	12.50	7.50
(24)	Johnny Mize (*)	45.00	22.00	13.50
(25)	Buck Newson (Newsom)	15.00	7.50	4.50
(26)	Mel Ott (*)	45.00	22.00	13.50
(27)	Johnny Rizzo (*)	25.00	12.50	7.50
(28)	Red Ruffing (*)(Unconfirmed)	45.00	22.00	13.50
(29)	Cecil Travis	15.00	7.50	4.50
(30)	Johnny Vander Meer	15.00	7.50	4.50
(31)	Arky Vaughan (*)	45.00	22.00	13.50
(32)	Lon Warneke	15.00	7.50	4.50
(33)	Rudy York (*)(Unconfirmed)	25.00	12.50	7.50

1979 Diamond Greats

SENATORS
1ST BASE
Roy Sievers
Diamond Greats 1979 # 75
Life- H 2B HR RBI BA
time 1703 292 318 1147 .267

Card collector, dealer and later Donruss photographer Jack Wallin produced this collectors' issue. Cards are in the 2-1/2" x 3-1/2" format, printed in black-and-white and blank-backed. Besides the player photo on front, there is identification and a line of career stats. Four 100-card series were issued. Series 1 concentrates on Yankees, Giants, Senators and Dodgers. Series 2 comprises the Cubs, White Sox, Cardinals and Browns. The third series features Braves, Red Sox, Reds and Indians. Series 4 concentrates on the Phillies, A's, Pirates and Tigers.

		NM	EX	VG
Complete Set (400):		275.00	135.00	85.00
Series 1 (1-100):		60.00	30.00	18.00
Series 2 (101-200):		50.00	25.00	15.00
Series 3 (201-300):		50.00	25.00	15.00
Series 4 (301-400):		50.00	25.00	15.00
Common Player:		2.00	1.00	.60
1	Joe DiMaggio	12.00	6.00	3.50
2	Ben Chapman	2.00	1.00	.60
3	Joe Dugan	2.00	1.00	.60
4	Bobby Shawkey	2.00	1.00	.60
5	Joe Sewell	2.00	1.00	.60
6	George Pipgras	2.00	1.00	.60
7	George Selkirk	2.00	1.00	.60
8	Babe Dahlgren	2.00	1.00	.60
9	Spud Chandler	2.00	1.00	.60
10	Duffy Lewis	2.00	1.00	.60
11	Lefty Gomez	3.00	1.50	.90
12	Atley Donald	2.00	1.00	.60
13	Whitey Witt	2.00	1.00	.60
14	Marius Russo	2.00	1.00	.60
15	Buddy Rosar	2.00	1.00	.60
16	Russ Van Atta	2.00	1.00	.60
17	Johnny Lindell	2.00	1.00	.60
18	Bobby Brown	2.00	1.00	.60
19	Tony Kubek	2.50	1.25	.70
20	Joe Beggs	2.00	1.00	.60
21	Don Larsen	2.50	1.25	.70
22	Andy Carey	2.00	1.00	.60
23	Johnny Kucks	2.00	1.00	.60
24	Elston Howard	2.50	1.25	.70
25	Roger Maris	4.00	2.00	1.25
26	Rube Marquard	2.50	1.25	.70
27	Sam Leslie	2.00	1.00	.60
28	Freddy Leach	2.00	1.00	.60
29	Fred Fitzsimmons	2.00	1.00	.60
30	Bill Terry	2.50	1.25	.70
31	Joe Moore	2.00	1.00	.60
32	Waite Hoyt	2.00	1.00	.60
33	Travis Jackson	2.00	1.00	.60
34	Gus Mancuso	2.00	1.00	.60
35	Carl Hubbell	3.00	1.50	.90
36	Bill Voiselle	2.00	1.00	.60
37	Hank Leiber	2.00	1.00	.60
38	Burgess Whitehead	2.00	1.00	.60
39	Johnny Mize	3.00	1.50	.90
40	Bill Lohrman	2.00	1.00	.60
41	Bill Rigney	2.00	1.00	.60
42	Cliff Melton	2.00	1.00	.60
43	Willard Marshall	2.00	1.00	.60
44	Wes Westrum	2.00	1.00	.60
45	Monte Irvin	3.00	1.50	.90
46	Marv Grissom	2.00	1.00	.60
47	Clyde Castleman	2.00	1.00	.60
48	Harry Gumbert	2.00	1.00	.60
49	Daryl Spencer	2.00	1.00	.60
50	Willie Mays	9.00	4.50	2.75
51	Sam West	2.00	1.00	.60
52	Fred Schulte	2.00	1.00	.60
53	Cecil Travis	2.00	1.00	.60
54	Tommy Thomas	2.00	1.00	.60
55	Dutch Leonard	2.00	1.00	.60
56	Jimmy Wasdell	2.00	1.00	.60
57	Doc Cramer	2.00	1.00	.60
58	Harland Clift (Harlond)	2.00	1.00	.60
59	Ken Chase	2.00	1.00	.60
60	Buddy Lewis	2.00	1.00	.60
61	Ossie Bluege	2.00	1.00	.60
62	Chuck Stobbs	2.00	1.00	.60
63	Jimmy DeShong	2.00	1.00	.60
64	Roger Wolff	2.00	1.00	.60
65	Luke Sewell	2.00	1.00	.60
66	Sid Hudson	2.00	1.00	.60
67	Jack Russell	2.00	1.00	.60
68	Walt Masterson	2.00	1.00	.60
69	George Myatt	2.00	1.00	.60
70	Monte Weaver	2.00	1.00	.60
71	Cliff Bolton	2.00	1.00	.60
72	Ray Scarborough	2.00	1.00	.60
73	Albie Pearson	2.00	1.00	.60
74	Gil Coan	2.00	1.00	.60
75	Roy Sievers	2.00	1.00	.60
76	Burleigh Grimes	2.00	1.00	.60
77	Charlie Hargreaves	2.00	1.00	.60
78	Babe Herman	2.00	1.00	.60
79	Fred Frankhouse	2.00	1.00	.60
80	Al Lopez	2.00	1.00	.60
81	Lonny Frey	2.00	1.00	.60
82	Dixie Walker	2.00	1.00	.60
83	Kirby Higbe	2.00	1.00	.60
84	Bobby Bragan	2.00	1.00	.60
85	Leo Durocher	2.00	1.00	.60
86	Woody English	2.00	1.00	.60
87	Preacher Roe	2.00	1.00	.60
88	Vic Lombardi	2.00	1.00	.60
89	Clyde Sukeforth	2.00	1.00	.60
90	Pee Wee Reese	5.00	2.50	1.50
91	Joe Hatten	2.00	1.00	.60
92	Gene Hermanski	2.00	1.00	.60
93	Ray Benge	2.00	1.00	.60
94	Duke Snider	5.00	2.50	1.50
95	Walter Alston	2.00	1.00	.60
96	Don Drysdale	3.00	1.50	.90
97	Andy Pafko	2.00	1.00	.60
98	Don Zimmer	2.00	1.00	.60
99	Carl Erskine	2.00	1.00	.60
100	Dick Williams	2.00	1.00	.60
101	Charlie Grimm	2.00	1.00	.60
102	Clarence Blair	2.00	1.00	.60
103	Johnny Moore	2.00	1.00	.60
104	Clay Bryant	2.00	1.00	.60
105	Billy Herman	2.00	1.00	.60
106	Hy Vandenberg	2.00	1.00	.60
107	Lennie Merullo	2.00	1.00	.60
108	Hank Wyse	2.00	1.00	.60
109	Dom Dallessandro	2.00	1.00	.60
110	Al Epperly	2.00	1.00	.60
111	Bill Nicholson	2.00	1.00	.60
112	Vern Olsen	2.00	1.00	.60
113	Johnny Schmitz	2.00	1.00	.60
114	Bob Scheffing	2.00	1.00	.60
115	Bob Rush	2.00	1.00	.60
116	Roy Smalley	2.00	1.00	.60
117	Ransom Jackson	2.00	1.00	.60
118	Cliff Chambers	2.00	1.00	.60
119	Harry Chiti	2.00	1.00	.60
120	Johnny Klippstein	2.00	1.00	.60
121	Gene Baker	2.00	1.00	.60
122	Walt Moryn	2.00	1.00	.60
123	Dick Littlefield	2.00	1.00	.60
124	Bob Speake	2.00	1.00	.60
125	Hank Sauer	2.00	1.00	.60
126	Monty Stratton	2.50	1.25	.70
127	Johnny Kerr	2.00	1.00	.60
128	Milt Gaston	2.00	1.00	.60
129	Eddie Smith	2.00	1.00	.60
130	Larry Rosenthal	2.00	1.00	.60
131	Orval Grove	2.00	1.00	.60
132	Johnny Hodapp	2.00	1.00	.60
133	Johnny Rigney	2.00	1.00	.60
134	Willie Kamm	2.00	1.00	.60
135	Ed Lopat	2.00	1.00	.60
136	Smead Jolley	2.00	1.00	.60
137	Ralph Hodgin	2.00	1.00	.60
138	Ollie Bejma	2.00	1.00	.60
139	Zeke Bonura	2.00	1.00	.60
140	Al Hollingsworth	2.00	1.00	.60
141	Thurman Tucker	2.00	1.00	.60
142	Cass Michaels	2.00	1.00	.60
143	Bill Wight	2.00	1.00	.60
144	Don Lenhardt	2.00	1.00	.60
145	Sammy Esposito	2.00	1.00	.60
146	Jack Harshman	2.00	1.00	.60
147	Turk Lown	2.00	1.00	.60
148	Jim Landis	2.00	1.00	.60
149	Bob Shaw	2.00	1.00	.60
150	Minnie Minoso	2.50	1.25	.70
151	Les Bell	2.00	1.00	.60
152	Taylor Douthit	2.00	1.00	.60
153	Jack Rothrock	2.00	1.00	.60
154	Terry Moore	2.00	1.00	.60
155	Max Lanier	2.00	1.00	.60
156	Don Gutteridge	2.00	1.00	.60
157	Stu Martin	2.00	1.00	.60
158	Stan Musial	5.00	2.50	1.50
159	Frank Crespi	2.00	1.00	.60
160	Johnny Hopp	2.00	1.00	.60
161	Ernie Koy	2.00	1.00	.60
162	Joe Garagiola	3.00	1.50	.90
163	Ed Kazak	2.00	1.00	.60
164	Joe Orengo	2.00	1.00	.60
165	Howie Krist	2.00	1.00	.60
166	Enos Slaughter	3.00	1.50	.90
167	Ray Sanders	2.00	1.00	.60
168	Walker Cooper	2.00	1.00	.60
169	Nippy Jones	2.00	1.00	.60
170	Dick Sisler	2.00	1.00	.60
171	Harvey Haddix	2.00	1.00	.60
172	Solly Hemus	2.00	1.00	.60
173	Ray Jablonski	2.00	1.00	.60
174	Alex Grammas	2.00	1.00	.60
175	Joe Cunningham	2.00	1.00	.60
176	Debs Garms	2.00	1.00	.60
177	Chief Hogsett	2.00	1.00	.60
178	Alan Strange	2.00	1.00	.60
179	Rick Ferrell	2.00	1.00	.60
180	Jack Kramer	2.00	1.00	.60
181	Jack Knott	2.00	1.00	.60
182	Bob Harris	2.00	1.00	.60
183	Billy Hitchcock	2.00	1.00	.60
184	Jim Walkup	2.00	1.00	.60
185	Roy Cullenbine	2.00	1.00	.60
186	Bob Muncrief	2.00	1.00	.60
187	Chet Laabs	2.00	1.00	.60
188	Vern Kennedy	2.00	1.00	.60
189	Bill Trotter	2.00	1.00	.60
190	Denny Galehouse	2.00	1.00	.60
191	Al Zarilla	2.00	1.00	.60
192	Hank Arft	2.00	1.00	.60
193	Nelson Potter	2.00	1.00	.60
194	Ray Coleman	2.00	1.00	.60
195	Bob Dillinger	2.00	1.00	.60
196	Dick Kokos	2.00	1.00	.60
197	Bob Cain	2.00	1.00	.60
198	Virgil Trucks	2.00	1.00	.60
199	Duane Pillette	2.00	1.00	.60
200	Bob Turley	2.00	1.00	.60
201	Wally Berger	2.00	1.00	.60
202	John Lanning	2.00	1.00	.60
203	Buck Jordan	2.00	1.00	.60
204	Jim Turner	2.00	1.00	.60
205	Johnny Cooney	2.00	1.00	.60
206	Hank Majeski	2.00	1.00	.60
207	Phil Masi	2.00	1.00	.60
208	Tony Cuccinello	2.00	1.00	.60
209	Whitey Wietelmann	2.00	1.00	.60
210	Lou Fette	2.00	1.00	.60
211	Vince DiMaggio	2.50	1.25	.70
212	Huck Betts	2.00	1.00	.60
213	Red Barrett	2.00	1.00	.60
214	Pinkey Whitney	2.00	1.00	.60
215	Tommy Holmes	2.00	1.00	.60
216	Ray Berres	2.00	1.00	.60
217	Mike Sandlock	2.00	1.00	.60
218	Max Macon	2.00	1.00	.60
219	Sibby Sisti	2.00	1.00	.60
220	Johnny Beazley	2.00	1.00	.60
221	Bill Posedel	2.00	1.00	.60
222	Connie Ryan	2.00	1.00	.60
223	Del Crandall	2.00	1.00	.60
224	Bob Addis	2.00	1.00	.60
225	Warren Spahn	3.00	1.50	.90
226	Johnny Pesky	2.00	1.00	.60
227	Dom DiMaggio	2.50	1.25	.70
228	Emerson Dickman	2.00	1.00	.60
229	Bobby Doerr	2.00	1.00	.60
230	Tony Lupien	2.00	1.00	.60
231	Roy Partee	2.00	1.00	.60
232	Stan Spence	2.00	1.00	.60
233	Jim Bagby	2.00	1.00	.60
234	Buster Mills	2.00	1.00	.60
235	Fabian Gaffke	2.00	1.00	.60
236	George Metkovich	2.00	1.00	.60
237	Tom McBride	2.00	1.00	.60
238	Charlie Wagner	2.00	1.00	.60
239	Eddie Pellagrini	2.00	1.00	.60
240	Harry Dorish	2.00	1.00	.60
241	Ike Delock	2.00	1.00	.60
242	Mel Parnell	2.00	1.00	.60
243	Matt Batts	2.00	1.00	.60
244	Gene Stephens	2.00	1.00	.60
245	Milt Bolling	2.00	1.00	.60
246	Charlie Maxwell	2.00	1.00	.60
247	Willard Nixon	2.00	1.00	.60
248	Sammy White	2.00	1.00	.60
249	Dick Gernert	2.00	1.00	.60
250	Rico Petrocelli	2.00	1.00	.60
251	Edd Roush	2.00	1.00	.60
252	Mark Koenig	2.00	1.00	.60
253	Jimmy Outlaw	2.00	1.00	.60
254	Ethan Allen	2.00	1.00	.60
255	Tony Freitas	2.00	1.00	.60
256	Frank McCormick	2.00	1.00	.60
257	Bucky Walters	2.00	1.00	.60
258	Harry Craft	2.00	1.00	.60
259	Nate Andrews	2.00	1.00	.60
260	Ed Lukon	2.00	1.00	.60
261	Elmer Riddle	2.00	1.00	.60
262	Lee Grissom	2.00	1.00	.60
263	Johnny Vander Meer	2.00	1.00	.60
264	Eddie Joost	2.00	1.00	.60
265	Kermit Wahl	2.00	1.00	.60
266	Ival Goodman	2.00	1.00	.60
267	Clyde Vollmer	2.00	1.00	.60
268	Grady Hatton	2.00	1.00	.60
269	Ted Kluszewski	3.00	1.50	.90
270	Johnny Pramesa	2.00	1.00	.60
271	Joe Black	2.50	1.25	.70
272	Roy McMillan	2.00	1.00	.60
273	Wally Post	2.00	1.00	.60
274	Joe Nuxhall	2.00	1.00	.60
275	Jerry Lynch	2.00	1.00	.60
276	Stan Coveleski	2.00	1.00	.60
277	Bill Wambsganss	2.00	1.00	.60
278	Bruce Campbell	2.00	1.00	.60
279	George Uhle	2.00	1.00	.60
280	Earl Averill	2.00	1.00	.60
281	Whit Wyatt	2.00	1.00	.60
282	Oscar Grimes	2.00	1.00	.60

283	Roy Weatherly	2.00	1.00	.60
284	Joe Dobson	2.00	1.00	.60
285	Bob Feller	3.00	1.50	.90
286	Jim Hegan	2.00	1.00	.60
287	Mel Harder	2.00	1.00	.60
288	Ken Keltner	2.00	1.00	.60
289	Red Embree	2.00	1.00	.60
290	Al Milnar	2.00	1.00	.60
291	Lou Boudreau	2.00	1.00	.60
292	Ed Klieman	2.00	1.00	.60
293	Steve Gromek	2.00	1.00	.60
294	George Strickland	2.00	1.00	.60
295	Gene Woodling	2.00	1.00	.60
296	Hank Edwards	2.00	1.00	.60
297	Don Mossi	2.00	1.00	.60
298	Eddie Robinson	2.00	1.00	.60
299	Sam Dente	2.00	1.00	.60
300	Herb Score	2.00	1.00	.60
301	Dolf Camilli	2.00	1.00	.60
302	Jack Warner	2.00	1.00	.60
303	Ike Pearson	2.00	1.00	.60
304	Johnny Peacock	2.00	1.00	.60
305	Gene Corbett	2.00	1.00	.60
306	Walt Millies	2.00	1.00	.60
307	Vance Dinges	2.00	1.00	.60
308	Joe Marty	2.00	1.00	.60
309	Hugh Mulcahey	2.00	1.00	.60
310	Boom Boom Beck	2.00	1.00	.60
311	Charley Schanz	2.00	1.00	.60
312	John Bolling	2.00	1.00	.60
313	Danny Litwhiler	2.00	1.00	.60
314	Emil Verban	2.00	1.00	.60
315	Andy Semenick	2.00	1.00	.60
316	John Antonelli	2.00	1.00	.60
317	Robin Roberts	3.00	1.50	.90
318	Richie Ashburn	3.00	1.50	.90
319	Curt Simmons	2.00	1.00	.60
320	Murry Dickson	2.00	1.00	.60
321	Jim Greengrass	2.00	1.00	.60
322	Gene Freese	2.00	1.00	.60
323	Bobby Morgan	2.00	1.00	.60
324	Don Demeter	2.00	1.00	.60
325	Eddie Sawyer	2.00	1.00	.60
326	Bob Johnson	2.00	1.00	.60
327	Ace Parker	3.00	1.50	.90
328	Joe Hauser	2.00	1.00	.60
329	Walt French	2.00	1.00	.60
330	Tom Ferrick	2.00	1.00	.60
331	Bill Werber	2.00	1.00	.60
332	Walt Masters	2.00	1.00	.60
333	Les McCrabb	2.00	1.00	.60
334	Ben McCoy	2.00	1.00	.60
335	Eric Tipton	2.00	1.00	.60
336	Al Rubeling	2.00	1.00	.60
337	Nick Etten	2.00	1.00	.60
338	Carl Scheib	2.00	1.00	.60
339	Dario Lodigiani	2.00	1.00	.60
340	Earle Brucker	2.00	1.00	.60
341	Al Brancato	2.00	1.00	.60
342	Lou Limmer	2.00	1.00	.60
343	Elmer Valo	2.00	1.00	.60
344	Bob Hooper	2.00	1.00	.60
345	Joe Astroth	2.00	1.00	.60
346	Pete Suder	2.00	1.00	.60
347	Dave Philley	2.00	1.00	.60
348	Gus Zernial	2.00	1.00	.60
349	Bobby Shantz	2.00	1.00	.60
350	Joe DeMaestri	2.00	1.00	.60
351	Fred Lindstrom	2.00	1.00	.60
352	Red Lucas	2.00	1.00	.60
353	Clyde Barnhart	2.00	1.00	.60
354	Nick Strincevich	2.00	1.00	.60
355	Lloyd Waner	2.00	1.00	.60
356	Guy Bush	2.00	1.00	.60
357	Joe Bowman	2.00	1.00	.60
358	Al Todd	2.00	1.00	.60
359	Mace Brown	2.00	1.00	.60
360	Larry French	2.00	1.00	.60
361	Elbie Fletcher	2.00	1.00	.60
362	Woody Jensen	2.00	1.00	.60
363	Rip Sewell	2.00	1.00	.60
364	Johnny Dickshot	2.00	1.00	.60
365	Pete Coscarart	2.00	1.00	.60
366	Bud Hafey	2.00	1.00	.60
367	Ken Heintzelman	2.00	1.00	.60
368	Wally Westlake	2.00	1.00	.60
369	Frank Gustine	2.00	1.00	.60
370	Smoky Burgess	2.00	1.00	.60
371	Dick Groat	2.00	1.00	.60
372	Vern Law	2.00	1.00	.60
373	Bob Skinner	2.00	1.00	.60
374	Don Cardwell	2.00	1.00	.60
375	Bob Friend	2.00	1.00	.60
376	Frank O'Rourke	2.00	1.00	.60
377	Birdie Tebbetts	2.00	1.00	.60
378	Charlie Gehringer	3.00	1.50	.90
379	Eldon Auker	2.00	1.00	.60
380	Tuck Stainback	2.00	1.00	.60
381	Chet Morgan	2.00	1.00	.60
382	Johnny Lipon	2.00	1.00	.60
383	Paul Richards	2.00	1.00	.60
384	Johnny Gorsica	2.00	1.00	.60
385	Ray Hayworth	2.00	1.00	.60
386	Jimmy Bloodworth	2.00	1.00	.60
387	Gene Desautels	2.00	1.00	.60
388	Jo Jo White	2.00	1.00	.60
389	Boots Poffenberger	2.00	1.00	.60
390	Barney McCosky	2.00	1.00	.60
391	Dick Wakefield	2.00	1.00	.60
392	Johnny Groth	2.00	1.00	.60
393	Steve Souchock	2.00	1.00	.60
394	George Vico	2.00	1.00	.60
395	Hal Newhouser	2.00	1.00	.60
396	Ray Herbert	2.00	1.00	.60
397	Jim Bunning	2.00	1.00	.60
398	Frank Lary	2.00	1.00	.60
399	Harvey Kuenn	2.00	1.00	.60
400	Eddie Mathews	3.00	1.50	.90

1911 Diamond Gum Pins (PE2)

The World's Champion Philadelphia A's are well represented and specially marked in this series of small 1" diameter pins. The sepia-toned center portion of the pin has a player portrait photo with his last name, team and league in white at left and right. Around that is a metallic blue border with a white inscription; either "World's Champions" on the A's players, or "Free with Diamond Gum" on the other players.

		NM	EX	VG
Complete Set (31):		30,000	15,000	9,000
Common Player:		500.00	250.00	150.00
(1)	Babe Adams	500.00	250.00	150.00
(2)	Home Run Baker	1,200	600.00	360.00
(3)	Chief Bender	1,200	600.00	360.00
(4)	Mordecai Brown	1,200	600.00	360.00
(5)	Donie Bush	500.00	250.00	150.00
(6)	Bill Carrigan	500.00	250.00	150.00
(7)	Frank Chance	1,200	600.00	360.00
(8)	Hal Chase	800.00	400.00	240.00
(9)	Ty Cobb	3,000	1,500	900.00
(10)	Eddie Collins	1,200	600.00	360.00
(11)	George Davis	500.00	250.00	150.00
(12)	Red Dooin	500.00	250.00	150.00
(13)	Larry Doyle	500.00	250.00	150.00
(14)	Johnny Evers	1,200	600.00	360.00
(15)	Miller Huggins	1,200	600.00	360.00
(16)	Hughie Jennings	1,200	600.00	360.00
(17)	Nap Lajoie	1,200	600.00	360.00
(18)	Harry Lord	500.00	250.00	150.00
(19)	Christy Mathewson	2,000	1,000	600.00
(20)	Dots Miller	500.00	250.00	150.00
(21)	George Mullen (Mullin)	500.00	250.00	150.00
(22)	Danny Murphy	500.00	250.00	150.00
(23)	Orval Overall	500.00	250.00	150.00
(24)	Eddie Plank	1,250	625.00	375.00
(25)	Ryan (Rochester)	500.00	250.00	150.00
(26)	Jimmie Savage (Rochester)	500.00	250.00	150.00
(27)	Hack Simmons	500.00	250.00	150.00
(28)	Ira Thomas	500.00	250.00	150.00
(29)	Joe Tinker	1,200	600.00	360.00
(30)	Honus Wagner	2,500	1,250	750.00
(31)	Cy Young	2,000	1,000	600.00

1934 Diamond Matchbooks - Silver Border

During much of the Great Depression, the hobby of matchbook collecting swept the country. Generally selling at two for a penny, the matchbooks began to feature photos and artwork to attract buyers. In the late 1930s, several series of sports subjects were issued by Diamond Match Co., of New York City. The first issue was a set of 200 baseball players known to collectors as "silver border" for the color of the photo frame on of the approximately 1-1/2" x 4-1/8" (open) matchbooks. Player portrait or posed photos are printed in sepia on front, and can be found bordered in either red, green, blue or orange (though it is unclear whether all players can actually be found in the red version), theoretically creating an 800-piece color variation set. The player's name and team are printed on the "saddle" and there is a career summary on back, along with a design of glove, ball and bats. Matchbooks are commonly collected with the matches removed and the striker at back-bottom intact. Pieces without the striker are valued at 50 percent of these listed prices. Complete covers with matches bring a premium of 2-3X. The players are listed here alphabetically.

		NM	EX	VG
Complete Set (200):		4,500	2,250	1,350
Common Player:		20.00	10.00	6.00
(1)	Earl Adams	20.00	10.00	6.00
(2)	Ethan Allen	20.00	10.00	6.00
(3)	Eldon L. Auker	20.00	10.00	6.00
(4)	Delmar David Baker	20.00	10.00	6.00
(5)	Richard "Dick" Bartell	20.00	10.00	6.00
(6)	Walter Beck	20.00	10.00	6.00
(7)	Herman Bell	20.00	10.00	6.00
(8)	Ray Benge	20.00	10.00	6.00
(9)	Larry J. Benton	20.00	10.00	6.00
(10)	Louis W. Berger	20.00	10.00	6.00
(11)	Walter "Wally" Berger	20.00	10.00	6.00
(12)	Ray Berres	20.00	10.00	6.00
(13)	Charlie Berry	20.00	10.00	6.00
(14)	Walter M. "Huck" Betts	20.00	10.00	6.00
(15)	Ralph Birkofer	20.00	10.00	6.00
(16)	George F. Blaeholder	20.00	10.00	6.00
(17)	Jim Bottomley	40.00	20.00	12.00
(18a)	Ralph Boyle (Photo actually Virgil Davis, white cap.)	20.00	10.00	6.00
(18b)	Ralph Boyle (Correct photo, cark cap.)	20.00	10.00	6.00
(19)	Ed Brandt	20.00	10.00	6.00
(20)	Don Brennan	20.00	10.00	6.00
(21)	Irving (Jack) Burns	20.00	10.00	6.00
(22)	Guy "Joe" Bush	20.00	10.00	6.00
(23)	Adolph Camilli	20.00	10.00	6.00
(24)	Ben Cantwell	20.00	10.00	6.00
(25)	Tex Carleton	20.00	10.00	6.00
(26)	Owen Carroll	20.00	10.00	6.00
(27)	Louis Chiozza	20.00	10.00	6.00
(28)	Watson Clark	20.00	10.00	6.00
(29)	James A. Collins	20.00	10.00	6.00
(30)	Phil Collins	20.00	10.00	6.00
(31)	Edward J. Connolly	20.00	10.00	6.00
(32)	Raymond F. Coombs	20.00	10.00	6.00
(33)	Roger Cramer	20.00	10.00	6.00
(34)	Clifford Crawford	20.00	10.00	6.00
(35)	Hugh M. Critz	20.00	10.00	6.00
(36)	Alvin Crowder	20.00	10.00	6.00
(37)	Tony Cuccinello	20.00	10.00	6.00
(38)	Hazen "Kiki" Cuyler	40.00	20.00	12.00
(39)	Virgil Davis	20.00	10.00	6.00
(40)	Jerome "Dizzy" Dean	80.00	40.00	24.00
(41)	Paul Dean	35.00	17.50	10.50
(42)	Edward Delker	20.00	10.00	6.00
(43)	Paul Derringer	20.00	10.00	6.00
(44)	Eugene DeSautel	20.00	10.00	6.00
(45)	William J. Dietrich	20.00	10.00	6.00
(46)	Frank F. Doljack	20.00	10.00	6.00
(47)	Edward F. Durham	20.00	10.00	6.00
(48)	Leo Durocher	40.00	20.00	12.00
(49)	Jim Elliott	20.00	10.00	6.00
(50)	Charles D. English	20.00	10.00	6.00
(51)	Elwood G. English	20.00	10.00	6.00
(52)	Richard Ferrell	40.00	20.00	12.00
(53)	Wesley Ferrell (EXISTENCE DOUBTED)			
(54)	Charles W. Fischer	20.00	10.00	6.00
(55)	Freddy Fitzsimmons	20.00	10.00	6.00
(56)	Lew Fonseca	20.00	10.00	6.00
(57)	Fred Frankhouse	20.00	10.00	6.00
(58)	John Frederick	20.00	10.00	6.00
(59)	Benny Frey (Reds)	20.00	10.00	6.00
(60)	Linus Frey (Dodgers)	20.00	10.00	6.00
(61)	Frankie Frisch	45.00	22.00	13.50
(62)	Chick Fullis	20.00	10.00	6.00
(63)	August Galan	20.00	10.00	6.00
(64)	Milton Galatzer	120.00	60.00	36.00
(65)	Dennis W. Galehouse	20.00	10.00	6.00
(66)	Milton Gaston	20.00	10.00	6.00
(67)	Chas. Gehringer	45.00	22.00	13.50
(68)	Edward P. Gharrity	20.00	10.00	6.00
(69)	George Gibson	20.00	10.00	6.00
(70)	Isidore Goldstein	250.00	125.00	75.00
(71)	"Hank" Gowdy	20.00	10.00	6.00
(72)	Earl Grace	20.00	10.00	6.00
(73)	Chas. Grimm/Fldg	20.00	10.00	6.00
(74)	Chas. Grimm/Portrait	20.00	10.00	6.00
(75)	Frank T. Grube	20.00	10.00	6.00
(76)	Richard Gyselman	20.00	10.00	6.00
(77)	Stanley C. Hack	25.00	12.50	7.50
(78)	Irving Hadley	20.00	10.00	6.00
(79)	Charles "Chick" Hafey	40.00	20.00	12.00
(80)	Harold A. Haid	20.00	10.00	6.00
(81)	Jesse Haines	40.00	20.00	12.00
(82)	Odell A. Hale	20.00	10.00	6.00
(83)	Bill Hallahan	20.00	10.00	6.00
(84)	Luke D. Hamlin	20.00	10.00	6.00
(85)	Roy Hansen	20.00	10.00	6.00
(86)	Melvin Harder	20.00	10.00	6.00
(87)	William M. Harris	20.00	10.00	6.00
(88)	Gabby Hartnett	40.00	20.00	12.00
(89)	Harvey Hendrick	20.00	10.00	6.00
(90)	Floyd "Babe" Herman	25.00	12.50	7.50
(91)	William Herman	40.00	20.00	12.00
(92)	J. Francis Hogan	20.00	10.00	6.00
(93)	Elon Hogsett	20.00	10.00	6.00
(94)	Waite Hoyt	40.00	20.00	12.00
(95)	Carl Hubbell	50.00	25.00	15.00
(96)	Silas K. Johnson	20.00	10.00	6.00
(97)	Sylvester Johnson	20.00	10.00	6.00
(98)	Roy M. Joiner	20.00	10.00	6.00
(99)	Baxter Jordan	20.00	10.00	6.00
(100)	Arndt Jorgens	20.00	10.00	6.00
(101)	William F. Jurges	20.00	10.00	6.00
(102)	Vernon Kennedy	20.00	10.00	6.00
(103)	John F. Kerr	20.00	10.00	6.00
(104)	Charles "Chuck" Klein	40.00	20.00	12.00
(105)	Theodore Kleinhans	20.00	10.00	6.00
(106)	Bill Klem/Umpire	125.00	65.00	35.00

(107)	Robert G. Kline	20.00	10.00	6.00
(108)	William Knickerbocker	20.00	10.00	6.00
(109)	Jack H. Knott	20.00	10.00	6.00
(110)	Mark Koenig	20.00	10.00	6.00
(111)	William Lawrence	20.00	10.00	6.00
(112)	Thornton S. Lee	20.00	10.00	6.00
(113)	Wm. C. "Bill" Lee	20.00	10.00	6.00
(114)	Emil Leonard	20.00	10.00	6.00
(115)	Ernest Lombardi	40.00	20.00	12.00
(116)	Alfonso Lopez	40.00	20.00	12.00
(117)	Red Lucas	20.00	10.00	6.00
(118)	Ted Lyons	40.00	20.00	12.00
(119)	Daniel MacFayden	20.00	10.00	6.00
(120)	Ed. Majeski	20.00	10.00	6.00
(121)	Leroy Mahaffey	20.00	10.00	6.00
(122)	Pat Malone	20.00	10.00	6.00
(123)	Leo Mangum	20.00	10.00	6.00
(124)	Rabbit Maranville	40.00	20.00	12.00
(125)	Charles K. Marrow	20.00	10.00	6.00
(126)	William McKechnie	40.00	20.00	12.00
(127)	Justin McLaughlin	20.00	10.00	6.00
(128)	Marty McManus	20.00	10.00	6.00
(129)	Eric McNair	20.00	10.00	6.00
(130)	Joe Medwick	40.00	20.00	12.00
(131)	Jim Mooney	20.00	10.00	6.00
(132)	Joe Moore	20.00	10.00	6.00
(133)	John Moore	20.00	10.00	6.00
(134)	Randy Moore	20.00	10.00	6.00
(135)	Joe Morrissey	20.00	10.00	6.00
(136)	Joseph Mowrey	20.00	10.00	6.00
(137)	Fred W. Muller	20.00	10.00	6.00
(138)	Van Mungo	25.00	12.50	7.50
(139)	Glenn Myatt	20.00	10.00	6.00
(140a)	Lynn Nelson (Photo actually Eugene DeSautel, no "C" on cap.)	20.00	10.00	6.00
(140b)	Lynn Nelson (Correct photo, "C" on cap.)	20.00	10.00	6.00
(141)	Henry Oana	60.00	30.00	18.00
(142)	Lefty O'Doul	35.00	17.50	10.50
(143)	Robert O'Farrell	20.00	10.00	6.00
(144)	Ernest Orsatti	20.00	10.00	6.00
(145)	Fritz R. Ostermueller	20.00	10.00	6.00
(146)	Melvin Ott	45.00	22.00	13.50
(147)	Roy Parmelee	20.00	10.00	6.00
(148)	Ralph Perkins	20.00	10.00	6.00
(149)	Frank Pytlak	20.00	10.00	6.00
(150)	Ernest C. Quigley/Umpire	45.00	22.00	13.50
(151)	George Rensa	20.00	10.00	6.00
(152)	Harry Rice	20.00	10.00	6.00
(153)	Walter Roettger	20.00	10.00	6.00
(154)	William G. Rogell	20.00	10.00	6.00
(155)	Edwin A. Rommel	20.00	10.00	6.00
(156)	Charlie Root	20.00	10.00	6.00
(157)	John Rothrock	20.00	10.00	6.00
(158)	Jack Russell	20.00	10.00	6.00
(159)	Blondy Ryan	20.00	10.00	6.00
(160)	Alexander (Al) Schacht	35.00	17.50	10.50
(161)	Wesley Schultmerick	20.00	10.00	6.00
(162)	Truett B. Sewell	20.00	10.00	6.00
(163)	Gordon Slade	20.00	10.00	6.00
(164)	Bob Smith	20.00	10.00	6.00
(165)	Julius J. Solters	20.00	10.00	6.00
(166)	Glenn Spencer	20.00	10.00	6.00
(167)	Al Spohrer	20.00	10.00	6.00
(168)	George Stainback	20.00	10.00	6.00
(169)	Albert "Dolly" Stark/Umpire	40.00	20.00	12.00
(170)	Casey Stengel	50.00	25.00	15.00
(171)	Riggs Stephenson	20.00	10.00	6.00
(172)	Walter C. Stewart	20.00	10.00	6.00
(173)	Lin Storti	20.00	10.00	6.00
(174)	Allyn (Fish Hook) Stout	20.00	10.00	6.00
(175)	Joe Stripp	20.00	10.00	6.00
(176)	Gus Suhr	20.00	10.00	6.00
(177)	Billy Sullivan, Jr.	20.00	10.00	6.00
(178)	Benny Tate	20.00	10.00	6.00
(179)	Danny Taylor	20.00	10.00	6.00
(180)	Tommy Thevenow	20.00	10.00	6.00
(181)	Bud Tinning	20.00	10.00	6.00
(182)	Cecil Travis	20.00	10.00	6.00
(183)	Forest F. Twogood	20.00	10.00	6.00
(184)	Bill Urbanski	20.00	10.00	6.00
(185)	Dazzy Vance	40.00	20.00	12.00
(186)	Arthur Veltman/SP	100.00	50.00	30.00
(187)	John L. Vergez	20.00	10.00	6.00
(188)	Gerald (Jerry) Walker	20.00	10.00	6.00
(189)	William H. Walker	20.00	10.00	6.00
(190)	Lloyd Waner	40.00	20.00	12.00
(191)	Paul Waner	40.00	20.00	12.00
(192)	Lon Warnecke	20.00	10.00	6.00
(193)	Harold B. Warstler	20.00	10.00	6.00
(194)	Bill Werber	20.00	10.00	6.00
(195)	Joyner White	20.00	10.00	6.00
(196)	Arthur Whitney	20.00	10.00	6.00
(197)	James Wilson	20.00	10.00	6.00
(198)	Lewis (Hack) Wilson	40.00	20.00	12.00
(199)	Ralph L. Winegarner	20.00	10.00	6.00
(200)	Thomas Zachary	20.00	10.00	6.00

1935 Diamond Matchbooks - Black Border

Only 24 players were issued in the 1935 Diamond Matchbook baseball series. Similar in design to the 1934 issue, these 1-1/2" x 4-1/8" matchbooks have sepia player portrait photos on front, framed in either red, green or blue. The overall borders of the cover are black. Backs of the 1935 issue feature a career summary overprinted on a silhouetted batting figure. The "saddle" has the player name and team superimposed on a baseball. These matchbooks are commonly collected with the matches removed and the striker at back-bottom intact. Pieces without the striker are valued at 50 percent of these listed prices. Complete covers with matches bring a premium of 2-3X. The players are listed here alphabetically.

		NM	EX	VG
Complete Set (24):		850.00	425.00	250.00
Common Player:		25.00	12.50	7.50
(1)	Ethan Allen/Red	25.00	12.50	7.50
(2)	Walter Berger/Red	25.00	12.50	7.50
(3)	Tommy Carey/Blue	25.00	12.50	7.50
(4)	Louis Chiozza/Blue	25.00	12.50	7.50
(5)	Jerome (Dizzy) Dean/Green	65.00	32.50	20.00
(6)	Frankie Frisch/Red	50.00	25.00	15.00
(7)	Charles Grimm/Blue	25.00	12.50	7.50
(8)	Charles Hafey/Red	40.00	20.00	12.00
(9)	J. Francis Hogan/Red	25.00	12.50	7.50
(10)	Carl Hubbell/Green	50.00	25.00	15.00
(11)	Charles Klein/Green	40.00	20.00	12.00
(12)	Ernest Lombardi/Blue	40.00	20.00	12.00
(13)	Alfonso Lopez/Blue	40.00	20.00	12.00
(14)	Rabbit Maranville/Green	40.00	20.00	12.00
(15)	Joe Moore/Red	25.00	12.50	7.50
(16)	Van Mungo/Green	25.00	12.50	7.50
(17)	Melvin (Mel) Ott/Blue	50.00	25.00	15.00
(18)	Gordon Slade/Green	25.00	12.50	7.50
(19)	Casey Stengel/Green	50.00	25.00	15.00
(20)	Tommy Thevenow/Red	25.00	12.50	7.50
(21)	Lloyd Waner/Red	40.00	20.00	12.00
(22)	Paul Waner/Green	50.00	25.00	15.00
(23)	Lon Warnecke/Blue	25.00	12.50	7.50
(24)	James Wilson/Blue	25.00	12.50	7.50

1935-36 Diamond Matchbooks

By the career summaries on back of these covers it is evident this series was issued over a two-year period. Measuring about 1-1/2" x 4-1/8", the fronts have posed player photos printed in sepia. Borders can be found in red, green or blue, and it is believed that most, if not all, players, can be found in those three color varieties. Matchbooks in this series do not have the team name on back beneath the player name, as is the case on later series. Collectors generally prefer matchbooks to be complete with striker surface on bottom-back, though with matches removed. Values shown should be halved for covers without strikers. Complete with matches, covers will sell for a 2-3X premium over the values shown.

		NM	EX	VG
Complete Set (156):		3,500	1,750	1,000
Common Player:		20.00	10.00	6.00
(1)	Ethan Allen	20.00	10.00	6.00
(2)	Melo Almada	30.00	15.00	9.00
(3)	Eldon Auker	20.00	10.00	6.00
(4)	Dick Bartell	20.00	10.00	6.00
(5)	Aloysius Bejma	20.00	10.00	6.00
(6)	Ollie Bejma	20.00	10.00	6.00
(7)	Roy Chester Bell	20.00	10.00	6.00
(8)	Louis Berger	20.00	10.00	6.00
(9)	Walter Berger	20.00	10.00	6.00
(10)	Ralph Birkofer	20.00	10.00	6.00
(11)	Max Bishop	20.00	10.00	6.00
(12)	George Blaeholder	20.00	10.00	6.00
(13)	Henry (Zeke) Bonura	20.00	10.00	6.00
(14)	Jim Bottomley	35.00	17.50	10.50
(15)	Ed Brandt	20.00	10.00	6.00
(16)	Don Brennan	20.00	10.00	6.00
(17)	Lloyd Brown	20.00	10.00	6.00
(18)	Walter G. Brown	20.00	10.00	6.00
(19)	Claiborne Bryant	20.00	10.00	6.00
(20)	Jim Bucher	20.00	10.00	6.00
(21)	John Burnett	20.00	10.00	6.00
(22)	Irving Burns	20.00	10.00	6.00
(23)	Merritt Cain	20.00	10.00	6.00
(24)	Ben Cantwell	20.00	10.00	6.00
(25)	Tommy Carey	20.00	10.00	6.00
(26)	Tex Carleton	20.00	10.00	6.00
(27)	Joseph Cascarella	20.00	10.00	6.00
(28)	Thomas H. Casey	20.00	10.00	6.00
(29)	George Caster	20.00	10.00	6.00
(30)	Phil Cavarretta	20.00	10.00	6.00
(31)	Louis Chiozza	20.00	10.00	6.00
(32)	Edward Cihocki	20.00	10.00	6.00
(33)	Herman E. Clifton	20.00	10.00	6.00
(34)	Richard Coffman	20.00	10.00	6.00
(35)	Edward P. Coleman	20.00	10.00	6.00
(36)	James A. Collins	20.00	10.00	6.00
(37)	John Conlan	40.00	20.00	12.00
(38)	Roger Cramer	20.00	10.00	6.00
(39)	Hugh M. Critz	20.00	10.00	6.00
(40)	Alvin Crowder	20.00	10.00	6.00
(41)	Tony Cuccinello	20.00	10.00	6.00
(42)	Hazen "Kiki" Cuyler	35.00	17.50	10.50
(43)	Virgil Davis	20.00	10.00	6.00
(44)	Jerome Dean	75.00	37.00	22.00
(45)	Paul Derringer	20.00	10.00	6.00
(46)	James DeShong	20.00	10.00	6.00
(47)	William Dietrich	20.00	10.00	6.00
(48)	Leo Durocher	35.00	17.50	10.50
(49)	George Earnshaw	20.00	10.00	6.00
(50)	Elwood English	20.00	10.00	6.00
(51)	Louis Finney	20.00	10.00	6.00
(52)	Charles Fischer	20.00	10.00	6.00
(53)	Freddy Fitzsimmons	20.00	10.00	6.00
(54)	Benny Frey	20.00	10.00	6.00
(55)	Linus B. Frey	20.00	10.00	6.00
(56)	Frankie Frisch	40.00	20.00	12.00
(57)	August Galan	20.00	10.00	6.00
(58)	Milton Galatzer	20.00	10.00	6.00
(59)	Dennis Galehouse	20.00	10.00	6.00
(60)	Debs Garms	20.00	10.00	6.00
(61)	Angelo J. Giuliani	20.00	10.00	6.00
(62)	Earl Grace	20.00	10.00	6.00
(63)	Charles Grimm	20.00	10.00	6.00
(64)	Frank Grube	20.00	10.00	6.00
(65)	Stanley Hack	25.00	12.50	7.50
(66)	Irving "Bump" Hadley	20.00	10.00	6.00
(67)	Odell Hale	20.00	10.00	6.00
(68)	Bill Hallahan	20.00	10.00	6.00
(69)	Roy Hansen	20.00	10.00	6.00
(70)	Melvin Harder	20.00	10.00	6.00
(71)	Charles Hartnett	35.00	17.50	10.50
(72)	"Gabby" Hartnett	35.00	17.50	10.50
(73)	Clyde Hatter	20.00	10.00	6.00
(74)	Raymond Hayworth	20.00	10.00	6.00
(75)	Raymond Hayworth (W/chest protector.)	20.00	10.00	6.00
(76)	William Herman	35.00	17.50	10.50
(77)	Gordon Hinkle	20.00	10.00	6.00
(78)	George Hockette	20.00	10.00	6.00
(79)	James Holbrook	20.00	10.00	6.00
(80)	Alex Hooks	20.00	10.00	6.00
(81)	Waite Hoyt	35.00	17.50	10.50
(82)	Carl Hubbell	40.00	20.00	12.00
(83)	Roy M. Joiner	20.00	10.00	6.00
(84)	Sam Jones	20.00	10.00	6.00
(85)	Baxter Jordan	20.00	10.00	6.00
(86)	Arndt Jorgens	20.00	10.00	6.00
(87)	William F. Jurges	20.00	10.00	6.00
(88)	William Kamm	20.00	10.00	6.00
(89)	Vernon Kennedy	20.00	10.00	6.00
(90)	John Kerr	20.00	10.00	6.00
(91)	Charles Klein	40.00	20.00	12.00
(92)	Ted Kleinhans	20.00	10.00	6.00
(93)	Wm. Knickerbocker (Thighs-up.)	20.00	10.00	6.00
(94)	Wm. Knickerbocker (Waist-up.)	20.00	10.00	6.00
(95)	Jack Knott	20.00	10.00	6.00
(96)	Mark Koenig	20.00	10.00	6.00
(97)	Fabian L. Kowalik	20.00	10.00	6.00
(98)	Ralph Kress	20.00	10.00	6.00
(99)	Wm. C. "Bill" Lee	20.00	10.00	6.00
(100)	Louis Legett	20.00	10.00	6.00
(101)	Emil "Dutch" Leonard	20.00	10.00	6.00
(102)	Fred Lindstrom	35.00	17.50	10.50
(103)	Edward Linke (Pole in background.)	20.00	10.00	6.00
(104)	Edward Linke (No pole.)	20.00	10.00	6.00
(105)	Ernest Lombardi	35.00	17.50	10.50
(106)	Al Lopez	35.00	17.50	10.50
(107)	John Marcum	20.00	10.00	6.00
(108)	William McKechnie	35.00	17.50	10.50
(109)	Eric McNair	20.00	10.00	6.00
(110)	Joe Medwick	35.00	17.50	10.50
(111)	Oscar Melillo	20.00	10.00	6.00
(112)	John Michaels	20.00	10.00	6.00
(113)	Joe Moore	20.00	10.00	6.00
(114)	John Moore	20.00	10.00	6.00
(115)	Wallace Moses	20.00	10.00	6.00
(116)	Joseph Milligan	20.00	10.00	6.00
(117)	Van Mungo	25.00	12.50	7.50
(118)	Glenn Myatt	20.00	10.00	6.00
(119)	James O'Dea	20.00	10.00	6.00
(120)	Ernest Orsatti	20.00	10.00	6.00
(121)	Fred Ostermueller	20.00	10.00	6.00
(122)	Melvin "Mel" Ott	40.00	20.00	12.00
(123)	LeRoy Parmelee	20.00	10.00	6.00
(124)	Monte Pearson	20.00	10.00	6.00
(125)	Raymond Pepper	20.00	10.00	6.00
(126)	Raymond Phelps	20.00	10.00	6.00

(127)	George Pipgras	20.00	10.00	6.00
(128)	Frank Pytlak	20.00	10.00	6.00
(129)	Gordon Rhodes	20.00	10.00	6.00
(130)	Charlie Root	20.00	10.00	6.00
(131)	John Rothrock	20.00	10.00	6.00
(132)	Herold "Muddy" Ruel	20.00	10.00	6.00
(133)	Jack Saltzgaver	20.00	10.00	6.00
(134)	Fred Schulte	20.00	10.00	6.00
(135)	George Selkirk	20.00	10.00	6.00
(136)	Mervyn Shea	20.00	10.00	6.00
(137)	Al Spohrer	20.00	10.00	6.00
(138)	George Stainback	20.00	10.00	6.00
(139)	Casey Stengel	40.00	20.00	12.00
(140)	Walter Stephenson	20.00	10.00	6.00
(141)	Lee Stine	20.00	10.00	6.00
(142)	John Stone	20.00	10.00	6.00
(143)	Gus Suhr	20.00	10.00	6.00
(144)	Tommy Thevenow	20.00	10.00	6.00
(145)	Fay Thomas	20.00	10.00	6.00
(146)	Leslie Tietje	20.00	10.00	6.00
(147)	Bill Urbanski	20.00	10.00	6.00
(148)	William H. Walker	20.00	10.00	6.00
(149)	Lloyd Waner	40.00	20.00	12.00
(150)	Paul Waner	40.00	20.00	12.00
(151)	Lon Warnecke	20.00	10.00	6.00
(152)	Harold Warstler	20.00	10.00	6.00
(153)	Bill Werber	20.00	10.00	6.00
(154)	Vernon Wiltshere	20.00	10.00	6.00
(155)	James Wilson	20.00	10.00	6.00
(156)	Ralph Winegarner	20.00	10.00	6.00

1936 Diamond Matchbooks - Team on Back

This is the smallest series of baseball player matchbooks, with only 13 subjects, each found with borders of red, green or blue. Player poses on front are printed in sepia (except one variation of Grimm that is in black-and-white). This series can be differentiated from contemporary series by the appearance of the player's team name on back, beneath his name. Backs have a career summary. About 1-1/2" x 4-1/8", these matchbooks are commonly collected with the matches removed and the striker at back bottom intact. Pieces without the striker are valued at 50 percent of these listed prices. Complete covers with matches bring a premium of 2-3X. The players are listed here alphabetically.

		NM	EX	VG
Complete Set (13):		350.00	175.00	100.00
Common Player:		20.00	10.00	6.00
(1)	Tommy Carey	20.00	10.00	6.00
(2)	Tony Cuccinello	20.00	10.00	6.00
(3)	Freddy Fitzsimmons	20.00	10.00	6.00
(4)	Frank Frisch	45.00	22.00	13.50
(5a)	Charles Grimm (Home uniform, b/w.)	20.00	10.00	6.00
(5b)	Charlie Grimm (Home uniform, sepia.)	20.00	10.00	6.00
(6)	Charlie Grimm (Road uniform.)	20.00	10.00	6.00
(7)	Carl Hubbell	45.00	22.00	13.50
(8)	Baxter Jordan	20.00	10.00	6.00
(9)	Chuck Klein	45.00	22.00	13.50
(10)	Al Lopez	35.00	17.50	10.50
(11)	Joe Medwick	35.00	17.50	10.50
(12)	Van Lingle Mungo	25.00	12.50	7.50
(13)	Mel Ott	45.00	22.00	13.50

1936 Diamond Matchbooks - Chicago Cubs

This short series of baseball player matchbooks can each be found with borders of red, green or blue. Except for Dean, all photos are portraits, printed in sepia or black-and-white. Dean and Paul Waner are the only subjects in the set who were not members of the Chicago Cubs. This series can be differentiated from 1935-36 Diamond Matchbooks only by studying the career summary and stats on back. About 1-1/2" x 4-1/8", these matchbooks are commonly collected with the matches removed and the striker at back-bottom intact. Pieces without the striker are valued at 50 percent of these listed prices. Complete covers with matches bring a premium of 2-3X. The players are listed here alphabetically.

		NM	EX	VG
Complete Set (23):		350.00	175.00	100.00
Common Player:		12.50	6.25	3.75
(1)	Claiborne Bryant	12.50	6.25	3.75
(2)	Tex Carleton	12.50	6.25	3.75
(3)	Phil Cavarretta	12.50	6.25	3.75
(4)	James A. Collins	12.50	6.25	3.75
(5)	Curt Davis	12.50	6.25	3.75
(6)	Jerome "Dizzy" Dean	50.00	25.00	15.00
(7)	Frank Demaree	12.50	6.25	3.75
(8)	Larry French	12.50	6.25	3.75
(9)	Linus R. Frey	12.50	6.25	3.75
(10)	August Galan	12.50	6.25	3.75
(11)	Bob Garbark	12.50	6.25	3.75
(12)	Stanley Hack	15.00	7.50	4.50
(13)	Charles Hartnett	30.00	15.00	9.00
(14)	William Herman	30.00	15.00	9.00
(15)	William F. Jurges	12.50	6.25	3.75
(16)	William C. "Bill" Lee	12.50	6.25	3.75
(17)	Joe Marty	12.50	6.25	3.75
(18)	James K. O'Dea	12.50	6.25	3.75
(19)	LeRoy Parmelee	12.50	6.25	3.75
(20)	Charlie Root	12.50	6.25	3.75
(21)	Clyde Shoun	12.50	6.25	3.75
(22)	George Stainback	12.50	6.25	3.75
(23)	Paul Waner	40.00	20.00	12.00

1889 Diamond S Cigars Boston N.L.

(See 1889 Number 7 Cigars for checklist and value information.)

1934-36 Diamond Stars (R327)

Issued from 1934-36, the Diamond Stars set (ACC designation R327) consists of 108 cards. Produced by National Chicle, the cards measure 2-3/8" x 2-7/8" and are color art renderings of actual photographs on art deco backgrounds. The year of issue can usually be determined by the player's statistics found on the reverse of the card. Backs also feature either a player biography or a playing tip. Some cards can be found with either green or blue printing on the backs. The complete set price does not include the higher priced variations which make up the 170-card "master" set.

		NM	EX	VG
Complete Set (108):		22,500	9,000	4,000
Complete Set (170):		35,000	14,000	6,250
Common Player (1-84):		100.00	35.00	20.00
Common Player (85-96):		200.00	85.00	45.00
Common Player (97-108):		500.00	245.00	120.00
1a	"Lefty" Grove (1934 green back)	5,040	770.00	245.00
1b	"Lefty" Grove (1935 green back)	5,040	770.00	245.00
2a	Al Simmons (1934 green back)	840.00	225.00	155.00
2b	Al Simmons (1935 green back)	840.00	225.00	155.00
2c	Al Simmons (1936 blue back)	910.00	365.00	180.00
3a	"Rabbit" Maranville (1934 green back)	455.00	180.00	90.00
3b	"Rabbit" Maranville (1935 green back)	455.00	180.00	90.00
4a	"Buddy" Myer (1934 green back)	100.00	35.00	20.00
4b	"Buddy" Myer (1935 green back)	100.00	35.00	20.00
4c	"Buddy" Myer (1936 blue back)	105.00	45.00	20.00
5a	Tom Bridges (1934 green back)	100.00	35.00	20.00
5b	Tom Bridges (1935 green back)	100.00	35.00	20.00
5c	Tom Bridges (1936 blue back)	105.00	45.00	20.00
6a	Max Bishop (1934 green back)	100.00	35.00	20.00
6b	Max Bishop (1935 green back)	100.00	35.00	20.00
7a	Lew Fonseca (1934 green back)	100.00	35.00	20.00
7b	Lew Fonseca (1935 green back)	100.00	35.00	20.00
8a	Joe Vosmik (1934 green back)	100.00	35.00	20.00
8b	Joe Vosmik (1935 green back)	100.00	35.00	20.00
8c	Joe Vosmik (1936 blue back)	105.00	45.00	20.00
9a	"Mickey" Cochrane (1934 green back)	455.00	180.00	90.00
9b	"Mickey" Cochrane (1935 green back)	455.00	180.00	90.00
9c	"Mickey" Cochrane (1936 blue back)	525.00	210.00	105.00
10a	Roy Mahaffey (1934 green back)	100.00	35.00	20.00
10b	Roy Mahaffey (1935 green back)	100.00	35.00	20.00
10c	Roy Mahaffey (1936 blue back)	105.00	45.00	20.00
11a	Bill Dickey (1934 green back)	525.00	210.00	105.00
11b	Bill Dickey (1935 green back)	525.00	210.00	105.00
12a	Dixie Walker (1934 green back)	100.00	35.00	20.00
12b	Dixie Walker (1935 green back)	100.00	35.00	20.00
12c	Dixie Walker (1936 blue back)	105.00	45.00	20.00
13a	George Blaeholder (1934 green back)	100.00	35.00	20.00
13b	George Blaeholder (1935 green back)	100.00	35.00	20.00
14a	Bill Terry (1934 green back)	455.00	180.00	90.00
14b	Bill Terry (1935 green back)	455.00	180.00	90.00
15a	Dick Bartell (1934 green back)	100.00	35.00	20.00
15b	Dick Bartell (1935 green back)	100.00	35.00	20.00
16a	Lloyd Waner (1934 green back)	455.00	180.00	90.00
16b	Lloyd Waner (1935 green back)	455.00	180.00	90.00
16c	Lloyd Waner (1936 blue back)	560.00	225.00	115.00
17a	Frankie Frisch (1934 green back)	455.00	180.00	90.00
17b	Frankie Frisch (1935 green back)	455.00	180.00	90.00
18a	"Chick" Hafey (1934 green back)	455.00	180.00	90.00
18b	"Chick" Hafey (1935 green back)	455.00	180.00	90.00
19a	Van Mungo (1934 green back)	315.00	125.00	65.00
19b	Van Mungo (1935 green back)	315.00	125.00	65.00
20a	"Shanty" Hogan (1934 green back)	100.00	35.00	20.00
20b	"Shanty" Hogan (1935 green back)	100.00	35.00	20.00
21a	Johnny Vergez (1934 green back)	100.00	35.00	20.00
21b	Johnny Vergez (1935 green back)	100.00	35.00	20.00
22a	Jimmy Wilson (1934 green back)	100.00	35.00	20.00
22b	Jimmy Wilson (1935 green back)	100.00	35.00	20.00
22c	Jimmy Wilson (1936 blue back)	105.00	45.00	20.00
23a	Bill Hallahan (1934 green back)	100.00	35.00	20.00
23b	Bill Hallahan (1935 green back)	100.00	35.00	20.00
24a	"Sparky" Adams (1934 green back)	100.00	35.00	20.00
24b	"Sparky" Adams (1935 green back)	100.00	35.00	20.00
25	Walter Berger	100.00	35.00	20.00
26a	"Pepper" Martin (1935 green back)	160.00	65.00	30.00
26b	"Pepper" Martin (1936 blue back)	175.00	70.00	35.00
27	"Pie" Traynor	200.00	85.00	45.00
28	"Al" Lopez	200.00	85.00	45.00
29	Robert Rolfe	100.00	35.00	20.00
30a	"Heinie" Manush (1935 green back)	200.00	85.00	45.00
30b	"Heinie" Manush (1936 blue back)	245.00	100.00	50.00
31a	"Kiki" Cuyler (1935 green back)	200.00	85.00	45.00

31b	"Kiki" Cuyler (1936 blue back)	245.00	100.00	50.00
32	Sam Rice	200.00	85.00	45.00
33	"Schoolboy" Rowe	125.00	50.00	20.00
34	Stanley Hack	125.00	50.00	20.00
35	Earle Averill	200.00	85.00	45.00
36a	Earnie Lombardi	560.00	225.00	115.00
36b	Ernie Lombardi	245.00	100.00	50.00
37	"Billie" Urbanski	100.00	35.00	20.00
38	Ben Chapman	100.00	35.00	20.00
39	Carl Hubbell	295.00	120.00	55.00
40	"Blondy" Ryan	100.00	35.00	20.00
41	Harvey Hendrick	100.00	35.00	20.00
42	Jimmy Dykes	100.00	35.00	20.00
43	Ted Lyons	200.00	85.00	45.00
44	Rogers Hornsby	525.00	210.00	105.00
45	"Jo Jo" White	100.00	35.00	20.00
46	"Red" Lucas	100.00	35.00	20.00
47	Cliff Bolton	100.00	35.00	20.00
48	"Rick" Ferrell	200.00	85.00	45.00
49	"Buck" Jordan	100.00	35.00	20.00
50	"Mel" Ott	310.00	120.00	55.00
51	John Whitehead	100.00	35.00	20.00
52	George Stainback	100.00	35.00	20.00
53	Oscar Melillo	100.00	35.00	20.00
54a	"Hank" Greenburg (Greenberg)	1,260	505.00	250.00
54b	"Hank" Greenberg	805.00	325.00	160.00
55	Tony Cuccinello	100.00	35.00	20.00
56	"Gus" Suhr	100.00	35.00	20.00
57	Cy Blanton	100.00	35.00	20.00
58	Glenn Myatt	100.00	35.00	20.00
59	Jim Bottomley	200.00	85.00	45.00
60	Charley "Red" Ruffing	200.00	85.00	45.00
61	"Billie" Werber	100.00	35.00	20.00
62	Fred M. Frankhouse	100.00	35.00	20.00
63	"Stonewall" Jackson	200.00	85.00	45.00
64	Jimmie Foxx	560.00	225.00	115.00
65	"Zeke" Bonura	100.00	35.00	20.00
66	"Ducky" Medwick	200.00	85.00	45.00
67	Marvin Owen	100.00	35.00	20.00
68	"Sam" Leslie	100.00	35.00	20.00
69	Earl Grace	100.00	35.00	20.00
70	"Hal" Trosky	100.00	35.00	20.00
71	"Ossie" Bluege	100.00	35.00	20.00
72	"Tony" Piet	100.00	35.00	20.00
73a	"Fritz" Ostermueller (1935 green back)	100.00	35.00	20.00
73b	"Fritz" Ostermueller (1935 blue back)	100.00	35.00	20.00
73c	"Fritz" Ostermueller (1936 blue back)	105.00	45.00	20.00
74a	Tony Lazzeri (1935 green back)	365.00	140.00	70.00
74b	Tony Lazzeri (1935 blue back)	365.00	140.00	70.00
74c	Tony Lazzeri (1936 blue back)	385.00	155.00	77.00
75a	Irving Burns (1935 green back)	100.00	35.00	20.00
75b	Irving Burns (1936 blue back)	100.00	35.00	20.00
75c	Irving Burns (1936 blue back)	105.00	45.00	20.00
76a	Bill Rogell (1935 green back)	100.00	35.00	20.00
76b	Bill Rogell (1935 blue back)	105.00	45.00	20.00
76c	Bill Rogell (1936 blue back)	105.00	45.00	20.00
77a	Charlie Gehringer (1935 green back)	350.00	140.00	70.00
77b	Charlie Gehringer (1935 blue back)	350.00	140.00	70.00
77c	Charlie Gehringer (1936 blue back)	370.00	140.00	70.00
78a	Joe Kuhel (1935 green back)	100.00	35.00	20.00
78b	Joe Kuhel (1935 blue back)	100.00	35.00	20.00
78c	Joe Kuhel (1936 blue back)	105.00	45.00	20.00
79a	Willis Hudlin (1935 green back)	100.00	35.00	20.00
79b	Willis Hudlin (1935 blue back)	100.00	35.00	20.00
79c	Willis Hudlin (1936 blue back)	105.00	45.00	20.00
80a	Louis Chiozza (1935 green back)	100.00	35.00	20.00
80b	Louis Chiozza (1935 blue back)	100.00	35.00	20.00
80c	Louis Chiozza (1936 blue back)	105.00	45.00	20.00
81a	Bill DeLancey (1935 green back)	100.00	35.00	20.00
81b	Bill DeLancey (1935 blue back)	100.00	35.00	20.00
81c	Bill DeLancey (1936 blue back)	105.00	45.00	20.00
82a	John Babich (1935 green back)	100.00	35.00	20.00
82b	John Babich (1935 blue back)	100.00	35.00	20.00
q2c	John Babich (1936 blue back)	105.00	45.00	20.00
83a	Paul Waner (1935 green back)	200.00	85.00	45.00
83b	Paul Waner (1935 blue back)	200.00	85.00	45.00
83c	Paul Waner (1936 blue back)	225.00	85.00	45.00
84a	Sam Byrd (1935 green back)	100.00	35.00	20.00
84b	Sam Byrd (1935 blue back)	100.00	35.00	20.00
84c	Sam Byrd (1936 blue back)	105.00	45.00	20.00
85	Julius Solters	200.00	85.00	45.00
86	Frank Crosetti	350.00	140.00	70.00
87	Steve O'Neil (O'Neill)	200.00	85.00	45.00
88	Geo. Selkirk	200.00	85.00	45.00
89	Joe Stripp	200.00	85.00	45.00
90	Ray Hayworth	200.00	85.00	45.00
91	Bucky Harris	455.00	185.00	90.00
92	Ethan Allen	200.00	85.00	45.00
93	Alvin Crowder	200.00	85.00	45.00
94	Wes Ferrell	200.00	85.00	45.00
95	Luke Appling	455.00	185.00	90.00
96	Lew Riggs	200.00	85.00	45.00
97	"Al" Lopez	840.00	335.00	170.00
98	"Schoolboy" Rowe	500.00	245.00	120.00
99	"Pie" Traynor	805.00	325.00	160.00
100	Earle Averill (Earl)	805.00	325.00	160.00
101	Dick Bartell	500.00	245.00	120.00
102	Van Mungo	665.00	265.00	135.00
103	Bill Dickey	1,085	435.00	215.00
104	Robert Rolfe	500.00	245.00	120.00
105	"Ernie" Lombardi	840.00	335.00	170.00
106	"Red" Lucas	500.00	245.00	120.00
107	Stanley Hack	630.00	250.00	125.00
108	Walter Berger	1,120	280.00	135.00

1924 Diaz Cigarettes

Because they were printed in Cuba and feature only pitchers, the 1924 Diaz Cigarette cards are among the rarest and most intriguing of all tobacco issues. Produced in Havana for the Diaz brand, the black-and-white cards measure 1-3/4" x 2-1/2" and were printed on a semi-gloss stock. The player's name and position are listed at the bottom of the card, while his team and league appear at the top. According to the card backs, printed in Spanish, the set consists of 136 cards - all major league pitchers. But to date only the cards checklisted here have been discovered, and several of them never played in the major leagues.

		NM	EX	VG
Common Player:		900.00	360.00	180.00
1	Walter P. Johnson	5,250	2,200	1,100
2	Waite C. Hoyt	1,500	600.00	300.00
3	Grover C. Alexander	2,250	900.00	450.00
4	Thomas Sheehan	900.00	360.00	180.00
5	Pete Donohue	900.00	360.00	180.00
6	Herbert J. Pennock	1,350	550.00	275.00
7				
8	Carl Mays	1,100	450.00	225.00
9				
10	Allan S. Sothoron (Allen)	900.00	360.00	180.00
11	Wm. Piercy	900.00	360.00	180.00
12	Curtis Fullerton	900.00	360.00	180.00
13	Hollis Thurston	900.00	360.00	180.00
14	George Walberg	900.00	360.00	180.00
15	Fred Heimach	900.00	360.00	180.00
16	Sherrod M. Smith	900.00	360.00	180.00
17	Warren H. Ogden	900.00	360.00	180.00
18	Ernest P. Osborne (Earnest)	900.00	360.00	180.00
19	Walter H. Ruether	900.00	360.00	180.00
20	Burleigh A. Grimes	1,350	550.00	275.00
21	Joseph Genewich	900.00	360.00	180.00
22	Victor Aldridge	900.00	360.00	180.00
23	Arnold E. Stone	900.00	360.00	180.00
24	Lester C. Howe	900.00	360.00	180.00
25	George K. Murry (Murray)	900.00	360.00	180.00
26	Herman Pillette	900.00	360.00	180.00
27	John D. Couch	900.00	360.00	180.00
28	Tony C. Kaufmann	900.00	360.00	180.00
29	Frank (Jake) May	900.00	360.00	180.00
30	Howard J. Ehmke	900.00	360.00	180.00
31				
32				
33	Gorham V. Leverett	900.00	360.00	180.00
34	Bryan Harris	900.00	360.00	180.00
35	Paul F. Schreiber	900.00	360.00	180.00
36	Dewey Hinkle	900.00	360.00	180.00
37	Arthur C. Vance	1,350	550.00	275.00
38	Jesse J. Haines	1,350	550.00	275.00
39	Earl Hamilton	900.00	360.00	180.00
40	A. Wilbur Cooper	900.00	360.00	180.00
41	Thomas F. Long	900.00	360.00	180.00
42	Alex Ferguson	900.00	360.00	180.00
43	Chester Ross	900.00	360.00	180.00
44	John J. Quinn (Middle initial actually P.)	900.00	360.00	180.00
45	Ray C. Kolp	900.00	360.00	180.00
46	Arthur N. Nehf	900.00	360.00	180.00
47				
48				
49	Edwin A. Rommel	900.00	360.00	180.00
50	Theodore A. Lyons	1,350	550.00	275.00
51	Roy Meeker	900.00	360.00	180.00
52	John D. Stuart	900.00	360.00	180.00
53	Joseph Oeschger	900.00	360.00	180.00
54	Wayland Dean	900.00	360.00	180.00
55	Guy Morton	900.00	360.00	180.00
56	William L. Doak	900.00	360.00	180.00
57	Edward J. Pfeffer	900.00	360.00	180.00
58	Sam Gray	900.00	360.00	180.00
59				
60	Godfrey Brogan	900.00	360.00	180.00
61				
62	Howard E. Baldwin	900.00	360.00	180.00
63	Bert Lewis	900.00	360.00	180.00
64				
65	Dennis Burns	900.00	360.00	180.00
66	Roline C. Naylor (Roleine)	900.00	360.00	180.00
67	Walter H. Huntzinger	900.00	360.00	180.00
68	S. F. Baumgartner	900.00	360.00	180.00
69				
70	Clarence E. Mitchell	900.00	360.00	180.00
71				
72	Charles F. Clazner (Glazner)	900.00	360.00	180.00
73				
74				
75	Dennis J. Gearin	900.00	360.00	180.00
76	Jonathan T. Zachary	900.00	360.00	180.00
77				
78	Jess F. Winter (Jesse Winters)	900.00	360.00	180.00
79	Charles Ruffing	1,350	550.00	275.00
80	John W. Cooney	900.00	360.00	180.00
81	Leslie J. Bush (Middle initial A.)	900.00	360.00	180.00
82	William Harris	900.00	360.00	180.00
83	Joseph B. Shaute	900.00	360.00	180.00
84				
85	Eppa J. Rixey	1,350	550.00	275.00
86	William L. Sherdel	900.00	360.00	180.00
87	John C. Benton	900.00	360.00	180.00
88	Arthur R. Decatur	900.00	360.00	180.00
89	Harry G. Shriver	900.00	360.00	180.00
90	John D. Morrison	900.00	360.00	180.00
91	Walter M. Betts	900.00	360.00	180.00
92	Oscar Roettger	900.00	360.00	180.00
93				
94	Mike Cvengros	900.00	360.00	180.00
95	Leo L. Dickerman	900.00	360.00	180.00
96	Philip B. Weinart	2,400	960.00	480.00
97	Nicholas Dumovich	900.00	360.00	180.00
98				
99	Timothy A. McNamara	900.00	360.00	180.00
100	Allan Russell	900.00	360.00	180.00
101	Ted Blankenship	900.00	360.00	180.00
102	Howard E. Baldwin	900.00	360.00	180.00
103	Frank T. Davis	900.00	360.00	180.00
104	James C. Edwards	900.00	360.00	180.00
105	Hubert F. Pruett	900.00	360.00	180.00
106	Richard Rudolph	900.00	360.00	180.00
107				
108	Claude Jonnard	900.00	360.00	180.00
109				
110				
111	John M. Bentley (Initial actually N.)	900.00	360.00	180.00
112	Wilfred D. Ryan	900.00	360.00	180.00
113	George D. Metivier	900.00	360.00	180.00
114				
115	Sylvester Johnson	900.00	360.00	180.00
116	O.L. Fuhr	900.00	360.00	180.00
117				
118	Stanley Coveleski	1,350	550.00	275.00
119	Dave C. Danforth	900.00	360.00	180.00
120	Elam Van Gilder	900.00	360.00	180.00
121	Bert Cole	900.00	360.00	180.00
122	Kenneth E. Holoway (Holloway)	900.00	360.00	180.00
123	Charles Robertson	900.00	360.00	180.00
124				
125	George Dauss	900.00	360.00	180.00
126				
127				
128				
129	Phillip Bedgood	900.00	360.00	180.00
130	Fred Wingfield	900.00	360.00	180.00
131	George Mogridge	900.00	360.00	180.00
132	J. Martina	900.00	360.00	180.00
133	B.F. Speece	900.00	360.00	180.00
134	Harold Carlson	900.00	360.00	180.00
135	Wilbert W. Hubbell	900.00	360.00	180.00
136	Milton Gaston	900.00	360.00	180.00

(The following pitchers are known to have been included in the set, though their card numbers are unknown. They are listed here alphabetically, though the names may be different on the cards.)

---	Jess L. Barnes	900.00	360.00	180.00
---	Virgil E. Barnes	900.00	360.00	180.00
---	William Bayne	900.00	360.00	180.00
---	Lawrence J. Benton	900.00	360.00	180.00
---	Warren Collins (Rip)	900.00	360.00	180.00
---	Joubert Davenport (Lum)	900.00	360.00	180.00
---	Urban C. Faber	900.00	360.00	180.00
---	Robert K. Hasty	900.00	360.00	180.00
---	Frank J. Henry	900.00	360.00	180.00
---	Samuel P. Jones	900.00	360.00	180.00
---	Adolfo Luque	900.00	360.00	180.00
---	Fred Marberry	900.00	360.00	180.00
---	Richard W. Marquard	900.00	360.00	180.00
---	Walter H. McGrew (Slim)	900.00	360.00	180.00
---	Herbert McQuaid	900.00	360.00	180.00
---	Hugh A. McQuillan	900.00	360.00	180.00
---	Lee Meadows	900.00	360.00	180.00
---	Louis A. North	900.00	360.00	180.00
---	George W. Pipgras	900.00	360.00	180.00
---	James J. Ring	900.00	360.00	180.00
---	Robert Shawkey	900.00	360.00	180.00
---	Urban J. Shocker	900.00	360.00	180.00
---	George Uhle	900.00	360.00	180.00
---	John R. Watson	900.00	360.00	180.00
---	Ed L. Wells	900.00	360.00	180.00
---	Byron W. Yarrison	900.00	360.00	180.00
---	Paul V. Zahniser	900.00	360.00	180.00

1962 Dickson Orde & Co.

One of several English tobacco cards to include baseball among a series of world's sports, this card is of marginal interest to U.S. collectors because its color front pictures (from the back) a batter who could be Babe Ruth as part of a baseball scene on the front of the 2-5/8" x 1-3/8" card. The short description of baseball on the card's black-and-white back does mention Ruth. The "Sports of the Countries" series comprises 25 cards.

SPORTS OF THE COUNTRIES (A Series of 25)

No. 11
AMERICA
Everyone knows that America is a great Baseball playing country, where an almost fanatical enthusiasm is displayed. The game is very similar to "Rounders" in its basic rules but it requires players of great strength and skill in judgment. The best known Baseball player of all time is Babe Ruth, whose record of 714 home runs has never been equalled.

DICKSON ORDE & CO. LTD.
Farnham : Surrey : England

		NM	EX	VG
11	America (Babe Ruth)	25.00	12.50	7.50

1980 Did You Know . . . ?

DID YOU KNOW.................?
Mickey WITEK–
THE N.Y. GIANTS 2ND BASEMAN IN 1943 — BANGED OUT 196 HITS!

This collectors' edition was produced by artist Mel (?) Anderson. The blank-backed 3-1/4" x 6-3/8" cards have black-and-white drawings of ballplayers and a "Did You Know" trivia fact. The unnumbered cards are checklisted here alphabetically.

		NM	EX	VG
Complete Set (30):		25.00	12.50	7.50
Common Player:		2.00	1.00	.60
(1)	Richie Ashburn	4.00	2.00	1.25
(2)	Hank Bauer	2.50	1.25	.70
(3)	Ewell "The Whip" Blackwell	2.50	1.25	.70
(4)	Johnny Callison	2.00	1.00	.60
(5)	Roger "Doc" Cramer	2.00	1.00	.60
(6)	Harry Danning	2.00	1.00	.60
(7)	Ferris Fain	2.00	1.00	.60
(8)	Ned Garver	2.00	1.00	.60
(9)	Harvey Haddix	2.00	1.00	.60
(10)	Clint Hartung	2.00	1.00	.60
(11)	"Bobo" Holloman	2.00	1.00	.60
(12)	Ron Hunt	2.00	1.00	.60
(13)	Howard "Spud" Krist	2.00	1.00	.60
(14)	Emil "Dutch" Leonard	2.00	1.00	.60
(15)	Buddy Lewis	2.00	1.00	.60
(16)	Jerry Lynch	2.00	1.00	.60
(17)	Roy McMillan	2.00	1.00	.60
(18)	Johnny Mize	3.00	1.50	.90
(19)	Hugh Mulcahy	2.00	1.00	.60
(20)	Hal Newhouser	2.00	1.00	.60
(21)	Jim Perry	2.00	1.00	.60
(22)	Phil Rizzuto	4.00	2.00	1.25
(23)	Bobby Shantz	2.00	1.00	.60
(24)	Roy Sievers	2.00	1.00	.60
(25)	Nick Testa	3.00	1.50	.90
(26)	Cecil Travis	2.00	1.00	.60
(27)	Elmer "Valient" Valo	2.00	1.00	.60
(28)	Bill Werber	2.00	1.00	.60
(29)	Mickey Witek	2.00	1.00	.60
(30)	Hal Woodeshick	2.00	1.00	.60

1907-09 Dietsche Detroit Tigers Postcards (PC765-1)

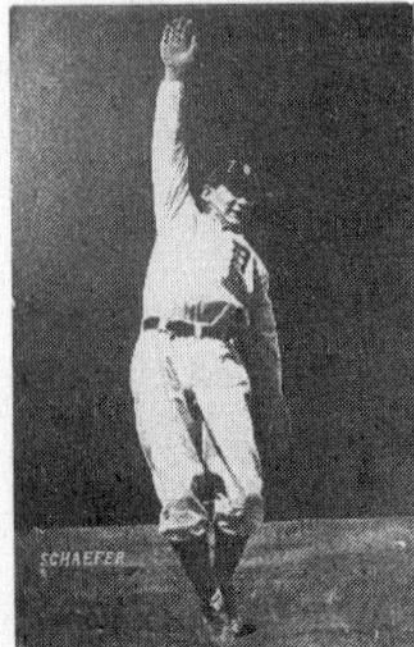

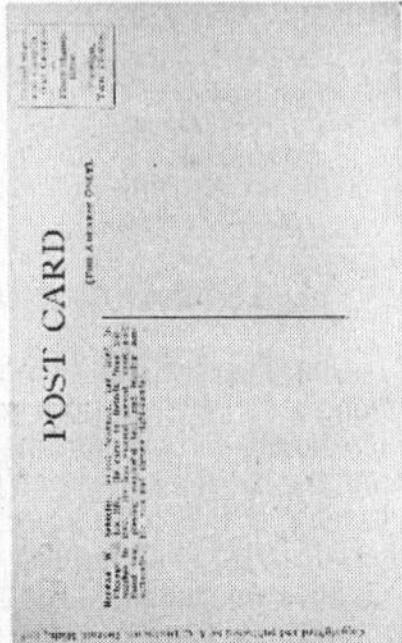

Three apparent annual issues (1907-09) of the home team by Detroit postcard publisher A.C. Dietsche, these 3-1/2" x 5-1/2" black-and-white postcards have most of the photographic background on front blackened out. The player's last name usually appears on the front. On back, along with the postcard legalities are a short player biography and a dated copyright line. The postcards were sold in sets of 15 cards for 25 cents.

		NM	EX	VG
Common Player:		150.00	60.00	30.00
Series 1 - 1907				
	Complete Set (16):	7,000	2,800	1,400
(1)	Tyrus R. Cobb/Btg	2,000	800.00	400.00
(2)	Tyrus R. Cobb/Fldg	3,000	1,200	600.00
(3)	William Coughlin	150.00	60.00	30.00
(4)	Samuel S. Crawford	325.00	130.00	65.00
(5)	William E. Donovan	150.00	60.00	30.00
(6)	Jerome W. Downs	150.00	60.00	30.00
(7)	Hughie A. Jennings	325.00	130.00	65.00
(8)	David Jones	150.00	60.00	30.00
(9)	Edward H. Killian	150.00	60.00	30.00
(10)	George J. Mullin	150.00	60.00	30.00
(11)	Charles O'Leary	150.00	60.00	30.00
(12)	Fred T. Payne	150.00	60.00	30.00
(13)	Claude Rossman	150.00	60.00	30.00
(14)	Herman W. Schaefer	150.00	60.00	30.00
(15)	Charles Schmidt	150.00	60.00	30.00
(16)	Edward Siever	150.00	60.00	30.00
Series 2 - 1908				
	Complete Set (22):	6,000	2,400	1,200
(1)	Henry Beckendorf	180.00	70.00	35.00
(2)	Owen Bush	180.00	70.00	35.00
(3)	Tyrus R. Cobb	2,500	1,000	500.00
(4)	William Coughlin	180.00	70.00	35.00
(5)	Sam Crawford	350.00	140.00	70.00
(6)	William E. Donovan	180.00	70.00	35.00
(7)	Jerome W. Downs	180.00	70.00	35.00
(8)	Hughie A. Jennings	350.00	140.00	70.00
(9)	Tom Jones	180.00	70.00	35.00
(10)	Edward H. Killian	180.00	70.00	35.00
(11)	Matthew McIntyre	180.00	70.00	35.00
(12)	George J. Moriarty	180.00	70.00	35.00
(13)	George J. Mullin	180.00	70.00	35.00
(14)	Charles O'Leary	180.00	70.00	35.00
(15)	Fred T. Payne	180.00	70.00	35.00
(16)	Germany Schaefer	180.00	70.00	35.00
(17)	Charles Schmidt	180.00	70.00	35.00
(18)	Oscar Stanage	180.00	70.00	35.00
(19)	Oren Edgar Summers	180.00	70.00	35.00
(20)	Ira Thomas	180.00	70.00	35.00
(21)	Edgar Willett	180.00	70.00	35.00
(22)	George Winter	180.00	70.00	35.00
Series 3 - 1909				
	Complete Set (4):	750.00	300.00	150.00
(1)	James Delehanty	200.00	80.00	40.00
(2)	Tom Jones	180.00	70.00	35.00
(3)	Ralph Works	180.00	70.00	35.00
(4)	Detroit Tigers Team	300.00	125.00	60.00

1907 Dietsche Chicago Cubs Postcards (PC765-2)

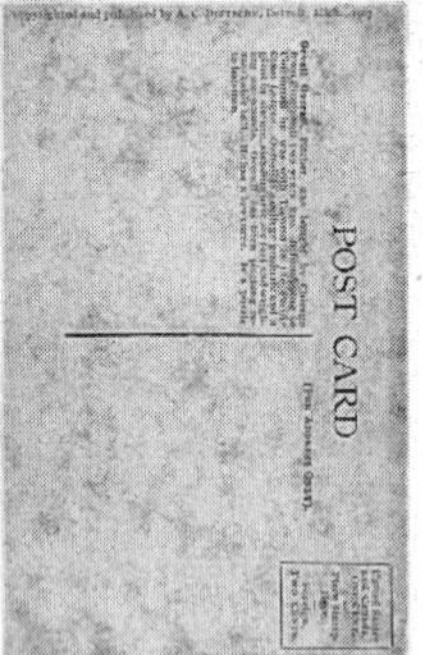

This series of early Cubs postcards was published by the same Detroit printer who issued Tigers postcard series from 1907-09. The Dietsche Cubs postcards are scarcer than the Tigers issues because they were only offered for sale in Detroit in conjunction with the 1907 World Series between the Tigers and Cubs, and few people bought the visiting team's cards. The 3-1/2" x 5-1/2" black-and-white cards have most of the photographic background blacked out on front. The player's last name may or may not appear on the front. Postcard style backs include a short career summary and a dated copyright line. The 15-card sets originally sold for 25 cents.

		NM	EX	VG
Complete Set (15):		5,500	2,200	1,100
Common Player:		340.00	135.00	65.00
(1)	Mordecai Brown	500.00	200.00	100.00
(2)	Frank L. Chance	500.00	200.00	100.00
(3)	John Evers	500.00	200.00	100.00
(4)	Arthur F. Hoffman (Hofman)	340.00	135.00	65.00
(5)	John Kling	340.00	135.00	65.00
(6)	Carl Lundgren	340.00	135.00	65.00
(7)	Patrick J. Moran	340.00	135.00	65.00
(8)	Orval Overall	340.00	135.00	65.00
(9)	John A. Pfeister	340.00	135.00	65.00
(10)	Edw. M. Ruelbach	340.00	135.00	65.00
(11)	Frank M. Schulte	340.00	135.00	65.00
(12)	James T. Sheckard	340.00	135.00	65.00
(13)	James Slagle	340.00	135.00	65.00
(14)	Harry Steinfeldt	340.00	135.00	65.00
(15)	Joseph B. Tinker	500.00	200.00	100.00

1907 Dietsche Posters

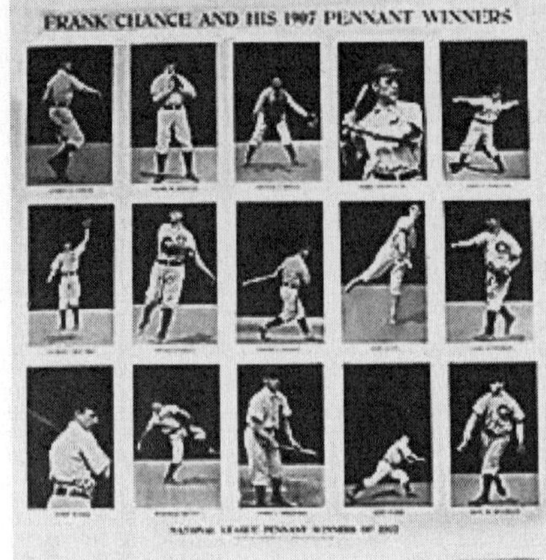

The images found on the Dietsche postcards were conglomerated on a pair of black-and-white cardboard posters. About 22" square, the posters are headlined: "FRANK CHANCE AND HIS 1907 PENNANT WINNERS" and "HUGHIE JENNINGS AND HIS GREA 1970 TIGERS."

	NM	EX	VG
1907 Chicago Cubs	1,000	500.00	300.00
1907 Detroit Tigers	1,000	500.00	300.00

1934 Dietz Gum Ball Players in Action

See 1934 Al Demaree Die-cuts (R304).

1942 Joe DiMaggio Candy Box Card

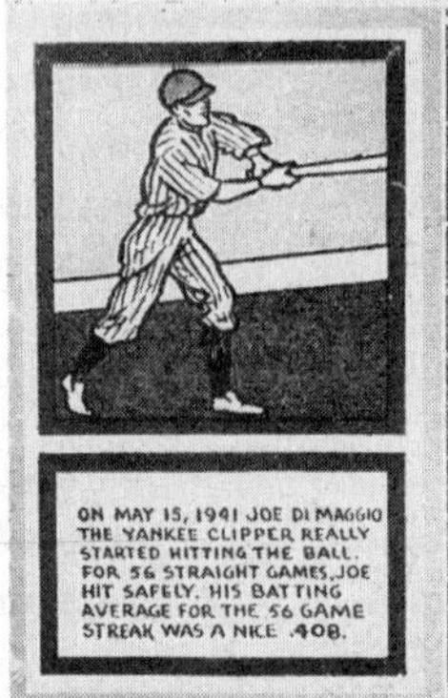

ON MAY 15, 1941 JOE DI MAGGIO THE YANKEE CLIPPER REALLY STARTED HITTING THE BALL. FOR 56 STRAIGHT GAMES, JOE HIT SAFELY. HIS BATTING AVERAGE FOR THE 56 GAME STREAK WAS A NICE .408.

With no maker's name visible, this crudely executed war-era card is believed to have been printed on a candy box. In a format of 2-7/16" x 3-3/16" it is printed in blue and orange on white, is perforated on the sides and blank-backed.

	NM	EX	VG
Joe DiMaggio	150.00	75.00	45.00

1950 Joe DiMaggio Oriental Tour Postcard

In the post-season of 1950, during the Korean War, Joe DiMaggio led a goodwill tour of the Orient, including stops to visit the troops and to baseball-related destinations in Japan. This Italian postcard shows DiMaggio and Lefty O'Doul in a colorized photo surrounded by Japanese schoolboy ballplayers. The postcard-style back describes the scene. The card measures about 6" x 4".

	NM	EX	VG
Joe DiMaggio	125.00	65.00	40.00

1951 Joe DiMaggio Baseball Shoes

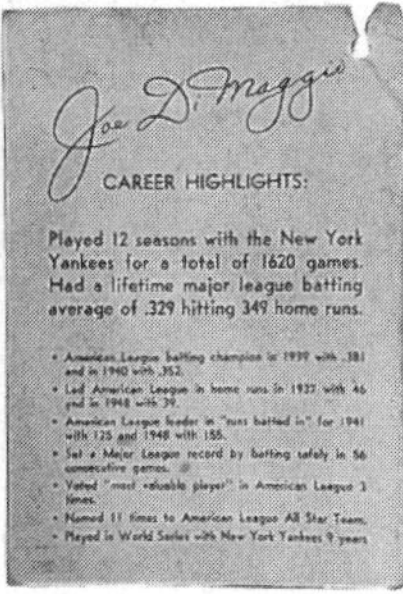

This 2-1/2" x 3-1/2" card was included with DiMaggio brand baseball shoes. A hole punched in the upper-left corner allowed the card to be attached to the shoe strings. Front has an action pose of DiMaggio printed in black-and-white on a dark green background. A facsimile autograph is at center. At bottom is printed: "THE YANKEE CLIPPER." The back has another facsimile signature and the player's career highlights through the 1950 season.

	NM	EX	VG
Joe DiMaggio (Hang-tag card.)	140.00	70.00	40.00
Joe DiMaggio (Complete box, shoes, tag.)	650.00	325.00	200.00

1972-83 Dimanche/Derniere Heure Photos

From 1972-74, and 1977-83, the Montreal magazine Dimanche / Derniere Heure (loosely translated, "Sunday / Latest Hour," issued color photos of Expos (and a few other) players. The 8-1/2" x 11" photos are printed on semi-gloss paper stock that is punched for a three-ring binder. Fronts have a large color photo with player data, stats and career highlights printed in black beneath - all in French. At left or top is usually the issue date in which the photo was included in the magazine. Backs are blank.

	NM	EX	VG
Common Player:	5.00	2.50	1.50
(Stars are valued up to $50.)			

1972 Dimanche/Derniere Heure Expos

		NM	EX	VG
Complete Set (27):		155.00	78.00	47.00
Common Player:		5.00	2.50	1.50
(1)	Bill Stoneman (April 9)	5.00	2.50	1.50
(2)	John Boccabella (April 16)	5.00	2.50	1.50
(3)	Gene Mauch (April 23)	5.00	2.50	1.50
(4)	Ron Hunt (April 30)	5.00	2.50	1.50
(5)	Steve Renko (May 7)	5.00	2.50	1.50
(6)	Boots Day (May 14)	5.00	2.50	1.50
(7)	Bob Bailey (May 21)	5.00	2.50	1.50
(8)	Ernie McAnally (May 28)	5.00	2.50	1.50
(9)	Ken Singleton (June 4)	5.00	2.50	1.50
(10)	Ron Fairly (June 11)	5.00	2.50	1.50
(11)	Ron Woods (June 18)	5.00	2.50	1.50
(12)	Mike Jorgensen (June 25)	5.00	2.50	1.50
(13)	Bobby Wine (July 2)	5.00	2.50	1.50
(14)	Mike Torrez (July 9)	5.00	2.50	1.50
(15)	Terry Humphrey (July 16)	5.00	2.50	1.50
(16)	Jim Fairey (July 23)	5.00	2.50	1.50
(17)	Tim Foli (July 30)	5.00	2.50	1.50
(18)	Clyde Mashore (Aug. 6)	5.00	2.50	1.50
(19)	Tim McCarver (Aug. 13)	9.00	4.50	2.75
(20)	Hector Torres (Aug. 20)	5.00	2.50	1.50
(21)	Tom Walker (Aug. 27)	5.00	2.50	1.50
(22)	Cal McLish (Sept. 3)	5.00	2.50	1.50
(23)	Balor Moore (Sept. 10)	5.00	2.50	1.50
(24)	John Strohmayer (Sept. 17)	5.00	2.50	1.50
(25)	Larry Doby (Sept. 24)	12.00	6.00	3.50
(26)	Hal Breeden (Oct. 1)	5.00	2.50	1.50
(27)	Mike Marshall (Oct. 8)	5.00	2.50	1.50

1973 Dimanche/Derniere Heure National Leaguers

		NM	EX	VG
Complete Set (16):		185.00	90.00	55.00
Common Player:		6.00	3.00	1.75
(1)	Roberto Clemente (April 15)	25.00	12.50	7.50
(2)	Coco Laboy (April 22)	6.00	3.00	1.75
(3)	Rusty Staub (April 29)	8.00	4.00	2.50
(4)	Johnny Bench (May 6)	12.50	6.25	3.75
(5)	Ferguson Jenkins (May 13)	9.00	4.50	2.75
(6)	Bob Gibson (May 20)	10.00	5.00	3.00
(7)	Hank Aaron (May 27)	20.00	10.00	6.00
(8)	Willie Montanez (June 3)	6.00	3.00	1.75
(9)	Willie McCovey (June 10)	10.00	5.00	3.00
(10)	Willie Davis (June 17)	6.00	3.00	1.75
(11)	Steve Carlton (June 24)	10.00	5.00	3.00
(12)	Willie Stargell (July 1)	10.00	5.00	3.00
(13)	Dave Bristol (July 8)	6.00	3.00	1.75
(14)	Larry Bowa (July 15)	6.00	3.00	1.75
(15)	Pete Rose (July 22)	20.00	10.00	6.00
(16)	Pepe Frias (July 29)	6.00	3.00	1.75

1974 Dimanche/Derniere Heure Expos

		NM	EX	VG
Complete Set (10):		40.00	20.00	12.00
Common Player:		5.00	2.50	1.50
(1)	Dennis Blair	5.00	2.50	1.50
(2)	Don Carrithers	5.00	2.50	1.50
(3)	Jim Cox	5.00	2.50	1.50
(4)	Willie Davis	5.00	2.50	1.50
(5)	Don Demola	5.00	2.50	1.50
(6)	Barry Foote	5.00	2.50	1.50
(7)	Larry Lintz	5.00	2.50	1.50
(8)	John Montague	5.00	2.50	1.50
(9)	Steve Rogers	5.00	2.50	1.50
(10)	Chuck Taylor	5.00	2.50	1.50

1977 Dimanche/Derniere Heure Expos

		NM	EX	VG
Complete Set (26):		125.00	62.00	37.00
Common Player:		5.00	2.50	1.50
(1)	Steve Rogers (April 24)	5.00	2.50	1.50
(2)	Tim Foli (May 1)	5.00	2.50	1.50
(3)	Dick Williams (May 8)	5.00	2.50	1.50
(4)	Larry Parrish (May 15)	5.00	2.50	1.50
(5)	Jose Morales (May 22)	5.00	2.50	1.50
(6)	Don Stanhouse (May 29)	5.00	2.50	1.50
(7)	Gary Carter (June 5)	10.00	5.00	3.00
(8)	Ellis Valentine (June 12)	5.00	2.50	1.50
(9)	Dave Cash (June 19)	5.00	2.50	1.50
(10)	Jackie Brown (June 26)	5.00	2.50	1.50
(11)	Barry Foote (July 3)	5.00	2.50	1.50
(12)	Dan Warthen (July 10)	5.00	2.50	1.50
(13)	Tony Perez (July 17)	10.00	5.00	3.00
(14)	Wayne Garrett (July 24)	5.00	2.50	1.50
(15)	Bill Atkinson (July 31)	5.00	2.50	1.50
(16)	Joe Kerrigan (Aug. 7)	5.00	2.50	1.50
(17)	Mickey Vernon (Aug. 14)	5.00	2.50	1.50
(18)	Jeff Terpko (Aug. 21)	5.00	2.50	1.50
(19)	Andre Dawson (Aug. 28)	10.00	5.00	3.00
(20)	Del Unser (Sept. 4)	5.00	2.50	1.50
(21)	Stan Bahnsen (Sept. 11)	5.00	2.50	1.50
(22)	Warren Cromartie (Sept. 18)	5.00	2.50	1.50
(23)	Santo Alcala (Sept. 25)	5.00	2.50	1.50
(24)	Wayne Twitchell (Oct. 2)	5.00	2.50	1.50
(25)	Pepe Frias (Oct. 9)	5.00	2.50	1.50
(26)	Sam Mejias (Oct. 16)	5.00	2.50	1.50

1978 Dimanche/Derniere Heure Expos

		NM	EX	VG
Complete Set (13):		62.00	31.00	18.50
Common Player:		5.00	2.50	1.50
(1)	Ross Grimsley (May 7)	5.00	2.50	1.50
(2)	Chris Speier (May 14)	5.00	2.50	1.50
(3)	Norm Sherry (May 21)	5.00	2.50	1.50
(4)	Hal Dues (May 28)	5.00	2.50	1.50
(5)	Rudy May (June 4)	5.00	2.50	1.50
(6)	Stan Papi (June 11)	5.00	2.50	1.50
(7)	Darold Knowles (June 18)	5.00	2.50	1.50
(8)	Bob Reece (June 25)	5.00	2.50	1.50
(9)	Dan Schatzeder (July 2)	5.00	2.50	1.50
(10)	Jim Brewer (July 9)	5.00	2.50	1.50
(11)	Mike Garman (July 16)	5.00	2.50	1.50
(12)	Woodie Fryman (July 23)	5.00	2.50	1.50
(13)	Ed Hermann	5.00	2.50	1.50

1979 Dimanche/Derniere Heure Expos

		NM	EX	VG
Complete Set (8):		35.00	17.50	10.50
Common Player:		5.00	2.50	1.50
(1)	Bill Lee (May 6)	5.00	2.50	1.50
(2)	Elias Sosa (May 13)	5.00	2.50	1.50
(3)	Tommy Hutton (May 20)	5.00	2.50	1.50
(4)	Tony Solaita (May 27)	5.00	2.50	1.50
(5)	Rodney Scott (June 3)	5.00	2.50	1.50
(6)	Duffy Dyer (June 10)	5.00	2.50	1.50
(7)	Jim Mason (June 17)	5.00	2.50	1.50
(8)	Ken Macha (June 24)	5.00	2.50	1.50

1980 Dimanche/Derniere Heure Expos

		NM	EX	VG
Complete Set (23):		125.00	62.00	37.00
Common Player:		5.00	2.50	1.50
(1)	Steve Rogers (April 20)	5.00	2.50	1.50
(2)	Dick Williams (April 27)	5.00	2.50	1.50
(3)	Bill Lee (May 4)	5.00	2.50	1.50
(4)	Jerry White (May 11)	5.00	2.50	1.50
(5)	Scott Sanderson (May 18)	5.00	2.50	1.50
(6)	Ron LeFlore (May 25)	5.00	2.50	1.50
(7)	Elias Sosa (June 1)	5.00	2.50	1.50

(8)	Ellis Valentine (June 8)	5.00	2.50	1.50
(9)	Rodney Scott (June 22)	5.00	2.50	1.50
(10)	Woodie Fryman (June 29)	5.00	2.50	1.50
(11)	Chris Speier (July 6)	5.00	2.50	1.50
(12)	Warren Cromartie (July 13)	5.00	2.50	1.50
(13)	Stan Bahnsen (July 20)	5.00	2.50	1.50
(14)	Tommy Hutton (July 27)	5.00	2.50	1.50
(15)	Bill Almon (Aug. 3)	5.00	2.50	1.50
(16)	Fred Norman (Aug. 10)	5.00	2.50	1.50
(17)	Andre Dawson (Aug. 17)	10.00	5.00	3.00
(18)	John Tamargo (Aug. 24)	5.00	2.50	1.50
(19)	Larry Parrish (Aug. 31)	5.00	2.50	1.50
(20)	David Palmer (Sept. 7)	5.00	2.50	1.50
(21)	Tony Bernazard (Sept. 14)	5.00	2.50	1.50
(22)	Gary Carter (Sept. 21)	10.00	5.00	3.00
(23)	Ken Macha (Sept. 28)	5.00	2.50	1.50

1888 Dixie Cigarettes Girl Baseball Players (N48)

(See 1888 Allen & Ginter Girl Baseball Players.)

1937 Dixie Lids

This unnumbered set of Dixie cup ice cream tops was issued in 1937 and consists of 24 different lids, although only six picture sports stars; four of whom are baseball players. The lids are found in two different sizes, either 2-11/16" in diameter or 2-5/16" in diameter. The 1937 Dixie lids have their "picture" side printed in black or dark red. The reverse carries the advertising of one of many local dairies which packaged the ice cream treats. The lids must have the small tab still intact to command top value.

		NM	EX	VG
Complete Set (4):		700.00	350.00	210.00
Common Player:		180.00	90.00	55.00
(1)	Charles Gehringer	180.00	90.00	55.00
(2)	Charles ("Gabby") Hartnett	180.00	90.00	55.00
(3)	Carl Hubbell (Mouth closed.)	195.00	95.00	55.00
(4)	Joe Medwick	180.00	90.00	55.00

1937 Dixie Lids Premiums

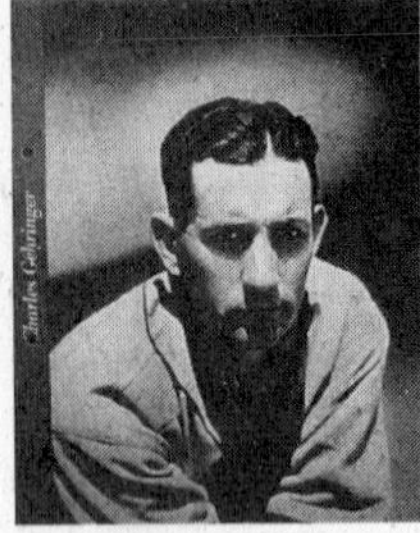

Issued as a premium offer in conjunction with the 1937 Dixie lids, this unnumbered set of color 8" x 10" pictures was printed on heavy paper and features the same subjects as the Dixie lids set. The 1937 Dixie premiums have a distinctive dark green band along the left margin containing the player's name. The back has smaller photos of the player in action with a large star at the top and a player write-up. The 1937 premiums are easily distinguished from the 1938 issue by the use of yellow ink for the names in the left border. A "My Scrapbook of Stars" album was issued in which to house the 24 sports and movie stars issued in the series.

		NM	EX	VG
Complete Set (4):		500.00	250.00	150.00
Common Player:		150.00	75.00	45.00
Album:		300.00	150.00	90.00
(2)	Charles Gehringer	150.00	75.00	45.00
(3)	Charles (Gabby) Hartnett	150.00	75.00	45.00
(4)	Carl Hubbell	175.00	87.00	52.00
(5)	Joe (Ducky) Medwick	150.00	75.00	45.00

1938 Dixie Lids

Similar to its set of the previous year, the 1938 Dixie lids set is a 24-subject set that includes six sports stars - four of whom are baseball players. The lids are found in two sizes, either 2-11/16" in diameter or 2-5/16" in diameter. The 1938 Dixie Lids have their "picture" side printed in blue ink. The reverse carries advertising from one of many local dairies which packaged the ice cream cups. Dixie lids must have the small tab still intact to command top value.

		NM	EX	VG
Complete Set (4):		600.00	300.00	180.00
Common Player:		80.00	40.00	25.00
(1)	Bob Feller	200.00	100.00	60.00
(2)	Jimmie Foxx	200.00	100.00	60.00
(3)	Carl Hubbell (Mouth open.)	175.00	85.00	50.00
(4)	Wally Moses	80.00	40.00	25.00

1938 Dixie Lids Premiums

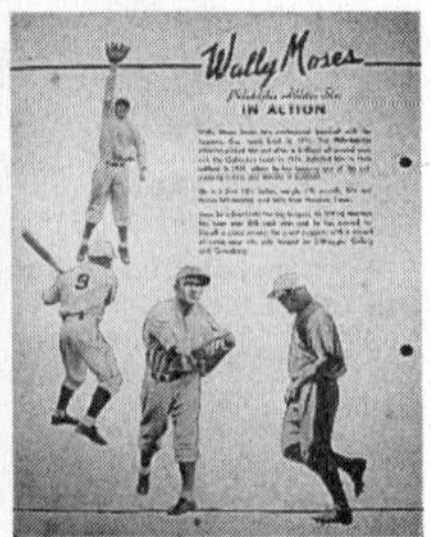

Issued in conjunction with the 1938 Dixie cup lids, this unnumbered set of 8" x 10" pictures contains the same subjects. A colored border surrounds the entire picture with the player's name in black at left. The back contains smaller photos of the player in action with his name in script at the top and a short write-up. A "My Scrapbook of Stars" album was issued in which to house the 24 sports and movie stars that comprise the complete series.

		NM	EX	VG
Complete Set (4):		425.00	210.00	125.00
Common Player:		62.00	31.00	18.50
Album:		300.00	150.00	90.00
(1)	Bob Feller	125.00	62.00	37.00
(2)	Jimmy Foxx	125.00	62.00	37.00
(3)	Carl Hubbell	125.00	62.00	37.00
(4)	Wally Moses	60.00	30.00	18.00

1952 Dixie Lids

After a 14-year break, another Dixie lid set, featuring 24 baseball players, appeared in 1952. The unnumbered lids are found in three sizes, the most common being 2-11/16" in diameter. Somewhat scarcer, and carrying a modest premium over the values listed, are lids in sizes of 2-1/4" or 3-3/16". All are printed with a blue tint on their "picture" side. The backs carry advertising from one of the many local or regional dairies which packaged the ice cream treats. The Dixie lids of the 1950s can be distinguished from earlier issues because the bottom of the photo is squared off to accomodate the player's name. Dixie lids must contain the small tab to command top value.

		NM	EX	VG
Complete Set (24):		5,500	2,750	1,650
Common Player:		200.00	100.00	60.00
(1)	Richie Ashburn	325.00	160.00	95.00
(2)	Tommy Byrne	200.00	100.00	60.00
(3)	Chico Carrasquel	200.00	100.00	60.00
(4)	Pete Castiglione	200.00	100.00	60.00
(5)	Walker Cooper	200.00	100.00	60.00
(6)	Billy Cox	225.00	110.00	65.00
(7)	Ferris Fain	200.00	100.00	60.00
(8)	Bobby Feller	350.00	175.00	100.00
(9)	Nelson Fox	325.00	160.00	95.00
(10)	Monte Irvin	275.00	135.00	80.00
(11)	Ralph Kiner	275.00	135.00	80.00
(12)	Cass Michaels	200.00	100.00	60.00
(13)	Don Mueller	200.00	100.00	60.00
(14)	Mel Parnell	200.00	100.00	60.00
(15)	Allie Reynolds	225.00	110.00	65.00
(16)	Preacher Roe	225.00	110.00	65.00
(17)	Connie Ryan	200.00	100.00	60.00
(18)	Hank Sauer	200.00	100.00	60.00
(19)	Al Schoendienst	275.00	135.00	80.00
(20)	Andy Seminick	200.00	100.00	60.00
(21)	Bobby Shantz	200.00	100.00	60.00
(22)	Enos Slaughter	275.00	135.00	80.00
(23)	Virgil Trucks	200.00	100.00	60.00
(24)	Gene Woodling	250.00	125.00	75.00

1952 Dixie Lids Premiums

This unnumbered set of 24 player photos was issued as a premium in conjunction with the 1952 Dixie cup lids and features the same subjects. The player's team and facsimile autograph appear along the bottom of the 8" x 10" blank-backed photo, which was printed on heavy paper. The 1952 Dixie premiums show the player's 1951 season statistics in the lower right corner.

		NM	EX	VG
Complete Set (24):		2,250	1,125	675.00
Common Player:		90.00	45.00	25.00
(1)	Richie Ashburn	225.00	110.00	65.00
(2)	Tommy Byrne	90.00	45.00	25.00
(3)	Chico Carrasquel	90.00	45.00	25.00
(4)	Pete Castiglione	90.00	45.00	25.00
(5)	Walker Cooper	90.00	45.00	25.00
(6)	Billy Cox	100.00	50.00	30.00
(7)	Ferris Fain	90.00	45.00	25.00
(8)	Bob Feller	225.00	110.00	65.00
(9)	Nelson Fox	200.00	100.00	60.00
(10)	Monte Irvin	125.00	60.00	35.00
(11)	Ralph Kiner	125.00	60.00	35.00
(12)	Cass Michaels	90.00	45.00	25.00
(13)	Don Mueller	90.00	45.00	25.00
(14)	Mel Parnell	90.00	46.00	25.00
(15)	Allie Reynolds	100.00	50.00	30.00
(16)	Preacher Roe	100.00	50.00	30.00
(17)	Connie Ryan	90.00	45.00	25.00
(18)	Hank Sauer	90.00	45.00	25.00
(19)	Al Schoendienst	125.00	60.00	35.00
(20)	Andy Seminick	90.00	45.00	25.00
(21)	Bobby Shantz	90.00	45.00	25.00
(22)	Enos Slaughter	125.00	60.00	35.00
(23)	Virgil Trucks	90.00	45.00	25.00
(24)	Gene Woodling	100.00	50.00	30.00

1953 Dixie Lids

The 1953 Dixie lids set again consists of 24 unnumbered players and is identical in design to the 1952 set. Lids are either 2-1/4" or 2-11/16" in diameter and must include the small tab to command top value. Backs of the lids may be found with advertising of many local or regional dairies which packaged the ice cream cups.

		NM	EX	VG
Complete Set (24):		4,000	2,000	1,200
Common Player:		120.00	60.00	35.00
(1)	Richie Ashburn	250.00	125.00	75.00
(2)	Chico Carrasquel	120.00	60.00	35.00
(3)	Billy Cox	130.00	65.00	40.00
(4)	Ferris Fain	120.00	60.00	35.00
(5)	Nelson Fox	200.00	100.00	60.00
(6a)	Sid Gordon (Boston)	240.00	120.00	70.00
(6b)	Sid Gordon (Milwaukee)	120.00	60.00	35.00
(7)	Warren Hacker	120.00	60.00	35.00
(8)	Monte Irvin	200.00	100.00	60.00
(9)	Jackie Jensen	180.00	90.00	55.00
(10a)	Ralph Kiner (Pittsburgh)	350.00	175.00	100.00
(10b)	Ralph Kiner (Chicago)	200.00	100.00	60.00
(11)	Ted Kluszewski	200.00	100.00	60.00
(12)	Bob Lemon	200.00	100.00	60.00
(13)	Don Mueller	120.00	60.00	35.00
(14)	Mel Parnell	120.00	60.00	35.00
(15)	Jerry Priddy	120.00	60.00	35.00
(16)	Allie Reynolds	130.00	65.00	40.00
(17)	Preacher Roe	130.00	65.00	40.00
(18)	Hank Sauer	120.00	60.00	35.00
(19)	Al Schoendienst	200.00	100.00	60.00
(20)	Bobby Shantz	120.00	60.00	35.00
(21)	Enos Slaughter	200.00	100.00	60.00
(22a)	Warren Spahn (Boston)	550.00	275.00	165.00
(22b)	Warren Spahn (Milwaukee)	500.00	250.00	150.00
(23a)	Virgil Trucks (Chicago)	250.00	125.00	75.00
(23b)	Virgil Trucks (St. Louis)	150.00	75.00	45.00
(24)	Gene Woodling	130.00	65.00	40.00

1953 Dixie Lids Premiums

This set of 8" x 10" photos was issued as a premium in conjunction with the 1953 Dixie lids set and includes the same subjects. A premium picture could be obtained in exchange for 12 lids. The player's team and facsimile autograph are at the bottom of the unnumbered, blank-backed photos. His 1952 season stats are shown in the lower right corner.

	NM	EX	VG
Complete Set (24):	3,000	1,500	900.00
Common Player:	100.00	50.00	30.00
(1) Richie Ashburn	250.00	125.00	75.00
(2) Chico Carrasquel	100.00	50.00	30.00
(3) Billy Cox	120.00	60.00	35.00
(4) Ferris Fain	100.00	50.00	30.00
(5) Nelson Fox	200.00	100.00	60.00
(6) Sid Gordon	100.00	50.00	30.00
(7) Warren Hacker	100.00	50.00	30.00
(8) Monte Irvin	180.00	90.00	55.00
(9) Jack Jensen	120.00	60.00	35.00
(10) Ralph Kiner	180.00	90.00	55.00
(11) Ted Kluszewski	180.00	90.00	55.00
(12) Bob Lemon	180.00	90.00	55.00
(13) Don Mueller	100.00	50.00	30.00
(14) Mel Parnell	100.00	50.00	30.00
(15) Jerry Priddy	100.00	50.00	30.00
(16) Allie Reynolds	120.00	60.00	35.00
(17) Preacher Roe	120.00	60.00	35.00
(18) Hank Sauer	100.00	50.00	30.00
(19) Al Schoendienst	180.00	90.00	55.00
(20) Bobby Shantz	120.00	60.00	35.00
(21) Enos Slaughter	180.00	90.00	55.00
(22) Warren Spahn	260.00	130.00	75.00
(23) Virgil Trucks	100.00	50.00	30.00
(24) Gene Woodling	120.00	60.00	35.00

1954 Dixie Lids

The 1954 Dixie lids set consists of 18 players. Each player is foind in both a "left" and "right" version. The picture side features a black-and-white photo. The lids usually measure 2-11/16" in diameter, although two other sizes (2-1/4" and 3-3/16") also exist and are valued at a significant premium above the prices listed. The 1954 Dixie lids are similar to earlier issues, except they carry an offer for a "3-D Star-viewer" around the outside edge. The small tabs must be attached to command top value. The lids are unnumbered. Backs can be found with advertising from many local or regional dairies which packaged the ice cream cups.

	NM	EX	VG
Complete Set (18):	2,000	1,000	600.00
Common Player:	120.00	60.00	35.00
2-1/4" or 3-3/16": 2-3X			
(1) Richie Ashburn	250.00	125.00	75.00
(2) Clint Courtney	120.00	60.00	35.00
(3) Sid Gordon	120.00	60.00	35.00
(4) Billy Hoeft	120.00	60.00	35.00
(5) Monte Irvin	200.00	100.00	60.00
(6) Jackie Jensen	130.00	65.00	40.00
(7) Ralph Kiner	200.00	100.00	60.00
(8) Ted Kluszewski	200.00	100.00	60.00
(9) Gil McDougald	130.00	65.00	40.00
(10) Minny Minoso	130.00	65.00	40.00
(11) Danny O'Connell	120.00	60.00	35.00
(12) Mel Parnell	120.00	60.00	35.00
(13) Preacher Roe	130.00	65.00	40.00
(14) Al Rosen	130.00	65.00	40.00
(15) Al Schoendienst	200.00	100.00	60.00
(16) Enos Slaughter	200.00	100.00	60.00
(17) Gene Woodling	130.00	65.00	40.00
(18) Gus Zernial	120.00	60.00	35.00

1909 Dockman & Sons Gum (E92)

Once cataloged as a part of the E92 compendium, the John Dockman & Sons Gum card issue differs from the Croft's Candy/Cocoa sets in that it has 10 fewer cards. Otherwise the format (1-1/2" x 2-3/4") and color litho player pictures are identical. Beneath the player picture on front is his last name, position and team. Backs, which describe the set as having 50 cards, are an ad for the gum company. Cards are checklisted here alphabetically.

Base Ball Gum.

THIS CARD IS ONE OF A SET OF

50 Base Ball Players

PROMINENT MEMBERS OF NATIONAL AND AMERICAN LEAGUES, ONE OF WHICH IS WRAPPED WITH EVERY PACKAGE OF BASE BALL GUM.

Manufactured only by JOHN H. DOCKMAN & SONS

	NM	EX	VG
Complete Set (40):	50,000	20,000	10,000
Common Player:	910.00	365.00	180.00
(1) Harry Bemis	910.00	365.00	180.00
(2) Chief Bender	1,620	660.00	330.00
(3) Bill Bergen	910.00	365.00	180.00
(4) Bob Bescher	910.00	365.00	180.00
(5) Al Bridwell	910.00	365.00	180.00
(6) Doc Casey	910.00	365.00	180.00
(7) Frank Chance	1,800	720.00	360.00
(8) Hal Chase	1,110	450.00	220.00
(9) Sam Crawford	1,620	660.00	330.00
(10) Harry Davis	910.00	365.00	180.00
(11) Art Devlin	910.00	365.00	180.00
(12) Wild Bill Donovan	910.00	365.00	180.00
(13) Mickey Doolan	910.00	365.00	180.00
(14) Patsy Dougherty	910.00	365.00	180.00
(15) Larry Doyle/Throwing	910.00	365.00	180.00
(16) Larry Doyle (With bat.)	910.00	365.00	180.00
(17) George Gibson	910.00	365.00	180.00
(18) Topsy Hartsel	910.00	365.00	180.00
(19) Hugh Jennings	1,620	660.00	330.00
(20) Red Kleinow	910.00	365.00	180.00
(21) Nap Lajoie	1,800	720.00	360.00
(22) Hans Lobert	910.00	365.00	180.00
(23) Sherry Magee	910.00	365.00	180.00
(24) Christy Matthewson (Mathewson)	5,400	2,160	1,080
(25) John McGraw	1,620	660.00	330.00
(26) Larry McLean	910.00	365.00	180.00
(27) Dots Miller	910.00	365.00	180.00
(28) Danny Murphy	910.00	365.00	180.00
(29) Bill O'Hara	910.00	365.00	180.00
(30) Germany Schaefer	910.00	365.00	180.00
(31) Admiral Schlei	910.00	365.00	180.00
(32) Boss Schmidt	910.00	365.00	180.00
(33) Johnny Seigle	910.00	365.00	180.00
(34) Dave Shean	910.00	365.00	180.00
(35) Boss Smith (Schmidt)	910.00	365.00	180.00
(36) Joe Tinker	1,620	660.00	330.00
(37) Honus Wagner/Btg	10,000	2,880	1,440
(38) Honus Wagner/Throwing	10,000	2,880	1,440
(39) Cy Young	4,200	1,680	840.00
(40) Heinie Zimmerman	910.00	365.00	180.00

1969-1972 Dodge Postcards

Between 1969-1972 Dodge issued a series of black-and-white promotional postcards featuring sports figures endorsing the car company's line-up. Player portrait photos on front are combined with a photo of one of the cars and some extraneous sales copy. Divided backs of the 5-1/2" x 3-1/2" cards have a couple sentences of career summary or highlights and a sales pitch. Only the baseball players are listed here, though stars from football, basketball, golf, hockey and racing were also included in the series.

	NM	EX	VG
Common Player:	15.00	7.50	4.50
(1) Lou Brock/1970	40.00	20.00	12.00
(2) Lou Brock/1971	40.00	20.00	12.00
(3) Bill Freehan/1969	30.00	15.00	9.00
(4) Bill Freehan/1971	15.00	7.50	4.50
(5) Bill Freehan/1972	15.00	7.50	4.50
(6) Joe Garagiola/1970	20.00	10.00	6.00
(7) Mickey Lolich/1969	15.00	7.50	4.50

1888-1889 Dogs Head Cabinets (N173)

(See 1888-1889 Old Judge Cabinets.)

1950 Dominican Republic

Selection of known Major League players makes 1950 the best guess for year of issue of this Caribbean card set. Like many contemporary Latin issues, these were probably produced to be collected in an accompanying album. Printed on fragile paper in blue, red or green duo-tones, the cards measure about 1-5/8" x 2-3/8" and are blank-backed. The set may or may not be complete at 292, the highest number currenly known. Players featured in the issue are drawn from the Dominican and Cuban winter leagues (including Negro Leagues and minor league players) as well as the majors. In the bottom border beneath the player photo is a card number and name. Names are frequently misspelled and this list may not have succeeded in correcting all of them, particularly the Latino players. It is hoped that gaps in the checklist will eventually be filled with confirmed specimens. Many of the photos on these cards appear to have been lifted - some even with the typeography intact - from Bowman baseball cards of the era. Some, perhaps all, of the cards were printed in more than one color.

	NM	EX	VG
Common Player:			
1 Guillermo Estrella			10.00
2 Benitez Redondo			10.00
3 Vidal Lopez			10.00
4 R. del Monte y C.			10.00
5			
6			
7 Juan Delfin Garcia			10.00
8 J. Raf. Carretero			10.00
9 J. Benjamin (Papo)			10.00
10			
11 Rufo E. Felix			10.00
12 Gallego Munoz			10.00
13 Julio A. Lara			10.00
14			
15			
16 Rafael Espada			10.00
17 Aladino Paez			10.00
18			
19 Pepe Lucas			10.00
20 Manolete Caceres			10.00
21 E.A. Lantigua			10.00
22 Olmedo Suarez			10.00
23 Chucho Ramos			10.00
24 Gullabin Olivo			10.00
25 Jose Luis Velazquez			10.00
26			
27 Felle Delgado			10.00
28			
29			
30 Alcibades Colon			10.00
31 Horacio Martinez			10.00
32 Ramon Burgos			10.00
33 Carlos A. Piallo			10.00
34 W.E. Springfield			10.00
35 Fiquito Suarez			10.00
36			
37			
38 Rafael Ortiz			10.00
39			
40			

41 Tetelo Vargas 10.00
42 Miguel Rueda 10.00
43 Hector Salazar 10.00
44
45 Rafael Vargas 10.00
46
47
48
49
50 Gerard Thorne 10.00
51 Bienvenido Arias 10.00
52 Son Howell 15.00
53
54
55
56
57 P. Mateo (Richard) 10.00
58
59
60 Martin Dihigo 150.00
61
62
63
64
65 Octavio Blanco 10.00
66 Daniel Rodriguez 10.00
67
68 Luis Villodas 10.00
69 Miguel Aracena 10.00
70 Amor Diaz 10.00
71 Juan B. Perdomo 10.00
72 Julio Martinez 10.00
73 Fernando Bueno 10.00
74 Rene Gutierrez 10.00
75 Israel Hernandez 10.00
76 Tomas Gomez Checo 10.00
77
78 Miguel Tian Tineo 10.00
79 Rafael Valdez 10.00
80 Calampio Leon 10.00
81 Leonardo Coicochea 10.00
82 Herberto Blanco 10.00
83
84 Rogelio Martinez 10.00
85
86
87 Silvio Garcia 10.00
88
89 Napoleon Reyes 15.00
90
91
92
93 Claro Duane (Duany) 10.00
94
95
96 Regino Otero 10.00
97 Avelino Canizares 10.00
98 Sandalio Consuegra 25.00
99 Roberto R. Topane 10.00
100 Jaok Cassin (Jack Cassini) 20.00
101 Jaime B. Prendesgart (Jim Prendergast) 20.00
102 Pablo Garcia 10.00
103
104
105
106 Alejandro Crespo 20.00
107 Hiran Gonzalez 10.00
108 Rafael Noble 20.00
109
110 Jose R. Lopez 10.00
111
112
113 Gilberto Torres 10.00
114
115 Patato Pascual 10.00
116
117
118
119 Gilberto Valdivia 10.00
120 Svdor. Hernandoz 10.00
121
122
123
124 Pedro Formental (Formenthal) 10.00
125
126
127
128
129
130
131
132
133
134
135 H. Wilson 25.00
136
137
138
139 Carl Hubbell 35.00
140
141
142 Cocaina Garcia 10.00
143
144
145
146
147
148
149
150
151 Phill Rizzuto (Phil) 75.00
152 Bill Mc Cahan 20.00
153
154 Allie Reynolds 55.00
155 Gill Coan (Gil) 20.00
156
157 Mizell Platt 20.00
158
159 Al S. "Red" (Schoendienst) 50.00
160 Jack Lorke (Lohrke) 20.00
161
162
163 Bill Nicholson 20.00
164 Sam Mele 20.00
165 Bob Schiffino (Scheffing) 20.00
166
167
168
169 Harri Gumbert (Harry) 20.00
170
171 Johnny Wyrostek 20.00
172
173
174
175
176
177 Ken Keltner 25.00
178
179 Harry Walker 25.00
180
181
182
183
184
185 Sibby Sisti 20.00
186
187 Eddie Waiticus (Waitkus) 25.00
188 Eddie Lake 20.00
189
190 Hank Arft 20.00
191
192
193
194 Walker Cooper 20.00
195 Al Brazle 20.00
196 Sam Champmann (Chapman) 20.00
197
198 Doyle Lade 20.00
199
200 Henry Eduards (Edwards) 20.00
201
202
203 N.Y. "Baby" (Norman "Babe" Young) 20.00
204
205
206 Bob Feller 75.00
207 Ralph Branca 35.00
208
209
210
211 Larry (Yogi) Berra 75.00
212 Eddie Joost 20.00
213
214
215
216
217
218
219 Gil Hodges 55.00
220
221
222
223 James, Vernon (Mickey) 25.00
224
225
226
227
228
229
230
231
232
233
234 Pete Raiser (Reiser) 30.00
235
236 Bob Elliot 20.00
237
238 Lou Boudreau 45.00
239 Danny Murtany (Photo is Joe Gordon.) 25.00
240 Jakie Robinson (Jackie) 125.00
241
242
243 Tommy Henrick (Henrich) 25.00
244 Pee Wee Reese 55.00
245 Bobby Brower (Brown) 25.00
246
247
248 Enos Slaughter 35.00
249
250
251 Tommy Henrich 25.00
252 George Koslo (Dave) 20.00
253 Frank Gustino (Gustine) 20.00
254
255
256
257 Bill Rigney 20.00
258
259 Rex Barney 25.00
260
261 Mark Christman 20.00
262 Whetey Lockman (Whitey) 20.00
263
264 Ralph Kiner 55.00
265
266 Cliff Fannin 20.00
267 Joe Page 25.00
268
269
270
271 Johnny Sain 30.00
272
273
274
275
276
277
278
279 Joe Dobson 20.00
280
281 Carrol Lockman (Whitey) 20.00
282
283 Monte Kennedy 20.00
284
285
286 Carlos Bernier 20.00
287
288
289 Buster Clarkson 20.00
290 Williard Brown (Willard) 25.00
291 Jim Rivera 25.00
292 Saturnino Escalera 20.00

1958 Dominican Republic

The date of issue is speculative, based on the known winter ball career of the sole card known. The identity of the issuer and manner of distribution is unknown, though from their wide borders it is possible these were printed on some type of box or package and intended to be cut out and possibly placed into an album, as is customary with many Latin American baseball card issues. The cards are nominally about 2" x 2-1/2" and are printed in sepia on thin, blank-back cardboard. As with many issues of the era and area, when these cards are found they are usually in wretched condition.

	NM	EX	VG
Felipe R. Alou			35.00

1959 Dominican Republic

The date of issue is speculative. The identity of the issuer and manner of distribution is unknown, though they appear to have been sold in strips or panels and intended to be separated and possibly placed into an album, as is customary with many Latin American baseball cards. The cards are nominally about 2-1/8" x 3-1/4" and printed in black or blue on thin, blank-back cardboard. As with many issues of the era and area, when these cards are found they are usually in wretched condition. These players certainly represent only a portion of the checklist.

	NM	EX	VG
Walter James			15.00
Osvaldo Virgil			25.00

1966 Dominican Republic

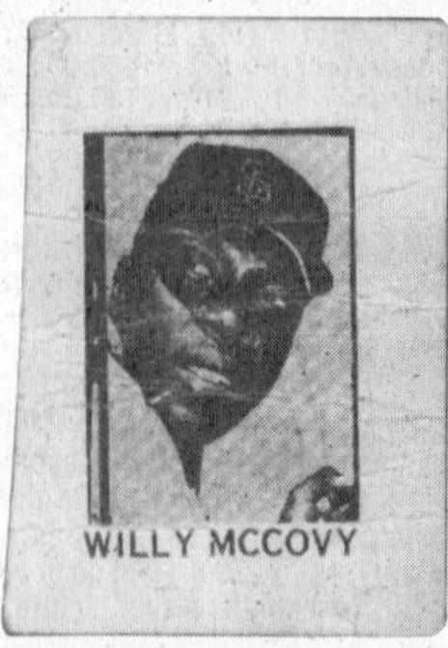

The date of issue is speculative, based on the fact these cards "borrowed" their images from 1965 Topps cards. The identity of the issuer and manner of distribution is unknown, though from their wide borders it is possible these were printed on some type of box or package and intended to be cut out and possibly placed into an album, as is customary with many Latin American baseball card issues. The cards are nominally about 1-3/4" x 2-1/2" and are printed in red on thin, blank-back cardboard. As with many issues of the era and area, when these cards are found they are usually in wretched condition. These players probably represent only a portion of the checklist which may or may not comprise only Major League players.

		NM	EX	VG
(1)	Sandy Koufax			200.00
(2)	Juan Marichal			100.00
(3)	Willy Mays (Willie)			200.00
(4)	Willy McCovy (Willie McCovey)			45.00

1937 Donut Co. of American Thrilling Moments

The official title of this multi-subject card set is "Thrilling Moments in the Lives of Famous Americans." The cards, about 1-7/8" x 2-7/8", were printed in groups of 18 on donut boxes. Each card is printed in black-and-white on a single background color. The cards themselves do not name the famous American depicted, but his biography is found in the album which was issued to house the set. Cards are blank-backed. There is only a single baseball playered in the 72-card set.

	NM	EX	VG
Beloved Baseball Idol of All Boys (Babe Ruth)	4,000	1,600	800.00

1953-55 Dormand Postcards

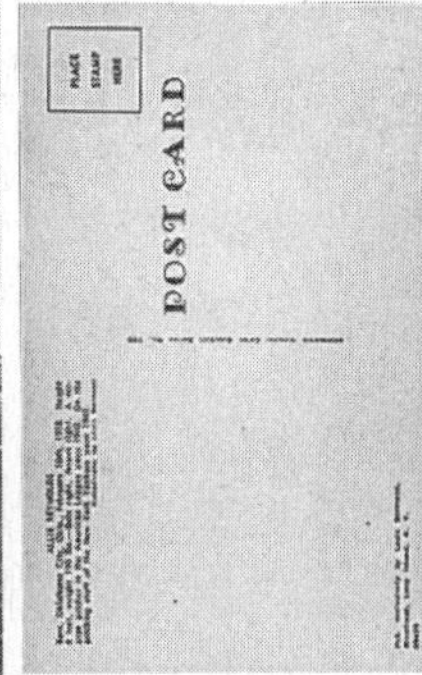

This mid-1950s issue features only selected players from the Yankees, Brooklyn Dodgers, White Sox and Philadelphia A's. Apparently produced on order by the players by Louis Dormand, a Long Island, N.Y., photographer, the cards were used to honor fan requests for photos and autographs. All cards have a facsimile autograph printed in front. Otherwise the fronts of these 3-1/2" x 5-1/2" postcards feature only sharp color photos with no border. Backs, printed in blue or green, feature a few player biographical and career details, one or two lines identifying the producer and usually product and series numbers. Most have a Kodachrome logo. Some cards do not have all of these elements and several are found blank-backed. The Gil Hodges card is considerably scarcer than the others in the set, with those of Jim Konstanty, Elston Howard, and Casey Stengel also seldom seen. Besides the standard-sized cards listed below, there are oversize versions of Rizzuto's and Mantle's cards. A variation of Johnny Sain's card shows his Arkansas Chevrolet dealership in a photo above the player's picture. The complete set price includes only the standard-size cards.

		NM	EX	VG
	Common Player:	25.00	12.50	7.50
101a	Phil Rizzuto (Large autograph parallel to top.)	40.00	20.00	12.00
101b	Phil Rizzuto (Small autograph parallel to top.)	45.00	22.50	13.50
101c	Phil Rizzuto (Autograph angles downward.)	50.00	25.00	15.00
101d	Phil Rizzuto (9" x 12")	55.00	27.50	16.50
102	Yogi Berra	65.00	32.50	20.00
103	Ed Lopat	30.00	15.00	9.00
104	Hank Bauer (Small autograph.)	30.00	15.00	9.00
104	Hank Bauer (Large autograph.)	35.00	17.50	10.50
105	Joe Collins (Patch on sleeve, autograph at top.)	60.00	30.00	18.00
105	Joe Collins (Patch on sleeve, autograph at bottom.)	60.00	30.00	18.00
105	Joe Collins (No patch on sleeve.)	40.00	20.00	12.00
106	Ralph Houk	30.00	15.00	9.00
107	Bill Miller	27.50	13.50	8.25
108	Ray Scarborough	35.00	17.50	10.00
109	Allie Reynolds	25.00	12.50	7.50
110	Gil McDougald (Small autograph.)	25.00	12.50	7.50
110	Gil McDougald (Large autograph.)	25.00	12.50	7.50
111	Mickey Mantle (Bat on shoulder.)	100.00	50.00	30.00
111	Mickey Mantle (Batting stance, 3-1/2" x 5-1/2".)	75.00	37.50	22.50
111	Mickey Mantle (Bat on shoulder, 6" x 9".)	550.00	275.00	165.00
111	Mickey Mantle (Bat on shoulder, 9" x 12".)	1,200	600.00	360.00
112	Johnny Mize	90.00	45.00	27.50
113	Casey Stengel (Autograph at top.)	165.00	80.00	50.00
113	Casey Stengel (Autograph at bottom.)	165.00	80.00	50.00
114	Bobby Shantz (Autograph parallel to top.)	40.00	20.00	12.00
114	Bobby Shantz (Autograph angles downward.)	40.00	20.00	12.00
115	Whitey Ford	60.00	30.00	18.00
116	Johnny Sain (Beginning windup.)	35.00	17.50	10.00
116	Johnny Sain (Leg kick.)	25.00	12.50	7.50
116	Johnny Sain (With auto dealership ad.)	150.00	75.00	45.00
117	Jim McDonald	25.00	12.50	7.50
118	Gene Woodling	25.00	12.50	7.50
119	Charlie Silvera	30.00	15.00	9.00
120	Don Bollweg	25.00	12.50	7.50
121	Billy Pierce	30.00	15.00	9.00
122	Chico Carrasquel	25.00	12.50	7.50
123	Willie Miranda	25.00	12.50	7.50
124	Carl Erskine	65.00	32.50	20.00
125	Roy Campanella	150.00	75.00	45.00
126	Jerry Coleman	25.00	12.50	7.50
127	Pee Wee Reese	50.00	25.00	15.00
128	Carl Furillo	50.00	25.00	15.00
129	Gil Hodges	75.00	37.50	22.50
130	Billy Martin	30.00	15.00	9.00
131	NOT ISSUED			
132	Irv Noren	35.00	17.50	10.50
133	Enos Slaughter	65.00	32.50	20.00
134	Tom Gorman	25.00	12.50	7.50
135	Ed Robinson	35.00	17.50	10.00
136	Frank Crosetti	35.00	17.50	10.00
137	NOT ISSUED			
138	Jim Konstanty	150.00	75.00	45.00
139	Elston Howard	150.00	75.00	45.00
140	Bill Skowron	150.00	75.00	45.00

1941 Double Play (R330)

JOE DI MAGGIO
New York Yankees. Center fielder. Born Nov. 25, 1914. Bats right. Throws right. Height 6 ft. Weight 195 lbs. Batted .352.
No. 63 Double Play
CHARLEY KELLER
New York Yankees. Left fielder. Born Sept. 12, 1916. Bats left. Throws right. Height 5 ft. 10 in. Wt. 190 lbs. Batted .286.
No. 64 Double Play

Issued by Gum Products Inc., Cambridge, Mass., this set comprises 75 numbered cards with two consecutive numbers per card featuring 150 (130 different) players. The blank-backed cards measure about 3-1/8" x 2-1/2". Most feature sepia-toned portrait photos. Cards 81-82 through 99-100 have vertical "in action" photos of 40 of the players who also appear in portraits. The last 50 cards in the series are scarcer than the early numbers. Cards which have been cut in half to form single cards have little collector value.

		NM	EX	VG
	Complete Set (75):	10,000	4,000	2,000
	Common Player (1/2-99/100):	70.00	25.00	12.50
	Common Player (101/102-149/150):	90.00	35.00	15.00
1-2	Larry French, Vance Page	90.00	30.00	15.00
3-4	Billy Herman, Stanley Hack	125.00	50.00	25.00
5-6	Linus Frey, John Vander Meer	75.00	30.00	15.00
7-8	Paul Derringer, Bucky Walters	70.00	25.00	12.50
9-10	Frank McCormick, Bill Werber	70.00	25.00	12.50
11-12	Jimmy Ripple, Ernie Lombardi	85.00	35.00	15.00
13-14	Alex Kampouris, John Wyatt	70.00	25.00	12.50
15-16	Mickey Owen, Paul Waner	110.00	45.00	20.00
17-18	Cookie Lavagetto, Harold Reiser	75.00	30.00	15.00
19-20	Jimmy Wasdell, Dolph Camilli	70.00	25.00	12.50
21-22	Dixie Walker, Ducky Medwick	110.00	45.00	20.00
23-24	Harold Reese, Kirby Higbe	600.00	240.00	120.00
25-26	Harry Danning, Cliff Melton	70.00	25.00	12.50
27-28	Harry Gumbert, Burgess Whitehead	70.00	25.00	12.50
29-30	Joe Orengo, Joe Moore	70.00	25.00	12.50
31-32	Mel Ott, Babe Young	200.00	80.00	40.00
33-34	Lee Handley, Arky Vaughan	110.00	45.00	20.00
35-36	Bob Klinger, Stanley Brown	70.00	25.00	12.50
37-38	Terry Moore, Gus Mancuso	70.00	25.00	12.50
39-40	Johnny Mize, Enos Slaughter	700.00	280.00	140.00
41-42	John Cooney, Sibby Sisti	70.00	25.00	12.50
43-44	Max West, Carvel Rowell	70.00	25.00	12.50
45-46	Danny Litwhiler, Merrill May	70.00	25.00	12.50
47-48	Frank Hayes, Al Brancato	70.00	25.00	12.50
49-50	Bob Johnson, Bill Nagel	70.00	25.00	12.50
51-52	Buck Newsom, Hank Greenberg	200.00	80.00	40.00
53-54	Barney McCosky, Charley Gehringer	140.00	55.00	25.00
55-56	Pinky Higgins, Dick Bartell	70.00	25.00	12.50
57-58	Ted Williams, Jim Tabor	650.00	260.00	130.00
59-60	Joe Cronin, Jimmy Foxx	275.00	110.00	55.00
61-62	Lefty Gomez, Phil Rizzuto	675.00	275.00	135.00
63-64	Joe DiMaggio, Charley Keller	750.00	300.00	150.00
65-66	Red Rolfe, Bill Dickey	125.00	50.00	25.00
67-68	Joe Gordon, Red Ruffing	120.00	45.00	25.00
69-70	Mike Tresh, Luke Appling	110.00	45.00	20.00
71-72	Moose Solters, John Rigney	70.00	25.00	12.50
73-74	Buddy Meyer, Ben Chapman (Myer)	70.00	25.00	12.50
75-76	Cecil Travis, George Case	70.00	25.00	12.50
77-78	Joe Krakauskas, Bob Feller	200.00	80.00	40.00
79-80	Ken Keltner, Hal Trosky	70.00	25.00	12.50
81-82	Ted Williams, Joe Cronin/IA	550.00	220.00	110.00
83-84	Joe Gordon, Charley Keller/IA	90.00	35.00	15.00
85-86	Hank Greenberg, Red Ruffing/IA	225.00	90.00	45.00
87-88	Hal Trosky, George Case/IA	70.00	25.00	12.50
89-90	Mel Ott, Burgess Whitehead/IA	210.00	85.00	40.00
91-92	Harry Danning, Harry Gumbert/IA	70.00	25.00	12.50
93-94	Babe Young, Cliff Melton/IA	70.00	25.00	12.50
95-96	Jimmy Ripple, Bucky Walters/IA	70.00	25.00	12.50
97-98	Stanley Hack, Bob Klinger/IA	70.00	25.00	12.50
99-100	Johnny Mize, Dan Litwhiler/IA	135.00	55.00	25.00
101-102	Dom Dallessandro, Augie Galan	70.00	25.00	12.50
103-104	Bill Lee, Phil Cavarretta	90.00	35.00	15.00
105-106	Lefty Grove, Bobby Doerr	210.00	85.00	40.00
107-108	Frank Pytlak, Dom DiMaggio	115.00	45.00	20.00
109-110	Gerald Priddy, John Murphy	90.00	35.00	15.00
111-112	Tommy Henrich, Marius Russo	100.00	40.00	20.00
113-114	Frank Crosetti, John Sturm	100.00	40.00	20.00
115-116	Ival Goodman, Myron McCormick	90.00	35.00	15.00
117-118	Eddie Joost, Ernie Koy	90.00	35.00	15.00
119-120	Lloyd Waner, Hank Majeski	125.00	50.00	25.00
121-122	Buddy Hassett, Eugene Moore	90.00	35.00	15.00
123-124	Nick Etten, John Rizzo	90.00	35.00	15.00
125-126	Sam Chapman, Wally Moses	90.00	35.00	15.00
127-128	John Babich, Richard Siebert	90.00	35.00	15.00
129-130	Nelson Potter, Benny McCoy	90.00	25.00	15.00
131-132	Clarence Campbell, Louis Boudreau	125.00	50.00	25.00
133-134	Rolly Hemsley, Mel Harder	90.00	35.00	15.00
135-136	Gerald Walker, Joe Heving	90.00	35.00	15.00
137-138	John Rucker, Ace Adams	90.00	35.00	15.00
139-140	Morris Arnovich, Carl Hubbell	225.00	90.00	45.00
141-142	Lew Riggs, Leo Durocher	135.00	55.00	25.00
143-144	Fred Fitzsimmons, Joe Vosmik	90.00	35.00	15.00
145-146	Frank Crespi, Jim Brown	90.00	35.00	15.00
147-148	Don Heffner, Harland Clift (Harlond)	90.00	35.00	15.00
149-150	Debs Garms, Elbie Fletcher	90.00	35.00	15.00

1976 Douglas Cool Papa Bell

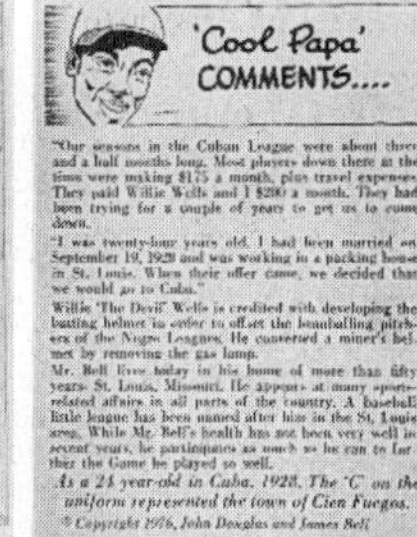

This collectors' issue was produced following the 1974 induction of James "Cool Papa" Bell into the Hall of Fame. Collector John Douglas collaborated with Bell to produce the set chronicling Bell's career (1922-46) in the Negro and Latin

American pro leagues. Fronts have vintage sepia-toned photos of Bell surrounded by a yellow, green or orange woodgrain frame with a title plaque at bottom. Backs are in brown-and-white with a drawing of Bell at top and autobiographical material at center. A description of the photo and copyright data are at bottom. The unnumbered cards are checklisted here alphabetically by their titles.

		NM	EX	VG
Complete Set (13):		10.00	5.00	3.00
Common Card:		1.00	.50	.30
(1)	Amazing Speed	1.00	.50	.30
(2)	Brock Sets SB Record	1.00	.50	.30
(3)	Cool Papa	1.00	.50	.30
(4)	Cuba, 1928	1.00	.50	.30
(5)	Great Fielder, Too	1.00	.50	.30
(6)	HOF, Cooperstown	1.00	.50	.30
(7)	HOF Favorite	1.00	.50	.30
(8)	Induction Day, 1974	1.00	.50	.30
(9)	Monarchs' Manager	1.00	.50	.30
(10)	On Deck in Cuba	1.00	.50	.30
(11)	The Mexican Leagues	1.00	.50	.30
(12)	Touring Havana	1.00	.50	.30
(13)	With Josh Gibson	1.00	.50	.30

1977 Douglas Johnny Mize

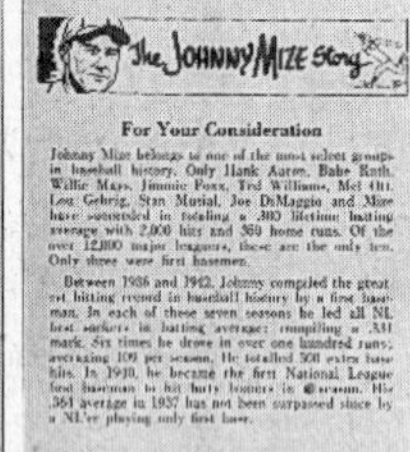

In an effort to promote Johnny Mize for induction to the Hall of Fame, John Douglas created this collectors' issue. The Big Cat's career is traced on a series of 3-1/4" x 3-7/8" cards with black-and-white photos on a greenish-brown background. Black-and-white backs have a drawing of Mize at top with lengthy narrative below. The unnumbered cards are checklisted here by the title which appears on the front. Mize was selected for the Hall of Fame in 1981.

		NM	EX	VG
Complete Set (20):		9.00	4.50	2.75
Common Card:		1.00	.50	.30
(1)	Blattner, Gordon, Lombardi, Mize, Marshall	1.00	.50	.30
(2)	Call for Phillip Morris	1.00	.50	.30
(3)	Cardinal Slugger	1.00	.50	.30
(4)	Card's Big Stick	1.00	.50	.30
(5)	Early Photo - 1913	1.00	.50	.30
(6)	51 Homers, 1947	1.00	.50	.30
(7)	Home Run, 1952 Series	1.00	.50	.30
(8)	June 16, 1953	1.00	.50	.30
(9)	Louisville Poster - 1947	1.00	.50	.30
(10)	Mize, Happy Chandler, Bucky Harris	1.00	.50	.30
(11)	Mize, Reynolds, Johnson	1.00	.50	.30
(12)	N.L. Homer Champ 1948	1.00	.50	.30
(13)	Series MVP - 1952	1.00	.50	.30
(14)	St. Louis Star	1.00	.50	.30
(15)	The Navy - 1943	1.00	.50	.30
(16)	Vu-Master Slide	1.00	.50	.30
(17)	With Enos Slaughter	1.00	.50	.30
(18)	With Roy Rogers	1.00	.50	.30
(19)	With Terry Moore	1.00	.50	.30
(20)	Woodling, Raschi, Mize - 1952	1.00	.50	.30

1978 Dover Publications Great Players Postcards

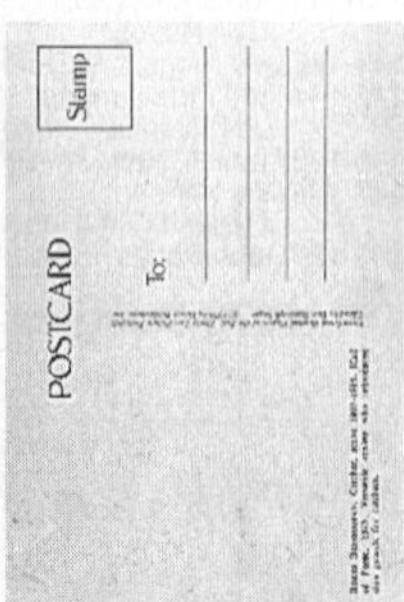

This set of 32 collectors' issue postcards was originally issued in the form of an 8" x 11" booklet from which individual cards could be separated. The 3-7/8" x 5-1/2" cards are perforated on two sides, depending on their placement on a four-card page. Fronts have borderless sepia photos. Black-and-white backs have standard postcard indicia, copyright data, player identification and a brief career summary. The unnumbered cards are checklisted here alphabetically.

		NM	EX	VG
Complete Set, Booklet:		7.50	3.75	2.25
Complete Set, Singles (32):		7.50	3.75	2.25
Common Player:		.50	.25	.15
(1)	Grover Cleveland Alexander	.60	.30	.20
(2)	Chief Bender	.50	.25	.15
(3)	Roger Bresnahan	.50	.25	.15
(4)	Bullet Joe Bush	.50	.25	.15
(5)	Frank Chance	.50	.25	.15
(6)	Ty Cobb	1.25	.60	.40
(7)	Eddie Collins	.50	.25	.15
(8)	Stan Coveleski	.50	.25	.15
(9)	Sam Crawford	.50	.25	.15
(10)	Frankie Frisch	.50	.25	.15
(11)	Goose Goslin	.50	.25	.15
(12)	Harry Heilmann	.50	.25	.15
(13)	Rogers Hornsby	.75	.40	.25
(14)	Joe Jackson	4.00	2.00	1.25
(15)	Hughie Jennings	.50	.25	.15
(16)	Walter Johnson	1.00	.50	.30
(17)	Sad Sam Jones	.50	.25	.15
(18)	Rabbit Maranville	.50	.25	.15
(19)	Rube Marquard	.50	.25	.15
(20)	Christy Mathewson	1.00	.50	.30
(21)	John McGraw	.50	.25	.15
(22)	Herb Pennock	.50	.25	.15
(23)	Eddie Plank	.50	.25	.15
(24)	Edd Roush	.50	.25	.15
(25)	Babe Ruth	4.00	2.00	1.25
(26)	George Sisler	.50	.25	.15
(27)	Tris Speaker	.75	.40	.25
(28)	Casey Stengel	.50	.25	.15
(29)	Joe Tinker	.50	.25	.15
(30)	Pie Traynor	.50	.25	.15
(31)	Dazzy Vance	.50	.25	.15
(32)	Cy Young	.75	.40	.25

1925 Drake's

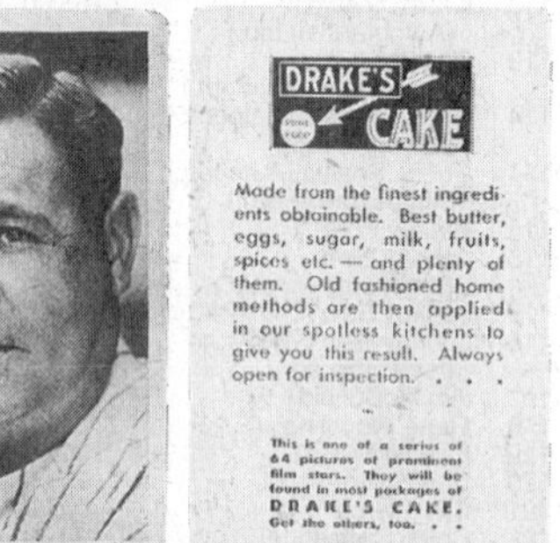

Among a series of 64 movie stars packaged with Drake's Cake in the mid-1920s was a card of Babe Ruth, who did some movie work for Universal Pictures at the time. The 2-7/16" x 4-3/16" black-and-white card has a portrait of Ruth on front, with his name, studio and card number in the bottom border. Backs have been seen with at least two styles of advertising, one for Drake's Cake and one for Yankee Cake.

		NM	EX	VG
61	Babe Ruth	3,750	1,875	1,125

1950 Drake's

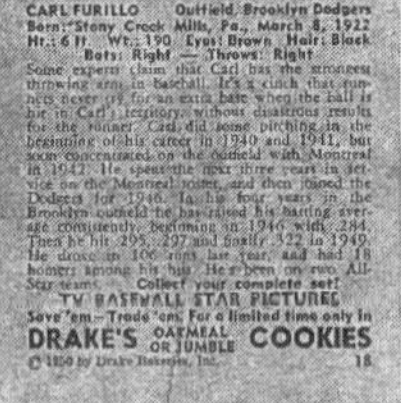

Entitled "TV Baseball Series," the 1950 Drake's Bakeries set pictures 36 different players on a television screen format. The cards, 2-1/2" x 2-1/2", contain black-and-white photos surrounded by a black border. Backs carry a player biography plus an advertisement advising collectors to look for the cards in packages of Oatmeal or Jumble cookies.

		NM	EX	VG
Complete Set (36):		7,500	3,000	1,500
Common Player:		150.00	60.00	30.00
1	Elwin "Preacher" Roe	250.00	100.00	50.00
2	Clint Hartung	150.00	60.00	30.00
3	Earl Torgeson	150.00	60.00	30.00
4	Leland "Lou" Brissie	150.00	60.00	30.00
5	Edwin "Duke" Snider	500.00	200.00	100.00
6	Roy Campanella	500.00	200.00	100.00
7	Sheldon "Available" Jones	150.00	60.00	30.00
8	Carroll "Whitey" Lockman	150.00	60.00	30.00
9	Bobby Thomson	175.00	70.00	35.00
10	Dick Sisler	150.00	60.00	30.00
11	Gil Hodges	300.00	120.00	60.00
12	Eddie Waitkus	150.00	60.00	30.00
13	Bobby Doerr	250.00	100.00	50.00
14	Warren Spahn	300.00	120.00	60.00
15	John "Buddy" Kerr	150.00	60.00	30.00
16	Sid Gordon	150.00	60.00	30.00
17	Willard Marshall	150.00	60.00	30.00
18	Carl Furillo	300.00	120.00	60.00
19	Harold "Pee Wee" Reese	400.00	160.00	80.00
20	Alvin Dark	150.00	60.00	30.00
21	Del Ennis	150.00	60.00	30.00
22	Ed Stanky	150.00	60.00	30.00
23	Tommy "Old Reliable" Henrich	175.00	70.00	35.00
24	Larry "Yogi" Berra	500.00	200.00	100.00
25	Phil "Scooter" Rizzuto	500.00	200.00	100.00
26	Jerry Coleman	150.00	60.00	30.00
27	Joe Page	150.00	60.00	30.00
28	Allie Reynolds	175.00	70.00	35.00
29	Ray Scarborough	150.00	60.00	30.00
30	George "Birdie" Tebbetts	150.00	60.00	30.00
31	Maurice "Lefty" McDermott	150.00	60.00	30.00
32	Johnny Pesky	150.00	60.00	30.00
33	Dom "Little Professor" DiMaggio	190.00	75.00	35.00
34	Vern "Junior" Stephens	150.00	60.00	30.00
35	Bob Elliott	150.00	60.00	30.00
36	Enos "Country" Slaughter	325.00	130.00	65.00

1909-11 Drum Cigarettes

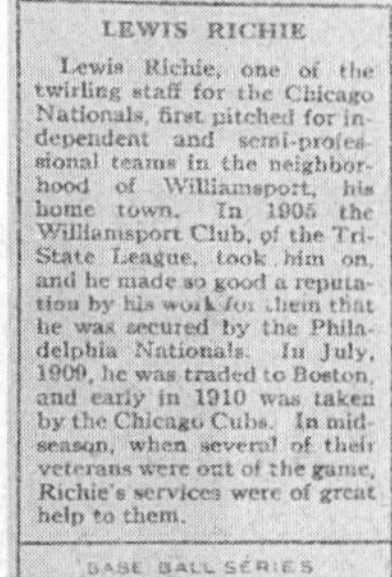

Other than Ty Cobb brand, Drum is the rarest of the various cigarette advertisements to be found on the backs of T206. Typography on the back is printed in a plum color. Multipliers shown are for "common" players; Hall of Fame players and other high-demand cards command a lesser premium relative to common-brand backs. Among T205 backs, Drum, printed in brown, ranks as the scarcest of the brands.

PREMIUMS
T205: 25X
T206: 40X
(See T205, T206 for checklists and base card values.)

1972 Don Drysdale's Restaurant Postcards

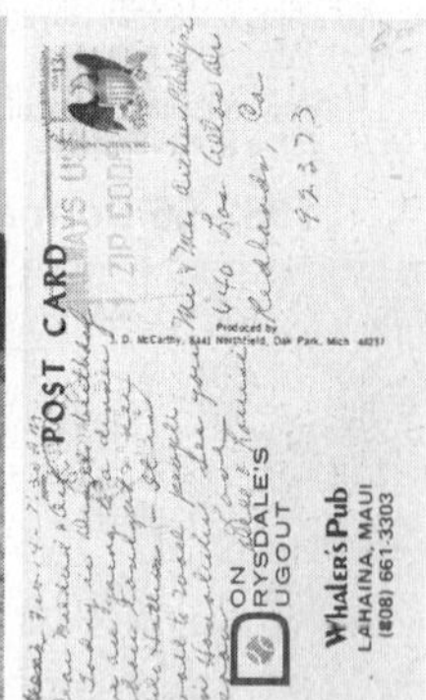

The date cited is taken from the postmark of an observed example. The actual span during which the cards were current is unknown. These versions of J.D. McCarthy postcards have on their 3-1/4" x 5-1/2" fronts a borderless black-and-white pose. The salutation and facsimile autograph are incuse printed in blue ink. Postcard style backs are known in three styles. One advertises Don Drysdale's Dugout in Santa Ana, Calif., another advertises his Club 53 in Kona, Hawaii, while a third advertizes Don Drysdale's Dugout and the Whaler's Pub on Maui.

	NM	EX	VG
Don Drysdale	16.00	8.00	4.75

1965 Dugan Bros. Casey Stengel

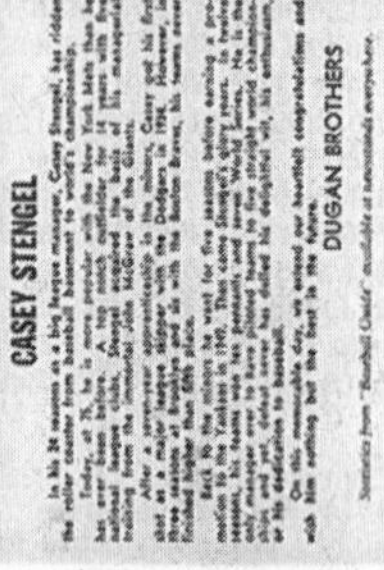

In celebration of the Ol' Perfesser's 75th birthday, the N.Y. Mets held a birthday party for him at Shea Stadium on July 25. This approximately 2-1/2" x 3-1/2" card was given to each of the 40,000+ fans in attendance, sponsored by Dugan Bros., a local bakery which also provided a birthday cake for the occasion. Unfortunately, Stengel was unable to attend the fete; early that morning he broke his hip leaving a nightclub, ending his managerial career. The card is printed in blue on white. The back provides career highlights.

	NM	EX	VG
Casey Stengel	25.00	12.50	7.50

1888 Duke Talk of the Diamond (N135)

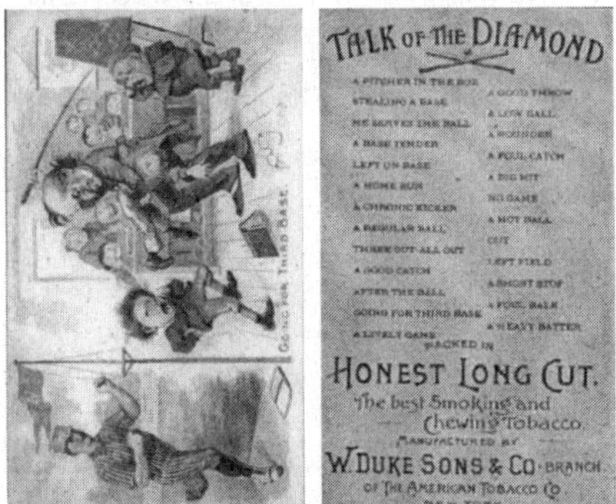

One of the more obscure 19th Century tobacco issues is a 25-card set issued by Honest Long Cut Tobacco in the late 1880's. Titled "Talk of the Diamond," the set features full-color cards measuring 4-1/8" x 2-1/2". Each card features a cartoon-like drawing illustrating a popular baseball term or expression. The left portion of the card pictures an unspecified player in a fielding position, and some of the artwork for that part of the set was borrowed from the more popular Buchner Gold Coin set (N284) issued about the same time. Because the "Talk of the Diamond" set does not feature individual players, it has never really captured the attention of baseball card collectors. It does, however, hold interest as a novelty item of the period. It carries an N135 American Card Catalog designation.

		NM	EX	VG
Complete Set (25):		9,350	3,850	1,925
Common Card:		385.00	155.00	75.00
(1)	A Base Tender	400.00	155.00	75.00
(2)	A Big Hit	400.00	155.00	75.00
(3)	A Chronic Kicker	400.00	155.00	75.00
(4)	A Foul Balk	400.00	155.00	75.00
(5)	A Foul Catch	400.00	155.00	75.00
(6)	A Good Catch	400.00	155.00	75.00
(7)	A Good Throw	400.00	155.00	75.00
(8)	A Heavy Batter	400.00	155.00	75.00
(9)	A Home Run	400.00	155.00	75.00
(10)	A Hot Ball	400.00	155.00	75.00
(11)	A Low Ball	400.00	155.00	75.00
(12)	A Pitcher in the Box	400.00	155.00	75.00
(13)	A Regular Ball	400.00	155.00	75.00
(14)	A Rounder	400.00	155.00	75.00
(15)	A Short Stop	400.00	155.00	75.00
(16)	After the Ball	400.00	155.00	75.00
(17)	Going for Third Base	400.00	155.00	75.00
(18)	He Serves the Ball	400.00	155.00	75.00
(19)	Left Field	400.00	155.00	75.00
(20)	Left on Base	400.00	155.00	75.00
(21)	Lively Game	400.00	155.00	75.00
(22)	No Game	400.00	155.00	75.00
(23)	Out	400.00	155.00	75.00
(24)	Stealing a Base	400.00	155.00	75.00
(25)	Three out-All out	400.00	155.00	75.00

1889 Duke's Terrors of America

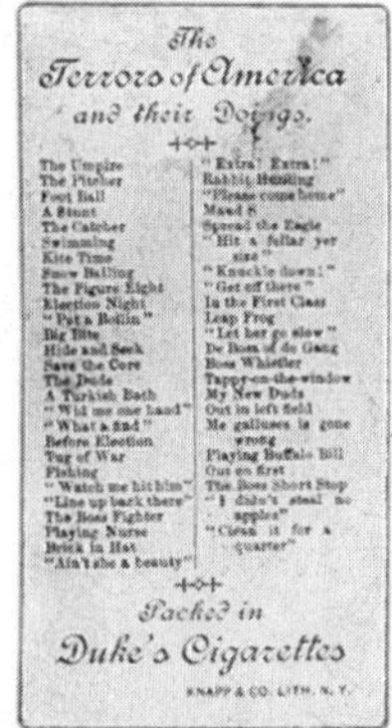

Officially titled "The Terrors of America and their Doings," this set of tobacco inserts features color artwork of boys in all manners of activities, some mischievous. Several of the cards picture the lads playing sports, including baseball. The cards were issued in three sizes. The smallest measure 1-7/16" x 2-3/4" and have an ad on the checklist back for Duke's Cigarettes. A slightly larger 1-3/4" x 3-1/8" version advertises Duke's Mixture. The largest features the card design on an ornate background and measures 2-1/2" x 4-3/16", advertising Honest Long Cut on back.

	NM	EX	VG
Duke's Cigarettes	80.00	40.00	24.00
Duke's Mixture	100.00	50.00	30.00
Honest Long Cut	200.00	100.00	60.00

1969 Dunkin' Donuts Chicago Cubs Bumper Stickers

This series of Cubs novelty collectibles was the first of two annual presentations. The stickers measure about 8" x 4" and have at their left end a photographic portrait of a player at one end of an artwork bat on a black background. At right is a baseball design with the sponsor's logo. A second version exists with "Cub Power" in place of the DD advertising. The unnumbered stickers are checklisted here alphabetically.

		NM	EX	VG
Complete Set (6):		350.00	175.00	100.00
Common Player:		30.00	15.00	9.00
(1)	Ernie Banks	125.00	65.00	35.00
(2)	Glenn Beckert	30.00	15.00	9.00
(3)	Randy Hundley	30.00	15.00	9.00
(4)	Don Kessinger	30.00	15.00	9.00
(5)	Ron Santo	60.00	30.00	18.00
(6)	Billy Williams	75.00	37.00	22.00

1970 Dunkin' Donuts Chicago Cubs Bumper Stickers

This series of Cubs novelty collectibles was the second of two annual presentations. The stickers measure about 8" x 4" and have at their left end a photographic portrait (without cap) of a player in a vaguely baseball-like design. In upper-left is a blue facsimile autograph. At right is "Cubs are no. 1," at bottom is a DD credit line. Basic color scheme of the graphics is red, white and blue. The unnumbered stickers are checklisted here alphabetically.

		NM	EX	VG
Complete Set (6):		350.00	175.00	100.00
Common Player:		30.00	15.00	9.00
(1)	Ernie Banks	125.00	62.00	37.00
(2)	Glenn Beckert	30.00	15.00	9.00
(3)	Randy Hundley	30.00	15.00	9.00
(4)	Don Kessinger	30.00	15.00	9.00
(5)	Ron Santo	60.00	30.00	18.00
(6)	Billy Williams	75.00	37.00	22.00

1937 Dupont Cavalcade of America Premium

This 6" x 9" black-and-white card was distributed by NBC radio in conjunction with one of its weekly programs, which featured Babe Ruth on Sept. 29, 1937. The front has a bordered photo of Ruth in his classic batting follow-through. The back has information about the broadcast and details "The Babe's 54 Major League Records."

	NM	EX	VG
Babe Ruth	500.00	250.00	150.00

1972 Durochrome Chicago White Sox Decals

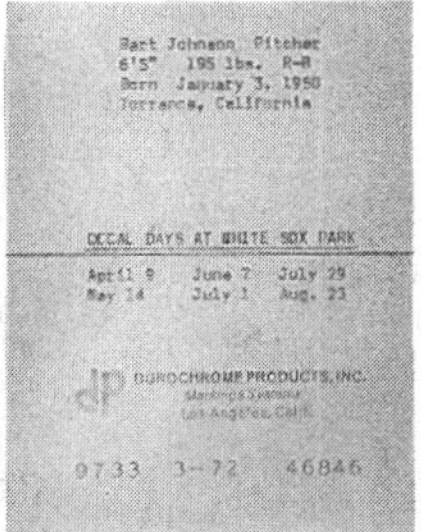

While they are technically stickers rather than decals, this set of six White Sox was given away during the course of half a dozen "Decal Days" at Comiskey Park, as listed on the peel-off back. The stickers measure 3-9/16" x 4-9/16" and feature posed action photos of the players in their vintage red-trimmed uniforms. Fronts have a facsimile autograph and, in the bottom border, the team name. Backs are printed in green and have a few vital statistics, an ad by the manufacturer and an enigmatic row of numbers at the bottom. The unnumbered stickers are checklisted here in alphabetical order.

		NM	EX	VG
Complete Set (6):		60.00	30.00	18.00
Common Player:		9.00	4.50	2.75
(1)	Richard Allen	25.00	12.50	7.50
(2)	Ed Hermann	9.00	4.50	2.75
(3)	Bart Johnson	9.00	4.50	2.75
(4)	Carlos May	9.00	4.50	2.75
(5)	Bill Melton	9.00	4.50	2.75
(6)	Wilbur Wood	9.00	4.50	2.75

E

1914 E. & S. Publishing Co.

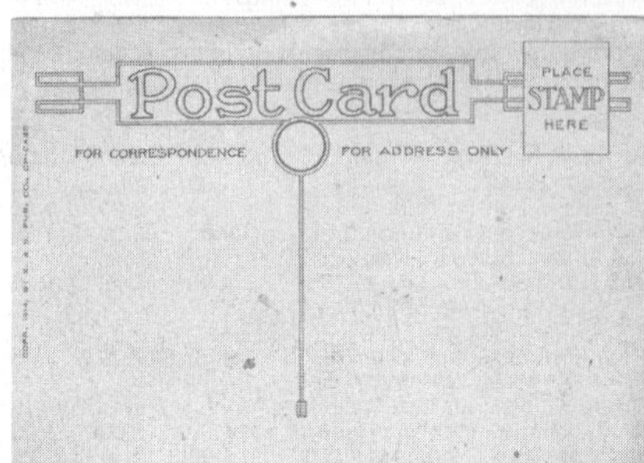

Currently, a dozen players have been reported from this issue. Front of the 5-/1/2" x 3-3/4" postcards has a large portrait or action picture of the player at center, with a number of cartoons around. The printing is in blue ink. The back is done in ornate typography with copyright line, stamp box, etc. Other players may yet be discovered.

		NM	EX	VG
(1)	"Jimmie" Archer	300.00	150.00	90.00
(2)	Joe Benz	300.00	150.00	90.00
(3)	Frank Chance	300.00	150.00	90.00

		NM	EX	VG
(4)	Ty Cobb	4,500	2,250	1,350
(5)	Miller Huggins	600.00	300.00	180.00
(6)	Joe Jackson	6,000	3,000	1,800
(7)	James Lavender	300.00	150.00	90.00
(8)	Christy Mathewson	2,500	1,250	750.00
(9)	"Tex" Russell	300.00	150.00	90.00
(10)	Frank Schulte	300.00	150.00	90.00
(11)	Jim Scott	300.00	150.00	90.00
(12)	Art Wilson	300.00	150.00	90.00

1940s Eagle Hall of Fame

The date of this issue can only be approximated, probably in the late 1940s. The 9-1/4" x 11-1/4" cards have high-gloss sepia photos on thick cardboard. A wood-look frame and identification plaques are pictured around the central photo. Backs are blank. The pictures were issued by the Carnegie (Pa.) Aerie of the Eagles, lodge #1134, according to the bottom "plaque." At top is "Eagle Hall of Fame." Presumably the four ballplayers and two boxers known were all members of that fraternal order. The unnumbered pieces are checklisted alphabetically.

		NM	EX	VG
Complete Set (6):		700.00	350.00	210.00
Common Player:		40.00	20.00	12.00
(1)	Bob Fitzsimmons (Boxer)	40.00	20.00	12.00
(2)	Lefty Grove	150.00	75.00	45.00
(3)	Stan Musial	200.00	100.00	60.00
(4)	John Sullivan (Boxer)	75.00	37.00	22.00
(5)	Honus Wagner	175.00	87.00	52.00
(6)	Cy Young	175.00	87.00	52.00

1979 Early Red Sox Favorites

This collectors' issue from Maine features players of the 1920s-1930s Red Sox. Cards are printed in black-and-white in a 2-5/8" x 3-3/4" format. Front photos are bordered in white and have identification of the players overprinted in black. Backs have a few stats, highlights or an explanation of the photo on front. Many cards feature more than one player.

		NM	EX	VG
Complete Set (24):		40.00	20.00	12.00
Common Player:		4.00	2.00	1.25
1	New Fenway Park	4.00	2.00	1.25
2	Mrs. Tom Yawkey and Mrs. Eddie Collins	4.00	2.00	1.25
3	Red Sox Outfielders - 1932 (Tom Oliver, Earl Webb, Jack Rothrock)	4.00	2.00	1.25
4	Red Sox Ace Pitchers (John Marcum, Wes Ferrell, Lefty Grove, Fritz Ostermueller)	4.00	2.00	1.25
5	John Gooch	4.00	2.00	1.25
6	Red Sox Recruits at Sarasota, Fla. (Joe Cronin)	4.00	2.00	1.25
7	Danny MacFayden	4.00	2.00	1.25
8	Dale Alexander	4.00	2.00	1.25
9	Robert (Fatsy) Fothergill	4.00	2.00	1.25
10	Red Sox Sunday Morning Workout	4.00	2.00	1.25
11	Jimmie Foxx (Signing ball for Mrs. Yawkey.)	6.00	3.00	1.75
12	Lefty Grove (Presented keys to new car.)	6.00	3.00	1.75
13	"Fireball" Lefty Grove	6.00	3.00	1.75
14	Praciticng Base Stealing (Jack Rothrock, Urban Pickering)	4.00	2.00	1.25
15	Tom Daly, Al Schacht, Herb Pennock	4.00	2.00	1.25
16	Eddie Collins, Heinie Manush	6.00	3.00	1.75
17	Tris Speaker	6.00	3.00	1.75
18	Home Run Star (Jimmie Foxx)	6.00	3.00	1.75
19	Smead Jolley	4.00	2.00	1.25
20	Hal Trosky, Jimmie Foxx	4.00	2.00	1.25
21	Herold "Muddy" Ruel, Wilcy "Fireman" Moore	4.00	2.00	1.25
22	Bob Quinn, Shano Collins	4.00	2.00	1.25
23	Tom Oliver	4.00	2.00	1.25
24	Joe Cronin, Herb Pennock, Buetter	4.00	2.00	1.25

1966 East Hills Pirates

Stores in the East Hills Shopping Center, a large mall located in suburban Pittsburgh, distributed cards from this 25-card full-color set in 1966. The cards, which measure 3-1/4" x 4-1/4", are blank-backed and are numbered by the players' uniform numbers. The numbers appear in the lower right corners of the cards.

		NM	EX	VG
Complete Set (25):		50.00	25.00	15.00
Common Player:		2.50	1.25	.70
3	Harry Walker	2.50	1.25	.70
7	Bob Bailey	2.50	1.25	.70
8	Willie Stargell	10.00	5.00	3.00
9	Bill Mazeroski	10.00	5.00	3.00
10	Jim Pagliaroni	2.50	1.25	.70
11	Jose Pagan	2.50	1.25	.70
12	Jerry May	2.50	1.25	.70
14	Gene Alley	2.50	1.25	.70
15	Manny Mota	2.50	1.25	.70
16	Andy Rodgers	2.50	1.25	.70
17	Donn Clendenon	2.50	1.25	.70
18	Matty Alou	2.50	1.25	.70
19	Pete Mikkelsen	2.50	1.25	.70
20	Jesse Gonder	2.50	1.25	.70
21	Bob Clemente	30.00	15.00	9.00
22	Woody Fryman	2.50	1.25	.70
24	Jerry Lynch	2.50	1.25	.70
25	Tommie Sisk	2.50	1.25	.70
26	Roy Face	2.50	1.25	.70
28	Steve Blass	2.50	1.25	.70
32	Vernon Law	3.50	1.75	1.00
34	Al McBean	2.50	1.25	.70
39	Bob Veale	2.50	1.25	.70
43	Don Cardwell	2.50	1.25	.70
45	Gene Michael	2.50	1.25	.70

1933 Eclipse Import

No. 410
This is one of a series of 24 cards
JIMMY DYKES
Chicago White Sox
He is one of the few players who can play every position in the field but catch. A timely batter and dependable fielder, he hit 265 in over 150 games and played three infield positions in 1932. Played with Philadelphia Athletics for over 12 years, finally traded to White Sox this year. Dykes is 36 years old, about five feet nine inches tall and weighs 175 lbs.

Issued in 1933, this set was sold in eight-card strips. Numbered from 401 through 424, the cards measure 2-7/16" x 2-7/8". The design features a crude colored drawing of the player on the front. The back of the card displays the card number at the top followed by the player's name, team and a brief write-up. Card numbers 403, 413, and 414 are missing and probably correspond to the three unnumbered cards in the set. The set carries an American Card Catalog designation of R337.

		NM	EX	VG
Complete Set (24):		7,500	3,000	1,500
Common Player:		165.00	65.00	30.00
401	Johnny Vergez	165.00	65.00	30.00
402	Babe Ruth	1,200	480.00	240.00
403	Not Issued			
404	George Pipgras	165.00	65.00	30.00
405	Bill Terry	425.00	170.00	85.00
406	George Connally	165.00	65.00	30.00
407	Watson Clark	165.00	65.00	30.00
408	"Lefty" Grove	500.00	200.00	100.00
409	Henry Johnson	165.00	65.00	30.00
410	Jimmy Dykes	165.00	65.00	30.00
411	Henry Hine Schuble	165.00	65.00	30.00
412	Bucky Harris	425.00	170.00	85.00
413	Not Issued			
414	Not Issued			
415	Al Simmons	425.00	170.00	85.00
416	Henry "Heinie" Manush	425.00	170.00	85.00
417	Glen Myatt (Glenn)	165.00	65.00	30.00
418	Babe Herman	175.00	70.00	35.00
419	Frank Frisch	425.00	170.00	85.00
420	Tony Lazzeri	425.00	170.00	85.00
421	Paul Waner	425.00	170.00	85.00
422	Jimmy Wilson	165.00	65.00	30.00
423	Charles Grimm	165.00	65.00	30.00
424	Dick Bartell	165.00	65.00	30.00
----	Jimmy Fox (Jimmie Foxx)	600.00	240.00	120.00
----	Roy Johnson	165.00	65.00	30.00
----	Pie Traynor	425.00	170.00	85.00

1942 Editorial Bruguera Babe Ruth

The Babe is the only baseball player appearing is this 12-card series of "Figuras deportivas de fama mundial" (World famous sports figures) issued in Spain. The cards are blank-backed, about 4-3/4" x 3-1/2", with color artwork on front.

	NM	EX	VG
Babe Ruth	175.00	90.00	50.00

1930s Edwards, Ringer & Bigg Cigarettes

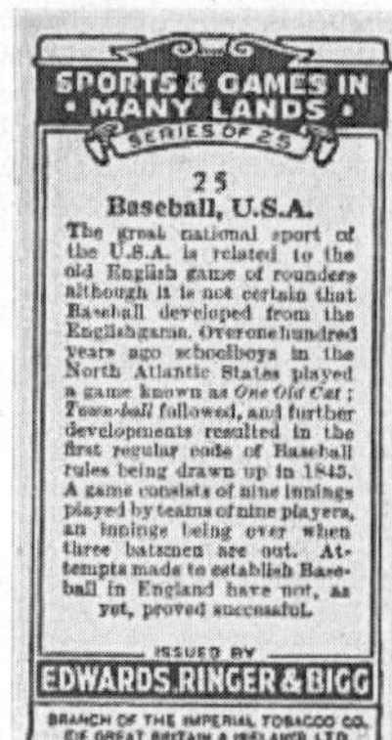

SPORTS & GAMES IN MANY LANDS
SERIES OF 25

25
Baseball, U.S.A.

The great national sport of the U.S.A. is related to the old English game of rounders although it is not certain that Baseball developed from the Englishgame. Overonehundred years ago schoolboys in the North Atlantic States played a game known as *One Old Cat*; *Town-ball* followed, and further developments resulted in the first regular code of Baseball rules being drawn up in 1845. A game consists of nine innings played by teams of nine players, an innings being over when three batsmen are out. Attempts made to establish Baseball in England have not, as yet, proved successful.

ISSUED BY
EDWARDS, RINGER & BIGG
BRANCH OF THE IMPERIAL TOBACCO CO. OF GREAT BRITAIN & IRELAND, LTD.

Though he is identified nowhere on this English cigarette card, the home run swing of Babe Ruth on the front is unmistakable. The last card in a set of 25 "Sports & Games in Many Lands" series, the approximately 2-5/8" x 1-3/8" cards have color artwork on the front and green-and-white backs. The back of the baseball card provides a short history of "The great national sport of the U.S.A." The card is nearly identical to the much more common 1929 Churchman's brand, except for the ads on back and the lack on the later card of the Churchman's name on top-right front.

		NM	EX	VG
25	Baseball, U.S.A. (Babe Ruth)	400.00	200.00	120.00

1909-11 El Principe de Gales Cigarettes

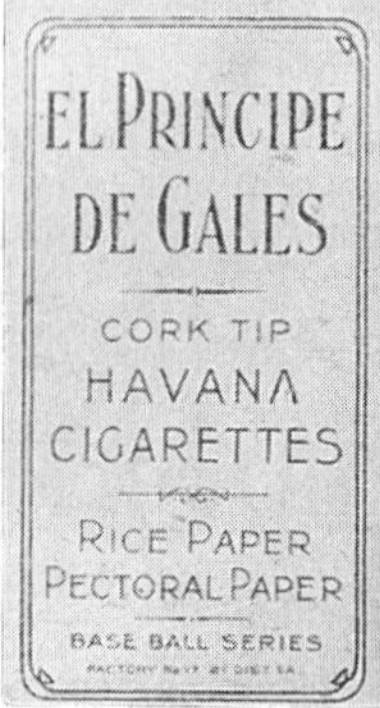

PREMIUMS:
Commons: 1-2X

Hall of Famers: 1-2X
(See T206 for checklist and base card values.)

1976 English's Chicken Baltimore Orioles Lids

It is uncertain whether the checklist presented here is complete. These 8-3/8" diameter fried chicken bucket lids are printed on heavy waxed cardboard in black-and-white. Cap logos have been airbrushed off. A few previous seasons' stats are printed to the left and right of the player photo.

		NM	EX	VG
Complete Set (4):		45.00	22.50	13.50
Common Player:		9.00	4.50	2.75
(1)	Mike Cuellar	9.00	4.50	1.75
(2)	Ken Holtzman	9.00	4.50	1.75
(3)	Lee May	9.00	4.50	1.75
(4)	Jim Palmer	20.00	10.00	6.00

1963-1973 Equitable Sports Hall of Fame

This series of black-and-white art prints was produced over more than a decade. About 8" x 11", the prints feature the artwork of Robert Riger or George Loh, reproduced from ads for the life insurance company. Nearly 95 pieces honoring athletes from many sports were produced. Only the baseball players are listed here.

		NM	EX	VG
Common Player:		6.00	3.00	1.80
(1)	Ernie Banks	7.50	3.75	2.25
(2)	Roy Campanella	7.50	3.75	2.25
(3)	Johnny Evers	6.00	3.00	1.80
(4)	Bob Feller	6.00	3.00	1.80
(5)	Lou Gehrig	10.00	5.00	3.00
(6)	Lefty Grove	6.00	3.00	1.80
(7)	Tommy Henrich	6.00	3.00	1.80
(8)	Carl Hubbell	6.00	3.00	1.80
(9)	Al Kaline	6.00	3.00	1.80
(10)	Jerry Koosman	6.00	3.00	1.80
(11)	Mickey Mantle	15.00	7.50	4.50
(12)	Eddie Mathews	6.00	3.00	1.80
(13)	Willie Mays	9.00	4.50	2.75
(14)	Stan Musial	9.00	4.50	2.75
(15)	Pee Wee Reese	6.00	3.00	1.80
(16)	Allie Reynolds	6.00	3.00	1.80
(17)	Robin Roberts	6.00	3.00	1.80
(18)	Brooks Robinson	6.00	3.00	1.80
(19)	Red Ruffing	6.00	3.00	1.80
(20)	Babe Ruth	12.50	6.25	3.75
(21)	Warren Spahn	6.00	3.00	1.80

1954 Esskay Hot Dogs Orioles

Measuring 2-1/4" x 3-1/2", the 1954 Esskay Hot Dogs set features the Baltimore Orioles. The unnumbered color cards were issued in panels of two on packages of hot dogs and are usually found with grease stains. The cards have waxed fronts with blank backs on a white stock. Complete boxes of Esskay Hot Dogs are scarce and command a price of 2-3 times greater than the single card values.

		NM	EX	VG
Complete Set (34):		45,000	18,000	9,000
Common Player:		1,500	600.00	300.00
(1)	Neil Berry	1,500	600.00	300.00
(2)	Michael Blyzka	1,500	600.00	300.00
(3)	Harry Brecheen	1,500	600.00	300.00
(4)	Gil Coan	1,500	600.00	300.00
(5)	Joe Coleman	1,500	600.00	300.00
(6)	Clinton Courtney	1,500	600.00	300.00
(7)	Charles E. Diering	1,500	600.00	300.00
(8)	Jimmie Dykes	1,500	600.00	300.00
(9)	Frank J. Fanovich	1,500	600.00	300.00
(10)	Howard Fox	1,500	600.00	300.00
(11)	Jim Fridley	1,500	600.00	300.00
(12)	Vinicio "Chico" Garcia	1,500	600.00	300.00
(13)	Jehosie Heard	2,000	800.00	400.00
(14)	Darrell Johnson	1,500	600.00	300.00
(15)	Bob Kennedy	1,500	600.00	300.00
(16)	Dick Kokos	1,500	600.00	300.00
(17)	Dave Koslo	1,500	600.00	300.00
(18)	Lou Kretlow	1,500	600.00	300.00
(19)	Richard D. Kryhoski	1,500	600.00	300.00
(20)	Don Larsen	2,500	1,000	500.00
(21)	Donald E. Lenhardt	1,500	600.00	300.00
(22)	Richard Littlefield	1,500	600.00	300.00
(23)	Sam Mele	1,500	600.00	300.00
(24)	Les Moss	1,500	600.00	300.00
(25)	Ray L. Murray	1,500	600.00	300.00
(26a)	"Bobo" Newsom (No stadium lights in background.)	1,750	700.00	350.00
(26b)	"Bobo" Newson (Stadium lights in background.)	1,750	700.00	350.00
(27)	Tom Oliver	1,500	600.00	300.00
(28)	Duane Pillette	1,500	600.00	300.00
(29)	Francis M. Skaff	1,500	600.00	300.00
(30)	Marlin Stuart	1,500	600.00	300.00
(31)	Robert L. Turley	2,250	900.00	450.00
(32)	Eddie Waitkus	1,500	600.00	300.00
(33)	Vic Wertz	1,500	600.00	300.00
(34)	Robert G. Young	1,500	600.00	300.00

1955 Esskay Hot Dogs Orioles

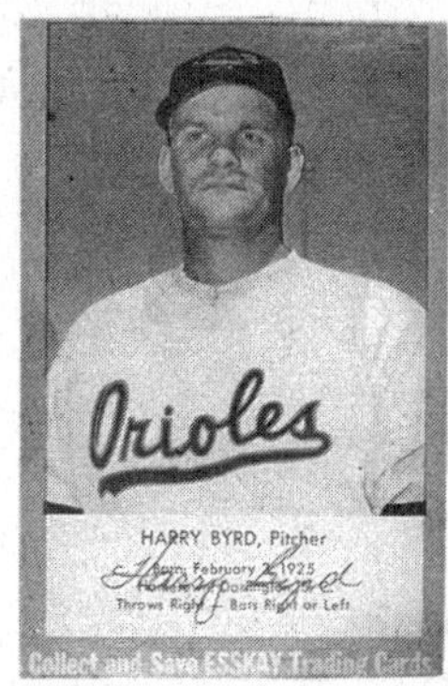

For the second consecutive year, Esskay Meats placed baseball cards of Orioles players on their boxes of hot dogs. The unnumbered, color cards measure 2-1/4" x 3-1/2" and can be distinguished from the previous year by their unwaxed fronts and blank gray backs. Many of the same photos from 1954 were used with only minor picture-cropping differences. For 1955, only one player card per box was printed. The space which was occupied by the second player card in 1954 carried a prize redemption coupon on 1955 boxes.

		NM	EX	VG
Complete Set (26):		37,500	15,000	7,500
Common Player:		1,500	600.00	300.00
(1)	Cal Abrams	1,500	600.00	300.00
(2)	Robert S. Alexander	1,500	600.00	300.00
(3)	Harry Byrd	1,500	600.00	300.00
(4)	Gil Coan	1,500	600.00	300.00
(5)	Joseph P. Coleman	1,500	600.00	300.00
(6)	William R. Cox	1,500	600.00	300.00
(7)	Charles E. Diering	1,500	600.00	300.00
(8)	Walter A. Evers	1,500	600.00	300.00
(9)	Don Johnson	1,500	600.00	300.00
(10)	Robert D. Kennedy	1,500	600.00	300.00
(11)	Lou Kretlow	1,500	600.00	300.00
(12)	Robert L. Kuzava	1,500	600.00	300.00
(13)	Fred Marsh	1,500	600.00	300.00
(14)	Charles Maxwell	1,500	600.00	300.00
(15)	Jimmie McDonald	1,500	600.00	300.00
(16)	Bill Miller	1,500	600.00	300.00
(17)	Willy Miranda	1,500	600.00	300.00
(18)	Raymond L. Moore	1,500	600.00	300.00
(19)	John Lester Moss	1,500	600.00	300.00
(20)	"Bobo" Newsom	1,500	600.00	300.00
(21)	Duane Pillette	1,500	600.00	300.00
(22)	Edward S. Waitkus	1,500	600.00	300.00
(23)	Harold W. Smith	1,500	600.00	300.00
(24)	Gus Triandos	1,500	600.00	300.00
(25)	Eugene R. Woodling	1,750	700.00	350.00
(26)	Robert G. Young	1,500	600.00	300.00

1972 Esso Hispanic Coins

Little is known of these coins, except that they were distributed in Puerto Rico. Even the sponsor, Esso Oil Co., is not mentioned anywhere on the pieces. Made of aluminum and 1-1/4" in diameter, coin fronts have a portrait of the player with his name above. Backs are in Spanish and have the player's position, team, height, weight, date and place of birth. The coins of Tony Perez and, to a lesser extent, Rod Carew are scarcer than the others. A person receiving a Perez coin was able to exchange it for a full tank of gas. In 2006, a brass-finish Roberto Clemente coin was first reported, probably also a short-printed exchange coin.

		NM	EX	VG
Complete Set (13):		325.00	160.00	95.00
Common Player:		9.00	4.50	2.75
(1)	Luis Aparicio	15.00	7.50	4.50
(2)	Rod Carew	50.00	25.00	15.00
(3)	Rico Carty	9.00	4.50	2.75
(4)	Cesar Cedeno	9.00	4.50	2.75
(5)	Orlando Cepeda	15.00	7.50	4.50
(6)	Roberto Clemente	110.00	55.00	35.00
(7)	Mike Cuellar	9.00	4.50	2.75
(8)	Juan Marichal	15.00	7.50	4.50
(9)	Felix Millan	9.00	4.50	2.75
(10)	Guillermo Montanez	9.00	4.50	2.75
(11)	Tony Oliva	12.00	6.00	3.50
(12a)	Tany Perez (Tony)	75.00	37.50	22.50
(12b)	Tony Perez	75.00	37.50	22.50
(13)	Manny Sanguillen	9.00	4.50	2.75

1949 Eureka Sportstamps

The commissioner of baseball, president of the National League and 198 N.L. players are included in this issue. The stamps were issued on team sheets measuring 7-1/2" x 10", with individual stamps measuring 1-1/2" x 2". An album issued with the set provided short player biographies. The stamps feature colorized posed player action photos. At bottom is a yellow strip with the player's name, stamp number and copyright line. Stamps are numbered alphabetically within teams.

		NM	EX	VG
Complete Set (200):		900.00	450.00	275.00
Common Player:		5.00	2.50	1.50
Album w/mounted stamps:		400.00	200.00	120.00
Album:		75.00	37.50	22.00
1	Albert B. (Happy) Chandler	15.00	7.50	4.50
2	Ford Frick	5.00	2.50	1.50
3	Billy Southworth	5.00	2.50	1.50
4	Johnny Antonelli	5.00	2.50	1.50
5	Red Barrett	5.00	2.50	1.50
6	Clint Conatser	5.00	2.50	1.50
7	Alvin Dark	5.00	2.50	1.50
8	Bob Elliott	5.00	2.50	1.50
9	Glenn Elliott	5.00	2.50	1.50
10	Elbie Fletcher	5.00	2.50	1.50
11	Bob Hall	5.00	2.50	1.50
12	Jeff Heath	5.00	2.50	1.50
13	Bobby Hogue	5.00	2.50	1.50
14	Tommy Holmes	5.00	2.50	1.50
15	Al Lakeman	5.00	2.50	1.50
16	Phil Masi	5.00	2.50	1.50
17	Nelson Potter	5.00	2.50	1.50
18	Pete Reiser	10.00	5.00	3.00
19	Rick Rickert	5.00	2.50	1.50
20	Connie Ryan	5.00	2.50	1.50
21	Jim Russell	5.00	2.50	1.50
22	Johnny Sain	10.00	5.00	3.00
23	Bill Salkeld	5.00	2.50	1.50
24	Sibby Sisti	5.00	2.50	1.50
25	Warren Spahn	25.00	12.50	7.50
26	Eddie Stanky	5.00	2.50	1.50
27	Bill Voiselle	5.00	2.50	1.50
28	Bert Shotton	5.00	2.50	1.50

29	Jack Banta	5.00	2.50	1.50
30	Rex Barney	7.50	3.75	2.25
31	Ralph Branca	15.00	7.50	4.50
32	Tommy Brown	5.00	2.50	1.50
33	Roy Campanella	40.00	20.00	12.00
34	Billy Cox	7.50	3.75	2.25
35	Bruce Edwards	5.00	2.50	1.50
36	Carl Furillo	20.00	10.00	6.00
37	Joe Hatten	5.00	2.50	1.50
38	Gene Hermanski	5.00	2.50	1.50
39	Gil Hodges	25.00	12.50	7.50
40	Johnny Jorgensen	5.00	2.50	1.50
41	Lefty Martin	5.00	2.50	1.50
42	Mike McCormick	5.00	2.50	1.50
43	Eddie Miksis	5.00	2.50	1.50
44	Paul Minner	5.00	2.50	1.50
45	Sam Narron	10.00	5.00	3.00
46	Don Newcombe	20.00	10.00	6.00
47	Jake Pitler	5.00	2.50	1.50
48	Pee Wee Reese	35.00	17.50	10.50
49	Jackie Robinson	50.00	25.00	15.00
50	Duke Snider	40.00	20.00	12.00
51	Dick Whitman	5.00	2.50	1.50
52	Forrest Burgess	10.00	5.00	3.00
53	Phil Cavaretta	5.00	2.50	1.50
54	Bob Chipman	5.00	2.50	1.50
55	Walter Dubiel	5.00	2.50	1.50
56	Hank Edwards	5.00	2.50	1.50
57	Frankie Gustine	5.00	2.50	1.50
58	Hal Jeffcoat	5.00	2.50	1.50
59	Emil Kush	5.00	2.50	1.50
60	Doyle Lade	5.00	2.50	1.50
61	Dutch Leonard	5.00	2.50	1.50
62	Peanuts Lowrey	5.00	2.50	1.50
63	Gene Mauch	7.50	3.75	2.25
64	Cal McLish	5.00	2.50	1.50
65	Rube Novotney	5.00	2.50	1.50
66	Andy Pafko	5.00	2.50	1.50
67	Bob Ramozzotti	5.00	2.50	1.50
68	Herman Reich	5.00	2.50	1.50
69	Bob Rush	5.00	2.50	1.50
70	Johnny Schmitz	5.00	2.50	1.50
71	Bob Scheffing	5.00	2.50	1.50
72	Roy Smalley	5.00	2.50	1.50
73	Emil Verban	5.00	2.50	1.50
74	Al Walker	5.00	2.50	1.50
75	Harry Walker	5.00	2.50	1.50
76	Bucky Walters	5.00	2.50	1.50
77	Bob Adams	5.00	2.50	1.50
78	Ewell Blackwell	5.00	2.50	1.50
79	Jimmy Bloodworth	5.00	2.50	1.50
80	Walker Cooper	5.00	2.50	1.50
81	Tony Cuccinello	5.00	2.50	1.50
82	Jess Dobernic	5.00	2.50	1.50
83	Eddie Erautt	5.00	2.50	1.50
84	Frank Fanovich	5.00	2.50	1.50
85	Howie Fox	5.00	2.50	1.50
86	Grady Hatton	5.00	2.50	1.50
87	Homer Howell	5.00	2.50	1.50
88	Ted Kluszewski	20.00	10.00	6.00
89	Danny Litwhiler	5.00	2.50	1.50
90	Everett Lively	5.00	2.50	1.50
91	Lloyd Merriman	5.00	2.50	1.50
92	Phil Page	5.00	2.50	1.50
93	Kent Peterson	5.00	2.50	1.50
94	Ken Raffensberger	5.00	2.50	1.50
95	Luke Sewell	5.00	2.50	1.50
96	Virgil Stallcup	5.00	2.50	1.50
97	Johnny Vander Meer	10.00	5.00	3.00
98	Herman Wehmeier	5.00	2.50	1.50
99	Johnny Wyrostek	5.00	2.50	1.50
100	Benny Zientara	5.00	2.50	1.50
101	Leo Durocher	12.50	6.25	3.75
102	Hank Behrman	5.00	2.50	1.50
103	Augie Galan	5.00	2.50	1.50
104	Sid Gordon	5.00	2.50	1.50
105	Bert Haas	5.00	2.50	1.50
106	Andy Hansen	5.00	2.50	1.50
107	Clint Hartung	5.00	2.50	1.50
108	Kirby Higbe	5.00	2.50	1.50
109	George Hausman	5.00	2.50	1.50
110	Larry Jansen	5.00	2.50	1.50
111	Sheldon Jones	5.00	2.50	1.50
112	Monte Kennedy	5.00	2.50	1.50
113	Buddy Kerr	5.00	2.50	1.50
114	Dave Koslo	5.00	2.50	1.50
115	Joe Lafata	5.00	2.50	1.50
116	Whitey Lockman	5.00	2.50	1.50
117	Jack Lohrke	5.00	2.50	1.50
118	Willard Marshall	5.00	2.50	1.50
119	Bill Milne	5.00	2.50	1.50
120	Johnny Mize	15.00	7.50	4.50
121	Don Mueller	5.00	2.50	1.50
122	Ray Mueller	5.00	2.50	1.50
123	Bill Rigney	5.00	2.50	1.50
124	Bobby Thomson	7.50	3.75	2.25
125	Sam Webb	5.00	2.50	1.50
126	Wesley Westrum	5.00	2.50	1.50
127	Eddie Sawyer	5.00	2.50	1.50
128	Richie Ashburn	30.00	15.00	9.00
129	Benny Bengough	5.00	2.50	1.50
130	Charlie Bicknell	5.00	2.50	1.50
131	Buddy Blattner	5.00	2.50	1.50
132	Hank Borowy	5.00	2.50	1.50
133	Ralph Caballero	5.00	2.50	1.50
134	Blix Donnelly	5.00	2.50	1.50
135	Del Ennis	5.00	2.50	1.50
136	Granville Hamner	5.00	2.50	1.50
137	Ken Heintzelman	5.00	2.50	1.50
138	Stan Hollmig	5.00	2.50	1.50
139	Willie Jones	5.00	2.50	1.50
140	Jim Konstanty	5.00	2.50	1.50
141	Stan Lopata	5.00	2.50	1.50
142	Jackie Mayo	5.00	2.50	1.50
143	Bill Nicholson	5.00	2.50	1.50
144	Robin Roberts	60.00	30.00	18.00
145	Schoolboy Rowe	5.00	2.50	1.50
146	Andy Seminick	5.00	2.50	1.50
147	Ken Silvestri	5.00	2.50	1.50
148	Curt Simmons	5.00	2.50	1.50
149	Dick Sisler	5.00	2.50	1.50
150	Ken Trinkle	5.00	2.50	1.50
151	Eddie Waitkus	5.00	2.50	1.50
152	Bill Meyer	5.00	2.50	1.50
153	Monte Basgall	5.00	2.50	1.50
154	Eddie Bockman	5.00	2.50	1.50
155	Ernie Bonham	5.00	2.50	1.50
156	Hugh Casey	5.00	2.50	1.50
157	Pete Castiglione	5.00	2.50	1.50
158	Cliff Chambers	5.00	2.50	1.50
159	Murry Dickson	5.00	2.50	1.50
160	Ed Fitz Gerald	5.00	2.50	1.50
161	Les Fleming	5.00	2.50	1.50
162	Hal Gregg	5.00	2.50	1.50
163	Goldie Holt	5.00	2.50	1.50
164	Johnny Hopp	5.00	2.50	1.50
165	Ralph Kiner	20.00	10.00	6.00
166	Vic Lombardi	5.00	2.50	1.50
167	Clyde McCullough	5.00	2.50	1.50
168	Danny Murtaugh	5.00	2.50	1.50
169	Bill Posedel	5.00	2.50	1.50
170	Elmer Riddle	5.00	2.50	1.50
171	Stan Rojek	5.00	2.50	1.50
172	Rip Sewell	5.00	2.50	1.50
173	Eddie Stevens	5.00	2.50	1.50
174	Dixie Walker	5.00	2.50	1.50
175	Bill Werle	5.00	2.50	1.50
176	Wally Westlake	5.00	2.50	1.50
177	Eddie Dyer	5.00	2.50	1.50
178	Bill Baker	5.00	2.50	1.50
179	Al Brazle	5.00	2.50	1.50
180	Harry Brecheen	5.00	2.50	1.50
181	Chuck Diering	5.00	2.50	1.50
182	Joe Garagiola	13.50	6.75	4.00
183	Tom Galviano	5.00	2.50	1.50
184	Jim Hearn	5.00	2.50	1.50
185	Ken Johnson	5.00	2.50	1.50
186	Nippy Jones	5.00	2.50	1.50
187	Ed Kazak	5.00	2.50	1.50
188	Lou Klein	5.00	2.50	1.50
189	Marty Marion	5.00	2.50	1.50
190	George Munger	5.00	2.50	1.50
191	Stan Musial	45.00	22.00	13.50
192	Spike Nelson	5.00	2.50	1.50
193	Howie Pollet	5.00	2.50	1.50
194	Bill Reeder	5.00	2.50	1.50
195	Del Rice	5.00	2.50	1.50
196	Ed Sauer	5.00	2.50	1.50
197	Red Schoendienst	20.00	10.00	6.00
198	Enos Slaughter	20.00	10.00	6.00
199	Ted Wilks	5.00	2.50	1.50
200	Ray Yochim	5.00	2.50	1.50

1914 Evening Sun N.Y. Giants

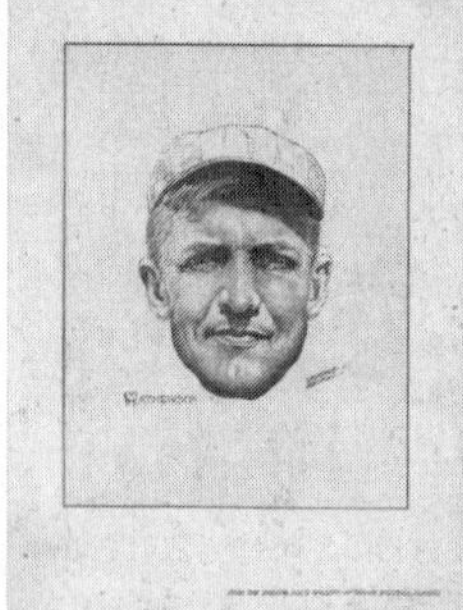

The World's Champion 1913 N.Y. Giants are featured in this set of newspaper supplements titled, "Evening Sun's Gallery of Famous Baseball Players." It is believed the paper was published in Norwich, N.Y. Slightly larger than 9" x 12", the supplements feature black-and-white portraits by Lawrence Semon, who also produced a contemporary series of baseball postcards.

		NM	EX	VG
Complete Set (21):		7,000	3,500	2,100
Common Player:		200.00	100.00	60.00
(1)	George Burns	200.00	100.00	60.00
(2)	Doc Crandall	200.00	100.00	60.00
(3)	Al Demaree	200.00	100.00	60.00
(4)	Art Fletcher	200.00	100.00	60.00
(5)	Art Fromme	200.00	100.00	60.00
(6)	Grover Hartley	200.00	100.00	60.00
(7)	Buck Herzog	200.00	100.00	60.00
(8)	Rube Marquard	400.00	200.00	120.00
(9)	Christy Mathewson	1,200	600.00	360.00
(10)	Moose McCormick	200.00	100.00	60.00
(11)	John McGraw	400.00	200.00	120.00
(12)	Fred Merkle	200.00	100.00	60.00
(13)	Chief Meyers	200.00	100.00	60.00
(14)	Red Murray	200.00	100.00	60.00
(15)	Wilbert Robinson	400.00	200.00	120.00
(16)	Arthur Shafer	200.00	100.00	60.00
(17)	Fred Snodgrass	200.00	100.00	60.00
(18)	Jeff Tesreau	200.00	100.00	60.00
(19)	Jim Thorpe	1,750	875.00	525.00
(20)	Art Wilson	200.00	100.00	60.00
(21)	Hooks Wiltse	200.00	100.00	60.00

1916 Everybody's

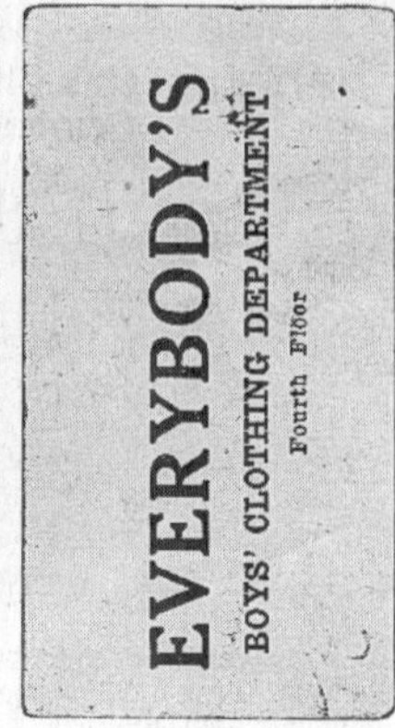

Where "Everybody's" department store was located is unknown, but in 1916 they chose to use baseball cards to promote their boy's wear department. The approximately 1-5/8" x 3" black-and-white cards share the format and checklist with the much more common M101-4 blank-back version and several other regional advertisers. Everybody's is one of the scarcest advertising backs to be found in this issue and the cards command a premium from type-card and superstar collectors. There are four styles of typography on back.

Premium: 6-9X

(See 1916 M101-4 Blank Backs for checklist and base card values.)

1921 Exhibits

The Exhibit Supply Company of Chicago issued the first in a long series of postcard-size (3-3/8" x 5-3/8") baseball cards in 1921. The Exhibit cards were commonly sold in "penny arcade" vending machines. The 1921 series consists of 64 cards and includes four players from each of the 16 major league teams. The cards feature black-and-white photos with the player's name printed in a fancy script. The player's position and team appear below the name in small, hand-lettered capital letters. American League is designated as "AM.L.," which can help differentiate the 1921 series from future years. Some of the cards contain white borders while others do not. All have blank backs. There are various spelling errors in the picture legends.

		NM	EX	VG
Complete Set (64):		11,000	5,500	3,250
Common Player:		75.00	35.00	20.00
(1)	Chas. B. Adams	75.00	35.00	20.00
(2)	Grover C. Alexander	275.00	135.00	80.00
(3)	David Bancroft	175.00	85.00	50.00
(4)	Geo. J. Burns	75.00	35.00	20.00
(5)	Owen Bush	75.00	35.00	20.00
(6)	Max J. Carey	175.00	85.00	50.00
(7)	Ty R. Cobb	1,000	500.00	300.00
(8)	Eddie T. Collins	175.00	85.00	50.00
(9)	John Collins	75.00	35.00	20.00
(10)	Stanley Coveleskie (Coveleski)	200.00	100.00	60.00
(11)	Walton E. Cruise	75.00	35.00	20.00
(12)	Jacob E. Daubert	75.00	35.00	20.00
(13)	George Dauss	75.00	35.00	20.00
(14)	Charles A. Deal	75.00	35.00	20.00
(15)	Joe A. Dugan	75.00	35.00	20.00
(16)	James Dykes	75.00	35.00	20.00
(17)	U.C. "Red" Faber	175.00	85.00	50.00
(18)	J.F. Fournier	75.00	35.00	20.00
(19)	Frank F. Frisch	175.00	85.00	50.00
(20)	W.L. Gardner	75.00	35.00	20.00
(21)	H.M. "Hank" Gowdy	75.00	35.00	20.00
(22)	Burleigh A. Grimes	200.00	100.00	60.00
(23)	Heinie Groh	75.00	35.00	20.00
(24)	Jesse Haines	200.00	100.00	60.00
(25)	Sam Harris (Stanley)	200.00	100.00	60.00
(26)	Walter L. Holke	75.00	35.00	20.00
(27)	Charles J. Hollicher (Hollocher)	75.00	35.00	20.00
(28)	Rogers Hornsby	325.00	160.00	95.00
(29)	James H. Johnson (Johnston)	75.00	35.00	20.00
(30)	Walter P. Johnson	750.00	375.00	225.00
(31)	Sam P. Jones	75.00	35.00	20.00
(32)	Geo. L. Kelly	200.00	100.00	60.00
(33)	Dick Kerr	75.00	35.00	20.00
(34)	William L. Killifer (Killefer)	75.00	35.00	20.00
(35)	Ed Konetchy	75.00	35.00	20.00

(36)	John "Doc" Lavan	75.00	35.00	20.00
(37)	Walter J. Maranville	175.00	85.00	50.00
(38)	Carl W. Mays	75.00	35.00	20.00
(39)	J. "Stuffy" McInnis	75.00	35.00	20.00
(40)	Rollie C. Naylor	75.00	35.00	20.00
(41)	A. Earl Neale (Earle)	125.00	60.00	35.00
(42)	Ivan M. Olsen	75.00	35.00	20.00
(43)	S.F. "Steve" O'Neil (O'Neill)	75.00	35.00	20.00
(44)	Robert (Roger) Peckinpaugh	75.00	35.00	20.00
(45)	Ralph "Cy" Perkins	75.00	35.00	20.00
(46)	Raymond R. Powell	75.00	35.00	20.00
(47)	Joe "Goldie" Rapp	75.00	35.00	20.00
(48)	Edgar S. Rice	175.00	85.00	50.00
(49)	Jimmy Ring	75.00	35.00	20.00
(50)	Geo. H. "Babe" Ruth	2,750	1,375	825.00
(51)	Ray W. Schalk	175.00	85.00	50.00
(52)	Wallie Schang	75.00	35.00	20.00
(53)	Everett Scott	75.00	35.00	20.00
(54)	H.S. Shanks (Photo actually Wally Schang.)	75.00	35.00	20.00
(55)	Urban Shocker	75.00	35.00	20.00
(56)	Geo. H. Sisler	175.00	85.00	50.00
(57)	Tris Speaker	325.00	160.00	95.00
(58)	John Tobin	75.00	35.00	20.00
(59)	Robt. Veach	75.00	35.00	20.00
(60)	Zack D. Wheat	175.00	85.00	50.00
(61)	Geo. B. Whitted	75.00	35.00	20.00
(62)	Cy Williams	75.00	35.00	20.00
(63)	Kenneth R. Williams	75.00	35.00	20.00
(64)	Ivy B. Wingo	75.00	35.00	20.00

1922 Exhibits

The Exhibit Supply Co. continued the 3-3/8" x 5-3/8" format in 1922 but doubled the number of cards in the series to 128, including eight players from each team. All but nine of the players who appeared in the 1921 series are pictured in the 1922 set, along with 74 new players. The cards again display black-and-white photos with blank backs. Some photos have white borders. The player's name appears in script with the postition and team below in small block capital letters. American League is designated as "A.L." Again, there are several spelling errors and incorrect player identifications. Only the 74 new additions are included in this checklist.

		NM	EX	VG
Complete Set (74):		7,500	3,750	2,250
Common Player:		85.00	40.00	25.00
(1)	Jim Bagby	85.00	40.00	25.00
(2)	J. Frank Baker	150.00	75.00	45.00
(3)	Walter Barbare	85.00	40.00	25.00
(4)	Turner Barber	85.00	40.00	25.00
(5)	John Bassler	85.00	40.00	25.00
(6)	Carlson L. Bigbee (Carson)	85.00	40.00	25.00
(7)	Sam Bohne	85.00	42.00	25.00
(8)	Geo. Burns	85.00	40.00	25.00
(9)	George Burns	85.00	40.00	25.00
(10)	Jeo Bush (Joe)	85.00	40.00	25.00
(11)	Leon Cadore	85.00	40.00	25.00
(12)	Jim Caveney	85.00	40.00	25.00
(13)	Wilbur Cooper	85.00	40.00	25.00
(14)	George Cutshaw	85.00	40.00	25.00
(15)	Dave Danforth	85.00	40.00	25.00
(16)	Bill Doak	85.00	40.00	25.00
(17)	Joe Dugan	85.00	40.00	25.00
(18)	Pat Duncan	85.00	40.00	25.00
(19)	Howard Emke (Ehmke)	85.00	40.00	25.00
(20)	Wm. Evans/Umpire	375.00	185.00	110.00
(21)	Bib Falk (Bibb)	85.00	40.00	25.00
(22)	Dana Fillingin (Fillingim)	85.00	40.00	25.00
(23)	Ira Flagstead	85.00	40.00	25.00
(24)	(Art) Fletcher	85.00	40.00	25.00
(25)	(Wally) Gerber	85.00	40.00	25.00
(26)	Ray Grimes	85.00	40.00	25.00
(27)	Harry Heilman (Heilmann)	150.00	75.00	45.00
(28)	George Hildebrand/Umpire	200.00	100.00	60.00
(29)	Wibur Hubbell (Wilbert)	85.00	40.00	25.00
(30)	Bill Jacobson	85.00	40.00	25.00
(31)	E.R. Johnson	85.00	40.00	25.00
(32)	Joe Judge	85.00	40.00	25.00
(33)	Bill Klem/Umpire	375.00	185.00	110.00
(34)	Harry Liebold (Leibold)	85.00	40.00	25.00
(35)	Walter Mails	85.00	40.00	25.00
(36)	Geo. Maisel	85.00	40.00	25.00
(37)	Lee Meadows	85.00	40.00	25.00
(38)	Clyde Milam (Milan)	85.00	40.00	25.00
(39)	Ed (Bing) Miller	85.00	40.00	25.00
(40)	Hack Miller	85.00	40.00	25.00
(41)	George Moriarty/Umpire	200.00	100.00	60.00
(42)	Robert Muesel (Meusel)	85.00	40.00	25.00
(43)	Harry Myers	85.00	40.00	25.00
(44)	Arthur Nehf	85.00	40.00	25.00
(45)	Joe Oeschger	85.00	40.00	25.00
(46)	Geo. O'Neil	85.00	40.00	25.00
(47)	Roger Peckinpaugh	85.00	40.00	25.00
(48)	Val Picinich	85.00	40.00	25.00
(49)	Bill Piercy	85.00	40.00	25.00
(50)	Derrill Pratt	85.00	40.00	25.00
(51)	Jack Quinn	85.00	40.00	25.00
(52)	Walter Reuther (Ruether)	85.00	40.00	25.00
(53)	Charles Rigler/Umpire	200.00	100.00	60.00
(54)	Eppa Rixey	150.00	75.00	45.00
(55)	Chas. Robertson	85.00	40.00	25.00
(56)	Everett Scott	85.00	40.00	25.00
(57)	Earl Sheely	85.00	40.00	25.00
(58)	Earl Smith/Portrait	85.00	40.00	25.00
(59)	Earl Smith/Standing (Photo actually Brad Kocher.)	85.00	40.00	25.00
(60)	Elmer Smith	85.00	40.00	25.00
(61)	Jack Smith (Photo actually Jimmy Smith.)	85.00	40.00	25.00
(62)	Sherrod Smith	85.00	40.00	25.00
(63)	Frank Snyder	85.00	40.00	25.00
(64)	Allan Sothoron (Allen)	85.00	40.00	25.00
(65)	Arnold Statz	85.00	40.00	25.00
(66)	Milton Stock	85.00	40.00	25.00
(67)	James Tierney	85.00	40.00	25.00
(68)	George Toporcer	85.00	40.00	25.00
(69)	Clarence (Tilly) Walker	85.00	40.00	25.00
(70)	Curtis Walker	85.00	40.00	25.00
(71)	Aaron Ward	85.00	40.00	25.00
(72)	Joe Wood	100.00	50.00	30.00
(73)	Moses Yellowhorse	300.00	150.00	90.00
(74)	Ross Young (Youngs)	150.00	75.00	45.00

1922 Eastern Exhibit Supply Co.

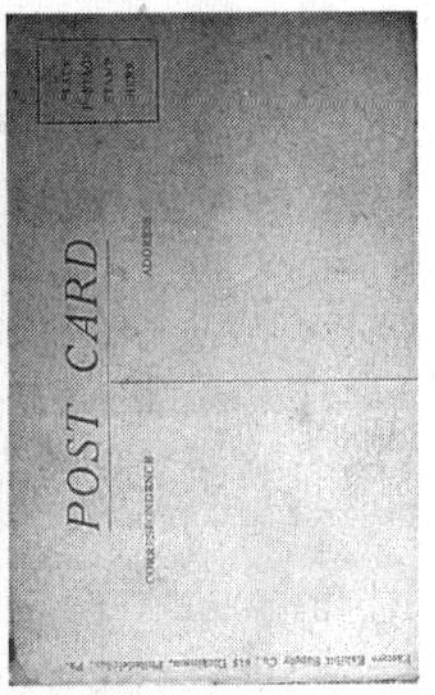

Postcard-style backs differentiate these cards from the more common Exhibit Supply Co., cards from Chicago. This 20-card series was produced by a Philadelphia company, although on some cards, the Eastern Exhibit copyright line on back has been blacked out and that of the Chicago company printed beneath it. The black-and-white cards measure 3-3/8" x 5-5/8".

		NM	EX	VG
Complete Set (20):		4,200	2,100	1,250
Common Player:		80.00	40.00	20.00
(1)	Grover Alexander	200.00	100.00	60.00
(2)	Dave Bancroft	125.00	65.00	35.00
(3)	Jesse Barnes	80.00	40.00	20.00
(4)	Joe Bush	80.00	40.00	20.00
(5)	Ty Cobb	750.00	375.00	225.00
(6)	Eddie Collins	125.00	65.00	35.00
(7)	Urban Faber	125.00	65.00	35.00
(8)	Clarence Galloway	80.00	40.00	20.00
(9)	Heinie Groh	80.00	40.00	20.00
(10)	Harry Heilmann	125.00	65.00	35.00
(11)	Charlie Hollocher	80.00	40.00	20.00
(12)	Rogers Hornsby	200.00	100.00	60.00
(13)	Walter Johnson	375.00	185.00	110.00
(14)	Eddie Rommel	80.00	40.00	20.00
(15)	Babe Ruth	1,550	775.00	465.00
(16)	Ray Schalk	125.00	65.00	35.00
(17)	Wallie Schang	80.00	40.00	20.00
(18)	Tris Speaker	200.00	100.00	60.00
(19)	Zach Wheat	125.00	65.00	35.00
(20)	Kenneth Williams	80.00	40.00	20.00

1923-24 Exhibits

The Exhibit cards for 1923 and 1924 are generally collected as a single 128-card series. The format remained basically the same as the previous year, 3-3/8" x 5-3/8", with black-and-white photos (some surrounded by a white border) and blank backs. The player's name is again shown in script with the position and team printed below in a small, square block-type style. Many of the same photos were used from previous years, although some are cropped differently, and some players have new team designations, background changes, team emblems removed, borders added or taken away, and other minor changes. Fifty-eight new cards are featured, including 38 players pictured for the first time in an Exhibit set. Only the 58 new cards are included in this checklist.

		NM	EX	VG
Complete Set (59):		20,000	10,000	6,000
Common Player:		225.00	110.00	65.00
(1)	Clyde Barnhart	225.00	110.00	65.00
(2)	Ray Blades	225.00	110.00	65.00
(3)	James Bottomley	400.00	200.00	120.00
(4)	George Burns	225.00	110.00	65.00
(5)	Dan Clark	225.00	110.00	65.00
(6)	Bill Doak	225.00	110.00	65.00
(7)	Joe Dugan	225.00	110.00	65.00
(8)	Howard J. Ehmke	225.00	110.00	65.00
(9)	Ira Flagstead	225.00	110.00	65.00
(10)	J.F. Fournier	225.00	110.00	65.00
(11)	Howard Freigan (Freigau)	225.00	110.00	65.00
(12)	C.E. Galloway	225.00	110.00	65.00
(13)	Joe Genewich	225.00	110.00	65.00
(14)	Mike Gonzales (Gonzalez)	275.00	135.00	82.00
(15)	H.M. "Hank" Gowdy	225.00	110.00	65.00
(16)	Charles Grimm	225.00	110.00	65.00
(17)	Heinie Groh	225.00	110.00	65.00
(18)	Chas. L. Harnett (Hartnett)	400.00	200.00	120.00
(19)	George Harper	225.00	110.00	65.00
(20)	Slim Harris (Harriss)	225.00	110.00	65.00
(21)	Clifton Heathcote	225.00	110.00	65.00
(22)	Andy High	225.00	110.00	65.00
(23)	Walter L. Holke	225.00	110.00	65.00
(24)	Charles D. Jamieson	225.00	110.00	65.00
(25)	Willie Kamm	225.00	110.00	65.00
(26)	Tony Kaufmann	225.00	110.00	65.00
(27)	Dudley Lee	225.00	110.00	65.00
(28)	Harry Liebold (Leibold)	225.00	110.00	65.00
(29)	Aldofo Luque	225.00	110.00	65.00
(30)	W.C. (Wid) Matthews	225.00	110.00	65.00
(31)	John J. McGraw	400.00	200.00	120.00
(32)	J. "Stuffy" McInnis	225.00	110.00	65.00
(33)	Johnny Morrison	225.00	110.00	65.00
(34)	John A. Mostil	225.00	110.00	65.00
(35)	J.F. O'Neill (Should be S.F.)	225.00	110.00	65.00
(36)	Ernest Padgett	225.00	110.00	65.00
(37)	Val Picinich	225.00	110.00	65.00
(38)	Bill Piercy	225.00	110.00	65.00
(39)	Herman Pillette	225.00	110.00	65.00
(40)	Wallie Pipp	275.00	135.00	82.00
(41)	Raymond R. Powell (Black background.)	225.00	110.00	65.00
(42)	Raymond R. Powell (Stands in background.)	225.00	110.00	65.00
(43)	Del. Pratt	225.00	110.00	65.00
(44)	E.E. Rigney	225.00	110.00	65.00
(45)	Eddie Rommel	225.00	110.00	65.00
(46)	Geo. H. "Babe" Ruth	7,500	3,750	2,250
(47)	Muddy Ruel	225.00	110.00	65.00
(48)	J.H. Sand	225.00	110.00	65.00
(49)	Henry Severeid	225.00	110.00	65.00
(50)	Joseph Sewell	400.00	200.00	120.00
(51)	Al. Simmons	450.00	225.00	135.00
(52)	R.E. Smith	225.00	110.00	65.00
(53)	Sherrod Smith	225.00	110.00	65.00
(54)	Casey Stengel	450.00	225.00	135.00
(55)	J.R. Stevenson (Stephenson)	225.00	110.00	65.00
(56)	James Tierney	225.00	110.00	65.00
(57)	Robt. Veach	225.00	110.00	65.00
(58)	L. Woodall	225.00	110.00	65.00
(59)	Russell G. Wrighstone	225.00	110.00	65.00

1925 Exhibits

The 1925 series of Exhibits contains 128 unnumbered cards, each measuring 3-3/8" x 5-3/8". The player's name (in all capital letters), position and team (along with a line reading "Made in U.S.A.") are printed in a small white box in a lower corner of the card. Most of the photos are vertical, however a few are horizontal. There are several misspellings in the set. Lou Gehrig's first baseball card appears in this issue. The cards are listed here in alphabetical order.

		NM	EX	VG
Complete Set (128):		32,500	16,000	9,750
Common Player:		125.00	65.00	35.00
(1)	Sparky Adams	125.00	65.00	35.00
(2)	Grover C. Alexander	300.00	150.00	90.00
(3)	David Bancroft	200.00	100.00	60.00
(4)	Jesse Barnes	125.00	65.00	35.00
(5)	John Bassler	125.00	65.00	35.00
(6)	Lester Bell	125.00	65.00	35.00
(7)	Lawrence Benton	125.00	65.00	35.00
(8)	Carson Bigbee	125.00	65.00	35.00
(9)	Max Bishop	125.00	65.00	35.00
(10)	Raymond Blates (Blades)	125.00	65.00	35.00
(11)	Oswald Bluege	125.00	65.00	35.00
(12)	James Bottomly (Bottomley)	200.00	100.00	60.00
(13)	Raymond Bressler	125.00	65.00	35.00
(14)	John Brooks	125.00	65.00	35.00
(15)	Maurice Burrus	125.00	65.00	35.00
(16)	Max Carey	200.00	100.00	60.00
(17)	Tyrus Cobb	1,100	550.00	330.00
(18)	Eddie Collins	200.00	100.00	60.00
(19)	Stanley Coveleski	200.00	100.00	60.00
(20)	Hugh M. Critz	125.00	65.00	35.00
(21)	Hazen Cuyler	225.00	110.00	65.00
(22)	George Dauss	125.00	65.00	35.00
(23)	I.M. Davis	125.00	65.00	35.00
(24)	John H. DeBerry	125.00	65.00	35.00
(25)	Art Decatur	125.00	65.00	35.00
(26)	Peter Donohue	125.00	65.00	35.00
(27)	Charles Dressen	125.00	65.00	35.00
(28)	James J. Dykes	125.00	65.00	35.00
(29)	Howard Ehmke	125.00	65.00	35.00
(30)	Bib Falk (Bibb)	125.00	65.00	35.00
(31)	Wilson Fewster	125.00	65.00	35.00
(32)	Max Flack	125.00	65.00	35.00
(33)	Ira Flagstead	125.00	65.00	35.00
(34)	Jacques F. Fournier	125.00	65.00	35.00
(35)	Howard Freigau	125.00	65.00	35.00
(36)	Frank Frisch	200.00	100.00	60.00
(37)	Henry L. Gehrig	12,000	6,000	3,600
(38)	Joseph Genewich	125.00	65.00	35.00
(39)	Walter Gerber	125.00	65.00	35.00
(40)	Frank Gibson	125.00	65.00	35.00
(41)	Leon Goslin	200.00	100.00	60.00
(42)	George Grantham	125.00	65.00	35.00
(43)	Samuel Gray	125.00	65.00	35.00
(44)	Burleigh A. Grimes	200.00	100.00	60.00
(45)	Charles Grimm	125.00	65.00	35.00
(46)	Heine Groh (Heinie)	125.00	65.00	35.00
(47)	Samuel Hale	125.00	65.00	35.00
(48)	George Harper	125.00	65.00	35.00
(49)	David Harris	125.00	65.00	35.00
(50)	Stanley Harris	200.00	100.00	60.00
(51)	Leo Hartnett	200.00	100.00	60.00
(52)	Nelson Hawks	125.00	65.00	35.00
(53)	Harry Heilmann	200.00	100.00	60.00
(54)	Walter Henline	125.00	65.00	35.00
(55)	Walter Holke	125.00	65.00	35.00
(56)	Harry Hooper	200.00	100.00	60.00
(57)	Rogers Hornsby	300.00	150.00	90.00
(58)	Wilbur Hubbell	125.00	65.00	35.00
(59)	Travis C. Jackson	200.00	100.00	60.00
(60)	William Jacobson	125.00	65.00	35.00
(61)	Charles Jamieson	125.00	65.00	35.00
(62)	James H. Johnson (Johnston)	125.00	65.00	35.00
(63)	Walter Johnson	400.00	200.00	120.00
(64)	Joseph Judge	125.00	65.00	35.00
(65)	Willie Kamm	125.00	65.00	35.00
(66)	Ray Kremer	125.00	65.00	35.00
(67)	Walter Lutzke	125.00	65.00	35.00
(68)	Walter Maranville	200.00	100.00	60.00
(69)	John ("Stuffy") McInnes (McInnis)	125.00	65.00	35.00
(70)	Martin McManus	125.00	65.00	35.00
(71)	Earl McNeely	125.00	65.00	35.00
(72)	Emil Meusel	125.00	65.00	35.00
(73)	Edmund (Bing) Miller	125.00	65.00	35.00
(74)	John Mokan	125.00	65.00	35.00
(75)	Clarence Mueller	125.00	65.00	35.00
(76)	Robert W. Muesel (Meusel)	125.00	65.00	35.00
(77)	Glenn Myatt	125.00	65.00	35.00
(78)	Arthur Nehf	125.00	65.00	35.00
(79)	George O'Neil	125.00	65.00	35.00
(80)	Frank O'Rourke	125.00	65.00	35.00
(81)	Ralph Perkins	125.00	65.00	35.00
(82)	Valentine Picinich	125.00	65.00	35.00
(83)	Walter C. Pipp	125.00	65.00	35.00
(84)	John Quinn	125.00	65.00	35.00
(85)	Emory Rigney	125.00	65.00	35.00
(86)	Eppa Rixey	200.00	100.00	60.00
(87)	Edwin Rommel	125.00	65.00	35.00
(88)	Ed (Edd) Roush	200.00	100.00	60.00
(89)	Harold Ruel (Herold)	125.00	65.00	35.00
(90)	Charles Ruffing	200.00	100.00	60.00
(91)	George H. "Babe" Ruth	1,700	850.00	510.00
(92)	John Sand	125.00	65.00	35.00
(93)	Henry Severid (Severeid)	125.00	65.00	35.00
(94)	Joseph Sewell	200.00	100.00	60.00
(95)	Ray Shalk (Schalk)	200.00	100.00	60.00
(96)	Walter H. Shang (Schang)	125.00	65.00	35.00
(97)	J.R. Shawkey	125.00	65.00	35.00
(98)	Earl Sheely	125.00	65.00	35.00
(99)	William Sherdell (Sherdel)	125.00	65.00	35.00
(100)	Urban J. Shocker	125.00	65.00	35.00
(101)	George Sissler (Sisler)	200.00	100.00	60.00
(102)	Earl Smith	125.00	65.00	35.00
(103)	Sherrod Smith	125.00	65.00	35.00
(104)	Frank Snyder	125.00	65.00	35.00
(105)	Wm. H. Southworth	125.00	65.00	35.00
(106)	Tristram Speaker	300.00	150.00	90.00
(107)	Milton J. Stock	125.00	65.00	35.00
(108)	Homer Summa	125.00	65.00	35.00
(109)	William Terry	225.00	110.00	65.00
(110)	Hollis Thurston	125.00	65.00	35.00
(111)	John Tobin	125.00	65.00	35.00
(112)	Philip Todt	125.00	65.00	35.00
(113)	George Torporcer (Toporcer)	125.00	65.00	35.00
(114)	Harold Traynor	200.00	100.00	60.00
(115)	A.C. "Dazzy" Vance	200.00	100.00	60.00
(116)	Robert Veach (Photo actually Ernest Vache.)	125.00	65.00	35.00
(117)	William Wambsganss	125.00	65.00	35.00
(118)	Aaron Ward	125.00	65.00	35.00
(119)	A.J. Weis	125.00	65.00	35.00
(120)	Frank Welch	125.00	65.00	35.00
(121)	Zack Wheat	200.00	100.00	60.00
(122)	Fred Williams	125.00	65.00	35.00
(123)	Kenneth Williams	125.00	65.00	35.00
(124)	Ernest Wingard	125.00	65.00	35.00
(125)	Ivy Wingo	125.00	65.00	35.00
(126)	Al Wings (Wingo)	125.00	65.00	35.00
(127)	Larry Woodall	125.00	65.00	35.00
(128)	Glen Wright (Glenn)	125.00	65.00	35.00

1925 Champions Babe Ruth Exhibit

This is part of a (presumably) 32-card multi-sport "World's Champions" issue and the only baseball player in the set. The 3-3/8" x 5-3/8" card is printed in black-and-white and has a blank back.

	NM	EX	VG
Babe Ruth	2,250	1,125	675.00

1926 Exhibits

The 1926 Exhibit cards are the same size (3-3/8" x 5-3/8") as previous Exhibit issues but are easily distinguished because of their blue-gray color. The set consists of 128 cards, 91 of which are identical to the photos in the 1925 series. The 37 new photos do not include the boxed caption used in 1925. The cards are unnumbered and are listed here alphabetically.

		NM	EX	VG
Complete Set (128):		22,500	11,250	6,750
Common Player:		125.00	60.00	35.00
(1)	Sparky Adams	125.00	60.00	35.00
(2)	David Bancroft	200.00	100.00	60.00
(3)	John Bassler	125.00	60.00	35.00
(4)	Lester Bell	125.00	60.00	35.00
(5)	John M. Bentley	125.00	60.00	35.00
(6)	Lawrence Benton	125.00	60.00	35.00
(7)	Carson Bigbee	125.00	60.00	35.00
(8)	George Bischoff (Team actually Boston A.L.)	125.00	60.00	35.00
(9)	Max Bishop	125.00	60.00	35.00
(10)	J. Fred Blake	125.00	60.00	35.00
(11)	Ted Blankenship	125.00	60.00	35.00
(12)	Raymond Blates (Blades)	125.00	60.00	35.00
(13)	Lucerne A. Blue (Luzerne)	125.00	60.00	35.00
(14)	Oswald Bluege	125.00	60.00	35.00
(15)	James Bottomly (Bottomley)	200.00	100.00	60.00
(16)	Raymond Bressler	125.00	60.00	35.00
(17)	Geo. H. Burns	125.00	60.00	35.00
(18)	Maurice Burrus	125.00	60.00	35.00
(19)	John Butler	125.00	60.00	35.00
(20)	Max Carey	200.00	100.00	60.00
(21)	Tyrus Cobb	1,400	700.00	425.00
(22)	Eddie Collins	200.00	100.00	60.00
(23)	Patrick T. Collins	125.00	60.00	35.00
(24)	Earl B. Combs (Earle)	225.00	110.00	65.00
(25)	James E. Cooney	125.00	60.00	35.00
(26)	Stanley Coveleski	200.00	100.00	60.00
(27)	Hugh M. Critz	125.00	60.00	35.00
(28)	Hazen Cuyler	200.00	100.00	60.00
(29)	George Dauss	125.00	60.00	35.00
(30)	Peter Donohue	125.00	60.00	35.00
(31)	Charles Dressen	125.00	60.00	35.00
(32)	James J. Dykes	125.00	60.00	35.00
(33)	Bib Falk (Bibb)	125.00	60.00	35.00
(34)	Edward S. Farrell	125.00	60.00	35.00
(35)	Wilson Fewster	125.00	60.00	35.00
(36)	Ira Flagstead	125.00	60.00	35.00
(37)	Howard Freigau	125.00	60.00	35.00
(38)	Bernard Friberg	125.00	60.00	35.00
(39)	Frank Frisch	200.00	100.00	60.00
(40)	Jacques F. Furnier (Fournier)	125.00	60.00	35.00
(41)	Joseph Galloway (Clarence) (Photo reversed)	125.00	60.00	35.00
(42)	Henry L. Gehrig	2,350	1,175	725.00
(43)	Charles Gehringer	250.00	125.00	75.00
(44)	Joseph Genewich	125.00	60.00	35.00
(45)	Walter Gerber	125.00	60.00	35.00
(46)	Leon Goslin	200.00	100.00	60.00
(47)	George Grantham	125.00	60.00	35.00
(48)	Burleigh A. Grimes	200.00	100.00	60.00
(49)	Charles Grimm	125.00	60.00	35.00
(50)	Fred Haney	125.00	60.00	35.00
(51)	Wm. Hargrave	125.00	60.00	35.00
(52)	George Harper	125.00	60.00	35.00
(53)	Stanley Harris	200.00	100.00	60.00
(54)	Leo Hartnett	200.00	100.00	60.00
(55)	Joseph Hauser	125.00	60.00	35.00
(56)	C.E. Heathcote	125.00	60.00	35.00
(57)	Harry Heilmann	200.00	100.00	60.00
(58)	Walter Henline	125.00	60.00	35.00
(59)	Ramon Herrera	125.00	60.00	35.00
(60)	Andrew A. High	125.00	60.00	35.00
(61)	Rogers Hornsby	210.00	105.00	65.00
(62)	Clarence Huber	125.00	60.00	35.00
(63)	Wm. Hunnefield (Photo actually Tommy Thomas.)	125.00	60.00	35.00
(64)	William Jacobson	125.00	60.00	35.00
(65)	Walter Johnson	300.00	150.00	90.00
(66)	Joseph Judge	125.00	60.00	35.00
(67)	Willie Kamm	125.00	60.00	35.00
(68)	Ray Kremer	125.00	60.00	35.00
(69)	Anthony Lazzeri	250.00	125.00	75.00
(70)	Frederick Lindstrom	225.00	110.00	65.00
(71)	Walter Lutzke	125.00	60.00	35.00
(72)	John Makan (Mokan)	125.00	60.00	35.00
(73)	Walter Maranville	200.00	100.00	60.00
(74)	Martin McManus	125.00	60.00	35.00
(75)	Earl McNeely	125.00	60.00	35.00
(76)	Hugh A. McQuillan	125.00	60.00	35.00
(77)	Douglas McWeeny	125.00	60.00	35.00
(78)	Oscar Melillo	125.00	60.00	35.00
(79)	Edmund (Bind)(Bing) Miller	125.00	60.00	35.00
(80)	Clarence Mueller	125.00	60.00	35.00
(81)	Robert W. Muesel (Meusel)	125.00	60.00	35.00
(82)	Joseph W. Munson	125.00	60.00	35.00
(83)	Emil Musel (Meusel)	125.00	60.00	35.00
(84)	Glenn Myatt	125.00	60.00	35.00
(85)	Bernie F. Neis	125.00	60.00	35.00
(86)	Robert O'Farrell	125.00	60.00	35.00
(87)	George O'Neil	125.00	60.00	35.00
(88)	Frank O'Rourke	125.00	60.00	35.00
(89)	Ralph Perkins	125.00	60.00	35.00
(90)	Walter C. Pipp	135.00	65.00	40.00
(91)	Emory Rigney	125.00	60.00	35.00
(92)	James J. Ring	125.00	60.00	35.00
(93)	Eppa Rixey	200.00	100.00	60.00
(94)	Edwin Rommel	125.00	60.00	35.00
(95)	Ed. Roush	200.00	100.00	60.00
(96)	Harold Ruel (Herold)	125.00	60.00	35.00
(97)	Charles Ruffing	200.00	100.00	60.00
(98)	Geo. H. "Babe" Ruth	1,875	935.00	560.00
(99)	John Sand	125.00	60.00	35.00
(100)	Joseph Sewell	200.00	100.00	60.00
(101)	Ray Shalk (Schalk)	200.00	100.00	60.00
(102)	J.R. Shawkey	125.00	60.00	35.00
(103)	Earl Sheely	125.00	60.00	35.00
(104)	William Sherdell (Sherdel)	125.00	60.00	35.00
(105)	Urban J. Shocker	125.00	60.00	35.00
(106)	George Sissler (Sisler)	200.00	100.00	60.00
(107)	Earl Smith	125.00	60.00	35.00
(108)	Sherrod Smith	125.00	60.00	35.00
(109)	Frank Snyder	125.00	60.00	35.00
(110)	Tristram Speaker	210.00	105.00	65.00
(111)	Fred Spurgeon	125.00	60.00	35.00
(112)	Homer Summa	125.00	60.00	35.00
(113)	Edward Taylor	125.00	60.00	35.00
(114)	J. Taylor	125.00	60.00	35.00
(115)	William Terry	200.00	100.00	60.00
(116)	Hollis Thurston	125.00	60.00	35.00
(117)	Philip Todt	125.00	60.00	35.00
(118)	George Torporcer (Toporcer)	125.00	60.00	35.00
(119)	Harold Traynor	200.00	100.00	60.00
(120)	Wm. Wambsganss	125.00	60.00	35.00
(121)	John Warner	125.00	60.00	35.00
(122)	Zach Wheat	200.00	100.00	60.00
(123)	Kenneth Williams	125.00	60.00	35.00
(124)	Ernest Wingard	125.00	60.00	35.00
(125)	Fred Wingfield	125.00	60.00	35.00
(126)	Ivy Wingo	125.00	60.00	35.00
(127)	Glen Wright (Glenn)	125.00	60.00	35.00
(128)	Russell Wrightstone	125.00	60.00	35.00

1926-29 Postcard-back Exhibits

Probably issued in the Philadelphia area, these cards can be found with plain backs, with postcard backs including the legend: "This Side for Correspondence," and with postcard backs including the legend, "Not for use in Exhibit machines." Some printings also have the legend, "Made in U.S.A." added to the backs. The fronts are borderless photos which generally

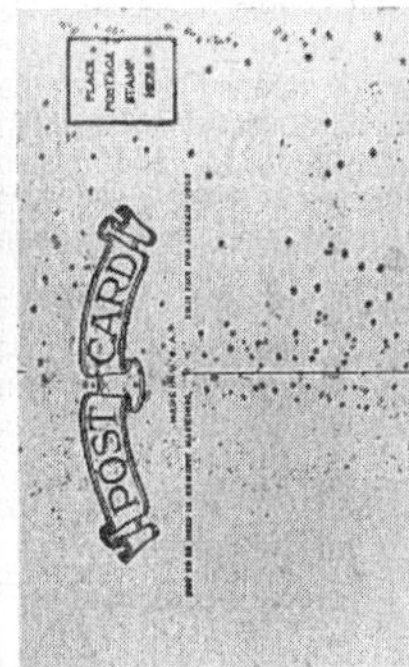

have the player's name, team and league designation printed in a hand-writing style; several variations in style have been noted. Five cards have typeset, rather than handwritten identification appearing in a white box: Cobb (Philadelphia), Frisch (N.Y.), Hornsby (Boston), Rouch (N.Y.) and Peckinpaugh (Cleveland), reflecting trades during the period of issue. Cards can be found printed in one of several different colors, and some or all players can be found in more than one color. Some subjects also appear with the photographic background removed. Cards size is about 3-3/8" x 5-3/8". The checklist below has been arranged alphabetically and is probably incomplete. Gaps have been left in the assigned numbers to accommodate future additions.

		NM	EX	VG
Common Player:		90.00	45.00	25.00
(1)	Virgie Barnes	90.00	45.00	25.00
(2)	Johnny Bassler	90.00	45.00	25.00
(3)	Sammy Bohne	200.00	100.00	60.00
(4)	Jim Bottomley	250.00	125.00	75.00
(5)	Ty Cobb (Detroit)	900.00	450.00	270.00
(6)	Ty Cobb (Athletics)	900.00	450.00	270.00
(7)	Mickey Cochrane	250.00	125.00	75.00
(8)	Urban Faber (Photo background.)	250.00	125.00	75.00
(9)	Urban Faber (Plain background.)	250.00	125.00	75.00
(10)	Jack Fournier	90.00	45.00	25.00
(11)	Jimmy Foxx	600.00	300.00	180.00
(12)	Frank Frisch (New York)	250.00	125.00	75.00
(13)	Frank Frisch (St. Louis)	275.00	135.00	80.00
(14)	Lou Gehrig/Btg (Photo background.)	2,000	1,000	600.00
(15)	Lou Gehrig/Btg (Plain background.)	2,000	1,000	600.00
(16)	Lou Gehrig/Portrait	2,000	1,000	600.00
(17)	Tom Griffith	90.00	45.00	25.00
(18)	Heinie Groh	90.00	45.00	25.00
(19)	Lefty Grove	500.00	250.00	150.00
(20)	George Haas	90.00	45.00	25.00
(21)	Stanley Harris	250.00	125.00	75.00
(22)	Charlie Hartnett (Photo background.)	250.00	125.00	75.00
(23)	Charlie Hartnett (Plain background.)	250.00	125.00	75.00
(24)	Harry Heilmann	250.00	125.00	75.00
(25)	Rogers Hornsby (St. Louis)	400.00	200.00	120.00
(26)	Rogers Hornsby (Boston)	600.00	300.00	180.00
(27)	Rogers Hornsby (Chicago)	400.00	200.00	120.00
(28)	Walter Johnson	600.00	300.00	180.00
(29)	Jimmy Johnston	90.00	45.00	25.00
(30)	Joe Judge	90.00	45.00	25.00
(31)	George Kelly	250.00	125.00	75.00
(32)	Chuck Klein	250.00	125.00	75.00
(33)	Hugh McQuillan	90.00	45.00	25.00
(34)	"Bob" Meusel	90.00	45.00	25.00
(35)	Bing Miller	90.00	45.00	25.00
(36)	Lefty O'Doul	150.00	75.00	45.00
(37)	Roger Peckinpaugh (Washington)	90.00	45.00	25.00
(38)	Roger Peckinpaugh (Cleveland)	90.00	45.00	25.00
(39)	Ralph Pinelli	90.00	45.00	25.00
(40)	Walter Pipp	125.00	60.00	35.00
(41)	Jimmy Ring	90.00	45.00	25.00
(42)	Eppa Rixey	250.00	125.00	75.00
(43)	Ed Rouch (Edd Roush)(Cincinnati)	250.00	125.00	75.00
(44)	Ed Rouch (Edd Roush) (New York)	250.00	125.00	75.00
(45)	Babe Ruth (Pose)	2,200	1,100	660.00
(46)	Babe Ruth (Batting follow-through.)	2,200	1,100	660.00
(47)	John Sand	90.00	45.00	25.00
(48)	Everett Scott	90.00	45.00	25.00
(49)	Al Simmons (View from side, "AM.L.")	250.00	125.00	75.00
(50)	Al Simmons (View from front, "A.L.")	250.00	125.00	75.00
(51)	George Sisler (Photo background.)	250.00	125.00	75.00
(52)	George Sisler (Plain background.)	250.00	125.00	75.00
(53)	Jack Smith	90.00	45.00	25.00
(54)	Tris Speaker (Photo background.)	350.00	175.00	100.00
(55)	Tris Speaker (Plain background.)	350.00	175.00	100.00
(56)	Phil Todt (Photo background.)	90.00	45.00	25.00
(57)	Phil Todt (Plain background.)	90.00	45.00	25.00
(58)	Specs Toporcer	90.00	45.00	25.00
(59)	Pie Traynor	250.00	125.00	75.00
(60)	Dazzy Vance	250.00	125.00	75.00
(61)	Rube Walberg	90.00	45.00	25.00
(62)	Paul Waner/Btg (Photo background.)	250.00	125.00	75.00
(63)	Paul Waner/Btg (Plain background.)	250.00	125.00	75.00
(64)	Paul Waner/Portrait	250.00	125.00	75.00
(65)	Zack Wheat	250.00	125.00	75.00
(66)	Cy Williams	90.00	45.00	25.00
(67)	Hack Wilson	250.00	125.00	75.00
(68)	Jimmy Wilson (Photo background.)	90.00	45.00	25.00
(69)	Jimmy Wilson (Plain background.)	90.00	45.00	25.00

1926-31 Postcard-back Four-on-One Exhibits

In the same format as Exhibit Supply Co.'s Four-on-One series which debuted in 1929, this set differs in that players from different teams (or sports, or the entertainment world) are represented. The photos of most players are the same as those found on 1926-1929 Postcard-back Exhibits, though some team indications show that at least some of the cards could not have been printed prior to 1931. As with the single-player cards, examples have been found with blank backs, as well as postcard backs.

		NM	EX	VG
(1)	Lou Gehrig, Lefty Grove, Pete Donahue, Gordon Cochrane	2,200	1,100	650.00
(2)	Lefty O'Doul, Dazzy Vance, Hughey Critz, Art Shires	650.00	325.00	195.00
(3)	Eugene Criqui/Boxer, Dave Shade/Boxer, Joe Judge, Ty Cobb	3,000	1,500	900.00
(4)	Joe Judge, Ty Cobb, Charlie Chaplin/Actor, Marie Prevost/Actress	2,500	1,250	750.00
(5)	Joe Judge, Paul Waner, Willie Kamm, Travis Jackson	750.00	375.00	225.00
(6)	Bucky Harris, Heinie Groh, Jack Dempsey/Boxer, Rocky Kansas/Boxer	750.00	375.00	225.00
(7)	Walter Johnson, Al Simmons, Gene Tunney/ Boxer, Benny Leonard/Boxer	2,500	1,250	750.00
(8)	Babe Ruth, Rogers Hornsby, Mickey Walker/Boxer, Georges Carpentier/Boxer	3,500	1,750	1,000

1927 Exhibits

The Exhibit Supply Co. issued a set of 64 cards in 1927, each measuring 3-3/8" x 5-3/8". The set can be identified from earlier issues by its light green tint. The player's name and team appear in capital letters in one lower corner, while "Ex. Sup. Co., Chgo." and "Made in U.S.A." appear in the other. All 64 photos used in the 1927 set were borrowed from previous issues, but 13 players are listed with new teams. There are several misspellings and other labeling errors in the set. The unnumbered cards are listed here in alphabetical order.

		NM	EX	VG
Complete Set (64):		11,000	5,500	3,250
Common Player:		75.00	35.00	20.00
(1)	Sparky Adams	75.00	35.00	20.00
(2)	Grover C. Alexander	250.00	125.00	75.00
(3)	David Bancroft	150.00	75.00	45.00
(4)	John Bassler	75.00	35.00	20.00
(5)	John M. Bentley (Middle initial actually N.)	75.00	35.00	20.00
(6)	Fred Blankenship (Ted)	75.00	35.00	20.00
(7)	James Bottomly (Bottomley)	150.00	75.00	45.00
(8)	Raymond Bressler	75.00	35.00	20.00
(9)	Geo. H. Burns	75.00	35.00	20.00
(10)	John Buttler (Butler)	75.00	35.00	20.00
(11)	Tyrus Cobb	1,100	550.00	330.00
(12)	Eddie Collins	150.00	75.00	45.00
(13)	Hazen Cuyler	150.00	75.00	45.00
(14)	George Daus (Dauss)	75.00	35.00	20.00
(15)	A.R. Decatur	75.00	35.00	20.00
(16)	Wilson Fewster	75.00	35.00	20.00
(17)	Ira Flagstead	75.00	35.00	20.00
(18)	Henry L. Gehrig	1,200	600.00	360.00
(19)	Charles Gehringer	150.00	75.00	45.00
(20)	Joseph Genewich	75.00	35.00	20.00
(21)	Leon Goslin	150.00	75.00	45.00
(22)	Burleigh A. Grimes	150.00	75.00	45.00
(23)	Charles Grimm	75.00	35.00	20.00
(24)	Fred Haney	75.00	35.00	20.00
(25)	Wm. Hargrave	75.00	35.00	20.00
(26)	George Harper	75.00	35.00	20.00
(27)	Leo Hartnett	150.00	75.00	45.00
(28)	Clifton Heathcote	75.00	35.00	20.00
(29)	Harry Heilman (Heillmann)	150.00	75.00	45.00
(30)	Walter Henline	75.00	35.00	20.00
(31)	Andrew High	75.00	35.00	20.00
(32)	Rogers Hornsby	250.00	125.00	75.00
(33)	Wm. Hunnefield (Photo actually Tommy Thomas.)	75.00	35.00	20.00
(34)	Walter Johnson	650.00	325.00	195.00
(35)	Willie Kamm	75.00	35.00	20.00
(36)	Ray Kremer	75.00	35.00	20.00
(37)	Anthony Lazzeri	150.00	75.00	45.00
(38)	Fredrick Lindstrom (Frederick)	150.00	75.00	45.00
(39)	Walter Lutzke	75.00	35.00	20.00
(40)	John "Stuffy" McInnes (McInnis)	75.00	35.00	20.00
(41)	John Mokan	75.00	35.00	20.00
(42)	Robert W. Muesel (Meusel)	75.00	35.00	20.00
(43)	Glenn Myatt	75.00	35.00	20.00
(44)	Bernie Neis	75.00	35.00	20.00
(45)	Robert O'Farrell	75.00	35.00	20.00
(46)	Walter C. Pipp	100.00	50.00	30.00
(47)	Eppa Rixey	150.00	75.00	45.00
(48)	Harold Ruel (Herold)	75.00	35.00	20.00
(49)	Geo. H. "Babe" Ruth	2,100	1,100	630.00
(50)	Ray Schalk	150.00	75.00	45.00
(51)	George Sissler (Sisler)	150.00	75.00	45.00
(52)	Earl Smith	75.00	35.00	20.00
(53)	Wm. H. Southworth	75.00	35.00	20.00
(54)	Tristam Speaker (Tristram)	250.00	125.00	75.00
(55)	J. Taylor	75.00	35.00	20.00
(56)	Philip Todt	75.00	35.00	20.00
(57)	Harold Traynor	150.00	75.00	45.00
(58)	William Wambsgganns (Wambsganss)	75.00	35.00	20.00
(59)	Zach Wheat	150.00	75.00	45.00
(60)	Kenneth Williams	75.00	35.00	20.00
(61)	Ernest Wingard	75.00	35.00	20.00
(62)	Fred Wingfield	75.00	35.00	20.00
(63)	Ivy Wingo	75.00	35.00	20.00
(64)	Russell Wrightstone	75.00	35.00	20.00

1928 Exhibits

The Exhibit Supply Co. switched to a blue tint for the photos in its 64-card set in 1928. There are 36 new photos in the set, including 24 new players. Four players from the previous year are shown with new teams and 24 of the cards are identical to the 1927 series, except for the color of the card. Cards are found with either blank backs or postcard backs. The photos are captioned in the same style as the 1927 set. The set again includes some misspelling and incorrect labels. The cards are unnumbered and are listed here in alphabetical order.

		NM	EX	VG
Complete Set (64):		9,500	4,750	2,750
Common Player:		80.00	40.00	20.00
(1)	Grover C. Alexander	400.00	200.00	120.00
(2)	David Bancroft	200.00	100.00	60.00
(3)	Virgil Barnes	80.00	40.00	20.00
(4)	Francis R. Blades	80.00	40.00	20.00
(5)	L.A. Blue	80.00	40.00	20.00
(6)	Edward W. Brown	80.00	40.00	20.00
(7)	Max G. Carey	200.00	100.00	60.00
(8)	Chalmer W. Cissell	80.00	40.00	20.00
(9)	Gordon S. Cochrane	200.00	100.00	60.00
(10)	Pat Collins	80.00	40.00	20.00
(11)	Hugh M. Critz	80.00	40.00	20.00
(12)	Howard Ehmke	80.00	40.00	20.00
(13)	E. English	80.00	40.00	20.00
(14)	Bib Falk (Bibb)	80.00	40.00	20.00
(15)	Ira Flagstead	80.00	40.00	20.00
(16)	Robert Fothergill	80.00	40.00	20.00
(17)	Frank Frisch	200.00	100.00	60.00
(18)	Lou Gehrig	1,200	600.00	360.00
(19)	Leon Goslin	200.00	100.00	60.00
(20)	Eugene Hargrave	80.00	40.00	20.00
(21)	Charles R. Hargraves (Hargreaves)	80.00	40.00	20.00
(22)	Stanley Harris	200.00	100.00	60.00
(23)	Bryan "Slim" Harriss	80.00	40.00	20.00
(24)	Leo Hartnett	200.00	100.00	60.00
(25)	Joseph Hauser	80.00	40.00	20.00
(26)	Fred Hoffman (Hofmann)	80.00	40.00	20.00

(27)	J. Francis Hogan	80.00	40.00	20.00
(28)	Rogers Hornsby	300.00	150.00	90.00
(29)	Chas. Jamieson	80.00	40.00	20.00
(30)	Sam Jones	80.00	40.00	20.00
(31)	Ray Kremer	80.00	40.00	20.00
(32)	Fred Leach	80.00	40.00	20.00
(33)	Fredrick Lindstrom (Frederick)	200.00	100.00	60.00
(34)	Adolph Luque (Adolfo)	100.00	50.00	30.00
(35)	Theodore Lyons	200.00	100.00	60.00
(36)	Harry McCurdy	80.00	40.00	20.00
(37)	Glenn Myatt	80.00	40.00	20.00
(38)	John Ogden (Photo actually Warren Ogden.)	80.00	40.00	20.00
(39)	James Ring	80.00	40.00	20.00
(40)	A.C. Root (Should be C.H.)	80.00	40.00	20.00
(41)	Edd. Roush	200.00	100.00	60.00
(42)	Harold Ruel (Herold)	80.00	40.00	20.00
(43)	Geo. H. "Babe" Ruth	1,350	675.00	400.00
(44)	Henry Sand	80.00	40.00	20.00
(45)	Fred Schulte	80.00	40.00	20.00
(46)	Joseph Sewell	200.00	100.00	60.00
(47)	Walter Shang (Schang)	80.00	40.00	20.00
(48)	Urban J. Shocker	80.00	40.00	20.00
(49)	Al. Simmons	200.00	100.00	60.00
(50)	Earl Smith	80.00	40.00	20.00
(51)	Robert Smith	80.00	40.00	20.00
(52)	Jack Tavener	80.00	40.00	20.00
(53)	J. Taylor	80.00	40.00	20.00
(54)	Philip Todt	80.00	40.00	20.00
(55)	Geo. Uhle	80.00	40.00	20.00
(56)	Arthur "Dazzy" Vance	200.00	100.00	60.00
(57)	Paul Waner	200.00	100.00	60.00
(58)	Earl G. Whitehill (Middle intial actually O.)	80.00	40.00	20.00
(59)	Fred Williams	80.00	40.00	20.00
(60)	James Wilson	80.00	40.00	20.00
(61)	L.R. (Hack) Wilson	200.00	100.00	60.00
(62)	Lawrence Woodall	80.00	40.00	20.00
(63)	Glen Wright (Glenn)	80.00	40.00	20.00
(64)	William A. Zitzman (Zitzmann)	80.00	40.00	20.00

1929-30 Four-on-One Exhibits

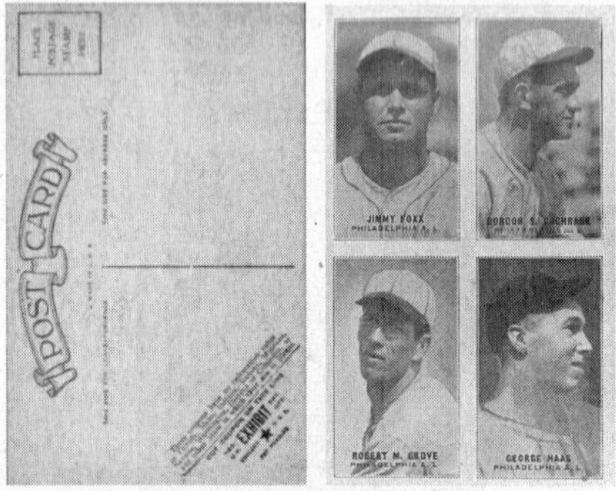

Although the size of the card remained the same, the Exhibit Supply Co. of Chicago began putting four players' pictures on each card in 1929 - a practice that would continue for the next decade. Known as "four-on-one" cards, the players are identified by name and team at the bottom of the photos, which are separated by borders. The 32 cards in the 1929-30 series have postcard backs and were printed in a wide range of color combinations of black, brown and blue ink on blue, orange, green, red, white, and yellow backgrounds. Most of the backs are uncolored, however, cards with a black on red front have been seen with red backs, and cards with blue on yellow fronts have been seen with yellow backs. There are numerous spelling and caption errors in the set, and the player identified as Babe Herman is actually Jesse Petty.

		NM	EX	VG
Complete Set (32):		5,500	2,750	1,600
Common Card:		65.00	32.00	20.00
(1)	Earl J. Adams, R. Bartell, Earl Sheely, Harold Traynor	150.00	75.00	45.00
(2)	Dale Alexander, C. Gehringer, G.F. McManus (Should be M.J.), H.F. Rice	150.00	75.00	45.00
(3)	Grover C. Alexander, James Bottomly (Bottomley), Frank Frisch, James Wilson	250.00	125.00	75.00
(4)	Martin G. Autrey (Autry), Alex Metzler, Carl Reynolds, Alphonse Thomas	65.00	32.50	20.00
(5)	Earl Averill, B.A. Falk, K. Holloway, L. Sewell	150.00	75.00	45.00
(6)	David Bancroft, Del L. Bisonette (Bissonette), John H. DeBerry, Floyd C. Herman (Photo actually Jesse Petty.)	150.00	75.00	45.00
(7)	C.E. Beck, Leo Hartnett, Rogers Hornsby, L.R. (Hack) Wilson	200.00	100.00	60.00
(8)	Ray Benge, Lester L. Sweetland, A.C. Whitney, Cy. Williams	65.00	32.50	20.00
(9)	Benny Bengough, Earl B. Coombs (Combs), Waite Hoyt, Anthony Lazzeri	200.00	100.00	60.00
(10)	L. Benton, Melvin Ott, Andrew Reese, William Terry	150.00	75.00	45.00
(11)	Max Bishop, James Dykes, Samuel Hale, Homer Summa	65.00	32.50	20.00
(12)	L.A. Blue, O. Melillo, F.O. Rourke (Frank O'Rourke), F. Schulte	65.00	32.50	20.00
(13)	Oswald Bluege, Leon Goslin, Joseph Judge, Harold Ruel (Herold)	150.00	75.00	45.00
(14)	Chalmer W. Cissell, John W. Clancy, Willie Kamm, John L. Kerr (Kerr's middle initial actually "F.")	65.00	32.50	20.00
(15)	Gordon S. Cochrane, Jimmy Foxx, Robert M. Grove, George Haas	250.00	125.00	75.00
(16)	Pat Collins, Joe Dugan, Edward Farrel (Farrell), George Sisler	150.00	75.00	45.00
(17)	H.M. Critz, G.L. Kelly, V.J. Picinich, W.C. Walker	150.00	75.00	45.00
(18)	Nick Cullop, D'Arcy Flowers, Harvey Hendrick, Arthur "Dazzy" Vance	150.00	75.00	45.00
(19)	Hazen Cuyler, E. English, C.J. Grimm, C.H. Root	150.00	75.00	45.00
(20)	Taylor Douthit, Chas. M. Gilbert (Gelbert), Chas. J. Hafey, Fred G. Haney	150.00	75.00	45.00
(21)	Leo Durocher, Henry L. Gohrig, Mark Koenig, Geo. H. "Babe" Ruth	1,400	700.00	400.00
(22)	L.A. Fonseca, Carl Lind, J. Sewell, J. Tavener	150.00	75.00	45.00
(23)	H.E. Ford, C.F. Lucas, C.A. Pittenger, E.V. Purdy	65.00	32.50	20.00
(24)	Bernard Friberg, Donald Hurst, Frank O'Doul, Fresco Thompson	65.00	32.50	20.00
(25)	S. Gray, R. Kress, H. Manush, W.H. Shang (Schang)	150.00	75.00	45.00
(26)	Charles R. Hargreaves, Ray Kremer, Lloyd Waner, Paul Waner	150.00	75.00	45.00
(27)	George Harper, Fred Maguire, Lance Richbourg, Robert Smith	65.00	32.50	20.00
(28)	Jack Hayes, Sam P. Jones, Chas. M. Myer, Sam Rice	150.00	75.00	45.00
(29)	Harry E. Heilman (Heilmann), C.N. Richardson, M.J. Shea, G.E. Uhle	150.00	75.00	45.00
(30)	J.A. Heving, R.R. Reeves (Should be R.E.), J. Rothrock, C.H. Ruffing	150.00	75.00	45.00
(31)	J.F. Hogan, T.C. Jackson, Fred Lindstrom, J.D. Welsh	150.00	75.00	45.00
(32)	W.W. Regan, H. Rhyne, D. Taitt, P.J. Todt	65.00	32.50	20.00

1929 Exhibit "Star Picture Stamps"

This series of movie star Exhibit cards includes pictures of other celebrities who were featured in contemporary movies. Produced by Exhibit Supply Co. of Chicago, whose advertising appears on the postcard-style back, the 5-3/8" x 3-3/8" card has a red monochrome front which pictures the stars in the format of eight "Star Pictures Stamps." On this card, Ruth is pictured in the uniform he wore in the 1927 film "The Babe Comes Home."

	NM	EX	VG
Babe Ruth (W/Tom Mix, Charles Lindbergh, Charlie Chaplin, Jack Dempsey, Harold Lloyd, Douglas Fairbanks and Al Jolson.)	750.00	375.00	225.00

1931-32 Four-on-One Exhibits

The 1931-1932 series issued by the Exhibit Co. again consisted of 32 cards, each picturing four players. The series can be differentiated from the previous year by the coupon backs, which list various premiums available (including kazoos, toy pistols and other prizes). The cards again were printed in various color combinations, including; black on green, blue on green, black on orange, black on red, blue on white and black on yellow. There are numerous spelling and caption errors in the series. The Babe Herman/Jesse Petty error of the previous year was still not corrected, and the card of Rick Ferell not only misspells his name ("Farrel"), but also pictures the wrong player (Edward Farrell).

		NM	EX	VG
Complete Set (32):		5,500	2,750	1,600
Common Card:		90.00	45.00	27.00
(1)	Earl J. Adams, James Bottomly (Bottomley), Frank Frisch, James Wilson	150.00	75.00	45.00
(2)	Dale Alexander, C. Gehringer, G.F. McManus (Should be M.J.), G.E. Uhle	150.00	75.00	45.00
(3)	L.L. Appling (Should be L.B.), Chalmer W. Cissell, Willie Kamm, Ted Lyons	150.00	75.00	45.00
(4)	Buzz Arlett, Ray Benge, Chuck Klein, A.C. Whitney	150.00	75.00	45.00
(5)	Earl Averill, B.A. Falk, L.A. Fonseca, L. Sewell	150.00	75.00	45.00
(6)	Richard Bartell, Bernard Friberg, Donald Hurst, Harry McCurdy	90.00	45.00	27.00
(7)	Walter Berger, Fred Maguire, Lance Richbourg, Earl Sheely	90.00	45.00	27.00
(8)	Chas. Berry, Robt. Reeves, R.R. Reeves (Should be R.E.), J. Rothrock	90.00	45.00	27.00
(9)	Del L. Bisonette (Bissonette), Floyd C. Herman (Photo - J. Petty, Jack Quinn, Glenn Wright)	90.00	45.00	27.00
(10)	L.A. Blue, Smead Jolley, Carl Reynolds, Henry Tate	90.00	45.00	27.00
(11)	O. Bluege, Joe Judge, Chas. M. Myer, Sam Rice	150.00	75.00	45.00
(12)	John Boley, James Dykes, E.J. Miller, Al. Simmons	150.00	75.00	45.00
(13)	Gordon S. Cochrane, Jimmy Foxx, Robert M. Grove, George Haas	325.00	160.00	95.00
(14)	Adam Comorosky, Gus Suhr, T.J. Thevenow, Harold Traynor	150.00	75.00	45.00
(15)	Earl B. Coombs (Combs), W. Dickey, Anthony Lazzeri, H. Pennock	225.00	110.00	65.00
(16)	H.M. Critz, J.F. Hogan, T.C. Jackson, Fred Lindstrom	150.00	75.00	45.00
(17)	Joe Cronin, H. Manush, F. Marberry, Roy Spencer	150.00	75.00	45.00
(18)	Nick Cullop, Les Durocher (Leo), Harry Heilmann, W.C. Walker	150.00	75.00	45.00
(19)	Hazen Cuyler, E. English, C.J. Grimm, C.H. Root	150.00	75.00	45.00
(20)	Taylor Douthit, Chas. M. Gilbert (Gelbert), Chas. J. Hafey, Bill Hallahan	90.00	45.00	27.00
(21)	Richard Farrel (Ferrell), S. Gray, R. Kress, W. Stewart (Photo actually Ed Farrell.)	90.00	45.00	27.00
(22)	W. Ferrell, J. Goldman, Hunnefield, Ed Morgan	90.00	45.00	27.00
(23)	Fred Fitzsimmons, Robert O'Farrell, Melvin Ott, William Terry	150.00	75.00	45.00
(24)	D'Arcy Flowers, Frank O'Doul, Fresco Thompson, Arthur "Dazzy" Vance	150.00	75.00	45.00
(25)	H.E. Ford (Should be H.H.), Gooch, C.F. Lucas, W. Roettger	90.00	45.00	27.00
(26)	E. Funk, W. Hoyt, Mark Koenig, Wallie Schang	90.00	45.00	27.00
(27)	Henry L. Gehrig, Lyn Lary, James Reese (Photo actually Andy Reese.), Geo. H. "Babe" Ruth	1,150	575.00	345.00
(28)	George Grantham, Ray Kremer, Lloyd Waner, Paul Waner	150.00	75.00	45.00
(29)	Leon Goslin, O. Melillo, F.O. Rourke (Frank O'Rourke), F. Schulte	150.00	75.00	45.00
(30)	Leo Hartnett, Rogers Hornsby, J.R. Stevenson (Stephenson), L.R. (Hack) Wilson	200.00	100.00	60.00
(31)	D. MacFayden, H. Rhyne, Bill Sweeney, E.W. Webb	90.00	45.00	27.00
(32)	Walter Maranville, Randolph Moore, Alfred Spohrer, J.T. Zachary	150.00	75.00	45.00

1931-32 Babe Ruth Exhibit

The rarest Exhibit card to feature Babe Ruth, this circa 1931 issue has a photographic portrait of him in dress clothes, and is part of a 32-card movie stars series. Found in black-and-white or various color tints, this approximately 3-1/2" x 5-1/2" card has a facsimile autograph in white on front. It can be found with either a postcard-style back or a back offering premium merchandise.

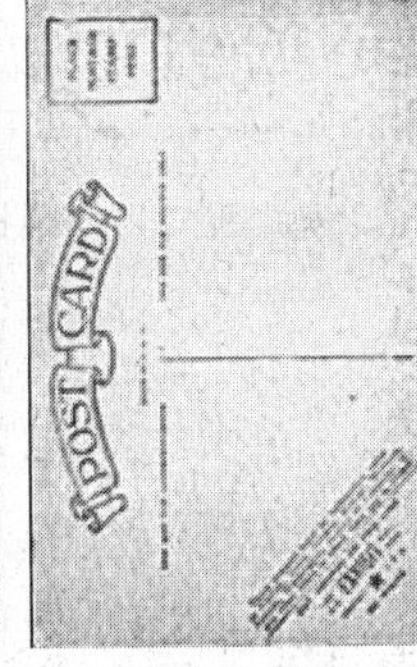

	NM	EX	VG
Babe Ruth	900.00	450.00	270.00

1933 Four-on-One Exhibits

The 1933 series of four-on-one Exhibits consists of 16 cards with blank backs. Color combinations include: blue on green, black on orange, black on red, blue on white and black on yellow. Most have a plain, white back, although the black on yellow cards are also found with a yellow back. Most of the pictures used are reprinted from previous series, and there are some spelling and caption errors, including the Richard Ferrell/Edward Farrel mixup from the previous year. Al Lopez is shown as "Vincent" Lopez.

		NM	EX	VG
Complete Set (16):		4,000	2,000	1,200
Common Card:		85.00	40.00	25.00
(1)	Earl J. Adams, Frank Frisch, Chas. Gilbert (Gelbert), Bill Hallahan	150.00	75.00	45.00
(2)	Earl Averill, W. Ferrell, Ed Morgan, L. Sewell	150.00	75.00	45.00
(3)	Richard Bartell, Ray Benge, Donald Hurst, Chuck Klein	150.00	75.00	45.00
(4)	Walter Berger, Walter Maranville, Alfred Spohrer, J.T. Zachary	150.00	75.00	45.00
(5)	Charles Berry, L.A. Blue, Ted Lyons, Bob Seeds	150.00	75.00	45.00
(6)	Chas. Berry, D. MacFayden, H. Rhyne, E.W. Webb	85.00	40.00	25.00
(7)	Mickey Cochrane, Jimmy Foxx, Robert M. Grove, Al. Simmons	450.00	225.00	135.00
(8)	H.M. Critz, Fred Fitzsimmons, Fred Lindstrom, Robert O'Farrell	150.00	75.00	45.00
(9)	W. Dickey, Anthony Lazzeri, H. Pennock, George H. "Babe" Ruth	2,000	1,000	600.00
(10)	Taylor Douthit, George Grantham, Chas. J. Hafey, C.F. Lucas	150.00	75.00	45.00
(11)	E. English, C.J. Grimm, C.H. Root, J.R. Stevenson (Stephenson)	85.00	40.00	25.00
(12)	Richard Farrel (Farrell), Leon Goslin, S. Gray, O. Melillo (photo actually Ed Farrell)	150.00	75.00	45.00
(13)	C. Gehringer, "Muddy" Ruel, Jonathan Stone (first name - John, G.E. Uhle	150.00	75.00	45.00
(14)	Joseph Judge, H. Manush, F. Marberry, Roy Spencer	150.00	75.00	45.00
(15)	Vincent Lopez (Al), Frank O'Doul, Arthur "Dazzy" Vance, Glenn Wright	150.00	75.00	45.00
(16)	Gus Suhr, Tom J. Thevenow, Lloyd Waner, Paul Waner	150.00	75.00	45.00

1934 Four-on-One Exhibits

This 16-card series issued by the Exhibit Co. in 1934 is again blank-backed and continues the four-on-one format in a 3-3/8" x 5-3/8" size. The 1934 series can be differentiated from previous years by the more subdued colors of the cards, which include lighter shades of blue, brown, green and violet - all printed on white card stock. Many new photos were also used in the 1934 series. Of the 64 players included, 25 appear for the first time and another 16 were given new poses. Spelling was improved, but Al Lopez is still identified as "Vincent."

		NM	EX	VG
Complete Set (16):		2,750	1,350	825.00
Common Card:		75.00	35.00	20.00
(1)	Luke Appling, George Earnshaw, Al Simmons, Evar Swanson	125.00	60.00	35.00
(2)	Earl Averill, W. Ferrell, Willie Kamm, Frank Pytlak	125.00	60.00	35.00
(3)	Richard Bartell, Donald Hurst, Wesley Schulmerich, Jimmy Wilson	75.00	35.00	20.00
(4)	Walter Berger, Ed Brandt, Frank Hogan, Bill Urbanski	75.00	35.00	20.00
(5)	Jim Bottomley, Chas. J. Hafey, Botchi Lombardi, Tony Piet	125.00	60.00	35.00
(6)	Irving Burns, Irving Hadley, Rollie Hemsley, O. Melillo	75.00	35.00	20.00
(7)	Bill Cissell, Rick Ferrell, Lefty Grove, Roy Johnson	125.00	60.00	35.00
(8)	Mickey Cochrane, C. Gehringer, Goose Goslin, Fred Marberry	125.00	60.00	35.00
(9)	George Cramer (Roger), Jimmy Foxx, Frank Higgins, Slug Mahaffey	150.00	75.00	45.00
(10)	Joe Cronin, Alvin Crowder, Joe Kuhel, H. Manush	125.00	60.00	35.00
(11)	W. Dickey, Lou Gehrig, Vernon Gomez, Geo. H. "Babe" Ruth	1,400	700.00	425.00
(12)	E. English, C.J. Grimm, Chas. Klein, Lon Warneke	125.00	60.00	35.00
(13)	Frank Frisch, Bill Hallahan, Pepper Martin, John Rothrock	125.00	60.00	35.00
(14)	Carl Hubbell, Mel Ott, Blondy Ryan, Bill Terry	150.00	75.00	45.00
(15)	Leonard Koenecke, Sam Leslie, Vincent Lopez (Al), Glenn Wright	125.00	60.00	35.00
(16)	T.J. Thevenow, Pie Traynor, Lloyd Waner, Paul Waner	125.00	60.00	35.00

1935 Four-on-One Exhibits

Continuing with the same four-on-one format, the Exhibit Supply Co. issued another 16-card series in 1935. All cards were printed in a slate-blue color with a blank back. Seventeen of the players included in the 1935 series appear for the first time. While another 11 are shown with new poses. There are several spelling and caption errors. Babe Ruth appears in a regular Exhibit issue for the last time.

		NM	EX	VG
Complete Set (16):		4,000	2,000	1,200
Common Card:		75.00	35.00	20.00
(1)	Earl Averill, Mel Harder, Willie Kamm, Hal Trosky	125.00	60.00	35.00
(2)	Walter Berger, Ed Brandt, Frank Hogan, "Babe" Ruth	1,300	650.00	350.00
(3)	Henry Bonura, Jimmy Dykes, Ted Lyons, Al Simmons	125.00	60.00	35.00
(4)	Jimmy Bottomley, Paul Derringer, Chas. J. Hafey, Botchi Lombardi	125.00	60.00	35.00
(5)	Irving Burns, Rollie Hemsley, O. Melillo, L.N. Newson	75.00	35.00	20.00
(6)	Guy Bush, Pie Traynor, Floyd Vaughn (Vaughan), Paul Waner	125.00	60.00	35.00
(7)	Mickey Cochrane, C. Gehringer, Goose Goslin, Linwood Rowe (Lynwood)	125.00	60.00	35.00
(8)	Phil Collins, John "Blondy" Ryan, Geo. Watkins, Jimmy Wilson	75.00	35.00	20.00
(9)	George Cramer (Roger), Jimmy Foxx, Bob Johnson, Slug Mahaffey	150.00	75.00	45.00
(10)	Hughie Critz, Carl Hubbell, Mel Ott, Bill Terry	150.00	75.00	45.00
(11)	Joe Cronin, Rick Ferrell, Lefty Grove, Billy Werber	145.00	70.00	40.00
(12)	Tony Cuccinello, Vincent Lopez (Al), Van Mungo, Dan Taylor (photo actually George Puccinelli)	125.00	60.00	35.00
(13)	Jerome "Dizzy" Dean, Paul Dean, Frank Frisch, Pepper Martin	325.00	160.00	95.00
(14)	W. Dickey, Lou Gehrig, Vernon Gomez, Tony Lazzeri	900.00	450.00	275.00
(15)	C.J. Grimm, Gabby Hartnett, Chas. Klein, Lon Warneke	125.00	60.00	35.00
(16)	H. Manush, Buddy Meyer (Myer), Fred Schulte, Earl Whitehill	125.00	60.00	35.00

1936 Four-on-One Exhibits

The 1936 series of four-on-one cards again consisted of 16 cards in either green or slate blue with plain, blank backs. The series can be differentiated from the previous year's Exhibit cards by the line "PTD. IN U.S.A." at the bottom. Of the 64 players pictured, 16 appear for the first time and another nine are shown in new poses. The series is again marred by several spelling and caption errors.

		NM	EX	VG
Complete Set (16):		3,000	1,500	900.00
Common Card:		80.00	40.00	25.00
(1)	Paul Andrews, Harland Clift (Harlond), Rollie Hemsley, Sammy West	80.00	40.00	25.00
(2)	Luke Appling, Henry Bonura, Jimmy Dykes, Ted Lyons	100.00	50.00	30.00
(3)	Earl Averill, Mel Harder, Hal Trosky, Joe Vosmik	100.00	50.00	30.00
(4)	Walter Berger, Danny MacFayden, Bill Urbanski, Pinky Whitney	80.00	40.00	25.00
(5)	Charles Berry, Frank Higgins, Bob Johnson, Puccinelli	80.00	40.00	25.00
(6)	Ossie Bluege, Buddy Meyer (Myer), L.N. Newsom, Earl Whitehill	80.00	40.00	25.00
(7)	Stan. Bordagaray, Dutch Brandt, Fred Lindstrom, Van Mungo	100.00	50.00	30.00
(8)	Guy Bush, Pie Traynor, Floyd Vaughn (Vaughan), Paul Waner	100.00	50.00	30.00
(9)	Dolph Camilli, Curt Davis, Johnny Moore, Jimmy Wilson	80.00	40.00	25.00
(10)	Mickey Cochrane, C. Gehringer, Goose Goslin, Linwood Rowe (Lynwood)	100.00	50.00	30.00
(11)	Joe Cronin, Rick Ferrell, Jimmy Foxx, Lefty Grove	175.00	85.00	50.00
(12)	Jerome "Dizzy" Dean, Paul Dean, Frank Frisch, Joe "Ducky" Medwick	300.00	150.00	90.00
(13)	Paul Derringer, Babe Herman, Alex Kampouris, Botchi Lombardi	100.00	50.00	30.00
(14)	Augie Galan, Gabby Hartnett, Billy Herman, Lon Warneke	100.00	50.00	30.00
(15)	Lou Gehrig, Vernon Gomez, Tony Lazzeri, Red Ruffing	1,300	650.00	390.00
(16)	Carl Hubbell, Gus Mancuso, Mel Ott, Bill Terry	125.00	60.00	35.00

1937 Four-on-One Exhibits

The 1937 four-on-one Exhibit cards were printed in either green or bright blue. The backs are again blank. The 1937 cards are difficult to distinguish from the 1936 series, because both contain the "PTD. IN U.S.A." line along the bottom. Of the 64 photos, 47 are re-issues from previous series.

		NM	EX	VG
Complete Set (16):		2,750	1,350	825.00
Common Card:		60.00	30.00	18.00
(1)	Earl Averill, Bob Feller, Frank Pytlak, Hal Trosky	150.00	75.00	45.00
(2)	Luke Appling, Henry Bonura, Jimmy Dykes, Vernon Kennedy	125.00	60.00	35.00
(3)	Walter Berger, Alfonso Lopez, Danny MacFayden, Bill Urbanski	125.00	60.00	35.00
(4)	Cy Blanton, Gus Suhr, Floyd Vaughn (Vaughan), Paul Waner	125.00	60.00	35.00
(5)	Dolph Camilli, Johnny Moore, Wm. Walters, Pinky Whitney	60.00	30.00	18.00
(6)	Harland Clift (Harlond), Rollie Hemsley, Orval Hildebrand (Oral), Sammy West	60.00	30.00	18.00
(7)	Mickey Cochrane, C. Gehringer, Goose Goslin, Linwood Rowe (Lynwood)	125.00	60.00	35.00
(8)	Joe Cronin, Rick Ferrell, Jimmy Foxx, Lefty Grove	150.00	75.00	45.00
(9)	Jerome "Dizzy" Dean, Stuart Martin, Joe "Ducky" Medwick, Lon Warneke	175.00	85.00	50.00
(10)	Paul Derringer, Botchi Lombardi, Lew Riggs, Phil Weintraub	125.00	60.00	35.00
(11)	Joe DiMaggio, Lou Gehrig, Vernon Gomez, Tony Lazzeri	1,325	660.00	375.00
(12)	E. English, Johnny Moore, Van Mungo, Gordon Phelps	60.00	30.00	18.00
(13)	Augie Galan, Gabby Hartnett, Billy Herman, Bill Lee	125.00	60.00	35.00
(14)	Carl Hubbell, Sam Leslie, Gus. Mancuso, Mel Ott	125.00	60.00	35.00
(15)	Bob Johnson, Harry Kelly (Kelley), Wallace Moses, Billy Weber (Werber)	60.00	30.00	18.00
(16)	Joe Kuhel, Buddy Meyer (Myer), L.N. Newsom, Jonathan Stone (first name actually John)	60.00	30.00	18.00

1938 Four-on-One Exhibits

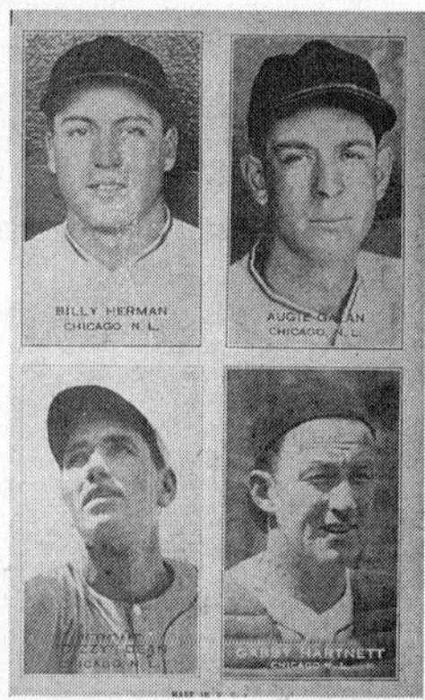

The Exhibit Co. used its four-on-one format for the final time in 1938, issuing another 16-card series. The cards feature brown printing on white stock with the line "MADE IN U.S.A." appearing along the bottom. The backs are blank. Twelve players appeared for the first time and three others are shown in new poses. Again, there are several spelling and caption mistakes.

		NM	EX	VG
Complete Set (16):		3,250	1,600	975.00
Common Card:		83.00	41.00	25.00
(1)	Luke Appling, Mike Kreevich, Ted Lyons, L. Sewell	125.00	60.00	35.00
(2)	Morris Arnovich, Chas. Klein, Wm. Walters, Pinky Whitney	125.00	60.00	35.00
(3)	Earl Averill, Bob Feller, Odell Hale, Hal Trosky	165.00	80.00	50.00
(4)	Beau Bell, Harland Clift (Harlond), L.N. Newsom, Sammy West	80.00	40.00	25.00
(5)	Cy Blanton, Gus Suhr, Floyd Vaughn (Vaughan), Paul Waner	125.00	60.00	35.00
(6)	Tom Bridges, C. Gehringer, Hank Greenberg, Rudy York	125.00	60.00	35.00
(7)	Dolph Camilli, Leo Durocher, Van Mungo, Gordon Phelps	125.00	60.00	35.00
(8)	Joe Cronin, Jimmy Foxx, Lefty Grove, Joe Vosmik	165.00	80.00	50.00
(9)	Tony Cuccinello, Vince DiMaggio, Roy Johnson, Danny MacFayden (photo actually George Puccinelli)	90.00	45.00	25.00
(10)	Jerome "Dizzy" Dean, Augie Galan, Gabby Hartnett, Billy Herman	200.00	100.00	60.00
(11)	Paul Derringer, Ival Goodman, Botchi Lombardi, Lew Riggs	125.00	60.00	35.00
(12)	W. Dickey, Joe DiMaggio, Lou Gehrig, Vernon Gomez	1,375	685.00	400.00
(13)	Rick Ferrell, W. Ferrell, Buddy Meyer (Myer), Jonathan Stone (first name actually John)	125.00	60.00	35.00
(14)	Carl Hubbell, Hank Leiber, Mel Ott, Jim Ripple	130.00	65.00	40.00
(15)	Bob Johnson, Harry Kelly (Kelley), Wallace Moses, Billy Weber (Werber)	80.00	40.00	25.00
(16)	Stuart Martin, Joe "Ducky" Medwick, Johnny Mize, Lon Warneke	125.00	60.00	35.00

1939-46 Salutation Exhibits

Referred to as "Exhibits" because they were issued by the Exhibit Supply Co. of Chicago, Ill., the bulk of this group was produced over an eight-year span, though production and sale of some players' cards continued well into the period of the 1947-66 Exhibits. These cards are frequently called "Salutations" because of the personalized greeting found on the card. The black-and-white cards, which measure 3-3/8" x 5-3/8", are unnumbered and blank-backed. Most Exhibits were sold through vending machines for a penny. The complete set price includes all variations.

		NM	EX	VG
Complete Set (83):		6,500	3,250	1,950
Common Player:		15.00	7.50	4.50
(1)	Luke Appling ("Made In U.S.A." in left corner.)	20.00	10.00	6.00
(2)	Luke Appling ("Made In U.S.A." in right corner.)	45.00	22.50	13.50
(3)	Earl Averill	400.00	200.00	120.00
(4)	Charles "Red" Barrett	20.00	10.00	6.00
(5)	Henry "Hank" Borowy	15.00	7.50	4.50
(6)	Lou Boudreau	25.00	12.50	7.50
(7)	Adolf Camilli	30.00	15.00	9.00
(8)	Phil Cavarretta	15.00	7.50	4.50
(9)	Harland Clift (Harlond)	20.00	10.00	6.00
(10)	Tony Cuccinello	40.00	20.00	12.00
(11)	Dizzy Dean	140.00	70.00	45.00
(12)	Paul Derringer	20.00	10.00	6.00
(13)	Bill Dickey ("Made In U.S.A." in left corner.)	35.00	17.50	10.00
(14)	Bill Dickey ("Made In U.S.A." in right corner.)	55.00	27.50	16.50
(15)	Joe DiMaggio (Issued into the 1950s.)	150.00	75.00	45.00
(16)	Bob Elliott	15.00	7.50	4.50
(17)	Bob Feller/Portrait	120.00	60.00	35.00
(18)	Bob Feller/Pitching	50.00	25.00	15.00
(19)	Dave Ferriss	45.00	22.50	13.50
(20)	Jimmy Foxx	75.00	37.50	22.50
(21)	Lou Gehrig	1,750	875.00	525.00
(22)	Charlie Gehringer	100.00	50.00	30.00
(23)	Vernon Gomez	175.00	85.00	50.00
(24)	Joe Gordon (Cleveland)	27.50	13.50	8.25
(25)	Joe Gordon (New York)	15.00	7.50	4.50
(26)	Hank Greenberg (Truly yours.)	35.00	17.50	10.00
(27)	Hank Greenberg (Very truly yours.)	160.00	80.00	50.00
(28)	Robert Grove	50.00	25.00	15.00
(29)	Gabby Hartnett	175.00	85.00	50.00
(30)	Buddy Hassett	20.00	10.00	6.00
(31)	Jeff Heath (Large projection.)	25.00	12.50	7.50
(32)	Jeff Heath (Small projection.)	25.00	12.50	7.50
(33)	Kirby Higbe	20.00	10.00	6.00
(34)	Tommy Holmes (Yours truly.)	15.00	7.50	4.50
(35)	Tommy Holmes (Sincerely yours.)	130.00	65.00	40.00
(36)	Carl Hubbell	40.00	20.00	12.00
(37)	Bob Johnson	40.00	20.00	12.00
(38)	Charles Keller ("MADE IN U.S.A." left corner.)	25.00	12.50	7.50
(39)	Charles Keller ("MADE IN U.S.A." right corner.)	15.00	7.50	4.50
(40)	Ken Keltner	25.00	12.50	7.50
(41)	Chuck Klein	165.00	85.00	50.00
(42)	Mike Kreevich	85.00	40.00	20.00
(43)	Joe Kuhel	20.00	10.00	6.00
(44)	Bill Lee	20.00	10.00	6.00
(45)	Ernie Lombardi (Cordially)	325.00	160.00	95.00
(46)	Ernie Lombardi (Cordially yours.)	20.00	10.00	6.00
(47)	Martin Marion ("An Exhibit Card" in lower-left.)	20.00	10.00	6.00
(48)	Marty Marion (No "An Exhibit Card.")	20.00	10.00	6.00
(49)	Merrill May	25.00	12.50	7.50
(50)	Frank McCormick ("Made In U.S.A." in left corner.)	30.00	15.00	9.00
(51)	Frank McCormick ("Made In U.S.A." in right corner.)	15.00	7.50	4.50
(52)	George McQuinn ("Made In U.S.A." in left corner.)	20.00	10.00	6.00
(53)	George McQuinn ("Made In U.S.A." in right corner.)	15.00	7.50	4.50
(54)	Joe Medwick	55.00	27.50	16.50
(55)	Johnny Mize ("Made In U.S.A." in left corner.)	35.00	17.50	10.00
(56)	Johnny Mize ("Made In U.S.A." in right corner.)	20.00	10.00	6.00
(57)	Hugh Mulcahy	150.00	75.00	45.00
(58)	Hal Newhouser	30.00	15.00	9.00
(59)	Buck Newson (Newsom)	275.00	135.00	80.00
(60)	Louis (Buck) Newsom	15.00	7.50	4.50
(61)	Mel Ott ("Made In U.S.A." in left corner.)	40.00	20.00	12.00
(62)	Mel Ott ("Made In U.S.A." in right corner.)	25.00	12.50	7.50
(63)	Andy Pafko ("C" on cap.)	20.00	10.00	6.00
(64)	Andy Pafko (Plain cap.)	15.00	7.50	4.50
(65)	Claude Passeau	15.00	7.50	4.50
(66)	Howard Pollet ("Made In U.S.A." in left corner.)	20.00	10.00	6.00
(67)	Howard Pollet ("Made In U.S.A." in right corner.)	15.00	7.50	4.50
(68)	Pete Reiser ("Made In U.S.A." in left corner.)	45.00	22.50	13.50
(69)	Pete Reiser ("Made In U.S.A." in right corner.)	20.00	10.00	6.00
(70)	Johnny Rizzo	125.00	65.00	35.00
(71)	Glenn Russell	75.00	37.50	22.00
(72)	George Stirnweiss	20.00	10.00	6.00
(73)	Cecil Travis	45.00	20.00	12.50
(74)	Paul Trout	15.00	7.50	4.50
(75)	Johnny Vander Meer	65.00	32.50	20.00
(76)	Arky Vaughn (Vaughan)	22.50	11.00	6.75
(77)	Fred "Dixie" Walker ("D" on cap.)	20.00	10.00	6.00
(78)	Fred "Dixie" Walker ("D" blanked out.)	60.00	30.00	18.00
(79)	"Bucky" Walters	15.00	7.50	4.50
(80)	Lon Warneke	20.00	10.00	6.00
(81)	Ted Williams (#9 shows)	375.00	185.00	110.00
(82)	Ted Williams (#9 not showing, issued at least through 1960)	45.00	22.50	13.50
(83)	Rudy York	20.00	10.00	6.00

1947-66 Exhibits

Produced by the Exhibit Supply Co. of Chicago, these issues cover a span of 20 years. Each unnumbered, black-and-white card is printed on heavy cardboard measuring 3-3/8" x 5-3/8" and is blank-backed. The company issued new sets each year, with many players being repeated year after year. Other players appeared in only one or two years, thereby creating levels of scarcity. Many cards can be found with minor variations in the wording and placement of the credit line at bottom. Some pieces have been found printed on a semi-gloss paper stock, perhaps as proofs. Their value is 50 percent or less than the issued version.

		NM	EX	VG
Common Player:		9.00	4.50	2.75
(1)	Hank Aaron	30.00	15.00	9.00
(2)	Joe Adcock (Script signature.)	9.00	4.50	2.75
(3)	Joe Adcock (Plain signature.)	10.00	5.00	3.00
(4)	Max Alvis	30.00	15.00	9.00
(5)	Johnny Antonelli (Braves)	9.00	4.50	2.75
(6)	Johnny Antonelli (Giants)	10.00	5.00	3.00
(7)	Luis Aparicio/Portrait	12.00	6.00	3.50
(8)	Luis Aparicio/Btg	17.50	8.75	5.25
(9)	Luke Appling	20.00	10.00	6.00
(10)	Ritchie Ashburn (Phillies, first name incorrect.)	12.00	6.00	3.50
(11)	Richie Ashburn (Phillies, first name correct.)	12.00	6.00	3.50
(12)	Richie Ashburn (Cubs)	17.50	8.75	5.25
(13)	Bob Aspromonte	9.00	4.50	2.75
(14)	Toby Atwell	9.00	4.50	2.75

(15) Ed Bailey (With cap.) 10.00 5.00 3.00
(16) Ed Bailey (No cap.) 9.00 4.50 2.75
(17) Gene Baker 9.00 4.50 2.75
(18) Ernie Banks (Bat on shoulder, script signature.) 55.00 27.50 16.50
(19) Ernie Banks (Bat on shoulder, plain signature.) 17.50 8.75 5.25
(20) Ernie Banks/Portrait 30.00 15.00 9.00
(21) Steve Barber 9.00 4.50 2.75
(22) Earl Battey 10.00 5.00 3.00
(23) Matt Batts 9.00 4.50 2.75
(24) Hank Bauer (N.Y. cap.) 10.00 5.00 3.00
(25) Hank Bauer (Plain cap.) 12.00 6.00 3.50
(26) Frank Baumholtz 9.00 4.50 2.75
(27) Gene Bearden 9.00 4.50 2.75
(28) Joe Beggs 15.00 7.50 4.50
(29) Larry "Yogi" Berra 60.00 30.00 18.00
(30a) Yogi Berra ("MADE IN U.S.A." lower-right.) 35.00 17.50 10.00
(30b) Yogi Berra ("PRINTED IN U.S.A." lower-right.) 35.00 17.50 10.00
(31) Steve Bilko 10.00 5.00 3.00
(32) Ewell Blackwell/Pitching 10.00 5.00 3.00
(33) Ewell Blackwell/Portrait 9.00 4.50 2.75
(34) Don Blasingame (St. Louis cap.) 9.00 4.50 2.75
(35) Don Blasingame (Plain cap.) 17.50 8.75 5.25
(36) Ken Boyer 12.00 6.00 3.50
(37) Ralph Branca 12.00 6.00 3.50
(38) Jackie Brandt 40.00 20.00 12.00
(39) Harry Brecheen 9.00 4.50 2.75
(40) Tom Brewer 13.50 6.75 4.00
(41) Lou Brissie 10.00 5.00 3.00
(42) Bill Bruton 9.00 4.50 2.75
(43) Lew Burdette/Pitching (Side view.) 9.00 4.50 2.75
(44) Lew Burdette/Pitching (Front view.) 10.00 5.00 3.00
(45) Johnny Callison 12.50 6.25 3.75
(46) Roy Campanella 25.00 12.50 7.50
(47) Chico Carrasquel/Portrait 15.00 7.50 4.50
(48) Chico Carrasquel/Leaping 9.00 4.50 2.75
(49) George Case 13.50 6.75 4.00
(50) Hugh Casey 12.50 6.25 3.75
(51) Norm Cash 12.00 6.00 3.50
(52) Orlando Cepeda/Portrait 15.00 7.50 4.50
(53) Orlando Cepeda/Btg 15.00 7.50 4.50
(54) Bob Cerv (A's cap.) 12.00 6.00 3.50
(55) Bob Cerv (Plain cap.) 20.00 10.00 6.00
(56) Dean Chance 9.00 4.50 2.75
(57) Spud Chandler 15.00 7.50 4.50
(58) Tom Cheney 9.00 4.50 2.75
(59) Bubba Church 10.00 5.00 3.00
(60) Roberto Clemente 40.00 20.00 12.00
(61) Rocky Colavito/Portrait 35.00 17.50 10.00
(62) Rocky Colavito/Btg 25.00 12.50 7.50
(63) Choo Choo Coleman 12.00 6.00 3.50
(64) Gordy Coleman 30.00 15.00 9.00
(65) Jerry Coleman 10.00 5.00 3.00
(66) Mort Cooper 35.00 17.50 10.00
(67) Walker Cooper 9.00 4.50 2.75
(68) Roger Craig 12.00 6.00 3.50
(69) Delmar Crandall 9.00 4.50 2.75
(70) Joe Cunningham/Btg 40.00 20.00 12.00
(71) Joe Cunningham/Portrait 65.00 32.00 19.50
(72) Guy Curtwright (Curtright) 10.00 5.00 3.00
(73) Bud Daley 35.00 17.50 10.00
(74) Alvin Dark (Braves) 12.00 6.00 3.50
(75) Alvin Dark (Giants) 10.00 5.00 3.00
(76) Alvin Dark (Cubs) 12.00 6.00 3.50
(77) Murray Dickson (Murry) 25.00 12.50 7.50
(78) Bob Dillinger 12.00 6.00 3.50
(79) Dom DiMaggio 25.00 12.50 7.50
(80) Joe Dobson 30.00 15.00 9.00
(81a) Larry Doby (Bat on right border.) 40.00 20.00 12.00
(81b) Larry Doby (Bat well off right border.) 25.00 12.50 7.50
(82a) Bobby Doerr ("AN EXHIBIT CARD" lower-left.) 15.00 7.50 4.50
(82b) Bobby Doerr (No "AN EXHIBIT CARD.") 15.00 7.50 4.50
(83) Dick Donovan (Plain cap.) 12.00 6.00 3.50
(84) Dick Donovan (Sox cap.) 9.00 4.50 2.75
(85) Walter Dropo 9.00 4.50 2.75
(86) Don Drysdale (Glove at waist.) 20.00 10.00 6.00
(87) Don Drysdale/Portrait 35.00 17.50 10.00
(88) Luke Easter 15.00 7.50 4.50
(89) Bruce Edwards 15.00 7.50 4.50
(90) Del Ennis 15.00 7.50 4.50
(91) Al Evans 10.00 5.00 3.00
(92) Walter Evers 9.00 4.50 2.75
(93) Ferris Fain/Fldg 12.00 6.00 3.50
(94) Ferris Fainv 15.00 7.50 4.50
(95) Dick Farrell 9.00 4.50 2.75
(96) Ed "Whitey" Ford 30.00 15.00 9.00
(97) Whitey Ford/Pitching 30.00 15.00 9.00
(98) Whitey Ford/Portrait 175.00 85.00 50.00
(99) Dick Fowler 12.50 6.25 3.75
(100) Nelson Fox 25.00 12.50 7.50
(101) Tito Francona 9.00 4.50 2.75
(102) Bob Friend 9.00 4.50 2.75
(103) Carl Furillo 25.00 12.50 7.50
(104) Augie Galan 30.00 15.00 9.00
(105) Jim Gentile 9.00 4.50 2.75
(106) Tony Gonzalez 9.00 4.50 2.75
(107) Billy Goodman/Leaping 17.50 8.75 5.25
(108) Billy Goodman/Btg 12.00 6.00 3.50
(109) Ted Greengrass (Jim) 9.00 4.50 2.75
(110) Dick Groat 10.00 5.00 3.00
(111) Steve Gromek 9.00 4.50 2.75
(112) Johnny Groth 9.00 4.50 2.75
(113) Orval Grove 15.00 7.50 4.50
(114) Frank Gustine (Pirates uniform.) 20.00 10.00 6.00
(115) Frank Gustine (Plain uniform.) 10.00 5.00 3.00
(116) Berthold Haas 20.00 10.00 6.00
(117) Grady Hatton 10.00 5.00 3.00
(118) Jim Hegan 9.00 4.50 2.75
(119) Tom Henrich 12.00 6.00 3.50
(120) Ray Herbert 15.00 7.50 4.50
(121) Gene Hermanski 10.00 5.00 3.00
(122) Whitey Herzog 12.00 6.00 3.50
(123) Kirby Higbe 30.00 15.00 9.00
(124) Chuck Hinton 9.00 4.50 2.75
(125) Don Hoak 15.00 7.50 4.50
(126) Gil Hodges ("B" on cap.) 12.50 6.25 3.75
(127) Gil Hodges ("LA" on cap.) 25.00 12.50 7.50
(128) Johnny Hopp 13.50 6.75 4.00
(129) Elston Howard 12.00 6.00 3.50
(130) Frank Howard 15.00 7.50 4.50
(131) Ken Hubbs 30.00 15.00 9.00
(132) Tex Hughson 13.50 6.75 4.00
(133) Fred Hutchinson 60.00 30.00 18.00
(134) Monty Irvin (Monte) 12.00 6.00 3.50
(135) Joey Jay 9.00 4.50 2.75
(136) Jackie Jensen 45.00 22.50 13.50
(137) Sam Jethroe 10.00 5.00 3.00
(138) Bill Johnson 30.00 15.00 9.00
(139) Walter Judnich 13.50 6.75 4.00
(140) Al Kaline/Kneeling 25.00 12.50 7.50
(141) Al Kaline (Portrait w/ two bats.) 17.50 8.75 5.25
(142) George Kell 20.00 10.00 6.00
(143) Charley Keller 12.50 6.25 3.75
(144) Alex Kellner 9.00 4.50 2.75
(145) Kenn (Ken) Keltner 10.00 5.00 3.00
(146) Harmon Killebrew (With bat.) 50.00 25.00 15.00
(147) Harmon Killebrew/Throwing 40.00 20.00 12.00
(148) Harmon Killibrew/Portrait (Killebrew) 50.00 25.00 15.00
(149) Ellis Kinder 9.00 4.50 2.75
(150) Ralph Kiner 25.00 12.50 7.50
(151) Billy Klaus 30.00 15.00 9.00
(152) Ted Kluzewski/Btg (Kluszewski) 17.50 8.75 5.25
(153) Ted Kluzewski (Kluszewski) (Pirates uniform.) 12.00 6.00 3.50
(154) Ted Kluzewski (Kluszewski) (Plain uniform.) 17.50 8.75 5.25
(155) Don Kolloway 20.00 10.00 6.00
(156) Jim Konstanty 10.00 5.00 3.00
(157) Sandy Koufax 40.00 20.00 12.00
(158) Ed Kranepool 55.00 27.50 16.50
(159) Tony Kubek (Light background.) 16.00 8.00 4.75
(160) Tony Kubek (Dark background.) 45.00 22.50 13.50
(161) Harvey Kuenn ("D" on cap.) 30.00 15.00 9.00
(162) Harvey Kuenn (Plain cap.) 16.00 8.00 4.75
(163) Harvey Kuenn ("SF" on cap.) 15.00 7.50 4.50
(164) Whitey Kurowski 30.00 15.00 9.00
(165) Eddie Lake 12.00 6.00 3.50
(166) Jim Landis 9.00 4.50 2.75
(167) Don Larsen 10.00 5.00 3.00
(168) Bob Lemon (Glove not visible.) 15.00 7.50 4.50
(169) Bob Lemon (Glove partially visible.) 25.00 12.50 7.50
(170) Buddy Lewis 25.00 12.50 7.50
(171) Johnny Lindell 35.00 17.50 10.00
(172) Phil Linz 25.00 12.50 7.50
(173) Don Lock 25.00 12.50 7.50
(174) Whitey Lockman 9.00 4.50 2.75
(175) Johnny Logan 9.00 4.50 2.75
(176) Dale Long ("P" on cap.) 9.00 4.50 2.75
(177) Dale Long ("C" on cap.) 20.00 10.00 6.00
(178) Ed Lopat 10.00 5.00 3.00
(179) Harry Lowery (Name misspelled.) 10.00 5.00 3.00
(180) Harry Lowrey (Name correct.) 10.00 5.00 3.00
(181) Sal Maglie 9.00 4.50 2.75
(182) Art Mahaffey 10.00 5.00 3.00
(183) Hank Majeski 9.00 4.50 2.75
(184) Frank Malzone 16.00 8.00 4.75
(185) Mickey Mantle/Btg (Full-length.) 140.00 70.00 40.00
(186) Mickey Mantle/Btg (Waist-up, "ck" in "Mickey" connected.) 120.00 60.00 35.00
(187) Mickey Mantle/Btg (Waist-up, "c k" in "Mickey" connected.) 175.00 85.00 50.00
(188) Mickey Mantle/Portrait 600.00 300.00 180.00
(189) Martin Marion 20.00 10.00 6.00
(190) Roger Maris 25.00 12.50 7.50
(191) Willard Marshall 10.00 5.00 3.00
(192) Eddie Matthews (Name incorrect.) 16.00 8.00 4.75
(193) Eddie Mathews (Name correct.) 30.00 15.00 9.00
(194) Ed Mayo 10.00 5.00 3.00
(195) Willie Mays/Btg 45.00 22.50 13.50
(196) Willie Mays/Portrait 60.00 30.00 18.00
(197) Bill Mazeroski/Portrait 16.00 8.00 4.75
(198) Bill Mazeroski/Btg 16.00 8.00 4.75
(199) Ken McBride 15.00 7.50 4.50
(200) Barney McCaskey (McCosky) 13.50 6.75 4.00
(201) Barney McCoskey (McCosky) 100.00 50.00 30.00
(202) Lindy McDaniel 9.00 4.50 2.75
(203a) Gil McDougald ("MADE IN U.S.A." lower-right.) 15.00 7.50 4.50
(203b) Gil McDougald ("PRINTED IN U.S.A." lower-right.) 15.00 7.50 4.50
(204) Albert Mele 30.00 15.00 9.00
(205) Sam Mele 20.00 10.00 6.00
(206) Orestes Minoso ("C" on cap.) 12.50 6.25 3.75
(207) Orestes Minoso (Sox on cap.) 9.00 4.50 2.75
(208) Dale Mitchell 9.00 4.50 2.75
(209) Wally Moon 12.00 6.00 3.50
(210) Don Mueller 10.00 5.00 3.00
(211) Stan Musial/Kneeling 60.00 30.00 18.00
(212) Stan Musial/Btg 70.00 35.00 20.00
(213) Charley Neal 15.00 7.50 4.50
(214) Don Newcombe (Shaking hands.) 25.00 12.50 7.50
(215) Don Newcombe (Dodgers on jacket.) 9.00 4.50 2.75
(216) Don Newcombe (Plain jacket.) 10.00 5.00 3.00
(217) Hal Newhouser 35.00 17.50 10.00
(218) Ron Northey 20.00 10.00 6.00
(219) Bill O'Dell 9.00 4.50 2.75
(220) Joe Page 20.00 10.00 6.00
(221) Satchel Paige 90.00 45.00 25.00
(222) Milt Pappas 9.00 4.50 2.75
(223) Camilo Pascual 9.00 4.50 2.75
(224) Albie Pearson 25.00 12.50 7.50
(225) Johnny Pesky 9.00 4.50 2.75
(226) Gary Peters 25.00 12.50 7.50
(227) Dave Philley 9.00 4.50 2.75
(228) Billy Pierce 9.00 4.50 2.75
(229) Jimmy Piersall 15.00 7.50 4.50
(230) Vada Pinson 12.50 6.25 3.75
(231) Bob Porterfield 9.00 4.50 2.75
(232) John "Boog" Powell 45.00 22.50 13.50
(233) Vic Raschi 15.00 7.50 4.50
(234) Harold "Peewee" Reese/Fldg (Ball partially visible.) 35.00 17.50 10.00
(235) Harold "Peewee" Reese/Fldg (Ball not visible.) 25.00 12.50 7.50
(236) Del Rice 12.50 6.25 3.75
(237) Bobby Richardson 125.00 60.00 35.00
(238) Phil Rizzuto 25.00 12.50 7.50
(239) Robin Roberts (Script signature.) 14.50 7.25 4.25
(240) Robin Roberts (Plain signature.) 25.00 12.50 7.50
(241) Brooks Robinson 17.50 8.75 5.25
(242) Eddie Robinson 9.00 4.50 2.75
(243) Floyd Robinson 17.50 8.75 5.25
(244) Frankie Robinson 60.00 30.00 18.00
(245) Jackie Robinson 50.00 25.00 15.00
(246) Preacher Roe 35.00 17.50 10.00
(247) Bob Rogers (Rodgers) 30.00 15.00 9.00
(248) Richard Rollins 25.00 12.50 7.50
(249) Pete Runnels 13.50 6.75 4.00
(250) John Sain 12.50 6.25 3.75
(251) Ron Santo 25.00 12.50 7.50
(252) Henry Sauer 10.00 5.00 3.00
(253) Carl Sawatski ("M" on cap.) 9.00 4.50 2.75
(254) Carl Sawatski ("P" on cap.) 9.00 4.50 2.75
(255) Carl Sawatski (Plain cap.) 17.50 8.75 5.25
(256) Johnny Schmitz 10.00 5.00 3.00
(257) Red Schoendeinst/Fldg (Schoendienst) (Name in white.) 25.00 12.50 7.50
(258) Red Schoendeinst/Fldg (Schoendienst) (Name in red-brown.) 30.00 15.00 9.00
(259) Red Schoendinst/Btg (Schoendienst) 12.50 6.25 3.75
(260) Herb Score ("C" on cap.) 15.00 7.50 4.50
(261) Herb Score (Plain cap.) 17.50 8.75 5.25
(262) Andy Seminick 9.00 4.50 2.75
(263) Rip Sewell 20.00 10.00 6.00
(264) Norm Siebern 9.00 4.50 2.75
(265) Roy Sievers/Btg 15.00 7.50 4.50
(266) Roy Sievers/Portrait ("W" on cap, light background.) 12.00 6.00 3.50
(267) Roy Sievers/Portrait ("W" on cap, dark background.) 10.00 5.00 3.00
(268) Roy Sievers/Portrait (Plain cap.) 20.00 10.00 6.00
(269) Curt Simmons 10.00 5.00 3.00
(270) Dick Sisler 10.00 5.00 3.00
(271) Bill Skowron 12.50 6.25 3.75
(272) Bill "Moose" Skowron 65.00 32.50 20.00
(273) Enos Slaughter 20.00 10.00 6.00
(274) Duke Snider ("B" on cap.) 22.50 11.00 6.75
(275) Duke Snider ("LA" on cap.) 20.00 10.00 6.00
(276) Warren Spahn ("B" on cap.) 20.00 10.00 6.00
(277) Warren Spahn ("M" on cap.) 20.00 10.00 6.00
(278) Stanley Spence 16.00 8.00 4.75
(279) Ed Stanky (Plain uniform.) 17.50 8.75 5.25
(280) Ed Stanky (Giants uniform.) 10.00 5.00 3.00
(281) Vern Stephens/Btg 10.00 5.00 3.00
(282) Vern Stephens/Portrait 10.00 5.00 3.00
(283) Ed Stewart 10.00 5.00 3.00
(284) Snuffy Stirnweiss 12.50 6.25 3.75
(285) George "Birdie" Tebbetts 17.50 8.75 5.25
(286) Frankie Thomas (Photo actually Bob Skinner.) 35.00 17.50 10.00
(287) Frank Thomas/Portrait "Best Wishes.") 16.00 8.00 4.75
(288) Lee Thomas 9.00 4.50 2.75
(289) Bobby Thomson 25.00 12.50 7.50
(290) Earl Torgeson (Braves uniform.) 9.00 4.50 2.75
(291) Earl Torgeson (Plain uniform.) 10.00 5.00 3.00
(292) Gus Triandos 12.00 6.00 3.50
(293) Virgil Trucks 9.00 4.50 2.75
(294) Johnny Vandermeer (VanderMeer) 25.00 12.50 7.50
(295) Emil Verban 12.00 6.00 3.50
(296) Mickey Vernon/Throwing 15.00 7.50 4.50
(297) Mickey Vernon/Btg 9.00 4.50 2.75
(298) Bill Voiselle 30.00 15.00 9.00
(299) Leon Wagner 6.50 3.25 1.75
(300) Eddie Waitkus/Throwing (Chicago uniform.) 40.00 20.00 12.00
(301) Eddie Waitkus/Throwing (Plain uniform.) 10.00 5.00 3.00
(302) Eddie Waitkus/Portrait 15.00 7.50 4.50
(303) Dick Wakefield 10.00 5.00 3.00
(304) Harry Walker 40.00 20.00 12.00
(305) Bucky Walters 20.00 10.00 6.00
(306) Pete Ward 75.00 37.50 22.50
(307) Herman Wehmeier 10.00 5.00 3.00
(308) Vic Wertz/Btg 9.00 4.50 2.75
(309) Vic Wertz/Portrait 9.00 4.50 2.75
(310) Wally Westlake 10.00 5.00 3.00
(311) Wes Westrum 17.50 8.75 5.25

(312)	Billy Williams	20.00	10.00	6.00
(313)	Maurice Wills	15.00	7.50	4.50
(314)	Gene Woodling (Script signature.)	9.00	4.50	2.75
(315)	Gene Woodling (Plain signature.)	12.00	6.00	3.50
(316)	Taffy Wright	10.00	5.00	3.00
(317)	Carl Yastrazemski (Yastrzemski)	200.00	100.00	60.00
(318)	Al Zarilla	12.50	6.25	3.75
(319)	Gus Zernial (Script signature.)	9.00	4.50	2.75
(320)	Gus Zernial (Plain signature.)	12.00	6.00	3.50
(321)	Braves Team - 1948	50.00	25.00	15.00
(322)	Dodgers Team - 1949	75.00	37.50	22.50
(323)	Dodgers Team - 1952	65.00	32.50	20.00
(324)	Dodgers Team - 1955	125.00	60.00	35.00
(325)	Dodgers Team - 1956	60.00	30.00	18.00
(326)	Giants Team - 1951	60.00	30.00	18.00
(327a)	Giants Team - 1954 (Plain back.)	50.00	25.00	15.00
(328)	Indians Team - 1948	55.00	27.50	16.50
(329)	Indians Team - 1954	50.00	25.00	15.00
(330)	Phillies Team - 1950	40.00	20.00	12.00
(331)	Yankees Team - 1949	60.00	30.00	18.00
(332)	Yankees Team - 1950	65.00	32.50	20.00
(333)	Yankees Team - 1951	65.00	32.50	20.00
(334)	Yankees Team - 1952	70.00	35.00	20.00
(335)	Yankees Team - 1955	70.00	35.00	20.00
(336)	Yankees Team - 1956	70.00	35.00	20.00

1948 Baseball's Great Hall of Fame Exhibits

Titled "Baseball's Great Hall of Fame," this 32-player set features black and white player photos against a gray background. The photos are accented by Greek columns on either side with brief player information printed at the bottom. The blank-backed cards are unnumbered and are listed here alphabetically. The cards measure 3-3/8" x 5-3/8". Collectors should be aware that 24 cards from this set were reprinted on whiter stock in 1974.

		NM	EX	VG
Complete Set (33):		500.00	250.00	150.00
Common Player:		7.50	3.75	2.25
(1)	Grover Cleveland Alexander	15.00	7.50	4.50
(2)	Roger Bresnahan	7.50	3.75	2.25
(3)	Frank Chance	7.50	3.75	2.25
(4)	Jack Chesbro	7.50	3.75	2.25
(5)	Fred Clarke	7.50	3.75	2.25
(6)	Ty Cobb	55.00	27.50	16.50
(7)	Mickey Cochrane	7.50	3.75	2.25
(8)	Eddie Collins	7.50	3.75	2.25
(9)	Hugh Duffy	7.50	3.75	2.25
(10)	Johnny Evers	7.50	3.75	2.25
(11)	Frankie Frisch	7.50	3.75	2.25
(12)	Lou Gehrig	35.00	17.50	10.00
(13)	Clark Griffith	7.50	3.75	2.25
(14)	Robert "Lefty" Grove	7.50	3.75	2.25
(15)	Rogers Hornsby	10.00	5.00	3.00
(16)	Carl Hubbell	7.50	3.75	2.25
(17)	Hughie Jennings	7.50	3.75	2.25
(18)	Walter Johnson	15.00	7.50	4.50
(19)	Willie Keeler	7.50	3.75	2.25
(20)	Napolean Lajoie	7.50	3.75	2.25
(21)	Connie Mack	7.50	3.75	2.25
(22)	Christy Matthewson (Mathewson)	20.00	10.00	6.00
(23)	John J. McGraw	7.50	3.75	2.25
(24)	Eddie Plank	7.50	3.75	2.25
(25)	Babe Ruth/Btg	60.00	30.00	18.00
(26)	Babe Ruth (Standing with bats.)	250.00	125.00	75.00
(27)	George Sisler	7.50	3.75	2.25
(28)	Tris Speaker	10.00	5.00	3.00
(29)	Joe Tinker	7.50	3.75	2.25
(30)	Rube Waddell	7.50	3.75	2.25
(31)	Honus Wagner	25.00	12.50	7.50
(32)	Ed Walsh	7.50	3.75	2.25
(33)	Cy Young	15.00	7.50	4.50

1953 Canadian Exhibits

This Canadian-issued set consists of 64 cards and includes both major leaguers and players from the Montreal Royals of the International League. The cards are slightly smaller than the U.S. exhibit cards, measuring 3-1/4" x 5-1/4", and are numbered. The blank-backed cards were printed on gray stock. Card numbers 1-32 have a green or red tint, while card numbers 33-64 have a blue or reddish-brown tint.

		NM	EX	VG
Complete Set (64):		1,750	875.00	525.00
Common Player (1-32):		15.00	7.50	4.50
Common Player (33-64):		9.00	4.50	2.75
1	Preacher Roe	20.00	10.00	6.00
2	Luke Easter	20.00	10.00	6.00
3	Gene Bearden	15.00	7.50	4.50
4	Chico Carrasquel	20.00	10.00	6.00
5	Vic Raschi	20.00	10.00	6.00
6	Monty (Monte) Irvin	30.00	15.00	9.00
7	Henry Sauer	15.00	7.50	4.50
8	Ralph Branca	20.00	10.00	6.00
9	Ed Stanky	20.00	10.00	6.00
10	Sam Jethroe	15.00	7.50	4.50
11	Larry Doby	30.00	15.00	9.00
12	Hal Newhouser	30.00	15.00	9.00
13	Gil Hodges	50.00	25.00	15.00
14	Harry Brecheen	15.00	7.50	4.50
15	Ed Lopat	20.00	10.00	6.00
16	Don Newcombe	25.00	12.50	7.50
17	Bob Feller	60.00	30.00	18.00
18	Tommy Holmes	15.00	7.50	4.50
19	Jackie Robinson	65.00	35.00	20.00
20	Roy Campanella	55.00	25.00	15.00
21	Harold "Peewee" Reese	50.00	25.00	15.00
22	Ralph Kiner	40.00	20.00	12.00
23	Dom DiMaggio	25.00	12.50	7.50
24	Bobby Doerr	30.00	15.00	9.00
25	Phil Rizzuto	50.00	25.00	15.00
26	Bob Elliott	15.00	7.50	4.50
27	Tom Henrich	20.00	10.00	6.00
28	Joe DiMaggio	200.00	100.00	60.00
29	Harry Lowery (Lowrey)	15.00	7.50	4.50
30	Ted Williams	75.00	37.50	22.50
31	Bob Lemon	40.00	20.00	12.00
32	Warren Spahn	50.00	25.00	15.00
33	Don Hoak	25.00	12.50	7.50
34	Bob Alexander	15.00	7.50	4.50
35	John Simmons	15.00	7.50	4.50
36	Steve Lembo	15.00	7.50	4.50
37	Norman Larker	20.00	10.00	6.00
38	Bob Ludwick	15.00	7.50	4.50
39	Walter Moryn	20.00	10.00	6.00
40	Charlie Thompson	15.00	7.50	4.50
41	Ed Roebuck	20.00	10.00	6.00
42	Russell Rose	15.00	7.50	4.50
43	Edmundo (Sandy) Amoros	25.00	12.50	7.50
44	Bob Milliken	15.00	7.50	4.50
45	Art Fabbro	15.00	7.50	4.50
46	Spook Jacobs	15.00	7.50	4.50
47	Carmen Mauro	15.00	7.50	4.50
48	Walter Fiala	15.00	7.50	4.50
49	Rocky Nelson	15.00	7.50	4.50
50	Tom La Sorda (Lasorda)	60.00	30.00	18.00
51	Ronnie Lee	15.00	7.50	4.50
52	Hampton Coleman	15.00	7.50	4.50
53	Frank Marchio	15.00	7.50	4.50
54	William Sampson	15.00	7.50	4.50
55	Gil Mills	15.00	7.50	4.50
56	Al Ronning	15.00	7.50	4.50
57	Stan Musial	75.00	37.50	22.50
58	Walker Cooper	9.00	4.50	2.75
59	Mickey Vernon	9.00	4.50	2.75
60	Del Ennis	9.00	4.50	2.75
61	Walter Alston	40.00	20.00	12.00
62	Dick Sisler	9.00	4.50	2.75
63	Billy Goodman	9.00	4.50	2.75
64	Alex Kellner	9.00	4.50	2.75

1955 Exhibits - Post Card Backs

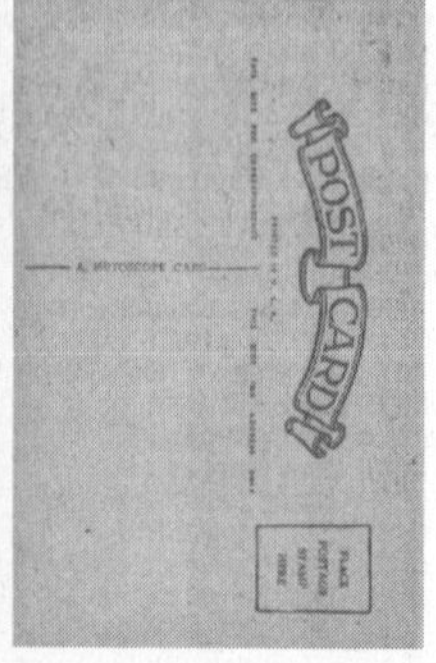

For an unknkown purpose, the 64 Exhibit cards issued in 1955 (including many re-issued from earlier years) were produced in a very limited edition with a post card back, as opposed to the blank-back format usually found on the 3-3/8" x 5-3/8" cards.

		NM	EX	VG
Complete Set (64):		3,000	1,500	900.00
Common Player:		25.00	12.50	7.50
(1)	Joe Adcock	25.00	12.50	7.50
(2)	Ritchie (Richie) Ashburn	45.00	22.50	13.50
(3)	Toby Atwell	25.00	12.50	7.50
(4)	Gene Baker	25.00	12.50	7.50
(5)	Ernie Banks (Bat on shoulder, printed name.)	75.00	37.50	22.50
(6)	Matt Batts	25.00	12.50	7.50
(7)	Frank Baumholtz	25.00	12.50	7.50
(8)	Yogi Berra	125.00	65.00	35.00
(9)	Steve Bilko	25.00	12.50	7.50
(10)	Roy Campanella	60.00	30.00	18.00
(11)	Chico Carrasquel/Leaping	25.00	12.50	7.50
(12)	Alvin Dark (Giants)	25.00	12.50	7.50
(13)	Larry Doby	45.00	22.50	13.50
(14)	Walter Dropo	25.00	12.50	7.50
(15)	Del Ennis	25.00	12.50	7.50
(16)	Ferris Fain/Portrait	45.00	22.50	13.50
(17)	Bob Feller (Yours truly.)	100.00	50.00	30.00
(18)	Billy Goodman/Leaping	45.00	22.50	13.50
(19)	Ted (Jim) Greengrass	25.00	12.50	7.50
(20)	Steve Gromek	25.00	12.50	7.50
(21)	Johnny Groth	25.00	12.50	7.50
(22)	Jim Hegan	25.00	12.50	7.50
(23)	Gene Hermanski	25.00	12.50	7.50
(24)	Gil Hodges (B on cap.)	50.00	25.00	15.00
(25)	Monty (Monte) Irvin	45.00	22.50	13.50
(26)	Al Kaline/Kneeling	75.00	37.50	22.50
(27)	George Kell	45.00	22.50	13.50
(28)	Alex Kellner	25.00	12.50	7.50
(29)	Ted Kluzewski/Btg (Kluszewski)	60.00	30.00	18.00
(30)	Bob Lemon (Glove not showing.)	45.00	22.50	13.50
(31)	Whitey Lockman	25.00	12.50	7.50
(32)	Ed Lopat	30.00	15.00	9.00
(33)	Sal Maglie	25.00	12.50	7.50
(34)	Mickey Mantle/Btg (Waist-up.)	400.00	200.00	120.00
(35)	Ed Matthews (Mathews)	60.00	30.00	18.00
(36)	Willie Mays/Btg	200.00	100.00	60.00
(37)	Gil McDougald	30.00	15.00	9.00
(38)	Sam Mele	25.00	12.50	7.50
(39)	Orestes Minoso (C on cap.)	45.00	22.50	13.50
(40)	Dale Mitchell	25.00	12.50	7.50
(41)	Stan Musial/Kneeling	100.00	50.00	30.00
(42)	Andy Pafko (Yours truly.) (C on cap.)	25.00	12.50	7.50
(43)	Bob Porterfield	25.00	12.50	7.50
(44)	Vic Raschi	25.00	12.50	7.50
(45)	Harold "Peewee" Reese	60.00	30.00	18.00
(46)	Phil Rizzuto	60.00	30.00	18.00
(47)	Robin Roberts	45.00	22.50	13.50
(48)	Jackie Robinson	150.00	75.00	45.00
(49)	Henry Sauer	25.00	12.50	7.50
(50)	Johnny Schmitz	25.00	12.50	7.50
(51)	Red Schoendinst (Schoendienst)	45.00	22.50	13.50
(52)	Andy Seminick	25.00	12.50	7.50
(53)	Duke Snider (B on cap.)	60.00	30.00	18.00
(54)	Warren Spahn (B on cap.)	60.00	30.00	18.00
(55)	Vern Stephens/Portrait	25.00	12.50	7.50
(56)	Earl Torgeson (Braves uniform.)	25.00	12.50	7.50
(57)	Virgil Trucks	25.00	12.50	7.50
(58)	Mickey Vernon/Btg	25.00	12.50	7.50
(59)	Eddie Waitkus	25.00	12.50	7.50
(60)	Vic Wertz/Btg	25.00	12.50	7.50
(61)	Gene Woodling	25.00	12.50	7.50
(62)	Gus Zernial	25.00	12.50	7.50
(63)	Cleveland Indians 1954 American League Champions	150.00	75.00	45.00
(64)	New York Giants 1954 National League Champions	150.00	75.00	45.00

1959 Exhibits - Dad's Cookies

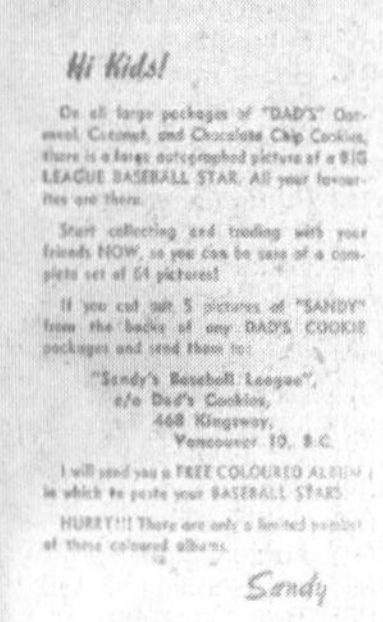

(See 1959 Dad's Cookies.)

1961 Exhibits - Wrigley Field

Distributed at Chicago's Wrigley Field circa 1961, this 24-card set features members of the Baseball Hall of Fame. The cards measure 3-3/8" x 5-3/8" and include the player's full name along the bottom. They were printed on gray stock and have a postcard back. The set is unnumbered.

	NM	EX	VG
Complete Set (24):	750.00	375.00	225.00
Common Player:	10.00	5.00	3.00
(1) Grover Cleveland Alexander	15.00	7.50	4.50
(2) Adrian Constantine Anson	12.50	6.25	3.75
(3) John Franklin Baker	10.00	5.00	3.00
(4) Roger Phillip Bresnahan	10.00	5.00	3.00
(5) Mordecai Peter Brown	10.00	5.00	3.00
(6) Frank Leroy Chance	10.00	5.00	3.00
(7) Tyrus Raymond Cobb	145.00	75.00	45.00
(8) Edward Trowbridge Collins	10.00	5.00	3.00
(9) James J. Collins	10.00	5.00	3.00
(10) John Joseph Evers	10.00	5.00	3.00
(11) Henry Louis Gehrig	145.00	75.00	45.00
(12) Clark C. Griffith	10.00	5.00	3.00
(13) Walter Perry Johnson	25.00	12.50	7.50
(14) Anthony Michael Lazzeri	10.00	5.00	3.00
(15) James Walter Vincent Maranville	10.00	5.00	3.00
(16) Christopher Mathewson	30.00	15.00	9.00
(17) John Joseph McGraw	10.00	5.00	3.00
(18) Melvin Thomas Ott	10.00	5.00	3.00
(19) Herbert Jeffries Pennock	10.00	5.00	3.00
(20) George Herman Ruth	180.00	90.00	55.00
(21) Aloysius Harry Simmons	10.00	5.00	3.00
(22) Tristram Speaker	25.00	12.50	7.50
(23) Joseph B. Tinker	10.00	5.00	3.00
(24) John Peter Wagner	40.00	20.00	12.00

1962 Pittsburgh Exhibits

The attributed date is approximate since none is shown on the cards; nor is a credit line to the manufacturer. Player content suggests Pittsburgh was the center of distribution and veteran collectors report having received the cards in penny arcade vending machines at Kennywood Amusement Park near there. It has also been reported that the cards were given over the counter as prizes for getting a winning gumball from a machine. The 3-1/4" x 5-1/4" cards are printed in black-and-white, or red, black and white. They are usually blank-backed, but examples have been seen with apprarent prize references printed on back. Most of the card "denominations" can be found with more than one subject. Besides the ballplayers listed here, the set contained TV and movie cowboys, rock-and-roll stars, boxers, wrestlers and cartoon characters.

	NM	EX	VG
Complete Set (81):	2,500	1,250	750.00
Common Player:	5.00	2.50	1.50
AC Bill Mazeroski	25.00	12.50	7.50
2C Whitey Ford	30.00	15.00	9.00
2C Al Kaline	20.00	10.00	6.00
2C Pirates logo cartoon	5.00	2.50	1.50
4C Frank Robinson	20.00	10.00	6.00
4C Babe Ruth	125.00	65.00	35.00
5C Wilmer Mizell	5.00	2.50	1.50
5C Mickey Mantle	175.00	85.00	50.00
5C Honus Wagner	35.00	17.50	10.00
6C Eddie Mathews	20.00	10.00	6.00
6C Willie Mays	90.00	45.00	27.00
7C Dodgers' "Bum" cartoon logo	5.00	2.50	1.50
7C Eddie Mathews	20.00	10.00	6.00
7C Willie Mays	90.00	45.00	27.00
8C Walter Johnson	20.00	10.00	6.00
8C Mickey Mantle	175.00	85.00	50.00
8C Wilmer Mizell	5.00	2.50	1.50
9C Hank Aaron	90.00	45.00	27.00
9C Frank Robinson	20.00	10.00	6.00
10C Lew Burdette	5.00	2.50	1.50
JC Harvey Haddix	5.00	2.50	1.50
JC Bill Mazeroski	25.00	12.50	7.50
JC Al McBean	5.00	2.50	1.50
QC Ty Cobb	60.00	30.00	18.00
QC Whitey Ford	30.00	15.00	9.00
QC Don Leppert	5.00	2.50	1.50
KC Al Kaline	20.00	10.00	6.00
KC Honus Wagner	35.00	17.50	10.00
AS Lew Burdette	5.00	2.50	1.50
AS Ty Cobb	60.00	30.00	18.00
2S Smoky Burgess	5.00	2.50	1.50
3S Don Hoak	5.00	2.50	1.50
4S Roy Face	5.00	2.50	1.50
5S Roberto Clemente	125.00	65.00	35.00
5S Danny Murtaugh	5.00	2.50	1.50
6S Christy Mathewson	25.00	12.50	7.50
6S Dick Stuart	5.00	2.50	1.50
7S Christy Mathewson	25.00	12.50	7.50
7S Dick Stuart	5.00	2.50	1.50
8S Danny Murtaugh	5.00	2.50	1.50
9S Roy Face	5.00	2.50	1.50
10S Don Hoak	5.00	2.50	1.50
JS Smoky Burgess	5.00	2.50	1.50
QS Walter Johnson	20.00	10.00	6.00
QS Babe Ruth	125.00	65.00	35.00
KS Hank Aaron	90.00	45.00	27.00
KS Harvey Haddix	5.00	2.50	1.50
AH Don Drysdale	20.00	10.00	6.00
AH Ken Boyer	5.00	2.50	1.50
2H Satchel Paige	60.00	30.00	18.00
3H Rocky Colavito	20.00	10.00	6.00
4H Stan Musial	50.00	25.00	15.00
4H Bobby Richardson	15.00	7.50	4.50
5H Ken Boyer	5.00	2.50	1.50
5H Harmon Killebrew	20.00	10.00	6.00
6H Luis Aparicio	20.00	10.00	6.00
6H Ralph Kiner	20.00	10.00	6.00
7H Sandy Koufax	75.00	37.50	22.00
8H Warren Spahn	20.00	10.00	6.00
9H Jimmy Piersall	5.00	2.50	1.50
10H Yogi Berra	30.00	15.00	9.00
10H Ralph Kiner	20.00	10.00	6.00
JH Orlando Cepeda	20.00	10.00	6.00
JH Ken Boyer	5.00	2.50	1.50
QH Roger Maris	75.00	37.50	22.00
QH Stan Musial	50.00	25.00	15.00
KH Bob Purkey	5.00	2.50	1.50
AD Don Drysdale	20.00	10.00	6.00
AD Don Hoak	5.00	2.50	1.50
2D Satchel Paige	60.00	30.00	18.00
6D Luis Aparicio	20.00	10.00	6.00
6D Ernie Banks	25.00	12.50	7.50
7D Bill Virdon	5.00	2.50	1.50
7D Sandy Koufax	75.00	37.50	22.00
8D Bob Skinner	5.00	2.50	1.50
9D Dick Groat	5.00	2.50	1.50
10D Vernon Law	5.00	2.50	1.50
JD Joe Adcock	5.00	2.50	1.50
JD Orlando Cepeda	20.00	10.00	6.00
QD Roger Maris	75.00	37.50	22.00
KD Bob Friend	5.00	2.50	1.50

1962 Statistic Back Exhibits

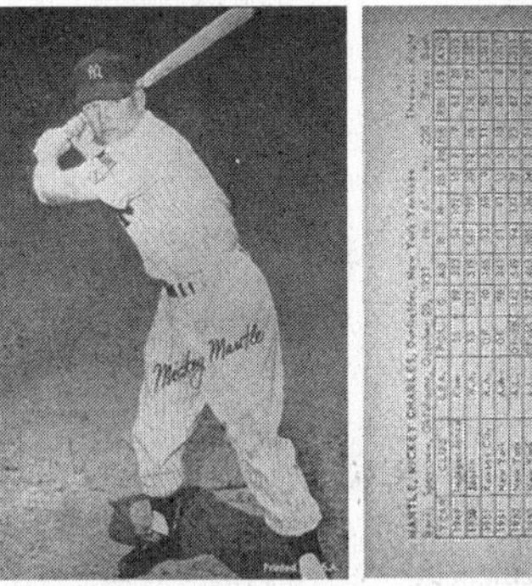

In 1962, the Exhibit Supply Co. added career statistics to the yearly set they produced. The black-and-white, unnumbered cards measure 3-3/8" x 5-3/8". The statistics found on the back are printed in black or red.

	NM	EX	VG
Complete Set (32):	500.00	250.00	150.00
Common Player:	6.00	3.00	1.75
Red Backs: 1.5X			
(1) Hank Aaron	35.00	17.50	10.00
(2) Luis Aparicio	15.00	7.50	4.50
(3) Ernie Banks	25.00	12.50	7.50
(4) Larry "Yogi" Berra	25.00	12.50	7.50
(5) Ken Boyer	7.50	3.75	2.25
(6) Lew Burdette	6.00	3.00	1.75
(7) Norm Cash	7.50	3.75	2.25
(8) Orlando Cepeda	15.00	7.50	4.50
(9) Roberto Clemente	50.00	25.00	15.00
(10) Rocky Colavito	15.00	7.50	4.50
(11) Ed "Whitey" Ford	17.50	8.75	5.25
(12) Nelson Fox	15.00	7.50	4.50
(13) Tito Francona	6.00	3.00	1.75
(14) Jim Gentile	6.00	3.00	1.75
(15) Dick Groat	6.00	3.00	1.75
(16) Don Hoak	6.00	3.00	1.75
(17) Al Kaline	17.50	8.75	5.25
(18) Harmon Killebrew	17.50	8.75	5.25
(19) Sandy Koufax	30.00	15.00	9.00
(20) Jim Landis	6.00	3.00	1.75
(21) Art Mahaffey	6.00	3.00	1.75
(22) Frank Malzone	6.00	3.00	1.75
(23) Mickey Mantle	100.00	50.00	30.00
(24) Roger Maris	17.50	8.75	5.25
(25) Eddie Mathews	17.50	8.75	5.25
(26) Willie Mays	35.00	17.50	10.00
(27) Wally Moon	6.00	3.00	1.75
(28) Stan Musial	30.00	15.00	9.00
(29) Milt Pappas	6.00	3.00	1.75
(30) Vada Pinson	7.50	3.75	2.25
(31) Norm Siebern	6.00	3.00	1.75
(32) Warren Spahn	17.50	8.75	5.25

1963 Statistic Back Exhibits

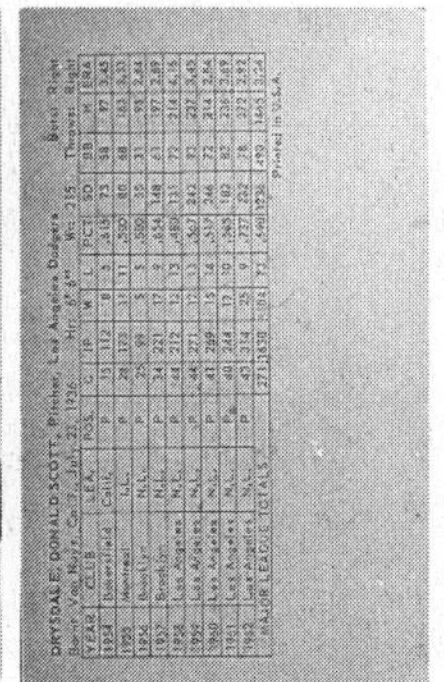

The Exhibit Supply Co. issued a 64-card set with career statistics on the backs of the cards in 1963. The unnumbered, black-and-white cards are printed on thick cardboard and measure 3-3/8" x 5-3/8" in size. The statistics on the back are only found printed in red.

	NM	EX	VG
Complete Set (64):	900.00	450.00	275.00
Common Player:	7.50	3.75	2.25
(1) Hank Aaron	35.00	17.50	10.00
(2) Luis Aparicio	15.00	7.50	4.50
(3) Bob Aspromonte	7.50	3.75	2.25
(4) Ernie Banks	25.00	12.50	7.50
(5) Steve Barber	7.50	3.75	2.25
(6) Earl Battey	7.50	3.75	2.25
(7) Larry "Yogi" Berra	25.00	12.50	7.50
(8) Ken Boyer	9.00	4.50	2.75
(9) Lew Burdette	7.50	3.75	2.25
(10) Johnny Callison	7.50	3.75	2.25
(11) Norm Cash	9.00	4.50	2.75
(12) Orlando Cepeda	15.00	7.50	4.50
(13) Dean Chance	7.50	3.75	2.25
(14) Tom Cheney	7.50	3.75	2.25
(15) Roberto Clemente	40.00	20.00	12.00
(16) Rocky Colavito	15.00	7.50	4.50
(17) Choo Choo Coleman	7.50	3.75	2.25
(18) Roger Craig	7.50	3.75	2.25
(19) Joe Cunningham	7.50	3.75	2.25
(20) Don Drysdale	15.00	7.50	4.50
(21) Dick Farrell	7.50	3.75	2.25
(22) Ed "Whitey" Ford	20.00	10.00	6.00
(23) Nelson Fox	15.00	7.50	4.50
(24) Tito Francona	7.50	3.75	2.25
(25) Jim Gentile	7.50	3.75	2.25
(26) Tony Gonzalez	7.50	3.75	2.25
(27) Dick Groat	7.50	3.75	2.25
(28) Ray Herbert	7.50	3.75	2.25
(29) Chuck Hinton	7.50	3.75	2.25
(30) Don Hoak	7.50	3.75	2.25
(31) Frank Howard	9.00	4.50	2.75
(32) Ken Hubbs	12.00	6.00	3.50
(33) Joey Jay	7.50	3.75	2.25
(34) Al Kaline	15.00	7.50	4.50
(35) Harmon Killebrew	15.00	7.50	4.50
(36) Sandy Koufax	30.00	15.00	9.00
(37) Harvey Kuenn	7.50	3.75	2.25
(38) Jim Landis	7.50	3.75	2.25
(39) Art Mahaffey	7.50	3.75	2.25
(40) Frank Malzone	7.50	3.75	2.25
(41) Mickey Mantle	150.00	75.00	45.00
(42) Roger Maris	15.00	7.50	4.50
(43) Eddie Mathews	15.00	7.50	4.50
(44) Willie Mays	35.00	17.50	10.00
(45) Bill Mazeroski	15.00	7.50	4.50
(46) Ken McBride	7.50	3.75	2.25
(47) Wally Moon	7.50	3.75	2.25
(48) Stan Musial	30.00	15.00	9.00
(49) Charlie Neal	7.50	3.75	2.25
(50) Bill O'Dell	7.50	3.75	2.25
(51) Milt Pappas	7.50	3.75	2.25
(52) Camilo Pascual	7.50	3.75	2.25
(53) Jimmy Piersall	9.00	4.50	2.75
(54) Vada Pinson	9.00	4.50	2.75
(55) Brooks Robinson	20.00	10.00	6.00
(56) Frankie Robinson	20.00	10.00	6.00
(57) Pete Runnels	7.50	3.75	2.25
(58) Ron Santo	9.00	4.50	2.75
(59) Norm Siebern	7.50	3.75	2.25
(60) Warren Spahn	20.00	10.00	6.00
(61) Lee Thomas	7.50	3.75	2.25
(62) Leon Wagner	7.50	3.75	2.25
(63) Billy Williams	15.00	7.50	4.50
(64) Maurice Wills	13.50	6.75	4.00

1974 Baseball's Great Hall of Fame Exhibits

Two dozen of the cards from the 1948 issue were reprinted in 1974 by the original publisher, Exhibit Supply Co., Chicago. The 1974 reissues are in the same 3-3/8" x 5-3/8"

format as the originals, and in the same design. They are blank-backed and printed on a thinner, slicker cardboard stock than the 1948 cards. The reprints can be found printed in black, blue or brown. The unnumbered cards are checklisted here alphabetically.

		NM	EX	VG
Complete Set (24):		20.00	10.00	6.00
Common Player:		3.00	1.50	.90
(1)	Grover Cleveland Alexander	3.50	1.75	1.00
(2)	Roger Bresnahan	3.00	1.50	.90
(3)	Frank Chance	3.00	1.50	.90
(4)	Jack Chesbro	3.00	1.50	.90
(5)	Fred Clarke	3.00	1.50	.90
(6)	Ty Cobb	10.00	5.00	3.00
(7)	Mickey Cochrane	3.00	1.50	.90
(8)	Eddie Collins	3.00	1.50	.90
(9)	Johnny Evers	3.00	1.50	.90
(10)	Frankie Frisch	3.00	1.50	.90
(11)	Clark Griffith	3.00	1.50	.90
(12)	Robert "Lefty" Grove	3.00	1.50	.90
(13)	Rogers Hornsby	4.00	2.00	1.25
(14)	Hughie Jennings	3.00	1.50	.90
(15)	Walter Johnson	5.00	2.50	1.50
(16)	Connie Mack	3.00	1.50	.90
(17)	Christy Mathewson	5.00	2.50	1.50
(18)	John McGraw	3.00	1.50	.90
(19)	George Sisler	3.00	1.50	.90
(20)	Joe Tinker	3.00	1.50	.90
(21)	Rube Waddell	3.00	1.50	.90
(22)	Honus Wagner	6.00	3.00	1.75
(23)	Ed Walsh	3.00	1.50	.90
(24)	Cy Young	5.00	2.50	1.50

1977 Baseball's Great Hall of Fame Exhibits

A second set of "Baseball's Great Hall of Fame" exhibit cards was produced in 1977, most cards featuring more recent players than the 1948 issue. The cards were produced in the same 3-3/8" x 5-3/8" blank-back, black-and-white design as the 1948 cards, and are a genuine product of Exhibit Supply Co., Chicago. The new cards were printed on an extremely high grade of semi-gloss cardboard, in contrast to the earlier versions. Production was announced at 500,000 cards. The unnumbered cards are checklisted here alphabetically.

		NM	EX	VG
Complete Set (32):		35.00	17.50	10.00
Common Player:		2.00	1.00	.60
(1)	Luke Appling	2.00	1.00	.60
(2)	Ernie Banks	3.00	1.50	.90
(3)	Yogi Berra	3.00	1.50	.90
(4)	Roy Campanella	3.00	1.50	.90
(5)	Roberto Clemente	9.00	4.50	2.75
(6)	Alvin Dark	2.00	1.00	.60
(7)	Joe DiMaggio	9.00	4.50	2.75
(8)	Bob Feller	2.00	1.00	.60
(9)	Whitey Ford	2.00	1.00	.60
(10)	Jimmie Foxx	2.00	1.00	.60
(11)	Lou Gehrig	9.00	4.50	2.75
(12)	Charlie Gehringer	2.00	1.00	.60
(13)	Hank Greenberg	2.50	1.25	.70
(14)	Gabby Hartnett	2.00	1.00	.60
(15)	Carl Hubbell	2.00	1.00	.60
(16)	Al Kaline	2.00	1.00	.60
(17)	Mickey Mantle	15.00	7.50	4.50
(18)	Willie Mays	6.00	3.00	1.75
(19)	Johnny Mize	2.00	1.00	.60
(20)	Stan Musial	4.00	2.00	1.25
(21)	Mel Ott	2.00	1.00	.60
(22)	Satchel Paige	2.50	1.25	.70
(23)	Robin Roberts	2.00	1.00	.60
(24)	Jackie Robinson	6.00	3.00	1.75
(25)	Babe Ruth	12.00	6.00	3.50
(26)	Duke Snider	2.00	1.00	.60
(27)	Warren Spahn	2.00	1.00	.60
(28)	Tris Speaker	2.00	1.00	.60
(29)	Honus Wagner	3.00	1.50	.90
(30)	Ted Williams	6.00	3.00	1.75
(31)	Rudy York	2.00	1.00	.60
(32)	Cy Young	2.00	1.00	.60

1980 Exhibits

Following the purchase of the "remains" of the Exhibit Supply Co., by a collector in the late 1970s, this set of Exhibits was issued in 1980. The set utilized photos from earlier issues in the same 3-3/8" x 5-3/8" size. Each card carries a notation in white at the bottom, "An Exhibit Card 1980," to distinguish them from the older version. Sets could be purchased printed in sepia, red or blue, at $4.50 per set. A total of 5,000 sets were reported printed. The unnumbered cards are checklisted here alphabetically.

		NM	EX	VG
Complete Set (32):		40.00	20.00	12.00
Common Player:		2.00	1.00	.60
(1)	Johnny Antonelli	2.00	1.00	.60
(2)	Richie Ashburn	2.00	1.00	.60
(3)	Earl Averill	2.00	1.00	.60
(4)	Ernie Banks	4.00	2.00	1.25
(5)	Ewell Blackwell	2.00	1.00	.60
(6)	Lou Brock	2.00	1.00	.60
(7)	Dean Chance	2.00	1.00	.60
(8)	Roger Craig	2.00	1.00	.60
(9)	Lou Gehrig	20.00	10.00	6.00
(10)	Gil Hodges	2.00	1.00	.60
(11)	Jack Jensen	2.00	1.00	.60
(12)	Willie Keeler	2.00	1.00	.60
(13)	George Kell	2.00	1.00	.60
(14)	Alex Kellner	2.00	1.00	.60
(15)	Harmon Killebrew	2.00	1.00	.60
(16)	Dale Long	2.00	1.00	.60
(17)	Sal Maglie	2.00	1.00	.60
(18)	Roger Maris	4.00	2.00	1.25
(19)	Willie Mays	13.50	6.75	4.00
(20)	Minnie Minoso	2.00	1.00	.60
(21)	Stan Musial	10.00	5.00	3.00
(22)	Billy Pierce	2.00	1.00	.60
(23)	Jimmy Piersall	2.00	1.00	.60
(24)	Eddie Plank	2.00	1.00	.60
(25)	Pete Reiser	2.00	1.00	.60
(26)	Brooks Robinson	2.00	1.00	.60
(27)	Pete Runnels	2.00	1.00	.60
(28)	Herb Score	2.00	1.00	.60
(29)	Warren Spahn	2.00	1.00	.60
(30)	Billy Williams	2.00	1.00	.60
(31)	1948 Boston Braves Team	3.00	1.50	.90
(32)	1948 Cleveland Indians Team	3.00	1.50	.90

1980 Hall of Fame Exhibits

Following the purchase of the "remains" of the Exhibit Supply Co., by a collector in the late 1970s, this set of Exhibits was issued in 1980. The set utilizies photos from earlier issues in the same 3-3/8" x 5-3/8" size. Each card has a notation in white at the bottom, "An Exhibit Card 1980 Hall Of Fame," to distinguish them from the older version. Sets could be purchased printed in sepia, red or blue for $5. The unnumbered cards are checklisted here alphabetically.

		NM	EX	VG
Complete Set (32):		25.00	12.50	7.50
Common Player:		2.00	1.00	.60
(1)	Grover Cleveland Alexander	2.50	1.25	.70
(2)	Lou Boudreau	2.00	1.00	.60
(3)	Roger Bresnahan	2.00	1.00	.60
(4)	Roy Campanella	2.00	1.00	.60
(5)	Frank Chance	2.00	1.00	.60
(6)	Ty Cobb	5.00	2.50	1.50
(7)	Mickey Cochrane	2.00	1.00	.60
(8)	Dizzy Dean	2.50	1.25	.70
(9)	Joe DiMaggio	6.00	3.00	1.75
(10)	Bill Dickey	2.00	1.00	.60
(11)	Johnny Evers	2.00	1.00	.60
(12)	Jimmy Foxx	2.50	1.25	.70
(13)	Vernon Gomez	2.00	1.00	.60
(14)	Robert "Lefty" Grove	2.00	1.00	.60
(15)	Hank Greenberg	2.50	1.25	.70
(16)	Rogers Hornsby	2.00	1.00	.60
(17)	Carl Hubbell	2.00	1.00	.60
(18)	Hughie Jennings	2.00	1.00	.60
(19)	Walter Johnson	2.50	1.25	.70
(20)	Napoleon Lajoie	2.00	1.00	.60
(21)	Bob Lemon	2.00	1.00	.60
(22)	Mickey Mantle	12.00	6.00	3.50
(23)	Christy Mathewson	2.00	1.00	.60
(24)	Mel Ott	2.00	1.00	.60
(25)	Satchel Paige	2.50	1.25	.70
(26)	Jackie Robinson	4.00	2.00	1.25
(27)	Babe Ruth	9.00	4.50	2.75
(28)	Tris Speaker	2.00	1.00	.60
(29)	Joe Tinker	2.00	1.00	.60
(30)	Honus Wagner	3.00	1.50	.90
(31)	Ted Williams	4.00	2.00	1.25
(32)	Cy Young	2.50	1.25	.70

1990s Exhibit Card Unauthorized Reprints

Sometime during the 1990s (and possibly continuing today), unauthorized reprints of 16 popular Exhibit cards from the 1940s and 1950s were made. Besides printing anomalies on front resulting from re-screening genuine cards, the reprints are on the wrong weight (too thin) and color (too white on back) of cardboard. Collectors should use caution when purchasing any of the cards found in this group. Because the reprints are unauthorized, they have no collector value.

Complete Set (16):
(1) Hank Aaron
(2) Yogi Berra
(3) Roy Campanella
(4) Whitey Ford/Pitching
(5) Nelson Fox
(6) Gil Hodges ("B"on cap.)
(7) Mickey Mantle/Btg (Waist-up, "ck" in "Mickey" connected.)
(8) Willie Mays/Btg
(9) Stan Musial/Kneeling
(10) Don Newcombe ("Dodgers" on jacket.)
(11) Harold "Peewee" Reese (Ball partially visible.)
(12) Duke Snider ("B" on cap.)
(13) Warren Spahn ("B" on cap.)
(14) Ted Williams (#9 not showing)
(15) 1956 Brooklyn Dodgers
(16) 1956 N.Y. Yankees

1910 E-UNC Candy

Little is known about these 1910-era cards except that they appear to have been cut from a candy box. Printed in blue or red duo-tone and blank-backed, the cards measure about 2-3/4" per side. A 1-3/8" x 2-1/2" central image has a player photo with a diamond design around. Player identification is in a white strip at bottom.

	NM	EX	VG
Common Player:	715.00	360.00	210.00
(1) "Ty" Cobb	3,000	1,500	900.00
(2) Eddie Collins	715.00	360.00	210.00
(3) Johnny Evers	715.00	360.00	210.00
(4) "Christy" Mathewson	1,425	715.00	430.00
(5) "Honus" Wagner	1,800	900.00	540.00
(6) "Cy" Young	1,425	715.00	430.00

1936 E-UNC Candy

These cards appear to be a secondary use of the center portions of the 1936 S and S Game cards, having the same player photos and data in a size which varies from about 1-3/4" to 1-7/8" wide and between 2-3/8" and 2-1/2" tall. These differ in that instead of the green backs found on most of the game cards, these have plain backs which are sometimes found with a rubber-stamped message to present the card for a free gift or candy bar. These stamps indicate the cards were used as a prize premium in an as yet unidentified candy company's promotion. With more than half of the S and S players known in this candy company version, it is not unreasonable to assume the checklists for both sets are the same.

	NM	EX	VG
Complete Set (52):	3,000	1,500	900.00
Common Player:	45.00	22.50	13.50
(1) Luke Appling	90.00	45.00	25.00
(2) Earl Averill	90.00	45.00	25.00
(3) Zeke Bonura	45.00	22.50	13.50
(4) Dolph Camilli	45.00	22.50	13.50
(5) Ben Cantwell	45.00	22.50	13.50
(6) Phil Cavaretta (Cavarretta)	45.00	22.50	13.50
(7) Rip Collins	45.00	22.50	13.50
(8) Joe Cronin	90.00	45.00	25.00
(9) Frank Crosetti	60.00	30.00	18.00
(10) Kiki Cuyler	90.00	45.00	25.00
(11) Virgil Davis	45.00	22.50	13.50
(12) Frank Demaree	45.00	22.50	13.50
(13) Paul Derringer	45.00	22.50	13.50
(14) Bill Dickey	120.00	60.00	35.00
(15) Woody English	45.00	22.50	13.50
(16) Fred Fitzsimmons	45.00	22.50	13.50
(17) Richard Ferrell	90.00	45.00	25.00
(18) Pete Fox	45.00	22.50	13.50
(19) Jimmy Foxx	150.00	75.00	45.00
(20) Larry French	45.00	22.50	13.50
(21) Frank Frisch	100.00	50.00	30.00
(22) August Galan	45.00	22.50	13.50
(23) Chas. Gehringer	100.00	50.00	30.00
(24) John Gill	45.00	22.50	13.50
(25) Charles Grimm	45.00	22.50	13.50
(26) Mule Haas	45.00	22.50	13.50
(27) Stanley Hack	45.00	22.50	13.50
(28) Bill Hallahan	45.00	22.50	13.50
(29) Melvin Harder	45.00	22.50	13.50
(30) Gabby Hartnett	90.00	45.00	25.00
(31) Ray Hayworth	45.00	22.50	13.50
(32) Ralston Hemsley	45.00	22.50	13.50
(33) Bill Herman	90.00	45.00	25.00
(34) Frank Higgins	45.00	22.50	13.50
(35) Carl Hubbell	120.00	60.00	35.00
(36) Bill Jurges	45.00	22.50	13.50
(37) Vernon Kennedy	45.00	22.50	13.50
(38) Chuck Klein	90.00	45.00	25.00
(39) Mike Kreevich	45.00	22.50	13.50
(40) Bill Lee	45.00	22.50	13.50
(41) Jos. Medwick	90.00	45.00	25.00
(42) Van Mungo	45.00	22.50	13.50
(43) James O'Dea	45.00	22.50	13.50
(44) Mel Ott	120.00	60.00	35.00
(45) Rip Radcliff	45.00	22.50	13.50
(46) Pie Traynor	90.00	45.00	25.00
(47) Arky Vaughan (Vaughn)	90.00	45.00	25.00
(48) Joe Vosmik	45.00	22.50	13.50
(49) Lloyd Waner	90.00	45.00	25.00
(50) Paul Waner	90.00	45.00	25.00
(51) Lon Warneke	45.00	22.50	13.50
(52) Floyd Young	45.00	22.50	13.50

1909-11 E90-1, E90-2, E90-3 American Caramel

(See 1909-11 American Caramel Co. for checklists, values.)

1908-09 E91 American Caramel Co.

(See 1908-09 American Caramel Co. for checklists, values.)

1909 E92 Nadja Caramels

(See 1909 Nadja Caramels.)

1910 E93 Standard Caramel Co.

(See 1910 Standard Caramel Co. for checklist, values.)

1911 E94

(See 1911 George Close Candy Co. for checklist and value data.)

1909 E95 Philadelphia Caramel

(See 1909 Philadelphia Caramel for checklist, price guide.)

1910 E96 Philadelphia Caramel

(See 1910 Philadelphia Caramel for checklist, values.)

1910 E98 "Set of 30"

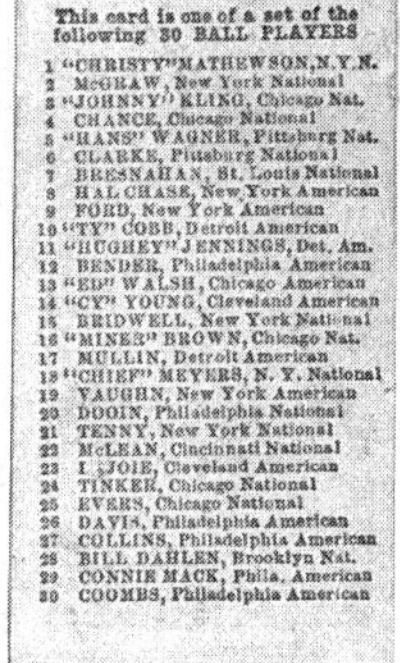
This card is one of a set of the following 30 BALL PLAYERS

1 "CHRISTY" MATHEWSON, N.Y.N.
2 McGRAW, New York National
3 "JOHNNY" KLING, Chicago Nat.
4 CHANCE, Chicago National
5 "HANS" WAGNER, Pittsburg Nat.
6 CLARKE, Pittsburg National
7 BRESNAHAN, St. Louis National
8 HAL CHASE, New York American
9 FORD, New York American
10 "TY" COBB, Detroit American
11 "HUGHEY" JENNINGS, Det. Am.
12 BENDER, Philadelphia American
13 "ED" WALSH, Chicago American
14 "CY" YOUNG, Cleveland American
15 BRIDWELL, New York National
16 "MINER" BROWN, Chicago Nat.
17 MULLIN, Detroit American
18 "CHIEF" MEYERS, N. Y. National
19 VAUGHN, New York American
20 DOOIN, Philadelphia National
21 TENNY, New York National
22 McLEAN, Cincinnati National
23 LAJOIE, Cleveland American
24 TINKER, Chicago National
25 EVERS, Chicago National
26 DAVIS, Philadelphia American
27 COLLINS, Philadelphia American
28 BILL DAHLEN, Brooklyn Nat.
29 CONNIE MACK, Phila. American
30 COOMBS, Philadelphia American

This set of 30 subjects was issued in 1910 and is closely related to several other early candy issues that are nearly identical. The cards measure 1-1/2" x 2-3/4" and feature color lithograph player pictures. The backs, printed in brown, contain a checklist of the set but no advertising or other information indicating the manufacturer. The set was designated E98 by the "American Card Catalog." While the cards are unnumbered, they are listed here according to the numbers on the back checklist. Some or all of the cards may be found with different colored backgrounds.

	NM	EX	VG
Complete Set (30):	75,000	30,000	15,000
Common Player:	1,500	480.00	240.00
(1) Christy Matthewson (Mathewson)	15,000	7,500	4,500
(2) John McGraw	2,500	860.00	430.00
(3) Johnny Kling	1,500	480.00	240.00
(4) Frank Chance	2,150	860.00	430.00
(5) "Hans" Wagner	15,000	3,400	2,000
(6) Fred Clarke	2,150	860.00	430.00
(7) Roger Bresnahan	2,150	860.00	430.00
(8) Hal Chase	2,000	800.00	400.00
(9) Russ Ford	1,200	480.00	240.00
(10) "Ty" Cobb	9,000	3,600	2,000
(11) Hughey Jennings	2,150	860.00	430.00
(12) Chief Bender	2,150	860.00	430.00
(13) Ed Walsh	2,150	860.00	430.00
(14) "Cy" Young (Picture actually Irv Young.)	9,000	3,000	1,500
(15) Al Bridwell	1,500	480.00	240.00
(16) Miner Brown	2,150	860.00	430.00
(17) George Mullin	1,500	480.00	240.00
(18) Chief Meyers	1,500	480.00	240.00
(19) Hippo Vaughn	3,500	1,750	650.00
(20) Red Dooin	1,500	480.00	240.00
(21) Fred Tenny (Tenney)	3,000	1,500	750.00
(22) Larry McLean	1,500	480.00	240.00
(23) Nap Lajoie	5,000	2,500	1,000
(24) Joe Tinker	2,150	860.00	430.00
(25) Johnny Evers	2,150	860.00	430.00
(26) Harry Davis	1,500	480.00	240.00
(27) Eddie Collins	2,150	860.00	430.00
(28) Bill Dahlen	3,000	1,500	750.00
(29) "Connie" Mack	5,000	2,500	1,000
(30) Jack Coombs	3,500	1,750	650.00

1909 E101 "Set of 50"

THIS CARD IS ONE OF A SET OF 50 Base Ball Players PROMINENT MEMBERS OF NATIONAL AND AMERICAN LEAGUES,

This 50-card set is closely related to the E92 issues by Nadja, Croft's, Dockman, etc. The fronts of the E101 cards are identical to the E92 set, but the back is "anonymous," containing no advertising or other information regarding the set's sponsor. The backs read simply "This card is one of a set of 50 Base Ball Players Prominent Members of National and American Leagues."

	NM	EX	VG
Complete Set (50):	75,000	30,000	15,000
Common Player:	950.00	400.00	200.00
(1) Jack Barry	950.00	400.00	200.00
(2) Harry Bemis	950.00	400.00	200.00
(3) Chief Bender (White hat.)	3,700	1,500	750.00
(4) Chief Bender (Striped hat.)	4,200	1,700	850.00
(5) Bill Bergen	950.00	400.00	200.00
(6) Bob Bescher	950.00	400.00	200.00
(7) Al Bridwell	1,500	600.00	300.00
(8) Doc Casey	950.00	400.00	200.00
(9) Frank Chance	3,700	1,500	750.00
(10) Hal Chase	3,200	1,300	650.00
(11) Ty Cobb	20,000	8,000	4,000
(12) Eddie Collins	3,700	1,500	750.00
(13) Sam Crawford	3,700	1,500	750.00
(14) Harry Davis	1,500	600.00	300.00
(15) Art Devlin	950.00	400.00	200.00
(16) Wild Bill Donovan	950.00	400.00	200.00
(17) Red Dooin	950.00	400.00	200.00
(18) Mickey Doolan	950.00	400.00	200.00
(19) Patsy Dougherty	950.00	400.00	200.00
(20) Larry Doyle (With bat.)	950.00	400.00	200.00
(21) Larry Doyle/Throwing	950.00	400.00	200.00
(22) Johnny Evers	3,700	1,500	750.00
(23) George Gibson	950.00	400.00	200.00
(24) Topsy Hartsel	950.00	400.00	200.00
(25) Fred Jacklitsch	950.00	400.00	200.00
(26) Hugh Jennings	3,700	1,500	750.00
(27) Red Kleinow	950.00	400.00	200.00
(28) Otto Knabe	950.00	400.00	200.00
(29) Jack Knight	950.00	400.00	200.00
(30) Nap Lajoie	3,700	1,500	750.00
(31) Hans Lobert	950.00	400.00	200.00
(32) Sherry Magee	950.00	400.00	200.00
(33) Christy Matthewson (Mathewson)	13,500	5,400	2,700
(34) John McGraw	3,700	1,500	750.00
(35) Larry McLean	950.00	400.00	200.00
(36) Dots Miller/Btg	950.00	400.00	200.00
(37) Dots Miller?Fldg	950.00	400.00	200.00
(38) Danny Murphy	950.00	400.00	200.00
(39) Bill O'Hara	950.00	400.00	200.00
(40) Germany Schaefer	1,500	600.00	300.00
(41) Admiral Schlei	950.00	400.00	200.00
(42) Boss Schmidt	950.00	400.00	200.00
(43) Johnny Seigle	1,500	600.00	300.00
(44) Dave Shean	950.00	400.00	200.00
(45) Boss Smith (Schmidt)	950.00	400.00	200.00
(46) Joe Tinker	3,700	1,500	750.00
(47) Honus Wagner/Btg	17,500	7,000	3,500
(48) Honus Wagner/Throwing	17,500	7,000	3,500
(49) Cy Young	12,500	5,000	2,500
(50) Heinie Zimmerman	950.00	400.00	200.00

1909 E102 "Set of 25"

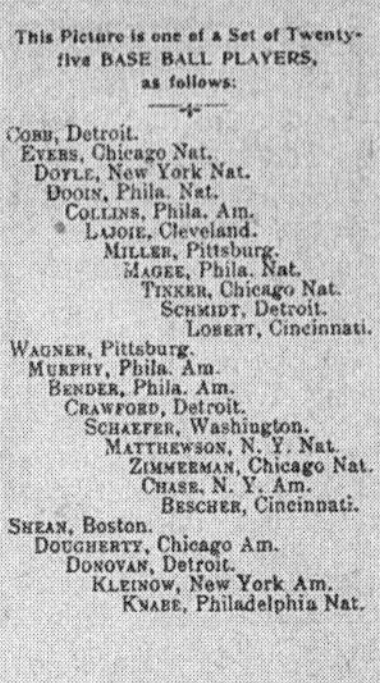
This Picture is one of a Set of Twenty-five BASE BALL PLAYERS, as follows:

Cobb, Detroit.
Evers, Chicago Nat.
Doyle, New York Nat.
Dooin, Phila. Nat.
Collins, Phila. Am.
Lajoie, Cleveland.
Miller, Pittsburg.
Magee, Phila. Nat.
Tinker, Chicago Nat.
Schmidt, Detroit.
Lobert, Cincinnati.
Wagner, Pittsburg.
Murphy, Phila. Am.
Bender, Phila. Am.
Crawford, Detroit.
Schaefer, Washington.
Matthewson, N. Y. Nat.
Zimmerman, Chicago Nat.
Chase, N. Y. Am.
Bescher, Cincinnati.
Shean, Boston.
Dougherty, Chicago Am.
Donovan, Detroit.
Kleinow, New York Am.
Knabe, Philadelphia Nat.

One of many similar early candy card sets, this set - designated as E102 in the American Card Catalog - was published no earlier than mid-1909. The producer of the set is unknown. Measuring approximately 1-1/2" x 2-3/4", the set is almost identical in design to the E101 set and other closely related issues. The set consists of 25 players, which are checklisted on the back of the card. Four of the players have been found in two variations, resulting in 29 different cards. Because there is no advertising on the cards, the set can best be identified by the words - "This Picture is one of a Set of Twenty-five Base Ball Players, as follows" - which appears on the back of each card.

	NM	EX	VG
Complete Set (29):	55,000	22,000	11,000
Common Player:	850.00	350.00	175.00
(1) Chief Bender	1,450	575.00	290.00
(2) Bob Bescher	850.00	350.00	175.00
(3) Hal Chase	900.00	360.00	180.00
(4) Ty Cobb	15,000	6,000	3,000
(5) Eddie Collins	1,450	575.00	290.00
(6) Sam Crawford	1,450	575.00	290.00
(7) Wild Bill Donovan	850.00	350.00	175.00
(8) Red Dooin	850.00	350.00	175.00
(9) Patsy Dougherty	850.00	350.00	175.00
(10) Larry Doyle/Btg	850.00	350.00	175.00
(11) Larry Doyle/Throwing	850.00	350.00	175.00
(12) Johnny Evers	1,450	575.00	290.00
(13) Red Kleinow	850.00	350.00	175.00
(14) Otto Knabe	850.00	350.00	175.00
(15) Nap Lajoie	1,825	725.00	365.00
(16) Hans Lobert	850.00	350.00	175.00
(17) Sherry Magee	850.00	350.00	175.00
(18) Christy Matthewson (Mathewson)	5,000	2,000	1,000
(19) Dots Miller/Btg	850.00	350.00	175.00
(20) Dots Miller/Fldg	1,650	650.00	325.00
(21) Danny Murphy	850.00	350.00	175.00
(22) Germany Schaefer	850.00	350.00	175.00
(23) Boss Schmidt	850.00	350.00	175.00
(24) Dave Shean	850.00	350.00	175.00
(25) Boss Smith (Schmidt)	850.00	350.00	175.00
(26) Joe Tinker	1,450	575.00	290.00
(27) Honus Wagner/Btg	10,000	2,600	1,300
(28) Honus Wagner /Throwing	10,000	2,600	1,300
(29) Heinie Zimmerman	850.00	350.00	175.00

1910 E104 Nadja Caramels

(See 1910 Nadja Caramels.)

1915 E106 American Caramel Co.

(See 1915 American Caramel Co.)

1903-1904 E107 Type 1

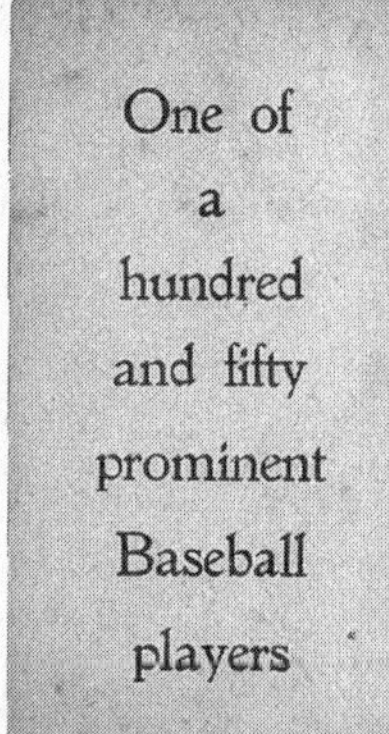

Identified by the American Card Catalog as E107, this set is significant because it was one of the first major baseball card sets since the 1880s. It established the pattern for most of the tobacco and candy cards that followed over the next two decades. Measuring approximately 1-3/8" x 2-5/8", cards feature black-and-white player photos with the name, position and team in the bottom border. Most are found either with black back printing reading, "One of a hundred and fifty prominent Baseball players," or blank-backed, in about equal numbers. Also found are cards with a purple diagonal overprint stating "THE BREISCH-WILLIAMS CO." Type 1 consists of 147 known different players, plus 11 additional variations. The Type 2 cards are thicker than those of Type 1 and some (Keeler and Delehanty) cards have captions different from those found in Type 1. Values shown for EX and NM grades are mostly theoretical, as few cards are known in better than VG condition.

	NM	EX	VG
Common Player:	10,200	4,080	2,040
Breisch-Williams Overprint: 2-3X			
(1a) John Anderson (St. Louis)	10,200	4,080	2,040
(1b) John Anderson (New York)	10,200	4,080	2,040
(2) Jimmy Barret (Barrett)	10,200	4,080	2,040
(3) Ginger Beaumont	10,200	4,080	2,040
(4) Fred Beck	10,200	4,080	2,040
(5) Jake Beckley	30,000	15,000	9,000
(6) Harry Bemis	10,200	4,080	2,040
(7) Chief Bender	30,000	15,000	9,000
(8) Bill Bernhard	10,200	4,080	2,040
(9) Harry Bey (Bay)	10,200	4,080	2,040
(10) Bill Bradley	10,200	4,080	2,040
(11) Fritz Buelow	10,200	4,080	2,040
(12) Nixey Callahan	10,200	4,080	2,040
(13) Scoops Carey	10,200	4,080	2,040
(14) Charley Carr	10,200	4,080	2,040
(15) Bill Carrick	10,200	4,080	2,040
(16) Doc Casey	10,500	4,080	2,040
(17) Frank Chance	30,000	15,000	9,000
(18) Jack Chesbro	30,000	15,000	9,000
(19) Boileryard Clark (Clarke)	10,200	4,080	2,040
(20) Fred Clarke	30,000	15,000	9,000
(21) Jimmy Collins	30,000	15,000	9,000
(22) Duff Cooley	10,200	4,080	2,040
(23) Tommy Corcoran	10,200	4,080	2,040
(24) Bill Coughlan (Coughlin)	10,200	4,080	2,040
(25) Lou Criger	10,200	4,080	2,040
(26) Lave Cross	10,200	4,080	2,040
(27) Monte Cross	10,200	4,080	2,040
(28a) Bill Dahlen (Brooklyn)	10,200	4,080	2,040
(28b) Bill Dahlen (New York)	17,000	4,080	2,040
(29) Tom Daly	10,200	4,080	2,040
(30) George Davis	30,000	15,000	9,000
(31) Harry Davis	10,200	4,080	2,040
(32) Ed Delehanty (Delahanty)	30,000	15,000	9,000
(33) Gene DeMont (DeMontreville)	10,200	4,080	2,040
(34a) Pop Dillon (Detroit)	10,200	4,080	2,040
(34b) Pop Dillon (Brooklyn)	16,200	8,100	4,800
(35) Bill Dineen (Dinneen)	10,200	4,080	2,040
(36) Red Donahue	10,200	4,080	2,040
(37) Mike Donlin	10,200	4,080	2,040
(38) Patsy Donovan	10,200	4,080	2,040
(39) Patsy Dougherty (Photo actually Tom Hughes.)	10,200	4,080	2,040
(40) Klondike Douglass	10,200	4,080	2,040
(41a) Jack Doyle (Brooklyn)	10,200	4,080	2,040
(41b) Jack Doyle (Philadelphia)	10,200	4,080	2,040
(42) Lew Drill	10,200	4,080	2,040
(43) Jack Dunn	10,200	4,080	2,040
(44a) Kid Elberfield (Elberfeld) (Detroit)	10,200	4,080	2,040
(44b) Kid Elberfield (Elberfeld) (No team designation.)	10,200	4,080	2,040
(45) Duke Farrell	10,200	4,080	2,040
(46) Hobe Ferris	10,200	4,080	2,040
(47) Elmer Flick	30,000	15,000	9,000
(48) Buck Freeman	10,200	4,080	2,040
(49) Bill Freil (Friel)	10,200	4,080	2,040
(50) Dave Fultz	10,200	4,080	2,040
(51) Ned Garvin	10,200	4,080	2,040
(52) Billy Gilbert	10,200	4,080	2,040
(53) Harry Gleason	10,200	4,080	2,040
(54a) Kid Gleason (New York)	10,200	4,080	2,040
(54b) Kid Gleason (Philadelphia)	10,200	4,080	2,040
(55) John Gochnauer (Gochnaur)	10,200	4,080	2,040
(56) Danny Green	10,200	4,080	2,040
(57) Noodles Hahn	10,200	4,080	2,040
(58) Bill Hallman	10,200	4,080	2,040
(59) Ned Hanlon	30,000	15,000	9,000
(60) Dick Harley	10,200	4,080	2,040
(61) Jack Harper	10,200	4,080	2,040
(62) Topsy Hartsell (Hartsel)	10,200	4,080	2,040
(63) Emmet Heidrick	10,200	4,080	2,040
(64) Charlie Hemphill	10,200	4,080	2,040
(65) Weldon Henley	10,200	4,080	2,040
(66) Piano Legs Hickman	10,200	4,080	2,040
(67) Harry Howell	10,200	4,080	2,040
(68) Frank Iasbel (Isbell)	10,200	4,080	2,040
(69) Fred Jacklitzch (Jacklitsch)	10,200	4,080	2,040
(70) Fielder Jones (Chicago)	10,200	4,080	2,040
(71) Charlie Jones (Boston)	10,200	4,080	2,040
(72) Addie Joss	30,000	15,000	9,000
(73) Mike Kahoe	10,200	4,080	2,040
(74) Wee Willie Keeler	30,000	15,000	9,000
(75) Joe Kelley	30,000	15,000	9,000
(76) Brickyard Kennedy	10,200	4,080	2,040
(77) Frank Kitson	10,200	4,080	2,040
(78a) Malachi Kittredge (Boston)	10,200	4,080	2,040
(78b) Malachi Kittredge (Washington)	10,200	4,080	2,040
(79) Candy LaChance	10,200	4,080	2,040
(80) Nap Lajoie	30,000	15,000	9,000
(81) Tommy Leach	10,200	4,080	2,040
(82a) Watty Lee (Washington)	10,200	4,080	2,040
(82b) Watty Lee (Pittsburg)	10,200	4,080	2,040
(83) Sam Leever	10,200	4,080	2,040
(84) Herman Long	10,200	4,080	2,040
(85a) Billy Lush (Detroit)	10,200	4,080	2,040
(85b) Billy Lush (Cleveland)	10,200	4,080	2,040
(86) Christy Mathewson	78,000	39,000	24,000
(87) Sport McAllister	10,200	4,080	2,040
(88) Jack McCarthy	10,200	4,080	2,040
(89) Barry McCormick	10,200	4,080	2,040
(90) Ed McFarland (Chicago)	10,200	4,080	2,040
(91) Herm McFarland (New York)	10,200	4,080	2,040
(92) Joe McGinnity	30,000	15,000	9,000
(93) John McGraw	30,000	15,000	9,000
(94a) Deacon McGuire (Brooklyn)	10,200	4,080	2,040
(94b) Deacon McGuire (New York)	17,000	4,080	2,040
(95) Jock Menefee	10,200	4,080	2,040
(96) Sam Mertes	10,200	4,080	2,040
(97) Roscoe Miller (Picture actually George Mullin.)	10,200	4,080	2,040
(98) Fred Mitchell	10,200	4,080	2,040
(99) Earl Moore	10,200	4,080	2,040
(100) Danny Murphy	10,200	4,080	2,040
(101) Jack O'Connor	10,200	4,080	2,040
(102) Al Orth	10,200	4,080	2,040
(103) Dick Padden	10,200	4,080	2,040
(104) Freddy Parent	10,200	4,080	2,040
(105) Roy Patterson	10,200	4,080	2,040
(106) Heinie Peitz	10,200	4,080	2,040
(107) Deacon Phillipi (Phillippe)	10,200	4,080	2,040
(108) Wiley Piatt	10,200	4,080	2,040
(109) Ollie Pickering	10,200	4,080	2,040
(110) Eddie Plank	78,000	39,000	24,000
(111a) Ed Poole (Cincinnati)	10,200	4,080	2,040
(111b) Ed Poole (Brooklyn)	10,200	4,080	2,040
(112a) Jack Powell (St. Louis)	10,200	4,080	2,040
(112b) Jack Powell (New York)	10,200	4,080	2,040
(113) Mike Powers	10,200	4,080	2,040
(114) Claude Ritchie (Ritchey)	10,200	4,080	2,040
(115) Jimmy Ryan	10,200	4,080	2,040
(116) Ossee Schreckengost	10,200	4,080	2,040
(117) Kip Selbach	10,200	4,080	2,040
(118) Socks Seybold	10,200	4,080	2,040
(119) Jimmy Sheckard	10,200	4,080	2,040
(120) Ed Siever	10,200	4,080	2,040
(121) Harry Smith	10,200	4,080	2,040
(122) Tully Sparks	10,200	4,080	2,040
(123) Jake Stahl	10,200	4,080	2,040
(124) Harry Steinfeldt	10,200	4,080	2,040
(125) Sammy Strang	10,200	4,080	2,040
(126) Willie Sudhoff	10,200	4,080	2,040
(127) Joe Sugden	10,200	4,080	2,040
(128) Billy Sullivan	10,200	4,080	2,040
(129) Jack Taylor	10,200	4,080	2,040
(130) Fred Tenney	10,200	4,080	2,040
(131) Roy Thomas	10,200	4,080	2,040
(132a) Jack Thoney (Cleveland)	10,200	4,080	2,040
(132b) Jack Thoney (New York)	10,200	4,080	2,040
(133) Jack Townsend	10,200	4,080	2,040
(134) George Van Haltren	10,200	4,080	2,040
(135) Rube Waddell	30,000	15,000	9,000
(136) Honus Wagner	360,000	180,000	108,000
(137) Bobby Wallace	30,000	15,000	9,000
(138) Jack Warner	10,200	4,080	2,040
(139) Jimmy Wiggs	10,200	4,080	2,040
(140) Jimmy Williams	10,200	4,080	2,040
(141) Vic Willis	30,000	15,000	9,000
(142) Hooks Wiltse	10,200	4,080	2,040
(143) George Winters (Winter)	10,200	4,080	2,040
(144) Bob Wood	10,200	4,080	2,040
(145) Joe Yeager	9,600	4,800	2,880
(146) Cy Young	90,000	45,000	27,000
(147) Chief Zimmer	10,200	4,080	2,040

1903-1904 E107 Type 2

Many of the Type 2 E107 cards seen to date do not measure the nominal 1-3/8" x 2-5/8" of the Type 1 cards, often having been cut more narrowly. Once thought to have been cut from an advertising piece, it now appears these were a regular production issue, as at least one specimen has been found with the purple diagonal overprint stating "THE BREISCH-WILLIAMS CO." Type 2 cards are printed on a thicker and more gray card stock than Type 1 and at least a few (Keeler and Delehanty) cards have captions different from those found in Type 1. NM values are principally theoretical as few cards in known in conditions better than EX.

	NM	EX	VG
Common Player:	9,000	3,600	1,800
(1) Ed Delehanty (Delahanty)	50,000	20,000	10,000
(2) Jack Doyle	9,000	3,600	1,800
(3) Wee Willie Keeler	50,000	20,000	10,000
(4) Nap Lajoie	50,000	20,000	10,000
(5) Tommy Leach	9,000	3,600	1,800
(6) Socks Seybold	9,000	3,600	1,800
(7) Fred Tenney	9,000	3,600	1,800
(8) Rube Waddell	50,000	20,000	10,000

1922 E120 American Caramel Series of 240

(See 1922 American Caramel Series of 240.)

1921-22 E121 American Caramel Series of 80/120

(See 1921 American Caramel Series of 80, Series of 120.)

1922 E122 American Caramel Series of 80

(See 1922 American Caramel Series of 80 for checklist, values.)

1910 E125 American Caramel Die-Cuts

(See 1910 American Caramel Die-Cuts for checklist, values.)

1927 E126 American Caramel Series of 60

(See 1927 American Caramel Series of 60.)

1927 E210 York Caramels

(See York Caramels.)

1921 E253 Oxford Confectionery

(See 1921 Oxford Confectionery.)

1961 F & M Bank Minnesota Twins Matchbook Covers

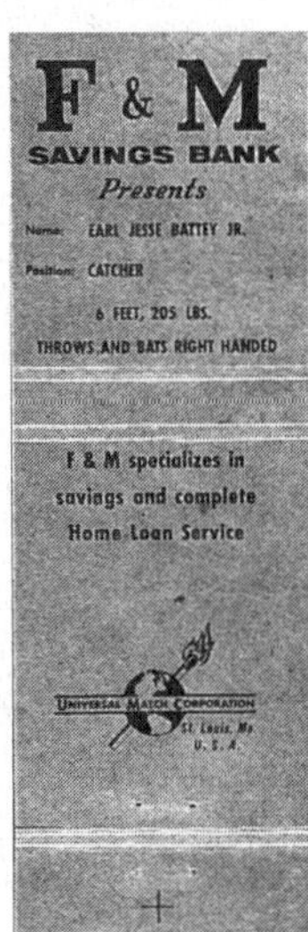

The star players on the inaugural Twins team are featured in this series of matchbook covers. The 1-1/2" x 4-7/16" matchbooks are printed in black, red and blue on white, and include a player portrait (players are shown wearing Washington Senators caps) and team logo on front. The sponsoring bank's picture and logo are on back. Inside the front cover are a few details about the player. Values shown are for complete but empty covers, with the striker surface intact. Complete matchbooks with matches bring about 2X the values quoted.

		NM	EX	VG
Complete Set (10):		70.00	35.00	20.00
Common Player:		7.50	3.75	2.25
(1)	Bob Allison	12.00	6.00	3.50
(2)	Earl Battey	9.00	4.50	2.75
(3)	Reno Bertoia	7.50	3.75	2.25
(4)	Billy Gardner	7.50	3.75	2.25
(5)	Lenny Green	7.50	3.75	2.25
(6)	Harmon Killebrew	20.00	10.00	6.00
(7)	Cookie Lavagetto	7.50	3.75	2.25
(8)	Jim Lemon	12.00	6.00	3.50
(9)	Camilo Pascual	12.00	6.00	3.50
(10)	Pedro Ramos	7.50	3.75	2.25

1962 F & M Bank Minnesota Twins Matchbook Covers

The '62 Twins are featured in this series of matchbook covers. The 1-1/2" x 4-7/16" matchbooks are printed in black, red and blue on white, and include a player portrait (new players who did not appear in the 1961 set are shown in Twins caps) and team logo on front. The sponsoring bank's picture and logo are on back. Inside the front cover are a few details about the player. Values shown are for complete but empty covers, with the striker surface intact. Complete matchbooks with matches bring about 2X the values quoted.

		NM	EX	VG
Complete Set (10):		75.00	37.00	22.00
Common Player:		7.50	3.75	2.25
(1)	Bob Allison	12.00	6.00	3.50
(2)	Earl Battey	9.00	4.50	2.75
(3)	Lenny Green	7.50	3.75	2.25
(4)	Jim Kaat	12.00	6.00	3.50
(5)	Harmon Killebrew	20.00	10.00	6.00
(6)	Jack Kralick	7.50	3.75	2.25
(7)	Jim Lemon	12.00	6.00	3.50
(8)	Camilo Pascual	12.00	6.00	3.50
(9)	Pedro Ramos	7.50	3.75	2.25
(10)	Zoilo Versalles	12.00	6.00	3.50

1966 Fairway Minnesota Twins

Color portraits of Twins favorites comprise this regional issue from a local grocery chain. The 8" x 10" glossy pictures have blue facsimile autographs on front and a white border. Black-and-white backs have a lengthy career summary, biographical data and full major and minor league stats. The unnumbered pictures are checklisted here in alphabetical order. There are no markings on the picture to identify the Fairway store.

		NM	EX	VG
Complete Set (17):		175.00	85.00	55.00
Common Player:		7.50	3.75	2.25
(1)	Bernie Allen	7.50	3.75	2.25
(2)	Bob Allison	13.50	6.75	4.00
(3)	Earl Battey	10.00	5.00	3.00
(4)	Jim Grant	7.50	3.75	2.25
(5)	Jimmie Hall	7.50	3.75	2.25
(6)	Jim Kaat	15.00	7.50	4.50
(7)	Harmon Killebrew	30.00	15.00	9.00
(8)	Jim Merritt	7.50	3.75	2.25
(9)	Don Mincher	7.50	3.75	2.25
(10)	Tony Oliva	15.00	7.50	4.50
(11)	Camilo Pascual	10.00	5.00	3.00
(12)	Jim Perry	10.00	5.00	3.00
(13)	Frank Quilici	7.50	3.75	2.25
(14)	Rich Rollins	7.50	3.75	2.25
(15)	Sandy Valdespino	7.50	3.75	2.25
(16)	Zoilo Versalles	13.50	6.75	4.00
(17)	Al Worthington	7.50	3.75	2.25

1964 Falstaff Beer

This 6" x 4" black-and-white postcard pictures the principal radio announcers for the CBS "Game of the Week" sponsored by the brewing company and was probably used to respond to fan requests for autographs. Facsimile signatures of the Hall of Famers are featured on front.

	NM	EX	VG
"Dizzy" Dean, "Pee Wee Reese"	20.00	10.00	6.00

1977 Family Fun Centers Padres

For 1977, Family Fun Centers, a chain of mini theme parks, took over sponsorship of the Padres annual issue of black-and-white player photos. The 5-1/2" x 8-1/2" photos have a large player pose at top-center, with his name and position below. In the bottom corners are team and sponsor logos. Backs have biographical data, complete stats and career highlights. Players are checklisted here alphabetically.

		NM	EX	VG
Complete Set (33):		90.00	45.00	27.50
Common Player:		4.50	2.25	1.25
(1)	Billy Almon	4.50	2.25	1.25
(2)	Joey Amalfitano	4.50	2.25	1.25
(3)	Tucker Ashford	4.50	2.25	1.25
(4)	Mike Champion	4.50	2.25	1.25
(5)	Roger Craig	4.50	2.25	1.25
(6)	Alvin Dark	4.50	2.25	1.25
(7)	Bob Davis	4.50	2.25	1.25
(8)	Rollie Fingers	12.50	6.25	3.75
(9)	Dave Freisleben	4.50	2.25	1.25
(10)	Tom Griffin	4.50	2.25	1.25
(11)	George Hendrick	4.50	2.25	1.25
(12)	Mike Ivie	4.50	2.25	1.25
(13)	Randy Jones	4.50	2.25	1.25
(14)	John McNamara	4.50	2.25	1.25
(15)	Bob Owchinko	4.50	2.25	1.25
(16)	Merv Rettenmund	4.50	2.25	1.25
(17)	Gene Richards	4.50	2.25	1.25
(18)	Dave Roberts	4.50	2.25	1.25
(19)	Jackie Robinson (Blank back.)	25.00	12.50	7.50
(20)	Rick Sawyer	4.50	2.25	1.25
(21)	Pat Scanlon	4.50	2.25	1.25
(22)	Bob Shirley	4.50	2.25	1.25
(23)	Bob Skinner	4.50	2.25	1.25
(24)	Dan Spillner	4.50	2.25	1.25
(25)	Gary Sutherland	4.50	2.25	1.25
(26)	Gene Tenace	4.50	2.25	1.25
(27)	Dave Tomlin	4.50	2.25	1.25
(28)	Jerry Turner	4.50	2.25	1.25
(29)	Bobby Valentine	4.50	2.25	1.25
(30)	Dave Wehrmeister	4.50	2.25	1.25
(31)	Whitey Wietelmann	4.50	2.25	1.25
(32)	Don Williams	4.50	2.25	1.25
(33)	Dave Winfield	15.00	7.50	4.50

1978 Family Fun Centers Angels

The players, manager and coaches of the '78 Angels are featured in this set of 3-1/2" x 5-1/2" sepia-tone cards. The unnumbered cards are checklisted here alphabetically.

		NM	EX	VG
Complete Set (38):		90.00	45.00	25.00
Common Player:		2.50	1.25	.70
(1)	Don Aase	2.50	1.25	.70
(2)	Mike Barlow	2.50	1.25	.70
(3)	Don Baylor	3.50	1.75	1.00
(4)	Lyman Bostock	2.50	1.25	.70
(5)	Ken Brett	2.50	1.25	.70
(6)	Dave Chalk	2.50	1.25	.70
(7)	Bob Clear	2.50	1.25	.70
(8)	Brian Downing	2.50	1.25	.70
(9)	Ron Fairly	2.50	1.25	.70
(10)	Gil Flores	2.50	1.25	.70
(11)	Dave Frost	2.50	1.25	.70
(12)	Dave Garcia	2.50	1.25	.70
(13)	Bobby Grich	2.50	1.25	.70
(14)	Tom Griffin	2.50	1.25	.70
(15)	Marv Grissom	2.50	1.25	.70
(16)	Ike Hampton	2.50	1.25	.70
(17)	Paul Hartzell	2.50	1.25	.70
(18)	Terry Humphrey	2.50	1.25	.70
(19)	Ron Jackson	2.50	1.25	.70
(20)	Chris Knapp	2.50	1.25	.70
(21)	Ken Landreaux	2.50	1.25	.70
(22)	Carney Lansford	2.50	1.25	.70
(23)	Dave LaRoche	2.50	1.25	.70
(24)	John McNamara	2.50	1.25	.70
(25)	Dyar Miller	2.50	1.25	.70
(26)	Rick Miller	2.50	1.25	.70
(27)	Balor Moore	2.50	1.25	.70
(28)	Rance Mulliniks	2.50	1.25	.70
(29)	Floyd Rayford	2.50	1.25	.70
(30)	Jimmie Reese	4.00	2.00	1.25
(31)	Merv Rettenmund	2.50	1.25	.70
(32)	Joe Rudi	2.50	1.25	.70
(33)	Nolan Ryan	45.00	22.50	13.50
(34)	Bob Skinner	2.50	1.25	.70
(35)	Tony Solaita	2.50	1.25	.70
(36)	Frank Tanana	2.50	1.25	.70
(37)	Dickie Thon	2.50	1.25	.70
---	Header Card	.70	.35	.20

1978 Family Fun Centers Padres

In conjunction with the Padres' hosting of the 1978 All-Star Game, Family Fun Centers issued this set of cards covering the players, coaches, announcers and even the owner. The 3-1/2" x 5-1/2" cards have a plaque look with a 3" x 3-1/4" posed color photo set on a wood background. The player's name is in a gold

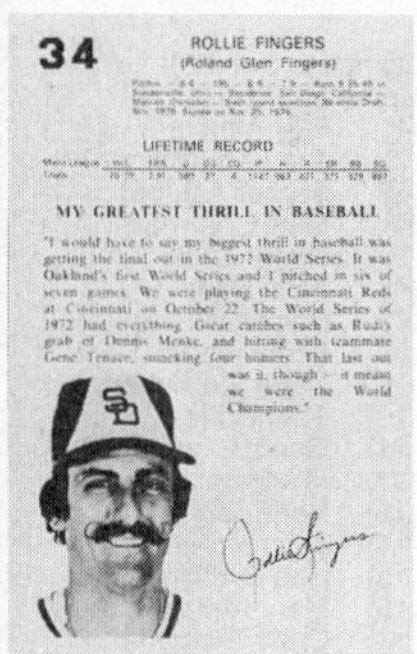

box at bottom, with the team and sponsor's logos in between. Backs are in black-and-white with a player portrait photo and facsimile autograph at bottom, a few biographical details and career stats at top and an essay in the middle titled, "My Greatest Thrill in Baseball." A uniform number appears at top-left. The set is checklisted here in alphabetical order.

		NM	EX	VG
Complete Set (39):		75.00	37.50	22.50
Common Player:		3.00	1.50	.90
(1)	Bill Almon	3.00	1.50	.90
(2)	Tucker Ashford	3.00	1.50	.90
(3)	Chuck Baker	3.00	1.50	.90
(4)	Dave Campbell (Announcer)	3.00	1.50	.90
(5)	Mike Champion	3.00	1.50	.90
(6)	Jerry Coleman (Announcer)	3.00	1.50	.90
(7)	Roger Craig	3.00	1.50	.90
(8)	John D'Acquisto	3.00	1.50	.90
(9)	Bob Davis	3.00	1.50	.90
(10)	Chuck Estrada	3.00	1.50	.90
(11)	Rollie Fingers	9.00	4.50	2.75
(12)	Dave Freisleben	3.00	1.50	.90
(13)	Oscar Gamble	3.00	1.50	.90
(14)	Fernando Gonzalez	3.00	1.50	.90
(15)	Billy Herman	4.00	2.00	1.25
(16)	Randy Jones	3.00	1.50	.90
(17)	Ray Kroc (owner)	5.00	2.50	1.50
(18)	Mark Lee	3.00	1.50	.90
(19)	Mickey Lolich	3.00	1.50	.90
(20)	Bob Owchinko	3.00	1.50	.90
(21)	Broderick Perkins	3.00	1.50	.90
(22)	Gaylord Perry	9.00	4.50	2.75
(23)	Eric Rasmussen	3.00	1.50	.90
(24)	Don Reynolds	3.00	1.50	.90
(25)	Gene Richards	3.00	1.50	.90
(26)	Dave Roberts	3.00	1.50	.90
(27)	Phil Roof	3.00	1.50	.90
(28)	Bob Shirley	3.00	1.50	.90
(29)	Ozzie Smith	60.00	30.00	18.00
(30)	Dan Spillner	3.00	1.50	.90
(31)	Rick Sweet	3.00	1.50	.90
(32)	Gene Tenace	3.00	1.50	.90
(33)	Derrel Thomas	3.00	1.50	.90
(34)	Jerry Turner	3.00	1.50	.90
(35)	Dave Wehrmeister	3.00	1.50	.90
(36)	Whitey Wietelmann	3.00	1.50	.90
(37)	Don Williams	3.00	1.50	.90
(38)	Dave Winfield	15.00	7.50	4.50
(39)	All-Star Game	3.00	1.50	.90

1979 Family Fun Centers Padres

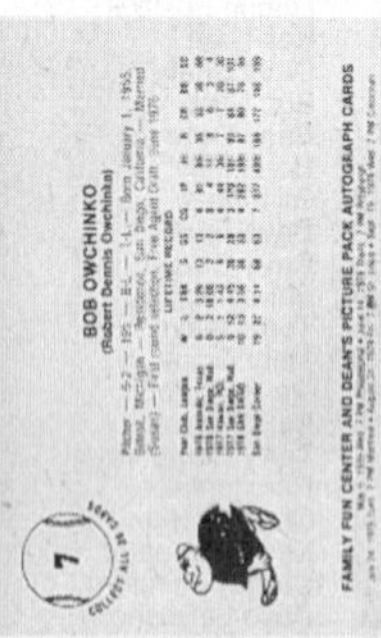

Each card features a posed color photo against a woodgrain border. Fronts have player identification, the Padres mascot and the logo of one of the sponsors - Family Fun Centers or Dean's Photo Service. Black-and-white backs have player personal data, major and minor league stats, a notation to "COLLECT ALL 36 CARDS" and a list of distribution dates. The 3-1/4" x 4-3/4" cards were issued in 12-1/2" x 9-1/2" perforated panels of six cards plus a coupon from each sponsor. Panels were given out one per month May through September at promotional games, making the set difficult to complete. Cards #25-30 have not been confirmed as issued.

		NM	EX	VG
Complete Set (30):		60.00	30.00	18.00
Common Player:		3.00	1.50	.90
1	Roger Craig	3.00	1.50	.90
2	John D'Acquisto	3.00	1.50	.90
3	Ozzie Smith	25.00	12.50	7.50
4	KGB Chicken	4.00	2.00	1.25
5	Gene Richards	3.00	1.50	.90
6	Jerry Turner	3.00	1.50	.90
7	Bob Owchinko	3.00	1.50	.90
8	Gene Tenace	3.00	1.50	.90
9	Whitey Wietelmann	3.00	1.50	.90
10	Bill Almon	3.00	1.50	.90
11	Dave Winfield	15.00	7.50	4.50
12	Mike Hargrove	3.00	1.50	.90
13	Fernando Gonzalez	3.00	1.50	.90
14	Barry Evans	3.00	1.50	.90
15	Steve Mura	3.00	1.50	.90
16	Chuck Estrada	3.00	1.50	.90
17	Bill Fahey	3.00	1.50	.90
18	Gaylord Perry	6.00	3.00	1.75
19	Dan Briggs	3.00	1.50	.90
20	Billy Herman	4.00	2.00	1.25
21	Mickey Lolich	3.00	1.50	.90
22	Broderick Perkins	3.00	1.50	.90
23	Fred Kendall	3.00	1.50	.90
24	Rollie Fingers	6.00	3.00	1.75
31	Bobby Tolan	3.00	1.50	.90
32	Doug Rader	3.00	1.50	.90
33	Dave Campbell	3.00	1.50	.90
34	Jay Johnstone	3.00	1.50	.90
35	Mark Lee	3.00	1.50	.90
36	Bob Shirley	3.00	1.50	.90

1980 Family Fun Centers Padres

Six Padres players or staff are featured on these 13" x 10" or 12-1/2" x 9-1/2" coupon sheets. At the right end of each glossy paper sheet is a group of coupons and advertising for the recreation centers, printed in black, yellow and green. At left are six photos. Each of the 3" x 4" photos has a color player pose. At either top or bottom, depending on placement on the sheet, is the player name in black, "FAMILY FUN CENTER" in green and a red building logo. Backs are blank and the sheets are not perforated.

		NM	EX	VG
Complete Set (7):		80.00	40.00	24.00
Common Sheet:		7.00	3.50	2.00
(1)	Kurt Bevacqua, Dave Cash, Paul Dade, Rollie Fingers, Don Williams, Dave Winfield	20.00	10.00	6.00
(2)	Ed Brinkman, Dave Edwards, Jack Krol, Luis Salazar, Craig Stimac, John Urrea	7.00	3.50	2.00
(3)	Jerry Coleman, John D'Acquisto, Bill Fahey, Randy Jones, Gene Richards, Ozzie Smith	30.00	15.00	9.00
(4)	Dave Campbell, Juan Eichelberger, Barry Evans, Bobby Tolan, Jerry Turner, Rick Wise	7.00	3.50	2.00
(5)	John Curtis, Al Heist, Gary Lucas, Willie Montanez, Aurelio Rodriguez, Gene Tenace	7.00	3.50	2.00
(6)	Eddie Doucette, Chuck Estrada, Tim Flannery, Eric Rasmussen, Bob Shirley, San Diego Chicken	10.00	5.00	3.00
(7)	Von Joshua, Fred Kendall, Dennis Kinney, Jerry Mumphrey, Steve Mura, Dick Phillips	7.00	3.50	2.00

1916 Famous and Barr Clothiers

The advertisement for this St. Louis clothier is among the most commonly found on the backs of this 200-player set that parallels the more common M101-5 Blank Backs issue. Famous and Barr was one of many regional advertisers to use the cards for local promotions. Premiums over the same cards in M101-5 Blank Backs are modest for most players, but can be substantial for the top stars. The cards are printed in black-and-white and measure 1-5/8" x 3".

		NM	EX	VG
Complete Set (200):		143,750	57,500	28,750
Common Player:		125.00	50.00	25.00
1	Babe Adams	190.00	65.00	25.00
2	Sam Agnew	125.00	50.00	25.00
3	Eddie Ainsmith	125.00	50.00	25.00
4	Grover Alexander	2,065	825.00	415.00
5	Leon Ames	125.00	50.00	25.00
6	Jimmy Archer	125.00	50.00	25.00
7	Jimmy Austin	125.00	50.00	25.00
8	J. Franklin Baker	720.00	290.00	145.00
9	Dave Bancroft	720.00	290.00	145.00
10	Jack Barry	125.00	50.00	25.00
11	Zinn Beck	125.00	50.00	25.00
12	Lute Boone	125.00	50.00	25.00
13	Joe Benz	125.00	50.00	25.00
14	Bob Bescher	125.00	50.00	25.00
15	Al Betzel	125.00	50.00	25.00
16	Roger Bresnahan	720.00	290.00	145.00
17	Eddie Burns	125.00	50.00	25.00
18	Geo. J. Burns	125.00	50.00	25.00
19	Joe Bush	125.00	50.00	25.00
20	Owen Bush	125.00	50.00	25.00
21	Art Butler	125.00	50.00	25.00
22	Bobbie Byrne	125.00	50.00	25.00
23a	Forrest Cady (MAY NOT EXIST)			
23b	Mordecai Brown	720.00	290.00	145.00
24	Jimmy Callahan	125.00	50.00	25.00
25	Ray Caldwell	125.00	50.00	25.00
26	Max Carey	720.00	290.00	145.00
27	George Chalmers	125.00	50.00	25.00
28	Frank Chance	720.00	290.00	145.00
29	Ray Chapman	155.00	65.00	30.00
30	Larry Cheney	125.00	50.00	25.00
31	Eddie Cicotte	720.00	290.00	145.00
32	Tom Clarke	125.00	50.00	25.00
33	Eddie Collins	720.00	290.00	145.00
34	"Shauno" Collins	125.00	50.00	25.00
35	Charles Comisky (Comiskey)	720.00	290.00	145.00
36	Joe Connolly	125.00	50.00	25.00
37	Luther Cook	125.00	50.00	25.00
38	Jack Coombs	125.00	50.00	25.00
39	Dan Costello	125.00	50.00	25.00
40	Harry Coveleskie (Coveleski)	125.00	50.00	25.00
41	Gavvy Cravath	125.00	50.00	25.00
42	Sam Crawford	720.00	290.00	145.00
43	Jean Dale	125.00	50.00	25.00
44	Jake Daubert	125.00	50.00	25.00
45	Geo. A. Davis Jr.	125.00	50.00	25.00
46	Charles Deal	125.00	50.00	25.00
47	Al Demaree	125.00	50.00	25.00
48	William Doak	125.00	50.00	25.00
49	Bill Donovan	125.00	50.00	25.00
50	Charles Dooin	125.00	50.00	25.00
51	Mike Doolan	125.00	50.00	25.00
52	Larry Doyle	125.00	50.00	25.00
53	Jean Dubuc	125.00	50.00	25.00
54	Oscar Dugey	125.00	50.00	25.00
55	Johnny Evers	720.00	290.00	145.00
56	Urban Faber	720.00	290.00	145.00
57	"Hap" Felsch	1,000	400.00	200.00
58	Bill Fischer	125.00	50.00	25.00
59	Ray Fisher	125.00	50.00	25.00
60	Max Flack	125.00	50.00	25.00
61	Art Fletcher	125.00	50.00	25.00
62	Eddie Foster	125.00	50.00	25.00
63	Jacques Fournier	125.00	50.00	25.00
64	Del Gainer (Gainor)	125.00	50.00	25.00
65	Larry Gardner	125.00	50.00	25.00
66	Joe Gedeon	125.00	50.00	25.00
67	Gus Getz	125.00	50.00	25.00
68	Geo. Gibson	125.00	50.00	25.00
69	Wilbur Good	125.00	50.00	25.00
70	Hank Gowdy	125.00	50.00	25.00
71	John Graney	125.00	50.00	25.00
72	Tom Griffith	125.00	50.00	25.00
73	Heinie Groh	125.00	50.00	25.00
74	Earl Hamilton	125.00	50.00	25.00
75	Bob Harmon	125.00	50.00	25.00
76	Roy Hartzell	125.00	50.00	25.00
77	Claude Hendrix	125.00	50.00	25.00
78	Olaf Henriksen	125.00	50.00	25.00
79	John Henry	125.00	50.00	25.00
80	"Buck" Herzog	125.00	50.00	25.00
81	Hugh High	125.00	50.00	25.00
82	Dick Hoblitzell	125.00	50.00	25.00
83	Harry Hooper	720.00	290.00	145.00
84	Ivan Howard	125.00	50.00	25.00
85	Miller Huggins	720.00	290.00	145.00
86	Joe Jackson	25,000	10,000	5,000
87	William James	125.00	50.00	25.00
88	Harold Janvrin	125.00	50.00	25.00
89	Hugh Jennings	720.00	290.00	145.00
90	Walter Johnson	2,190	875.00	440.00
91	Fielder Jones	125.00	50.00	25.00
92	Bennie Kauff	125.00	50.00	25.00
93	Wm. Killefer Jr.	125.00	50.00	25.00
94	Ed. Konetchy	125.00	50.00	25.00
95	Napoleon Lajoie	720.00	290.00	145.00
96	Jack Lapp	125.00	50.00	25.00
97a	John Lavan (Correct spelling.)	125.00	50.00	25.00
97b	John Lavin ((Incorret spelling.) (MAY NOT EXIST)			
98	Jimmy Lavender	125.00	50.00	25.00
99	"Nemo" Leibold	125.00	50.00	25.00
100	H.B. Leonard	125.00	50.00	25.00

101	Duffy Lewis	125.00	50.00	25.00
102	Hans Lobert	125.00	50.00	25.00
103	Tom Long	125.00	50.00	25.00
104	Fred Luderus	125.00	50.00	25.00
105	Connie Mack	720.00	290.00	145.00
106	Lee Magee	125.00	50.00	25.00
107	Al. Mamaux	125.00	50.00	25.00
108	Leslie Mann	125.00	50.00	25.00
109	"Rabbit" Maranville	720.00	290.00	145.00
110	Rube Marquard	720.00	290.00	145.00
111	Armando Marsans	155.00	65.00	30.00
112	J. Erskine Mayer	155.00	65.00	30.00
113	George McBride	125.00	50.00	25.00
114	John J. McGraw	720.00	290.00	145.00
115	Jack McInnis	125.00	50.00	25.00
116	Fred Merkle	125.00	50.00	25.00
117	Chief Meyers	125.00	50.00	25.00
118	Clyde Milan	125.00	50.00	25.00
119	Otto Miller	125.00	50.00	25.00
120	Willie Mitchel (Mitchell)	125.00	50.00	25.00
121	Fred Mollwitz	125.00	50.00	25.00
122	J. Herbert Moran	125.00	50.00	25.00
123	Pat Moran	125.00	50.00	25.00
124	Ray Morgan	125.00	50.00	25.00
125	Geo. Moriarty	125.00	50.00	25.00
126	Guy Morton	125.00	50.00	25.00
127	Ed. Murphy (Photo actually Danny Murphy.)	125.00	50.00	25.00
128	John Murray	125.00	50.00	25.00
129	"Hy" Myers	125.00	50.00	25.00
130	J.A. Niehoff	125.00	50.00	25.00
131	Leslie Nunamaker	125.00	50.00	25.00
132	Rube Oldring	125.00	50.00	25.00
133	Oliver O'Mara	125.00	50.00	25.00
134	Steve O'Neill	125.00	50.00	25.00
135	"Dode" Paskert	125.00	50.00	25.00
136	Roger Peckinpaugh (Photo actually Gavvy Cravath.)	125.00	50.00	25.00
137	E.J. Pfeffer (Photo actually Jeff Pfeffer.)	125.00	50.00	25.00
138	Geo. Pierce (Pearce)	125.00	50.00	25.00
139	Walter Pipp	125.00	50.00	25.00
140	Derril Pratt (Derrill)	125.00	50.00	25.00
141	Bill Rariden	125.00	50.00	25.00
142	Eppa Rixey	720.00	290.00	145.00
143	Davey Robertson	125.00	50.00	25.00
144	Wilbert Robinson	720.00	290.00	145.00
145	Bob Roth	125.00	50.00	25.00
146	Ed. Roush	720.00	290.00	145.00
147	Clarence Rowland	125.00	50.00	25.00
148	"Nap" Rucker	125.00	50.00	25.00
149	Dick Rudolph	125.00	50.00	25.00
150	Reb Russell	125.00	50.00	25.00
151	Babe Ruth	68,750	27,500	13,750
152	Vic Saier	125.00	50.00	25.00
153	"Slim" Sallee	125.00	50.00	25.00
154	"Germany" Schaefer	125.00	50.00	25.00
155	Ray Schalk	720.00	290.00	145.00
156	Walter Schang	125.00	50.00	25.00
157	Chas. Schmidt	125.00	50.00	25.00
158	Frank Schulte	125.00	50.00	25.00
159	Jim Scott	125.00	50.00	25.00
160	Everett Scott	125.00	50.00	25.00
161	Tom Seaton	125.00	50.00	25.00
162	Howard Shanks	125.00	50.00	25.00
163	Bob Shawkey (Photo actually Jack McInnis.)	125.00	50.00	25.00
164	Ernie Shore	125.00	50.00	25.00
165	Burt Shotton	125.00	50.00	25.00
166	George Sisler	720.00	290.00	145.00
167	J. Carlisle Smith	125.00	50.00	25.00
168	Fred Snodgrass	125.00	50.00	25.00
169	Geo. Stallings	125.00	50.00	25.00
170	Oscar Stanage (Photo actually Chas. Schmidt.)	125.00	50.00	25.00
171	Charles Stengel	815.00	325.00	165.00
172	Milton Stock	125.00	50.00	25.00
173	Amos Strunk (Photo actually Olaf Henriksen.)	125.00	50.00	25.00
174	Billy Sullivan	125.00	50.00	25.00
175	Chas. Tesreau	125.00	50.00	25.00
176	Jim Thorpe	13,750	5,500	2,750
177	Joe Tinker	720.00	290.00	145.00
178	Fred Toney	125.00	50.00	25.00
179	Terry Turner	125.00	50.00	25.00
180	Jim Vaughn	125.00	50.00	25.00
181	Bob Veach	125.00	50.00	25.00
182	James Voix	125.00	50.00	25.00
183	Oscar Vitt	125.00	50.00	25.00
184	Hans Wagner	5,000	1,065	530.00
185	Clarence Walker (Photo not Walker.)	125.00	50.00	25.00
186	Zach Wheat	720.00	290.00	145.00
187	Ed. Walsh	720.00	290.00	145.00
188	Buck Weaver	720.00	290.00	145.00
189	Carl Weilman	125.00	50.00	25.00
190	Geo. Whitted	125.00	50.00	25.00
191	Fred Williams	125.00	50.00	25.00
192	Art Wilson	125.00	50.00	25.00
193	J. Owen Wilson	125.00	50.00	25.00
194	Ivy Wingo	125.00	50.00	25.00
195	"Mel" Wolfgang	125.00	50.00	25.00
196	Joe Wood	220.00	90.00	45.00
197	Steve Yerkes	125.00	50.00	25.00
198	Rollie Zeider	125.00	50.00	25.00
199	Heiny Zimmerman	125.00	50.00	25.00
200	Ed. Zwilling	125.00	50.00	25.00

1906 Fan Craze - American League

One of the earliest 20th Century baseball card sets, this issue from the Fan Craze Co. of Cincinnati was designed as a deck of playing cards and was intended to be used as a baseball table game. Separate sets were issued for the National League, with backs printed in red, and the American League, which are blue-backed. Both sets feature black-and-white player portraits in an oval vignette with the player's name and team below. The top of the card indicates one of many various baseball plays, such as "Single," "Out at First," "Strike," "Stolen Base," etc. The unnumbered cards measure 2-1/2" x 3-1/2". An ad card identifies the set as "An Artistic Constellation of Great Stars." Sears sold the set for 48 cents, postpaid.

		NM	EX	VG
Complete Set (51):		8,250	4,125	2,475
Complete Boxed Set:		9,350	4,675	2,750
Common Player:		90.00	45.00	25.00
(1)	Nick Altrock	110.00	55.00	35.00
(2)	Jim Barrett	90.00	45.00	25.00
(3)	Harry Bay	90.00	45.00	25.00
(4)	Albert Bender	330.00	165.00	100.00
(5)	Bill Bernhardt	90.00	45.00	25.00
(6)	W. Bradley	90.00	45.00	25.00
(7)	Jack Chesbro	330.00	165.00	100.00
(8)	Jimmy Collins	330.00	165.00	100.00
(9)	Sam Crawford	330.00	165.00	100.00
(10)	Lou Criger	90.00	45.00	25.00
(11)	Lave Cross	90.00	45.00	25.00
(12)	Monte Cross	90.00	45.00	25.00
(13)	Harry Davis	90.00	45.00	25.00
(14)	Bill Dinneen	90.00	45.00	25.00
(15)	Pat (Bill) Donovan	90.00	45.00	25.00
(16)	Pat Dougherty	90.00	45.00	25.00
(17)	Norman Elberfield (Elberfeld)	90.00	45.00	25.00
(18)	Hoke Ferris (Hobe)	90.00	45.00	25.00
(19)	Elmer Flick	330.00	165.00	100.00
(20)	Buck Freeman	90.00	45.00	25.00
(21)	Fred Glade	90.00	45.00	25.00
(22)	Clark Griffith	330.00	165.00	100.00
(23)	Charley Hickman	90.00	45.00	25.00
(24)	Wm. Holmes	90.00	45.00	25.00
(25)	Harry Howell	90.00	45.00	25.00
(26)	Frank Isbel (Isbell)	90.00	45.00	25.00
(27)	Albert Jacobson	90.00	45.00	25.00
(28)	Ban Johnson	330.00	165.00	100.00
(29)	Fielder Jones	90.00	45.00	25.00
(30)	Adrian Joss	330.00	165.00	100.00
(31)	Billy Keeler	330.00	165.00	100.00
(32)	Napolean Lajoie	330.00	165.00	100.00
(33)	Connie Mack	330.00	165.00	100.00
(34)	Jimmy McAleer	90.00	45.00	25.00
(35)	Jim McGuire	90.00	45.00	25.00
(36)	Earl Moore	90.00	45.00	25.00
(37)	George Mullen (Mullin)	90.00	45.00	25.00
(38)	Billy Owen (Frank Owens)	90.00	45.00	25.00
(39)	Fred Parent	90.00	45.00	25.00
(40)	Case Patten	90.00	45.00	25.00
(41)	Ed Plank	550.00	275.00	165.00
(42)	Ossie Schreckengost	90.00	45.00	25.00
(43)	Jake Stahl	90.00	45.00	25.00
(44)	Fred (George) Stone	90.00	45.00	25.00
(45)	Wm. Sudhoff	90.00	45.00	25.00
(46)	Roy (Terry) Turner	90.00	45.00	25.00
(47)	G.E. Waddell	330.00	165.00	100.00
(48)	Bob Wallace	330.00	165.00	100.00
(49)	G. Harris White	90.00	45.00	25.00
(50)	Geo. Winters (Winter)	90.00	45.00	25.00
(51)	Cy Young	1,320	660.00	395.00

1906 Fan Craze - National League

Identical in size and format to the American League set of two years previous, this set of unnumbered cards was issued by the Fan Craze Co. of Cincinnati in 1906 and was designed like a deck of playing cards. The cards were intended to be used in playing a baseball table game. The National League cards are printed with red backs and black-and-white player photos on front. Sears sold the set for 48 cents postpaid.

		NM	EX	VG
Complete Set (54):		11,000	5,500	3,300
Complete Boxed Set:		17,600	8,800	5,225
Common Player:		65.00	35.00	20.00
(1)	Leon Ames	65.00	35.00	20.00
(2)	Clarence Beaumont	65.00	35.00	20.00
(3)	Jake Beckley	330.00	165.00	100.00
(4)	Billy Bergen	65.00	35.00	20.00
(5)	Roger Bresnahan	330.00	165.00	100.00
(6)	George Brown (Browne)	65.00	35.00	20.00
(7)	Mordacai Brown	330.00	165.00	100.00
(8)	Jas. Casey	65.00	35.00	20.00
(9)	Frank Chance	330.00	165.00	100.00
(10)	Fred Clarke	330.00	165.00	100.00
(11)	Thos. Corcoran	65.00	35.00	20.00
(12)	Bill Dahlen	65.00	35.00	20.00
(13)	Mike Donlin	65.00	35.00	20.00
(14)	Charley Dooin	65.00	35.00	20.00
(15)	Mickey Doolin (Doolan)	65.00	35.00	20.00
(16)	Hugh Duffy	330.00	165.00	100.00
(17)	John E. Dunleavy	65.00	35.00	20.00
(18)	Bob Ewing	65.00	35.00	20.00
(19)	"Chick" Fraser	65.00	35.00	20.00
(20)	J. Edward (Edward H.) Hanlon	330.00	165.00	100.00
(21)	G.E. Howard	65.00	35.00	20.00
(22)	Miller Huggins	330.00	165.00	100.00
(23)	Joseph Kelley	330.00	165.00	100.00
(24)	John Kling	65.00	35.00	20.00
(25)	Tommy Leach	65.00	35.00	20.00
(26)	Harry Lumley	65.00	35.00	20.00
(27)	Carl Lundgren	65.00	35.00	20.00
(28)	Bill Maloney	65.00	35.00	20.00
(29)	Dan McGann	65.00	35.00	20.00
(30)	Joe McGinnity	330.00	165.00	100.00
(31)	John J. McGraw	330.00	165.00	100.00
(32)	Harry McIntire (McIntyre)	65.00	35.00	20.00
(33)	Charley Nichols	550.00	275.00	165.00
(34)	Mike O'Neil (O'Neill)	65.00	35.00	20.00
(35)	Orville (Orval) Overall	65.00	35.00	20.00
(36)	Frank Pfeffer	65.00	35.00	20.00
(37)	Deacon Phillippe	65.00	35.00	20.00
(38)	Charley Pittinger	65.00	35.00	20.00
(39)	Harry C. Pulliam	65.00	35.00	20.00
(40)	Claude Ritchey	65.00	35.00	20.00
(41)	Ed Ruelbach (Reulbach)	65.00	35.00	20.00
(42)	J. Bentley Seymour	65.00	35.00	20.00
(43)	Jim Sheckard	65.00	35.00	20.00
(44)	Jack Taylor	65.00	35.00	20.00
(45)	Luther H. Taylor	220.00	110.00	65.00
(46)	Fred Tenny (Tenney)	65.00	35.00	20.00
(47)	Harry Theilman (Jake Thielman)	65.00	35.00	20.00
(48)	Roy Thomas	65.00	35.00	20.00
(49)	Hans Wagner	5,000	2,065	1,240
(50)	Jake Weimer	65.00	35.00	20.00
(51)	Bob Wicker	65.00	35.00	20.00
(52)	Victor Willis	330.00	165.00	100.00
(53)	Lew (George "Hooks") Wiltsie	65.00	35.00	20.00
(54)	Irving Young	65.00	35.00	20.00

1922 Fans Cigarettes (T231)

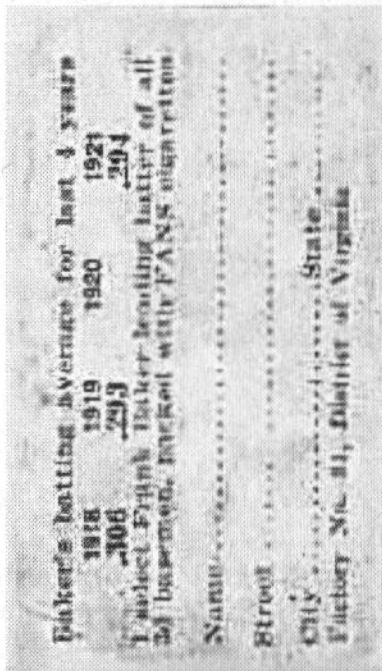

More mystery surrounds this obscure set than any other tobacco issue. In fact, the only evidence of its existence until 1992 was a photocopy of a single card of Pittsburgh Pirates outfielder Carson Bigbee. Even the owner of the card is unknown. Cards measure approximately 2-1/2" x 1-1/2" and are black-and-white. Adding to the mystery is the number "85" which appears in the lower right corner on the front of the card, apparently indicating there were at least that many cards in the set. In 1992 card "61" was reported. Card backs displays the player's batting averages for each season from 1918 through 1921 and includes the line: "I select (name) leading batter of all (position), packed with FANS cigarettes." The statement is followed by blanks for a person to fill in his name and address, as if the card were some sort of "ballot." With only one specimen known of each, these are among the rarest baseball cards in the hobby. Their American Card Catalog designation is T231.

Values Undetermined

61	Frank Baker
85	Carson Bigbee

1939 Father & Son Shoes

This set features Phillies and A's players and was distributed in the Philadelphia area in 1939 by Father & Son Shoes stores. The unnumbered black and white cards measure 3" x 4". The player's name, position and team appear below the photo, along with the line "Compliments of Fathers & Son Shoes." The backs are blank. The checklist, arranged here alphabetically, may be incomplete.

Chuck Klein, outfielder, Phillies
Compliments Father & Son Shoes

		NM	EX	VG
Complete Set (17):		5,000	2,500	1,500
Common Player:		300.00	150.00	90.00
(1)	Morrie Arnovich	300.00	150.00	90.00
(2)	Earl Brucker	300.00	150.00	90.00
(3)	George Caster	300.00	150.00	90.00
(4)	Sam Chapman	300.00	150.00	90.00
(5)	Spud Davis	300.00	150.00	90.00
(6)	Joe Gantenbein	300.00	150.00	90.00
(7)	Bob Johnson	300.00	150.00	90.00
(8)	Chuck Klein	750.00	375.00	225.00
(9)	Herschel Martin	300.00	150.00	90.00
(10)	Merrill May	300.00	150.00	90.00
(11)	Wally Moses	300.00	150.00	90.00
(12)	Emmett Mueller	300.00	150.00	90.00
(13)	Hugh Mulcahy	300.00	150.00	90.00
(14)	Skeeter Newsome	300.00	150.00	90.00
(15)	Claude Passeau	300.00	150.00	90.00
(16)	George Scharien (Scharein)	300.00	150.00	90.00
(17)	Dick Siebert	300.00	150.00	90.00

1913 Fatima Team Cards (T200)

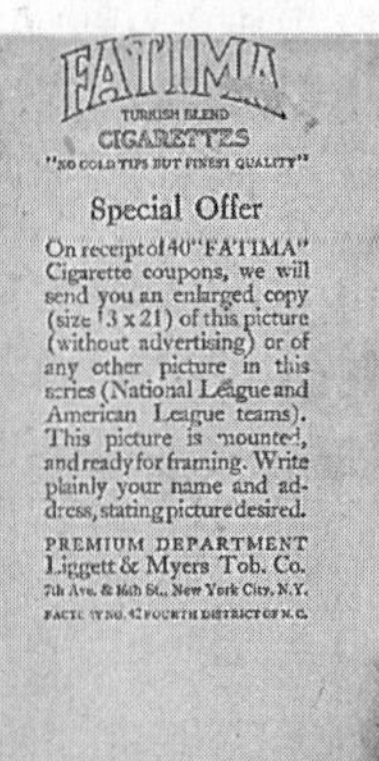

Issued by the Ligget & Myers Tobacco Co. in 1913 with Fatima brand cigarettes, the T200 set consists of eight National and eight American League team cards. The cards measure 2-5/8" x 4-3/4" and are glossy photographs on paper stock. Although it is unknown why, several of the cards are more difficult to obtain than others. The team cards feature 369 different players, managers and mascots. The card backs contain an offer for an enlarged copy (13" x 21") of a team card, minus the advertising on front, in exchange for 40 Fatima cigarette coupons.

		NM	EX	VG
Complete Set (16):		20,000	10,000	6,000
Common Card:		575.00	285.00	175.00
(1)	Boston Nationals	2,000	500.00	300.00
(2)	Brooklyn Nationals	950.00	475.00	285.00
(3)	Chicago Nationals	575.00	285.00	175.00
(4)	Cincinnati Nationals	700.00	350.00	210.00
(5)	New York Nationals	1,100	550.00	330.00
(6)	Philadelphia Nationals	575.00	285.00	175.00
(7)	Pittsburgh Nationals	750.00	375.00	225.00
(8)	St. Louis Nationals	1,750	875.00	525.00
(9)	Boston Americans	1,650	825.00	500.00
(10)	Chicago Americans	1,000	500.00	300.00
(11)	Cleveland Americans	1,900	950.00	575.00
(12)	Detroit Americans	3,750	1,875	1,125
(13)	New York Americans	2,250	1,125	675.00
(14)	Philadelphia Americans	650.00	325.00	200.00
(15)	St. Louis Americans	1,600	800.00	480.00
(16)	Washington Americans	2,100	1,050	625.00

1913 Fatima Premiums

Among the rarest of the tobacco cards are the large-format (21" x 13") versions of the T200 Fatima team photos which could be obtained by redeeming 40 coupons from cigarette packs. The premium-size team photos are virtually identical to the smaller cards, except they do not carry the Fatima advertising on the front. Because of their large size, the premiums are seldom seen in top grade. The complete set price is quoted as a hypothetical proposition only; none is known.

		NM	EX	VG
Common Card:		7,500	3,500	2,000
(1)	Boston Nationals	8,000	4,000	2,400
(2)	Brooklyn Nationals	8,000	4,000	2,400
(3)	Chicago Nationals	9,500	4,750	2,850
(4)	Cincinnati Nationals	7,500	3,500	2,000
(5)	New York Nationals	8,000	4,000	2,400
(6)	Philadelphia Nationals	7,500	3,500	2,000
(7)	Pittsburg Nationals	10,000	5,000	3,000
(8)	St. Louis Nationals	7,500	3,750	2,250
(9)	Boston Americans	12,500	6,250	3,750
(10)	Chicago Americans	8,000	4,000	2,400
(11)	Cleveland Americans	15,000	7,500	4,500
(12)	Detroit Americans	15,000	7,500	4,500
(13)	New York Americans	12,500	6,250	3,750
(14)	Philadelphia Americans	9,250	4,625	2,775
(15)	St. Louis Americans	9,000	4,500	2,700
(16)	Washington Americans	7,500	3,500	2,000

1913-1915 Fatima Posters

These blank-back, black-and-white (1913) or b/w with a color picture of a cigarette pack (1914-15) window posters were produced by Pictorial News Co. of New York for distribution by Fatima Cigarettes, whose advertising appears in the lower-right corner of the 12-1/2" x 19" pictures. To the left of the advertising are a couple of sentences about the player(s) pictured (usually in an action pose). The pictures are numbered, but there is currently no idea as to the extent of the issue.

		NM	EX	VG
6	Frank Chance's New York Americans in Bermuda	1,200	600.00	360.00
15	Christy Mathewson	6,000	3,000	2,000
22	Ty Cobb	7,500	3,500	2,500
31	Pittsburgh Pirates Only Hope of West in National Race	1,000	500.00	300.00
33	Joe Jackson	4,500	2,250	1,350
35	Athletics' Star Pitchers the Giants Will Have to Beat (Chief Bender, Jack Coombs, Eddie Plank)	450.00	225.00	135.00
36	Cleveland Strong Second in the American League Race	650.00	325.00	200.00
43	Chicago Cubs team	1,200	600.00	360.00
45	Plays that Made Baseball History (Various action photos.)	250.00	125.00	75.00
51	Walter Johnson	5,500	2,750	1,650
56	Opposing Pitchers in the Coming World's Series Battles (Christy Mathewson, Rube Marquard, Jeff Tesreau, Al Demaree, Chief Bender, Boardwalk Brown, Byron Houck, Eddie Plank)	650.00	325.00	195.00
105	Giants 'Clearing the Deck for Action' Down in Marlin (Mathewson, Snodgrass, Fletcher, etc.)	325.00	160.00	95.00
153	American League Pennant Winners Ready For the World's Series (1914 Philadelphia A's)	1,500	750.00	450.00
226	Ty Cobb, The Most Talked About Man in Big League Baseball	7,500	3,750	2,250
259	(1915 Philadelphia Phillies)	2,500	1,250	750.00
260	Red Sox Ready to do Battle for World's Championship (1915 Red Sox)	3,500	1,750	1,050

1914 Fatima (T222)

Alexander-Phila. Nationals

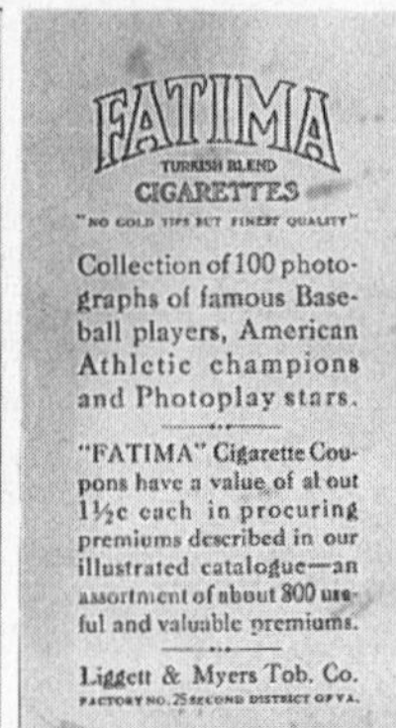

Unlike the typical 20th Century tobacco card issues, the T222 Fatima cards are glossy photographs on a thin paper stock and measure a larger 2-1/2" x 4-1/2". According to the back of the card, the set includes "100 photographs of famous Baseball Players, American Athletic Champions and Photoplay stars." The baseball portion of the set appears to be complete at 52. The set includes players from 13 of the 16 major league teams (no Red Sox, White Sox or Pirates). Most cards are seen with a small black number from 2-9 or 12-15 beneath the player's name. The same number can be found on up to seven cards. Cards with numbers 12-15 are considered shortprints and so designated in this alphabetical checklist.

		NM	EX	VG
Complete Set (52):		137,500	56,250	28,125
Common Player:		1,440	565.00	280.00
(1)	Grover Alexander	20,000	4,500	2,250
(2)	Jimmy Archer	1,440	565.00	280.00
(3)	Jimmy Austin/SP	3,440	1,375	690.00
(4)	Jack Barry	1,440	565.00	280.00
(5)	George Baumgardner/SP	3,440	1,375	690.00
(6)	Rube Benton	1,440	565.00	280.00
(7)	Roger Bresnahan	4,500	1,815	905.00
(8)	Boardwalk Brown	1,440	565.00	280.00
(9)	George Burns	1,440	565.00	280.00
(10)	Bullet Joe Bush	1,440	565.00	280.00
(11)	George Chalmers	1,440	565.00	280.00
(12)	Frank Chance	4,500	1,815	905.00
(13)	Al Demaree	1,440	565.00	280.00
(14)	Art Fletcher	1,440	565.00	280.00
(15)	Earl Hamilton/SP	3,440	1,375	690.00
(16)	John Henry/SP	3,440	1,375	690.00
(17)	Byron Houck	1,440	565.00	280.00
(18)	Miller Huggins	4,500	1,815	905.00
(19)	Hughie Jennings	4,500	1,815	905.00
(20)	Walter Johnson/SP	15,625	6,250	3,125
(21)	Ray Keating/SP	3,440	1,375	690.00
(22)	Jack Lapp	1,440	565.00	280.00
(23)	Tommy Leach	1,440	565.00	280.00
(24)	Nemo Leibold/SP	3,440	1,375	690.00
(25)	Jack Lelivelt/SP	3,440	1,375	690.00
(26)	Hans Lobert/SP	3,440	1,375	690.00
(27)	Lee Magee/SP	3,440	1,375	690.00
(28)	Sherry Magee/SP	3,440	1,375	690.00
(29)	Fritz Maisel	1,440	565.00	280.00
(30)	Rube Marquard	4,500	1,815	905.00
(31)	George McBride/SP	3,440	1,375	690.00
(32)	Stuffy McInnis	1,440	565.00	280.00
(33)	Larry McLean	1,440	565.00	280.00
(34)	Ray Morgan/SP	3,440	1,375	690.00
(35)	Eddie Murphy	1,440	565.00	280.00
(36)	Red Murray	1,440	565.00	280.00
(37)	Rube Oldring	1,440	565.00	280.00
(38)	Bill Orr	1,440	565.00	280.00
(39)	Hub Perdue	1,440	565.00	280.00
(40)	Art Phelan	1,440	565.00	280.00
(41)	Ed Reulbach	1,440	565.00	280.00
(42)	Vic Saier	1,140	565.00	280.00
(43)	Slim Sallee	1,440	565.00	280.00
(44)	Wally Schang	1,440	565.00	280.00
(45)	Wildfire Schulte/SP	3,440	1,375	690.00
(46)	J.C. "Red" Smith/SP	3,440	1,375	690.00
(47)	Amos Strunk	1,440	565.00	280.00
(48)	Bill Sweeney	1,440	565.00	280.00
(49)	Lefty Tyler	1,440	565.00	280.00
(50)	Ossie Vitt	1,440	565.00	280.00
(51)	Ivy Wingo	1,440	565.00	280.00
(52)	Heinie Zimmerman	1,440	565.00	280.00

1955 Felin's Franks

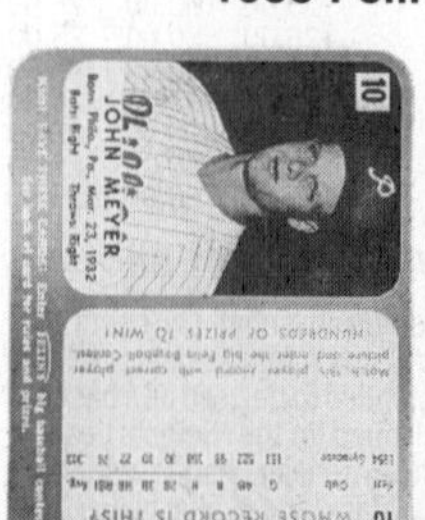

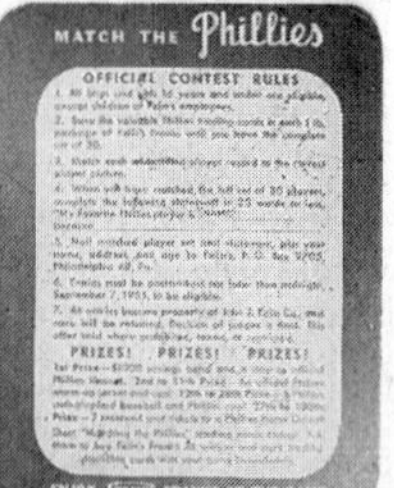

Because of the relatively few specimens in collectors' hands, it is believed this hot dog issue was never actually released. The 4" x 3-5/8" round-cornered panels have a red border front and back with a color player photo on the left side of the front. At right-front are the 1954 stats of a player different than that pictured. Each half of the front shares a large black number. According to the card back, hot dog buyers were supposed to match the pictures and stats of 30 different players to have a chance to win prizes.

		NM	EX	VG
Common Player:		1,250	625.00	375.00
1	Mayo Smith	1,250	625.00	375.00
2	Unknown (Probably coach Benny Bengough.)			
3	Wally Moses	1,250	625.00	375.00
4	Whit Wyatt	1,250	625.00	375.00
5	Maje McDonnell	1,250	625.00	375.00
6	Wiechec (Trainer)	750.00	375.00	225.00
7	Murry Dickson	1,250	625.00	375.00
8	Earl Torgeson	1,250	625.00	375.00
9	Bobby Morgan	1,250	625.00	375.00
10	John Meyer	1,250	625.00	375.00
11	Bob Miller	1,250	625.00	375.00
12	Jim Owens	1,250	625.00	375.00
13	Steve Ridzik	1,250	625.00	375.00
14	Robin Roberts	2,000	1,000	600.00
15	Unknown (Probably Curt Simmons.)			
16	Herm Wehmeier	1,250	625.00	375.00
17	Smoky Burgess	1,250	625.00	375.00
18	Stan Lopata	1,250	625.00	375.00
19	Gus Niarhos	1,250	625.00	375.00
20	Floyd Baker	1,250	625.00	375.00
21	Marv Blaylock	1,250	625.00	375.00
22	Granny Hamner	1,250	625.00	375.00
23	Willie Jones	1,250	625.00	375.00
24	Unknown			
25	Unknown			
26	Richie Ashburn	2,250	1,125	675.00
27	Joe Lonnett	1,250	625.00	375.00
28	Mel Clark	1,250	625.00	375.00
29	Bob Greenwood	1,250	625.00	375.00
30	Unknown			

1913 Fenway Breweries/ Tom Barker Game

Presumably distributed as a promotion for its Fenway brand of beer, a specially labeled boxed set of the Tom Barker baseball game cards was issued. Only the box, the Score Card and the card of Frank "Home Run" Baker are found bearing the red advertising overprint.

	NM	EX	VG
Complete Set (54):	6,000	3,000	1,800
Frank Baker	175.00	90.00	55.00
Score Card	40.00	20.00	12.00

1916 Ferguson Bakery Felt Pennants (BF2)

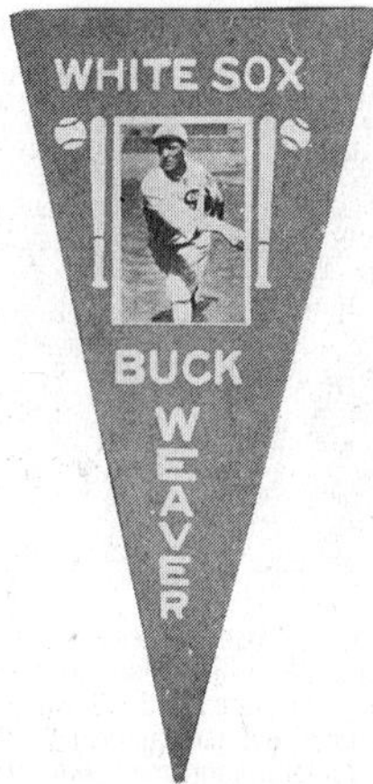

Issued circa 1916, this unnumbered set consists of 97 felt pennants with a small black-and-white player photo glued to each. The triangular pennants measure approximately 2-7/8" across the wide top and taper to a length of about 6". The photos are about 1-1/4" x 1-3/4" and appear to be identical to photos used for The Sporting News issues of the same period. The pennants list the player's name and team. The pennants were given away as premiums with the purchase of five-cent loaves of Ferguson Bakery Bread in the Roxbury, Mass. area. It is believed that each player can be found on several different colors of background felt.

		NM	EX	VG
Complete Set (97):		27,500	13,500	8,250
Common Player:		175.00	85.00	50.00
(1)	Grover Alexander	600.00	300.00	180.00
(2)	Jimmy Archer	175.00	85.00	50.00
(3)	J. Franklin Baker	450.00	225.00	135.00
(4)	Dave Bancroft	450.00	225.00	135.00
(5)	Jack Barry	175.00	85.00	50.00
(6)	"Chief" Bender	450.00	225.00	135.00
(7)	Joe Benz	175.00	85.00	50.00
(8)	Mordecai Brown	450.00	225.00	135.00
(9)	Geo. J. Burns	175.00	85.00	50.00
(10)	"Donie" Bush	175.00	85.00	50.00
(11)	Forrest Cady	175.00	85.00	50.00
(12)	Max Carey	450.00	225.00	135.00
(13)	Ray Chapman	300.00	150.00	90.00
(14)	Ty Cobb	1,800	900.00	550.00
(15)	Eddie Collins	450.00	225.00	135.00
(16)	"Shauno" Collins	175.00	85.00	50.00
(17)	Charles Comiskey	450.00	225.00	135.00
(18)	Harry Coveleskie (Coveleski)	175.00	85.00	50.00
(19)	Gavvy Cravath	175.00	85.00	50.00
(20)	Sam Crawford	450.00	225.00	135.00
(21)	Jake Daubert	175.00	85.00	50.00
(22)	Josh Devore	175.00	85.00	50.00
(23)	Charles Dooin	175.00	85.00	50.00
(24)	Larry Doyle	175.00	85.00	50.00
(25)	Jean Dubuc	175.00	85.00	50.00
(26)	Johnny Evers	450.00	225.00	135.00
(27)	Urban Faber	450.00	225.00	135.00
(28)	Eddie Foster	175.00	85.00	50.00
(29)	Del Gainer (Gainor)	175.00	85.00	50.00
(30)	"Chic" Gandil	375.00	185.00	110.00
(31)	Joe Gedeon	175.00	85.00	50.00
(32)	Hank Gowdy	175.00	85.00	50.00
(33)	Earl Hamilton	175.00	85.00	50.00
(34)	Claude Hendrix	175.00	85.00	50.00
(35)	Buck Herzog	175.00	85.00	50.00
(36)	Harry Hooper	450.00	225.00	135.00
(37)	Miller Huggins	450.00	225.00	135.00
(38)	Joe Jackson	3,500	1,750	1,000
(39)	William James	175.00	85.00	50.00
(40)	Hugh Jennings	450.00	225.00	135.00
(41)	Walter Johnson	900.00	450.00	275.00
(42)	Fielder Jones	175.00	85.00	50.00
(43)	Joe Judge	175.00	85.00	50.00
(44)	Benny Kauff	175.00	85.00	50.00
(45)	Wm. Killefer	175.00	85.00	50.00
(46)	Napoleon Lajoie	450.00	225.00	135.00
(47)	Jack Lapp	175.00	85.00	50.00
(48)	John Lavan	175.00	85.00	50.00
(49)	Jimmy Lavender	175.00	85.00	50.00
(50)	"Dutch" Leonard	175.00	85.00	50.00
(51)	Duffy Lewis	175.00	85.00	50.00
(52)	Hans Lobert	175.00	85.00	50.00
(53)	Fred Luderus	175.00	85.00	50.00
(54)	Connie Mack	450.00	225.00	135.00
(55)	Sherwood Magee	175.00	85.00	50.00
(56)	Al Mamaux	175.00	85.00	50.00
(57)	"Rabbit" Maranville	450.00	225.00	135.00
(58)	Rube Marquard	450.00	225.00	135.00
(59)	George McBride	175.00	85.00	50.00
(60)	John J. McGraw	450.00	225.00	135.00
(61)	Jack McInnis	175.00	85.00	50.00
(62)	Fred Merkle	175.00	85.00	50.00
(63)	Chief Meyers	175.00	85.00	50.00
(64)	Clyde Milan	175.00	85.00	50.00
(65)	Otto Miller	175.00	85.00	50.00
(66)	Pat Moran	175.00	85.00	50.00
(67)	Ray Morgan	175.00	85.00	50.00
(68)	Guy Morton	175.00	85.00	50.00
(69)	Ed. Murphy	175.00	85.00	50.00
(70)	Rube Oldring	175.00	85.00	50.00
(71)	"Dode" Paskert	175.00	85.00	50.00
(72)	Walter Pipp	175.00	85.00	50.00
(73)	Clarence Rowland	175.00	85.00	50.00
(74)	"Nap" Rucker	175.00	85.00	50.00
(75)	Dick Rudolph	175.00	85.00	50.00
(76)	Reb Russell	175.00	85.00	50.00
(77)	Vic Saier	175.00	85.00	50.00
(78)	"Slim" Sallee	175.00	85.00	50.00
(79)	Ray Schalk	450.00	225.00	135.00
(80)	Walter Schang	175.00	85.00	50.00
(81)	Frank Schulte	175.00	85.00	50.00
(82)	Jim Scott	175.00	85.00	50.00
(83)	George Sisler	450.00	225.00	135.00
(84)	Geo. Stallings	175.00	85.00	50.00
(85)	Oscar Stanage	175.00	85.00	50.00
(86)	"Jeff" Tesreau	175.00	85.00	50.00
(87)	Joe Tinker	450.00	225.00	135.00
(88)	Geo. Tyler	175.00	85.00	50.00
(89)	Jim Vaughn	175.00	85.00	50.00
(90)	Bobby Veach	175.00	85.00	50.00
(91)	Hans Wagner	1,350	675.00	400.00
(92)	Ed. Walsh	450.00	225.00	135.00
(93)	Buck Weaver	750.00	375.00	225.00
(94)	Ivy Wingo	175.00	85.00	50.00
(95)	Joe Wood	350.00	175.00	100.00
(96)	"Pep" Young	175.00	85.00	50.00
(97)	Heiny Zimmerman	175.00	85.00	50.00

1916 Ferguson Bakery Photo Prize Pennants

As part of its baseball insert and premium program, the Roxbury, Mass., bakery issued this series of large (9" x 24") felt pennants bearing a black-and-white player photo (3" x 5").

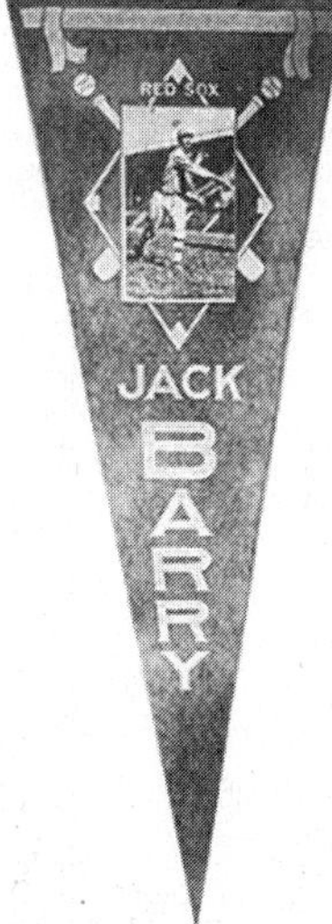

The colorful pennants are decorated with baseball graphics and have player and team identification. The pennants were a premium for redeeming 50 tickets from five-cent loaves of bread. Examples of the large-format pennants are so scarce only a handful of players are checklisted thus far.

		NM	EX	VG
Common Player:		9,000	4,500	2,750
(1)	Grover Alexander	15,000	7,500	4,500
(2)	Jack Barry	9,000	4,500	2,750
(3)	Ty Cobb	20,000	10,000	6,000
(4)	Bill Donovan	9,000	4,500	2,750
(5)	Miller Huggins	12,500	6,250	3,750
(6)	John McGraw	12,500	6,250	3,750

1957 Fine Arts Studio

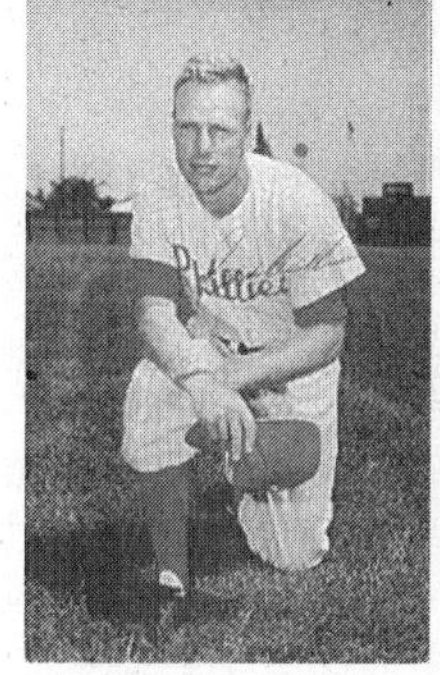

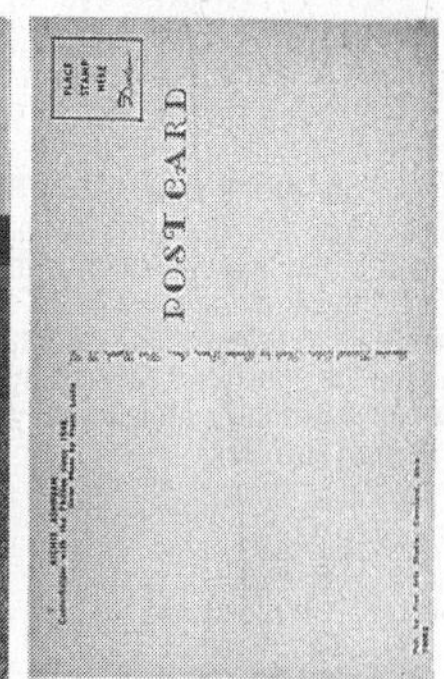

The date of issue on this card is theoretical with no real evidence present on the piece. Published by Fine Arts Studio of Cleveland, the 3-1/2" x 5-1/2" card has a borderless color photo on front. Player identification is on back with standard postcard markings and credit lines to the publisher and printer (Dexter Press of New York).

	NM	EX	VG
75062 Richie Ashburn	100.00	50.00	30.00

1959 First Federal Savings Famous Senators Matchbooks

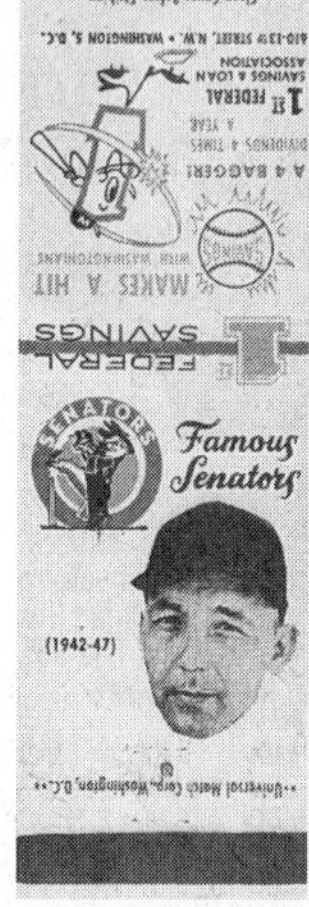

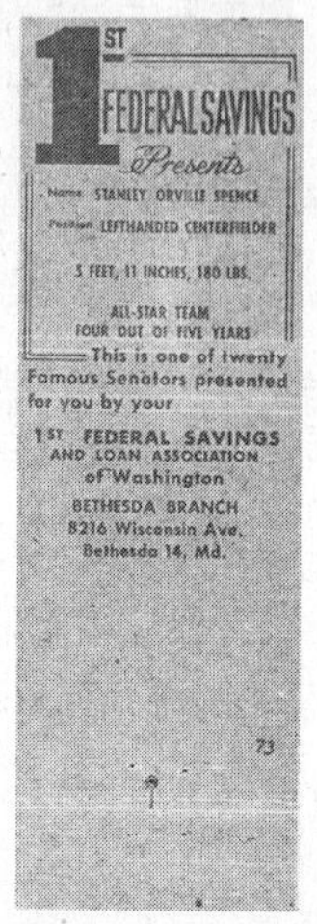

Star Senators of the 20th Century are featured in this series of matchbook covers. The 1-1/2" x 4-1/2" matchbooks include a black-and-white player portrait photo and team logo on front. The sponsoring bank's advertising is on back. Player identification and information are printed inside. Values shown are for complete but empty covers, with the striker surface intact. Complete matchbooks with matches bring about 2X the values quoted.

	NM	EX	VG
Complete Set (20):	325.00	160.00	95.00
Common Player:	15.00	7.50	4.50
(1) Nick Altrock	15.00	7.50	4.50
(2) Ossie Bluege	15.00	7.50	4.50
(3) Joe Cronin	20.00	10.00	6.00
(4) Alvin Crowder	15.00	7.50	4.50
(5) Goose Goslin	20.00	10.00	6.00
(6) Clark Griffith	20.00	10.00	6.00
(7) Bucky Harris	20.00	10.00	6.00
(8) Walter Johnson	45.00	22.00	13.50
(9) Joe Judge	15.00	7.50	4.50
(10) Harmon Killebrew	25.00	12.50	7.50
(11) Joe Kuhel	15.00	7.50	4.50
(12) Buddy Lewis	15.00	7.50	4.50
(13) Clyde Milan	15.00	7.50	4.50
(14) Buddy Myer	15.00	7.50	4.50
(15) Roger Peckinpaugh	15.00	7.50	4.50
(16) Sam Rice	20.00	10.00	6.00
(17) Roy Sievers	15.00	7.50	4.50
(18) Stanley Spence	15.00	7.50	4.50
(19) Mickey Vernon	15.00	7.50	4.50
(20) Samuel West	15.00	7.50	4.50

1953 First National Super Market Boston Red Sox

Four of the early 1950s Red Sox appear in this series issued by a Boston grocery chain. The cards may have been distributed in conjunction with players' in-store appearances. The cards measure 3-3/4" x 5" and are printed in black-and-white. A facsimile autograph appears on the front. Backs have the sponsor's advertising. The unnumbered cards are checklisted here alphabetically. See also 1953 Stop & Shop Boston Red Sox.

	NM	EX	VG
Complete Set (4):	2,500	1,250	750.00
Common Player:	750.00	375.00	225.00
(1) Billy Goodman	750.00	375.00	225.00
(2) Ellis Kinder	750.00	375.00	225.00
(3) Mel Parnell	750.00	375.00	225.00
(4) Sammy White	750.00	375.00	225.00

1951 Fischer's Bread Labels

This set of end-labels from loaves of bread consists of 32 player photos, each measuring approximately 2-3/4" square. The labels include the player's name, team and position, along with a few words about him. The bakery's slogan "Bread For Energy" appears in a dark band along the bottom. The set, which is unnumbered, was distributed in the Northeast.

	NM	EX	VG
Complete Set (32):	25,000	10,000	5,000
Common Player:	750.00	375.00	225.00
(1) Vern Bickford	750.00	300.00	150.00
(2) Ralph Branca	825.00	325.00	175.00
(3) Harry Brecheen	750.00	300.00	150.00
(4) "Chico" Carrasquel	750.00	300.00	150.00
(5) Cliff Chambers	750.00	300.00	150.00
(6) "Hoot" Evers	750.00	300.00	150.00
(7) Ned Garver	750.00	300.00	150.00
(8) Billy Goodman	750.00	300.00	150.00
(9) Gil Hodges	1,350	550.00	275.00
(10) Larry Jansen	750.00	300.00	150.00
(11) Willie Jones	750.00	300.00	150.00
(12) Eddie Joost	750.00	300.00	150.00
(13) George Kell	1,250	500.00	250.00
(14) Alex Kellner	750.00	300.00	150.00
(15) Ted Kluszewski	1,200	480.00	240.00
(16) Jim Konstanty	750.00	300.00	150.00
(17) Bob Lemon	1,250	500.00	250.00
(18) Cass Michaels	750.00	300.00	150.00
(19) Johnny Mize	1,250	500.00	250.00
(20) Irv Noren	750.00	300.00	150.00
(21) Andy Pafko	750.00	300.00	150.00
(22) Joe Page	750.00	300.00	150.00
(23) Mel Parnell	750.00	300.00	150.00
(24) Johnny Sain	825.00	330.00	165.00
(25) "Red" Schoendienst	1,250	500.00	250.00
(26) Roy Sievers	750.00	300.00	150.00
(27) Roy Smalley	750.00	300.00	150.00
(28) Herman Wehmeier	750.00	300.00	150.00
(29) Bill Werle	750.00	300.00	150.00
(30) Wes Westrum	750.00	300.00	150.00
(31) Early Wynn	1,250	500.00	250.00
(32) Gus Zernial	750.00	300.00	150.00

1970 Flavor-est Milk Milwaukee Brewers

While purporting to be a dairy issue, this is actually a collectors' set produced by Illinois hobbyist Bob Solon. The cards picture members of the 1970 Brewers in their first year in Milwaukee. Posed action photos and portraits are printed in blue-and-white on a 2-3/8" x 4-1/4" format. The pictures are borderless at top and sides. At bottom is a white strip with the player name. Backs have a dairy ad. The unnumbered cards are checklisted here alphabetically. Ironically, this set was later reissued in a marked reprint.

	NM	EX	VG
Complete Set (24):	25.00	12.50	7.50
Common Player:	2.50	1.25	.70
(1) Gene Brabender	2.50	1.25	.70
(2) Dave Bristol	2.50	1.25	.70
(3) Wayne Comer	2.50	1.25	.70
(4) Cal Ermer	2.50	1.25	.70
(5) Greg Goossen	2.50	1.25	.70
(6) Tom Harper	3.50	1.75	1.00
(7) Mike Hegan	3.50	1.75	1.00
(8) Mike Hershberger	2.50	1.25	.70
(9) Steve Hovley	2.50	1.25	.70
(10) John Kennedy	2.50	1.25	.70
(11) Lew Krausse	2.50	1.25	.70
(12) Ted Kubiak	2.50	1.25	.70
(13) Bob Locker	2.50	1.25	.70
(14) Roy McMillan	2.50	1.25	.70
(15) Jerry McNertney	2.50	1.25	.70
(16) Bob Meyer	2.50	1.25	.70
(17) John Morris	2.50	1.25	.70
(18) John O'Donoghue	2.50	1.25	.70
(19) Marty Pattin	2.50	1.25	.70
(20) Rich Rollins	2.50	1.25	.70
(21) Phil Roof	2.50	1.25	.70
(22) Ted Savage	2.50	1.25	.70
(23) Russ Snyder	2.50	1.25	.70
(24) Dan Walton	3.50	1.75	1.00

1923 Fleer

While only a few specimens are known to date, from the print on the back it can be presumed that all 60 of the baseball players from the blank-back strip card set cataloged as W515 were also issued with Fleer advertising on the verso. Several cards are also known with boxers, indicating another 60 cards of non-baseball athletes and other famous people were also produced. The 1-5/8" x 2-3/8" cards feature crude color line art of the player on front, with a black-and-white ad on back. The cards pre-date by more than a decade Fleer's "Cops and Robbers" set of 1935, and are some 35 years in advance of Fleer's first modern baseball issue.

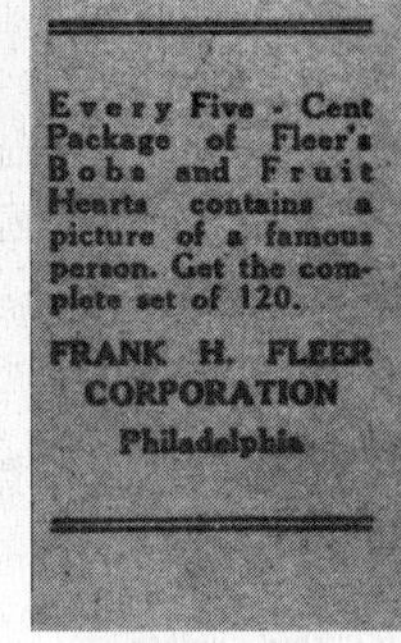

	NM	EX	VG
Complete Set (60):	15,000	7,500	4,500
Common Player:	175.00	85.00	50.00
1 Bill Cunningham	175.00	85.00	50.00
2 Al Mamaux	175.00	85.00	50.00
3 "Babe" Ruth	1,325	660.00	400.00
4 Dave Bancroft	350.00	175.00	105.00
5 Ed Rommel	175.00	85.00	50.00
6 "Babe" Adams	175.00	85.00	50.00
7 Clarence Walker	175.00	85.00	50.00
8 Waite Hoyt	350.00	175.00	105.00
9 Bob Shawkey	175.00	85.00	50.00
10 "Ty" Cobb	1,000	500.00	300.00
11 George Sisler	350.00	175.00	105.00
12 Jack Bentley	175.00	85.00	50.00
13 Jim O'Connell	175.00	85.00	50.00
14 Frank Frisch	350.00	175.00	105.00
15 Frank Baker	350.00	175.00	105.00
16 Burleigh Grimes	350.00	175.00	105.00
17 Wally Schang	175.00	85.00	50.00
18 Harry Heilman (Heilmann)	350.00	175.00	105.00
19 Aaron Ward	175.00	85.00	50.00
20 Carl Mays	200.00	100.00	60.00
21 The Meusel Bros. (Bob Meusel, Irish Meusel)	225.00	110.00	67.00
22 Arthur Nehf	175.00	85.00	50.00
23 Lee Meadows	175.00	85.00	50.00
24 "Casey" Stengel	375.00	185.00	110.00
25 Jack Scott	175.00	85.00	50.00
26 Kenneth Williams	175.00	85.00	50.00
27 Joe Bush	175.00	85.00	50.00
28 Tris Speaker	400.00	200.00	120.00
29 Ross Young (Youngs)	350.00	175.00	105.00
30 Joe Dugan	175.00	85.00	50.00
31 The Barnes Bros. (Jesse Barnes, Virgil Barnes)	200.00	100.00	60.00
32 George Kelly	350.00	175.00	105.00
33 Hugh McQuillen (McQuillan)	175.00	85.00	50.00
34 Hugh Jennings	350.00	175.00	105.00
35 Tom Griffith	175.00	85.00	50.00
36 Miller Huggins	350.00	175.00	105.00
37 "Whitey" Witt	175.00	85.00	50.00
38 Walter Johnson	500.00	250.00	150.00
39 "Wally" Pipp	200.00	100.00	60.00
40 "Dutch" Reuther (Ruether)	175.00	85.00	50.00
41 Jim Johnston	175.00	85.00	50.00
42 Willie Kamm	175.00	85.00	50.00
43 Sam Jones	175.00	85.00	50.00
44 Frank Snyder	175.00	85.00	50.00
45 John McGraw	350.00	175.00	105.00
46 Everett Scott	175.00	85.00	50.00
47 "Babe" Ruth	1,325	660.00	400.00
48 Urban Shocker	175.00	85.00	50.00
49 Grover Alexander	400.00	200.00	120.00
50 "Rabbit" Maranville	350.00	175.00	105.00
51 Ray Schalk	350.00	175.00	105.00
52 "Heinie" Groh	175.00	85.00	50.00
53 Wilbert Robinson	350.00	175.00	105.00
54 George Burns	175.00	85.00	50.00
55 Rogers Hornsby	400.00	200.00	120.00
56 Zack Wheat	350.00	175.00	105.00
57 Eddie Roush	350.00	175.00	105.00
58 Eddie Collins	350.00	175.00	105.00
59 Charlie Hollocher	175.00	85.00	50.00
60 Red Faber	350.00	175.00	105.00

1959 Fleer Ted Williams

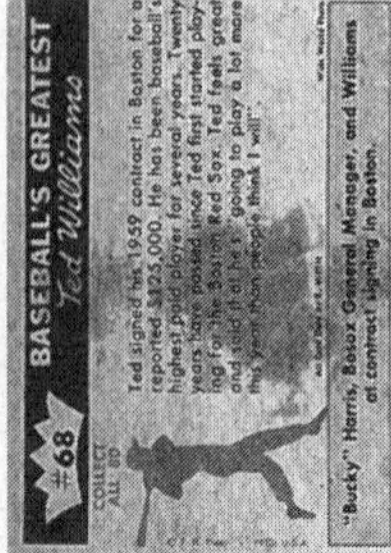

This 80-card 1959 Fleer set tells of the life of baseball great Ted Williams, from his childhood years up to 1958. The full-color cards measure 2-1/2" x 3-1/2" in size and make use of both horizontal and vertical formats. The card backs, all designed horizontally, contain a continuing biography of Williams. Card #68 was withdrawn from the set early in production and is scarce. Counterfeit cards of #68 have been produced and can be distinguished by a cross-hatch pattern which appears over the photo on the card fronts.

		NM	EX	VG
Complete Set (80):		2,100	1,000	500.00
Common Card:		12.50	6.25	3.75
Wax Pack (6):		550.00		
1	The Early Years	95.00	20.00	7.50
2	Ted's Idol (Babe Ruth)	65.00	32.50	20.00
3	Practice Makes Perfect	12.50	6.25	3.75
4	1934 - Ted Learns The Fine Points	12.50	6.25	3.75
5	Ted's Fame Spreads - 1935-36	12.50	6.25	3.75
6	Ted Turns Professional	20.00	10.00	6.00
7	1936 - From Mound To Plate	12.50	6.25	3.75
8	1937 - First Full Season	12.50	6.25	3.75
9	1937 - First Step To The Majors (With Eddie Collins.)	12.50	6.25	3.75
10	1938 - Gunning As A Pastime	12.50	6.25	3.75
11	1938 - First Spring Training (With Jimmie Foxx.)	30.00	15.00	9.00
12	1939 - Burning Up The Minors	20.00	10.00	6.00
13	1939 - Ted Shows He Will Stay	12.50	6.25	3.75
14	Outstanding Rookie of 1939	20.00	10.00	6.00
15	1940 - Williams Licks Sophomore Jinx	20.00	10.00	6.00
16	1941 - Williams' Greatest Year	12.50	6.25	3.75
17	1941 - How Ted Hit .400	30.00	15.00	9.00
18	1941 - All-Star Hero	12.50	6.25	3.75
19	1942 - Ted Wins Triple Crown	12.50	6.25	3.75
20	1942 - On To Naval Training	12.50	6.25	3.75
21	1943 - Honors For Williams	12.50	6.25	3.75
22	1944 - Ted Solos	12.50	6.25	3.75
23	1944 - Williams Wins His Wings	12.50	6.25	3.75
24	1945 - Sharpshooter	12.50	6.25	3.75
25	1945 - Ted Is Discharged	12.50	6.25	3.75
26	1946 - Off To A Flying Start	12.50	6.25	3.75
27	July 9, 1946 - One Man Show	12.50	6.25	3.75
28	July 14, 1946 - The Williams Shift	12.50	6.25	3.75
29	July 21, 1946, Ted Hits For The Cycle	20.00	10.00	6.00
30	1946 - Beating The Williams Shift	12.50	6.25	3.75
31	Oct. 1946 - Sox Lose The Series	12.50	6.25	3.75
32	1946 - Most Valuable Player	12.50	6.25	3.75
33	1947 - Another Triple Crown For Ted	12.50	6.25	3.75
34	1947 - Ted Sets Runs-Scored Record	12.50	6.25	3.75
35	1948 - The Sox Miss The Pennant	12.50	6.25	3.75
36	1948 - Banner Year For Ted	12.50	6.25	3.75
37	1949 - Sox Miss Out Again	12.50	6.25	3.75
38	1949 - Power Rampage	12.50	6.25	3.75
39	1950 - Great Start (With Joe Cronin and Eddie Collins.)	12.50	6.25	3.75
40	July 11, 1950 - Ted Crashes Into Wall	12.50	6.25	3.75
41	1950 - Ted Recovers	12.50	6.25	3.75
42	1951 - Williams Slowed By Injury	12.50	6.25	3.75
43	1951 - Leads Outfielders In Double Play	12.50	6.25	3.75
44	1952 - Back To The Marines	12.50	6.25	3.75
45	1952 - Farewell To Baseball?	12.50	6.25	3.75
46	1952 - Ready For Combat	12.50	6.25	3.75
47	1953 - Ted Crash Lands Jet	12.50	6.25	3.75
48	July 14, 1953 - Ted Returns	12.50	6.25	3.75
49	1953 - Smash Return	12.50	6.25	3.75
50	March 1954 - Spring Injury	12.50	6.25	3.75
51	May 16, 1954 - Ted Is Patched Up	12.50	6.25	3.75
52	1954 - Ted's Comeback	12.50	6.25	3.75
53	1954 - Ted's Comeback Is A Sucess	12.50	6.25	3.75
54	Dec. 1954, Fisherman Ted Hooks a Big On	12.50	6.25	3.75
55	1955 - Ted Decides Retirement Is "No Go (With Joe Cronin.)	12.50	6.25	3.75
56	1955 - 2,000th Major League Hit	12.50	6.25	3.75
57	1956 - Ted Reaches 400th Homer	12.50	6.25	3.75
58	1957 - Williams Hits .388	12.50	6.25	3.75
59	1957 - Hot September For Ted	12.50	6.25	3.75
60	1957 - More Records For Ted	12.50	6.25	3.75
61	1957 - Outfielder Ted	12.50	6.25	3.75
62	1958 - 6th Batting Title For Ted	12.50	6.25	3.75
63	Ted's All-Star Record	35.00	17.50	10.00
64	1958 - Daughter And Famous Daddy	12.50	6.25	3.75
65	August 30, 1958	12.50	6.25	3.75
66	1958 - Powerhouse	12.50	6.25	3.75
67	Two Famous Fishermen (With Sam Snead.)	20.00	10.00	6.00
68	Jan. 23, 1959 - Ted Signs For 1959	600.00	300.00	175.00
69	A Future Ted Williams?	12.50	6.25	3.75
70	Ted Williams & Jim Thorpe	30.00	15.00	9.00
71	Ted's Hitting Fundamentals #1	12.50	6.25	3.75
72	Ted's Hitting Fundamentals #2	12.50	6.25	3.75
73	Ted's Hitting Fundamentals #3	12.50	6.25	3.75
74	Here's How!	12.50	6.25	3.75
75	Williams' Value To Red Sox (With Babe Ruth, Eddie Collins.)	30.00	15.00	9.00
76	Ted's Remarkable "On Base" Record	12.50	6.25	3.75
77	Ted Relaxes	12.50	6.25	3.75
78	Honors For Williams	12.50	6.25	3.75
79	Where Ted Stands	25.00	12.50	7.50
80	Ted's Goals For 1959	40.00	15.00	9.00

1960 Fleer Baseball Greats

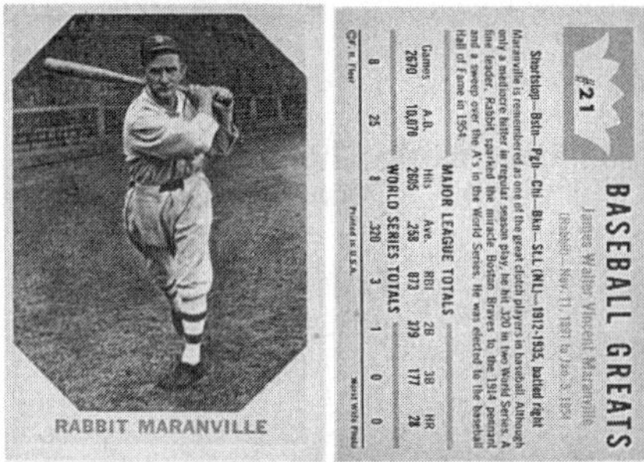

The 1960 Fleer Baseball Greats set consists of 78 cards of the game's top players from the past, plus a card of Ted Williams, who was in his final major league season. The cards are standard size (2-1/2" x 3-1/2") and feature color photos inside blue, green, red or yellow borders. The card backs carry a short player biography plus career hitting or pitching statistics. Unissued cards with a Pepper Martin back (#80), but with another player pictured on the front, exist. All have been either cancelled with a slit cut out of the bottom, or show evidence of having been hand-cut from a sheet.

		NM	EX	VG
Complete Set (79):		850.00	425.00	250.00
Common Player:		9.00	4.50	2.75
Wax Pack:		550.00		
1	Nap Lajoie	22.50	7.50	4.00
2	Christy Mathewson	16.00	8.00	5.00
3	Babe Ruth	60.00	30.00	18.00
4	Carl Hubbell	9.00	4.50	2.75
5	Grover Cleveland Alexander	15.00	7.50	4.50
6	Walter Johnson	20.00	10.00	6.00
7	Chief Bender	9.00	4.50	2.75
8	Roger Bresnahan	9.00	4.50	2.75
9	Mordecai Brown	9.00	4.50	2.75
10	Tris Speaker	9.00	4.50	2.75
11	Arky Vaughan	9.00	4.50	2.75
12	Zack Wheat	9.00	4.50	2.75
13	George Sisler	9.00	4.50	2.75
14	Connie Mack	9.00	4.50	2.75
15	Clark Griffith	9.00	4.50	2.75
16	Lou Boudreau	9.00	4.50	2.75
17	Ernie Lombardi	9.00	4.50	2.75
18	Heinie Manush	9.00	4.50	2.75
19	Marty Marion	9.00	4.50	2.75
20	Eddie Collins	9.00	4.50	2.75
21	Rabbit Maranville	9.00	4.50	2.75
22	Joe Medwick	9.00	4.50	2.75
23	Ed Barrow	9.00	4.50	2.75
24	Mickey Cochrane	9.00	4.50	2.75
25	Jimmy Collins	9.00	4.50	2.75
26	Bob Feller	13.50	6.75	4.00
27	Luke Appling	9.00	4.50	2.75
28	Lou Gehrig	50.00	25.00	15.00
29	Gabby Hartnett	9.00	4.50	2.75
30	Chuck Klein	9.00	4.50	2.75
31	Tony Lazzeri	9.00	4.50	2.75
32	Al Simmons	9.00	4.50	2.75
33	Wilbert Robinson	9.00	4.50	2.75
34	Sam Rice	9.00	4.50	2.75
35	Herb Pennock	9.00	4.50	2.75
36	Mel Ott	9.00	4.50	2.75
37	Lefty O'Doul	9.00	4.50	2.75
38	Johnny Mize	9.00	4.50	2.75
39	Bing Miller	9.00	4.50	2.75
40	Joe Tinker	9.00	4.50	2.75
41	Frank Baker	9.00	4.50	2.75
42	Ty Cobb	30.00	15.00	9.00
43	Paul Derringer	9.00	4.50	2.75
44	Cap Anson	9.00	4.50	2.75
45	Jim Bottomley	9.00	4.50	2.75
46	Eddie Plank	9.00	4.50	2.75
47	Cy Young	16.00	8.00	5.00
48	Hack Wilson	9.00	4.50	2.75
49	Ed Walsh	9.00	4.50	2.75
50	Frank Chance	9.00	4.50	2.75
51	Dazzy Vance	9.00	4.50	2.75
52	Bill Terry	9.00	4.50	2.75
53	Jimmy Foxx	15.00	7.50	4.50
54	Lefty Gomez	9.00	4.50	2.75
55	Branch Rickey	9.00	4.50	2.75
56	Ray Schalk	9.00	4.50	2.75
57	Johnny Evers	9.00	4.50	2.75
58	Charlie Gehringer	9.00	4.50	2.75
59	Burleigh Grimes	9.00	4.50	2.75
60	Lefty Grove	9.00	4.50	2.75
61	Rube Waddell	9.00	4.50	2.75
62	Honus Wagner	15.00	7.50	4.50
63	Red Ruffing	9.00	4.50	2.75
64	Judge Landis	9.00	4.50	2.75
65	Harry Heilmann	9.00	4.50	2.75
66	John McGraw	9.00	4.50	2.75
67	Hughie Jennings	9.00	4.50	2.75
68	Hal Newhouser	9.00	4.50	2.75
69	Waite Hoyt	9.00	4.50	2.75
70	Bobo Newsom	9.00	4.50	2.75
71	Earl Averill	9.00	4.50	2.75
72	Ted Williams	50.00	25.00	15.00
73	Warren Giles	9.00	4.50	2.75
74	Ford Frick	9.00	4.50	2.75
75	Ki Ki Cuyler	9.00	4.50	2.75
76	Paul Waner	9.00	4.50	2.75
77	Pie Traynor	9.00	4.50	2.75
78	Lloyd Waner	9.00	4.50	2.75
79	Ralph Kiner	9.00	4.50	2.75
80	Pepper Martin (Unissued, slit-cancelled proof, Lefty Grove, Joe Tinker or Eddie Collins on front.)	2,000	800.00	400.00
80	Pepper Martin (Unissued hand-cut proof. Lefty Grove, Eddie Collins or Joe Tinker on front.)	2,750	1,350	825.00

1960-62 Fleer Team Logo Decals

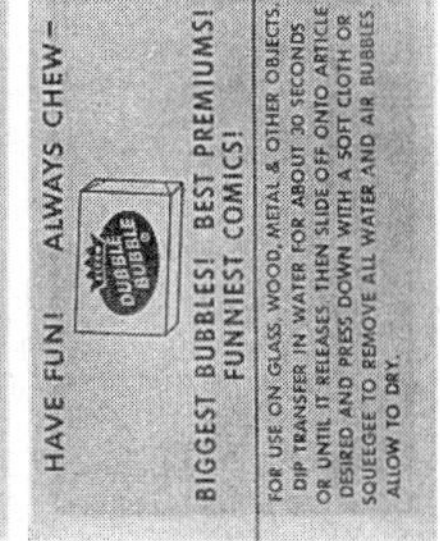

These colorful team logo decals were pack inserts in Fleer's 1960-62 baseball card issues. The decals measure 2-1/4" x 3". Those issued in 1960 have a blue background on front. The 1961-62 decals have a white background on front. Backs have advertising for Fleer bubblegum and instructions on applying the decals. The 1961 decals have back printing in blue; the 1962s are in red.

	NM	EX	VG
Complete Set, 1960 (16):	100.00	50.00	30.00
Complete Set, 1961 (18):	100.00	50.00	30.00
Complete Set, 1962 (20):	250.00	125.00	75.00
1960 team decal, blue background	9.00	4.50	2.75
1961 decal, white background, blue back	4.50	2.25	1.25
1962 decal, white background, red back	9.00	4.50	2.75

1961 Fleer Baseball Greats

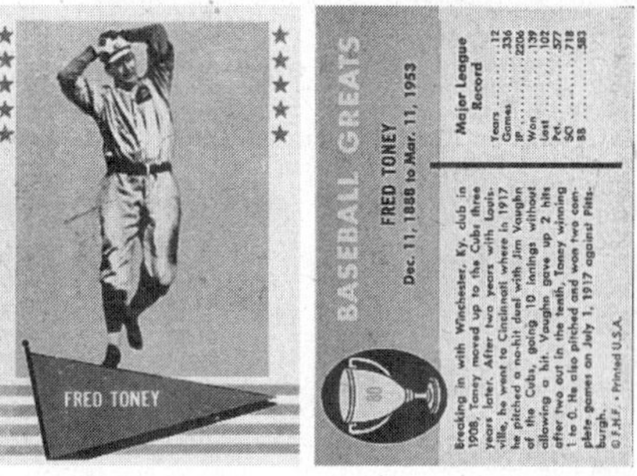

In 1961, Fleer issued another set utilizing the Baseball Greats theme. The 154-card set was issued in two series and features a color (or colorized) player portrait against a colored background. The player's name is located in a pennant at bottom. Card backs feature orange and black on white stock and contain player biographical and statistical information. The cards measure 2-1/2" x 3-1/2" in size. Five-cent wax packs included five cards plus a team logo decal and sticker.

		NM	EX	VG
Complete Set (154):		1,000	500.00	300.00
Common Player:		6.00	3.00	1.75
Wax Pack (5+1+1):		225.00		
1	Checklist (Frank Baker, Ty Cobb, Zach Wheat)	25.00	12.50	7.50
2	G.C. Alexander	7.50	3.75	2.25
3	Nick Altrock	6.00	3.00	1.75
4	Cap Anson	6.00	3.00	1.75
5	Earl Averill	6.00	3.00	1.75
6	Home Run Baker	6.00	3.00	1.75
7	Dave Bancroft	6.00	3.00	1.75
8	Chief Bender	6.00	3.00	1.75
9	Jim Bottomley	6.00	3.00	1.75
10	Roger Bresnahan	6.00	3.00	1.75
11	Mordecai Brown	6.00	3.00	1.75
12	Max Carey	6.00	3.00	1.75
13	Jack Chesbro	6.00	3.00	1.75
14	Ty Cobb	25.00	12.50	7.50
15	Mickey Cochrane	6.00	3.00	1.75
16	Eddie Collins	6.00	3.00	1.75
17	Earle Combs	6.00	3.00	1.75
18	Charles Comiskey	6.00	3.00	1.75
19	Ki Ki Cuyler	6.00	3.00	1.75
20	Paul Derringer	6.00	3.00	1.75
21	Howard Ehmke	6.00	3.00	1.75
22	Billy Evans	6.00	3.00	1.75
23	Johnny Evers	6.00	3.00	1.75
24	Red Faber	6.00	3.00	1.75
25	Bob Feller	10.00	5.00	3.00
26	Wes Ferrell	6.00	3.00	1.75
27	Lew Fonseca	6.00	3.00	1.75
28	Jimmy Foxx	7.50	3.75	2.25
29	Ford Frick	6.00	3.00	1.75
30	Frankie Frisch	6.00	3.00	1.75
31	Lou Gehrig	45.00	22.50	13.50

32	Charlie Gehringer	6.00	3.00	1.75
33	Warren Giles	6.00	3.00	1.75
34	Lefty Gomez	6.00	3.00	1.75
35	Goose Goslin	6.00	3.00	1.75
36	Clark Griffith	6.00	3.00	1.75
37	Burleigh Grimes	6.00	3.00	1.75
38	Lefty Grove	6.00	3.00	1.75
39	Chick Hafey	6.00	3.00	1.75
40	Jesse Haines	6.00	3.00	1.75
41	Gabby Hartnett	6.00	3.00	1.75
42	Harry Heilmann	6.00	3.00	1.75
43	Rogers Hornsby	6.00	3.00	1.75
44	Waite Hoyt	6.00	3.00	1.75
45	Carl Hubbell	6.00	3.00	1.75
46	Miller Huggins	6.00	3.00	1.75
47	Hughie Jennings	6.00	3.00	1.75
48	Ban Johnson	6.00	3.00	1.75
49	Walter Johnson	12.00	6.00	3.50
50	Ralph Kiner	6.00	3.00	1.75
51	Chuck Klein	6.00	3.00	1.75
52	Johnny Kling	6.00	3.00	1.75
53	Judge Landis	6.00	3.00	1.75
54	Tony Lazzeri	6.00	3.00	1.75
55	Ernie Lombardi	6.00	3.00	1.75
56	Dolf Luque	6.00	3.00	1.75
57	Heinie Manush	6.00	3.00	1.75
58	Marty Marion	6.00	3.00	1.75
59	Christy Mathewson	12.00	6.00	3.50
60	John McGraw	6.00	3.00	1.75
61	Joe Medwick	6.00	3.00	1.75
62	Bing Miller	6.00	3.00	1.75
63	Johnny Mize	6.00	3.00	1.75
64	Johnny Mostil	6.00	3.00	1.75
65	Art Nehf	6.00	3.00	1.75
66	Hal Newhouser	6.00	3.00	1.75
67	Bobo Newsom	6.00	3.00	1.75
68	Mel Ott	6.00	3.00	1.75
69	Allie Reynolds	6.00	3.00	1.75
70	Sam Rice	6.00	3.00	1.75
71	Eppa Rixey	6.00	3.00	1.75
72	Edd Roush	6.00	3.00	1.75
73	Schoolboy Rowe	6.00	3.00	1.75
74	Red Ruffing	6.00	3.00	1.75
75	Babe Ruth	65.00	32.50	20.00
76	Joe Sewell	6.00	3.00	1.75
77	Al Simmons	6.00	3.00	1.75
78	George Sisler	6.00	3.00	1.75
79	Tris Speaker	6.00	3.00	1.75
80	Fred Toney	6.00	3.00	1.75
81	Dazzy Vance	6.00	3.00	1.75
82	Jim Vaughn	6.00	3.00	1.75
83	Big Ed Walsh	6.00	3.00	1.75
84	Lloyd Waner	6.00	3.00	1.75
85	Paul Waner	6.00	3.00	1.75
86	Zach Wheat	6.00	3.00	1.75
87	Hack Wilson	6.00	3.00	1.75
88	Jimmy Wilson	6.00	3.00	1.75
89	Checklist (George Sisler, Pie Traynor)	20.00	10.00	6.00
90	Babe Adams	6.00	3.00	1.75
91	Dale Alexander	6.00	3.00	1.75
92	Jim Bagby	6.00	3.00	1.75
93	Ossie Bluege	6.00	3.00	1.75
94	Lou Boudreau	6.00	3.00	1.75
95	Tommy Bridges	6.00	3.00	1.75
96	Donnie Bush (Donie)	6.00	3.00	1.75
97	Dolph Camilli	6.00	3.00	1.75
98	Frank Chance	6.00	3.00	1.75
99	Jimmy Collins	6.00	3.00	1.75
100	Stanley Coveleskie (Coveleski)	6.00	3.00	1.75
101	Hughie Critz	6.00	3.00	1.75
102	General Crowder	6.00	3.00	1.75
103	Joe Dugan	6.00	3.00	1.75
104	Bibb Falk	6.00	3.00	1.75
105	Rick Ferrell	6.00	3.00	1.75
106	Art Fletcher	6.00	3.00	1.75
107	Dennis Galehouse	6.00	3.00	1.75
108	Chick Galloway	6.00	3.00	1.75
109	Mule Haas	6.00	3.00	1.75
110	Stan Hack	6.00	3.00	1.75
111	Bump Hadley	6.00	3.00	1.75
112	Billy Hamilton	6.00	3.00	1.75
113	Joe Hauser	6.00	3.00	1.75
114	Babe Herman	6.00	3.00	1.75
115	Travis Jackson	6.00	3.00	1.75
116	Eddie Joost	6.00	3.00	1.75
117	Addie Joss	6.00	3.00	1.75
118	Joe Judge	6.00	3.00	1.75
119	Joe Kuhel	6.00	3.00	1.75
120	Nap Lajoie	6.00	3.00	1.75
121	Dutch Leonard	6.00	3.00	1.75
122	Ted Lyons	6.00	3.00	1.75
123	Connie Mack	6.00	3.00	1.75
124	Rabbit Maranville	6.00	3.00	1.75
125	Fred Marberry	6.00	3.00	1.75
126	Iron Man McGinnity	6.00	3.00	1.75
127	Oscar Melillo	6.00	3.00	1.75
128	Ray Mueller	6.00	3.00	1.75
129	Kid Nichols	6.00	3.00	1.75
130	Lefty O'Doul	6.00	3.00	1.75
131	Bob O'Farrell	6.00	3.00	1.75
132	Roger Peckinpaugh	6.00	3.00	1.75
133	Herb Pennock	6.00	3.00	1.75
134	George Pipgras	6.00	3.00	1.75
135	Eddie Plank	6.00	3.00	1.75
136	Ray Schalk	6.00	3.00	1.75
137	Hal Schumacher	6.00	3.00	1.75
138	Luke Sewell	6.00	3.00	1.75
139	Bob Shawkey	6.00	3.00	1.75
140	Riggs Stephenson	6.00	3.00	1.75
141	Billy Sullivan	6.00	3.00	1.75
142	Bill Terry	6.00	3.00	1.75
143	Joe Tinker	6.00	3.00	1.75
144	Pie Traynor	6.00	3.00	1.75
145	George Uhle	6.00	3.00	1.75
146	Hal Troskey (Trosky)	6.00	3.00	1.75
147	Arky Vaughan	6.00	3.00	1.75
148	Johnny Vander Meer	6.00	3.00	1.75
149	Rube Waddell	6.00	3.00	1.75
150	Honus Wagner	25.00	12.50	7.50
151	Dixie Walker	6.00	3.00	1.75
152	Ted Williams	60.00	30.00	18.00
153	Cy Young	12.00	6.00	3.50
154	Ross Young (Youngs)	6.00	3.00	1.75

1961 Fleer World Champions Pennant Decals

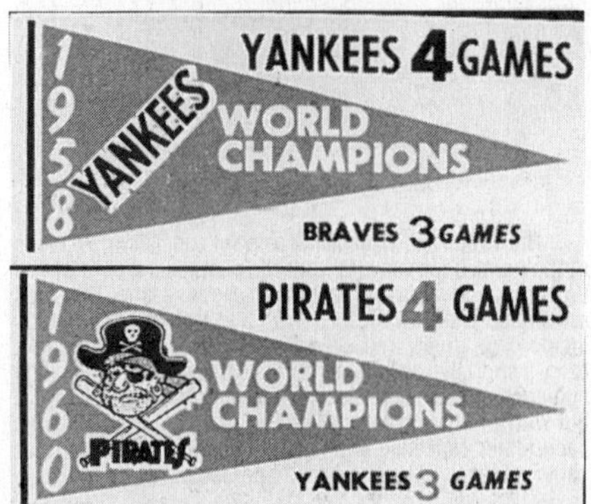

The winner of each World Series from 1913-1960 is honored in this pack insert. The 3" x 1-1/4" decals have a large red or blue pennant at center, with a team name or logo and the "WORLD CHAMPIONS" notation. The year of the Series win is at left on the pennant. The number of games won by each team is at top and botom on right. Backs offer instructions for applying the decals.

		NM	EX	VG
Complete Set (48):		300.00	150.00	90.00
Common Decal:		6.00	3.00	1.75
(1)	1913 - A's	6.00	3.00	1.75
(2)	1914 - Braves	6.00	3.00	1.75
(3)	1915 - Red Sox	6.00	3.00	1.75
(4)	1916 - Red Sox	6.00	3.00	1.75
(5)	1917 - White Sox	6.00	3.00	1.75
(6)	1918 - Red Sox	6.00	3.00	1.75
(7)	1919 - Reds	9.00	4.50	2.75
(8)	1920 - Indians	6.00	3.00	1.75
(9)	1921 - Giants	6.00	3.00	1.75
(10)	1922 - Giants	6.00	3.00	1.75
(11)	1923 - Yankees	7.50	3.75	2.25
(12)	1924 - Senators	6.00	3.00	1.75
(13)	1925 - Yankees	7.50	3.75	2.25
(14)	1926 - Cardinals	6.00	3.00	1.75
(15)	1927 - Yankees	7.50	3.75	2.25
(14)	1928 - Yankees	7.50	3.75	2.25
(15)	1929 - A's	6.00	3.00	1.75
(16)	1930 - A's	6.00	3.00	1.75
(17)	1931 - Cardinals	6.00	3.00	1.75
(18)	1932 - Yankees	7.50	3.75	2.25
(19)	1933 - Giants	6.00	3.00	1.75
(20)	1934 - Cardinals	6.00	3.00	1.75
(21)	1935 - Tigers	6.00	3.00	1.75
(22)	1936 - Yankees	7.50	3.75	2.25
(23)	1937 - Yankees	7.50	3.75	2.25
(24)	1938 - Yankees	7.50	3.75	2.25
(25)	1939 - Yankees	7.50	3.75	2.25
(26)	1940 - Reds	6.00	3.00	1.75
(27)	1941 - Yankees	7.50	3.75	2.25
(28)	1942 - Cardinals	6.00	3.00	1.75
(29)	1943 - Yankees	7.50	3.75	2.25
(30)	1944 - Cardinals	6.00	3.00	1.75
(31)	1945 - Tigers	6.00	3.00	1.75
(32)	1946 - Cardinals	6.00	3.00	1.75
(33)	1947 - Yankees	7.50	3.75	2.25
(34)	1948 - Indians	6.00	3.00	1.75
(35)	1949 - Yankees	7.50	3.75	2.25
(36)	1950 - Yankees	7.50	3.75	2.25
(37)	1951 - Yankees	7.50	3.75	2.25
(38)	1952 - Yankees	7.50	3.75	2.25
(41)	1953 - Yankees	7.50	3.75	2.25
(42)	1954 - Giants	6.00	3.00	1.75
(43)	1955 - Dodgers	9.00	4.50	2.75
(44)	1956 - Yankees	7.50	3.75	2.25
(45)	1957 - Braves	7.50	3.75	2.25
(46)	1958 - Yankees	7.50	3.75	2.25
(47)	1959 - Dodgers	9.00	4.50	2.75
(48)	1960 - Pirates	9.00	4.50	2.75

1963 Fleer

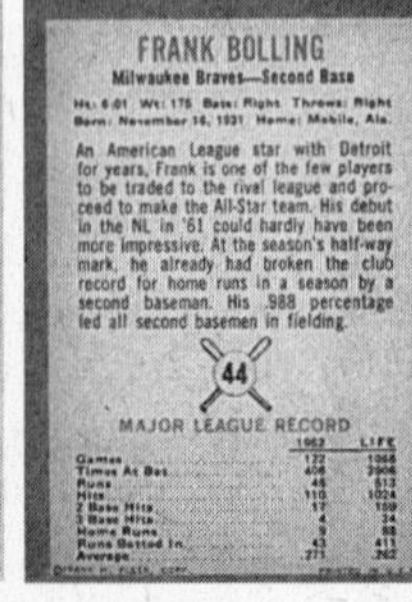

A lawsuit by Topps stopped Fleer's 1963 set at one series of 66 cards. Issued with a cookie rather than gum, the set features color photos of current players. The card backs include statistical information for 1962 and career plus a brief player biography. The cards, which measure 2-1/2" x 3-1/2", are numbered 1-66. An unnumbered checklist was issued with the set and is included in the complete set price in the checklist that follows. The checklist and #46 Adcock are scarce.

		NM	EX	VG
Complete Set (67):		1,500	750.00	450.00
Common Player:		10.00	5.00	3.00
Wax Pack:		1,000		
1	Steve Barber	40.00	10.00	5.00
2	Ron Hansen	10.00	5.00	3.00
3	Milt Pappas	10.00	5.00	3.00
4	Brooks Robinson	50.00	25.00	15.00
5	Willie Mays	90.00	45.00	27.50
6	Lou Clinton	10.00	5.00	3.00
7	Bill Monbouquette	10.00	5.00	3.00
8	Carl Yastrzemski	50.00	25.00	15.00
9	Ray Herbert	10.00	5.00	3.00
10	Jim Landis	10.00	5.00	3.00
11	Dick Donovan	10.00	5.00	3.00
12	Tito Francona	10.00	5.00	3.00
13	Jerry Kindall	10.00	5.00	3.00
14	Frank Lary	10.00	5.00	3.00
15	Dick Howser	10.00	5.00	3.00
16	Jerry Lumpe	10.00	5.00	3.00
17	Norm Siebern	10.00	5.00	3.00
18	Don Lee	10.00	5.00	3.00
19	Albie Pearson	10.00	5.00	3.00
20	Bob Rodgers	10.00	5.00	3.00
21	Leon Wagner	10.00	5.00	3.00
22	Jim Kaat	15.00	7.50	4.50
23	Vic Power	10.00	5.00	3.00
24	Rich Rollins	10.00	5.00	3.00
25	Bobby Richardson	17.50	9.00	5.00
26	Ralph Terry	10.00	5.00	3.00
27	Tom Cheney	10.00	5.00	3.00
28	Chuck Cottier	10.00	5.00	3.00
29	Jimmy Piersall	12.50	6.25	3.75
30	Dave Stenhouse	10.00	5.00	3.00
31	Glen Hobbie	10.00	5.00	3.00
32	Ron Santo	25.00	12.50	7.50
33	Gene Freese	10.00	5.00	3.00
34	Vada Pinson	12.50	6.25	3.75
35	Bob Purkey	10.00	5.00	3.00
36	Joe Amalfitano	10.00	5.00	3.00
37	Bob Aspromonte	10.00	5.00	3.00
38	Dick Farrell	10.00	5.00	3.00
39	Al Spangler	10.00	5.00	3.00
40	Tommy Davis	10.00	5.00	3.00
41	Don Drysdale	35.00	17.50	10.00
42	Sandy Koufax	100.00	50.00	30.00
43	*Maury Wills*	55.00	27.50	16.50
44	Frank Bolling	10.00	5.00	3.00
45	Warren Spahn	40.00	20.00	12.00
46	Joe Adcock/SP	80.00	40.00	24.00
47	Roger Craig	10.00	5.00	3.00
48	Al Jackson	10.00	5.00	3.00
49	Rod Kanehl	10.00	5.00	3.00
50	Ruben Amaro	10.00	5.00	3.00
51	John Callison	10.00	5.00	3.00
52	Clay Dalrymple	10.00	5.00	3.00
53	Don Demeter	10.00	5.00	3.00
54	Art Mahaffey	10.00	5.00	3.00
55	"Smoky" Burgess	10.00	5.00	3.00
56	Roberto Clemente	95.00	47.50	28.00
57	Elroy Face	10.00	5.00	3.00
58	Vernon Law	10.00	5.00	3.00
59	Bill Mazeroski	20.00	10.00	6.00
60	Ken Boyer	12.50	6.25	3.75
61	Bob Gibson	40.00	20.00	12.00
62	Gene Oliver	10.00	5.00	3.00
63	Bill White	13.50	6.75	4.00
64	Orlando Cepeda	22.50	11.00	6.75
65	Jimmy Davenport	10.00	5.00	3.00
66	Billy O'Dell	20.00	7.50	4.00
---	Checklist/SP	300.00	150.00	90.00

1966 Fleer All Star Match Baseball

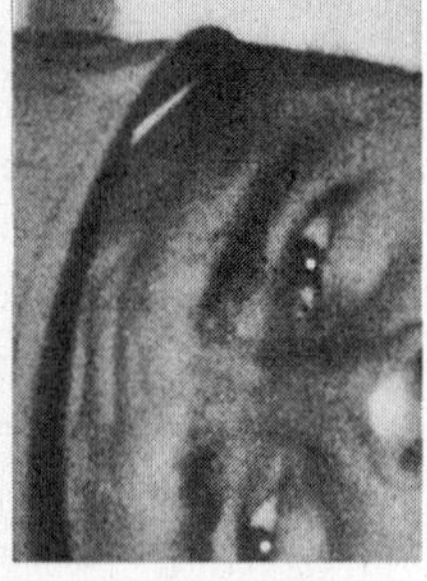

This seldom-seen issue was produced in the years when Fleer was locked out of the "regular" baseball card market. Standard 2-1/2" x 3-1/2" format cards are designed for playing a baseball match game. Backs have a portion of a black-and-white photo of Dodger pitcher Don Drysdale, which can be assembled in jigsaw puzzle fashion. Fronts are printed in red, blue, yellow and black, and numbered F1-F66. Because single cards have little collector appeal, the value of a set is considerably higher than the sum of the parts.

	NM	EX	VG
Complete Set (66):	400.00	200.00	120.00

Common Card:	6.00	3.00	1.75
Wax Pack:	200.00		
Don Drysdale			

1968-70 Fleer Major League Baseball Patches

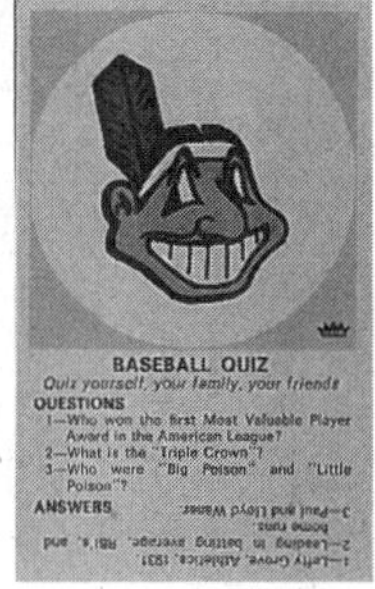

From 1968-70, Fleer sold bubblegum in wax packs which also included four team logo/quiz cards and half a dozen cloth patches, all for a dime. The 2-9/16" x 4-1/16" cards are blank-back and have on front a color team logo at top and three baseball trivia questions at bottom. The cloth patches are about 2-1/2" x 3-5/16" and are die-cut to allow the team logos and nameplates to be removed from the paper backing and stuck on jackets, etc.

		NM	EX	VG
Complete Set Logo Cards (24):		18.00	9.00	5.50
Common Logo Card:		1.50	.70	.45
Complete Set Cloth Patches (29):		35.00	17.50	10.00
Common Cloth Patch:		1.50	.75	.45
Wax Pack:		2.00		
Wax Box (24):		30.00		
	LOGO/QUIZ CARDS			
(1)	Atlanta Braves	1.50	.70	.45
(2)	Baltimore Orioles	1.50	.70	.45
(3)	Boston Red Sox	1.50	.70	.45
(4)	California Angels	1.50	.70	.45
(5)	Chicago Cubs	1.50	.70	.45
(6)	Chicago White Sox	1.50	.70	.45
(7)	Cincinnati Reds	1.50	.70	.45
(8)	Cleveland Indians	1.50	.70	.45
(9)	Detroit Tigers	1.50	.70	.45
(10)	Houston Astros	1.50	.70	.45
(11)	Kansas City Royals	1.50	.70	.45
(12)	Los Angeles Dodgers	1.50	.70	.45
(13)	Minnesota Twins	1.50	.70	.45
(14)	Montreal Expos	2.50	1.25	.70
(15)	New York Mets	3.00	1.50	.90
(16)	New York Yankees	4.00	2.00	1.25
(17)	Oakland A's	2.50	1.25	.70
(18)	Philadelphia Phillies	1.50	.70	.45
(19)	Pittsburgh Pirates	1.50	.70	.45
(20)	San Diego Padres	2.50	1.25	.70
(21)	San Francisco Giants	1.50	.70	.45
(22)	Seattle Pilots	6.00	3.00	1.75
(23)	St. Louis Cardinals	1.50	.70	.45
(24)	Washington Senators	1.50	.70	.45
	TEAM LOGO CLOTH PATCHES			
(1)	Atlanta Braves	1.50	.70	.45
(2)	Baltimore Orioles	1.50	.70	.45
(3)	Boston Red Sox	1.50	.70	.45
(4)	California Angels	1.50	.70	.45
(5)	Chicago Cubs	1.50	.70	.45
(6)	Chicago White Sox	1.50	.70	.45
(7)	Cincinnati Reds	1.50	.70	.45
(8)	Cleveland Indians (Indian head)	1.50	.70	.45
(9)	Cleveland Indians (Batting Indian.)	1.50	.70	.45
(10)	Detroit Tigers	1.50	.70	.45
(11)	Houston Astros	1.50	.70	.45
(12)	Kansas City Royals	1.50	.70	.45
(13)	Los Angeles Dodgers	1.50	.70	.45
(14)	Milwaukee Brewers (M)	1.50	.70	.45
(15)	Milwaukee Brewers (Batting keg.)	1.50	.70	.45
(16)	Minnesota Twins	1.50	.70	.45
(17)	Montreal Expos	2.00	1.00	.60
(18)	New York Mets	2.00	1.00	.60
(19)	New York Yankees	3.00	1.50	.90
(20)	Oakland A's (Plain ball.)	2.00	1.00	.60
(21)	Oakland A's ("The SWINGIN,'" white shoes, on ball.)	1.50	.70	.45
(22)	Philadelphia Phillies	1.50	.70	.45
(23)	Pittsburgh Pirates	1.50	.70	.45
(24)	San Diego Padres	2.00	1.00	.60
(25)	San Francisco Giants	1.50	.70	.45
(26)	Seattle Pilots	3.00	1.50	.90
(27)	St. Louis Cardinals	1.50	.70	.45
(28)	Washington Senators	1.50	.70	.45
(29)	Major League Baseball	1.50	.70	.45

1969 Fleer Cap Plaques

This set of novelty plaques features 3D impressions of each team's cap on thin plastic stock in a 3" x 4" format. Each cap plaque was sold in a wrapper with an easel backing board, surviving specimens of which are quite scarce.

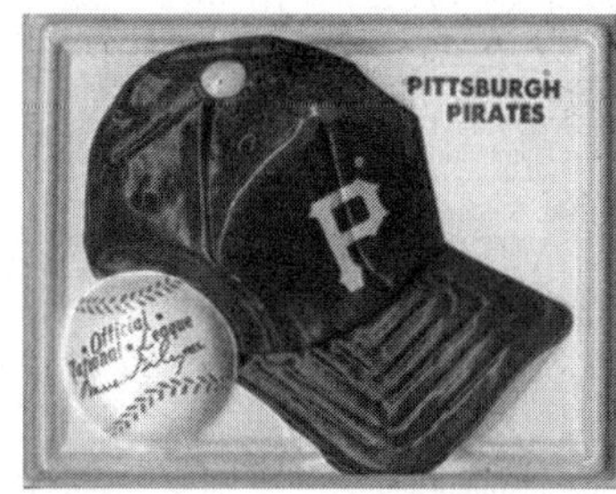

		NM	EX	VG
Complete Set (24):		1,200	600.00	350.00
Common Plaque:		45.00	22.50	13.50
Easel Backing Board:		22.00	11.00	6.50
Unopened Pack:		45.00		
(1)	Atlanta Braves	50.00	25.00	15.00
(2)	Baltimore Orioles	60.00	30.00	18.00
(3)	Boston Red Sox	50.00	25.00	15.00
(4)	California Angels	45.00	22.50	13.50
(5)	Chicago Cubs	60.00	30.00	18.00
(6)	Chicago White Sox	45.00	22.50	13.50
(7)	Cincinnati Reds	45.00	22.50	13.50
(8)	Cleveland Indians	45.00	22.50	13.50
(9)	Detroit Tigers	45.00	22.50	13.50
(10)	Houston Astros	45.00	22.50	13.50
(11)	Kansas City Royals	45.00	22.50	13.50
(12)	Los Angeles Dodgers	50.00	25.00	15.00
(13)	Minnesota Twins	45.00	22.50	13.50
(14)	Montreal Expos	45.00	22.50	13.50
(15)	New York Mets	75.00	37.50	22.50
(16)	New York Yankees	115.00	55.00	35.00
(17)	Oakland A's	60.00	30.00	18.00
(18)	Philadelphia Phillies	45.00	22.50	13.50
(19)	Pittsburgh Pirates	50.00	25.00	15.00
(20)	San Diego Padres	45.00	22.50	13.50
(21)	San Francisco Giants	45.00	22.50	13.50
(22)	Seattle Pilots	125.00	62.50	37.00
(23)	St. Louis Cardinals	50.00	25.00	15.00
(24)	Washington Senators	50.00	25.00	15.00

1970 Fleer Team Logo Decals

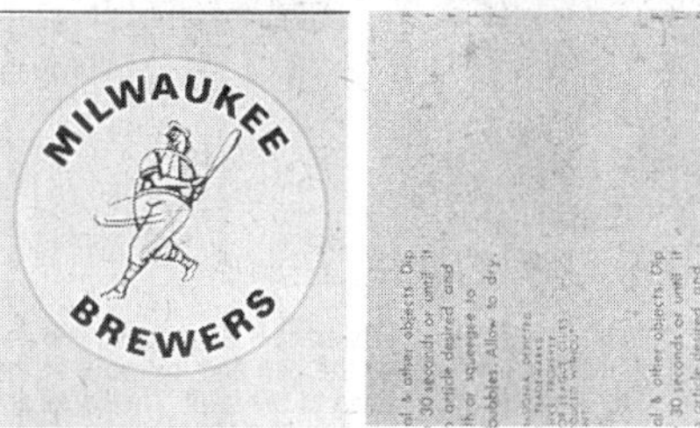

These colorful team logo decals were pack inserts in Fleer's 1970 World Series issue. The decals measure 2-7/16" x 2-3/4". Backs have instructions for applying the decals.

		NM	EX	VG
Complete Set (24):		90.00	45.00	27.50
Common Team:		7.50	3.75	2.25
(1)	Atlanta Braves	7.50	3.75	2.25
(2)	Baltimore Orioles	9.00	4.50	2.75
(3)	Boston Red Sox	7.50	3.75	2.25
(4)	California Angels	7.50	3.75	2.25
(5)	Chicago Cubs	7.50	3.75	2.25
(6)	Chicago White Sox	7.50	3.75	2.25
(7)	Cincinnati Reds	7.50	3.75	2.25
(8)	Cleveland Indians	7.50	3.75	2.25
(9)	Detroit Tigers	7.50	3.75	2.25
(10)	Houston Astros	7.50	3.75	2.25
(11)	Kansas City Royals	7.50	3.75	2.25
(12)	Los Angeles Dodgers	7.50	3.75	2.25
(13)	Milwaukee Brewers	7.50	3.75	2.25
(14)	Minnesota Twins	7.50	3.75	2.25
(15)	Montreal Expos	7.50	3.75	2.25
(16)	New York Mets	7.50	3.75	2.25
(17)	New York Yankees	9.00	4.50	2.75
(18)	Oakland A's	7.50	3.75	2.25
(19)	Philadelphia Phillies	7.50	3.75	2.25
(20)	Pittsburgh Pirates	9.00	4.50	2.75
(21)	San Diego Padres	7.50	3.75	2.25
(22)	San Francisco Giants	7.50	3.75	2.25
(23)	St. Louis Cardinals	7.50	3.75	2.25
(24)	Washington Senators	10.00	5.00	3.00

1970 Fleer World Series

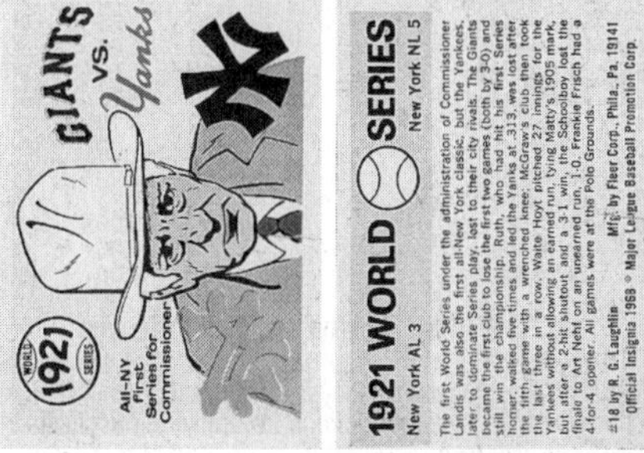

Utilizing the artwork done by Robert Laughlin a few years earlier for a privately marketed set, Fleer offered the first of two World Series highlights sets in 1970. Cards have color front with light blue backs. No card was issued for the 1904 World Series because no Series was played. Cards are checklisted in chronological order.

		NM	EX	VG
Complete Set (66):		150.00	75.00	45.00
Common Card:		1.50	.70	.45
Wax Pack:		35.00		
1	1903 Red Sox/Pirates	2.50	1.25	.70
2	1905 Giants/A's (Christy Mathewson)	2.50	1.25	.70
3	1906 White Sox/Cubs	1.50	.70	.45
4	1907 Cubs/Tigers	1.50	.70	.45
5	1908 Cubs/Tigers (Tinker/Evers/Chance)	3.00	1.50	.90
6	1909 Pirates/Tigers (Honus Wagner/Ty Cobb)	7.50	3.75	2.25
7	1910 A's/Cubs (Chief Bender/Jack Coombs)	2.00	1.00	.60
8	1911 A's/Giants (John McGraw)	2.00	1.00	.60
9	1912 Red Sox/Giants	2.00	1.00	.60
10	1913 A's/Giants	1.50	.70	.45
11	1914 Braves/A's	2.00	1.00	.60
12	1915 Red Sox/Phillies (Babe Ruth)	5.00	2.50	1.50
13	1916 Red Sox/Dodgers (Babe Ruth)	5.00	2.50	1.50
14	1917 White Sox/Giants	1.50	.70	.45
15	1918 Red Sox/Cubs	1.50	.70	.45
16	1919 Reds/White Sox	3.00	1.50	.90
17	1920 Indians/Dodgers (Stan Coveleski)	2.00	1.00	.60
18	1921 Giants/Yankees (Kenesaw Landis)	2.00	1.00	.60
19	1922 Giants/Yankees (Heinie Groh)	2.00	1.00	.60
20	1923 Yankees/Giants (Babe Ruth)	7.50	3.75	2.25
21	1924 Senators/Giants (John McGraw)	2.50	1.25	.70
22	1925 Pirates/Senators (Walter Johnson)	3.00	1.50	.90
23	1926 Cardinals/Yankees (Grover Cleveland Alexander/Tony Lazzeri)	3.00	1.50	.90
24	1927 Yankees/Pirates	2.50	1.25	.70
25	1928 Yankees/Cardinals (Babe Ruth/Lou Gehrig)	7.50	3.75	2.25
26	1929 A's/Cubs	1.50	.70	.45
27	1930 A's/Cardinals	1.50	.70	.45
28	1931 Cardinals/A's (Pepper Martin)	2.00	1.00	.60
29	1932 Yankees/Cubs (Babe Ruth/Lou Gehrig)	7.50	3.75	2.25
30	1933 Giants/Senators (Mel Ott)	2.50	1.25	.70
31	1934 Cardinals/Tigers	1.50	.70	.45
32	1935 Tigers/Cubs (Charlie Gehringer/Tommy Bridges)	2.00	1.00	.60
33	1936 Yankees/Giants	2.00	1.00	.60
34	1937 Yankees/Giants (Carl Hubbell)	2.50	1.25	.70
35	1938 Yankees/Cubs (Lou Gehrig)	4.00	2.00	1.25
36	1939 Yankees/Reds	1.50	.70	.45
37	1940 Reds/Tigers (Mike McCormick)	1.50	.70	.45
38	1941 Yankees/Dodgers	2.00	1.00	.60
39	1942 Cardinals/Yankees	1.50	.70	.45
40	1943 Yankees/Cardinals	1.50	.70	.45
41	1944 Cardinals/Browns	2.00	1.00	.60
42	1945 Tigers/Cubs (Hank Greenberg)	2.50	1.25	.70
43	1946 Cardinals/Red Sox (Enos Slaughter)	2.00	1.00	.60
44	1947 Yankees/Dodgers (Al Gionfriddo)	2.00	1.00	.60
45	1948 Indians/Braves	1.50	.70	.45
46	1949 Yankees/Dodgers (Allie Reynolds/ Preacher Roe)	2.00	1.00	.60
47	1950 Yankees/Phillies	2.00	1.00	.60
48	1951 Yankees/Giants	1.50	.70	.45
49	1952 Yankees/Dodgers (Johnny Mize/ Duke Snider)	2.50	1.25	.70
50	1953 Yankees/Dodgers (Carl Erskine)	2.00	1.00	.60
51	1954 Giants/Indians (Johnny Antonelli)	1.50	.70	.45
52	1955 Dodgers/Yankees	2.00	1.00	.60
53	1956 Yankees/Dodgers	2.00	1.00	.60
54	1957 Braves/Yankees (Lew Burdette)	3.00	1.50	.90
55	1958 Yankees/Braves (Bob Turley)	1.50	.70	.45
56	1959 Dodgers/White Sox (Chuck Essegian)	2.00	1.00	.60
57	1960 Pirates/Yankees	2.00	1.00	.60
58	1961 Yankees/Reds (Whitey Ford)	2.00	1.00	.60
59	1962 Yankees/Giants	1.50	.70	.45
60	1963 Dodgers/Yankees (Bill Skowron)	1.50	.70	.45
61	1964 Cardinals/Yankees (Bobby Richardson)	2.00	1.00	.60
62	1965 Dodgers/Twins	2.00	1.00	.60
63	1966 Orioles/Dodgers	1.50	.70	.45
64	1967 Cardinals/Red Sox	1.50	.70	.45
65	1968 Tigers/Cardinals	2.00	1.00	.60
66	1969 Mets/Orioles	4.50	2.25	1.25

1971-80 Fleer World Series

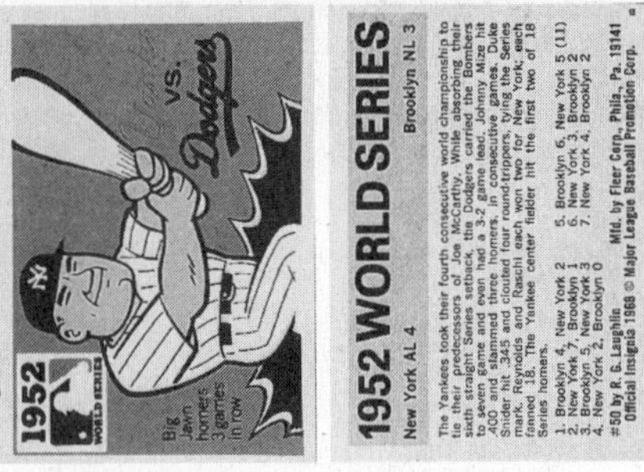

New artwork by Robert Laughlin is featured in the second of Fleer's World Series highlights sets. Fronts feature color art with backs printed in black. It appears as if the original set issued in 1971 was updated intermittently.

		NM	EX	VG
Complete Set (68):		135.00	65.00	40.00
Complete Set (75):		350.00	175.00	100.00
Common Card:		2.00	1.00	.60
Wax Pack:		30.00		
1	1903 Red Sox/Pirates (Cy Young)	6.00	3.00	1.75
2	1904 No World Series (John McGraw)	5.00	2.50	1.50
3	1905 Giants/A's (Christy Mathewson/Chief Bender)	5.00	2.50	1.50
4	1906 White Sox/Cubs	2.00	1.00	.60
5	1907 Cubs/Tigers	2.00	1.00	.60
6	1908 Cubs/Tigers (Ty Cobb)	5.00	2.50	1.50
7	1909 Pirates/Tigers	2.50	1.25	.70
8	1910 A's/Cubs (Eddie Collins)	2.50	1.25	.70
9	1911 A's/Giants (Home Run Baker)	2.50	1.25	.70
10	1912 Red Sox/Giants	2.00	1.00	.60
11	1913 A's/Giants (Christy Mathewson)	3.00	1.50	.90
12	1914 Braves/A's	2.00	1.00	.60
13	1915 Red Sox/Phillies (Grover Cleveland Alexander)	3.00	1.50	.90
14	1916 Red Sox/Dodgers (Jack Coombs)	2.00	1.00	.60
15	1917 White Sox/Giants (Red Faber)	2.50	1.25	.70
16	1918 Red Sox/Cubs (Babe Ruth)	6.00	3.00	1.75
17	1919 Reds/White Sox	4.00	2.00	1.25
18	1920 Indians/Dodgers (Elmer Smith)	2.50	1.25	.70
19	1921 Giants/Yankees (Waite Hoyt)	4.00	2.00	1.25
20	1922 Giants/Yankees (Art Nehf)	2.50	1.25	.70
21	1923 Yankees/Giants (Herb Pennock)	2.50	1.25	.70
22	1924 Senators/Giants (Walter Johnson)	4.00	2.00	1.25
23	1925 Pirates/Senators (Walter Johnson/Ki Ki Cuyler)	4.00	2.00	1.25
24	1926 Cardinals/Yankees (Rogers Hornsby)	4.00	2.00	1.25
25	1927 Yankees/Pirates	2.50	1.25	.70
26	1928 Yankees/Cardinals (Lou Gehrig)	5.00	2.50	1.50
27	1929 A's/Cubs (Howard Ehmke)	2.00	1.00	.60
28	1930 A's/Cardinals (Jimmie Foxx)	3.00	1.50	.90
29	1931 Cardinals/A's (Pepper Martin)	2.50	1.25	.70
30	1932 Yankees/Cubs (Babe Ruth)	6.00	3.00	1.75
31	1933 Giants/Senators (Carl Hubbell)	3.00	1.50	.90
32	1934 Cardinals/Tigers	2.00	1.00	.60
33	1935 Tigers/Cubs (Mickey Cochrane)	2.50	1.25	.70
34	1936 Yankees/Giants (Red Rolfe)	2.50	1.25	.70
35	1937 Yankees/Giants (Tony Lazerri)	4.00	2.00	1.25
36	1938 Yankees/Cubs	3.00	1.50	.90
37	1939 Yankees/Reds	3.00	1.50	.90
38	1940 Reds/Tigers (Mike McCormick)	2.00	1.00	.60
39	1941 Yankees/Dodgers (Charlie Keller)	2.50	1.25	.70
40	1942 Cardinals/Yankees (Whitey Kurowski/ Johnny Beazley)	2.00	1.00	.60
41	1943 Yankees/Cardinals (Spud Chandler)	2.00	1.00	.60
42	1944 Cardinals/Browns (Mort Cooper)	2.50	1.25	.70
43	1945 Tigers/Cubs (Hank Greenberg)	3.00	1.50	.90
44	1946 Cardinals/Red Sox (Enos Slaughter)	2.50	1.25	.70
45	1947 Yankees/Dodgers (Johnny Lindell/ Hugh Casey)	2.50	1.25	.70
46	1948 Indians/Braves	2.00	1.00	.60
47	1949 Yankees/Dodgers (Preacher Roe)	2.00	1.00	.60
48	1950 Yankees/Phillies (Allie Reynolds)	2.50	1.25	.70
49	1951 Yankees/Giants (Ed Lopat)	2.50	1.25	.70
50	1952 Yankees/Dodgers (Johnny Mize)	2.50	1.25	.70
51	1953 Yankees/Dodgers	2.50	1.25	.70
52	1954 Giants/Indians	2.00	1.00	.60
53	1955 Dodgers/Yankees (Duke Snider)	4.00	2.00	1.25
54	1956 Yankees/Dodgers	2.50	1.25	.70
55	1957 Braves/Yankees	2.50	1.25	.70
56	1958 Yankees/Braves (Hank Bauer)	2.50	1.25	.70
57	1959 Dodgers/White Sox (Duke Snider)	3.00	1.50	.90
58	1960 Pirates/Yankees (Bill Skowron/Bobby Richardson)	2.50	1.25	.70
59	1961 Yankees/Reds (Whitey Ford)	2.50	1.25	.70
60	1962 Yankees/Giants	2.00	1.00	.60
61	1963 Dodgers/Yankees	2.00	1.00	.60
62	1964 Cardinals/Yankees	2.50	1.25	.70
63	1965 Dodgers/Twins	2.50	1.25	.70
64	1966 Orioles/Dodgers	2.00	1.00	.60
65	1967 Cardinals/Red Sox	2.00	1.00	.60
66	1968 Tigers/Cardinals	2.50	1.25	.70
67	1969 Mets/Orioles	6.00	3.00	1.75
68	1970 Orioles/Reds	5.00	2.50	1.50
69	1971 Pirates/Orioles (Roberto Clemente)	35.00	17.50	10.00
70	1972 A's/Reds	15.00	7.50	4.50
71	1973 A's/Mets	15.00	7.50	4.50
(72)	1974 A's/Dodgers	50.00	25.00	15.00
(73)	1975 Reds/Red Sox	50.00	25.00	15.00
(74)	1976 Reds/Yankees	50.00	25.00	15.00
(75)	1977 Yankees/Dodgers	50.00	25.00	15.00

1972 Fleer Famous Feats

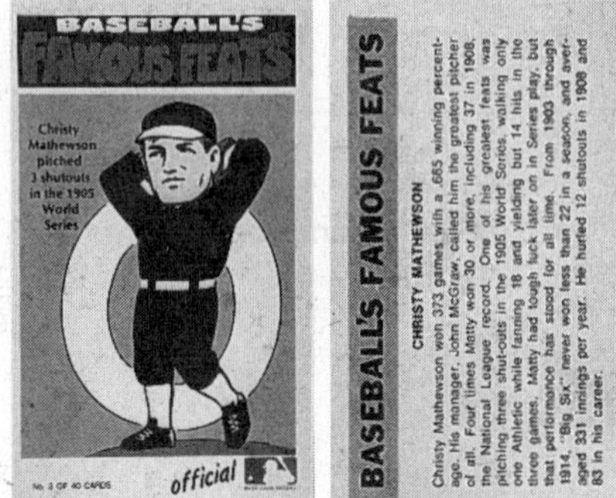

This 40-card set by sports artist R.G. Laughlin is oversized, 2-1/2" x 4". It features the pen and ink work of the artist, with several colors added to the front. The backs are printed in blue on white card stock. The Major League Baseball logo appears on the front of the card, one of the few Laughlin issues to do so. Selling price at issue was about $3.

		NM	EX	VG
Complete Set (40):		40.00	20.00	12.00
Common Player:		1.50	.75	.45
1	Joe McGinnity	2.00	1.00	.60
2	Rogers Hornsby	3.50	1.75	1.00
3	Christy Mathewson	4.00	2.00	1.25
4	Dazzy Vance	2.00	1.00	.60
5	Lou Gehrig	7.50	3.75	2.25
6	Jim Bottomley	2.00	1.00	.60
7	Johnny Evers	2.00	1.00	.60
8	Walter Johnson	4.00	2.00	1.25
9	Hack Wilson	2.00	1.00	.60
10	Wilbert Robinson	2.00	1.00	.60
11	Cy Young	3.50	1.75	1.00
12	Rudy York	1.50	.75	.45
13	Grover C. Alexander	2.00	1.00	.60
14	Fred Toney, Hippo Vaughn	1.50	.75	.45
15	Ty Cobb	7.50	3.75	2.25
16	Jimmie Foxx	3.50	1.75	1.00
17	Hub Leonard	1.50	.75	.45
18	Eddie Collins	2.00	1.00	.60
19	Joe Oeschger, Leon Cadore	1.50	.75	.45
20	Babe Ruth	9.00	4.50	2.75
21	Honus Wagner	4.00	2.00	1.25
22	Red Rolfe	1.50	.75	.45
23	Ed Walsh	2.00	1.00	.60
24	Paul Waner	2.00	1.00	.60
25	Mel Ott	2.50	1.25	.70
26	Eddie Plank	2.00	1.00	.60
27	Sam Crawford	2.00	1.00	.60
28	Napoleon Lajoie	2.00	1.00	.60
29	Ed Reulbach	1.50	.75	.45
30	Pinky Higgins	1.50	.75	.45
31	Bill Klem	2.00	1.00	.60
32	Tris Speaker	3.00	1.50	.90
33	Hank Gowdy	1.50	.75	.45
34	Lefty O'Doul	1.50	.75	.45
35	Lloyd Waner	2.00	1.00	.60
36	Chuck Klein	2.00	1.00	.60
37	Deacon Phillippe	1.50	.75	.45
38	Ed Delahanty	2.00	1.00	.60
39	Jack Chesbro	2.00	1.00	.60
40	Willie Keeler	2.00	1.00	.60

1973 Fleer Team Logo Decals

These colorful team logo decals were pack inserts in Fleer's "Wildest Days and Plays." The decals measure 4" x 2-11/16". Backs have instructions for applying the decals.

		NM	EX	VG
Complete Set (24):		110.00	55.00	33.00
Common Team:		9.00	4.50	2.75
(1)	Atlanta Braves	9.00	4.50	2.75
(2)	Baltimore Orioles	9.00	4.50	2.75
(3)	Boston Red Sox	9.00	4.50	2.75
(4)	California Angels	9.00	4.50	2.75
(5)	Chicago Cubs	9.00	4.50	2.75
(6)	Chicago White Sox	9.00	4.50	2.75
(7)	Cincinnati Reds	9.00	4.50	2.75
(8)	Cleveland Indians	9.00	4.50	2.75
(9)	Detroit Tigers	9.00	4.50	2.75
(10)	Houston Astros	9.00	4.50	2.75
(11)	Kansas City Royals	9.00	4.50	2.75
(12)	Los Angeles Dodgers	9.00	4.50	2.75
(13)	Milwaukee Brewers	9.00	4.50	2.75
(14)	Minnesota Twins	9.00	4.50	2.75
(15)	Montreal Expos	9.00	4.50	2.75
(16)	New York Mets	12.00	6.00	3.50
(17)	New York Yankees	10.00	5.00	3.00
(18)	Oakland A's	10.00	5.00	3.00
(19)	Philadelphia Phillies	9.00	4.50	2.75
(20)	Pittsburgh Pirates	11.00	5.50	3.25
(21)	San Diego Padres	9.00	4.50	2.75
(22)	San Francisco Giants	9.00	4.50	2.75
(23)	St. Louis Cardinals	9.00	4.50	2.75
(24)	Texas Rangers	12.00	6.00	3.50

1973 Fleer Team Signs

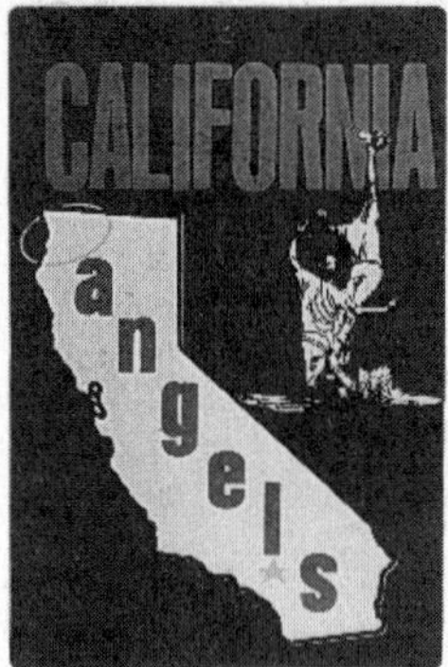

Each of the major league teams was represented in this issue of thick oversized (7-3/4" x 11-1/2") team logo signs. The blank-back signs have rounded corners and a grommeted hole at top-center for hanging. The unnumbered signs are checklisted here alphabetically.

		NM	EX	VG
Complete Set (24):		35.00	17.50	10.00
Common Team:		4.00	2.00	1.25
(1)	Atlanta Braves	4.00	2.00	1.25
(2)	Baltimore Orioles	4.00	2.00	1.25
(3)	Boston Red Sox	4.00	2.00	1.25
(4)	California Angels	4.00	2.00	1.25
(5)	Chicago Cubs	4.00	2.00	1.25
(6)	Chicago White Sox	4.00	2.00	1.25
(7)	Cincinnati Reds	5.00	2.50	1.50
(8)	Cleveland Indians	4.00	2.00	1.25
(9)	Detroit Tigers	4.00	2.00	1.25
(10)	Houston Astros	4.00	2.00	1.25
(11)	Kansas City Royals	4.00	2.00	1.25
(12)	Los Angeles Dodgers	4.00	2.00	1.25
(13)	Milwaukee Brewers	4.00	2.00	1.25
(14)	Minnesota Twins	4.00	2.00	1.25
(15)	Montreal Expos	4.00	2.00	1.25
(16)	New York Mets	5.00	2.50	1.50
(17)	New York Yankees	5.00	2.50	1.50
(18)	Oakland A's	5.00	2.50	1.50
(19)	Philadelphia Phillies	4.00	2.00	1.25
(20)	Pittsburgh Pirates	4.00	2.00	1.25
(21)	St. Louis Cardinals	4.00	2.00	1.25
(22)	San Francisco Giants	4.00	2.00	1.25
(23)	San Diego Padres	4.00	2.00	1.25
(24)	Texas Rangers	4.00	2.00	1.25

1973 Fleer Wildest Days and Plays

This 42-card set highlights unusual plays and happenings in baseball history, with the fronts featuring artwork by R.G. Laughlin. The cards are 2-1/2" x 4" and printed with color on the front and in red on the back. Original retail price was about $3.25.

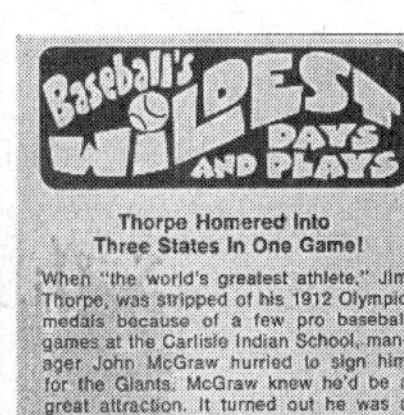

		NM	EX	VG
Complete Set (42):		35.00	17.50	10.00
Common Player:		1.50	.70	.45
1	Cubs and Phillies Score 49 Runs in Game	1.50	.70	.45
2	Frank Chance Five HBP's in One Day	2.00	1.00	.60
3	Jim Thorpe Homered Into Three States	2.00	1.00	.60
4	Eddie Gaedel Midget in Majors	2.00	1.00	.60
5	Most Tied Game Ever	1.50	.70	.45
6	Seven Errors in One Inning	1.50	.70	.45
7	Four 20-Game Winners But No Pennant	1.50	.70	.45
8	Dummy Hoy Umpire Signals Strikes	2.00	1.00	.60
9	Fourteen Hits in One Inning	1.50	.70	.45
10	Yankees Not Shut Out for Two Years	1.50	.70	.45
11	Buck Weaver 17 Straight Fouls	2.00	1.00	.60
12	George Sisler Greatest Thrill	1.50	.70	.45
13	Wrong-Way Baserunner	1.50	.70	.45
14	Kiki Cuyler Sits Out Series	1.50	.70	.45
15	Grounder Climbed Wall	1.50	.70	.45
16	Gabby Street Washington Monument	1.50	.70	.45
17	Mel Ott Ejected Twice	2.00	1.00	.60
18	Shortest Pitching Career	1.50	.70	.45
19	Three Homers in One Inning	1.50	.70	.45
20	Bill Byron Singing Umpire	1.50	.70	.45
21	Fred Clarke Walking Steal of Home	1.50	.70	.45
22	Christy Mathewson 373rd Win Discovered	2.00	1.00	.60
23	Hitting Through the Unglaub Arc	1.50	.70	.45
24	Jim O'Rourke Catching at 52	1.50	.70	.45
25	Fired for Striking Out in Series	1.50	.70	.45
26	Eleven Run Inning on One Hit	1.50	.70	.45
27	58 Innings in 3 Days	1.50	.70	.45
28	Homer on Warm-up Pitch	1.50	.70	.45
29	Giants Win 26 Straight But Finish Fourth	1.50	.70	.45
30	Player Who Stole First Base	1.50	.70	.45
31	Ernie Shore Perfect Game in Relief	1.50	.70	.45
32	Greatest Comeback	1.50	.70	.45
33	All-Time Flash-in-the-Pan	1.50	.70	.45
34	Pruett Fanned Ruth 19 Out of 31	2.00	1.00	.60
35	Fixed Batting Race (Ty Cobb, Nap Lajoie)	2.00	1.00	.60
36	Wild Pitch Rebound Play	1.50	.70	.45
37	17 Straight Scoring Innings	1.50	.70	.45
38	Wildest Opening Day	1.50	.70	.45
39	Baseball's Strike One	1.50	.70	.45
40	Opening Day No-Hitter That Didn't Count	1.50	.70	.45
41	Jimmie Foxx 6 Straight Walks in One Game	2.00	1.00	.60
42	Entire Team Hit and Scored in Inning	1.50	.70	.45

1974 Fleer Baseball Firsts

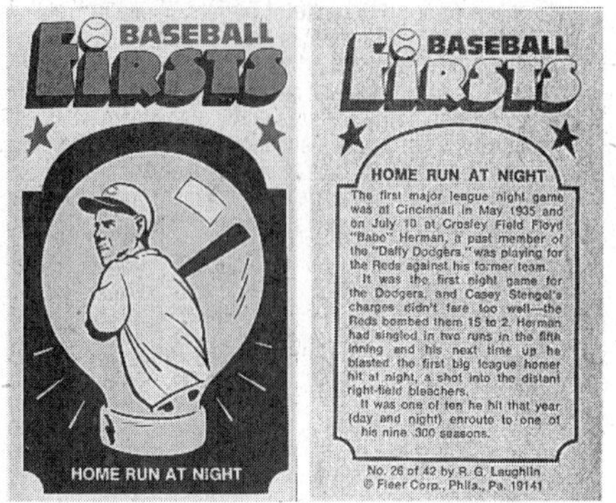

This 42-card set from Fleer is titled "Baseball Firsts" and features several historical moments in baseball, as captured through the artwork of sports artist R.G. Laughlin. The cards are 2-1/2" x 4" and are numbered on the back, which is gray card stock with black printing. The set is not licensed by Major League Baseball.

		NM	EX	VG
Complete Set (42):		80.00	40.00	25.00
Common Player:		2.00	1.00	.60
1	Slide	2.00	1.00	.60
2	Spring Training	2.00	1.00	.60
3	Bunt	2.00	1.00	.60
4	Catcher's Mask	2.00	1.00	.60
5	Four Straight Homers (Lou Gehrig)	10.00	5.00	3.00
6	Radio Broadcast	2.00	1.00	.60
7	Numbered Uniforms	2.00	1.00	.60
8	Shin Guards	2.00	1.00	.60
9	Players Association	2.00	1.00	.60
10	Knuckleball	2.00	1.00	.60
11	Player With Glasses	2.00	1.00	.60
12	Baseball Cards	12.00	6.00	3.50
13	Standardized Rules	2.00	1.00	.60
14	Grand Slam	2.00	1.00	.60
15	Player Fined	2.00	1.00	.60
16	Presidential Opener	2.00	1.00	.60
17	Player Transaction	2.00	1.00	.60
18	All-Star Game	2.00	1.00	.60
19	Scoreboard	2.00	1.00	.60
20	Cork-center Ball	2.00	1.00	.60
21	Scorekeeping	2.00	1.00	.60
22	Domed Stadium	2.00	1.00	.60
23	Batting Helmet	2.00	1.00	.60
24	Fatality	4.00	2.00	1.25
25	Unassisted Triple Play	2.00	1.00	.60
26	Home Run at Night	2.00	1.00	.60
27	Black Major Leaguer	4.00	2.00	1.25
28	Pinch Hitter	2.00	1.00	.60
29	Million Dollar World Series	2.00	1.00	.60
30	Tarpaulin	2.00	1.00	.60
31	Team Initials	2.00	1.00	.60
32	Pennant Playoff	2.00	1.00	.60
33	Glove	2.00	1.00	.60
34	Curve Ball	2.00	1.00	.60
35	Night Game	2.00	1.00	.60
36	Admission Charge	2.00	1.00	.60
37	Farm System	2.00	1.00	.60
38	Telecast	2.00	1.00	.60
39	Commissioner	2.00	1.00	.60
40	.400 Hitter	2.00	1.00	.60
41	World Series	2.00	1.00	.60
42	Player Into Service	2.00	1.00	.60

1975 Fleer Pioneers of Baseball

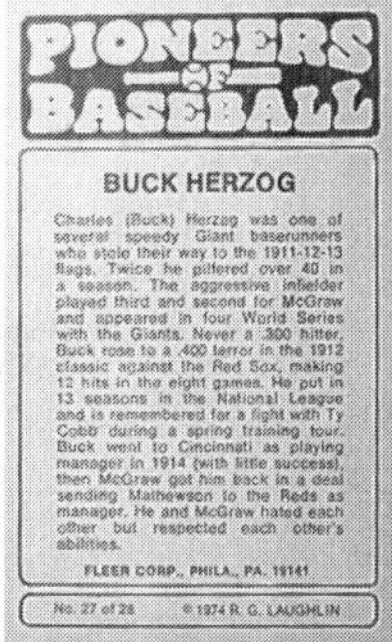

This 28-card set did not draw a great deal of interest in the hobby. The cards are slightly oversized (2-1/2" x 4") and feature sepia-toned photographs of old baseball players. The backs feature information about the player and the card number. A "Pioneers of Baseball" banner appears at the top of the card back. Each 10-cent pack included one card and one each cloth team pennant and patch, plus a stick of gum.

		NM	EX	VG
Complete Set (28):		20.00	10.00	6.00
Common Player:		1.50	.75	.45
Wax Pack:		6.00		
Wax Box (24):		65.00		
1	Cap Anson	1.50	.75	.45
2	Harry Wright	1.50	.75	.45
3	Buck Ewing	1.50	.75	.45
4	A.G. Spalding	1.50	.75	.45
5	Old Hoss Radbourn	1.50	.75	.45
6	Dan Brouthers	1.50	.75	.45
7	Roger Bresnahan	1.50	.75	.45
8	Mike Kelly	1.50	.75	.45
9	Ned Hanlon	1.50	.75	.45
10	Ed Delahanty	1.50	.75	.45
11	Pud Galvin	1.50	.75	.45
12	Amos Rusie	1.50	.75	.45
13	Tommy McCarthy	1.50	.75	.45
14	Ty Cobb	6.00	3.00	1.75
15	John McGraw	1.50	.75	.45
16	Home Run Baker	1.50	.75	.45
17	Johnny Evers	1.50	.75	.45
18	Nap Lajoie	1.50	.75	.45
19	Cy Young	2.50	1.25	.70
20	Eddie Collins	1.50	.75	.45
21	John Glasscock	1.50	.75	.45
22	Hal Chase	1.50	.75	.45
23	Mordecai Brown	1.50	.75	.45
24	Jake Daubert	1.50	.75	.45
25	Mike Donlin	1.50	.75	.45
26	John Clarkson	1.50	.75	.45
27	Buck Herzog	1.50	.75	.45
28	Art Nehf	1.50	.75	.45

1980 Fleer Baseball's Famous Feats

Yet another incarnation of Robert Laughlin's "Baseball's Famous Feats" cartoon artwork is this 22-card issue, in standard 2-1/2" x 3-1/2" format. The player art is backed with

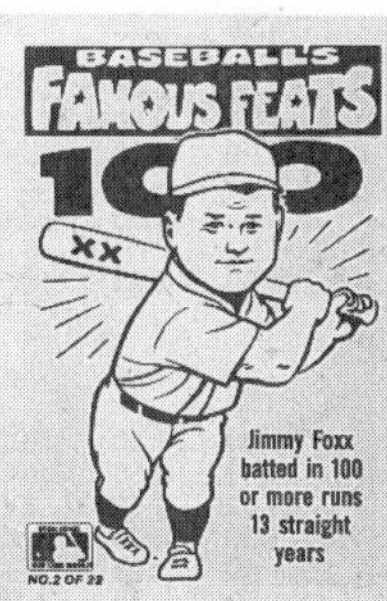

team logo and pennant stickers, creating a huge variety of possible front/back combinations. The cards are licensed by Major League Baseball and numbered on the front.

		NM	EX	VG
Complete Set (22):		6.00	3.00	1.75
Common Player:		.75	.40	.25
1	Grover Cleveland Alexander	.75	.40	.25
2	Jimmy (Jimmie) Foxx	1.00	.50	.30
3	Ty Cobb	1.50	.70	.45
4	Walter Johnson	1.00	.50	.30
5	Hack Wilson	.75	.40	.25
6	Tris Speaker	1.00	.50	.30
7	Hank Gowdy	.75	.40	.25
8	Bill Klem	.75	.40	.25
9	Ed Reulbach	.75	.40	.25
10	Fred Toney, Hippo Vaughn	.75	.40	.25
11	Joe Oeschger, Leon Cadore	.75	.40	.25
12	Lloyd Waner	.75	.40	.25
13	Eddie Plank	.75	.40	.25
14	Deacon Phillippe	.75	.40	.25
15	Ed Dalahanty (Delahanty)	.75	.40	.25
16	Eddie Collins	.75	.40	.25
17	Jack Chesbro	.75	.40	.25
18	Red Rolfe	.75	.40	.25
19	Ed Walsh	.75	.40	.25
20	Honus Wagner	1.25	.60	.40
21	Nap Lajoie	.75	.40	.25
22	Cy Young	1.00	.50	.30

1980 Fleer World Series/Team Logo Stickers

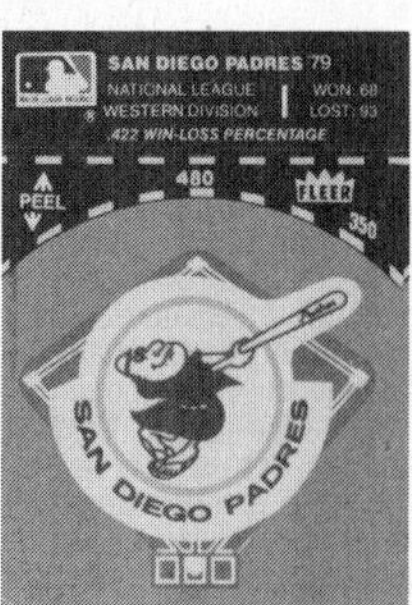

World Series cards similar to previous Fleer issues of the 1970s were issued in a new version in 1980. Wax packs containing five stickercards and a piece of bubblegum were offered for a nickel. Each card/sticker combination carried a World Series cartoon card from one of the Autumn Classics from 1940-1979. Unlike the earlier Fleer-Laughlin W.S. cards, these are backed with a team-logo sticker, some of which bear the team's 1979 record, and some of which do not.

		NM	EX	VG
Complete Set (40):		50.00	25.00	15.00
Common Card:		1.50	.75	.45
Wax Pack (5):		4.00		
Wax Box (36):		80.00		
(1)	1940 Reds/Tigers (Mike McCormick)	1.50	.75	.45
(2)	1941 Yankees/Dodgers (Charlie Keller)	2.25	1.25	.75
(3)	1942 Cardinals/Yankees (Whitey Kurowski/ Johnny Beazley)	2.25	1.25	.75
(4)	1943 Yankees/Cardinals (Spud Chandler)	2.25	1.25	.75
(5)	1944 Cardinals/Browns (Mort Cooper)	2.25	1.25	.75
(6)	1945 Tigers/Cubs (Hank Greenberg)	3.00	1.50	.90
(7)	1946 Cardinals/Red Sox (Enos Slaughter)	1.50	.75	.45
(8)	1947 Yankees/Dodgers (Johnny Lindell/Hugh Casey)	3.00	1.50	.90
(9)	1948 Indians/Braves	1.50	.75	.45
(10)	1949 Yankees/Dodgers (Preacher Roe)	3.00	1.50	.90
(11)	1950 Yankees/Phillies (Allie Reynolds)	3.00	1.50	.90
(12)	1951 Yankees/Giants (Ed Lopat)	3.00	1.50	.90
(13)	1952 Yankees/Dodgers (Johnny Mize)	4.00	2.00	1.25
(14)	1953 Yankees/Dodgers	4.00	2.00	1.25
(15)	1954 Giants/Indians	3.00	1.50	.90

(16)	1955 Dodgers/Yankees (Duke Snider)	4.50	2.25	1.25
(17)	1956 Yankees/Dodgers	4.00	2.00	1.25
(18)	1957 Braves/Yankees	4.00	2.00	1.25
(19)	1958 Yankees/Braves (Hank Bauer)	3.00	1.50	.90
(20)	1959 Dodgers/White Sox (Duke Snider)	3.00	1.50	.90
(21)	1960 Pirates/Yankees (Bill Skowron/ Bobby Richardson)	4.50	2.25	1.25
(22)	1961 Yankees/Reds (Whitey Ford)	3.00	1.50	.90
(23)	1962 Yankees/Giants	3.00	1.50	.90
(24)	1963 Dodgers/Yankees	3.00	1.50	.90
(25)	1964 Cardinals/Yankees	3.00	1.50	.90
(26)	1965 Dodgers/Twins	1.50	.75	.45
(27)	1966 Orioles/Dodgers	1.50	.75	.45
(28)	1967 Cardinals/Red Sox	1.50	.75	.45
(29)	1968 Tigers/Cardinals	1.50	.75	.45
(30)	1969 Mets/Orioles	4.00	2.00	1.25
(31)	1970 Orioles/Reds	1.50	.75	.45
(32)	1971 Pirates/Orioles	1.50	.75	.45
(33)	1972 A's/Reds	1.50	.75	.45
(34)	1973 A's/Mets	1.50	.75	.45
(35)	1974 A's/Dodgers	1.50	.75	.45
(36)	1975 Reds/Red Sox	2.25	1.25	.75
(37)	1976 Reds/Yankees	1.50	.75	.45
(38)	1977 Yankees/Dodgers	2.25	1.25	.75
(39)	1978 Yankees/Dodgers	2.25	1.25	.75
(40)	1979 Pirates/Orioles	2.25	1.25	.75

1916 Fleischmann Bakery (D381)

These cards were issued by a New York City bakery, presumably given away with the purchase of bread or other goods. The blank-back cards are printed in black-and-white in a 2-3/4" x 5-3/8" format. Fronts have player photos with the name, team and position in two lines beneath. Most cards have an Underwood & Underwood copyright notice on the picture. At bottom is a coupon that could be redeemed for an album to house the cards. Prices shown here are for cards without the coupon. Cards with coupon are valued at about the premium shown below. Cards are checklisted here in alphabetical order. Some cards can be found with differing sizes of the player's photo and/or with wrong and corrected photos. A nearly identical issue was produced contemporarily by Ferguson Bread. The two can be distinguished by the two-line identification on front of the Fleischmann cards, and one-line identification on Fergusons.

		NM	EX	VG
Common Player:		400.00	200.00	100.00
With Coupon: 4-6X				
(1)	Babe Adams	400.00	200.00	100.00
(2)	Grover Alexander	700.00	300.00	150.00
(3)	Walt E. Alexander	400.00	200.00	100.00
(4)	Frank Allen	400.00	200.00	100.00
(5)	Fred Anderson	400.00	200.00	100.00
(6)	Dave Bancroft	550.00	225.00	110.00
(7)	Jack Barry	400.00	200.00	100.00
(8a)	Beals Becker (No uniform logo.)	400.00	200.00	100.00
(8b)	Beals Becker (Partial uniform logo.)	400.00	200.00	100.00
(9)	Eddie Burns	400.00	200.00	100.00
(10)	George J. Burns	400.00	200.00	100.00
(11)	Bobby Byrne	400.00	200.00	100.00
(12)	Ray Caldwell	400.00	200.00	100.00
(13)	James Callahan	400.00	200.00	100.00
(14)	William Carrigan	400.00	200.00	100.00
(15)	Larry Cheney	400.00	200.00	100.00
(16a)	Tom Clark (No hand/glove.)	400.00	200.00	100.00
(16b)	Tom Clark (Hand and glove show.)	400.00	200.00	100.00
(17)	Ty Cobb	2,900	1,450	725.00
(18a)	Ray W. Collins (Partial top button.)	400.00	200.00	100.00
(18b)	Ray W. Collins (Full top button.)	400.00	200.00	100.00
(19)	Jack Coombs	400.00	200.00	100.00
(20)	A. Wilbur Cooper	400.00	200.00	100.00
(21)	George Cutshaw	400.00	200.00	100.00
(22)	Jake Daubert	400.00	200.00	100.00
(23)	Wheezer Dell	400.00	200.00	100.00
(24)	Bill Donovan	400.00	200.00	100.00
(25)	Larry Doyle	400.00	200.00	100.00
(26)	R.J. Egan	400.00	200.00	100.00
(27)	Johnny Evers	550.00	225.00	110.00
(28)	Ray Fisher	400.00	200.00	100.00
(29)	Harry Gardner (Larry)	400.00	200.00	100.00
(30)	Joe Gedeon	400.00	200.00	100.00
(31)	Larry Gilbert	400.00	200.00	100.00
(32)	Frank Gilhooley	400.00	200.00	100.00
(33)	Hank Gowdy	400.00	200.00	100.00
(34)	Sylvanus Gregg	400.00	200.00	100.00
(35)	Tom Griffith	400.00	200.00	100.00
(36)	Heinie Groh	400.00	200.00	100.00
(37)	Bob Harmon	400.00	200.00	100.00
(38)	Roy A. Hartzell	400.00	200.00	100.00
(39)	Claude Hendrix	400.00	200.00	100.00
(40)	Olaf Henriksen	400.00	200.00	100.00
(41)	Buck Herzog	400.00	200.00	100.00
(42)	Hugh High	400.00	200.00	100.00
(43)	Dick Hoblitzell	400.00	200.00	100.00
(44)	Herb Hunter	400.00	200.00	100.00
(45)	Harold Janvrin	400.00	200.00	100.00
(46)	Hugh Jennings	550.00	225.00	110.00
(47)	John Johnston	400.00	200.00	100.00
(48)	Erving Kantlehner	400.00	200.00	100.00
(49)	Benny Kauff	400.00	200.00	100.00
(50a)	Ray Keating (Error, striped cap, photo is Kocher.)	400.00	200.00	100.00
(50b)	Ray Keating (Correct, "NY" on cap.)	400.00	200.00	100.00
(51)	Wade Killefer	400.00	200.00	100.00
(52a)	Elmer Knetzer (Error, no "B" on cap, photo is Konetchy.)	400.00	200.00	100.00
(52b)	Elmer Knetzer (Correct, "B" on cap.)	400.00	200.00	100.00
(53a)	B.W. Kocher (Error, "NY" on cap, photo is Keating.)	400.00	200.00	100.00
(53b)	B.W. Kocher (Correct, striped cap.)	400.00	200.00	100.00
(54a)	Ed. Konetchy (Error, "B" on cap, photo is Knetzer.)	400.00	200.00	100.00
(54b)	Ed. Konetchy (Correct, no "B" on cap.)	400.00	200.00	100.00
(55)	Fred Lauderous (Luderous)	400.00	200.00	100.00
(56)	Dutch Leonard	400.00	200.00	100.00
(57)	Duffy Lewis	400.00	200.00	100.00
(58)	Slim Love	400.00	200.00	100.00
(59)	Albert L. Mamaux	400.00	200.00	100.00
(60)	Rabbit Maranville	550.00	225.00	110.00
(61)	Rube Marquard	540.00	215.00	110.00
(62)	Christy Mathewson	1,900	950.00	475.00
(63)	Bill McKechnie	550.00	225.00	110.00
(64)	Chief Meyer (Meyers)	400.00	200.00	100.00
(65)	Otto Miller	400.00	200.00	100.00
(66)	Fred Mollwitz	400.00	200.00	100.00
(67)	Herbie Moran	400.00	200.00	100.00
(68)	Mike Mowrey	400.00	200.00	100.00
(69)	Dan Murphy	400.00	200.00	100.00
(70)	Art Nehf	400.00	200.00	100.00
(71)	Rube Oldring	400.00	200.00	100.00
(72)	Oliver O'Mara	400.00	200.00	100.00
(73)	Dode Paskert	400.00	200.00	100.00
(74)	D.C. Pat Ragan	400.00	200.00	100.00
(75)	William A. Rariden	400.00	200.00	100.00
(76)	Davis Robertson	400.00	200.00	100.00
(77)	Wm. Rodgers	400.00	200.00	100.00
(78)	Edw. F. Rousch (Roush)	550.00	225.00	110.00
(79)	Nap Rucker	400.00	200.00	100.00
(80)	Dick Rudolph	400.00	200.00	100.00
(81)	Wally Schang	400.00	200.00	100.00
(82)	Rube Schauer	400.00	200.00	100.00
(83)	Pete Schneider	400.00	200.00	100.00
(84)	Ferd Schupp	400.00	200.00	100.00
(85)	Ernie Shore	400.00	200.00	100.00
(86)	Red Smith	400.00	200.00	100.00
(87)	Fred Snodgrass	400.00	200.00	100.00
(88)	Tris Speaker	700.00	350.00	175.00
(89)	George Stallings	400.00	200.00	100.00
(90)	Casey Stengel	600.00	300.00	150.00
(91)	Sailor Stroud	400.00	200.00	100.00
(92)	Amos Strunk	400.00	200.00	100.00
(93)	Chas. (Jeff) Tesreau	400.00	200.00	100.00
(94a)	Chester D. Thomas (One button shows.)	400.00	200.00	100.00
(94b)	Chester D. Thomas (Two buttons.)	400.00	200.00	100.00
(95)	Fred Toney	400.00	200.00	100.00
(96)	Walt Tragesser	400.00	200.00	100.00
(97)	Honus Wagner	5,000	1,000	500.00
(98)	Carl Weilman	400.00	200.00	100.00
(99)	Zack Wheat	550.00	225.00	110.00
(100)	George Whitted	400.00	200.00	100.00
(101)	Arthur Wilson	400.00	200.00	100.00
(102)	Ivy Wingo	400.00	200.00	100.00
(103)	Joe Wood	500.00	250.00	125.00

1940s Ford Babe Ruth Premium

The exact date of this premium photo's issue is unknown. The approximately 5" x 6-1/2" blank-back, black-and-white photo features Ruth in an oft-seen batting pose. In the wide white border at bottom is printed, "CONSULTANT / FORD MOTOR COMPANY / AMERICAN LEGION JUNIOR BASEBALL."

	NM	EX	VG
Babe Ruth	300.00	150.00	90.00

1961 Ford Pittsburgh Pirates Prints

The year after the team's dramatic World Series win over the Yankees, Pittsburgh area Ford dealers distributed a set of six player prints. The blank-back, 11-7/8" x 14-3/4" prints feature action drawings of the players by artist Robert Riger. Some of the prints are horizontal in format, some are vertical. A Ford Motor Co. copyright line appears in the lower-left corner and a line at bottom center identifies the player in the form of a title for the picture. The unnumbered prints are listed here in alphabetical order. The pictures were reprinted by an unauthorized party circa 1998.

		NM	EX	VG
Complete Set (6):		125.00	65.00	35.00
Common Player:		15.00	7.50	4.50
(1)	BOB FRIEND COMES IN WITH THE FAST ONE (Bob Friend)	15.00	7.50	4.50
(2)	CLEMENTE LINES ONE OVER SECOND (Roberto Clemente)	75.00	37.50	22.00
(3)	GROAT CUTS DOWN A BRAVE STEAL (Dick Groat)	15.00	7.50	4.50
(4)	HOAK HANDLES A HOT SHOT AT THIRD (Don Hoak)	15.00	7.50	4.50
(5)	MAZ GETS THE BIG HIT (Bill Mazeroski)	30.00	15.00	9.00
(6)	THE LAW (Vern Law)	15.00	7.50	4.50

1962 Ford Detroit Tigers Postcards

Because baseball card collectors have to compete with auto memorabilia hobbyists for these scarce cards, they are among the most valuable postcard issues of the early 1960s. In 3-1/4" x 5-1/2" postcard format, the full-color cards feature photos taken on a golf course of players posed in front of various new Fords. White backs have a name, position and team, with a box for a stamp. Probably given out in conjunction with autograph appearances at car dealers (they are frequently found autographed), the set lacks some of the team's biggest stars (Al Kaline, Norm Cash), and includes coaches and even trainer Jack Homel. Probably because of lack of demand, the coaches' and trainer's cards are the scarcest to find today. The unnumbered cards are checklisted here alphabetically.

		NM	EX	VG
Complete Set (16):		1,425	710.00	425.00
Common Player:		60.00	30.00	18.00
(1)	Hank Aguirre	90.00	45.00	27.50
(2)	Steve Boros	120.00	60.00	35.00
(3)	Dick Brown	90.00	45.00	27.50
(4)	Jim Bunning	150.00	75.00	45.00
(5)	Phil Cavaretta	135.00	65.00	40.00
(6)	Rocky Colavito	185.00	90.00	55.00
(7)	Terry Fox	60.00	30.00	18.00
(8)	Purn Goldy	75.00	37.50	22.50
(9)	Jack Homel	135.00	65.00	40.00
(10)	Ron Kline	90.00	45.00	27.50
(11)	Don Mossi	60.00	30.00	18.00
(12)	George Myatt	120.00	60.00	35.00
(13)	Ron Nischwitz	90.00	45.00	27.50
(14)	Larry Osborne	60.00	30.00	18.00
(15)	Phil Regan	90.00	45.00	27.50
(16)	Mike Roarke	135.00	65.00	40.00

1938 Foto Fun

An early attempt at a self-developing player photocard (a technology that Topps used in the 1940s-50s) used a black-and-white negative and a piece of photo paper to create a blue-tint photo that could be placed in a gold cardboard frame. The back of the 2-3/4" x 3-5/8" frame is printed in brown and gives instructions for developing the photo. The checklist of the unnumbered cards, presented here alphabetically, may or may not be complete at 93.

		NM	EX	VG
Common Player:		160.00	80.00	45.00
(1)	Luke Appling	375.00	185.00	110.00
(2)	Morris Arnovich	160.00	80.00	45.00
(3)	Eldon Auker	160.00	80.00	45.00
(4)	Jim Bagby	160.00	80.00	45.00
(5)	Red Barrett	160.00	80.00	45.00
(6)	Roy Bell	160.00	80.00	45.00
(7)	Wally Berger	160.00	80.00	45.00
(8)	Oswald Bluege	160.00	80.00	45.00
(9)	Frenchy Bordagaray	160.00	80.00	45.00
(10)	Tom Bridges	160.00	80.00	45.00
(11)	Dolf Camilli	160.00	80.00	45.00
(12)	Ben Chapman	160.00	80.00	45.00
(13)	Harland Clift (Harlond)	160.00	80.00	45.00
(14)	Harry Craft	160.00	80.00	45.00
(15)	Roger Cramer	160.00	80.00	45.00
(16)	Joe Cronin	375.00	185.00	110.00
(17)	Tony Cuccinello	160.00	80.00	45.00
(18)	Kiki Cuyler	375.00	185.00	110.00
(19)	Ellsworth Dahlgren	160.00	80.00	45.00
(20)	Harry Danning	160.00	80.00	45.00
(21)	Frank Demaree	160.00	80.00	45.00
(22)	Gene Desautels	160.00	80.00	45.00
(23)	Jim Deshong	160.00	80.00	45.00
(24)	Bill Dickey	450.00	225.00	135.00
(25)	Lou Fette	160.00	80.00	45.00
(26)	Lou Finney	160.00	80.00	45.00
(27)	Larry French	160.00	80.00	45.00
(28)	Linus Frey	160.00	80.00	45.00
(29)	Augie Galan	160.00	80.00	45.00
(30)	Debs Garms	160.00	80.00	45.00
(31)	Charles Gehringer	450.00	225.00	135.00
(32)	Lefty Gomez	450.00	225.00	135.00
(33)	Ival Goodman	160.00	80.00	45.00
(34)	Lee Grissom	160.00	80.00	45.00
(35)	Stan Hack	180.00	90.00	55.00
(36)	Irving Hadley	160.00	80.00	45.00
(37)	Rollie Hemsley	160.00	80.00	45.00
(38)	Tommy Henrich	160.00	80.00	45.00
(39)	Billy Herman	375.00	185.00	110.00
(40)	Willard Hershberger	160.00	80.00	45.00
(41)	Michael Higgins	160.00	80.00	45.00
(42)	Oral Hildebrand	160.00	80.00	45.00
(43)	Carl Hubbell	450.00	225.00	135.00
(44)	Willis Hudlin	160.00	80.00	45.00
(45)	Mike Kreevich	160.00	80.00	45.00
(46)	Ralph Kress	160.00	80.00	45.00
(47)	John Lanning	160.00	80.00	45.00
(48)	Lyn Lary	160.00	80.00	45.00
(49)	Cookie Lavagetto	160.00	80.00	45.00
(50)	Thornton Lee	160.00	80.00	45.00
(51)	Ernie Lombardi	375.00	185.00	110.00
(52)	Al Lopez	375.00	185.00	110.00
(53)	Ted Lyons	375.00	185.00	110.00
(54)	Danny MacFayden	160.00	80.00	45.00
(55)	Max Macon	160.00	80.00	45.00
(56)	Pepper Martin	250.00	125.00	75.00
(57)	Joe Marty	160.00	80.00	45.00
(58)	Frank McCormick	160.00	80.00	45.00
(59)	Bill McKechnie	375.00	185.00	110.00
(60)	Joe Medwick	375.00	185.00	110.00
(61)	Cliff Melton	160.00	80.00	45.00
(62)	Charley Meyer (Myer)	160.00	80.00	45.00
(63)	John Mize	450.00	225.00	135.00
(64)	Terry Moore	180.00	90.00	55.00
(65)	Whitey Moore	160.00	80.00	45.00
(66)	Emmett Mueller	160.00	80.00	45.00
(67)	Hugh Mulcahy	160.00	80.00	45.00
(68)	Van L. Mungo	160.00	80.00	45.00
(69)	Johnny Murphy	160.00	80.00	45.00
(70)	Lynn Nelson	160.00	80.00	45.00
(71)	Mel Ott	450.00	225.00	135.00
(72)	Monte Pearson	160.00	80.00	45.00
(73)	Bill Rogell	160.00	80.00	45.00
(74)	George Selkirk	160.00	80.00	45.00
(75)	Milt Shofner	160.00	80.00	45.00
(76)	Al Simmons	375.00	185.00	110.00
(77)	Clyde Shoun	160.00	80.00	45.00
(78)	Gus Suhr	160.00	80.00	45.00
(79)	Billy Sullivan	160.00	80.00	45.00
(80)	Cecil Travis	160.00	80.00	45.00
(81)	Pie Traynor	375.00	185.00	110.00
(82)	Hal Trosky	160.00	80.00	45.00
(83)	Jim Turner	160.00	80.00	45.00
(84)	Johnny Vander Meer	160.00	80.00	45.00
(85)	Oscar Vitt	160.00	80.00	45.00
(86)	Gerald Walker	160.00	80.00	45.00
(87)	Paul Waner	375.00	185.00	110.00
(88)	Rabbit Warstler	160.00	80.00	45.00
(89)	Bob Weiland	160.00	80.00	45.00
(90)	Burgess Whitehead	160.00	80.00	45.00
(91)	Earl Whitehill	160.00	80.00	45.00
(92)	Rudy York	160.00	80.00	45.00
(93)	Del Young	160.00	80.00	45.00

1887 Four Base Hits

Although the exact origin of this set is still in doubt, the Four Base Hits cards are among the rarest and most sought after of all 19th century tobacco issues. There is some speculation that the cards, measuring 2-1/4" x 3-7/8", were produced by Charles Gross & Co. because of their similarity to the Kalamazoo Bats issues, but there is also some evidence to support the theory that they were issued by August Beck & Co., producer of the Yum Yum set. The Four Base Hits cards feature sepia-toned photos with the player's name and position below the picture, and the words "Smoke Four Base Hits. Four For 10 Cents." along the bottom. The card labeled "Daily" is a double error. The name should have been spelled "Daly," but the card actually pictures Billy Sunday. Many of the cards on this surely incomplete checklist are known to survive in only a single example; few in grades above VG.

		NM	EX	VG
Common Player:			35,000	15,000
(1)	John Clarkson		150,000	80,000
(2)	Tido Daily (Daly) (Photo is Billy Sunday.)		60,000	24,000
(3)	Pat Deasley		35,000	15,000
(4)	Mike Dorgan		35,000	15,000
(5)	Buck Ewing		175,000	80,000
(6)	Pete Gillespie		35,000	15,000
(7)	Frank Hankinson		35,000	15,000
(8)	King Kelly		250,000	120,000
(9)	Al Mays		35,000	15,000
(10)	Jim Mutrie		35,000	15,000
(11)	Chief Roseman		35,000	15,000
(12)	Marty Sullivan		35,000	15,000
(13)	Rip Van Haltren		35,000	15,000
(14)	John Ward		150,000	80,000
(15)	Mickey Welch		150,000	80,000

1960s Nellie Fox Bowl Postcard

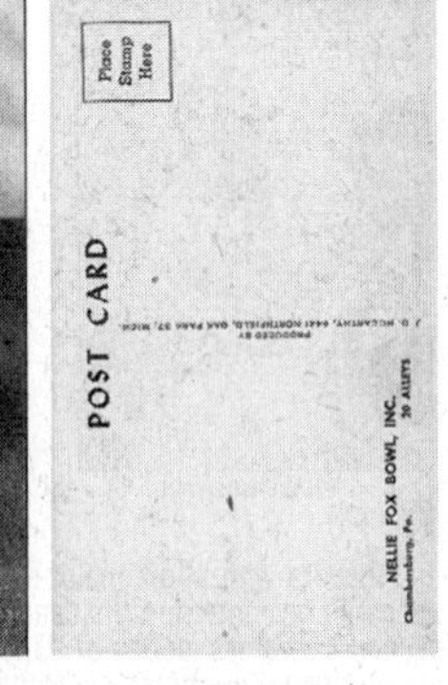

This specially marked version of a typical J.D. McCarthy postcard advertises on back the White Sox second baseman's bowling enterprise in Chambersburg, Pa. The card is black-and-white with a facsimile autograph on front.

	NM	EX	VG
Nellie Fox	35.00	17.50	10.50

1980 Franchise Babe Ruth

The first in a series of collectors' issues relative to Maryland baseball, this 80-card set chronicles the life - on and off the field - of Babe Ruth. Fronts of the 2-1/2" x 3-1/2" cards have black-and-white photos surrounded by wide white borders. Backs are printed in red and black and include a caption and description of the front photo. At the time of issue, the set sold for about $8.

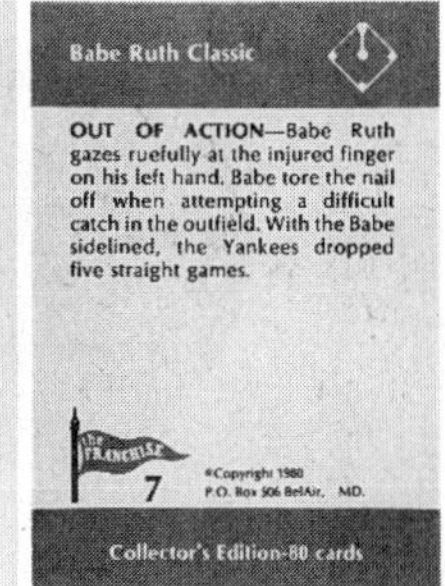

	NM	EX	VG
Complete Set (80):	35.00	17.50	10.00
Common Card:	1.00	.50	.30
1-80 Babe Ruth			

1961 Franklin Milk

While it is not part of the contemporary Cloverleaf Dairy milk carton Minnesota Twins issues, this carton is often collected alongside the others. Printed in red and blue, the portion of the milk carton advertising Harmon Killebrew's radio show measures about 4" x 4-1/2".

		NM	EX	VG
(1)	Harmon Killebrew (Complete carton.)	1,600	800.00	480.00
(1)	Harmon Killebrew (Cut panel.)	250.00	125.00	75.00

1964 Freihofer's Philadelphia Phillies

The attributed date is speculative, based on the players checklisted from this issue. These 8" x 10" pictures feature studio poses and are printed on heavy, non-glossy paper. A white border surrounds the photo, with the player name in typewriter-style all-caps at bottom. Backs are blank. Two styles of advertising have been seen imprinted on the pictures. Type 1 pictures have a bakery logo as part of the legend "ANOTHER FAVORITE / FROM FREIHOFER'S / that's who!" Type 2 pictures have a script inscription: "Best WISHES to a / Fellow Freihofer's Booster."

	NM	EX	VG
TYPE 1 (Logo)			
Ruben Amaro	50.00	25.00	15.00
Wes Covington	50.00	25.00	15.00
TYPE 2 (No logo.)			
Wes Covington	30.00	15.00	9.00

1963 French Bauer Reds Milk Caps

This regional set of cardboard milk bottle caps was issued in the Cincinnati area in 1963 and features 30 members of the Cincinnati Reds. The unnumbered, blank-backed discs are approximately 1-1/4" in diameter and feature rather crude drawings of the players with their names in script alongside the artwork and the words "Visit Beautiful Crosley Field/See The Reds in Action" along the outside. An album was issued to house the set. Some caps have been seen with incorrect picture/name combinations.

		NM	EX	VG
Complete Set (30):		1,300	650.00	400.00
Common Player:		25.00	12.50	7.50
Album:		100.00	50.00	30.00
(1)	Don Blasingame	25.00	12.50	7.50
(2)	Leo Cardenas	25.00	12.50	7.50
(3)	Gordon Coleman	25.00	12.50	7.50
(4)	Wm. O. DeWitt	25.00	12.50	7.50
(5)	John Edwards	25.00	12.50	7.50
(6)	Jesse Gonder	25.00	12.50	7.50
(7)	Tommy Harper	25.00	12.50	7.50
(8)	Bill Henry	25.00	12.50	7.50
(9)	Fred Hutchinson	25.00	12.50	7.50
(10)	Joey Jay	25.00	12.50	7.50
(11)	Eddie Kasko	25.00	12.50	7.50
(12)	Marty Keough	25.00	12.50	7.50
(13)	Jim Maloney	25.00	12.50	7.50
(14)	Joe Nuxhall	30.00	15.00	9.00
(15)	Reggie Otero	25.00	12.50	7.50
(16)	Jim O'Toole	25.00	12.50	7.50
(17)	Jim Owens	25.00	12.50	7.50
(18)	Vada Pinson	30.00	15.00	9.00
(19)	Bob Purkey	25.00	12.50	7.50
(20)	Frank Robinson	125.00	60.00	35.00
(21)	Dr. Richard Rohde	25.00	12.50	7.50
(22)	Pete Rose	500.00	250.00	150.00
(23)	Ray Shore	25.00	12.50	7.50
(24)	Dick Sisler	25.00	12.50	7.50
(25)	Bob Skinner	25.00	12.50	7.50
(26)	John Tsitorius	25.00	12.50	7.50
(27)	Jim Turner	25.00	12.50	7.50
(28)	Ken Walters	25.00	12.50	7.50
(29)	Al Worthington	25.00	12.50	7.50
(30)	Dom Zanni	25.00	12.50	7.50

1946 Friedman's Dodger Aces Postcard

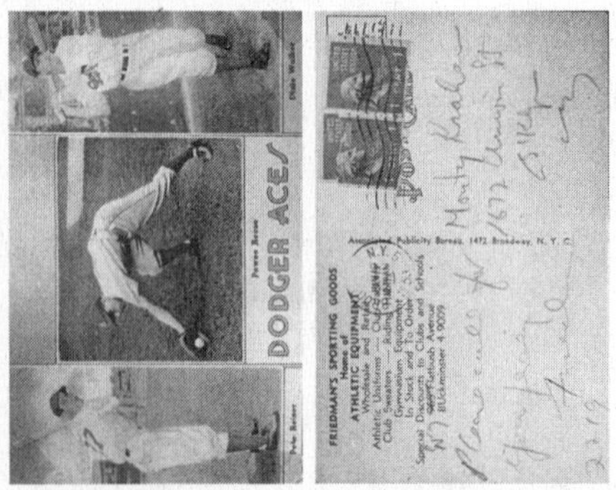

The date of issue is conjectural and could actually have been anytime in the 1940s until 1947, though the cards continued to be used at least into 1953 according to postally used examples. The 5-1/2" x 3-1/2" postcard has a linen finish on front and features color posed action photos of three Dodgers stars. Backs have information about the sporting goods store, a postage stamp box and a credit line to Associated Publicity Bureau.

	NM	EX	VG
Dodger Aces (Pete Reiser, Pewee (Pee Wee) Reese, Dixie Walker)	35.00	17.50	10.50

1960-61 Fritos Ticket Folders

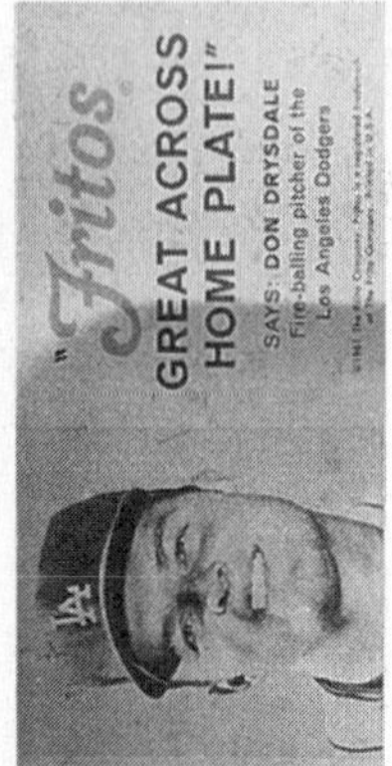

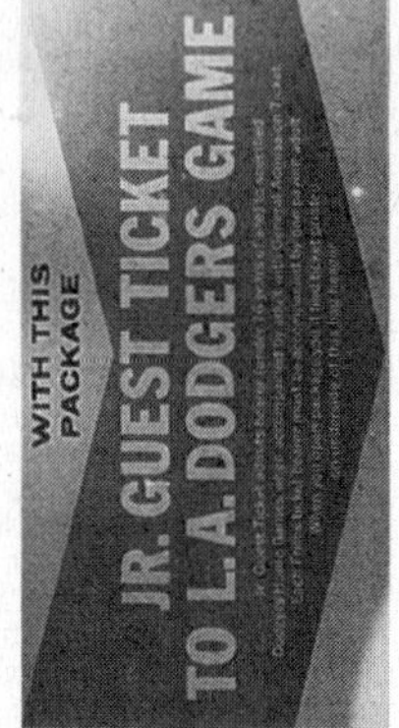

Only a few players are known in this issue of folders which includes a "Jr. Guest Ticket" to selected Dodgers games. About 5-5/8" x 3", the folder has a black-and-white player portrait on front and is highlighted in red and yellow. When opened, the folder has advertising for Fritos corn chips (or other Firtos-Lay brands) and a Dodgers home schedule. Others may exist.

		NM	EX	VG
Common Player:		90.00	45.00	25.00
(1)	Don Drysdale/1960 (Crispies advertising.)	250.00	125.00	75.00
(1)	Don Drysdale/1961	200.00	100.00	60.00
(2)	Gil Hodges/1960	200.00	100.00	60.00
(3)	Frank Howard/1961	90.00	45.00	25.00
(4)	Wally Moon/1960	150.00	75.00	45.00
(5)	Charley Neal/1960	150.00	75.00	45.00

1977 Fritsch One-Year Winners

First printed in 1977, this collector's issue features players with brief, but often well-known, major league baseball careers. Because of the timing or duration of their playing days, few ever appeared on a major baseball card issue. The 2-1/2" x 3-1/2" cards have black-and-white photos on front, bordered in green, with the player name in white within a green strip at bottom. Backs are printed in black, red and white in similitude of the 1953 Bowman backs and contain personal data, stats and career highlights.

		NM	EX	VG
Complete Set (18):		12.00	6.00	3.50
Common Player:		1.00	.50	.30
1	Eddie Gaedel	5.00	2.50	1.50
2	Chuck Connors	3.00	1.50	.90
3	Joe Brovia	1.00	.50	.30
4	Ross Grimsley	1.00	.50	.30
5	Bob Thorpe	1.00	.50	.30
6	Pete Gray	5.00	2.50	1.50
7	Cy Buker	1.00	.50	.30
8	Ted Fritsch	2.00	1.00	.60
9	Ron Necciai	1.00	.50	.30
10	Nino Escalera	1.00	.50	.30
11	Bobo Holloman	1.00	.50	.30
12	Tony Roig	1.00	.50	.30
13	Paul Pettit	1.00	.50	.30
14	Paul Schramka	1.00	.50	.30
15	Hal Trosky	1.00	.50	.30
16	Floyd Wooldridge	1.00	.50	.30
17	Jim Westlake	1.00	.50	.30
18	Leon Brinkopf	1.00	.50	.30

1979 Fritsch One-Year Winners

Players with short major-league careers, few of whom appeared on contemporary baseball cards, are featured in the second collectors' series of "One-Year Winners." The cards are numbered contiguously from the end of the 1977 issue and share a back format printed in red, white and black. Fronts of the 1979 issue have a white border and feature color player photos with a shadow box beneath carrying the name.

		NM	EX	VG
Complete Set (36):		40.00	20.00	12.00
Common Player:		3.00	1.50	.90
19	Daryl Robertson	3.00	1.50	.90
20	Gerry Schoen	3.00	1.50	.90
21	Jim Brenneman	3.00	1.50	.90
22	Pat House	3.00	1.50	.90
23	Ken Poulsen	3.00	1.50	.90
24	Arlo Brunsberg	3.00	1.50	.90
25	Jay Hankins	3.00	1.50	.90
26	Chuck Nieson	3.00	1.50	.90
27	Dick Joyce	3.00	1.50	.90
28	Jim Ellis	3.00	1.50	.90
29	John Duffie	3.00	1.50	.90
30	Vern Holtgrave	3.00	1.50	.90
31	Bill Bethea	3.00	1.50	.90
32	Joe Moock	3.00	1.50	.90
33	John Hoffman	3.00	1.50	.90
34	Jorge Rubio	3.00	1.50	.90
35	Fred Rath	3.00	1.50	.90
36	Jess Hickman	3.00	1.50	.90
37	Tom Fisher	3.00	1.50	.90
38	Dick Scott	3.00	1.50	.90
39	Jim Hibbs	3.00	1.50	.90
40	Paul Gilliford	3.00	1.50	.90
41	Bob Botz	3.00	1.50	.90
42	Jack Kubiszyn	3.00	1.50	.90
43	Rich Rusteck	3.00	1.50	.90
44	Roy Gleason	3.00	1.50	.90
45	Glenn Vaughn	3.00	1.50	.90
46	Bill Graham	3.00	1.50	.90
47	Dennis Musgraves	3.00	1.50	.90
48	Ron Henry	3.00	1.50	.90
49	Mike Jurewicz	3.00	1.50	.90
50	Pidge Browne	3.00	1.50	.90
51	Ron Keller	3.00	1.50	.90
52	Doug Gallagher	3.00	1.50	.90
53	Dave Thies	3.00	1.50	.90
54	Don Eaddy	3.00	1.50	.90

1928 Fro-joy (F52)

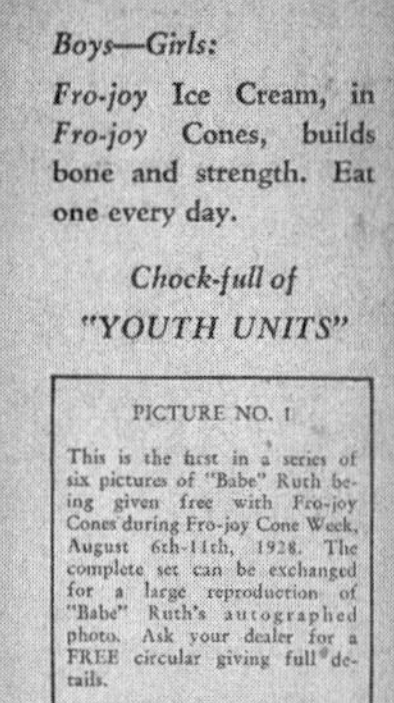

Capitalizing on the extreme popularity of Babe Ruth, these cards were given away with ice cream cones during the Aug. 6-11, 1928, "Fro-joy Cone Week." The 2-1/16" x 4" cards have black-and-white photos on front with a title and a few sentences explaining the photo. Backs contain advertising for Fro-joy Ice Cream and Cones. An uncut sheet along with a large-format action photo of Ruth was available in a mail-in redemption offer. Virtually all uncut sheets offered in the market today, and all color Fro-joy cards are modern counterfeits. Purchase of an uncut sheet without the original mailing envelope and/or premium picture is not advised. Cards graded by a major authentication firm carry a significant premium due to the prevalence of single-card counterfeits in the market.

		NM	EX	VG
Complete Set (6):		3,250	1,625	975.00
Uncut Sheet:		2,575	1,275	775.00
1	George Herman ("Babe") Ruth	750.00	375.00	225.00
2	Look Out, Mr. Pitcher!	500.00	250.00	150.00
3	Bang! The Babe Lines One Out!	500.00	250.00	150.00
4	When the "Babe" Comes Home	500.00	250.00	150.00
5	"Babe" Ruth's Grip!	200.00	100.00	60.00
6	Ruth is a Crack Fielder	500.00	250.00	150.00

1928 Fro-joy Premium Photo

This 8-1/2" x 10" photo of Babe Ruth was given away when a complete set of individual Fro-joy Babe Ruth cards was sent in for redemption. It is extremely scarce in its own right and is vital for verification of the authenticity of uncut Fro-joy card sheets. The premium photo is printed in blue in the debossed center area of a cream-colored card. A facsimile autograph of Ruth adorns the image.

	NM	EX	VG
Babe Ruth	1,200	600.00	360.00

1969 Fud's Photography Montreal Expos

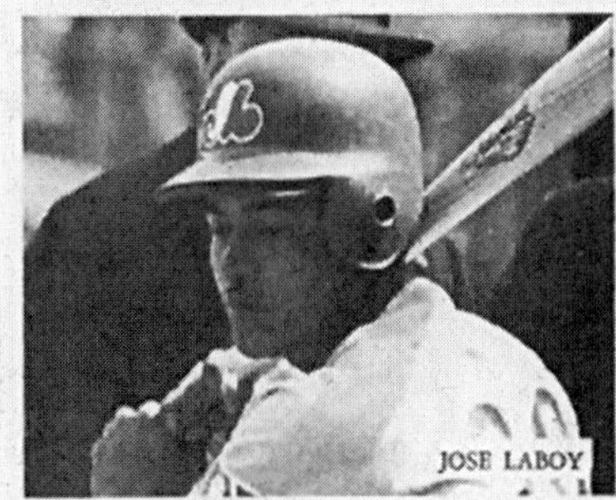

This collectors' issue was produced by Bob Solon sometime after 1969. The 3-1/2" x 3" black-and-white horizontal cards have action photos of the players with a white strip in the lower-right corner bearing the name. In the white border at top is "Compliments of," while the purported photo studio name is centered at bottom. Backs are blank. The unnumbered cards are checklisted here alphabetically.

		NM	EX	VG
Complete Set (14):		40.00	20.00	12.00
Common Player:		4.00	2.00	1.25
(1)	Bob Bailey	4.00	2.00	1.25
(2)	John Bateman	4.00	2.00	1.25
(3)	Don Bosch	4.00	2.00	1.25
(4)	Jim Grant	4.00	2.00	1.25
(5)	Mack Jones	4.00	2.00	1.25
(6)	Jose Laboy	4.00	2.00	1.25
(7)	Dan McGinn	4.00	2.00	1.25
(8)	Cal McLish	4.00	2.00	1.25
(9)	Carl Morton	4.00	2.00	1.25
(10)	Manny Mota	6.00	3.00	1.75
(11)	Rusty Staub	9.00	4.50	2.75
(12)	Gary Sutherland	4.00	2.00	1.25
(13)	Mike Wegener	4.00	2.00	1.25
(14)	Floyd Wicker	4.00	2.00	1.25

G

1888 G & B Chewing Gum (E223)

This set, issued with G&B Chewing Gum, is the first baseball card issued with candy or gum and the only 19th Century candy issue. The cards in the G&B set are small, measuring approximately 1-1/16" x 2-1/8", and nearly identical in format to the August Beck Yum Yum tobacco issue (N403). Many of the photos and pictures were shared between the sets. The player's name and position appear in thin capital letters below the photo, followed by either "National League" or "American League" (actually referring to the American Association). At the very bottom of the card, the manufacturer, "G & B N.Y." is indicated. Some of the "National League" cards also include the words "Chewing Gum" under the league designation. The set was assigned the ACC number E223. All of the action poses and some of the portraits are line drawings rather than photographs. Gaps have been left in the assigned numbering to accommodate future additions.

		NM	EX	VG
Common Player:		10,000	4,000	2,500
(3)	Cap Anson/Btg	25,000	10,000	6,250
(4)	Cap Anson (Photo portrait.)	37,500	15,000	9,375
(7)	Lady Baldwin (Detroit) (Left arm extended.)	10,000	4,000	2,500
(9)	Mark Baldwin (Chicago) (Bat at side.)	10,000	4,000	2,500
(10)	Mark Baldwin (Chicago) (Photo portrait.)	31,250	12,500	7,815
(13)	Sam Barkley (Line portrait.)	10,000	4,000	2,500
(15)	Steve Brady (Photo portrait.)	31,250	12,500	7,815
(17)	Dan Brouthers (Pose unrecorded.)	31,250	12,500	7,815
(19)	Willard (California) Brown (Photo portrait.)	31,250	12,500	7,815
(20)	Willard (California) Brown (Line art.)	10,000	4,000	2,500
(23)	Charles Buffington (Buffinton) (Photo portrait.)	31,250	12,500	7,815
(25)	Tom Burns (Photo portrait.)	31,250	12,500	7,815
(27)	Doc Bushong (Line portrait.)	10,000	4,000	2,500
(29)	Bob Caruthers (Line portrait.)	10,000	4,000	2,500
(33)	John Clarkson (Photo portrait.)	37,500	15,000	9,375
(35)	John Coleman (Photo portrait.)	31,250	12,500	7,815
(37)	Charlie Comiskey (Line portrait.)	18,750	7,500	4,690
(39)	Roger Connor/Btg	18,750	7,500	4,690
(40)	Roger Connor (Photo portrait.)	37,500	15,000	9,375
(43)	Con Daily (Photo portrait.)	31,250	12,500	7,815
(45)	Tom Deasley (Photo portrait.)	31,250	12,500	7,815
(47)	Jim Donahue (Photo portrait.)	31,250	12,500	7,815
(49)	Mike Dorgan (Photo portrait.)	31,250	12,500	7,815
(51)	Dude Esterbrook (Photo portrait.)	31,250	12,500	7,815
(53)	Buck Ewing (Photo portrait.)	37,500	15,000	9,375
(54)	Buck Ewing (With bat.)	18,750	7,500	4,690
(57)	Charlie Ferguson (Right arm head-high.)	10,000	4,000	2,500
(59)	Silver Flint (Line portrait.)	15,625	6,250	3,905
(61)	Pud Galvin (Ball in hands at front.)	18,750	7,500	4,690
(63)	Charlie Getzein (Getzien)/Throwing	10,000	4,000	2,500
(65)	Jack Glasscock (Line art.)	10,000	4,000	2,500
(67)	Will Gleason/Btg	10,000	4,000	2,500
(69)	Ed Greer (Photo portrait.)	31,250	12,500	7,815
(71)	Frank Hankinson (Photo portrait.)	31,250	12,500	7,815
(73)	Ned Hanlon/Btg	18,750	7,500	4,690
(75)	Pete Hotaling/Btg	15,625	6,250	3,905
(77)	Spud Johnson/Btg	10,000	4,000	2,500
(79)	Tim Keefe (Ball in hands above waist.)	18,750	7,500	4,690
(80)	Tim Keefe/Btg	18,750	7,500	4,690
(81)	Tim Keefe (Photo portrait.)	37,500	15,000	9,375
(83)	King Kelly/Btg	25,000	10,000	6,250
(84)	King Kelly (Photo, standing by urn.)	100,000	20,000	12,500
(87)	Gus Krock (Photo portrait.)	31,250	12,500	7,815
(89)	Arlie Latham (Line portrait.)	10,000	4,000	2,500
(91)	Connie Mack (Throwing)	37,500	15,000	9,375
(93)	Kid Madden (Pitching)	10,000	4,000	2,500
(95)	Al Mays (Photo portrait.)	31,250	12,500	7,815
(97)	Jumbo McGinnis (Line portrait.)	10,000	4,000	2,500
(99)	Doggie Miller (Leaning on bat.)	10,000	4,000	2,500
(101)	John Morrill (Bat at side.)	10,000	4,000	2,500
(103)	James Mutrie (Photo portrait.)	31,250	12,500	7,815
(105)	Hugh Nicoll (Nicol) (Line portrait.))	10,000	4,000	2,500
(107)	Tip O'Neill (Line portrait.)	10,000	4,000	2,500
(109)	Jim O'Rourke (Photo portrait.)	37,500	15,000	9,375
(111)	Dave Orr/Btg	10,000	4,000	2,500
(112)	Dave Orr (Photo portrait.)	31,250	12,500	7,815
(115)	Fred Pfeffer (Bat on shoulder.)	10,000	4,000	2,500
(117)	Henry Porter (Pitching)	10,000	4,000	2,500
(119)	Al Reache (Reach) (Line portrait.) (Possibly unique; value undetermined.))			
(121)	Danny Richardson/Btg	10,000	4,000	2,500
(122)	Danny Richardson (Photo portrait.)	31,250	12,500	7,815
(125)	Yank Robinson (Line portrait.)	10,000	4,000	2,500
(127)	Chief Roseman (Photo portrait.)	31,250	12,500	7,815
(129)	Jimmy Ryan (Photo portrait.)	31,250	12,500	7,815
(130)	Jimmy Ryan/Throwing	10,000	4,000	2,500
(133)	Pop Smith (Photo portrait.)	31,250	12,500	7,815
(137)	Bill Sowders (Ball in hands at chest.)	10,000	4,000	2,500
(138)	Bill Sowders/Throwing	10,000	4,000	2,500
(139)	Albert Spaulding (Spalding) (Line portrait.) (Possibly unique; value undetermined.)			
(141)	Marty Sullivan (Line portrait.)	10,000	4,000	2,500
(143)	Billy Sunday/Fldg	15,620	6,250	3,905
(144)	Billy Sunday (Photo portrait.)	34,375	13,750	8,595
(145)	Ezra Sutton/Btg	10,000	4,000	2,500
(149)	Sam Thompson/Btg	18,750	7,500	4,690
(153)	Mike Tiernan/Btg	10,000	4,000	2,500
(154)	Mike Tiernan (Photo portrait.)	31,250	12,500	7,815
(157)	Larry Twitchell (Photo portrait.)	31,250	12,500	7,815
(159)	Rip Van Haltren (Photo portrait.)	31,250	12,500	7,815
(161)	Chris Von Der Ahe (Line portrait.)	10,000	4,000	2,500
(165)	John Ward (Photo portrait.)	37,500	15,000	9,375
(169)	Mickey Welch (Ball in hands above waist.)	18,750	7,500	4,690
(170)	Mickey Welch (Right arm extended forward.)	18,750	7,500	4,690
(171)	Mickey Welch (Photo portrait.)	37,500	15,000	9,375
(173)	Curt Welsh (Welch)	10,000	4,000	2,500
(177)	Jim Whitney	10,000	4,000	2,500
(181)	Pete Wood/Throwing	10,000	4,000	2,500

1966 H.F. Gardner Postcards

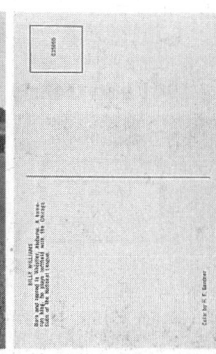

Baseball players (and track legend Jesse Owens) who were born in Alabama are featured in this issue credited on some of the cards' backs to a Bessemer, Ala., firm, Scenic South Card Co. Fronts feature borderless color photos attributed to H.F. Gardner. The date given is somewhat arbitrary based on the mention of the Atlanta Braves on the back of a card. Cards are in standard 3-1/2" x 5-1/2" postcard size and format. A brief biography of the athletes appears on the back, along with the credits. A quantity of the Aarons and Williams cards were found in a warehouse in 1999, driving down their prices.

		NM	EX	VG
Complete Set (5):		15.00	7.50	4.50
Common Player:		3.00	1.50	.90
(1)	Hank Aaron, Tommie Aaron	6.00	3.00	1.75
(2)	Bill Bruton	3.50	1.75	1.00
(3)	Lee Maye	3.50	1.75	1.00
(4)	Jesse Owens	4.50	2.25	1.25
(5)	Billy Williams	3.00	1.50	.90

1922 Gassler's American Maid Bread

These 2" x 3-1/4" black-and-white cards are one of several versions of the W575-1 strip cards with custom-printed advertising on the backs. It is unknown whether each card in the W575-1 checklist can be found with the Gassler's back.

	NM	EX	VG
Common Player:	150.00	75.00	45.00
Stars: 4-6X			

(See W575-1 for checklist; Gassler values 3X-4X.)

1962 Gehl's Ice Cream

Issued only in the Milwaukee area to promote sales of Gold-Mine brand ice cream, the six cards in this black-and-white set all feature Roger Maris, who the previous year had broken Babe Ruth's season home run record. The 4" x 5" cards are blank backed and each has a facsimile autograph on front reading "To My / Gold Mine Pal / Roger Maris." The cards are unnumbered; a description of each is provided in the checklist.

		NM	EX	VG
Complete Set (6):		1,600	800.00	480.00
Common Card:		400.00	200.00	120.00
(1)	Roger Maris (Bat on shoulder, close-up.)	400.00	200.00	120.00
(2)	Roger Maris (Bat on shoulder, photo to waist.)	400.00	200.00	120.00
(3)	Roger Maris (Batting stance.)	400.00	200.00	120.00
(4)	Roger Maris ("Hitting My 61st," ballpark photo.)	325.00	160.00	100.00

		NM	EX	VG
(5)	Roger Maris (Holding bat in hands.)	400.00	200.00	120.00
(6)	Roger Maris (Portrait in warm-up jacket.)	400.00	200.00	120.00

1941 Lou Gehrig Memorial Ticket

On July 4, 1941, just a month after his death, the N.Y. Yankees scheduled special memorial ceremonies for the Iron Horse. Tickets for the event picture Gehrig and were issued in several colors and price ranges based on seat location. Most often found in stub form of about 3-3/8" x 2-1/2", full tickets are also occasionally seen, probably because a rain-out on July 4 forced the ceremonies to the following Sunday.

	NM	EX	VG
Lou Gehrig (Ticket stub.)	1,300	650.00	390.00
Lou Gehrig (Full ticket.)	3,250	1,625	975.00

1911-14 General Baking Co. (D304)

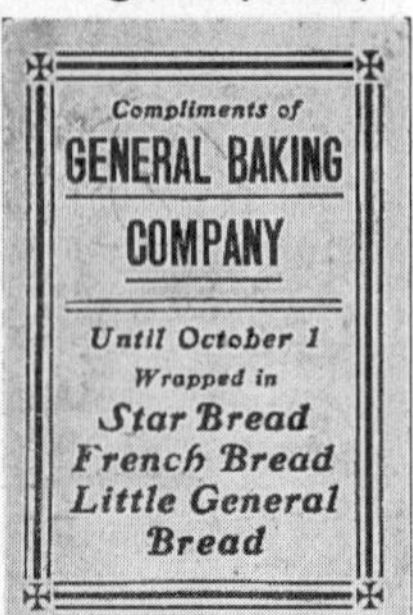

This issue by a bakery based in Buffalo, N.Y., is similar in design to contemporary tobacco and candy cards, but is larger in size, at 1-3/4" x 2-1/2". Fronts feature a color lithograph with the player's name and team below in capital letters. Some players who changed teams in 1913-14 are found with the team name obliterated at bottom by a black line. Five different back styles are known, listed here by the principal brand name: 1) Brunners, 2) Butter Krust, 3) General Baking Co., 4) Weber Bakery, 5) Martens Bakery. The complete set price does not include "no-team" variations. Modern counterfeits of the issue are widely seen in the hobby market.

		NM	EX	VG
Complete Set (25):		270,000	108,000	54,000
Common Player:		3,600	1,425	720.00
(1)	J. Frank Baker	11,250	4,500	2,250
(2)	Jack Barry	3,600	1,425	720.00
(3)	George Bell	3,600	1,425	720.00
(4)	Charles Bender	11,250	4,500	2,250
(5a)	Frank Chance (Chicago)	11,250	4,500	2,250
(5b)	Frank Chance (No team.)	15,000	6,000	3,000
(6a)	Hal Chase (N.Y.)	4,500	2,100	900.00
(6b)	Hal Chase (No team.)	5,400	2,400	1,200
(7)	Ty Cobb	60,000	30,000	10,000
(8)	Eddie Collins	11,250	4,500	2,250
(9a)	Otis Crandall (N.Y.)	3,600	1,425	720.00
(9b)	Otis Crandall (No team.)	5,250	2,250	1,050
(10)	Sam Crawford	11,250	4,500	2,250
(11a)	John Evers (Chicago)	11,250	4,500	2,250
(11b)	John Evers (No team.)	15,000	6,000	3,000
(12)	Arthur Fletcher	3,600	1,425	720.00
(13a)	Charles Herzog (N.Y.)	3,600	1,425	720.00
(13b)	Charles Herzog (No team.)	5,250	2,250	1,050
(14)	M. (Billy) Kelly	3,600	1,425	720.00
(15)	Napoleon Lajoie	15,000	6,750	3,750
(16)	Rube Marquard	11,250	4,500	2,250
(17)	Christy Mathewson	44,000	21,000	6,600
(18)	Fred Merkle	3,600	1,425	720.00
(19)	"Chief" Meyers	3,600	1,425	720.00
(20)	Marty O'Toole	3,600	1,425	720.00
(21)	Nap. Rucker	3,600	1,425	720.00
(22)	Arthur Shafer	3,600	1,425	720.00
(23)	Fred Tenny (Tenney)	9,000	6,500	3,500
(24)	Honus Wagner	44,000	21,000	6,600
(25)	Cy Young	40,000	18,000	6,000

1915 General Baking Co. (D303)

Issued in 1915 by the General Baking Co., these unnumbered cards measure 1-1/2" x 2-3/4". The player pictures and format of the cards are identical to the E106 set, but the D303 cards are easily identified by the advertisement for General Baking on the back.

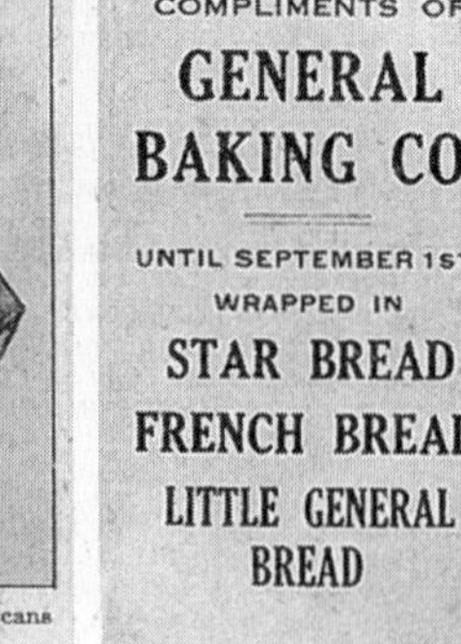

		NM	EX	VG
Complete Set (51):		80,000	32,000	16,000
Common Player:		1,600	800.00	300.00
(1)	Jack Barry	1,600	800.00	300.00
(2)	Chief Bender (Blue background.)	3,000	1,700	800.00
(3)	Chief Bender (Green background.)	3,000	1,750	800.00
(4)	Bob Bescher (New York)	1,600	800.00	300.00
(5)	Bob Bescher (St. Louis)	1,600	800.00	300.00
(6)	Roger Bresnahan	3,000	1,750	800.00
(7)	Al Bridwell	1,600	800.00	300.00
(8)	Donie Bush	1,600	800.00	300.00
(9)	Hal Chase/Catching	1,800	800.00	360.00
(10)	Hal Chase/Portrait	1,800	900.00	360.00
(11)	Ty Cobb/Btg	20,000	10,000	3,000
(12)	Ty Cobb (Leaning on bat.)	30,000	15,000	5,000
(13)	Eddie Collins	3,000	1,700	800.00
(14)	Sam Crawford	3,000	1,700	800.00
(15)	Ray Demmitt	1,600	800.00	300.00
(16)	Wild Bill Donovan	1,600	800.00	300.00
(17)	Red Dooin	1,600	800.00	300.00
(18)	Mickey Doolan	1,600	800.00	300.00
(19)	Larry Doyle	1,600	800.00	300.00
(20)	Clyde Engle	1,600	800.00	300.00
(21)	Johnny Evers	3,000	1,700	800.00
(22)	Art Fromme	1,600	800.00	300.00
(23)	George Gibson/Catching (Back view.)	1,600	800.00	300.00
(24)	George Gibson/Catching (Front view.)	1,600	800.00	300.00
(25)	Roy Hartzell	1,600	800.00	300.00
(26)	Fred Jacklitsch	1,600	800.00	300.00
(27)	Hugh Jennings	3,000	1,750	800.00
(28)	Otto Knabe	1,600	800.00	300.00
(29)	Nap Lajoie	4,000	2,000	1,000
(30)	Hans Lobert	1,600	800.00	300.00
(31)	Rube Marquard	1,500	850.00	400.00
(32)	Christy Mathewson	6,000	3,500	1,250
(33)	John McGraw	1,500	850.00	400.00
(34)	George McQuillan	1,600	800.00	300.00
(35)	Dots Miller	1,600	800.00	300.00
(36)	Danny Murphy	1,600	800.00	300.00
(37)	Rebel Oakes	1,600	800.00	300.00
(38)	Eddie Plank (No position on front.)	3,000	1,700	750.00
(39)	Eddie Plank (Position on front.)	6,000	3,000	1,500
(40)	Germany Schaefer	1,600	800.00	300.00
(41)	Boss Smith (Schmidt)	1,600	800.00	300.00
(42)	Tris Speaker	3,000	1,700	750.00
(43)	Oscar Stanage	1,600	800.00	300.00
(44)	George Stovall	1,600	800.00	300.00
(45)	Jeff Sweeney	1,600	800.00	300.00
(46)	Joe Tinker/Btg	2,000	1,200	600.00
(47)	Joe Tinker/Portrait	2,000	1,200	600.00
(48)	Honus Wagner/Btg	20,000	10,000	3,000
(49)	Honus Wagner/Throwing	30,000	15,000	5,000
(50)	Hooks Wiltse	1,600	800.00	300.00
(51)	Heinie Zimmerman	1,600	800.00	300.00

1908 General Photo Co. St. Louis Browns Postcards

The extent of this postcard issue by a hometown printer is unknown. It is likely other single-player postcards were issued. Approximately 3-1/2" x 5-1/2", the cards are black-and-white with a credit line on bottom: "Photo by General Photo Co., 610 Granite Bldg., St. Louis." On the team photo card, players are identified below the group photo.

		NM	EX	VG
(1)	"Rube" Waddell	500.00	250.00	150.00
(2)	St. Louis Browns - 1908	750.00	375.00	225.00

1948 Gentle's Bread Boston Braves

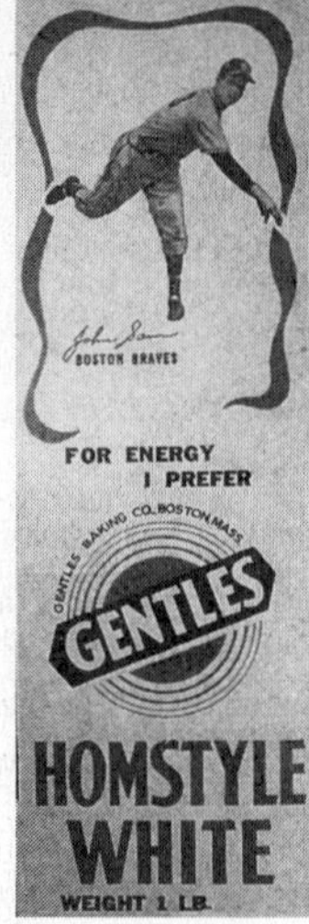

These 3" x 9" waxed-paper end labels were found on loaves of Gentle's bread. Printed in blue and red, the labels depict action poses of the National League Champion '48 Braves. A facsimile autograph appears with the photo. Backs are blank. The unnumbered labels are checklisted here alphabetically.

		NM	EX	VG
Complete Set (9):		3,000	1,500	900.00
Common Player:		400.00	200.00	120.00
(1)	Alvin Dark	450.00	225.00	135.00
(2)	Bob Elliott	400.00	200.00	120.00
(3)	Tommy Heath	400.00	200.00	120.00
(4)	Tommy Holmes	400.00	200.00	120.00
(5)	Phil Masi	400.00	200.00	120.00
(6)	John Sain	450.00	225.00	135.00
(7)	Warren Spahn	600.00	300.00	180.00
(8)	Eddie Stanky	450.00	225.00	135.00
(9)	Earl Torgeson	400.00	200.00	120.00

1956 Gentry Magazine Ty Cobb

In issue #20 of Gentry magazine, dated Fall, 1956, a feature article on card collecting was enhanced with the inclusion of an original Ty Cobb card tipped onto an interior page. Measuring about 4" x 2-1/4" and blank-backed, the color card is similar in design to the T205 tobacco card issue.

	NM	EX	VG
Complete Magazine:	125.00	65.00	40.00
Ty Cobb	90.00	45.00	27.00

1909-10 German Baseball Stamps

A marginal notation "Made in Germany" on one of the stamps in this series identifies its origins. Little else in known of them. The stamps measure about 1-3/8" to 1-1/2" by 1-3/4" to 1-7/8". They are printed in bright colors on a pink background with name and team in blue. Because of their European origins, there are many mistakes in player and team names. The crude pictures are not representative of the player named. Unnumbered stamps are listed here in alphabetical order. It is evident several different configurations of 35-stamp sheets must have been issued.

Checklists showing are card numbers in parentheses ( ) indicates the numbers do not appear on the cards.

		NM	EX	VG
Complete Sheet (35):		1,150	575.00	345.00
Complete Set (41):		1,300	650.00	400.00
Common Player:		65.00	32.50	20.00
(1)	Ginger Beaumont	65.00	32.50	20.00
(2)	Frank Bowerman	65.00	32.50	20.00
(3)	Kitty Bransfield	65.00	32.50	20.00
(4)	Al Bridwell	65.00	32.50	20.00
(5a)	Roger Bresnahan (Light shirt.)	100.00	50.00	30.00
(5b)	Roger Bresnahan (Dark shirt.)	100.00	50.00	30.00
(6)	Bill Carrigan	65.00	32.50	20.00
(7)	Hal Chase	80.00	40.00	24.00
(8)	Eddie Collins	100.00	50.00	30.00
(9)	Harry Davis	65.00	32.50	20.00
(10)	Wild Bill Donovan	65.00	32.50	20.00
(11)	Larry Doyle	65.00	32.50	20.00
(12)	Jean Dubuc	65.00	32.50	20.00
(13)	Kid Elberfield (Elberfeld)	65.00	32.50	20.00
(14)	Dick Hoblitzell	65.00	32.50	20.00
(15)	Solly Hoffman (Hofman)	65.00	32.50	20.00
(16)	Tim Jordan	65.00	32.50	20.00
(17)	Willie Keeler	100.00	50.00	30.00
(18)	Nap Lajoie	100.00	50.00	30.00
(19)	Tommy Leach	65.00	32.50	20.00
(20)	Christy Mathewson	325.00	160.00	100.00
(21)	Dots Miller	65.00	32.50	20.00
(22)	John McGraw	100.00	50.00	30.00
(23)	Eddie Plank	100.00	50.00	30.00
(24)	Jack Rowan	65.00	32.50	20.00
(25)	Nap Rucker	65.00	32.50	20.00
(26)	Shannon (Boston)	65.00	32.50	20.00
(27)	Frank Smith	65.00	32.50	20.00
(28)	Tris Speaker	120.00	60.00	35.00
(29)	Jake Stahl	65.00	32.50	20.00
(30)	Lee Tannehill	65.00	32.50	20.00
(31)	Fred Tenney	65.00	32.50	20.00
(32)	Ira Thomas	65.00	32.50	20.00
(33)	Joe Tinker	100.00	50.00	30.00
(34)	Honus Wagner	285.00	140.00	85.00
(35)	Jimmy Williams	65.00	32.50	20.00
(36)	Cy Young	165.00	85.00	50.00
(37)	Baseball	15.00	7.50	4.50
(38)	Bat	15.00	7.50	4.50
(39)	Body Protector	15.00	7.50	4.50
(40)	Catcher's Mask	15.00	7.50	4.50
(41)	Crossed Bats	15.00	7.50	4.50
(42)	Glove	15.00	7.50	4.50

1923 German Baseball Transfers

With crude artwork lifted from the W515 strip card set, this issue of baseball player (and boxer) transfers was produced in Germany. Approximately 1-3/16" x 1-1/2", the stamps are printed in red on a green background. All of the design, except for the "MADE IN GERMANY" notation in the white bottom margin, is in mirror-image, befitting their use as tattoos or transfers. Two of the baseball players are double-prints. The unnumbered stamps (baseball only) are checklisted here alphabetically.

		NM	EX	VG
Complete Baseball Set (13):		350.00	175.00	105.00
Complete Sheet (25):		400.00	200.00	120.00
Common Player:		40.00	20.00	12.00
(1)	Grover Alexander	45.00	22.00	13.50
(2)	Dave Bancroft	40.00	20.00	12.00
(3)	George (J.) Burns	30.00	15.00	9.00
(4)	"Ty" Cobb	100.00	50.00	30.00
(5)	Red Faber/DP	25.00	12.50	7.50
(6)	Arthur Nehf	30.00	15.00	9.00
(7)	"Babe" Ruth	200.00	100.00	60.00
(8)	Ray Schalk	40.00	20.00	12.00
(9)	Everett Scott	30.00	15.00	9.00
(10)	Bob Shawkey	30.00	15.00	9.00
(11)	Tris Speaker	45.00	22.00	13.50
(12)	"Casey" Stengel	45.00	22.00	13.50
(13)	Zack Wheat/DP	30.00	15.00	9.00

1922 Lou Gertenrich

One of the most attractive advertising backs of the 1920s is found on this version of the 1922 issue which is most often found with American Caramel ads on back. Gertenrich had a three-game major league career between 1901-1903, supporting his advertising claim of "The Baseball Player Candy Manufacturer." Probably originating in Chicago, these cards are 2" x 3-1/2" black-and-white. The set shares the checklist with the American Caramel Co. (E121) set of 120. Because of the scarcity and appeal of this regional issue, the Gertenrich versions carry a substantial premium for type-card and superstar collectors.

	NM	EX	VG
Common Player:	600.00	300.00	175.00

Stars: 3-4X

(See 1922 American Caramel Series of 120 for checklist.)

1888 Gilbert & Bacon Cabinets

The known range of this cabinet card issue comprises mostly members of the 1888 Philadelphia Athletics and Phillies. The posed action photos on the approximately 4-1/4" x 6-1/2" cards are the same pictures seen on many of the players' Old Judge and Old Judge cabinet cards. The G&B cabinets have an embossed Goodwin & Co. copyright seal. An elaborate typescript Gilbert & Bacon studio logo is found in the bottom-left border, with the city named at right. Backs have an ornate studio logo.

		NM	EX	VG
Common Player:		3,000	1,200	700.00
(1)	Louis Bierbauer	3,000	1,200	700.00
(2)	Bill Blair	3,000	1,200	700.00
(3)	Charlie Ferguson (Ball in hands at chest.)	3,000	1,200	700.00
(4)	Charlie Ferguson/Btg	3,000	1,200	700.00
(5)	Charlie Ferguson/Throwing	3,000	1,200	700.00
(6)	Kid Gleason	3,000	1,200	700.00
(7)	John Henry	3,000	1,200	700.00
(8)	Henry Larkin	3,000	1,200	700.00
(9)	Denny Lyons	3,000	1,200	700.00
(11)	Deacon McGuire (Bat behind head.)	3,000	1,200	700.00
(12)	Deacon McGuire (Bat on shoulder.)	3,000	1,200	700.00
(13)	Deacon McGuire/Fldg (Hands at waist.)	3,000	1,200	700.00
(14)	Deacon McGuire/Fldg (Hands head-high.)	3,000	1,200	700.00
(15)	Deacon McGuire/Throwing	3,000	1,200	700.00
(16)	George Pinkney (Bat at 45-degree angle.)	3,000	1,200	700.00
(17)	George Pinkney (Bat at 60-degree angle.)	3,000	1,200	700.00
(18)	George Pinkney (Bat nearly horizontal.)	3,000	1,200	700.00
(19)	George Pinkney (Fielding fly ball.)	3,000	1,200	700.00
(21)	George Pinkney (Fielding line drive.)	3,000	1,200	700.00
(22)	George Pinkney/Throwing	3,000	1,200	700.00
(23)	Ben Sanders (Ball in hands at chest.)	3,000	1,200	700.00
(24)	Ben Sanders/Btg	3,000	1,200	700.00
(25)	Ben Sanders (Fielding fly ball.)	3,000	1,200	700.00
(26)	Ben Sanders/Throwing	3,000	1,200	700.00
(27)	Harry Stovey	3,000	1,200	700.00
(28)	Michael Sullivan	3,000	1,200	700.00
(29)	Gus Weyhing	3,000	1,200	700.00
(31)	John Weyhing	3,000	1,200	700.00

1916 Gimbels

This version of the 1916 M101-5 and M101-4 Blank Backs can be found with three slightly different styles of typography on back.

	NM	EX	VG
Common Player:	130.00	65.00	40.00

Stars: 1-2X

(See 1916 M101-5 and M101-4 Blank Backs for checklists and base pricing.)

1953 Glendale Hot Dogs Tigers

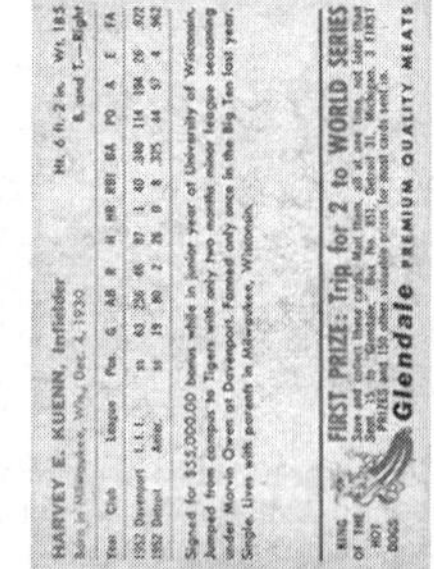

Glendale Meats issued these unnumbered, full- color cards (2-5/8" x 3-3/4") in packages of hot dogs Featuring only Detroit Tigers players, the card fronts contain a player picture with his name, a facsimile autograph, and the Tigers logo. Backs carry player statistical and biographical information plus an offer for a trip for two to the World Series. Collectors were advised to mail all the cards they had saved to Glendale Meats. The World Series trip plus 150 other prizes were to be given to the individuals sending in the most cards. As with most cards issued with food products, high-grade cards are tough to find because of the cards' susceptibilty to stains. The Houtteman card is extremely scarce.

		NM	EX	VG
Complete Set (28):		27,500	11,000	5,500
Common Player:		900.00	365.00	180.00
(1)	Matt Batts	900.00	365.00	180.00
(2)	Johnny Bucha	900.00	365.00	180.00
(3)	Frank Carswell	900.00	365.00	180.00
(4)	Jim Delsing	900.00	365.00	180.00
(5)	Walt Dropo	900.00	365.00	180.00
(6)	Hal Erickson	900.00	365.00	180.00
(7)	Paul Foytack	900.00	365.00	180.00
(8)	Owen Friend	900.00	365.00	180.00
(9)	Ned Garver	900.00	365.00	180.00
(10)	Joe Ginsberg	900.00	365.00	180.00
(11)	Ted Gray	900.00	365.00	180.00
(12)	Fred Hatfield	900.00	365.00	180.00
(13)	Ray Herbert	900.00	365.00	180.00
(14)	Bill Hitchcock	900.00	365.00	180.00
(15)	Bill Hoeft	900.00	365.00	180.00
(16)	Art Houtteman	5,000	2,000	1,000
(17)	Milt Jordan	900.00	365.00	180.00
(18)	Harvey Kuenn	1,200	480.00	240.00
(19)	Don Lund	900.00	365.00	180.00
(20)	Dave Madison	900.00	365.00	180.00
(21)	Dick Marlowe	900.00	365.00	180.00
(22)	Pat Mullin	900.00	365.00	180.00
(23)	Bob Nieman	900.00	365.00	180.00
(24)	Johnny Pesky	900.00	365.00	180.00
(25)	Jerry Priddy	900.00	365.00	180.00
(26)	Steve Souchock	900.00	365.00	180.00
(27)	Russ Sullivan	900.00	365.00	180.00
(28)	Bill Wight	1,100	450.00	225.00

1916 Globe Clothing Store (H801-9)

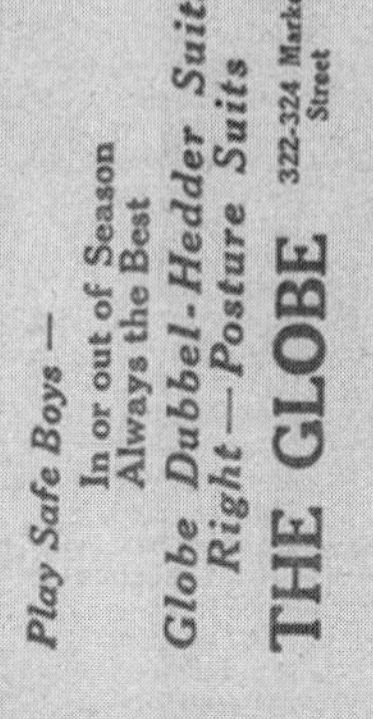

This 200-card set can be found with ads on the back for several local and regional businesses. Among them is the Globe clothing store in St. Louis. Type card, team- and single-player collectors may pay a modest premium for individual cards with the Globe store's advertising over the parallel 1916 M101-4 Blank Backs values. This version carries an "American Card Catalog" designation of H801-9. Cards measure 1-5/8" x 3" and are printed in black-and-white.

	NM	EX	VG
Common Player:	225.00	110.00	65.00
Stars: 2-3X			

(See 1916 M101-4 Blank Backs for checklist and base values.)

1969 Globe Imports Playing Cards

Largely ignored by collectors for more than 35 years, this issue has little to offer any but the most avid superstar collector. Printed in black-and-white on very thin white cardboard, either with blank backs, or with red-and-white checkerboard patterned backs, the cards measure 1-5/8" x 2-1/4". Muddy player action photos are at center of each card, with the player's name reversed out of a black strip at the bottom. It is likely this set was issued over a period of more than one year. The plain-back version was probably issued first, and has photos which include cap and jersey logos. The checked-back version seems to have been a later issue with many of the cards showing uniform logos airbrushed away. The photo quality of the checked-back cards is also much poorer than the plain-backs. A few players were substituted between the issues, and there may be more yet to be reported. The Babe Ruth AD card listed here is actually part of a multi-topic deck in similar format issued contemprarily with the baseball decks.

		NM	EX	VG
Complete Set (52+Joker):		20.00	10.00	6.00
Common Player:		.25	.15	.10
	PLAIN BACK HEARTS			
2	Chris Short	.25	.15	.10
3	Tony Conigliaro	.75	.40	.25
4	Bill Freehan	.25	.15	.10
5	Willie McCovey	2.00	1.00	.60
6	Joel Horlen	.25	.15	.10
7	Ernie Banks	2.00	1.00	.60
8	Jim Wynn	.25	.15	.10
9	Brooks Robinson	2.00	1.00	.60
10	Orlando Cepeda	1.00	.50	.30
J	Al Kaline	2.00	1.00	.60
Q	Gene Alley	.25	.15	.10
K	Rusty Staub	.75	.40	.25
A	Willie Mays	4.00	2.00	1.25
	CLUBS			
2	Reggie Smith	.25	.15	.10
3	Mike McCormick	.25	.15	.10
4	Tony Oliva	.50	.25	.15
5	Bud Harrelson	.25	.15	.10
6	Rick Reichardt	.25	.15	.10
7	Billy Williams	1.00	.50	.30
8	Pete Rose	6.00	3.00	1.75
9	Jim Maloney	.25	.15	.10
10	Tim McCarver	.75	.40	.25
J	Max Alvis	.25	.15	.10
Q	Ron Swoboda	.25	.15	.10
K	Johnny Callison	.25	.15	.10
A	Richie Allen	.75	.40	.25
	DIAMONDS			
2	Paul Casanova	.25	.15	.10
3	Juan Marichal	1.00	.50	.30
4	Jim Fregosi	.25	.15	.10
5	Earl Wilson	.25	.15	.10
6	Tony Horton	.25	.15	.10
7	Harmon Killebrew	2.00	1.00	.60
8	Tom Seaver	3.00	1.50	.90
9	Curt Flood	.75	.40	.25
10	Frank Robinson	2.00	1.00	.60
J	Bob Aspromonte	.25	.15	.10
Q	Lou Brock	2.00	1.00	.60
K	Jim Lonborg	.25	.15	.10
A(a)	Bob Gibson	2.00	1.00	.60
A(b)	Babe Ruth	12.00	6.00	3.60
	SPADES			
2	Cesar Tovar	.25	.15	.10
3	Rick Monday	.25	.15	.10
4	Richie Allen	.75	.40	.25
5	Mel Stottlemyre	.50	.25	.15
6	Tommy John	.75	.40	.25
7	Don Mincher	.25	.15	.10
8	Chico Cardenas	.25	.15	.10
9	Willie Davis	.25	.15	.10
10	Bert Campaneris	.25	.15	.10
J	Ron Santo	.75	.40	.25
Q	Al Ferrera	.25	.15	.10
K	Clete Boyer	.50	.25	.15
A(a)	Don Drysdale	3.00	1.50	.90
A(b)	Mickey Mantle	40.00	20.00	12.00
	CHECKERBOARD BACK HEARTS			
2	Chris Short	.25	.15	.10
3	Tony Conigliaro	.75	.40	.25
4	Bill Freehan	.25	.15	.10
5	Willie McCovey	2.00	1.00	.60
6	Joel Horlen	.25	.15	.10
7	Ernie Banks	2.00	1.00	.60
8	Jim Wynn	.25	.15	.10
9	Brooks Robinson	2.00	1.00	.60
10	Orlando Cepeda	1.00	.50	.30
J	Al Kaline	2.00	1.00	.60
Q	Gene Alley	.25	.15	.10
K	Rusty Staub	.75	.40	.25
A	Willie Mays	6.00	3.00	1.75
	CLUBS			
2	Reggie Smith	.25	.15	.10
3	Jerry Koosman	.25	.15	.10
4	Tony Oliva	.50	.25	.15
5	Bud Harrelson	.25	.15	.10
6	Rick Reichardt	.25	.15	.10
7	Billy Williams	1.00	.50	.30
8	Pete Rose	6.00	3.00	1.75
9	Jim Maloney	.25	.15	.10
10	Tim McCarver	.75	.40	.25
J	Max Alvis	.25	.15	.10
Q	Ron Swoboda	.25	.15	.10
K	Johnny Callison	.25	.15	.10
A	Richie Allen	.75	.40	.25
	DIAMONDS			
2	Paul Casanova	.25	.15	.10
3	Juan Marichal	1.00	.50	.30
4	Jim Fregosi	.25	.15	.10
5	Earl Wilson	.25	.15	.10
6	Tony Horton	.25	.15	.10
7	Harmon Killebrew	2.00	1.00	.60
8	Tom Seaver	3.00	1.50	.90
9	Curt Flood	.75	.40	.25
10	Frank Robinson	2.00	1.00	.60
J	Bob Aspromonte	.25	.15	.10
Q	Lou Brock	2.00	1.00	.60
K	Jim Lonborg	.25	.15	.10
A	Bob Gibson	2.00	1.00	.60
	SPADES			
2	Denny McLain	.50	.25	.15
3	Rick Monday	.25	.15	.10
4	Richie Allen	.75	.40	.25
5	Mel Stottlemyre	.50	.25	.15
6	Tommy John	.75	.40	.25
7	Don Mincher	.25	.15	.10
8	Chico Cardenas	.25	.15	.10
9	Willie Davis	.25	.15	.10
10	Bert Campaneris	.25	.15	.10
J	Ron Santo	.75	.40	.25
Q	Al Ferrera	.25	.15	.10
K	Clete Boyer	.50	.25	.15
A	Ken Harrelson	.25	.15	.10

1887 Gold Coin (Buchner) (N284)

KENNEDY, PITCHER, LACROSSE

WE WILL PACK IN THE CELEBRATED GOLD COIN CHEWING TOBACCO THE PORTRAITS OF ALL THE LEADING BASE-BALL PLAYERS IN THE COUNTRY IN FULL UNIFORM CONTINUE TO SAVE THE WRAPPERS THEY ARE VALUABLE.

Issued circa 1887, the N284 issue was produced by D. Buchner & Co.for its Gold Coin brand of chewing tobacco. Actually, the series was not comprised only of baseball players - actors, jockeys, firemen and policemen were also included. The cards, which measure 1-3/4" x 3", are color drawings. The set is not a popular one among collectors as the drawings do not in all cases represent the players designated on the cards. In most instances, players at a given position share the same drawing depicted on the card front. Three different card backs are found, all advising collectors to save the valuable chewing tobacco wrappers. Wrappers could be redeemed for various prizes.

		NM	EX	VG
Complete Set (143):		135,000	60,000	27,500
Common Player:		815.00	365.00	165.00
(1)	Ed Andrews (Hands at neck.)	815.00	365.00	165.00
(2)	Ed Andrews (Hands waist high.)	815.00	365.00	165.00
(3)	Cap Anson (Hands outstretched.)	4,065	1,815	815.00
(4)	Cap Anson (Left hand on hip.)	5,315	2,375	1,065
(5)	Tug Arundel	815.00	365.00	165.00
(6)	Sam Barkley (Pittsburg)	815.00	365.00	165.00
(7)	Sam Barkley (St. Louis)	815.00	365.00	165.00
(8)	Charley Bassett	815.00	365.00	165.00
(9)	Charlie Bastian	815.00	365.00	165.00
(10)	Ed Beecher	815.00	365.00	165.00
(11)	Charlie Bennett	815.00	365.00	165.00
(12)	Henry Boyle	815.00	365.00	165.00
(13)	Dan Brouthers (Hands outstretched.)	3,125	1,405	625.00
(14)	Dan Brouthers (With bat.)	3,125	1,405	625.00
(15)	Tom Brown	815.00	365.00	165.00
(16)	Jack Burdock	815.00	365.00	165.00
(17)	Oyster Burns (Baltimore)	815.00	365.00	165.00
(18)	Tom Burns (Chicago)	815.00	365.00	165.00
(19)	Doc Bushong	815.00	365.00	165.00
(20)	John Cahill	815.00	365.00	165.00
(21)	Cliff Carroll (Washington)	815.00	365.00	165.00
(22)	Fred Carroll (Pittsburgh)	815.00	365.00	165.00
(23)	Bob Carruthers (Caruthers)	815.00	365.00	165.00
(24)	Dan Casey	815.00	365.00	165.00
(25)	John Clarkson (Ball at chest.)	2,815	1,250	565.00
(26)	John Clarkson (Arm outstretched.)	3,125	1,405	625.00
(27)	Jack Clements	815.00	365.00	165.00
(28)	John Coleman	815.00	365.00	165.00
(29)	Charles Comiskey	3,440	1,530	690.00
(30)	Roger Connor (Hands outstretched chest-level, "New York.")	2,815	1,250	565.00
(31)	Roger Connor (Hands oustreteched face-level, "N.Y.")	3,125	1,405	625.00
(32)	John Corbett	815.00	365.00	165.00
(33)	Sam Craig (Crane)	815.00	365.00	165.00
(34)	Sam Crane	815.00	365.00	165.00
(35)	John Crowley	815.00	365.00	165.00
(36)	Ed Cushmann (Cushman)	815.00	365.00	165.00
(37)	Ed Dailey (Daily)	815.00	365.00	165.00
(38)	Con Daley (Daily)	815.00	365.00	165.00
(39)	Pat Deasley	815.00	365.00	165.00
(40)	Jerry Denny (Hands on knees.)	815.00	365.00	165.00
(41)	Jerry Denny (Hands on thighs.)	815.00	365.00	165.00
(42)	Jim Donnelly	815.00	365.00	165.00
(43)	Jim Donohue (Donahue)	815.00	365.00	165.00
(44)	Mike Dorgan (Right field.)	815.00	365.00	165.00
(45)	Mike Dorgan (Batter)	815.00	365.00	165.00
(46)	Fred Dunlap	815.00	365.00	165.00
(47)	Dude Esterbrook	815.00	365.00	165.00
(48)	Buck Ewing (Ready to tag.)	2,815	1,250	565.00
(49)	Buck Ewing (Hands at neck.)	3,125	1,405	625.00
(50)	Sid Farrar	815.00	365.00	165.00
(51)	Jack Farrell (Ready to tag.)	815.00	365.00	165.00
(52)	Jack Farrell (Hands at knees.)	815.00	365.00	165.00
(53)	Charlie Ferguson	815.00	365.00	165.00
(54)	Silver Flint	815.00	365.00	165.00
(55)	Jim Fogerty (Fogarty)	815.00	365.00	165.00
(56)	Tom Forster	815.00	365.00	165.00
(57)	Dave Foutz	815.00	365.00	165.00
(58)	Chris Fulmer	815.00	365.00	165.00
(59)	Joe Gerhardt	815.00	365.00	165.00
(60)	Charlie Getzein (Getzien)	815.00	365.00	165.00
(61)	Pete Gillespie (Left field.)	815.00	365.00	165.00
(62)	Pete Gillespie (Batter)	815.00	365.00	165.00
(63)	Barney Gilligan	815.00	365.00	165.00
(64)	Jack Glasscock (Fielding grounder.)	815.00	365.00	165.00
(65)	Jack Glasscock (Hands on knees.)	815.00	365.00	165.00
(66)	Will Gleason	815.00	365.00	165.00
(67)	George Gore	815.00	365.00	165.00
(68)	Frank Hankinson	815.00	365.00	165.00
(69)	Ned Hanlon	2,815	1,250	565.00
(70)	Jim Hart	815.00	365.00	165.00
(71)	Egyptian Healy	815.00	365.00	165.00
(72)	Paul Hines (Centre field.)	815.00	365.00	165.00
(73)	Paul Hines (Batter)	815.00	365.00	165.00
(74)	Joe Hornung	815.00	365.00	165.00
(75)	Arthur Irwin	815.00	365.00	165.00
(76)	Dick Johnston	815.00	365.00	165.00
(77)	Tim Keefe (Ball in hand.)	2,815	1,250	565.00
(78)	Tim Keefe (Ball out of hand.)	3,125	1,405	625.00
(79)	King Kelly (Right field.)	3,440	1,530	690.00
(80)	King Kelly (Catcher)	3,440	1,530	690.00
(81)	Ted Kennedy	815.00	365.00	165.00
(82)	Matt Kilroy	815.00	365.00	165.00
(83)	Arlie Latham	815.00	365.00	165.00
(84)	Jimmy Manning	815.00	365.00	165.00
(85)	Bill McClellan	815.00	365.00	165.00
(86)	Jim McCormick	815.00	365.00	165.00
(87)	Jack McGeachy	815.00	365.00	165.00
(88)	Jumbo McGinnis	815.00	365.00	165.00
(89)	George Meyers (Myers)	815.00	365.00	165.00
(90)	Doggie Miller	815.00	365.00	165.00
(91)	John Morrill (Hands outstretched.)	815.00	365.00	165.00
(92)	John Morrill (Hands at neck.)	815.00	365.00	165.00
(93)	Tom Morrissy (Morrissey)	815.00	365.00	165.00
(94)	Joe Mulvey (Hands on knees.)	815.00	365.00	165.00
(95)	Joe Mulvey (Hands above head.)	815.00	365.00	165.00
(96)	Al Myers	815.00	365.00	165.00
(97)	Candy Nelson	815.00	365.00	165.00
(98)	Hugh Nichol	815.00	365.00	165.00
(99)	Billy O'Brien	815.00	365.00	165.00
(100)	Tip O'Neil (O'Neill)	815.00	365.00	165.00
(101)	Orator Jim O'Rourke (Hands cupped.)	3,125	1,405	625.00
(102)	Orator Jim O'Rourke (Hands on thighs.)	3,125	1,405	625.00
(103)	Dave Orr	815.00	365.00	165.00
(104)	Jimmy Peoples	815.00	365.00	165.00
(105)	Fred Pfeffer	815.00	365.00	165.00
(106)	Bill Phillips	815.00	365.00	165.00
(107)	Mark Polhemus	815.00	365.00	165.00
(108)	Henry Porter	815.00	365.00	165.00
(109)	Blondie Purcell	815.00	365.00	165.00
(110)	Old Hoss Radbourn (Hands at chest.)	2,815	1,250	565.00
(111)	Old Hoss Radbourn (Hands above waist.)	3,125	1,405	625.00
(112)	Danny Richardson (New York, hands at knees.)	815.00	365.00	165.00
(113)	Danny Richardson (New York, foot on base.)	815.00	365.00	165.00

(114)	Hardy Richardson (Detroit, hands at right shoulder.)	815.00	365.00	165.00
(115)	Hardy Richardson (Detroit, right hand above head.)	815.00	365.00	165.00
(116)	Yank Robinson	815.00	365.00	165.00
(117)	George Rooks	815.00	365.00	165.00
(118)	Chief Rosemann (Roseman)	815.00	365.00	165.00
(119)	Jimmy Ryan	815.00	365.00	165.00
(120)	Emmett Seery (Hands at right shoulder.)	815.00	365.00	165.00
(121)	Emmett Seery (Hands outstretched.)	815.00	365.00	165.00
(122)	Otto Shomberg (Schomberg)	815.00	365.00	165.00
(123)	Pap Smith	815.00	365.00	165.00
(124)	Joe Strauss	815.00	365.00	165.00
(125)	Danny Sullivan (St. Louis)	815.00	365.00	165.00
(126)	Marty Sullivan (Chicago)	815.00	365.00	165.00
(127)	Billy Sunday	1,565	700.00	315.00
(128)	Ezra Sutton	815.00	365.00	165.00
(129)	Sam Thompson (Hand at belt.)	2,815	1,250	565.00
(130)	Sam Thompson (Hands chest high.)	3,125	1,405	625.00
(131)	Chris Von Der Ahe	2,815	1,250	565.00
(132)	John Ward (Fielding grounder.)	2,815	1,250	565.00
(133)	John Ward (Hands by knee.)	3,125	1,405	625.00
(134)	John Ward (Hands on knees.)	3,125	1,405	625.00
(135)	Curt Welch	815.00	365.00	165.00
(136)	Deacon White	815.00	365.00	165.00
(137)	Art Whitney (Pittsburgh)	815.00	365.00	165.00
(138)	Jim Whitney (Washington)	815.00	365.00	165.00
(139)	Ned Williamson (Fielding grounder.)	815.00	365.00	165.00
(140)	Ned Williamson (Hands at chest.)	815.00	365.00	165.00
(141)	Medoc Wise	815.00	365.00	165.00
(142)	George Wood (Hands at right shoulder.)	815.00	365.00	165.00
(143)	George Wood (Stealing base.)	815.00	365.00	165.00

1961 Golden Press

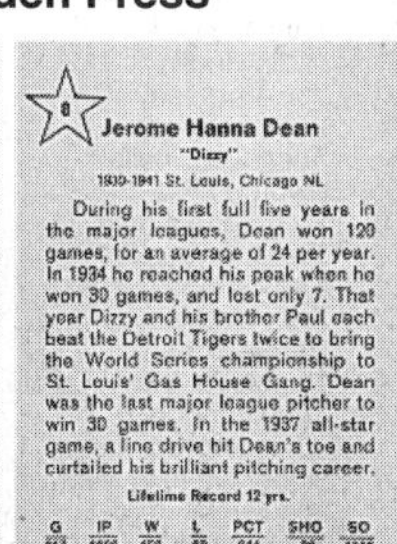

The 1961 Golden Press set features 33 players, all enshrined in the Baseball Hall of Fame. The full color cards measure 2-1/2" x 3-1/2" and came in a booklet with perforations so that they could be easily removed. Full books with the cards intact would command 50 percent over the set price in the checklist that follows. Card numbers 1-3 and 28-33 are slightly higher in price as they were located on the book's front and back covers, making them more susceptible to scuffing and wear. Cards in a larger (2-3/4" x 3-5/8"), apparently unperforated format are also known, though their method of distribution is unclear.

		NM	EX	VG
Complete Set (33):		100.00	50.00	30.00
Complete Set in Book:		175.00	85.00	50.00
Common Player:		3.00	1.50	.90
1	Mel Ott	3.00	1.50	.90
2	Grover Cleveland Alexander	5.00	2.50	1.50
3	Babe Ruth	40.00	20.00	12.00
4	Hank Greenberg	5.00	2.50	1.50
5	Bill Terry	3.00	1.50	.90
6	Carl Hubbell	3.00	1.50	.90
7	Rogers Hornsby	4.00	2.00	1.25
8	Dizzy Dean	5.00	2.50	1.50
9	Joe DiMaggio	20.00	10.00	6.00
10	Charlie Gehringer	3.00	1.50	.90
11	Gabby Hartnett	3.00	1.50	.90
12	Mickey Cochrane	3.00	1.50	.90
13	George Sisler	3.00	1.50	.90
14	Joe Cronin	3.00	1.50	.90
15	Pie Traynor	3.00	1.50	.90
16	Lou Gehrig	20.00	10.00	6.00
17	Lefty Grove	3.00	1.50	.90
18	Chief Bender	3.00	1.50	.90
19	Frankie Frisch	3.00	1.50	.90
20	Al Simmons	3.00	1.50	.90
21	Home Run Baker	3.00	1.50	.90
22	Jimmy Foxx	4.00	2.00	1.25
23	John McGraw	3.00	1.50	.90
24	Christy Mathewson	10.00	5.00	3.00
25	Ty Cobb	20.00	10.00	6.00
26	Dazzy Vance	3.00	1.50	.90
27	Bill Dickey	3.00	1.50	.90
28	Eddie Collins	3.00	1.50	.90
29	Walter Johnson	9.00	4.50	2.75
30	Tris Speaker	4.00	2.00	1.25
31	Nap Lajoie	3.00	1.50	.90
32	Honus Wagner	12.00	6.00	3.50
33	Cy Young	9.00	4.50	2.75

1955 Golden Stamp Books

The 1954 World Series contestants, Cleveland and the Giants, along with the popular Dodgers and Braves are featured in this set of stamp books. The 32-page albums mea-

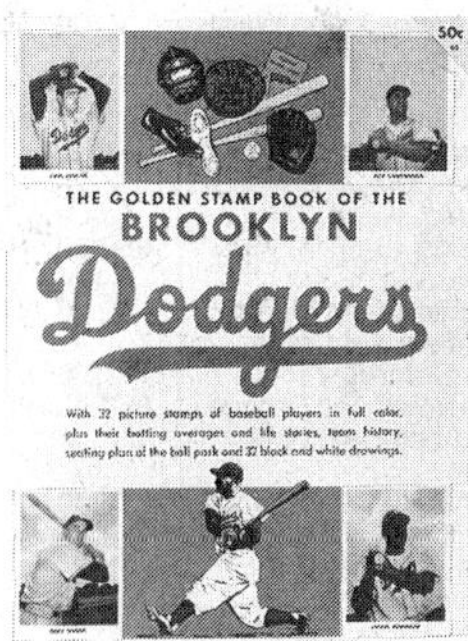

sure about 8-1/2" x 11" and include drawings and write-ups for each of the 32 players and managers featured. Other pages of the album include team histories, stats, etc. Sheets of 16 color stamps each are bound into the front and back of the album. Individual stamps measure about 2" x 2-5/8" and are unnumbered. Values shown are for complete albums with the stamps not pasted in; albums with stamps affixed to the pages are worth about 50 percent. The players for each team are listed in the order in which they appear in the album.

		NM	EX	VG
Complete Set (4):		500.00	250.00	150.00
Common Stamp:		5.00	2.50	1.50
S-1	**NEW YORK GIANTS ALBUM**	125.00	65.00	35.00
(1)	1954 Team Photo	5.00	2.50	1.50
(2)	Leo Durocher	6.00	3.00	1.75
(3)	Johnny Antonelli	5.00	2.50	1.50
(4)	Sal Maglie	5.00	2.50	1.50
(5)	Ruben Gomez	5.00	2.50	1.50
(6)	Hoyt Wilhelm	6.00	3.00	1.75
(7)	Marv Grissom	5.00	2.50	1.50
(8)	Jim Hearn	5.00	2.50	1.50
(9)	Paul Giel	5.00	2.50	1.50
(10)	Al Corwin	5.00	2.50	1.50
(11)	George Spencer	5.00	2.50	1.50
(12)	Don Liddle	5.00	2.50	1.50
(13)	Windy McCall	5.00	2.50	1.50
(14)	Al Worthington	5.00	2.50	1.50
(15)	Wes Westrum	5.00	2.50	1.50
(16)	Whitey Lockman	5.00	2.50	1.50
(17)	Dave Williams	5.00	2.50	1.50
(18)	Hank Thompson	5.00	2.50	1.50
(19)	Alvin Dark	5.00	2.50	1.50
(20)	Monte Irvin	7.50	3.75	2.25
(21)	Willie Mays	50.00	25.00	15.00
(22)	Don Mueller	5.00	2.50	1.50
(23)	Dusty Rhodes	5.00	2.50	1.50
(24)	Ray Katt	5.00	2.50	1.50
(25)	Joe Amalfitano	5.00	2.50	1.50
(26)	Bill Gardner	5.00	2.50	1.50
(27)	Foster Castleman	5.00	2.50	1.50
(28)	Bobby Hofman	5.00	2.50	1.50
(29)	Bill Taylor	5.00	2.50	1.50
(30)	Manager and Coaches	5.00	2.50	1.50
(31)	Bobby Weinstein (Batboy)	5.00	2.50	1.50
(32)	Polo Grounds	5.00	2.50	1.50
S-2	**MILWAUKEE BRAVES ALBUM**	125.00	65.00	35.00
(1)	1954 Team Photo	5.00	2.50	1.50
(2)	Charlie Grimm	5.00	2.50	1.50
(3)	Warren Spahn	7.50	3.75	2.25
(4)	Lew Burdette	5.00	2.50	1.50
(5)	Chet Nichols	5.00	2.50	1.50
(6)	Gene Conley	5.00	2.50	1.50
(7)	Bob Buhl	5.00	2.50	1.50
(8)	Jim Wilson	5.00	2.50	1.50
(9)	Dave Jolly	5.00	2.50	1.50
(10)	Ernie Johnson	5.00	2.50	1.50
(11)	Joey Jay	5.00	2.50	1.50
(12)	Dave Koslo	5.00	2.50	1.50
(13)	Charlie Gorin	5.00	2.50	1.50
(14)	Ray Crone	5.00	2.50	1.50
(15)	Del Crandall	5.00	2.50	1.50
(16)	Joe Adcock	5.00	2.50	1.50
(17)	Jack Dittmer	5.00	2.50	1.50
(18)	Eddie Mathews	15.00	7.50	4.50
(19)	Johnny Logan	5.00	2.50	1.50
(20)	Andy Pafko	5.00	2.50	1.50
(21)	Bill Bruton	5.00	2.50	1.50
(22)	Bobby Thomson	5.00	2.50	1.50
(23)	Charlie White	5.00	2.50	1.50
(24)	Danny O'Connell	5.00	2.50	1.50
(25)	Hank Aaron	50.00	25.00	15.00
(26)	Jim Pendleton	5.00	2.50	1.50
(27)	George Metkovich	5.00	2.50	1.50
(28)	Mel Roach	5.00	2.50	1.50
(29)	John Cooney	5.00	2.50	1.50
(30)	Bucky Walters	5.00	2.50	1.50
(31)	Charles Lacks (Trainer)	5.00	2.50	1.50
(32)	Milwaukee County Stadium	5.00	2.50	1.50
S-3	**BROOKLYN DODGERS ALBUM**	200.00	100.00	60.00
(1)	Walter Alston	6.00	3.00	1.75
(2)	Don Newcombe	6.00	3.00	1.75
(3)	Carl Erskine	5.00	2.50	1.50
(4)	Johnny Podres	5.00	2.50	1.50
(5)	Billy Loes	5.00	2.50	1.50
(6)	Russ Meyer	5.00	2.50	1.50
(7)	Jim Hughes	5.00	2.50	1.50
(8)	Sandy Koufax	100.00	50.00	30.00
(9)	Joe Black	5.00	2.50	1.50
(10)	Karl Spooner	5.00	2.50	1.50
(11)	Clem Labine	5.00	2.50	1.50
(12)	Roy Campanella	15.00	7.50	4.50
(13)	Gil Hodges	12.00	6.00	3.50
(14)	Jim Gilliam	6.00	3.00	1.75
(15)	Jackie Robinson	50.00	25.00	15.00
(16)	Pee Wee Reese	15.00	7.50	4.50
(17)	Duke Snider	15.00	7.50	4.50
(18)	Carl Furillo	6.00	3.00	1.75
(19)	Sandy Amoros	5.00	2.50	1.50
(20)	Frank Kellert	5.00	2.50	1.50
(21)	Don Zimmer	6.00	3.00	1.75
(22)	Al Walker	5.00	2.50	1.50
(23)	Tommy Lasorda	7.50	3.75	2.25
(24)	Ed Roebuck	5.00	2.50	1.50
(25)	Don Hoak	5.00	2.50	1.50
(26)	George Shuba	5.00	2.50	1.50
(27)	Billy Herman	6.00	3.00	1.75
(28)	Jake Pitler	5.00	2.50	1.50
(29)	Joe Becker	5.00	2.50	1.50
(30)	Doc Wendler (Trainer), Carl Furillo	5.00	2.50	1.50
(31)	Charlie Di Giovanna (Batboy)	5.00	2.50	1.50
(32)	Ebbets Field	5.00	2.50	1.50
S-4	**CLEVELAND INDIANS ALBUM**	100.00	50.00	30.00
(1)	Al Lopez	6.00	3.00	1.75
(2)	Bob Lemon	6.00	3.00	1.75
(3)	Early Wynn	6.00	3.00	1.75
(4)	Mike Garcia	5.00	2.50	1.50
(5)	Bob Feller	12.00	6.00	3.50
(6)	Art Houtteman	5.00	2.50	1.50
(7)	Herb Score	7.50	3.75	2.25
(8)	Don Mossi	7.50	3.75	2.25
(9)	Ray Narleski	5.00	2.50	1.50
(10)	Jim Hegan	5.00	2.50	1.50
(11)	Vic Wertz	5.00	2.50	1.50
(12)	Bobby Avila	5.00	2.50	1.50
(13)	George Strickland	5.00	2.50	1.50
(14)	Al Rosen	5.00	2.50	1.50
(15)	Larry Doby	6.00	3.00	1.75
(16)	Ralph Kiner	7.50	3.75	2.25
(17)	Al Smith	5.00	2.50	1.50
(18)	Wally Westlake	5.00	2.50	1.50
(19)	Hal Naragon	5.00	2.50	1.50
(20)	Hank Foiles	5.00	2.50	1.50
(21)	Hank Majeski	5.00	2.50	1.50
(22)	Bill Wight	5.00	2.50	1.50
(23)	Sam Dente	5.00	2.50	1.50
(24)	Dave Pope	5.00	2.50	1.50
(25)	Dave Philley	5.00	2.50	1.50
(26)	Dale Mitchell	5.00	2.50	1.50
(27)	Hank Greenberg (GM)	10.00	5.00	3.00
(28)	Mel Harder	5.00	2.50	1.50
(29)	Ralph Kress	5.00	2.50	1.50
(30)	Tony Cuccinello	5.00	2.50	1.50
(31)	Bill Lobe	5.00	2.50	1.50
(32)	Cleveland Municipal Stadium	5.00	2.50	1.50

1934 Gold Medal Foods (R313A)

This set of unnumbered, blank-backed cards was issued by Gold Medal Foods (the Minneapolis parent company of Wheaties) to commemorate the 1934 World Series. The black-and-white cards measure 3-1/4" x 5-3/8". The checklist comprises six members each of the Detroit Tigers and St. Louis Cardinals, who were participants in the '34 World Series.

		NM	EX	VG
Complete Set (12):		1,000	500.00	300.00
Common Player:		60.00	30.00	18.00
(1)	Tommy Bridges	60.00	30.00	18.00
(2)	Mickey Cochrane	90.00	45.00	27.50
(3)	Dizzy Dean	350.00	175.00	100.00
(4)	Paul Dean	75.00	37.50	22.50
(5)	Frank Frisch	90.00	45.00	27.50
(6)	"Goose" Goslin	90.00	45.00	27.50
(7)	William Hallahan	60.00	30.00	18.00
(8)	Fred Marberry	60.00	30.00	18.00
(9)	Johnny "Pepper" Martin	60.00	30.00	18.00
(10)	Joe Medwick	90.00	45.00	27.50
(11)	William Rogell	60.00	30.00	18.00
(12)	"Jo Jo" White	60.00	30.00	18.00

1930s Goodrich Tire Mickey Cochrane

Without postmarked examples for verification, the issue date of this promotional postcard can only be estimated. Front of the 5-1/4" x 3-1/4" postcard has line art of Cochrane and his endorsement for the company's tires. The card is printed in yellow, orange and black. The lower-right quadrant was likely left blank to allow local tire retailers to place their advertisement. Back of the card has a pre-printed one-cent stamp.

	NM	EX	VG
Mickey Cochrane	100.00	50.00	30.00

1888 Goodwin Champions (N162)

Issued in 1888 by New York's Goodwin & Co., the 50-card "Champions" set includes eight baseball players - seven from the National League and one from the American Association. The full-color cards, which measure 1-1/2" x 2-5/8", were inserted in packages of Old Judge and Gypsy Queen Cigarettes. A small ad for the cards lists all 50 subjects of the "Champions" set, which also included popular billiards players, bicyclists, marksmen, pugilists, runners, wrestlers, college football stars, weightlifters, and Wild West star Buffalo Bill Cody. Four of the eight baseball players in the set (Anson, Kelly, Keefe and Brouthers) are Hall of Famers. The cards feature very attractive player portraits, making the "Champions" set among the most beautiful of all the 19th Century tobacco inserts. All cards can be found with or without a tiny line of type at the bottom of the back which reads, "Geo. S. Harris & Sons, Lith, Phila."

		NM	EX	VG
Complete Set (8):		44,000	17,000	7,700
Common Player:		3,850	1,600	725.00
Album:		7,500	3,750	2,250
(1)	Ed Andrews	3,850	1,600	725.00
(2)	Cap Anson	14,000	4,950	2,200
(3)	Dan Brouthers	5,500	3,325	1,050
(4)	Bob Caruthers	3,850	1,600	725.00
(5)	Fred Dunlap	3,850	1,600	725.00
(6)	Jack Glasscock	3,850	1,600	725.00
(7)	Tim Keefe	5,775	3,325	1,050
(8)	King Kelly	8,525	3,300	1,600

1889 Goodwin & Co. Baseball Album (A35)

As a mail-in redemption premium for 75 coupons from its Old Judge and Dog's Head cigarette brands, Goodwin offered this 12-page lithographed album. In an unusual 8-1/4" diameter format, the pages have a single hole punched at the side and are attached by a fancy tasseled cord allowing them to be fanned out for viewing. Front and back covers of the album depict a baseball, with the inside covers advertising the cigarettes, as does the sixth page of the album. The nine other pages depict in vivid color either single stars of the game or groups of four players, with an emphasis on the N.Y. Giants champions of 1888. Backs of the pages offer player stats for the previous season and schedules for various leagues for 1889. Because these albums are sometimes offered as single pages, they are priced as such here.

		NM	EX	VG
Complete Album:		20,000	10,000	6,000
(1)	Front Cover	225.00	110.00	65.00
(2)	Mickey Welch, John Ward, Buck Ewing, Tim Keefe	1,100	550.00	330.00
(3)	Cap Anson	4,000	1,500	900.00
(4)	Jim O'Rourke, Danny Richardson, Roger Connor, George Gore	1,200	460.00	275.00
(5)	Mike "King" Kelly	3,000	1,500	900.00
(6)	Advertising	350.00	100.00	60.00
(7)	John Ward	2,125	1,050	635.00
(8)	Mike Slattery, Pat Murphy, Gil Hatfield, Ed Crane	750.00	375.00	225.00
(9)	Charles Comiskey	2,125	1,050	635.00
(10)	Willard Brown, Bill George, Elmer Foster, Michael Tiernan	850.00	425.00	255.00
(11)	Jim Mutrie, Lidell Titcomb, Art Whitney, Willie Breslin - Mascot	875.00	435.00	260.00
(12)	Back Cover	200.00	100.00	60.00

1933 Goudey (R319)

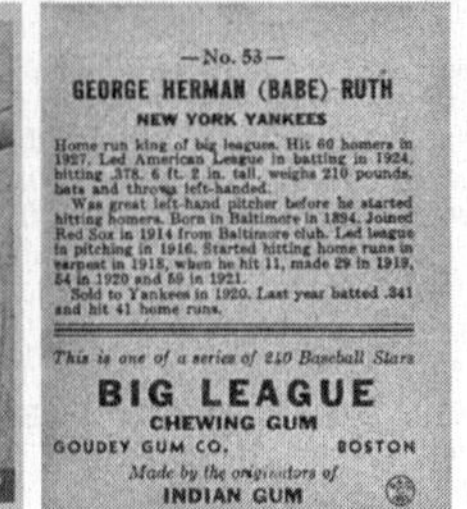

Goudey Gum Co.'s first baseball card issue was a 239-card effort in 1933. The cards are color art reproductions of either portrait or action photos. The numbered cards measure 2-3/8" x 2-7/8" and carry a short player biography on the reverse. Card #106 (Napoleon Lajoie) is listed in the set though it was not actually issued until 1934. The card is very scarce and is unique in that it carries a 1934 design front and a 1933 back. The Lajoie card is not included in the complete set prices quoted here. The ACC designation for the set is R319.

		NM	EX	VG
Complete Set (239):		110,000	37,500	19,500
Common Player (1-40):		250.00	85.00	45.00
Common Player (41-44):		165.00	55.00	30.00
Common Player (45-52):		200.00	70.00	35.00
Common Player (53-240):		165.00	55.00	30.00
1	Benny Bengough	5,500	900.00	100.00
2	Arthur (Dazzy) Vance	1,300	465.00	165.00
3	Hugh Critz	300.00	100.00	50.00
4	Henry "Heinie" Schuble	250.00	85.00	45.00
5	Floyd (Babe) Herman	500.00	175.00	90.00
6a	Jimmy Dykes (Age is 26 in bio.)	375.00	130.00	65.00
6b	Jimmy Dykes (Age is 36 in bio.)	375.00	130.00	65.00
7	Ted Lyons	925.00	325.00	165.00
8	Roy Johnson	250.00	85.00	45.00
9	Dave Harris	250.00	85.00	45.00
10	Glenn Myatt	250.00	85.00	45.00
11	Billy Rogell	250.00	85.00	45.00
12	George Pipgras	260.00	90.00	50.00
13	Lafayette Thompson	250.00	85.00	45.00
14	Henry Johnson	250.00	85.00	45.00
15	Victor Sorrell	250.00	85.00	45.00
16	George Blaeholder	250.00	85.00	45.00
17	Watson Clark	250.00	85.00	45.00
18	Herold (Muddy) Ruel	250.00	85.00	45.00
19	Bill Dickey	1,000	350.00	180.00
20	Bill Terry	925.00	325.00	165.00
21	Phil Collins	250.00	85.00	45.00
22	Harold (Pie) Traynor	925.00	325.00	165.00
23	Hazen (Ki-Ki) Cuyler	925.00	325.00	165.00
24	Horace Ford	250.00	85.00	45.00
25	Paul Waner	1,000	350.00	180.00
26	Chalmer Cissell	250.00	85.00	45.00
27	George Connally	250.00	85.00	45.00
28	Dick Bartell	250.00	85.00	45.00
29	Jimmy Foxx	2,000	700.00	300.00
30	Frank Hogan	250.00	85.00	45.00
31	Tony Lazzeri	925.00	325.00	165.00
32	John (Bud) Clancy	250.00	85.00	45.00
33	Ralph Kress	250.00	85.00	45.00
34	Bob O'Farrell	250.00	85.00	45.00
35	Al Simmons	925.00	325.00	165.00
36	Tommy Thevenow	250.00	85.00	45.00
37	Jimmy Wilson	250.00	85.00	45.00
38	Fred Brickell	250.00	85.00	45.00
39	Mark Koenig	260.00	90.00	50.00
40	Taylor Douthit	250.00	85.00	45.00
41	Gus Mancuso	165.00	55.00	30.00
42	Eddie Collins	475.00	165.00	85.00
43	Lew Fonseca	165.00	55.00	30.00
44	Jim Bottomley	415.00	145.00	75.00
45	Larry Benton	200.00	70.00	35.00
46	Ethan Allen	200.00	70.00	35.00
47a	Henry "Heinie" Manush (Chain-link fence at top left.)	600.00	210.00	110.00
47b	Henry "Heinie" Manush (No fence.)	600.00	210.00	110.00
48	Marty McManus	200.00	70.00	35.00
49	Frank Frisch	800.00	280.00	145.00
50	Ed Brandt	200.00	70.00	35.00
51	Charlie Grimm	200.00	70.00	35.00
52	Andy Cohen	225.00	80.00	40.00
53	George Herman (Babe) Ruth	11,350	3,600	1,825
54	Ray Kremer	165.00	55.00	30.00
55	Perce (Pat) Malone	165.00	55.00	30.00
56	Charlie Ruffing	425.00	150.00	80.00
57	Earl Clark	165.00	55.00	30.00
58	Frank (Lefty) O'Doul	250.00	85.00	45.00
59	Edmund (Bing) Miller	165.00	55.00	30.00
60	Waite Hoyt	415.00	145.00	75.00
61	Max Bishop	165.00	55.00	30.00
62	"Pepper" Martin	275.00	90.00	50.00
63	Joe Cronin	415.00	145.00	75.00
64	Burleigh Grimes	415.00	145.00	75.00
65	Milton Gaston	165.00	55.00	30.00
66	George Grantham	165.00	55.00	30.00
67	Guy Bush	165.00	55.00	30.00
68	Horace Lisenbee	165.00	55.00	30.00
69	Randy Moore	165.00	55.00	30.00
70	Floyd (Pete) Scott	165.00	55.00	30.00
71	Robert J. Burke	165.00	55.00	30.00
72	Owen Carroll	165.00	55.00	30.00
73	Jesse Haines	415.00	145.00	75.00
74	Eppa Rixey	415.00	145.00	75.00
75	Willie Kamm	165.00	55.00	30.00
76	Gordon (Mickey) Cochrane	475.00	165.00	85.00
77	Adam Comorosky	165.00	55.00	30.00
78	Jack Quinn	165.00	55.00	30.00
79	Urban (Red) Faber	415.00	145.00	75.00
80	Clyde Manion	165.00	55.00	30.00
81	Sam Jones	165.00	55.00	30.00
82	Dibrell Williams	165.00	55.00	30.00
83	Pete Jablonowski	165.00	55.00	30.00
84	Glenn Spencer	165.00	55.00	30.00
85	John Henry "Heinie" Sand	165.00	55.00	30.00
86	Phil Todt	165.00	55.00	30.00
87	Frank O'Rourke	165.00	55.00	30.00
88	Russell Rollings	165.00	55.00	30.00
89	Tris Speaker	550.00	190.00	95.00
90	Jess Petty	165.00	55.00	30.00
91	Tom Zachary	165.00	55.00	30.00
92	Lou Gehrig	3,200	1,475	700.00
93	John Welch	165.00	55.00	30.00
94	Bill Walker	165.00	55.00	30.00
95	Alvin Crowder	165.00	55.00	30.00
96	Willis Hudlin	165.00	55.00	30.00
97	Joe Morrissey	165.00	55.00	30.00
98	Walter Berger	165.00	55.00	30.00
99	Tony Cuccinello	165.00	55.00	30.00
100	George Uhle	165.00	55.00	30.00
101	Richard Coffman	165.00	55.00	30.00
102	Travis C. Jackson	415.00	145.00	75.00
103	Earl Combs (Earle)	415.00	145.00	75.00
104	Fred Marberry	165.00	55.00	30.00
105	Bernie Friberg	165.00	55.00	30.00
106	Napoleon (Larry) Lajoie	37,500	24,000	8,500
106p	Leo Durocher (Unique proof card.)	.00	.00	4,000
107	Henry (Heinie) Manush	415.00	145.00	75.00
108	Joe Kuhel	165.00	55.00	30.00
109	Joe Cronin	415.00	145.00	75.00
110	Leon (Goose) Goslin/Portrait	415.00	145.00	75.00
110p	Leon (Goose) Goslin (Proof card, batting - same as #168 - name in two lines on front.)	800.00	280.00	145.00
111	Monte Weaver	165.00	55.00	30.00
112	Fred Schulte	165.00	55.00	30.00
113	Oswald Bluege	165.00	55.00	30.00
114	Luke Sewell	165.00	55.00	30.00
115	Cliff Heathcote	165.00	55.00	30.00
116	Eddie Morgan	165.00	55.00	30.00
117	Walter (Rabbit) Maranville	415.00	145.00	75.00
118	Valentine J. (Val) Picinich	165.00	55.00	30.00
119	Rogers Hornsby	1,100	385.00	200.00
120	Carl Reynolds	165.00	55.00	30.00
121	Walter Stewart	165.00	55.00	30.00
122	Alvin Crowder	165.00	55.00	30.00
123	Jack Russell (Orange background, white cap.)	165.00	55.00	30.00
123(pa)	Jack Russell (Proof card, red background, dark cap - same as #167 - name in one line on front.)	400.00	140.00	70.00
123(pb)	Luke Sewell (Proof card, otherwise identical to #163.)	8,000	2,800	1,450
124	Earl Whitehill	165.00	55.00	30.00
125	Bill Terry	415.00	145.00	75.00
126	Joe Moore	165.00	55.00	30.00
127	Melvin Ott	725.00	250.00	125.00
128	Charles (Chuck) Klein	415.00	145.00	75.00
129	Harold Schumacher	165.00	55.00	30.00
130	Fred Fitzsimmons	165.00	55.00	30.00
131	Fred Frankhouse	165.00	55.00	30.00
132	Jim Elliott	165.00	55.00	30.00
133	Fred Lindstrom	415.00	145.00	75.00
134	Edgar (Sam) Rice	415.00	145.00	75.00
135	Elwood (Woody) English	165.00	55.00	30.00
136	Flint Rhem	165.00	55.00	30.00
137	Fred (Red) Lucas	165.00	55.00	30.00
138	Herb Pennock	415.00	145.00	75.00
139	Ben Cantwell	165.00	55.00	30.00
140	Irving (Bump) Hadley	165.00	55.00	30.00
141	Ray Benge	165.00	55.00	30.00
142	Paul Richards	165.00	55.00	30.00
143	Glenn Wright	165.00	55.00	30.00
144	George Herman (Babe) Ruth (Double-print; replaced card #106 on press sheet.)	6,500	2,575	1,175
145	George Walberg	165.00	55.00	30.00
146	Walter Stewart	165.00	55.00	30.00
147	Leo Durocher	415.00	145.00	75.00
148	Eddie Farrell	165.00	55.00	30.00
149	George Herman (Babe) Ruth	7,500	3,400	1,450
150	Ray Kolp	165.00	55.00	30.00
151	D'Arcy (Jake) Flowers	165.00	55.00	30.00
152	James (Zack) Taylor	165.00	55.00	30.00
153	Charles (Buddy) Myer	165.00	55.00	30.00
154	Jimmy Foxx	1,600	500.00	200.00
155	Joe Judge	165.00	55.00	30.00

156	Danny Macfayden (MacFayden)	165.00	55.00	30.00
157	Sam Byrd	165.00	55.00	30.00
158	Morris (Moe) Berg	700.00	250.00	150.00
159	Oswald Bluege	165.00	55.00	30.00
160	Lou Gehrig	4,000	1,200	625.00
161	Al Spohrer	165.00	55.00	30.00
162	Leo Mangum	165.00	55.00	30.00
163	Luke Sewell	165.00	55.00	30.00
164	Lloyd Waner	415.00	145.00	75.00
165	Joe Sewell	415.00	145.00	75.00
166	Sam West	165.00	55.00	30.00
167	Jack Russell (Name on two lines, see also #123p.)	165.00	55.00	30.00
168	Leon (Goose) Goslin (Name on one line, see also #110p.)	600.00	210.00	110.00
169	Al Thomas	165.00	55.00	30.00
170	Harry McCurdy	165.00	55.00	30.00
171	Charley Jamieson	165.00	55.00	30.00
172	Billy Hargrave	165.00	55.00	30.00
173	Roscoe Holm	165.00	55.00	30.00
174	Warren (Curley) Ogden	165.00	55.00	30.00
175	Dan Howley	165.00	55.00	30.00
176	John Ogden	165.00	55.00	30.00
177	Walter French	165.00	55.00	30.00
178	Jackie Warner	165.00	55.00	30.00
179	Fred Leach	165.00	55.00	30.00
180	Eddie Moore	165.00	55.00	30.00
181	George Herman (Babe) Ruth	7,000	3,200	1,350
182	Andy High	165.00	55.00	30.00
183	George Walberg	165.00	55.00	30.00
184	Charley Berry	165.00	55.00	30.00
185	Bob Smith	165.00	55.00	30.00
186	John Schulte	165.00	55.00	30.00
187	Henry (Heinie) Manush	415.00	145.00	75.00
188	Rogers Hornsby	1,200	425.00	215.00
189	Joe Cronin	415.00	145.00	75.00
190	Fred Schulte	165.00	55.00	30.00
191	Ben Chapman	165.00	55.00	30.00
192	Walter Brown	165.00	55.00	30.00
193	Lynford Lary	165.00	55.00	30.00
194	Earl Averill	415.00	145.00	75.00
195	Evar Swanson	165.00	55.00	30.00
196	Leroy Mahaffey	165.00	55.00	30.00
197	Richard (Rick) Ferrell	415.00	145.00	75.00
198	Irving (Jack) Burns	165.00	55.00	30.00
199	Tom Bridges	165.00	55.00	30.00
200	Bill Hallahan	165.00	55.00	30.00
201	Ernie Orsatti	165.00	55.00	30.00
202	Charles Leo (Gabby) Hartnett	415.00	145.00	75.00
203	Lonnie Warneke	165.00	55.00	30.00
204	Jackson Riggs Stephenson	165.00	55.00	30.00
205	Henry (Heinie) Meine	165.00	55.00	30.00
206	Gus Suhr	165.00	55.00	30.00
207	Melvin Ott	1,150	400.00	200.00
208	Byrne (Bernie) James	165.00	44.00	22.00
209	Adolfo Luque	200.00	70.00	36.00
210	Virgil Davis	165.00	55.00	30.00
211	Lewis (Hack) Wilson	700.00	250.00	140.00
212	Billy Urbanski	165.00	55.00	30.00
213	Earl Adams	165.00	55.00	30.00
214	John Kerr	165.00	55.00	30.00
215	Russell Van Atta	165.00	55.00	30.00
216	Vernon Gomez	415.00	145.00	75.00
217	Frank Crosetti	275.00	96.00	49.00
218	Wesley Ferrell	165.00	55.00	30.00
219	George (Mule) Haas	165.00	55.00	30.00
220	Robert (Lefty) Grove	775.00	275.00	140.00
221	Dale Alexander	165.00	55.00	30.00
222	Charley Gehringer	600.00	210.00	110.00
223	Jerome (Dizzy) Dean	1,500	500.00	275.00
224	Frank Demaree	165.00	55.00	30.00
225	Bill Jurges	165.00	55.00	30.00
226	Charley Root	165.00	55.00	30.00
227	Bill Herman	415.00	145.00	75.00
228	Tony Piet	165.00	55.00	30.00
229	Floyd Vaughan	415.00	145.00	75.00
230	Carl Hubbell	600.00	210.00	110.00
231	Joe Moore	165.00	55.00	30.00
232	Frank (Lefty) O'Doul	250.00	85.00	45.00
233	Johnny Vergez	165.00	55.00	30.00
234	Carl Hubbell	575.00	200.00	100.00
235	Fred Fitzsimmons	165.00	55.00	30.00
236	George Davis	165.00	55.00	30.00
237	Gus Mancuso	165.00	55.00	30.00
238	Hugh Critz	165.00	55.00	30.00
239	Leroy Parmelee	165.00	55.00	30.00
240	Harold Schumacher	350.00	75.00	35.00

1934 Goudey (R320)

—No. 10 — 1934 Series—
CHARLES (CHUCK) KLEIN
CHICAGO CUBS
BIG LEAGUE
CHEWING GUM
GOUDEY GUM CO. BOSTON
INDIAN GUM

The 1934 Goudey set contains 96 cards (2-3/8" x 2-7/8") that feature color art reproductions of player photographs. Card fronts have two different designs; one featuring a small portrait photo of Lou Gehrig with the the words "Lou Gehrig says..." inside a blue strip at the bottom, while the other design carries a red "Chuck Klein says..." strip and also has his photo. The card backs contain a short player biography that purports to have been written by Gehrig or Klein. The ACC designation for the set is R320. Albums, blue for N.L., magenta for A.L., were given away to the person who bought the last penny pack in each box of high-numbers or who mailed 50 wrappers to the gum company.

		NM	EX	VG
Complete Set (96):		30,000	11,000	5,250
Common Player (1-48):		120.00	45.00	20.00
Common Player (49-72):		160.00	55.00	25.00
Common Player (73-96):		300.00	100.00	50.00
Album:		500.00	250.00	150.00
1	Jimmy Foxx	3,000	600.00	210.00
2	Gordon (Mickey) Cochrane	425.00	175.00	85.00
3	Charlie Grimm	120.00	45.00	20.00
4	Elwood (Woody) English	120.00	45.00	20.00
5	Ed Brandt	120.00	45.00	20.00
6	Jerome (Dizzy) Dean	1,700	400.00	190.00
7	Leo Durocher	325.00	130.00	65.00
8	Tony Piet	120.00	45.00	20.00
9	Ben Chapman	120.00	45.00	20.00
10	Charles (Chuck) Klein	325.00	130.00	65.00
11	Paul Waner	325.00	130.00	65.00
12	Carl Hubbell	325.00	130.00	65.00
13	Frank Frisch	325.00	130.00	65.00
14	Willie Kamm	120.00	45.00	20.00
15	Alvin Crowder	120.00	45.00	20.00
16	Joe Kuhel	120.00	45.00	20.00
17	Hugh Critz	120.00	45.00	20.00
18	Henry (Heinie) Manush	325.00	130.00	65.00
19	Robert (Lefty) Grove	675.00	225.00	110.00
20	Frank Hogan	120.00	45.00	20.00
21	Bill Terry	325.00	130.00	65.00
22	Floyd Vaughan	325.00	130.00	65.00
23	Charley Gehringer	375.00	150.00	75.00
24	Ray Benge	120.00	45.00	20.00
25	Roger Cramer	120.00	45.00	20.00
26	Gerald Walker	120.00	45.00	20.00
27	Luke Appling	325.00	130.00	65.00
28	Ed. Coleman	120.00	45.00	20.00
29	Larry French	120.00	45.00	20.00
30	Julius Solters	120.00	45.00	20.00
31	Baxter Jordan	120.00	45.00	20.00
32	John (Blondy) Ryan	120.00	45.00	20.00
33	Frank (Don) Hurst	120.00	45.00	20.00
34	Charles (Chick) Hafey	325.00	130.00	65.00
35	Ernie Lombardi	325.00	130.00	65.00
36	Walter (Huck) Betts	120.00	45.00	20.00
37	Lou Gehrig	4,000	1,800	900.00
38	Oral Hildebrand	120.00	45.00	20.00
39	Fred Walker	120.00	45.00	20.00
40	John Stone	120.00	45.00	20.00
41	George Earnshaw	120.00	45.00	20.00
42	John Allen	120.00	45.00	20.00
43	Dick Porter	120.00	45.00	20.00
44	Tom Bridges	120.00	45.00	20.00
45	Oscar Melillo	120.00	45.00	20.00
46	Joe Stripp	120.00	45.00	20.00
47	John Frederick	120.00	45.00	20.00
48	James (Tex) Carleton	120.00	45.00	20.00
49	Sam Leslie	160.00	55.00	25.00
50	Walter Beck	160.00	55.00	25.00
51	Jim (Rip) Collins	160.00	55.00	25.00
52	Herman Bell	160.00	55.00	25.00
53	George Watkins	160.00	55.00	25.00
54	Wesley Schulmerich	160.00	55.00	25.00
55	Ed Holley	160.00	55.00	25.00
56	Mark Koenig	160.00	55.00	25.00
57	Bill Swift	160.00	55.00	25.00
58	Earl Grace	160.00	55.00	25.00
59	Joe Mowry	160.00	55.00	25.00
60	Lynn Nelson	160.00	55.00	25.00
61	Lou Gehrig	3,800	1,500	800.00
62	Henry Greenberg	1,350	550.00	275.00
63	Minter Hayes	160.00	55.00	25.00
64	Frank Grube	160.00	55.00	25.00
65	Cliff Bolton	160.00	55.00	25.00
66	Mel Harder	160.00	55.00	25.00
67	Bob Weiland	160.00	55.00	25.00
68	Bob Johnson	160.00	55.00	25.00
69	John Marcum	160.00	55.00	25.00
70	Ervin (Pete) Fox	160.00	55.00	25.00
71	Lyle Tinning	160.00	55.00	25.00
72	Arndt Jorgens	160.00	55.00	25.00
73	Ed Wells	300.00	100.00	50.00
74	Bob Boken	300.00	100.00	50.00
75	Bill Werber	300.00	100.00	50.00
76	Hal Trosky	300.00	100.00	50.00
77	Joe Vosmik	300.00	100.00	50.00
78	Frank (Pinkey) Higgins	300.00	100.00	50.00
79	Eddie Durham	300.00	100.00	50.00
80	Marty McManus	300.00	100.00	50.00
81	Bob Brown	300.00	100.00	50.00
82	Bill Hallahan	300.00	100.00	50.00
83	Jim Mooney	300.00	100.00	50.00
84	Paul Derringer	300.00	100.00	50.00
85	Adam Comorosky	300.00	100.00	50.00
86	Lloyd Johnson	300.00	100.00	50.00
87	George Darrow	300.00	100.00	50.00
88	Homer Peel	300.00	100.00	50.00
89	Linus Frey	300.00	100.00	50.00
90	Hazen (Ki-Ki) Cuyler	600.00	240.00	120.00
91	Dolph Camilli	300.00	100.00	50.00
92	Steve Larkin	300.00	100.00	50.00
93	Fred Ostermueller	300.00	100.00	50.00
94	Robert A. (Red) Rolfe	400.00	160.00	80.00
95	Myril Hoag	300.00	100.00	50.00
96	Jim DeShong	525.00	160.00	60.00

1933-34 Goudey Premiums (R309-1)

Consisting of just four unnumbered cards, this set of black-and-white photos was printed on heavy cardboard and issued as a premium by the Goudey Gum Co. in 1933. Cards (1), (2), and (4) were issued in 1933 and card (3) was issued in 1933. The cards measure 5-1/2" x 8-13/16" and are ac-

cented with a gold, picture-frame border and an easel on the back. Besides the game's greatest player, the set has team photos of the 1933 All-Star squads from each league and the World's Champion 1933 N.Y. Giants.

		NM	EX	VG
Complete Set (4):		3,250	1,625	975.00
Common Card:		600.00	300.00	180.00
(1)	American League All Stars	650.00	325.00	195.00
(2)	National League All Stars	600.00	300.00	180.00
(3)	"Worlds Champions 1933" (New York Giants)	750.00	375.00	225.00
(4)	George Herman (Babe) Ruth	1,250	625.00	375.00

1935 Goudey 4-in-1 (R321)

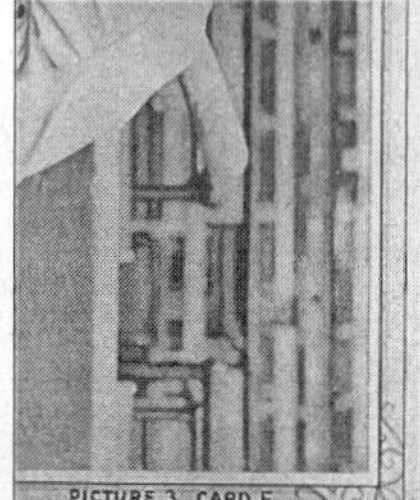

The 1935 Goudey set features color portraits of four players (usually) from the same team on each card. Thirty-six card fronts make up the set with 114 front/back combinations existing. The card backs form nine different puzzles: 1) Tigers Team, 2) Chuck Klein, 3) Frankie Frisch, 4) Mickey Cochrane, 5) Joe Cronin, 6) Jimmy Foxx, 7) Al Simmons, 8) Indians Team, and 9) Senators Team. The cards, which measure 2-3/8" x 2-7/8", have an ACC designation of R321. The numbering has been assigned for this checklist on the basis of alphabetical order of the players found on each card front.

		NM	EX	VG
Complete Set (36):		11,000	4,400	2,200
Common Card:		125.00	50.00	25.00
(1)	Sparky Adams, Jim Bottomley, Adam Comorosky, Tony Piet	300.00	120.00	60.00
(2)	Ethan Allen, Fred Brickell, Bubber Jonnard, Jimmie Wilson	125.00	30.00	15.00
(3)	Johnny Allen, Jimmie Deshong, Red Rolfe, Dixie Walker (DeShong)	125.00	30.00	15.00
(4)	Luke Appling, Jimmie Dykes, George Earnshaw, Luke Sewell	300.00	120.00	60.00
(5)	Earl Averill, Oral Hildebrand, Willie Kamm, Hal Trosky	300.00	120.00	60.00
(6)	Dick Bartell, Hughie Critz, Gus Mancuso, Mel Ott	300.00	120.00	60.00
(7)	Ray Benge, Fred Fitzsimmons, Mark Koenig, Tom Zachary	125.00	30.00	15.00
(8)	Larry Benton, Ben Cantwell, Flint Rhem, Al Spohrer	125.00	30.00	15.00
(9)	Charlie Berry, Bobby Burke, Red Kress, Dazzy Vance	300.00	120.00	60.00
(10)	Max Bishop, Bill Cissell, Joe Cronin, Carl Reynolds	300.00	120.00	60.00
(11)	George Blaeholder, Dick Coffman, Oscar Melillo, Sammy West	125.00	30.00	15.00
(12)	Cy Blanton, Babe Herman, Tom Padden, Gus Suhr	125.00	30.00	15.00
(13)	Zeke Bonura, Mule Haas, Jackie Hayes, Ted Lyons	300.00	120.00	60.00
(14)	Jim Bottomley, Adam Comorosky, Willis Hudlin, Glenn Myatt	300.00	120.00	60.00
(15)	Ed Brandt, Fred Frankhouse, Shanty Hogan, Gene Moore	125.00	50.00	25.00
(16)	Ed Brandt, Rabbit Maranville, Marty McManus, Babe Ruth	2,900	900.00	400.00

(17)	Tommy Bridges, Mickey Cochrane, Charlie Gehringer, Billy Rogell	350.00	140.00	70.00
(18)	Jack Burns, Frank Grube, Rollie Hemsley, Bob Weiland	125.00	30.00	15.00
(19)	Guy Bush, Waite Hoyt, Lloyd Waner, Paul Waner	350.00	140.00	70.00
(20)	Sammy Byrd, Danny MacFayden, Pepper Martin, Bob O'Farrell	125.00	30.00	15.00
(21a)	Gilly Campbell, Ival Goodman, Alex Kampouris, Billy Meyers (Myers) (no "Meyers")	200.00	80.00	40.00
(21b)	Gilly Campbell, Ival Goodman, Alex Kampouris, Billy Meyers (Myers)	150.00	60.00	30.00
(22)	Tex Carleton, Dizzy Dean, Frankie Frisch, Ernie Orsatti	650.00	260.00	130.00
(23)	Watty Clark, Lonny Frey, Sam Leslie, Joe Stripp	125.00	30.00	15.00
(24)	Mickey Cochrane, Willie Kamm, Muddy Ruel, Al Simmons	350.00	140.00	70.00
(25)	Ed Coleman, Doc Cramer, Bob Johnson, Johnny Marcum	125.00	30.00	15.00
(26)	General Crowder, Goose Goslin, Firpo Marberry, Heinie Schuble	300.00	120.00	60.00
(27)	Kiki Cuyler, Woody English, Burleigh Grimes, Chuck Klein	350.00	140.00	70.00
(28)	Bill Dickey, Tony Lazzeri, Pat Malone, Red Ruffing	400.00	160.00	80.00
(29)	Rick Ferrell, Wes Ferrell, Fritz Ostermueller, Bill Werber	300.00	120.00	60.00
(30)	Pete Fox, Hank Greenberg, Schoolboy Rowe, Gee Walker	350.00	140.00	70.00
(31)	Jimmie Foxx, Pinky Higgins, Roy Mahaffey, Dib Williams	400.00	160.00	80.00
(32)	Bump Hadley, Lyn Lary, Heinie Manush, Monte Weaver	300.00	120.00	60.00
(33)	Mel Harder, Bill Knickerbocker, Lefty Stewart, Joe Vosmik	125.00	30.00	15.00
(34)	Travis Jackson, Gus Mancuso, Hal Schumacher, Bill Terry	300.00	120.00	60.00
(35)	Joe Kuhel, Buddy Meyer, John Stone, Earl Whitehill (Myer)	125.00	30.00	15.00
(36)	Red Lucas, Tommy Thevenow, Pie Traynor, Glenn Wright	300.00	120.00	60.00

1935 Goudey Puzzle-Backs

Each of the 36 card fronts in 1935 Goudey can be found with from two to four different backs that could be used to assemble a six-piece (single player) or 12-piece (team photo or composite) puzzle. This listing checklists the different backs found with each front as well as the cards that comprise each of the nine puzzles. The numbers given for each puzzle piece correspond to the assigned numbers of the card fronts.

Sparky Adams, Jim Bottomley, Adam Comorosky, Tony Piet
1H Tigers, H
3F Frisch, F
4F Cochrane, F
5F Cronin, F

Ethan Allen, Fred Brickell, Bubber Jonnard, Jimmie Wilson
1E Tigers, E
3C Frisch, C
5C Cronin, C
6C Foxx, C

Johnny Allen, Jimmie Deshong, Red Rolfe, Dixie Walker (DeShong)
8E Indians, E
9E Senators, E

Luke Appling, Jimmie Dykes, George Earnshaw, Luke Sewell
1I Tigers, I
2F Klein, F
6F Foxx, F
7F Simmons, F

Earl Averill, Oral Hildebrand, Willie Kamm, Hal Trosky
1L Tigers, L
2E Klein, E
6E Foxx, E
7E Simmons, E

Dick Bartell, Hughie Critz, Gus Mancuso, Mel Ott
2A Klein, A
4A Cochrane, A
7A Simmons, A

Ray Benge, Fred Fitzsimmons, Mark Koenig, Tom Zachary
8A Indians, A
9A Senators, A

Larry Benton, Ben Cantwell, Flint Rhem, Al Spohrer
8L Indians, L
9L Senators, L

Charlie Berry, Bobby Burke, Red Kress, Dazzy Vance
2C Klein, C
4C Cochrane, C
7C Simmons, C

Max Bishop, Bill Cissell, Joe Cronin, Carl Reynolds
1G Tigers, G
3E Frisch, E
5E Cronin, E
6E Foxx, E

George Blaeholder, Dick Coffman, Oscar Melillo, Sammy West
1F Tigers, F
3D Frisch, D
5D Cronin, D
6D Foxx, D

Cy Blanton, Babe Herman, Tom Padden, Gus Suhr
8K Indians, K
9K Senators, K

Zeke Bonura, Mule Haas, Jackie Hayes, Ted Lyons
8B Indians, B
9B Senators, B

Jim Bottomley, Adam Comorosky, Willis Hudlin, Glenn Myatt
1K Tigers, K
3B Frisch, B
5B Cronin, B
6B Foxx, B

Ed Brandt, Fred Frankhouse, Shanty Hogan, Gene Moore
2E Klein, E
4E Cochrane, E
7E Simmons, E

Ed Brandt, Rabbit Maranville, Marty McManus, Babe Ruth
1J Tigers, J
3A Frisch, A
4A Cochrane, A
5A Cronin, A

Tommy Bridges, Mickey Cochrane, Charlie Gehringer, Billy Rogell
1D Tigers, D
2D Klein, D
6D Foxx, D
7D Simmons, D

Jack Burns, Frank Grube, Rollie Hemsley, Bob Weiland
8C Indians, C
9C Senators, C

Guy Bush, Waite Hoyt, Lloyd Waner, Paul Waner
1E Tigers, E
3C Frisch, C
4C Cochrane, C
5C Cronin, C

Sammy Byrd, Danny MacFayden, Pepper Martin, Bob O'Farrell
2F Klein, F
4F Cochrane, F
7F Simmons, F

Alex Kampouris, Billy Meyers (Myers), Gilly Campbell, Ival Goodman
8D Indians, D
9D Senators, D

Tex Carleton, Dizzy Dean, Frankie Frisch, Ernie Orsatti
1A Tigers, A
2A Klein, A
6A Foxx, A
7A Simmons, A

Watty Clark, Lonny Frey, Sam Leslie, Joe Stripp
1G Tigers, G
3E Frisch, E
4E Cochrane, E
5E Cronin, E

Mickey Cochrane, Willie Kamm, Muddy Ruel, Al Simmons
1J Tigers, J
3A Frisch, A
5A Cronin, A
6A Foxx, A

Ed Coleman, Doc Cramer, Bob Johnson, Johnny Marcum
8J Indians, J
9J Senators, J

General Crowder, Goose Goslin, Firpo Marberry, Heinie Schuble
1H Tigers, H
3F Frisch, F
5F Cronin, F
6F Foxx, F

Kiki Cuyler, Woody English, Burleigh Grimes, Chuck Klein
1F Tigers, F
3D Frisch, D
4D Cochrane, D
5D Cronin, D

Bill Dickey, Tony Lazzeri, Pat Malone, Red Ruffing
2D Klein, D
4D Cochrane, D
7D Simmons, D

Rick Ferrell, Wes Ferrell, Fritz Ostermueller, Bill Werber
8G Indians, G
9G Senators, G

Pete Fox, Hank Greenberg, Schoolboy Rowe, Gee Walker
8F Indians, F
9F Senators, F

Jimmie Foxx, Pinky Higgins, Roy Mahaffey, Dib Williams
1B Tigers, B
2B Klein, B
6B Foxx, B
7B Simmons, B

Bump Hadley, Lyn Lary, Heinie Manush, Monte Weaver
1C Tigers, C
2C Klein, C
6C Foxx, C
7C Simmons, C

Mel Harder, Bill Knickerbocker, Lefty Stewart, Joe Vosmik
8I Indians, I
9I Senators, I

Travis Jackson, Gus Mancuso, Hal Schumacher, Bill Terry
1K Tigers, K
3B Frisch, B
4B Cochrane, B
5B Cronin, B

Joe Kuhel, Buddy Meyer, John Stone, Earl Whitehill (Myer)
8H Indians, H
9H Senators, H

Red Lucas, Tommy Thevenow, Pie Traynor, Glenn Wright
2B Klein, B
4B Cochrane, B
7B Simmons, B

Picture 1, Detroit Tigers Team Photo
A (22)
B (31)
C (32)
D (17)
E (2)
E (19)
F (11)
F (27)
G (10)
G (23)
H (1)
H (26)
I (4)
J (16)
J (24)
K (14)
K (34)
L (5)

Picture 2, Chuck Klein
A (6)
A (22)
B (31)
B (36)
C (9)
C (32)
D (17)
D (28)
E (5)
E (15)
F (4)
F (20)

Picture 3, Frankie Frisch
A (16)
A (24)
B (14))
B (34)
C (2)
C (19)
D (11)
D (27)
E (10)
E (23)
F (1)
F (26)

Picture 4, Gordon (Mickey) Cochrane
A (6)
A (16)
B (34)
B (36)
C (9)
C (19)
D (27)
D (28)
E (15)
E (23)
F (1)
F (20)

Picture 5, Joe Cronin
A (16)
A (24)
B (14)
B (34)
C (2)
C (19)
D (11)
D (27)
E (10)
E (23)
F (1)
F (26)

Picture 6, Jimmy (Jimmie) Foxx
A (22)
A (24)
B (14)
B (31)
C (2)
C (32)
D (11)
D (17)
E (5)
E (10)
F (4)
F (26)

Picture 7, Al Simmons
A (6)
A (22)
B (31)
B (36)
C (9)
C (32)
D (17)

D (28)
E (5)
E (15)
F (4)
F (20)

Picture 8, Cleve. Indians Composite
A (7)
B (13)
C (18)
D (21)
E (3)
F (30)
G (34)
H (35)
I (32)
J (25)
K (12)
L (8)

Picture 9, Wash. Senators Composite
A (7)
B (13)
C (18)
D (21)
E (3)
F (30)
G (29)
H (35)
I (33)
J (25)
K (12)
L (8)

1935 Goudey Premiums (R309-2)

The black-and-white photos in this set were issued as a premium by retailers in exchange for coupons from 10 Goudey wrappers in 1935. The pictures measure 5-1/2" x 9" (or a bit longer), and are printed on thin, glossy paper. The unnumbered set includes three team collages and players, whose names are written in script in the "wide pen" style.

		NM	EX	VG
Complete Set (16):		5,000	2,500	1,500
Common Player:		275.00	135.00	82.00
(1)	Elden Auker	275.00	135.00	82.00
(2)	Johnny Babich	275.00	135.00	82.00
(3)	Dick Bartell	275.00	135.00	82.00
(4)	Lester R. Bell	275.00	135.00	82.00
(5)	Wally Berger	275.00	135.00	82.00
(6)	Mickey Cochrane	400.00	200.00	120.00
(7)	Ervin Fox, Leon "Goose" Goslin, Gerald Walker	325.00	160.00	97.00
(8)	Vernon Gomez	400.00	200.00	120.00
(9)	Hank Greenberg	500.00	250.00	150.00
(10)	Oscar Melillo	275.00	135.00	82.00
(11)	Mel Ott	400.00	200.00	120.00
(12)	Schoolboy Rowe	275.00	135.00	82.00
(13)	Vito Tamulis	275.00	135.00	82.00
(14)	Boston Red Sox	300.00	150.00	90.00
(15)	Cleveland Indians	300.00	150.00	90.00
(16)	Washington Senators	300.00	150.00	90.00

1936 Goudey (R322)

The 1936 Goudey set consists of black-and-white cards measuring 2-3/8" x 2-7/8". A facsimile autograph is positioned on the card fronts. Backs contain a brief player biography and were designed to be used to play a baseball game. Different game situations (out, single, double, etc.) are given on each card. Numerous front/back combinations exist in the set. The ACC designation for the set is R322.

		NM	EX	VG
Complete Set (25):		2,625	1,300	785.00
Common Player:		80.00	40.00	25.00
(1)	Walter Berger	80.00	40.00	25.00
(2)	Henry Bonura	80.00	40.00	25.00
(3)	Stan Bordagaray	80.00	40.00	25.00
(4)	Bill Brubaker	80.00	40.00	25.00
(5)	Dolf Camilli	80.00	40.00	25.00
(6)	Clydell Castleman	80.00	40.00	25.00
(7)	"Mickey" Cochrane	175.00	85.00	50.00
(8)	Joe Coscarart	80.00	40.00	25.00
(9)	Frank Crosetti	110.00	55.00	30.00
(10)	"Kiki" Cuyler	140.00	70.00	40.00
(11)	Paul Derringer	80.00	40.00	25.00
(12)	Jimmy Dykes	80.00	40.00	25.00
(13)	"Rick" Ferrell	140.00	70.00	40.00
(14)	"Lefty" Gomez	175.00	85.00	50.00
(15)	Hank Greenberg	275.00	135.00	80.00
(16)	"Bucky" Harris	140.00	70.00	40.00
(17)	"Rolly" Hemsley	80.00	40.00	25.00
(18)	Frank Higgins	80.00	40.00	25.00
(19)	Oral Hildebrand	80.00	40.00	25.00
(20)	"Chuck" Klein	140.00	70.00	40.00
(21)	"Pepper" Martin	110.00	55.00	30.00
(22)	"Buck" Newsom	80.00	40.00	25.00
(23)	Joe Vosmik	80.00	40.00	25.00
(24)	Paul Waner	140.00	70.00	40.00
(25)	Bill Werber	80.00	40.00	25.00

1936 Goudey "Wide Pen" Premiums (R314)

The premium cards originally listed in the American Card Catalog as R314 are known to generations of collectors as "Wide Pens" because of the distinctive, thick style of cursive printing used for the facsimile autographs. Current thinking is that the issue is actually comprised of several distinct types issued over the course of at least two years and sharing a basic 3-1/4" x 5-1/2" black-and-white unnumbered format. Dates attributed are speculative.

1936 Goudey "Wide Pen" Premiums - Type 1

These in-store premiums are known to collectors as "Wide Pens" because of the distinctive, thick style of cursive printing used for the facsimile autographs. Cards have a 3-1/4" x 5-1/2" black-and-white, unnumbered format. Type 1 cards have bordered photos with "LITHO IN U.S.A." in the bottom border.

		NM	EX	VG
Complete Set (120):		6,000	2,500	1,500
Common Player:		40.00	17.50	10.00
(1)	Ethan Allen/Kneeling	40.00	17.50	10.00
(2)	Earl Averill/Portrait	60.00	25.00	15.00
(3)	Dick Bartell/Portrait	40.00	17.50	10.00
(4)	Dick Bartell/Sliding	40.00	17.50	10.00
(5)	Walter Berger/Portrait	40.00	17.50	10.00
(6)	Geo. Blaeholder/Portrait	40.00	17.50	10.00
(7)	"Cy" Blanton/Portrait	40.00	17.50	10.00
(8)	"Cliff" Bolton/Portrait	40.00	17.50	10.00
(9)	Stan Bordagaray/Portrait	40.00	17.50	10.00
(10)	Tommy Bridges/Portrait	40.00	17.50	10.00
(11)	Bill Brubaker/Portrait	40.00	17.50	10.00
(12)	Sam Byrd/Portrait	40.00	17.50	10.00
(13)	Dolph Camilli/Portrait	40.00	17.50	10.00
(14)	Clydell Castleman/Pitching	40.00	17.50	10.00
(15)	Clydell Castleman/Portrait	40.00	17.50	10.00
(16)	"Phil" Cavaretta (Cavarretta)/Fldg	40.00	17.50	10.00
(17)	Ben Chapman, Bill Werber	50.00	20.00	15.00
(18)	"Mickey" Cochrane/Portrait	65.00	25.00	15.00
(19)	Earl Coombs (Earle Combs)/Btg	60.00	25.00	15.00
(20)	Joe Coscarart/Portrait	40.00	17.50	10.00
(21)	Joe Cronin/Kneeling	60.00	25.00	15.00
(22)	Frank Crosetti/Btg	45.00	20.00	12.00
(23)	Tony Cuccinello/Portrait	40.00	17.50	10.00
(24)	"Kiki" Cuyler/Portrait	60.00	25.00	15.00
(25)	Curt Davis/Pitching	40.00	17.50	10.00
(26)	Virgil Davis/Catching	40.00	17.50	10.00
(27)	Paul Derringer/Portrait	40.00	17.50	10.00
(28)	"Bill" Dickey/Catching	65.00	25.00	15.00
(29)	Joe DiMaggio, Joe McCarthy	575.00	240.00	150.00
(30)	Jimmy Dykes/Kneeling	40.00	17.50	10.00
(31)	"Rick" Ferrell/Catching	60.00	25.00	15.00
(32)	"Wes" Ferrell/Portrait	40.00	17.50	10.00
(33)	Rick Ferrell, Wes Ferrell	70.00	30.00	17.50
(34)	Lou Finney/Portrait	40.00	17.50	10.00
(35)	Ervin "Pete" Fox/Portrait	40.00	17.50	10.00
(36)	Tony Freitas/Portrait	40.00	17.50	10.00
(37)	Lonnie Frey/Btg	40.00	17.50	10.00
(38)	Frankie Frisch/Portrait	60.00	25.00	15.00
(39)	"Augie" Galan/Portrait	40.00	17.50	10.00
(40)	Charles Gehringer/Portrait	70.00	30.00	17.50
(41)	Charlie Gelbert/Portrait	40.00	17.50	10.00
(42)	"Lefty" Gomez/Portrait	70.00	30.00	17.50
(43)	"Goose" Goslin/Portrait	60.00	25.00	15.00
(44)	Earl Grace/Catching	40.00	17.50	10.00
(45)	Hank Greenberg/Portrait	175.00	75.00	45.00
(46)	"Mule" Haas/Btg	40.00	17.50	10.00
(47)	Odell Hale/Portrait	40.00	17.50	10.00
(48)	Bill Hallahan/Portrait	40.00	17.50	10.00
(49)	"Mel" Harder/Portrait	40.00	17.50	10.00
(50)	"Bucky" Harris/Portrait	60.00	25.00	15.00
(51)	"Gabby" Hartnett/Catching	60.00	25.00	15.00
(52)	Ray Hayworth/Catching	40.00	17.50	10.00
(53)	"Rolly" Hemsley/Catching	40.00	17.50	10.00
(54)	Babe Herman/Portrait	50.00	20.00	12.50
(55)	Frank Higgins/Portrait	40.00	17.50	10.00
(56)	Oral Hildebrand/Portrait	40.00	17.50	10.00
(57)	Myril Hoag/Portrait	40.00	17.50	10.00
(58)	Waite Hoyt/Pitching	60.00	25.00	15.00
(59)	Woody Jensen/Btg	40.00	17.50	10.00
(60)	Bob Johnson/Btg	40.00	17.50	10.00
(61)	"Buck" Jordan/Portrait	40.00	17.50	10.00
(62)	Alex Kampouris/Portrait	40.00	17.50	10.00
(63)	"Chuck" Klein/Portrait	60.00	25.00	15.00
(64)	Joe Kuhel/Portrait	40.00	17.50	10.00
(65)	Lyn Lary/Portrait	40.00	17.50	10.00
(66)	Harry Lavagetto/Portrait	40.00	17.50	10.00
(67)	Sam Leslie/Portrait	40.00	17.50	10.00
(68)	Freddie Lindstrom/Portrait	60.00	25.00	15.00
(69)	Ernie Lombardi/Throwing	60.00	25.00	15.00
(70)	"Al" Lopez/Throwing	60.00	25.00	15.00
(71)	Dan MacFayden/Portrait	40.00	17.50	10.00
(72)	John Marcum/Pitching	40.00	17.50	10.00
(73)	"Pepper" Martin/Portrait	50.00	20.00	12.50
(74)	Eric McNair/Portrait	40.00	17.50	10.00
(75)	"Ducky" Medwick/Kneeling	60.00	25.00	15.00
(76)	Gene Moore/Portrait	40.00	17.50	10.00
(77)	Randy Moore/Portrait	40.00	17.50	10.00
(78)	Terry Moore/Portrait	40.00	17.50	10.00
(79)	Edw. Moriarty/Portrait	40.00	17.50	10.00
(80)	"Wally" Moses/Portrait	40.00	17.50	10.00
(81)	"Buddy" Myer/Btg	40.00	17.50	10.00
(82)	"Buck" Newsom/Portrait	40.00	17.50	10.00
(83)	Steve O'Neill, Frank Pytlak	40.00	17.50	10.00
(84)	Fred Ostermueller/Portrait	40.00	17.50	10.00
(85)	Marvin Owen/Portrait	40.00	17.50	10.00
(86)	Tommy Padden/Portrait	40.00	17.50	10.00
(87)	Ray Pepper/Btg	40.00	17.50	10.00
(88)	Tony Piet/Portrait	40.00	17.50	10.00
(89)	"Rabbit" Pytlak/Throwing	40.00	17.50	10.00
(90)	"Rip" Radcliff/Portrait	40.00	17.50	10.00
(91)	Bobby Reis/Portrait	40.00	17.50	10.00
(92)	"Lew" Riggs/Fldg	40.00	17.50	10.00
(93)	Bill Rogell/Portrait	40.00	17.50	10.00
(94)	"Red" Rolfe/Portrait	40.00	17.50	10.00
(95)	"Schoolboy" Rowe/Portrait	45.00	20.00	12.00
(96)	Al Schacht/Portrait	50.00	20.00	12.50
(97)	"Luke" Sewell/Catching	40.00	17.50	10.00
(98)	Al Simmons/Portrait	60.00	25.00	15.00
(99)	John Stone/Portrait	40.00	17.50	10.00
(100)	Gus Suhr/Fldg	40.00	17.50	10.00
(101)	Joe Sullivan/Portrait	40.00	17.50	10.00
(102)	Bill Swift/Portrait	40.00	17.50	10.00
(103)	Vito Tamulis/Portrait	40.00	17.50	10.00
(104)	Dan Taylor/Portrait	40.00	17.50	10.00
(105)	Cecil Travis/Portrait	40.00	17.50	10.00
(106)	Hal Trosky/Portrait	40.00	17.50	10.00
(107)	"Bill" Urbanski/Portrait	40.00	17.50	10.00
(108)	Russ Van Atta/Portrait	40.00	17.50	10.00
(109)	"Arky" Vaughan/Portrait	60.00	25.00	15.00
(110)	Gerald Walker/Portrait	40.00	17.50	10.00
(111)	"Buck" Walter (Walters)/Portrait	40.00	17.50	10.00
(112a)	Lloyd Waner (Portrait) (No "LITHO IN U.S.A.)	60.00	25.00	15.00
(112b)	Lloyd Waner/Portrait ("LITHO IN U.S.A.)	60.00	25.00	15.00
(113)	Paul Waner/Portrait	60.00	25.00	15.00
(114)	"Lon" Warneke/Portrait	40.00	17.50	10.00
(115)	"Rabbit" Warstler/Btg	40.00	17.50	10.00
(116)	Bill Werber/Portrait	40.00	17.50	10.00
(117)	"Jo Jo" White/Portrait	40.00	17.50	10.00
(118)	Burgess Whitehead/Portrait	40.00	17.50	10.00
(119)	John Whitehead/Portrait	40.00	17.50	10.00
(120)	Whitlow Wyatt/Portrait	40.00	17.50	10.00

1936 Goudey "Wide Pen" Premiums - Type 2

These 3-1/4" x 5-1/2" black-and-white, unnumbered cards are known as "Wide Pens" because of the distinctive cursive printing of the facsimile autographs. Type 2 and Type 3 cards share their photos. Type 2 cards have borders, but no "LITHO IN U.S.A." line. Some Type 2 cards also share their photos with Type 1, but have a different projection (size). Those are indicated parenthetically with an asterisk.

		NM	EX	VG
Complete Set (24):		1,800	850.00	500.00
Common Player:		60.00	27.50	15.00
(1)	Mel Almada/Kneeling	75.00	35.00	20.00
(2)	Lucius Appling/Portrait	90.00	40.00	22.50
(3)	Henry Bonura/Portrait	60.00	27.50	15.00
(4)	Ben Chapman, Bill Werber	80.00	35.00	20.00
(5)	Herman Clifton/Btg	60.00	27.50	15.00
(6)	Roger "Doc" Cramer/Portrait	60.00	27.50	15.00
(7)	Joe Cronin/Kneeling*	90.00	40.00	22.50

		NM	EX	VG
(8)	Jimmy Dykes/Kneeling*	60.00	27.50	15.00
(9)	Erwin "Pete" Fox (Ervin)/ Portrait	60.00	27.50	15.00
(10)	Jimmy Foxx/Portrait	175.00	80.00	45.00
(11)	Hank Greenberg/Portrait*	235.00	100.00	60.00
(12)	Oral Hildebrand/Portrait*	60.00	27.50	15.00
(13)	Alex Hooks/Fldg	60.00	27.50	15.00
(14)	Willis Hudlin/Throwing	60.00	27.50	15.00
(15)	Bill Knickerbocker/Portrait	60.00	27.50	15.00
(16)	Heine (Heinie) Manush/ Portrait	90.00	40.00	22.50
(17)	Steve O'Neill/Portrait	60.00	27.50	15.00
(18)	Marvin Owen/Portrait*	60.00	27.50	15.00
(19)	Al Simmons (Bats on shoulder.)	90.00	40.00	22.50
(20)	Lem "Moose" Solters/Btg (First name actually Julius.)	60.00	27.50	15.00
(21)	Hal Trosky/Btg	60.00	27.50	15.00
(22)	Joe Vosmik/Btg	60.00	27.50	15.00
(23)	Joe Vosmik/Portrait	60.00	27.50	15.00
(24)	Earl Whitehill/Throwing	60.00	27.50	15.00

1936 Goudey "Wide Pen" Premiums - Type 3

These 3-1/4" x 5-1/2" black-and-white, unnumbered cards are known as "Wide Pens" because of the distinctive cursive printing of the facsimile autographs. Type 2 and Type 3 cards share their photos. Type 3 cards are borderless and some also share their photos with Type 1, but have a different projection (size). Those are indicated parenthetically with an asterisk.

		NM	EX	VG
Complete Set (24):		1,800	850.00	500.00
Common Player:		60.00	27.50	15.00
(1)	Mel Almada/Kneeling	75.00	35.00	20.00
(2)	Lucius Appling/Portrait	90.00	40.00	22.50
(3)	Henry Bonura/Portrait	60.00	27.50	15.00
(4)	Ben Chapman, Bill Werber	80.00	35.00	20.00
(5)	Herman Clifton/Btg	60.00	27.50	15.00
(6)	Roger "Doc" Cramer/Portrait	60.00	27.50	15.00
(7)	Joe Cronin/Kneeling*	90.00	40.00	22.50
(8)	Jimmy Dykes/Kneeling*	60.00	27.50	15.00
(9)	Erwin "Pete" Fox (Ervin)/ Portrait*	60.00	27.50	15.00
(10)	Jimmy Foxx/Portrait	175.00	80.00	45.00
(11)	Hank Greenberg/Portrait*	235.00	100.00	60.00
(12)	Oral Hildebrand/Portrait*	60.00	27.50	15.00
(13)	Alex Hooks/Fldg	60.00	27.50	15.00
(14)	Willis Hudlin/Throwing	60.00	27.50	15.00
(15)	Bill Knickerbocker/Portrait	60.00	27.50	15.00
(16)	Heine (Heinie) Manush/ Portrait	90.00	40.00	22.50
(17)	Steve O'Neill/Portrait	60.00	27.50	15.00
(18)	Marvin Owen/Portrait*	60.00	27.50	15.00
(19)	Al Simmons (Bats on shoulder.)	90.00	40.00	22.50
(20)	Lem "Moose" Solters/Btg (First name actually Julius.)	60.00	27.50	15.00
(21)	Hal Trosky/Btg	60.00	27.50	15.00
(22)	Joe Vosmik/Btg	60.00	27.50	15.00
(23)	Joe Vosmik/Portrait	60.00	27.50	15.00
(24)	Earl Whitehill/Throwing	60.00	27.50	15.00

1937 Goudey "Wide Pen" Premiums - Type 4

These premium cards are known to generations of collectors as "Wide Pens" because of the distinctive, thick style of cursive typography used for the facsimile autographs. They have a 3-1/4" x 5-1/2" black-and-white, unnumbered format. Type 4 cards are printed on a paper stock usually described as "creamy." They are bordered, but do not have a "LITHO IN U.S.A." line. Type 5 cards share the creamy paper stock of Type 4, and may have been part of the same issue, which would indicate Canadian origins. An asterisk after the pose indicates a photo shared with Type 1, though possibly of a larger or smaller projection.

		NM	EX	VG
Complete Set (36):		4,500	2,000	1,200
Common Player:		60.00	25.00	15.00
(1)	"Luke" Appling/Btg	90.00	40.00	22.50
(2)	Earl Averill/Portrait*	90.00	40.00	22.50
(3)	"Cy" Blanton/Pitching	60.00	25.00	15.00
(4)	"Zeke" Bonura/Btg	60.00	25.00	15.00
(5)	Tom Bridges/Throwing	60.00	25.00	15.00
(6)	Tommy Bridges/Portrait*	60.00	25.00	15.00
(7)	Mickey Cochrane/Portrait*	90.00	40.00	22.50
(8)	Joe Cronin/Kneeling*	90.00	40.00	22.50
(9)	"Joe" DiMaggio/Portrait	2,000	900.00	500.00
(10)	"Bobby" Doeer (Doerr)/Btg	90.00	40.00	22.50
(11)	Jimmy Dykes/Fldg	60.00	25.00	15.00
(12)	"Bob" Feller/Pitching	200.00	90.00	50.00
(13)	"Elbie" Fletcher/Fldg	60.00	25.00	15.00
(14)	Erwin "Pete" Fox (Ervin)/ Portrait*	60.00	25.00	15.00
(15)	Pete Fox/Btg	60.00	25.00	15.00
(16)	"Gus" Galan/Btg	60.00	25.00	15.00
(17)	Charles Gehringer/Portrait*	90.00	40.00	22.50
(18)	Hank Greenberg/Portrait*	150.00	65.00	35.00
(19)	"Goose" Goslin/Portrait	90.00	40.00	22.50
(20)	Mel Harder/Portrait	60.00	25.00	15.00
(21)	"Gabby" Hartnett/Catching*	90.00	40.00	22.50
(22)	Ray Hayworth/Catching*	60.00	25.00	15.00
(23)	"Pinky" Higgins/Btg	60.00	25.00	15.00
(24)	Carl Hubbell (Pitching)	90.00	40.00	22.50
(25)	"Wally" Moses/Btg	60.00	25.00	15.00
(26)	Lou Newsom/Portrait	60.00	25.00	15.00
(27)	Marvin Owen/Portrait*	60.00	25.00	15.00
(28)	Bill Rogell (Portrait*)	60.00	25.00	15.00
(29)	"Schoolboy" Rowe/Pitching	60.00	25.00	15.00
(30)	"Schoolboy" Rowe/Portrait*	60.00	25.00	15.00
(31)	Al Simmons/Portrait*	90.00	40.00	22.50
(32)	Julius Solters/Btg	60.00	25.00	15.00
(33)	"Hal" Trosky/Btg	60.00	25.00	15.00
(34)	Joe Vosmik/Kneeling	60.00	25.00	15.00
(35)	"Jo Jo" White/Portrait*	60.00	25.00	15.00
(36)	Johnnie Whitehead/Pitching	60.00	25.00	15.00

1937 Goudey "Wide Pen" Premiums - Type 5

These premium cards are known as "Wide Pens" because of the distinctive, thick style of cursive printing used for the facsimile autographs. they have a 3-1/4" x 5-1/2" black-and-white, unnumbered format. The photos are bordered, but do not have a "LITHO IN U.S.A." line. Type 5 cards are printed on a paper stock usually described as "creamy" and may have been part of the same issue as Type 4. Type 5 is comprised only of Toronto and Montreal (International League) players.

		NM	EX	VG
Complete Set (39):		3,500	1,600	900.00
Common Player:		90.00	40.00	25.00
(1)	Buddy Bates	90.00	40.00	25.00
(2)	Del Bisonette/Portrait	90.00	40.00	25.00
(3)	Lincoln Blakely	90.00	40.00	25.00
(4)	Isaac J. Boone	90.00	40.00	25.00
(5)	John H. Burnett/Btg	90.00	40.00	25.00
(6)	Leon Chagon	90.00	40.00	25.00
(7)	Gus Dugas/Portrait	90.00	40.00	25.00
(8)	Henry N. Erickson/Catching	90.00	40.00	25.00
(9)	Art Funk/Portrait	90.00	40.00	25.00
(10)	George Granger/Portrait	90.00	40.00	25.00
(11)	Thomas G. Heath	90.00	40.00	25.00
(12)	Phil Hensiek/Portrait	90.00	40.00	25.00
(13)	Leroy Herrmann/Throwing	90.00	40.00	25.00
(14)	Henry Johnson	90.00	40.00	25.00
(15)	Hal King/Portrait	90.00	40.00	25.00
(16)	Charles F. Lucas/Portrait	90.00	40.00	25.00
(17)	Edward S. Miller/Btg (Middle initial actually R.)	90.00	40.00	25.00
(18)	Jake F. Mooty/Pitching	90.00	40.00	25.00
(19)	Guy Moreau/Portrait (Street clothes.)	90.00	40.00	25.00
(20)	George Murray/Portrait	90.00	40.00	25.00
(21)	Glenn Myatt	90.00	40.00	25.00
(22)	Lauri Myllykangas	90.00	40.00	25.00
(23)	Francis J. Nicholas/Pitching	90.00	40.00	25.00
(24)	Bill O'Brien/Portrait (Street clothes.)	90.00	40.00	25.00
(25)	Thomas Oliver/Btg	90.00	40.00	25.00
(26)	James Pattison	90.00	40.00	25.00
(27)	Crip Polli/Portrait	90.00	40.00	25.00
(28)	Harlan Pool/Bats	90.00	40.00	25.00
(29)	Walter Purcey/Pitching	90.00	40.00	25.00
(30)	Bill Rhiel	90.00	40.00	25.00
(31)	Ben Sankey	90.00	40.00	25.00
(32)	Les Scarcella (Scarsella)/ Kneeling	90.00	40.00	25.00
(33)	Bob Seeds/Portrait	90.00	40.00	25.00
(34)	Frank Shaugnessy/Portrait	90.00	40.00	25.00
(35)	Harry Smythe/Portrait	90.00	40.00	25.00
(36)	Ben Tate/Portrait	90.00	40.00	25.00
(37)	Fresco Thompson/Portrait	90.00	40.00	25.00
(38)	Charles Wilson/Portrait	90.00	40.00	25.00
(39)	Francis Wistert/Pitching	90.00	40.00	25.00

1937 Goudey Knot Hole League

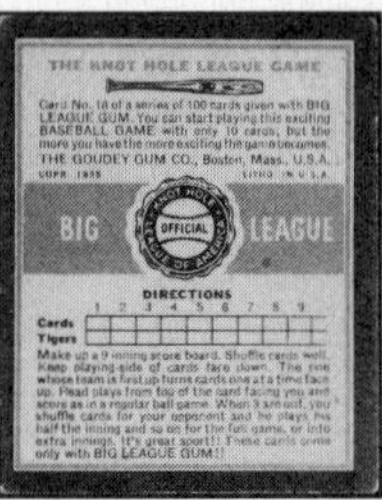

Though they do not picture or name any players, the fact these game cards were issued by Goudey makes them collectible for many hobbyists. While they carry a copyright date of 1935, the cards were not issued until 1937. About 2-3/8" x 2-7/8", and printed in red, white and blue, the cards were intended to be used to play a baseball game using the situations printed on the fronts. Despite advertising a series of 100 cards, only 24 were actually issued. The cards were designated R325 in the American Card Catalog.

		NM	EX	VG
Complete Set (24):		450.00	180.00	90.00
Common Card:		25.00	10.00	5.00
1	Double / Foul	25.00	10.00	5.00
2	Steals Home!! / Strike	25.00	10.00	5.00
3	Ball / Out	25.00	10.00	5.00
4	Strike / Ball	25.00	10.00	5.00
5	Strike / Wild Pitch	25.00	10.00	5.00
6	Ball / Out	25.00	10.00	5.00
7	Bunt - Scratch Hit!! / Stolen Base !!	25.00	10.00	5.00
8	Hit by Pitched Ball / Out	25.00	10.00	5.00
9	Foul / Ball	25.00	10.00	5.00
10	Foul / Double!	25.00	10.00	5.00
11	Out / Ball	25.00	10.00	5.00
12	Foul / Force Out	25.00	10.00	5.00
13	Out / Single	25.00	10.00	5.00
14	Strike / Ball	25.00	10.00	5.00
15	Foul Tip / Strike!	25.00	10.00	5.00
16	Three Bagger / Out	25.00	10.00	5.00
17	Ball / Out	25.00	10.00	5.00
18	Out!! / Error!!!	25.00	10.00	5.00
19	Strike / Foul	25.00	10.00	5.00
20	Out / Double Play	25.00	10.00	5.00
21	!!Home Run!! / Ball	25.00	10.00	5.00
22	Out / Strike	25.00	10.00	5.00
23	Ball / Out	25.00	10.00	5.00
24	Lout!! / Error!!!	25.00	10.00	5.00

1937 Goudey Thum Movies

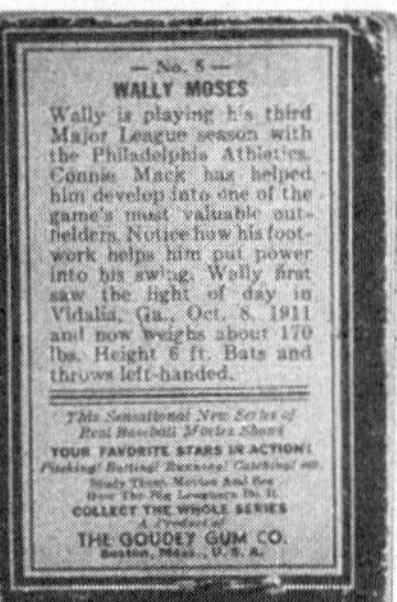

These 2" x 3" baseball novelty booklets create the illusion of baseball action in motion when the pages are rapidly flipped. The booklets are numbered on the top of the back page. Thum Movies were listed in the American Card Catalog as R342.

		NM	EX	VG
Complete Set (13):		1,750	875.00	525.00
Common Player:		70.00	35.00	20.00
1	John Irving Burns	70.00	35.00	20.00
2	Joe Vosmik	70.00	35.00	20.00
3	Mel Ott	225.00	110.00	65.00
4	Joe DiMaggio	525.00	260.00	155.00
5	Wally Moses	70.00	35.00	20.00
6	Van Lingle Mungo	70.00	35.00	20.00
7	Luke Appling	100.00	50.00	30.00
8	Bob Feller	225.00	110.00	65.00
9	Paul Derringer	70.00	35.00	20.00
10	Paul Waner	100.00	50.00	30.00
11	Joe Medwick	100.00	50.00	30.00
12	James Emory Foxx	225.00	110.00	65.00
13	Wally Berger	70.00	35.00	20.00

1938 Goudey (R323)

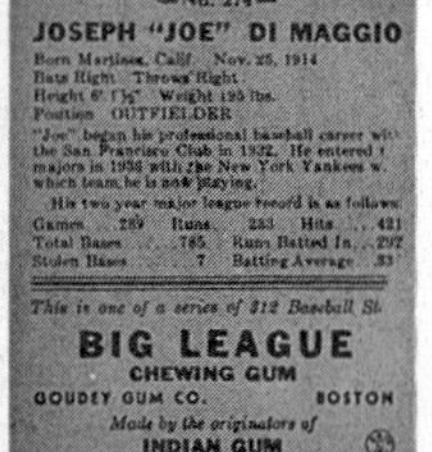

Sometimes referred to as the Goudey Heads-Up set, this issue begins numbering (#241) where the 1933 Goudey set left off. On the card fronts, a photo is used for the player's head with the body being a cartoon drawing. Twenty-four different players are pictured twice in the set. Cards #241-264 feature plain backgrounds on the fronts. Cards #265-288 contain the same basic design and photo but include small drawings and comments within the background. Backs have player statistical and biographical information. The ACC designation for the issue is R323.

		NM	EX	VG
Complete Set (48):		29,000	11,500	5,750
Common Player (241-264):		200.00	85.00	30.00
Common Player (265-288):		225.00	100.00	35.00
241	Charlie Gehringer	600.00	250.00	100.00
242	Ervin Fox	300.00	100.00	40.00
243	Joe Kuhel	200.00	85.00	30.00
244	Frank DeMaree	200.00	85.00	30.00
245	Frank Pytlak	200.00	85.00	30.00
246a	Ernie Lombardi (Red Sox)	675.00	270.00	135.00
246b	Ernie Lombardi (Reds followed by black baseball.)	425.00	200.00	85.00
246c	Ernie Lombardi (Reds)	350.00	140.00	70.00
247	Joe Vosmik	200.00	85.00	30.00
248	Dick Bartell	200.00	85.00	30.00
249	Jimmy Foxx	900.00	350.00	150.00
250	Joe DiMaggio	5,000	2,000	800.00
251	Bump Hadley	200.00	85.00	30.00
252	Zeke Bonura	200.00	85.00	30.00
253	Hank Greenberg	1,100	450.00	225.00
254	Van Lingle Mungo	400.00	100.00	40.00
255	Julius Solters	200.00	85.00	30.00
256	Vernon Kennedy	200.00	85.00	30.00
257	Al Lopez	425.00	200.00	85.00
258	Bobby Doerr	500.00	200.00	85.00
259	Bill Werber	200.00	85.00	30.00
260	Rudy York	200.00	85.00	30.00
261	Rip Radcliff	200.00	85.00	30.00
262	Joe Ducky Medwick	425.00	200.00	85.00
263	Marvin Owen	200.00	85.00	30.00
264	Bob Feller	2,000	700.00	300.00
265	Charlie Gehringer	600.00	200.00	100.00
266	Ervin Fox	225.00	100.00	35.00
267	Joe Kuhel	225.00	100.00	35.00
268	Frank DeMaree	225.00	100.00	35.00
269	Frank Pytlak	225.00	100.00	35.00
270	Ernie Lombardi	500.00	225.00	100.00
271	Joe Vosmik	225.00	100.00	35.00
272	Dick Bartell	225.00	100.00	35.00
273	Jimmy Foxx	1,200	500.00	200.00
274	Joe DiMaggio	6,750	2,900	1,100
275	Bump Hadley	225.00	100.00	35.00
276	Zeke Bonura	225.00	100.00	35.00
277	Hank Greenberg	1,300	600.00	300.00
278	Van Lingle Mungo	225.00	100.00	35.00
279	Julius Solters	225.00	100.00	35.00
280	Vernon Kennedy	225.00	100.00	35.00
281	Al Lopez	500.00	225.00	90.00
282	Bobby Doerr	550.00	250.00	100.00
283	Bill Werber	225.00	100.00	35.00
284	Rudy York	225.00	100.00	35.00
285	Rip Radcliff	225.00	100.00	35.00
286	Joe Ducky Medwick	600.00	250.00	100.00
287	Marvin Owen	225.00	100.00	35.00
288	Bob Feller	2,500	800.00	400.00

1938 Goudey Big League Baseball Movies

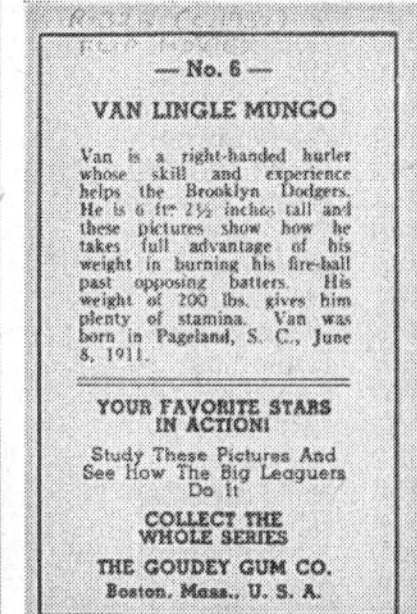

Probably issued in both 1937-38, according to the biographies on back, this set of "flip movies" was comprised of small (2" x 3") booklets whose pages produced a movie effect when flipped rapidly, similar to a penny arcade novelty popular at the time. There are 13 players in the set; each movie having two cleary labeled parts. The cover of the booklets identify the set as "Big League Baseball Movies." They carry the American Card Catalog designation R326.

		NM	EX	VG
Complete Set (26):		3,750	1,875	1,125
Common Player:		75.00	37.50	22.50
1a	John Irving Burns (Part 1)	75.00	37.50	22.50
1b	John Irving Burns (Part 2)	75.00	37.50	22.50
2a	Joe Vosmik (Part 1)	75.00	37.50	22.50
2b	Joe Vosmik (Part 2)	75.00	37.50	22.50
3a	Mel Ott (Part 1)	185.00	95.00	55.00
3b	Mel Ott (Part 2)	185.00	95.00	55.00
4a	Joe DiMaggio (Part 1, Joe DiMaggio cover photo.)	475.00	235.00	140.00
4aa	Joe DiMaggio (Part 1, Vince DiMaggio cover photo.)	375.00	185.00	110.00
4b	Joe DiMaggio (Part 2, Joe DiMaggio cover photo.)	475.00	235.00	140.00
4ba	Joe DiMaggio (Part 2, Vince DiMaggio cover photo.)	375.00	185.00	110.00
5a	Wally Moses (Part 1)	75.00	37.50	22.50
5b	Wally Moses (Part 2)	75.00	37.50	22.50
6a	Van Lingle Mungo (Part 1)	75.00	37.50	22.50
6b	Van Lingle Mungo (Part 2)	75.00	37.50	22.50
7a	Luke Appling (Part 1)	110.00	55.00	35.00
7b	Luke Appling (Part 2)	110.00	55.00	35.00
8a	Bob Feller (Part 1)	225.00	110.00	65.00
8b	Bob Feller (Part 2)	225.00	110.00	65.00
9a	Paul Derringer (Part 1)	75.00	37.50	22.50
9b	Paul Derringer (Part 2)	75.00	37.50	22.50
10a	Paul Waner (Part 1)	110.00	55.00	35.00
10b	Paul Waner (Part 2)	110.00	55.00	35.00
11a	Joe Medwick (Part 1)	110.00	55.00	35.00
11b	Joe Medwick (Part 2)	110.00	55.00	35.00
12a	James Emory Foxx (Part 1)	260.00	130.00	75.00
12b	James Emory Foxx (Part 2)	260.00	130.00	75.00
13a	Wally Berger (Part 1)	75.00	37.50	22.50
13b	Wally Berger (Part 2)	75.00	37.50	22.50

1939 Goudey Premiums (R303-A)

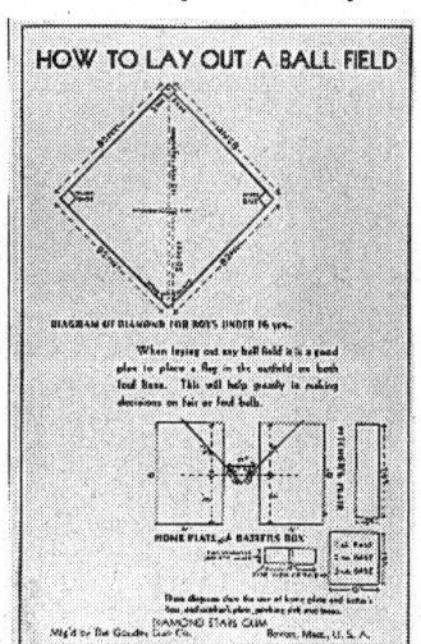

Although this unnumbered set of paper premiums has the name "Diamond Stars Gum" on the back, it is not related to National Chicle's Diamond Stars card sets. Rather, this 48-player set was a premium issued by the Goudey Gum Co. Each premium photo measures 4" x 6-3/16" and is printed in a brown-toned sepia. The front of the photo includes a facsimile autograph, while the back contains drawings that illustrate various baseball tips. These pictures are soemtimes found with top and bottom border trimmed to a depth of 5-3/4" for distribution in Canada.

		NM	EX	VG
Complete Set (48):		6,000	2,400	1,200
Common Player:		75.00	30.00	15.00
(1)	Luke Appling	135.00	55.00	25.00
(2)	Earl Averill	135.00	55.00	25.00
(3)	Wally Berger	75.00	30.00	15.00
(4)	Darrell Blanton	75.00	30.00	15.00
(5)	Zeke Bonura	75.00	30.00	15.00
(6)	Mace Brown	75.00	30.00	15.00
(7)	George Case	75.00	30.00	15.00
(8)	Ben Chapman	75.00	30.00	15.00
(9)	Joe Cronin	135.00	55.00	25.00
(10)	Frank Crosetti	90.00	36.00	18.00
(11)	Paul Derringer	75.00	30.00	15.00
(12)	Bill Dickey	150.00	60.00	30.00
(13)	Joe DiMaggio	650.00	260.00	130.00
(14)	Bob Feller	225.00	90.00	45.00
(15)	Jimmy (Jimmie) Foxx	235.00	95.00	45.00
(16)	Charles Gehringer	135.00	55.00	25.00
(17)	Lefty Gomez	135.00	55.00	25.00
(18)	Ival Goodman	75.00	30.00	15.00
(19)	Joe Gordon	75.00	30.00	15.00
(20)	Hank Greenberg	175.00	70.00	35.00
(21)	Buddy Hassett	75.00	30.00	15.00
(22)	Jeff Heath	75.00	30.00	15.00
(23)	Tom Henrich	75.00	30.00	15.00
(24)	Billy Herman	135.00	54.00	27.00
(25)	Frank Higgins	75.00	30.00	15.00
(26)	Fred Hutchinson	75.00	30.00	15.00
(27)	Bob Johnson	75.00	30.00	15.00
(28)	Ken Keltner	75.00	30.00	15.00
(29)	Mike Kreevich	75.00	30.00	15.00
(30)	Ernie Lombardi	135.00	55.00	25.00
(31)	Gus Mancuso	75.00	30.00	15.00
(32)	Eric McNair	75.00	30.00	15.00
(33)	Van Mungo	75.00	30.00	15.00
(34)	Buck Newsom	75.00	30.00	15.00
(35)	Mel Ott	150.00	55.00	25.00
(36)	Marvin Owen	75.00	30.00	15.00
(37)	Frank Pytlak	75.00	30.00	15.00
(38)	Woodrow Rich	75.00	30.00	15.00
(39)	Charley Root	75.00	30.00	15.00
(40)	Al Simmons	135.00	55.00	25.00
(41)	James Tabor	75.00	30.00	15.00
(42)	Cecil Travis	75.00	30.00	15.00
(43)	Hal Trosky	75.00	30.00	15.00
(44)	Arky Vaughan	135.00	55.00	25.00
(45)	Joe Vosmik	75.00	30.00	15.00
(46)	Lon Warneke	75.00	30.00	15.00
(47)	Ted Williams	1,050	420.00	210.00
(48)	Rudy York	75.00	30.00	15.00

1939 Goudey Premiums (R303-B)

Although larger (4-3/4" x 7-1/4" to 7-3/8"), the photos in this 24-player set are identical to those in the R303-A issue of the same year, and the format of the set is unchanged. The set, designated as R303-B in the American Card Catalog, can be found in both black-and-white and sepia-toned, with backs printed in brown.

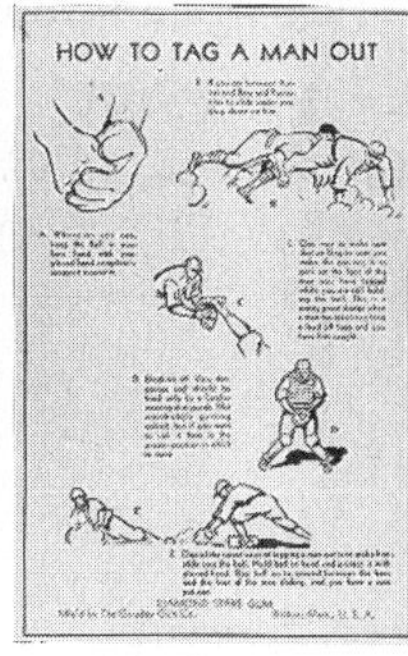

		NM	EX	VG
Complete Set (24):		2,500	1,000	500.00
Common Player:		60.00	24.00	12.00
(1)	Luke Appling	90.00	35.00	15.00
(2)	George Case	60.00	25.00	12.00
(3)	Ben Chapman	60.00	25.00	12.00
(4)	Joe Cronin	90.00	35.00	15.00
(5)	Bill Dickey	110.00	45.00	20.00
(6)	Joe DiMaggio	600.00	240.00	120.00
(7)	Bob Feller	150.00	60.00	30.00
(8)	Jimmy (Jimmie) Foxx	175.00	70.00	35.00
(9)	Lefty Gomez	90.00	35.00	15.00
(10)	Ival Goodman	60.00	25.00	12.00
(11)	Joe Gordon	60.00	25.00	12.00
(12)	Hank Greenberg	125.00	50.00	25.00
(13)	Jeff Heath	60.00	25.00	12.00
(14)	Billy Herman	90.00	35.00	15.00
(15)	Frank Higgins	60.00	25.00	12.00
(16)	Ken Keltner	60.00	25.00	12.00
(17)	Mike Kreevich	60.00	25.00	12.00
(18)	Ernie Lombardi	90.00	35.00	15.00
(19)	Gus Mancuso	60.00	25.00	12.00
(20)	Mel Ott	110.00	45.00	20.00
(21)	Al Simmons	90.00	35.00	15.00
(22)	Arky Vaughan	90.00	35.00	15.00
(23)	Joe Vosmik	60.00	25.00	12.00
(24)	Rudy York	60.00	25.00	12.00

1941 Goudey (R324)

Goudey Gum's last set was issued in 1941. The 2-3/8" x 2-7/8" (size approximate due to imprecise cutting) cards feature black-and-white photos set against blue, green, red or yellow backgrounds. The player's name, team and position plus the card number are supposed to be situated in a box at the bottom of the card. However, due to vagaries of cutting, some or all of the bottom printing might appear at the top of the card, greatly reducing its value. The card backs are blank. The ACC designation for the set is R324.

		NM	EX	VG
Complete Set (33):		8,500	3,400	1,700
Common Player:		250.00	100.00	50.00
1	Hugh Mulcahy	250.00	100.00	50.00
2	Harlond Clift	250.00	100.00	50.00
3	Louis Chiozza	250.00	100.00	50.00
4	Warren (Buddy) Rosar	250.00	100.00	50.00
5	George McQuinn	250.00	100.00	50.00
6	Emerson Dickman	250.00	100.00	50.00
7	Wayne Ambler	250.00	100.00	50.00
8	Bob Muncrief	250.00	100.00	50.00
9	Bill Dietrich	250.00	100.00	50.00
10	Taft Wright	250.00	100.00	50.00
11	Don Heffner	250.00	100.00	50.00
12	Fritz Ostermueller	250.00	100.00	50.00
13	Frank Hayes	250.00	100.00	50.00
14	John (Jack) Kramer	250.00	100.00	50.00
15	Dario Lodigiani	275.00	110.00	55.00
16	George Case	250.00	100.00	50.00
17	Vito Tamulis	250.00	100.00	50.00
18	Whitlow Wyatt	250.00	100.00	50.00
19	Bill Posedel	250.00	100.00	50.00
20	Carl Hubbell	675.00	275.00	125.00
21	Harold Warstler/SP	400.00	175.00	85.00
22	Joe Sullivan/SP	400.00	175.00	85.00
23	Norman (Babe) Young/SP	400.00	175.00	85.00
24	Stanley Andrews/SP	400.00	175.00	85.00
25	Morris Arnovich/SP	700.00	260.00	90.00
26	Elburt Fletcher	250.00	100.00	50.00
27	Bill Crouch	275.00	110.00	55.00
28	Al Todd	250.00	100.00	50.00
29	Debs Garms	250.00	100.00	50.00
30	Jim Tobin	250.00	100.00	50.00
31	Chester Ross	250.00	100.00	50.00
32	George Coffman	250.00	100.00	50.00
33	Mel Ott	600.00	240.00	120.00

1955 Robert Gould All Stars Cards

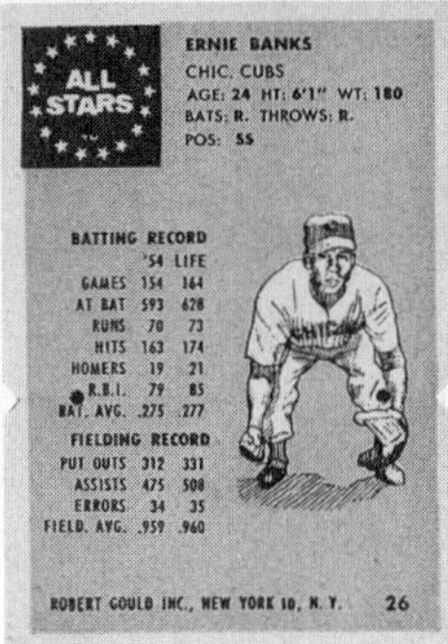

One of three issues of miniature plastic player statues issued in the mid-Fifties was the All Stars series by Robert Gould Inc. of New York. The white plastic statues, which sold for about a quarter, came rubber-banded to a baseball card. The card measures 2-1/2" x 3-1/2" with a white border. A rather crude black-and-white line drawing of the player is set against a green background. There are a few biographical details and 1954 and lifetime stats. An "All Stars" logo is in an upper corner, while the card number is at lower-right. The cards are blank-backed. All cards have a pair of notches at the sides and two punch holes to hold the rubber band. Prices shown here are for the cards alone. A 2-5/8" x 3-5/8" album reproducing all 28 player cards was also issued.

		NM	EX	VG
Complete Set, Cards (28):		8,500	4,250	2,500
Common Player:		250.00	125.00	75.00
Album:		200.00	100.00	50.00
1	Willie Mays	1,100	550.00	325.00
2	Gus Zernial	250.00	125.00	75.00
3	Red Schoendienst	325.00	160.00	95.00
4	Chico Carrasquel	250.00	125.00	75.00
5	Jim Hegan	250.00	125.00	75.00
6	Curt Simmons	250.00	125.00	75.00
7	Bob Porterfield	250.00	125.00	75.00
8	Jim Busby	250.00	125.00	75.00
9	Don Mueller	250.00	125.00	75.00
10	Ted Kluszewski	275.00	135.00	80.00
11	Ray Boone	250.00	125.00	75.00
12	Smoky Burgess	250.00	125.00	75.00
13	Bob Rush	250.00	125.00	75.00
14	Early Wynn	300.00	150.00	90.00
15	Bill Bruton	250.00	125.00	75.00
16	Gus Bell	250.00	125.00	75.00
17	Jim Finigan	250.00	125.00	75.00
18	Granny Hamner	250.00	125.00	75.00
19	Hank Thompson	250.00	125.00	75.00
20	Joe Coleman	250.00	125.00	75.00
21	Don Newcombe	275.00	135.00	80.00
22	Richie Ashburn	325.00	160.00	95.00
23	Bobby Thomson	250.00	125.00	75.00
24	Sid Gordon	250.00	125.00	75.00
25	Gerry Coleman	250.00	125.00	75.00
26	Ernie Banks	850.00	425.00	255.00
27	Billy Pierce	250.00	125.00	75.00
28	Mel Parnell	250.00	125.00	75.00

1955 Robert Gould All Stars Statues

One of three issues of miniature plastic player statues issued in the mid-Fifties was the All Stars series by Robert Gould Inc. of New York. The white plastic statues, which sold for about a quarter, came rubber-banded to a baseball card. Depending on pose, they vary in size from around 2" to 2-1/2". The figures have a round base with the player's name. Prices shown here are for the statues alone. The statues were also sold in seven-player boxed sets labeled "A" through "D."

		NM	EX	VG
Complete Set, Statues (28):		1,500	750.00	450.00
Common Player:		40.00	20.00	12.00
1	Willie Mays	300.00	150.00	90.00
2	Gus Zernial	40.00	20.00	12.00
3	Red Schoendienst	75.00	37.00	22.00
4	Chico Carrasquel	40.00	20.00	12.00
5	Jim Hegan	40.00	20.00	12.00
6	Curt Simmons	40.00	20.00	12.00
7	Bob Porterfield	40.00	20.00	12.00
8	Jim Busby	40.00	20.00	12.00
9	Don Mueller	40.00	20.00	12.00
10	Ted Kluszewski	50.00	25.00	15.00
11	Ray Boone	40.00	20.00	12.00
12	Smoky Burgess	40.00	20.00	12.00
13	Bob Rush	40.00	20.00	12.00
14	Early Wynn	60.00	30.00	18.00
15	Bill Bruton	40.00	20.00	12.00
16	Gus Bell	40.00	20.00	12.00
17	Jim Finigan	40.00	20.00	12.00
18	Granny Hamner	40.00	20.00	12.00
19	Hank Thompson	40.00	20.00	12.00
20	Joe Coleman	40.00	20.00	12.00
21	Don Newcombe	45.00	22.00	13.50
22	Richie Ashburn	75.00	37.00	22.00
23	Bobby Thomson	45.00	22.00	13.50
24	Sid Gordon	40.00	20.00	12.00
25	Gerry Coleman	40.00	20.00	12.00
26	Ernie Banks	240.00	120.00	72.00
27	Billy Pierce	40.00	20.00	12.00
28	Mel Parnell	40.00	20.00	12.00

1978 Grand Slam

This collectors' edition card set was produced by Jack Wallin. The black-and-white 2-1/4" x 3-1/4" cards have player poses or action photos on front, with the name in the white border at bottom. Backs have a career summary.

		NM	EX	VG
Complete Set (200):		120.00	60.00	35.00
Common Player:		2.00	1.00	.60
1	Leo Durocher	2.00	1.00	.60
2	Bob Lemon	2.00	1.00	.60
3	Earl Averill	2.00	1.00	.60
4	Dale Alexander	2.00	1.00	.60
5	Hank Greenberg	12.00	6.00	3.50
6	Waite Hoyt	2.00	1.00	.60
7	Al Lopez	2.00	1.00	.60
8	Lloyd Waner	2.00	1.00	.60
9	Bob Feller	2.00	1.00	.60
10	Guy Bush	2.00	1.00	.60
11	Stan Hack	2.00	1.00	.60
12	Zeke Bonura	2.00	1.00	.60
13	Wally Moses	2.00	1.00	.60
14	Fred Fitzsimmons	2.00	1.00	.60
15	Johnny Vander Meer	2.00	1.00	.60
16	Riggs Stephenson	2.00	1.00	.60
17	Bucky Walters	2.00	1.00	.60
18	Charlie Grimm	2.00	1.00	.60
19	Phil Cavarretta	2.00	1.00	.60
20	Wally Berger	2.00	1.00	.60
21	Joe Sewell	2.00	1.00	.60
22	Edd Roush	2.00	1.00	.60
23	Johnny Mize	2.00	1.00	.60
24	Bill Dickey	2.00	1.00	.60
25	Lou Boudreau	2.00	1.00	.60
26	Bill Terry	2.00	1.00	.60
27	Willie Kamm	2.00	1.00	.60
28	Charlie Gehringer	2.00	1.00	.60
29	Stan Coveleski	2.00	1.00	.60
30	Larry French	2.00	1.00	.60
31	George Kelly	2.00	1.00	.60
32	Terry Moore	2.00	1.00	.60
33	Billy Herman	2.00	1.00	.60
34	Babe Herman	2.00	1.00	.60
35	Carl Hubbell	2.00	1.00	.60
36	Buck Leonard	2.00	1.00	.60
37	Gus Suhr	2.00	1.00	.60
38	Burleigh Grimes	2.00	1.00	.60
39	Al Fonseca	2.00	1.00	.60
40	Travis Jackson	2.00	1.00	.60
41	Enos Slaughter	2.00	1.00	.60
42	Fred Lindstrom	2.00	1.00	.60
43	Rick Ferrell	2.00	1.00	.60
44	Cookie Lavagetto	2.00	1.00	.60
45	Stan Musial	12.00	6.00	3.50
46	Hal Trosky	2.00	1.00	.60
47	Hal Newhouser	2.00	1.00	.60
48	Paul Dean	2.00	1.00	.60
49	George Halas	6.00	3.00	1.75
50	Jocko Conlan	2.00	1.00	.60
51	Joe DiMaggio	30.00	15.00	9.00
52	Bobby Doerr	2.00	1.00	.60
53	Carl Reynolds	2.00	1.00	.60
54	Pete Reiser	2.00	1.00	.60
55	Frank McCormick	2.00	1.00	.60
56	Mel Harder	2.00	1.00	.60
57	George Uhle	2.00	1.00	.60
58	Doc Cramer	2.00	1.00	.60
59	Taylor Douthit	2.00	1.00	.60
60	Cecil Travis	2.00	1.00	.60
61	James Bell	2.00	1.00	.60
62	Charlie Keller	2.00	1.00	.60
63	Bill Hallahan	2.00	1.00	.60
64	Debs Garms	2.00	1.00	.60
65	Rube Marquard	2.00	1.00	.60
66	Rube Walberg	2.00	1.00	.60
67	Augie Galan	2.00	1.00	.60
68	George Pipgras	2.00	1.00	.60
69	Hal Schumacher	2.00	1.00	.60
70	Dolf Camilli	2.00	1.00	.60
71	Paul Richards	2.00	1.00	.60
72	Judy Johnson	2.00	1.00	.60
73	Frank Crosetti	2.00	1.00	.60
74	Harry Lowery	2.00	1.00	.60
75	Walter Alston	2.00	1.00	.60
76	Dutch Leonard	2.00	1.00	.60
77	Barney McCosky	2.00	1.00	.60
78	Joe Dobson	2.00	1.00	.60
79	George Kell	2.00	1.00	.60
80	Ted Lyons	2.00	1.00	.60
81	Johnny Pesky	2.00	1.00	.60
82	Hank Borowy	2.00	1.00	.60
83	Ewell Blackwell	2.00	1.00	.60
84	Pee Wee Reese	12.00	6.00	3.50
85	Monte Irvin	2.00	1.00	.60
86	Joe Moore	2.00	1.00	.60
87	Joe Wood	2.00	1.00	.60
88	Babe Dahlgren	2.00	1.00	.60
89	Bibb Falk	2.00	1.00	.60
90	Ed Lopat	2.00	1.00	.60
91	Rip Sewell	2.00	1.00	.60
92	Marty Marion	2.00	1.00	.60
93	Taft Wright	2.00	1.00	.60
94	Allie Reynolds	2.00	1.00	.60
95	Harry Walker	2.00	1.00	.60
96	Tex Hughson	2.00	1.00	.60
97	George Selkirk	2.00	1.00	.60
98	Dom DiMaggio	10.00	5.00	3.00
99	Walker Cooper	2.00	1.00	.60
100	Phil Rizzuto	10.00	5.00	3.00
101	Robin Roberts	2.00	1.00	.60
102	Joe Adcock	2.00	1.00	.60
103	Hank Bauer	2.00	1.00	.60
104	Frank Baumholtz	2.00	1.00	.60
105	Ray Boone	2.00	1.00	.60
106	Smoky Burgess	2.00	1.00	.60
107	Walt Dropo	2.00	1.00	.60
108	Alvin Dark	2.00	1.00	.60
109	Carl Erskine	2.00	1.00	.60
110	Dick Donovan	2.00	1.00	.60
111	Dee Fondy	2.00	1.00	.60
112	Mike Garcia	2.00	1.00	.60
113	Bob Friend	2.00	1.00	.60
114	Ned Garver	2.00	1.00	.60
115	Billy Goodman	2.00	1.00	.60
116	Larry Jansen	2.00	1.00	.60
117	Jackie Jensen	2.00	1.00	.60
118	John Antonelli	2.00	1.00	.60
119	Ted Kluszewski	2.00	1.00	.60
120	Harvey Kuenn	2.00	1.00	.60
121	Clem Labine	2.00	1.00	.60
122	Red Schoendienst	2.00	1.00	.60
123	Don Larsen	2.00	1.00	.60
124	Vern Law	2.00	1.00	.60
125	Charlie Maxwell	2.00	1.00	.60
126	Wally Moon	2.00	1.00	.60
127	Bob Nieman	2.00	1.00	.60
128	Don Newcombe	2.00	1.00	.60
129	Wally Post	2.00	1.00	.60
130	Johnny Podres	2.00	1.00	.60
131	Vic Raschi	2.00	1.00	.60
132	Dusty Rhodes	2.00	1.00	.60
133	Jim Rivera	2.00	1.00	.60
134	Pete Runnels	2.00	1.00	.60
135	Hank Sauer	2.00	1.00	.60
136	Roy Sievers	2.00	1.00	.60
137	Bobby Shantz	2.00	1.00	.60
138	Curt Simmons	2.00	1.00	.60
139	Bob Skinner	2.00	1.00	.60
140	Bill Skowron	2.00	1.00	.60
141	Warren Spahn	2.00	1.00	.60
142	Gerry Staley	2.00	1.00	.60
143	Frank Thomas	2.00	1.00	.60
144	Bobby Thomson	2.00	1.00	.60
145	Bob Turley	2.00	1.00	.60
146	Vic Wertz	2.00	1.00	.60
147	Bill Virdon	2.00	1.00	.60
148	Gene Woodling	2.00	1.00	.60
149	Eddie Yost	2.00	1.00	.60
150	Sandy Koufax	25.00	12.50	7.50
151	Lefty Gomez	2.00	1.00	.60
152	Al Rosen	2.00	1.00	.60
153	Vince DiMaggio	2.00	1.00	.60
154	Bill Nicholson	2.00	1.00	.60
155	Mark Koenig	2.00	1.00	.60
156	Max Lanier	2.00	1.00	.60
157	Ken Keltner	2.00	1.00	.60
158	Whit Wyatt	2.00	1.00	.60
159	Marv Owen	2.00	1.00	.60
160	Red Lucas	2.00	1.00	.60
161	Babe Phelps	2.00	1.00	.60
162	Pete Donohue	2.00	1.00	.60
163	Johnny Cooney	2.00	1.00	.60
164	Glenn Wright	2.00	1.00	.60
165	Willis Hudlin	2.00	1.00	.60
166	Tony Cuccinello	2.00	1.00	.60
167	Bill Bevens	2.00	1.00	.60
168	Dave Ferris	2.00	1.00	.60
169	Whitey Kurowski	2.00	1.00	.60
170	Buddy Hassett	2.00	1.00	.60
171	Ossie Bluege	2.00	1.00	.60
172	Hoot Evers	2.00	1.00	.60
173	Thornton Lee	2.00	1.00	.60
174	Virgil Davis	2.00	1.00	.60
175	Bob Shawkey	2.00	1.00	.60
176	Smead Jolley	2.00	1.00	.60
177	Andy High	2.00	1.00	.60
178	George McQuinn	2.00	1.00	.60
179	Mickey Vernon	2.00	1.00	.60
180	Birdie Tebbetts	2.00	1.00	.60
181	Jack Kramer	2.00	1.00	.60
182	Don Kolloway	2.00	1.00	.60

		NM	EX	VG
183	Claude Passeau	2.00	1.00	.60
184	Frank Shea	2.00	1.00	.60
185	Bob O'Farrell	2.00	1.00	.60
186	Bob Johnson	2.00	1.00	.60
187	Ival Goodman	2.00	1.00	.60
188	Mike Kreevich	2.00	1.00	.60
189	Joe Stripp	2.00	1.00	.60
190	Mickey Owen	2.00	1.00	.60
191	Hughie Critz	2.00	1.00	.60
192	Ethan Allen	2.00	1.00	.60
193	Billy Rogell	2.00	1.00	.60
194	Joe Kuhel	2.00	1.00	.60
195	Dale Mitchell	2.00	1.00	.60
196	Eldon Auker	2.00	1.00	.60
197	Johnny Beazley	2.00	1.00	.60
198	Spud Chandler	2.00	1.00	.60
199	Ralph Branca	2.00	1.00	.60
200	Joe Cronin	2.00	1.00	.60

1957-58 Graphics Arts Service Detroit Tigers Postcards

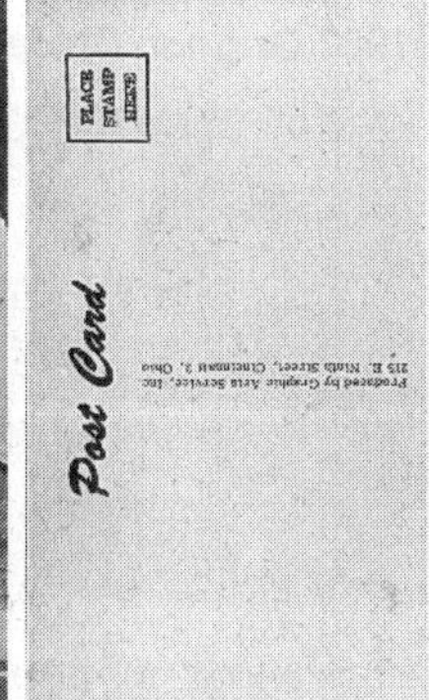

This series of Tigers postcards was issued over a two-year span by a Cincinnati printer. The 3-3/16" x 5-7/16" cards have a black-and-white borderless player photo on front with or without a facsimile autograph. Backs have standard post-card indicia, including the producer's name and address.

		NM	EX	VG
Complete Set (22):		1,500	750.00	450.00
Common Player:		60.00	30.00	18.00
(1)	Al Aber	60.00	30.00	18.00
(2)	Hank Aguirre	60.00	30.00	18.00
(3)	Reno Bertoia/Fldg	60.00	30.00	18.00
(4)	Reno Bertoia/Portrait	60.00	30.00	18.00
(5)	Frank Bolling	60.00	30.00	18.00
(6)	Jim Bunning	120.00	60.00	35.00
(7)	Jack Dittmer	60.00	30.00	18.00
(8)	Paul Foytack	60.00	30.00	18.00
(9)	Jim Hegan	60.00	30.00	18.00
(10)	Tommy Henrich	80.00	40.00	24.00
(11)	Billy Hoeft	60.00	30.00	18.00
(12)	Frank House	60.00	30.00	18.00
(13)	Al Kaline	180.00	90.00	55.00
(14)	Harvey Kuenn	80.00	40.00	24.00
(15)	Don Lee	60.00	30.00	18.00
(16)	Billy Martin	90.00	45.00	25.00
(17)	Tom Morgan	60.00	30.00	18.00
(18)	J.W. Porter	60.00	30.00	18.00
(19)	Ron Samford	60.00	30.00	18.00
(20)	Bob Shaw	60.00	30.00	18.00
(21)	Lou Sleater	60.00	30.00	18.00
(22)	Tim Thompson	60.00	30.00	18.00

1888 Gray Studio Cabinets

The posed action photos on the approximately 4-1/4" x 6-1/2" cards are the same pictures seen on many of the players' Old Judge and Old Judge cabinet cards. Gray cabinets are found with two fancy logotypes at lower-left. On one, the tail of the "y" underscores the "Gra," while on the other, fancy decorations bookend the studio name. The Boston address of the studio is at lower-right. Players are not identified on the cards, and the backs are blank.

		NM	EX	VG
Common Player:		1,500	700.00	450.00
(1)	Charlie Buffinton/Btg	1,500	700.00	450.00
(2)	Charlie Buffinton (Right arm forward.)	1,500	700.00	450.00
(3)	Dan Casey (Arms at sides.)	1,500	700.00	450.00
(4)	Dan Casey (Ball in hands at chest.)	1,500	700.00	450.00
(5)	Dan Casey (Left arm outstretched.)	1,500	700.00	450.00
(6)	Jack Clements/Btg	1,500	700.00	450.00
(7)	Jack Clements/Fldg (Hands chest-high.)	1,500	700.00	450.00
(8)	Jack Clements (Hands on knees.)	1,500	700.00	450.00
(12)	Ed Daily/Btg	1,500	700.00	450.00
(13)	Ed Daily (Holding ball in front of face.)	1,500	700.00	450.00
(14)	Ed Daily/Throwing	1,500	700.00	450.00
(16)	Sid Farrar (Arms crossed.)	1,500	700.00	450.00
(17)	Sid Farrar (Fielding grounder.)	1,500	700.00	450.00
(18)	Sid Farrar (Fielding fly ball.)	1,500	700.00	450.00
(19)	Sid Farrar (Right hand on belt buckle.)	1,500	700.00	450.00
(21)	Charlie Ferguson (Ball in hands at chest.)	1,500	700.00	450.00
(22)	Charlie Ferguson/Btg	1,500	700.00	450.00
(23)	Charlie Ferguson (Tagging Tommy McCarthy.)	1,800	900.00	550.00
(24)	Charlie Ferguson/Throwing (Right arm back.)	1,500	700.00	450.00
(26)	Jim Fogarty/Btg	1,500	700.00	450.00
(27)	Jim Fogarty (Fielding grounder.)	1,500	700.00	450.00
(28)	Jim Fogarty/Fldg (Hands at neck.)	1,500	700.00	450.00
(29)	Jim Fogarty (Fielding on the run.)	1,500	700.00	450.00
(32)	Tom Gunning/Fldg (Hands at knees.)	1,500	700.00	450.00
(33)	Arthur Irwin/Btg	1,500	700.00	450.00
(34)	Arthur Irwin/Fldg (Hands chest-high.)	1,500	700.00	450.00
(35)	Arthur Irwin/Throwing	1,500	700.00	450.00
(39)	Tommy McCarthy/Btg	3,000	1,500	900.00
(40)	Tommy McCarthy/Fldg (Hands chest-high.)	3,000	1,500	900.00
(41)	Tommy McCarthy (Tagging baserunner.)	3,000	1,500	900.00
(42)	Tommy McCarthy/Throwing	3,000	1,500	900.00
(44)	Deacon McGuire/Btg	1,500	700.00	450.00
(45)	Deacon McGuire/Fldg (Hands chest-high.)	1,500	700.00	450.00
(48)	Joe Mulvey/Btg	1,500	700.00	450.00
(49)	Joe Mulvey/Fldg (Hands at waist.)	1,500	700.00	450.00
(50)	Joe Mulvey (Watching ball.)	1,500	700.00	450.00
(60)	George Wood/Btg	1,500	700.00	450.00
(61)	George Wood (Fielding fly ball.)	1,500	700.00	450.00
(62)	George Wood (Fielding grounder.)	1,500	700.00	450.00
(63)	George Wood/Throwing	1,500	700.00	450.00

1975-76 Great Plains Greats

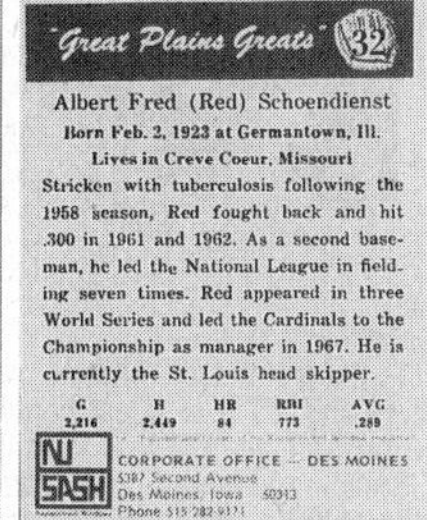

This collectors' issue was issued in two series in conjunction with shows conducted by the Great Plains Sports Collectors Association. Cards are about 2-5/8" x 3-3/4". Fronts have black-and-white photos with heavy colored frames and white borders. Player name is overprinted on a diamond at bottom. Backs have a career summary and stats, and a sponsor's ad. The 1975 issue (#1-24) was sponsored by Sheraton Inns; the 1976 cards (#25-42) were sponsored by Nu-Sash Corp.

		NM	EX	VG
Complete Set (43):		20.00	10.00	6.00
Common Player:		1.00	.50	.30
1	Bob Feller	2.00	1.00	.60
2	Carl Hubbell	1.00	.50	.30
3	Jocko Conlan	1.00	.50	.30
4	Hal Trosky	1.00	.50	.30
5	Allie Reynolds	1.00	.50	.30
6	Burleigh Grimes	1.00	.50	.30
7	Jake Beckley	1.00	.50	.30
8	Al Simmons	1.00	.50	.30
9	Paul Waner	1.00	.50	.30
10	Chief Bender	1.00	.50	.30
11	Fred Clarke	1.00	.50	.30
12	Jim Bottomley	1.00	.50	.30
13	Dave Bancroft	1.00	.50	.30
14	Bing Miller	1.00	.50	.30
15	Walter Johnson	2.50	1.25	.70
16	Grover Alexander	2.50	1.25	.70
17	Bob Johnson	1.00	.50	.30
18	Roger Maris	2.50	1.25	.70
19	Ken Keltner	1.00	.50	.30
20	Red Faber	1.00	.50	.30
21	"Cool Papa" Bell	1.00	.50	.30
22	Yogi Berra	2.50	1.25	.70
23	Fred Lindstrom	1.00	.50	.30
24	Ray Schalk	1.00	.50	.30
---	Checklist	.10	.05	.03
25	Lloyd Waner	1.00	.50	.30
26	Johnny Hopp	1.00	.50	.30
27	Mel Harder	1.00	.50	.30
28	Dutch Leonard	1.00	.50	.30
29	Bob O'Farrell	1.00	.50	.30
30	Cap Anson	1.00	.50	.30
31	Dazzy Vance	1.00	.50	.30
32	Red Schoendienst	1.00	.50	.30
33	George Pipgras	1.00	.50	.30
34	Harvey Kuenn	1.00	.50	.30
35	Red Ruffing	1.00	.50	.30
36	Roy Sievers	1.00	.50	.30
37	Ken Boyer	1.00	.50	.30
38	Al Smith	1.00	.50	.30
39	Casey Stengel	1.00	.50	.30
40	Bob Gibson	1.50	.70	.45
41	Mickey Mantle	10.00	5.00	3.00
42	Denny McLain	1.00	.50	.30

1908-1909 Greenfield's Chocolates Postcards

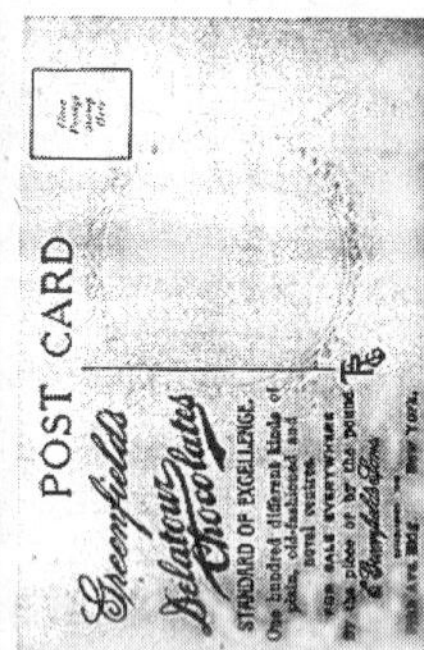

These special advertising versions of the Rose Co. postcards were produced circa 1908-09. The 3-1/2" x 5-1/2" cards feature a black-and-white player portrait photo at center, surrounded by an embossed round gold frame. The player's surname and (usually) team are in a white panel under the photo. The background is green and includes crossed bats and a baseball, a diamond diagram and pictures of a fielder and batter. The postcard-format back is printed in black-and-white with a TRC logo at bottom-center. Printed at left in ornate typography is advertising for the New York confectioner. Two back styles are known apparently the result of the candy company's move from Fifth Ave. to Barclay St. (or vice versa) during the issuing period. It is unknown how many of the player postcards in the Rose Co. series can be found with this advertising on back. While much rarer than Rose Co. cards without the advertising, the Greenfield's version currently carries only modest premium value, perhaps 10-20 percent higher than the regular version.

(See 1908-1909 Rose Company Postcards for checklist and base values.)

1916 Green-Joyce

Best known for its use as a promotional medium for The Sporting News, this 200-card set can be found with blank backs or with ads on the back for several local and regional businesses. Among them is Green-Joyce "Department of Sports, " location Columbus, OH. Type-card and superstar collectors can expect to pay a premiu, for individual cards with Green- Joyce advertising as opposed to the more common M101-4 blank-back values. Cards measure 1-5/8" x 3" and are printed in black-and-white.

PREMIUM: 3-4X

(See 1916 M101-4 Blank Backs for checklist and base values.)

1969 Greiner Tires Pittsburgh Pirates

Good Luck to Roberto Clemente and Pittsburgh Pirates
from
GREINER TIRE SERVICE
Route 30 West Phone 527-2841 Jeannette, Pa.

One of the scarcer of the many Pirates regionals of the late 1960s is this eight-card issue. Printed on heavy paper in black-and-white, the 5-1/2" x 8-1/2" cards are blank-backed and unnumbered. They are checklisted here alphabetically. Some sources say the Matty Alou card is scarcer than the rest of the set.

	NM	EX	VG
Complete Set (8):	80.00	40.00	24.00
Common Player:	4.50	2.25	1.25
(1) Gene Alley	4.50	2.25	1.25
(2) Matty Alou	30.00	15.00	9.00
(3) Steve Blass	4.50	2.25	1.25
(4) Roberto Clemente	30.00	15.00	9.00
(5) Jerry May	4.50	2.25	1.25
(6) Bill Mazeroski	12.50	6.25	3.75
(7) Larry Shepard	4.50	2.25	1.25
(8) Willie Stargell	12.50	6.25	3.75

1928 Greiners Bread

This set of about 1-3/8" x 2-1/2" black-and-white cards is a parallel of the strip card set cataloged as 1928 W502. The difference lies in advertising on the back of this version for an unidentified bakery's product.

	NM	EX	VG
Complete Set (60):	8,500	3,500	1,750
Common Player:	75.00	30.00	15.00
1 Burleigh Grimes	125.00	50.00	25.00
2 Walter Reuther (Ruether)	75.00	30.00	15.00
3 Joe Dugan	75.00	30.00	15.00
4 Red Faber	125.00	50.00	25.00
5 Gabby Hartnett	125.00	50.00	25.00
6 Babe Ruth	1,350	550.00	275.00
7 Bob Meusel	75.00	30.00	15.00
8 Herb Pennock	125.00	50.00	25.00
9 George Burns	75.00	30.00	15.00
10 Joe Sewell	125.00	50.00	25.00
11 George Uhle	75.00	30.00	15.00
12 Bob O'Farrell	75.00	30.00	15.00
13 Rogers Hornsby	150.00	60.00	30.00
14 "Pie" Traynor	125.00	50.00	25.00
15 Clarence Mitchell	75.00	30.00	15.00
16 Eppa Jepha Rixey	125.00	50.00	25.00
17 Carl Mays	90.00	35.00	18.00
18 Adolfo Luque	75.00	30.00	15.00
19 Dave Bancroft	125.00	50.00	25.00
20 George Kelly	125.00	50.00	25.00
21 Earl (Earle) Combs	125.00	50.00	25.00
22 Harry Heilmann	125.00	50.00	25.00
23 Ray W. Schalk	125.00	50.00	25.00
24 Johnny Mostil	75.00	30.00	15.00
25 Hack Wilson	125.00	50.00	25.00
26 Lou Gehrig	900.00	360.00	180.00
27 Ty Cobb	900.00	360.00	180.00
28 Tris Speaker	150.00	60.00	30.00
29 Tony Lazzeri	125.00	50.00	25.00
30 Waite Hoyt	125.00	50.00	25.00
31 Sherwood Smith	75.00	30.00	15.00
32 Max Carey	125.00	50.00	25.00
33 Eugene Hargrave	75.00	30.00	15.00
34 Miguel L. Gonzales (Miguel A. Gonzalez)	75.00	30.00	15.00
35 Joe Judge	75.00	30.00	15.00
36 E.C. (Sam) Rice	125.00	50.00	25.00
37 Earl Sheely	75.00	30.00	15.00
38 Sam Jones	75.00	30.00	15.00
39 Bib (Bibb) A. Falk	75.00	30.00	15.00
40 Willie Kamm	75.00	30.00	15.00
41 Stanley Harris	125.00	50.00	25.00
42 John J. McGraw	125.00	50.00	25.00
43 Artie Nehf	75.00	30.00	15.00
44 Grover Alexander	150.00	60.00	30.00
45 Paul Waner	125.00	50.00	25.00
46 William H. Terry	125.00	50.00	25.00
47 Glenn Wright	75.00	30.00	15.00
48 Earl Smith	75.00	30.00	15.00
49 Leon (Goose) Goslin	125.00	50.00	25.00
50 Frank Frisch	125.00	50.00	25.00
51 Joe Harris	75.00	30.00	15.00
52 Fred (Cy) Williams	75.00	30.00	15.00
53 Eddie Roush	125.00	50.00	25.00
54 George Sisler	125.00	50.00	25.00
55 Ed. Rommel	75.00	30.00	15.00
56 Rogers Peckinpaugh (Roger)	75.00	30.00	15.00
57 Stanley Coveleskie (Coveleski)	125.00	50.00	25.00
58 Lester Bell	75.00	30.00	15.00
59 L. Waner	125.00	50.00	25.00
60 John P. McInnis	75.00	30.00	15.00

1974 Greyhound Heroes on the Base Paths

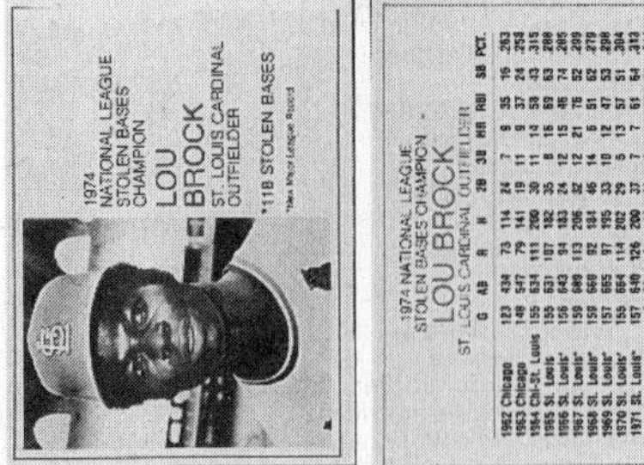

The first of three annual baseball card folders honoring the stolen base leaders and runners-up in each league, this 20" x 9" five-panel sheet features six 4" x 3" cards printed in black-and-white with sepia graphics. Backs are printed in black, brown and white. Besides the cards, the folder contains information about the bus company's award, as well as major league stolen base records and base-stealing tips. Besides individual cards of the 1974 winner and runner-up in each league, the folder has cards picturing all winners and runners-up since 1965.

	NM	EX	VG
Complete Set, Folder:	10.00	5.00	3.00
Complete Set, Singles:	8.00	4.00	2.50
Common Player:	2.00	1.00	.60
(1) Lou Brock	4.00	2.00	1.25
(2) Rod Carew	4.00	2.00	1.25
(3) Davey Lopes	2.00	1.00	.60
(4) Bill North	2.00	1.00	.60
(5) A.L. Winners/Runners-Up (Don Buford, Bert Campaneris, Rod Carew, Tommy Harper, Dave Nelson, Bill North, Amos Otis, Fred Patek)	2.00	1.00	.60
(6) N.L. Winners/Runners-Up (Lou Brock, Jose Cardenal, Sonny Jackson, Davey Lopes, Joe Morgan, Bobby Tolan, Maury Wills)	2.00	1.00	.60

1975 Greyhound Heroes on the Base Paths

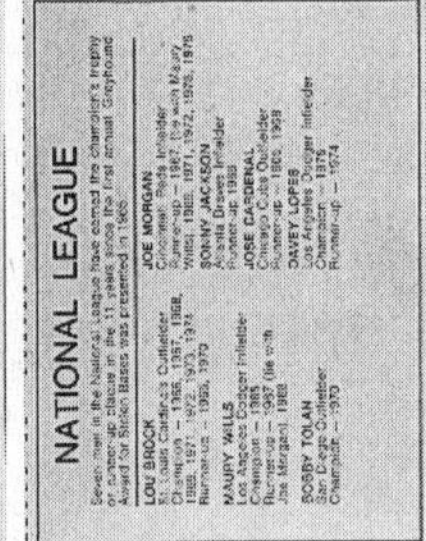

Six perforated 3-7/8" x 3" cards are featured on this folded five-panel 20" x 9" sheet honoring top base stealers in both leagues for the 1975 season. Four of the cards have each league's SB leader and runner-up in a black-and-white portrait photo with blue background. Backs are printed in black, blue and white and include major league stats. There are also two action photo cards with lists on the back of each year's winner and runner-up for the Greyhound Stolen Base Awards since 1965.

	NM	EX	VG
Complete Set, Folder:	7.00	3.50	2.00
Complete Set, Singles:	4.00	2.00	1.25
Common Player:	1.50	.70	.45
(1) Davey Lopes	1.50	.70	.45
(2) Davey Lopes (Action)	1.50	.70	.45
(3) Joe Morgan	2.50	1.25	.70
(4) Bill North (Action)	1.50	.70	.45
(5) Mickey Rivers	1.50	.70	.45
(6) Claudell Washington	1.50	.70	.45

1976 Greyhound Heroes on the Base Paths

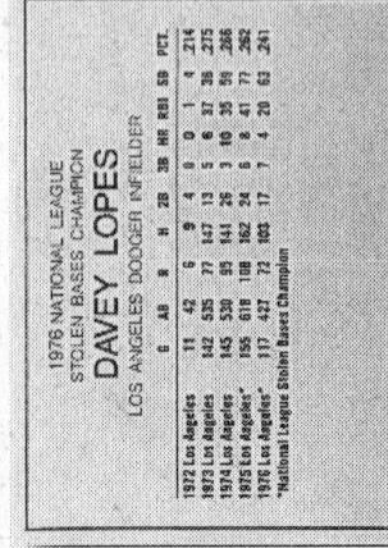

The last of three annual baseball card folders honoring the stolen base leaders and runners-up in each league, this 20" x 9" five-panel sheet features six 4" x 3" cards printed in black-and-white with sepia graphics. Backs are printed in black, brown and white. Besides the cards, the folder contains information about the bus company's award, as well as major league stolen base records and base-stealing tips. Besides individual cards of the 1974 winner and runner-up in each league, the folder includes two action-photo cards listing all winners and runners-up since 1965.

	NM	EX	VG
Complete Set, Folder:	6.00	3.00	1.75
Complete Set, Singles:	5.00	2.50	1.50
Common Player:	1.50	.70	.45
(1) Ronald Le Flore	1.50	.70	.45
(2) Davey Lopes	1.50	.70	.45
(3) Davey Lopes/Action	1.50	.70	.45
(4) Joe Morgan	3.00	1.50	.90
(5) Bill North	1.50	.70	.45
(6) Bill North/Action	1.50	.70	.45

1907 Grignon Chicago Cubs Postcards

The eventual 1907 World Champion Cubs are featured in this set of novelty postcards. Fronts of the 3-1/2" x 5-1/2" horizontal cards have a green background with white border. The central figure on each is a teddy bear in a baseball pose. In an upper corner is a black-and-white circular portrait of one of the Cubs, with identification below. A line of infield chatter - i.e., "This is a Cinch" - completes the design. Backs have standard postcard markings and some have been seen with advertising for local businesses. The unnumbered cards are checklisted here alphabetically.

	NM	EX	VG
Complete Set (16):	12,000	6,000	3,500
Common Player:	475.00	235.00	140.00
(1) Mordecai Brown	1,600	800.00	480.00
(2) Frank Chance	1,600	800.00	480.00
(3) John Evers	1,600	800.00	480.00
(4) Arthur Hofman	475.00	235.00	140.00
(5) John Kling	475.00	235.00	140.00
(6) Carl Lundgren	475.00	235.00	140.00
(7) Pat Moran	475.00	235.00	140.00
(8) Orvie Overall	475.00	235.00	140.00
(9) Jack Pfeister	475.00	235.00	140.00
(10) Ed Reulbach	475.00	235.00	140.00
(11) Frank Schulte	475.00	235.00	140.00
(12) James Sheckard	475.00	235.00	140.00
(13) James Slagle	475.00	235.00	140.00
(14) Harry Steinfeldt	475.00	235.00	140.00
(15) Jack Taylor	475.00	235.00	140.00
(16) Joe Tinker	1,600	800.00	480.00

"1959-60" Gulf Oil Corporation

These fantasy/fraud cards were first reported in the hobby in 1999, though the copyright line on back purports to date them from 1959-1960. Two types of cards were produced, one series of eight featuring line-art portraits, the other featuring re-screened photos taken from team photo packs and similar sources. Cards are 2-1/2" x 3-1/2" printed in black-and-white. The unnumbered cards are checklisted here alphabetically within series. Because the cards were illegally produced in violation of player rights and team copyrights, no collector value is attributed.

Complete Set (16):

Artwork Series

(1) Ty Cobb
(2) Bill Dickey
(3) Joe DiMaggio
(4) Lou Gehrig
(5) Rogers Hornsby
(6) Walter Johnson

(7) Babe Ruth
(8) Pie Traynor

Photo Series

(1) Don Drysdale
(2) Bob Gibson
(3) Sandy Koufax
(4) Mickey Mantle
(5) Roger Maris
(6) Willie Mays
(7) Willie McCovey
(8) Stan Musial

1956 Gum Products Adventure

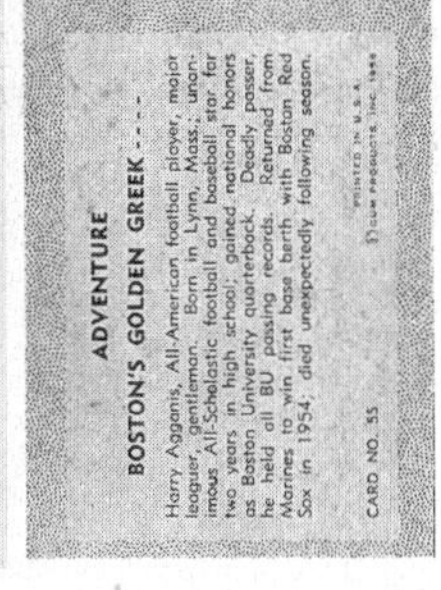

This series of 100 cards depicts all manner of action and adventure scenes, including several sports subjects, one of which is a baseball player. The card depicts Boston U. quarterback and Boston Red Sox prospect Harry Agganis, who died unexpectedly in 1955. The 3-1/2" x 2-1/2" horizontal card has a central portrait artwork of Agganis as a Red Sox, surrounded by other scenes from his personal and sporting life. The black-and-white back has a short biography.

		NM	EX	VG
55	Harry Agganis (Boston's Golden Greek)	25.00	12.50	7.50

1948 Gunther Beer Washington Senators Postcards

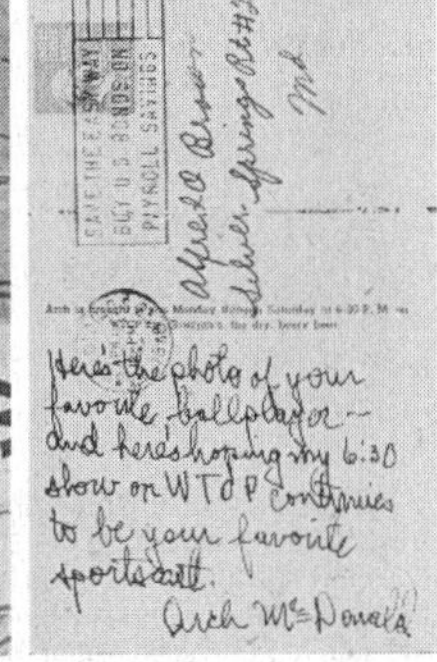

These postcards were apparently made available by writing to the radio voice of the Senators, Arch McDonald. A pre-printed message on the left side of the back urges the fan to keep listening to McDonald's program, sponsored by "Gunther's, the dry, beery beer." The black-and-white cards measure 3-1/2" x 5-1/2" and feature portrait photos of the Washington players. Most cards have two players side-by-side while manager Joe Kuhel has his own card. Player names are in heavy black letters across their chests. The cards are unnumbered and it is possible others will surface.

		NM	EX	VG
Complete Set (11):		3,000	1,500	900.00
Common Card:		285.00	140.00	85.00
(1)	Joe Kuhel	285.00	140.00	85.00
(2)	Gil Coan, Mickey Vernon	285.00	140.00	85.00
(3)	Al Evans, Scott Cary	285.00	140.00	85.00
(4)	Tom Ferrick, Harold Keller	285.00	140.00	85.00
(5)	Mickey Haefner, Forrest Thompson	285.00	140.00	85.00
(6)	Sid Hudson, Al Kozar	285.00	140.00	85.00
(7)	Walter Masterson, Rick Ferrell	325.00	160.00	95.00
(8)	Marino Pieretti, Leon Culberson	285.00	140.00	85.00
(9)	Sherrard Robertson, Eddie Lyons	285.00	140.00	85.00
(10)	Ray Scarborough, Kenneth McCreight	285.00	140.00	85.00
(11)	Early Wynn, Eddie Yost	400.00	200.00	120.00

1923-1924 Tomas Gutierrez

The largest of the Cuban baseball card issues of the 1920s, this is also one of the scarcest and most popular. Printed in dark brown (some backs are in black) on sepia paper, the 1-5/8" x 2-3/8" cards were inserted into packs of Diaz cigarettes. Cards have portrait photos on front with team name at top and the player name (sometimes misspelled and sometimes a nickname) and position below. Backs, which can be found in three styles, have the card number and an offer for an album. It is the album offer which accounts for much of this issue's scarcity.

No. 46.
Cigarros Tomás Gutiérrez
La persona que nos entregue la colección completa de los clubs HABANA, MARIANAO, STA. CLARA y ALMENDARES, consistente en 86 postales del número 1 al 85 será gratificada con un lujoso Album con iguales postales ya impresas.
Cia. Cigarrera Diaz, S. A.
Finlay núm. 66
Antes Zanja-Habana.

The album was a hardcover, ornate book with pictures of each card pre-printed. It is believed that the album was available by turning in a complete set of the cards, which were not returned. Adding to the set's popularity is its inclusion of many Negro Leagues players including future Hall of Famers Oscar Charleston and Pop Lloyd. Following the checklist are the names of cards known to exist from their presence in the album, but whose number is unknkown.

		NM	EX	VG
Complete Set (85): Value Undetermined				
Common Player:		350.00	140.00	70.00
Album:		4,500	2,250	1,350
	SANTA CLARA			
1	Agustin "Tinti" Molina	350.00	140.00	70.00
2	Julio Rojo	450.00	180.00	90.00
3	Frank Duncan	1,750	700.00	350.00
4	Eustaquio "Bombin" Pedroso	2,250	900.00	450.00
5	Dave Brown	2,250	900.00	450.00
6	Pedro Dibut	450.00	180.00	90.00
7	Rube Currie	1,750	700.00	350.00
8	Jose Mendez	6,000	2,400	1,200
9	Esteban "Mayari" Montalvo	850.00	340.00	170.00
10	Frank Warfield	1,750	700.00	350.00
11	Oliver Marcelle	2,250	900.00	450.00
12	Dobie Moore	1,750	700.00	350.00
13	Herman Matias Rios	350.00	140.00	70.00
14	Oscar Charleston	20,000	8,000	4,000
15	Alejandro Oms	2,250	900.00	450.00
16	Pablo "Champion" Mesa	850.00	340.00	170.00
17	Bill Holland	2,250	900.00	450.00
18	Oscar "Heavy" Johnson	2,250	900.00	450.00
	ALMENDARES			
19	Eugenio Morin	350.00	140.00	70.00
20	Snake Henry	350.00	140.00	70.00
21	Manuel Cueto	350.00	140.00	70.00
22	Jesse Hubbard	850.00	340.00	170.00
23	Kakin Gonzalez	350.00	140.00	70.00
24	Jose Maria Fernandez	350.00	140.00	70.00
25	Oscar Rodriguez	350.00	140.00	70.00
26	Lucas Boada	350.00	140.00	70.00
27	Eusebio "Papo" Gonzalez	350.00	140.00	70.00
28	Ramon "Paito" Herrera	350.00	140.00	70.00
29	Bernardo Baro	850.00	340.00	170.00
30	Armando Marsans	1,200	480.00	240.00
31	Isidro Fabre	850.00	340.00	170.00
32				
33	Valentin Dreke	850.00	340.00	170.00
34	Joseito Rodriguez	350.00	140.00	70.00
35	Jose "Cheo" Ramos	350.00	140.00	70.00
36	Willis "Pud" Flournoy	1,200	480.00	240.00
37	Oscar Tuero	350.00	140.00	70.00
38	Rafael Almeida	850.00	340.00	170.00
39	Almendares Pennant	350.00	140.00	70.00
---	Oscar Fuhr	350.00	140.00	70.00
	MARIANAO			
40				
41	Don Brown	350.00	140.00	70.00
42				
43	(Ed) Morris	350.00	140.00	70.00
44	Ernie Krueger	350.00	140.00	70.00
45				
46	(Harry) McCurdy	350.00	140.00	70.00
47	Jose "Acostica" Acosta	350.00	140.00	70.00
48	Jacinto Calvo	350.00	140.00	70.00
49	(Eddie) Brown	350.00	140.00	70.00
50	(Rosy) Ryan	350.00	140.00	70.00
51	Rogelio Crespo	350.00	140.00	70.00
52	Hank Deberry	350.00	140.00	70.00
53	(Art) Phelan	350.00	140.00	70.00
54				
55	(Jimmy) Cooney	350.00	140.00	70.00
56a	H. Scheiber (Hank Schreiber) (Infielder)	350.00	140.00	70.00
56b	H. Scheiber (Hank Schreiber) (Infielder)	350.00	140.00	70.00
57				
58				
59				
---	Marianao Pennant	350.00	140.00	70.00
---	Merito Acosta	350.00	140.00	70.00
---	Otis Brannan	350.00	140.00	70.00
---	Charlie Dressen	450.00	180.00	90.00
---	Emilio Palmero	350.00	140.00	70.00
---	Jose "Pepin" Perez	350.00	140.00	70.00
---	Jess Petty	450.00	180.00	90.00
	HAVANA			
60	Buster Ross	350.00	140.00	70.00
61	Juanelo Mirabal	350.00	140.00	70.00
62	Cristobal Torriente	17,500	7,000	3,500
63	John Henry "Pop" Lloyd	20,000	8,000	4,000
64	Oscar Levis	700.00	280.00	140.00
65	Pelayo Chacon	850.00	340.00	170.00
66	Eufemio Abreu	350.00	140.00	70.00
67	Mack Eggleston	850.00	340.00	170.00
68	(Tauca "Manzanillo") Campos	350.00	140.00	70.00
69	Raphael "Busta" Quintana	350.00	140.00	70.00
70	Merven "Red" Ryan	850.00	340.00	170.00
71	(Danny) Clark	350.00	140.00	70.00
72	Clint Thomas	1,000	400.00	200.00
73	Adolfo Luque	1,200	480.00	240.00
74	Marcelino Guerra	350.00	140.00	70.00
75	Bartolo Portuondo	850.00	340.00	170.00
76	Andy Cooper	6,000	2,400	1,200
77	(John) Bischoff	350.00	140.00	70.00
78	Edgar Wesley	1,750	700.00	350.00
79	Havana Pennant	350.00	140.00	70.00
---	Jacinto Calvo	300.00	120.00	60.00
---	Bienvenido "Hooks" Jimenez	250.00	100.00	50.00
	MISCELLANEOUS			
80	Hector Magrinat (Umpire)	350.00	140.00	70.00
81	Valentin "Sirique" Gonzalez (Umpire)	350.00	140.00	70.00
82	Slim Love (Marianao)	350.00	140.00	70.00
83	Cristobal Torriente (Marianao)	17,500	7,000	3,500
84				
85	Jakie May (Almendares)	450.00	180.00	90.00

1887 Gypsy Queen (N175)

The 1887 Gypsy Queen set is very closely related to the N172 Old Judge set and employs the same photos. Gypsy Queens are easily identified by the advertising along the top. A line near the bottom lists the player's name, position and team, followed by an 1887 copyright line and words "Cigarettes" and "Goodwin & Co. N.Y." Although the checklist is still considered incomplete, some 140 different poses have been discovered so far. Gypsy Queens were issued in two distinct sizes, the more common version measuring 1-1/2" x 2-1/2" (same as Old Judge) and a larger size measuring 2" x 3-1/2" which are considered extremely rare. The large Gypsy Queens are identical in format to the smaller size; the nine known examples are designated here.

		NM	EX	VG
Common Player:		3,300	1,650	1,100
(13)	J. (Tug) Arundel/Fldg	3,300	1,650	1,100
(17)	Mark Baldwin	3,300	1,650	1,100
(19 1)	Sam Barkley/Fldg	3,300	1,650	1,100
(19 2)	Sam Barkley (Tagging player.)	3,300	1,650	1,100
(19 3)	Sam Barkley/Throwing	3,300	1,650	1,100
(35)	Henry Boyle (Right arm outstretched.)	3,300	1,650	1,100
(43 1)	Dan Brouthers (Looking at ball.)	8,250	4,125	2,475
(43 2)	Dan Brouthers (Looking to right.)	8,250	4,125	2,475
(44 1)	Tom Brown (Pittsburgh, bat at side.)	3,300	1,650	1,100
(44 2)	Tom Brown/Catching (Pittsburgh)	3,300	1,650	1,100
(45L)	Willard (California) Brown/ Throwing (N.Y., large)	20,625	10,300	6,200
(45 1)	Willard (California) Brown/ Throwing (N.Y.)	3,300	1,650	1,100
(45 2)	Willard (California) Brown (N.Y., wearing mask.)	3,800	1,900	1,125
(50)	Charlie Buffington (Buffinton) (Bat at 45 degrees.)	3,300	1,650	1,100
(51)	Ernie Burch/Fldg (Hands above head, outdoors.)	4,000	1,650	1,200
(53)	Jack Burdock (Fielding grounder.)	4,000	1,650	1,200
(55)	Watch Burnham	3,300	1,650	1,100
(59)	Tom Burns	3,300	1,650	1,100
(60)	Doc Bushong (Brown's Champions)	5,850	2,925	1,750
(61)	John (Patsy) Cahill	3,300	1,650	1,100
(68)	Fred Carroll (Bat at side.)	3,300	1,650	1,100
(71)	Bob Caruthers	3,300	1,650	1,100
(72 1)	Dan Casey (Hands at chest.)	3,800	1,900	1,125
(72 2)	Dan Casey (Left arm extended.)	3,300	1,650	1,100
(79 1)	Jack Clements (Hands on knees.)	3,300	1,650	1,100
(79 2)	Jack Clements (With bat.)	3,300	1,650	1,100

(83)	John Coleman (Bat at side.)	3,300	1,650	1,100
(86)	Charlie Comiskey	8,250	4,125	2,475
(88 1)	Roger Connor (Hands on knees.)	29,150	15,450	9,300
(88 2)	Roger Connor (Bat at 45 degrees.)	8,250	4,125	2,475
(89)	Dick Conway	3,300	1,650	1,100
(94)	Larry Corcoran	3,300	1,650	1,100
(97 1)	Sam Crane (Fielding grounder.)	3,300	1,650	1,100
(97 2)	Sam Crane (With bat.)	3,300	1,650	1,100
(109)	Ed Dailey	3,300	1,650	1,100
(113)	Abner Dalrymple (Right arm cap-high.)	3,300	1,650	1,100
(117)	Dell Darling	3,300	1,650	1,100
(121 1)	Pat Dealey (Bat at side.)	3,300	1,650	1,100
(121 2)	Pat Dealey (Bat on shoulder.)	3,300	1,650	1,100
(125L)	Jerry Denny (Large, with bat.)	20,625	10,300	6,200
(125 1)	Jerry Denny/Catching	3,300	1,650	1,100
(125 2)	Jerry Denny (With bat.)	3,300	1,650	1,100
(130)	Jim Donnelly (Bat at 45 degrees.)	3,300	1,650	1,100
(133)	Mike Dorgan (Arms crossed.)	3,300	1,650	1,100
(149L)	Buck Ewing (Large, catching fly ball.)	32,000	15,450	9,300
(149 1)	Buck Ewing (Bat at 45 degrees.)	8,250	4,125	2,475
(149 2)	Buck Ewing (Fielding fly ball.)	8,250	4,125	2,475
(149 3)	Buck Ewing (Fielding ground ball.)	8,250	4,125	2,475
(156 1)	Jack Farrell (Bat at side.)	3,300	1,650	1,100
(156 2)	Jack Farrell (Bat in air.)	3,300	1,650	1,100
(156 3)	Jack Farrell/Fldg	3,300	1,650	1,100
(156 4)	Jack Farrell (Hands on thighs.)	3,300	1,650	1,100
(158 1)	Charlie Ferguson (Hands at chest.)	4,000	1,650	1,200
(158 2)	Charlie Ferguson (Right arm extended back.)	4,000	1,650	1,200
(158 3)	Charlie Ferguson (Tagging player.)	3,300	1,650	1,100
(158 4)	Charlie Ferguson (With bat.)	3,300	1,650	1,100
(161 1)	Jocko Fields/Catching	3,300	1,650	1,100
(161 2)	Jocko Fields (Tagging player.)	3,800	1,900	1,125
(161 3)	Jocko Fields/Throwing	3,300	1,650	1,100
(167 1)	Jim Fogarty (Bat on shoulder.)	3,300	1,650	1,100
(167 2)	Jim Fogarty (Fielding fly ball.)	3,300	1,650	1,100
(171)	Dave Foutz (Brown's Champions)	5,850	2,925	1,750
(178)	John Gaffney (Bending to right.)	3,300	1,650	1,100
(171 1)	Pud Galvin (Leaning on bat.)	8,250	4,125	2,475
(171 2)	Pud Galvin (Without bat.)	8,250	4,125	2,475
(184 1)	Emil Geiss (Hands above waist.)	3,300	1,650	1,100
(184 2)	Emil Geiss (Right hand extended.)	3,300	1,650	1,100
(191 1)	Pete Gillespie/Fldg	3,300	1,650	1,100
(191 2)	Pete Gillespie (With bat.)	3,300	1,650	1,100
(192)	Barney Gilligan	3,300	1,650	1,100
(194 1)	Jack Glasscock (Hands on knees.)	3,300	1,650	1,100
(194 2)	Jack Glasscock/Throwing	3,300	1,650	1,100
(194 3)	Jack Glasscock (With bat.)	3,300	1,650	1,100
(195)	Bill Gleason (Brown's Champions)	5,850	2,925	1,700
(199 1)	George Gore (Fielding)	3,300	1,650	1,100
(199 2)	George Gore (Hand at head level.)	3,300	1,650	1,100
(202)	Ed Greer/Btg (Outdoors)	5,150	2,600	1,550
(207 1)	Tom Gunning (Stooping to catch low ball on left.)	3,300	1,650	1,100
(207 2)	Tom Gunning (Bending, hands by right knee.)	3,300	1,650	1,100
(215 1)	Ned Hanlon/Catching	8,250	4,125	2,475
(215 2)	Ned Hanlon (Bat at 45 degrees.)	8,250	4,125	2,475
(218 1)	John Harkins (Hands above waist, outdoors.)	4,000	1,650	1,200
(218 2)	John Harkins/Throwing (Outdoors)	5,150	2,600	1,550
(223)	Egyptian Healey (Healy)/Btg	3,300	1,650	1,100
(232)	Paul Hines (Hands at sides.)	3,300	1,650	1,100
(241)	Joe Horning (Hornung) (Bat at 45 degrees.)	3,300	1,650	1,100
(244)	Nat Hudson (Brown's Champions)	5,850	2,925	1,700
(248 1)	Arthur Irwin/Btg	3,300	1,650	1,100
(248 2)	Arthur Irwin/Fldg (Hands below knees.)	3,300	1,650	1,100
(253 1)	Dick Johnston/Catching	3,300	1,650	1,100
(253 2)	Dick Johnston (With bat.)	3,300	1,650	1,100
(256L)	Tim Keefe (Large, ball in hands at chest.)	33,000	16,500	10,000
(256 1)	Tim Keefe (Ball in hands at chest.)	8,250	4,125	2,475
(256 2)	Tim Keefe (Hands above waist, facing front.)	8,250	4,125	2,475
(256 3)	Tim Keefe (Right hand extended at head level.)	8,250	4,125	2,475
(256 4)	Tim Keefe (With bat.)	8,250	4,125	2,475
(261L)	King Kelly (Large, bat horizontal.)	34,800	16,900	10,100
(261 1)	King Kelly/Fldg (Hands chest-high.)	12,375	6,200	3,700
(261 2)	King Kelly/Portrait	12,375	6,200	3,700
(261 4)	King Kelly (With bat.)	11,700	5,850	3,500
(262)	Rudy Kemmler	3,300	1,650	1,100
(273 1)	Bill Krieg (Fielding thigh-high ball.)	3,300	1,650	1,100
(273 2)	Bill Krieg (With bat.)	3,300	1,650	1,100
(278)	Arlie Latham	3,300	1,650	1,100
(302 1)	Mike Mattimore (Hands above head.)	3,300	1,650	1,100
(302 2)	Mike Mattimore (Hands at neck.)	3,300	1,650	1,100
(302 3)	Mike Mattimore/Sliding	3,300	1,650	1,100
(307 1)	Tommy McCarthy/Catching	8,250	4,125	2,475
(307 2)	Tommy McCarthy/Sliding	8,250	4,125	2,475
(307 3)	Tommy McCarthy (With bat.)	8,250	4,125	2,475
(309)	Bill McClellan	3,300	1,650	1,100
(311 1)	Jim McCormick (Ball in hands at chest.)	3,300	1,650	1,100
(311 2)	Jim McCormick (Bat at 45 degrees.)	3,300	1,650	1,100
(316 1)	Jack McGeachy (Bat at 45 degrees.)	4,000	1,650	1,125
(316 2)	Jack McGeachy (Fielding ball over head.)	5,150	2,600	1,550
(318 1)	Deacon McGuire/Btg	3,300	1,650	1,100
(318 2)	Deacon McGuire/Catching	3,300	1,650	1,100
(321)	Alex McKinnon/Fldg (Hands waist-high.)	3,300	1,650	1,100
(326 1)	Jim McTamany (Bat on shoulder, outdoors.)	4,000	1,650	1,125
(326 2)	Jim McTamany/Fldg (Outdoors)	4,000	1,650	1,125
(330)	Doggie Miller	3,300	1,650	1,100
(336)	John Morrell (Morrill) (Hands on hips.)	3,800	1,900	1,125
(339)	Joe Mulvey (Fiedling ball at waist.)	3,300	1,650	1,100
(344 1)	Al Myers (Washington, bat vertical.)	3,300	1,650	1,100
(344 2)	Al Myers (Washington, hands on knees.)	3,300	1,650	1,100
(344 3)	Al Myers/Portrait (With arms folded.)	3,300	1,650	1,100
(345 1)	George Myers (Indianapolis, stooping.)	3,300	1,650	1,100
(345 2)	George Myers (Indianapolis, with bat.)	3,300	1,650	1,100
(347)	Billy Nash/Portrait	3,300	1,650	1,100
(353)	Hugh Nicol (Brown's Champions)	5,850	2,925	1,700
(358)	Jack O'Brien (Bat over shoulder, outdoors.)	3,300	1,650	1,100
(362 1)	Hank O'Day (Ball in hand.)	3,300	1,650	1,100
(362 2)	Hank O'Day (With bat.)	3,300	1,650	1,100
(365)	Tip O'Neill (Brown's Champions)	6,425	3,200	1,900
(366)	Orator Jim O'Rourke/Fldg	6,200	3,100	1,850
(367)	Tom O'Rourke (Bat at 45 degrees.)	3,300	1,650	1,100
(371)	Jimmy Peeples/Catching (Outdoors)	3,300	1,650	1,100
(374)	Fred Pfeffer/Throwing	3,300	1,650	1,100
(378)	George Pinkney (Pinckney)	3,300	1,650	1,100
(380)	Henry Porter/Throwing (Right hand cap-high, outdoors.)	4,000	1,650	1,125
(386)	Old Hoss Radbourn (With bat.)	8,250	4,125	2,475
(393L)	Danny Richardson (N.Y., large, bat at 45 degrees.)	24,200	12,000	7,200
(393 1)	Danny Richardson (N.Y., bat at 45 degrees.)	3,300	1,650	1,100
(393 2)	Danny Richardson (N.Y., moving to left, arms at sides.)	3,300	1,650	1,100
(394)	Hardy Richardson (Detroit)	3,300	1,650	1,100
(396)	John Roach/Btg	3,300	1,650	1,100
(399)	Yank Robinson (Brown's Champions)	5,850	2,925	1,700
(403)	Jack Rowe (Bat at side.)	3,300	1,650	1,100
(405)	Jimmy Ryan (Ball in hands at chest.)	3,300	1,650	1,100
(415 1)	Emmett Seery (Arms folded.)	3,300	1,650	1,100
(415 2)	Emmett Seery (Ball in hands.)	3,300	1,650	1,100
(415 3)	Emmett Seery/Catching	3,300	1,650	1,100
(425 1)	George Shoch/Btg (W/umpire.)	3,300	1,650	1,100
(425 2)	George Schoch (Shoch) (Fielding, hands head high.)	3,300	1,650	1,100
(426)	Otto Shomberg (Schomberg) (Ball in hands at shoulder.)	3,300	1,650	1,100
(435)	Pop Smith	3,300	1,650	1,100
(446 1)	Bill Stemmyer (Stemmeyer) (Ball in hands at chest.)	3,300	1,650	1,100
(446 2)	Bill Stemmyer (Stemmeyer) (With bat.)	3,300	1,650	1,100
(459 1)	Ezra Sutton/Fldg	3,300	1,650	1,100
(459 2)	Ezra Sutton/Throwing	3,300	1,650	1,100
(459 3)	Ezra Sutton (With bat.)	3,300	1,650	1,100
(460)	Ed Swartwood (Kneeling to field, outdoors.)	5,150	2,600	1,550
(464)	Pop Tate/Fldg	3,300	1,650	1,100
(467)	William "Adonis" Terry ((Batting outdoors.))	3,300	1,650	1,100
(468 1)	Sam Thompson (Arms folded.)	8,250	4,125	2,475
(468 2)	Sam Thompson (Bat at side.)	8,250	4,125	2,475
(468 3)	Sam Thompson (Swinging at ball.)	8,250	4,125	2,475
(469L)	Mike Tiernan (Large, fielding fly ball.)	20,625	10,300	6,200
(469)	Mike Tiernan (Fielding grounder.)	3,300	1,650	1,100
(472)	Steve Toole (With bat, outdoors.)	5,150	2,600	1,550
(480 1)	Larry Twitchell (Hands by chest.)	3,300	1,650	1,100
(480 2)	Larry Twitchell (Right hand extended.)	3,300	1,650	1,100
(489)	Chris Von Der Ahe	4,800	2,400	1,375
(491L)	John Ward/Throwing (Large)	32,000	15,450	9,300
(491)	John Ward	8,250	4,125	2,475
(493)	Bill Watkins/Portrait	3,300	1,650	1,100
(498)	Curt Welch	3,300	1,650	1,100
(511 1)	Art Whitney/Bending (Pittsburgh)	3,300	1,650	1,100
(511 2)	Art Whitney (Pittsburgh, with bat.)	3,300	1,650	1,100
(513)	Jim Whitney (Washington, throwing, r. hand waist-high.)	3,300	1,650	1,100
(515)	Ned Williamson/Throwing	4,000	1,650	1,125
(519)	Sam Wise	3,300	1,650	1,100
(521 1)	George Wood/Btg	3,300	1,650	1,100
(521 2)	George Wood/Throwing	3,300	1,650	1,100

H

1953 H-O Instant Oatmeal Records

Baseball playing tips from several star New York players are featured in this set of box-top premium records. For 25 cents and two oatmeal box tops, a set of three of the four records could be ordered by mail. The records are 4-3/4" in diameter and have a color player portrait with facsimile autograph on the back side, while the grooved recording side has an action pose in black-and-white.

		NM	EX	VG
Complete Set (4):		1,050	525.00	315.00
Common Player:		160.00	80.00	48.00
(1)	Roy Campanella	350.00	175.00	105.00
(2)	"Whitey" Lockman	175.00	87.00	52.00
(3)	Allie Reynolds	225.00	110.00	67.00
(4)	Duke Snider	350.00	175.00	105.00

1922 Haffner's Big-Tayto-Loaf Bread

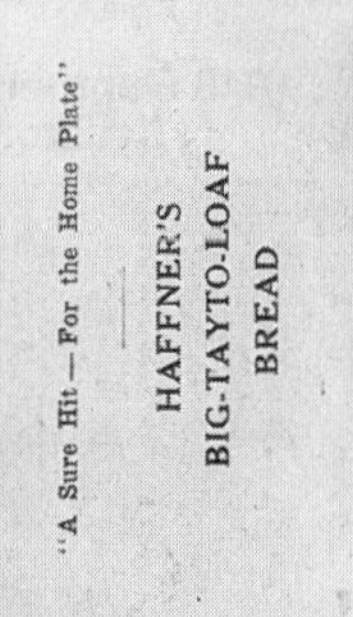

The bakery ad on the back is all that sets this issue apart from the blank-back W575-1 and several other versions with different sponsors named on back. The cards are 2" x 3-1/4" black-and-white. It is unknown whether each of the cards in the W575-1 checklist can be found in the Haffner's version.

PREMIUMS:
Common Players: 5-6X
Hall of Famers: 3-4X
(See W575-1 for checklist and card values.)

1951 Hage's Ice Cream Cleveland Indians

Similar in format to the Pacific Coast League cards produced by the dairy from 1949-51, these cards feature former members of the San Diego Padres, then a farm club of the Indians. Cards measure 2-5/8" x 3-1/8" and are printed in tones of sepia and green. Fronts have posed action photos similar to those found on contemporary Num Num and team photo pack pictures. A small white box on front has the player name and "CLEVELAND." There is a white border around the front photo. Backs are blank and unnumbered; the cards are presented here in alphabetical order.

		NM	EX	VG
Complete Set (6):		5,000	2,500	1,500
Common Player:		850.00	425.00	250.00
(1)	Ray Boone	850.00	425.00	250.00

		NM	EX	VG
(2)	Allie Clark	850.00	425.00	250.00
(3)	Jesse Flores	850.00	425.00	250.00
(4)	Al Olsen	850.00	425.00	250.00
(5)	Al Rosen	900.00	450.00	270.00
(6)	George Zuverink	850.00	425.00	250.00

1888 Joseph Hall Cabinets

These cabinet-sized (6-1/2" x 4-1/2") cards feature team photos taken by Joseph Hall, a well-known photographer of the day. Extremely rare, all have Hall's name beneath the photo and some include his Brooklyn address. The team is identified in large capital letters with the individual players identified in smaller type on both sides. Fourteen teams are known to date, but others may also exist, and Hall may have produced similar team cabinets in other years as well.

		NM	EX	VG
	Common Team:	6,000	3,000	1,800
(1)	Athletic Ball Club, 1888	12,000	6,000	3,600
(2)	Baltimore Ball Club, 1888	16,800	8,400	5,000
(3)	Boston Ball Club, 1888	18,000	9,000	5,400
(4)	Brooklyn Ball Club, 1888	21,000	10,500	6,300
(5)	Chicago Ball Club, 1888	42,000	21,000	12,000
(6)	Cincinnati Ball Club, 1888	18,000	9,000	5,400
(7)	Cleveland Ball Club, 1888	15,000	7,500	4,500
(8)	Detroit Ball Club, 1888	19,200	9,600	5,800
(9)	Indianapolis Ball Club, 1888	18,000	9,000	5,400
(10)	Kansas City Ball Club, 1888	21,000	10,500	6,300
(11)	Louisville Ball Club, 1888	15,000	7,500	4,500
(12)	New York Ball Club, League Champions - 1889 (Wearing baseball uniforms.)	27,000	13,500	8,100
(13)	New York Ball Club, 1888 (Wearing tuxedos.)	22,000	11,000	6,660
(14)	St. Louis Baseball Club, 1888	15,000	7,500	4,500
(15)	Washington Baseball Club, 1888	48,000	24,000	14,400

1888 Joseph Hall Imperial Cabinets

Besides the standard-sized team-photo cabinet cards, super-sized versions of some (possibly all) teams were also available in a format known to collectors as an imperial cabinet. The large pictures use the same photos as the regular cabinets, enlarged to sizes as diverse as approximately 13" x 10" and 24" x 19" and mounted on heavy black or white backing boards. Printed on the mount in gold are the team name, date, player names and the Joseph Hall studio identification. Only those teams which have actually been observed in this format are listed here, with values generally set by their infrequent appearances in hobby auctions.

	NM	EX	VG
Cincinnati Ball Club, 1888 (13" x 10")	13,750	6,350	3,750
New York Ball Club/1888 (13" x 10")	20,625	9,525	5,625
St. Louis Ball Club - 1888 (24" x 19")	13,750	6,350	3,750

1908 Hall's Studio N.Y. Giants Cabinets

Members of the N.Y. Giants are pictured in this series of approximately 4-1/2" x 6-1/2" cabinet photos from New York City photographer, Hall's Studio. The players are all identically posed bare-headed in white shirts buttoned at the collar. It is unknown whether this checklist is complete.

		NM	EX	VG
	Common Player:	600.00	300.00	180.00
(1)	Al Bridwell	600.00	300.00	180.00
(2)	Doc Crandall	600.00	300.00	180.00
(3)	Larry Doyle	600.00	300.00	180.00
(4)	Buck Herzog	600.00	300.00	180.00
(5)	Rube Marquard	800.00	400.00	240.00
(6)	John McGraw	800.00	400.00	240.00
(7)	Fred Merkle	600.00	300.00	180.00

1939-43 Hall of Fame Sepia Postcards

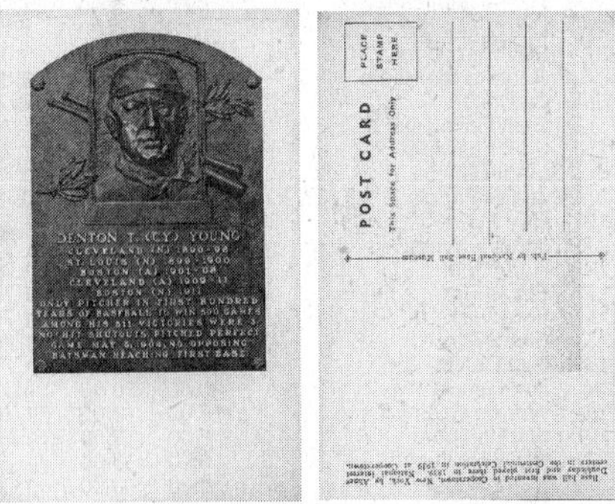

The first Hall of Fame postcards were issued in two types between 1939-1943. They share an identical format and are differentiated by the typography on back, one set having been issued prior to the Hall of Fame's opening in June, 1939, and a later version issued after the opening. The 3-1/2" x 5-1/2" cards are similar in format to the later series printed in black-and-white and various colors, but this initial effort is printed in sepia on a cream-colored background. Most fronts picture the plaque of one of the 25 first inductees, with a wide bottom border to accomodate an autograph. Designated Type 1, this issue has a back caption which ends with, "National interest centers in the Centennial Celebration in 1939 at Cooperstown." The later version, Type 2, ends its description, "The National Base Ball Museum and Hall of Fame and Doubleday Field are maintained here as a Shrine to the national game." On both types, vertically at centers is a credit line "Pub. by National Base Ball Museum." At right are a stamp box and line for the mailing address. The unnumbered cards are listed here in alphabetical order within type.

		NM	EX	VG
	Complete Set, Type 1 (35):	2,800	1,400	840.00
	Complete Set, Type 2 (37):	3,250	1,625	975.00
	Common Card:	60.00	30.00	18.00
	TYPE 1			
(1)	G.C. Alexander	100.00	50.00	30.00
(2)	Adrian Anson	100.00	50.00	30.00
(3)	Morgan Bulkeley	100.00	50.00	30.00
(4)	Alexander Cartwright	100.00	50.00	30.00
(5)	Henry Chadwick	100.00	50.00	30.00
(6)	Ty Cobb	225.00	110.00	65.00
(7)	Eddie Collins	100.00	50.00	30.00
(8)	Chas. Comiskey	100.00	50.00	30.00
(9)	Candy Cummings	100.00	50.00	30.00
(10)	Buck Ewing	100.00	50.00	30.00
(11)	Ban Johnson	100.00	50.00	30.00
(12)	Walter Johnson	175.00	85.00	50.00
(13)	Willie Keeler	100.00	50.00	30.00
(14)	Napoleon Lajoie	100.00	50.00	30.00
(15)	Connie Mack	100.00	50.00	30.00
(16)	Christy Mathewson	175.00	85.00	50.00
(17)	John McGraw	100.00	50.00	30.00
(18)	Chas. Radbourne	100.00	50.00	30.00
(19)	Babe Ruth	450.00	225.00	135.00
(20)	George Sisler	100.00	50.00	30.00
(21)	Al Spalding	100.00	50.00	30.00
(22)	Tris Speaker	100.00	50.00	30.00
(23)	Honus Wagner	200.00	100.00	60.00
(24)	George Wright	100.00	50.00	30.00
(25)	Cy Young	150.00	75.00	45.00
(26)	The Abner Doubleday Baseball	50.00	25.00	15.00
(27)	Abner Doubleday, Major Gen'l	50.00	25.00	15.00
(28)	Doubleday Field in its Original State	50.00	25.00	15.00
(29)	Doubleday Field in 1938	50.00	25.00	15.00
(30)	Exhibition Game on Doubleday Field	50.00	25.00	15.00
(31)	Exterior - Ntl. Baseball Hall of Fame (no title on front)	50.00	25.00	15.00
(32)	Interior - Ntl. Baseball Museum	50.00	25.00	15.00
(33)	The Bust of Christy Mathewson	50.00	25.00	15.00
(34)	Entrance of the Hall of Fame	50.00	25.00	15.00
(35)	Ntl. Baseball Museum "Immortals"	50.00	25.00	15.00
	TYPE 2			
(1)	G.C. Alexander	100.00	50.00	30.00
(2)	Adrian Anson	100.00	50.00	30.00
(3)	Morgan Bulkeley	100.00	50.00	30.00
(4)	Alexander Cartwright	100.00	50.00	30.00
(5)	Henry Chadwick	100.00	50.00	30.00
(6)	Ty Cobb	225.00	110.00	65.00
(7)	Eddie Collins	100.00	50.00	30.00
(8)	Charles Comiskey	100.00	50.00	30.00
(9)	Candy Cummings	100.00	50.00	30.00
(10)	Buck Ewing	100.00	50.00	30.00
(11)	Lou Gehrig	300.00	150.00	90.00
(12)	Rogers Hornsby	125.00	65.00	35.00
(13)	Ban Johnson	100.00	50.00	30.00
(14)	Walter Johnson	175.00	85.00	50.00
(15)	Willie Keeler	100.00	50.00	30.00
(16)	Napoleon Lajoie	100.00	50.00	30.00
(17)	Connie Mack	100.00	50.00	30.00
(18)	Christy Mathewson	175.00	85.00	50.00
(19)	John McGraw	100.00	50.00	30.00
(20)	Chas. Radbourne	100.00	50.00	30.00
(21)	Babe Ruth	450.00	225.00	135.00
(22)	George Sisler	100.00	50.00	30.00
(23)	Al Spalding	100.00	50.00	30.00
(24)	Tris Speaker	100.00	50.00	30.00
(25)	Honus Wagner	200.00	100.00	60.00
(26)	George Wright	100.00	50.00	30.00
(27)	Cy Young	150.00	75.00	45.00
(28)	The Abner Doubleday Baseball	50.00	25.00	15.00
(29)	Abner Doubleday, Major Gen'l	50.00	25.00	15.00
(30)	Doubleday Field in its Original State	50.00	25.00	15.00
(31)	Doubleday Field in 1938	50.00	25.00	15.00
(32)	Exhibition Game on Doubleday Field	50.00	25.00	15.00
(33)	Exterior - Ntl. Baseball Hall of Fame	50.00	25.00	15.00
(34)	Interior - Ntl. Baseball Hall of Fame	50.00	25.00	15.00
(35)	The Bust of Christy Mathewson	50.00	25.00	15.00
(36)	Entrance of the Hall of Fame	50.00	25.00	15.00
(37)	Ntl. Baseball Museum - "Immortals"	50.00	25.00	15.00

1944-63 Hall of Fame Black-and-White Plaque Postcards

(See listings cataloged under Albertype and Artvue.)

1939-63 Hall of Fame B/W Plaque Postcards - Autographed

Collecting Hall of Fame plaque postcards autographed by inductees has long been popular in the hobby. Obviously, completion of a set is impossible because many Hall of Famers have been inducted posthumously. Generally, the value of a genuinely autographed HoF plaque postcard is not so much dependent on star status of the player, but on the perception of how many such cards could have been autographed in his remaining lifetime. Players who died within months of their induction or who were un-cooperative with autograph requests have cards that are far more valuable than many players of greater renown. While the majority of the players checklisted here could have signed both Albertye and Artvue cards, some players are possible only on the latter brand because their induction or death happened after 1952. Values quoted are for cards signed on the front. Cards signed on back can be worth 50 percent less .

	NM	EX	VG
Complete Set (55): Value Undetermined			
G.C. Alexander	1,250	1,125	935.00
Frank Baker	1,600	1,450	1,200
Ed Barrow	1,500	1,350	1,125
Chief Bender	550.00	500.00	410.00
Jesse Burkett	1,100	990.00	825.00
Max Carey	100.00	90.00	75.00
Fred Clarke	1,700	1,525	1,275
Ty Cobb	2,500	2,250	1,875
Mickey Cochrane	1,500	1,350	1,125
Eddie Collins	8,000	7,200	6,000
Tom Connolly	3,000	2,700	2,250
Sam Crawford	550.00	500.00	410.00
Joe Cronin	200.00	180.00	150.00
Dizzy Dean	325.00	290.00	245.00
Bill Dickey	150.00	135.00	110.00
Joe DiMaggio	550.00	500.00	410.00
Hugh Duffy	1,500	1,350	1,125
Johnny Evers	450.00	400.00	335.00
Bob Feller	35.00	30.00	25.00
Elmer Flick	500.00	450.00	375.00
Jimmie Foxx	4,000	3,600	3,000
Frankie Frisch	400.00	360.00	300.00
Lou Gehrig (Sepia only.)	2,000	1,800	1,500
Charlie Gehringer	60.00	55.00	45.00
Hank Greenberg	325.00	290.00	245.00
Clark Griffith	2,750	2,475	2,050
Lefty Grove	250.00	225.00	185.00
Gabby Hartnett	475.00	425.00	355.00
Rogers Hornsby	1,600	1,450	1,200
Carl Hubbell (Deduct 33 percent for post-stroke signature.)	65.00	58.00	49.00
Walter Johnson	1,400	1,250	1,050

	NM	EX	VG
Nap Lajoie	2,500	2,250	1,875
Ted Lyons	300.00	275.00	225.00
Connie Mack	1,450	1,300	1,100
Joe McCarthy	200.00	180.00	150.00
Bill McKechnie	900.00	810.00	675.00
Kid Nichols	3,500	3,150	2,625
Mel Ott	1,600	1,450	1,200
Sam Rice	175.00	155.00	130.00
Eppa Rixey (Possible but unlikely.)			
Jackie Robinson	2,250	2,025	1,675
Edd Roush	75.00	65.00	55.00
Babe Ruth (Value Undetermined)			
Ray Schalk	500.00	450.00	375.00
Al Simmons	1,750	1,575	1,300
George Sisler	500.00	450.00	375.00
Tris Speaker	1,500	1,350	1,125
Bill Terry	60.00	55.00	45.00
Joe Tinker	550.00	500.00	410.00
Pie Traynor	850.00	765.00	635.00
Dazzy Vance	1,700	1,525	1,275
Honus Wagner	2,800	2,525	2,100
Bobby Wallace	2,000	1,800	1,500
Ed Walsh	1,250	1,125	935.00
Paul Waner	1,550	1,400	1,150
Zack Wheat	650.00	585.00	485.00
Cy Young	2,400	2,150	1,800

1963 Hall of Fame Picture Pack

The attributed date is only approximate for this set of 5" x 7" black-and-white, blank-back pictures sold by the Hall of Fame. In the wide border beneath the player photo are identification, teams and years played, a few stats and induction year along with an HoF logo. Some of the same pictures were repeated in the later version of the issue.

		NM	EX	VG
Complete Set (24):		40.00	20.00	12.00
Common Player:		3.00	1.50	.90
(1)	Grover Alexander	4.00	2.00	1.25
(2)	Ty Cobb	6.00	3.00	1.75
(3)	Mickey Cochrane	3.00	1.50	.90
(4)	Eddie Collins	3.00	1.50	.90
(5)	Joe Cronin	3.00	1.50	.90
(6)	Bill Dickey	3.00	1.50	.90
(7)	Joe DiMaggio	7.50	3.75	2.25
(8)	Bob Feller	4.00	2.00	1.25
(9)	Frank Frisch	3.00	1.50	.90
(10)	Lou Gehrig	7.50	3.75	2.25
(11)	Rogers Hornsby	3.00	1.50	.90
(12)	Walter Johnson	4.00	2.00	1.25
(13)	Connie Mack	3.00	1.50	.90
(14)	Christy Mathewson	4.00	2.00	1.25
(15)	John McGraw	3.00	1.50	.90
(16)	Jackie Robinson	5.00	2.50	1.50
(17)	Babe Ruth	10.00	5.00	3.00
(18)	George Sisler	3.00	1.50	.90
(19)	Tris Speaker	3.00	1.50	.90
(20)	Bill Terry	3.00	1.50	.90
(21)	Pie Traynor	3.00	1.50	.90
(22)	Honus Wagner	4.00	2.00	1.25
(23)	Paul Waner	3.00	1.50	.90
(24)	Cy Young	4.00	2.00	1.25

1973 Hall of Fame Picture Pack

This set of 5" x 6-3/4" black-and-white player photos picture "Baseball's Greats Enshrined at Cooperstown, N.Y." Player career data is printed in the wide white border at bottom and there is a Hall of Fame logo at lower-left. The unnumbered pictures are listed here in alphabetical order.

		NM	EX	VG
Complete Set (20):		20.00	10.00	6.00
Common Player:		2.00	1.00	.60
(1)	Yogi Berra	3.00	1.50	.90
(2)	Roy Campanella	3.00	1.50	.90
(3)	Ty Cobb	4.00	2.00	1.25
(4)	Joe Cronin	2.50	1.25	.70
(5)	Dizzy Dean	3.00	1.50	.90
(6)	Joe DiMaggio	7.50	3.75	2.25
(7)	Bob Feller	3.00	1.50	.90
(8)	Lou Gehrig	7.50	3.75	2.25
(9)	Rogers Hornsby	3.00	1.50	.90
(10)	Sandy Koufax	5.00	2.50	1.50
(11)	Christy Mathewson	3.00	1.50	.90
(12)	Stan Musial	3.00	1.50	.90
(13)	Satchel Paige	3.00	1.50	.90
(14)	Jackie Robinson	5.00	2.50	1.50
(15)	Babe Ruth	10.00	5.00	3.00
(16)	Warren Spahn	2.50	1.25	.70
(17)	Casey Stengel	3.00	1.50	.90
(18)	Honus Wagner	3.00	1.50	.90
(19)	Ted Williams	5.00	2.50	1.50
(20)	Cy Young	3.00	1.50	.90

1979 Hall of Fame (Dexter Press) Plaque Postcards

This short-lived series, begun no later than 1979, features the Hall of Fame inductees' plaques on bright backgrounds of red, orange, blue and green. Because of the cards' color and finish, they are difficult to autograph.

		NM	EX	VG
Complete Set (53):		350.00	175.00	105.00
Common Player:		6.00	3.00	1.75
(1)	Grover Alexander	6.00	3.00	1.75
(2)	Lou Boudreau	6.00	3.00	1.75
(3)	Roy Campanella	10.00	5.00	3.00
(4)	Roberto Clemente	20.00	10.00	6.00
(5)	Ty Cobb	15.00	7.50	4.50
(6)	Stan Coveleski	6.00	3.00	1.75
(7)	Sam Crawford	6.00	3.00	1.75
(8)	Martin Dihigo	6.00	3.00	1.75
(9)	Joe DiMaggio	22.50	11.00	6.75
(10)	Billy Evans	6.00	3.00	1.75
(11)	Johnny Evers	6.00	3.00	1.75
(12)	Red Faber	6.00	3.00	1.75
(13)	Elmer Flick	6.00	3.00	1.75
(14)	Ford Frick	6.00	3.00	1.75
(15)	Frank Frisch	6.00	3.00	1.75
(16)	Pud Galvin	6.00	3.00	1.75
(17)	Lou Gehrig	20.00	10.00	6.00
(18)	Warren Giles	6.00	3.00	1.75
(19)	Will Harridge	6.00	3.00	1.75
(20)	Harry Heilmann	6.00	3.00	1.75
(21)	Harry Hooper	6.00	3.00	1.75
(22)	Waite Hoyt	6.00	3.00	1.75
(23)	Miller Huggins	6.00	3.00	1.75
(24)	Judy Johnson	6.00	3.00	1.75
(25)	Addie Joss	6.00	3.00	1.75
(26)	Tim Keefe	6.00	3.00	1.75
(27)	Willie Keeler	6.00	3.00	1.75
(28)	George Kelly	6.00	3.00	1.75
(29)	Sandy Koufax	15.00	7.50	4.50
(30)	Nap Lajoie	6.00	3.00	1.75
(31)	Pop Lloyd	6.00	3.00	1.75
(32)	Connie Mack	6.00	3.00	1.75
(33)	Larry MacPhail	6.00	3.00	1.75
(34)	Mickey Mantle	25.00	12.50	7.50
(35)	Heinie Manush	6.00	3.00	1.75
(36)	Eddie Mathews	6.00	3.00	1.75
(37)	Willie Mays	15.00	7.50	4.50
(38)	Ducky Medwick	6.00	3.00	1.75
(39)	Stan Musial	12.00	6.00	3.50
(40)	Herb Pennock	6.00	3.00	1.75
(41)	Edd Roush	6.00	3.00	1.75
(42)	Babe Ruth	25.00	12.50	7.50
(43)	Amos Rusie	6.00	3.00	1.75
(44)	Ray Schalk	6.00	3.00	1.75
(45)	Al Simmons	6.00	3.00	1.75
(46)	Albert Spalding	6.00	3.00	1.75
(47)	Joe Tinker	6.00	3.00	1.75
(48)	Pie Traynor	6.00	3.00	1.75
(49)	Dazzy Vance	6.00	3.00	1.75
(50)	Lloyd Waner	6.00	3.00	1.75
(51)	Ted Williams	20.00	10.00	6.00
(52)	Hack Wilson	6.00	3.00	1.75
(53)	Ross Youngs	6.00	3.00	1.75

1979 HoF (Dexter Press) Plaque Postcards - Autographed

		NM	EX	VG
(2)	Lou Boudreau	30.00	27.00	22.00
(3)	Roy Campanella(Value Undetermined)			
(6)	Stan Coveleski	50.00	45.00	37.00
(9)	Joe DiMaggio	350.00	315.00	260.00
(22)	Waite Hoyt	100.00	90.00	75.00
(24)	Judy Johnson	65.00	60.00	50.00
(28)	George Kelly	75.00	65.00	55.00
(29)	Sandy Koufax	150.00	135.00	110.00
(34)	Mickey Mantle	400.00	360.00	300.00
(36)	Eddie Mathews	50.00	45.00	37.00
(37)	Willie Mays	50.00	45.00	37.00
(39)	Stan Musial	25.00	22.00	18.50
(41)	Edd Roush	50.00	45.00	37.00
(50)	Lloyd Waner	50.00	45.00	37.00
(51)	Ted Williams	300.00	270.00	225.00

1964-Date Hall of Fame Yellow Plaque Postcards

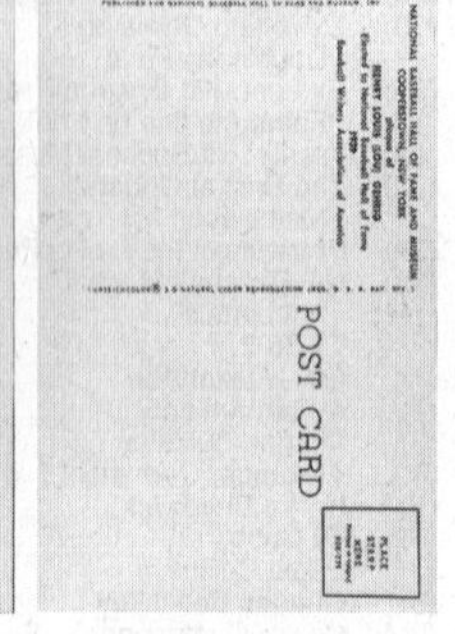

Since 1964 a number of related series of Hall of Fame Plaque Postcards have been produced by a pair of printers. The 3-1/2" x 5-1/2" postcards were first produced by Curteichcolor and, later, by Mike Roberts Color Productions. Like earlier HoF postcards, these series feature a color photo of an inductee's plaque on a yellow background. Black-and-white backs have a variety of player information, postcard indicia, copyright data and credit lines. Few hobbyists attempt to collect these by issuer, rather trying to assemble a complete set of each player regardless of who did the printing and when. Prior to 1977, single postcards sold for five cents at the HoF gift shop; in 1977 the price doubled to a dime, with complete sets (about 150) selling for $6. Today a complete set is available from the Hall of Fame for about $45, with singles at 25 cents apiece.

	NM	EX	VG
Complete Set (256)	45.00	22.00	13.50
Common Player:	.50	.25	.15
Hank Aaron	.50	.25	.15
Grover Alexander	.50	.25	.15
Walter Alston	.50	.25	.15
Sparky Anderson	.50	.25	.15
Cap Anson	.50	.25	.15
Luis Aparicio	.50	.25	.15
Luke Appling	.50	.25	.15
Richie Ashburn	.50	.25	.15
Earl Averill	.50	.25	.15
Frank Baker	.50	.25	.15
Dave Bancroft	.50	.25	.15
Ernie Banks	.50	.25	.15
Al Barlick	.50	.25	.15
Ed Barrow	.50	.25	.15
Jake Beckley	.50	.25	.15
Cool Papa Bell	.50	.25	.15
Johnny Bench	.50	.25	.15
Chief Bender	.50	.25	.15
Yogi Berra	.50	.25	.15
Wade Boggs	.50	.25	.15
Jim Bottomley	.50	.25	.15
Lou Boudreau	.50	.25	.15
Roger Bresnahan	.50	.25	.15
George Brett	.50	.25	.15
Lou Brock	.50	.25	.15
Dan Brouthers	.50	.25	.15
Mordecai Brown	.50	.25	.15
Ray Brown	.50	.25	.15
Willard Brown	.50	.25	.15
Morgan Bulkeley	.50	.25	.15
Jim Bunning	.50	.25	.15
Jesse Burkett	.50	.25	.15
Roy Campanella	.50	.25	.15
Rod Carew	.50	.25	.15
Max Carey	.50	.25	.15
Steve Carlton	.50	.25	.15
Gary Carter	.50	.25	.15
Alexander Cartwright	.50	.25	.15
Orlando Cepeda	.50	.25	.15
Henry Chadwick	.50	.25	.15
Frank Chance	.50	.25	.15
A.B. (Happy) Chandler	.50	.25	.15
Oscar Charleston	.50	.25	.15
Jack Chesbro	.50	.25	.15
Nestor Chylak	.50	.25	.15
Fred Clarke	.50	.25	.15
John Clarkson	.50	.25	.15
Roberto Clemente	.50	.25	.15
Ty Cobb	.50	.25	.15
Mickey Cochrane	.50	.25	.15
Eddie Collins	.50	.25	.15
Jimmy Collins	.50	.25	.15
Earle Combs	.50	.25	.15
Charles Comiskey	.50	.25	.15
Jocko Conlan	.50	.25	.15
Tom Connolly	.50	.25	.15
Roger Connor	.50	.25	.15
Andy Cooper	.50	.25	.15
Stan Coveleski	.50	.25	.15
Sam Crawford	.50	.25	.15
Joe Cronin	.50	.25	.15
Candy Cummings	.50	.25	.15
Kiki Cuyler	.50	.25	.15
Ray Dandridge	.50	.25	.15
George Davis	.50	.25	.15
Leon Day	.50	.25	.15
Dizzy Dean	.50	.25	.15
Ed Delahanty	.50	.25	.15
Bill Dickey	.50	.25	.15
Martin Dihigo	.50	.25	.15
Joe DiMaggio	.50	.25	.15
Larry Doby	.50	.25	.15
Bobby Doerr	.50	.25	.15
Barney Dreyfuss	.50	.25	.15
Don Drysdale	.50	.25	.15
Hugh Duffy	.50	.25	.15
Leo Durocher	.50	.25	.15
Dennis Eckersley	.50	.25	.15
Billy Evans	.50	.25	.15
Johnny Evers	.50	.25	.15
Buck Ewing	.50	.25	.15
Red Faber	.50	.25	.15
Bob Feller	.50	.25	.15
Rick Ferrell	.50	.25	.15
Rollie Fingers	.50	.25	.15
Carlton Fisk	.50	.25	.15
Elmer Flick	.50	.25	.15
Whitey Ford	.50	.25	.15
Bill Foster	.50	.25	.15
Rube Foster	.50	.25	.15
Nellie Fox	.50	.25	.15
Jimmie Foxx	.50	.25	.15
Ford Frick	.50	.25	.15
Frank Frisch	.50	.25	.15
Pud Galvin	.50	.25	.15
Lou Gehrig	.50	.25	.15
Charlie Gehringer	.50	.25	.15
Bob Gibson	.50	.25	.15
Josh Gibson	.50	.25	.15
Warren Giles	.50	.25	.15
Lefty Gomez	.50	.25	.15
Goose Goslin	.50	.25	.15
Rich Gossage	.50	.25	.15
Frank Grant	.50	.25	.15

Hank Greenberg	.50	.25	.15
Clark Griffith	.50	.25	.15
Burleigh Grimes	.50	.25	.15
Lefty Grove	.50	.25	.15
Tony Gwynn	.50	.25	.15
Chick Hafey	.50	.25	.15
Jesse Haines	.50	.25	.15
Billy Hamilton	.50	.25	.15
Ned Hanlon	.50	.25	.15
Will Harridge	.50	.25	.15
Bucky Harris	.50	.25	.15
Gabby Hartnett	.50	.25	.15
Harry Heilmann	.50	.25	.15
Billy Herman	.50	.25	.15
Pete Hill	.50	.25	.15
Harry Hooper	.50	.25	.15
Rogers Hornsby	.50	.25	.15
Waite Hoyt	.50	.25	.15
Cal Hubbard	.50	.25	.15
Carl Hubbell	.50	.25	.15
Miller Huggins	.50	.25	.15
William Hulbert	.50	.25	.15
Catfish Hunter	.50	.25	.15
Monte Irvin	.50	.25	.15
Reggie Jackson	.50	.25	.15
Travis Jackson	.50	.25	.15
Fergie Jenkins	.50	.25	.15
Hughie Jennings	.50	.25	.15
Ban Johnson	.50	.25	.15
Judy Johnson	.50	.25	.15
Walter Johnson	.50	.25	.15
Addie Joss	.50	.25	.15
Al Kaline	.50	.25	.15
Tim Keefe	.50	.25	.15
Willie Keeler	.50	.25	.15
George Kell	.50	.25	.15
Joe Kelley	.50	.25	.15
George Kelly	.50	.25	.15
Mike "King" Kelly	.50	.25	.15
Harmon Killebrew	.50	.25	.15
Ralph Kiner	.50	.25	.15
Chuck Klein	.50	.25	.15
Bill Klem	.50	.25	.15
Sandy Koufax	.50	.25	.15
Bowie kuhn	.50	.25	.15
Nap Lajoie	.50	.25	.15
Kenesaw M. Landis	.50	.25	.15
Tommy Lasorda	.50	.25	.15
Tony Lazzeri	.50	.25	.15
Bob Lemon	.50	.25	.15
Buck Leonard	.50	.25	.15
Freddie Lindstrom	.50	.25	.15
Pop Lloyd	.50	.25	.15
Ernie Lombardi	.50	.25	.15
Al Lopez	.50	.25	.15
Ted Lyons	.50	.25	.15
Connie Mack	.50	.25	.15
Biz Mackey	.50	.25	.15
Larry MacPhail	.50	.25	.15
Effa Manley	.50	.25	.15
Mickey Mantle	.50	.25	.15
Heinie Manush	.50	.25	.15
Rabbit Maranville	.50	.25	.15
Juan Marichal	.50	.25	.15
Rube Marquard	.50	.25	.15
Eddie Mathews	.50	.25	.15
Christy Mathewson	.50	.25	.15
Willie Mays	.50	.25	.15
Bill Mazeroski	.50	.25	.15
Joe McCarthy	.50	.25	.15
Tommy McCarthy	.50	.25	.15
Willie McCovey	.50	.25	.15
Joe McGinnity	.50	.25	.15
Bill McGowan	.50	.25	.15
John McGraw	.50	.25	.15
Bill McKechnie	.50	.25	.15
Lee MacPhail	.50	.25	.15
Bid McPhee	.50	.25	.15
Ducky Medwick	.50	.25	.15
José Méndez	.50	.25	.15
Johnny Mize	.50	.25	.15
Paul Molitor	.50	.25	.15
Joe Morgan	.50	.25	.15
Eddie Murray	.50	.25	.15
Stan Musial	.50	.25	.15
Hal Newhouser	.50	.25	.15
Kid Nichols	.50	.25	.15
Phil Niekro	.50	.25	.15
Walter O'Malley	.50	.25	.15
Jim O'Rourke	.50	.25	.15
Mel Ott	.50	.25	.15
Satchel Paige	.50	.25	.15
Jim Palmer	.50	.25	.15
Herb Pennock	.50	.25	.15
Tony Perez	.50	.25	.15
Gaylord Perry	.50	.25	.15
Ed Plank	.50	.25	.15
Alex Pompez	.50	.25	.15
Cum Posey	.50	.25	.15
Kirby Puckett	.50	.25	.15
Charles Radbourne	.50	.25	.15
Pee Wee Reese	.50	.25	.15
Sam Rice	.50	.25	.15
Cal Ripken Jr.	.50	.25	.15
Branch Rickey	.50	.25	.15
Eppa Rixey	.50	.25	.15
Phil Rizzuto	.50	.25	.15
Robin Roberts	.50	.25	.15
Brooks Robinson	.50	.25	.15
Frank Robinson	.50	.25	.15
Jackie Robinson	.50	.25	.15
Wilbert Robinson	.50	.25	.15
Bullet Rogan	.50	.25	.15
Edd Roush	.50	.25	.15
Red Ruffing	.50	.25	.15
Amos Rusie	.50	.25	.15
Babe Ruth	.50	.25	.15
Nolan Ryan	.50	.25	.15
Ryne Sandberg	.50	.25	.15
Louis Santop	.50	.25	.15
Ray Schalk	.50	.25	.15
Mike Schmidt	.50	.25	.15
Red Schoendienst	.50	.25	.15
Tom Seaver	.50	.25	.15
Frank Selee	.50	.25	.15
Joe Sewell	.50	.25	.15
Al Simmons	.50	.25	.15
George Sisler	.50	.25	.15
Enos Slaughter	.50	.25	.15
Hilton Smith	.50	.25	.15
Ozzie Smith	.50	.25	.15
Duke Snider	.50	.25	.15
Billy Southworth	.50	.25	.15
Warren Spahn	.50	.25	.15
Albert Spalding	.50	.25	.15
Tris Speaker	.50	.25	.15
Willie Stargell	.50	.25	.15
Turkey Stearnes	.50	.25	.15
Casey Stengel	.50	.25	.15
Mule Suttles	.50	.25	.15
Don Sutton	.50	.25	.15
Ben Taylor	.50	.25	.15
Bill Terry	.50	.25	.15
Sam Thompson	.50	.25	.15
Joe Tinker	.50	.25	.15
Cristóbal Torriente	.50	.25	.15
Paul Traynor	.50	.25	.15
Dazzy Vance	.50	.25	.15
Arky Vaughan	.50	.25	.15
Bill Veeck	.50	.25	.15
Rube Waddell	.50	.25	.15
Honus Wagner	.50	.25	.15
Bobby Wallace	.50	.25	.15
Ed Walsh	.50	.25	.15
Lloyd Waner	.50	.25	.15
Paul Waner	.50	.25	.15
Monte Ward	.50	.25	.15
Earl Weaver	.50	.25	.15
George Weiss	.50	.25	.15
Mickey Welch	.50	.25	.15
Willie Wells	.50	.25	.15
Zack Wheat	.50	.25	.15
Sol White	.50	.25	.15
Hoyt Wilhelm	.50	.25	.15
J.L. Wilkinson	.50	.25	.15
Billy Williams	.50	.25	.15
Dick Williams	.50	.25	.15
Joe Williams	.50	.25	.15
Ted Williams	.50	.25	.15
Vic Willis	.50	.25	.15
Hack Wilson	.50	.25	.15
Jud Wilson	.50	.25	.15
Dave Winfield	.50	.25	.15
George Wright	.50	.25	.15
Harry Wright	.50	.25	.15
Early Wynn	.50	.25	.15
Carl Yastrzemski	.50	.25	.15
Tom Yawkey	.50	.25	.15
Cy Young	.50	.25	.15
Ross Youngs	.50	.25	.15
Robin Yount	.50	.25	.15

1964-Date Hall of Fame Yellow Plaque Postcards - Autographed

This listing represents the Curteichcolor and Mike Roberts yellow Hall of Fame plaque postcards which are known to exist, or in a few cases are theoretically possible. Value of genuinely autographed HoF plaque postcards is not so much dependent on star status of the player, but on perception of how many such cards could exist given the time the player remained alive and in good health following his selection at Cooperstown. Players who died or were incapacitated shortly after induction may have more valuable autographed cards than currently living players of greater renown. Values quoted are for cards autographed on front; cards signed on the back can be worth 50 percent less.

	NM	EX	VG
Hank Aaron	55.00	45.00	35.00
Walter Alston	150.00	120.00	90.00
Sparky Anderson	55.00	45.00	35.00
Luis Aparicio	15.00	12.00	9.00
Luke Appling	20.00	16.00	12.00
Richie Ashburn	55.00	45.00	35.00
Earl Averill	50.00	40.00	30.00
Dave Bancroft	2,250	1,800	1,350
Ernie Banks	45.00	35.00	25.00
Al Barlick	15.00	12.00	9.00
Cool Papa Bell	50.00	40.00	30.00
Johnny Bench	45.00	36.00	27.00
Yogi Berra	25.00	20.00	15.00
Wade Boggs	50.00	40.00	30.00
Lou Boudreau	15.00	12.00	9.00
George Brett	125.00	100.00	75.00
Lou Brock	30.00	24.00	18.00
Jim Bunning	40.00	32.00	24.00
Roy Campanella (Value Undetermined)			
Rod Carew	50.00	40.00	30.00
Max Carey	60.00	50.00	35.00
Steve Carlton	35.00	30.00	20.00
Gary Carter	100.00	80.00	60.00
Orlando Cepeda	35.00	30.00	20.00
A.B. (Happy) Chandler	20.00	16.00	12.00
Earle Combs	300.00	240.00	180.00
Jocko Conlan	25.00	20.00	15.00
Stan Coveleski	30.00	24.00	18.00
"Stanislaus Kowalewski"	150.00	120.00	90.00
Sam Crawford	600.00	480.00	360.00
Joe Cronin	50.00	40.00	30.00
Ray Dandridge	15.00	12.00	9.00
Dizzy Dean	300.00	240.00	180.00
Bill Dickey	50.00	40.00	30.00
Joe DiMaggio	225.00	180.00	135.00
Larry Doby	90.00	70.00	55.00
Bobby Doerr	7.50	6.00	4.50
Don Drysdale	45.00	35.00	25.00
Dennis Eckersley	75.00	60.00	45.00
Red Faber	165.00	130.00	100.00
Bob Feller	7.50	6.00	4.50
Rick Ferrell	15.00	12.00	9.00
Rollie Fingers	20.00	16.00	12.00
Carlton Fisk	80.00	65.00	45.00
Elmer Flick	600.00	480.00	360.00
Whitey Ford	35.00	30.00	20.00
Jimmie Foxx (Usually signed on back.)	1,750	1,400	1,050
Ford Frick	225.00	180.00	135.00
Frank Frisch	300.00	240.00	180.00
Charlie Gehringer	30.00	24.00	18.00
Bob Gibson	30.00	24.00	18.00
Lefty Gomez	35.00	30.00	20.00
Goose Goslin (Usually signed on back; value of such $750-1,000.)	2,250	1,800	1,350
Hank Greenberg	175.00	140.00	100.00
Burleigh Grimes	35.00	30.00	20.00
Lefty Grove	160.00	130.00	95.00
Tony Gwynn	150.00	120.00	90.00
Chick Hafey	725.00	580.00	435.00
Jesse Haines	125.00	100.00	75.00
Bucky Harris	325.00	260.00	195.00
Gabby Hartnett	725.00	580.00	435.00
Billy Herman	12.00	9.50	7.25
Harry Hooper	235.00	190.00	140.00
Waite Hoyt	40.00	32.00	24.00
Cal Hubbard	1,250	1,000	750.00
Carl Hubbell (Pre-stroke.)	40.00	32.00	24.00
Carl Hubbell (Post-stroke.)	25.00	20.00	15.00
Catfish Hunter	30.00	24.00	18.00
Monte Irvin	10.00	8.00	6.00
Reggie Jackson	75.00	60.00	45.00
Travis Jackson	30.00	24.00	18.00
Fergie Jenkins	15.00	12.00	9.00
Judy Johnson	30.00	24.00	18.00
Al Kaline	20.00	16.00	12.00
George Kell	7.50	6.00	4.50
George Kelly	40.00	32.00	24.00
Harmon Killebrew	25.00	20.00	15.00
Ralph Kiner	15.00	12.00	9.00
Sandy Koufax	125.00	100.00	75.00
Tommy Lasorda	100.00	80.00	60.00
Bob Lemon	12.00	9.50	7.25
Buck Leonard (Post-stroke autographed cards worth 50 percent.)	15.00	12.00	9.00
Freddie Lindstrom	75.00	60.00	45.00
Al Lopez	40.00	32.00	24.00
Ted Lyons	45.00	35.00	25.00
Lee MacPhail	35.00	28.00	21.00
Mickey Mantle	235.00	190.00	140.00
Heinie Manush	325.00	260.00	195.00
Juan Marichal	15.00	12.00	9.00
Rube Marquard	40.00	32.00	24.00
Eddie Mathews	25.00	20.00	15.00
Willie Mays	50.00	40.00	30.00
Bill Mazeroski	50.00	40.00	30.00
Joe McCarthy	80.00	65.00	45.00
Willie McCovey	35.00	28.00	21.00
Bill McKechnie (Possible, not likely.)			
Ducky Medwick	185.00	150.00	110.00
Johnny Mize	15.00	12.00	9.00
Paul Molitor	90.00	75.00	55.00
Joe Morgan	30.00	24.00	18.00
Eddie Murray	125.00	100.00	75.00
Stan Musial	25.00	20.00	15.00
Hal Newhouser	15.00	12.00	9.00
Phil Niekro	35.00	30.00	20.00
Satchel Paige	235.00	190.00	140.00
Jim Palmer	20.00	16.00	12.00
Tony Perez	50.00	40.00	30.00
Gaylord Perry	25.00	20.00	15.00
Kirby Puckett	125.00	100.00	75.00
Pee Wee Reese	45.00	35.00	25.00
Sam Rice	185.00	150.00	110.00
Cal Ripken Jr.	100.00	80.00	60.00
Phil Rizzuto	30.00	24.00	18.00
Robin Roberts	12.50	10.00	7.50
Brooks Robinson	12.50	10.00	7.50
Frank Robinson	25.00	20.00	15.00

Jackie Robinson (Often signed on back; value of such $550.)	1,600	1,275	960.00
Edd Roush	30.00	24.00	18.00
Red Ruffing	200.00	160.00	120.00
Nolan Ryan	65.00	50.00	40.00
Ryne Sandberg	60.00	45.00	35.00
Ray Schalk	450.00	360.00	270.00
Mike Schmidt	80.00	65.00	50.00
Red Schoendienst	30.00	24.00	18.00
Tom Seaver	40.00	32.00	24.00
Joe Sewell	15.00	12.00	9.00
George Sisler	200.00	160.00	120.00
Enos Slaughter	10.00	8.00	6.00
Ozzie Smith	95.00	75.00	55.00
Duke Snider	20.00	16.00	12.00
Warren Spahn	20.00	16.00	12.00
Willie Stargell	50.00	40.00	30.00
Casey Stengel	225.00	180.00	135.00
Bruce Sutter	60.00	45.00	35.00
Don Sutton	40.00	32.00	24.00
Bill Terry	25.00	20.00	15.00
Pie Traynor	850.00	680.00	510.00
Lloyd Waner	30.00	24.00	18.00
Paul Waner (Possible, not likely.)			
Earl Weaver	35.00	30.00	20.00
George Weiss (Possible, not likely.)			
Zack Wheat	450.00	360.00	270.00
Hoyt Wilhelm	15.00	12.00	9.00
Billy Williams	15.00	12.00	9.00
Ted Williams	200.00	160.00	120.00
Dave Winfield	100.00	80.00	60.00
Early Wynn	25.00	20.00	15.00
Carl Yastrzemski	55.00	45.00	35.00
Robin Yount	150.00	120.00	90.00

1973 Jack Hamilton's "The Pzazz" Postcard

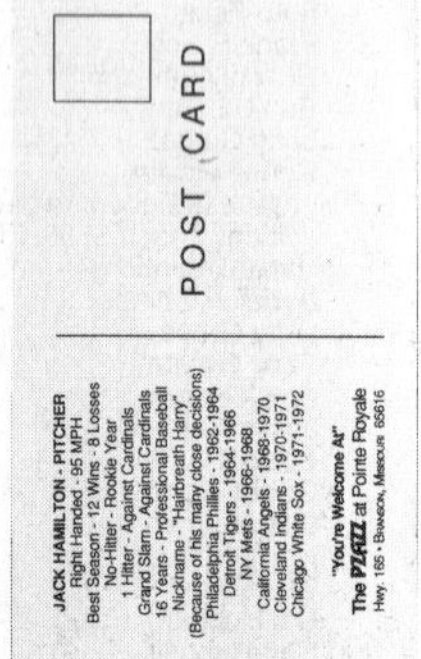

The date attributed is speculative, based on the not totally honest major league career summary printed on the back of this standard-size, black-and-white postcard. The front reproduces a J.D. McCarthy postcard of the pitcher in a New York Mets uniform. There is a white border all around and a facsimile autograph in blue. The back has a few career highlights and advertisement for Hamilton's "The Pzazz" restaurant in Branson, Mo.

	NM	EX	VG
Jack Hamilton	6.00	3.00	1.75

1961 Harmony Milk Pittsburgh Pirates

The attributed year of issue is approximate and subject to change if and when further players are added to the checklist. These premium photos are 8" x 10" in format, round-cornered with blank backs.

		NM	EX	VG
Common Player:		175.00	90.00	50.00
(1)	Roberto Clemente	600.00	300.00	180.00
(2)	Dick Groat	175.00	90.00	50.00
(3)	Don Hoak	175.00	90.00	50.00
(4)	Vern Law	175.00	90.00	50.00
(5)	Danny Murtaugh	175.00	90.00	50.00

1928 Harrington's Ice Cream

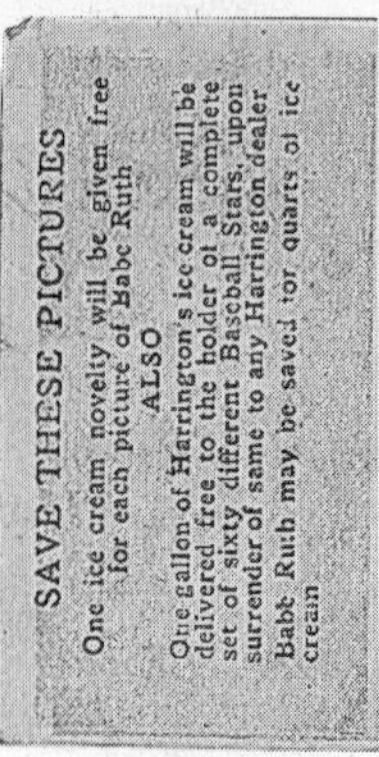

Sharing the same format and checklist with several other (Tharp's, Yeungling's, Sweetman, etc.) contemporary ice cream sets this 60-card set includes all of the top stars of the day. Cards are printed in black-and-white on a 1-3/8" x 2-1/2" format. The player's name and a card number appear either in a strip within the frame of the photo, or printed in the border beneath the photo. Card backs have a redemption offer that includes an ice cream bar in exchange for a Babe Ruth card, or a gallon of ice cream for a complete set of 60.

		NM	EX	VG
Complete Set (60):		20,000	8,000	4,000
Common Player:		90.00	35.00	20.00
1	Burleigh Grimes	350.00	140.00	70.00
2	Walter Reuther (Ruether)	90.00	35.00	20.00
3	Joe Dugan	90.00	35.00	20.00
4	Red Faber	350.00	140.00	70.00
5	Gabby Hartnett	350.00	140.00	70.00
6	Babe Ruth	5,000	2,000	1,000
7	Bob Meusel	90.00	35.00	20.00
8	Herb Pennock	350.00	140.00	70.00
9	George Burns	90.00	35.00	20.00
10	Joe Sewell	350.00	140.00	70.00
11	George Uhle	90.00	35.00	20.00
12	Bob O'Farrell	90.00	35.00	20.00
13	Rogers Hornsby	450.00	180.00	90.00
14	"Pie" Traynor	350.00	140.00	70.00
15	Clarence Mitchell	90.00	35.00	20.00
16	Eppa Jepha Rixey	350.00	140.00	70.00
17	Carl Mays	125.00	50.00	25.00
18	Adolfo Luque	100.00	40.00	20.00
19	Dave Bancroft	350.00	140.00	70.00
20	George Kelly	350.00	140.00	70.00
21	Earl (Earle) Combs	350.00	140.00	70.00
22	Harry Heilmann	350.00	140.00	70.00
23	Ray W. Schalk	350.00	140.00	70.00
24	Johnny Mostil	90.00	35.00	20.00
25	Hack Wilson	350.00	140.00	70.00
26	Lou Gehrig	6,000	1,400	700.00
27	Ty Cobb	1,500	600.00	300.00
28	Tris Speaker	450.00	180.00	90.00
29	Tony Lazzeri	350.00	140.00	70.00
30	Waite Hoyt	350.00	140.00	70.00
31	Sherwood Smith	90.00	35.00	20.00
32	Max Carey	350.00	140.00	70.00
33	Eugene Hargrave	90.00	35.00	20.00
34	Miguel L. Gonzalez (Middle initial A.)	100.00	40.00	20.00
35	Joe Judge	90.00	35.00	20.00
36	E.C. (Sam) Rice	350.00	140.00	70.00
37	Earl Sheely	90.00	35.00	20.00
38	Sam Jones	90.00	35.00	20.00
39	Bib (Bibb) A. Falk	90.00	35.00	20.00
40	Willie Kamm	90.00	35.00	20.00
41	Stanley Harris	350.00	140.00	70.00
42	John J. McGraw	350.00	140.00	70.00
43	Artie Nehf	90.00	35.00	20.00
44	Grover Alexander	450.00	180.00	90.00
45	Paul Waner	350.00	140.00	70.00
46	William H. Terry	350.00	140.00	70.00
47	Glenn Wright	90.00	35.00	20.00
48	Earl Smith	90.00	35.00	20.00
49	Leon (Goose) Goslin	350.00	140.00	70.00
50	Frank Frisch	350.00	140.00	70.00
51	Joe Harris	90.00	35.00	20.00
52	Fred (Cy) Williams	90.00	35.00	20.00
53	Eddie Roush	350.00	140.00	70.00
54	George Sisler	350.00	140.00	70.00
55	Ed. Rommel	90.00	35.00	20.00
56	Rogers Peckinpaugh (Roger)	90.00	35.00	20.00
57	Stanley Coveleskie (Coveleski)	350.00	140.00	70.00
58	Lester Bell	90.00	35.00	20.00
59	L. Waner	350.00	140.00	70.00
60	John P. McInnis	90.00	35.00	20.00

1930-1931 Harrison Studio Homestead Grays Postcards

Whether the famed Negro League powerhouse team, the Homestead Grays, were in Little Rock, Ark., for spring training or on a barnstorming tour, they became the subjects of a series of postcards from the local photographer, Harrison Studio. The cards are in standard postcard format, featuring borderless black-and-white photographic poses. It is likely the checklist here is incomplete.

(1)	Josh Gibson (Front/back autographed card sold at auction 4/06 for $81,200.)
(2)	Ted Page
(3)	Ambrose Reed
(4)	Homestead Grays 1930 Team Photo
(5)	Homestead Grays 1931 Team Photo

1911-12 Hassan Cigarettes

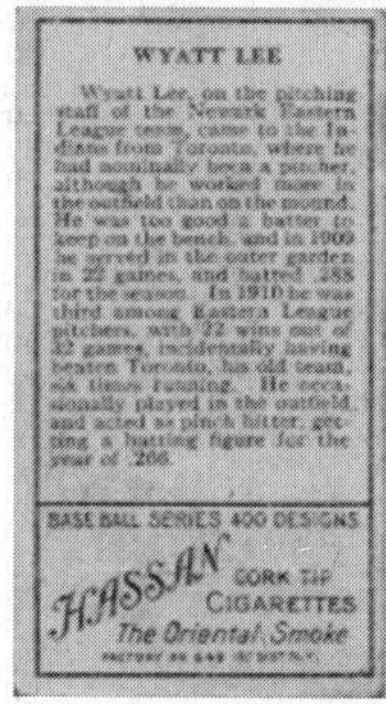

Prior to its sole sponsorship of the T202 Triplefolders set of 1912, Hassan was one of 10 American Tobacco Co. brands advertising on the backs of 1911 T205 Gold Borders. Two different factories are noted on these backs, No. 30 and No. 649, the former being slightly scarcer, though currently no more valuable. Hassan backs in T205 are printed in green and do not command any significant premium in the market.

(See T202, T205.)

1887 Hastings Cabinets

From the Boston studio of G.H. Hastings, this standard-format (about 3-3/4" x 5-3/4") cabinet card depicts the 19th Century's most popular star in stylish street clothers. Printed beneath the portrait is a copyright line, player and team identification and the logo and address of the studio. Back is blank. It is unknown whether other ballplayers' portraits were produced, though it is likely.

	NM	EX	VG
M.J. Kelly	12,500	5,000	2,500

1952 Hawthorn-Mellody Chicago White Sox Pins

This issue was sponsored by a local dairy. The 1-3/8" diameter pins have sepia lithographs of the players with "Club of Champs" printed above. A non-pictorial membership button is also part of the set. The unnumbered pins are listed here in alphabetical order.

		NM	EX	VG
Complete Set (11):		400.00	200.00	120.00
Common Player:		35.00	17.50	10.50
(1)	Ray Coleman	35.00	17.50	10.50
(2)	Sam Dente	35.00	17.50	10.50
(3)	Joe Dobson	35.00	17.50	10.50
(4)	Nelson Fox	80.00	40.00	24.00
(5)	Sherman Lollar	45.00	22.00	13.50
(6)	Bill Pierce	45.00	22.00	13.50
(7)	Eddie Robinson	35.00	17.50	10.50
(8)	Hector Rodriguez	35.00	17.50	10.50
(9)	Eddie Stewart	35.00	17.50	10.50
(10)	Al Zarilla	35.00	17.50	10.50
(11)	Member's pin	15.00	7.50	4.50

1959 R.H. Hayes Postcards

Whether there are any other player postcards distributed by R.H. Hayes of Kansas is unknown. Produced for Hayes by Dexter Press, which issued cards for Coke in later years, the 3-1/2" x 5-1/2" postcard has a borderless color photo on front with a facsimile autograph at bottom. The postcard back has credit lines for Hayes and Dexter and a short biography of the player.

		NM	EX	VG
(1)	Hank Bauer	45.00	22.50	13.50

1911 Helmar Stamps (T332)

A collectible departure from the traditional tobacco cards of the period, Helmar Cigarettes in 1911 issued a series of small major league baseball player "stamps." The stamps, each measuring approximately 1-1/8" x 1-3/8", feature a black and white player portrait surrounded by a colorful, ornate frame. The stamps were originally issued in a 2" x 2-1/2" glassine envelope which advertised the Helmar brand and promoted "Philately - the Popular European Rage." To date, 181 different player stamps have been found. The set includes as many as 50 different frame designs. The Helmar stamp set has been assigned a T332 designation by the American Card Catalog.

		NM	EX	VG
Complete Set (180):		8,000	4,000	2,400
Common Player:		50.00	25.00	15.00
(1)	Babe Adams	50.00	25.00	15.00
(2)	Red Ames	50.00	25.00	15.00
(3)	Jimmy Archer	50.00	25.00	15.00
(4)	Jimmy Austin	50.00	25.00	15.00
(5)	Home Run Baker	100.00	50.00	30.00
(6)	Neal Ball	50.00	25.00	15.00
(7)	Cy Barger	50.00	25.00	15.00
(8)	Jack Barry	50.00	25.00	15.00
(9)	Johnny Bates	50.00	25.00	15.00
(10)	Fred Beck	50.00	25.00	15.00
(11)	Beals Becker	50.00	25.00	15.00
(12)	George Bell	50.00	25.00	15.00
(13)	Chief Bender	100.00	50.00	30.00
(14)	Bob Bescher	50.00	25.00	15.00
(15)	Joe Birmingham	50.00	25.00	15.00
(16)	John Bliss	50.00	25.00	15.00
(17)	Bruno Block	50.00	25.00	15.00
(18)	Ping Bodie	50.00	25.00	15.00
(19)	Roger Bresnahan	100.00	50.00	30.00
(20)	Al Bridwell	50.00	25.00	15.00
(21)	Lew Brockett	50.00	25.00	15.00
(22)	Mordecai Brown	100.00	50.00	30.00
(23)	Bill Burns	50.00	25.00	15.00
(24)	Donie Bush	50.00	25.00	15.00
(25)	Bobby Byrne	50.00	25.00	15.00
(26)	Nixey Callahan	50.00	25.00	15.00
(27)	Howie Camnitz	50.00	25.00	15.00
(28)	Max Carey	100.00	50.00	30.00
(29)	Bill Carrigan	50.00	25.00	15.00
(30)	Frank Chance	100.00	50.00	30.00
(31)	Hal Chase	50.00	25.00	15.00
(32)	Ed Cicotte	80.00	40.00	24.00
(33)	Fred Clarke	100.00	50.00	30.00
(34)	Tommy Clarke	50.00	25.00	15.00
(35)	Ty Cobb	750.00	375.00	225.00
(36)	King Cole	50.00	25.00	15.00
(37)	Eddie Collins (Philadelphia)	100.00	50.00	30.00
(38)	Shano Collins (Chicago)	50.00	25.00	15.00
(39)	Wid Conroy	50.00	25.00	15.00
(40)	Doc Crandall	50.00	25.00	15.00
(41)	Sam Crawford	100.00	50.00	30.00
(42)	Birdie Cree	50.00	25.00	15.00
(43)	Bill Dahlen	50.00	25.00	15.00
(44)	Jake Daubert	50.00	25.00	15.00
(45)	Harry Davis	50.00	25.00	15.00
(46)	Jim Delahanty	50.00	25.00	15.00
(47)	Art Devlin	50.00	25.00	15.00
(48)	Josh Devore	50.00	25.00	15.00
(49)	Mike Donlin	50.00	25.00	15.00
(50)	Wild Bill Donovan	50.00	25.00	15.00
(51)	Red Dooin	50.00	25.00	15.00
(52)	Mickey Doolan	50.00	25.00	15.00
(53)	Patsy Dougherty	50.00	25.00	15.00
(54)	Tom Downey	50.00	25.00	15.00
(55)	Larry Doyle	50.00	25.00	15.00
(56)	Louis Drucke	50.00	25.00	15.00
(57)	Clyde Engle	50.00	25.00	15.00
(58)	Tex Erwin	50.00	25.00	15.00
(59)	Steve Evans	50.00	25.00	15.00
(60)	Johnny Evers	100.00	50.00	30.00
(61)	Jack Ferry	50.00	25.00	15.00
(62)	Ray Fisher	50.00	25.00	15.00
(63)	Art Fletcher	50.00	25.00	15.00
(64)	Russ Ford	50.00	25.00	15.00
(65)	Art Fromme	50.00	25.00	15.00
(66)	Earl Gardner	50.00	25.00	15.00
(67)	Harry Gaspar	50.00	25.00	15.00
(68)	George Gibson	50.00	25.00	15.00
(69)	Roy Golden	50.00	25.00	15.00
(70)	Hank Gowdy	50.00	25.00	15.00
(71)	Peaches Graham	50.00	25.00	15.00
(72)	Eddie Grant	50.00	25.00	15.00
(73)	Dolly Gray	50.00	25.00	15.00
(74)	Clark Griffith	100.00	50.00	30.00
(75)	Bob Groom	50.00	25.00	15.00
(76)	Bob Harmon	50.00	25.00	15.00
(77)	Grover Hartley	50.00	25.00	15.00
(78)	Arnold Hauser	50.00	25.00	15.00
(79)	Buck Herzog	50.00	25.00	15.00
(80)	Dick Hoblitzell	50.00	25.00	15.00
(81)	Solly Hoffman (Hofman)	50.00	25.00	15.00
(82)	Miller Huggins	100.00	50.00	30.00
(83)	Long Tom Hughes	50.00	25.00	15.00
(84)	John Hummel	50.00	25.00	15.00
(85)	Hughie Jennings	100.00	50.00	30.00
(86)	Walter Johnson	275.00	135.00	82.00
(87)	Davy Jones	50.00	25.00	15.00
(88)	Johnny Kling	50.00	25.00	15.00
(89)	Otto Knabe	50.00	25.00	15.00
(90)	Jack Knight	50.00	25.00	15.00
(91)	Ed Konetchy	50.00	25.00	15.00
(92)	Harry Krause	50.00	25.00	15.00
(93)	Nap Lajoie	100.00	50.00	30.00
(94)	Joe Lake	50.00	25.00	15.00
(95)	Frank LaPorte	50.00	25.00	15.00
(96)	Tommy Leach	50.00	25.00	15.00
(97)	Lefty Leifield	50.00	25.00	15.00
(98)	Ed Lennox	50.00	25.00	15.00
(99)	Paddy Livingston	50.00	25.00	15.00
(100)	Hans Lobert	50.00	25.00	15.00
(101)	Harry Lord	50.00	25.00	15.00
(102)	Fred Luderus	50.00	25.00	15.00
(103)	Sherry Magee	50.00	25.00	15.00
(104)	Rube Marquard	100.00	50.00	30.00
(105)	Christy Mathewson	300.00	150.00	90.00
(106)	Al Mattern	50.00	25.00	15.00
(107)	George McBride	50.00	25.00	15.00
(108)	Amby McConnell	50.00	25.00	15.00
(109)	John McGraw	100.00	50.00	30.00
(110)	Harry McIntire (McIntyre)	50.00	25.00	15.00
(111)	Matty McIntyre	50.00	25.00	15.00
(112)	Larry McLean	50.00	25.00	15.00
(113)	Fred Merkle	50.00	25.00	15.00
(114)	Chief Meyers	50.00	25.00	15.00
(115)	Clyde Milan	50.00	25.00	15.00
(116)	Dots Miller	50.00	25.00	15.00
(117)	Mike Mitchell	50.00	25.00	15.00
(118)	Earl Moore	50.00	25.00	15.00
(119)	Pat Moran	50.00	25.00	15.00
(120)	George Moriarty	50.00	25.00	15.00
(121)	Mike Mowrey	50.00	25.00	15.00
(122)	George Mullin	50.00	25.00	15.00
(123)	Danny Murphy	50.00	25.00	15.00
(124)	Red Murray	50.00	25.00	15.00
(125)	Tom Needham	50.00	25.00	15.00
(126)	Rebel Oakes	50.00	25.00	15.00
(127)	Rube Oldring	50.00	25.00	15.00
(128)	Marty O'Toole	50.00	25.00	15.00
(129)	Fred Parent	50.00	25.00	15.00
(130)	Dode Paskert	50.00	25.00	15.00
(131)	Barney Pelty	50.00	25.00	15.00
(132)	Eddie Phelps	50.00	25.00	15.00
(133)	Jack Powell	50.00	25.00	15.00
(134)	Jack Quinn	50.00	25.00	15.00
(135)	Ed Reulbach	50.00	25.00	15.00
(136)	Lew Richie	50.00	25.00	15.00
(137)	Reggie Richter	50.00	25.00	15.00
(138)	Jack Rowan	50.00	25.00	15.00
(139)	Nap Rucker	50.00	25.00	15.00
(140)	Slim Sallee	50.00	25.00	15.00
(141)	Doc Scanlan	50.00	25.00	15.00
(142)	Germany Schaefer	50.00	25.00	15.00
(143)	Boss Schmidt	50.00	25.00	15.00
(144)	Wildfire Schulte	50.00	25.00	15.00
(145)	Jim Scott	50.00	25.00	15.00
(146)	Tillie Shafer	50.00	25.00	15.00
(147)	Dave Shean	50.00	25.00	15.00
(148)	Jimmy Sheckard	50.00	25.00	15.00
(149)	Mike Simon	50.00	25.00	15.00
(150)	Fred Snodgrass	50.00	25.00	15.00
(151)	Tris Speaker	125.00	62.00	37.00
(152)	Oscar Stanage	50.00	25.00	15.00
(153)	Bill Steele	50.00	25.00	15.00
(154)	Harry Stovall	50.00	25.00	15.00
(155)	Gabby Street	50.00	25.00	15.00
(156)	George Suggs	50.00	25.00	15.00
(157)	Billy Sullivan	50.00	25.00	15.00
(158)	Bill Sweeney	50.00	25.00	15.00
(159)	Jeff Sweeney	50.00	25.00	15.00
(160)	Lee Tannehill	50.00	25.00	15.00
(161)	Ira Thomas	50.00	25.00	15.00
(162)	Joe Tinker	100.00	50.00	30.00
(163)	John Titus	50.00	25.00	15.00
(164)	Fred Toney	50.00	25.00	15.00
(165)	Terry Turner	50.00	25.00	15.00
(166)	Hippo Vaughn	50.00	25.00	15.00
(167)	Heinie Wagner	50.00	25.00	15.00
(168)	Bobby Wallace	100.00	50.00	30.00
(169)	Ed Walsh	100.00	50.00	30.00
(170)	Jack Warhop	50.00	25.00	15.00
(171)	Zach Wheat	100.00	50.00	30.00
(172)	Doc White	50.00	25.00	15.00
(173)	Ed Willett	50.00	25.00	15.00
(174)	Art Wilson (New York)	50.00	25.00	15.00
(175)	Owen Wilson (Pittsburgh)	50.00	25.00	15.00
(176)	Hooks Wiltse	50.00	25.00	15.00
(177)	Harry Wolter	50.00	25.00	15.00
(178)	Harry Wolverton	50.00	25.00	15.00
(179)	Cy Young	400.00	200.00	120.00
(180)	Irv Young	50.00	25.00	15.00

1910 Hermes Ice Cream Pirates Pins

The World's Champion Pittsburgh Pirates are featured on this colorful set of 1-1/4" pins. Sepia player portraits at center have a yellow border around with a blue banner at bottom and a skull and crossbones. The players are not identified on the buttons, making them difficult to collect.

		NM	EX	VG
Complete Set (12):		11,000	5,500	3,250
Common Player:		450.00	225.00	135.00
(1)	Bill Abstein	450.00	225.00	135.00
(2)	Red Adams	450.00	225.00	135.00
(3)	Bobby Byrne	450.00	225.00	135.00
(4)	Howie Camnitz	450.00	225.00	135.00
(5)	Fred Clarke	450.00	225.00	135.00
(6)	George Gibson	450.00	225.00	135.00
(7)	Tommy Leach	450.00	225.00	135.00
(8)	Sam Leever	450.00	225.00	135.00
(9)	Dots Miller	450.00	225.00	135.00
(10)	Mike Simon	450.00	225.00	135.00
(11)	Honus Wagner	6,500	3,250	2,000
(12)	Owen Wilson	450.00	225.00	135.00

1916 Herpolsheimer Co.

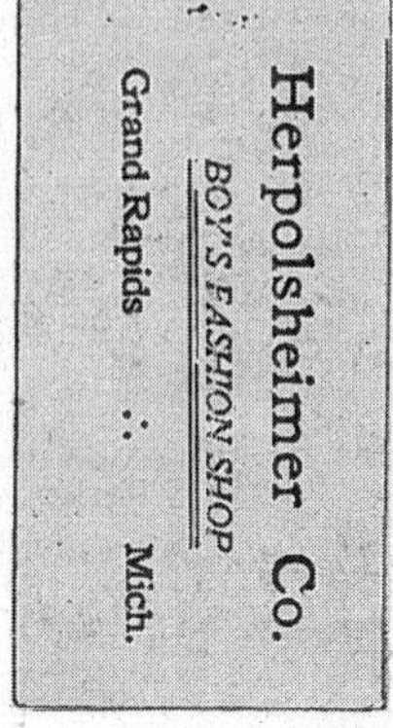

Advertising for a Michigan clothier is all that differentiates these cards from the more common Sporting News or blank-back M101-4 versions and those of other regional advertisers. The cards are black-and-white in 1-5/8" x 3" format. The Herpolsheimer cards command a significant premium from type-card and superstar collectors.

PREMIUMS:
Common Players: 3-4X
Hall of Famers: 2-3X
(See 1916 M101-4 Blank Backs for checklist and price guide.)

1921 Herpolsheimer's

Issued by a Grand Rapids, Mich., department store that also produced a card set in 1916, this issue shares a basic format with the blank-backed strip-card set designated W575-1, though the known checklist of the Herpolsheimers includes cards that have not yet been verified in W575-1. It is also not known to what extent the variations listed among W575-1 are found among the Michigan store's version. The Herpolsheimer's cards differ from the strip cards in the inclusion of the advertising on the back and sometimes in photo and/or caption details. The 2-1/16" x 3-3/8" black-and-white cards are much scarcer than the strip-card version. The checklist presented here is incomplete. Gaps have been left in the assgned numbering to accomodate future additions. This set only game to the hobby's attention late in 2004 through a series of eBay auctions. Currently only a single example is known of each card. All known examples have a pencilled figure and dollar sign on back.

		NM	EX	VG
Common Player:				450.00
(3)	Grover Alexander			1,100
(5)	J. Franklin Baker			750.00
(11)	Jim Bagby			450.00
(13)	Ping Bodie			450.00
(15)	George Burns			450.00
(16)	Geo. J. Burns			450.00
(18)	Owen Bush			450.00
(21)	Ty Cobb			4,000
(22)	Eddie Collins			750.00
(28)	George Dauss			450.00
(29)	Dave Davenport			450.00
(30)	Charles Deal			450.00
(33)	William Doak			450.00
(34)	Bill Donovan/Pitching			450.00
(39)	Urban Faber (Dark uniform.)			750.00
(45)	Art Fletcher			450.00
(47)	Jacques Fournier			450.00
(49)	W.L. Gardner			450.00
(52)	"Kid" Gleason			450.00
(54)	Hank Gowdy			450.00
(55)	John Graney (L.F.)			450.00
(57)	Tom Griffith			450.00
(67)	John Henry			450.00
(74)	Rogers Hornsby (2nd B.)			2,000
(79)	Hugh Jennings			450.00
(80)	Walter Johnson			4,500
(82)	James Johnston			450.00
(84)	Joe Judge/Btg			450.00
(89)	P.J. Kilduff			450.00
(93)	"Nemo" Leibold			450.00
(94)	Duffy Lewis			450.00
(95)	Al Mamaux			450.00
(96)	"Rabbit" Maranville			750.00
(101)	John McGraw (Manager)			750.00
(102)	Jack McInnis			450.00
(107)	Clyde Milan			450.00
(109)	Otto Miller			450.00
(112)	Guy Morton			450.00
(115)	Eddie Murphy			450.00
(116)	"Hy" Myers (C.F.)			450.00
(123)	Steve O'Neill			450.00
(124)	Roger Peckinbaugh (Peckinpaugh)			450.00
(125)	Jeff Pfeffer (Brooklyn)			450.00
(133)	E.C. Rice			750.00
(134)	Eppa Rixey, Jr.			750.00
(145)	Babe Ruth (R.F.)			10,000
(149)	"Slim" Sallee (Glove showing.)			450.00
(151)	Ray Schalk (Bunting)			750.00
(153)	Walter Schang			450.00
(155)	Everett Scott (Boston)			450.00
(173)	Tris Speaker (Manager)			1,250
(175)	Charles Stengel/Btg			750.00
(177)	Milton Stock			450.00
(178)	Amos Strunk (R.F.)			450.00
(181)	Zeb Terry (White uniform.)			450.00
(182)	Chester Thomas			450.00
(183)	Fred Toney (Both feet on ground.)			450.00
(186)	George Tyler			450.00
(187)	Jim Vaughn (Dark cap.)			450.00
(190)	Bob Veach (Arms folded.)			450.00
(191)	Oscar Vitt (3rd B.)			450.00
(193)	W. Wambsganss			450.00
(194)	Carl Weilman			450.00
(195)	Zach Wheat			750.00
(196)	George Whitted			450.00
(198)	Ivy B. Wingo			450.00
(200)	Joe Wood			675.00
(202)	"Pep" (Ralph) Young			450.00

1888 S.F. Hess (N338-2)

The most popular of the S.F. Hess & Co. issues, this 21-card set was issued in 1889 and pictures 16 players from the New York Giants, two New York Mets players, two from St. Louis and one from Detroit. The cards measure 2-3/4" x 1-1/2" and feature sepia-toned photographs, most of which are enclosed in ovals with a dark background. The player's name is printed in capital letters just beneath the photo, and the S.F. Hess & Co. logo appears at the bottom (without using the Creole Cigarette brand name).

		NM	EX	VG
Common Player:		7,900	3,950	2,375
(1)	Bill Brown	7,900	3,950	2,375
(2)	Roger Conner (Connor)	20,000	10,000	6,000
(3)	Ed Crane	7,900	3,950	2,375
(4)	Buck Ewing	21,000	10,500	6,200
(5)	Elmer Foster	7,900	3,950	2,375
(6)	Wm. George	7,900	3,950	2,375
(7)	Joe Gerhardt	7,900	3,950	2,375
(8)	Chas. Getzein (Getzien)	7,900	3,950	2,375
(9)	Geo. Gore	7,900	3,950	2,375
(10)	Gil Hatfield	7,900	3,950	2,375
(11)	Tim Keefe	20,000	10,000	6,000
(12)	Arlie Latham	7,900	3,950	2,375
(13)	Pat Murphy	7,900	3,950	2,375
(14)	Jim Mutrie	7,900	3,950	2,375
(15)	Dave Orr	7,900	3,950	2,375
(16)	Danny Richardson	7,900	3,950	2,375
(17)	Mike Slattery	7,900	3,950	2,375
(18)	Silent Mike Tiernan	7,900	3,950	2,375
(19)	Lidell Titcomb	7,900	3,950	2,375
(20)	Johnny Ward	20,000	10,000	6,000
(21)	Curt Welch	7,900	3,950	2,375
(22)	Mickey Welch	20,000	10,000	6,000
(23)	Arthur Whitney	7,900	3,950	2,375

1909-11 Hindu Cigarettes

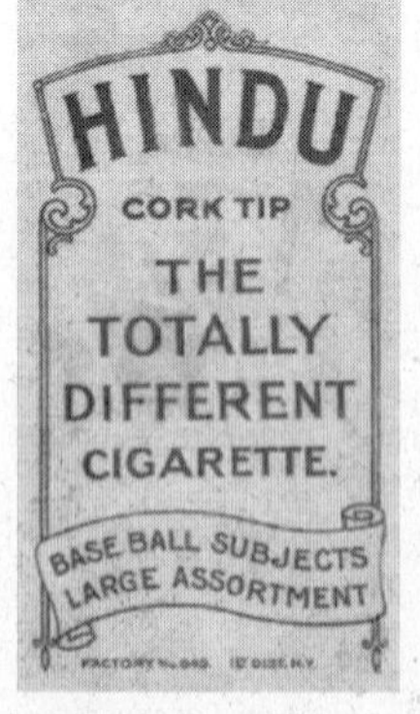

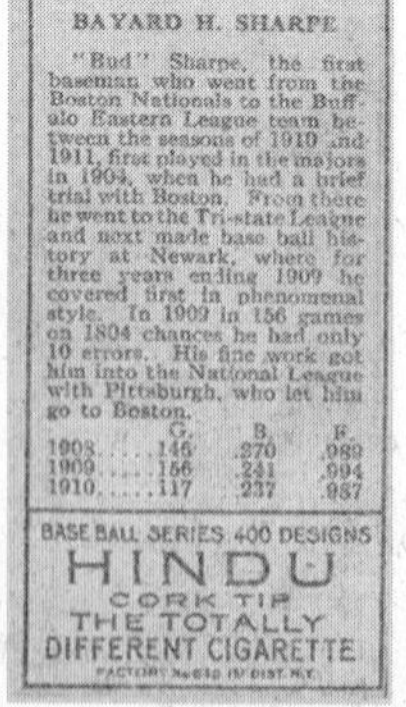

Hindu backs are among the more difficult to find among the various cigarette-brand ads seen on T205 and T206 cards. T206s are usually found with the ad printed in brown ink. Much scarcer are those with the ad in red. Fewer than 50 T205s have ever been seen with the Hindu ad on back, printed in brown. Multipliers shown are for "common" player cards. Cards of Hall of Famers or other high-demand cards are usually figured by using a multiplier of about one-half those shown here.

PREMIUMS
T205: 15-20X
T206 Brown Commons: 8-10X
T206 Brown Hall of Famers: 5-7X
T206 Brown Southern Leaguers: 3-4X
T206 Red Commons: 15X
T206 Red Hall of Famers: 10X
(See T205, T206 for checklists and base card values.)

1958 Hires Root Beer Test Set

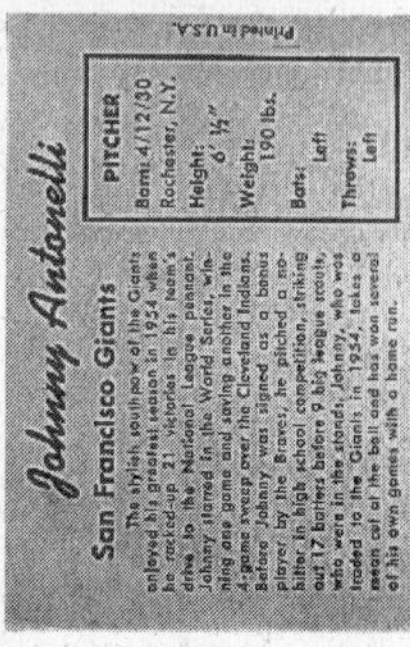

Among the scarcest of the regional issues of the late 1950s is the eight-card test issue which preceded the Hires Root Beer set of 66 cards. The test cards differ from the regular issue in that they have sepia-toned, rather than color pictures, which are set against plain yellow or orange backgrounds (much like the 1958 Topps), instead of viewed through a knothole. Like the regular Hires cards, the 2-5/16" x 3-1/2" cards were issued with an attached wedge-shaped tab of like size. The tab offered membership in Hires' baseball fan club, and served to hold the card into the carton of bottled root beer with which it was given away.

		NM	EX	VG
Complete Set, W/Tab (8):		10,000	4,000	2,000
Common Player, W/Tab:		725.00	290.00	145.00
Complete Set, No Tab (8):		3,000	1,200	600.00
Common Player, No Tab:		250.00	100.00	50.00
	WITH TAB			
(1)	Johnny Antonelli	725.00	290.00	145.00
(2)	Jim Busby	725.00	290.00	145.00
(3)	Chico Fernandez	725.00	290.00	145.00
(4)	Bob Friend	725.00	290.00	145.00
(5)	Vern Law	725.00	290.00	145.00
(6)	Stan Lopata	725.00	290.00	145.00
(7)	Willie Mays	5,000	2,000	1,000
(8)	Al Pilarcik	725.00	290.00	145.00
	NO TAB			
(1)	Johnny Antonelli	250.00	100.00	50.00
(2)	Jim Busby	250.00	100.00	50.00
(3)	Chico Fernandez	250.00	100.00	50.00
(4)	Bob Friend	250.00	100.00	50.00
(5)	Vern Law	250.00	100.00	50.00
(6)	Stan Lopata	250.00	100.00	50.00
(7)	Willie Mays	1,300	525.00	250.00
(8)	Al Pilarcik	250.00	100.00	50.00

1958 Hires Root Beer

Like most baseball cards issued with a tab in the 1950s, the Hires cards are extremely scarce today in their original form. The basic card was attached to a wedge-shaped tab that served the dual purpose of offering a fan club membership and of holding the card into the cardboard carton of soda bottles with which it was distributed. Measurements of the card vary somewhat, from about 2-3/8" to 2-5/8" wide and 3-3/8" to 3-5/8" tall (without tab). The tab extends for another 3-1/2". Numbering of the Hires set begins at 10 and goes through 76, with card #69 never issued, making a set complete at 66 cards.

		NM	EX	VG
Complete Set, W/Tab (66):		5,250	2,650	1,550
Common Player, W/Tab:		60.00	30.00	18.00
Complete Set, No Tab (66):		3,250	1,600	975.00
Common Player, No Tab:		35.00	17.50	10.00
	WITH TAB			
10	Richie Ashburn	165.00	80.00	50.00
11	Chico Carrasquel	60.00	30.00	18.00
12	Dave Philley	60.00	30.00	18.00
13	Don Newcombe	110.00	55.00	35.00
14	Wally Post	60.00	30.00	18.00
15	Rip Repulski	60.00	30.00	18.00
16	Chico Fernandez	60.00	30.00	18.00
17	Larry Doby	95.00	50.00	25.00
18	Hector Brown	60.00	30.00	18.00

19	Danny O'Connell	60.00	30.00	18.00
20	Granny Hamner	60.00	30.00	18.00
21	Dick Groat	60.00	30.00	18.00
22	Ray Narleski	60.00	30.00	18.00
23	Pee Wee Reese	165.00	85.00	50.00
24	Bob Friend	60.00	30.00	18.00
25	Willie Mays	500.00	250.00	150.00
26	Bob Nieman	60.00	30.00	18.00
27	Frank Thomas	60.00	30.00	18.00
28	Curt Simmons	60.00	30.00	18.00
29	Stan Lopata	60.00	30.00	18.00
30	Bob Skinner	60.00	30.00	18.00
31	Ron Kline	60.00	30.00	18.00
32	Willie Miranda	60.00	30.00	18.00
33	Bob Avila	60.00	30.00	18.00
34	Clem Labine	90.00	45.00	27.50
35	Ray Jablonski	60.00	30.00	18.00
36	Bill Mazeroski	110.00	55.00	35.00
37	Billy Gardner	60.00	30.00	18.00
38	Pete Runnels	60.00	30.00	18.00
39	Jack Sanford	60.00	30.00	18.00
40	Dave Sisler	60.00	30.00	18.00
41	Don Zimmer	90.00	45.00	27.00
42	Johnny Podres	90.00	45.00	27.50
43	Dick Farrell	60.00	30.00	18.00
44	Hank Aaron	425.00	210.00	125.00
45	Bill Virdon	60.00	30.00	18.00
46	Bobby Thomson	75.00	37.50	22.50
47	Willard Nixon	60.00	30.00	18.00
48	Billy Loes	60.00	30.00	18.00
49	Hank Sauer	60.00	30.00	18.00
50	Johnny Antonelli	60.00	30.00	18.00
51	Daryl Spencer	60.00	30.00	18.00
52	Ken Lehman	75.00	37.50	22.50
53	Sammy White	60.00	30.00	18.00
54	Charley Neal	75.00	37.50	22.50
55	Don Drysdale	165.00	80.00	50.00
56	Jack Jensen	65.00	32.50	20.00
57	Ray Katt	60.00	30.00	18.00
58	Franklin Sullivan	60.00	30.00	18.00
59	Roy Face	60.00	30.00	18.00
60	Willie Jones	60.00	30.00	18.00
61	Duke Snider/SP	250.00	125.00	75.00
62	Whitey Lockman	60.00	30.00	18.00
63	Gino Cimoli	75.00	37.00	22.50
64	Marv Grissom	60.00	30.00	18.00
65	Gene Baker	60.00	30.00	18.00
66	George Zuverink	60.00	30.00	18.00
67	Ted Kluszewski	135.00	70.00	40.00
68	Jim Busby	60.00	30.00	18.00
69	Not issued			
70	Curt Barclay	60.00	30.00	18.00
71	Hank Foiles	60.00	30.00	18.00
72	Gene Stephens	60.00	30.00	18.00
73	Al Worthington	60.00	30.00	18.00
74	Al Walker	60.00	30.00	18.00
75	Bob Boyd	60.00	30.00	18.00
76	Al Pilarcik	60.00	30.00	18.00

NO TAB

10	Richie Ashburn	110.00	55.00	35.00
11	Chico Carrasquel	35.00	17.50	10.00
12	Dave Philley	35.00	17.50	10.00
13	Don Newcombe	65.00	32.50	20.00
14	Wally Post	35.00	17.50	10.00
15	Rip Repulski	35.00	17.50	10.00
16	Chico Fernandez	35.00	17.50	10.00
17	Larry Doby	75.00	37.50	22.50
18	Hector Brown	35.00	17.50	10.00
19	Danny O'Connell	35.00	17.50	10.00
20	Granny Hamner	35.00	17.50	10.00
21	Dick Groat	35.00	17.50	10.00
22	Ray Narleski	35.00	17.50	10.00
23	Pee Wee Reese	100.00	50.00	30.00
24	Bob Friend	35.00	17.50	10.00
25	Willie Mays	200.00	100.00	60.00
26	Bob Nieman	35.00	17.50	10.00
27	Frank Thomas	35.00	17.50	10.00
28	Curt Simmons	35.00	17.50	10.00
29	Stan Lopata	35.00	17.50	10.00
30	Bob Skinner	35.00	17.50	10.00
31	Ron Kline	35.00	17.50	10.00
32	Willie Miranda	35.00	17.50	10.00
33	Bob Avila	35.00	17.50	10.00
34	Clem Labine	45.00	22.50	13.50
35	Ray Jablonski	35.00	17.50	10.00
36	Bill Mazeroski	75.00	37.50	22.50
37	Billy Gardner	35.00	17.50	10.00
38	Pete Runnels	35.00	17.50	10.00
39	Jack Sanford	35.00	17.50	10.00
40	Dave Sisler	35.00	17.50	10.00
41	Don Zimmer	45.00	22.50	13.50
42	Johnny Podres	45.00	22.50	13.50
43	Dick Farrell	35.00	17.50	10.00
44	Hank Aaron	200.00	100.00	60.00
45	Bill Virdon	35.00	17.50	10.00
46	Bobby Thomson	45.00	22.50	13.50
47	Willard Nixon	35.00	17.50	10.00
48	Billy Loes	35.00	17.50	10.00
49	Hank Sauer	35.00	17.50	10.00
50	Johnny Antonelli	35.00	17.50	10.00
51	Daryl Spencer	35.00	17.50	10.00
52	Ken Lehman	40.00	20.00	12.00
53	Sammy White	35.00	17.50	10.00
54	Charley Neal	40.00	20.00	12.00
55	Don Drysdale	75.00	37.50	22.50
56	Jack Jensen	40.00	20.00	12.00
57	Ray Katt	35.00	17.50	10.00
58	Franklin Sullivan	35.00	17.50	10.00
59	Roy Face	35.00	17.50	10.00
60	Willie Jones	35.00	17.50	10.00
61	Duke Snider/SP	180.00	90.00	55.00
62	Whitey Lockman	35.00	17.50	10.00
63	Gino Cimoli	40.00	20.00	10.00
64	Marv Grissom	35.00	17.50	10.00
65	Gene Baker	35.00	17.50	10.00
66	George Zuverink	35.00	17.50	10.00
67	Ted Kluszewski	75.00	37.50	22.50
68	Jim Busby	35.00	17.50	10.00
69	NOT ISSUED			
70	Curt Barclay	35.00	17.50	10.00
71	Hank Foiles	35.00	17.50	10.00
72	Gene Stephens	35.00	17.50	10.00
73	Al Worthington	35.00	17.50	10.00
74	Al Walker	35.00	17.50	10.00
75	Bob Boyd	35.00	17.50	10.00
76	Al Pilarcik	35.00	17.50	10.00

1951-52 Hit Parade of Champions

(See 1951-52 Berk Ross.)

1977 Holiday Inn Discs

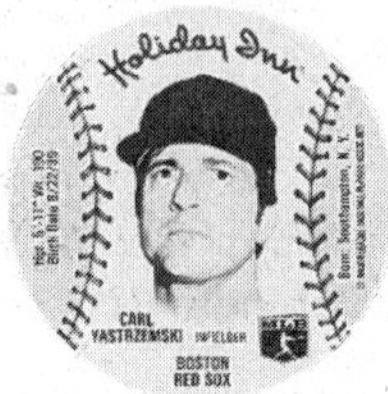

Virtually identical in format to the several locally sponsored disc sets of the previous year, these 3-3/8" diameter player discs were given away five at a time with the purchase of a children's dinner at some 72 participating Holiday Inns in the Midwest. Discs once again feature black-and-white player portrait photos in the center of a baseball design. The left and right panels are in one of several bright colors. Licensed by the Players Association through Mike Schechter Associates, the player photos carry no uniform logos. Backs are printed in green. The unnumbered discs are checklisted here alphabetically.

		NM	EX	VG
Complete Set (70):		160.00	80.00	45.00
Common Player:		2.00	1.00	.60
(1)	Sal Bando	2.00	1.00	.60
(2)	Buddy Bell	2.00	1.00	.60
(3)	Johnny Bench	6.00	3.00	1.75
(4)	Larry Bowa	2.00	1.00	.60
(5)	Steve Braun	2.00	1.00	.60
(6)	George Brett	20.00	10.00	6.00
(7)	Lou Brock	6.00	3.00	1.75
(8)	Jeff Burroughs	2.00	1.00	.60
(9)	Bert Campaneris	2.00	1.00	.60
(10)	John Candelaria	2.00	1.00	.60
(11)	Jose Cardenal	2.00	1.00	.60
(12)	Rod Carew	6.00	3.00	1.75
(13)	Steve Carlton	6.00	3.00	1.75
(14)	Dave Cash	2.00	1.00	.60
(15)	Cesar Cedeno	2.00	1.00	.60
(16)	Ron Cey	2.00	1.00	.60
(17)	Dave Concepcion	2.00	1.00	.60
(18)	Dennis Eckersley	5.00	2.50	1.50
(19)	Mark Fidrych	3.00	1.50	.90
(20)	Rollie Fingers	5.00	2.50	1.50
(21)	Carlton Fisk	6.00	3.00	1.75
(22)	George Foster	2.00	1.00	.60
(23)	Wayne Garland	2.00	1.00	.60
(24)	Ralph Garr	2.00	1.00	.60
(25)	Steve Garvey	4.00	2.00	1.25
(26)	Cesar Geronimo	2.00	1.00	.60
(27)	Bobby Grich	2.00	1.00	.60
(28)	Ken Griffey Sr.	2.50	1.25	.70
(29)	Don Gullett	2.00	1.00	.60
(30)	Mike Hargrove	2.00	1.00	.60
(31)	Al Hrabosky	2.00	1.00	.60
(32)	Jim Hunter	5.00	2.50	1.50
(33)	Reggie Jackson	10.00	5.00	3.00
(34)	Randy Jones	2.00	1.00	.60
(35a)	Dave Kingman (Mets)	2.50	1.25	.70
(35b)	Dave Kingman (Padres)	4.00	2.00	1.25
(36)	Jerry Koosman	2.00	1.00	.60
(37)	Dave LaRoche	2.00	1.00	.60
(38)	Greg Luzinski	2.00	1.00	.60
(39)	Fred Lynn	2.00	1.00	.60
(40)	Bill Madlock	2.00	1.00	.60
(41)	Rick Manning	2.00	1.00	.60
(42)	Jon Matlock	2.00	1.00	.60
(43)	John Mayberry	2.00	1.00	.60
(44)	Hal McRae	2.00	1.00	.60
(45)	Andy Messersmith	2.00	1.00	.60
(46)	Rick Monday	2.00	1.00	.60
(47)	John Montefusco	2.00	1.00	.60
(48)	Joe Morgan	6.00	3.00	1.75
(49)	Thurman Munson	4.00	2.00	1.25
(50)	Bobby Murcer	2.00	1.00	.60
(51)	Bill North	2.00	1.00	.60
(52)	Jim Palmer	6.00	3.00	1.75
(53)	Tony Perez	5.00	2.50	1.50
(54)	Jerry Reuss	2.00	1.00	.60
(55)	Brooks Robinson	6.00	3.00	1.75
(56)	Pete Rose	15.00	7.50	4.50
(57)	Joe Rudi	2.00	1.00	.60
(58)	Nolan Ryan	40.00	20.00	12.00
(59)	Manny Sanguillen	2.00	1.00	.60
(60)	Mike Schmidt	15.00	7.50	4.50
(61)	Tom Seaver	6.00	3.00	1.75
(62)	Bill Singer	2.00	1.00	.60
(63)	Willie Stargell	6.00	3.00	1.75
(64)	Rusty Staub	3.00	1.50	.90
(65)	Luis Tiant	2.00	1.00	.60
(66)	Bob Watson	2.00	1.00	.60
(67)	Butch Wynegar	2.00	1.00	.60
(68)	Carl Yastrzemski	7.50	3.75	2.25
(69)	Robin Yount	6.00	3.00	1.75
(70)	Richie Zisk	2.00	1.00	.60

1925 Holland World's Champions Washington Senators

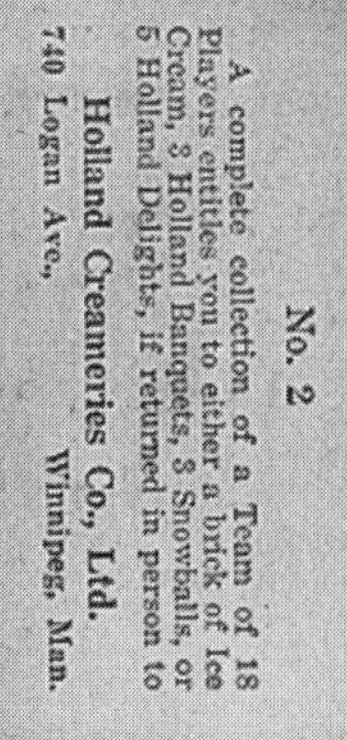

The World's Champion Washington Senators were featured on a set issued in Winnipeg, Manitoba, of all places. The 1-1/2" x 3" cards have player portrait photos printed in blue on front. The black-printed back has a card number and details of a redemption offer of cards for ice cream. Like many such offers it appears as if card #16 was intentionally withheld or minimally distributed, making it very scarce today.

		NM	EX	VG
Complete Set, No #16 (17):		17,500	8,750	5,250
Common Player:		800.00	400.00	240.00
1	Ralph Miller	800.00	400.00	240.00
2	Earl McNeely	800.00	400.00	240.00
3	Allan Russell	800.00	400.00	240.00
4	Ernest Shirley	800.00	400.00	240.00
5	Sam Rice	1,200	600.00	360.00
6	Muddy Ruel	800.00	400.00	240.00
7	Ossie Bluege	800.00	400.00	240.00
8	Nemo Leibold	800.00	400.00	240.00
9	Paul Zahniser	800.00	400.00	240.00
10	Firpo Marberry	800.00	400.00	240.00
11	Warren Ogden	800.00	400.00	240.00
12	George Mogridge	800.00	400.00	240.00
13	Tom Zachary	800.00	400.00	240.00
14	Goose Goslin	1,200	600.00	360.00
15	Joe Judge	800.00	400.00	240.00
16	Roger Peckinpaugh	2,500	1,250	750.00
17	Bucky Harris	1,200	600.00	360.00
18	Walter Johnson	3,500	1,750	1,000

1916 Holmes to Homes Bread

Most often found with blank backs, this 200-card set can also be found with ads on the back for several local and regional businesses. Among them is Holmes to Homes Milk-Made Bread, location unknown. Type card collectors and superstar collectors can expect to pay a significant premium for individual cards with Holmes to Homes advertising. Cards measure 1-5/8" x 3" and are printed in black-and-white.

(See 1916 M101-5 Blank Backs for checklist and base value information.)

1921 Holsum Bread

Issued by the Weil Baking Co., New Orleans, which produced several sets in the 1910s, this issue shares a format, but not the checklist of the 1921 American Caramel Co. set known as E121, Series of 80, and the contemporary W575-1 blank-back strip cards. To what extent the base cards and known variations in those set are found among the Holsum version is unknown. The Holsum cards differ from E121 primarily in the advertising on the back and sometimes in photo

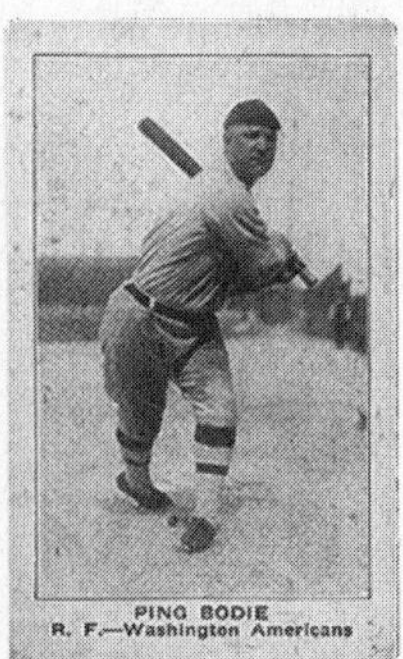

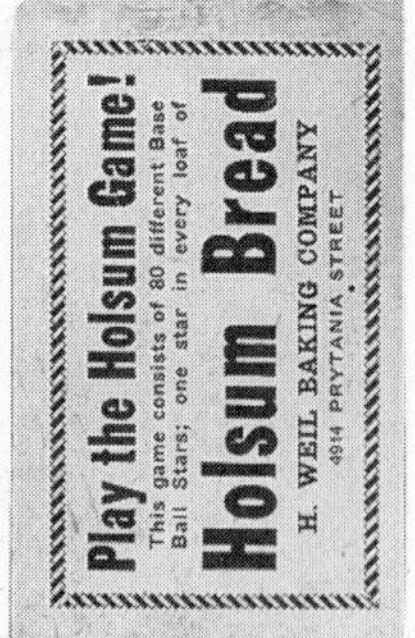

and/or caption details. The approximately 2" x 3-1/4" black-and-white cards are much scarcer than the caramel version. The trial checklist presented here is incomplete.

		NM	EX	VG
Common Player:		350.00	175.00	100.00
(4)	Jimmy Austin	350.00	175.00	100.00
(7)	Dave Bancroft	600.00	300.00	180.00
(13)	Jack Barry	350.00	175.00	100.00
(16)	Ping Bodie	350.00	175.00	100.00
(19)	George Burns	350.00	175.00	100.00
(26)	Ray Chapman	425.00	210.00	125.00
(28)	Eddie Cicotte	600.00	300.00	180.00
(37)	Geo. Cutshaw	350.00	175.00	100.00
(39)	Charles Deal (Dark uniform.)	350.00	175.00	100.00
(42)	Johnny Evers	600.00	300.00	180.00
(46)	Urban Faber (Dark uniform.)	600.00	300.00	180.00
(50)	Art Fletcher	350.00	175.00	100.00
(51)	Eddie Foster	350.00	175.00	100.00
(52)	Jacques Fournier	350.00	175.00	100.00
(53)	Hank Gowdy	350.00	175.00	100.00
(54)	Tom Griffith	350.00	175.00	100.00
(80)	Rogers Hornsby	1,250	625.00	375.00
(85)	Joe Jackson (Value Undetermined)			
(88)	Walter Johnson (Hands at chest.)	2,000	1,000	600.00
(93)	Wm. Killefer Jr.	350.00	175.00	100.00
(95)	John Lavan	350.00	175.00	100.00
(97)	H.B. Leonard	350.00	175.00	100.00
(99)	Duffy Lewis	350.00	175.00	100.00
(105)	Al Mamaux	350.00	175.00	100.00
(107)	"Rabbit" Maranville	600.00	300.00	180.00
(116)	Otto Miller	350.00	175.00	100.00
(122)	Guy Morton	350.00	175.00	100.00
(124)	"Hy" Myers	350.00	175.00	100.00
(127)	Arthur Nehf	350.00	175.00	100.00
(129)	Steve O'Neill	350.00	175.00	100.00
(133)	Jeff Pfeffer	350.00	175.00	100.00
(136)	Bill Rariden	350.00	175.00	100.00
(137)	Bob Roth	350.00	175.00	100.00
(153)	Walter Schang	350.00	175.00	100.00
(155)	Scott Everett	350.00	175.00	100.00
(162)	Geo. Sisler	600.00	300.00	180.00
(164)	J. Carlisle Smith	350.00	175.00	100.00
(168)	Charles Stengel	600.00	300.00	180.00
(170)	Amos Strunk/Btg (Chicago Americans.)	350.00	175.00	100.00
(171)	Amos Strunk (Arms at side, Chicago White Sox.)	350.00	175.00	100.00
(173)	Chester Thomas	350.00	175.00	100.00
(174)	Fred Toney	350.00	175.00	100.00
(175)	Jim Vaughn	350.00	175.00	100.00
(178)	Bob Veach	350.00	175.00	100.00
(184)	W. Wambsganss	350.00	175.00	100.00
(186)	Carl Weilman	350.00	175.00	100.00
(187)	Zack Wheat	600.00	300.00	180.00
(190)	Claude Williams (White stockings, correct photo.)	2,500	1,250	750.00
(202)	Pep Young	350.00	175.00	100.00

1959 Home Run Derby

This 20-card unnumbered set was produced by American Motors to publicize the Home Run Derby television program. The cards measure approximately 3-1/4" x 5-1/4" and feature black-and-white player photos on blank-backed white stock. The player name and team are printed beneath the photo. This set was reprinted (marked as such) in 1988 by Card Collectors' Co. of New York. An advertising poster is sometimes seen which is essentially an uncut sheet of the cards with a promotional message at bottom.

		NM	EX	VG
Complete Set (20):		10,000	5,000	3,000
Common Player:		175.00	85.00	50.00
Advertising Poster:		3,500	1,750	1,000
(1)	Hank Aaron	900.00	450.00	275.00
(2)	Bob Allison	175.00	85.00	50.00
(3)	Ernie Banks	700.00	350.00	210.00
(4)	Ken Boyer	200.00	100.00	60.00
(5)	Bob Cerv	175.00	85.00	50.00
(6)	Rocky Colavito	325.00	160.00	100.00
(7)	Gil Hodges	325.00	160.00	100.00
(8)	Jackie Jensen	175.00	85.00	50.00
(9)	Al Kaline	600.00	300.00	180.00
(10)	Harmon Killebrew	600.00	300.00	180.00
(11)	Jim Lemon	175.00	85.00	50.00
(12)	Mickey Mantle	2,250	1,125	675.00
(13)	Ed Mathews	550.00	275.00	165.00
(14)	Willie Mays	900.00	450.00	270.00
(15)	Wally Post	175.00	85.00	50.00
(16)	Frank Robinson	550.00	275.00	165.00
(17)	Mark Scott (Host)	350.00	175.00	100.00
(18)	Duke Snider	600.00	300.00	180.00
(19)	Dick Stuart	175.00	85.00	50.00
(20)	Gus Triandos	175.00	85.00	50.00

1894 Honest (Duke) Cabinets (N142)

These color cabinet cards, which measure 6" x 9-1/2", were produced by W.H. Duke for its Honest tobacco brand. The player name is centered at the bottom of the card front. The brand name "Honest" is located in the lower-left corner with the words "New York" in the lower-right corner. Three bicyclists are also part of the set.

		NM	EX	VG
Complete Set (4):		49,500	24,750	14,850
Common Player:		9,350	4,675	2,750
(1)	G.S. Davis	12,100	6,050	3,630
(2)	E.J. Delahanty	17,600	8,800	5,280
(3)	W.M. Nash	9,350	4,675	2,750
(4)	W. Robinson	18,425	9,215	5,530

1911-12 Honest Long Cut Tobacco

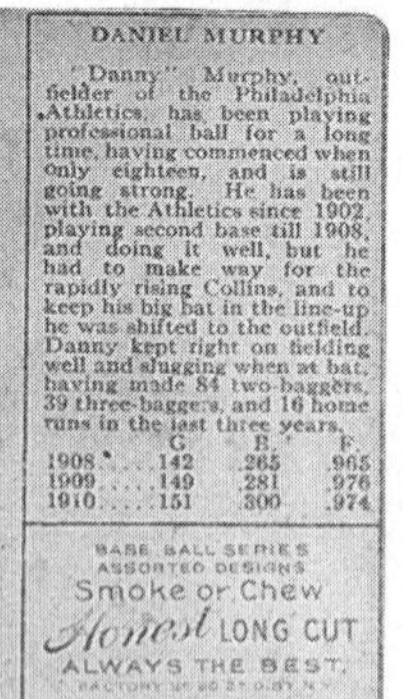

DANIEL MURPHY

"Danny" Murphy, outfielder of the Philadelphia Athletics, has been playing professional ball for a long time, having commenced when only eighteen, and is still going strong. He has been with the Athletics since 1902, playing second base till 1908, and doing it well, but he had to make way for the rapidly rising Collins, and to keep his big bat in the line-up he was shifted to the outfield. Danny kept right on fielding well and slugging when at bat, having made 84 two-baggers, 39 three-baggers, and 16 home runs in the last three years.

	G.	B.	F.
1908	142	.265	.965
1909	149	.281	.976
1910	151	.300	.974

BASE BALL SERIES
ASSORTED DESIGNS
Smoke or Chew
Honest LONG CUT
ALWAYS THE BEST.

Advertising, printed in black, for Honest Long Cut tobacco is among the more commonly found on the backs of T205 Gold Border cards of 1911. The brand also advertised on the multi-sport T227 Series of Champions in 1912.

(See T205, T227 for checklists and values.)

1927 Honey Boy

—19—
SAVE THESE PICTURES
The complete series of 21 photographs of baseball players will entitle the holder to a brick of Delicious Honey Boy Ice Cream
These pictures are redeemable at our plant, 234 Pritchard Ave.
Issued by
The PURITY ICE CREAM Co., Ltd.
Manufacturers of
"HONEY BOY" ICE CREAM
In packages, bricks and bulk for all occasions

The date of issue for this rare Canadian issue is conjectural. These black-and-white 1-5/8" x 2-3/8" cards were issued by the Purity Ice Cream Company in Winnipeg, Canada, and were redeemable as a set of 21 for a brick of "Delicious Honey Boy Ice Cream." Besides the major leaguers in the set, there are also cards of local amateurs and semi-pros, including hockey Hall of Famer Steamer Maxwell and Chicago Blackhawks star Cecil Browne. The major leaguers are not identified by team, nor do their photos have team insignias present. When redeemed, cards were punch-cancelled. Values shown are for uncancelled cards; cards exhibiting the punch-holes would be worth about 50 percent of the indicated figures.

		NM	EX	VG
Complete Set (21):		24,000	12,000	7,500
Common (Major League) Player:		900.00	450.00	275.00
1	"Steamer" Maxwell (Arenas)	2,000	1,000	600.00
2	Cecil Browne (Dominion Express)	400.00	200.00	120.00
3	Carson McVey (Transcona)	400.00	200.00	120.00
4	Sam Perlman (Tigers)	400.00	200.00	120.00
5	"Snake" Siddle (Arenas)	400.00	200.00	120.00
6	Eddie Cass (Columbus)	400.00	200.00	120.00
7	Jimmy Bradley (Columbus)	400.00	200.00	120.00
8	Gordon Caslake (Dominion Express)	400.00	200.00	120.00
9	Ward McVey (Tigers)	400.00	200.00	120.00
10	"Tris" Speaker	1,800	900.00	540.00
11	George Sisler	1,500	750.00	450.00
12	E. Meusel	900.00	450.00	275.00
13	Ed. Roush	1,500	750.00	450.00
14	"Babe" Ruth	8,500	4,250	2,550
15	Harry Heilmann	1,500	750.00	450.00
16	Heinie Groh	900.00	450.00	275.00
17	Eddie Collins	1,500	750.00	450.00
18	Grover Alexander	1,650	825.00	495.00
19	Dave Bancroft	1,500	750.00	450.00
20	Frank Frisch	1,500	750.00	450.00
21	George Burns	900.00	450.00	275.00

1905-1909 Carl Horner Cabinets

Carl Horner was the premier baseball portraitist of the early 20th Century. From his Boston studio came the images of the day's stars and journeymen which live on today on some of the most popular baseball cards of the era - including the famed T206 Honus Wagner. Highly collectible in their own right are the cabinet photos produced by the studio. Because of rarity, values can be determined only on those rare occasions when an example comes onto the market. Because the body of his work was accomplished over a number of years, mounting style and other technical details of the generally 5-1/2" x 7" cabinets may vary. Because the players are not identified on the cabinet, identification can be a problem, though quite often a contemporary notation of the player's name can be found written on back.

	NM	EX	VG
Common Player:	1,000	500.00	300.00
Nick Altrock	2,500	1,250	750.00
Frank Arrelanes (Arellanes)	2,000	1,000	600.00
Frank Baker	3,500	1,750	1,050
Harry Barton	2,000	1,000	600.00
Jake Beckley	3,500	1,750	1,050
Frank Chance	3,500	1,750	1,050
Eddie Collins	3,500	1,750	1,050
Bill Dahlen	2,000	1,000	600.00
Frank Delahanty	2,250	1,125	675.00
Kid Elberfeld	2,000	1,000	600.00
Billy Gilbert	2,000	1,000	600.00
Danny Green	2,000	1,000	600.00
Walter Johnson	15,000	3,250	1,950
Addie Joss	4,000	2,000	1,200
Harry Krause	2,000	1,000	600.00
Rube Kroh	2,000	1,000	600.00
Bris Lord	2,000	1,000	600.00
Charlie Lush	2,000	1,000	600.00
Earl Moore	2,000	1,000	600.00
Harry Niles	2,000	1,000	600.00
Billy Sullivan	2,000	1,000	600.00
Joe Tinker	3,500	1,750	1,050
Honus Wagner	20,000	4,500	2,700
Victor Willis	3,500	1,750	1,050

1959 Hostess Bob Turley

The date attributed to this card is speculative. The 3-1/2" x 4-3/8" black-and-white card has an action pose of the Yankees pitcher on front surrounded by a white border. On back is a list of Hostess Cakes products.

BOB TURLEY
Now Pitching For
HOSTESS CAKES
Cup Cakes—Sno-Balls—Twinkies
Li'l Angels—Fruit Pies
Hostess Finer Pastries
Hostess Donuts and Donettes
and
WONDER BREAD
The bread that helps build
strong bodies 12 ways

	NM	EX	VG
Bob Turley	125.00	60.00	40.00

1975 Hostess

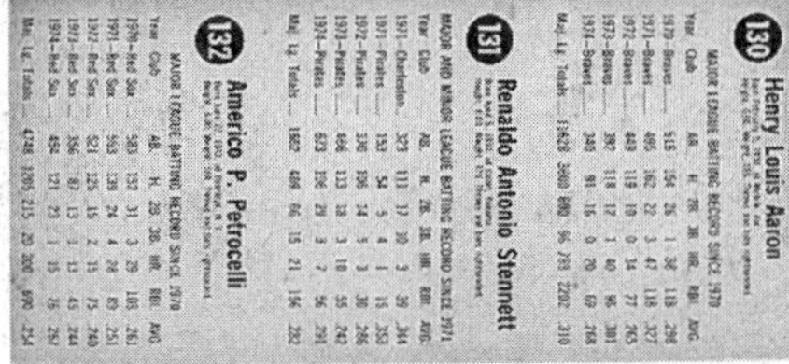

The first of what would become five annual issues, the 1975 Hostess set consists of 50 three-card panels which formed the bottom of boxes of family-size snack cake products. Unlike many similar issues, the Hostess cards do not share common borders, so it was possible to cut them neatly and evenly from the box. Well-cut single cards measure 2-1/4" x 3-1/4", while a three-card panel measures 7-1/4" x 3-1/4". Because some of the panels were issued on packages of less popular snack cakes, they are somewhat scarcer today. Since the hobby was quite well-developed when the Hostess cards were first issued, there is no lack of complete panels. Even unused complete boxes are available today. Some of the photos in this issue also appear on Topps cards of the era.

		NM	EX	VG
	Complete Panel Set (50):	350.00	175.00	100.00
	Complete Set, Singles (150):	165.00	80.00	50.00
	Common Panel:	5.00	2.50	1.50
	Common Player:	1.00	.50	.30
	Panel (1)	5.00	2.50	1.50
1	Bobby Tolan	1.00	.50	.30
2	Cookie Rojas	1.00	.50	.30
3	Darrell Evans	1.25	.60	.40
	Panel (2)	10.00	5.00	3.00
4	Sal Bando	1.00	.50	.30
5	Joe Morgan	5.00	2.50	1.50
6	Mickey Lolich	1.25	.60	.40
	Panel (3)	10.00	5.00	3.00
7	Don Sutton	4.50	2.25	1.25
8	Bill Melton	1.00	.50	.30
9	Tim Foli	1.00	.50	.30
	Panel (4)	5.00	2.50	1.50
10	Joe Lahoud	1.00	.50	.30
11a	Bert Hooten (Incorrect spelling.)	1.50	.70	.45
11b	Burt Hooton (Corrected)	1.00	.50	.30
12	Paul Blair	1.00	.50	.30
	Panel (5)	5.00	2.50	1.50
13	Jim Barr	1.00	.50	.30
14	Toby Harrah	1.00	.50	.30
15	John Milner	1.00	.50	.30
	Panel (6)	5.00	2.50	1.50
16	Ken Holtzman	1.00	.50	.30
17	Cesar Cedeno	1.00	.50	.30
18	Dwight Evans	1.00	.50	.30
	Panel (7)	10.00	5.00	3.00
19	Willie McCovey	5.00	2.50	1.50
20	Tony Oliva	1.25	.60	.40
21	Manny Sanguillen	1.00	.50	.30
	Panel (8)	10.00	5.00	3.00
22	Mickey Rivers	1.00	.50	.30
23	Lou Brock	5.00	2.50	1.50
24	Graig Nettles	1.50	.70	.45
	Panel (9)	5.00	2.50	1.50
25	Jim Wynn	1.00	.50	.30
26	George Scott	1.00	.50	.30
27	Greg Luzinski	1.00	.50	.30
	Panel (10)	15.00	7.50	4.50
28	Bert Campaneris	1.00	.50	.30
29	Pete Rose	12.50	6.25	3.75
30	Buddy Bell	1.00	.50	.30
	Panel (11)	5.00	2.50	1.50
31	Gary Matthews	1.00	.50	.30
32	Fred Patek	1.00	.50	.30
33	Mike Lum	1.00	.50	.30
	Panel (12)	5.00	2.50	1.50
34	Ellie Rodriguez	1.00	.50	.30
35	Milt May	1.00	.50	.30
36	Willie Horton	1.00	.50	.30
	Panel (13)	10.00	5.00	3.00
37	Dave Winfield	5.00	2.50	1.50
38	Tom Grieve	1.00	.50	.30
39	Barry Foote	1.00	.50	.30
	Panel (14)	5.00	2.50	1.50
40	Joe Rudi	1.00	.50	.30
41	Bake McBride	1.00	.50	.30
42	Mike Cuellar	1.00	.50	.30
	Panel (15)	5.00	2.50	1.50
43	Garry Maddox	1.00	.50	.30
44	Carlos May	1.00	.50	.30
45	Bud Harrelson	1.00	.50	.30
	Panel (16)	10.00	5.00	3.00
46	Dave Chalk	1.00	.50	.30
47	Dave Concepcion	1.00	.50	.30
48	Carl Yastrzemski	7.50	3.75	2.25
	Panel (17)	10.00	5.00	3.00
49	Steve Garvey	3.00	1.50	.90
50	Amos Otis	1.00	.50	.30
51	Ricky Reuschel	1.00	.50	.30
	Panel (18)	10.00	5.00	3.00
52	Rollie Fingers	4.50	2.25	1.25
53	Bob Watson	1.00	.50	.30
54	John Ellis	1.00	.50	.30
	Panel (19)	10.00	5.00	3.00
55	Bob Bailey	1.00	.50	.30
56	Rod Carew	6.00	3.00	1.75
57	Richie Hebner	1.00	.50	.30
	Panel (20)	20.00	10.00	6.00
58	Nolan Ryan	15.00	7.50	4.50
59	Reggie Smith	1.00	.50	.30
60	Joe Coleman	1.00	.50	.30
	Panel (21)	10.00	5.00	3.00
61	Ron Cey	1.00	.50	.30
62	Darrell Porter	1.00	.50	.30
63	Steve Carlton	5.00	2.50	1.50
	Panel (22)	5.00	2.50	1.50
64	Gene Tenace	1.00	.50	.30
65	Jose Cardenal	1.00	.50	.30
66	Bill Lee	1.00	.50	.30
	Panel (23)	5.00	2.50	1.50
67	Davey Lopes	1.00	.50	.30
68	Wilbur Wood	1.00	.50	.30
69	Steve Renko	1.00	.50	.30
	Panel (24)	10.00	5.00	3.00
70	Joe Torre	3.00	1.50	.90
71	Ted Sizemore	1.00	.50	.30
72	Bobby Grich	1.00	.50	.30
	Panel (25)	12.50	6.25	3.75
73	Chris Speier	1.00	.50	.30
74	Bert Blyleven	1.25	.60	.40
75	Tom Seaver	6.00	3.00	1.75
	Panel (26)	5.00	2.50	1.50
76	Nate Colbert	1.00	.50	.30
77	Don Kessinger	1.00	.50	.30
78	George Medich	1.00	.50	.30
	Panel (27)	20.00	10.00	6.00
79	Andy Messersmith	1.00	.50	.30
80	Robin Yount	12.50	6.25	3.75
81	Al Oliver	1.25	.60	.40
	Panel (28)	15.00	7.50	4.50
82	Bill Singer	1.00	.50	.30
83	Johnny Bench	6.00	3.00	1.75
84	Gaylord Perry	4.50	2.25	1.25
	Panel (29)	5.00	2.50	1.50
85	Dave Kingman	1.00	.50	.30
86	Ed Herrmann	1.00	.50	.30
87	Ralph Garr	1.00	.50	.30
	Panel (30)	12.50	6.25	3.75
88	Reggie Jackson	7.50	3.75	2.25
89a	Doug Radar (Incorrect spelling.)	1.50	.70	.45
89b	Doug Rader (Corrected)	1.00	.50	.30
90	Elliott Maddox	1.00	.50	.30
	Panel (31)	5.00	2.50	1.50
91	Bill Russell	1.00	.50	.30
92	John Mayberry	1.00	.50	.30
93	Dave Cash	1.00	.50	.30
	Panel (32)	5.00	2.50	1.50
94	Jeff Burroughs	1.00	.50	.30
95	Ted Simmons	1.00	.50	.30
96	Joe Decker	1.00	.50	.30
	Panel (33)	10.00	5.00	3.00
97	Bill Buckner	1.25	.60	.40
98	Bobby Darwin	1.00	.50	.30
99	Phil Niekro	4.50	2.25	1.25
	Panel (34)	5.00	2.50	1.50
100	Mike Sundberg (Jim)	1.00	.50	.30
101	Greg Gross	1.00	.50	.30
102	Luis Tiant	1.00	.50	.30
	Panel (35)	5.00	2.50	1.50
103	Glenn Beckert	1.00	.50	.30
104	Hal McRae	1.00	.50	.30
105	Mike Jorgensen	1.00	.50	.30
	Panel (36)	5.00	2.50	1.50
106	Mike Hargrove	1.00	.50	.30
107	Don Gullett	1.00	.50	.30
108	Tito Fuentes	1.00	.50	.30
	Panel (37)	5.00	2.50	1.50
109	Johnny Grubb	1.00	.50	.30
110	Jim Kaat	1.25	.60	.40
111	Felix Millan	1.00	.50	.30
	Panel (38)	5.00	2.50	1.50
112	Don Money	1.00	.50	.30
113	Rick Monday	1.00	.50	.30
114	Dick Bosman	1.00	.50	.30
	Panel (39)	10.00	5.00	3.00
115	Roger Metzger	1.00	.50	.30
116	Fergie Jenkins	4.50	2.25	1.25
117	Dusty Baker	1.25	.60	.40
	Panel (40)	10.00	5.00	3.00
118	Billy Champion	1.00	.50	.30
119	Bob Gibson	5.00	2.50	1.50
120	Bill Freehan	1.00	.50	.30
	Panel (41)	5.00	2.50	1.50
121	Cesar Geronimo	1.00	.50	.30
122	Jorge Orta	1.00	.50	.30
123	Cleon Jones	1.00	.50	.30
	Panel (42)	10.00	5.00	3.00
124	Steve Busby	1.00	.50	.30
125a	Bill Madlock/Pitcher	1.50	.70	.45
125b	Bill Madlock (Infield)	1.00	.50	.30
126	Jim Palmer	5.00	2.50	1.50
	Panel (43)	10.00	5.00	3.00
127	Tony Perez	5.00	2.50	1.50
128	Larry Hisle	1.00	.50	.30
129	Rusty Staub	1.25	.60	.40
	Panel (44)	20.00	10.00	6.00
130	Hank Aaron	13.50	6.75	4.00
131	Rennie Stennett	1.00	.50	.30
132	Rico Petrocelli	1.00	.50	.30
	Panel (45)	15.00	7.50	4.50
133	Mike Schmidt	12.50	6.25	3.75
134	Sparky Lyle	1.00	.50	.30
135	Willie Stargell	5.00	2.50	1.50
	Panel (46)	10.00	5.00	3.00
136	Ken Henderson	1.00	.50	.30
137	Willie Montanez	1.00	.50	.30
138	Thurman Munson	5.00	2.50	1.50
	Panel (47)	5.00	2.50	1.50
139	Richie Zisk	1.00	.50	.30
140	George Hendricks (Hendrick)	1.00	.50	.30
141	Bobby Murcer	1.50	.70	.45
	Panel (48)	15.00	7.50	4.50
142	Lee May	1.00	.50	.30
143	Carlton Fisk	5.00	2.50	1.50
144	Brooks Robinson	6.00	3.00	1.75
	Panel (49)	5.00	2.50	1.50
145	Bobby Bonds	1.25	.60	.40
146	Gary Sutherland	1.00	.50	.30
147	Oscar Gamble	1.00	.50	.30
	Panel (50)	10.00	5.00	3.00
148	Jim Hunter	4.50	2.25	1.25
149	Tug McGraw	1.25	.60	.40
150	Dave McNally	1.00	.50	.30

1975 Hostess Twinkies

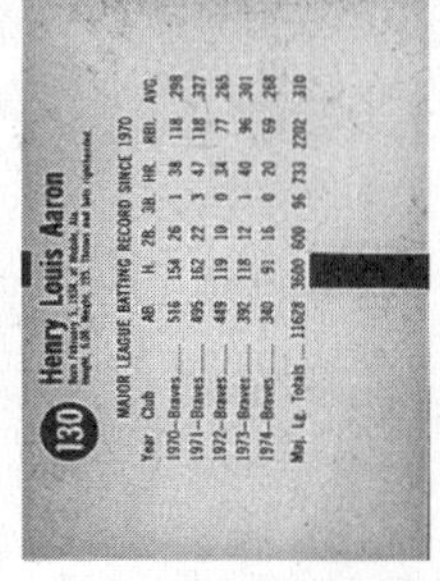

Believed to have been issued only in selected markets, and on a limited basis at that, the 1975 Hostess Twinkie set features 60 of the cards from the "regular" Hostess set of that year. The cards were issued one per pack with the popular snack cake. Cards #1-36 are a direct pick-up from the Hostess set, while the remaining 24 cards in the set were selected from the more popular names in the remainder of the Hostess issue - with an emphasis on West Coast players. Thus, after card #36, the '75 Twinkie cards are skip-numbered from 40-136. In identical 2-1/4" x 3-1/4" size, the Twinkie cards differ from the Hostess issue only in the presence of small black bars at top and bottom center of the back of the card. While cards actually issued with snack cakes are virtually always found with brown stains, enough unissued cards were leaked into the hobby to provide clean examples for those willing to search them out and pay the price.

		NM	EX	VG
	Complete Set (60):	800.00	325.00	80.00
	Common Player:	4.00	1.50	.40
1	Bobby Tolan	4.00	1.50	.40
2	Cookie Rojas	4.00	1.50	.40
3	Darrell Evans	4.00	1.50	.40
4	Sal Bando	4.00	1.50	.40
5	Joe Morgan	24.00	9.50	2.50
6	Mickey Lolich	6.00	2.50	.60
7	Don Sutton	20.00	8.00	2.00
8	Bill Melton	4.00	1.50	.40
9	Tim Foli	4.00	1.50	.40
10	Joe Lahoud	4.00	1.50	.40
11	Bert Hooten (Burt Hooton)	4.00	1.50	.40
12	Paul Blair	4.00	1.50	.40
13	Jim Barr	4.00	1.50	.40
14	Toby Harrah	4.00	1.50	.40
15	John Milner	4.00	1.50	.40
16	Ken Holtzman	4.00	1.50	.40
17	Cesar Cedeno	4.00	1.50	.40
18	Dwight Evans	4.00	1.50	.40
19	Willie McCovey	24.00	9.50	2.50
20	Tony Oliva	8.00	3.25	.80
21	Manny Sanguillen	4.00	1.50	.40
22	Mickey Rivers	4.00	1.50	.40
23	Lou Brock	24.00	9.50	2.50
24	Graig Nettles	6.00	2.50	.60
25	Jim Wynn	4.00	1.50	.40
26	George Scott	4.00	1.50	.40
27	Greg Luzinski	4.00	1.50	.40
28	Bert Campaneris	4.00	1.50	.40
29	Pete Rose	80.00	32.00	8.00
30	Buddy Bell	4.00	1.50	.40
31	Gary Matthews	4.00	1.50	.40
32	Fred Patek	4.00	1.50	.40
33	Mike Lum	4.00	1.50	.40

#	Player	NM	EX	VG
34	Ellie Rodriguez	4.00	1.50	.40
35	Milt May (Photo actually Lee May.)	4.00	1.50	.40
36	Willie Horton	4.00	1.50	.40
40	Joe Rudi	4.00	1.50	.40
43	Garry Maddox	4.00	1.50	.40
46	Dave Chalk	4.00	1.50	.40
49	Steve Garvey	15.00	6.00	1.50
52	Rollie Fingers	20.00	8.00	2.00
58	Nolan Ryan	100.00	40.00	10.00
61	Ron Cey	4.00	1.50	.40
64	Gene Tenace	4.00	1.50	.40
65	Jose Cardenal	4.00	1.50	.40
67	Dave Lopes	4.00	1.50	.40
68	Wilbur Wood	4.00	1.50	.40
73	Chris Speier	4.00	1.50	.40
77	Don Kessinger	4.00	1.50	.40
79	Andy Messersmith	4.00	1.50	.40
80	Robin Yount	40.00	16.00	4.00
82	Bill Singer	4.00	1.50	.40
103	Glenn Beckert	4.00	1.50	.40
110	Jim Kaat	6.00	2.50	.60
112	Don Money	4.00	1.50	.40
113	Rick Monday	4.00	1.50	.40
122	Jorge Orta	4.00	1.50	.40
125	Bill Madlock	4.00	1.50	.40
130	Hank Aaron	75.00	30.00	7.50
136	Ken Henderson	4.00	1.50	.40

1976 Hostess

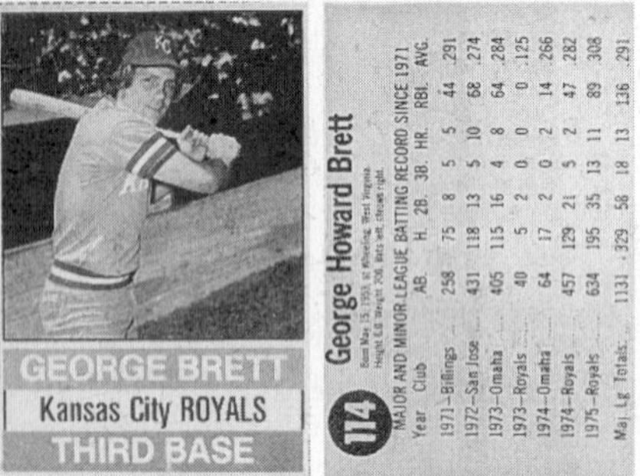

The second of five annual Hostess issues, the 1976 cards carried a "Bicentennial" color theme, with red, white and blue stripes at the bottom of the 2-1/4" x 3-1/4" cards. Like other Hostess issues, the cards were printed in panels of three as the bottom of family-size boxes of snack cake products. This leads to a degree of scarcity for some of the 150 cards in the set; those which were found on less-popular brands. A well-trimmed three-card panel measures 7-1/4" x 3-1/4". Some of the photos used in the 1976 Hostess set can also be found on Topps issues of the era. A "Hostess All-Star Team" album with spaces for 18 cards was available.

#	Player	NM	EX	VG
	Complete Panel Set (50):	300.00	150.00	90.00
	Complete Set, Singles (150):	250.00	125.00	75.00
	Common Panel:	5.00	2.50	1.50
	Common Player:	.75	.40	.25
	Album:	20.00	10.00	6.00
	Panel (1)	20.00	10.00	6.00
1	Fred Lynn	1.00	.50	.30
2	Joe Morgan	5.00	2.50	1.50
3	Phil Niekro	4.00	2.00	1.25
	Panel (2)	10.00	5.00	3.00
4	Gaylord Perry	4.00	2.00	1.25
5	Bob Watson	.75	.40	.25
6	Bill Freehan	.75	.40	.25
	Panel (3)	10.00	5.00	3.00
7	Lou Brock	5.00	2.50	1.50
8	Al Fitzmorris	.75	.40	.25
9	Rennie Stennett	.75	.40	.25
	Panel (4)	10.00	5.00	3.00
10	Tony Oliva	1.00	.50	.30
11	Robin Yount	5.00	2.50	1.50
12	Rick Manning	.75	.40	.25
	Panel (5)	7.00	3.50	2.00
13	Bobby Grich	.75	.40	.25
14	Terry Forster	.75	.40	.25
15	Dave Kingman	1.00	.50	.30
	Panel (6)	10.00	5.00	3.00
16	Thurman Munson	4.50	2.25	1.25
17	Rick Reuschel	.75	.40	.25
18	Bobby Bonds	1.00	.50	.30
	Panel (7)	10.00	5.00	3.00
19	Steve Garvey	3.50	1.75	1.00
20	Vida Blue	.75	.40	.25
21	Dave Rader	.75	.40	.25
	Panel (8)	10.00	5.00	3.00
22	Johnny Bench	5.00	2.50	1.50
23	Luis Tiant	.75	.40	.25
24	Darrell Evans	.75	.40	.25
	Panel (9)	7.00	3.50	2.00
25	Larry Dierker	.75	.40	.25
26	Willie Horton	.75	.40	.25
27	John Ellis	.75	.40	.25
	Panel (10)	7.00	3.50	2.00
28	Al Cowens	.75	.40	.25
29	Jerry Reuss	.75	.40	.25
30	Reggie Smith	.75	.40	.25
	Panel (11)	10.00	5.00	3.00
31	Bobby Darwin	.75	.40	.25
32	Fritz Peterson	.75	.40	.25
33	Rod Carew	5.00	2.50	1.50
	Panel (12)	20.00	10.00	6.00
34	Carlos May	.75	.40	.25
35	Tom Seaver	6.00	3.00	1.75
36	Brooks Robinson	6.00	3.00	1.75
	Panel (13)	7.00	3.50	2.00
37	Jose Cardenal	.75	.40	.25
38	Ron Blomberg	.75	.40	.25
39	Lee Stanton	.75	.40	.25
	Panel (14)	7.00	3.50	2.00
40	Dave Cash	.75	.40	.25
41	John Montefusco	.75	.40	.25
42	Bob Tolan	.75	.40	.25
	Panel (15)	7.00	3.50	2.00
43	Carl Morton	.75	.40	.25
44	Rick Burleson	.75	.40	.25
45	Don Gullett	.75	.40	.25
	Panel (16)	7.00	3.50	2.00
46	Vern Ruhle	.75	.40	.25
47	Cesar Cedeno	.75	.40	.25
48	Toby Harrah	.75	.40	.25
	Panel (17)	10.00	5.00	3.00
49	Willie Stargell	5.00	2.50	1.50
50	Al Hrabosky	.75	.40	.25
51	Amos Otis	.75	.40	.25
	Panel (18)	7.00	3.50	2.00
52	Bud Harrelson	.75	.40	.25
53	Jim Hughes	.75	.40	.25
54	George Scott	.75	.40	.25
	Panel (19)	10.00	5.00	3.00
55	Mike Vail	.75	.40	.25
56	Jim Palmer	5.00	2.50	1.50
57	Jorge Orta	.75	.40	.25
	Panel (20)	7.00	3.50	2.00
58	Chris Chambliss	.75	.40	.25
59	Dave Chalk	.75	.40	.25
60	Ray Burris	.75	.40	.25
	Panel (21)	10.00	5.00	3.00
61	Bert Campaneris	.75	.40	.25
62	Gary Carter	5.00	2.50	1.50
63a	Ron Cey	.75	.40	.25
63b	Ron Cey (Reversed negatives, unissued proof.)	35.00	17.50	10.50
	Panel (22)	27.50	13.50	8.25
64	Carlton Fisk	5.00	2.50	1.50
65	Marty Perez	.75	.40	.25
66	Pete Rose	12.00	6.00	3.50
	Panel (23)	7.00	3.50	2.00
67	Roger Metzger	.75	.40	.25
68	Jim Sundberg	.75	.40	.25
69	Ron LeFlore	.75	.40	.25
	Panel (24)	7.00	3.50	2.00
70	Ted Sizemore	.75	.40	.25
71	Steve Busby	.75	.40	.25
72	Manny Sanguillen	.75	.40	.25
	Panel (25)	10.00	5.00	3.00
73	Larry Hisle	.75	.40	.25
74	Pete Broberg	.75	.40	.25
75	Boog Powell	3.00	1.50	.90
	Panel (26)	8.00	4.00	2.50
76	Ken Singleton	.75	.40	.25
77	Rich Gossage	1.25	.60	.40
78	Jerry Grote	.75	.40	.25
	Panel (27)	35.00	17.50	10.50
79	Nolan Ryan	16.00	8.00	4.75
80	Rick Monday	.75	.40	.25
81	Graig Nettles	1.25	.60	.40
	Panel (28)	27.50	13.50	8.25
82	Chris Speier	.75	.40	.25
83	Dave Winfield	5.00	2.50	1.50
84	Mike Schmidt	7.50	3.75	2.25
	Panel (29)	10.00	5.00	3.00
85	Buzz Capra	.75	.40	.25
86	Tony Perez	5.00	2.50	1.50
87	Dwight Evans	.75	.40	.25
	Panel (30)	7.00	3.50	2.00
88	Mike Hargrove	.75	.40	.25
89	Joe Coleman	.75	.40	.25
90	Greg Gross	.75	.40	.25
	Panel (31)	7.00	3.50	2.00
91	John Mayberry	.75	.40	.25
92	John Candelaria	.75	.40	.25
93	Bake McBride	.75	.40	.25
	Panel (32)	20.00	10.00	6.00
94	Hank Aaron	12.00	6.00	3.50
95	Buddy Bell	.75	.40	.25
96	Steve Braun	.75	.40	.25
	Panel (33)	7.00	3.50	2.00
97	Jon Matlack	.75	.40	.25
98	Lee May	.75	.40	.25
99	Wilbur Wood	.75	.40	.25
	Panel (34)	7.00	3.50	2.00
100	Bill Madlock	.75	.40	.25
101	Frank Tanana	.75	.40	.25
102	Mickey Rivers	.75	.40	.25
	Panel (35)	10.00	5.00	3.00
103	Mike Ivie	.75	.40	.25
104	Rollie Fingers	4.00	2.00	1.25
105	Davey Lopes	.75	.40	.25
	Panel (36)	7.00	3.50	2.00
106	George Foster	.75	.40	.25
107	Denny Doyle	.75	.40	.25
108	Earl Williams	.75	.40	.25
	Panel (37)	7.00	3.50	2.00
109	Tom Veryzer	.75	.40	.25
110	J.R. Richard	.75	.40	.25
111	Jeff Burroughs	.75	.40	.25
	Panel (38)	17.50	8.75	5.25
112	Al Oliver	1.00	.50	.30
113	Ted Simmons	.75	.40	.25
114	George Brett	7.50	3.75	2.25
	Panel (39)	7.00	3.50	2.00
115	Frank Duffy	.75	.40	.25
116	Bert Blyleven	.75	.40	.25
117	Darrell Porter	.75	.40	.25
	Panel (40)	8.00	4.00	2.50
118	Don Baylor	1.00	.50	.30
119	Bucky Dent	.75	.40	.25
120	Felix Millan	.75	.40	.25
	Panel (41)	8.00	4.00	2.50
121a	Mike Cuellar	.75	.40	.25
121b	Andy Messersmith (Unissued proof.)	25.00	12.50	7.50
122	Gene Tenace	.75	.40	.25
123	Bobby Murcer	1.25	.60	.40
	Panel (42)	10.00	5.00	3.00
124	Willie McCovey	5.00	2.50	1.50
125	Greg Luzinski	.75	.40	.25
126	Larry Parrish	.75	.40	.25
	Panel (43)	8.00	4.00	2.50
127	Jim Rice	2.00	1.00	.60
128	Dave Concepcion	.75	.40	.25
129	Jim Wynn	.75	.40	.25
	Panel (44)	7.00	3.50	2.00
130	Tom Grieve	.75	.40	.25
131	Mike Cosgrove	.75	.40	.25
132	Dan Meyer	.75	.40	.25
	Panel(45)	7.00	3.50	2.00
133	Dave Parker	1.00	.50	.30
134	Don Kessinger	.75	.40	.25
135	Hal McRae	.75	.40	.25
	Panel (46)	13.50	6.75	4.00
136	Don Money	.75	.40	.25
137	Dennis Eckersley	5.00	2.50	1.50
138a	Fergie Jenkins	4.00	2.00	1.25
138b	Johnny Briggs (Unissued proof.)	25.00	12.50	7.50
	Panel (47)	10.00	5.00	3.00
139	Mike Torrez	.75	.40	.25
140	Jerry Morales	.75	.40	.25
141	Jim Hunter	4.00	2.00	1.25
	Panel (48)	7.00	3.50	2.00
142	Gary Matthews	.75	.40	.25
143	Randy Jones	.75	.40	.25
144	Mike Jorgensen	.75	.40	.25
	Panel (49)	17.50	8.75	5.25
145	Larry Bowa	.75	.40	.25
146	Reggie Jackson	7.50	3.75	2.25
147	Steve Yeager	.75	.40	.25
	Panel (50)	13.50	6.75	4.00
148	Dave May	.75	.40	.25
149	Carl Yastrzemski	6.00	3.00	1.75
150	Cesar Geronimo	.75	.40	.25

1976 Hostess Twinkies

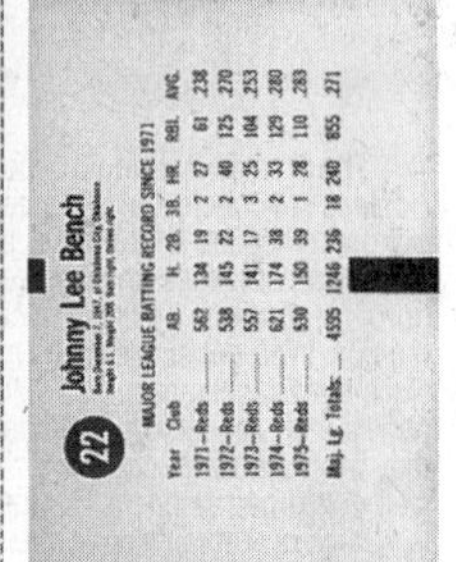

The 60 cards in this regionally issued (test markets only) set closely parallel the first 60 cards in the numerical sequence of the "regular" 1976 Hostess issue. The singular difference is the appearance on the back of a black band toward the center of the card at top and bottom. Also unlike the three-card panels of the regular Hostess issue, the 2-1/4" x 3-1/4" Twinkie cards were issued singly, as the cardboard stiffener for the cellophane-wrapped snack cakes. While cards actually issued with snack cakes are virtually always found with brown stains, enough unissued cards were leaked into the hobby to provide clean examples for those willing to search them out and pay the price.

#	Player	NM	EX	VG
	Complete Set (60):	500.00	200.00	50.00
	Common Player:	4.00	1.50	.40
1	Fred Lynn	4.00	1.50	.40
2	Joe Morgan	24.00	9.50	2.50
3	Phil Niekro	20.00	8.00	2.00
4	Gaylord Perry	20.00	8.00	2.00
5	Bob Watson	4.00	1.50	.40
6	Bill Freehan	4.00	1.50	.40
7	Lou Brock	24.00	9.50	2.50
8	Al Fitzmorris	4.00	1.50	.40
9	Rennie Stennett	4.00	1.50	.40
10	Tony Oliva	6.00	2.50	.60
11	Robin Yount	24.00	9.50	2.50
12	Rick Manning	4.00	1.50	.40
13	Bobby Grich	4.00	1.50	.40
14	Terry Forster	4.00	1.50	.40
15	Dave Kingman	5.00	2.00	.50
16	Thurman Munson	15.00	6.00	1.50
17	Rick Reuschel	4.00	1.50	.40
18	Bobby Bonds	4.00	1.50	.40
19	Steve Garvey	12.00	4.75	1.25
20	Vida Blue	4.00	1.50	.40
21	Dave Rader	4.00	1.50	.40
22	Johnny Bench	24.00	9.50	2.50
23	Luis Tiant	4.00	1.50	.40
24	Darrell Evans	4.00	1.50	.40
25	Larry Dierker	4.00	1.50	.40
26	Willie Horton	4.00	1.50	.40
27	John Ellis	4.00	1.50	.40
28	Al Cowens	4.00	1.50	.40
29	Jerry Reuss	4.00	1.50	.40
30	Reggie Smith	4.00	1.50	.40
31	Bobby Darwin	4.00	1.50	.40
32	Fritz Peterson	4.00	1.50	.40
33	Rod Carew	24.00	9.50	2.50
34	Carlos May	4.00	1.50	.40
35	Tom Seaver	30.00	12.00	3.00

#	Player	NM	EX	VG
36	Brooks Robinson	24.00	9.50	2.50
37	Jose Cardenal	4.00	1.50	.40
38	Ron Blomberg	4.00	1.50	.40
39	Lee Stanton	4.00	1.50	.40
40	Dave Cash	4.00	1.50	.40
41	John Montefusco	4.00	1.50	.40
42	Bob Tolan	4.00	1.50	.40
43	Carl Morton	4.00	1.50	.40
44	Rick Burleson	4.00	1.50	.40
45	Don Gullett	4.00	1.50	.40
46	Vern Ruhle	4.00	1.50	.40
47	Cesar Cedeno	4.00	1.50	.40
48	Toby Harrah	4.00	1.50	.40
49	Willie Stargell	24.00	9.50	2.50
50	Al Hrabosky	4.00	1.50	.40
51	Amos Otis	4.00	1.50	.40
52	Bud Harrelson	4.00	1.50	.40
53	Jim Hughes	4.00	1.50	.40
54	George Scott	4.00	1.50	.40
55	Mike Vail	4.00	1.50	.40
56	Jim Palmer	20.00	8.00	2.00
57	Jorge Orta	4.00	1.50	.40
58	Chris Chambliss	4.00	1.50	.40
59	Dave Chalk	4.00	1.50	.40
60	Ray Burris	4.00	1.50	.40

1976 Hostess Unissued Proofs

To help prevent a recurrance of the errors which plagued Hostess' debut set in 1975, the company prepared proof sheets of the cards before they were printed onto the bottoms of snack cake boxes. Probably to have ready substitutes in case problems were found, or a card had to be withdrawn at the last minute, there were seven players printed in proof version that were never issued on boxes. In addition, changes to cards #61, 121 and 138 were made between the proof stage and issued versions (they are detailed in the 1976 Hostess listings). The proofs share the format and 2-1/4" x 3-1/4" size of the issued cards.

		NM	EX	VG
	Complete Set (9):	400.00	200.00	120.00
	Common Player:	40.00	20.00	12.00
151	Fergie Jenkins (Issued as #138.)	75.00	37.50	22.50
152	Mike Cuellar (Issued as #121.)	40.00	20.00	12.00
153	Tom Murphy	40.00	20.00	12.00
154	Dusty Baker	40.00	20.00	12.00
155	Barry Foote	40.00	20.00	12.00
156	Steve Carlton	100.00	50.00	30.00
157	Richie Zisk	40.00	20.00	12.00
158	Ken Holtzman	40.00	20.00	12.00
159	Cliff Johnson	40.00	20.00	12.00

1977 Hostess

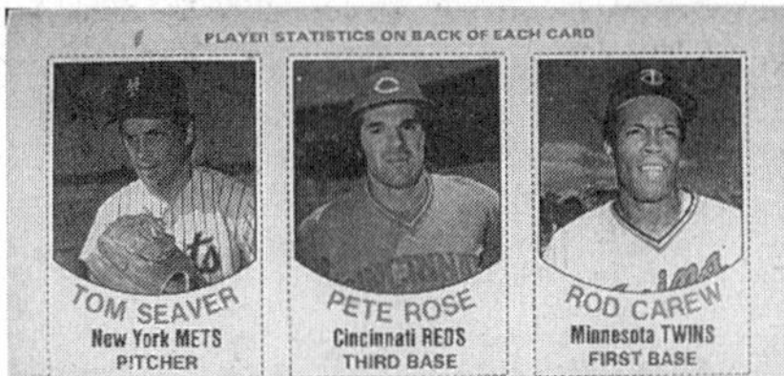

The third of five consecutive annual issues, the 1977 Hostess cards retained the same card size - 2-1/4" x 3-1/4", set size - 150 cards, and mode of issue - three cards on a 7-1/4" x 3-1/4" panel, as the previous two efforts. Because they were issued as the bottom panel of snack cake boxes, and because some brands of Hostess products were more popular than others, certain cards in the set are scarcer than others. A fold-out (to 8-1/2" x 22") All-Star Team album was available.

		NM	EX	VG
	Complete Panel Set (50):	250.00	125.00	75.00
	Complete Set, Singles (150):	200.00	100.00	60.00
	Common Panel:	4.00	2.00	1.25
	Common Player:	.75	.40	.25
	Album:	20.00	10.00	6.00
	Panel (1)	20.00	10.00	6.00
1	Jim Palmer	3.00	1.50	.90
2	Joe Morgan	3.00	1.50	.90
3a	Reggie Jackson	5.00	2.50	1.50
3b	Rod Carew (Unissued proof.)	20.00	10.00	6.00
	Panel (2)	25.00	12.50	7.50
4	Carl Yastrzemski	3.50	1.75	1.00
5	Thurman Munson	2.50	1.25	.70
6	Johnny Bench	3.50	1.75	1.00
	Panel (3)	30.00	15.00	9.00
7	Tom Seaver	3.00	1.50	.90
8	Pete Rose	7.50	3.75	2.25
9a	Rod Carew	3.00	1.50	.90
9b	Reggie Jackson (Unissued proof.)	75.00	37.00	22.00
	Panel (4)	4.00	2.00	1.25
10	Luis Tiant	.75	.40	.25
11	Phil Garner	.75	.40	.25
12	Sixto Lezcano	.75	.40	.25
	Panel (5)	4.00	2.00	1.25
13	Mike Torrez	.75	.40	.25
14	Davey Lopes	.75	.40	.25
15	Doug DeCinces	.75	.40	.25
	Panel (6)	4.00	2.00	1.25
16	Jim Spencer	.75	.40	.25
17	Hal McRae	.75	.40	.25
18	Mike Hargrove	.75	.40	.25
	Panel (7)	4.00	2.00	1.25
19	Willie Montanez	.75	.40	.25
20	Roger Metzger	.75	.40	.25
21	Dwight Evans	.75	.40	.25
	Panel (8)	5.00	2.50	1.50
22	Steve Rogers	.75	.40	.25
23	Jim Rice	1.25	.60	.40
24	Pete Falcone	.75	.40	.25
	Panel (9)	6.00	3.00	1.75
25	Greg Luzinski	.75	.40	.25
26	Randy Jones	.75	.40	.25
27	Willie Stargell	3.00	1.50	.90
	Panel (10)	5.00	2.50	1.50
28	John Hiller	.75	.40	.25
29	Bobby Murcer	.75	.40	.25
30	Rick Monday	.75	.40	.25
	Panel (11)	6.00	3.00	1.75
31	John Montefusco	.75	.40	.25
32	Lou Brock	3.00	1.50	.90
33	Bill North	.75	.40	.25
	Panel (12)	15.00	7.50	4.50
34	Robin Yount	3.00	1.50	.90
35	Steve Garvey	1.00	.50	.30
36	George Brett	5.00	2.50	1.50
	Panel (13)	4.00	2.00	1.25
37	Toby Harrah	.75	.40	.25
38	Jerry Royster	.75	.40	.25
39	Bob Watson	.75	.40	.25
	Panel (14)	5.00	2.50	1.50
40	George Foster	.75	.40	.25
41	Gary Carter	3.00	1.50	.90
42	John Denny	.75	.40	.25
	Panel (15)	20.00	10.00	6.00
43	Mike Schmidt	5.00	2.50	1.50
44	Dave Winfield	3.00	1.50	.90
45	Al Oliver	.90	.45	.25
	Panel (16)	4.00	2.00	1.25
46	Mark Fidrych	.75	.40	.25
47	Larry Herndon	.75	.40	.25
48	Dave Goltz	.75	.40	.25
	Panel (17)	4.00	2.00	1.25
49	Jerry Morales	.75	.40	.25
50	Ron LeFlore	.75	.40	.25
51	Fred Lynn	.75	.40	.25
	Panel (18)	4.00	2.00	1.25
52	Vida Blue	.75	.40	.25
53	Rick Manning	.75	.40	.25
54	Bill Buckner	.75	.40	.25
	Panel (19)	4.00	2.00	1.25
55	Lee May	.75	.40	.25
56	John Mayberry	.75	.40	.25
57	Darrel Chaney	.75	.40	.25
	Panel (20)	4.00	2.00	1.25
58	Cesar Cedeno	.75	.40	.25
59	Ken Griffey	.75	.40	.25
60	Dave Kingman	.75	.40	.25
	Panel (21)	4.00	2.00	1.25
61	Ted Simmons	.75	.40	.25
62	Larry Bowa	.75	.40	.25
63	Frank Tanana	.75	.40	.25
	Panel (22)	4.00	2.00	1.25
64	Jason Thompson	.75	.40	.25
65	Ken Brett	.75	.40	.25
66	Roy Smalley	.75	.40	.25
	Panel (23)	4.00	2.00	1.25
67	Ray Burris	.75	.40	.25
68	Rick Burleson	.75	.40	.25
69	Buddy Bell	.75	.40	.25
	Panel (24)	5.00	2.50	1.50
70	Don Sutton	2.50	1.25	.70
71	Mark Belanger	.75	.40	.25
72	Dennis Leonard	.75	.40	.25
	Panel (25)	5.00	2.50	1.50
73	Gaylord Perry	2.50	1.25	.70
74	Dick Ruthven	.75	.40	.25
75	Jose Cruz	.75	.40	.25
	Panel (26)	4.00	2.00	1.25
76	Cesar Geronimo	.75	.40	.25
77	Jerry Koosman	.75	.40	.25
78	Garry Templeton	.75	.40	.25
	Panel (27)	25.00	12.50	7.50
79	Jim Hunter	2.50	1.25	.70
80	John Candelaria	.75	.40	.25
81	Nolan Ryan	10.00	5.00	3.00
	Panel (28)	4.00	2.00	1.25
82	Rusty Staub	.90	.45	.25
83	Jim Barr	.75	.40	.25
84	Butch Wynegar	.75	.40	.25
	Panel (29)	4.00	2.00	1.25
85	Jose Cardenal	.75	.40	.25
86	Claudell Washington	.75	.40	.25
87	Bill Travers	.75	.40	.25
	Panel (30)	4.00	2.00	1.25
88	Rick Waits	.75	.40	.25
89	Ron Cey	.75	.40	.25
90	Al Bumbry	.75	.40	.25
	Panel (31)	4.00	2.00	1.25
91	Bucky Dent	.90	.45	.25
92	Amos Otis	.75	.40	.25
93	Tom Grieve	.75	.40	.25
	Panel (32)	4.00	2.00	1.25
94	Enos Cabell	.75	.40	.25
95	Dave Concepcion	.75	.40	.25
96	Felix Millan	.75	.40	.25
	Panel (33)	4.00	2.00	1.25
97	Bake McBride	.75	.40	.25
98	Chris Chambliss	.75	.40	.25
99	Butch Metzger	.75	.40	.25
	Panel (34)	4.00	2.00	1.25
100	Rennie Stennett	.75	.40	.25
101	Dave Roberts	.75	.40	.25
102	Lyman Bostock	.75	.40	.25
	Panel (35)	6.00	3.00	1.75
103	Rick Reuschel	.75	.40	.25
104	Carlton Fisk	3.00	1.50	.90
105	Jim Slaton	.75	.40	.25
	Panel (36)	5.00	2.50	1.50
106	Dennis Eckersley	2.50	1.25	.70
107	Ken Singleton	.75	.40	.25
108	Ralph Garr	.75	.40	.25
	Panel (37)	5.00	2.50	1.50
109	Freddie Patek	.75	.40	.25
110	Jim Sundberg	.75	.40	.25
111	Phil Niekro	2.50	1.25	.70
	Panel (38)	4.00	2.00	1.25
112	J.R. Richard	.75	.40	.25
113	Gary Nolan	.75	.40	.25
114	Jon Matlack	.75	.40	.25
	Panel (39)	7.50	3.75	2.25
115	Keith Hernandez	.75	.40	.25
116	Graig Nettles	.90	.45	.25
117	Steve Carlton	3.00	1.50	.90
	Panel (40)	4.00	2.00	1.25
118	Bill Madlock	.75	.40	.25
119	Jerry Reuss	.75	.40	.25
120	Aurelio Rodriguez	.75	.40	.25
	Panel (41)	4.00	2.00	1.25
121	Dan Ford	.75	.40	.25
122	Ray Fosse	.75	.40	.25
123	George Hendrick	.75	.40	.25
	Panel (42)	4.00	2.00	1.25
124	Alan Ashby	.75	.40	.25
125	Joe Lis	.75	.40	.25
126	Sal Bando	.75	.40	.25
	Panel (43)	5.00	2.50	1.50
127	Richie Zisk	.75	.40	.25
128	Rich Gossage	.75	.40	.25
129	Don Baylor	.75	.40	.25
	Panel (44)	4.00	2.00	1.25
130	Dave McKay	.75	.40	.25
131	Bobby Grich	.75	.40	.25
132	Dave Pagan	.75	.40	.25
	Panel (45)	4.00	2.00	1.25
133	Dave Cash	.75	.40	.25
134	Steve Braun	.75	.40	.25
135	Dan Meyer	.75	.40	.25
	Panel (46)	5.00	2.50	1.50
136	Bill Stein	.75	.40	.25
137	Rollie Fingers	2.50	1.25	.70
138	Brian Downing	.75	.40	.25
	Panel (47)	4.00	2.00	1.25
139	Bill Singer	.75	.40	.25
140	Doyle Alexander	.75	.40	.25
141	Gene Tenace	.75	.40	.25
	Panel (48)	4.00	2.00	1.25
142	Gary Matthews	.75	.40	.25
143	Don Gullett	.75	.40	.25
144	Wayne Garland	.75	.40	.25
	Panel (49)	4.00	2.00	1.25
145	Pete Broberg	.75	.40	.25
146	Joe Rudi	.75	.40	.25
147	Glenn Abbott	.75	.40	.25
	Panel (50)	4.00	2.00	1.25
148	George Scott	.75	.40	.25
149	Bert Campaneris	.75	.40	.25
150	Andy Messersmith	.75	.40	.25

1977 Hostess Twinkies

The 1977 Hostess Twinkie issue, at 150 different cards, is the largest of the single-panel Twinkie sets. It is also the most obscure. The cards, which measure 2-1/4" x 3-1/4" but are part of a larger panel, were found not only with Twinkies, but with Hostess Cupcakes as well. Cards #1-30 and 111-150 are Twinkies panels and #31-135 are Cupcakes panels. Complete Cupcakes panels are approximately 2-1/4" x 4-1/2" in size, while complete Twinkies panels measure 3-1/8" x 4-1/4". The photos used in the set are identical to those in the 1977 Hostess three-card panel set. The main difference is the appearance of a black band at the center of the card back. While cards actually issued with snack cakes are virtually always found with brown stains, enough unissued cards were leaked into the hobby to provide clean examples for those willing to search them out and pay the price.

Checklists showing are card numbers in parentheses ( ) indicates the numbers do not appear on the cards.

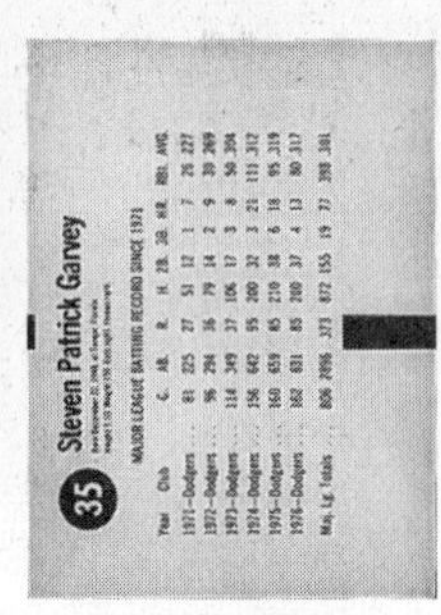

#	Player	NM	EX	VG
	Complete Set (150):	725.00	300.00	75.00
	Common Player:	4.00	1.50	.40
1	Jim Palmer	25.00	10.00	2.50
2	Joe Morgan	25.00	10.00	2.50
3	Reggie Jackson	40.00	16.00	4.00
4	Carl Yastrzemski	32.50	13.00	3.25
5	Thurman Munson	15.00	6.00	1.50
6	Johnny Bench	25.00	10.00	2.50
7	Tom Seaver	25.00	10.00	2.50
8	Pete Rose	65.00	26.00	6.50
9	Rod Carew	25.00	10.00	2.50
10	Luis Tiant	4.00	1.50	.40
11	Phil Garner	4.00	1.50	.40
12	Sixto Lezcano	4.00	1.50	.40
13	Mike Torrez	4.00	1.50	.40
14	Dave Lopes	4.00	1.50	.40
15	Doug DeCinces	4.00	1.50	.40
16	Jim Spencer	4.00	1.50	.40
17	Hal McRae	4.00	1.50	.40
18	Mike Hargrove	4.00	1.50	.40
19	Willie Montanez	4.00	1.50	.40
20	Roger Metzger	4.00	1.50	.40
21	Dwight Evans	4.00	1.50	.40
22	Steve Rogers	4.00	1.50	.40
23	Jim Rice	12.50	5.00	1.25
24	Pete Falcone	4.00	1.50	.40
25	Greg Luzinski	4.00	1.50	.40
26	Randy Jones	4.00	1.50	.40
27	Willie Stargell	25.00	10.00	2.50
28	John Hiller	4.00	1.50	.40
29	Bobby Murcer	4.00	1.50	.40
30	Rick Monday	4.00	1.50	.40
31	John Montefusco	4.00	1.50	.40
32	Lou Brock	25.00	10.00	2.50
33	Bill North	4.00	1.50	.40
34	Robin Yount	25.00	10.00	2.50
35	Steve Garvey	12.50	5.00	1.25
36	George Brett	40.00	16.00	4.00
37	Toby Harrah	4.00	1.50	.40
38	Jerry Royster	4.00	1.50	.40
39	Bob Watson	4.00	1.50	.40
40	George Foster	4.00	1.50	.40
41	Gary Carter	25.00	10.00	2.50
42	John Denny	4.00	1.50	.40
43	Mike Schmidt	40.00	16.00	4.00
44	Dave Winfield	25.00	10.00	2.50
45	Al Oliver	4.00	1.50	.40
46	Mark Fidrych	6.50	2.50	.60
47	Larry Herndon	4.00	1.50	.40
48	Dave Goltz	4.00	1.50	.40
49	Jerry Morales	4.00	1.50	.40
50	Ron LeFlore	4.00	1.50	.40
51	Fred Lynn	4.00	1.50	.40
52	Vida Blue	4.00	1.50	.40
53	Rick Manning	4.00	1.50	.40
54	Bill Buckner	4.00	1.50	.40
55	Lee May	4.00	1.50	.40
56	John Mayberry	4.00	1.50	.40
57	Darrel Chaney	4.00	1.50	.40
58	Cesar Cedeno	4.00	1.50	.40
59	Ken Griffey	4.00	1.50	.40
60	Dave Kingman	6.50	2.50	.60
61	Ted Simmons	4.00	1.50	.40
62	Larry Bowa	4.00	1.50	.40
63	Frank Tanana	4.00	1.50	.40
64	Jason Thompson	4.00	1.50	.40
65	Ken Brett	4.00	1.50	.40
66	Roy Smalley	4.00	1.50	.40
67	Ray Burris	4.00	1.50	.40
68	Rick Burleson	4.00	1.50	.40
69	Buddy Bell	4.00	1.50	.40
70	Don Sutton	20.00	8.00	2.00
71	Mark Belanger	4.00	1.50	.40
72	Dennis Leonard	4.00	1.50	.40
73	Gaylord Perry	20.00	8.00	2.00
74	Dick Ruthven	4.00	1.50	.40
75	Jose Cruz	4.00	1.50	.40
76	Cesar Geronimo	4.00	1.50	.40
77	Jerry Koosman	4.00	1.50	.40
78	Garry Templeton	4.00	1.50	.40
79	Catfish Hunter	20.00	8.00	2.00
80	John Candelaria	4.00	1.50	.40
81	Nolan Ryan	100.00	40.00	10.00
82	Rusty Staub	6.50	2.50	.60
83	Jim Barr	4.00	1.50	.40
84	Butch Wynegar	4.00	1.50	.40
85	Jose Cardenal	4.00	1.50	.40
86	Claudell Washington	4.00	1.50	.40
87	Bill Travers	4.00	1.50	.40
88	Rick Waits	4.00	1.50	.40
89	Ron Cey	4.00	1.50	.40
90	Al Bumbry	4.00	1.50	.40
91	Bucky Dent	4.00	1.50	.40
92	Amos Otis	4.00	1.50	.40
93	Tom Grieve	4.00	1.50	.40
94	Enos Cabell	4.00	1.50	.40
95	Dave Concepcion	4.00	1.50	.40
96	Felix Millan	4.00	1.50	.40
97	Bake McBride	4.00	1.50	.40
98	Chris Chambliss	4.00	1.50	.40
99	Butch Metzger	4.00	1.50	.40
100	Rennie Stennett	4.00	1.50	.40
101	Dave Roberts	4.00	1.50	.40
102	Lyman Bostock	4.00	1.50	.40
103	Rick Reuschel	4.00	1.50	.40
104	Carlton Fisk	25.00	10.00	2.50
105	Jim Slaton	4.00	1.50	.40
106	Dennis Eckersley	20.00	8.00	2.00
107	Ken Singleton	4.00	1.50	.40
108	Ralph Garr	4.00	1.50	.40
109	Freddie Patek	4.00	1.50	.40
110	Jim Sundberg	4.00	1.50	.40
111	Phil Niekro	20.00	8.00	2.00
112	J. R. Richard	4.00	1.50	.40
113	Gary Nolan	4.00	1.50	.40
114	Jon Matlack	4.00	1.50	.40
115	Keith Hernandez	4.00	1.50	.40
116	Graig Nettles	4.00	1.50	.40
117	Steve Carlton	25.00	10.00	2.50
118	Bill Madlock	4.00	1.50	.40
119	Jerry Reuss	4.00	1.50	.40
120	Aurelio Rodriguez	4.00	1.50	.40
121	Dan Ford	4.00	1.50	.40
122	Ray Fosse	4.00	1.50	.40
123	George Hendrick	4.00	1.50	.40
124	Alan Ashby	4.00	1.50	.40
125	Joe Lis	4.00	1.50	.40
126	Sal Bando	4.00	1.50	.40
127	Richie Zisk	4.00	1.50	.40
128	Rich Gossage	4.00	1.50	.40
129	Don Baylor	6.50	2.50	.60
130	Dave McKay	4.00	1.50	.40
131	Bob Grich	4.00	1.50	.40
132	Dave Pagan	4.00	1.50	.40
133	Dave Cash	4.00	1.50	.40
134	Steve Braun	4.00	1.50	.40
135	Dan Meyer	4.00	1.50	.40
136	Bill Stein	4.00	1.50	.40
137	Rollie Fingers	20.00	8.00	2.00
138	Brian Downing	4.00	1.50	.40
139	Bill Singer	4.00	1.50	.40
140	Doyle Alexander	4.00	1.50	.40
141	Gene Tenace	4.00	1.50	.40
142	Gary Matthews	4.00	1.50	.40
143	Don Gullett	4.00	1.50	.40
144	Wayne Garland	4.00	1.50	.40
145	Pete Broberg	4.00	1.50	.40
146	Joe Rudi	4.00	1.50	.40
147	Glenn Abbott	4.00	1.50	.40
148	George Scott	4.00	1.50	.40
149	Bert Campaneris	4.00	1.50	.40
150	Andy Messersmith	4.00	1.50	.40

1977 Hostess Unissued Proofs

The reason for the existence of these rare Hostess proofs is unknown, but there seems little doubt that they were never actually circulated; perhaps being held in reserve in case the cards actually printed on product boxes had to be replaced. The 10 cards were printed on a sheet in three-card panels, like the issued Hostess cards, plus a single of Briles. The proofs share the format of the issued cards, and the 2-1/4" x 3-1/4" size. Besides these "high number" proofs, there also exist numbering-variation proofs of cards #3, 9, 65 and 119 (see 1977 Hostess listings).

#	Player	NM	EX	VG
	Complete Set (10):	400.00	200.00	120.00
	Common Single:	40.00	20.00	12.00
151	Ed Kranepool	40.00	20.00	12.00
152	Ross Grimsley	40.00	20.00	12.00
153	Ken Brett (#65 in regular-issue set)	40.00	20.00	12.00
154	Rowland Office	40.00	20.00	12.00
155	Rick Wise	40.00	20.00	12.00
156	Paul Splittorff	40.00	20.00	12.00
157	Jerry Augustine	40.00	20.00	12.00
158	Ken Forsch	40.00	20.00	12.00
159	Jerry Reuss	40.00	20.00	12.00
160	Nelson Briles	40.00	20.00	12.00

1978 Hostess

Other than the design on the front of the card, there was little different about the 1978 Hostess cards from the three years' issues which had preceded it, or the one which followed. The 2-1/4" x 3-1/4" cards were printed in panels of three (7-1/4" x 3-1/4") as the bottom of family-sized boxes of snack cakes. The 1978 set was again complete at 150 cards. Like other years of Hostess issues, there are scarcities within the 1978 set that are the result of those panels having been issued with less-popular brands of snack cakes.

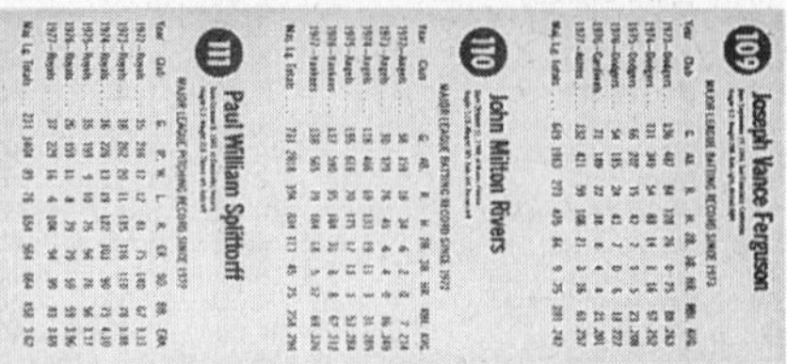

#	Player	NM	EX	VG
	Complete Panel Set (50):	275.00	135.00	80.00
	Complete Set, Singles (150):	225.00	110.00	65.00
	Common Panel:	6.00	3.00	1.75
	Common Player:	.75	.40	.25
	Album:	25.00	12.50	7.50
	Panel (1)	6.00	3.00	1.75
1	Butch Hobson	.75	.40	.25
2	George Foster	.75	.40	.25
3	Bob Forsch	.75	.40	.25
	Panel (2)	13.50	6.75	4.00
4	Tony Perez	4.00	2.00	1.25
5	Bruce Sutter	4.00	2.00	1.25
6	Hal McRae	.75	.40	.25
	Panel (3)	7.50	3.75	2.25
7	Tommy John	1.25	.60	.40
8	Greg Luzinski	.75	.40	.25
9	Enos Cabell	.75	.40	.25
	Panel (4)	10.00	5.00	3.00
10	Doug DeCinces	.75	.40	.25
11	Willie Stargell	4.50	2.25	1.25
12	Ed Halicki	.75	.40	.25
	Panel (5)	6.00	3.00	1.75
13	Larry Hisle	.75	.40	.25
14	Jim Slaton	.75	.40	.25
15	Buddy Bell	.75	.40	.25
	Panel (6)	6.00	3.00	1.75
16	Earl Williams	.75	.40	.25
17	Glenn Abbott	.75	.40	.25
18	Dan Ford	.75	.40	.25
	Panel (7)	6.00	3.00	1.75
19	Gary Matthews	.75	.40	.25
20	Eric Soderholm	.75	.40	.25
21	Bump Wills	.75	.40	.25
	Panel (8)	6.00	3.00	1.75
22	Keith Hernandez	.75	.40	.25
23	Dave Cash	.75	.40	.25
24	George Scott	.75	.40	.25
	Panel (9)	20.00	10.00	6.00
25	Ron Guidry	1.25	.60	.40
26	Dave Kingman	.75	.40	.25
27	George Brett	9.00	4.50	2.75
	Panel (10)	6.00	3.00	1.75
28	Bob Watson	.75	.40	.25
29	Bob Boone	.90	.45	.25
30	Reggie Smith	.75	.40	.25
	Panel (11)	45.00	22.00	13.50
31	Eddie Murray	18.50	9.25	5.50
32	Gary Lavelle	.75	.40	.25
33	Rennie Stennett	.75	.40	.25
	Panel (12)	6.00	3.00	1.75
34	Duane Kuiper	.75	.40	.25
35	Sixto Lezcano	.75	.40	.25
36	Dave Rozema	.75	.40	.25
	Panel (13)	6.00	3.00	1.75
37	Butch Wynegar	.75	.40	.25
38	Mitchell Page	.75	.40	.25
39	Bill Stein	.75	.40	.25
	Panel (14)	6.00	3.00	1.75
40	Elliott Maddox	.75	.40	.25
41	Mike Hargrove	.75	.40	.25
42	Bobby Bonds	.75	.40	.25
	Panel (15)	20.00	10.00	6.00
43	Garry Templeton	.75	.40	.25
44	Johnny Bench	4.50	2.25	1.25
45	Jim Rice	1.50	.70	.45
	Panel (16)	17.50	8.75	5.25
46	Bill Buckner	.75	.40	.25
47	Reggie Jackson	9.00	4.50	2.75
48	Freddie Patek	.75	.40	.25
	Panel (17)	10.00	5.00	3.00
49	Steve Carlton	4.50	2.25	1.25
50	Cesar Cedeno	.75	.40	.25
51	Steve Yeager	.75	.40	.25
	Panel (18)	6.00	3.00	1.75
52	Phil Garner	.75	.40	.25
53	Lee May	.75	.40	.25
54	Darrell Evans	.75	.40	.25
	Panel (19)	6.00	3.00	1.75
55	Steve Kemp	.75	.40	.25
56a	Dusty Baker	.90	.45	.25
56b	Andre Thornton (Unissued proof.)	18.00	9.00	5.50
57	Ray Fosse	.75	.40	.25
	Panel (20)	6.00	3.00	1.75
58	Manny Sanguillen	.75	.40	.25
59	Tom Johnson	.75	.40	.25
60	Lee Stanton	.75	.40	.25
	Panel (21)	10.00	5.00	3.00
61	Jeff Burroughs	.75	.40	.25
62	Bobby Grich	.75	.40	.25

63	Dave Winfield	4.50	2.25	1.25
	Panel (22)	6.00	3.00	1.75
64	Dan Driessen	.75	.40	.25
65	Ted Simmons	.75	.40	.25
66	Jerry Remy	.75	.40	.25
	Panel (23)	6.00	3.00	1.75
67	Al Cowens	.75	.40	.25
68	Sparky Lyle	.75	.40	.25
69	Manny Trillo	.75	.40	.25
	Panel (24)	9.00	4.50	2.75
70	Don Sutton	4.00	2.00	1.25
71	Larry Bowa	.75	.40	.25
72	Jose Cruz	.75	.40	.25
	Panel (25)	10.00	5.00	3.00
73	Willie McCovey	4.50	2.25	1.25
74	Bert Blyleven	.75	.40	.25
75	Ken Singleton	.75	.40	.25
	Panel (26)	6.00	3.00	1.75
76	Bill North	.75	.40	.25
77	Jason Thompson	.75	.40	.25
78	Dennis Eckersley	4.00	2.00	1.25
	Panel (27)	6.00	3.00	1.75
79	Jim Sundberg	.75	.40	.25
80	Jerry Koosman	.75	.40	.25
81	Bruce Bochte	.75	.40	.25
	Panel (28)	45.00	22.00	13.50
82	George Hendrick	.75	.40	.25
83	Nolan Ryan	20.00	10.00	6.00
84	Roy Howell	.75	.40	.25
	Panel (29)	10.00	5.00	3.00
85	Butch Metzger	.75	.40	.25
86	George Medich	.75	.40	.25
87	Joe Morgan	4.50	2.25	1.25
	Panel (30)	6.00	3.00	1.75
88	Dennis Leonard	.75	.40	.25
89	Willie Randolph	.90	.45	.25
90	Bobby Murcer	.90	.45	.25
	Panel (31)	6.00	3.00	1.75
91	Rick Manning	.75	.40	.25
92	J.R. Richard	.75	.40	.25
93	Ron Cey	.75	.40	.25
	Panel (32)	6.00	3.00	1.75
94	Sal Bando	.75	.40	.25
95	Ron LeFlore	.75	.40	.25
96	Dave Goltz	.75	.40	.25
	Panel (33)	6.00	3.00	1.75
97	Dan Meyer	.75	.40	.25
98	Chris Chambliss	.75	.40	.25
99	Biff Pocoroba	.75	.40	.25
	Panel (34)	6.00	3.00	1.75
100	Oscar Gamble	.75	.40	.25
101	Frank Tanana	.75	.40	.25
102	Lenny Randle	.75	.40	.25
	Panel (35)	6.00	3.00	1.75
103	Tommy Hutton	.75	.40	.25
104	John Candelaria	.75	.40	.25
105	Jorge Orta	.75	.40	.25
	Panel (36)	6.00	3.00	1.75
106	Ken Reitz	.75	.40	.25
107	Bill Campbell	.75	.40	.25
108	Dave Concepcion	.75	.40	.25
	Panel (37)	6.00	3.00	1.75
109	Joe Ferguson	.75	.40	.25
110	Mickey Rivers	.75	.40	.25
111	Paul Splittorff	.75	.40	.25
	Panel (38)	20.00	10.00	6.00
112	Davey Lopes	.75	.40	.25
113	Mike Schmidt	9.00	4.50	2.75
114	Joe Rudi	.75	.40	.25
	Panel (39)	10.00	5.00	3.00
115	Milt May	.75	.40	.25
116	Jim Palmer	4.50	2.25	1.25
117	Bill Madlock	.75	.40	.25
	Panel (40)	6.00	3.00	1.75
118	Roy Smalley	.75	.40	.25
119	Cecil Cooper	.75	.40	.25
120	Rick Langford	.75	.40	.25
	Panel (41)	9.00	4.50	2.75
121	Ruppert Jones	.75	.40	.25
122	Phil Niekro	4.00	2.00	1.25
123	Toby Harrah	.75	.40	.25
	Panel (42)	6.00	3.00	1.75
124	Chet Lemon	.75	.40	.25
125	Gene Tenace	.75	.40	.25
126	Steve Henderson	.75	.40	.25
	Panel (43)	35.00	17.50	10.50
127	Mike Torrez	.75	.40	.25
128	Pete Rose	10.00	5.00	3.00
129	John Denny	.75	.40	.25
	Panel (44)	6.00	3.00	1.75
130	Darrell Porter	.75	.40	.25
131	Rick Reuschel	.75	.40	.25
132	Graig Nettles	.90	.45	.25
	Panel (45)	6.00	3.00	1.75
133	Garry Maddox	.75	.40	.25
134	Mike Flanagan	.75	.40	.25
135	Dave Parker	.75	.40	.25
	Panel (46)	10.00	5.00	3.00
136	Terry Whitfield	.75	.40	.25
137	Wayne Garland	.75	.40	.25
138	Robin Yount	4.50	2.25	1.25
	Panel (47)	20.00	10.00	6.00
139a	Gaylord Perry (San Diego)	4.00	2.00	1.25
139b	Gaylord Perry (Texas, unissued proof.)	30.00	15.00	9.00
140	Rod Carew	4.50	2.25	1.25
141	Wayne Gross	.75	.40	.25
	Panel (48)	9.00	4.50	2.75
142	Barry Bonnell	.75	.40	.25
143	Willie Montanez	.75	.40	.25
144	Rollie Fingers	4.00	2.00	1.25
	Panel (49)	35.00	17.50	10.50
145	Lyman Bostock	.75	.40	.25
146	Gary Carter	4.50	2.25	1.25
147	Ron Blomberg	.75	.40	.25
	Panel (50)	30.00	15.00	9.00
148	Bob Bailor	.75	.40	.25
149	Tom Seaver	5.00	2.50	1.50
150	Thurman Munson	4.00	2.00	1.25

1978 Hostess Unissued Proofs

Different versions of two of the issued cards (see 1978 Hostess #56, 139) plus 10 players who do not appear on the snack cake boxes constitute the proof set for '78 Hostess. The unissued proofs are identical in format to the cards actually issued and measure 2-1/4" x 3-1/4" at the dotted lines.

		NM	EX	VG
	Complete Set (10):	450.00	225.00	135.00
	Common Player:	50.00	25.00	15.00
151	Bill Robinson	50.00	25.00	15.00
152	Lou Piniella	75.00	37.50	22.50
153	Lamar Johnson	50.00	25.00	15.00
154	Mark Belanger	50.00	25.00	15.00
155	Ken Griffey	75.00	37.50	22.50
156	Ken Forsch	50.00	25.00	15.00
157	Ted Sizemore	50.00	25.00	15.00
158	Don Baylor	50.00	25.00	15.00
159	Dusty Baker	60.00	30.00	18.00
160	Al Oliver	75.00	37.50	22.50

1979 Hostess

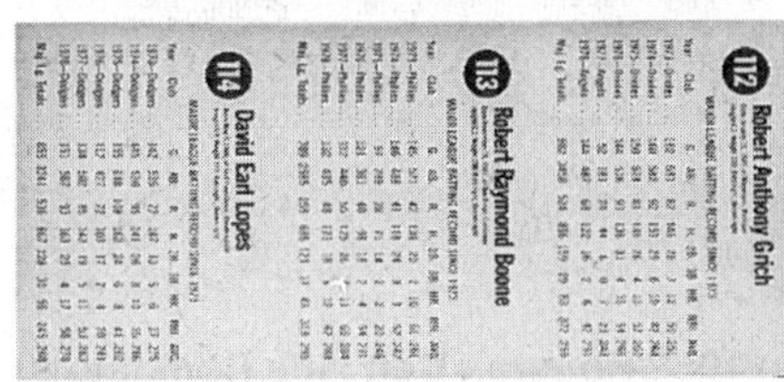

The last of five consecutive annual issues, the 1979 Hostess set retained the 150-card set size, 2-1/4" x 3-1/4" single-card size and 7-1/4" x 3-1/4" three-card panel format from the previous years. The cards were printed as the bottom panel on family-size boxes of Hostess snack cakes. Some panels, which were printed on less-popular brands, are somewhat scarcer today than the rest of the set. Like all Hostess issues, because the hobby was in a well-developed state at the time of issue, the 1979s survive today in complete panels and complete unused boxes for collectors who like original packaging.

		NM	EX	VG
	Complete Panel Set (50):	250.00	125.00	75.00
	Complete Singles Set (150):	175.00	85.00	50.00
	Common Panel:	4.50	2.25	1.25
	Common Single Player:	.75	.40	.25
	Panel (1)	7.50	3.75	2.25
1	John Denny	.75	.40	.25
2a	Jim Rice ("d-of", unissued proof)	15.00	7.50	4.50
2b	Jim Rice ("dh-of")	1.50	.70	.45
3	Doug Bair	.75	.40	.25
	Panel (2)	6.00	3.00	1.75
4	Darrell Porter	.75	.40	.25
5	Ross Grimsley	.75	.40	.25
6	Bobby Murcer	1.00	.50	.30
	Panel (3)	25.00	12.50	7.50
7	Lee Mazzilli	.75	.40	.25
8	Steve Garvey	1.50	.70	.45
9	Mike Schmidt	6.00	3.00	1.75
	Panel (4)	12.00	6.00	3.50
10	Terry Whitfield	.75	.40	.25
11	Jim Palmer	2.50	1.25	.70
12	Omar Moreno	.75	.40	.25
	Panel (5)	5.00	2.50	1.50
13	Duane Kuiper	.75	.40	.25
14	Mike Caldwell	.75	.40	.25
15	Steve Kemp	.75	.40	.25
	Panel (6)	5.00	2.50	1.50
16	Dave Goltz	.75	.40	.25
17	Mitchell Page	.75	.40	.25
18	Bill Stein	.75	.40	.25
	Panel (7)	5.00	2.50	1.50
19	Gene Tenace	.75	.40	.25
20	Jeff Burroughs	.75	.40	.25
21	Francisco Barrios	.75	.40	.25
	Panel (8)	7.50	3.75	2.25
22	Mike Torrez	.75	.40	.25
23	Ken Reitz	.75	.40	.25
24	Gary Carter	2.50	1.25	.70
	Panel (9)	9.00	4.50	2.75
25	Al Hrabosky	.75	.40	.25
26	Thurman Munson	1.50	.70	.45
27	Bill Buckner	.75	.40	.25
	Panel (10)	6.00	3.00	1.75
28	Ron Cey	.75	.40	.25
29	J.R. Richard	.75	.40	.25
30	Greg Luzinski	.75	.40	.25
	Panel (11)	5.00	2.50	1.50
31	Ed Ott	.75	.40	.25
32	Denny Martinez	.75	.40	.25
33	Darrell Evans	.75	.40	.25
	Panel (12)	5.00	2.50	1.50
34	Ron LeFlore	.75	.40	.25
35	Rick Waits	.75	.40	.25
36	Cecil Cooper	.75	.40	.25
	Panel (13)	15.00	7.50	4.50
37	Leon Roberts	.75	.40	.25
38a	Rod Carew (Large head.) (Botton of collar trim does not show.)	3.00	1.50	.90
38b	Rod Carew (Small head.) (Bottom of collar trim shows.)	3.00	1.50	.90
39	John Henry Johnson	.75	.40	.25
	Panel (14)	5.00	2.50	1.50
40	Chet Lemon	.75	.40	.25
41	Craig Swan	.75	.40	.25
42	Gary Matthews	.75	.40	.25
	Panel (15)	5.00	2.50	1.50
43	Lamar Johnson	.75	.40	.25
44	Ted Simmons	.75	.40	.25
45	Ken Griffey	.75	.40	.25
	Panel (16)	6.00	3.00	1.75
46	Freddie Patek	.75	.40	.25
47	Frank Tanana	.75	.40	.25
48	Rich Gossage	1.00	.50	.30
	Panel (17)	5.00	2.50	1.50
49	Burt Hooton	.75	.40	.25
50	Ellis Valentine	.75	.40	.25
51	Ken Forsch	.75	.40	.25
	Panel (18)	6.00	3.00	1.75
52	Bob Knepper	.75	.40	.25
53	Dave Parker	.75	.40	.25
54	Doug DeCinces	.75	.40	.25
	Panel (19)	20.00	10.00	6.00
55	Robin Yount	3.00	1.50	.90
56	Rusty Staub	1.00	.50	.30
57	Gary Alexander	.75	.40	.25
	Panel (20)	5.00	2.50	1.50
58	Julio Cruz	.75	.40	.25
59	Matt Keough	.75	.40	.25
60	Roy Smalley	.75	.40	.25
	Panel (21)	15.00	7.50	4.50
61	Joe Morgan	3.00	1.50	.90
62	Phil Niekro	2.00	1.00	.60
63	Don Baylor	.75	.40	.25
	Panel (22)	20.00	10.00	6.00
64	Dwight Evans	.75	.40	.25
65	Tom Seaver	3.00	1.50	.90
66	George Hendrick	.75	.40	.25
	Panel (23)	25.00	12.50	7.50
67	Rick Reuschel	.75	.40	.25
68	George Brett	6.00	3.00	1.75
69	Lou Piniella	1.00	.50	.30
	Panel (24)	12.00	6.00	3.50
70	Enos Cabell	.75	.40	.25
71	Steve Carlton	2.50	1.25	.70
72	Reggie Smith	.75	.40	.25
	Panel (25)	5.00	2.50	1.50
73	Rick Dempsey	.75	.40	.25
74	Vida Blue	.75	.40	.25
75	Phil Garner	.75	.40	.25
	Panel (26)	5.00	2.50	1.50
76	Rick Manning	.75	.40	.25
77	Mark Fidrych	1.00	.50	.30
78	Mario Guerrero	.75	.40	.25
	Panel (27)	5.00	2.50	1.50
79	Bob Stinson	.75	.40	.25
80	Al Oliver	.75	.40	.25
81	Doug Flynn	.75	.40	.25
	Panel (28)	7.50	3.75	2.25
82	John Mayberry	.75	.40	.25
83	Gaylord Perry	2.00	1.00	.60
84	Joe Rudi	.75	.40	.25
	Panel (29)	5.00	2.50	1.50
85	Dave Concepcion	.75	.40	.25
86	John Candelaria	.75	.40	.25
87	Pete Vuckovich	.75	.40	.25
	Panel (30)	5.00	2.50	1.50
88	Ivan DeJesus	.75	.40	.25
89	Ron Guidry	.75	.40	.25
90	Hal McRae	.75	.40	.25
	Panel (31)	6.00	3.00	1.75
91	Cesar Cedeno	.75	.40	.25
92	Don Sutton	2.00	1.00	.60
93	Andre Thornton	.75	.40	.25
	Panel (32)	5.00	2.50	1.50
94	Roger Erickson	.75	.40	.25
95	Larry Hisle	.75	.40	.25
96	Jason Thompson	.75	.40	.25
	Panel (33)	5.00	2.50	1.50
97	Jim Sundberg	.75	.40	.25
98	Bob Horner	.75	.40	.25
99	Ruppert Jones	.75	.40	.25
	Panel (34)	60.00	30.00	18.00
100	Willie Montanez	.75	.40	.25
101	Nolan Ryan	12.00	6.00	3.50
102	Ozzie Smith	15.00	7.50	4.50
	Panel (35)	12.00	6.00	3.50
103	Eric Soderholm	.75	.40	.25
104	Willie Stargell	2.50	1.25	.70
105a	Bob Bailor (Photo reversed, unissued proof.)	.75	.40	.25
105b	Bob Bailor (Photo corrected.)	.75	.40	.25
	Panel (36)	12.50	6.25	3.75
106	Carlton Fisk	2.50	1.25	.70
107	George Foster	.75	.40	.25
108	Keith Hernandez	.75	.40	.25
	Panel (37)	5.00	2.50	1.50
109	Dennis Leonard	.75	.40	.25
110	Graig Nettles	1.00	.50	.30
111	Jose Cruz	.75	.40	.25
	Panel (38)	5.00	2.50	1.50
112	Bobby Grich	.75	.40	.25
113	Bob Boone	.75	.40	.25
114	Davey Lopes	.75	.40	.25
	Panel (39)	15.00	7.50	4.50
115	Eddie Murray	3.00	1.50	.90
116	Jack Clark	.75	.40	.25

		NM	EX	VG
117	Lou Whitaker	.75	.40	.25
	Panel (40)	20.00	10.00	6.00
118	Miguel Dilone	.75	.40	.25
119	Sal Bando	.75	.40	.25
120	Reggie Jackson	6.00	3.00	1.75
	Panel (41)	15.00	7.50	4.50
121	Dale Murphy	2.00	1.00	.60
122	Jon Matlack	.75	.40	.25
123	Bruce Bochte	.75	.40	.25
	Panel (42)	12.50	6.25	3.75
124	John Stearns	.75	.40	.25
125	Dave Winfield	3.00	1.50	.90
126	Jorge Orta	.75	.40	.25
	Panel (43)	25.00	12.50	7.50
127	Garry Templeton	.75	.40	.25
128	Johnny Bench	3.00	1.50	.90
129	Butch Hobson	.75	.40	.25
	Panel (44)	6.00	3.00	1.75
130	Bruce Sutter	2.50	1.25	.70
131	Bucky Dent	.75	.40	.25
132	Amos Otis	.75	.40	.25
	Panel (45)	5.00	2.50	1.50
133	Bert Blyleven	.75	.40	.25
134	Larry Bowa	.75	.40	.25
135	Ken Singleton	.75	.40	.25
	Panel (46)	5.00	2.50	1.50
136	Sixto Lezcano	.75	.40	.25
137	Roy Howell	.75	.40	.25
138	Bill Madlock	.75	.40	.25
	Panel (47)	5.00	2.50	1.50
139	Dave Revering	.75	.40	.25
140	Richie Zisk	.75	.40	.25
141	Butch Wynegar	.75	.40	.25
	Panel (48)	25.00	12.50	7.50
142	Alan Ashby	.75	.40	.25
143	Sparky Lyle	.75	.40	.25
144	Pete Rose	7.50	3.75	2.25
	Panel (49)	6.00	3.00	1.75
145	Dennis Eckersley	2.50	1.25	.70
146	Dave Kingman	.75	.40	.25
147	Buddy Bell	.75	.40	.25
	Panel (50)	5.00	2.50	1.50
148	Mike Hargrove	.75	.40	.25
149	Jerry Koosman	.75	.40	.25
150	Toby Harrah	.75	.40	.25

1979 Hostess Unissued Proofs

Identical in format to the 150 cards which were issued on boxes of Hostess snack cakes, these cards were possibly prepared in the event trades of players in the issued set required quick replacement. The reason these cards were never released is unknown. Cards measure 2-1/4" x 3-1/4" at the dotted-line borders. While some of the proofs are numbered on back, others have no card number.

		NM	EX	VG
Complete Set (17):		1,100	550.00	330.00
Common Player:		50.00	25.00	15.00
151	Dusty Baker	60.00	30.00	18.00
152	Mark Belanger	60.00	30.00	18.00
154	Al Cowens	50.00	25.00	15.00
155	Dan Driessen	50.00	25.00	15.00
157	Steve Henderson	50.00	25.00	15.00
159	Tommy John	75.00	37.50	22.50
160	Garry Maddox	50.00	25.00	15.00
(161)	Willie McCovey	250.00	125.00	75.00
(162)	Scott McGregor	50.00	25.00	15.00
(163)	Bill Nahorodny	50.00	25.00	15.00
(164)	Terry Puhl	50.00	25.00	15.00
(165)	Willie Randolph	50.00	25.00	15.00
(166)	Jim Slaton	50.00	25.00	15.00
(167)	Paul Splittorff	50.00	25.00	15.00
(168)	Frank Taveras	50.00	25.00	15.00
(169)	Alan Trammell	125.00	65.00	35.00
(170)	Bump Wills	50.00	25.00	15.00

1971 House of Jazz

Controversy has dogged this card set since the first reports of its existence in the early 1970s. The legitimacy of the issue has been questioned though certain hobby journalists traced the cards to a record store which supposedly gave them away with music purchases, along with similar cards depicting musicians. The 2-3/8" x 3-1/2" cards are printed in black-and-white with round corners. Backs of some, but not all, cards have a blue-and-white address sticker for "HOUSE OF JAZZ, LTD." The unnumbered cards are checklisted here in alphabetical order.

		NM	EX	VG
Complete Set (35):		200.00	100.00	60.00
Common Player:		5.00	2.50	1.50
(1)	John Antonelli	5.00	2.50	1.50
(2)	Richie Ashburn	6.00	3.00	1.75
(3)	Ernie Banks	6.50	3.25	2.00
(4)	Hank Bauer	5.00	2.50	1.50
(5)	Joe DiMaggio	15.00	7.50	4.50
(6)	Bobby Doerr	5.00	2.50	1.50
(7)	Herman Franks	5.00	2.50	1.50
(8)	Lou Gehrig	15.00	7.50	4.50
(9)	Granny Hamner	5.00	2.50	1.50
(10)	Al Kaline	6.50	3.25	2.00
(11)	Harmon Killebrew	6.00	3.00	1.75
(12)	Jim Konstanty	5.00	2.50	1.50
(13)	Bob Lemon	5.00	2.50	1.50
(14)	Ed Lopat	5.00	2.50	1.50
(15)	Stan Lopata	5.00	2.50	1.50
(16)	Peanuts Lowrey	5.00	2.50	1.50
(17)	Mickey Mantle	35.00	17.50	10.00
(18)	Phil Marchildon	5.00	2.50	1.50
(19)	Walt Masterson	5.00	2.50	1.50
(20)	Ed Mathews	6.00	3.00	1.75
(21)	Willie Mays	10.00	5.00	3.00
(22)	Don Newcombe	5.00	2.50	1.50
(23)	Joe Nuxhall	5.00	2.50	1.50
(24)	Satchel Paige	7.50	3.75	2.25
(25)	Roy Partee	5.00	2.50	1.50
(26)	Jackie Robinson	7.50	3.75	2.25
(27)	Babe Ruth	20.00	10.00	6.00
(28)	Carl Scheib	5.00	2.50	1.50
(29)	Bobby Shantz	5.00	2.50	1.50
(30)	Burt Shotton	5.00	2.50	1.50
(31)	Duke Snider	6.50	3.25	2.00
(32)	Warren Spahn	6.00	3.00	1.75
(33)	Johnny Temple	5.00	2.50	1.50
(34)	Ted Williams	10.00	5.00	3.00
(35)	Early Wynn	5.00	2.50	1.50

1962 Houston Colt .45s Booklets

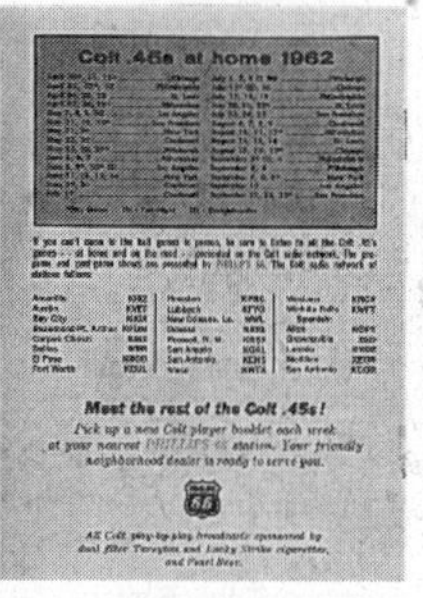

To introduce the members of the new Houston National League team, Phillips 66 gasoline sponsored (along with the team's cigarette and beer broadcast sponsors) this set of 24 player profile booklets given away one per week during the season. Fronts of the 16-page 5-3/8" x 7-7/16" booklets feature a blue and white action photo of the player on a bright orange background. Black and white graphics complete the design. The player's name appears in a Texas map outline. Backs have the 1962 Houston Colt .45s home-game schedule and details of the team's statewide radio network. Inside the booklet are a complete biography, stats and both posed and action photos of the players, along with families, teammates, etc. Because of player trades during the season, and lessened demand for some of the non-player booklets, some of the series are quite scarce. Each of the booklets can be found with different sponsors logos on front.

		NM	EX	VG
Complete Set (24):		240.00	120.00	72.00
Common Booklet:		15.00	7.50	4.50
(1)	Joe Amalfitano	15.00	7.50	4.50
(2)	Bob Aspromonte	15.00	7.50	4.50
(3)	Bob Bruce	15.00	7.50	4.50
(4)	Jim Campbell	18.00	9.00	5.50
(5)	Harry Craft	15.00	7.50	4.50
(6)	Dick Farrell	15.00	7.50	4.50
(7)	Dave Giusti	15.00	7.50	4.50
(8)	Jim Golden	15.00	7.50	4.50
(9)	J.C. Hartman	18.00	9.00	5.50
(10)	Ken Johnson	15.00	7.50	4.50
(11)	Norm Larker	15.00	7.50	4.50
(12)	Bob Lillis	15.00	7.50	4.50
(13)	Don McMahon	15.00	7.50	4.50
(14)	Roman Mejias	15.00	7.50	4.50
(15)	Jim Pendleton	18.00	9.00	5.50
(16)	Paul Richards (GM)	15.00	7.50	4.50
(17)	Bobby Shantz	30.00	15.00	9.00
(18)	Hal Smith	15.00	7.50	4.50
(19)	Al Spangler	15.00	7.50	4.50
(20)	Jim Umbricht	15.00	7.50	4.50
(21)	Carl Warwick	15.00	7.50	4.50
(22)	Hal Woodeshick	15.00	7.50	4.50
(23)	Coaches (James Adair, Bobby Bragan, Cot Deal, Luman Harris)	25.00	12.50	7.50
(24)	Announcers (Rene Cardenas, Orlando Diego, Gene Elston, Al Helfer, Lowell Passe, Guy Savage)	19.00	9.50	5.75

1967 Houston Astros Team Issue

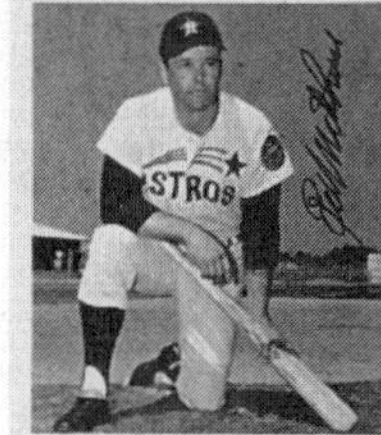

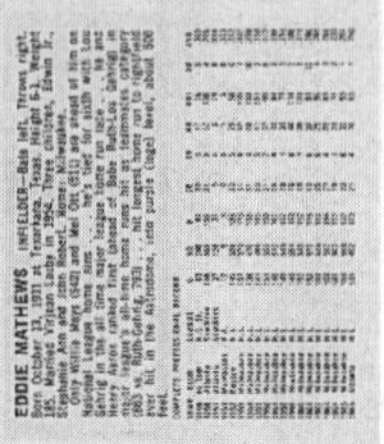

This set of 12 player cards was issued by the Houston Astros, though the exact nature of the promotion is not known. Individual cards of 2-5/8" x 3-1/8" were printed on a perforated sheet about 9" x 10-1/2". Fronts have a posed color photo with a black facsimile autograph. Backs are printed in black on white with a yellow color block behind the player data and career notes. Full major and minor league stats are at bottom. The unnumbered cards are checklisted here in alphabetical order.

		NM	EX	VG
Complete Set, Sheet:		65.00	32.50	20.00
Complete Set, Singles (12):		65.00	32.50	20.00
Common Player:		8.00	4.00	2.50
(1)	Bob Aspromonte	8.00	4.00	2.50
(2)	John Bateman	8.00	4.00	2.50
(3)	Mike Cuellar	8.00	4.00	2.50
(4)	Larry Dierker	8.00	4.00	2.50
(5)	Dave Giusti	8.00	4.00	2.50
(6)	Grady Hatton	8.00	4.00	2.50
(7)	Bill Heath	8.00	4.00	2.50
(8)	Sonny Jackson	8.00	4.00	2.50
(9)	Ed Mathews	20.00	10.00	6.00
(10)	Joe Morgan	20.00	10.00	6.00
(11)	Rusty Staub	12.50	6.25	3.75
(12)	Jim Wynn	8.00	4.00	2.50

1953-1955 Howard Photo Service Postcards

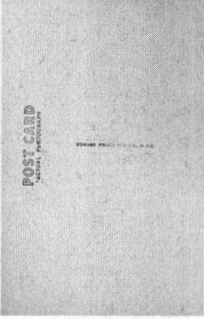

Little is known about these postcards. Player and team combinations on the known pieces suggest a range of issue dates between 1953 and 1955. The 3-1/2" x 5-5/8" cards have a glossy black-and-white front photo. A rubber-stamp on the back attributes the card to "Howard Photo Service, N.Y.C." The specific pose on the second Turley card is not known. It is possible other cards may yet be discovered.

		NM	EX	VG
Common Player:		20.00	10.00	6.00
(1)	Ned Garver	20.00	10.00	6.00
(2)	Billy Hitchcock	20.00	10.00	6.00
(3)	Dave Madison	20.00	10.00	6.00
(4)	Willie Mays	165.00	85.00	50.00
(5)	Willie Mays (Seven-Up ad on back.)	200.00	100.00	60.00
(6)	Bob Turley (Follow-through.)	30.00	15.00	9.00
(7)	Bob Turley (Wind-up.)	30.00	15.00	9.00

1976 HRT/RES 1942 Play Ball

This "phantom" continuation of the Play Ball series of 1939-41 was the creation of Ted Taylor and Bob Schmierer, whose initials appear in the copyright line on back. The 2-1/2" x 3-1/8" cards feature black-and-white photos on front and were printed on gray clay-content cardboard in a near replication of the stock found on the vintage Play Ball series. Backs were also done in style reminiscent of 1940s issues. Besides player data and career summaries, backs have a "1942 PLAY BALL - U.S.A." title line and either a "Buy War Bonds" or "'Keep Baseball Going' - FDR" slogan above the 1976 copyright line. The pair produced a number of other original and reprint issues in the 1970s. All of the others carry advertisements for their "Philly" card shows.

	NM	EX	VG
Complete Set (36):	30.00	15.00	9.00
Common Card:	1.00	.50	.30
1 Lou Gehrig	7.50	3.75	2.25
2 Joe DiMaggio	7.50	3.75	2.25
3 Phil Rizzuto	3.00	1.50	.90
4 Ted Williams	6.00	3.00	1.75
5 Charles Wagner	1.00	.50	.30
6 Thornton Lee	1.00	.50	.30
7 Taft Wright	1.00	.50	.30
8 Jeff Heath	1.00	.50	.30
9 Roy Mack	1.00	.50	.30
10 Pat Mullin	1.00	.50	.30
11 Al Benton	1.00	.50	.30
12 Bob Harris	1.00	.50	.30
13 Roy Cullenbine	1.00	.50	.30
14 Cecil Travis	1.00	.50	.30
15 Buck Newsom	1.00	.50	.30
16 Eddie Collins Jr.	1.00	.50	.30
17 Dick Siebert	1.00	.50	.30
18 Dee Miles	1.00	.50	.30
19 Pete Reiser	1.00	.50	.30
20 Dolph Camilli	1.00	.50	.30
21 Curt Davis	1.00	.50	.30
22 Spud Krist	1.00	.50	.30
23 Frank Crespi	1.00	.50	.30
24 Elmer Riddle	1.00	.50	.30
25 Bucky Walters	1.00	.50	.30
26 Vince DiMaggio	1.50	.70	.45
27 Max Butcher	1.00	.50	.30
28 Mel Ott	3.00	1.50	.90
29 Bob Carpenter	1.00	.50	.30
30 Claude Passeau	1.00	.50	.30
31 Dom Dallessandro	1.00	.50	.30
32 Casey Stengel	3.00	1.50	.90
33 Alva Javery	1.00	.50	.30
34 Hans Lobert	1.00	.50	.30
35 Nick Etten	1.00	.50	.30
36 John Podgajny	1.00	.50	.30

1976-77 HRT/RES 1947 Bowman

Advertised as "The Set That Never Was," this collectors' issue from Ted Taylor and Bob Schmierer used a 2-1/8" x 2-1/2" black-and-white format and gray cardboard stock to replicate the feel of the first post-WWII baseball cards. The set was issued in three series with advertising on back promoting the second (1976) and third (1977) annual EPSCC "Philly" shows. Series one (#1-49) was issued in 1976; series two (#50-81) and three (#82-113) were 1977 issues.

	NM	EX	VG
Complete Set (113):	90.00	45.00	27.50
Common Player:	1.00	.50	.30
1 Bobby Doerr	1.00	.50	.30
2 Stan Musial	3.00	1.50	.90
3 Babe Ruth	7.50	3.75	2.25
4 Joe DiMaggio	6.00	3.00	1.75
5 Andy Pafko	1.00	.50	.30
6 Johnny Pesky	1.00	.50	.30
7 Gil Hodges	1.50	.70	.45
8 Tommy Holmes	1.00	.50	.30
9 Ralph Kiner	1.00	.50	.30
10 Yogi Berra	2.00	1.00	.60
11 Bob Feller	1.50	.70	.45
12 Joe Gordon	1.00	.50	.30
13 Eddie Joost	1.00	.50	.30
14 Del Ennis	1.00	.50	.30
15 Johnny Mize	1.00	.50	.30
16 Pee Wee Reese	1.25	.60	.40
17 Jackie Robinson	4.00	2.00	1.25
18 Enos Slaughter	1.00	.50	.30
19 Vern Stephens	1.00	.50	.30
20 Bobby Thomson	1.00	.50	.30
21 Ted Williams	6.00	3.00	1.75
22 Bob Elliott	1.00	.50	.30
23 Mickey Vernon	1.00	.50	.30
24 Ewell Blackwell	1.00	.50	.30
25 Lou Boudreau	1.00	.50	.30
26 Ralph Branca	1.00	.50	.30
27 Harry Breechen (Brecheen)	1.00	.50	.30
28 Dom DiMaggio	1.00	.50	.30
29 Bruce Edwards	1.00	.50	.30
30 Sam Chapman	1.00	.50	.30
31 George Kell	1.00	.50	.30
32 Jack Kramer	1.00	.50	.30
33 Hal Newhouser	1.00	.50	.30
34 Charlie Keller	1.00	.50	.30
35 Ken Keltner	1.00	.50	.30
36 Hank Greenberg	1.25	.60	.40
37 Howie Pollet	1.00	.50	.30
38 Luke Appling	1.00	.50	.30
39 Pete Suder	1.00	.50	.30
40 Johnny Sain	1.00	.50	.30
41 Phil Cavaretta (Cavarretta)	1.00	.50	.30
42 Johnny Vander Meer	1.00	.50	.30
43 Mel Ott	1.00	.50	.30
44 Walker Cooper	1.00	.50	.30
45 Birdie Tebbetts	1.00	.50	.30
46 George Stirnweiss	1.00	.50	.30
47 Connie Mack	1.00	.50	.30
48 Jimmie Foxx	1.00	.50	.30
49 Checklist (Joe DiMaggio, Babe Ruth)	1.50	.70	.45
(50) Honus Wagner T206 Card (First series.)	1.00	.50	.30
51 Ted Taylor (First series.)	1.00	.50	.30
52 Bob Schmierer (First series.)	1.00	.50	.30
50 Schoolboy Rowe (Second series.)	1.00	.50	.30
51 Andy Seminick (Second series.)	1.00	.50	.30
52 Fred Walker (Second series.)	1.00	.50	.30
53 Virgil Trucks	1.00	.50	.30
54 Dizzy Trout	1.00	.50	.30
55 Walter Evers	1.00	.50	.30
56 Thurman Tucker	1.00	.50	.30
57 Fritz Ostermueller	1.00	.50	.30
58 Augie Galan	1.00	.50	.30
59 Norman Young	1.00	.50	.30
60 Skeeter Newsome	1.00	.50	.30
61 Jack Lohrke	1.00	.50	.30
62 Rudy York	1.00	.50	.30
63 Tex Hughson	1.00	.50	.30
64 Sam Mele	1.00	.50	.30
65 Fred Hutchinson	1.00	.50	.30
66 Don Black	1.00	.50	.30
67 Les Fleming	1.00	.50	.30
68 George McQuinn	1.00	.50	.30
69 Mike McCormick	1.00	.50	.30
70 Mickey Witek	1.00	.50	.30
71 Blix Donnelly	1.00	.50	.30
72 Elbie Fletcher	1.00	.50	.30
73 Hal Gregg	1.00	.50	.30
74 Dick Whitman	1.00	.50	.30
75 Johnny Neun	1.00	.50	.30
76 Doyle Lade	1.00	.50	.30
77 Ron Northey	1.00	.50	.30
78 Walker Cooper	1.00	.50	.30
79 Warren Spahn	1.00	.50	.30
80 Happy Chandler	1.00	.50	.30
81 Checklist (Connie Mack, Roy Mack, Connie Mack III)	1.00	.50	.30
82 Earle Mack	1.00	.50	.30
83 Buddy Rosar	1.00	.50	.30
84 Walt Judnich	1.00	.50	.30
85 Bob Kennedy	1.00	.50	.30
86 Mike Tresh	1.00	.50	.30
87 Sid Hudson	1.00	.50	.30
88 Eugene Thompson	1.00	.50	.30
89 Bill Nicholson	1.00	.50	.30
90 Stan Hack	1.00	.50	.30
91 Terry Moore	1.00	.50	.30
92 Ted Lyons	1.00	.50	.30
93 Barney McCosky	1.00	.50	.30
94 Stan Spence	1.00	.50	.30
95 Larry Jansen	1.00	.50	.30
96 Whitey Kurowski	1.00	.50	.30
97 Honus Wagner	1.50	.70	.45
98 Billy Herman	1.00	.50	.30
99 Jim Tabor	1.00	.50	.30
100 Phil Marchildon	1.00	.50	.30
101 Dave Ferriss	1.00	.50	.30
102 Al Zarilla	1.00	.50	.30
103 Bob Dillinger	1.00	.50	.30
104 Bob Lemon	1.00	.50	.30
105 Jim Hegan	1.00	.50	.30
106 Johnny Lindell	1.00	.50	.30
107 Willard Marshall	1.00	.50	.30
108 Walt Masterson	1.00	.50	.30
109 Carl Scheib	1.00	.50	.30
110 Bobby Brown	1.00	.50	.30
111 Cy Block	1.00	.50	.30
112 Sid Gordon	1.00	.50	.30
113 Checklist (Ty Cobb, Babe Ruth, Tris Speaker)	1.50	.70	.45

1977 HRT/RES Philadelphia 'Favorites'

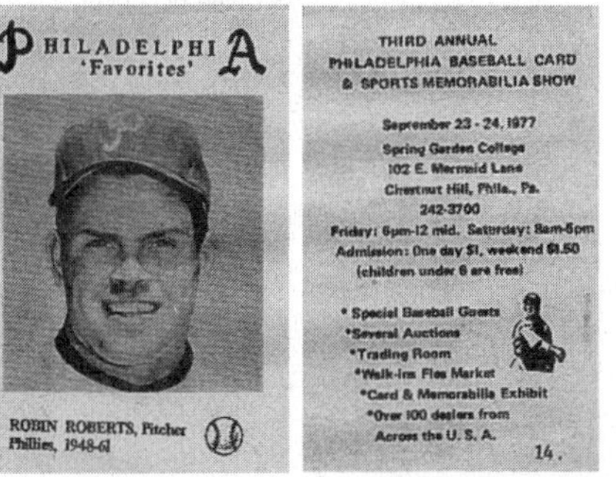

PHILADELPHIA
'Favorites'
ROBIN ROBERTS, Pitcher
Phillies, 1948-61
THIRD ANNUAL
PHILADELPHIA BASEBALL CARD
& SPORTS MEMORABILIA SHOW
September 23 - 24, 1977
Spring Garden College
102 E. Mermaid Lane
Chestnut Hill, Phila., Pa.
242-3700
Friday: 6pm-12 mid. Saturday: 8am-6pm
Admission: One day $1, weekend $1.50
(children under 6 are free)
* Special Baseball Guests
*Several Auctions
*Trading Room
*Walk-ins Flea Market
*Card & Memorabilia Exhibit
*Over 100 dealers from
Across the U. S. A.
14.

This collectors' issue was produced by promoters Ted Taylor and Bob Schmierer to promote their third annual "Philly Show" in 1977. Printed in black-and-white on front and back, the 2-3/8" x 3-5/8" cards feature former Philadelphia A's and Phillies player photos on front, and an ad for the show on back. Cards were given away at area malls and sporting events to promote the show. Complete sets were originally sold for $2.75.

	NM	EX	VG
Complete Set (25):	30.00	15.00	9.00
Common Player:	2.00	1.00	.60
1 Connie Mack	2.00	1.00	.60
2 Larry Lajoie	2.50	1.25	.70
3 Eddie Collins	2.00	1.00	.60
4 Lefty Grove	2.50	1.25	.70
5 Al Simmons	2.00	1.00	.60
6 Jimmie Foxx	3.00	1.50	.90
7 Frank Baker	2.00	1.00	.60
8 Ferris Fain	2.00	1.00	.60
9 Jimmy Dykes	2.00	1.00	.60
10 Willie Jones	2.00	1.00	.60
11 Del Ennis	2.00	1.00	.60
12 Granny Hamner	2.00	1.00	.60
13 Andy Seminick	2.00	1.00	.60
14 Robin Roberts	4.00	2.00	1.25
15 Ed Delahanty	2.00	1.00	.60
16 Gavvy Cravath	2.00	1.00	.60
17 Cy Williams	2.00	1.00	.60
18 Chuck Klein	2.00	1.00	.60
19 Rich Ashburn	4.00	2.00	1.25
20 Bobby Shantz	2.00	1.00	.60
21 Gus Zernial	2.00	1.00	.60
22 Eddie Sawyer	2.00	1.00	.60
23 Grover Alexander	2.00	1.00	.60
24 Wally Moses	2.00	1.00	.60
25 Connie Mack Stadium	2.00	1.00	.60

1978 HRT/RES 1939 Father and Son Reprints

Wally Moses, outfielder, Phila. Athletics

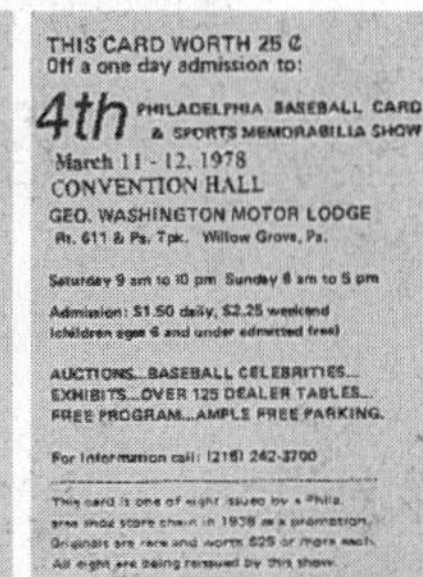

THIS CARD WORTH 25 ¢
Off a one day admission to:
4th PHILADELPHIA BASEBALL CARD & SPORTS MEMORABILIA SHOW
March 11 - 12, 1978
CONVENTION HALL
GEO. WASHINGTON MOTOR LODGE
Rt. 611 & Pa. Tpk. Willow Grove, Pa.
Saturday 9 am to 10 pm Sunday 8 am to 5 pm
Admission: $1.50 daily, $2.25 weekend
(children ages 6 and under admitted free)
AUCTIONS...BASEBALL CELEBRITIES...
EXHIBITS...OVER 125 DEALER TABLES...
FREE PROGRAM...AMPLE FREE PARKING.
For information call: (215) 242-3700

Reprints of scarce 1939 Father and Son Shoes stores cards of local ballplayers (minus the original advertising on front) were created by Ted Taylor and Bob Schmierer to promote their fourth "Philly Show" in March, 1978. The 3" x 4" cards have black-and-white player photos on front. Backs carry an ad for the show and information about the reprints.

	NM	EX	VG
Complete Set (8):	7.50	3.75	2.25
Common Player:	1.00	.50	.30
(1) Sam Chapman	1.00	.50	.30
(2) Chuck Klein	1.50	.70	.45
(3) Herschel Martin	1.00	.50	.30
(4) Wally Moses	1.00	.50	.30
(5) Hugh Mulcahy	1.00	.50	.30
(6) Skeeter Newsome	1.00	.50	.30
(7) George Scharien (Scharein)	1.00	.50	.30
(8) Dick Siebert	1.00	.50	.30

1979 HRT/RES 1950 Phillies/ A's "Doubleheaders"

Stan Lopata, Catcher

Eddie Waitkus, Infield

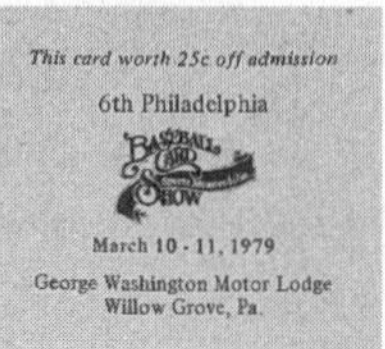

Though their names or initials do not appear on the cards, this collectors' set was issued by Ted Taylor and Bob Schmierer to promote the March and September 1979, "Philly Shows," the sixth and seventh in the show's history. Borrowing from the format of the 1941 "Doubleheaders" bubblegum card issue, these 2-1/2" x 2-1/8" cards depict members of the 1950 Phillies "Whiz Kids" and the 1950 A's, the last team managed by Connie Mack. Fronts are printed in blue and white, backs in maroon and white. The dual-player cards feature various ads on back, while the managers' cards have a team narrative. The unnumbered cards are checklisted here alphabetically within team, by the last name of the player on the left.

	NM	EX	VG
Complete Set (30):	25.00	12.50	7.50
Common Card:	1.50	.70	.45
(1) Joe Astroth, Dick Fowler	1.50	.70	.45

(2)	Sam Chapman, Lou Brissie	1.50	.70	.45
(3)	Bob Dillinger, Billy Hitchcock	1.50	.70	.45
(4)	Ben Guintini, Joe Tipton	1.50	.70	.45
(5)	Bob Hooper, Barney McCosky	1.50	.70	.45
(6)	Eddie Joost, Kermit Wahl	1.50	.70	.45
(7)	Ed Klieman, Mike Guerra	1.50	.70	.45
(8)	Paul Lehner, Ferris Fain	1.50	.70	.45
(9)	Connie Mack	1.50	.70	.45
(10)	Earle Mack, Mickey Cochrane	1.50	.70	.45
(11)	Wally Moses, Carl Scheib	1.50	.70	.45
(12)	Pete Suder, Alex Kellner	1.50	.70	.45
(13)	Elmer Valo, Bobby Shantz	1.50	.70	.45
(14)	Bob Wellman, Joe Coleman	1.50	.70	.45
(15)	Hank Wyse, Gene Markland	1.50	.70	.45
(16)	Johnny Blatnik, Ed Wright	1.50	.70	.45
(17)	Ralph Caballero, Bubba Church	1.50	.70	.45
(18)	Milo Candini, Hank Borowy	1.50	.70	.45
(19)	Blix Donnelly, Bill Nicholson	1.50	.70	.45
(20)	Del Ennis, Ken Heintzelman	1.50	.70	.45
(21)	Mike Goliat, Dick Whitman	1.50	.70	.45
(22)	Granny Hamner, Rich Ashburn	3.50	1.75	1.00
(23)	Willie Jones, Russ Meyer	1.50	.70	.45
(24)	Jim Konstanty, Ken Silvestri	1.50	.70	.45
(25)	Stan Lopata, Eddie Waitkus	1.50	.70	.45
(26)	Ed Sanicki, Robin Roberts	3.50	1.75	1.00
(27)	Eddie Sawyer	1.50	.70	.45
(28)	Andy Seminick, Ken Trinkle	1.50	.70	.45
(29)	Dick Sisler, Stan Hollmig/DP	1.50	.70	.45
(30)	Jocko Thompson, Curt Simmons	1.50	.70	.45

1957-1959 Hudepohl Beer Cincinnati Reds

These 8" x 10" black-and-white photos were distributed by Hudepohl Beer, although the brewery or brand is not mentioned on the pictures. They are identical in format to the team-issued publicity photos. The Hudepohl pictures differ from the team-issue in that the beer pictures have a semi-gloss finish and no printing on the back, while the team pictures have a glossy surface and a four-line warning on back not to use them for advertising purposes. The pictures have portrait or posed action photos, sometimes with the background removed. They are bordered in white with the player and team name at bottom. The type style is sans-serif for 1957 pictures, and serifed in 1959. Years of issue have been attributed according to corresponding team-issue photos and uniforms pictured. Because so many of the Hudepohl pictures are found autographed, it is possible they were distributed in conjunction with player promotional appearances. This checklist may well not be complete.

	NM	EX	VG
Common Player:	20.00	10.00	6.00
1957 (Redlegs, sans-serif.)			
Ed. Bailey/Btg	20.00	10.00	6.00
George Crowe/Btg	20.00	10.00	6.00
Ted Kluszewski/Btg	35.00	17.50	10.50
Brooks Lawrence (Follow-through.)	20.00	10.00	6.00
Roy McMillan/Btg	20.00	10.00	6.00
Joe Nuxhall (Follow-through.)	25.00	12.50	7.50
Manager "Birdie" Tebbetts/ Portrait	20.00	10.00	6.00
1959 (Reds, serif.)			
Brooks Lawrence/Portrait	20.00	10.00	6.00

1960 Hudepohl Beer Cincinnati Reds

These 8" x 10" black-and-white photos were distributed by Hudepohl Beer, although the brewery or brand is not mentioned on the pictures. Similar in format to the team-issued publicity photos, the Hudepohl pictures differ in that they have a semi-gloss finish and no printing on the back, while the team pictures have a glossy surface and a four-line warning on back not to use them for advertising purposes. The pictures have portrait or posed action photos, sometimes with the background removed. They are bordered in white with the player and team name at bottom in a light sans-serif type. Years of issue have been attributed according to corresponding team-issue photos and uniforms pictured. Because so many of the Hudepohl pictures are found autographed, it is possible they were distributed in conjunction with player promotional appearances. This checklist may not be complete.

		NM	EX	VG
	Common Player:	20.00	10.00	6.00
(1)	Ed. Bailey	20.00	10.00	6.00
(2)	Gus Bell	20.00	10.00	6.00
(3)	Jerry Lynch	20.00	10.00	6.00
(4)	Roy McMillan	20.00	10.00	6.00

(5)	Don Newcombe	20.00	10.00	6.00
(6)	Joe Nuxhall	25.00	12.50	7.50
(7)	Vada Pinson	30.00	15.00	9.00
(8)	Frank Robinson	85.00	42.00	25.00

1907 Geo. W. Hull Chicago White Sox Postcards

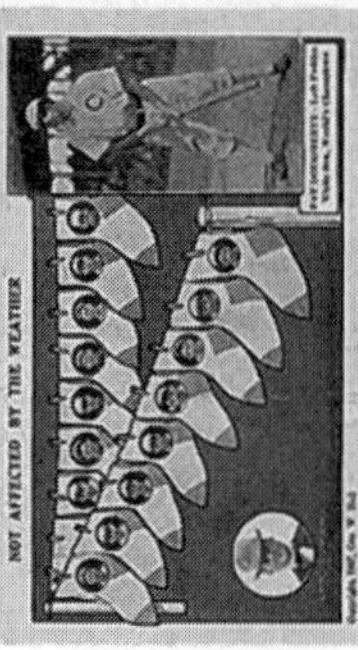

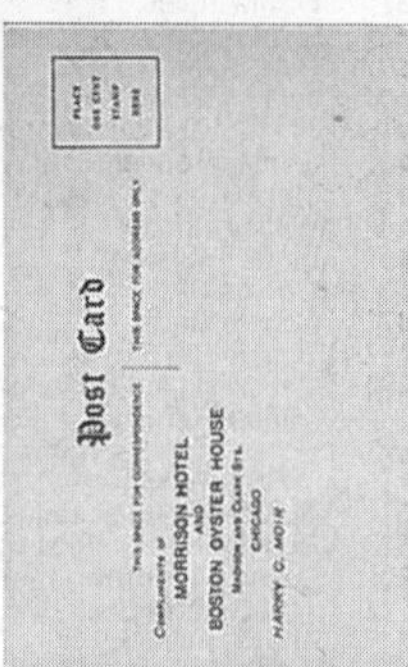

Members of the World Champion White Sox are featured on this single-team issue. Horizontal in format, the black-and-white cards measure about 5-1/2" x 3-1/2". All of the cards share a basic design of a player action posed photo at right, with his name, position, and "White Sox, World's Champions" in a white box beneath. The main part of the card pictures a clothesline full of white socks, each of which has a small round portrait photo of one of the players - 15 in all. In a larger portrait at lower-left is team owner Charles Comiskey. In the white border at top, each card has a witty statement such as "String of World-Beaters" and "Not Worn By Ladies, But Admired By Them." In the bottom border is, "Copyright 1907, Geo. W. Hull." Backs have been seen with a schedule of home games and with an ad from the Morrison Hotel and Boston Oyster House of Chicago.

		NM	EX	VG
	Complete Set (16):	10,000	5,000	3,000
	Common Player:	600.00	300.00	180.00
(1)	Nick Altrock	600.00	300.00	180.00
(2)	George Davis	950.00	475.00	285.00
(3)	Jiggs Donahue	600.00	300.00	180.00
(4)	Pat Dougherty	600.00	300.00	180.00
(5)	Eddie Hahn	600.00	300.00	180.00
(6)	Frank Isbell	600.00	300.00	180.00
(7)	Fielder Jones	600.00	300.00	180.00
(8)	Ed McFarland	600.00	300.00	180.00
(9)	Frank Owens	600.00	300.00	180.00
(10)	Roy Patterson	600.00	300.00	180.00
(11)	George Rohe	600.00	300.00	180.00
(12)	Frank Smith	600.00	300.00	180.00
(13)	Billy Sullivan	600.00	300.00	180.00
(14)	Lee Tannehill	600.00	300.00	180.00
(15)	Eddie Walsh	950.00	475.00	285.00
(16)	Doc White	600.00	300.00	180.00

1953 Hunter Wieners Cardinals

From the great era of the regionally issued hot dog cards in the mid-1950s, the 1953 Hunter wieners set of St. Louis Cardinals is among the rarest today. Originally issued in two-card panels, the cards are most often found as 2-1/4" x 3-1/4" singles today when they can be found at all. The cards feature a light blue facsimile autograph printed over the stat box at the bottom. They are blank-backed.

		NM	EX	VG
	Complete Set (26):	10,000	5,000	3,000
	Common Player:	300.00	150.00	90.00
(1)	Steve Bilko	300.00	150.00	90.00
(2)	Cloyd Boyer	300.00	150.00	90.00
(3)	Al Brazle	300.00	150.00	90.00
(4)	Cliff Chambers	300.00	150.00	90.00
(5)	Michael Clark	300.00	150.00	90.00
(6)	Jack Crimian	300.00	150.00	90.00
(7)	Lester Fusselman	300.00	150.00	90.00
(8)	Harvey Haddix	325.00	160.00	100.00
(9)	Solly Hemus	300.00	150.00	90.00
(10)	Ray Jablonski	300.00	150.00	90.00
(11)	William Johnson	300.00	150.00	90.00
(12)	Harry Lowrey	300.00	150.00	90.00
(13)	Lawrence Miggins	300.00	150.00	90.00
(14)	Stuart Miller	300.00	150.00	90.00
(15)	Wilmer Mizell	300.00	150.00	90.00
(16)	Stanley Musial	3,000	1,500	900.00
(17)	Joseph Presko	300.00	150.00	90.00
(18)	Delbert Rice	300.00	150.00	90.00
(19)	Harold Rice	300.00	150.00	90.00
(20)	Willard Schmidt	300.00	150.00	90.00
(21)	Albert Schoendienst	650.00	325.00	195.00
(22)	Richard Sisler	300.00	150.00	90.00
(23)	Enos Slaughter	650.00	325.00	195.00
(24)	Gerald Staley	300.00	150.00	90.00
(25)	Edward Stanky	325.00	160.00	97.00
(26)	John Yuhas	300.00	150.00	90.00

1954 Hunter Wieners Cardinals

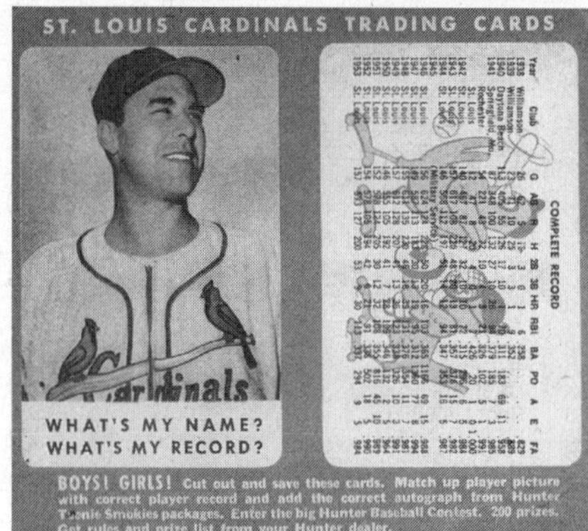

A nearly impossible set to complete today by virtue of the method of its issue, the 1954 Hunter hot dog set features what would traditionally be the front and back of a normal baseball card on two different cards. The "front," has a color photo with a box at bottom challenging the the collector to name the player and quote his stats. The "back" features cartoon Cardinals in action, and contains the answers. However, because both parts were printed on a single panel. Because most of the back (non-picture) portions of the panels were thrown away years ago, it is a formidable challenge to complete a '54 Hunter set today. There is no back printing on the 2-1/4" x 3-1/2" cards.

		NM	EX	VG
	Complete Set (30):	9,000	4,500	2,700
	Common Player:	250.00	125.00	75.00
(1)	Tom Alston	250.00	125.00	75.00
(2)	Steve Bilko	250.00	125.00	75.00
(3)	Al Brazle	250.00	125.00	75.00
(4)	Tom Burgess	250.00	125.00	75.00
(5)	Cot Deal	250.00	125.00	75.00
(6)	Alex Grammas	250.00	125.00	75.00
(7)	Harvey Haddix	250.00	125.00	75.00
(8)	Solly Hemus	250.00	125.00	75.00
(9)	Ray Jablonski	250.00	125.00	75.00
(10)	Royce Lint	250.00	125.00	75.00
(11)	Peanuts Lowrey	250.00	125.00	75.00
(12)	Memo Luna	250.00	125.00	75.00
(13)	Stu Miller	250.00	125.00	75.00
(14)	Stan Musial	2,000	1,000	600.00
(15)	Tom Poholsky	250.00	125.00	75.00
(16)	Bill Posedel	250.00	125.00	75.00
(17)	Joe Presko	250.00	125.00	75.00
(18)	Dick Rand	250.00	125.00	75.00
(19)	Vic Raschi	250.00	125.00	75.00
(20)	Rip Repulski	250.00	125.00	75.00
(21)	Del Rice	250.00	125.00	75.00
(22)	John Riddle	250.00	125.00	75.00
(23)	Mike Ryba	250.00	125.00	75.00
(24)	Red Schoendienst	500.00	250.00	150.00
(25)	Dick Schofield	275.00	135.00	82.00
(26)	Enos Slaughter	500.00	250.00	150.00
(27)	Gerry Staley	250.00	125.00	75.00
(28)	Ed Stanky	250.00	125.00	75.00
(29)	Ed Yuhas	250.00	125.00	75.00
(30)	Sal Yvars	250.00	125.00	75.00

1955 Hunter Wieners Cardinals

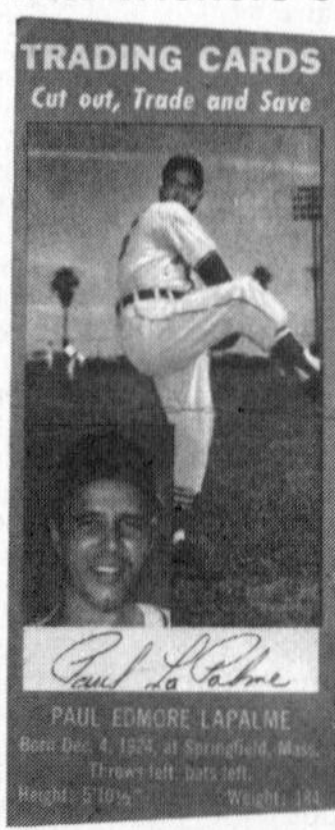

The 1955 team set of St. Louis Cardinals, included with packages of Hunter hot dogs, features the third format change in three years of issue. For 1955, the cards were printed in a tall, narrow (2" wide with the height tapering from 4-3/4" at left to 4-1/2" at right) format, two to a panel. The cards feature both a posed action photo and a portrait photo, along with a facsimile autograph and brief biographical data on the front. There is no back printing, as the cards were part of the wrapping for packages of hot dogs.

		NM	EX	VG
Complete Set (30):		11,000	5,500	3,250
Common Player:		250.00	125.00	75.00
(1)	Thomas Edison Alston	250.00	125.00	75.00
(2)	Kenton Lloyd Boyer	675.00	335.00	200.00
(3)	Harry Lewis Elliott	250.00	125.00	75.00
(4)	John Edward Faszholz	250.00	125.00	75.00
(5)	Joseph Filmore Frazier	250.00	125.00	75.00
(6)	Alexander Pete Grammas	250.00	125.00	75.00
(7)	Harvey Haddix	250.00	125.00	75.00
(8)	Solly Joseph Hemus	250.00	125.00	75.00
(9)	Lawrence Curtis Jackson	250.00	125.00	75.00
(10)	Tony R. Jacobs	250.00	125.00	75.00
(11)	Gordon Bassett Jones	250.00	125.00	75.00
(12)	Paul Edmore LaPalme	250.00	125.00	75.00
(13)	Brooks Ulysses Lawrence	250.00	125.00	75.00
(14)	Wallace Wade Moon	400.00	200.00	120.00
(15)	Stanley Frank Musial	2,700	1,350	810.00
(16)	Thomas George Poholsky	250.00	125.00	75.00
(17)	William John Posedel	250.00	125.00	75.00
(18)	Victor Angelo John Raschi	250.00	125.00	75.00
(19)	Eldon John Repulski	250.00	125.00	75.00
(20)	Delbert Rice	250.00	125.00	75.00
(21)	John Ludy Riddle	250.00	125.00	75.00
(22)	William F. Sarni	250.00	125.00	75.00
(23)	Albert Fred Schoendienst	550.00	275.00	165.00
(24)	Richard John Schofield (Actually John Richard.)	250.00	125.00	75.00
(25)	Frank Thomas Smith	250.00	125.00	75.00
(26)	Edward R. Stanky	275.00	135.00	82.00
(27)	Bobby Gene Tiefenauer	250.00	125.00	75.00
(28)	William Charles Virdon	400.00	200.00	120.00
(29)	Frederick E. Walker	250.00	125.00	75.00
(30)	Floyd Lewis Woolridge	250.00	125.00	75.00

1941 Huskies

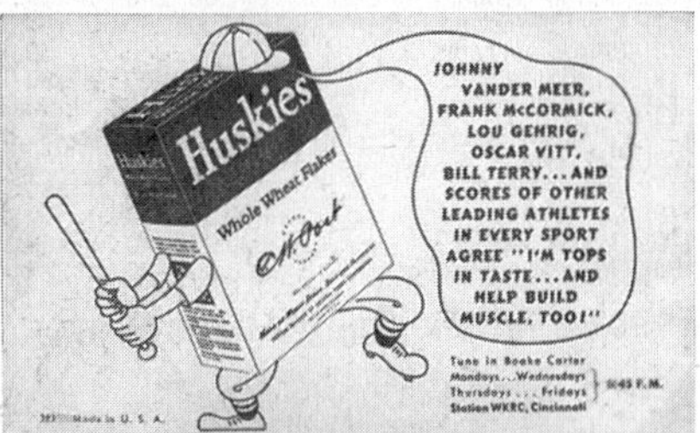

This advertising card was issued by Huskies Whole Wheat Flakes cereal. In black-and-white, the card measures about 5-1/2" x 3-1/2". Facsimile autographs appear on the borderless front photo.

	NM	EX	VG
John Vander Meer, Frank McCormick	125.00	65.00	40.00

1976 Icee Drinks Reds

Issued in 1976 in the Cincinnati area by Icee Drinks, this 12-card set of semi-circular cards features members of the Reds. The cards measure approximately 2" in diameter with the bottom of the disc squared off. The cards were originally issued as soft drink lids. Fronts have a portrait photo in black-and-white, with uniform logos removed. Backs are blank. The cards are unnumbered. A 7" x 12" cap saver sheet was also available; it does not picture the players.

		NM	EX	VG
Complete Set (12):		60.00	30.00	18.00
Common Player:		2.00	1.00	.60
Saver Sheet:		27.00	13.50	8.00
(1)	Johnny Bench	10.00	5.00	3.00
(2)	Dave Concepcion	2.25	1.25	.70
(3)	Rawly Eastwick	2.00	1.00	.60
(4)	George Foster	2.25	1.25	.70
(5)	Cesar Geronimo	2.00	1.00	.60
(6)	Ken Griffey	2.50	1.25	.70
(7)	Don Gullett	2.00	1.00	.60
(8)	Will McEnaney	2.00	1.00	.60
(9)	Joe Morgan	6.00	3.00	1.75
(10)	Gary Nolan	2.00	1.00	.60
(11)	Tony Perez	4.00	2.00	1.25
(12)	Pete Rose	27.50	13.50	8.25

1963 I.D.L. Drug Store Pittsburgh Pirates

This set of 26 black-and-white cards was regionally distributed. The 4" x 5" semi-gloss cards are blank-backed and unnumbered. The checklist is arranged alphabetically. Johnny Logan's card is considered scarce and may have been pulled from distribution early.

		NM	EX	VG
Complete Set (27):		225.00	115.00	65.00
Common Player:		7.50	3.75	2.25
(1)	Bob Bailey	7.50	3.75	2.25
(2)	Forrest "Smoky" Burgess	7.50	3.75	2.25
(3)	Don Cardwell	7.50	3.75	2.25
(4)	Roberto Clemente	75.00	37.00	22.00
(5)	Donn Clendenon	10.00	5.00	3.00
(6)	Roy Face	7.50	3.75	2.25
(7)	Earl Francis	7.50	3.75	2.25
(8)	Bob Friend	7.50	3.75	2.25
(9)	Joe Gibbon	7.50	3.75	2.25
(10)	Julio Gotay	7.50	3.75	2.25
(11)	Harvey Haddix	7.50	3.75	2.25
(12)	Johnny Logan/SP	15.00	7.50	4.50
(13)	Bill Mazeroski	25.00	12.50	7.50
(14)	Al McBean	7.50	3.75	2.25
(15)	Danny Murtaugh	7.50	3.75	2.25
(16)	Sam Narron	7.50	3.75	2.25
(17)	Ron Northey	7.50	3.75	2.25
(18)	Frank Oceak	7.50	3.75	2.25
(19)	Jim Pagliaroni	7.50	3.75	2.25
(20)	Ted Savage	7.50	3.75	2.25
(21)	Dick Schofield	7.50	3.75	2.25
(22)	Bob Skinner/SP	15.00	7.50	4.50
(23)	Willie Stargell	25.00	12.50	7.50
(24)	Tom Sturdivant	7.50	3.75	2.25
(25)	Virgil "Fire" Trucks	7.50	3.75	2.25
(26)	Bob Veale	7.50	3.75	2.25
(27)	Bill Virdon	7.50	3.75	2.25

1916 Indianapolis Brewing Co.

THIS is one of a series of 200 pictures of Major League Baseball Players — all action pictures.

Complete set will be sent to you upon receipt of 25 cents

INDIANAPOLIS BREWING CO.
INDIANAPOLIS, INDIANA

LIEBER'S GOLD MEDAL
PROGRESS BEER
LIEBER'S SPECIAL BREW

World's Standard of Perfection

Best known in blank-back form or with ads on back for The Sporting News, this 200-card set can be found with the imprint of several other local and regional businesses. Among them is the Indianapolis Brewing Co. Type-card and superstar collectors can expect to pay a significant premium for individual cards with Indianapolis Brewing advertising. The checklist parallels that of the 1916 M101-4 Blank Backs. Cards measure 1-5/8" x 3" and are printed in black-and-white. The brewery originally advertised the set on its "Facts for Fans" booklet, at a cost of 25 cents.

		NM	EX	VG
Complete Set (200):		96,000	48,000	28,800
Common Player:		240.00	120.00	75.00
1	Babe Adams	360.00	120.00	75.00
2	Sam Agnew	240.00	120.00	75.00
3	Eddie Ainsmith	240.00	120.00	75.00
4	Grover Alexander	720.00	360.00	215.00
5	Leon Ames	240.00	120.00	75.00
6	Jimmy Archer	240.00	120.00	75.00
7	Jimmy Austin	240.00	120.00	75.00
8	H.D. Baird	240.00	120.00	75.00
9	J. Franklin Baker	540.00	270.00	160.00
10	Dave Bancroft	540.00	270.00	160.00
11	Jack Barry	240.00	120.00	75.00
12	Zinn Beck	240.00	120.00	75.00
13	"Chief" Bender	540.00	270.00	160.00
14	Joe Benz	240.00	120.00	75.00
15	Bob Bescher	240.00	120.00	75.00
16	Al Betzel	240.00	120.00	75.00
17	Mordecai Brown	540.00	270.00	160.00
18	Eddie Burns	240.00	120.00	75.00
19	George Burns	240.00	120.00	75.00
20	Geo. J. Burns	240.00	120.00	70.00
21	Joe Bush	240.00	120.00	75.00
22	"Donie" Bush	240.00	120.00	75.00
23	Art Butler	240.00	120.00	75.00
24	Bobbie Byrne	240.00	120.00	75.00
25	Forrest Cady	240.00	120.00	75.00
26	Jimmy Callahan	240.00	120.00	75.00
27	Ray Caldwell	240.00	120.00	75.00
28	Max Carey	540.00	270.00	160.00
29	George Chalmers	240.00	120.00	75.00
30	Ray Chapman	270.00	135.00	80.00
31	Larry Cheney	240.00	120.00	75.00
32	Eddie Cicotte	540.00	270.00	160.00
33	Tom Clarke	240.00	120.00	75.00
34	Eddie Collins	540.00	270.00	160.00
35	"Shauno" Collins	240.00	120.00	75.00
36	Charles Comiskey	540.00	270.00	160.00
37	Joe Connolly	240.00	120.00	75.00
38	Ty Cobb	3,600	1,800	1,080
39	Harry Coveleskie (Coveleski)	240.00	120.00	75.00
40	Gavvy Cravath	240.00	120.00	75.00
41	Sam Crawford	540.00	270.00	160.00
42	Jean Dale	240.00	120.00	75.00
43	Jake Daubert	240.00	120.00	75.00
44	Charles Deal	240.00	120.00	75.00
45	Al Demaree	240.00	120.00	75.00
46	Josh Devore	240.00	120.00	75.00
47	William Doak	240.00	120.00	75.00
48	Bill Donovan	240.00	120.00	75.00
49	Charles Dooin	240.00	120.00	75.00
50	Mike Doolan	240.00	120.00	75.00
51	Larry Doyle	240.00	120.00	75.00
52	Jean Dubuc	240.00	120.00	75.00
53	Oscar Dugey	240.00	120.00	75.00
54	Johnny Evers	540.00	270.00	160.00
55	Urban Faber	540.00	270.00	160.00
56	"Hap" Felsch	720.00	360.00	215.00
57	Bill Fischer	240.00	120.00	75.00
58	Ray Fisher	240.00	120.00	75.00
59	Max Flack	240.00	120.00	75.00
60	Art Fletcher	240.00	120.00	75.00
61	Eddie Foster	240.00	100.00	75.00
62	Jacques Fournier	240.00	120.00	75.00
63	Del Gainer (Gainor)	240.00	120.00	75.00
64	"Chic" Gandil	540.00	270.00	160.00
65	Larry Gardner	240.00	120.00	75.00
66	Joe Gedeon	240.00	120.00	75.00
67	Gus Getz	240.00	120.00	75.00
68	Geo. Gibson	240.00	120.00	75.00
69	Wilbur Good	240.00	120.00	75.00
70	Hank Gowdy	240.00	120.00	75.00
71	John Graney	240.00	120.00	75.00
72	Clark Griffith	540.00	270.00	160.00
73	Tom Griffith	240.00	120.00	75.00
74	Heinie Groh	240.00	120.00	75.00
75	Earl Hamilton	240.00	120.00	75.00
76	Bob Harmon	240.00	120.00	75.00
77	Roy Hartzell	240.00	120.00	75.00
78	Claude Hendrix	240.00	120.00	75.00
79	Olaf Henriksen	240.00	120.00	75.00
80	John Henry	240.00	120.00	75.00
81	"Buck" Herzog	240.00	120.00	75.00
82	Hugh High	240.00	120.00	75.00
83	Dick Hoblitzell	240.00	120.00	75.00
84	Harry Hooper	540.00	270.00	160.00
85	Ivan Howard	240.00	120.00	75.00
86	Miller Huggins	540.00	270.00	160.00
87	Joe Jackson	20,000	7,500	4,500
88	William James	240.00	120.00	75.00
89	Harold Janvrin	240.00	120.00	75.00
90	Hugh Jennings	540.00	270.00	160.00
91	Walter Johnson	1,800	900.00	540.00
92	Fielder Jones	240.00	120.00	75.00
93	Joe Judge	240.00	120.00	75.00
94	Bennie Kauff	240.00	120.00	75.00
95	Wm. Killefer Jr.	240.00	120.00	75.00
96	Ed. Konetchy	240.00	120.00	75.00
97	Napoleon Lajoie	600.00	300.00	180.00
98	Jack Lapp	240.00	120.00	75.00
99	John Lavan	240.00	120.00	75.00
100	Jimmy Lavender	240.00	120.00	75.00
101	"Nemo" Leibold	240.00	120.00	75.00
102	H.B. Leonard	240.00	120.00	75.00
103	Duffy Lewis	240.00	120.00	75.00
104	Hans Lobert	240.00	120.00	75.00
105	Tom Long	240.00	120.00	75.00
106	Fred Luderus	240.00	120.00	75.00
107	Connie Mack	540.00	270.00	160.00
108	Lee Magee	240.00	120.00	75.00
109	Sherwood Magee	240.00	120.00	75.00
110	Al. Mamaux	240.00	120.00	75.00
111	Leslie Mann	240.00	120.00	75.00
112	"Rabbit" Maranville	540.00	270.00	160.00
113	Rube Marquard	540.00	270.00	160.00
114	J. Erskine Mayer	360.00	180.00	110.00

115	George McBride	240.00	120.00	75.00
116	John J. McGraw	540.00	270.00	160.00
117	Jack McInnis	240.00	120.00	75.00
118	Fred Merkle	240.00	120.00	75.00
119	Chief Meyers	240.00	120.00	75.00
120	Clyde Milan	240.00	120.00	75.00
121	John Miller	240.00	120.00	75.00
122	Otto Miller	240.00	120.00	75.00
123	Willie Mitchell	240.00	120.00	75.00
124	Fred Mollwitz	240.00	120.00	75.00
125	Pat Moran	240.00	120.00	75.00
126	Ray Morgan	240.00	120.00	75.00
127	Geo. Moriarty	240.00	120.00	75.00
128	Guy Morton	240.00	120.00	75.00
129	Mike Mowrey	240.00	120.00	75.00
130	Ed. Murphy	240.00	120.00	75.00
131	"Hy" Myers	240.00	120.00	75.00
132	J.A. Niehoff	240.00	120.00	75.00
133	Rube Oldring	240.00	120.00	75.00
134	Oliver O'Mara	240.00	120.00	75.00
135	Steve O'Neill	240.00	120.00	75.00
136	"Dode" Paskert	240.00	120.00	75.00
137	Roger Peckinpaugh	240.00	120.00	75.00
138	Walter Pipp	240.00	120.00	75.00
139	Derril Pratt (Derrill)	240.00	120.00	75.00
140	Pat Ragan	240.00	120.00	75.00
141	Bill Rariden	240.00	120.00	75.00
142	Eppa Rixey	540.00	270.00	160.00
143	Davey Robertson	240.00	120.00	75.00
144	Wilbert Robinson	540.00	270.00	160.00
145	Bob Roth	240.00	120.00	75.00
146	Ed. Roush	540.00	270.00	160.00
147	Clarence Rowland	240.00	120.00	75.00
148	"Nap" Rucker	240.00	120.00	75.00
149	Dick Rudolph	240.00	120.00	75.00
150	Reb Russell	240.00	120.00	75.00
151	Babe Ruth	24,000	12,000	7,200
152	Vic Saier	240.00	120.00	75.00
153	"Slim" Sallee	240.00	120.00	75.00
154	Ray Schalk	540.00	270.00	160.00
155	Walter Schang	240.00	120.00	75.00
156	Frank Schulte	240.00	120.00	75.00
157	Everett Scott	240.00	120.00	75.00
158	Jim Scott	240.00	120.00	75.00
159	Tom Seaton	240.00	120.00	75.00
160	Howard Shanks	240.00	120.00	75.00
161	Bob Shawkey	240.00	120.00	75.00
162	Ernie Shore	240.00	120.00	75.00
163	Burt Shotton	240.00	120.00	75.00
164	Geo. Sisler	540.00	270.00	160.00
165	J. Carlisle Smith	240.00	120.00	75.00
166	Fred Snodgrass	240.00	120.00	75.00
167	Geo. Stallings	240.00	120.00	75.00
168	Oscar Stanage	240.00	120.00	75.00
169	Charles Stengel	540.00	270.00	160.00
170	Milton Stock	240.00	120.00	75.00
171	Amos Strunk	240.00	120.00	75.00
172	Billy Sullivan	240.00	120.00	75.00
173	"Jeff" Tesreau	240.00	120.00	75.00
174	Joe Tinker	540.00	270.00	160.00
175	Fred Toney	240.00	120.00	75.00
176	Terry Turner	240.00	120.00	75.00
177	George Tyler	240.00	120.00	75.00
178	Jim Vaughn	240.00	120.00	75.00
179	Bob Veach	240.00	120.00	75.00
180	James Viox	240.00	120.00	75.00
181	Oscar Vitt	240.00	120.00	75.00
182	Hans Wagner	5,000	1,200	720.00
183	Clarence Walker	240.00	120.00	75.00
184	Ed. Walsh	540.00	270.00	160.00
185	W. Wambsganss (Photo actually Fritz Coumbe.)	240.00	120.00	75.00
186	Buck Weaver	2,000	450.00	270.00
187	Carl Weilman	240.00	120.00	75.00
188	Zach Wheat	540.00	270.00	160.00
189	Geo. Whitted	240.00	120.00	75.00
190	Fred Williams	240.00	120.00	75.00
191	Art Wilson	240.00	120.00	75.00
192	J. Owen Wilson	240.00	120.00	75.00
193	Ivy Wingo	240.00	120.00	75.00
194	"Mel" Wolfgang	240.00	120.00	75.00
195	Joe Wood	360.00	180.00	110.00
196	Steve Yerkes	240.00	120.00	75.00
197	"Pep" Young	240.00	120.00	75.00
198	Rollie Zeider	240.00	120.00	75.00
199	Heiny Zimmerman	240.00	120.00	75.00
200	Ed. Zwilling	240.00	120.00	75.00

1923 Curtis Ireland Candy (E123)

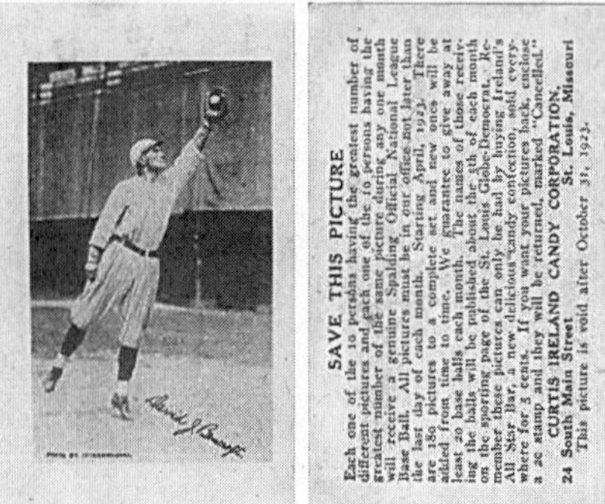

SAVE THIS PICTURE
Each one of the 10 persons having the greatest number of different pictures and each one of the 10 persons having the greatest number of the same picture during any one month will receive a genuine Spalding Official National League Base Ball. All pictures must be in our office not later than the last day of each month. Starting April, 1923. There are 180 pictures to a complete set and new ones will be added from time to time. We guarantee to give away at least 20 base balls each month. The names of those receiving the balls will be published about the 5th of each month on the sporting page of the St. Louis Globe-Democrat. Remember these pictures can only be had by buying Ireland's All Star Bar, a new delicious candy confection, sold everywhere for 5 cents. If you want your pictures back, enclose a 2c stamp and they will be returned, marked "Cancelled."
CURTIS IRELAND CANDY CORPORATION.
24 South Main Street St. Louis, Missouri
This picture is void after October 31, 1923.

This set, identified in the ACC as E123, was issued in 1923 by the Curtis Ireland Candy Corp. of St. Louis and was distributed with Ireland's "All Star Bars." Except for the backs, the Ireland set is identical to the Willard Chocolate V100 set of the same year. Measuring 3-1/4" x 2-1/16", the cards feature sepia-toned photos with the player's name in script on the front. The backs advertise a contest which required the collector to mail in the cards in exchange for prizes, which probably explains their relative scarcity today.

		NM	EX	VG
Complete Set (180):		125,000	50,000	30,000
Common Player:		600.00	240.00	150.00
(1)	Chas. B Adams	600.00	240.00	150.00
(2)	Grover C. Alexander	1,000	400.00	250.00
(3)	J.P. Austin	600.00	240.00	150.00
(4)	J.C. Bagby	600.00	240.00	150.00
(5)	J. Franklin Baker	900.00	360.00	225.00
(6)	David J. Bancroft	900.00	360.00	225.00
(7)	Turner Barber	600.00	240.00	150.00
(8)	Jesse L. Barnes	600.00	240.00	150.00
(9)	J.C. Bassler	600.00	240.00	150.00
(10)	L.A. Blue	600.00	240.00	150.00
(11)	Norman D. Boeckel	600.00	240.00	150.00
(12)	F.L. Brazil (Brazill)	600.00	240.00	150.00
(13)	G.H. Burns	600.00	240.00	150.00
(14)	Geo. J. Burns	600.00	240.00	150.00
(15)	Leon Cadore	600.00	240.00	150.00
(16)	Max G. Carey	900.00	360.00	225.00
(17)	Harold G. Carlson	600.00	240.00	150.00
(18)	Lloyd R. Christenberry (Christenbury)	600.00	240.00	150.00
(19)	Vernon J. Clemons	600.00	240.00	150.00
(20)	T.R. Cobb	8,500	3,400	2,125
(21)	Bert Cole	600.00	240.00	150.00
(22)	John F. Collins	600.00	240.00	150.00
(23)	S. Coveleskie (Coveleski)	900.00	360.00	225.00
(24)	Walton E. Cruise	600.00	240.00	150.00
(25)	G.W. Cutshaw	600.00	240.00	150.00
(26)	Jacob E. Daubert	600.00	240.00	150.00
(27)	Geo. Dauss	600.00	240.00	150.00
(28)	F.T. Davis	600.00	240.00	150.00
(29)	Chas. A. Deal	600.00	240.00	150.00
(30)	William L. Doak	600.00	240.00	150.00
(31)	William E. Donovan	600.00	240.00	150.00
(32)	Hugh Duffy	900.00	360.00	225.00
(33)	J.A. Dugan	600.00	240.00	150.00
(34)	Louis B. Duncan	600.00	240.00	150.00
(35)	James Dykes	600.00	240.00	150.00
(36)	H.J. Ehmke	600.00	240.00	150.00
(37)	F.R. Ellerbe	600.00	240.00	150.00
(38)	E.G. Erickson	600.00	240.00	150.00
(39)	John J. Evers	900.00	360.00	225.00
(40)	U.C. Faber	900.00	360.00	225.00
(41)	B.A. Falk	600.00	240.00	150.00
(42)	Max Flack	600.00	240.00	150.00
(43)	Lee Fohl	600.00	240.00	150.00
(44)	Jacques F. Fournier	600.00	240.00	150.00
(45)	Frank F. Frisch	900.00	360.00	225.00
(46)	C.E. Galloway	600.00	240.00	150.00
(47)	W.C. Gardner	600.00	240.00	150.00
(48)	E.P. Gharrity	600.00	240.00	150.00
(49)	Geo. Gibson	600.00	240.00	150.00
(50)	Wm. Gleason	600.00	240.00	150.00
(51)	William Gleason	600.00	240.00	150.00
(52)	Henry M. Gowdy	600.00	240.00	150.00
(53)	I.M. Griffin	600.00	240.00	150.00
(54)	Thomas Griffith	600.00	240.00	150.00
(55)	Burleigh A. Grimes	900.00	360.00	225.00
(56)	Charles J. Grimm	600.00	240.00	150.00
(57)	Jesse J. Haines	900.00	360.00	225.00
(58)	S.R. Harris	900.00	360.00	225.00
(59)	W.B. Harris	600.00	240.00	150.00
(60)	R.K. Hasty	600.00	240.00	150.00
(61)	H.E. Heilman (Heilmann)	900.00	360.00	225.00
(62)	Walter J. Henline	600.00	240.00	150.00
(63)	Walter L. Holke	600.00	240.00	150.00
(64)	Charles J. Hollocher	600.00	240.00	150.00
(65)	H.B. Hooper	900.00	360.00	225.00
(66)	Rogers Hornsby	1,250	500.00	310.00
(67)	W.C. Hoyt	900.00	360.00	225.00
(68)	Miller Huggins	900.00	360.00	225.00
(69)	W.C. Jacobsen (Jacobson)	600.00	240.00	150.00
(70)	C.D. Jamieson	600.00	240.00	150.00
(71)	Ernest Johnson	600.00	240.00	150.00
(72)	W.P. Johnson	2,250	900.00	560.00
(73)	James H. Johnston	600.00	240.00	150.00
(74)	R.W. Jones	600.00	240.00	150.00
(75)	Samuel Pond Jones	600.00	240.00	150.00
(76)	J.I. Judge	600.00	240.00	150.00
(77)	James W. Keenan	600.00	240.00	150.00
(78)	Geo. L. Kelly	900.00	360.00	225.00
(79)	Peter J. Kilduff	600.00	240.00	150.00
(80)	William Killefer	600.00	240.00	150.00
(81)	Lee King	600.00	240.00	150.00
(82)	Ray Kolp	600.00	240.00	150.00
(83)	John Lavan	600.00	240.00	150.00
(84)	H.L. Leibold	600.00	240.00	150.00
(85)	Connie Mack	900.00	360.00	225.00
(86)	J.W. Mails	600.00	240.00	150.00
(87)	Walter J. Maranville	900.00	360.00	225.00
(88)	Richard W. Marquard	900.00	360.00	225.00
(89)	C.W. Mays	650.00	260.00	160.00
(90)	Geo. F. McBride	600.00	240.00	150.00
(91)	H.M. McClellan	600.00	240.00	150.00
(92)	John J. McGraw	900.00	360.00	225.00
(93)	Austin B. McHenry	600.00	240.00	150.00
(94)	J. McInnis	600.00	240.00	150.00
(95)	Douglas McWeeney (McWeeny)	600.00	240.00	150.00
(96)	M. Menosky	600.00	240.00	150.00
(97)	Emil F. Meusel	600.00	240.00	150.00
(98)	R. Meusel	600.00	240.00	150.00
(99)	Henry W. Meyers	600.00	240.00	150.00
(100)	J.C. Milan	600.00	240.00	150.00
(101)	John K. Miljus	600.00	240.00	150.00
(102)	Edmund J. Miller	600.00	240.00	150.00
(103)	Elmer Miller	600.00	240.00	150.00
(104)	Otto L. Miller	600.00	240.00	150.00
(105)	Fred Mitchell	600.00	240.00	150.00
(106)	Geo. Mogridge	600.00	240.00	150.00
(107)	Patrick J. Moran	600.00	240.00	150.00
(108)	John D. Morrison	600.00	240.00	150.00
(109)	J.A. Mostil	600.00	240.00	150.00
(110)	Clarence F. Mueller	600.00	240.00	150.00
(111)	A. Earle Neale	650.00	260.00	160.00
(112)	Joseph Oeschger	600.00	240.00	150.00
(113)	Robert J. O'Farrell	600.00	240.00	150.00
(114)	J.C. Oldham	600.00	240.00	150.00
(115)	I.M. Olson	600.00	240.00	150.00
(116)	Geo. M. O'Neil	600.00	240.00	150.00
(117)	S.F. O'Neill	600.00	240.00	150.00
(118)	Frank J. Parkinson	600.00	240.00	150.00
(119)	Geo. H. Paskert	600.00	240.00	150.00
(120)	R.T. Peckinpaugh	600.00	240.00	150.00
(121)	H.J. Pennock	900.00	360.00	225.00
(122)	Ralph Perkins	600.00	240.00	150.00
(123)	Edw. J. Pfeffer	600.00	240.00	150.00
(124)	W.C. Pipp	600.00	240.00	150.00
(125)	Charles Elmer Ponder	600.00	240.00	150.00
(126)	Raymond R. Powell	600.00	240.00	150.00
(127)	D.B. Pratt	600.00	240.00	150.00
(128)	Joseph Rapp	600.00	240.00	150.00
(129)	John H. Rawlings	600.00	240.00	150.00
(130)	E.S. Rice (Should be E.C.)	900.00	360.00	225.00
(131)	Branch Rickey	1,000	400.00	250.00
(132)	James J. Ring	600.00	240.00	150.00
(133)	Eppa J. Rixey	900.00	360.00	225.00
(134)	Davis A. Robertson	600.00	240.00	150.00
(135)	Edwin Rommel	600.00	240.00	150.00
(136)	Edd J. Roush	900.00	360.00	225.00
(137)	Harold Ruel (Herold)	600.00	240.00	150.00
(138)	Allen Russell	600.00	240.00	150.00
(139)	G.H. Ruth	12,500	5,000	3,125
(140)	Wilfred D. Ryan	600.00	240.00	150.00
(141)	Henry F. Sallee	600.00	240.00	150.00
(142)	W.H. Schang	600.00	240.00	150.00
(143)	Raymond H. Schmandt	600.00	240.00	150.00
(144)	Everett Scott	600.00	240.00	150.00
(145)	Henry Severeid	600.00	240.00	150.00
(146)	Jos. W. Sewell	900.00	360.00	225.00
(147)	Howard S. Shanks	600.00	240.00	150.00
(148)	E.H. Sheely	600.00	240.00	150.00
(149)	Ralph Shinners	600.00	240.00	150.00
(150)	U.J. Shocker	600.00	240.00	150.00
(151)	G.H. Sisler	900.00	360.00	225.00
(152)	Earl L. Smith	600.00	240.00	150.00
(153)	Earl S. Smith	600.00	240.00	150.00
(154)	Geo. A. Smith	600.00	240.00	150.00
(155)	J.W. Smith	600.00	240.00	150.00
(156)	Tris E. Speaker	1,350	540.00	335.00
(157)	Arnold Staatz	600.00	240.00	150.00
(158)	J.R. Stephenson	600.00	240.00	150.00
(159)	Milton J. Stock	600.00	240.00	150.00
(160)	John L. Sullivan	600.00	240.00	150.00
(161)	H.F. Tormahlen	600.00	240.00	150.00
(162)	Jas. A. Tierney	600.00	240.00	150.00
(163)	J.T. Tobin	600.00	240.00	150.00
(164)	Jas. L. Vaughn	600.00	240.00	150.00
(165)	R.H. Veach	600.00	240.00	150.00
(166)	C.W. Walker	600.00	240.00	150.00
(167)	A.L. Ward	600.00	240.00	150.00
(168)	Zack D. Wheat	900.00	360.00	225.00
(169)	George B. Whitted	600.00	240.00	150.00
(170)	Irvin K. Wilhelm	600.00	240.00	150.00
(171)	Roy H. Wilkinson	600.00	240.00	150.00
(172)	Fred C. Williams	600.00	240.00	150.00
(173)	K.R. Williams	600.00	240.00	150.00
(174)	Sam'l W. Wilson	600.00	240.00	150.00
(175)	Ivy B. Wingo	600.00	240.00	150.00
(176)	L.W. Witt	600.00	240.00	150.00
(177)	Joseph Wood	650.00	260.00	160.00
(178)	E. Yaryan	600.00	240.00	150.00
(179)	R.S. Young	600.00	240.00	150.00
(180)	Ross Young (Youngs)	900.00	360.00	225.00

1967 Irvindale Dairy Atlana Braves

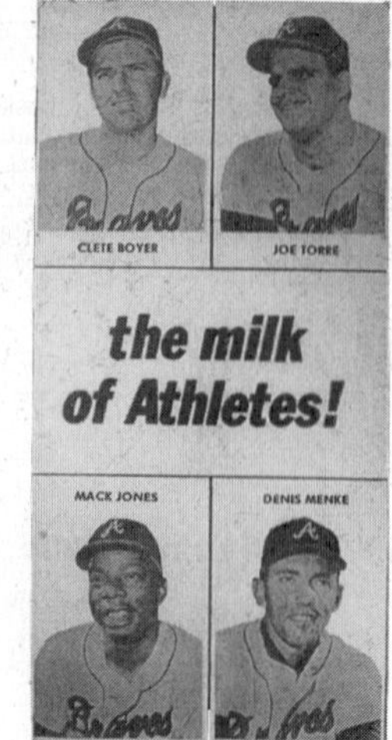

This quartet of Braves was printed in shades of deep red on the white background of a milk carton panel. Well-cut individual pieces measure 1-3/4" x 2-5/8" and are blank-backed.

		NM	EX	VG
Complete Set, Panel:		250.00	125.00	75.00
Complete Set, Singles:		175.00	85.00	45.00
Common Player:		40.00	20.00	12.00
(1)	Clete Boyer	40.00	20.00	12.00

		NM	EX	VG
(2)	Mack Jones	40.00	20.00	12.00
(3)	Denis Menke	40.00	20.00	12.00
(4)	Joe Torre	60.00	30.00	18.00

1976 Isaly's/Sweet William discs

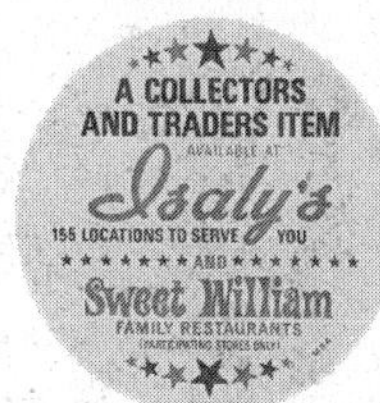

One of several regional sponsors of player disc sets in 1976 was the Pittsburgh area dairy store chain, Isaly's, and the Sweet William restaurants. The discs are 3-3/8" diameter with a black-and-white player portrait photo in the center of the baseball design. A line of red stars is above, while the left and right panels feature one of several bright colors. Produced by Michael Schecter Associates under license from the Major League Baseball Players Association, the player photos have had uniform and cap logos removed. Backs are printed in red and purple. The unnumbered checklist here is presented in alphabetical order.

		NM	EX	VG
Complete Set (70):		15.00	7.50	4.50
Common Player:		.50	.25	.15
(1)	Henry Aaron	4.00	2.00	1.25
(2)	Johnny Bench	2.00	1.00	.60
(3)	Vida Blue	.50	.25	.15
(4)	Larry Bowa	.50	.25	.15
(5)	Lou Brock	2.00	1.00	.60
(6)	Jeff Burroughs	.50	.25	.15
(7)	John Candelaria	.50	.25	.15
(8)	Jose Cardenal	.50	.25	.15
(9)	Rod Carew	2.00	1.00	.60
(10)	Steve Carlton	2.00	1.00	.60
(11)	Dave Cash	.50	.25	.15
(12)	Cesar Cedeno	.50	.25	.15
(13)	Ron Cey	.50	.25	.15
(14)	Carlton Fisk	2.00	1.00	.60
(15)	Tito Fuentes	.50	.25	.15
(16)	Steve Garvey	1.50	.70	.45
(17)	Ken Griffey	.50	.25	.15
(18)	Don Gullett	.50	.25	.15
(19)	Willie Horton	.50	.25	.15
(20)	Al Hrabosky	.50	.25	.15
(21)	Catfish Hunter	2.00	1.00	.60
(22)	Reggie Jackson (A's)	3.00	1.50	.90
(23)	Randy Jones	.50	.25	.15
(24)	Jim Kaat	.50	.25	.15
(25)	Don Kessinger	.50	.25	.15
(26)	Dave Kingman	.50	.25	.15
(27)	Jerry Koosman	.50	.25	.15
(28)	Mickey Lolich	.50	.25	.15
(29)	Greg Luzinski	.50	.25	.15
(30)	Fred Lynn	.50	.25	.15
(31)	Bill Madlock	.50	.25	.15
(32)	Carlos May (White Sox)	.50	.25	.15
(33)	John Mayberry	.50	.25	.15
(34)	Bake McBride	.50	.25	.15
(35)	Doc Medich	.50	.25	.15
(36)	Andy Messersmith (Dodgers)	.50	.25	.15
(37)	Rick Monday	.50	.25	.15
(38)	John Montefusco	.50	.25	.15
(39)	Jerry Morales	.50	.25	.15
(40)	Joe Morgan	2.00	1.00	.60
(41)	Thurman Munson	2.00	1.00	.60
(42)	Bobby Murcer	.50	.25	.15
(43)	Al Oliver	.50	.25	.15
(44)	Jim Palmer	2.00	1.00	.60
(45)	Dave Parker	.50	.25	.15
(46)	Tony Perez	2.00	1.00	.60
(47)	Jerry Reuss	.50	.25	.15
(48)	Brooks Robinson	2.00	1.00	.60
(49)	Frank Robinson	2.00	1.00	.60
(50)	Steve Rogers	.50	.25	.15
(51)	Pete Rose	6.00	3.00	1.75
(52)	Nolan Ryan	12.00	6.00	3.50
(53)	Manny Sanguillen	.50	.25	.15
(54)	Mike Schmidt	3.00	1.50	.90
(55)	Tom Seaver	2.00	1.00	.60
(56)	Ted Simmons	.50	.25	.15
(57)	Reggie Smith	.50	.25	.15
(58)	Willie Stargell	2.00	1.00	.60
(59)	Rusty Staub	.75	.40	.25
(60)	Rennie Stennett	.50	.25	.15
(61)	Don Sutton	2.00	1.00	.60
(62)	Andy Thornton (Cubs)	.50	.25	.15
(63)	Luis Tiant	.50	.25	.15
(64)	Joe Torre	1.50	.70	.45
(65)	Mike Tyson	.50	.25	.15
(66)	Bob Watson	.50	.25	.15
(67)	Wilbur Wood	.50	.25	.15
(68)	Jimmy Wynn	.50	.25	.15
(69)	Carl Yastrzemski	2.50	1.25	.70
(70)	Richie Zisk	.50	.25	.15

1976 ISCA Hoosier Hot-Stove All-Stars

Famous native Hoosier ballplayers are featured in this collectors' issue from the Indiana Sports Collectors Assn. The 2-5/8" x 3-5/8" cards have black-and-white player photos on front framed in the state's outline. Red and blue graphics on a white background complete the design. Backs are in black and blue on white and include a career summary. A star on the state map at bottom indicates where the player was born.

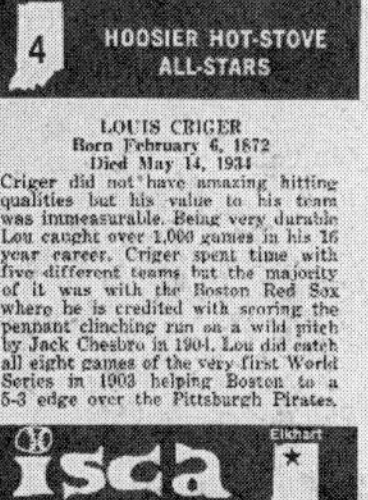
4 HOOSIER HOT-STOVE ALL-STARS

LOUIS CRIGER
Born February 6, 1872
Died May 14, 1934

Criger did not have amazing hitting qualities but his value to his team was immeasurable. Being very durable Lou caught over 1,000 games in his 16 year career. Criger spent time with five different teams but the majority of it was with the Boston Red Sox where he is credited with scoring the pennant clinching run on a wild pitch by Jack Chesbro in 1904. Lou did catch all eight games of the very first World Series in 1903 helping Boston to a 5-3 edge over the Pittsburgh Pirates.

Elkhart

isca
INDIANA SPORTS COLLECTORS ASSOCIATION

		NM	EX	VG
Complete Set (26):		15.00	7.50	4.50
Common Player:		2.00	1.00	.60
1	Edd Roush	2.00	1.00	.60
2	Sam Thompson	2.00	1.00	.60
3	Chuck Klein	2.00	1.00	.60
4	Lou Criger	2.00	1.00	.60
5	Amos Rusie	2.00	1.00	.60
6	Billy Herman	2.00	1.00	.60
7	George Dauss	2.00	1.00	.60
8	Tom Thevenow	2.00	1.00	.60
9	Mordecai Brown	2.00	1.00	.60
10	Freddie Fitzsimmons	2.00	1.00	.60
11	Art Nehf	2.00	1.00	.60
12	Carl Erskine	3.00	1.50	.90
13	Don Larsen	3.00	1.50	.90
14	Gil Hodges	6.00	3.00	1.75
15	Pete Fox	2.00	1.00	.60
16	Butch Henline	2.00	1.00	.60
17	Doc Crandall	2.00	1.00	.60
18	Dizzy Trout	2.00	1.00	.60
19	Donie Bush	2.00	1.00	.60
20	Max Carey	2.00	1.00	.60
21	Eugene Hargrave, William Hargrave	2.00	1.00	.60
22	Sam Rice	2.00	1.00	.60
23	Babe Adams	2.00	1.00	.60
24	Cy Williams	2.00	1.00	.60
25	1913 Indianapolis Federal League Team	2.00	1.00	.60
26	Paul Frisz	2.00	1.00	.60

J

1912 J=K Candy

Originally printed on the front and back of candy boxes which advertised "100 Principal League Players," the extent of this series is currently unknown and the checklist presented here is almost certainly incomplete. The blank-back, black-and-white (some have a bit of color tinting) cards can be found in two sizes, 1-7/8" x 3-1/2" if printed on the box front, or 1-7/8" x 2-7/8" if printed on back. Player photos are framed with an ornate-cornered border. In a plaque at bottom, all in capital letters, are the player's name, position, team and league; the latter three designations are abbreviated. Gaps have been left in the assigned numbering to accommodate future discoveries.

		NM	EX	VG
Common Player:		2,000	1,000	600.00
(1)	Hugh Bedient	2,000	1,000	600.00
(2)	Hick Cady	2,000	1,000	600.00
(3)	Bill Carrigan	2,000	1,000	600.00
(4)	Hal Chase	2,500	1,250	750.00
(5)	Eddie Collins	3,000	1,500	900.00
(6)	Doc Crandall	2,000	1,000	600.00
(7)	Lou Criger	2,000	1,000	600.00
(8)	Harry Davis	2,000	1,000	600.00
(9)	Jim Delahanty	2,000	1,000	600.00
(10)	Art Devlin	2,000	1,000	600.00
(11)	Josh Devore	2,000	1,000	600.00
(12)	Larry Doyle	2,000	1,000	600.00
(13)	Larry Gardner	2,000	1,000	600.00
(14)	George Gibson	2,000	1,000	600.00
(15)	Charley Hall	2,000	1,000	600.00
(16)	Topsy Hartsel	2,000	1,000	600.00
(17)	Buck Herzog	2,000	1,000	600.00
(18)	Solly Hofman	2,000	1,000	600.00
(19)	Marty Krug	2,000	1,000	600.00
(20)	Duffy Lewis	2,000	1,000	600.00
(21)	Rube Marquard	3,000	1,500	900.00
(22)	Christy Mathewson	6,000	3,000	1,800
(23)	John McGraw	3,000	1,500	900.00
(24)	Red Murray	2,000	1,000	600.00
(25)	Harry Niles	2,000	1,000	600.00
(26)	Orval Overall	2,000	1,000	600.00
(27)	Larry Pape	2,000	1,000	600.00
(28)	Ed Reulbach	2,000	1,000	600.00
(29)	Cy Seymour	2,000	1,000	600.00
(30)	Jimmy Sheckard	2,000	1,000	600.00
(31)	Hack Simmons	2,000	1,000	600.00
(33)	Tris Speaker	4,800	2,400	1,450
(34)	Jake Stahl	2,000	1,000	600.00
(35)	Oscar Stanage	2,000	1,000	600.00
(36)	Harry Steinfeldt	2,000	1,000	600.00
(37)	Jeff Tesreau	2,000	1,000	600.00
(38)	Ira Thomas	2,000	1,000	600.00
(39)	Joe Tinker	3,000	1,500	900.00
(40)	Honus Wagner	12,000	6,000	3,600
(41)	Ed Walsh	3,000	1,500	900.00
(43)	Owen Wilson	2,000	1,000	600.00

1969 Jack In The Box California Angels

This regional issue was distributed a few cards per week at the chain's fast food restaurants. Blank-back cards are printed in black-and-white on thin white stock in a 1-15/16" x 3-1/2" format. The checklist for the unnumbered cards is presented here alphabetically.

		NM	EX	VG
Complete Set (13):		30.00	15.00	9.00
Common Player:		3.00	1.50	.90
(1)	Sandy Alomar	3.00	1.50	.90
(2)	Joe Azcue	3.00	1.50	.90
(3)	Jim Fregosi	3.50	1.75	1.00
(4)	Lou Johnson	3.00	1.50	.90
(5)	Jay Johnstone	6.00	3.00	1.75
(6)	Rudy May	3.00	1.50	.90
(7)	Jim McGlothlin	3.00	1.50	.90
(8)	Andy Messersmith	3.00	1.50	.90
(9)	Tom Murphy	3.00	1.50	.90
(10)	Rick Reichardt	3.00	1.50	.90
(11)	Aurelio Rodriguez	3.00	1.50	.90
(12)	Jim Spencer	3.00	1.50	.90
(13)	Hoyt Wilhelm	10.00	5.00	3.00

1971 Jack In The Box California Angels

Unlike the legitimate issue of 1969, this is an unauthorized collectors issue with no official connection to either the team of the fast food restaurant chain. The cards are printed in horizontal format on 4" x 2-1/2" manila paper in black ink. Fronts have a player portrait photo at left. Stacked at right are the player's name, team, position and Jack in the Box logo. Backs are blank. The set is checklisted here in alphabetical order.

		NM	EX	VG
Complete Set (10):		25.00	12.50	7.50
Common Player:		3.00	1.50	.90
(1)	Sandy Alomar	3.00	1.50	.90
(2)	Ken Berry	3.00	1.50	.90

(3)	Tony Conigliaro	15.00	7.50	4.50
(4)	Jim Fregosi	3.00	1.50	.90
(5)	Alex Johnson	3.00	1.50	.90
(6)	Rudy May	3.00	1.50	.90
(7)	Andy Messersmith	3.00	1.50	.90
(8)	"Lefty" Phillips	3.00	1.50	.90
(9)	Jim Spencer	3.00	1.50	.90
(10)	Clyde Wright	3.00	1.50	.90

1970 Jack in the Box Pittsburgh Pirates

Though this set is known within the hobby as the "Jack in the Box" Pirates, it bears no such advertising and has no actual connection to the restaurant chain; they are a collector's issue. The black-and-white cards measure 2" x 3-1/2" and are blank-backed. Beneath the photo on front is the player identification and a few stats from the 1969 season.

		NM	EX	VG
Complete Set (12):		35.00	17.50	10.00
Common Player:		3.00	1.50	.90
(1)	Gene Alley	3.00	1.50	.90
(2)	Dave Cash	3.00	1.50	.90
(3)	Dock Ellis	3.00	1.50	.90
(4)	Dave Giusti	3.00	1.50	.90
(5)	Jerry May	3.00	1.50	.90
(6)	Bill Mazeroski	12.50	6.25	3.75
(7)	Al Oliver	6.00	3.00	1.75
(8)	Jose Pagan	3.00	1.50	.90
(9)	Fred Patek	3.00	1.50	.90
(10)	Bob Robertson	3.00	1.50	.90
(11)	Manny Sanguillen	4.50	2.25	1.25
(12)	Willie Stargell	12.50	6.25	3.75

1954 Bill Jacobellis N.Y. Giants

In the Giants' championship season, New York photographer Bill Jacobellis produced this set of player/team pictures, probably to be sold at the Polo Grounds souvenir stands. The black-and-white pictures are blank-backed and measure about 8-1/4" x 10-1/2", printed on semi-gloss paper. The player name is centered in bold type in the white bottom border; at right is "Bill Jacobellis Photo." The unnumbred pictures are listed here in alphabetical order.

		NM	EX	VG
Complete Set (8):		110.00	55.00	32.50
Common Player:		12.50	6.25	3.75
(1)	John Antonelli	12.50	6.25	3.75
(2)	Alvin Dark	12.50	6.25	3.75
(3)	Ruben Gomez	12.50	6.25	3.75
(4)	Whitey Lockman	12.50	6.25	3.75
(5)	Willie Mays	60.00	30.00	18.00
(6)	Don Mueller	12.50	6.25	3.75
(7)	James (Dusty) Rhodes	12.50	6.25	3.75
(8)	N.Y. Giants of 1954	20.00	10.00	6.00

1968 Jamesway Trucking Co.

Although it doesn't say so in the red logo which decorates this black-and-white card, Jamesway was a Southern Ohio trucking company. The 4" x 5-1/4" card is blank-backed. The purpose for which the card was created and its manner of distribution is unknown.

	NM	EX	VG
Pete Rose	275.00	135.00	85.00

1958-1965 Jay Publishing Picture Packs

The name "Picture Packs" has been used to describe this massive series of 5" x 7" black-and-white player photos issued by Jay Publishing's Big League Books division over the eight-year period from 1958-1965. The company also produced yearbooks for various major league teams during that period; many of the photos used in the yearbooks also appear in the Picture Packs. Picture Pack sets consist of 12 player/manager photos with name, city and team nickname in the bottom border. They were available by mail, at the ballparks and in stores. They were sold in either plain brown or white envelopes, or in clear plastic. Most were printed on a glossy, slick paper stock, although the quality of the paper may vary from team to team and year to year. The photos were issued anonymously, with no indication of the producer or year of issue. Two different types were issued, differentiated by the typeface used in the captions. Type 1 photos, issued from 1958 through 1961, were printed with a sans-serif style typeface, while Type 2 photos, issued from 1962 through 1965, used a serif typeface. Besides team sets there were a few special picture packs such as All-Stars, old-timers and World Series participants. Some years' team-set packs were updated (sometimes more than once) to reflect roster changes. Many pictures were reused from year to year.

	NM	EX	VG
Typical Team Set:	40.00	20.00	12.00
Common Player:	3.00	1.50	.90
Typical Hall of Famer:	10.00	5.00	3.00
Superstars:	20.00	10.00	6.00

1962 Jell-O

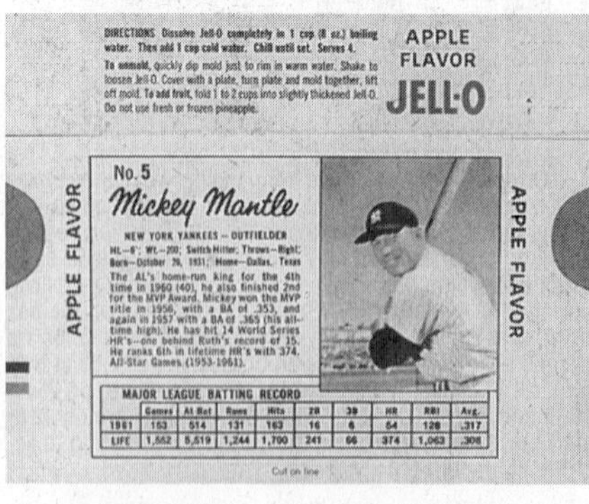

Virtually identical in content to the 1962 Post cereal cards, the '62 Jell-O set of 197 was only issued in the Midwest. Players and card numbers are identical in the two sets, except Brooks Robinson (#29), Ted Kluszewski (#82) and Smoky Burgess (#176) were not issued in the Jell-O version. The Jell-O cards are easy to distinguish from the Post of that year by the absence of the red oval Post logo and red or blue border around the stat box. Cards which have been neatly trimmed from the box on which they were printed will measure 3-1/2" x 2-1/2". Cards of some non-star players can be very scarce because they originally appeared on a limited number of boxes, or unpopular flavors or sizes.

		NM	EX	VG
Complete Set (197):		7,000	2,750	1,750
Common Player:		12.50	5.00	3.25
1	Bill Skowron	30.00	12.00	7.50
2	Bobby Richardson	500.00	200.00	125.00
3	Cletis Boyer	30.00	12.00	7.50
4	Tony Kubek	35.00	14.00	9.00
5	Mickey Mantle	350.00	140.00	90.00
6	Roger Maris	125.00	50.00	30.00
7	Yogi Berra	75.00	30.00	17.50
8	Elston Howard	30.00	12.00	7.50
9	Whitey Ford	60.00	25.00	15.00
10	Ralph Terry	25.00	10.00	6.25
11	John Blanchard	30.00	12.00	7.50
12	Luis Arroyo	15.00	6.00	3.75
13	Bill Stafford	30.00	12.00	7.50
14	Norm Cash	20.00	8.00	5.00
15	Jake Wood	12.50	5.00	3.25
16	Steve Boros	12.50	5.00	3.25
17	Chico Fernandez	12.50	5.00	3.25
18	Billy Bruton	12.50	5.00	3.25
19	Ken Aspromonte	12.50	5.00	3.25
20	Al Kaline	75.00	30.00	17.50
21	Dick Brown	12.50	5.00	3.25
22	Frank Lary	12.50	5.00	3.25
23	Don Mossi	12.50	5.00	3.25
24	Phil Regan	12.50	5.00	3.25
25	Charley Maxwell	12.50	5.00	3.25
26	Jim Bunning	30.00	12.00	7.50
27	Jim Gentile	12.50	5.00	3.25
28	Marv Breeding	12.50	5.00	3.25
29	Not Issued			
30	Ron Hansen	12.50	5.00	3.25
31	Jackie Brandt	50.00	20.00	12.50
32	Dick Williams	12.50	5.00	3.25
33	Gus Triandos	12.50	5.00	3.25
34	Milt Pappas	12.50	5.00	3.25
35	Hoyt Wilhelm	30.00	12.00	7.50
36	Chuck Estrada	12.50	5.00	3.25
37	Vic Power	12.50	5.00	3.25
38	Johnny Temple	12.50	5.00	3.25
39	Bubba Phillips	30.00	12.00	7.50
40	Tito Francona	12.50	5.00	3.25
41	Willie Kirkland	12.50	5.00	3.25
42	John Romano	12.50	5.00	3.25
43	Jim Perry	15.00	6.00	3.75
44	Woodie Held	12.50	5.00	3.25
45	Chuck Essegian	12.50	5.00	3.25
46	Roy Sievers	15.00	6.00	3.75
47	Nellie Fox	40.00	16.00	10.00
48	Al Smith	15.00	6.00	3.75
49	Luis Aparicio	40.00	16.00	10.00
50	Jim Landis	12.50	5.00	3.25
51	Minnie Minoso	25.00	10.00	6.25
52	Andy Carey	30.00	12.00	7.50
53	Sherman Lollar	12.50	5.00	3.25
54	Bill Pierce	12.50	5.00	3.25
55	Early Wynn	50.00	20.00	12.50
56	Chuck Schilling	75.00	30.00	18.50
57	Pete Runnels	12.50	5.00	3.25
58	Frank Malzone	20.00	8.00	5.00
59	Don Buddin	15.00	6.00	3.75
60	Gary Geiger	12.50	5.00	3.25
61	Carl Yastrzemski	250.00	100.00	60.00
62	Jackie Jensen	60.00	24.00	15.00
63	Jim Pagliaroni	30.00	12.00	7.50
64	Don Schwall	12.50	5.00	3.25
65	Dale Long	12.50	5.00	3.25
66	Chuck Cottier	20.00	8.00	5.00
67	Billy Klaus	30.00	12.00	7.50
68	Coot Veal	12.50	5.00	3.25
69	Marty Keough	60.00	25.00	15.00
70	Willie Tasby	60.00	25.00	15.00
71	Gene Woodling	12.50	5.00	3.25
72	Gene Green	60.00	25.00	15.00
73	Dick Donovan	15.00	6.00	3.75
74	Steve Bilko	25.00	10.00	6.25
75	Rocky Bridges	30.00	12.00	7.50
76	Eddie Yost	15.00	6.00	3.75
77	Leon Wagner	15.00	6.00	3.75
78	Albie Pearson	15.00	6.00	3.75
79	Ken Hunt	20.00	8.00	5.00
80	Earl Averill	75.00	30.00	17.50
81	Ryne Duren	15.00	6.00	3.75
82	Not Issued			
83	Bob Allison	15.00	6.00	3.75
84	Billy Martin	20.00	8.00	5.00
85	Harmon Killebrew	75.00	30.00	17.50
86	Zoilo Versalles	15.00	6.00	3.75
87	Lennie Green	90.00	35.00	20.00
88	Bill Tuttle	60.00	25.00	15.00
89	Jim Lemon	60.00	25.00	15.00
90	Earl Battey	30.00	12.00	7.50
91	Camilo Pascual	25.00	10.00	6.25
92	Norm Siebern	12.50	5.00	3.25
93	Jerry Lumpe	12.50	5.00	3.25
94	Dick Howser	15.00	6.00	3.75
95	Gene Stephens	60.00	25.00	15.00
96	Leo Posada	15.00	6.00	3.75
97	Joe Pignatano	15.00	6.00	3.75
98	Jim Archer	15.00	6.00	3.75
99	Haywood Sullivan	30.00	12.00	7.50
100	Art Ditmar	12.50	5.00	3.25
101	Gil Hodges	100.00	40.00	25.00
102	Charlie Neal	15.00	6.00	3.75
103	Daryl Spencer	15.00	6.00	3.75
104	Maury Wills	30.00	12.00	7.50
105	Tommy Davis	30.00	12.00	7.50
106	Willie Davis	15.00	6.00	3.75
107	John Roseboro	60.00	25.00	15.00
108	John Podres	30.00	12.00	7.50
109	Sandy Koufax	100.00	40.00	25.00
110	Don Drysdale	125.00	50.00	30.00
111	Larry Sherry	90.00	35.00	20.00
112	Jim Gilliam	30.00	12.00	7.50
113	Norm Larker	60.00	25.00	15.00
114	Duke Snider	90.00	35.00	20.00
115	Stan Williams	60.00	25.00	15.00
116	Gordon Coleman	80.00	30.00	20.00
117	Don Blasingame	30.00	12.00	7.50

118	Gene Freese	50.00	20.00	12.50
119	Ed Kasko	60.00	25.00	15.00
120	Gus Bell	30.00	12.00	7.50
121	Vada Pinson	15.00	6.00	3.75
122	Frank Robinson	40.00	15.00	10.00
123	Bob Purkey	15.00	6.00	3.75
124	Joey Jay	15.00	6.00	3.75
125	Jim Brosnan	15.00	6.00	3.75
126	Jim O'Toole	15.00	6.00	3.75
127	Jerry Lynch	15.00	6.00	3.75
128	Wally Post	15.00	6.00	3.75
129	Ken Hunt	15.00	6.00	3.75
130	Jerry Zimmerman	15.00	6.00	3.75
131	Willie McCovey	60.00	25.00	15.00
132	Jose Pagan	30.00	12.00	7.50
133	Felipe Alou	15.00	6.00	3.75
134	Jim Davenport	15.00	6.00	3.75
135	Harvey Kuenn	15.00	6.00	3.75
136	Orlando Cepeda	50.00	20.00	12.50
137	Ed Bailey	15.00	6.00	3.75
138	Sam Jones	15.00	6.00	3.75
139	Mike McCormick	15.00	6.00	3.75
140	Juan Marichal	60.00	25.00	15.00
141	Jack Sanford	15.00	6.00	3.75
142	Willie Mays	125.00	50.00	30.00
143	Stu Miller	90.00	35.00	20.00
144	Joe Amalfitano	15.00	6.00	3.75
145	Joe Adcock	15.00	6.00	3.75
146	Frank Bolling	30.00	12.00	7.50
147	Ed Mathews	90.00	35.00	20.00
148	Roy McMillan	12.50	5.00	3.25
149	Hank Aaron	60.00	25.00	15.00
150	Gino Cimoli	30.00	12.00	7.50
151	Frank J. Thomas	12.50	5.00	3.25
152	Joe Torre	60.00	25.00	15.00
153	Lou Burdette	15.00	6.00	3.75
154	Bob Buhl	12.50	5.00	3.25
155	Carlton Willey	12.50	5.00	3.25
156	Lee Maye	50.00	20.00	12.50
157	Al Spangler	60.00	25.00	15.00
158	Bill White	90.00	35.00	20.00
159	Ken Boyer	75.00	30.00	17.50
160	Joe Cunningham	15.00	6.00	3.75
161	Carl Warwick	15.00	6.00	3.75
162	Carl Sawatski	75.00	30.00	17.50
163	Lindy McDaniel	12.50	5.00	3.25
164	Ernie Broglio	15.00	6.00	3.75
165	Larry Jackson	12.50	5.00	3.25
166	Curt Flood	25.00	10.00	6.25
167	Curt Simmons	60.00	25.00	15.00
168	Alex Grammas	30.00	12.00	7.50
169	Dick Stuart	15.00	6.00	3.75
170	Bill Mazeroski	60.00	25.00	15.00
171	Don Hoak	15.00	6.00	3.75
172	Dick Groat	15.00	6.00	3.75
173	Roberto Clemente	180.00	70.00	45.00
174	Bob Skinner	30.00	12.00	7.50
175	Bill Virdon	60.00	25.00	15.00
176	Not Issued			
177	Elroy Face	15.00	6.00	3.75
178	Bob Friend	15.00	6.00	3.75
179	Vernon Law	30.00	12.00	7.50
180	Harvey Haddix	60.00	25.00	15.00
181	Hal Smith	30.00	12.00	7.50
182	Ed Bouchee	50.00	20.00	12.50
183	Don Zimmer	60.00	25.00	15.00
184	Ron Santo	35.00	15.00	9.00
185	Andre Rodgers	12.50	5.00	3.25
186	Richie Ashburn	50.00	20.00	12.50
187	George Altman	12.50	5.00	3.25
188	Ernie Banks	50.00	20.00	12.50
189	Sam Taylor	12.50	5.00	3.25
190	Don Elston	12.50	5.00	3.25
191	Jerry Kindall	50.00	20.00	12.50
192	Pancho Herrera	12.50	5.00	3.25
193	Tony Taylor	12.50	5.00	3.25
194	Ruben Amaro	30.00	12.00	7.50
195	Don Demeter	12.50	5.00	3.25
196	Bobby Gene Smith	60.00	25.00	15.00
197	Clay Dalrymple	12.50	5.00	3.25
198	Robin Roberts	60.00	25.00	15.00
199	Art Mahaffey	12.50	5.00	3.25
200	John Buzhardt	12.50	5.00	3.25

1963 Jell-O

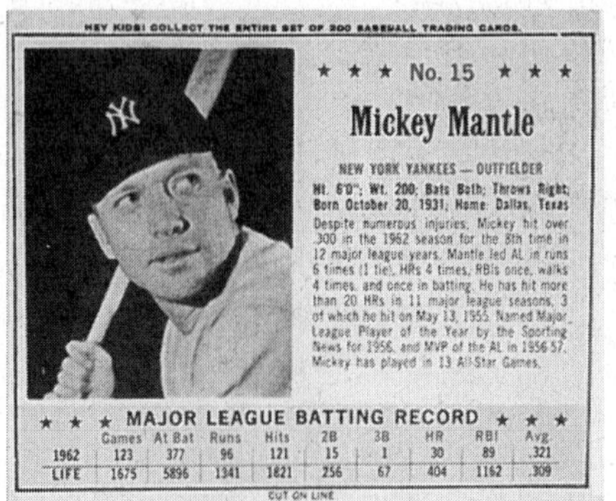

Like the other Post and Jell-O issues of the era, the '63 Jell-O set includes many scarce cards; primarily those which were printed as the backs of less popular brands and sizes of the gelatin dessert. Slightly smaller than the virtually identical Post cereal cards of the same year, the 200 cards in the Jell-O issue measure 3-3/8" x 2-1/2". The easiest way to distinguish 1963 Jell-O cards from Post cards is by the red line that separates the 1962 stats from the lifetime stats. On Post cards, the line extends almost all the way to the side borders, on the Jell-O cards, the line begins and ends much closer to the stats. The high value of some non-star players' cards can be attributed to scarcity caused by the cards having originally been printed on unpopular flavors or sizes.

		NM	EX	VG
Complete Set (200):		5,500	2,200	1,325
Common Player:		7.50	3.00	2.00
1	Vic Power	15.00	6.00	3.50
2	Bernie Allen	65.00	25.00	15.00
3	Zoilo Versalles	65.00	25.00	15.00
4	Rich Rollins	7.50	3.00	2.00
5	Harmon Killebrew	50.00	20.00	12.50
6	Lenny Green	35.00	15.00	10.00
7	Bob Allison	15.00	6.00	3.50
8	Earl Battey	55.00	22.50	13.50
9	Camilo Pascual	10.00	4.00	2.50
10	Jim Kaat	60.00	25.00	15.00
11	Jack Kralick	7.50	3.00	2.00
12	Bill Skowron	65.00	25.00	15.00
13	Bobby Richardson	10.00	4.00	2.50
14	Cletis Boyer	7.50	3.00	2.00
15	Mickey Mantle	175.00	60.00	40.00
16	Roger Maris	40.00	15.00	10.00
17	Yogi Berra	30.00	12.00	7.50
18	Elston Howard	35.00	15.00	10.00
19	Whitey Ford	20.00	8.00	5.00
20	Ralph Terry	7.50	3.00	2.00
21	John Blanchard	30.00	12.00	7.50
22	Bill Stafford	25.00	10.00	6.00
23	Tom Tresh	7.50	3.00	2.00
24	Steve Bilko	7.50	3.00	2.00
25	Bill Moran	7.50	3.00	2.00
26	Joe Koppe	7.50	3.00	2.00
27	Felix Torres	7.50	3.00	2.00
28	Leon Wagner	10.00	4.00	2.50
29	Albie Pearson	7.50	3.00	2.00
30	Lee Thomas	7.50	3.00	2.00
31	Bob Rodgers	65.00	25.00	15.00
32	Dean Chance	7.50	3.00	2.00
33	Ken McBride	35.00	15.00	10.00
34	George Thomas	35.00	15.00	10.00
35	Joe Cunningham	60.00	25.00	15.00
36	Nelson Fox	12.50	5.00	3.00
37	Luis Aparicio	12.50	5.00	3.00
38	Al Smith	7.50	3.00	2.00
39	Floyd Robinson	7.50	3.00	2.00
40	Jim Landis	7.50	3.00	2.00
41	Charlie Maxwell	7.50	3.00	2.00
42	Sherman Lollar	15.00	6.00	3.50
43	Early Wynn	20.00	8.00	5.00
44	Juan Pizarro	75.00	30.00	17.50
45	Ray Herbert	50.00	20.00	12.50
46	Norm Cash	17.50	7.00	4.50
47	Steve Boros	35.00	15.00	10.00
48	Dick McAuliffe	7.50	3.00	2.00
49	Bill Bruton	15.00	6.00	3.75
50	Rocky Colavito	25.00	10.00	6.00
51	Al Kaline	30.00	12.00	7.50
52	Dick Brown	35.00	15.00	10.00
53	Jim Bunning	15.00	6.00	3.50
54	Hank Aguirre	7.50	3.00	2.00
55	Frank Lary	40.00	15.00	10.00
56	Don Mossi	40.00	15.00	10.00
57	Jim Gentile	7.50	3.00	2.00
58	Jackie Brandt	7.50	3.00	2.00
59	Brooks Robinson	30.00	12.00	7.50
60	Ron Hansen	7.50	3.00	2.00
61	Jerry Adair	175.00	70.00	45.00
62	John Powell	9.00	3.50	2.25
63	Russ Snyder	35.00	15.00	10.00
64	Steve Barber	7.50	3.00	2.00
65	Milt Pappas	40.00	15.00	10.00
66	Robin Roberts	10.00	4.00	2.50
67	Tito Francona	7.50	3.00	2.00
68	Jerry Kindall	35.00	15.00	10.00
69	Woodie Held	7.50	3.00	2.00
70	Bubba Phillips	7.50	3.00	2.00
71	Chuck Essegian	7.50	3.00	2.00
72	Willie Kirkland	35.00	15.00	10.00
73	Al Luplow	35.00	15.00	10.00
74	Ty Cline	75.00	30.00	17.50
75	Dick Donovan	7.50	3.00	2.00
76	John Romano	7.50	3.00	2.00
77	Pete Runnels	12.50	5.00	3.00
78	Ed Bressoud	100.00	40.00	25.00
79	Frank Malzone	7.50	3.00	2.00
80	Carl Yastrzemski	100.00	40.00	25.00
81	Gary Geiger	7.50	3.00	2.00
82	Lou Clinton	40.00	15.00	10.00
83	Earl Wilson	7.50	3.00	2.00
84	Bill Monbouquette	7.50	3.00	2.00
85	Norm Siebern	7.50	3.00	2.00
86	Jerry Lumpe	9.00	3.50	2.00
87	Manny Jimenez	9.00	3.50	2.25
88	Gino Cimoli	12.50	5.00	3.00
89	Ed Charles	75.00	30.00	17.50
90	Ed Rakow	7.50	3.00	2.00
91	Bob Del Greco	165.00	65.00	40.00
92	Haywood Sullivan	40.00	15.00	10.00
93	Chuck Hinton	7.50	3.00	2.00
94	Ken Retzer	35.00	15.00	10.00
95	Harry Bright	30.00	12.00	7.50
96	Bob Johnson	10.00	4.00	2.50
97	Dave Stenhouse	35.00	15.00	10.00
98	Chuck Cottier	7.50	3.00	2.00
99	Tom Cheney	9.00	3.50	2.00
100	Claude Osteen	75.00	30.00	17.50
101	Orlando Cepeda	15.00	6.00	3.50
102	Charley Hiller	35.00	15.00	10.00
103	Jose Pagan	35.00	15.00	10.00
104	Jim Davenport	7.50	3.00	2.00
105	Harvey Kuenn	7.50	3.00	2.00
106	Willie Mays	50.00	20.00	12.50
107	Felipe Alou	7.50	3.00	2.00
108	Tom Haller	35.00	15.00	10.00
109	Juan Marichal	25.00	10.00	6.00
110	Jack Sanford	12.50	5.00	3.00
111	Bill O'Dell	7.50	3.00	2.00
112	Willie McCovey	100.00	40.00	25.00
113	Lee Walls	35.00	15.00	10.00
114	Jim Gilliam	60.00	25.00	15.00
115	Maury Wills	10.00	4.00	2.50
116	Ron Fairly	7.50	3.00	2.00
117	Tommy Davis	7.50	3.00	2.00
118	Duke Snider	20.00	8.00	5.00
119	Willie Davis	20.00	8.00	5.00
120	John Roseboro	7.50	3.00	2.00
121	Sandy Koufax	50.00	20.00	12.50
122	Stan Williams	30.00	12.00	7.50
123	Don Drysdale	12.50	5.00	3.00
124	Daryl Spencer	7.50	3.00	2.00
125	Gordy Coleman	7.50	3.00	2.00
126	Don Blasingame	50.00	20.00	12.50
127	Leo Cardenas	7.50	3.00	2.00
128	Eddie Kasko	80.00	35.00	20.00
129	Jerry Lynch	7.50	3.00	2.00
130	Vada Pinson	7.50	3.00	2.00
131	Frank Robinson	20.00	8.00	5.00
132	John Edwards	40.00	15.00	10.00
133	Joey Jay	7.50	3.00	2.00
134	Bob Purkey	7.50	3.00	2.00
135	Marty Keough	100.00	40.00	25.00
136	Jim O'Toole	40.00	15.00	10.00
137	Dick Stuart	7.50	3.00	2.00
138	Bill Mazeroski	12.50	5.00	3.00
139	Dick Groat	7.50	3.00	2.00
140	Don Hoak	7.50	3.00	2.00
141	Bob Skinner	12.50	5.00	3.00
142	Bill Virdon	7.50	3.00	2.00
143	Roberto Clemente	100.00	40.00	25.00
144	Smoky Burgess	7.50	3.00	2.00
145	Bob Friend	7.50	3.00	2.00
146	Al McBean	50.00	20.00	12.50
147	ElRoy Face	7.50	3.00	2.00
148	Joe Adcock	7.50	3.00	2.00
149	Frank Bolling	7.50	3.00	2.00
150	Roy McMillan	7.50	3.00	2.00
151	Eddie Mathews	12.50	5.00	3.00
152	Hank Aaron	50.00	20.00	12.50
153	Del Crandall	35.00	15.00	10.00
154	Bob Shaw	7.50	3.00	2.00
155	Lew Burdette	7.50	3.00	2.00
156	Joe Torre	50.00	20.00	12.50
157	Tony Cloninger	200.00	80.00	50.00
158	Bill White	7.50	3.00	2.00
159	Julian Javier	60.00	25.00	15.00
160	Ken Boyer	9.00	3.50	2.00
161	Julio Gotay	75.00	30.00	17.50
162	Curt Flood	25.00	10.00	6.00
163	Charlie James	65.00	25.00	15.00
164	Gene Oliver	50.00	20.00	12.50
165	Ernie Broglio	15.00	6.00	3.50
166	Bob Gibson	125.00	50.00	30.00
167	Lindy McDaniel	35.00	15.00	10.00
168	Ray Washburn	7.50	3.00	2.00
169	Ernie Banks	40.00	15.00	10.00
170	Ron Santo	15.00	6.00	3.50
171	George Altman	7.50	3.00	2.00
172	Billy Williams	100.00	40.00	25.00
173	Andre Rodgers	75.00	30.00	17.50
174	Ken Hubbs	15.00	6.00	3.75
175	Don Landrum	60.00	25.00	15.00
176	Dick Bertell	65.00	25.00	15.00
177	Roy Sievers	7.50	3.00	2.00
178	Tony Taylor	35.00	15.00	10.00
179	John Callison	7.50	3.00	2.00
180	Don Demeter	7.50	3.00	2.00
181	Tony Gonzalez	125.00	50.00	30.00
182	Wes Covington	50.00	20.00	12.50
183	Art Mahaffey	7.50	3.00	2.00
184	Clay Dalrymple	7.50	3.00	2.00
185	Al Spangler	7.50	3.00	2.00
186	Roman Mejias	7.50	3.00	2.00
187	Bob Aspromonte	250.00	100.00	60.00
188	Norm Larker	7.50	3.00	2.00
189	Johnny Temple	7.50	3.00	2.00
190	Carl Warwick	35.00	15.00	10.00
191	Bob Lillis	35.00	15.00	10.00
192	Dick Farrell	150.00	60.00	35.00
193	Gil Hodges	15.00	6.00	3.50
194	Marv Throneberry	7.50	3.00	2.00
195	Charlie Neal	75.00	30.00	17.50
196	Frank Thomas	25.00	10.00	6.00
197	Richie Ashburn	15.00	6.00	3.50
198	Felix Mantilla	60.00	25.00	15.00
199	Rod Kanehl	35.00	15.00	10.00
200	Roger Craig	75.00	30.00	17.50

1969 Jewel Food Chicago Cubs

This set of premium pictures was issued by the midwest regional home-delivery food service. The pictures are 6" x 9" color poses with white borders and blank backs. A facsimile autograph appears on front.

		NM	EX	VG
Complete Set (20):		125.00	65.00	35.00
Common Player:		6.00	3.00	1.80
(1)	Ted Abernathy	6.00	3.00	1.80
(2)	Hank Aguirre	6.00	3.00	1.80
(3)	Ernie Banks	30.00	15.00	9.00
(4)	Glenn Beckert	7.50	3.75	2.25
(5)	Bill Hands	6.00	3.00	1.80
(6)	Jim Hickman	6.00	3.00	1.80
(7)	Kenny Holtzman	6.00	3.00	1.75
(8)	Randy Hundley	7.50	3.75	2.25
(9)	Fergie Jenkins	12.50	6.25	3.75
(10)	Don Kessinger	7.50	3.75	2.25
(11)	Rich Nye	6.00	3.00	1.80
(12)	Paul Popovich	6.00	3.00	1.80
(13)	Jim Qualls	6.00	3.00	1.80
(14)	Phil Regan	6.00	3.00	1.80
(15)	Ron Santo	15.00	7.50	4.50
(16)	Dick Selma	6.00	3.00	1.80
(17)	Willie Smith	6.00	3.00	1.80
(18)	Al Spangler	6.00	3.00	1.80
(19)	Billy Williams	15.00	7.50	4.50
(20)	Don Young	6.00	3.00	1.80

1973 Jewel Food Baseball Photos

Jewel Food Stores, a midwestern grocery chain, issued three team sets of large-format baseball player photos in 1973. The 5-7/8" x 9" blank-back photos are full color and feature a facsimile autograph. Photos were sold in groups of four or five per week at five or ten cents per picture. There are 24 Milwaukee Brewers in the issue, and 16 each Chicago Cubs and Chicago White Sox. The unnumbered cards are alphabetized by team in the checklist below.

		NM	EX	VG
CHICAGO CUBS				
Complete Set (16):		40.00	20.00	12.00
Common Player:		4.00	2.00	1.25
(1)	Jack Aker	4.00	2.00	1.25
(2)	Glenn Beckert	5.00	2.50	1.50
(3)	Jose Cardenal	4.00	2.00	1.25
(4)	Carmen Fanzone	4.00	2.00	1.25
(5)	Burt Hooton	4.00	2.00	1.25
(6)	Fergie Jenkins	10.00	5.00	3.00
(7)	Don Kessinger	5.00	2.50	1.50
(8)	Jim Hickman	4.00	2.00	1.25
(9)	Randy Hundley	5.00	2.50	1.50
(10)	Bob Locker	4.00	2.00	1.25
(11)	Rick Monday	4.00	2.00	1.25
(12)	Milt Pappas	4.00	2.00	1.25
(13)	Rick Reuschel	4.00	2.00	1.25
(14)	Ken Rudolph	4.00	2.00	1.25
(15)	Ron Santo	10.00	5.00	3.00
(16)	Billy Williams	15.00	7.50	4.50
CHICAGO WHITE SOX				
Complete Set (16):		30.00	15.00	9.00
Common Player:		4.00	2.00	1.25
(17)	Dick Allen	7.50	3.75	2.25
(18)	Mike Andrews	4.00	2.00	1.25
(19)	Stan Bahnsen	4.00	2.00	1.25
(20)	Eddie Fisher	4.00	2.00	1.25
(21)	Terry Forster	4.00	2.00	1.25
(22)	Ken Henderson	4.00	2.00	1.25
(23)	Ed Hermann	4.00	2.00	1.25
(24)	John Jeter	4.00	2.00	1.25
(25)	Pat Kelly	4.00	2.00	1.25
(26)	Eddie Leon	4.00	2.00	1.25
(27)	Carlos May	4.00	2.00	1.25
(28)	Bill Melton	4.00	2.00	1.25
(29)	Tony Muser	4.00	2.00	1.25
(30)	Jorge Orta	4.00	2.00	1.25
(31)	Rick Reichardt	4.00	2.00	1.25
(32)	Wilbur Wood	4.00	2.00	1.25
MILWAUKEE BREWERS				
Complete Set (25):		35.00	17.50	10.00
Common Player:		4.00	2.00	1.25
(33)	Jerry Bell	4.00	2.00	1.25
(34)	John Briggs	4.00	2.00	1.25
(35)	Ollie Brown	4.00	2.00	1.25
(36)	Billy Champion	4.00	2.00	1.25
(37)	Jim Colborn	4.00	2.00	1.25
(38)	Bob Coluccio	4.00	2.00	1.25
(39)	John Felske	4.00	2.00	1.25
(40)	Pedro Garcia	4.00	2.00	1.25
(41)	Rob Gardner	4.00	2.00	1.25
(42)	Bob Heise	4.00	2.00	1.25
(43)	Tim Johnson	4.00	2.00	1.25
(44)	Joe Lahoud	4.00	2.00	1.25
(45)	Frank Linzy	4.00	2.00	1.25
(46)	Skip Lockwood	4.00	2.00	1.25
(47)	Dave May	4.00	2.00	1.25
(48)	Bob Mitchell	4.00	2.00	1.25
(49)	Don Money	4.00	2.00	1.25
(50)	Bill Parsons	4.00	2.00	1.25
(51)	Darrell Porter	4.00	2.00	1.25
(52)	Eduardo Rodriguez	4.00	2.00	1.25
(53)	Ellie Rodriguez	4.00	2.00	1.25
(54)	George Scott	5.00	2.50	1.50
(55)	Chris Short	4.00	2.00	1.25
(56)	Jim Slaton	4.00	2.00	1.25
(57)	John Vukovich	4.00	2.00	1.25

1977 Jewel Food Chicago Cubs/ White Sox

Once again in 1977, Jewel grocery stores in the Chicago area offered photos of local players with specific product purchases over a four-week period. The 5-7/8" x 9" color photos are printed on heavy paper. Fronts have player poses, a facsimile signature and the MLB Players Association logo in the upper-left corner. Backs are blank. The pictures are not numbered and are checklisted here alphabetically within team. It was reported 12,000 of each picture were produced.

		NM	EX	VG
Complete Set, Cubs (16):		12.00	6.00	3.50
Complete Set, White Sox (16):		12.00	6.00	3.50
Common Player:		1.50	.70	.45
	CHICAGO CUBS			
(1)	Larry Biittner	1.50	.70	.45
(2)	Bill Bonham	1.50	.70	.45
(3)	Bill Buckner	2.50	1.25	.70
(4)	Ray Burris	1.50	.70	.45
(5)	Jose Cardenal	1.50	.70	.45
(6)	Gene Clines	1.50	.70	.45
(7)	Ivan DeJesus	1.50	.70	.45
(8)	Willie Hernandez	1.50	.70	.45
(9)	Mike Krukow	1.50	.70	.45
(10)	George Mitterwald	1.50	.70	.45
(11)	Jerry Morales	1.50	.70	.45
(12)	Bobby Murcer	2.50	1.25	.70
(13)	Steve Ontiveros	1.50	.70	.45
(14)	Rick Reuschel	1.50	.70	.45
(15)	Bruce Sutter	3.50	1.75	1.00
(16)	Manny Trillo	1.50	.70	.45
	CHICAGO WHITE SOX			
(1)	Alan Bannister	1.50	.70	.45
(2)	Francisco Barrios	1.50	.70	.45
(3)	Jim Essian	1.50	.70	.45
(4)	Oscar Gamble	1.50	.70	.45
(5)	Ralph Garr	1.50	.70	.45
(6)	Lamar Johnson	1.50	.70	.45
(7)	Chris Knapp	1.50	.70	.45
(8)	Ken Kravec	1.50	.70	.45
(9)	Lerrin LaGrow	1.50	.70	.45
(10)	Chet Lemon	1.50	.70	.45
(11)	Jorge Orta	1.50	.70	.45
(12)	Eric Soderholm	1.50	.70	.45
(13)	Jim Spencer	1.50	.70	.45
(14)	Steve Stone	2.50	1.25	.70
(15)	Wilbur Wood	1.50	.70	.45
(16)	Richie Zisk	1.50	.70	.45

1949 Jimmy Fund Boston Braves Die-Cuts

The reigning National League champions undertook the support of the Jimmy Fund, a Boston charity for children's cancer research, with a set of die-cut counter cards accompanying contributions boxes. Between about 6" and 8" at the base, and up to a foot tall, these heavy cardboard pieces feature sepia-toned player action photos in front of a large baseball on which is written, "THANK YOU! in behalf of 'JIMMY.'" with a facsimile signature below. Backs have a fold-out easel to stand the card up, and a notation that following the fund drive, the card should be given to the largest contributor at that location.

		NM	EX	VG
Complete Set (20):		15,000	7,500	4,500
Common Player:		750.00	375.00	225.00
(1)	Johnny Antonelli	750.00	375.00	225.00
(2)	Red Barrett	750.00	375.00	225.00
(3)	Vern Bickford	750.00	375.00	225.00
(4)	Clint Conatser	750.00	375.00	225.00
(5)	Al Dark	750.00	375.00	225.00
(6)	Bob Elliott	750.00	375.00	225.00
(7)	Glenn Elliott	750.00	375.00	225.00
(8)	Bobby Hogue	750.00	375.00	225.00
(9)	Tommy Holmes	750.00	375.00	225.00
(10)	Pete Reiser	750.00	375.00	225.00
(11)	Marv Rickert	750.00	375.00	225.00
(12)	Jim Russell	750.00	375.00	225.00
(13)	Connie Ryan	750.00	375.00	225.00
(14)	Johnny Sain	850.00	425.00	255.00
(15)	Bill Salkeld	750.00	375.00	225.00
(16)	Sibby Sisti	750.00	375.00	225.00
(17)	Warren Spahn	1,200	600.00	360.00
(18)	Don Thompson	750.00	375.00	225.00
(19)	Earl Torgeson	750.00	375.00	225.00
(20)	Bill Voiselle	750.00	375.00	225.00

1978 JJH Reading Remembers

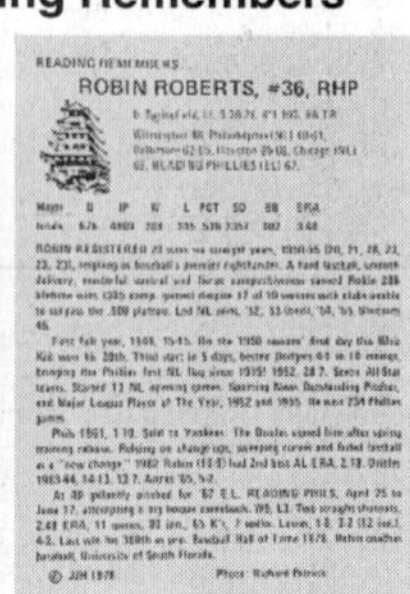

This collectors' issue was created to honor baseball players (and a few others) who were born, lived in or played in Berks County, Pa., particularly in Reading. The cards are 3" x 4" featuring borderless sepia photos on front. Most of the photos picture players in big league uniforms. Backs are in black-and-white and have career stats and summaries. A number of major leaguers who did not have cards contemporary with their careers are found in this set. Cards are numbered by uniform number. Production was reported as 1,000 sets.

		NM	EX	VG
Complete Set (23):		25.00	12.50	7.50
Common Player:		2.00	1.00	.60
1	Whitey Kurowski	2.00	1.00	.60
6	Carl Furillo	5.00	2.50	1.50
9	Roger Maris	10.00	5.00	3.00
12	Stan Wetzel	2.00	1.00	.60
17	Doug Clemens	2.00	1.00	.60
18	Randy Gumpert	2.00	1.00	.60
18	Ty Stofflet (Softball)	2.00	1.00	.60
21	George Eyrich	2.00	1.00	.60
23	Vic Wertz	2.00	1.00	.60
24	Lenny Moore (Football)	2.00	1.00	.60
25	Dick Gernert	2.00	1.00	.60
27	Herb Score	2.00	1.00	.60
27	Charlie Wagner	2.00	1.00	.60
28	Carl Mathias	2.00	1.00	.60
32	Jesse Levan	2.00	1.00	.60
34	Betz Klopp	2.00	1.00	.60
36	Robin Roberts	9.00	4.50	2.75
39	Bob Katz	2.00	1.00	.60
39	Harry Schaeffer	2.00	1.00	.60
40	Tommy Brown (Baseball/Football)	1.50	.70	.45
46	Dom Dallessandro	2.00	1.00	.60
---	Lauer's Park	2.00	1.00	.60
---	John Updike (Author)	2.00	1.00	.60

1950s J.J.K. Copyart Postcards

Issued from about 1950 through at least 1956, this series of glossy black-and-white player postcards appears to have been produced on order of the individual players to respond to fan requests for pictures and/or autographs. Fronts have player poses bordered in white in about 3-1/2" x 5-1/2" format; most have facsimile autographs. Backs have typical postcard layout with a credit line to J.J.K. Copyart Photographers of New York City. Some players are known in more than one pose.

		NM	EX	VG
Common Player:		15.00	7.50	4.50
	BOSTON/MILWAUKEE BRAVES			
(1)	Del Crandall	15.00	7.50	4.50
(2)	Tommy Holmes	15.00	7.50	4.50
(3)	Willard Marshall	15.00	7.50	4.50
(4)	Eddie Mathews	60.00	30.00	18.00
(5)	Eddie Mathews	60.00	30.00	18.00
(6)	Danny O'Connell	15.00	7.50	4.50
(7)	Sibby Sisti	15.00	7.50	4.50
(8)	Eddie Stanky	25.00	12.50	7.50
	BROOKLYN DODGERS			
(1)	Jackie Robinson	200.00	100.00	60.00
	NEW YORK GIANTS			
(1)	Johnny Antonelli	15.00	7.50	4.50
(2)	Johnny Antonelli	15.00	7.50	4.50
(3)	Sam Calderone	15.00	7.50	4.50
(4)	Jim Hearn	15.00	7.50	4.50
(5)	Jim Hearn	15.00	7.50	4.50
(6)	Larry Jansen	15.00	7.50	4.50
(7)	Whitey Lockman	15.00	7.50	4.50
(8)	Whitey Lockman	15.00	7.50	4.50
(9)	Don Mueller	15.00	7.50	4.50
(10)	Bill Rigney	15.00	7.50	4.50
(11)	Bill Rigney	15.00	7.50	4.50
(12)	Hank Sauer	15.00	7.50	4.50
(13)	Red Schoendienst	30.00	15.00	9.00
(14)	Daryl Spencer	15.00	7.50	4.50
(15)	Eddie Stanky	25.00	12.50	7.50
(16)	Wes Westrum	15.00	7.50	4.50
(17)	Wes Westrum	15.00	7.50	4.50
(18)	Hoyt Wilhelm	30.00	15.00	9.00
(19)	Al Worthington	15.00	7.50	4.50
	PHILADELPHIA PHILLIES			
(1)	Del Ennis	15.00	7.50	4.50
(2)	Robin Roberts	30.00	15.00	9.00
(3)	Curt Simmons	15.00	7.50	4.50

1973 Johnny Pro Orioles

This regional set of large (4-1/4" x 7-1/4") die-cut cards was issued by Johnny Pro Enterprises Inc. of Baltimore and features only Orioles. The cards were designed to be punched out and folded to make baseball player figures that can stand up. The full-color die-cut figures appear against a green background. The cards are numbered according to the player's uniform number, which appears in a white box along with his name and position. The backs are blank. Three players (Robinson, Grich, and Palmer) appear in two poses each, and cards of Orlando Pena were not die-cut. Values listed are for complete cards not punched out. Cards originally sold for 15 cents apiece.

		NM	EX	VG
Complete Set (28):		135.00	65.00	40.00
Common Player:		3.00	1.50	.90
1	Al Bumbry	3.00	1.50	.90
2	Rich Coggins	3.00	1.50	.90
3a	Bobby Grich/Btg	5.00	2.50	1.50
3b	Bobby Grich/Fldg	5.00	2.50	1.50
4	Earl Weaver	6.00	3.00	1.75
5a	Brooks Robinson/Btg	25.00	12.50	7.50
5b	Brooks Robinson/Fldg	25.00	12.50	7.50
6	Paul Blair	4.00	2.00	1.25
7	Mark Belanger	4.00	2.00	1.25
8	Andy Etchebarren	3.00	1.50	.90
10	Elrod Hendricks	3.00	1.50	.90
11	Terry Crowley	3.00	1.50	.90
12	Tommy Davis	4.00	2.00	1.25
13	Doyle Alexander	3.00	1.50	.90
14	Merv Rettenmund	3.00	1.50	.90
15	Frank Baker	3.00	1.50	.90
19	Dave McNally	4.00	2.00	1.25
21	Larry Brown	3.00	1.50	.90
22a	Jim Palmer (Follow-through.)	15.00	7.50	4.50
22b	Jim Palmer (Wind-up)	15.00	7.50	4.50
23	Grant Jackson	3.00	1.50	.90
25	Don Baylor	6.00	3.00	1.75
26	Boog Powell	7.00	3.50	2.00
27	Orlando Pena	8.00	4.00	2.50
32	Earl Williams	3.00	1.50	.90
34	Bob Reynolds	3.00	1.50	.90
35	Mike Cuellar	5.00	2.50	1.50
39	Eddie Watt	3.00	1.50	.90

1974 Johnny Pro Phillies

Although slightly smaller (3-3/4" x 7-1/8") and featuring members of the Phillies, this set is very similar to the 1973 Johnny Pro Orioles set. The full-color die-cut player figures are set against a white background. Again, the set is numbered according to the player's uniform number. The values listed are for complete cards.

		NM	EX	VG
Complete Set (12):		150.00	75.00	45.00
Common Player:		3.00	1.50	.90
8	Bob Boone	7.50	3.75	2.25
10	Larry Bowa	7.50	3.75	2.25
16	Dave Cash	3.00	1.50	.90
19	Greg Luzinski	5.00	2.50	1.50
20	Mike Schmidt	100.00	50.00	30.00
22	Mike Anderson	3.00	1.50	.90
24	Bill Robinson	3.00	1.50	.90
25	Del Unser	3.00	1.50	.90
27	Willie Montanez	3.00	1.50	.90
32	Steve Carlton	25.00	12.50	7.50
37	Ron Schueler	3.00	1.50	.90
41	Jim Lonborg	3.00	1.50	.90

1922 Henry A. Johnson Wholesale Confectioner

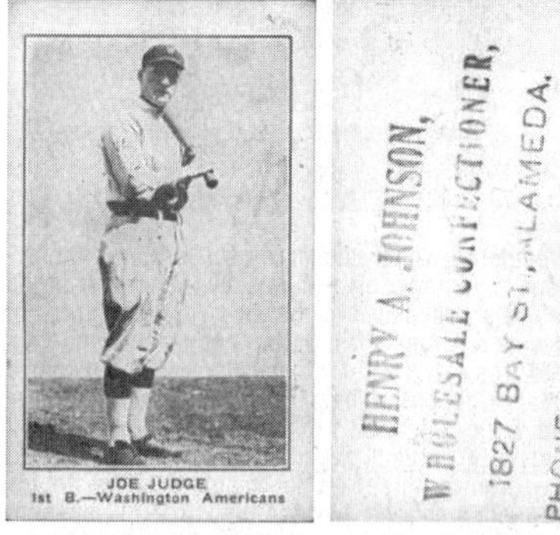

To compete with other candy issues featuring baseball cards as premiums, Alameda, Calif., confectioner Henry A. Johnson purchased uncut sheets of the blank-back strip cards known as W575-1, overprinted their backs and packaged them with his Likem brand candy bars. The advertising on back gives the firm's name, address and telephone number. Collectors can expect to pay a premium of about 3X for this version. Only the type style shown here can definitely be traced to the 1920s. Other styles of typography are known to have been applied in the 1980s and later.

	NM	EX	VG
Common Player:	85.00	42.50	25.00
Stars: 2-3X			

(See W575-1 for checklist and base card values.)

1953 Johnston Cookies Braves

The first and most common of three annual issues, the '53 Johnstons were inserted into boxes of cookies on a regional basis. Complete sets were also available via a mail-in offer from the company, whose factory sits in the shadow of Milwaukee County Stadium. While at first glance appearing to be color photos, the pictures on the 25 cards in the

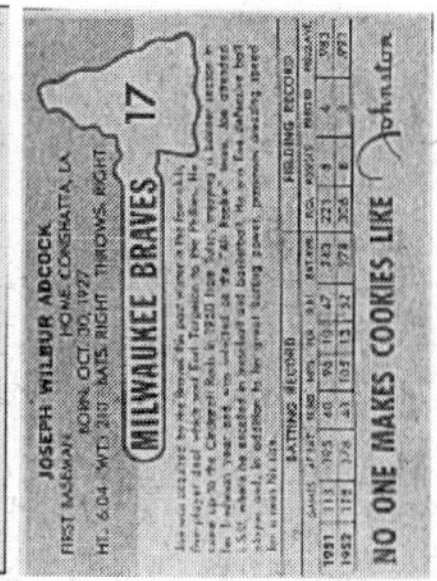

set are actually well-done colorizations of black-and-white photos. Cards measure 2-9/16" x 3-5/8". Write-ups on the backs were "borrowed" from the Braves' 1953 yearbook.

		NM	EX	VG
Complete Set (25):		500.00	250.00	150.00
Common Player:		15.00	7.50	4.50
1	Charlie Grimm	15.00	7.50	4.50
2	John Antonelli	15.00	7.50	4.50
3	Vern Bickford	15.00	7.50	4.50
4	Bob Buhl	15.00	7.50	4.50
5	Lew Burdette	15.00	7.50	4.50
6	Dave Cole	15.00	7.50	4.50
7	Ernie Johnson	15.00	7.50	4.50
8	Dave Jolly	15.00	7.50	4.50
9	Don Liddle	15.00	7.50	4.50
10	Warren Spahn	150.00	75.00	45.00
11	Max Surkont	15.00	7.50	4.50
12	Jim Wilson	15.00	7.50	4.50
13	Sibby Sisti	15.00	7.50	4.50
14	Walker Cooper	15.00	7.50	4.50
15	Del Crandall	15.00	7.50	4.50
16	Ebba St. Claire	15.00	7.50	4.50
17	Joe Adcock	15.00	7.50	4.50
18	George Crowe	15.00	7.50	4.50
19	Jack Dittmer	15.00	7.50	4.50
20	Johnny Logan	15.00	7.50	4.50
21	Ed Mathews	150.00	75.00	45.00
22	Bill Bruton	15.00	7.50	4.50
23	Sid Gordon	15.00	7.50	4.50
24	Andy Pafko	15.00	7.50	4.50
25	Jim Pendleton	15.00	7.50	4.50

1954 Johnston Cookies Braves

In its second of three annual issues, Johnston's increased the number of cards in its 1954 Braves issue to 35, and switched to an unusual size, a narrow format, 2" x 3-7/8". Cards are listed here by uniform number. After his early-season injury (which gave Hank Aaron a chance to play regularly), Bobby Thomson's card was withdrawn, accounting for its scarcity and high value. Uncut sheets of 42 cards (including seven double-prints) in a size of about 12-1/2" x 27-3/4" are not uncommon. A 21-1/2" x 31" wall-hanging display poster with die-cuts into which cards could be inserted was available as a premium offer.

		NM	EX	VG
Complete Set (35):		1,500	750.00	450.00
Common Player:		20.00	10.00	6.00
Uncut Sheet:		4,750	2,400	1,400
Display Poster:		500.00	250.00	150.00
1	Del Crandall	20.00	10.00	6.00
3	Jim Pendleton	20.00	10.00	6.00
4	Danny O'Connell	20.00	10.00	6.00
5	Henry Aaron	750.00	375.00	225.00
6	Jack Dittmer	20.00	10.00	6.00
9	Joe Adcock	20.00	10.00	6.00
10	Robert Buhl	20.00	10.00	6.00
11	Phillip Paine/DP (Phillips)	20.00	10.00	6.00
12	Ben Johnson	20.00	10.00	6.00
13	Sibby Sisti	20.00	10.00	6.00
15	Charles Gorin	20.00	10.00	6.00
16	Chet Nichols	20.00	10.00	6.00
17	Dave Jolly/DP	20.00	10.00	6.00
19	Jim Wilson/DP	20.00	10.00	6.00
20	Ray Crone	20.00	10.00	6.00
21	Warren Spahn/DP	100.00	50.00	30.00
22	Gene Conley	20.00	10.00	6.00
23	Johnny Logan/DP	20.00	10.00	6.00

24	Charlie White	20.00	10.00	6.00
27	George Metkovich	20.00	10.00	6.00
28	John Cooney	20.00	10.00	6.00
29	Paul Burris	20.00	10.00	6.00
31	Wm. Walters/DP	20.00	10.00	6.00
32	Ernest T. Johnson	20.00	10.00	6.00
33	Lew Burdette	20.00	10.00	6.00
34	Bob Thomson/SP	165.00	80.00	50.00
35	Robert Keely	20.00	10.00	6.00
38	Billy Bruton	20.00	10.00	6.00
40	Charles Grimm	20.00	10.00	6.00
41	Ed Mathews	100.00	50.00	30.00
42	Sam Calderone/DP	20.00	10.00	6.00
47	Joey Jay	20.00	10.00	6.00
48	Andy Pafko	20.00	10.00	6.00
---	Dr. Charles Lacks (Asst. trainer.)	20.00	10.00	6.00
---	Joseph F. Taylor (Asst. trainer.)	20.00	10.00	6.00

1955 Johnston Cookies Braves

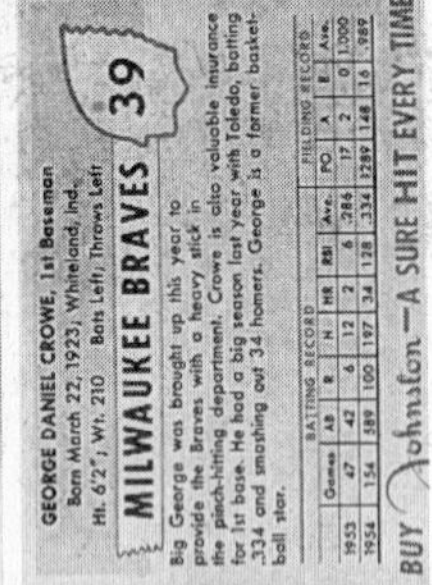

A third change in size and format was undertaken in the final year of Braves sets produced by Johnston's. The 35 cards in the 1955 set were issued in six fold-out panels of six cards each (Andy Pafko was double-printed). As in 1954, cards are numbered by uniform number, except those of the team equipment manager, trainer and road secretary (former Boston star Duffy Lewis). Single cards measure 2-7/8" x 4". Besides including panels in boxes of cookies, the '55 Johnstons could be ordered for five cents per panel by mail. The scarcest of the Johnston's issues, the 1955 set can be found today still in complete panels, or as single cards.

		NM	EX	VG
Complete Folder Set (6):		1,250	625.00	375.00
Complete Singles Set (35):		1,500	750.00	450.00
Common Player:		30.00	20.00	12.00
Common Folder:		200.00	100.00	60.00
1	Del Crandall	30.00	20.00	12.00
3	Jim Pendleton	30.00	20.00	12.00
4	Danny O'Connell	30.00	20.00	12.00
6	Jack Dittmer	30.00	20.00	12.00
9	Joe Adcock	30.00	20.00	12.00
10	Bob Buhl	30.00	20.00	12.00
11	Phil Paine	30.00	20.00	12.00
12	Ray Crone	30.00	20.00	12.00
15	Charlie Gorin	30.00	20.00	12.00
16	Dave Jolly	30.00	20.00	12.00
17	Chet Nichols	30.00	20.00	12.00
18	Chuck Tanner	30.00	20.00	12.00
19	Jim Wilson	30.00	20.00	12.00
20	Dave Koslo	30.00	20.00	12.00
21	Warren Spahn	100.00	50.00	30.00
22	Gene Conley	30.00	20.00	12.00
23	John Logan	30.00	20.00	12.00
24	Charlie White	30.00	20.00	12.00
28	Johnny Cooney	30.00	20.00	12.00
30	Roy Smalley	30.00	20.00	12.00
31	Bucky Walters	30.00	20.00	12.00
32	Ernie Johnson	30.00	20.00	12.00
33	Lew Burdette	30.00	20.00	12.00
34	Bobby Thomson	35.00	17.50	10.50
35	Bob Keely	30.00	20.00	12.00
38	Billy Bruton	30.00	20.00	12.00
39	George Crowe	30.00	20.00	12.00
40	Charlie Grimm	30.00	20.00	12.00
41	Eddie Mathews	100.00	50.00	30.00
44	Hank Aaron	450.00	225.00	135.00
47	Joe Jay	30.00	20.00	12.00
48	Andy Pakfo	30.00	20.00	12.00
----	Dr. Charles K. Lacks	30.00	20.00	12.00
---	Duffy Lewis	30.00	20.00	12.00
---	Joe Taylor	30.00	20.00	12.00

	NM	EX	VG
Series 1 Folder Hank Aaron, Lew Burdette, Del Crandall, Charlie Gorin, Bob Keely, Danny O'Connell	475.00	240.00	140.00
Series 2 Folder Joe Adcock, Joe Jay, Dr. Charles K. Lacks, Chet Nichols, Andy Pafko, Charlie White	160.00	80.00	45.00
Series 3 Folder Gene Conley, George Crowe, Jim Pendleton, Roy Smalley, Warren Spahn, Joe Taylor	175.00	90.00	50.00
Series 4 Folder Billy Bruton, John Cooney, Dave Jolly, Dave Koslo, Johnny Logan, Andy Pafko	160.00	80.00	45.00
Series 5 Folder Ray Crone, Ernie Johnson, Duffy Lewis, Eddie Mathews, Phil Paine, Chuck Tanner	190.00	95.00	55.00
Series 6 Folder Bob Buhl, Jack Dittmer, Charlie Grimm, Bobby Thomson, Bucky Walters, Jim Wilson	160.00	80.00	45.00

1976 Jerry Jonas Productions All Time Greats

This card set was produced only in prototype form with an estimated 50 of each printed. The cards were designed to introduce a baseball card promotion to team executives at their annual World Series meeting. The 2-3/4" x 3-3/4" cards have black-and-white player photos at center with colored borders reminiscent of the 1975 Topps cards. Backs are printed in black on blue and feature biographical data, career highlights and stats along with a credit line to Jerry Jones Productions. The proposed promotion was never adopted. The unnumbered cards are checklisted here in alphabetical order.

		NM	EX	VG
Complete Set, Uncut Sheet:		450.00	225.00	135.00
Complete Set, Singles (8):		450.00	225.00	135.00
Common Player:		30.00	15.00	9.00
(1)	Grover Alexander	30.00	15.00	9.00
(2)	Rogers Hornsby	30.00	15.00	9.00
(3)	Sandy Koufax	150.00	75.00	45.00
(4)	Willie Mays	100.00	50.00	30.00
(5)	Stan Musial	50.00	25.00	15.00
(6)	Mel Ott	30.00	15.00	9.00
(7)	Robin Roberts	30.00	15.00	9.00
(8)	Honus Wagner	30.00	15.00	9.00

1911 Jones, Keyser & Arras Cabinets

Contemporary with the better-known Sporting Life, Turkey Red and Pinkerton cabinet photos, this series of baseball player cabinets was issued by the New York City studio of Jones, Keyser & Arras, whose address appears on the back of the card. The 4-1/2" x 7-1/4" cabinets have photos glued to stiff gray cardboard mounts. Both photo and mount are numbered within the known range of 301-349, making it likely there are 50 baseball players in the series. Most known subjects are from the three New York teams of the era. Photos carry at bottom a stylized J, K & A logo, a 1911 copyright and a number. That number is repeated in the bottom border of the mount, along with the player's last name and the team/league. Several photos are known which have been removed from the mount, making identification difficult.

		NM	EX	VG
Common Player:		2,400	1,200	720.00
301	Russ Ford	2,400	1,200	720.00
303	John Warhop	2,400	1,200	720.00
304	Bill Dahlen	2,400	1,200	720.00
306	Zack Wheat	4,000	2,000	1,200
307	Al Bridwell	2,400	1,200	720.00
308	Red Murray	2,400	1,200	720.00
310	Fred Snodgrass	2,400	1,200	720.00
311	Red Ames	2,400	1,200	720.00
312	Fred Merkle	2,400	1,200	720.00
313	Art Devlin	2,400	1,200	720.00
314	Hooks Wiltse	2,400	1,200	720.00
315	Josh Devore	2,400	120.00	720.00
316	Eddie Collins	4,000	2,000	1,200
317	Ed Reulbach	2,400	1,200	720.00
318	Jimmy Scheckard (Sheckard)	2,400	120.00	720.00
320	Frank Schulte	2,400	1,200	720.00
321	Solly Hofman	2,400	1,200	720.00
322	Bill Bergen	2,400	1,200	720.00
323	George Bell	2,400	1,200	720.00
324	Nap Rucker	2,400	120.00	720.00
325	Fred Clarke	4,000	2,000	1,200
326	Clark Griffith, Mgr.	4,000	2,000	1,200
327	Roger Bresnahan	4,000	2,000	1,200
328	Fred Tenney	2,400	1,200	720.00
329	Harry Lord	2,400	1,200	720.00
331	Walter Johnson	12,000	6,000	3,600
332	Nap Lajoie	4,000	2,000	1,200
333	Joe Tinker	4,000	2,000	1,200
334	Mordecai Brown	4,000	2,000	1,200
336	Jimmy Archer	2,400	1,200	720.00
338	Nixey Callahan	2,400	1,200	720.00
340	Hal Chase	3,500	1,750	1,050
341	Larry Doyle	2,400	1,200	720.00
342	Chief Meyers	2,400	1,200	720.00
343	Christy Mathewson	12,000	6,000	3,600
344	Bugs Raymond	2,400	1,200	720.00
345	John J. McGraw, Mgr.	4,000	2,000	1,200
346	Honus Wagner	15,000	7,500	4,500
347	Ty Cobb	25,000	12,500	7,500
348	Johnny Evers	4,000	2,000	1,200
349	Frank Chance	4,000	2,000	1,200

1863 Jordan & Co.

Because this card pictures a ballplayer on front with advertising on back, it has been described as the world's first baseball card. The 2-7/16" x 4-1/16" card doubled as a ticket to a benefit (to the players!) series of matches between New York and Brooklyn teams and all-stars at Hoboken, N.J., in Sept., 1863. The ticket cards were sold for 50 cents apiece, twice the cost of regular admission. According to surviving records, photos of four different players were used on the tickets.

(1) William Crossley (Ball in hands at chest.) (1/08 auction, $7,100)
(2) William Hammond (12/04 auction, $19,364)
(3) Sam Wright (Unknown)
(4) Harry Wright (Clipped-corners, 7/00 auction, $83,545.)

1931 Josetti Tobacco

This is one of several early 1930s German cigarette cards to picture Babe Ruth. In this case he is pictured on the 1-5/8" x 2-3/8" black-and-white card with American comedic actor Harold Lloyd. The card is part of a numbered set of 272 movie star cards. Backs are printed in German. The card can be found with Ruth's first name printed as George or as Babe.

		NM	EX	VG
151a	George Ruth, Harold Lloyd	450.00	225.00	135.00
151b	Babe Ruth, Harold Lloyd	450.00	225.00	135.00

1910 Ju-Ju Drums (E286)

Issued in 1910 with Ju Ju Drum Candy, this extremely rare set of circular baseball cards is very similar in design to the more common Colgan's Chips cards. About the size of a silver dollar (1-7/16" in diameter) the cards display a player photo on the front with the player's name and team printed below in a semi-circle design. The backs carry advertising for Ju-Ju Drums. The checklist contains 45 different players to date, but the issue - known as E286 in the American Card Catalog - is so rare that others are likely to exist.

		NM	EX	VG
Complete Set (45):		40,000	16,000	8,000
Common Player:		750.00	300.00	175.00
(1)	Eddie Ainsmith	750.00	300.00	175.00
(2)	Jimmy Austin	750.00	300.00	175.00
(3)	Chief Bender	1,500	600.00	360.00
(4)	Bob Bescher	750.00	300.00	175.00
(5)	Bruno Bloch (Block)	750.00	300.00	175.00
(6)	Frank Burke	750.00	300.00	175.00
(7)	Donie Bush	750.00	300.00	175.00
(8)	Frank Chance	1,500	600.00	360.00
(9)	Harry Cheek	750.00	300.00	175.00
(10)	Ed Cicotte	1,500	600.00	360.00
(11)	Ty Cobb	6,500	2,600	1,550
(12)	King Cole	750.00	300.00	175.00
(13)	Jack Coombs	750.00	300.00	175.00
(14)	Bill Dahlen	750.00	300.00	175.00
(15)	Bert Daniels	750.00	300.00	175.00
(16)	Harry Davis	750.00	300.00	175.00
(17)	Larry Doyle	750.00	300.00	175.00
(18)	Rube Ellis	750.00	300.00	175.00
(19)	Cecil Ferguson	750.00	300.00	175.00
(20)	Russ Ford	750.00	300.00	175.00
(21)	Bob Harnion (Harmon)	750.00	300.00	175.00
(22)	Ham Hyatt	750.00	300.00	175.00
(23)	Red Kellifer (Killifer)	750.00	300.00	175.00
(24)	Art Kruger (Krueger)	750.00	300.00	175.00
(25)	Tommy Leach	750.00	300.00	175.00
(26)	Harry Lumley	750.00	300.00	175.00
(27)	Christy Mathewson	3,500	1,400	840.00
(28)	John McGraw	1,500	600.00	360.00
(29)	Deacon McGuire	750.00	300.00	175.00
(30)	Chief Meyers	750.00	300.00	175.00
(31)	Otto Miller	750.00	300.00	175.00
(32)	Charlie Mullen	750.00	300.00	175.00
(33)	Tom Needham	750.00	300.00	175.00
(34)	Rube Oldring	750.00	300.00	175.00
(35)	Barney Pelty	750.00	300.00	175.00
(36)	Ed Reulbach	750.00	300.00	175.00
(37)	Jack Rowan	750.00	300.00	175.00
(38)	Dave Shean	750.00	300.00	175.00
(39)	Tris Speaker	2,000	800.00	480.00
(40)	Ed Sweeney	750.00	300.00	175.00
(41)	Honus Wagner	4,500	1,800	1,075
(42)	Jimmy Walsh	750.00	300.00	175.00
(43)	Kirby White	750.00	300.00	175.00
(44)	Ralph Works	750.00	300.00	175.00
(45)	Elmer Zacher	750.00	300.00	175.00

1893 Just So Tobacco

This set is so rare that only a dozen or so examples are known, although it is possible others remain to be reported. The set features only members of the Cleveland club, known then as the "Spiders." Measuring 2-1/2" x 3-7/8", these sepia-colored cards were printed on heavy paper. The player appears in a portrait photo with his name beneath and an ad for Just So Tobacco at bottom. The existence of this set wasn't even established until the 1960s, and for 15 years only two subjects were known. In 1981 and 1989 several more cards were discovered. To date only one or two copies of each of the known cards have turned up in collectors' hands, making it among the rarest of all baseball card issues.

		NM	EX	VG
Common Player:			30,000	19,000
(1)	F.W. Boyd		30,000	19,000
(2)	Burkette (Jesse Burkett) (Unique. Trimmed and restored. Value undetermined.)			
(3)	C.L. Childs ("Cupid")		30,000	19,000
(4)	John Clarkson		100,000	18,000
(5)	J.O. Connor (John O'Connor)		30,000	19,000
(6)	G. Cuppy		30,000	19,000
(7)	G.W. Davies		30,000	19,000
(8)	C.M. Hastings		30,000	19,000
(9)	E.J. McKean		30,000	19,000
(10)	CAPt Tebeau ("Patsy")		30,000	19,000
(11)	J.K. Virtue		30,000	19,000
(12)	T.C. Williams		30,000	19,000
(13)	D.T. Young (Cy)(Unique. Value undetermined.)			
(14)	C.L. Zimmer ("Chief")		30,000	19,000

1950s Kabaya Caramel Babe Ruth

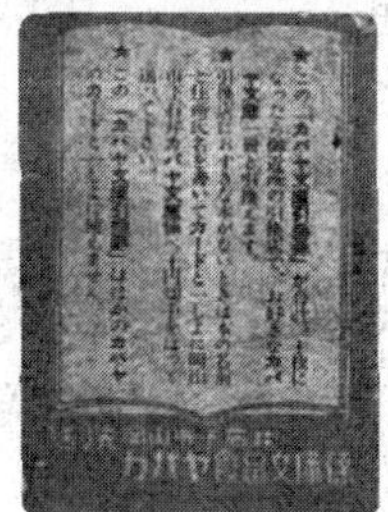

This card was part of a series produced by an Okayama, Japan candy company. The card measures about 1-1/2" x 2-1/8" with color artwork of Ruth on front. On back is Japanese script within the design of an open book.

	NM	EX	VG
Babe Ruth	1,200	600.00	350.00

1955 Kahn's Wieners Reds

The first of what would become 15 successive years of baseball card issues by the Kahn's meat company of Cincinnati is also the rarest. The set consists of six Cincinnati Redlegs player cards, 3-1/4" x 4". Printed in black and white, with blank backs, the '55 Kahn's cards were distributed at a one-day promotional event at a Cincinnati amusement park, where the featured players were on hand to sign autographs. Like the other Kahn's issues through 1963, the '55 cards have a 1/2" white panel containing an advertising message below the player photo. These cards are sometimes found with this portion cut off, greatly reducing the value of the card.

		NM	EX	VG
Complete Set (6):		6,500	3,250	2,000
Common Player:		1,000	500.00	300.00
(1)	Gus Bell	1,250	625.00	375.00
(2)	Ted Kluszewski	1,450	725.00	435.00
(3)	Roy McMillan	1,000	500.00	300.00
(4)	Joe Nuxhall	1,000	500.00	300.00
(5)	Wally Post	1,000	500.00	300.00
(6)	Johnny Temple	1,000	500.00	300.00

1956 Kahn's Wieners Reds

In 1956, Kahn's expanded its baseball card program to include 15 Redlegs players, and began issuing the cards one per pack in packages of hot dogs. Because the cards were packaged in direct contact with the meat, they are often found today in stained condition. In 3-1/4" x 4" format, black and white with blank backs, the '56 Kahn's cards can be distinguished from later issues by the presence of full stadium photographic backgrounds behind the player photos. Like all Kahn's issues, the 1956 set is unnumbered; the checklists are arranged alphabetically for convenience. The set features the first-ever baseball card of Hall of Famer Frank Robinson.

		NM	EX	VG
Complete Set (15):		3,250	1,625	1,000
Common Player:		150.00	75.00	45.00
(1)	Ed Bailey	150.00	75.00	45.00
(2)	Gus Bell	175.00	90.00	55.00
(3)	Joe Black	225.00	110.00	65.00
(4)	"Smoky" Burgess	200.00	100.00	60.00
(5)	Art Fowler	150.00	75.00	45.00
(6)	Hershell Freeman	150.00	75.00	45.00
(7)	Ray Jablonski	150.00	75.00	45.00
(8)	John Klippstein	150.00	75.00	45.00
(9)	Ted Kluszewski	365.00	180.00	110.00
(10)	Brooks Lawrence	150.00	75.00	45.00
(11)	Roy McMillan	150.00	75.00	45.00
(12)	Joe Nuxhall	150.00	75.00	45.00
(13)	Wally Post	150.00	75.00	45.00
(14)	Frank Robinson	1,000	500.00	300.00
(15)	Johnny Temple	150.00	75.00	45.00

1957 Kahn's Wieners

In its third season of baseball card issue, Kahn's kept the basic 3-1/4" x 4" format, with black-and-white photos and blank backs. The issue was expanded to 28 players, all Pirates or Reds. The last of the blank-backed Kahn's sets until 1966, the 1957 Reds players can be distinguished from the 1956 issue by the general lack of background photo detail, in favor of a neutral light gray background. The Dick Groat card appears with two name variations, a facsimile autograph, "Richard Groat," and a printed "Dick Groat." Both Groat varieties are included in the complete set price.

		NM	EX	VG
Complete Set (29):		4,000	2,000	1,200
Common Player:		80.00	40.00	24.00
(1)	Tom Acker	80.00	40.00	24.00
(2)	Ed Bailey	80.00	40.00	24.00
(3)	Gus Bell	100.00	50.00	30.00
(4)	Smoky Burgess	100.00	50.00	30.00
(5)	Roberto Clemente	1,250	625.00	375.00
(6)	George Crowe	80.00	40.00	24.00
(7)	Elroy Face	80.00	40.00	24.00
(8)	Hershell Freeman	80.00	40.00	24.00
(9)	Robert Friend	80.00	40.00	24.00
(10a)	Dick Groat	190.00	95.00	55.00
(10b)	Richard Groat	190.00	95.00	55.00
(11)	Don Gross	80.00	40.00	24.00
(12)	Warren Hacker	80.00	40.00	24.00
(13)	Don Hoak	80.00	40.00	24.00
(14)	Hal Jeffcoat	80.00	40.00	24.00
(15)	Ron Kline	80.00	40.00	24.00
(16)	John Klippstein	80.00	40.00	24.00
(17)	Ted Kluszewski	225.00	110.00	65.00
(18)	Brooks Lawrence	80.00	40.00	24.00
(19)	Dale Long	80.00	40.00	24.00
(20)	Bill Mazeroski	325.00	160.00	95.00
(21)	Roy McMillan	80.00	40.00	24.00
(22)	Joe Nuxhall	80.00	40.00	24.00
(23)	Wally Post	80.00	40.00	24.00
(24)	Frank Robinson	300.00	150.00	90.00
(25)	Johnny Temple	80.00	40.00	24.00
(26)	Frank Thomas	80.00	40.00	24.00
(27)	Bob Thurman	80.00	40.00	24.00
(28)	Lee Walls	80.00	40.00	24.00

1958 Kahn's Wieners

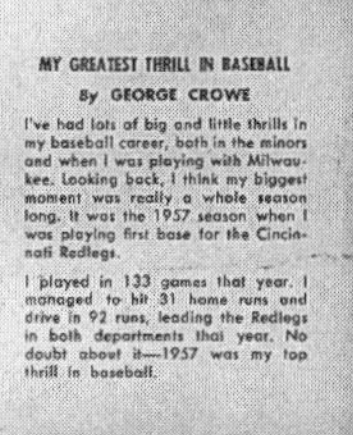

MY GREATEST THRILL IN BASEBALL

By GEORGE CROWE

I've had lots of big and little thrills in my baseball career, both in the minors and when I was playing with Milwaukee. Looking back, I think my biggest moment was really a whole season long. It was the 1957 season when I was playing first base for the Cincinnati Redlegs.

I played in 133 games that year. I managed to hit 31 home runs and drive in 92 runs, leading the Redlegs in both departments that year. No doubt about it—1957 was my top thrill in baseball.

Long-time Cincinnati favorite Wally Post became the only Philadelphia Phillies ballplayer to appear in the 15-year run of Kahn's issues when he was traded in 1958, but included as part of the otherwise exclusively Pirates-Reds set. Like previous years, the '58 Kahn's were 3-1/4" x 4", with black and white player photos. Unlike previous years, however, the cards had printing on the back, a story by the pictured player, titled "My Greatest Thrill in Baseball." Quite similar to the 1959 issue, the '58 Kahn's can be distinguished by the fact that the top line of the advertising panel at bottom has the word "Wieners" in 1958, but not in 1959. Several of cards in the set appear to have been short-printed.

	NM	EX	VG
Complete Set (29):	4,500	2,250	1,350
Common Player:	100.00	50.00	30.00
(1) Ed Bailey	100.00	50.00	30.00
(2) Gene Baker	100.00	50.00	30.00
(3) Gus Bell	110.00	55.00	35.00
(4) Smoky Burgess	110.00	55.00	35.00
(5) Roberto Clemente	900.00	450.00	275.00
(6) George Crowe	100.00	50.00	30.00
(7) Elroy Face	100.00	50.00	30.00
(8) Henry Foiles	100.00	50.00	30.00
(9) Dee Fondy	100.00	50.00	30.00
(10) Robert Friend	100.00	50.00	30.00
(11) Richard Groat	110.00	55.00	35.00
(12) Harvey Haddix	100.00	50.00	30.00
(13) Don Hoak	110.00	55.00	35.00
(14) Hal Jeffcoat	110.00	55.00	35.00
(15) Ronald L. Kline	110.00	55.00	35.00
(16) Ted Kluszewski	200.00	100.00	60.00
(17) Vernon Law	100.00	50.00	30.00
(18) Brooks Lawrence	100.00	50.00	30.00
(19) Bill Mazeroski	300.00	150.00	90.00
(20) Roy McMillan	100.00	50.00	30.00
(21) Joe Nuxhall	100.00	50.00	30.00
(22) Wally Post	300.00	150.00	90.00
(23) John Powers	100.00	50.00	30.00
(24) Robert T. Purkey	100.00	50.00	30.00
(25) Charles Rabe	300.00	150.00	90.00
(26) Frank Robinson	600.00	300.00	180.00
(27) Robert Skinner	100.00	50.00	30.00
(28) Johnny Temple	100.00	50.00	30.00
(29) Frank Thomas	300.00	150.00	90.00

1959 Kahn's Wieners

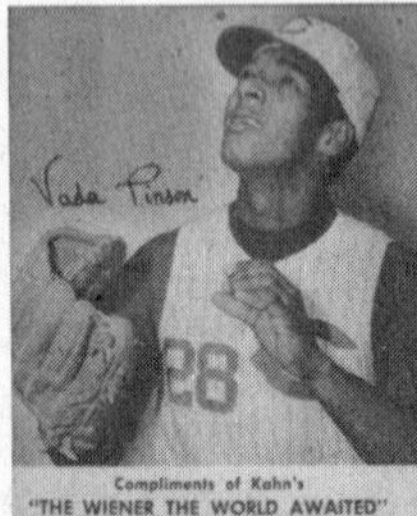

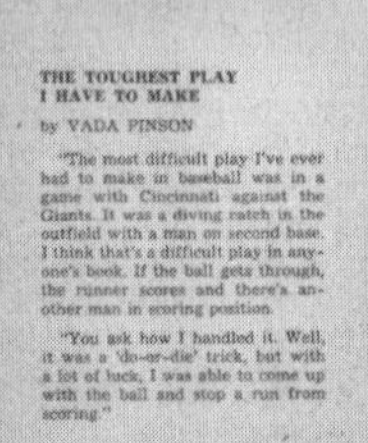

A third team was added to the Kahn's lineup in 1959, the Cleveland Indians joining the Pirates and Reds. Again printed in black-and-white in the 3-1/4" x 4" size, the 1959 Kahn's cards can be differentiated from the previous issue by the lack of the word "Wieners" on the top line of the advertising panel at bottom. Backs again featured a story written by the pictured player, such as "The Toughest Play I Had to Make," "My Most Difficult Moment in Baseball," etc. A number of the cards were short-printed.

	NM	EX	VG
Complete Set (38):	6,000	3,000	1,800
Common Player:	75.00	37.50	22.50
(1) Ed Bailey	75.00	37.50	22.50
(2) Gary Bell	75.00	37.50	22.50
(3) Gus Bell	75.00	37.50	22.50
(4) Richard Brodowski	500.00	250.00	150.00
(5) Forrest Burgess	75.00	37.50	22.50
(6) Roberto Clemente	850.00	425.00	255.00
(7) Rocky Colavito	325.00	160.00	100.00
(8) ElRoy Face	75.00	37.50	22.50
(9) Robert Friend	75.00	37.50	22.50
(10) Joe Gordon	75.00	37.50	22.50
(11) Jim Grant	75.00	37.50	22.50
(12) Richard M. Groat	90.00	45.00	27.00
(13) Harvey Haddix	450.00	225.00	135.00
(14) Woodie Held	450.00	225.00	135.00
(15) Don Hoak	75.00	37.50	22.50
(16) Ronald Kline	75.00	37.50	22.50
(17) Ted Kluszewski	200.00	100.00	60.00
(18) Vernon Law	75.00	37.50	22.50
(19) Jerry Lynch	75.00	37.50	22.50
(20) Billy Martin	115.00	55.00	35.00
(21) Bill Mazeroski	250.00	125.00	75.00
(22) Cal McLish	450.00	225.00	135.00
(23) Roy McMillan	75.00	37.50	22.50
(24) Minnie Minoso	80.00	40.00	24.00
(25) Russell Nixon	75.00	37.50	22.50
(26) Joe Nuxhall	75.00	37.50	22.50
(27) Jim Perry	75.00	37.50	22.50
(28) Vada Pinson	200.00	100.00	60.00
(29) Vic Power	75.00	37.50	22.50
(30) Robert Purkey	75.00	37.50	22.50
(31) Frank Robinson	235.00	120.00	75.00
(32) Herb Score	75.00	37.50	22.50
(33) Robert Skinner	75.00	37.50	22.50
(34) George Strickland	275.00	135.00	85.00
(35) Richard L. Stuart	75.00	37.50	22.50
(36) John Temple	75.00	37.50	22.50
(37) Frank Thomas	75.00	37.50	22.50
(38) George A. Witt	75.00	37.50	22.50

1960 Kahn's Wieners

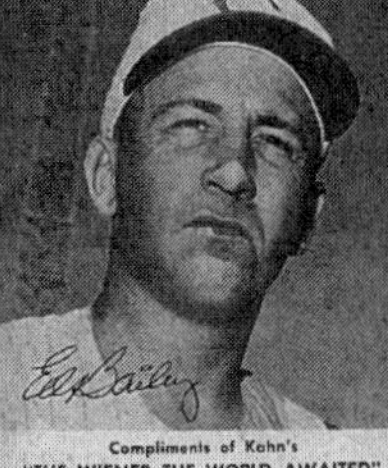

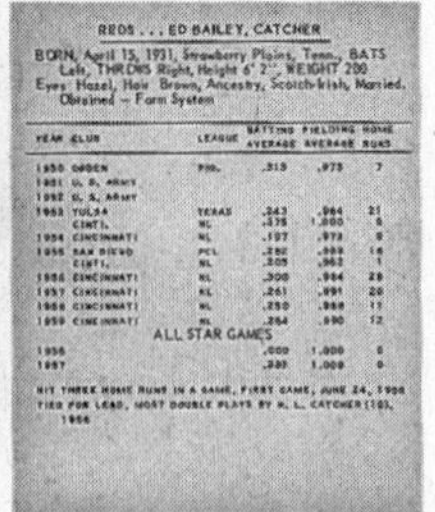

Three more teams joined the Kahn's roster in 1960, the Chicago Cubs, Chicago White Sox and St. Louis Cardinals. Again 3-1/4" x 4" with black-and-white photos, the 1960 Kahn's cards featured for the first time player stats and personal data on the back, except Harvey Kuenn, which was issued with blank back, probably because of the lateness of his trade to the Indians.

	NM	EX	VG
Complete Set (42):	3,000	1,500	900.00
Common Player:	40.00	20.00	12.00
(1) Ed Bailey	40.00	20.00	12.00
(2) Gary Bell	40.00	20.00	12.00
(3) Gus Bell	45.00	22.50	13.50
(4) Forrest Burgess	45.00	22.50	13.50
(5) Gino N. Cimoli	40.00	20.00	12.00
(6) Roberto Clemente	725.00	360.00	215.00
(7) ElRoy Face	40.00	20.00	12.00
(8) Tito Francona	40.00	20.00	12.00
(9) Robert Friend	40.00	20.00	12.00
(10) Jim Grant	40.00	20.00	12.00
(11) Richard Groat	40.00	20.00	12.00
(12) Harvey Haddix	40.00	20.00	12.00
(13) Woodie Held	40.00	20.00	12.00
(14) Bill Henry	40.00	20.00	12.00
(15) Don Hoak	40.00	20.00	12.00
(16) Jay Hook	40.00	20.00	12.00
(17) Eddie Kasko	40.00	20.00	12.00
(18) Ronnie Kline	50.00	25.00	15.00
(19) Ted Kluszewski	300.00	150.00	90.00
(20) Harvey Kuenn	200.00	100.00	60.00
(21) Vernon S. Law	45.00	22.50	13.50
(22) Brooks Lawrence	40.00	20.00	12.00
(23) Jerry Lynch	40.00	20.00	12.00
(24) Billy Martin	90.00	45.00	27.00
(25) Bill Mazeroski	150.00	75.00	45.00
(26) Cal McLish	40.00	20.00	12.00
(27) Roy McMillan	40.00	20.00	12.00
(28) Don Newcombe	45.00	22.50	13.50
(29) Russ Nixon	40.00	20.00	12.00
(30) Joe Nuxhall	40.00	20.00	12.00
(31) James J. O'Toole	40.00	20.00	12.00
(32) Jim Perry	45.00	22.00	13.50
(33) Vada Pinson	65.00	32.50	20.00
(34) Vic Power	40.00	20.00	12.00
(35) Robert T. Purkey	40.00	20.00	12.00
(36) Frank Robinson	200.00	100.00	60.00
(37) Herb Score	45.00	22.50	13.50
(38) Robert R. Skinner	40.00	20.00	12.00
(39) Richard L. Stuart	40.00	20.00	12.00
(40) John Temple	40.00	20.00	12.00
(41) Frank Thomas	50.00	25.00	15.00
(42) Lee Walls	40.00	20.00	12.00

1961 Kahn's Wieners

After a single season, the Chicago and St. Louis teams dropped out of the Kahn's program, but the 1961 set was larger than ever, at 43 cards. The same basic format - 3-1/4" x 4" size, black-and-white photos and statistical information on the back - was retained. For the first time in '61, the meat company made complete sets of the Kahn's cards available to collectors via a mail-in offer. This makes the 1961 and later Kahn's cards considerably easier to obtain than the earlier issues.

	NM	EX	VG
Complete Set (43):	2,650	1,300	800.00
Common Player:	40.00	20.00	12.00
(1) John A. Antonelli	40.00	20.00	12.00
(2) Ed Bailey	40.00	20.00	12.00
(3) Gary Bell	40.00	20.00	12.00
(4) Gus Bell	45.00	22.00	13.50
(5) James P. Brosnan	40.00	20.00	12.00
(6) Forrest Burgess	45.00	22.00	13.50
(7) Gino Cimoli	40.00	20.00	12.00
(8) Roberto Clemente	825.00	410.00	245.00
(9) Gordon Coleman	40.00	20.00	12.00
(10) Jimmie Dykes	40.00	20.00	12.00
(11) ElRoy Face	40.00	20.00	12.00
(12) Tito Francona	40.00	20.00	12.00
(13) Gene L. Freese	40.00	20.00	12.00
(14) Robert Friend	40.00	20.00	12.00
(15) Jim Grant	40.00	20.00	12.00
(16) Richard M. Groat	40.00	20.00	12.00
(17) Harvey Haddix	40.00	20.00	12.00
(18) Woodie Held	40.00	20.00	12.00
(19) Don Hoak	40.00	20.00	12.00
(20) Jay Hook	40.00	20.00	12.00
(21) Joe Jay	40.00	20.00	12.00
(22) Eddie Kasko	40.00	20.00	12.00
(23) Willie Kirkland	40.00	20.00	12.00
(24) Vernon S. Law	40.00	20.00	12.00
(25) Jerry Lynch	40.00	20.00	12.00
(26) Jim Maloney	40.00	20.00	12.00
(27) Bill Mazeroski	150.00	75.00	45.00
(28) Wilmer D. Mizell	40.00	20.00	12.00
(29) Glenn R. Nelson	40.00	20.00	12.00
(30) James J. O'Toole	40.00	20.00	12.00
(31) Jim Perry	40.00	20.00	12.00
(32) John M. Phillips	40.00	20.00	12.00
(33) Vada E. Pinson Jr.	55.00	27.00	16.50
(34) Wally Post	40.00	20.00	12.00
(35) Vic Power	40.00	20.00	12.00
(36) Robert T. Purkey	40.00	20.00	12.00
(37) Frank Robinson	250.00	125.00	75.00
(38) John A. Romano Jr.	40.00	20.00	12.00
(39) Dick Schofield	40.00	20.00	12.00
(40) Robert Skinner	40.00	20.00	12.00
(41) Hal Smith	40.00	20.00	12.00
(42) Richard Stuart	40.00	20.00	12.00
(43) John E. Temple	40.00	20.00	12.00

1962 Kahn's Wieners

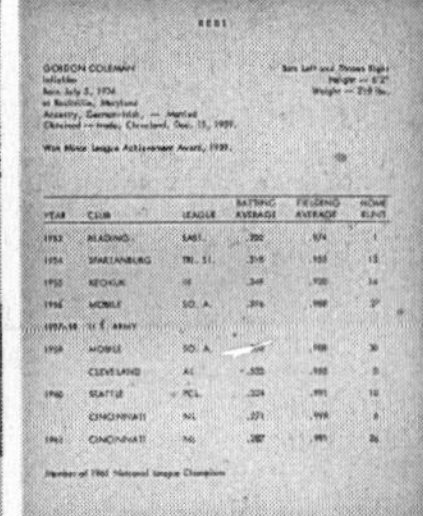

Besides the familiar Reds, Pirates and Indians players in the 1962 Kahn's set, a fourth team was added, the Minnesota Twins, though the overall size of the set was decreased from the previous year, to 38 players in 1962. The cards retained the 3-1/4" x 4" black-and-white format of previous years. The '62 Kahn's set is awash in variations. Besides the photo and front design variations on the Bell, Purkey and Power cards, each Cleveland player can be found with two back variations, listing the team either as "Cleveland" or "Cleveland Indians." The complete set values listed below include all variations.

	NM	EX	VG
Complete Set (51):	2,250	1,125	675.00
Common Player:	15.00	7.50	4.50
(1a) Gary Bell (Cleveland Indians back.)	100.00	50.00	30.00
(1b) Gary Bell (Cleveland back.)	35.00	17.50	10.00
(2) James P. Brosnan	15.00	7.50	4.50
(3) Forrest Burgess	30.00	15.00	9.00
(4) Leonardo Cardenas	15.00	7.50	4.50
(5) Roberto Clemente	250.00	125.00	75.00
(6a) Ty Cline (Cleveland Indians back.)	70.00	35.00	20.00
(6b) Ty Cline (Cleveland back.)	30.00	15.00	9.00
(7) Gordon Coleman	15.00	7.50	4.50
(8) Dick Donovan	30.00	15.00	9.00
(9) John Edwards	15.00	7.50	4.50
(10a) Tito Francona (Cleveland Indians back.)	70.00	35.00	20.00
(10b) Tito Francona (Cleveland back.)	30.00	15.00	9.00
(11) Gene Freese	15.00	7.50	4.50
(12) Robert B. Friend	20.00	10.00	6.00
(13) Joe Gibbon	75.00	37.50	22.50
(14a) Jim Grant (Cleveland Indians back.)	70.00	35.00	20.00
(14b) Jim Grant (Cleveland back.)	30.00	15.00	9.00
(15) Richard M. Groat	40.00	20.00	12.00
(16) Harvey Haddix	15.00	7.50	4.50
(17a) Woodie Held (Cleveland Indians back.)	70.00	35.00	20.00
(17b) Woodie Held (Cleveland back.)	30.00	15.00	9.00
(18) Bill Henry	15.00	7.50	4.50
(19) Don Hoak	15.00	7.50	4.50
(20) Ken Hunt	15.00	7.50	4.50
(21) Joseph R. Jay	15.00	7.50	4.50
(22) Eddie Kasko	15.00	7.50	4.50
(23a) Willie Kirkland (Cleveland Indians back.)	70.00	35.00	20.00
(23b) Willie Kirkland (Cleveland back.)	30.00	15.00	9.00
(24a) Barry Latman (Cleveland Indians back.)	70.00	35.00	20.00
(24b) Barry Latman (Cleveland back.)	30.00	15.00	9.00
(25) Jerry Lynch	15.00	7.50	4.50
(26) Jim Maloney	20.00	10.00	6.00
(27) Bill Mazeroski	100.00	50.00	30.00
(28) Jim O'Toole	15.00	7.50	4.50
(29a) Jim Perry (Cleveland Indians back.)	70.00	35.00	20.00

		NM	EX	VG
(29b)	Jim Perry (Cleveland back.)	30.00	15.00	9.00
(30a)	John M. Phillips (Cleveland Indians back.)	70.00	35.00	20.00
(30b)	John M. Phillips (Cleveland back.)	30.00	15.00	9.00
(31)	Vada E. Pinson	30.00	15.00	9.00
(32)	Wally Post	15.00	7.50	4.50
(33a)	Vic Power (Cleveland Indians back.)	70.00	35.00	20.00
(33b)	Vic Power (Cleveland back.)	30.00	15.00	9.00
(33c)	Vic Power (Minnesota Twins back.)	150.00	75.00	45.00
(34a)	Robert T. Purkey (No autograph.)	150.00	75.00	45.00
(34b)	Robert T. Purkey (With autograph.)	35.00	17.50	10.00
(35)	Frank Robinson	100.00	50.00	30.00
(36a)	John Romano (Cleveland Indians back.)	70.00	35.00	20.00
(36b)	John Romano (Cleveland back.)	30.00	15.00	9.00
(37)	Dick Stuart	15.00	7.50	4.50
(38)	Bill Virdon	15.00	7.50	4.50

1963 Kahn's Wieners

In 1963, for the first time since Kahn's began issuing baseball cards in 1955, the design underwent a significant change, white borders were added to the top and sides of player photo. Also, the card size was changed to 3-3/16" x 4-1/4". Statistical and personal data continued to be printed on the card backs. Joining traditional Reds, Pirates and Indians personnel in the 1963 set were a handful of New York Yankees and Dick Groat, in his new identity as a St. Louis Cardinal.

		NM	EX	VG
Complete Set (30):		2,000	1,000	600.00
Common Player:		50.00	25.00	15.50
(1)	Robert Bailey	50.00	25.00	15.50
(2)	Don Blasingame	50.00	25.00	15.50
(3)	Clete Boyer	90.00	45.00	27.00
(4)	Forrest Burgess	60.00	30.00	18.00
(5)	Leonardo Cardenas	50.00	25.00	15.50
(6)	Roberto Clemente	350.00	175.00	105.00
(7)	Don Clendennon (Donn Clendenon)	50.00	25.00	15.50
(8)	Gordon Coleman	50.00	25.00	15.50
(9)	John A. Edwards	50.00	25.00	15.50
(10)	Gene Freese	50.00	25.00	15.50
(11)	Robert B. Friend	50.00	25.00	15.00
(12)	Joe Gibbon	50.00	25.00	15.50
(13)	Dick Groat	90.00	45.00	27.00
(14)	Harvey Haddix	50.00	25.00	15.00
(15)	Elston Howard	100.00	50.00	30.00
(16)	Joey Jay	50.00	25.00	15.50
(17)	Eddie Kasko	50.00	25.00	15.50
(18)	Tony Kubek	100.00	50.00	30.00
(19)	Jerry Lynch	50.00	25.00	15.50
(20)	Jim Maloney	60.00	30.00	18.00
(21)	Bill Mazeroski	150.00	75.00	45.00
(22)	Joe Nuxhall	60.00	30.00	18.00
(23)	Jim O'Toole	50.00	25.00	15.50
(24)	Vada E. Pinson	90.00	45.00	27.00
(25)	Robert T. Purkey	50.00	25.00	15.50
(26)	Bob Richardson	100.00	50.00	30.00
(27)	Frank Robinson	200.00	100.00	60.00
(28)	Bill Stafford	60.00	30.00	18.00
(29)	Ralph W. Terry	60.00	30.00	18.00
(30)	Bill Virdon	60.00	30.00	18.00

1964 Kahn's Wieners

After nearly a decade of virtually identical card issues, the 1964 Kahn's issue was an abrupt change. In a new size, 3" x 3-1/2", the nearly square cards featured a borderless color photo. The only other design element on the front of the card was a facsimile autograph. The advertising slogan which had traditionally appeared on the front of the card was moved to the back, where it joined the player's stats and personal data. The teams in the 1964 issue once again reverted to the Reds, Pirates and Indians.

		NM	EX	VG
Complete Set (31):		1,150	600.00	350.00
Common Player:		20.00	10.00	6.00
(1)	Max Alvis	20.00	10.00	6.00
(2)	Bob Bailey	20.00	10.00	6.00
(3)	Leonardo Cardenas	20.00	10.00	6.00
(4)	Roberto Clemente	300.00	150.00	90.00
(5)	Donn A. Clendenon	20.00	10.00	6.00
(6)	Victor Davalillo	20.00	10.00	6.00
(7)	Dick Donovan	20.00	10.00	6.00
(8)	John A. Edwards	20.00	10.00	6.00
(9)	Robert Friend	20.00	10.00	6.00
(10)	Jim Grant	20.00	10.00	6.00
(11)	Tommy Harper	20.00	10.00	6.00
(12)	Woodie Held	20.00	10.00	6.00
(13)	Joey Jay	20.00	10.00	6.00
(14)	Jack Kralick	20.00	10.00	6.00
(15)	Jerry Lynch	20.00	10.00	6.00
(16)	Jim Maloney	20.00	10.00	6.00
(17)	Bill Mazeroski	75.00	37.50	22.00
(18)	Alvin McBean	20.00	10.00	6.00
(19)	Joe Nuxhall	20.00	10.00	6.00
(20)	Jim Pagliaroni	20.00	10.00	6.00
(21)	Vada E. Pinson Jr.	35.00	17.50	10.00
(22)	Robert T. Purkey	20.00	10.00	6.00
(23)	Pedro Ramos	20.00	10.00	6.00
(24)	Frank Robinson	75.00	37.50	22.50
(25)	John Romano	20.00	10.00	6.00
(26)	Pete Rose	250.00	125.00	75.00
(27)	John Tsitouris	20.00	10.00	6.00
(28)	Robert A. Veale Jr.	20.00	10.00	6.00
(29)	Bill Virdon	20.00	10.00	6.00
(30)	Leon Wagner	20.00	10.00	6.00
(31)	Fred Whitfield	20.00	10.00	6.00

1965 Kahn's Wieners

There was little change for the Kahn's issue in 1965 beyond the addition of Milwaukee Braves players to the Reds, Pirates and Indians traditionally included in the set. At 45 players, the 1965 issue was the largest of the Kahn's sets. Once again in 3" x 3-1/2" size, the 1965s retained the borderless color photo design of the previous season. A look at the stats on the back will confirm the year of issue, allowing differentiation between the 1964 and 1965 cards.

		NM	EX	VG
Complete Set (45):		1,250	625.00	400.00
Common Player:		15.00	7.50	4.50
(1)	Hank Aaron	125.00	65.00	35.00
(2)	Max Alvis	15.00	7.50	4.50
(3)	Jose Azcue	15.00	7.50	4.50
(4)	Bob Bailey	15.00	7.50	4.50
(5)	Frank Bolling	15.00	7.50	4.50
(6)	Leonardo Cardenas	15.00	7.50	4.50
(7)	Rico Ricardo Carty	15.00	7.50	4.50
(8)	Donn A. Clendenon	15.00	7.50	4.50
(9)	Tony Cloninger	15.00	7.50	4.50
(10)	Gordon Coleman	15.00	7.50	4.50
(11)	Victor Davalillo	15.00	7.50	4.50
(12)	John A. Edwards	15.00	7.50	4.50
(13)	Sam Ellis	15.00	7.50	4.50
(14)	Robert Friend	15.00	7.50	4.50
(15)	Tommy Harper	15.00	7.50	4.50
(16)	Chuck Hinton	15.00	7.50	4.50
(17)	Dick Howser	15.00	7.50	4.50
(18)	Joey Jay	15.00	7.50	4.50
(19)	Deron Johnson	15.00	7.50	4.50
(20)	Jack Kralick	15.00	7.50	4.50
(21)	Denny Lemaster	15.00	7.50	4.50
(22)	Jerry Lynch	15.00	7.50	4.50
(23)	Jim Maloney	15.00	7.50	4.50
(24)	Lee Maye	15.00	7.50	4.50
(25)	Bill Mazeroski	60.00	30.00	18.00
(26)	Alvin McBean	15.00	7.50	4.50
(27)	Bill McCool	15.00	7.50	4.50
(28)	Sam McDowell	20.00	10.00	6.00
(29)	Donald McMahon	15.00	7.50	4.50
(30)	Denis Menke	15.00	7.50	4.50
(31)	Joe Nuxhall	15.00	7.50	4.50
(32)	Gene Oliver	15.00	7.50	4.50
(33)	Jim O'Toole	15.00	7.50	4.50
(34)	Jim Pagliaroni	15.00	7.50	4.50
(35)	Vada E. Pinson Jr.	25.00	12.50	7.50
(36)	Frank Robinson	100.00	50.00	30.00
(37)	Pete Rose	300.00	150.00	90.00
(38)	Willie Stargell	60.00	30.00	18.00
(39)	Ralph W. Terry	15.00	7.50	4.50
(40)	Luis Tiant	20.00	10.00	6.00
(41)	Joe Torre	25.00	12.50	7.50
(42)	John Tsitouris	15.00	7.50	4.50
(43)	Robert A. Veale Jr.	15.00	7.50	4.50
(44)	Bill Virdon	15.00	7.50	4.50
(45)	Leon Wagner	15.00	7.50	4.50

1966 Kahn's Wieners

The fourth new format in five years greeted collectors with the introduction of Kahn's 1966 issue. The design consists of a color photo bordered by white and yellow vertical stripes. The player's name is printed above the photo, and a facsimile autograph appears across the photo. As printed, the cards are 2-13/16" x 4-9/16" in size. The player photo area is about 2-13/16" x x 2-11/16", separated at top by a dotted line from an advertising panel with a red rose logo and the word "Kahn's" and by a dotted line at bottom from an irregularly shaped piece marked "CUT ALONG DOTTED LINES." Naturally, many of the cards are found today with the top and/or bottom portion cut off. Values listed here are for complete uncut cards; those without the ad portion and bottom panel are valued at 50 percent or less. Players from the Cincinnati Reds, Pittsburgh Pirates, Cleveland Indians and Atlanta Braves were included in the set. Since the cards are blank-backed, collectors must learn to differentiate player poses to determine year of issue for some cards.

		NM	EX	VG
Complete Set (32):		1,250	625.00	375.00
Common Player:		15.00	7.50	4.50
(1)	Henry Aaron	200.00	100.00	60.00
(2)	Felipe Alou	20.00	10.00	6.00
(3)	Max Alvis	15.00	7.50	4.50
(4)	Robert Bailey	15.00	7.50	4.50
(5)	Wade Blasingame	15.00	7.50	4.50
(6)	Frank Bolling	15.00	7.50	4.50
(7)	Leo Cardenas	15.00	7.50	4.50
(8)	Roberto Clemente	400.00	200.00	120.00
(9)	Tony Cloninger	15.00	7.50	4.50
(10)	Vic Davalillo	15.00	7.50	4.50
(11)	John Edwards	15.00	7.50	4.50
(12)	Sam Ellis (White cap.)	15.00	7.50	4.50
(13)	Pedro Gonzalez	15.00	7.50	4.50
(14)	Tommy Harper	15.00	7.50	4.50
(15)	Deron Johnson	15.00	7.50	4.50
(16)	Mack Jones	15.00	7.50	4.50
(17)	Denny Lemaster	15.00	7.50	4.50
(18)	Jim Maloney (White cap.)	15.00	7.50	4.50
(19)	Bill Mazeroski	90.00	45.00	27.00
(20)	Bill McCool	15.00	7.50	4.50
(21)	Sam McDowell	25.00	12.50	7.50
(22)	Denis Menke	15.00	7.50	4.50
(23)	Joe Nuxhall	15.00	7.50	4.50
(24)	Jim Pagliaroni	15.00	7.50	4.50
(25)	Milt Pappas	15.00	7.50	4.50
(26)	Vada Pinson	25.00	12.50	7.50
(27)	Pete Rose (Right hand in glove.)	250.00	125.00	75.00
(28)	Sonny Siebert	15.00	7.50	4.50
(29)	Willie Stargell	90.00	45.00	27.00
(30)	Joe Torre	25.00	12.50	7.50
(31)	Bob Veale	15.00	7.50	4.50
(32)	Fred Whitfield	15.00	7.50	4.50

1967 Kahn's Wieners

Retaining the 1966 format, the '67 Kahn's set was expanded to 41 players by adding several New York Mets to the previous season's lineup of Reds, Pirates, Indians and Braves. Making this set especially challenging for collectors is the fact that some cards are found in a smaller size and/or with different colored stripes bordering the color player photo. On the majority of cards, the size remained about 2-13/16" x 4-9/16" (with ad at top and bottom panel; about 2-13/16" x 2-11/16" when cut on dotted lines). However, because of packing in different products, some cards can be found in 2-13/16" x 3-1/4" size (with ad; 2-13/16" x 2-1/8" without ad). The border stripe variations are listed below. Values quoted are for complete uncut cards; values drop by 50 percent or more for cards without the ad and/or bottom panels. All variation cards are included in the valuations given for the complete set.

		NM	EX	VG
Complete Set (51):		1,800	900.00	550.00
Common Player:		20.00	10.00	6.00
(1a)	Henry Aaron (Large size.)	125.00	65.00	35.00
(1b)	Henry Aaron (Small size.)	125.00	65.00	35.00
(2)	Gene Alley	20.00	10.00	6.00
(3a)	Felipe Alou (Large size.)	25.00	12.50	7.50
(3b)	Felipe Alou (Small size.)	25.00	12.50	7.50
(4a)	Matty Alou (Yellow & white striped border.)	25.00	12.50	7.50
(4b)	Matty Alou (Red & white striped border.)	30.00	15.00	9.00
(5)	Max Alvis	20.00	10.00	6.00
(6a)	Ken Boyer (Yellow & white striped border.)	30.00	15.00	9.00
(6b)	Ken Boyer (Red, white & green striped border.)	35.00	17.50	10.00
(7)	Leo Cardenas	20.00	10.00	6.00
(8)	Rico Carty	20.00	10.00	6.00
(9)	Tony Cloninger	20.00	10.00	6.00
(10)	Tommy Davis	20.00	10.00	6.00
(11)	John Edwards	20.00	10.00	6.00
(12a)	Sam Ellis (Large size.) (Red cap.)	20.00	10.00	6.00
(12b)	Sam Ellis (Small size.) (Red cap.)	30.00	15.00	9.00
(13)	Jack Fisher	20.00	10.00	6.00
(14)	Steve Hargan	20.00	10.00	6.00
(15)	Tom Harper	20.00	10.00	6.00
(16a)	Tom Helms (Large size.)	20.00	10.00	6.00
(16b)	Tom Helms (Small size.)	35.00	17.50	10.00
(17)	Deron Johnson	20.00	10.00	6.00
(18)	Ken Johnson	20.00	10.00	6.00
(19)	Cleon Jones	20.00	10.00	6.00
(20a)	Ed Kranepool (Yellow & white striped border.)	20.00	10.00	6.00
(20b)	Ed Kranepool (Red & white striped border.)	30.00	15.00	9.00
(21a)	James Maloney (Yellow & white striped border.)	25.00	12.50	7.50
(21b)	James Maloney (Red & white striped border.)	30.00	15.00	9.00
(22)	Lee May	20.00	10.00	6.00
(23a)	Wm. Mazeroski (Large size.)	75.00	37.50	22.50
(23b)	Wm. Mazeroski (Small size.)	75.00	37.50	22.50
(24)	Wm. McCool	20.00	10.00	6.00
(25)	Sam McDowell (Blue sleeves.)	25.00	12.50	7.50
(26)	Dennis Menke (Denis)	20.00	10.00	6.00
(27)	Jim Pagliaroni	20.00	10.00	6.00
(28)	Don Pavletich	20.00	10.00	6.00
(29)	Tony Perez	60.00	30.00	18.00
(30)	Vada Pinson	30.00	15.00	9.00
(31)	Dennis Ribant	20.00	10.00	6.00
(32)	Pete Rose/Btg	275.00	135.00	85.00
(33)	Art Shamsky	20.00	10.00	6.00
(34)	Bob Shaw	20.00	10.00	6.00
(35)	Sonny Siebert	20.00	10.00	6.00
(36)	Wm. Stargell (First name actually Wilver.)	80.00	40.00	24.00
(37a)	Joe Torre (Large size.)	35.00	17.50	10.00
(37b)	Joe Torre (Small size.)	35.00	17.50	10.00
(38)	Bob Veale	20.00	10.00	6.00
(39)	Leon Wagner	20.00	10.00	6.00
(40a)	Fred Whitfield (Large size.)	20.00	10.00	6.00
(40b)	Fred Whitfield (Small size.)	20.00	10.00	6.00
(41)	Woody Woodward	20.00	10.00	6.00

1968 Kahn's Wieners

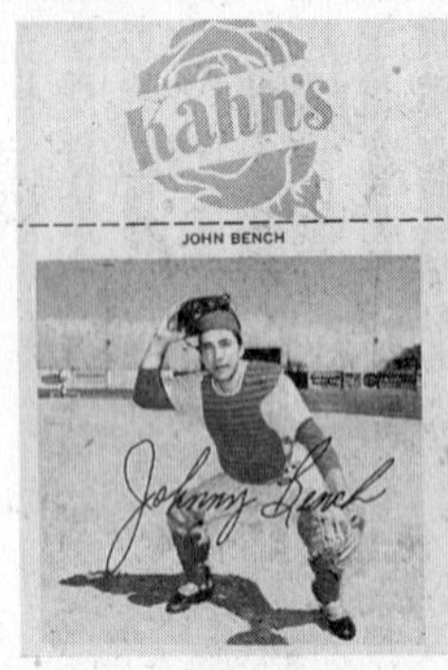

The number of card size and stripe color variations increased with the 1968 Kahn's issue, though the basic card format was retained. Basic size is about 2-13/16" x 4-9/16" with top ad panel and bottom panel intact; 2-13/16" x 2-11/16" with ad and bottom panels cut off. Color photos are bordered by yellow and white vertical stripes. In addition to the basic issue, a number of the cards appear in a smaller, 2-13/16" x 3-1/4", size, while some appear with variations in the color of border stripes. One card, Maloney, can be found with a top portion advertising Blue Mountain brand meats, as well as Kahn's. The 1968 set features the largest number of teams represented in any Kahn's issue: Braves, Cubs, White Sox, Reds, Indians, Tigers, Mets and Pirates. Values quoted are for complete uncut cards, those without the ad and/or bottom panel are worth 50 percent or less. Complete set prices include all variations.

		NM	EX	VG
Complete Set (56):		2,250	1,125	675.00
Common Player:		20.00	10.00	6.00
(1a)	Hank Aaron (Large size.)	100.00	50.00	30.00
(1b)	Hank Aaron (Small size.)	125.00	62.00	37.00
(2)	Tommy Agee	20.00	10.00	6.00
(3a)	Gene Alley (Large size.)	20.00	10.00	6.00
(3b)	Gene Alley (Small size.)	30.00	15.00	9.00
(4)	Felipe Alou	25.00	12.50	7.50
(5a)	Matty Alou (Yellow striped border.)	25.00	12.50	7.50
(5b)	Matty Alou (Red striped border.)	25.00	12.50	7.50
(6a)	Max Alvis (Large size.)	20.00	10.00	6.00
(6b)	Max Alvis (Small size.)	30.00	15.00	9.00
(7)	Gerry Arrigo	20.00	10.00	6.00
(8)	John Bench	550.00	275.00	165.00
(9a)	Clete Boyer (Large size.)	20.00	10.00	6.00
(9b)	Clete Boyer (Small size.)	30.00	15.00	9.00
(10)	Larry Brown	20.00	10.00	6.00
(11a)	Leo Cardenas (Large size.)	20.00	10.00	6.00
(11b)	Leo Cardenas (Small size.)	30.00	15.00	9.00
(12a)	Bill Freehan (Large size.)	30.00	15.00	9.00
(12b)	Bill Freehan (Small size.)	30.00	15.00	9.00
(13)	Steve Hargan	20.00	10.00	6.00
(14)	Joel Horlen	20.00	10.00	6.00
(15)	Tony Horton	30.00	15.00	9.00
(16)	Willie Horton	25.00	12.50	7.50
(17)	Ferguson Jenkins	75.00	37.00	22.00
(18)	Deron Johnson	20.00	10.00	6.00
(19)	Mack Jones	20.00	10.00	6.00
(20)	Bob Lee	20.00	10.00	6.00
(21a)	Jim Maloney (Large size, rose logo.)	25.00	12.50	7.50
(21b)	Jim Maloney (Large size, Blue Mountain logo.)	60.00	30.00	18.00
(21c)	Jim Maloney (Small size, yellow & white striped border.)	30.00	15.00	9.00
(21d)	Jim Maloney (Small size, yellow, white & green striped border.)	30.00	15.00	9.00
(22a)	Lee May (Large size.)	25.00	12.50	7.50
(22b)	Lee May (Small size.)	30.00	15.00	9.00
(23a)	Wm. Mazeroski (Large size.)	50.00	25.00	15.00
(23b)	Wm. Mazeroski (Small size.)	65.00	32.50	20.00
(24)	Dick McAuliffe	20.00	10.00	6.00
(25)	Bill McCool	20.00	10.00	6.00
(26a)	Sam McDowell (Yellow striped border.)	25.00	12.50	7.50
(26b)	Sam McDowell (Red striped border.)	30.00	15.00	9.00
(27a)	Tony Perez (Yellow striped border.)	45.00	22.00	13.50
(27b)	Tony Perez (Red striped border.)	50.00	25.00	15.00
(28)	Gary Peters	20.00	10.00	6.00
(29a)	Vada Pinson (Large size.)	30.00	15.00	9.00
(29b)	Vada Pinson (Small size.)	30.00	15.00	9.00
(30)	Chico Ruiz	20.00	10.00	6.00
(31a)	Ron Santo (Yellow striped border.)	30.00	15.00	9.00
(31b)	Ron Santo (Red striped border.)	40.00	20.00	12.00
(32)	Art Shamsky	20.00	10.00	6.00
(33)	Luis Tiant (Arms above head.)	20.00	10.00	6.00
(34a)	Joe Torre (Large size.)	30.00	15.00	9.00
(34b)	Joe Torre (Small size.)	35.00	17.50	10.50
(35a)	Bob Veale (Large size.)	20.00	10.00	6.00
(35b)	Bob Veale (Small size.)	30.00	15.00	9.00
(36)	Leon Wagner	20.00	10.00	6.00
(37)	Billy Williams	75.00	37.00	22.00
(38)	Earl Wilson	20.00	10.00	6.00

1969 Kahn's Wieners

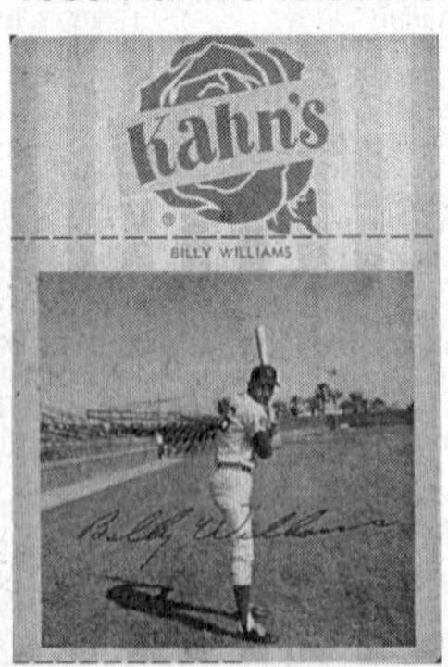

In its 15th consecutive year of baseball card issue, Kahn's continued the format adopted in 1966. The basic 22 players' cards were printed in about 2-13/16" x 4-9/16" size (with ad panel at top and bottom panel; 2-13/16" x 2-11/16" without panels) and are blanked-backed. Teams represented in the set are the Braves, Cubs, White Sox, Reds, Cardinals, Indians and Pirates. Cards feature a color photo and facsimile autograph bordered by yellow and white vertical stripes. At top is an ad panel consisting of the Kahn's red rose logo. However, because some cards were produced for inclusion in packages other than the standard hot dogs, a number of variations in card size and stripe color were created, as noted in the listings. The smaller size cards, 2-13/16" x 3-1/4" with top and bottom panels; 3/16" x 2-1/8" without panels, were created by more closely cropping the player photo at top and bottom. Values quoted are for complete uncut cards with both panels intact; deduct a minimum 50 percent for cards wihtout the ad and/or bottom panel. Complete set values include all variations. For years an (18b) (red-striped border) Ron Santo had been documented. Recent evidence now suggests that such a variation does not exist.

		NM	EX	VG
Complete Set (29):		1,200	600.00	375.00
Common Player:		25.00	12.50	7.50
(1a)	Hank Aaron (Large size.)	125.00	62.00	37.00
(1b)	Hank Aaron (Small size.)	140.00	70.00	42.00
(2)	Matty Alou	25.00	12.50	7.50
(3)	Max Alvis	25.00	12.50	7.50
(4)	Gerry Arrigo	25.00	12.50	7.50
(5)	Steve Blass	25.00	12.50	7.50
(6)	Clay Carroll (Follow-through.)	25.00	12.50	7.50
(7)	Tony Cloninger	25.00	12.50	7.50
(8)	George Culver	25.00	12.50	7.50
(9)	Joel Horlen (Follow-through.)	25.00	12.50	7.50
(10)	Tony Horton/Btg	35.00	17.50	10.50
(11)	Alex Johnson	25.00	12.50	7.50
(12a)	Jim Maloney (Large size.) (Arms at sides.)	30.00	15.00	9.00
(12b)	Jim Maloney (Small size.) (Arms at sides.)	35.00	17.50	10.50
(13a)	Lee May (Yellow striped border.) (Foot on bag.)	30.00	15.00	9.00
(13b)	Lee May (Red striped border.) (Foot on bag.)	35.00	17.50	10.50
(14a)	Bill Mazeroski (Yellow striped border.)	50.00	25.00	15.00
(14b)	Bill Mazeroski (Red striped border.)	55.00	27.00	16.50
(15a)	Sam McDowell (Yellow striped border.) (Right leg raised.)	30.00	15.00	9.00
(15b)	Sam McDowell (Red striped border.) (Right leg raised.)	35.00	17.50	10.50
(16a)	Tony Perez (Large size.) (Glove on base.)	60.00	30.00	18.00
(16b)	Tony Perez (Small size.) (Glove on base.)	75.00	37.50	22.50
(17)	Gary Peters (Follow-through.)	25.00	12.50	7.50
(18a)	Ron Santo (Yellow striped border.)	50.00	25.00	15.00
(18b)	Ron Santo (Red striped border. Now believed not to exist.)			
(19)	Luis Tiant (Arms at knees.)	25.00	12.50	7.50
(20)	Joe Torre	35.00	17.50	10.50
(21)	Bob Veale	25.00	12.50	7.50
(22)	Billy Williams (Bat behind head.)	80.00	40.00	24.00

1970s Kahn's Kielbasa Singles Carl Yastrzemski

The exact year or years of this label's issue are not known. The 4-7/8" x 3-1/8" cardboard package insert has a color portrait photo of baseball's most famous Polish player endorsing the polish sausage product.

	NM	EX	VG
Carl Yastrzemski	15.00	7.50	4.50

1887 Kalamazoo Bats (N690)

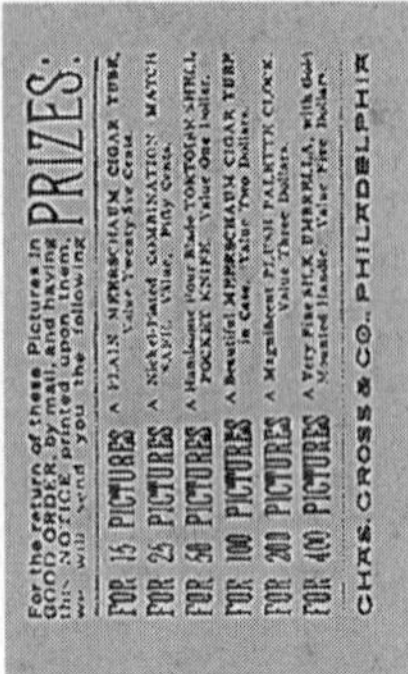

This set, issued circa 1887 by Charles Gross & Co. Phila., is one of the most difficult of all 19th Century tobacco issues. The cards measure a rather large 2-1/4" x 4" and feature a sepia-toned photograph on heavy cardboard. The player's name and team appear inside a white strip at the bottom of the photo, while a small ad for Kalamazoo Bats cigarettes is printed at the very bottom of the card. Some cards carry an

1887 copyright line, but there are indications that some of the cards date from 1886 or 1888. The unnumbered set pictures players from four teams - two from New York (Giants and Mets) and two from Philadelphia (Athletics and Phillies). A few of the cards picture more than one player, and some Philadelphia cards have been found with an ad on the back offering various prizes in exchange for saving the cards. The set has been assigned the American Card Catalog number N690. This checklist is likely not complete. Players from the New York teams are significantly rarer than those of the Philadelphia teams.

		NM	EX	VG
Common Player:		6,250	3,750	2,500
Advertising-back: 1.5X				
(1)	Ed Andrews	6,250	3,750	2,500
(2)	Charles Bastian, Lyons	7,000	4,200	2,800
(3)	Lou Bierbauer	7,000	4,200	2,800
(4)	Lou Bierbauer, Gallagher	7,000	4,200	2,800
(5)	Charles Buffington (Buffinton)	6,250	3,750	2,500
(6)	Dan Casey	6,250	3,750	2,500
(7)	Jack Clements	7,000	4,200	2,800
(8)	Roger Connor (Three known.)	65,000	24,000	16,000
(9)	Larry Corcoran	7,500	4,500	3,000
(10)	Ed Cushman	17,500	10,500	7,000
(11)	Pat Deasley	17,500	10,500	7,000
(12)	Jim Devlin	6,250	3,750	2,500
(13)	Jim Donahue	17,500	10,500	7,000
(14)	Mike Dorgan	11,500	6,900	4,600
(15)	Dude Esterbrooke (Esterbrook)	17,500	10,500	7,000
(16)	Buck Ewing (Possibly unique.)	85,000	27,000	18,000
(17)	Sid Farrar	6,250	3,750	2,500
(18)	Charlie Ferguson	6,250	3,750	2,500
(19)	Jim Fogarty	6,250	3,750	2,500
(20)	Jim Fogarty, Deacon McGuire	7,000	4,200	2,800
(21)	Elmer Foster	17,500	10,500	7,000
(22)	Whitey Gibson	7,000	4,200	2,800
(23)	Pete Gillespie	17,500	10,500	7,000
(24)	Tom Gunning	6,250	3,750	2,500
(25)	Arthur Irwin	6,250	3,750	2,500
(26)	Arthur Irwin, Al Maul	7,000	4,200	2,800
(27)	Tim Keefe	65,000	21,000	14,000
(28)	Henry Larkin	7,000	4,200	2,800
(29)	Henry Larkins (Larkin), Jocko Milligan	7,000	4,200	2,800
(30)	Jack Lynch	17,500	10,500	7,000
(31)	Denny Lyons ((Athletics))	35,000	21,000	14,000
(32)	Harry Lyons (Phila.)	7,000	4,200	2,800
(33)	Harry Lyons (Phila.), Billy Taylor	7,000	4,200	2,800
(34)	Fred Mann	7,000	4,200	2,800
(35)	Charlie Mason	7,000	4,200	2,800
(36)	Bobby Mathews	7,000	4,200	2,800
(37)	Al Maul	6,250	3,750	2,500
(38)	Al Mays	17,500	10,500	7,000
(39)	Chippy McGan (McGarr)	7,000	4,200	2,800
(40)	Deacon McGuire/Catching	6,250	3,750	2,500
(41)	Deacon McGuire/Throwing	6,250	3,750	2,500
(42)	Tom McLaughlin	17,500	10,500	7,000
(43)	Jocko Milligan, Harry Stowe (Stovey)	7,000	4,200	2,800
(44)	Joseph Mulvey	6,250	3,750	2,500
(45)	Candy Nelson	17,500	10,500	7,000
(46)	Orator Jim O'Rourke (Possibly unique.)	75,000	21,000	14,000
(47)	Dave Orr	17,500	10,500	7,000
(48)	Tom Poorman	6,250	3,750	2,500
(49)	Danny Richardson	17,500	10,500	7,000
(50)	Wilbert Robinson	10,500	6,300	4,200
(51)	Wilbert Robinson, Fred Mann	10,500	6,300	4,200
(52)	Chief Roseman	17,500	10,500	7,000
(53)	Ed Seward (Possibly unique.)	14,000	8,400	5,600
(54)	Harry Stowe (Stovey) (Hands on hips.)	75,000	21,000	14,000
(55)	Harry Stowe (Stovey) (Hands outstretched.)	7,000	4,200	2,800
(56)	George Townsend	7,000	4,200	2,800
(57)	Jocko Milligan, George Townsend	7,900	4,750	3,150
(58)	John Ward (Possibly unique.)	100,000	28,500	19,000
(59)	Gus Weyhing	24,000	14,500	9,500
(60)	George Wood	6,250	3,750	2,500
(61)	Harry Wright	40,000	25,000	15,000

1887 Kalamazoo Bats Cabinets (N690-1)

This extremely rare issue of cabinet cards was issued as a premium by Charles Gross & Co. of Philadelphia, makers of the Kalamazoo Bats brand of cigarettes. Two distinct types have been found, both measuring 4-1/4" x 6-1/2". One variety displays the photo on a black mount with the words "Smoke Kalamazoo Bats" embossed in gold to the left. The other contains no advertising, although there is an oval embossment on the card, along with the words "Chas. Gross & Co." and an 1887 copyright line. These cards also have a distinctive pink color on the back of the cardboard mount. Because of the rarity of Kalamazoo Bats cabinets, and uncertainty as to completeness of this checklist, gaps have been left in the assigned numbering.

		NM	EX	VG
Common Player:		7,500	3,750	2,250
(1)	Ed Andrews	7,500	3,750	2,250
(2)	Charles Bastian, Daniel Casey, Billy Taylor	7,500	3,750	2,250
(3)	Charles Bastian, Denny Lyons	7,500	3,750	2,250
(4)	Louis Bierbauer, Gallagher	7,500	3,750	2,250
(5)	Charles Buffington (Buffinton)	7,500	3,750	2,250
(6)	Daniel Casey	7,500	3,750	2,250
(7)	Jack Clements	7,500	3,750	2,250
(8)	Jim Devlin	7,500	3,750	2,250
(9)	Sid Farrar	7,500	3,750	2,250
(10)	Charlie Ferguson	7,500	3,750	2,250
(11)	Jim Fogarty	7,500	3,750	2,250
(12)	Whitey Gibson	7,500	3,750	2,250
(13)	Tom Gunning	7,500	3,750	2,250
(14)	Arthur Irwin	7,500	3,750	2,250
(15)	Arthur Irwin, Al Maul	7,500	3,750	2,250
(16)	Henry Larkins (Larkin), Jocko Milligan	7,500	3,750	2,250
(17)	Harry Lyons	7,500	3,750	2,250
(18)	Harry Lyons, Billy Taylor	7,500	3,750	2,250
(19)	Fred Mann	7,500	3,750	2,250
(20)	Fred Mann, Wilbert Robinson	12,500	3,750	2,250
(21)	Bobby Mathews	7,500	3,750	2,250
(22)	Al Maul	7,500	3,750	2,250
(23)	Chippy McCan (McGarr)	7,500	3,750	2,250
(24)	Deacon McGuire/Fldg	7,500	3,750	2,250
(25)	Deacon McGuire/Throwing	7,500	3,750	2,250
(26)	Jocko Milligan, Harry Stowe (Stovey)	7,500	3,750	2,250
(27)	Joseph Mulvey	7,500	3,750	2,250
(28)	Tom Poorman	7,500	3,750	2,250
(29)	Ed Seward	7,500	3,750	2,250
(30)	Harry Stowe (Stovey)	7,500	3,750	2,250
(31)	George Townsend	7,500	3,750	2,250
(32)	George Wood	7,500	3,750	2,250
(33)	Harry Wright	31,250	5,625	3,425
(35)	Athletic Club (Three known, $9,031 paid in 12/04 auction for Good example.)			
(36)	Boston B.B.C. (Believed unique, mount restored, brought $14,434 in 5/05 auction.)			
(37)	Detroit B.B.C. (Believed unique)			
(38)	Philadelphia B.B.C. (Believed unique, VG, brought $9,935 in 12/04 auction.)			
(39)	Pittsburg B.B.C. (Believed unique, sold for $62,299 in Excellent in 12/05 auction.)			

1887 Kalamazoo Bats Team Cards (N693)

The team photos in this set were issued by Charles Gross & Co. of Philadelphia as a promotion for its Kalamazoo Bats brand of cigarettes. The cards, which are similar in design and size (about 4" x 2-1/4") to the related N690 series, are extremely rare. They feature a team photo with the caption in a white box at the bottom of the photo and an ad for Kalamazoo Bats to the left.

		NM	EX	VG
Common Team:		10,000	3,575	2,175
(1)	Athletic Club	10,000	3,575	2,175
(2)	Baltimore B.B.C.	33,000	12,000	7,250
(3)	Boston B.B.C.	26,400	9,500	5,800
(4)	Detroit B.B.C.	27,500	10,000	6,000
(5)	Philadelphia B.B.C.	13,200	4,750	2,900
(6)	Pittsburg B.B.C.	33,000	3,575	2,275

1955 Kansas City Athletics Photo Pack

In the first year following the team's move from Philadelphia to K.C., this set of player pictures was issued, probably sold as a souvenir stand item. The black-and-white photos are in an 8" x 10" format on heavy cardboard. Player poses or portraits are bordered in white with the player name in all-caps at bottom. Backs are blank. This checklist may be incomplete.

		NM	EX	VG
Complete Set (29):		200.00	100.00	60.00
Common Player:		9.00	4.50	2.75
(1)	Joe Astroth	9.00	4.50	2.75
(2)	Lou Boudreau	25.00	12.50	7.50
(3)	Cloyd Boyer	9.00	4.50	2.75
(4)	Art Ceccarelli	9.00	4.50	2.75
(5)	Harry Craft	9.00	4.50	2.75
(6)	Joe DeMaestri	9.00	4.50	2.75
(7)	Art Ditmar	9.00	4.50	2.75
(8)	Jim Finigan	9.00	4.50	2.75
(9)	Tom Gorman	9.00	4.50	2.75
(10)	Ray Herbert	9.00	4.50	2.75
(11)	Alex Kellner	9.00	4.50	2.75
(12)	Dick Kryhoski	9.00	4.50	2.75
(13)	Jack Littrell	9.00	4.50	2.75
(14)	Hector Lopez	9.00	4.50	2.75
(15)	Oscar Melillo	9.00	4.50	2.75
(16)	Arnie Portocarrero	9.00	4.50	2.75
(17)	Vic Power	15.00	7.50	4.50
(18)	Vic Raschi	12.00	6.00	3.50
(19)	Bill Renna	9.00	4.50	2.75
(20)	Johnny Sain	12.00	6.00	3.50
(21)	Bobby Shantz	12.00	6.00	3.50
(22)	Wilmer Shantz	9.00	4.50	2.75
(23)	Harry Simpson	15.00	7.50	4.50
(24)	Enos Slaughter	30.00	15.00	9.00
(25)	Lou Sleator	9.00	4.50	2.75
(26)	George Susce	9.00	4.50	2.75
(27)	Elmer Valo	9.00	4.50	2.75
(28)	Bill Wilson	9.00	4.50	2.75
(29)	Gus Zernial	15.00	7.50	4.50

1956-61 Kansas City Athletics Photocards

Issued over a period of several years these black-and-white photocards share an identical format. The cards are 3-1/4" x 5-1/2" with borderless poses and facsimile autographs on front. Backs are blank. The unnumbered cards are checklisted here in alphabetical order, though the list is surely not complete. Gaps have been left in the assigned numbering for future additions.

		NM	EX	VG
Common Player:		15.00	7.50	4.50
(1)	Jim Archer	15.00	7.50	4.50
(2)	Mike Baxes	15.00	7.50	4.50
(3)	Zeke Bella	15.00	7.50	4.50
(4)	Lou Boudreau	30.00	15.00	9.00
(5)	Cletis Boyer	20.00	10.00	6.00
(6)	Wally Burnette	15.00	7.50	4.50
(7)	Chico Carrasquel	17.50	8.75	5.25
(8)	Bob Cerv	15.00	7.50	4.50
(9)	Harry Chiti	15.00	7.50	4.50
(10)	Harry Craft	15.00	7.50	4.50
(11)	Jack Crimian	15.00	7.50	4.50
(12)	Bud Daley	15.00	7.50	4.50
(13)	Bob Davis	15.00	7.50	4.50
(14)	Joe DeMaestri	15.00	7.50	4.50
(15)	Art Ditmar	15.00	7.50	4.50
(16)	Jim Ewell (Trainer)	15.00	7.50	4.50
(17)	Jim Finigan	15.00	7.50	4.50
(18)	Hank Foiles	15.00	7.50	4.50
(19)	Ned Garver	17.50	8.75	5.25
(20)	Joe Ginsberg	15.00	7.50	4.50
(21)	Tom Gorman (Cap-to-knees.)	15.00	7.50	4.50
(22)	Tom Gorman/Ptchg	15.00	7.50	4.50
(23)	Bob Grim	15.00	7.50	4.50
(24)	Johnny Groth	15.00	7.50	4.50
(25)	Kent Hadley	15.00	7.50	4.50
(26)	Ray Herbert	15.00	7.50	4.50
(27)	Troy Herriage	15.00	7.50	4.50
(28)	Whitey Herzog	20.00	10.00	6.00
(29)	Frank House	15.00	7.50	4.50
(32)	Alex Kellner	15.00	7.50	4.50
(33)	Lou Kretlow	15.00	7.50	4.50
(34)	Hec Lopez	15.00	7.50	4.50
(35)	Roger Maris	125.00	62.00	37.00
(36)	Oscar Melillo	15.00	7.50	4.50
(37)	Rance Pless	15.00	7.50	4.50
(38)	Vic Power	20.00	10.00	6.00

(39)	Jose Santiago	15.00	7.50	4.50
(40)	Bobby Shantz	25.00	12.50	7.50
(41)	Harry Simpson	17.50	8.75	5.25
(42)	Lou Skizas	15.00	7.50	4.50
(43)	Enos Slaughter	45.00	22.00	13.50
(44)	Hal Smith	15.00	7.50	4.50
(45)	George Susce	15.00	7.50	4.50
(46)	Wayne Terwilliger	15.00	7.50	4.50
(47)	Charles Thompson	15.00	7.50	4.50
(48)	Dick Tomanek	15.00	7.50	4.50
(49)	Bill Tuttle	15.00	7.50	4.50
(52)	Jack Urban	15.00	7.50	4.50
(53)	Preston Ward	15.00	7.50	4.50
(54)	Dick Williams	17.50	8.75	5.25
(55)	Gus Zernial/Btg	17.50	8.75	5.25
(56)	Gus Zernial/Fldg	17.50	8.75	5.25

1929 Kashin Publications (R316)

This set of 101 unnumbered cards was issued in 25-card boxed series, with cards measuring 3-1/2" x 4-1/2". The cards feature black-and-white photos with the player's name printed in script near the bottom of the photo. Team and league are designated at bottom in printed letters. The backs of the cards are blank. Four of the cards (Hadley, Haines, Siebold and Todt) are considered to be scarcer than the rest of the set. Some cards have been seen with "MADE IN U.S.A." in one of the picture's lower corners; their significance and value are undetermined.

		NM	EX	VG
Complete Set (101):		9,500	4,750	2,750
Common Player:		40.00	20.00	12.00
(1)	Dale Alexander	40.00	20.00	12.00
(2)	Ethan N. Allen	40.00	20.00	12.00
(3)	Larry Benton	40.00	20.00	12.00
(4)	Moe Berg	250.00	125.00	75.00
(5)	Max Bishop	40.00	20.00	12.00
(6)	Del Bissonette	40.00	20.00	12.00
(7)	Lucerne A. Blue	40.00	20.00	12.00
(8)	James Bottomley	100.00	50.00	30.00
(9)	Guy T. Bush	40.00	20.00	12.00
(10)	Harold G. Carlson	40.00	20.00	12.00
(11)	Owen Carroll	40.00	20.00	12.00
(12)	Chalmers W. Cissell (Chalmer)	40.00	20.00	12.00
(13)	Earl Combs	100.00	50.00	30.00
(14)	Hugh M. Critz	40.00	20.00	12.00
(15)	H.J. DeBerry	40.00	20.00	12.00
(16)	Pete Donohue	40.00	20.00	12.00
(17)	Taylor Douthit	40.00	20.00	12.00
(18)	Chas. W. Dressen	40.00	20.00	12.00
(19)	Jimmy Dykes	40.00	20.00	12.00
(20)	Howard Ehmke	40.00	20.00	12.00
(21)	Elwood English	40.00	20.00	12.00
(22)	Urban Faber	100.00	50.00	30.00
(23)	Fred Fitzsimmons	40.00	20.00	12.00
(24)	Lewis A. Fonseca	40.00	20.00	12.00
(25)	Horace H. Ford	40.00	20.00	12.00
(26)	Jimmy Foxx	235.00	115.00	70.00
(27)	Frank Frisch	100.00	50.00	30.00
(28)	Lou Gehrig	1,125	560.00	335.00
(29)	Charles Gehringer	100.00	50.00	30.00
(30)	Leon Goslin	100.00	50.00	30.00
(31)	George Grantham	40.00	20.00	12.00
(32)	Burleigh Grimes	100.00	50.00	30.00
(33)	Robert Grove	200.00	100.00	60.00
(34)	Bump Hadley	150.00	75.00	45.00
(35)	Charlie Hafey	100.00	50.00	30.00
(36)	Jesse J. Haines	250.00	125.00	75.00
(37)	Harvey Hendrick	40.00	20.00	12.00
(38)	Floyd C. Herman	40.00	20.00	12.00
(39)	Andy High	40.00	20.00	12.00
(40)	Urban J. Hodapp	40.00	20.00	12.00
(41)	Frank Hogan	40.00	20.00	12.00
(42)	Rogers Hornsby	175.00	85.00	50.00
(43)	Waite Hoyt	100.00	50.00	30.00
(44)	Willis Hudlin	40.00	20.00	12.00
(45)	Frank O. Hurst	40.00	20.00	12.00
(46)	Charlie Jamieson	40.00	20.00	12.00
(47)	Roy C. Johnson	40.00	20.00	12.00
(48)	Percy Jones	40.00	20.00	12.00
(49)	Sam Jones	40.00	20.00	12.00
(50)	Joseph Judge	40.00	20.00	12.00
(51)	Willie Kamm	40.00	20.00	12.00
(52)	Charles Klein	100.00	50.00	30.00
(53)	Mark Koenig	40.00	20.00	12.00
(54)	Ralph Kress	40.00	20.00	12.00
(55)	Fred M. Leach	40.00	20.00	12.00
(56)	Fred Lindstrom	100.00	50.00	30.00
(57)	Ad Liska	40.00	20.00	12.00
(58)	Fred Lucas (Red)	40.00	20.00	12.00
(59)	Fred Maguire	40.00	20.00	12.00
(60)	Perce L. Malone	40.00	20.00	12.00
(61)	Harry Manush (Henry)	100.00	50.00	30.00
(62)	Walter Maranville	100.00	50.00	30.00
(63)	Douglas McWeeney (McWeeny)	40.00	20.00	12.00
(64)	Oscar Melillo	40.00	20.00	12.00
(65)	Ed "Bing" Miller	40.00	20.00	12.00
(66)	Frank O'Doul	80.00	40.00	24.00
(67)	Melvin Ott	200.00	100.00	60.00
(68)	Herbert Pennock	100.00	50.00	30.00
(69)	William W. Regan	40.00	20.00	12.00
(70)	Harry F. Rice	40.00	20.00	12.00
(71)	Sam Rice	100.00	50.00	30.00
(72)	Lance Richbourgh (Richbourg)	40.00	20.00	12.00
(73)	Eddie Rommel	40.00	20.00	12.00
(74)	Chas. H. Root	40.00	20.00	12.00
(75)	Ed (Edd) Roush	100.00	50.00	30.00
(76)	Harold Ruel (Herold)	40.00	20.00	12.00
(77)	Charles Ruffing	125.00	65.00	35.00
(78)	Jack Russell	40.00	20.00	12.00
(79)	Babe Ruth	1,650	825.00	500.00
(80)	Fred Schulte	40.00	20.00	12.00
(81)	Harry Seibold	150.00	75.00	45.00
(82)	Joe Sewell	100.00	50.00	30.00
(83)	Luke Sewell	40.00	20.00	12.00
(84)	Art Shires	40.00	20.00	12.00
(85)	Al Simmons	100.00	50.00	30.00
(86)	Bob Smith	40.00	20.00	12.00
(87)	Riggs Stephenson	40.00	20.00	12.00
(88)	Wm. H. Terry	100.00	50.00	30.00
(89)	Alphonse Thomas	40.00	20.00	12.00
(90)	Lafayette F. Thompson	40.00	20.00	12.00
(91)	Phil Todt	150.00	75.00	45.00
(92)	Harold J. Traynor	100.00	50.00	30.00
(93)	Dazzy Vance	100.00	50.00	30.00
(94)	Lloyd Waner	100.00	50.00	30.00
(95)	Paul Waner	100.00	50.00	30.00
(96)	Jimmy Welsh	40.00	20.00	12.00
(97)	Earl Whitehill	40.00	20.00	12.00
(98)	A.C. Whitney	40.00	20.00	12.00
(99)	Claude Willoughby	40.00	20.00	12.00
(100)	Hack Wilson	200.00	100.00	60.00
(101)	Tom Zachary	40.00	20.00	12.00

1964 KDKA Pittsburgh Pirates Portraits

Issued prior to the radio/TV stations' much more common color player cards of 1968, this seldom-seen regional issue presents the 1964 Pittsburgh Pirates in a set of 28 large-format (8" x 11-7/8") schedule cards. The cards are printed in sepia tones on blank-backed cardboard. Fronts present a player pose and a '64 Pirates schedule. A redemption offer states that a pair of Bucs' tickets will be given in exchange for a complete set of the portraits, and the pictures will be returned, presumably cancelled in some fashion. The unnumbered cards are checklisted here alphabetically. While the cards advertise the Pirates' broadcasting partners, they were actually issued by Sweet Clean laundry as stiffeners for men's shirts that had been washed. The laundry's name is not mentioned anywhere on the cards.

		NM	EX	VG
Complete Set (28):		3,500	1,750	1,000
Common Player:		100.00	50.00	30.00
(1)	Gene Alley	100.00	50.00	30.00
(2)	Bob Bailey	100.00	50.00	30.00
(3)	Frank Bork	100.00	50.00	30.00
(4)	Smoky Burgess	100.00	50.00	30.00
(5)	Tom Butters	100.00	50.00	30.00
(6)	Don Cardwell	100.00	50.00	30.00
(7)	Roberto Clemente	600.00	300.00	180.00
(8)	Donn Clendenon	100.00	50.00	30.00
(9)	Elroy Face	100.00	50.00	30.00
(10)	Gene Freese	100.00	50.00	30.00
(11)	Bob Friend	100.00	50.00	30.00
(12)	Joe Gibbon	100.00	50.00	30.00
(13)	Julio Gotay	100.00	50.00	30.00
(14)	Rex Johnston	100.00	50.00	30.00
(15)	Vernon Law	100.00	50.00	30.00
(16)	Jerry Lynch	100.00	50.00	30.00
(17)	Bill Mazeroski	250.00	125.00	75.00
(18)	Al McBean	100.00	50.00	30.00
(19)	Orlando McFarlane	100.00	50.00	30.00
(20)	Manny Mota	100.00	50.00	30.00
(21)	Danny Murtaugh	100.00	50.00	30.00
(22)	Jim Pagliaroni	100.00	50.00	30.00
(23)	Dick Schofield	100.00	50.00	30.00
(24)	Don Schwall	100.00	50.00	30.00
(25)	Tommie Sisk	100.00	50.00	30.00
(26)	Willie Stargell	250.00	125.00	75.00
(27)	Bob Veale	100.00	50.00	30.00
(28)	Bill Virdon	100.00	50.00	30.00

1968 KDKA Pittsburgh Pirates

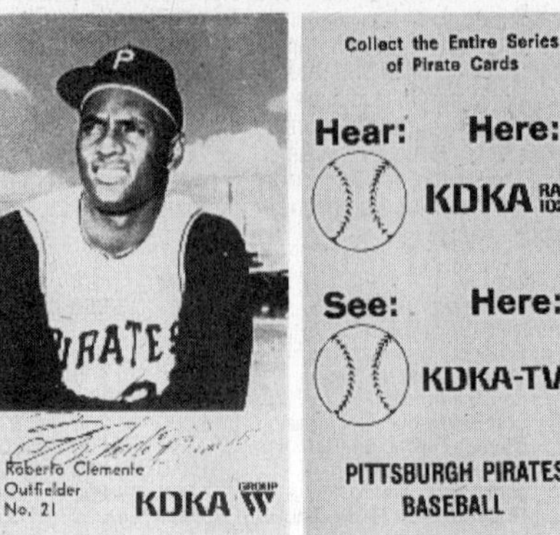

The most common of the many Pirates regional issues of the late 1960s, this 23-card set was sponsored by the Pirates' TV and radio flagship stations, KDKA in Pittsburgh. Cards measure 2-1/2" x 4" and feature at top front a color posed photo of the player, with no top or side borders. In the white panel beneath the photo are a facsimile autograph, the player's name, position and uniform number and the broadcasters' logo. Backs are printed in black on white and feature advertising for the radio and TV station. The checklist is presented here by uniform number.

		NM	EX	VG
Complete Set (23):		125.00	65.00	35.00
Common Player:		5.00	2.50	1.50
7	Larry Shepard	5.00	2.50	1.50
8	Willie Stargell	15.00	7.50	4.50
9	Bill Mazeroski	15.00	7.50	4.50
10	Gary Kolb	5.00	2.50	1.50
11	Jose Pagan	5.00	2.50	1.50
12	Gerry May (Jerry)	5.00	2.50	1.50
14	Jim Bunning	10.00	5.00	3.00
15	Manny Mota	5.00	2.50	1.50
17	Donn Clendenon	5.00	2.50	1.50
18	Matty Alou	5.00	2.50	1.50
21	Roberto Clemente	40.00	20.00	12.00
22	Gene Alley	5.00	2.50	1.50
25	Tommy Sisk	5.00	2.50	1.50
26	Roy Face	5.00	2.50	1.50
27	Ron Kline	5.00	2.50	1.50
28	Steve Blass	5.00	2.50	1.50
29	Juan Pizarro	5.00	2.50	1.50
30	Maury Wills	6.50	3.25	2.00
34	Al McBean	5.00	2.50	1.50
35	Manny Sanguillen	5.00	2.50	1.50
38	Bob Moose	5.00	2.50	1.50
39	Bob Veale	5.00	2.50	1.50
40	Dave Wickersham	5.00	2.50	1.50

1922 Keating Candy Co.

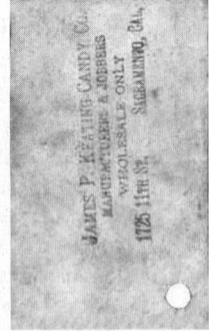

To compete with other candy issues featuring baseball cards as premiums, Sacramento, Calif., wholesale candy merchant James P. Keating appears to have purchased uncut sheets of the blank-back strip cards known as W575-1, over-printed their backs and packaged them with his product. The advertising on back is rubber-stamped. The fact that examples are known that have been cancelled with a hole punch probably indicates there was some sort of prize redemption program attached to the issue. Collectors can expect to pay a premium of about 3X for this version.

	NM	EX	VG
Common Player:	85.00	45.00	25.00
Stars: 3X			

(See 1922 W575-1 for checklist and base card values.)

1971 Keds Kedcards

These (usually) 2-1/4" x 2-1/8" cards were printed on the side of Keds athletic shoe boxes. The cards have colorful drawings of various athletes, with dotted lines for cutting. Backs are blank.

		NM	EX	VG
Complete Panel Set (3):		150.00	75.00	45.00
Complete Set (10):		120.00	60.00	35.00
Common Player:		8.00	4.00	2.50
	PANEL 1	40.00	20.00	12.00
(1)	Dave Bing (Basketball)	8.00	4.00	2.50
(2)	Clark Graebner (Tennis)	8.00	4.00	2.50
(3)	Jim Maloney	10.00	5.00	3.00
(4)	Bubba Smith (Football)	10.00	5.00	3.00
	PANEL 2	65.00	32.00	19.50
(5)	Johnny Bench	30.00	15.00	9.00
(6)	Willis Reed (Basketball)	10.00	5.00	3.00
(7)	Bubba Smith (Football)	10.00	5.00	3.00
(8)	Stan Smith (Tennis)	8.00	4.00	2.50
	PANEL 3	50.00	25.00	15.00
(9)	Willis Reed (Basketball) (5-1/4" x 3-1/2")	15.00	7.50	4.50
(10)	Johnny Bench (5-1/4" x 3-1/2")	30.00	15.00	9.00

1937 Kellogg's Pep Sports Stamps

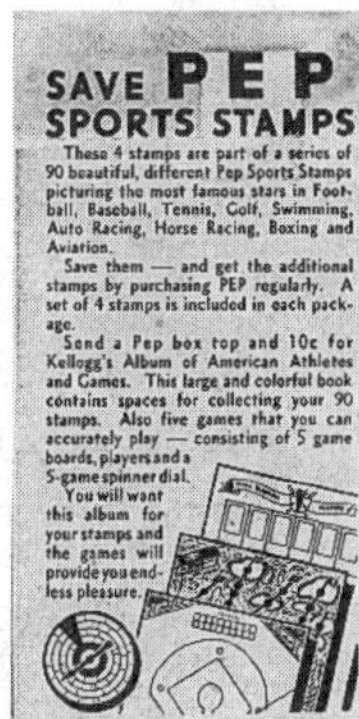

Kellogg's packaged a four-stamp panel of "Sports Stamps" in boxes of Pep cereal. While 24 panels comprise a complete set, six of the stamps were double-printed, creating a set of 90. Backs of the stamp panels gave details for ordering an album and game boards for playing with the stamps. The color-tinted stamps measure 1-1/8" x 2-3/4" individually, and 2-1/4" x 4-1/4" as a panel. Besides the ballplayers checklisted here, the Kellogg's/Pep stamps included football, tennis and golf players, swimmers, boxers, avaiators and race horses. Baseball player stamps are listed here according to the number of the four-stamp panel on which they appeared. Prices for complete panels would be considerably higher, factoring in the other stamps on the sheet.

		NM	EX	VG
Complete Set (18):		900.00	450.00	275.00
Common Player:		60.00	30.00	18.00
Album:		300.00	150.00	100.00
1	Joe Medwick	60.00	30.00	18.00
3	Leo Durocher	60.00	30.00	18.00
5	Gabby Hartnett	60.00	30.00	18.00
6	Billy Herman	60.00	30.00	18.00
7	Luke Appling	60.00	30.00	18.00
8	Floyd Vaughan	60.00	30.00	18.00
9	Paul Waner	60.00	30.00	18.00
11	Bill Terry	60.00	30.00	18.00
12	George Selkirk	60.00	30.00	18.00
13	Walter Johnson	120.00	60.00	36.00
15	Lew Fonseca	60.00	30.00	18.00
16	Richard Ferrell	60.00	30.00	18.00
17	Johnny Evers	60.00	30.00	18.00
18	Sam West	60.00	30.00	18.00
19	Buddy Myer	60.00	30.00	18.00
20	Tris Speaker (Double print, also on Panel 23.)	60.00	30.00	18.00
21	Joe Tinker	60.00	30.00	18.00
22	Mordecai Brown	60.00	30.00	18.00
23	Tris Speaker (Double-print, also on Panel 20.)	60.00	30.00	18.00

1948 Kellogg's Corn Flakes Cuban Postcards

These advertising postcards were issued in Cuba. The approximately 3-1/2" x 5-3/8" black-and-white cards have a portrait photo on front. A small logo for the cereal appears

in the lower-left corner, while a facsimile autograph is at lower-right. The back is in traditional postcard format, printed in English. This checklist is likely incomplete.

		NM	EX	VG
(1)	Tomas de la Cruz	400.00	200.00	120.00
(2)	Salvador Hernandez	400.00	200.00	120.00
(3)	Adolfo Luque	600.00	300.00	180.00
(4)	Roberto Ortiz	400.00	200.00	120.00
(5)	Napoleon Reyes	400.00	200.00	120.00
(6)	Lazaro Salazar	400.00	200.00	120.00

1948 Kellogg's Pep Celebrities

PHIL CAVARETTA
First baseman and outfielder, Chicago Cubs. National league batting champion and most valuable player in 1945. Joined Cubs at age of 17 and has lifetime batting average of .292. Bats and throws left-handed.
Get Complete Series with Kellogg's PEP

Five baseball players are included among the 18 athletes in this set of 1-3/8" x 1-5/8" cards. Fronts have player photos bordered in white. Backs have player name at top, a short career summary and a Kellogg's ad. The baseball players from the unnumbered set are listed here alphabetically.

		NM	EX	VG
Complete Set (5):		175.00	90.00	55.00
Common Player:		40.00	20.00	12.00
(1)	Phil Cavarretta	40.00	20.00	12.00
(2)	Orval Grove	40.00	20.00	12.00
(3)	Mike Tresh	40.00	20.00	12.00
(4)	Paul "Dizzy" Trout	40.00	20.00	12.00
(5)	Dick Wakefield	40.00	20.00	12.00

1970 Kellogg's

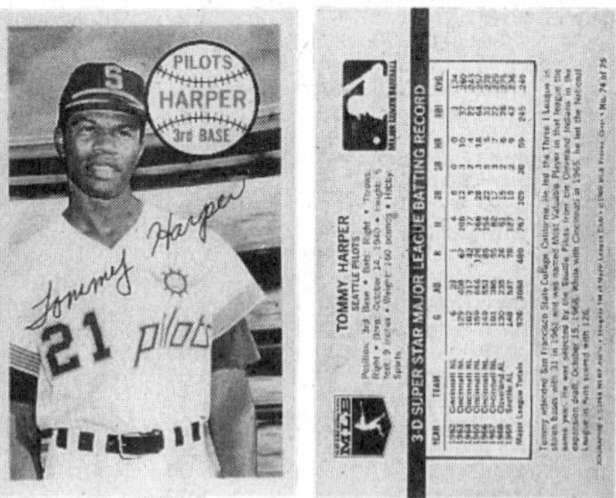

For 14 years in the 1970s and early 1980s, the Kellogg's cereal company provided Topps with virtually the only meaningful national competition in the baseball card market. Kellogg's kicked off its baseball card program in 1970 with a 75-player set of simulated 3-D cards. Single cards were available in selected brands of the company's cereal, while a mail-in program offered complete sets. The 3-D effect was achieved by the sandwiching of a clear color player photo between a purposely blurred stadium background scene and a layer of ribbed plastic. The relatively narrow dimension of the card, 2-1/4" x 3-1/2" and the nature of the plastic overlay seem to conspire to cause the cards to curl, often cracking the plastic layer, if not stored properly. Cards with major cracks in the plastic can be considered in Fair condition, at best.

		NM	EX	VG
Complete Set (75):		300.00	150.00	90.00
Common Player:		3.50	1.75	1.00
1	Ed Kranepool	3.50	1.75	1.00
2	Pete Rose	20.00	10.00	6.00
3	Cleon Jones	3.50	1.75	1.00
4	Willie McCovey	10.00	5.00	3.00
5	Mel Stottlemyre	3.50	1.75	1.00
6	Frank Howard	3.50	1.75	1.00
7	Tom Seaver	15.00	7.50	4.50
8	Don Sutton	10.00	5.00	3.00
9	Jim Wynn	3.50	1.75	1.00
10	Jim Maloney	3.50	1.75	1.00
11	Tommie Agee	3.50	1.75	1.00
12	Willie Mays	25.00	12.50	7.50
13	Juan Marichal	10.00	5.00	3.00
14	Dave McNally	3.50	1.75	1.00
15	Frank Robinson	15.00	7.50	4.50
16	Carlos May	3.50	1.75	1.00
17	Bill Singer	3.50	1.75	1.00
18	Rick Reichardt	3.50	1.75	1.00
19	Boog Powell	4.50	2.25	1.25
20	Gaylord Perry	10.00	5.00	3.00
21	Brooks Robinson	15.00	7.50	4.50
22	Luis Aparicio	10.00	5.00	3.00
23	Joel Horlen	3.50	1.75	1.00
24	Mike Epstein	3.50	1.75	1.00
25	Tom Haller	3.50	1.75	1.00
26	Willie Crawford	3.50	1.75	1.00
27	Roberto Clemente	35.00	17.50	10.00
28	Matty Alou	3.50	1.75	1.00
29	Willie Stargell	12.50	6.25	3.75
30	Tim Cullen	3.50	1.75	1.00
31	Randy Hundley	3.50	1.75	1.00
32	Reggie Jackson	20.00	10.00	6.00
33	Rich Allen	4.25	2.25	1.25
34	Tim McCarver	3.50	1.75	1.00
35	Ray Culp	3.50	1.75	1.00
36	Jim Fregosi	3.50	1.75	1.00
37	Billy Williams	12.50	6.25	3.75
38	Johnny Odom	3.50	1.75	1.00
39	Bert Campaneris	3.50	1.75	1.00
40	Ernie Banks	20.00	10.00	6.00
41	Chris Short	3.50	1.75	1.00
42	Ron Santo	6.00	3.00	1.75
43	Glenn Beckert	3.50	1.75	1.00
44	Lou Brock	12.50	6.25	3.75
45	Larry Hisle	3.50	1.75	1.00
46	Reggie Smith	3.50	1.75	1.00
47	Rod Carew	15.00	7.50	4.50
48	Curt Flood	3.50	1.75	1.00
49	Jim Lonborg	3.50	1.75	1.00
50	Sam McDowell	3.50	1.75	1.00
51	Sal Bando	3.50	1.75	1.00
52	Al Kaline	15.00	7.50	4.50
53	Gary Nolan	3.50	1.75	1.00
54	Rico Petrocelli	3.50	1.75	1.00
55	Ollie Brown	3.50	1.75	1.00
56	Luis Tiant	3.50	1.75	1.00
57	Bill Freehan	3.50	1.75	1.00
58	Johnny Bench	15.00	7.50	4.50
59	Joe Pepitone	3.50	1.75	1.00
60	Bobby Murcer	3.50	1.75	1.00
61	Harmon Killebrew	15.00	7.50	4.50
62	Don Wilson	3.50	1.75	1.00
63	Tony Oliva	3.50	1.75	1.00
64	Jim Perry	3.50	1.75	1.00
65	Mickey Lolich	3.50	1.75	1.00
66	Coco Laboy	3.50	1.75	1.00
67	Dean Chance	3.50	1.75	1.00
68	Ken Harrelson	3.50	1.75	1.00
69	Willie Horton	3.50	1.75	1.00
70	Wally Bunker	3.50	1.75	1.00
71a	Bob Gibson (1959 IP blank)	12.50	6.25	3.75
71b	Bob Gibson (1959 IP 76)	12.50	6.25	3.75
72	Joe Morgan	12.50	6.25	3.75
73	Denny McLain	3.50	1.75	1.00
74	Tommy Harper	3.50	1.75	1.00
75	Don Mincher	3.50	1.75	1.00

1971 Kellogg's

The scarcest and most valuable of the Kellogg's editions, the 75-card 1971 set was the only one not offered by the company on a mail-in basis. The only way to complete it was to buy ... and buy and buy ... boxes of cereal. Kellogg's again used the simulated 3-D effect in the cards' design, with the same result being many of the 2-1/4" x 3-1/2" cards are found today with cracks resulting from the cards' curling. A number of scarcer back variations are checklisted below. In addition, all 75 cards can be found with and without the 1970 date before the "Xograph" copyright line on the back; though there is no difference in value.

		NM	EX	VG
Complete Set (75):		1,000	500.00	300.00
Common Player:		13.50	6.75	4.00
1a	Wayne Simpson (SO 120)	13.50	6.75	4.00
1b	Wayne Simpson (SO 119)	20.00	10.00	6.00
2	Tom Seaver	30.00	15.00	9.00
3a	Jim Perry (IP 2238)	13.50	6.75	4.00
3b	Jim Perry (IP 2239)	20.00	10.00	6.00

		NM	EX	VG
4a	Bob Robertson (RBI 94)	13.50	6.75	4.00
4b	Bob Robertson (RBI 95)	20.00	10.00	6.00
5	Roberto Clemente	70.00	35.00	20.00
6a	Gaylord Perry (IP 2014)	25.00	12.50	7.50
6b	Gaylord Perry (IP 2015)	30.00	15.00	9.00
7a	Felipe Alou (1970 Oakland NL)	20.00	10.00	6.00
7b	Felipe Alou (1970 Oakland AL)	25.00	12.50	7.50
8	Denis Menke	13.50	6.75	4.00
9a	Don Kessinger (Hits 849)	13.50	6.75	4.00
9b	Don Kessinger (Hits 850)	20.00	10.00	6.00
10	Willie Mays	45.00	22.00	13.50
11	Jim Hickman	13.50	6.75	4.00
12	Tony Oliva	17.50	8.75	5.25
13	Manny Sanguillen	13.50	6.75	4.00
14a	Frank Howard (1968 Washington NL)	30.00	15.00	9.00
14b	Frank Howard (1968 Washington AL)	20.00	10.00	6.00
15	Frank Robinson	30.00	15.00	9.00
16	Willie Davis	13.50	6.75	4.00
17	Lou Brock	25.00	12.50	7.50
18	Cesar Tovar	13.50	6.75	4.00
19	Luis Aparicio	25.00	12.50	7.50
20	Boog Powell	17.50	8.75	5.25
21a	Dick Selma (SO 584)	13.50	6.75	4.00
21b	Dick Selma (SO 587)	20.00	10.00	6.00
22	Danny Walton	13.50	6.75	4.00
23	Carl Morton	13.50	6.75	4.00
24a	Sonny Siebert (SO 1054)	13.50	6.75	4.00
24b	Sonny Siebert (SO 1055)	20.00	10.00	6.00
25	Jim Merritt	13.50	6.75	4.00
26a	Jose Cardenal (Hits 828)	13.50	6.75	4.00
26b	Jose Cardenal (Hits 829)	20.00	10.00	6.00
27	Don Mincher	13.50	6.75	4.00
28a	Clyde Wright (California state logo.)	13.50	6.75	4.00
28b	Clyde Wright (Angels crest logo.)	20.00	10.00	6.00
29	Les Cain	13.50	6.75	4.00
30	Danny Cater	13.50	6.75	4.00
31	Don Sutton	25.00	12.50	7.50
32	Chuck Dobson	13.50	6.75	4.00
33	Willie McCovey	25.00	12.50	7.50
34	Mike Epstein	13.50	6.75	4.00
35a	Paul Blair (Runs 386)	13.50	6.75	4.00
35b	Paul Blair (Runs 385)	20.00	10.00	6.00
36a	Gary Nolan (SO 577)	13.50	6.75	4.00
36b	Gary Nolan (SO 581)	20.00	10.00	6.00
37	Sam McDowell	13.50	6.75	4.00
38	Amos Otis	13.50	6.75	4.00
39a	Ray Fosse (RBI 69)	13.50	6.75	4.00
39b	Ray Fosse (RBI 70)	20.00	10.00	6.00
40	Mel Stottlemyre	13.50	6.75	4.00
41	Cito Gaston	13.50	6.75	4.00
42	Dick Dietz	13.50	6.75	4.00
43	Roy White	13.50	6.75	4.00
44	Al Kaline	30.00	15.00	9.00
45	Carlos May	13.50	6.75	4.00
46a	Tommie Agee (RBI 313)	13.50	6.75	4.00
46b	Tommie Agee (RBI 314)	20.00	10.00	6.00
47	Tommy Harper	13.50	6.75	4.00
48	Larry Dierker	13.50	6.75	4.00
49	Mike Cuellar	13.50	6.75	4.00
50	Ernie Banks	30.00	15.00	9.00
51	Bob Gibson	25.00	12.50	7.50
52	Reggie Smith	13.50	6.75	4.00
53a	Matty Alou (RBI 273)	13.50	6.75	4.00
53b	Matty Alou (RBI 274)	20.00	10.00	6.00
54a	Alex Johnson (California state logo.)	13.50	6.75	4.00
54b	Alex Johnson (Angels crest logo.)	20.00	10.00	6.00
55	Harmon Killebrew	30.00	15.00	9.00
56	Billy Grabarkewitz	13.50	6.75	4.00
57	Rich Allen	17.50	8.75	5.25
58	Tony Perez	25.00	12.50	7.50
59a	Dave McNally (SO 1065)	13.50	6.75	4.00
59b	Dave McNally (SO 1067)	20.00	10.00	6.00
60a	Jim Palmer (SO 564)	25.00	12.50	7.50
60b	Jim Palmer (SO 567)	30.00	15.00	9.00
61	Billy Williams	25.00	12.50	7.50
62	Joe Torre	20.00	10.00	6.00
63a	Jim Northrup (AB 2773)	13.50	6.75	4.00
63b	Jim Northrup (AB 2772)	20.00	10.00	6.00
64a	Jim Fregosi (Calif. state logo - Hits 1326)	13.50	6.75	4.00
64b	Jim Fregosi (Calif. state logo - Hits 1327)	20.00	10.00	6.00
64c	Jim Fregosi (Angels crest logo.)	20.00	10.00	6.00
65	Pete Rose	60.00	30.00	18.00
66a	Bud Harrelson (RBI 112)	13.50	6.75	4.00
66b	Bud Harrelson (RBI 113)	20.00	10.00	6.00
67	Tony Taylor	13.50	6.75	4.00
68	Willie Stargell	25.00	12.50	7.50
69	Tony Horton	25.00	12.50	7.50
70a	Claude Osteen (No number.)	25.00	12.50	7.50
70b	Claude Osteen (#70 on back)	13.50	6.75	4.00
71	Glenn Beckert	13.50	6.75	4.00
72	Nate Colbert	13.50	6.75	4.00
73a	Rick Monday (AB 1705)	13.50	6.75	4.00
73b	Rick Monday (AB 1704)	20.00	10.00	6.00
74a	Tommy John (BB 444)	20.00	10.00	6.00
74b	Tommy John (BB 443)	25.00	12.50	7.50
75	Chris Short	13.50	6.75	4.00

1972 Kellogg's

For 1972, Kellogg's reduced both the number of cards in its set and the dimensions of each card, moving to a 2-1/8" x 3-1/4" size and fixing the set at 54 cards. Once again, the cards were produced to simulate a 3-D effect (see description for 1970 Kellogg's). The set was available via a mail-in offer. The checklist includes variations which resulted from the correction of erroneous statistics on the backs of some cards. The complete set values quoted do not include the scarcer variations.

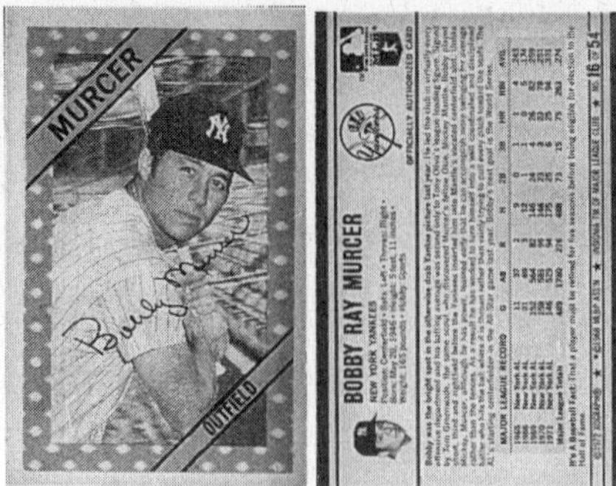

		NM	EX	VG
Complete Set (54):		125.00	65.00	35.00
Common Player:		1.00	.50	.30
1a	Tom Seaver (1970 ERA 2.85)	10.00	5.00	3.00
1b	Tom Seaver (1970 ERA 2.81)	7.50	3.75	2.25
2	Amos Otis	1.00	.50	.30
3a	Willie Davis (Runs 842)	2.00	1.00	.60
3b	Willie Davis (Runs 841)	1.25	.60	.40
4	Wilbur Wood	1.00	.50	.30
5	Bill Parsons	1.00	.50	.30
6	Pete Rose	15.00	7.50	4.50
7a	Willie McCovey (HR 360)	6.00	3.00	1.75
7b	Willie McCovey (HR 370)	5.00	2.50	1.50
8	Fergie Jenkins	3.50	1.75	1.00
9a	Vida Blue (ERA 2.35)	2.00	1.00	.60
9b	Vida Blue (ERA 2.31)	1.25	.60	.40
10	Joe Torre	2.50	1.25	.70
11	Merv Rettenmund	1.00	.50	.30
12	Bill Melton	1.00	.50	.30
13a	Jim Palmer (Games 170)	6.00	3.00	1.75
13b	Jim Palmer (Games 168)	4.50	2.25	1.25
14	Doug Rader	1.00	.50	.30
15a	Dave Roberts (...Seaver, the NL leader...)	2.00	1.00	.60
15b	Dave Roberts (...Seaver, the league leader...)	1.25	.60	.40
16	Bobby Murcer	1.25	.60	.40
17	Wes Parker	1.00	.50	.30
18a	Joe Coleman (BB 394)	2.00	1.00	.60
18b	Joe Coleman (BB 393)	1.25	.60	.40
19	Manny Sanguillen	1.00	.50	.30
20	Reggie Jackson	10.00	5.00	3.00
21	Ralph Garr	1.00	.50	.30
22	Jim "Catfish" Hunter	3.50	1.75	1.00
23	Rick Wise	1.00	.50	.30
24	Glenn Beckert	1.00	.50	.30
25	Tony Oliva	1.00	.50	.30
26a	Bob Gibson (SO 2577)	6.00	3.00	1.75
26b	Bob Gibson (SO 2578)	4.50	2.25	1.25
27a	Mike Cuellar (1971 ERA 3.80)	2.00	1.00	.60
27b	Mike Cuellar (1971 ERA 3.08)	1.25	.60	.40
28	Chris Speier	1.00	.50	.30
29a	Dave McNally (ERA 3.18)	2.00	1.00	.60
29b	Dave McNally (ERA 3.15)	1.25	.60	.40
30	Chico Cardenas	1.00	.50	.30
31a	Bill Freehan (AVG. .263)	2.00	1.00	.60
31b	Bill Freehan (AVG. .262)	1.25	.60	.40
32a	Bud Harrelson (Hits 634)	2.00	1.00	.60
32b	Bud Harrelson (Hits 624)	1.25	.60	.40
33a	Sam McDowell (...less than 200 innings...)	2.00	1.00	.60
33b	Sam McDowell (...less than 225 innings...)	1.25	.60	.40
34a	Claude Osteen (1971 ERA 3.25)	2.00	1.00	.60
34b	Claude Osteen (1971 ERA 3.51)	1.25	.60	.40
35	Reggie Smith	1.00	.50	.30
36	Sonny Siebert	1.00	.50	.30
37	Lee May	1.00	.50	.30
38	Mickey Lolich	1.00	.50	.30
39a	Cookie Rojas (2B 149)	2.00	1.00	.60
39b	Cookie Rojas (2B 150)	1.25	.60	.40
40	Dick Drago	1.00	.50	.30
41	Nate Colbert	1.00	.50	.30
42	Andy Messersmith	1.00	.50	.30
43a	Dave Johnson (AVG. .262)	2.00	1.00	.60
43b	Dave Johnson (AVG. .264)	1.25	.60	.40
44	Steve Blass	1.00	.50	.30
45	Bob Robertson	1.00	.50	.30
46a	Billy Williams (...missed only one last season...)	6.00	3.00	1.75
46b	Billy Williams (Phrase omitted.)	4.50	2.25	1.25
47	Juan Marichal	4.00	2.00	1.25
48	Lou Brock	4.00	2.00	1.25
49	Roberto Clemente	17.50	8.75	5.25
50	Mel Stottlemyre	1.00	.50	.30
51	Don Wilson	1.00	.50	.30
52a	Sal Bando (RBI 355)	2.00	1.00	.60
52b	Sal Bando (RBI 356)	1.25	.60	.40
53a	Willie Stargell (2B 197)	6.00	3.00	1.75
53b	Willie Stargell (2B 196)	4.50	2.25	1.25
54a	Willie Mays (RBI 1855)	15.00	7.50	4.50
54b	Willie Mays (RBI 1856)	12.00	6.00	3.50

1972 Kellogg's All-Time Baseball Greats

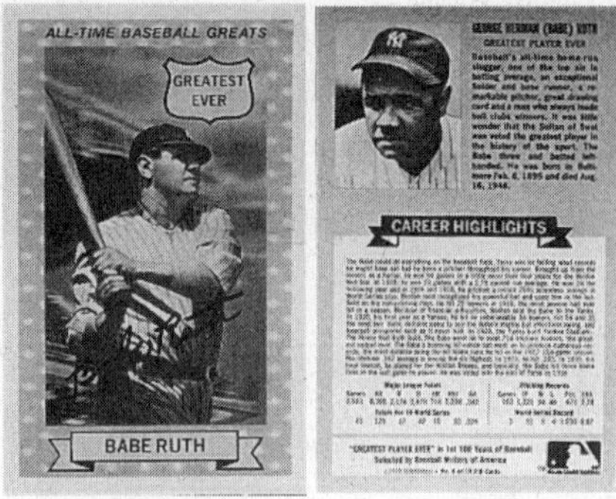

Kellogg's issued a second baseball card set in 1972, inserted into packages of breakfast rolls. The 2-1/4" x 3-1/2" cards also featured a simulated 3-D effect, but the 15 players in the set were "All-Time Baseball Greats," rather than current players. The set is virtually identical to a Rold Gold pretzel issue of 1970; the only difference being the 1972 copyright date on the back of the Kellog's cards, while the pretzel issue bears a 1970 date. The pretzel cards are considerably scarcer than the Kellogg's.

		NM	EX	VG
Complete Set (15):		45.00	22.50	13.50
Common Player:		2.50	1.25	.70
1	Walter Johnson	3.50	1.75	1.00
2	Rogers Hornsby	2.50	1.25	.70
3	John McGraw	2.50	1.25	.70
4	Mickey Cochrane	2.50	1.25	.70
5	George Sisler	2.50	1.25	.70
6	Babe Ruth (Portrait photo on back.)	15.00	7.50	4.50
7	Robert "Lefty" Grove	2.50	1.25	.70
8	Harold "Pie" Traynor	2.50	1.25	.70
9	Honus Wagner	5.00	2.50	1.50
10	Eddie Collins	2.50	1.25	.70
11	Tris Speaker	2.50	1.25	.70
12	Cy Young	3.50	1.75	1.00
13	Lou Gehrig	10.00	5.00	3.00
14	Babe Ruth (Action photo on back.)	15.00	7.50	4.50
15	Ty Cobb	10.00	5.00	3.00

1973 Kellogg's

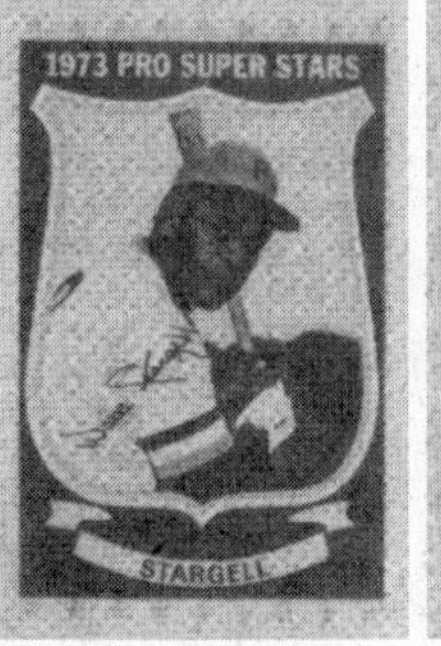

The lone exception to Kellogg's long run of simulated 3-D effect cards came in 1973, when the cereal company's 54-card set was produced by "normal" printing methods. In 2-1/4" x 3-1/2" size, the design was otherwise quite compatible with the issues which preceded and succeeded it. Because it was available via a mail-in offer ($1.25 and two Raisin Bran boxtops), it is not as scarce as the earlier Kellogg's issues.

		NM	EX	VG
Complete Set (54):		65.00	32.50	20.00
Common Player:		.90	.45	.25
1	Amos Otis	.90	.45	.25
2	Ellie Rodriguez	.90	.45	.25
3	Mickey Lolich	.90	.45	.25
4	Tony Oliva	1.25	.60	.40
5	Don Sutton	3.50	1.75	1.00
6	Pete Rose	12.00	6.00	3.50
7	Steve Carlton	4.50	2.25	1.25
8	Bobby Bonds	.90	.45	.25
9	Wilbur Wood	.90	.45	.25
10	Billy Williams	4.50	2.25	1.25
11	Steve Blass	.90	.45	.25
12	Jon Matlack	.90	.45	.25
13	Cesar Cedeno	.90	.45	.25
14	Bob Gibson	4.50	2.25	1.25
15	Sparky Lyle	.90	.45	.25
16	Nolan Ryan	17.50	8.75	5.25
17	Jim Palmer	4.50	2.25	1.25
18	Ray Fosse	.90	.45	.25
19	Bobby Murcer	.90	.45	.25
20	Jim "Catfish" Hunter	3.50	1.75	1.00
21	Tug McGraw	.90	.45	.25
22	Reggie Jackson	9.00	4.50	2.75
23	Bill Stoneman	.90	.45	.25
24	Lou Piniella	.90	.45	.25
25	Willie Stargell	4.50	2.25	1.25
26	Dick Allen	2.50	1.25	.70
27	Carlton Fisk	4.50	2.25	1.25
28	Fergie Jenkins	3.50	1.75	1.00
29	Phil Niekro	3.50	1.75	1.00
30	Gary Nolan	.90	.45	.25
31	Joe Torre	2.50	1.25	.70
32	Bobby Tolan	.90	.45	.25
33	Nate Colbert	.90	.45	.25

34	Joe Morgan	4.50	2.25	1.25
35	Bert Blyleven	.90	.45	.25
36	Joe Rudi	.90	.45	.25
37	Ralph Garr	.90	.45	.25
38	Gaylord Perry	3.50	1.75	1.00
39	Bobby Grich	.90	.45	.25
40	Lou Brock	4.00	2.00	1.25
41	Pete Broberg	.90	.45	.25
42	Manny Sanguillen	.90	.45	.25
43	Willie Davis	.90	.45	.25
44	Dave Kingman	.90	.45	.25
45	Carlos May	.90	.45	.25
46	Tom Seaver	6.00	3.00	1.75
47	Mike Cuellar	.90	.45	.25
48	Joe Coleman	.90	.45	.25
49	Claude Osteen	.90	.45	.25
50	Steve Kline	.90	.45	.25
51	Rod Carew	4.50	2.25	1.25
52	Al Kaline	6.00	3.00	1.75
53	Larry Dierker	.90	.45	.25
54	Ron Santo	2.50	1.25	.70

1974 Kellogg's

For 1974, Kellogg's returned to the use of simulated 3-D for its 54-player baseball card issue (see 1970 Kellogg's listing for description). In 2-1/8" x 3-1/4" size, the cards were available as a complete set via a mail-in offer. The complete set price listed here does not include the more expensive variations.

		NM	EX	VG
Complete Set (54):		65.00	32.50	20.00
Common Player:		.90	.45	.25
1	Bob Gibson	3.50	1.75	1.00
2	Rick Monday	.90	.45	.25
3	Joe Coleman	.90	.45	.25
4	Bert Campaneris	.90	.45	.25
5	Carlton Fisk	4.00	2.00	1.25
6	Jim Palmer	3.50	1.75	1.00
7a	Ron Santo (Chicago Cubs)	2.25	1.25	.70
7b	Ron Santo (Chicago White Sox)	1.25	.60	.40
8	Nolan Ryan	16.00	8.00	4.75
9	Greg Luzinski	.90	.45	.25
10a	Buddy Bell (Runs 134)	2.25	1.25	.70
10b	Buddy Bell (Runs 135)	1.00	.50	.30
11	Bob Watson	.90	.45	.25
12	Bill Singer	.90	.45	.25
13	Dave May	.90	.45	.25
14	Jim Brewer	.90	.45	.25
15	Manny Sanguillen	.90	.45	.25
16	Jeff Burroughs	.90	.45	.25
17	Amos Otis	.90	.45	.25
18	Ed Goodson	.90	.45	.25
19	Nate Colbert	.90	.45	.25
20	Reggie Jackson	6.50	3.25	2.00
21	Ted Simmons	.90	.45	.25
22	Bobby Murcer	1.00	.50	.30
23	Willie Horton	1.00	.50	.30
24	Orlando Cepeda	3.50	1.75	1.00
25	Ron Hunt	.90	.45	.25
26	Wayne Twitchell	.90	.45	.25
27	Ron Fairly	.90	.45	.25
28	Johnny Bench	4.50	2.25	1.25
29	John Mayberry	.90	.45	.25
30	Rod Carew	4.00	2.00	1.25
31	Ken Holtzman	.90	.45	.25
32	Billy Williams	3.50	1.75	1.00
33	Dick Allen	1.50	.70	.45
34a	Wilbur Wood (SO 959)	1.50	.70	.45
34b	Wilbur Wood (SO 960)	1.00	.50	.30
35	Danny Thompson	.90	.45	.25
36	Joe Morgan	3.50	1.75	1.00
37	Willie Stargell	3.50	1.75	1.00
38	Pete Rose	10.00	5.00	3.00
39	Bobby Bonds	.90	.45	.25
40	Chris Speier	.90	.45	.25
41	Sparky Lyle	.90	.45	.25
42	Cookie Rojas	.90	.45	.25
43	Tommy Davis	.90	.45	.25
44	Jim "Catfish" Hunter	3.50	1.75	1.00
45	Willie Davis	.90	.45	.25
46	Bert Blyleven	.90	.45	.25
47	Pat Kelly	.90	.45	.25
48	Ken Singleton	.90	.45	.25
49	Manny Mota	.90	.45	.25
50	Dave Johnson	.90	.45	.25
51	Sal Bando	.90	.45	.25
52	Tom Seaver	4.50	2.25	1.25
53	Felix Millan	.90	.45	.25
54	Ron Blomberg	.90	.45	.25

1975 Kellogg's

While the card size remained the same at 2-1/8" x 3-1/4", the size of the 1975 Kellogg's "3-D" set was increased by three, to 57 cards. Despite the fact cards could be obtained

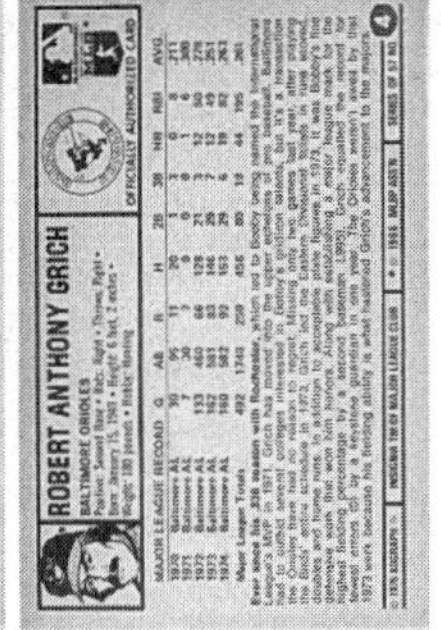

by a mail-in offer, as well as in cereal boxes, the '75 Kellogg's are noticeably scarcer than the company's other issues, with the exception of the 1971 set. Also helping to raise the value of the cards is the presence of an unusually large number of current and future Hall of Famers.

		NM	EX	VG
Complete Set (57):		175.00	90.00	55.00
Common Player:		2.00	1.00	.60
1	Roy White	2.00	1.00	.60
2	Ross Grimsley	2.00	1.00	.60
3	Reggie Smith	2.00	1.00	.60
4a	Bob Grich ("...1973 work..." in last line)	3.00	1.50	.90
4b	Bob Grich (no "...1973 work...")	2.00	1.00	.60
5	Greg Gross	2.00	1.00	.60
6	Bob Watson	2.00	1.00	.60
7	Johnny Bench	10.00	5.00	3.00
8	Jeff Burroughs	2.00	1.00	.60
9	Elliott Maddox	2.00	1.00	.60
10	Jon Matlack	2.00	1.00	.60
11	Pete Rose	25.00	12.50	7.50
12	Leroy Stanton	2.00	1.00	.60
13	Bake McBride	2.00	1.00	.60
14	Jorge Orta	2.00	1.00	.60
15	Al Oliver	2.50	1.25	.70
16	John Briggs	2.00	1.00	.60
17	Steve Garvey	4.50	2.25	1.25
18	Brooks Robinson	10.00	5.00	3.00
19	John Hiller	2.00	1.00	.60
20	Lynn McGlothen	2.00	1.00	.60
21	Cleon Jones	2.00	1.00	.60
22	Fergie Jenkins	6.00	3.00	1.75
23	Bill North	2.00	1.00	.60
24	Steve Busby	2.00	1.00	.60
25	Richie Zisk	2.00	1.00	.60
26	Nolan Ryan	35.00	17.50	10.50
27	Joe Morgan	7.50	3.75	2.25
28	Joe Rudi	2.00	1.00	.60
29	Jose Cardenal	2.00	1.00	.60
30	Andy Messersmith	2.00	1.00	.60
31	Willie Montanez	2.00	1.00	.60
32	Bill Buckner	2.00	1.00	.60
33	Rod Carew	7.50	3.75	2.25
34	Lou Piniella	2.50	1.25	.70
35	Ralph Garr	2.00	1.00	.60
36	Mike Marshall	2.00	1.00	.60
37	Garry Maddox	2.00	1.00	.60
38	Dwight Evans	2.00	1.00	.60
39	Lou Brock	7.50	3.75	2.25
40	Ken Singleton	2.00	1.00	.60
41	Steve Braun	2.00	1.00	.60
42	Dick Allen	3.50	1.75	1.00
43	Johnny Grubb	2.00	1.00	.60
44a	Jim Hunter (Oakland)	9.00	4.50	2.75
44b	Jim Hunter (New York)	7.50	3.75	2.25
45	Gaylord Perry	6.00	3.00	1.75
46	George Hendrick	2.00	1.00	.60
47	Sparky Lyle	2.00	1.00	.60
48	Dave Cash	2.00	1.00	.60
49	Luis Tiant	2.00	1.00	.60
50	Cesar Geronimo	2.00	1.00	.60
51	Carl Yastrzemski	12.00	6.00	3.50
52	Ken Brett	2.00	1.00	.60
53	Hal McRae	2.00	1.00	.60
54	Reggie Jackson	15.00	7.50	4.50
55	Rollie Fingers	6.00	3.00	1.75
56	Mike Schmidt	15.00	7.50	4.50
57	Richie Hebner	2.00	1.00	.60

1976 Kellogg's

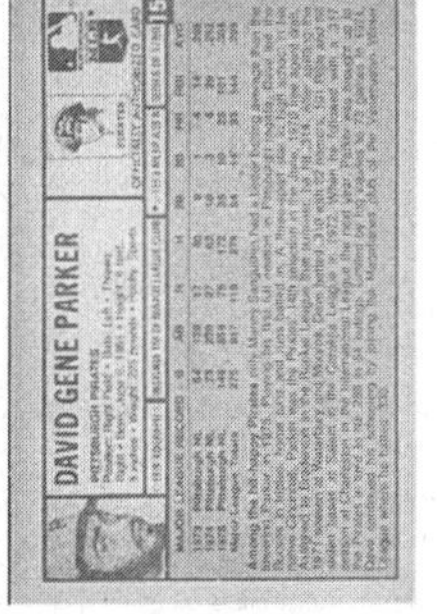

A sizeable list of corrected errors and other variation cards dots the checklist for the 57-card 1976 Kellogg's 3-D set. Again containing 57 cards, the first three cards in the set are found far less often than cards #4-57, indicating they were short-printed in relation to the rest of the set. The complete set values quoted below do not include the scarcer variation cards. Card size remained at 2-1/8" x 3-1/4". Cards #1-3 were significantly short-printed.

		NM	EX	VG
Complete Set (57):		70.00	35.00	20.00
Common Player:		1.25	.60	.40
1	Steve Hargan	10.00	5.00	3.00
2	Claudell Washington	10.00	5.00	3.00
3	Don Gullett	10.00	5.00	3.00
4	Randy Jones	1.25	.60	.40
5	Jim "Catfish" Hunter	3.50	1.75	1.00
6a	Clay Carroll (Cincinnati)	2.25	1.25	.70
6b	Clay Carroll (Chicago)	1.25	.60	.40
7	Joe Rudi	1.25	.60	.40
8	Reggie Jackson	9.00	4.50	2.75
9	Felix Millan	1.25	.60	.40
10	Jim Rice	2.00	1.00	.60
11	Bert Blyleven	1.25	.60	.40
12	Ken Singleton	1.25	.60	.40
13	Don Sutton	3.50	1.75	1.00
14	Joe Morgan	4.00	2.00	1.25
15	Dave Parker	1.50	.70	.45
16	Dave Cash	1.25	.60	.40
17	Ron LeFlore	1.25	.60	.40
18	Greg Luzinski	1.25	.60	.40
19	Dennis Eckersley	6.00	3.00	1.75
20	Bill Madlock	1.25	.60	.40
21	George Scott	1.25	.60	.40
22	Willie Stargell	4.00	2.00	1.25
23	Al Hrabosky	1.25	.60	.40
24	Carl Yastrzemski	7.50	3.75	2.25
25a	Jim Kaat (White Sox logo on back.)	3.00	1.50	.90
25b	Jim Kaat (Phillies logo on back.)	1.50	.70	.45
26	Marty Perez	1.25	.60	.40
27	Bob Watson	1.25	.60	.40
28	Eric Soderholm	1.25	.60	.40
29	Bill Lee	1.25	.60	.40
30a	Frank Tanana (1975 ERA 2.63)	2.00	1.00	.60
30b	Frank Tanana (1975 ERA 2.62)	1.25	.60	.40
31	Fred Lynn	1.50	.70	.45
32a	Tom Seaver (1967 PCT. 552)	7.50	3.75	2.25
32b	Tom Seaver (1967 Pct. .552)	6.00	3.00	1.75
33	Steve Busby	1.25	.60	.40
34	Gary Carter	4.00	2.00	1.25
35	Rick Wise	1.25	.60	.40
36	Johnny Bench	5.00	2.50	1.50
37	Jim Palmer	4.00	2.00	1.25
38	Bobby Murcer	1.50	.70	.45
39	Von Joshua	1.25	.60	.40
40	Lou Brock	4.00	2.00	1.25
41a	Mickey Rivers (last line begins "In three...")	2.00	1.00	.60
41b	Mickey Rivers (last line begins "The Yankees...")	1.25	.60	.40
42	Manny Sanguillen	1.25	.60	.40
43	Jerry Reuss	1.25	.60	.40
44	Ken Griffey	1.25	.60	.40
45a	Jorge Orta (AB 1616)	1.75	.90	.50
45b	Jorge Orta (AB 1615)	1.25	.60	.40
46	John Mayberry	1.25	.60	.40
47a	Vida Blue (2nd line reads "...pitched more innings ...")	2.25	1.25	.70
47b	Vida Blue (2nd line reads "...struck out more...")	1.25	.60	.40
48	Rod Carew	4.00	2.00	1.25
49a	Jon Matlack (1975 ER 87)	1.75	.90	.50
49b	Jon Matlack (1975 ER 86)	1.25	.60	.40
50	Boog Powell	2.25	1.25	.70
51a	Mike Hargrove (AB 935)	1.75	.90	.50
51b	Mike Hargrove (AB 934)	1.25	.60	.40
52a	Paul Lindblad (1975 ERA 2.72)	1.75	.90	.50
52b	Paul Lindblad (1975 ERA 2.73)	1.25	.60	.40
53	Thurman Munson	4.00	2.00	1.25
54	Steve Garvey	2.50	1.25	.70
55	Pete Rose	12.50	6.25	3.75
56a	Greg Gross (Games 302)	1.75	.90	.50
56b	Greg Gross (Games 334)	1.25	.60	.40
57	Ted Simmons	1.25	.60	.40

1977 Kellogg's

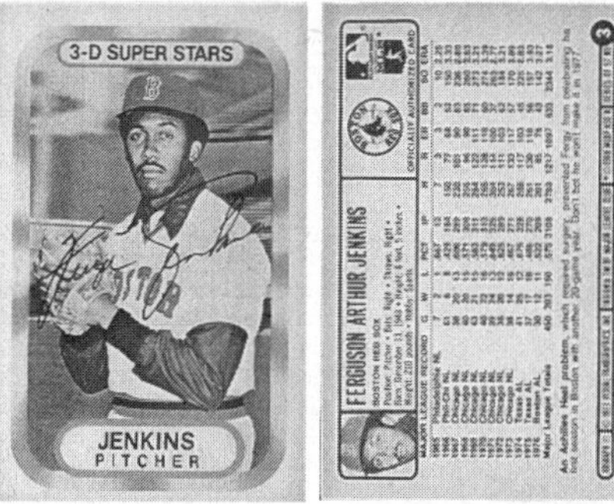

Other than another innovative card design to complement the simulated 3-D effect, there was little change in the 1977 Kellogg's issue. Set size remained at 57 cards, the set remained in the 2-1/8" x 3-1/4" format, and the cards were available either individually in boxes of cereal, or as a complete set via a mail-in box top offer. The 1977 set is the last in which Kellogg's used a player portrait photo on the back of the card.

		NM	EX	VG
Complete Set (57):		60.00	30.00	18.00
Common Player:		.75	.40	.25
1	George Foster	.75	.40	.25
2	Bert Campaneris	.75	.40	.25
3	Fergie Jenkins	2.50	1.25	.70
4	Dock Ellis	.75	.40	.25
5	John Montefusco	.75	.40	.25
6	George Brett	12.50	6.25	3.75
7	John Candelaria	.75	.40	.25
8	Fred Norman	.75	.40	.25
9	Bill Travers	.75	.40	.25
10	Hal McRae	.75	.40	.25
11	Doug Rau	.75	.40	.25
12	Greg Luzinski	.75	.40	.25
13	Ralph Garr	.75	.40	.25
14	Steve Garvey	1.50	.70	.45
15	Rick Manning	.75	.40	.25
16a	Lyman Bostock (Back photo is N.Y. Yankee Dock Ellis.)	7.50	3.75	2.25
16b	Lyman Bostock (Correct back photo.)	.75	.40	.25
17	Randy Jones	.75	.40	.25
18a	Ron Cey (58 homers in first sentence)	1.00	.50	.30
18b	Ron Cey (48 homers in first sentence)	.75	.40	.25
19	Dave Parker	.75	.40	.25
20	Pete Rose	15.00	7.50	4.50
21a	Wayne Garland (Last line begins "Prior to...")	1.00	.50	.30
21b	Wayne Garland (Last line begins "There he...")	.75	.40	.25
22	Bill North	.75	.40	.25
23	Thurman Munson	4.50	2.25	1.25
24	Tom Poquette	.75	.40	.25
25	Ron LeFlore	.75	.40	.25
26	Mark Fidrych	1.00	.50	.30
27	Sixto Lezcano	.75	.40	.25
28	Dave Winfield	7.50	3.75	2.25
29	Jerry Koosman	.75	.40	.25
30	Mike Hargrove	.75	.40	.25
31	Willie Montanez	.75	.40	.25
32	Don Stanhouse	.75	.40	.25
33	Jay Johnstone	.75	.40	.25
34	Bake McBride	.75	.40	.25
35	Dave Kingman	.75	.40	.25
36	Freddie Patek	.75	.40	.25
37	Garry Maddox	.75	.40	.25
38a	Ken Reitz (Last line begins "The previous...")	1.00	.50	.30
38b	Ken Reitz (Last line begins "In late...")	.75	.40	.25
39	Bobby Grich	.75	.40	.25
40	Cesar Geronimo	.75	.40	.25
41	Jim Lonborg	.75	.40	.25
42	Ed Figueroa	.75	.40	.25
43	Bill Madlock	.75	.40	.25
44	Jerry Remy	.75	.40	.25
45	Frank Tanana	.75	.40	.25
46	Al Oliver	1.00	.50	.30
47	Charlie Hough	.75	.40	.25
48	Lou Piniella	1.00	.50	.30
49	Ken Griffey	.75	.40	.25
50	Jose Cruz	.75	.40	.25
51	Rollie Fingers	2.50	1.25	.70
52	Chris Chambliss	.75	.40	.25
53	Rod Carew	4.50	2.25	1.25
54	Andy Messersmith	.75	.40	.25
55	Mickey Rivers	.75	.40	.25
56	Butch Wynegar	.75	.40	.25
57	Steve Carlton	3.50	1.75	1.00

1978 Kellogg's

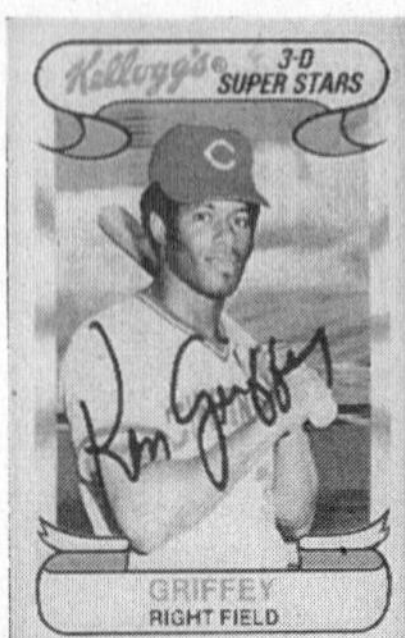

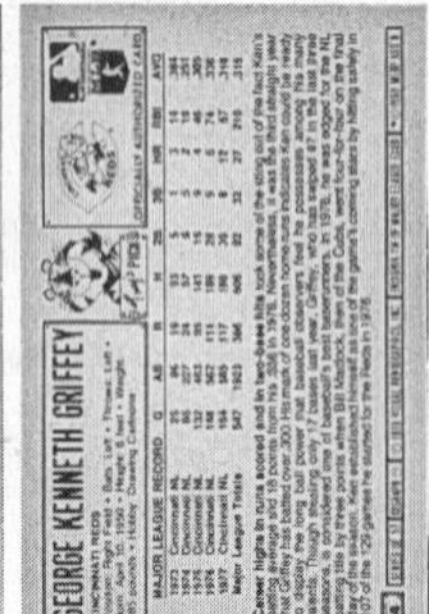

Besides the substitution of a Tony the Tiger drawing for a player portrait photo on the back of the card, the 1978 Kellogg's set offered no major changes from the previous few years issues. Cards were once again in the 2-1/8" x 3-1/4" format, with 57 cards comprising a complete set. Single cards were available in selected brands of the company's cereal, while complete sets could be obtained by a mail-in offer.

		NM	EX	VG
Complete Set (57):		60.00	30.00	18.00
Common Player:		.90	.45	.25
1	Steve Carlton	4.50	2.25	1.25
2	Bucky Dent	1.25	.60	.40
3	Mike Schmidt	13.50	6.75	4.00
4	Ken Griffey	.90	.45	.25
5	Al Cowens	.90	.45	.25
6	George Brett	13.50	6.75	4.00
7	Lou Brock	4.50	2.25	1.25
8	Rich Gossage	1.25	.60	.40
9	Tom Johnson	.90	.45	.25
10	George Foster	.90	.45	.25
11	Dave Winfield	4.50	2.25	1.25
12	Dan Meyer	.90	.45	.25
13	Chris Chambliss	.90	.45	.25
14	Paul Dade	.90	.45	.25
15	Jeff Burroughs	.90	.45	.25
16	Jose Cruz	.90	.45	.25
17	Mickey Rivers	.90	.45	.25
18	John Candelaria	.90	.45	.25
19	Ellis Valentine	.90	.45	.25
20	Hal McRae	.90	.45	.25
21	Dave Rozema	.90	.45	.25
22	Lenny Randle	.90	.45	.25
23	Willie McCovey	4.50	2.25	1.25
24	Ron Cey	.90	.45	.25
25	Eddie Murray	17.50	8.75	5.25
26	Larry Bowa	.90	.45	.25
27	Tom Seaver	5.00	2.50	1.50
28	Garry Maddox	.90	.45	.25
29	Rod Carew	4.50	2.25	1.25
30	Thurman Munson	4.50	2.25	1.25
31	Garry Templeton	.90	.45	.25
32	Eric Soderholm	.90	.45	.25
33	Greg Luzinski	.90	.45	.25
34	Reggie Smith	.90	.45	.25
35	Dave Goltz	.90	.45	.25
36	Tommy John	1.25	.60	.40
37	Ralph Garr	.90	.45	.25
38	Alan Bannister	.90	.45	.25
39	Bob Bailor	.90	.45	.25
40	Reggie Jackson	12.00	6.00	3.50
41	Cecil Cooper	.90	.45	.25
42	Burt Hooton	.90	.45	.25
43	Sparky Lyle	.90	.45	.25
44	Steve Ontiveros	.90	.45	.25
45	Rick Reuschel	.90	.45	.25
46	Lyman Bostock	.90	.45	.25
47	Mitchell Page	.90	.45	.25
48	Bruce Sutter	3.50	1.75	1.00
49	Jim Rice	2.50	1.25	.70
50	Bob Forsch	.90	.45	.25
51	Nolan Ryan	17.50	8.75	5.25
52	Dave Parker	.90	.45	.25
53	Bert Blyleven	.90	.45	.25
54	Frank Tanana	.90	.45	.25
55	Ken Singleton	.90	.45	.25
56	Mike Hargrove	.90	.45	.25
57	Don Sutton	3.50	1.75	1.00

1979 Kellogg's

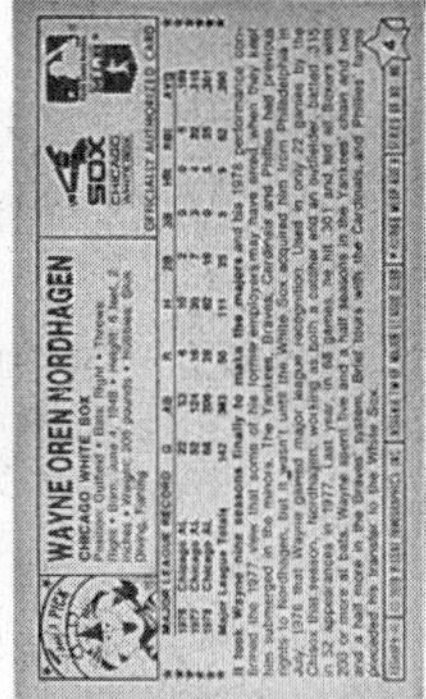

For its 1979 3-D issue, Kellogg's increased the size of the set to 60 cards, but reduced the width of the cards to 1-15/16". Depth stayed the same as in previous years, 3-1/4". The narrower card format seems to have compounded the problem of curling and subsequent cracking of the ribbed plastic surface which helps give the card a 3-D effect. Cards with major cracks can be graded no higher than VG. The complete set price in the checklist that follows does not include the scarcer variations. Numerous minor variations featuring copyright and trademark logos can be found in the set.

		NM	EX	VG
Complete Set (60):		30.00	15.00	9.00
Common Player:		.60	.30	.20
1	Bruce Sutter	2.50	1.25	.70
2	Ted Simmons	.60	.30	.20
3	Ross Grimsley	.60	.30	.20
4	Wayne Nordhagen	.60	.30	.20
5a	Jim Palmer (PCT. .649)	3.00	1.50	.90
5b	Jim Palmer (PCT. .650)	3.00	1.50	.90
6	John Henry Johnson	.60	.30	.20
7	Jason Thompson	.60	.30	.20
8	Pat Zachry	.60	.30	.20
9	Dennis Eckersley	3.00	1.50	.90
10a	Paul Splittorff (IP 1665)	.60	.30	.20
10b	Paul Splittorff (IP 1666)	.60	.30	.20
11a	Ron Guidry (Hits 397)	.60	.30	.20
11b	Ron Guidry (Hits 396)	.60	.30	.20
12	Jeff Burroughs	.60	.30	.20
13	Rod Carew	3.00	1.50	.90
14a	Buddy Bell (No trade line in bio.)	1.00	.50	.30
14b	Buddy Bell (Trade line in bio.)	.60	.30	.20
15	Jim Rice	1.00	.50	.30
16	Garry Maddox	.60	.30	.20
17	Willie McCovey	3.00	1.50	.90
18	Steve Carlton	3.00	1.50	.90
19a	J. R. Richard (Stats begin with 1972.)	.60	.30	.20
19b	J. R. Richard (Stats begin with 1971.)	.60	.30	.20
20	Paul Molitor	3.00	1.50	.90
21a	Dave Parker (AVG. .281)	.60	.30	.20
21b	Dave Parker (AVG. .318)	.60	.30	.20
22a	Pete Rose (1978 3B 3)	7.50	3.75	2.25
22b	Pete Rose (1978 3B 33)	7.50	3.75	2.25
23a	Vida Blue (Runs 819)	.60	.30	.20
23b	Vida Blue (Runs 818)	.60	.30	.20
24	Richie Zisk	.60	.30	.20
25a	Darrell Porter (2B 101)	.60	.30	.20
25b	Darrell Porter (2B 111)	.60	.30	.20
26a	Dan Driessen (Games 642)	.60	.30	.20
26b	Dan Driessen (Games 742)	.60	.30	.20
27a	Geoff Zahn (1978 Minnesota)	.60	.30	.20
27b	Geoff Zahn (1978 Minnesota)	.60	.30	.20
28	Phil Niekro	2.50	1.25	.70
29	Tom Seaver	3.00	1.50	.90
30	Fred Lynn	.60	.30	.20
31	Bill Bonham	.60	.30	.20
32	George Foster	.60	.30	.20
33a	Terry Puhl (Last line of bio begins "Terry...")	.60	.30	.20
33b	Terry Puhl (Last line of bio begins "His...")	.60	.30	.20
34a	John Candelaria (Age is 24.)	.60	.30	.20
34b	John Candelaria (Age is 25.)	.60	.30	.20
35	Bob Knepper	.60	.30	.20
36	Freddie Patek	.60	.30	.20
37	Chris Chambliss	.60	.30	.20
38a	Bob Forsch (1977 Games 86)	.60	.30	.20
38b	Bob Forsch (1977 Games 35)	.60	.30	.20
39a	Ken Griffey (1978 AB 674)	.60	.30	.20
39b	Ken Griffey (1978 AB 614)	.60	.30	.20
40	Jack Clark	.60	.30	.20
41a	Dwight Evans (1978 Hits 13)	.60	.30	.20
41b	Dwight Evans (1978 Hits 123)	.60	.30	.20
42	Lee Mazzilli	.60	.30	.20
43	Mario Guerrero	.60	.30	.20
44	Larry Bowa	.60	.30	.20
45a	Carl Yastrzemski (Games 9930)	4.00	2.00	1.25
45b	Carl Yastrzemski (Games 9929)	4.00	2.00	1.25
46a	Reggie Jackson (1978 Games 162)	6.00	3.00	1.75
46b	Reggie Jackson (1978 Games 139)	6.00	3.00	1.75
47	Rick Reuschel	.60	.30	.20
48a	Mike Flanagan (1976 SO 57)	.60	.30	.20
48b	Mike Flanagan (1976 SO 56)	.60	.30	.20
49a	Gaylord Perry (1973 Hits 325)	2.50	1.25	.70
49b	Gaylord Perry (1973 Hits 315)	2.50	1.25	.70
50	George Brett	6.00	3.00	1.75
51a	Craig Reynolds (Last line of bio begins "He spent...")	.60	.30	.20
51b	Craig Reynolds (Last line of bio begins "In those...")	.60	.30	.20
52	Davey Lopes	.60	.30	.20
53a	Bill Almon (2B 31)	.60	.30	.20
53b	Bill Almon (2B 41)	.60	.30	.20
54	Roy Howell	.60	.30	.20
55	Frank Tanana	.60	.30	.20
56a	Doug Rau (1978 PCT. .577)	.60	.30	.20
56b	Doug Rau (1978 PCT. .625)	.60	.30	.20
57a	Rick Monday (1976 Runs 197)	.60	.30	.20
57b	Rick Monday (1976 Runs 107)	.60	.30	.20
58	Jon Matlack	.60	.30	.20
59a	Ron Jackson (Last line of bio begins "His best...")	.60	.30	.20
59b	Ron Jackson (Last line of bio begins "The Twins...")	.60	.30	.20
60	Jim Sundberg	.60	.30	.20

1980 Kellogg's

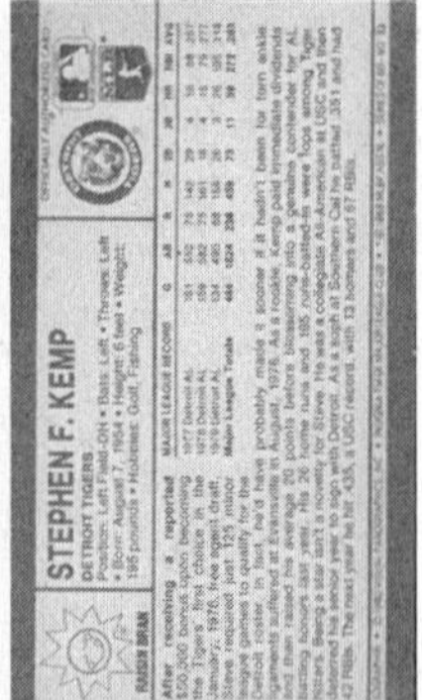

The 1980 cereal company issue featured the narrowest format of any Kellogg's card, 1-7/8" x 3-1/4". For the second straight year, set size remained at 60 cards, available either singly in boxes of cereal, or as complete sets by a mail-in offer.

		NM	EX	VG
Complete Set (60):		25.00	12.50	7.50
Common Player:		.60	.30	.20
1	Ross Grimsley	.60	.30	.20
2	Mike Schmidt	4.00	2.00	1.25
3	Mike Flanagan	.60	.30	.20
4	Ron Guidry	.60	.30	.20
5	Bert Blyleven	.60	.30	.20
6	Dave Kingman	.60	.30	.20
7	Jeff Newman	.60	.30	.20

8	Steve Rogers	.60	.30	.20
9	George Brett	4.00	2.00	1.25
10	Bruce Sutter	2.00	1.00	.60
11	Gorman Thomas	.60	.30	.20
12	Darrell Porter	.60	.30	.20
13	Roy Smalley	.60	.30	.20
14	Steve Carlton	2.00	1.00	.60
15	Jim Palmer	2.00	1.00	.60
16	Bob Bailor	.60	.30	.20
17	Jason Thompson	.60	.30	.20
18	Graig Nettles	.60	.30	.20
19	Ron Cey	.60	.30	.20
20	Nolan Ryan	7.50	3.75	2.25
21	Ellis Valentine	.60	.30	.20
22	Larry Hisle	.60	.30	.20
23	Dave Parker	.60	.30	.20
24	Eddie Murray	2.00	1.00	.60
25	Willie Stargell	2.00	1.00	.60
26	Reggie Jackson	4.00	2.00	1.25
27	Carl Yastrzemski	2.50	1.25	.70
28	Andre Thornton	.60	.30	.20
29	Davey Lopes	.60	.30	.20
30	Ken Singleton	.60	.30	.20
31	Steve Garvey	1.00	.50	.30
32	Dave Winfield	2.00	1.00	.60
33	Steve Kemp	.60	.30	.20
34	Claudell Washington	.60	.30	.20
35	Pete Rose	6.00	3.00	1.75
36	Cesar Cedeno	.60	.30	.20
37	John Stearns	.60	.30	.20
38	Lee Mazzilli	.60	.30	.20
39	Larry Bowa	.60	.30	.20
40	Fred Lynn	.60	.30	.20
41	Carlton Fisk	2.00	1.00	.60
42	Vida Blue	.60	.30	.20
43	Keith Hernandez	.60	.30	.20
44	Jim Rice	1.00	.50	.30
45	Ted Simmons	.60	.30	.20
46	Chet Lemon	.60	.30	.20
47	Fergie Jenkins	2.00	1.00	.60
48	Gary Matthews	.60	.30	.20
49	Tom Seaver	2.50	1.25	.70
50	George Foster	.60	.30	.20
51	Phil Niekro	2.00	1.00	.60
52	Johnny Bench	2.50	1.25	.70
53	Buddy Bell	.60	.30	.20
54	Lance Parrish	.60	.30	.20
55	Joaquin Andujar	.60	.30	.20
56	Don Baylor	.60	.30	.20
57	Jack Clark	.60	.30	.20
58	J.R. Richard	.60	.30	.20
59	Bruce Bochte	.60	.30	.20
60	Rod Carew	2.00	1.00	.60

1969 Kelly's Potato Chips Pins

Consisting of 20 pins, each measuring approximately 1-3/16" in diameter, this set was issued by Kelly's Potato Chips in 1969 and has a heavy emphasis on St. Louis Cardinals. The pin has a black-and-white player photo in the center surrounded by either a red border (for A.L. players) or a blue border (for N.L. players) that displays the player's team and name at the top and bottom. "Kelly's" appears to the left while the word "Zip!" is printed to the right. The pins are unnumbered.

		NM	EX	VG
Complete Set (20):		350.00	175.00	100.00
Common Player:		5.00	2.50	1.50
(1)	Luis Aparicio	25.00	12.50	7.50
(2)	Ernie Banks	45.00	22.00	13.50
(3)	Glenn Beckert	5.00	2.50	1.50
(4)	Lou Brock	25.00	12.50	7.50
(5)	Curt Flood	5.00	2.50	1.50
(6)	Bob Gibson	25.00	12.50	7.50
(7)	Joel Horlen	5.00	2.50	1.50
(8)	Al Kaline	45.00	22.00	13.50
(9)	Don Kessinger	5.00	2.50	1.50
(10)	Mickey Lolich	5.00	2.50	1.50
(11)	Juan Marichal	25.00	12.50	7.50
(12)	Willie Mays	75.00	37.00	22.00
(13)	Tim McCarver	7.50	3.75	2.25
(14)	Denny McLain	6.00	3.00	1.75
(15)	Pete Rose	65.00	32.00	19.50
(16)	Ron Santo	7.50	3.75	2.25
(17)	Joe Torre	15.00	7.50	4.50
(18)	Pete Ward	5.00	2.50	1.50
(19)	Billy Williams	25.00	12.50	7.50
(20)	Carl Yastrzemski	60.00	30.00	18.00

1887 W.S. Kimball Champions (N184)

Similar to sets issued by Allen & Ginter and Goodwin, the Kimball tobacco company of Rochester, N.Y., issued its own 50-card set of "Champions of Games and Sport" in 1887, and included four baseball players among the "billiardists, girl riders, tight-rope walkers" and other popular celebrities featured in the series. Measuring 1-1/2" x 2-3/4", the color lithograped artwork on the card features a posed portrait, which occupies the top three-fourths, and a drawing of the player in action at the bottom. The back of the card contains an ad for Kimball Cigarettes along with a list of the various sports and activities depicted in the set. The Kimball promotion also included an album to house the card set.

		NM	EX	VG
Complete Set (4):		5,500	2,200	1,650
Common Player:		1,100	440.00	330.00
Album:		4,125	1,650	1,000
(1)	E.A. Burch	1,650	550.00	425.00
(2)	Dell Darling	1,375	550.00	425.00
(3)	Hardie Henderson	1,375	550.00	425.00
(4)	James O'Neil (O'Neill)	1,375	550.00	425.00

1957-1959 Kiwanis Orioles Clinic

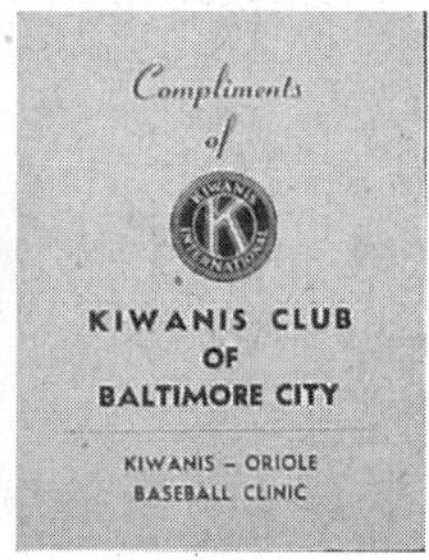

Details are lacking on this card which may or may not have been part of a series. Unless or until further players are checklisted, it is impossible to date the issue any more precisely. The front of the 2-7/8" x 3-1/4" card has a sepia photo that appears to have been copied from a team-issued postcard or picture. On back is the Kiwanis International logo with "Compliments / of" above and "KIWANIS CLUB / OF / BALTIMORE CITY / KIWANIS - ORIOLE / BASEBALL CLINIC" below.

	NM	EX	VG
Bob Nieman	40.00	20.00	12.00

1955-1957 Ted Kluszewski Steak House

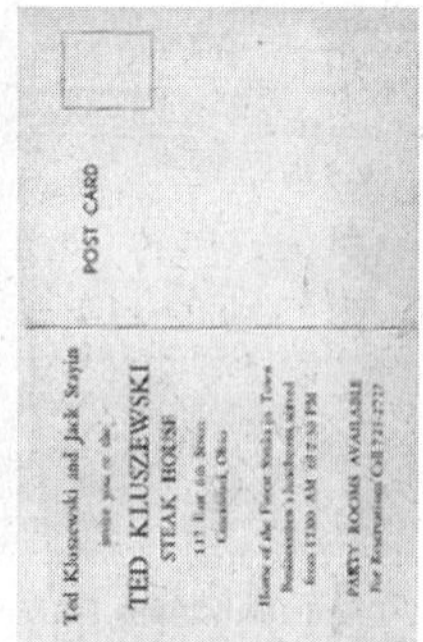

The true scope of this issue combined with the related Charcoal Steak House card (see also) is not known. Based on cards showing Klu in Reds and Angels uniforms, it is possible examples may yet be seen in Pirates and White Sox uniforms. Measuring about 3-1/2" x 5-1/2", the black-and-white cards have a facsimile signature of Kluszewski on front. The back is postcard style and advertises the Cincinnati restaurant he operated with Jack Stayin.

	NM	EX	VG
Ted Kluszewski/Fldg (Reds, white cap.)	75.00	37.50	22.50
Ted Kluszewski/Portrait (Reds, dark cap.)	100.00	50.00	30.00

1930s Knickerbocker Beer Yankees Premium

Jacob Ruppert, who owned both the Yankees and the Knickerbocker Brewing Co., is pictured on this 10" x 8" black-and-white, blank-backed premium photo with a trio of his Italian stars. Facsimile autographs of all are printed on front.

	NM	EX	VG
Tony Lazzeri, Jacob Ruppert, Joe DiMaggio, Frank Crosetti	150.00	75.00	45.00

1921 Koester Bread N.Y. Giants/Yankees

CHAS. STENGEL
Outf.—New York Nationals

The 1921 World Series was the first of many for the N.Y. Yankees, and it was the first "subway series," as their opponents were the Giants. This special card issue, a blank-backed version of the American Caramel Series of 120 (E121), featured the players, managers and coaches of each team. The 2" x about 3-1/4" cards feature black-and-white photos on front. They were distributed in October 1921, by E.H. Koester, a New York bakery. The unnumbered cards are checklisted here alphabetically within team. Several of the players in this issue do not appear in the contemporary American Caramel sets. A rarely seen album was issued to house the cards.

		NM	EX	VG
Complete Set (52):		45,000	22,500	13,500
Common Player:		500.00	250.00	150.00
Album:		800.00	400.00	240.00
	N.Y. Giants Team Set:	19,000	9,500	5,700
(1)	Dave Bancroft	1,500	750.00	450.00
(2)	Jesse Barnes	500.00	250.00	150.00
(3)	Howard Berry	500.00	250.00	150.00
(4)	"Ed." Brown	500.00	250.00	150.00
(5)	Jesse Burkett	1,875	940.00	565.00
(6)	Geo. J. Burns	500.00	250.00	150.00
(7)	Cecil Causey	500.00	250.00	150.00
(8)	"Bill" Cunningham	500.00	250.00	150.00
(9)	"Phil" Douglas	500.00	250.00	150.00
(10)	Frank Frisch	1,500	750.00	450.00
(11)	Alexander Gaston	500.00	250.00	150.00
(12)	"Mike" Gonzalez	600.00	300.00	180.00
(13)	Hugh Jennings	1,500	750.00	450.00
(14)	George Kelly	1,500	750.00	450.00
(15)	John McGraw	1,500	750.00	450.00
(16)	Emil Meusel	500.00	250.00	150.00
(17)	Arthur Nehf	500.00	250.00	150.00
(18)	John Rawlings	500.00	250.00	150.00
(19)	"Bill" Ryan	500.00	250.00	150.00
(20)	"Slim" Sallee	500.00	250.00	150.00
(21)	"Pat" Shea	500.00	250.00	150.00
(22)	Earl Smith	500.00	250.00	150.00
(23)	Frank Snyder	500.00	250.00	150.00
(24)	Chas. Stengel	1,875	940.00	565.00
(25)	Fred Toney	500.00	250.00	150.00
(26)	Ross Young (Youngs)	1,875	940.00	565.00
	N.Y. Yankees Team Set:	26,000	13,000	7,800
(1)	Frank Baker	1,500	750.00	450.00
(2)	"Rip" Collins	500.00	250.00	150.00
(3)	Lou De Vormer	500.00	250.00	150.00
(4)	Alex Ferguson	500.00	250.00	150.00
(5)	William Fewster	500.00	250.00	150.00
(6)	Harry Harper	500.00	250.00	150.00
(7)	"Chicken" Hawks	500.00	250.00	150.00
(8)	Fred Hoffmann (Hofmann)	500.00	250.00	150.00

(9)	Waite Hoyt	1,500	750.00	450.00
(10)	Miller Huggins	1,500	750.00	450.00
(11)	Carl Mays	500.00	250.00	150.00
(12)	M.J. McNally	500.00	250.00	150.00
(13)	R. Meusel	500.00	250.00	150.00
(14)	Elmer Miller	500.00	250.00	150.00
(15)	John Mitchell	500.00	250.00	150.00
(16)	Chas. O'Leary	500.00	250.00	150.00
(17)	Roger Peckinpaugh	500.00	250.00	150.00
(18)	William Piercy	500.00	250.00	150.00
(19)	Walter Pipp	500.00	250.00	150.00
(20)	Jack Quinn	500.00	250.00	150.00
(21)	Tom Rogers	500.00	250.00	150.00
(22)	Robert Roth	500.00	250.00	150.00
(23)	George Ruth	15,000	7,500	4,500
(24)	Walter Schang	500.00	250.00	150.00
(25)	Robert Shawkey	500.00	250.00	150.00
(26)	Aaron Ward	500.00	250.00	150.00

1911-16 Kotton Tobacco

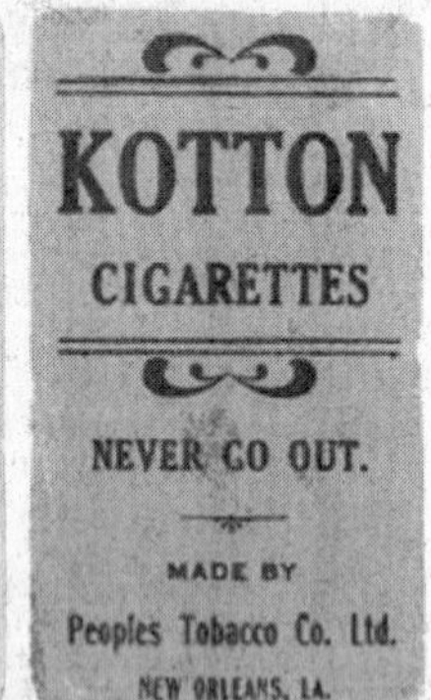

The T216 baseball card set, issued with several brands by the People's Tobacco Co., is the last of the Louisiana cigarette sets and the most confusing. Issued over a period of several years between 1911 and 1916, the set employs the same pictures as several contemporary caramel and bakery sets. Cards measure a nominal 1-1/2" x 2-5/8", though reasonable allowance must be made for original cutting variances. Positive identification can be made by the back of the cards. The Peoples Tobacco cards carry advertising for one of three brands of cigarettes: Kotton, Mino or Virginia Extra. The Kotton brand is the most common, with cards found in two types; one has a glossy front finish, while a second scarcer type is printed on a thin paper. The thin paper cards command an additional 15 percent premium. The glossy-front cards can be found with either of two ad styles on back: "KOTTON / TOBACCO" (Factory No. 11) or "KOTTON / CIGARETTES" (Factory No. 4). The cards include players from the American, National and Federal Leagues. The complete set price includes only the least expensive of each variation.

		NM	EX	VG
Common Player:		990.00	495.00	300.00
(1)	Jack Barry/Btg	990.00	495.00	300.00
(2)	Jack Barry/Fldg	990.00	495.00	300.00
(3)	Harry Bemis	990.00	495.00	300.00
(4a)	Chief Bender (Philadelphia, striped cap.)	1,800	900.00	540.00
(4b)	Chief Bender (Baltimore, striped cap.)	1,800	900.00	540.00
(5a)	Chief Bender (Philadelphia, white cap.)	1,800	900.00	540.00
(5b)	Chief Bender (Baltimore, white cap.)	1,800	900.00	540.00
(6)	Bill Bergen	990.00	495.00	300.00
(7a)	Bob Bescher (Cincinnati)	990.00	495.00	300.00
(7b)	Bob Bescher (St. Louis)	990.00	495.00	300.00
(8)	Roger Bresnahan	1,800	900.00	540.00
(9)	Al Bridwell/Btg	990.00	495.00	300.00
(10a)	Al Bridwell/Sliding (New York)	990.00	495.00	300.00
(10b)	Al Bridwell/Slidging (St. Louis)	990.00	495.00	300.00
(11)	Donie Bush	990.00	495.00	300.00
(12)	Doc Casey	990.00	495.00	300.00
(13)	Frank Chance	1,800	900.00	540.00
(14a)	Hal Chase/Fldg (New York)	990.00	495.00	300.00
(14b)	Hal Chase/Fldg (Buffalo)	1,800	900.00	540.00
(15)	Hal Chase/Portrait	1,440	720.00	430.00
(16a)	Ty Cobb/Standing (Detroit Am.)	24,000	12,000	7,200
(16b)	Ty Cobb/Standing (Detroit Americans)	21,000	10,500	6,300
(17)	Ty Cobb/Btg (Detroit Americans)	24,000	12,000	7,200
(18a)	Eddie Collins (Phila. Am.)	1,800	900.00	540.00
(18b)	Eddie Collins (Phila. Amer.)	1,800	900.00	540.00
(19)	Eddie Collins (Chicago)	1,800	900.00	540.00
(20a)	Sam Crawford (Small print.)	1,800	900.00	540.00
(20b)	Sam Crawford (Large print.)	1,800	900.00	540.00
(21)	Harry Davis	990.00	495.00	300.00
(22)	Ray Demmitt	990.00	495.00	300.00
(23)	Art Devlin	990.00	495.00	300.00
(24a)	Wild Bill Donovan (Detroit)	990.00	495.00	300.00
(24b)	Wild Bill Donovan (New York)	990.00	495.00	300.00
(25a)	Red Dooin (Philadelphia)	990.00	495.00	300.00
(25b)	Red Dooin (Cincinnati)	990.00	495.00	300.00
(26a)	Mickey Doolan (Philadelphia)	990.00	495.00	300.00
(26b)	Mickey Doolan (Baltimore)	990.00	495.00	300.00
(27)	Patsy Dougherty	990.00	495.00	300.00
(28a)	Larry Doyle, Larry Doyle/Btg (N.Y. Nat'l)	990.00	495.00	300.00
(28b)	Larry Doyle/Btg (New York Nat'l)	990.00	495.00	300.00
(29)	Larry Doyle/Throwing	990.00	495.00	300.00
(30)	Clyde Engle	990.00	495.00	300.00
(31a)	Johnny Evers (Chicago)	1,800	900.00	540.00
(31b)	Johnny Evers (Boston)	1,800	900.00	540.00
(32)	Art Fromme	990.00	495.00	300.00
(33a)	George Gibson (Pittsburg Nat'l, back view.)	990.00	495.00	300.00
(33b)	George Gibson (Pittsburgh Nat'l., back view.)	990.00	495.00	300.00
(34a)	George Gibson (Pittsburg Nat'l, front view.)	990.00	495.00	300.00
(34b)	George Gibson (Pittsburgh Nat'l., front view.)	990.00	495.00	300.00
(35a)	Topsy Hartsel (Phila. Am.)	990.00	495.00	300.00
(35b)	Topsy Hartsel (Phila. Amer.)	990.00	495.00	300.00
(36)	Roy Hartzell/Btg	990.00	495.00	300.00
(37)	Roy Hartzell/Catching	990.00	495.00	300.00
(38a)	Fred Jacklitsch (Philadelphia)	990.00	495.00	300.00
(38b)	Fred Jacklitsch (Baltimore)	990.00	495.00	300.00
(39a)	Hughie Jennings (Orange background.)	1,800	900.00	540.00
(39b)	Hughie Jennings (Red background.)	1,800	900.00	540.00
(40)	Red Kleinow	990.00	495.00	300.00
(41a)	Otto Knabe (Philadelphia)	990.00	495.00	300.00
(41b)	Otto Knabe (Baltimore)	990.00	495.00	300.00
(42)	Jack Knight	990.00	495.00	300.00
(43a)	Nap Lajoie/Fldg (Philadelphia)	1,800	900.00	540.00
(43b)	Nap Lajoie/Fldg (Cleveland)	1,800	900.00	540.00
(44)	Nap Lajoie/Portrait	1,800	900.00	540.00
(45a)	Hans Lobert (Cincinnati)	990.00	495.00	300.00
(45b)	Hans Lobert (New York)	990.00	495.00	300.00
(46)	Sherry Magee	990.00	495.00	300.00
(47)	Rube Marquard	1,800	900.00	540.00
(48a)	Christy Matthewson (Mathewson) (Large print.)	5,400	2,700	1,620
(48b)	Christy Matthewson (Mathewson) (Small print.)	5,400	2,700	1,620
(49a)	John McGraw (Large print.)	1,800	900.00	540.00
(49b)	John McGraw (Small print.)	1,800	900.00	540.00
(50)	Larry McLean	990.00	495.00	300.00
(51)	George McQuillan	990.00	495.00	300.00
(52)	Dots Miller/Btg	990.00	495.00	300.00
(53a)	Dots Miller/Fldg (Pittsburg)	990.00	495.00	300.00
(53b)	Dots Miller/Fldg (St. Louis)	990.00	495.00	300.00
(54a)	Danny Murphy (Philadelphia)	990.00	495.00	300.00
(54b)	Danny Murphy (Brooklyn)	990.00	495.00	300.00
(55)	Rebel Oakes	990.00	495.00	300.00
(56)	Bill O'Hara	990.00	495.00	300.00
(57)	Eddie Plank	2,400	1,200	720.00
(58a)	Germany Schaefer (Washington)	990.00	495.00	300.00
(58b)	Germany Schaefer (Newark)	990.00	495.00	300.00
(59)	Admiral Schlei	990.00	495.00	300.00
(60)	Boss Schmidt	990.00	495.00	300.00
(61)	Johnny Seigle	990.00	495.00	300.00
(62)	Dave Shean	990.00	495.00	300.00
(63)	Boss Smith (Schmidt)	990.00	495.00	300.00
(64)	Tris Speaker	2,400	1,200	720.00
(65)	Oscar Stanage	990.00	495.00	300.00
(66)	George Stovall	990.00	495.00	300.00
(67)	Jeff Sweeney	990.00	495.00	300.00
(68a)	Joe Tinker/Btg (Chicago Nat'l)	1,800	900.00	540.00
(68b)	Joe Tinker/Btg (Chicago Feds)	2,400	1,200	720.00
(69)	Joe Tinker/Portrait	1,800	900.00	540.00
(70a)	Honus Wagner/Btg (S.S.)	18,000	9,000	5,400
(70b)	Honus Wagner/Btg (2b.)	18,000	9,000	5,400
(71a)	Honus Wagner/Throwing (S.S.)	18,000	9,000	5,400
(71b)	Honus Wagner/Throwinig (2b.)	18,000	9,000	5,400
(72)	Hooks Wiltse	990.00	495.00	300.00
(73)	Cy Young	4,200	2,100	1,260
(74a)	Heinie Zimmerman (2b.)	990.00	495.00	300.00
(74b)	Heinie Zimmerman (3b.)	990.00	495.00	300.00

1964 Sandy Koufax's Tropicana Postcard

In the early 1960s, Dodgers pitcher Sandy Koufax owned the Tropicana Motor Hotel in Hollywood. Among the collectible souvenirs of that venture are a pair of color postcards picturing the player overlooking the pool. The original version pictures Koufax in civilian clothes. A later version uses the same photo, but has a Dodgers uniform crudely drawn on Koufax' photo.

	NM	EX	VG
Sandy Koufax (Civilian)	175.00	90.00	50.00
Sandy Koufax (Uniform)	150.00	75.00	45.00

1907 Krieg & Co. Chicago Cubs Base Ball Mail Card

Distributed by a shoe retailers' supply firm, this foldout black-and-white postcard features the World Champion Cubs. About 5-1/4" x 3-1/2" closed, the foldout opens to reveal portrait photos of 16 of the players, two per post-card size panel. Manager Frank Chance and the team president each have their own panel. The back cover of the mailer has a composite photo of the team, with a 1907 National League schedule on its flip side.

	NM	EX	VG
1907 Chicago Cubs Foldout	2,000	1,000	600.00

1976 Kroger Cincinnati Reds

These 5-7/8" x 9" color photos were grocery store giveaways. Blank-backed and unnumbered, they are checklisted here alphabetically. Because the photos were licensed only by the players' union, and not Major League Baseball, photos do not show uniform logos.

		NM	EX	VG
Complete Set (16):		45.00	22.50	13.50
Common Player:		3.00	1.50	.90
(1)	Ed Armbrister	3.00	1.50	.90
(2)	Bob Bailey	3.00	1.50	.90
(3)	Johnny Bench	15.00	7.50	4.50
(4)	Jack Billingham	3.00	1.50	.90
(5)	Dave Concepcion	3.00	1.50	.90
(6)	Dan Driessen	3.00	1.50	.90
(7)	Rawly Eastwick	3.00	1.50	.90
(8)	George Foster	3.50	1.75	1.00
(9)	Cesar Geronimo	3.00	1.50	.90
(10)	Ken Griffey	3.00	1.50	.90
(11)	Don Gullett	3.00	1.50	.90
(12)	Joe Morgan	12.50	6.25	3.75
(13)	Gary Nolan	3.00	1.50	.90
(14)	Fred Norman	3.00	1.50	.90
(15)	Tony Perez	7.50	3.75	2.25
(16)	Pete Rose	24.00	12.00	7.25

1977 Kurland Tom Seaver

These large-format (4-3/16" x 5-1/2") black-and-white cards appear to have been produced in conjunction with promotional appearances by Seaver for Kurland Cadillac-Oldsmobile, a metropolitan New York auto dealer. Most of the cards seen are autographed by Seaver. The back is blank.

		NM	EX	VG
Complete Set (2):		150.00	75.00	45.00
Common Card:		75.00	37.00	22.00
(1)	Tom Seaver (N.Y. Mets)	75.00	37.00	22.00
(2)	Tom Seaver (Cincinnati Reds)	75.00	37.00	22.00

1926 Kut Outs Giants/Yankees Die-Cuts

These black-and-white, blank-back, die-cut cards were sold as complete sets for 10 cents per team. The size varies with the pose depicted, but the cards are generally about 2" wide and 4-1/2" tall. The player's name is printed at the bottom of his photo. The unnumbered cards are checklisted here in alphabetical order by team. The issue is very similar to the Middy Bread Cardinals/Browns cards of 1927.

		NM	EX	VG
Complete Set (20):		14,500	5,800	2,900
Common Player:		350.00	140.00	70.00
	N.Y. Giants Team Set:	4,500	1,800	900.00
(1)	Ed Farrell	350.00	140.00	70.00
(2)	Frank Frisch	600.00	240.00	120.00
(3)	George Kelly	600.00	240.00	120.00
(4)	Freddie Lindstrom	600.00	240.00	120.00
(5)	John McGraw	600.00	240.00	120.00
(6)	Emil Meusel	350.00	140.00	70.00
(7)	John Scott	350.00	140.00	70.00
(8)	Frank Snyder	350.00	140.00	70.00
(9)	Billy Southworth	350.00	140.00	70.00
(10)	Ross Young (Youngs)	600.00	240.00	120.00
	N.Y. Yankees Team Set:	10,000	4,000	2,000
(11)	Pat Collins	350.00	140.00	70.00
(12)	Earle Combs	600.00	240.00	120.00
(13)	Joe Dugan	350.00	140.00	70.00
(14)	Lou Gehrig	2,500	1,000	500.00
(15)	Miller Huggins	600.00	240.00	120.00
(16)	Mark Koenig	350.00	140.00	70.00
(17)	Tony Lazzeri	600.00	240.00	120.00
(18)	Bob Meusel	350.00	140.00	70.00
(19)	Herb Pennock	600.00	240.00	120.00
(20)	Babe Ruth	5,000	2,000	1,000

L

1912 La Azora Cigars

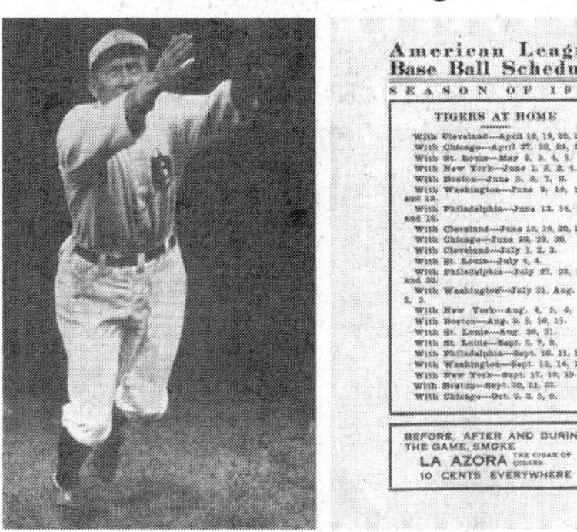
American League
Base Ball Schedule
SEASON OF 1912

TIGERS AT HOME

BEFORE, AFTER AND DURING THE GAME, SMOKE
LA AZORA
10 CENTS EVERYWHERE

These postcard-size (about 3-3/8" x 5-3/8") ad cards were issued by a Detroit cigar maker. Both cards feature of their front a borderless sepia photo of Ty Cobb, though he is not named. The backs differ somewhat in format and content, but basically provide the Tigers' home and road schedules for the season.

		NM	EX	VG
Complete Set (2):		5,000	2,500	1,500
(1)	Ty Cobb/Fldg (Home schedule.)	3,000	1,500	900.00
(2)	Ty Cobb/Sliding (Road schedule.)	3,000	1,500	900.00

1958-60 L.A. Dodgers Premium Pictures

Apparently issued over a period of years from 1958 through at least 1960, these black-and-white, 8-1/2" x 11" premium pictures were sold as a set through Dodgers souvenir outlets, though the make-up of a set changed with the comings and goings of players. The blank-backed pictures feature on front a pencil portrait of the player, with his name printed towards the bottom. The signature of sports artist Nicholas Volpe also appears on front. The unnumbered pictures are checklisted here alphabetically.

		NM	EX	VG
Complete Set (16):		300.00	150.00	90.00
Common Player:		15.00	7.50	4.50
(1)	Walter Alston	17.50	8.75	5.25
(2)	Roy Campanella	30.00	15.00	9.00
(3)	Gino Cimoli	15.00	7.50	4.50
(4)	Don Drysdale	30.00	15.00	9.00
(5)	Carl Erskine	15.00	7.50	4.50
(6)	Carl Furillo	20.00	10.00	6.00
(7)	Jim Gilliam	17.50	8.75	5.25
(8)	Gil Hodges	30.00	15.00	9.00
(9)	Clem Labine	15.00	7.50	4.50
(10)	Wally Moon	15.00	7.50	4.50
(11)	Don Newcombe	17.50	8.75	5.25
(12)	Johnny Podres	17.50	8.75	5.25
(13)	Pee Wee Reese	30.00	15.00	9.00
(14)	Rip Repulski	15.00	7.50	4.50
(15)	Vin Scully, Jerry Doggett (Announcers)	15.00	7.50	4.50
(16)	Duke Snider	30.00	15.00	9.00

1959 L.A. Dodgers Postcards

In the team's second year in California, the Dodgers began production of an on-going set of color player postcards. Cards were usually sold in 10-card packs in stadium souvenir stands. The makeup of the packs sold varied as players came and went and cards were issued or withdrawn. When supplies of any player's cards were exhausted, he would be included in the current printing. Various photographers and printers were responsible for the issue over the years, but all utilized a similar format of 3-1/2" x 5-1/2" glossy borderless fronts and postcard style backs. The initial effort in 1959 has no player identification on the front. Backs are printed in brown, including player ID, birthdate and place, copyright date and credits to Mirro Krome and Crocker Co. Cards are numbered as shown here, but with an "LA-D-" prefix. The set was also available in the form of an accordian-foldout.

		NM	EX	VG
Complete Set (12):		400.00	200.00	125.00
Common Player:		30.00	15.00	9.00
901	Duke Snider	40.00	20.00	12.00
902	Gil Hodges	35.00	17.50	10.00
903	Johnny Podres	30.00	15.00	9.00
904	Carl Furillo	30.00	15.00	9.00
905	Don Drysdale	40.00	20.00	12.00
906	Sandy Koufax	75.00	37.50	22.50
907	Jim Gilliam	30.00	15.00	9.00
908	Don Zimmer	30.00	15.00	9.00
909	Charlie Neal	30.00	15.00	9.00
910	Norm Larker (Photo actually Joe Pignatano.)	30.00	15.00	9.00
911	Clem Labine (Photo actually Stan Williams.)	30.00	15.00	9.00
912	John Roseboro	30.00	15.00	9.00

1960 L.A. Dodgers Postcards

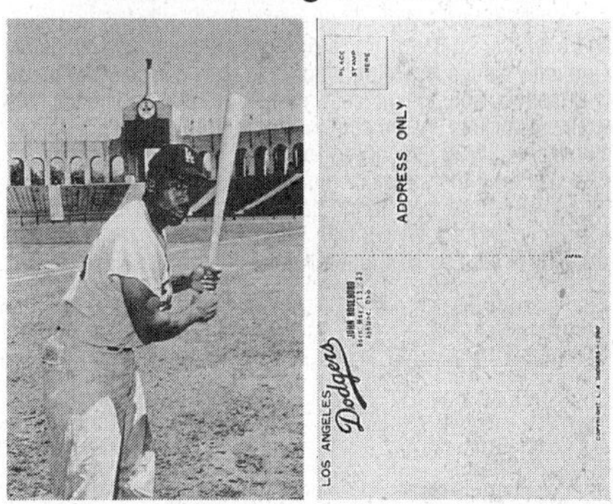

Like many baseball souvenirs, this set of team-issued postcards was "Made in Japan." The 3-1/2" x 5-1/2" cards share the basic format of the 1959 premiere issue with borderless color poses on front and postcard-style back. Backs are printed in blue with player ID and copyright date, but the cards are unnumbered. They are checklisted here alphabetically. The Carl Furillo card is scarce because it was withdrawn when he retired after playing only eight games in 1960.

		NM	EX	VG
Complete Set (12):		250.00	125.00	75.00
Common Player:		12.50	6.25	3.75
(1)	Walt Alston	12.50	6.25	3.75
(2)	Roger Craig	12.50	6.25	3.75
(3)	Don Drysdale	15.00	7.50	4.50
(4)	Carl Furillo	75.00	37.00	22.00
(5)	Gil Hodges	15.00	7.50	4.50
(6)	Sandy Koufax	60.00	30.00	18.00
(7)	Wally Moon	12.50	6.25	3.75
(8)	Charlie Neal	12.50	6.25	3.75
(9)	Johnny Podres	12.50	6.25	3.75
(10)	John Roseboro	12.50	6.25	3.75
(11)	Larry Sherry	12.50	6.25	3.75
(12)	Duke Snider	15.00	7.50	4.50

1962 L.A. Dodgers Pins

The attributed date is speculative based on available checklist information. This series of, presumably, stadium souvenir pinback buttons is in an unusually large 3-1/2" format. The pins have black-and-white photos on a white or light blue background. Two styles of name presentation are known, those with names in a white strip at the bottom of the pin and those with the names overprinted on the photo and more towards the center.

	NM	EX	VG
Common Player:	75.00	37.50	22.00
NAME IN STRIP			
Don Drysdale	60.00	30.00	18.00
Duke Snider	125.00	62.00	37.00
NAME OVERPRINTED			
Gil Hodges	95.00	47.00	28.00
Sandy Koufax	500.00	250.00	150.00
Maury Wills	75.00	37.50	22.00

1963 L.A. Dodgers Pin-Ups

Borrowing on the concept of the 1938 Goudey Heads-up cards, this set was sold, probably at the stadium souvenir stands, in a white envelope labeled "Los Angeles Dodgers Pin-Ups." The cards feature large full-color head-and-cap photos set atop cartoon ballplayers' bodies. Cards are printed on 7-1/4" x 8-1/2" semi-gloss cardboard with blank backs. The player's name appears in black on the front, along with the instructions, "Push out character carefully. Take scissors and trim white around player's head." Each figure was die-cut to allow its easy removal from the background.

		NM	EX	VG
Complete Set (10):		75.00	35.00	25.00
Common Player:		6.00	3.00	1.75
(1)	Tommy Davis	7.50	3.75	2.25
(2)	Willie Davis	7.50	3.75	2.25
(3)	Don Drysdale	10.00	5.00	3.00
(4)	Ron Fairly	6.00	3.00	1.75
(5)	Frank Howard	7.50	3.75	2.25
(6)	Sandy Koufax	25.00	12.50	7.50
(7)	Joe Moeller	6.00	3.00	1.75
(8)	Ron Perranoski	6.00	3.00	1.75
(9)	John Roseboro	6.00	3.00	1.75
(10)	Maury Wills	7.50	3.75	2.25

1965 L.A. Dodgers Motion Pins

These "flasher" pins were issued in conjunction with the Dodgers' World Series appearance and ultimate victory in 1965. The 2-1/2" diameter pins feature player portraits on a seamed blue background resembling a baseball. When the angle of view is changed, the player's name and team logo and the starbursts pop in and out of sight.

	NM	EX	VG
Don Drysdale	15.00	7.50	4.50
Sandy Koufax	25.00	12.50	7.50
Dodgers Logo - "Our Champs"	15.00	7.50	4.50

1979 L.A. Dodgers

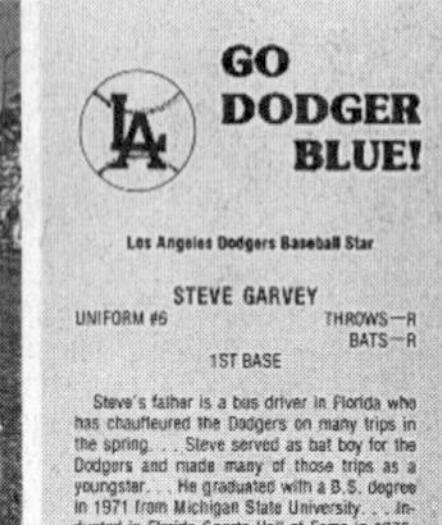

Presumed to be a collectors' issue due to lack of sponsors or licensors logos, this set features the top players of the '79 Dodgers. Fronts of the 2-1/2" x 3-3/8" cards are borderless color photos. Backs are printed in blue and white with career highlights and personal data. Cards are checklisted here in alphabetical order.

		NM	EX	VG
Complete Set (15):		15.00	7.50	4.50
Common Player:		2.00	1.00	.60
(1)	Dusty Baker	3.00	1.50	.90
(2)	Ron Cey	2.00	1.00	.60
(3)	Terry Forster	2.00	1.00	.60
(4)	Steve Garvey	4.00	2.00	1.25
(5)	Burt Hooton	2.00	1.00	.60
(6)	Charlie Hough	2.00	1.00	.60
(7)	Tommy Lasorda	3.00	1.50	.90
(8)	Dave Lopes	2.00	1.00	.60
(9)	Rick Monday	2.00	1.00	.60
(10)	Manny Mota	2.00	1.00	.60
(11)	Doug Rau	2.00	1.00	.60
(12)	Bill Russell	2.00	1.00	.60
(13)	Reggie Smith	2.00	1.00	.60
(14)	Don Sutton	4.00	2.00	1.25
(15)	Steve Yeager	2.00	1.00	.60

1980 L.A. Dodgers Police

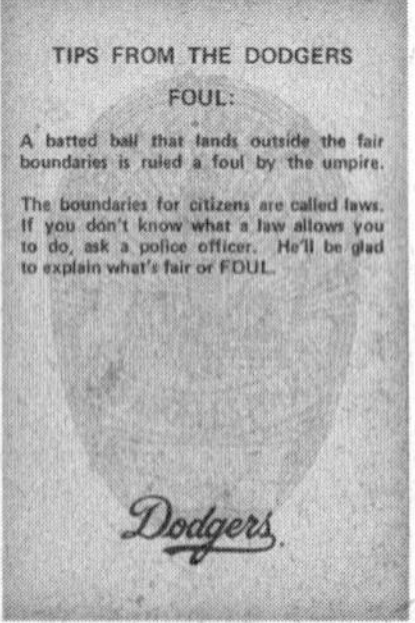

Producers of one of the most popular police and safety sets in the hobby, the Dodgers began this successful promotion in 1980. The 2-13/16" x 4-1/8" cards feature full-color photos on front, along with brief personal statistics. Backs include "Tips from the Dodgers" along with the team and LAPD logos. Cards are numbered by player uniform number, with an unnumbered team card also included in the set.

		NM	EX	VG
Complete Set (30):		6.00	3.00	1.75
Common Player:		.50	.25	.15
5	Johnny Oates	.50	.25	.15
6	Steve Garvey	2.00	1.00	.60
7	Steve Yeager	.50	.25	.15
8	Reggie Smith	.50	.25	.15
9	Gary Thomasson	.50	.25	.15
10	Ron Cey	.60	.30	.20
12	Dusty Baker	.60	.30	.20
13	Joe Ferguson	.50	.25	.15
15	Davey Lopes	.50	.25	.15
16	Rick Monday	.50	.25	.15
18	Bill Russell	.50	.25	.15
20	Don Sutton	2.00	1.00	.60
21	Jay Johnstone	.50	.25	.15
23	Teddy Martinez	.50	.25	.15
27	Joe Beckwith	.50	.25	.15
28	Pedro Guerrero	.50	.25	.15
29	Don Stanhouse	.50	.25	.15
30	Derrel Thomas	.50	.25	.15
31	Doug Rau	.50	.25	.15
34	Ken Brett	.50	.25	.15
35	Bob Welch	.50	.25	.15
37	Robert Castillo	.50	.25	.15
38	Dave Goltz	.50	.25	.15
41	Jerry Reuss	.50	.25	.15
43	Rick Sutcliffe	.60	.30	.20
44	Mickey Hatcher	.50	.25	.15
46	Burt Hooton	.50	.25	.15
49	Charlie Hough	.50	.25	.15
51	Terry Forster	.50	.25	.15
---	Team Photo	.50	.25	.15

1913 Napoleon Lajoie Game

1	Out on Strikes	1
2	Fly Out	2
3	Three Base Hit	4
4	One Base Hit	2
5	Home Run	1
6	Infield Hit—Out Home	6
7	Triple Play	1
8	Out—Sacrifice Fly	7

Although individual cards are not marked, these cards were produced as part of a Parker Bros. baseball board game called "The National American Baseball Game." Each of the approximately 2-3/8" x 3-1/4", round-cornered cards has a borderless photo on front picturing the Hall of Famer at bat. Backs have a chart of various baseball plays used in the game. Cards can be found with the Lajoie photo tinted either blue or red, the latter being somewhat scarcer.

	NM	EX	VG
Complete Game Set:	1,500	750.00	450.00
SINGLE CARD			
Napoleon Lajoie/Blue	25.00	12.50	7.50
Napoleon Lajoie/Red	45.00	22.50	13.50

1960 Lake To Lake Dairy Braves

This 28-card set of unnumbered 2-1/2" x 3-1/4" cards offers a special challenge for the condition-conscious collector. Originally issued by being stapled to milk cartons, the cards were redeemable for prizes ranging from pen and pencil sets to Braves tickets. When sent in for redemption, the cards had a hole punched in the corner. Naturally, collectors most desire cards without the staple or punch holes. Cards are printed in blue ink on front, red ink on back. Because he was traded in May, and his card withdrawn, the Ray Boone card is scarce; the Billy Bruton card is unaccountably scarcer still.

		NM	EX	VG
Complete Set (28):		2,250	1,125	650.00
Common Player:		35.00	17.50	10.00
(1)	Henry Aaron	500.00	250.00	150.00
(2)	Joe Adcock	35.00	17.50	10.00
(3)	Ray Boone	250.00	125.00	75.00
(4)	Bill Bruton	500.00	250.00	150.00
(5)	Bob Buhl	35.00	17.50	10.00
(6)	Lou Burdette	35.00	17.50	10.00
(7)	Chuck Cottier	35.00	17.50	10.00
(8)	Wes Covington	35.00	17.50	10.00
(9)	Del Crandall	35.00	17.50	10.00
(10)	Charlie Dressen	35.00	17.50	10.00
(11)	Bob Giggie	35.00	17.50	10.00
(12)	Joey Jay	35.00	17.50	10.00
(13)	Johnny Logan	35.00	17.50	10.00
(14)	Felix Mantilla	35.00	17.50	10.00
(15)	Lee Maye	35.00	17.50	10.00
(16)	Don McMahon	35.00	17.50	10.00
(17)	George Myatt	35.00	17.50	10.00
(18)	Andy Pafko	35.00	17.50	10.00
(19)	Juan Pizarro	35.00	17.50	10.00
(20)	Mel Roach	35.00	17.50	10.00
(21)	Bob Rush	35.00	17.50	10.00
(22)	Bob Scheffing	35.00	17.50	10.00
(23)	Red Schoendienst	75.00	37.50	22.50
(24)	Warren Spahn	150.00	75.00	45.00
(25)	Al Spangler	35.00	17.50	10.00
(26)	Frank Torre	35.00	17.50	10.00
(27)	Carl Willey	35.00	17.50	10.00
(28)	Whitlow Wyatt	35.00	17.50	10.00

1923-24 La Moda

This is appears to be a parallel to the more frequently encountered Cuban cigar cards advertising the Billiken brand. Specialists feel that the La Moda ("The Fashion") branded cards survive at a rate about one per 10 Billikens, though demand is not such that prices follow such a ratio.

	NM	EX	VG
Common Player:	1,000	400.00	200.00
Stars: 2X			

(See 1923-24 Billiken for checklist and base card values.)

1970 La Pizza Royale Expos

This colorful collectors' issue features only Montreal Expos. Each of the 2-1/2" x 5" cards can be found printed in red, yellow, blue of green duo-tones. "La Pizza Royale" is printed in white above the player photo. Below the photo is the player's name and, in French, his position. Backs are blank and the cards are unnumbered. The checklist is presented here alphabetically. The La Pizza Royale cards are a fantasy issue produced by a collector for sale within the hobby.

		NM	EX	VG
Complete Set (14):		20.00	10.00	6.00
Common Player:		2.00	1.00	.60
(1)	Bob Bailey	2.00	1.00	.60
(2)	John Boccabella	2.00	1.00	.60
(3)	Ron Fairly	3.00	1.50	.90
(4)	Jim Gosger	2.00	1.00	.60
(5)	Coco Laboy	2.00	1.00	.60
(6)	Gene Mauch	3.00	1.50	.90
(7)	Rich Nye	2.00	1.00	.60
(8)	John O'Donoghue	2.00	1.00	.60
(9)	Adolfo Phillips	2.00	1.00	.60
(10)	Howie Reed	2.00	1.00	.60
(11)	Marv Staehle	2.00	1.00	.60
(12)	Rusty Staub	4.50	2.25	1.25
(13)	Gary Sutherland	2.00	1.00	.60
(14)	Bobby Wine	2.00	1.00	.60

1967 Laughlin World Series

Apparently a prototype set for subsequent offerings by the sports artist R.G. Laughlin that were produced by Fleer, this set of 64 cards was printed in black-and-white with the cartoon line drawings for which Laughlin was noted. The cards

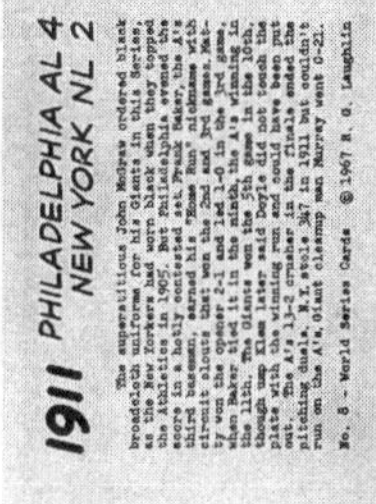

are an odd size, 2-3/4" x 3-1/2", like so many of the Laughlin/Fleer issues of the period. The text on the back is printed in red and offer details of the World Series from that year.

		NM	EX	VG
Complete Set (64):		450.00	225.00	135.00
Common Card:		9.00	4.50	2.75
1	1903 Red Sox/Pirates	9.00	4.50	2.75
2	1905 Giants/A's (Christy Mathewson)	20.00	10.00	6.00
3	1906 White Sox/Cubs	9.00	4.50	2.75
4	1907 Cubs/Tigers	9.00	4.50	2.75
5	1908 Cubs/Tigers (Joe Tinker, Evers, Frank Chance)	20.00	10.00	6.00
6	1909 Pirates/Tigers (Honus Wagner, Ty Cobb)	30.00	15.00	9.00
7	1910 A's/Cubs	9.00	4.50	2.75
8	1911 A's/Giants (John McGraw)	9.00	4.50	2.75
9	1912 Red Sox/Giants	9.00	4.50	2.75
10	1913 A's/Giants	9.00	4.50	2.75
11	1914 Braves/A's	9.00	4.50	2.75
12	1915 Red Sox/Phillies (Babe Ruth)	35.00	17.50	10.00
13	1916 White Sox/Dodgers (Babe Ruth)	35.00	17.50	10.00
14	1917 White Sox/Giants	9.00	4.50	2.75
15	1918 Red Sox/Cubs	9.00	4.50	2.75
16	1919 Reds/White Sox	35.00	17.50	10.00
17	1920 Indians/Dodgers (Bill Wambsganss)	9.00	4.50	2.75
18	1921 Giants/Yankees (Waite Hoyt)	9.00	4.50	2.75
19	1922 Giants/Yankees (Frank Frisch, Heinie Groh)	9.00	4.50	2.75
20	1923 Yankees/Giants (Babe Ruth)	35.00	17.50	10.00
21	1924 Senators/Giants (Walter Johnson)	15.00	7.50	4.50
22	1925 Pirates/Senators (Walter Johnson)	15.00	7.50	4.50
23	1926 Cardinals/Yankees (Grover Alexander, Anthony Lazzeri)	15.00	7.50	4.50
24	1927 Yankees/Pirates	9.00	4.50	2.75
25	1928 Yankees/Cardinals (Babe Ruth, Lou Gehrig)	35.00	17.50	10.00
26	1929 A's/Cubs	9.00	4.50	2.75
27	1930 A's/Cardinals	9.00	4.50	2.75
28	1931 Cardinals/A's (Pepper Martin)	9.00	4.50	2.75
29	1932 Yankees/Cubs (Babe Ruth)	35.00	17.50	10.00
30	1933 Giants/Senators (Mel Ott)	12.50	6.25	3.75
31	1934 Cardinals/Tigers (Dizzy Dean, Paul Dean)	20.00	10.00	6.00
32	1935 Tigers/Cubs	9.00	4.50	2.75
33	1936 Yankees/Giants	9.00	4.50	2.75
34a	1937 Yankees/Giants (Carl Hubbell) (#11 on uniform)	12.50	6.25	3.75
34b	1937 Yankees/Giants (Carl Hubbell) (#14 on uniform)	12.50	6.25	3.75
35	1938 Yankees/Cubs	9.00	4.50	2.75
36	1939 Yankees/Reds (Joe DiMaggio)	30.00	15.00	9.00
37	1940 Reds/Tigers	9.00	4.50	2.75
38	1941 Yankees/Dodgers (Mickey Owen)	9.00	4.50	2.75
39	1942 Cardinals/Yankees	9.00	4.50	2.75
40	1943 Yankees/Cardinals (Joe McCarthy)	9.00	4.50	2.75
41	1944 Cardinals/Browns	9.00	4.50	2.75
42	1945 Tigers/Cubs (Hank Greenberg)	15.00	7.50	4.50
43	1946 Cardinals/Red Sox (Enos Slaughter)	9.00	4.50	2.75
44	1947 Yankees/Dodgers (Al Gionfriddo)	9.00	4.50	2.75
45	1948 Indians/Braves (Bob Feller)	12.50	6.25	3.75
46	1949 Yankees/Dodgers (Allie Reynolds, Preacher Roe)	20.00	10.00	6.00
47	1950 Yankees/Phillies	9.00	4.50	2.75
48	1951 Yankees/Giants	9.00	4.50	2.75
49	1952 Yankees/Dodgers (Johnny Mize, Duke Snider)	20.00	10.00	6.00
50	1953 Yankees/Dodgers (Casey Stengel)	20.00	10.00	6.00
51	1954 Giants/Indians (Dusty Rhodes)	9.00	4.50	2.75
52	1955 Dodgers/Yankees (Johnny Podres)	20.00	10.00	6.00
53	1956 Yankees/Dodgers (Don Larsen)	25.00	12.50	7.50
54	1957 Braves/Yankees (Lew Burdette)	9.00	4.50	2.75
55	1958 Yankees/Braves (Hank Bauer)	9.00	4.50	2.75
56	1959 Dodgers/White Sox (Larry Sherry)	9.00	4.50	2.75
57	1960 Pirates/Yankees	25.00	12.50	7.50
58	1961 Yankees/Reds (Whitey Ford)	20.00	10.00	6.00
59	1962 Yankees/Giants	9.00	4.50	2.75
60	1963 Dodgers/Yankees (Sandy Koufax)	20.00	10.00	6.00
61	1964 Cardinals/Yankees (Mickey Mantle)	35.00	17.50	10.00
62	1965 Dodgers/Twins (Sandy Koufax)	9.00	4.50	2.75
63	1966 Orioles/Dodgers	9.00	4.50	2.75
64	1967 Cardinals/Red Sox (Bob Gibson)	9.00	4.50	2.75

1972 Laughlin Great Feats

Sports artist R.G. Laughlin created this set of 50 numbered cards and one unnumbered title card highlighting top performances by stars over the years. The cards depict the player in pen and ink, with one variation of the set adding flesh tones to the players. One variation of the set has red borders, the other (with the flesh tones) blue. The cards are blank backed and numbered on the front with a brief caption. Cards measure about 2-9/16" x 3-9/16". Sets originally sold for about $3.

		NM	EX	VG
Complete Set, Red (51):		45.00	22.50	13.50
Complete Set, Blue (51):		60.00	30.00	18.00
Common Player (Red):		1.50	.70	.45
Common Player (Blue): 1.5-2X				
1	Joe DiMaggio	12.00	6.00	3.50
2	Walter Johnson	4.50	2.25	1.25
3	Rudy York	1.50	.70	.45
4	Sandy Koufax	9.00	4.50	2.75
5	George Sisler	1.50	.70	.45
6	Iron Man McGinnity	1.50	.70	.45
7	Johnny VanderMeer	1.50	.70	.45
8	Lou Gehrig	12.00	6.00	3.50
9	Max Carey	1.50	.70	.45
10	Ed Delahanty	1.50	.70	.45
11	Pinky Higgins	1.50	.70	.45
12	Jack Chesbro	1.50	.70	.45
13	Jim Bottomley	1.50	.70	.45
14	Rube Marquard	1.50	.70	.45
15	Rogers Hornsby	1.50	.70	.45
16	Lefty Grove	1.50	.70	.45
17	Johnny Mize	1.50	.70	.45
18	Lefty Gomez	1.50	.70	.45
19	Jimmie Fox (Foxx)	1.50	.70	.45
20	Casey Stengel	1.50	.70	.45
21	Dazzy Vance	1.50	.70	.45
22	Jerry Lynch	1.50	.70	.45
23	Hughie Jennings	1.50	.70	.45
24	Stan Musial	4.50	2.25	1.25
25	Christy Mathewson	4.50	2.25	1.25
26	Elroy Face	1.50	.70	.45
27	Hack Wilson	1.50	.70	.45
28	Smoky Burgess	1.50	.70	.45
29	Cy Young	3.00	1.50	.90
30	Wilbert Robinson	1.50	.70	.45
31	Wee Willie Keeler	1.50	.70	.45
32	Babe Ruth	15.00	7.50	4.50
33	Mickey Mantle	15.00	7.50	4.50
34	Hub Leonard	1.50	.70	.45
35	Ty Cobb	7.50	3.75	2.25
36	Carl Hubbell	1.50	.70	.45
37	Joe Oeschger, Leon Cadore	1.50	.70	.45
38	Don Drysdale	1.50	.70	.45
39	Fred Toney, Hippo Vaughn	1.50	.70	.45
40	Joe Sewell	1.50	.70	.45
41	Grover Cleveland Alexander	1.50	.70	.45
42	Joe Adcock	1.50	.70	.45
43	Eddie Collins	1.50	.70	.45
44	Bob Feller	2.00	1.00	.60
45	Don Larsen	2.00	1.00	.60
46	Dave Philley	1.50	.70	.45
47	Bill Fischer	1.50	.70	.45
48	Dale Long	1.50	.70	.45
49	Bill Wambsganss	1.50	.70	.45
50	Roger Maris	4.50	2.25	1.25
---	Title Card	1.50	.70	.45

1973 Laughlin Super Stand-Ups

A dozen Hall of Famers are featured in this collectors' issue of stand-up figures. Printed in color on heavy cardboard, each is die-cut around the player action picture with typical measurements being 7" x 11". The stand-ups are

much scarcer than most of the artist's other baseball issues. They are listed here alphabetically. The stand-ups originally retailed for $3.50 apiece.

		NM	EX	VG
Complete Set (13):		7,500	3,750	2,250
Common Player:		300.00	150.00	90.00
(1)	Hank Aaron	650.00	325.00	195.00
(2)	Johnny Bench	450.00	225.00	135.00
(3)	Roberto Clemente	750.00	375.00	225.00
(4)	Joe DiMaggio	750.00	375.00	225.00
(5)	Lou Gehrig	750.00	375.00	225.00
(6)	Gil Hodges	450.00	225.00	135.00
(7)	Sandy Koufax	750.00	375.00	225.00
(8)	Mickey Mantle	1,500	750.00	450.00
(9)	Willie Mays	650.00	325.00	195.00
(10)	Stan Musial	500.00	250.00	150.00
(11)	Babe Ruth	1,200	600.00	360.00
(12)	Tom Seaver	450.00	225.00	135.00
(13)	Ted Williams	650.00	325.00	195.00

1974 Laughlin All-Star Games

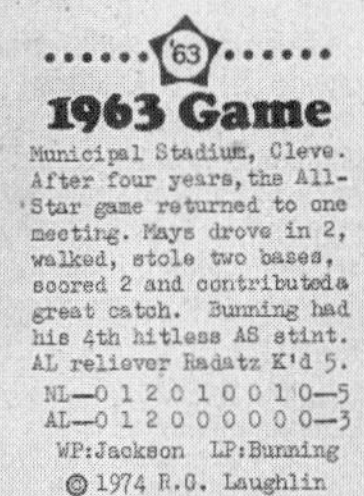

With pen and ink drawings by R.G. Laughlin on the fronts, this set (40 cards) features one card from each year of the game from 1933 to 1973. The 2-3/4" x 3-3/8" cards show a player in black ink in front of a light blue background with a glossy finish, with red printing for the title of the set and the year. The backs are printed in blue, with the year of the All-Star Game serving as the card number. Issue price was $3.50.

		NM	EX	VG
Complete Set (40):		60.00	30.00	18.00
Common Player:		3.00	1.50	.90
33	Babe's Homer (Babe Ruth)	25.00	12.50	7.50
34a	Hub Fans Five (Carl Hubbell) (Uniform #11.)	4.50	2.25	1.25
34b	Hub Fans Five (Carl Hubbell) (Uniform #14.)	4.50	2.25	1.25
35	Foxx Smashes HR (Jimmie Foxx)	4.50	2.25	1.25
36	Ol' Diz Fogs 'Em (Dizzy Dean)	4.50	2.25	1.25
37	Four Hits for Ducky (Ducky Medwick)	3.00	1.50	.90
38	No-Hit Vandy (John VanderMeer)	3.00	1.50	.90
39	DiMaggio Homers (Joe DiMaggio)	20.00	10.00	6.00
40	West's 3-Run Shot (Max West)	3.00	1.50	.90
41	Vaughan Busts Two (Arky Vaughan)	3.00	1.50	.90
42	York's 2-Run Smash (Rudy York)	3.00	1.50	.90
43	Doerr's 3-Run Blast (Bobby Doerr)	3.00	1.50	.90
44	Cavarretta Reaches (Phil Cavarretta)	3.00	1.50	.90
46	Field Day for Ted (Ted Williams)	15.00	7.50	4.50
47	Big Cat Plants One (Johnny Mize)	3.00	1.50	.90
48	Raschi Pitches (Vic Raschi)	3.00	1.50	.90
49	Jackie Scores (Jackie Robinson)	12.00	6.00	3.50
50	Schoendienst Breaks (Red Schoendienst)	3.00	1.50	.90
51	Kiner Homers (Ralph Kiner)	3.00	1.50	.90
52	Sauer's Shot (Hank Sauer)	3.00	1.50	.90
53	Slaughter Hustles (Enos Slaughter)	3.00	1.50	.90
54	Rosen Hits (Al Rosen)	3.00	1.50	.90

		NM	EX	VG
55	Stan the Man's HR (Stan Musial)	7.50	3.75	2.25
56	Boyer Super (Ken Boyer)	3.00	1.50	.90
57	Kaline's Hits (Al Kaline)	4.50	2.25	1.25
58	Nellie Gets Two (Nellie Fox)	3.00	1.50	.90
59	Robbie Perfect (Frank Robinson)	4.50	2.25	1.25
60	Willie 3-for-4 (Willie Mays)	12.00	6.00	3.50
61	Bunning Hitless (Jim Bunning)	3.00	1.50	.90
62	Roberto Perfect (Roberto Clemente)	15.00	7.50	4.50
63	Monster Strikeouts (Dick Radatz)	3.00	1.50	.90
64	Callison's Homer (Johnny Callison)	3.00	1.50	.90
65	Stargell's Big Day (Willie Stargell)	3.00	1.50	.90
66	Brooks Gets Triple (Brooks Robinson)	4.50	2.25	1.25
67	Fergie Fans Six (Fergie Jenkins)	3.00	1.50	.90
68	Tom Terrific (Tom Seaver)	5.00	2.50	1.50
69	Stretch Belts Two (Willie McCovey)	3.00	1.50	.90
70	Yaz' Four Hits (Carl Yastrzemski)	4.50	2.25	1.25
71	Reggie Unloads (Reggie Jackson)	6.00	3.00	1.75
72	Henry Hammers (Hank Aaron)	12.00	6.00	3.50
73	Bonds Perfect (Bobby Bonds)	3.00	1.50	.90

1974 Laughlin Old-Time Black Stars

This set of slightly oversized cards (2-5/8" x 3-1/2") features drawings by R.G. Laughlin. The artwork is printed in brown and a light tan; backs are printed in brown on white stock. The set features many of the greatest players from the Negro Leagues. The cards carry no copyright date and no mention of the prolific Laughlin, but the simple line drawings are obviously his work, and a subsequent issue four years later by Laughlin removes any doubt. Original retail price at time of issue was about $3.25.

		NM	EX	VG
Complete Set (36):		60.00	30.00	18.00
Common Player:		2.00	1.00	.60
1	Smokey Joe Williams	5.00	2.50	1.50
2	Rap Dixon	2.00	1.00	.60
3	Oliver Marcelle	2.00	1.00	.60
4	Bingo DeMoss	4.00	2.00	1.25
5	Willie Foster	2.50	1.25	.70
6	John Beckwith	2.00	1.00	.60
7	Floyd (Jelly) Gardner	2.00	1.00	.60
8	Josh Gibson	10.00	5.00	3.00
9	Jose Mendez	5.00	2.50	1.50
10	Pete Hill	5.00	2.50	1.50
11	Buck Leonard	5.00	2.50	1.50
12	Jud Wilson	5.00	2.50	1.50
13	Willie Wells	5.00	2.50	1.50
14	Jimmie Lyons	2.00	1.00	.60
15	Satchel Paige	10.00	5.00	3.00
16	Louis Santop	5.00	2.50	1.50
17	Frank Grant	7.50	3.75	2.25
18	Christobel Torrienti	5.00	2.50	1.50
19	Bullet Rogan	4.00	2.00	1.25
20	Dave Malarcher	2.50	1.25	.70
21	Spot Poles	2.00	1.00	.60
22	Home Run Johnson	2.50	1.25	.70
23	Charlie Grant	4.00	2.00	1.25
24	Cool Papa Bell	5.00	2.50	1.50
25	Cannonball Dick Redding	2.00	1.00	.60
26	Ray Dandridge	5.00	2.50	1.50
27	Biz Mackey	7.50	3.75	2.25
28	Fats Jenkins	2.00	1.00	.60
29	Martin Dihigo	5.00	2.50	1.50
30	Mule Suttles	5.00	2.50	1.50
31	Bill Monroe	2.00	1.00	.60
32	Dan McClellan	2.00	1.00	.60
33	Pop Lloyd	5.00	2.50	1.50
34	Oscar Charleston	5.00	2.50	1.50
35	Andrew "Rube" Foster	5.00	2.50	1.50
36	William (Judy) Johnson	5.00	2.50	1.50

1974 Laughlin Sportslang

Featuring the cartoon artwork of R.G. Laughlin, this 41-card set features 40 cards (plus one unnumbered title card) detailing the history and derivation of slang terms from several sports. The cards are 2-3/4" x 3-1/4", with red and blue printing on the front and red on the back. The cards are numbered on the back.

		NM	EX	VG
Complete Set (41):		80.00	40.00	24.00
Common Card:		3.00	1.50	.80
1	Bull Pen	3.00	1.50	.80
2	Charley Horse	3.00	1.50	.80
3	Derby	3.00	1.50	.80
4	Anchor Man	3.00	1.50	.80
5	Mascot	3.00	1.50	.80
6	Annie Oakley	3.00	1.50	.80
7	Taxi Squad	3.00	1.50	.80
8	Dukes	3.00	1.50	.80
9	Rookie	3.00	1.50	.80
10	Jinx	3.00	1.50	.80
11	Dark Horse	3.00	1.50	.80
12	Hat Trick	3.00	1.50	.80
13	Bell Wether	3.00	1.50	.80
14	Love	3.00	1.50	.80
15	Red Dog	3.00	1.50	.80
16	Barnstorm	3.00	1.50	.80
17	Bull's Eye	3.00	1.50	.80
18	Rabbit Punch	3.00	1.50	.80
19	The Upper Hand	3.00	1.50	.80
20	Handi Cap	3.00	1.50	.80
21	Marathon	3.00	1.50	.80
22	Southpaw	3.00	1.50	.80
23	Boner	3.00	1.50	.80
24	Gridiron	3.00	1.50	.80
25	Fan	3.00	1.50	.80
26	Moxie	3.00	1.50	.80
27	Birdie	3.00	1.50	.80
28	Sulky	3.00	1.50	.80
29	Dribble	3.00	1.50	.80
30	Donnybrook	3.00	1.50	.80
31	The Real McCoy	3.00	1.50	.80
32	Even Stephen	3.00	1.50	.80
33	Chinese Homer	3.00	1.50	.80
34	English	3.00	1.50	.80
35	Garrison Finish	3.00	1.50	.80
36	Foot in the Bucket	3.00	1.50	.80
37	Steeple Chase	3.00	1.50	.80
38	Long Shot	3.00	1.50	.80
39	Nip and Tuck	3.00	1.50	.80
40	Battery	3.00	1.50	.80
----	Header Card	3.00	1.50	.80

1975 Laughlin Batty Baseball

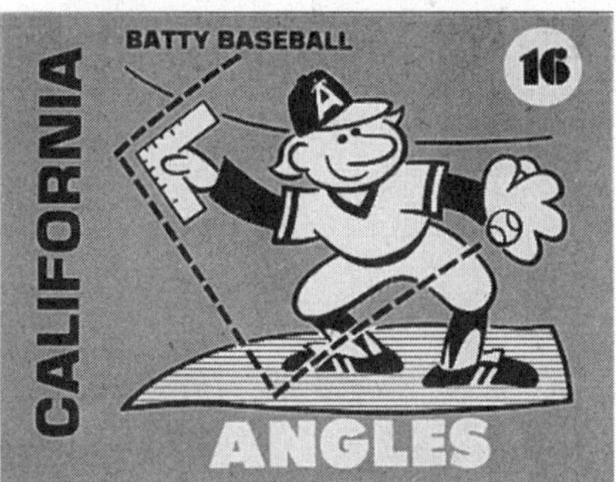

This 25-card set depicts one humorous nickname for each of 24 Major League teams, plus one unnumbered title card. The cards are approximately standard size at 2-1/2" x 3-1/2", with simple black and white cartoon drawings on the front with orange back- grounds. The backs are blank and the cards are numbered on front.

		NM	EX	VG
Complete Set (25):		60.00	30.00	18.00
Common Card:		3.00	1.50	.90
1	Oakland Daze	3.00	1.50	.90
2	Boston Wet Sox	3.00	1.50	.90
3	Cincinnati Dreads	3.00	1.50	.90
4	Chicago Wide Sox	3.00	1.50	.90
5	Milwaukee Boozers	3.00	1.50	.90
6	Philadelphia Fillies	3.00	1.50	.90
7	Cleveland Engines	3.00	1.50	.90
8	New York Mitts	3.00	1.50	.90
9	Texas Ranchers	3.00	1.50	.90
10	San Francisco Gents	3.00	1.50	.90
11	Houston Disastros	3.00	1.50	.90
12	Chicago Clubs	3.00	1.50	.90
13	Minnesota Wins	3.00	1.50	.90
14	St. Louis Gardeners	3.00	1.50	.90
15	New York Yankers	3.00	1.50	.90
16	California Angles	3.00	1.50	.90
17	Pittsburgh Irates	3.00	1.50	.90
18	Los Angeles Smoggers	3.00	1.50	.90
19	Baltimore Oreos	3.00	1.50	.90
20	Montreal Expose	3.00	1.50	.90
21	San Diego Parties	3.00	1.50	.90
22	Detroit Taggers	3.00	1.50	.90
23	Kansas City Broils	3.00	1.50	.90
24	Atlanta Briefs	3.00	1.50	.90
----	Header Card	3.00	1.50	.90

1976 Laughlin Diamond Jubilee

This set of 32 oversized cards (2-3/4" x 4") features Laughlin's drawings of baseball stars highlighting specific events or records. The fronts are printed in black and blue

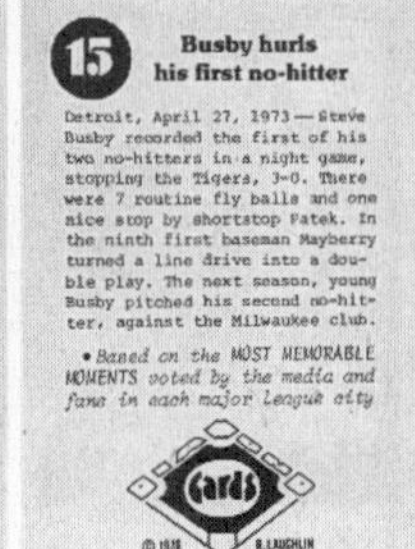

over a red background; the backs are numbered and printed in blue with information about the specific event. Sets originally sold for $3.50.

		NM	EX	VG
Complete Set (32):		90.00	45.00	25.00
Common Player:		2.00	1.00	.60
1	Nolan Ryan	30.00	15.00	9.00
2	Ernie Banks	4.50	2.25	1.25
3	Mickey Lolich	2.00	1.00	.60
4	Sandy Koufax	9.00	4.50	2.75
5	Frank Robinson	3.00	1.50	.90
6	Bill Mazeroski	3.00	1.50	.90
7	Catfish Hunter	2.00	1.00	.60
8	Hank Aaron	9.00	4.50	2.75
9	Carl Yastrzemski	3.00	1.50	.90
10	Jim Bunning	2.00	1.00	.60
11	Brooks Robinson	3.00	1.50	.90
12	John VanderMeer	2.00	1.00	.60
13	Harmon Killebrew	3.00	1.50	.90
14	Lou Brock	2.50	1.25	.70
15	Steve Busby	2.00	1.00	.60
16	Nate Colbert	2.00	1.00	.60
17	Don Larsen	2.50	1.25	.70
18	Willie Mays	9.00	4.50	2.75
19	David Clyde	2.00	1.00	.60
20	Mack Jones	2.00	1.00	.60
21	Mike Hegan	2.00	1.00	.60
22	Jerry Koosman	2.00	1.00	.60
23	Early Wynn	2.50	1.25	.70
24	Nellie Fox	2.50	1.25	.70
25	Joe DiMaggio	15.00	7.50	4.50
26	Jackie Robinson	12.00	6.00	3.50
27	Ted Williams	12.00	6.00	3.50
28	Lou Gehrig	12.00	6.00	3.50
29	Bobby Thomson	2.50	1.25	.70
30	Roger Maris	7.50	3.75	2.25
31	Harvey Haddix	2.00	1.00	.60
32	Babe Ruth	20.00	10.00	6.00

1976 Laughlin Indianapolis Clowns

In a departure from the style of most Laughlin issues, this 42-card set does not use his artwork but rather black and white photos framed by a light blue border. The cards are oversized at 2-5/8" x 4-1/4", with red printing on front and back. The cards are numberd on the front.

		NM	EX	VG
Complete Set (42):		30.00	15.00	9.00
Common Player:		.60	.30	.20
1	Ed Hamman (Ed the Clown)	1.00	.50	.30
2	Dero Austin	.60	.30	.20
3	James Williams (Natureboy)	.60	.30	.20
4	Sam Brison (Birmingham)	.60	.30	.20
5	Richard King (King Tut)	.60	.30	.20
6	Syd Pollock (Founder)	.60	.30	.20
7	Nataniel (Lefty) Small	.60	.30	.20
8	Grant Greene (Double Duty)	.60	.30	.20
9	Nancy Miller (Lady Umpire)	.60	.30	.20
10	Billy Vaughn	.60	.30	.20
11	Sam Brison (Putout for Sam)	.60	.30	.20
12	Ed Hamman	.60	.30	.20
13	Dero Austin (Home Delivery)	.60	.30	.20
14	Steve (Nub) Anderson	.60	.30	.20
15	Joe Cherry	.60	.30	.20
16	Reece (Goose) Tatum	3.00	1.50	.90
17	James Williams (Natureboy)	.60	.30	.20
18	Byron Purnell	.60	.30	.20
19	Bat Boy	.60	.30	.20
20	Spec BeBop	.60	.30	.20
21	Satchel Paige	5.00	2.50	1.50
22	Prince Jo Henry	.60	.30	.20
23	Ed Hamman, Syd Pollock	.60	.30	.20

24	Paul Casanova	.60	.30	.20
25	Steve (Nub) Anderson (Nub Singles)	.60	.30	.20
26	Comiskey Park	.60	.30	.20
27	Toni Stone (Second Basewoman)	1.50	.70	.45
28	Dero Austin (Small Target)	.60	.30	.20
29	Calling Dr. Kildare (Sam Brison, Natureboy Williams)	.60	.30	.20
30	Oscar Charleston	2.00	1.00	.60
31	Richard King (King Tut)	.60	.30	.20
32	Ed and Prospects (Ed Hamman, Joe Cherry, Hal King)	.60	.30	.20
33	Team Bus	.60	.30	.20
34	Hank Aaron	6.00	3.00	1.75
35	The Greta Yogi	1.50	.70	.45
36	W.H. (Chauff) Wilson	.60	.30	.20
37	Doin' Their Thing (Sam Brison, Sonny Jackson)	.60	.30	.20
38	Billy Vaughn (The Hard Way)	.60	.30	.20
39	James Williams (18 the easy way)	.60	.30	.20
40	Casey & Ed (Ed Hamman, Casey Stengel)	1.25	.60	.40
---	Header Card	.60	.30	.20
---	Baseball Laff Book	.60	.30	.20

1978 Laughlin Long Ago Black Stars

2. LARRY BROWN C

This sparkplug came from Birmingham to join the Pitt Keystones in 1921, and became one of the great defensive catchers of black baseball. He caught for the two Chicago teams of '26 and '27 that won the black World Series. After he threw out Ty Cobb five successive times in a '26 game in Havana, Ty asked the light-skinned Brown to join the Tigers—as a Cuban—but Larry declined. In '30 "Iron Man" Brown caught 234 games! He never pulled off his mask on a foul. A .300 hitter, Larry played longest for the Memphis Red Sox and also managed. He was voted catcher on many All-Star teams. Died in '72.

©1978 R.G. Laughlin

In what appears very much like a second series save for slight title alteration, sports artist R.G. Laughlin produced this 36-card set in a format very similar to his 1974 issue highlighting Negro League stars. This set is printed in dark and light green on a non-glossy front, with printing on the back in black. Most of the more widely known Negro League stars appeared in the 1974 issue.

		NM	EX	VG
Complete Set (36):		60.00	30.00	18.00
Common Player:		1.50	.70	.45
1	Ted Trent	1.50	.70	.45
2	Larry Brown	1.50	.70	.45
3	Newt Allen	3.00	1.50	.90
4	Norman Stearns	4.50	2.25	1.25
5	Leon Day	6.00	3.00	1.75
6	Dick Lundy	1.50	.70	.45
7	Bruce Petway	1.50	.70	.45
8	Bill Drake	1.50	.70	.45
9	Chaney White	1.50	.70	.45
10	Webster McDonald	2.50	1.25	.70
11	Tommy Butts	1.50	.70	.45
12	Ben Taylor	4.50	2.25	1.25
13	James (Joe) Greene	1.50	.70	.45
14	Dick Seay	1.50	.70	.45
15	Sammy Hughes	1.50	.70	.45
16	Ted Page	3.00	1.50	.90
17	Willie Cornelius	1.50	.70	.45
18	Pat Patterson	1.50	.70	.45
19	Frank Wickware	1.50	.70	.45
20	Albert Haywood	1.50	.70	.45
21	Bill Holland	1.50	.70	.45
22	Sol White	4.50	2.25	1.25
23	Chet Brewer	3.00	1.50	.90
24	Crush Holloway	1.50	.70	.45
25	George Johnson	1.50	.70	.45
26	George Scales	1.50	.70	.45
27	Dave Brown	1.50	.70	.45
28	John Donaldson	1.50	.70	.45
29	William Johnson	3.00	1.50	.90
30	Bill Yancey	3.00	1.50	.90
31	Sam Bankhead	4.00	2.00	1.25
32	Leroy Matlock	1.50	.70	.45
33	Quincy Troupe	2.50	1.25	.70
34	Hilton Smith	3.00	1.50	.90
35	Jim Crutchfield	3.00	1.50	.90
36	Ted Radcliffe	4.00	2.00	1.25

1980 Laughlin Famous Feats

A set of 40 cards, this Famous Feats set by sports artist R.G. Laughlin carries a subtitle as the Second Series, apparently a reference to a 1972 issue of the same name by Laughlin that was produced by Fleer. Unlike many of the odd sized Laughlin issues, this one is the standard 2-1/2" x 3-1/2", with full color used with the artist's pen and ink drawings on the front. The cards are numbered on the front and the backs are blank.

		NM	EX	VG
Complete Set (40):		15.00	7.50	4.50
Common Player:		.75	.35	.20
1	Honus Wagner	2.50	1.25	.70
2	Herb Pennock	.75	.35	.20
3	Al Simmons	.75	.35	.20
4	Hack Wilson	.75	.35	.20
5	Dizzy Dean	1.50	.70	.45
6	Chuck Klein	.75	.35	.20
7	Nellie Fox	.75	.40	.25
8	Lefty Grove	.75	.35	.20
9	George Sisler	.75	.35	.20
10	Lou Gehrig	3.50	1.75	1.00
11	Rube Waddell	.75	.35	.20
12	Max Carey	.75	.35	.20
13	Thurman Munson	2.00	1.00	.60
14	Mel Ott	.75	.35	.20
15	Doc White	.75	.35	.20
16	Babe Ruth	6.00	3.00	1.75
17	Schoolboy Rowe	.75	.35	.20
18	Jackie Robinson	3.50	1.75	1.00
19	Joe Medwick	.75	.35	.20
20	Casey Stengel	.75	.35	.20
21	Roberto Clemente	4.50	2.25	1.25
22	Christy Mathewson	1.50	.70	.45
23	Jimmie Foxx	1.25	.60	.40
24	Joe Jackson	6.00	3.00	1.75
25	Walter Johnson	1.50	.70	.45
26	Tony Lazzeri	.75	.35	.20
27	Hugh Casey	.75	.35	.20
28	Ty Cobb	3.50	1.75	1.00
29	Stuffy McInnis	.75	.35	.20
30	Cy Young	1.25	.60	.40
31	Lefty O'Doul	.75	.35	.20
32	Eddie Collins	.75	.35	.20
33	Joe McCarty	.75	.35	.20
34	Ed Walsh	.75	.35	.20
35	George Burns	.75	.35	.20
36	Walt Dropo	.75	.35	.20
37	Connie Mack	.75	.35	.20
38	Babe Adams	.75	.35	.20
39	Rogers Hornsby	1.00	.50	.30
40	Grover C. Alexander	.75	.35	.20

1980 Laughlin 300/400/500

This unusual set features a combination of the line drawings of R.G. Laughlin and a photo head shot of the player depicted. The cards are actually square, 3-1/4" x 3-1/4", with a background in color depicting a baseball diamond. The set is based on 300 wins, batting .400 or better and 500 homers, with a total of 30 cards in the blank backed set. The cards are numbered on the front.

		NM	EX	VG
Complete Set (30):		25.00	12.50	7.50
Common Player:		1.50	.75	.45
1	Header Card	1.50	.75	.45
2	Babe Ruth	10.00	5.00	3.00
3	Walter Johnson	3.00	1.50	.90
4	Ty Cobb	6.00	3.00	1.75
5	Christy Mathewson	3.00	1.50	.90
6	Ted Williams	4.00	2.00	1.25
7	Bill Terry	1.50	.75	.45
8	Grover C. Alexander	1.50	.75	.45
9	Napoleon Lajoie	1.50	.75	.45
10	Willie Mays	4.00	2.00	1.25
11	Cy Young	3.00	1.50	.90
12	Mel Ott	1.50	.75	.45
13	Joe Jackson	10.00	5.00	3.00
14	Harmon Killebrew	1.50	.75	.45
15	Warren Spahn	1.50	.75	.45
16	Hank Aaron	4.00	2.00	1.25
17	Rogers Hornsby	1.50	.75	.45
18	Mickey Mantle	10.00	5.00	3.00
19	Lefty Grove	1.50	.75	.45
20	Ted Williams	4.00	2.00	1.25
21	Jimmie Fox	1.50	.75	.45
22	Eddie Plank	1.50	.75	.45
23	Frank Robinson	1.50	.75	.45
24	George Sisler	1.50	.75	.45
25	Eddie Mathews	1.50	.75	.45
26	Early Wynn	1.50	.75	.45
27	Ernie Banks	1.50	.75	.45
28	Harry Heilmann	1.50	.75	.45
29	Lou Gehrig	7.50	3.75	2.25
30	Willie McCovey	1.50	.75	.45

1929 Leader Novelty Candy Co.

Though unmarked as such, these cards are believed to have been an insert in boxes of Leader Novelty Candy, or at least were so advertised in the famous Copeland Collection auction of 1991. They are one of two "mini" versions of the R316 Kashin Publications cards (see also W553), though it is not known whether the entire 101-card Kashin set was so paralleled. While sizes seem to vary significantly, nominal measurements for this version are about 1-3/4" x 2-5/8". Cards have been seen in duotones of red, sepia, purple and green. They are unnumbered and blank-backed. This checklist is known to be incomplete. Gaps have been left in the assigned numbering to accommodate additions.

		NM	EX	VG
Common Player:		75.00	37.50	22.50
(7)	Lucerne A. Blue	75.00	37.00	22.00
(8)	James Bottomley	150.00	75.00	45.00
(13)	Earl (Earle) Combs	150.00	75.00	45.00
(26)	Jimmy Foxx	250.00	125.00	75.00
(27)	Frank Frisch	150.00	75.00	45.00
(33)	Robert Grove	175.00	87.00	52.00
(42)	Rogers Hornsby	200.00	100.00	60.00
(45)	Sam Jones	75.00	37.50	22.50
(50)	Joseph Judge	75.00	37.50	22.50
(52)	Charles Klein	150.00	75.00	45.00
(62)	Walter Maranville	150.00	75.00	45.00
(65)	Ed "Bing" Miller	75.00	37.00	22.00
(66)	Frank O'Doul	100.00	50.00	30.00
(67)	Melvin Ott	175.00	87.00	52.00
(74)	Eddie Rommel	75.00	37.00	22.00
(85)	Al Simmons	150.00	75.00	45.00
(92)	Harold J. Traynor	150.00	75.00	45.00
(93)	Dazzy Vance	150.00	75.00	45.00
(95)	Paul Waner	150.00	75.00	45.00
(100)	Hack Wilson	175.00	87.00	52.00

1922 Leader Theatre

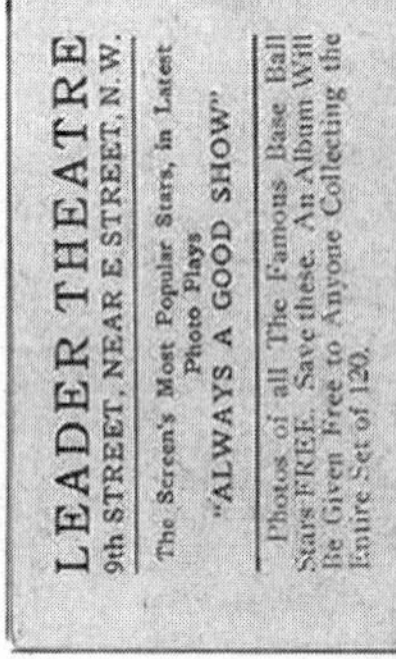

LEADER THEATRE
9th STREET, NEAR E STREET, N.W.

The Screen's Most Popular Stars, in Latest Photo Plays
"ALWAYS A GOOD SHOW"

Photos of all The Famous Base Ball Stars FREE. Save these. An Album Will Be Given Free to Anyone Collecting the Entire Set of 120.

This issue by a Washington, D.C. moviehouse is a version of the W573 and W575-1 strip card sets on which at least two forms of customized advertising were printed on the card backs. The ads state that 120 cards (paralleling W573 and/or W575-1) were originally issued in this version. An album was also offered.

	NM	EX	VG
Common Player:	500.00	250.00	150.00

(See 1922 W573 and W575-1 for checklists and base card values. Add 5X premium for non-commons.)

1949 Leaf

The first color baseball cards of the post-World War II era were the 98-card, 2-3/8" x 2-7/8", set produced by Chicago's Leaf Gum Co. for issue in 1949. One of the toughest postwar sets to complete, exactly half of the issue - 49 cards - are significantly harder to find than the others. Probably intended to confound bubblegum buyers of the day, the set is skip-numbered between 1-168. Card backs contain offers of felt pennants, an album for the cards or 5-1/2" x 7-1/2" premium photos of Hall of Famers. While some cards carry

76---TED (The Kid) WILLIAMS
Right Fielder--Boston Red Sox
Age--31 Bats--left handed
Ht.--6' 3" Throws--right handed
Wgt.--190 lbs. Home--San Diego, Calif.

One of the greatest hitters of all time. Won 4th American league batting title in 1948 with .369 mark. Captured other swat crowns in 1941 (.406); 1942 (.356) and 1947 (.343). Hit 25 home runs last year. In 1946 won home run championship with 38 round toppers. Has all-time batting average of .351.

ALL-STAR BASEBALL GUM

Collect this series of Diamond Greats

LEAF GUM CO., Box 5907 CHICAGO 80, ILL.

a 1948 copyright date on back, it is now believed the issue was not released until 1949. The complete set price does not include the higher value in the variation pairs.

		NM	EX	VG
Complete Set (98):		85,000	35,000	17,500
Common Player:		125.00	45.00	22.50
Common Short-print:		900.00	360.00	180.00
Album:		900.00	450.00	275.00
1	Joe DiMaggio	3,000	725.00	400.00
3	Babe Ruth	3,300	1,650	1,000
4	***Stan Musial***	1,700	850.00	510.00
5	***Virgil Trucks***/SP	1,150	460.00	230.00
8	***Satchel Paige*** /SP	17,500	7,000	3,500
10	Paul Trout	125.00	45.00	22.50
11	***Phil Rizzuto***	325.00	130.00	65.00
13	Casimer Michaels/SP	900.00	360.00	180.00
14	Billy Johnson	125.00	45.00	22.50
17	Frank Overmire	125.00	45.00	22.50
19	John Wyrostek/SP	900.00	360.00	180.00
20	***Hank Sauer***/SP	1,000	400.00	200.00
22	Al Evans	125.00	45.00	22.50
26	Sam Chapman	125.00	45.00	22.50
27	Mickey Harris	125.00	45.00	22.50
28	***Jim Hegan***	125.00	45.00	22.50
29	***Elmer Valo***	125.00	45.00	22.50
30	***Bill Goodman***/SP	900.00	360.00	180.00
31	Lou Brissie	125.00	45.00	22.50
32	***Warren Spahn***	450.00	180.00	90.00
33	Harry Lowrey/SP	900.00	360.00	180.00
36	Al Zarilla/SP	900.00	360.00	180.00
38	***Ted Kluszewski***	300.00	120.00	60.00
39	***Ewell Blackwell***	130.00	50.00	25.00
42a	Kent Peterson (Red cap.)	1,100	440.00	220.00
42b	Kent Peterson (Black cap.)	125.00	45.00	22.50
43	Eddie Stevens/SP	900.00	360.00	180.00
45	Ken Keltner/SP	900.00	360.00	180.00
46	Johnny Mize	300.00	120.00	60.00
47	George Vico	125.00	45.00	22.50
48	Johnny Schmitz/SP	900.00	360.00	180.00
49	***Del Ennis***	130.00	50.00	25.00
50	Dick Wakefield	125.00	45.00	22.50
51	***Alvin Dark***/SP	1,750	700.00	350.00
53	John Vandermeer (Vander Meer)	225.00	90.00	45.00
54	Bobby Adams/SP	900.00	360.00	180.00
55	Tommy Henrich/SP	2,000	800.00	400.00
56	***Larry Jensen***	130.00	50.00	25.00
57	Bob McCall	125.00	45.00	22.50
59	Luke Appling	200.00	80.00	40.00
61	Jake Early	125.00	45.00	22.50
62	Eddie Joost/SP	900.00	360.00	180.00
63	Barney McCosky/SP	900.00	360.00	180.00
65	Bob Elliot (Elliott)	125.00	45.00	22.50
66	Orval Grove/SP	900.00	360.00	180.00
68	Ed Miller/SP	900.00	360.00	180.00
70	Honus Wagner	500.00	200.00	100.00
72	Hank Edwards	125.00	45.00	22.50
73	Pat Seerey	125.00	45.00	22.50
75	Dom DiMaggio/SP	1,400	560.00	280.00
76	Ted Williams	2,600	1,300	780.00
77	Roy Smalley	125.00	45.00	22.50
78	Walter Evers/SP	900.00	360.00	180.00
79	***Jackie Robinson***	1,800	550.00	325.00
81	George Kurowski/SP	900.00	360.00	180.00
82	Johnny Lindell	125.00	45.00	22.50
83	Bobby Doerr	225.00	90.00	45.00
84	Sid Hudson	125.00	45.00	22.50
85	***Dave Philley***/SP	900.00	360.00	180.00
86	Ralph Weigel	125.00	45.00	22.50
88	Frank Gustine/SP	900.00	360.00	180.00
91	***Ralph Kiner***	175.00	70.00	35.00
93	Bob Feller/SP	3,250	1,300	650.00
95	George Stirnweiss	125.00	45.00	22.50
97	***Martin Marion***	150.00	60.00	30.00
98	***Hal Newhouser***/SP	1,800	725.00	360.00
102a	Gene Hermansk (Incorrect spelling.)	2,750	1,100	550.00
102b	Gene Hermanski (Correct spelling.)	135.00	55.00	25.00
104	Edward Stewart/SP	900.00	360.00	180.00
106	Lou Boudreau	200.00	80.00	40.00
108	Matthew Batts/SP	900.00	360.00	180.00
111	Gerald Priddy	125.00	45.00	22.50
113	Emil Leonard/SP	900.00	360.00	180.00
117	Joe Gordon	125.00	45.00	22.50
120	***George Kell***/SP	1,100	440.00	220.00
121	***John Pesky***/SP	1,000	400.00	200.00
123	Clifford Fannin/SP	900.00	360.00	180.00
125	***Andy Pafko***	160.00	65.00	30.00
127	Enos Slaughter/SP	1,750	700.00	350.00
128	Warren Rosar	125.00	45.00	22.50
129	Kirby Higbe/SP	900.00	360.00	180.00
131	Sid Gordon/SP	900.00	360.00	180.00
133	Tommy Holmes/SP	1,000	400.00	200.00
136a	Cliff Aberson (Full sleeve.)	125.00	50.00	25.00
136b	Cliff Aberson (Short sleeve.)	175.00	70.00	35.00
137	Harry Walker/SP	900.00	360.00	180.00
138	***Larry Doby***/SP	3,000	1,200	600.00
139	Johnny Hopp	125.00	45.00	22.50
142	***Danny Murtaugh***/SP	1,000	400.00	200.00
143	Dick Sisler/SP	900.00	360.00	180.00
144	Bob Dillinger/SP	900.00	360.00	180.00
146	Harold Reiser/SP	1,000	400.00	200.00
149	Henry Majeski/SP	900.00	360.00	180.00
153	Floyd Baker/SP	900.00	360.00	180.00
158	***Harry Brecheen***/SP	900.00	360.00	180.00
159	Mizell Platt	125.00	45.00	22.50
160	Bob Scheffing/SP	900.00	360.00	180.00
161	***Vernon Stephens***/SP	1,000	400.00	200.00
163	***Freddy Hutchinson***/SP	1,000	400.00	200.00
165	***Dale Mitchell***/SP	1,000	400.00	200.00
168	Phil Cavaretta/SP	900.00	360.00	180.00

1949 Leaf Premiums

These blank-back, sepia photos were available with the purchase of 1948 Leaf baseball cards. Measuring 5-5/8" x 7-1/4", the pictures have a facsimile autograph and a black box labeled "BASEBALL'S IMMORTALS" at bottom containing a short biography. The unnumbered pictures are checklisted alphabetically.

		NM	EX	VG
Complete Set (9):		6,000	3,000	1,800
Common Player:		400.00	200.00	120.00
(1)	Grover Alexander	450.00	225.00	135.00
(2)	Mickey Cochrane	400.00	200.00	120.00
(3)	Lou Gehrig	1,200	600.00	360.00
(4)	Walter Johnson	450.00	225.00	135.00
(5)	Christy Mathewson	525.00	260.00	155.00
(6)	John McGraw	400.00	200.00	120.00
(7)	Babe Ruth (Dark background, text boxes.)	1,200	600.00	360.00
(8)	Babe Ruth (Light background, no text.)	1,200	600.00	360.00
(9)	Ed Walsh	400.00	200.00	120.00

1960 Leaf Pre-production

Evidently produced prior to final approval for the design of the 1960 Leaf set, these cards all feature much larger player photos than the issued versions. Generally the issued cards have cap-to-waist photos while the pre-production cards have to cap-to-chin shots. Backs of the pre-production cards are virtually identical to the regular cards. The pre-production cards were never publically issued and show evidence of having been hand-cut. The cards of Donovan and Jay appear to be more common than the others.

		NM	EX	VG
Complete Set (8):		15,000	7,500	4,500
Common Player:		1,500	750.00	450.00
1	Luis Aparicio	4,500	2,250	1,350
12	Ken Boyer	2,150	1,075	645.00
17	Walt Moryn	1,250	625.00	375.00
23	Joey Jay	1,250	625.00	375.00
35	Jim Coates	2,250	1,125	675.00
58	Hal Smith	1,950	975.00	585.00
61	Vic Rehm	1,500	750.00	450.00
72	Dick Donovan	1,250	625.00	375.00

1960 Leaf

While known to the hobby as "Leaf" cards, this set of 144 carries the copyright of Sports Novelties Inc., Chicago. The 2-1/2" x 3-1/2" cards feature black-and-white player portrait photos, with plain background. Cards were sold in nickel wax packs with a marble, rather than a piece of bubble gum. The second half of the set, #73-144, are quite scarce. Card #25, Jim Grant, is found in two versions, with his own picture (black cap) and with a photo of Brooks Lawrence (white cap). Three back variations of Hal Smith card #58 are also known.

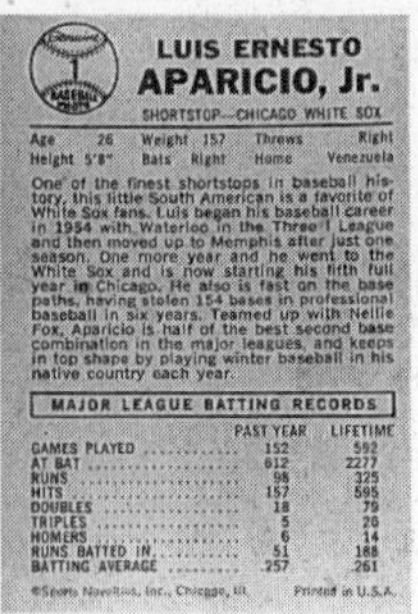

LUIS ERNESTO
APARICIO, Jr.
SHORTSTOP—CHICAGO WHITE SOX

Age 26 Weight 157 Throws Right
Height 5'8" Bats Right Home Venezuela

One of the finest shortstops in baseball history, this little South American is a favorite of White Sox fans. Luis began his baseball career in 1954 with Waterloo in the Three I League and then moved up to Memphis after just one season. One more year and he went to the White Sox and is now starting his fifth full year in Chicago. He also is fast on the base paths, having stolen 154 bases in professional baseball in six years. Teamed up with Nellie Fox, Aparicio is half of the best second base combination in the major leagues, and keeps in top shape by playing winter baseball in his native country each year.

MAJOR LEAGUE BATTING RECORDS

	PAST YEAR	LIFETIME
GAMES PLAYED	152	592
AT BAT	612	2277
RUNS	98	325
HITS	157	595
DOUBLES	18	79
TRIPLES	5	26
HOMERS	6	14
RUNS BATTED IN	51	188
BATTING AVERAGE	.257	.261

Printed in U.S.A.

Complete set prices do not include variations. In the late 1990s, a large group of high-number (Series 2) boxes - in excess of 4,000 cards - was added to the surviving supply.

		NM	EX	VG
Complete Set (144):		2,000	1,000	500.00
Common Player (1-72):		9.00	4.50	2.75
Common Player (73-144):		12.00	6.00	3.50
Wax Pack, Series 1 (5):		120.00		
Wax Box, Series 1 (24):		2,400		
Wax Pack, Series 2 (5):		190.00		
Wax Box, Series 2 (24):		3,250		
1	Luis Aparicio	55.00	15.00	9.00
2	Woody Held	9.00	4.50	2.75
3	Frank Lary	9.00	4.50	2.75
4	Camilo Pascual	9.00	4.50	2.75
5	Frank Herrera	9.00	4.50	2.75
6	Felipe Alou	8.00	4.00	2.50
7	Bennie Daniels	9.00	4.50	2.75
8	Roger Craig	9.00	4.50	2.75
9	Eddie Kasko	9.00	4.50	2.75
10	Bob Grim	9.00	4.50	2.75
11	Jim Busby	9.00	4.50	2.75
12	Ken Boyer	17.50	8.75	5.25
13	Bob Boyd	9.00	4.50	2.75
14	Sam Jones	9.00	4.50	2.75
15	Larry Jackson	9.00	4.50	2.75
16	Roy Face	9.00	4.50	2.75
17	Walt Moryn	9.00	4.50	2.75
18	Jim Gilliam	8.00	4.00	2.50
19	Don Newcombe	8.00	4.00	2.50
20	Glen Hobbie	9.00	4.50	2.75
21	Pedro Ramos	9.00	4.50	2.75
22	Ryne Duren	8.00	4.00	2.50
23	Joe Jay	9.00	4.50	2.75
24	Lou Berberet	9.00	4.50	2.75
25a	Jim Grant (White cap, photo actually Brooks Lawrence.)	15.00	7.50	4.50
25b	Jim Grant (Dark cap, correct photo.)	22.50	11.00	6.75
26	Tom Borland	9.00	4.50	2.75
27	Brooks Robinson	25.00	12.50	7.50
28	Jerry Adair	9.00	4.50	2.75
29	Ron Jackson	9.00	4.50	2.75
30	George Strickland	9.00	4.50	2.75
31	Rocky Bridges	9.00	4.50	2.75
32	Bill Tuttle	9.00	4.50	2.75
33	Ken Hunt	9.00	4.50	2.75
34	Hal Griggs	9.00	4.50	2.75
35	Jim Coates	9.00	4.50	2.75
36	Brooks Lawrence	9.00	4.50	2.75
37	Duke Snider	30.00	15.00	9.00
38	Al Spangler	9.00	4.50	2.75
39	Jim Owens	9.00	4.50	2.75
40	Bill Virdon	9.00	4.50	2.75
41	Ernie Broglio	9.00	4.50	2.75
42	Andre Rodgers	9.00	4.50	2.75
43	Julio Becquer	9.00	4.50	2.75
44	Tony Taylor	9.00	4.50	2.75
45	Jerry Lynch	9.00	4.50	2.75
46	Clete Boyer	8.00	4.00	2.50
47	Jerry Lumpe	9.00	4.50	2.75
48	Charlie Maxwell	9.00	4.50	2.75
49	Jim Perry	9.00	4.50	2.75
50	Danny McDevitt	9.00	4.50	2.75
51	Juan Pizarro	9.00	4.50	2.75
52	***Dallas Green***	20.00	10.00	6.00
53	Bob Friend	9.00	4.50	2.75
54	Jack Sanford	9.00	4.50	2.75
55	Jim Rivera	9.00	4.50	2.75
56	Ted Wills	9.00	4.50	2.75
57	Milt Pappas	9.00	4.50	2.75
58a	Hal Smith (Team & position on back.)	9.00	4.50	2.75
58b	Hal Smith (Team blackened out on back.)	750.00	375.00	225.00
58c	Hal Smith (Team missing on back.)	75.00	37.50	22.50
59	Bob Avila	9.00	4.50	2.75
60	Clem Labine	9.00	4.50	2.75
61	Vic Rehm	9.00	4.50	2.75
62	John Gabler	9.00	4.50	2.75
63	John Tsitouris	9.00	4.50	2.75
64	Dave Sisler	9.00	4.50	2.75
65	Vic Power	9.00	4.50	2.75
66	Earl Battey	9.00	4.50	2.75
67	Bob Purkey	9.00	4.50	2.75
68	Moe Drabowsky	9.00	4.50	2.75
69	Hoyt Wilhelm	15.00	7.50	4.50
70	Humberto Robinson	9.00	4.50	2.75
71	Whitey Herzog	9.00	4.50	2.75
72	Dick Donovan	9.00	4.50	2.75
73	Gordon Jones	12.00	6.00	3.50
74	Joe Hicks	12.00	6.00	3.50
75	***Ray Culp***	12.00	6.00	3.50
76	Dick Drott	12.00	6.00	3.50
77	Bob Duliba	12.00	6.00	3.50

78	Art Ditmar	12.00	6.00	3.50
79	Steve Korcheck	12.00	6.00	3.50
80	Henry Mason	12.00	6.00	3.50
81	Harry Simpson	12.00	6.00	3.50
82	Gene Green	12.00	6.00	3.50
83	Bob Shaw	12.00	6.00	3.50
84	Howard Reed	12.00	6.00	3.50
85	Dick Stigman	12.00	6.00	3.50
86	Rip Repulski	12.00	6.00	3.50
87	Seth Morehead	12.00	6.00	3.50
88	Camilo Carreon	12.00	6.00	3.50
89	John Blanchard	17.50	8.75	5.25
90	Billy Hoeft	12.00	6.00	3.50
91	Fred Hopke	12.00	6.00	3.50
92	Joe Martin	12.00	6.00	3.50
93	Wally Shannon	12.00	6.00	3.50
94	Baseball's Two Hal Smiths	50.00	25.00	15.00
95	Al Schroll	12.00	6.00	3.50
96	John Kucks	12.00	6.00	3.50
97	Tom Morgan	12.00	6.00	3.50
98	Willie Jones	12.00	6.00	3.50
99	Marshall Renfroe	12.00	6.00	3.50
100	Willie Tasby	12.00	6.00	3.50
101	Irv Noren	12.00	6.00	3.50
102	Russ Snyder	12.00	6.00	3.50
103	Bob Turley	17.50	8.75	5.25
104	Jim Woods	12.00	6.00	3.50
105	Ronnie Kline	12.00	6.00	3.50
106	Steve Bilko	12.00	6.00	3.50
107	Elmer Valo	12.00	6.00	3.50
108	Tom McAvoy	12.00	6.00	3.50
109	Stan Williams	12.00	6.00	3.50
110	Earl Averill	12.00	6.00	3.50
111	Lee Walls	12.00	6.00	3.50
112	Paul Richards	12.00	6.00	3.50
113	Ed Sadowski	12.00	6.00	3.50
114	Stover McIlwain (Photo actually Jim McAnany.)	17.50	8.75	5.25
115	Chuck Tanner (Photo actually Ken Kuhn.)	17.50	8.75	5.25
116	Lou Klimchock	12.00	6.00	3.50
117	Neil Chrisley	12.00	6.00	3.50
118	Johnny Callison	12.00	6.00	3.50
119	Hal Smith	12.00	6.00	3.50
120	Carl Sawatski	12.00	6.00	3.50
121	Frank Leja	12.00	6.00	3.50
122	Earl Torgeson	12.00	6.00	3.50
123	Art Schult	12.00	6.00	3.50
124	Jim Brosnan	12.00	6.00	3.50
125	Sparky Anderson	60.00	30.00	18.00
126	Joe Pignatano	12.00	6.00	3.50
127	Rocky Nelson	12.00	6.00	3.50
128	Orlando Cepeda	45.00	22.50	13.50
129	Daryl Spencer	12.00	6.00	3.50
130	Ralph Lumenti	12.00	6.00	3.50
131	Sam Taylor	12.00	6.00	3.50
132	Harry Brecheen	12.00	6.00	3.50
133	Johnny Groth	12.00	6.00	3.50
134	Wayne Terwilliger	12.00	6.00	3.50
135	Kent Hadley	12.00	6.00	3.50
136	Faye Throneberry	12.00	6.00	3.50
137	Jack Meyer	12.00	6.00	3.50
138	***Chuck Cottier***	12.00	6.00	3.50
139	Joe DeMaestri	12.00	6.00	3.50
140	Gene Freese	12.00	6.00	3.50
141	Curt Flood	30.00	15.00	9.00
142	Gino Cimoli	12.00	6.00	3.50
143	Clay Dalrymple	12.00	6.00	3.50
144	Jim Bunning	50.00	25.00	15.00

1923 Lections

This series of cards was virtually unknown in the hobby until 1997 when 28 cards turned up in Albany, N.Y. The cards measure about 4" x 2-1/2" with rounded corners and are printed on very thick cardboard. At left front is an oval black-and-white player photo with name and team below. At right is green or orange art of a baseball game with the issuer's logo and trademark information. It is unknown with what, if any, product these cards were issued; a candy premium seems the most likely source. Most of the cards seen so far are in grades from Fair-Good, though a few are known in Ex-Mt.

		NM	EX	VG
Complete Set (10):		30,000	15,000	9,000
Common Player:		2,000	1,000	600.00
(1)	Frank Chance	3,500	1,750	1,050
(2)	Howard Ehmke	2,000	1,000	600.00
(3)	Frank Frisch	3,500	1,750	1,050
(4)	Roger (Rogers) Hornsby	5,000	2,500	1,500
(5)	Charles Jamieson	2,000	1,000	600.00
(6)	"Bob" Meusel	2,000	1,000	600.00
(7)	Emil Meusel	2,000	1,000	600.00
(8)	"Babe" Ruth	9,000	4,500	2,700
(9)	Charles Schmidt	2,000	1,000	600.00
(10)	"Bob" Shawkey	2,000	1,000	600.00

1975 Lee's Sweets

Baseball Greats

A series of 68 cards, of baseball's greatest players. Baseball is America's greatest game, a way of life. Most every child has at one time played baseball, and most every child has their favorite ballplayer.

Baseball is played in almost every corner of the world, by both young and old. These cards represent some of the greatest ballplayers that ever lived.

Lee's Sweets
Camp Hill, Ala.

Professing to be an issue of 68 cards of "Baseball Greats," this collectors' issue first appeared about 1975. Only four players are known. Fronts of the 2-1/2" x 3-3/16" cards have crudely printed black-and-white player photos. Backs describe the series and give the Lee's Sweets address as Camp Hill, Ala.

		NM	EX	VG
Complete Set (4):		25.00	12.50	7.50
Common Player:		6.00	3.00	1.75
(1)	Ty Cobb	6.00	3.00	1.75
(2)	Joe DiMaggio	6.00	3.00	1.75
(3)	Lou Gehrig	6.00	3.00	1.75
(4)	Babe Ruth	12.00	6.00	3.50

1909-11 Lenox Cigarettes

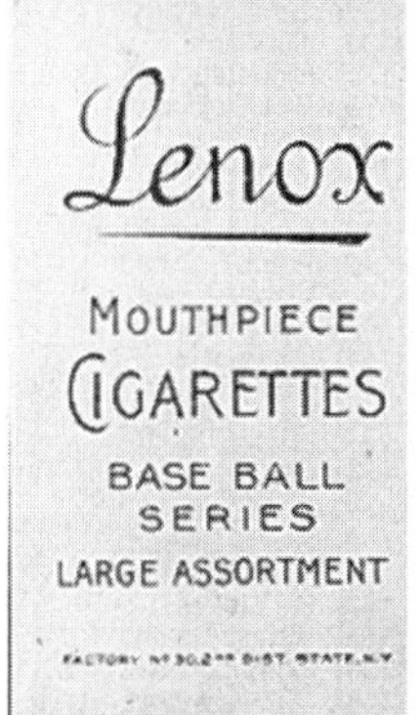

Many collectors rank the Lenox back as the third rarest among T206, behind only Ty Cobb and Drum. Lenox cards can be found with the back printing in either black or brown.

PREMIUMS
Black, Common Players: 12-15X
Black, Hall of Famers: 8-10X
Brown, Common Players: 75-100X
Brown, Hall of Famers: 40-60X
(See T206 for checklist and base card values.)

1969 Lincoln-Mercury Sports Panel Postcards

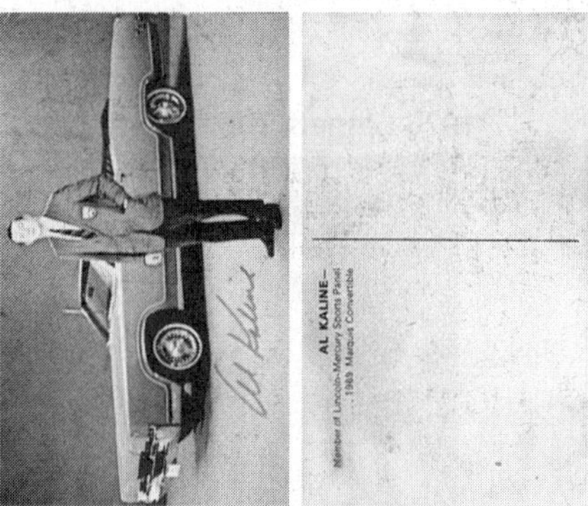

Various celebrity spokesmen on the Lincoln-Mercury Sports Panel can be found on a series of color postcards. In standard 5-1/2" x 3-1/2" format, cards have borderless color photos on front of the spokesman standing with one of the company's new cars; a facsimile autograph also appears. Divided backs identify the player and the automobile.

	NM	EX	VG
Al Kaline	80.00	40.00	25.00

1906 Lincoln Publishing Philadelphia A's

Members of the American League Champions (says so right at the top) Philadelphia A's, decked out in their Sunday-best, are featured in this set of black-and-white postcards.

The portraits are framed in fancy graphics which include a baseball, the dates 1905 and 1906 and the player's name in a banner beneath the photo. At bottom is a box with "ATHLETIC BASE BALL TEAM." Back of the approximately 3-1/2" x 5-1/2" cards has a box at upper-left enclosing "POST CARD." The unnumbered cards are listed here alphabetically.

		NM	EX	VG
Complete Set (20):		10,000	5,000	3,000
Common Player:		300.00	150.00	90.00
(1)	Chief Bender	1,500	750.00	450.00
(2)	Andy Coakley	300.00	150.00	90.00
(3)	Lave Cross	300.00	150.00	90.00
(4)	Monte Cross	300.00	150.00	90.00
(5)	Harry Davis	300.00	150.00	90.00
(6)	Jimmy Dygert	300.00	150.00	90.00
(7)	Topsy Hartsel	300.00	150.00	90.00
(8)	Weldon Henley	300.00	150.00	90.00
(9)	Danny Hoffman	300.00	150.00	90.00
(10)	John Knight	300.00	150.00	90.00
(11)	Bris Lord	300.00	150.00	90.00
(12)	Connie Mack	1,500	750.00	450.00
(13)	Danny Murphy	300.00	150.00	90.00
(14)	Joe Myers	300.00	150.00	90.00
(15)	Rube Oldring	300.00	150.00	90.00
(16)	Eddie Plank	2,000	1,000	600.00
(17)	Mike Powers	300.00	150.00	90.00
(18)	Ossee Schreckengost	300.00	150.00	90.00
(19)	Ralph Seybold	300.00	150.00	90.00
(20)	Rube Waddell	1,500	750.00	450.00

1975 Linnett MLB All-Stars

This series of pencil-portrait prints was done by sports artist Charles Linnett of Walpole, Mass. The black-and-white prints are on 8-1/2" x 11" textured paper, featuring a facsimile autograph of the player. Because the portraits are licensed only by the Players Association, the players are pictured capless with no uniform logos visible. Backs are blank. The 1975 pictures differ from the 1976 issue in that they include a printed player name, besides the facsimile autograph. At least some of the portraits were given away in a ballpark "Portrait Day" promotion at Fenway Park, sponsored by Grant City (W.T. Grant Co.) department stores. A coupon accompanying the SGA portraits offered a discount on a package of three pictures, apparently the standard retail offering that carried a $1.19 price tag. This rudimentary checklist is certainly incomplete.

		NM	EX	VG
Common Player:		6.00	3.00	1.75
(25)	Fred Lynn	9.00	4.50	2.75
(50)	Tom Seaver	9.00	4.50	2.75
(75)	Carl Yastrzemski	12.00	6.00	3.50

1976 Linnett Portraits

This series of pencil-portrait prints was done by sports artist Charles Linnett of Walpole, Mass., and includes baseball, football, hockey, NBA and Harlem Globetrotters players (only baseball listed here). The black-and-white prints are on 8-1/2" x 11" textured paper, featuring a facsimile autograph of the player. Because the portraits are licensed only by the Players Association, the players are pictured capless with no uniform logos visible. Backs are blank. The portraits originally sold for 50 cents apiece by mail.

		NM	EX	VG
Complete Baseball Set (176):		300.00	150.00	90.00
Common Player:		2.50	1.25	.75
(1)	Hank Aaron	10.00	5.00	3.00
(2)	Dick Allen	4.00	2.00	1.25
(3)	Matty Alou	2.50	1.25	.75
(4)	Mike Anderson	2.50	1.25	.75
(5)	Luis Aparicio	5.00	2.50	1.50
(6)	Sal Bando	2.50	1.25	.75
(7)	Mark Belanger	2.50	1.25	.70
(8)	Buddy Bell	2.50	1.25	.75
(9)	Johnny Bench	6.00	3.00	1.75
(10)	Jim Bibby	2.50	1.25	.75
(11)	Paul Blair	2.50	1.25	.75
(12)	Bert Blyleven	3.00	1.50	.90
(13)	Ron Blomberg	2.50	1.25	.75
(14)	Bob Bolin	2.50	1.25	.75
(15)	Bill Bonham	2.50	1.25	.75
(16)	Pedro Borbon	2.50	1.25	.75
(17)	Bob Boone	3.00	1.50	.90
(18)	Larry Bowa	2.50	1.25	.75
(19)	Steve Braun	2.50	1.25	.75
(20)	Ken Brett	2.50	1.25	.75
(21)	John Briggs	2.50	1.25	.75
(22)	Lou Brock	5.00	2.50	1.50
(23)	Jack Brohamer	2.50	1.25	.75
(24)	Steve Brye	2.50	1.25	.75
(25)	Bill Buckner	2.50	1.25	.70
(26)	Jeff Burroughs	2.50	1.25	.75
(27)	Steve Busby	2.50	1.25	.75
(28)	Bert Campaneris	2.50	1.25	.75
(29)	Bernie Carbo	2.50	1.25	.75
(30)	Jose Cardenal	2.50	1.25	.75
(31)	Steve Carlton	5.00	2.50	1.50
(32)	Rod Carew	5.00	2.50	1.50
(33)	Dave Cash	2.50	1.25	.75
(34)	Norm Cash	3.00	1.50	.90
(35)	Danny Cater	2.50	1.25	.75
(36)	Cesar Cedeno	2.50	1.25	.75
(37)	Orlando Cepeda	5.00	2.50	1.50
(38)	Ron Cey	2.50	1.25	.70
(39)	Chris Chambliss	2.50	1.25	.75
(40)	David Clyde	2.50	1.25	.75
(41)	Rich Coggins	2.50	1.25	.75
(42)	Jim Colborn	2.50	1.25	.75
(43)	Dave Concepcion	3.00	1.50	.90
(44)	Willie Crawford	2.50	1.25	.75
(45)	John Curtis	2.50	1.25	.75
(46)	Bobby Darwin	2.50	1.25	.75
(47)	Dan Driessen	2.50	1.25	.75
(48)	Duffy Dyer	2.50	1.25	.75
(49)	John Ellis	2.50	1.25	.75
(50)	Darrell Evans	2.50	1.25	.70
(51)	Dwight Evans	2.50	1.25	.70
(52)	Joe Ferguson	2.50	1.25	.75
(53)	Rollie Fingers	4.00	2.00	1.25
(54)	Carlton Fisk	5.00	2.50	1.50
(55)	Bill Freehan	2.50	1.25	.70
(56)	Jim Fregosi	2.50	1.25	.75
(57)	Oscar Gamble	2.50	1.25	.75
(58)	Pedro Garcia	2.50	1.25	.75
(59)	Ralph Garr	2.50	1.25	.75
(60)	Wayne Garrett	2.50	1.25	.75
(61)	Steve Garvey	2.50	1.25	.70
(62)	Cesar Geronimo	2.50	1.25	.75
(63)	Bob Gibson	5.00	2.50	1.50
(64)	Dave Giusti	2.50	1.25	.75
(65)	Bobby Grich	2.50	1.25	.75
(66)	Doug Griffin	2.50	1.25	.75
(67)	Mario Guerrero	2.50	1.25	.75
(68)	Don Gullett	2.50	1.25	.75
(69)	Tommy Harper	2.50	1.25	.75
(70)	Toby Harrah	2.50	1.25	.75
(71)	Bud Harrelson	2.50	1.25	.75
(72)	Vic Harris	2.50	1.25	.75
(73)	Richie Hebner	2.50	1.25	.75
(74)	George Hendrick	2.50	1.25	.75
(75)	Ed Hermann	2.50	1.25	.75
(76)	John Hiller	2.50	1.25	.75
(77)	Willie Horton	2.50	1.25	.75
(78)	Jim Hunter	4.00	2.00	1.25
(79)	Tommy Hutton	2.50	1.25	.75
(80)	Reggie Jackson	7.50	3.75	2.25
(81)	Fergie Jenkins	4.00	2.00	1.25
(82)	Dave Johnson	2.50	1.25	.75
(83)	Cleon Jones	2.50	1.25	.75
(84)	Al Kaline	6.00	3.00	1.75
(85)	John Kennedy	2.50	1.25	.75
(86)	Steve Kline	2.50	1.25	.75
(87)	Jerry Koosman	2.50	1.25	.75
(88)	Bill Lee	2.50	1.25	.75
(89)	Eddie Leon	2.50	1.25	.75
(90)	Bob Locker	2.50	1.25	.75
(91)	Mickey Lolich	3.00	1.50	.90
(92)	Jim Lonborg	2.50	1.25	.75
(93)	Davey Lopes	2.50	1.25	.75
(94)	Mike Lum	2.50	1.25	.75
(95)	Greg Luzinski	2.50	1.25	.75
(96)	Sparky Lyle	2.50	1.25	.75
(97)	Teddy Martinez	2.50	1.25	.75
(98)	Jon Matlack	2.50	1.25	.75
(99)	Dave May	2.50	1.25	.75
(100)	John Mayberry	2.50	1.25	.75
(101)	Willie Mays	10.00	5.00	3.00
(102)	Jim McAndrew	2.50	1.25	.75
(103)	Dick McAuliffe	2.50	1.25	.75
(104)	Sam McDowell	2.50	1.25	.70
(105)	Lynn McGlothen	2.50	1.25	.75
(106)	Tug McGraw	2.50	1.25	.70
(107)	Hal McRae	2.50	1.25	.75
(108)	Bill Melton	2.50	1.25	.75
(109)	Andy Messersmith	2.50	1.25	.75
(110)	Gene Michael	2.50	1.25	.75
(111)	Felix Millan	2.50	1.25	.75
(112)	Rick Miller	2.50	1.25	.75
(113)	John Milner	2.50	1.25	.75
(114)	Rick Monday	2.50	1.25	.75
(115)	Don Money	2.50	1.25	.75
(116)	Bob Montgomery	2.50	1.25	.75
(117)	Joe Morgan	5.00	2.50	1.50
(118)	Carl Morton	2.50	1.25	.75
(119)	Thurman Munson	4.00	2.00	1.25
(120)	Bobby Murcer	2.50	1.25	.75
(121)	Graig Nettles	3.00	1.50	.90
(122)	Jim Northrup	2.50	1.25	.75
(123)	Ben Oglivie	2.50	1.25	.75
(124)	Al Oliver	3.00	1.50	.90
(125)	Bob Oliver	2.50	1.25	.75
(126)	Jorge Orta	2.50	1.25	.75
(127)	Amos Otis	2.50	1.25	.75
(128)	Jim Palmer	5.00	2.50	1.50
(129)	Harry Parker	2.50	1.25	.75
(130)	Fred Patek	2.50	1.25	.75
(131)	Marty Pattin	2.50	1.25	.75
(132)	Tony Perez	4.00	2.00	1.25
(133)	Gaylord Perry	4.00	2.00	1.25
(134)	Jim Perry	2.50	1.25	.75
(135)	Rico Petrocelli	2.50	1.25	.75
(136)	Rick Reichardt	2.50	1.25	.75
(137)	Ken Reitz	2.50	1.25	.75
(138)	Jerry Reuss	2.50	1.25	.75
(139)	Bill Robinson	2.50	1.25	.75
(140)	Brooks Robinson	5.00	2.50	1.50
(141)	Frank Robinson	5.00	2.50	1.50
(142)	Cookie Rojas	2.50	1.25	.75
(143)	Pete Rose	9.00	4.50	2.75
(144)	Bill Russell	2.50	1.25	.75
(145)	Nolan Ryan	15.00	7.50	4.50
(146)	Manny Sanguillen	2.50	1.25	.75
(147)	George Scott	2.50	1.25	.75
(148)	Mike Schmidt	7.50	3.75	2.25
(149)	Tom Seaver	6.00	3.00	1.75
(150)	Sonny Siebert	2.50	1.25	.75
(151)	Ted Simmons	2.50	1.25	.75
(152)	Bill Singer	2.50	1.25	.75
(153)	Reggie Smith	2.50	1.25	.75
(154)	Chris Speier	2.50	1.25	.75
(155)	Charlie Spikes	2.50	1.25	.75
(156)	Paul Splittorff	2.50	1.25	.75
(157)	Mickey Stanley	2.50	1.25	.75
(158)	Lee Stanton	2.50	1.25	.75
(159)	Willie Stargell	5.00	2.50	1.50
(160)	Rusty Staub	3.00	1.50	.90
(161)	Rennie Stennett	2.50	1.25	.75
(162)	Steve Stone	3.00	1.50	.90
(163)	Mel Stottlemyre	2.50	1.25	.75
(164)	Don Sutton	4.00	2.00	1.25
(165)	George Theodore	2.50	1.25	.75
(166)	Danny Thompson	2.50	1.25	.75
(167)	Luis Tiant	3.00	1.50	.90
(168)	Joe Torre	3.50	1.75	1.00
(169)	Bobby Valentine	2.50	1.25	.75
(170)	Bob Veale	2.50	1.25	.75
(171)	Billy Williams	5.00	2.50	1.50
(172)	Wilbur Wood	2.50	1.25	.75
(173)	Jim Wynn	2.50	1.25	.75
(174)	Carl Yastrzemski	6.00	3.00	1.75
(175)	Robin Yount	5.00	2.50	1.50
(175)	Richie Zisk	2.50	1.25	.75

1976 Linnett Superstars

This frequently encountered set of 36 cards has enjoyed little collector interest since its issue in 1976. Officially known as "Pee-Wee Superstars," the cards measure 4" x 5-5/8". Player portraits by artist Charles Linnett are rendered in black-and-white pencil and set against a pale yellow background. Players are shown without caps or uniforms (most appear to be wearing white T-shirts). According to the logos at top the set was fully licensed by both the Players Association and Major League Baseball, and team logos do appear in the lower-left corner. A facsimile autograph in red or purple appears on each card. Front borders are bright purple, red, green, dark brown, or white. Card backs feature either a photo of an antique auto or a drawing of an historic sailing ship. Each of the 12 different back designs appears on one card from each team set. The Linnetts were sold in panels of six perforated cards. An offer on the back of each card makes 8" x 10" premium portraits of each player available for 95 cents. The premium pictures have about the same value as the cards. Inexplicably, the cards are numbered from 90-125. Only the World's Champion Cincinnati Reds, A.L. Champion Boston Red Sox and N.L. runner-up Dodgers are represented in the issue.

		NM	EX	VG
Complete Panel Set (6):		15.00	7.50	4.50
Complete Singles Set (36):		15.00	7.50	4.50
Common Player:		.60	.30	.20
Panel 1		7.50	3.75	2.25
90	Don Gullett	.60	.30	.20
91	Johnny Bench	2.50	1.25	.70
92	Tony Perez	1.25	.60	.40
93	Mike Lum	.60	.30	.20
94	Ken Griffey	.60	.30	.20
95	George Foster	.60	.30	.20
Panel 2		9.00	4.50	2.75
96	Joe Morgan	2.50	1.25	.70
97	Pete Rose	6.00	3.00	1.75
98	Dave Concepcion	.60	.30	.20
99	Cesar Geronimo	.60	.30	.20
100	Dan Driessen	.60	.30	.20
101	Pedro Borbon	.60	.30	.20
Panel 3		7.50	3.75	2.25
102	Carl Yastrzemski	2.50	1.25	.70
103	Fred Lynn	.60	.30	.20
104	Dwight Evans	.60	.30	.20
105	Ferguson Jenkins	1.25	.60	.40
106	Rico Petrocelli	.60	.30	.20
107	Denny Doyle	.60	.30	.20
Panel 4		6.00	3.00	1.75
108	Luis Tiant	.60	.30	.20
109	Carlton Fisk	2.50	1.25	.70
110	Rick Burleson	.60	.30	.20
111	Bill Lee	.60	.30	.20
112	Rick Wise	.60	.30	.20
113	Jim Rice	1.00	.50	.30
Panel 5		6.00	3.00	1.75
114	Davey Lopes	.60	.30	.20
115	Steve Garvey	1.25	.60	.40
116	Bill Russell	.60	.30	.20
117	Ron Cey	.60	.30	.20
118	Steve Yaeger	.60	.30	.20
119	Doug Rau	.60	.30	.20
Panel 6		6.00	3.00	1.75
120	Don Sutton	1.75	.90	.50
121	Joe Ferguson	.60	.30	.20
122	Mike Marshall	.60	.30	.20
123	Bill Buckner	.60	.30	.20
124	Rick Rhoden	.60	.30	.20
125	Ted Sizemore	.60	.30	.20

1923 Little Wonder Picture Series

Some versions of the W515-2 strip cards are found with part of a line of type in the top border that reads "THE LITTLE WONDER PICTURE SERIES" and includes a Underwood (U&U) logo.

(See W515-2.)

1887 Lone Jack St. Louis Browns (N370)

The Lone Jack set is among the rarest of all 19th Century tobacco issues. Issued by the Lone Jack Cigarette Co. of Lynchburg, Va., the set consists of 13 subjects, all members of the American Association champion St. Louis Browns. Photos for the set are enlarged versions of those used in the more popular N172 Old Judge series. Cards in the set measure 2-1/2" x 1-1/2" and carry an ad for Lone Jack Cigarettes along the bottom of the front. The set features the Browns' starting lineup for 1886 along with their two top pitchers, backup catcher and owner, Chris Von Der Ahe.

		NM	EX	VG
Common Player:		12,000	7,150	4,950
(1)	Doc Bushong	12,000	7,150	4,950
(2)	Parisian Bob Caruthers	12,000	7,150	4,950
(3)	Charles Commiskey (Comiskey)	75,000	12,000	8,000
(4)	Dave Foutz	12,000	7,150	4,950
(5)	Will Gleason	12,000	7,150	4,950
(6)	Nat Hudson	12,000	7,150	4,950
(7)	Rudy Kimler (Kemmler)	12,000	7,150	4,950
(8)	Arlie Latham	12,000	7,150	4,950
(9)	Little Nick Nicol	12,000	7,150	4,950
(10)	Tip O'Neil (O'Neill)	12,000	7,150	4,950
(11)	Yank Robinson	11,000	6,500	4,500
(12)	Chris Von Der Ahe	18,000	10,800	7,200
(13)	Curt Welsh (Welch)	12,000	7,150	4,950

1886 Lorillard Team Cards

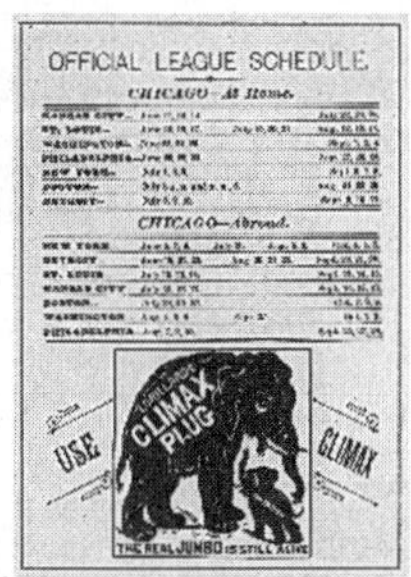

Issued in 1886 by Lorillard Tobacco Co., these 4" x 5-1/2" cards were issued for the Chicago, Detroit and New York baseball clubs. Each card carries the team's schedule (starting with June) on one side and features 11 player portraits enclosed in circles on the other. Each side has advertising for one of Lorillard's tobacco brands - Climax, Rebecca, etc.

		NM	EX	VG
Complete Set (4):		45,000	22,500	13,500
Common Team:		7,500	3,750	2,200
(1)	Chicago League Base Ball Club	13,500	6,750	4,050
(2)	Detroit League Base Ball Club	12,000	6,000	3,600
(3)	New York League Base Ball Club	10,000	5,000	3,000
(4)	Philadelphia League Base Ball Club	7,500	3,750	2,250

1949 Lummis Peanut Butter Phillies

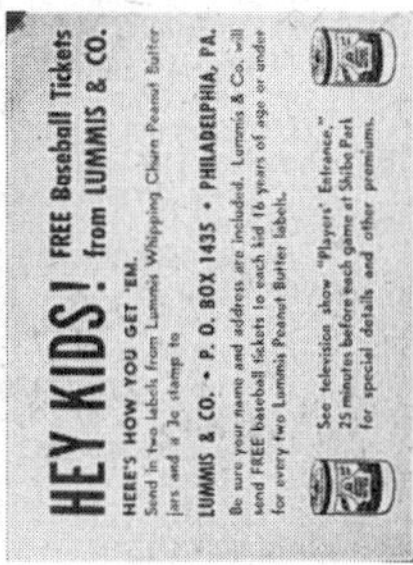

This 12-card regional set featuring the Phillies was issued in the Philadelphia area by Lummis Peanut Butter in 1949. The cards measure 3-1/4" x 4-1/4" and are unnumbered. The fronts feature an action photo with a facsimile autograph, while the backs advertise a game ticket promotion by Lummis Peanut Butter. The same photos and checklist were also used for a regional sticker set issued by Sealtest Dairy the same year.

		NM	EX	VG
Complete Set (12):		22,500	11,250	6,750
Common Player:		1,350	675.00	400.00
(1)	Rich Ashburn	4,500	2,250	1,350
(2)	Hank Borowy	1,350	675.00	400.00
(3)	Del Ennis	1,500	750.00	450.00
(4)	Granny Hamner	1,350	675.00	400.00
(5)	Puddinhead Jones	1,350	675.00	400.00
(6)	Russ Meyer	1,350	675.00	400.00
(7)	Bill Nicholson	1,350	675.00	400.00
(8)	Robin Roberts	4,500	2,250	1,350
(9)	"Schoolboy" Rowe	1,350	675.00	400.00
(10)	Andy Seminick	1,350	675.00	400.00
(11)	Curt Simmons	1,500	750.00	450.00
(12)	Eddie Waitkus	1,350	675.00	400.00

1910 Luxello Cigars A's/Phillies Pins (P13)

Players from the two Philadelphia teams are pictured in this series of 7/8" black-and-white pins. The player's last name, team and position are printed below the photo; the Luxello Cigar name at top. On left and right are a horseshoe with monogram inside.

		NM	EX	VG
Complete Set (21):		17,500	8,750	5,250
Common Player:		750.00	375.00	225.00
	Philadelphia Athletics			
(1)	Franklin Baker	1,500	750.00	450.00
(2)	Jack Barry	750.00	375.00	225.00
(3)	Eddie Collins	1,500	750.00	450.00
(4)	John W. Coombs	750.00	375.00	225.00
(5)	Harry Davis	750.00	375.00	225.00
(6)	James Dygert	750.00	375.00	225.00
(7)	Heinie Heitmuller	750.00	375.00	225.00
(8)	Harry Krause	750.00	375.00	225.00
(9)	Paddy Livingston	750.00	375.00	225.00
(10)	Danny Murphy	750.00	375.00	225.00
(11)	Ed Plank	1,500	750.00	450.00
	Philadelphia Phillies			
(12)	John W. Bates	750.00	375.00	225.00
(13)	Chas. S. Dooin	750.00	375.00	225.00
(14)	Mike Doolan	750.00	375.00	225.00
(15)	Eddie Grant	750.00	375.00	225.00
(16)	Otto Knabe	750.00	375.00	225.00
(17)	Geo. McQuillan	750.00	375.00	225.00
(18)	Earl Moore	750.00	375.00	225.00
(19)	Lew Moren	750.00	375.00	225.00
(20)	Tully Sparks	750.00	375.00	225.00
(21)	John Titus	750.00	375.00	225.00

1912 L1 Leathers

One of the more unusual baseball collectibles of the tobacco era, the L1 "Leathers" were issued by Helmar Tobacco Co. in 1912 as a premium with its "Turkish Trophies" brand of cigarettes. The set featured 25 of the top baseball players and shared a checklist with the closely-related S81 "Silks," which were another part of the same promotion. The "Leathers," advertised as being 10" x 12", featured drawings of baseball players on horsehide-shaped pieces of leather. The drawings were based on the pictures used for the popular T3 Turkey Red series issued a year earlier. Twenty of the 25 players in the "Leathers" set are from the T3 set. Five pitchers (Rube Marquard, Rube Benton, Marty O'Toole, Grover Alexander and Russ Ford) not pictured in T3 were added to the "Leathers" set, and the Frank Baker error was corrected. According to the promotion, each "Leather" was available in exchange for 50 Helmar coupons. In addition to the 25 baseball stars, the "Leathers" set also included more than 100 other subjects, including female athletes and bathing beauties, famous generals, Indian chiefs, actresses, national flags, college mascots, and others.

		NM	EX	VG
Common Player:		3,000	1,500	900.00
86	Rube Marquard	7,500	3,750	2,250
87	Marty O'Toole	3,000	1,500	900.00
88	Rube Benton	3,000	1,500	900.00
89	Grover Alexander	8,500	4,250	2,550
90	Russ Ford	3,000	1,500	900.00
91	John McGraw	7,500	3,750	2,250
92	Nap Rucker	3,000	1,500	900.00
93	Mike Mitchell	3,000	1,500	900.00
94	Chief Bender	7,500	3,750	2,250
95	Home Run Baker	7,500	3,750	2,250
96	Nap Lajoie	7,500	3,750	2,250
97	Joe Tinker	7,500	3,750	2,250
98	Sherry Magee	3,000	1,500	900.00
99	Howie Camnitz	3,000	1,500	900.00
100	Eddie Collins	7,500	3,750	2,250
101	Red Dooin	3,000	1,500	900.00
102	Ty Cobb	45,000	22,500	13,500
103	Hugh Jennings	7,500	3,750	2,250
104	Roger Bresnahan	7,000	3,500	2,100
105	Jake Stahl	3,000	1,500	900.00
106	Tris Speaker	8,500	4,250	2,550
107	Ed Walsh	7,000	3,500	2,100
108	Christy Mathewson	15,000	7,500	4,500
109	Johnny Evers	7,000	3,500	2,100
110	Walter Johnson	15,000	7,500	4,500

M

1947 Mabley & Carew Cincinnati Reds

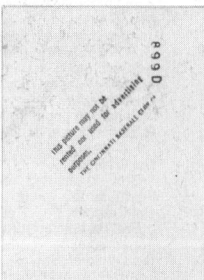

Pictures of Reds players and staff were given away and sold by the boys' shop of the Cincinnati department store. The black-and-white glossy photos measure 3-5/8" x 5-1/16" and have a white border. Backs have a rubber-stamped alpha-numeric identifier and the notice: "This picture may not be rented nor used for advertising purposes. The Cincinnati Baseball Club." The players are not named on the pictures. Small groups of pictures were apparently given away in a tan-and-orange paper folder measuring about 3-7/8" x 5-1/4". The folder pictures the store, has a team roster and schedule and a coupon for purchasing addtional photos at a relatively hefty 10 cents apiece. The pictures are listed here alphabetically.

		NM	EX	VG
Complete Set (28):		850.00	425.00	250.00
Common Player:		30.00	15.00	9.00
Folder:		60.00	30.00	18.00
(1)	Bob Adams	30.00	15.00	9.00
(2)	Frank Baumholtz	30.00	15.00	9.00
(3)	Ewell Blackwell	40.00	20.00	12.00
(4)	Ed Erautt	30.00	15.00	9.00
(5)	Augie Galan	30.00	15.00	9.00
(6)	Harry Gumbert	30.00	15.00	9.00
(7)	Bert Haas	30.00	15.00	9.00
(8)	Grady Hatton	30.00	15.00	9.00
(9)	John Hetki	30.00	15.00	9.00
(10)	George Kelly	30.00	15.00	9.00
(11)	Ray Lamanno	30.00	15.00	9.00
(12)	Everett Lively	30.00	15.00	9.00
(13)	Ed Lukon	30.00	15.00	9.00
(14)	Eddie Miller	30.00	15.00	9.00
(15)	Ray Mueller	30.00	15.00	9.00
(16)	John Neun	30.00	15.00	9.00
(17)	Phil Page	30.00	15.00	9.00
(18)	Kent Peterson	30.00	15.00	9.00
(19)	Hugh Poland	30.00	15.00	9.00
(20)	Ken Raffensberger	30.00	15.00	9.00
(21)	Elmer Riddle	30.00	15.00	9.00
(22)	Tom Tatum	30.00	15.00	9.00
(23)	Johnny Vander Meer	40.00	20.00	12.00
(24)	Clyde Vollmer	30.00	15.00	9.00
(25)	Kermit Wahl	30.00	15.00	9.00
(26)	Bucky Walters	30.00	15.00	9.00
(27)	Babe Young	30.00	15.00	9.00
(28)	Ben Zientara	30.00	15.00	9.00

1950s-70s MacGregor Advisory Staff Photos

Advisory staff photos were a promotional item which debuted in the early 1950s, flourished in the Sixties and died in the early 1970s. Generally 8" x 10" (sometimes a little larger), these black-and-white (a few later were color) glossy photos picture players who had contracted with a major baseball equipment company to endorse and use their product. Usually the product - most often a glove - was prominently displayed in the photo. The pictures were often displayed in the windows of sporting goods stores or the walls of sports departments and were sometimes made available to customers. Because the companies tended to stick with players over the years, some photos were reissued, sometimes with and sometimes without a change of team, pose or typography. All MacGregor staff photos of the era are checklisted here in alphabetical order. Team designation and pose description is given for each known picture. The photos are checklisted here in alphabetical order. It is unlikely this list is complete. Several arrangements of typography in the bottom border are seen and some photos have a facsimile autograph.

	NM	EX	VG
Common Player:	15.00	7.50	4.50
Hank Aaron/Btg (Atlanta, color.)	25.00	12.50	7.50
Richie Ashburn (Cubs, full-length, hands on knees.)	25.00	12.50	7.50
Richie Ashburn (Phillies, full-length, hands on knees.)	40.00	20.00	12.00
Gus Bell/Kneeling (Reds)	15.00	7.50	4.50
Ed Bouchee (Phillies, upper body.)	15.00	7.50	4.50
Ed Brinkman (Senators, upper body.)	15.00	7.50	4.50
Roberto Clemente (Full-length.)	125.00	65.00	35.00
Del Crandall (Braves, catching crouch in gear, large.)	15.00	7.50	4.50
Del Crandall (Braves, catching crouch in gear, small.)	15.00	7.50	4.50
Del Crandall (Braves, catching crouch, no gear.)	15.00	7.50	4.50
Del Crandall (Braves, kneeling, glove on knee.)	15.00	7.50	4.50
Al Downing (Dodgers, glove at waist.)	15.00	7.50	4.50
Al Downing (Yankees, upper body.)	15.00	7.50	4.50
Ron Hansen/Fldg (White Sox)	15.00	7.50	4.50
Tommy Helms (Reds, full-length.)	15.00	7.50	4.50
Randy Hundley (Cubs, upper body.)	15.00	7.50	4.50
Jackie Jensen (Red Sox, chest-up.)	15.00	7.50	4.50
Jack Jensen/Btg (Red Sox,full-length)	15.00	7.50	4.50
Jack Jensen (Red Sox, full-length, hands on knees.)	15.00	7.50	4.50
Ralph Kiner (Cubs, hands on knees.)	30.00	15.00	9.00
Ralph Kiner (Pirates, full-length.)	25.00	12.50	7.50
Ted Kluszewski/Btg (Reds)	25.00	12.50	7.50
Ted Kluszewski/Fldg (White Sox)	25.00	12.50	7.50
Ted Kluszewski/Portrait (Reds)	35.00	17.50	10.00
Johnny Kucks/Pitching (Yankees)	15.00	7.50	4.50
Willie Mays (Giants, full-length.)	90.00	45.00	27.00
Bill Mazeroski/Btg (Pirates)	30.00	15.00	9.00
Mike McCormick (Giants, follow-through.)	15.00	7.50	4.50
Gil McDougald/Throwing (Yankees)	15.00	7.50	4.50
Gil McDougald (Yankees, upper-body portrait.)	15.00	7.50	4.50
Tony Oliva/Btg (Twins)	15.00	7.50	4.50
Tony Oliva (Twins, upper body.)	15.00	7.50	4.50
Claude Osteen/Pitching (Dodgers)	15.00	7.50	4.50
Claude Osteen/Portrait (Dodgers)	15.00	7.50	4.50
Juan Pizzaro (White Sox, follow-through.)	15.00	7.50	4.50
Robin Roberts/Portrait (Phillies)	25.00	12.50	7.50
Robin Roberts (Phillies, follow-through.)	25.00	12.50	7.50
Frank Robinson/Portrait (Orioles)	25.00	12.50	7.50
Pete Rose (Reds, kneeling.)	35.00	17.50	10.00
Pete Rose (Reds, leading off, color.)	65.00	32.50	20.00
Pete Rose (Reds, chest-to-cap portrait.)	35.00	17.50	10.00
Al Schoendienst/Kneeling (Cardinals)	25.00	12.50	7.50
Warren Spahn (Boston Braves, follow-through.)	25.00	12.50	7.50
Daryl Spencer (Cardinals, fielding grounder.)	15.00	7.50	4.50
Don Sutton (Dodgers, color, ready to pitch.)	20.00	10.00	6.00
Frank Torre (Braves, ready to throw.)	15.00	7.50	4.50

1960 MacGregor

The MacGregor Sporting Goods Co. was one of the pioneers in celebrity marketing, creating an advisory staff in 1960 to promote its products. The 25-card set features black-and-white photography of several stars and lesser lights, and even a couple of managers. The cards are 3-3/4" x 5" with a thin white border and the words "MacGregor Baseball Advisory Staff of Champions" on the bottom panel. The cards are not numbered and are blank-backed, and include a facsimile

autograph in white on the front photo. The checklist is arranged here alphabetically.

		NM	EX	VG
Complete Set (25):		700.00	350.00	210.00
Common Player:		15.00	7.50	4.50
1	Hank Aaron	110.00	55.00	35.00
2	Richie Ashburn	35.00	17.50	10.00
3	Gus Bell	15.00	7.50	4.50
4	Lou Berberet	15.00	7.50	4.50
5	Jerry Casale	15.00	7.50	4.50
6	Del Crandall	15.00	7.50	4.50
7	Art Ditmar	15.00	7.50	4.50
8	Gene Freese	15.00	7.50	4.50
9	James Gilliam	17.50	8.75	5.25
10	Ted Kluszewski	35.00	17.50	10.00
11	Jim Landis	15.00	7.50	4.50
12	Al Lopez	30.00	15.00	9.00
13	Willie Mays	110.00	55.00	35.00
14	Bill Mazeroski	35.00	17.50	10.00
15	Mike McCormick	15.00	7.50	4.50
16	Gil McDougald	15.00	7.50	4.50
17	Russ Nixon	15.00	7.50	4.50
18	Bill Rigney	15.00	7.50	4.50
19	Robin Roberts	35.00	17.50	10.00
20	Frank Robinson	45.00	22.50	13.50
21	John Roseboro	15.00	7.50	4.50
22	Red Schoendienst	35.00	17.50	10.00
23	Bill Skowron	20.00	10.00	6.00
24	Daryl Spencer	15.00	7.50	4.50
25	Johnny Temple	15.00	7.50	4.50

1960-70s MacGregor Pete Rose

Besides the several series of card issues and Advisory Staff photos issued over the years, MacGregor produced a number of special Pete Rose cards to promote its relationship with one of baseball's top stars of the 1960s and 1970s. All cards in this listing are in black-and-white with blank backs. The 1965-66 cards are 3-1/2" x 5". The later cards are 5" x 7-1/4" to 7-1/2".

		NM	EX	VG
1965	Pete Rose (Full-length photo, crouching w/glove.)	200.00	100.00	60.00
1966	Pete Rose (Half-length photo, crouching w/glove.)	200.00	100.00	60.00
1969	Pete Rose (Portrait to chest.)	100.00	50.00	30.00
1970	Pete Rose/Fldg (White background.)	75.00	37.50	22.00
1973	Pete Rose/Portrait	75.00	37.50	22.00
1974	Pete Rose (Portrait to waist, w/glove.)	75.00	37.50	22.00

1965 MacGregor

The 1965 MacGregor set is similar to earlier issues, with only a slight change in dimension to 3-1/2" x 5-1/8" and reduced in size to only 10 players. The cards are blank-backed and unnumbered and have a glossy finish. They are checklisted here alphabetically.

		NM	EX	VG
Complete Set (10):		375.00	185.00	110.00
Common Player:		10.00	5.00	3.00
(1)	Roberto Clemente	150.00	75.00	45.00
(2)	Al Downing	10.00	5.00	3.00
(3)	Johnny Edwards	10.00	5.00	3.00
(4)	Ron Hansen	10.00	5.00	3.00
(5)	Deron Johnson	10.00	5.00	3.00
(6)	Willie Mays	135.00	65.00	40.00
(7)	Tony Oliva	15.00	7.50	4.50
(8)	Claude Osteen	10.00	5.00	3.00
(9)	Bobby Richardson	15.00	7.50	4.50
(10)	Zoilo Versalles	10.00	5.00	3.00

1970s MacGregor Advisory Staff Photos

This advisory staff photo series was among the last in a line of promotional items which debuted in the early 1950s, flourished in the Sixties and died in the 1970s. While earlier advisory staff photos were generally 8" x 10", this later series of black-and-white glossy photos is in a 5" x 7" format. They picture players who had contracted with MacGregor to endorse and use its product. The pictures were often displayed in the windows of sporting goods stores or the walls of sports departments and were sometimes made available to customers. Because the companies tended to stick with players over the years, some photos were reissued, sometimes with a change of team, pose or typography. Known MacGregor staff photos of the era are checklisted here in alphabetical order. Team designation and pose description is given for each picture. It is unlikely this list is complete. Gaps have been left in the assigned numbering to accommodate future additions.

		NM	EX	VG
Common Player:		15.00	7.50	4.50
(1)	Hank Aaron (Braves, chest-to-cap.)	40.00	20.00	12.00
(2)	Rod Carew (Twins, chest-to-cap.)	25.00	12.50	7.50
(3)	Rod Carew (Twins, chin-to-cap.)	25.00	12.50	7.50
(5)	George Foster (Reds, chest-to-cap.)	15.00	7.50	4.50
(8)	Lee May (Orioles, chest-to-cap.)	15.00	7.50	4.50
(10)	Joe Morgan (Reds, neck-to-cap.)	25.00	12.50	7.50
(11)	Joe Morgan (Reds, waist-to-cap.)	25.00	12.50	7.50
(12)	Thurman Munson (Yankees, neck-to-cap.)	27.50	13.50	8.25
(15)	Tony Perez (Reds, neck-to-cap.)	25.00	12.50	7.50
(16)	Tony Perez (Expos, chest-to-cap.)	25.00	12.50	7.50
(20)	Don Sutton (Dodgers, chest-to-cap.)	20.00	10.00	6.00
(21)	Don Sutton (Dodgers, neck-to-cap.)	20.00	10.00	6.00

1975 MacGregor Advisory Staff Poster

This 19-1/2" x 26" color poster features Pete Rose in a game-action photo, leading off at first base. Two lines of type, "Winners Play MacGregor" and "The Greatest Name In Sports" are centered above the picture. Back is blank.

	NM	EX	VG
Pete Rose	50.00	25.00	15.00

1886 MacIntire Studio Cabinets

The number of baseball players who found themselves in front of the lens at the MacIntire photography studio in Philadelphia is unknown, but all those thus far seen were members of the 1886 Philadelphia National League team. In standard cabinet-card format of about 3-3/4" x 5-3/4", the pieces feature a cream-colored mount with a sepia photo.

	NM	EX	VG
Common Player:	4,500	3,000	2,000
(1) Tony Cusick	4,500	3,000	2,000
(2) Edward Dailey	4,500	3,000	2,000
(3) Jack Farrell	4,500	3,000	2,000
(4) Charlie Ganzel	4,500	3,000	2,000
(5) Deacon McGuire	4,500	3,000	2,000
(6) Cannonball Titcomb	4,500	3,000	2,000
(7) Harry Wright (Facing his right.)	10,000	4,500	2,800
(8) Harry Wright (Pose unrecorded.)	10,000	4,500	2,800
(9) Team Photo	6,500	4,500	2,800

1951 Connie Mack Book

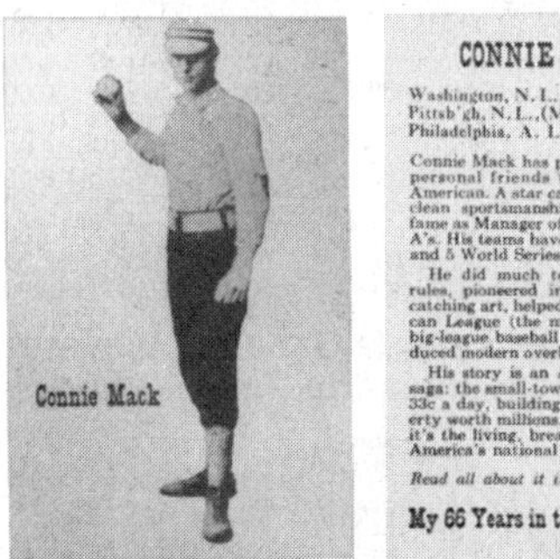

Connie Mack
CONNIE MACK
Washington, N.L., (Buffalo, P.L.), Pittsb'gh, N.L., (M'waukee, W.L.) Philadelphia, A.L. 1886-present
Connie Mack has perhaps had more personal friends than any living American. A star catcher, a model of clean sportsmanship, he made his fame as Manager of the Philadelphia A's. His teams have won 9 pennants and 5 World Series.
He did much to shape baseball rules, pioneered in developing the catching art, helped form the American League (the move which made big-league baseball big), and introduced modern overhand pitching.
His story is an American success saga: the small-town boy starting at 33c a day, building a business property worth millions. More than that, it's the living, breathing, history of America's national sport.
Read all about it in Connie Mack's
My 66 Years in the Big Leagues

In conjunction with the publication of Connie Mack's book "My 66 Years in the Big Leagues," a folder of cards titled, "Four Mighty Heroes" was also issued. The folder contained a quartet of black-and-white player cards. Fronts feature a player photo against a white background. Backs have a bit of player career data and an ad for Mack's book. Cards measure 2-1/4" x 3-1/2".

	NM	EX	VG
Complete Set (4):	1,900	950.00	575.00
Common Player:	275.00	135.00	80.00
Book:	60.00	30.00	18.00
(1) Connie Mack	275.00	135.00	80.00
(2) Christy Mathewson	400.00	200.00	120.00
(3) Babe Ruth	1,000	500.00	300.00
(4) Rube Waddell	275.00	135.00	80.00

1924 Walter Mails Card Game (WG7)

This set of playing cards features 56 subjects. Card backs are printed in either red or blue, featuring player and umpire figures in each corner. At center is the picture of a pitcher with the name of the game's creator beneath. Walter Mails was a major league pitcher between 1915-26. Fronts feature a black-and-white player photo with a facsimile autograph. Printed beneath are the player's name, position and team. At bottom is the designation of a play used in the card game. Both major and minor league players are included in the set. Cards are round-cornered and measure 2-5/16" x 3-1/2". The unnumbered cards are checklisted here alphabetically. It appears as if the blue-back set was issued first and in lesser quantities than those with red backs. Many variations of player personal data between the two colors of backs are reported.

	NM	EX	VG
Complete Set (56):	12,000	6,000	3,500
Common Player, Major Leaguer:	250.00	100.00	60.00
Common Player, Minor Leaguer:	200.00	80.00	50.00
Rules Card:	50.00	20.00	10.00
(1) Russell "Buzz" Arlett	200.00	80.00	50.00
(2) J.C. "Jim" Bagby	200.00	80.00	50.00
(3) Dave "Beauty" Bancroft	500.00	200.00	125.00
(4) Johnny Basseler (Bassler)	250.00	100.00	60.00
(5) Jack Bentley	250.00	100.00	60.00
(6) J.C. "Rube" Benton	250.00	100.00	60.00
(7) Geo. Burns	250.00	100.00	60.00
(8) "Bullet Joe" Bush	250.00	100.00	60.00
(9) Harold P. Chavezo	200.00	80.00	50.00
(10) Hugh Critz	200.00	80.00	50.00
(11) "Jake" E. Daubert	250.00	100.00	60.00
(12) Wheezer Dell	200.00	80.00	50.00
(13) Joe Dugan	250.00	100.00	60.00
(14) Pat Duncan	250.00	100.00	60.00
(15) Howard J. Ehmke	250.00	100.00	60.00
(16) Lewis Fonseca	250.00	100.00	60.00
(17) Ray French	250.00	100.00	60.00
(18) Ed Gharity (Gharrity)	250.00	100.00	60.00
(19) Heinie Groh	250.00	100.00	60.00
(20) George N. Groves	250.00	100.00	60.00
(21) E.F. "Red" Hargrave	250.00	100.00	60.00
(22) Elmer Jacobs	250.00	100.00	60.00
(23) Walter Johnson	1,200	480.00	300.00
(24) WM. "Duke" Kenworthy	250.00	100.00	60.00
(25) Harry Krause	200.00	80.00	50.00
(26) Ray Kremer	250.00	100.00	60.00
(27) Walter Mails	250.00	100.00	60.00
(28) Walter "Rabbitt" Maranville	500.00	200.00	125.00
(29) John "Stuffy" McInnis	250.00	100.00	60.00
(30) Marty McManus	250.00	100.00	60.00
(31) Bob Meusel	250.00	100.00	60.00
(32) Hack Miller	250.00	100.00	60.00
(33) Pat J. Moran	250.00	100.00	60.00
(34) Guy Morton	250.00	100.00	60.00
(35) Johnny Mostil	250.00	100.00	60.00
(36) Rod Murphy	200.00	80.00	50.00
(37) Jimmy O'Connell	250.00	100.00	60.00
(38) Steve O'Neil	250.00	100.00	60.00
(39) Joe Oeschger	250.00	100.00	60.00
(40) Roger Peckinpaugh	250.00	100.00	60.00
(41) Ralph "Babe" Pinelli	250.00	100.00	60.00
(42) Wally Pipp	250.00	100.00	60.00
(43) Elmer Ponder	200.00	80.00	50.00
(44) Sam Rice	500.00	200.00	125.00
(45) Edwin Rommell (Rommel)	250.00	100.00	60.00
(46) Walter Schmidt	250.00	100.00	60.00
(47) Wilford Shupes	200.00	80.00	50.00
(48) Joe Sewell	500.00	200.00	125.00
(49) Pat Shea	200.00	80.00	50.00
(50) W. "Paddy" Siglin	200.00	80.00	50.00
(51) Geo. H. Sisler	500.00	200.00	125.00
(52) William "Bill" Skiff	200.00	80.00	50.00
(53) J. Smith	250.00	100.00	60.00
(54) Harry "Suds" Sutherland	200.00	80.00	50.00
(55) James A. Tierney	250.00	100.00	60.00
(56) Geo. Uhle	250.00	100.00	60.00

1921-1930 Major League Ball Die-Cuts

These die-cut, blank-back player cards were issued over the period 1921-30 for use with a board game called, "Major League Ball - The Indoor Baseball Game Supreme," from The National Game Makers of Washington, D.C. Measuring about 2-1/2" to 2-3/4" tall x 1" to 1-1/4" wide, the cards were originally printed on a sheet of 14 from which they were punched out to play the game. The cards were issued in team sets with on-field roster changes reflected in the player cards over the years. Individual cards are generic, liberally sharing the same poses and portraits with identification possible only by changes to the uniform and the player ID printed in the box below the figure. That player data changed from year to year and the only way to determine exact year of issue is when the player card is found with a complete team set, often in a small pre-printed manila envelope. It is unknown whether all teams were issued in all years. According to information found with the game, stickers could be purchased each year to update the game's figures with new player identification. Beginning in at least 1925 player cards were numbered at bottom within team set.

	NM	EX	VG
Typical Team Set:	300.00	150.00	90.00
Common Player:	50.00	25.00	15.00
Typical Hall of Famer:	75.00	37.50	22.50
Ty Cobb	150.00	75.00	45.00
Lou Gehrig	200.00	100.00	60.00
Walter Johnson	125.00	65.00	40.00
Babe Ruth	350.00	175.00	100.00

1969 Major League Baseball Photostamps

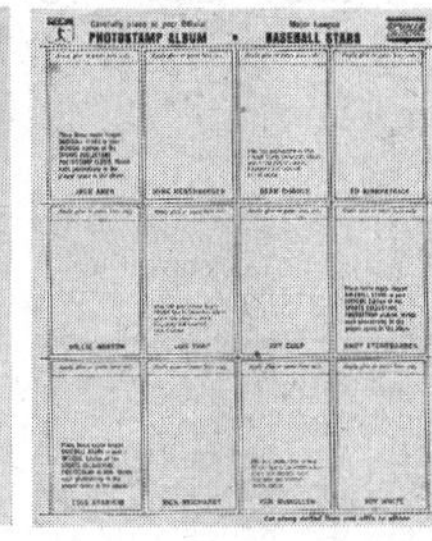

This set of 216 player stamps, sponsored by the Major League Baseball Players Association (not authorized by MLB, thus the lack of team uniform insignia) was issued in professional baseball's centennial year of 1969 and was sold in 18 different uncut sheets, with 12 stamps on each sheet. Each individual stamp measured 2" x 3-1/4". There were nine sheets picturing National League players and nine picturing American Leaguers. The full-color stamps display facsimilie autographs on the fronts. The backs carry instructions to moisten the stamps and place them in a special album that was also available. Many sheets of these stamps were uncovered by a dealer in the early 1980s and they were available at inexpensive prices.

	NM	EX	VG
Complete Sheet Set (18):	60.00	30.00	18.00
Complete Singles Set (216):	60.00	30.00	18.00
A.L. Album and Sheets:	25.00	12.50	7.50
N.L. Album and Sheets:	35.00	17.50	10.00
Common Sheet:	3.50	1.75	1.00
Common Player:	.50	.25	.15
Sheet A.L. 1	3.75	2.00	1.00
(1) Don Buford	.50	.25	.15
(2) Mike Andrews	.50	.25	.15
(3) Max Alvis	.50	.25	.15
(4) Bill Freehan	.50	.25	.15
(5) Horace Clarke	.50	.25	.15
(6) Bernie Allen	.50	.25	.15
(7) Jim Fregosi	.50	.25	.15
(8) Joe Horlen	.50	.25	.15
(9) Jerry Adair	.50	.25	.15
(10) Harmon Killebrew	3.00	1.50	.90
(11) Johnny Odom	.50	.25	.15
(12) Steve Barber	.50	.25	.15
Sheet A.L. 2	2.50	1.25	.75
(13) Tom Harper	.50	.25	.15
(14) Boog Powell	1.00	.50	.30
(15) Jose Santiago	.50	.25	.15
(16) Sonny Siebert	.50	.25	.15
(17) Mickey Lolich	.75	.40	.25
(18) Tom Tresh	.75	.40	.25
(19) Camilo Pascual	.50	.25	.15
(20) Bob Rodgers	.50	.25	.15
(21) Pete Ward	.50	.25	.15
(22) Dave Morehead	.50	.25	.15
(23) John Roseboro	.50	.25	.15
(24) Bert Campaneris	.50	.25	.15
Sheet A.L. 3	3.75	2.00	1.00
(25) Danny Cater	.50	.25	.15
(26) Rich Rollins	.50	.25	.15
(27) Brooks Robinson	3.00	1.50	.90
(28) Rico Petrocelli	.50	.25	.15
(29) Larry Brown	.50	.25	.15
(30) Norm Cash	.75	.40	.25
(31) Jake Gibbs	.50	.25	.15
(32) Mike Epstein	.50	.25	.15
(33) George Brunet	.50	.25	.15
(34) Tom McCraw	.50	.25	.15
(35) Steve Whitaker	.50	.25	.15
(36) Bob Allison	.50	.25	.15
Sheet A.L. 4	2.50	1.25	.75
(37) Jim Kaat	.65	.35	.20
(38) Sal Bando	.50	.25	.15
(39) Ray Oyler	.50	.25	.15
(40) Dave McNally	.50	.25	.15
(41) George Scott	.50	.25	.15
(42) Joe Azcue	.50	.25	.15
(43) Jim Northrup	.50	.25	.15
(44) Fritz Peterson	.50	.25	.15
(45) Paul Casanova	.50	.25	.15
(46) Roger Repoz	.50	.25	.15
(47) Tommy John	.75	.40	.25
(48) Moe Drabowsky	.50	.25	.15
Sheet A.L. 5	2.50	1.25	.75
(49) Ed Kirkpatrick	.50	.25	.15
(50) Dean Chance	.50	.25	.15
(51) Mike Hershberger	.50	.25	.15
(52) Jack Aker	.50	.25	.15
(53) Andy Etchebarren	.50	.25	.15
(54) Ray Culp	.50	.25	.15
(55) Luis Tiant	.65	.35	.20
(56) Willie Horton	.50	.25	.15
(57) Roy White	.50	.25	.15
(58) Ken McMullen	.50	.25	.15
(59) Rick Reichardt	.50	.25	.15

(60) Luis Aparicio	3.00	1.50	.90
Sheet A.L. 6	2.50	1.25	.75
(61) Ken Berry	.50	.25	.15
(62) Wally Bunker	.50	.25	.15
(63) Tony Oliva	1.00	.50	.30
(64) Rick Monday	.50	.25	.15
(65) Chico Salmon	.50	.25	.15
(66) Paul Blair	.50	.25	.15
(67) Jim Lonborg	.50	.25	.15
(68) Zoilo Versalles	.50	.25	.15
(69) Denny McLain	.75	.40	.25
(70) Mel Stottlemyre	.50	.25	.15
(71) Joe Coleman	.50	.25	.15
(72) Bob Knoop	.50	.25	.15
Sheet A.L. 7	2.50	1.25	.75
(73) Chuck Hinton	.50	.25	.15
(74) Duane Josephson	.50	.25	.15
(75) Roger Nelson	.50	.25	.15
(76) Ted Uhlaender	.50	.25	.15
(77) John Donaldson	.50	.25	.15
(78) Tommy Davis	.50	.25	.15
(79) Frank Robinson	3.00	1.50	.90
(80) Dick Ellsworth	.50	.25	.15
(81) Sam McDowell	.50	.25	.15
(82) Dick McAuliffe	.50	.25	.15
(83) Bill Robinson	.50	.25	.15
(84) Frank Howard	.75	.40	.25
Sheet A.L. 8	5.00	2.50	1.50
(85) Ed Brinkman	.50	.25	.15
(86) Vic Davalillo	.50	.25	.15
(87) Gary Peters	.50	.25	.15
(88) Joe Foy	.50	.25	.15
(89) Rod Carew	3.00	1.50	.90
(90) Jim "Catfish" Hunter	2.00	1.00	.60
(91) Gary Bell	.50	.25	.15
(92) Dave Johnson	.50	.25	.15
(93) Ken Harrelson	.50	.25	.15
(94) Tony Horton	.50	.25	.15
(95) Al Kaline	3.00	1.50	.90
(96) Steve Hamilton	.50	.25	.15
Sheet A.L. 9	2.50	1.25	.75
(97) Joseph Pepitone	.75	.40	.25
(98) Ed Stroud	.50	.25	.15
(99) Jim McGlothlin	.50	.25	.15
(100) Wilbur Wood	.50	.25	.15
(101) Paul Schaal	.50	.25	.15
(102) Cesar Tovar	.50	.25	.15
(103) Jim Nash	.50	.25	.15
(104) Don Mincher	.50	.25	.15
(105) Thomas Phoebus	.50	.25	.15
(106) Reggie Smith	.50	.25	.15
(107) Jose Cardenal	.50	.25	.15
(108) Mickey Stanley	.50	.25	.15
Sheet N.L. 1	5.00	2.50	1.50
(109) Billy Williams	2.00	1.00	.60
(110) Mack Jones	.50	.25	.15
(111) Tom Seaver	3.00	1.50	.90
(112) Rich Allen	1.50	.70	.45
(113) Bob Veale	.50	.25	.15
(114) Curt Flood	.65	.35	.20
(115) Pat Jarvis	.50	.25	.15
(116) Jim Merritt	.50	.25	.15
(117) Joe Morgan	2.50	1.25	.70
(118) Tom Haller	.50	.25	.15
(119) Larry Stahl	.50	.25	.15
(120) Willie McCovey	2.50	1.25	.70
Sheet N.L. 2	6.00	3.00	1.75
(121) Ron Hunt	.50	.25	.15
(122) Ernie Banks	3.00	1.50	.90
(123) Jim Fairey	.50	.25	.15
(124) Tommy Agee	.50	.25	.15
(125) Cookie Rojas	.50	.25	.15
(126) Mateo Alou	.50	.25	.15
(127) Mike Shannon	.50	.25	.15
(128) Milt Pappas	.50	.25	.15
(129) Johnny Bench	3.00	1.50	.90
(130) Larry Dierker	.50	.25	.15
(131) Willie Davis	.50	.25	.15
(132) Tony Gonzalez	.50	.25	.15
Sheet N.L. 3	3.75	2.00	1.00
(133) Dick Selma	.50	.25	.15
(134) Jim Ray Hart	.50	.25	.15
(135) Phil Regan	.50	.25	.15
(136) Manny Mota	.50	.25	.15
(137) Cleon Jones	.50	.25	.15
(138) Rick Wise	.50	.25	.15
(139) Willie Stargell	2.50	1.25	.70
(140) Robert Gibson	2.50	1.25	.70
(141) Rico Carty	.50	.25	.15
(142) Gary Nolan	.50	.25	.15
(143) Doug Rader	.50	.25	.15
(144) Wes Parker	.50	.25	.15
Sheet N.L. 4	2.50	1.25	.75
(145) Bill Singer	.50	.25	.15
(146) Bill McCool	.50	.25	.15
(147) Juan Marichal	2.00	1.00	.60
(148) Randy Hundley	.50	.25	.15
(149) "Mudcat" Grant	.50	.25	.15
(150) Ed Kranepool	.50	.25	.15
(151) Tony Taylor	.50	.25	.15
(152) Gene Alley	.50	.25	.15
(153) Dal Maxvill	.50	.25	.15
(154) Felipe Alou	.65	.35	.20
(155) Jim Maloney	.50	.25	.15
(156) Jesus Alou	.50	.25	.15
Sheet N.L. 5	8.00	4.00	2.50
(157) Curt Blefary	.50	.25	.15
(158) Ron Fairly	.50	.25	.15
(159) Dick Kelley	.50	.25	.15
(160) Frank Linzy	.50	.25	.15
(161) Fergie Jenkins	2.00	1.00	.60
(162) Maury Wills	.75	.40	.25
(163) Jerry Grote	.50	.25	.15
(164) Chris Short	.50	.25	.15
(165) Jim Bunning	2.00	1.00	.60
(166) Nelson Briles	.50	.25	.15
(167) Orlando Cepeda	2.50	1.25	.70
(168) Pete Rose	8.00	4.00	2.50
Sheet N.L. 6	3.00	1.50	.90
(169) Tony Cloninger	.50	.25	.15
(170) Jim Wynn	.50	.25	.15
(171) Jim Lefebvre	.50	.25	.15
(172) Ron Davis	.50	.25	.15
(173) Mike McCormick	.50	.25	.15
(174) Ron Santo	.75	.40	.25
(175) Ty Cline	.50	.25	.15
(176) Jerry Koosman	.50	.25	.15
(177) Mike Ryan	.50	.25	.15
(178) Jerry May	.50	.25	.15
(179) Tim McCarver	.75	.40	.25
(180) Phil Niekro	2.00	1.00	.60
Sheet N.L. 7	15.00	7.50	4.50
(181) Hank Aaron	5.00	2.50	1.50
(182) Tommy Helms	.50	.25	.15
(183) Denis Menke	.50	.25	.15
(184) Don Sutton	2.00	1.00	.60
(185) Al Ferrera	.50	.25	.15
(186) Willie Mays	5.00	2.50	1.50
(187) Bill Hands	.50	.25	.15
(188) Rusty Staub	.70	.35	.20
(189) Bud Harrelson	.50	.25	.15
(190) Johnny Callison	.50	.25	.15
(191) Roberto Clemente	8.00	4.00	2.50
(192) Julian Javier	.50	.25	.15
Sheet N.L. 8	2.50	1.25	.75
(193) Joe Torre	1.25	.60	.40
(194) Bob Aspromonte	.50	.25	.15
(195) Lee May	.50	.25	.15
(196) Don Wilson	.50	.25	.15
(197) Claude Osteen	.50	.25	.15
(198) Ed Spiezio	.50	.25	.15
(199) Hal Lanier	.50	.25	.15
(200) Glenn Beckert	.50	.25	.15
(201) Bob Bailey	.50	.25	.15
(202) Ron Swoboda	.50	.25	.15
(203) John Briggs	.50	.25	.15
(204) Bill Mazeroski	2.50	1.25	.70
Sheet N.L. 9	3.75	2.00	1.00
(205) Tommie Sisk	.50	.25	.15
(206) Lou Brock	2.50	1.25	.70
(207) Felix Millan	.50	.25	.15
(208) Tony Perez	2.00	1.00	.60
(209) John Edwards	.50	.25	.15
(210) Len Gabrielson	.50	.25	.15
(211) Ollie Brown	.50	.25	.15
(212) Gaylord Perry	2.00	1.00	.60
(213) Don Kessinger	.50	.25	.15
(214) John Bateman	.50	.25	.15
(215) Ed Charles	.50	.25	.15
(216) Woodie Fryman	.50	.25	.15

1969 Major League Baseball Player Pins

Black-and-white or color player portraits (noted parenthetically) are featured in the center of a red, white and blue design on these 3-1/2" diameter pins. The existing checklist, which may be incomplete, shows a mix of contemporary and retired players. The celluloid pinback buttons were sold at concession stands around the Major Leagues. Production continued at least into 1970, based on some observed player/team combinations.

	NM	EX	VG
Common Player:	20.00	12.00	6.00
(1) Hank Aaron (B/W)	60.00	30.00	18.00
(2) Tommie Agee (B/W)	20.00	10.00	6.00
(3) Mike Andrews (B/W)	20.00	10.00	6.00
(4) Mike Andrews (Color)	20.00	10.00	6.00
(5) Luis Aparicio (B/W)	25.00	12.50	7.50
(6) Ernie Banks (B/W)	60.00	30.00	18.00
(7) Ernie Banks (B/W, 2-1/2")	60.00	30.00	18.00
(8) Ernie Banks (Color)	60.00	30.00	18.00
(9) Glenn Beckert (B/W)	20.00	10.00	6.00
(10) Curt Blefary (B/W)	20.00	10.00	6.00
(11) Ken Boswell (B/W)	20.00	10.00	6.00
(12) Lou Brock (B/W)	30.00	15.00	9.00
(13) John Callison (B/W)	20.00	10.00	6.00
(14) Orlando Cepeda (B/W)	25.00	12.50	7.50
(15) Ed Charles (B/W)	20.00	10.00	6.00
(16) Horace Clarke (B/W)	20.00	10.00	6.00
(17) Roberto Clemente (B/W)	75.00	37.00	22.00
(18) Donn Clendenon (B/W)	20.00	10.00	6.00
(19) Billy Conigliaro (B/W)	20.00	10.00	6.00
(20) Tony Conigliaro (B/W)	25.00	12.50	7.50
(21) Tony Conigliaro (Color)	25.00	12.50	7.50
(22) Ray Culp (Color)	20.00	10.00	6.00
(23) Joe DiMaggio (B/W)	50.00	25.00	15.00
(24) Don Drysdale (B/W)	30.00	15.00	9.00
(25) Frank Fernandez (Color)	20.00	10.00	6.00
(26) Curt Flood (B/W)	20.00	10.00	6.00
(27) Lou Gehrig (B/W)	50.00	25.00	15.00
(28) Bob Gibson (B/W)	30.00	15.00	9.00
(29) Jerry Grote (B/W)	20.00	10.00	6.00
(30) Jim Hickman (B/W)	20.00	10.00	6.00
(31) Ken Holtzman (B/W)	20.00	10.00	6.00
(32) Frank Howard (B/W)	22.50	11.00	6.75
(33) Randy Hundley (B/W)	20.00	10.00	6.00
(34) Reggie Jackson (Color)	60.00	30.00	18.00
(35) Ferguson Jenkins (B/W)	30.00	15.00	9.00
(36) Dalton Jones (B/W)	20.00	10.00	6.00
(37) Al Kaline (B/W)	60.00	30.00	18.00
(38) Don Kessinger (B/W)	20.00	10.00	6.00
(39) Harmon Killebrew (B/W)	30.00	15.00	9.00
(40) Jerry Koosman (Color)	20.00	10.00	6.00
(41) Jim Lonborg (B/W)	20.00	10.00	6.00
(42) Mickey Mantle (B/W)	100.00	50.00	30.00
(43) Carlos May (B/W)	20.00	10.00	6.00
(44) Willie Mays (B/W)	75.00	37.00	22.00
(45) Willie McCovey (B/W)	25.00	12.50	7.50
(46) Denny McLain (B/W)	22.50	11.00	6.75
(47) Gene Michael (B/W)	20.00	10.00	6.00
(48) Gene Michael (Color)	20.00	10.00	6.00
(49) Bobby Murcer (Color)	22.50	11.00	6.75
(50) Joe Pepitone (B/W)	25.00	12.50	7.50
(51) Rico Petrocelli (B/W)	20.00	10.00	6.00
(52) Rico Petrocelli (Color)	20.00	10.00	6.00
(53) Pete Rose (B/W)	75.00	37.00	22.00
(54) Babe Ruth (B/W)	50.00	25.00	15.00
(55) Ron Santo (B/W)	22.50	11.00	6.75
(56) Ron Santo (Color)	22.50	11.00	6.75
(57) Ron Santo (B/W, 2-1/2")	60.00	30.00	18.00
(58) George Scott (B/W)	20.00	10.00	6.00
(59) Tom Seaver (B/W)	45.00	22.00	13.50
(60) Tom Seaver (Color)	45.00	22.00	13.50
(61) Reggie Smith (B/W)	20.00	10.00	6.00
(62) Reggie Smith (Color)	20.00	10.00	6.00
(63) Mel Stottlemyre (Color)	20.00	10.00	6.00
(64) Tony Taylor (B/W, 2-1/2")	20.00	10.00	6.00
(65) Joe Torre (B/W)	22.50	11.00	6.75
(66) Tom Tresh (Color)	20.00	10.00	6.00
(67) Pete Ward (B/W)	20.00	10.00	6.00
(68) Roy White (B/W)	20.00	10.00	6.00
(69) Billy Williams (B/W)	25.00	12.50	7.50
(70) Carl Yastrzemski (B/W)	60.00	30.00	18.00
(71) Carl Yastrzemski (Color)	60.00	30.00	18.00

1969 Major League Baseball Players Association Pins

Issued by the Major League Baseball Players Association in 1969, this unnumbered set consists of 60 pins - 30 players from the N.L. and 30 from the A.L. Each pin measures approximately 7/8" in diameter and features a black-and-white player photo. A.L. players are surrounded by a red border, while N.L. players are framed in blue. The player's name and team appear at the top and bottom. Also along the bottom is a line reading "1969 MLBPA MFG. R.R. Winona, MINN."

	NM	EX	VG
Complete Set (60):	250.00	125.00	75.00
Common Player:	6.00	3.00	1.75
(1) Hank Aaron	30.00	15.00	9.00
(2) Richie Allen	10.00	5.00	3.00
(3) Felipe Alou	7.50	3.75	2.25
(4) Max Alvis	6.00	3.00	1.75
(5) Luis Aparicio	12.50	6.25	3.75
(6) Ernie Banks	15.00	7.50	4.50
(7) Johnny Bench	15.00	7.50	4.50
(8) Lou Brock	15.00	7.50	4.50
(9) George Brunet	6.00	3.00	1.75
(10) Johnny Callison	6.00	3.00	1.75
(11) Rod Carew	15.00	7.50	4.50
(12) Orlando Cepeda	12.50	6.25	3.75
(13) Dean Chance	6.00	3.00	1.75
(14) Roberto Clemente	40.00	20.00	12.00
(15) Willie Davis	6.00	3.00	1.75
(16) Don Drysdale	15.00	7.50	4.50
(17) Ron Fairly	6.00	3.00	1.75
(18) Curt Flood	6.00	3.00	1.75
(19) Bill Freehan	6.00	3.00	1.75
(20) Jim Fregosi	6.00	3.00	1.75
(21) Bob Gibson	15.00	7.50	4.50
(22) Ken Harrelson	6.00	3.00	1.75
(23) Bud Harrelson	6.00	3.00	1.75
(24) Jim Ray Hart	6.00	3.00	1.75
(25) Tommy Helms	6.00	3.00	1.75
(26) Joe Horlen	6.00	3.00	1.75
(27) Tony Horton	7.50	3.75	2.25
(28) Willie Horton	6.00	3.00	1.75
(29) Frank Howard	7.50	3.75	2.25
(30) Al Kaline	15.00	7.50	4.50
(31) Don Kessinger	6.00	3.00	1.75
(32) Harmon Killebrew	15.00	7.50	4.50

(33)	Jerry Koosman	6.00	3.00	1.75
(34)	Mickey Lolich	6.00	3.00	1.75
(35)	Jim Lonborg	6.00	3.00	1.75
(36)	Jim Maloney	6.00	3.00	1.75
(37)	Juan Marichal	12.50	6.25	3.75
(38)	Willie Mays	30.00	15.00	9.00
(39)	Tim McCarver	7.50	3.75	2.25
(40)	Willie McCovey	15.00	7.50	4.50
(41)	Sam McDowell	6.00	3.00	1.75
(42)	Denny McLain	7.50	3.75	2.25
(43)	Rick Monday	6.00	3.00	1.75
(44)	Tony Oliva	7.50	3.75	2.25
(45)	Joe Pepitone	7.50	3.75	2.25
(46)	Boog Powell	7.50	3.75	2.25
(47)	Rick Reichardt	6.00	3.00	1.75
(48)	Pete Richert	6.00	3.00	1.75
(49)	Brooks Robinson	15.00	7.50	4.50
(50)	Frank Robinson	15.00	7.50	4.50
(51)	Pete Rose	25.00	12.50	7.50
(52)	Ron Santo	9.00	4.50	2.75
(53)	Mel Stottlemyre	6.00	3.00	1.75
(54)	Ron Swoboda	6.00	3.00	1.75
(55)	Luis Tiant	6.00	3.00	1.75
(56)	Joe Torre	9.00	4.50	2.75
(57)	Pete Ward	6.00	3.00	1.75
(58)	Billy Williams	12.50	6.25	3.75
(59)	Jim Wynn	6.00	3.00	1.75
(60)	Carl Yastrzemski	15.00	7.50	4.50

1983 "1969" MLBPA Pins

Virtually identical in format to the 60-pin 1969 MLBPA issue, these pins were probably not issued prior to 1983 and despite what is printed thereon, are not a licensed issue of the Players Association. The 7/8" diameter pins have a black-and-white player portrait photo on a white background at center. The photo is bordered in red or blue with the player name at top and team at bottom in white. A copyright line on back reads, "1969 MLBPA MFG IN U.S.A." Latter-day pins can be distinguished from the 1969s by the absence of mention of Winona, Minn., on the replicas.

Complete Set (36):
(1) Hank Aaron
(2) Bob Allison
(3) Yogi Berra
(4) Roy Campanella
(5) Norm Cash
(6) Orlando Cepeda
(7) Roberto Clemente
(8) Joe DiMaggio
(9) Bobby Doerr
(10) Don Drysdale
(11) Bob Feller
(12) Whitey Ford
(13) Nellie Fox
(14) Frank Howard
(15) Jim "Catfish" Hunter
(16) Al Kaline
(17) Sandy Koufax
(18) Mickey Mantle
(19) Juan Marichal
(20) Eddie Mathews
(21) Willie Mays
(22) Willie McCovey
(23) Stan Musial
(24) Tony Oliva
(25) Satchel Paige
(26) Phil Rizzuto
(27) Robin Roberts
(28) Brooks Robinson
(29) Jackie Robinson
(30) Ron Santo
(31) Duke Snider
(32) Warren Spahn
(33) Bill Skowron
(34) Billy Williams
(35) Ted Williams
(36) Maury Wills

1970 Major League Baseball Photostamps

For a second year, ballplayer "stamps" were sold in conjunction with team albums. Approximately 1-7/8" x 3", the pieces are printed on glossy paper in full color with a white border and facsimile autograph. Backs, which are not gummed, have gluing instructions and the players name at bottom. The 1970 issue can be differentiated from the 1969 issue in that they have uniform insignia present on the photos whereas the 1969 stamps do not. The unnumbered stamps are checklisted here alphabetically within team.

		NM	EX	VG
Complete Set (288):		200.00	100.00	60.00
Common Player:		1.00	.50	.30
	ATLANTA BRAVES			
(1)	Hank Aaron	15.00	7.50	4.50
(2)	Bob Aspromonte	1.00	.50	.30
(3)	Rico Carty	1.00	.50	.30
(4)	Orlando Cepeda	6.00	3.00	1.75
(5)	Bob Didier	1.00	.50	.30
(6)	Tony Gonzalez	1.00	.50	.30
(7)	Pat Jarvis	1.00	.50	.30
(8)	Felix Millan	1.00	.50	.30
(9)	Jim Nash	1.00	.50	.30
(10)	Phil Niekro	4.00	2.00	1.25
(11)	Milt Pappas	1.00	.50	.30
(12)	Ron Reed	1.00	.50	.30
	BALTIMORE ORIOLES			
(1)	Mark Belanger	1.00	.50	.30
(2)	Paul Blair	1.00	.50	.30
(3)	Don Buford	1.00	.50	.30
(4)	Mike Cuellar	1.00	.50	.30
(5)	Andy Etchebarren	1.00	.50	.30
(6)	Dave Johnson	1.00	.50	.30
(7)	Dave McNally	1.00	.50	.30
(8)	Tom Phoebus	1.00	.50	.30
(9)	Boog Powell	2.00	1.00	.60
(10)	Brooks Robinson	6.00	3.00	1.75
(11)	Frank Robinson	6.00	3.00	1.75
(12)	Chico Salmon	1.00	.50	.30
	BOSTON RED SOX			
(1)	Mike Andrews	1.00	.50	.30
(2)	Ray Culp	1.00	.50	.30
(3)	Jim Lonborg	1.00	.50	.30
(4)	Sparky Lyle	1.00	.50	.30
(5)	Gary Peters	1.00	.50	.30
(6)	Rico Petrocelli	1.00	.50	.30
(7)	Vicente Romo	1.00	.50	.30
(8)	Tom Satriano	1.00	.50	.30
(9)	George Scott	1.00	.50	.30
(10)	Sonny Seibert	1.00	.50	.30
(11)	Reggie Smith	1.00	.50	.30
(12)	Carl Yastrzemski	6.00	3.00	1.75
	CALIFORNIA ANGELS			
(1)	Sandy Alomar	1.00	.50	.30
(2)	Jose Azcue	1.00	.50	.30
(3)	Tom Egan	1.00	.50	.30
(4)	Jim Fregosi	1.00	.50	.30
(5)	Alex Johnson	1.00	.50	.30
(6)	Jay Johnstone	1.00	.50	.30
(7)	Rudy May	1.00	.50	.30
(8)	Andy Messersmith	1.00	.50	.30
(9)	Rick Reichardt	1.00	.50	.30
(10)	Roger Repoz	1.00	.50	.30
(11)	Aurelio Rodriguez	1.00	.50	.30
(12)	Ken Tatum	1.00	.50	.30
	CHICAGO CUBS			
(1)	Ernie Banks	7.50	3.75	2.25
(2)	Glenn Beckert	1.00	.50	.30
(3)	Johnny Callison	1.00	.50	.30
(4)	Bill Hands	1.00	.50	.30
(5)	Randy Hundley	1.00	.50	.30
(6)	Ken Holtzman	1.00	.50	.30
(7)	Fergie Jenkins	4.00	2.00	1.25
(8)	Don Kessinger	1.00	.50	.30
(9)	Phil Regan	1.00	.50	.30
(10)	Ron Santo	2.00	1.00	.60
(11)	Dick Selma	1.00	.50	.30
(12)	Billy Williams	5.00	2.50	1.50
	CHICAGO WHITE SOX			
(1)	Luis Aparicio	5.00	2.50	1.50
(2)	Ken Berry	1.00	.50	.30
(3)	Buddy Bradford	1.00	.50	.30
(4)	Ron Hansen	1.00	.50	.30
(5)	Joel Horlen	1.00	.50	.30
(6)	Tommy John	1.50	.70	.45
(7)	Duane Josephson	1.00	.50	.30
(8)	Bobby Knoop	1.00	.50	.30
(9)	Tom McCraw	1.00	.50	.30
(10)	Bill Melton	1.00	.50	.30
(11)	Walt Williams	1.00	.50	.30
(12)	Wilbur Wood	1.00	.50	.30
	CINCINNATI REDS			
(1)	Johnny Bench	7.50	3.75	2.25
(2)	Tony Cloninger	1.00	.50	.30
(3)	Wayne Granger	1.00	.50	.30
(4)	Tommy Helms	1.00	.50	.30
(5)	Jim Maloney	1.00	.50	.30
(6)	Lee May	1.00	.50	.30
(7)	Jim McGlothlin	1.00	.50	.30
(8)	Jim Merritt	1.00	.50	.30
(9)	Gary Nolan	1.00	.50	.30
(10)	Tony Perez	5.00	2.50	1.50
(11)	Pete Rose	12.50	6.25	3.75
(12)	Bobby Tolan	1.00	.50	.30
	CLEVELAND INDIANS			
(1)	Max Alvis	1.00	.50	.30
(2)	Larry Brown	1.00	.50	.30
(3)	Dean Chance	1.00	.50	.30
(4)	Dick Ellsworth	1.00	.50	.30
(5)	Vern Fuller	1.00	.50	.30
(6)	Ken Harrelson	1.00	.50	.30
(7)	Chuck Hinton	1.00	.50	.30
(8)	Tony Horton	1.00	.50	.30
(9)	Sam McDowell	1.00	.50	.30
(10)	Vada Pinson	1.50	.70	.45
(11)	Duke Sims	1.00	.50	.30
(12)	Ted Uhlaender	1.00	.50	.30
	DETROIT TIGERS			
(1)	Norm Cash	1.50	.70	.45
(2)	Bill Freehan	1.00	.50	.30
(3)	Willie Horton	1.00	.50	.30
(4)	Al Kaline	7.50	3.75	2.25
(5)	Mike Kilkenny	1.00	.50	.30
(6)	Mickey Lolich	1.00	.50	.30
(7)	Dick McAuliffe	1.00	.50	.30
(8)	Denny McLain	1.50	.70	.45
(9)	Jim Northrup	1.00	.50	.30
(10)	Mickey Stanley	1.00	.50	.30
(11)	Tom Tresh	1.00	.50	.30
(12)	Earl Wilson	1.00	.50	.30
	HOUSTON ASTROS			
(1)	Jesus Alou	1.00	.50	.30
(2)	Tommy Davis	1.00	.50	.30
(3)	Larry Dierker	1.00	.50	.30
(4)	Johnny Edwards	1.00	.50	.30
(5)	Fred Gladding	1.00	.50	.30
(6)	Denver Lemaster	1.00	.50	.30
(7)	Denis Menke	1.00	.50	.30
(8)	Joe Morgan	6.00	3.00	1.75
(9)	Joe Pepitone	1.50	.70	.45
(10)	Doug Rader	1.00	.50	.30
(11)	Don Wilson	1.00	.50	.30
(12)	Jim Wynn	1.00	.50	.30
	KANSAS CITY ROYALS			
(1)	Jerry Adair	1.00	.50	.30
(2)	Wally Bunker	1.00	.50	.30
(3)	Bill Butler	1.00	.50	.30
(4)	Moe Drabowsky	1.00	.50	.30
(5)	Jackie Hernandez	1.00	.50	.30
(6)	Pat Kelly	1.00	.50	.30
(7)	Ed Kirkpatrick	1.00	.50	.30
(8)	Dave Morehead	1.00	.50	.30
(9)	Roger Nelson	1.00	.50	.30
(10)	Bob Oliver	1.00	.50	.30
(11)	Lou Piniella	1.50	.70	.45
(12)	Paul Schaal	1.00	.50	.30
	LOS ANGELES DODGERS			
(1)	Willie Davis	1.00	.50	.30
(2)	Len Gabrielson	1.00	.50	.30
(3)	Tom Haller	1.00	.50	.30
(4)	Jim Lefebvre	1.00	.50	.30
(5)	Manny Mota	1.00	.50	.30
(6)	Claude Osteen	1.00	.50	.30
(7)	Wes Parker	1.00	.50	.30
(8)	Bill Russell	1.00	.50	.30
(9)	Bill Singer	1.00	.50	.30
(10)	Ted Sizemore	1.00	.50	.30
(11)	Don Sutton	4.00	2.00	1.25
(12)	Maury Wills	1.00	.50	.30
	MINNESOTA TWINS			
(1)	Bob Allison	1.00	.50	.30
(2)	Dave Boswell	1.00	.50	.30
(3)	Leo Cardenas	1.00	.50	.30
(4)	Rod Carew	6.00	3.00	1.75
(5)	Jim Kaat	1.50	.70	.45
(6)	Harmon Killebrew	6.00	3.00	1.75
(7)	Tony Oliva	1.50	.70	.45
(8)	Jim Perry	1.00	.50	.30
(9)	Ron Perranoski	1.00	.50	.30
(10)	Rich Reese	1.00	.50	.30
(11)	Luis Tiant	1.00	.50	.30
(12)	Cesar Tovar	1.00	.50	.30
	MONTREAL EXPOS			
(1)	John Bateman	1.00	.50	.30
(2)	Bob Bailey	1.00	.50	.30
(3)	Ron Brand	1.00	.50	.30
(4)	Ty Cline	1.00	.50	.30
(5)	Ron Fairly	1.00	.50	.30
(6)	Mack Jones	1.00	.50	.30
(7)	Jose Laboy	1.00	.50	.30
(8)	Claude Raymond	1.00	.50	.30
(9)	Joe Sparma	1.00	.50	.30
(10)	Rusty Staub	1.50	.70	.45
(11)	Bill Stoneman	1.00	.50	.30
(12)	Bobby Wine	1.00	.50	.30
	NEW YORK METS			
(1)	Tommie Agee	1.00	.50	.30
(2)	Donn Clendenon	1.00	.50	.30
(3)	Joe Foy	1.00	.50	.30
(4)	Jerry Grote	1.00	.50	.30
(5)	Bud Harrelson	1.00	.50	.30
(6)	Cleon Jones	1.00	.50	.30
(7)	Jerry Koosman	1.00	.50	.30
(8)	Ed Kranepool	1.00	.50	.30
(9)	Nolan Ryan	25.00	12.50	7.50
(10)	Tom Seaver	6.00	3.00	1.75
(11)	Ron Swoboda	1.00	.50	.30
(12)	Al Weis	1.00	.50	.30
	NEW YORK YANKEES			
(1)	Jack Aker	1.00	.50	.30
(2)	Curt Blefary	1.00	.50	.30
(3)	Danny Cater	1.00	.50	.30
(4)	Horace Clarke	1.00	.50	.30
(5)	Jake Gibbs	1.00	.50	.30
(6)	Steve Hamilton	1.00	.50	.30
(7)	Bobby Murcer	1.50	.70	.45
(8)	Fritz Peterson	1.00	.50	.30
(9)	Bill Robinson	1.00	.50	.30
(10)	Mel Stottlemyre	1.00	.50	.30
(11)	Pete Ward	1.00	.50	.30
(12)	Roy White	1.50	.70	.45
	OAKLAND A's			
(1)	Felipe Alou	1.50	.70	.45
(2)	Sal Bando	1.00	.50	.30

(3)	Bert Campaneris	1.00	.50	.30
(4)	Chuck Dobson	1.00	.50	.30
(5)	Tito Francona	1.00	.50	.30
(6)	Dick Green	1.00	.50	.30
(7)	Catfish Hunter	4.00	2.00	1.25
(8)	Reggie Jackson	10.00	5.00	3.00
(9)	Don Mincher	1.00	.50	.30
(10)	Rick Monday	1.00	.50	.30
(11)	John Odom	1.00	.50	.30
(12)	Ray Oyler	1.00	.50	.30
	PHILADELPHIA PHILLIES			
(1)	Johnny Briggs	1.00	.50	.30
(2)	Jim Bunning	4.00	2.00	1.25
(3)	Curt Flood	1.50	.70	.45
(4)	Woodie Fryman	1.00	.50	.30
(5)	Larry Hisle	1.00	.50	.30
(6)	Joe Hoerner	1.00	.50	.30
(7)	Grant Jackson	1.00	.50	.30
(8)	Tim McCarver	1.50	.70	.45
(9)	Mike Ryan	1.00	.50	.30
(10)	Chris Short	1.00	.50	.30
(11)	Tony Taylor	1.00	.50	.30
(12)	Rick Wise	1.00	.50	.30
	PITTSBURGH PIRATES			
(1)	Gene Alley	1.00	.50	.30
(2)	Matty Alou	1.00	.50	.30
(3)	Roberto Clemente	20.00	10.00	6.00
(4)	Ron Davis	1.00	.50	.30
(5)	Richie Hebner	1.00	.50	.30
(6)	Jerry May	1.00	.50	.30
(7)	Bill Mazeroski	6.00	3.00	1.75
(8)	Bob Moose	1.00	.50	.30
(9)	Al Oliver	1.50	.70	.45
(10)	Manny Sanguillen	1.00	.50	.30
(11)	Willie Stargell	5.00	2.50	1.50
(12)	Bob Veale	1.00	.50	.30
	SAN DIEGO PADRES			
(1)	Ollie Brown	1.00	.50	.30
(2)	Dave Campbell	1.00	.50	.30
(3)	Nate Colbert	1.00	.50	.30
(4)	Pat Dobson	1.00	.50	.30
(5)	Al Ferrera	1.00	.50	.30
(6)	Dick Kelley	1.00	.50	.30
(7)	Clay Kirby	1.00	.50	.30
(8)	Bill McCool	1.00	.50	.30
(9)	Frank Reberger	1.00	.50	.30
(10)	Tommie Sisk	1.00	.50	.30
(11)	Ed Spiezio	1.00	.50	.30
(12)	Larry Stahl	1.00	.50	.30
	SAN FRANCISCO GIANTS			
(1)	Bobby Bonds	1.50	.70	.45
(2)	Jim Davenport	1.00	.50	.30
(3)	Dick Dietz	1.00	.50	.30
(4)	Jim Ray Hart	1.00	.50	.30
(5)	Ron Hunt	1.00	.50	.30
(6)	Hal Lanier	1.00	.50	.30
(7)	Frank Linzy	1.00	.50	.30
(8)	Juan Marichal	5.00	2.50	1.50
(9)	Willie Mays	15.00	7.50	4.50
(10)	Mike McCormick	1.00	.50	.30
(11)	Willie McCovey	6.00	3.00	1.75
(12)	Gaylord Perry	4.00	2.00	1.25
	SEATTLE PILOTS			
(1)	Steve Barber	1.00	.50	.30
(2)	Bobby Bolin	1.00	.50	.30
(3)	George Brunet	1.00	.50	.30
(4)	Wayne Comer	1.00	.50	.30
(5)	John Donaldson	1.00	.50	.30
(6)	Tommy Harper	1.00	.50	.30
(7)	Mike Hegan	1.00	.50	.30
(8)	Mike Hershberger	1.00	.50	.30
(9)	Steve Hovley	1.00	.50	.30
(10)	Bob Locker	1.00	.50	.30
(11)	Gerry McNertney	1.00	.50	.30
(12)	Rich Rollins	1.00	.50	.30
	ST. LOUIS CARDINALS			
(1)	Richie Allen	2.50	1.25	.70
(2)	Nelson Briles	1.00	.50	.30
(3)	Lou Brock	6.00	3.00	1.75
(4)	Jose Cardenal	1.00	.50	.30
(5)	Steve Carlton	6.00	3.00	1.75
(6)	Vic Davalillo	1.00	.50	.30
(7)	Bob Gibson	6.00	3.00	1.75
(8)	Julian Javier	1.00	.50	.30
(9)	Dal Maxvill	1.00	.50	.30
(10)	Cookie Rojas	1.00	.50	.30
(11)	Mike Shannon	1.00	.50	.30
(12)	Joe Torre	3.00	1.50	.90
	WASHINGTON SENATORS			
(1)	Bernie Allen	1.00	.50	.30
(2)	Dick Bosman	1.00	.50	.30
(3)	Ed Brinkman	1.00	.50	.30
(4)	Paul Casanova	1.00	.50	.30
(5)	Joe Coleman	1.00	.50	.30
(6)	Mike Epstein	1.00	.50	.30
(7)	Frank Howard	1.50	.70	.45
(8)	Ken McMullen	1.00	.50	.30
(9)	John Roseboro	1.00	.50	.30
(10)	Ed Stroud	1.00	.50	.30
(11)	Del Unser	1.00	.50	.30
(12)	Zoilo Versalles	1.00	.50	.30

1910 Makaroff Cigarettes World Series Postcard

The text on this postcard indicates it may have been given out at World Series games in Philadelphia and Chicago. Two versions are known, one with Connie Mack's portrait at left and the Athletics score listed first, and one with Frank Chance's portrait at left and the Cubs score listed first. On the black-and-white address side are photographic portraits of the A's and Cubs managers with appropriate team pennants. Below is scripted, "Saw the world's championship game to-day." Beneath that are lines to record the score. The front of the card is printed in black, white and red and has a picture of a smoking cigarette and a two-headed Russian

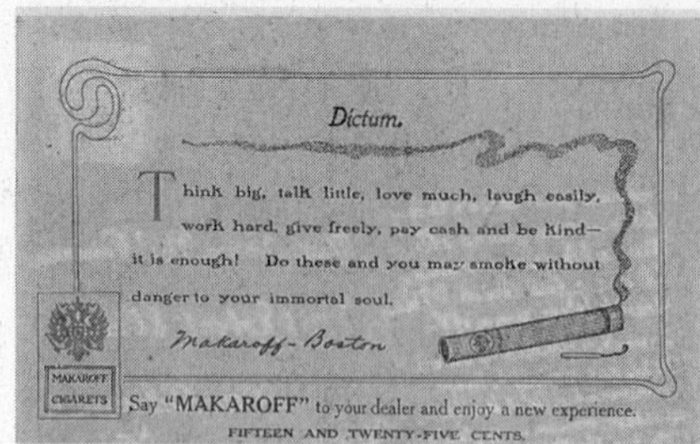

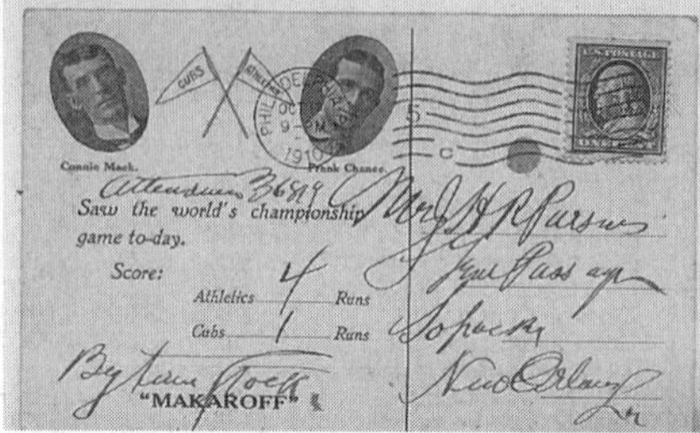

eagle logo. At center is this "Dictum. / Think big, talk little, love much, laugh easily, / work hard, give freely, pay cash and be kind - / it is enough! Do these and you may smoke without / danger to your immortal soul."

	NM	EX	VG
Frank Chance, Connie Mack	350.00	175.00	100.00
Connie Mack, Frank Chance	350.00	175.00	100.00

1916 Mall Theatre

DAVE BANCROFT
S.S.—Philadelphia Nationals
10

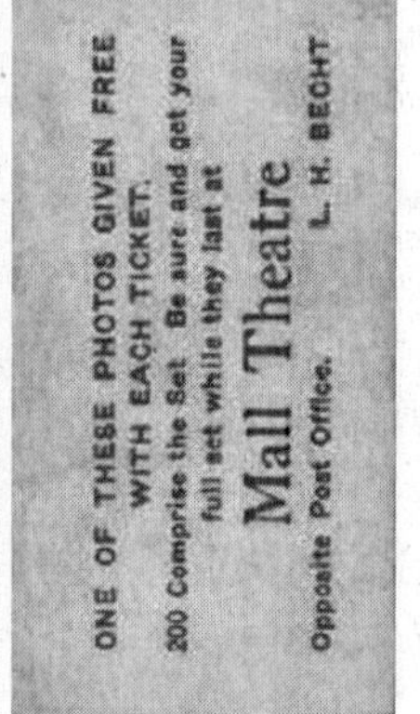

Best known for its use as a promotional medium for The Sporting News, this 200-card set can be found with ads on the back for several local and regional businesses. Among them is the Mall Theatre, location unknown. Type-card and superstar collectors can expect to pay a significant premium for individual cards with this advertising over generic 1916 M101-4 Blank Backs values. Cards measure 1-5/8" x 3" and are printed in black-and-white.

PREMIUM: 2-3X
(See 1916 M101-4 Blank Backs for checklist and base card values.)

1926-1927 Mallorquina Caramels

These tiny (about 3/4" x 1-1/8") cards were distributed with Mallorquina brand caramels in Cuba. The black-and-white images are printed on hard photographic paper stock. The bordered portrait photos on front have a box at bottom with player identification and card number. Backs are printed in dark blue with the wording "LA MALLORQUINA / CARAMELOS / PELOTEROS" and a few graphic flourishes. The set's first 17 cards feature professional players, including a number of Negro Leagues stars. The last 83 cards in the set are Cuban amateurs. While there was probably some sort of album issued to house the set, none has been reported to date. Because the card of Hall of Famer Willie Foster is his only known career-contemporary issue, and that of Martin Dihigo is his earliest known, "book" values have not been assigned.

		NM	EX	VG
Common Player:		200.00	100.00	60.00
1	Adolfo Luque	750.00	375.00	225.00
2	Alfredo Cabrera	250.00	125.00	75.00
3	George Scales	350.00	175.00	105.00
4	Jose Maria Fernandez	250.00	125.00	75.00
5	Oliver Marcelle	3,000	1,500	900.00
6	Oscar Rodriguez	200.00	100.00	60.00
7	Martin Dihigo (Value Undetermined)			
8	Cheo Ramos	250.00	125.00	75.00
9	Pop Lloyd	4,500	2,250	1,350
10	Joe Olivares	200.00	100.00	60.00
11	Brujo Rosell	200.00	100.00	60.00
12	Willie Foster (Value Undetermined)			
13	Cho Cho Correa	250.00	125.00	75.00
14	Larry Brown	350.00	175.00	105.00
15	Oscar Levis	250.00	125.00	75.00
16	Raul Alvarez	250.00	125.00	75.00
17	Juan Eckelson	250.00	125.00	75.00
18	Quesada	200.00	100.00	60.00
19	J. Rosado	200.00	100.00	60.00
20	A. Unanuo	200.00	100.00	60.00
21	A. Echavarria	200.00	100.00	60.00
22	C. Beltran	200.00	100.00	60.00
23	J. Beltran	200.00	100.00	60.00
24	G. Orama	200.00	100.00	60.00
25	E. Carrillo	200.00	100.00	60.00
26	A. Casuso	200.00	100.00	60.00
27	A. Consuegra	200.00	100.00	60.00
28	R. Gallardo	200.00	100.00	60.00
29	M. Sotolongo	200.00	100.00	60.00
30	M. Llano	200.00	100.00	60.00
31	H. Rocamora	200.00	100.00	60.00
32	Calvo	200.00	100.00	60.00
33	R. Inclan	200.00	100.00	60.00
34	Mendizabal	200.00	100.00	60.00
35	H. Alonso	200.00	100.00	60.00
36	C. Leonard	200.00	100.00	60.00
37	Cap Cordova	200.00	100.00	60.00
38	Cordova	200.00	100.00	60.00
39	Sarasua	200.00	100.00	60.00
40	E. Cubillas	200.00	100.00	60.00
41	B. Wilryc	200.00	100.00	60.00
42	Morera	200.00	100.00	60.00
43	C. Fernandez	200.00	100.00	60.00
44	Milian	200.00	100.00	60.00
45	P. Espinosa	200.00	100.00	60.00
46	Macia	200.00	100.00	60.00
47	J. Lagueruela	200.00	100.00	60.00
48	Bernal	200.00	100.00	60.00
49	J.A. Ruiz	200.00	100.00	60.00
50	Unknown			
51	J. Gayoso	200.00	100.00	60.00
52	Castro	200.00	100.00	60.00
53	C. Hernandez	200.00	100.00	60.00
54	Reynolds	200.00	100.00	60.00
55	M. Rodriguez	200.00	100.00	60.00
56	P. Flores	200.00	100.00	60.00
57	A. Collazo	200.00	100.00	60.00
58	R. Gonzalez	200.00	100.00	60.00
59	A. Casas	200.00	100.00	60.00
60	Barcena	200.00	100.00	60.00
61	Quesada	200.00	100.00	60.00
62	Riquerin	200.00	100.00	60.00
63	Carbonere	200.00	100.00	60.00
64	Vega	200.00	100.00	60.00
65	Rodriguez	200.00	100.00	60.00
66	A. Castillo	200.00	100.00	60.00
67	Y. Balleste	200.00	100.00	60.00
68	Fernandez	200.00	100.00	60.00
69	Garros	200.00	100.00	60.00
70	Cabada	200.00	100.00	60.00
71	R.P. Fernandez	200.00	100.00	60.00
72	R. Cejas	200.00	100.00	60.00
73	Gros	200.00	100.00	60.00
74	Mendez	200.00	100.00	60.00
75	M. Sotolongo	200.00	100.00	60.00
76	E. Vela	200.00	100.00	60.00
77	A. Vela	200.00	100.00	60.00
78	F. Pinera	200.00	100.00	60.00
79	M. Valdes	200.00	100.00	60.00
80	L. Romero	200.00	100.00	60.00
81	A. Febles	200.00	100.00	60.00
82	Lugo	200.00	100.00	60.00
83	Polo Calvo	200.00	100.00	60.00
84	Silvio O. Farrill	200.00	100.00	60.00
85	Zalazar	200.00	100.00	60.00
86	Tapia	200.00	100.00	60.00
87	Hernandez	200.00	100.00	60.00
88	Manrrara	200.00	100.00	60.00
89	J. Deschapelle	200.00	100.00	60.00
90	Arguelles	200.00	100.00	60.00
91	E. Arechaede	200.00	100.00	60.00
92	E. Quintanal	200.00	100.00	60.00
93	M. Valdes	200.00	100.00	60.00
94	J. Martinez	200.00	100.00	60.00
95	R. Martinez	200.00	100.00	60.00
96	F. Gali	200.00	100.00	60.00
97	A. Martinez	200.00	100.00	60.00
98	G. Hernandez	200.00	100.00	60.00
99	A. Fernandez	200.00	100.00	60.00
100	Armando Figarola	200.00	100.00	60.00

1961 Manny's Baseball Land 8x10s

In 1961, Manny's Baseball Land issued 18 10-piece 8" x 10" printed black-and-white photo packs, arranged by team. Manny's was a next-door neighbor of Yankee Stadium and the

nation's largest purveyor of baseball souvenirs. These photo sets were sold for $1.50 per team. The blank-back photos were printed on semi-gloss paper. Portraits or posed action photos were surrounded by a white border which contains the player's name in all caps at bottom. The unnumbered pictures are checklisted here alphabetically by and within team.

		NM	EX	VG
Complete Set (180):		2,500	1,250	750.00
Common Player:		10.00	5.00	3.00
	BALTIMORE ORIOLES			
(1)	Jackie Brandt	10.00	5.00	3.00
(2)	Marv Breeding	10.00	5.00	3.00
(3)	Chuck Estrada	10.00	5.00	3.00
(4)	Jack Fisher	10.00	5.00	3.00
(5)	Jim Gentile	10.00	5.00	3.00
(6)	Ron Hansen	10.00	5.00	3.00
(7)	Milt Pappas	10.00	5.00	3.00
(8)	Brooks Robinson	30.00	15.00	9.00
(9)	Gus Triandos	10.00	5.00	3.00
(10)	Jerry Walker	10.00	5.00	3.00
	BOSTON RED SOX			
(11)	Tom Brewer	10.00	5.00	3.00
(12)	Don Buddin	10.00	5.00	3.00
(13)	Gene Conley	10.00	5.00	3.00
(14)	Mike Fornieles	10.00	5.00	3.00
(15)	Gary Geiger	10.00	5.00	3.00
(16)	Pumpsie Green	10.00	5.00	3.00
(17)	Jackie Jensen	15.00	7.50	4.50
(18)	Frank Malzone	10.00	5.00	3.00
(19)	Pete Runnels	10.00	5.00	3.00
(20)	Vic Wertz	10.00	5.00	3.00
	CHICAGO CUBS			
(21)	George Altman	10.00	5.00	3.00
(22)	Bob Anderson	10.00	5.00	3.00
(23)	Richie Ashburn	30.00	15.00	9.00
(24)	Ernie Banks	35.00	17.50	10.00
(25)	Don Cardwell	10.00	5.00	3.00
(26)	Moe Drabowsky	10.00	5.00	3.00
(27)	Don Elston	10.00	5.00	3.00
(28)	Jerry Kindall	10.00	5.00	3.00
(29)	Ron Santo	15.00	7.50	4.50
(30)	Bob Will	10.00	5.00	3.00
	CHICAGO WHITE SOX			
(31)	Luis Aparicio	25.00	12.50	7.50
(32)	Frank Baumann	10.00	5.00	3.00
(33)	Sam Esposito	10.00	5.00	3.00
(34)	Nellie Fox	30.00	15.00	9.00
(35)	Jim Landis	10.00	5.00	3.00
(36)	Sherman Lollar	10.00	5.00	3.00
(37)	Minnie Minoso	20.00	10.00	6.00
(38)	Billy Pierce	10.00	5.00	3.00
(39)	Bob Shaw	10.00	5.00	3.00
(40)	Early Wynn	25.00	12.50	7.50
	CINCINNATI REDLEGS			
(41)	Ed Bailey	10.00	5.00	3.00
(42)	Gus Bell	10.00	5.00	3.00
(43)	Gordon Coleman	10.00	5.00	3.00
(44)	Bill Henry	10.00	5.00	3.00
(45)	Jerry Lynch	10.00	5.00	3.00
(46)	Claude Osteen	10.00	5.00	3.00
(47)	Vada Pinson	12.50	6.25	3.75
(48)	Wally Post	10.00	5.00	3.00
(49)	Bob Purkey	10.00	5.00	3.00
(50)	Frank Robinson	35.00	17.50	10.00
	CLEVELAND INDIANS			
(51)	Mike de la Hoz	10.00	5.00	3.00
(52)	Tito Francona	10.00	5.00	3.00
(53)	Woody Held	10.00	5.00	3.00
(54)	Barry Latman	10.00	5.00	3.00
(55)	Jim Perry	10.00	5.00	3.00
(56)	Bubba Phillips	10.00	5.00	3.00
(57)	Jim Piersall	12.50	6.25	3.75
(58)	Vic Power	10.00	5.00	3.00
(59)	John Romano	10.00	5.00	3.00
(60)	Johnny Temple	10.00	5.00	3.00
	DETROIT TIGERS			
(61)	Hank Aguirre	10.00	5.00	3.00
(62)	Billy Bruton	10.00	5.00	3.00
(63)	Jim Bunning	25.00	12.50	7.50
(64)	Norm Cash	20.00	10.00	6.00
(65)	Rocky Colavito	25.00	12.50	7.50
(66)	Chico Fernandez	10.00	5.00	3.00
(67)	Paul Foytack	10.00	5.00	3.00
(68)	Al Kaline	35.00	17.50	10.00
(69)	Frank Lary	10.00	5.00	3.00
(70)	Don Mossi	10.00	5.00	3.00
	KANSAS CITY ATHLETICS			
(71)	Hank Bauer	10.00	5.00	3.00
(72)	Andy Carey	10.00	5.00	3.00
(73)	Leo "Bud" Daley	10.00	5.00	3.00
(74)	Ray Herbert	10.00	5.00	3.00
(75)	John Kucks	10.00	5.00	3.00
(76)	Jerry Lumpe	10.00	5.00	3.00
(77)	Norm Siebern	10.00	5.00	3.00
(78)	Haywood Sullivan	10.00	5.00	3.00
(79)	Marv Throneberry	10.00	5.00	3.00
(80)	Dick Williams	10.00	5.00	3.00
	LOS ANGELES ANGELS			
(81)	Ken Aspromonte	10.00	5.00	3.00
(82)	Steve Bilko	10.00	5.00	3.00
(83)	Bob Cerv	10.00	5.00	3.00
(84)	Ned Garver	10.00	5.00	3.00
(85)	Ken Hunt	10.00	5.00	3.00
(86)	Ted Kluszewski	25.00	12.50	7.50
(87)	Jim McAnany	10.00	5.00	3.00
(88)	Duke Maas	10.00	5.00	3.00
(89)	Albie Pearson	10.00	5.00	3.00
(90)	Eddie Yost	10.00	5.00	3.00
	LOS ANGELES DODGERS			
(91)	Don Drysdale	30.00	15.00	9.00
(92)	Jim Gilliam	12.50	6.25	3.75
(93)	Frank Howard	12.50	6.25	3.75
(94)	Sandy Koufax	50.00	25.00	15.00
(95)	Norm Larker	10.00	5.00	3.00
(96)	Wally Moon	10.00	5.00	3.00
(97)	Charles Neal	10.00	5.00	3.00
(98)	Johnny Podres	12.50	6.25	3.75
(99)	Larry Sherry	10.00	5.00	3.00
(100)	Maury Wills	12.50	6.25	3.75
	MILWAUKEE BRAVES			
(101)	Hank Aaron	50.00	25.00	15.00
(102)	Joe Adcock	10.00	5.00	3.00
(103)	Frank Bolling	10.00	5.00	3.00
(104)	Bob Buhl	10.00	5.00	3.00
(105)	Lew Burdette	10.00	5.00	3.00
(106)	Del Crandall	10.00	5.00	3.00
(107)	Ed Mathews	35.00	17.50	10.00
(108)	Roy McMillan	10.00	5.00	3.00
(109)	Warren Spahn	35.00	17.50	10.00
(110)	Al Spangler	10.00	5.00	3.00
	MINNESOTA TWINS			
(111)	Bob Allison	10.00	5.00	3.00
(112)	Earl Battey	10.00	5.00	3.00
(113)	Reno Bertola (Bertoia)	10.00	5.00	3.00
(114)	Billy Consolo	10.00	5.00	3.00
(115)	Billy Gardner	10.00	5.00	3.00
(116)	Harmon Killebrew	35.00	17.50	10.00
(117)	Jim Lemon	10.00	5.00	3.00
(118)	Camilo Pascual	10.00	5.00	3.00
(119)	Pedro Ramos	10.00	5.00	3.00
(120)	Chuck Stobbs	10.00	5.00	3.00
	NEW YORK YANKEES			
(121)	Larry "Yogi" Berra	35.00	17.50	10.00
(122)	John Blanchard	10.00	5.00	3.00
(123)	Ed "Whitey" Ford	35.00	17.50	10.00
(124)	Elston Howard	15.00	7.50	4.50
(125)	Tony Kubek	15.00	7.50	4.50
(126)	Mickey Mantle	65.00	32.50	20.00
(127)	Roger Maris	40.00	20.00	12.00
(128)	Bobby Richardson	15.00	7.50	4.50
(129)	Bill Skowron	15.00	7.50	4.50
(130)	Bob Turley	10.00	5.00	3.00
	PHILADELPHIA PHILLIES			
(131)	John Callison	10.00	5.00	3.00
(132)	Dick Farrell	10.00	5.00	3.00
(133)	Pancho Herrera	10.00	5.00	3.00
(134)	Joe Koppe	10.00	5.00	3.00
(135)	Art Mahaffey	10.00	5.00	3.00
(136)	Gene Mauch	10.00	5.00	3.00
(137)	Jim Owens	10.00	5.00	3.00
(138)	Robin Roberts	30.00	15.00	9.00
(139)	Frank Sullivan	10.00	5.00	3.00
(140)	Tony Taylor	10.00	5.00	3.00
	PITTSBURGH PIRATES			
(141)	Roberto Clemente	60.00	30.00	18.00
(142)	Roy Face	10.00	5.00	3.00
(143)	Bob Friend	10.00	5.00	3.00
(144)	Dick Groat	10.00	5.00	3.00
(145)	Harvey Haddix	10.00	5.00	3.00
(146)	Don Hoak	10.00	5.00	3.00
(147)	Vern Law	10.00	5.00	3.00
(148)	Bill Mazeroski	30.00	15.00	9.00
(149)	Wilmer Mizell	10.00	5.00	3.00
(150)	Bill Virdon	10.00	5.00	3.00
	SAN FRANCISCO GIANTS			
(151)	Felipe Alou	12.50	6.25	3.75
(152)	Orlando Cepeda	30.00	15.00	9.00
(153)	Sam Jones	10.00	5.00	3.00
(154)	Harvey Kuenn	10.00	5.00	3.00
(155)	Willie Mays	50.00	25.00	15.00
(156)	Mike McCormick	10.00	5.00	3.00
(157)	Willie McCovey	30.00	15.00	9.00
(158)	Stu Miller	10.00	5.00	3.00
(159)	Billy O'Dell	10.00	5.00	3.00
(160)	Jack Sanford	10.00	5.00	3.00
	ST. LOUIS CARDINALS			
(161)	Ernie Broglio	10.00	5.00	3.00
(162)	Ken Boyer	12.50	6.25	3.75
(163)	Joe Cunningham	10.00	5.00	3.00
(164)	Alex Grammas	10.00	5.00	3.00
(165)	Larry Jackson	10.00	5.00	3.00
(166)	Julian Javier	10.00	5.00	3.00
(167)	Lindy McDaniel	10.00	5.00	3.00
(168)	Stan Musial	45.00	22.50	13.50
(169)	Hal Smith	10.00	5.00	3.00
(170)	Daryl Spencer	10.00	5.00	3.00
	WASHINGTON SENATORS			
(171)	Pete Daley	10.00	5.00	3.00
(172)	Dick Donovan	10.00	5.00	3.00
(173)	Bob Johnson	10.00	5.00	3.00
(174)	Marty Keough	10.00	5.00	3.00
(175)	Billy Klaus	10.00	5.00	3.00
(176)	Dale Long	10.00	5.00	3.00
(177)	Carl Mathias	10.00	5.00	3.00
(178)	Willie Tasby	10.00	5.00	3.00
(179)	Mickey Vernon	10.00	5.00	3.00
(180)	Gene Woodling	10.00	5.00	3.00

1959 Mickey Mantle's Holiday Inn Postcard

The attributed date is speculative. Much rarer than the more common pose of Mantle in civvies in his Joplin, Mo. motel's lounge, this approximately 3-1/2" x 5-1/2" card features two color poses of the Mick in Yankees uniform on its front. The postcard-style back is printed in blue and gives motel information and features.

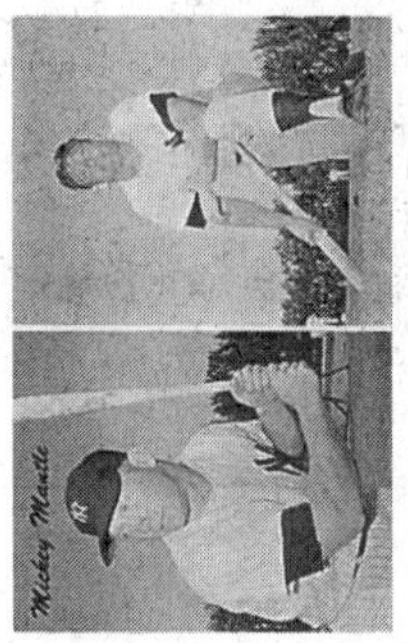

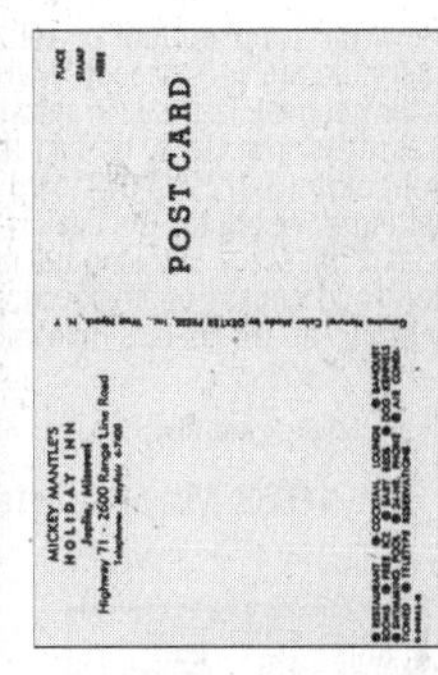

	NM	EX	VG
Mickey Mantle	100.00	50.00	30.00

1962 Mickey Mantle's Holiday Inn Postcard

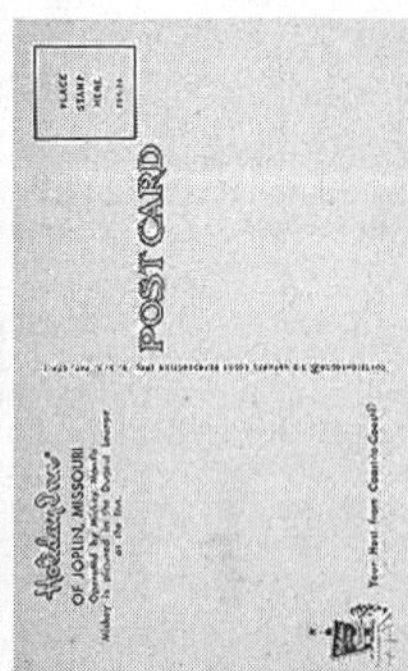

This color postcard pictures Mantle in civilian clothes. On the back of the standard-size (about 3-1/2" x 5-1/2") card it says the Mick is "pictured in the Dugout Lounge at the Inn." The "Inn" is the Joplin, Mo., Holiday Inn which Mantle owned. This was one of the more popular, and thus more common, of the souvenirs issued in conjunction with Mantle's motel.

	NM	EX	VG
Mickey Mantle	30.00	15.00	9.00

1962 Mickey Mantle's Holiday Inn Premium Photo

Probably issued in 1962, though not dated, this 8" x 10" photo pictures the M&M Boys in the lounge of Mantle's motel. Back is blank.

	NM	EX	VG
Mickey Mantle, Roger Maris	600.00	300.00	180.00

1963 Mickey Mantle Hospital Postcard

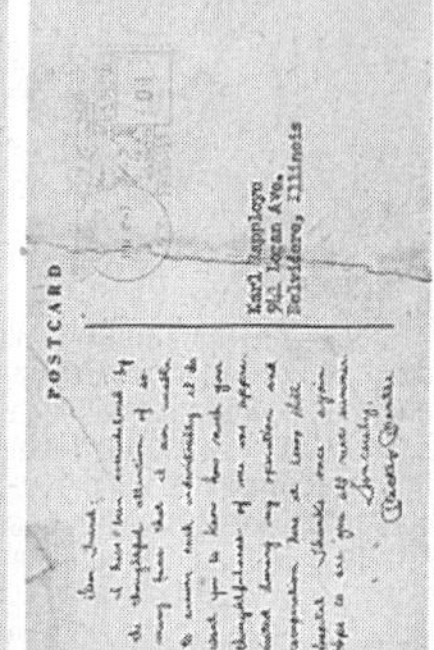

With a broken foot in 1963 following hard on a knee injury the previous season, Mantle spent considerable time in the hospital. To assist in answering a mountain of goodwill messages from fans, he had these postcards created. On front of the 3-1/2" x 5-1/2" card is a glossy black-and-white batting-pose photo. The back is printed in blue with a "Dear Friend" message thanking the fan for "the thoughtful attention" and ending optimistically, "Hope to see you all next season," above his facsimile autograph.

	NM	EX	VG
Mickey Mantle	450.00	225.00	135.00

1923 Maple Crispette (V117)

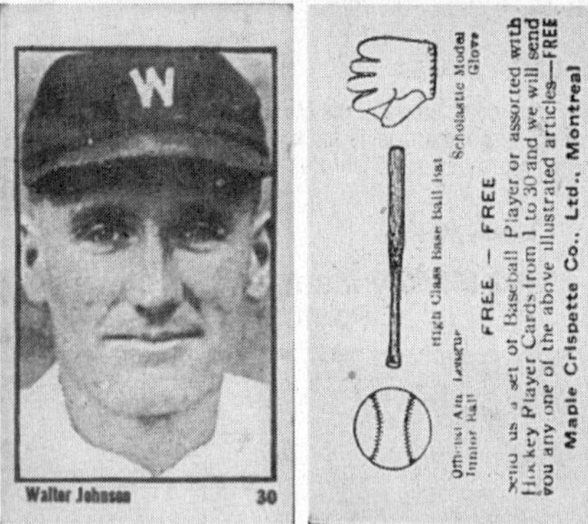

Issued by a Montreal candy company, these small (1-3/8" x 2-1/4") black-and-white cards were redeemable for baseball equipment, accounting for their scarcity today. Card #15, Stengel, was only discovered in 1992 and was obviously short-printed by the issuer to avoid giving away many bats, balls and gloves. Only a single specimen of the Stengel card is currently known; it is not included in the complete set prices.

		NM	EX	VG
Complete Set, no Stengel (29):		27,000	10,800	6,720
Common Player:		420.00	170.00	110.00
1	Jesse Barnes	420.00	170.00	110.00
2	Harold Traynor	720.00	290.00	180.00
3	Ray Schalk	720.00	290.00	180.00
4	Eddie Collins	720.00	290.00	180.00
5	Lee Fohl	420.00	170.00	110.00
6	Howard Summa	420.00	170.00	110.00
7	Waite Hoyt	720.00	290.00	180.00
8	Babe Ruth	8,700	3,600	1,920
9	Cozy Dolan	420.00	170.00	110.00
10	Johnny Bassler	420.00	170.00	110.00
11	George Dauss	420.00	170.00	110.00
12	Joe Sewell	720.00	290.00	180.00
13	Syl Johnson	420.00	170.00	110.00
14a	Wingo	420.00	170.00	110.00
14b	Ivy Wingo	420.00	170.00	110.00
15	Casey Stengel	18,000	9,000	4,500
16	Arnold Statz	420.00	170.00	110.00
17	Emil Meusel	420.00	170.00	110.00
18	Bill Jacobson	420.00	170.00	11.00
19	Jim Bottomley	2,000	290.00	180.00
20	Sam Bohne	540.00	215.00	130.00
21	Bucky Harris	720.00	290.00	180.00
22	Ty Cobb	3,000	1,200	750.00
23	Roger Peckinpaugh	420.00	170.00	110.00
24	Muddy Ruel	420.00	170.00	110.00
25	Bill McKechnie	720.00	290.00	180.00
26	Riggs Stephenson	420.00	170.00	110.00
27	Herb Pennock	720.00	290.00	180.00
28	Edd Roush	720.00	290.00	180.00
29	Bill Wambsganss	420.00	170.00	110.00
30	Walter Johnson	2,400	960.00	600.00

1962 Roger Maris Action Baseball Game

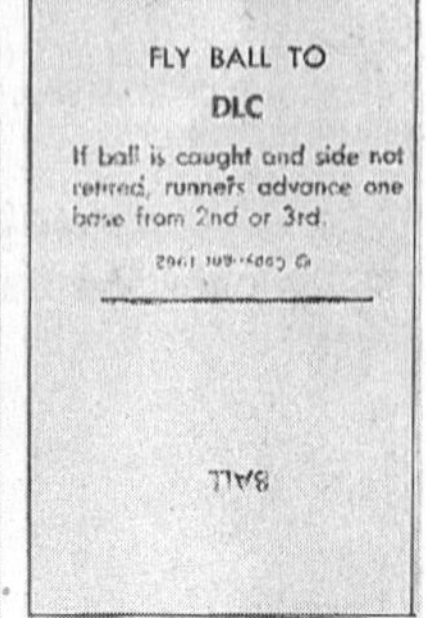

Baseball's new home run king was featured in this board game by Pressman Toy Co. Besides the colorful metal game board and other pieces, the set contains 88 playing cards. Each 2-1/4" x 3-1/2" card has a black-and-white photo on front of Maris in a batting pose, along with a white facsimile autograph. Backs have two possible game action plays printed, along with a copyright line.

	NM	EX	VG
Complete Game:	150.00	75.00	45.00
Single Card: Roger Maris	15.00	7.50	4.50

1913-14 Martens Bakery

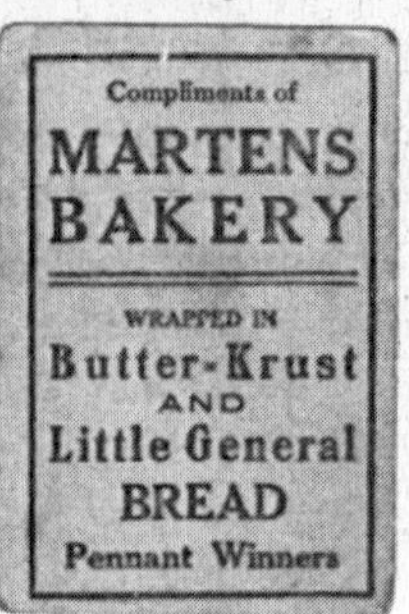

(See 1911-14 General Baking Co. (D304).)

1955 Mascot Dog Food

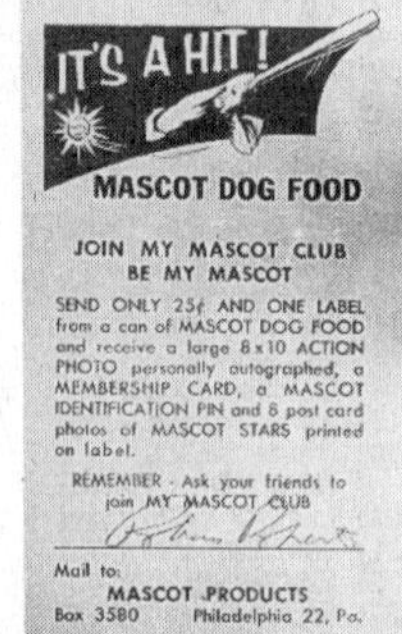

The date of issue shown is approximate. It is likely other players' cards exist, since the back mentions eight stars printed on the label, presumably of the dog food can. In black-and-white, the 3-1/2" x 5-1/2" card has on front a glossy action pose with a facsimile autograph personalized, "To My Mascot" and the player name and position printed in black in the bottom border. The back has an ad for a fan club offering an autographed 8" x 10" membership card and and set of eight postcards for a quarter and a label. label.

		NM	EX	VG
(1)	Robin Roberts	450.00	225.00	135.00

1971 Mattel Instant Replay Records

These 2-3/8" diameter plastic records were produced in conjunction with a hand-held, battery-operated record player. Paper inserts featured illustrations of players in baseball, football and basketball, as well as various racing vehicles and airplanes. The audio recounts career highlights of the depicted player. Additional records were sold in sets of four.

		NM	EX	VG
Complete Set (12):		250.00	125.00	75.00
Common Player:		10.00	5.00	3.00
(1)	Hank Aaron	30.00	15.00	9.00
(2)	Ernie Banks	15.00	7.50	4.50
(3)	Roberto Clemente	50.00	25.00	15.00
(4)	Al Kaline	15.00	7.50	4.50
(5)	Sandy Koufax	40.00	20.00	12.00
(6)	Roger Maris	15.00	7.50	4.50
(7)	Willie Mays (Plays one side only; came with record player purchase.)	12.00	6.00	3.50
(8)	Willie McCovey	12.00	6.00	3.50
(9)	Tony Oliva	10.00	5.00	3.00
(10)	Frank Robinson	13.50	6.75	4.00
(11)	Tom Seaver	15.00	7.50	4.50
(12)	Willie Stargell	12.00	6.00	3.50

1895 Mayo's Cut Plug (N300)

These 1-5/8" x 2-7/8" cards were issued by the Mayo Tobacco Works of Richmond, Va. There are 48 cards in the set, with 40 different players pictured. Twenty-eight of the players are pictured in uniform and 12 are shown in street clothes. Eight players appear both ways. Eight of the uniformed players also appear in two variations, creating the 48-card total. Card

fronts are black-and-white or sepia portraits on black cardboard, with a Mayo's Cut Plug ad at the bottom of each card. Cards have a blank black back and are unnumbered.

		NM	EX	VG
Complete Set (48):		264,000	132,000	80,000
Common Player:		2,400	950.00	500.00
(1)	Charlie Abbey	2,400	950.00	500.00
(2)	Cap Anson	21,000	8,450	4,225
(3)	Jimmy Bannon	2,400	950.00	500.00
(4a)	Dan Brouthers (Baltimore on shirt.)	11,900	4,750	2,375
(4b)	Dan Brouthers (Louisville on shirt.)	13,200	5,300	2,650
(5)	Ed Cartwright	2,400	950.00	500.00
(6)	John Clarkson	7,900	3,150	1,600
(7)	Tommy Corcoran	2,400	950.00	500.00
(8)	Lave Cross	2,400	950.00	500.00
(9)	Bill Dahlen	3,000	1,200	600.00
(10)	Tom Daly	2,400	950.00	500.00
(11)	E.J. Delehanty (Delahanty)	15,800	6,325	3,150
(12)	Hugh Duffy	7,900	3,200	1,600
(13a)	Buck Ewing (Cleveland on shirt.)	13,200	5,300	2,650
(13b)	Buck Ewing (Cincinnati on shirt.)	10,000	4,000	2,000
(14)	Dave Foutz	2,400	950.00	500.00
(15)	Charlie Ganzel	2,400	950.00	500.00
(16a)	Jack Glasscock (Pittsburg on shirt.)	3,000	1,200	600.00
(16b)	Jack Glasscock (Louisville on shirt.)	2,400	950.00	500.00
(17)	Mike Griffin	2,400	950.00	500.00
(18a)	George Haddock (No team on shirt.)	3,300	1,300	650.00
(18b)	George Haddock (Philadelphia on shirt.)	2,400	950.00	500.00
(19)	Bill Hallman	2,400	950.00	500.00
(20)	Billy Hamilton	7,900	3,200	1,600
(21)	Bill Joyce	2,400	950.00	500.00
(22)	Brickyard Kennedy	2,400	950.00	500.00
(23a)	Tom Kinslow (No team on shirt.)	3,300	1,300	650.00
(23b)	Tom Kinslow (Pittsburg on shirt.)	2,400	950.00	500.00
(24)	Arlie Latham	2,400	950.00	500.00
(25)	Herman Long	2,400	950.00	500.00
(26)	Tom Lovett	2,400	950.00	500.00
(27)	Bobby Lowe	2,400	950.00	500.00
(28)	Tommy McCarthy	7,900	3,200	1,600
(29)	Yale Murphy	2,400	950.00	500.00
(30)	Billy Nash	2,400	950.00	500.00
(31)	Kid Nichols	13,200	5,300	2,650
(32a)	Fred Pfeffer (2nd Base)	2,400	950.00	500.00
(32b)	Fred Pfeffer (Retired)	2,400	950.00	500.00
(33)	Wilbert Robinson	7,900	3,200	1,600
(34a)	Amos Russie (Incorrect spelling.)	16,500	6,600	3,300
(34b)	Amos Rusie (Correct)	11,900	4,750	2,375
(35)	Jimmy Ryan	2,400	950.00	500.00
(36)	Bill Shindle	2,400	950.00	500.00
(37)	Germany Smith	2,400	950.00	500.00
(38)	Otis Stocksdale (Stockdale)	2,400	950.00	500.00
(39)	Tommy Tucker	2,400	950.00	500.00
(40a)	Monte Ward (2nd Base)	11,900	4,750	2,370
(40b)	Monte Ward (Retired)	10,000	4,000	2,000

1896 Mayo's Die-Cut Game Cards (N301)

Mayo Tobacco Works of Richmond, Va., issued an innovative, if not very popular, series of die-cut baseball player figures in 1896. These tiny (1-1/2" long by just 3/16" wide) cardboard figures were inserted in packages of Mayo's Cut Plug Tobacco and were designed to be used as part of a baseball board game. A "grandstand, base and teetotum" were available free by mail to complete the game pieces. Twenty-eight different die-cut figures were available, representing 26 unspecified New York and Boston players along with two umpires. The players are shown in various action poses - either running, batting, pitching or fielding. The backs carry an ad for Mayo's Tobacco. The players shown do not relate to any actual members of the New York or Boston clubs, diminishing the popularity of this issue, which has an American Card Catalog designation of N301.

		NM	EX	VG
Complete Set (28):		4,000	1,600	800.00
Common Player:		150.00	60.00	30.00
(1a)	Pitcher (Boston)	150.00	60.00	30.00
(1b)	Pitcher (New York)	150.00	60.00	30.00
(2a)	1st Baseman (Boston)	150.00	60.00	30.00
(2b)	1st Baseman (New York)	150.00	60.00	30.00
(3a)	2nd Baseman (Boston)	150.00	60.00	30.00
(3b)	2nd Baseman (New York)	150.00	60.00	30.00
(4a)	3rd Baseman (Boston)	150.00	60.00	30.00
(4b)	3rd Baseman (New York)	150.00	60.00	30.00
(5a)	Right Fielder (Boston)	150.00	60.00	30.00
(5b)	Right Fielder (New York)	150.00	60.00	30.00
(6a)	Center Fielder (Boston)	150.00	60.00	30.00
(6b)	Center Fielder (New York)	150.00	60.00	30.00
(7a)	Left Fielder (Boston)	150.00	60.00	30.00
(7b)	Left Fielder (New York)	150.00	60.00	30.00
(8a)	Short Stop (Boston)	150.00	60.00	30.00
(8b)	Short Stop (New York)	150.00	60.00	30.00
(9a)	Catcher (Boston)	150.00	60.00	30.00
(9b)	Catcher (New York)	150.00	60.00	30.00
(10a)	Batman (Boston)	150.00	60.00	30.00
(10b)	Batman (New York)	150.00	60.00	30.00
(11a)	Runner (Boston, standing upright.)	150.00	60.00	30.00
(11b)	Runner (New York, standing upright.)	150.00	60.00	30.00
(12a)	Runner (Boston, bent slightly forward)	150.00	60.00	30.00
(12b)	Runner (New York, bent slightly forward)	150.00	60.00	30.00
(13a)	Runner (Boston, bent well forward.)	150.00	60.00	30.00
(13b)	Runner (New York, bent well forward.)	150.00	60.00	30.00
(14)	Umpire (Facing front.)	150.00	60.00	30.00
(15)	Field Umpire (Rear view.)	150.00	60.00	30.00

1900 Mayo's Baseball Comics (T203)

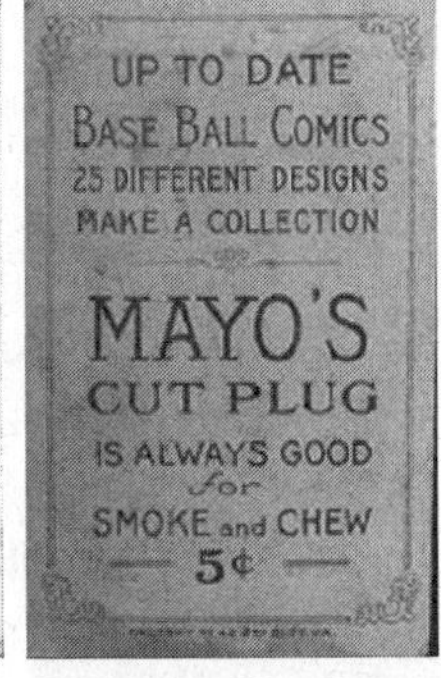

As their name implies, the T203 Baseball Comics feature cartoon-like drawings that illustrate various baseball phrases and terminology. Issued with Winner Cut Plug and Mayo Cut Plug tobacco products, the complete set consists of 25 different comics, each measuring approximately 2-1/16" x 3-1/8". Because they do not picture individual players, these cards have never attracted much of a following among serious baseball card collectors. They do, however, hold some interest as a novelty item of the period.

		NM	EX	VG
Complete Set (25):		3,000	1,500	650.00
Common Card:		150.00	75.00	30.00
(1)	"A Crack Outfielder"	150.00	75.00	30.00
(2)	"A Fancy Twirler"	150.00	75.00	30.00
(3)	"A Fine Slide"	150.00	75.00	30.00
(4)	"A Fowl Bawl"	150.00	75.00	30.00
(5)	"A Great Game"	150.00	75.00	30.00
(6)	"A Home Run"	150.00	75.00	30.00
(7)	"An All Star Battery"	150.00	75.00	30.00
(8)	"A Short Stop"	150.00	75.00	30.00
(9)	"A Star Catcher"	150.00	75.00	30.00
(10)	"A White Wash"	150.00	75.00	30.00
(11)	"A Tie Game"	150.00	75.00	30.00
(12)	"A Two Bagger"	150.00	75.00	30.00
(13)	"A Wild Pitch"	150.00	75.00	30.00
(14)	"Caught Napping"	150.00	75.00	30.00
(15)	"On To The Curves"	150.00	75.00	30.00
(16)	"Out"	150.00	75.00	30.00
(17)	"Put Out On 1st"	150.00	75.00	30.00
(18)	"Right Over The Plate"	150.00	75.00	30.00
(19)	"Rooting For The Home Team"	150.00	75.00	30.00
(20)	"Stealing A Base"	150.00	75.00	30.00
(21)	"Stealing Home"	150.00	75.00	30.00
(22)	"Strike One"	150.00	75.00	30.00
(23)	"The Bleacher"	150.00	75.00	30.00
(24)	"The Naps"	150.00	75.00	30.00
(25)	"The Red Sox"	150.00	75.00	30.00

1948 Thom McAn Bob Feller Premium

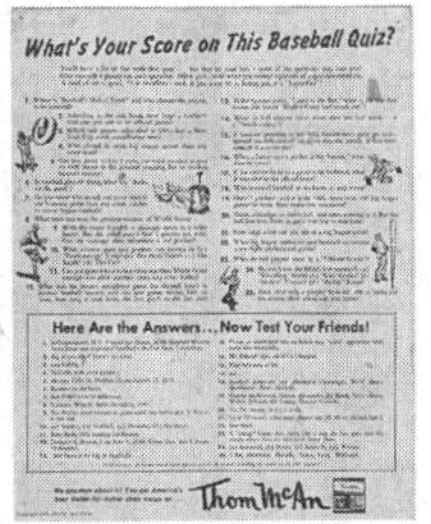

This black-and-white 8" x 10" premium picture has on front a posed action photo and facsimile autograph. On back is a 25-question baseball quiz and advertising for the shoe store chain, along with a copyright for Melville Shoe Co.

	NM	EX	VG
Bob Feller	150.00	75.00	45.00

1950s-80s J.D. McCarthy Player Postcards

From the 1950s into the 1980s, Detroit area photographer J.D. McCarthy produced black-and-white postcards to order for hundreds of ballplayers to use in answering fan mail requests for pictures and autographs. Sizes and formats differed through the years, but most are about standard postcard size (3-1/2" x 5-1/2") with borderless poses on front. Some cards have a white strip with printed name on front, others have a facsimile autograph, while others have no identification at all. Some card fronts carry his stylized JcMD monogram. Backs, likewise, differ in the style and manner of their markings. Printing was generally done on thin, semigloss cardboard. Many players are found in more than one pose, or in cropping variations of a pose. Many players continued to re-order postcards long after their careers were over. Following McCarthy's death, archives of his negatives were sold into the hobby, making it theoretically possible for many cards to be reproduced in perpetuity. That mitigates against many of these cards attaining any great degree of collectible value, though they are popular with team and single-player collectors. Postally-used cards which carry a dated postmark are of the greatest value. Many cards, as the one pictured here, are autographed.

	NM	EX	VG
Common Player:	3.00	1.50	.90

1970 McDonald's Brewers

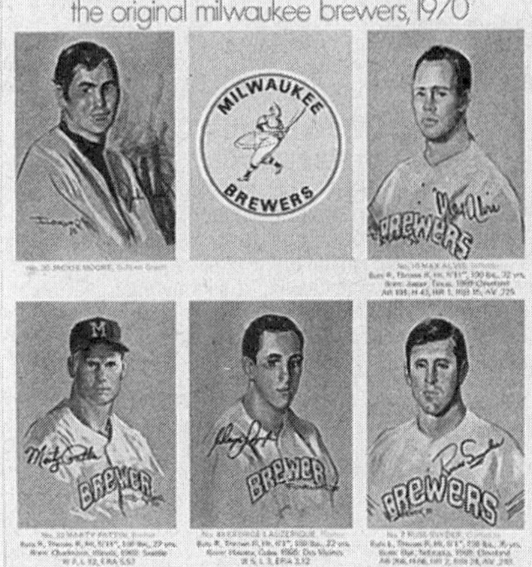

McDonald's welcomed the American League Brewers to Milwaukee in 1970 by issuing a set of six baseball card panels. Five of the panels picture five players and a team logo, while the sixth panel contains six players, resulting in 31 different players. The panels measure 9" x 9-1/2" and feature full-color paintings of the players. Each sheet displays the heading, "the original milwaukee brewers, 1970." The cards are numbered by uniform number and the backs are blank. Although distributed by McDonald's, their name does not appear on the cards.

		NM	EX	VG
Complete Sheet Set (6):		15.00	7.50	4.50
Complete Singles Set (32):		15.00	7.50	4.50
Common Player:		.50	.25	.15
1	Ted Kubiak	.50	.25	.15
2	Ted Savage	.50	.25	.15
4	Dave Bristol	.50	.25	.15
5	Phil Roof	.50	.25	.15
6	Mike Hershberger	.50	.25	.15
7	Russ Snyder	.50	.25	.15
8	Mike Hegan	.50	.25	.15
9	Rich Rollins	.50	.25	.15
10	Max Alvis	.50	.25	.15
11	John Kennedy	.50	.25	.15
12	Dan Walton	.50	.25	.15
15	Jerry McNertney	.50	.25	.15
18	Wes Stock	.50	.25	.15
20	Wayne Comer	.50	.25	.15
21	Tommy Harper	.50	.25	.15
23	Bob Locker	.50	.25	.15
24	Lew Krausse	.50	.25	.15
25	John Gelnar	.50	.25	.15
26	Roy McMillan	.50	.25	.15
27	Cal Ermer	.50	.25	.15
28	Sandy Valdespino	.50	.25	.15
30	Jackie Moore	.50	.25	.15
32	Gene Brabender	.50	.25	.15
33	Marty Pattin	.50	.25	.15
34	Greg Goossen	.50	.25	.15
35	John Morris	.50	.25	.15
36	Steve Hovley	.50	.25	.15
38	Bob Meyer	.50	.25	.15
39	Bob Bolin	.50	.25	.15
43	John O'Donoghue	.50	.25	.15
49	George Lauzerique	.50	.25	.15
---	Logo Card	.50	.25	.15

1974 McDonald's Gene Michael

Though there is no advertising or logo on this one-card "set," this black-and-white card of "The Stick" in his last year as a Yankee was distributed by a Staten Island McDonald's restaurant during an autograph appearance. The card measures 2-5/8" x 4-3/8" and is blank-backed.

	NM	EX	VG
Gene "The Stick" Michael	25.00	12.50	7.50

1974 McDonald's Padres Discs

Envisioned as part of a line of sports promotional sets, this concept died following the test with San Diego area McDonalds. At the July 30, 1974, game, Padres fans were given a hinged plastic baseball containing five Padres player photo discs plus a disc with the team's schedule and a Ronald

McDonald disc which listed the dates on which the remaining eight player cards would be distributed at area McDonalds. Only 60,000 of the "starter set" discs were made, while 180,000 of each of the other player discs were printed. The 2-3/8" diameter discs feature a color photo on front and player stats on back. The promotion was the work of Photo Sports, Inc., of Los Angeles.

		NM	EX	VG
Complete Set (15):		25.00	12.50	7.50
Common Player:		1.00	.50	.30
(1)	Matty Alou	1.00	.50	.30
(2)	Glenn Beckert	3.00	1.50	.90
(3)	Nate Colbert	1.00	.50	.30
(4)	Bill Grief	1.00	.50	.30
(5)	John Grubb	1.00	.50	.30
(6)	Enzo Hernandez	3.00	1.50	.90
(7)	Randy Jones	3.00	1.50	.90
(8)	Fred Kendall	3.00	1.50	.90
(9)	Willie McCovey	6.00	3.00	1.75
(10)	John McNamara	3.00	1.50	.90
(11)	Dave Roberts	1.00	.50	.30
(12)	Bobby Tolan	1.00	.50	.30
(13)	Dave Winfield	15.00	7.50	4.50
(14)	Padres home game schedule	1.50	.70	.45
(15)	Ronald McDonald	1.50	.70	.45

1978 McDonald's Boston Red Sox

Reportedly because of a production problem, distribution of these cards was limited to a few Boston-area McDonald's restaurants for a very limited time. The blank-back, approximately 3-1/2" x 6" color cards have borderless portraits on front with the player's facsimile autograph. The cards were reportedly distributed in Treasure Chest meals for kids under 12.

		NM	EX	VG
Complete Set (6):		450.00	225.00	135.00
Common Player:		35.00	17.50	10.00
(1)	Rick Burleson	35.00	17.50	10.00
(2)	Carlton Fisk	125.00	60.00	35.00
(3)	Fred Lynn	75.00	37.50	22.50
(4)	Jim Rice	100.00	50.00	30.00
(5)	Luis Tiant	50.00	25.00	15.00
(6)	Carl Yastrzemski	150.00	75.00	45.00

1950-1952 Bill McGowan's School for Umpires

Over a period of at least three years in the early 1950s, Hall of Fame American League umpire Bill McGowan issued a series of black-and-white postcards to promote his umpires' school in Florida. The 3-1/2" x 5-1/2" cards have bordered or borderless photos on front, some of which bear the imprint of Grogan Photo, Danville, Ill.

		NM	EX	VG
(1)	Bill McGowan's Umpire School Cocoa - 1950 - Florida (Students on bleachers.)	60.00	30.00	20.00
(2)	Bill McGowman's Umpire School - 1950 - Florida (Students standing on field.)	60.00	30.00	20.00
(3)	Bill McGowan/1951	500.00	250.00	150.00
(4)	Donatelli Instructs/1952 (Augie Donatelli)	65.00	32.50	20.00
(5)	Guglielmo Instructs/1952 (Augie Guglielmo)	65.00	32.50	20.00

1970s-80s Doug McWilliams Postcards

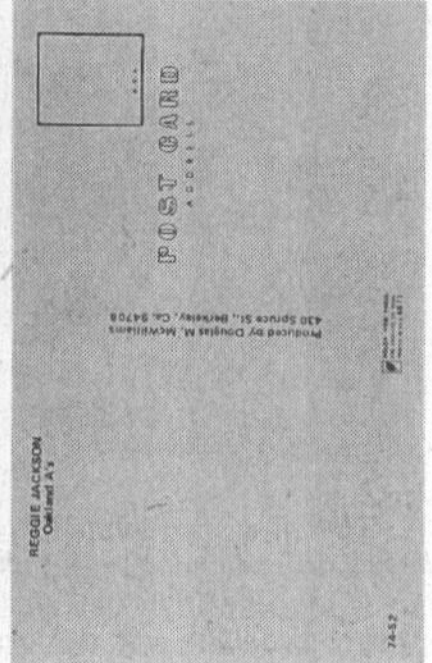

For more than two decades, California photographer Doug McWilliams (who also worked for Topps for 23 years) produced a series of black-and-white and color postcards for individual use by ballplayers, mostly members of the Oakland A's. Almost uniformly, the 3-1/2" x 5-1/2" cards have no graphics on front (a few have facsimile autographs), just a player pose or portrait. Backs have standard postcard markings, player identification, and McWilliams' credit lines. Backs carry a two-digit year of issue prefix to the card number. Postcards are printed in black-and-white unless noted.

	NM	EX	VG
Common Player:	3.00	1.50	.90
(See individual years for checklists and values.)			

1970 Doug McWilliams Postcards

		NM	EX	VG
1	Jim Roland	1.00	.50	.30
2a	Mudcat Grant, Mudcat Grant	1.50	.75	.45
2b	Mudcat Grant	1.50	.75	.45
3	Reggie Jackson (Color - only 50 produced.)	150.00	75.00	45.00
4	Darrell Osteen	1.00	.50	.30
5a	Tom Hafey (First printing.)	1.00	.50	.30
5b	Tom Hafey (Second printing.)	1.00	.50	.30
6	Chick Hafey	1.50	.75	.45

1970 Doug McWilliams Collectors' Issue Postcards

This set of black-and-white player postcards was produced by San Fransisco art photographer Doug McWilliams as a custom order for an Eastern collector. Fewer than 50 sets were reportedly produced. The 3-1/2" x 5-1/2" cards have glossy photographic fronts and standard postcard backs with player identification. The unnumbered cards are checklisted here in alphabetical order.

		NM	EX	VG
Complete Set (22):		400.00	200.00	125.00
Common Player:		20.00	10.00	6.00
(1)	Jerry Adair	20.00	10.00	6.00
(2)	Brant Alyea	20.00	10.00	6.00
(3)	Brant Alyea	20.00	10.00	6.00
(4)	Dwain Anderson	20.00	10.00	6.00
(5)	Curt Blefary	20.00	10.00	6.00
(6)	Bill Daniels	20.00	10.00	6.00
(7)	Mike Epstein	22.50	11.00	6.75
(8)	Adrian Garrett	20.00	10.00	6.00
(9)	Frank Fernandez	20.00	10.00	6.00
(10)	Mike Hegan	20.00	10.00	6.00
(11)	George Hendrick	20.00	10.00	6.00
(12)	Reggie Jackson	125.00	62.00	37.00
(13)	Reggie Jackson	125.00	62.00	37.00
(14)	Ron Klimkowski	20.00	10.00	6.00
(15)	Darold Knowles	20.00	10.00	6.00
(16)	Jerry Lumpe	20.00	10.00	6.00
(17)	Angel Mangual	20.00	10.00	6.00
(18)	Denny McLain	30.00	15.00	9.00
(19)	Denny McLain	30.00	15.00	9.00
(20)	Irv Noren	20.00	10.00	6.00
(21)	Ramon Webster	20.00	10.00	6.00
(22)	Dick Williams	20.00	10.00	6.00

1970 Doug McWilliams Oakland A's Postcards

These 3-1/2" x 5-1/2" black-and-white player postcards were produced by San Francisco photographer Doug McWilliams for sale by Sports Cards for Collectors, a forerunner of TCMA. Each card can be found either with or without borders on front, the latter having a slightly enlarged image. Player identification is on back. The unnumbered cards are checklisted here alphabetically. Fewer than 50 sets were reported produced.

		NM	EX	VG
Complete Set (42):		400.00	200.00	125.00
Common Player:		15.00	7.50	4.50
(1)	Felipe Alou	20.00	10.00	6.00
(2)	Sal Bando	20.00	10.00	6.00
(3)	Vida Blue	25.00	12.50	7.50
(4)	Bobby Brooks	15.00	7.50	4.50
(5)	Bert Campaneris	25.00	12.50	7.50
(6)	"Babe" Dahlgren	15.00	7.50	4.50
(7)	Tommy Davis	17.50	8.75	5.25
(8)	Chuck Dobson	15.00	7.50	4.50
(9)	John Donaldson	15.00	7.50	4.50
(10)	Al Downing	15.00	7.50	4.50
(11)	Jim Driscoll	15.00	7.50	4.50
(12)	Dave Duncan	15.00	7.50	4.50
(13)	Frank Fernandez	15.00	7.50	4.50
(14)	Rollie Fingers	45.00	22.00	13.50
(15)	Tito Francona	15.00	7.50	4.50
(16)	Jim Grant	20.00	10.00	6.00
(17)	Dick Green	15.00	7.50	4.50
(18)	Larry Haney	15.00	7.50	4.50
(19)	Bobby Hofman	15.00	7.50	4.50
(20)	Steve Hovley	15.00	7.50	4.50
(21)	Jim Hunter	45.00	22.00	13.50
(22)	Reggie Jackson	125.00	62.00	37.00
(23)	Dave Johnson	15.00	7.50	4.50
(24)	Marcel Lacheman	15.00	7.50	4.50
(25)	Tony LaRussa	40.00	20.00	12.00
(26)	Paul Lindblad	15.00	7.50	4.50
(27)	Bob Locker	15.00	7.50	4.50
(28)	John McNamara	15.00	7.50	4.50
(29)	Don Mincher	15.00	7.50	4.50
(30)	Rick Monday	15.00	7.50	4.50
(31)	"Blue Moon" Odom	17.50	8.75	5.25
(32)	Darrell Osteen	15.00	7.50	4.50
(33)	Ray Oyler	15.00	7.50	4.50
(34)	Roberto Pena	15.00	7.50	4.50
(35)	Bill Posedel	15.00	7.50	4.50
(36)	Roberto Rodriguez	15.00	7.50	4.50
(37)	Jim Roland	15.00	7.50	4.50
(38)	Joe Rudi	20.00	10.00	6.00
(39)	Diego Segui	15.00	7.50	4.50
(40)	Jose Tartabull	15.00	7.50	4.50
(41)	Gene Tenace	15.00	7.50	4.50
(42)	Dooley Womack	15.00	7.50	4.50

1971 Doug McWilliams Postcards

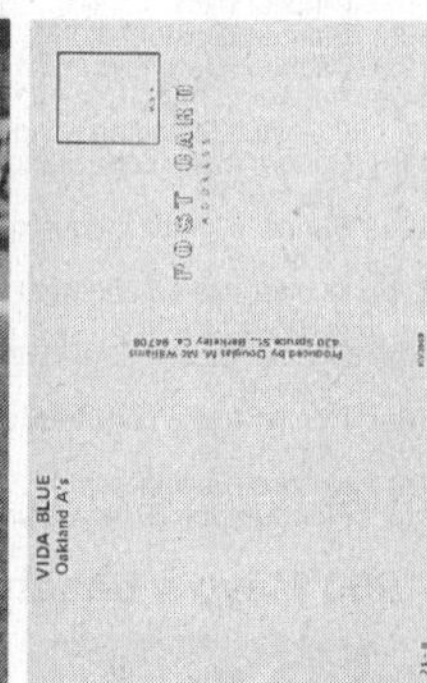

		NM	EX	VG
7	Larry Brown	3.00	1.50	.90
8a	Vida Blue/Color (First printing - KV3321.)	6.00	3.00	1.75
8b	Vida Blue/Color (Second printing - KV3509.)	6.00	3.00	1.75
8c	Vida Blue/Color (Third printing - KV4403.)	6.00	3.00	1.75
9	Dave Duncan	3.00	1.50	.90
10	George Hendrick/Color	9.00	4.50	2.75
11	Mudcat Grant	3.00	1.50	.90
12	Mudcat Grant	3.00	1.50	.90

1972 Doug McWilliams Postcards

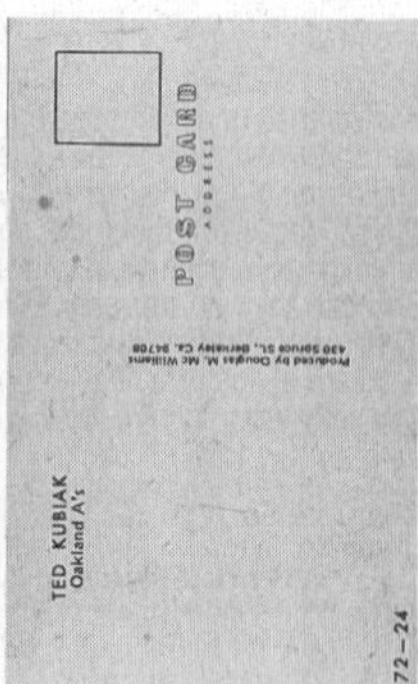

		NM	EX	VG
13	John Odom (Color)	6.00	3.00	1.75
14	Reggie Jackson (Color)	20.00	10.00	6.00
15	Sal Bando (Color)	6.00	3.00	1.75
16	Dan Cater	3.00	1.50	.90
17	Bob Locker	3.00	1.50	.90
18a	Joe Rudi (Equal edges to player.)	3.00	1.50	.90
18b	Joe Rudi (Bat close at bottom.)	3.00	1.50	.90
18c	Joe Rudi (Hand close to edge.)	3.00	1.50	.90
19	Larry Brown	3.00	1.50	.90
20a	Dick Green (First printing - glossy.)	3.00	1.50	.90
20b	Dick Green (Second printing - glossy, more contrast.)	3.00	1.50	.90

		NM	EX	VG
20c	Dick Green/Matte (Third printing.)	3.00	1.50	.90
21	Vida Blue/Color	6.00	3.00	1.75
22a	Joe Horlen/Bright (First printing.)	3.00	1.50	.90
22b	Joe Horlen/Dark (Second printing.)	3.00	1.50	.90
23	Gene Tenace/Color	6.00	3.00	1.75
24a	Ted Kubiak/Glossy	3.00	1.50	.90
24b	Ted Kubiak/Matte	3.00	1.50	.90
A	Emeryville Ball Park	3.00	1.50	.90
B	Oakland Coliseum	3.00	1.50	.90

1973 Doug McWilliams Postcards

		NM	EX	VG
25	Rene Lachemann	3.00	1.50	.90
26	Tom Greive	3.00	1.50	.90
27	John Odom/Color	6.00	3.00	1.75
28a	Rollie Fingers (First printing.)	9.00	4.50	2.75
28b	Rollie Fingers (Second printing - thinner stock.)	9.00	4.50	2.75
29	Jim Hunter/Color	9.00	4.50	2.75
30	Ray Fosse/Color	6.00	3.00	1.75
31	Charley Pride/Color	15.00	7.50	4.50
32	Charley Pride/Color	15.00	7.50	4.50
33	Bill North	3.00	1.50	.90
34	Damasco Blanco	3.00	1.50	.90
35	Paul Lindblad	3.00	1.50	.90
36	Rollie Fingers/Color	9.00	4.50	2.75
37	Horacio Pina	3.00	1.50	.90
38	Bert Campaneris/Color	7.50	3.75	2.25
39	Jim Holt/Color	6.00	3.00	1.75
40	Sal Bando/Color	6.00	3.00	1.75
41	Joe Rudi/Color	6.00	3.00	1.75
42	Dick Williams/Color	6.00	3.00	1.75
43	Jesus Alou	3.00	1.50	.90
44	Joe Niekro	3.75	2.00	1.25
45	Johnny Oates	3.00	1.50	.90

1974 Doug McWilliams Postcards

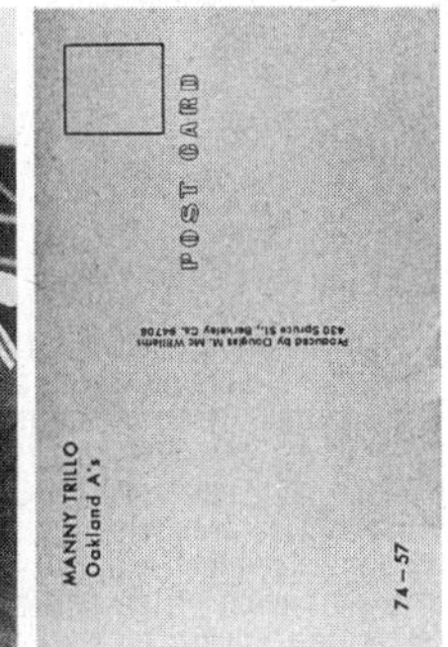

		NM	EX	VG
46a	Ray Fosse/Color (First printing - w/signature.)	6.00	3.00	1.75
46b	Ray Fosse/Color (Second printing - no signature.)	6.00	3.00	1.75
46c	Ray Fosse/Color (Third printing - no sig., very green grass.)	6.00	3.00	1.75
47	Jesus Alou	3.00	1.50	.90
48	John Summers	3.00	1.50	.90
49	Dal Maxvill	3.00	1.50	.90
50	Joe Rudi/Color	6.00	3.00	1.75
51	Sal Bando/Color	6.00	3.00	1.75
52	Reggie Jackson/Color	20.00	10.00	6.00
53	Ted Kubiak/Color	6.00	3.00	1.75
54	Dave Hamilton	3.00	1.50	.90
55	Gene Tenace/Color	6.00	3.00	1.75
56a	Bob Locker (First printing - back foot near edge.)	3.00	1.50	.90
56b	Bob Locker (Second printing - foot 3/4" from edge.)	3.00	1.50	.90
57	Manny Trillo	3.00	1.50	.90

1975 Doug McWilliams Postcards

		NM	EX	VG
58a	Dan Godby (First printing.)	3.00	1.50	.90
58b	Dan Godby (Second printing - blank back.)	3.00	1.50	.90
58c	Dan Godby (Third printing - flat contrast.)	3.00	1.50	.90
59	Bob Locker	3.00	1.50	.90
60	Rollie Fingers/Color	9.00	4.50	2.75
61	Glenn Abbott	3.00	1.50	.90
62	Jim Todd	3.00	1.50	.90
63	Phil Garner	3.00	1.50	.90
64	Paul Lindblad	3.00	1.50	.90
65	Bill North/Color	6.00	3.00	1.75
66	Dick Sisler	3.00	1.50	.90
67	Angel Mangual	3.00	1.50	.90
68	Claudell Washington	3.00	1.50	.90

1976 Doug McWilliams Postcards

		NM	EX	VG
69	Oakland Coliseum/Color	6.00	3.00	1.75
70	Sal Bando/Color	6.00	3.00	1.75
71	Mike Torrez/Color	6.00	3.00	1.75
72	Joe Lonnett	3.00	1.50	.90
73	Chuck Tanner	3.00	1.50	.90
74	Tommy Sandt	3.00	1.50	.90
75	Dick Bosman/Color	6.00	3.00	1.75
76	Bert Campaneris/Color	6.00	3.00	1.75
77	Ken Brett	6.00	3.00	1.75
78	Jim Todd/Color	6.00	3.00	1.75
79	Jeff Newman	3.00	1.50	.90
80	John McCall	3.00	1.50	.90

1977 Doug McWilliams Postcards

		NM	EX	VG
81	Don Baylor/Color	9.00	4.50	2.75
82	Lee Stange	3.00	1.50	.90
83	Rob Picciolo	3.00	1.50	.90
84	Jack Mc Keon/Color	6.00	3.00	1.75
85	Rollie Fingers/Color	9.00	4.50	2.75
86	Manny Sanguillen	3.00	1.50	.90
87	Tony Armas	3.00	1.50	.90
88	Jim Tyrone	3.00	1.50	.90
89	Wayne Gross	3.00	1.50	.90
90	Rick Langford	3.00	1.50	.90
91	Rich Gossage	3.00	1.50	.90
92	Phil Garner/Color	6.00	3.00	1.75
93	Del Alston	3.00	1.50	.90
94	Bert Blyleven/Color	7.50	3.75	2.25
95	Willie McCovey/Color	9.00	4.50	2.75
96	Ken Brett/Color	6.00	3.00	1.75
97	Doyle Alexander/Color	6.00	3.00	1.75

1978 Doug McWilliams Postcards

		NM	EX	VG
98	Rene Lacheman	3.00	1.50	.90
99	Del Alston	3.00	1.50	.90
100	Lee Stange/Color	6.00	3.00	1.75
101	Taylor Duncan	3.00	1.50	.90
102	Matt Keough	3.00	1.50	.90
103	Bruce Robinson	3.00	1.50	.90
104	Sal Bando/Color	6.00	3.00	1.75

1979 Doug McWilliams Postcards

		NM	EX	VG
105	Alan Wirth	3.00	1.50	.90
106	Mike Edwards	3.00	1.50	.90
107	Craig Minetto	3.00	1.50	.90
108	Mike Morgan	3.00	1.50	.90
109	Brian Kingman	3.00	1.50	.90

1980 Doug McWilliams Postcards

		NM	EX	VG
110	Jim Essian	3.00	1.50	.90
111a	Willie McCovey/Color (First printing - no signature.)	9.00	4.50	2.75
111b	Willie McCovey/Color (Second printing - w/signature, stamp at top.)	9.00	4.50	2.75
111c	Willie McCovey/Color (Third printing - w/sig., stamp at bottom.)	9.00	4.50	2.75
112a	Willie McCovey/Color (First printing - no signature.)	9.00	4.50	2.75
112b	Willie McCovey/Color (Second printing - w/signature.)	9.00	4.50	2.75

1964 Meadowgold Dairy

Four of the mid-60s' biggest stars appear as a panel on this milk carton issue. The four-player portion measures about 3-3/4" x 4-1/4" and is printed in shades of blue on the white background. Individual cards measure about 1-1/8" x 2-1/16" and are, of course, blank-backed. In 1998, a complete milk carton was sold at auction for $2,475.

		NM	EX	VG
	Complete Set, Panel:	600.00	300.00	180.00
	Complete Set, Singles (4):	475.00	250.00	150.00
	Common Player:	60.00	30.00	18.00
(1)	Sandy Koufax	85.00	42.00	25.00
(2)	Mickey Mantle	260.00	130.00	78.00
(3)	Willie Mays	80.00	40.00	24.00
(4)	Bill Mazeroski	60.00	30.00	18.00

1911 Mecca Cigarettes

(See 1911 T201 Double Folders.)

1937 Joe "Ducky" Medwick

Little is known about these cards featuring the perennial All-Star of the Gashouse Gang. Both styles are in a round-cornered playing card format, about 2-1/4" x 3-1/2". Fronts have black-and-white artwork of Medwick swinging a bat against a large baseball. The background is black-and-orange with a facsimile autograph at bottom. Most cards are found with some sort of card-game baseball scenario on back, while another type has a black-and-white photo of Medwick signing autographs amid a gaggle of children. His name and the date appear at bottom. It is not known whether the two types of cards were distributed together.

	NM	EX	VG
Joe "Ducky" Medwick (Game card.)	45.00	22.50	13.50
Joe "Ducky" Medwick (Photo back.)	90.00	45.00	25.00

1910 Mello-Mint (E105)

Issued circa 1910 by Smith's Mello-Mint, "The Texas Gum," this set of 50 cards shares the same checklist and artwork as the better known E101 set. Mello-Mint cards are slightly smaller, measuring approximately 1-3/8" x 2-5/8", and are printed on thin paper, making them difficult to find in top condition. Also contributing to condition problems is the fact that many cards were folded vertically to fit the packaging. The backs contain advertising, printed in green, for Mello-Mint Gum. The set carries an ACC designation of E105. Two finds of multiple examples of about eight cards in the 1980s can mislead collectors into thinking the rest of the cards in the set are more common than is actually the case. The cards most heavily over-represented in those finds are indicated with an asterisk.

		NM	EX	VG
	Complete Set (50):	195,000	75,000	35,000
	Common Player:	1,400	550.00	275.00
(1)	Jack Barry	3,200	1,300	650.00
(2)	Harry Bemis	3,200	1,300	650.00
(3)	Chief Bender (White hat.)	6,400	2,600	1,300
(4)	Chief Bender (Striped hat.)	6,400	2,600	1,300
(5)	Bill Bergen	3,200	1,300	650.00
(6)	Bob Bescher (*)	1,400	550.00	275.00
(7)	Al Bridwell	3,200	1,300	650.00
(8)	Doc Casey (*)	1,400	550.00	275.00
(9)	Frank Chance	7,200	2,900	1,450
(10)	Hal Chase	4,600	1,850	925.00
(11)	Ty Cobb	11,000	7,500	5,500
(12)	Eddie Collins	7,200	2,900	1,450
(13)	Sam Crawford	7,200	2,900	1,450
(14)	Harry Davis	3,200	1,300	650.00
(15)	Art Devlin	3,200	1,300	650.00
(16)	Wild Bill Donovan	3,200	1,300	650.00
(17)	Red Dooin	3,200	1,300	650.00
(18)	Mickey Doolan	3,200	1,300	650.00
(19)	Patsy Dougherty	3,200	1,300	650.00
(20)	Larry Doyle (With bat.)	3,200	1,300	650.00
(21)	Larry Doyle/Throwing	3,200	1,300	650.00
(22)	Johnny Evers	7,200	2,900	1,450
(23)	George Gibson	3,200	1,300	650.00
(24)	Topsy Hartsel (*)	1,400	550.00	275.00
(25)	Fred Jacklitsch	3,200	1,300	650.00
(26)	Hugh Jennings	7,200	2,900	1,450
(27)	Red Kleinow	3,200	1,300	650.00
(28)	Otto Knabe	3,200	1,300	650.00
(29)	Jack Knight (*)	1,400	550.00	275.00
(30)	Nap Lajoie (*)	5,100	2,000	1,000
(31)	Hans Lobert	3,200	1,300	650.00
(32)	Sherry Magee	3,200	1,300	650.00
(33)	Christy Matthewson (Mathewson)	11,000	4,500	2,250
(34)	John McGraw	7,200	2,900	1,450
(35)	Larry McLean	3,200	1,300	650.00
(36)	Dots Miller/Btg	3,200	1,300	650.00
(37)	Dots Miller/Fldg	3,200	1,300	650.00
(38)	Danny Murphy (*)	1,400	550.00	275.00
(39)	Bill O'Hara	3,200	1,300	650.00
(40)	Germany Schaefer	3,200	1,300	650.00
(41)	Admiral Schlei	3,200	1,300	650.00
(42)	Boss Schmidt	3,200	1,300	650.00

(43)	Johnny Seigle	3,200	1,300	650.00
(44)	Dave Shean (*)	1,400	550.00	275.00
(45)	Boss Smith (Schmidt)	3,200	1,300	650.00
(46)	Joe Tinker	7,200	2,900	1,450
(47)	Honus Wagner/Btg	10,500	4,200	2,100
(48)	Honus Wagner/Throwing	11,000	7,500	5,500
(49)	Cy Young (*)	9,600	3,900	1,900
(50)	Heinie Zimmerman	3,200	1,300	650.00

1916 Felix Mendelsohn

This Chicago printing and publishing firm was the originator of the card set often found bearing the advertising of The Sporting News on back, or less frequently with ads from other concerns. Mendelsohn is not mentioned on the cards, which are blank-backed. Fronts of the 1-5/8" x 3" black-and-white cards have a player photo, name, position abbreviation, team and card number. The first version of the set, designated M101-5 in the ACC, was prepared in advance of the 1916 season and offered in ads in The Sporting News for $1, or a framed uncut sheet for $2.50. An updated version, designated M101-4 in the American Card Catalog, was released later in the summer.

(See 1916 M101-4 and M101-5 Blank Backs and 1917 M-UNC.)

1917 Felix Mendelsohn (M101-UNC)

These 2-1/4" x 4" blank-back, black-and-white cards may have been prototypes for a "Hall of Fame" card set advertised early in 1917 by Felix Mendelsohn in The Sporting News. A set of 200 was offered for $1, but may not have actually been produced. Each example of this set is believed to be unique.

(1) Walter Johnson (Value Undetermined)
(2) Christy Mathewson (Value Undetermined)
(3) Ray Schalk (Brought $1,464 in 4/05 auction, in Excellent condition.)

1917-1920 Felix Mendelsohn

This set of glossy black-and-white player photos was produced by Chicago publisher Felix Mendelsohn, whose initials appear beneath the copyright logo. The photos measure about 4-3/8" x 6-3/8" and feature action poses of the player whose name, position and team appear at the bottom of the borderless pictures. Four of the players in the checklist appear with two different teams, indicating the photos were issued over a period of several seasons. The set was offered in ads in The Sporting News at $5 for 100 pictures. This checklist may not be complete. Gaps have been left in the assigned numbering to accommodate future additions.

		NM	EX	VG
Complete Set (119):		40,000	20,000	12,000
Common Player:		125.00	60.00	35.00
(1)	Grover C. Alexander (Philadelphia)	600.00	300.00	180.00
(2)	Grover C. Alexander (Chicago)	600.00	300.00	180.00
(3)	Jim Bagby	125.00	60.00	35.00
(4)	Doug Baird	125.00	60.00	35.00
(5)	Franklin Baker	300.00	150.00	90.00
(6)	Dave Bancroft	300.00	150.00	90.00
(7)	Jack Barry	125.00	60.00	35.00
(8)	Johnny Bates	125.00	60.00	35.00
(9)	Carson Bigbee	125.00	60.00	35.00
(10)	"Ping" Bodie	125.00	60.00	35.00
(11)	George Burns	125.00	60.00	35.00
(12)	Joe Bush	125.00	60.00	35.00
(13)	Owen Bush	125.00	60.00	35.00
(14)	Ray Caldwell	125.00	60.00	35.00
(15)	Max Carey	300.00	150.00	90.00
(16)	Ray Chapman	150.00	75.00	45.00
(17)	Hal Chase	250.00	125.00	75.00
(18)	Eddie Cicotte	300.00	150.00	90.00
(19)	Ty Cobb	3,500	1,750	1,050
(20)	Eddie Collins	300.00	150.00	90.00
(21)	Harry Coveleskie (Coveleskie)	125.00	60.00	35.00
(22)	"Gavvy" Cravath	125.00	60.00	35.00
(23)	Sam Crawford	300.00	150.00	90.00
(24)	Walton Cruise	125.00	60.00	35.00
(26)	George Cutshaw	125.00	60.00	35.00
(27)	Jake Daubert	125.00	60.00	35.00
(28)	George Dauss	125.00	60.00	35.00
(29)	Dave Davenport	125.00	60.00	35.00
(30)	Bill Doak	125.00	60.00	35.00
(31)	Larry Doyle	125.00	60.00	35.00
(32)	George Dumont	125.00	60.00	35.00
(33)	Howard Ehmke	125.00	60.00	35.00
(34)	Urban Faber	300.00	150.00	90.00
(35)	Happy Felsch	600.00	300.00	180.00
(36)	Art Fletcher	125.00	60.00	35.00
(37)	Del Gainer (Gainor)	125.00	60.00	35.00
(38)	Chick Gandil	300.00	150.00	90.00
(39)	Larry Gardner	125.00	60.00	35.00
(40)	Mike Gonzales (Gonzalez)	125.00	60.00	35.00
(41)	Jack Graney	125.00	60.00	35.00
(42)	Heinie Groh	125.00	60.00	35.00
(43)	Earl Hamilton	125.00	60.00	35.00
(44)	Harry Heilmann	300.00	150.00	90.00
(45)	Buck Herzog	125.00	60.00	35.00
(46)	Hugh High (New York, photo actually Bob Shawkey.)	125.00	60.00	35.00
(47)	Hugh High (Detroit, correct photo.)	125.00	60.00	35.00
(48)	Bill Hinchman	125.00	60.00	35.00
(49)	Dick Hoblitzell	125.00	60.00	35.00
(51)	Walter Holke (New York)	125.00	60.00	35.00
(52)	Walter Holke (Boston)	125.00	60.00	35.00
(53)	Harry Hooper	300.00	150.00	90.00
(54)	Rogers Hornsby	400.00	200.00	120.00
(55)	Joe Jackson	5,000	2,500	1,500
(56)	Bill Jacobson	125.00	60.00	35.00
(57)	Walter Johnson	900.00	450.00	270.00
(58)	Sam Jones	125.00	60.00	35.00
(59)	Joe Judge	125.00	60.00	35.00
(60)	Benny Kauff	125.00	60.00	35.00
(61)	Bill Killefer	125.00	60.00	35.00
(62)	Ed Konetchy (Boston)	125.00	60.00	35.00
(63)	Ed Konetchy (Brooklyn)	125.00	60.00	35.00
(64)	Nemo Leibold	125.00	60.00	35.00
(65)	Duffy Lewis	125.00	60.00	35.00
(66)	Fred Luderas (Luderus)	125.00	60.00	35.00
(67)	Fred Luderus	125.00	60.00	35.00
(68)	Al Mamaux	125.00	60.00	35.00
(69)	Les Mann	125.00	60.00	35.00
(70)	"Rabbit" Maranville	300.00	150.00	90.00
(71)	Armando Marsans	125.00	60.00	35.00
(72)	John McGraw	300.00	150.00	90.00
(73)	Stuffy McInnis	125.00	60.00	35.00
(74)	Lee Meadows	125.00	60.00	35.00
(76)	Fred Merkle	125.00	60.00	35.00
(77)	Clyde Milan	125.00	60.00	35.00
(78)	Otto Miller	125.00	60.00	35.00
(79)	Guy Morton	125.00	60.00	35.00
(80)	Hy Myers	125.00	60.00	35.00
(81)	Greasy Neale	150.00	75.00	45.00
(82)	Dode Paskert	125.00	60.00	35.00
(83)	Roger Peckinpaugh	125.00	60.00	35.00
(84)	Jeff Pfeffer	125.00	60.00	35.00
(85)	Walter Pipp	125.00	60.00	35.00
(86)	Bill Rariden	125.00	60.00	35.00
(87)	Johnny Rawlings	125.00	60.00	35.00
(88)	Sam Rice	300.00	150.00	90.00
(89)	Dave Robertson	125.00	60.00	35.00
(90)	Bob Roth	125.00	60.00	35.00
(91)	Ed Roush	300.00	150.00	90.00
(92)	Dick Rudolph	125.00	60.00	35.00
(93)	Babe Ruth (Red Sox)	4,500	2,250	1,350
(94)	Babe Ruth (New York)	5,000	2,500	1,500
(95)	Vic Saier	125.00	60.00	35.00
(96)	Ray Schalk	300.00	150.00	90.00
(97)	Hank Severeid	125.00	60.00	35.00
(98)	Ernie Shore	125.00	60.00	35.00
(99)	Burt Shotton	125.00	60.00	35.00
(101)	George Sisler	300.00	150.00	90.00
(102)	Jack Smith	125.00	60.00	35.00
(103)	Frank Snyder	125.00	60.00	35.00
(104)	Tris Speaker	400.00	200.00	120.00
(105)	Oscar Stanage	125.00	60.00	35.00
(106)	Casey Stengel	300.00	150.00	90.00
(107)	Amos Strunk	125.00	60.00	35.00
(108)	Jeff Tesreau	125.00	60.00	35.00
(109)	Fred Toney	125.00	60.00	35.00
(110)	Terry Turner	125.00	60.00	35.00
(111)	Jim Vaughn	125.00	60.00	35.00
(112)	Bobby Veach	125.00	60.00	35.00
(113)	Oscar Vitt	125.00	60.00	35.00
(114)	"Honus" Wagner	3,000	1,500	900.00
(115)	Tilly Walker	125.00	60.00	35.00
(116)	Bill Wambsganss	125.00	60.00	35.00
(117)	"Buck" Weaver	600.00	300.00	180.00
(118)	Zack Wheat	300.00	150.00	90.00
(119)	George Whitted	125.00	60.00	35.00
(120)	Cy Williams	125.00	60.00	35.00
(121)	Ivy Wingo	125.00	60.00	35.00
(122)	Pep ("Pep" Young)	125.00	60.00	35.00
(123)	Heinie Zimmerman	125.00	60.00	35.00

1975 Clarence Mengler Baseball's Best

This collectors' issue art set holds the distinction of being one of the first whose distribution was halted by the Major League Baseball Players Association for lack of a license to depict current players. Produced as an autograph medium by Illinois collector Clarence Mengler, the 5" x 3" blank-back cards have portraits drawn by Keith Peterson. Of the original production of 200 sets, fewer than half were sold before the union intervened with threatened legal action. Because of a spelling error, the Ralph Garr card was withdrawn early. Hal McRae's card, also misspelled, was not withdrawn. Originally sold in five series, the unnumbered cards are checklisted alphabetically within series.

		NM	EX	VG
Complete Set (125):		150.00	75.00	45.00
Common Player:		1.00	.50	.30
	SERIES A			
(1)	Sal Bando	1.00	.50	.30
(2)	Johnny Bench	4.00	2.00	1.25
(3)	Jack Billingham	1.00	.50	.30
(4)	Paul Blair	1.00	.50	.30
(5)	Bert Blyleven	1.50	.70	.45
(6)	Lou Brock	2.50	1.25	.70
(7)	Jeff Burroughs	1.00	.50	.30
(8)	Nate Colbert	1.00	.50	.30
(9)	Carlton Fisk	2.50	1.25	.70
(10)	Bob Gibson	2.50	1.25	.70
(11)	Ferguson Jenkins	2.00	1.00	.60
(12)	Bob Johnson	1.00	.50	.30
(13)	Dave McNally	1.00	.50	.30
(14)	Bobby Murcer	1.50	.70	.45
(15)	Tony Muser	1.00	.50	.30
(16)	Phil Niekro	2.00	1.00	.60
(17)	Brooks Robinson	3.00	1.50	.90
(18)	Frank Robinson	3.00	1.50	.90
(19)	Nolan Ryan	12.00	6.00	3.50
(20)	Mike Schmidt	6.00	3.00	1.75
(21)	Willie Stargell	2.50	1.25	.70
(22)	Andre Thornton	1.00	.50	.30
(23)	Bobby Tolan	1.00	.50	.30
(24)	Jim Wynn	1.00	.50	.30
(25)	Richie Zisk	1.00	.50	.30
	SERIES B			
(26)	Hank Aaron	9.00	4.50	2.75
(27)	Larry Bowa	1.00	.50	.30
(28)	Steve Carlton	2.50	1.25	.70
(29)	Cesar Cedeno	1.00	.50	.30
(30)	Jim Colborn	1.00	.50	.30
(31)	Tim Foli	1.00	.50	.30
(32)	Steve Garvey	1.50	.70	.45
(33)	Bud Harrelson	1.00	.50	.30
(34)	Willie Horton	1.00	.50	.30
(35)	Jim Hunter	2.00	1.00	.60
(36)	Reggie Jackson	6.00	3.00	1.75
(37)	Billy Martin	1.50	.70	.45
(38)	Bake McBride	1.00	.50	.30
(39)	Andy Messersmith	1.00	.50	.30
(40)	Rick Monday	1.00	.50	.30
(41)	Joe Morgan	2.50	1.25	.70
(42)	Tony Oliva	1.50	.70	.45
(43)	Amos Otis	1.00	.50	.30
(44)	Gaylord Perry	2.00	1.00	.60
(45)	Tom Seaver	5.00	2.50	1.50
(46)	Ken Singleton	1.00	.50	.30

		NM	EX	VG
(47)	Chris Speier	1.00	.50	.30
(48)	Gene Tenace	1.00	.50	.30
(49)	Del Unser	1.00	.50	.30
(50)	Carl Yastrzemski	5.00	2.50	1.50
	SERIES C			
(51)	Steve Busby	1.00	.50	.30
(52)	Jose Cardenal	1.00	.50	.30
(53)	Rod Carew	2.50	1.25	.70
(54)	Ron Cey	1.00	.50	.30
(55)	Willie Davis	1.00	.50	.30
(56)	Barry Foote	1.00	.50	.30
(57)	Ken Holtzman	1.00	.50	.30
(58)	Davey Lopes	1.00	.50	.30
(59)	Greg Luzinski	1.00	.50	.30
(60)	Sparky Lyle	1.00	.50	.30
(61)	Dave May	1.00	.50	.30
(62)	Lee May	1.00	.50	.30
(63)	Doc Medich	1.00	.50	.30
(64)	Bill Melton	1.00	.50	.30
(65)	Randy Moffitt	1.00	.50	.30
(66)	Don Money	1.00	.50	.30
(67)	Al Oliver	1.50	.70	.45
(68)	George Scott	1.00	.50	.30
(69)	Ted Simmons	1.00	.50	.30
(70)	Charlie Spikes	1.00	.50	.30
(71)	Rusty Staub	1.25	.60	.40
(72)	Jim Sundberg	1.00	.50	.30
(73)	Bob Watson	1.00	.50	.30
(74)	Dick Williams	1.00	.50	.30
(75)	Dave Winfield	2.50	1.25	.70
	SERIES D			
(76)	Vida Blue	1.00	.50	.30
(77)	Bobby Bonds	1.00	.50	.30
(78)	Jerry Coleman	1.00	.50	.30
(79)	Bob Coluccio	1.00	.50	.30
(80)	Joe Decker	1.00	.50	.30
(81)	Darrell Evans	1.00	.50	.30
(82)	Ralph Gaar/SP (Garr)	4.00	2.00	1.25
(83)	Richie Hebner	1.00	.50	.30
(84)	Ken Henderson	1.00	.50	.30
(85)	Bill Madlock	1.00	.50	.30
(86)	Jon Matlack	1.00	.50	.30
(87)	Carlos May	1.00	.50	.30
(88)	John Mayberry	1.00	.50	.30
(89)	Willie McCovey	2.50	1.25	.70
(90)	Lynn McGlothen	1.00	.50	.30
(91)	Tug McGraw	1.00	.50	.30
(92)	Roger Metzger	1.00	.50	.30
(93)	Jim Palmer	2.00	1.00	.60
(94)	Rico Petrocelli	1.00	.50	.30
(95)	Ellie Rodriguez	1.00	.50	.30
(96)	Steve Rogers	1.00	.50	.30
(97)	Pete Rose	9.00	4.50	2.75
(98)	Bill Singer	1.00	.50	.30
(99)	Don Sutton	2.00	1.00	.60
(100)	Billy Williams	2.50	1.25	.70
	SERIES E			
(101)	Mark Belanger	1.00	.50	.30
(102)	Buddy Bell	1.00	.50	.30
(103)	Jim Bibby	1.00	.50	.30
(104)	Bob Boone	1.00	.50	.30
(105)	Ken Brett	1.00	.50	.30
(106)	Ron Bryant	1.00	.50	.30
(107)	Bill Buckner	1.00	.50	.30
(108)	Buzz Capra	1.00	.50	.30
(109)	Dave Concepcion	1.00	.50	.30
(110)	Rollie Fingers	2.00	1.00	.60
(111)	Bill Freehan	1.00	.50	.30
(112)	Bobby Grich	1.00	.50	.30
(113)	Fred Kendall	1.00	.50	.30
(114)	Don Kessinger	1.00	.50	.30
(115)	Hal McCrae (McRae)	1.00	.50	.30
(116)	Thurman Munson	2.50	1.25	.70
(117)	Fred Patek	1.00	.50	.30
(118)	Doug Rader	1.00	.50	.30
(119)	A. (Aurelio) Rodriguez	1.00	.50	.30
(120)	Manny Sanguillen	1.00	.50	.30
(121)	Reggie Smith	1.00	.50	.30
(122)	Danny Thompson	1.00	.50	.30
(123)	Luis Tiant	1.00	.50	.30
(124)	Joe Torre	1.50	.70	.45
(125)	Wilbur Wood	1.00	.50	.30

1953-54 Marshall Merrell Milwaukee Braves Portfolio

One of several portfolios of Milwaukee Braves artwork produced during the team's first few years, this issue of 8" x 10" black-and-white lithographs was sold at County Stadium for 25 cents apiece. The player checklist here is believed to be complete, but it is possible other poses may yet be reported. The cards are blank-backed and unnumbered; the checklist here has been arranged alphabetically.

		NM	EX	VG
Complete Set (25):		900.00	450.00	275.00
Common Player:		25.00	12.50	7.50
(1)	Henry Aaron	200.00	100.00	60.00
(2)	Joe Adcock	25.00	12.50	7.50
(3)	Johnny Antonelli	25,00	12.50	7.50
(4)	Billy Bruton	25.00	12.50	7.50
(5)	Bob Buhl	25.00	12.50	7.50
(6)	Lou Burdette (Follow-through.)	25.00	12.50	7.50
(7)	Lew Burdette (Wind-up.)	25.00	12.50	7.50
(8)	Gene Conley	25.00	12.50	7.50
(9)	Del Crandall	25.00	12.50	7.50
(10)	Jack Dittmer	25.00	12.50	7.50
(11)	Sid Gordon/Btg	25.00	12.50	7.50
(12)	Sid Gordon/Standing	25.00	12.50	7.50
(13)	Charlie Grimm (Tomahawk on jersey.)	25.00	12.50	7.50
(14)	Charlie Grimm (No tomahawk.)	25.00	12.50	7.50
(15)	Don Liddle	25.00	12.50	7.50
(16)	Johnny Logan	25.00	12.50	7.50
(17)	Ed Mathews/Btg	75.00	37.50	22.50
(18)	Ed Mathews/Standing	75.00	37.50	22.50
(19)	Danny O'Connell	25.00	12.50	7.50
(20)	Andy Pafko	25.00	12.50	7.50
(21)	Jim Pendleton	25.00	12.50	7.50
(22)	Warren Spahn	75.00	37.50	22.50
(23)	Max Surkont	25.00	12.50	7.50
(24)	Bobby Thomson	45.00	22.50	13.50
(25)	Jim Wilson	25.00	12.50	7.50

1979 Metallic Creations Signature Miniatures

This collectors' issue was created by combining an approximately 3-1/2" tall pewter statue with a 3-5/8" x 5" baseball card. The statues were released in pewter at about $10 apiece and silver-plate at $20. The black-bordered cards feature color portraits in front of a pair of sepia action pictures. The artwork was by J. Payette. Fronts also feature a facsimile autograph. Backs have basic player personal data and career stats. It was reported that 5,000 of each card were printed, though most were never issued due to failure of the venture. The remaining cards and statues were sold into the hobby as remainders. It is unclear whether a Munson card exists, although the Munson statue and the Ryan card have been confirmed.

		NM	EX	VG
Complete Set, Cards (20):		240.00	120.00	70.00
Common Card:		7.50	3.75	2.25
Complete Set, Pewter Statues (20):		200.00	100.00	60.00
Common Statue:		7.50	3.75	2.25
Silver-plate Statues: 2X				
(1)	Hank Aaron (Card)	12.50	6.25	3.75
(1)	Hank Aaron (Statue)	12.50	6.25	3.75
(2)	Rod Carew (Card)	7.50	3.75	2.25
(2)	Rod Carew (Statue)	7.50	3.75	2.25
(3)	Cesar Cedeno (Card)	7.50	3.75	2.25
(4)	Ty Cobb (Card)	15.00	7.50	4.50
(4)	Ty Cobb (Statue)	12.50	6.25	3.75
(5)	Steve Garvey (Card)	15.00	7.50	4.50
(5)	Steve Garvey (Statue)	15.00	7.50	4.50
(6)	Lou Gehrig (Card)	15.00	7.50	4.50
(6)	Lou Gehrig (Statue)	15.00	7.50	4.50
(7)	Ron Guidry (Card)	7.50	3.75	2.25
(7)	Ron Guidry (Statue)	7.50	3.75	2.25
(8)	Rogers Hornsby (Card)	7.50	3.75	2.25
(8)	Rogers Hornsby (Statue)	7.50	3.75	2.25
(9)	Walter Johnson (Card)	10.00	5.00	3.00
(9)	Walter Johnson (Statue)	10.00	5.00	3.00
(10)	Ralph Kiner (Card)	7.50	3.75	2.25
(10)	Ralph Kiner (Statue)	7.50	3.75	2.25
(11)	Sandy Koufax (Card)	20.00	10.00	6.00
(11)	Sandy Koufax (Statue)	20.00	10.00	6.00
(12)	Davey Lopes (Card)	7.50	3.75	2.25
(12)	Davey Lopes (Statue)	7.50	3.75	2.25
(13)	Christy Mathewson (Card)	10.00	5.00	3.00
(13)	Christy Mathewson (Statue)	10.00	5.00	3.00
(14)	Willie Mays (Card)	15.00	7.50	4.50
(14)	Willie Mays (Statue)	15.00	7.50	4.50
(15)	Willie McCovey (Card)	10.00	5.00	3.00
(15)	Willie McCovey (Statue)	10.00	5.00	3.00
(16)	Thurman Munson (Statue)	10.00	5.00	3.00
(17)	Mel Ott (Card)	7.50	3.75	2.25
(17)	Mel Ott (Statue)	7.50	3.75	2.25
(18)	Babe Ruth (Card)	12.50	6.25	3.75
(18)	Babe Ruth (Statue)	12.50	6.25	3.75
(19)	Nolan Ryan (Card)	30.00	15.00	9.00
(20)	Tris Speaker (Card)	7.50	3.75	2.25
(20)	Tris Speaker (Statue)	7.50	3.75	2.25
(21)	Honus Wagner (Card)	10.00	5.00	3.00
(21)	Honus Wagner (Statue)	10.00	5.00	3.00

Checklists showing are card numbers in parentheses ( ) indicates the numbers do not appear on the cards.

1938-39 Metropolitan Clothing Cincinnati Reds Postcards

(See 1937-39 Orcajo Cincinnati Reds postcards for checklist, values.)

1968 Metropolitan Museum of Art Burdick Collection

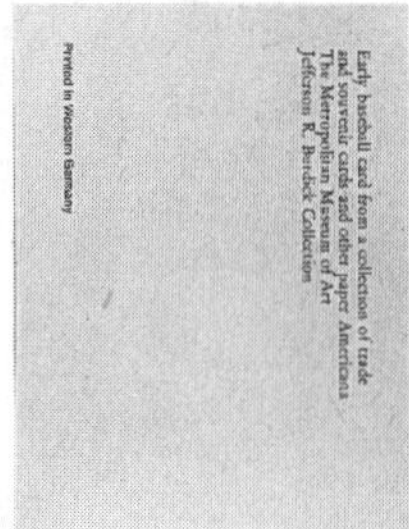

The date of issue is approximate for this set promoting New York's Metropolitan Museum of Art as the repository for the Jefferson Burdick collection, once the world's premier accumulation of trading cards. Burdick, author of the once-standard "American Card Catalog" donated his collection to the Met. The 2-3/4" x 3-5/8" black-and-white glossy card fronts reproduce 1928 R315 cards of major leaguers and earlier Zeenuts cards of minor leaguers. Backs have a few words about the museum and a "Printed in Western Germany" line. The unnumbered cards are checklisted here in alphabetical order.

		NM	EX	VG
Complete Set (8):		125.00	65.00	35.00
Common Player:		10.00	5.00	3.00
(1)	Max Bishop	10.00	5.00	3.00
(2)	Lou Gehrig	40.00	20.00	12.00
(3)	Carl Hubbell	15.00	7.50	4.50
(4)	Art Kores	10.00	5.00	3.00
(5)	Bill Leard	10.00	5.00	3.00
(6)	Babe Ruth	50.00	25.00	15.00
(7)	Dazzy Vance	10.00	5.00	3.00
(8)	Elmer Zacher	10.00	5.00	3.00

1931 Metropolitan Studio St. Louis Cardinals

Members of the St. Louis Cardinals are featured in this 30-card set. The cards were printed on heavy paper and feature sepia-toned photos. The player's name appears along the bottom white border below the photo. The cards measure 6-1/4" x 9-1/2" and are not numbered. Most cards feature the logo of Metropolitan Studio in a bottom corner, while others have "Sid Whiting St. Louis MO," and a few have no sponsor's credit.

	NM	EX	VG
Complete Set (30):	1,800	810.00	450.00

Common Player:	45.00	20.00	12.00
(1) Earl "Sparky" Adams	45.00	20.00	12.00
(2) Ray Blades	45.00	20.00	12.00
(3) James Bottomley	95.00	45.00	25.00
(4) Sam Breadon	45.00	20.00	12.00
(5) James "Rip" Collins	45.00	20.00	12.00
(6) Dizzy Dean	225.00	100.00	55.00
(7) Paul Derringer	45.00	20.00	12.00
(8) Jake Flowers	45.00	20.00	12.00
(9) Frank Frisch	95.00	45.00	25.00
(10) Charles Gelbert	45.00	20.00	12.00
(11) Miguel Gonzales (Gonzalez)	80.00	35.00	20.00
(12) Burleigh Grimes	95.00	45.00	25.00
(13) Charles "Chick" Hafey	95.00	45.00	25.00
(14) William Hallahan	45.00	20.00	12.00
(15) Jesse Haines	95.00	45.00	25.00
(16) Andrew High	45.00	20.00	12.00
(17) Sylvester Johnson	45.00	20.00	12.00
(18) Tony Kaufmann	45.00	20.00	12.00
(19) James Lindsey	45.00	20.00	12.00
(20) Gus Mancuso	45.00	20.00	12.00
(21) John Leonard "Pepper" Martin	80.00	35.00	20.00
(22) Ernest Orsatti	45.00	20.00	12.00
(23) Charles Flint Rhem	45.00	20.00	12.00
(24) Branch Rickey	125.00	55.00	35.00
(25) Walter Roettger	45.00	20.00	12.00
(26) Allyn Stout	45.00	20.00	12.00
(27) "Gabby" Street	45.00	20.00	12.00
(28) Clyde Wares	45.00	20.00	12.00
(29) George Watkins	45.00	20.00	12.00
(30) James Wilson	45.00	20.00	12.00

1979 Michigan Sports Collectors

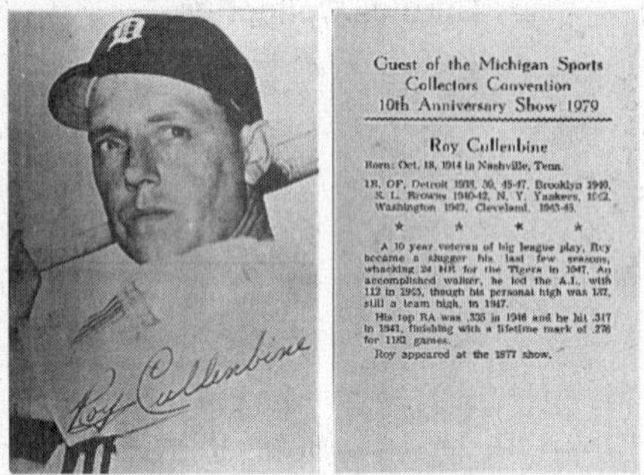

Former Detroit Tigers, along with several baseball writers and announcers, including some who were appearing as autograph guests were featured in this collectors set issued in conjunction with the 1979 Troy, Mich. show. Cards are 3-1/2" x 5-1/16" black-and-white. Backs have personal data and a career summary of the pictured player, along with mention of the show. The unnumbered cards are checklisted here alphabetically.

	NM	EX	VG
Complete Set (20):	20.00	10.00	6.00
Common Player:	3.00	1.50	.90
(1) Gates Brown	3.00	1.50	.90
(2) Norm Cash	5.00	2.50	1.50
(3) Al Cicotte	3.00	1.50	.90
(4) Roy Cullenbine	3.00	1.50	.90
(5) Gene Desautels	3.00	1.50	.90
(6) Hoot Evers	3.00	1.50	.90
(7) Joe Falls	3.00	1.50	.90
(8) Joe Ginsberg	3.00	1.50	.90
(9) Ernie Harwell	3.00	1.50	.90
(10) Ray Herbert	3.00	1.50	.90
(11) John Hiller	3.00	1.50	.90
(12) Billy Hoeft	3.00	1.50	.90
(13) Ralph Houk	4.00	2.00	1.25
(14) Cliff Kachline	3.00	1.50	.90
(15) George Kell	5.00	2.50	1.50
(16) Ron LeFlore	4.00	2.00	1.25
(17) Barney McCosky	3.00	1.50	.90
(18) Jim Northrup	3.00	1.50	.90
(19) Dick Radatz	3.00	1.50	.90
(20) Tom Timmermann	3.00	1.50	.90

1940 Michigan Sportservice Detroit Tigers

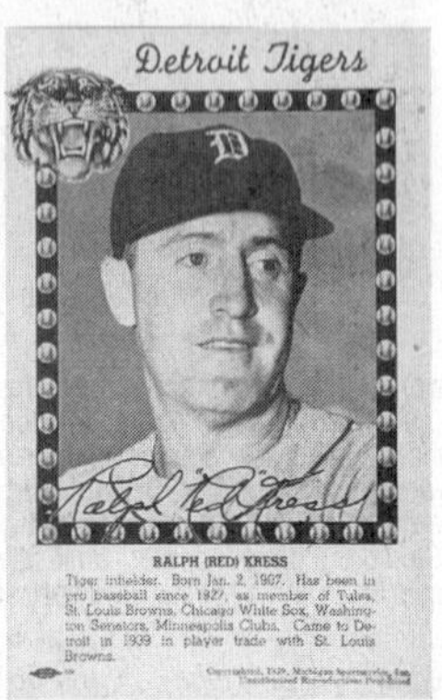

Apparently a team issue sent to persons who wrote the team or players for photos, these blank-back cards measure 4-1/8" x 6-1/4" and are printed in black-and-white. A facsimile autograph is printed over the central portrait, which is surrounded by a border of baseballs. A few career notes are printed under the photo. At bottom-left is a union printing label. At bottom-right is printed, "Copyrighted 1939, Michigan Sportservice, Inc. Unauthorized Reproduction Prohibited." The unnumbered cards are checklisted here alphabetically.

	NM	EX	VG
Complete Set (21):	5,400	2,700	1,650
Common Player:	300.00	150.00	90.00
(1) Earl Averill	350.00	175.00	105.00
(2) Dick Bartell	300.00	150.00	90.00
(3) Roy "Beau" Bell	300.00	150.00	90.00
(4) Al Benton	300.00	150.00	90.00
(5) Tommy Bridges	300.00	150.00	90.00
(6) Frank Croucher	300.00	150.00	90.00
(7) Pete Fox	300.00	150.00	90.00
(8) Charlie Gehringer	400.00	200.00	120.00
(9) Hank Greenberg	550.00	275.00	165.00
(10) John Gorsica	300.00	150.00	90.00
(11) Pinky Higgins	300.00	150.00	90.00
(12) Fred Hutchinson	300.00	150.00	90.00
(13) Ralph "Red" Kress	300.00	150.00	90.00
(14) Barney McCosky	300.00	150.00	90.00
(15) Archie R. McKain	300.00	150.00	90.00
(16) Hal Newhouser	350.00	175.00	105.00
(17) Louis "Buck" Newsom	300.00	150.00	90.00
(18) Schoolboy Rowe	300.00	150.00	90.00
(19) Birdie Tebbetts	300.00	150.00	90.00
(20) Dizzy Trout	300.00	150.00	90.00
(21) Rudy York	300.00	150.00	90.00

1975 Mid-Atlantic Sports Collectors Assn.

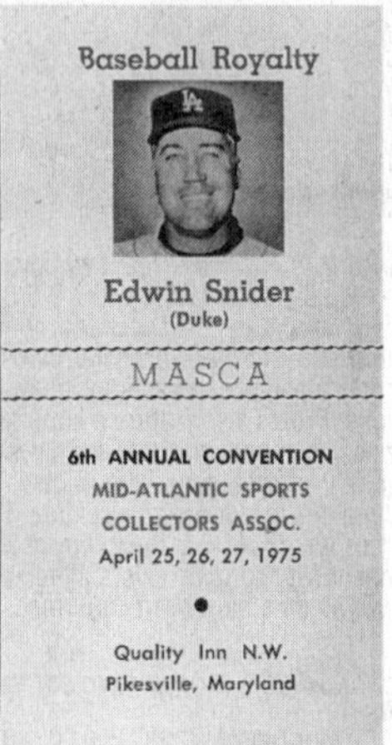

This "Baseball Royalty" collectors' set was issued in conjunction with the 1975 convention of the Mid-Atlantic Sports Collectors Association in Pikesville, Md. The blank-backed, 2-1/2" x 4-3/4" cards are printed in red and blue on white with player photos in blue. Each of the players in the set has a name or nickname pertaining to royalty. The unnumbered cards are checklisted here in alphabetical order.

	NM	EX	VG
Complete Set (8):	20.00	10.00	6.00
Common Player:	3.00	1.50	.90
(1) Paul (Duke) Derringer	3.00	1.50	.90
(2) Elroy (Baron of the Bullpen) Face	3.00	1.50	.90
(3) Rogers (Rajah) Hornsby	5.00	2.50	1.50
(4) (King) Carl Hubbell	4.00	2.00	1.25
(5) Charley (King Kong) Keller	3.00	1.50	.90
(6) Babe (Sultan of Swat) Ruth	10.00	5.00	3.00
(7) (Prince) Hal Schumacher	3.00	1.50	.90
(8) Edwin (Duke) Snider	7.50	3.75	2.25

1927 Middy Bread Browns/Cardinals Die-Cuts

St. Louis Cardinals and St. Louis Browns players comprise this set. Black-and-white, blank-backed and unnumbered, the cards are known only in die-cut form, and vary in size according to the player pose, with a typical card measuring 2-1/4" x 4" or so. The checklist, arranged here alphabetically, consists of 22 players from each team, but may be subject to future additions. Similar to the previous year's issue of Kut Outs Yankees and Giants die-cut cards, this issue features posed action photos with the backgrounds cut away and the player and team name printed at the bottom of the photo. Unlike the earlier New York issue, however, these cards carry an advertisement at bottom for Midday Bread, and were presumably issued in the St. Louis area, though the exact method of their distribution is unknown. Cards are blank-backed and unnumbered. As with all die-cut cards, various appendages and bat ends were easily torn off and cards with such defects suffer severe loss of value.

	NM	EX	VG
Complete Set (44):	13,500	6,750	4,250
Common Player:	300.00	120.00	60.00
St. Louis Browns			
(1) Spencer Adams	450.00	180.00	90.00
(2) Win Ballou	300.00	120.00	60.00
(3) Walter Beck	300.00	120.00	60.00
(4) Herschel Bennett	300.00	120.00	60.00
(5) Stewart Bolen	300.00	120.00	60.00
(6) Leo Dixon	300.00	120.00	60.00
(7) Chester Falk	300.00	120.00	60.00
(8) Milton Gaston	300.00	120.00	60.00
(9) Walter Gerber	300.00	120.00	60.00
(10) Sam Jones	300.00	120.00	60.00
(11) Oscar Melillo	300.00	120.00	60.00
(12) Bing Miller	300.00	120.00	60.00
(13) Otis Miller	300.00	120.00	60.00
(14) Billie Mullen	300.00	120.00	60.00
(15) Ernie Nevers	600.00	240.00	120.00
(16) Steve O'Neill	300.00	120.00	60.00
(17) Harry Rice	300.00	120.00	60.00
(18) George Sisler	500.00	200.00	100.00
(19) Walter Stewart	300.00	120.00	60.00
(20) Elam VanGilder	300.00	120.00	60.00
(21) Ken Williams	300.00	120.00	60.00
(22) Ernie Wingard	300.00	120.00	60.00
St. Louis Cardinals			
(1) Grover Alexander	600.00	240.00	120.00
(2) Herman Bell	300.00	120.00	60.00
(3) Lester Bell	300.00	120.00	60.00
(4) Ray Blades	300.00	120.00	60.00
(5) Jim Bottomley	500.00	200.00	100.00
(6) Danny Clark	300.00	120.00	60.00
(7) Taylor Douthit	300.00	120.00	60.00
(8) Frank Frisch	500.00	200.00	100.00
(9) Chick Hafey	500.00	200.00	100.00
(10) Jesse Haines	500.00	200.00	100.00
(11) Vic Keen	300.00	120.00	60.00
(12) Carlise Littlejohn	300.00	120.00	60.00
(13) Bob McGraw	300.00	120.00	60.00
(14) Bob O'Farrell	300.00	120.00	60.00
(15) Art Reinhardt	300.00	120.00	60.00
(16) Jimmy Ring	300.00	120.00	60.00
(17) Walter Roettger	300.00	120.00	60.00
(18) Robert Schang	300.00	120.00	60.00
(19) Willie Sherdel	300.00	120.00	60.00
(20) Billy Southworth	300.00	120.00	60.00
(21) Tommy Thevenow	300.00	120.00	60.00
(22) George Toporcer	300.00	120.00	60.00

1976 Midwest Sports Collectors Convention

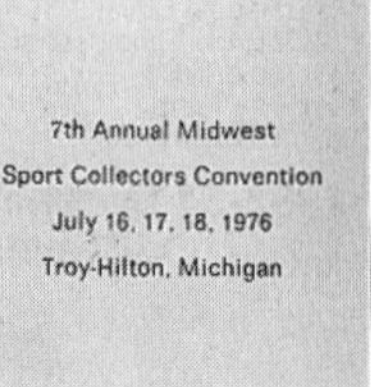

This collectors' issue was produced in conjunction with the 7th annual convention of the Midwest Sports Collectors in Troy, Mich. Former members of the Detroit Tigers, with an emphasis on the 1930s, are featured on the black-and-white, 2-3/8" x 2-7/8" cards. Players are depicted in portrait and action drawings, with personal data and career highlights added in either written or comic form. Backs advertise the show. The unnumbered cards are checklisted here in alphabetical order.

	NM	EX	VG
Complete Set (23):	15.00	7.50	4.50
Common Player:	3.00	1.50	.90
(1) Eldon Auker	3.00	1.50	.90
(2) Tommy Bridges	3.00	1.50	.90
(3) Flea Clifton	3.00	1.50	.90
(4) Mickey Cochrane	7.50	3.75	2.25
(5) General Crowder	3.00	1.50	.90
(6) Frank Doljack	3.00	1.50	.90
(7) Carl Fischer	3.00	1.50	.90
(8) Pete Fox	3.00	1.50	.90
(9) Charlie Gehringer	6.00	3.00	1.75
(10) Goose Goslin	4.50	2.25	1.25
(11) Hank Greenberg	9.00	4.50	2.75

(12)	Luke Hamlin	3.00	1.50	.90
(13)	Ray Hayworth	3.00	1.50	.90
(14)	Chief Hogsett	3.00	1.50	.90
(15)	Firpo Marberry	3.00	1.50	.90
(16)	Marvin Owen	3.00	1.50	.90
(17)	Cy Perkins	3.00	1.50	.90
(18)	Bill Rogell	3.00	1.50	.90
(19)	Schoolboy Rowe	3.00	1.50	.90
(20)	Heinie Schuble	3.00	1.50	.90
(21)	Vic Sorrell	3.00	1.50	.90
(22)	Gee Walker	3.00	1.50	.90
(23)	Jo Jo White	3.00	1.50	.90

1980 Midwest Sports Collectors Convention

Reprints of a number of the player postcards of J.D. McCarthy were produced in conjunction with the 1980 Detroit show. The blank-backed, black-and-white postcards are 3-1/4" x 5-1/2" and all feature former Detroit Tigers. The unnumbered cards are checklisted here alphabetically.

		NM	EX	VG
Complete Set (11):		7.50	3.75	2.25
Common Player:		1.00	.50	.30
(1)	Bob Anderson	1.00	.50	.30
(2)	Babe Birrer	1.00	.50	.30
(3)	Frank Bolling	1.00	.50	.30
(4)	Jim Bunning	2.00	1.00	.60
(5)	Al Cicotte	1.00	.50	.30
(6)	Paul Foytack	1.00	.50	.30
(7)	Joe Ginsberg	1.00	.50	.30
(8)	Steve Gromek	1.00	.50	.30
(9)	Art Houtteman	1.00	.50	.30
(10)	Al Kaline	5.00	2.50	1.50
(11)	Harvey Kuenn	2.00	1.00	.60

1971 Milk Duds

These cards were issued on the backs of five-cent packages of Milk Duds candy. Most collectors prefer complete boxes, rather than cut-out cards, which measure approximately 1-13/16" x 2-5/8" when trimmed tightly. Values quoted below are for complete boxes. Cut cards will bring 50-75 percent of the quoted values. The set includes 37 National League and 32 American League players. Card numbers appear on the box flap, with each number from 1 through 24 being shared by three different players. A suffix (a, b and c) has been added for the collector's convenience. Harmon Killebrew, Brooks Robinson and Pete Rose were double-printed.

		NM	EX	VG
Complete Set, Boxes:		1,000	500.00	300.00
Complete Set, Singles (72):		500.00	250.00	150.00
Common Player:		10.00	5.00	3.00
1a	Frank Howard	12.00	6.00	3.50
1b	Fritz Peterson	10.00	5.00	3.00
1c	Pete Rose	55.00	27.50	16.50
2a	Johnny Bench	15.00	7.50	4.50
2b	Rico Carty	10.00	5.00	3.00
2c	Pete Rose	55.00	27.50	16.50
3a	Ken Holtzman	10.00	5.00	3.00
3b	Willie Mays	50.00	25.00	15.00
3c	Cesar Tovar	10.00	5.00	3.00
4a	Willie Davis	10.00	5.00	3.00
4b	Harmon Killebrew	15.00	7.50	4.50
4c	Felix Millan	10.00	5.00	3.00
5a	Billy Grabarkewitz	10.00	5.00	3.00
5b	Andy Messersmith	10.00	5.00	3.00
5c	Thurman Munson	45.00	22.50	13.50
6a	Luis Aparicio	13.50	6.75	4.00
6b	Lou Brock	13.50	6.75	4.00
6c	Bill Melton	10.00	5.00	3.00
7a	Ray Culp	10.00	5.00	3.00
7b	Willie McCovey	20.00	10.00	6.00
7c	Luke Walker	10.00	5.00	3.00
8a	Roberto Clemente	115.00	55.00	35.00
8b	Jim Merritt	10.00	5.00	3.00
8c	Claud Osteen (Claude)	10.00	5.00	3.00
9a	Stan Bahnsen	10.00	5.00	3.00
9b	Sam McDowell	10.00	5.00	3.00
9c	Billy Williams	15.00	7.50	4.50
10a	Jim Hickman	10.00	5.00	3.00
10b	Dave McNally	10.00	5.00	3.00
10c	Tony Perez	20.00	10.00	6.00
11a	Hank Aaron	40.00	20.00	12.00
11b	Glen Beckert (Glenn)	10.00	5.00	3.00
11c	Ray Fosse	10.00	5.00	3.00
12a	Alex Johnson	10.00	5.00	3.00
12b	Gaylord Perry	13.50	6.75	4.00
12c	Wayne Simpson	10.00	5.00	3.00
13a	Dave Johnson	10.00	5.00	3.00
13b	George Scott	10.00	5.00	3.00
13c	Tom Seaver	25.00	12.50	7.50
14a	Bill Freehan	10.00	5.00	3.00
14b	Bud Harrelson	10.00	5.00	3.00
14c	Manny Sanguillen	10.00	5.00	3.00
15a	Bob Gibson	15.00	7.50	4.50
15b	Rusty Staub	12.00	6.00	3.50
15c	Roy White	10.00	5.00	3.00
16a	Jim Fregosi	10.00	5.00	3.00
16b	Catfish Hunter	13.50	6.75	4.00
16c	Mel Stottlemyer (Stottlemyre)	10.00	5.00	3.00
17a	Tommy Harper	10.00	5.00	3.00
17b	Frank Robinson	20.00	10.00	6.00
17c	Reggie Smith	10.00	5.00	3.00
18a	Orlando Cepeda	20.00	10.00	6.00
18b	Rico Petrocelli	10.00	5.00	3.00
18c	Brooks Robinson	20.00	10.00	6.00
19a	Tony Oliva	12.00	6.00	3.50
19b	Milt Pappas	10.00	5.00	3.00
19c	Bobby Tolan	10.00	5.00	3.00
20a	Ernie Banks	30.00	15.00	9.00
20b	Don Kessinger	10.00	5.00	3.00
20c	Joe Torre	12.00	6.00	3.50
21a	Fergie Jenkins	13.50	6.75	4.00
21b	Jim Palmer	15.00	7.50	4.50
21c	Ron Santo	12.00	6.00	3.50
22a	Randy Hundley	10.00	5.00	3.00
22b	Dennis Menke (Denis)	10.00	5.00	3.00
22c	Boog Powell	12.00	6.00	3.50
23a	Dick Dietz	10.00	5.00	3.00
23b	Tommy John	10.00	5.00	3.00
23c	Brooks Robinson	20.00	10.00	6.00
24a	Danny Cater	10.00	5.00	3.00
24b	Harmon Killebrew	15.00	7.50	4.50
24c	Jim Perry	12.00	6.00	3.50

1933 George C. Miller (R300)

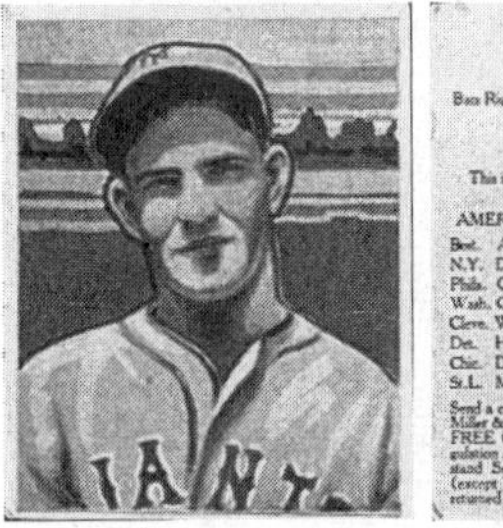

Jimmy Dykes, Infield
Born, Philadelphia, Pa., Nov. 10, 1896
Home, Oakmont, Pa.
Bats Right - Throws Right - Hgt. 5 ft. 9 in. - Wgt. 180 lbs.
1932 Batting Average .265
Major League Batting Average .283

This is one of a set of 32 of Am. & Natl. League Stars
--- consisting of ---

AMERICAN LEAGUE			NATIONAL LEAGUE		
Bost.	Andrews	Alexander	Bost.	Maranville	Berger
N.Y.	Dickey	Ruffing	N.Y.	Terry	Ott
Phila.	Grove	Fox	Bkln.	Stripp	O'Doul
Wash.	Cronin	Goslin	Phila.	Bartell	Klien
Cleve.	W. Ferrell	Averill	Cinn.	Bottomley	Hafey
Det.	Hayworth	Gehringer	Pitts.	P. Waner	L. Waner
Chic.	Dykes	Simmons	Chic.	Warneke	Grimm
St.L.	Melillo	Reynolds	St.L.	Dean	Frisch

Send a complete uncancelled set of 32 pictures to George C. Miller & Co., Inc., 927 Washington St., Boston, and receive FREE OF CHARGE, your choice of Fielder's Mitt, regulation American or National League Baseball or 1 Grandstand Seat to any American or National League Game (except World's Series) at any Park. Your pictures will be returned cancelled, with the Baseball, Mitt or Ticket.

George C. Miller & Co. of Boston, Mass., issued a 32-card set in one-cent packs of toffee1933. The set, which received limited distribution, consists of 16 National League and 16 American League players. The cards are color art reproductions of actual photographs and measure 2-3/8" x 2-7/8". Two distinct variations can be found for each card in the set. Type 1 cards have the names "Fox" and "Klien" misspelled on the back, while Type 2 cards have them correctly as "Foxx" and "Klein." Collectors were advised on the card backs to collect all 32 cards and return them for prizes. (Ivy Andrews' card was short-printed to avoid giving out too many prizes.) The cancelled cards were returned to the collector with the prize. Two forms of cancellation were used; one involved the complete trimming of the bottom one-quarter of the card, the other a diamond-shaped series of punch holes. Cancelled cards have a significantly decreased value.

		NM	EX	VG
Complete Set (32):		65,000	30,000	16,000
Common Player:		1,200	550.00	300.00
(1)	Dale Alexander	1,200	550.00	300.00
(2)	"Ivy" Paul Andrews	5,500	2,475	1,375
	Cut-cancelled: 1150.00			
	Punch-cancelled: 2,400			
(3)	Earl Averill	2,500	1,125	625.00
(4)	Dick Bartell	1,200	550.00	300.00
(5)	Walter Berger	1,200	550.00	300.00
(6)	Jim Bottomley	2,500	1,125	625.00
(7)	Joe Cronin	2,500	1,125	625.00
(8)	Jerome "Dizzy" Dean	3,000	1,350	750.00
(9)	William Dickey	2,500	1,125	625.00
(10)	Jimmy Dykes	1,200	550.00	300.00
(11)	Wesley Ferrell	1,200	550.00	300.00
(12)	Jimmy Foxx	3,500	1,575	875.00
(13)	Frank Frisch	2,500	1,125	625.00
(14)	Charlie Gehringer	2,500	1,125	625.00
(15)	Leon "Goose" Goslin	2,500	1,125	625.00
(16)	Charlie Grimm	1,200	550.00	300.00
(17)	Bob "Lefty" Grove	3,000	1,350	750.00
(18)	Charles "Chick" Hafey	2,500	1,125	625.00
(19)	Ray Hayworth	1,200	550.00	300.00
(20)	Charles "Chuck" Klein	2,500	1,125	625.00
(21)	Walter "Rabbit" Maranville	2,500	1,125	625.00
(22)	Oscar Melillo	1,200	550.00	300.00
(23)	Frank "Lefty" O'Doul	2,000	900.00	500.00
(24)	Melvin Ott	2,750	1,225	685.00
(25)	Carl Reynolds	1,200	550.00	300.00
(26)	Charles Ruffing	2,500	1,125	625.00
(27)	Al Simmons	2,500	1,125	625.00
(28)	Joe Stripp	1,200	550.00	300.00
(29)	Bill Terry	2,500	1,125	625.00
(30)	Lloyd Waner	2,500	1,125	625.00
(31)	Paul Waner	2,500	1,125	625.00
(32)	Lonnie Warneke	1,200	550.00	300.00

1969 Milton Bradley

The first of three sets issued by Milton Bradley over a four-year period, these cards were part of a baseball board game. The unnumbered cards measure 2" x 3" and have a white border surrounding the black-and-white player photo. The player's name appears above the photo in upper case letters. There are no team designations and the photos are airbrushed to eliminate team logos. Backs display biographical data along the top followed by a list of various game situations used in playing the board game. The cards have square corners. The 1969 and 1972 game cards are virtually identical in format. They can be differentiated by looking on the back at any numeral "1" in a line of red type. If the "1" does not have a base, it is a 1969 card; if there is a base, the card is a 1972. Besides individual player cards, there was a non-photographic team cards for each of the contemporary 24 Major League teams.

		NM	EX	VG
Complete Boxed Set:		400.00	200.00	120.00
Complete Set (296):		150.00	75.00	45.00
Common Player:		.50	.25	.15
Team Card:		2.00	1.00	.60
(1)	Hank Aaron	30.00	15.00	9.00
(2)	Ted Abernathy	.50	.25	.15
(3)	Jerry Adair	.50	.25	.15
(4)	Tommy Agee	.50	.25	.15
(5)	Bernie Allen	.50	.25	.15
(6)	Hank Allen	.50	.25	.15
(7)	Richie Allen	5.00	2.50	1.50
(8)	Gene Alley	.50	.25	.15
(9)	Bob Allison	.50	.25	.15
(10)	Felipe Alou	1.00	.50	.30
(11)	Jesus Alou	.50	.25	.15
(12)	Matty Alou	.50	.25	.15
(13)	Max Alvis	.50	.25	.15
(14)	Mike Andrews	.50	.25	.15
(15)	Luis Aparicio	10.00	5.00	3.00
(16)	Jose Arcia	.50	.25	.15
(17)	Bob Aspromonte	.50	.25	.15
(18)	Joe Azcue	.50	.25	.15
(19)	Ernie Banks	20.00	10.00	6.00
(20)	Steve Barber	.50	.25	.15
(21)	John Bateman	.50	.25	.15
(22)	Glen Beckert (Glenn)	.50	.25	.15
(23)	Gary Bell	.50	.25	.15
(24)	John Bench	15.00	7.50	4.50
(25)	Ken Berry	.50	.25	.15
(26)	Frank Bertaina	.50	.25	.15
(27)	Paul Blair	.50	.25	.15
(28)	Wade Blasingame	.50	.25	.15
(29)	Curt Blefary	.50	.25	.15
(30)	John Boccabella	.50	.25	.15
(31)	Bobby Lee Bonds	1.00	.50	.30
(32)	Sam Bowens	.50	.25	.15
(33)	Ken Boyer	1.00	.50	.30
(34)	Charles Bradford	.50	.25	.15
(35)	Darrell Brandon	.50	.25	.15
(36)	Jim Brewer	.50	.25	.15
(37)	John Briggs	.50	.25	.15
(38)	Nelson Briles	.50	.25	.15
(39)	Ed Brinkman	.50	.25	.15
(40)	Lou Brock	10.00	5.00	3.00
(41)	Gates Brown	.50	.25	.15
(42)	Larry Brown	.50	.25	.15
(43)	George Brunet	.50	.25	.15

(44)	Jerry Buchek	.50	.25	.15
(45)	Don Buford	.50	.25	.15
(46)	Jim Bunning	7.50	3.75	2.25
(47)	Johnny Callison	.50	.25	.15
(48)	Campy Campaneris	.50	.25	.15
(49)	Jose Cardenal	.50	.25	.15
(50)	Leo Cardenas	.50	.25	.15
(51)	Don Cardwell	.50	.25	.15
(52)	Rod Carew	12.50	6.25	3.75
(53)	Paul Casanova	.50	.25	.15
(54)	Norm Cash	1.50	.70	.45
(55)	Danny Cater	.50	.25	.15
(56)	Orlando Cepeda	10.00	5.00	3.00
(57)	Dean Chance	.50	.25	.15
(58)	Ed Charles	.50	.25	.15
(59)	Horace Clarke	.50	.25	.15
(60)	Roberto Clemente	45.00	22.00	13.50
(61)	Donn Clendenon	.50	.25	.15
(62)	Ty Cline	.50	.25	.15
(63)	Nate Colbert	.50	.25	.15
(64)	Joe Coleman	.50	.25	.15
(65)	Bob Cox	.50	.25	.15
(66)	Mike Cuellar	.50	.25	.15
(67)	Ray Culp	.50	.25	.15
(68)	Clay Dalrymple	.50	.25	.15
(69)	Vic Davalillo	.50	.25	.15
(70)	Jim Davenport	.50	.25	.15
(71)	Ron Davis	.50	.25	.15
(72)	Tommy Davis	.50	.25	.15
(73)	Willie Davis	.50	.25	.15
(74)	Chuck Dobson	.50	.25	.15
(75)	John Donaldson	.50	.25	.15
(76)	Al Downing	.50	.25	.15
(77)	Moe Drabowsky	.50	.25	.15
(78)	Dick Ellsworth	.50	.25	.15
(79)	Mike Epstein	.50	.25	.15
(80)	Andy Etchebarren	.50	.25	.15
(81)	Ron Fairly	.50	.25	.15
(82)	Dick Farrell	.50	.25	.15
(83)	Curt Flood	1.00	.50	.30
(84)	Joe Foy	.50	.25	.15
(85)	Tito Francona	.50	.25	.15
(86)	Bill Freehan	.75	.40	.25
(87)	Jim Fregosi	.50	.25	.15
(88)	Woodie Fryman	.50	.25	.15
(89)	Len Gabrielson	.50	.25	.15
(90)	Cito Gaston	.50	.25	.15
(91)	Jake Gibbs	.50	.25	.15
(92)	Russ Gibson	.50	.25	.15
(93)	Dave Giusti	.50	.25	.15
(94)	Tony Gonzalez	.50	.25	.15
(95)	Jim Gosger	.50	.25	.15
(96)	Julio Gotay	.50	.25	.15
(97)	Dick Green	.50	.25	.15
(98)	Jerry Grote	.50	.25	.15
(99)	Jimmie Hall	.50	.25	.15
(100)	Tom Haller	.50	.25	.15
(101)	Steve Hamilton	.50	.25	.15
(102)	Ron Hansen	.50	.25	.15
(103)	Jim Hardin	.50	.25	.15
(104)	Tommy Harper	.50	.25	.15
(105)	Bud Harrelson	.50	.25	.15
(106)	Ken Harrelson	.50	.25	.15
(107)	Jim Hart	.50	.25	.15
(108)	Woodie Held	.50	.25	.15
(109)	Tommy Helms	.50	.25	.15
(110)	Elrod Hendricks	.50	.25	.15
(111)	Mike Hershberger	.50	.25	.15
(112)	Jack Hiatt	.50	.25	.15
(113)	Jim Hickman	.50	.25	.15
(114)	John Hiller	.50	.25	.15
(115)	Chuck Hinton	.50	.25	.15
(116)	Ken Holtzman	.50	.25	.15
(117)	Joel Horlen	.50	.25	.15
(118)	Tony Horton	.50	.25	.15
(119)	Willie Horton	.50	.25	.15
(120)	Frank Howard	1.00	.50	.30
(121)	Dick Howser	.50	.25	.15
(122)	Randy Hundley	.50	.25	.15
(123)	Ron Hunt	.50	.25	.15
(124)	Catfish Hunter	7.50	3.75	2.25
(125)	Al Jackson	.50	.25	.15
(126)	Larry Jackson	.50	.25	.15
(127)	Reggie Jackson	30.00	15.00	9.00
(128)	Sonny Jackson	.50	.25	.15
(129)	Pat Jarvis	.50	.25	.15
(130)	Julian Javier	.50	.25	.15
(131)	Ferguson Jenkins	7.50	3.75	2.25
(132)	Manny Jimenez	.50	.25	.15
(133)	Tommy John	1.00	.50	.30
(134)	Bob Johnson	.50	.25	.15
(135)	Dave Johnson	.50	.25	.15
(136)	Deron Johnson	.50	.25	.15
(137)	Lou Johnson	.50	.25	.15
(138)	Jay Johnstone	.50	.25	.15
(139)	Cleon Jones	.50	.25	.15
(140)	Dalton Jones	.50	.25	.15
(141)	Duane Josephson	.50	.25	.15
(142)	Jim Kaat	1.50	.70	.45
(143)	Al Kaline	15.00	7.50	4.50
(144)	Don Kessinger	.50	.25	.15
(145)	Harmon Killebrew	12.50	6.25	3.75
(146)	Harold King	.50	.25	.15
(147)	Ed Kirkpatrick	.50	.25	.15
(148)	Fred Klages	.50	.25	.15
(149)	Ron Kline	.50	.25	.15
(150)	Bobby Knoop	.50	.25	.15
(151)	Gary Kolb	.50	.25	.15
(152)	Andy Kosco	.50	.25	.15
(153)	Ed Kranepool	.50	.25	.15
(154)	Lew Krausse	.50	.25	.15
(155)	Harold Lanier	.50	.25	.15
(156)	Jim Lefebvre	.50	.25	.15
(157)	Denny Lemaster	.50	.25	.15
(158)	Dave Leonhard	.50	.25	.15
(159)	Don Lock	.50	.25	.15
(160)	Mickey Lolich	1.50	.70	.45
(161)	Jim Lonborg	.75	.40	.25
(162)	Mike Lum	.50	.25	.15
(163)	Al Lyle	.50	.25	.15
(164)	Jim Maloney	.50	.25	.15
(165)	Juan Marichal	8.00	4.00	2.50
(166)	J.C. Martin	.50	.25	.15
(167)	Marty Martinez	.50	.25	.15
(168)	Tom Matchick	.50	.25	.15
(169)	Ed Mathews	12.50	6.25	3.75
(170)	Dal Maxvill	.50	.25	.15
(171)	Jerry May	.50	.25	.15
(172)	Lee May	.50	.25	.15
(173)	Lee Maye	.50	.25	.15
(174)	Willie Mays	30.00	15.00	9.00
(175)	Bill Mazeroski	12.50	6.25	3.75
(176)	Richard McAuliffe	.50	.25	.15
(177)	Al McBean	.50	.25	.15
(178)	Tim McCarver	.75	.40	.25
(179)	Bill McCool	.50	.25	.15
(180)	Mike McCormick	.50	.25	.15
(181)	Willie McCovey	12.50	6.25	3.75
(182)	Tom McCraw	.50	.25	.15
(183)	Lindy McDaniel	.50	.25	.15
(184)	Sam McDowell	.75	.40	.25
(185)	Orlando McFarlane	.50	.25	.15
(186)	Jim McGlothlin	.50	.25	.15
(187)	Denny McLain	1.25	.60	.40
(188)	Ken McMullen	.50	.25	.15
(189)	Dave McNally	.50	.25	.15
(190)	Gerry McNertney	.50	.25	.15
(191)	Dennis Menke (Denis)	.50	.25	.15
(192)	Felix Millan	.50	.25	.15
(193)	Don Mincher	.50	.25	.15
(194)	Rick Monday	.50	.25	.15
(195)	Joe Morgan	10.00	5.00	3.00
(196)	Bubba Morton	.50	.25	.15
(197)	Manny Mota	.50	.25	.15
(198)	Jim Nash	.50	.25	.15
(199)	Dave Nelson	.50	.25	.15
(200)	Dick Nen	.50	.25	.15
(201)	Phil Niekro	7.50	3.75	2.25
(202)	Jim Northrup	.50	.25	.15
(203)	Richard Nye	.50	.25	.15
(204)	Johnny Odom	.50	.25	.15
(205)	Tony Oliva	1.00	.50	.30
(206)	Gene Oliver	.50	.25	.15
(207)	Phil Ortega	.50	.25	.15
(208)	Claude Osteen	.50	.25	.15
(209)	Ray Oyler	.50	.25	.15
(210)	Jose Pagan	.50	.25	.15
(211)	Jim Pagliaroni	.50	.25	.15
(212)	Milt Pappas	.50	.25	.15
(213)	Wes Parker	.50	.25	.15
(214)	Camilo Pascual	.50	.25	.15
(215)	Don Pavletich	.50	.25	.15
(216)	Joe Pepitone	.50	.25	.15
(217)	Tony Perez	10.00	5.00	3.00
(218)	Gaylord Perry	7.50	3.75	2.25
(219)	Jim Perry	.50	.25	.15
(220)	Gary Peters	.50	.25	.15
(221)	Rico Petrocelli	.50	.25	.15
(222)	Adolfo Phillips	.50	.25	.15
(223)	Tom Phoebus	.50	.25	.15
(224)	Vada Pinson	2.00	1.00	.60
(225)	Boog Powell	2.00	1.00	.60
(226)	Frank Quilici	.50	.25	.15
(227)	Doug Rader	.50	.25	.15
(228)	Rich Reese	.50	.25	.15
(229)	Phil Regan	.50	.25	.15
(230)	Rick Reichardt	.50	.25	.15
(231)	Rick Renick	.50	.25	.15
(232)	Roger Repoz	.50	.25	.15
(233)	Dave Ricketts	.50	.25	.15
(234)	Bill Robinson	.50	.25	.15
(235)	Brooks Robinson	15.00	7.50	4.50
(236)	Frank Robinson	15.00	7.50	4.50
(237)	Bob Rodgers	.50	.25	.15
(238)	Cookie Rojas	.50	.25	.15
(239)	Rich Rollins	.50	.25	.15
(240)	Phil Roof	.50	.25	.15
(241)	Pete Rose	30.00	15.00	9.00
(242)	John Roseboro	.50	.25	.15
(243)	Chico Ruiz	.50	.25	.15
(244)	Ray Sadecki	.50	.25	.15
(245)	Chico Salmon	.50	.25	.15
(246)	Jose Santiago	.50	.25	.15
(247)	Ron Santo	2.50	1.25	.70
(248)	Tom Satriano	.50	.25	.15
(249)	Paul Schaal	.50	.25	.15
(250)	Tom Seaver	15.00	7.50	4.50
(251)	Art Shamsky	.50	.25	.15
(252)	Mike Shannon	.50	.25	.15
(253)	Chris Short	.50	.25	.15
(254)	Dick Simpson	.50	.25	.15
(255)	Duke Sims	.50	.25	.15
(256)	Reggie Smith	.50	.25	.15
(257)	Willie Smith	.50	.25	.15
(258)	Russ Snyder	.50	.25	.15
(259)	Al Spangler	.50	.25	.15
(260)	Larry Stahl	.50	.25	.15
(261)	Lee Stange	.50	.25	.15
(262)	Mickey Stanley	.50	.25	.15
(263)	Willie Stargell	10.00	5.00	3.00
(264)	Rusty Staub	1.00	.50	.30
(265)	Mel Stottlemyre	.50	.25	.15
(266)	Ed Stroud	.50	.25	.15
(267)	Don Sutton	7.50	3.75	2.25
(268)	Ron Swoboda	.50	.25	.15
(269)	Jose Tartabull	.50	.25	.15
(270)	Tony Taylor	.50	.25	.15
(271)	Luis Tiant	1.00	.50	.30
(272)	Bob Tillman	.50	.25	.15
(273)	Bobby Tolan	.50	.25	.15
(274)	Jeff Torborg	.50	.25	.15
(275)	Joe Torre	2.50	1.25	.70
(276)	Cesar Tovar	.50	.25	.15
(277)	Dick Tracewski	.50	.25	.15
(278)	Tom Tresh	.75	.40	.25
(279)	Ted Uhlaender	.50	.25	.15
(280)	Del Unser	.50	.25	.15
(281)	Hilario Valdespino	.50	.25	.15
(282)	Fred Valentine	.50	.25	.15
(283)	Bob Veale	.50	.25	.15
(284)	Zoilo Versalles	.50	.25	.15
(285)	Pete Ward	.50	.25	.15
(286)	Al Weis	.50	.25	.15
(287)	Don Wert	.50	.25	.15
(288)	Bill White	.50	.25	.15
(289)	Roy White	.50	.25	.15
(290)	Fred Whitfield	.50	.25	.15
(291)	Hoyt Wilhelm	7.50	3.75	2.25
(292)	Billy Williams	10.00	5.00	3.00
(293)	Maury Wills	.75	.40	.25
(294)	Earl Wilson	.50	.25	.15
(295)	Wilbur Wood	.50	.25	.15
(296)	Jerry Zimmerman	.50	.25	.15

1970 Milton Bradley

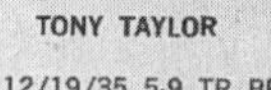

TONY TAYLOR
IF 12/19/35 5-9 TR BR

TONY TAYLOR
3 CATCHER
4 1ST BASEMAN
5 LEFT FIELDER
6 2ND BASEMAN
8 3RD BASEMAN
9 SHORTSTOP
10 CENTER FIELDER
11 RIGHT FIELDER
12 PITCHER

Except for the slightly larger (2-3/8" x 3-1/2") size, the format of the 1970 Milton Bradley set is similar to the 1969 Milton Bradley issue. Again designed for use with a baseball board game, the unnumbered black-and-white cards have rounded corners and wide white borders. The player's name appears in capital letters beneath the photo with his position, birthdate, height and batting and throwing preference on a line below. The back of the card shows the player's name along the top followed by a list of possible game situations used in playing the board game. There are no team designations on the cards and all team insignias have been airbrushed from the photos.

		NM	EX	VG
Complete Boxed Set:		175.00	85.00	45.00
Complete Card Set (28):		120.00	55.00	30.00
Common Player:		1.50	.70	.45
(1)	Hank Aaron	15.00	7.50	4.50
(2)	Ernie Banks	10.00	5.00	3.00
(3)	Lou Brock	7.50	3.75	2.25
(4)	Rod Carew	9.00	4.50	2.75
(5)	Roberto Clemente	15.00	7.50	4.50
(6)	Tommy Davis	1.50	.70	.45
(7)	Bill Freehan	1.50	.70	.45
(8)	Jim Fregosi	1.50	.70	.45
(9)	Tom Haller	1.50	.70	.45
(10)	Frank Howard	2.00	1.00	.60
(11)	Reggie Jackson	10.00	5.00	3.00
(12)	Harmon Killebrew	9.00	4.50	2.75
(13)	Mickey S. Lolich	1.50	.70	.45
(14)	Juan Marichal	6.00	3.00	1.75
(15)	Willie Mays	15.00	7.50	4.50
(16)	Willie McCovey	7.50	3.75	2.25
(17)	Sam McDowell	1.50	.70	.45
(18)	Dennis Menke (Denis)	1.50	.70	.45
(19)	Don Mincher	1.50	.70	.45
(20)	Phil Niekro	6.00	3.00	1.75
(21)	Rico Petrocelli	1.50	.70	.45
(22)	Boog Powell	2.00	1.00	.60
(23)	Frank Robinson	9.00	4.50	2.75
(24)	Pete Rose	15.00	7.50	4.50
(25)	Ron Santo	3.00	1.50	.90
(26)	Tom Seaver	9.00	4.50	2.75
(27)	Mel Stottlemyre	1.50	.70	.45
(28)	Tony Taylor	1.50	.70	.45

1972 Milton Bradley

The 1972 Milton Bradley set was again designed for use with a baseball table game. The 1972 cards are similar to the 1969 and 1970 issues. The unnumbered black-and-white cards measure 2" x 3" and display the player's name along the top of the card. Again, all team insignias have been eliminated by airbrushing, and there are no team designations indicated. Backs carry the player's name and personal data followed by a list of possible game situations used in playing the game. To differentiate a 1972 card from a 1969, look on back for a line of red type which contains the numeral "1." If the digit has a base, the card is a '72; if there is no base to the red "1," it is a 1969. Besides individual player cards, non-photographic team cards were issued for each of the contemporary 24 Major League teams.

		NM	EX	VG
Complete Boxed Set:		400.00	200.00	120.00
Complete Card Set (378):		350.00	175.00	110.00
Common Player:		.50	.25	.15
Team Card:		2.00	1.00	.60
(1)	Hank Aaron	25.00	12.50	7.50
(2)	Tommie Aaron	.50	.25	.15
(3)	Ted Abernathy	.50	.25	.15
(4)	Jerry Adair	.50	.25	.15
(5)	Tommy Agee	.50	.25	.15
(6)	Bernie Allen	.50	.25	.15
(7)	Hank Allen	.50	.25	.15
(8)	Richie Allen	1.50	.70	.45
(9)	Gene Alley	.50	.25	.15
(10)	Bob Allison	.50	.25	.15
(11)	Sandy Alomar	.50	.25	.15
(12)	Felipe Alou	.75	.40	.25
(13)	Jesus Alou	.50	.25	.15
(14)	Matty Alou	.50	.25	.15
(15)	Max Alvis	.50	.25	.15
(16)	Brant Alyea	.50	.25	.15
(17)	Mike Andrews	.50	.25	.15
(18)	Luis Aparicio	9.00	4.50	2.75
(19)	Jose Arcia	.50	.25	.15
(20)	Gerald Arrigo	.50	.25	.15
(21)	Bob Aspromonte	.50	.25	.15
(22)	Joe Azcue	.50	.25	.15
(23)	Robert Bailey	.50	.25	.15
(24)	Sal Bando	.50	.25	.15
(25)	Ernie Banks	17.50	8.75	5.25
(26)	Steve Barber	.50	.25	.15
(27)	Robert Barton	.50	.25	.15
(28)	John Bateman	.50	.25	.15
(29)	Glen Beckert (Glenn)	.50	.25	.15
(30)	John Bench	12.50	6.25	3.75
(31)	Ken Berry	.50	.25	.15
(32)	Frank Bertaina	.50	.25	.15
(33)	Paul Blair	.50	.25	.15
(34)	Stephen Blass	.50	.25	.15
(35)	Curt Blefary	.50	.25	.15
(36)	Bobby Bolin	.50	.25	.15
(37)	Bobby Lee Bonds	1.00	.50	.30
(38)	Donald Bosch	.50	.25	.15
(39)	Richard Bosman	.50	.25	.15
(40)	Dave Boswell	.50	.25	.15
(41)	Kenneth Boswell	.50	.25	.15
(42)	Cletis Boyer	.50	.25	.15
(43)	Ken Boyer	1.25	.60	.40
(44)	Charles Bradford	.50	.25	.15
(45)	Ronald Brand	.50	.25	.15
(46)	Ken Brett	.50	.25	.15
(47)	Jim Brewer	.50	.25	.15
(48)	John Briggs	.50	.25	.15
(49)	Nelson Briles	.50	.25	.15
(50)	Ed Brinkman	.50	.25	.15
(51)	James Britton	.50	.25	.15
(52)	Lou Brock	9.00	4.50	2.75
(53)	Gates Brown	.50	.25	.15
(54)	Larry Brown	.50	.25	.15
(55)	Ollie Brown	.50	.25	.15
(56)	George Brunet	.50	.25	.15
(57)	Don Buford	.50	.25	.15
(58)	Wallace Bunker	.50	.25	.15
(59)	Jim Bunning	6.00	3.00	1.75
(60)	William Butler	.50	.25	.15
(61)	Johnny Callison	.50	.25	.15
(62)	Campy Campaneris	.50	.25	.15
(63)	Jose Cardenal	.50	.25	.15
(64)	Leo Cardenas	.50	.25	.15
(65)	Don Cardwell	.50	.25	.15
(66)	Rod Carew	9.00	4.50	2.75
(67)	Cisco Carlos	.50	.25	.15
(68)	Steve Carlton	9.00	4.50	2.75
(69)	Clay Carroll	.50	.25	.15
(70)	Paul Casanova	.50	.25	.15
(71)	Norm Cash	1.50	.70	.45
(72)	Danny Cater	.50	.25	.15
(73)	Orlando Cepeda	9.00	4.50	2.75
(74)	Dean Chance	.50	.25	.15
(75)	Horace Clarke	.50	.25	.15
(76)	Roberto Clemente	30.00	15.00	9.00
(77)	Donn Clendenon	.50	.25	.15
(78)	Ty Cline	.50	.25	.15
(79)	Nate Colbert	.50	.25	.15
(80)	Joe Coleman	.50	.25	.15
(81)	William Conigliaro	.75	.40	.25
(82)	Casey Cox	.50	.25	.15
(83)	Mike Cuellar	.50	.25	.15
(84)	Ray Culp	.50	.25	.15
(85)	George Culver	.50	.25	.15
(86)	Vic Davalillo	.50	.25	.15
(87)	Jim Davenport	.50	.25	.15
(88)	Tommy Davis	.50	.25	.15
(89)	Willie Davis	.50	.25	.15
(90)	Larry Dierker	.50	.25	.15
(91)	Richard Dietz	.50	.25	.15
(92)	Chuck Dobson	.50	.25	.15
(93)	Pat Dobson	.50	.25	.15
(94)	John Donaldson	.50	.25	.15
(95)	Al Downing	.50	.25	.15
(96)	Moe Drabowsky	.50	.25	.15
(97)	John Edwards	.50	.25	.15
(98)	Thomas Egan	.50	.25	.15
(99)	Dick Ellsworth	.50	.25	.15
(100)	Mike Epstein	.50	.25	.15
(101)	Andy Etchebarren	.50	.25	.15
(102)	Ron Fairly	.50	.25	.15
(103)	Frank Fernandez	.50	.25	.15
(104)	Alfred Ferrara	.50	.25	.15
(105)	Michael Fiore	.50	.25	.15
(106)	Curt Flood	1.00	.50	.30
(107)	Vern Fuller	.50	.25	.15
(108)	Joe Foy	.50	.25	.15
(109)	Tito Francona	.50	.25	.15
(110)	Bill Freehan	.50	.25	.15
(111)	Jim Fregosi	.50	.25	.15
(112)	Woodie Fryman	.50	.25	.15
(113)	Len Gabrielson	.50	.25	.15
(114)	Philip Gagliano	.50	.25	.15
(115)	Cito Gaston	.50	.25	.15
(116)	Jake Gibbs	.50	.25	.15
(117)	Russ Gibson	.50	.25	.15
(118)	Dave Giusti	.50	.25	.15
(119)	Fred Gladding	.50	.25	.15
(120)	Tony Gonzalez	.50	.25	.15
(121)	Jim Gosger	.50	.25	.15
(122)	James Grant	.50	.25	.15
(123)	Thomas Griffin	.50	.25	.15
(124)	Dick Green	.50	.25	.15
(125)	Jerry Grote	.50	.25	.15
(126)	Tom Hall	.50	.25	.15
(127)	Tom Haller	.50	.25	.15
(128)	Steve Hamilton	.50	.25	.15
(129)	William Hands	.50	.25	.15
(130)	James Hannan	.50	.25	.15
(131)	Ron Hansen	.50	.25	.15
(132)	Jim Hardin	.50	.25	.15
(133)	Steve Hargan	.50	.25	.15
(134)	Tommy Harper	.50	.25	.15
(135)	Bud Harrelson	.50	.25	.15
(136)	Ken Harrelson	.50	.25	.15
(137)	Jim Hart	.50	.25	.15
(138)	Rich Hebner	.50	.25	.15
(139)	Michael Hedlund	.50	.25	.15
(140)	Tommy Helms	.50	.25	.15
(141)	Elrod Hendricks	.50	.25	.15
(142)	Ronald Herbel	.50	.25	.15
(143)	Jack Hernandez	.50	.25	.15
(144)	Mike Hershberger	.50	.25	.15
(145)	Jack Hiatt	.50	.25	.15
(146)	Jim Hickman	.50	.25	.15
(147)	Dennis Higgins	.50	.25	.15
(148)	John Hiller	.50	.25	.15
(149)	Chuck Hinton	.50	.25	.15
(150)	Larry Hisle	.50	.25	.15
(151)	Ken Holtzman	.50	.25	.15
(152)	Joel Horlen	.50	.25	.15
(153)	Tony Horton	.50	.25	.15
(154)	Willie Horton	.50	.25	.15
(155)	Frank Howard	.75	.40	.25
(156)	Robert Humphreys	.50	.25	.15
(157)	Randy Hundley	.50	.25	.15
(158)	Ron Hunt	.50	.25	.15
(159)	Catfish Hunter	6.00	3.00	1.75
(160)	Grant Jackson	.50	.25	.15
(161)	Reggie Jackson	15.00	7.50	4.50
(162)	Sonny Jackson	.50	.25	.15
(163)	Pat Jarvis	.50	.25	.15
(164)	Larry Jaster	.50	.25	.15
(165)	Julian Javier	.50	.25	.15
(166)	Ferguson Jenkins	6.00	3.00	1.75
(167)	Tommy John	1.00	.50	.30
(168)	Alexander Johnson	.50	.25	.15
(169)	Bob Johnson	.50	.25	.15
(170)	Dave Johnson	.50	.25	.15
(171)	Deron Johnson	.50	.25	.15
(172)	Jay Johnstone	.50	.25	.15
(173)	Cleon Jones	.50	.25	.15
(174)	Dalton Jones	.50	.25	.15
(175)	Mack Jones	.50	.25	.15
(176)	Richard Joseph	.50	.25	.15
(177)	Duane Josephson	.50	.25	.15
(178)	Jim Kaat	2.00	1.00	.60
(179)	Al Kaline	12.50	6.25	3.75
(180)	Richard Kelley	.50	.25	.15
(181)	Harold Kelly	.50	.25	.15
(182)	Gerald Kenney	.50	.25	.15
(183)	Don Kessinger	.50	.25	.15
(184)	Harmon Killebrew	9.00	4.50	2.75
(185)	Ed Kirkpatrick	.50	.25	.15
(186)	Bobby Knoop	.50	.25	.15
(187)	Calvin Koonce	.50	.25	.15
(188)	Jerry Koosman	.50	.25	.15
(189)	Andy Kosco	.50	.25	.15
(190)	Ed Kranepool	.50	.25	.15
(191)	Ted Kubiak	.50	.25	.15
(192)	Jose Laboy	.50	.25	.15
(193)	Joseph Lahoud	.50	.25	.15
(194)	William Landis	.50	.25	.15
(195)	Harold Lanier	.50	.25	.15
(196)	Fred Lasher	.50	.25	.15
(197)	John Lazar	.50	.25	.15
(198)	Jim Lefebvre	.50	.25	.15
(199)	Denny Lemaster	.50	.25	.15
(200)	Dave Leonhard	.50	.25	.15
(201)	Frank Linzy	.50	.25	.15
(202)	Mickey Lolich	.50	.25	.15
(203)	Jim Lonborg	.50	.25	.15
(204)	Mike Lum	.50	.25	.15
(205)	Al Lyle	.50	.25	.15
(206)	Jim Maloney	.50	.25	.15
(207)	Juan Marichal	7.50	3.75	2.25
(208)	David Marshall	.50	.25	.15
(209)	J.C. Martin	.50	.25	.15
(210)	Marty Martinez	.50	.25	.15
(211)	Tom Matchick	.50	.25	.15
(212)	Dal Maxvill	.50	.25	.15
(213)	Carlos May	.50	.25	.15
(214)	Jerry May	.50	.25	.15
(215)	Lee May	.50	.25	.15
(216)	Lee Maye	.50	.25	.15
(217)	Willie Mays	25.00	12.50	7.50
(218)	Bill Mazeroski	9.00	4.50	2.75
(219)	Richard McAuliffe	.50	.25	.15
(220)	Al McBean	.50	.25	.15
(221)	Tim McCarver	.75	.40	.25
(222)	Bill McCool	.50	.25	.15
(223)	Mike McCormick	.50	.25	.15
(224)	Willie McCovey	9.00	4.50	2.75
(225)	Tom McCraw	.50	.25	.15
(226)	Lindy McDaniel	.50	.25	.15
(227)	Sam McDowell	.50	.25	.15
(228)	Leon McFadden	.50	.25	.15
(229)	Daniel McGinn	.50	.25	.15
(230)	Jim McGlothlin	.50	.25	.15
(231)	Fred McGraw	.50	.25	.15
(232)	Denny McLain	.75	.40	.25
(233)	Ken McMullen	.50	.25	.15
(234)	Dave McNally	.50	.25	.15
(235)	Gerry McNertney	.50	.25	.15
(236)	William Melton	.50	.25	.15
(237)	Dennis Menke (Denis)	.50	.25	.15
(238)	John Messersmith	.50	.25	.15
(239)	Felix Millan	.50	.25	.15
(240)	Norman Miller	.50	.25	.15
(241)	Don Mincher	.50	.25	.15
(242)	Rick Monday	.50	.25	.15
(243)	Donald Money	.50	.25	.15
(244)	Barry Moore	.50	.25	.15
(245)	Bob Moose	.50	.25	.15
(246)	David Morehead	.50	.25	.15
(247)	Joe Morgan	9.00	4.50	2.75
(248)	Curt Motton	.50	.25	.15
(249)	Manny Mota	.50	.25	.15
(250)	Bob Murcer	.50	.25	.15
(251)	Thomas Murphy	.50	.25	.15
(252)	Ivan Murrell	.50	.25	.15
(253)	Jim Nash	.50	.25	.15
(254)	Joe Niekro	1.25	.60	.40
(255)	Phil Niekro	6.00	3.00	1.75
(256)	Gary Nolan	.50	.25	.15
(257)	Jim Northrup	.50	.25	.15
(258)	Richard Nye	.50	.25	.15
(259)	Johnny Odom	.50	.25	.15
(260)	John O'Donaghue	.50	.25	.15
(261)	Tony Oliva	1.00	.50	.30
(262)	Al Oliver	1.00	.50	.30
(263)	Robert Oliver	.50	.25	.15
(264)	Claude Osteen	.50	.25	.15
(265)	Ray Oyler	.50	.25	.15
(266)	Jose Pagan	.50	.25	.15
(267)	Jim Palmer	9.00	4.50	2.75
(268)	Milt Pappas	.50	.25	.15
(269)	Wes Parker	.50	.25	.15
(270)	Fred Patek	.50	.25	.15
(271)	Mike Paul	.50	.25	.15
(272)	Joe Pepitone	.50	.25	.15
(273)	Tony Perez	7.50	3.75	2.25
(274)	Gaylord Perry	6.00	3.00	1.75
(275)	Jim Perry	.50	.25	.15
(276)	Gary Peters	.50	.25	.15
(277)	Rico Petrocelli	.50	.25	.15
(278)	Tom Phoebus	.50	.25	.15
(279)	Lou Piniella	1.00	.50	.30
(280)	Vada Pinson	1.50	.70	.45
(281)	Boog Powell	1.50	.70	.45
(282)	Jim Price	.50	.25	.15
(283)	Frank Quilici	.50	.25	.15
(284)	Doug Rader	.50	.25	.15
(285)	Ron Reed	.50	.25	.15
(286)	Rich Reese	.50	.25	.15
(287)	Phil Regan	.50	.25	.15
(288)	Rick Reichardt	.50	.25	.15
(289)	Rick Renick	.50	.25	.15
(290)	Roger Repoz	.50	.25	.15
(291)	Mervin Rettenmund	.50	.25	.15
(292)	Dave Ricketts	.50	.25	.15
(293)	Juan Rios	.50	.25	.15
(294)	Bill Robinson	.50	.25	.15
(295)	Brooks Robinson	12.50	6.25	3.75
(296)	Frank Robinson	12.50	6.25	3.75
(297)	Aurelio Rodriguez	.50	.25	.15
(298)	Ellie Rodriguez	.50	.25	.15
(299)	Cookie Rojas	.50	.25	.15
(300)	Rich Rollins	.50	.25	.15
(301)	Vicente Romo	.50	.25	.15
(302)	Phil Roof	.50	.25	.15
(303)	Pete Rose	25.00	12.50	7.50
(304)	John Roseboro	.50	.25	.15
(305)	Chico Ruiz	.50	.25	.15
(306)	Mike Ryan	.50	.25	.15
(307)	Ray Sadecki	.50	.25	.15
(308)	Chico Salmon	.50	.25	.15
(309)	Manuel Sanguillen	.50	.25	.15
(310)	Ron Santo	3.00	1.50	.90
(311)	Tom Satriano	.50	.25	.15
(312)	Theodore Savage	.50	.25	.15
(313)	Paul Schaal	.50	.25	.15
(314)	Dick Schofield	.50	.25	.15
(315)	George Scott	.50	.25	.15
(316)	Tom Seaver	12.50	6.25	3.75
(317)	Art Shamsky	.50	.25	.15
(318)	Mike Shannon	.50	.25	.15
(319)	Chris Short	.50	.25	.15
(320)	Sonny Siebert	.50	.25	.15
(321)	Duke Sims	.50	.25	.15
(322)	William Singer	.50	.25	.15
(323)	Reggie Smith	.50	.25	.15
(324)	Willie Smith	.50	.25	.15
(325)	Russ Snyder	.50	.25	.15
(326)	Al Spangler	.50	.25	.15
(327)	James Spencer	.50	.25	.15
(328)	Ed Spiezio	.50	.25	.15
(329)	Larry Stahl	.50	.25	.15
(330)	Lee Stange	.50	.25	.15
(331)	Mickey Stanley	.50	.25	.15
(332)	Willie Stargell	9.00	4.50	2.75
(333)	Rusty Staub	2.00	1.00	.60
(334)	James Stewart	.50	.25	.15
(335)	George Stone	.50	.25	.15
(336)	William Stoneman	.50	.25	.15

(337) Mel Stottlemyre	.50	.25	.15
(338) Ed Stroud	.50	.25	.15
(339) Ken Suarez	.50	.25	.15
(340) Gary Sutherland	.50	.25	.15
(341) Don Sutton	6.00	3.00	1.75
(342) Ron Swoboda	.50	.25	.15
(343) Fred Talbot	.50	.25	.15
(344) Jose Tartabull	.50	.25	.15
(345) Kenneth Tatum	.50	.25	.15
(346) Tony Taylor	.50	.25	.15
(347) Luis Tiant	.75	.40	.25
(348) Bob Tillman	.50	.25	.15
(349) Bobby Tolan	.50	.25	.15
(350) Jeff Torborg	.50	.25	.15
(351) Joe Torre	3.00	1.50	.90
(352) Cesar Tovar	.50	.25	.15
(353) Tom Tresh	.75	.40	.25
(354) Ted Uhlaender	.50	.25	.15
(355) Del Unser	.50	.25	.15
(356) Bob Veale	.50	.25	.15
(357) Zoilo Versalles	.50	.25	.15
(358) Luke Walker	.50	.25	.15
(359) Pete Ward	.50	.25	.15
(360) Eddie Watt	.50	.25	.15
(361) Ramon Webster	.50	.25	.15
(362) Al Weis	.50	.25	.15
(363) Don Wert	.50	.25	.15
(364) Bill White	.50	.25	.15
(365) Roy White	.50	.25	.15
(366) Hoyt Wilhelm	6.00	3.00	1.75
(367) Billy Williams	9.00	4.50	2.75
(368) Walter Williams	.50	.25	.15
(369) Maury Wills	.75	.40	.25
(370) Don Wilson	.50	.25	.15
(371) Earl Wilson	.50	.25	.15
(372) Robert Wine	.50	.25	.15
(373) Richard Wise	.50	.25	.15
(374) Wilbur Wood	.50	.25	.15
(375) William Woodward	.50	.25	.15
(376) Clyde Wright	.50	.25	.15
(377) James Wynn	.50	.25	.15
(378) Jerry Zimmerman	.50	.25	.15

1957 Milwaukee Braves Picture Pack

HENRY AARON, Outfielder

Prior to the Jay Publishing Co. photo packs which dominated the market from 1958-62, the Braves issued this souvenir stand picture pack of 5" x 7" black-and-white, blank-back, player pictures. In the wide bottom border player names are printed in all-caps with the position indicated in upper- and lower-case letters. The unnumbered pictures are listed here in alphabetical order.

	NM	EX	VG
Complete Set (12):	100.00	50.00	30.00
Common Player:	7.50	3.75	2.25
(1) Hank Aaron	30.00	15.00	9.00
(2) Joe Adcock	7.50	3.75	2.25
(3) Lew Burdette	7.50	3.75	2.25
(4) Wes Covington	7.50	3.75	2.25
(5) Del Crandall	7.50	3.75	2.25
(6) Bob Hazle	7.50	3.75	2.25
(7) Johnny Logan	7.50	3.75	2.25
(8) Edwin Mathews	12.50	6.25	3.75
(9) Don McMahon	7.50	3.75	2.25
(10) Andy Pafko	7.50	3.75	2.25
(11) Red Schoendienst	10.00	5.00	3.00
(12) Warren Spahn	12.50	6.25	3.75

1965 Milwaukee Braves Picture Pack

HANK AARON, Braves

These 4-7/8" x 7-1/8" blank-back, black-and-white pictures were sold in groups of 12 in a white paper window envelope and possibly also as a complete set of 24. Besides the slight size difference, the team-issued pictures differ from the contemporary Jay Publishing pictures in that the city name is not included in the typography in the bottom border.

	NM	EX	VG
Complete Set (24):	75.00	37.50	22.50
Common Player:	3.00	1.50	.90
(1) Hank Aaron	15.00	7.50	4.50
(2) Sandy Alomar	3.00	1.50	.90
(3) Felipe Alou	3.00	1.50	.90
(4) Wade Blasingame	3.00	1.50	.90
(5) Frank Bolling	3.00	1.50	.90
(6) Bobby Bragan	3.00	1.50	.90
(7) Rico Carty	3.00	1.50	.90
(8) Ty Cline	3.00	1.50	.90
(9) Tony Cloninger	3.00	1.50	.90
(10) Mike de la Hoz	3.00	1.50	.90
(11) Hank Fischer	3.00	1.50	.90
(12) Mack Jones	3.00	1.50	.90
(13) Gary Kolb	3.00	1.50	.90
(14) Denny LeMaster	3.00	1.50	.90
(15) Eddie Mathews	6.00	3.00	1.75
(16) Lee Maye	3.00	1.50	.90
(17) Denis Menke	3.00	1.50	.90
(18) Billy O'Dell	3.00	1.50	.90
(19) Gene Oliver	3.00	1.50	.90
(20) Chi Chi Olivo	3.00	1.50	.90
(21) Dan Osinki (Osinski)	3.00	1.50	.90
(22) Bob Sadowski	3.00	1.50	.90
(23) Bobby Tiefenauer	3.00	1.50	.90
(24) Joe Torre	4.50	2.25	1.25

1980 Milwaukee Brewers/ Pepsi Fan Club

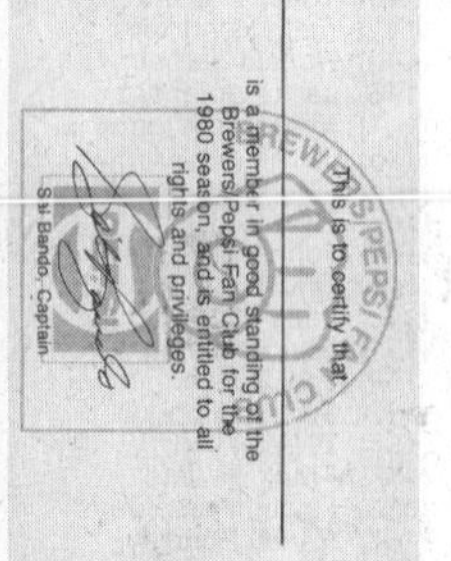

Star Milwaukee infielder Sal Bando is featured on this 2-1/2" x 3-1/2" membership card in a blue-bordered action pose. The back is printed in blue on white with both the team and soda logo.

	NM	EX	VG
Sal Bando	6.00	3.00	1.80

1912 Miner's Extra Series of Champions (T227)

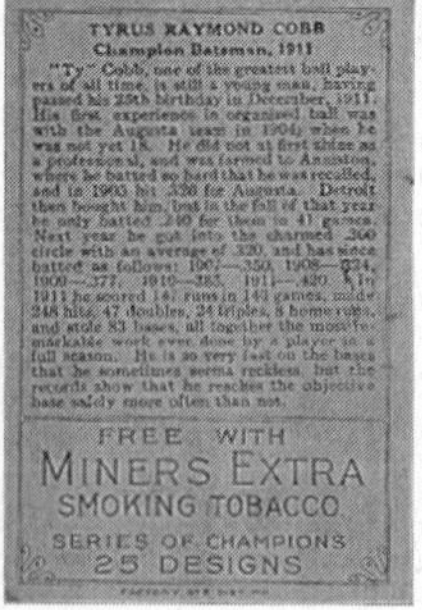

(See 1912 T227 Series of Champions for checklist, price guide.

1977 Minneapolis Star Twins Scrapbook

Between July 4-August 12, the Star printed one player "Scrapbook" picture each day in the sports section. While sizes vary somewhat, most are about 4-3/16" x 10-3/16". Enclosed in a dotted-line border are a player portrait photo, facsimile autograph, position, uniform number, team logo, career highlights and full stats. Because they are printed on newsprint, the pictures are subject to rapid deterioration.

	NM	EX	VG
Complete Set (36):	100.00	50.00	30.00
Common Player:	4.00	2.00	1.25
7/4 Rod Carew	12.00	6.00	3.50
7/5 Geoff Zahn	4.00	2.00	1.25
7/6 Luis Gomez	4.00	2.00	1.25
7/7 Glenn Adams	4.00	2.00	1.25
7/8 Lyman Bostock	6.00	3.00	1.75
7/9 Bob Gorinski	4.00	2.00	1.25
7/11 Butch Wynegar	4.00	2.00	1.25
7/12 Rob Wilfong	4.00	2.00	1.25
7/13 Dave Goltz	4.00	2.00	1.25
7/14 Bill Butler	4.00	2.00	1.25
7/15 Bob Randall	4.00	2.00	1.25
7/16 Jeff Holly	4.00	2.00	1.25
7/18 Gene Mauch	4.00	2.00	1.25
7/19 Walt Terrell	4.00	2.00	1.25
7/20 Rich Chiles	4.00	2.00	1.25
7/21 Paul Thormodsgard	4.00	2.00	1.25
7/22 Dave Johnson	4.00	2.00	1.25
7/23 Mike Cubbage	4.00	2.00	1.25
7/25 Larry Hisle	4.00	2.00	1.25
7/26 Don McMahon	4.00	2.00	1.25
7/27 Glenn Borgmann	4.00	2.00	1.25
7/28 Craig Kusick	4.00	2.00	1.25
7/29 Ron Schueler	4.00	2.00	1.25
7/30 Karl Kuehl	4.00	2.00	1.25
8/1 Roy Smalley	4.00	2.00	1.25
8/2 Tony Oliva	7.50	3.75	2.25
8/3 Jerry Zimmerman	4.00	2.00	1.25
8/4 Dan Ford	4.00	2.00	1.25
8/5 Don Carrithers	4.00	2.00	1.25
8/6 Tom Johnson	4.00	2.00	1.25
8/8 Pete Redfern	4.00	2.00	1.25
8/9 Tom Burgmeier	4.00	2.00	1.25
8/10 Bud Bulling	4.00	2.00	1.25
8/11 Gary Serum	4.00	2.00	1.25
8/12 Calvin Griffith	4.00	2.00	1.25

1977-78 Minnesota Twins Team Issue

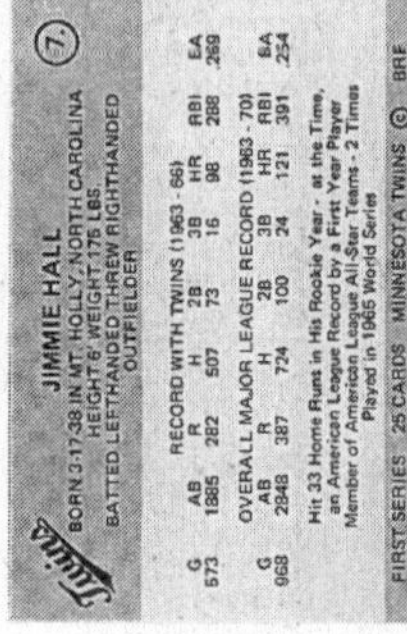

Produced by collector Barry Fritz, and sold by the team through its normal concession outlets, this set consists of two 25-card series. Cards 1-25 were issued in 1977; cards 26-50 in 1978. Measuring 2-5/8" x 3-3/4", card fronts feature quality color player poses with no other graphics. Backs are in black-and-white and have all player data, stats with the Twins and overall major league numbers, plus career highlights. Besides being sold as sets, the cards were also offered in uncut sheet form.

	NM	EX	VG
Complete Set (50):	35.00	17.50	10.00
Common Player:	1.00	.50	.30
1 Bob Allison	1.00	.50	.30
2 Earl Battey	1.00	.50	.30
3 Dave Boswell	1.00	.50	.30
4 Dean Chance	1.25	.60	.40
5 Jim Grant	1.25	.60	.40
6 Calvin Griffith	1.25	.60	.40
7 Jimmie Hall	1.00	.50	.30
8 Harmon Killebrew	6.00	3.00	1.75
9 Jim Lemon	1.00	.50	.30
10 Billy Martin	3.00	1.50	.90
11 Gene Mauch	1.00	.50	.30
12 Sam Mele	1.00	.50	.30
13 Metropolitan Stadium	1.50	.70	.45
14 Don Mincher	1.00	.50	.30
15 Tony Oliva	3.00	1.50	.90
16 Camilo Pascual	1.00	.50	.30
17 Jim Perry	1.25	.60	.40
18 Frank Quilici	1.00	.50	.30
19 Rich Reese	1.00	.50	.30
20 Bill Rigney	1.00	.50	.30
21 Cesar Tovar	1.00	.50	.30
22 Zoilo Versalles	1.00	.50	.30
23 Al Worthington	1.00	.50	.30
24 Jerry Zimmerman	1.00	.50	.30
25 Checklist / Souvenir List	1.00	.50	.30
26 Bernie Allen	1.00	.50	.30
27 Leo Cardenas	1.00	.50	.30
28 Ray Corbin	1.00	.50	.30
29 Joe Decker	1.00	.50	.30
30 Johnny Goryl	1.00	.50	.30
31 Tom Hall	1.00	.50	.30
32 Bill Hands	1.00	.50	.30

33	Jim Holt	1.00	.50	.30
34	Randy Hundley	1.00	.50	.30
35	Jerry Kindall	1.00	.50	.30
36	Johnny Klippstein	1.00	.50	.30
37	Jack Kralick	1.00	.50	.30
38	Jim Merritt	1.00	.50	.30
39	Joe Nossek	1.00	.50	.30
40	Ron Perranoski	1.00	.50	.30
41	Bill Pleis	1.00	.50	.30
42	Rick Renick	1.00	.50	.30
43	Jim Roland	1.00	.50	.30
44	Lee Stange	1.00	.50	.30
45	Dick Stigman	1.00	.50	.30
46	Danny Thompson	1.00	.50	.30
47	Ted Uhlaender	1.00	.50	.30
48	Sandy Valdespino	1.00	.50	.30
49	Dick Woodson	1.00	.50	.30
50	Checklist #26-50	1.00	.50	.30

1911-16 Mino Cigarettes (T216)

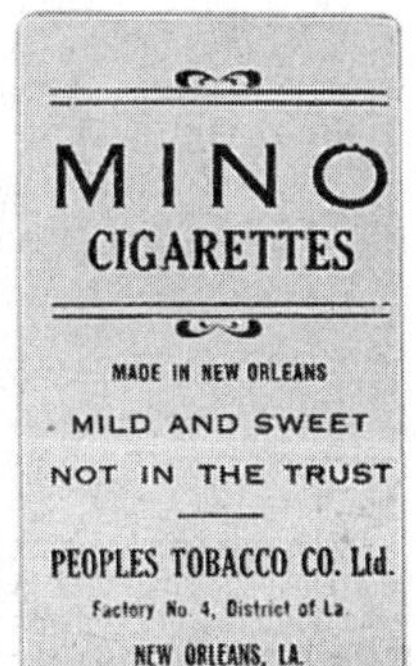

The T216 baseball card set, issued by several brands of the Peoples Tobacco Co., is the last of the Louisiana cigarette sets and the most confusing. Apparently issued over a period of several years between 1911 and 1916, the set employs the same pictures as several contemporary caramel and bakery sets. Positive identification can be made by the back of the cards. The Peoples Tobacco cards carry advertising for one of three brands of cigarettes: Kotton, Mino or Virginia Extra. The Kotton brand is the most common, while the Virginia Extra and Mino backs command a premium. T216 cards are found in two types; one has a glossy front finish, while a second scarcer type is printed on a thin paper. The thin paper cards command an additional 15% premium. The cards represent players from the American, National and Federal Leagues. Cards measure a nominal 1-1/2" x 2-5/8", though reasonable allowance for variance must be made on consideration of original standards for cutting.

		NM	EX	VG
	Common Player:	1,920	870.00	480.00
(1)	Jack Barry/Btg	1,920	870.00	480.00
(2)	Jack Barry/Fldg	1,920	870.00	480.00
(3)	Harry Bemis	1,920	870.00	480.00
(4a)	Chief Bender (Philadelphia, striped cap.)	4,200	1,890	1,050
(4b)	Chief Bender (Baltimore, striped cap.)	4,200	1,890	1,050
(5a)	Chief Bender (Philadelphia, white cap.)	4,200	1,890	1,050
(5b)	Chief Bender (Baltimore, white cap.)	4,200	1,890	1,050
(6)	Bill Bergen	1,920	870.00	480.00
(7a)	Bob Bescher (Cincinnati)	1,920	870.00	480.00
(7b)	Bob Bescher (St. Louis)	1,920	870.00	480.00
(8)	Roger Bresnahan	4,200	1,890	1,050
(9)	Al Bridwell/Btg	1,920	870.00	480.00
(10a)	Al Bridwell/Sliding (New York)	1,920	870.00	480.00
(10b)	Al Bridwell/Sliding (St. Louis)	1,920	870.00	480.00
(11)	Donie Bush	1,920	870.00	480.00
(12)	Doc Casey	1,920	870.00	480.00
(13)	Frank Chance	4,200	1,890	1,050
(14a)	Hal Chase/Fldg (New York)	1,920	870.00	480.00
(14b)	Hal Chase/Fldg (Buffalo)	1,920	870.00	480.00
(15)	Hal Chase/Portrait	1,920	870.00	480.00
(16a)	Ty Cobb/Standing (Detroit Am.)	36,000	16,200	9,000
(16b)	Ty Cobb/Standing (Detroit Americans)	36,000	16,200	9,000
(17)	Ty Cobb/Btg (Detroit Americans)	36,000	16,200	9,000
(18a)	Eddie Collins (Phila. Am.)	4,200	1,890	1,050
(18b)	Eddie Collins (Phila. Amer.)	4,200	1,890	1,050
(19)	Eddie Collins (Chicago)	4,200	1,890	1,050
(20a)	Sam Crawford (Small print.)	4,200	1,890	1,050
(20b)	Sam Crawford (Large print.)	4,200	1,890	1,050
(21)	Harry Davis	1,920	870.00	480.00
(22)	Ray Demmitt	1,920	870.00	480.00
(23)	Art Devlin	1,920	870.00	480.00
(24a)	Wild Bill Donovan (Detroit)	1,920	870.00	480.00
(24b)	Wild Bill Donovan (New York)	1,920	870.00	480.00
(25a)	Red Dooin (Philadelphia)	1,920	870.00	480.00
(25b)	Red Dooin (Cincinnati)	1,920	870.00	480.00
(26a)	Mickey Doolan (Philadelphia)	1,920	870.00	480.00
(26b)	Mickey Doolan (Baltimore)	1,920	870.00	480.00
(27)	Patsy Dougherty	1,920	870.00	480.00
(28a)	Larry Doyle (N.Y. Nat'l,) (W/bat.)	1,920	870.00	480.00
(28b)	Larry Doyle (New York Nat'l) (W/bat.)	1,920	870.00	480.00
(29)	Larry Doyle/Throwing	1,920	870.00	480.00
(30)	Clyde Engle	1,920	870.00	480.00
(31a)	Johnny Evers (Chicago)	4,200	1,890	1,050
(31b)	Johnny Evers (Boston)	4,200	1,890	1,050
(32)	Art Fromme	1,920	870.00	480.00
(33a)	George Gibson (Pittsburg Nat'l, back view.)	1,920	870.00	480.00
(33b)	George Gibson (Pittsburgh Nat'l., back view.)	1,920	870.00	480.00
(34a)	George Gibson (Pittsburg Nat'l, front view.)	1,920	870.00	480.00
(34b)	George Gibson (Pittsburgh Nat'l., front view.)	1,920	870.00	480.00
(35a)	Topsy Hartsel (Phila. Am.)	1,920	870.00	480.00
(35b)	Topsy Hartsel (Phila. Amer.)	1,920	870.00	480.00
(36)	Roy Hartzell/Btg	1,920	870.00	480.00
(37)	Roy Hartzell/Catching	1,920	870.00	480.00
(38a)	Fred Jacklitsch (Philadelphia)	1,920	870.00	480.00
(38b)	Fred Jacklitsch (Baltimore)	1,920	870.00	480.00
(39a)	Hughie Jennings (Orange background.)	4,200	1,890	1,050
(39b)	Hughie Jennings (Red background.)	4,200	1,890	1,050
(40)	Red Kleinow	1,920	870.00	480.00
(41a)	Otto Knabe (Philadelphia)	1,920	870.00	480.00
(41b)	Otto Knabe (Baltimore)	1,920	870.00	480.00
(42)	Jack Knight	1,920	870.00	480.00
(43a)	Nap Lajoie/Fldg (Philadelphia)	4,800	2,160	1,200
(43b)	Nap Lajoie/Fldg (Cleveland)	4,800	2,160	1,200
(44)	Nap Lajoie/Portrait	4,800	2,160	1,200
(45a)	Hans Lobert (Cincinnati)	1,920	870.00	480.00
(45b)	Hans Lobert (New York)	1,920	870.00	480.00
(46)	Sherry Magee	1,920	870.00	480.00
(47)	Rube Marquard	4,200	1,890	1,050
(48a)	Christy Matthewson (Mathewson) (Large print.)	18,000	8,100	4,500
(48b)	Christy Matthewson (Mathewson) (Small print.)	18,000	8,100	4,550
(49a)	John McGraw (Large print.)	4,200	1,890	1,050
(49b)	John McGraw (Small print.)	4,200	1,890	1,050
(50)	Larry McLean	1,920	870.00	480.00
(51)	George McQuillan	1,920	870.00	480.00
(52)	Dots Miller/Btg	1,920	870.00	480.00
(53a)	Dots Miller/Fldg (Pittsburg)	1,920	870.00	480.00
(53b)	Dots Miller/Fldg (St. Louis)	1,920	870.00	480.00
(54a)	Danny Murphy (Philadelphia)	1,920	870.00	480.00
(54b)	Danny Murphy (Brooklyn)	1,920	870.00	480.00
(55)	Rebel Oakes	1,920	870.00	480.00
(56)	Bill O'Hara	1,920	870.00	480.00
(57)	Eddie Plank	5,400	2,430	1,350
(58a)	Germany Schaefer (Washington)	1,920	870.00	480.00
(58b)	Germany Schaefer (Newark)	1,920	870.00	480.00
(59)	Admiral Schlei	1,920	870.00	480.00
(60)	Boss Schmidt	1,920	870.00	480.00
(61)	Johnny Seigle	1,920	870.00	480.00
(62)	Dave Shean	1,920	870.00	480.00
(63)	Boss Smith (Schmidt)	1,920	870.00	480.00
(64)	Tris Speaker	7,800	3,510	1,950
(65)	Oscar Stanage	1,920	870.00	480.00
(66)	George Stovall	1,920	870.00	480.00
(67)	Jeff Sweeney	1,920	870.00	480.00
(68a)	Joe Tinker/Btg (Chicago Nat'l)	4,200	1,890	1,050
(68b)	Joe Tinker/Btg (Chicago Feds)	4,200	1,890	1,050
(69)	Joe Tinker/Portrait	4,200	1,890	1,050
(70a)	Honus Wagner/Btg (S.S.)	30,000	13,500	7,500
(70b)	Honus Wagner/Btg (2b)	30,000	13,500	7,500
(71a)	Honus Wagner/Throwing (S.S.)	30,000	13,500	7,500
(71b)	Honus Wagner/Throwing (2b)	30,000	13,500	7,500
(72)	Hooks Wiltse	1,920	870.00	480.00
(73)	Cy Young	15,000	6,750	3,750
(74a)	Heinie Zimmerman (2b.)	1,920	870.00	480.00
(74b)	Heinie Zimmerman (3b.)	1,920	870.00	480.00

1962 Molinari's Restaurant Frank Malzone

This black-and-white J.D. McCarthy postcard of the former Red Sox infielder was given to patrons of an Oneonta, N.Y., restaurant in which Malzone was a partner with his brother-in-law. The card measures 3-1/4" x 5-1/2" and has a facsimile autograph on front. A similar promotional postcard is listed under Ticoa Tires.

	NM	EX	VG
Frank Malzone	15.00	7.50	4.50

1911 Monarch Typewriter Philadelphia A's

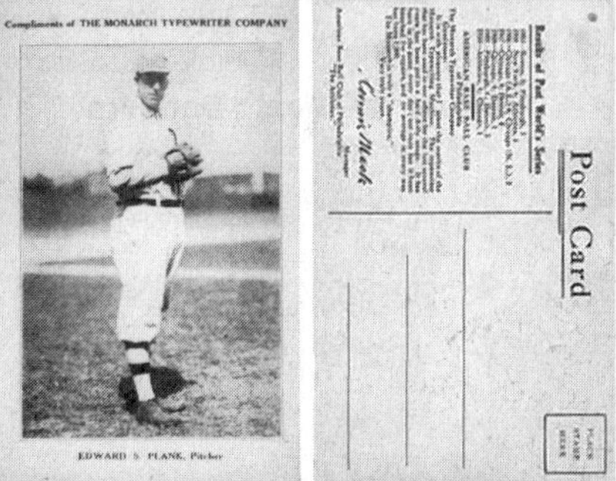

These black-and-white postcards (about 3-1/2" x 5") depict the World Champion 1910 Philadelphia A's. Fronts have posed player photos with a black pin stripe and white borders. The player's name and position are printed in the bottom border. "Compliments of THE MONARCH TYPEWRITER COMPANY" appears in the top border. Backs are rather standard postcard fare, but include data about the World Series between 1903-1910.

		NM	EX	VG
	Complete Set (6):	8,000	4,000	2,400
	Common Player:	1,150	575.00	350.00
(1)	John J. Barry	1,150	575.00	350.00
(2)	Chief Bender	1,650	825.00	500.00
(3)	Eddie Collins	1,650	825.00	500.00
(4)	Rube Oldring	1,150	575.00	350.00
(5)	Eddie Plank	1,650	825.00	500.00
(6)	Ira Thomas	1,150	575.00	350.00

1970 Montreal Expos Player Pins

Produced by "Best in Sports" for sale in the Montreal area for 35¢ apiece, these 1-3/4" diameter pinbacks feature action poses of the players set against a white background. The player's name at top is in black.

		NM	EX	VG
	Complete Set (16):	350.00	175.00	100.00
	Common Player:	25.00	12.50	7.50
(1)	John Bateman	25.00	12.50	7.50
(2)	Ron Brand	25.00	12.50	7.50
(3)	Ron Fairly	25.00	12.50	7.50
(4)	Mack Jones	25.00	12.50	7.50
(5)	Coco Laboy	25.00	12.50	7.50
(6)	Gene Mauch	25.00	12.50	7.50
(7)	Dan McGinn	25.00	12.50	7.50
(8)	Adolfo Phillips	25.00	12.50	7.50
(9)	Claude Raymond	25.00	12.50	7.50
(10)	Steve Renko	25.00	12.50	7.50
(11)	Marv Staehle	25.00	12.50	7.50
(12)	Rusty Staub	40.00	20.00	12.00
(13)	Bill Stoneman	25.00	12.50	7.50
(14)	Gary Sutherland	25.00	12.50	7.50
(15)	Bobby Wine	25.00	12.50	7.50
(16)	Expos Team Logo	10.00	5.00	3.00

1972-76 Montreal Expos Matchbook Covers

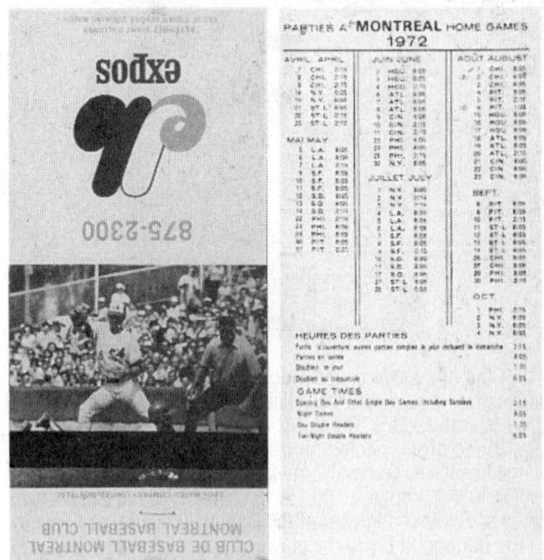

In 1972, 1973 and 1976, the Eddy Match Co., Montreal, issued series of seven matchbook covers featuring action photos. Fronts have a red, white and blue team logo on a white background. Backs have a bluetone action photo with the match-striking surface across the lower portion. The player in the photo is not identified on the matchbook. Inside of the 2-1/8" x 4-3/8" cover, printed in blue, is the team home schedule for that season. The unnumbered matchbook covers are checklisted here alphabetically by year. Values shown are for empty matchbooks; full matchbooks would be valued at 2-3X.

		NM	EX	VG
	Complete Set (21):	40.00	20.00	12.00
	Common Player:	4.00	2.00	1.25
	1972			
(1)	Boots Day	4.00	2.00	1.25
(2)	Ron Fairly	4.00	2.00	1.25
(3)	Ron Hunt	4.00	2.00	1.25
(4)	Steve Renko	4.00	2.00	1.25
(5)	Rusty Staub	6.00	3.00	1.75
(6)	Bobby Wine	4.00	2.00	1.25
(7)	Hunt's 50th HBP (Scoreboard)	4.00	2.00	1.25

		NM	EX	VG
	1973			
(1)	Tim Foli	4.00	2.00	1.25
(2)	Ron Hunt	4.00	2.00	1.25
(3)	Mike Jorgensen	4.00	2.00	1.25
(4)	Gene Mauch	4.00	2.00	1.25
(5)	Balor Moore	4.00	2.00	1.25
(6)	Ken Singleton	4.00	2.00	1.25
(7)	Bill Stoneman	4.00	2.00	1.25
	1976			
(1)	Barry Foote	4.00	2.00	1.25
(2)	Mike Jorgensen	4.00	2.00	1.25
(3)	Pete Mackanin	4.00	2.00	1.25
(4)	Dale Murray	4.00	2.00	1.25
(5)	Larry Parrish	4.00	2.00	1.25
(6)	Steve Rogers	4.00	2.00	1.25
(7)	Dan Warthen	4.00	2.00	1.25

1916 Morehouse Baking Co.

BOYS and GIRLS

Here's your chance to get a complete set of 200 of the Best Ball Players in the Big Leagues. These photos will be wrapped in

SUNLIGHT 10c BREAD

When you get fifty, with no two alike, you may keep the photos but show them at our office and get a Dandy baseball and bat, or a nice long jumprope FREE

MOREHOUSE BAKING CO.
OFFICE 7 MILL STREET
LAWRENCE : MASS.

While this 200-card set is most often found with blank backs or with the advertising of "The Sporting News" on the back, a number of scarcer regional advertisers also can be found. This Massachusetts baker inserted the cards into bread loaves and offered a redemption program. Since cards are known that correspond to both versions of the parent M101 Blank Backs, it not known whether the bakery's version parallels M101-4 and M101-5 or is a hybrid of the two.

PREMIUM: 2X

(See 1916 M101-4 and M101-5 Blank Backs for checklist and price guide.)

1907 Morgan Stationery "Red Belt" Postcards

Only one player is individually identified in this series of postcards, though the identities of others have been discovered over the years. The 3-1/2" x 5-1/2" cards have colorized player and group photos on front with a title printed in white in the lower-left corner. Some photos were taken at the Reds ballpark, then known as the Palace of Fans. Cards include pictures of Reds and Pirates of the National League, and Toledo of the minors. Many of the players have bright red belts, thus the set's nickname. Postcard backs have a credit line: "The Morgan Stationery Co., Cincinnati, O., Publishers." The unnumbered cards are checklisted here alphabetically by title.

		NM	EX	VG
Complete Set (12):		3,250	1,625	950.00
Common Card:		275.00	135.00	80.00
(1)	After A High One	275.00	135.00	80.00
(2)	A Home Run	275.00	135.00	80.00
(3)	Hit & Run	275.00	135.00	80.00
(4)	In Consultation	275.00	135.00	80.00
(5)	It's All in the Game - "Noise" (Pat Moran)	275.00	135.00	80.00
(6)	Huggins Second Baseman Par Excellence (Miller Huggins) (Stadium background.)	325.00	160.00	95.00
(7)	Huggins Second Baseman Par Excellance (Miller Huggins) (Low buildings in background.)	325.00	160.00	95.00
(8)	Opening of the Season 1907	275.00	135.00	80.00
(9)	Out to the Long Green	275.00	135.00	80.00
(10)	Practise (Practice) Makes Perfect (Sam Leever)	275.00	135.00	80.00
(11)	Safe	275.00	135.00	80.00
(12)	Use Two If Necessary (Hans Lobert)	275.00	135.00	80.00

1959 Morrell Meats Dodgers

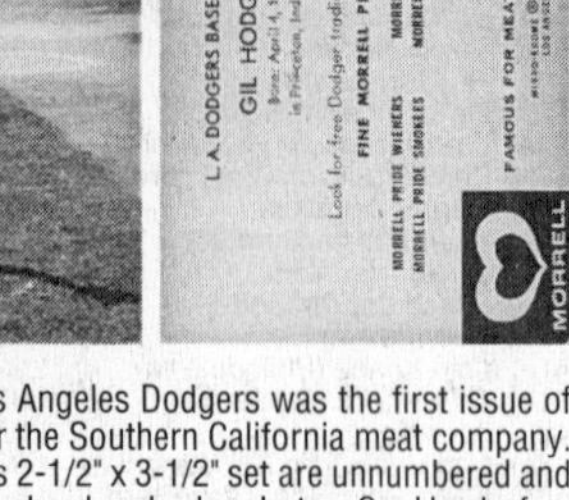

This set of Los Angeles Dodgers was the first issue of a three-year run for the Southern California meat company. The 12 cards in this 2-1/2" x 3-1/2" set are unnumbered and feature full-frame, unbordered color photos. Card backs feature a company ad and list only the player's name, birthdate and birthplace. Two errors exist in the set; the cards naming Clem Labine and Norm Larker show photos of Stan Williams and Joe Pignatano, respectively.

		NM	EX	VG
Complete Set (12):		3,500	1,750	1,000
Common Player:		100.00	50.00	30.00
(1)	Don Drysdale	200.00	100.00	60.00
(2)	Carl Furillo	150.00	75.00	45.00
(3)	Jim Gilliam	125.00	60.00	35.00
(4)	Gil Hodges	200.00	100.00	60.00
(5)	Sandy Koufax	2,000	1,000	600.00
(6)	Clem Labine (Photo actually Stan Williams.)	100.00	50.00	30.00
(7)	Norm Larker (Photo actually Joe Pignatano.)	100.00	50.00	30.00
(8)	Charlie Neal	100.00	50.00	30.00
(9)	Johnny Podres	125.00	60.00	35.00
(10)	John Roseboro	100.00	50.00	30.00
(11)	Duke Snider	200.00	100.00	60.00
(12)	Don Zimmer	125.00	60.00	35.00

1960 Morrell Meats Dodgers

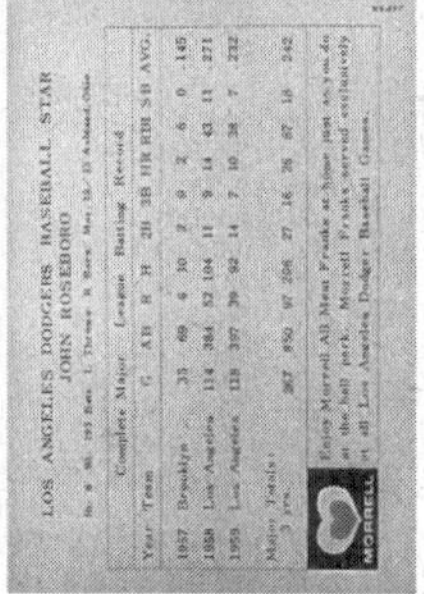

This 12-card set is the same 2-1/2" x 3-1/2" size as the 1959 set, and again features unbordered color card fronts. Five of the players included are new to the Morrell's sets. Card backs in 1960 list player statistics and brief personal data on each player. Cards of Gil Hodges, Carl Furillo and Duke Snider are apparently scarcer than others in the set.

		NM	EX	VG
Complete Set (12):		2,200	1,100	650.00
Common Player:		80.00	40.00	24.00
(1)	Walt Alston	90.00	45.00	27.50
(2)	Roger Craig	80.00	40.00	24.00
(3)	Don Drysdale	120.00	60.00	35.00
(4)	Carl Furillo	225.00	110.00	65.00
(5)	Gil Hodges	400.00	200.00	120.00
(6)	Sandy Koufax	500.00	250.00	150.00
(7)	Wally Moon	80.00	40.00	24.00
(8)	Charlie Neal	80.00	40.00	24.00
(9)	Johnny Podres	80.00	40.00	24.00
(10)	John Roseboro	80.00	40.00	24.00
(11)	Larry Sherry	80.00	40.00	24.00
(12)	Duke Snider	450.00	225.00	135.00

1961 Morrell Meats Dodgers

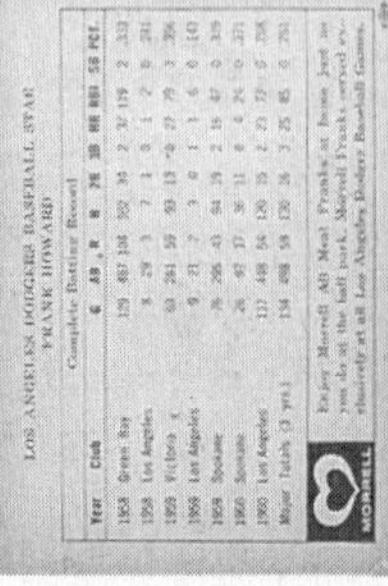

The Morrell set shrunk to just six cards in 1961, with a format almost identical to the 1960 cards. Card fronts are again full-color, unbordered photos. Player statistics appear on the backs. The unnumbered cards measure a slightly smaller 2-1/4" x 3-1/4", and comparison of statistical information can also distinguish the cards from the 1960 version.

		NM	EX	VG
Complete Set (6):		900.00	450.00	275.00
Common Player:		90.00	45.00	27.50
(1)	Tommy Davis	90.00	45.00	27.50
(2)	Don Drysdale	120.00	60.00	36.00
(3)	Frank Howard	90.00	45.00	27.50
(4)	Sandy Koufax	450.00	225.00	135.00
(5)	Norm Larker	90.00	45.00	27.50
(6)	Maury Wills	90.00	45.00	27.00

1910 Morton's Buster Brown Bread Tigers Pins (PD2)

Dating of these two issues is arbitrary, since there is no indication on the pins of vintage. Both sets feature members of the Detroit Tigers, American League champions of 1907-09. The Buster Brown Bread pins measure 1-1/4" in diameter and have a small black-and-white player portrait photo surrounded by a yellow border. Artwork to the left depicts Buster Brown with a tiger holding a blue banner with the Morton's name. The player photos carry no identification, which may make the checklist presented here somewhat tentative.

		NM	EX	VG
Complete Set (15):		10,000	5,000	3,000
Common Player:		450.00	225.00	135.00
(1)	Jimmy Archer	450.00	225.00	135.00
(2)	Heinie Beckendorf	450.00	225.00	135.00
(3)	Donie Bush	450.00	225.00	135.00
(4)	Ty Cobb	4,000	2,000	1,200
(5)	Sam Crawford	750.00	375.00	225.00
(6)	Wild Bill Donovan	450.00	225.00	135.00
(7)	Hughie Jennings	750.00	375.00	225.00
(8)	Tom Jones	450.00	225.00	135.00
(9)	Red Killefer	450.00	225.00	135.00
(10)	George Moriarty	450.00	225.00	135.00
(11)	George Mullin	450.00	225.00	135.00
(12)	Claude Rossman	450.00	225.00	135.00
(13)	"Germany" Schaefer	450.00	225.00	135.00
(14)	Ed Summers	450.00	225.00	135.00
(15)	Ed Willett	450.00	225.00	135.00

1910 Morton's Pennant Winner Bread Tigers Pins

The American League champion Detroit Tigers (1907-1909) are featured on this set of pins advertising -- appropriately -- Pennant Winner Bread. The 1-1/4" pins have black-and-white player photos surrounded by a yellow border. A Detroit banner with tiger head superimposed is at bottom. The players are not identified anywhere on the pins, which may make this checklist somewhat arbitrary.

		NM	EX	VG
Complete Set (16):		12,000	6,000	3,500
Common Player:		500.00	250.00	150.00
(1)	Jimmy Archer	500.00	250.00	150.00
(2)	Heinie Beckendorf	500.00	250.00	150.00
(3)	Donie Bush	500.00	250.00	150.00
(4)	Ty Cobb	4,000	2,000	1,200
(5)	Sam Crawford	750.00	375.00	225.00
(6)	Wild Bill Donovan	500.00	250.00	150.00
(7)	Hughie Jennings	750.00	375.00	225.00
(8)	Davy Jones	500.00	250.00	150.00
(9)	Matty McIntyre	500.00	250.00	150.00
(10)	George Moriarty	500.00	250.00	150.00
(11)	George Mullin	500.00	250.00	150.00
(12)	Claude Rossman	500.00	250.00	150.00
(13)	Herman Schaeffer (Schaefer)	500.00	250.00	150.00
(14)	Charles Schmidt	500.00	250.00	150.00

		NM	EX	VG
(15)	Ed Summers	500.00	250.00	150.00
(16)	Ed Willett	500.00	250.00	150.00

1916 Mothers' Bread (D303)

Apparently issued in 1916 by the New Orleans branch of the General Baking Co., these unnumbered cards measure 1-1/2" x 2-3/4". The player pictures and format of the cards are identical to the 1915 American Caramel (E106) and 1914 General Baking Co. (D303) sets, but this issue carries an advertisement for Mothers' Bread on back. This version is much scarcer than the General Baking or American Caramel types. It is known that at least one player appears in this set who is not found in E106/D303 and many players are found with team, league and postion changes. The checklist here is incomplete and additions are welcome. Gaps have been left in the assigned numbering for future additions.

		NM	EX	VG
Common Player:		2,500	1,500	900.00
(1)	Chief Bender (Brooklyn Nat'l.)	6,000	2,700	1,500
(2)	Bob Bescher (St. Louis Nat'l)	2,500	1,500	900.00
(3)	Rube Bressler (Phila. Am.)	2,500	1,500	900.00
(4)	Donie Bush (Detroit American)	2,500	1,500	900.00
(5)	Hal Chase/Portrait (Cincinnati Nat'l.)	3,900	1,750	950.00
(6)	Bill Donovan (N.Y. Amer.)	2,500	1,500	900.00
(7)	Larry Doyle (N.Y. Nat'l)	2,500	1,500	900.00
(8)	Happy Felsch (Chicago Am.) (Picture actually Ray Demmitt.)	7,500	3,375	1,875
(9)	George Gibson	2,500	1,500	900.00
(11)	Roy Hartzell	2,500	1,500	900.00
(15)	Nap Lajoie (Phila. Americans)	6,000	2,700	1,500
(16)	Hans Lobert (New York Nat'l)	2,500	1,500	900.00
(17)	William Louden (Cincinnati Nat'l)(Picture is Otto Knabe.)	2,500	1,500	900.00
(20)	Rube Marquard (Brooklyn Nat'l)	6,000	2,700	1,500
(21)	Christy Matthewson (Mathewson)	12,500	5,625	3,125
(22)	Billy Meyer (Phila. Am.) (Picture is Fred Jacklitsch.)	2,500	1,500	900.00
(24)	Ray Morgan (Washington Am.) (Picture is Mike Doolan.)	2,500	1,500	900.00
(26)	Eddie Plank (St. Louis Am.)	10,000	4,500	2,500
(28)	Tris Speaker (Cleveland Am.)	7,500	3,375	1,875
(30)	Joe Tinker/Portrait (Mgr. Chicago Am.)	6,000	2,700	1,500
(33)	Honus Wagner/Btg	30,000	15,000	5,000
(35)	Buck Weaver/Btg (Picture is Joe Tinker.)	5,000	2,250	1,250

1919 Mother's Bread

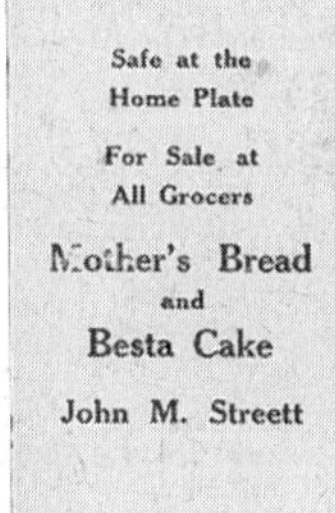

Essentially a version of the W514 strip cards with an advertisement on the back, the Mother's Bread cards are much scarcer than the blank-backs with which they share a checklist. The cards are 1-1/2" x 2-1/2" with color drawings of the players on front, along with name, position, team, league and card number.

(See 1919 W514 for checklist; cards valued at 2.5X-3X W514 version.)

1955 Motorola Bob Feller Premium Photo

Dating of this promotional photo is approximate, based on the uniform details. The 8" x 10" glossy black-and-white

photo features a facsimile autograph. Feller is described on the picture as "CONSULTANT ON YOUTH ACTIVITIES" for Motorola, Inc. The picture is blank-backed and its method of distribution is unknown.

	NM	EX	VG
Bob Feller	60.00	30.00	18.00

1976 Motorola

This set of (mostly) Hall of Famers was issued in conjunction with the annual convention of Motorola electronics dealers. Cards were issued singly in a wax wrapper with a piece of bubblegum. Sepia player photos are featured in an oval at center. Player identification and a career highlight are in the white frame around the photo. A sales message appears in a white box at bottom. Overall borders are rust colored. Backs have information about various Motorola products.

		NM	EX	VG
Complete Set (11):		25.00	12.50	7.50
Common Player:		2.50	1.25	.70
1	Honus Wagner	4.00	2.00	1.25
2	Nap Lajoie	2.50	1.25	.70
3	Ty Cobb	7.50	3.75	2.25
4	William Wambsganss	2.50	1.25	.70
5	Three Finger Brown	2.50	1.25	.70
6	Ray Schalk	2.50	1.25	.70
7	Frank Frisch	2.50	1.25	.70
8	Pud Galvin	2.50	1.25	.70
9	Babe Ruth	15.00	7.50	4.50
10	Grover Cleveland Alexander	3.00	1.50	.90
11	Frank L. Chance	2.50	1.25	.70

1943 M.P. & Co. (R302-1)

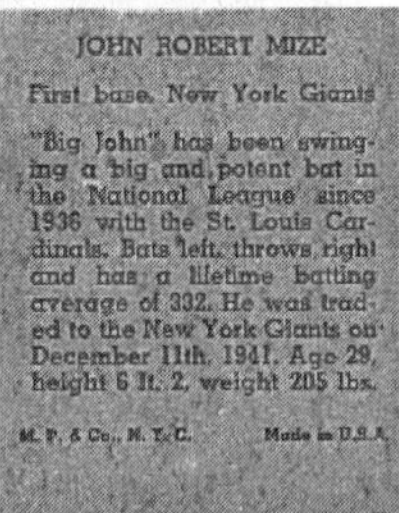
JOHN ROBERT MIZE

First base, New York Giants

"Big John" has been swinging a big and potent bat in the National League since 1936 with the St. Louis Cardinals. Bats left, throws right and has a lifetime batting average of 332. He was traded to the New York Giants on December 11th, 1941. Age 29, height 6 ft. 2, weight 205 lbs.

M. P. & Co., N. Y. C. Made in U.S.A.

One of the few baseball card sets issued during World War II, this set of unnumbered cards, measuring approximately 2-5/8" x 2-1/4" was produced in two major types and at least five subtypes. The cards feature crude color drawings that have little resemblance to the player named. They were originally produced in strips and sold inexpensively in candy stores. The backs contain brief player write-ups. One major type has the player's full name, team and position on back. The second type has only the player's first and last name and position on back; no team. Variations in ink color and wording of the biographies on back are also seen. M.P. & Co. stands for Michael Pressner and Co., a New York City novelty and carnival supply firm.

		NM	EX	VG
Complete Set (24):		1,750	625.00	275.00
Common Player:		40.00	15.00	5.00
(1)	Ernie Bonham	40.00	15.00	5.00
(2)	Lou Boudreau	60.00	20.00	10.00
(3)	Dolph Camilli	40.00	15.00	5.00
(4)	Mort Cooper	40.00	15.00	5.00
(5)	Walker Cooper	40.00	15.00	5.00
(6)	Joe Cronin	60.00	20.00	10.00
(7)	Hank Danning	40.00	15.00	5.00
(8)	Bill Dickey	75.00	25.00	10.00
(9)	Joe DiMaggio	300.00	100.00	45.00
(10)	Bobby Feller	100.00	35.00	15.00
(11)	Jimmy Foxx	75.00	25.00	10.00
(12)	Hank Greenberg	100.00	35.00	15.00
(13)	Stan Hack	40.00	15.00	5.00
(14)	Tom Henrich	40.00	15.00	5.00
(15)	Carl Hubbell	60.00	20.00	10.00
(16)	Joe Medwick	60.00	20.00	10.00
(17)	John Mize	60.00	20.00	10.00
(18)	Lou Novikoff	40.00	15.00	5.00
(19)	Mel Ott	60.00	20.00	10.00
(20)	Pee Wee Reese	75.00	25.00	10.00
(21)	Pete Reiser	40.00	15.00	5.00
(22)	Charlie Ruffing	60.00	20.00	10.00
(23)	Johnny VanderMeer	40.00	15.00	5.00
(24)	Ted Williams	250.00	85.00	35.00

1949 M.P. & Co. (R302-2)

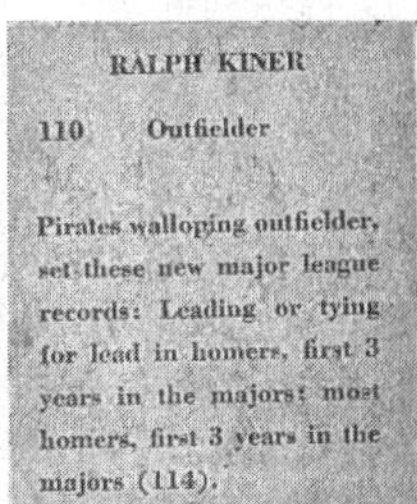

This set appears to be a re-issue of M.P. & Co.'s 1943 cards with several different players (although reusing the same pictures as the '43s). The cards, which measure about 2-11/16" x 2-1/4", feature crude drawings of generic baseball players which have little resemblance to the player named. Most backs include card number and player information. The numbering sequence begins with card 100. Numbers 104, 118, and 120 are unknown, while three of the cards are unnumbered. The set is assigned the American Card Catalog number R302-2.

		NM	EX	VG
Complete Set (25):		1,750	575.00	275.00
Common Player:		45.00	16.00	7.00
100	Lou Boudreau	60.00	20.00	9.00
101	Ted Williams	250.00	85.00	35.00
102	Buddy Kerr	45.00	16.00	7.00
103	Bobby Feller	75.00	25.00	10.00
104	Unknown			
105	Joe DiMaggio	325.00	115.00	50.00
106	Pee Wee Reese	75.00	25.00	10.00
107	Ferris Fain	45.00	16.00	7.00
108	Andy Pafko	45.00	16.00	7.00
109	Del Ennis	45.00	16.00	7.00
110	Ralph Kiner	60.00	20.00	9.00
111	Nippy Jones	45.00	16.00	7.00
112	Del Rice	45.00	16.00	7.00
113	Hank Sauer	45.00	16.00	7.00
114	Gil Coan	45.00	16.00	7.00
115	Eddie Joost	45.00	16.00	7.00
116	Alvin Dark	45.00	16.00	7.00
117	Larry Berra	75.00	25.00	10.00
118	Unknown			
119	Bob Lemon	60.00	20.00	9.00
120	Unknown			
121	Johnny Pesky	45.00	16.00	7.00
122	Johnny Sain	45.00	16.00	7.00
123	Hoot Evers	45.00	16.00	7.00
124	Larry Doby	60.00	20.00	9.00
----	Jimmy Foxx	100.00	35.00	15.00
----	Tom Henrich	45.00	16.00	7.00
----	Al Kozar	45.00	16.00	7.00

1948-49 M.P. & Co. Photoprints

One of several 1930s-1940s kits for do-it-yourself production of photos, this issue was produced in New York City by the novelty firm M.P. & Co. A complete outfit consists of a film negative and a piece of light-sensitive paper for producing the photo. The negative and resulting print measure about 2" x 2-1/4". The issue includes 13 subjects, mostly non-sport, but includes Babe Ruth.

	NM	EX	VG
Babe Ruth (Negative)	300.00	150.00	90.00
Babe Ruth (Print)	75.00	37.50	22.00

1976 Mr. Softee Iron-Ons

Anecdotal evidence connects these iron-on transfers with the Mr. Softee dairy chain. About 4-1/2" x 6" inches, the color transfers have a player portrait on a baseball background, very similar in format to the 1978 Royal Crown Cola iron-ons. Like the RC pieces, the pictures have team logos removed from caps. The Mr. Softees include the team nickname beneath the player picture, along with a Players Association logo and an undated Quaker copyright line. The extent of the checklist is unknown.

		NM	EX	VG
Common Player:		4.00	2.00	1.25
(1)	George Brett	10.00	5.00	3.00
(2)	Jim Hunter	6.00	3.00	1.75
(3)	Randy Jones	4.00	2.00	1.25
(4)	Dave Kingman	5.00	2.50	1.50
(5)	Jerry Koosman	4.00	2.00	1.25
(6)	Fred Lynn	5.00	2.50	1.50
(7)	Joe Morgan	6.00	3.00	1.75
(8)	Thurman Munson	10.00	5.00	3.00
(9)	Amos Otis	4.00	2.00	1.25
(10)	Bill Russell	4.00	2.00	1.25
(11)	Nolan Ryan	12.00	6.00	3.60
(12)	Mike Schmidt	10.00	5.00	3.00
(13)	Tom Seaver	10.00	5.00	3.00

1977 Mrs. Carter's Bread Sports Illustrated Covers

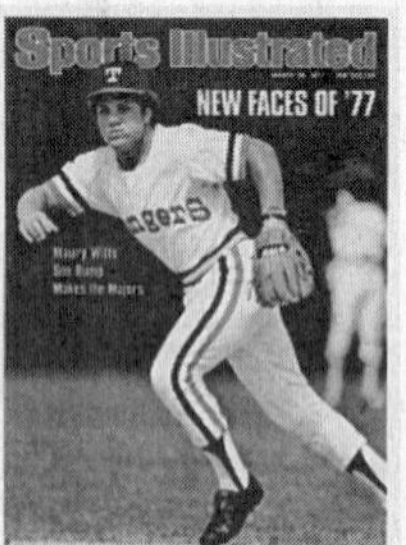

This two-sport set was issued by Mrs. Carter's Bread. Fronts of the 3-1/2" x 4-3/4" cards reproduce SI covers in full color, surrounded by a white border. Backs have a special offer for SI subscriptions, and are printed in black and blue on white. Despite the higher card numbers, it does not appear any more than five were ever issued.

		NM	EX	VG
Complete Set (5):		35.00	17.50	10.00
Common Card:		3.00	1.50	.90
(1)	George Brett	25.00	12.50	7.50
(2)	George Foster	4.00	2.00	1.25
(3)	Bump Wills	4.00	2.00	1.25
(4)	Oakland Wins a Big One (Football)	4.00	2.00	1.25
(5)	Michigan is No. 1 (Football)	6.00	3.00	1.75

1921 Mrs. Sherlock's Bread Pins

The date of issue for these pins is uncertain. The 7/8" diameter pins feature black-and-white player photos with a red border. The player's last name and team are printed beneath the photo; above is "Mrs. Sherlock's Home Made Bread." The set is one of several sponsored by the Toledo bakery. The Babe Ruth pin was reproduced circa 1999 in 1-3/4" size; it has no collectible value.

		NM	EX	VG
Complete Set (10):		4,750	2,400	1,400
Common Player:		100.00	50.00	30.00
(1)	Grover Alexander	350.00	175.00	100.00
(2)	Ty Cobb	1,700	850.00	425.00
(3)	Rogers Hornsby	375.00	185.00	110.00
(4)	Walter Johnson	375.00	185.00	110.00
(5)	Rabbit Maranville	300.00	150.00	90.00
(6)	Pat Moran	100.00	50.00	30.00
(7)	"Babe" Ruth	2,200	1,100	650.00
(8)	George Sisler	300.00	150.00	90.00
(9)	Tris Speaker	375.00	185.00	110.00
(10)	Honus Wagner	700.00	350.00	210.00

1975-96 MSA

(See listings under Michael Schechter Associates.)

1916 M101-5 Blank Backs

The Chicago printing and publishing firm of Felix Mendelsohn was the originator of this card set, which is often

found bearing advertising on back of several businesses from around the country. Mendelsohn is not mentioned on the cards, which are blank-backed. Fronts of the 1-5/8" x 3" black-and-white cards have a player photo, name, position abbreviation, team and card number. The set was prepared in advance of the 1916 season and offered in ads in The Sporting News for $1, or a framed uncut sheet for $2.50. The blank-backs are the most common version of M101-5. There were at least two printings of the set, creating several variations to correct errors or replace players.

		NM	EX	VG
Complete Set (200):		82,500	41,250	24,200
Common Player:		90.00	45.00	30.00
1	Babe Adams	100.00	35.00	20.00
2	Sam Agnew	90.00	45.00	30.00
3	Eddie Ainsmith	90.00	45.00	30.00
4	Grover Alexander	550.00	275.00	165.00
5	Leon Ames	90.00	45.00	30.00
6	Jimmy Archer	90.00	45.00	30.00
7	Jimmy Austin	90.00	45.00	30.00
8	J. Franklin Baker	360.00	175.00	105.00
9	Dave Bancroft	360.00	175.00	105.00
10	Jack Barry	90.00	45.00	30.00
11	Zinn Beck	90.00	45.00	30.00
12a	Beals Becker	275.00	135.00	80.00
12b	Lute Boone	90.00	45.00	30.00
13	Joe Benz	90.00	45.00	30.00
14	Bob Bescher	90.00	45.00	30.00
15	Al Betzel	90.00	45.00	30.00
16	Roger Bresnahan	360.00	175.00	105.00
17	Eddie Burns	90.00	45.00	30.00
18	Geo. J. Burns	90.00	45.00	30.00
19	Joe Bush	90.00	45.00	30.00
20	Owen Bush	90.00	45.00	30.00
21	Art Butler	90.00	45.00	30.00
22	Bobbie Byrne	90.00	45.00	30.00
23a	Forrest Cady	330.00	165.00	100.00
23b	Mordecai Brown	360.00	175.00	105.00
24	Jimmy Callahan	90.00	45.00	30.00
25	Ray Caldwell	90.00	45.00	30.00
26	Max Carey	360.00	175.00	105.00
27	George Chalmers	90.00	45.00	30.00
28	Frank Chance	360.00	175.00	105.00
29	Ray Chapman	110.00	55.00	35.00
30	Larry Cheney	90.00	45.00	30.00
31	Eddie Cicotte	360.00	175.00	105.00
32	Tom Clarke	90.00	45.00	30.00
33	Eddie Collins	360.00	175.00	105.00
34	"Shauno" Collins	90.00	45.00	30.00
35	Charles Comisky (Comiskey)	360.00	175.00	105.00
36	Joe Connolly	90.00	45.00	30.00
37	Luther Cook	90.00	45.00	30.00
38	Jack Coombs	90.00	45.00	30.00
39	Dan Costello	90.00	45.00	30.00
40	Harry Coveleskie (Coveleski)	90.00	45.00	30.00
41	Gavvy Cravath	90.00	45.00	30.00
42	Sam Crawford	360.00	175.00	105.00
43	Jean Dale	90.00	45.00	30.00
44	Jake Daubert	90.00	45.00	30.00
45	Geo. A. Davis Jr.	90.00	45.00	30.00
46	Charles Deal	90.00	45.00	30.00
47	Al Demaree	90.00	45.00	30.00
48	William Doak	90.00	45.00	30.00
49	Bill Donovan	90.00	45.00	30.00
50	Charles Dooin	90.00	45.00	30.00
51	Mike Doolan	90.00	45.00	30.00
52	Larry Doyle	90.00	45.00	30.00
53	Jean Dubuc	90.00	45.00	30.00
54	Oscar Dugey	90.00	45.00	30.00
55	Johnny Evers	360.00	175.00	105.00
56	Urban Faber	360.00	175.00	105.00
57	"Hap" Felsch	2,000	415.00	250.00
58	Bill Fischer	90.00	45.00	30.00
59	Ray Fisher	90.00	45.00	30.00
60	Max Flack	90.00	45.00	30.00
61	Art Fletcher	90.00	45.00	30.00
62	Eddie Foster	90.00	45.00	30.00
63	Jacques Fournier	90.00	45.00	30.00
64	Del Gainer (Gainor)	90.00	45.00	30.00
65	Larry Gardner	90.00	45.00	30.00
66	Joe Gedeon	90.00	45.00	30.00
67	Gus Getz	90.00	45.00	30.00
68	Geo. Gibson	90.00	45.00	30.00
69	Wilbur Good	90.00	45.00	30.00
70	Hank Gowdy	90.00	45.00	30.00
71	John Graney	90.00	45.00	30.00
72	Tom Griffith	90.00	45.00	30.00
73	Heinie Groh	90.00	45.00	30.00
74	Earl Hamilton	90.00	45.00	30.00
75	Bob Harmon	90.00	45.00	30.00
76	Roy Hartzell	90.00	45.00	30.00
77	Claude Hendrix	90.00	45.00	30.00
78	Olaf Henriksen	90.00	45.00	30.00
79	John Henry	90.00	45.00	30.00
80	"Buck" Herzog	90.00	45.00	30.00
81	Hugh High	90.00	45.00	30.00
82	Dick Hoblitzell	90.00	45.00	30.00
83	Harry Hooper	360.00	175.00	105.00
84	Ivan Howard	90.00	45.00	30.00
85	Miller Huggins	360.00	175.00	105.00
86	Joe Jackson	15,000	4,950	2,970
87	William James	90.00	45.00	30.00
88	Harold Janvrin	90.00	45.00	30.00
89	Hugh Jennings	360.00	175.00	105.00
90	Walter Johnson	1,500	550.00	330.00
91	Fielder Jones	90.00	45.00	30.00
92	Bennie Kauff	90.00	45.00	30.00
93	Wm. Killefer Jr.	90.00	45.00	30.00
94	Ed. Konetchy	90.00	45.00	30.00
95	Napoleon Lajoie	360.00	175.00	105.00
96	Jack Lapp	90.00	45.00	30.00
97a	John Lavan (Correct spelling.)	90.00	45.00	30.00
97b	John Lavin (Incorrect spelling.)	90.00	45.00	30.00
98	Jimmy Lavender	90.00	45.00	30.00
99	"Nemo" Leibold	90.00	45.00	30.00
100	H.B. Leonard	90.00	45.00	30.00
101	Duffy Lewis	90.00	45.00	30.00
102	Hans Lobert	90.00	45.00	30.00
103	Tom Long	90.00	45.00	30.00
104	Fred Luderus	90.00	45.00	30.00
105	Connie Mack	360.00	175.00	105.00
106	Lee Magee	90.00	45.00	30.00
107	Al. Mamaux	90.00	45.00	30.00
108	Leslie Mann	90.00	45.00	30.00
109	"Rabbit" Maranville	360.00	175.00	105.00
110	Rube Marquard	360.00	175.00	105.00
111	Armando Marsans	100.00	50.00	30.00
112	J. Erskine Mayer	90.00	45.00	30.00
113	George McBride	90.00	45.00	30.00
114	John J. McGraw	360.00	175.00	105.00
115	Jack McInnis	90.00	45.00	30.00
116	Fred Merkle	90.00	45.00	30.00
117	Chief Meyers	90.00	45.00	30.00
118	Clyde Milan	90.00	45.00	30.00
119	Otto Miller	90.00	45.00	30.00
120	Willie Mitchel (Mitchell)	90.00	45.00	30.00
121	Fred Mollwitz	90.00	45.00	30.00
122	J. Herbert Moran	90.00	45.00	30.00
123	Pat Moran	90.00	45.00	30.00
124	Ray Morgan	90.00	45.00	30.00
125	Geo. Moriarty	90.00	45.00	30.00
126	Guy Morton	90.00	45.00	30.00
127	Ed. Murphy (Photo actually Danny Murphy.)	90.00	45.00	30.00
128	John Murray	90.00	45.00	30.00
129	"Hy" Myers	90.00	45.00	30.00
130	J.A. Niehoff	90.00	45.00	30.00
131	Leslie Nunamaker	90.00	45.00	30.00
132	Rube Oldring	90.00	45.00	30.00
133	Oliver O'Mara	90.00	45.00	30.00
134	Steve O'Neill	90.00	45.00	30.00
135	"Dode" Paskert	90.00	45.00	30.00
136	Roger Peckinpaugh (Photo actually Gavvy Cravath.)	90.00	45.00	30.00
137	E.J. Pfeffer (Photo actually Jeff Pfeffer.)	90.00	45.00	30.00
138	Geo. Pierce (Pearce)	90.00	45.00	30.00
139	Walter Pipp	90.00	45.00	30.00
140	Derril Pratt (Derrill)	90.00	45.00	30.00
141	Bill Rariden	90.00	45.00	30.00
142	Eppa Rixey	360.00	175.00	105.00
143	Davey Robertson	90.00	45.00	30.00
144	Wilbert Robinson	360.00	175.00	105.00
145	Bob Roth	90.00	45.00	30.00
146	Ed. Roush	360.00	175.00	105.00
147	Clarence Rowland	90.00	45.00	30.00
148	"Nap" Rucker	90.00	45.00	30.00
149	Dick Rudolph	90.00	45.00	30.00
150	Reb Russell	90.00	45.00	30.00
151	Babe Ruth	30,000	13,750	8,250
152	Vic Saier	90.00	45.00	30.00
153	"Slim" Sallee	90.00	45.00	30.00
154	"Germany" Schaefer	90.00	45.00	30.00
155	Ray Schalk	360.00	175.00	105.00
156	Walter Schang	90.00	45.00	30.00
157	Chas. Schmidt	90.00	45.00	30.00
158	Frank Schulte	90.00	45.00	30.00
159	Jim Scott	90.00	45.00	30.00
160	Everett Scott	90.00	45.00	30.00
161	Tom Seaton	90.00	45.00	30.00
162	Howard Shanks	90.00	45.00	30.00
163	Bob Shawkey (Photo actually Jack McInnis.)	90.00	45.00	30.00
164	Ernie Shore	90.00	45.00	30.00
165	Burt Shotton	90.00	45.00	30.00
166	George Sisler	360.00	175.00	105.00
167	J. Carlisle Smith	90.00	45.00	30.00
168	Fred Snodgrass	90.00	45.00	30.00
169	Geo. Stallings	90.00	45.00	30.00
170	Oscar Stanage (Photo actually Chas. Schmidt.)	90.00	45.00	30.00
171	Charles Stengel	360.00	175.00	105.00
172	Milton Stock	90.00	45.00	30.00
173	Amos Strunk (Photo actually Olaf Henriksen.)	90.00	45.00	30.00
174	Billy Sullivan	90.00	45.00	30.00
175	Chas. Tesreau	90.00	45.00	30.00
176	Jim Thorpe	19,250	9,625	5,775
177	Joe Tinker	360.00	175.00	105.00
178	Fred Toney	90.00	45.00	30.00
179	Terry Turner	90.00	45.00	30.00
180	Jim Vaughn	90.00	45.00	30.00
181	Bob Veach	90.00	45.00	30.00
182	James Viox	90.00	45.00	30.00
183	Oscar Vitt	90.00	45.00	30.00
184	Hans Wagner	3,000	660.00	395.00
185	Clarence Walker (Photo not Walker.)	90.00	45.00	30.00
186a	Bobby Wallace	5,500	2,750	1,650
186b	Zach Wheat	360.00	175.00	105.00

187	Ed. Walsh	360.00	175.00	105.00
188	Buck Weaver	2,000	360.00	215.00
189	Carl Weilman	90.00	45.00	30.00
190	Geo. Whitted	90.00	45.00	30.00
191	Fred Williams	90.00	45.00	30.00
192	Art Wilson	90.00	45.00	30.00
193	J. Owen Wilson	90.00	45.00	30.00
194	Ivy Wingo	90.00	45.00	30.00
195	"Mel" Wolfgang	90.00	45.00	30.00
196	Joe Wood	500.00	110.00	65.00
197	Steve Yerkes	90.00	45.00	30.00
198	Rollie Zeider	90.00	45.00	30.00
199	Heiny Zimmerman	90.00	45.00	30.00
200	Ed. Zwilling	90.00	45.00	30.00

1916 M101-4 Blank Backs

The "update" version of this set is nearly identical to the earlier cards. The 200 black-and-white cards once again are printed with player photo, name, position, team and card number on front and blank backs. This version appears to have been sold directly to consumers by the manufacturer, Felix Mendelsohn of Chicago. The same cards can be found with advertising on back from several businesses around the country. Most of the players included on the 1-5/8" x 3" cards also appear in the prior edition. Despite being labeled in the American Card Catalog as M101-4, this version was issued after the M101-5 version, with the first advertising appearing in August 1916. The complete set price does not include variations.

		NM	EX	VG
Complete Set (200):		45,000	22,500	13,500
Common Player:		60.00	30.00	18.00
1	Babe Adams	75.00	30.00	18.00
2	Sam Agnew	60.00	30.00	18.00
3	Eddie Ainsmith	60.00	30.00	18.00
4	Grover Alexander	375.00	185.00	110.00
5	Leon Ames	60.00	30.00	18.00
6	Jimmy Archer	60.00	30.00	18.00
7	Jimmy Austin	60.00	30.00	18.00
8	H.D. Baird	60.00	30.00	18.00
9	J. Franklin Baker	300.00	150.00	90.00
10	Dave Bancroft	300.00	150.00	90.00
11	Jack Barry	60.00	30.00	18.00
12	Zinn Beck	60.00	30.00	18.00
13	"Chief" Bender	300.00	150.00	90.00
14	Joe Benz	60.00	30.00	18.00
15	Bob Bescher	60.00	30.00	18.00
16	Al Betzel	60.00	30.00	18.00
17	Mordecai Brown	300.00	150.00	90.00
18	Eddie Burns	60.00	30.00	18.00
19	George Burns	60.00	30.00	18.00
20	Geo. J. Burns	60.00	30.00	18.00
21	Joe Bush	60.00	30.00	18.00
22	"Donie" Bush	60.00	30.00	18.00
23	Art Butler	60.00	30.00	18.00
24	Bobbie Byrne	60.00	30.00	18.00
25	Forrest Cady	60.00	30.00	18.00
26	Jimmy Callahan	60.00	30.00	18.00
27	Ray Caldwell	60.00	30.00	18.00
28	Max Carey	300.00	150.00	90.00
29	George Chalmers	60.00	30.00	18.00
30	Ray Chapman	90.00	45.00	25.00
31	Larry Cheney	60.00	30.00	18.00
32	Eddie Cicotte	300.00	150.00	90.00
33	Tom Clarke	60.00	30.00	18.00
34	Eddie Collins	300.00	150.00	90.00
35	"Shauno" Collins	60.00	30.00	18.00
36	Charles Comiskey	300.00	150.00	90.00
37	Joe Connolly	60.00	30.00	18.00
38	Ty Cobb	2,500	1,250	750.00
39	Harry Coveleskie (Coveleski)	60.00	30.00	18.00
40	Gavvy Cravath	60.00	30.00	18.00
41	Sam Crawford	300.00	150.00	90.00
42	Jean Dale	60.00	30.00	18.00
43	Jake Daubert	60.00	30.00	18.00
44	Charles Deal	60.00	30.00	18.00
45	Al Demaree	60.00	30.00	18.00
46	Josh Devore	60.00	30.00	18.00
47	William Doak	60.00	30.00	18.00
48	Bill Donovan	60.00	30.00	18.00
49	Charles Dooin	60.00	30.00	18.00
50	Mike Doolan	60.00	30.00	18.00
51	Larry Doyle	60.00	30.00	18.00
52	Jean Dubuc	60.00	30.00	18.00
53	Oscar Dugey	60.00	30.00	18.00
54	Johnny Evers	300.00	150.00	90.00
55	Urban Faber	300.00	150.00	90.00
56	"Hap" Felsch	2,000	375.00	225.00
57	Bill Fischer	60.00	30.00	18.00
58	Ray Fisher	60.00	30.00	18.00
59	Max Flack	60.00	30.00	18.00
60	Art Fletcher	60.00	30.00	18.00
61	Eddie Foster	60.00	30.00	18.00
62	Jacques Fournier	60.00	30.00	18.00
63	Del Gainer (Gainor)	60.00	30.00	18.00
64	"Chic" Gandil	500.00	250.00	150.00
65	Larry Gardner	60.00	30.00	18.00
66	Joe Gedeon	60.00	30.00	18.00
67	Gus Getz	60.00	30.00	18.00
68	Geo. Gibson	60.00	30.00	18.00
69	Wilbur Good	60.00	30.00	18.00
70	Hank Gowdy	60.00	30.00	18.00
71	John Graney	60.00	30.00	18.00
72	Clark Griffith	300.00	150.00	90.00
73	Tom Griffith	60.00	30.00	18.00
74	Heinie Groh	60.00	30.00	18.00
75	Earl Hamilton	60.00	30.00	18.00
76	Bob Harmon	60.00	30.00	18.00
77	Roy Hartzell	60.00	30.00	18.00
78	Claude Hendrix	60.00	30.00	18.00
79	Olaf Henriksen	60.00	30.00	18.00
80	John Henry	60.00	30.00	18.00
81	"Buck" Herzog	60.00	30.00	18.00
82	Hugh High	60.00	30.00	18.00
83	Dick Hoblitzell	60.00	30.00	18.00
84	Harry Hooper	300.00	150.00	90.00
85	Ivan Howard	60.00	30.00	18.00
86	Miller Huggins	300.00	150.00	90.00
87	Joe Jackson	15,000	4,000	2,400
88	William James	60.00	30.00	18.00
89	Harold Janvrin	60.00	30.00	18.00
90	Hugh Jennings	300.00	150.00	90.00
91	Walter Johnson	800.00	400.00	240.00
92	Fielder Jones	60.00	30.00	18.00
93	Joe Judge	60.00	30.00	18.00
94	Bennie Kauff	60.00	30.00	18.00
95	Wm. Killefer Jr.	60.00	30.00	18.00
96	Ed. Konetchy	60.00	30.00	18.00
97	Napoleon Lajoie	375.00	185.00	110.00
98	Jack Lapp	60.00	30.00	18.00
99	John Lavan	60.00	30.00	18.00
100	Jimmy Lavender	60.00	30.00	18.00
101	"Nemo" Leibold	60.00	30.00	18.00
102	H.B. Leonard	60.00	30.00	18.00
103	Duffy Lewis	60.00	30.00	18.00
104	Hans Lobert	60.00	30.00	18.00
105	Tom Long	60.00	30.00	18.00
106	Fred Luderus	60.00	30.00	18.00
107	Connie Mack	300.00	150.00	90.00
108	Lee Magee	60.00	30.00	18.00
109	Sherwood Magee	60.00	30.00	18.00
110	Al. Mamaux	60.00	30.00	18.00
111	Leslie Mann	60.00	30.00	18.00
112	"Rabbit" Maranville	300.00	150.00	90.00
113	Rube Marquard	300.00	150.00	90.00
114	J. Erskine Mayer	125.00	65.00	35.00
115	George McBride	60.00	30.00	18.00
116	John J. McGraw	300.00	150.00	90.00
117	Jack McInnis	60.00	30.00	18.00
118	Fred Merkle	60.00	30.00	18.00
119	Chief Meyers	60.00	30.00	18.00
120	Clyde Milan	60.00	30.00	18.00
121	John Miller	60.00	30.00	18.00
122	Otto Miller	60.00	30.00	18.00
123	Willie Mitchell	60.00	30.00	18.00
124	Fred Mollwitz	60.00	30.00	18.00
125	Pat Moran	60.00	30.00	18.00
126	Ray Morgan	60.00	30.00	18.00
127	Geo. Moriarty	60.00	30.00	18.00
128	Guy Morton	60.00	30.00	18.00
129	Mike Mowrey	60.00	30.00	18.00
130	Ed. Murphy	60.00	30.00	18.00
131	"Hy" Myers	60.00	30.00	18.00
132	J.A. Niehoff	60.00	30.00	18.00
133	Rube Oldring	60.00	30.00	18.00
134	Oliver O'Mara	60.00	30.00	18.00
135	Steve O'Neill	60.00	30.00	18.00
136	"Dode" Paskert	60.00	30.00	18.00
137	Roger Peckinpaugh	60.00	30.00	18.00
138	Walter Pipp	75.00	37.50	22.50
139	Derril Pratt (Derrill)	60.00	30.00	18.00
140	Pat Ragan	60.00	30.00	18.00
141	Bill Rariden	60.00	30.00	18.00
142	Eppa Rixey	300.00	150.00	90.00
143	Davey Robertson	60.00	30.00	18.00
144	Wilbert Robinson	300.00	150.00	90.00
145	Bob Roth	60.00	30.00	18.00
146	Ed. Roush	300.00	150.00	90.00
147	Clarence Rowland	60.00	30.00	18.00
148	"Nap" Rucker	60.00	30.00	18.00
149	Dick Rudolph	60.00	30.00	18.00
150	Reb Russell	60.00	30.00	18.00
151	Babe Ruth	15,000	7,500	4,500
152	Vic Saier	60.00	30.00	18.00
153	"Slim" Sallee	60.00	30.00	18.00
154	Ray Schalk	300.00	150.00	90.00
155	Walter Schang	60.00	30.00	18.00
156	Frank Schulte	60.00	30.00	18.00
157	Everett Scott	60.00	30.00	18.00
158	Jim Scott	60.00	30.00	18.00
159	Tom Seaton	60.00	30.00	18.00
160	Howard Shanks	60.00	30.00	18.00
161	Bob Shawkey	60.00	30.00	18.00
162	Ernie Shore	60.00	30.00	18.00
163	Burt Shotton	60.00	30.00	18.00
164	Geo. Sisler	300.00	150.00	90.00
165	J. Carlisle Smith	60.00	30.00	18.00
166	Fred Snodgrass	60.00	30.00	18.00
167	Geo. Stallings	60.00	30.00	18.00
168a	Oscar Stanage/Catching	60.00	30.00	24.00
168b	Oscar Stanage (Portrait to thighs.)	750.00	375.00	225.00
169	Charles Stengel	375.00	185.00	110.00
170	Milton Stock	60.00	30.00	18.00
171	Amos Strunk	60.00	30.00	18.00
172	Billy Sullivan	60.00	30.00	18.00
173	"Jeff" Tesreau	60.00	30.00	18.00
174	Joe Tinker	300.00	150.00	90.00
175	Fred Toney	60.00	30.00	18.00
176	Terry Turner	60.00	30.00	18.00
177	George Tyler	60.00	30.00	18.00
178	Jim Vaughn	60.00	30.00	18.00
179	Bob Veach	60.00	30.00	18.00
180	James Viox	60.00	30.00	18.00
181	Oscar Vitt	60.00	30.00	18.00
182	Hans Wagner	1,200	600.00	360.00
183	Clarence Walker	60.00	30.00	18.00
184	Ed. Walsh	300.00	150.00	90.00
185	W. Wambsganss (Photo actually Fritz Coumbe.)	60.00	30.00	18.00
186	Buck Weaver	600.00	300.00	180.00
187	Carl Weilman	60.00	30.00	18.00
188	Zach Wheat	300.00	150.00	90.00
189	Geo. Whitted	60.00	30.00	18.00
190	Fred Williams	60.00	30.00	18.00
191	Art Wilson	60.00	30.00	18.00
192	J. Owen Wilson	60.00	30.00	18.00
193	Ivy Wingo	60.00	30.00	18.00
194	"Mel" Wolfgang	60.00	30.00	18.00
195	Joe Wood	175.00	85.00	50.00
196	Steve Yerkes	60.00	30.00	18.00
197	"Pep" Young	60.00	30.00	18.00
198	Rollie Zeider	60.00	30.00	18.00
199	Heiny Zimmerman	60.00	30.00	18.00
200	Ed. Zwilling	60.00	30.00	18.00

N

1969 Nabisco Team Flakes

This set of cards is seen in two different sizes: 1-15/16" x 3" and 1-3/4" x 2-15/16". This is explained by the varying widths of the card borders on the backs of Nabisco cereal packages. Cards are action color photos bordered in yellow. Twenty-four of the top players in the game are included in the set, which was issued in three series of eight cards each. No team insignias are visible on any of the cards. Packages described the cards as "Mini Posters."

		NM	EX	VG
Complete Set (24):		475.00	240.00	140.00
Common Player:		8.00	4.00	2.50
(1)	Hank Aaron	45.00	22.50	13.50
(2)	Richie Allen	12.50	6.25	3.75
(3)	Lou Brock	20.00	10.00	6.00
(4)	Paul Casanova	8.00	4.00	2.50
(5)	Roberto Clemente	95.00	47.50	28.00
(6)	Al Ferrara	8.00	4.00	2.50
(7)	Bill Freehan	8.00	4.00	2.50
(8)	Jim Fregosi	8.00	4.00	2.50
(9)	Bob Gibson	20.00	10.00	6.00
(10)	Tony Horton	8.00	4.00	2.50
(11)	Tommy John	8.00	4.00	2.50
(12)	Al Kaline	25.00	12.50	7.50
(13)	Jim Lonborg	8.00	4.00	2.50
(14)	Juan Marichal	20.00	10.00	6.00
(15)	Willie Mays	45.00	22.50	13.50
(16)	Rick Monday	8.00	4.00	2.50
(17)	Tony Oliva	8.00	4.00	2.50
(18)	Brooks Robinson	25.00	12.50	7.50
(19)	Frank Robinson	25.00	12.50	7.50
(20)	Pete Rose	35.00	17.50	10.00
(21)	Ron Santo	12.50	6.25	3.75
(22)	Tom Seaver	25.00	12.50	7.50
(23)	Rusty Staub	8.00	4.00	2.50
(24)	Mel Stottlemyre	8.00	4.00	2.50

1923-1924 Nacionales Cigarros

The baseball players in this mid-20s Cuban issue are part of a larger set which included boxers, actresses, actors, nudes, soccer players and others. The cards measure about 1-5/8" x 2-1/4" and have a distinctive wide black border on front. Backs identify the issue. An album was issued to house the set. The cards are printed on thin cardboard with a glossy finish.

		NM	EX	VG
Complete Baseball Set (40):		60,000	24,000	12,000
Common Player:		500.00	200.00	100.00
21	Rafael Almeida	1,500	600.00	300.00
22	Isidro Fabre	1,125	450.00	225.00
23	Eugenio Morin	500.00	200.00	100.00
24	Oscar Rodriguez	500.00	200.00	100.00
25	Joseito Rodriguez	500.00	200.00	100.00
26	Papo Gonzalez	500.00	200.00	100.00
27	Gutierrez	500.00	200.00	100.00
28	Valentin Dreke (Photo actually Lucas Boada.)	1,125	450.00	225.00
29	Jose Maria Fernandez	750.00	300.00	150.00
30	(Cheo) Ramos	500.00	200.00	100.00
31	Paito (Ramon Herrera)	500.00	200.00	100.00
32	Bernardo Baro	1,125	450.00	225.00
33	Manuel Cueto	750.00	300.00	150.00
34	(Oscar) Tuero	500.00	200.00	100.00
35	Kakin Gonzalez	500.00	200.00	100.00
36	Armando Marsans	1,500	600.00	300.00
37	Andy Cooper	9,000	3,600	1,800
38	Dolf Luque	2,500	1,000	500.00
39	Marcelino Guerra	500.00	200.00	100.00
40	Manzanillo (Tatic Campos)	500.00	200.00	100.00
41	Oscar Levis	750.00	300.00	150.00
42	Eufemio Abreu	500.00	200.00	100.00
43	Cristobal Torriente	12,000	4,800	2,400
44	Juanelo Mirabal	750.00	300.00	150.00
45	Merito Acosta	500.00	200.00	100.00
46	Jose Acostica (Acosta)	500.00	200.00	100.00
47	Rogelio Crespo	500.00	200.00	100.00
48	(Jacinto) Calvo	750.00	300.00	150.00
49	(Emilio) Palmero	750.00	300.00	150.00
50	Jose Mendez	9,000	3,600	1,800
51	Alejandro Oms	3,750	1,500	750.00
52	Pedro Dibut	750.00	300.00	150.00
53	Strike (Valentin "Sirique" Gonzalez)	500.00	200.00	100.00
54	Magrinat (Hector Magrinut)	500.00	200.00	100.00
55	Raphael Quintana	500.00	200.00	100.00
56	Bienvenido Jimenez	750.00	300.00	150.00
57	Bartolo Portuando (Portuondo)	1,500	600.00	300.00
58	(Pelayo) Chacon	1,500	600.00	300.00
59	Riant (Red Ryan)	1,500	600.00	300.00
60	Perico El Mano (Mascot)	500.00	200.00	100.00

1909 Nadja Caramels (E92)

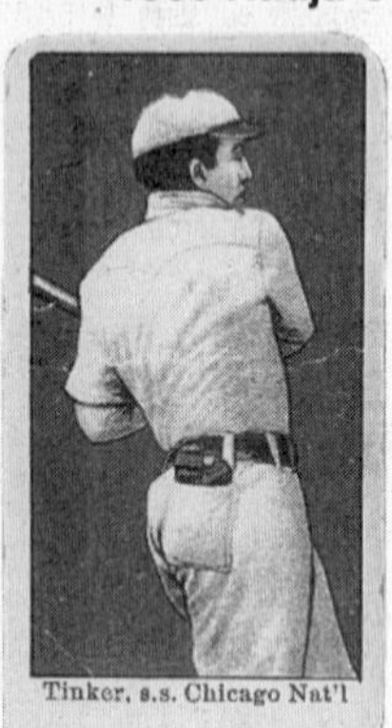
Tinker, s.s. Chicago Nat'l

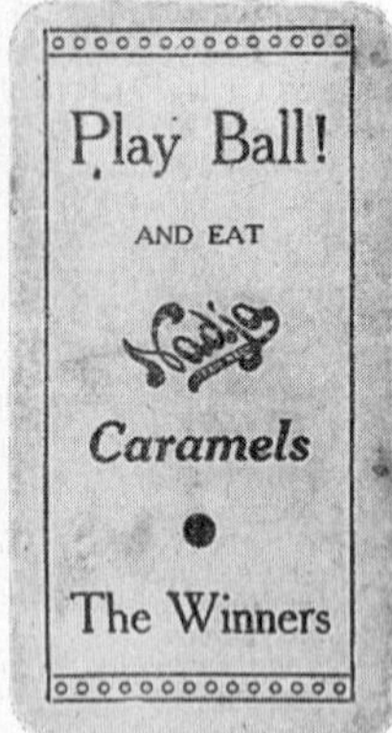

One of several 1909-10 issues produced for Nadja Caramels, this set can be distinguished by the players in the checklist (alphabetized here) and the type beneath the color player lithograph. In this set, the player's last name is in upper- and lower-case letters, and his position is given, along with the team. Backs of these 1-1/2" x 2-3/4" cards are identical to later Nadja issues, featuring an ad for the candy brand. Cataloged (along with the cards of Croft's Candy/Cocoa and Dockman Gum) as E92 in the "American Card Catalog," the Nadja set checklist differs from those issues in that it is larger and contains a group of St. Louis players not found in the other sets. Nadja was a brand name of the Blake-Wenneker Candy Co. of St. Louis.

		NM	EX	VG
Complete Set (62):		50,000	22,500	12,500
Common Player:		550.00	220.00	110.00
(1)	Bill Bailey	550.00	220.00	110.00
(2)	Jack Barry	550.00	220.00	110.00
(3)	Harry Bemis	550.00	220.00	110.00
(4)	Chief Bender (Striped cap.)	1,020	455.00	305.00
(5)	Chief Bender (White cap.)	1,020	455.00	305.00
(6)	Bill Bergen	550.00	220.00	110.00
(7)	Bob Bescher	550.00	220.00	110.00
(8)	Roger Bresnahan	1,020	455.00	305.00
(9)	Al Bridwell	550.00	220.00	110.00
(10)	Doc Casey	550.00	220.00	110.00
(11)	Frank Chance	1,020	455.00	305.00
(12)	Hal Chase	780.00	350.00	235.00
(13)	Ty Cobb	7,500	3,360	2,250
(14)	Eddie Collins	1,020	455.00	305.00
(15)	Sam Crawford	1,020	455.00	305.00
(16)	Harry Davis	550.00	220.00	110.00
(17)	Art Devlin	550.00	220.00	110.00
(18)	Bill Donovan	550.00	220.00	110.00
(19)	Red Dooin	550.00	220.00	110.00
(20)	Mickey Doolan	550.00	220.00	110.00
(21)	Patsy Dougherty	550.00	220.00	110.00
(22)	Larry Doyle/Throwing	550.00	220.00	110.00
(23)	Larry Doyle (With bat.)	550.00	220.00	110.00
(24)	Rube Ellis	550.00	220.00	110.00
(25)	Johnny Evers	1,020	455.00	305.00
(26)	George Gibson	550.00	220.00	110.00
(27)	Topsy Hartsel	550.00	220.00	110.00
(28)	Roy Hartzell/Btg	550.00	220.00	110.00
(29)	Roy Hartzell/Fldg	550.00	220.00	110.00
(30)	Harry Howell (Ready to pitch.)	550.00	220.00	110.00
(31)	Harry Howell (Follow-through.)	550.00	220.00	110.00
(32)	Fred Jacklitsch	550.00	220.00	110.00
(33)	Hugh Jennings	1,020	455.00	305.00
(34)	Red Kleinow	550.00	220.00	110.00
(35)	Otto Knabe	550.00	220.00	110.00
(36)	Jack Knight	550.00	220.00	110.00
(37)	Nap Lajoie	1,020	455.00	305.00
(38)	Hans Lobert	550.00	220.00	110.00
(39)	Sherry Magee	550.00	220.00	110.00
(40)	Christy Matthewson (Mathewson)	3,900	1,740	1,170
(41)	John McGraw	1,020	455.00	305.00
(42)	Larry McLean	550.00	220.00	110.00
(43)	Dots Miller/Btg	550.00	220.00	110.00
(44)	Dots Miller/Fldg	550.00	220.00	110.00
(45)	Danny Murphy	550.00	220.00	110.00
(46)	Rebel Oakes	550.00	220.00	110.00
(47)	Bill O'Hara	550.00	220.00	110.00
(48)	Eddie Phelps	550.00	220.00	110.00
(49)	Germany Schaefer	550.00	220.00	110.00
(50)	Admiral Schlei	550.00	220.00	110.00
(51)	Boss Schmidt	550.00	220.00	110.00
(52)	Johnny Seigle (Siegle)	550.00	220.00	110.00
(53)	Dave Shean	550.00	220.00	110.00
(54)	Boss Smith (Schmidt)	550.00	220.00	110.00
(55)	George Stone (Blue background.)	550.00	220.00	110.00
(56)	George Stone (Green background.)	550.00	220.00	110.00
(57)	Joe Tinker	1,020	455.00	305.00
(58)	Honus Wagner/Btg	6,000	2,700	1,800
(59)	Honus Wagner/Throwing	7,200	3,240	2,160
(60)	Bobby Wallace	1,020	455.00	305.00
(61)	Cy Young	2,520	1,140	750.00
(62)	Heinie Zimmerman	550.00	220.00	110.00

1910 Nadja Caramels Philadelphia Athletics (E104-1)

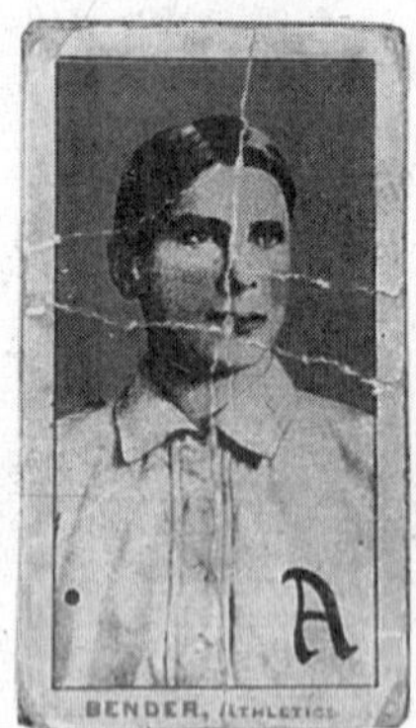
BENDER, ATHLETICS

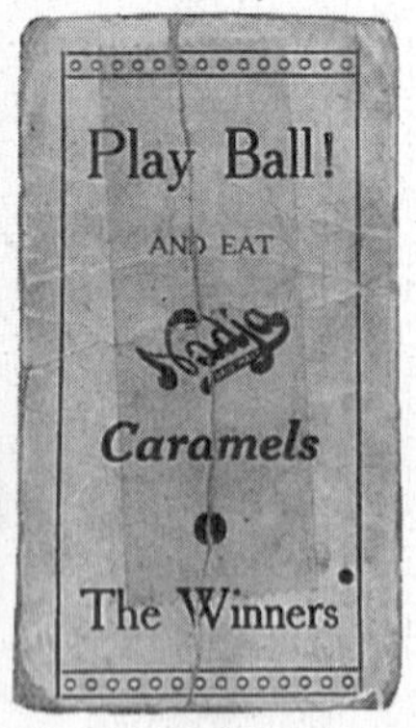

The 18 Philadelphia Athletics players in this set, can each be found in three different variations. Each of the approximately 1-1/2" x 2-3/4" cards can be found with a plain portrait lithograph on front, and either a blank back or a back containing a Nadja ad. Each player can also be found with a black overprint on front, comprised of a white elephant figure on the uniform and the notation "World's Champions 1910" above. The overprinted cards are known only with blank backs, and are somewhat scarcer than the plain cards of either type. Nadja-back cards should be valued about the same as the overprinted type.

		NM	EX	VG
Complete Set, No O/P, Blank Back (18):		20,000	9,000	6,000
Complete Set, With O/P or Ad Back:		25,000	12,500	7,250
Common Player:		1,000	450.00	300.00
(1a)	Home Run Baker	1,750	800.00	500.00
(1b)	Home Run Baker ("World's Champions")	3,600	1,800	900.00
(2a)	Jack Barry	1,000	450.00	300.00
(2b)	Jack Barry ("World's Champions")	3,600	1,800	900.00
(3a)	Chief Bender	1,750	800.00	500.00
(3b)	Chief Bender ("World's Champions")	3,600	1,800	900.00
(4a)	Eddie Collins	1,750	800.00	500.00
(4b)	Eddie Collins ("World's Champions")	3,600	1,800	900.00
(5a)	Harry Davis	1,000	450.00	300.00
(5b)	Harry Davis ("World's Champions")	3,600	1,800	900.00
(6a)	Jimmy Dygert (1910 above head)	1,000	450.00	300.00
(6b-1)	Jimmy Dygert ("World's Champions" (1910 above head))	3,600	1,800	900.00
(6b-2)	Jimmy Dygert (1910 at right)	3,600	1,800	900.00
(7a)	Topsy Hartsel	1,000	450.00	300.00
(7b)	Topsy Hartel ("World's Champions")	3,600	1,800	900.00
(8a)	Harry Krause	1,000	450.00	300.00
(8b)	Harry Krause ("World's Champions")	3,600	1,800	900.00
(9a)	Jack Lapp	1,000	450.00	300.00
(9b)	Jack Lapp ("World's Champions")	3,600	1,800	900.00
(10a)	Paddy Livingstone (Livingston)	1,000	450.00	300.00
(10b)	Paddy Livingstone (Livingston) ("World's Champions")	3,600	1,800	900.00
(11a)	Bris Lord	1,000	450.00	300.00
(11b)	Bris Lord ("World's Champions")	3,600	1,800	900.00
(12a)	Connie Mack	5,250	2,400	1,500
(12b)	Connie Mack ("World's Champions")	12,000	6,000	3,000
(13a)	Cy Morgan	1,000	450.00	300.00
(13b)	Cy Morgan ("World's Champions")	3,600	1,800	900.00
(14a)	Danny Murphy	1,000	450.00	300.00
(14b)	Danny Murphy ("World's Champions")	3,600	1,800	900.00
(15a)	Rube Oldring	1,000	450.00	300.00
(15b)	Rube Oldring ("World's Champions")	3,600	1,800	900.00
(16a)	Eddie Plank	8,100	3,600	2,400
(16b)	Eddie Plank ("World's Champions")	15,000	7,500	3,750
(17a)	Amos Strunk	1,000	450.00	300.00
(17b)	Amos Strunk ("World's Champions")	3,600	1,800	900.00
(18a)	Ira Thomas	1,000	450.00	300.00
(18b-1)	Ira Thomas ("World's Champions" (1910 above head))	3,600	1,800	900.00
(18b-2)	Ira Thomas (1910 at right)	3,600	1,800	900.00

1910 Nadja Caramels Pittsburgh Pirates (E104-2)

WAGNER, PITTSBURG

Similar to the contemporary American Caramel issue, this set of 1-1/2" x 2-3/4" cards features portrait color lithographs of the 1909 World's Champion Pittsburgh (spelled "Pittsburg") Pirates. Each card was issued with both blank back and with a back bearing a Nadja ad. The Nadja-backed cards are scarcer but command little premium.

		NM	EX	VG
Complete Set (11):		17,500	7,900	5,250
Common Player:		780.00	360.00	240.00
Ad Back: 1.25X				
(1)	Babe Adams	780.00	360.00	240.00
(2)	Fred Clarke	1,800	810.00	540.00
(3)	George Gibson	780.00	360.00	240.00
(4)	Ham Hyatt	780.00	360.00	240.00
(5)	Tommy Leach	780.00	360.00	240.00
(6)	Sam Leever	780.00	360.00	240.00
(7)	Nick Maddox	780.00	360.00	240.00
(8)	Dots Miller	780.00	360.00	240.00
(9)	Deacon Phillippe	780.00	360.00	240.00
(10)	Honus Wagner	12,000	5,400	3,600
(11)	Owen Wilson	780.00	360.00	240.00

1910 Nadja Caramels (E104-3)

The cards in this issue can each be found with or without a Nadja ad on back; the latter being somewhat scarcer and car-

MOORE, PHILADELPHIA

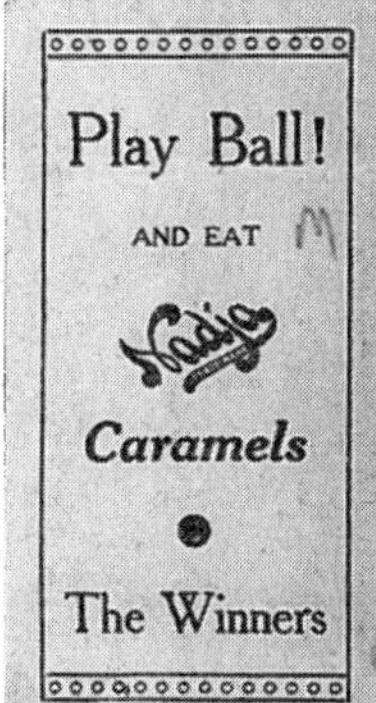
Play Ball!
AND EAT
Nadja
Caramels
The Winners

rying a premium over the values shown. These 1-1/2" x 2-3/4" cards can be distinguished from the 1909 issue by the line of type beneath the player portrait. On the 1910 cards, the player's last name is in all blue capital letters and there is no position designation given. This checklist is likely incomplete.

		NM	EX	VG
Common Player:		1,440	660.00	420.00
Ad Back: 1.25X				
(1)	Bill Abstein	1,440	660.00	420.00
(2)	Red Ames	1,440	660.00	420.00
(3)	Johnny Bates	1,440	660.00	420.00
(4)	Kitty Bransfield	1,440	660.00	420.00
(5)	Al Bridwell	1,440	660.00	420.00
(6)	Hal Chase	1,920	870.00	600.00
(7)	Doc Crandall	1,440	660.00	420.00
(8)	Sam Crawford	2,400	1,080	720.00
(9)	Jim Delehanty (Delahanty)	1,440	660.00	420.00
(10)	Art Devlin	1,440	660.00	420.00
(11)	Red Dooin	1,440	660.00	420.00
(12)	Mickey Doolan	1,440	660.00	420.00
(13)	Larry Doyle	1,440	660.00	420.00
(14)	Eddie Grant	1,440	660.00	420.00
(15)	Fred Jacklitsch	1,440	660.00	420.00
(16)	Hugh Jennings	2,400	1,080	720.00
(17)	Davy Jones	1,440	660.00	420.00
(18)	Tom Jones	1,440	660.00	420.00
(19)	Otto Knabe	1,440	660.00	420.00
(201	Sherry Magee	1,440	660.00	420.00
(21)	John McGraw	2,400	1,080	720.00
(22)	Matty McIntyre	1,440	660.00	420.00
(23)	Earl Moore	1,440	660.00	420.00
(24)	Pat Moren (Moran)	1,440	660.00	420.00
(25)	George Moriarity	1,440	660.00	420.00
(26)	George Mullin	1,440	660.00	420.00
(27)	Red Murray	1,440	660.00	420.00
(28)	Simon Nicholls	1,440	660.00	420.00
(29)	Charley O'Leary	1,440	660.00	420.00
(30)	Admiral Schlei	1,440	660.00	420.00
(31)	Boss Schmidt	1,440	660.00	420.00
(32)	Cy Seymore (Seymour)	1,440	660.00	420.00
(33)	Tully Sparks	1,440	660.00	420.00
(34)	Ed Summers	1,440	660.00	420.00
(35)	Ed Willetts (Willett)	1,440	660.00	420.00
(36)	Vic Willis	2,400	1,080	720.00
(37)	Hooks Wiltse	1,440	660.00	420.00

1912 Napoleon Little Cigars

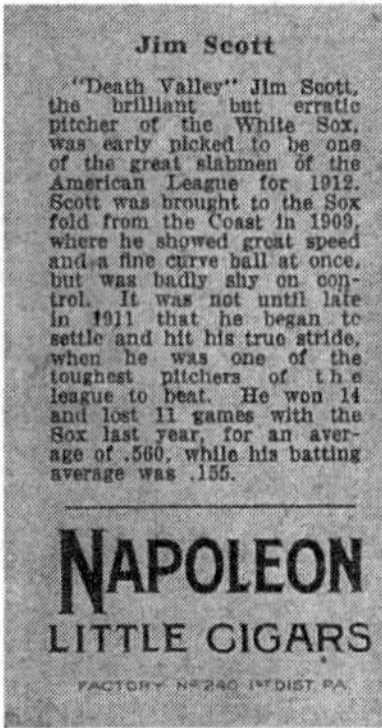
Jim Scott

"Death Valley" Jim Scott, the brilliant but erratic pitcher of the White Sox, was early picked to be one of the great slabmen of the American League for 1912. Scott was brought to the Sox fold from the Coast in 1909, where he showed great speed and a fine curve ball at once, but was badly shy on control. It was not until late in 1911 that he began to settle and hit his true stride, when he was one of the toughest pitchers of the league to beat. He won 14 and lost 11 games with the Sox last year, for an average of .560, while his batting average was .155.

NAPOLEON
LITTLE CIGARS

While this cigarette brand advertising on the backs of T207 cards is less commonly encountered than Recruit, collectors do not attach a commensurate premium to them, largely because each of the players can be found with more common back ads.

PREMIUM: 2X
(See T207 for checklist and base card values.)

1963 Nassau County Boy Scouts

According to the text on the back, six cards were issued in this set. The other subjects are unknown, and may not feature any additional baseball players. The standard-size cards are printed in blue-and-white, both front and back, including a duo-tone photo of Snider in his only season with the Mets.

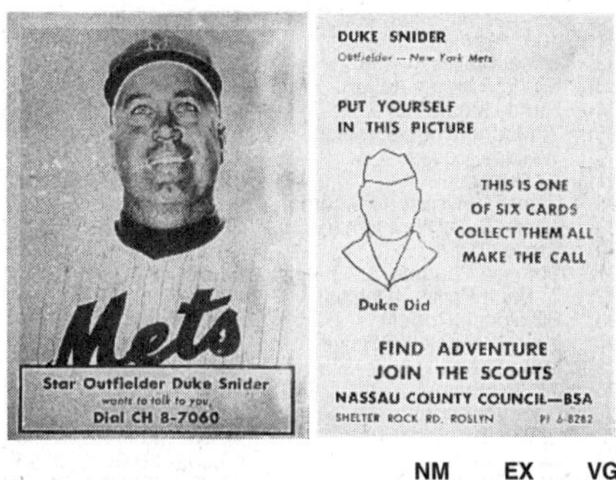
Mets
Star Outfielder Duke Snider
wants to talk to you,
Dial CH 8-7060
DUKE SNIDER
Outfielder — New York Mets
PUT YOURSELF
IN THIS PICTURE
THIS IS ONE
OF SIX CARDS
COLLECT THEM ALL
MAKE THE CALL
Duke Did
FIND ADVENTURE
JOIN THE SCOUTS
NASSAU COUNTY COUNCIL—BSA
SHELTER ROCK RD. ROSLYN

		NM	EX	VG
(1)	Duke Snider	150.00	75.00	45.00

1974 Nassau Tuberculosis and Respiratory Disease Assn.

The date attributed to these cards is arbitrary. The black-and-white 2-1/2" x 3-1/2" cards have a photo of the Yankees pitcher on front and a career summary on back, along with an anti-smoking message.

	NM	EX	VG
Whitey Ford (Facing his right.)	45.00	22.50	13.50
Whitey Ford (Follow-through.)	45.00	22.50	13.50

1921-23 National Caramel (E220)

FRANKLIN 'HOME RUN' BAKER
3rd B. N.Y. Yankees

Issued circa 1921 to 1923, this 120-card set is sometimes confused with contemporary American Caramel issues, but is easy to identify because of the words "Made only by National Caramel Company" on the back. With due consideration to normal cutting variances on cards of this era and type, E220s measure about 2" x 3-1/4" and feature black-and-white photos with the player's name, position and team at the bottom. In addition to the line indicating the manufacturer, the backs read "This set consists of pictures of 120 of the leading Base Ball Stars of the American and National Leagues." There are 115 different players included in the set, with five players shown on two cards each. About half of the photos in the set are identical to those used in various American Caramel sets, leading to some confusion regarding the three sets.

		NM	EX	VG
Complete Set (120):		27,500	13,500	8,250
Common Player:		100.00	50.00	30.00
(1)	Charles "Babe" Adams	100.00	50.00	30.00
(2)	G.C. Alexander	400.00	200.00	120.00
(3)	James Austin	100.00	50.00	30.00
(4)	Jim Bagbyk (Bagby)	100.00	50.00	30.00
(5)	Franklin "Home Run" Baker	300.00	150.00	90.00
(6)	Dave Bancroft	300.00	150.00	90.00
(7)	Turner Barber	100.00	50.00	30.00
(8)	George Burns (Cincinnati)	100.00	50.00	30.00
(9)	George Burns (Cleveland)	100.00	50.00	30.00
(10)	Joe Bush	100.00	50.00	30.00
(11)	Leon Cadore	100.00	50.00	30.00
(12)	Max Carey	300.00	150.00	90.00
(13)	Ty Cobb	1,750	875.00	525.00
(14)	Eddie Collins	300.00	150.00	90.00
(15)	John Collins	100.00	50.00	30.00
(16)	Wilbur Cooper	100.00	50.00	30.00
(17)	S. Coveleskie (Coveleski)	300.00	150.00	90.00
(18)	Walton Cruise	100.00	50.00	30.00
(19)	Wm. Cunningham	100.00	50.00	30.00
(20)	George Cutshaw	100.00	50.00	30.00
(21)	Jake Daubert	100.00	50.00	30.00
(22)	Chas. A. Deal	100.00	50.00	30.00
(23)	Bill Doak	100.00	50.00	30.00
(24)	Joe Dugan	100.00	50.00	30.00
(25)	Jimmy Dykes/Btg	100.00	50.00	30.00
(26)	Jimmy Dykes/Fldg	100.00	50.00	30.00
(27)	"Red" Faber	300.00	150.00	90.00
(28)	"Chick" Fewster	100.00	50.00	30.00
(29)	Wilson Fewster	100.00	50.00	30.00
(30)	Ira Flagstead	100.00	50.00	30.00
(31)	Arthur Fletcher	100.00	50.00	30.00
(32)	Frank Frisch	300.00	150.00	90.00
(33)	Larry Gardner	100.00	50.00	30.00
(34)	Walter Gerber	100.00	50.00	30.00
(35)	Charles Glazner	100.00	50.00	30.00
(36)	Hank Gowdy	100.00	50.00	30.00
(37)	J.C. Graney (Should be J.G.)	100.00	50.00	30.00
(38)	Tommy Griffith	100.00	50.00	30.00
(39)	Charles Grimm	100.00	50.00	30.00
(40)	Heinie Groh	100.00	50.00	30.00
(41)	Byron Harris	100.00	50.00	30.00
(42)	Sam Harris (Bucky)	300.00	150.00	90.00
(43)	Harry Heilman (Heilmann)	300.00	150.00	90.00
(44)	Claude Hendrix	100.00	50.00	30.00
(45)	Walter Henline	100.00	50.00	30.00
(46)	Chas. Hollocher	100.00	50.00	30.00
(47)	Harry Hooper	300.00	150.00	90.00
(48)	Rogers Hornsby	400.00	200.00	120.00
(49)	Waite Hoyt	300.00	150.00	90.00
(50)	Wilbert Hubbell	100.00	50.00	30.00
(51)	Wm. Jacobson	100.00	50.00	30.00
(52)	Walter Johnson	850.00	425.00	255.00
(53)	Jimmy Johnston	100.00	50.00	30.00
(54)	Joe Judge	100.00	50.00	30.00
(55)	Geo. "Bingo" Kelly	300.00	150.00	90.00
(56)	Dick Kerr	100.00	50.00	30.00
(57)	Pete Kilduff/Bending	100.00	50.00	30.00
(58)	Pete Kilduff/Leaping	100.00	50.00	30.00
(59)	Larry Kopf	100.00	50.00	30.00
(60)	H.B. Leonard	100.00	50.00	30.00
(61)	Harry Liebold (Leibold)	100.00	50.00	30.00
(62)	Walter "Buster" Mails ("Duster")	100.00	50.00	30.00
(63)	Walter "Rabbit" Maranville	300.00	150.00	90.00
(64)	Carl Mays	100.00	50.00	30.00
(65)	Lee Meadows	100.00	50.00	30.00
(66)	Bob Meusel	100.00	50.00	30.00
(67)	Emil Meusel	100.00	50.00	30.00
(68)	J.C. Milan	100.00	50.00	30.00
(69)	Earl Neale	125.00	60.00	35.00
(70)	Robert Nehf (Arthur)	100.00	50.00	30.00
(71)	Bernie Neis	100.00	50.00	30.00
(72)	Joe Oeschger	100.00	50.00	30.00
(73)	Robert O'Farrell	100.00	50.00	30.00
(74)	Ivan Olson	100.00	50.00	30.00
(75)	Steve O'Neill	100.00	50.00	30.00
(76)	Geo. Paskert	100.00	50.00	30.00
(77)	Roger Peckinpaugh	100.00	50.00	30.00
(78)	Herb Pennock	300.00	150.00	90.00
(79)	Ralph "Cy" Perkins	100.00	50.00	30.00
(80)	Scott Perry (Photo actually Ed Rommel.)	100.00	50.00	30.00
(81)	Jeff Pfeffer	100.00	50.00	30.00
(82)	V.J. Picinich	100.00	50.00	30.00
(83)	Walter Pipp	115.00	55.00	35.00
(84)	Derrill Pratt	100.00	50.00	30.00
(85)	Goldie Rapp	100.00	50.00	30.00
(86)	Edgar Rice	300.00	150.00	90.00
(87)	Jimmy Ring	100.00	50.00	30.00
(88)	Eddie Rousch (Roush)	300.00	150.00	90.00
(89)	Babe Ruth	8,000	4,000	2,400
(90)	Raymond Schmandt	100.00	50.00	30.00
(91)	Everett Scott	100.00	50.00	30.00
(92)	Joe Sewell	300.00	150.00	90.00
(93)	Wally Shang (Schang)	100.00	50.00	30.00
(94)	Maurice Shannon	100.00	50.00	30.00
(95)	Bob Shawkey	100.00	50.00	30.00
(96)	Urban Shocker	100.00	50.00	30.00
(97)	George Sisler	300.00	150.00	90.00
(98)	Earl Smith	100.00	50.00	30.00
(99)	John Smith	100.00	50.00	30.00
(100)	Sherrod Smith	100.00	50.00	30.00
(101)	Frank Snyder/Crouching	100.00	50.00	30.00
(102)	Frank Snyder/Standing	100.00	50.00	30.00
(103)	Tris Speaker	400.00	200.00	120.00
(104)	Vernon Spencer	100.00	50.00	30.00
(105)	Chas. "Casey" Stengle (Stengel)	350.00	175.00	100.00
(106)	Milton Stock/Btg	100.00	50.00	30.00
(107)	Milton Stock/Fldg	100.00	50.00	30.00
(108)	James Vaughn	100.00	50.00	30.00
(109)	Robert Veach	100.00	50.00	30.00
(110)	Wm. Wambsgauss (Wambsganss)	100.00	50.00	30.00
(111)	Aaron Ward	100.00	50.00	30.00
(112)	Zach Wheat	300.00	150.00	90.00
(113)	George Whitted/Btg	100.00	50.00	30.00
(114)	George Whitted/Fldg	100.00	50.00	30.00
(115)	Fred C. Williams	100.00	50.00	30.00
(116)	Arthur Wilson	100.00	50.00	30.00
(117)	Ivy Wingo	100.00	50.00	30.00
(118)	Lawton Witt	100.00	50.00	30.00
(119)	"Pep" Young (Photo actually Ralph Young.)	100.00	50.00	30.00
(120)	Ross Young (Youngs)	300.00	150.00	90.00

1936 National Chicle "Fine Pens" (R313)

Issued in 1936 by the National Chicle Co., this set consists of 120 cards, measuring 3-1/4" x 5-3/8". The black-and-white cards are blank-backed and unnumbered. Although issued by National Chicle, the name of the company does not appear on the cards. The set includes individual player portraits with facsimilie autographs, multi-player cards and

action photos. The cards, known in the hobby as "Fine Pen" because of the thin style of writing used for the facsimilie autographs, were originally available as an in-store premium.

		NM	EX	VG
Complete Set (120):		6,500	3,250	1,950
Common Player:		40.00	20.00	12.00
(1)	Melo Almada	45.00	22.50	13.50
(2)	Nick Altrock, Al Schacht	40.00	20.00	12.00
(3)	Paul Andrews	40.00	20.00	12.00
(4)	Elden Auker (Eldon)	40.00	20.00	12.00
(5)	Earl Averill	75.00	37.50	22.50
(6)	John Babich, James Bucher	40.00	20.00	12.00
(7)	Jim Becher (Bucher)	40.00	20.00	12.00
(8)	Moe Berg	150.00	75.00	45.00
(9)	Walter Berger	40.00	20.00	12.00
(10)	Charles Berry	40.00	20.00	12.00
(11)	Ralph Birkhofer (Birkofer)	40.00	20.00	12.00
(12)	Cy Blanton	40.00	20.00	12.00
(13)	O. Bluege	40.00	20.00	12.00
(14)	Cliff Bolton	40.00	20.00	12.00
(15)	Zeke Bonura	40.00	20.00	12.00
(16)	Stan Bordagaray, George Earnshaw	40.00	20.00	12.00
(17)	Jim Bottomley, Charley Gelbert	50.00	25.00	15.00
(18)	Thos. Bridges	40.00	20.00	12.00
(19)	Sam Byrd	40.00	20.00	12.00
(20)	Dolph Camilli	40.00	20.00	12.00
(21)	Dolph Camilli, Billy Jurges	40.00	20.00	12.00
(22)	Bruce Campbell	40.00	20.00	12.00
(23)	Walter "Kit" Carson	40.00	20.00	12.00
(24)	Ben Chapman	40.00	20.00	12.00
(25)	Harlond Clift, Luke Sewell	40.00	20.00	12.00
(26)	Mickey Cochrane, Jimmy Fox (Foxx), Al Simmons	90.00	45.00	27.50
(27)	"Rip" Collins	40.00	20.00	12.00
(28)	Joe Cronin	75.00	37.50	22.50
(29)	Frank Crossetti (Crosetti)	40.00	20.00	12.00
(30)	Frank Crosetti, Jimmy Dykes	40.00	20.00	12.00
(31)	Kiki Cuyler, Gabby Hartnett	85.00	40.00	25.00
(32)	Paul Derringer	40.00	20.00	12.00
(33)	Bill Dickey, Hank Greenberg	90.00	45.00	27.50
(34)	Bill Dietrich	40.00	20.00	12.00
(35)	Joe DiMaggio, Hank Erickson	750.00	375.00	225.00
(36)	Carl Doyle	40.00	20.00	12.00
(37)	Charles Dressen, Bill Myers	40.00	20.00	12.00
(38)	Jimmie Dykes	40.00	20.00	12.00
(39)	Rick Ferrell, Wess Ferrell (Wes)	75.00	37.50	22.50
(40)	Pete Fox	40.00	20.00	12.00
(41)	Frankie Frisch	75.00	37.50	22.50
(42)	Milton Galatzer	40.00	20.00	12.00
(43)	Chas. Gehringer	75.00	37.50	22.50
(44)	Charley Gelbert	40.00	20.00	12.00
(45)	Joe Glenn	40.00	20.00	12.00
(46)	Jose Gomez	40.00	20.00	12.00
(47)	Lefty Gomez, Red Ruffing	90.00	45.00	27.50
(48)	Vernon Gomez	75.00	37.50	22.50
(49)	Leon Goslin	75.00	37.50	22.50
(50)	Hank Gowdy	40.00	20.00	12.00
(51)	"Hank" Greenberg	90.00	45.00	27.50
(52)	"Lefty" Grove	90.00	45.00	27.50
(53)	Stan Hack	40.00	20.00	12.00
(54)	Odell Hale	40.00	20.00	12.00
(55)	Wild Bill Hallahan	40.00	20.00	12.00
(56)	Mel Harder	40.00	20.00	12.00
(57)	Stanley Bucky Harriss (Harris)	75.00	37.50	22.50
(58)	Gabby Hartnett, Rip Radcliff	40.00	20.00	12.00
(59)	Gabby Hartnett, L. Waner	45.00	22.50	13.50
(60)	Gabby Hartnett, Lon Warnecke (Warneke)	40.00	20.00	12.00
(61)	Buddy Hassett	40.00	20.00	12.00
(62)	Babe Herman	40.00	20.00	12.00
(63)	Frank Higgins	40.00	20.00	12.00
(64)	Oral C. Hildebrand	40.00	20.00	12.00
(65)	Myril Hoag	40.00	20.00	12.00
(66)	Rogers Hornsby	90.00	45.00	27.50
(67)	Waite Hoyt	75.00	37.50	22.50
(68)	Willis G. Hudlin	40.00	20.00	12.00
(69)	"Woody" Jensen	40.00	20.00	12.00
(70)	Woody Jenson (Jensen)	40.00	20.00	12.00
(71)	William Knickerbocker	40.00	20.00	12.00
(72)	Joseph Kuhel	40.00	20.00	12.00
(73)	Cookie Lavagetto	40.00	20.00	12.00
(74)	Thornton Lee	40.00	20.00	12.00
(75)	Ernie Lombardi	75.00	37.50	22.50
(76)	Red Lucas	40.00	20.00	12.00
(77)	Connie Mack, John McGraw	75.00	37.50	22.50
(78)	Pepper Martin	40.00	20.00	12.00
(79)	George McQuinn	40.00	20.00	12.00
(80)	George McQuinn, Lee Stine	40.00	20.00	12.00
(81)	Joe Medwick	75.00	37.50	22.50
(82)	Oscar Melillo	40.00	20.00	12.00
(83)	"Buddy" Meyer (Myer)	40.00	20.00	12.00
(84)	Randy Moore	40.00	20.00	12.00
(85)	T. Moore, Jimmie Wilson	40.00	20.00	12.00
(86)	Wallace Moses	40.00	20.00	12.00
(87)	V. Mungo	40.00	20.00	12.00
(88)	Lamar Newsom (Newsome)	40.00	20.00	12.00
(89)	Lewis "Buck" Newsom (Louis)	40.00	20.00	12.00
(90)	Steve O'Neill	40.00	20.00	12.00
(91)	Tommie Padden	40.00	20.00	12.00
(92)	E. Babe Philips (Phelps)	40.00	20.00	12.00
(93)	Bill Rogel (Rogell)	40.00	20.00	12.00
(94)	Lynn "Schoolboy" Rowe	40.00	20.00	12.00
(95)	Luke Sewell	40.00	20.00	12.00
(96)	Al Simmons	75.00	37.50	22.50
(97)	Casey Stengel	80.00	40.00	24.00
(98)	Bill Swift	40.00	20.00	12.00
(99)	Cecil Travis	40.00	20.00	12.00
(100)	"Pie" Traynor	75.00	37.50	22.50
(101)	William Urbansky (Urbanski)	40.00	20.00	12.00
(102)	Arky Vaughn (Vaughan)	75.00	37.50	22.50
(103)	Joe Vosmik	40.00	20.00	12.00
(104)	Honus Wagner	135.00	65.00	40.00
(105)	Rube Walberg	40.00	20.00	12.00
(106)	Bill Walker	40.00	20.00	12.00
(107)	Gerald Walker	40.00	20.00	12.00
(108)	L. Waner, P. Waner, Big Jim Weaver	75.00	37.50	22.50
(109)	George Washington	40.00	20.00	12.00
(110)	Bill Werber	40.00	20.00	12.00
(111)	Sam West	40.00	20.00	12.00
(112)	Pinkey Whitney	40.00	20.00	12.00
(113)	Vernon Wiltshere (Wilshere)	40.00	20.00	12.00
(114)	"Pep" Young	40.00	20.00	12.00
(115)	Chicago White Sox 1936	40.00	20.00	12.00
(116)	Fence Busters	40.00	20.00	12.00
(117)	Talking It Over (Leo Durocher)	40.00	20.00	12.00
(118)	There She Goes! Chicago City Series	40.00	20.00	12.00
(119)	Ump Says No - Cleveland vs. Detroit	40.00	20.00	12.00
(120)	World Series 1935 (Phil Cavarretta, Goose Goslin, Lon Warneke)	40.00	20.00	12.00

1936 National Chicle Rabbit Maranville 'How To'

Issued by National Chicle in 1936, this 20-card set was a paper issue distributed with Batter-Up Gum. Unfolded, each paper measured 3-5/8" x 6". The numbered set featured a series of baseball tips from Rabbit Maranville and are illustrated with line drawings. American Card Catalog designation was R344.

		NM	EX	VG
Complete Set (20):		700.00	350.00	210.00
Common Card:		35.00	17.50	10.00
1	How to Pitch the Out Shoot	35.00	17.50	10.00
2	How to Throw the In Shoot	35.00	17.50	10.00
3	How to Pitch the Drop	35.00	17.50	10.00
4	How to Pitch the Floater	35.00	17.50	10.00
5	How to Run Bases	35.00	17.50	10.00
6	How to Slide	35.00	17.50	10.00
7	How to Catch Flies	35.00	17.50	10.00
8	How to Field Grounders	35.00	17.50	10.00
9	How to Tag A Man Out	35.00	17.50	10.00
10	How to Cover A Base	35.00	17.50	10.00
11	How to Bat	35.00	17.50	10.00
12	How to Steal Bases	35.00	17.50	10.00
13	How to Bunt	35.00	17.50	10.00
14	How to Coach Base Runner	35.00	17.50	10.00
15	How to Catch Behind the Bat	35.00	17.50	10.00
16	How to Throw to Bases	35.00	17.50	10.00
17	How to Signal	35.00	17.50	10.00
18	How to Umpire Balls and Strikes	35.00	17.50	10.00
19	How to Umpire Bases	35.00	17.50	10.00
20	How to Lay Out a Ball Field	35.00	17.50	10.00

1898-99 National Copper Plate Co. Portraits

Besides supplying The Sporting News with the player portrait supplements issued during 1899-1900, this Grand Rapids, Mich., firm also sold nearly identical pieces in portfolios of 50 in a hard-cover, string-bound book. Approximately 10" x 13", the pictures feature the players at the turn of the century in formal portrait poses; some are in uniform, some in civilian clothes. The pictures are vignetted on a white background with the player's full name, team and year of issue printed at bottom. At lower-left on most, but not all, of the pictures is National Copper Plate's credit line. Backs have a player biographies in elaborate scrollwork frames.

		NM	EX	VG
Complete Set (50):		60,000	30,000	18,000
Common Player:		1,100	425.00	200.00
(1)	M.F. Amole (M.G. "Doc")	1,100	425.00	200.00
(2)	A.C. Anson	2,400	950.00	480.00
(3)	Robert Becker	1,100	425.00	200.00
(4)	Martin Bergen	1,100	425.00	200.00
(5)	James A. Collins	2,100	850.00	425.00
(6)	Joe Corbett	1,100	425.00	200.00
(7)	Louis Criger	1,100	425.00	200.00
(8)	Lave Cross	1,100	425.00	200.00
(9)	Montford Cross	1,100	425.00	200.00
(10)	Eugene DeMontreville	1,100	425.00	200.00
(11)	Charles Dexter	1,100	425.00	200.00
(12)	P.J. Donovan	1,100	425.00	200.00
(13)	Thomas Dowd	1,100	425.00	200.00
(14)	John J. Doyle	1,100	425.00	200.00
(15)	Hugh Duffy	1,800	700.00	350.00
(16)	Frank Dwyer	1,100	425.00	200.00
(17)	Fred Ely ("Bones")	1,100	425.00	200.00
(18)	A.F. Esterquest	1,100	425.00	200.00
(19)	Wm. Ewing	1,800	700.00	350.00
(20)	Elmer Flick	1,800	700.00	350.00
(21)	Daniel Friend	1,100	425.00	200.00
(22)	George F. Gilpatrick (Gillpatrick)	1,100	425.00	200.00
(23)	J.M. Goar	1,100	425.00	200.00
(24)	Michael Griffin	1,100	425.00	200.00
(25)	Clark C. Griffith	1,800	700.00	350.00
(26)	William Hill	1,100	425.00	200.00
(27)	Dummy Hoy	2,100	850.00	400.00
(28)	James Hughes	1,100	425.00	200.00
(29)	William Joyce	1,100	425.00	200.00
(30)	William Keeler	1,800	700.00	350.00
(31)	Joseph J. Kelley	1,800	700.00	350.00
(32)	William Kennedy	1,100	425.00	200.00
(33)	William Lange	1,100	425.00	200.00
(34)	John J. McGraw	1,800	700.00	350.00
(35)	W.B. Mercer (George B. "Win")	1,100	425.00	200.00
(36)	Charles A. Nichols	2,100	850.00	400.00
(37)	Jerry Nops	1,100	425.00	200.00
(38)	John O'Connor	1,100	425.00	200.00
(39)	Richard Padden	1,100	425.00	200.00
(40)	Wilbert Robinson	1,800	700.00	350.00
(41)	William Shindle	1,000	425.00	200.00
(42)	Charles Stahl	1,000	425.00	200.00
(43)	E.F. Stein	1,100	425.00	200.00
(44)	S.L. Thompson	2,100	850.00	400.00
(45)	John Wagner	2,900	1,150	575.00
(46)	R.J. Wallace	1,800	700.00	350.00
(47)	Victor Willis	1,800	700.00	350.00
(48)	Parke Wilson	1,100	425.00	200.00
(49)	George Yeager	1,100	425.00	200.00
(50)	C.L. Zimmer	1,100	425.00	200.00

1913 National Game (WG5)

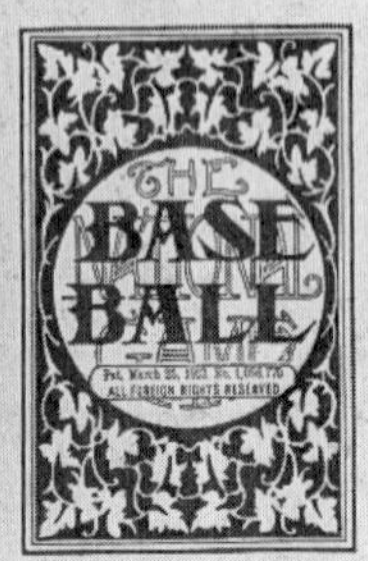

The patent date on the ornate red-and-white backs identify this as a 1913 issue. Fronts of the 2-1/2" x 3-1/2" cards have a black-and-white photo and a pair of baseball play scenarios used to play the card game. Corners are rounded. The set contains 43 identified player cards, a group of nine action photos in which the players are not identified and two header cards. The unnumbered cards are checklisted in alphabetical order. This set carries the ACC designation of WG5.

		NM	EX	VG
Complete Set (54):		6,000	3,000	1,800
Common Player:		55.00	30.00	20.00
Action Photo Card:		16.50	8.25	5.00
(1)	Grover Alexander	800.00	100.00	60.00
(2)	Frank Baker	150.00	50.00	30.00
(3)	Chief Bender	150.00	50.00	30.00
(4)	Bob Bescher	55.00	30.00	20.00
(5)	Joe Birmingham	55.00	30.00	20.00

(6)	Roger Bresnahan	150.00	50.00	30.00
(7)	Nixey Callahan	55.00	30.00	20.00
(8)	Frank Chance	150.00	50.00	30.00
(9)	Hal Chase	75.00	37.50	22.50
(10)	Fred Clarke	150.00	50.00	30.00
(11)	Ty Cobb	1,000	300.00	180.00
(12)	Sam Crawford	150.00	50.00	30.00
(13)	Bill Dahlen	55.00	30.00	20.00
(14)	Jake Daubert	55.00	30.00	20.00
(15)	Red Dooin	55.00	30.00	20.00
(16)	Johnny Evers	150.00	50.00	30.00
(17)	Vean Gregg	55.00	30.00	20.00
(18)	Clark Griffith	150.00	50.00	30.00
(19)	Dick Hoblitzel	55.00	30.00	20.00
(20)	Miller Huggins	150.00	50.00	30.00
(21)	Joe Jackson	3,500	800.00	480.00
(22)	Hughie Jennings	150.00	50.00	30.00
(23)	Walter Johnson	500.00	125.00	75.00
(24)	Ed Konetchy	55.00	30.00	20.00
(25)	Nap Lajoie	150.00	50.00	30.00
(26)	Connie Mack	150.00	50.00	30.00
(27)	Rube Marquard	150.00	50.00	30.00
(28)	Christy Mathewson	500.00	125.00	75.00
(29)	John McGraw	150.00	50.00	30.00
(30)	Larry McLean	55.00	30.00	20.00
(31)	Clyde Milan	55.00	30.00	20.00
(32)	Marty O'Toole	55.00	30.00	20.00
(33)	Nap Rucker	55.00	30.00	20.00
(34)	Tris Speaker	200.00	75.00	45.00
(35)	Jake Stahl	55.00	30.00	20.00
(36)	George Stallings	55.00	30.00	20.00
(37)	George Stovall	55.00	30.00	20.00
(38)	Bill Sweeney	55.00	30.00	20.00
(39)	Joe Tinker	150.00	50.00	30.00
(40)	Honus Wagner	1,000	200.00	120.00
(41)	Ed Walsh	150.00	50.00	30.00
(42)	Joe Wood	55.00	30.00	20.00
(43)	Cy Young	500.00	125.00	75.00
(---)	Rules Card	55.00	30.00	20.00
(---)	Score Card	55.00	30.00	20.00
(1A)	Batter swinging, looking forward	15.00	7.50	4.50
(2A)	Batter swinging, looking back	15.00	7.50	4.50
(3A)	Runner sliding, fielder at bag	15.00	7.50	4.50
(4A)	Runner sliding, umpire behind (Some collectors believe the player in the picture is Ty Cobb and are willing to pay a premium for this card.)	75.00	37.50	22.50
(5A)	Runner sliding, hugging base	15.00	7.50	4.50
(6A)	Sliding play at plate, umpire at left	15.00	7.50	4.50
(7A)	Sliding play at plate, umpire at right	15.00	7.50	4.50
(8A)	Play at plate, runner standing	15.00	7.50	4.50
(9A)	Runner looking backwards	15.00	7.50	4.50

1952 National Tea Labels

Another set of bread end-labels, this checklist now comprises 44 players, although there is speculation that others remain to be cataloged. The unnumbered labels measure approximately 2-3/4" x 2-11/16" and are sometimes referred to as "Red Borders" because of their wide, red margins. The player's name and team are printed alongside his photo, and the slogan "Eat More Bread for Health" also appears on some labels.

		NM	EX	VG
Complete Set (44):		10,000	5,000	3,000
Common Player:		200.00	100.00	60.00
(1)	Gene Bearden	200.00	100.00	60.00
(2)	Yogi Berra	450.00	225.00	135.00
(3)	Lou Brissie	200.00	100.00	60.00
(4)	Sam Chapman	200.00	100.00	60.00
(5)	Chuck Diering	200.00	100.00	60.00
(6)	Dom DiMaggio	250.00	125.00	75.00
(7)	Bruce Edwards	200.00	100.00	60.00
(8)	Del Ennis	200.00	100.00	60.00
(9)	Ferris Fain	200.00	100.00	60.00
(10)	Bob Feller	375.00	185.00	110.00
(11)	Howie Fox	200.00	100.00	60.00
(12)	Sid Gordon	200.00	100.00	60.00
(13)	John Groth	200.00	100.00	60.00
(14)	Granny Hamner	200.00	100.00	60.00
(15)	Jim Hegan	200.00	100.00	60.00
(16)	Sheldon Jones	200.00	100.00	60.00
(17)	Howie Judson	200.00	100.00	60.00
(18)	Sherman Lollar	200.00	100.00	60.00
(19)	Clarence Marshall	200.00	100.00	60.00
(20)	Don Mueller	200.00	100.00	60.00
(21)	Danny Murtaugh	200.00	100.00	60.00
(22)	Dave Philley	200.00	100.00	60.00
(23)	Jerry Priddy	200.00	100.00	60.00
(24)	Bill Rigney	200.00	100.00	60.00
(25)	Robin Roberts	350.00	175.00	100.00
(26)	Eddie Robinson	200.00	100.00	60.00
(27)	Preacher Roe	225.00	110.00	65.00
(28)	Stan Rojek	200.00	100.00	60.00
(29)	Al Rosen	225.00	110.00	65.00
(30)	Bob Rush	200.00	100.00	60.00
(31)	Hank Sauer	200.00	100.00	60.00
(32)	Johnny Schmitz	200.00	100.00	60.00
(33)	Enos Slaughter	350.00	175.00	100.00
(34)	Duke Snider	400.00	200.00	120.00
(35)	Warren Spahn	375.00	185.00	110.00
(36)	Gerry Staley	200.00	100.00	60.00
(37)	Virgil Stallcup	200.00	100.00	60.00
(38)	George Stirnweiss	200.00	100.00	60.00
(39)	Earl Torgeson	200.00	100.00	60.00
(40)	Dizzy Trout	200.00	100.00	60.00
(41)	Mickey Vernon	200.00	100.00	60.00
(42)	Wally Westlake	200.00	100.00	60.00
(43)	Johnny Wyrostek	200.00	100.00	60.00
(44)	Eddie Yost	200.00	100.00	60.00

1922 Neilson's Chocolate Type 1 (V61)

This set is closely related to the popular 1922 American Caramels (E120). The 120-card set was issued in Canada by Neilson's Chocolate Bars and carries the American Card Catalog designation V61. The front of the approximately 2" x 3-1/2" black-and-white cards has oval posed action photos with a decorative border. In the bottom border is the player name, position and team. Backs contain an ad for Neilson's Chocolates. Two types of cards exist. Type 1 is printed on heavy paper (similar to E120), has a card number in the lower-left corner and features Old English typography of the sponsor's name on back. Type 2 is printed on cardboard, has no card numbers and has no Old English typography on back.

		NM	EX	VG
Complete Set (120):		27,500	11,000	5,500
Common Player:		115.00	45.00	22.50
1	George Burns	115.00	45.00	22.50
2	John Tobin	115.00	45.00	22.50
3	J.T. Zachary	115.00	45.00	22.50
4	"Bullet" Joe Bush	115.00	45.00	22.50
5	Lu Blue	115.00	45.00	22.50
6	Clarence (Tillie) Walker	115.00	45.00	22.50
7	Carl Mays	115.00	45.00	22.50
8	Leon Goslin	300.00	120.00	60.00
9	Ed Rommel	115.00	45.00	22.50
10	Charles Robertson	115.00	45.00	22.50
11	Ralph (Cy) Perkins	115.00	45.00	22.50
12	Joe Sewell	300.00	120.00	60.00
13	Harry Hooper	300.00	120.00	60.00
14	Urban (Red) Faber	300.00	120.00	60.00
15	Bib Falk (Bibb)	115.00	45.00	22.50
16	George Uhle	115.00	45.00	22.50
17	Emory Rigney	115.00	45.00	22.50
18	George Dauss	115.00	45.00	22.50
19	Herman Pillette	115.00	45.00	22.50
20	Wallie Schang	115.00	45.00	22.50
21	Lawrence Woodall	115.00	45.00	22.50
22	Steve O'Neill	115.00	45.00	22.50
23	Edmund (Bing) Miller	115.00	45.00	22.50
24	Sylvester Johnson	115.00	45.00	22.50
25	Henry Severeid	115.00	45.00	22.50
26	Dave Danforth	115.00	45.00	22.50
27	Harry Heilmann	300.00	120.00	60.00
28	Bert Cole	115.00	45.00	22.50
29	Eddie Collins	300.00	120.00	60.00
30	Ty Cobb	3,500	1,400	700.00
31	Bill Wambsganss	115.00	45.00	22.50
32	George Sisler	300.00	120.00	60.00
33	Bob Veach	115.00	45.00	22.50
34	Earl Sheely	115.00	45.00	22.50
35	T.P. (Pat) Collins	115.00	45.00	22.50
36	Frank (Dixie) Davis	115.00	45.00	22.50
37	Babe Ruth	6,000	2,400	1,200
38	Bryan Harris	115.00	45.00	22.50
39	Bob Shawkey	115.00	45.00	22.50
40	Urban Shocker	115.00	45.00	22.50
41	Martin McManus	115.00	45.00	22.50
42	Clark Pittenger	115.00	45.00	22.50
43	"Deacon" Sam Jones	115.00	45.00	22.50
44	Waite Hoyt	300.00	120.00	60.00
45	Johnny Mostil	115.00	45.00	22.50
46	Mike Menosky	115.00	45.00	22.50
47	Walter Johnson	600.00	240.00	120.00
48	Wallie Pipp (Wally)	115.00	45.00	22.50
49	Walter Gerber	115.00	45.00	22.50
50	Ed Gharrity	115.00	45.00	22.50
51	Frank Ellerbe	115.00	45.00	22.50
52	Kenneth Williams	115.00	45.00	22.50
53	Joe Hauser	175.00	70.00	35.00
54	Carson Bigbee	115.00	45.00	22.50
55	Emil (Irish) Meusel	115.00	45.00	22.50
56	Milton Stock	115.00	45.00	22.50
57	Wilbur Cooper	115.00	45.00	22.50
58	Tom Griffith	115.00	45.00	22.50
59	Walter (Butch) Henline	115.00	45.00	22.50
60	Gene (Bubbles) Hargrave	115.00	45.00	22.50
61	Russell Wrightstone	115.00	45.00	22.50
62	Frank Frisch	300.00	120.00	60.00
63	Frank Parkinson	115.00	45.00	22.50
64	Walter (Dutch) Reuther (Ruether)	115.00	45.00	22.50
65	Bill Doak	115.00	45.00	22.50
66	Marty Callaghan	115.00	45.00	22.50
67	Sammy Bohne	175.00	70.00	35.00
68	Earl Hamilton	115.00	45.00	22.50
69	Grover C. Alexander	325.00	130.00	65.00
70	George Burns	115.00	45.00	22.50
71	Max Carey	300.00	120.00	60.00
72	Adolfo Luque	145.00	58.00	29.00
73	Dave (Beauty) Bancroft	300.00	120.00	60.00
74	Vic Aldridge	115.00	45.00	22.50
75	Jack Smith	115.00	45.00	22.50
76	Bob O'Farrell	115.00	45.00	22.50
77	Pete Donohue	115.00	45.00	22.50
78	Ralph Pinelli	115.00	45.00	22.50
79	Eddie Roush	300.00	120.00	60.00
80	Norman Boeckel	115.00	45.00	22.50
81	Rogers Hornsby	400.00	160.00	80.00
82	George Toporcer	115.00	45.00	22.50
83	Ivy Wingo	115.00	45.00	22.50
84	Virgil Cheeves	115.00	45.00	22.50
85	Vern Clemons	115.00	45.00	22.50
86	Lawrence (Hack) Miller	115.00	45.00	22.50
87	Johnny Kelleher	115.00	45.00	22.50
88	Heinie Groh	115.00	45.00	22.50
89	Burleigh Grimes	300.00	120.00	60.00
90	"Rabbit" Maranville	300.00	120.00	60.00
91	Charles (Babe) Adams	115.00	45.00	22.50
92	Lee King	115.00	45.00	22.50
93	Art Nehf	115.00	45.00	22.50
94	Frank Snyder	115.00	45.00	22.50
95	Raymond Powell	115.00	45.00	22.50
96	Wilbur Hubbell	115.00	45.00	22.50
97	Leon Cadore	115.00	45.00	22.50
98	Joe Oeschger	115.00	45.00	22.50
99	Jake Daubert	115.00	45.00	22.50
100	Will Sherdel	115.00	45.00	22.50
101	Hank DeBerry	115.00	45.00	22.50
102	Johnny Lavan	115.00	45.00	22.50
103	Jesse Haines	300.00	120.00	60.00
104	Joe (Goldie) Rapp	115.00	45.00	22.50
105	Oscar Ray Grimes	115.00	45.00	22.50
106	Ross Young (Youngs)	300.00	120.00	60.00
107	Art Fletcher	115.00	45.00	22.50
108	Clyde Barnhart	115.00	45.00	22.50
109	Louis (Pat) Duncan	115.00	45.00	22.50
110	Charlie Hollocher	115.00	45.00	22.50
111	Horace Ford	115.00	45.00	22.50
112	Bill Cunningham	115.00	45.00	22.50
113	Walter Schmidt	115.00	45.00	22.50
114	Joe Schultz	115.00	45.00	22.50
115	John Morrison	115.00	45.00	22.50
116	Jimmy Caveney	115.00	45.00	22.50
117	Zach Wheat	300.00	120.00	60.00
118	Fred (Cy) Williams	115.00	45.00	22.50
119	George Kelly	300.00	120.00	60.00
120	Jimmy Ring	115.00	45.00	22.50

1922 Neilson's Chocolate Type 2 (V61)

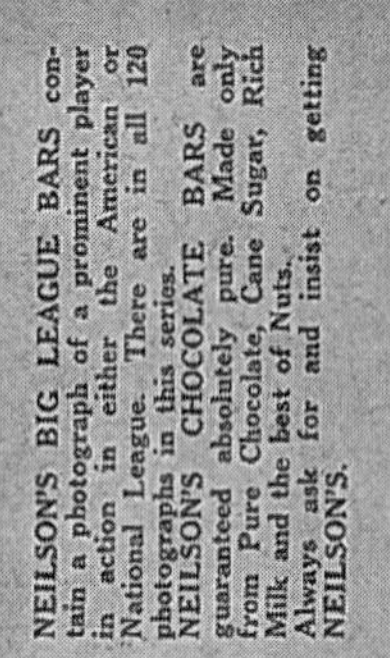

This set is closely related to the popular 1922 American Caramels (E120). The 120-card set was issued in Canada by Neilson's Chocolate Bars and carries the American Card Catalog designation V61. The front of the approximately 2" x 3-1/2" black-and-white cards has oval posed action photos with a decorative border. In the bottom border is the player name, position and team. Backs contain and ad for Neilson's Chocolates. Two types of cards exist. Type 1 is printed on heavy paper (similar to E120), has a card number in the lower-left corner and features Old English typography of the sponsor's name on back. Type 2 is printed on cardboard, has no card numbers and has no Old English typography on back.

		NM	EX	VG
Complete Set (120):		42,500	17,000	8,500
Common Player:		200.00	85.00	40.00
(1)	Charles (Babe) Adams	200.00	85.00	40.00
(2)	Vic Aldridge	200.00	85.00	40.00
(3)	Grover C. Alexander	750.00	300.00	150.00
(4)	Dave (Beauty) Bancroft	450.00	180.00	90.00
(5)	Clyde Barnhart	200.00	85.00	40.00
(6)	Carson Bigbee	200.00	85.00	40.00
(7)	Lu Blue	200.00	85.00	40.00
(8)	Norman Boeckel	200.00	85.00	40.00
(9)	Sammy Bohne	250.00	100.00	50.00

(10)	George Burns (Boston)	200.00	85.00	40.00
(11)	George Burns (Cincinnati)	200.00	85.00	40.00
(12)	""Bullet" Joe Bush	200.00	85.00	40.00
(13)	Leon Cadore	200.00	85.00	40.00
(14)	Marty Callaghan	200.00	85.00	40.00
(15)	Max Carey	450.00	180.00	90.00
(16)	Jimmy Caveney	200.00	85.00	40.00
(17)	Virgil Cheeves	200.00	85.00	40.00
(18)	Vern Clemons	200.00	85.00	40.00
(19)	Ty Cobb	5,500	2,200	1,100
(20)	Bert Cole	200.00	85.00	40.00
(21)	Eddie Collins	450.00	180.00	90.00
(22)	T.P. (Pat) Collins	200.00	85.00	40.00
(23)	Wilbur Cooper	200.00	85.00	40.00
(24)	Bill Cunningham	200.00	85.00	40.00
(25)	Dave Danforth	200.00	85.00	40.00
(26)	Jake Daubert	200.00	85.00	40.00
(27)	George Dauss	200.00	85.00	40.00
(28)	Frank (Dixie) Davis	200.00	85.00	40.00
(29)	Hank DeBerry	200.00	85.00	40.00
(30)	Bill Doak	200.00	85.00	40.00
(31)	Pete Donohue	200.00	85.00	40.00
(32)	Louis (Pat) Duncan	200.00	85.00	40.00
(33)	Frank Ellerbe	200.00	85.00	40.00
(34)	Urban (Red) Faber	450.00	180.00	90.00
(35)	Bib (Bibb) Falk	200.00	85.00	40.00
(36)	Art Fletcher	200.00	85.00	40.00
(37)	Horace Ford	200.00	85.00	40.00
(38)	Frank Frisch	450.00	180.00	90.00
(39)	Walter Gerber	200.00	85.00	40.00
(40)	Ed Gharrity	200.00	85.00	40.00
(41)	Leon Goslin	450.00	180.00	90.00
(42)	Tom Griffith	200.00	85.00	40.00
(43)	Burleigh Grimes	450.00	180.00	90.00
(44)	Oscar Ray Grimes	200.00	85.00	40.00
(45)	Heinie Groh	200.00	85.00	40.00
(46)	Jesse Haines	450.00	180.00	90.00
(47)	Earl Hamilton	200.00	85.00	40.00
(48)	Gene (Bubbles) Hargrave	200.00	85.00	40.00
(49)	Bryan Harris	200.00	85.00	40.00
(50)	Joe Hauser	350.00	140.00	70.00
(51)	Harry Heilmann	450.00	180.00	90.00
(52)	Walter (Butch) Henline	200.00	85.00	40.00
(53)	Charlie Hollocher	200.00	85.00	40.00
(54)	Harry Hooper	450.00	180.00	90.00
(55)	Rogers Hornsby	550.00	220.00	110.00
(56)	Waite Hoyt	450.00	180.00	90.00
(57)	Wilbert Hubbell	200.00	85.00	40.00
(58)	Sylvester Johnson	200.00	85.00	40.00
(59)	Walter Johnson	800.00	320.00	160.00
(60)	"Deacon" Sam Jones	200.00	85.00	40.00
(61)	Johnny Kelleher	200.00	85.00	40.00
(62)	George Kelly	450.00	180.00	90.00
(63)	Lee King	200.00	85.00	40.00
(64)	Johnny Lavan	200.00	85.00	40.00
(65)	Adolfo Luque	250.00	100.00	50.00
(66)	"Rabbit" Maranville	450.00	180.00	90.00
(67)	Carl Mays	200.00	85.00	40.00
(68)	Martin McManus	200.00	85.00	40.00
(69)	Mike Menosky	200.00	85.00	40.00
(70)	Emil (Irish) Meusel	200.00	85.00	40.00
(71)	Edmund (Bing) Miller	200.00	85.00	40.00
(72)	Lawrence (Hack) Miller	200.00	85.00	40.00
(73)	John Morrison	200.00	85.00	40.00
(74)	Johnny Mostil	200.00	85.00	40.00
(75)	Art Nehf	200.00	85.00	40.00
(76)	Joe Oeschger	200.00	85.00	40.00
(77)	Bob O'Farrell	200.00	85.00	40.00
(78)	Steve O'Neill	200.00	85.00	40.00
(79)	Frank Parkinson	200.00	85.00	40.00
(80)	Ralph (Cy) Perkins	200.00	85.00	40.00
(81)	Herman Pillette	200.00	85.00	40.00
(82)	Ralph Pinelli	200.00	85.00	40.00
(83)	Wallie (Wally) Pipp	200.00	85.00	40.00
(84)	Clark Pittinger	200.00	85.00	40.00
(85)	Raymond Powell	200.00	85.00	40.00
(86)	Joe (Goldie) Rapp	200.00	85.00	40.00
(87)	Walter (Dutch) Reuther	200.00	85.00	40.00
(88)	Emory Rigney	200.00	85.00	40.00
(89)	Jimmy Ring	200.00	85.00	40.00
(90)	Charles Robertson	200.00	85.00	40.00
(91)	Ed Rommel	200.00	85.00	40.00
(92)	Eddie Roush	450.00	180.00	90.00
(93)	Babe Ruth	7,500	3,000	1,500
(94)	Wallie (Wally) Schang	200.00	85.00	40.00
(95)	Walter Schmidt	200.00	85.00	40.00
(96)	Joe Schultz	200.00	85.00	40.00
(97)	Hank Severeid	200.00	85.00	40.00
(98)	Joe Sewell	450.00	180.00	90.00
(99)	Bob Shawkey	200.00	85.00	40.00
(100)	Earl Sheely	200.00	85.00	40.00
(101)	Will Sherdel	200.00	85.00	40.00
(102)	Urban Shocker	200.00	85.00	40.00
(103)	George Sisler	450.00	180.00	90.00
(104)	Jack Smith	200.00	85.00	40.00
(105)	Frank Snyder	200.00	85.00	40.00
(106)	Milton Stock	200.00	85.00	40.00
(107)	John Tobin	200.00	85.00	40.00
(108)	George Torporcer	200.00	85.00	40.00
(109)	George Uhle	200.00	85.00	40.00
(110)	Bob Veach	200.00	85.00	40.00
(111)	Clarence (Tillie) Walker	200.00	85.00	40.00
(112)	Bill Wambsganss	200.00	85.00	40.00
(113)	Zach Wheat	450.00	180.00	90.00
(114)	Fred (Cy) Williams	200.00	85.00	40.00
(115)	Kenneth Williams	200.00	85.00	40.00
(116)	Ivy Wingo	200.00	85.00	40.00
(117)	Lawrence Woodall	200.00	85.00	40.00
(118)	Russell Wrightstone	200.00	85.00	40.00
(119)	Ross Young (Youngs)	450.00	180.00	90.00
(120)	J.T. Zachary	200.00	85.00	40.00

1923 "Neilson's Chocolates"

This issue, purporting to come from the Canadian candy maker which had produced a 1922 set, was first reported in 1996. The cards appear to be genuine W572 strip cards which have had a Neilson's ad overprinted on the back many

years later in an apparent effort to defraud collectors. These altered W572s would have to be significantly downgraded to adjust for the defacing. It can be expected that any card that appears in W572 can be found with the Neilson's back, but the "discovery" contained only 47 different players.

(See W572 for checklist.)

1959 Neptune Sardines Jimmy Piersall

Like the earlier advertising postcards he did for various Cain's food products, this 3-1/2" x 5-1/2" black-and-white postcard carries the endorsement of the popular Indians outfielder for Neptune brand sardines. The front has a borderless photo of the player in a batting pose with a facsimile autograph at top. The back has standard postcard indicia along with the ad message and a product picture.

	NM	EX	VG
Jimmy Piersall	50.00	25.00	15.00

1976-81 New England Sports Collectors

From the period 1976-81, the New England Sports Collectors club issued a series of postcard-size (3-1/2" x 5-1/4") black-and-white card promoting their annual shows in Nashua, N.H. No card was issued in 1978.

		NM	EX	VG
Complete Set (5):		30.00	15.00	9.00
Common Player:		6.00	3.00	1.75
1	Joe DiMaggio (1976)	8.00	4.00	2.50
2	Jackie Robinson (1977)	6.00	3.00	1.75
3	Ted Williams (1979)	7.00	3.50	2.00
4	Vince DiMaggio, Joe DiMaggio, Dom DiMaggio (1980)	6.00	3.00	1.75
5	Mickey Mantle (1981)	9.00	4.50	2.75

1895 Newsboy Cabinets (N566)

Issued in the 1890s by the National Tobacco Works, this massive cabinet card set was distributed as a premium with the Newsboy tobacco brand. Although the set contained over 500 popular actresses, athletes, politicians and other celebrities of the day, only about a dozen cards of baseball players have been found. The cards measure 4-1/4" x 6-1/2" and feature sepia-toned photographs mounted on a backing that usually has "Newsboy New York" printed at bottom. Each portrait photograph is numbered and a few of the photos are round. The ballplayers in the set are mostly members of the 1894 New York Giants with a couple of Brooklyn players. There are two known poses of John Ward. Cards have been seen with advertising on the back for Keystone cigars and Red Indian tobacco.

		NM	EX	VG
Common Player:		6,000	3,000	1,800
174	W.H. Murphy	6,000	3,000	1,800
175	Amos Rusie	15,000	4,500	2,750
176	Michael Tiernan	6,000	3,000	1,800
177	E.D. Burke	6,000	3,000	1,800
178	J.J. Doyle	6,000	3,000	1,800
179	W.B. Fuller	6,000	3,000	1,800
180	George Van Haltren	6,000	3,000	1,800
181	Dave Foutz	6,000	3,000	1,800
182	Jouett Meekin	6,000	3,000	1,800
183	Michael Griffin	6,000	3,000	1,800
201	W.H. (Dad) Clark (Clarke)	6,000	3,000	1,800
202	Parke Wilson	6,000	3,000	1,800
586	John Ward (Arms folded.)	9,250	4,625	2,775
587	John Ward (Bat at side.)	8,000	4,000	2,400

1886 New York Baseball Club (H812)

This rare 19th Century baseball issue can be classified under the general category of "trade" cards, a popular advertising vehicle of the period. The cards measure 3" x 4-3/4" and feature blue line-drawing portraits of members of the "New York Base Ball Club," which is printed along the top. As was common with this type of trade card, the bottom was left blank to accomodate various messages. The known examples of this set carry ads for local tobacco merchants and other businesses. The portraits are all based on the photographs used in the 1886 Old Judge set. The cards, which have been assigned an ACC designation of H812, are printed on thin paper rather than cardboard.

		NM	EX	VG
Complete Set (8):		84,000	37,200	20,400
Common Player:		7,200	3,200	1,450
(1)	T. Dealsey	7,200	3,200	1,450
(2)	M. Dorgan	7,200	3,200	1,450
(3)	T. Esterbrook	7,200	3,200	1,450
(4)	W. Ewing	16,200	8,100	4,800
(5)	J. Gerhardt	7,200	3,200	1,450
(6)	J. O'Rourke	16,200	8,100	4,800
(7)	D. Richardson	7,200	3,200	1,450
(8)	M. Welch	16,200	8,100	4,800

1969 N.Y. Boy Scouts

Cards featuring N.Y. Mets and Yankees players were used as a recruitment incentive in 1969. Cards are 2-1/2" x 3-1/2" and printed in black-and-white on thin cardboard. It is unknown, but likely, that players other than those checklisted here were also issued.

		NM	EX	VG
Common Player:		140.00	70.00	40.00
(1)	Tommy Agee	175.00	85.00	50.00
(2)	Bud Harrelson	175.00	85.00	50.00
(3)	Cleon Jones	175.00	85.00	50.00
(4)	Bobby Murcer	260.00	130.00	75.00
(5)	Art Shamsky	140.00	70.00	40.00
(6)	Tom Seaver	700.00	350.00	210.00
(7)	Mel Stottlemyre	260.00	130.00	75.00
(8)	Ron Swoboda	175.00	85.00	50.00

1879-80 N.Y. Clipper Woodcuts

The N.Y. Clipper was a weekly newspaper devoted to theater and sports (primarily baseball) coverage in New York City between 1853-1923. Like many contemporary papers, the Clipper featured woodcut engravings in its pages in a time before photographic reproduction of pictures was feasible. Between April 1879, and November 1880, the paper printed a series of baseball player portraits. The early pieces were titled "The Clipper Prize Winners." and numbered. All of the woodcuts are about 4-1/2" x 5-3/4" in size featuring portraits within ornate frames with identification and biographical details below. Collectors prefer the woodcuts to be neatly trimmed from the newspaper page, with the biography at bottom intact. Because of the rarity of surviving examples, catalog values are undetermined. Many of these early stars of the game appear on no other contemprary cards or memorabilia issues.

1879

1 M.C. Dorgan (4/12)
2 H.F. McCormick (4/19)
3 Stephen A. Libby (4/26)
4 Roscoe C. Barnes (5/3)
5 David W. Force (5/10)
6 Herman Doescher (Dosher) (5/17)
7a Joseph Hornung (5/24)
7b William H. McGunnigle (5/31)
9 Harding Richardson (6/7)
(10) James L. White (7/14)
(11) Levi S. Meyerle (6/21)
(12) Joe Start (6/28)
(13) T.H. Murnam (Murnane) (7/5)
(14) Thomas York (7/12)
(15) Fred Dunlap (7/19)
(16) A.J. Leonard (7/26)
(17) J. Lee Richmond (8/2)
(18) Charles N. Snyder (8/9)
(19) John Cassidy (8/16)
(20) Charles Fulmer (8/23)
(21) Thomas Poorman (8/30)
(22) John Ward (9/6)
(23) Larry Corcoran (9/13)
(24) Douglas Allison (9/20)
(25) John J. Farrow (9/27)
(26) E.N. Williamson (10/4)
(27) George Wright (10/11)
(28) John J. Burdock (10/18)
(29) James O'Rourke (10/25)
(30) Philip Baker (11/1)
(31) Samuel W. Trott (11/8)
(32) John Lynch (11/15)
(33) A.G. Spalding (11/22)
(34) John C. Chapman (11/29)
(35) Paul A. Hines (12/6)
(36) Frank C. Bancroft (12/13)
(37) John T. O'Conner (12/20)
(38) Andrew J. Piercy (12/27)

1880

(39) Harold M. McClure (1/3)
(40) J.H. Gifford (1/24)
(41) Sam Wright (5/15)
(42) T.J. Keefe (5/22)
(43) M.J. Kelly (5/29)
(44) John Troy (6/5)
(45) Joe Quest (6/12)
(46) Alonzo Knight (6/19)
(47) Charles E. Mason (6/26)
(48) F.E. Goldsmith (7/3)
(49) R.E. McKelvy (7/10)
(50) Wm. McLean (Umpire)(7/17)
(51) C.A. McVey (7/24)
(52) John Manning (7/31)
(53) Harry D. Stovey (8/7)
(54) George A. Wood (8/14)
(55) Robert T. Mathews (8/21)
(56) D. Brouthers (8/28)
(57) C.M. Smith (9/4)
(58) James L. Clinton (9/11)
(59) A.J. Bushong (9/18)
(60) William J. Sweeney (9/25)
(61) Roger Connor (10/2)
(62) William Hawes (10/9)
(63) Frank S. Flint (10/16)
(64) William L. Haug (10/23)
(65) M. Welch (10/30)
(66) Aaron B. Clapp (11/6)
(67) John J. Smith (11/13)
(68) George Creamer (11/20)

1905 N.Y. Giants Scorecard Postcard

Two versions, black-and-white and color, of this standard size (about 5-1/2" x 3-1/2") postcard were apparently available for several years as it is copyrighted 1905 but postally used examples from years later are often seen. The card has a black background with large cut-out letters "GIANTS" at center featuring action poses of six players. A grid at bottom allows by-inning scores of a game to be posted before mailing. The undivided back has an embellished double-ruled stamp box and a large ornate "Post Card" at top-center.

	NM	EX	VG
Black-and-White:	300.00	150.00	90.00
Color:	400.00	200.00	125.00

Frank Bowerman, Red Ames, Sam Mertes, Christy Mathewson, Iron Man McGinnity, Luther Taylor

1932 N.Y. Giants Schedule Postcards

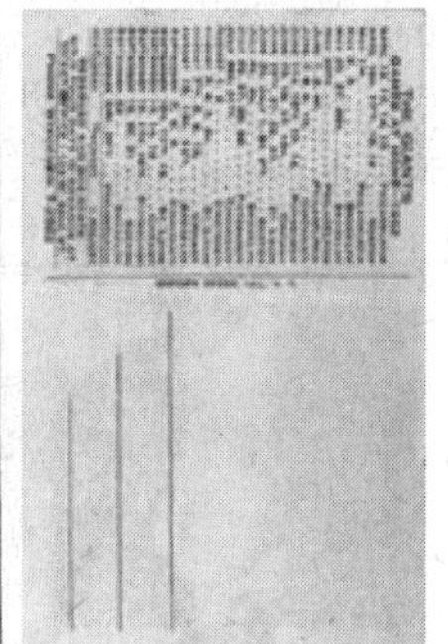

These postcard-size (3-1/2" x 5-1/2") black-and-white cards have an action pose on front with the player's identification and previous season's stats. At bottom is information about ladies' days, directions to the Polo Grounds and an offer to receive a free picture of a favorite player. The divided back has the team's 1932 schedule at left and space for addressing at right. There is also a credit line to Minden Press. The Carl Hubbell card is far more common than all others and can be found on either a thick or thin card stock that is unlike the stock on which the other players are found.

		NM	EX	VG
Common Player:		300.00	150.00	90.00
(1)	Ethan Allen	300.00	150.00	90.00
(2)	Herman Bell	300.00	150.00	90.00
(3)	Hugh Critz	300.00	150.00	90.00
(4)	Freddie Fitzsimmons	300.00	150.00	90.00
(5)	Chick Fullis	300.00	150.00	90.00
(6)	Sam Gibson	300.00	150.00	90.00
(7)	Fran Healey (Healy)	300.00	150.00	90.00
(8)	Frank Hogan	300.00	150.00	90.00
(9a)	Carl Hubbell (Thin stock.)	100.00	50.00	30.00
(9b)	Carl Hubbell (Thick stock.)	450.00	225.00	135.00
(10)	Travis Jackson	450.00	225.00	135.00
(11)	Len Koenecke	300.00	150.00	90.00
(12)	Sam Leslie	300.00	150.00	90.00
(13)	Freddy Lindstrom	450.00	225.00	135.00
(14)	Dolf Luque	325.00	160.00	97.00
(15)	Clarence Mitchell	300.00	150.00	90.00
(16)	Jim Mooney	300.00	150.00	90.00
(17)	Bob O'Farrell	300.00	150.00	90.00
(18)	Mel Ott	600.00	300.00	180.00
(19)	Roy Parmelee	300.00	150.00	90.00
(20)	Bill Terry	450.00	225.00	135.00
(21)	Johnny Vergez	300.00	150.00	90.00
(22)	Bill Walker	300.00	150.00	90.00

1948 N.Y. Giants Photo Pack

This set of player photos was sold at Polo Grounds souvenir stands. Pictures have player portraits in a 6-1/2" x 9" format. The black-and-white photos are blank-backed and have facsimile autographs printed near the bottom on front. A white border surrounds the front. The unnumbered photos are checklisted here in alphabetical order. It is possible the specific lineup of the packs changed over the course of the season to reflect roster moves.

		NM	EX	VG
Complete Set (27):		200.00	100.00	60.00
Common Player:		5.00	2.50	1.50
(1)	Jack Conway	5.00	2.50	1.50
(2)	Walker Cooper	5.00	2.50	1.50
(3)	Leo Durocher	9.00	4.50	2.75
(4)	Sid Gordon	7.50	3.75	2.25
(5)	Andy Hansen	5.00	2.50	1.50
(6)	Clint Hartung	5.00	2.50	1.50
(7)	Larry Jansen	5.00	2.50	1.50
(8)	Sheldon Jones	5.00	2.50	1.50
(9)	Monte Kennedy	5.00	2.50	1.50
(10)	Buddy Kerr	5.00	2.50	1.50
(11)	Dave Koslo	5.00	2.50	1.50
(12)	Thornton Lee	5.00	2.50	1.50
(13)	Mickey Livingston	5.00	2.50	1.50
(14)	Whitey Lockman	5.00	2.50	1.50
(15)	Jack Lohrke	5.00	2.50	1.50
(16)	Willard Marshall	5.00	2.50	1.50
(17)	Johnnie McCarthy	5.00	2.50	1.50
(18)	Earl McGowan	7.50	3.75	2.25
(19)	Johnny Mize	12.50	6.25	3.75
(20)	Bobo Newsom	5.00	2.50	1.50
(21)	Mel Ott	25.00	12.50	7.50
(22)	Ray Poat	5.00	2.50	1.50
(23)	Bobby Rhawn	5.00	2.50	1.50
(24)	Bill Rigney	5.00	2.50	1.50
(25)	Bobby Thomson	10.00	5.00	3.00
(26)	Ken Trinkle	5.00	2.50	1.50
(27)	Wesley N. Westrum	5.00	2.50	1.50

1949 N.Y. Giants Photo Pack

This set of player photos was sold at Polo Grounds souvenir stands. Pictures have player portraits in a 6-1/2" x 9" format. The black-and-white photos are blank-backed and have facsimile autographs printed near the bottom on front. A white border surrounds the front. The unnumbered photos are checklisted here in alphabetical order.

		NM	EX	VG
Complete Set (25):		200.00	100.00	60.00
Common Player:		5.00	2.50	1.50
(1)	Hank Behrman	5.00	2.50	1.50
(2)	Walker Cooper	5.00	2.50	1.50
(3)	Leo Durocher	9.00	4.50	2.75
(4)	Fred Fitzsimmons	5.00	2.50	1.50
(5)	Frank Frisch	12.50	6.25	3.75
(6)	Augie Galan	5.00	2.50	1.50
(7)	Sid Gordon	7.50	3.75	2.25
(8)	Bert Haas	5.00	2.50	1.50
(9)	Andy Hansen	5.00	2.50	1.50
(10)	Clint Hartung	5.00	2.50	1.50
(11)	Bob Hofman	5.00	2.50	1.50
(12)	Larry Jansen	5.00	2.50	1.50
(13)	Sheldon Jones	5.00	2.50	1.50
(14)	Monte Kennedy	5.00	2.50	1.50
(15)	Buddy Kerr	5.00	2.50	1.50
(16)	Dave Koslo	5.00	2.50	1.50
(17)	Mickey Livingston	5.00	2.50	1.50
(18)	Whitey Lockman	5.00	2.50	1.50
(19)	Willard Marshall	5.00	2.50	1.50
(20)	Johnny Mize	12.50	6.25	3.75
(21)	Don Mueller	5.00	2.50	1.50
(22)	Ray Poat	5.00	2.50	1.50
(23)	Bobby Rhawn	5.00	2.50	1.50
(24)	Bill Rigney	5.00	2.50	1.50
(25)	Bobby Thomson	10.00	5.00	3.00

1954 N.Y. Journal-American

Issued during the Golden Age of baseball in New York City, this 59-card set features only players from the Giants, Yankees and Dodgers. The 2" x 4" cards were issued at newsstands with the purchase of the now-extinct newspaper. Card fronts have promotional copy and a contest serial number in addition to the player's name. Cards are printed in black-and-white on colored stock and unnumbered. Backs feature team schedules. It has been theorized that a 60th card should exist, probably a Brooklyn Dodger. Each card can be found with the word "OFFERS" printed in either red or black, depending on the contest number at bottom. Numbers beginning with "0" have the word in black. Numbers 100000-150000 have the word in red or black, and numbers over 150000 have the word in red.

		NM	EX	VG
Complete Set (59):		4,750	2,400	1,400
Common Player:		20.00	10.00	6.00
(1)	Johnny Antonelli	40.00	20.00	12.00
(2)	Hank Bauer	45.00	22.50	13.50
(3)	Yogi Berra	125.00	65.00	35.00
(4)	Joe Black	65.00	32.50	20.00
(5)	Harry Byrd	40.00	20.00	12.00
(6)	Roy Campanella	200.00	100.00	60.00
(7)	Andy Carey	40.00	20.00	12.00
(8)	Jerry Coleman	40.00	20.00	12.00
(9)	Joe Collins	40.00	20.00	12.00
(10)	Billy Cox	65.00	32.50	20.00
(11)	Al Dark	40.00	20.00	12.00
(12)	Carl Erskine	65.00	32.50	20.00
(13)	Whitey Ford	125.00	65.00	35.00
(14)	Carl Furillo	90.00	45.00	27.50
(15)	Junior Gilliam	90.00	45.00	27.50
(16)	Ruben Gomez	40.00	20.00	12.00
(17)	Marv Grissom	40.00	20.00	12.00
(18)	Jim Hearn	40.00	20.00	12.00
(19)	Gil Hodges	125.00	65.00	35.00
(20)	Bobby Hofman	40.00	20.00	12.00
(21)	Jim Hughes	65.00	32.50	20.00
(22)	Monte Irvin	90.00	45.00	27.50
(23)	Larry Jansen	40.00	20.00	12.00
(24)	Ray Katt	40.00	20.00	12.00
(25)	Steve Kraly	40.00	20.00	12.00
(26)	Bob Kuzava	40.00	20.00	12.00
(27)	Clem Labine	65.00	32.50	20.00
(28)	Frank Leja	40.00	20.00	12.00
(29)	Don Liddle	40.00	20.00	12.00
(30)	Whitey Lockman	40.00	20.00	12.00
(31)	Billy Loes	65.00	32.50	20.00
(32)	Eddie Lopat	40.00	20.00	12.00
(33)	Sal Maglie	40.00	20.00	12.00
(34)	Mickey Mantle	650.00	325.00	200.00
(35)	Willie Mays	375.00	185.00	110.00
(36)	Gil McDougald	45.00	22.50	13.50
(37)	Russ Meyer	65.00	32.50	20.00
(38)	Bill Miller	40.00	20.00	12.00
(39)	Tom Morgan	40.00	20.00	12.00
(40)	Don Mueller	40.00	20.00	12.00
(41)	Don Newcombe	75.00	37.50	22.50
(42)	Irv Noren	40.00	20.00	12.00
(43)	Erv Palica	65.00	32.50	20.00
(44)	Pee Wee Reese	130.00	65.00	40.00
(45)	Allie Reynolds	40.00	20.00	12.00
(46)	Dusty Rhodes	40.00	20.00	12.00
(47)	Phil Rizzuto	125.00	65.00	35.00
(48)	Ed Robinson	40.00	20.00	12.00
(49)	Jackie Robinson	235.00	115.00	70.00
(50)	Preacher Roe	65.00	32.50	20.00
(51)	George Shuba	65.00	32.50	20.00
(52)	Duke Snider	200.00	100.00	60.00
(53)	Hank Thompson	40.00	20.00	12.00
(54)	Wes Westrum	40.00	20.00	12.00
(55)	Hoyt Wilhelm	110.00	55.00	32.50
(56)	Davey Williams	40.00	20.00	12.00
(57)	Dick Williams	65.00	32.50	20.00
(58)	Gene Woodling	45.00	22.50	13.50
(59)	Al Worthington	40.00	20.00	12.00

1969 N.Y. News Mets Portfolio of Stars

To commemorate the N.Y. Mets miracle season of 1969, one of the city's daily newspapers, The News, issued a portfolio of player portraits done by editorial cartoonist Bruce Stark. The 9" x 12" pencil drawings are printed on heavy textured paper and were sold as a set in a folder labeled, "The 1969 Mets / A Portfolio of Stars." The black-and-white drawings are on a white background. A facsimile player autograph is printed at lower-left. At lower-right is the signature of the artist, Stark, along with the paper's logo and a union label. The blank-backed, unnumbered pieces are checklisted here alphabetically.

		NM	EX	VG
Complete Set (20):		225.00	110.00	70.00
Common Player:		7.50	3.75	2.25
(1)	Tommie Agee	7.50	3.75	2.25
(2)	Ken Boswell	7.50	3.75	2.25
(3)	Don Cardwell	7.50	3.75	2.25
(4)	Donn Clendenon	10.00	5.00	3.00
(5)	Wayne Garrett	7.50	3.75	2.25
(6)	Gary Gentry	7.50	3.75	2.25
(7)	Jerry Grote	7.50	3.75	2.25
(8)	Bud Harrelson	10.00	5.00	3.00
(9)	Gil Hodges	20.00	10.00	6.00
(10)	Cleon Jones	7.50	3.75	2.25
(11)	Jerry Koosman	7.50	3.75	2.25
(12)	Ed Kranepool	7.50	3.75	2.25
(13)	Jim McAndrew	7.50	3.75	2.25
(14)	Tug McGraw	10.00	5.00	3.00
(15)	Nolan Ryan	150.00	75.00	45.00
(16)	Tom Seaver	40.00	20.00	12.00
(17)	Art Shamsky	7.50	3.75	2.25
(18)	Ron Swoboda	7.50	3.75	2.25
(19)	Ron Taylor	7.50	3.75	2.25
(20)	Al Weis	7.50	3.75	2.25

1973 N.Y. News Mets/Yankees Caricatures

Between June 17 and August 26, the Sunday color comics section of the N.Y. News carried a centerspread picturing one Mets and one Yankees player as caricatured by artist Bruce Stark. Each player picture is printed on newsprint in approximately 10-1/2" x 14-1/2", the pictures have a page of comics or other matter on their backs. Values shown are for single pages. Intact pairs or complete comics section would command a premium.

		NM	EX	VG
Complete Set (22):		200.00	100.00	60.00
Common Player:		6.00	3.00	1.75
	METS			
(1)	Yogi Berra (6/17)	17.50	8.75	5.25
(2)	Tom Seaver (6/24)	15.00	7.50	4.50
(3)	John Milner (7/1)	6.00	3.00	1.75
(4)	Felix Millan (7/8)	6.00	3.00	1.75
(5)	Bud Harrelson (7/15)	6.00	3.00	1.75
(6)	Jim Fregosi (7/22)	6.00	3.00	1.75
(7)	Jerry Grote (7/29)	6.00	3.00	1.75
(8)	Cleon Jones (8/5)	6.00	3.00	1.75
(9)	Willie Mays (8/12)	25.00	12.50	7.50
(10)	Rusty Staub (8/19)	9.00	4.50	2.75
(11)	Tug McGraw (8/26)	7.50	3.75	2.25
	YANKEES			
(12)	Ralph Houk (6/17)	7.50	3.75	2.25
(13)	Mel Stottlemyre (6/24)	7.50	3.75	2.25
(14)	Ron Blomberg (7/1)	6.00	3.00	1.75
(15)	Horace Clarke (7/8)	6.00	3.00	1.75
(16)	Gene Michael (7/15)	6.00	3.00	1.75
(17)	Graig Nettles (7/22)	7.50	3.75	2.25
(18)	Thurman Munson (7/29)	15.00	7.50	4.50
(19)	Roy White (8/5)	9.00	4.50	2.75
(20)	Bobby Murcer (8/12)	9.00	4.50	2.75
(21)	Matty Alou (8/19)	6.00	3.00	1.75
(22)	Sparky Lyle (8/26)	9.00	4.50	2.75

1916 N.Y. World Leaders in Baseball

This set of large-format (about 9" x 4") sepia-tone cards was issued to demonstrate the dominance of the World in New York City's newspaper wars. Each card has a portrait photo of a New York player. Most of the card is devoted to stats to boost the paper's claim as the "Pennant Winner in Advertising and Circulation." A note at left identifies the series as "'Leaders in Baseball' Series II." It is not known whether this checklist is complete.

		NM	EX	VG
Common Player:		600.00	300.00	180.00
(1)	Home Run Baker	750.00	375.00	225.00
(2)	Jake Daubert	600.00	300.00	180.00
(3)	Buck Herzog	600.00	300.00	180.00
(4)	Dave Robertson	600.00	300.00	180.00

1944 N.Y. Yankees Stamps

One of the few paper collectibles issued during World War II, this set includes several players who do not appear on any other contemporary baseball card issue. The 1-3/4" x 2-3/8" stamps were issued on a single sheet with an album marking the Yankees 1943 World Series win. Stamps are in full color with the player's name in white on a red strip at bottom. The unnumbered stamps are checklisted here alphabetically. An album, about 6-1/2" x 3-1/2", was issued to display the stamps.

		NM	EX	VG
Complete Set (30):		100.00	50.00	30.00
Common Player:		12.00	6.00	3.50
Uncut Sheet:		145.00	75.00	45.00
Album:		40.00	20.00	12.00
(1)	Ernie Bonham	12.00	6.00	3.50
(2)	Hank Borowy	12.00	6.00	3.50
(3)	Marvin Breuer	12.00	6.00	3.50
(4)	Tommy Byrne	12.00	6.00	3.50
(5)	Spud Chandler	15.00	7.50	4.50
(6)	Earl Combs (Earle)	25.00	12.50	7.50
(7)	Frank Crosetti	20.00	10.00	6.00
(8)	Bill Dickey	35.00	17.50	10.50
(9)	Atley Donald	12.00	6.00	3.50
(10)	Nick Etten	12.00	6.00	3.50
(11)	Art Fletcher	12.00	6.00	3.50
(12)	Joe Gordon	15.00	7.50	4.50
(13)	Oscar Grimes	12.00	6.00	3.50
(14)	Rollie Hemsley	12.00	6.00	3.50
(15)	Bill Johnson	12.00	6.00	3.50
(16)	Charlie Keller	15.00	7.50	4.50
(17)	John Lindell	15.00	7.50	4.50
(18)	Joe McCarthy	25.00	12.50	7.50
(19)	Bud Metheny	12.00	6.00	3.50
(20)	Johnny Murphy	12.00	6.00	3.50
(21)	Pat O'Daugherty	12.00	6.00	3.50
(22)	Marius Russo	12.00	6.00	3.50
(23)	John Schulte	12.00	6.00	3.50
(24)	Ken Sears	12.00	6.00	3.50
(25)	Tuck Stainbeck	12.00	6.00	3.50
(26)	George Stirnweiss	12.00	6.00	3.50
(27)	Jim Turner	12.00	6.00	3.50
(28)	Roy Weatherly	12.00	6.00	3.50
(29)	Charley Wensloff	12.00	6.00	3.50
(30)	Bill Zuber	12.00	6.00	3.50

1947-50 N.Y. Yankees Picture Pack

These team-issued sets offered fans at the souvenir stand more than two dozen pictures of the players and staff. The 6-1/2" x 9" pictures are in black-and-white with a white border and a facsimile autograph. Backs are blank. Players repeated over the years were represented by the same picture. The unnumbered pictures are listed in aphabetical order by year of issue.

		NM	EX	VG
Common Player:		4.00	2.00	1.25
	Complete 1947 Set (25):	100.00	50.00	30.00
(1)	Yogi Berra	20.00	10.00	6.00
(2)	Bill Bevens	4.00	2.00	1.25
(3)	Bobby Brown	4.00	2.00	1.25
(4)	Spud Chandler	4.00	2.00	1.25
(5)	Frank Colman	4.00	2.00	1.25
(6)	John Corriden	4.00	2.00	1.25
(7)	Frank Crosetti	5.00	2.50	1.50
(8)	Joe DiMaggio	40.00	20.00	12.00
(9)	Chuck Dressen	4.00	2.00	1.25
(10)	Randy Gumpert	4.00	2.00	1.25
(11)	Bucky Harris	5.00	2.50	1.50
(12)	Tommy Henrich	4.00	2.00	1.25
(13)	Ralph Houk	5.00	2.50	1.50
(14)	Don Johnson	4.00	2.00	1.25
(15)	Bill Johnson	4.00	2.00	1.25
(16)	Charlie Keller	5.00	2.50	1.50
(17)	John Lindell	4.00	2.00	1.25
(18)	George McQuinn	4.00	2.00	1.25

(19)	Joe Page	4.00	2.00	1.25
(20)	Allie Reynolds	5.00	2.50	1.50
(21)	Phil Rizzuto	12.50	6.25	3.75
(22)	Aaron Robinson	4.00	2.00	1.25
(23)	Frank Shea	4.00	2.00	1.25
(24)	Ken Silvestri	4.00	2.00	1.25
(25)	George Stirnweiss	4.00	2.00	1.25
	Complete 1948 Set (26):	100.00	50.00	30.00
(1)	Yogi Berra	20.00	10.00	6.00
(2)	Bobby Brown	4.00	2.00	1.25
(3)	Red Corriden	4.00	2.00	1.25
(4)	Frank Crosetti	5.00	2.50	1.50
(5)	Joe DiMaggio	40.00	20.00	12.00
(6)	Chuck Dressen	4.00	2.00	1.25
(7)	Karl Drews	4.00	2.00	1.25
(8)	Red Embree	4.00	2.00	1.25
(9)	Randy Gumpert	4.00	2.00	1.25
(10)	Bucky Harris	5.00	2.50	1.50
(11)	Tommy Henrich	4.00	2.00	1.25
(12)	Frank Hiller	4.00	2.00	1.25
(13)	Bill Johnson	4.00	2.00	1.25
(14)	Charlie Keller	5.00	2.50	1.50
(15)	John Lindell	4.00	2.00	1.25
(16)	Eddie Lopat	5.00	2.50	1.50
(17)	Cliff Mapes	4.00	2.00	1.25
(18)	George McQuinn	4.00	2.00	1.25
(19)	Gus Niarhos	4.00	2.00	1.25
(20)	George McQuinn	4.00	2.00	1.25
(21)	Joe Page	4.00	2.00	1.25
(22)	Vic Raschi	5.00	2.50	1.50
(23)	Allie Reynolds	5.00	2.50	1.50
(24)	Phil Rizzuto	12.50	6.25	3.75
(25)	Frank Shea	4.00	2.00	1.25
(26)	Snuffy Stirnweiss	4.00	2.00	1.25
	Complete 1949 Set (25):	100.00	50.00	30.00
(1)	Mel Allen	8.00	4.00	2.50
(2)	Larry Berra	20.00	10.00	6.00
(3)	Bobby Brown	4.00	2.00	1.25
(4)	Tommy Byrne	4.00	2.00	1.25
(5)	Jerry Coleman	4.00	2.00	1.25
(6)	Frank Crosetti	5.00	2.50	1.50
(7)	Bill Dickey	10.00	5.00	3.00
(8)	Joe DiMaggio	40.00	20.00	12.00
(9)	Tommy Henrich	4.00	2.00	1.25
(10)	Bill Johnson	4.00	2.00	1.25
(11)	Charlie Keller	5.00	2.50	1.50
(12)	John Lindell	4.00	2.00	1.25
(13)	Ed Lopat	5.00	2.50	1.50
(14)	Gus Niarhos	4.00	2.00	1.25
(15)	Joe Page	4.00	2.00	1.25
(16)	Bob Porterfield	4.00	2.00	1.25
(17)	Vic Raschi	4.00	2.00	1.25
(18)	Allie Reynolds	5.00	2.50	1.50
(19)	Phil Rizzuto	12.50	6.25	3.75
(20)	Fred Sanford	4.00	2.00	1.25
(21)	Frank Shea	4.00	2.00	1.25
(22)	Casey Stengel	15.00	7.50	4.50
(23)	George Stirnweiss	4.00	2.00	1.25
(24)	Jim Turner	4.00	2.00	1.25
(25)	Gene Woodling	5.00	2.50	1.50
	Complete 1950 Set (25):	100.00	50.00	30.00
(1)	Mel Allen	8.00	4.00	2.50
(2)	Hank Bauer	5.00	2.50	1.50
(3)	Larry Berra	20.00	10.00	6.00
(4)	Bobby Brown	4.00	2.00	1.25
(5)	Tommy Byrne	4.00	2.00	1.25
(6)	Jerry Coleman	4.00	2.00	1.25
(7)	Frank Crosetti	5.00	2.50	1.50
(8)	Bill Dickey	10.00	5.00	3.00
(9)	Joe DiMaggio	40.00	20.00	12.00
(10)	Tommy Henrich	4.00	2.00	1.25
(11)	Jack Jensen	7.50	3.75	2.25
(12)	Bill Johnson	4.00	2.00	1.25
(13)	Ed Lopat	5.00	2.50	1.50
(14)	Cliff Mapes	4.00	2.00	1.25
(15)	Joe Page	4.00	2.00	1.25
(16)	Bob Porterfield	4.00	2.00	1.25
(17)	Vic Raschi	5.00	2.50	1.50
(18)	Allie Reynolds	5.00	2.50	1.50
(19)	Phil Rizzuto	12.50	6.25	3.75
(20)	Fred Sanford	4.00	2.00	1.25
(21)	Charlie Silvera	5.00	2.50	1.50
(22)	Casey Stengel	15.00	7.50	4.50
(23)	George Stirnweiss	4.00	2.00	1.25
(24)	Jim Turner	4.00	2.00	1.25
(25)	Gene Woodling	5.00	2.50	1.50

1955-1957 N.Y. Yankees Picture Pack

The checklist for this set of 5" x 7" black-and-white, blank-back pictures does not allow pinpointing its year of issue more closely. Similar in format to the later Jay Publishing photo packs, this issue differs in that only the team name (in upper- and lower-case letters), and not the city, is presented along with the player name (all-caps) in the identification line in the bottom border. The set was sold for 25 cents in a manila envelope. The unnumbered pictures are listed here alphabetically.

		NM	EX	VG
	Complete Set (12):	75.00	37.50	22.50
	Common Player:	4.00	2.00	1.25
(1)	Hank Bauer	5.00	2.50	1.50
(2)	Yogi Berra	7.50	3.75	2.25
(3)	Tommy Byrne	4.00	2.00	1.25
(4)	Andy Carey	4.00	2.00	1.25
(5)	Joe Collins	4.00	2.00	1.25
(6)	Whitey Ford	7.50	3.75	2.25
(7)	Elston Howard	5.00	2.50	1.50
(8)	Mickey Mantle	35.00	17.50	10.00
(9)	Billy Martin	5.00	2.50	1.50
(10)	Gil McDougald	4.00	2.00	1.25
(11)	Casey Stengel	7.50	3.75	2.25
(12)	Bob Turley	4.00	2.00	1.25

1956 N.Y. Yankees "Action Pictures"

This set of 8" x 10" black-and-white pictures was sold for 75 cents in a paper envelope marked "12 ACTION / PIC-

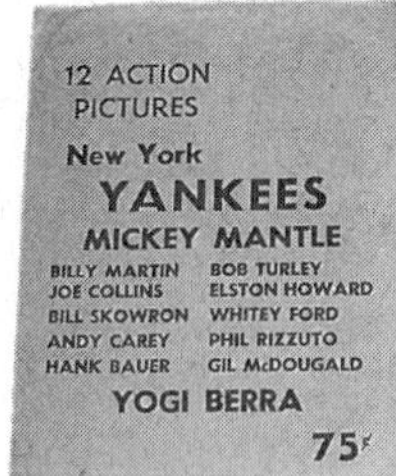

TURES." The white-bordered pictures have facsimile autographs or printed names on front and are blank-backed.

		NM	EX	VG
	Complete Set (12):	125.00	65.00	49.00
	Common Player:	6.00	3.00	1.75
(1)	Hank Bauer	7.50	3.75	2.25
(2)	Yogi Berra	15.00	7.50	4.50
(3)	Andy Carey	6.00	3.00	1.75
(4)	Joe Collins	6.00	3.00	1.75
(5)	Whitey Ford	15.00	7.50	4.50
(6)	Elston Howard	9.00	4.50	2.75
(7)	Mickey Mantle	75.00	37.00	22.00
(8)	Billy Martin	9.00	4.50	2.75
(9)	Gil McDougald	7.50	3.75	2.25
(10)	Phil Rizzuto	15.00	7.50	4.50
(11)	Bill Skowron	9.00	4.50	2.75
(12)	Bob Turley	7.50	3.75	2.25

1956 N.Y. Yankees Picture Pack

This set was issued, probably for sale at Yankee Stadium souvenir stands, in 1956, though some of the photos date as far back as 1951, and a few appear to have been taken during the 1955 World Series at Ebbets Field. Printed in black-and-white on semi-gloss paper, the pictures measure about 6" x 8-7/8". There is a 1/4" white border around the photo and a white strip at the bottom of each photo with the player's name. Backs are blank. The pictures are checklisted here in alphabetical order, but the list may not be complete. Some of the photos are familiar from their use on baseball cards, including the 1951 Bowman Mantle.

		NM	EX	VG
	Complete Set (22):	275.00	135.00	80.00
	Common Player:	8.00	4.00	2.50
(1)	Hank Bauer	10.00	5.00	3.00
(2)	Larry "Yogi" Berra	20.00	10.00	6.00
(3)	Tommy Byrne	8.00	4.00	2.50
(4)	Andy Carey	8.00	4.00	2.50
(5)	Bob Cerv	8.00	4.00	2.50
(6)	Gerry Coleman	8.00	4.00	2.50
(7)	Joe Collins	8.00	4.00	2.50
(8)	Ed "Whitey" Ford	20.00	10.00	6.00
(9)	Bob Grim	8.00	4.00	2.50
(10)	Elston Howard	10.00	5.00	3.00
(11)	Johnny Kucks	8.00	4.00	2.50
(12)	Don Larsen	12.50	6.25	3.75
(13)	Jerry Lumpe	8.00	4.00	2.50
(14)	Mickey Mantle	130.00	65.00	39.00
(15)	Billy Martin	15.00	7.50	4.50
(16)	Mickey McDermott	8.00	4.00	2.50
(17)	Gil McDougald	10.00	5.00	3.00
(18)	Tom Morgan	8.00	4.00	2.50
(19)	Irv Noren	8.00	4.00	2.50
(20)	Charlie Silvera	8.00	4.00	2.50
(21)	Bill Skowron	10.00	5.00	3.00
(22)	Bob Turley	10.00	5.00	3.00

1957 N.Y. Yankees Picture Pack

Nominally 8" x 10", the actual size on these blank-back, black-and-white pictures varies from about 7-1/2" to 8" wide by 9-7/8" x 10-1/8" tall. The player poses are surrounded with a white border. The player name is printed within the picture. Some of the photos used considerably pre-date the period of issue.

		NM	EX	VG
	Complete Set (12):	125.00	65.00	40.00
	Common Player:	10.00	5.00	3.00
(1)	Hank Bauer	12.50	6.25	3.75
(2)	Larry Berra	20.00	10.00	6.00
(3)	Andy Carey	10.00	5.00	3.00
(4)	Whitey Ford	20.00	10.00	6.00
(5)	Elston Howard	12.50	6.25	3.75
(6)	Tony Kubek	15.00	7.50	4.50
(7)	Don Larsen	12.50	6.25	3.75
(8)	Mickey Mantle	60.00	30.00	18.00
(9)	Gil McDougald	12.50	6.25	3.75
(10)	Bill Skowron	12.50	6.25	3.75
(11)	Bob Turley	12.50	6.25	3.75
(12)	Frank Crosetti, Bill Dickey, Casey Stengel, Jim Turner	10.00	5.00	3.00

1960 N.Y. Yankees "Action Pictures"

This set of 8" x 10" black-and-white pictures was sold for 75 cents in a paper envelope marked "12 ACTION / PICTURES." The white bordered pictures have facsimile autographs or printed names on front and are blank-backed.

		NM	EX	VG
	Complete Set (12):	200.00	100.00	60.00
	Common Player:	10.00	5.00	3.00
(1)	Larry Berra	20.00	10.00	6.00
(2)	Art Ditmar	10.00	5.00	3.00
(3)	Whitey Ford	20.00	10.00	6.00
(4)	Elston Howard	12.50	6.25	3.75
(5)	Tony Kubek	15.00	7.50	4.50
(6)	Hector Lopez	10.00	5.00	3.00
(7)	Mickey Mantle	60.00	30.00	18.00
(8)	Roger Maris	35.00	17.50	10.50
(9)	Bobby Richardson	12.50	6.25	3.75
(10)	Bill Skowron	12.50	6.25	3.75
(11)	Casey Stengel	15.00	7.50	4.50
(12)	Bob Turley	12.50	6.25	3.75

1970 N.Y. Yankees Clinic Schedule Postcards

This series of postcards was issued in conjunction with a series of baseball clinics which the Yankees put on for youngsters prior to selected home games. Fronts of the 3-1/2 x 5-1/2" glossy color cards have player portraits with a facsimile autograph in a white panel at bottom. Backs have player identification and career highlights, a schedule of the clinic days and credit line for Howard Photo Service. White and Murcer cards are scarce because of rainouts on their scheduled clinic appearance days. Cards are checklisted here in alphabetical order.

		NM	EX	VG
	Complete Set (13):	130.00	65.00	40.00
	Common Player:	3.00	1.50	.90
(1)	Stan Bahnsen	3.00	1.50	.90
(2)	Curt Blefary	3.00	1.50	.90
(3)	Danny Cater	3.00	1.50	.90
(4)	Horace Clarke	3.00	1.50	.90
(5)	Joe DiMaggio, Mickey Mantle	25.00	12.50	7.50
(6)	John Ellis	3.00	1.50	.90
(7)	Jerry Kenney	3.00	1.50	.90
(8)	Gene Michael	3.00	1.50	.90

Checklists showing are card numbers in parentheses ( ) indicates the numbers do not appear on the cards.

		NM	EX	VG
(9)	Thurman Munson	30.00	15.00	9.00
(10)	Bobby Murcer	15.00	7.50	4.50
(11)	Fritz Peterson	3.00	1.50	.90
(12)	Mel Stottlemyre	4.50	2.25	1.25
(13)	Roy White	35.00	17.50	10.50

1971 N.Y. Yankees Clinic Schedule Postcards

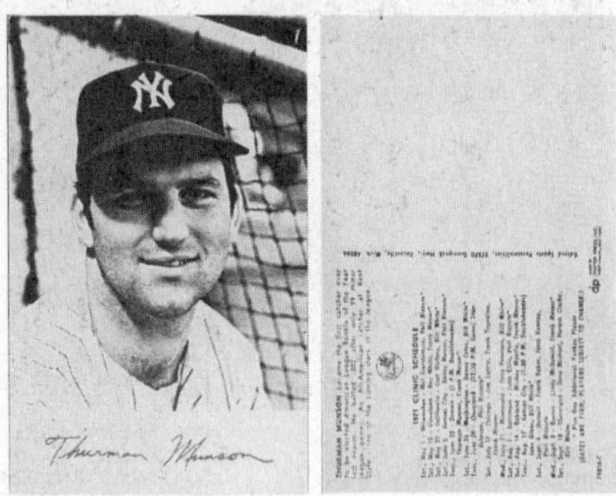

These postcards were issued in conjunction with a series of baseball clinics which the Yankees put on for youngsters prior to selected home games. Fronts of the 3-1/2" x 5-1/2" glossy color cards have player portraits with a facsimile autograph in a white panel at bottom. Backs are printed in blue, have player identification and career highlights and a schedule of the clinic days. Cards are checklisted here in alphabetical order.

		NM	EX	VG
Complete Set (16):		90.00	45.00	27.00
Common Player:		3.00	1.50	.90
(1)	Felipe Alou, Jim Lyttle	3.00	1.50	.90
(2)	Stan Bahnsen	3.00	1.50	.90
(3)	Frank Baker, Jerry Kenney	3.00	1.50	.90
(4)	Curt Blefary	3.00	1.50	.90
(5)	Danny Cater	3.00	1.50	.90
(6)	Horace Clarke, Gene Michael	3.00	1.50	.90
(7)	John Ellis	3.00	1.50	.90
(8)	Jake Gibbs	3.00	1.50	.90
(9)	Ralph Houk	3.00	1.50	.90
(10)	Mickey Mantle	30.00	15.00	9.00
(11)	Lindy McDaniel	3.00	1.50	.90
(12)	Thurman Munson	15.00	7.50	4.50
(13)	Bobby Murcer	4.50	2.25	1.25
(14)	Fritz Peterson	3.00	1.50	.90
(15)	Mel Stottlemyre	3.00	1.50	.90
(16)	Roy White	3.00	1.50	.90

1972 N.Y. Yankees Schedule Cards

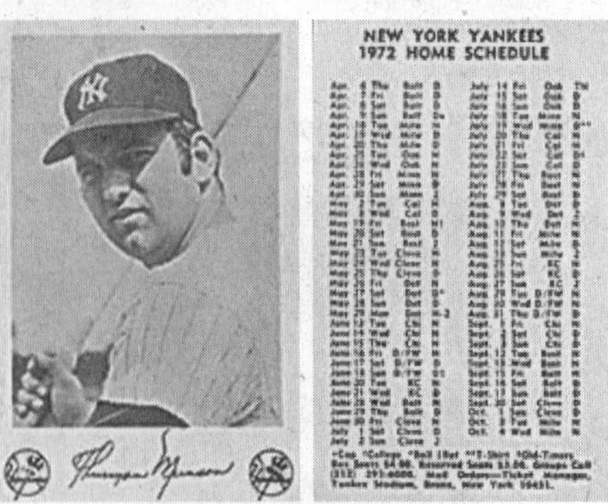

The origins and distribution of these cards is unclear. They may have been a collector issue. The 2-1/4" x 3-1/2" cards are printed in blue and sepia. Fronts have player photos with a facsimile autograph in the white border at bottom, between a pair of team insignia. Backs have the team schedule. The unnumbered cards are listed here alphabetically.

		NM	EX	VG
Complete Set (8):		350.00	175.00	100.00
Common Player:		30.00	15.00	9.00
(1)	Felipe Alou	35.00	17.50	10.50
(2)	Ron Blomberg	30.00	15.00	9.00
(3)	Thurman Munson	225.00	110.00	67.00
(4)	Bobby Murcer	35.00	17.50	10.50
(5)	Mel Stottlemyre	30.00	15.00	9.00
(6)	Ron Swoboda	30.00	15.00	9.00
(7)	Roy White	35.00	17.50	10.50
(8)	Frank Messer, Phil Rizzuto, Bill White (Announcers)	30.00	15.00	9.00

1909 Niagara Baking Co.

This is a version of the set known as E101 "Set of 50" which has been rubber-stamped on back with an advertisement for Niagara Baking Co., of Lockport, N.Y. It is unclear whether all 50 cards in E101 can be found with the overprint. Because of the ease with which this regional variation could be faked, collectors must exercise extreme caution. Collectors can expect to pay a considerable premium over E101 prices for this version, especially for common players.

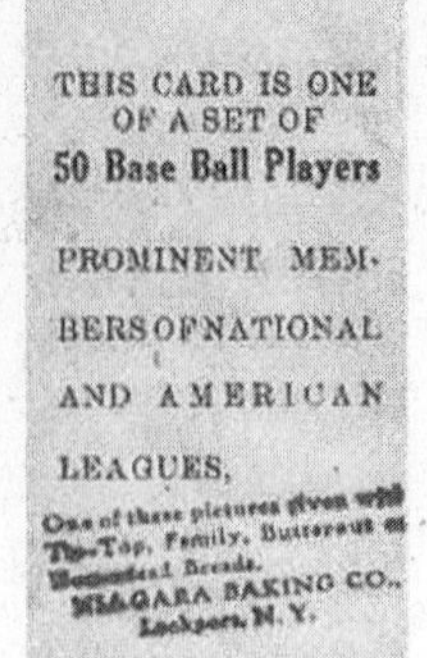
THIS CARD IS ONE OF A SET OF 50 Base Ball Players PROMINENT MEMBERS OF NATIONAL AND AMERICAN LEAGUES.

One of these pictures given with Tip-Top, Family, Butternut or Homestead Breads. NIAGARA BAKING CO., Lockport, N. Y.

Values Undetermined
(See 1909 E101 for checklist.)

1953 Northland Bread Labels

This bread end-label set consists of 32 players - two from each major league team. The unnumbered black and white labels measure approximately 2-11/16" square and include the slogan "Bread for Energy" along the top. An album to house the labels was also part of the promotion.

		NM	EX	VG
Complete Set (32):		8,250	4,250	2,500
Common Player:		200.00	100.00	60.00
(1)	Cal Abrams	200.00	100.00	60.00
(2)	Richie Ashburn	400.00	200.00	120.00
(3)	Gus Bell	200.00	100.00	60.00
(4)	Jim Busby	200.00	100.00	60.00
(5)	Clint Courtney	200.00	100.00	60.00
(6)	Billy Cox	200.00	100.00	60.00
(7)	Jim Dyck	200.00	100.00	60.00
(8)	Nellie Fox	400.00	200.00	120.00
(9)	Sid Gordon	200.00	100.00	60.00
(10)	Warren Hacker	200.00	100.00	60.00
(11)	Jim Hearn	200.00	100.00	60.00
(12)	Fred Hutchinson	200.00	100.00	60.00
(13)	Monte Irvin	400.00	200.00	120.00
(14)	Jackie Jensen	225.00	110.00	65.00
(15)	Ted Kluszewski	350.00	175.00	100.00
(16)	Bob Lemon	400.00	200.00	120.00
(17)	Maury McDermott	200.00	100.00	60.00
(18)	Minny Minoso	350.00	175.00	105.00
(19)	Johnny Mize	400.00	200.00	120.00
(20)	Mel Parnell	200.00	100.00	60.00
(21)	Howie Pollet	200.00	100.00	60.00
(22)	Jerry Priddy	200.00	100.00	60.00
(23)	Allie Reynolds	200.00	100.00	60.00
(24)	Preacher Roe	250.00	125.00	75.00
(25)	Al Rosen	225.00	110.00	65.00
(26)	Connie Ryan	200.00	100.00	60.00
(27a)	Hank Sauer (Bread for Energy at top.)	200.00	100.00	60.00
(27b)	Hank Sauer (Top Taste at top.)	375.00	185.00	110.00
(28)	Red Schoendienst	400.00	200.00	120.00
(29)	Bobby Shantz	200.00	100.00	60.00
(30)	Enos Slaughter	400.00	200.00	120.00
(31)	Warren Spahn	400.00	200.00	120.00
(32)	Gus Zernial	200.00	100.00	60.00

1978 North Shore Dodge Cecil Cooper

As part of his work as promotional spokesman for a local auto dealership, popular Brewers first baseman Cecil Cooper appears on a one-card set which was given to fans and collectors during public appearances. The card is printed in black-and-white in standard 2-1/2" x 3-1/2" size and is often found with a genuine autograph on the front.

	NM	EX	VG
Cecil Cooper	6.00	3.00	1.75
Cecil Cooper (Autographed)	15.00	7.50	4.50

1980 Nostalgic Enterprises 1903 N.Y. Highlanders

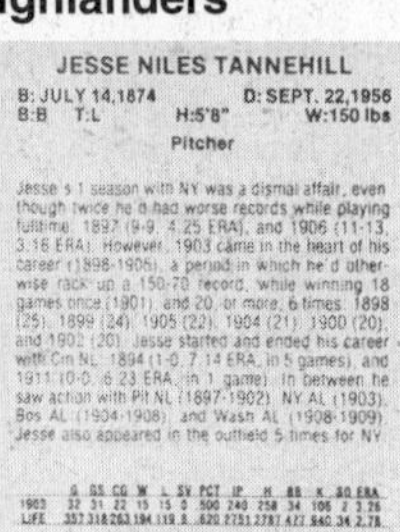

New York City's first team in the American League, the 1903 Highlanders, are featured in this collectors' issue. Fronts of the 2-1/2" x 3-1/2" cards have black-and-white portrait photos with ornate graphics, highlighted in yellow, and a white border. Backs have season and lifetime stats, player data and an extensive career summary. The unnumbered cards are checklisted here in alphabetical order. Sets originally sold for about $2.50.

		NM	EX	VG
Complete Set (17):		15.00	7.50	4.50
Common Player:		2.00	1.00	.60
(1)	Monte Beville	2.50	1.25	.70
(2)	Jack Chesbro	2.00	1.00	.60
(3)	Wid Conroy	2.00	1.00	.60
(4)	Lefty Davis	2.00	1.00	.60
(5)	John Deering	2.50	1.25	.70
(6)	Kid Elberfeld	2.00	1.00	.60
(7)	Dave Fultz	2.00	1.00	.60
(8)	John Ganzel	2.00	1.00	.60
(9)	Clark Griffith	2.00	1.00	.60
(10)	Harry Howell	2.00	1.00	.60
(11)	Willie Keeler	2.00	1.00	.60
(12)	Herm McFarland	2.00	1.00	.60
(13)	Jack O'Connor	2.00	1.00	.60
(14)	Jesse Tannehill	2.00	1.00	.60
(15)	Jimmy Williams	2.00	1.00	.60
(16)	Jack Zalusky	2.50	1.25	.70
(17)	Header Card/Checklist	2.00	1.00	.60

1907-09 Novelty Cutlery Postcards (PC805)

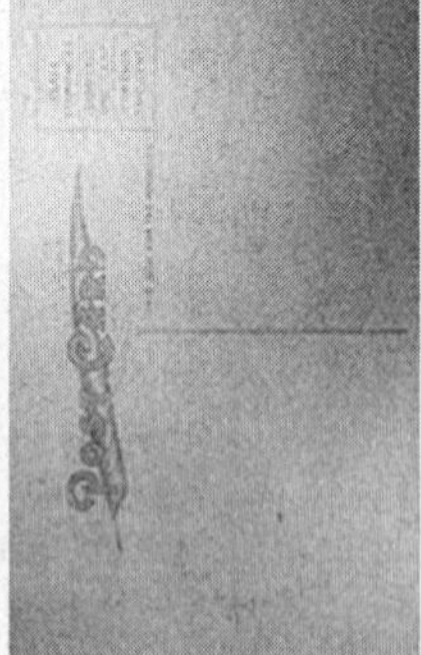

An ornately bordered black-and-white or sepia portrait or action pose of the day's great players identifies these postcards from a Canton, Ohio, knife company. Cards measure the standard 3-1/2" x 5-1/2" size with postcard indicia on the back. The sponsor is identified in a tiny line of type beneath the lower-right corner of the player photo.

		NM	EX	VG
Complete Set (26):		60,000	30,000	18,000
Common Player:		1,400	560.00	280.00
(1)	Roger Bresnahan	1,800	720.00	360.00
(2)	Al Bridwell	1,400	560.00	280.00
(3)	Three Finger Brown	1,800	720.00	360.00
(4)	Frank Chance	1,800	720.00	360.00
(5)	Hal Chase	1,600	640.00	320.00
(6)	Ty Cobb	9,000	3,600	1,800
(7)	Eddie Collins	1,800	720.00	360.00
(8)	Sam Crawford	1,800	720.00	360.00
(9)	Art Devlin	1,400	560.00	280.00
(10)	Red Dooin	1,400	560.00	280.00
(11)	Elmer Flick	1,800	720.00	360.00
(12)	Sam Frock	1,400	560.00	280.00
(13)	George Gibson	1,400	560.00	280.00
(14)	Solly Hofman	1,400	560.00	280.00
(15)	Walter Johnston (Johnson)	3,000	1,200	600.00

(16)	Nap Lajoie	1,800	720.00	360.00
(17)	Bris Lord	1,400	560.00	280.00
(18)	Christy Mathewson	3,000	1,200	600.00
(19)	Orval Overall	1,400	560.00	280.00
(20)	Eddie Plank	1,800	720.00	360.00
(21)	Tris Speaker	2,500	1,000	500.00
(22)	Gabby Street	1,400	560.00	280.00
(23)	Honus Wagner	6,000	2,400	1,200
(24)	Ed Walsh	1,800	720.00	360.00
(25)	Ty Cobb, Honus Wagner	6,500	2,600	1,300
(26)	Johnny Evers, Germany Schaefer	1,600	640.00	320.00

1960 Nu-Card Baseball Hi-Lites

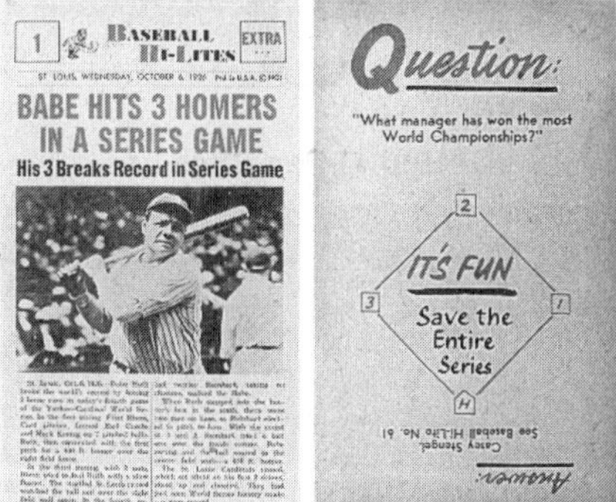

These large, 3-1/4" x 5-3/8" cards are printed in a mock newspaper format, with a headline, picture and story describing one of baseball's greatest moments. Cards #1-18 can be found either printed entirely in black, or in red-and-black, like the rest of the set. Each card is numbered in the upper-left corner. Backs offer a quiz question and answer.

		NM	EX	VG
Complete Set (72):		500.00	250.00	150.00
Common Player:		6.00	3.00	1.75
1	Babe Hits 3 Homers In A Series Game	40.00	20.00	12.00
2	Podres Pitching Wins Series	9.00	4.50	2.75
3	Bevans Pitches No Hitter, Almost	6.00	3.00	1.75
4	Box Score Devised By Reporter	6.00	3.00	1.75
5	VanderMeer Pitches 2 No Hitters	6.00	3.00	1.75
6	Indians Take Bums	6.00	3.00	1.75
7	DiMag Comes Thru	25.00	12.50	7.50
8	Mathewson Pitches 3 W.S. Shutouts	7.50	3.75	2.25
9	Haddix Pitches 12 Perfect Innings	6.00	3.00	1.75
10	Thomson's Homer Sinks Dodgers	9.00	4.50	2.75
11	Hubbell Strikes Out 5 A.L. Stars	6.00	3.00	1.75
12	Pickoff Ends Series (Marty Marion)	6.00	3.00	1.75
13	Cards Take Series From Yanks (Grover Cleveland Alexander)	6.00	3.00	1.75
14	Dizzy And Daffy Win Series	10.00	5.00	3.00
15	Owen Drops 3rd Strike	6.00	3.00	1.75
16	Ruth Calls His Shot	40.00	20.00	12.00
17	Merkle Pulls Boner	6.00	3.00	1.75
18	Larsen Hurls Perfect World Series Game	10.00	5.00	3.00
19	Bean Ball Ends Career of Mickey Cochrane	6.00	3.00	1.75
20	Banks Belts 47 Homers, Earns MVP Honors	6.00	3.00	1.75
21	Stan Musial Hits 5 Homers In 1 Day	12.50	6.25	3.75
22	Mickey Mantle Hits Longest Homer	60.00	30.00	18.00
23	Sievers Captures Home Run Title	6.00	3.00	1.75
24	Gehrig Consecutive Game Record Ends	25.00	12.50	7.50
25	Red Schoendienst Key Player In Victory	6.00	3.00	1.75
26	Midget Pinch-Hits For St. Louis Browns (Eddie Gaedel)	10.00	5.00	3.00
27	Willie Mays Makes Greatest Catch	25.00	12.50	7.50
28	Homer By Berra Puts Yanks In 1st Place	6.00	3.00	1.75
29	Campy National League's MVP	6.00	3.00	1.75
30	Bob Turley Hurls Yanks To Championship	6.00	3.00	1.75
31	Dodgers Take Series From Sox In Six	6.00	3.00	1.75
32	Furillo Hero As Dodgers Beat Chicago	6.00	3.00	1.75
33	Adcock Gets Four Homers And A Double	6.00	3.00	1.75
34	Dickey Chosen All Star Catcher	6.00	3.00	1.75
35	Burdette Beats Yanks In 3 Series Games	6.00	3.00	1.75
36	Umpires Clear White Sox Bench	6.00	3.00	1.75
37	Reese Honored As Greatest Dodger S.S.	7.50	3.75	2.25
38	Joe DiMaggio Hits In 56 Straight Games	30.00	15.00	9.00
39	Ted Williams Hits .406 For Season	25.00	12.50	7.50
40	Johnson Pitches 56 Scoreless Innings	6.00	3.00	1.75
41	Hodges Hits 4 Home Runs In Nite Game	6.00	3.00	1.75
42	Greenberg Returns To Tigers From Army	10.00	5.00	3.00
43	Ty Cobb Named Best Player Of All Time	15.00	7.50	4.50
44	Robin Roberts Wins 28 Games	6.00	3.00	1.75
45	Rizzuto's 2 Runs Save 1st Place	6.00	3.00	1.75
46	Tigers Beat Out Senators For Pennant (Hal Newhouser)	6.00	3.00	1.75
47	Babe Ruth Hits 60th Home Run	40.00	20.00	12.00
48	Cy Young Honored	6.00	3.00	1.75
49	Killebrew Starts Spring Training	6.00	3.00	1.75
50	Mantle Hits Longest Homer At Stadium	60.00	30.00	18.00
51	Braves Take Pennant (Hank Aaron)	6.00	3.00	1.75
52	Ted Williams Hero Of All Star Game	30.00	15.00	9.00
53	Robinson Saves Dodgers For Playoffs (Jackie Robinson)	12.50	6.25	3.75
54	Snodgrass Muffs A Fly Ball	6.00	3.00	1.75
55	Snider Belts 2 Homers	6.00	3.00	1.75
56	New York Giants Win 26 Straight Games (Christy Mathewson)	6.00	3.00	1.75
57	Ted Kluszewski Stars In 1st Game Win	6.00	3.00	1.75
58	Ott Walks 5 Times In A Single Game (Mel Ott)	6.00	3.00	1.75
59	Harvey Kuenn Takes Batting Title	6.00	3.00	1.75
60	Bob Feller Hurls 3rd No-Hitter Of Career	6.00	3.00	1.75
61	Yanks Champs Again! (Casey Stengel)	6.00	3.00	1.75
62	Aaron's Bat Beats Yankees In Series	10.00	5.00	3.00
63	Warren Spahn Beats Yanks in World Series	6.00	3.00	1.75
64	Ump's Wrong Call Helps Dodgers	6.00	3.00	1.75
65	Kaline Hits 3 Homers, 2 In Same Inning	6.00	3.00	1.75
66	Bob Allison Named A.L. Rookie of Year	6.00	3.00	1.75
67	McCovey Blasts Way Into Giant Lineup	6.00	3.00	1.75
68	Colavito Hits Four Homers In One Game	10.00	5.00	3.00
69	Erskine Sets Strike Out Record In W.S.	6.00	3.00	1.75
70	Sal Maglie Pitches No-Hit Game	6.00	3.00	1.75
71	Early Wynn Victory Crushes Yanks	6.00	3.00	1.75
72	Nellie Fox American League's M.V.P.	6.00	3.00	1.75

1961 Nu-Card Baseball Scoops

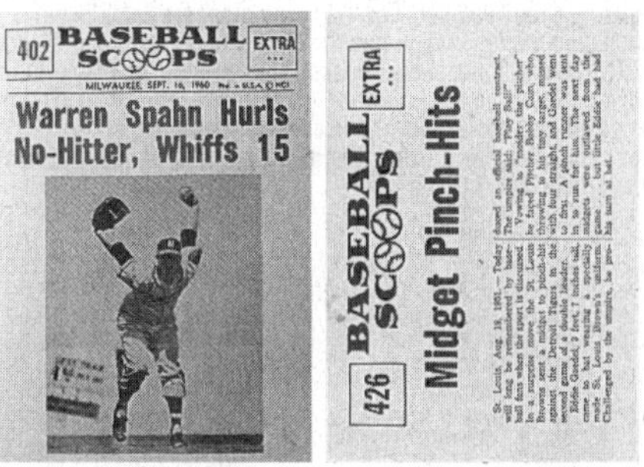

Very similar in style to their set of the year before, the Nu-Card Baseball Scoops were issued in a smaller 2-1/2" x 3-1/2" size, but still featured the mock newspaper card front. This 80-card set is numbered from 401 to 480, with numbers shown on both the card front and back. These cards, which commemorate great moments in individual players' careers, included only the headline and black and white photo on the fronts, with the descriptive story on the card backs. Cards are again printed in red and black. It appears the set may have been counterfeited, though when is not known. These cards can be determined by examining the card photo for unusual blurring and fuzziness.

		NM	EX	VG
Complete Set (80):		400.00	200.00	120.00
Common Player:		3.00	1.50	.90
Wax Pack (7):		100.00		
401	Gentile Powers Birds Into 1st	6.00	3.00	1.75
402	Warren Spahn Hurls No-Hitter, Whiffs 15	5.00	2.50	1.50
403	Mazeroski's Homer Wins Series For Bucs	10.00	5.00	3.00
404	Willie Mays' 3 Triples Paces Giants	15.00	7.50	4.50
405	Woodie Held Slugs 2 Homers, 6 RBIs	3.00	1.50	.90
406	Vern Law Winner Of Cy Young Award	3.00	1.50	.90
407	Runnels Makes 9 Hits in Twin-Bill	3.00	1.50	.90
408	Braves' Lew Burdette Wins No-Hitter	3.00	1.50	.90
409	Dick Stuart Hits 3 Homers, Single	3.00	1.50	.90
410	Don Cardwell Of Cubs Pitches No-Hit Game	3.00	1.50	.90
411	Camilo Pascual Strikes Out 15 Bosox	3.00	1.50	.90
412	Eddie Mathews Blasts 300th Big League HR	3.00	1.50	.90
413	Groat, NL Bat King, Named Loop's MVP	3.00	1.50	.90
414	AL Votes To Expand To 10 Teams (Gene Autry)	3.00	1.50	.90
415	Bobby Richardson Sets Series Mark	3.00	1.50	.90
416	Maris Nips Mantle For AL MVP Award	10.00	5.00	3.00
417	Merkle Pulls Boner	3.00	1.50	.90
418	Larsen Hurls Perfect World Series Game	5.00	2.50	1.50
419	Bean Ball Ends Career Of Mickey Cochrane	3.00	1.50	.90
420	Banks Belts 47 Homers, Earns MVP Award	6.00	3.00	1.75
421	Stan Musial Hits 5 Homers In 1 Day	9.00	4.50	2.75
422	Mickey Mantle Hits Longest Homer	35.00	17.50	10.50
423	Sievers Captures Home Run Title	3.00	1.50	.90
424	Gehrig Consecutive Game Record Ends	15.00	7.50	4.50
425	Red Schoendienst Key Player In Victory	3.00	1.50	.90
426	Midget Pinch-Hits For St. Louis Browns (Eddie Gaedel)	5.00	2.50	1.50
427	Willie Mays Makes Greatest Catch	20.00	10.00	6.00
428	Robinson Saves Dodgers For Playoffs	9.00	4.50	2.75
429	Campy Most Valuable Player	3.00	1.50	.90
430	Turley Hurls Yanks To Championship	3.00	1.50	.90
431	Dodgers Take Series From Sox In Six (Larry Sherry)	3.00	1.50	.90
432	Furillo Hero In 3rd World Series Game	3.00	1.50	.90
433	Adcock Gets Four Homers, Double	3.00	1.50	.90
434	Dickey Chosen All Star Catcher	3.00	1.50	.90
435	Burdette Beats Yanks In 3 Series Games	3.00	1.50	.90
436	Umpires Clear White Sox Bench	3.00	1.50	.90
437	Reese Honored As Greatest Dodgers S.S.	3.00	1.50	.90
438	Joe DiMaggio Hits In 56 Straight Games	20.00	10.00	6.00
439	Ted Williams Hits .406 For Season	20.00	10.00	6.00
440	Johnson Pitches 56 Scoreless Innings	3.00	1.50	.90
441	Hodges Hits 4 Home Runs In Nite Game	3.00	1.50	.90
442	Greenberg Returns To Tigers From Army	3.00	1.50	.90
443	Ty Cobb Named Best Player Of All Time	10.00	5.00	3.00
444	Robin Roberts Wins 28 Games	3.00	1.50	.90
445	Rizzuto's 2 Runs Save 1st Place	3.00	1.50	.90
446	Tigers Beat Out Senators For Pennant (Hal Newhouser)	3.00	1.50	.90
447	Babe Ruth Hits 60th Home Run	20.00	10.00	6.00
448	Cy Young Honored	4.50	2.25	1.25
449	Killebrew Starts Spring Training	3.00	1.50	.90
450	Mantle Hits Longest Homer At Stadium	35.00	17.50	10.50
451	Braves Take Pennant	3.00	1.50	.90
452	Ted Williams Hero Of All Star Game	20.00	10.00	6.00
453	Homer By Berra Puts Yanks In 1st Place	3.00	1.50	.90
454	Snodgrass Muffs A Fly Ball	3.00	1.50	.90
455	Babe Hits 3 Homers In A Series Game	25.00	12.50	7.50
456	New York Wins 26 Straight Games	3.00	1.50	.90
457	Ted Kluszewski Stars In 1st Series Win	3.00	1.50	.90
458	Ott Walks 5 Times In A Single Game	3.00	1.50	.90
459	Harvey Kuenn Takes Batting Title	3.00	1.50	.90
460	Bob Feller Hurls 3rd No-Hitter Of Career	3.00	1.50	.90
461	Yanks Champs Again! (Casey Stengel)	3.00	1.50	.90
462	Aaron's Bat Beats Yankees In Series	10.00	5.00	3.00
463	Warren Spahn Beats Yanks In World Series	3.00	1.50	.90
464	Ump's Wrong Call Helps Dodgers	3.00	1.50	.90
465	Kaline Hits 3 Homers, 2 In Same Inning	3.00	1.50	.90

466	Bob Allison Named A.L. Rookie Of Year	3.00	1.50	.90
467	DiMag Comes Thru	20.00	10.00	6.00
468	Colavito Hits Four Homers In One Game	3.50	1.75	1.00
469	Erskine Sets Strike Out Record In W.S.	3.00	1.50	.90
470	Sal Maglie Pitches No-Hit Game	3.00	1.50	.90
471	Early Wynn Victory Crushes Yanks	3.00	1.50	.90
472	Nellie Fox American League's MVP	3.00	1.50	.90
473	Pickoff Ends Series (Marty Marion)	3.00	1.50	.90
474	Podres Pitching Wins Series	3.00	1.50	.90
475	Owen Drops 3rd Strike	3.00	1.50	.90
476	Dizzy And Daffy Win Series	9.00	4.50	2.75
477	Mathewson Pitches 3 W.S. Shutouts	10.00	5.00	3.00
478	Haddix Pitches 12 Perfect Innings	3.00	1.50	.90
479	Hubbell Strike Out 5 A.L. Stars	3.00	1.50	.90
480	Homer Sinks Dodgers (Bobby Thomson)	6.00	3.00	1.75

1889 Number 7 Cigars (N526)

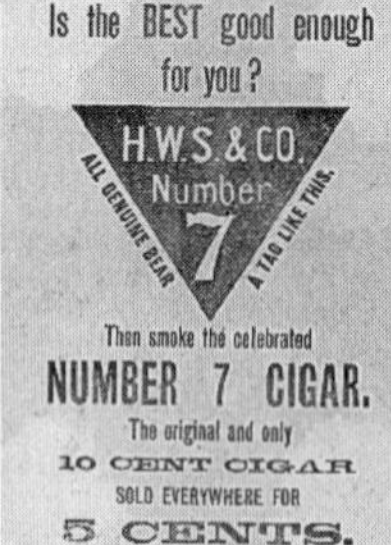

Three versions of this set picturing Boston Beaneaters (N.L.) players were issued in 1889. Number 7 and Diamond S brand cigars are the most commonly encountered advertising printed on the cards' backs. Cards with "C.S. White & Co." at top front are also known. The cards measure approximately 3-1/8" x 4-1/2" and feature black-and-white portrait drawings of the players with their name printed below in capital letters along with the team name. Backs carry ads for either Number 7 Cigars, a product of H.W.S. & Co. Howard W. Spurr & Co.), or Diamond S Cigars, advertised as the "Best 10 cent Cigar in America."

		NM	EX	VG
Complete Set (15):		20,000	8,000	4,000
Common Player:		1,100	450.00	225.00
(1)	C.W. Bennett	1,100	450.00	225.00
(2)	Dennis Brouthers	2,500	800.00	400.00
(3)	T.T. Brown	1,100	450.00	225.00
(4)	John G. Clarkson	2,500	800.00	400.00
(5)	C.W. Ganzel	1,100	450.00	225.00
(6)	James A. Hart	1,100	450.00	225.00
(7)	R.F. Johnston	1,100	450.00	225.00
(8)	M.J. Kelly	3,500	1,000	500.00
(9)	M.J. Madden	1,100	450.00	225.00
(10)	Wm. Nash	1,100	450.00	225.00
(11)	Jos. Quinn	1,100	450.00	225.00
(12)	Chas. Radbourn	2,500	800.00	400.00
(13)	J.B. Ray (Should be I.B.)	1,100	450.00	225.00
(14)	Hardie Richardson	1,100	450.00	225.00
(15)	Wm. Sowders	1,100	450.00	225.00

1949-1950 Num Num Cleveland Indians

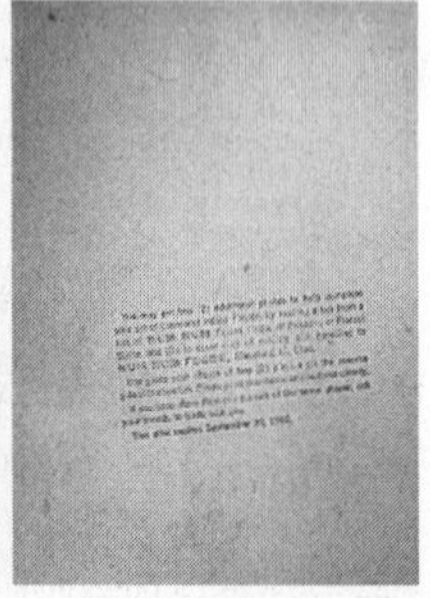

The 6-1/2" x 9" photopack pictures sold at Municipal Stadium in 1949 did double duty when they were also used as a premium for Num Num snack foods. A rubber-stamped notice on the back of the black-and-white photos offered two pictures for 10 cents and a box top, while encouraging trading. The pictures generally feature posed action shots with a facsimile autograph and white border. Backs are blank except for the rubber stamping. The unnumbered cards are checklisted here alphabetically.

		NM	EX	VG
Complete Set (36):		1,850	925.00	550.00
Common Player:		35.00	17.50	10.00
(1)	Bob Avila	35.00	17.50	10.00
(2)	Gene Bearden	35.00	17.50	10.00
(3)	Al Benton	35.00	17.50	10.00
(4)	John Berardino	45.00	22.50	13.50
(5)	Ray Boone	35.00	17.50	10.00
(6)	Lou Boudreau	65.00	30.00	15.00
(7)	Allie Clark	35.00	17.50	10.00
(8)	Larry Doby	65.00	30.00	15.00
(9)	Luke Easter	35.00	17.50	10.00
(10)	Bob Feller	125.00	60.00	30.00
(11)	Jess Flores	35.00	17.50	10.00
(12)	Mike Garcia	35.00	17.50	10.00
(13)	Joe Gordon	35.00	17.50	10.00
(14)	Hank Greenberg	125.00	65.00	35.00
(15)	Steve Gromek	35.00	17.50	10.00
(16)	Jim Hegan	35.00	17.50	10.00
(17)	Ken Keltner	35.00	17.50	10.00
(18)	Bob Kennedy	35.00	17.50	10.00
(19)	Bob Lemon	65.00	30.00	15.00
(20)	Dale Mitchell	35.00	17.50	10.00
(21)	Ray Murray	35.00	17.50	10.00
(22)	Satchell Paige	200.00	90.00	50.00
(23)	Frank Papish	35.00	17.50	10.00
(24)	Hal Peck	35.00	17.50	10.00
(25)	Chick Pieretti	35.00	17.50	10.00
(26)	Al Rosen	45.00	22.50	13.50
(27)	Dick Rozek (Glove out front.)	35.00	17.50	10.00
(28)	Dick Rozek (Glove under leg.)	35.00	17.50	10.00
(29)	Mike Tresh	35.00	17.50	10.00
(30)	Thurman Tucker	35.00	17.50	10.00
(31)	Bill Veeck	65.00	30.00	15.00
(32)	Mickey Vernon	35.00	17.50	10.00
(33)	Early Wynn	65.00	30.00	15.00
(34)	Sam Zoldak	35.00	17.50	10.00
(35)	Coaches (George Susce, Herold Ruel, Bill McKechnie, Steve O'Neill, Mel Harder)	35.00	17.50	10.00
(36)	Municipal Stadium	35.00	17.50	10.00

1952 Num Num Cleveland Indians

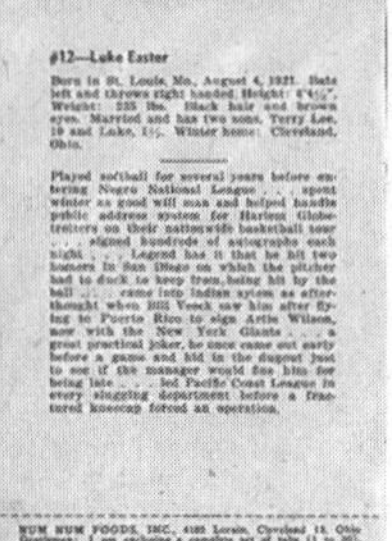

Distributed with packages of Num Num potato chips, pretzels and other snack foods, this black-and-white set, like the 1950 issue, was also issued in a slightly different format directly by the team. The Num Num cards have a 1" tab at the bottom which could be redeemed, when a complete set was collected, for an autographed baseball. The team-issued version of the cards was printed without the tabs. Also like the 1950 Num Nums, Bob Kennedy's card is unaccountably scarce in the 1952 set. The '52 cards measure 3-1/2" x 5-1/2" including the tab, which has the card number on front, along with redemption details. Backs, also printed in black-and-white, repeat the card number in the upper-left corner. There is significant player biographical information and some 1951 season highlights. Cards with no tabs are worth about 1/3 less than the values quoted.

		NM	EX	VG
Complete Set, With Tabs (20):		5,750	2,300	1,150
Common Player, With Tab:		125.00	50.00	25.00
Complete Set, No Tabs (20):		3,250	1,300	650.00
Common Player, No Tab:		110.00	45.00	22.50
	WITH TABS			
1	Lou Brissie	150.00	60.00	30.00
2	Jim Hegan	150.00	60.00	30.00
3	Birdie Tebbetts	150.00	60.00	30.00
4	Bob Lemon	300.00	120.00	60.00
5	Bob Feller	900.00	360.00	180.00
6	Early Wynn	300.00	120.00	60.00
7	Mike Garcia	150.00	60.00	30.00
8	Steve Gromek	150.00	60.00	30.00
9	Bob Chakales	150.00	60.00	30.00
10	Al Rosen	175.00	70.00	35.00
11	Dick Rozek	150.00	60.00	30.00
12	Luke Easter	175.00	70.00	35.00
13	Ray Boone	150.00	60.00	30.00
14	Bobby Avila	150.00	60.00	30.00
15	Dale Mitchell	150.00	60.00	30.00
16	Bob Kennedy/SP	1,600	640.00	320.00
17	Harry Simpson	150.00	60.00	30.00
18	Larry Doby	300.00	120.00	60.00
19	Sam Jones	150.00	60.00	30.00
20	Al Lopez	300.00	120.00	60.00
	NO TABS			
1	Lou Brissie	100.00	40.00	20.00
2	Jim Hegan	100.00	40.00	20.00
3	Birdie Tebbetts	100.00	40.00	20.00
4	Bob Lemon	200.00	80.00	40.00
5	Bob Feller	600.00	240.00	120.00
6	Early Wynn	200.00	80.00	40.00
7	Mike Garcia	100.00	40.00	20.00
8	Steve Gromek	100.00	40.00	20.00
9	Bob Chakales	100.00	40.00	20.00
10	Al Rosen	125.00	50.00	25.00
11	Dick Rozek	100.00	40.00	20.00
12	Luke Easter	125.00	50.00	25.00
13	Ray Boone	100.00	40.00	20.00
14	Bobby Avila	100.00	40.00	20.00
15	Dale Mitchell	100.00	40.00	20.00
16	Bob Kennedy/SP	1,250	500.00	250.00
17	Harry Simpson	100.00	40.00	20.00
18	Larry Doby	200.00	80.00	40.00
19	Sam Jones	100.00	40.00	20.00
20	Al Lopez	200.00	80.00	40.00

1937 O-Pee-Chee

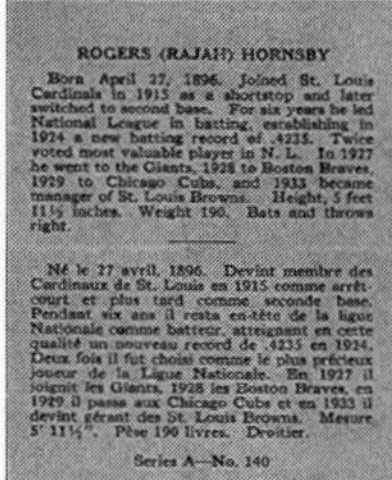

Kind of a combination of 1934 Goudeys and 1934-36 Batter Ups, the '37 OPC "Baseball Stars" set features black-and-white action photos against a stylized ballpark. About halfway up the 2-5/8" x 2-15/16" cards, the background was die-cut to allow it to be folded back to create a stand-up card. Backs are printed in English and French. The 40 cards in "Series A" are all American Leaguers, leading to speculation that a Series B of National League players was to have been issued at a later date. The set carries the American Card Catalog designation of V300.

		NM	EX	VG
Complete Set (40):		17,500	8,750	5,250
Common Player:		275.00	135.00	85.00
101	John Lewis	275.00	135.00	85.00
102	"Jack" Hayes	275.00	135.00	85.00
103	Earl Averill	400.00	200.00	120.00
104	Harland Clift (Harlond)	275.00	135.00	85.00
105	"Beau" Bell	275.00	135.00	85.00
106	Jimmy Foxx (Jimmie)	1,050	525.00	315.00
107	Hank Greenberg	1,325	660.00	400.00
108	George Selkirk	275.00	135.00	85.00
109	Wally Moses	275.00	135.00	85.00
110	"Gerry" Walker	275.00	135.00	85.00
111	"Goose" Goslin	400.00	200.00	120.00
112	Charlie Gehringer	425.00	210.00	125.00
113	Hal Trosky	275.00	135.00	85.00
114	"Buddy" Myer	275.00	135.00	85.00
115	Luke Appling	400.00	200.00	120.00
116	"Zeke" Bonura	275.00	135.00	85.00
117	Tony Lazzeri	425.00	210.00	125.00
118	Joe DiMaggio	4,100	2,050	1,225
119	Bill Dickey	600.00	300.00	180.00
120	Bob Feller	1,600	800.00	480.00
121	Harry Kelley	275.00	135.00	85.00
122	Johnny Allen	275.00	135.00	85.00
123	Bob Johnson	275.00	135.00	85.00
124	Joe Cronin	400.00	200.00	120.00
125	"Rip" Radcliff	275.00	135.00	85.00
126	Cecil Travis	275.00	135.00	85.00
127	Joe Kuhel	275.00	135.00	85.00
128	Odell Hale	275.00	135.00	85.00
129	Sam West	275.00	135.00	85.00
130	Ben Chapman	275.00	135.00	85.00
131	Monte Pearson	275.00	135.00	85.00
132	"Rick" Ferrell	400.00	200.00	120.00
133	Tommy Bridges	275.00	135.00	85.00
134	"Schoolboy" Rowe	275.00	135.00	85.00
135	Vernon Kennedy	275.00	135.00	85.00
136	"Red" Ruffing	400.00	200.00	120.00
137	"Lefty" Grove	500.00	250.00	150.00
138	Wes Farrell	275.00	135.00	85.00
139	"Buck" Newsom	275.00	135.00	85.00
140	Rogers Hornsby	750.00	375.00	225.00

1960 O-Pee-Chee Tattoos

Though much scarcer than the contemporary Topps version, this Canadian specialty bubblegum issue does not currently enjoy any price premium. The OPC type is identifiable by its imprint on the outside of the wrapper.

(See 1960 Topps Tattoos for description, checklist and price guide.)

1965 O-Pee-Chee

Identical in design to the 1965 Topps set, the Canadian-issued 1965 O-Pee-Chee set was printed on gray stock and consists of 283 cards, each measuring the standard 2-1/2" x 3-1/2". The words "Printed in Canada" appear along the bottom of the back of the cards. The checklist for '65 OPC parallels the first 283 cards in 1965 Topps.

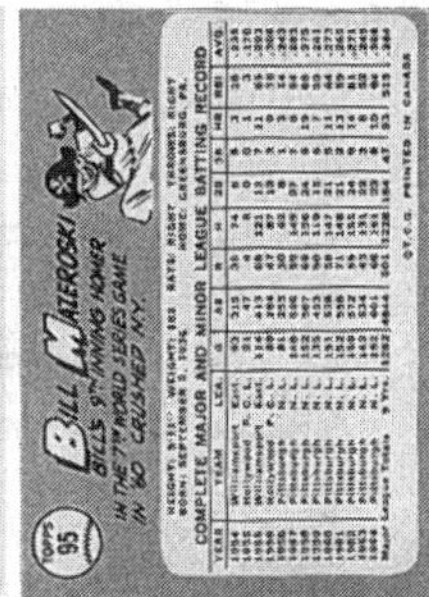

	NM	EX	VG
Complete Set (283):	3,150	1,575	950.00
Common Player (1-196):	3.00	1.50	9.00
Common Player (197-283):	6.00	3.00	1.80

Stars: 2-3X Topps

(See 1965 Topps #1-283 for checklist and star card values.)

1966 O-Pee-Chee

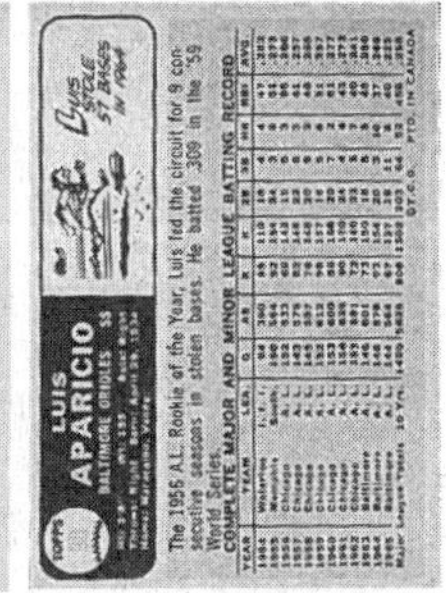

Utilizing the same design as the 1966 Topps set, the 1966 O-Pee-Chee set consists of 196 cards, measuring 2-1/2" x 3-1/2". The words "Ptd. in Canada" appear along the bottom on the back of the cards. The '66 OPC checklist parallels the first 196 cards in the Topps version.

	NM	EX	VG
Complete Set (196):	1,600	800.00	475.00
Common Player (1-196):	2.50	1.25	.75

Stars: 2-3X Topps

(See 1966 Topps #1-196 for checklist and base star card values.)

1967 O-Pee-Chee

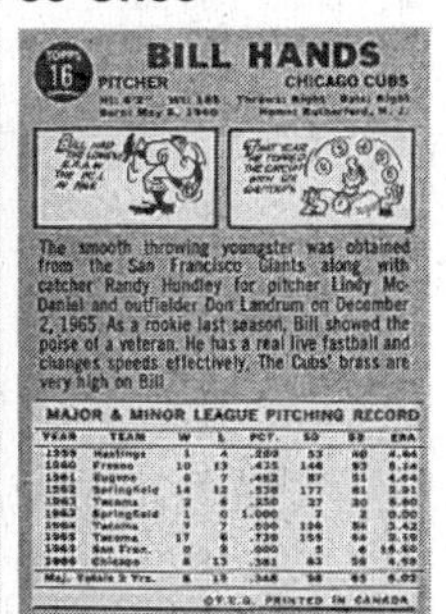

Cards in the 196-card Canadian set are nearly identical in design to the 1967 Topps set, except the words "Printed in Canada" are found on the back in the lower-right corner. Cards measure 2-1/2" x 3-1/2". The '67 OPC set parallels the first 196 cards on the Topps checklist, including "corrected" versions of the checklists and McCormick card.

	NM	EX	VG
Complete Set (196):	1,100	550.00	330.00
Common Player (1-109):	2.00	1.00	.60
Common Player (110-196):	2.50	1.25	.75

Stars: 2-3X Topps

(See 1967 Topps #1-196 for checklist and base star card values.

1968 O-Pee-Chee

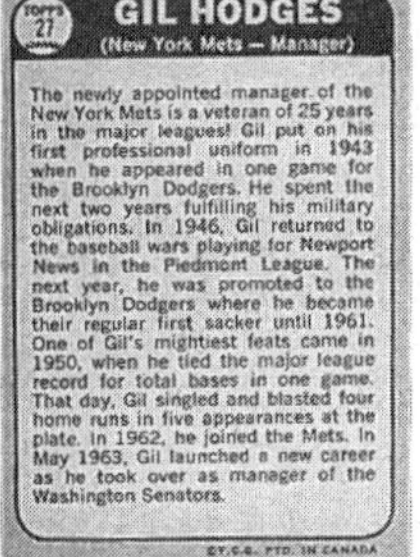

The O-Pee-Chee set for 1968 again consists of 196 cards, in the standard 2-1/2" x 3-1/2". The design is identical to the 1968 Topps set, except the color of the backs is slightly different and the words "Prd. in Canada" appear in the lower-right corner of the back. The checklist parallels the first 196 cards in '68 Topps, though only the "b" versions of the checklists and name-color variations are found in OPC.

		NM	EX	VG
	Complete Set (196):	2,000	1,000	600.00
	Common Player:	2.00	1.00	.60
	Stars: 2-3X Topps			
	(See 1968 Topps #1-196 for checklist and base star card values.)			
177	Mets Rookies (Jerry Koosman, Nolan Ryan)	825.00	410.00	245.00

1968 O-Pee-Chee Posters

The 5" x 7" "All Star Pin-ups" were inserts to 1968 OPC wax packs, but are virtually identical to the Topps version issued in 1967. The OPC posters have a small "Ptd. in Canada" line at bottom. They feature a full- color picture with the player's name, position and team in a circle in the lower-right corner on front. The numbered set consists of 32 players (generally big names). Because the large paper pin-ups had to be folded several times to fit into the wax packs, they are almost never found in technical Mint or NM condition.

		NM	EX	VG
	Complete Set (32):	300.00	150.00	90.00
	Common Player:	3.00	1.50	.90
1	Brooks Robinson	12.00	6.00	3.50
2	Bert Campaneris	3.00	1.50	.90
3	Carl Yastrzemski	12.00	6.00	3.50
4	Roberto Clemente	25.00	12.50	7.50
5	Cleon Jones	3.00	1.50	.90
6	Don Drysdale	12.00	6.00	3.50
7	Orlando Cepeda	9.00	4.50	2.75
8	Hank Aaron	25.00	12.50	7.50
9	Tommie Agee	6.00	3.00	1.75
10	Boog Powell	4.50	2.25	1.25
11	Mickey Mantle	40.00	20.00	12.00
12	Chico Cardenas	3.00	1.50	.90
13	John Callison	3.00	1.50	.90
14	Frank Howard	3.75	2.00	1.25
15	Willie Mays	25.00	12.50	7.50
16	Sam McDowell	4.50	2.25	1.25
17	Al Kaline	12.00	6.00	3.50
18	Juan Marichal	9.00	4.50	2.75
19	Denny McLain	4.50	2.25	1.25
20	Matty Alou	3.00	1.50	.90
21	Felipe Alou	4.50	2.25	1.25
22	Joe Pepitone	4.50	2.25	1.25
23	Leon Wagner	3.00	1.50	.90
24	Bobby Knoop	3.00	1.50	.90
25	Tony Oliva	4.50	2.25	1.25
26	Joe Torre	4.50	2.25	1.25
27	Ron Santo	6.00	3.00	1.75
28	Willie McCovey	12.00	6.00	3.50
29	Frank Robinson	12.00	6.00	3.50
30	Ron Hunt	3.00	1.50	.90
31	Harmon Killebrew	12.00	6.00	3.50
32	Joe Morgan	12.00	6.00	3.50

1969 O-Pee-Chee

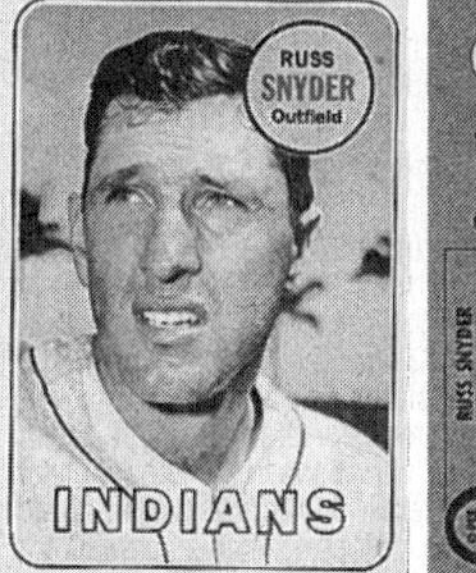

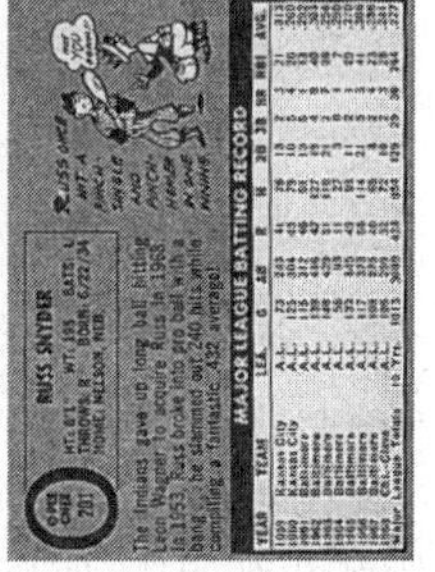

O-Pee-Chee increased the number of cards in its 1969 set to 218, maintaining the standard 2-1/2" x 3-1/2" size. The card design is identical to the 1969 Topps set, except for the appearance of an OPC logo on back, a slightly different color on the back and the words "Ptd. in Canada," which appear along the bottom. The checklist for '69 OPC parallels the Topps version, but includes only the later-printed "b" versions of the variation cards. This was the first year for the N.L. expansion Montreal Expos, and the Canadian versions of their cards generally sell for a modest premium.

	NM	EX	VG
Complete Set (218):	775.00	375.00	225.00
Common Player:	2.50	1.25	.75

Stars: 1-2X Topps

Expos: 1.5X Topps

(See 1969 Topps #1-218 for checklist and base star card values.)

1969 O-Pee-Chee Deckle

Very similar in design to the Topps Deckle Edge set of the same year, the 1969 O-Pee-Chee set consists of 24 (rather than Topps' 33) unnumbered black-and-white cards. The Canadian version measures 2-1/8" x 3-1/8", slightly smaller than the Topps set, but features the same "deckle cut" borders. The OPC set is blank-backed and has the facsimile autographs in black ink, rather than blue.

		NM	EX	VG
	Complete Set (24):	160.00	80.00	45.00
	Common Player:	2.50	1.25	.75
(1)	Rich Allen	3.00	1.50	.90
(2)	Luis Aparicio	7.50	3.75	2.25
(3)	Rodney Carew	12.50	6.25	3.75
(4)	Roberto Clemente	30.00	15.00	9.00
(5)	Curt Flood	2.50	1.25	.75
(6)	Bill Freehan	2.50	1.25	.75
(7)	Robert Gibson	7.50	3.75	2.25
(8)	Ken Harrelson	2.50	1.25	.75
(9)	Tommy Helms	2.50	1.25	.75
(10)	Tom Haller	2.50	1.25	.75
(11)	Willie Horton	2.50	1.25	.70
(12)	Frank Howard	2.50	1.25	.75
(13)	Willie McCovey	10.00	5.00	3.00
(14)	Denny McLain	2.50	1.25	.75
(15)	Juan Marichal	7.50	3.75	2.25
(16)	Willie Mays	25.00	12.50	7.50
(17)	John "Boog" Powell	3.00	1.50	.90
(18)	Brooks Robinson	12.50	6.25	3.75
(19)	Ronald Santo	3.00	1.50	.90
(20)	Rusty Staub	3.00	1.50	.90
(21)	Mel Stottlemyre	2.50	1.25	.75
(22)	Luis Tiant	2.50	1.25	.75
(23)	Maurie Wills	2.50	1.25	.75
(24)	Carl Yastrzemski	12.50	6.25	3.75

1970 O-Pee-Chee

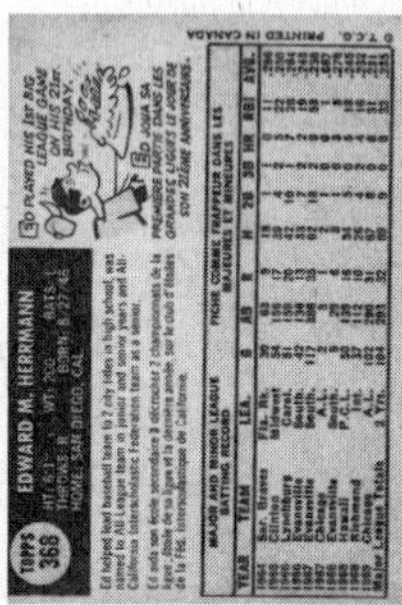

The 1970 O-Pee-Chee set, identical in design to the 1970 Topps set, expanded to 546 cards, measuring 2-1/2" x 3-1/2". The Canadian-issued O-Pee-Chee set is easy to distinguish because the backs are printed in both French and English and include the words "Printed in Canada." The '70 OPC checklist parallels the Topps versions. Besides the star cards generally bringing a premium over the Topps version due to scarcity, collectors pay a modest premium for OPC cards of Expos players.

	NM	EX	VG
Complete Set (546):	1,750	875.00	525.00
Common Player (1-459):	1.50	.75	.45
Common Player (460-546):	2.50	1.25	.75

Stars: 1-2X Topps

Expos: 1.5X Topps

(See 1970 Topps #1-546 for checklist and base card values.)

1971 O-Pee-Chee

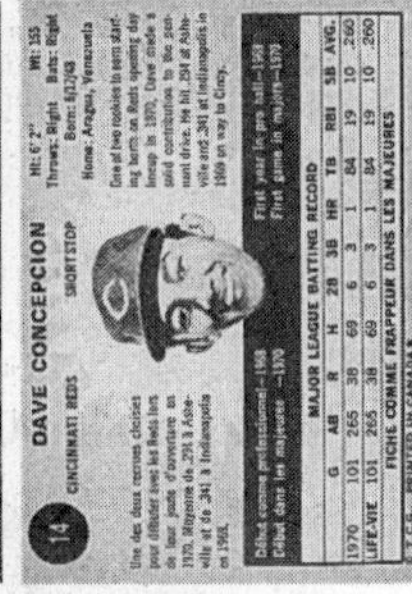

For 1971 O-Pee-Chee increased the number of cards in its set to 752, the same as the 1971 Topps set, which shares the same black-bordered design. The backs of the OPC are printed in yellow, rather than green, in a slightly different format and (except card numbers 524-752) are printed in both French and English. The words "Printed in Canada" appear on the back. Fourteen of the OPC cards have different photos from their corresponding Topps' cards or list the player with a different team. The '71 OPC checklist paralells the Topps version. Because of relative scarcity, superstars in the OPC set command a premium, as do cards of the "local" Expos players.

	NM	EX	VG
Complete Set (752):	3,000	1,500	900.00
Common Player (1-523):	2.75	1.50	.80
Common Player (524-643):	4.50	2.25	1.25
Common Player (644-752):	6.50	3.25	2.00
Stars: 1-2X Topps			
Expos: 1.5X Topps			

(See 1971 Topps for checklist and base card values.)

1972 O-Pee-Chee

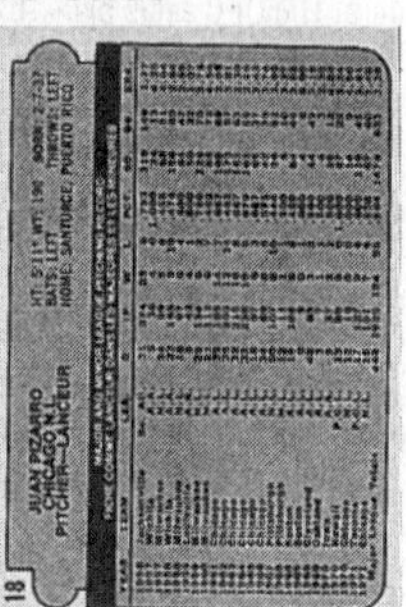

Identical in design to the Topps cards of the same year, the Canadian-issued 1972 O-Pee-Chee set numbers 525 cards, measuring 2-1/2" x 3-1/2". The backs state "Printed in Canada" and are written in both French and English. The O-Pee-Chee card of Gil Hodges notes the Mets' manager's death. The '72 OPC set parallels the first 525 cards on the '72 Topps checklist, though without any of the scarcer "a" variations. Because of relative scarcity, superstars in the OPC brand bring a premium over Topps cards, while increased demand for Expos players causes their cards to bring a similar modest premium.

	NM	EX	VG
Complete Set (525):	875.00	425.00	250.00
Common Player (1-263):	.60	.30	.20
Common Player (264-394):	.90	.45	.25
Common Player (395-525):	1.00	.50	.30
Stars: 1-2X Topps			
Expos: 1.5X Topps			

(See 1972 Topps #1-525 for checklist and base card values.)

1973 O-Pee-Chee

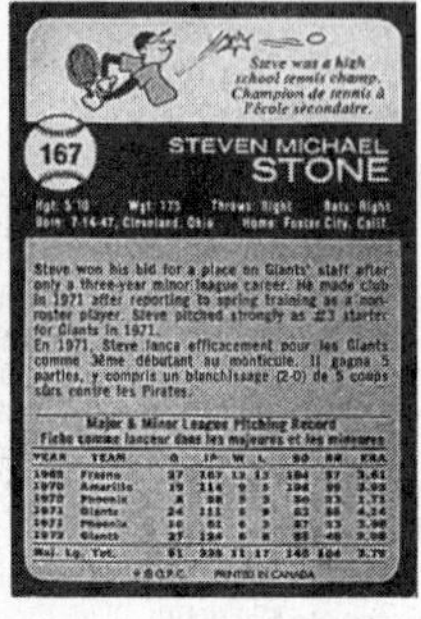

The 1973 Canadian-issued O-Pee-Chee set numbers 660 cards and is identical in design and checklist (including only the later-printed "b" variations) to the 1973 Topps set. The backs of the OPC cards are written in both French and English and contain the line "Printed in Canada" along the bottom. The cards measure 2-1/2" x 3-1/2". Unlike the '73 Topps set, which was issued in series of increasing scarcity throughout the summer, the '73 OPC cards were issued in a single series, with cards #529-660 being somewhat short-printed. OPC star cards generally sell for more than the Topps version due to relative scarcity, while Expos players in OPC rate a similar premium due to increased "local" demand.

	NM	EX	VG
Complete Set (660):	500.00	250.00	150.00
Common Player (1-528):	.75	.35	.20
Common Player (529-660):	1.25	.60	.40
Stars/Expos: 1.5X Topps			
Wax Pack (10):	55.00		
Wax Box (36):	1,900		

(See 1973 Topps for checklist and base card values.)

1973 O-Pee-Chee Team Checklists

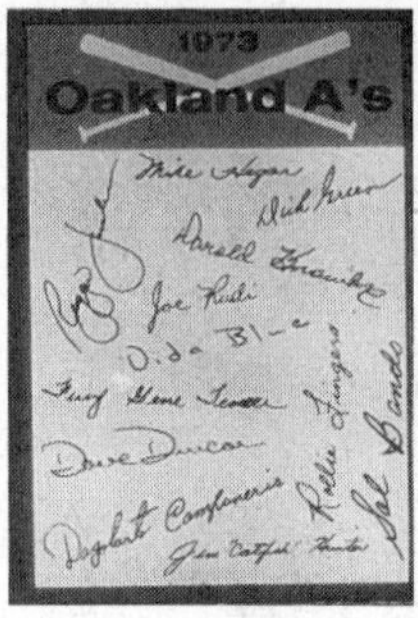

Similar to the 1973 Topps team checklist cards, this set was produced in Canada. The set consists of 24 unnumbered cards (2-1/2" x 3-1/2") with blue borders. The card fronts contain facsimile autographs of players from the same team. The backs contain team checklists of players found in the 1973 O-Pee-Chee regular issue set. The card backs contain the French translation for Team Checklist plus a copyright line "O.P.C. Printed in Canada."

		NM	EX	VG
Complete Set (24):		40.00	20.00	12.00
Common Card:		3.00	1.50	.90
(1)	Atlanta Braves	3.00	1.50	.90
(2)	Baltimore Orioles	3.00	1.50	.90
(3)	Boston Red Sox	3.00	1.50	.90
(4)	California Angels	3.00	1.50	.90
(5)	Chicago Cubs	3.00	1.50	.90
(6)	Chicago White Sox	3.00	1.50	.90
(7)	Cincinnati Reds	4.00	2.00	1.25
(8)	Cleveland Indians	3.00	1.50	.90
(9)	Detroit Tigers	4.00	2.00	1.25
(10)	Houston Astros	3.00	1.50	.90
(11)	Kansas City Royals	3.00	1.50	.90
(12)	Los Angeles Dodgers	3.00	1.50	.90
(13)	Milwaukee Brewers	3.00	1.50	.90
(14)	Minnesota Twins	3.00	1.50	.90
(15)	Montreal Expos	6.00	3.00	1.75
(16)	New York Mets	4.00	2.00	1.25
(17)	New York Yankees	3.00	1.50	.90
(18)	Oakland A's	4.50	2.25	1.25
(19)	Philadelphia Phillies	3.00	1.50	.90
(20)	Pittsburgh Pirates	3.00	1.50	.90
(21)	St. Louis Cardinals	3.00	1.50	.90
(22)	San Diego Padres	3.00	1.50	.90
(23)	San Francisco Giants	3.00	1.50	.90
(24)	Texas Rangers	3.00	1.50	.90

1974 O-Pee-Chee

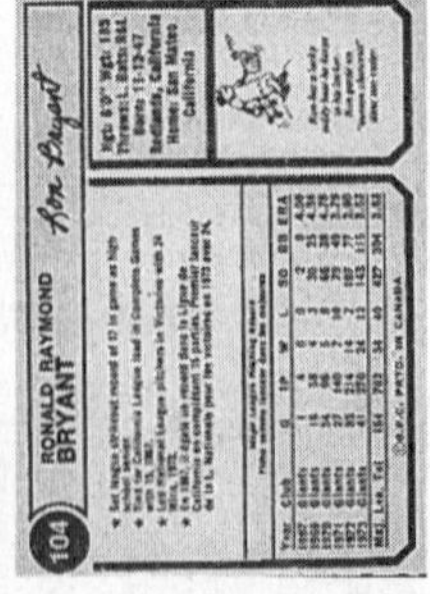

Again numbering 660 cards, the 1974 O-Pee-Chee set borrows its design and, except for 10 of the cards, shares its checklist with the Topps set of the same year. The cards measure the standard 2-1/2" x 3-1/2" and the backs are printed in both French and English and state "Printed in Canada." Because the OPC cards were printed later than Topps, there are no "Washington, Nat'l. League" variations in the Canadian set. Superstar cards and Expos players in OPC command a modest premium over the Topps version due to relative scarcity and increased local demand, respectively. Those OPC cards which differ from Topps are listed below, with the Topps version of each card number shown parenthetically.

		NM	EX	VG
Complete Set (660):		950.00	475.00	275.00
Common Player:		.50	.25	.15
Stars/Expos: 1.5X Topps				
Wax Pack (8):		65.00		
Wax Box (36):		2,150		
3	Aaron Special 1958-1959 (Aaron Special 1958-1961)	7.00	3.50	2.00
4	Aaron Special 1960-1961 (Aaron Special 1962-1965)	7.00	3.50	2.00
5	Aaron Special 1962-1963 (Aaron Special 1966-1969)	7.00	3.50	2.00
6	Aaron Special 1964-1965 (Aaron Special 1970-1973)	7.00	3.50	2.00
7	Aaron Special 1966-1967 (Jim Hunter)	7.00	3.50	2.00
8	Aaron Special 1968-1969 (George Theodore)	7.00	3.50	2.00
9	Aaron Special 1970-1973 (Mickey Lolich)	7.00	3.50	2.00
99	George Theodore (Brewers Mgr./Coaches)	1.50	.70	.45
166	Mickey Lolich (Royals Mgr./Coaches)	2.00	1.00	.60
196	Jim Hunter (Jim Fregosi)	7.50	3.75	2.25

(See 1974 Topps for checklist and base card values.)

1974 O-Pee-Chee Team Checklists

The 1974 O-Pee-Chee Team Checklists set is nearly identical to its Topps counterpart of the same year. Twenty-four unnumbered cards that measure 2-1/2" x 3-1/2" make up the set. The card fronts contain facsimile autographs while the backs carry a team checklist of players found in the regular issue O-Pee-Chee set of 1974. The cards have red borders and can be differentiated from the U.S. version by the "O.P.C. Printed in Canada" line on the back.

		NM	EX	VG
Complete Set (24):		25.00	12.50	7.50
Common Checklist:		1.50	.70	.40
(1)	Atlanta Braves	1.50	.70	.45
(2)	Baltimore Orioles	1.50	.70	.45
(3)	Boston Red Sox	1.50	.70	.45
(4)	California Angels	1.50	.70	.45
(5)	Chicago Cubs	1.50	.70	.45
(6)	Chicago White Sox	1.50	.70	.45
(7)	Cincinnati Reds	1.50	.70	.45
(8)	Cleveland Indians	1.50	.70	.45
(9)	Detroit Tigers	1.50	.70	.45
(10)	Houston Astros	1.50	.70	.45
(11)	Kansas City Royals	1.50	.70	.45
(12)	Los Angeles Dodgers	1.50	.70	.45
(13)	Milwaukee Brewers	1.50	.70	.45
(14)	Minnesota Twins	1.50	.70	.45
(15)	Montreal Expos	3.00	1.50	.90
(16)	New York Mets	1.50	.70	.45
(17)	New York Yankees	1.50	.70	.45
(18)	Oakland A's	1.50	.70	.45
(19)	Philadelphia Phillies	1.50	.70	.45
(20)	Pittsburgh Pirates	1.50	.70	.45
(21)	St. Louis Cardinals	1.50	.70	.45
(22)	San Diego Padres	1.50	.70	.45
(23)	San Francisco Giants	1.50	.70	.45
(24)	Texas Rangers	1.50	.70	.45

1975 O-Pee-Chee

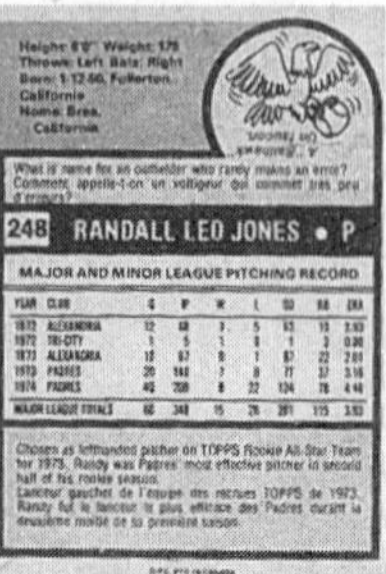

The 1975 O-Pee-Chee set was again complete at 660 cards, each measuring 2-1/2" x 3-1/2", and using the same design as the 1975 Topps set. The backs of the O-Pee-Chee cards are written in both French and English and state that the cards were printed in Canada. The checklist for OPC and Topps are identical in '75. Because they are relatively scarcer, OPC superstars sell for a premium over Topps. Expos players also enjoy a premium due to increased local demand.

	NM	EX	VG
Complete Set (660):	625.00	325.00	200.00

	NM	EX	VG
Common Player:	.45	.25	.15
Stars: 2X Topps			
Expos: 1.5X Topps			
Wax Pack (8):	30.00		
Wax Box (48):	1,200		

(See 1975 Topps for checklist and base card values.)

1976 O-Pee-Chee

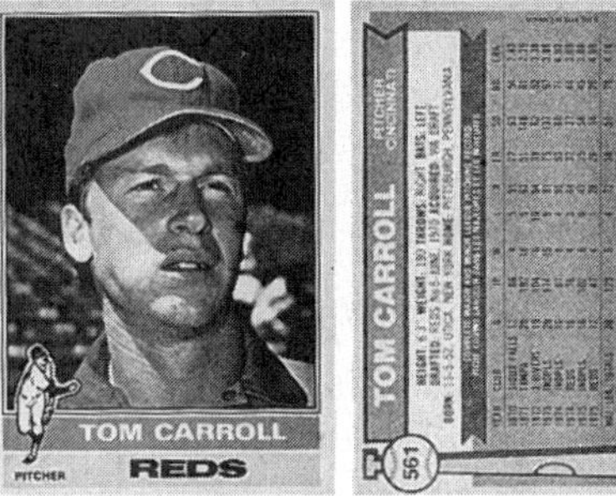

Identical in design to, and sharing a checklist with, the 1976 Topps set, the Canadian-issued 1976 O-Pee-Chees comprise 660 cards, each 2-1/2" x 3-1/2". The backs are printed in both French and English and state "Ptd. in Canada." Stars and Expos players enjoy a modest premium over the Topps versions due to relative scarcity and increased local demand, respectively.

	NM	EX	VG
Complete Set (660):	700.00	350.00	210.00
Common Player:	.20	.10	.05
Stars/Expos 2X Topps			
Wax Pack (8):	30.00		
Wax Box (48):	750.00		

(See 1976 Topps for checklist and base card values.)

1977 O-Pee-Chee

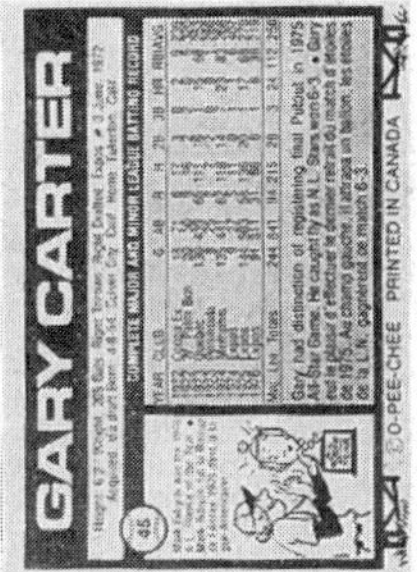

The 1977 O-Pee-Chee set represents a change in philosophy for the Canadian company. The design of the set is still identical to the Topps set of the same year, but the number of cards was reduced to 264 with more emphasis on players from the two Canadian teams. The backs are printed in both French and English and state "O-Pee-Chee Printed in Canada." About 1/3 of the photos in the OPC set differ from the corresponding Topps cards either with entirely different photos, airbrushed uniform changes, the removal of All-Star and Rookie Team designations, or significant photo cropping variations. Cards measure the standard 2-1/2" x 3-1/2".

		NM	EX	VG
Complete Set (264):		125.00	65.00	40.00
Common Player:		.25	.13	.08
Wax Pack (8):		12.00		
Wax Box (48):		285.00		
1	Batting Leaders (George Brett, Bill Madlock)	4.00	2.00	1.25
2	Home Run Leaders (Graig Nettles, Mike Schmidt)	2.75	1.50	.80
3	Runs Batted In Leaders (George Foster, Lee May)	.25	.13	.08
4	Stolen Base Leaders (Dave Lopes, Bill North)	.25	.13	.08
5	Victory Leaders (Randy Jones, Jim Palmer)	1.00	.50	.30
6	Strikeout Leaders (Nolan Ryan, Tom Seaver)	12.50	6.25	3.75
7	Earned Run Avg. Leaders (John Denny, Mark Fidrych)	.25	.13	.08
8	Leading Firemen (Bill Campbell, Rawly Eastwick)	.25	.13	.08
9	Mike Jorgensen	.25	.13	.08
10	Jim Hunter	4.00	2.00	1.25
11	Ken Griffey	.25	.13	.08
12	Bill Campbell	.25	.13	.08
13	Otto Velez	.25	.13	.08
14	Milt May	.25	.13	.08
15	Dennis Eckersley	4.00	2.00	1.25
16	John Mayberry	.25	.13	.08
17	Larry Bowa	.25	.13	.08
18	Don Carrithers	.25	.13	.08
19	Ken Singleton	.25	.13	.08
20	Bill Stein	.25	.13	.08
21	Ken Brett	.25	.13	.08
22	Gary Woods	.25	.13	.08
23	Steve Swisher	.25	.13	.08
24	Don Sutton	4.00	2.00	1.25
25	Willie Stargell	4.00	2.00	1.25
26	Jerry Koosman	.25	.13	.08
27	Del Unser	.25	.13	.08
28	Bob Grich	.25	.13	.08
29	Jim Slaton	.25	.13	.08
30	Thurman Munson	4.00	2.00	1.25
31	Dan Driessen	.25	.13	.08
32	Tom Bruno (Not in Topps.)	.25	.13	.08
33	Larry Hisle	.25	.13	.08
34	Phil Garner	.25	.13	.08
35	Mike Hargrove	.25	.13	.08
36	Jackie Brown	.25	.13	.08
37	Carl Yastrzemski	7.50	3.75	2.25
38	Dave Roberts	.25	.13	.08
39	Ray Fosse	.25	.13	.08
40	Dave McKay	.25	.13	.08
41	Paul Splittorff	.25	.13	.08
42	Garry Maddox	.25	.13	.08
43	Phil Niekro	4.00	2.00	1.25
44	Roger Metzger	.25	.13	.08
45	Gary Carter	7.50	3.75	2.25
46	Jim Spencer	.25	.13	.08
47	Ross Grimsley	.25	.13	.08
48	Bob Bailor	.25	.13	.08
49	Chris Chambliss	.25	.13	.08
50	Will McEnaney	.25	.13	.08
51	Lou Brock	4.50	2.25	1.25
52	Rollie Fingers	4.00	2.00	1.25
53	Chris Speier	.25	.13	.08
54	Bombo Rivera	.25	.13	.08
55	Pete Broberg	.25	.13	.08
56	Bill Madlock	.25	.13	.08
57	Rick Rhoden	.25	.13	.08
58	Blue Jay Coaches (Don Leppert, Bob Miller, Jackie Moore, Harry Warner)	.50	.25	.15
59	John Candelaria	.25	.13	.08
60	Ed Kranepool	.25	.13	.08
61	Dave LaRoche	.25	.13	.08
62	Jim Rice	.75	.40	.25
63	Don Stanhouse	.25	.13	.08
64	Jason Thompson	.25	.13	.08
65	Nolan Ryan	25.00	12.50	7.50
66	Tom Poquette	.25	.13	.08
67	Leon Hooten	.25	.13	.08
68	Bob Boone	.25	.13	.08
69	Mickey Rivers	.25	.13	.08
70	Gary Nolan	.25	.13	.08
71	Sixto Lezcano	.25	.13	.08
72	Larry Parrish	.25	.13	.08
73	Dave Goltz	.25	.13	.08
74	Bert Campaneris	.25	.13	.08
75	Vida Blue	.25	.13	.08
76	Rick Cerone	.25	.13	.08
77	Ralph Garr	.25	.13	.08
78	Ken Forsch	.25	.13	.08
79	Willie Montanez	.25	.13	.08
80	Jim Palmer	4.50	2.25	1.25
81	Jerry White	.25	.13	.08
82	Gene Tenace	.25	.13	.08
83	Bobby Murcer	.25	.13	.08
84	Garry Templeton	.25	.13	.08
85	Bill Singer	.25	.13	.08
86	Buddy Bell	.25	.13	.08
87	Luis Tiant	.25	.13	.08
88	Rusty Staub	.25	.13	.08
89	Sparky Lyle	.25	.13	.08
90	Jose Morales	.25	.13	.08
91	Dennis Leonard	.25	.13	.08
92	Tommy Smith	.25	.13	.08
93	Steve Carlton	5.50	2.75	1.75
94	John Scott	.25	.13	.08
95	Bill Bonham	.25	.13	.08
96	Dave Lopes	.25	.13	.08
97	Jerry Reuss	.25	.13	.08
98	Dave Kingman	.35	.20	.11
99	Dan Warthen	.25	.13	.08
100	Johnny Bench	7.50	3.75	2.25
101	Bert Blyleven	.25	.13	.08
102	Cecil Cooper	.25	.13	.08
103	Mike Willis	.25	.13	.08
104	Dan Ford	.25	.13	.08
105	Frank Tanana	.25	.13	.08
106	Bill North	.25	.13	.08
107	Joe Ferguson	.25	.13	.08
108	Dick Williams	.25	.13	.08
109	John Denny	.25	.13	.08
110	Willie Randolph	.25	.13	.08
111	Reggie Cleveland	.25	.13	.08
112	Doug Howard	.25	.13	.08
113	Randy Jones	.25	.13	.08
114	Rico Carty	.25	.13	.08
115	Mark Fidrych	2.75	1.50	.80
116	Darrell Porter	.25	.13	.08
117	Wayne Garrett	.25	.13	.08
118	Greg Luzinski	.25	.13	.08
119	Jim Barr	.25	.13	.08
120	George Foster	.25	.13	.08
121	Phil Roof	.25	.13	.08
122	Bucky Dent	.25	.13	.08
123	Steve Braun	.25	.13	.08
124	Checklist 1-132	.40	.20	.12
125	Lee May	.25	.13	.08
126	Woodie Fryman	.25	.13	.08
127	Jose Cardenal	.25	.13	.08
128	Doug Rau	.25	.13	.08
129	Rennie Stennett	.25	.13	.08
130	Pete Vuckovich	.25	.13	.08
131	Cesar Cedeno	.25	.13	.08
132	Jon Matlack	.25	.13	.08
133	Don Baylor	.30	.15	.09
134	Darrel Chaney	.25	.13	.08
135	Tony Perez	4.00	2.00	1.25
136	Aurelio Rodriguez	.25	.13	.08
137	Carlton Fisk	4.00	2.00	1.25
138	Wayne Garland	.25	.13	.08
139	Dave Hilton	.25	.13	.08
140	Rawly Eastwick	.25	.13	.08
141	Amos Otis	.25	.13	.08
142	Tug McGraw	.25	.13	.08
143	Rod Carew	5.50	2.75	1.75
144	Mike Torrez	.25	.13	.08
145	Sal Bando	.25	.13	.08
146	Dock Ellis	.25	.13	.08
147	Jose Cruz	.25	.13	.08
148	Alan Ashby	.25	.13	.08
149	Gaylord Perry	4.00	2.00	1.25
150	Keith Hernandez	.25	.13	.08
151	Dave Pagan	.25	.13	.08
152	Richie Zisk	.25	.13	.08
153	Steve Rogers	.25	.13	.08
154	Mark Belanger	.25	.13	.08
155	Andy Messersmith	.25	.13	.08
156	Dave Winfield	6.00	3.00	1.75
157	Chuck Hartenstein	.25	.13	.08
158	Manny Trillo	.25	.13	.08
159	Steve Yeager	.25	.13	.08
160	Cesar Geronimo	.25	.13	.08
161	Jim Rooker	.25	.13	.08
162	Tim Foli	.25	.13	.08
163	Fred Lynn	.25	.13	.08
164	Ed Figueroa	.25	.13	.08
165	Johnny Grubb	.25	.13	.08
166	Pedro Garcia	.25	.13	.08
167	Ron LeFlore	.25	.13	.08
168	Rich Hebner	.25	.13	.08
169	Larry Herndon	.25	.13	.08
170	George Brett	15.00	7.50	4.50
171	Joe Kerrigan	.25	.13	.08
172	Bud Harrelson	.25	.13	.08
173	Bobby Bonds	.25	.13	.08
174	Bill Travers	.25	.13	.08
175	John Lowenstein	.25	.13	.08
176	Butch Wynegar	.25	.13	.08
177	Pete Falcone	.25	.13	.08
178	Claudell Washington	.25	.13	.08
179	Checklist 133-264	.40	.20	.12
180	Dave Cash	.25	.13	.08
181	Fred Norman	.25	.13	.08
182	Roy White	.25	.13	.08
183	Marty Perez	.25	.13	.08
184	Jesse Jefferson	.25	.13	.08
185	Jim Sundberg	.25	.13	.08
186	Dan Meyer	.25	.13	.08
187	Fergie Jenkins	6.00	3.00	1.75
188	Tom Veryzer	.25	.13	.08
189	Dennis Blair	.25	.13	.08
190	Rick Manning	.25	.13	.08
191	Doug Bird	.25	.13	.08
192	Al Bumbry	.25	.13	.08
193	Dave Roberts	.25	.13	.08
194	Larry Christenson	.25	.13	.08
195	Chet Lemon	.25	.13	.08
196	Ted Simmons	.25	.13	.08
197	Ray Burris	.25	.13	.08
198	Expos Coaches (Jim Brewer, Billy Gardner, Mickey Vernon, Ozzie Virgil)	.25	.13	.08
199	Ron Cey	.25	.13	.08
200	Reggie Jackson	12.50	6.25	3.75
201	Pat Zachry	.25	.13	.08
202	Doug Ault	.25	.13	.08
203	Al Oliver	.25	.13	.08
204	Robin Yount	5.50	2.75	1.75
205	Tom Seaver	7.50	3.75	2.25
206	Joe Rudi	.25	.13	.08
207	Barry Foote	.25	.13	.08
208	Toby Harrah	.25	.13	.08
209	Jeff Burroughs	.25	.13	.08
210	George Scott	.25	.13	.08
211	Jim Mason	.25	.13	.08
212	Vern Ruhle	.25	.13	.08
213	Fred Kendall	.25	.13	.08
214	Rick Reuschel	.25	.13	.08
215	Hal McRae	.25	.13	.08
216	Chip Lang	.25	.13	.08
217	Graig Nettles	.30	.15	.09
218	George Hendrick	.25	.13	.08
219	Glenn Abbott	.25	.13	.08
220	Joe Morgan	4.50	2.25	1.25
221	Sam Ewing	.25	.13	.08
222	George Medich	.25	.13	.08
223	Reggie Smith	.25	.13	.08
224	Dave Hamilton	.25	.13	.08
225	Pepe Frias	.25	.13	.08
226	Jay Johnstone	.25	.13	.08
227	J.R. Richard	.25	.13	.08
228	Doug DeCinces	.25	.13	.08
229	Dave Lemanczyk	.25	.13	.08
230	Rick Monday	.25	.13	.08
231	Manny Sanguillen	.25	.13	.08
232	John Montefusco	.25	.13	.08
233	Duane Kuiper	.25	.13	.08
234	Ellis Valentine	.25	.13	.08
235	Dick Tidrow	.25	.13	.08
236	Ben Oglivie	.25	.13	.08
237	Rick Burleson	.25	.13	.08
238	Roy Hartsfield	.25	.13	.08
239	Lyman Bostock	.25	.13	.08
240	Pete Rose	13.50	6.75	4.00
241	Mike Ivie	.25	.13	.08
242	Dave Parker	.35	.20	.11
243	Bill Greif	.25	.13	.08
244	Freddie Patek	.25	.13	.08
245	Mike Schmidt	15.00	7.50	4.50
246	Brian Downing	.25	.13	.08
247	Steve Hargan	.25	.13	.08
248	Dave Collins	.25	.13	.08
249	Felix Millan	.25	.13	.08
250	Don Gullett	.25	.13	.08
251	Jerry Royster	.25	.13	.08
252	Earl Williams	.25	.13	.08
253	Frank Duffy	.25	.13	.08
254	Tippy Martinez	.25	.13	.08
255	Steve Garvey	2.75	1.50	.80
256	Alvis Woods	.25	.13	.08

		NM	EX	VG
257	John Hiller	.25	.13	.08
258	Dave Concepcion	.25	.13	.08
259	Dwight Evans	.25	.13	.08
260	Pete MacKanin	.25	.13	.08
261	George Brett (Record Breaker)	5.00	2.50	1.50
262	Minnie Minoso (Record Breaker)	.25	.13	.08
263	Jose Morales (Record Breaker)	.25	.13	.08
264	Nolan Ryan (Record Breaker)	12.50	6.25	3.75

1978 O-Pee-Chee

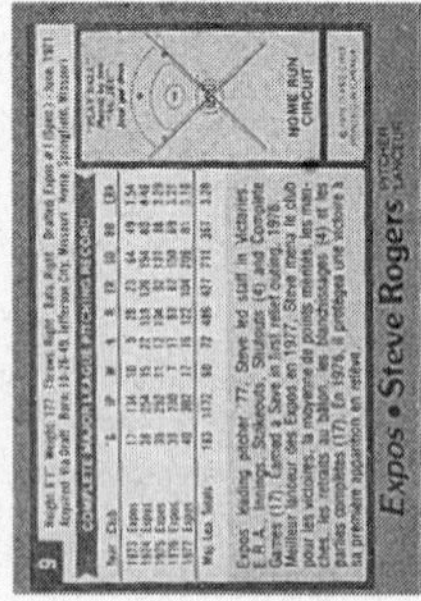

The 1978 O-Pee-Chee set was further reduced to 242 cards and again had heavy representation from the two Canadian teams. The cards measure the standard 2-1/2" x 3-1/2" and the backs are printed in both French and English. The cards use the same design as the 1978 Topps set. Some of the cards contain an extra line on the front indicating a team change.

		NM	EX	VG
Complete Set (242):		120.00	60.00	35.00
Common Player:		.25	.13	.08
Wax Pack (10):		8.00		
Wax Box (36):		200.00		
1	Batting Leaders (Rod Carew, Dave Parker)	.75	.40	.25
2	Home Run Leaders (George Foster, Jim Rice)	.25	.13	.08
3	Runs Batted In Leaders (George Foster, Larry Hisle)	.25	.13	.08
4	Stolen Base Leaders (Freddie Patek, Frank Taveras)	.25	.13	.08
5	Victory Leaders (Steve Carlton, Dave Goltz, Dennis Leonard, Jim Palmer)	.45	.25	.14
6	Strikeout Leaders (Phil Niekro, Nolan Ryan)	1.50	.70	.45
7	Earned Run Avg. Ldrs. (John Candelaria, Frank Tanana)	.25	.13	.08
8	Leading Firemen (Bill Campbell, Rollie Fingers)	.45	.25	.14
9	Steve Rogers	.25	.13	.08
10	Graig Nettles	.25	.13	.08
11	Doug Capilla	.25	.13	.08
12	George Scott	.25	.13	.08
13	Gary Woods	.25	.13	.08
14	Tom Veryzer	.25	.13	.08
15	Wayne Garland	.25	.13	.08
16	Amos Otis	.25	.13	.08
17	Larry Christenson	.25	.13	.08
18	Dave Cash	.25	.13	.08
19	Jim Barr	.25	.13	.08
20	Ruppert Jones	.25	.13	.08
21	Eric Soderholm	.25	.13	.08
22	Jesse Jefferson	.25	.13	.08
23	Jerry Morales	.25	.13	.08
24	Doug Rau	.25	.13	.08
25	Rennie Stennett	.25	.13	.08
26	Lee Mazzilli	.25	.13	.08
27	Dick Williams	.25	.13	.08
28	Joe Rudi	.25	.13	.08
29	Robin Yount	2.00	1.00	.60
30	Don Gullett	.25	.13	.08
31	Roy Howell	.25	.13	.08
32	Cesar Geronimo	.25	.13	.08
33	Rick Langford	.25	.13	.08
34	Dan Ford	.25	.13	.08
35	Gene Tenace	.25	.13	.08
36	Santo Alcala	.25	.13	.08
37	Rick Burleson	.25	.13	.08
38	Dave Rozema	.25	.13	.08
39	Duane Kulper	.25	.13	.08
40	Ron Fairly	.25	.13	.08
41	Dennis Leonard	.25	.13	.08
42	Greg Luzinski	.25	.13	.08
43	Willie Montanez	.25	.13	.08
44	Enos Cabell	.25	.13	.08
45	Ellis Valentine	.25	.13	.08
46	Steve Stone	.25	.13	.08
47	Lee May	.25	.13	.08
48	Roy White	.25	.13	.08
49	Jerry Garvin	.25	.13	.08
50	Johnny Bench	2.00	1.00	.60
51	Garry Templeton	.25	.13	.08
52	Doyle Alexander	.25	.13	.08
53	Steve Henderson	.25	.13	.08
54	Stan Bahnsen	.25	.13	.08
55	Dan Meyer	.25	.13	.08
56	Rick Reuschel	.25	.13	.08
57	Reggie Smith	.25	.13	.08
58	Blue Jays Team	.50	.25	.15
59	John Montefusco	.25	.13	.08
60	Dave Parker	.25	.13	.08
61	Jim Bibby	.25	.13	.08
62	Fred Lynn	.25	.13	.08
63	Jose Morales	.25	.13	.08
64	Aurelio Rodriguez	.25	.13	.08
65	Frank Tanana	.25	.13	.08
66	Darrell Porter	.25	.13	.08
67	Otto Velez	.25	.13	.08
68	Larry Bowa	.25	.13	.08
69	Jim Hunter	1.50	.70	.45
70	George Foster	.25	.13	.08
71	Cecil Cooper	.25	.13	.08
72	Gary Alexander	.25	.13	.08
73	Paul Thormodsgard	.25	.13	.08
74	Toby Harrah	.25	.13	.08
75	Mitchell Page	.25	.13	.08
76	Alan Ashby	.25	.13	.08
77	Jorge Orta	.25	.13	.08
78	Dave Winfield	3.00	1.50	.90
79	Andy Messersmith	.25	.13	.08
80	Ken Singleton	.25	.13	.08
81	Will McEnaney	.25	.13	.08
82	Lou Piniella	.25	.13	.08
83	Bob Forsch	.25	.13	.08
84	Dan Driessen	.25	.13	.08
85	Dave Lemanczyk	.25	.13	.08
86	Paul Dade	.25	.13	.08
87	Bill Campbell	.25	.13	.08
88	Ron LeFlore	.25	.13	.08
89	Bill Madlock	.25	.13	.08
90	Tony Perez	.25	.13	.08
91	Freddie Patek	.25	.13	.08
92	Glenn Abbott	.25	.13	.08
93	Garry Maddox	.25	.13	.08
94	Steve Staggs	.25	.13	.08
95	Bobby Murcer	.25	.13	.08
96	Don Sutton	1.50	.70	.45
97	Al Oliver	.25	.13	.08
98	Jon Matlack	.25	.13	.08
99	Sam Mejias	.25	.13	.08
100	Pete Rose	6.00	3.00	1.75
101	Randy Jones	.25	.13	.08
102	Sixto Lezcano	.25	.13	.08
103	Jim Clancy	.25	.13	.08
104	Butch Wynegar	.25	.13	.08
105	Nolan Ryan	15.00	7.50	4.50
106	Wayne Gross	.25	.13	.08
107	Bob Watson	.25	.13	.08
108	Joe Kerrigan	.25	.13	.08
109	Keith Hernandez	.25	.13	.08
110	Reggie Jackson	5.00	2.50	1.50
111	Denny Doyle	.25	.13	.08
112	Sam Ewing	.25	.13	.08
113	Bert Blyleven	.25	.13	.08
114	Andre Thornton	.25	.13	.08
115	Milt May	.25	.13	.08
116	Jim Colborn	.25	.13	.08
117	Warren Cromartie	.25	.13	.08
118	Ted Sizemore	.25	.13	.08
119	Checklist 1-121	.35	.20	.11
120	Tom Seaver	2.50	1.25	.70
121	Luis Gomez	.25	.13	.08
122	Jim Spencer	.25	.13	.08
123	Leroy Stanton	.25	.13	.08
124	Luis Tiant	.25	.13	.08
125	Mark Belanger	.25	.13	.08
126	Jackie Brown	.25	.13	.08
127	Bill Buckner	.25	.13	.08
128	Bill Robinson	.25	.13	.08
129	Rick Cerone	.25	.13	.08
130	Ron Cey	.25	.13	.08
131	Jose Cruz	.25	.13	.08
132	Len Randle	.25	.13	.08
133	Bob Grich	.25	.13	.08
134	Jeff Burroughs	.25	.13	.08
135	Gary Carter	6.00	3.00	1.75
136	Milt Wilcox	.25	.13	.08
137	Carl Yastrzemski	2.50	1.25	.70
138	Dennis Eckersley	1.50	.70	.45
139	Tim Nordbrook	.25	.13	.08
140	Ken Griffey	.25	.13	.08
141	Bob Boone	.25	.13	.08
142	Dave Goltz	.25	.13	.08
143	Al Cowens	.25	.13	.08
144	Bill Atkinson	.25	.13	.08
145	Chris Chambliss	.25	.13	.08
146	Jim Slaton	.25	.13	.08
147	Bill Stein	.25	.13	.08
148	Bob Bailor	.25	.13	.08
149	J.R. Richard	.25	.13	.08
150	Ted Simmons	.25	.13	.08
151	Rick Manning	.25	.13	.08
152	Lerrin LaGrow	.25	.13	.08
153	Larry Parrish	.25	.13	.08
154	Eddie Murray	15.00	7.50	4.50
155	Phil Niekro	1.50	.70	.45
156	Bake McBride	.25	.13	.08
157	Pete Vuckovich	.25	.13	.08
158	Ivan DeJesus	.25	.13	.08
159	Rick Rhoden	.25	.13	.08
160	Joe Morgan	2.00	1.00	.60
161	Ed Ott	.25	.13	.08
162	Don Stanhouse	.25	.13	.08
163	Jim Rice	.50	.25	.15
164	Bucky Dent	.25	.13	.08
165	Jim Kern	.25	.13	.08
166	Doug Rader	.25	.13	.08
167	Steve Kemp	.25	.13	.08
168	John Mayberry	.25	.13	.08
169	Tim Foli	.25	.13	.08
170	Steve Carlton	2.00	1.00	.60
171	Pepe Frias	.25	.13	.08
172	Pat Zachry	.25	.13	.08
173	Don Baylor	.25	.13	.08
174	Sal Bando	.25	.13	.08
175	Alvis Woods	.25	.13	.08
176	Mike Hargrove	.25	.13	.08
177	Vida Blue	.25	.13	.08
178	George Hendrick	.25	.13	.08
179	Jim Palmer	2.00	1.00	.60
180	Andre Dawson	10.00	5.00	3.00
181	Paul Moskau	.25	.13	.08
182	Mickey Rivers	.25	.13	.08
183	Checklist 122-242	.35	.20	.11
184	Jerry Johnson	.25	.13	.08
185	Willie McCovey	2.00	1.00	.60
186	Enrique Romo	.25	.13	.08
187	Butch Hobson	.25	.13	.08
188	Rusty Staub	.45	.25	.14
189	Wayne Twitchell	.25	.13	.08
190	Steve Garvey	1.00	.50	.30
191	Rick Waits	.25	.13	.08
192	Doug DeCinces	.25	.13	.08
193	Tom Murphy	.25	.13	.08
194	Rich Hebner	.25	.13	.08
195	Ralph Garr	.25	.13	.08
196	Bruce Sutter	1.50	.70	.45
197	Tom Poquette	.25	.13	.08
198	Wayne Garrett	.25	.13	.08
199	Pedro Borbon	.25	.13	.08
200	Thurman Munson	2.00	1.00	.60
201	Rollie Fingers	1.50	.70	.45
202	Doug Ault	.25	.13	.08
203	Phil Garner	.25	.13	.08
204	Lou Brock	2.00	1.00	.60
205	Ed Kranepool	.25	.13	.08
206	Bobby Bonds	.25	.13	.08
207	Expos Team	.25	.13	.08
208	Bump Wills	.25	.13	.08
209	Gary Matthews	.25	.13	.08
210	Carlton Fisk	2.00	1.00	.60
211	Jeff Byrd	.25	.13	.08
212	Jason Thompson	.25	.13	.08
213	Larvell Blanks	.25	.13	.08
214	Sparky Lyle	.25	.13	.08
215	George Brett	6.00	3.00	1.75
216	Del Unser	.25	.13	.08
217	Manny Trillo	.25	.13	.08
218	Roy Hartsfield	.25	.13	.08
219	Carlos Lopez	.25	.13	.08
220	Dave Concepcion	.25	.13	.08
221	John Candelaria	.25	.13	.08
222	Dave Lopes	.25	.13	.08
223	Tim Blackwell	.25	.13	.08
224	Chet Lemon	.25	.13	.08
225	Mike Schmidt	6.00	3.00	1.75
226	Cesar Cedeno	.25	.13	.08
227	Mike Willis	.25	.13	.08
228	Willie Randolph	.25	.13	.08
229	Doug Bair	.25	.13	.08
230	Rod Carew	2.00	1.00	.60
231	Mike Flanagan	.25	.13	.08
232	Chris Speier	.25	.13	.08
233	Don Aase	.25	.13	.08
234	Buddy Bell	.25	.13	.08
235	Mark Fidrych	.30	.15	.09
236	Lou Brock (Record Breaker)	.75	.40	.25
237	Sparky Lyle (Record Breaker)	.25	.13	.08
238	Willie McCovey (Record Breaker)	.45	.25	.14
239	Brooks Robinson (Record Breaker)	.90	.45	.25
240	Pete Rose (Record Breaker)	2.00	1.00	.60
241	Nolan Ryan (Record Breaker)	10.00	5.00	3.00
242	Reggie Jackson (Record Breaker)	1.50	.70	.45

1979 O-Pee-Chee

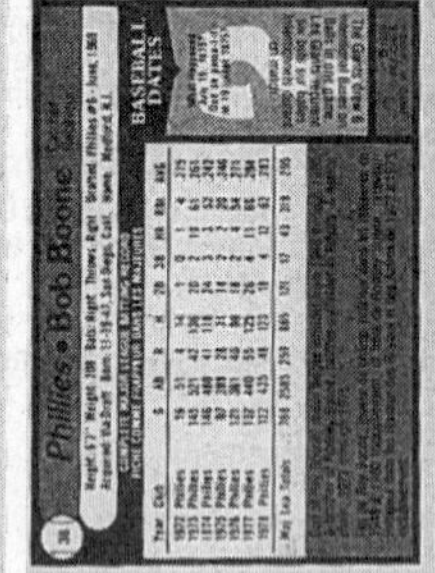

The 1979 O-Pee-Chee cards are nearly identical in design to the Topps set of the same year, but display the O-Pee-Chee logo inside the baseball in the lower-left corner of the front. The number of cards in the set was increased to 374, each measuring 2-1/2" x 3-1/2".

		NM	EX	VG
Complete Set (374):		80.00	40.00	24.00
Common Player:		.25	.13	.08
Wax Pack (10):		10.00		
Wax Box (36):		175.00		
1	Lee May	.25	.13	.08
2	Dick Drago	.25	.13	.08
3	Paul Dade	.25	.13	.08
4	Ross Grimsley	.25	.13	.08
5	Joe Morgan	2.00	1.00	.60
6	Kevin Kobel	.25	.13	.08
7	Terry Forster	.25	.13	.08
8	Paul Molitor	12.00	6.00	3.50
9	Steve Carlton	2.00	1.00	.60
10	Dave Goltz	.25	.13	.08
11	Dave Winfield	3.00	1.50	.90
12	Dave Rozema	.25	.13	.08
13	Ed Figueroa	.25	.13	.08
14	Alan Ashby	.25	.13	.08
15	Dale Murphy	2.50	1.25	.70
16	Dennis Eckersley	1.50	.70	.45
17	Ron Blomberg	.25	.13	.08
18	Wayne Twitchell	.25	.13	.08

19	Al Hrabosky	.25	.13	.08
20	Fred Norman	.25	.13	.08
21	Steve Garvey	1.00	.50	.30
22	Willie Stargell	2.00	1.00	.60
23	John Hale	.25	.13	.08
24	Mickey Rivers	.25	.13	.08
25	Jack Brohamer	.25	.13	.08
26	Tom Underwood	.25	.13	.08
27	Mark Belanger	.25	.13	.08
28	Elliott Maddox	.25	.13	.08
29	John Candelaria	.25	.13	.08
30	Shane Rawley	.25	.13	.08
31	Steve Yeager	.25	.13	.08
32	Warren Cromartie	.25	.13	.08
33	Jason Thompson	.25	.13	.08
34	Roger Erickson	.25	.13	.08
35	Gary Matthews	.25	.13	.08
36	Pete Falcone	.25	.13	.08
37	Dick Tidrow	.25	.13	.08
38	Bob Boone	.25	.13	.08
39	Jim Bibby	.25	.13	.08
40	Len Barker	.25	.13	.08
41	Robin Yount	2.00	1.00	.60
42	Sam Mejias	.25	.13	.08
43	Ray Burris	.25	.13	.08
44	Tom Seaver	2.50	1.25	.70
45	Roy Howell	.25	.13	.08
46	Jim Todd	.25	.13	.08
47	Frank Duffy	.25	.13	.08
48	Joel Youngblood	.25	.13	.08
49	Vida Blue	.25	.13	.08
50	Cliff Johnson	.25	.13	.08
51	Nolan Ryan	15.00	7.50	4.50
52	Ozzie Smith	20.00	10.00	6.00
53	Jim Sundberg	.25	.13	.08
54	Mike Paxton	.25	.13	.08
55	Lou Whitaker	1.00	.50	.30
56	Dan Schatzeder	.25	.13	.08
57	Rick Burleson	.25	.13	.08
58	Doug Bair	.25	.13	.08
59	Ted Martinez	.25	.13	.08
60	Bob Watson	.25	.13	.08
61	Jim Clancy	.25	.13	.08
62	Rowland Office	.25	.13	.08
63	Bobby Murcer	.25	.13	.08
64	Don Gullett	.25	.13	.08
65	Tom Paciorek	.25	.13	.08
66	Rick Rhoden	.25	.13	.08
67	Duane Kuiper	.25	.13	.08
68	Bruce Boisclair	.25	.13	.08
69	Manny Sarmiento	.25	.13	.08
70	Wayne Cage	.25	.13	.08
71	John Hiller	.25	.13	.08
72	Rick Cerone	.25	.13	.08
73	Dwight Evans	.25	.13	.08
74	Buddy Solomon	.25	.13	.08
75	Roy White	.25	.13	.08
76	Mike Flanagan	.25	.13	.08
77	Tom Johnson	.25	.13	.08
78	Glenn Burke	.25	.13	.08
79	Frank Taveras	.25	.13	.08
80	Don Sutton	1.50	.70	.45
81	Leon Roberts	.25	.13	.08
82	George Hendrick	.25	.13	.08
83	Aurelio Rodriguez	.25	.13	.08
84	Ron Reed	.25	.13	.08
85	Alvis Woods	.25	.13	.08
86	Jim Beattie	.25	.13	.08
87	Larry Hisle	.25	.13	.08
88	Mike Garman	.25	.13	.08
89	Tim Johnson	.25	.13	.08
90	Paul Splittorff	.25	.13	.08
91	Darrel Chaney	.25	.13	.08
92	Mike Torrez	.25	.13	.08
93	Eric Soderholm	.25	.13	.08
94	Ron Cey	.25	.13	.08
95	Randy Jones	.25	.13	.08
96	Bill Madlock	.25	.13	.08
97	Steve Kemp	.25	.13	.08
98	Bob Apodaca	.25	.13	.08
99	Johnny Grubb	.25	.13	.08
100	Larry Milbourne	.25	.13	.08
101	Johnny Bench	2.00	1.00	.60
102	Dave Lemanczyk	.25	.13	.08
103	Reggie Cleveland	.25	.13	.08
104	Larry Bowa	.25	.13	.08
105	Denny Martinez	1.00	.50	.30
106	Bill Travers	.25	.13	.08
107	Willie McCovey	2.00	1.00	.60
108	Wilbur Wood	.25	.13	.08
109	Dennis Leonard	.25	.13	.08
110	Roy Smalley	.25	.13	.08
111	Cesar Geronimo	.25	.13	.08
112	Jesse Jefferson	.25	.13	.08
113	Dave Revering	.25	.13	.08
114	Rich Gossage	.30	.15	.09
115	Steve Stone	.25	.13	.08
116	Doug Flynn	.25	.13	.08
117	Bob Forsch	.25	.13	.08
118	Paul Mitchell	.25	.13	.08
119	Toby Harrah	.25	.13	.08
120	Steve Rogers	.25	.13	.08
121	Checklist 1-125	.25	.13	.08
122	Balor Moore	.25	.13	.08
123	Rick Reuschel	.25	.13	.08
124	Jeff Burroughs	.25	.13	.08
125	Willie Randolph	.25	.13	.08
126	Bob Stinson	.25	.13	.08
127	Rick Wise	.25	.13	.08
128	Luis Gomez	.25	.13	.08
129	Tommy John	.25	.13	.08
130	Richie Zisk	.25	.13	.08
131	Mario Guerrero	.25	.13	.08
132	Oscar Gamble	.25	.13	.08
133	Don Money	.25	.13	.08
134	Joe Rudi	.25	.13	.08
135	Woodie Fryman	.25	.13	.08
136	Butch Hobson	.25	.13	.08
137	Jim Colborn	.25	.13	.08
138	Tom Grieve	.25	.13	.08
139	Andy Messersmith	.25	.13	.08
140	Andre Thornton	.25	.13	.08
141	Kevin Kravec	.25	.13	.08
142	Bobby Bonds	.25	.13	.08
143	Jose Cruz	.25	.13	.08
144	Dave Lopes	.25	.13	.08
145	Jerry Garvin	.25	.13	.08
146	Pepe Frias	.25	.13	.08
147	Mitchell Page	.25	.13	.08
148	Ted Sizemore	.25	.13	.08
149	Rich Gale	.25	.13	.08
150	Steve Ontiveros	.25	.13	.08
151	Rod Carew	2.00	1.00	.60
152	Lary Sorensen	.25	.13	.08
153	Willie Montanez	.25	.13	.08
154	Floyd Bannister	.25	.13	.08
155	Bert Blyleven	.25	.13	.08
156	Ralph Garr	.25	.13	.08
157	Thurman Munson	1.00	.50	.30
158	Bob Robertson	.25	.13	.08
159	Jon Matlack	.25	.13	.08
160	Carl Yastrzemski	2.50	1.25	.70
161	Gaylord Perry	1.50	.70	.45
162	Mike Tyson	.25	.13	.08
163	Cecil Cooper	.25	.13	.08
164	Pedro Borbon	.25	.13	.08
165	Art Howe	.25	.13	.08
166	Joe Coleman	.25	.13	.08
167	George Brett	6.00	3.00	1.75
168	Gary Alexander	.25	.13	.08
169	Chet Lemon	.25	.13	.08
170	Craig Swan	.25	.13	.08
171	Chris Chambliss	.25	.13	.08
172	John Montague	.25	.13	.08
173	Ron Jackson	.25	.13	.08
174	Jim Palmer	2.00	1.00	.60
175	Willie Upshaw	.75	.40	.25
176	Tug McGraw	.25	.13	.08
177	Bill Buckner	.25	.13	.08
178	Doug Rau	.25	.13	.08
179	Andre Dawson	3.50	1.75	1.00
180	Jim Wright	.25	.13	.08
181	Garry Templeton	.25	.13	.08
182	Bill Bonham	.25	.13	.08
183	Lee Mazzilli	.25	.13	.08
184	Alan Trammell	2.00	1.00	.60
185	Amos Otis	.25	.13	.08
186	Tom Dixon	.25	.13	.08
187	Mike Cubbage	.25	.13	.08
188	Sparky Lyle	.25	.13	.08
189	Juan Bernhardt	.25	.13	.08
190	Bump Wills	.25	.13	.08
191	Dave Kingman	.25	.13	.08
192	Lamar Johnson	.25	.13	.08
193	Lance Rautzhan	.25	.13	.08
194	Ed Herrmann	.25	.13	.08
195	Bill Campbell	.25	.13	.08
196	Gorman Thomas	.25	.13	.08
197	Paul Moskau	.25	.13	.08
198	Dale Murray	.25	.13	.08
199	John Mayberry	.25	.13	.08
200	Phil Garner	.25	.13	.08
201	Dan Ford	.25	.13	.08
202	Gary Thomasson	.25	.13	.08
203	Rollie Fingers	1.50	.70	.45
204	Al Oliver	.25	.13	.08
205	Doug Ault	.25	.13	.08
206	Scott McGregor	.25	.13	.08
207	Dave Cash	.25	.13	.08
208	Bill Plummer	.25	.13	.08
209	Ivan DeJesus	.25	.13	.08
210	Jim Rice	.75	.40	.25
211	Ray Knight	.25	.13	.08
212	Paul Hartzell	.25	.13	.08
213	Tim Foli	.25	.13	.08
214	Butch Wynegar	.25	.13	.08
215	Darrell Evans	.25	.13	.08
216	Ken Griffey	.25	.13	.08
217	Doug DeCinces	.25	.13	.08
218	Ruppert Jones	.25	.13	.08
219	Bob Montgomery	.25	.13	.08
220	Rick Manning	.25	.13	.08
221	Chris Speier	.25	.13	.08
222	Bobby Valentine	.25	.13	.08
223	Dave Parker	.25	.13	.08
224	Larry Biittner	.25	.13	.08
225	Ken Clay	.25	.13	.08
226	Gene Tenace	.25	.13	.08
227	Frank White	.25	.13	.08
228	Rusty Staub	.35	.20	.11
229	Lee Lacy	.25	.13	.08
230	Doyle Alexander	.25	.13	.08
231	Bruce Bochte	.25	.13	.08
232	Steve Henderson	.25	.13	.08
233	Jim Lonborg	.25	.13	.08
234	Dave Concepcion	.25	.13	.08
235	Jerry Morales	.25	.13	.08
236	Len Randle	.25	.13	.08
237	Bill Lee	.25	.13	.08
238	Bruce Sutter	1.50	.70	.45
239	Jim Essian	.25	.13	.08
240	Graig Nettles	.25	.13	.08
241	Otto Velez	.25	.13	.08
242	Checklist 126-250	.25	.13	.08
243	Reggie Smith	.25	.13	.08
244	Stan Bahnsen	.25	.13	.08
245	Garry Maddox	.25	.13	.08
246	Joaquin Andujar	.25	.13	.08
247	Dan Driessen	.25	.13	.08
248	Bob Grich	.25	.13	.08
249	Fred Lynn	.25	.13	.08
250	Skip Lockwood	.25	.13	.08
251	Craig Reynolds	.25	.13	.08
252	Willie Horton	.25	.13	.08
253	Rick Waits	.25	.13	.08
254	Bucky Dent	.25	.13	.08
255	Bob Knepper	.25	.13	.08
256	Miguel Dilone	.25	.13	.08
257	Bob Owchinko	.25	.13	.08
258	Al Cowens	.25	.13	.08
259	Bob Bailor	.25	.13	.08
260	Larry Christenson	.25	.13	.08
261	Tony Perez	1.50	.70	.45
262	Blue Jays Team	.25	.13	.08
263	Glenn Abbott	.25	.13	.08
264	Ron Guidry	.50	.25	.15
265	Ed Kranepool	.25	.13	.08
266	Charlie Hough	.25	.13	.08
267	Ted Simmons	.25	.13	.08
268	Jack Clark	.25	.13	.08
269	Enos Cabell	.25	.13	.08
270	Gary Carter	6.00	3.00	1.75
271	Sam Ewing	.25	.13	.08
272	Tom Burgmeier	.25	.13	.08
273	Freddie Patek	.25	.13	.08
274	Frank Tanana	.25	.13	.08
275	Leroy Stanton	.25	.13	.08
276	Ken Forsch	.25	.13	.08
277	Ellis Valentine	.25	.13	.08
278	Greg Luzinski	.25	.13	.08
279	Rick Bosetti	.25	.13	.08
280	John Stearns	.25	.13	.08
281	Enrique Romo	.25	.13	.08
282	Bob Bailey	.25	.13	.08
283	Sal Bando	.25	.13	.08
284	Matt Keough	.25	.13	.08
285	Biff Pocoroba	.25	.13	.08
286	Mike Lum	.25	.13	.08
287	Jay Johnstone	.25	.13	.08
288	John Montefusco	.25	.13	.08
289	Ed Ott	.25	.13	.08
290	Dusty Baker	.25	.13	.08
291	Rico Carty	.25	.13	.08
292	Nino Espinosa	.25	.13	.08
293	Rich Hebner	.25	.13	.08
294	Cesar Cedeno	.25	.13	.08
295	Darrell Porter	.25	.13	.08
296	Rod Gilbreath	.25	.13	.08
297	Jim Kern	.25	.13	.08
298	Claudell Washington	.25	.13	.08
299	Luis Tiant	.25	.13	.08
300	Mike Parrott	.25	.13	.08
301	Pete Broberg	.25	.13	.08
302	Greg Gross	.25	.13	.08
303	Darold Knowles	.25	.13	.08
304	Paul Blair	.25	.13	.08
305	Julio Cruz	.25	.13	.08
306	Hal McRae	.25	.13	.08
307	Ken Reitz	.25	.13	.08
308	Tom Murphy	.25	.13	.08
309	Terry Whitfield	.25	.13	.08
310	J.R. Richard	.25	.13	.08
311	Mike Hargrove	.25	.13	.08
312	Rick Dempsey	.25	.13	.08
313	Phil Niekro	1.50	.70	.45
314	Bob Stanley	.25	.13	.08
315	Jim Spencer	.25	.13	.08
316	George Foster	.25	.13	.08
317	Dave LaRoche	.25	.13	.08
318	Rudy May	.25	.13	.08
319	Jeff Newman	.25	.13	.08
320	Rick Monday	.25	.13	.08
321	Omar Moreno	.25	.13	.08
322	Dave McKay	.25	.13	.08
323	Mike Schmidt	6.00	3.00	1.75
324	Ken Singleton	.25	.13	.08
325	Jerry Remy	.25	.13	.08
326	Bert Campaneris	.25	.13	.08
327	Pat Zachry	.25	.13	.08
328	Larry Herndon	.25	.13	.08
329	Mark Fidrych	.25	.13	.08
330	Del Unser	.25	.13	.08
331	Gene Garber	.25	.13	.08
332	Bake McBride	.25	.13	.08
333	Jorge Orta	.25	.13	.08
334	Don Kirkwood	.25	.13	.08
335	Don Baylor	.25	.13	.08
336	Bill Robinson	.25	.13	.08
337	Manny Trillo	.25	.13	.08
338	Eddie Murray	3.00	1.50	.90
339	Tom Hausman	.25	.13	.08
340	George Scott	.25	.13	.08
341	Rick Sweet	.25	.13	.08
342	Lou Piniella	.25	.13	.08
343	Pete Rose	15.00	7.50	4.50
344	Stan Papi	.25	.13	.08
345	Jerry Koosman	.25	.13	.08
346	Hosken Powell	.25	.13	.08
347	George Medich	.25	.13	.08
348	Ron LeFlore	.25	.13	.08
349	Expos Team	.75	.40	.25
350	Lou Brock	2.00	1.00	.60
351	Bill North	.25	.13	.08
352	Jim Hunter	1.50	.70	.45
353	Checklist 251-374	.25	.13	.08
354	Ed Halicki	.25	.13	.08
355	Tom Hutton	.25	.13	.08
356	Mike Caldwell	.25	.13	.08
357	Larry Parrish	.25	.13	.08
358	Geoff Zahn	.25	.13	.08
359	Derrel Thomas	.25	.13	.08
360	Carlton Fisk	2.00	1.00	.60
361	John Henry Johnson	.25	.13	.08
362	Dave Chalk	.25	.13	.08
363	Dan Meyer	.25	.13	.08
364	Sixto Lezcano	.25	.13	.08
365	Rennie Stennett	.25	.13	.08
366	Mike Willis	.25	.13	.08
367	Buddy Bell	.25	.13	.08
368	Mickey Stanley	.25	.13	.08
369	Dave Rader	.25	.13	.08
370	Burt Hooton	.25	.13	.08
371	Keith Hernandez	.25	.13	.08
372	Bill Stein	.25	.13	.08

373	Hal Dues	.25	.13	.08
374	Reggie Jackson	3.00	1.50	.90

1980 O-Pee-Chee

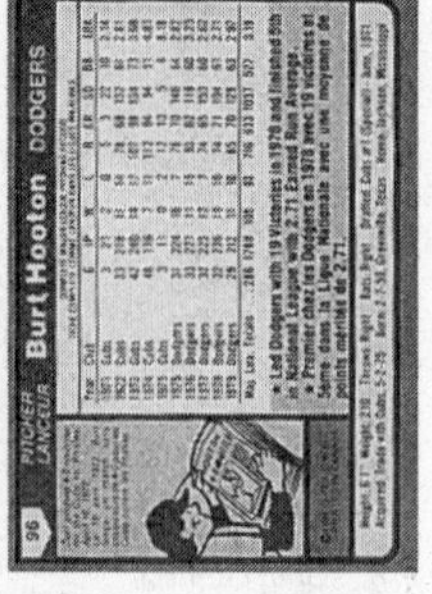

The 1980 Canadian-issued O-Pee-Chee set was again complete at 374 cards, which measure 2-1/2" x 3-1/2" and share the same design as the 1980 Topps set. The OPC cards are printed on a white stock, rather than the traditional gray stock used by Topps, and their backs are written in both French and English. Some of the cards include an extra line on the front indicating a new team designation.

		NM	EX	VG
Complete Set (374):		110.00	55.00	32.50
Common Player:		.15	.08	.05
Wax Pack (10):		10.00		
Wax Box (36):		290.00		
1	Craig Swan	.15	.08	.05
2	Denny Martinez	.15	.08	.05
3	Dave Cash	.15	.08	.05
4	Bruce Sutter	1.50	.70	.45
5	Ron Jackson	.15	.08	.05
6	Balor Moore	.15	.08	.05
7	Dan Ford	.15	.08	.05
8	Pat Putnam	.15	.08	.05
9	Derrel Thomas	.15	.08	.05
10	Jim Slaton	.15	.08	.05
11	Lee Mazzilli	.15	.08	.05
12	Del Unser	.15	.08	.05
13	Mark Wagner	.15	.08	.05
14	Vida Blue	.15	.08	.05
15	Jay Johnstone	.15	.08	.05
16	Julio Cruz	.15	.08	.05
17	Tony Scott	.15	.08	.05
18	Jeff Newman	.15	.08	.05
19	Luis Tiant	.15	.08	.05
20	Carlton Fisk	1.50	.70	.45
21	Dave Palmer	.15	.08	.05
22	Bombo Rivera	.15	.08	.05
23	Bill Fahey	.15	.08	.05
24	Frank White	.15	.08	.05
25	Rico Carty	.15	.08	.05
26	Bill Bonham	.15	.08	.05
27	Rick Miller	.15	.08	.05
28	J.R. Richard	.15	.08	.05
29	Joe Ferguson	.15	.08	.05
30	Bill Madlock	.15	.08	.05
31	Pete Vuckovich	.15	.08	.05
32	Doug Flynn	.15	.08	.05
33	Bucky Dent	.15	.08	.05
34	Mike Ivie	.15	.08	.05
35	Bob Stanley	.15	.08	.05
36	Al Bumbry	.15	.08	.05
37	Gary Carter	5.00	2.50	1.50
38	John Milner	.15	.08	.05
39	Sid Monge	.15	.08	.05
40	Bill Russell	.15	.08	.05
41	John Stearns	.15	.08	.05
42	Dave Stieb	1.25	.60	.40
43	Ruppert Jones	.15	.08	.05
44	Bob Owchinko	.15	.08	.05
45	Ron LeFlore	.15	.08	.05
46	Ted Sizemore	.15	.08	.05
47	Ted Simmons	.15	.08	.05
48	Pepe Frias	.15	.08	.05
49	Ken Landreaux	.15	.08	.05
50	Manny Trillo	.15	.08	.05
51	Rick Dempsey	.15	.08	.05
52	Cecil Cooper	.15	.08	.05
53	Bill Lee	.15	.08	.05
54	Victor Cruz	.15	.08	.05
55	Johnny Bench	1.50	.70	.45
56	Rich Dauer	.15	.08	.05
57	Frank Tanana	.15	.08	.05
58	Francisco Barrios	.15	.08	.05
59	Bob Horner	.30	.15	.09
60	Fred Lynn	.15	.08	.05
61	Bob Knepper	.15	.08	.05
62	Sparky Lyle	.15	.08	.05
63	Larry Cox	.15	.08	.05
64	Dock Ellis	.15	.08	.05
65	Phil Garner	.15	.08	.05
66	Greg Luzinski	.15	.08	.05
67	Checklist 1-125	.25	.13	.08
68	Dave Lemanczyk	.15	.08	.05
69	Tony Perez	1.50	.70	.45
70	Gary Thomasson	.15	.08	.05
71	Craig Reynolds	.15	.08	.05
72	Amos Otis	.15	.08	.05
73	Biff Pocoroba	.15	.08	.05
74	Matt Keough	.15	.08	.05
75	Bill Buckner	.15	.08	.05
76	John Castino	.15	.08	.05
77	Rich Gossage	.25	.13	.08
78	Gary Alexander	.15	.08	.05
79	Phil Huffman	.15	.08	.05
80	Bruce Bochte	.15	.08	.05
81	Darrell Evans	.15	.08	.05
82	Terry Puhl	.15	.08	.05
83	Jason Thompson	.15	.08	.05
84	Lary Sorenson	.15	.08	.05
85	Jerry Remy	.15	.08	.05
86	Tony Brizzolara	.15	.08	.05
87	Willie Wilson	.15	.08	.05
88	Eddie Murray	3.00	1.50	.90
89	Larry Christenson	.15	.08	.05
90	Bob Randall	.15	.08	.05
91	Greg Pryor	.15	.08	.05
92	Glenn Abbott	.15	.08	.05
93	Jack Clark	.15	.08	.05
94	Rick Waits	.15	.08	.05
95	Luis Gomez	.15	.08	.05
96	Burt Hooton	.15	.08	.05
97	John Henry Johnson	.15	.08	.05
98	Ray Knight	.15	.08	.05
99	Rick Reuschel	.15	.08	.05
100	Champ Summers	.15	.08	.05
101	Ron Davis	.15	.08	.05
102	Warren Cromartie	.15	.08	.05
103	Ken Reitz	.15	.08	.05
104	Hal McRae	.15	.08	.05
105	Alan Ashby	.15	.08	.05
106	Kevin Kobel	.15	.08	.05
107	Buddy Bell	.15	.08	.05
108	Dave Goltz	.15	.08	.05
109	John Montefusco	.15	.08	.05
110	Lance Parrish	.65	.35	.20
111	Mike LaCoss	.15	.08	.05
112	Jim Rice	.30	.15	.09
113	Steve Carlton	1.50	.70	.45
114	Sixto Lezcano	.15	.08	.05
115	Ed Halicki	.15	.08	.05
116	Jose Morales	.15	.08	.05
117	Dave Concepcion	.15	.08	.05
118	Joe Cannon	.15	.08	.05
119	Willie Montanez	.15	.08	.05
120	Lou Piniella	.15	.08	.05
121	Bill Stein	.15	.08	.05
122	Dave Winfield	3.00	1.50	.90
123	Alan Trammell	.30	.15	.09
124	Andre Dawson	4.00	2.00	1.25
125	Marc Hill	.15	.08	.05
126	Don Aase	.15	.08	.05
127	Dave Kingman	.15	.08	.05
128	Checklist 126-250	.25	.13	.08
129	Dennis Lamp	.15	.08	.05
130	Phil Niekro	1.00	.50	.30
131	Tim Foli	.15	.08	.05
132	Jim Clancy	.15	.08	.05
133	Bill Atkinson	.15	.08	.05
134	Paul Dade	.15	.08	.05
135	Dusty Baker	.15	.08	.05
136	Al Oliver	.15	.08	.05
137	Dave Chalk	.15	.08	.05
138	Bill Robinson	.15	.08	.05
139	Robin Yount	1.50	.70	.45
140	Dan Schatzeder	.15	.08	.05
141	Mike Schmidt	5.00	2.50	1.50
142	Ralph Garr	.15	.08	.05
143	Dale Murphy	1.00	.50	.30
144	Jerry Koosman	.15	.08	.05
145	Tom Veryzer	.15	.08	.05
146	Rick Bosetti	.15	.08	.05
147	Jim Spencer	.15	.08	.05
148	Gaylord Perry	1.00	.50	.30
149	Paul Blair	.15	.08	.05
150	Don Baylor	.15	.08	.05
151	Dave Rozema	.15	.08	.05
152	Steve Garvey	.50	.25	.15
153	Elias Sosa	.15	.08	.05
154	Larry Gura	.15	.08	.05
155	Tim Johnson	.15	.08	.05
156	Steve Henderson	.15	.08	.05
157	Ron Guidry	.20	.10	.06
158	Mike Edwards	.15	.08	.05
159	Butch Wynegar	.15	.08	.05
160	Randy Jones	.15	.08	.05
161	Denny Walling	.15	.08	.05
162	Mike Hargrove	.15	.08	.05
163	Dave Parker	.15	.08	.05
164	Roger Metzger	.15	.08	.05
165	Johnny Grubb	.15	.08	.05
166	Steve Kemp	.15	.08	.05
167	Bob Lacey	.15	.08	.05
168	Chris Speier	.15	.08	.05
169	Dennis Eckersley	1.00	.50	.30
170	Keith Hernandez	.15	.08	.05
171	Claudell Washington	.15	.08	.05
172	Tom Underwood	.15	.08	.05
173	Dan Driessen	.15	.08	.05
174	Al Cowens	.15	.08	.05
175	Rich Hebner	.15	.08	.05
176	Willie McCovey	1.50	.70	.45
177	Carney Lansford	.15	.08	.05
178	Ken Singleton	.15	.08	.05
179	Jim Essian	.15	.08	.05
180	Mike Vail	.15	.08	.05
181	Randy Lerch	.15	.08	.05
182	Larry Parrish	.15	.08	.05
183	Checklist 251-374	.25	.13	.08
184	George Hendrick	.15	.08	.05
185	Bob Davis	.15	.08	.05
186	Gary Matthews	.15	.08	.05
187	Lou Whitaker	.15	.08	.05
188	Darrell Porter	.15	.08	.05
189	Wayne Gross	.15	.08	.05
190	Bobby Murcer	.15	.08	.05
191	Willie Aikens	.15	.08	.05
192	Jim Kern	.15	.08	.05
193	Cesar Cedeno	.15	.08	.05
194	Joel Youngblood	.15	.08	.05
195	Ross Grimsley	.15	.08	.05
196	Jerry Mumphrey	.15	.08	.05
197	Kevin Bell	.15	.08	.05
198	Garry Maddox	.15	.08	.05
199	Dave Freisleben	.15	.08	.05
200	Ed Ott	.15	.08	.05
201	Enos Cabell	.15	.08	.05
202	Pete LaCock	.15	.08	.05
203	Fergie Jenkins	1.50	.70	.45
204	Milt Wilcox	.15	.08	.05
205	Ozzie Smith	5.00	2.50	1.50
206	Ellis Valentine	.15	.08	.05
207	Dan Meyer	.15	.08	.05
208	Barry Foote	.15	.08	.05
209	George Foster	.15	.08	.05
210	Dwight Evans	.15	.08	.05
211	Paul Molitor	5.00	2.50	1.50
212	Tony Solaita	.15	.08	.05
213	Bill North	.15	.08	.05
214	Paul Splittorff	.15	.08	.05
215	Bobby Bonds	.15	.08	.05
216	Butch Hobson	.15	.08	.05
217	Mark Belanger	.15	.08	.05
218	Grant Jackson	.15	.08	.05
219	Tom Hutton	.15	.08	.05
220	Pat Zachry	.15	.08	.05
221	Duane Kuiper	.15	.08	.05
222	Larry Hisle	.15	.08	.05
223	Mike Krukow	.15	.08	.05
224	Johnnie LeMaster	.15	.08	.05
225	Billy Almon	.15	.08	.05
226	Joe Niekro	.15	.08	.05
227	Dave Revering	.15	.08	.05
228	Don Sutton	1.00	.50	.30
229	John Hiller	.15	.08	.05
230	Alvis Woods	.15	.08	.05
231	Mark Fidrych	.15	.08	.05
232	Duffy Dyer	.15	.08	.05
233	Nino Espinosa	.15	.08	.05
234	Doug Bair	.15	.08	.05
235	George Brett	5.00	2.50	1.50
236	Mike Torrez	.15	.08	.05
237	Frank Taveras	.15	.08	.05
238	Bert Blyleven	.15	.08	.05
239	Willie Randolph	.15	.08	.05
240	Mike Sadek	.15	.08	.05
241	Jerry Royster	.15	.08	.05
242	John Denny	.15	.08	.05
243	Rick Monday	.15	.08	.05
244	Jesse Jefferson	.15	.08	.05
245	Aurelio Rodriguez	.15	.08	.05
246	Bob Boone	.15	.08	.05
247	Cesar Geronimo	.15	.08	.05
248	Bob Shirley	.15	.08	.05
249	Expos Team	.25	.13	.08
250	Bob Watson	.15	.08	.05
251	Mickey Rivers	.15	.08	.05
252	Mike Tyson	.15	.08	.05
253	Wayne Nordhagen	.15	.08	.05
254	Roy Howell	.15	.08	.05
255	Lee May	.15	.08	.05
256	Jerry Martin	.15	.08	.05
257	Bake McBride	.15	.08	.05
258	Silvio Martinez	.15	.08	.05
259	Jim Mason	.15	.08	.05
260	Tom Seaver	2.00	1.00	.60
261	Rick Wortham	.15	.08	.05
262	Mike Cubbage	.15	.08	.05
263	Gene Garber	.15	.08	.05
264	Bert Campaneris	.15	.08	.05
265	Tom Buskey	.15	.08	.05
266	Leon Roberts	.15	.08	.05
267	Ron Cey	.15	.08	.05
268	Steve Ontiveros	.15	.08	.05
269	Mike Caldwell	.15	.08	.05
270	Nelson Norman	.15	.08	.05
271	Steve Rogers	.15	.08	.05
272	Jim Morrison	.15	.08	.05
273	Clint Hurdle	.15	.08	.05
274	Dale Murray	.15	.08	.05
275	Jim Barr	.15	.08	.05
276	Jim Sundberg	.15	.08	.05
277	Willie Horton	.15	.08	.05
278	Andre Thornton	.15	.08	.05
279	Bob Forsch	.15	.08	.05
280	Joe Strain	.15	.08	.05
281	Rudy May	.15	.08	.05
282	Pete Rose	9.00	4.50	2.75
283	Jeff Burroughs	.15	.08	.05
284	Rick Langford	.15	.08	.05
285	Ken Griffey	.15	.08	.05
286	Bill Nahorodny	.15	.08	.05
287	Art Howe	.15	.08	.05
288	Ed Figueroa	.15	.08	.05
289	Joe Rudi	.15	.08	.05
290	Alfredo Griffin	.15	.08	.05
291	Dave Lopes	.15	.08	.05
292	Rick Manning	.15	.08	.05
293	Dennis Leonard	.15	.08	.05
294	Bud Harrelson	.15	.08	.05
295	Skip Lockwood	.15	.08	.05
296	Roy Smalley	.15	.08	.05
297	Kent Tekulve	.15	.08	.05
298	Scot Thompson	.15	.08	.05
299	Ken Kravec	.15	.08	.05
300	Blue Jays Team	.25	.13	.08
301	Scott Sanderson	.15	.08	.05
302	Charlie Moore	.15	.08	.05
303	Nolan Ryan	20.00	10.00	6.00
304	Bob Bailor	.15	.08	.05
305	Bob Stinson	.15	.08	.05
306	Al Hrabosky	.15	.08	.05
307	Mitchell Page	.15	.08	.05
308	Garry Templeton	.15	.08	.05
309	Chet Lemon	.15	.08	.05
310	Jim Palmer	1.50	.70	.45
311	Rick Cerone	.15	.08	.05
312	Jon Matlack	.15	.08	.05
313	Don Money	.15	.08	.05
314	Reggie Jackson	5.00	2.50	1.50
315	Brian Downing	.15	.08	.05

316	Woodie Fryman	.15	.08	.05
317	Alan Bannister	.15	.08	.05
318	Ron Reed	.15	.08	.05
319	Willie Stargell	1.50	.70	.45
320	Jerry Garvin	.15	.08	.05
321	Cliff Johnson	.15	.08	.05
322	Doug DeCinces	.15	.08	.05
323	Gene Richards	.15	.08	.05
324	Joaquin Andujar	.15	.08	.05
325	Richie Zisk	.15	.08	.05
326	Bob Grich	.15	.08	.05
327	Gorman Thomas	.15	.08	.05
328	Chris Chambliss	.15	.08	.05
329	Blue Jays Future Stars (Butch Edge, Pat Kelly, Ted Wilborn)	.25	.13	.08
330	Larry Bowa	.15	.08	.05
331	Barry Bonnell	.15	.08	.05
332	John Candelaria	.15	.08	.05
333	Toby Harrah	.15	.08	.05
334	Larry Biittner	.15	.08	.05
335	Mike Flanagan	.15	.08	.05
336	Ed Kranepool	.15	.08	.05
337	Ken Forsch	.15	.08	.05
338	John Mayberry	.15	.08	.05
339	Rick Burleson	.15	.08	.05
340	Milt May	.15	.08	.05
341	Roy White	.15	.08	.05
342	Joe Morgan	1.50	.70	.45
343	Rollie Fingers	1.00	.50	.30
344	Mario Mendoza	.15	.08	.05
345	Stan Bahnsen	.15	.08	.05
346	Tug McGraw	.15	.08	.05
347	Rusty Staub	.15	.08	.05
348	Tommy John	.15	.08	.05
349	Ivan DeJesus	.15	.08	.05
350	Reggie Smith	.15	.08	.05
351	Expos Future Stars (Tony Bernazard, Randy Miller, John Tamargo)	.40	.20	.12
352	Floyd Bannister	.15	.08	.05
353	Rod Carew	1.50	.70	.45
354	Otto Velez	.15	.08	.05
355	Gene Tenace	.15	.08	.05
356	Freddie Patek	.15	.08	.05
357	Elliott Maddox	.15	.08	.05
358	Pat Underwood	.15	.08	.05
359	Graig Nettles	.15	.08	.05
360	Rodney Scott	.15	.08	.05
361	Terry Whitfield	.15	.08	.05
362	Fred Norman	.15	.08	.05
363	Sal Bando	.15	.08	.05
364	Greg Gross	.15	.08	.05
365	Carl Yastrzemski	2.00	1.00	.60
366	Paul Hartzell	.15	.08	.05
367	Jose Cruz	.15	.08	.05
368	Shane Rawley	.15	.08	.05
369	Jerry White	.15	.08	.05
370	Rick Wise	.15	.08	.05
371	Steve Yeager	.15	.08	.05
372	Omar Moreno	.15	.08	.05
373	Bump Wills	.15	.08	.05
374	Craig Kusick	.15	.08	.05

1969 Oakland A's (Andersen)

Though they are sometimes identified as an issue of Jack in the Box restaurants, there is no identifier of that nature on these cards. In fact, they are a collectors' fantasy issue sold only within the hobby by Boston photographer Mike Andersen. The blank-back black-and-white cards measure 2-1/8" x 3-5/8". Beneath the portrait photo on front is the player's name, position and uniform number. The team name is in gothic script at bottom. Cards are checklisted here by uniform number.

		NM	EX	VG
Complete Set (21):		80.00	40.00	24.00
Common Player:		2.50	1.25	.75
1	Dick Green	2.50	1.25	.75
2	Danny Cater	2.50	1.25	.75
3	Mike Hershberger	2.50	1.25	.75
4	Phil Roof	2.50	1.25	.75
5	Joe DiMaggio (Coach)	30.00	15.00	9.00
6	Sal Bando	2.50	1.25	.75
7	Rick Monday	2.50	1.25	.75
9a	Bert Campaneris	5.00	2.50	1.50
9b	Reggie Jackson	45.00	22.00	13.50
13	Blue Moon Odom	3.50	1.75	1.00
17	Jim Pagliaroni	2.50	1.25	.75
19	Bert Campaneris	2.50	1.25	.75
20	Lew Krausse	2.50	1.25	.75
24	Joe Nossek	2.50	1.25	.75
25	Paul Lindblad	2.50	1.25	.75
27	Catfish Hunter	7.50	3.75	2.25
29	Chuck Dobson	2.50	1.25	.75
30	Jim Nash	2.50	1.25	.75
31	Ramon Webster	2.50	1.25	.75
35	Tom Reynolds	2.50	1.25	.75
42	Hank Bauer	2.50	1.25	.70

1969 Oakland A's (Broder)

A second issue of black-and-white collector cards featuring the 1969 A's was produced by West Coast collector/dealer Ed Broder. In larger (2-3/4" x 4") format the Broder issue is considerably scarcer than that produced by Mike Andersen. Availability of the Broders was advertised at 100 sets. The blank-back Broder cards have the player name in the wide white border beneath the photo. At bottom the city name is in gothic script with the A's logo on a baseball flying out of a stadium. The unnumbered cards are checklisted here alphabetically.

		NM	EX	VG
Complete Set (14):		65.00	32.50	20.00
Common Player:		2.00	1.00	.60
(1)	Sal Bando	2.00	1.00	.60
(2)	Hank Bauer	2.00	1.00	.60
(3)	Bert Campaneris	3.00	1.50	.90
(4)	Dan Cater	2.00	1.00	.60
(5)	Joe DiMaggio	15.00	7.50	4.50
(6)	Chuck Dobson	2.00	1.00	.60
(7)	Dick Green	2.00	1.00	.60
(8)	Mike Hershberger	2.00	1.00	.60
(9)	Jim Hunter	8.00	4.00	2.50
(10)	Reggie Jackson	25.00	12.50	7.50
(11)	Bob Johnson	2.00	1.00	.60
(12)	Rick Monday	2.00	1.00	.60
(13)	Johnny Moon Odom	4.00	2.00	1.25
(14)	Phil Roof	2.00	1.00	.60

1970 Oakland A's (Andersen)

Boston baseball photographer Mike Andersen produced a second collectors' issue of Oakland A's cards in 1970. Nearly identical in format to his 1969 issue, the '70 team set measures 2-1/4" x 3-5/8" with black-and-white player poses at center. Uniform number, name and team are in the bottom border. Backs are blank. Cards are checklisted here by uniform number.

		NM	EX	VG
Complete Set (24):		30.00	15.00	9.00
Common Player:		1.50	.75	.45
1	Dick Green	1.50	.75	.45
6	Sal Bando	1.50	.75	.45
7	Rick Monday	1.50	.75	.45
8	Felipe Alou	2.00	1.00	.60
9	Reggie Jackson	15.00	7.50	4.50
10	Dave Duncan	1.50	.75	.45
11	John McNamera (McNamara)	1.50	.75	.45
12	Larry Haney	1.50	.75	.45
13	Blue Moon Odom	2.00	1.00	.60
17	Roberto Pena	1.50	.75	.45
19	Bert Campaneris	2.00	1.00	.60
24	Diego Segui	1.50	.75	.45
25	Paul Lindblad	1.50	.75	.45
27	Catfish Hunter	4.00	2.00	1.25
28	Mudcat Grant	1.50	.75	.45
29	Chuck Dobson	1.50	.75	.45
30	Don Mincher	1.50	.75	.45
31	Jose Tartabull	1.50	.75	.45
33	Jim Roland	1.50	.75	.45
34	Rollie Fingers	4.00	2.00	1.25
36	Tito Francona	1.50	.75	.45
38	Al Downing	1.50	.75	.45
39	Frank Fernandez	1.50	.75	.45
45	Roberto Rodriguez	1.50	.75	.45

1968 Official Major League Players Baseball Marbles

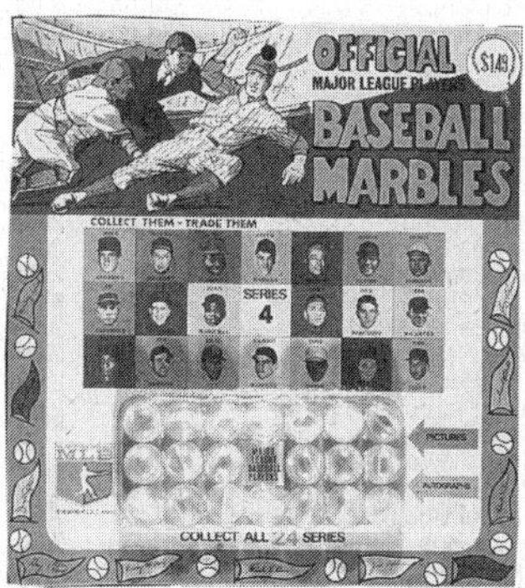

Produced by Creative Creations Inc., though not so identified on the marbles themselves, these approximately 3/4" hard plastic marbles have a player portrait photo (with cap logos removed) on one side and a facsimile autograph on the other, with "JAPAN" beneath. The marbles were issued in series of 20 on colorful cardboard packaging which pictures each player in the series. While the packaging says "Collect All 24 Series" only 120 marbles were actually issued. Suggested retail price at issue was $1.49 per series.

		NM	EX	VG
Complete Set (115):		675.00	325.00	200.00
Common Player:		4.00	2.00	1.25
(1)	Hank Aaron	40.00	20.00	12.00
(2)	Tommie Aaron	4.00	2.00	1.25
(3)	Tommy Agee	4.00	2.00	1.25
(4)	Richie Allen	7.00	3.50	2.00
(5)	Gene Alley	4.00	2.00	1.25
(6)	Bob Allison	4.00	2.00	1.25
(7)	Felipe Alou	5.00	2.50	1.50
(8)	Jesus Alou	4.00	2.00	1.25
(9)	Matty Alou	4.00	2.00	1.25
(10)	Max Alvis	4.00	2.00	1.25
(11)	Mike Andrews	4.00	2.00	1.25
(12)	Luis Aparicio	12.50	6.25	3.75
(13)	Bob Aspromonte	4.00	2.00	1.25
(14)	Stan Bahnsen	4.00	2.00	1.25
(15)	Bob Bailey	4.00	2.00	1.25
(16)	Ernie Banks	25.00	12.50	7.50
(17)	Glenn Beckert	4.00	2.00	1.25
(18)	Gary Bell	4.00	2.00	1.25
(19)	Johnny Bench	30.00	15.00	9.00
(20)	Ken Berry	4.00	2.00	1.25
(21)	Paul Blair	4.00	2.00	1.25
(22)	Bob Bolin	4.00	2.00	1.25
(23)	Dave Boswell	4.00	2.00	1.25
(24)	Nelson Briles	4.00	2.00	1.25
(25)	Lou Brock	12.50	6.25	3.75
(26)	Wally Bunker	4.00	2.00	1.25
(27)	Johnny Callison	4.00	2.00	1.25
(28)	Norm Cash	5.00	2.50	1.50
(29)	Orlando Cepeda	12.50	6.25	3.75
(30)	Dean Chance	4.00	2.00	1.25
(31)	Roberto Clemente	50.00	25.00	15.00
(32)	Donn Clendenon	4.00	2.00	1.25
(33)	Tony Cloninger	4.00	2.00	1.25
(34)	Tommy Davis	4.00	2.00	1.25
(35)	Al Downing	4.00	2.00	1.25
(36)	Curt Flood	4.00	2.00	1.25
(37)	Bill Freehan	4.00	2.00	1.25
(38)	Jim Fregosi	4.00	2.00	1.25
(39)	Bob Gibson	12.50	6.25	3.75
(40)	Jim "Mudcat" Grant	4.00	2.00	1.25
(41)	Jerry Grote	4.00	2.00	1.25
(42)	Jimmie Hall	4.00	2.00	1.25
(43)	Tom Haller	4.00	2.00	1.25
(44)	Ron Hansen	4.00	2.00	1.25
(45)	Steve Hargan	4.00	2.00	1.25
(46)	Ken Harrelson	4.00	2.00	1.25
(47)	Jim Hart	4.00	2.00	1.25
(48)	Jimmie Holt	4.00	2.00	1.25
(49)	Joe Horlen	4.00	2.00	1.25
(50)	Willie Horton	4.00	2.00	1.25
(51)	Frank Howard	5.00	2.50	1.50
(52)	Dick Hughes	4.00	2.00	1.25
(53)	Randy Hundley	4.00	2.00	1.25
(54)	Ron Hunt	4.00	2.00	1.25
(55)	Jim "Catfish" Hunter	12.50	6.25	3.75
(56)	Pat Jarvis	4.00	2.00	1.25
(57)	Julian Javier	4.00	2.00	1.25
(58)	Tommy John	6.00	3.00	1.75
(59)	Deron Johnson	4.00	2.00	1.25
(60)	Mack Jones	4.00	2.00	1.25
(61)	Jim Kaat	5.00	2.50	1.50
(62)	Al Kaline	20.00	10.00	6.00
(63)	Don Kessinger	4.00	2.00	1.25
(64)	Harmon Killebrew	20.00	10.00	6.00

(65)	Jerry Koosman	4.00	2.00	1.25
(66)	Jim Lefebvre	4.00	2.00	1.25
(67)	Mickey Lolich	4.00	2.00	1.25
(68)	Jim Lonborg	4.00	2.00	1.25
(69)	Juan Marichal	12.50	6.25	3.75
(70)	Roger Maris	30.00	15.00	9.00
(71)	Ed Mathews	20.00	10.00	6.00
(72)	Jerry May	4.00	2.00	1.25
(73)	Willie Mays	40.00	20.00	12.00
(74)	Dick McAuliffe	4.00	2.00	1.25
(75)	Tim McCarver	5.00	2.50	1.50
(76)	Willie McCovey	12.50	6.25	3.75
(77)	Sam McDowell	4.00	2.00	1.25
(78)	Denny McLain	5.00	2.50	1.50
(79)	Dave McNally	4.00	2.00	1.25
(80)	Denis Menke	4.00	2.00	1.25
(81)	Jim Merritt	4.00	2.00	1.25
(82)	Bob Miller	4.00	2.00	1.25
(83)	Rick Monday	4.00	2.00	1.25
(84)	Joe Morgan	12.50	6.25	3.75
(85)	Gary Nolan	4.00	2.00	1.25
(86)	Jim Northrup	4.00	2.00	1.25
(87)	Rich Nye	4.00	2.00	1.25
(88)	Tony Oliva	5.00	2.50	1.50
(89)	Milt Pappas	4.00	2.00	1.25
(90)	Camilo Pascual	4.00	2.00	1.25
(91)	Joe Pepitone	5.00	2.50	1.50
(92)	Tony Perez	12.50	6.25	3.75
(93)	Jim Perry	4.00	2.00	1.25
(94)	Gary Peters	4.00	2.00	1.25
(95)	Fritz Peterson	4.00	2.00	1.25
(96)	Rico Petrocelli	4.00	2.00	1.25
(97)	Vada Pinson	5.00	2.50	1.50
(98)	Boog Powell	5.00	2.50	1.50
(99)	Rick Reichardt	4.00	2.00	1.25
(100)	Brooks Robinson	15.00	7.50	4.50
(101)	Frank Robinson	15.00	7.50	4.50
(102)	Pete Rose	40.00	20.00	12.00
(103)	Chico Salmon	4.00	2.00	1.25
(104)	Ron Santo	5.00	2.50	1.50
(105)	George Scott	4.00	2.00	1.25
(106)	Tom Seaver	15.00	7.50	4.50
(107)	Dick Selma	4.00	2.00	1.25
(108)	Mike Shannon	4.00	2.00	1.25
(109)	Joe Sparma	4.00	2.00	1.25
(110)	Willie Stargell	12.50	6.25	3.75
(111)	Mel Stottlemyre	4.00	2.00	1.25
(113)	Luis Tiant	4.00	2.00	1.25
(114)	Cesar Tovar	4.00	2.00	1.25
(115)	Tom Tresh	4.50	2.25	1.25
(116)	Pete Ward	4.00	2.00	1.25
(117)	Billy Williams	12.50	6.25	3.75
(118)	Maury Wills	4.00	2.00	1.25
(119)	Earl Wilson	4.00	2.00	1.25
(120)	Dooley Womack	4.00	2.00	1.25

1974 Oh Henry! Henry Aaron Premium Photo

This 8" x 10" black-and-white photo was prepared as a premium for Oh Henry! candy. It features a full-length pose of Aaron and has a facsimile inscribed autographed on front.

	NM	EX	VG
Henry Aaron	20.00	10.00	6.00

1959 Oklahoma Today Major Leaguers

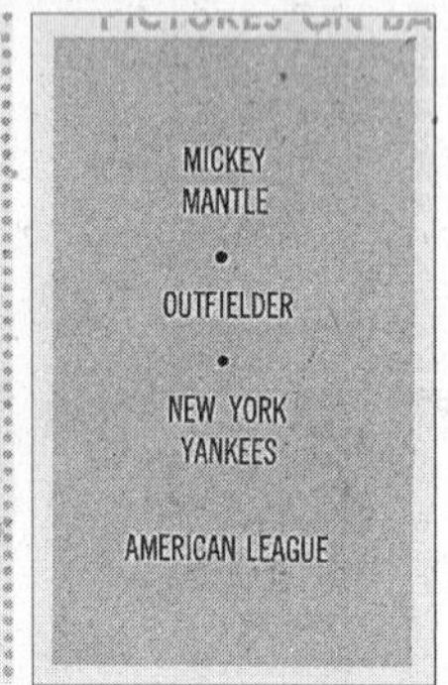

Contemporary and former ballplayers from the Sooner State were featured in this "card set" which was printed on the back cover of the Summer, 1959, issue of "Oklahoma Today" magazine. If cut from the cover, the cards measure about 1-11/16" x 2-3/4". Fronts have black-and-white photos on green, gold or aqua backgrounds. A white strip at bottom has the player name in red. Gray backs have the player name, position, team and league. The unnumbered cards are checklisted here in alphabetical order.

		NM	EX	VG
Complete Magazine:		1,350	675.00	400.00
Complete Set, Singles (20):		1,350	675.00	400.00
Common Player:		45.00	22.50	13.50
(1)	Jerry Adair	45.00	22.00	13.50
(2)	Harry Brecheen	45.00	22.00	13.50
(3)	Johnny Callison	45.00	22.00	13.50
(4)	Alvin Dark	45.00	22.50	13.50
(5)	"Dizzy" Dean	60.00	30.00	18.00
(6)	Paul Dean	45.00	22.00	13.50
(7)	Don Demeter	45.00	22.50	13.50
(8)	Carl Hubbell	50.00	25.00	15.00
(9)	Mickey Mantle	500.00	250.00	150.00
(10)	"Pepper" Martin	45.00	22.00	13.50
(11)	Lindy McDaniel	45.00	22.50	13.50
(12)	Von McDaniel	45.00	22.50	13.50
(13)	Cal McLish	45.00	22.50	13.50
(14)	Dale Mitchel (Mitchell)	45.00	22.50	13.50
(15)	Allie Reynolds	45.00	22.00	13.50
(16)	Warren Spahn	45.00	22.00	13.50
(17)	Tom Sturdivant	45.00	22.50	13.50
(18)	Jerry Walker	45.00	22.50	13.50
(19)	Lloyd Waner	45.00	22.00	13.50
(20)	Paul Waner	45.00	22.00	13.50

1948 Old Gold Jackie Robinson

JACKIE ROBINSON, first baseman of the Brooklyn Dodgers, was born in Cairo, Georgia, 28 years ago. After his family moved to Pasadena, Calif., he entered the University of California, where he distinguished himself as a star athlete in baseball, football, basketball and track.

At 23, Jackie entered the Army, rising to second lieutenant. For 31 months he served overseas, and then joined the Kansas City Monarchs baseball team, for which he fielded so sensationally that he attracted the attention of organized baseball. Impressed with his performance, Branch Rickey, president of the Brooklyn Dodgers, signed him for the Montreal Royals, a Dodger "farm."

So outstanding was Jackie's record with the Montreal Royals that President Rickey signed him to the Dodgers early in 1947. In that way, he became the first Negro to enter the big leagues. He is noted for his speed and batting skill.

A good-looking six-footer, Jackie weighs about 185, and is even-tempered and modest. Off season he lives in Los Angeles with his wife, a former trained nurse, and their young son, Jackie, Jr. His chief ambition is "an earnest desire to contribute to the advancement and recognition of the Negro race."

These postcard-size (3-1/2" x 5-1/2") advertising pieces picture Jackie Robinson and a pack of Old Gold cigarettes on their black-and-white fronts, along with an endorsement from the player and his facsimile autograph. Each back has a different presentation of biography and career summary.

	NM	EX	VG
Jackie Robinson (Fielding)	400.00	200.00	120.00
Jackie Robinson (In dugout.)	200.00	100.00	60.00

1886 Old Judge New York Giants (N167)

Produced in 1886, the rare N167 Old Judge tobacco cards were the first to be issued by New York's Goodwin & Co., the parent firm of Old Judge Cigarettes. The 1-1/2" x 2-1/2" sepia-toned cards were printed on thin paper and featured only members of the New York National League club. Twelve subjects are known to exist, six of whom are Hall of Famers. The front of each card lists the player's name, position and team and has the words "Old Judge" at the top. The backs contain another ad for the Old Judge brand and also include a line noting that the player poses were "copied from photo by J. Wood, 208 Bowery, N.Y."

		NM	EX	VG
Common Player:		50,000	25,000	15,000
(1)	Roger Connor	112,500	56,250	33,750
(2)	Larry Corcoran	50,000	25,000	15,000
(3)	Mike Dorgan	50,000	25,000	15,000
(4)	Dude Esterbrook	50,000	25,000	15,000
(5)	Buck Ewing	120,000	60,000	30,000
(6)	Joe Gerhardt	50,000	25,000	15,000
(7)	Pete Gillespie	50,000	25,000	15,000
(8)	Tim Keefe	112,500	56,250	33,750
(9)	Orator Jim O'Rourke	112,500	56,250	33,750
(10)	Danny Richardson	50,000	25,000	15,000
(11)	John Ward	112,500	56,250	33,750
(12)	Mickey Welsh (Welch)	112,500	56,250	33,750

1887-1890 Old Judge (N172)

This is one of the most fascinating of all card sets, being not only one of the first, but also the largest ever. The number of cards issued may never be finally determined. These cards were issued by the Goodwin & Co. tobacco firm in their Old Judge and, to a lesser extent, Gypsy Queen cigarettes. Players from more than 40 major and minor league teams are pictured on the nominally 1-7/16" x 2-1/2" cards (actual size varies), with some 500 different players known to exist. Up to 20 different pose, team and caption variations exist for some players. Cards were issued both with and without dates, numbered and unnumbered, and with both script and machine-printed identification. Known variations number over 3,500. The cards themselves are black-and-white (many now toned sepia or even pink) photographs pasted onto thick cardboard. They are blank-backed. Values shown here are for the most common examples of a specific player's cards, unless otherwise indicated. Demand for various photo, team, league, etc., variations can significantly affect value and, because of the relatively "thin" nature of the market for Old Judge cards, is subject to rapid fluctuations as collectors enter and leave the arena. These listings are presented alphabetically. Few Old Judge cards were issued with the player's first name, or even initial. Where verifiable, the first names have been added to these listings in the form most often encountered at the time of issue. Misspellings were common among the issue. Cases in which all of a player's cards were incorrectly spelled are listed by the misspelling, with the correct spelling in parentheses following. In cases where the name was sometimes spelled correctly, and sometimes not, the incorrect spellings are provided thus: "(Also: ...)." For each player, the number of different photo/team combinations known is indicated. Minor changes in the player identification caption, such as addition of an initial, presence or absence of period or comma, abbreviation of position, or spelling of team name, are not included in the number of cards listed. Team designations for each player are listed, where known. Pose/designation variations which have historically attracted increased collector interest are specified. These include such subsets as the Brown's Champions and Mets "spotted tie" portrait cards of 1887, the Player's League designations of 1890 and some other popularly collected subsets, such as the dual-player cards. Cards which depict and name both players are listed here under each player's name and are numbered with a "DP" prefix. League designations found in the listings include: AA - American Association; NL - National League; PL - Player's League; WA - Western Association. Gaps have been left in the assigned numbering to accommodate future additions.

		NM	EX	VG
Common Card:		700.00	300.00	175.00
(1)	Gus Albert (Alberts) 7			
1 (a)	(Cleveland)	700.00	300.00	175.00
1 (b)	(Milwaukee)	700.00	300.00	175.00
(2)	Charles Alcott 6			
2 (a)	(Mansfield)	1,500	300.00	175.00
2 (b)	(St. Louis Whites WA)	975.00	425.00	250.00
(3)	Daniel Alexander 4			
3 (a)	(Des Moines)	920.00	400.00	230.00
(4)	Bob Allen 7			
4 (a)	(Philadelphia NL)	700.00	300.00	175.00
4 (a)	(Pittsburgh)	700.00	300.00	175.00
(5)	Myron Allen 6			
5 (a)	(Kansas City)	700.00	300.00	175.00
(6)	Billy Alvord 3			
6 (a)	(Des Moines)	700.00	300.00	175.00
6 (b)	(Toledo)	975.00	425.00	250.00
(7)	Varney Anderson 3			
7 (a)	(St. Paul)	11,500	300.00	175.00
(8)	Ed Andrews 6			

8 (a) (Philadelphia NL) 700.00 300.00 175.00
DP 1 (Being tagged by Buster Hoover.) 920.00 400.00 230.00

(9) Wally Andrews 3
9 (a) (Omaha) 850.00 375.00 200.00

(10) Bill Annis 4
10 (a) (Omaha) 900.00 400.00 230.00
10 (b) (Worcester) 700.00 300.00 175.00

(11) Cap Anson
SEE HALL OF FAME SECTION FOLLOWING

(12) Joe Ardner 4
12 (a) (Kansas City) 700.00 300.00 175.00
12 (b) (St. Joseph) 1,150 500.00 275.00

(13) Tug Arundel 5
13 (a) (Indianapolis) 700.00 300.00 175.00

(14) Jersey Bakley (Bakely) 5
14 (a) (Cleveland) 850.00 375.00 200.00

(15) Kid Baldwin 5
15 (a) (Cincinnati) 700.00 300.00 175.00

(16) Lady Baldwin 4
16 (a) (Detroit) 2,200 975.00 550.00

(17) Mark Baldwin 10
17 (a) (Chicago NL) 850.00 375.00 200.00
17 (b) (Chicago NL)/Portrait 1,400 600.00 350.00
17 (c) (Chicago PL) 2,250 1,000 550.00
17 (d) (Columbus) 700.00 300.00 175.00

(18) Jim Banning 5
18 (a) (Washington) 700.00 300.00 175.00

(19) Sam Barkley 8
19 (a) (Kansas City) 975.00 425.00 250.00
19 (b) (Pittsburgh) 920.00 400.00 230.00
DP 6 (Watching Jocko Fields field.) 1,250 575.00 300.00
DP 7 (Tagged by Jocko Fields.) 1,250 575.00 300.00

(20) John Barnes (Also: Barns) 2
20 (a) (St. Paul) 1,400 600.00 350.00

(21) Billy Barnie 1
21 (a) (Baltimore) 920.00 400.00 250.00

(22) Charley Bassett 3
22 (a) (Indianapolis) 700.00 300.00 175.00
22 (b) (New York NL) 700.00 300.00 175.00

(23) Charlie Bastian 6
23 (a) (Chicago NL) 700.00 300.00 175.00
23 (b) (Chicago PL) 2,700 1,200 600.00
23 (c) (Philadelphia NL) 600.00 275.00 150.00
DP 2 (Being tagged by Pop Schriver.) 1,150 500.00 275.00

(24) Ed Beatin (Also: Beattin) 3
24 (a) (Cleveland) 700.00 300.00 175.00

(25) Jake Beckley
SEE HALL OF FAME SECTION FOLLOWING

(26) Stephen Behel 1
26 (a) (New York AA "dotted tie") 24,750 11,125 6,200

(27) Charlie Bennett 1
27 (a) (Boston NL) 700.00 300.00 175.00

(28) Lou Bierbauer (Also: Bierbaur) 5
28 (a) (Philadelphia AA) 1,025 450.00 250.00
DP 3 (Tagging Bob Gamble.) 1,600 725.00 400.00

(29) Bill Bishop 4
29 (a) (Pittsburgh) 700.00 300.00 175.00
29 (b) (Syracuse) 700.00 300.00 175.00

(30) Bill Blair 5
30 (a) (Hamilton) 1,025 450.00 250.00
30 (b) (Philadelphia AA) 700.00 300.00 175.00

(31) Ned Bligh 6
31 (a) (Columbus) 700.00 300.00 175.00

(32) Walter Bogart 5
32 (a) (Indianapolis) 700.00 300.00 175.00

(33) Boyce 4
33 (a) (Washington) (Never played for Wash.) 920.00 400.00 230.00

(34) Boyd 2
34 (a) (Chicago Maroons WA) 2,000 900.00 500.00

(35) Henry Boyle 6
35 (a) (Indianapolis) 750.00 325.00 175.00
35 (b) (New York NL) (Never played for N.Y.) 700.00 300.00 175.00

(36) Jack Boyle 6
36 (a) (Chicago PL) 6,000 2,700 1,500
36 (b) (St. Louis AA) 875.00 350.00 200.00

(37) George Bradley 5
37 (a) (Sioux City) 700.00 300.00 175.00

(38) Nick Bradley 4
38 (a) (Kansas City) 700.00 300.00 175.00
38 (b) (Worcester) 700.00 300.00 175.00

(39) Steve Brady 1
39 (a) (New York AA "dotted tie") 3,375 1,525 850.00

(40) E.L. Breckenridge 1
40 (a) (Sacramento) (VALUE UNDETERMINED)

Willie Breslin - See Mascot

(41) Timothy Brosnan (Also: Brosman) 8
41 (a) (Minneapolis) 700.00 300.00 175.00
41 (b) (Sioux City) 700.00 300.00 175.00

(42) Cal Broughton 5
42 (a) (St. Paul) 700.00 300.00 175.00

(43) Dan Brouthers
SEE HALL OF FAME SECTION FOLLOWING

(44) Tom Brown 7
44 (a) (Boston NL) 700.00 300.00 175.00
44 (b) (Boston PL) 2,700 1,200 700.00
44 (c) (Pittsburgh) 600.00 275.00 150.00

(45) Willard (California) Brown 6
45 1 (New York NL) 700.00 300.00 175.00
45 1 (New York PL) 2,250 1,000 550.00

(46) Pete Browning 5
46 (a) (Louisville) 5,450 2,425 1,350

(47) Charlie Brynan (Also: Bryn) 6
47 (a) (Chicago NL) 750.00 325.00 200.00
47 (b) (Des Moines) 800.00 350.00 200.00

(48) Al Buckenberger 2
48 (a) (Columbus) 700.00 300.00 175.00

(49) Dick Buckley 7
49 (a) (Indianapolis) 700.00 300.00 175.00
49 (b) (New York NL) 700.00 300.00 175.00

(50) Charlie Buffinton (Also: Buffington) 4
50 (a) (Philadelphia NL) 700.00 300.00 175.00
50 (b) (Philadelphia PL) 2,700 1,200 600.00

(51) Ernie Burch 8
51 (a) (Brooklyn) 2,300 1,025 575.00
51 (b) (St. Louis Whites WA) 700.00 300.00 175.00

(52) Bill Burdick 4
52 (a) (Indianapolis) 700.00 300.00 175.00
52 (b) (Omaha) 850.00 375.00 200.00

(53) Jack Burdock 5
53 (a) (Boston NL) 1,250 550.00 300.00

(54) Bob Burks (Burk) 3
54 (a) (Sioux City) 920.00 400.00 230.00

(55) Watch Burnham 1
55 (a) (Indianapolis) 800.00 350.00 200.00

(56) Jim Burns 8
56 (a) (Kansas City) 850.00 375.00 200.00
56 (b) (Omaha) 700.00 300.00 175.00

(58) Oyster Burns 5
58 (a) (Baltimore) 700.00 300.00 175.00
58 (b) (Brooklyn) 850.00 375.00 200.00
DP 22 (Being tagged by Sam Trott.) 1,150 500.00 275.00

(59) Tom Burns (Also: "E. Burns") 4
59 (a) (Chicago NL) 700.00 300.00 175.00

(60) Doc Bushong 6
60 (a) (Brooklyn) 850.00 375.00 200.00
60 2 (St. Louis AA "Brown's Champions") 1,000 450.00 250.00

(61) John (Patsy) Cahill 2
61 (a) (Indianapolis) 700.00 300.00 175.00

(62) Count Campau 7
62 (a) (Detroit) 700.00 300.00 175.00
62 (b) (Kansas City) 700.00 300.00 175.00

(63) Jimmy Canavan 3
63 (a) (Omaha) 700.00 300.00 175.00

(64) Bart Cantz (Also: McCantz) 5
64 (a) (Baltimore) 700.00 300.00 175.00
64 (b) (St. Louis Whites WA) 700.00 300.00 175.00

(65) Jack Carney 5
65 (a) (Washington) 700.00 300.00 175.00

(66) Hick Carpenter 5
66 (a) (Cincinnati) 700.00 300.00 175.00
66 (b) (Tagging player.) 1,425 650.00 350.00

(67) Cliff Carroll 2
67 (a) (Washington) 700.00 300.00 175.00

(68) Fred Carroll 3
68 (a) (Pittsburgh) 700.00 300.00 175.00

(69) Scrappy Carroll 8
69 (a) (Chicago NL) 700.00 300.00 175.00
69 (b) (St. Paul) 700.00 300.00 175.00

(70) Ed Cartwright 5
70 (a) (Kansas City) 700.00 300.00 175.00
70 (b) (St. Joseph) 700.00 300.00 175.00

(71) Bob Caruthers 7
71 (a) (Brooklyn) 750.00 325.00 200.00
71 (b) (St. Louis AA "Brown's Champions") 1,875 850.00 450.00

(72) Dan Casey 3
72 (a) (Philadelphia NL) 700.00 300.00 175.00

(73) Elton Chamberlain 6
73 (a) (St. Louis) 700.00 300.00 175.00

(74) Cupid Childs 5
74 (a) (Philadelphia NL) 1,150 500.00 275.00
74 (b) (Syracuse) 920.00 400.00 230.00

Chreve - See Shreve

(75) Bob Clark 6
75 (a) (Brooklyn) 700.00 300.00 175.00
DP 4 (Tagging Mickey Hughes.) 2,300 1,025 575.00

(76) Spider Clark 4
76 (a) (Washington) 750.00 325.00 200.00

(77) Dad Clarke (Also: Clark) 11
77 (a) (Chicago NL) 700.00 300.00 175.00
77 (b) (Omaha) 850.00 375.00 200.00

(78) John Clarkson
SEE HALL OF FAME SECTION FOLLOWING

(79) Jack Clements 3
79 (a) (Philadelphia NL) 700.00 300.00 175.00

(80) Elmer Cleveland 6
80 (a) (New York NL) 700.00 300.00 175.00

(81) Monk Cline 5
81 (a) (Sioux City) 700.00 300.00 175.00

(82) Mike Cody 4
82 (a) (Des Moines) 920.00 400.00 230.00

(83) John Coleman 5
83 (a) (Pittsburgh) 700.00 300.00 175.00

(84) Bill Collins 13
84 (a) (Lowell) 700.00 300.00 175.00
84 (b) (Newark) 825.00 375.00 200.00
84 (c) (New York) (Never played for N.Y.) 900.00 400.00 230.00

(85) Hub Collins 6
85 (a) (Brooklyn) 700.00 300.00 175.00
85 (b) (Louisville) 975.00 425.00 250.00

(86) Charlie Comiskey (Also: Commiskey)
86 (a) SEE HALL OF FAME SECTION FOLLOWING

(87) Pete Connell 2
87 (a) (Des Moines, 3B, dark uniform.) 700.00 325.00 175.00
87 (b) (Des Moines, 1B, light uniform. Photo actually P.J. O'Connell.) 700.00 300.00 175.00

(88) Roger Connor (Also: Conner)
SEE HALL OF FAME SECTION FOLLOWING

(89) Dick Conway 6
89 (a) (Boston NL) 1,025 450.00 250.00
89 (b) (Worcester) 700.00 300.00 175.00

(90) Jim Conway 5
90 (a) (Kansas City) 800.00 350.00 200.00

(91) Pete Conway 10
91 (a) (Detroit) 800.00 350.00 200.00
91 (b) (Pittsburgh) 700.00 300.00 175.00
91 (c) (Indianapolis) 700.00 300.00 175.00

(92) Paul Cook 4
92 (a) (Louisville) 700.00 300.00 175.00

(93) Jimmy Cooney 5
93 (a) (Chicago NL) 700.00 300.00 175.00
93 (b) (Omaha) 850.00 375.00 200.00

(94) Larry Corcoran 4
94 (a) (Indianapolis) 850.00 375.00 200.00
94 (b) (London) 850.00 375.00 200.00

(95) Pop Corkhill 7
95 (a) (Brooklyn) 700.00 300.00 175.00
95 (b) (Cincinnati) 800.00 350.00 200.00

(96) Cannonball Crane 7
96 (a) (New York NL) 700.00 300.00 175.00
96 (b) (New York PL) 2,700 1,200 600.00

(97) Sam Crane 3
97 (a) (Washington) 700.00 300.00 175.00

(98) Jack Crogan (Croghan) 5
98 (a) (Chicago Maroons WA) 2,000 900.00 500.00

(99) John Crooks 7
99 (a) (Omaha) 850.00 375.00 200.00
99 (b) (St. Louis Whites WA) 700.00 300.00 175.00

(100) Lave Cross 6
100 (a)(Louisville) 700.00 300.00 175.00
100 (b)(Philadelphia AA) 920.00 400.00 230.00
100 (c)(Philadelphia PL) 2,700 1,200 600.00

(101) William Crossley 5
101 (a)(Milwaukee) 750.00 325.00 200.00

(102) Joe Crotty 5
102 (a)(New York AA "dotted tie") 2,800 1,250 700.00
102 (b)(Sioux City) 700.00 300.00 175.00

(103) Billy Crowell 9
103 (a)(Cleveland) 700.00 300.00 175.00

103 (b)(St. Joseph) 700.00 300.00 175.00

(104) Jim Cudworth 4
104 (a)(Worcester) 700.00 300.00 175.00

(105) Bert Cunningham 6
105 (a)(Baltimore) 850.00 375.00 200.00
105 (b)(Philadelphia PL) 2,700 1,200 600.00

(106) Tacks Curtis 5
106 (a)(St. Joseph) 920.00 400.00 230.00

(107) Ed Cushman 3
107 (a)(New York AA "dotted tie") 2,800 1,250 600.00
107 (b)(New York AA) 2,300 300.00 175.00
107 (c)(Toledo) 3,500 775.00 425.00

(108) Tony Cusick 2
108 (a)(Milwaukee) 5,750 300.00 175.00

(109) Edward Dailey (Also: Daley) 7
109 (a)(Columbus) 700.00 300.00 175.00
109 (b)(Philadelphia NL) 700.00 300.00 175.00
109 (c)(Washington) 700.00 300.00 175.00

(110) Vincent Dailey 1
110 (a)(Oakland) (SGC-graded Poor auctioned for $101,100 12/05.)

(111) Bill Daley 2
111 (a)(Boston NL) 750.00 325.00 200.00
111 (b)(Boston PL) 2,400 1,100 600.00

(112) Con Daley (Daily) 9
112 (a)(Boston NL) 700.00 300.00 175.00
112 (b)(No name, team, etc.) 2,600 1,150 650.00
112 (c)(Indianapolis) 700.00 300.00 175.00

(113) Abner Dalrymple 7
113 (a)(Denver) 1,050 475.00 250.00
113 (b)(Pittsburgh) 800.00 350.00 200.00

(114) Sun Daly 5
114 (a)(Minneapolis) 900.00 400.00 225.00

(115) Tom Daly 7
115 (a)(Chicago NL) 800.00 350.00 200.00
115 (b)(Chicago NL)/Portrait 1,400 625.00 350.00
115 (c)(Cleveland) 700.00 300.00 175.00
(Never played with Cleveland.)

(116) Law Daniels 5
116 (a)(Kansas City) 700.00 300.00 175.00

(117) Dell Darling 6
117 (a)(Chicago NL) 700.00 300.00 175.00
117 (b)(Portrait) 1,400 625.00 350.00
117 (c)(Chicago PL) 2,700 1,200 600.00

(118) William Darnbrough 2
118 (a)(Denver) 850.00 375.00 200.00

(119) D.J. Davin 2
119 (a)(Milwaukee) 5,750 300.00 175.00

(120) Jumbo Davis 5
120 (a)(Kansas City) 700.00 300.00 175.00

(121) Pat Dealey (Also: Dealy) 6
121 (a)(Washington) 775.00 350.00 200.00

(122) Tom Deasley 20
122 (a)(New York NL) 700.00 300.00 175.00
122 (b)(Washington) 700.00 300.00 175.00

(123) Harry Decker 5
123 (a)(Philadelphia NL) 750.00 325.00 200.00

(124) Ed Delahanty
SEE HALL OF FAME SECTION FOLLOWING

(125) Jerry Denny 4
125 (a)(Indianapolis) 700.00 300.00 175.00
125 (b)(New York NL) 700.00 300.00 175.00

(126) Jim Devlin (Also: Delvin) 5
126 (a)(St. Louis AA) 700.00 300.00 175.00

(127) Tom Dolan 5
127 (a)(Denver) 700.00 300.00 175.00
127 (b)(St. Louis AA) 700.00 300.00 175.00

(128) Jack Donahue 1
128 (a)(San Francisco) (SGC-certified Poor, $52,240, 12/04 auction.)

(129) Jim Donahue (Also: Donohue) 7
129 (a)(New York AA "dotted tie") 3,375 1,525 850.00
129 (b)(Kansas City) 700.00 300.00 175.00

(130) Jim Donnelly 3
130 (a)(Washington) 850.00 375.00 200.00

(131) Charlie Dooley 1
131 (a)(Oakland)(SGC-certified Poor, $52,240, 12/04 auction.)

(132) John Doran 2
132 (a)(Omaha) 920.00 400.00 230.00

(133) Mike Dorgan 17
133 (a)(New York NL) 700.00 300.00 175.00
(Sliding) 1,100 500.00 250.00

(134) Con Doyle 1
134 (a)(San Francisco) (VALUE UNDETERMINED)

(135) Charlie Duffe (Duffee) 5
135 (a)(St. Louis AA) 850.00 375.00 200.00

(136) Hugh Duffy
SEE HALL OF FAME SECTION FOLLOWING

(137) Dan Dugdale 7
137 (a)(Chicago Maroons WA) 1,025 450.00 250.00
137 (b)(Minneapolis) 750.00 335.00 185.00

(138) Martin Duke 5
138 (a)(Minneapolis) 700.00 300.00 175.00

(139) Fred Dunlap 9
139 (b)(Pittsburgh) 825.00 375.00 200.00

(140) J.E. Dunn 5
140 (a)(Chicago Maroons WA) 2,300 1,100 600.00

(141) Jesse Duryea 4
141 (a)(Cincinnati) 800.00 350.00 200.00
141 (b)(St. Paul) 700.00 300.00 175.00

(142) Frank Dwyer 5
142 (a)(Chicago NL) 700.00 300.00 175.00
142 (b)(Chicago Maroons WA) 2,300 1,100 600.00

(143) Billy Earle (Also: Earl) 4
143 (a)(Cincinnati) 700.00 300.00 175.00
143 (b)(St. Paul) 700.00 300.00 175.00

(144) Hi Ebright 2
144 (a)(Washington) 700.00 300.00 175.00

(145) Red Ehret 4
145 (a)(Louisville) 700.00 300.00 175.00

Eidner - See Weidner

(146) R. Emmerke 5
146 (a)(Des Moines) 800.00 350.00 200.00

(147) Dude Esterbrook 11
147 (a)(Indianapolis) 700.00 300.00 175.00
147 (b)(Louisville) 700.00 300.00 175.00
147 (c)(New York AA) 1,300 575.00 325.00
147 (d)(New York NL) 700.00 300.00 175.00

(148) Henry Esterday (Easterday) 6
148 (a)(Columbus) 700.00 300.00 175.00
148 (b)(Kansas City) 700.00 300.00 175.00

(149) Buck Ewing
SEE HALL OF FAME SECTION FOLLOWING

(150) John Ewing 4
150 (a)(Louisville) 800.00 350.00 200.00

(151) Jay Faatz 3
151 (a)(Cleveland) 800.00 350.00 200.00

(152) Bill Fagan 5
152 (a)(Denver) 850.00 375.00 200.00
152 (b)(Kansas City) 750.00 325.00 200.00

(153) Bill Farmer 7
153 (a)(Pittsburgh) 700.00 300.00 175.00
153 (b)(St. Paul) 850.00 375.00 200.00

(154) Sid Farrar (Also: Farrer, Faraer) 8
154 (a)(Philadelphia NL) 700.00 300.00 175.00
154 (b)(Philadelphia PL) 2,700 1,200 600.00

(155) Duke Farrell (Also: Farrel) 5
155 (a)(Chicago NL) 700.00 300.00 175.00
155 (b)(Chicago PL) 2,700 1,200 600.00

(156) Jack Farrell 12
156 (a)(Baltimore) 700.00 300.00 175.00
156 (b)(Washington) 700.00 300.00 175.00
156 (c)(Washington) 875.00 400.00 230.00
(Tagging Paul Hines.)

(157) Frank Fennelly 5
157 (a)(Cincinnati) 700.00 300.00 175.00
157 (b)(Philadelphia AA) 700.00 300.00 175.00

(158) Charlie Ferguson 4
158 (a)(Philadelphia NL) 700.00 300.00 175.00

(159) Alex Ferson 5
159 (a)(Washington) 850.00 375.00 200.00

(160) Wallace Fessenden 4
160 1 (Umpire) 1,850 825.00 450.00

(161) Jocko Fields (Also: Field) 6
161 (a)(Pittsburgh) 700.00 300.00 175.00
DP 6 (Fielding, Sam Barkley looking on.) 1,250 575.00 300.00
DP 7 (Tagging Sam Barkley.) 1,250 575.00 300.00

(162) Fischer 3
162 (a)(Chicago Maroons WA) 25,875 11,500 6,475

(163) Thomas Flanigan (Flanagan) 4
163 (a)(Cleveland) 920.00 400.00 230.00
(Never played for Cleveland.)
163 (b)(Sioux City) 700.00 300.00 175.00

(164) Silver Flint 5
164 (a)(Chicago NL) 1,025 450.00 250.00

(165) Thomas Flood 5
165 (a)(St. Joseph) 700.00 300.00 175.00

(166) Jocko Flynn 2
166 (a)(Omaha)(Two known.)) 11,500

(167) Jim Fogarty (Also: Fogerty) 5
167 (a)(Philadelphia NL) 700.00 300.00 175.00

(168) Frank Foreman 6
168 (a)(Baltimore) 700.00 300.00 175.00
168 (b)(Cincinnati) 1,250 575.00 300.00

(169) Tom Forster (Also: "F.W. Foster") 3
169 (a)(Hartford) 700.00 300.00 175.00
169 (b)(Milwaukee, squatting.)) 850.00 375.00 200.00
169 (c)(New York AA "dotted tie") 3,375 1,525 850.00
169 (d)Tom Forester (Milwaukee, standing.) 750.00 335.00 185.00

(170) Elmer Foster 7
170 (a)(New York AA "dotted tie") 6,200 2,750 1,550
170 (b)(New York NL) 700.00 300.00 175.00
170 (c)(Minneapolis) 700.00 300.00 175.00

(171) Dave Foutz 5
171 (a)(Brooklyn) 920.00 400.00 230.00
171 (b)(St. Louis AA "Brown's Champions") 1,700 750.00 400.00

(172) Julie Freeman 5
172 (a)(Milwaukee) 850.00 375.00 200.00

(173) Will Fry 4
173 (a)(St. Joseph) 850.00 375.00 200.00

(174) Frank Fudger 1
174 (a)(Oakland)(VALUE UNDETERMINED)

(175) Shorty Fuller 5
175 (a)(St. Louis AA) 850.00 375.00 200.00

(176) William Fuller 5
176 (a)(Milwaukee) 920.00 400.00 230.00

(177) Chris Fulmer (Also: Fullmer) 6
177 (a)(Baltimore) 700.00 300.00 175.00
DP 8 (Tagging Tom Tucker.) 2,000 900.00 500.00

(178) John Gaffney 1
178 (a)(Washington) 875.00 400.00 225.00
DP 21 (Behind George Shoch.) 1,150 500.00 300.00

(179) Pud Galvin
SEE HALL OF FAME SECTION FOLLOWING

(180) Bob Gamble 3
180 (a)(Philadelphia AA) 700.00 300.00 175.00
DP 3 (Being tagged by Lou Bierbaur.) (Bierbauer)) 1,600 725.00 400.00

(181) Charlie Ganzel (Also: Gauzel) 5
181 (a)(Boston) 700.00 300.00 175.00
181 (b)(Detroit) 700.00 300.00 175.00

(182) Gid Gardner 5
182 (a)(Philadelphia NL) 700.00 300.00 175.00
182 (b)(Washington) 1,025 450.00 250.00
DP 9 (Tagging Miah Murray.) 2,875 1,300 700.00

(183) Hank Gastreich (Gastright) 5
183 (a)(Columbus) 700.00 300.00 175.00

(184) Emil Geiss 6
184 (a)(Chicago NL) 700.00 300.00 175.00

(185) Frank Genins (Also: Genius) 5
185 (a)(Sioux City) 750.00 325.00 200.00

(186) Bill George 5
186 (a)(New York NL) 800.00 350.00 200.00

(187) Joe Gerhardt 4
187 (a)(Jersey City) 800.00 325.00 200.00
187 (b)(New York NL) 1,400 625.00 350.00

(188) Charlie Getzein (Getzien) 6
188 (a)(Detroit) 700.00 300.00 175.00
188 (b)(Indianapolis) 700.00 300.00 175.00

(189) Whitey Gibson 1
189 (a)(Philadelphia AA, two known.) (2003 auction) 11,500 3,800

(190) Bob Gilks 6
190 (a)(Cleveland) 800.00 350.00 200.00

(191) Pete Gillespie 5
191 (a)(New York NL) 850.00 375.00 200.00

(192) Barney Gilligan 3
192 (a)(Detroit) 700.00 300.00 175.00
192 (b)(Washington) 725.00 325.00 200.00

(193) Frank Gilmore 5
193 (a)(Washington) 1,025 450.00 250.00

(194) Jack Glasscock (Also: Glassock, Glass, Cock) 5
194 (a)(Indianapolis) 775.00 350.00 200.00
194 (b)(New York NL) 700.00 300.00 175.00

(195) Bill Gleason 5
195 (a)(Louisville) 700.00 300.00 175.00
195 (b)(Philadelphia AA) 700.00 300.00 175.00
195 (c)(St. Louis AA "Brown's Champions") 2,200 1,000 550.00
DP 23 (W/ Curt Welch.) 2,300 1,100 600.00

(196) Kid Gleason 5
196 (a)(Philadelphia NL) 700.00 300.00 175.00

(197) Ed Glenn 5
197 (a)(Sioux City) 850.00 375.00 200.00

(198) Mike Goodfellow 9
198 (a)(Cleveland) 920.00 400.00 230.00

198 (b)(Detroit) 825.00 375.00 200.00

(199) George Gore 10
199 (a)(New York NL) 1,025 450.00 250.00
199 (b)(New York PL) 2,700 1,200 600.00

(200) Frank Graves 6
200 (a)(Minneapolis) 700.00 300.00 175.00

(201) Bill Greenwood 8
201 (a)(Baltimore) 1,250 575.00 300.00
201 (b)(Columbus) 800.00 350.00 200.00

(202) Ed Greer 3
202 (a)(Brooklyn) 850.00 375.00 200.00
DP 10 (Catching, Hardie Henderson batting.) 1,150 500.00 300.00

(203) Mike Griffin 6
203 (a)(Baltimore) 1,150 500.00 300.00
203 (b)(Philadelphia PL) 2,700 1,200 600.00

(204) Clark Griffith
SEE HALL OF FAME SECTION FOLLOWING

(205) Henry Gruber 4
205 (a)(Cleveland) 700.00 300.00 175.00

(206) Ad Gumbert 5
206 (a)(Chicago NL) 700.00 300.00 175.00
206 (b)(Boston PL) 2,700 1,200 600.00

(207) Tom Gunning 4
207 (a)(Philadelphia AA) 700.00 300.00 175.00
207 (b)(Philadelphia NL) 700.00 300.00 175.00

(208) Joe Gunson 4
208 (a)(Kansas City) 750.00 325.00 200.00

(209) George Haddock 5
209 (a)(Washington) 700.00 300.00 175.00

(210) Frank Hafner 5
210 (a)(Kansas City) 750.00 325.00 200.00

(211) Willie Hahn (Mascot)
211 (a)(Chicago NL) 850.00 375.00 200.00
DP 24 (W/ Ned Williamson.) 4,000 1,800 1,000

Halliday - See Holliday

(212) Bill Hallman 6
212 (a)(Philadelphia NL) 850.00 375.00 200.00
212 (b)(Philadelphia PL) 2,700 1,200 600.00

(213) Billy Hamilton
SEE HALL OF FAME SECTION FOLLOWING

(214) Frank Hankinson 1
214 (a)(New York AA "dotted tie") 27,000 12,150 6,750

(215) Ned Hanlon 6
SEE HALL OF FAME SECTION FOLLOWING

Hannon - See Shannon

(216) Bill Hanrahan 9
216 (a)(Chicago Maroons WA) 1,025 450.00 250.00
216 (b)(Minneapolis) 700.00 300.00 175.00

(217) Al Hapeman 1
217 (a)(Sacramento)(VALUE UNDETERMINED)

(218) John Harkins (Also: Harkens) 9
218 (a)(Baltimore) 800.00 350.00 200.00
218 (b)(Brooklyn) 700.00 300.00 175.00

(219) Bill Hart 5
219 (a)(Cincinnati) (Never played for Cincinnati.) 700.00 300.00 175.00
219 (b)(Des Moines) 850.00 375.00 200.00

(220) Bill Hasamdear (Hassamaer) 3
220 (a)(Kansas City) 800.00 350.00 200.00

(221) Gil Hatfield 5
221 (a)(New York NL) 800.00 350.00 200.00
221 (b)(New York PL) 2,700 1,200 600.00

(222) Bill Hawes (Also Howes) 5
222 (a)(Minneapolis) 800.00 350.00 200.00
222 (b)(St. Paul) 875.00 400.00 225.00

(223) John J. "Egyptian" Healey (Healy) 5
223 (a)(Indianapolis) 750.00 325.00 200.00
223 (b)(Washington) 920.00 400.00 230.00
223 (c)(Washington, portrait, w/ moustache, no cap, possibly unique.) 34,500 15,525 8,625

(224) John C. "Jack" Healy (Also: Healey) 8
224 (a)(Denver) 1,050 475.00 275.00
224 (b)(Omaha) 850.00 375.00 200.00

(225) Guy Hecker 5
225 (a)(Louisville) 2,200 975.00 550.00

(226) Tony Hellman 5
226 (a)(Sioux City) 800.00 375.00 200.00

(227) Hardie Henderson 13
227 (a)(Brooklyn) 700.00 300.00 175.00
227 (b)(Pittsburgh) 700.00 300.00 175.00
DP 10 (Batting, Ed Greer catching.) 1,150 500.00 300.00
DP 11 (Tagging Jimmy Peoples.) 1,600 725.00 400.00

(228) Moxie Hengle 10
228 (a)(Chicago Maroons WA) 1,425 650.00 350.00
228 (b)(Minneapolis) 920.00 400.00 230.00

(229) John Henry 5
229 (a)(Philadelphia) 700.00 300.00 175.00
(Never actually played for Philadelphia.)

(230) Ed Herr 7
230 (a)(Milwaukee) 920.00 400.00 230.00
230 (b)(St. Louis Whites WA) 700.00 300.00 175.00

(231) Hunkey Hines 4
231 (a)(St. Louis Whites WA) 1,400 600.00 350.00

(232) Paul Hines 7
232 (a)(Indianapolis) 920.00 400.00 230.00
232 (b)(Washington) 850.00 375.00 200.00

(233) Frank Hoffman 4
233 (a)(Denver) 975.00 425.00 250.00

(234) Eddie Hogan 5
234 (a)(Cleveland) 775.00 350.00 200.00

(235) Bill Holbert 10
235 (a)(Brooklyn) 1,025 450.00 250.00
235 (b)(Jersey City) 1,025 450.00 250.00
235 (c)(New York AA "dotted tie") 10,700 4,800 2,650
235 (d)(New York AA) 700.00 300.00 175.00

(236) Bug Holliday (Also: Halliday) 7
236 (a)(Cincinnati) 700.00 300.00 175.00
236 (b)(Des Moines) 700.00 300.00 175.00

(238) Buster Hoover 3
238 (a)(Philadelphia) 700.00 300.00 175.00
238 (b)(Toronto) 775.00 350.00 200.00
(Never played for Phila. in N172 era.)
DP 1 (Hoover tagging Ed Andrews.) 1,150 500.00 300.00

(239) Charlie Hoover 7
239 (a)(Chicago) 700.00 300.00 175.00
(Never played for Chicago.)
239 (b)(Kansas City) 800.00 350.00 200.00

(240) Jack Horner (Also: Hodner) 6
240 (a)(Milwaukee) 700.00 300.00 175.00
240 (b)(New Haven) 700.00 300.00 175.00
240 (c)(Photo actually E.H. Warner.) 700.00 300.00 175.00
DP 5 (W/ Ed Warner.) 1,150 500.00 300.00

(241) Joe Hornung (Also: Horning) 6
241 (a)(Baltimore) 700.00 300.00 175.00
241 (b)(Boston) 850.00 375.00 200.00
241 (c)(New York NL) 700.00 300.00 175.00

(242) Pete Hotaling (Also: Hotoling) 4
242 (a)(Cleveland) 700.00 300.00 175.00

Howes - See Hawes

(243) Dummy Hoy 5
243 (a)(Washington) 8,625 3,900 2,150

(244) Nat Hudson 6
244 (a)(St. Louis AA "Brown's Champions") 1,800 800.00 450.00
244 (b)(St. Louis AA) 700.00 300.00 175.00

(245) Mickey Hughes 7
245 (a)(Brooklyn) 700.00 300.00 175.00
DP 4 (Being tagged by Bob Clark.) 2,300 1,100 600.00

(246) Al Hungler 4
246 (a)(Sioux City) 800.00 350.00 200.00

(247) Bill Hutchinson 4
247 (a)(Chicago NL) 1,400 600.00 350.00

(248) Arthur Irwin 13
248 (a)(Boston PL) 1,200 550.00 300.00
248 (b)(Philadelphia NL) 875.00 400.00 225.00
(Portrait, cap off.) 2,300 1,100 600.00
248 (c)(Washington) 700.00 300.00 175.00

(249) John Irwin 5
249 (a)(Washington) 700.00 300.00 175.00
249 (b)(Wilkes-Barre) 875.00 400.00 225.00

(250) A.C. Jantzen 5
250 (a)(Minneapolis) 800.00 350.00 200.00

(251) Frederick Jevne 5
251 (a)(Minneapolis) 825.00 375.00 200.00

(252) Spud Johnson 6
252 (a)(Columbus) 700.00 300.00 175.00
252 (b)(Kansas City) 920.00 400.00 230.00

(253) Dick Johnston 7
253 (a)(Boston NL) 750.00 325.00 200.00
253 (b)(Boston PL) 2,700 1,200 600.00

(254) W.T. Jordan 5
254 (a)(Minneapolis) 920.00 400.00 230.00

(255) Heinie Kappell (Kappel) 8
255 (a)(Cincinnati) 700.00 300.00 175.00
255 (b)(Columbus) 700.00 300.00 175.00

(256) Tim (Also: Jim) Keefe, (Also: Keef, Keefep)
SEE HALL OF FAME SECTION FOLLOWING

(257) George Keefe 5
257 (a)(Washington) 700.00 300.00 175.00

(258) Jim Keenan 5
258 (a)(Cincinnati) 700.00 300.00 175.00

(259) Charlie Kelly 5
259 (a)(Philadelphia AA) 1,850 825.00 450.00

(260) Honest John Kelly 4
260 (a)(Louisville) 700.00 300.00 175.00
260 (b)(Umpire WA) 1,800 800.00 450.00
DP 14 (W/ Jim Powell.) 1,150 500.00 275.00

(261) King Kelly
SEE HALL OF FAME SECTION FOLLOWING

(262) Rudy Kemmler (Also: Kemler) 2
262 (a)(St. Louis AA "Brown's Champions") 1,425 650.00 350.00
262 (b)(St. Paul) 700.00 300.00 175.00

(263) Ted Kennedy 9
263 (a)(Des Moines) 850.00 375.00 200.00
263 (b)(Omaha) 1,150 500.00 275.00

(264) J.J. Kenyon 7
264 (a)(Des Moines) 700.00 300.00 175.00
264 (b)(St. Louis Whites WA) 775.00 350.00 200.00

(265) John Kerins 6
265 (a)(Louisville) 850.00 375.00 200.00

(266) Matt Kilroy 7
266 (a)(Baltimore) 1,400 600.00 350.00
266 (b)(Boston PL) 2,700 1,200 600.00

(267) Silver King 3
267 (a)(Chicago PL) 2,700 1,200 600.00
267 (b)(St. Louis AA) 700.00 300.00 175.00

(268) Gus Kloff (Klopf) 7
268 (a)(Minneapolis) 700.00 300.00 175.00
268 (b)(St. Joseph) 700.00 300.00 175.00
DP 15 (W/ Bill Krieg.) 1,150 500.00 275.00

(269) Billy Klusman 7
269 (a)(Denver) 1,100 500.00 250.00
269 (b)(Milwaukee) 700.00 300.00 175.00

(270) Phil Knell 5
270 (a)(St. Joseph) 800.00 350.00 200.00

(271) Ed Knouff 5
271 (a)(St. Louis AA) 800.00 350.00 200.00

(272) Charles Kremmeyer (Krehmeyer) 1
272 (a)(Sacramento)(SGC-certified Fair, $50,233 12/04 auction.)

(273) Bill Krieg (Also: Kreig) 14
273 (a)(Minneapolis) 775.00 350.00 200.00
273 (b)(St. Joseph) 750.00 325.00 200.00
273 (c)(Washington) 700.00 300.00 175.00
DP 15 (W/ Gus Kloff.) (Klopf)) 1,150 500.00 300.00

(274) Gus Krock 5
274 (a)(Chicago NL) 700.00 300.00 175.00

(275) Willie Kuehne (Also: Kuchne) 5
275 (a)(Pittsburgh) 700.00 300.00 175.00

(276) Fred Lange 5
276 (a)(Chicago Maroons WA) 2,100 900.00 500.00

(277) Henry Larkin 4
277 (a)(Philadelphia AA) 700.00 300.00 175.00

(278) Arlie Latham 7
278 (a)(St. Louis AA "Brown's Champions") 1,625 725.00 400.00
278 (b)(St. Louis AA) 700.00 325.00 200.00
278 (c)(Chicago PL) 2,700 1,200 600.00

(279) Chuck Lauer 4
279 (a)(Pittsburgh) 700.00 300.00 175.00

(280) John Leighton 5
280 (a)(Omaha) 850.00 375.00 200.00

(281) Levy 1
281 (a)(San Francisco)(VALUE UNDETERMINED)

(282) Tom Loftus 2
282 (a)(Cleveland) 700.00 300.00 175.00
282 (b)(St. Louis Whites WA) 700.00 300.00 175.00

(283) Danny Long 1
283 (a)(Oakland)(VALUE UNDETERMINED)

(284) Herman Long 7
284 (a)(Chicago Maroons WA) 3,100 1,400 775.00
284 (b)(Kansas City) 900.00 400.00 250.00

(285) Tom Lovett 6
285 (a)(Brooklyn) 900.00 400.00 250.00
285 (b)(Omaha) 850.00 375.00 200.00

(286) Bobby Lowe 6
286 (a)(Milwaukee) 1,100 500.00 300.00
DP 18 (About to be tagged by Pat Pettee.) 1,400 600.00 350.00

(287) Jack Lynch 5
287 (a)(New York AA "dotted tie") 3,375 1,500 850.00
287 (b)(New York AA) 700.00 300.00 175.00

(288) Denny Lyons 4
288 (a)(Philadelphia AA) 700.00 300.00 175.00

(289) Harry Lyons 6

289 (a)(St. Louis AA) 700.00 300.00 175.00
289 (b)(Jersey City) 700.00 300.00 175.00

(290) Connie Mack 3
SEE HALL OF FAME SECTION FOLLOWING

(291) Reddy Mack 6
291 (a)(Baltimore) 800.00 350.00 200.00
291 (b)(Louisville) 700.00 300.00 175.00

(292) Jimmy Macullar 7
292 (a)(Des Moines) 1,400 600.00 350.00
292 (b)(Milwaukee) 700.00 300.00 175.00

(293) Kid Madden 9
293 (a)(Boston NL) 700.00 300.00 175.00
293 (b)(Boston NL)(Portrait) 2,875 1,300 700.00
293 (c)(Boston PL) 2,700 1,200 600.00

(294) Danny Mahoney 1
294 (a)(St. Joseph) 2,525 1,125 600.00

(295) Willard Maines (Mains) 5
295 (a)(St. Paul) 700.00 300.00 175.00

(296) Fred Mann 5
296 (a)(Hartford) 700.00 300.00 175.00
296 (b)(St. Louis AA) 700.00 300.00 175.00
(Never played for St. Louis.)

(297) Jimmy Manning 6
297 (a)(Kansas City) 850.00 375.00 200.00

(298) Lefty Marr 7
298 (a)(Cincinnati) 700.00 300.00 175.00
298 (b)(Columbus) 775.00 350.00 200.00

(299) Mascot (Willie Breslin 1)
299 (a)New York NL (Caption reads "New York Mascot.") 1,850 825.00 450.00

(300) Leech Maskrey 5
300 (a)(Des Moines) 700.00 300.00 175.00
300 (b)(Milwaukee) 700.00 300.00 175.00
300 (c)(Photo actually Jimmy Macullar.) 700.00 300.00 175.00

Massitt - See Messitt

(301) Bobby Mathews 3
301 (a)(Philadelphia AA) 900.00 400.00 250.00

(302) Mike Mattimore (Also: Mattemore) 19
302 (a)(New York NL) 800.00 350.00 200.00
302 (b)(Philadelphia AA) 725.00 325.00 200.00

(303) Al Maul 7
303 (a)(Pittsburgh) 700.00 300.00 175.00

(304) Al Mays 5
304 (a)(New York AA "dotted tie") 3,375 1,525 850.00
304 (b)(Columbus) 700.00 300.00 175.00

(305) Jimmy McAleer 4
305 (a)(Cleveland) 700.00 300.00 175.00

(306) John McCarthy (McCarty) 3
306 (a)(Kansas City) 900.00 400.00 250.00

(307) Tommy McCarthy
SEE HALL OF FAME SECTION FOLLOWING

(308) Jim McCauley 3
308 (a)(Chicago Maroons WA) 2,100 900.00 500.00

(309) Bill McClellan (Also: McClennan) 3
309 (a)(Brooklyn) 700.00 300.00 175.00
309 (b)(Denver) 1,400 600.00 350.00

(310) Jim McCormack 4
310 (a)(St. Louis Whites WA) 700.00 300.00 175.00

(311) Jim McCormick 10
311 (a)(Chicago) 1,400 600.00 350.00
311 (b)(Portrait) 4,600 2,100 1,150
311 (c)(Pittsburgh) 850.00 375.00 200.00

(312) McCreachery 1
312 (a)(Indianapolis)(VALUE UNDETEREMINED)
(Nobody named McCreachery ever managed Indianapolis. Photo actually Deacon White.)

(313) Tom McCullum (McCallum) 4
313 (a)(Minneapolis) 700.00 300.00 175.00

(314) Jim McDonald 1
314 (a)(Oakland)(VALUE UNDETERMINED)

(315) Chippy McGarr 5
315 (a)(Kansas City) 700.00 300.00 175.00
315 (b)(St. Louis AA) 700.00 300.00 175.00
315 (c)(St. Louis AA, batting, umpire behind.) 875.00 400.00 225.00

(316) Jack McGeachy 4
316 (a)(Indianapolis) 850.00 375.00 200.00

(317) John McGlone 7
317 (a)(Cleveland) 700.00 300.00 175.00
317 (b)(Detroit) 700.00 300.00 175.00

(318) Deacon McGuire 5
318 (a)(Philadelphia NL) 750.00 325.00 200.00
318 (b)(Toronto) 825.00 375.00 200.00

(319) Bill McGunnigle 1
319 (a)(Brooklyn) 1,800 775.00 425.00

(320) Ed McKean 5
320 (a)(Cleveland) 700.00 300.00 175.00

(321) Alex McKinnon 4
321 (a)(Pittsburgh) 700.00 300.00 175.00

(322) Tom McLaughlin 1
322 (a)(New York AA "dotted tie") 7,875 3,550 1,975

(323) Bid McPhee
SEE HALL OF FAME SECTION FOLLOWING

(324) Jack McQuaid 1
324 (a)(Umpire) 2,300 1,025 575.00

(325) James McQuaid 3
325 (a)(Denver) 1,800 775.00 425.00

(326) Jim McTamany (Also: McTammany) 6
326 (a)(Brooklyn)) 1,800 775.00 425.00
326 (b)(Columbus) 1,800 775.00 425.00
326 (c)(Kansas City) 1,800 775.00 425.00

(327) George McVey 9
327 (a)(Denver) 700.00 300.00 175.00
327 (b)(Milwaukee) 700.00 300.00 175.00
327 (c)(St. Joseph) 750.00 325.00 200.00

(328) Pete Meegan 1
328 (a)(San Francisco)(VALUE UNDETERMINED)

(329) John Messitt (Also: Massitt, Wassitt) 3
329 (a)(Omaha) 1,325 600.00 325.00

Micholson - See Nicholson

(330) Doggie Miller 5
330 (a)(Pittsburgh) 700.00 300.00 175.00

(331) Joe Miller 3
331 (a)(Minneapolis) 700.00 300.00 175.00
331 (b)(Omaha) 750.00 325.00 200.00

(332) Jocko Milligan 6
332 (a)(Philadelphia PL) 2,700 1,200 600.00
332 (b)(St. Louis AA) 700.00 300.00 175.00

(333) E.L. Mills 5
333 (a)(Milwaukee) 700.00 300.00 175.00

(334) Daniel Minnehan (Minahan) 4
334 (a)(Minneapolis) 700.00 300.00 175.00

(335) Sam Moffet 3
335 (a)(Indianapolis) 700.00 300.00 175.00

(336) John Morrill (Also: Morrell) 4
336 (a)(Boston NL) 1,250 550.00 300.00
336 (b)(Boston NL)/Portrait 2,100 900.00 500.00
336 (c)(Washington) 1,025 450.00 250.00

(337) Ed Morris 6
337 (a)(Pittsburgh) 700.00 300.00 175.00

(338) Tony Mullane 7
338 (a)(Cincinnati) 1,600 700.00 400.00

(339) Joe Mulvey 4
339 (a)(Philadelphia NL) 700.00 300.00 175.00
339 (b)(Philadelphia PL) 2,700 1,200 600.00

(340) Pat Murphy 3
340 (a)(New York NL) 700.00 300.00 175.00

(341) P.L. Murphy 5
341 (a)(St. Paul) 700.00 300.00 175.00

(342) Miah Murray 5
342 (a)(Washington) 700.00 300.00 175.00
DP 9 (Being tagged by Gid Gardner.) 2,875 1,300 700.00

(343) Jim Mutrie 3
343 (a)(New York NL) 2,100 900.00 500.00

(344) Al Myers 6
344 (a)(Philadelphia NL) 700.00 300.00 175.00
344 (b)(Washington) 775.00 350.00 200.00

(345) George Myers 3
345 (a)(Indianapolis) 700.00 300.00 175.00

(346) Tom Nagle 6
346 (a)(Chicago NL) 700.00 300.00 175.00
346 (b)(Omaha) 775.00 350.00 200.00

(347) Billy Nash 7
347 (a)(Boston NL) 900.00 400.00 250.00
347 (b)(Tagging (unnamed) Old Hoss Radbourn.) 2,750 1,225 700.00
347 (c)(Boston PL) 2,700 1,200 600.00

(348) Jack Nelson 1
348 (a)(New York AA "dotted tie") 7,875 3,550 1,975

(349) Kid Nichols
SEE HALL OF FAME SECTION FOLLOWING

(350) Samuel Nichols (Nichol) 4
350 (a)(Pittsburgh) 700.00 300.00 175.00

(351) J.W. Nicholson 6
351 (a)(Chicago Maroons WA) 2,100 900.00 500.00

(352) Parson Nicholson (Also: Micholson) 7
352 (a)(Cleveland) 700.00 300.00 175.00
(Never played for Cleveland.)
352 (b)(St. Louis Whites WA) 700.00 300.00 175.00

(353) Hugh Nicol (Also: Nicoll) 8
353 (a)(St. Louis AA "Brown's Champions") 1,000 450.00 250.00
353 (b)(Cincinnati) 825.00 375.00 200.00
DP 16 (Side by side w/ John Reilly.) 2,300 1,025 575.00
DP 17 (Facing John Reilly.) 2,525 1,125 625.00

(354) Frederick Nyce 4
354 (a)(Burlington) 700.00 300.00 175.00
354 (b)(St. Louis Whites WA) 700.00 300.00 175.00

(355) Doc Oberlander 8
355 (a)(Cleveland) 700.00 300.00 175.00
355 (b)(Syracuse) 700.00 300.00 175.00

(356) Billy O'Brien 5
356 (a)(Washington) 900.00 400.00 250.00

(357) Darby O'Brien 5
357 (a)("Brooklyns" or "Bk'ns") 700.00 300.00 175.00

(358) Jack O'Brien 8
358 (a)(Baltimore) 700.00 300.00 175.00
358 (b)("Brooklyn") 700.00 300.00 175.00
358 (c)("Mini" photo.) 5,750 2,600 1,425

(359) John O'Brien 4
359 (a)(Cleveland) 900.00 400.00 250.00

(360) P.J. O'Connell 5
360 (a)(Des Moines) 750.00 325.00 200.00
360 (b)(Omaha) 800.00 350.00 200.00

(361) Jack O'Connor 8
361 (a)(Cincinnati) 700.00 300.00 175.00
361 (b)(Columbus) 700.00 300.00 175.00

(362) Hank O'Day 3
362 (a)(Washington) 800.00 350.00 200.00

(363) Harry O'Day 1
363 (a)(Sacramento)(VALUE UNDETERMINED)

(364) Norris O'Neill 1
364 (a)(Oakland)(VALUE UNDETERMINED)

(365) Tip O'Neill (Also: O'Neil) 11
365 (a)(Chicago PL) 2,500 1,100 625.00
365 (b)(St. Louis AA "Brown's Champions") 1,875 850.00 475.00
365 (c)(St. Louis AA) 700.00 300.00 175.00
365 (d)(Photo actually Bill White.) (W/moustasche, stooping to field grounder.)) 975.00 425.00 250.00

(366) Orator Jim O'Rourke
SEE HALL OF FAME SECTION FOLLOWING

(367) Tom O'Rourke (Also: Rourke) 8
367 (a)(Boston NL) 850.00 375.00 200.00
367 (b)(Jersey City) 700.00 300.00 175.00

(368) Dave Orr 10
368 (a)(Brooklyn) 900.00 400.00 250.00
368 (b)(Columbus) 975.00 425.00 250.00
368 (c)(New York AA "dotted tie") 15,750 7,100 3,925
368 (d)(New York AA) 700.00 300.00 175.00

(369) Charlie Parsons 4
369 (a)(Minneapolis) 700.00 300.00 175.00

(370) Owen Patton 8
370 (a)(Des Moines) 700.00 300.00 175.00
370 (b)(Minneapolis) 850.00 375.00 200.00

(371) Jimmy Peeples (Peoples) 4
371 (a)(Brooklyn) 700.00 300.00 175.00
371 (b)(Columbus) 800.00 350.00 200.00
DP 11 (Being tagged by Hardie Henderson.) 1,600 725.00 400.00

(372) Hip Perrier 1
372 (a)(San Francisco)(VALUE UNDETERMINED)

(373) Pat Pettee 4
373 (a)(London) 700.00 300.00 175.00
373 (b)(Milwaukee) 700.00 300.00 175.00
DP 18 (About to tag Bobby Lowe.) 1,400 600.00 350.00

(374) Fred Pfeffer 5
374 (a)(Chicago NL) 1,050 500.00 275.00

(375) Dick Phelan 5
375 (a)(Des Moines) 700.00 300.00 175.00

(376) Bill Phillips 7
376 (a)(Brooklyn, large photo.) 1,400 600.00 350.00
376 (b)(Brooklyn, mini photo.) 5,175 2,325 1,300
376 (c)(Kansas City) 800.00 350.00 200.00

(377) John Pickett 12
377 (a)(Kansas City) 700.00 300.00 175.00
377 (b)(Philadelphia PL) 900.00 400.00 225.00
377 (c)(St. Paul) 700.00 300.00 175.00

(378) George Pinkney (Pinckney) 5
378 (a)(Brooklyn) 700.00 300.00 175.00

(379) Tom Poorman (Also: Poor Man, Porrman) 7
379 (a)(Milwaukee) 800.00 350.00 200.00
379 (b)(Philadelphia AA) 700.00 300.00 175.00

(380) Henry Porter 7
380 (a)(Brooklyn) 1,500 675.00 375.00
380 (b)(Kansas City) 1,125 500.00 275.00

(381) Jim Powell 5

381 (a)(Sioux City) 900.00 400.00 250.00
DP 14 (w/ Honest John Kelly.) 1,600 725.00 400.00

(382) Thomas Powers (Power) 1
382 (a)(San Francisco)(VALUE UNDETERMINED)

(383) Blondie Purcell 7
383 (b)(Baltimore) 700.00 300.00 175.00
383 (b)(Philadelphia AA) 700.00 300.00 175.00

(384) Tom Quinn 5
384 (a)(Baltimore) 875.00 400.00 250.00

(385) Joe Quinn 3
385 (a)(Boston NL) 1,400 600.00 350.00
385 (b)(Des Moines) 700.00 300.00 175.00

(386) Old Hoss Radbourn
SEE HALL OF FAME SECTION FOLLOWING

(387) Paul Radford 8
387 (a)(Brooklyn) 700.00 300.00 175.00
387 (b)(Cleveland) 700.00 300.00 175.00

(388) Tom Ramsey 3
388 (a)(Louisville) 1,050 450.00 300.00

(389) Rehse 5
389 (a)(Minneapolis) 800.00 350.00 200.00

(390) Charlie Reilly (Also: Riley) 4
390 (a)(St. Paul) 700.00 300.00 175.00

(391) Long John Reilly 3
391 (a)(Cincinnati) 1,050 450.00 250.00
DP 16 (Side by side w/ Hugh Nicol.) 2,300 1,125 575.00
DP 17 (Facing Hugh Nicol.) 2,600 1,150 625.00

(392) Charlie Reynolds 4
392 (a)(Kansas City) 800.00 350.00 200.00

(393) Danny Richardson (Also: Richards) 5
393 (a)(New York NL) 700.00 300.00 175.00
393 (b)(New York PL) 2,700 1,200 600.00
DP 12 (Being tagged by Tim Keefe.) 2,600 1,150 625.00
DP 13 (Sliding, Tim Keefe fielding ball.) 2,600 1,150 625.00

(394) Hardy Richardson 5
394 (a)(Boston NL) 700.00 300.00 175.00
394 (b)(Detroit) 700.00 300.00 175.00

(395) Charlie Ripslager (Reipschlager) 1
395 (a)(New York AA "dotted tie") 9,000 4,050 2,250

(396) John Roach 6
396 (a)(New York NL) 775.00 350.00 200.00

(397) M.C. Robinson 6
397 (a)(Minneapolis) 700.00 300.00 175.00

(398) Wilbert Robinson
SEE HALL OF FAME SECTION FOLLOWING

(399) Yank Robinson 6
399 (a)(St. Louis AA "Brown's Champions") 1,500 675.00 375.00
399 (b)(St. Louis AA) 700.00 300.00 175.00

(400) George Rooks 6
400 (a)(Chicago Maroons WA) 1,050 450.00 250.00
400 (b)(Detroit) 700.00 300.00 175.00
(Never played for Detroit.)

(401) Chief Roseman 1
401 (a)(New York AA "dotted tie") 7,850 3,525 1,950

Rourke - See Tom O'Rourke

(402) Dave Rowe 8
402 (a)(Denver) 1,600 725.00 400.00
402 (b)(Kansas City, portrait.) 6,325 2,850 1,600
402 (c)(Kansas City) 1,050 450.00 250.00

(403) Jack Rowe 3
403 (a)(Detroit) 875.00 400.00 225.00

(404) Amos Rusie (Also: Russie)
SEE HALL OF FAME SECTION FOLLOWING

(405) Jimmy Ryan 8
405 (a)(Chicago NL) 700.00 300.00 175.00
405 (b)(Chicago PL) 2,700 1,200 600.00
405 (c)(Philadelphia)(Never player for Phila.) 700.00 300.00 175.00

(406) Harry Sage 6
406 (a)(Des Moines) 700.00 300.00 175.00
406 (b)(Toledo) 1,750 800.00 425.00
DP 19 (W/ Bill Van Dyke.) (Des Moines)) 1,150 500.00 300.00
DP 20 (W/ Bill Van Dyke.) (Toledo) 1,150 500.00 300.00

(407) Ben Sanders 5
407 (a)(Philadelphia NL) 700.00 300.00 175.00
407 (b)(Philadelphia PL) 2,700 1,200 600.00

(408) Frank Scheibeck 4
408 (a)(Detroit) 850.00 375.00 200.00

(409) Al Schellhase 5
409 (a)(St. Joseph) 900.00 400.00 250.00

(410) Bill Schenkel (Also: Schenkle) 4
410 (a)(Milwaukee) 700.00 300.00 175.00

(411) L. Schildknecht 4
411 (a)(Des Moines) 700.00 300.00 175.00
411 (b)(Milwaukee) 700.00 300.00 175.00

(412) Gus Schmelz 2
412 (a)(Cincinnati) 1,800 775.00 425.00

Schoch - See Shoch

(413) Jumbo Schoeneck 8
413 (a)(Chicago Maroons WA) 2,325 1,125 600.00
413 (b)(Indianapolis) 700.00 300.00 175.00

(414) Pop Schriver 5
414 (a)(Philadelphia NL) 700.00 300.00 175.00
DP 2 (Tagging Charlie Bastian.) 1,150 500.00 300.00

Schwartwood - See Swartwood

(415) Emmett Seery 4
415 (a)(Indianapolis) 700.00 300.00 175.00

(416) Billy Serad 5
416 (a)(Cincinnati) 700.00 300.00 175.00
416 (b)(Toronto) 850.00 375.00 200.00

(417) Ed Seward 3
417 (a)(Philadelphia AA) 700.00 300.00 175.00

(418) Orator Shafer (Shaffer) 4
418 (a)(Des Moines) 700.00 300.00 175.00

(419) Taylor Shafer (Shaffer) 3
419 (a)(St. Louis Whites WA) 700.00 300.00 175.00
419 (b)(St. Paul) 700.00 300.00 175.00

(420) Daniel Shannon (Also: Hannon) 6
420 (a)(Louisville) 700.00 300.00 175.00
420 (b)(Omaha) 800.00 350.00 200.00
420 (c)(Philadelphia PL) 2,700 1,200 600.00

(421) Bill Sharsig 1
421 (a)(Philadelphia AA) 700.00 300.00 175.00

(422) John Shaw 5
422 (a)(Minneapolis) 700.00 300.00 175.00

(423) Samuel Shaw 4
423 (a)(Baltimore) 1,050 450.00 250.00
423 (b)(Newark) 1,150 500.00 300.00

(424) Bill Shindle (Also: Shindel) 7
424 (a)(Baltimore) 850.00 375.00 200.00
424 (b)(Philadelphia PL) 3,300 1,500 825.00
("PL" not on card.))

(425) George Shoch (Also: Schoch) 4
425 (a)(Washington) 700.00 300.00 175.00
DP 21 (Batting, John Gaffney behind.) 1,150 500.00 300.00

(426) Otto Shomberg (Schomberg) 3
426 (a)(Indianapolis) 700.00 300.00 175.00

(427) Lev Shreve 7
427 (a)(Indianapolis) 800.00 350.00 200.00

(428) Ed Silch 8
428 (a)(Brooklyn) 700.00 300.00 175.00
428 (b)(Denver) 825.00 375.00 225.00

(429) Mike Slattery 6
429 (a)(New York NL) 700.00 300.00 175.00
429 (b)(New York PL) 2,700 1,200 600.00

(430) Elmer Smith 5
430 (a)(Cincinnati) 700.00 300.00 175.00

(431) Fred Smith 5
431 (a)(Des Moines) 700.00 300.00 175.00

(432) Germany (Geo.) Smith 5
432 (a)(Brooklyn) 700.00 300.00 175.00

(433) Nick Smith 5
433 (a)(St. Joseph) 750.00 325.00 200.00

(434) Phenomenal Smith 10
434 (a)(Baltimore) 775.00 350.00 200.00
434 (b)(Baltimore, portrait.) 9,775 4,400 2,450
(No team designation.)
434 (c)(Philadelphia AA) 1,250 550.00 300.00

(435) Pop Smith 5
435 (a)(Boston NL) 775.00 350.00 200.00
435 (b)(Pittsburgh) 700.00 300.00 175.00

(436) Skyrocket (Sam) Smith 4
436 (a)(Louisville) 700.00 300.00 175.00

(437) Pete Somers 5
437 (a)(St. Louis AA) 700.00 300.00 175.00
(Never played for St. Louis.)

(438) Joe Sommer (Also: Sommers) 5
438 (a)(Baltimore) 1,050 450.00 250.00

(439) Pete Sommers 7
439 (a)(Chicago NL) 700.00 300.00 175.00
439 (b)(New York NL) 700.00 300.00 175.00

(440) Bill Sowders 7
440 (a)(Boston NL) 700.00 300.00 175.00

(441) John Sowders 4
441 (a)(Kansas City) 750.00 325.00 200.00
441 (b)(St. Paul) 700.00 300.00 175.00

(442) Charlie Sprague 9
442 (a)(Chicago NL) 700.00 300.00 175.00
442 (b)(Chicago Maroons WA) 1,050 450.00 250.00
442 (c)(Cleveland) 775.00 350.00 200.00

(443) Ed Sproat 5
443 (a)(St. Louis Whites WA) 975.00 425.00 250.00

(444) Harry Staley (Also: Stoley) 7
444 (a)(Pittsburgh) 700.00 300.00 175.00
444 (b)(St. Louis Whites WA) 775.00 350.00 200.00

(445) Dan Stearns (Also: Tearns) 4
445 (a)(Des Moines) 700.00 300.00 175.00
445 (b)(Kansas City) 850.00 375.00 225.00

(446) Bill Stemmeyer (Also: Stemmyer) 6
446 (a)(Boston NL) 700.00 300.00 175.00
446 (b)(Cleveland) 1,050 450.00 250.00

(447) B.F. Stephens 3
447 (a)(Milwaukee) 700.00 300.00 175.00

(448) John Sterling 4
448 (a)(Minneapolis) 700.00 300.00 175.00

(449) Len Stockwell 1
449 (a)(San Francisco)(VALUE UNDETERMINED)

Stoley - See Staley

(450) Harry Stovey 9
450 (a)(Boston PL) 2,700 1,200 600.00
450 (b)(Philadelphia AA) 1,600 725.00 400.00

(451) Scott Stratton 5
451 (a)(Louisville) 700.00 300.00 175.00

(452) Joe Strauss (Also: Straus) 8
452 (a)(Milwaukee) 700.00 300.00 175.00
452 (b)(Omaha) 825.00 375.00 225.00

(453) Cub Stricker 3
453 (a)(Cleveland) 700.00 300.00 175.00

(454) Marty Sullivan 7
454 (a)(Chicago NL) 700.00 300.00 175.00
454 (b)(Indianapolis) 700.00 300.00 175.00

(455) Mike Sullivan 3
455 (a)(Philadelphia AA) 700.00 300.00 175.00

(457) Billy Sunday 10
457 (a)(Chicago NL) 2,100 900.00 500.00
457 (b)(Pittsburgh) 1,800 775.00 425.00

(458) Sy Sutcliffe 5
458 (a)(Cleveland) 900.00 400.00 250.00

(459) Ezra Sutton 8
459 (a)(Boston NL) 700.00 300.00 175.00
459 (b)(Milwaukee) 725.00 325.00 200.00

(460) Ed Swartwood (Also: Schwartwood) 7
460 (a)(Brooklyn) 700.00 300.00 175.00
460 (b)(Des Moines) 700.00 300.00 175.00
460 (c)(Hamilton) 825.00 375.00 225.00

(461) Park Swartzel 6
461 (a)(Kansas City) 700.00 300.00 175.00

(462) Pete Sweeney (Also: Sweeny) 5
462 (a)(Washington) 1,050 450.00 250.00

(463) Louis Sylvester 1
463 (a)(Sacramento)(VALUE UNDETERMINED)

(464) Pop Tate 6
464 (a)(Baltimore) 700.00 300.00 175.00
464 (b)(Boston NL) 700.00 300.00 175.00

(465) Patsy (Oliver) Tebeau 8
465 (a)(Chicago NL) 700.00 300.00 175.00
465 (b)(Cleveland) 800.00 350.00 200.00

Tearns - See Stearns

(466) John Tener 5
466 (a)(Chicago NL) 1,425 650.00 350.00

(467) Adonis Terry 5
467 (a)(Brooklyn) 700.00 300.00 175.00

(468) Sam Thompson
SEE HALL OF FAME SECTION FOLLOWING

(469) Mike Tiernan 6
469 (a)(New York NL) 700.00 300.00 175.00

(470) Cannonball Titcomb 5
470 (a)(New York NL) 700.00 300.00 175.00

(471) Phil Tomney 4
471 (a)(Louisville) 700.00 300.00 175.00

(472) Steve Toole 7
472 (a)(Brooklyn) 850.00 375.00 225.00
472 (b)(Kansas City) 700.00 300.00 175.00
472 (c)(Rochester) 775.00 350.00 200.00

(473) George Townsend 3
473 (a)(Philadelphia AA) 700.00 300.00 175.00

(474) Bill Traffley 4
474 (a)(Des Moines) 700.00 300.00 175.00

(475) George Treadway (Also: Tredway) 6
475 (a)(Denver) 775.00 350.00 200.00
475 (b)(St. Paul) 775.00 350.00 200.00

(476) Sam Trott 10

476 (a)(Baltimore) 700.00 300.00 175.00
476 (b)(Newark) 700.00 300.00 175.00
DP 22 (Tagging Oyster Burns.) 1,150 500.00 300.00

(477) Tommy Tucker 5
477 (a)(Baltimore) 1,400 600.00 350.00
DP 8 (Being tagged by Chris Fulmer.) 2,100 900.00 500.00

(478) A.M. Tuckerman 5
478 (a)(St. Paul) 700.00 300.00 175.00

(479) George Turner 5
479 (a)(Minneapolis) 700.00 300.00 175.00

(480) Larry Twitchell 6
480 (a)(Cleveland) 700.00 300.00 175.00
480 (b)(Detroit) 700.00 300.00 175.00

(481) Jim Tyng 3
481 (a)(Philadelphia NL) 700.00 300.00 175.00

(482) Bill Van Dyke 3
482 (a)(Des Moines) 700.00 300.00 175.00
482 (b)(Toledo) 700.00 300.00 175.00
DP 19 (W/ Harry Sage.) (Des Moines) 1,150 500.00 300.00
DP 20 (W/ Harry Sage.) (Toledo)) 1,150 500.00 300.00

(483) George Van Haltren 4
483 (a)(Chicago NL) 1,500 675.00 375.00

(484) Farmer Vaughn 7
484 (a)(Louisville) 700.00 300.00 175.00
484 (b)(New York PL) 2,700 1,200 600.00

(485) Peek-A-Boo Veach 4
485 (a)(Sacramento)(VALUE UNDETERMINED)
485 (b)(St. Paul) 700.00 300.00 175.00

(486) Leon Viau 5
486 (a)(Cincinnati) 775.00 350.00 200.00

(487) Bill Vinton 4
487 (a)(Minneapolis) 800.00 350.00 200.00

(488) Joe Visner 5
488 (a)(Brooklyn) 700.00 300.00 175.00

(489) Chris Von Der Ahe 1
489 (a)(St. Louis AA "Brown's Champions") 4,050 1,800 1,000

(490) Reddy Walsh 5
490 (a)(Omaha) 850.00 375.00 225.00

(491) John Ward
SEE HALL OF FAME SECTION FOLLOWING

(492) Ed Warner 2
492 (a)(Milwaukee) 700.00 300.00 175.00
DP 5 (W/ Jack Horner.) 1,150 500.00 300.00

Wassitt - See Messitt

(493) Bill Watkins 2
493 (a)(Detroit) 700.00 300.00 175.00
493 (b)(Kansas City) 900.00 400.00 250.00

(494) Farmer Weaver 4
494 (a)(Louisville) 1,800 900.00 450.00

(495) Charlie Weber 5
495 (a)(Sioux City) 900.00 400.00 250.00

(496) Stump Weidman (Wiedman) 4
496 (a)(Detroit) 700.00 300.00 175.00

(497) Wild Bill Weidner (Widner) 5
497 (a)(Columbus) 900.00 400.00 250.00

(498) Curt Welch (Also: Welsh) 7
498 (a)(St. Louis AA "Brown's Champions") 1,875 850.00 475.00
498 (b)(Philadelphia AA) 800.00 350.00 200.00
DP 23 (W/ Bill Gleason.) 2,300 1,050 575.00

(499) Mickey Welch (Also: Welsh)
SEE HALL OF FAME SECTION FOLLOWING

(500) Jake Wells 2
500 (a)(Kansas City) 1,325 600.00 325.00

(501) Frank Wells 1
501 (a)(Milwaukee) 850.00 375.00 225.00

(502) Joe Werrick 5
502 (a)(Louisville) 700.00 300.00 175.00
502 (b)(St. Paul) 975.00 450.00 250.00

(503) Buck West 5
503 (a)(Minneapolis) 850.00 375.00 225.00

(504) Gus Weyhing 3
504 (a)(Philadelphia AA) 800.00 350.00 200.00

(505) John Weyhing 4
505 (a)(Columbus) 700.00 300.00 175.00
505 (b)(Philadelphia AA) (Never played for Phila.) 1,100 500.00 300.00

(506) Bobby Wheelock 9
506 (a)(Boston NL) 700.00 300.00 175.00
506 (b)(Detroit) (Never played for Detroit.) 700.00 300.00 175.00
506 (c)(Photo actually Con Daily.) 700.00 300.00 175.00

(508) Pat Whitaker (Also: Whitacre) 7
508 (a)(Baltimore) 700.00 300.00 175.00
508 (b)(Philadelphia AA) (Never played for Philadelphia.) 700.00 300.00 175.00

(509) Bill White 5
509 (a)(Louisville) 700.00 300.00 175.00

(510) Deacon White 10
510 (a)(Detroit) 1,550 700.00 375.00
510 (b)(Pittsburgh) 700.00 300.00 175.00

(511) Art Whitney 7
511 (a)(New York NL) 700.00 300.00 175.00
511 (b)(New York PL) 2,700 1,200 600.00
511 (c)(Pittsburgh) 700.00 300.00 175.00
511 (d)(W/dog.) 4,800 2,150 1,200

(512) G. Whitney 5
512 (a)(St. Joseph) 850.00 375.00 225.00

(513) Jim Whitney 4
513 (a)(Indianapolis) 700.00 300.00 175.00
513 (b)(Washington) 750.00 325.00 200.00

E. Williams, W. Williams - See Ned Williamson

(514) Jimmy Williams 2
514 (a)(Cleveland) 1,050 450.00 250.00

(515) Ned Williamson 8
515 (a)(Chicago NL) 1,400 600.00 350.00
515 (c)(in dress clothes) 5,175 2,325 1,300
515 (c)(Chicago PL) 3,000 1,350 750.00
DP 24 (W/ Willie Hahn. (Mascot)) 4,000 1,800 1,000

(516) Tit Willis 5
516 (a)(Omaha) 800.00 350.00 200.00

(517) Walt Wilmot 8
517 (a)(Chicago NL) 700.00 300.00 175.00
517 (b)(Washington) 750.00 325.00 200.00

(518) George Winkleman (Winkelman) 4
518 (a)(Hartford) 2,500 400.00 225.00
518 (b)(Minneapolis) 2,500 400.00 225.00

(519) Sam Wise 5
519 (a)(Boston NL) 1,050 450.00 250.00
519 (b)(Washington) 700.00 300.00 175.00

(520) Chicken Wolf 5
520 (a)(Louisville) 750.00 325.00 200.00

(521) George Wood 5 (L.F.)
521 (a)(Philadelphia NL) 700.00 300.00 175.00
521 (b)(Philadelphia PL) 2,700 1,200 600.00

(522) Pete Wood 5 (P)
522 (a)(Philadelphia NL) 875.00 400.00 225.00

(523) Harry Wright
SEE HALL OF FAME SECTION FOLLOWING

(524) Chief Zimmer 4
524 (a)(Cleveland) 725.00 325.00 200.00

(525) Frank Zinn 3
525 (a)(Philadelphia AA) 700.00 300.00 175.00

1887-1890 Old Judge Hall of Famers Pose Variations

Because of the popularity of collecting Old Judge cards of Hall of Famers, and the sometimes widely varying market values of different poses for those players, this appendix lists each known pose and/or caption variation. These listings disregard the presence, absence or placement of Old Judge advertising within the photo area. Caption variations consider only those machine-printed captions outside of the photo area.

NM EX VG

(11) Cap Anson
11 (a) Street Clothes
(A.C. ANSON, Chicagoes) 10,200 4,600 2,550
(Chicago's) 10,200 4,600 2,550
(ANSON, CAPT., Chicagos (N L)) 15,000 6,750 3,750
11 (b) In Uniform
(Chicago N L) 250,000 75,000 40,000

(25) Jake Beckley
25 (a) Pittsburgh
(Batting, "O" just visible on jersey, Pittsburghs.) 5,400 2,430 1,350
(Batting, "O" just visible on jersey, Pittsburgs.) 5,400 2,425 1,350
(Fielding, ball knee-high, "BECKLEY, 1st B., Pittsburgs.") 5,400 2,430 1,350
(Fielding, hands neck-high, Pittsburgh.) 5,400 2,430 1,350
(Fielding, hands neck-high, "J. BECKLEY, 1st B., Pittsburghs.") 7,800 3,500 1,950
(Fielding, hands neck-high, Pittsburgs.) 5,400 2,430 1,350
25 (b) St. Louis Whites
(Batting, "O" just visible on jersey.) 7,800 3,500 1,950
(Batting, "TLO" visible on jersey.) 7,800 3,500 1,950
(Fielding, ball knee-high, "J. BECKLEY, 1st B., St. Louis Whites.") 10,200 4,600 2,550
(Fielding, hands neck-high, "J. BECKLEY.") 6,000 2,700 1,500

(43) Dan Brouthers
43 (a) Boston, N.L.
(Bat at ready, looking to right, "1st B., Bostons.") 3,600 1,620 900.00
(Fielding, Brouthers on front, Bostons.) 3,120 1,400 780.00
43 (b) Boston, P.L.
(Pose unrecorded.) 7,200 3,240 1,800
43 (c) Detroit
(Bat at ready, looking down at ball.) 4,800 2,160 1,200
(Bat at ready, looking to right, "1st B., Detroits.") 4,500 2,000 1,125
(Fielding, "BROUTHERS, 1st B. Detroits.") 5,100 2,280 1,260
(Fielding, "D. BROUTHERS.") 4,800 2,160 1,200

(78) John Clarkson
78 (a) Boston
(Batting, Bostons.) 2,280 1,025 570.00
(Right arm forward, left hand on thigh, Boston.) 2,280 1,025 570.00
(Right arm forward, left hand on thigh, "P., Bostons.") 2,280 1,025 570.00
(Right arm back, left hand clear of thigh, "P., Bostons.") 3,300 1,470 825.00
(Right hand hip-high, Bostons.) 1,620 725.00 400.00
78 (b) Chicago
(Ball in hands at chest, "P. Chicago.") 3,000 1,350 750.00
(Batting, "P. Chicago.") 3,600 1,620 900.00
(Fielding, hands head-high, "P. Chicago.") 3,600 1,620 900.00
(Right arm forward, left hand on thigh, "P. Chicago.") 4,080 1,830 1,020
(Right arm back, left hand clear of thigh, "P. Chicago.") 3,000 1,350 750.00
(Right arm back, left hand on thigh, "P. Chicago.") 3,000 1,350 750.00
(Right hand hip-high, "P. Chicago.") 3,000 1,350 750.00

(86) Charlie Comiskey
86 (a) St. Louis Browns
("Brown's Champions") 7,620 3,420 1,890
86 (b) St. Louis Browns
(Arms folded.) 5,100 2,300 1,275
(Batting, "COMISKEY, Capt. St. Louis Browns.") 6,720 3,030 1,680
(Fielding, hands head-high, "CHAS. COMISKEY, 1st B., Capt. St. Louis Browns.") 5,100 2,280 1,260
(Fielding, hands shoulder-high, "COMISKEY, Capt. St. Louis.") 5,100 2,280 1,260
(Fielding, hands shoulder-high, "C. COMMISKEY, 1st B., St. L. B's.") 4,800 2,160 1,200
(Sliding, "CHAS. COMISKEY, 1st B., Capt. St. Louis Brown.") 4,800 2,160 1,200
(Sliding, "COMISKEY, Capt., St. Louis.") 4,800 2,160 1,200
86 (c) Chicago, P.L.
(Arms folded, "COMMISKEY, 1st B., Chicagos.") 24,000 10,800 6,000

(88) Roger Connor
88 (a) New York, N.L.
(Batter's box on floor, script name.) 6,900 3,100 1,700
(Bat on shoulder, name in script.) 6,900 3,100 1,700
(Bat on shoulder, N Y's.) 5,100 2,400 1,200
(Fielding, "B. CONNOR," New Yorks.) 5,100 2,400 1,200
(Fielding, hands at waist, "CONNER, 1st B., New Yorks.") 5,100 2,400 1,200
(Hands on knees, name in script.) 6,900 3,100 1,700
(Hands on knees, New York.) 4,800 2,160 1,200
(Hands on knees, New Yorks.) 4,800 2,160 1,200
(Hands on knees, N Y's.) 4,800 2,160 1,200

(124) Ed Delahanty
124 (a)Philadelphia
(Bat on right shoulder, "2d B., Phila.") 14,000 10,000 6,000

(Bat on right shoulder, "2d B., Phila's") 14,000 10,000 6,000
(Bat nearly horizontal, "2d B., Phila.") 14,000 10,000 6,000
(Fielding grounder, Phila.) 13,000 9,000 4,800
(Fielding, hands at waist, "2d B., Phila.") 12,000 7,600 4,200
(Fielding, hands at waist, Phila's.) 13,000 7,600 4,200
(Throwing, "2d B., Phila.") 15,000 10,500 5,900
(Throwing, Phila's.) 15,000 10,500 5,900

(136) Hugh Duffy
136 (a)Chicago, N.L.
(Batting, S.S. Chicago.) 3,600 1,620 900.00
(Batting, "H. DUFFY, S.S., Chicagos.") 3,600 1,625 900.00
(Batting, "DUFFY, S.S., Chicago's.") 3,600 1,620 900.00
(Fielding grounder, "H. DUFFY, S.S., Chicago.") 3,600 1,620 900.00
(Fielding grounder, Chicagos.) 3,600 1,620 900.00
(Fielding, hands chin-high, right heel behind left leg, Chicago.) 3,600 1,620 900.00
(Fielding, hands chin-high, right heel behind left leg, Chicagos.) 3,600 1,620 900.00
(Fielding, hands chin-high, right heel behind left leg, Chicago's.) 3,600 1,620 900.00
(Fielding, hands neck-high, feet apart, Chicago.) 3,600 1,620 900.00
(Throwing, right hand head-high, Chicago.) 3,600 1,620 900.00
(Throwing, right hand head-high, Chicago's.) 3,600 1,620 900.00
136 (b)Chicago, P.L.
(Pose unrecorded.) (VALUE UNDETERMINED)

(149) Buck Ewing
149 (a)New York, N.L.
(Bat at 45 degrees, New Yorks.) 3,300 1,475 825.00
(Bat at 45 degrees, N Y's.) 3,300 1,470 825.00
(Bat in hand at side, New Yorks.) 3,300 1,470 825.00
(Bat nearly horizontal, Capt. New Yorks.) 3,300 1,470 825.00
(Bat nearly horizontal, Captain, New Yorks.) 3,300 1,470 825.00
(Fielding grounder, "BUCK EWING, Capt., New Yorks.") 3,300 1,470 825.00
(Fielding grounder, "EWING, C., New Yorks.") 3,300 1,470 825.00
(Fielding, hands head-high, New Yorks.) 3,300 1,470 825.00
(Fielding, hands head-high, N Y's.) 3,300 1,470 825.00
(Hands on knees, C. New Yorks.) 3,600 1,620 900.00
(Hands on knees, Captain, New Yorks.) 3,600 1,620 900.00
(Hands on knees, Capt. N Y's.) 3,600 1,620 900.00
(Running to left, C., New Yorks.) 3,600 1,620 900.00
(Running to left, Captain, New Yorks.) 3,600 1,620 900.00
(Sliding, C., New York.) 3,600 1,620 900.00
(Sliding, C., New Yorks.) 3,600 1,620 900.00
(Sliding, Capt., New York.) 3,600 1,620 900.00
(Throwing, right arm forward, C., New Yorks.) 4,200 1,900 1,050
(Throwing, right arm forward, Captain, New Yorks.) 4,200 1,900 1,050
(Throwing, right hand waist-high at side, "EWING, Captain, New Yorks.") 4,800 2,160 1,200
149 (b)New York, P.L.
(Hands on knees, C. New York.(PL)) 7,800 3,500 1,950
149 (c)With mascot Willie Breslin.
("EWING & MASCOT, New Yorks") 9,000 4,050 2,250
(N. Y's) 9,000 4,050 2,250
149 (c)"EWING, MASCOT New York P L" (A Fair-Good example sold at auction 5/05 for $7,475.)

(179) Pud Galvin
179 (a)Pittsburgh
(Arms at sides, P. Pittsburg.) 5,400 2,430 1,350
(Arms at sides, P. Pittsburgs.) 5,400 2,430 1,350
(Arms at sides, P. Pittsburgh.) 5,400 2,430 1,350
(Arms at sides, Pitcher.) 5,400 2,430 1,350
(Ball in hands above waist, P.) 4,500 2,000 1,125
(Ball in hands above waist, Pitcher.) 4,500 2,000 1,125
(Bat at ready, P.) 4,500 2,000 1,125
(Bat at ready, Pitcher.) 4,500 2,000 1,125
(Bat in hand at side, "GALVIN, P. Pittsburg.") 8,700 3,900 2,160
(Bat in hand at side, "GALVIN, Pitcher Pittsburg.") 8,750 3,900 2,160
(Bat in hand at side "GALVIN, P., Pittsburgs.") 8,700 3,900 2,160
(Bat in hand at side, "J. GALVIN, P., Pittsburghs.") 8,700 3,900 2,160
(Bat in hand at side, "JIM GALVIN.") 8,700 3,900 2,160

(204) Clark Griffith
204 (a)Milwaukee
(Ball in hands at chest.) 5,100 2,280 1,260
(Batting, looking at ball.) 5,100 2,300 1,275
(Batting, looking at camera, Milwaukee.) 5,100 2,280 1,260
(Batting, looking at camera, Milwaukees.) 6,000 2,700 1,500
(Pitching, hands at neck, Milwaukees.) 5,400 2,430 1,350
(Pitching, right hand head-high, Milwaukees.) 5,100 2,280 1,260

(213) Billy Hamilton
213 (a)Kansas City
(Batting, looking at camera, Kansas Citys.) 3,900 1,750 975.00
(Batting, looking up at ball, "L.F. KANSAS CITYS.") 3,900 1,740 975.00
(Batting, looking up at ball, K.C.s.) 3,900 1,740 975.00
(Fielding grounder.) 3,900 1,740 975.00
(Fielding, hands above waist, "L.F. Kansas Citys.") 3,900 1,740 975.00
(Fielding, hands neck-high, "L.F. Kansas Citys.") 3,900 1,740 975.00
213 (b)Philadelphia, N.L.
(Fielding, hands above waist, Philadelphia N.L.) 2,880 1,300 720.00
(Fielding, hands neck-high, Philadelphia N.L.) 2,880 1,300 720.00

(215) Ned Hanlon
215 (a)Boston
(Never played for Boston.)
(Bat in hand at sides, Bostons.) 3,600 1,620 900.00
215 (b)Detroit
(Bat in hand at side, C.F. Detroits.) 3,600 1,620 900.00
(Batting, Detroits.) 3,600 1,620 900.00
(Fielding, Detroits.) 3,600 1,620 900.00
215 (c)Pittsburgh
(Batting, Pittsburgs.) 3,900 1,620 975.00
(Fielding, C.F., Pittsburghs.) 3,900 1,620 975.00

(256) Tim Keefe
256 (a)New York, N.L.
(Ball in hands, front view, "KEEFE, P., New Yorks.") 3,360 1,500 840.00
(Ball in hands, front view, TIM KEEFE, P. N.Y's.") 3,360 1,500 840.00
(Ball in hands, side view, "JIM KEEFE," New Yorks.) 3,360 1,500 840.00
(Ball in hands, side view, "TIM KEEFE," New Yorks.) 3,360 1,500 840.00
(Ball in hands, side view, "TIM KEEFE, P. N.Y's.") 3,360 1,500 840.00
(Bat nearly horizontal, "KEEFE, P., New Yorks.") 3,360 1,500 840.00
(Bat nearly horizontal, "TIM KEEF," New Yorks.) 3,360 1,500 840.00
(Bat nearly horizontal, "TIM KEEFE," New Yorks.) 3,360 1,500 840.00
(Bat nearly horizontal, "TIM KEEFE," N. Y's.) 3,360 1,500 840.00
(Bat nearly vertical, "TIM KEEFE, P. N.Y's.") 3,360 1,500 840.00
(Pitching, right hand at back, "JIM KEEFE," New Yorks.) 3,600 1,620 900.00
(Pitching, right hand at back, "TIM KEEF," New Yorks.) 3,600 1,620 900.00
(Pitching, right hand at back, "TIM KEEFE," New Yorks.) 3,600 1,620 900.00
(Pitching, right hand at back, "TIM KEEFE," N. Y's.) 3,600 1,620 900.00
(Pitching, right hand head-high, "KEEFE P., New Yorks.") 3,600 1,620 900.00
(Pitching, right hand head-high, "TIM KEEFE, P. N. Y's.") 3,600 1,620 900.00
(Pitching, right hand waist-high, "KEEFE, P., New Yorks.") 2,880 1,300 720.00
(Pitching, right hand waist-high, "TIM KEEFE, P. N.Y's.") 2,880 1,300 720.00
256 (b)New York, P.L.
(Pose unrecorded.) (VALUE UNDETERMINED))
DP 12 Tagging Danny Richardson.
("KEEFE, P., New Yorks") 2,700 1,225 675.00
("Keefe & Richardson") 2,700 1,200 675.00
("Keefe and Richardson Stealing 2d, N.Y's") 2,700 1,200 675.00
DP 13 Fielding Ball, Danny Richardson Sliding.
("Keefe and Richardson Stealing 2d, N.Y's") 3,600 1,620 900.00

(261) King Kelly
261 (a)Chicago
(Bat at 45 degrees, left-handed, "$10,000 KELLY" Chicago on jersey.) 7,500 3,375 1,875
(Portrait, bare head, "$10,000 KELLY," Chicago on jersey.) 9,300 3,970 2,300
(Portrait in cap, "$10,000 KELLY," Chicago on jersey.) 7,800 3,500 1,950
261 (b)Boston, N.L.
(Bat at 45 degrees, "$10,000 KELLY.") 7,200 3,240 1,800
(Bat at 45 degrees, no position, Boston.) 6,000 2,700 1,500
(Bat at 45 degrees, "Kelly, C., Boston.") 4,800 2,160 1,200
(Bat at 45 degrees, "Kelly, C., Bostons.") 4,800 2,160 1,200
(Bat horizontal, "$10,000 KELLY.") 6,000 2,700 1,500
(Bat in left hand at side, "$10,000 KELLY.") 6,000 2,700 1,500
(Bat on right shoulder, "$10,000 KELLY.") 7,200 3,240 1,800
(Fielding, hands chest-high, "$10,000 KELLY.") 6,000 2,700 1,500
(Fielding, hands head-high, "$10,000 KELLY.") 6,000 2,700 1,500
(Portrait, bare head, "$10,000 KELLY," Boston on jersey.) 11,400 5,130 2,850
261 (c)Boston, P.L.
(Bat at 45 degrees, no position, Boston. (PL) (VALUE UNDETERMINED)

(290) Connie Mack
290 (a)Washington
(Batting, C.) 10,800 4,860 2,700
(Batting, Catcher.) 10,800 4,860 2,700
(Stooping, hands on knees, C. Washington.) 10,800 4,860 2,700
(Stooping, hands on knees, Catcher.) 10,800 4,860 2,700
(Throwing, C.) 10,800 4,860 2,700
(Throwing, Catcher, "C. MACK.") 10,800 4,860 2,700
(Throwing, Catcher, "MACK.") 10,800 4,860 2,700

(307) Tommy McCarthy
307 (a)Philadelphia, N.L.
(Batting, indoor background, "2d B. Phila.") 4,200 1,900 1,050
(Batting, indoor background, "McCARTHY, Second Base, Philadelphia.") 4,200 1,900 1,050
(Fielding, hands chest-high, "McCARTHY, 2d B. Phila.") 5,400 2,430 1,350
(Fielding, hands chest-high, Philadelphia.) 5,400 2,430 1,350
(Sliding, indoor background, 2d B. Phila.) 4,800 2,160 1,200
(Sliding, Philadelphia.) 4,800 2,160 1,200
(Tagging player, Phila.) 4,200 1,900 1,050
(Tagging player, Philadelphia.) 4,200 1,900 1,050
(Throwing, 2d B. Phila.) 4,200 1,900 1,050
(Throwing, Philadelphia.) 4,200 1,900 1,050
307 (b)St. Louis Browns
(Batting, indoor background, St. Louis Browns.) 3,300 1,470 825.00
(Batting, outdoor background, St. Louis.) 3,300 1,470 825.00
(Batting, outdoor background, St. Louis Browns.) 3,300 1,470 825.00
(Fielding, hands chest-high, 2d B. St. Louis.) 3,300 1,470 825.00
(Fielding, hands chest-high, C.F.) 3,300 1,470 825.00
(Fielding, hands head-high, "TOMMY CARTHY," St. Louis Brown.) 3,300 1,470 825.00
(Fielding, hands head-high, "TOMMY McCARTHY," St. Louis Brown.) 3,300 1,470 825.00
(Fielding, hands head-high, "cCARTHY, C. F. St. Louis Brown.") 3,300 1,470 825.00
(Fielding, hands head-high, "TOMMY McCARTHY" St. Louis Browns.) 3,300 1,470 825.00
(Fielding, hands head-high, "T. McCARTHY, C.F., St. Louis Browns.) 3,300 1,470 825.00
(Sliding, indoor background, "McCARTHY, 2d B. St. Louis.") 3,300 1,470 825.00
(Sliding, indoor background, C.F., St. Louis.) 3,300 1,470 825.00
(Sliding, outdoor background, St. Louis.) 3,300 1,470 825.00
(Sliding, outdoor background, C.F. St. Louis Browns.) 3,300 1,470 825.00
(Tagging player, 2d B.) 3,300 1,470 825.00
(Tagging player, C.F.) 3,300 1,470 825.00
(Throwing, "T. McCARTHY," St. Louis.) 3,600 1,620 900.00
(Throwing, "T. McCARTHY," St. Louis Browns.) 3,600 1,620 900.00
(Throwing, "McCARTHY," St. Louis Browns.) 3,600 1,620 900.00
(Throwing, "McCARTHY, C.F., St. Louis.") 3,600 1,620 900.00

(323) Bid McPhee
323 (a)Cincinnati
(Batting, looking at ball, "McPHEE.") 22,500 10,125 5,625
(Batting, looking at ball, "JOHN McPHEE.") 22,500 10,125 5,625
(Batting, looking at camera, Cincinnati.) 22,500 10,125 5,625
(Batting, looking at camera, Cincinnati. (NL)) 22,500 10,125 5,625
(Batting, looking at camera, Cincinnatti.) 22,500 10,125 5,625
(Fielding, hands ankle-high, "McPHEE, 2d B., Cincinnat.") 22,500 10,125 5,625
(Fielding, hands ankle-high, "JOHN McPHEE, 2d B., Cincinnatis.") 22,500 10,125 5,625
(Fielding, hands head-high, "McPHEE, 2d B., Cincinnati.") 22,500 10,125 5,625
(Fielding, hands head-high, "JOHN McPHEE, 2d B. Cincinnati.") 22,500 10,125 5,625
(Fielding, hands head-high, "McPHEE, 2d B., Cincinnatis.") 22,500 10,125 5,625

(Fielding, hands head-high, Cincinnati.)	22,500	10,125	5,625
(Throwing, Cincinnati.)	22,500	10,125	5,625
(Throwing, Cincinnati.)	22,500	10,125	5,625
(349) Kid Nichols			
349 (a)Omaha			
(Batting, looking at ball, Omaha.)	9,000	4,050	2,250
(Batting, looking at camera, Omaha.)	9,000	4,050	2,250
(Batting, looking at camera, "NICHOLS, P., Omahas.")	9,000	4,050	2,250
(Pitching, hands at chest, Omaha.)	9,000	4,050	2,250
(Pitching, right hand behind back, Omaha.)	9,600	4,320	2,400
(Pitching, right hand behind back, "NICHOLS, P., Omahas.")	9,600	4,320	2,400
(Pitching, right hand forward, P., Omaha.)	9,600	4,320	2,400
(Pitching, right hand forward, P., Omahas.)	9,600	4,320	2,400
(366) Orator Jim O'Rourke			
366 (a)New York, N.L.			
(Bat in hand at side, C., New Yorks.)	6,000	2,700	1,500
(Bat in hand at side, 3d B., New Yorks.)	6,000	2,700	1,500
(Bat in hand at side, 3d B. N.Y's.)	6,000	2,700	1,500
(Bat in hand at side, 3d B., N. Y's.)	6,000	2,700	1,500
(Batting, 3d B., New Yorks.)	6,000	2,700	1,500
(Batting, 3d B., N. Y's.)	6,000	2,700	1,500
(Fielding, "JIM O'ROURKE, 3d B. N. Y's.")	4,200	1,900	1,050
(Throwing, 3d B., N. Y's.)	4,800	2,160	1,200
(386) Old Hoss Radbourn			
386 (a)Boston, N.L.			
(Bat on shoulder, P., Boston.)	3,900	1,740	975.00
(Bat on shoulder, P., Bostons.)	3,900	1,750	975.00
(Bat on shoulder, Pitcher, Boston.)	3,900	1,740	975.00
(Bat on shoulder, Pitcher, Bostons.)	3,900	1,740	975.00
(Hands at waist, no space visible between hands and belt, P.)	3,600	1,620	900.00
(Hands at waist, no space visible between hands and belt, Pitcher.)	3,600	1,620	900.00
(Hands at waist, white uniform visible between hands and belt, P.)	4,800	2,160	1,200
(Hands at waist, white uniform visible between hands and belt, Pitcher.)	4,800	2,160	1,200
(Hands on hips, P.)	10,800	4,860	2,700
(Hands on hips, Pitcher.)	10,800	4,860	2,700
(Portrait, P., Boston.)	9,600	4,320	2,400
(Portrait, Pitcher, Boston.)	9,900	4,440	2,430
(Tagging Billy Nash, P., Boston.)	5,400	2,430	1,350
(Tagging Billy Nash, Pitcher.)	5,400	2,430	1,350
386 (b)Boston, P.L.			
(Hands on hips, Pitcher, Boston.(PL) (VALUE UNDETERMINED)			
(398) Wilbert Robinson			
398 (a)Philadelphia Athletics			
(Batting)	4,800	2,150	1,200
(Fielding, hands above head, C. Athletics.)	4,800	2,160	1,200
(Fielding, hands above head, C., Athletics.)	4,800	2,160	1,200
(Fielding, hands neck-high, C. Athletics.)	4,800	2,160	1,200
(Fielding, hands thigh-high.)	4,800	2,160	1,200
(Throwing)	4,800	2,160	1,200
(404) Amos Rusie			
404 (a)Indianapolis			
(Batting, P., Indianapolis.)	4,200	1,900	1,050
(Pitching, hands at neck.)	4,200	1,900	1,050
(Pitching, right hand forward chin-high.)	4,200	1,900	1,050
(Pitching, right hand head-high to side, "RUSIE, P., Indianapolis.")	6,000	2,700	1,500
(Pitching, right hand head-high to side, "RUSSIE.")	6,000	2,700	1,500
(Ball in right hand, thigh-high "P., Indianapolis.")	6,300	2,820	1,560
404 (b)New York, N.L.			
(Pitching, hands at neck, New Yorks.(NL))	24,000	10,800	6,000
(Pitching, right hand forward chin-high, New Yorks.(NL))	24,000	10,800	6,000
(468) Sam Thompson			
468 (a)Detroit			
(Arms folded, R.F. Detroits.)	3,300	1,475	825.00
(Bat at 45 degrees, Detroits.)	3,900	1,740	975.00
(Bat in hand at side, Detroits.)	4,200	1,900	1,050
(Batting, ball above head, Detroits.)	3,000	1,350	750.00
(Batting, ball chest-high, R.F. Detroits.)	3,000	1,350	750.00
468 (b)Philadelphia, N.L.			
(Arms folded, Phil'a.(NL))	2,640	1,190	660.00
(Bat in hand at side, Philadelphia.)	2,640	1,190	660.00
(Bat in hand at side, R.F., Philadelphias.)	2,640	1,190	660.00
(Bat in hand at side, Phila's.)	2,640	1,190	660.00
(491) John Ward			
491 (a)New York, N.L.			
(Batting, New Yorks.)	2,880	1,300	720.00
(Batting, "Capt. JOHN WARD, S.S. N Y's.")	2,880	1,300	720.00
(Cap in hand at side, "Capt. JOHN WARD.")	4,200	1,900	1,050
(Cap in hand at side, "J. WARD, S.S., New Yorks.")	4,200	1,900	1,050
(Cap in hand at side, "JOHN WARD.")	4,200	1,900	1,050
(Hands behind back, New Yorks.)	3,000	1,350	750.00
(Hands behind back, "Capt. JOHN WARD, S.S. N. Y's.")	3,000	1,350	750.00
(Hands on hips, "J.M. WARD, S.S. New Yorks.")	4,500	2,000	1,125
(Hands on hips, "Capt. JOHN WARD, S.S. N. Y's.")	6,600	2,970	1,650
(Portrait, "Capt. JOHN WARD.")	5,400	2,430	1,350
(Portrait, "J. WARD, S.S., New Yorks.")	5,400	2,430	1,350
(Portrait, "J.M. WARD, S.S., New Yorks.")	5,400	2,430	1,350
(Sliding, left hand raised, "Capt. JOHN WARD, S.S. N Y's.")	2,640	1,190	660.00
(Sliding, left hand raised, "J.M. WARD, S.S., New Yorks.")	2,640	1,190	660.00
(Sliding, left hand raised, "WARD.")	2,640	1,190	660.00
(Sliding, right hand raised, New Yorks.)	3,000	1,350	750.00
(Sliding, right hand raised, "Capt. JOHN WARD, S.S. N Y's.")	3,000	1,350	750.00
(Throwing, left profile, New Yorks.)	4,200	1,900	1,050
(Throwing, left profile, "Capt. JOHN WARD, S.S. N. Y's.")	4,200	1,900	1,050
(Throwing, right profile, "Capt. JOHN WARD, S.S. N. Y's.")	4,200	1,900	1,050
(Throwing, right profile, "JOHN WARD.")	4,200	1,900	1,050
(499) Mickey Welch			
499 (a)New York, N.L.			
(Ball in hands above waist, "SMILING MICKEY.")	5,400	2,425	1,350
(Ball in hands above waist, "WELSH.")	5,400	2,430	1,350
(Right arm extended forward, "SMILING MICKEY.")	5,400	2,430	1,350
(Right hand at right thigh, "WELCH," New Yorks.)	5,400	2,430	1,350
(Right hand at right thigh, "WELCH," New Yorks.(NL))	5,400	2,430	1,350
(Right hand at right thigh, "WELSH," New Yorks.)	5,400	2,430	1,350
(Right hand head-high, "WELCH," New York.)	5,400	2,430	1,350
(Right hand head-high, "WELCH", N.Y's.)	5,400	2,430	1,350
(Right hand head-high, "WELSH," New York.)	5,400	2,430	1,350
(523) Harry Wright			
523 (a)Philadelphia, N.L.			
(Portrait, looking to his right, beard clear of right side of collar, "HARRY WRIGHT, Man'g. Philas.")	18,000	8,100	4,500
(Portrait, looking to his right, beard just over right side of collar, "Mgr., Phila. N L.")	18,000	8,100	4,500
(Portrait, looking to his right, beard just over right side of collar, "Man'g. Phila.")	18,000	8,100	4,500
(Portrait, looking to his right, beard just over right side of collar, "Mgr. Phila's.")	18,000	8,100	4,500
(Portrait, looking to his left, "Man'g. Phila.")	18,000	8,100	4,500
(Portrait, looking to his left, "Man'g. Philas.")	18,000	8,100	4,500
(Portrait, looking to his left, Phila. (NL))	19,200	8,640	4,800
(Portrait, looking to his left, "Mgr. Phila's.")	18,000	8,100	5,400

1888-1889 Old Judge Cabinets (N173)

These cabinet cards were issued by Goodwin & Co. in 1888-89 as a premium available by exchanging coupons found in Old Judge or Dogs Head brand cigarettes. The cabinet cards consist of 3-3/4" x 5-3/4" photographs affixed to a cardboard backing that measures approximately 4-1/4" x 6-1/2". The mounting is usually pale yellow with gold-leaf trimmings, but backings have also been found in red, blue or black. An ad for Old Judge Cigarettes appears along the bottom of the cabinet. Cabinets obtained by exchanging coupons from Dogs Head cigarettes include an ad for both Old Judge and Dogs Head, and are scarcer. According to an advertising sheet, cabinets were available of "every prominent player in the National League, Western League and American Association." There will continue to be additions to this checklist. This list includes all confirmed photo and team variations; minor differences in

spelling of team name, position abbreviations or punctuation are not recorded, except in the case of Hall of Famers. Several Old Judge cabinets are not known to exist in the standard N172 format.

		NM	EX	VG
	Common Player:	2,200	1,300	925.00
	Black or Colored Mount: 2X			
	Unlisted Dogs Head: 2-3X			
(4)	Bob Allen			
4 (a)	Pittsburgh, hands clasped at waist	2,200	1,300	925.00
4 (b)	Pittsburgh, batting, Dogs Head	5,250	3,150	2,250
(7)	Varney Anderson			
7 (a)	pitching, right hand head-high	2,200	1,300	925.00
(8)	Ed Andrews			
8 (a)	Philadelphia, both hands shoulder-high	2,200	1,300	925.00
8 (b)	Philadelphia, one hand above head	2,200	1,300	925.00
DP 1	being tagged by Buster Hoover	3,750	2,250	1,625
(9)	Wally Andrews			
9 (a)	Omaha, hands shoulder-high	2,200	1,300	925.00
(11)	Cap Anson			
11 (a)	portrait	20,250	12,150	8,700
11 (b)	portrait, Dogs Head	45,000	27,000	18,750
(15)	Kid Baldwin			
15 (a)	ball in right hand, head-high	2,200	1,300	925.00
(16)	Lady Baldwin			
16 (a)	Detroit, pitching, left hand head-high	2,200	1,300	925.00
(17)	Mark Baldwin			
17 (a)	Chicago, batting, heels together	2,200	1,300	925.00
17 (b)	Chicago, pitching, right hand above head	2,200	1,300	925.00
17 (c)	Chicago, pitching, right hand waist-high	2,200	1,300	925.00
(20)	John Barnes			
20 (a)	portrait	2,200	1,300	925.00
(21)	Billy Barnie			
21 (a)	portrait	3,000	1,800	1,300
(22)	Charley Bassett			
22 (a)	Indianapolis, bat at ready	2,200	1,300	925.00
(23)	Charlie Bastian			
23 (a)	Chicago, bat over shoulder	2,200	1,300	925.00
23 (b)	Chicago, fielding, hands chest-high	2,200	1,300	925.00
23 (c)	Philadelphia, stooping to field low ball	2,200	1,300	925.00
DP 2	Philadelphia, tagging Pop Schriver	3,750	2,250	1,625
(24)	Ed Beatin			
24 (a)	pitching, right arm forward	2,200	1,300	925.00
(27)	Charlie Bennett			
27 (a)	batting	2,200	1,300	925.00
27 (b)	batting, Dogs Head	5,250	3,150	2,250
(28)	Lou Bierbauer			
28 (a)	fielding grounder	2,200	1,300	925.00
28 (b)	fielding, hands chest-high	3,375	2,000	1,450
28 (c)	throwing	3,750	2,250	1,650
(31)	Ned Bligh			
31 (a)	fielding, hands head-high	2,200	1,300	925.00
(32)	Bogart			
32 (a)	fielding, hands chest-high	2,200	1,300	925.00
(35)	Henry Boyle			
35 (a)	Indianapolis, pitch., right arm extended	2,200	1,300	925.00
(36)	Jack Boyle			
36 (a)	St. Louis, bat at side	2,200	1,300	925.00
36 (b)	St. Louis, bat at ready	2,200	1,300	925.00

36 (c)	St. Louis, catching, hands knee-high	2,200	1,300	925.00
(37)	George Bradley			
37 (a)	Sioux City, fielding, looking up at ball	2,200	1,300	925.00
(43)	Dan Brouthers			
43 (a)	Boston, batting	5,625	3,375	2,400
43 (b)	Boston, batting, Dogs Head	9,750	5,850	4,200
43 (c)	Boston, fielding, hands at waist	5,625	3,375	2,400
43 (d)	Boston, throwing, horizontal format	6,000	3,600	2,600
43 (e)	Detroit, batting	5,625	3,375	2,400
(44)	Tom Brown			
44 (a)	Boston, bat at ready	2,200	1,300	925.00
44 (b)	Boston, fielding	2,200	1,300	925.00
(45)	Willard (California) Brown			
45 (a)	New York, bat at side	2,200	1,300	925.00
45 (b)	New York, throwing, mask in left hand	2,200	1,300	925.00
(46)	Pete Browning			
46 (a)	batting, feet together	5,625	3,375	2,400
(47)	Charlie Brynan			
47 (a)	Chicago, pitching, right arm neck-high	2,200	1,300	925.00
47 (b)	Des Moines, pitching, right arm forward	2,200	1,300	925.00
(48)	Al Buckenberger			
48 (a)	portrait, looking right	2,200	1,300	925.00
(49)	Dick Buckley			
49 (a)	Indianapolis, fielding, hands chest-high	2,200	1,300	925.00
(50)	Charlie Buffinton			
50 (a)	fielding, hands chest-high	2,200	1,300	925.00
50 (b)	pitch., right hand above head, Dogs Head	9,000	5,400	3,850
(52)	Jack Burdock			
52 (a)	fielding grounder	2,200	1,300	925.00
(56)	Jim Burns			
56 (a)	Kansas City, fielding grounder	2,200	1,300	925.00
(58)	Oyster Burns			
58 (a)	Brooklyn, bat at ready vertically	2,200	1,300	925.00
58 (b)	Brooklyn, throwing, right hand head-high	2,200	1,300	925.00
(59)	Tom Burns			
59 (a)	Chicago, bat at side	2,200	1,300	925.00
59 (b)	Chicago, bat at ready	2,200	1,300	925.00
59 (b)	Chicago, fielding	2,200	1,300	925.00
59 (c)	Chicago, tagging player	2,850	1,725	1,225
(60)	Doc Bushong			
60 (a)	stooping, hands waist-high	2,200	1,300	925.00
60 (b)	throwing	3,750	2,250	1,625
(63)	Jimmy Canavan			
63 (a)	batting	2,200	1,300	925.00
(66)	Hick Carpenter			
66 (a)	batting	2,200	1,300	925.00
(68)	Fred Carroll			
68 (a)	Pittsburgh, throwing	2,200	1,300	925.00
(69)	Scrappy Carroll			
69 (a)	St. Paul, fielding, hands chest-high	3,375	2,000	1,450
(70)	Ed Cartwright			
70 (a)	St. Joseph, throwing	2,200	1,300	925.00
(71)	Bob Caruthers			
71 (a)	batting, feet apart	2,200	1,300	925.00
71 (b)	holding ball in left hand, neck-high	7,125	4,275	3,000
(72)	Daniel Casey			
72 (a)	pitching, left hand shoulder-high	2,200	1,300	925.00
(73)	Elton Chamberlain			
73 (a)	batting, looking at camera	2,200	1,300	925.00
73 (b)	pitching, hands chest-high	2,200	1,300	925.00
73 (c)	pitching, right hand head-high	2,200	1,300	925.00
(74)	Cupid Childs			
74 (a)	fielding	2,200	1,300	925.00
(75)	Bob Clark			
75 (a)	Brookyln, fielding, hands shoulder-high	2,200	1,300	925.00
75 (b)	Brooklyn, throwing	2,200	1,300	925.00
DP 4	Brooklyn, tagging Mickey Hughes	6,750	4,050	2,875
DP 4	Brooklyn, tagging M. Hughes, Dogs Head	8,250	4,950	3,550
	Clark, Chicago - See Dad Clarke			
(76)	Spider Clark			
76 (a)	Washington, pose unrecorded	2,200	1,300	925.00
(77)	Dad Clark (Clarke)			
77 (a)	Chicago, right arm extended forward	2,200	1,300	925.00
77 (b)	Omaha, batting	2,200	1,300	925.00
(78)	John Clarkson			
78 (a)	Boston, batting	5,250	3,150	2,250
78 (b)	Boston, right arm forward, left on thigh	7,125	4,275	3,075
78 (c)	Boston, pitching, right arm back	5,250	3,150	2,250
78 (d)	Boston, pitching, arm back, Dogs Head	10,500	6,300	4,500
(79)	Jack Clements			
79 (a)	batting	2,200	1,300	925.00
79 (b)	fielding	3,225	1,950	1,375
79 (c)	hands on knees	2,200	1,300	925.00
(80)	Elmer Cleveland			
80 (a)	pose unrecorded	2,200	1,300	925.00
(81)	Monk Cline			
81 (a)	bat nearly vertical	2,200	1,300	925.00
(83)	John Coleman			
83 (a)	ball in hands at waist	2,200	1,300	925.00
83 (b)	bat in hands below waist	2,200	1,300	925.00
(85)	Hub Collins			
85 (a)	Brooklyn, batting	2,200	1,300	925.00
85 (b)	Brooklyn, fielding, hands chest-high	2,200	1,300	925.00
(86)	Charlie Comiskey			
86 (a)	arms folded	7,500	4,500	3,225
86 (b)	fielding, hands neck-high, ball visible	7,500	4,500	3,225
86 (c)	fielding, hands shoulder-high, no ball	11,250	6,750	4,825
86 (d)	sliding	14,250	8,550	6,100
(88)	Roger Connor			
88 (a)	batting, home plate, batter's boxes on floor	11,250	6,750	4,825
88 (b)	batting, outdoors scene on backdrop	9,750	6,000	4,200
88 (c)	fielding, hands at waist	7,500	4,500	3,225
88 (d)	hands on knees	7,500	4,500	3,225
(89)	Dick Conway			
90 (a)	Boston, bat in hand at side	4,500	2,700	1,950
(90)	Jim Conway			
90 (a)	Kansas City, pitching, left ear visible	2,200	1,300	925.00
90 (b)	K.C., pitching, left ear not visible	2,200	1,300	925.00
(91)	Pete Conway			
91 (a)	Detroit, pitching, right hand extended	2,200	1,300	925.00
(92)	Paul Cook			
92 (a)	fielding in mask	2,200	1,300	925.00
92 (b)	tagging baserunner	2,200	1,300	925.00
(93)	Jimmy Cooney			
93 (a)	batting, Omaha, Dogs Head	5,250	3,150	2,250
(95)	Pop Corkhill			
95 (a)	Brooklyn, batting	2,200	1,300	925.00
95 (b)	Brooklyn, fielding, hands neck-high	2,200	1,300	925.00
(96)	Cannonball Crane			
96 (a)	New York, pitching, right hand head-high	2,200	1,300	925.00
(99)	John Crooks			
99 (a)	Omaha, pose unrecorded	2,200	1,300	925.00
(100)	Lave Cross			
100 (a)	Louisville, hands on thighs	2,200	1,300	925.00
(105)	Bert Cunningham			
105 (a)	both arms waist level	2,200	1,300	925.00
(109)	Edward Dailey			
109 (a)	Columbus, pitching, right hand head-high	2,200	1,300	925.00
109 (b)	Washington, pitch., right hand head-high	2,200	1,300	925.00
(111)	Bill Daley			
111 (a)	Boston, pitching, hands above waist	2,200	1,300	925.00
(112)	Con Daley (Daily)			
112 (a)	Indianapolis, right hand on hip	2,200	1,300	925.00
(113)	Abner Dalrymple			
113 (a)	Pittsburgh, hands on hips, feet apart	2,200	1,300	925.00
(114)	Sun Daly			
114 (a)	Minneapolis, fielding, hands chest-high	2,200	1,300	925.00
(115)	Tom Daly			
115 (a)	Chicago, fielding, hands chest-high	2,200	1,300	925.00
115 (b)	Chicago, hands on knees	2,200	1,300	925.00
115 (c)	Washington, fielding, hands chest-high	2,200	1,300	925.00
(117)	Dell Darling			
117 (a)	fielding, hands waist-high	2,200	1,300	925.00
(118)	William Darnbrough			
118 (a)	pitching	2,200	1,300	925.00
(123)	Harry Decker			
123 (a)	bat nearly horizontal	2,200	1,300	925.00
(124)	Ed Delehanty			
124 (a)	bat by shoulder	31,250	5,400	3,875
124 (b)	bat horizontal	9,000	5,400	3,875
124 (c)	fielding	22,500	13,500	9,675
(125)	Jerry Denny			
125 (a)	Indianapolis, batting	2,200	1,300	925.00
125 (b)	Indianapolis, fielding	2,200	1,300	925.00
(126)	Jim Devlin			
126 (a)	pitching, left hand shoulder-high	2,200	1,300	925.00
126 (b)	sliding	2,200	1,300	925.00
(130)	Jim Donnelly			
130 (a)	batting	2,200	1,300	925.00
(133)	Mike Dorgan			
133 (a)	sliding, horizontal format	3,375	2,000	1,450
(135)	Charlie Duffe (Duffee)			
135 (a)	batting	2,200	1,300	925.00
135 (b)	fielding, bending to left	2,200	1,300	925.00
135 (c)	fielding grounder	2,200	1,300	925.00
135 (d)	fielding, standing upright	2,200	1,300	925.00
(136)	Hugh Duffy			
136 (a)	batting	4,875	2,925	2,100
136 (b)	fielding, hands chin-high	4,875	2,925	2,100
136 (c)	fielding grounder	6,000	3,600	2,600
(138)	Martin Duke			
138 (a)	ball in hands, chest-high	3,750	2,250	1,625
(139)	Fred Dunlap			
139 (a)	arms at side	2,200	1,300	925.00
139 (b)	holding ball aloft	2,200	1,300	925.00
139 (c)	holding ball aloft, Dogs Head	4,500	2,700	1,950
(141)	Jesse Duryea			
141 (a)	batting	2,200	1,300	925.00
(142)	Frank Dwyer			
142 (a)	bat at side	3,750	2,250	1,625
142 (b)	bat in air	2,200	1,300	925.00
142 (c)	fielding	2,200	1,300	925.00
(143)	Billy Earle			
143 (a)	Cincinnati, fielding, hands over head	2,200	1,300	925.00
(145)	Red Ehret			
145 (a)	batting	2,200	1,300	925.00
(147)	Dude Esterbrook			
147 (a)	Indianapolis, fielding grounder	2,200	1,300	925.00
147 (b)	Indianapolis, fielding, hands chest-high	2,200	1,300	925.00
147 (c)	Louisville, fielding, hands chest high	2,200	1,300	925.00
(149)	Buck Ewing			
149 (a)	New York, bat at side	6,000	3,600	2,600
149 (b)	New York, bat in air	6,000	3,600	2,600
149 (c)	New York, fielding, hands head-high	6,000	3,600	2,600
149 (d)	New York, hands on knees	6,000	3,600	2,600
149 (e)	New York, throwing, right arm extended forward	9,000	5,400	3,875
149 (f)	New York, with mascot Willie Breslin	22,500	13,500	9,675
149 (g)	New York, w/ mascot, Dogs Head	26,250	15,750	11,275
(150)	John Ewing			
150 (a)	Louisville, bat almost vertical	2,200	1,300	925.00
(151)	Jay Faatz			
151 (a)	throwing	2,200	1,300	925.00
151 (b)	batting	2,200	1,300	925.00
(152)	Bill Farmer			
152 (a)	Pittsburgh, hands on knees	2,200	1,300	925.00
(154)	Sid Farrar			
154 (a)	fielding grounder	2,200	1,300	925.00
154 (b)	fielding, hands head-high	2,200	1,300	925.00
(155)	Duke Farrell			
155 (a)	Chicago, fielding grounder	2,200	1,300	925.00
155 (b)	Chicago, hands on knees	2,200	1,300	925.00
(157)	Frank Fennelly			
157 (a)	Cincinnati, fielding grounder	2,200	1,300	925.00
(158)	Charlie Ferguson			
158 (a)	pitching, hands at chest	2,200	1,300	925.00
(159)	Alex Ferson			
159 (a)	pitching, hands neck-high, looking front	2,200	1,300	925.00
(161)	Jocko Fields			
161 (a)	hands on thighs	2,200	1,300	925.00
(164)	Silver Flint			
164 (a)	batting	2,200	1,300	925.00
164 (b)	catching, with mask, hands waist-high	3,000	1,800	1,300
(167)	Jim Fogarty			
167 (a)	batting	2,200	1,300	925.00

167 (b) fielding, hands neck-high 2,200 1,300 925.00
167 (c) running to left 2,200 1,300 925.00
167 (d) sliding 2,200 1,300 925.00

(168) Frank Foreman
168 (a) Baltimore, ball in hands by right thigh 3,375 2,000 1,450

(170) Elmer Foster
170 (a) Minneapolis, batting 2,200 1,300 925.00
170 (b) New York, fielding 2,200 1,300 925.00

(171) Dave Foutz
171 (a) bat at 45 degrees 2,200 1,300 925.00
171 (b) throwing 2,200 1,300 925.00

(175) Shorty Fuller
175 (a) St. Louis, fielding 2,200 1,300 925.00
175 (b) St. Louis, hands on knees 2,200 1,300 925.00
175 (c) St. Louis, swinging bat 2,200 1,300 925.00

(177) Chris Fulmer
DP 8 tagging Tom Tucker, Dogs Head 6,750 4,050 2,875

(179) Pud Galvin
179 (a) batting 5,625 3,375 2,400
.00 .00 .00

(181) Charlie Ganzel .00 .00 .00
181 (a) Boston, batting 2,200 1,300 925.00
181 (b) Boston, fielding, hands shoulder-high 3,750 2,250 1,625
181 (c) Boston, fielding, hands thigh-high 2,200 1,300 925.00

(182) Gid Gardner
182 (a) Philadelphia, fielding low ball 2,200 1,300 925.00

(183) Hank Gastreich
183 (a) pitching, left hand by thigh 2,200 1,300 925.00

(185) Frank Genins
185 (a) batting, looking at ball 2,200 1,300 925.00
185 (b) batting, looking at camera 2,200 1,300 925.00

(186) Bill George
186 (a) bat at side 2,200 1,300 925.00

(188) Charlie Getzein (Getzien)
188 (a) pitching, hands above waist 2,200 1,300 925.00

(190) Bobby Gilks
190 (a) batting 2,200 1,300 925.00

(192) Barney Gilligan
192 (a) Washington, fielding 2,200 1,300 925.00

(193) Frank Gilmore
193 (a) pitching, hands neck-high 2,200 1,300 925.00

(194) Jack Glasscock
194 (a) Indianapolis, bat at side, Dogs Head 5,250 3,150 2,250
194 (b) Indianapolis, hands on knees 2,200 1,300 925.00
194 (c) Indianapolis, throwing 2,200 1,300 925.00

(195) Bill Gleason
195 (a) Louisville, batting 2,200 1,300 925.00
195 (b) Louisville, stooping, hands clasped 2,200 1,300 925.00
DP 23 with Curt Welch 3,375 2,025 1,450

(196) Kid Gleason
196 (a) Philadelphia, fielding grounder 3,375 2,025 1,450
196 (b) Philadelphia, ball in hands at chin 3,375 2,025 1,450

(197) Ed Glenn
197 (a) fielding, hands neck-high 2,200 1,300 925.00

(199) George Gore
199 (a) bat nearly horizontal 2,200 1,300 925.00
199 (b) bat at ready over left shoulder 2,200 1,300 925.00
199 (c) fielding grounder 2,200 1,300 925.00

(205) Henry Gruber
205 (a) pitching, right hand chin-high 2,200 1,300 925.00

(206) Ad Gumbert
206 (a) pitching, right hand eye-high 3,150 1,875 1,350
206 (b) pitching, right hand waist-high 2,200 1,300 925.00

(207) Tom Gunning
207 (a) bending forward, hands by right knee 2,200 1,300 925.00

(208) Joe Gunson
208 (a) wearing jacket 2,200 1,300 925.00

(212) Bill Hallman
212 (a) leaning left to catch ball chest-high 2,200 1,300 925.00

(213) Billy Hamilton
213 (a) Kansas City, batting: looking at camera 9,000 5,400 3,875
213 (b) Kansas City, fielding, hands neck-high 9,000 5,400 3,875
213 (c) Kansas City, fielding grounder 9,000 5,400 3,875

(215) Ned Hanlon
215 (a) Detroit, batting 4,500 2,700 1,950
215 (b) Pittsburgh, fielding 4,875 2,925 2,100

(216) Bill Hanrahan
216 (a) bat at side 2,200 1,300 925.00

(221) Gil Hatfield
221 (a) bat at waist 2,200 1,300 925.00
221 (b) bat over shoulder 2,200 1,300 925.00
221 (c) fielding, hands chest-high 2,200 1,300 925.00

(223) Egyptian Healey (Healy)
223 (a) Indianapolis, pitching, hands at chest 2,200 1,300 925.00

(227) Hardie Henderson
227 (a) Brooklyn, outdoors, throwing, right hand head-high 3,000 1,800 1,300

(228) Moxie Hengle
228 (a) Minneapolis, hands on knees 2,200 1,300 925.00

(229) John Henry
229 (a) throwing, right hand neck-high 2,200 1,300 925.00

(231) Hunkey Hines
231 (a) St. Louis Whites, fielding 2,200 1,300 925.00

(232) Paul Hines
232 (a) Washington, arms at side 2,200 1,300 925.00

(233) Frank Hoffman
233 (a) pitching, right hand head-high 2,200 1,300 925.00

(235) Bill Holbert
235 (a) throwing 2,200 1,300 925.00

(236) Bug Holliday
236 (a) Cincinnati, arms at side 2,200 1,300 925.00
236 (b) Cincinnati, ball in hands at shoulder 2,200 1,300 925.00

(238) Buster Hoover
238 (a) Philadelphia, fielding, hands head-high 2,200 1,300 925.00
DP 1 being tagged by Ed Andrews 3,750 2,250 1,625

(239) Charlie Hoover
239 (a) Chicago, fielding grounder (Never played for Chicago) 2,200 1,300 925.00
239 (b) Kansas City, pose unrecorded 2,200 1,300 925.00

(241) Joe Hornung
241 (a) Boston, batting 2,200 1,300 925.00

(243) Dummy Hoy
243 (a) fielding grounder 6,750 4,050 2,875

(244) Nat Hudson
244 (a) ball in hands waist-high 2,200 1,300 925.00
244 (b) pitching, right hand head-high 2,200 1,300 925.00
244 (c) pitching, right hand waist-high 2,200 1,300 925.00

(245) Mickey Hughes
245 (a) holding ball at chest 2,200 1,300 925.00
245 (b) holding ball at side 2,200 1,300 925.00
245 (c) right hand extended 2,200 1,300 925.00
DP 4 being tagged by Bob Clark 5,625 3,375 2,400

(247) Bill Hutchinson
247 (a) ball in hand, right heel hidden 2,200 1,300 925.00
247 (b) ball in hand, right heel visible 2,200 1,300 925.00
247 (c) batting 2,200 1,300 925.00

(248) Arthur Irwin
248 (a) Philadelphia, fielding, hands chest-high 2,200 1,300 925.00
248 (b) Phila., throwing, right hand head-high 2,200 1,300 925.00

(249) John Irwin
249 (a) Washington, hands on knees 2,200 1,300 925.00
249 (b) Washington, throwing 2,200 1,300 925.00

(250) A.C. Jantzen
250 (a) batting, looking at camera 2,200 1,300 925.00

(252) Spud Johnson
252 (a) Columbus, pose unrecorded 2,200 1,300 925.00

(253) Dick Johnston
253 (a) batting, looking at ball 2,200 1,300 925.00
253 (b) hands on hips 2,200 1,300 925.00
253 (c) throwing right hand head high 2,200 1,300 925.00

(256) Tim Keefe
256 (a) bat nearly horizontal, Old Judge 4,500 2,700 1,950
256 (b) bat nearly horizontal, Dogs Head 18,750 11,250 8,100
256 (c) ball in hands at chest 3,750 2,250 1,625
256 (d) pitching, right hand head-high 4,500 2,700 1,950
256 (e) pitching, right hand waist-high 4,500 2,700 1,950

(259) Charlie Kelly
259 (a) Philadelphia, fielding, hands head-high 2,200 1,300 925.00

(261) King Kelly
261 (a) "Kelly, Boston.", bat at 45-degree angle 9,000 5,400 3,875
261 (b) "Kelly, Boston.", bat at 45-degree angle, Dogs Head 12,000 7,200 5,175
261 (c) "Mike Kelly, C, Bostons", bat at 45-degree angle 9,000 5,400 3,875
261 (d) "Kelly, Capt.", bat at 45-degree angle 9,000 5,400 3,875

(262) Rudy Kemmler
262 (a) fielding, hands chest-high 2,200 1,300 925.00

(263) Ted Kennedy
263 (a) Omaha, pose unrecorded 2,200 1,300 925.00

(264) J.J. Kenyon
264 (a) Des Moines, right hand in glove, head-high 2,200 1,300 925.00

(265) John Kerins
265 (a) hands on thighs 2,200 1,300 925.00

(266) Matt Kilroy
266 (a) pitching, hands waist-high to left 2,200 1,300 925.00

(267) Silver King
267 (a) St. Louis, pitching, hands chest-high 2,200 1,300 925.00
267 (b) St. Louis, pitching, hands chin-high 2,200 1,300 925.00

(269) Billy Klusman
269 (a) fielding grounder 2,200 1,300 925.00

(274) Gus Krock
274 (a) ball in hands above waist 2,200 1,300 925.00
274 (b) batting 2,200 1,300 925.00
274 (c) pitching, right hand chin-high 2,200 1,300 925.00

(275) Willie Kuehne
275 (a) fielding grounder 2,200 1,300 925.00

(277) Henry Larkin
277 (a) fielding, hands thigh-high 2,200 1,300 925.00
277 (b) right hand shoulder-high 2,200 1,300 925.00

(278) Arlie Latham
278 (a) batting 2,200 1,300 925.00
278 (b) throwing 4,125 2,475 1,750

(279) Chuck Lauer
279 (a) fielding, hands chest-high 2,200 1,300 925.00

(280) John Leighton
280 (a) batting 2,200 1,300 925.00
280 (b) fielding 2,200 1,300 925.00

(284) Herman Long
284 (a) Kansas City, bat at side 2,200 1,300 925.00
284 (b) Kansas City, fielding, hands chest-high 2,200 1,300 925.00

(285) Tom Lovett
285 (a) Brooklyn, bat on shoulder 2,200 1,300 925.00
285 (b) Brooklyn, pitching, hands over head 2,200 1,300 925.00
285 (c) Brooklyn, right hand extended 2,200 1,300 925.00

(288) Denny Lyons
288 (a) Philadelphia AA, bat at ready 2,200 1,300 925.00
288 (b) Phila. AA, fielding, left hand over head 2,200 1,300 925.00

(289) Harry Lyons
289 (a) St. Louis, at first base 2,200 1,300 925.00

(290) Connie Mack
290 (a) Washington, batting 31,250 11,250 8,100
290 (b) Washington, squatting, hands on knees 31,250 13,500 9,675

(292) Jimmy Macullar
292 (a) Des Moines, fielding, hands head-high 2,200 1,300 925.00

(293) Kid Madden
293 (a) ball in hand over head 2,200 1,300 925.00
293 (b) ball in hands, neck-high 2,200 1,300 925.00
293 (c) ball in left hand, eye-high 2,200 1,300 925.00

(297) Jimmy Manning
297 (a) bat at side 2,200 1,300 925.00
297 (b) fielding grounder 2,200 1,300 925.00

(298) Lefty Marr
298 (a) Columbus, left hand neck-high 2,200 1,300 925.00

(299) Mascot (Willie Breslin)
299 (a) New York 4,125 2,475 1,750

(300) Leech Maskrey
300 (a) Des Moines, ball in hands chin-high 2,200 1,300 925.00

(302) Mike Mattimore
302 (a) Phila. AA, sliding, left hand raised 2,200 1,300 925.00

(303) Al Maul
303 (a) pitching, hands at chest 2,200 1,300 925.00

(304) Al Mays
304 (a) pitching, hands chest-high 2,200 1,300 925.00

(305) Jimmy McAleer
305 (a) batting, looking at ball 2,200 1,300 925.00

(307) Tommy McCarthy
307 (a) St. Louis, batting, indoors 5,250 3,150 2,250
307 (b) St. Louis, right hand head-high, indoors 5,250 3,150 2,250
307 (c) tagging player 6,900 4,125 2,950

(318) Deacon McGuire
318 (a) Phila., fielding, hands shoulder-high 2,200 1,300 925.00

(319) Bill McGunnigle
319 (a) looking to right 2,200 1,300 925.00

(320) Ed McKean
320 (a) batting, looking at camera 2,200 1,300 925.00
320 (b) fielding, hands over head 2,200 1,300 925.00

(325) James McQuaid
325 (a) fielding, hands near chin 2,200 1,300 925.00

(330) Doggie Miller
330 (a) Pittsburgh, ball in hands, Dogs Head 8,250 4,950 3,550
330 (b) Pittsburgh, bat at side 2,200 1,300 925.00
330 (c) fielding, hands chest-high 2,200 1,300 925.00

(331) Joe Miller
331 (a) Minneapolis, bat at side 2,200 1,300 925.00
331 (b) Minneapolis, fielding 2,200 1,300 925.00

(332) Jocko Milligan
332 (a) bat at side 2,200 1,300 925.00
332 (b) bat in air 2,200 1,300 925.00
332 (c) fielding 2,200 1,300 925.00
332 (d) throwing 2,200 1,300 925.00

(334) Daniel Minnehan (Minahan)
334 (a) batting, looking at camera 2,200 1,300 925.00

(335) Sam Moffet
335 (a) pose unrecorded 2,200 1,300 925.00

(336) John Morrill
336 (a) Boston, batting 2,200 1,300 925.00

(338) Tony Mullane
338 (a) ball in hands above waist 4,125 2,475 1,750

(339) Joe Mulvey
339 (a) batting 2,200 1,300 925.00
339 (b) fielding 2,200 1,300 925.00

(340) Pat Murphy
340 (a) New York, fielding, hands chin-high 2,200 1,300 925.00

(341) P.L. Murphy
341 (a) St. Paul, batting 3,000 1,800 1,300

(342) Miah Murray
342 (a) on knee, hands at shoulder 2,200 1,300 925.00

(343) Jim Mutrie
343 (a) seated 2,200 1,300 925.00
343 (b) standing 2,200 1,300 925.00

(344) Al Myers
344 (a) Wash., right hand at side, left at back 2,200 1,300 925.00

(345) George Myers
345 (a) Indianpolis, batting 2,200 1,300 925.00

(346) Tom Nagle
346 (a) Omaha, batting 2,200 1,300 925.00
346 (b) fielding, Dogs Head 9,000 5,400 3,875

(347) Billy Nash
347 (a) hands on knees 3,375 2,025 1,450
347 (b) throwing 2,200 1,300 925.00

(349) Kid Nichols
349 (a) Omaha, batting, looking at ball 6,375 3,825 2,750
349 (b) Omaha, pitching, right hand forward 6,375 3,825 2,750

(353) Hugh Nicol
DP 16 side by side with Reilly, "Long & Short" 3,375 2,025 1,450

(357) Darby O'Brien
357 (a) Brooklyn, batting, looking at camera 2,200 1,300 925.00

(359) John O'Brien
359 (a) Cleveland, batting 2,200 1,300 925.00
359 (b) Cleveland, pose unrecorded, Dogs Head 7,125 4,275 3,075

(361) Jack O'Connor
361 (a) Columbus, throwing 2,200 1,300 925.00

(362) Hank O'Day
362 (a) ball in right hand, head-high 2,200 1,300 925.00

(365) Tip O'Neill
365 (a) bat held horizontally 2,200 1,300 925.00
365 (b) bat over shoulder 2,200 1,300 925.00
365 (c) fielding grounder 2,200 1,300 925.00
365 (d) throwing 4,350 2,625 1,875

(366) Orator Jim O'Rourke
366 (a) New York, bat in hand at side 6,000 3,600 2,600
366 (b) New York, batting 7,125 4,275 3,075
366 (c) New York, throwing, hand head-high 5,250 3,150 2,250

(367) Tom O'Rourke
367 (a) Boston, fielding, hands thigh-high 3,375 2,025 1,450

(368) Dave Orr
368 (a) Columbus, bat at ready, nearly vertical 2,200 1,300 925.00
(370) Owen Patton
370 (a) Des Moines, bat at head 2,200 1,300 925.00

(374) Fred Pfeffer
374 (a) batting, looking at ball 2,200 1,300 925.00
374 (b) tagging player 2,850 1,725 1,225
374 (c) throwing, right-hand neck-high 2,200 1,300 925.00

(375) Dick Phelan
375 (a) batting, looking at ball 2,200 1,300 925.00
(377) Jack Pickett
377 (a) St. Paul, bat over shoulder 2,200 1,300 925.00
377 (b) St. Paul, fielding grounder 2,200 1,300 925.00
377 (c) St. Paul, throwing, right hand head-high 2,200 1,300 925.00

(378) George Pinkney
378 (a) bat in air, nearly vertical 2,200 1,300 925.00
378 (b) bat over shoulder 2,200 1,300 925.00
DP 25 (w/ Steve Toole) 6,750 4,050 2,875

(381) Jim Powell
381 (a) batting, looking at camera 2,200 1,300 925.00

(383) Blondie Purcell
383 (a) throwing 2,200 1,300 925.00

(385) Joe Quinn
385 (a) ball in hands by chin 2,200 1,300 925.00
385 (b) ready to run 2,200 1,300 925.00

(386) Old Hoss Radbourn
386 (a) hands at waist, Dogs Head 9,750 5,850 4,200
386 (b) hands on hips, bat on left 4,500 2,700 1,950
386 (c) tagging player 5,250 3,150 2,250

(388) Tom Ramsey
388 (a) bat at ready, nearly vertical 2,200 1,300 925.00
388 (b) bat over right shoulder, Dogs Head 6,000 3,600 2,600

(390) Charlie Reilly
390 (a) St. Paul, throwing 2,200 1,300 925.00

(391) Long John Reilly
391 (a) Cincinnati, fielding 2,200 1,300 925.00
DP 16 side by side w/Nicol, "Long & Short" 3,375 2,025 1,450

(393) Danny Richardson
393 (a) New York, moving left, arms at side 2,200 1,300 925.00
393 (b) New York, throwing 2,200 1,300 925.00

(394) Hardy Richardson
394 (a) Boston, bat over shoulder 2,200 1,300 925.00
394 (b) Detroit, bat over shoulder 2,200 1,300 925.00
394 (c) Boston, fielding, hands head-high 2,200 1,300 925.00

(398) Wilbert Robinson
398 (a) Philadelphia AA, batting 5,625 3,375 2,475
398 (b) Phila. AA, catching, hands neck-high 5,625 3,375 2,475
398 (c) Philadelphia AA, throwing 5,625 3,375 2,475

(399) Yank Robinson
399 (a) St. Louis, batting 3,150 1,875 1,350
399 (b) St. Louis, fielding grounder 3,150 1,875 1,350
399 (c) St. Louis, hands at chest 3,150 1,875 1,350

(402) Dave Rowe
402 (a) Kansas City, fielding, Dogs Head 5,250 3,150 2,250

(403) Jack Rowe
403 (a) Detroit, batting, looking at camera 2,200 1,300 925.00
403 (b) Detroit, bat on shoulder, looking at ball 2,200 1,300 925.00

(404) Amos Rusie
404 (a) Indianapolis, ball in right hand, thigh-high 11,250 6,750 4,875

(405) Jimmy Ryan
405 (a) bat at side 3,150 1,875 1,350
405 (b) batting 3,375 2,025 1,450
405 (c) stooping for knee-high catch 3,150 1,875 1,350
405 (d) throwing, left hand head-high 3,150 1,875 1,350

(407) Ben Sanders
407 (a) batting 2,200 1,300 925.00
407 (b) fielding 2,200 1,300 925.00
407 (c) right hand head-high 2,200 1,300 925.00

(408) Frank Scheibeck
408 (a) fielding, hand over head 2,200 1,300 925.00

(412) Gus Schmelz
412 (a) portrait 2,200 1,300 925.00

(413) Jumbo Schoeneck
413 (a) fielding, hands chin-high 2,200 1,300 925.00

(414) Pop Schriver
414 (a) fielding, hands ankle-high 2,200 1,300 925.00
414 (b) hands cupped chest-high 1,750 1,050 750.00
DP 2 being tagged by Charlie Bastian 3,750 2,250 1,750

(415) Emmett Seery
415 (a) arms folded 2,200 1,300 925.00

(417) Ed Seward
417 (a) ball in hands neck-high 2,200 1,300 925.00

(420) Daniel Shannon
420 (a) Louisville, leaning to tag player 2,200 1,300 925.00

(421) Bill Sharsig
421 (a) full length in bowler hat 2,200 1,300 925.00

(425) George Shoch
425 (a) fielding grounder 2,200 1,300 925.00

(426) Otto Shomberg (Schomberg)
426 (a) fielding, hands head-high 2,200 1,300 925.00
(427) Lev Shreve
427 (a) right hand eye-high, looking at camera 2,200 1,300 925.00

(429) Mike Slattery
429 (a) fielding, hands chest-high 2,200 1,300 925.00

(430) Elmer Smith
(431) Germany Smith
431 (a) Cincinnati, pitching, left hand head-high, looking at camera 2,200 1,300 925.00
431 (a) Brooklyn, batting, looking at ball 2,200 1,300 925.00
431 (b) Brooklyn, hands on knees 2,200 1,300 925.00
431 (c) Brooklyn, right hand head-high 2,200 1,300 925.00

(435) Pop Smith
435 (a) Boston, batting 2,200 1,300 925.00
435 (b) Pittsburgh, batting 2,200 1,300 925.00
435 (c) hands on knees 2,200 1,300 925.00

(439) Pete Sommers
439 (a) portrait 3,375 2,025 1,450

(440) Bill Sowders
440 (a) Boston, pitching, hands at throat 2,200 1,300 925.00
440 (b) Boston, pitching, right hand cap-high, left hand waist-high 3,000 1,800 1,300

(442) Charlie Sprague
442 (a) Chicago, left hand at back head-high 2,200 1,300 925.00
442 (b) Cleveland, left hand at back head-high 2,200 1,300 925.00

(444) Harry Staley
444 (a) pitching, right hand chest-high 2,200 1,300 925.00

(445) Dan Stearns
445 (a) Kansas City, fielding, hands neck-high 3,750 2,250 1,750

(450) Harry Stovey
450 (a) bat at ready by head 3,375 2,025 1,450
450 (b) fielding, hands chest-high, Dogs Head 18,000 10,800 7,725
450 (c) hands on knees 2,200 1,300 925.00

(451) Scott Stratton
451 (a) batting 2,200 1,300 925.00

(452) Joe Straus (Strauss)
452 (a) Milwaukee, kneeling, looking to right 2,200 1,300 925.00
452 (b) Omaha, throwing 2,200 1,300 925.00

(453) Cub Stricker
453 (a) fielding, hands over head 2,200 1,300 925.00

(454) Marty Sullivan
454 (a) Chicago, batting, looking at ball 2,200 1,300 925.00
454 (b) Indianapolis, hands chest-high 2,200 1,300 925.00

(457) Billy Sunday
457 (a) Pittsburgh, bat at side 5,250 3,150 2,250
457 (b) Pittsburgh, batting 7,500 4,500 3,225
457 (c) Pittsburgh, fielding, hands thigh-high 5,250 3,150 2,250

(459) Ezra Sutton
459 (a) batting, looking down at ball 2,200 1,300 925.00
459 (b) fielding, hands shoulder-high 2,200 1,300 925.00

(461) Park Swartzel
461 (a) arms at side 2,200 1,300 925.00

(464) Pop Tate
464 (a) Boston, batting 2,200 1,300 925.00

(465) Patsy Tebeau
465 (a) Chicago, fielding grounder 2,200 1,300 925.00

(466) John Tener
466 (a) ball in right hand chin-high 3,750 2,250 1,750
466 (b) batting 3,750 2,250 1,750

(467) Adonis Terry
467 (a) arms extended horizontally 2,200 1,300 925.00
467 (b) bat on shoulder 2,200 1,300 925.00

(468) Sam Thompson
468 (a) Detroit, bat ready at 45 degree angle 9,750 5,850 4,200
468 (b) Philadelphia, batting, ball above head 9,750 5,850 4,200

(469) Mike Tiernan
469 (a) batting 2,200 1,300 925.00
469 (b) sliding 3,375 2,025 1,450
469 (c) throwing, left hand chin-high 2,200 1,300 925.00

(470) Cannonball Titcomb
470 (a) pitching, hands chin-high 2,200 1,300 925.00

(471) Phil Tomney
471 (a) fielding, hands over head 2,200 1,300 925.00

(472) Steve Toole
DP 25 (w/ George Pinkney (Pinckney)) 6,750 4,050 2,875

(473) George Townsend
473 (a) bat at ready by head 2,200 1,300 925.00
473 (b) fielding. hands chest-high 2,200 1,300 925.00

(474) Bill Traffley
474 (a) hands on thighs 2,200 1,300 925.00

(477) Tommy Tucker
477 (a) ball in hands at chest 2,200 1,300 925.00
DP 8 being tagged by Chris Fulmer 6,750 4,050 2,875

(479) George Turner
479 (a) fielding, hands head-high 2,200 1,300 925.00

(480) Larry Twitchell
480 (a) Cleveland, pitching, hands at chest 2,200 1,300 925.00
480 (b) Detroit, pitching, hands at chest 2,200 1,300 925.00

(481) Jim Tyng
481 (a) pitching 2,200 1,300 925.00

(483) George Van Haltren
483 (a) batting 4,500 2,700 1,950
483 (b) ball in hands at waist 4,500 2,700 1,950
482 (c) right hand at thigh 4,500 2,700 1,950

(484) Farmer Vaughn
484 (a) bat at ready, looking at camera 2,200 1,300 925.00

(488) Joe Visner
488 (a) arms at side 2,200 1,300 925.00
488 (b) batting 2,200 1,300 925.00
488 (c) throwing 2,200 1,300 925.00

(490) Reddy Walsh
490 (a) batting 2,200 1,300 925.00

(491) John Ward
491 (a) hands behind back 6,000 3,600 2,600
491 (b) hands on hips 10,500 6,300 4,500
491 (c) portrait in dress clothes)(VALUE UNDETERMINED
491 (d) sliding, left arm in air 6,000 3,600 2,600
491 (e) throwing, right profile 6,000 3,600 2,600
491 (f) cap in right hand at side 6,000 3,600 2,600
491 (g) cap in right hand at side, Dogs Head 9,000 5,400 3,875

(493) Bill Watkins
493 (a) Detroit, portrait 2,200 1,300 925.00
493 (b) Kansas City, portrait 2,200 1,300 925.00

(494) Farmer Weaver
494 (a) fielding, left hand over head 2,200 1,300 925.00

(496) Stump Weidman (Wiedman)
496 (a) New York, batting 2,200 1,300 925.00

(497) Wild Bill Weidner (Widner)
497 (a) batting 2,200 1,300 925.00

(498) Curt Welch
498 (a) Philadelphia AA, fielding grounder 2,200 1,300 925.00
DP 23 with Will Gleason 3,375 2,025 1,450

(499) Mickey Welch
499 (a) N.Y., pitching, right arm extended forward, name incorrect (Welsh) 4,500 2,700 1,950
499 (b) N.Y., pitching, right arm extended forward, name correct 4,500 2,700 1,950
499 (c) N.Y., pitching, right arm behind head, Dogs Head 22,500 13,500 9,675

(504) A.C. (Gus) Weyhing
504 (a) Philadelphia AA, right hand chest-high 2,200 1,300 925.00

(505) John Weyhing
505 (a) Philadelphia AA, left hand chest-high (Never played for Philadelphia) 2,200 1,300 925.00

(510) Deacon White
510 (a) Detroit, hands above head 2,200 1,300 925.00
510 (b) looking down at ball 2,200 1,300 925.00

(511) Art Whitney
511 (a) New York, with dog 18,750 11,250 8,100
511 (b) New York, fielding, hands thigh-high 2,200 1,300 925.00
511 (c) Pittsburgh, fielding, hands thigh-high 2,200 1,300 925.00

(512) G. Whitney
512 (a) St. Joseph, batting, looking at ball 2,200 1,300 925.00

(513) Jim Whitney
513 (a) Wash., pitching, right hand waist-high 2,200 1,300 925.00

(515) Ned Williamson
515 (a) arms folded 2,200 1,300 925.00
515 (b) batting, looking at ball 2,200 1,300 925.00
515 (c) fielding 2,200 1,300 925.00
515 (d) throwing 2,200 1,300 925.00

(516) Tit Willis
516 (a) pitching, arms head-high 2,200 1,300 925.00

(517) Walt Wilmot
517 (a) Washington, fielding, hands at chest 2,200 1,300 925.00

(519) Sam Wise
519 (a) Boston, bat at side 2,200 1,300 925.00
519 (b) Boston, hands on knees 3,000 1,800 1,300

(520) Chicken Wolf
520 (a) bat at ready, team name visible on shirt 2,200 1,300 925.00

(521) George Wood (L.F.)
521 (a) both hands neck-high 2,200 1,300 925.00
521 (b) right hand head-high 2,200 1,300 925.00

(522) Pete Wood (P.)
522 (a) bat on shoulder 2,200 1,300 925.00

(523) Harry Wright
523 (a) portrait, looking to his left 30,000 18,000 13,000

(524) Chief Zimmer
524 (a) fielding, hands at chest 2,200 1,300 925.00
524 (b) throwing 2,200 1,300 925.00

1965 Old London Coins

These 1-1/2" diameter metal coins were included in Old London snack food packages. The 40 coins in this set feature two players from each of the major leagues' 20 teams, except St. Louis (3) and the New York Mets (1). Coin fronts have color photos and player names, while the silver-colored backs give a brief biography. An Old London logo is also displayed on each coin back. Space Magic Ltd. produced the coins. This is the same company which produced similar sets for Topps in 1964 and 1971.

	NM	EX	VG
Complete Set (40):	475.00	240.00	140.00
Common Player:	3.00	1.50	.90
(1) Henry Aaron	35.00	17.50	10.50
(2) Richie Allen	7.50	3.75	2.25
(3) Bob Allison	3.00	1.50	.90
(4) Ernie Banks	25.00	12.50	7.50
(5) Ken Boyer	4.50	2.25	1.25
(6) Jim Bunning	15.00	7.50	4.50
(7) Orlando Cepeda	12.50	6.25	3.75
(8) Dean Chance	3.00	1.50	.90
(9) Rocky Colavito	10.00	5.00	3.00
(10) Vic Davalillo	3.00	1.50	.90
(11) Tommy Davis	3.00	1.50	.90
(12) Ron Fairly	3.00	1.50	.90
(13) Dick Farrell	3.00	1.50	.90
(14) Jim Fregosi	3.00	1.50	.90
(15) Bob Friend	3.00	1.50	.90
(16) Dick Groat	3.00	1.50	.90
(17) Ron Hunt	3.00	1.50	.90
(18) Chuck Hinton	3.00	1.50	.90
(19) Ken Johnson	3.00	1.50	.90
(20) Al Kaline	20.00	10.00	6.00
(21) Harmon Killebrew	20.00	10.00	6.00
(22) Don Lock	3.00	1.50	.90
(23) Mickey Mantle	100.00	50.00	30.00
(24) Roger Maris	30.00	15.00	9.00
(25) Willie Mays	35.00	17.50	10.50
(26) Bill Mazeroski	12.50	6.25	3.75
(27) Gary Peters	3.00	1.50	.90
(28) Vada Pinson	3.50	1.75	1.00
(29) Boog Powell	4.50	2.25	1.25
(30) Dick Radatz	3.00	1.50	.90
(31) Brooks Robinson	20.00	10.00	6.00
(32) Frank Robinson	20.00	10.00	6.00
(33) Tracy Stallard	3.00	1.50	.90
(34) Joe Torre	7.50	3.75	2.25
(35) Leon Wagner	3.00	1.50	.90
(36) Pete Ward	3.00	1.50	.90
(37) Dave Wickersham	3.00	1.50	.90
(38) Billy Williams	15.00	7.50	4.50
(39) John Wyatt	3.00	1.50	.90
(40) Carl Yastrzemski	25.00	12.50	7.50

1909-11 Old Mill Cigarettes

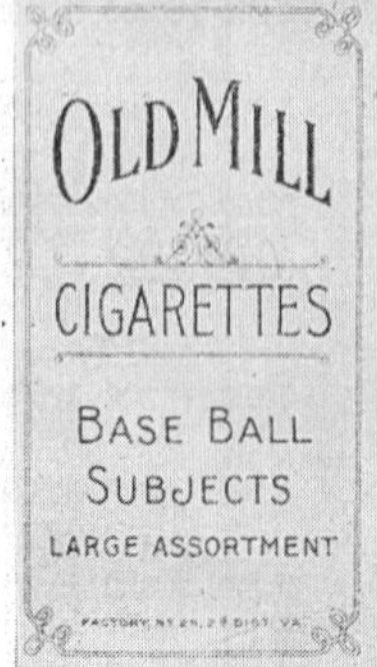

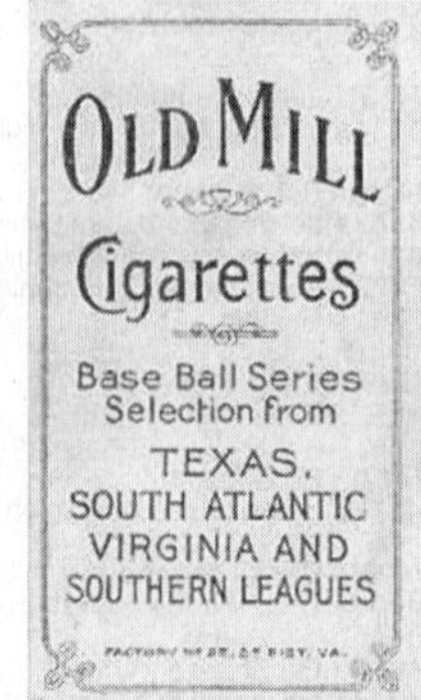

T206 cards bearing the Old Mill advertising are, with a major exception, among the most common of the set's back variations. Two styles of Old Mill T206 backs are found. One, which appears on cards of major league players and minor leaguers other than those from the Southern leagues, mentions a "BASE BALL / SUBJECTS / LARGE ASSORTMENT." The other specifies the four Southern leagues from which the players depicted originate. In recent years advanced T206 specialists have become aware of a brown-ink version of the Southern leagues back, much rarer than the black-ink version usually found on both types of Old Mill backs. All of the confirmed brown-ink cards appear to have been hand-cut from a sheet, leading to speculation as to whether they represent an actual issued variation or were salvaged from a scrapped printing. Contemporary with the T206 issues, Old Mill also produced a lengthy series of red-bordered minor league player cards in 1910. Those are listed in the minor league section of this book.

PREMIUMS
Common: 1.25X
Stars/So. Leagues: 1X
Brown-ink So. Leagues: 10X
(See S74, T3, T206.)

1910 Old Put Cigar

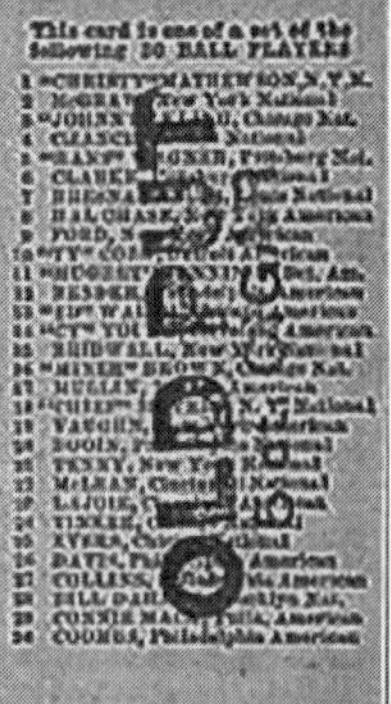

This is a version of the anonymous E98 "Set of 30" on which an advertisement for "OLD PUT / 5 ct. CIGAR" has been rubber-stamped in purple. Because of the ease with which these could be faked, collectors must exercise extreme caution.

	NM	EX	VG
Common Player:	3,750	1,875	1,125
(1) Christy Matthewson (Mathewson)	12,000	6,000	3,600
(2) John McGraw	6,000	3,000	1,800
(3) Johnny Kling	3,750	1,875	1,025
(4) Frank Chance	6,000	3,000	1,800
(5) Hans Wagner	13,500	6,750	4,050
(6) Fred Clarke	3,000	1,500	900.00
(7) Roger Bresnahan	3,000	1,500	900.00
(8) Hal Chase	6,000	3,000	1,800
(9) Russ Ford	3,750	1,875	1,025
(10) "Ty" Cobb	16,500	8,250	4,950
(11) Hughey Jennings	3,000	1,500	900.00
(12) Chief Bender	6,000	3,000	1,800
(13) Ed Walsh	3,000	1,500	900.00
(14) Cy Young	12,000	6,000	3,600
(15) Al Bridwell	3,750	1,875	1,025
(16) Miner Brown	3,000	1,500	900.00
(17) George Mullin	3,750	1,875	1,025
(18) Chief Meyers	3,750	1,875	1,025
(19) Hippo Vaughn	3,750	1,875	1,025
(20) Red Dooin	3,750	1,875	1,025
(21) Fred Tenny (Tenney)	3,750	1,875	1,025
(22) Larry McLean	3,750	1,875	1,025
(23) Nap Lajoie	6,000	3,000	1,800
(24) Joe Tinker	6,000	3,000	1,800
(25) Johnny Evers	6,000	3,000	1,800
(26) Harry Davis	3,750	1,875	1,025
(27) Eddie Collins	6,000	3,000	1,800
(28) Bill Dahlen	3,750	1,875	1,025
(29) Connie Mack	6,000	3,000	1,800
(30) Jack Coombs	3,750	1,875	1,025

1951 Olmes Studio Postcards

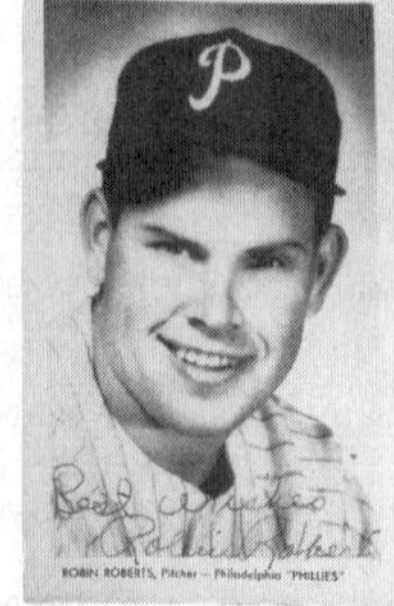

This line of Philadelphia player postcards (all but one from the A's) was produced by a local photographer, probably for player use in satisfying fans' autograph requests. The 3-1/2" x 5-1/2" cards have a glossy black-and-white player photo on front. Backs have only standard postcard indicia and the Olmes credit line. Other players may remain to be checklisted. The unnumbered cards are listed here alphabetically.

	NM	EX	VG
Common Player:	75.00	37.50	22.50
(1) Sam Chapman	75.00	37.50	22.50
(2) Ferris Fain (Ready to hit, on grass.)	100.00	50.00	30.00
(3) Ferris Fain/Btg (Choking up.)	100.00	50.00	30.00
(4) Ferris Fain/Btg (Follow-through.)	100.00	50.00	30.00
(5) Ferris Fain/Kneeling	100.00	50.00	30.00
(6) Dick Fowler	75.00	37.50	22.50
(7) Bob Hooper	75.00	37.50	22.50
(8) Skeeter Kell	75.00	37.00	22.50
(9) Paul Lehner	75.00	37.50	22.50
(10) Lou Limmer	75.00	37.50	22.50
(11) Barney McCosky	75.00	37.50	22.50
(12) Robin Roberts	275.00	135.00	80.00
(13) Carl Scheib	75.00	37.50	22.50
(14) Bobby Shantz	75.00	37.50	22.50
(15) Joe Tipton	75.00	37.50	22.50
(16) Gus Zernial/Btg	100.00	50.00	30.00
(17) Gus Zernial/Kneeling	100.00	50.00	30.00

1979 Open Pantry/Lake to Lake MACC

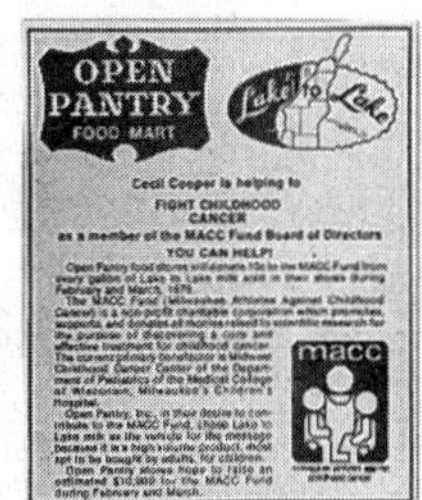

To benefit Milwaukee Athletes Against Childhood Cancer the Open Pantry convenience stores in Wisconsin teamed with Lake to Lake Dairy to produce this card set. Red, white and black fronts of the 5" x 6" cards have a player photo, facsimile autograph and team logo. Backs are printed in red with a message from the player about the MACC fund. Besides members of the Milwaukee Brewers listed here, the set features Green Bay Packers and Milwaukee Bucks players. The unnumbered cards are checklisted here alphabetically.

	NM	EX	VG
Complete Set (12):	10.00	5.00	3.00
Common (Baseball) Player:	2.00	1.00	.60
(1) Jerry Augustine	3.00	1.50	.90
(2) Sal Bando	3.00	1.50	.90
(3) Cecil Cooper	4.00	2.00	1.25
(4) Larry Hisle	3.00	1.50	.90
(5) Lary Sorensen	3.00	1.50	.90

1910 "Orange Borders"

Known in the hobby as "Orange Borders," these 1-1/2" x 2-7/16" cards were issued in 1910 and were printed on candy boxes that displayed the words "American Sports and Candy and Jewelry." The end flaps indicate the producers as the "Geo. Davis Co., Inc." and the "P.R. Warren Co., Warrenville Lowell, Mass." According to the box, the complete set includes "144 leading ballplayers," but to date just over two dozen different subjects are known. When found today, these black and white photos are often surrounded by orange borders which, in reality, were part of the candy box. Similar in format to the "Baseball Bats" cards, Orange Borders have player names which are hand-lettered, rather than typeset. Gaps have been left in the assigned numbering to accomodate future additions to the checklist.

	NM	EX	VG
Common Player:	960.00	390.00	190.00
(1) Bill Bergen	960.00	390.00	190.00
(2) Bill Bradley	960.00	390.00	190.00
(3) Bill Carrigan	960.00	390.00	190.00
(4) Hal Chase	1,140	455.00	230.00
(5) Fred Clark (Clarke)	1,440	575.00	290.00
(6) Ty Cobb	12,000	4,800	2,400
(7) Sam Crawford	1,440	575.00	290.00
(8) Lou Criger	960.00	390.00	190.00
(9) Harry Davis	960.00	390.00	190.00
(11) Art Devlin	960.00	390.00	190.00
(12) Mickey Doolan	960.00	390.00	190.00
(13) George Gibson	960.00	390.00	190.00
(14) Addie Joss	1,560	625.00	315.00
(15) Nap Lajoie	1,440	575.00	290.00
(16) Frank LaPorte	960.00	390.00	190.00
(17) Harry Lord	960.00	390.00	190.00
(18) Christy Mathewson	5,400	2,160	1,080
(19) Amby McConnell	960.00	390.00	190.00
(21) John McGraw	1,440	575.00	290.00
(22) Dots Miller	960.00	390.00	190.00
(23) George Mullin	960.00	390.00	190.00
(24) Eddie Plank	1,440	575.00	290.00
(25) Tris Speaker	1,680	675.00	335.00
(26) Jake Stahl	960.00	390.00	190.00
(27) Honus Wagner/Btg	9,000	3,600	1,800
(28) Honus Wagner/Portrait	9,000	3,600	1,800
(29) Jack Warhop	960.00	390.00	190.00
(31) American League Champions, 1909 (Detroit)	2,400	960.00	480.00
(32) National League Champions, 1909 (Pittsburgh)	2,400	960.00	480.00

1976 Orbaker's Discs

One of several regional sponsors of player disc sets in 1976 was the Orbaker's restaurant chain. The discs are 3-3/8" diameter with a black-and-white player portrait photo in the center of the baseball design. A line of red stars is above, while the left and right panels feature one of several bright colors. Produced by Michael Schecter Associates under license from the Major League Baseball Players Association, the player photos have had uniform and cap logos removed. Backs are printed in red and purple. The unnumbered checklist here is presented in alphabetical order.

	NM	EX	VG
Complete Set (70):	50.00	25.00	15.00
Common Player:	1.00	.50	.30
(1) Henry Aaron	20.00	10.00	6.00
(2) Johnny Bench	6.00	3.00	1.75
(3) Vida Blue	1.00	.50	.30
(4) Larry Bowa	1.00	.50	.30
(5) Lou Brock	4.00	2.00	1.25
(6) Jeff Burroughs	1.00	.50	.30
(7) John Candelaria	1.00	.50	.30
(8) Jose Cardenal	1.00	.50	.30
(9) Rod Carew	4.00	2.00	1.25
(10) Steve Carlton	4.00	2.00	1.25
(11) Dave Cash	1.00	.50	.30
(12) Cesar Cedeno	1.00	.50	.30
(13) Ron Cey	1.00	.50	.30
(14) Carlton Fisk	4.00	2.00	1.25
(15) Tito Fuentes	1.00	.50	.30
(16) Steve Garvey	2.00	1.00	.60
(17) Ken Griffey	1.00	.50	.30
(18) Don Gullett	1.00	.50	.30
(19) Willie Horton	1.00	.50	.30
(20) Al Hrabosky	1.00	.50	.30
(21) Catfish Hunter	3.00	1.50	.90
(22) Reggie Jackson (A's)	12.00	6.00	3.50
(23) Randy Jones	1.00	.50	.30
(24) Jim Kaat	1.00	.50	.30
(25) Don Kessinger	1.00	.50	.30
(26) Dave Kingman	1.00	.50	.30
(27) Jerry Koosman	1.00	.50	.30
(28) Mickey Lolich	1.00	.50	.30
(29) Greg Luzinski	1.00	.50	.30
(30) Fred Lynn	1.00	.50	.30
(31) Bill Madlock	1.00	.50	.30
(32) Carlos May	1.00	.50	.30
(33) John Mayberry	1.00	.50	.30
(34) Bake McBride	1.00	.50	.30
(35) Doc Medich	1.00	.50	.30
(36) Andy Messersmith	1.00	.50	.30
(37) Rick Monday	1.00	.50	.30
(38) John Montefusco	1.00	.50	.30
(39) Jerry Morales	1.00	.50	.30
(40) Joe Morgan	4.00	2.00	1.25
(41) Thurman Munson	3.00	1.50	.90
(42) Bobby Murcer	1.00	.50	.30
(43) Al Oliver	1.00	.50	.30
(44) Jim Palmer	4.00	2.00	1.25
(45) Dave Parker	1.00	.50	.30
(46) Tony Perez	3.00	1.50	.90
(47) Jerry Reuss	1.00	.50	.30
(48) Brooks Robinson	6.00	3.00	1.75
(49) Frank Robinson	6.00	3.00	1.75
(50) Steve Rogers	1.00	.50	.30
(51) Pete Rose	17.50	8.75	5.25
(52) Nolan Ryan	25.00	12.50	7.50
(53) Manny Sanguillen	1.00	.50	.30
(54) Mike Schmidt	15.00	7.50	4.50
(55) Tom Seaver	6.00	3.00	1.75
(56) Ted Simmons	1.00	.50	.30
(57) Reggie Smith	1.00	.50	.30
(58) Willie Stargell	4.00	2.00	1.25
(59) Rusty Staub	1.50	.70	.45
(60) Rennie Stennett	1.00	.50	.30
(61) Don Sutton	3.00	1.50	.90
(62) Andy Thornton	1.00	.50	.30
(63) Luis Tiant	1.00	.50	.30
(64) Joe Torre	1.00	.50	.30
(65) Mike Tyson	1.00	.50	.30
(66) Bob Watson	1.00	.50	.30
(67) Wilbur Wood	1.00	.50	.30
(68) Jimmy Wynn	1.00	.50	.30
(69) Carl Yastrzemski	6.00	3.00	1.75
(70) Richie Zisk	1.00	.50	.30

1932 Orbit Gum Pins - Numbered (PR2)

Issued circa 1932, this skip-numbered set of small (13/16" diameter) pins was produced by Orbit Gum and carries the American Card Catalog designation of PR2. A color player lithograph is set against a green background with the player's name and team printed on a strip of yellow below. The pin number is at the very bottom; pins after #40 are skip-numbered.

	NM	EX	VG
Complete Set (53):	2,500	1,250	750.00
Common Player:	30.00	15.00	9.00
1 Ivy Andrews	30.00	15.00	9.00
2 Carl Reynolds	30.00	15.00	9.00
3 Riggs Stephenson	30.00	15.00	9.00
4 Lon Warneke	30.00	15.00	9.00
5 Frank Grube	30.00	15.00	9.00
6 "Kiki" Cuyler	60.00	30.00	18.00
7 Marty McManus	30.00	15.00	9.00
8 Lefty Clark	30.00	15.00	9.00
9 George Blaeholder	30.00	15.00	9.00
10 Willie Kamm	30.00	15.00	9.00
11 Jimmy Dykes	30.00	15.00	9.00
12 Earl Averill	60.00	30.00	18.00
13 Pat Malone	30.00	15.00	9.00
14 Dizzy Dean	200.00	100.00	60.00
15 Dick Bartell	30.00	15.00	9.00
16 Guy Bush	30.00	15.00	9.00
17 Bud Tinning	30.00	15.00	9.00
18 Jimmy Foxx	150.00	75.00	45.00
19 Mule Haas	30.00	15.00	9.00
20 Lew Fonseca	30.00	15.00	9.00
21 Pepper Martin	40.00	20.00	12.00
22 Phil Collins	30.00	15.00	9.00
23 Bill Cissell	30.00	15.00	9.00
24 Bump Hadley	30.00	15.00	9.00
25 Smead Jolley	30.00	15.00	9.00
26 Burleigh Grimes	60.00	30.00	18.00
27 Dale Alexander	30.00	15.00	9.00
28 Mickey Cochrane	60.00	30.00	18.00
29 Mel Harder	30.00	15.00	9.00
30 Mark Koenig	30.00	15.00	9.00
31a Lefty O'Doul (Dodgers)	50.00	25.00	15.00
31b Lefty O'Doul (Giants)	90.00	45.00	27.00
32a Woody English (With bat.)	30.00	15.00	9.00
32b Woody English (Without bat.)	80.00	40.00	24.00
33a Billy Jurges (With bat.)	30.00	15.00	9.00
33b Billy Jurges (Without bat.)	80.00	40.00	24.00
34 Bruce Campbell	30.00	15.00	9.00
35 Joe Vosmik	30.00	15.00	9.00
36 Dick Porter	30.00	15.00	9.00
37 Charlie Grimm	30.00	15.00	9.00
38 George Earnshaw	30.00	15.00	9.00
39 Al Simmons	60.00	30.00	18.00
40 Red Lucas	30.00	15.00	9.00
51 Wally Berger	30.00	15.00	9.00
55 Jim Levey	30.00	15.00	9.00
58 Ernie Lombardi	60.00	30.00	18.00
64 Jack Burns	30.00	15.00	9.00
67 Billy Herman	60.00	30.00	18.00
72 Bill Hallahan	30.00	15.00	9.00
92 Don Brennan	30.00	15.00	9.00
96 Sam Byrd	30.00	15.00	9.00
99 Ben Chapman	30.00	15.00	9.00
103 John Allen	30.00	15.00	9.00
107 Tony Lazzeri	60.00	30.00	18.00
111 Earl Combs (Earle)	60.00	30.00	18.00
116 Joe Sewell	60.00	30.00	18.00
120 Vernon Gomez	60.00	30.00	18.00

1932 Orbit Gum Pins - Unnumbered (PR3)

This set, issued by Orbit Gum circa 1932, has the American Card Catalog designation PR3. The pins are identical to the PR2 set, except they are unnumbered.

		NM	EX	VG
Complete Set (60):		3,750	1,850	1,100
Common Player:		60.00	30.00	18.00
(1)	Dale Alexander	60.00	30.00	18.00
(2)	Ivy Andrews	60.00	30.00	18.00
(3)	Earl Averill	100.00	50.00	30.00
(4)	Dick Bartell	60.00	30.00	18.00
(5)	Wally Berger	60.00	30.00	18.00
(6)	George Blaeholder	60.00	30.00	18.00
(7)	Jack Burns	60.00	30.00	18.00
(8)	Guy Bush	60.00	30.00	18.00
(9)	Bruce Campbell	60.00	30.00	18.00
(10)	Bill Cissell	60.00	30.00	18.00
(11)	Lefty Clark	60.00	30.00	18.00
(12)	Mickey Cochrane	100.00	50.00	30.00
(13)	Phil Collins	60.00	30.00	18.00
(14)	"Kiki" Cuyler	100.00	50.00	30.00
(15)	Dizzy Dean	175.00	87.00	52.00
(16)	Jimmy Dykes	60.00	30.00	18.00
(17)	George Earnshaw	60.00	30.00	18.00
(18)	Woody English	60.00	30.00	18.00
(19)	Lew Fonseca	60.00	30.00	18.00
(20)	Jimmy (Jimmie) Foxx	175.00	87.00	52.00
(21)	Burleigh Grimes	100.00	50.00	30.00
(22)	Charlie Grimm	60.00	30.00	18.00
(23)	Lefty Grove	100.00	50.00	30.00
(24)	Frank Grube	60.00	30.00	18.00
(25)	Mule Haas	60.00	30.00	18.00
(26)	Bump Hadley	60.00	30.00	18.00
(27)	Chick Hafey	100.00	50.00	30.00
(28)	Jesse Haines	100.00	50.00	30.00
(29)	Bill Hallahan	60.00	30.00	18.00
(30)	Mel Harder	60.00	30.00	18.00
(31)	Gabby Hartnett	100.00	50.00	30.00
(32)	Babe Herman	65.00	32.00	19.50
(33)	Billy Herman	100.00	50.00	30.00
(34)	Rogers Hornsby	135.00	67.00	40.00
(35)	Roy Johnson	60.00	30.00	18.00
(36)	Smead Jolley	60.00	30.00	18.00
(37)	Billy Jurges	60.00	30.00	18.00
(38)	Willie Kamm	60.00	30.00	18.00
(39)	Mark Koenig	60.00	30.00	18.00
(40)	Jim Levey	60.00	30.00	18.00
(41)	Ernie Lombardi	100.00	50.00	30.00
(42)	Red Lucas	60.00	30.00	18.00
(43)	Ted Lyons	100.00	50.00	30.00
(44)	Connie Mack	100.00	50.00	30.00
(45)	Pat Malone	60.00	30.00	18.00
(46)	Pepper Martin	75.00	37.00	22.00
(47)	Marty McManus	60.00	30.00	18.00
(48)	Lefty O'Doul	80.00	40.00	24.00
(49)	Dick Porter	60.00	30.00	18.00
(50)	Carl Reynolds	60.00	30.00	18.00
(51)	Charlie Root	60.00	30.00	18.00
(52)	Bob Seeds	60.00	30.00	18.00
(53)	Al Simmons	100.00	50.00	30.00
(54)	Riggs Stephenson	60.00	30.00	18.00
(55)	Bud Tinning	60.00	30.00	18.00
(56)	Joe Vosmik	60.00	30.00	18.00
(57)	Rube Walberg	60.00	30.00	18.00
(58)	Paul Waner	100.00	50.00	30.00
(59)	Lon Warneke	60.00	30.00	18.00
(60)	Pinky Whitney	60.00	30.00	18.00

1937-39 Orcajo Cincinnati Reds Postcards (PC786)

Orcajo, a Dayton, Ohio, photo firm, issued a series of Reds player postcards (plus, inexplicably, Joe DiMaggio) from 1937-39. Besides those found with just the issuer's imprint on the back, some or all of the players' cards can be found with the advertising on front of the Val Decker Packing Co., a meat dealer, Metropolitan Clothing Co., and an inset photo of WHIO radio announcer Si Burick (the latter are the 1937 cards and have no Orcajo imprint on back, utilizing different photos than the 1938-39 cards). The 3-1/2" x 5-1/2" cards have glossy black-and-white player poses on front with the player's name overprinted. Backs have standard postcard indicia. A number of spelling errors and several variations exist. The unnumbered cards are checklisted here alphabetically; those with ads for the meat company, men's store or radio station are appropriately noted.

		NM	EX	VG
Complete Set (37):		3,775	1,700	945.00
Common Player:		100.00	45.00	25.00
(1)	Wally Berger	100.00	45.00	25.00
(2)	Bongiovanni (First name Nino.)	100.00	45.00	25.00
(3)	Frenchy Bordagaray	100.00	45.00	25.00
(4)	Joe Cascarella, Gene Schott (Val Decker only.)	100.00	45.00	25.00
(5)	Allan Cooke (Allen) (Val Decker only.))	100.00	45.00	25.00
(6)	Harry Craft (Also Val Decker.)	100.00	45.00	25.00
(7)	Kiki Cuyler (WHIO only.)	160.00	72.00	40.00
(8)	Ray Davis	100.00	45.00	25.00
(9)	Virgil Davis (Val Decker only.)	100.00	45.00	25.00
(10)	Paul Derringer (Also Val Decker.)	100.00	45.00	25.00
(11)	Joe DiMaggio	825.00	370.00	205.00
(12a)	Linus Frey (Also Val Decker.) (No right foot, large caption.)	100.00	45.00	25.00
(12b)	Linus Frey (Also Val Decker.) (Right foot shows, small caption.)	100.00	45.00	25.00
(13)	Lee Gamble	100.00	45.00	25.00
(14)	Ivan Goodman (Ival) (Also Val Decker.)	100.00	45.00	25.00
(15)	Hank Gowdy	100.00	45.00	25.00
(16)	Lee Grissom	100.00	45.00	25.00
(17a)	Willard Hershberger (Hershberger, name in white.) (Also Val Decker.))	100.00	45.00	25.00
(17b)	Willard Hershberger (Name in black.)	100.00	45.00	25.00
(18a)	Al Hollingsworth	100.00	45.00	25.00
(18b)	Al Hollingsworth (WHIO)	100.00	45.00	25.00
(18c)	Al Hollingsworth (Val Decker)	100.00	45.00	25.00
(19)	Hank Johnson	100.00	45.00	25.00
(20)	Edwin Joost	100.00	45.00	25.00
(21a)	Ernie Lombardi (Plain letters.) (Also Val Decker, Metro.)	160.00	72.00	40.00
(21b)	Ernie Lombardi (Fancy letters.) (Also Val Decker, Metro.)	160.00	72.00	40.00
(22)	Frank McCormick (Also Val Decker, Metro.)	100.00	45.00	25.00
(23)	Bill McKecknie (McKechnie)	145.00	65.00	36.00
(24)	Billy Meyers (Myers) (Also Val Decker.))	100.00	45.00	25.00
(25a)	Whitey Moore (Photo actually Bucky Walters.)	100.00	45.00	25.00
(25b)	Whitey Moore (Correct photo.)	100.00	45.00	25.00
(26)	Lew Riggs	100.00	45.00	25.00
(27)	Edd Roush (Val Decker only.)	145.00	65.00	36.00
(28a)	Leo Scarsella (Les)	160.00	72.00	40.00
(28b)	Les Scarcella (WHIO)	100.00	45.00	25.00
(29)	Gene Schott (WHIO)	100.00	45.00	25.00
(30)	Milburn Shoffner	100.00	45.00	25.00
(31)	Junior Thompson	100.00	45.00	25.00
(32a)	Johnny VanderMeer/ Throwing (Also Metro, Val Decker.)	175.00	79.00	44.00
(32b)	Johnny VanderMeer/Fldg (Also Metro.)	175.00	79.00	44.00
(33)	Bucky Walters	100.00	45.00	25.00
(34)	Bill Werber	100.00	45.00	25.00
(35)	Dick West	100.00	45.00	25.00
(36)	Jimmie Wilson	100.00	45.00	25.00
(37)	Cincinnati Reds composite team card.	100.00	45.00	25.00

1933 Oriental Theatre

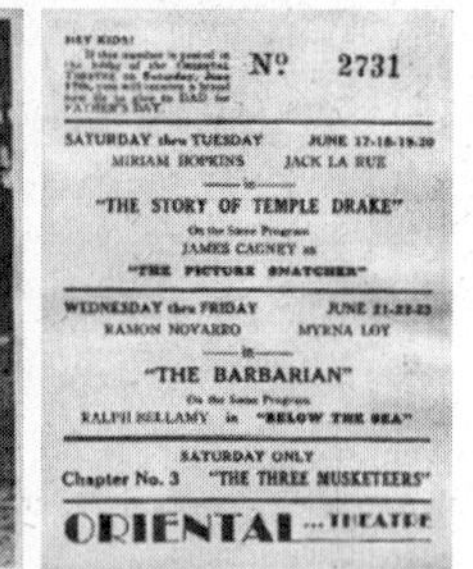
HEY KIDS!

Nº 2731

SATURDAY thru TUESDAY JUNE 17-18-19-20

MIRIAM HOPKINS JACK LA RUE

in

"THE STORY OF TEMPLE DRAKE"

On the Same Program

JAMES CAGNEY in

"THE PICTURE SNATCHER"

WEDNESDAY thru FRIDAY JUNE 21-22-23

RAMON NOVARRO MYRNA LOY

in

"THE BARBARIAN"

On the Same Program

RALPH BELLAMY in "BELOW THE SEA"

SATURDAY ONLY

Chapter No. 3 "THE THREE MUSKETEERS"

ORIENTAL ...THEATRE

To advertise its movie schedule for the week of June 17-23, as well as a Father's Day prize drawing, the Oriental Theatre (location unknown) printed its message on the back of a 1929 Kashin Publications (R316) card or cards. The extent to which this overprinting was undertaken is unknown.

	NM	EX	VG
Ed "Bing" Miller	125.00	62.50	37.50

1912 A.F. Orr Louis Sockalexis Photocard

This 3-1/2" x 5-1/2" sepia photocard carries the copyright of A.F. Orr of Old Town, Maine, hometown of the original Cleveland Indian. At the time of the card's issue, the fallen diamond star was operating a ferry and probably commissioned this image for sale to tourists.

	NM	EX	VG
Louis Sockalexis	2,000	1,000	600.00

1963 Otto Milk

The attributed issue date of this commemorative milk carton is approximate. A 4" x 8" panel on the front of the milk carton has a picture and history of Honus Wagner printed in red and blue. Wagner is the only ballplayer in the milk carton series honoring Western Pennsylvania celebrities.

		NM	EX	VG
(1)	Honus Wagner (Complete carton.)	250.00	125.00	75.00
(1)	Honus Wagner (Cut panel.)	60.00	30.00	18.00

1938 Our National Game Pins

This unnumbered 30-pin set issued circa 1938 carries the American Card Catalog designation of PM8. The pins, which measure 7/8" in diameter, have a bendable "tab" rather than a pin back. The player photo is printed in blue-and-white. The player's name and team are printed at bottom. The pins were originally sold on a square of cardboard decorated with stars and stripes and imprinted "OUR NATIONAL GAME" above the pin, and "A BASEBALL HERO" below. A large number of the pins, complete with their cardboard backing, were found in a hoard in Oklahoma in the early 1990s.

		NM	EX	VG
Complete Set (30):		1,200	600.00	350.00
Common Player:		20.00	10.00	6.00
(1)	Wally Berger	20.00	10.00	6.00
(2)	Lou Chiozza	20.00	10.00	6.00
(3)	Joe Cronin	40.00	20.00	12.00
(4)	Frank Crosetti	25.00	12.50	7.50
(5)	Jerome (Dizzy) Dean	75.00	37.00	22.00
(6)	Frank DeMaree (Demaree)	20.00	10.00	6.00
(7)	Joe DiMaggio	100.00	50.00	30.00
(8)	Bob Feller	65.00	32.00	19.50
(9)	Jimmy Foxx (Jimmie)	75.00	37.00	22.00
(10)	Lou Gehrig	100.00	50.00	30.00
(11)	Charles Gehringer	50.00	25.00	15.00
(12)	Lefty Gomez	40.00	20.00	12.00
(13)	Hank Greenberg	65.00	32.00	19.50
(14)	Irving (Bump) Hadley	20.00	10.00	6.00
(15)	Leo Hartnett	40.00	20.00	12.00
(16)	Carl Hubbell	50.00	25.00	15.00
(17)	John (Buddy) Lewis	20.00	10.00	6.00
(18)	Gus Mancuso	20.00	10.00	6.00
(19)	Joe McCarthy	40.00	20.00	12.00
(20)	Joe Medwick	40.00	20.00	12.00
(21)	Joe Moore	20.00	10.00	6.00
(22)	Mel Ott	50.00	25.00	15.00
(23)	Jake Powell	20.00	10.00	6.00
(24)	Jimmy Ripple	20.00	10.00	6.00
(25)	Red Ruffing	40.00	20.00	12.00
(26)	Hal Schumacher	20.00	10.00	6.00
(27)	George Selkirk	20.00	10.00	6.00
(28)	"Al" Simmons	40.00	20.00	12.00
(29)	Bill Terry	40.00	20.00	12.00
(30)	Harold Trosky	20.00	10.00	6.00

1936 Overland Candy Co. (R301)

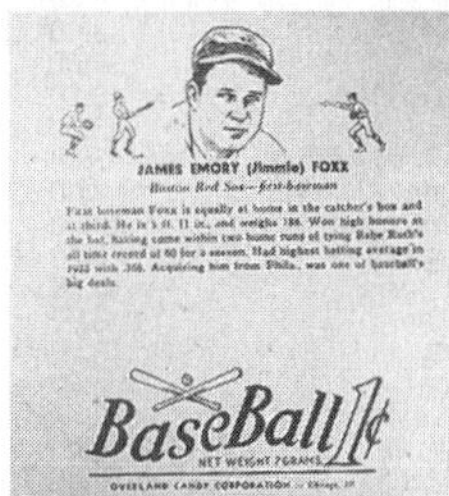

Used as wrappers for a piece of penny candy, these 5" x 5-1/4" waxed papers are usually found with resultant folds and creases, though unfolded examples are known. Printed in dark blue, the top of the wrapper features a line drawing portrait of the player, his formal name and nickname, team, position and career summary. The unnumbered wrappers are checklisted here alphabetically.

		NM	EX	VG
Complete Set (60):		45,000	20,000	9,000
Common Player:		650.00	300.00	130.00
(1)	Melo (Mel) Almada	650.00	300.00	130.00
(2)	Lucius B. (Luke) Appling	900.00	400.00	180.00
(3)	Howard Earl Averill	900.00	400.00	180.00
(4)	Walter Antone (Wally) Berger	650.00	300.00	130.00
(5)	Henry John (Zeke) Bonura	650.00	300.00	130.00
(6)	Dolph Camilli	650.00	300.00	130.00
(7)	Philip Joseph (Phil) Cavarretta	650.00	300.00	130.00
(8)	William Ben (Chappy) Chapman	650.00	300.00	130.00
(9)	Harland Clift (First name Harlond.)	650.00	300.00	130.00
(10a)	John Walter (Johnny) Cooney (Bees)	650.00	300.00	130.00
(10b)	John Walter (Johnny) Cooney (Dodgers)	650.00	300.00	130.00
(11)	Harry Danning	650.00	300.00	130.00
(12)	William N. (Bill) Dickey (Middle initial is N.)	950.00	425.00	190.00
(13a)	William J. (Bill) Dietrich (Athletics)	650.00	300.00	130.00
(13b)	William J. (Bill) Dietrich (White Sox)	650.00	300.00	130.00
(14)	Joseph (Deadpan Joe) DiMaggio	3,000	1,350	600.00
(15)	Wesley Cheek Ferrell	650.00	300.00	130.00
(16)	James Emory (Jimmie) Foxx	1,200	540.00	240.00
(17)	Henry Louis (Lou) Gehrig	3,150	1,425	630.00
(18)	Charles Leonard (Charley) Gehringer	900.00	400.00	180.00
(19)	Jose Luis (Chile) Gomez	650.00	300.00	130.00
(20)	Vernon (Lefty) Gomez	900.00	400.00	180.00
(21)	Joe Gordon	650.00	300.00	130.00
(22)	Henry (Hank) Greenberg	1,200	540.00	240.00
(23)	Robert Moses (Lefty) Grove	950.00	425.00	190.00
(24)	George W. (Mule) Haas	650.00	300.00	130.00
(25)	Ralston Burdett (Rollie) Hemsley	650.00	300.00	130.00
(26)	Michael Francis (Pinky) Higgins (Middle name Franklin.)	650.00	300.00	130.00
(27)	Oral Clyde (Hildy) Hildebrand	650.00	300.00	130.00
(28)	Robert Lee (Cherokee) Johnson	650.00	300.00	130.00
(29)	Baxter Byerly (Buck) Jordan	650.00	300.00	130.00
(30)	Ken Keltner	650.00	300.00	130.00
(31)	Fabian Kowalik	650.00	300.00	130.00
(32)	Harry A. Lavagetto	650.00	300.00	130.00
(33)	Anthony Michael (Poosh 'em Up) Lazzeri	900.00	400.00	180.00
(34)	Samuel A. Leslie	650.00	300.00	130.00
(35)	Dan (Slug) Lithwhiler (Last name Litwhiler.)	650.00	300.00	130.00
(36)	Theodore A. (Ted) Lyons	900.00	400.00	180.00
(37)	George McQuinn	650.00	300.00	130.00
(38)	John Robert (Skippy) Mize	900.00	400.00	180.00
(39)	Terry Moore	650.00	300.00	130.00
(40)	Charles Solomon (Buddy) Myer	650.00	300.00	130.00
(41)	Louis Norman (Buck) Newsom	650.00	300.00	130.00
(42)	Bill Nicholson	650.00	300.00	130.00
(43)	Raymond Pepper	650.00	300.00	130.00
(44)	Frank A. (Pity) Pytlak	650.00	300.00	130.00
(45)	Raymond Allen (Rip) Radcliff	650.00	300.00	130.00
(46)	Peter (Pete) Reiser (Correct name Harold Patrick.)	650.00	300.00	130.00
(47)	Carl Nettles (Sheeps) Reynolds	650.00	300.00	130.00
(48)	Robert Abial (Red) Rolfe	650.00	300.00	130.00
(49)	Lynwood Thomas (Schoolboy) Rowe	650.00	300.00	130.00
(50)	Aloysius Harry (Al) Simmons	900.00	400.00	180.00
(51)	Cecil Howard Travis (Middle name is Howell.)	650.00	300.00	130.00
(52)	Harold Arthus (Hal) Trosky	650.00	300.00	130.00
(53)	Joseph Franklin (Joe) Vosmik	650.00	300.00	130.00
(54)	Harold Burton (Rabbit) Warstler	650.00	300.00	130.00
(55)	William M. (Bill) Werber	650.00	300.00	130.00
(56)	Max West	650.00	300.00	130.00
(57)	Samuel F. (Sam) West	650.00	300.00	130.00
(58)	Whitlow (Whit) Wyatt	650.00	300.00	130.00

1921 Oxford Confectionery (E253)

Issued in 1921 by Oxford Confectionery of Oxford, Pa., this 20-card set was printed on thin paper and distributed with caramels. Each card measures 1-5/8" x 2-3/4" and features a

black-and-white player photo with the player's name and team printed in a white band along the bottom. The back carries a checklist of the players in the set, 14 of whom are now in the Hall of Fame. The set is designated as E253 in the ACC.

		NM	EX	VG
Complete Set (20):		35,000	15,750	7,000
Common Player:		1,000	450.00	200.00
(1)	Grover Alexander	1,800	810.00	360.00
(2)	Dave Bancroft	1,200	540.00	240.00
(3)	Max Carey	1,200	540.00	240.00
(4)	Ty Cobb	6,000	2,700	1,200
(5)	Eddie Collins	1,200	540.00	240.00
(6)	Frankie Frisch	1,200	540.00	240.00
(7)	Burleigh Grimes	1,200	540.00	240.00
(8)	"Bill" Holke (Walter)	1,000	450.00	200.00
(9)	Rogers Hornsby	1,800	810.00	360.00
(10)	Walter Johnson	3,000	1,350	600.00
(11)	Lee Meadows	1,000	450.00	200.00
(12)	Cy Perkins	1,000	450.00	200.00
(13)	Derrill Pratt	1,000	450.00	200.00
(14)	Ed Rousch (Roush)	1,200	540.00	240.00
(15)	"Babe" Ruth	12,000	5,400	2,400
(16)	Ray Schalk	1,200	540.00	240.00
(17)	George Sisler	1,200	540.00	240.00
(18)	Tris Speaker	1,800	810.00	360.00
(19)	Cy Williams	1,000	450.00	200.00
(20)	Whitey Witt	1,000	450.00	200.00

P

1958 Packard-Bell

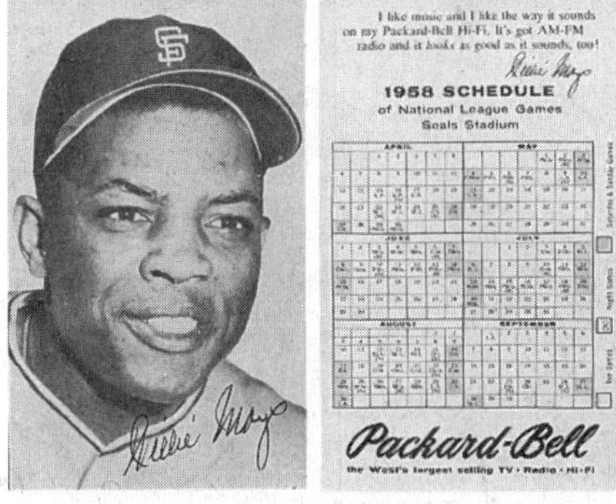

Issued by the "world's largest seller of TVs, radios and hi-fis," this set was distributed in California and features members of the newly arrived Los Angeles Dodgers and San Francisco Giants. The 3-1/2" x 5-1/2" black-and-white cards are unnumbered, checklisted here alphabetically.

		NM	EX	VG
Complete Set (7):		1,500	750.00	450.00
Common Player:		100.00	50.00	30.00
(1)	Walter Alston	125.00	65.00	35.00
(2)	John A. Antonelli	100.00	50.00	30.00
(3)	Jim Gilliam	125.00	65.00	35.00
(4)	Gil Hodges	200.00	100.00	60.00
(5)	Willie Mays	800.00	400.00	240.00
(6)	Bill Rigney	100.00	50.00	30.00
(7)	Hank Sauer	100.00	50.00	30.00

1978 Papa Gino's Discs

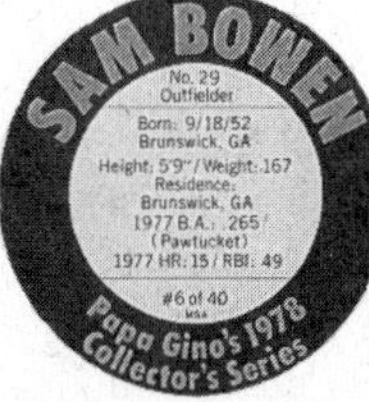

This promotion was largely confined to the Boston area, as 25 of the 40 players represented are Red Sox, the other 15 are all from American League teams. The 3-3/8" discs were given away with the purchase of soft drinks at the restaurant chain. Fronts have player portraits at center with name in the dark blue border at top and team below. Photos have the uniform logos airbrushed away because the discs were licensed only by the players' union, not MLB. Backs retain the color scheme with player data, previous season's stats, uniform and card numbers, sponsor's ad, etc.

		NM	EX	VG
Complete Set (40):		20.00	10.00	6.00
Common Player:		2.00	1.00	.60
1	Allen Ripley	2.00	1.00	.60
2	Jerry Remy	2.00	1.00	.60
3	Jack Brohamer	2.00	1.00	.60
4	Butch Hobson	2.00	1.00	.60
5	Dennis Eckersley	3.50	1.75	1.00
6	Sam Bowen	2.00	1.00	.60
7	Rick Burleson	2.00	1.00	.60
8	Carl Yastrzemski	5.00	2.50	1.50
9	Bill Lee	2.00	1.00	.60
10	Bob Montgomery	2.00	1.00	.60
11	Dick Drago	2.00	1.00	.60
12	Bob Stanley	2.00	1.00	.60
13	Fred Kendall	2.00	1.00	.60
14	Jim Rice	3.00	1.50	.90
15	George Scott	2.00	1.00	.60
16	Tom Burgmeier	2.00	1.00	.60
17	Frank Duffy	2.00	1.00	.60
18	Jim Wright	2.00	1.00	.60
19	Fred Lynn	2.00	1.00	.60
20	Bob Bailey	2.00	1.00	.60
21	Mike Torrez	2.00	1.00	.60
22	Bill Campbell	2.00	1.00	.60
23	Luis Tiant	2.00	1.00	.60
24	Dwight Evans	2.00	1.00	.60
25	Carlton Fisk	4.00	2.00	1.25
26	Reggie Jackson	5.00	2.50	1.50
27	Thurman Munson	3.50	1.75	1.00
28	Ron Guidry	2.00	1.00	.60
29	Bruce Bochte	2.00	1.00	.60
30	Richie Zisk	2.00	1.00	.60
31	Jim Palmer	4.00	2.00	1.25
32	Mark Fidrych	2.50	1.25	.70
33	Frank Tanana	2.00	1.00	.60
34	Buddy Bell	2.00	1.00	.60
35	Rod Carew	4.00	2.00	1.25
36	George Brett	7.50	3.75	2.25
37	Ralph Garr	2.00	1.00	.60
38	Larry Hisle	2.00	1.00	.60
39	Mitchell Page	2.00	1.00	.60
40	John Mayberry	2.00	1.00	.60

1974 Bob Parker 2nd Best

Star players who came in second, often to lesser-known players, in various statistical categories between 1899-1955 are featured in this collectors issue from Bob Parker. The blank-backed, black-and-white cards measure an unusual 3" x 8" and feature the story of the 1-2 finish in cartoon form. The unnumbered cards are listed here in chronological order.

		NM	EX	VG
Complete Set (25):		55.00	25.00	15.00
Common Player:		3.00	1.50	.90
(1)	Jesse Burkett, Ed Delahanty/1899	3.00	1.50	.90
(2)	Hans Wagner, Cy Seymour/1905	4.00	2.00	1.25
(3)	Gavvy Cravath, Jake Daubert/1913	3.00	1.50	.90
(4)	Joe Jackson, Ty Cobb/1913	10.00	5.00	3.00
(5)	Eddie Collins, Ty Cobb/1914	4.00	2.00	1.25
(6)	Babe Ruth, Heinie Manush/1926	7.50	3.75	2.25
(7)	Chick Hafey, Jim Bottomley, Hack Wilson/1928	3.00	1.50	.90
(8)	Paul Waner, Rogers Hornsby/1928	3.00	1.50	.90
(9)	Babe Herman, Lefty O'Doul/1929	3.00	1.50	.90
(10)	Al Simmons, Lew Fonseca/1929	3.00	1.50	.90
(11)	Lou Gehrig, Babe Ruth/1930	10.00	5.00	3.00

(12)	Babe Herman, Bill Terry/1930	3.00	1.50	.90
(13)	Chuck Klein, Hack Wilson/ 1930	3.00	1.50	.90
(14)	Jim Bottomley, Bill Terry, Chick Hafey/1931	3.00	1.50	.90
(15)	Jimmy (Jimmie) Foxx, Dale Alexander/1932	3.00	1.50	.90
(16)	Spud Davis, Chuck Klein/1933	3.00	1.50	.90
(17)	Heinie Manush, Jimmy Foxx/ 1933	3.00	1.50	.90
(18)	Mel Ott, Wally Berger/1935	3.00	1.50	.90
(19)	Joe Vosmik, Buddy Myer/ 1935	3.00	1.50	.90
(20)	Blimp Phelps, Paul Waner/ 1936	3.00	1.50	.90
(21)	Bobby Doerr, Lou Boudreau/ 1944	3.00	1.50	.90
(22)	Stan Musial, Dixie Walker/ 1944	4.00	2.00	1.25
(23)	George Kell, Billy Goodman/ 1950	3.00	1.50	.90
(24)	Al Rosen, Mickey Vernon/ 1953	3.00	1.50	.90
(25)	Vic Power, Al Kaline/1955	3.00	1.50	.90

1976 Bob Parker More Baseball Cartoons

This collectors' issue showcased the pen and ink artwork of Ohio cartoonist Bob Parker on cards featuring current and former ballplayers from the great to the obscure. Cards are in 3-1/2" x 5" format with black-and-white fronts and blank backs.

		NM	EX	VG
Complete Set (24):		65.00	32.50	20.00
Common Card:		3.00	1.50	.90
1	Hank Aaron, Babe Ruth (All-Time HR Specialists)	7.50	3.75	2.25
2	Ernie Banks	4.00	2.00	1.25
3	Rod Carew	3.00	1.50	.90
4	Joe DiMaggio	15.00	7.50	4.50
5	Doug Flynn	3.00	1.50	.90
6	Mike Garcia	3.00	1.50	.90
7	Steve Garvey, Greg Luzinski/ AS	3.00	1.50	.90
8	Lou Gehrig	15.00	7.50	4.50
9	Chuck Klein, Hack Wilson (Hall of Famers?)	3.00	1.50	.90
10	Don Larsen	3.00	1.50	.90
11	Fred Lynn	3.00	1.50	.90
12	Roy Majtyka	3.00	1.50	.90
13	Pepper Martin	3.00	1.50	.90
14	Christy Mathewson	5.00	2.50	1.50
15	Cal McVey	3.00	1.50	.90
16	Tony Perez	3.00	1.50	.90
17	Lou Gehrig, Babe Ruth (Great Moments)	15.00	7.50	4.50
18	Everett Scott	3.00	1.50	.90
19	Bobby Thomson	3.00	1.50	.90
20	Ted Williams/1939	7.50	3.75	2.25
21	Ted Williams (Great Moments)	7.50	3.75	2.25
22	Bill Madlock	3.00	1.50	.90
23	Henry Chadwick, Buck Ewing, Albert Spalding, Honus Wagner (Hall of Famers)	3.00	1.50	.90
---	Checklist	3.00	1.50	.90

1977 Bob Parker Cincinnati Reds

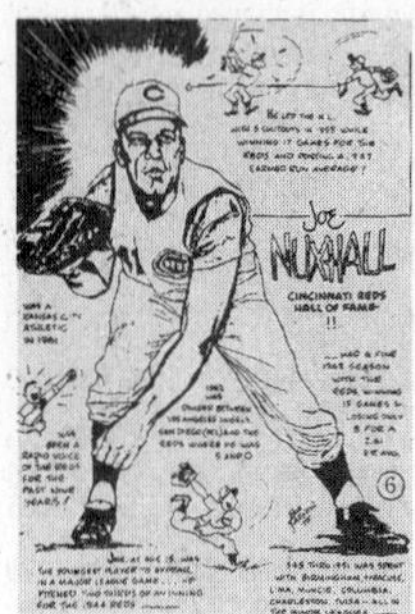

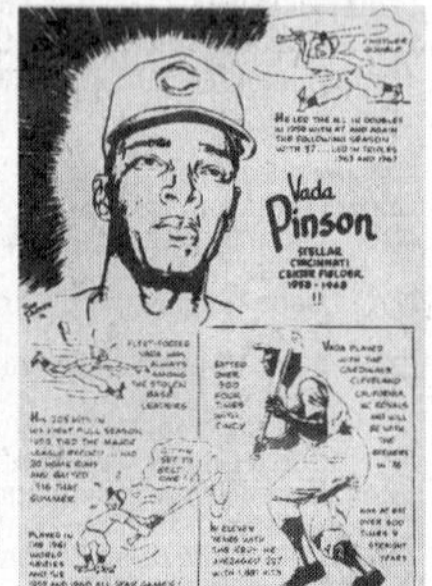

In the late 1970s, Ohio cartoonist Bob Parker drew a series of Reds feature cartoons for the weekly "Reds Alert." Later, he assembled two groups of those cartoons into collectors' issue card sets. The cards are black-and-white with blank backs. Fronts have portraits and/or action main drawings, usually with some cartoon figures included to draw attention to the player's career highlights. Size is 3-1/2" x 5". The unnumbered series is listed in alphabetical order.

		NM	EX	VG
Complete Set (48):		110.00	55.00	32.50
Common Player:		3.00	1.50	.90
	UNNUMBERED SERIES (24):	55.00	25.00	15.00
(1)	Sparky Anderson	4.00	2.00	1.25
(2)	Wally Berger	3.00	1.50	.90
(3)	Pedro Borbon	3.00	1.50	.90
(4)	Rube Bressler	3.00	1.50	.90
(5)	Gordy Coleman	3.00	1.50	.90
(6)	Dave Concepcion	3.00	1.50	.90
(7)	Harry Craft	3.00	1.50	.90
(8)	Hugh Critz	3.00	1.50	.90
(9)	Dan Driessen	3.00	1.50	.90
(10)	Pat Duncan	3.00	1.50	.90
(11)	Lonnie Frey	3.00	1.50	.90
(12)	Ival Goodman	3.00	1.50	.90
(13)	Heinie Groh	3.00	1.50	.90
(14)	Noodles Hahn	3.00	1.50	.90
(15)	Mike Lum	3.00	1.50	.90
(16)	Bill McKechnie	3.00	1.50	.90
(17)	Pat Moran	3.00	1.50	.90
(18)	Billy Myers	3.00	1.50	.90
(19)	Gary Nolan	3.00	1.50	.90
(20)	Fred Norman	3.00	1.50	.90
(21)	Jim O'Toole	3.00	1.50	.90
(22)	Vada Pinson	4.00	2.00	1.25
(23)	Bucky Walters	3.00	1.50	.90
(24)	Checklist	3.00	1.50	.90
	NUMBERED SERIES (24):	60.00	30.00	18.00
1	Ted Kluszewski	6.00	3.00	1.75
2	Johnny Bench	10.00	5.00	3.00
3	Jim Maloney	3.00	1.50	.90
4	Bubbles Hargrave	3.00	1.50	.90
5	Don Gullett	3.00	1.50	.90
6	Joe Nuxhall	4.00	2.00	1.25
7	Edd Roush	3.00	1.50	.90
8	Wally Post	3.00	1.50	.90
9	George Wright	3.00	1.50	.90
10	George Foster	3.00	1.50	.90
11	Pete Rose	15.00	7.50	4.50
12	Red Lucas	3.00	1.50	.90
13	Joe Morgan	4.00	2.00	1.25
14	Eppa Rixey	3.00	1.50	.90
15	Bill Werber	3.00	1.50	.90
16	Frank Robinson	6.00	3.00	1.75
17	Dolf Luque	4.00	2.00	1.25
18	Paul Derringer	3.00	1.50	.90
19	Frank McCormick	3.00	1.50	.90
20	Ken Griffey	3.00	1.50	.90
21	Jack Billingham	3.00	1.50	.90
22	Larry Kopf	3.00	1.50	.90
23	Ernie Lombardi	3.00	1.50	.90
24	Johnny Vander Meer	3.00	1.50	.90

1977-81 Bob Parker Hall of Fame

This is one of many collectors issues produced in the mid to late 1970s by midwestern sports artist Bob Parker. The 3-3/8" x 5-1/2" cards are printed in sepia on tan cardboard; they are blank-backed. Fronts have a portrait drawing of the player, with career highlights in cartoon form. Three series were issued: #1-54 in 1977; #55-77 in 1980 and #78-100 in 1981. A header card was issued with each series.

		NM	EX	VG
Complete Set (103):		125.00	65.00	35.00
Common Player:		3.00	1.50	.90
	First Series Set (55):	50.00	25.00	15.00
---	First Series Header	1.00	.50	.30
1	Grover Alexander	3.00	1.50	.90
2	Cap Anson	3.00	1.50	.90
3	Luke Appling	3.00	1.50	.90
4	Ernie Banks	4.00	2.00	1.25
5	Chief Bender	3.00	1.50	.90
6	Jim Bottomley	3.00	1.50	.90
7	Dan Brouthers	3.00	1.50	.90
8	Morgan Bulkeley	3.00	1.50	.90
9	Roy Campanella	7.50	3.75	2.25
10	Alexander Cartwright	3.00	1.50	.90
11	Henry Chadwick	3.00	1.50	.90
12	John Clarkson	3.00	1.50	.90
13	Ty Cobb	10.00	5.00	3.00
14	Eddie Collins	3.00	1.50	.90
16	Charles Comiskey	3.00	1.50	.90
17	Sam Crawford	3.00	1.50	.90
18	Dizzy Dean	4.00	2.00	1.25
19	Joe DiMaggio	16.00	8.00	4.75
20	Buck Ewing	3.00	1.50	.90
21	Bob Feller	4.00	2.00	1.25
22	Lou Gehrig	16.00	8.00	4.75
23	Goose Goslin	3.00	1.50	.90
24	Burleigh Grimes	3.00	1.50	.90
25	Chick Hafey	3.00	1.50	.90
26	Rogers Hornsby	3.00	1.50	.90
27	Carl Hubbell	3.00	1.50	.90
28	Miller Huggins	3.00	1.50	.90
29	Tim Keefe	3.00	1.50	.90
30	Mike Kelly	3.00	1.50	.90
31	Nap Lajoie	3.00	1.50	.90
32	Freddie Lindstrom	3.00	1.50	.90
33	Connie Mack	3.00	1.50	.90
34	Mickey Mantle	25.00	12.50	7.50
35	Heinie Manush	3.00	1.50	.90
36	Joe McGinnity	3.00	1.50	.90
37	John McGraw	3.00	1.50	.90
38	Ed Plank	3.00	1.50	.90
39	Eppa Rixey	3.00	1.50	.90
40	Jackie Robinson	12.00	6.00	3.50
41	Edd Roush	3.00	1.50	.90
42	Babe Ruth	20.00	10.00	6.00
43	Al Simmons	3.00	1.50	.90
44	Al Spalding	3.00	1.50	.90
45	Tris Speaker	3.00	1.50	.90
46	Casey Stengel	3.00	1.50	.90
47	Bill Terry	3.00	1.50	.90
48	Rube Waddell	3.00	1.50	.90
49	Honus Wagner	5.00	2.50	1.50
50	Paul Waner	3.00	1.50	.90
51	John Montgomery Ward	3.00	1.50	.90
52	Ted Williams	10.00	5.00	3.00
53	George Wright	3.00	1.50	.90
54	Harry Wright	3.00	1.50	.90
	Second Series Set (24):	40.00	20.00	12.00
---	Second Series Header	1.00	.50	.30
55	Mordecai Brown	3.00	1.50	.90
56	Frank Chance	3.00	1.50	.90
57	Candy Cummings	3.00	1.50	.90
58	Frank Frisch	3.00	1.50	.90
59	Gabby Hartnett	3.00	1.50	.90
60	Billy Herman	3.00	1.50	.90
61	Waite Hoyt	3.00	1.50	.90
62	Walter Johnson	5.00	2.50	1.50
63	Kenesaw Landis	3.00	1.50	.90
64	Rube Marquard	3.00	1.50	.90
65	Christy Mathewson	6.00	3.00	1.75
66	Eddie Mathews	3.00	1.50	.90
67	Willie Mays	10.00	5.00	3.00
68	Bill McKechnie	3.00	1.50	.90
69	Stan Musial	7.50	3.75	2.25
70	Mel Ott	3.00	1.50	.90
71	Satchel Paige	7.50	3.75	2.25
72	Robin Roberts	3.00	1.50	.90
73	George Sisler	3.00	1.50	.90
74	Warren Spahn	3.00	1.50	.90
75	Joe Tinker	3.00	1.50	.90
76	Dazzy Vance	3.00	1.50	.90
77	Cy Young	6.00	3.00	1.75
	Third Series Set (24):	40.00	20.00	12.00
---	Third Series Header	1.00	.50	.30
78	Home Run Baker	3.00	1.50	.90
79	Yogi Berra	4.00	2.00	1.25
80	Max Carey	3.00	1.50	.90
81	Roberto Clemente	16.00	8.00	4.75
82	Mickey Cochrane	3.00	1.50	.90
83	Roger Connor	3.00	1.50	.90
84	Joe Cronin	3.00	1.50	.90
85	Kiki Cuyler	3.00	1.50	.90
86	Johnny Evers	3.00	1.50	.90
87	Jimmie Foxx	3.00	1.50	.90
88	Charlie Gehringer	3.00	1.50	.90
89	Lefty Gomez	3.00	1.50	.90
90	Jesse Haines	3.00	1.50	.90
91	Will Harridge	3.00	1.50	.90
92	Monte Irvin	3.00	1.50	.90
93	Addie Joss	3.00	1.50	.90
94	Al Kaline	3.00	1.50	.90
95	Sandy Koufax	10.00	5.00	3.00
96	Rabbit Maranville	3.00	1.50	.90
97	Jim O'Rourke	3.00	1.50	.90
98	Wilbert Robinson	3.00	1.50	.90
99	Pie Traynor	3.00	1.50	.90
100	Zack Wheat	3.00	1.50	.90

1968-70 Partridge Meats Reds

These cards were produced in conjunction with Reds' autograph appearances at Kroger food stores in the Cincinnati area. Players' service with the Reds indicates this set was issued over a period of several years. Similar cards are known for other Cincinnati pro sports teams. The 1968 cards measure 4" x 5" and feature a black-and-white player photo set against a borderless white background. The player's name and team and the word "Likes" are printed in black, the ad for the issuing meat company at bottom is printed in red. Cards have a blank back. The 1969-70 cards are in the same format but in 3-3/4" x 5-1/2" format. The unnumbered cards are checklisted here in alphabetical order.

	NM	EX	VG
Complete Set (11):	500.00	250.00	150.00
Common Player:	20.00	10.00	6.00
(1) Ted Abernathy	40.00	20.00	12.00
(2) John Bench	50.00	25.00	15.00
(3) Jimmy Bragan	20.00	10.00	6.00
(4) Dave Bristol	40.00	20.00	12.00
(5) Tommy Helms	40.00	20.00	12.00
(6) Gary Nolan	20.00	10.00	6.00
(7) Milt Pappas	40.00	20.00	12.00
(8) Don Pavletich	40.00	20.00	12.00
(9) Mel Queen	40.00	20.00	12.00
(10) Pete Rose	150.00	75.00	45.00
(11) Jim Stewart	40.00	20.00	12.00

1972 Partridge Meats Reds

Similar in format to the meat company's 1968-70 issue, these later cards are in a slightly different size - 3-3/4" x 5-1/2". The ad on the '72 cards reads "Photo courtesy of Partridge Meats."

	NM	EX	VG
Complete Set (7):	225.00	110.00	65.00
Common Player:	30.00	15.00	9.00
(1) Don Gullett	30.00	15.00	9.00
(2) Lee May	30.00	15.00	9.00
(3) Denis Menke	30.00	15.00	9.00
(4) Jim Merritt	30.00	15.00	9.00
(5) Gary Nolan	30.00	15.00	9.00
(6) Tony Perez	60.00	30.00	18.00
(7) Bob Tolan	30.00	15.00	9.00

1922 Wm. Paterson

Believed to have been a Canadian candy premium, this 50-card set of 2" x 3-1/4" cards features portrait or posed action photos with wide white borders. Beneath the photo is a card number, player name, team, and in two lines, "Wm. Paterson, Limited / Brantford, Canada." Backs are blank. Two distinct types are seen, black-and-white and sepia, though the reason for the variations is unknown.

	NM	EX	VG
Complete Set (50):	60,000	24,000	12,000
Common Player:	475.00	200.00	100.00
1 Eddie Roush	1,000	400.00	200.00
2 Rube Marquard	1,000	400.00	200.00
3 Del Gainor	475.00	200.00	100.00
4 George Sisler	1,000	400.00	200.00
5 Joe Bush	475.00	200.00	100.00
6 Joe Oeschger	475.00	200.00	100.00
7 Willie Kamm	475.00	200.00	100.00
8 John Watson	475.00	200.00	100.00
9 Dolf Luque	550.00	225.00	110.00
10 Miller Huggins	1,000	400.00	200.00
11 Wally Schang	475.00	200.00	100.00
12 Bob Shawkey	475.00	200.00	100.00
13 Tris Speaker	1,750	700.00	350.00
14 Hugh McQuillan	475.00	200.00	100.00
15 "Long George" Kelly	1,000	400.00	200.00
16 Ray Schalk	1,000	400.00	200.00
17 Sam Jones	475.00	200.00	100.00
18 Grover Alexander	1,750	700.00	350.00
19 Bob Meusel	475.00	200.00	100.00
20 "Irish" Emil Meusel	475.00	200.00	100.00
21 Rogers Hornsby	1,750	700.00	350.00
22 Harry Heilmann	1,000	400.00	200.00
23 Heinie Groh	475.00	200.00	100.00
24 Frank Frisch	1,000	400.00	200.00
25 Babe Ruth	15,000	6,000	3,000
26 Jack Bentley	475.00	200.00	100.00
27 Everett Scott	475.00	200.00	100.00
28 Max Carey	1,000	400.00	200.00
29 Chick Fewster	475.00	200.00	100.00
30 Cy Williams	475.00	200.00	100.00
31 Burleigh Grimes	1,000	400.00	200.00
32 Waite Hoyt	1,000	400.00	200.00
33 Frank Snyder	475.00	200.00	100.00
34 Clyde Milan	475.00	200.00	100.00
35 Eddie Collins	1,000	400.00	200.00
36 Travis Jackson	1,000	400.00	200.00
37 Ken Williams	475.00	200.00	100.00
38 Dave Bancroft	1,000	400.00	200.00
39 Mike McNally	475.00	200.00	100.00
40 John McGraw	1,000	400.00	200.00
41 Art Nehf	475.00	200.00	100.00
42 "Rabbit" Maranville	1,000	400.00	200.00
43 Charlie Grimm	475.00	200.00	100.00
44 Joe Judge	475.00	200.00	100.00
45 Wally Pipp	475.00	200.00	100.00
46 Ty Cobb	10,000	4,000	2,000
47 Walter Johnson	3,000	1,200	600.00
48 Jake Daubert	475.00	200.00	100.00
49 Zack Wheat	1,000	400.00	200.00
50 Herb Pennock	1,000	400.00	200.00

1921 Pathe Freres Phonograph Co.

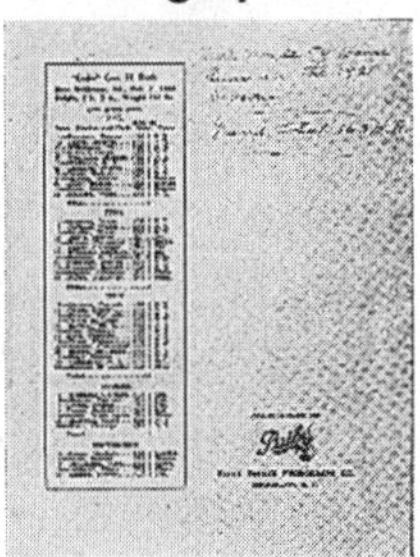

One of the rarest early-1920s Babe Ruth items is this premium photo issued by Pathe Freres Phonograph Co. of Brooklyn. Ruth is pictured bare-headed in a pinstriped uniform on the front of this approximately 7" x 9-1/4" card, printed in green and gray tones with a white border. A photo credit to White Studios of New York is given on the front and there is a facsimile autograph at bottom front. The black-and-white back has a listing of Ruth's 1920 homers in a box at left, and a Pathe ad at bottom-right.

	NM	EX	VG
Babe Ruth	3,500	1,750	1,050

1910 PC796 Sepia Postcards

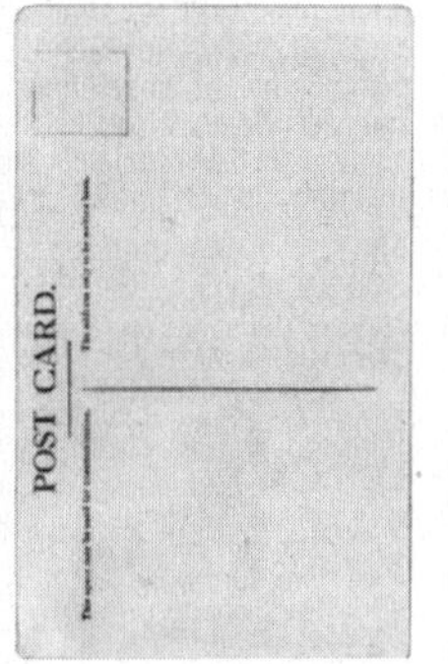

The manufacturer of these sepia-toned 3-1/2" x 5-1/2" postcards is unknown, but most of the photos utilized are familiar from other card issues of the era. Fronts have the player name at bottom in fancy capital letters. Backs have a standard divided postcard indicia. The set was given the PC796 designation in the "American Card Catalog." The unnumbered cards are checklisted here alphabetically.

	NM	EX	VG
Complete Set (25):	22,500	9,000	4,500
Common Player:	300.00	120.00	60.00
(1) Roger Bresnahan	600.00	240.00	120.00
(2) Al Bridwell	300.00	120.00	60.00
(3) Mordecai Brown	600.00	240.00	120.00
(4) Frank Chance	600.00	240.00	120.00
(5) Hal Chase	450.00	180.00	90.00
(6) Ty Cobb	4,250	1,700	850.00
(7) Ty Cobb, Hanus Wagner	3,750	1,500	750.00
(8) Eddie Collins	600.00	240.00	120.00
(9) Sam Crawford	600.00	240.00	120.00
(10) Art Devlin	300.00	120.00	60.00
(11) Red Dooin	300.00	120.00	60.00
(12) Johnny Evers, Germany Schaefer	400.00	160.00	80.00
(13) Sam Frock	300.00	120.00	60.00
(14) George Gibson	300.00	120.00	60.00
(15) Artie Hoffman (Hofman)	300.00	120.00	60.00
(16) Walter Johnson	1,200	480.00	240.00
(17) Nap Lajoie	600.00	240.00	120.00
(18) Harry Lord	300.00	120.00	60.00
(19) Christy Mathewson	2,000	800.00	400.00
(20) Orval Overall	300.00	120.00	60.00
(21) Eddie Plank	600.00	240.00	120.00
(22) Tris Speaker	750.00	300.00	150.00
(23) Gabby Street	300.00	120.00	60.00
(24) Honus Wagner	3,000	1,200	600.00
(25) Ed Walsh	600.00	240.00	120.00

1869 Peck & Snyder Cincinnati Red Stockings - Small

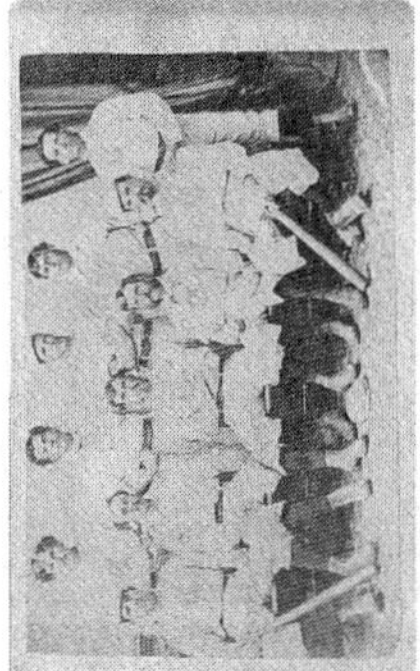

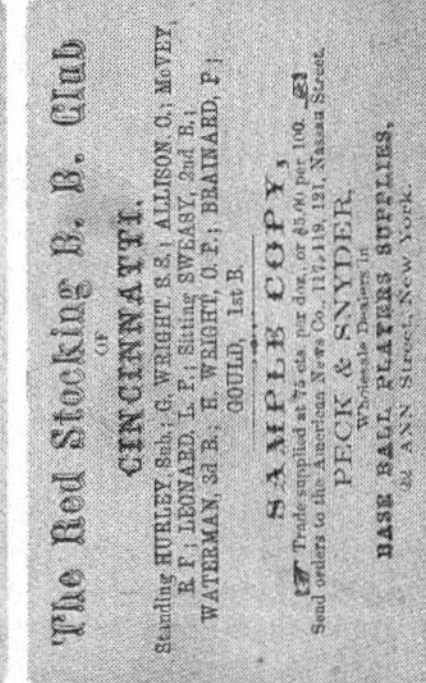

Many consider this to be the first true baseball card in that it was produced in large quantities (relative to the cabinets and carte de visites of the era) and offered to firms wishing to place their advertising on the back. The 3-15/16" x 2-3/8" card features a sepia team photo on front of baseball's first real professional team, including Hall of Famers George and Harry Wright. The Peck & Snyder ad back is the most commonly found, but others are known, including a back which lists only the team's line-up.

	NM	EX	VG
Cincinnati Red Stocking Team	25,000	12,000	7,000

1869 Peck & Snyder Cincinnati Red Stockings - Large

Many consider this to be the first true baseball card in that it was produced in large quantities (relative to the cabinets and carte de visites of the era) and offered to firms wishing to place their advertising on the back. The 4-3/16" x 3-5/16" card features a sepia team photo on front of baseball's first real professional team, including Hall of Famers George and Harry Wright. On this larger format, the players are identified on front with the team name in ornate black or red (slightly scarcer) type at bottom. Backs have been seen with ads for New York "Sportsman's "Emporium" along with a caricature of a bearded ballplayer, and for "The New York City Base Ball & Skate Emporium," with a large illsutration of an ice skate.

	NM	EX	VG
Cincinnati Red Stocking Team	35,000	20,000	12,000

1870 Peck & Snyder Chicago White Stockings

Using popular baseball teams of the day as an advertising medium, this apporoximately 4" x 2-3/4" black-and-white card pictures and identifies on front the 1870 Chicago White Stockings of pre-National Association days. On back is an ad for Peck & Snyder of New York City.

	NM	EX	VG
Chicago White Stockings	20,000	10,000	6,000

1870 Peck & Snyder New York Mutuals

Using popular baseball teams of the day as an advertising medium, this apporoximately 4" x 2-3/4" black-and-white card pictures and identifies on front the 1870 New York Mutuals of pre-National Association days. On back is a cartoon ad for Peck & Snyder of New York City.

	NM	EX	VG
New York Mutuals	20,000	10,000	6,000
James Creighton			

1870 Peck & Snyder Philadelphia Athletics

A composite photo of the players in street clothes is featured on this promotional card for the New York City sporting goods dealer whose advertising appears on back.

Philadelphia Athletics (Sold for $2,780 in 10/01 auction in Poor condition.)

1963 Pepsi-Cola Colt .45's

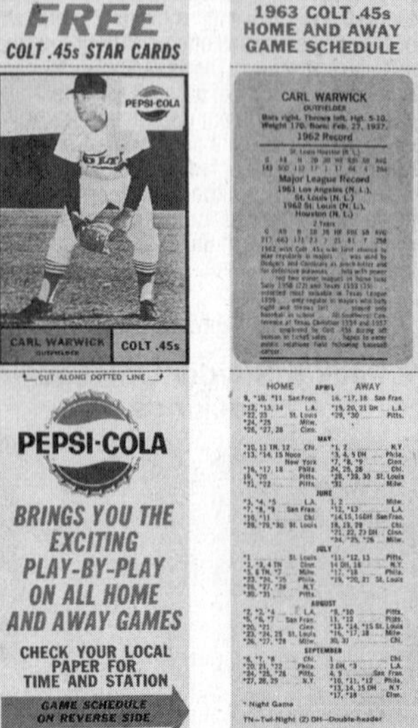

This issue was distributed regionally in Texas in bottled six-packs of Pepsi. The cards were issued on 2-3/8" x 9-1/8" panels. A 2-3/8" x 3-3/4" card was printed on each panel, which also included promos for Pepsi and the Colt .45's, as well as a team schedule. Card fronts are black-and-white posed action photos with blue and red trim. Backs offer player statistics and career highlights. The John Bateman card was apparently never distributed publicly and is among the rarest baseball cards of the 1960s. The unnumbered cards are checklisted here alphabetically. Values shown are for complete panels with top and bottom tabs; those without are valued about 25 percent.

		NM	EX	VG
Complete Set (16):		800.00	400.00	240.00
Common Player:		10.00	5.00	3.00
(1)	Bob Aspromonte	10.00	5.00	3.00
(2)	John Bateman/SP	2,500	1,250	750.00
(3)	Bob Bruce	10.00	5.00	3.00
(4)	Jim Campbell	10.00	5.00	3.00
(5)	Dick Farrell	10.00	5.00	3.00
(6)	Ernie Fazio	10.00	5.00	3.00
(7)	Carroll Hardy	10.00	5.00	3.00
(8)	J.C. Hartman	10.00	5.00	3.00
(9)	Ken Johnson	10.00	5.00	3.00
(10)	Bob Lillis/SP	375.00	185.00	110.00
(11)	Don McMahon	10.00	5.00	3.00
(12)	Pete Runnels	10.00	5.00	3.00
(13)	Al Spangler	10.00	5.00	3.00
(14)	Rusty Staub	35.00	17.50	10.00
(15)	Johnny Temple	10.00	5.00	3.00
(16)	Carl Warwick/SP	300.00	150.00	90.00

1977 Pepsi-Cola Baseball Stars

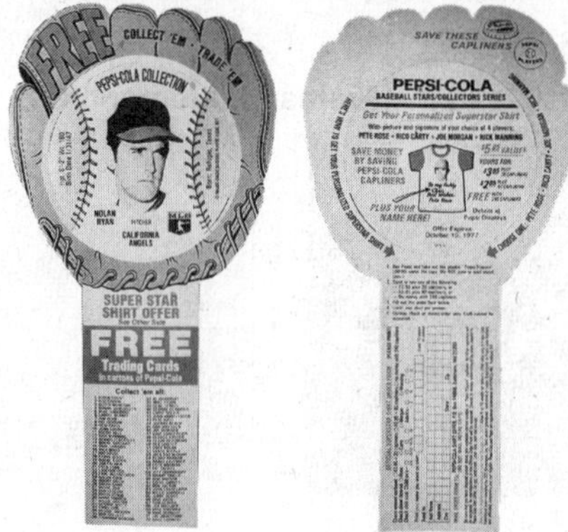

An Ohio regional promotion (the checklist is extra heavy with Indians and Reds players), large numbers of these cards found their way into hobby dealers' hands. Designed to be inserted into cartons of soda, the cards have a 3-3/8" diameter central disc attached with perforations to a baseball glove design. A tab beneath the glove contains the checklist (the card discs themselves are unnumbered) and a coupon on back for ordering a player t-shirt, the offer for which is made on the back of the player disc. The Players Association logo appears on front, but the producer, Mike Schechter Associates, did not seek licensing by Major League Baseball, with the result that uniform logos have been removed from the black-and-white player photos. Prices shown are for complete glove/disc/tab cards. Values for unattached player discs would be no more than one-half of those shown. The discs of Reggie Jackson and Mike Schmidt can be found with either orange, green, purple, light blue or sky blue side panels; the other player discs are known in only one color each.

		NM	EX	VG
Complete Set (72):		35.00	17.50	10.00
W/Color Variations (80):		75.00	37.50	22.50
Common Player:		1.00	.50	.30
1	Robin Yount	4.00	2.00	1.25
2	Rod Carew	4.00	2.00	1.25
3	Butch Wynegar	1.00	.50	.30
4	Manny Sanguillen	1.00	.50	.30
5	Mike Hargrove	1.00	.50	.30
6	Larvel (Larvell) Blanks	1.00	.50	.30
7	Jim Kern	1.00	.50	.30
8	Pat Dobson	1.00	.50	.30
9	Rico Carty	1.00	.50	.30
10	John Grubb	1.00	.50	.30
11	Buddy Bell	1.00	.50	.30
12	Rick Manning	1.00	.50	.30
13	Dennis Eckersley	4.00	2.00	1.25
14	Wayne Garland	1.00	.50	.30
15	Dave LaRoche	1.00	.50	.30
16	Rick Waits	1.00	.50	.30
17	Ray Fosse	1.00	.50	.30
18	Frank Duffy	1.00	.50	.30
19	Duane Kuiper	1.00	.50	.30
20	Jim Palmer	4.00	2.00	1.25
21	Fred Lynn	1.00	.50	.30
22	Carlton Fisk	4.00	2.00	1.25
23	Carl Yastrzemski	6.00	3.00	1.75
24	Nolan Ryan	17.50	8.75	5.25
25	Bobby Grich	1.00	.50	.30
26	Ralph Garr	1.00	.50	.30
27	Richie Zisk	1.00	.50	.30
28	Ron LeFlore	1.00	.50	.30
29	Rusty Staub	1.00	.50	.30
30	Mark Fidrych	1.50	.70	.45
31	Willie Horton	1.00	.50	.30
32	George Brett	10.00	5.00	3.00
33	Amos Otis	1.00	.50	.30
34a	Reggie Jackson (Green)	7.50	3.75	2.25
34b	Reggie Jackson (Light blue.)	7.50	3.75	2.25
34c	Reggie Jackson (Orange)	7.50	3.75	2.25
34d	Reggie Jackson (Purple)	7.50	3.75	2.25
34e	Reggie Jackson (Sky blue.)	7.50	3.75	2.25
35	Don Gullett	1.00	.50	.30
36	Thurman Munson	3.00	1.50	.90
37	Al Hrabosky	1.00	.50	.30
38	Mike Tyson	1.00	.50	.30
39	Gene Tenace	1.00	.50	.30
40	George Hendrick	1.00	.50	.30
41	Chris Speier	1.00	.50	.30
42	John Montefusco	1.00	.50	.30
43	Pete Rose	10.00	5.00	3.00
44	Johnny Bench	5.00	2.50	1.50
45	Dan Driessen	1.00	.50	.30
46	Joe Morgan	4.00	2.00	1.25
47	Dave Concepcion	1.00	.50	.30
48	George Foster	1.00	.50	.30
49	Cesar Geronimo	1.00	.50	.30
50	Ken Griffey	1.00	.50	.30
51	Gary Nolan	1.00	.50	.30
52	Santo Alcala	1.00	.50	.30
53	Jack Billingham	1.00	.50	.30
54	Pedro Borbon	1.00	.50	.30
55	Rawly Eastwick	1.00	.50	.30
56	Fred Norman	1.00	.50	.30
57	Pat Zachary (Zachry)	1.00	.50	.30
58	Jeff Burroughs	1.00	.50	.30
59	Manny Trillo	1.00	.50	.30
60	Bob Watson	1.00	.50	.30
61	Steve Garvey	1.50	.70	.45
62	Don Sutton	4.00	2.00	1.25
63	John Candelaria	1.00	.50	.30
64	Willie Stargell	4.00	2.00	1.25
65	Jerry Reuss	1.00	.50	.30
66	Dave Cash	1.00	.50	.30
67	Tom Seaver	5.00	2.50	1.50
68	Jon Matlock	1.00	.50	.30
69	Dave Kingman	1.00	.50	.30
70a	Mike Schmidt (Green)	7.50	3.75	2.25
70b	Mike Schmidt (Light blue.)	7.50	3.75	2.25
70c	Mike Schmidt (Orange)	7.50	3.75	2.25
70d	Mike Schmidt (Purple)	7.50	3.75	2.25
70e	Mike Schmidt (Sky blue.)	7.50	3.75	2.25
71	Jay Johnstone	1.00	.50	.30
72	Greg Luzinski	1.00	.50	.30

1977 Pepsi-Cola Cincinnati Reds Playing Cards

Similar to a multi-sport series produced by Cubic Corp. (see also), these playing cards sets feature on back the pencil drawings of Al Landsman. Each boxed deck featured one Reds star player within a red border. Also on each card back are a facsimile autograph and Pepsi logo. Cards are standard bridge size (2-1/4" x 3-1/2") with rounded corners. Decks were available by sending in 250 16-oz. Pepsi cap liners or a combination of cash and cap liners.

		NM	EX	VG
(1)	Johnny Bench (Boxed deck.)	35.00	17.50	10.00
(1)	Johnny Bench (Single card.)	1.50	.70	.45
(2)	Joe Morgan (Boxed deck.)	20.00	10.00	6.00
(2)	Joe Morgan (Single card.)	1.00	.50	.30
(3)	Pete Rose (Boxed deck.)	55.00	27.50	16.50
(3)	Pete Rose (Single card.)	4.00	2.00	1.25

1978 Pepsi-Cola Superstars

In its second year of producing carton-stuffer baseball cards, Cincinnati area Pepsi bottlers issued a 40-card set featuring 25 Reds players and 15 other major league stars. The entire carton insert measures 2-1/8" x 9-1/2". Besides the baseball card at top, there is a checklist and mail-in offer for playing cards featuring Johnny Bench, Joe Morgan and Pete Rose. The card element at the top measures 2-1/8" x 2-1/2". A player portrait, with uniform logos airbrushed off, is featured in black-and-white in a white star on a red background. The Major League Baseball Players Association logo appears in dark blue in the upper-left. Printed in black below are the player's name, team, position, birthdate and place and a few 1977 stats. In back, printed in red, white and blue, is part of the offer for the playing cards. Large quantities of this set found their way into hobby hands and they remain common today.

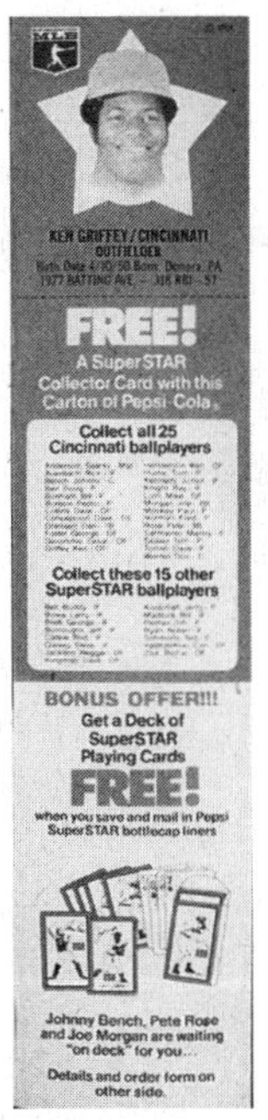

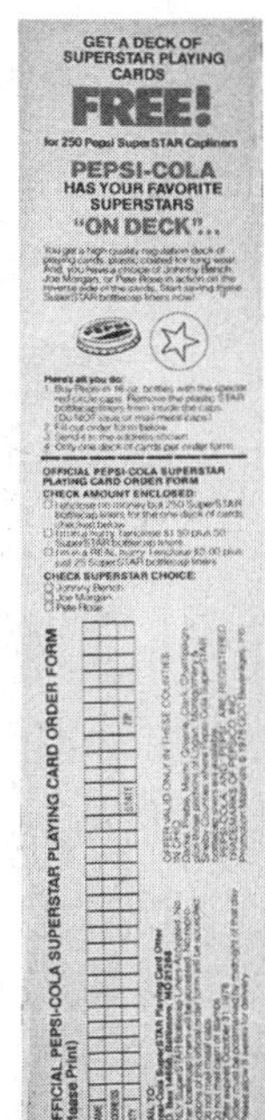

		NM	EX	VG
Complete Set (40):		30.00	15.00	9.00
Common Player:		.75	.35	.20
(1)	Sparky Anderson	2.00	1.00	.60
(2)	Rick Auerbach	.75	.35	.20
(3)	Doug Bair	.75	.35	.20
(4)	Buddy Bell	.75	.35	.20
(5)	Johnny Bench	4.00	2.00	1.25
(6)	Bill Bonham	.75	.35	.20
(7)	Pedro Borbon	.75	.35	.20
(8)	Larry Bowa	.75	.35	.20
(9)	George Brett	7.50	3.75	2.25
(10)	Jeff Burroughs	.75	.35	.20
(11)	Rod Carew	3.00	1.50	.90
(12)	Dave Collins	.75	.35	.20
(13)	Dave Concepcion	.75	.35	.20
(14)	Dan Driessen	.75	.35	.20
(15)	George Foster	.75	.35	.20
(16)	Steve Garvey	1.50	.70	.45
(17)	Cesar Geronimo	.75	.35	.20
(18)	Ken Griffey	.75	.35	.20
(19)	Ken Henderson	.75	.35	.20
(20)	Tom Hume	.75	.35	.20
(21)	Reggie Jackson	7.50	3.75	2.25
(22)	Junior Kennedy	.75	.35	.20
(23)	Dave Kingman	.75	.40	.25
(24)	Ray Knight	.75	.35	.20
(25)	Jerry Koosman	.75	.35	.20
(26)	Mike Lum	.75	.35	.20
(27)	Bill Madlock	.75	.35	.20
(28)	Joe Morgan	3.00	1.50	.90
(29)	Paul Moskau	.75	.35	.20
(30)	Fred Norman	.75	.35	.20
(31)	Jim Palmer	3.00	1.50	.90
(32)	Pete Rose	10.00	5.00	3.00
(33)	Nolan Ryan	12.50	6.25	3.75
(34)	Manny Sarmiento	.75	.35	.20
(35)	Tom Seaver	4.00	2.00	1.25
(36)	Ted Simmons	.75	.35	.20
(37)	Dave Tomlin	.75	.35	.20
(38)	Don Werner	.75	.35	.20
(39)	Carl Yastrzemski	4.00	2.00	1.25
(40)	Richie Zisk	.75	.35	.20

1980 Pepsi-Cola All-Stars Prototypes

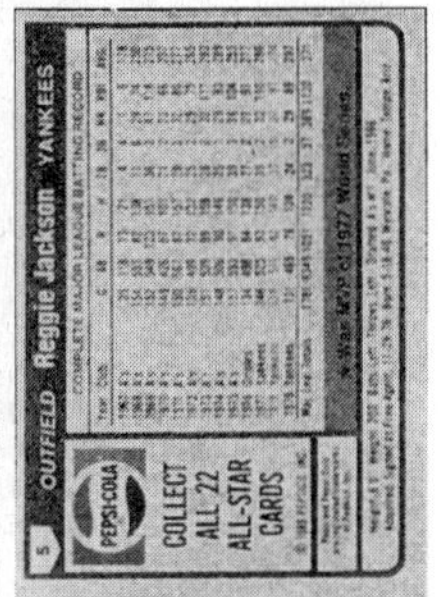

These prototype cards were prepared by Topps and Mike Schechter Associates for a proposed Pepsi promotion. Three sets of the cards were given to Pepsi officials for consideration but only two were returned when the deal fell through. The third sheet was cut up and sold into the hobby. The Pepsi cards share the format of Topps' regular 1980 issue, although Pepsi logos have been added on front and back, name and banner colors changed on front and a position circle added. In 2005, a number of the individual cards were offered on eBay by Topps.

		NM	EX	VG
Common Player:		250.00	125.00	75.00
1	Rod Carew	1,000	500.00	300.00
2	Paul Molitor	1,000	500.00	300.00
3	George Brett	1,500	750.00	450.00
4	Robin Yount	1,000	500.00	300.00
5	Reggie Jackson	1,500	750.00	450.00
6	Fred Lynn	250.00	125.00	75.00
7	Ken Landreaux	250.00	125.00	75.00
8	Jim Sundberg	250.00	125.00	75.00
9	Ron Guidry (One known, other two cut from sheets and destroyed; negatives reversed.)	1,450	725.00	435.00
10	Jim Palmer	1,000	500.00	300.00
11	Goose Gossage	250.00	125.00	75.00
12	Keith Hernandez	250.00	125.00	75.00
13	Dave Lopes	250.00	125.00	75.00
14	Mike Schmidt	1,500	750.00	450.00
15	Garry Templeton	250.00	125.00	75.00
16	Dave Parker	250.00	125.00	75.00
17	George Foster	250.00	125.00	75.00
18	Dave Winfield	1,000	500.00	300.00
19	Ted Simmons	250.00	125.00	75.00
20	Steve Carlton	1,000	500.00	300.00
21	J.R. Richard	400.00	200.00	120.00
22	Bruce Sutter	1,000	500.00	300.00

1966 Gaylord Perry Insurance

The attributed date is arbitrary, near the middle of his stay with the S.F. Giants in whose uniform he is pictured on this approximately 3-1/2" x 5-1/2", blank-backed, black-and-white "business" card for his insurance agency.

	NM	EX	VG
Gaylord Perry	40.00	20.00	12.00

1971 Pete Rose & Johnny Bench Lincoln-Mercury Postcards

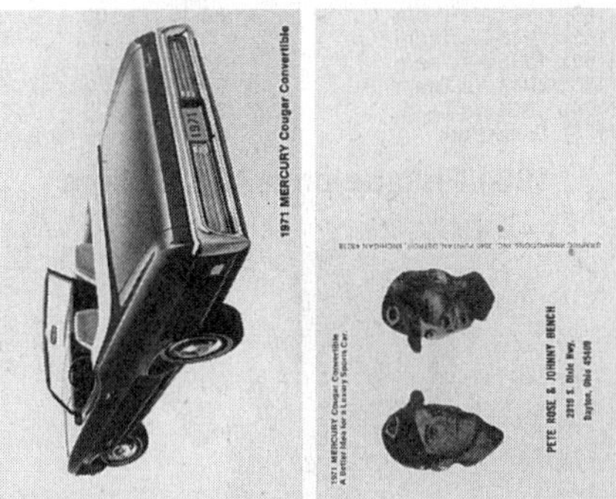

This series of promotional postcards was issued in 1970-71 in conjunction with a Dayton, Ohio, Lincoln-Mercury auto dealership owned by Reds teammates Rose and Bench. Fronts of the 5-1/2" x 3-1/2" postcards feature color photos of new cars. Black-and-white backs have portraits of the players, a description of the auto, the address of the dealership and a credit line for the postcard's printer. Besides those listed here, other auto fronts may exist.

		NM	EX	VG
Common Card:		25.00	12.50	7.50
(1)	Johnny Bench, Pete Rose (1971 Lincoln Continental Sedan)	25.00	12.50	7.50
(2)	Johnny Bench, Pete Rose (1971 Mercury Cougar Convertible)	25.00	12.50	7.50
(3)	Johnny Bench, Pete Rose (1971 Mercury Montego)	25.00	12.50	7.50

1972 Pete Rose & Johnny Bench Lincoln-Mercury Postcards

This series of promotional postcards was issued in 1971-72 in conjunction with a Dayton, Ohio, Lincoln-Mercury auto dealership owned by Reds teammates Rose and

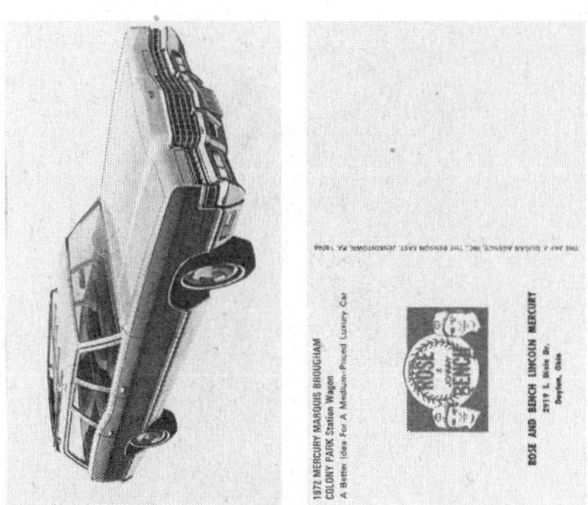

Bench. Fronts of the 5-1/2" x 3-1/2" postcards feature color photos of new cars. Black, white and backs have portraits of the players, a description of the auto, the address of the dealership and a credit line for the postcard's printer. Besides those listed here, other auto fronts may exist.

		NM	EX	VG
(1)	Pete Rose, Johnny Bench (1972 Mercury Marquis Brougham Colony Park Station Wagon)	25.00	12.50	7.50

1961 Peters Meats Twins

This set, featuring the first-year 1961 Minnesota Twins, is in a large, 4-5/8" x 3-1/2", format. Cards are on thick cardboard and heavily waxed, as they were used as partial packaging for the company's meat products. Card fronts feature full-color photos, team and Peters logos, and biographical information. The cards are blank-backed. Prices shown are for cards with the surrounding packaging panel. Cut cards are worth about 50-75 percent of the prices shown.

		NM	EX	VG
Complete Set, Panels (26):		1,600	800.00	475.00
Complete Set, Cards (26):		1,500	750.00	450.00
Common Player, Panel:		80.00	40.00	24.00
Common Player, Card:		50.00	25.00	15.00
1	Zoilo Versalles	160.00	80.00	48.00
2	Eddie Lopat	80.00	40.00	24.00
3	Pedro Ramos	160.00	80.00	48.00
4	Charles "Chuck" Stobbs	80.00	40.00	24.00
5	Don Mincher	80.00	40.00	24.00
6	Jack Kralick	80.00	40.00	24.00
7	Jim Kaat	125.00	65.00	35.00
8	Hal Naragon	80.00	40.00	24.00
9	Don Lee	80.00	40.00	24.00
10	Harry "Cookie" Lavagetto	80.00	40.00	24.00
11	Tom "Pete" Whisenant	80.00	40.00	24.00
12	Elmer Valo	80.00	40.00	24.00
13	Ray Moore	80.00	40.00	24.00
14	Billy Gardner	80.00	40.00	24.00
15	Lenny Green	80.00	40.00	24.00
16	Sam Mele	80.00	40.00	24.00
17	Jim Lemon	80.00	40.00	24.00
18	Harmon "Killer" Killebrew	400.00	200.00	120.00
19	Paul Giel	80.00	40.00	24.00
20	Reno Bertoia	80.00	40.00	24.00
21	Clyde McCullough	80.00	40.00	24.00
22	Earl Battey	80.00	40.00	24.00
23	Camilo Pascual	160.00	80.00	48.00
24	Dan Dobbek	80.00	40.00	24.00
25	Joe "Valvy" Valdivielso	80.00	40.00	24.00
26	Billy Consolo	80.00	40.00	24.00

1938-53 Philadelphia A's Team-Issue Photos

For a decade and a half the Philadelphia A's issued souvenir sets of black-and-white player photos. All are in a 7" x 10" format but the size of picture, the use of posed action and portrait photos and the type style of the name printed in the bottom border differ among the years. In many cases, pictures were re-issued year after year making it impossible 50 years later to reconstruct the composition of any partic-

ular year's issue. The unnumbered pictures are checklisted here alphabetically. Multiple player listings are the result of known pose variations. Gaps have been left in the assigned numbering for future additions.

		NM	EX	VG
Common Player:		12.00	6.00	3.50
(1)	Joe Astroth	12.00	6.00	3.50
(2)	Loren Babe	12.00	6.00	3.50
(3)	Johnny Babich	12.00	6.00	3.50
(4)	Bill Beckman	12.00	6.00	3.50
(5)	Joe Berry	12.00	6.00	3.50
(6)	Herman Besse	12.00	6.00	3.50
(7)	Hal Bevan	12.00	6.00	3.50
(8)	Henry Biasatti	12.00	6.00	3.50
(9)	Don Black	12.00	6.00	3.50
(10)	Lena Blackburne	12.00	6.00	3.50
(11)	Buddy Blair	12.00	6.00	3.50
(12)	Don Bollweg	12.00	6.00	3.50
(13)	Al Brancato	12.00	6.00	3.50
(14)	Lou Brissie	12.00	6.00	3.50
(15)	Earle Brucker	12.00	6.00	3.50
(16)	Earle Brucker	12.00	6.00	3.50
(17)	Earle Brucker	12.00	6.00	3.50
(18)	William Burgo	15.00	7.50	4.50
(19)	Joe Burns	12.00	6.00	3.50
(20)	Ed Burtschy	12.00	6.00	3.50
(21)	Edgar Busch	12.00	6.00	3.50
(22)	Harry Byrd	12.00	6.00	3.50
(23)	Fred Caligiuri	18.00	9.00	5.50
(24)	George Caster	12.00	6.00	3.50
(25)	Jim Castiglia	12.00	6.00	3.50
(27)	Sam Chapman	12.00	6.00	3.50
(28)	Sam Chapman	12.00	6.00	3.50
(29)	Sam Chapman	12.00	6.00	3.50
(30)	Russ Christopher	12.00	6.00	3.50
(31)	Joe Coleman	12.00	6.00	3.50
(32)	Eddie Collins Jr.	15.00	7.50	4.50
(33)	Lawrence Davis	12.00	6.00	3.50
(34)	Tom Davis	12.00	6.00	3.50
(35)	Chubby Dean	12.00	6.00	3.50
(36)	Joe DeMaestri	12.00	6.00	3.50
(37)	Russ Derry	12.00	6.00	3.50
(38)	Gene Desautels	12.00	6.00	3.50
(39)	Art Ditmar	12.00	6.00	3.50
(40)	Jimmy Dykes	12.00	6.00	3.50
(41)	Bob Estalella	12.00	6.00	3.50
(42)	Nick Etten	12.00	6.00	3.50
(43)	Ferris Fain	18.00	9.00	5.50
(44)	Tom Ferrick	12.00	6.00	3.50
(45)	Jim Finigan	12.00	6.00	3.50
(46)	Lewis Flick	12.00	6.00	3.50
(47)	Jesse Flores	12.00	6.00	3.50
(48)	Richard Fowler	12.00	6.00	3.50
(49)	Nelson Fox	30.00	15.00	9.00
(51)	Marion Fricano	12.00	6.00	3.50
(52)	Joe Gantenbein	12.00	6.00	3.50
(53)	Ford Garrison	12.00	6.00	3.50
(54)	Mike Guerra	12.00	6.00	3.50
(55)	Irv Hadley	12.00	6.00	3.50
(56)	Irv Hall	12.00	6.00	3.50
(57)	Luke Hamlin	12.00	6.00	3.50
(58)	Gene Handley	12.00	6.00	3.50
(59)	Bob Harris	12.00	6.00	3.50
(60)	Charlie Harris	12.00	6.00	3.50
(61)	Luman C. Harris (Full-length.)	12.00	6.00	3.50
(62)	Luman Harris	12.00	6.00	3.50
(63)	Frank Hayes	12.00	6.00	3.50
(64)	Bob Johnson	15.00	7.50	4.50
(65)	Bob Johnson	15.00	7.50	4.50
(66)	Eddie Joost	12.00	6.00	3.50
(67)	David Keefe	12.00	6.00	3.50
(68)	George Kell	20.00	10.00	6.00
(69)	Everett Kell	15.00	7.50	4.50
(70)	Alex Kellner	12.00	6.00	3.50
(71)	Alex Kellner	12.00	6.00	3.50
(72)	Lou Klein	12.00	6.00	3.50
(73)	Bill Knickerbocker	12.00	6.00	3.50
(74)	Jack Knott	12.00	6.00	3.50
(75)	Mike Kreevich	12.00	6.00	3.50
(76)	John Kucab	12.00	6.00	3.50
(77)	Paul Lehner	12.00	6.00	3.50
(78)	Bill Lillard	12.00	6.00	3.50
(79)	Lou Limmer	12.00	6.00	3.50
(80)	Lou Limmer	12.00	6.00	3.50
(81)	Dario Lodigiani	12.00	6.00	3.50
(82)	Connie Mack	20.00	10.00	6.00
(83)	Connie Mack	20.00	10.00	6.00
(84)	Connie Mack	20.00	10.00	6.00
(85)	Connie Mack	20.00	10.00	6.00
(86)	Earle Mack	15.00	7.50	4.50
(87)	Earle Mack	15.00	7.50	4.50
(88)	Felix Mackiewicz	12.00	6.00	3.50
(89)	Hank Majeski	12.00	6.00	3.50
(90)	Hank Majeski	12.00	6.00	3.50
(91)	Phil Marchildon	12.00	6.00	3.50
(92)	Phil Marchildon	12.00	6.00	3.50
(93)	Phil Marchildon	12.00	6.00	3.50
(94)	Morris Martin	12.00	6.00	3.50
(95)	Barney McCosky	12.00	6.00	3.50
(96)	Bennie McCoy	12.00	6.00	3.50
(97)	Les McCrabb	12.00	6.00	3.50
(98)	Bill McGhee	18.00	9.00	5.50
(99)	George McQuinn	12.00	6.00	3.50
(101)	Charlie Metro	12.00	6.00	3.50
(102)	Cass Michaels	12.00	6.00	3.50
(103)	Dee Miles	12.00	6.00	3.50
(104)	Wally Moses	12.00	6.00	3.50
(105)	Wally Moses	12.00	6.00	3.50
(106)	Ray Murray	12.00	6.00	3.50
(107)	Bill Nagel	12.00	6.00	3.50
(108)	Bobo Newsom	12.00	6.00	3.50
(109)	Skeeter Newsome	12.00	6.00	3.50
(110)	Hal Peck	12.00	6.00	3.50
(111)	Dave Philley	12.00	6.00	3.50
(112)	Cotton Pippen	12.00	6.00	3.50
(113)	Arnie Portocarrero	12.00	6.00	3.50
(114)	Nelson Potter	12.00	6.00	3.50
(115)	Vic Power	15.00	7.50	4.50
(116)	Jim Pruett	12.00	6.00	3.50
(117)	Bill Renna	12.00	6.00	3.50
(118)	Al Robertson	12.00	6.00	3.50
(119)	Ed Robinson	12.00	6.00	3.50
(120)	Buddy Rosar	12.00	6.00	3.50
(121)	Buddy Rosar	12.00	6.00	3.50
(122)	Al Rubeling	12.00	6.00	3.50
(123)	Joseph Rullo	18.00	9.00	5.50
(124)	Carl Scheib	12.00	6.00	3.50
(125)	Bill Shantz	15.00	7.50	4.50
(126)	Bob Shantz	18.00	9.00	5.50
(127)	Newman Shirley	12.00	6.00	3.50
(128)	Dick Siebert (Thigh-to-cap.)	12.00	6.00	3.50
(129)	Dick Siebert	12.00	6.00	3.50
(130)	Al Simmons	25.00	12.50	7.50
(131)	Al Simmons	25.00	12.50	7.50
(132)	Tuck Stainback	12.00	6.00	3.50
(133)	Pete Suder (Waist-to-cap.)	12.00	6.00	3.50
(134)	Pete Suder	12.00	6.00	3.50
(135)	Bob Swift	12.00	6.00	3.50
(136)	Keith Thomas	12.00	6.00	3.50
(137)	Eric Tipton	12.00	6.00	3.50
(138)	Bob Trice	12.00	6.00	3.50
(139)	Elmer Valo (Portrait to waist.)	12.00	6.00	3.50
(140)	Elmer Valo	12.00	6.00	3.50
(141)	Ozzie Van Brabant	18.00	9.00	5.50
(142)	Porter Vaughan	12.00	6.00	3.50
(143)	Harold Wagner	12.00	6.00	3.50
(144)	Harold Wagner	12.00	6.00	3.50
(145)	Jack Wallaesa	12.00	6.00	3.50
(146)	Johnny Welaj	12.00	6.00	3.50
(147)	Elwood Wheaton	15.00	7.50	4.50
(148)	Don White	12.00	6.00	3.50
(149)	Jo Jo White	12.00	6.00	3.50
(151)	Roger Wolff	12.00	6.00	3.50
(152)	Tom Wright	12.00	6.00	3.50
(153)	Gus Zernial	17.50	8.75	5.25
(154)	1938 A's Team	30.00	15.00	9.00
(155)	1939 A's Team	30.00	15.00	9.00
(156)	1940 A's Team	30.00	15.00	9.00
(157)	1941 A's Team	30.00	15.00	9.00
(158)	1942 A's Team	30.00	15.00	9.00
(159)	1943 A's Team	30.00	15.00	9.00
(160)	1944 A's Team	30.00	15.00	9.00
(161)	1945 A's Team	30.00	15.00	9.00
(162)	1946 A's Team	24.00	12.00	7.25
(163)	1948 A's Team	24.00	12.00	7.25
(164)	1949 A's Team	24.00	12.00	7.25
(165)	Shibe Park	30.00	15.00	9.00

1954 Philadelphia A's Stickers

The issuer of this novelty set and the exact scope of its checklist are currently unknown. The pieces are printed in black-and-white on 4-1/2" x 8-1/4" gummed-back paper. Instructions on front say, "(Moisten back. Paste on Cardboard and cut out.)" Only the player name is printed beneath the photo.

		NM	EX	VG
Common Player:		25.00	12.50	7.50
(1)	Joe Astroth	25.00	12.50	7.50
(2)	Marion Fricano	25.00	12.50	7.50
(3)	Forrest Jacobs	25.00	12.50	7.50
(4)	Eddie Joost	25.00	12.50	7.50
(5)	Morrie Martin	25.00	12.50	7.50
(6)	Vic Power	35.00	17.50	10.50
(7)	Jim Robertson	25.00	12.50	7.50
(8)	Bob Shantz	35.00	17.50	10.50
(9)	Pete Suder	25.00	12.50	7.50
(10)	Bob Trice	25.00	12.50	7.50

1952 Philadelphia A's/Phillies Player Pins

Only players on the Philadelphia A's and Phillies are found in this series of player pinbacks. The 1-3/4" diameter celluloid pins have black-and-white player portraits on front. The player name is printed in block letters across his shoulders, while the team name is printed in script across the chest. It is possible other player pins may exist. The unnumbered pieces are checklisted here in alphabetical order.

		NM	EX	VG
Common Player:		150.00	75.00	45.00
	Philadelphia Athletics			
(1)	Ferris Fain	200.00	100.00	60.00
(2)	Bobby Shantz	200.00	100.00	60.00
(3)	Gus Zernial	200.00	100.00	60.00
	Philadelphia Phillies			
(1)	Richie Ashburn	300.00	150.00	90.00
(2)	Del Ennis	150.00	75.00	45.00
(3)	Granny Hamner	150.00	75.00	45.00
(4)	Willie Jones	150.00	75.00	45.00
(5)	Jim Konstanty	150.00	75.00	45.00
(6)	Robin Roberts	300.00	150.00	90.00
(7)	Andy Seminick	150.00	75.00	45.00
(8)	Curt Simmons	150.00	75.00	45.00
(9)	Eddie Waitkus	150.00	75.00	45.00

1948 Philadelphia Bulletin Stand-Ups

These player pictures were printed in the "Fun Book" color section of the Sunday paper. The full-body pose cutouts carry facsimile autographs and were printed four per week on a page of about 9-1/2" x 14". While the individual pictures vary is size according to the pose, most are about 3" to 4" x 6-1/2" to 7". The player pictures are in black-and-white with a blue background and red base. They were intended to be cut out around the heavy black line, pasted to cardboard and folded at their base to create a stand-up figure. Values shown here are for well trimmed pieces without evidence of mounting. Complete pages carry a premium somewhat greater than the sum of the players present.

		NM	EX	VG
Common Player:		15.00	7.50	4.50
	PHILADELPHIA A'S			
	June 13	75.00	37.00	22.00
(1)	Ferris Fain	15.00	7.50	4.50
(2)	Eddie Joost	15.00	7.50	4.50
(3)	Hank Majeski	15.00	7.50	4.50
(4)	Pete Suder	15.00	7.50	4.50
	June 20	75.00	37.00	22.00
(5)	Sam Chapman	15.00	7.50	4.50
(6)	Barney McCosky	15.00	7.50	4.50

		NM	EX	VG
(7)	Buddy Rosar	15.00	7.50	4.50
(8)	Elmer Valo	15.00	7.50	4.50
	June 27	75.00	37.00	22.00
(9)	Mike Guerra	15.00	7.50	4.50
(10)	Dick Fowler	15.00	7.50	4.50
(11)	Phil Marchildon	15.00	7.50	4.50
(12)	Carl Sheib	15.00	7.50	4.50
	July 4	75.00	37.00	22.00
(13)	Joe Coleman	15.00	7.50	4.50
(14)	Bob Savage	15.00	7.50	4.50
(15)	Don White	15.00	7.50	4.50
(16)	Rudy York	15.00	7.50	4.50
	July 11	75.00	37.00	22.00
(17)	Herman Franks	15.00	7.50	4.50
(18)	Charlie Harris	15.00	7.50	4.50
(19)	Bill McCahan	15.00	7.50	4.50
(20)	Skeeter Webb	15.00	7.50	4.50
	July 18	75.00	37.00	22.00
(21)	Lou Brissie	15.00	7.50	4.50
(22)	Ray Coleman	15.00	7.50	4.50
(23)	Billy DeMars	15.00	7.50	4.50
(24)	Webb?	15.00	7.50	4.50
	PHILADELPHIA PHILLIES			
	July 25	90.00	45.00	27.00
(1)	Don Padgett	15.00	7.50	4.50
(2)	Schoolboy Rowe	15.00	7.50	4.50
(3)	Andy Seminick	15.00	7.50	4.50
(4)	Curt Simmons	20.00	10.00	6.00
	August 1	225.00	110.00	67.00
(5)	Richie Ashburn	150.00	75.00	45.00
(6)	Johnny Blatnik	15.00	7.50	4.50
(7)	Del Ennis	20.00	10.00	6.00
(8)	Harry Walker	15.00	7.50	4.50
	August 8	75.00	37.00	22.00
(9)	Bert Haas	15.00	7.50	4.50
(10)	Granny Hamner	15.00	7.50	4.50
(11)	Eddie Miller	15.00	7.50	4.50
(12)	Dick Sisler	15.00	7.50	4.50
	August 15	200.00	100.00	60.00
(13)	Ralph Caballero	15.00	7.50	4.50
(14)	Ed Heusser	15.00	7.50	4.50
(15)	Robin Roberts	125.00	62.00	37.00
(16)	Emil Verban	15.00	7.50	4.50
	August 22	75.00	37.00	22.00
(17)	Blix Donnelly	15.00	7.50	4.50
(18)	Walt Dubiel	15.00	7.50	4.50
(19)	Ken Heintzelman	15.00	7.50	4.50
(20)	"Dutch" Leonard	15.00	7.50	4.50
	August 29	75.00	37.00	22.00
(21)	Charlie Bicknell	15.00	7.50	4.50
(22)	Al Lakeman	15.00	7.50	4.50
(23)	Sam Nahem	15.00	7.50	4.50
(24)	Bama Rowell	15.00	7.50	4.50

1949 Philadelphia Bulletin A's/Phillies

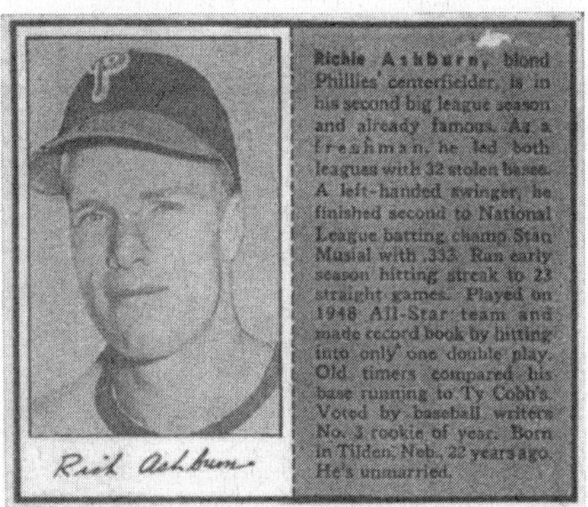

Each Sunday between May 22 and July 24, 1949, the "Fun Book" rotogravure section of the Bulletin included a page of (usually) six baseball "cards" of the hometeam A's and Phillies which could be cut out and pasted to cardboard. The left side (front) of each card has a sepia portrait of the player, while a colored box at right (back) has biographical and career information. Uncut and unfolded, each card measures about 4-1/2" x 3-5/8". If cut out and pasted onto cardboard, the created cards would measure about 2-1/4" x 3-5/8". Complete pages measure about 9-1/2" x 13-3/8". Values shown are for single "cards" which have been cut off the page, but not pasted onto a backing.

		NM	EX	VG
Complete Set (59):		1,600	800.00	480.00
Common Player:		25.00	12.50	7.50
	MAY 22			
(1)	Richie Ashburn	265.00	130.00	79.00
(2)	Granny Hamner	25.00	12.50	7.50
(3)	Eddie Joost	25.00	12.50	7.50
(4)	Bill Nicholson	25.00	12.50	7.50
(5)	Buddy Rosar	25.00	12.50	7.50
(6)	Pete Suder	25.00	12.50	7.50
	MAY 29			
(7)	Hank Borowy	25.00	12.50	7.50
(8)	Del Ennis	35.00	17.50	10.50
(9)	Ferris Fain	35.00	17.50	10.50
(10)	Phil Marchildon	25.00	12.50	7.50
(11)	Wally Moses	25.00	12.50	7.50
(12)	Eddie Waitkus	25.00	12.50	7.50
	JUNE 5			
(13)	Dick Fowler	25.00	12.50	7.50
(14)	Willie Jones	25.00	12.50	7.50
(15)	Stan Lopata	25.00	12.50	7.50
(16)	Hank Majeski	25.00	12.50	7.50
(17)	Schoolboy Rowe	25.00	12.50	7.50
(18)	Elmer Valo	25.00	12.50	7.50
	JUNE 12			
(19)	Joe Coleman	25.00	12.50	7.50
(20)	Charley Harris	25.00	12.50	7.50
(21)	Russ Meyer	25.00	12.50	7.50
(22)	Eddie Miller	25.00	12.50	7.50
(23)	Robin Roberts	265.00	130.00	79.00
(24)	Taft Wright	25.00	12.50	7.50
	JUNE 19			
(25)	Lou Brissie	25.00	12.50	7.50
(26)	Ralph Caballero	25.00	12.50	7.50
(27)	Sam Chapman	25.00	12.50	7.50
(28)	Fermin (Mike) Guerra	25.00	12.50	7.50
(29)	Jim Konstanty	35.00	17.50	10.50
(30)	Curt Simmons	35.00	17.50	10.50
	JUNE 26			
(31)	Charles Bicknell	25.00	12.50	7.50
(32)	Ken Heintzelman	25.00	12.50	7.50
(33)	Alex Kellner	25.00	12.50	7.50
(34)	Barney McCosky	25.00	12.50	7.50
(35)	Bobby Shantz	35.00	17.50	10.50
(36)	Ken Trinkle	25.00	12.50	7.50
	JULY 3			
(37)	Blix Donnelly	25.00	12.50	7.50
(38)	Bill McCahan	25.00	12.50	7.50
(39)	Carl Scheib	25.00	12.50	7.50
(40)	Andy Seminick	25.00	12.50	7.50
(41)	Dick Sisler	25.00	12.50	7.50
(42)	Don White	25.00	12.50	7.50
	JULY 10			
(43)	Joe Astroth	25.00	12.50	7.50
(44)	Henry Biasetti	25.00	12.50	7.50
(45)	Buddy Blattner	25.00	12.50	7.50
(46)	Thomas O. Davis	25.00	12.50	7.50
(47)	Stan Hollmig	25.00	12.50	7.50
(48)	Jackie Mayo	25.00	12.50	7.50
	JULY 17			
(49)	Benny Bengough	25.00	12.50	7.50
(50)	Earle Brucker	25.00	12.50	7.50
(51)	Dusty Cooke	25.00	12.50	7.50
(52)	Jimmy Dykes	25.00	12.50	7.50
(53)	Cy Perkins	25.00	12.50	7.50
(54)	Al Simmons	40.00	20.00	12.00
	JULY 24			
(55)	Nellie Fox	265.00	130.00	79.00
(56)	Connie Mack	200.00	100.00	60.00
(57)	Earle Mack	25.00	12.50	7.50
(58)	Eddie Sawyer	25.00	12.50	7.50
(59)	Ken Silvestri	25.00	12.50	7.50

1950 Philadelphia Bulletin Pin-Ups

This series of 8" x 10" black-and-white portraits of Phillies players, coaches, and manager was produced in two versions. A (mostly) numbered newsprint version was issued one per day in the paper, between September 13-30. A premium version, printed on heavy paper with a semi-gloss finish and blank back, was made available to fans for a nickel at the newspaper's office or a dime by mail. Each of the pictures is a cap-less portrait with facsimile autograph on front. A number of players in the premium version were not issued in the newsprint style.

		NM	EX	VG
Complete Set (26):		900.00	450.00	275.00
Common Player:		40.00	20.00	12.00
(1)	Rich Ashburn	75.00	37.00	22.00
(2)	Jimmy Bloodworth	40.00	20.00	12.00
(3)	Ralph Caballero	40.00	20.00	12.00
(4)	Milo Candini	40.00	20.00	12.00
(5)	Emory Church	40.00	20.00	12.00
(6)	Sylvester (Blix) Donnelly	40.00	20.00	12.00
(7)	Del Ennis	50.00	25.00	15.00
(8)	Mike Goliat	40.00	20.00	12.00
(9)	Gran Hamner	40.00	20.00	12.00
(10)	Ken Heintzelman	40.00	20.00	12.00
(11)	Stan Hollmig	40.00	20.00	12.00
(12)	Ken Johnson	40.00	20.00	12.00
(13)	Willie Jones	40.00	20.00	12.00
(14)	Jim Konstanty	40.00	20.00	12.00
(15)	Stan Lopata	40.00	20.00	12.00
(16)	Russ Meyer	40.00	20.00	12.00
(17)	Bob Miller	40.00	20.00	12.00
(18)	Bill Nicholson	40.00	20.00	12.00
(19)	Robin Roberts	65.00	32.00	19.50
(20)	Eddie Sawyer	40.00	20.00	12.00
(21)	Andy Seminick	40.00	20.00	12.00
(22)	Ken Silvestri	40.00	20.00	12.00
(23)	Curtis T. Simmons	50.00	25.00	15.00
(24)	Dick Sisler	40.00	20.00	12.00
(25)	Eddie Waitkus	40.00	20.00	12.00
(26)	Dick Whitman	40.00	20.00	12.00

1964 Philadelphia Bulletin Phillies Album (Paper)

This series of newspaper features was the basis for the more often-encountered mail-in premiums. About 5-1/2" x 9", these pieces were printed in black-and-white in the sports section of the daily paper. The artwork is by staff artist Jim Porter. While the newspaper pieces are numbered, they are checklisted here in alphabetical order due to uncertainty about the original issue sequence.

		NM	EX	VG
Complete Set (27):		400.00	200.00	120.00
Common Player:		15.00	7.50	4.50
(1)	Richie Allen	40.00	20.00	12.00
(2)	Ruben Amaro	15.00	7.50	4.50
(3)	Jack Baldschun	15.00	7.50	4.50
(4)	Dennis Bennett	15.00	7.50	4.50
(5)	John Boozer	15.00	7.50	4.50
(6)	Johnny Briggs	15.00	7.50	4.50
(7)	Jim Bunning	50.00	25.00	15.00
(8)	Johnny Callison	15.00	7.50	4.50
(9)	Danny Cater	15.00	7.50	4.50
(10)	Wes Covington	15.00	7.50	4.50
(11)	Ray Culp	15.00	7.50	4.50
(12)	Clay Dalrymple	15.00	7.50	4.50
(13)	Tony Gonzalez	15.00	7.50	4.50
(14)	John Herrnstein	15.00	7.50	4.50
(15)	Alex Johnson	15.00	7.50	4.50
(16)	Art Mahaffey	15.00	7.50	4.50
(17)	Gene Mauch	15.00	7.50	4.50
(18)	Vic Power	15.00	7.50	4.50
(19)	Ed Roebuck	15.00	7.50	4.50
(20)	Cookie Rojas	15.00	7.50	4.50
(21)	Bobby Shantz	15.00	7.50	4.50
(22)	Chris Short	15.00	7.50	4.50
(23)	Tony Taylor	15.00	7.50	4.50
(24)	Frank Thomas	15.00	7.50	4.50
(25)	Gus Triandos	15.00	7.50	4.50
(26)	Bobby Wine	15.00	7.50	4.50
(27)	Rick Wise	15.00	7.50	4.50

1964 Philadelphia Bulletin Phillies Album

Color artwork by Jim Ponter is featured in this series of newspaper inserts. Portrait and action figures are combined on a blank-backed 8" x 10" format, along with a facsimile autograph. The unnumbered pictures are checklisted here alphabetically, two varieties of Jim Bunning's picture have been reported.

		NM	EX	VG
Complete Set (28):		550.00	275.00	175.00
Common Player:		20.00	10.00	6.00
(1)	Richie Allen	60.00	30.00	18.00
(2)	Ruben Amaro	20.00	10.00	6.00
(3)	Jack Baldschun	20.00	10.00	6.00
(4)	Dennis Bennett	20.00	10.00	6.00
(5)	John Boozer	20.00	10.00	6.00
(6)	Johnny Briggs	20.00	10.00	6.00
(7)	Jim Bunning/Pitching	75.00	37.00	22.00
(8)	Jim Bunning/Portrait	60.00	30.00	18.00
(9)	Johnny Callison	20.00	10.00	6.00
(10)	Danny Cater	20.00	10.00	6.00
(11)	Wes Covington	20.00	10.00	6.00
(12)	Ray Culp	20.00	10.00	6.00
(13)	Clay Dalrymple	20.00	10.00	6.00
(14)	Tony Gonzalez	20.00	10.00	6.00
(15)	John Herrnstein	20.00	10.00	6.00
(16)	Alex Johnson	20.00	10.00	6.00
(17)	Art Mahaffey	20.00	10.00	6.00
(18)	Gene Mauch	20.00	10.00	6.00
(19)	Vic Power	20.00	10.00	6.00
(20)	Ed Roebuck	20.00	10.00	6.00
(21)	Cookie Rojas	20.00	10.00	6.00

		NM	EX	VG
(22)	Bobby Shantz	20.00	10.00	6.00
(23)	Chris Short	20.00	10.00	6.00
(24)	Tony Taylor	20.00	10.00	6.00
(25)	Frank Thomas	20.00	10.00	6.00
(26)	Gus Triandos	20.00	10.00	6.00
(27)	Bobby Wine	20.00	10.00	6.00
(28)	Rick Wise	20.00	10.00	6.00

1909 Philadelphia Caramel (E95)

MORGAN, ATHLETICS AMER.
This card is one of a set of
25 BALL PLAYERS
Cards, as follows:
1. WAGNER, Pittsburg National
2. MADDOX, Pittsburg National
3. MERKLE, New York National
4. MORGAN, Athletics American
5. BENDER, Athletics American
6. KRAUSE, Athletics American
7. DEVLIN, New York National
8. McINTYRE, Detroit American
9. COBB, Detroit American
10. WILLETTS, Detroit American
11. CRAWFORD, Detroit Amer.
12. MATTHEWSON, N. Y. Nat'l
13. WILTSE, New York National
14. DOYLE, New York National
15. LEACH, Pittsburg National
16. LORD, Boston American
17. CICOTTE, Boston American
18. CARRIGAN, Boston American
19. WILLIS, Pittsburg National
20. EVERS, Chicago National
21. CHANCE, Chicago National
22. HOFFMAN, Chicago National
23. PLANK, Athletics American
24. COLLINS, Athletics American
25. REULBACH, Chicago Nat'l
Made by
PHILADELPHIA CARAMEL CO.
Camden, New Jersey

Similar in style to several other early candy and caramel cards, the set designated as E95 by the American Card Catalog is a 25-card issue produced by the Philadelphia Caramel Co., Camden, N.J., in 1909. The cards measure approximately 1-1/2" x 2-5/8" and contain a full-color player drawing. The back, which differentiates the set from other similar issues, checklists the 25 players in black ink and displays the Philadelphia Caramel Co. name at the bottom. Blank-back cards printed on thinner stock exist; these are not proofs, but were cut off a "Base Ball Series" notebook cover, they are valued about 25-50 percent of a corresponding regular-issue card.

		NM	EX	VG
Complete Set (25):		50,000	20,000	10,000
Common Player:		850.00	350.00	165.00
1	Honus Wagner	13,000	5,200	2,600
2	Nick Maddox	850.00	350.00	165.00
3	Fred Merkle	850.00	350.00	165.00
4	Cy Morgan	850.00	350.00	165.00
5	Chief Bender	1,950	780.00	390.00
6	Harry Krause	850.00	350.00	165.00
7	Art Devlin	850.00	350.00	165.00
8	Matty McIntyre	850.00	350.00	165.00
9	Ty Cobb	15,600	5,200	2,600
10	Ed Willetts (Willett)	850.00	350.00	165.00
11	Sam Crawford	1,950	780.00	360.00
12	Christy Matthewson (Mathewson)	9,750	2,600	1,300
13	Hooks Wiltse	850.00	350.00	165.00
14	Larry Doyle	850.00	350.00	165.00
15	Tommy Leach	850.00	350.00	165.00
16	Harry Lord	850.00	350.00	165.00
17	Ed Cicotte	2,730	780.00	470.00
18	Bill Carrigan	850.00	350.00	165.00
19	Vic Willis	1,950	780.00	360.00
20	Johnny Evers	1,950	780.00	360.00
21	Frank Chance	1,950	780.00	360.00
22	Solly Hoffman (Hofman)	850.00	350.00	165.00
23	Eddie Plank	3,120	1,170	650.00
24	Eddie Collins	1,950	780.00	360.00
25	Ed Reulbach	850.00	350.00	165.00

1910 Philadelphia Caramel (E96)

LAJOIE, CLEVELAND, A. L.
This Card is one of a New Set of
30 BALL PLAYERS
1. DAVIS, Athletics
2. CONNIE MACK, Athletics
3. THOMAS, Athletics
4. BAKER, Athletics
5. DOOIN, Phila. Natl.
6. McQUILLAN, Phila. Natl.
7. KONETCHY, St. Louis Natl
8. KARGER, St. Louis Natl.
9. MOWRAY, St. Louis Natl.
10. MURRAY, St. Louis Natl.
11. LAJOIE, Cleveland
12. ROSSMAN, Cleveland
13. RUCKER, Brooklyn
14. JENNINGS, Detroit
15. DONOVAN, Detroit
16. DELAHANTY, Detroit
17. MULLIN, Detroit
18. ARRELANES, Boston Am
19. SPENCER, Boston Am.
20. KLING, Chicago
21. PFISTER, Chicago
22. BROWN, Chicago
23. TINKER, Chicago
24. CLARK, Pittsburg
25. GIBSON, Pittsburg
26. ADAMS, Pittsburg
27. AMES, N. Y. Natl.
28. MARQUARD, N. Y. Natl.
29. HERZOG, N. Y. Natl.
30. MYERS, N. Y. Natl.
Previous Series 25, making total issue 55 Cards
PHILADELPHIA CARAMEL CO.
Camden, N. J.

This set of 30 subjects, known by the ACC designation E96, was issued in 1910 by the Philadelphia Caramel Co. The approximately 1-1/2" x 2-5/8" size and front design remained the same, but the two issues can be identified by the backs. The backs of E96 cards are printed in red and carry a checklist of 30 players. There is also a line at the bottom advising "Previous series 25, making total issue 55 cards." Just below that appears "Philadelphia Caramel Co./Camden, N.J." Blank-back cards printed on thinner stock are not proofs, but rather were cut off a "Base Ball Series" notebook cover. They are valued about 25-50 percent of a corresponding regular-issue card.

		NM	EX	VG
Complete Set (30):		38,500	15,500	9,500
Common Player:		1,100	400.00	200.00
1	Harry Davis	1,100	400.00	200.00
2	Connie Mack	2,000	1,000	500.00
3	Ira Thomas	1,100	400.00	200.00
4	Home Run Baker	2,000	800.00	400.00
5	Red Dooin	1,100	400.00	200.00
6	George McQuillan	1,100	400.00	200.00
7	Ed Konetchy	1,100	400.00	200.00
8	Ed Karger	1,100	400.00	200.00
9	Mike Mowrey	1,100	400.00	200.00
10	Red Murray	1,100	400.00	200.00
11	Nap Lajoie	2,700	1,100	550.00
12	Claude Rossman	1,100	400.00	200.00
13	Nap Rucker	1,100	400.00	200.00
14	Hugh Jennings	2,000	800.00	400.00
15	Wild Bill Donovan	1,100	400.00	200.00
16	Jim Delahanty	1,100	400.00	200.00
17	George Mullin	1,100	400.00	200.00
18	Frank Arrelanes (Arellanes)	1,100	400.00	200.00
19	Tubby Spencer	1,100	400.00	200.00
20	Johnny Kling	1,100	400.00	200.00
21	Jack Pfister (Pfiester)	1,500	750.00	400.00
22	Mordecai Brown	2,500	1,250	600.00
23	Joe Tinker	2,500	1,250	600.00
24	Fred Clark (Clarke)	2,000	800.00	400.00
25	George Gibson	1,100	400.00	200.00
26	Babe Adams	1,100	400.00	200.00
27	Red Ames	1,100	400.00	200.00
28	Rube Marquard	2,000	800.00	400.00
29	Buck Herzog	1,100	400.00	200.00
30	Chief Myers (Meyers)	1,100	400.00	200.00

1913 Philadelphia Caramel Proofs

The attribution of these cards to Philadelphia Caramel is speculative, since no advertising is found on their blank backs. The three known pieces, however, have pictures and color identical to the players' cards in the 1910 E96 Philadelphia Caramel issue. These proofs differ only in the team designations. Nominally 1-1/2" x 2-5/8", the known examples were hand-cut from a sheet and are, at present, each unique. The Kling card was offered at auction in 2003 without meeting a $500 reserve.

Frank Chance (New York, A.L.)
Harry Davis (Cleveland)
Johnny Kling (Boston, A.L.)

1913 Philadelphia Evening Telegraph Postcards

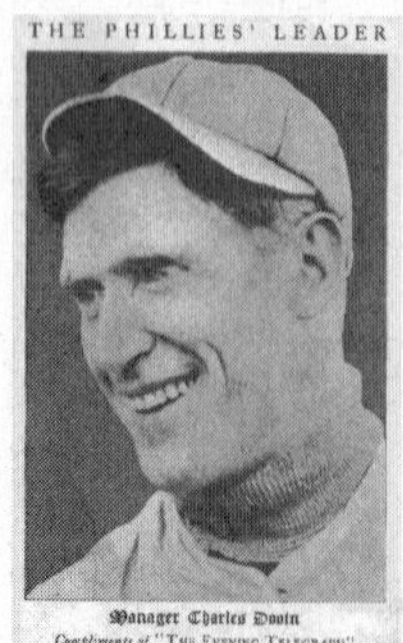

The attributed date of issue is speculative, about midway through Phillies manager Red Dooin's tenure. Issued by one of the city's daily newspapers, these 3-1/2" x 5-1/2" black-and-white postcards picture the managers of the Phils and A's in large portrait photos. The postcard-style back has ornate typography and embellishments.

		NM	EX	VG
Complete Set (2):		1,100	550.00	325.00
Common Card:		500.00	250.00	150.00
(1)	Charles Dooin	500.00	250.00	150.00
(2)	Connie Mack	650.00	325.00	200.00

1913 Philadelphia Evening Times Supplements

The checklist comprised almost entirely of Connie Mack's A's and John McGraw's Giants suggests this series of newspaper supplements was issued around World Series time. The blank-backed, sepia-toned pictures have posed action photos, are printed on light cardboard stock and measure about 7-1/2" x 9-1/2". This checklist may be incomplete.

		NM	EX	VG
Common Player:		200.00	100.00	60.00
(1)	Home Run Baker	400.00	200.00	120.00
(2)	Jack Barry	200.00	100.00	60.00
(3)	Chief Bender	400.00	200.00	120.00
(4)	George Burns	200.00	100.00	60.00
(5)	Ty Cobb	1,200	600.00	360.00
(6)	Eddie Collins	400.00	200.00	120.00
(7)	Al Demaree	200.00	100.00	60.00
(8)	Larry Doyle	200.00	100.00	60.00
(9)	Walter Johnson	800.00	400.00	240.00
(10)	Rube Marquard	400.00	200.00	120.00
(11)	Christy Mathewson	800.00	400.00	240.00
(12)	Stuffy McInnis	200.00	100.00	60.00
(13)	Chief Meyers	200.00	100.00	60.00
(14)	Rube Oldring	200.00	100.00	60.00
(15)	Eddie Plank	400.00	200.00	120.00
(16)	Jeff Tesreau	200.00	100.00	60.00

1950 Philadelphia Inquirer Fightin' Phillies

As the Whiz Kids battled to a National League pennant the "Philadelphia Inquirer" instituted a set of cut-out baseball cards in the Sunday rotogravure editions during September. The 4-7/8" x 6-7/8" cards have colored portrait photos surrounded with a white border. A facsimile autograph is printed across the chest. In the bottom border are the player's formal name, position, career summary and the line, "Inquirer Fightin' Phillies Album." Backs have whatever articles or ads were on the next page. The unnumbered cards are printed here in alphabetical order.

		NM	EX	VG
Complete Set (24):		350.00	175.00	105.00
Common Player:		15.00	7.50	4.50
(1)	Richie Ashburn	35.00	17.50	10.50
(2)	James Henry Bloodworth	15.00	7.50	4.50
(3)	Ralph Joseph Caballero	15.00	7.50	4.50
(4)	Milo Candini	15.00	7.50	4.50
(5)	Emory Church	15.00	7.50	4.50
(6)	Sylvester Urban Donnelly	15.00	7.50	4.50
(7)	Delmer Ennis	15.00	7.50	4.50
(8)	Mike Mitchel Goliat (Mitchell)	15.00	7.50	4.50
(9)	Granville Wilbur Hamner	15.00	7.50	4.50
(10)	Kenneth Alphonse Heintzelman	15.00	7.50	4.50
(11)	Stanley Ernst Hollmig	15.00	7.50	4.50
(12)	Kenneth W. Johnson	15.00	7.50	4.50
(13)	Willie Edward Jones	15.00	7.50	4.50
(14)	Stanley Edward Lopata	15.00	7.50	4.50
(15)	Russell Charles Meyer	15.00	7.50	4.50
(16)	Robert Miller	15.00	7.50	4.50
(17)	William Beck Nicholson	15.00	7.50	4.50
(18)	Robin Evan Roberts	35.00	17.50	10.50
(19)	Andrew Wasal Seminick	15.00	7.50	4.50
(20)	Kenneth Joseph Silvestri	15.00	7.50	4.50
(21)	Curtis Thomas Simmons	15.00	7.50	4.50
(22)	Richard Alan Sisler	15.00	7.50	4.50
(23)	Edward Stephen Waitkus	15.00	7.50	4.50
(24)	Dick Whitman	15.00	7.50	4.50

1954 Philadelphia Inquirer Album of Baseball Stars

A series of four baseball players from each of Philadelphia's teams appeared on a pair of pages in the Colorama color rotogravure section of the Sunday. Philadelphia Inquirer. Each picture is about 6-3/4" x 9-3/4" and was separated from the other three on its "ALBUM OF SPORTS" page by a black dotted line, indicative of an intention for them to be cut out and saved. Under the portrait is a brief career summary. Backs have other newspaper content as printed each Sunday.

		NM	EX	VG
Complete Set (8):		75.00	37.50	22.50
Common Player:		8.00	4.00	2.50
	JULY 25			
(1)	Richie Ashburn	25.00	12.50	7.50
(2)	Jim Finigan	8.00	4.00	2.50
(3)	Gran Hamner	8.00	4.00	2.50
(4)	Bill Shantz	8.00	4.00	2.50
	SEPT. 12			
(1)	Smoky Burgess	10.00	5.00	3.00
(2)	Arnold Portocarrero	8.00	4.00	2.50
(3)	Robin Roberts	16.00	8.00	4.75
(4)	Curt Simmons	10.00	5.00	3.00

1940 Philadelphia Phillies Photo Pack

This set of 25 photos show players in poses on the field with the Quaker figure and "PHILADELPHIA NATIONAL LEAGUE BASE BALL CLUB" around it in a circular logo in the upper right hand corner. Size is 6" x 8-1/2".

		NM	EX	VG
Complete Set (25):		150.00	75.00	30.00
Common Player:		7.50	3.75	2.25
(1)	Morrie Arnovich	7.50	3.75	2.25
(2)	Bill Atwood	7.50	3.75	2.25
(3)	Walter Beck	7.50	3.75	2.25
(4)	Stan Benjamin	7.50	3.75	2.25
(5)	Bob Bragan	7.50	3.75	2.25
(6)	Roy Bruner	7.50	3.75	2.25
(7)	Kirby Higbie	7.50	3.75	2.25
(8)	Si Johnson	7.50	3.75	2.25
(9)	Syl Johnson	7.50	3.75	2.25
(10)	Chuck Klein	7.50	3.75	2.25
(11)	Ed Levy	7.50	3.75	2.25
(12)	Dan Litwhiler	7.50	3.75	2.25
(13)	Hans Lobert	7.50	3.75	2.25
(14)	Herschel Martin	7.50	3.75	2.25
(15)	Joe Marty	7.50	3.75	2.25
(16)	Maerrill May	7.50	3.75	2.25
(17)	Walk Millies	7.50	3.75	2.25
(18)	Hugh Mulcahy	7.50	3.75	2.25
(19)	Ike Pearson	7.50	3.75	2.25
(20)	Doc Prothro	7.50	3.75	2.25
(21)	George Scharen	7.50	3.75	2.25
(22)	Clyde Smoll	7.50	3.75	2.25
(23)	Gus Suhr	7.50	3.75	2.25
(24)	Ben Warren	7.50	3.75	2.25
(25)	Del Young	7.50	3.75	2.25

1943 Philadelphia Phillies Photo Pack

Like many teams in that era, the Phillies issued souvenir photo packs for sale at the stadium and by mail-order. This team issue is in a 6" x 8-1/2", blank-back, black-and-white format. The player picture is bordered in white with the player name in all-caps in the bottom border. From the large number of players known, it is evident that the composition of the photo packs was changed from time to time as the team roster changed. It is possible this checklist is not complete. The unnumbered pictures have been listed here alphabetically.

		NM	EX	VG
Complete Set (40):		300.00	150.00	90.00
Common Player:		8.00	4.00	2.50
(1)	Buster Adams	8.00	4.00	2.50
(2)	Walter Beck	8.00	4.00	2.50
(3)	Stan Benjamin	8.00	4.00	2.50
(4)	Cy Blanton	8.00	4.00	2.50
(5)	Bobby Bragan	8.00	4.00	2.50
(6)	Charlie Brewster	8.00	4.00	2.50
(7)	Paul Busby	8.00	4.00	2.50
(8)	Ben Culp	8.00	4.00	2.50
(9)	Babe Dahlgren	8.00	4.00	2.50
(10)	Lloyd Dietz	8.00	4.00	2.50
(11)	Nick Etten	8.00	4.00	2.50
(12)	George Eyrich	8.00	4.00	2.50
(13)	Charlie Fuchs	8.00	4.00	2.50
(14)	Al Glossop	8.00	4.00	2.50
(15)	Al Gerheauser	8.00	4.00	2.50
(16)	"Bucky" Harris	12.00	6.00	3.50
(17)	Frank Hoerst	8.00	4.00	2.50
(18)	Si Johnson	8.00	4.00	2.50
(19)	Chuck Klein	15.00	7.50	4.50
(20)	Ernie Koy	8.00	4.00	2.50
(21)	Tex Kraus	8.00	4.00	2.50
(22)	Danny Litwhiler	8.00	4.00	2.50
(23)	Mickey Livingston	8.00	4.00	2.50
(24)	Hans Lobert	8.00	4.00	2.50
(25)	Henry Marnie	8.00	4.00	2.50
(26)	Merrill May	8.00	4.00	2.50
(27)	Rube Melton	8.00	4.00	2.50
(28)	Danny Murtaugh	10.00	5.00	3.00
(29)	Sam Nahem	8.00	4.00	2.50
(30)	Earl Naylor	8.00	4.00	2.50
(31)	Ron Northey	8.00	4.00	2.50
(32)	Tommy Padden	8.00	4.00	2.50
(33)	Ike Pearson	8.00	4.00	2.50
(34)	Johnny Podgajny	8.00	4.00	2.50
(35)	Schoolboy Rowe	10.00	5.00	3.00
(36)	Glen Stewart	8.00	4.00	2.50
(37)	Coaker Triplett	8.00	4.00	2.50
(38)	Lloyd Waner	15.00	7.50	4.50
(39)	Ben Warren	8.00	4.00	2.50
(40)	Jimmy Wasdell	8.00	4.00	2.50

1958 Philadelphia Phillies Picture Pack

This set of 5" x 7" blank-backed, black-and-white player pictures was most likely issued in 1958, though it is also possible the set was issued in 1957 (or both). This team-issue set differs from the contemporary Jay Publishing picture packs in that it does not have the city name in the identication line, only the player name in all-caps and "Phillies." The unnumbered pictures are listed here alphabetically.

		NM	EX	VG
Complete Set (12):		75.00	40.00	22.50
Common Player:		7.50	3.75	2.25
(1)	Harry Anderson	7.50	3.75	2.25
(2)	Richie Ashburn	15.00	7.50	4.50
(3)	Bob Bowman	7.50	3.75	2.25
(4)	Turk Farrell	7.50	3.75	2.25
(5)	Chico Fernandez	7.50	3.75	2.25
(6)	Granny Hamner	7.50	3.75	2.25
(7)	Stan Lopata	7.50	3.75	2.25
(8)	Rip Repulski	7.50	3.75	2.25
(9)	Robin Roberts	15.00	7.50	4.50
(10)	Jack Sanford	7.50	3.75	2.25
(11)	Curt Simmons	7.50	3.75	2.25
(12)	Mayo Smith	7.50	3.75	2.25

1958-60 Philadelphia Phillies Team Issue

Thus far 22 different cards have been discovered in this format; it is likely the checklist here is not yet complete. Like many teams, the Phillies issued these cards to players and staff to honor fan requests for photos and autographs. The cards are 3-1/4" x 5-1/2" and have black-and-white portrait photos with white borders. Backs are blank. The unnumbered cards are listed here alphabetically.

		NM	EX	VG
Common Player:		6.00	3.00	1.75
(1)	Harry Anderson	6.00	3.00	1.75
(2)	Richie Ashburn	12.00	6.00	3.50
(3)	Ed Bouchee	6.00	3.00	1.75
(4)	Smoky Burgess	7.50	3.75	2.25
(5)	Johnny Callison	8.00	4.00	2.50
(6)	Jim Coker	6.00	3.00	1.75
(7)	Clay Dalrymple	6.00	3.00	1.75
(8)	Del Ennis	7.50	3.75	2.25
(9)	Tony Gonzalez	6.00	3.00	1.75
(10)	Granny Hamner	6.00	3.00	1.75
(11)	Willie Jones	6.00	3.00	1.75
(12)	Stan Lopata	6.00	3.00	1.75
(13)	Art Mahaffey	6.00	3.00	1.75
(14)	Gene Mauch	6.00	3.00	1.75
(15)	Bob Morgan	6.00	3.00	1.75
(16)	Wally Post	6.00	3.00	1.75
(17)	Robin Roberts	12.00	6.00	3.50
(18)	Eddie Sawyer	6.00	3.00	1.75
(19)	Andy Seminick	6.00	3.00	1.50
(20)	Ray Semproch	6.00	3.00	1.75
(21)	Chris Short	6.00	3.00	1.75
(22)	Curt Simmons	8.00	4.00	2.50
(23)	Earl Torgeson	6.00	3.00	1.75

1964 Philadelphia Phillies Player Pins

Only four players are checklisted in this series, but it is expected more will be added in the future. These pinbacks are 2-3/16" in diameter and have black-and-white player portraits on front, on a white background. The player's name is printed at bottom in block letters.

		NM	EX	VG
Common Player:		45.00	22.50	13.50
(1)	Dick Allen	90.00	45.00	27.50
(2)	Jim Bunning	90.00	45.00	27.50
(3)	Chris Short	45.00	22.50	13.50
(4)	Roy Sievers	45.00	22.50	13.50

1965 Go! Phillies Go! Pins

These large (3-1/2" diameter) pinback buttons feature a dozen members of the '65 Phils. Player portraits are on a white background and have had the cap and pinstripes colored in red. At top, the title is printed in red and blue. The facsimile autograph at bottom is printed in blue.

		NM	EX	VG
Complete Set (12):		750.00	375.00	225.00
Common Player:		50.00	25.00	15.00
(1)	Rich Allen	100.00	50.00	30.00
(2)	Ruben Amaro	50.00	25.00	15.00
(3)	Bo Belinsky	65.00	32.50	20.00
(4)	Jim Bunning	100.00	50.00	30.00
(5)	Johnny Callison	65.00	32.50	20.00
(6)	Wes Covington	50.00	25.00	15.00
(7)	Ray Culp	50.00	25.00	15.00
(8)	Cookie Rojas	50.00	25.00	15.00
(9)	Chris Short	50.00	25.00	15.00
(10)	Dick Stuart	50.00	25.00	15.00
(11)	Tony Taylor	50.00	25.00	15.00
(12)	Bobby Wine	50.00	25.00	15.00

1965 Philadelphia Phillies Tiles

These decorative heavy ceramic tiles feature color portraits and facsimile autographs on a white background. In 6" x 6" format the tiles were made in England, but decorated in the U.S. They appear to have been originally issued with cork backing and some have been seen with a hangar attached on back.

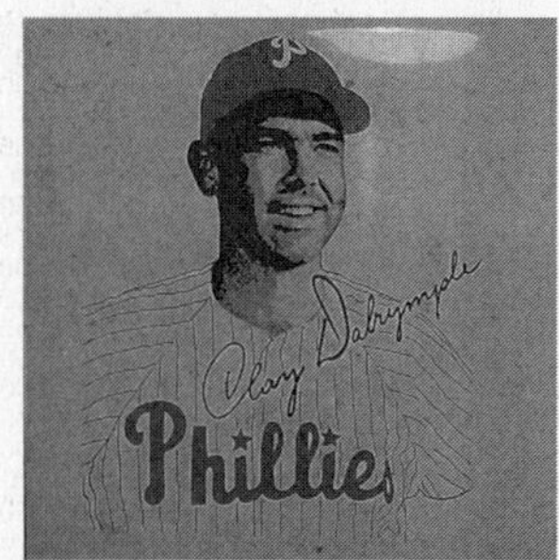

	NM	EX	VG
Complete Set (12):	600.00	300.00	180.00
Common Player:	40.00	20.00	12.00
(1) Richie Allen	100.00	50.00	30.00
(2) Bo Belinsky	60.00	30.00	18.00
(3) Jim Bunning	125.00	65.00	35.00
(4) Johnny Callison	60.00	30.00	18.00
(5) Wes Covington	40.00	20.00	12.00
(6) Clay Dalrymple	40.00	20.00	12.00
(7) Gene Mauch	40.00	20.00	12.00
(8) Cookie Rojas	40.00	20.00	12.00
(9) Tony Taylor	40.00	20.00	12.00
(10) Chris Short	40.00	20.00	12.00
(11) Dick Stuart	40.00	20.00	12.00
(12) Bobby Wine	40.00	20.00	12.00

1967 Philadelphia Phillies Safe Driving

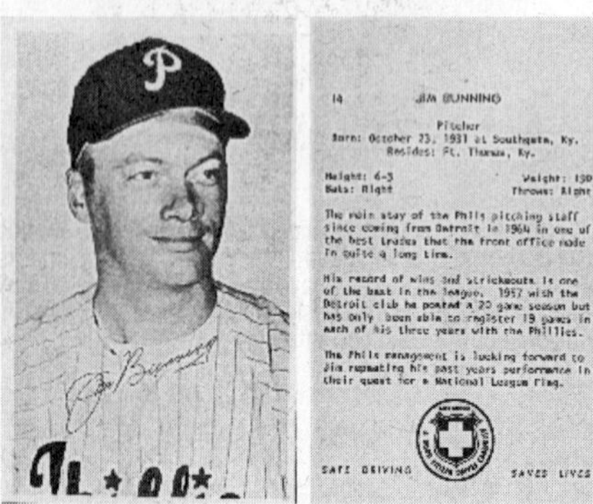

The honor of producing the only safety set of the 1960s goes to the Phillies for this traffic safety set. Measuring 2-3/4" x 4-1/2", the cards have a black-and-white front featuring the standard publicity photo of the player, with a facsimile autograph superimposed. Backs are printed in blue and include a few career and biographical details, along with the player's uniform number, by which the set is checklisted here. At bottom is a circle and shield design with the safety message.

	NM	EX	VG
Complete Set (13):	95.00	47.00	28.00
Common Player:	8.00	4.00	2.50
4 Gene Mauch	8.00	4.00	2.50
6 Johnny Callison	10.00	5.00	3.00
10 Bill White	10.00	5.00	3.00
11 Clay Dalrymple	8.00	4.00	2.50
12 Johnny Briggs	8.00	4.00	2.50
14 Jim Bunning	20.00	10.00	6.00
15 Dick Allen	18.00	9.00	5.50
16 Cookie Rojas	8.00	4.00	2.50
24 Dick Groat	10.00	5.00	3.00
25 Tony Gonzalez	8.00	4.00	2.50
37 Dick Ellsworth	8.00	4.00	2.50
41 Chris Short	8.00	4.00	2.50
46 Larry Jackson	8.00	4.00	2.50

1975 Philadelphia Phillies Photocards

These 3-1/4" x 5-1/2" blank-back, black-and-white cards feature player portrait photos with only the player name in the white border at bottom. Fronts have a semi-gloss finish. It is likely the checklist, presented here alphabetically, is incomplete.

	NM	EX	VG
Common Player:	3.00	1.50	.90
(1) Tom Hilgendorf	3.00	1.50	.90
(2) Terry Harmon	3.00	1.50	.90
(3) Joe Hoerner	3.00	1.50	.90
(4) Tommy Hutton	3.00	1.50	.90
(5) Jim Lonborg	4.00	2.00	1.25
(6) John Oates	3.00	1.50	.90

1961 Phillies Cigar Mickey Mantle

This 6-1/2" x 9" blank-back color photo card of Mickey Mantle was part of a redemption program for Phillies cigars. For $3.39 and 20 cigar bands, a person could receive a Mickey Mantle model baseball glove and this "autographed" (facsimile) photo.

	NM	EX	VG
Mickey Mantle	125.00	62.50	37.50

1912 Photo Art Shop Boston Red Sox

Two postcards are currently known to have been produced, according to the legend on the back, by The Photo Art Shop of Swampscott, Mass. The standard-size (about 3-1/2" x 5-1/2") cards are printed in black-and-white. A vertically formatted card shows opposing World Series aces Joe Wood and Walter Johnson. A horizontal team-photo card has each player's last name printed over his picture and describes the team as "Champions of the American League." The Red Sox went on to defeat the Giants in the World Series.

	NM	EX	VG
Joe Wood, Walter Johnson	1,800	900.00	540.00
1912 Boston Red Sox	900.00	450.00	275.00

1964 Photo Linen Emblems

The attributed date of issue is only approximate. About 3-1/2" x 4-1/2", these sew-on patches feature black-and-white photos with an embroidered red border. The patches were sold in a cello-wrapped package. The checklist presented here in alphabetical order is not complete.

	NM	EX	VG
Complete Set (10):	625.00	300.00	180.00
Common Player:	30.00	15.00	9.00
(1) Yogi Berra	50.00	25.00	15.00
(2) Clete Boyer	30.00	15.00	9.00
(3) Elston Howard	30.00	15.00	9.00
(4) Sandy Koufax	175.00	87.00	52.00
(5) Tony Kubek	30.00	15.00	9.00
(6) Mickey Mantle	250.00	125.00	75.00
(7) Roger Maris	90.00	45.00	27.00
(8) Joe Pepitone	30.00	15.00	9.00
(9) Bobby Richardson	30.00	15.00	9.00
(10) Tom Tresh	30.00	15.00	9.00

1972 Photo Sports Co. L.A. Dodgers

This is the first known issue of a sports novelty marketed by Photo Sports Co., Los Angeles. The company is best known to collectors for its 1974 McDonald's promotional "Foto Balls" with player discs. The Dodgers set is similar in concept with a hinged plastic baseball which opens to reveal player discs. A "keyhole" punched at the bottom of the discs keeps them in place within the ball. The Dodgers never rolled out the project and surviving sets are extremely rare. Discs are 2-5/8" diameter with borderless color photos on front. Backs have player stats and the team logo. The unnumbered discs are checklisted here in alphabetical order.

	NM	EX	VG
Complete Set (Ball and Discs):	300.00	150.00	90.00
Common Player:	16.00	8.00	4.75
(1) Red Adams	16.00	8.00	4.75
(2) Walt Alston	35.00	17.50	10.50
(3) Willie Crawford	16.00	8.00	4.75
(4) Willie Davis	24.00	12.00	7.25
(5) Al Downing	16.00	8.00	4.75
(6) Jim Gilliam	24.00	12.00	7.25
(7) Bill Grabarkewitz	16.00	8.00	4.75
(8) Jim Lefebvre	16.00	8.00	4.75
(9) Pete Mikkelsen	16.00	8.00	4.75
(10) Manny Mota	18.00	9.00	5.50
(11) Claude Osteen	16.00	8.00	4.75
(12) Wes Parker	16.00	8.00	4.75
(13) Duke Sims	16.00	8.00	4.75
(14) Bill Singer	16.00	8.00	4.75
(15) Bill Sudakis	16.00	8.00	4.75
(16) Don Sutton	30.00	15.00	9.00
(17) Bob Valentine	18.00	9.00	5.50
(18) Maury Wills	22.00	11.00	6.50

1953 Pictsweet Milwaukee Braves

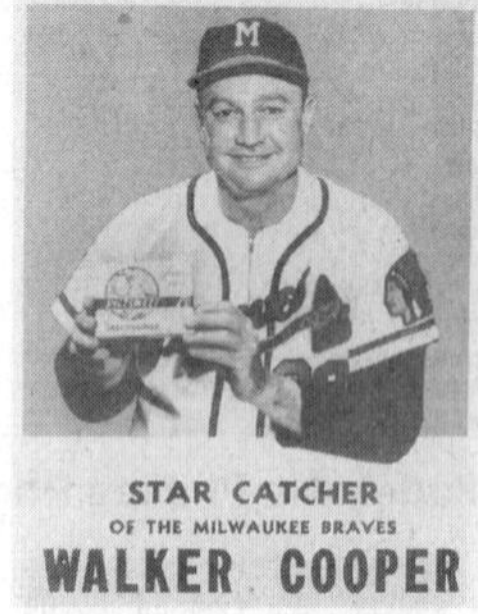

This black-and-white mini-poster (8-1/2" x 11-1/4") depicts a player holding a package of frozen vegetables. They were probably intended for grocery store window or aisle display. Backs are blank. It's unknown how many players are in the set. See also, Top Taste Bread.

	NM	EX	VG
Common Player:	150.00	75.00	45.00
(1) "Bullet Bill" Bruton	150.00	75.00	45.00
(2) Walker Cooper	150.00	75.00	45.00
(3) Sid Gordon	150.00	75.00	45.00
(4) Charlie Grimm	150.00	75.00	45.00
(5) Sibby Sisti	150.00	75.00	45.00
(6) Max Surkont	150.00	75.00	45.00

1970 Pictures of Champions Baltimore Orioles

Issued in 1970 in the Baltimore area, this 16-card set pictures members of the Baltimore Orioles. The 2-1/8" x 2-3/4" cards feature black and white player photos on orange card stock. The method of distribution is unknown.

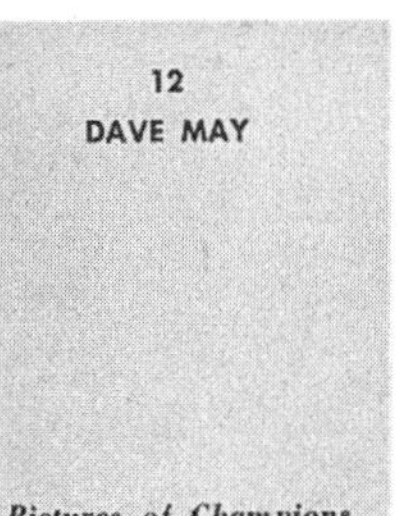

		NM	EX	VG
Complete Set (16):		80.00	40.00	25.00
Common Player:		2.00	1.00	.60
4	Earl Weaver	7.50	3.75	2.25
5	Brooks Robinson	25.00	12.50	7.50
7	Mark Belanger	2.00	1.00	.60
8	Andy Etchebarren	2.00	1.00	.60
9	Don Buford	2.00	1.00	.60
10	Ellie Hendricks	2.00	1.00	.60
12	Dave May	2.00	1.00	.60
15	Dave Johnson	2.00	1.00	.60
16	Dave McNally	2.00	1.00	.60
20	Frank Robinson	20.00	10.00	6.00
22	Jim Palmer	20.00	10.00	6.00
24	Pete Richert	2.00	1.00	.60
29	Dick Hall	2.00	1.00	.60
35	Mike Cuellar	2.00	1.00	.60
39	Eddie Watt	2.00	1.00	.60
40	Dave Leonhard	2.00	1.00	.60

1909-11 Piedmont Cigarettes

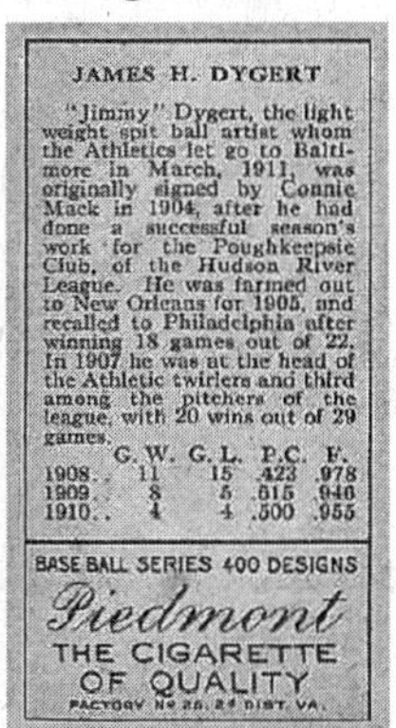

JAMES H. DYGERT
"Jimmy" Dygert, the light weight spit ball artist whom the Athletics let go to Baltimore in March, 1911, was originally signed by Connie Mack in 1904, after he had done a successful season's work for the Poughkeepsie Club, of the Hudson River League. He was farmed out to New Orleans for 1905, and recalled to Philadelphia after winning 18 games out of 22. In 1907 he was at the head of the Athletic twirlers and third among the pitchers of the league, with 20 wins out of 29 games.
G. W. G. L. P.C. F.
1908.. 11 15 .423 .978
1909.. 8 5 .615 .946
1910.. 4 4 .500 .955
BASE BALL SERIES 400 DESIGNS
Piedmont
THE CIGARETTE OF QUALITY

In both T205 and T206, Piedmont is the brand found most often on the cards' backs. In T205, Piedmonts backs are printed in blue with either Factory 25 and 42 designation, the latter of which is much scarcer but commands little premium, more due to collector indifference than relative scarcity. In T206, the familiar blue Piedmont logo is found in all three series. In the "150 Subjects" and "350 Subjects" series, only Factory 25 (Va.) is seen. In the "350-460 Subjects" series, both Factory 25 and Factory 42 (N.C.) are seen. The latter is much scarcer and commands a premium over the more common Factory 25 version.

FACTORY 42 OVERPRINTS PREMIUM:
Common Players: 5-7X
Hall of Famers: 2X
(See T205, T206)

1914 Piedmont Art Stamps (T330-2)

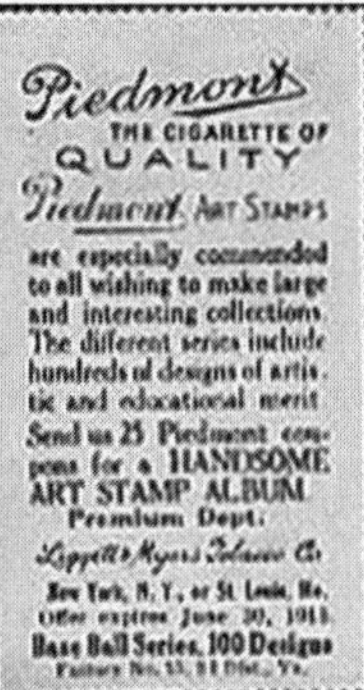

Piedmont
THE CIGARETTE OF QUALITY
Piedmont Art Stamps
are especially commended to all wishing to make large and interesting collections. The different series include hundreds of designs of artistic and educational merit.
Send us 25 Piedmont coupons for a HANDSOME ART STAMP ALBUM.
Premium Dept:
Liggett & Myers Tobacco Co.
New York, N.Y., or St. Louis, Mo.
Offer expires June 30, 1915.
Base Ball Series, 100 Designs

This series of "Piedmont Art Stamps" looks like a fragile version of the more popular T205 Gold Border tobacco cards of 1911, employing the same basic design on front. The Piedmont stamps measure 1-1/2" x 2-5/8". Though the backs advertise "100 designs," more than 110 different players are known. And, because some of the players are pictured in two separate poses, there are actually 118 different stamps known, with new discoveries still being made. All but three of the subjects in the Piedmont set were taken from the T205 set; the exceptions being Joe Wood, Walt Blair and Bill Killifer. Because of their fragile composition, and since they are stamps that were frequently stuck to album pages, examples of Piedmont Art Stamps in Near Mint or better condition are very scarce. The back of the stamps offered a "handsome" album in exchange for 25 Piedmont coupons. The set has an American Card Catalog designation of T330-2. Gaps have been left in the assigned numbering to accommodate future additions.

		NM	EX	VG
Common Player:		150.00	60.00	30.00
(1)	Leon K. Ames	150.00	60.00	30.00
(2)	Jimmy Archer	150.00	60.00	30.00
(3)	Jimmy Austin	150.00	60.00	30.00
(4)	Home Run Baker	450.00	180.00	90.00
(5)	Cy Barger (Full "B" on cap.)	150.00	60.00	30.00
(6)	Cy Barger (Partial "B" on cap.)	150.00	60.00	30.00
(7)	Jack Barry	150.00	60.00	30.00
(8)	Johnny Bates	150.00	60.00	30.00
(9)	Fred Beck	150.00	60.00	30.00
(10)	Beals Becker	150.00	60.00	30.00
(11)	Chief Bender	450.00	180.00	90.00
(12)	Bob Bescher	150.00	60.00	30.00
(13)	Joe Birmingham	150.00	60.00	30.00
(14)	Walt Blair	150.00	60.00	30.00
(15)	Roger Bresnahan	450.00	180.00	90.00
(16)	Al Bridwell	150.00	60.00	30.00
(17)	Mordecai Brown	450.00	180.00	90.00
(18)	Bobby Byrne	150.00	60.00	30.00
(19)	Howie Camnitz	150.00	60.00	30.00
(20)	Bill Carrigan	150.00	60.00	30.00
(21)	Frank Chance	450.00	180.00	90.00
(22)	Hal Chase ("Chase" on front.)	250.00	100.00	50.00
(23)	Hal Chase ("Hal Chase" on front.)	300.00	120.00	60.00
(24)	Ed Cicotte	375.00	150.00	75.00
(25)	Fred Clarke	450.00	180.00	90.00
(26)	Ty Cobb	5,500	2,200	1,100
(27)	Eddie Collins (Mouth closed.)	450.00	180.00	90.00
(28)	Eddie Collins (Mouth open.)	450.00	180.00	90.00
(29)	Otis "Doc" Crandall	150.00	60.00	30.00
(30)	Bill Dahlen	150.00	60.00	30.00
(31)	Jake Daubert	150.00	60.00	30.00
(32)	Jim Delahanty	150.00	60.00	30.00
(33)	Josh Devore	150.00	60.00	30.00
(34)	Red Dooin	150.00	60.00	30.00
(35)	Mickey Doolan	150.00	60.00	30.00
(36)	Tom Downey	150.00	60.00	30.00
(37)	Larry Doyle	150.00	60.00	30.00
(38)	Dick Egan	150.00	60.00	30.00
(39)	Kid Elberfield (Elberfeld)	150.00	60.00	30.00
(40)	Clyde Engle	150.00	60.00	30.00
(41)	Louis Evans	150.00	60.00	30.00
(42)	Johnny Evers	450.00	180.00	90.00
(43)	Ray Fisher	150.00	60.00	30.00
(44)	Art Fletcher	150.00	60.00	30.00
(45)	Russ Ford (Dark cap.)	150.00	60.00	30.00
(46)	Russ Ford (White cap.)	150.00	60.00	30.00
(47)	Art Fromme	150.00	60.00	30.00
(48)	George Gibson	150.00	60.00	30.00
(49)	William Goode (Wilbur Good)	150.00	60.00	30.00
(51)	Eddie Grant	225.00	90.00	45.00
(52)	Clark Griifith	450.00	180.00	90.00
(53)	Bob Groom	150.00	60.00	30.00
(54)	Bob Harmon	150.00	60.00	30.00
(55)	Arnold Hauser	150.00	60.00	30.00
(56)	Buck Herzog	150.00	60.00	30.00
(57)	Dick Hoblitzell	150.00	60.00	30.00
(58)	Miller Huggins	450.00	180.00	90.00
(59)	John Hummel	150.00	60.00	30.00
(60)	Hughie Jennings	450.00	180.00	90.00
(61)	Walter Johnson	750.00	300.00	150.00
(62)	Davy Jones	150.00	60.00	30.00
(63)	Bill Killifer (Killefer)	150.00	60.00	30.00
(64)	Jack Knight	150.00	60.00	30.00
(65)	Ed Konetchy	150.00	60.00	30.00
(66)	Frank LaPorte	150.00	60.00	30.00
(67)	Thomas Leach	150.00	60.00	30.00
(68)	Edgar Lennox	150.00	60.00	30.00
(69)	Hans Lobert	150.00	60.00	30.00
(70)	Harry Lord	150.00	60.00	30.00
(71)	Sherry Magee	150.00	60.00	30.00
(72)	Rube Marquard	450.00	180.00	90.00
(73)	Christy Mathewson	1,250	500.00	250.00
(74)	George McBride	150.00	60.00	30.00
(76)	J.J. McGraw	450.00	180.00	90.00
(77)	Larry McLean	150.00	60.00	30.00
(78)	Fred Merkle	150.00	60.00	30.00
(79)	Chief Meyers	150.00	60.00	30.00
(80)	Clyde Milan	150.00	60.00	30.00
(81)	Dots Miller	150.00	60.00	30.00
(82)	Mike Mitchell	150.00	60.00	30.00
(83)	Pat Moran	150.00	60.00	30.00
(84)	George Moriarity (Moriarty)	150.00	60.00	30.00
(85)	George Mullin	150.00	60.00	30.00
(86)	Danny Murphy	150.00	60.00	30.00
(87)	Jack "Red" Murray	150.00	60.00	30.00
(88)	Tom Needham	150.00	60.00	30.00
(89)	Rebel Oakes	150.00	60.00	30.00
(90)	Rube Oldring	150.00	60.00	30.00
(91)	Fred Parent	150.00	60.00	30.00
(92)	Dode Paskert	150.00	60.00	30.00
(93)	Jack Quinn	150.00	60.00	30.00
(94)	Ed Reulbach	150.00	60.00	30.00
(95)	Lewis Ritchie	150.00	60.00	30.00
(96)	Jack Rowan	150.00	60.00	30.00
(97)	Nap Rucker	150.00	60.00	30.00
(98)	Germany Schaefer	150.00	60.00	30.00
(99)	Wildfire Schulte	150.00	60.00	30.00
(101)	Jim Scott	150.00	60.00	30.00
(102)	Fred Snodgrass	150.00	60.00	30.00
(103)	Tris Speaker	600.00	240.00	120.00
(104)	Oscar Stamage (Stanage)	150.00	60.00	30.00
(105)	George Stovall	150.00	60.00	30.00
(106)	George Suggs	150.00	60.00	30.00
(107)	Jeff Sweeney	150.00	60.00	30.00
(108)	Ira Thomas	150.00	60.00	30.00
(109)	Joe Tinker	450.00	180.00	90.00
(110)	Terry Turner	150.00	60.00	30.00
(111)	Hippo Vaughn	150.00	60.00	30.00
(112)	Heinie Wagner	150.00	60.00	30.00
(113)	Bobby Wallace (No cap.)	450.00	180.00	90.00
(114)	Bobby Wallace (With cap.)	450.00	180.00	90.00
(115)	Ed Walsh	450.00	180.00	90.00
(116)	Zach Wheat	450.00	180.00	90.00
(117)	Irwin "Kaiser" Wilhelm	150.00	60.00	30.00
(118)	Ed Willett	150.00	60.00	30.00
(119)	Owen Wilson	150.00	60.00	30.00
(120)	Hooks Wiltse	150.00	60.00	30.00
(121)	Joe Wood	150.00	60.00	30.00

1939 Piel's Beer Coasters

PIEL'S
BEER
"IT SURE MAKES A HIT WITH ME"
Bill Terry

New York Giants manager Bill Terry was the only baseball player among a trio of local celebrities endoring the beer brand in this series of approximately 4" diameter bar coasters. The printing is in black-and-red.

	NM	EX	VG
Bill Terry	30.00	15.00	9.00

1913-1915 Pinkerton Score/Photo/Post Cards

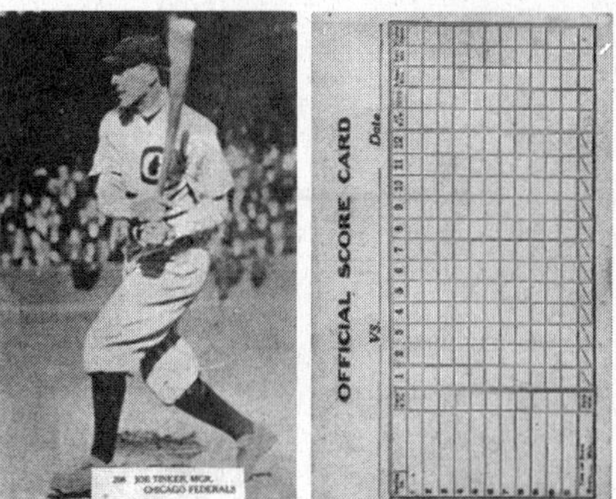

The picture portions of the T5 Pinkerton cabinets have also been seen in other formats, in printed rather than photographic presentation. The most desirable of these have backs printed for use as baseball scorecards. These measure a nominal 3-1/2" x 5-1/2", give or take 1/4". They are believed to have been printed some years after the cabinet cards. It is unknown to what extent the checklist of T5 can be found in this format. Postcard-style backs have also been seen for some Pinkerton pictures, as well as blank-backed versions; they are considerably discounted from the scorecard type. Confirmed examples are listed here.

		NM	EX	VG
Common Player:		250.00	125.00	75.00
	SCORECARD BACKS			
153	Hughie Jennings	500.00	250.00	150.00
159	Ty Cobb	2,500	1,250	750.00
203	King Cole	250.00	125.00	75.00
205	Heinie Zimmerman	250.00	125.00	75.00
206	Wildfire Schulte	250.00	125.00	75.00
208	Joe Tinker	500.00	250.00	150.00
251	Christy Mathewson	1,500	750.00	450.00
252	Fred Merkle	250.00	125.00	75.00
260	Larry Doyle	250.00	125.00	75.00
303	Red Dooin	250.00	125.00	75.00
420	R.C. Hoblitzell	250.00	125.00	75.00
424	Mike Mitchell	250.00	125.00	75.00
505	Connie Mack	500.00	250.00	150.00
511	Eddie Collins	500.00	250.00	150.00
512	Frank Baker	500.00	250.00	150.00
872	Hans Wagner	800.00	400.00	240.00
	POSTCARD OR BLANK BACKS			
159	Ty Cobb	1,500	750.00	450.00
203	King Cole	150.00	75.00	45.00
206	Frank Schulte	150.00	75.00	45.00
208	Joe Tinker	250.00	125.00	75.00
251	Christy Mathewson	350.00	175.00	105.00
260	Larry Doyle	150.00	75.00	45.00
264	Chief Myers (Meyers)	150.00	75.00	45.00
419	Clark Griffith	250.00	125.00	75.00
424	Mike Mitchell	150.00	75.00	45.00
501	Chas. Bender	250.00	125.00	75.00

511	Eddie Collins	250.00	125.00	75.00
512	Frank Baker	250.00	125.00	75.00
627	Napoleon Lajoie	250.00	125.00	75.00
855	Fred Clarke	250.00	125.00	75.00
865	Babe Adams	150.00	75.00	45.00
872	Hans Wagner	600.00	300.00	180.00

1912 Pirate Cigarettes (T215)

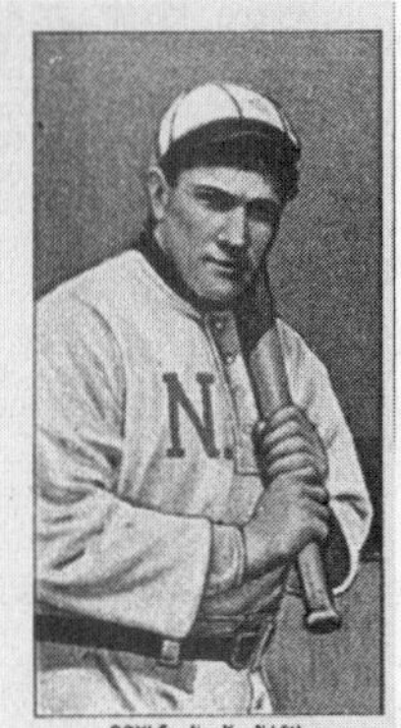

This set can be considered a British version of the T215 Red Cross Type 1 set. Distributed by Pirate brand cigarettes of Bristol and London, England, the fronts of the cards are identical to the Red Cross cards, but the green backs carry advertising for Pirate Cigarettes. It is believed that the Pirate cards were printed for distribution to U.S. servicemen in the South Seas. There is reason to believe the "standard" tobacco card length of 2-5/8" (width 1-7/16") may not be universally applicable to the Pirate cards, possibly because of packaging considerations.

		NM	EX	VG
Common Player:		11,000	5,500	3,300
(1)	Red Ames	11,000	5,500	3,300
(2)	Home Run Baker	16,000	8,000	4,800
(3)	Neal Ball	11,000	5,500	3,300
(4)	Chief Bender	16,000	8,000	4,800
(5)	Al Bridwell	11,000	5,500	3,300
(6)	Bobby Byrne (St. Louis)	11,000	5,500	3,300
(7)	Mordecai Brown (Chicago on shirt.)	16,000	8,000	4,800
(8)	Howie Camnitz	11,000	5,500	3,300
(9)	Frank Chance	9,800	4,900	2,950
(10)	Hal Chase	14,500	7,250	4,350
(11)	Eddie Collins	16,000	8,000	4,800
(12)	Doc Crandall	11,000	5,500	3,300
(13)	Sam Crawford	16,000	8,000	4,800
(14)	Birdie Cree	11,000	5,500	3,300
(15)	Harry Davis	11,000	5,500	3,300
(16)	Josh Devore	11,000	5,500	3,300
(17)	Mike Donlin	11,000	5,500	3,300
(18)	Mickey Doolan/Btg	11,000	5,500	3,300
(19)	Mickey Doolan/Fldg	11,000	5,500	3,300
(20)	Patsy Dougherty	11,000	5,500	3,300
(21)	Larry Doyle/Btg	11,000	5,500	3,300
(22)	Larry Doyle/Portrait	11,000	5,500	3,300
(23)	Jean Dubuc	11,000	5,500	3,300
(24)	Kid Elberfeld	11,000	5,500	3,300
(25)	Steve Evans	11,000	5,500	3,300
(26)	Johnny Evers	16,000	8,000	4,800
(27)	Russ Ford	11,000	5,500	3,300
(28)	Art Fromme	11,000	5,500	3,300
(29)	Clark Griffith	16,000	8,000	4,800
(30)	Bob Groom	11,000	5,500	3,300
(31)	Topsy Hartsel	11,000	5,500	3,300
(32)	Buck Herzog	11,000	5,500	3,300
(33)	Dick Hoblitzell	11,000	5,500	3,300
(34)	Solly Hofman	11,000	5,500	3,300
(35)	Del Howard	11,000	5,500	3,300
(36)	Miller Huggins (Hands at mouth.)	16,000	8,000	4,800
(37)	Miller Huggins/Portrait	16,000	8,000	4,800
(38)	John Hummel	11,000	5,500	3,300
(39)	Hughie Jennings (Both hands showing.)	16,000	8,000	4,800
(40)	Hughie Jennings (One hand showing.)	16,000	8,000	4,800
(41)	Walter Johnson	35,000	17,500	10,500
(42)	Joe Kelley	16,000	8,000	4,800
(43)	Ed Konetchy	11,000	5,500	3,300
(44)	Harry Krause	11,000	5,500	3,300
(45)	Nap Lajoie	16,000	8,000	4,800
(46)	Joe Lake	11,000	5,500	3,300
(47)	Lefty Leifield	11,000	5,500	3,300
(48)	Harry Lord	11,000	5,500	3,300
(49)	Sherry Magee	11,000	5,500	3,300
(50)	Rube Marquard/Pitching	16,000	8,000	4,800
(51)	Rube Marquard/Portrait	16,000	8,000	4,800
(52)	Christy Mathewson (Black cap.)	20,000	10,000	5,000
(53)	Joe McGinnity	16,000	8,000	4,800
(54)	John McGraw (Glove at side.)	16,000	8,000	4,800
(55)	John McGraw/Portrait	16,000	8,000	4,800
(56)	Harry McIntyre (Chicago)	11,000	5,500	3,300
(57)	Harry McIntyre (Brooklyn & Chicago)	11,000	5,500	3,300
(58)	Matty McIntyre (Detroit)	11,000	5,500	3,300
(59)	Larry McLean	11,000	5,500	3,300
(60)	Fred Merkle	11,000	5,500	3,300
(61)	Chief Meyers	11,000	5,500	3,300
(62)	Mike Mitchell	11,000	5,500	3,300
(63)	Dots Miller	11,000	5,500	3,300
(64)	Mike Mowrey	11,000	5,500	3,300
(65)	George Mullin	11,000	5,500	3,300
(66)	Danny Murphy	11,000	5,500	3,300
(67)	Red Murray	11,000	5,500	3,300
(68)	Rebel Oakes	11,000	5,500	3,300
(69)	Rube Oldring	11,000	5,500	3,300
(70)	Charley O'Leary	11,000	5,500	3,300
(71)	Dode Paskert	11,000	5,500	3,300
(72)	Barney Pelty	11,000	5,500	3,300
(73)	Billy Purtell	11,000	5,500	3,300
(74)	Jack Quinn	11,000	5,500	3,300
(75)	Ed Reulbach	11,000	5,500	3,300
(76)	Nap Rucker	11,000	5,500	3,300
(77)	Germany Schaefer	11,000	5,500	3,300
(78)	Wildfire Schulte	11,000	5,500	3,300
(79)	Jimmy Sheckard	11,000	5,500	3,300
(80)	Frank Smith	11,000	5,500	3,300
(81)	Tris Speaker	18,000	9,000	5,400
(82)	Jake Stahl	11,000	5,500	3,300
(83)	Harry Steinfeldt	11,000	5,500	3,300
(84)	Gabby Street	11,000	5,500	3,300
(85)	Ed Summers	11,000	5,500	3,300
(86)	Jeff Sweeney	11,000	5,500	3,300
(87)	Lee Tannehill	11,000	5,500	3,300
(88)	Ira Thomas	11,000	5,500	3,300
(89)	Joe Tinker	16,000	8,000	4,800
(90)	Heinie Wagner	11,000	5,500	3,300
(91)	Jack Warhop	11,000	5,500	3,300
(92)	Zack Wheat	16,000	8,000	4,800
(93)	Ed Willetts (Willett)	11,000	5,500	3,300
(94)	Owen Wilson	11,000	5,500	3,300
(95)	Hooks Wiltse/Pitching	11,000	5,500	3,300
(96)	Hooks Wiltse/Portrait	11,000	5,500	3,300

1910 Pittsburgh Gazette Times Honus Wagner Postcard

Describing him as "The Worlds' Greatest Base Ball Player," the local newspaper published this black-and-white standard size, typically marked, photographic postcard picturing the Flying Dutchman and landmarks from his Carnegie, Pa., hometown.

	NM	EX	VG
Honus Wagner	650.00	325.00	200.00

1904 Pittsburg Leader Honus Wagner Schedule

BASE BALL SCHEDULE
NATIONAL LEAGUE
1904
PITTSBURG CLUB AT HOME
COMPLIMENTS OF THE
Pittsburg Leader.
THE BEST BASE BALL NEWSPAPER

This 3-3/4" x 1-3/4" celluloid pocket schedule for the 1904 Pirates features on its front a black-and-white photographic portrait of the "KING OF BALL PLAYERS," Honus Wagner. Much of the remainder of the front and back printing is in regal purple typography.

	NM	EX	VG
Honus Wagner	3,500	1,750	1,100

1908 Pittsburgh Pirates Vignette Postcards

It has been reliably reported that 15 postcards and an album were produced for this souvenir issue sold at Pittsburgh's Exhibition Field. Only Pirates are pictured in this series of black-and-white standard-format postcards published locally by J.B. Coyle. Cards have an irregularly shaped posed photo of the player at center with his last name (or nickname), position and "PGH-08" crudely printed in white. Divided postcard backs have a stamp box and publisher's

credit line. The incomplete checklist presented here is alphabetically arranged. Later editions of the American Card Catalog listed this set as PC800.

		NM	EX	VG
Common Player:		250.00	125.00	75.00
(1)	Abby (Ed Abbaticchio)	250.00	125.00	75.00
(2)	Howie Camnitz	250.00	125.00	75.00
(3)	Fred Clarke	350.00	175.00	105.00
(4)	George Gibson	250.00	125.00	75.00
(5)	Tommy Leach	250.00	125.00	75.00
(6)	Dan Moeller	250.00	125.00	75.00
(10)	Allen Storke	250.00	125.00	75.00
(14)	Honus Wagner	1,000	500.00	300.00
(15)	Owen Wilson	250.00	125.00	75.00

1909 Pittsburgh Pirates Extension Postcard

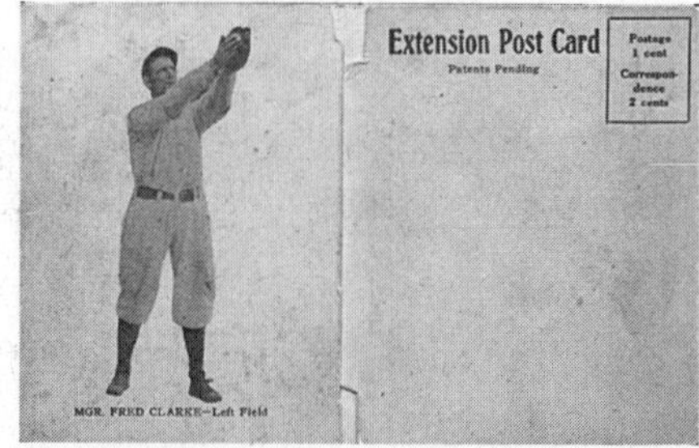

One of many novelty souvenirs commemorating the Bucs' World Championship season of 1909 was this uniquely formatted postcard. Picturing manager Fred Clarke on front, the 3-1/4" x 5-1/2" postcard opens up accordian fashion to a length of 14", revealing small action photos of 17 players each on a white background and identified by last name and position.

	NM	EX	VG
1909 Pittsburgh Pirates	3,000	1,500	900.00

1950-60s Pittsburgh Pirates Postcards

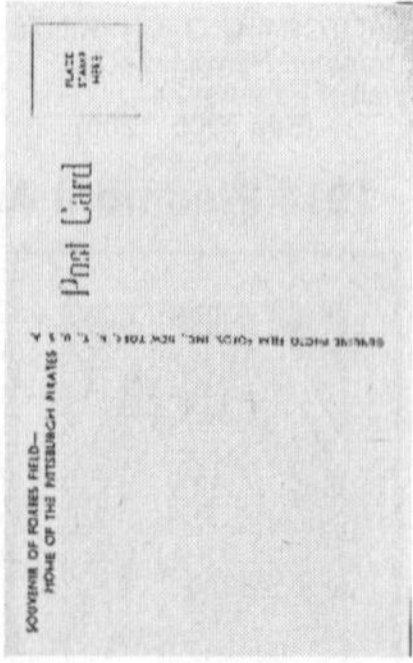

This listing encompasses the issues of several different postcard publishers who supplied black-and-white cards to the players for use in answering fan mail. Several different types of card stock are found, both matte and glossy. Some cards have postcard markings on back, others do not, especially those picturing players in the 1960s style sleeveless style uniforms. Because it is likely other players and poses will be reported, a description of each pose is included.

		NM	EX	VG
Common Player:		15.00	7.50	4.50
(1)	Gair Allie (Ready to hit.)	15.00	7.50	4.50
(2)	Toby Atwell (Squatting w/glove.)	15.00	7.50	4.50
(3)	Tony Bartirome (Stretching at 1B.)	15.00	7.50	4.50

(4)	Carlos Bernier/Btg	15.00	7.50	4.50
(5)	Ron Blackburn/Pitching (Left leg up.)	15.00	7.50	4.50
(6)	Ron Brand (Kneeling w/glove.)	15.00	7.50	4.50
(7)	Jim Bunning/Pitching (To letters.)	25.00	12.50	7.50
(8)	Don (Swede) Carlson (Pitching, by wall.)	15.00	7.50	4.50
(9)	Pete Castiglione (Ready to hit.)	15.00	7.50	4.50
(10)	Pete Castiglione (Kneeling w/bat.)	15.00	7.50	4.50
(12)	Cliff Chambers/Pitching (Leg up.)	15.00	7.50	4.50
(13)	Bob Chesnes (Follow-through.)	15.00	7.50	4.50
(14)	Roberto Clemente (Kneeling w/bat.)	125.00	65.00	35.00
(15)	Dick Cole /Fldg	15.00	7.50	4.50
(16)	Dale Coogan (Ready to hit.)	15.00	7.50	4.50
(18)	Bobby Del Greco (Batting follow-through.)	15.00	7.50	4.50
(20)	Elroy Face (Follow-through, cloth cap, sleeves.)	17.50	8.75	5.25
(21)	Elroy Face (Follow-through, cloth cap, no sleeves.)	17.50	8.75	5.25
(22)	Elroy Face (Follow-through, helmet, sleeves.)	17.50	8.75	5.25
(23)	Elroy Face (Follow-through, helmet, no sleeves.)	17.50	8.75	5.25
(24)	Hank Foiles/Squatting	15.00	7.50	4.50
(25)	Gene Freese (Ready to hit.)	15.00	7.50	4.50
(26)	Bob Friend (Follow-through.)	15.00	7.50	4.50
(27)	Bob Friend/Pitchign (Leg up.)	15.00	7.50	4.50
(28)	Bob Friend (Standing in dugout.)	15.00	7.50	4.50
(29)	Dick Groat (Ready to hit.)	17.50	8.75	5.25
(30)	Fred Haney (Arms folded.)	15.00	7.50	4.50
(31)	John Hetki (Follow-through.)	15.00	7.50	4.50
(32)	Johnny Hopp (Stretching at 1B.)	15.00	7.50	4.50
(34)	Ralph Kiner/Btg (Two decks.)	25.00	12.50	7.50
(35)	Nellie King (Follow-through.)	15.00	7.50	4.50
(36)	Ron Kline (Follow-through.)	15.00	7.50	4.50
(37)	Ron Kline/Pitching (Leg up.)	15.00	7.50	4.50
(38)	Ted Kluszewski (Kneeling with bat.)	20.00	10.00	6.00
(39)	Ted Kluszewski (Pose to chest.)	20.00	10.00	6.00
(41)	Nick Koback/Kneeling	15.00	7.50	4.50
(42)	Clem Koshorek/Fldg	15.00	7.50	4.50
(43)	Danny Kravitz (Ready to hit.)	15.00	7.50	4.50
(44)	Vern Law (Follow-through, bleachers.)	17.50	8.75	5.25
(45)	Vern Law (Follow-through, trees.)	17.50	8.75	5.25
(46)	Vern Law (Follow-through, right foot cut off.)	17.50	8.75	5.25
(47)	Vern Law/Kneeling	17.50	8.75	5.25
(48)	Vern Law/Pitching (Leg up.)	17.50	8.75	5.25
(49)	Lenny Levy/Catching	15.00	7.50	4.50
(50)	Lenny Levy (Standing in dugout.)	15.00	7.50	4.50
(51)	Dale Long/Btg	15.00	7.50	4.50
(52)	Dale Long (Kneeling w/bat.)	15.00	7.50	4.50
(53)	Jerry Lynch/Btg (Sleeves)	15.00	7.50	4.50
(54)	Jerry Lynch/Btg (No sleeves.)	15.00	7.50	4.50
(55)	Bill MacDonald/Pitching (Leg up.)	15.00	7.50	4.50
(56)	Bill Mazeroski/Fldg (Ball in glove, horizontal.)	25.00	12.50	7.50
(57)	Bill Mazeroski/Fldg (Ball in hand.)	25.00	12.50	7.50
(58)	Danny Murtaugh/Fldg	15.00	7.50	4.50
(59)	Danny Murtaugh/Portrait (Helmet)	15.00	7.50	4.50
(60)	George "Red" Munger/ Pitching	15.00	7.50	4.50
(61)	Johnny O'Brien/Jumping	15.00	7.50	4.50
(63)	Danny O'Connell/Btg	15.00	7.50	4.50
(64)	Bob Oldis (Portrait to belt.)	15.00	7.50	4.50
(65)	Laurin Pepper (Follow-through.)	15.00	7.50	4.50
(66)	Pete Peterson/Catching	15.00	7.50	4.50
(68)	Buddy Pritchard/Btg	15.00	7.50	4.50
(69)	Bob Purkey (Follow-through.)	15.00	7.50	4.50
(70)	Bob Purkey/Portrait	15.00	7.50	4.50
(71)	Mel Queen/Pitching (Leg up.)	15.00	7.50	4.50
(72)	Curt Raydon (Follow-through, horizontal.)	15.00	7.50	4.50
(74)	Dino Restelli/Btg	15.00	7.50	4.50
(75)	Stan Rojek/Btg	15.00	7.50	4.50
(76)	Stan Rojek (Standing in dugout.)	15.00	7.50	4.50
(78)	Tom Saffell/Btg	15.00	7.50	4.50
(80)	Don Schwall/Pitching (No cap.)	15.00	7.50	4.50
(81)	Bob Skinner/Btg	15.00	7.50	4.50
(82)	Bob Smith (Follow-through.)	15.00	7.50	4.50
(83)	Paul Smith/Btg	15.00	7.50	4.50
(84)	Art Swanson (Hands on hips.)	15.00	7.50	4.50
(86)	Frank Thomas/Btg (Cap)	17.50	8.75	5.25
(87)	Frank Thomas/Btg (Helmet)	17.50	8.75	5.25
(90)	Bill Virdon/Btg (Matte)	17.50	8.75	5.25
(91)	Bill Virdon/Btg (Glossy)	17.50	8.75	5.25
(92)	Bill Virdon/Kneeling	17.50	8.75	5.25
(93)	Harry Walker/Portrait	15.00	7.50	4.50
(94)	Lee Walls/Btg (Glove in pocket.)	15.00	7.50	4.50
(95)	Lee Walls/Btg (Trees)	15.00	7.50	4.50
(96)	Jim Walsh (Follow-through, horizontal.)	15.00	7.50	4.50
(97)	Preston Ward/Btg (#44 in background.)	15.00	7.50	4.50
(98)	Preston Ward/Btg (No #44.)	15.00	7.50	4.50
(99)	Fred Waters/Pitching (Leg up.)	15.00	7.50	4.50
(100)	Bill Werle/Pitching	15.00	7.50	4.50

1950 Pittsburgh Pirates Photo Pack

The player photos in this picture pack that was sold at Forbes Field measure 6-1/2" x 9" and are printed in black-and-white on heavy, blank-backed paper. A facsimile "autograph" is printed on front of each picture, though all were written in the same hand. Several of the photos from this set were the basis for the color paintings found on 1951 Bowman cards. The unnumbered pictures are checklisted here alphabetically.

		NM	EX	VG
Complete Set (26):		250.00	125.00	75.00
Common Player:		12.00	6.00	3.50
(1)	Ted Beard	12.00	6.00	3.50
(2)	Gus Bell	20.00	10.00	6.00
(3)	Pete Castiglione	12.00	6.00	3.50
(4)	Cliff Chambers	12.00	6.00	3.50
(5)	Dale Coogan	12.00	6.00	3.50
(6)	Murry Dickson	12.00	6.00	3.50
(7)	Bob Dillinger	12.00	6.00	3.50
(8)	Froilan Fernandez	12.00	6.00	3.50
(9)	Johnny Hopp	12.00	6.00	3.50
(10)	Ralph Kiner	30.00	15.00	9.00
(11)	Vernon Law	20.00	10.00	6.00
(12)	Vic Lombardi	12.00	6.00	3.50
(13)	Bill MacDonald	12.00	6.00	3.50
(14)	Clyde McCullough	12.00	6.00	3.50
(15)	Bill Meyer	12.00	6.00	3.50
(16)	Ray Mueller	12.00	6.00	3.50
(17)	Danny Murtaugh	12.00	6.00	3.50
(18)	Jack Phillips	12.00	6.00	3.50
(19)	Mel Queen	12.00	6.00	3.50
(20)	Stan Rojek	12.00	6.00	3.50
(21)	Henry Schenz	12.00	6.00	3.50
(22)	George Strickland	12.00	6.00	3.50
(23)	Earl Turner	12.00	6.00	3.50
(24)	Jim Walsh	12.00	6.00	3.50
(25)	Bill Werle	12.00	6.00	3.50
(26)	Wally Westlake	12.00	6.00	3.50

1967 Pittsburgh Pirates Autograph Cards

A souvenir stand item introduced by the Pirates in 1967 was a series of color player cards bearing facsimile autographs. The 3-1/4" x 4-1/4" cards identify the player with a line of type beneath the photo giving name, position and uniform number. Backs are blank. The cards are checklisted here in alphabetical order.

		NM	EX	VG
Complete Set (24):		100.00	50.00	30.00
Common Player:		4.00	2.00	1.25
	SERIES A			
(1)	Gene Alley	4.00	2.00	1.25
(2)	Steve Blass	4.00	2.00	1.25
(3)	Roberto Clemente	35.00	17.50	10.00
(4)	Donn Clendenon	5.00	2.50	1.50
(5)	Roy Face	5.00	2.50	1.50
(6)	Jesse Gonder	4.00	2.00	1.25
(7)	Jerry May	4.00	2.00	1.25
(8)	Manny Mota	5.00	2.50	1.50
(9)	Jose Pagan	4.00	2.00	1.25
(10)	Dennis Ribant	4.00	2.00	1.25
(11)	Tommie Sisk	4.00	2.00	1.25
(12)	Bob Veale	4.00	2.00	1.25
	SERIES B			
(13)	Matty Alou	4.00	2.00	1.25
(14)	Woody Fryman	4.00	2.00	1.25
(15)	Vernon Law	5.00	2.50	1.50
(16)	Bill Mazeroski	17.50	8.75	5.25
(17)	Al McBean	4.00	2.00	1.25
(18)	Pete Mikkelsen	4.00	2.00	1.25
(19)	Jim Pagliaroni	4.00	2.00	1.25
(20)	Juan Pizarro	4.00	2.00	1.25
(21)	Andy Rodgers	4.00	2.00	1.25
(22)	Willie Stargell	15.00	7.50	4.50
(23)	Harry Walker	4.00	2.00	1.25
(24)	Maury Wills	6.50	3.25	2.00

1968 Pittsburgh Pirates Autograph Cards

These team-issued autograph cards were sold in packages at Forbes Field. The 3-1/4" x 4-1/4" cards feature a color player photo and facsimile autograph. They are blank-backed. Cards were issued in Series A and Series B, with header cards in each series providing a checklist. Cards are listed here by series according to the uniform number found on the card.

		NM	EX	VG
Complete Set (26):		45.00	22.00	13.50
Common Player:		2.00	1.00	.60
	SERIES A			
7	Larry Shepard	2.00	1.00	.60
11	Jose Pagan	2.00	1.00	.60
12	Jerry May	2.00	1.00	.60
14	Jim Bunning	7.50	3.75	2.25
15	Manny Mota	2.00	1.00	.60
17	Donn Clendenon	3.00	1.50	.90
21	Roberto Clemente	15.00	7.50	4.50
22	Gene Alley	2.00	1.00	.60
25	Tommie Sisk	2.00	1.00	.60
26	Roy Face	2.00	1.00	.60
28	Steve Blass	2.00	1.00	.60
39	Bob Veale	2.00	1.00	.60
--	Checklist Card, Series A	2.00	1.00	.60
	SERIES B			
8	Willie Stargell	8.00	4.00	2.50
9	Bill Mazeroski	9.00	4.50	2.75
10	Gary Kolb	2.00	1.00	.60
18	Matty Alou	2.50	1.25	.70
27	Ronnie Kline	2.00	1.00	.60
29	Juan Pizzaro	2.00	1.00	.60
30	Maury Wills	4.00	2.00	1.25
34	Al McBean	2.00	1.00	.60
35	Manny Sanguillen	2.00	1.00	.60
38	Bob Moose	2.00	1.00	.60
40	Dave Wickersham	2.00	1.00	.60
--	Jim Shellenback	2.00	1.00	.60
--	Checklist Card, Series B	2.00	1.00	.60

1969 Pittsburgh Pirates Autograph Cards

Sold in Series A with a blue header card/checklist and Series B with a pink header card/checklist, these team-issue autograph cards were available at Forbes Field. Identical in format to the previous year's issue, the 3-1/4" x 4-1/4" cards are blank-backed and feature a color player photo on front with a facsimile autograph in the wide white bottom border. Cards are checklisted here by series and uniform number (found on card fronts) within series.

		NM	EX	VG
Complete Set:		50.00	25.00	15.00
Common Player:		2.00	1.00	.60
	Series A			
2	Fred Patek	2.00	1.00	.60
4	Larry Shepard	2.00	1.00	.60
8	Willie Stargell	6.00	3.00	1.75
9	Bill Mazeroski	9.00	4.50	2.75
10	Gary Kolb	2.00	1.00	.60
23	Luke Walker	2.00	1.00	.60

#	Player	NM	EX	VG
28	Steve Blass	2.00	1.00	.60
29	Al Oliver	4.00	2.00	1.25
35	Manny Sanguillen	2.50	1.25	.70
38	Bob Moose	2.00	1.00	.60
39	Bob Veale	2.00	1.00	.60
42	Chuck Hartenstein	2.00	1.00	.60
Series B				
7	Bill Virdon	2.50	1.25	.70
11	Jose Pagan	2.00	1.00	.60
12	Jerry May	2.00	1.00	.60
14	Jim Bunning	7.50	3.75	2.25
18	Matty Alou	2.50	1.25	.70
20	Richie Hebner	3.00	1.50	.90
21	Roberto Clemente	15.00	7.50	4.50
22	Gene Alley	2.00	1.00	.60
32	Vernon Law	2.50	1.25	.70
36	Carl Taylor	2.00	1.00	.60
40	Dock Ellis	2.50	1.25	.70
43	Bruce Dal Canton	2.00	1.00	.60

1970 Pittsburgh Pirates (Andersen)

Boston baseball photographer Mike Andersen is believed to have produced this collectors' issue of Pirates cards. Nearly identical in format to his 1969-70 Oakland A's issues, the '70 Pirates measures 2-1/4" x 3-5/8" with black-and-white player poses at center. Player identification and 1969 stats are in the bottom border. Backs are blank. Cards are checklisted here alphabetically.

		NM	EX	VG
Complete Set (12):		40.00	20.00	12.00
Common Player:		2.00	1.00	.60
(1)	Gene Alley	2.00	1.00	.60
(2)	Dave Cash	2.00	1.00	.60
(3)	Dock Ellis	2.00	1.00	.60
(4)	Dave Giusti	2.00	1.00	.60
(5)	Jerry May	2.00	1.00	.60
(6)	Bill Mazeroski	12.00	6.00	3.50
(7)	Al Oliver	4.00	2.00	1.25
(8)	Jose Pagan	2.00	1.00	.60
(9)	Fred Patek	2.00	1.00	.60
(10)	Bob Robertson	2.00	1.00	.60
(11)	Manny Sanguillen	2.00	1.00	.60
(12)	Willie Stargell	12.00	6.00	3.50

1970 Pittsburgh Pirates Autograph Cards

Retaining the 3-1/4" x 4-1/4" format from previous years, these team-issued autograph cards can be distinguished from the 1968-69 issues by the Three Rivers Stadium photo background on each card. The Pirates moved from Forbes Field in June, 1970. The set is checklisted here by uniform number without regard to Series A and B.

		NM	EX	VG
Complete Set (25):		90.00	45.00	27.50
Common Player:		3.00	1.50	.80
2	Fred Patek	3.00	1.50	.80
5	Dave Ricketts	3.00	1.50	.80
8	Willie Stargell	12.00	6.00	3.50
9	Bill Mazeroski	12.00	6.00	3.50
10	Richie Hebner	3.00	1.50	.90
11	Jose Pagan	3.00	1.50	.80
12	Jerry May	3.00	1.50	.80
16	Al Oliver	5.00	2.50	1.50
17	Dock Ellis	3.00	1.50	.80
18	Matty Alou	3.00	1.50	.80
19	Joe Gibbon	3.00	1.50	.80
21	Roberto Clemente	25.00	12.50	7.50
22	Gene Alley	3.00	1.50	.80
22	Orlando Pena	3.00	1.50	.80
23	Luke Walker	3.00	1.50	.80
25	John Jeter	3.00	1.50	.80
25	Bob Robertson	3.00	1.50	.80
30	Dave Cash	3.00	1.50	.80
31	Dave Giusti	3.00	1.50	.80
35	Manny Sanguillen	3.00	1.50	.90
36	Dick Calpaert (Colpaert)	3.00	1.50	.80
38	Bob Moose	3.00	1.50	.80
39	Bob Veale	3.00	1.50	.80
40	Danny Murtaugh	3.00	1.50	.80
50	Jim Nelson	3.00	1.50	.80

1971 Pittsburgh Pirates Autograph Cards

The '71 team-issued Pirates autograph cards are distinguished by the appearance of mustard-yellow caps on the players' portraits. Otherwise the blank-back 3-1/4" x 4-1/2" photocards are identical in format to those of earlier seasons. Players are checklisted here alphabetically within series.

		NM	EX	VG
Complete Set (20):		45.00	22.50	13.50
Common Player:		2.00	1.00	.60
	Series A			
(1)	Gene Alley	2.00	1.00	.60
(2)	Nelson Briles	2.00	1.00	.60
(3)	Dave Cash	2.00	1.00	.60
(4)	Dock Ellis	2.00	1.00	.60
(5)	Mudcat Grant	2.50	1.25	.70
(6)	Bill Mazeroski	9.00	4.50	2.75
(7)	Jim Nelson	2.00	1.00	.60
(8)	Al Oliver	4.00	2.00	1.25
(9)	Manny Sanguillen	2.50	1.25	.70
(10)	Luke Walker	2.00	1.00	.60
	Series B			
(11)	Steve Blass	2.00	1.00	.60
(12)	Bob Clemente	15.00	7.50	4.50
(13)	Dave Giusti	2.00	1.00	.60
(14)	Richie Hebner	2.50	1.25	.70
(15)	Bob Johnson	2.00	1.00	.60
(16)	Bob Moose	2.00	1.00	.60
(17)	Jose Pagan	2.00	1.00	.60
(18)	Bob Robertson	2.00	1.00	.60
(19)	Willie Stargell	8.00	4.00	2.50
(20)	Bob Veale	2.00	1.00	.60

1973 Pittsburgh Post-Gazette Pirates

This set of Pirates pictures was printed on newspaper stock one per day in the sports section of the daily paper. The black-bordered black-and-white photos are 5-1/4" x 9-1/4". At top is "'73 Pirate Album" and a short career summary. At bottom are 1972 and career stats. The first six pictures are unnumbered, the others are numbered alphabetically.

		NM	EX	VG
Complete Set (25):		125.00	60.00	35.00
Common Player:		6.00	3.00	1.75
	Gene Alley	6.00	3.00	1.75
	Steve Blass	6.00	3.00	1.75
	Nellie Briles	6.00	3.00	1.75
	Dave Cash	6.00	3.00	1.75
	Roberto Clemente	40.00	20.00	12.00
	Gene Clines	6.00	3.00	1.75
6	Vic Davalillo	6.00	3.00	1.75
7	Dock Ellis	6.00	3.00	1.75
8	Dave Giusti	6.00	3.00	1.75
9	Richie Hebner	6.00	3.00	1.75
10	Jackie Hernandez	6.00	3.00	1.75
11	Ramon Hernandez	6.00	3.00	1.75
12	Bob Johnson	6.00	3.00	1.75
13	Bruce Kison	6.00	3.00	1.75
14	Milt May	6.00	3.00	1.75
15	Bob Miller	6.00	3.00	1.75
16	Bob Moose	6.00	3.00	1.75
17	Al Oliver	7.50	3.75	2.25
18	Bob Robertson	6.00	3.00	1.75
19	Charlie Sands	6.00	3.00	1.75
20	Manny Sanguillen	6.00	3.00	1.75
21	Willie Stargell	12.00	6.00	3.50
22	Rennie Stennett	6.00	3.00	1.75
23	Luke Walker	6.00	3.00	1.75
24	Bill Virdon	7.50	3.75	2.25

1972 Pittsburgh Press "Buc-A-Day" Pirates

Through the month of March 1972, the daily Pittsburgh Press carried a "Buc-A-Day" feature highlighting members of the team. The feature was intended to be cut out of the paper and saved. Individual pieces measure 3-3/8" wide and vary in length from 9-1/4" to 11-1/16" depending on the length of the biographical information provided. Each player is pictured in a black-and-white photo in street clothes. Some are pictured with golf clubs, fishing poles, with their children, etc. Because of the nature of their distribution and their fragile nature, complete sets are very scarce.

		NM	EX	VG
Complete Set (25):		100.00	50.00	30.00
Common Player:		2.50	1.25	.70
1	Willie Stargell	7.50	3.75	2.25
2	Steve Blass	2.50	1.25	.70
3	Al Oliver	3.00	1.50	.90
4	Bob Moose	2.50	1.25	.70
5	Dave Cash	2.50	1.25	.70
6	Bill Mazeroski	7.50	3.75	2.25
7	Bob Johnson	2.50	1.25	.70
8	Nellie Briles	2.50	1.25	.70
9	Manny Sanguillen	3.00	1.50	.90
10	Vic Davalillo	2.50	1.25	.70
11	Dave Giusti	2.50	1.25	.70
12	Luke Walker	2.50	1.25	.70
13	Gene Clines	2.50	1.25	.70
14	Milt May	2.50	1.25	.70
15	Bob Robertson	2.50	1.25	.70
16	Roberto Clemente	15.00	7.50	4.50
17	Gene Alley	2.50	1.25	.70
18	Bruce Kison	2.50	1.25	.70
19	Jose Pagan	2.50	1.25	.70
20	Dock Ellis	2.50	1.25	.70
21	Richie Hebner	2.50	1.25	.70
22	Bob Miller	2.50	1.25	.70
23	Jackie Hernandez	2.50	1.25	.70
24	Rennie Stennett	2.50	1.25	.70
25	Bob Veale	2.50	1.25	.70

1948 Pittsburgh Provision & Packing Co.

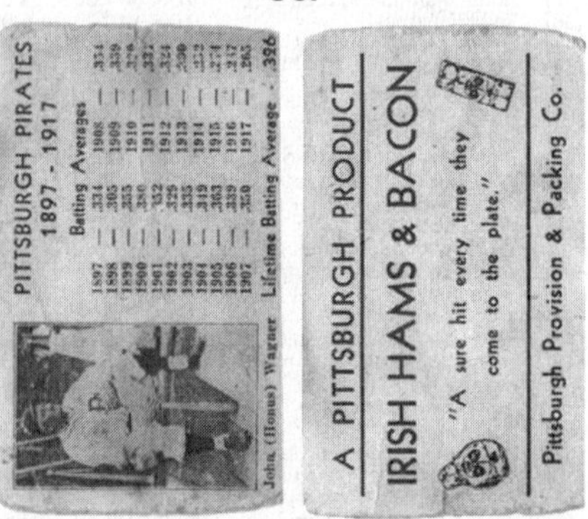

The attributed date is totally arbitrary, based on the photo shown. Also unknown are the scope of the issue and its manner of distribution. Hobby history would suggest the card was created to promote Wagner's ties to the meat company as a spokesman, or perhaps the card was created for Wagner to distribute at appearances on behalf of the packing company. The dark green-printed card measures about 4" x 2-1/2" and is printed on rather thin cardboard. It is not known whether similar cards exist for other players.

	NM	EX	VG
Honus Wagner	400.00	200.00	120.00

1936 Pittsburgh Sun-Telegraph Sport Stamps

Similar to several contemporary issues, the Sport Stamps were printed in a single edition of the daily newspaper. Thirteen players were printed for each of the 16 Major League teams. About 2" x 3", depending on the length of the biography and how well they were cut off the paper, they are printed in black-and-white. A tightly cropped player portrait is centered on a 1-3/4" x 2-1/4" stamp design with the paper's name above and the player's name, position and team below. This checklist is incomplete.

		NM	EX	VG
Complete Set (208):				
Common Player:		12.00	6.00	3.50
(1)	Ralph Birkofer	12.00	6.00	3.50
(2)	Cy Blanton	12.00	6.00	3.50
(3)	Bill Brubaker	12.00	6.00	3.50
(4)	Guy Bush	12.00	6.00	3.50
(5)	Ty Cobb	25.00	12.50	7.50
(6)	Jerome "Dizzy" Dean	25.00	12.50	7.50
(7)	Joe DiMaggio	75.00	37.00	22.00
(8)	Hank Greenberg	25.00	12.50	7.50
(9)	Waite Hoyt	20.00	10.00	6.00
(10)	Carl Hubbell	20.00	10.00	6.00
(11)	Woody Jensen	12.00	6.00	3.50
(12)	Red Lucas	12.00	6.00	3.50
(13)	Joe Medwick	20.00	10.00	6.00
(13)	Tommy Padden	12.00	6.00	3.50
(14)	Casey Stengel	20.00	10.00	6.00
(15)	Clarence Strass	12.00	6.00	3.50
(16)	Gus Suhr	12.00	6.00	3.50
(17)	Bill Swift	12.00	6.00	3.50
(18)	John Tising	12.00	6.00	3.50
(19)	Al Todd	12.00	6.00	3.50
(20)	Pie Traynor	20.00	10.00	6.00
(21)	Honus Wagner	25.00	12.50	7.50
(22)	Lloyd Waner	20.00	10.00	6.00
(23)	Paul Waner	20.00	10.00	6.00
(24)	Jim Weaver	12.00	6.00	3.50
(25)	Floyd Young	12.00	6.00	3.50

1954 Plankinton Milwaukee Braves Playing Tips

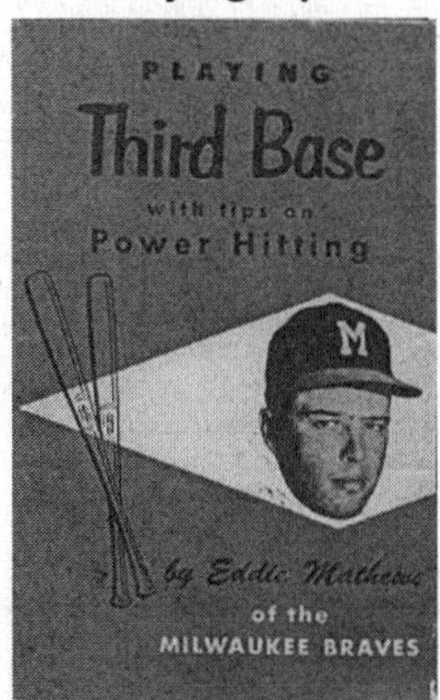

This set of "How to Play Better Baseball" poster booklets was apparently distributed in packages of hot dogs on a regional basis. Folded, the booklet measures 2-7/8" x 4-3/8" and has a black-and-white player portrait photo with a red background. When opened, the booklet forms an 11" x 17" poster offering big league tips from Braves players. The tips are well illustrated with many photos. There is a booklet for each position as well as one for right- and left-handed pitchers, a coach and even a team trainer.

		NM	EX	VG
Complete Set (12):		800.00	400.00	240.00
Common Player:		75.00	37.50	22.50
1	Joe Adcock	90.00	45.00	27.50
2	Danny O'Connell	75.00	37.50	22.50
3	Eddie Mathews	150.00	75.00	45.00
4	Johnny Logan	75.00	37.50	22.50
5	Bobby Thomson	90.00	45.00	27.50
6	Bill Bruton	75.00	37.50	22.50
7	Andy Pafko	75.00	37.50	22.50
8	Del Crandall	75.00	37.50	22.50
9	Warren Spahn	150.00	75.00	45.00
10	Gene Conley	75.00	37.50	22.50
11	Charlie Grimm	75.00	37.50	22.50
12	Joe Taylor	75.00	37.50	22.50

1939 Play Ball Samples

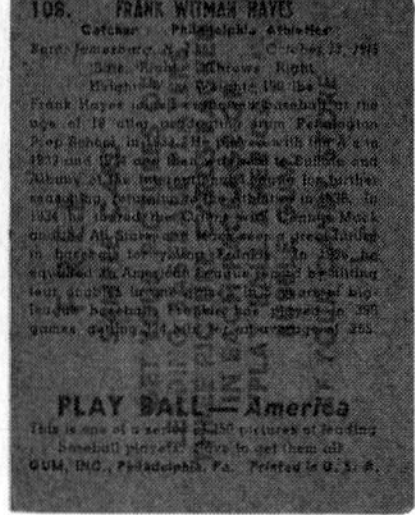

Each of the first 115 cards in the 1939 Play Ball set can be found with red overprinting on the back indicating sample card status. The overprint reads: FREE / SAMPLE CARD / GET YOUR PICTURES OF / LEADING BASEBALL PLAYERS. / THREE PICTURE CARDS PACKED / IN EACH PACKAGE OF / "PLAY BALL AMERICA" / BUBBLE GUM. / AT YOUR CANDY STORE / 1c." Collectors will pay a small premium for a type card of a common player. Sample cards of most star players sell for about double the price of the regular-issue cards, while DiMaggio and Williams samples sell for about the same price as their regular-issue cards.

		NM	EX	VG
Common Player:		35.00	17.50	10.00
26	Joe DiMaggio	1,300	650.00	390.00
92	Ted Williams	1,400	700.00	420.00

1939 Play Ball (R334)

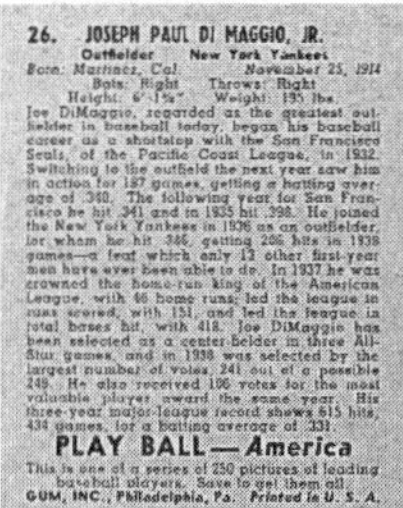

26. JOSEPH PAUL DI MAGGIO, JR.
Outfielder New York Yankees
Born: Martinez, Cal. November 25, 1914
Bats: Right Throws: Right
Height: 6' 1½" Weight: 193 lbs.
Joe DiMaggio, regarded as the greatest outfielder in baseball today, began his baseball career as a shortstop with the San Francisco Seals, of the Pacific Coast League, in 1932. Switching to the outfield the next year saw him in action for 187 games, getting a batting average of .340. The following year for San Francisco he hit .341 and in 1935 hit .398. He joined the New York Yankees in 1936 as an outfielder, for whom he hit .346, getting 206 hits in 1938 games—a feat which only 12 other first-year men have ever been able to do. In 1937 he was crowned the home-run king of the American League, with 46 home runs; led the league in runs scored, with 151, and led the league in total bases hit, with 418. Joe DiMaggio has been selected as a center fielder in three All-Star games, and in 1938 was selected by the largest number of votes, 241 out of a possible 249. He also received 106 votes for the most valuable player award the same year. His three-year major-league record shows 615 hits, 434 games, for a batting average of .331.
PLAY BALL — America
This is one of a series of 250 pictures of leading baseball players. Save to get them all.
GUM, INC., Philadelphia, Pa. Printed in U. S. A.

With the issue of this card set by Gum Inc., a new era of baseball cards was born. Although the cards are black-and-white, the photos on front are of better quality than previously seen, and the 2-1/2" x 3-1/8" size was larger than virtually all of the tobacco and caramel cards of the early 20th Century. Card backs feature full player names, "Joseph Paul DiMaggio" instead of "Joe DiMaggio" and extensive biographies. Players are listed here by their most commonly used name. There are 161 cards in the set; card #126 was never issued. The complete set price does not include all back variations found in the low-numbered series. Many of the cards between #2-115 (indicated with an asterisk) can be found with the player name either in all capital letters, or in both upper- and lower-case letters. Minor differences in typography, along with variations in details of the biographical data, or within the wording of the career summary may be found on those cards that exist in two versions. No premium currently attaches to either version, though the cards with name in upper- and lower-case are somewhat scarcer.

		NM	EX	VG
Complete Set (161):		10,000	4,750	2,750
Common Player (1-115):		25.00	12.50	7.50
Common Player (116-162):		55.00	27.50	16.50
1	Jake Powell	135.00	15.00	7.50
2	Lee Grissom	25.00	12.50	7.50
3	Red Ruffing (*)	100.00	50.00	30.00
4	Eldon Auker (*)	25.00	12.50	7.50
5	Luke Sewell (*)	25.00	12.50	7.50
6	Leo Durocher (*)	100.00	50.00	30.00
7	Bobby Doerr (*)	100.00	50.00	30.00
8	Cotton Pippen	25.00	12.50	7.50
9	Jim Tobin (*)	25.00	12.50	7.50
10	Jimmie DeShong	25.00	12.50	7.50
11	Johnny Rizzo	25.00	12.50	7.50
12	Hersh Martin	25.00	12.50	7.50
13	Luke Hamlin (*)	25.00	12.50	7.50
14	Jim Tabor (*)	25.00	12.50	7.50
15	Paul Derringer (*)	25.00	12.50	7.50
16	Johnny Peacock	25.00	12.50	7.50
17	Emerson Dickman	25.00	12.50	7.50
18	Harry Danning (*)	25.00	12.50	7.50
19	Paul Dean	50.00	25.00	15.00
20	Joe Heving	25.00	12.50	7.50
21	Dutch Leonard (*)	25.00	12.50	7.50
22	Bucky Walters (*)	25.00	12.50	7.50
23	Burgess Whitehead	25.00	12.50	7.50
24	Dick Coffman (*)	25.00	12.50	7.50
25	George Selkirk (*)	25.00	12.50	7.50
26	Joe DiMaggio (*)	1,400	575.00	300.00
27	Fritz Ostermueller (*)	25.00	12.50	7.50
28	Syl Johnson	25.00	12.50	7.50
29	Jack Wilson (*)	25.00	12.50	7.50
30	Bill Dickey (*)	175.00	85.00	55.00
31	Sammy West (*)	25.00	12.50	7.50
32	Bob Seeds	25.00	12.50	7.50
33	Del Young	25.00	12.50	7.50
34	Frank Demaree (*)	25.00	12.50	7.50
35	Bill Jurges (*)	25.00	12.50	7.50
36	Frank McCormick (*)	25.00	12.50	7.50
37	Spud Davis	25.00	12.50	7.50
38	Billy Myers (*)	25.00	12.50	7.50
39	Rick Ferrell (*)	100.00	50.00	30.00
40	Jim Bagby Jr.	25.00	12.50	7.50
41	Lon Warneke (*)	25.00	12.50	7.50
42	Arndt Jorgens	25.00	12.50	7.50
43	Mel Almada	35.00	17.50	10.00
44	Don Heffner	25.00	12.50	7.50
45	Pinky May (*)	25.00	12.50	7.50
46	Morrie Arnovich (*)	40.00	20.00	12.00
47	Buddy Lewis (*)	25.00	12.50	7.50
48	Lefty Gomez (*)	100.00	50.00	30.00
49	Eddie Miller	25.00	12.50	7.50
50	Charlie Gehringer (*)	110.00	55.00	35.00
51	Mel Ott (*)	135.00	65.00	40.00
52	Tommy Henrich (*)	60.00	30.00	18.00
53	Carl Hubbell (*)	125.00	65.00	35.00
54	Harry Gumbert (*)	25.00	12.50	7.50
55	Arky Vaughan (*)	100.00	50.00	30.00
56	Hank Greenberg (*)	250.00	125.00	75.00
57	Buddy Hassett (*)	25.00	12.50	7.50
58	Lou Chiozza	25.00	12.50	7.50
59	Ken Chase	25.00	12.50	7.50
60	Schoolboy Rowe (*)	25.00	12.50	7.50
61	Tony Cuccinello (*)	25.00	12.50	7.50
62	Tom Carey	25.00	12.50	7.50
63	Heinie Mueller	25.00	12.50	7.50
64	Wally Moses (*)	25.00	12.50	7.50
65	Harry Craft (*)	25.00	12.50	7.50
66	Jimmy Ripple	25.00	12.50	7.50
67	Eddie Joost	25.00	12.50	7.50
68	Fred Sington	25.00	12.50	7.50
69	Elbie Fletcher	25.00	12.50	7.50
70	Fred Frankhouse	25.00	12.50	7.50
71	Monte Pearson (*)	25.00	12.50	7.50
72	Debs Garms (*)	25.00	12.50	7.50
73	Hal Schumacher (*)	25.00	12.50	7.50
74	Cookie Lavagetto (*)	25.00	12.50	7.50
75	Frenchy Bordagaray (*)	25.00	12.50	7.50
76	Goody Rosen	40.00	20.00	12.00
77	Lew Riggs	25.00	12.50	7.50
78	Moose Solters (*)	25.00	12.50	7.50
79	Joe Moore (*)	25.00	12.50	7.50
80	Pete Fox (*)	25.00	12.50	7.50
81	Babe Dahlgren (*)	25.00	12.50	7.50
82	Chuck Klein (*)	100.00	50.00	30.00
83	Gus Suhr (*)	25.00	12.50	7.50
84	Skeeter Newsome	25.00	12.50	7.50
85	Johnny Cooney	25.00	12.50	7.50
86	Dolph Camilli (*)	25.00	12.50	7.50
87	Milt Shoffner	25.00	12.50	7.50
88	Charlie Keller	35.00	17.50	10.00
89	Lloyd Waner (*)	100.00	50.00	30.00
90	Bob Klinger (*)	25.00	12.50	7.50
91	Jack Knott (*)	25.00	12.50	7.50
92	Ted Williams (*)	2,100	1,000	500.00
93	Charley Gelbert	25.00	12.50	7.50
94	Heinie Manush	100.00	50.00	30.00
95	Whit Wyatt (*)	25.00	12.50	7.50
96	Babe Phelps (*)	25.00	12.50	7.50
97	Bob Johnson (*)	25.00	12.50	7.50
98	Pinky Whitney	25.00	12.50	7.50
99	Wally Berger (*)	25.00	12.50	7.50
100	Buddy Myer (*)	25.00	12.50	7.50
101	Doc Cramer (*)	25.00	12.50	7.50
102	Pep Young (*)	25.00	12.50	7.50
103	Moe Berg	140.00	75.00	45.00
104	Tommy Bridges (*)	25.00	12.50	7.50
105	Eric McNair (*)	25.00	12.50	7.50
106	Dolly Stark	50.00	25.00	15.00
107	Joe Vosmik	25.00	12.50	7.50
108	Frankie Hayes (*)	25.00	12.50	7.50
109	Myril Hoag (*)	25.00	12.50	7.50
110	Freddie Fitzsimmons	25.00	12.50	7.50
111	Van Lingle Mungo (*)	35.00	17.50	10.00
112	Paul Waner (*)	100.00	50.00	30.00
113	Al Schacht	50.00	25.00	15.00
114	Cecil Travis (*)	25.00	12.50	7.50
115	Red Kress (*)	25.00	12.50	7.50
116	Gene Desautels	55.00	27.50	16.50
117	Wayne Ambler	55.00	27.50	16.50
118	Lynn Nelson	55.00	27.50	16.50
119	Will Hershberger	55.00	27.50	16.50
120	Rabbit Warstler	55.00	27.50	16.50
121	Bill Posedel	55.00	27.50	16.50
122	George McQuinn	55.00	27.50	16.50
123	Peaches Davis	55.00	27.50	16.50
124	Jumbo Brown	55.00	27.50	16.50
125	Cliff Melton	55.00	27.50	16.50
126	Not issued			
127	Gil Brack	55.00	27.50	16.50
128	Joe Bowman	55.00	27.50	16.50
129	Bill Swift	55.00	27.50	16.50
130	Bill Brubaker	55.00	27.50	16.50
131	Mort Cooper	55.00	27.50	16.50
132	Jimmy Brown	55.00	27.50	16.50
133	Lynn Myers	55.00	27.50	16.50
134	Tot Pressnell	55.00	27.50	16.50
135	Mickey Owen	55.00	27.50	16.50
136	Roy Bell	55.00	27.50	16.50
137	Pete Appleton	55.00	27.50	16.50
138	George Case	55.00	27.50	16.50
139	Vito Tamulis	55.00	27.50	16.50
140	Ray Hayworth	55.00	27.50	16.50
141	Pete Coscarart	55.00	27.50	16.50
142	Ira Hutchinson	55.00	27.50	16.50
143	Earl Averill	225.00	110.00	65.00
144	Zeke Bonura	55.00	27.50	16.50
145	Hugh Mulcahy	55.00	27.50	16.50
146	Tom Sunkel	55.00	27.50	16.50
147	George Coffman	55.00	27.50	16.50
148	Bill Trotter	55.00	27.50	16.50
149	Max West	55.00	27.50	16.50
150	Jim Walkup	55.00	27.50	16.50
151	Hugh Casey	55.00	27.50	16.50
152	Roy Weatherly	55.00	27.50	16.50
153	Dizzy Trout	55.00	27.50	16.50
154	Johnny Hudson	55.00	27.50	16.50
155	Jimmy Outlaw	55.00	27.50	16.50
156	Ray Berres	55.00	27.50	16.50
157	Don Padgett	55.00	27.50	16.50
158	Bud Thomas	55.00	27.50	16.50
159	Red Evans	55.00	27.50	16.50
160	Gene Moore Jr.	55.00	27.50	16.50
161	Lonny Frey	60.00	27.50	17.50
162	Whitey Moore	200.00	30.00	17.50

1940 Play Ball (R335)

Following the success of its initial effort in 1939, Gum Inc. issued a bigger and better set in 1940. The 240 black-and-white cards are once again in 2-1/2" x 3-1/8" size, but the front photos are enclosed by a frame with the player's name. Backs again offer extensive biographies and are dated. A number of former stars were issued along with contemporary players, and many Hall of Famers are included. The final 60 cards of the set are more difficult to obtain.

		NM	EX	VG
Complete Set (240):		22,500	11,000	6,500
Common Player (1-180):		35.00	17.50	10.00
Common Player (181-240):		60.00	30.00	18.00
1	Joe DiMaggio	3,000	1,100	675.00
2	"Art" Jorgens	35.00	17.50	10.00
3	"Babe" Dahlgren	35.00	17.50	10.00
4	"Tommy" Henrich	60.00	30.00	18.00
5	"Monte" Pearson	35.00	17.50	10.00
6	"Lefty" Gomez	130.00	65.00	40.00
7	"Bill" Dickey	160.00	80.00	45.00
8	"Twinkletoes" Selkirk	35.00	17.50	10.00
9	"Charley" Keller	35.00	17.50	10.00
10	"Red" Ruffing	130.00	65.00	40.00
11	"Jake" Powell	35.00	17.50	10.00
12	"Johnny" Schulte	35.00	17.50	10.00
13	"Jack" Knott	35.00	17.50	10.00
14	"Rabbit" McNair	35.00	17.50	10.00
15	George Case	35.00	17.50	10.00
16	Cecil Travis	35.00	17.50	10.00
17	"Buddy" Myer	35.00	17.50	10.00
18	"Charley" Gelbert	35.00	17.50	10.00
19	Ken Chase	35.00	17.50	10.00
20	"Buddy" Lewis	35.00	17.50	10.00
21	"Rick" Ferrell	130.00	65.00	40.00
22	"Sammy" West	35.00	17.50	10.00
23	"Dutch" Leonard	35.00	17.50	10.00
24	Frank "Blimp" Hayes	35.00	17.50	10.00
25	"Cherokee" Bob Johnson	35.00	17.50	10.00
26	"Wally" Moses	35.00	17.50	10.00
27	"Ted" Williams	1,950	550.00	280.00
28	"Gene" Desautels	35.00	17.50	10.00
29	"Doc" Cramer	35.00	17.50	10.00
30	"Moe" Berg	160.00	80.00	45.00
31	Jack Wilson	35.00	17.50	10.00
32	"Jim" Bagby	35.00	17.50	10.00
33	"Fritz" Ostermueller	35.00	17.50	10.00
34	John Peacock	35.00	17.50	10.00
35	"Joe" Heving	35.00	17.50	10.00
36	"Jim" Tabor	35.00	17.50	10.00
37	Emerson Dickman	35.00	17.50	10.00
38	"Bobby" Doerr	130.00	65.00	40.00
39	"Tom" Carey	35.00	17.50	10.00
40	"Hank" Greenberg	450.00	225.00	135.00
41	"Charley" Gehringer	180.00	90.00	55.00
42	"Bud" Thomas	35.00	17.50	10.00
43	Pete Fox	35.00	17.50	10.00
44	"Dizzy" Trout	35.00	17.50	10.00
45	"Red" Kress	35.00	17.50	10.00
46	Earl Averill	130.00	65.00	40.00
47	"Old Os" Vitt	35.00	17.50	10.00
48	"Luke" Sewell	35.00	17.50	10.00
49	"Stormy Weather" Weatherly	35.00	17.50	10.00
50	"Hal" Trosky	35.00	17.50	10.00
51	"Don" Heffner	35.00	17.50	10.00
52	Myril Hoag	35.00	17.50	10.00
53	"Mac" McQuinn	35.00	17.50	10.00
54	"Bill" Trotter	35.00	17.50	10.00
55	"Slick" Coffman	35.00	17.50	10.00
56	"Eddie" Miller	35.00	17.50	10.00
57	Max West	35.00	17.50	10.00
58	"Bill" Posedel	35.00	17.50	10.00
59	"Rabbit" Warstler	35.00	17.50	10.00
60	John Cooney	35.00	17.50	10.00
61	"Tony" Cuccinello	35.00	17.50	10.00
62	"Buddy" Hassett	35.00	17.50	10.00
63	"Pete" Cascarart (Coscarart)	35.00	17.50	10.00
64	"Van" Mungo	40.00	20.00	12.00
65	"Fitz" Fitzsimmons	35.00	17.50	10.00
66	"Babe" Phelps	35.00	17.50	10.00
67	"Whit" Wyatt	35.00	17.50	10.00
68	"Dolph" Camilli	35.00	17.50	10.00
69	"Cookie" Lavagetto	35.00	17.50	10.00
70	"Hot Potato" Hamlin	35.00	17.50	10.00
71	Mel Almada	40.00	20.00	12.00
72	"Chuck" Dressen	35.00	17.50	10.00
73	"Bucky" Walters	35.00	17.50	10.00
74	"Duke" Derringer	35.00	17.50	10.00
75	"Buck" McCormick	35.00	17.50	10.00
76	"Lonny" Frey	35.00	17.50	10.00
77	"Bill" Hershberger	60.00	30.00	18.00
78	"Lew" Riggs	35.00	17.50	10.00
79	"Wildfire" Craft	35.00	17.50	10.00
80	"Bill" Myers	35.00	17.50	10.00
81	"Wally" Berger	35.00	17.50	10.00
82	"Hank" Gowdy	35.00	17.50	10.00
83	"Clif" Melton (Cliff)	35.00	17.50	10.00
84	"Jo-Jo" Moore	35.00	17.50	10.00
85	"Hal" Schumacher	35.00	17.50	10.00
86	Harry Gumbert	35.00	17.50	10.00
87	Carl Hubbell	160.00	80.00	45.00
88	"Mel" Ott	225.00	110.00	65.00
89	"Bill" Jurges	35.00	17.50	10.00
90	Frank Demaree	35.00	17.50	10.00
91	Bob "Suitcase" Seeds	35.00	17.50	10.00
92	"Whitey" Whitehead	35.00	17.50	10.00
93	Harry "The Horse" Danning	35.00	17.50	10.00
94	"Gus" Suhr	35.00	17.50	10.00
95	"Mul" Mulcahy	35.00	17.50	10.00
96	"Heinie" Mueller	35.00	17.50	10.00
97	"Morry" Arnovich	35.00	17.50	10.00
98	"Pinky" May	35.00	17.50	10.00
99	"Syl" Johnson	35.00	17.50	10.00
100	"Hersh" Martin	35.00	17.50	10.00
101	"Del" Young	35.00	17.50	10.00
102	"Chuck" Klein	130.00	65.00	40.00
103	"Elbie" Fletcher	35.00	17.50	10.00
104	"Big Poison" Waner	130.00	65.00	40.00
105	"Little Poison" Waner	130.00	65.00	40.00
106	"Pep" Young	35.00	17.50	10.00
107	"Arky" Vaughan	130.00	65.00	40.00
108	"Johnny" Rizzo	35.00	17.50	10.00
109	Don Padgett	35.00	17.50	10.00
110	"Tom" Sunkel	35.00	17.50	10.00
111	"Mickey" Owen	35.00	17.50	10.00
112	"Jimmy" Brown	35.00	17.50	10.00
113	"Mort" Cooper	35.00	17.50	10.00
114	"Lon" Warneke	35.00	17.50	10.00
115	"Mike" Gonzales (Gonzalez)	40.00	20.00	12.00
116	"Al" Schacht	60.00	30.00	18.00
117	"Dolly" Stark	75.00	37.50	22.50
118	"Schoolboy" Hoyt	130.00	65.00	40.00
119	"Ol Pete" Alexander	130.00	65.00	40.00
120	Walter "Big Train" Johnson	275.00	135.00	80.00
121	Atley Donald	35.00	17.50	10.00
122	"Sandy" Sundra	35.00	17.50	10.00
123	"Hildy" Hildebrand	35.00	17.50	10.00
124	"Colonel" Combs	120.00	60.00	35.00
125	"Art" Fletcher	35.00	17.50	10.00
126	"Jake" Solters	35.00	17.50	10.00
127	"Muddy" Ruel	35.00	17.50	10.00
128	"Pete" Appleton	35.00	17.50	10.00
129	"Bucky" Harris	120.00	60.00	35.00
130	"Deerfoot" Milan	35.00	17.50	10.00
131	"Zeke" Bonura	35.00	17.50	10.00
132	Connie Mack	120.00	60.00	35.00
133	"Jimmie" Foxx	300.00	150.00	90.00
134	"Joe" Cronin	130.00	65.00	40.00
135	"Line Drive" Nelson	35.00	17.50	10.00
136	"Cotton" Pippen	35.00	17.50	10.00
137	"Bing" Miller	35.00	17.50	10.00
138	"Beau" Bell	35.00	17.50	10.00
139	Elden Auker (Eldon)	35.00	17.50	10.00
140	"Dick" Coffman	35.00	17.50	10.00
141	"Casey" Stengel	175.00	85.00	50.00
142	"Highpockets" Kelly	120.00	60.00	35.00
143	"Gene" Moore	35.00	17.50	10.00
144	"Joe" Vosmik	35.00	17.50	10.00
145	"Vito" Tamulis	35.00	17.50	10.00
146	"Tot" Pressnell	35.00	17.50	10.00
147	"Johnny" Hudson	35.00	17.50	10.00
148	"Hugh" Casey	35.00	17.50	10.00
149	"Pinky" Shoffner	35.00	17.50	10.00
150	"Whitey" Moore	35.00	17.50	10.00
151	Edwin Joost	35.00	17.50	10.00
152	Jimmy Wilson	35.00	17.50	10.00
153	"Bill" McKechnie	120.00	60.00	35.00
154	"Jumbo" Brown	35.00	17.50	10.00
155	"Ray" Hayworth	35.00	17.50	10.00
156	"Daffy" Dean	65.00	32.50	20.00
157	"Lou" Chiozza	35.00	17.50	10.00
158	"Stonewall" Jackson	120.00	60.00	35.00
159	"Pancho" Snyder	35.00	17.50	10.00
160	"Hans" Lobert	35.00	17.50	10.00
161	"Debs" Garms	35.00	17.50	10.00
162	Joe Bowman	35.00	17.50	10.00
163	"Spud" Davis	35.00	17.50	10.00
164	"Ray" Berres	35.00	17.50	10.00
165	"Bob" Klinger	35.00	17.50	10.00
166	"Bill" Brubaker	35.00	17.50	10.00
167	"Frankie" Frisch	130.00	65.00	40.00
168	"Honus" Wagner	300.00	150.00	90.00
169	"Gabby" Street	35.00	17.50	10.00
170	"Tris" Speaker	135.00	70.00	40.00
171	Harry Heilmann	120.00	60.00	35.00
172	"Chief" Bender	120.00	60.00	35.00
173	"Larry" Lajoie	120.00	60.00	35.00
174	"Johnny" Evers	120.00	60.00	35.00
175	"Christy" Mathewson	250.00	125.00	75.00
176	"Heinie" Manush	130.00	65.00	40.00
177	Frank "Homerun" Baker	120.00	60.00	35.00
178	Max Carey	120.00	60.00	35.00
179	George Sisler	120.00	60.00	35.00
180	"Mickey" Cochrane	130.00	65.00	40.00
181	"Spud" Chandler	60.00	30.00	18.00
182	"Knick" Knickerbocker	60.00	30.00	18.00
183	Marvin Breuer	60.00	30.00	18.00
184	"Mule" Haas	60.00	30.00	18.00
185	"Joe" Kuhel	60.00	30.00	18.00
186	Taft Wright	60.00	30.00	18.00
187	"Jimmy" Dykes	60.00	30.00	18.00
188	"Joe" Krakauskas	60.00	30.00	18.00
189	"Jim" Bloodworth	60.00	30.00	18.00
190	"Charley" Berry	60.00	30.00	18.00
191	John Babich	60.00	30.00	18.00
192	"Dick" Siebert	60.00	30.00	18.00
193	"Chubby" Dean	60.00	30.00	18.00
194	Sam Chapman	60.00	30.00	18.00
195	"Dee" Miles	60.00	30.00	18.00
196	"Nonny" Nonnenkamp	60.00	30.00	18.00
197	"Lou" Finney	60.00	30.00	18.00
198	"Denny" Galehouse	60.00	30.00	18.00
199	"Pinky" Higgins	60.00	30.00	18.00
200	"Soupy" Campbell	60.00	30.00	18.00
201	Barney McCosky	60.00	30.00	18.00
202	Al Milnar	60.00	30.00	18.00
203	"Bad News" Hale	60.00	30.00	18.00
204	Harry Eisenstat	75.00	37.50	22.50
205	"Rollie" Hemsley	60.00	30.00	18.00
206	"Chet" Laabs	60.00	30.00	18.00
207	"Gus" Mancuso	60.00	30.00	18.00
208	Lee Gamble	60.00	30.00	18.00
209	"Hy" Vandenberg	60.00	30.00	18.00
210	"Bill" Lohrman	60.00	30.00	18.00
211	"Pop" Joiner	60.00	30.00	18.00
212	"Babe" Young	60.00	30.00	18.00
213	John Rucker	60.00	30.00	18.00
214	"Ken" O'Dea	60.00	30.00	18.00
215	"Johnnie" McCarthy	60.00	30.00	18.00
216	"Joe" Marty	60.00	30.00	18.00
217	Walter Beck	60.00	30.00	18.00
218	"Wally" Millies	60.00	30.00	18.00
219	Russ Bauers	60.00	30.00	18.00
220	Mace Brown	60.00	30.00	18.00
221	Lee Handley	60.00	30.00	18.00
222	"Max" Butcher	60.00	30.00	18.00
223	Hugh "Ee-Yah" Jennings	140.00	70.00	40.00
224	"Pie" Traynor	140.00	70.00	40.00
225	"Shoeless Joe" Jackson	2,900	1,250	700.00
226	Harry Hooper	140.00	70.00	40.00
227	"Pop" Haines	140.00	70.00	40.00
228	"Charley" Grimm	60.00	30.00	18.00
229	"Buck" Herzog	60.00	30.00	18.00
230	"Red" Faber	140.00	70.00	40.00
231	"Dolf" Luque	75.00	37.50	22.50
232	"Goose" Goslin	140.00	70.00	40.00
233	"Moose" Earnshaw	60.00	30.00	18.00
234	Frank "Husk" Chance	140.00	70.00	40.00
235	John J. McGraw	140.00	70.00	40.00
236	"Sunny Jim" Bottomley	140.00	70.00	40.00
237	"Wee Willie" Keeler	140.00	70.00	40.00
238	"Poosh 'Em Up Tony" Lazzeri	175.00	85.00	50.00
239	George Uhle	60.00	30.00	18.00
240	"Bill" Atwood	120.00	40.00	20.00

1940 Play Ball Colorized Proofs

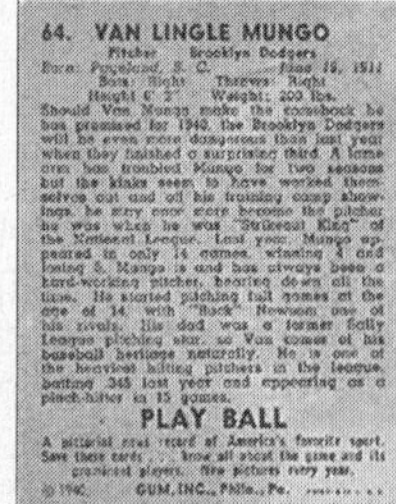

Probably created as part of the process which resulted in the introduction of color cards in 1941, these 1940 Play Balls have very muted color tones. It is unknown how many other players' cards from 1940 PB were created or survive in this form. The Mungo and Dean cards, authenticated and graded Excellent by SGC, sold in a 12/04 auction for $2,221.

64	"Van" Mungo
76	"Lonny" Frey
90	Frank Demaree
141	"Casey" Stengel
156	"Daffy" Dean

1941 Play Ball (R336)

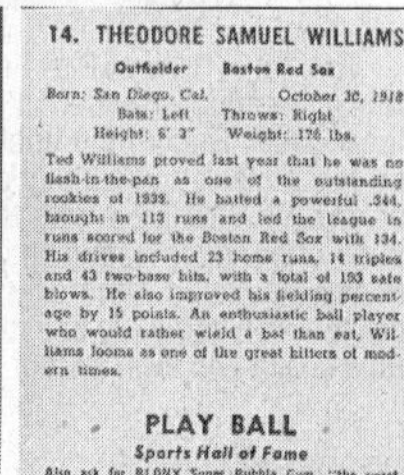

While the backs are quite similar to the black-and-white cards Gum Inc. issued in 1940, the card fronts in the 1941 set are printed in color. Many of the card photos, however, are just colorized versions of the player's 1940 card. The cards are still in the 2-1/2" x 3-1/8" size, but only 72 cards are included in the set. Card numbers 49-72 are rarer than the lower-numbered cards. The cards were printed in sheets of 12, and can still be found that way. Cards #1-48 can be found with or without the 1941 copyright date at lower-left; cards 49-72 are not found with the 1941 date. Some believe this indicates that a revised (no copyright) version of the low numbers and all of the high numbers were issued in 1942.

		NM	EX	VG
Complete Set (72):		15,000	7,500	4,500
Common Player (1-48):		75.00	37.50	22.50
Common Player (49-72):		100.00	50.00	30.00
1	"Eddie" Miller	340.00	60.00	25.00
2	Max West	110.00	37.50	22.50
3	"Bucky" Walters	75.00	37.50	22.50
4	"Duke" Derringer	75.00	37.50	22.50
5	"Buck" McCormick	75.00	37.50	22.50
6	Carl Hubbell	260.00	130.00	75.00
7	"The Horse" Danning	75.00	37.50	22.50
8	"Mel" Ott	340.00	170.00	100.00
9	"Pinky" May	75.00	37.50	22.50
10	"Arky" Vaughan	190.00	95.00	55.00
11	Debs Garms	75.00	37.50	22.50
12	"Jimmy" Brown	75.00	37.50	22.50
13	"Jimmie" Foxx	500.00	250.00	150.00
14	"Ted" Williams	2,200	1,000	400.00
15	"Joe" Cronin	190.00	95.00	55.00
16	"Hal" Trosky	75.00	37.50	22.50
17	"Stormy" Weatherly	75.00	37.50	22.50
18	"Hank" Greenberg	500.00	250.00	150.00
19	"Charley" Gehringer	250.00	125.00	75.00

20	"Red" Ruffing	190.00	95.00	55.00
21	"Charlie" Keller	150.00	75.00	45.00
22	"Indian Bob" Johnson	75.00	37.50	22.50
23	"Mac" McQuinn	75.00	37.50	22.50
24	"Dutch" Leonard	75.00	37.50	22.50
25	"Gene" Moore	75.00	37.50	22.50
26	Harry "Gunboat" Gumbert	75.00	37.50	22.50
27	"Babe" Young	75.00	37.50	22.50
28	"Joe" Marty	75.00	37.50	22.50
29	Jack Wilson	75.00	37.50	22.50
30	"Lou" Finney	75.00	37.50	22.50
31	"Joe" Kuhel	75.00	37.50	22.50
32	Taft Wright	75.00	37.50	22.50
33	"Happy" Milnar	75.00	37.50	22.50
34	"Rollie" Hemsley	75.00	37.50	22.50
35	"Pinky" Higgins	75.00	37.50	22.50
36	Barney McCosky	75.00	37.50	22.50
37	"Soupy" Campbell	75.00	37.50	22.50
38	Atley Donald	75.00	37.50	22.50
39	"Tommy" Henrich	150.00	75.00	45.00
40	"Johnny" Babich	75.00	37.50	22.50
41	Frank "Blimp" Hayes	75.00	37.50	22.50
42	"Wally" Moses	75.00	37.50	22.50
43	Albert "Bronk" Brancato	75.00	37.50	22.50
44	Sam Chapman	75.00	37.50	22.50
45	Elden Auker (Eldon)	75.00	37.50	22.50
46	"Sid" Hudson	75.00	37.50	22.50
47	"Buddy" Lewis	75.00	37.50	22.50
48	Cecil Travis	75.00	37.50	22.50
49	"Babe" Dahlgren	100.00	50.00	30.00
50	"Johnny" Cooney	100.00	50.00	30.00
51	"Dolph" Camilli	100.00	50.00	30.00
52	Kirby Higbe	100.00	50.00	30.00
53	Luke "Hot Potato" Hamlin	100.00	50.00	30.00
54	"Pee Wee" Reese	600.00	300.00	180.00
55	"Whit" Wyatt	100.00	50.00	30.00
56	"Vandy" Vander Meer	100.00	50.00	30.00
57	"Moe" Arnovich	125.00	65.00	35.00
58	"Frank" Demaree	100.00	50.00	30.00
59	"Bill" Jurges	100.00	50.00	30.00
60	"Chuck" Klein	300.00	150.00	90.00
61	"Vince" DiMaggio	300.00	150.00	90.00
62	"Elbie" Fletcher	100.00	50.00	30.00
63	"Dom" DiMaggio	400.00	200.00	120.00
64	"Bobby" Doerr	300.00	150.00	90.00
65	"Tommy" Bridges	100.00	50.00	30.00
66	Harland Clift (Harlond)	100.00	50.00	30.00
67	"Walt" Judnich	100.00	50.00	30.00
68	"Jack" Knott	100.00	50.00	30.00
69	George Case	100.00	50.00	30.00
70	"Bill" Dickey	350.00	175.00	100.00
71	"Joe" DiMaggio	3,000	1,300	700.00
72	"Lefty" Gomez	425.00	180.00	60.00

1941 Play Ball Paper Version

As cardboard became a critical commodity during the months prior to the United States' entry into WWII, Play Ball experimented by issuing a version of the first 24 cards in the 1941 set on paper sheets of 12, comprising the color-printed layer of the regular cards and the backs. These paper versions, understandably, did not stand up to handling as well as the cardboard cards and survivors are much scarcer today.

		NM	EX	VG
Complete Set (24):		10,000	5,000	3,000
Common Player:		160.00	55.00	30.00
Complete Sheet 1-12:		3,000	700.00	325.00
Complete Sheet 13-24:		7,000	3,500	2,100
1	Eddie Miller	160.00	55.00	30.00
2	Max West	160.00	55.00	30.00
3	Bucky Walters	160.00	55.00	30.00
4	"Duke" Derringer	160.00	55.00	30.00
5	"Buck" McCormick	160.00	55.00	30.00
6	Carl Hubbell	600.00	210.00	120.00
7	"The Horse" Danning	160.00	55.00	30.00
8	Mel Ott	650.00	225.00	130.00
9	"Pinky" May	160.00	55.00	30.00
10	"Arky" Vaughan	400.00	140.00	80.00
11	Debs Garms	160.00	55.00	30.00
12	"Jimmy" Brown	160.00	55.00	30.00
13	Jimmie Foxx	1,100	385.00	220.00
14	Ted Williams	3,200	1,125	640.00
15	Joe Cronin	400.00	140.00	80.00
16	Hal Trosky	160.00	55.00	30.00
17	Roy Weatherly	160.00	55.00	30.00
18	Hank Greenberg	1,100	385.00	220.00
19	Charley Gehringer	600.00	210.00	120.00
20	"Red" Ruffing	400.00	140.00	80.00
21	Charlie Keller	180.00	65.00	35.00
22	Bob Johnson	160.00	55.00	30.00
23	"Mac" McQuinn	160.00	55.00	30.00
24	Dutch Leonard	160.00	55.00	30.00

1976 Playboy Press Who Was Harry Steinfeldt?

(Babe Ruth)

This 12-card set was issued in 1976 by Playboy Press to promote author Bert Randolph Sugar's book "Who Was Harry Steinfeldt? & Other Baseball Trivia Questions." (Steinfeldt was the third baseman in the Cubs' famous infield that featured Hall of Famers Tinker, Evers and Chance). The black and white cards measure the standard 2-1/2" x 3-1/2" with a player photo on the front and a trivia question and ad for the book on the back.

		NM	EX	VG
Complete Set (12):		150.00	75.00	45.00
Common Player:		9.00	4.50	2.75
(1)	Frankie Baumholtz	9.00	4.50	2.75
(2)	Jim Bouton	12.00	6.00	3.50
(3)	Tony Conigliaro	9.00	4.50	2.75
(4)	Don Drysdale	17.50	8.75	5.25
(5)	Hank Greenberg	15.00	7.50	4.50
(6)	Walter Johnson	25.00	12.50	7.50
(7)	Billy Loes	9.00	4.50	2.75
(8)	Johnny Mize	15.00	7.50	4.50
(9)	Frank "Lefty" O'Doul	12.00	6.00	3.50
(10)	Babe Ruth	50.00	25.00	15.00
(11)	Johnny Sain	12.00	6.00	3.50
(12)	Jim Thorpe	40.00	20.00	12.00

1947 Pleetwood Slacks Jackie Robinson

The date of issue cited is conjectural. This card, about 5" x 8", depicts Jackie Robinson in a coat and tie in a black-and-white photo on front, along with a facsimile autograph. In a strip at bottom is his name and an endorsement for "Pleetwood Slacks." The back is blank. The card was probably used as an autograph vehicle for personal appearances by Robinson at clothing stores.

	NM	EX	VG
Jackie Robinson	600.00	300.00	180.00

1910-12 Plow Boy Tobacco

Plowboy Tobacco, a product of the Spaulding & Merrick Co., issued a set of cabinet-size cards in the Chicago area featuring members of the Cubs and White Sox. From the checklist, it appears the bulk of the set was originally issued in 1910 with a few additional cards appearing over the next several years. Measuring approximately 5-3/4" x 8", the Plow Boys feature sepia-toned player photos in poses not found on other tobacco issues. The player's name appears in the lower-left corner, while the team name appears in the lower-right. Two different backs are known. One consists of a simple advertisement for Plow Boy Tobacco, while a second, more difficult, variety includes a list of premiums available in exchange for coupons. The set is among the rarest of all 20th Century tobacco issues.

		NM	EX	VG
Common Player:		3,650	1,450	725.00
Premium Back: 1.5X				
(1)	Jimmy Archer	3,650	1,450	725.00
(2)	Ginger Beaumont	3,650	1,450	725.00
(3)	Lena Blackburne	3,650	1,450	725.00
(4)	Bruno Block	3,650	1,450	725.00
(5)	Ping Bodie	3,650	1,450	725.00
(6)	Mordecai Brown	5,500	2,200	1,100
(7)	Al Carson	3,650	1,450	725.00
(8)	Frank Chance	5,500	2,200	1,100
(9)	Ed Cicotte	5,250	2,100	1,050
(10)	King Cole	3,650	1,450	725.00
(11)	Shano Collins	3,650	1,450	725.00
(12)	George Davis	5,500	2,200	1,100
(13)	Patsy Dougherty	3,650	1,450	725.00
(14)	Johnny Evers	5,500	2,200	1,100
(15)	Chick Gandel (Gandil)	5,250	2,100	1,050
(16)	Ed Hahn	3,650	1,450	725.00
(17)	Solly Hoffman (Hofman)	3,650	1,450	725.00
(18)	Del Howard	3,650	1,450	725.00
(19)	Bill Jones	3,650	1,450	725.00
(20)	Johnny Kling	3,650	1,450	725.00
(21)	Rube Kroh	3,650	1,450	725.00
(22)	Frank Lange	3,650	1,450	725.00
(23)	Fred Luderus	3,650	1,450	725.00
(24)	Harry McIntyre (McIntire)	3,650	1,450	725.00
(25)	Ward Miller	3,650	1,450	725.00
(26)	Charlie Mullen	3,650	1,450	725.00
(27)	Tom Needham	3,650	1,450	725.00
(28)	Fred Olmstead	3,650	1,450	725.00
(29)	Orval Overall	3,650	1,450	725.00
(30)	Fred Parent	3,650	1,450	725.00
(31)	Fred Payne	3,650	1,450	725.00
(32)	Francis "Big Jeff" Pfeffer	3,650	1,450	725.00
(33)	Jake Pfeister	3,650	1,450	725.00
(34)	Billy Purtell	3,650	1,450	725.00
(35)	Ed Reulbach	3,650	1,450	725.00
(36)	Lew Richie	3,650	1,450	725.00
(37)	Jimmy Scheckard (Sheckard)	3,650	1,450	725.00
(38)	Wildfire Schulte	3,650	1,450	725.00
(39a)	Jim Scot (Name incorrect.)	3,650	1,450	725.00
(39b)	Jim Scott (Name correct.)	3,650	1,450	725.00
(40)	Frank Smith	3,650	1,450	725.00
(41)	Harry Steinfeldt	3,650	1,450	725.00
(42)	Billy Sullivan	3,650	1,450	725.00
(43)	Lee Tannehill	3,650	1,450	725.00
(44)	Joe Tinker	5,500	2,200	1,100
(45)	Ed Walsh	5,500	2,200	1,100
(46)	Doc White	3,650	1,450	725.00
(47)	Irv Young	3,650	1,450	725.00
(48)	Rollie Zeider	3,650	1,450	725.00
(49)	Heinie Zimmerman	3,650	1,450	725.00

1912 Plow's Candy (E300)

An extremely rare candy issue, cards in this 1912 set measure 3" x 4" and feature sepia-toned photos surrounded by a wide border. The player's name and team appear in the border below the photo, while the words "Plow's Candy Collection" appear at the top. The backs are blank. Not even known to exist until the late 1960s, this set has been assigned the designation of E300 and additions to the checklist continue to appear every few years.

		NM	EX	VG
Common Player:		3,000	1,500	900.00
(1)	Babe Adams	3,000	1,500	900.00
(2)	Home Run Baker	4,800	2,400	1,440
(3)	Cy Barger	3,000	1,500	900.00
(4)	Jack Barry	3,000	1,150	900.00
(5)	Johnny Bates	3,000	1,500	900.00
(7)	Joe Benz	3,000	1,150	900.00
(8)	Bill Berger (Bergen)	3,000	1,500	900.00
(9)	Roger Bresnahan	4,800	2,400	1,440
(10)	Mordecai Brown	4,800	2,400	1,440
(11)	Donie Bush	3,000	1,500	900.00
(12)	Bobby Byrne	3,000	1,500	900.00
(13)	Nixey Callahan	3,000	1,500	900.00
(14)	Hal Chase	4,500	2,250	1,350
(15)	Fred Clarke	4,800	2,400	1,440
(16)	Ty Cobb	40,000	16,500	9,900
(17)	King Cole	3,000	1,500	900.00

(18)	Eddie Collins	4,800	2,400	1,440
(19)	Jack Coombs	3,000	1,500	900.00
(20)	Bill Dahlen	3,000	1,500	900.00
(21)	Bert Daniels	3,000	1,500	900.00
(22)	Harry Davis	3,000	1,500	900.00
(23)	Jim Delehanty	3,000	1,500	900.00
(24)	Josh Devore	3,000	1,500	900.00
(25)	Wild Bill Donovan	3,000	1,500	900.00
(26)	Red Dooin	3,000	1,500	900.00
(27)	Larry Doyle	3,000	1,500	900.00
(28)	Johnny Evers	4,800	2,400	1,440
(29)	Russ Ford	3,000	1,500	900.00
(30)	Del Gainor	3,000	1,500	900.00
(31)	Vean Gregg	3,000	1,500	900.00
(32)	Bob Harmon	3,000	1,500	900.00
(33)	Arnold Hauser	3,000	1,500	900.00
(34)	Dick Hoblitzelle (Hoblitzell)	3,000	1,500	900.00
(35)	Solly Hofman	3,000	1,500	900.00
(36)	Miller Huggins	4,800	2,400	1,440
(37)	John Hummel	3,000	1,500	900.00
(38)	Walter Johnson	7,200	3,600	2,160
(39)	Johnny Kling	3,000	1,500	900.00
(41)	Nap Lajoie	5,400	2,700	1,620
(42)	Jack Lapp	3,000	1,500	900.00
(43)	Fred Luderus	3,000	1,500	900.00
(44)	Sherry Magee	3,000	1,500	900.00
(45)	Rube Marquard	4,800	2,400	1,440
(46)	Christy Mathewson	25,000	4,500	2,700
(47)	Stuffy McInnes (McInnis)	3,000	1,500	900.00
(48)	Larry McLean	3,000	1,500	900.00
(49)	Fred Merkle	3,000	1,500	900.00
(50)	Cy Morgan	3,000	1,500	900.00
(51)	George Moriarty	3,000	1,500	900.00
(52)	Mike Mowrey	3,000	1,500	900.00
(53)	Chief Myers (Meyers)	3,000	1,500	900.00
(54)	Rube Oldring	3,000	1,500	900.00
(55)	Marty O'Toole	3,000	1,500	900.00
(56)	Eddie Plank	5,400	2,700	1,620
(57)	Nap Rucker	3,000	1,500	900.00
(58)	Slim Sallee	3,000	1,500	900.00
(59)	Boss Schmidt	3,000	1,500	900.00
(60)	Jimmy Sheckard	3,000	1,500	900.00
(61)	Tris Speaker	5,400	2,700	1,620
(62)	Billy Sullivan	3,000	1,500	900.00
(63)	Ira Thomas	3,000	1,500	900.00
(64)	Joe Tinker	4,800	2,400	1,440
(65)	John Titus	3,000	1,500	900.00
(66)	Hippo Vaughan (Vaughn)	3,000	1,500	900.00
(67)	Honus Wagner	50,000	15,000	9,000
(68)	Ed Walsh	4,800	2,400	1,440
(69)	Bob Williams	3,000	1,500	900.00

1915 PM1 Ornate-Frame Pins

Little is known about these tiny (approximately 1-1/16" x 1") pins, such as who issued them, when and how they were distributed and how many are in the set. The pins feature a sepia-tone player photo surrounded by an ornate gilded metal frame. The player's name is usually printed in a black strip at the bottom of the photo. The pins were originally sold for 19 cents. Gaps have been left in the assigned numbering for future additions to the checklist.

		NM	EX	VG
Common Pin:		450.00	225.00	125.00
(1a)	Jimmy Archer	450.00	225.00	125.00
(1b)	Jimmy Archer (No name.)	575.00	285.00	175.00
(2)	Frank Baker	1,100	550.00	330.00
(3)	Jack Barry	450.00	225.00	135.00
(4a)	Chief Bender (No name.)	1,100	550.00	330.00
(4b)	Chief Bender (With name.)	1,100	550.00	330.00
(5)	Frank Chance	1,100	550.00	330.00
(6)	Ty Cobb	5,500	2,750	1,650
(7)	Jake Daubert	450.00	225.00	135.00
(8)	Al Demaree	450.00	225.00	125.00
(9a)	Johnny Evers (Name only.)	1,100	550.00	330.00
(9b)	Johnny Evers (Name and city.)	1,100	550.00	330.00
(10)	Rube Foster	450.00	225.00	125.00
(11)	Dick Hoblitzell	450.00	225.00	125.00
(12)	Walter Johnson	2,000	1,000	600.00
(13)	Benny Kauff	450.00	225.00	125.00
(14)	Johnny Kling (No name.)	450.00	225.00	135.00
(15)	Ed Konetchy	450.00	225.00	125.00
(16)	Nap Lajoie	1,100	550.00	330.00
(17)	Sherry Magee	450.00	225.00	135.00
(18)	Rube Marquard	1,100	550.00	330.00
(19)	Christy Mathewson	2,500	1,250	750.00
(21)	John McGraw	1,100	550.00	330.00
(22)	Ed Reulbach	450.00	225.00	135.00
(23)	Eppa Rixey	1,100	550.00	330.00
(24)	Babe Ruth	15,000	7,500	4,500
(25)	Tris Speaker/Btg (Facing forward.)	1,100	550.00	330.00
(26)	Tris Speaker/Btg (Side view.)	1,100	550.00	330.00
(27)	Jeff Tesreau	450.00	225.00	135.00
(28)	Joe Tinker	1,100	550.00	330.00
(29)	Honus Wagner	2,750	1,350	825.00

1928 PM6 Baseball Player Pins

The method of distribution for these small (3/8" diameter) pin-backs is unknown, but it has been reported they were given away in cereal boxes. The black-and-white photographic pins have the player name in a black arc at bottom. The extent of the checklist is unknown.

		NM	EX	VG
Common Player:		375.00	185.00	110.00
(1)	Grover Alexander	450.00	225.00	135.00
(2)	Ty Cobb	900.00	450.00	275.00
(3)	Bucky Harris	350.00	175.00	100.00
(4)	Rogers Hornsby	550.00	275.00	165.00
(5)	Walter Johnson	600.00	300.00	180.00
(6)	Babe Ruth	1,200	600.00	360.00
(7)	Geo. Sisler	350.00	175.00	100.00
(8)	Tris Speaker	450.00	225.00	135.00

1940 PM10 Baseball Player Pins

This was the first of two issues that share a nearly identical format. The 1-3/4" celluloid pin-back buttons feature a black-and-white player photo surrounded by a white border. The player's name is in black capital letters at bottom, and his team nickname in the same type size and style at top. These pins were originally sold at ballparks and other souvenir outlets. The checklist, arranged here in alphabetical order, is not complete.

	NM	EX	VG
Common Player:	30.00	15.00	9.00
Dick Bartell	30.00	15.00	9.00
Dolph Camilli	30.00	15.00	9.00
Bill Dickey	50.00	25.00	15.00
Joe DiMaggio	275.00	135.00	85.00
Lou Gehrig	700.00	350.00	210.00
Lou Gehrig (Black border, "NEVER FORGOTTEN" at top.)	650.00	325.00	195.00
Lefty Gomez	50.00	25.00	15.00
Carl Hubbell	100.00	50.00	30.00
Cliff Melton	30.00	15.00	9.00
Pete Reiser	30.00	15.00	9.00
Dixie Walker	30.00	15.00	9.00
Whitlow Wyatt	30.00	15.00	9.00

1951 PM10 Baseball Player Pins

This was the second of two issues that share a nearly identical format. The 1-3/4" celluloid pin-back buttons feature a black-and-white player photo surrounded by a white border. The player's name is in black capital letters at bottom, and full team name in the same type size and style at top. These pins were originally sold at ballparks and other souvenir outlets. The checklist, arranged here in alphabetical order, is likely not complete. Note that the woeful Pittsburgh Pirates represent more than half the known players in this issue.

	NM	EX	VG
Common Player:	50.00	25.00	15.00
Luke Easter	75.00	37.50	22.50
Ned Garver	50.00	25.00	15.00
Monte Irvin	100.00	50.00	30.00
Ralph Kiner	100.00	50.00	30.00
Bob Lemon	100.00	50.00	30.00
Willie Mays	175.00	87.00	52.00
Clyde McCullouhg (McCullough) ,	50.00	25.00	15.00
Billy Meyer	50.00	25.00	15.00
Danny Murtaugh	50.00	25.00	15.00
Don Newcombe	50.00	25.00	15.00
Saul Rogovin	50.00	25.00	15.00
Stan Rojek	50.00	25.00	15.00
Hank Thompson	50.00	25.00	15.00
Bill Werle	50.00	25.00	15.00

1950s-60s PM10 Baseball Player Pins - Name at Bottom

Issued over a period of years in a variety of styles, these celluloid pinback buttons have in common their approximately 1-3/4" diameter and the appearance of the player name at bottom. Black-and-white player portrait photos are found on a variety of backgrounds. In this checklist, the color of the background is listed, where known, immediately after the team name (where known). Other distinguishing characteristics may also be noted. The pins were usually originally sold with a red, white and blue swallow-tailed silk pennant attached and a brass chain with a baseball, bat or glove charms, or similar plastic toys. Values shown are for pins alone. The checklist here is incomplete.

	NM	EX	VG
Common Player:	20.00	10.00	6.00
Hank Aaron (Blue, script name, team above.)	100.00	50.00	30.00
Sandy Amoros (Brooklyn, blue.)	60.00	30.00	18.00
Harry Anderson (Phillies, photo.)	125.00	65.00	35.00
John Antonelli (NY cap, "floating head.")	20.00	10.00	6.00
John Antonelli (SF cap, ring around photo.)	20.00	10.00	6.00
Luis Aparicio (White Sox, white.)	75.00	37.00	22.00
Ernest Banks (Cubs, white, no cap logo.)	475.00	235.00	140.00
Bo Belinsky (Phillies, white.)	40.00	20.00	12.00
Gus Bell (White)	20.00	10.00	6.00
Gus Bell ("CINCINNATI REDLEGS" beneath name.)	100.00	50.00	30.00
Larry Berra (White)	90.00	45.00	27.00
Larry Berra (Blue)	100.00	50.00	30.00
Yogi Berra	80.00	40.00	24.00
Joe Black (Brooklyn, photo.)	40.00	20.00	12.00
Joe Black (Brooklyn, white, facing front.)	40.00	20.00	12.00
Joe Black (Brooklyn, white, facing his left.)	25.00	12.50	7.50
Don Bollweg (A's, photo.)	20.00	10.00	6.00
Lou Boudreau (Photo, script name.)	60.00	30.00	18.00
Lou Boudreau (Red Sox, white.)	50.00	25.00	15.00
Jackie Brandt (Orioles, photo.)	40.00	20.00	12.00
Eddie Bressoud	20.00	10.00	6.00
Bill Bruton (Braves, white.)	100.00	50.00	30.00
Jim Bunning (Phillies)	40.00	20.00	12.00
Roy Campanella (Brooklyn, blue.)	90.00	45.00	27.50
Roy Campanella (Brooklyn, yellow.)	80.00	40.00	24.00
Roy Campanella (Brooklyn, white, cap backwards.)	75.00	37.50	22.50
Roy Campanella (Brooklyn, white, name across photo.)	60.00	30.00	18.00
Roy Campanella (Brooklyn, white, name under photo.)	60.00	30.00	18.00

Roy Campanella (Brooklyn, white, name in strip.)	100.00	50.00	30.00
Roy Campanella (Brooklyn, white circle border, team at top.)	250.00	125.00	75.00
Chico Carrasquel (Name in script, team at top.)	50.00	25.00	15.00
Phil Cavarretta (Cubs, script name, stars above.)	150.00	75.00	45.00
Orlando Cepeda (Gray)	30.00	15.00	9.00
Orlando Cepeda (S.F., name in strip, photo.)	30.00	15.00	9.00
Gerry Coleman (Dark)	40.00	20.00	12.00
Gerry Coleman (Light)	40.00	20.00	12.00
Tony Conigliaro (Red Sox, gray.)	40.00	20.00	12.00
Morton Cooper (Cardinals, white/black background.)	40.00	20.00	12.00
Billy Cox (Brooklyn, white, neck-to-cap.)	95.00	47.50	28.00
Billy Cox (Brooklyn, white, chest-to-cap.)	60.00	30.00	18.00
Alvin Dark (NY cap, "floating head.")	20.00	10.00	6.00
Jerome (Dizzy) Dean (Black)	90.00	45.00	27.50
Dom DiMaggio (White)	40.00	20.00	12.00
Dom DiMaggio (Dark)	40.00	20.00	12.00
Joe DiMaggio (Black)	475.00	235.00	140.00
Joe DiMaggio (Dark blue, name beyond shoulders.)	250.00	125.00	75.00
Joe DiMaggio (Light blue, name within shoulders.)	150.00	75.00	45.00
Joe DiMaggio (Light blue, name "ear to ear" - modern fantasy, no collectible value.)			
Joe DiMaggio (Green border.)	325.00	160.00	100.00
Joe DiMaggio (White, name in strip.)	200.00	100.00	60.00
Joe DiMaggio (White, name not in strip.)	215.00	100.00	65.00
Joe DiMaggio (Yellow, "YANKEES" under name.)	350.00	175.00	100.00
Larry Doby (Dark)	60.00	30.00	18.00
Larry Doby (Indians, white.)	90.00	45.00	27.50
Carl Erskine (Brooklyn, white.)	75.00	37.50	22.50
Bob Feller (Indians, white.)	80.00	40.00	24.00
Bob Feller (Brown, name in script.)	325.00	160.00	100.00
Whitey Ford	80.00	40.00	24.00
Whitey Ford (White, name in strip, 3-1/2".)	200.00	100.00	60.00
Nelson Fox (White Sox, fox figures at top.)	350.00	175.00	100.00
Carl Furillo (Brooklyn, blue.)	75.00	37.50	22.50
Carl Furillo (Brooklyn, gray.)	65.00	32.50	20.00
Carl Furillo (Brooklyn, photo, dark sleeves.)	100.00	50.00	30.00
Carl Furillo (Brooklyn, photo, no sleeves.)	115.00	60.00	35.00
Ned Garver (Browns, white, belly-to-cap.)	30.00	15.00	9.00
Ned Garver (Browns, white, chest-to-cap.)	30.00	15.00	9.00
Junior Gilliam (Brooklyn, white.)	100.00	50.00	30.00
Junior Gilliam (Broklyn, photo.)	100.00	50.00	30.00
Ruben Gomez (SF cap, ring around photo.)	30.00	15.00	9.00
Billy Goodman (White)	100.00	50.00	30.00
Ron Hansen (Orioles, photo.)	40.00	20.00	12.00
Gabby Hartnett (Cubs, black.)	40.00	20.00	12.00
Mike Hegan (Indians, white border, script name.)	450.00	225.00	135.00
Tom Henrich (Gray)	40.00	20.00	12.00
Mike Higgins (Red Sox, dark.)	45.00	22.50	13.50
Gil Hodges (Brooklyn, blue.)	100.00	50.00	30.00
Gil Hodges (Brooklyn, red/orange.)	50.00	25.00	15.00
Gil Hodges (Brooklyn, photo.)	40.00	20.00	12.00
Gil Hodges (Brooklyn, white, name across photo.)	60.00	30.00	18.00
Gil Hodges (Brooklyn, white, name in strip.)	200.00	100.00	60.00
Gil Hodges (Brooklyn, white, name under photo.)	40.00	20.00	12.00
Gil Hodges (Mets, 3-1/2", name in strip.)	150.00	75.00	45.00
Roger Hornsby (Rogers) (Browns, white circle border.)	150.00	75.00	45.00
Monte Irvin (Giants, dark.)	80.00	40.00	24.00
Ransom Jackson (Cubs, stars above.)	150.00	75.00	45.00
Forrest "Spook" Jacobs (Gray)	20.00	10.00	6.00
Forrest "Spook" Jacobs (A's, photo.)	20.00	10.00	6.00
Jackie Jensen (Dark)	50.00	25.00	15.00
Jackie Jensen (White)	50.00	25.00	15.00
Ed Joost (A's, photo.)	20.00	10.00	6.00
Harmon Killebrew ("W" on cap, photo.)	375.00	185.00	110.00
Ralph Kiner (Color, facsimile autograph.)	40.00	20.00	12.00
Ralph Kiner (Cubs, hearts above.)	600.00	300.00	180.00
Ted Kluszewski (Dark, name overprinted horizontally.)	200.00	100.00	60.00
Ted Kluszewski (Reds, white, name in strip.)	40.00	20.00	12.00
Ed Kranepool (White)	50.00	25.00	15.00
Big Bill Lee (Cubs, black/gray.)	20.00	10.00	6.00
Bob Lemon (Light)	40.00	20.00	12.00
Whitey Lockman (NY cap, gray.)	25.00	12.50	7.50
Peanuts Lowrey (Cardinals, white.)	25.00	12.50	7.50
Sal Maglie (Brooklyn, photo.)	50.00	25.00	15.00
Frank Malzone	40.00	20.00	12.00
Mickey Mantle (White, batting to waist, name from elbow to armpit.)	275.00	135.00	80.00
Mickey Mantle (White, batting to waist, name from wrist to shoulder.)	300.00	150.00	90.00
Mickey Mantle (Blue, batting, left hand not visible, 1-3/4".)	350.00	175.00	100.00
Mickey Mantle (Baseball background, name in strip.)	200.00	100.00	60.00
Mickey Mantle (Blue, name in strip.)	250.00	125.00	75.00
(Modern replicas are commonly encountered .)			
Mickey Mantle (Blue, name in strip, looking over left shoulder, 3-1/2".)	150.00	75.00	45.00
Mickey Mantle (Yellow, name in strip, looking over left shoulder, 3-1/2".)	300.00	150.00	90.00
Mickey Mantle (White, portrait.)	300.00	150.00	90.00
Mickey Mantle (Blue, portrait, 3-1/2".)	1,750	875.00	525.00
Juan Marichal (SF cap, uncentered black border.)	60.00	30.00	18.00
Marty Marion (Browns, white circle border.)	300.00	150.00	90.00
Roger Maris (Blue, bat behind head, name in white strip, 3-1/2".)	100.00	50.00	30.00
Roger Maris (White, looking over shoulder, no cap insignia.)	125.00	60.00	35.00
Roger Maris (Orange, bat behind head, 3-1/2".)	100.00	50.00	30.00
Roger Maris (Yellow, bat behind head, 1-3/4".)	75.00	37.50	22.50
Roger Maris (Yellow, blue or purple, bat behind head, 2-1/4" - modern replica, no collectible value.)			
Roger Maris (Yellow, bat behind head, 3-1/2".)	100.00	50.00	30.00
Willie Mays (S.F. Giants, gray.)	325.00	160.00	97.00
Willie Mays (Photo, N.Y. cap.)	300.00	150.00	90.00
Willie Mays (Photo, grass background, S.F. cap.)	300.00	150.00	90.00
Willie Mays (Photo, stadium background, S.F. cap.)	300.00	150.00	90.00
Willie Mays (White, N.Y. cap.)	230.00	115.00	70.00
Willie Mays (White, S.F. cap.)	150.00	75.00	45.00
Willie McCovey (Pats on shoulder, no cap logo.)	200.00	100.00	60.00
Willie McCovey (SF cap, name in ear-to-ear white stripe.)	40.00	20.00	12.00
Gil McDougald (Yankees, gray.)	45.00	22.50	13.50
"Vinegar Bend" Mizell (Cardinals, white.)	30.00	15.00	9.00
Bill Monbouquette	40.00	20.00	12.00
Don Mueller (White, "floating head.")	40.00	20.00	12.00
Bobby Murcer (White)	30.00	15.00	9.00
Stan Musial (Cardinals, white, MUSIAL at bottom, "STAN" THE MAN at top.)	125.00	65.00	40.00
Stan Musial (Cardinals, white, piping shows.)	100.00	50.00	30.00
Stan Musial (Cardinals, white, no piping.)	100.00	50.00	30.00
Stan Musial (White, team name above photo, facsimile autograph.)	100.00	50.00	30.00
(Modern replica exists in 2-3/16" size; no collectible value.)			
Stan Musial (Yellow)	125.00	65.00	35.00
Don Newcombe (Brooklyn, blue.)	450.00	225.00	135.00
Don Newcombe (Brooklyn, white, name in strip.)	30.00	15.00	9.00
Don Newcombe (Brooklyn, white, name under photo.)	30.00	20.00	12.00
Don Newcombe (Brooklyn, white circle border, team at top.)	60.00	30.00	18.00
Don Newcombe (Yellow)	50.00	25.00	15.00
Dan O'Connell (SF cap, ring around photo.)	40.00	20.00	12.00
Andy Pafko (Brooklyn, black.)	30.00	15.00	9.00
Joe Page (White)	50.00	25.00	15.00
Leroy (Satchel) Paige (White)	175.00	85.00	50.00
Mel Parnell (Red Sox, white.)	45.00	22.50	13.50
Joe Pepitone (White)	30.00	15.00	9.00
Johnny Pesky (Red Sox, white.)	100.00	50.00	30.00
Billy Pierce (Name in serif type.)	40.00	20.00	12.00
Jimmy Piersall (Light)	50.00	25.00	15.00
Johnny Podres (Brooklyn, white.)	45.00	22.00	13.50
Wally Post ("CINCINNATI REDLEGS" beneath name.)	50.00	25.00	15.00
Vic Power (A's, photo.)	25.00	12.50	7.50
Dick Radatz (Red Sox, gray.)	30.00	15.00	9.00
Vic Raschi (Yankees, white.)	60.00	30.00	18.00
PeeWee Reese (Brooklyn, gray, name in strip.)	200.00	100.00	60.00
"Pee Wee" Reese (Brooklyn, gray, name across photo.)	60.00	30.00	18.00
"Pee Wee" Reese (Brooklyn, white, large photo.)	125.00	65.00	35.00
"Pee Wee" Reese (Brooklyn, white, small photo.)	100.00	50.00	30.00
"Pee Wee" Reese (Brooklyn, photo, name in strip.)	60.00	30.00	18.00
Bill Rigney (NY cap, dark background.)	20.00	10.00	6.00
Phil Rizzuto (White)	80.00	40.00	24.00
Robin Roberts (Phillies, photo.)	50.00	25.00	15.00
Frank Robinson ("Cincinnati Redlegs" at bottom.)	250.00	125.00	75.00
Jackie Robinson (Brooklyn, blue.)	300.00	150.00	90.00
Jackie Robinson (Brooklyn, yellow.)	190.00	95.00	55.00
Jackie Robinson (Brooklyn, white, chest-to-cap.)	200.00	100.00	60.00
Jackie Robinson (Brooklyn, white, neck-to-cap.)	250.00	125.00	75.00
Jackie Robinson (Brooklyn, white, name across bottom, facing his left.)	200.00	100.00	60.00
Jackie Robinson (Brooklyn, gray, name across photo, facing his left.)	200.00	100.00	60.00
Jackie Robinson (Brooklyn, white, name in strip, cap logo not visible.)	600.00	300.00	180.00
Jackie Robinson (Brooklyn, photo.)	275.00	135.00	80.00
Preacher Roe (Brooklyn, wind-up pose.)	90.00	45.00	27.50
Al Rosen (Light background.)	40.00	20.00	12.00
Charles Herbert Ruffing (Yankees, gray.)	40.00	20.00	12.00
Pete Runnels	40.00	20.00	12.00
Ron Santo (Cubs, white.)	40.00	20.00	12.00
Hank Sauer (Cubs, script name, stars above.)	150.00	75.00	45.00
Chuck Schilling	40.00	20.00	12.00
George Scott (White, "floating head.")	20.00	10.00	6.00
Bobby Shantz (A's, white.)	30.00	15.00	9.00
Frank Shea (Yankees, gray.)	50.00	25.00	15.00
Harry Simpson (Indians, white, team name at top, script name at bottom.)	650.00	325.00	195.00
Enos Slaughter (Cardinals, white.)	50.00	25.00	15.00
Enos Slaughter (Cardinals, black.)	50.00	25.00	15.00
Roy Smalley (Cubs, script name, stars above.)	150.00	75.00	45.00
Duke Snider (Brooklyn, white.)	80.00	40.00	24.00
Duke Snider (Brooklyn, blue.)	65.00	35.00	20.00
Duke Snider (Brooklyn, blue, 3-1/2".)	200.00	100.00	60.00
Duke Snider (Brooklyn, gray.)	75.00	37.50	22.50
Duke Snider (Brooklyn, photo.)	150.00	75.00	45.00
Gerald Staley (Cardinals, white.)	20.00	10.00	6.00
Bobby Thomson (NY cap, white, uniform shows.)	40.00	20.00	12.00
Bobby Thomson (NY cap, white, "floating head.")	30.00	15.00	9.00
Gus Triandos (Orioles, photo.)	40.00	20.00	12.00
Robt. Lee Trice (A's, photo.)	25.00	12.50	7.50
Sam White (Red Sox, white.)	30.00	15.00	9.00
James Hoyt Wilhelm (Orioles)	200.00	100.00	60.00
Ted Williams (Name beneath bust, white.)	200.00	100.00	60.00
Ted Williams (Name in strip, black.)	450.00	225.00	135.00
Ted Williams (Name in strip, white.)	400.00	200.00	120.00
Ted Williams (Name in strip, photo, belt-up.)	90.00	45.00	27.50
Ted Williams (Name in strip, photo, close-up.)	100.00	50.00	30.00
Carl Yastrzemski	100.00	50.00	30.00

1950s-60s PM10 Baseball Player Pins - Name at Top

This series of baseball player pins is similar to contemporary issues in its 1-3/4" (unless otherwise noted) black-and-white celluloid format, but differs in that the player name appears at top. Players known in the series indicate the buttons were issued over a period of several years, probably for sale in stadium concession stands and other souvenir outlets. The alphabetical checklist here is not complete.

	NM	EX	VG
Common Player:	60.00	30.00	18.00
Felipe Alou (Script name.)	40.00	20.00	12.00
Luis Arroyo	20.00	10.00	6.00
Hank Bauer	60.00	30.00	18.00
Yogi Berra	135.00	67.00	40.00
Johnny Blanchard	60.00	30.00	18.00
Cletis Boyer	75.00	37.00	22.00
Roy Campanella (2-1/4")	450.00	225.00	135.00
Andy Carey (2", Yankees, white)	125.00	65.00	37.50
Joe Collins	60.00	30.00	18.00
Del Crandall (2-1/8")	40.00	20.00	12.00

Whitey Ford (2")	150.00	75.00	45.00
Whitey Ford (3-1/2" diameter)	400.00	200.00	120.00
Carl Furillo (2", Brooklyn, white)	75.00	37.00	22.00
Junior Gilliam	75.00	37.00	22.00
Ruben Gomez	40.00	20.00	12.00
Ken Harrelson (Red Sox, white.)	50.00	25.00	15.00
Don Hoak (Brooklyn, white.)	60.00	30.00	18.00
Elston Howard	75.00	37.00	22.00
Jackie Jensen (Red Sox, white.)	75.00	37.00	22.00
Clem Labine (Brooklyn, white.)	60.00	30.00	18.00
Billy Loes (2", Brooklyn, white)	130.00	65.00	40.00
Ed Lopat	60.00	30.00	18.00
Hector Lopez	40.00	20.00	12.00
Frank Malzone (Red Sox, white.)	50.00	25.00	15.00
Mickey Mantle (1-5/8")	500.00	250.00	150.00
Mickey Mantle (2-1/4")	300.00	150.00	90.00
Roger Maris (2", yellow)	150.00	75.00	45.00
Roger Maris (2-1/4", white)	3.00	1.00	1.00
Billy Martin	75.00	37.00	22.00
Willie Mays (2-1/4", white)	450.00	225.00	135.00
Gil McDougald (2", Yankees, white)	100.00	50.00	30.00
Bill Monbouquette (Red Sox, white.)	50.00	25.00	15.00
Walt Moryn (1-1/2", Brooklyn, white)	250.00	125.00	75.00
Don Newcombe (2", Brooklyn, white)	125.00	62.00	37.00
Irv Noren	60.00	30.00	18.00
Johnny Podres (2", Brooklyn, white)	60.00	30.00	18.00
Allie Reynolds	60.00	30.00	18.00
Jackie Robinson (2-1/16", Brooklyn, white)	1,600	800.00	475.00
Preacher Roe (Brooklyn, white.)	60.00	30.00	18.00
Pete Runnels (Red Sox, white.)	50.00	25.00	15.00
Chuck Schilling (Red Sox, white.)	50.00	25.00	15.00
Bill Skowron	60.00	30.00	18.00
Enos Slaughter	60.00	30.00	18.00
Duke Snider (2-1/4", Brooklyn, white)	135.00	67.00	40.00
Warren Spahn	120.00	60.00	36.00
Don Thompson (2", Brooklyn, white)	200.00	100.00	60.00
Bob Turley	60.00	30.00	18.00
Ted Williams (1-3/4", name in strip at top, team in strip at bottom)	80.00	40.00	25.00
Gene Woodling	60.00	30.00	18.00
Carl Yastrzemski	200.00	100.00	60.00
Don Zimmer (Brooklyn, white.)	75.00	37.50	22.50

1956 PM15 Yellow Basepath Pins

These pins were issued circa 1956; the sponsor of this 32-pin set is not indicated. The set, which has been assigned the American Card Catalog designation PM15, is commonly called "Yellow Basepaths" because of the design of the pin, which features a black-and-white player photo set inside a green infield with yellow basepaths. The unnumbered pins measure 7/8" in diameter.

		NM	EX	VG
	Complete Set (32):	4,500	2,250	1,350
	Common Player:	85.00	40.00	25.00
(1)	Hank Aaron	400.00	200.00	120.00
(2)	Joe Adcock	85.00	40.00	25.00
(3)	Luis Aparicio	140.00	70.00	40.00
(4)	Richie Ashburn	150.00	75.00	45.00
(5)	Gene Baker	85.00	40.00	25.00
(6)	Ernie Banks	225.00	110.00	65.00
(7)	Yogi Berra	245.00	120.00	75.00
(8)	Bill Bruton	85.00	40.00	25.00
(9)	Larry Doby	140.00	70.00	40.00
(10)	Bob Friend	85.00	40.00	25.00
(11)	Nellie Fox	140.00	70.00	40.00
(12)	Ted Greengrass (Jim)	85.00	40.00	25.00
(13)	Steve Gromek	85.00	40.00	25.00
(14)	Johnny Groth	85.00	40.00	25.00
(15)	Gil Hodges	200.00	100.00	60.00
(16)	Al Kaline	150.00	75.00	45.00
(17)	Ted Kluzewski (Kluszewski)	140.00	70.00	40.00
(18)	Johnny Logan	85.00	40.00	25.00
(19)	Dale Long	85.00	40.00	25.00
(20)	Mickey Mantle	600.00	300.00	180.00
(21)	Ed Matthews (Mathews)	150.00	75.00	45.00
(22)	Minnie Minoso	100.00	50.00	30.00
(23)	Stan Musial	350.00	175.00	100.00
(24)	Don Newcombe	140.00	70.00	40.00
(25)	Bob Porterfield	85.00	40.00	25.00
(26)	Pee Wee Reese	200.00	100.00	60.00
(27)	Robin Roberts	140.00	70.00	40.00
(28)	Red Schoendienst	140.00	70.00	40.00
(29)	Duke Snider	225.00	110.00	65.00
(30)	Vern Stephens	85.00	40.00	25.00
(31)	Gene Woodling	100.00	50.00	30.00
(32)	Gus Zernial	85.00	40.00	25.00

1909-11 Polar Bear Tobacco

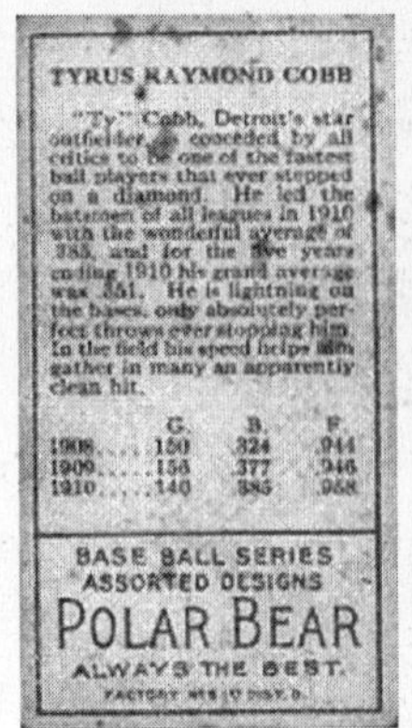

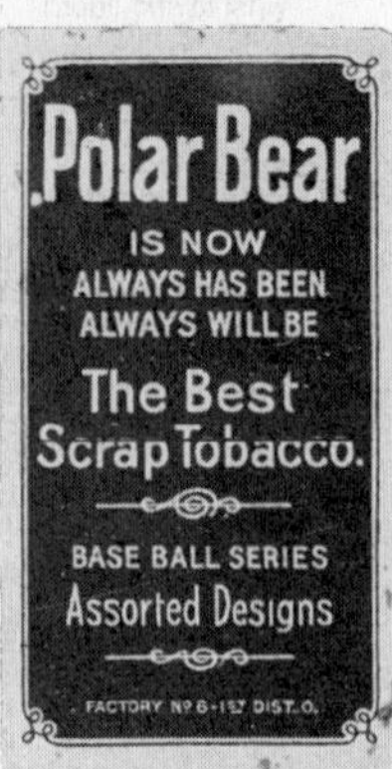

The most distinctive advertising-back found on 1909-11 T206 is that of Polar Bear with its dark blue background and white topography. A more conventional style of ad was used on 1911 T205 cards, also printed in blue. Because the cards were packaged loose among the tobacco leaves in Polar Bear pouches, stains on surviving cards are frequently seen. Polar Bear is among the most common brands found in both series.

PREMIUMS:
T205: 1X
T206: 1-1.5X
(See T205, T206 for checklists and card values.)

1889 Police Gazette Cabinets

Issued in the late 1880s through early 1890s as a premium by Police Gazette, a popular newspaper of the day, these cabinet cards are very rare. The 4-1/4" x 6-1/2" cards consist of sepia-toned photographs mounted on cardboard of various colors. Only about two dozen players are currently known. Some photographs correspond to those used in the S.F. Hess card series and many players are depicted in suit and tie, rather than baseball uniform. Each card displays the name of the player beneath his portrait, along with the signature of "Richard K. Fox" and a line identifying him as "Editor and Proprietor / Police Gazette / Franklin Square, New York."

	NM	EX	VG
Common Player:	16,000	8,000	4,800
Hick Carpenter	16,000	8,000	4,800
Fred Carroll	16,000	8,000	4,800
Bob Clark	16,000	8,000	4,800
John Coleman	16,000	8,000	4,800
Roger Conner (Connor)	20,000	10,000	6,000
Pete Conway	16,000	8,000	4,800
John Corkhill	16,000	8,000	4,800
Jerry Denny	16,000	8,000	4,800
Jas. A. Donohue (Donahue)	16,000	8,000	4,800
Buck Ewing	20,000	10,000	6,000
Bob Ferguson	16,000	8,000	4,800
Jocko Fields	16,000	8,000	4,800
Elmer Foster	16,000	8,000	4,800
Charlie Getzein (Getzien)	16,000	8,000	4,800
Pebbly Jack Glasscock	16,000	8,000	4,800
Bill Gleason	16,000	8,000	4,800
George Gore	16,000	8,000	4,800
Tim Keefe	20,000	10,000	6,000
Gus Krock	16,000	8,000	4,800
A.J. Maul	16,000	8,000	4,800
Ed Morris	16,000	8,000	4,800
Tip O'Neil (O'Neill)	16,000	8,000	4,800
N. (Fred) Pfeffer	16,000	8,000	4,800
Danny Richardson	16,000	8,000	4,800
A.B. Sanders	16,000	8,000	4,800
Charley (Pop) Smith	16,000	8,000	4,800
Elmer Smith	16,000	8,000	4,800
Harry Staley	16,000	8,000	4,800
William Swett (San Francisco)	20,000	10,000	6,000
George Tebeau	16,000	8,000	4,800
John Tener	18,000	9,000	5,400
Billy Terry (Adonis)	16,000	8,000	4,800
Sam Thompson	20,000	10,000	6,000
Curt Welch	16,000	8,000	4,800
Wheeler C. Wikoff (Wykoff) (Pres. American Association)	16,000	8,000	4,800

1895 Police Gazette Supplement

The 12 captains of the National League's teams, collectively termed "Our Baseball Heroes," are pictured in sepia lithographic portraits surrounding a colorful baseball action scene on this supplement issued with the June 1 edition of the men's newspaper. Overall the supplement measures about 21-1/2" x 15-1/2" and is the most impressive of the baseball items issued by the paper prior to the turn of the 20th Century.

	NM	EX	VG
Supplement:	15,000	7,000	4,000

Cap Anson
Jack Boyle
Ed Cartwright
George Davis
Buck Ewing
Jack Glasscock
Mike Griffin
Connie Mack
Doggie Miller
Billy Nash
Patsy Tebeau
Wilbert Robinson

1901-1917 Police Gazette Supplements

Each issue of the weekly men's magazine included a large-format (about 11-1/4" x 16-1/4") blank-backed, black-and-white supplement. In keeping with the publication's editorial focus at the time, the pictures featured baseball players, boxers, other atheletes, actresses and female models. The photos appear in a frame design and measure about 8-1/2" x 12-1/2". The supplements are designated as such by a line of type at top or bottom that names the publication, issue number and issue date. The subject is identified in capital letters beneath the photo and there are a few lines of information at bottom. The magazine sometimes printed the same pictures in nearly identical format within its regular pages. These can be differentiated from the supplements in that they are on pink paper, have advertising or other editorial material on back and are not marked as supplements. Such pages do not enjoy the same popularity and value as the supplements. In this possibly incomplete checklist, the card number shown is the issue number in which the supplement was inserted. The player name or title may not always exactly correspond to that printed on the piece. Because of their large size, the supplements are often found trimmed to remove evidence of corner creases and edge damage. This checklist includes only the baseball subjects.

		NM	EX	VG
	Common Player:	100.00	50.00	30.00
	1901			
	George Davis (Issue date unknown.)	200.00	100.00	60.00
1251	Christy Mathewson	2,000	1,000	600.00
	1903			
1351	Roy Thomas	100.00	50.00	30.00
1353	Red Dooin	100.00	50.00	30.00
1357	Tommy Leach	100.00	50.00	30.00
1359	John McGraw	200.00	100.00	60.00
1361	Cy Seymour	100.00	50.00	30.00

		NM	EX	VG
1363	Joe McGinnity	200.00	100.00	60.00
1365	Jack Cronin	100.00	50.00	30.00
	1904			
1400	Dan McGann	100.00	50.00	30.00
1403	Red Ames	100.00	50.00	30.00
1407	Jack Warner	100.00	50.00	30.00
1411	Frank Bowerman	100.00	50.00	30.00
1413	Roger Bresnahan	200.00	100.00	60.00
	1905			
1450	Joe McGinnity	200.00	100.00	60.00
1451	Napoleon Lajoie	250.00	125.00	75.00
1452	Hans Wagner	1,250	625.00	375.00
1453	Malachi Kittredge	100.00	50.00	30.00
1457	Jack Chesbro	200.00	100.00	60.00
1459	Roger Bresnahan	200.00	100.00	60.00
1461	1905 Pittsburg Team	900.00	450.00	275.00
1463	Willie Keeler	200.00	100.00	60.00
1465	Sam Mertes	100.00	50.00	30.00
1466	Dave Fultz	100.00	50.00	30.00
1467	Carlisle University Team	150.00	75.00	45.00
1468	Bill Hogg	100.00	50.00	30.00
	1906			
1502	Aleck Smith	100.00	50.00	30.00
1504	Jack Kleinow	100.00	50.00	30.00
1505	Rube Waddell	200.00	100.00	60.00
1507	Clark Griffith	200.00	100.00	60.00
1510	Nap Shea	100.00	50.00	30.00
1516	Jimmy Casey	100.00	50.00	30.00
1518	Hal Chase	200.00	100.00	60.00
	1907			
1548	Harry Davis	100.00	50.00	30.00
1549	Mike Powers	100.00	50.00	30.00
1551	Willie Keeler, Jack Kleinow	150.00	75.00	45.00
1554	Eddie Plank	250.00	125.00	75.00
1557	George Moriarty	100.00	50.00	30.00
1559	Bill Dahlen	100.00	50.00	30.00
1562	Cecil Ferguson	100.00	50.00	30.00
1564	Sammy Strang	100.00	50.00	30.00
1567	Hal Chase, Charlie Armbruster	150.00	75.00	45.00
1571	Mordecai Brown	200.00	100.00	60.00
1572	Danny Hoffman	100.00	50.00	30.00
	1908			
1607	Harry Bay	100.00	50.00	30.00
1613	Harry Lunn	100.00	50.00	30.00
1615	Charley Hemphill	100.00	50.00	30.00
	1909			
1655	Buck Herzog	100.00	50.00	30.00
1657	Al Bridwell	100.00	50.00	30.00
1660	Hans Lobert	100.00	50.00	30.00
1663	Bugs Raymond	100.00	50.00	30.00
1664	Harry Coveleski	100.00	50.00	30.00
1665	Chief Meyers	100.00	50.00	30.00
1667	Orval Overall	100.00	50.00	30.00
1673	Al Burch	100.00	50.00	30.00
1674	Mike Donlin	100.00	50.00	30.00
1676	Del Howard	100.00	50.00	30.00
1678	Dick Morris (Amateur)	100.00	50.00	30.00
	1910			
1716	Jack Warhop	100.00	50.00	30.00
1717	George Mullen (Mullin)	100.00	50.00	30.00
1720	Russ Ford	100.00	50.00	30.00
1721	Owen Bush	100.00	50.00	30.00
1722	Sherry Magee	100.00	50.00	30.00
1724	Jack Dalton	100.00	50.00	30.00
1726	Bert Daniels	100.00	50.00	30.00
1727	Birdie Cree	100.00	50.00	30.00
1729	Josh Devore	100.00	50.00	30.00
1730	Louis Drucke	100.00	50.00	30.00
	1911			
1771	Christy Mathewson	750.00	375.00	225.00
1779	Arthur Wilson	100.00	50.00	30.00
1782	Hans Wagner, Roger Bresnahan	750.00	375.00	225.00
1791	Home Run Baker	200.00	100.00	60.00
	1912			
1812	Zach Wheat	200.00	100.00	60.00
1814	Rube Marquard	200.00	100.00	60.00
1821	Tex Erwin	100.00	50.00	30.00
1823	Heinie Zimmerman	100.00	50.00	30.00
1825	Jake Stahl	100.00	50.00	30.00
	1913			
1856	Frank Chance	200.00	100.00	60.00
1861	Joe Wood	125.00	62.50	37.50
1867	Jim Thorpe	3,000	1,500	900.00
1872	Jake Daubert	100.00	50.00	30.00
1877	Nap Rucker	100.00	50.00	30.00
1883	Joe Jackson	2,000	1,000	600.00
1888	Walter Johnson	750.00	375.00	225.00
	1914			
1920	Ty Cobb	1,500	750.00	450.00
1926	Sam Crawford	200.00	100.00	60.00
1932	Dave Robertson	100.00	50.00	30.00
1938	Fritz Maisel	100.00	50.00	30.00
1942	Boston N.L. Team	200.00	100.00	60.00
1943	Philadelphia A.L. Team	200.00	100.00	60.00
	1915			
1961	Ray Caldwell	100.00	50.00	30.00
1966	Rabbit Maranville	200.00	100.00	60.00
1970	Sherry Magee	100.00	50.00	30.00
1975	Hans Lobert	100.00	50.00	30.00
1982	Eddie Collins	200.00	100.00	60.00
1985	Dick Hoblitzell	100.00	50.00	30.00
1989	Grover Alexander	500.00	250.00	150.00
	1916			
2011	Larry Doyle	100.00	50.00	30.00
2018	Fred Luderus	100.00	50.00	30.00
2020	Jimmy Archer	100.00	50.00	30.00
2023	Dick Rudolph	100.00	50.00	30.00
2026	Benny Kauff	100.00	50.00	30.00
2029	Sam Crawford	200.00	100.00	60.00
2035	Nick Cullop	100.00	50.00	30.00
2040	Clarence Mitchell	100.00	50.00	30.00
2042	George Sisler	200.00	100.00	60.00
2046	Pol Perritt	100.00	50.00	30.00
	1917			
2064	Ping Bodie	100.00	50.00	30.00
2070	Benny Kauff	100.00	50.00	30.00
2074	Hans Lobert	100.00	50.00	30.00
2078	Harry Coveleskie (Coveleski)	100.00	50.00	30.00
2081	Jack Coombs	100.00	50.00	30.00

1914 Polo Grounds Game (WG4)

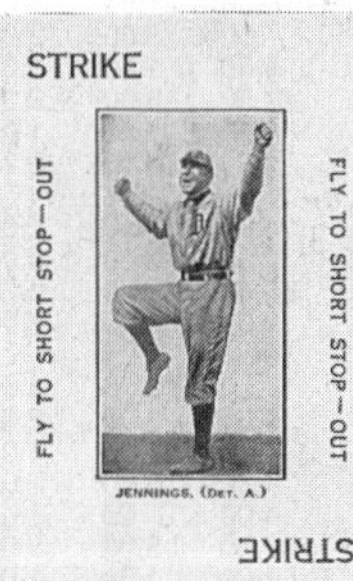

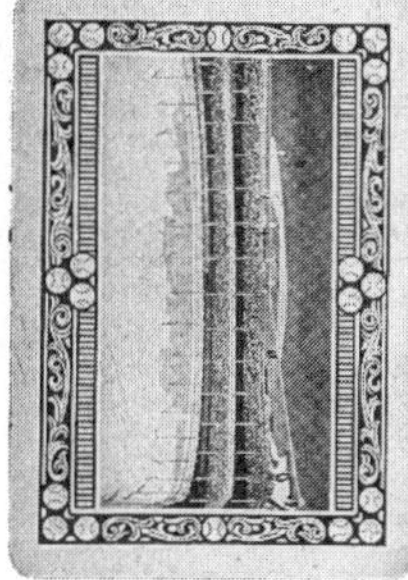

Called the "Polo Grounds Game" for the green-and-white photo of that stadium on each card's back, this set was officially issued as "All Star Card Base Ball" by The Card Baseball Co. of Norfolk, Va. Fronts of the round-cornered 2-1/2" x 3-1/2" cards have a black-and-white player photo and a baseball play scenario that is used to play the game. The set as issued includes 30 different players cards and 24 duplicate cards on which different game plays are displayed. The unnumbered cards are checklisted here alphabetically.

		NM	EX	VG
Complete Boxed Set (54):		6,650	3,325	2,000
Complete Set (30):		3,000	1,500	900.00
Common Player:		40.00	20.00	12.00
(1)	Jimmy Archer	40.00	20.00	12.00
(2)	Frank Baker	125.00	50.00	30.00
(3)	Frank Chance	125.00	50.00	30.00
(4)	Larry Cheney	40.00	20.00	12.00
(5)	Ty Cobb	1,000	275.00	165.00
(6)	Eddie Collins	100.00	50.00	30.00
(7)	Larry Doyle	40.00	20.00	12.00
(8)	Art Fletcher	40.00	20.00	12.00
(9)	Claude Hendrix	40.00	20.00	12.00
(10)	Joe Jackson	1,500	385.00	230.00
(11)	Hughie Jennings	125.00	50.00	30.00
(12)	Nap Lajoie	125.00	50.00	30.00
(13)	Jimmy Lavender	40.00	20.00	12.00
(14)	Fritz Maisel	40.00	20.00	12.00
(15)	Rabbit Maranville	125.00	50.00	30.00
(16)	Rube Marquard	125.00	50.00	30.00
(17)	Matty (Christy Mathewson)	500.00	100.00	60.00
(18)	John McGraw	125.00	50.00	30.00
(19)	Stuffy McInnis	40.00	20.00	12.00
(20)	Chief Meyers	40.00	20.00	12.00
(21)	Red Murray	40.00	20.00	12.00
(22)	Ed Plank	150.00	50.00	30.00
(23)	Nap Rucker	40.00	20.00	12.00
(24)	Reb Russell	40.00	20.00	12.00
(25)	Wildfire Schulte	40.00	20.00	12.00
(26)	Jim Scott	40.00	20.00	12.00
(27)	Tris Speaker	175.00	62.00	37.00
(28)	Honus Wagner	750.00	175.00	105.00
(29)	Ed Walsh	125.00	50.00	30.00
(30)	Joe Wood	100.00	30.00	18.00

1915 Postaco Stamps

A small find of these early stamps in complete sheets of 12 in the mid-1990s made the issue collectible, rather than impossibly rare. Individual stamps are 1-3/4" x 2-1/8" and feature black-and-white player portraits set against a bright background of either yellow or red-orange. The player name, position (in most cases), team and league are designated at the bottom of the picture. In the black frame between the picture and the perforated white border is a copyright symbol and "Postaco." Backs are, of course, blank. Stamps are checklisted here in alphabetical order within color group.

		NM	EX	VG
Complete Set, Sheets (3):		3,000	1,500	900.00
Complete Set, Singles (36):		2,500	1,250	750.00
Common Player:		30.00	15.00	9.00
	Red-orange background			
(1)	Home Run Baker	100.00	50.00	30.00
(2)	Chief Bender	100.00	50.00	30.00
(3)	George Burns	40.00	20.00	12.00
(4)	John Evers	100.00	50.00	30.00
(5)	Max Flack	40.00	20.00	12.00
(6)	Hank Gawdy (Gowdy)	40.00	20.00	12.00
(7)	Claude Ray Hendrix	40.00	20.00	12.00
(8)	Walter Johnson	200.00	100.00	60.00
(9)	Nap Lajoie	100.00	50.00	30.00
(10)	Hans Lobert	40.00	20.00	12.00
(11)	Sherwood Magee	40.00	20.00	12.00
(12)	Rabbit Maranville	100.00	50.00	30.00
(13)	Christy Mathewson	250.00	125.00	75.00
(14)	George McBride	40.00	20.00	12.00
(15)	John McGraw	100.00	50.00	30.00
(16)	Fred Merkle	40.00	20.00	12.00
(17)	Jack Miller	40.00	20.00	12.00
(18)	Emiliano Palmero	40.00	20.00	12.00
(19)	Pol Perritt	40.00	20.00	12.00
(20)	Derrill Pratt	40.00	20.00	12.00
(21)	Richard Rudolph	40.00	20.00	12.00
(22)	Butch Schmidt	40.00	20.00	12.00
(23)	Joe Tinker	100.00	50.00	30.00
(24)	Honus Wagner	300.00	150.00	90.00
	Yellow background			
(25)	G.C. Alexander	100.00	50.00	30.00
(26)	J.P. Archer	30.00	15.00	9.00
(27)	Ty Cobb	300.00	150.00	90.00
(28)	Eugene Cocreham	30.00	15.00	9.00
(29)	E.S. Cottrell	30.00	15.00	9.00
(30)	Josh Devore	30.00	15.00	9.00
(31)	A. Hartzell (Roy)	30.00	15.00	9.00
(32)	Wm. H. James (middle initial actually L)	30.00	15.00	9.00
(33)	Connie Mack	75.00	37.50	22.50
(34)	M. McHale	30.00	15.00	9.00
(35)	Geo. T. Stallings	30.00	15.00	9.00
(36)	Ed. Sweeney	30.00	15.00	9.00

1930 Post Cereal Famous North Americans

CHRISTY MATHEWSON (1880-1925)—Greatest of all baseball pitchers.

The year of issue is unconfirmed. Mathewson is the only baseball player from a group of cereal-box cards printed in panels of four and featuring presidents, generals, Indian chiefs, explorers, etc. The front is printed in red and blue, the back is blank. The card measures about 2-5/8" x 3-1/2".

	NM	EX	VG
Christy Mathewson	600.00	300.00	180.00

1960 Post Cereal

These cards were issued on the backs of Grape Nuts Flakes cereal and measure an oversized 7" x 8-3/4". The nine cards in the set include five baseball players two football (Frank Gifford and John Unitas) and two basketball players (Bob Cousy and Bob Pettit). The full-color photos are bordered by a wood frame design. The cards covered the entire back of the cereal box and are blank backed. Card fronts include the player's name, team and a facsimile autograph. A panel on the side of the box has biographical information.

		NM	EX	VG
Common Player:		400.00	200.00	120.00
(1)	Don Drysdale	400.00	200.00	120.00
(2)	Al Kaline	400.00	200.00	120.00
(3)	Harmon Killebrew	400.00	200.00	120.00
(4)	Ed Mathews	400.00	200.00	120.00
(5)	Mickey Mantle	2,500	1,250	750.00

1961 Post Cereal

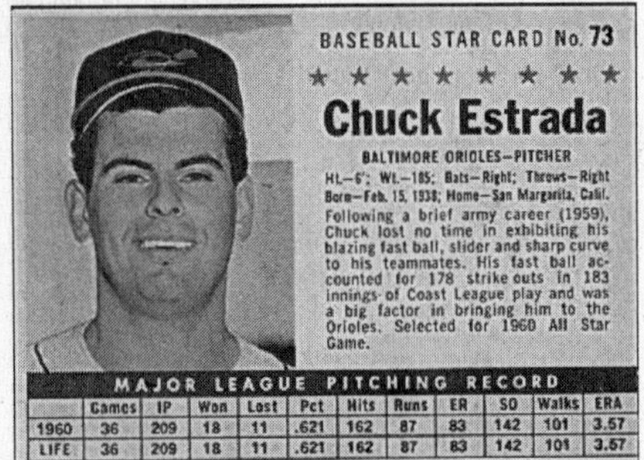

Two hundred different players are included in this set, but with variations the number of different cards exceeds 350. Cards were issued singly and in various panel configurations on the backs of cereal boxes, as well as on thinner stock in 10-card team sheets available from Post via a mail-in offer. Because of placement on less popular sizes and brands of cereal, or because they were issued only on box backs or company sheets, some cards were issued in significantly smaller quantities, making their prices much higher than other comparable players in the set. Well-cut individual cards measure about 3-1/2" x 2-1/2". All cards are numbered in the upper-left corner. Card fronts have full-color portait photos of the player, along with biographical information and 1960 and career statistics. Backs are blank. The complete set price includes only the most common variation of each player.

		NM	EX	VG
Complete Set (200):		1,600	650.00	375.00
Common Player:		4.00	2.00	1.25
1a	Yogi Berra (Box)	40.00	16.00	10.00
1b	Yogi Berra (Company)	25.00	10.00	6.00
2a	Elston Howard (Box)	7.50	3.00	2.00
2b	Elston Howard (Company)	7.50	3.00	2.00
3a	Bill Skowron (Box)	7.50	3.00	2.00
3b	Bill Skowron (Company)	7.50	3.00	2.00
4a	Mickey Mantle (Box)	160.00	65.00	40.00
4b	Mickey Mantle (Company)	110.00	45.00	25.00
5	Bob Turley (Company)	40.00	16.00	10.00
6a	Whitey Ford (Box)	20.00	8.00	5.00
6b	Whitey Ford (Company)	12.50	5.00	3.00
7a	Roger Maris (Box)	35.00	15.00	9.00
7b	Roger Maris (Company)	35.00	15.00	9.00
8a	Bobby Richardson (Box)	15.00	6.00	4.00
8b	Bobby Richardson (Company)	10.00	4.00	2.50
9a	Tony Kubek (Box)	25.00	10.00	6.25
9b	Tony Kubek (Company)	35.00	15.00	9.00
10	Gil McDougald (Box)	60.00	25.00	15.00
11	Cletis Boyer (Box)	6.00	2.50	1.50
12a	Hector Lopez (Box)	12.50	5.00	3.00
12b	Hector Lopez (Company)	7.50	3.00	2.00
13	Bob Cerv (Box)	4.00	1.50	1.00
14	Ryne Duren (Box)	4.00	1.50	1.00
15	Bobby Shantz (Box)	4.00	1.50	1.00
16	Art Ditmar (Box)	4.00	1.50	1.00
17	Jim Coates (Box)	4.00	1.50	1.00
18	John Blanchard (Box)	4.00	1.50	1.00
19a	Luis Aparicio (Box)	7.50	3.00	2.00
19b	Luis Aparicio (Company)	15.00	6.00	4.00
20a	Nelson Fox (Box)	22.50	9.00	5.75
20b	Nelson Fox (Company)	20.00	8.00	5.00
21a	Bill Pierce (Box)	20.00	8.00	5.00
21b	Bill Pierce (Company)	9.00	3.50	2.25
22a	Early Wynn (Box)	17.50	7.00	4.50
22b	Early Wynn (Company)	25.00	10.00	6.25
23	Bob Shaw (Box)	125.00	50.00	30.00
24a	Al Smith (Box)	20.00	8.00	5.00
24b	Al Smith (Company)	17.50	7.00	4.50
25a	Minnie Minoso (Box)	15.00	6.00	4.00
25b	Minnie Minoso (Company)	10.00	4.00	2.50
26a	Roy Sievers (Box)	4.00	1.50	1.00
26b	Roy Sievers (Company)	7.50	3.00	2.00
27a	Jim Landis (Box)	15.00	6.00	3.75
27b	Jim Landis (Company)	7.50	3.00	2.00
28a	Sherman Lollar (Box)	4.00	1.50	1.00
28b	Sherman Lollar (Company)	7.50	3.00	2.00
29	Gerry Staley (Box)	4.00	1.50	1.00
30a	Gene Freese (Box, White Sox.)	4.00	1.50	1.00
30b	Gene Freese (Company, Reds.)	9.00	3.50	2.25
31	Ted Kluszewski (Box)	15.00	6.00	4.00
32	Turk Lown (Box)	4.00	1.50	1.00
33a	Jim Rivera (Box)	4.00	1.50	1.00
33b	Jim Rivera (Company)	7.50	3.00	2.00
34	Frank Baumann (Box)	4.00	1.50	1.00
35a	Al Kaline (Box)	25.00	10.00	6.25
35b	Al Kaline (Company)	30.00	12.00	7.50
36a	Rocky Colavito (Box)	30.00	12.00	7.50
36b	Rocky Colavito (Company)	22.50	9.00	5.75
37a	Charley Maxwell (Box)	20.00	8.00	5.00
37b	Charley Maxwell (Company)	15.00	6.00	3.75
38a	Frank Lary (Box)	4.00	1.50	1.00
38b	Frank Lary (Company)	9.00	3.50	2.00
39a	Jim Bunning (Box)	20.00	8.00	5.00
39b	Jim Bunning (Company)	15.00	6.00	4.00
40a	Norm Cash (Box)	4.00	1.50	1.00
40b	Norm Cash (Company)	12.50	5.00	3.00
41a	Frank Bolling (Box, Tigers.)	15.00	6.00	3.75
41b	Frank Bolling (Company, Braves.)	9.00	3.50	2.00
42a	Don Mossi (Box)	10.00	4.00	2.50
42b	Don Mossi (Company)	9.00	3.50	2.00
43a	Lou Berberet (Box)	10.00	4.00	2.50
43b	Lou Berberet (Company)	9.00	3.50	2.00
44	Dave Sisler (Box)	4.00	1.50	1.00
45	Ed Yost (Box)	4.00	1.50	1.00
46	Pete Burnside (Box)	4.00	1.50	1.00
47a	Pete Runnels (Box)	20.00	8.00	5.00
47b	Pete Runnels (Company)	17.50	7.00	4.50
48a	Frank Malzone (Box)	12.50	5.00	3.00
48b	Frank Malzone (Company)	7.50	3.00	2.00
49a	Vic Wertz (Box)	15.00	6.00	3.75
49b	Vic Wertz (Company)	20.00	8.00	5.00
50a	Tom Brewer (Box)	4.00	1.50	1.00
50b	Tom Brewer (Company)	7.50	3.00	2.00
51a	Willie Tasby (Box, no sold line.)	7.50	3.00	2.00
51b	Willie Tasby (Company, sold line.)	15.00	6.00	4.00
52a	Russ Nixon (Box)	4.00	1.50	1.00
52b	Russ Nixon (Company)	7.50	3.00	2.00
53a	Don Buddin (Box)	4.00	1.50	1.00
53b	Don Buddin (Company)	7.50	3.00	2.00
54a	Bill Monbouquette (Box)	4.00	1.50	1.00
54b	Bill Monbouquette (Company)	7.50	3.00	2.00
55a	Frank Sullivan (Box, Red Sox.)	4.00	1.50	1.00
55b	Frank Sullivan (Company, Phillies.)	25.00	10.00	6.25
56a	Haywood Sullivan (Box)	4.00	1.50	1.00
56b	Haywood Sullivan (Company)	7.50	3.00	2.00
57a	Harvey Kuenn (Box, Indians.)	25.00	10.00	6.25
57b	Harvey Kuenn (Company, Giants.)	9.00	3.50	2.00
58a	Gary Bell (Box)	7.50	3.00	2.00
58b	Gary Bell (Company)	7.50	3.00	2.00
59a	Jim Perry (Box)	4.00	1.50	1.00
59b	Jim Perry (Company)	7.50	3.00	2.00
60a	Jim Grant (Box)	4.00	1.50	1.00
60b	Jim Grant (Company)	20.00	8.00	5.00
61a	Johnny Temple (Box)	4.00	1.50	1.00
61b	Johnny Temple (Company)	7.50	3.00	2.00
62a	Paul Foytack (Box)	4.00	1.50	1.00
62b	Paul Foytack (Company)	7.50	3.00	2.00
63a	Vic Power (Box)	15.00	6.00	3.75
63b	Vic Power (Company)	7.50	3.00	2.00
64a	Tito Francona (Box)	4.00	1.50	1.00
64b	Tito Francona (Company)	7.50	3.00	2.00
65a	Ken Aspromonte (Box, no sold line.)	9.00	3.50	2.00
65b	Ken Aspromonte (Company, sold line.)	9.00	3.50	2.00
66	Bob Wilson (Box)	4.00	1.50	1.00
67a	John Romano (Box)	4.00	1.50	1.00
67b	John Romano (Company)	7.50	3.00	2.00
68a	Jim Gentile (Box)	4.00	1.50	1.00
68b	Jim Gentile (Company)	9.00	3.50	2.00
69a	Gus Triandos (Box)	4.00	1.50	1.00
69b	Gus Triandos (Company)	9.00	3.50	2.00
70	Gene Woodling (Box)	30.00	12.00	7.50
71a	Milt Pappas (Box)	4.00	1.50	1.00
71b	Milt Pappas (Company)	17.50	7.00	4.50
72a	Ron Hansen (Box)	4.00	1.50	1.00
72b	Ron Hansen (Company)	9.00	3.50	2.00
73	Chuck Estrada (Company)	110.00	45.00	27.50
74a	Steve Barber (Box)	12.00	4.75	3.00
74b	Steve Barber (Company)	9.00	3.50	2.00
75a	Brooks Robinson (Box)	35.00	15.00	9.00
75b	Brooks Robinson (Company)	35.00	15.00	9.00
76a	Jackie Brandt (Box)	4.00	1.50	1.00
76b	Jackie Brandt (Company)	9.00	3.50	2.00
77a	Marv Breeding (Box)	4.00	1.50	1.00
77b	Marv Breedding (Company)	9.00	3.50	2.00
78	Hal Brown (Box)	4.00	1.50	1.00
79	Billy Klaus (Box)	4.00	1.50	1.00
80a	Hoyt Wilhelm (Box)	7.50	3.00	2.00
80b	Hoyt Wilhelm (Company)	12.50	5.00	3.00
81a	Jerry Lumpe (Box)	9.00	3.50	2.00
81b	Jerry Lumpe (Company)	7.50	3.00	2.00
82a	Norm Siebern (Box)	4.00	1.50	1.00
82b	Norm Siebern (Company)	7.50	3.00	2.00
83a	Bud Daley (Box)	15.00	6.00	4.00
83b	Bud Daley (Company)	25.00	10.00	6.25
84a	Bill Tuttle (Box)	4.00	1.50	1.00
84b	Bill Tuttle (Company)	7.50	3.00	2.00
85a	Marv Throneberry (Box)	4.00	1.50	1.00
85b	Marv Throneberry (Company)	7.50	3.00	2.00
86a	Dick Williams (Box)	15.00	6.00	3.75
86b	Dick Williams (Company)	7.50	3.00	2.00
87a	Ray Herbert (Box)	4.00	1.50	1.00
87b	Ray Herbert (Company)	7.50	3.00	2.00
88a	Whitey Herzog (Box)	4.00	1.50	1.00
88b	Whitey Herzog (Company)	7.50	3.00	2.00
89a	Ken Hamlin (Box, no sold line.)	4.00	1.50	1.00
89b	Ken Hamlin (Company, sold line.)	9.00	3.50	2.00
90a	Hank Bauer (Box)	15.00	6.00	3.75
90b	Hank Bauer (Company)	9.00	3.50	2.00
91a	Bob Allison (Box, Minneapolis.)	9.00	3.50	2.00
91b	Bob Allison (Company, Minnesota.)	20.00	8.00	5.00
92a	Harmon Killebrew (Box, Minneapolis.)	50.00	20.00	12.50
92b	Harmon Killebrew (Company, Minnesota.)	60.00	24.00	15.00
93a	Jim Lemon (Box, Minneapolis.)	65.00	25.00	15.00
93b	Jim Lemon (Company, Minnesota.)	30.00	12.00	7.50
94	Chuck Stobbs (Company)	150.00	60.00	35.00
95a	Reno Bertoia (Box, Minneapolis.)	4.00	1.50	1.00
95b	Reno Bertoia (Company, Minnesota.)	20.00	8.00	5.00
96a	Billy Gardner (Box, Minneapolis.)	4.00	1.50	1.00
96b	Billy Gardner (Company, Minnesota.)	20.00	8.00	5.00
97a	Earl Battey (Box, Minneapolis.)	6.00	2.50	1.50
97b	Earl Battey (Company, Minnesota.)	20.00	8.00	5.00
98a	Pedro Ramos (Box, Minneapolis.)	4.00	1.50	1.00
98b	Pedro Ramos (Company, Minnesota.)	20.00	8.00	5.00
99a	Camilio Pascual (Camilo) (Box, Minneapolis.)	4.00	1.50	1.00
99b	Camilio Pascual (Camilo) (Company, Minnesota.)	20.00	8.00	5.00
100a	Billy Consolo (Box, Minneapolis.)	4.00	1.50	1.00
100b	Billy Consolo (Company, Minnesota.)	22.50	9.00	5.75
101a	Warren Spahn (Box)	35.00	14.00	9.00
101b	Warren Spahn (Company)	25.00	10.00	6.00
102a	Lew Burdette (Box)	4.00	1.50	1.00
102b	Lew Burdette (Company)	7.50	3.00	2.00
103a	Bob Buhl (Box)	4.00	1.50	1.00
103b	Bob Buhl (Company)	12.50	5.00	3.25
104a	Joe Adcock (Box)	12.50	5.00	3.25
104b	Joe Adcock (Company)	7.50	3.00	2.00
105a	John Logan (Box)	6.00	2.50	1.50
105b	John Logan (Company)	15.00	6.00	4.00
106	Ed Mathews (Company)	40.00	16.00	10.00
107a	Hank Aaron (Box)	30.00	12.00	7.50
107b	Hank Aaron (Company)	30.00	12.00	7.50
108a	Wes Covington (Box)	4.00	1.50	1.00
108b	Wes Covington (Company)	7.50	3.00	2.00
109a	Bill Bruton (Box, Braves.)	25.00	10.00	6.25
109b	Bill Bruton (Company, Tigers.)	12.50	5.00	3.00
110a	Del Crandall (Box)	6.00	2.50	1.50
110b	Del Crandall (Company)	7.50	3.00	2.00
111	Red Schoendienst (Box)	12.50	5.00	3.00
112	Juan Pizarro (Box)	4.00	1.50	1.00
113	Chuck Cottier (Box)	15.00	6.00	4.00
114	Al Spangler (Cox)	4.00	1.50	1.00
115a	Dick Farrell (Box)	25.00	10.00	6.25
115b	Dick Farrell (Company)	7.50	3.00	2.00
116a	Jim Owens (Box)	15.00	6.00	3.75
116b	Jim Owens (Company)	7.50	3.00	2.00
117a	Robin Roberts (Box)	12.50	5.00	3.00
117b	Robin Roberts (Company)	12.50	5.00	3.00
118a	Tony Taylor (Box)	4.00	1.50	1.00
118b	Tony Taylor (Company)	7.50	3.00	2.00
119a	Lee Walls (Box)	4.00	1.50	1.00
119b	Lee Walls (Company)	7.50	3.00	2.00
120a	Tony Curry (Box)	4.00	1.50	1.00
120b	Tony Curry (Company)	7.50	3.00	2.00
121a	Pancho Herrera (Box)	4.00	1.50	1.00
121b	Pancho Herrera (Company)	7.50	3.00	2.00
122a	Ken Walters (Box)	4.00	1.50	1.00
122b	Ken Walters (Company)	7.50	3.00	2.00
123a	John Callison (Box)	4.00	1.50	1.00
123b	John Callison (Company)	7.50	3.00	2.00
124a	Gene Conley (Box, Phillies.)	4.00	1.50	1.00
124b	Gene Conley (Company, Red Sox.)	20.00	8.00	5.00
125a	Bob Friend (Box)	5.00	2.00	1.25
125b	Bob Friend (Company)	7.50	3.00	2.00
126a	Vernon Law (Box)	5.00	2.00	1.25
126b	Vernon Law (Company)	7.50	3.00	2.00
127a	Dick Stuart (Box)	4.00	1.50	1.00
127b	Dick Stuart (Company)	7.50	3.00	2.00
128a	Bill Mazeroski (Box)	20.00	8.00	5.00
128b	Bill Mazeroski (Company)	12.50	5.00	3.00
129a	Dick Groat (Box)	4.00	1.50	1.00
129b	Dick Groat (Company)	10.00	4.00	2.50
130a	Don Hoak (Box)	4.00	1.50	1.00
130b	Don Hoak (Company)	7.50	3.00	2.00
131a	Bob Skinner (Box)	4.00	1.50	1.00
131b	Bob Skinner (Company)	7.50	3.00	2.00
132a	Bob Clemente (Box)	50.00	20.00	12.50
132b	Bob Clemente (Company)	70.00	28.00	17.50
133	Roy Face (Box)	15.00	6.00	4.00
134	Harvey Haddix (Box)	10.00	4.00	2.50
135	Bill Virdon (Box)	40.00	16.00	10.00
136a	Gino Cimoli (Box)	4.00	1.50	1.00
136b	Gino Cimoli (Company)	7.50	3.00	2.00
137	Rocky Nelson (Box)	6.00	2.50	1.50
138a	Smoky Burgess (Box)	4.00	1.50	1.00
138b	Smoky Burgess (Company)	7.50	3.00	2.00
139	Hal Smith (Box)	6.00	2.50	1.50
140	Wilmer Mizell (Box)	12.00	4.75	3.00
141a	Mike McCormick (Box)	4.00	1.50	1.00
141b	Mike McCormick (Company)	7.50	3.00	2.00
142a	John Antonelli (Box, Giants.)	4.00	1.50	1.00
142b	John Antonelli (Company, Indians.)	9.00	3.50	2.00
143a	Sam Jones (Box)	5.00	2.00	1.25
143b	Sam Jones (Company)	7.50	3.00	2.00
144a	Orlando Cepeda (Box)	22.50	9.00	5.75
144b	Orlando Cepeda (Company)	12.50	5.00	3.00
145a	Willie Mays (Box)	55.00	22.50	13.50
145b	Willie Mays (Company)	45.00	18.00	10.00
146a	Willie Kirkland (Box, Giants.)	60.00	24.00	15.00
146b	Willie Kirkland (Company, Indians.)	25.00	10.00	6.25
147a	Willie McCovey (Box)	20.00	8.00	5.00
147b	Willie McCovey (Company)	25.00	10.00	6.00
148a	Don Blasingame (Box)	4.00	1.50	1.00
148b	Don Blasingame (Company)	7.50	3.00	2.00
149a	Jim Davenport (Box)	4.00	1.50	1.00
149b	Jim Davenport (Company)	7.50	3.00	2.00
150a	Hobie Landrith (Box)	4.00	1.50	1.00
150b	Hobie Landrith (Company)	7.50	3.00	2.00
151	Bob Schmidt (Box)	9.00	3.50	2.00
152a	Ed Bressoud (Box)	4.00	1.50	1.00
152b	Ed Bressoud (Company)	7.50	3.00	2.00
153a	Andre Rodgers (Box, no traded line.)	9.00	3.50	2.00
153b	Andre Rodgers (Box, traded line.)	4.00	1.50	1.00
154	Jack Sanford (Box)	20.00	8.00	5.00
155	Billy O'Dell (Box)	4.00	1.50	1.00
156a	Norm Larker (Box)	7.50	3.00	2.00
156b	Norm Larker (Company)	7.50	3.00	2.00
157a	Charlie Neal (Box)	4.00	1.50	1.00
157b	Charlie Neal (Company)	7.50	3.00	2.00
158a	Jim Gilliam (Box)	7.50	3.00	2.00

158b	Jim Gilliam (Company)	7.50	3.00	2.00
159a	Wally Moon (Box)	20.00	8.00	5.00
159b	Wally Moon (Company)	12.00	4.75	3.00
160a	Don Drysdale (Box)	20.00	8.00	5.00
160b	Don Drysdale (Company)	20.00	8.00	5.00
161a	Larry Sherry (Box)	4.00	1.50	1.00
161b	Larry Sherry (Company)	7.50	3.00	2.00
162	Stan Williams (Box)	7.50	3.00	2.00
163	Mel Roach (Box)	55.00	22.50	13.50
164a	Maury Wills (Box)	20.00	8.00	5.00
164b	Maury Wills (Company)	35.00	14.00	9.00
165	Tom Davis (Box)	4.00	1.50	1.00
166a	John Roseboro (Box)	4.00	1.50	1.00
166b	John Roseboro (Company)	7.50	3.00	2.00
167a	Duke Snider (Box)	15.00	6.00	3.75
167b	Duke Snider (Company)	20.00	8.00	5.00
168a	Gil Hodges (Box)	7.50	3.00	2.00
168b	Gil Hodges (Company)	12.50	5.00	3.00
169	John Podres (Box)	4.00	1.50	1.00
170	Ed Roebuck (Box)	4.00	1.50	1.00
171a	Ken Boyer (Box)	15.00	6.00	3.75
171b	Ken Boyer (Company)	7.50	3.00	2.00
172a	Joe Cunningham (Box)	12.50	5.00	3.00
172b	Joe Cunningham (Company)	9.00	3.50	2.00
173a	Daryl Spencer (Box)	4.00	1.50	1.00
173b	Daryl Spencer (Company)	7.50	3.00	2.00
174a	Larry Jackson (Box)	12.50	5.00	3.00
174b	Larry Jackson (Company)	7.50	3.00	2.00
175a	Lindy McDaniel (Box)	7.50	3.00	2.00
175b	Lindy McDaniel (Company)	7.50	3.00	2.00
176a	Bill White (Box)	4.00	1.50	1.00
176b	Bill White (Company)	7.50	3.00	2.00
177a	Alex Grammas (Box)	20.00	8.00	5.00
177b	Alex Grammas (Company)	7.50	3.00	2.00
178a	Curt Flood (Box)	4.00	1.50	1.00
178b	Curt Flood (Company)	12.50	5.00	3.00
179a	Ernie Broglio (Box)	4.00	1.50	1.00
179b	Ernie Broglio (Company)	8.00	3.25	2.00
180a	Hal Smith (Box)	8.00	3.25	2.00
180b	Hal Smith (Company)	12.50	5.00	3.00
181a	Vada Pinson (Box)	20.00	8.00	5.00
181b	Vada Pinson (Company)	7.50	3.00	2.00
182a	Frank Robinson (Box)	30.00	12.00	7.50
182b	Frank Robinson (Company)	35.00	15.00	9.00
183	Roy McMillan (Box)	100.00	40.00	25.00
184a	Bob Purkey (Box)	4.00	1.50	1.00
184b	Bob Purkey (Company)	7.50	3.00	2.00
185a	Ed Kasko (Box)	7.50	3.00	2.00
185b	Ed Kasko (Company)	7.50	3.00	2.00
186a	Gus Bell (Box)	4.00	1.50	1.00
186b	Gus Bell (Company)	7.50	3.00	2.00
187a	Jerry Lynch (Box)	4.00	1.50	1.00
187b	Jerry Lynch (Company)	7.50	3.00	2.00
188a	Ed Bailey (Box)	4.00	1.50	1.00
188b	Ed Bailey (Company)	7.50	3.00	2.00
189a	Jim O'Toole (Box)	4.00	1.50	1.00
189b	Jim O'Toole (Company)	7.50	3.00	2.00
190a	Billy Martin (Box, no sold line.)	6.00	2.50	1.50
190b	Billy Martin (Company, sold line.)	12.50	5.00	3.00
191a	Ernie Banks (Box)	35.00	15.00	9.00
191b	Ernie Banks (Company)	20.00	8.00	5.00
192a	Richie Ashburn (Box)	12.50	5.00	3.00
192b	Richie Ashburn (Company)	22.50	9.00	5.75
193a	Frank Thomas (Box)	100.00	40.00	25.00
193b	Frank Thomas (Company)	40.00	16.00	10.00
194a	Don Cardwell (Box)	6.00	2.50	1.50
194b	Don Cardwell (Company)	7.50	3.00	2.00
195a	George Altman (Box)	15.00	6.00	3.75
195b	George Altman (Company)	7.50	3.00	2.00
196a	Ron Santo (Box)	6.00	2.50	1.50
196b	Ron Santo (Company)	30.00	12.00	7.50
197a	Glen Hobbie (Box)	4.00	1.50	1.00
197b	Glen Hobbie (Company)	7.50	3.00	2.00
198a	Sam Taylor (Box)	4.00	1.50	1.00
198b	Sam Taylor (Company)	7.50	3.00	2.00
199a	Jerry Kindall (Box)	8.00	3.25	2.00
199b	Jerry Kindall (Company)	7.50	3.00	2.00
200a	Don Elston (Box)	12.00	4.75	3.00
200b	Don Elston (Company)	7.50	3.00	2.00

1961 Post Cereal Company Sheets

Via a mail-in offer, sheets of 10 cards from each team could be ordered from the cereal company. Known to collectors as "company" cards, the sheets were issued in a perforated format on cardboard that is somewhat thinner than box-back cards. Sheet cards have perforations on one, two, or three sides, depending on their original placement on the sheet. Because of player movements between the time the box-back cards and sheet cards were printed, some cards are only found on the mail-in sheets, while others could not be obtained via the mail-in offer, and some are shown on the sheets of the "wrong" team.

		NM	EX	VG
Complete Set (16):		5,250	2,625	1,575
Common Team:		300.00	150.00	90.00
(1)	Baltimore Orioles	300.00	150.00	90.00
(2)	Boston Red Sox	300.00	150.00	90.00
(3)	Chicago Cubs	300.00	150.00	90.00
(4)	Chicago White Sox	300.00	150.00	90.00
(5)	Cincinnati Reds	300.00	150.00	90.00
(6)	Cleveland Indians	300.00	150.00	90.00
(7)	Detroit Tigers	300.00	150.00	90.00
(8)	Kansas City Athletics	300.00	150.00	90.00
(9)	Los Angeles Dodgers	375.00	185.00	110.00
(10)	Milwaukee Braves	375.00	185.00	110.00
(11)	Minnesota Twins	475.00	235.00	140.00
(12)	New York Yankees	600.00	300.00	180.00
(13)	Philadelphia Phillies	300.00	150.00	90.00
(14)	Pittsburgh Pirates	375.00	185.00	110.00
(15)	San Francisco Giants	375.00	185.00	110.00
(16)	St. Louis Cardinals	300.00	150.00	90.00

1961 Post Cereal Display Pinwheel

Designed for use in grocery stores to promote sales of Post cereal with baseball cards on the back, this display features dou-

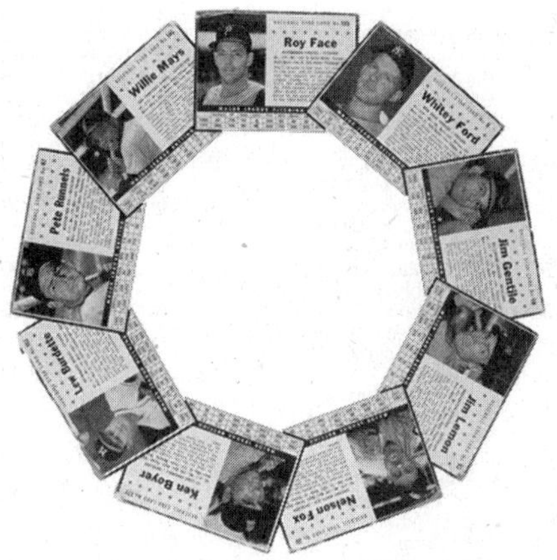

ble-sided, oversize (about 8-1/2" x 6") examples of nine of the cards arranged in a circle. At center was a cardboard cutout of a youngster and accommodation for an electric motor.

	NM	EX	VG
Complete Display:	6,500	3,750	2,000

Ken Boyer, Lew Burdette, Roy Face, Whitey Ford, Nellie Fox, Jim Gentile, Jim Lemon, Willie Mays, Pete Runnels

1962 Post Cereal

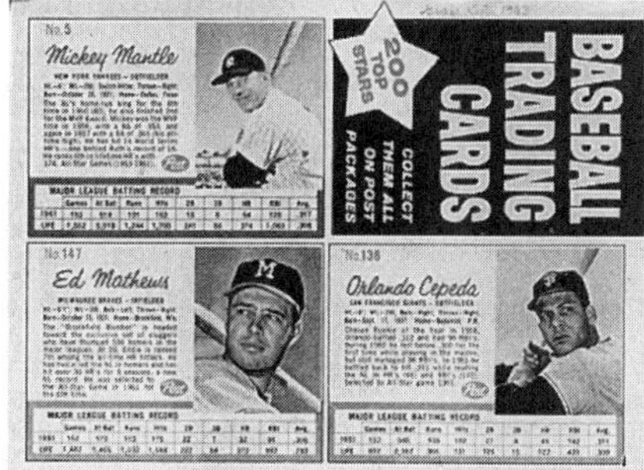

Like the 1961 Post set, there are 200 players pictured in this set of 3-1/2" x 2-1/2" cards. Differences include a Post logo on the card fronts and the player's name in script lettering. Cards are again blank backed and were issued in panels of five to seven cards on cereal boxes. American League players are numbered 1-100 and National League players 101-200. With variations there are 210 cards known. Some of the '62 cards, usually those printed on the backs of less popular brands or sizes, were issued in smaller quantities and sell for more than players of star caliber. The cards of Mickey Mantle and Roger Maris were reproduced in a special two-card panel for a Life magazine insert. The card stock for this insert is slightly thinner, with white margins. The 1962 Post Canadian and Jell-O sets have virtually the same checklist as this set. The complete set price does not include the scarcer variations. The #5 Mickey Mantle card has been extensively counterfeited in recent years by pasting a reproduction of the Life magazine promo card (no lines in the stats area) to a piece of blank cardboard. All genuine cereal-box Mantle cards have a grid of lines in the stats area.

		NM	EX	VG
Complete Set (200):		2,100	850.00	525.00
Common Player:		4.00	1.50	1.00
April 13 Life magazine w/ad panel:		90.00	50.00	30.00
1	Bill Skowron	10.00	4.00	2.50
2	Bobby Richardson	12.50	5.00	3.00
3	Cletis Boyer	7.50	3.00	2.00
4	Tony Kubek	9.00	3.50	2.00
5a	Mickey Mantle (From box, no printing on back.)	100.00	40.00	25.00
5b	Mickey Mantle (From ad, printing on back.)	60.00	25.00	15.00
6a	Roger Maris (From box, no printing on back.)	35.00	14.00	9.00
6b	Roger Maris (From ad, printing on back.)	30.00	12.00	7.50
7	Yogi Berra	27.50	11.00	7.00
8	Elston Howard	20.00	8.00	5.00
9	Whitey Ford	22.50	9.00	6.00
10	Ralph Terry	10.00	4.00	2.50
11	John Blanchard	4.00	1.50	1.00
12	Luis Arroyo	20.00	8.00	5.00
13	Bill Stafford	4.00	1.50	1.00
14a	Norm Cash (Throws: Right)	30.00	12.00	7.50
14b	Norm Cash (Throws: Left)	10.00	4.00	2.50
15	Jake Wood	7.50	3.00	2.00
16	Steve Boros	10.00	4.00	2.50
17	Chico Fernandez	4.00	1.50	1.00
18	Bill Bruton	4.00	1.50	1.00
19	Rocky Colavito	16.00	6.50	4.00
20	Al Kaline	20.00	8.00	5.00
21	Dick Brown	4.00	1.50	1.00
22	Frank Lary	4.00	1.50	1.00
23	Don Mossi	4.00	1.50	1.00
24	Phil Regan	4.00	1.50	1.00
25	Charley Maxwell	7.50	3.00	2.00
26	Jim Bunning	30.00	12.00	7.50
27a	Jim Gentile (Home: Baltimore)	4.00	1.50	1.00
27b	Jim Gentile (Home: San Lorenzo)	6.00	2.50	1.50
28	Marv Breeding	4.00	1.50	1.00
29	Brooks Robinson	17.50	7.00	4.50
30	Ron Hansen	4.00	1.50	1.00
31	Jackie Brandt	4.00	1.50	1.00
32	Dick Williams	4.00	1.50	1.00
33	Gus Triandos	4.00	1.50	1.00
34	Milt Pappas	7.50	3.00	2.00
35	Hoyt Wilhelm	15.00	6.00	3.50
36	Chuck Estrada	12.50	5.00	3.00
37	Vic Power	4.00	1.50	1.00
38	Johnny Temple	4.00	1.50	1.00
39	Bubba Phillips	4.00	1.50	1.00
40	Tito Francona	9.00	3.50	2.00
41	Willie Kirkland	4.00	1.50	1.00
42	John Romano	4.00	1.50	1.00
43	Jim Perry	4.00	1.50	1.00
44	Woodie Held	4.00	1.50	1.00
45	Chuck Essegian	4.00	1.50	1.00
46	Roy Sievers	4.00	1.50	1.00
47	Nellie Fox	7.50	3.00	2.00
48	Al Smith	4.00	1.50	1.00
49	Luis Aparicio	12.50	5.00	3.25
50	Jim Landis	7.50	3.00	2.00
51	Minnie Minoso	10.00	4.00	2.50
52	Andy Carey	7.50	3.00	2.00
53	Sherman Lollar	4.00	1.50	1.00
54	Bill Pierce	7.50	3.00	2.00
55	Early Wynn	50.00	20.00	12.50
56	Chuck Schilling	7.50	3.00	2.00
57	Pete Runnels	15.00	6.00	3.75
58	Frank Malzone	4.00	1.50	1.00
59	Don Buddin	4.00	1.50	1.00
60	Gary Geiger	25.00	10.00	6.25
61	Carl Yastrzemski	60.00	25.00	15.00
62	Jackie Jensen	7.50	3.00	2.00
63	Jim Pagliaroni	4.00	1.50	1.00
64	Don Schwall	4.00	1.50	1.00
65	Dale Long	4.00	1.50	1.00
66	Chuck Cottier	4.00	1.50	1.00
67	Billy Klaus	9.00	3.50	2.00
68	Coot Veal	9.00	3.50	2.00
69	Marty Keough	55.00	22.50	13.50
70	Willie Tasby	9.00	3.50	2.00
71	Gene Woodling	4.00	1.50	1.00
72	Gene Green	4.00	1.50	1.00
73	Dick Donovan	4.00	1.50	1.00
74	Steve Bilko	4.00	1.50	1.00
75	Rocky Bridges	4.00	1.50	1.00
76	Eddie Yost	4.00	1.50	1.00
77	Leon Wagner	4.00	1.50	1.00
78	Albie Pearson	7.50	3.00	2.00
79	Ken Hunt	4.00	1.50	1.00
80	Earl Averill	4.00	1.50	1.00
81	Ryne Duren	4.00	1.50	1.00
82	Ted Kluszewski	6.00	2.50	1.50
83	Bob Allison	90.00	35.00	20.00
84	Billy Martin	9.00	3.50	2.00
85	Harmon Killebrew	40.00	16.00	10.00
86	Zoilo Versalles	20.00	8.00	5.00
87	Lenny Green	10.00	4.00	2.50
88	Bill Tuttle	4.00	1.50	1.00
89	Jim Lemon	4.00	1.50	1.00
90	Earl Battey	4.00	1.50	1.00
91	Camilo Pascual	4.00	1.50	1.00
92	Norm Siebern	60.00	24.00	15.00
93	Jerry Lumpe	4.00	1.50	1.00
94	Dick Howser	4.00	1.50	1.00
95a	Gene Stephens (Born: Jan. 5)	4.00	1.50	1.00
95b	Gene Stephens (Born: Jan. 20)	20.00	8.00	5.00
96	Leo Posada	4.00	1.50	1.00
97	Joe Pignatano	7.50	3.00	2.00
98	Jim Archer	4.00	1.50	1.00
99	Haywood Sullivan	4.00	1.50	1.00
100	Art Ditmar	6.00	2.50	1.50
101	Gil Hodges	80.00	32.50	20.00
102	Charlie Neal	4.00	1.50	1.00
103	Daryl Spencer	25.00	10.00	6.00
104	Maury Wills	4.00	1.50	1.00
105	Tommy Davis	4.00	1.50	1.00
106	Willie Davis	4.00	1.50	1.00
107	John Roseboro	7.50	3.00	2.00
108	John Podres	4.00	1.50	1.00
109a	Sandy Koufax (Blue lines around stats.)	450.00	180.00	110.00
109b	Sandy Koufax (Red lines around stats.)	40.00	16.00	10.00
110	Don Drysdale	20.00	8.00	5.00
111	Larry Sherry	4.00	1.50	1.00
112	Jim Gilliam	7.50	3.00	2.00
113	Norm Larker	80.00	32.50	20.00
114	Duke Snider	20.00	8.00	5.00
115	Stan Williams	4.00	1.50	1.00
116	Gordy Coleman	75.00	30.00	18.50
117	Don Blasingame	12.50	5.00	3.00
118	Gene Freese	4.00	1.50	1.00
119	Ed Kasko	4.00	1.50	1.00
120	Gus Bell	4.00	1.50	1.00
121	Vada Pinson	7.50	3.00	2.00
122	Frank Robinson	50.00	20.00	12.50
123	Bob Purkey	4.00	1.50	1.00
124a	Joey Jay (Blue lines around stats.)	225.00	90.00	55.00
124b	Joey Jay (Red lines around stats.)	6.00	2.50	1.50
125	Jim Brosnan	35.00	14.00	9.00
126	Jim O'Toole	4.00	1.50	1.00
127	Jerry Lynch	65.00	25.00	15.00
128	Wally Post	4.00	1.50	1.00
129	Ken Hunt	4.00	1.50	1.00
130	Jerry Zimmerman	4.00	1.50	1.00

131	Willie McCovey	75.00	30.00	18.50
132	Jose Pagan	4.00	1.50	1.00
133	Felipe Alou	4.00	1.50	1.00
134	Jim Davenport	4.00	1.50	1.00
135	Harvey Kuenn	4.00	1.50	1.00
136	Orlando Cepeda	15.00	6.00	3.75
137	Ed Bailey	4.00	1.50	1.00
138	Sam Jones	4.00	1.50	1.00
139	Mike McCormick	4.00	1.50	1.00
140	Juan Marichal	80.00	32.00	20.00
141	Jack Sanford	4.00	1.50	1.00
142	Willie Mays	55.00	22.50	13.50
143	Stu Miller (Photo actually Chuck Hiller.)	5.00	2.00	1.25
144	Joe Amalfitano	35.00	14.00	9.00
145a	Joe Adock (Name incorrect.)	115.00	45.00	30.00
145b	Joe Adcock (Name correct.)	4.00	1.50	1.00
146	Frank Bolling	4.00	1.50	1.00
147	Ed Mathews	17.50	7.00	4.50
148	Roy McMillan	4.00	1.50	1.00
149	Hank Aaron	35.00	14.00	9.00
150	Gino Cimoli	4.00	1.50	1.00
151	Frank Thomas	4.00	1.50	1.00
152	Joe Torre	25.00	10.00	6.25
153	Lou Burdette	4.00	1.50	1.00
154	Bob Buhl	10.00	4.00	2.50
155	Carlton Willey	20.00	8.00	5.00
156	Lee Maye	20.00	8.00	5.00
157	Al Spangler	7.50	3.00	2.00
158	Bill White	45.00	18.00	10.00
159	Ken Boyer	6.00	2.50	1.50
160	Joe Cunningham	4.00	1.50	1.00
161	Carl Warwick	4.00	1.50	1.00
162	Carl Sawatski	4.00	1.50	1.00
163	Lindy McDaniel	4.00	1.50	1.00
164	Ernie Broglio	4.00	1.50	1.00
165	Larry Jackson	4.00	1.50	1.00
166	Curt Flood	4.00	1.50	1.00
167	Curt Simmons	4.00	1.50	1.00
168	Alex Grammas	4.00	1.50	1.00
169	Dick Stuart	10.00	4.00	2.50
170	Bill Mazeroski	20.00	8.00	5.00
171	Don Hoak	20.00	8.00	5.00
172	Dick Groat	4.00	1.50	1.00
173a	Roberto Clemente (Blue lines around stats.)	400.00	160.00	100.00
173b	Roberto Clemente (Red lines around stats.)	45.00	18.00	11.00
174	Bob Skinner	4.00	1.50	1.00
175	Bill Virdon	4.00	1.50	1.00
176	Smoky Burgess	9.00	3.50	2.25
177	Elroy Face	4.00	1.50	1.00
178	Bob Friend	4.00	1.50	1.00
179	Vernon Law	4.00	1.50	1.00
180	Harvey Haddix	4.00	1.50	1.00
181	Hal Smith	7.50	3.00	2.00
182	Ed Bouchee	4.00	1.50	1.00
183	Don Zimmer	4.00	1.50	1.00
184	Ron Santo	7.50	3.00	2.00
185	Andre Rodgers	4.00	1.50	1.00
186	Richie Ashburn	12.50	5.00	3.00
187a	George Altman (Last line is "...1955).")	6.00	2.50	1.50
187b	George Altman (Last line is "...1955.")	7.50	3.00	2.00
188	Ernie Banks	17.50	7.00	4.50
189	Sam Taylor	25.00	10.00	6.25
190	Don Elston	7.50	3.00	2.00
191	Jerry Kindall	4.00	1.50	1.00
192	Pancho Herrera	4.00	1.50	1.00
193	Tony Taylor	4.00	1.50	1.00
194	Ruben Amaro	9.00	3.50	2.00
195	Don Demeter	4.00	1.50	1.00
196	Bobby Gene Smith	4.00	1.50	1.00
197	Clay Dalrymple	4.00	1.50	1.00
198	Robin Roberts	10.00	4.00	2.50
199	Art Mahaffey	4.00	1.50	1.00
200	John Buzhardt	4.00	1.50	1.00

1962 Post Cereal - Canadian

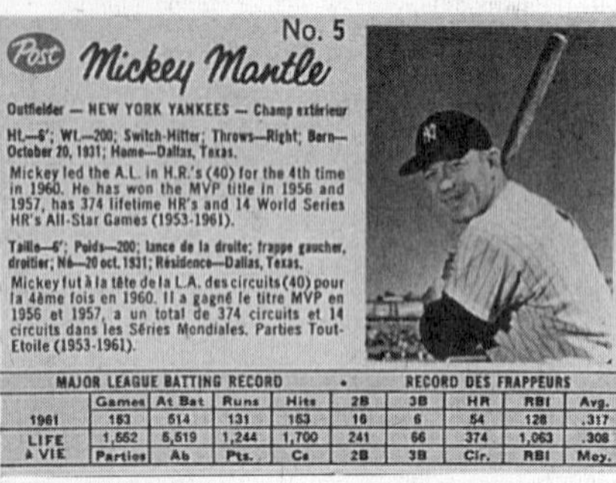

This Post set is scarce due to the much more limited distribution in Canada. Most cards were printed on the back of the cereal boxes and contain a full-color player photo with biography and statistics given in both French and English. Card backs are blank. Cards measure 3-1/2" x 2-1/2". This 200-card set is very similar to the Post Cereal cards printed in the United States. The Post logo appears at the upper-left corner in the Canadian issue. Several cards are scarce because of limited distribution and there are two Whitey Ford cards, the corrected version being the most scarce. The complete set price does not include the scarcer variations. Certain cereal brands had the cards packaged inside the box on perforated panels, and will be found with perforated edges on one side or other.

		NM	EX	VG
	Complete Set (200):	5,000	2,005	1,250
	Common Player:	8.00	3.25	2.00
1	Bill Skowron	35.00	15.00	9.00
2	Bobby Richardson	12.00	4.75	3.00
3	Cletis Boyer	10.00	4.00	2.50
4	Tony Kubek	12.00	4.75	3.00
5a	Mickey Mantle (Stats list 153 hits.)	215.00	85.00	55.00
5b	Mickey Mantle (163 hits; first line of bio ends: "4th time in")	120.00	50.00	30.00
5c	Mickey Mantle (163 hits; first line of bio ends: "4th time")	125.00	50.00	30.00
6a	Roger Maris (First line of French bio has large "P" in "Pour les circuits.")	65.00	25.00	15.00
6b	Roger Maris (French text reads, "Residence." Small "p" in "pour.")	55.00	22.50	13.50
6c	Roger Maris (French text reads, "a," not "Residence." Small "p" in "pour.")	55.00	22.50	13.50
7	Yogi Berra	40.00	16.00	10.00
8	Elston Howard	12.00	4.75	3.00
9a	Whitey Ford (Dodgers)	55.00	22.50	13.50
9b	Whitey Ford (Yankees)	80.00	32.00	20.00
10	Ralph Terry	95.00	38.00	24.00
11	John Blanchard	8.00	3.25	2.00
12	Luis Arroyo	8.00	3.25	2.00
13	Bill Stafford	8.00	3.25	2.00
14	Norm Cash	10.00	4.00	2.50
15	Jake Wood	8.00	3.25	2.00
16	Steve Boros	8.00	3.25	2.00
17	Chico Fernandez	8.00	3.25	2.00
18	Bill Bruton	8.00	3.25	2.00
19a	Rocky Colavito (Script name large.)	17.50	7.00	4.50
19b	Rocky Colavito (Script name small.)	17.50	7.00	4.50
20	Al Kaline	85.00	35.00	20.00
21	Dick Brown	12.00	4.75	3.00
22a	Frank Lary ("Residence-Northport, Alabama.")	17.50	7.00	4.50
22b	Frank Lary ("a Northport, Alabama.")	65.00	25.00	15.00
23	Don Mossi	8.00	3.25	2.00
24	Phil Regan	8.00	3.25	2.00
25	Charley Maxwell	8.00	3.25	2.00
26	Jim Bunning	25.00	10.00	6.25
27a	Jim Gentile (French bio begins "Le 8 mai, Jim ...")	13.50	5.50	3.50
27b	Jim Gentile (Begins, "Le 8 mai 1961, Jim ...")	13.50	5.50	3.50
28	Marv Breeding	17.50	7.00	4.50
29	Brooks Robinson	50.00	20.00	12.50
30	Ron Hansen	8.00	3.25	2.00
31	Jackie Brandt	8.00	3.25	2.00
32	Dick Williams	55.00	22.50	13.50
33	Gus Triandos	10.00	4.00	2.50
34	Milt Pappas	10.00	4.00	2.50
35	Hoyt Wilhelm	95.00	38.00	24.00
36	Chuck Estrada	8.00	3.25	2.00
37	Vic Power	8.00	3.25	2.00
38	Johnny Temple	8.00	3.25	2.00
39	Bubba Phillips	55.00	22.50	13.50
40	Tito Francona	55.00	22.50	13.50
41	Willie Kirkland	13.50	5.50	3.50
42	John Romano	13.50	5.50	3.50
43	Jim Perry	10.00	4.00	2.50
44	Woodie Held	8.00	3.25	2.00
45	Chuck Essegian	8.00	3.25	2.00
46	Roy Sievers	40.00	16.00	10.00
47	Nellie Fox	25.00	10.00	6.25
48	Al Smith	8.00	3.25	2.00
49	Luis Aparicio	100.00	40.00	25.00
50	Jim Landis	13.50	5.50	3.50
51	Minnie Minoso	55.00	22.50	13.50
52	Andy Carey	12.00	4.75	3.00
53	Sherman Lollar	8.00	3.25	2.00
54	Bill Pierce	10.00	4.00	2.50
55	Early Wynn	30.00	12.00	7.50
56	Chuck Schilling	10.00	4.00	2.50
57	Pete Runnels	10.00	4.00	2.50
58	Frank Malzone	8.00	3.25	2.00
59	Don Buddin	12.00	4.75	3.00
60	Gary Geiger	8.00	3.25	2.00
61	Carl Yastrzemski	60.00	25.00	15.00
62	Jackie Jensen	40.00	16.00	10.00
63	Jim Pagliaroni	8.00	3.25	2.00
64	Don Schwall	25.00	10.00	6.25
65	Dale Long	20.00	8.00	5.00
66	Chuck Cottier	8.00	3.25	2.00
67	Billy Klaus	8.00	3.25	2.00
68	Coot Veal	8.00	3.25	2.00
69	Marty Keough	8.00	3.25	2.00
70	Willie Tasby	125.00	50.00	30.00
71	Gene Woodling (Photo reversed.)	10.00	4.00	2.50
72	Gene Green	12.00	4.75	3.00
73	Dick Donovan	8.00	3.25	2.00
74	Steve Bilko	13.50	5.50	3.50
75	Rocky Bridges	12.00	4.75	3.00
76	Eddie Yost	8.00	3.25	2.00
77	Leon Wagner	65.00	25.00	15.00
78	Albie Pearson	13.50	5.50	3.50
79	Ken Hunt	8.00	3.25	2.00
80	Earl Averill	8.00	3.25	2.00
81	Ryne Duren	10.00	4.00	2.50
82	Ted Kluszewski	30.00	12.00	7.50
83	Bob Allison	13.50	5.50	3.50
84	Billy Martin	17.50	7.00	4.50
85	Harmon Killebrew	125.00	50.00	30.00
86	Zoilo Versalles	8.00	3.25	2.00
87	Lenny Green	95.00	38.00	24.00
88	Bill Tuttle	8.00	3.25	2.00
89	Jim Lemon	8.00	3.25	2.00
90	Earl Battey	13.50	5.50	3.50
91	Camilo Pascual	10.00	4.00	2.50
92	Norm Siebern	8.00	3.25	2.00
93	Jerry Lumpe	8.00	3.25	2.00
94	Dick Howser	80.00	32.00	20.00
95	Gene Stephens	8.00	3.25	2.00
96	Leo Posada	8.00	3.25	2.00
97	Joe Pignatano	8.00	3.25	2.00
98	Jim Archer	8.00	3.25	2.00
99	Haywood Sullivan	125.00	50.00	30.00
100	Art Ditmar	25.00	10.00	6.25
101	Gil Hodges	35.00	15.00	9.00
102	Charlie Neal	8.00	3.25	2.00
103	Daryl Spencer	8.00	3.25	2.00
104	Maury Wills	17.50	7.00	4.50
105	Tommy Davis	55.00	22.50	13.50
106	Willie Davis	12.00	4.75	3.00
107	John Rosboro (Roseboro)	10.00	4.00	2.50
108	John Podres	10.00	4.00	2.50
109	Sandy Koufax	80.00	32.00	20.00
110	Don Drysdale	35.00	15.00	9.00
111	Larry Sherry	55.00	22.50	13.50
112	Jim Gilliam	55.00	22.50	13.50
113	Norm Larker	8.00	3.25	2.00
114	Duke Snider	30.00	12.00	7.50
115	Stan Williams	13.50	5.50	3.50
116	Gordy Coleman	8.00	3.25	2.00
117	Don Blasingame	160.00	65.00	40.00
118	Gene Freese	40.00	16.00	10.00
119	Ed Kasko	13.50	5.50	3.50
120	Gus Bell	8.00	3.25	2.00
121	Vada Pinson	10.00	4.00	2.50
122	Frank Robinson	50.00	20.00	12.50
123	Bob Purkey	55.00	22.50	13.50
124	Joey Jay	8.00	3.25	2.00
125	Jim Brosnan	17.50	7.00	4.50
126	Jim O'Toole	8.00	3.25	2.00
127	Jerry Lynch	15.00	6.00	3.75
128	Wally Post	135.00	55.00	35.00
129	Ken Hunt	8.00	3.25	2.00
130	Jerry Zimmerman	8.00	3.25	2.00
131	Willie McCovey	40.00	16.00	10.00
132	Jose Pagan	12.00	4.75	3.00
133	Felipe Alou	10.00	4.00	2.50
134	Jim Davenport	8.00	3.25	2.00
135	Harvey Kuenn	10.00	4.00	2.50
136	Orlando Cepeda	25.00	10.00	6.25
137	Ed Bailey	75.00	30.00	18.50
138	Sam Jones	55.00	22.50	13.50
139	Mike McCormick	8.00	3.25	2.00
140	Juan Marichal	35.00	15.00	9.00
141	Jack Sanford	8.00	3.25	2.00
142a	Willie Mays (Big head.)	80.00	32.00	20.00
142b	Willie Mays (Small head.)	60.00	24.00	15.00
143	Stu Miller	8.00	3.25	2.00
144	Joe Amalfitano	100.00	40.00	25.00
145	Joe Adcock	13.50	5.50	3.50
146	Frank Bolling	13.50	5.50	3.50
147	Ed Mathews	30.00	12.00	7.50
148	Roy McMillan	24.00	9.50	6.00
149a	Hank Aaron (Script name large.)	80.00	32.00	20.00
149b	Hank Aaron (Script name small.)	60.00	24.00	15.00
150	Gino Cimoli	8.00	3.25	2.00
151	Frank Thomas	8.00	3.25	2.00
152	Joe Torre	25.00	10.00	6.25
153	Lou Burdette	25.00	10.00	6.25
154	Bob Buhl	10.00	4.00	2.50
155	Carlton Willey	12.00	4.75	3.00
156	Lee Maye	8.00	3.25	2.00
157	Al Spangler	8.00	3.25	2.00
158	Bill White	10.00	4.00	2.50
159	Ken Boyer	40.00	16.00	10.00
160	Joe Cunningham	8.00	3.25	2.00
161	Carl Warwick	55.00	22.50	13.50
162	Carl Sawatski	8.00	3.25	2.00
163	Lindy McDaniel	8.00	3.25	2.00
164	Ernie Broglio	8.00	3.25	2.00
165	Larry Jackson	8.00	3.25	2.00
166	Curt Flood	25.00	10.00	6.25
167	Curt Simmons	17.50	7.00	4.50
168	Alex Grammas	8.00	3.25	2.00
169	Dick Stuart	25.00	10.00	6.25
170	Bill Mazeroski	40.00	16.00	10.00
171	Don Hoak	8.00	3.25	2.00
172	Dick Groat	17.50	7.00	4.50
173	Roberto Clemente	100.00	40.00	25.00
174	Bob Skinner	8.00	3.25	2.00
175	Bill Virdon	10.00	4.00	2.50
176	Smoky Burgess	40.00	16.00	10.00
177	Elroy Face	17.50	7.00	4.50
178	Bob Friend	10.00	4.00	2.50
179	Vernon Law	10.00	4.00	2.50
180	Harvey Haddix	10.00	4.00	2.50
181	Hal Smith	85.00	35.00	20.00
182	Ed Bouchee	100.00	40.00	25.00
183	Don Zimmer	10.00	4.00	2.50
184	Ron Santo	13.50	5.50	3.50
185	Andre Rogers (Rodgers)	8.00	3.25	2.00
186	Richie Ashburn	30.00	12.00	7.50
187	George Altman	8.00	3.25	2.00
188	Ernie Banks	40.00	16.00	10.00
189	Sam Taylor	30.00	12.00	7.50
190	Don Elston	8.00	3.25	2.00
191	Jerry Kindall	8.00	3.25	2.00
192	Pancho Herrera	8.00	3.25	2.00
193	Tony Taylor	8.00	3.25	2.00
194	Ruben Amaro	8.00	3.25	2.00
195	Don Demeter	55.00	22.50	13.50
196	Bobby Gene Smith	8.00	3.25	2.00
197	Clay Dalrymple	8.00	3.25	2.00
198	Robin Roberts	45.00	18.00	11.00
199	Art Mahaffey	8.00	3.25	2.00
200	John Buzhardt	10.00	4.00	2.50

1963 Post Cereal

Another 200-player, 3-1/2" x 2-1/2" set that, with variations, totals more than 205 cards. Numerous color variations also exist due to the different cereal boxes on which the cards were printed. More than any of the other 1960s Post baseball issues, the set is rife with short-prints and other scarcities which make it more difficult to complete than earlier years' sets. The 1963 Post cards are almost identical to the '63 Jell-O set, which is a slight 1/4" narrower. Cards are blank-backed, with a color player photo, biographies and statistics on the numbered card fronts. No Post logo appears on the '63 cards. The complete set price does not include the scarcer variations. An album to hold the cards was given away at grocery stores in a display featuring Mickey Mantle.

		NM	EX	VG
Complete Set (200):		4,500	1,800	1,000
Common Player:		5.00	2.00	1.25
1	Vic Power	6.00	2.50	1.50
2	Bernie Allen	6.00	2.50	1.50
3	Zoilo Versalles	7.50	3.00	2.00
4	Rich Rollins	5.00	2.00	1.25
5	Harmon Killebrew	25.00	10.00	6.00
6	Lenny Green	35.00	15.00	9.00
7	Bob Allison	9.00	3.50	2.00
8	Earl Battey	12.50	5.00	3.00
9	Camilo Pascual	15.00	6.00	3.50
10a	Jim Kaat (Light pole in background.)	15.00	6.00	3.50
10b	Jim Kaat (No light pole.)	10.00	4.00	2.50
11	Jack Kralick	7.50	3.00	2.00
12	Bill Skowron	15.00	6.00	3.50
13	Bobby Richardson	15.00	6.00	3.50
14	Cletis Boyer	6.00	2.50	1.50
15	Mickey Mantle	300.00	120.00	75.00
16	Roger Maris	115.00	45.00	30.00
17	Yogi Berra	30.00	12.00	7.50
18	Elston Howard	13.50	5.50	3.50
19	Whitey Ford	15.00	6.00	3.50
20	Ralph Terry	6.00	2.50	1.50
21	John Blanchard	10.00	4.00	2.50
22	Bill Stafford	5.00	2.00	1.25
23	Tom Tresh	9.00	3.50	2.00
24	Steve Bilko	15.00	6.00	3.50
25	Bill Moran	5.00	2.00	1.25
26a	Joe Koppe (1962 Avg. is .277)	17.50	7.00	4.50
26b	Joe Koppe (1962 Avg. is .227)	35.00	15.00	9.00
27	Felix Torres	7.50	3.00	2.00
28a	Leon Wagner (Lifetime Avg. is .278.)	15.00	6.00	3.50
28b	Leon Wagner (Lifetime Avg. is .272.)	25.00	10.00	6.00
29	Albie Pearson	5.00	2.00	1.25
30	Lee Thomas (Photo actually George Thomas.)	75.00	30.00	18.50
31	Bob Rodgers	5.00	2.00	1.25
32	Dean Chance	5.00	2.00	1.25
33	Ken McBride	7.50	3.00	2.00
34	George Thomas (Photo actually Lee Thomas.)	9.00	3.50	2.00
35	Joe Cunningham	5.00	2.00	1.25
36a	Nelson Fox (No bat showing.)	30.00	12.00	7.50
36b	Nelson Fox (Part of bat showing.)	25.00	10.00	6.00
37	Luis Aparicio	15.00	6.00	3.75
38	Al Smith	50.00	20.00	12.50
39	Floyd Robinson	100.00	40.00	25.00
40	Jim Landis	5.00	2.00	1.25
41	Charlie Maxwell	5.00	2.00	1.25
42	Sherman Lollar	5.00	2.00	1.25
43	Early Wynn	9.00	3.50	2.00
44	Juan Pizarro	5.00	2.00	1.25
45	Ray Herbert	5.00	2.00	1.25
46	Norm Cash	25.00	10.00	6.25
47	Steve Boros	5.00	2.00	1.25
48	Dick McAuliffe	35.00	15.00	9.00
49	Bill Bruton	12.50	5.00	3.00
50	Rocky Colavito	25.00	10.00	6.25
51	Al Kaline	25.00	10.00	6.25
52	Dick Brown	5.00	2.00	1.25
53	Jim Bunning	100.00	40.00	25.00
54	Hank Aguirre	5.00	2.00	1.25
55	Frank Lary	5.00	2.00	1.25
56	Don Mossi	7.50	3.00	2.00
57	Jim Gentile	9.00	3.50	2.00
58	Jackie Brandt	7.50	3.00	2.00
59	Brooks Robinson	25.00	10.00	6.00
60	Ron Hansen	5.00	2.00	1.25
61	Jerry Adair	130.00	50.00	30.00
62	John (Boog) Powell	15.00	6.00	3.75
63	Russ Snyder	5.00	2.00	1.25
64	Steve Barber	7.50	3.00	2.00
65	Milt Pappas	5.00	2.00	1.25
66	Robin Roberts	10.00	4.00	2.50
67	Tito Francona	5.00	2.00	1.25
68	Jerry Kindall	12.50	5.00	3.00
69	Woodie Held	5.00	2.00	1.25
70	Bubba Phillips	25.00	10.00	6.00
71	Chuck Essegian	5.00	2.00	1.25
72	Willie Kirkland	5.00	2.00	1.25
73	Al Luplow	5.00	2.00	1.25
74	Ty Cline	5.00	2.00	1.25
75	Dick Donovan	5.00	2.00	1.25
76	John Romano	5.00	2.00	1.25
77	Pete Runnels	6.00	2.50	1.50
78	Ed Bressoud	5.00	2.00	1.25
79	Frank Malzone	10.00	4.00	2.50
80	Carl Yastrzemski	250.00	100.00	62.00
81	Gary Geiger	5.00	2.00	1.25
82	Lou Clinton	5.00	2.00	1.25
83	Earl Wilson	7.50	3.00	2.00
84	Bill Monbouquette	5.00	2.00	1.25
85	Norm Siebern	5.00	2.00	1.25
86	Jerry Lumpe	100.00	40.00	25.00
87	Manny Jimenez	150.00	60.00	37.50
88	Gino Cimoli	9.00	3.50	2.00
89	Ed Charles	5.00	2.00	1.25
90	Ed Rakow	5.00	2.00	1.25
91	Bob Del Greco	5.00	2.00	1.25
92	Haywood Sullivan	5.00	2.00	1.25
93	Chuck Hinton	5.00	2.00	1.25
94	Ken Retzer	12.50	5.00	3.00
95	Harry Bright	5.00	2.00	1.25
96	Bob Johnson	7.50	3.00	2.00
97	Dave Stenhouse	20.00	8.00	5.00
98	Chuck Cottier	25.00	10.00	6.25
99	Tom Cheney	7.50	3.00	2.00
100	Claude Osteen	35.00	15.00	9.00
101	Orlando Cepeda	7.50	3.00	2.00
102	Charley Hiller	7.50	3.00	2.00
103	Jose Pagan	5.00	2.00	1.25
104	Jim Davenport	5.00	2.00	1.25
105	Harvey Kuenn	15.00	6.00	3.50
106	Willie Mays	40.00	16.00	10.00
107	Felipe Alou	7.50	3.00	2.00
108	Tom Haller	100.00	40.00	25.00
109	Juan Marichal	10.00	4.00	2.50
110	Jack Sanford	5.00	2.00	1.25
111	Bill O'Dell	5.00	2.00	1.25
112	Willie McCovey	12.50	5.00	3.00
113	Lee Walls	10.00	4.00	2.50
114	Jim Gilliam	15.00	6.00	3.50
115	Maury Wills	17.50	7.00	4.50
116	Ron Fairly	5.00	2.00	1.25
117	Tommy Davis	5.00	2.00	1.25
118	Duke Snider	25.00	10.00	6.25
119	Willie Davis	225.00	90.00	55.00
120	John Roseboro	5.00	2.00	1.25
121	Sandy Koufax	50.00	20.00	12.50
122	Stan Williams	9.00	3.50	2.00
123	Don Drysdale	20.00	8.00	5.00
124a	Daryl Spencer (No arm showing.)	7.50	3.00	2.00
124b	Daryl Spencer (Part of arm showing.)	15.00	6.00	3.50
125	Gordy Coleman	7.50	3.00	2.00
126	Don Blasingame	5.00	2.00	1.25
127	Leo Cardenas	5.00	2.00	1.25
128	Eddie Kasko	200.00	80.00	50.00
129	Jerry Lynch	35.00	15.00	9.75
130	Vada Pinson	15.00	6.00	3.50
131a	Frank Robinson (No stripes on cap.)	30.00	12.00	7.50
131b	Frank Robinson (Stripes on cap.)	75.00	30.00	17.50
132	John Edwards	15.00	6.00	3.50
133	Joey Jay	5.00	2.00	1.25
134	Bob Purkey	5.00	2.00	1.25
135	Marty Keough	15.00	6.00	3.50
136	Jim O'Toole	5.00	2.00	1.25
137	Dick Stuart	7.50	3.00	2.00
138	Bill Mazeroski	12.50	5.00	3.00
139	Dick Groat	6.00	2.50	1.50
140	Don Hoak	25.00	10.00	6.00
141	Bob Skinner	25.00	10.00	6.25
142	Bill Virdon	5.00	2.00	1.25
143	Roberto Clemente	60.00	24.00	15.00
144	Smoky Burgess	15.00	6.00	3.50
145	Bob Friend	5.00	2.00	1.25
146	Al McBean	5.00	2.00	1.25
147	El Roy Face (Elroy)	20.00	8.00	5.00
148	Joe Adcock	13.50	5.50	3.50
149	Frank Bolling	5.00	2.00	1.25
150	Roy McMillan	7.50	3.00	2.00
151	Eddie Mathews	22.50	9.00	5.75
152	Hank Aaron	50.00	20.00	12.50
153	Del Crandall	25.00	10.00	6.25
154a	Bob Shaw (Third sentence has "In 1959" twice.)	10.00	4.00	2.50
154b	Bob Shaw (Third sentence has "In 1959" once.)	9.00	3.50	2.00
155	Lew Burdette	20.00	8.00	5.00
156	Joe Torre	7.50	3.00	2.00
157	Tony Cloninger	5.00	2.00	1.25
158a	Bill White (Ht. 6')	6.00	2.50	1.50
158b	Bill White (Ht. 6'0")	6.00	2.50	1.50
159	Julian Javier	5.00	2.00	1.25
160	Ken Boyer	7.50	3.00	2.00
161	Julio Gotay	5.00	2.00	1.25
162	Curt Flood	100.00	40.00	25.00
163	Charlie James	9.00	3.50	2.00
164	Gene Oliver	5.00	2.00	1.25
165	Ernie Broglio	15.00	6.00	3.50
166	Bob Gibson	45.00	18.00	11.00
167a	Lindy McDaniel (Asterisk before trade line.)	10.00	4.00	2.50
167b	Lindy McDaniel (No asterisk before trade line.)	12.50	5.00	3.25
168	Ray Washburn	5.00	2.00	1.25
169	Ernie Banks	17.50	7.00	4.50
170	Ron Santo	25.00	10.00	6.25
171	George Altman	7.50	3.00	2.00
172	Billy Williams	95.00	35.00	25.00
173	Andre Rodgers	10.00	4.00	2.50
174	Ken Hubbs	25.00	10.00	6.00
175	Don Landrum	5.00	2.00	1.25
176	Dick Bertell	20.00	8.00	5.00
177	Roy Sievers	7.50	3.00	2.00
178	Tony Taylor	12.50	5.00	3.50
179	John Callison	5.00	2.00	1.25
180	Don Demeter	5.00	2.00	1.25
181	Tony Gonzalez	25.00	10.00	6.25
182	Wes Covington	35.00	15.00	9.00
183	Art Mahaffey	5.00	2.00	1.25
184	Clay Dalrymple	7.50	3.00	2.00
185	Al Spangler	6.00	2.50	1.50
186	Roman Mejias	7.50	3.00	2.00
187	Bob Aspromonte	475.00	190.00	120.00
188	Norm Larker	25.00	10.00	6.00
189	Johnny Temple	7.50	3.00	2.00
190	Carl Warwick	15.00	6.00	3.50
191	Bob Lillis	9.00	3.50	2.00
192	Dick Farrell	5.00	2.00	1.25
193	Gil Hodges	15.00	6.00	3.50
194	Marv Throneberry	7.50	3.00	2.00
195	Charlie Neal	30.00	12.00	7.50
196	Frank Thomas	235.00	95.00	60.00
197	Richie Ashburn	35.00	15.00	9.00
198	Felix Mantilla	10.00	4.00	2.50
199	Rod Kanehl	60.00	25.00	15.00
200	Roger Craig	10.00	4.00	2.50

1963 Post/Jell-O Album

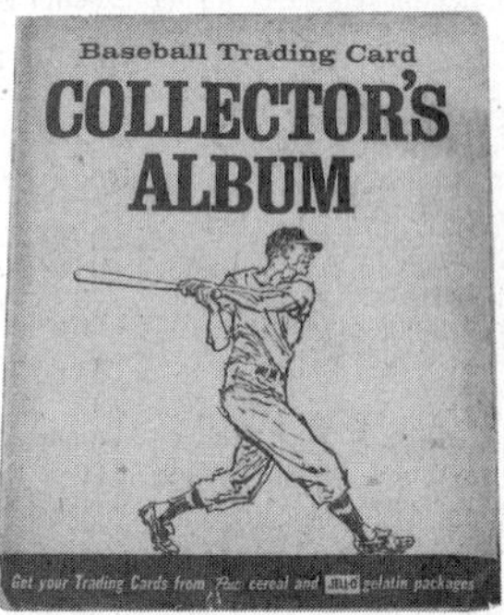

The baseball history and other printed matter in this 26-page 8-1/2" x 11" album seems to point to 1963 as the issue date, though 1962 would not be impossible. Each major league team has a page on which the box-back cards from Post cereals and Jell-O could be pasted. The front cover is printed in red-and-white while the interior pages are in black-and-white.

	NM	EX	VG
Post/Jell-O Album	90.00	45.00	25.00

1978 Post Cereal Steve Garvey Baseball Tips

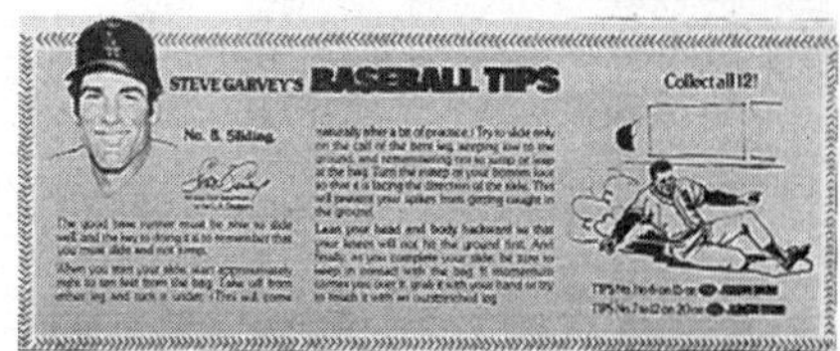

These 7-1/8" x 2-5/8" cut-out panels bordered in red "baseball" stitching were printed on the backs of 15-oz. (#1-6) and 20-oz. (#7-12) packages of Post Raisin Brand cereal. The panels have a green background with black-and-white artwork of a generic player illustrating the tip and a color portrait of Garvey.

		NM	EX	VG
Complete Set (12):		30.00	15.00	9.00
Common Panel:		3.00	1.50	.90
1	The Batting Stance	3.00	1.50	.90
2	Bunting	3.00	1.50	.90
3	Rounding First Base	3.00	1.50	.90
4	The Grip in Throwing	3.00	1.50	.90
5	Fielding a Pop-Up	3.00	1.50	.90
6	Proper Fielding Stances	3.00	1.50	.90
7	On-Deck Observation	3.00	1.50	.90
8	Sliding	3.00	1.50	.90
9	Hitting to the Opposite Field	3.00	1.50	.90
10	Throwing From the Outfield	3.00	1.50	.90
11	Mental Preparation for Each Play	3.00	1.50	.90
12	Total Conditioning	3.00	1.50	.90

1978 Post-Intelligencer 1969 Pilot Profiles

This series of cards of the one-year American League team states on its back they are reprinted from the Seattle Post-Intelligencer newspaper. The 2-3/8" x 5" cards are printed in black-and-white on semi-gloss cardboard. Fronts feature a

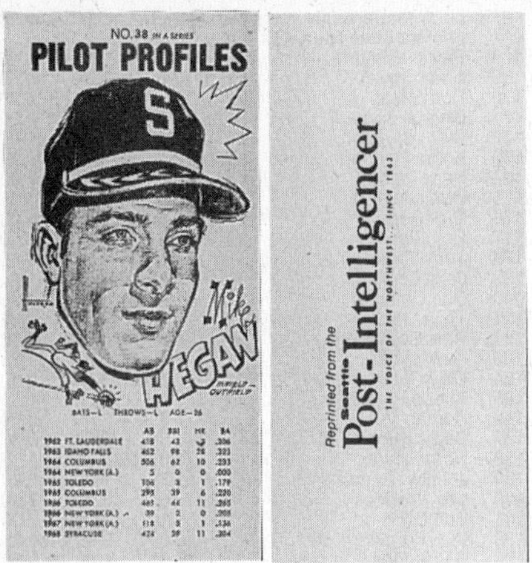

pencil caricature of the player and include major and minor league stats. A card number is at top. Backs have the newspaper's ad. The cards were a collectors' issue produced by long-time minor league card maker Frank Caruso, with the paper's permission. The cartoons originally ran in a 3" x 6-3/8" format within the pages of the newspaper and are themselves highly collectible, with values about 2X-3X those of the reprints listed here. Reprint sets were originally sold for $6.

		NM	EX	VG
Complete Set (39):		100.00	50.00	30.00
Common Player:		4.00	3.00	1.50
1	Don Mincher	4.00	3.00	1.50
2	Tommy Harper	5.00	2.50	1.50
3	Ray Oyler	4.00	3.00	1.50
4	Jerry McNertney	4.00	3.00	1.50
5	Not issued	4.00	3.00	1.50
6	Tommy Davis	5.00	2.50	1.50
7	Gary Bell	4.00	3.00	1.50
8	Chico Salmon	4.00	3.00	1.50
9	Jack Aker	4.00	3.00	1.50
10	Rich Rollins	4.00	3.00	1.50
11	Diego Segui	4.00	3.00	1.50
12	Steve Barber	5.00	2.50	1.50
13	Wayne Comer	4.00	3.00	1.50
14	John Kennedy	4.00	3.00	1.50
15	Buzz Stephen	4.00	3.00	1.50
16	Jim Gosger	4.00	3.00	1.50
17	Mike Ferraro	4.00	3.00	1.50
18	Marty Pattin	4.00	3.00	1.50
19	Gerry Schoen	4.00	3.00	1.50
20	Steve Hovely	4.00	3.00	1.50
21	Frank Crosetti	5.00	2.50	1.50
22	Charles Bates	4.00	3.00	1.50
23	Jose Vidal	4.00	3.00	1.50
24	Bob Richmond	4.00	3.00	1.50
25	Lou Piniella	6.00	3.00	1.75
26	John Miklos	4.00	3.00	1.50
27	John Morris	4.00	3.00	1.50
28	Larry Haney	4.00	3.00	1.50
29	Mike Marshall	5.00	2.50	1.50
30	Marv Staehle	4.00	3.00	1.50
31	Gus Gil	4.00	3.00	1.50
32	Sal Maglie	5.00	2.50	1.50
33	Ron Plaza	4.00	3.00	1.50
34	Ed O'Brien	4.00	3.00	1.50
35	Jim Bouton	6.00	3.00	1.75
36	Bill Stafford	4.00	3.00	1.50
37	Darrell Brandon	4.00	3.00	1.50
38	Mike Hegan	4.00	3.00	1.50
39	Dick Baney	4.00	3.00	1.50

1910 Doc Powers Day Postcard

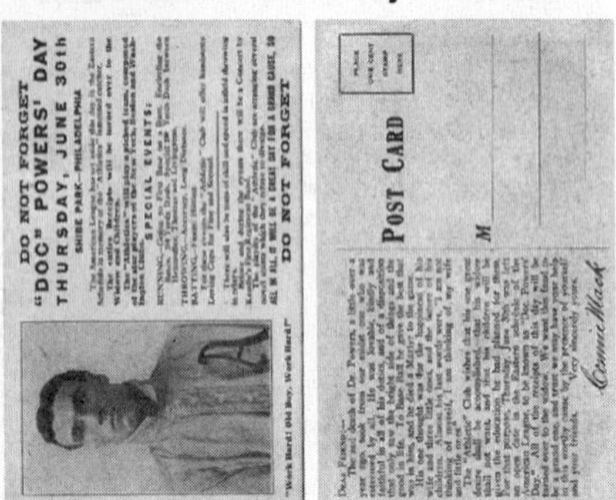

To announce to fans the forthcoming "'Doc' Powers' Day" benefit game, the Philadelphia A's produced this standard-sized (about 5-1/2" x 3-1/2") black-and-white postcard. Front has a photo of the late A's catcher and information about the special events to be held June 30. On back is a message over the facsimile autograph of Connie Mack asking fans to remember the widow and children of their fallen star.

	NM	EX	VG
Doc Powers	750.00	375.00	225.00

1975 Praeger Publishers Ty Cobb

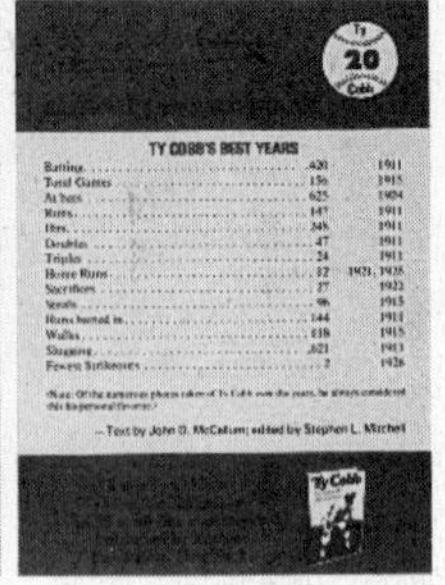

This set was produced by Washington state collector Stephen Mitchell in conjunction with Praeger Publishers of New York to promote the book "Ty Cobb" by John McCallum. Slightly larger than the current 2-1/2" x 3-1/2" standard, the cards featured black-and-white photos on front surrounded by a woodgrain-effect frame and with a plaque at bottom bearing the card title. Backs have an excerpt from the book, an ad for the book and a facsimile autograph. Cards are numbered in a baseball at upper-right. Sets originally sold for $3.25.

		NM	EX	VG
Complete Set (20):		25.00	12.50	7.50
Common Card:		2.00	1.00	.60
1	Ty Breaks In	3.00	1.50	.90
2	Four Inches of the Plate	2.00	1.00	.60
3	Slashing into Third	2.00	1.00	.60
4	Inking Another Contract	2.00	1.00	.60
5	Captain Tyrus R. Cobb	2.00	1.00	.60
6	Ty with "The Big Train" (With Walter Johnson.)	4.00	2.00	1.25
7	The End of an Era (With Babe Ruth.)	6.00	3.00	1.75
8	All-Time Centerfielder	2.00	1.00	.60
9	Ty Could "Walk 'em down"	2.00	1.00	.60
10	Menacing Batsman	2.00	1.00	.60
11	With Brother Paul	2.00	1.00	.60
12	Thomas Edison, Cobb Fan	3.00	1.50	.90
13	Ty Tangles with Muggsy McGraw	2.50	1.25	.70
14	Author McCallum with Cy Young	2.00	1.00	.60
15	Speaker - DiMaggio - Cobb	5.00	2.50	1.50
16	Ted Gets a Lesson (With Ted Williams.)	5.00	2.50	1.50
17	Five for Fivel	2.00	1.00	.60
18	"I have but one regret ..."	2.00	1.00	.60
19	Excellence: The Cobb Standard	2.00	1.00	.60
20	His Favorite Photo	3.00	1.50	.90

1954 Preferred Products Milwaukee Braves

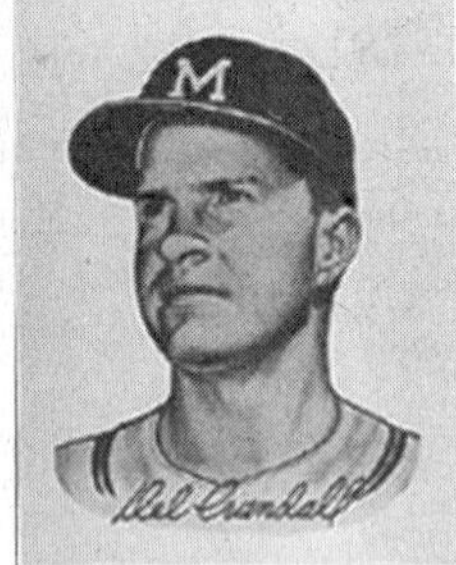

Sold as a 12-piece set in an envelope marked "Braves Team Autographed Portraits," this portfolio was one of several issued in the team's early years in Milwaukee. The artwork is apparently by Scott Douglas, whose copyright appears on the outer envelope. The same pictures can be found on Preferred Product felt patches and t-shirts. These 8" x 10" portraits are printed in sepia on cream-colored heavy textured paper and feature facsimile autographs. Backs are blank. The unnumbered portraits are checklisted here alphabetically.

		NM	EX	VG
Complete Set (12):		300.00	150.00	90.00
Common Player:		25.00	12.50	7.50
(1)	Joe Adcock	25.00	12.50	7.50
(2)	Bill Bruton	25.00	12.50	7.50
(3)	Bob Buhl	25.00	12.50	7.50
(4)	Lew Burdette	25.00	12.50	7.50
(5)	Del Crandall	25.00	12.50	7.50
(6)	Johnny Logan	25.00	12.50	7.50
(7)	Ed Mathews	40.00	20.00	12.00
(8)	Danny O'Connell	25.00	12.50	7.50
(9)	Andy Pafko	25.00	12.50	7.50
(10)	Jim Pendleton	25.00	12.50	7.50
(11)	Warren Spahn	40.00	20.00	12.00
(12)	Bob Thomson	25.00	12.50	7.50

1954 Preferred Products Milwaukee Braves Patches

While they are not so identified, the use of the same portraits and facsimile autographs found on the company's player pictures pinpoint this as a Preferred Products issue, as does

a paper tag enclosed in the cellophane wrapper in which the patch was sold. The patches are of heavy felt, with blue or sepia pictures and red "stitching" on the baseball background. At 4-7/8" in diameter, they were intended to be sewn to jackets, etc. While only a handful of players have been confirmed to date, it is possible, even likely, that all 12 of the players from the picture set were also issued in this format.

		NM	EX	VG
Common Player:		175.00	85.00	50.00
(1)	Joe Adcock	175.00	85.00	50.00
(2)	Bill Bruton	175.00	85.00	50.00
(3)	Lew Burdette	175.00	85.00	50.00
(5)	Del Crandall	175.00	85.00	50.00
(6)	Johnny Logan	175.00	85.00	50.00
(7)	Eddie Mathews	125.00	65.00	35.00
(8)	Danny O'Connell	175.00	85.00	50.00
(9)	Andy Pafko	175.00	85.00	50.00
(11)	Warren Spahn	125.00	65.00	35.00

1957-60 Preferred Products Milwaukee Braves

Similar in format to the company's 1954 issue, these 8" x 10" portraits are printed in sepia on cream-colored heavy textured paper with player names printed beneath. Backs are blank. The unnumbered portraits are checklisted here alphabetically, but the list may not be complete.

		NM	EX	VG
Common Player:		25.00	12.50	7.50
(1)	Hank Aaron	100.00	50.00	30.00
(2)	Joe Adcock	25.00	12.50	7.50
(3)	Bill Bruton	25.00	12.50	7.50
(4)	Lew Burdette	25.00	12.50	7.50
(5)	Wes Covington	25.00	12.50	7.50
(6)	Johnny Logan	25.00	12.50	7.50
(7)	Carl Sawatski	25.00	12.50	7.50
(8)	Red Schoendienst	35.00	17.50	10.50
(9)	Frank Torre	25.00	12.50	7.50

1950 Prest-O-lite

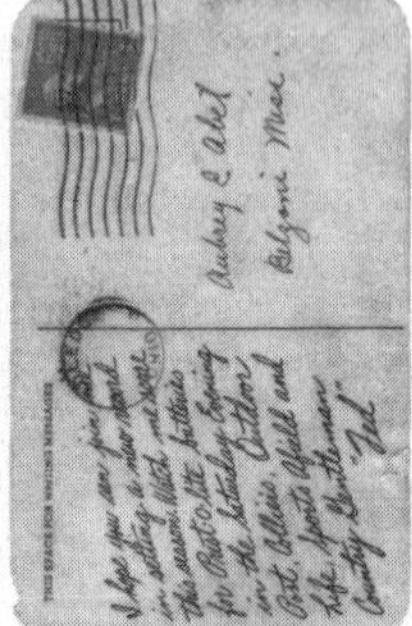

The attributed date of issue is approximate for this multi-sport promotional postcard issue. Besides the two baseball players, football stars Doak Walker and Leon Hart also exist. The black-and-white, approximately 3-1/2" x 5-1/2" cards on front have a borderless action pose with a salutation and facsimile autograph. The postcard-style divided back has a pre-printed message over the player's facsimile autograph, asking the recipient to view ads for the battery manufacturer in various magazines.

	NM	EX	VG
Tommy Henrich	200.00	100.00	60.00
Ted Williams	400.00	200.00	120.00

1914 Pritchard Publishing Giants/Yankees Stamps

These colorful large-format (about 1-7/8" x 2-5/8") stamps are copyrighted 1914 by Pritchard Publishing Co., New York. All players are N.Y. Giants or Yankees. A similar issue of Yale baseball players is listed in the minor league section. The unnumbered stamps are listed alphabetically by team.

		NM	EX	VG
Common Player:		200.00	100.00	60.00
	N.Y. GIANTS			
(1)	Bob Bescher	200.00	100.00	60.00
(2)	George Burns	200.00	100.00	60.00
(3)	Josh Devore	200.00	100.00	60.00
(4)	Larry Doyle	200.00	100.00	60.00
(5)	Art Fletcher	200.00	100.00	60.00
(6)	Christy Mathewson	900.00	450.00	270.00
(7)	Fred Merkle	200.00	100.00	60.00
(8)	Chief Meyers	200.00	100.00	60.00
(9)	Red Murray	200.00	100.00	60.00
(10)	Fred Snodgrass	200.00	100.00	60.00
	N.Y. YANKEES			
(1)	Ray Caldwell	200.00	100.00	60.00
(2)	Les Channell	200.00	100.00	60.00
(3)	Roy Hartzell	200.00	100.00	60.00
(4)	Bill Holden	200.00	100.00	60.00
(5)	Fritz Maisel	200.00	100.00	60.00
(6)	Roger Peckinpaugh	200.00	100.00	60.00
(7)	Jeff Sweeney	200.00	100.00	60.00
(8)	Jimmy Walsh	200.00	100.00	60.00
(9)	Harry Williams	200.00	100.00	60.00

1956 Prize Frankies Cleveland Indians

Though the back of the cards says 24 Indians' cards were issued, only one player has ever been seen - and precious few of him. The 2-1/4" x 3-3/8" cards have a black-and-white photo on front with the player's name and number in black in the white border at bottom. Backs have an Indian logo and instructions to redeem complete sets of the cards for a pair of box seats. It is unlikely this alone accounts for the scarcity of the cards. More likely this card was made as a prototype for a promotion that never materialized.

		NM	EX	VG
10	Vic Wertz	600.00	300.00	180.00

1924 Proctor's Theatre Babe Ruth

This 1-5/8" x 2-7/8" black-and-white card was issued to promote a vaudeville appearance by Babe Ruth in upstate New York during November 1924. The front has a photo with a facsimile autograph inscribed, "To My Mount Vernon Admirers." Back has details of his appearance.

COMPLIMENTS OF
Mr. F. F. Proctor
TO
BABE RUTH'S
MANY MT. VERNON
FRIENDS
APPEARING AT
PROCTOR'S
MOUNT VERNON
Nov. 3rd-4th-5th

	NM	EX	VG
Babe Ruth	9,000	4,500	2,700

1946-47 Propagandas Montiel Los Reyes del Deporte

Propagandas MONTIEL presenta
LOS REYES DEL DEPORTE
29
ADOLFO LUQUE
(Papá Montero)

Nació en la Habana, el 4 de Agosto de 1890. Batea y tira a la derecha. Debutó en las Grandes Ligas en 1914. En 1915 lanzó para el Toronto y en 1916, 1917 y parte de 1918 estuvo en el Louisville. A fines de 1918 pasó al Cincinnatti. En 1932 al New York Gigantes. En las Grandes Ligas ganó 194 juegos y perdió 179. En 1923 fué Champion Pitcher de la Liga Nacional. Participó en las Series Mundiales de 1919 y 1933. Recientemente firmó con su muy querido Almendares.

The 180 athletes in this issue of "Sporting Kings" cards are featured in a couple of different styles. Most cards from #1-101 have only the athlete's photo on front, surrounded by a yellow or orange border. Most cards #100-180 also have the card number and player ID on front, with a chest-to-cap photo set a colored frame. All are roughly 2-1/8" x 3-1/8". Backs have biographical data, the issuer's name and, sometimes, an ad for a Cuban novelty store or radio program. Most examples in the hobby today were once pasted in the colorful album accompanying the issue and it is rare to find cards in better than VG condition. The set opens with a run of boxers, then a group of Cuban baseball stars of the past and present, former big league greats and contemporary major leaguers, plus a few wrestlers. Cards #100-180 (except 101) feature players from the Florida International League, a Class B circuit within Organized Baseball with teams in Havana, Miami, Miami Beach, Lakeland and Tampa included. Curiously, the West Palm Beach team is not represented.

		NM	EX	VG
Complete Set (180):		20,000	8,800	4,000
Common Baseball Player:		45.00	20.00	9.00
Album:		300.00	135.00	60.00
1	John L. Sullivan (Boxer)	135.00	60.00	27.50
2	James J. Corbett (Boxer)	85.00	37.50	17.50
3	Bob Fitzsimmons (Boxer)	70.00	30.00	15.00
4	James J. Jeffries (Boxer)	85.00	37.50	17.50
5	Tommy Burns (Boxer)	70.00	30.00	15.00
6	Jack Johnson (Boxer)	90.00	40.00	18.00
7	Jess Willard (Boxer)	75.00	35.00	15.00
8	Jack Dempsey (Boxer)	135.00	60.00	27.50
9	Gene Tunney (Boxer)	75.00	35.00	15.00
10	Max Schmeling (Boxer)	75.00	35.00	15.00
11	Jack Sharkey (Boxer)	70.00	30.00	15.00
12	Primo Carnera (Boxer)	70.00	30.00	15.00
13	Max Baer (Boxer)	70.00	30.00	15.00
14	James J. Braddock (Boxer)	70.00	30.00	15.00
15	Joe Louis (Boxer)	135.00	60.00	27.50
16	Georges Carpentier (Boxer)	70.00	30.00	15.00
17	Tommy Loughran (Boxer)	70.00	30.00	15.00
18	Tony Zale (Boxer)	70.00	30.00	15.00
19	Johnny Dundee (Boxer)	55.00	25.00	10.00
20	Billy Conn (Boxer)	70.00	30.00	15.00
21	Holman Williams (Boxer)	55.00	25.00	10.00
22	Kid Tuncro (Tunero) (Boxer)	55.00	25.00	10.00
23	Lazaro Salazar	300.00	135.00	60.00
24	Napoleon Reyes	120.00	55.00	25.00
25	Roberto Estalella	110.00	50.00	22.50
26	Juan Oliva (Boxer)	55.00	25.00	10.00
27	Gilberto Torres	75.00	35.00	15.00
28	Heberto Blanco	75.00	35.00	15.00
29	Adolfo Luque	375.00	175.00	75.00
30	Luis Galvani (Boxer)	55.00	25.00	10.00
31	Miguel Angel Gonzalez	195.00	90.00	40.00
32	Chuck Klein	110.00	50.00	22.50
33	Joe Legon (Boxer)	55.00	25.00	10.00
34	Carlos Blanco	75.00	35.00	15.00
35	Santos Amaro	225.00	100.00	45.00
36	Kid Chocolate (Boxer)	85.00	37.50	17.50
37	Henry Armstrong (Boxer)	55.00	25.00	10.00
38	Silvio Garcia	300.00	135.00	60.00
39	Martin Dihigo	3,000	1,350	600.00
40	Fermin Guerra	120.00	55.00	25.00
41	Babe Ruth	1,250	560.00	250.00
42	Ty Cobb	450.00	200.00	90.00
43	Alejandro Crespo	75.00	35.00	15.00
44	Ted Williams	900.00	400.00	180.00
45	Jose Maria Fernandez	85.00	37.50	17.50
46	Dom DiMaggio	110.00	50.00	22.50
47	Julio Rojo	75.00	35.00	15.00
48	Armando Marsans	110.00	50.00	22.50
49	Dick Sisler	75.00	35.00	15.00
50	Antonio Rodriguez	75.00	35.00	15.00
51	Joscito Rodriguez	75.00	35.00	15.00
52	Antonio Ordenana	80.00	35.00	15.00
53	Armandito Pi (Boxer)	55.00	25.00	10.00
54	Paul Derringer	75.00	35.00	15.00
55	Bob Feller	185.00	85.00	37.50
56a	Bill Dickey (Photo is Gabby Hartnett.) (Light cap.)	150.00	65.00	30.00
56b	Bill Dickey (Corrected photo.) (Dark cap.)	225.00	100.00	45.00
57	Lou Gehrig	750.00	335.00	150.00
58	Joe DiMaggio	1,575	710.00	315.00
59	Hank Greenberg	165.00	75.00	35.00
60	Red Ruffing	110.00	50.00	22.50
61	Tex Hughson	75.00	35.00	15.00
62	Bucky Walters	75.00	35.00	15.00
63	Stanley Hack	75.00	35.00	15.00
64	Stanley Musial	600.00	275.00	125.00
65	Melvin Ott	135.00	60.00	27.50
66	Dutch Leonard	75.00	35.00	15.00
67	Frank Overmire	75.00	35.00	15.00
68	Mort Cooper	75.00	35.00	15.00
69	Edward Miller	75.00	35.00	15.00
70	Jimmie Foxx	165.00	75.00	35.00
71	Joseph Cronin	110.00	50.00	22.50
72	James Vernon	75.00	35.00	15.00
73	Carl Hubbell	165.00	75.00	35.00
74	Andrew Pafko	75.00	35.00	15.00
75	David Ferris	75.00	35.00	15.00
76	John Mize	110.00	50.00	22.50
77	Spud Chandler	75.00	35.00	15.00
78	Joseph Medwick	110.00	50.00	22.50
79	Christy Mathewson	450.00	200.00	90.00
80	Nelson Potter	75.00	35.00	15.00
81	James Tabor	75.00	35.00	15.00
82	Martin Marion	75.00	35.00	15.00
83	Rip Sewell	75.00	35.00	15.00
84	Philip Cavaretta (Cavarretta)	75.00	35.00	15.00
85	Al Lopez	110.00	50.00	22.50
86	Rudy York	75.00	35.00	15.00
87	Walter Masterson	75.00	35.00	15.00
88	Roger Wolff	75.00	35.00	15.00
89	Jacob Early	75.00	35.00	15.00
90	Oswald Bluege	75.00	35.00	15.00
91	Zoco Godoy (Wrestler)	45.00	20.00	9.00
92	John Kelly Lewis	75.00	35.00	15.00
93	Well Stewart (Wrestler)	45.00	20.00	9.00
94	Bruce Campbell	75.00	35.00	15.00
95	Sherrod Robertson	75.00	35.00	15.00
96	Rose Evans (Wrestler)	45.00	20.00	9.00
97	Maurice "El Angel" Tillet (Wrestler)	45.00	20.00	9.00
98	Nicholas Altrock	75.00	35.00	15.00
99	Helen Willis (Tennis)	70.00	30.00	15.00
100	Borrest Smith	45.00	20.00	9.00
101	Merito Acosta	80.00	35.00	15.00
102	Oscar Rodriguez	45.00	20.00	9.00
103	Octavio Rubert	45.00	20.00	9.00
104	Antonio Lorenzo	45.00	20.00	9.00
105	Agustin del Toro	45.00	20.00	9.00
106	Hector Arago	45.00	20.00	9.00
107	Agustin de la Ville	45.00	20.00	9.00
108	Valeriano (Lilo) Fano	45.00	20.00	9.00
109	Orlando Moreno	45.00	20.00	9.00
110	"Bicho" Dunabeitia	45.00	20.00	9.00
111	Rafael Rivas	45.00	20.00	9.00
112	Jose Traspuestro	45.00	20.00	9.00
113	Mario Diaz	45.00	20.00	9.00
114	Armando Valdes	45.00	20.00	9.00
115	Alberto Matos	45.00	20.00	9.00
116	Humberto Baez	45.00	20.00	9.00
117	Orlando (Tango) Suarez	45.00	20.00	9.00
118	Manuel (Chino) Hidalgo	45.00	20.00	9.00
119	Fernando Rodriguez	45.00	20.00	9.00
120	Jose Cendan	45.00	20.00	9.00
121	Francisco Gallardo	45.00	20.00	9.00
122	Orlando Mejido	45.00	20.00	9.00
123	Julio (Jiqui) Moreno	45.00	20.00	9.00
124	Efrain Vinajcras	45.00	20.00	9.00
125	Luis Suarez	45.00	20.00	9.00
126	Oscar del Calvo	45.00	20.00	9.00
127	Julio Gomez	45.00	20.00	9.00
128	Ernesto Morillas	45.00	20.00	9.00
129	Leonardo Goicochea	45.00	20.00	9.00
130	Max Rosenfeld	300.00	135.00	60.00
131	Oscar Garmendia	45.00	20.00	9.00
132	Fernando Solis	45.00	20.00	9.00
133	Oliverio Ortiz	55.00	25.00	10.00
134	Osmaro Blanco	45.00	20.00	9.00
135	Oral Ratliff	45.00	20.00	9.00
136	Deo Grose	45.00	20.00	9.00
137	Homer Daugherty	45.00	20.00	9.00
138	Frank Matthews	45.00	20.00	9.00
139	Roger LaFrance	45.00	20.00	9.00
140	Harold Cowan	45.00	20.00	9.00
141	Richard Henton	45.00	20.00	9.00
142	Banks McDowell	45.00	20.00	9.00
143	Harold Graham	45.00	20.00	9.00
144	Jack Sweeting	45.00	20.00	9.00
145	Bill Wixted	45.00	20.00	9.00
146	Larry Graham	45.00	20.00	9.00
147	Ralph Brown	45.00	20.00	9.00
148	Felipe Jimenez	45.00	20.00	9.00
149	John Ippolito	45.00	20.00	9.00
150	Joe Benito	45.00	20.00	9.00
151	Bernardo Fernandez	45.00	20.00	9.00
152	Buckey Winkler	45.00	20.00	9.00
153	Carl Armstrong	45.00	20.00	9.00
154	Jack Bearden	45.00	20.00	9.00
155	George Bucci	45.00	20.00	9.00
156	John Pere (Pare)	45.00	20.00	9.00
157	Mickey O'Brien	45.00	20.00	9.00

158	Lamar Murphy	45.00	20.00	9.00
159	Devon Chaptman (Choptman)	45.00	20.00	9.00
160	Hal Johnson	45.00	20.00	9.00
161	"Bitsy" Mott	45.00	20.00	9.00
162	Charles Cuellar	45.00	20.00	9.00
163	Chester Covington	45.00	20.00	9.00
164	Howard Ermisch	45.00	20.00	9.00
165	Bill Lewis	45.00	20.00	9.00
166	Roy Knepper	45.00	20.00	9.00
167	Bull Enos	45.00	20.00	9.00
168	Joe Wilder	45.00	20.00	9.00
169	Jake Baker	45.00	20.00	9.00
170	Joe Bodner	45.00	20.00	9.00
171	Jackie Myer	45.00	20.00	9.00
172	Mel Fisher	45.00	20.00	9.00
173	Larry Baldwin	45.00	20.00	9.00
174	Richard Farkas	45.00	20.00	9.00
175	Alston McGahgin	45.00	20.00	9.00
176	Ray Weiss	45.00	20.00	9.00
177	Paul Waner	400.00	180.00	80.00
178	Frank Miller	45.00	20.00	9.00
179	John Sabatie	45.00	20.00	9.00
180	John Maire	45.00	20.00	9.00

1966 Pro's Pizza Chicago Cubs

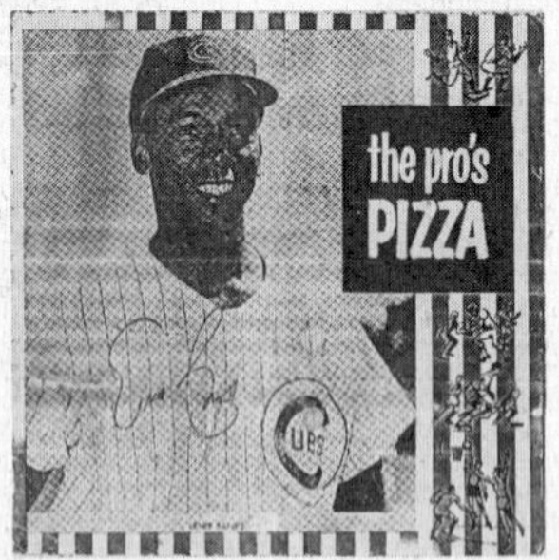

These black-and-white player cards were printed on boxes in which individual-serving pizzas were sold, reportedly only at Wrigley Field. The panel measures 6" x 6" and has a black-and-white player photo at left, with his name in a white strip at bottom. At right are drawn sports action scenes and toward the top is a black box with "the pro's PIZZA" in white. The backs are blank. The unnumbered pieces are listed here alphabetically. The example pictured was autographed by the player, no facsimile signature was printed originally.

		NM	EX	VG
Complete Set (15):		3,250	1,600	975.00
Common Player:		160.00	80.00	50.00
(1)	Ted Abernathy	160.00	80.00	50.00
(2)	Joe Amalfitano	160.00	80.00	50.00
(3)	George Altman	160.00	80.00	50.00
(4)	Ernie Banks	650.00	325.00	200.00
(5)	Ernie Broglio	160.00	80.00	50.00
(6)	Billy Connors	160.00	80.00	50.00
(7)	Dick Ellsworth	160.00	80.00	50.00
(8)	Bill Hoeft	160.00	80.00	50.00
(9)	Ken Holtzman	160.00	80.00	50.00
(10)	Randy Hundley	160.00	80.00	50.00
(11)	Ferguson Jenkins	325.00	160.00	100.00
(12)	Chris Krug	160.00	80.00	50.00
(13)	Ron Santo	245.00	120.00	75.00
(14)	Carl Warwick	160.00	80.00	50.00
(15)	Billy Williams	400.00	200.00	120.00

1967 Pro's Pizza - B & W

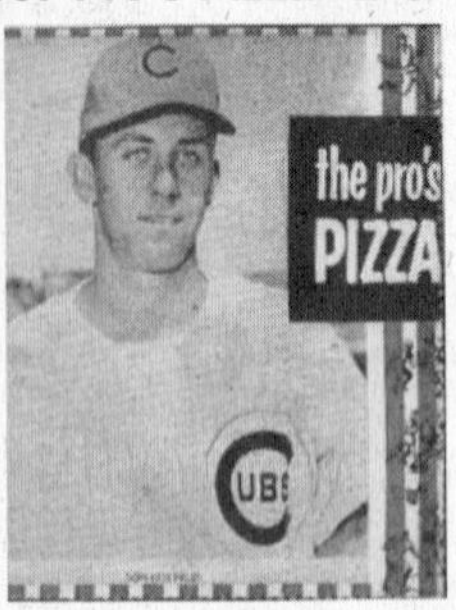

For a second year, Chicago players - Cubs and White Sox - were featured on boxes of individual-serving pizza reportedly sold only at the ballparks. The panel on which the player photos (black-and-white) are printed measures 4-3/4" x 5-3/4" and is similar in design to the 1966 issue, except there is a vertical perforation allowing most of the player photo to be torn away in a 3-1/16" x 5-3/4" size. Cards are unnumbered and listed here alphabetically. Values are for unseparated panels. Those separated at the perforation line are worth 60-75%.

		NM	EX	VG
Complete Set (10):		1,500	750.00	450.00
Common Player:		125.00	65.00	35.00
(1)	Ernie Banks	325.00	160.00	100.00
(2)	Glenn Beckert	125.00	65.00	35.00
(3)	Byron Browne	125.00	65.00	35.00
(4)	Don Buford	125.00	65.00	35.00
(5)	Joel Horlen	125.00	65.00	35.00
(6)	Randy Hundley	125.00	65.00	35.00
(7)	Don Kessinger	125.00	65.00	35.00
(8)	Gary Peters	125.00	65.00	35.00
(9)	Ron Santo	175.00	85.00	50.00
(10)	Billy Williams	200.00	100.00	60.00

1967 Pro's Pizza - Color

Only Chicago Cubs are included in this set of cards printed on the top of individual serving pizza boxes, reportedly sold only at Wrigley Field. The color player poses are printed in a 4-3/4" diameter circle on top of the box, with the player's name in a white panel at bottom. The player's name was also printed in large black letters on one side of the box. Values shown here for the unnumbered cards are for the complete box top. A similar issue of Chicago Bears players was also produced.

		NM	EX	VG
Complete Set (12):		5,000	2,500	1,500
Common Player:		400.00	200.00	120.00
(1)	Joe Amalfitano	400.00	200.00	120.00
(2)	Ernie Banks	1,100	550.00	330.00
(3)	Glenn Beckert	400.00	200.00	120.00
(4)	John Boccabella	400.00	200.00	120.00
(5)	Bill Hands	400.00	200.00	120.00
(6)	Ken Holtzman	400.00	200.00	120.00
(7)	Randy Hundley	400.00	200.00	120.00
(8)	Ferguson Jenkins	675.00	335.00	200.00
(9)	Don Kessinger	400.00	200.00	120.00
(10)	Adolfo Phillips	400.00	200.00	120.00
(11)	Ron Santo	600.00	300.00	180.00
(12)	Billy Williams	850.00	425.00	255.00

1972 Pro Star Promotions

This set of postcard-sized (3-1/2" x 5-1/2") color photo-cards features players from 14 major league teams, with a heavy emphasis on Montreal Expos. Uniforms in the photos have had team logos removed. Cards have a facsimile autograph on front. In the white border at bottom is the player name, league, copyright notice and "Printed in Canada." The unnumbered cards are checklisted here in alphabetical order.

		NM	EX	VG
Complete Set (40):		275.00	135.00	85.00
Common Player:		3.00	1.50	.90
(1)	Hank Aaron	17.50	8.75	5.25
(2)	Bob Bailey	3.00	1.50	.90
(3)	Johnny Bench	12.50	6.25	3.75
(4)	Vida Blue	3.00	1.50	.90
(5)	John Boccabella	3.00	1.50	.90
(6)	Roberto Clemente	20.00	10.00	6.00
(7)	Boots Day	3.00	1.50	.90
(8)	Jim Fairey	3.00	1.50	.90
(9)	Tim Foli	3.00	1.50	.90
(10)	Ron Hunt	3.00	1.50	.90
(11)	Catfish Hunter	7.50	3.75	2.25
(12)	Reggie Jackson	15.00	7.50	4.50
(13)	Fergy Jenkins	10.00	5.00	3.00
(14)	Mike Jorgensen	3.00	1.50	.90
(15)	Al Kaline	12.50	6.25	3.75
(16)	Harmon Killebrew	12.50	6.25	3.75
(17)	Mickey Lolich	3.00	1.50	.90
(18)	Juan Marichal	7.50	3.75	2.25
(19)	Willie Mays	17.50	8.75	5.25
(20)	Willie McCovey	10.00	5.00	3.00
(21)	Ernie McAnally	3.00	1.50	.90
(22)	Dave McNally	3.00	1.50	.90
(23)	Bill Melton	3.00	1.50	.90
(24)	Carl Morton	3.00	1.50	.90
(25)	Bobby Murcer	3.00	1.50	.90
(26)	Fritz Peterson	3.00	1.50	.90
(27)	Boog Powell	6.00	3.00	1.75
(28)	Steve Renko	3.00	1.50	.90
(29)	Merv Rettenmund	3.00	1.50	.90
(30)	Brooks Robinson	12.50	6.25	3.75
(31)	Frank Robinson	12.50	6.25	3.75
(32)	Pete Rose	17.50	8.75	5.25
(33)	Tom Seaver	12.50	6.25	3.75
(34)	Ken Singleton	3.00	1.50	.90
(35)	Willie Stargell	10.00	5.00	3.00
(36)	Bill Stoneman	3.00	1.50	.90
(37)	Joe Torre	6.00	3.00	1.75
(38)	Checklist - American League	1.50	.70	.45
(39)	Checklist - National League	1.50	.70	.45
(40)	Checklist - Montreal Expos	1.50	.70	.45

1971 Pro Stars Publications Montreal Expos

Posed action photos of the Expos are featured on this postcard-size (3-1/2" x 5-1/2") issue. The color photos are surrounded by a white border and have a facsimile autograph. Printed in the bottom border is, "Copyright Pro Stars Publications 1971 Printed in Canada." Backs are blank. The unnumbered cards are checklisted here in alphabetical order.

		NM	EX	VG
Complete Set (28):		175.00	85.00	50.00
Common Player:		6.00	3.00	1.80
(1)	Bob Bailey	6.00	3.00	1.80
(2)	John Bateman	6.00	3.00	1.80
(3)	John Boccabella	6.00	3.00	1.80
(4)	Ron Brand	6.00	3.00	1.80
(5)	Boots Day	6.00	3.00	1.80
(6)	Jim Fairey	6.00	3.00	1.80
(7)	Ron Fairly	7.50	3.75	2.25
(8)	Jim Gosger	6.00	3.00	1.80
(9)	Don Hahn	6.00	3.00	1.80
(10)	Ron Hunt	6.00	3.00	1.80
(11)	Mack Jones	6.00	3.00	1.80
(12)	Coco Laboy	6.00	3.00	1.80
(13)	Mike Marshall	7.50	3.75	2.25
(14)	Clyde Mashore	6.00	3.00	1.80
(15)	Gene Mauch	7.50	3.75	2.25
(16)	Dan McGinn	6.00	3.00	1.80
(17)	Carl Morton	6.00	3.00	1.80
(18)	John O'Donoghue	6.00	3.00	1.80
(19)	Adolfo Phillips	6.00	3.00	1.80
(20)	Claude Raymond	6.00	3.00	1.80
(21)	Howie Reed	6.00	3.00	1.80
(22)	Steve Renko	6.00	3.00	1.80
(23)	Rusty Staub	10.00	5.00	3.00
(24)	Bill Stoneman	6.00	3.00	1.80
(25)	John Strohmayer	6.00	3.00	1.80
(26)	Gary Sutherland	6.00	3.00	1.80
(27)	Mike Wegener	6.00	3.00	1.80
(28)	Bobby Wine	6.00	3.00	1.80

1950s Publix Markets

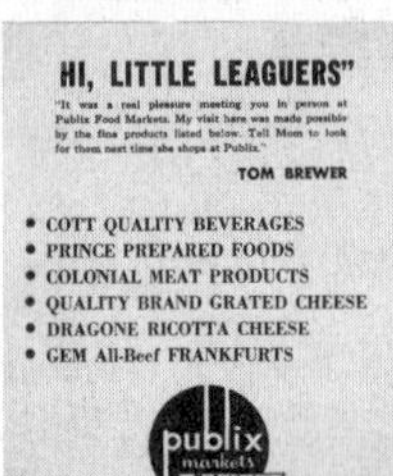

It is not known whether this is a one-card set or whether similar cards exist for other players. Without information on other subjects it is impossible to date the issue more precisely. The black-and-white card is printed on thin, semi-gloss cardboard in 4" x 4-3/4" format. The front has a facsimile autograph. The back has a message to Little Leaguers from the Red Sox pitcher and a list of sponsors, along with the Publix logo.

	NM	EX	VG
Tom Brewer	150.00	75.00	45.00

1972 Puerto Rican League Stickers

Often mistakenly called "minor league" cards, this issue consists of 231 ungummed stickers pertinent to the Puerto Rican winter baseball league. A colorful album was available

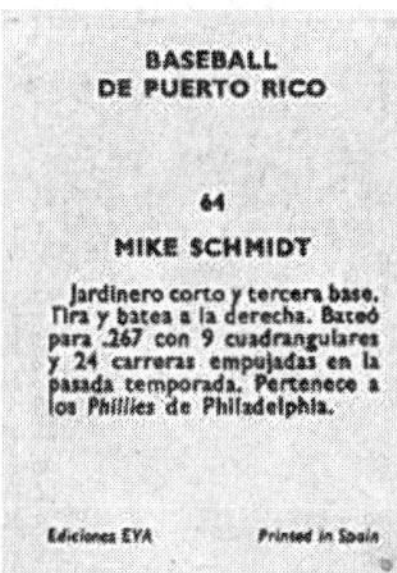

in which to paste the stickers, though obviously stickers that have evidence of glue or torn paper have little collector value. Besides individual player photos, there are stickers of "old-timers" and groups of stickers which make up composite photos of all-star teams and of the island's god of baseball, Roberto Clemente. Team emblem stickers are also included. Many big league stars who were either beginning or ending their pro careers can be found in the set, including some current and future Hall of Famers. Stickers have color photos on the front, with backs printed in Spanish. They measure 2-1/4" x 3".

		NM	EX	VG
Complete Set (231):		1,000	500.00	300.00
Complete Set in Album:		1,200	600.00	350.00
Common Player:		5.00	2.50	1.50
Album:		200.00	100.00	60.00
Unopened Pack:		50.00		
1	Santurce All-Star Team Composite Photo	10.00	5.00	3.00
2	Santurce All-Star Team Composite Photo	10.00	5.00	3.00
3	Santurce All-Star Team Composite Photo	10.00	5.00	3.00
4	Santurce All-Star Team Composite Photo	10.00	5.00	3.00
5	Santurce All-Star Team Composite Photo	10.00	5.00	3.00
6	Santurce All-Star Team Composite Photo	10.00	5.00	3.00
7	Santurce All-Star Team Composite Photo	10.00	5.00	3.00
8	Santurce All-Star Team Composite Photo	10.00	5.00	3.00
9	Santurce All-Star Team Composite Photo	10.00	5.00	3.00
10	Ponce All-Star Team Composite Photo	10.00	5.00	3.00
11	Ponce All-Star Team Composite Photo	10.00	5.00	3.00
12	Ponce All-Star Team Composite Photo	10.00	5.00	3.00
13	Ponce All-Star Team Composite Photo	10.00	5.00	3.00
14	Ponce All-Star Team Composite Photo	10.00	5.00	3.00
15	Ponce All-Star Team Composite Photo	10.00	5.00	3.00
16	Ponce All-Star Team Composite Photo	10.00	5.00	3.00
17	Ponce All-Star Team Composite Photo	10.00	5.00	3.00
18	Ponce All-Star Team Composite Photo	10.00	5.00	3.00
19	Arecibo Team Emblem	5.00	2.50	1.50
20	Caguas-Guayana Team Emblem	5.00	2.50	1.50
21	Mayaguez Team Emblem	5.00	2.50	1.50
22	Ponce Team Emblem	5.00	2.50	1.50
23	San Juan Team Emblem	5.00	2.50	1.50
24	Santurce Team Emblem	5.00	2.50	1.50
25	Steve Boros	5.00	2.50	1.50
26	Luis Isaac	5.00	2.50	1.50
27	Emmanuel Toledo	5.00	2.50	1.50
28	Gregorio Perez	5.00	2.50	1.50
29	Rosario Llanos	5.00	2.50	1.50
30	Jose Geigel	5.00	2.50	1.50
31	Eduardo Figueroa	5.00	2.50	1.50
32	Julian Muniz	5.00	2.50	1.50
33	Fernando Gonzalez	5.00	2.50	1.50
34	Bennie Ayala	5.00	2.50	1.50
35	Miguel Villaran	5.00	2.50	1.50
36	Efrain Vazquez	5.00	2.50	1.50
37	Ramon Ariles	5.00	2.50	1.50
38	Angel Alcaraz	5.00	2.50	1.50
39	Henry Cruz	5.00	2.50	1.50
40	Jose Silva	5.00	2.50	1.50
41	Jose Alcaide	5.00	2.50	1.50
42	Pepe Mangual	5.00	2.50	1.50
43	Mike Jackson	5.00	2.50	1.50
44	Lynn McGlothen	5.00	2.50	1.50
45	Frank Ortenzio	5.00	2.50	1.50
46	Norm Angelini	5.00	2.50	1.50
47	Richard Coggins	5.00	2.50	1.50
48	Lance Clemons	5.00	2.50	1.50
49	Mike Kelleher	5.00	2.50	1.50
50	Ken Wright	5.00	2.50	1.50
51	Buck Martinez	5.00	2.50	1.50
52	Billy De Mars	5.00	2.50	1.50
53	Elwood Huyke	5.00	2.50	1.50
54	Pedro Garcia	5.00	2.50	1.50
55	Bob Boone	15.00	7.50	4.50
56	Jose Laboy	5.00	2.50	1.50
57	Eduardo Rodriguez	5.00	2.50	1.50
58	Jesus Hernaiz	5.00	2.50	1.50
59	Joaquin Quintana	5.00	2.50	1.50
60	Domingo Figueroa	5.00	2.50	1.50
61	Juan Lopez	5.00	2.50	1.50
62	Luis Alvarado	5.00	2.50	1.50
63	Otoniel Velez	5.00	2.50	1.50
64	Mike Schmidt	300.00	150.00	90.00
65	Felix Millan	5.00	2.50	1.50
66	Guillermo Montanez	5.00	2.50	1.50
67	Ivan de Jesus	7.50	3.75	2.25
68	Sixto Lezcano	5.00	2.50	1.50
69	Jerry Morales	5.00	2.50	1.50
70	Bombo Rivera	5.00	2.50	1.50
71	Mike Ondina	5.00	2.50	1.50
72	Grant Jackson	5.00	2.50	1.50
73	Roger Freed	5.00	2.50	1.50
74	Steve Rogers	5.00	2.50	1.50
75	Mac Scarce	5.00	2.50	1.50
76	Mike Jorgensen	5.00	2.50	1.50
77	Jerry Crider	5.00	2.50	1.50
78	Fred Beene	5.00	2.50	1.50
79	Carl Ermer	5.00	2.50	1.50
80	Luis Marquez	5.00	2.50	1.50
81	Hector Valle	5.00	2.50	1.50
82	Ramon Vega	5.00	2.50	1.50
83	Cirito Cruz	5.00	2.50	1.50
84	Fernando Vega	5.00	2.50	1.50
85	Porfiro Sanchez	5.00	2.50	1.50
86	Jose Sevillano	5.00	2.50	1.50
87	Felix Roque	5.00	2.50	1.50
88	Enrique Rivera	5.00	2.50	1.50
89	Wildredo Rios	5.00	2.50	1.50
90	Javier Andino	5.00	2.50	1.50
91	Milton Ramirez	5.00	2.50	1.50
92	Max Oliveras	5.00	2.50	1.50
93	Jose Calero	5.00	2.50	1.50
94	Esteban Vazquez	5.00	2.50	1.50
95	Hector Cruz	5.00	2.50	1.50
96	Felix Arce	5.00	2.50	1.50
97	Gilberto Rivera	5.00	2.50	1.50
98	Rafael Rodriguez	5.00	2.50	1.50
99	Julio Gonzalez	5.00	2.50	1.50
100	Rosendo Cedeno	5.00	2.50	1.50
101	Pedro Cintron	5.00	2.50	1.50
102	Osvaldo Ortiz	5.00	2.50	1.50
103	Frank Verdi	5.00	2.50	1.50
104	Carlos Santiago	5.00	2.50	1.50
105	Ramon Conde	5.00	2.50	1.50
106	Pat Corrales	5.00	2.50	1.50
107	Jose Morales	5.00	2.50	1.50
108	Jack Whillock	5.00	2.50	1.50
109	Raul Mercado	5.00	2.50	1.50
110	Bonifacio Aponte	5.00	2.50	1.50
111	Angel Alicea	5.00	2.50	1.50
112	Santos Alomar	10.00	5.00	3.00
113	Francisco Libran	5.00	2.50	1.50
114	Edwin Pacheco	5.00	2.50	1.50
115	Luis Gonzalez	5.00	2.50	1.50
116	Juan Rios	5.00	2.50	1.50
117	Jorge Roque	5.00	2.50	1.50
118	Carlos Velez	5.00	2.50	1.50
119	David Gonzalez	5.00	2.50	1.50
120	Jose Cruz	7.50	3.75	2.25
121	Luis Melendez	5.00	2.50	1.50
122	Jose Ortiz	5.00	2.50	1.50
123	David Rosello	5.00	2.50	1.50
124	Juan Veintidos	5.00	2.50	1.50
125	Arnaldo Nazario	5.00	2.50	1.50
126	Dave Lemonds	5.00	2.50	1.50
127	Jim Magnuson	5.00	2.50	1.50
128	Tom Kelley	7.50	3.75	2.25
129	Chris Zachary	5.00	2.50	1.50
130	Hal Breeden	5.00	2.50	1.50
131	Jackie Hernandez	5.00	2.50	1.50
132	Rick Gossage	30.00	15.00	9.00
133	Frank Luchessi	5.00	2.50	1.50
134	Nino Escalera	5.00	2.50	1.50
135	Julio Navarro	5.00	2.50	1.50
136	Manny Sanguillen	15.00	7.50	4.50
137	Bob Johnson	5.00	2.50	1.50
138	Chuck Coggins	5.00	2.50	1.50
139	Orlando Gomez	5.00	2.50	1.50
140	William Melendez	5.00	2.50	1.50
141	Jose Del Moral	5.00	2.50	1.50
142	Jacinto Camacho	5.00	2.50	1.50
143	Emiliano Rivera	5.00	2.50	1.50
144	Luis Peraza	5.00	2.50	1.50
145	Carlos Velazquez	5.00	2.50	1.50
146	Luis Raul Garcia	5.00	2.50	1.50
147	Eliseo Rodriguez	5.00	2.50	1.50
148	Santiago Rosario	5.00	2.50	1.50
149	Ruben Castillo	5.00	2.50	1.50
150	Sergio Ferrer	5.00	2.50	1.50
151	Jose Pagan	5.00	2.50	1.50
152	Raul Colon	5.00	2.50	1.50
153	Robert Rauch	5.00	2.50	1.50
154	Luis Rosado	5.00	2.50	1.50
155	Francisco Lopez	5.00	2.50	1.50
156	Richard Zisk	5.00	2.50	1.50
157	Orlando Alvarez	5.00	2.50	1.50
158	Jaime Rosario	5.00	2.50	1.50
159	Rosendo Torres	5.00	2.50	1.50
160	Jim McKee	5.00	2.50	1.50
161	Mike Nagy	5.00	2.50	1.50
162	Brent Strom	5.00	2.50	1.50
163	Tom Walker	5.00	2.50	1.50
164	Angel Davila	5.00	2.50	1.50
165	Jose Cruz	5.00	2.50	1.50
166	Frank Robinson	25.00	12.50	7.50
167	German Rivera	5.00	2.50	1.50
168	Reinaldo Oliver	5.00	2.50	1.50
169	Geraldo Rodriguez	5.00	2.50	1.50
170	Elrod Hendricks	5.00	2.50	1.50
171	Gilberto Flores	5.00	2.50	1.50
172	Ruben Gomez	5.00	2.50	1.50
173	Juan Pizarro	5.00	2.50	1.50
174	William De Jesus	5.00	2.50	1.50
175	Rogelio Morel	5.00	2.50	1.50
176	Victor Agosto	5.00	2.50	1.50
177	Esteban Texidor	5.00	2.50	1.50
178	Ramon Hernandez	5.00	2.50	1.50
179	Gilberto Rondon Olivo	5.00	2.50	1.50
180	Juan Beniquez	5.00	2.50	1.50
181	Arturo Miranda	5.00	2.50	1.50
182	Manuel Ruiz	5.00	2.50	1.50
183	Julio Gotay	5.00	2.50	1.50
184	Arsenio Rodriguez	5.00	2.50	1.50
185	Luis Delgado	5.00	2.50	1.50
186	Jorge Rivera	5.00	2.50	1.50
187	Willie Crawford	5.00	2.50	1.50
188	Angel Mangual	5.00	2.50	1.50
189	Mike Strahler	5.00	2.50	1.50
190	Doyle Alexander	5.00	2.50	1.50
191	Bob Reynolds	5.00	2.50	1.50
192	Ron Cey	7.50	3.75	2.25
193	Jerr Da Vanon	5.00	2.50	1.50
194	Don Baylor	12.50	6.25	3.75
195	Tony Perez	25.00	12.50	7.50
196	Lloyd Allen	5.00	2.50	1.50
197	Orlando Cepeda	20.00	10.00	6.00
198	Roberto Clemente Composite Photo	15.00	7.50	4.50
199	Roberto Clemente Composite Photo	15.00	7.50	4.50
200	Roberto Clemente Composite Photo	15.00	7.50	4.50
201	Roberto Clemente Composite Photo	15.00	7.50	4.50
202	Roberto Clemente Composite Photo	15.00	7.50	4.50
203	Roberto Clemente Composite Photo	15.00	7.50	4.50
204	Roberto Clemente Composite Photo	15.00	7.50	4.50
205	Roberto Clemente Composite Photo	15.00	7.50	4.50
206	Roberto Clemente Composite Photo	15.00	7.50	4.50
207	Jaime Almendro	5.00	2.50	1.50
208	Jose R. Santiago	5.00	2.50	1.50
209	Luis Cabrera	5.00	2.50	1.50
210	Jorge Tirado	5.00	2.50	1.50
211	Radames Lopez	5.00	2.50	1.50
212	Juan Vargas	5.00	2.50	1.50
213	Francisco Coimbre	5.00	2.50	1.50
214	Freddie Thon	5.00	2.50	1.50
215	Manuel Alvarez	5.00	2.50	1.50
216	Luis Olmo	5.00	2.50	1.50
217	Jose Santiago	7.50	3.75	2.25
218	Hiram Bithorn	12.50	6.25	3.75
219	Willard Brown	30.00	15.00	9.00
220	Robert Thurman	10.00	5.00	3.00
221	Buster Clarkson	7.50	3.75	2.25
222	Satchel Paige	40.00	20.00	12.00
223	Raymond Brown	30.00	15.00	9.00
224	Alonso Perry	7.50	3.75	2.25
225	Quincy Trouppe	12.50	6.25	3.75
226	Santiago Muratti	5.00	2.50	1.50
227	Johnny Davis	5.00	2.50	1.50
228	Lino Suarez	5.00	2.50	1.50
229	Demetrio Pesante	5.00	2.50	1.50
230	Luis Arroyo	5.00	2.50	1.50
231	Jose Garcia	5.00	2.50	1.50

1905 Harry Pulliam Cigar Label

The attributed dated is speculative. Pulliam was the first president of the modern National League. These colorful gold-leaf highlighted lithographed cigar box labels measure 4-1/4" square with clipped corners. Since all examples seen appear to be unused it is believed that the cigar brand never materialized, possibly having been aborted when Pulliam commited suicide in 1909.

	NM	EX	VG
Harry Pulliam	100.00	50.00	30.00

1910 Punch Cigars

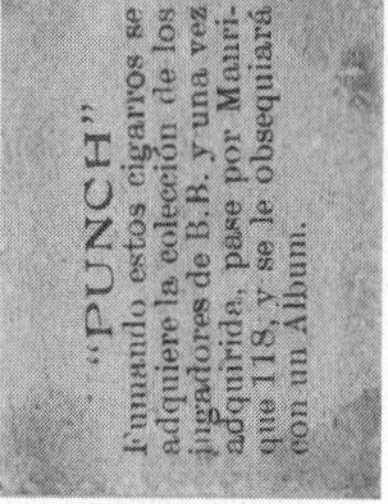

By virtue of its age, scarcity and checklist, this is among the most popular of the Cuban card sets. Issued contemporary with a visit by the Detroit Tigers and Philadelphia A's for an exhibition series in Cuba, these cards feature an approximately 1-1/4" x 1-7/8" black-and-white portrait photo attached to a decorative cardboard backing of about 1-3/4" x 2-1/4". Known cards include a dozen each of the Major League teams and, it is speculated, an equal number from Cuba's professional Almendares and Havana clubs; though the complete checklist remains unknown. The scarcity of surviving specimens may be traced to the copy on the original cardboard backing that offers an album for anybody turning in a complete set. Only a tiny percentage of Punch cards are known with their cardboard backing attached. Because most cards seen to date have been in wretched condition, no values are quoted above VG condition. Cards with backing should command a 3X premium.

		NM	EX	VG
Common Cuban Player:				750.00
Common Major Leaguer:				1,125
	ALMENDARES			
(1)	Armando Cabanas			1,125
(2)	Alfredo Cabrera			750.00
(3)	Gervasio Gonzalez			1,500
(4)	Eleadoro Hidalgo			1,500
(5)	Armando Marzans (Marsans)			2,250
(6)	Jose Mendez			30,000
(7)	Evaristo Pia (Trainer)			750.00
(8)	Carlos Roggers (Royer)			1,125
(9)	Rogelio Valdes			750.00
				500.00
	HAVANA			
(1)	P. (Pete) Hill			5,250
(2)	Carlos Moran			2,250
(3)	Agustin Molina			4,500
(4)	Luis Padron			2,250
(5)	Agustin Parpetti			1,500
				500.00
	DETROIT TIGERS			
(1)	Joe Casey			1,125
(2)	Ty Cobb			11,250
(3)	Sam Crawford			5,250
(4)	Tom Jones			1,125
(5)	Matty McIntyre			1,125
(6)	George Moriarty			1,125
(7)	George Mullin			1,125
(8)	Charley O'Leary			1,125
(9)	Germany Schaefer			1,125
(10)	Oscar Stanage			1,125
(11)	Ed Summers			1,125
(12)	Ed Willetts (Willett)			1,125
				500.00
	PHILADELPHIA A'S			
(1)	Jack Barry			1,125
(2)	Chief Bender			5,250
(3)	Jack Coombs			1,125
(4)	Harry Davis			1,125
(5)	Claude Derrick			1,125
(6)	Topsy Hartsel			1,125
(7)	Jack Lapp			1,125
(8)	Bris Lord			1,125
(9)	Stuffy McInnis			1,125
(10)	Danny Murphy			1,125
(11)	Eddie Plank			6,000
(12)	Ira Thomas			1,125

1966 Pure Oil Atlanta Braves

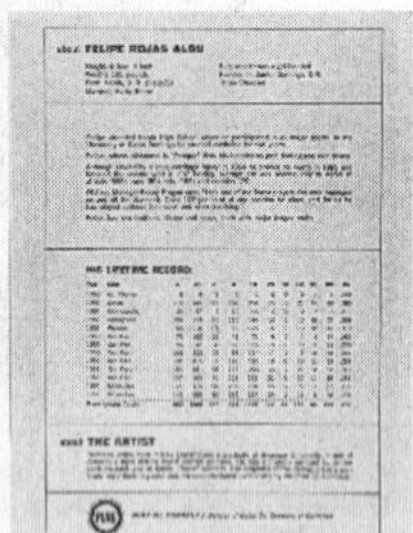

In their first year in Atlanta a set of Braves premium pictures done by noted portrait artist Nicholas Volpe was sponsored by Pure Oil. The 8-1/2" x 11" pictures were given away with gas purchases. Fronts featured a large pastel portrait and smaller full-figure action picture of the player set against a black background. A facsimile player autograph was pencilled at the bottom, along with the artist's signature. The player's name was printed in black in the white bottom border. Backs are printed in black-and-white and include biographical and career notes, full major and minor league stats, a short biography of the artist and the sponsoring company's logo. The unnumbered cards are checklisted here alphabetically.

		NM	EX	VG
Complete Set (12):		75.00	37.50	22.00
Common Player:		5.00	2.50	1.50
(1)	Hank Aaron	25.00	12.50	7.50
(2)	Felipe Alou	6.00	3.00	1.75
(3)	Frank Bolling	5.00	2.50	1.50
(4)	Bobby Bragan	5.00	2.50	1.50
(5)	Rico Carty	5.00	2.50	1.50
(6)	Tony Cloninger	5.00	2.50	1.50
(7)	Mack Jones	5.00	2.50	1.50
(8)	Denny LeMaster	5.00	2.50	1.50
(9)	Eddie Mathews	15.00	7.50	4.50
(10)	Denis Menke	5.00	2.50	1.50
(11)	Lee Thomas	5.00	2.50	1.50
(12)	Joe Torre	7.50	3.75	2.25

1933 PX3 Double Header Coins

Issued by Gum Inc. circa 1933, this unnumbered set consists of 43 metal discs approximately 1-1/4" in diameter. The front lists the player's name and team beneath his picture. The numbers "1" or "2" also appear inside a small circle at the bottom of the disc, and the wrapper advised collectors to "put 1 and 2 together and make a double header." Some players are found in more than one color. The set is designated as PX3 in the American Card Catalog.

		NM	EX	VG
Complete Set (43):		1,750	875.00	525.00
Common Player:		40.00	20.00	12.00
(1)	Sparky Adams	40.00	20.00	12.00
(2)	Dale Alexander	40.00	20.00	12.00
(3)	Earl Averill	75.00	37.00	22.00
(4)	Dick Bartell	40.00	20.00	12.00
(5)	Walter Berger	40.00	20.00	12.00
(6)	Jim Bottomley	75.00	37.00	22.00
(7)	Lefty Brandt	40.00	20.00	12.00
(8)	Owen Carroll	40.00	20.00	12.00
(9)	Lefty Clark	40.00	20.00	12.00
(10)	Mickey Cochrane	75.00	37.00	22.00
(11)	Joe Cronin	75.00	37.00	22.00
(12)	Jimmy Dykes	40.00	20.00	12.00
(13)	George Earnshaw	40.00	20.00	12.00
(14)	Wes Ferrell	40.00	20.00	12.00
(15)	Neal Finn	40.00	20.00	12.00
(16)	Lew Fonseca	40.00	20.00	12.00
(17)	Jimmy Foxx	100.00	50.00	30.00
(18)	Frankie Frisch	75.00	37.00	22.00
(19)	Chick Fullis	40.00	20.00	12.00
(20)	Charley Gehringer	75.00	37.00	22.00
(21)	Goose Goslin	75.00	37.00	22.00
(22)	Johnny Hodapp	40.00	20.00	12.00
(23)	Frank Hogan	40.00	20.00	12.00
(24)	Si Johnson	40.00	20.00	12.00
(25)	Joe Judge	40.00	20.00	12.00
(26)	Chuck Klein	75.00	37.00	22.00
(27)	Al Lopez	75.00	37.00	22.00
(28)	Ray Lucas	40.00	20.00	12.00
(29)	Red Lucas	40.00	20.00	12.00
(30)	Ted Lyons	75.00	37.00	22.00
(31)	Firpo Marberry	40.00	20.00	12.00
(32)	Oscar Melillo	40.00	20.00	12.00
(33)	Lefty O'Doul	50.00	25.00	15.00
(34)	George Pipgras	40.00	20.00	12.00
(35)	Flint Rhem	40.00	20.00	12.00
(36)	Sam Rice	75.00	37.00	22.00
(37)	Muddy Ruel	40.00	20.00	12.00
(38)	Harry Seibold	40.00	20.00	12.00
(39)	Al Simmons	75.00	37.00	22.00
(40)	Joe Vosmik	40.00	20.00	12.00
(41)	Gerald Walker	40.00	20.00	12.00
(42)	Pinky Whitney	40.00	20.00	12.00
(43)	Hack Wilson	75.00	37.00	22.00

Q

1934 Quaker Oats Babe Ruth Premium Photo (8x10)

Members of the cereal company's Babe Ruth Baseball Club could obtain this souvenir photo among many other promotional items endorsed by the slugger. This 8" x 10" black-and-white photo has a facsimile autograph and is inscribed, "To My Pal." Advertising for Quaker Oats appears in the white border at bottom.

	NM	EX	VG
Babe Ruth	600.00	350.00	150.00

1954 Quaker Sports Oddities

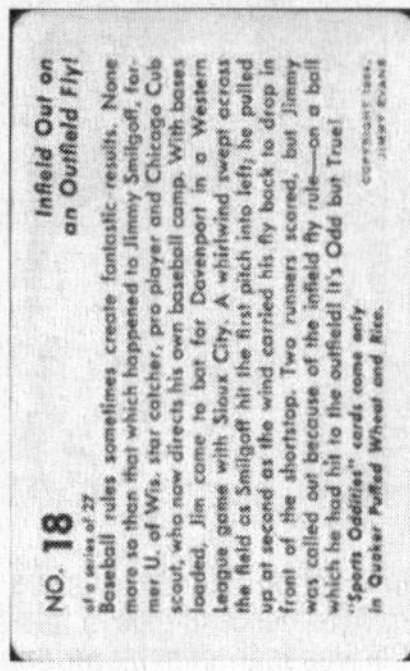

Available both as cereal-box premiums and a mail-away set, this issue of horizontal-format 3-1/2" x 2-1/2, round-corner cards depicts "Odd but True" moments in sports. Fronts of the multi-sports set feature portrait and action color art. Backs describe the sports oddity.

		NM	EX	VG
Complete Set (27):		200.00	100.00	60.00
Common Card:		3.00	1.50	.90
1	Johnny Miller (Football)	4.00	2.00	1.25
2	Fred Snite Jr. (Golf)	3.00	1.50	.90
3	George Quam (Handball)	3.00	1.50	.90
4	John B. Maypole (Speed boating.)	3.00	1.50	.90
5	Harold (Bunny) Leavitt (Basketball)	5.00	2.50	1.50
6	Wake Forest College (Football)	5.00	2.50	1.50
7	Amos Alonzo Stagg (Football)	20.00	10.00	6.00
8	Catherine Fellmuth (Bowling)	3.00	1.50	.90
9	Bill Wilson (Golf)	3.00	1.50	.90
10	Chicago Blackhawks (Hockey)	20.00	10.00	6.00
11	Betty Robinson (Track)	3.00	1.50	.90
12	Dartmouth College/University of Utah (Basketball)	5.00	2.50	1.50
13	Ab Jenkins (Auto racing.)	3.00	1.50	.90
14	Capt. Eddie Rickenbacker (Auto racing.)	5.00	2.50	1.50
15	Jackie LaVine (Swimming)	3.00	1.50	.90
16	Jack Riley (Wrestling)	3.00	1.50	.90
17	Carl Stockton (Biking)	3.00	1.50	.90
18	Jimmy Smilgoff (Baseball)	3.00	1.50	.90
19	George Halas (Football)	20.00	10.00	6.00
20	Joyce Rosenbom (Basketball)	5.00	2.50	1.50
21	Squatters Rights (Baseball)	3.00	1.50	.90
22	Richard Dwyer (Skating)	3.00	1.50	.90
23	Harlem Globetrotters (Basketball)	25.00	12.50	7.50
24	Everett Dean (Basketball)	3.00	1.50	.90
25	Texas U./Northwestern U. (Football)	5.00	2.50	1.50
26	Bronko Nagurski (Football)	25.00	12.50	7.50
27	Yankee Stadium (Baseball)	20.00	10.00	6.00

1909 Ramly Cigarettes (T204)

While issued with both Ramly and T.T.T. brand Turkish tobacco cigarettes, the cards in this set take their name from the more common of the two brands. By whatever name, the set is one of the more interesting and attractive of the early 20th Century. The 2" x 2-1/2" cards carry black-and-white photographic portraits with impressive gold embossed frames and borders on the front. Toward the bottom appears the player's last name, position, team and league. The backs carry only the most basic information on the cigarette company. The complete set price does not include the scarce variations of some players' cards on which the photos are square and surrounded by a heavy gold frame with white borders.

		NM	EX	VG
Complete Set (121):		125,000	50,000	25,000
Common Player:		1,000	250.00	125.00
T.T.T.: 4-5X				
(1)	Whitey Alperman	1,000	250.00	125.00

(2a)	John Anderson (Photo inside oval frame.)	1,000	250.00	125.00
(2b)	John Anderson (Photo inside square frame.)	22,500	9,000	4,500
(3)	Jimmy Archer	1,000	250.00	125.00
(4)	Frank Arrelanes (Arellanes)	1,000	250.00	125.00
(5)	Jim Ball	1,000	250.00	125.00
(6)	Neal Ball	1,000	250.00	125.00
(7a)	Frank C. Bancroft (Photo inside oval frame.)	1,000	250.00	125.00
(7b)	Frank C. Bancroft (Photo inside square frame.)	30,000	12,000	6,000
(8)	Johnny Bates	1,000	250.00	125.00
(9)	Fred Beebe	1,000	250.00	125.00
(10)	George Bell	1,000	250.00	125.00
(11)	Chief Bender	3,440	1,375	690.00
(12)	Walter Blair	1,000	250.00	125.00
(13)	Cliff Blankenship	1,000	250.00	125.00
(14)	Frank Bowerman	1,000	250.00	125.00
(15a)	Wm. Bransfield (Photo inside oval frame.)	1,000	250.00	125.00
(15b)	Wm. Bransfield (Photo inside square frame.)	22,500	9,000	4,500
(16)	Roger Bresnahan	3,440	1,375	690.00
(17)	Al Bridwell	1,000	250.00	125.00
(18)	Mordecai Brown	3,440	1,375	690.00
(19)	Fred Burchell	1,000	250.00	125.00
(20a)	Jesse C. Burkett (Photo inside oval frame.)	15,625	6,250	3,125
(20b)	Jesse C. Burkett (Photo inside square frame.)	22,500	9,000	4,500
(21)	Bobby Byrnes (Byrne)	1,000	250.00	125.00
(22)	Bill Carrigan	1,000	250.00	125.00
(23)	Frank Chance	3,440	1,375	690.00
(24)	Charlie Chech	1,000	250.00	125.00
(25)	Ed Cicolte (Cicotte)	3,000	1,200	600.00
(26)	Otis Clymer	1,000	250.00	125.00
(27)	Andy Coakley	1,000	250.00	125.00
(28)	Jimmy Collins	3,440	1,375	690.00
(29)	Ed. Collins	3,440	1,375	690.00
(30)	Wid Conroy	1,005	250.00	125.00
(31)	Jack Coombs	1,000	250.00	125.00
(32)	Doc Crandall	1,000	250.00	125.00
(33)	Lou Criger	1,000	250.00	125.00
(34)	Harry Davis	1,000	250.00	125.00
(35)	Art Devlin	1,000	250.00	125.00
(36a)	Wm. H. Dineen (Dinneen) (Photo inside oval frame.)	1,000	250.00	125.00
(36b)	Wm. H. Dineen (Dinneen) (Photo inside square frame.)	22,500	9,000	4,500
(37)	Jiggs Donahue	1,000	250.00	125.00
(38)	Mike Donlin	1,000	250.00	125.00
(39)	Wild Bill Donovan	1,000	250.00	125.00
(40)	Gus Dorner	1,000	250.00	125.00
(41)	Joe Dunn	1,000	250.00	125.00
(42)	Kid Elberfield (Elberfeld)	1,000	250.00	125.00
(43)	Johnny Evers	3,440	1,375	690.00
(44)	Bob Ewing	1,000	250.00	125.00
(45)	Cecil Ferguson	1,000	250.00	125.00
(46)	Hobe Ferris	1,000	250.00	125.00
(47)	Jerry Freeman	1,000	250.00	125.00
(48)	Art Fromme	1,000	250.00	125.00
(49)	Bob Ganley	1,000	250.00	125.00
(50)	Doc Gessler	1,000	250.00	125.00
(51)	Peaches Graham	1,000	250.00	125.00
(52)	Clark Griffith	3,440	1,375	690.00
(53)	Roy Hartzell	1,000	250.00	125.00
(54)	Charlie Hemphill	1,000	250.00	125.00
(55)	Dick Hoblitzel (Hoblitzell)	1,000	250.00	125.00
(56a)	Geo. Howard (Photo inside oval frame.)	1,000	250.00	125.00
(56b)	Geo. Howard (Photo inside square frame.)	22,500	9,000	4,500
(57)	Harry Howell	1,000	250.00	125.00
(58)	Miller Huggins	3,440	1,375	690.00
(59)	John Hummell (Hummel)	1,000	250.00	125.00
(60)	Walter Johnson	50,000	20,000	10,000
(61)	Thos. Jones	1,000	250.00	125.00
(62)	Mike Kahoe	1,000	250.00	125.00
(63)	Ed Kargar	1,000	250.00	125.00
(64)	Wee Willie Keeler	3,440	1,375	690.00
(65)	Red Kleinon (Kleinow)	1,000	250.00	125.00
(66)	Jack Knight	1,000	250.00	125.00
(67)	Ed Konetchey	1,000	250.00	125.00
(68)	Vive Lindaman	1,000	250.00	125.00
(69)	Hans Loebert (Lobert)	1,000	250.00	125.00
(70)	Harry Lord	1,000	250.00	125.00
(71)	Harry Lumley	1,000	250.00	125.00
(72)	Johnny Lush	1,000	250.00	125.00
(73)	Rube Manning	1,000	250.00	125.00
(74)	Jimmy McAleer	1,000	250.00	125.00
(75)	Amby McConnell	1,000	250.00	125.00
(76)	Moose McCormick	1,000	250.00	125.00
(77)	Harry McIntyre	1,000	250.00	125.00
(78)	Larry McLean	1,000	250.00	125.00
(79)	Fred Merkle	1,000	250.00	125.00
(80)	Clyde Milan	1,000	250.00	125.00
(81)	Mike Mitchell	1,005	250.00	125.00
(82a)	Pat Moran (Photo inside oval frame.)	1,000	250.00	125.00
(82b)	Pat Moran (Photo inside square frame.)	22,500	9,000	4,500
(83)	Cy Morgan	1,000	250.00	125.00
(84)	Tim Murname (Murnane)	1,005	250.00	125.00
(85)	Danny Murphy	1,000	250.00	125.00
(86)	Red Murray	1,000	250.00	125.00
(87)	Doc Newton	1,000	250.00	125.00
(88)	Simon Nichols (Nicholls)	1,000	250.00	125.00
(89)	Harry Niles	1,000	250.00	125.00
(90)	Bill O'Hare (O'Hara)	1,000	250.00	125.00
(91)	Charley O'Leary	1,000	250.00	125.00
(92)	Dode Paskert	1,000	250.00	125.00
(93)	Barney Pelty	1,000	250.00	125.00
(94)	Jake Pfeister	1,000	250.00	125.00
(95)	Ed Plank	9,375	3,750	1,875
(96)	Jack Powell	1,000	250.00	125.00
(97)	Bugs Raymond	1,000	250.00	125.00
(98)	Tom Reilly	1,000	250.00	125.00
(99)	Claude Ritchey	1,000	250.00	125.00
(100)	Nap Rucker	1,000	250.00	125.00
(101)	Ed Ruelbach (Reulbach)	1,000	250.00	125.00
(102)	Slim Sallee	1,000	250.00	125.00
(103)	Germany Schaefer	1,005	250.00	125.00
(104)	Jimmy Schekard (Sheckard)	1,000	250.00	125.00
(105)	Admiral Schlei	1,000	250.00	125.00
(106)	Wildfire Schulte	1,000	400.00	200.00
(107)	Jimmy Sebring	1,000	250.00	125.00
(108)	Bill Shipke	1,000	250.00	125.00
(109)	Charlie Smith	1,000	250.00	125.00
(110)	Tubby Spencer	1,000	250.00	125.00
(111)	Jake Stahl	1,000	250.00	125.00
(112)	Jim Stephens	1,000	250.00	125.00
(113)	Harry Stienfeldt (Steinfeldt)	1,000	250.00	125.00
(114)	Gabby Street	1,000	250.00	125.00
(115)	Bill Sweeney	1,000	250.00	125.00
(116)	Fred Tenney	1,000	250.00	125.00
(117)	Ira Thomas	1,000	250.00	125.00
(118)	Joe Tinker	3,440	1,375	690.00
(119)	Bob Unglane (Unglaub)	1,000	250.00	125.00
(120)	Heinie Wagner	1,000	250.00	125.00
(121)	Bobby Wallace	3,440	1,375	690.00

1910 Ramly Team Composite Premiums

At least two versions of coupons found in boxes of Ramly (and possibly T.T.T.) cigarettes offered a large-format (about 23" x 18-1/2") black-and-white photogravure premium featuring a composite of player portraits for five, or six, popular teams of the era. Players are identified in the bottom border, which also has a credit line for the tobacco company. To date, only the 1909 pennant winners' premiums have been confirmed as surviving.

(1) Boston Red Sox (Unconfirmed)
(2) Boston Rustlers
(3) Detroit Tigers
(4) New York Giants (Unconfirmed)
(5) Philadelphia A's (Unconfirmed)
(6) Pittsburgh Pirates (5/04 auction, trimmed, $3,163)

1881 Randall Studio Cabinets

What the players of the 1881 Boston Beaneaters were doing posing in their Sunday best suits at the Detroit studio of Randall the photographer is open to speculation, as is the question of whether other teams' players were also photographed there. These cabinets are about 4-1/4" x 6-1/2" and blank-backed. On most of them the player name and city and in small type on the portrait.

		NM	EX	VG
Common Player:		2,000	1,000	600.00
(1)	Tommy Bond	2,000	1,000	600.00
(2)	Tom Deasley	2,000	1,000	600.00
(3)	John Morrill	2,000	1,000	600.00
(4)	John Richmond	2,000	1,000	600.00
(5)	Ezra Sutton	2,000	1,000	600.00
(6)	Jim Whitney	2,000	1,000	600.00

1950s-70s Rawlings Advisory Staff Photos

Advisory staff photos were a promtional item which debuted in the early 1950s, flourished in the Sixties and died in the early 1970s. Generally 8" x 10" (sometimes a little larger), these black-and-white (a few later were color) glossy photos picture players who had contracted with a major baseball equipment company to endorse and use their product. Usually the product - most often a glove - was prominently displayed in the photo. The pictures were often displayed in the windows of sporting goods stores or the walls of sports departments and were sometimes made available to customers. Because the companies tended to stick with players over the years, some photos were reissued, sometimes with and sometimes without a change of team, pose or style. All advisory staff photos of the era are checklisted here in alphabetical order. A pose description is given for each known picture. The photos are checklisted here in alphabetical order. It is unlikely this list is complete. In general, Rawlings advisory staff photos feature a white box within the photo which contains the glove-company logo and a facsimile autograph of the player. Gaps have been left in the checklist numbering to accommodate possible additions.

		NM	EX	VG
Common Player:		25.00	12.50	7.50
(1)	Joe Adcock/Kneeling (Braves)	35.00	17.50	10.50
(2)	Joe Adcock (Braves, locker room.)	25.00	12.50	7.50
(3)	Joe Adcock (Braves, upper body.)	25.00	12.50	7.50
(4)	Hank Aguirre (Tigers, glove on knee.)	25.00	12.50	7.50
(5)	Bobby Avila (Indians, upper body.)	25.00	12.50	7.50
(6)	Bob Bailey/Kneeling (Pirates)	25.00	12.50	7.50
(7)	Ed Bailey (Reds, gearing up in dugout.)	25.00	12.50	7.50
(8)	Ed Bailey (Giants, catching crouch.)	25.00	12.50	7.50
(9)	Earl Battey (Twins, catching crouch.)	25.00	12.50	7.50
(10)	Earl Battey (Twins, kneeling w/bat.)	25.00	12.50	7.50
(11)	Johnny Bench (Crouching, no catcher's gear.)	45.00	22.00	13.50
(12)	Dick Bertell (Cubs, catching crouch.)	25.00	12.50	7.50
(13)	John Blanchard (Yankees, catching crouch.)	25.00	12.50	7.50
(14)	John Blanchard (Yankees, dugout step.)	25.00	12.50	7.50
(15)	"Clete" Boyer/Fldg (Yankees)	25.00	12.50	7.50
(16)	Ken Boyer (Cardinals, in front of locker.)	25.00	12.50	7.50
(17)	Ken Boyer/Kneeling (Cardinals, b/w)	25.00	12.50	7.50
(18)	Ken Boyer (Mets, b/w, full-length.)	25.00	12.50	7.50
(19)	Ken Boyer (Mets, color, leaning on bat.)	25.00	12.50	7.50
(20)	Ken Boyer (White Sox, upper body.)	30.00	15.00	9.00
(21)	Lew Burdette (Braves, beginning wind-up.)	25.00	12.50	7.50
(22)	Lew Burdette (Braves, upper body w/ball.)	35.00	17.50	10.50
(23)	Bob Cerv (A's, at bat rack.)	25.00	12.50	7.50
(24)	Gordon Coleman (Reds, kneeling w/bat.)	25.00	12.50	7.50
(25)	Tony Conigliaro (Red Sox, glove at chest.)	45.00	22.00	13.50
(26)	Wes Covington (Braves, upper body.)	25.00	12.50	7.50
(27)	Joe Cunningham (White Sox, glove at knee.)	25.00	12.50	7.50
(28)	Joe Cunningham (Cardinals, chest-up.)	25.00	12.50	7.50
(29)	Tommy Davis (Dodgers, dugout step.)	25.00	12.50	7.50
(30)	Don Demeter (Dodgers, upper body.)	25.00	12.50	7.50
(31)	Don Demeter (Phillies, hands on knees.)	25.00	12.50	7.50
(32)	Dick Dietz (Giants, catching pose.)	25.00	12.50	7.50
(33)	Tito Francona (Indians, sitting w/glove.)	25.00	12.50	7.50
(34)	Steve Garvey (Dodgers, horizontal, pose and action.)	25.00	12.50	7.50
(35)	Mudcat Grant (Indians, horizontal, upper body.)	25.00	12.50	7.50
(36)	Dick Groat (Pirates, b/w, full-length.)	25.00	12.50	7.50
(37)	Dick Groat (Pirates, b/w, upper body.)	25.00	12.50	7.50
(38)	Dick Groat (Cardinals, b/w, kneeling w/bat.)	25.00	12.50	7.50
(39)	Dick Groat (Cardinals, b/w, kneeling.)	25.00	12.50	7.50
(40)	Harvey Haddix/Kneeling (Pirates)	25.00	12.50	7.50
(41)	Harvey Haddix (Pirates, locker room.)	25.00	12.50	7.50
(42)	Ken Holtzman (Cubs, hands on knees.)	25.00	12.50	7.50
(43)	Ken Holtzman (A's, horizontal, two poses.)	25.00	12.50	7.50
(44)	Elston Howard (Yankees, catching crouch.)	30.00	15.000	9.00
(45)	Al Hrabosky (Cardinals, upper body.)	25.00	12.50	7.50
(46)	Larry Jackson/Kneeling (Cubs)	25.00	12.50	7.50
(47)	Larry Jackson/Fldg (Cardinals)	25.00	12.50	7.50
(48)	Larry Jackson (Cardinals, full-length on mound.)	25.00	12.00	7.50
(49)	Reggie Jackson (A's, full-length.)	40.00	20.00	12.00
(50)	Joey Jay (Reds, dugout step, glove on rail.)	25.00	12.50	7.50

(51)	Fergie Jenkins (Cubs, hands on knees.)	25.00	12.50	7.50
(52)	Ed Kranepool /Btg (Mets, color)	25.00	12.50	7.50
(53)	Tony Kubek/Fldg (Full-length)	25.00	12.50	7.50
(54)	Tony Kubek/Kneeling (No bat.)	25.00	12.50	7.50
(55)	Tony Kubek (Kneeling w/bat.)	25.00	12.50	7.50
(56)	Tony Kubek (Horizontal, upper body.)	25.00	12.50	7.50
(57)	Vern Law (Locker room.)	25.00	12.50	7.50
(58)	Jim Lefebvre (Dodgers, kneeling, bat on shoulder.)	25.00	12.50	7.50
(59)	Sherman Lollar (White Sox, throwing from crouch.)	25.00	12.50	7.50
(60)	Art Mahaffey (Phillies, upper body.)	25.00	12.50	7.50
(61)	Mickey Mantle (Upper body, road uniform.)	150.00	75.00	45.00
(62)	Mickey Mantle (Leaning, hands on knees.)	100.00	50.00	30.00
(63)	Mickey Mantle (Seated w/bat, glove on knee.)	130.00	65.00	40.00
(64)	Mickey Mantle/Kneeling	150.00	75.00	45.00
(65)	Mickey Mantle (Seated at locker, pointing to glove.)	150.00	75.00	45.00
(66)	Eddie Mathews (Braves, full-length.)	45.00	22.00	13.50
(67)	Eddie Mathews (Braves, sepia, upper body.)	45.00	22.00	13.50
(68)	Eddie Mathews (Braves, upper body, glove in front.)	45.00	22.00	13.50
(69)	Eddie Mathews (Braves, upper body, looking at glove.)	45.00	22.00	13.50
(70)	Dal Maxvill (Cardinals, bat on shoulder.)	25.00	12.50	7.50
(71)	Dal Maxvill/Fldg (Cardinals)	25.00	12.50	7.50
(72)	Charlie Maxwell (Tigers, horizontal, upper body.)	25.00	12.50	7.50
(73)	Tim McCarver (Cardinals, catching crouch.)	25.00	12.50	7.50
(74)	Lindy McDaniel (Cardinals, b/w, on dugout steps.)	25.00	12.50	7.50
(75)	Dave McNally (Orioles, upper body.)	25.00	12.50	7.50
(76)	Wilmer Mizell (Cardinals, upper body.)	25.00	12.50	7.50
(77)	Wally Moon/Kneeling (Dodgers)	25.00	12.50	7.50
(78)	Wally Moon/Standing (Dodgers)	25.00	12.50	7.50
(79)	Stan Musial (Upper body.)	50.00	25.00	15.00
(80)	Stan Musial/Btg (Horizontal)	50.00	25.00	15.00
(81)	Stan Musial (Full-length holding glove and bat.)	50.00	25.00	15.00
(82)	Stan Musial (Kneeling on bat.)	50.00	25.00	15.00
(83)	Stan Musial (Kneeling on bat, glove on ground.)	50.00	25.00	15.00
(84)	Stan Musial (Kneeling, glove in front, Busch Stadium.)	50.00	25.00	15.00
(85)	Stan Musial (Full-length, hands on knees.)	80.00	40.00	24.00
(86)	Stan Musial (Socks to cap, white background, in proposed '56 road uniform.)	125.00	62.00	37.00
(87)	Charlie Neal/Kneeling (Dodgers)	25.00	12.50	7.50
(88)	Charlie Neal (Dodgers, looking into glove.)	25.00	12.50	7.50
(89)	Rocky Nelson/Kneeling (Pirates)	25.00	12.50	7.50
(90)	Rocky Nelson/Fldg (Pirates)	25.00	12.50	7.50
(91)	Amos Otis (Royals, upper body.)	25.00	12.50	7.50
(92)	Jim Perry/Pitching (Indians)	25.00	12.50	7.50
(93)	Boog Powell (Orioles, full-length.)	25.00	12.50	7.50
(94)	Rick Reichardt (Angels, full-length.)	25.00	12.50	7.50
(95)	Brooks Robinson (Dugout step.)	45.00	22.00	13.50
(96)	Brooks Robinson/Throwing	45.00	22.00	13.50
(97)	Brooks Robinson (Standing w/glove.)	45.00	22.00	13.50
(98)	Brooks Robinson (Tying shoe.)	45.00	22.00	13.50
(99)	John Romano (Indians, adjusting shinguard.)	25.00	12.50	7.50
(101)	Manny Sanguillen (Pirates, catching crouch.)	25.00	12.50	7.50
(102)	Chuck Schilling (Full-length.)	25.00	12.50	7.50
(103)	Herb Score/Pitching (Indians)	25.00	12.50	7.50
(104)	Norm Siebern (A's, vest.)	25.00	12.50	7.50
(105)	Norm Siebern (A's, jersey.)	25.00	12.50	7.50
(106)	Roy Sievers (Senators, full-length.)	25.00	12.50	7.50
(107)	Roy Sievers (White Sox, drinking fountain.)	25.00	12.50	7.50
(108)	Roy Sievers/Kneeling (Phillies)	25.00	12.50	7.50
(109)	Bob Skinner (Pirates, upper body.)	25.00	12.50	7.50
(110)	Duke Snider (Brooklyn Dodgers, full-length.)	45.00	22.00	13.50
(111)	Duke Snider (L.A. Dodgers, upper body.)	45.00	22.00	13.50
(112)	Warren Spahn (Braves, b/w, wind-up.)	45.00	22.00	13.50
(114)	Willie Stargell (Upper body.)	35.00	17.50	10.50
(115)	Willie Stargell (Full-length.)	35.00	17.50	10.50
(116)	Tom Tresh/Fldg (Yankees)	25.00	12.50	7.50
(117)	Tom Tresh (Yankees, full-length.)	25.00	12.50	7.50
(119)	Bob Turley (Yankees, upper body.)	25.00	12.50	7.50
(120)	Bob Turley (At water fountain.)	25.00	12.50	7.50
(121)	Bill White (Cardinals, glove over rail.)	25.00	12.50	7.50
(122)	Bill White (Phillies, b/w, full-length.)	25.00	12.50	7.50
(123)	Bill White (Phillies, color, full-length.)	25.00	12.50	7.50
(124)	Billy Williams (Cubs, full-length.)	35.00	17.50	10.50
(126)	Steve Yeager (Dodgers, upper body.)	25.00	12.50	7.50

1952 Rawlings Stan Musial Premium Photo

In this black-and-white, blank-backed premium photo, Musial is shown in a batting stance superimposed over a game-action photo at Sportsman's Park. A white facsimile autograph is at lower-right. The wide bottom border of the 5" x 7" picture has the Rawlings logoscript and address.

	NM	EX	VG
Stan Musial	40.00	20.00	12.00

1954 Rawlings Stan Musial

The date of issue is speculation although the picture is certainly from 1955 or earlier. This 5-1/2" x 7-1/2" colorized photo is actually part of a cardboard Rawlings glove box. The panel at lower-right of the card identifies it as "A GENUINE RAWLINGS FACSIMILE AUTOGRAPH PICTURE." Back is blank.

	NM	EX	VG
Stan Musial	300.00	150.00	90.00

1955 Rawlings Stan Musial

Though missing from Topps and Bowman card sets from 1954-57, Cardinals superstar Stan Musial wasn't entirely unavailable on baseball cards. About 1955 he appeared on a series of six cards found on boxes of Rawlings baseball gloves carrying Musial's endorsement. The cards feature black-and-white photos of Musial set against a blue background. Because the cards were part of a display box, they are blank-backed. Depending on the position on the box, the cards measure approximately 2" x 3" (#1A and 2A) or 2-1/2" x 3-3/4" (#1-4). Cards are numbered in a yellow star at upper left.

		NM	EX	VG
	Complete Set (6):	2,500	1,250	750.00
	Complete Box:	3,000	1,500	900.00
	Common Card:	450.00	225.00	125.00
1	Stan Musial/Portrait	450.00	225.00	125.00
1A	Stan Musial (Portrait with bat.)	450.00	225.00	125.00
2	Stan Musial/Kneeling	450.00	225.00	125.00
2A	Stan Musial/Portrait	450.00	225.00	125.00
3	Stan Musial/Swinging (Horizontal)	450.00	225.00	125.00
4	Stan Musial (Batting pose.)	450.00	225.00	125.00

1963 Rawlings Stan Musial Premium

This premium was available by mail and commemorates the career of long-time Rawlings spokesman Stan Musial upon his retirement. The package contains an approximately 9" x 10" color portrait photo of Musial with a facsimile autograph, a sheet illustrated with four portraits of Musial during his career and listing his many records, and a note from the company indicating future availability of Musial gloves.

	NM	EX	VG
Complete Package:			
Stan Musial	60.00	30.00	18.00

1964 Rawlings Glove Box

Measuring about 2-3/8" x 4" when properly cut off the glove boxes on which they were printed, these full-color cards show stars of the day posing with their Rawlings glove prominently displayed. The blank-backed unnumbered cards are checklisted here alphabetically. The quality of cutting should be considered in grading these cards. In actuality, the cards were not meant to be cut from the boxes, but rather to show which premium photo was packed inside the glove box. Two cards of each player appear on the box.

		NM	EX	VG
	Complete Set (8):	450.00	225.00	135.00
	Common Player:	25.00	12.50	7.50
	Complete Box:	750.00	375.00	225.00
(1)	Ken Boyer	35.00	17.50	10.50
(2)	Tommy Davis	25.00	12.50	7.50
(3)	Dick Groat	25.00	12.50	7.50
(4)	Mickey Mantle	200.00	100.00	60.00
(5)	Brooks Robinson	60.00	30.00	18.00
(6)	Warren Spahn	50.00	25.00	15.00
(7)	Tom Tresh	25.00	12.50	7.50
(8)	Billy Williams	45.00	22.00	13.50

1964-66 Rawlings Premium Photos

One premium photo was inserted into each baseball glove box sold by Rawlings beginning in 1964 and continuing at least into 1966, when some changes in players and pictures were added. The 8" x 9-1/2" full-color photos were advertised on the outside of the boxes in miniature form. Each

of the photos pictures a player posed with his Rawlings leather prominently displayed. A black facsimile autograph is printed on the front.

		NM	EX	VG
Complete Set (12):		600.00	300.00	180.00
Common Player:		20.00	10.00	6.00
(1a)	Ken Boyer (Cardinals, 1964.)	25.00	12.50	7.50
(1b)	Ken Boyer (Mets, 1966.)	25.00	12.50	7.50
(2)	Tommy Davis	20.00	10.00	6.00
(3)	Dick Groat	20.00	10.00	6.00
(4a)	Mickey Mantle (No undershirt, 1964.)	150.00	75.00	45.00
(4b)	Mickey Mantle (Black undershirt, 1966.)	150.00	75.00	45.00
(5a)	Brooks Robinson (Full-bird cap, 1964.)	70.00	35.00	21.00
(5b)	Brooks Robinson (Bird's-head cap, 1966.)	85.00	42.00	25.00
(6)	Warren Spahn	75.00	37.00	22.00
(7)	Tom Tresh	20.00	10.00	6.00
(8)	Bill White (1966)	20.00	10.00	6.00
(9)	Billy Williams	50.00	25.00	15.00

1965 Rawlings MVP Premiums

The American and National League MVPs are featured in this pair of 8-1/8" x 10-1/4" premium pictures sponsored by the sporting goods manufacturer. The manner of their distribution is unknown. Printed on thin card stock, the premiums feature the artwork of Amadee Wohlschlaeger.

		NM	EX	VG
Complete Set (2):		125.00	65.00	40.00
(1)	Ken Boyer	65.00	35.00	20.00
(2)	Brooks Robinson	75.00	40.00	25.00

1969 Rawlings

How these cards were distributed is not certain today, nor is the extent of the series known. The approximately 3" x 5" black-and-white cards feature a portrait photo on front, with a wide white border at bottom that holds a facsimile autograph. The back has complete major and minor league stats, career highlights and a Rawlings ad.

	NM	EX	VG
Reggie Jackson	900.00	450.00	275.00
Mickey Mantle	2,500	1,250	750.00

1930 Ray-O-Print Photo Kits

This was one of several contemporary kits for do-it-yourself production of photo prints. The outfits were produced by M.P. & Co., of New York. The novelty kit consists of a 4-1/8" x 2-1/2" kraft paper envelope with production instructions printed on the outside and the name of the subject rubber-stamped on one end. Inside was a film negative, a piece of light-sensitive photo paper (each 1-7/8" x 2-15/16") and a tin stand for exposing and displaying the photo. Values shown are for complete kits. Individual components would be pro-rated, with the negative being the most valuable of the pieces. Anyone with a negative could make unlimited prints today, and even make them look old; collectors should use caution in purchasing prints alone.

		NM	EX	VG
Complete Set (8):		1,000	500.00	300.00
Common Kit:		125.00	67.00	38.00
Card: 20 Percent				
(1)	Lou Gehrig	250.00	125.00	75.00
(2)	Babe Ruth	400.00	200.00	120.00
(3)	Jack Dempsey (Boxer)	100.00	50.00	30.00
(4)	Herbert Hoover (President)	75.00	37.00	22.00
(5)	"Lindy" (Charles Lindbergh) (Aviator)	150.00	75.00	45.00
(6)	Mary Pickford (Actress)	50.00	25.00	15.00
(7)	Will Rogers (Humorist)	50.00	25.00	15.00
(8)	We (Charles Lindbergh) (W/ plane, Spirit of St. Louis.)	150.00	75.00	45.00

1899 Henry Reccius Cigars Honus Wagner

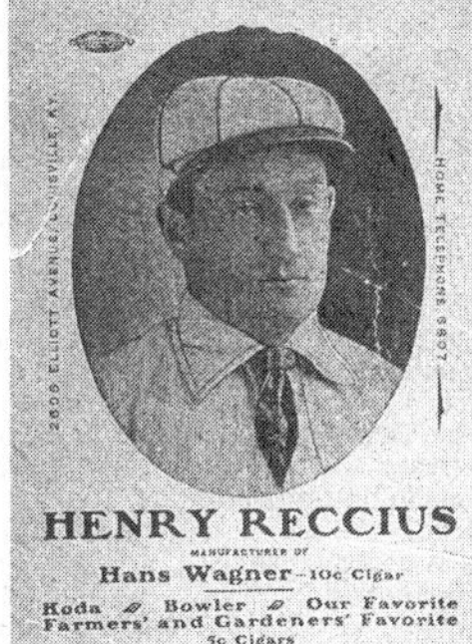

The date of this card's issue is probable, though it could have been issued anytime between 1897-99 during Wagner's stay in Louisville. The 3-3/8" x 4-11/16" card is printed in black-on-orange with an oval photograph of Wagner at center. Advertising for the company that marketed cigars under his name is around the border. The back has a lengthy pro-trade union poem. Only one example of the card is known. It was graded by PSA sometime after 1998 and given a Poor-Fair designation. The card was auctioned in November, 2001, for $21,850, and again in April, 2006, for $52,040.

Honus Wagner

1912 Recruit Little Cigars

This is the most common of the back advertisements found in T207. Factory 606 (Maryland) backs are much scarcer than those with Factory 240 (Pennsylvania), but currently carry little premium on that basis. Back printing is usually found in black, but several examples have been authenticated with brown ink printing on back. Their value is undetermined.

(See 1912 T207.)

1976 Red Barn Discs

The scarcest among the several regional sponsors of player disc sets issued in 1976 are those of the Red Barn family restaurant chain in Southeastern Wisconsin. The discs are 3-3/8" diameter with a black-and-white player portrait photo in the center of the baseball design. A line of red stars is above, while the left and right panels feature one of several bright colors. Produced by Michael Schecter Associates

under license from the Major League Baseball Players Association, the player photos have had uniform and cap logos removed. Backs are printed in red and purple. The unnumbered checklist here is presented in alphabetical order.

		NM	EX	VG
Complete Set (70):		500.00	250.00	150.00
Common Player:		8.00	4.00	2.50
(1)	Henry Aaron	65.00	32.00	19.50
(2)	Johnny Bench	25.00	12.50	7.50
(3)	Vida Blue	8.00	4.00	2.50
(4)	Larry Bowa	8.00	4.00	2.50
(5)	Lou Brock	20.00	10.00	6.00
(6)	Jeff Burroughs	8.00	4.00	2.50
(7)	John Candelaria	8.00	4.00	2.50
(8)	Jose Cardenal	8.00	4.00	2.50
(9)	Rod Carew	20.00	10.00	6.00
(10)	Steve Carlton	25.00	12.50	7.50
(11)	Dave Cash	8.00	4.00	2.50
(12)	Cesar Cedeno	8.00	4.00	2.50
(13)	Ron Cey	8.00	4.00	2.50
(14)	Carlton Fisk	20.00	10.00	6.00
(15)	Tito Fuentes	8.00	4.00	2.50
(16)	Steve Garvey	12.00	6.00	3.50
(17)	Ken Griffey	8.00	4.00	2.50
(18)	Don Gullett	8.00	4.00	2.50
(19)	Willie Horton	8.00	4.00	2.50
(20)	Al Hrabosky	8.00	4.00	2.50
(21)	Catfish Hunter	20.00	10.00	6.00
(22)	Reggie Jackson	40.00	20.00	12.00
(23)	Randy Jones	8.00	4.00	2.50
(24)	Jim Kaat	8.00	4.00	2.50
(25)	Don Kessinger	8.00	4.00	2.50
(26)	Dave Kingman	8.00	4.00	2.50
(27)	Jerry Koosman	8.00	4.00	2.50
(28)	Mickey Lolich	8.00	4.00	2.50
(29)	Greg Luzinski	8.00	4.00	2.50
(30)	Fred Lynn	10.00	5.00	3.00
(31)	Bill Madlock	8.00	4.00	2.50
(32)	Carlos May	8.00	4.00	2.50
(33)	John Mayberry	8.00	4.00	2.50
(34)	Bake McBride	8.00	4.00	2.50
(35)	Doc Medich	8.00	4.00	2.50
(36)	Andy Messersmith	8.00	4.00	2.50
(37)	Rick Monday	8.00	4.00	2.50
(38)	John Montefusco	8.00	4.00	2.50
(39)	Jerry Morales	8.00	4.00	2.50
(40)	Joe Morgan	20.00	10.00	6.00
(41)	Thurman Munson	15.00	7.50	4.50
(42)	Bobby Murcer	8.00	4.00	2.50
(43)	Al Oliver	8.00	4.00	2.50
(44)	Jim Palmer	20.00	10.00	6.00
(45)	Dave Parker	8.00	4.00	2.50
(46)	Tony Perez	20.00	10.00	6.00
(47)	Jerry Reuss	8.00	4.00	2.50
(48)	Brooks Robinson	25.00	12.50	7.50
(49)	Frank Robinson	25.00	12.50	7.50
(50)	Steve Rogers	8.00	4.00	2.50
(51)	Pete Rose	65.00	32.00	19.50
(52)	Nolan Ryan	100.00	50.00	30.00
(53)	Manny Sanguillen	8.00	4.00	2.50
(54)	Mike Schmidt	45.00	22.00	13.50
(55)	Tom Seaver	25.00	12.50	7.50
(56)	Ted Simmons	8.00	4.00	2.50
(57)	Reggie Smith	8.00	4.00	2.50
(58)	Willie Stargell	20.00	10.00	6.00
(59)	Rusty Staub	12.00	6.00	3.50
(60)	Rennie Stennett	8.00	4.00	2.50
(61)	Don Sutton	20.00	10.00	6.00
(62)	Andy Thornton	8.00	4.00	2.50
(63)	Luis Tiant	8.00	4.00	2.50
(64)	Joe Torre	12.00	6.00	3.50
(65)	Mike Tyson	8.00	4.00	2.50
(66)	Bob Watson	8.00	4.00	2.50
(67)	Wilbur Wood	8.00	4.00	2.50
(68)	Jimmy Wynn	8.00	4.00	2.50
(69)	Carl Yastrzemski	25.00	12.50	7.50
(70)	Richie Zisk	8.00	4.00	2.50

1912 Red Cross Tobacco (T207)

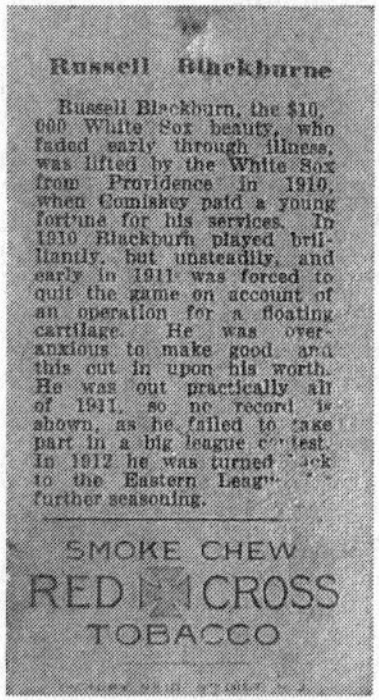

Among the rarest back variations known in the tobacco card series is the Red Cross back on T207. Only a handful of examples have ever been seen. Determination of values is an inexact science.

	NM	EX	VG
(See T207 for checklist. A Fair-condition "common" was bid to $3,500 in a 12/00 auction but was not sold.)			
Russell Blackburne (4/02 auction G-VG)			9,183
George Weaver (9/02 auction - Fair)			10,187

1910-12 Red Cross Tobacco Type 1 (T215)

The T215 set issued by Red Cross Tobacco is another of the Louisiana regional sets closely related to the T206 "White Border" tobacco cards. Very similar to the T213 Coupon cards, the Red Cross Tobacco cards are found in two distinct types, both featuring color player lithographs and measuring approximately 1-1/2" x 2-5/8", the standard tobacco card size. Type 1 Red Cross cards, issued from 1910 to 1912, have brown captions; while Type 2 cards, most of which appear to be from 1912-13, have blue printing. The backs of both types are identical, displaying the Red Cross name and emblem, which can be used to positively identify the set and differentiate it from the other Louisiana sets of the same period. Several variations have been found, most of them involving caption changes. Gaps have been left in the assigned numbering to accommodate future additions to these checklists.

		NM	EX	VG
Common Player:		825.00	330.00	165.00
(1)	Red Ames	825.00	330.00	165.00
(2)	Home Run Baker	2,500	1,000	500.00
(3)	Neal Ball	825.00	330.00	165.00
(4)	Chief Bender (No trees in background.)	2,500	1,000	500.00
(5)	Chief Bender (Trees in background.)	2,500	1,000	500.00
(6)	Al Bridwell	825.00	330.00	165.00
(7)	Bobby Byrne	825.00	330.00	165.00
(8)	Howie Camnitz	825.00	330.00	165.00
(9)	Frank Chance	2,500	1,000	500.00
(10)	Hal Chase	1,875	750.00	375.00
(11)	Ty Cobb	9,375	3,750	1,875
(12)	Eddie Collins	2,500	1,000	500.00
(13)	Wid Conroy	825.00	330.00	165.00
(14)	Doc Crandall	825.00	330.00	165.00
(15)	Sam Crawford	2,500	1,000	500.00
(16)	Birdie Cree	825.00	330.00	165.00
(17)	Harry Davis	825.00	330.00	165.00
(18)	Josh Devore	825.00	330.00	165.00
(19)	Mike Donlin	825.00	330.00	165.00
(20)	Mickey Doolan	825.00	330.00	165.00
(21)	Patsy Dougherty	825.00	330.00	165.00
(22)	Larry Doyle/Btg	825.00	330.00	165.00
(23)	Larry Doyle/Portrait	825.00	330.00	165.00
(24)	Kid Elberfeld	825.00	330.00	165.00
(25)	Russ Ford	825.00	330.00	165.00
(26)	Art Fromme	825.00	330.00	165.00
(27)	Clark Griffith	2,500	1,000	500.00
(28)	Topsy Hartsel	825.00	330.00	165.00
(29)	Dick Hoblitzell	825.00	330.00	165.00
(30)	Solly Hofman	825.00	330.00	165.00
(31)	Del Howard	825.00	330.00	165.00
(32)	Miller Huggins (Hands at mouth.)	2,500	1,000	500.00
(33)	Miller Huggins/Portrait	2,500	1,000	500.00
(34)	John Hummel	825.00	330.00	165.00
(35)	Hughie Jennings (Both hands showing.)	2,500	1,000	500.00
(36)	Hughie Jennings (One hand showing.)	2,500	1,000	500.00
(37)	Walter Johnson	4,375	1,750	875.00
(38)	Ed Konetchy	825.00	330.00	165.00
(39)	Harry Krause	825.00	330.00	165.00
(41)	Nap Lajoie	2,500	1,000	500.00
(42)	Joe Lake	825.00	330.00	165.00
(43)	Arlie Latham	825.00	330.00	165.00
(44)	Tommy Leach	825.00	330.00	165.00
(45)	Lefty Leifield	825.00	330.00	165.00
(46)	Harry Lord	825.00	330.00	165.00
(47)	Sherry Magee	825.00	330.00	165.00
(48)	Rube Marquard/Pitching	2,500	1,000	500.00
(49)	Rube Marquard/Portrait	2,500	1,000	500.00
(51)	Christy Mathewson (Dark cap.)	6,250	2,500	1,250
(52)	Christy Mathewson (White cap.)	6,250	2,500	1,250
(53)	Joe McGinnity	2,500	1,000	500.00
(54)	John McGraw (Glove at hip.)	2,500	1,000	500.00
(55)	John McGraw/Portrait	2,500	1,000	500.00
(56)	Harry McIntyre	825.00	330.00	165.00
(57)	Fred Merkle	825.00	330.00	165.00
(58)	Chief Meyers	825.00	330.00	165.00
(59)	Dots Miller	825.00	330.00	165.00
(61)	Mike Mowrey	825.00	330.00	165.00
(62)	Danny Murphy	825.00	330.00	165.00
(63)	Red Murray	825.00	330.00	165.00
(64)	Rebel Oakes	825.00	330.00	165.00
(65)	Charley O'Leary	825.00	330.00	165.00
(66)	Dode Paskert	825.00	330.00	165.00
(67)	Barney Pelty	825.00	330.00	165.00
(68)	Jack Quinn	825.00	330.00	165.00
(69)	Ed Reulbach	825.00	330.00	165.00
(71)	Nap Rucker	825.00	330.00	165.00
(72)	Germany Schaefer	825.00	330.00	165.00
(73)	Wildfire Schulte	825.00	330.00	165.00
(74)	Jimmy Sheckard	825.00	330.00	165.00
(75)	Frank Smith	825.00	330.00	165.00
(76)	Frank Smither (Smith)	825.00	330.00	165.00
(77)	Tris Speaker	3,125	1,250	625.00
(78)	Jake Stahl	825.00	330.00	165.00
(79)	Harry Steinfeldt	825.00	330.00	165.00
(81)	Gabby Street/Catching	825.00	330.00	165.00
(82)	Gabby Street/Portrait	825.00	330.00	165.00
(83)	Jeff Sweeney	825.00	330.00	165.00
(84)	Lee Tannehill	825.00	330.00	165.00
(85)	Joe Tinker (Bat off shoulder.)	2,500	1,000	500.00
(86)	Joe Tinker (Bat on shoulder.)	2,500	1,000	500.00
(87)	Heinie Wagner	825.00	330.00	165.00
(88)	Jack Warhop	825.00	330.00	165.00
(89)	Zach Wheat	2,500	1,000	500.00
(91)	Doc White	825.00	330.00	165.00
(92)	Ed Willetts (Willett)	825.00	330.00	165.00
(93)	Owen Wilson	825.00	330.00	165.00
(94)	Hooks Wiltse/Pitching	825.00	330.00	165.00
(95)	Hooks Wiltse/Portrait	825.00	330.00	165.00
(96)	Cy Young	6,250	2,500	1,250

1912-13 Red Cross Tobacco Type 2 (T215)

		NM	EX	VG
Common Player:		825.00	330.00	165.00
(1)	Red Ames	825.00	330.00	165.00
(2)	Neal Ball	825.00	330.00	165.00
(3)	Home Run Baker	2,375	950.00	475.00
(4)	Chief Bender (No trees in background.)	2,375	950.00	475.00
(5)	Chief Bender (Trees in background.)	2,375	950.00	475.00
(6)	Roger Bresnahan	2,375	950.00	475.00
(7)	Al Bridwell	825.00	330.00	165.00
(8)	Mordecai Brown	2,375	950.00	475.00
(9)	Bobby Byrne	825.00	330.00	165.00
(10)	Howie Camnitz	825.00	330.00	165.00
(11)	Frank Chance	2,375	950.00	475.00
(12)	Hal Chase	1,500	600.00	300.00
(13)	Ty Cobb	9,375	3,750	1,875
(14)	Eddie Collins	2,375	950.00	475.00
(15)	Doc Crandall	825.00	330.00	165.00
(16)	Sam Crawford	2,375	950.00	475.00
(17)	Birdie Cree	825.00	330.00	165.00
(18)	Harry Davis	825.00	330.00	165.00
(19)	Josh Devore	825.00	330.00	165.00
(21)	Mike Donlin	825.00	330.00	165.00
(22)	Mickey Doolan/Btg	825.00	330.00	165.00
(23)	Mickey Doolan/Fldg	825.00	330.00	165.00
(24)	Patsy Dougherty	825.00	330.00	165.00
(25)	Larry Doyle/Btg	825.00	330.00	165.00
(26)	Larry Doyle/Portrait	825.00	330.00	165.00
(27)	Jean Dubuc	825.00	330.00	165.00
(28)	Kid Elberfeld	825.00	330.00	165.00
(29)	Johnny Evers	2,375	950.00	475.00
(30)	Russ Ford	825.00	330.00	165.00
(31)	Art Fromme	825.00	330.00	165.00
(32)	Clark Griffith	2,375	950.00	475.00
(33)	Bob Groom	825.00	330.00	165.00
(34)	Topsy Hartsel	825.00	330.00	165.00
(35)	Buck Herzog	825.00	330.00	165.00
(36)	Dick Hoblitzell	825.00	330.00	165.00
(37)	Solly Hofman	825.00	330.00	165.00
(38)	Miller Huggins (Hands at mouth.)	2,375	950.00	475.00
(39)	Miller Huggins/Portrait	2,375	950.00	475.00
(41)	John Hummel	825.00	330.00	165.00
(42)	Hughie Jennings	2,375	950.00	475.00
(43)	Walter Johnson	3,125	1,250	625.00
(44)	Joe Kelley	2,375	950.00	475.00
(45)	Ed Konetchy	825.00	330.00	165.00
(46)	Harry Krause	825.00	330.00	165.00
(47)	Nap Lajoie	2,375	950.00	475.00
(48)	Joe Lake	825.00	330.00	165.00
(49)	Tommy Leach	825.00	330.00	165.00
(50)	Lefty Leifield	825.00	330.00	165.00
(51)	Harry Lord	825.00	330.00	165.00
(52)	Sherry Magee	825.00	330.00	165.00
(53)	Rube Marquard/Pitching	2,375	950.00	475.00
(54)	Rube Marquard/Portrait	2,375	950.00	475.00
(55)	Christy Mathewson	3,440	1,375	690.00
(56)	John McGraw (Glove at side.)	2,300	950.00	475.00
(57)	John McGraw/Portrait	2,375	950.00	475.00
(58)	Harry McIntire	825.00	330.00	165.00
(59)	Larry McLean	825.00	330.00	165.00
(61)	Fred Merkle	825.00	330.00	165.00
(62)	Dots Miller	825.00	330.00	165.00
(63)	Mike Mitchell	825.00	330.00	165.00
(64)	Mike Mowrey	825.00	330.00	165.00
(65)	George Mullin	825.00	330.00	165.00
(66)	Danny Murphy	825.00	330.00	165.00
(67)	Red Murray	825.00	330.00	165.00
(68)	Rebel Oakes	825.00	330.00	165.00
(69)	Rube Oldring	825.00	330.00	165.00
(70)	Charley O'Leary	825.00	330.00	165.00
(71)	Dode Paskert	825.00	330.00	165.00
(72)	Barney Pelty	825.00	330.00	165.00
(73)	Billy Purtell	825.00	330.00	165.00
(74)	Ed Reulbach	825.00	330.00	165.00
(75)	Nap Rucker	825.00	330.00	165.00
(76)	Germany Schaefer (Chicago)	825.00	330.00	165.00
(77)	Germany Schaefer (Washington)	825.00	330.00	165.00
(78)	Wildfire Schulte	825.00	330.00	165.00
(79)	Frank Smith	825.00	330.00	165.00
(80)	Frank Smither (Smith)	825.00	330.00	165.00
(82)	Tris Speaker	2,375	950.00	475.00
(83)	Jake Stahl	825.00	330.00	165.00
(84)	Harry Steinfeldt	825.00	330.00	165.00
(85)	Ed Summers	825.00	330.00	165.00
(86)	Jeff Sweeney	825.00	330.00	165.00
(87)	Ira Thomas	825.00	330.00	165.00
(88)	Joe Tinker (Bat off shoulder.)	2,375	950.00	475.00
(89)	Joe Tinker (Bat on shoulder.)	2,375	950.00	475.00
(90)	Heinie Wagner	825.00	330.00	165.00
(91)	Jack Warhop	825.00	330.00	165.00
(92)	Doc White	825.00	330.00	165.00
(93)	Hooks Wiltse/Pitching	825.00	330.00	165.00
(94)	Hooks Wiltse/Portrait	825.00	330.00	165.00

1954 Red Heart Dog Food

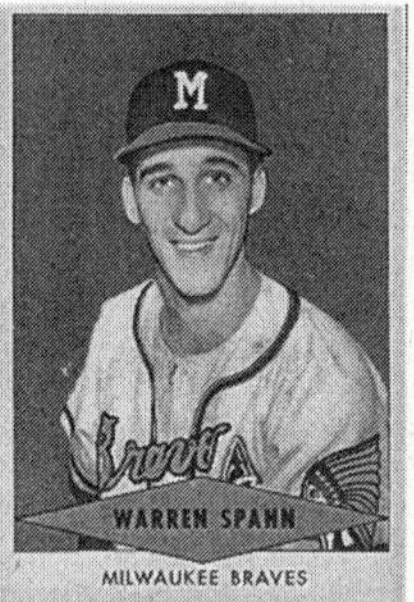

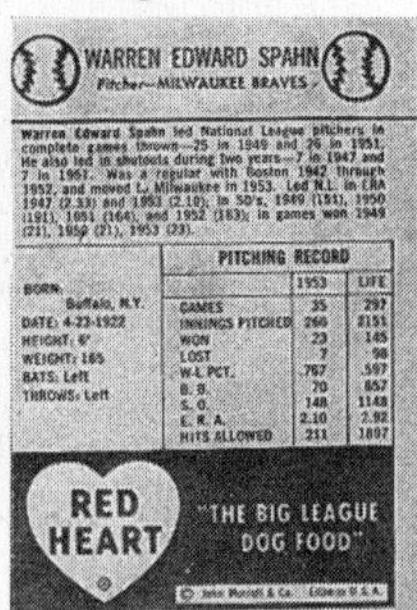

This set of 33 cards was issued in three color-coded series by the Red Heart Dog Food Co. Card fronts feature hand-colored photos on either a blue, green or red background. The 11 red-background cards are scarcer than the 11-card blue or green series. Backs of the 2-5/8" x 3-3/4" cards contain biographical and statistical information along with a Red Heart ad. Each 11-card series was available via a mail-in offer. As late as the early 1970s, the company was still sending cards to collectors who requested them.

		NM	EX	VG
Complete Set (33):		2,150	900.00	450.00
Common Player:		30.00	15.00	9.00
(1)	Richie Ashburn	100.00	40.00	20.00
(2)	Frankie Baumholtz	40.00	16.00	8.00
(3)	Gus Bell	30.00	15.00	9.00
(4)	Billy Cox	40.00	16.00	8.00
(5)	Alvin Dark	30.00	15.00	9.00
(6)	Carl Erskine	75.00	30.00	15.00
(7)	Ferris Fain	40.00	16.00	8.00
(8)	Dee Fondy	30.00	15.00	9.00
(9)	Nelson Fox	85.00	35.00	17.50
(10)	Jim Gilliam	50.00	20.00	10.00
(11)	Jim Hegan	40.00	16.00	8.00
(12)	George Kell	45.00	18.00	9.00
(13)	Ted Kluszewski	65.00	25.00	13.00
(14)	Ralph Kiner	60.00	24.00	12.00
(15)	Harvey Kuenn	30.00	12.00	6.00
(16)	Bob Lemon	55.00	22.50	11.00
(17)	Sherman Lollar	30.00	15.00	9.00
(18)	Mickey Mantle	430.00	175.00	90.00
(19)	Billy Martin	65.00	25.00	13.00
(20)	Gil McDougald	55.00	22.50	11.00
(21)	Roy McMillan	30.00	15.00	9.00
(22)	Minnie Minoso	50.00	20.00	10.00
(23)	Stan Musial	260.00	100.00	50.00
(24)	Billy Pierce	40.00	16.00	8.00
(25)	Al Rosen	45.00	18.00	9.00
(26)	Hank Sauer	30.00	15.00	9.00
(27)	Red Schoendienst	75.00	30.00	15.00
(28)	Enos Slaughter	65.00	25.00	13.00
(29)	Duke Snider	120.00	50.00	25.00
(30)	Warren Spahn	65.00	25.00	13.00
(31)	Sammy White	30.00	15.00	9.00
(32)	Eddie Yost	30.00	12.00	6.00
(33)	Gus Zernial	30.00	12.00	6.00

1952 Red Man Tobacco

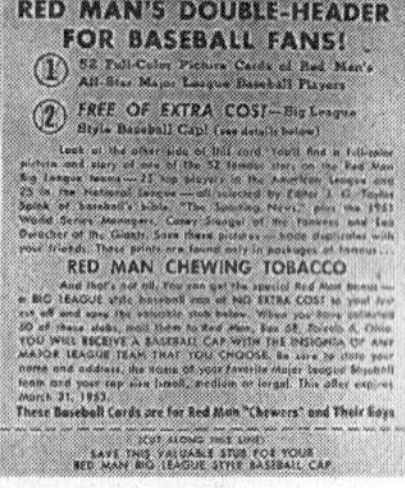

This was the first national set of tobacco cards produced since the golden days of tobacco sets in the early part of the century. There are 52 cards in the set, with 25 top players and one manager from each league. Player selection was made by editor J.G. Taylor Spink of The Sporting News. Cards measure 3-1/2" x 4", including a 1/2" tab at the bottom of each card. These tabs were redeemable for a free baseball cap from Red Man. Cards are harder to find with tabs intact, and thus more valuable in that form. Values quoted here are for cards with tabs. Cards with the tabs removed would be valued about 25-35 percent of the quoted figures. Card fronts are full color paintings of each player with biographical information inset in the portrait area. Card backs contain company advertising. Cards are numbered and dated only on the tabs. The 1952 Red Man cards can be found with either of two expiration dates on back, March 31 or June 1, 1953; neither commands a premium.

		NM	EX	VG
Complete Set, W/Tab (52):		10,000	4,000	2,000
Common Player, W/Tab:		100.00	40.00	20.00
Complete Set, No Tab (52):		2,250	550.00	275.00
Common Player, No Tab:		20.00	8.00	4.00
	WITH TAB			
1A	Casey Stengel	250.00	100.00	50.00
1N	Leo Durocher	200.00	80.00	40.00
2A	Roberto Avila	100.00	40.00	20.00
2N	Richie Ashburn	240.00	95.00	45.00
3A	Larry "Yogi" Berra	375.00	150.00	75.00
3N	Ewell Blackwell	120.00	45.00	25.00
4A	Gil Coan	100.00	40.00	20.00
4N	Cliff Chambers	100.00	40.00	20.00
5A	Dom DiMaggio	140.00	55.00	27.50
5N	Murry Dickson	100.00	40.00	20.00
6A	Larry Doby	215.00	85.00	45.00
6N	Sid Gordon	100.00	40.00	20.00
7A	Ferris Fain	100.00	40.00	20.00
7N	Granny Hamner	100.00	40.00	20.00
8A	Bob Feller	325.00	130.00	65.00
8N	Jim Hearn	100.00	40.00	20.00
9A	Nelson Fox	215.00	85.00	45.00
9N	Monte Irvin	215.00	85.00	45.00
10A	Johnny Groth	100.00	40.00	20.00
10N	Larry Jansen	100.00	40.00	20.00
11A	Jim Hegan	100.00	40.00	20.00
11N	Willie Jones	100.00	40.00	20.00
12A	Eddie Joost	100.00	40.00	20.00
12N	Ralph Kiner	215.00	85.00	45.00
13A	George Kell	215.00	85.00	45.00
13N	Whitey Lockman	100.00	40.00	20.00
14A	Gil McDougald	100.00	40.00	20.00
14N	Sal Maglie	100.00	40.00	20.00
15A	Orestes Minoso	100.00	40.00	20.00
15N	Willie Mays	600.00	240.00	120.00
16A	Bill Pierce	100.00	40.00	20.00
16N	Stan Musial	575.00	230.00	115.00
17A	Bob Porterfield	100.00	40.00	20.00
17N	Pee Wee Reese	340.00	135.00	65.00
18A	Eddie Robinson	100.00	40.00	20.00
18N	Robin Roberts	215.00	85.00	45.00
19A	Saul Rogovin	100.00	40.00	20.00
19N	Al Schoendienst	215.00	85.00	45.00
20A	Bobby Shantz	100.00	40.00	20.00
20N	Enos Slaughter	215.00	85.00	45.00
21A	Vern Stephens	100.00	40.00	20.00
21N	Duke Snider	275.00	110.00	55.00
22A	Vic Wertz	100.00	40.00	20.00
22N	Warren Spahn	215.00	85.00	45.00
23A	Ted Williams	1,800	725.00	360.00
23N	Eddie Stanky	100.00	40.00	20.00
24A	Early Wynn	215.00	85.00	45.00
24N	Bobby Thomson	100.00	40.00	20.00
25A	Eddie Yost	100.00	40.00	20.00
25N	Earl Torgeson	100.00	40.00	20.00
26A	Gus Zernial	100.00	40.00	20.00
26N	Wes Westrum	100.00	40.00	20.00
	NO TAB			
1A	Casey Stengel	45.00	18.00	9.00
1N	Leo Durocher	35.00	14.00	7.00
2A	Roberto Avila	20.00	8.00	4.00
2N	Richie Ashburn	55.00	22.00	11.00
3A	Larry "Yogi" Berra	85.00	35.00	17.50
3N	Ewell Blackwell	25.00	10.00	5.00
4A	Gil Coan	20.00	8.00	4.00
4N	Cliff Chambers	20.00	8.00	4.00
5A	Dom DiMaggio	30.00	12.00	6.00
5N	Murry Dickson	20.00	8.00	4.00
6A	Larry Doby	45.00	18.00	9.00
6N	Sid Gordon	20.00	8.00	4.00
7A	Ferris Fain	20.00	8.00	4.00
7N	Granny Hamner	20.00	8.00	4.00
8A	Bob Feller	80.00	32.00	16.00
8N	Jim Hearn	20.00	8.00	4.00
9A	Nelson Fox	50.00	20.00	10.00
9N	Monte Irvin	45.00	18.00	9.00
10A	Johnny Groth	20.00	8.00	4.00
10N	Larry Jansen	20.00	8.00	4.00
11A	Jim Hegan	20.00	8.00	4.00
11N	Willie Jones	20.00	8.00	4.00
12A	Eddie Joost	20.00	8.00	4.00
12N	Ralph Kiner	45.00	18.00	9.00
13A	George Kell	45.00	18.00	9.00
13N	Whitey Lockman	20.00	8.00	4.00
14A	Gil McDougald	25.00	10.00	5.00
14N	Sal Maglie	20.00	8.00	4.00
15A	Orestes Minoso	30.00	12.00	6.00
15N	Willie Mays	200.00	80.00	40.00
16A	Bill Pierce	20.00	8.00	4.00
16N	Stan Musial	175.00	70.00	35.00
17A	Bob Porterfield	20.00	8.00	4.00
17N	Pee Wee Reese	70.00	28.00	14.00
18A	Eddie Robinson	20.00	8.00	4.00
18N	Robin Roberts	45.00	18.00	9.00
19A	Saul Rogovin	20.00	8.00	4.00
19N	Al Schoendienst	45.00	18.00	9.00
20A	Bobby Shantz	20.00	8.00	4.00
20N	Enos Slaughter	45.00	18.00	9.00
21A	Vern Stephens	20.00	8.00	4.00
21N	Duke Snider	85.00	35.00	17.50
22A	Vic Wertz	20.00	8.00	4.00
22N	Warren Spahn	45.00	18.00	9.00
23A	Ted Williams	375.00	150.00	75.00
23N	Eddie Stanky	20.00	8.00	4.00
24A	Early Wynn	45.00	18.00	9.00
24N	Bobby Thomson	20.00	8.00	4.00
25A	Eddie Yost	20.00	8.00	4.00
25N	Earl Torgeson	20.00	8.00	4.00
26A	Gus Zernial	20.00	8.00	4.00
26N	Wes Westrum	20.00	8.00	4.00

1953 Red Man Tobacco

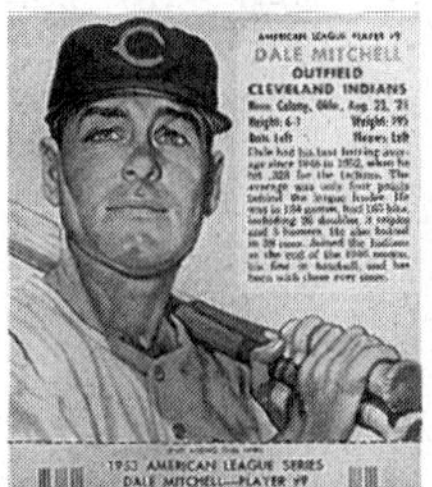

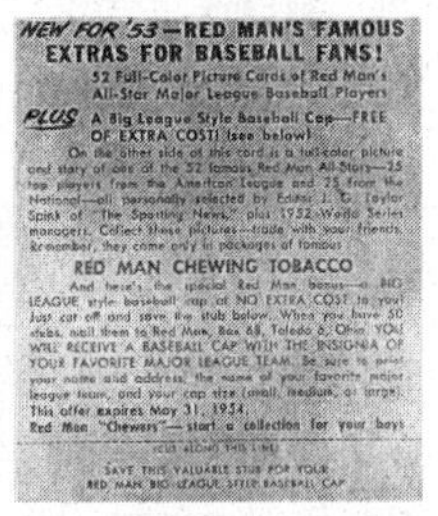

This was the chewing tobacco company's second annual set of 3-1/2" x 4" cards, including the tabs at the bottom of the cards. Formats for front and back are similar to the '52 edition. The 1953 Red Man cards, however, include card numbers within the player biographical section, and the card backs are headlined "New for '53." Once again, cards with intact tabs (which were redeemable for a free cap) are more valuable. Prices below are for cards with tabs. Cards with tabs removed are worth about 25-35 percent of the stated values. Each league is represented by 25 players and a manager on the full-color cards, a total of 52. Values quoted here are for cards with tabs. Cards with the tabs removed would be valued about 35-40 percent of the quoted figures. The 1953 Red Man cards can be found with either of two expiration dates on back, March 31 or May 31, 1954; neither commands a premium.

		NM	EX	VG
Complete Set, W/Tab (52):		5,500	2,200	1,100
Common Player:		60.00	24.00	12.00
Complete Set, No Tab (52):		1,400	550.00	275.00
Common Player, No Tab:		12.50	5.00	2.50
	WITH TAB			
1A	Casey Stengel	150.00	60.00	30.00
1N	Charlie Dressen	75.00	30.00	15.00
2A	Hank Bauer	75.00	30.00	15.00
2N	Bobby Adams	60.00	24.00	12.00
3A	Larry "Yogi" Berra	300.00	120.00	60.00
3N	Richie Ashburn	125.00	50.00	25.00
4A	Walt Dropo	60.00	24.00	12.00
4N	Joe Black	100.00	40.00	20.00
5A	Nelson Fox	125.00	50.00	25.00
5N	Roy Campanella	300.00	120.00	60.00
6A	Jackie Jensen	75.00	30.00	15.00
6N	Ted Kluszewski	95.00	40.00	20.00
7A	Eddie Joost	60.00	24.00	12.00
7N	Whitey Lockman	60.00	24.00	12.00
8A	George Kell	125.00	50.00	25.00
8N	Sal Maglie	60.00	24.00	12.00
9A	Dale Mitchell	60.00	24.00	12.00
9N	Andy Pafko	60.00	24.00	12.00
10A	Phil Rizzuto	225.00	90.00	45.00
10N	Pee Wee Reese	250.00	100.00	50.00
11A	Eddie Robinson	60.00	24.00	12.00
11N	Robin Roberts	125.00	50.00	25.00
12A	Gene Woodling	70.00	28.00	14.00
12N	Red Schoendienst	125.00	50.00	25.00
13A	Gus Zernial	60.00	24.00	12.00
13N	Enos Slaughter	125.00	50.00	25.00
14A	Early Wynn	125.00	50.00	25.00
14N	Edwin "Duke" Snider	300.00	120.00	60.00
15A	Joe Dobson	60.00	24.00	12.00
15N	Ralph Kiner	125.00	50.00	25.00
16A	Billy Pierce	60.00	24.00	12.00
16N	Hank Sauer	60.00	24.00	12.00
17A	Bob Lemon	125.00	50.00	25.00
17N	Del Ennis	60.00	24.00	12.00
18A	Johnny Mize	145.00	60.00	30.00
18N	Granny Hamner	60.00	24.00	12.00
19A	Bob Porterfield	60.00	24.00	12.00
19N	Warren Spahn	145.00	60.00	30.00
20A	Bobby Shantz	60.00	24.00	12.00
20N	Wes Westrum	60.00	24.00	12.00
21A	"Mickey" Vernon	60.00	24.00	12.00
21N	Hoyt Wilhelm	125.00	50.00	25.00
22A	Dom DiMaggio	75.00	30.00	15.00
22N	Murry Dickson	60.00	24.00	12.00
23A	Gil McDougald	70.00	28.00	14.00
23N	Warren Hacker	60.00	24.00	12.00
24A	Al Rosen	70.00	28.00	14.00
24N	Gerry Staley	60.00	24.00	12.00
25A	Mel Parnell	60.00	24.00	12.00
25N	Bobby Thomson	60.00	24.00	12.00
26A	Roberto Avila	60.00	24.00	12.00
26N	Stan Musial	700.00	280.00	140.00
	NO TAB			
1A	Casey Stengel	35.00	14.00	7.00
1N	Charlie Dressen	17.50	7.00	3.50
2A	Hank Bauer	17.50	7.00	3.50
2N	Bobby Adams	12.50	5.00	2.50
3A	Larry "Yogi" Berra	65.00	26.00	13.00
3N	Richie Ashburn	40.00	16.00	8.00
4A	Walt Dropo	12.50	5.00	2.50
4N	Joe Black	20.00	8.00	4.00
5A	Nelson Fox	40.00	16.00	8.00
5N	Roy Campanella	65.00	26.00	13.00
6A	Jackie Jensen	20.00	8.00	4.00
6N	Ted Kluszewski	25.00	10.00	5.00
7A	Eddie Joost	12.50	5.00	2.50
7N	Whitey Lockman	12.50	5.00	2.50
8A	George Kell	40.00	16.00	8.00
8N	Sal Maglie	15.00	6.00	3.00
9A	Dale Mitchell	12.50	5.00	2.50
9N	Andy Pafko	12.50	5.00	2.50
10A	Phil Rizzuto	50.00	20.00	10.00
10N	Pee Wee Reese	60.00	24.00	12.00
11A	Eddie Robinson	12.50	5.00	2.50
11N	Robin Roberts	40.00	16.00	8.00
12A	Gene Woodling	15.00	6.00	3.00
12N	Red Schoendienst	40.00	16.00	8.00
13A	Gus Zernial	12.50	5.00	2.50
13N	Enos Slaughter	40.00	16.00	8.00
14A	Early Wynn	40.00	16.00	8.00
14N	Edwin "Duke" Snider	75.00	30.00	15.00
15A	Joe Dobson	12.50	5.00	2.50
15N	Ralph Kiner	40.00	16.00	8.00
16A	Billy Pierce	15.00	6.00	3.00
16N	Hank Sauer	12.50	5.00	2.50
17A	Bob Lemon	40.00	16.00	8.00
17N	Del Ennis	12.50	5.00	2.50
18A	Johnny Mize	40.00	16.00	8.00
18N	Granny Hamner	12.50	5.00	2.50
19A	Bob Porterfield	12.50	5.00	2.50
19N	Warren Spahn	45.00	18.00	9.00
20A	Bobby Shantz	12.50	5.00	2.50
20N	Wes Westrum	12.50	5.00	2.50
21A	"Mickey" Vernon	12.50	5.00	2.50
21N	Hoyt Wilhelm	35.00	14.00	7.00
22A	Dom DiMaggio	25.00	10.00	5.00
22N	Murry Dickson	12.50	5.00	2.50
23A	Gil McDougald	15.00	6.00	3.00
23N	Warren Hacker	12.50	5.00	2.50
24A	Al Rosen	17.50	7.00	3.50
24N	Gerry Staley	12.50	5.00	2.50
25A	Mel Parnell	12.50	5.00	2.50
25N	Bobby Thomson	12.50	5.00	2.50
26A	Roberto Avila	12.50	5.00	2.50
26N	Stan Musial	125.00	50.00	25.00

1954 Red Man Tobacco

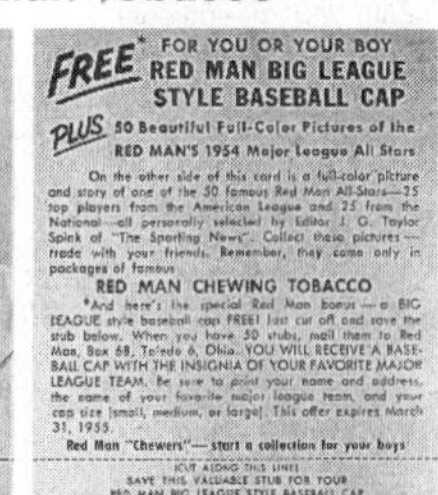

In 1954, the Red Man set eliminated managers from the set, and issued only 25 player cards for each league. There are, however, four variations which bring the total set size to 54 full-color cards. Two cards exist for Gus Bell and Enos Slaughter, while American Leaguers George Kell, Sam Mele and Dave Philley are each shown with two different teams. Complete set prices quoted below do not include the scarcer of the variation pairs. Cards measure 3-1/2" x 4" with tabs intact. Cards without tabs are worth about 25-35 percent of the values quoted below. Formats for the cards remain virtually unchanged, with card numbers included within the player information boxes as well as on the tabs. Cards can be found with either of two expiration dates on back, March 31 or May 31, 1955; neither commands a premium.

		NM	EX	VG
Complete Set, W/Tab (50):		4,000	1,600	800.00
Common Player, W/Tab:		45.00	18.00	9.00
Complete Set, No Tab (50):		1,400	550.00	275.00
Common Player, No Tab:		15.00	6.00	3.00
	WITH TAB			
1A	Bobby Avila	45.00	18.00	9.00
1N	Richie Ashburn	90.00	36.00	18.00
2A	Jim Busby	45.00	18.00	9.00
2N	Billy Cox	55.00	22.00	11.00
3A	Nelson Fox	90.00	36.00	18.00
3N	Del Crandall	45.00	18.00	9.00
4Aa	George Kell (Boston)	125.00	50.00	25.00
4Ab	George Kell (Chicago)	180.00	70.00	35.00
4N	Carl Erskine	60.00	24.00	12.00
5A	Sherman Lollar	45.00	18.00	9.00
5N	Monte Irvin	90.00	36.00	18.00
6Aa	Sam Mele (Baltimore)	90.00	36.00	18.00
6Ab	Sam Mele (Chicago)	110.00	44.00	22.00
6N	Ted Kluszewski	100.00	40.00	20.00
7A	Orestes Minoso	65.00	26.00	13.00
7N	Don Mueller	45.00	18.00	9.00
8A	Mel Parnell	45.00	18.00	9.00
8N	Andy Pafko	45.00	18.00	9.00
9Aa	Dave Philley (Cleveland)	75.00	30.00	15.00
9Ab	Dave Philley (Philadelphia)	145.00	60.00	30.00
9N	Del Rice	45.00	18.00	9.00
10A	Billy Pierce	45.00	18.00	9.00
10N	Al Schoendienst	90.00	36.00	18.00
11A	Jim Piersall	60.00	24.00	12.00
11N	Warren Spahn	100.00	40.00	20.00
12A	Al Rosen	50.00	20.00	10.00
12N	Curt Simmons	45.00	18.00	9.00
13A	"Mickey" Vernon	45.00	18.00	9.00
13N	Roy Campanella	215.00	85.00	45.00
14A	Sammy White	45.00	18.00	9.00
14N	Jim Gilliam	60.00	24.00	12.00
15A	Gene Woodling	60.00	24.00	12.00
15N	"Pee Wee" Reese	160.00	64.00	32.00
16A	Ed "Whitey" Ford	140.00	56.00	28.00
16N	Edwin "Duke" Snider	215.00	85.00	45.00
17A	Phil Rizzuto	140.00	56.00	28.00
17N	Rip Repulski	45.00	18.00	9.00
18A	Bob Porterfield	45.00	18.00	9.00

18N	Robin Roberts	90.00	36.00	18.00
19A	Al "Chico" Carrasquel	45.00	18.00	9.00
19Na	Enos Slaughter	215.00	85.00	45.00
19Nb	Gus Bell	190.00	75.00	35.00
20A	Larry "Yogi" Berra	200.00	80.00	40.00
20N	Johnny Logan	45.00	18.00	9.00
21A	Bob Lemon	90.00	36.00	18.00
21N	Johnny Antonelli	45.00	18.00	9.00
22A	Ferris Fain	45.00	18.00	9.00
22N	Gil Hodges	90.00	36.00	18.00
23A	Hank Bauer	50.00	20.00	10.00
23N	Eddie Mathews	100.00	40.00	20.00
24A	Jim Delsing	45.00	18.00	9.00
24N	Lew Burdette	45.00	18.00	9.00
25A	Gil McDougald	55.00	22.00	11.00
25N	Willie Mays	425.00	170.00	85.00
	NO TAB			
1A	Bobby Avila	15.00	6.00	3.00
1N	Richie Ashburn	35.00	14.00	7.00
2A	Jim Busby	15.00	6.00	3.00
2N	Billy Cox	20.00	8.00	4.00
3A	Nelson Fox	35.00	14.00	7.00
3N	Del Crandall	15.00	6.00	3.00
4Aa	George Kell (Boston)	50.00	20.00	10.00
4Ab	George Kell (Chicago)	65.00	26.00	13.00
4N	Carl Erskine	22.50	9.00	4.50
5A	Sherman Lollar	15.00	6.00	3.00
5N	Monte Irvin	35.00	14.00	7.00
6Aa	Sam Mele (Baltimore)	30.00	12.00	6.00
6Ab	Sam Mele (Chicago)	55.00	22.00	11.00
6N	Ted Kluszewski	30.00	12.00	6.00
7A	Orestes Minoso	25.00	10.00	5.00
7N	Don Mueller	15.00	6.00	3.00
8A	Mel Parnell	15.00	6.00	3.00
8N	Andy Pafko	15.00	6.00	3.00
9Aa	Dave Philley (Cleveland)	30.00	12.00	6.00
9Ab	Dave Philley (Philadelphia)	65.00	26.00	13.00
9N	Del Rice	15.00	6.00	3.00
10A	Billy Pierce	15.00	6.00	3.00
10N	Al Schoendienst	35.00	14.00	7.00
11A	Jim Piersall	20.00	8.00	4.00
11N	Warren Spahn	35.00	14.00	7.00
12A	Al Rosen	20.00	8.00	4.00
12N	Curt Simmons	15.00	6.00	3.00
13A	"Mickey" Vernon	15.00	6.00	3.00
13N	Roy Campanella	65.00	26.00	13.00
14A	Sammy White	15.00	6.00	3.00
14N	Jim Gilliam	22.50	9.00	4.50
15A	Gene Woodling	22.50	9.00	4.50
15N	"Pee Wee" Reese	55.00	22.00	11.00
16A	Ed "Whitey" Ford	45.00	18.00	9.00
16N	Edwin "Duke" Snider	65.00	26.00	13.00
17A	Phil Rizzuto	50.00	20.00	10.00
17N	Rip Repulski	15.00	6.00	3.00
18A	Bob Porterfield	15.00	6.00	3.00
18N	Robin Roberts	35.00	14.00	7.00
19A	Al "Chico" Carrasquel	20.00	8.00	4.00
19Na	Enos Slaughter	70.00	28.00	14.00
19Nb	Gus Bell	70.00	28.00	14.00
20A	Larry "Yogi" Berra	65.00	26.00	13.00
20N	Johnny Logan	15.00	6.00	3.00
21A	Bob Lemon	35.00	14.00	7.00
21N	Johnny Antonelli	15.00	6.00	3.00
22A	Ferris Fain	15.00	6.00	3.00
22N	Gil Hodges	35.00	14.00	7.00
23A	Hank Bauer	20.00	8.00	4.00
23N	Eddie Mathews	35.00	14.00	7.00
24A	Jim Delsing	15.00	6.00	3.00
24N	Lew Burdette	15.00	6.00	3.00
25A	Gil McDougald	20.00	8.00	4.00
25N	Willie Mays	130.00	55.00	25.00

1955 Red Man Tobacco

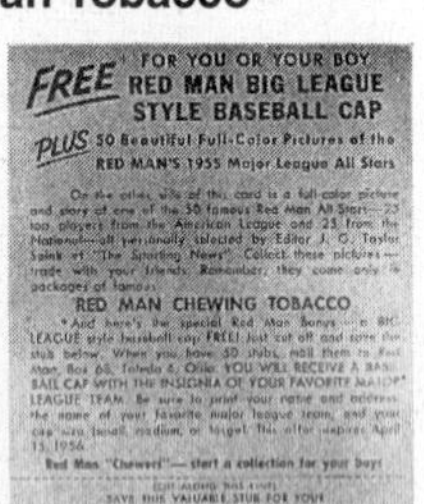

These 50 cards are quite similar to the 1954 edition, with card fronts virtually unchanged except for the data in the biographical box on the color picture area. This set of the 3-1/2" x 4" cards includes 25 players from each league, with no known variations. As with all Red Man sets, those cards complete with the redeemable tabs are more valuable. Values quoted below are for cards with tabs. Cards with the tabs removed are worth about 25-35 percent of those figures. Each card can be found with two different expiration dates on back, April 15 or June 15, 1956; neither version commands a premium.

		NM	EX	VG
Complete Set, W/Tab (50):		3,750	1,500	750.00
Common Player, W/Tab:		60.00	24.00	12.00
Complete Set, No Tab (50):		900.00	360.00	180.00
Common Player, No Tab:		10.00	4.00	2.00
	WITH TAB			
1A	Ray Boone	60.00	24.00	12.00
1N	Richie Ashburn	95.00	38.00	19.00
2A	Jim Busby	60.00	24.00	12.00
2N	Del Crandall	60.00	24.00	12.00
3A	Ed "Whitey" Ford	125.00	50.00	25.00
3N	Gil Hodges	90.00	36.00	18.00
4A	Nelson Fox	90.00	36.00	18.00
4N	Brooks Lawrence	60.00	24.00	12.00
5A	Bob Grim	60.00	24.00	12.00
5N	Johnny Logan	60.00	24.00	12.00
6A	Jack Harshman	60.00	24.00	12.00
6N	Sal Maglie	60.00	24.00	12.00
7A	Jim Hegan	60.00	24.00	12.00
7N	Willie Mays	250.00	100.00	50.00
8A	Bob Lemon	90.00	36.00	18.00
8N	Don Mueller	60.00	24.00	12.00
9A	Irv Noren	60.00	24.00	12.00
9N	Bill Sarni	60.00	24.00	12.00
10A	Bob Porterfield	60.00	24.00	12.00
10N	Warren Spahn	90.00	36.00	18.00
11A	Al Rosen	75.00	30.00	15.00
11N	Henry Thompson	60.00	24.00	12.00
12A	"Mickey" Vernon	60.00	24.00	12.00
12N	Hoyt Wilhelm	90.00	36.00	18.00
13A	Vic Wertz	60.00	24.00	12.00
13N	Johnny Antonelli	60.00	24.00	12.00
14A	Early Wynn	90.00	36.00	18.00
14N	Carl Erskine	75.00	30.00	15.00
15A	Bobby Avila	60.00	24.00	12.00
15N	Granny Hamner	60.00	24.00	12.00
16A	Larry "Yogi" Berra	165.00	65.00	35.00
16N	Ted Kluszewski	75.00	30.00	15.00
17A	Joe Coleman	60.00	24.00	12.00
17N	Pee Wee Reese	125.00	50.00	25.00
18A	Larry Doby	90.00	36.00	18.00
18N	Al Schoendienst	90.00	36.00	18.00
19A	Jackie Jensen	65.00	26.00	13.00
19N	Duke Snider	165.00	65.00	35.00
20A	Pete Runnels	60.00	24.00	12.00
20N	Frank Thomas	60.00	24.00	12.00
21A	Jim Piersall	60.00	24.00	12.00
21N	Ray Jablonski	60.00	24.00	12.00
22A	Hank Bauer	65.00	26.00	13.00
22N	James "Dusty" Rhodes	60.00	24.00	12.00
23A	"Chico" Carrasquel	60.00	24.00	12.00
23N	Gus Bell	60.00	24.00	12.00
24A	Orestes Minoso	75.00	30.00	15.00
24N	Curt Simmons	60.00	24.00	12.00
25A	Sandy Consuegra	60.00	24.00	12.00
25N	Marvin Grissom	60.00	24.00	12.00
	NO TAB			
1A	Ray Boone	10.00	4.00	2.00
1N	Richie Ashburn	30.00	12.00	6.00
2A	Jim Busby	10.00	4.00	2.00
2N	Del Crandall	10.00	4.00	2.00
3A	Ed "Whitey" Ford	35.00	14.00	7.00
3N	Gil Hodges	30.00	12.00	6.00
4A	Nelson Fox	30.00	12.00	6.00
4N	Brooks Lawrence	10.00	4.00	2.00
5A	Bob Grim	10.00	4.00	2.00
5N	Johnny Logan	10.00	4.00	2.00
6A	Jack Harshman	10.00	4.00	2.00
6N	Sal Maglie	10.00	4.00	2.00
7A	Jim Hegan	10.00	4.00	2.00
7N	Willie Mays	100.00	40.00	20.00
8A	Bob Lemon	30.00	12.00	6.00
8N	Don Mueller	10.00	4.00	2.00
9A	Irv Noren	10.00	4.00	2.00
9N	Bill Sarni	10.00	4.00	2.00
10A	Bob Porterfield	10.00	4.00	2.00
10N	Warren Spahn	30.00	12.00	6.00
11A	Al Rosen	13.50	5.50	2.75
11N	Henry Thompson	10.00	4.00	2.00
12A	"Mickey" Vernon	10.00	4.00	2.00
12N	Hoyt Wilhelm	30.00	12.00	6.00
13A	Vic Wertz	10.00	4.00	2.00
13N	Johnny Antonelli	10.00	4.00	2.00
14A	Early Wynn	30.00	12.00	6.00
14N	Carl Erskine	15.00	6.00	3.00
15A	Bobby Avila	10.00	4.00	2.00
15N	Granny Hamner	10.00	4.00	2.00
16A	Larry "Yogi" Berra	50.00	20.00	10.00
16N	Ted Kluszewski	20.00	8.00	4.00
17A	Joe Coleman	10.00	4.00	2.00
17N	Pee Wee Reese	50.00	20.00	10.00
18A	Larry Doby	30.00	12.00	6.00
18N	Al Schoendienst	30.00	12.00	6.00
19A	Jackie Jensen	13.50	5.50	2.75
19N	Duke Snider	55.00	22.00	11.00
20A	Pete Runnels	10.00	4.00	2.00
20N	Frank Thomas	10.00	4.00	2.00
21A	Jim Piersall	13.50	5.50	2.75
21N	Ray Jablonski	10.00	4.00	2.00
22A	Hank Bauer	13.50	5.50	2.75
22N	James "Dusty" Rhodes	10.00	4.00	2.00
23A	"Chico" Carrasquel	10.00	4.00	2.00
23N	Gus Bell	10.00	4.00	2.00
24A	Orestes Minoso	15.00	6.00	3.00
24N	Curt Simmons	10.00	4.00	2.00
25A	Sandy Consuegra	10.00	4.00	2.00
25N	Marvin Grissom	10.00	4.00	2.00

1952-1954 Red Man Posters

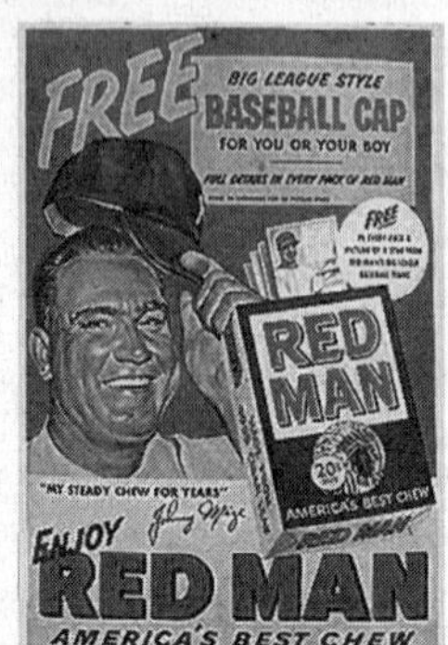

These colorful lithographed paper posters, 11" x 15-1/2", were intended as point-of-purchase displays to encourage sales of the chewing tobacco and offer a baseball cap in exchange for the tabs found on the bottom of each card. The posters were reproduced in 11" x 16" format on cardboard in the 1980s.

		NM	EX	VG
1952	Ralph Kiner (11" x 15")	200.00	100.00	60.00
1953	Enos Slaughter (11" x 15")	300.00	150.00	90.00
1954	Johnny Mize (12" x 15-1/2")	325.00	160.00	95.00

"1952-54" Red Man Posters

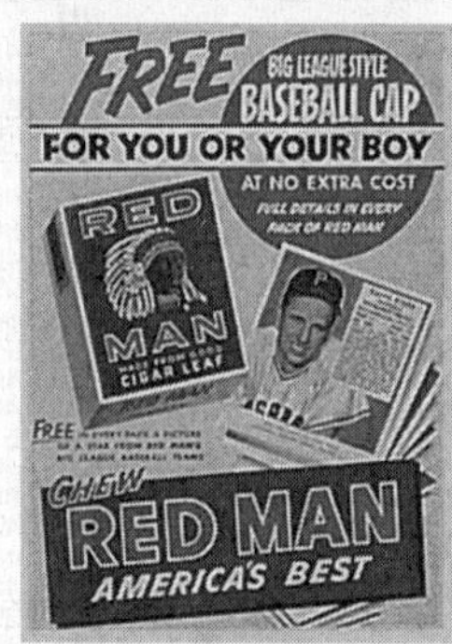

Some 30 years after the original 11" x 15-1/2" paper posters were used to advertise Red Man chewing tobacco and the baseball cards and caps available as premiums, three of the pieces were reproduced. Posters which are printed on cardboard and in a 11" x 16" size are modern reproductions with only decorative, rather than collectible, value.

NO COLLECTOR VALUE
1952 Ralph Kiner
1953 Enos Slaughter
1954 Johnny Mize

1976 Redpath Sugar Expos

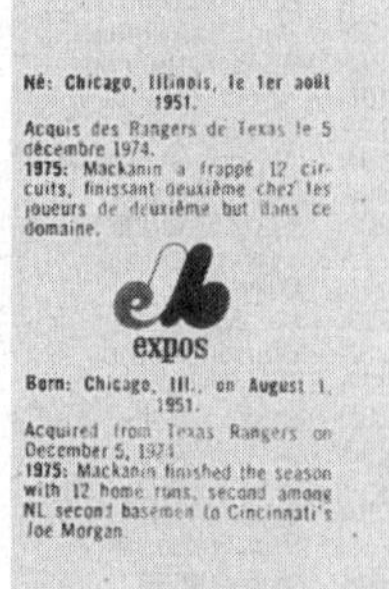

Among the more unusual baseball collectibles of the late 1970s are the Montreal Expos sugar packs produced by Redpath Sugar for distribution in Quebec. About 1-1/2" x 2-3/4" in size, the sugar packs feature color portraits of the players on front, along with bi-lingual personal information and a uniform number. Backs have a color team logo and career highlights. Uncut sheets or the packaging are known which indicate several players were double- or triple-printed. The checklist here is arranged by uniform number.

		NM	EX	VG
Complete Set (36):		75.00	37.00	22.00
Common Player:		2.00	1.00	.60
1	Osvaldo Jose Virgil	2.00	1.00	.60
5	Peter Mackanin, Jr.	2.00	1.00	.60
6	Karl Otto Kuehl	2.00	1.00	.60
8	Gary Edmund Carter	15.00	7.50	4.50
9	Barry Clifton Foote	2.00	1.00	.60
11	Jose Manuel Mangual	2.00	1.00	.60
14	Lawrence Eugene Doby	6.00	3.00	1.75
15	Larry Alton Parrish	2.00	1.00	.60
16	Michael Jorgensen	2.00	1.00	.60
17	Andre Thornton	4.00	2.00	1.25
18	Joseph Thomas Kerrigan	2.00	1.00	.60
19	Timothy John Foli/DP	2.00	1.00	.60
20	James Lawrence Lyttle, Jr.	2.00	1.00	.60
21	Frederick John Scherman, Jr.	2.00	1.00	.60
22	Ellis Clarence Valentine	2.00	1.00	.60
26	Donald Joseph Stanhouse	2.00	1.00	.60
27	Dale Albert Murray	2.00	1.00	.60
31	Clayton Laws Kirby, Jr.	2.00	1.00	.60
33	Robert David Lang	2.00	1.00	.60
34	Jose Manuel Morales	2.00	1.00	.60
35	Woodrow Thompson Fryman	3.00	1.50	.90
36	Steven John Dunning	2.00	1.00	.60
37	Jerome Cardell White	2.00	1.00	.60
38	Jesus Maria Frias (Andujar)	2.00	1.00	.60
39	Daniel Dean Warthen	2.00	1.00	.60
40	Donald George Carrithers (3P)	2.00	1.00	.60
41	Ronald Jacques Piche	2.00	1.00	.60
43	James Edward Dwyer	2.00	1.00	.60
44	Jesus Rivera (Torres), Jr.	2.00	1.00	.60
45	Stephen Douglas Rogers/DP	2.00	1.00	.60
46	Marion Danne Adair	2.00	1.00	.60

47	Wayne Allen Granger	2.00	1.00	.60
48	Lawrence Donald Bearnarth	2.00	1.00	.60
---	Roland Wayne Garrett	2.00	1.00	.60
---	Charles Gilbert Taylor	2.00	1.00	.60
---	Delbert Bernard Unser	2.00	1.00	.60

1977 Redpath Sugar Expos

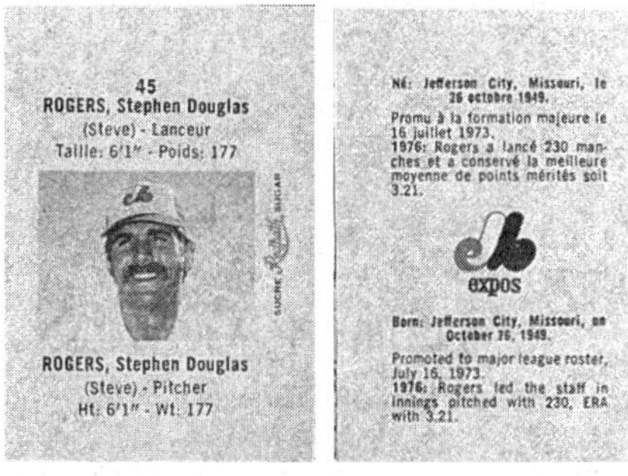

One of the more obscure regional Canadian issues, this 30-player set features members of the Expos and was printed on sugar packets distributed in the Montreal area in 1977. The front of the packet features a color photo of the player with his name, uniform number, position, height and weight listed in both English and French. A line identifying Redpath Sugar appears alongside the photo. The backs display the Expos logo and brief player highlights (again printed in both French and English). The set has been seen in uncut sheets, revealing that the packets of Steve Rogers and David Cash, Jr. were double printed.

		NM	EX	VG
Complete Set (30):		75.00	37.00	22.00
Common Player:		1.50	.70	.45
1	Osvaldo Jose Virgil	1.50	.70	.45
2	James Thomas Brewer	1.50	.70	.45
3	James Barton Vernon	1.50	.70	.45
4	Chris Edward Speier	1.50	.70	.45
5	Peter Mackanin Jr.	1.50	.70	.45
6	William Frederick Gardner	1.50	.70	.45
8	Gary Edmund Carter	15.00	7.50	4.50
9	Barry Clifton Foote	1.50	.70	.45
10	Andre Dawson	6.00	3.00	1.75
11	Ronald Wayne Garrett	1.50	.70	.45
14	Samuel Elias Mejias	1.50	.70	.45
15	Larry Alton Parrish	2.00	1.00	.60
16	Michael Jorgensen	1.50	.70	.45
17	Ellis Clarence Valentine	1.50	.70	.45
18	Joseph Thomas Kerrigan	1.50	.70	.45
20	William Henry McEnaney	1.50	.70	.45
23	Richard Hirshfield Williams	2.00	1.00	.60
24	Atanasio Rigal Perez	3.00	1.50	.90
25	Delbert Bernard Unser	1.50	.70	.45
26	Donald Joseph Stanhouse	1.50	.70	.45
30	David Cash, Jr.	1.50	.70	.45
31	Jackie Gene Brown	1.50	.70	.45
34	Jose Manual Morales	1.50	.70	.45
35	Gerald Ellis Hannahs	1.50	.70	.45
38	Jesus Maria Frias (Andujar)	1.50	.70	.45
39	Daniel Dean Warthen	1.50	.70	.45
42	William Cecil Glenn Atkinson	1.50	.70	.45
45	Stephen Douglas Rogers	2.25	1.25	.70
48	Jeffrey Michael Terpko	1.50	.70	.45
49	Warren Livingston Cromartie	1.50	.70	.45

1886 Red Stocking Cigars

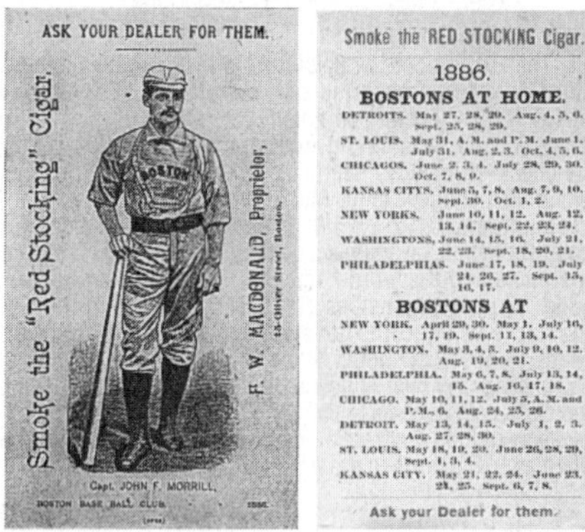

This set of Boston Red Stockings schedule cards was issued in 1886, and the three known cards measure 6-1/2" x 3-3/4". The cards were printed in black and red. One side carries the 1886 Boston schedule, while the other side features a full-length player drawing. Both sides include advertising for "Red Stocking" cigars. Only three different players are known.

		NM	EX	VG
Complete Set (3):		55,000	27,500	16,500
Common Player:		45,000	16,000	10,000
(1)	C.G. Buffington	45,000	16,000	10,000
(2)	Capt. John F. Morrill	45,000	16,000	10,000
(3)	Charles Radbourn	100,000	10,000	5,000

1972 Regent Glove Hang Tag

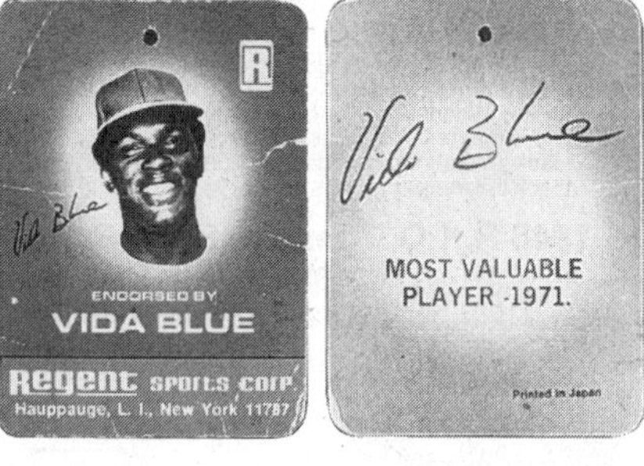

This 2-1/4" x 3" card was distributed as an attachment to baseball gloves sold at retail outlets. A hole punched at top allowed the card to be strung to the glove. Front has a blue background and black-and-white portrait photo of 1971 MVP Vida Blue. His facsimile autograph is on back.

	NM	EX	VG
Vida Blue	15.00	7.50	4.50

1964-68 Requena N.Y. Yankees Postcards

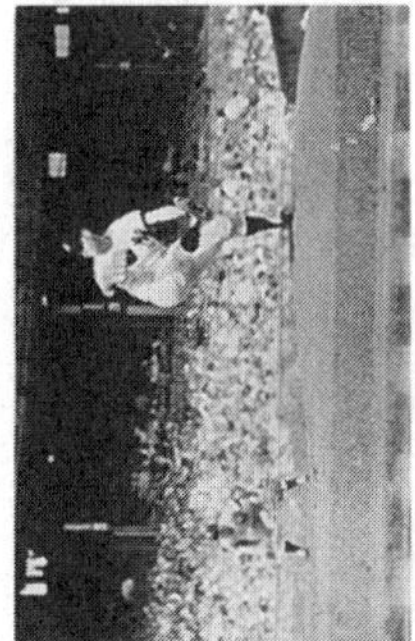

Over a period of several years in the 1960s a series of Yankee color player postcards was issued with the identifier "Photo by Requena." Similar in format, the 3-1/2" x 5-1/2" cards have borderless color photos on front. Except for facsimile autographs on some players' cards, there are no other front graphics. Backs are printed in dark green with player ID at upper-left, a "K"-within-diamond Kodachrome logo at bottom-left, a card number centered at bottom, the Requena line vertically at center and standard postcard markings at right.

		NM	EX	VG
Complete Set (17):		300.00	150.00	90.00
Common Player:		15.00	7.50	4.50
66443	Phil Linz	15.00	7.50	4.50
66880	Clete Boyer	15.00	7.50	4.50
66881	Jim Bouton	20.00	10.00	6.00
66882	Tom Tresh	20.00	10.00	6.00
66883	Joe Pepitone	20.00	10.00	6.00
66884	Tony Kubek	20.00	10.00	6.00
66885	Elston Howard	20.00	10.00	6.00
66886	Ralph Terry	15.00	7.50	4.50
66887	Bill Stafford	15.00	7.50	4.50
66888	Whitey Ford	30.00	15.00	9.00
66889	Bob Richardson	20.00	10.00	6.00
69891	Yogi Berra (Signature at top.)	30.00	15.00	9.00
69891	Yogi Berra (Signature at bottom.)	30.00	15.00	9.00
74284	John Blanchard	15.00	7.50	4.50
78909	Pedro Ramos	15.00	7.50	4.50
78910	Mel Stottlemyre	15.00	7.50	4.50
98553	Fritz Peterson	15.00	7.50	4.50
101461	Steve Barber	15.00	7.50	4.50

1964-66 Requena N.Y. Yankees 8x10s

Many of the same Yankees players and poses which appear in the standard (3-1/2" x 5-1/2") Requena postcard series can also be found, along with additional subjects, in an 8" x 10" blank-back format. The large format cards are listed here in alphabetical order.

		NM	EX	VG
Complete Set (21):		300.00	150.00	90.00
Common Player:		9.00	4.50	2.75
(1)	Yogi Berra	20.00	10.00	6.00
(2)	John Blanchard	9.00	4.50	2.75
(3)	Jim Bouton	12.50	6.25	3.75
(4)	Clete Boyer	9.00	4.50	2.75
(5)	Al Downing	9.00	4.50	2.75
(6)	Whitey Ford	20.00	10.00	6.00
(7)	Ralph Houk	9.00	4.50	2.75
(8)	Elston Howard	12.50	6.25	3.75
(9)	Tony Kubek	12.50	6.25	3.75
(10)	Phil Linz	9.00	4.50	2.75
(11)	Mickey Mantle	35.00	17.50	10.00
(12)	Mickey Mantle, Roger Maris	30.00	15.00	9.00
(13a)	Roger Maris (Facsimile autograph.)	25.00	12.50	7.50
(13b)	Roger Maris (No facsimile autograph.)	25.00	12.50	7.50
(14)	Joe Pepitone	12.50	6.25	3.75
(15)	Pedro Ramos	9.00	4.50	2.75
(16)	Bobby Richardson	12.50	6.25	3.75
(17)	Bill Stafford	9.00	4.50	2.75
(18)	Mel Stottlemyre	9.00	4.50	2.75
(19)	Ralph Terry	9.00	4.50	2.75
(20)	Tom Tresh	12.50	6.25	3.75

1953 R.G. Dun Cigars Milwaukee Braves

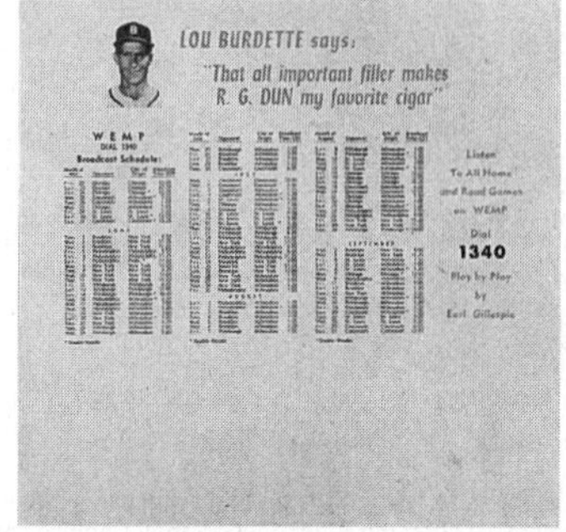

This series of counter cards was issued by a cigar company and features the radio schedule for the 1953 Braves. The cards are printed in red and black on cream cardboard and measure 10" x 9-1/2". They are unnumbered and blank-backed. The cards have vertical slits from bottom to about 1/3 the height of the cards, probably so they could be inserted into some type of counter display for Dun cigars. It's unknown how many players were represented in the series.

		NM	EX	VG
Common Player:		35.00	17.50	10.00
(1)	Lew Burdette	35.00	17.50	10.00
(2)	Jim Wilson	35.00	17.50	10.00

1935 Rice-Stix (UM7)

This two-card set was distributed in packages of shirts from a St. Louis firm. Measuring about 2-1/4" x 3", the cards feature color painting of the pitchers on front, along with a facsimile autograph and photo credits. Backs have a short career summary and an ad for the issuer.

		NM	EX	VG
Complete Set (2):		1,800	725.00	450.00
(1)	Dizzy Dean	1,200	475.00	300.00
(2)	Paul Dean	625.00	250.00	150.00

1927 Rinkeydink Stamps

These 1-1/4" x 1-1/2" pieces are not actually stamps, but rather are printed on newsprint with unrelated matter on back. The printing is in red, green and black and each stamp has a "denomination" of 2 in a baseball design at top. The "stamps" were featured in the heading of the "Winnie Winkle" comic strip in the Sunday funnies section of newspapers.

		NM	EX	VG
Complete Set (10):		450.00	225.00	135.00
Common Player:		30.00	15.00	9.00
(1)	Grover C. Alexander	40.00	20.00	12.00
(2)	Ty Cobb	75.00	37.50	22.00
(3)	Eddie Collins	30.00	15.00	9.00
(4)	Bucky Harris	30.00	15.00	9.00
(5)	Rogers Hornsby	40.00	20.00	12.00
(6)	Walter Johnson	50.00	25.00	15.00
(7)	George Kelly	30.00	15.00	9.00
(8)	Herb Pennock	30.00	15.00	9.00
(9)	Babe Ruth	100.00	50.00	30.00
(10)	Tris Speaker	40.00	20.00	12.00

1933 Rittenhouse Candy (E285)

Designed to resemble a set of playing cards, this set, issued circa 1933 by the Rittenhouse Candy Company of Philadelphia, carries the ACC designation E285 and is generally considered to be the last of the E-card issues. Each card measures 1-7/16" x 2-1/4" and features a small player photo in the center of the playing card design. Cards are known printed in red, orange, blue and green. The backs of the cards usually consist of just one large letter and were part of a promotion in which collectors were instructed to find enough different letters to spell "Rittenhouse Candy Co." Other backs explaining the contest and the prizes available were also issued, as were backs with numbers. Because it was designed as a deck of playing cards, the set is complete at 52 cards, featuring 46 different players (six are pictured on two cards each).

		NM	EX	VG
Complete Set (52):		9,000	3,600	1,800
Common Player:		100.00	40.00	20.00
(1)	Dick Bartell	100.00	40.00	20.00
(2)	Walter Berger	100.00	40.00	20.00
(3)	Max Bishop	100.00	40.00	20.00
(4)	James Bottomley	200.00	80.00	40.00
(5)	Fred Brickell	100.00	40.00	20.00
(6)	Sugar Cain	100.00	40.00	20.00
(7)	Ed. Cihocki	100.00	40.00	20.00
(8)	Phil Collins	100.00	40.00	20.00
(9)	Roger Cramer	100.00	40.00	20.00
(10)	Hughie Critz	100.00	40.00	20.00
(11)	Joe Cronin	200.00	80.00	40.00
(12)	Hazen (Kiki) Cuyler	200.00	80.00	40.00
(13)	Geo. Davis	100.00	40.00	20.00
(14)	Spud Davis	100.00	40.00	20.00
(15)	Jimmy Dykes	100.00	40.00	20.00
(16)	George Earnshaw	100.00	40.00	20.00
(17)	Jumbo Elliot	100.00	40.00	20.00
(18)	Lou Finney	100.00	40.00	20.00
(19)	Jimmy Foxx	275.00	110.00	55.00
(20)	Frankie Frisch (3 of Spades)	200.00	80.00	40.00
(21)	Frankie Frisch (7 of Spades)	200.00	80.00	40.00
(22)	Robert (Lefty) Grove	225.00	90.00	45.00
(23)	Mule Haas	100.00	40.00	20.00
(24)	Chick Hafey	200.00	80.00	40.00
(25)	Chas. Leo Hartnett	200.00	80.00	40.00
(26)	Babe Herman	110.00	45.00	25.00
(27)	Wm. Herman	200.00	80.00	40.00
(28)	Kid Higgins	100.00	40.00	20.00
(29)	Rogers Hornsby	235.00	95.00	45.00
(30)	Don Hurst (Jack of Diamonds)	100.00	40.00	20.00
(31)	Don Hurst (6 of Spades)	100.00	40.00	20.00
(32)	Chuck Klein	200.00	80.00	40.00
(33)	Leroy Mahaffey	100.00	40.00	20.00
(34)	Gus Mancuso	100.00	40.00	20.00
(35)	Rabbit McNair	100.00	40.00	20.00
(36)	Bing Miller	100.00	40.00	20.00
(37)	Frank (Lefty) O'Doul	115.00	45.00	25.00
(38)	Mel Ott	200.00	80.00	40.00
(39)	Babe Ruth (Ace of Spades)	1,000	400.00	200.00
(40)	Babe Ruth (King of Clubs)	1,000	400.00	200.00
(41)	Al Simmons	200.00	80.00	40.00
(42)	Bill Terry	200.00	80.00	40.00
(43)	Pie Traynor	200.00	80.00	40.00
(44)	Rube Wallberg (Walberg)	100.00	40.00	20.00
(45)	Lloyd Waner	200.00	80.00	40.00
(46)	Paul Waner	200.00	80.00	40.00
(47)	Lloyd Warner (Waner)	200.00	80.00	40.00
(48)	Paul Warner (Waner)	200.00	80.00	40.00
(49)	Pinkey Whitney	100.00	40.00	20.00
(50)	Dib Williams	100.00	40.00	20.00
(51)	Hack Wilson (9 of Spades)	200.00	80.00	40.00
(52)	Hack Wilson (9 of Clubs)	200.00	80.00	40.00

1948 R.K.O. Theaters Babe Ruth Premium

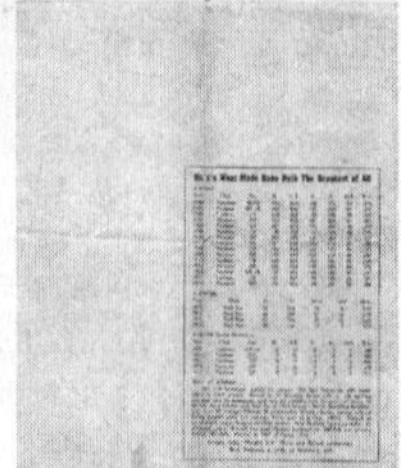

The attributed date is speculative, based on the similarity of the back copy to the 1948 American Association Babe Ruth memorial card. Apparently issued as a premium at moviehouses, this 8" x 9-1/2" picture is printed on thin cardboard. On front is a sepia action photo of Ruth in the 1932 World Series. In the bottom border is the R.K.O. attribution. Back has biographical details, career highlights and complete major league stats.

	NM	EX	VG
Babe Ruth	400.00	200.00	125.00

1951 Roadmaster Photos

Black-and-white glossy photos of at least two major league stars were available as a premium from Roadmaster bicycles. Contemporary ads said that for a dime, an 8" x 10" photo could be obtained. The photos show the uniformed players seated on Roadmaster bikes inside a ballpark. There is a facsimile autograph on each. Backs are blank. It's possible other player photos may yet be seen.

		NM	EX	VG
(1)	Bob Feller	200.00	100.00	60.00
(2)	Pee Wee Reese	250.00	125.00	75.00

1947 Jackie Robinson Pins

In his historic debut season with the Brooklyn Dodgers, a number of celluloid pinback buttons featuring Jackie Robinson were issued. Ranging in size from about 1-1/4" to 1-3/4", the pins usually feature a black-and-white portrait photo at center and were originally sold with a silk pennant and plastic or pot-metal baseball charms attached.

		NM	EX	VG
(1)	Brooklyn 1947 Dodgers Congratulations "Jackie" (1-1/4" white background)	600.00	300.00	180.00
(2)	HI TEAMMATES (1-3/8", batting, blue background)	250.00	125.00	75.00
(3)	I'M FOR JACKIE (Blue type on white ball, no photo.)	200.00	100.00	60.00
(4)	I'm Rooting for Jackie Robinson (1-3/4", red border)	275.00	135.00	80.00
(5)	I'm Rooting for Jackie Robinson (1-1/4", white background)	350.00	175.00	100.00
(6)	I'm Rooting for Jackie Robinson (1-3/4", gray background)	300.00	150.00	90.00
(7)	JACKIE ROBINSON / DODGERS (1-3/4", b/w photo batting in pinstripes and plain cap)	400.00	200.00	125.00
(8)	JACKIE ROBINSON / DODGERS (1-1/4", white background)	200.00	100.00	60.00
(9)	Jackie Robinson Outstanding Rookie (3-3/8" white border)	200.00	100.00	60.00
(10)	19 Rookie of the Year 47 (1-3/4" red border)(Modern reproductions exist.)	325.00	160.00	100.00

1950s Jackie Robinson WNBC Photocard

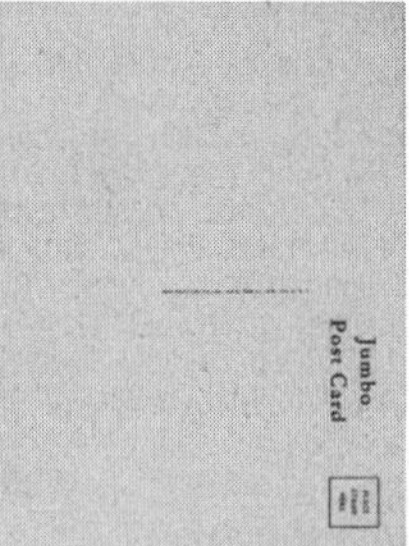

This black-and-white 5-3/4" x 7-1/2" photocard pictures Robinson in his post-playing days career as a broadcaster for the NBC radio network's flagship station in New York.

	NM	EX	VG
Jackie Robinson	35.00	17.50	10.50

1911 Rochester Baking Philadelphia A's (D359)

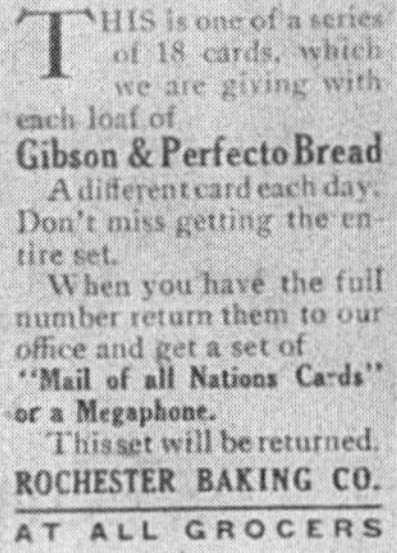

World's Championship Series

THIS is one of a series of 18 cards, which we are giving with each loaf of

Gibson & Perfecto Bread

A different card each day. Don't miss getting the entire set.

When you have the full number return them to our office and get a set of "Mail of all Nations Cards" or a Megaphone.

This set will be returned.

ROCHESTER BAKING CO.

AT ALL GROCERS

The 1911 Rochester Baking set, an 18-card Philadelphia Athletics set, is among the scarcest of early 20th Century bakery issues. The set commemorates the Athletics' 1910 Championship season, and, except for pitcher Jack Coombs, the checklist includes nearly all key members of the club, including manager Connie Mack. The cards are the standard size for the era, 1-1/2" x 2-5/8". The front of each card features a player portrait set against a colored background. The player's name and the word "Athletics" appear at the bottom, while "World's Champions 1910" is printed along the top. The backs of the cards advertise the set as the "Athletics Series." Collectors should be aware that the same checklist was used for a similar Athletics set issued by Williams Baking and Cullivan's Firesdie tobacco (T208), and also that blank-backed versions are also known to exist, but these are classified as E104 cards in the American Card Catalog.

		NM	EX	VG
Complete Set (18):		85,000	35,000	17,000
Common Player:		4,000	2,000	1,000
(1)	Home Run Baker	7,000	3,500	1,750
(2)	Jack Barry	4,000	2,000	1,000
(3)	Chief Bender	7,000	3,500	1,750
(4)	Eddie Collins	7,000	3,500	1,750
(5)	Harry Davis	4,000	2,000	1,000
(6)	Jimmy Dygert	4,000	2,000	1,000
(7)	Topsy Hartsel	4,000	2,000	1,000
(8)	Harry Krause	4,000	2,000	1,000
(9)	Jack Lapp	4,000	2,000	1,000
(10)	Paddy Livingston	4,000	2,000	1,000
(11)	Bris Lord	4,000	2,000	1,000
(12)	Connie Mack	14,000	7,900	4,575
(13)	Cy Morgan	4,000	2,000	1,000
(14)	Danny Murphy	4,000	2,000	1,000

		NM	EX	VG
(15)	Rube Oldring	4,000	2,000	1,000
(16)	Eddie Plank	14,000	7,900	4,575
(17)	Amos Strunk	4,000	2,000	1,000
(18)	Ira Thomas	4,000	2,000	1,000

1955 Rodeo Meats Athletics

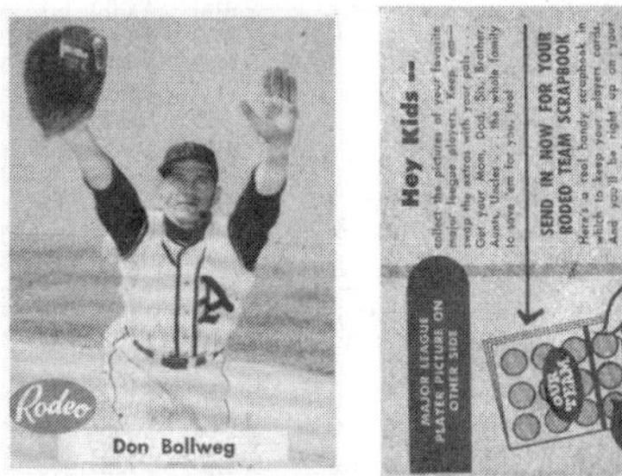

This set of 2-1/2" x 3-1/2" color cards was issued by a local meat company to commemorate the first year of the Athletics in Kansas City. There are 38 different players included in the set, with nine players known to apppear in two different variations for a total of 47 cards in the set. Most variations are in background colors, although Bobby Shantz is also listed incorrectly as "Schantz" on one variation. The cards are unnumbered, with the Rodeo logo and player name on the fronts, and an ad for a scrapbook album listed on the backs.

		NM	EX	VG
Complete Set (47):		12,500	6,250	3,750
Common Player:		225.00	110.00	45.00
Album:		550.00	275.00	125.00
(1)	Joe Astroth	225.00	110.00	45.00
(2)	Harold Bevan	275.00	135.00	55.00
(3)	Charles Bishop	275.00	135.00	55.00
(4)	Don Bollweg	275.00	135.00	55.00
(5)	Lou Boudreau	600.00	300.00	120.00
(6)	Cloyd Boyer (Blue background.)	275.00	135.00	55.00
(7)	Cloyd Boyer (Pink background.)	225.00	110.00	45.00
(8)	Ed Burtschy	275.00	135.00	55.00
(9)	Art Ceccarelli	225.00	110.00	45.00
(10)	Joe DeMaestri (Pea green background.)	275.00	135.00	55.00
(11)	Joe DeMaestri (Light green background.)	225.00	110.00	45.00
(12)	Art Ditmar	225.00	110.00	45.00
(13)	John Dixon	275.00	135.00	55.00
(14)	Jim Finigan	225.00	110.00	45.00
(15)	Marion Fricano	275.00	135.00	55.00
(16)	Tom Gorman	275.00	135.00	55.00
(17)	John Gray	225.00	110.00	45.00
(18)	Ray Herbert	225.00	110.00	45.00
(19)	Forest "Spook" Jacobs (Forrest)	275.00	135.00	55.00
(20)	Alex Kellner	275.00	135.00	55.00
(21)	Harry Kraft (Craft)	225.00	110.00	45.00
(22)	Jack Littrell	225.00	110.00	45.00
(23)	Hector Lopez	275.00	135.00	55.00
(24)	Oscar Melillo	225.00	110.00	45.00
(25)	Arnold Portocarrero (Purple background.)	275.00	135.00	55.00
(26)	Arnold Portocarrero (Gray background.)	225.00	110.00	45.00
(27)	Vic Power (Pink background.)	275.00	135.00	55.00
(28)	Vic Power (Yellow background.)	250.00	125.00	50.00
(29)	Vic Raschi	275.00	135.00	55.00
(30)	Bill Renna (Dark pink background.)	275.00	135.00	55.00
(31)	Bill Renna (Light pink background.)	225.00	110.00	45.00
(32)	Al Robertson	275.00	135.00	55.00
(33)	Johnny Sain	275.00	135.00	55.00
(34a)	Bobby Schantz (Incorrect spelling.)	900.00	450.00	180.00
(34b)	Bobby Shantz (Correct spelling.)	300.00	150.00	60.00
(35)	Wilmer Shantz (Orange background.)	275.00	135.00	55.00
(36)	Wilmer Shantz (Purple background.)	225.00	110.00	45.00
(37)	Harry Simpson	225.00	110.00	45.00
(38)	Enos Slaughter	650.00	325.00	130.00
(39)	Lou Sleater	225.00	110.00	45.00
(40)	George Susce	225.00	110.00	45.00
(41)	Bob Trice	275.00	135.00	55.00
(42)	Elmer Valo (Yellow background.)	275.00	135.00	55.00
(43)	Elmer Valo (Green background.)	225.00	110.00	45.00
(44)	Bill Wilson (Yellow background.)	275.00	135.00	55.00
(45)	Bill Wilson (Purple background.)	225.00	110.00	45.00
(46)	Gus Zernial	250.00	125.00	50.00

1956 Rodeo Meats Athletics

Rodeo Meats issued another Kansas City Athletics set in 1956, but this one was a much smaller 13-card set. The 2-1/2" x 3-1/2" cards are again unnumbered, with the player name and Rodeo logo on the fronts. Card backs feature some of the same graphics and copy as the 1955 cards, but the album offer is omitted. The full-color cards were only available in packages of Rodeo hot dogs.

		NM	EX	VG
Complete Set (12):		2,750	1,100	550.00
Common Player:		200.00	80.00	40.00
(1)	Joe Astroth	200.00	80.00	40.00
(2)	Lou Boudreau	350.00	140.00	70.00
(3)	Joe DeMaestri	200.00	80.00	40.00
(4)	Art Ditmar	200.00	80.00	40.00
(5)	Jim Finigan	200.00	80.00	40.00
(6)	Hector Lopez	200.00	80.00	40.00
(7)	Vic Power	200.00	80.00	40.00
(8)	Bobby Shantz	225.00	90.00	45.00
(9)	Harry Simpson	200.00	80.00	40.00
(10)	Enos Slaughter	475.00	190.00	95.00
(11)	Elmer Valo	200.00	80.00	40.00
(12)	Gus Zernial	200.00	80.00	40.00

1976 Rodeo Meats Athletics Commemorative

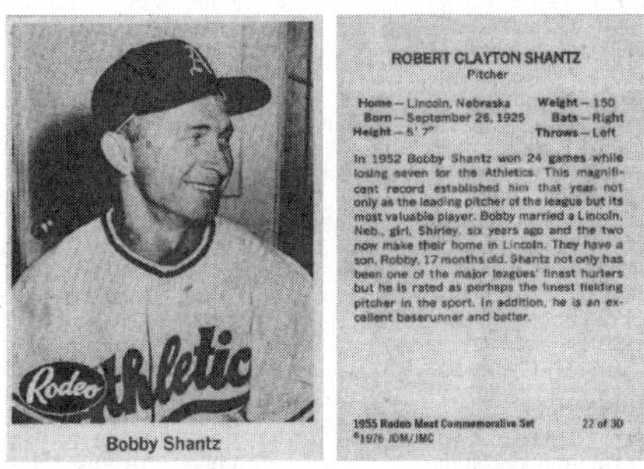

This collectors' issue essentially reprints many of the 1955-56 Rodeo Meats cards in a 2-1/2" x 3-1/2" black-and-white format. Fronts have player photos, the Rodeo logo and the player name in the white border at bottom. Backs, instead of the original Rodeo ads, have player identification, biographical information and career summary, along with a reprint notice.

		NM	EX	VG
Complete Set (30):		20.00	10.00	6.00
Common Player:		2.00	1.00	.60
1	Header Card	.50	.25	.15
2	Checklist Card	.50	.25	.15
3	Joe Astroth	2.00	1.00	.60
4	Lou Boudreau	3.00	1.50	.90
5	Cloyd Boyer	2.00	1.00	.60
6	Art Ceccarelli	2.00	1.00	.60
7	Harry Craft	2.00	1.00	.60
8	Joe DeMaestri	2.00	1.00	.60
9	Art Ditmar	2.00	1.00	.60
10	Jim Finigan	2.00	1.00	.60
11	Ray Herbert	2.00	1.00	.60
12	Tom Gorman	2.00	1.00	.60
13	Alex Kellner	2.00	1.00	.60
14	Jack Littrell	2.00	1.00	.60
15	Hector Lopez	2.00	1.00	.60
16	Oscar Melillo	2.00	1.00	.60
17	Arnie Portocarrero	2.00	1.00	.60
18	Vic Power	2.50	1.25	.70
19	Vic Raschi	2.50	1.25	.70
20	Bill Renna	2.00	1.00	.60
21	Johnny Sain	2.50	1.25	.70
22	Bobby Shantz	2.50	1.25	.70
23	Wilmer Shantz	2.00	1.00	.60
24	Harry Simpson	2.50	1.25	.70
25	Enos Slaughter	4.00	2.00	1.25
26	Lou Sleator	2.00	1.00	.60
27	George Susce	2.00	1.00	.60
28	Elmer Valo	2.00	1.00	.60
29	Bill Wilson	2.00	1.00	.60
30	Gus Zernial	2.50	1.25	.70

1930s Rogers Peet Sport Album

This is one of the scarcest multi-sport issues of the 1930s. It was the promotion of a New York-Boston chain of stores (boys' clothing?) in the form of a frequent customer program. Boys visiting the store with a parent could receive a set of four cards to be placed in a 14-page 4-1/2" x 7-1/4" album. Individual cards are about 1-7/8" x 2-1/2" and feature black-and-white photos with a white border. The athlete's name and card number are printed in the bottom border. Numbers correspond to spaces in the album. Only the "Baseball Stars" from the issue are checklisted here. Others include hockey, football, track, swimming, golf, tennis, aviation, etc.

18.— Herb Pennock

		NM	EX	VG
Complete Set (44):		7,500	3,750	2,250
Complete Set in Album:		5,000	2,500	1,500
Common Sticker:		30.00	15.00	9.00
Album:		500.00	250.00	150.00
5	Dazzy Vance	225.00	110.00	65.00
13	Walter Johnson	650.00	325.00	195.00
16	Rogers Hornsby	450.00	225.00	135.00
18	Herb Pennock	225.00	110.00	65.00
28	Lou Gehrig	2,400	1,200	725.00
34	Ty Cobb	1,100	550.00	330.00
38	Tris Speaker	450.00	225.00	135.00
48	Babe Ruth	2,600	1,300	780.00

1960s Rogers Printing Co. Postcards

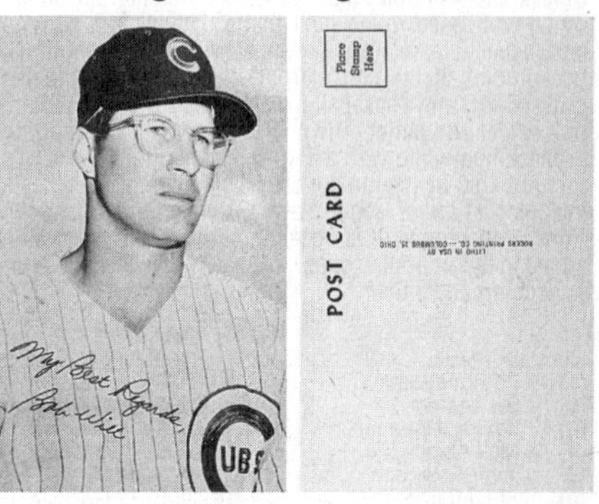

The extent to which this Columbus, Ohio, firm may have provided baseball players with postcards to answer fan mail requests is unknown. At present, only a single card is known, that of Bob Wills, who played his entire major league career (1957-63) with the Cubs. The card is printed in black-and-white on glossy stock in a 3-1/2" x 5-1/2" format. A facsimile autograph message is printed on front. Postcard-style backs have the imprint of the printer.

	NM	EX	VG
Bob Will	3.00	1.50	.90

1970 Rold Gold Pretzels

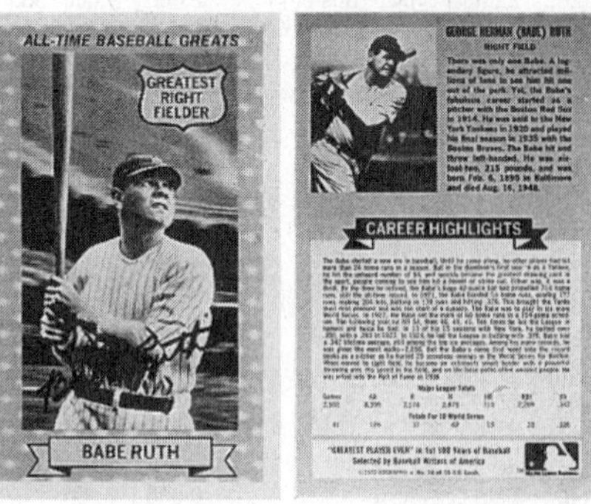

The 1970 Rold Gold Pretzels set of 15 cards honors the "Greatest Players Ever" in the first 100 years of baseball as chosen by the Baseball Writers of America. The cards, which measure 2-1/4" x 3-1/2" in size, feature a simulated 3-D effect. The set was re-released in 1972 by Kellogg's in packages of Danish-Go-Rounds. Rold Gold cards can be differentiated from the Kellogg's cards of 1972 by the 1970 copyright date found on the card reverse.

		NM	EX	VG
Complete Set (15):		50.00	25.00	15.00
Common Player:		2.00	1.00	.60
1	Walter Johnson	6.00	3.00	1.75
2	Rogers Hornsby	3.00	1.50	.90
3	John McGraw	2.00	1.00	.60
4	Mickey Cochrane	2.00	1.00	.60
5	George Sisler	2.00	1.00	.60
6	Babe Ruth ("Greatest Ever")	15.00	7.50	4.50
7	Robert "Lefty" Grove	2.00	1.00	.60

8	Harold "Pie" Traynor	2.00	1.00	.60
9	Honus Wagner	7.50	3.75	2.25
10	Eddie Collins	2.00	1.00	.60
11	Tris Speaker	3.00	1.50	.90
12	Cy Young	5.00	2.50	1.50
13	Lou Gehrig	10.00	5.00	3.00
14	Babe Ruth ("Greatest Right Fielder")	15.00	7.50	4.50
15	Ty Cobb	9.00	4.50	2.75

1908-1909 Rose Company Postcards

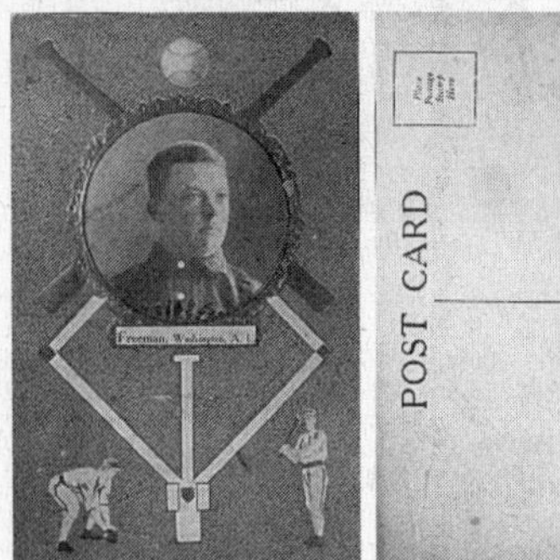

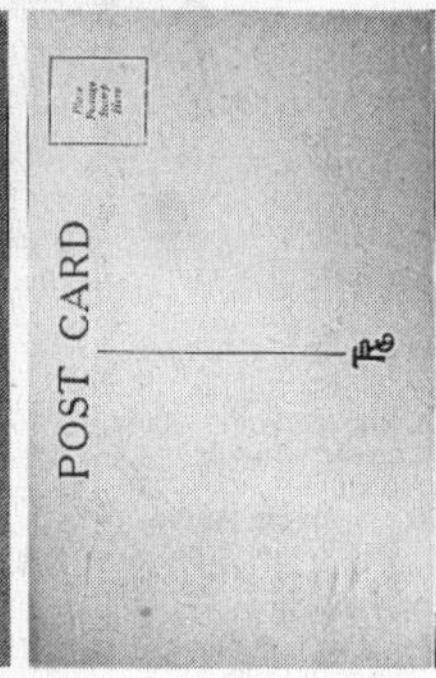

Among the most ornate and attractive baseball cards of the pre-1910 period is the set of postcards produced by The Rose Co., between 1908-09. The 3-1/2" x 5-1/2" cards feature a black-and-white player portrait photo at center, surrounded by an embossed round gold frame. The player's surname and (usually) team are in a white panel under the photo. The background of the card's front is in green and includes crossed bats and a baseball, a diamond diagram and pictures of a fielder and batter. The postcard-format back is printed in black-and-white with a TRC logo at bottom-center. The unnumbered postcards are checklisted here alphabetically; including 11 minor league players from Scranton in the New York State League. It is possible future discoveries will be added to this checklist; gaps have been left in the numbering to accommodate them.

		NM	EX	VG
Common Player:		2,400	1,000	500.00
(1)	Ed Abbaticchio	2,400	1,000	500.00
(2)	Bill Abstein	2,400	1,000	500.00
(3)	Whitey Alperman	2,400	1,000	500.00
(4)	Nick Altrock	2,400	1,000	500.00
(5)	John Anderson	2,400	1,000	500.00
(6)	Shad Barry	2,400	1,000	500.00
(7)	Ginger Beaumont	2,400	1,000	500.00
(8)	Heinie Beckendorf	2,400	1,000	500.00
(9)	Fred Beebe	2,400	1,000	500.00
(10)	Harry Bemis	2,400	1,000	500.00
(11)	Chief Bender	6,000	3,400	1,750
(12)	Bills	2,400	1,000	500.00
(13)	Joe Birmingham	2,400	1,000	500.00
(14)	Frank Bowerman	2,400	1,000	500.00
(15)	Bill Bradley	2,400	1,000	500.00
(16)	Kitty Bransfield	2,400	1,000	500.00
(17)	Roger Bresnahan	6,000	3,400	1,750
(18)	Al Bridwell	2,400	1,000	500.00
(19)	Buster Brown (Philadelphia) (Photo actually Mordecai Brown.)	2,400	1,000	500.00
(20)	Samuel Brown (Boston)	2,400	1,000	500.00
(21)	Mordecai Brown (Chicago)	6,000	3,400	1,750
(22)	Bobby Byrne	2,400	1,000	500.00
(23)	Howie Camnitz	2,400	1,000	500.00
(24)	Billy Campbell	2,400	1,000	500.00
(26)	Frank Chance	6,000	3,400	1,750
(27)	Hal Chase	2,400	1,000	500.00
(28)	Charlie Chech	2,400	1,000	500.00
(29)	Jack Chesbro	6,000	3,400	1,750
(30)	Fred Clarke (Pittsburg)	6,000	3,400	1,750
(31)	Nig Clarke (Cleveland)	2,400	1,000	500.00
(32)	Otis Clymer	2,400	1,000	500.00
(33a)	Andy Coakley (Cincinnati)	2,400	1,000	500.00
(33b)	Andy Coakley (No team name.)	2,400	1,000	500.00
(34)	Ty Cobb	24,000	13,600	7,000
(35)	Jimmy Collins	6,000	3,400	1,750
(36)	Wid Conroy	2,400	1,000	500.00
(37)	Jack Coombs	2,400	1,000	500.00
(38)	Frank Corridon	2,400	1,000	500.00
(39)	Bill Coughlin	2,400	1,000	500.00
(40)	Sam Crawford	6,000	3,400	1,750
(41a)	Lou Criger (Boston)	2,400	1,000	500.00
(41b)	Lou Criger (No team.)	2,400	1,000	500.00
(42)	Bill Dahlen	2,400	1,000	500.00
(43)	Harry Davis	2,400	1,000	500.00
(44)	Joe Delahanty (St. Louis)	2,400	1,000	500.00
(45)	Frank Delehanty (Delahanty) (Washington; team actually N.Y., A.L.)	2,400	1,000	500.00
(46)	Art Devlin	2,400	1,000	500.00
(47)	Mike Donlin	2,400	1,000	500.00
(48)	Jiggs Donohue (Donahue)	2,400	1,000	500.00
(49)	Wild Bill Donovan	2,400	1,000	500.00
(51)	Red Dooin	2,400	1,000	500.00
(52)	Mickey Doolan	2,400	1,000	500.00
(53)	Larry Doyle	2,400	1,000	500.00
(54)	Jimmy Dygert	2,400	1,000	500.00
(55)	Kid Elberfeld	2,400	1,000	500.00
(56)	Eley	2,400	1,000	500.00
(57)	Johnny Evers	6,000	3,400	1,750
(58)	Bob Ewing	2,400	1,000	500.00
(59)	George Ferguson	2,400	1,000	500.00
(60)	Hobe Ferris	2,400	1,000	500.00
(61)	Jerry Freeman	2,400	1,000	500.00
(62)	Bob Ganley	2,400	1,000	500.00
(63)	John Ganzel	2,400	1,000	500.00
(64)	Doc Gessler	2,400	1,000	500.00
(65)	George Gibson	2,400	1,000	500.00
(66)	Billy Gilbert	2,400	1,000	500.00
(67)	Fred Glade	2,400	1,000	500.00
(68)	Ralph Glaze	2,400	1,000	500.00
(69)	Graham	2,400	1,000	500.00
(70)	Eddie Grant	2,400	1,000	500.00
(71)	Groh	2,400	1,000	500.00
(72)	Charley Hale (Hall)	2,400	1,000	500.00
(73)	Halligan	2,400	1,000	500.00
(74)	Topsy Hartsel	2,400	1,000	500.00
(75)	Charlie Hemphill	2,400	1,000	500.00
(76)	Bill Hinchman	2,400	1,000	500.00
(77)	Art Hoelskoetter	2,400	1,000	500.00
(78)	Danny Hoffman	2,400	1,000	500.00
(79)	Solly Hofmann	2,400	1,000	500.00
(80)	Houser	2,400	1,000	500.00
(81)	Harry Howell	2,400	1,000	500.00
(82)	Miller Huggins	6,000	3,400	1,750
(83)	Rudy Hulswitt	2,400	1,000	500.00
(84)	John Hummel	2,400	1,000	500.00
(85a)	Frank Isbel (Isbell)(Chicago)	2,400	1,000	500.00
(85b)	Frank Isbel (Isbell)(No team.)	2,400	1,000	500.00
(86)	Walter Johnson	12,000	6,800	3,500
(87)	Fielder Jones (Chicago)	2,400	1,000	500.00
(88)	Tom Jones (St. Louis)	2,400	1,000	500.00
(89)	Tim Jordan	2,400	1,000	500.00
(90)	Addie Joss	12,000	6,800	3,500
(91)	Johnny Kane	2,400	1,000	500.00
(92)	Ed Karger	2,400	1,000	500.00
(93)	Wee Willie Keeler	6,000	3,400	1,750
(94)	Kellogg	2,400	1,000	500.00
(95)	Ed Killian	2,400	1,000	500.00
(96)	Malachi Kittredge (Kittridge)	2,400	1,000	500.00
(97)	Red Kleinow	2,400	1,000	500.00
(98)	Johnny Kling	2,400	1,000	500.00
(99)	Otto Knabe	2,400	1,000	500.00
(101)	John Knight	2,400	1,000	500.00
(102)	Ed Konetchy	2,400	1,000	500.00
(103)	Nap Lajoie	12,000	6,800	3,500
(104)	Frank LaPorte	2,400	1,000	500.00
(105)	Tommy Leach	2,400	1,000	500.00
(106)	Glenn Leibhardt (Liebhardt)	2,400	1,000	500.00
(107)	Phil Lewis	2,400	1,000	500.00
(108)	Vive Lindamann (Lindaman)	2,400	1,000	500.00
(109)	Hans Lobert	2,400	1,000	500.00
(110)	Harry Lord	2,400	1,000	500.00
(111)	Harry Lumley	2,400	1,000	500.00
(112)	Johnny Lush	2,400	1,000	500.00
(113)	Nick Maddox	2,400	1,000	500.00
(114)	Sherry Magee	2,400	1,000	500.00
(115)	Billy Maloney	2,400	1,000	500.00
(116)	Christy Mathewson	12,000	6,800	3,500
(117)	George McBride	2,400	1,000	500.00
(118)	Joe McGinnity	6,000	3,400	1,750
(119)	Stoney McGlynn	2,400	1,000	500.00
(120)	Harry McIntyre (McIntire) (Brooklyn)	2,400	1,000	500.00
(121)	Matty McIntyre (Detroit)	2,400	1,000	500.00
(122)	Larry McLean	2,400	1,000	500.00
(123)	George McQuillen (McQuillan)	2,400	1,000	500.00
(124)	Clyde Milan	2,400	1,000	500.00
(126)	Mike Mitchell	2,400	1,000	500.00
(127)	Moran	2,400	1,000	500.00
(128)	Mike Mowrey	2,400	1,000	500.00
(129)	George Mullin	2,400	1,000	500.00
(130)	Danny Murphy	2,400	1,000	500.00
(131)	J.J. Murray	2,400	1,000	500.00
(132)	Doc Newton	2,400	1,000	500.00
(133)	Simon Nicholls	2,400	1,000	500.00
(134)	Harry Niles	2,400	1,000	500.00
(135)	Rebel Oakes	2,400	1,000	500.00
(136)	Rube Oldring	2,400	1,000	500.00
(137)	Charley O'Leary	2,400	1,000	500.00
(138)	Patsy O'Rourke	2,400	1,000	800.00
(139)	Al Orth	2,400	1,000	800.00
(140)	Fred Osborne (Osborn)	2,400	1,000	500.00
(141)	Orval Overall	2,400	1,000	500.00
(142)	Freddy Parent	2,400	1,000	500.00
(143)	George Paskert	2,400	1,000	500.00
(144)	Case Patten	2,400	1,000	500.00
(145)	Deacon Phillippi (Phillippe)	2,400	1,000	500.00
(146)	Eddie Plank	12,000	6,800	3,500
(147)	Jack Powell	2,400	1,000	500.00
(148)	Tex Pruiett	2,400	1,000	500.00
(149)	Ed Reulbach	2,400	1,000	500.00
(151)	Bob Rhoades (Rhoads)	2,400	1,000	500.00
(152)	Claude Ritchey	2,400	1,000	500.00
(153)	Claude Rossman	2,400	1,000	500.00
(154)	Nap Rucker	2,400	1,000	500.00
(155)	Germany Schaefer	2,400	1,000	500.00
(156)	George Schlei	2,400	1,000	500.00
(157)	Boss Schmidt	2,400	1,000	500.00
(158)	Ossie Schreck	2,400	1,000	500.00
(159)	Wildfire Schulte	2,400	1,000	500.00
(160)	Schultz	2,400	1,000	500.00
(161)	Socks Seybold	2,400	1,000	500.00
(162)	Cy Seymour	2,400	1,000	500.00
(163)	Spike Shannon	2,400	1,000	500.00
(164)	Jimmy Sheckard	2,400	1,000	500.00
(165)	Tommy Sheehan	2,400	1,000	500.00
(166)	Bill Shipke	2,400	1,000	500.00
(167)	Jimmy Slagle	2,400	1,000	500.00
(168)	Charlie Smith (Chicago)	2,400	1,000	500.00
(169)	Frank Smith (Washington)	2,400	1,000	500.00
(170)	Bob Spade	2,400	1,000	500.00
(171)	Tully Sparks	2,400	1,000	500.00
(172)	Tris Speaker	6,000	3,400	1,750
(173)	Tubby Spencer	2,400	1,000	500.00
(174)	Jake Stahl	2,400	1,000	500.00
(176)	Steele	2,400	1,000	500.00
(177)	Harry Steinfeldt	2,400	1,000	500.00
(178)	George Stone	2,400	1,000	500.00
(179)	George Stovall	2,400	1,000	500.00
(180)	Billy Sullivan	2,400	1,000	500.00
(181)	Ed Summers	2,400	1,000	500.00
(182)	Bill Sweeney	2,400	1,000	500.00
(183)	Lee Tannehill	2,400	1,000	500.00
(184)	Dummy Taylor	2,400	1,000	500.00
(185)	Fred Tenney	2,400	1,000	500.00
(186)	Ira Thomas (No team.)	2,400	1,000	500.00
(187)	Roy Thomas (Pittsburg)	2,400	1,000	500.00
(188)	Jack Thoney	2,400	1,000	500.00
(189)	Joe Tinker	6,000	3,400	1,750
(190)	John Titus	2,400	1,000	500.00
(191)	Terry Turner	2,400	1,000	500.00
(192)	Bob Unglaub	2,400	1,000	500.00
(193)	Rube Waddell	6,000	3,400	1,750
(194)	Heinie Wagner (Boston)	2,400	1,000	500.00
(195)	Honus Wagner (Pittsburg)	24,000	13,600	7,000
(196)	Ed Walsh	6,000	3,400	1,750
(197)	Jack Warner	2,400	1,000	500.00
(198a)	Jake Weimer (Cincinnati)	2,400	1,000	500.00
(198b)	Jake Weimer (No team.)	2,400	1,000	500.00
(199)	Doc White	2,400	1,000	500.00
(201)	Jimmy Williams	2,400	1,000	500.00
(202)	Chief Wilson	2,400	1,000	500.00
(203)	Hooks Wiltse	2,400	1,000	500.00
(204)	George Winter	2,400	1,000	500.00
(205)	Cy Young (Boston)	12,000	6,800	3,500
(206)	Harley Young (Pittsburg)	2,400	1,000	500.00

1905 Rotograph Postcards

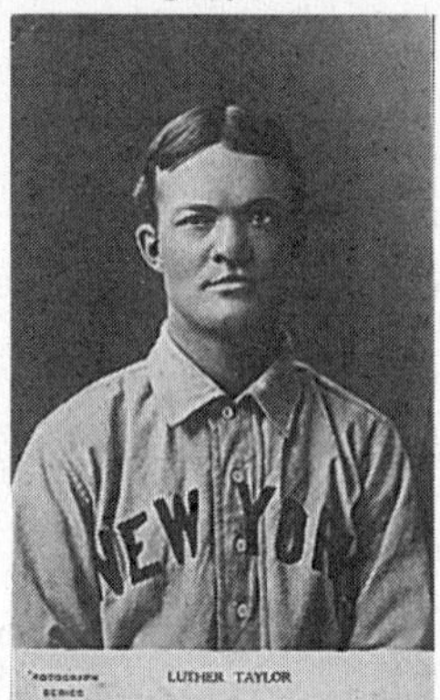

Only New York players have been seen on this series of 3-1/4" x 5-3/8" black-and-white or blue-and-white duotone postcards. Cards have player portrait photos with a white strip at bottom identifying the player; a "Rotograph / Series" notation is at left. Backs have typical postcard markings. This checklist may not be complete. The set was listed in the American Card Catalog under the number PC782.

		NM	EX	VG
Common Player:		800.00	400.00	250.00
(1)	Geo. Brown (Browne)	800.00	400.00	250.00
(2)	J.D. Chesbro	1,000	500.00	300.00
(3)	Wm. F. Dahlen	800.00	400.00	250.00
(4)	Clark Griffill (Griffith)	1,350	675.00	405.00
(5)	Joseph McGinnity	1,000	500.00	300.00
(6)	John McGraw	1,500	750.00	450.00
(7)	A. Puttmann	800.00	400.00	250.00
(8)	Luther Taylor	1,250	625.00	375.00

1977 Jim Rowe 4-on-1 Exhibits

This collectors' edition set harkens back to the four-player cards issued in the 1930s by Exhibit Supply Co. The 1977 version is printed in black on yellow in a 3-1/4" x 5-1/2" format. Backs are blank. Each of the four player photos on front is identified by name. The cards are checklisted here in order of team name.

		NM	EX	VG
Complete Set (16):		90.00	45.00	27.00
Common Card:		5.00	2.50	1.50
(1)	Boston Braves (Al Lopez, Rabbit Maranville, Warren Spahn, Casey Stengel)	5.00	2.50	1.50

		NM	EX	VG
(2)	Boston Red Sox (Joe Cronin, Herb Pennock, Babe Ruth, Ted Williams)	15.00	7.50	4.50
(3)	Brooklyn Dodgers (Max Carey, Burleigh Grimes, Joe Medwick, Dazzy Vance)	5.00	2.50	1.50
(4)	Chicago Cubs (Kiki Cuyler, Gabby Hartnett, Billy Herman, Freddy Lindstrom)	5.00	2.50	1.50
(5)	Chicago White Sox (Luke Appling, Red Faber, Ted Lyons, Red Ruffing)	5.00	2.50	1.50
(6)	Cincinnati Reds (Chick Hafey, George Kelly, Bill McKechnie, Edd Roush)	5.00	2.50	1.50
(7)	Cleveland Indians (Earl Averill, Lou Boudreau, Bob Feller, Bob Lemon)	5.00	2.50	1.50
(8)	Detroit Tigers (Ty Cobb, Charlie Gehringer, Goose Goslin, Hank Greenberg)	11.00	5.50	3.25
(9)	New York Giants (Dave Bancroft, Carl Hubbell, Mel Ott, Bill Terry)	5.00	2.50	1.50
(10)	New York Yankees (Bill Dickey, Joe DiMaggio, Lou Gehrig, Lefty Gomez)	12.00	6.00	3.50
(11)	Philadelphia Athletics (Mickey Cochrane, Eddie Collins, Lefty Grove, Al Simmons)	5.00	2.50	1.50
(12)	Philadelphia Phillies (Grover Alexander, Jimmie Foxx, Eppa Rixey, Robin Roberts)	5.00	2.50	1.50
(13)	Pittsburgh Pirates (Pie Traynor, Honus Wagner, Lloyd Waner, Paul Waner)	6.00	3.00	1.75
(14)	St. Louis Browns (Jim Bottomley, Earle Combs, Rogers Hornsby, George Sisler)	5.00	2.50	1.50
(15)	St. Louis Cardinals (Dizzy Dean, Frankie Frisch, Jesse Haines, Stan Musial)	5.00	2.50	1.50
(16)	Washington Senators (Bucky Harris, Walter Johnson, Heinie Manush, Sam Rice)	6.00	3.00	1.75

1977 Jim Rowe 1929 Cubs Postcards

Originally retailed for $3 per set, these collector-issue postcards feature on front borderless black-and-white photos in 3-1/2" x 5-7/16" format. Backs are standard Kodak postcard style, with no mention of the issuer. The player name is usually found penned at top.

		NM	EX	VG
Complete Set (13):		30.00	20.00	12.00
Common Player:		3.00	1.50	.90
(1)	Guy Bush	3.00	1.50	.90
(2)	Kiki Cuyler	3.00	1.50	.90
(3)	Woody English	3.00	1.50	.90
(4)	Charlie Grimm	3.00	1.50	.90
(5)	Gabby Hartnett	3.00	1.50	.90
(6)	Rogers Hornsby	3.00	1.50	.90
(7)	Pat Malone	3.00	1.50	.90
(8)	Norman McMillan	3.00	1.50	.90
(9)	Charlie Root	3.00	1.50	.90
(10)	Riggs Stephenson	3.00	1.50	.90
(11)	Zach Taylor	3.00	1.50	.90
(12)	Hack Wilson	3.00	1.50	.90
(13)	Team photo	3.00	1.50	.90

1977 Jim Rowe 1956 Braves Postcards

Originally retailed for $4 per set, these collector-issue postcards feature on front borderless black-and-white photos in 3-1/2" x 5-7/16" format. Backs are standard Kodak postcard style, with no mention of the issuer. The player name is usually found penned at top.

		NM	EX	VG
Complete Set (16):		35.00	17.50	10.50
Common Player:		3.00	1.50	.90
(1)	Hank Aaron	4.00	2.00	1.25
(2)	Joe Adcock	3.00	1.50	.90
(3)	Bill Bruton	3.00	1.50	.90
(4)	Bob Buhl	3.00	1.50	.90
(5)	Lew Burdette	3.00	1.50	.90
(6)	Gene Conley	3.00	1.50	.90
(7)	Del Crandall	3.00	1.50	.90
(8)	Charlie Grimm	3.00	1.50	.90
(9)	Fred Haney	3.00	1.50	.90
(10)	Joey Jay	3.00	1.50	.90
(11)	Johnny Logan	3.00	1.50	.90
(12)	Chet Nichols	3.00	1.50	.90
(13)	Danny O'Connell	3.00	1.50	.90
(14)	Andy Pafko	3.00	1.50	.90
(15)	Warren Spahn	3.00	1.50	.90
(16)	Bobby Thomson	3.00	1.50	.90

1978 Royal Crown Cola Iron-Ons

These iron-on color transfers were available in team strips of five players for 50 cents and six bottle cap liners. Because they were licensed only by the Players' Association, and not MLB, the approximately 4-1/4" x 6-1/4" transfers do not show team logos or nicknames.

		NM	EX	VG
Complete Set (130):		750.00	375.00	225.00
Common Player:		6.00	3.00	1.75
	Atlanta Strip	25.00	12.50	7.50
(1)	Jeff Burroughs	6.00	3.00	1.75
(2)	Gary Matthews	6.00	3.00	1.75
(3)	Phil Niekro	7.50	3.75	2.25
(4)	Biff Pocoroba	6.00	3.00	1.75
(5)	Dick Ruthven	6.00	3.00	1.75
	Baltimore Strip	50.00	25.00	15.00
(6)	Al Bumbry	6.00	3.00	1.75
(7)	Lee May	6.00	3.00	1.75
(8)	Eddie Murray	30.00	15.00	9.00
(9)	Jim Palmer	15.00	7.50	4.50
(10)	Ken Singleton	6.00	3.00	1.75
	Boston Strip	40.00	20.00	12.00
(11)	Bill Campbell	6.00	3.00	1.75
(12)	Fred Lynn	6.00	3.00	1.75
(13)	Jim Rice	7.50	3.75	2.25
(14)	George Scott	6.00	3.00	1.75
(15)	Carl Yastrzemski	25.00	12.50	7.50
	California Strip	75.00	37.50	22.50
(16)	Dave Chalk	6.00	3.00	1.75
(17)	Bobby Grich	6.00	3.00	1.75
(18)	Joe Rudi	6.00	3.00	1.75
(19)	Nolan Ryan	60.00	30.00	18.00
(20)	Frank Tanana	6.00	3.00	1.75
	Chicago (Cubs) Strip	30.00	15.00	9.00
(21)	Bill Buckner	6.00	3.00	1.75
(22)	Dave Kingman	6.00	3.00	1.75
(23)	Steve Ontiveros	6.00	3.00	1.75
(24)	Bruce Sutter	7.50	3.75	2.25
(25)	Manny Trillo	6.00	3.00	1.75
	Chicago (White Sox) Strip	25.00	12.50	7.50
(26)	Ron Blomberg	6.00	3.00	1.75
(27)	Bobby Bonds	6.00	3.00	1.75
(28)	Ralph Garr	6.00	3.00	1.75
(29)	Jorge Orta	6.00	3.00	1.75
(30)	Eric Soderholm	6.00	3.00	1.75
	Cincinnati Strip			
(31)	Johnny Bench	15.00	7.50	4.50
(32)	Unknown			
(33)	Joe Morgan	15.00	7.50	4.50
(34)	Unknown			
(35)	Pete Rose	40.00	20.00	12.00
	Cleveland Strip	25.00	12.50	7.50
(36)	Buddy Bell	6.00	3.00	1.75
(37)	Wayne Garland	6.00	3.00	1.75
(38)	Johnny Grubb	6.00	3.00	1.75
(39)	Rick Manning	6.00	3.00	1.75
(40)	Andre Thornton	6.00	3.00	1.75
	Detroit Strip	25.00	12.50	7.50
(41)	Mark Fidrych	6.00	3.00	1.75
(42)	John Hiller	6.00	3.00	1.75
(43)	Ron LeFlore	6.00	3.00	1.75
(44)	Milt May	6.00	3.00	1.75
(45)	Jason Thompson	6.00	3.00	1.75
	Houston Strip	25.00	12.50	7.50
(46)	Enos Cabell	6.00	3.00	1.75
(47)	Cesar Cedeno	6.00	3.00	1.75
(48)	Joe Ferguson	6.00	3.00	1.75
(49)	J.R. Richard	6.00	3.00	1.75
(50)	Bobby Watson	6.00	3.00	1.75
	Kansas City Strip	45.00	22.50	13.50
(51)	George Brett	30.00	15.00	9.00
(52)	Al Cowens	6.00	3.00	1.75
(53)	Hal McRae	6.00	3.00	1.75
(54)	Amos Otis	6.00	3.00	1.75
(55)	Fred Patek	6.00	3.00	1.75
	Los Angeles Strip	30.00	15.00	9.00
(56)	Ron Cey	6.00	3.00	1.75
(57)	Steve Garvey	7.50	3.75	2.25
(58)	Tommy John	6.00	3.00	1.75
(59)	Bill Russell	6.00	3.00	1.75
(60)	Don Sutton	7.50	3.75	2.25
	Milwaukee Strip	30.00	15.00	9.00
(61)	Sal Bando	6.00	3.00	1.75
(62)	Ray Fosse	6.00	3.00	1.75
(63)	Larry Hisle	6.00	3.00	1.75
(64)	Sixto Lezcano	6.00	3.00	1.75
(65)	Robin Yount	15.00	7.50	4.50
	Minnesota Strip	30.00	15.00	9.00
(66)	Rod Carew	15.00	7.50	4.50
(67)	Dan Ford	6.00	3.00	1.75
(68)	Dave Goltz	6.00	3.00	1.75
(69)	Roy Smalley	6.00	3.00	1.75
(70)	Butch Wynegar	6.00	3.00	1.75
	Montreal Strip	30.00	15.00	9.00
(71)	Dave Cash	6.00	3.00	1.75
(72)	Andre Dawson	7.50	3.75	2.25
(73)	Tony Perez	7.50	3.75	2.25
(74)	Steve Rogers	6.00	3.00	1.75
(75)	Ellis Valentine	6.00	3.00	1.75
	New York (Mets) Strip	25.00	12.50	7.50
(76)	Steve Henderson	6.00	3.00	1.75
(77)	Jerry Koosman	6.00	3.00	1.75
(78)	Elliott Maddox	6.00	3.00	1.75
(79)	Willie Montanez	6.00	3.00	1.75
(80)	Lenny Randle	6.00	3.00	1.75
	New York (Yankees) Strip	30.00	15.00	9.00
(81)	Sparky Lyle	6.00	3.00	1.75
(82)	Thurman Munson	7.50	3.75	2.25
(83)	Lou Piniella	6.00	3.00	1.75
(84)	Willie Randolph	6.00	3.00	1.75
(85)	Mickey Rivers	6.00	3.00	1.75
	Oakland Strip	25.00	12.50	7.50
(86)	Wayne Gross	6.00	3.00	1.75
(87)	Rick Langford	6.00	3.00	1.75
(88)	Bill North	6.00	3.00	1.75
(89)	Mitchell Page	6.00	3.00	1.75
(90)	Gary Thomasson	6.00	3.00	1.75
	Philadelphia Strip	60.00	30.00	18.00
(91)	Larry Bowa	6.00	3.00	1.75
(92)	Steve Carlton	15.00	7.50	4.50
(93)	Greg Luzinski	6.00	3.00	1.75
(94)	Garry Maddox	6.00	3.00	1.75
(95)	Mike Schmidt	35.00	17.50	10.50
	Pittsburgh Strip	30.00	15.00	9.00
(96)	John Candelaria	6.00	3.00	1.75
(97)	Dave Parker	6.00	3.00	1.75
(98)	Bill Robinson	6.00	3.00	1.75
(99)	Willie Stargell	15.00	7.50	4.50
(100)	Rennie Stennett	6.00	3.00	1.75
	San Diego Strip	35.00	17.50	10.00
(101)	Rollie Fingers	7.50	3.75	2.25
(102)	Oscar Gamble	6.00	3.00	1.75
(103)	Randy Jones	6.00	3.00	1.75
(104)	Gene Tenace	6.00	3.00	1.75
(105)	Dave Winfield	15.00	7.50	4.50
	San Francisco Strip	30.00	15.00	9.00
(106)	Vida Blue	6.00	3.00	1.75
(107)	Gary Lavelle	6.00	3.00	1.75
(108)	Bill Madlock	6.00	3.00	1.75
(109)	Willie McCovey	15.00	7.50	4.50
(110)	John Montefusco	6.00	3.00	1.75
	Seattle Strip	25.00	12.50	7.50
(111)	Bruce Bochte	6.00	3.00	1.75
(112)	Ruppert Jones	6.00	3.00	1.75
(113)	Dan Meyer	6.00	3.00	1.75
(114)	Lee Stanton	6.00	3.00	1.75
(115)	Bill Stein	6.00	3.00	1.75
	St. Louis Strip	30.00	15.00	9.00
(116)	Lou Brock	15.00	7.50	4.50
(117)	Bob Forsch	6.00	3.00	1.75
(118)	Ken Reitz	6.00	3.00	1.75
(119)	Ted Simmons	6.00	3.00	1.75
(120)	Garry Templeton	6.00	3.00	1.75
	Texas Strip	25.00	12.50	7.50
(121)	Mike Hargrove	6.00	3.00	1.75
(122)	Toby Harrah	6.00	3.00	1.75
(123)	Jon Matlack	6.00	3.00	1.75
(124)	Jim Sundberg	6.00	3.00	1.75
(125)	Richie Zisk	6.00	3.00	1.75
	Toronto Strip	25.00	12.50	7.50
(126)	Doug Ault	6.00	3.00	1.75
(127)	Bob Bailor	6.00	3.00	1.75
(128)	Jerry Garvin	6.00	3.00	1.75
(129)	Roy Howell	6.00	3.00	1.75
(130)	Al Woods	6.00	3.00	1.75

1950 Royal Desserts

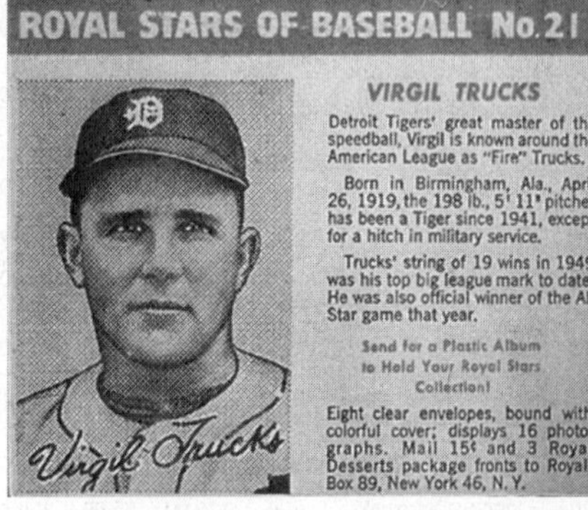

This set was issued one per box on the backs of various Royal Dessert products over a period of three years. The basic set contains 24 players, however a number of variations create the much higher total for the set. In 1950, Royal issued cards with two different tints - black and white with red, or blue and white with red. Over the next two years, various sentences of the cards' biographies were updated; up to three times in some cases. Some players from the set left the majors after 1950 and others were apparently never updated, but the 23 biography updates that do exist, added to the original 24 cards issued in 1950, give the set a total of 47 cards. The 2-5/8" x 3-1/4" cards are blank-backed with personal and playing biographies alongside the card front photos. Some sample cards can be found with advertising for the desserts on back; they are valued at about double regular card prices. A comb-bound album with seven pages to hold 14 cards was also issued in a 3-1/4" x 3-3/8" format with "Royal Stars" and a crown logo printed in red on white.

		NM	EX	VG
Common Player:		125.00	55.00	25.00
Album:		200.00	90.00	40.00
1a	Stan Musial (2nd paragraph begins "Musial's 207...")	525.00	235.00	100.00
1b	Stan Musial (2nd paragraph begins "Musial batted...")	525.00	235.00	100.00
2a	Pee Wee Reese (2nd paragraph begins "Pee Wee's...")	330.00	150.00	65.00
2b	Pee Wee Reese (2nd paragraph begins "Captain...")	330.00	150.00	65.00
2c	Pee Wee Reese (Ad card.)	330.00	150.00	65.00
3a	George Kell (2nd paragraph ends "...in 1945, '46.")	200.00	90.00	40.00
3b	George Kell (2nd paragraph ends "...two base hits, 56.")	200.00	90.00	40.00
3c	George Kell (Ad card.)	200.00	90.00	40.00
4a	Dom DiMaggio (2nd paragraph ends "...during 1947.")	165.00	75.00	35.00
4b	Dom DiMaggio (2nd paragraph ends "...with 11.")	165.00	75.00	35.00
5a	Warren Spahn (2nd paragraph ends "...shutouts 7.")	265.00	120.00	55.00
5b	Warren Spahn (2nd paragraph ends "...with 191.")	265.00	120.00	55.00
6a	Andy Pafko (2nd paragraph ends "...7 games.")	125.00	56.00	25.00
6b	Andy Pafko (2nd paragraph ends "...National League.")	125.00	55.00	25.00
6c	Andy Pafko (2nd paragraph ends "...weighs 190.")	125.00	55.00	25.00
7a	Andy Seminick (2nd paragraph ends "...as outfield.")	125.00	55.00	25.00
7b	Andy Seminick (2nd paragraph ends "...since 1916.")	125.00	55.00	25.00
7c	Andy Seminick (2nd paragraph ends "...in the outfield.")	125.00	55.00	25.00
7d	Andy Seminick (2nd paragraph ends "...right handed.")	125.00	55.00	25.00
8a	Lou Brissie (2nd paragraph ends "...when pitching.")	125.00	55.00	25.00
8b	Lou Brissie (2nd paragraph ends "...weighs 215.")	125.00	55.00	25.00
9a	Ewell Blackwell (2nd paragraph begins "Despite recent illness...")	145.00	65.00	30.00
9b	Ewell Blackwell (2nd paragraph begins "Blackwell's...")	145.00	65.00	30.00
10a	Bobby Thomson (2nd paragraph begins "In 1949...")	165.00	75.00	35.00
10b	Bobby Thomson (2nd paragraph begins "Thomson is...")	165.00	75.00	35.00
11a	Phil Rizzuto (2nd paragraph ends "...one 1942 game.")	330.00	150.00	65.00
11b	Phil Rizzuto (2nd paragraph ends "...Most Valuable Player.")	330.00	150.00	65.00
12	Tommy Henrich	155.00	70.00	30.00
13	Joe Gordon	125.00	55.00	25.00
14a	Ray Scarborough (Senators)	125.00	55.00	25.00
14b	Ray Scarborough (White Sox, 2nd paragraph ends "...military service.")	125.00	55.00	25.00
14c	Ray Scarborough (White Sox, 2nd paragraph ends "...the season.")	125.00	55.00	25.00
14d	Ray Scarborough (Red Sox)	125.00	55.00	25.00
15a	Stan Rojek (Pirates)	125.00	55.00	25.00
15b	Stan Rojek (Browns)	125.00	55.00	25.00
16	Luke Appling	180.00	80.00	35.00
17	Willard Marshall	125.00	55.00	25.00
18	Alvin Dark	125.00	55.00	25.00
19a	Dick Sisler (2nd paragraph ends "...service record.")	125.00	55.00	25.00
19b	Dick Sisler (2nd paragraph ends "...National League flag.")	125.00	55.00	25.00
19c	Dick Sisler (2nd paragraph ends "...Nov. 2, 1920.")	125.00	55.00	25.00
19d	Dick Sisler (2nd paragraph ends "...from '46 to '48. ")	125.00	55.00	25.00
20a	Johnny Ostrowski (White Sox)	125.00	55.00	25.00
20b	Johnny Ostrowski (Senators)	125.00	55.00	25.00
21a	Virgil Trucks (2nd paragraph ends "...in military service.")	125.00	55.00	25.00
21b	Virgil Trucks (2nd paragraph ends "...that year.")	125.00	55.00	25.00
21c	Virgil Trucks (2nd paragraph ends "...for military service.")	125.00	55.00	25.00
22	Eddie Robinson	125.00	55.00	25.00
23	Nanny Fernandez	125.00	55.00	25.00
24	Ferris Fain	125.00	55.00	25.00

1952 Royal Desserts

This set, issued as a premium by Royal Desserts in 1952, consists of 16 unnumbered black and white cards, each measuring 5" x 7". The cards include the inscription "To A Royal Fan" along with the player's facsimile autograph. Backs are blank.

		NM	EX	VG
Complete Set (16):		1,400	625.00	275.00
Common Player:		55.00	25.00	10.00
(1)	Ewell Blackwell	55.00	25.00	10.00
(2)	Leland V. Brissie Jr.	55.00	25.00	10.00
(3)	Alvin Dark	55.00	25.00	10.00
(4)	Dom DiMaggio	100.00	45.00	20.00
(5)	Ferris Fain	55.00	25.00	10.00
(6)	George Kell	100.00	45.00	20.00
(7)	Stan Musial	280.00	125.00	55.00
(8)	Andy Pafko	55.00	25.00	10.00
(9)	Pee Wee Reese	175.00	80.00	35.00
(10)	Phil Rizzuto	160.00	70.00	30.00
(11)	Eddie Robinson	55.00	25.00	10.00
(12)	Ray Scarborough	55.00	25.00	10.00
(13)	Andy Seminick	55.00	25.00	10.00
(14)	Dick Sisler	55.00	25.00	10.00
(15)	Warren Spahn	140.00	65.00	25.00
(16)	Bobby Thomson	80.00	35.00	15.00

1920 Babe Ruth "Headin' Home"

This was one of several series of promotional cards issued to advertise the Bambino's starring role in the 1920 silent film, "Headin' Home." The black-and-white cards measure about 1-1/2" x 2-7/16". They feature borderless photos with the three-line caption: BABE RUTH / IN / "HEADIN' HOME." The cards are frequently found miscut with a portion of another card showing at one or more of the edges. Backs may be blank or carry the advertising of a local theater.

		NM	EX	VG
Complete Set (6):		16,000	8,000	4,750
Common Card:		3,000	1,500	900.00
(1)	Babe Ruth (Bat at shoulder, crotch-to-cap.)	3,000	1,500	900.00
(2)	Babe Ruth (Bat extended to his right.)	3,000	1,500	900.00
(3)	Babe Ruth (Bat on shoulder, full-length.)	3,000	1,500	900.00
(4)	Babe Ruth (Follow-through, bat head-high.)	3,000	1,500	900.00
(5)	Babe Ruth (Follow-through, bat below waist.)	3,000	1,500	900.00
(6)	Babe Ruth (Horizontal card, holding bat.)	3,000	1,500	900.00

1920 Babe Ruth "Headin' Home" Theater Cards

To promote the showing of "Headin' Home," a silent movie starring Babe Ruth, theaters had these cards printed up with details of show dates. Fronts of the 1-3/4" x 3-1/4" cards have a sepia photo of Ruth swinging the bat. On back is an advertisement from a local theater. This is one of the first cards ever to picture Ruth as a N.Y. Yankee.

	NM	EX	VG
Babe Ruth (Both hands on bat.)	2,750	1,375	825.00
Babe Ruth (One hand on bat.)	2,750	1,375	825.00

1920 Babe Ruth "Headin' Home" (Tex Rickard)

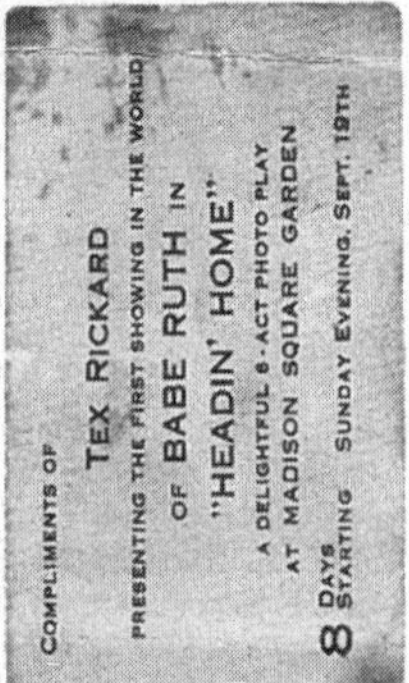

Taking advantage of the Babe's enormous popularity in the pinstripes of his new team, he was given a starring role in a 1920 silent movie titled "Headin Home." To promote the flick, a small set of cards was issued. The 1-7/8" x 3-1/4" black-and-white cards have posed photos of Ruth on front. Dropped out in white in the lower portion of the photo is his name and movie title. Backs have an ad for the movie (some cards are known with blank backs, as well). Tex Rickard was the Ebbets Field announcer for the Brooklyn Dodgers for over 30 years.

		NM	EX	VG
Common Card:		5,000	2,500	1,500
(1)	Babe Ruth (Bat on shoulder, crotch to cap.)	5,000	2,500	1,500
(2)	Babe Ruth (Bat on shoulder, full-length.)	5,000	2,500	1,500
(3)	Babe Ruth (Batting follow-through.)	5,000	2,500	1,500

1920s Babe Ruth Postcard

There is no indication of publisher or specific date of issue on this standard-size, typically marked black-and-white photo postcard which pictures the Babe in street clothes informally posed with a cane chair. The number "210" near the bottom of the photo indicates it was part of a series. The horizontal divided back has typical postcard markings.

		NM	EX	VG
210	Babe Ruth	750.00	375.00	225.00

1920s Babe Ruth Underwear Premium Photo

While the product itself and the boxes and display pieces are collectibles in their own right, among the scarcest pieces associated with the Babe Ruth brand underwear is this ap-

proximately 8" x 10" premium photo which was apparently only included in some forms of packaging. The blank-back photo shows a buff Babe in the product and has a facsimile autograph on his right bicep.

	NM	EX	VG
Babe Ruth	500.00	250.00	150.00

1927 "Babe Comes Home" Strip Cards (R94)

This strip card set of unknown scope (at least 75 known) was cataloged as "Movie Stars and Scenes (R94)" in the American Card Catalog. At least two of the cards depict Babe Ruth as "Babe Dugan" in scenes from his silent film. Cards are nominally about 2-7/8" x 2-5/16" and can be found printed in black-and-white or as red, blue or green duotones. The name of the movie is printed in white at bottom. Backs and blank.

	NM	EX	VG
Babe Ruth (In suit w/police.)	1,350	675.00	400.00
Babe Ruth (In uniform, locker room.)	1,350	675.00	400.00

1928 Babe Ruth Home Run Candy Club Membership Card

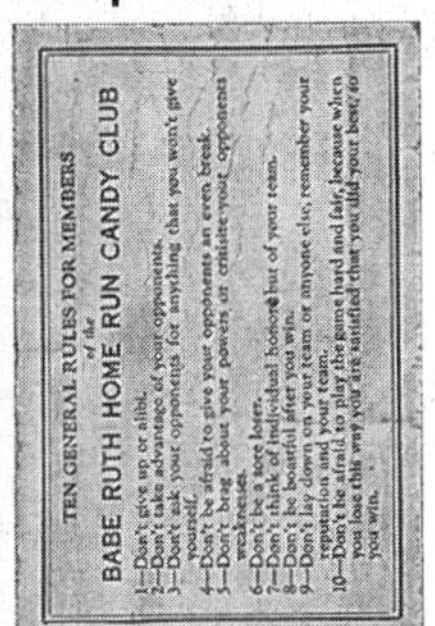

In conjunction with his candy bar, Ruth created the "Babe Ruth Home Run Candy Club," and issued this membership card. Front has a black-and-white portrait photo. Back of the 2-3/4" x 4" card has 10 rules of sportsmanship for members. The card folds open to reveal a membership certificate with a facsimile autograph.

	NM	EX	VG
Babe Ruth	2,500	1,250	750.00

1928 George Ruth Candy Co.

This circa 1928 issue features sepia-toned photos of Babe Ruth. According to the back of the cards, it was issued by the Geo. H. Ruth Candy Co. Cards measure 1-7/8" x 4" and picture Ruth during a 1924 promotional West Coast tour and in scenes from the movie "Babe Comes Home." The cards are numbered and include photo captions at the bottom. The backs of most cards contain an offer to exchange the six cards for an autographed baseball, which may explain their scarcity today. Cards have been seen with the address to mail for exchange as Cleveland and as San Francisco. Cards can also be found with blank backs. This issue was deceptively counterfeited in the early 21st Century.

		NM	EX	VG
Complete Set (6):		7,000	3,150	1,400
Common Card:		1,250	650.00	300.00
Wrapper:		3,500	2,000	1,250
1	"Babe" Ruth ("King of them all...")	1,250	650.00	300.00
2	"Babe" Ruth ("Knocked out 60 Home Runs...")	1,250	650.00	300.00
3	"Babe" Ruth ("The only player...")	1,250	650.00	300.00
4	"Babe" Ruth ("The Popular Bambino...")	1,250	650.00	300.00
5	"Babe" Ruth ("A favorite with the Kiddies...")	1,250	650.00	300.00
6	"Babe" Ruth ("The King of Swat...")	1,250	650.00	300.00

1948 Babe Ruth Memorial Pin

Likely issued following Ruth's death in 1948, this 1-3/4" celluloid pinback has a black-and-white photo of Ruth swinging a bat on a black background with his name in capital letters in a white arc below.

	NM	EX	VG
Babe Ruth	300.00	150.00	90.00

1936 R311 Glossy Finish

The cards in this 28-card set, which was available as a premium in 1936, measure 6" x 8" and were printed on a glossy cardboard. The photos are either black and white or sepia-toned and include a facsimile autograph. The unnumbered set includes individual players and team photos. The Boston Red Sox team card can be found in two varieties; one shows the sky above the building on the card's right side, while the other does not. Some of the cards are scarcer than others in the set and command a premium. Babe Ruth is featured on the Boston Braves team card.

		NM	EX	VG
Complete Set (27):		3,750	1,850	1,100
Common Player:		60.00	30.00	18.00
(1)	Earl Averill	100.00	50.00	30.00
(2)	James L. "Jim" Bottomley	100.00	50.00	30.00
(3)	Gordon S. "Mickey" Cochrane	100.00	50.00	30.00
(4)	Joe Cronin	100.00	50.00	30.00
(5)	Jerome "Dizzy" Dean	150.00	75.00	45.00
(6)	Jimmy Dykes	60.00	30.00	18.00
(7)	Jimmy Foxx	125.00	65.00	35.00
(8)	Frankie Frisch	100.00	50.00	30.00
(9)	Henry "Hank" Greenberg	120.00	60.00	35.00
(10)	Mel Harder/SP	120.00	60.00	35.00
(11)	Pepper Martin/SP	225.00	110.00	65.00
(12)	Lynwood "Schoolboy" Rowe/SP	120.00	60.00	35.00
(13)	William "Bill" Terry	100.00	50.00	30.00
(14)	Harold "Pie" Traynor	100.00	50.00	30.00
(15)	American League All-Stars/1935	275.00	135.00	80.00
(16)	American League Pennant Winners/1934 (Detroit Tigers)	125.00	65.00	35.00
(17)	Boston Braves/1935	300.00	150.00	90.00
(18a)	Boston Red Sox (Sky visible above building at right.)	100.00	50.00	30.00
(18b)	Boston Red Sox (No sky visible.)	180.00	90.00	55.00
(19)	Brooklyn Dodgers/1935/SP	225.00	110.00	65.00
(20)	Chicago White Sox/1935	100.00	50.00	30.00
(21)	Columbus Red Birds (1934 Pennant Winners of American Association)/SP	150.00	75.00	45.00
(22)	National League All-Stars/1935	180.00	90.00	55.00
(23)	National League Champions/1935 (Chicago Cubs)	100.00	50.00	30.00
(24)	New York Yankees/1935	180.00	90.00	55.00
(25)	Pittsburgh Pirates/1935/SP	200.00	100.00	60.00
(26)	St. Louis Browns/1935	100.00	50.00	30.00
(27)	The World Champions/1934 (St. Louis Cardinals)	100.00	50.00	30.00

1936 R311 Leather Finish

This set of 15 unnumbered cards, issued as a premium in 1936, is distinctive because of its uneven, leather-like surface. The cards measure 6" x 8" and display a facsimilie autograph on the black and white photo surrounded by a plain border. The cards are unnumbered and include individual player photos, multi-player photos and team photos of the 1935 pennant winners.

		NM	EX	VG
Complete Set (15):		2,750	1,325	825.00
Common Player:		90.00	45.00	25.00
(1)	Frank Crosetti, Joe DiMaggio, Tony Lazzeri	825.00	410.00	245.00
(2)	Paul Derringer	90.00	45.00	25.00
(3)	Wes Ferrell	90.00	45.00	25.00
(4)	Jimmy (Jimmie) Foxx	180.00	90.00	55.00
(5)	Charlie Gehringer	165.00	80.00	50.00
(6)	Mel Harder	90.00	45.00	25.00
(7)	Gabby Hartnett	165.00	80.00	50.00
(8)	Rogers Hornsby	190.00	95.00	55.00
(9)	Connie Mack	165.00	80.00	50.00
(10)	Van Mungo	90.00	45.00	25.00
(11)	Steve O'Neill	90.00	45.00	25.00
(12)	Charles Ruffing	165.00	80.00	50.00
(13)	Arky Vaughan, Honus Wagner	245.00	120.00	75.00
(14)	American League Pennant Winners/1935 (Detroit Tigers)	165.00	80.00	50.00
(15)	National League Pennant Winners/1935 (Chicago Cubs)	165.00	80.00	50.00

1936 R312

The 50 cards in this set of 4" x 5-3/8" point-of-purchase premiums are black-and-white photos that have been tinted in soft pastel colors. The set includes 25 individual player portraits, 14 multi-player cards and 11 action photos. Six of the action photos include facsimilie autographs, while the other five have printed legends. The Allen card is scarcer than the others in the set.

		NM	EX	VG
Complete Set (50):		8,500	4,250	2,500
Common Player:		90.00	35.00	20.00
(1)	John Thomas Allen	90.00	35.00	20.00

(2)	Nick Altrock, Al Schact	140.00	55.00	35.00
(3)	Ollie Bejma, Rolly Hemsley	90.00	35.00	20.00
(4)	Les Bell, Zeke Bonura	90.00	35.00	20.00
(5)	Cy Blanton	90.00	35.00	20.00
(6)	Cliff Bolton, Earl Whitehill	90.00	35.00	20.00
(7)	Frenchy Bordagaray, George Earnshaw	90.00	35.00	20.00
(8)	Mace Brown	90.00	35.00	20.00
(9)	Dolph Camilli	90.00	35.00	20.00
(10)	Phil Cavaretta (Cavarretta), Frank Demaree, Augie Galan, Stan Hack, Gabby Hartnett, Billy Herman, Billy Jurges, Chuck Klein, Fred Lindstrom	185.00	75.00	45.00
(11)	Phil Cavaretta (Cavarretta), Stan Hack, Billy Herman, Billy Jurges	185.00	75.00	45.00
(12)	Gordon Cochrane	185.00	75.00	45.00
(13)	Jim Collins, Stan Hack	90.00	35.00	20.00
(14)	Rip Collins	90.00	35.00	20.00
(15)	Joe Cronin, Buckey Harris (Bucky)	125.00	50.00	30.00
(16)	Alvin Crowder	90.00	35.00	20.00
(17)	Kiki Cuyler	185.00	75.00	45.00
(18)	Kiki Cuyler, Tris Speaker, Danny Taylor	225.00	90.00	55.00
(19)	"Bill" Dickey	185.00	75.00	45.00
(20)	Joe DiMagio (DiMaggio)	2,200	850.00	550.00
(21)	"Chas." Dressen	90.00	35.00	20.00
(22)	Rick Ferrell, Russ Van Atta	125.00	50.00	30.00
(23)	Pete Fox, Goose Goslin, "Jo Jo" White	165.00	65.00	40.00
(24)	Jimmey Foxx, Luke Sewell	215.00	85.00	55.00
(25)	Benny Frey	90.00	35.00	20.00
(26)	Augie Galan, "Pie" Traynor	165.00	65.00	40.00
(27)	Lefty Gomez, Myril Hoag	165.00	65.00	40.00
(28)	"Hank" Greenberg	185.00	75.00	45.00
(29)	Lefty Grove, Connie Mack	250.00	100.00	65.00
(30)	Muel Haas (Mule), Mike Kreevich, Dixie Walker	90.00	35.00	20.00
(31)	Mel Harder	90.00	35.00	20.00
(32)	Gabby Hartnett (Mickey Cochrane, Frank Demaree, Ernie Quigley (ump) in photo)	165.00	65.00	40.00
(33)	Gabby Hartnett, Lonnie Warnecke (Warneke)	135.00	55.00	35.00
(34)	Roger Hornsby (Rogers)	250.00	100.00	65.00
(35)	Rogers Hornsby, Allen Sothoren (Sothoron)	185.00	75.00	45.00
(36)	Ernie Lombardi	185.00	75.00	45.00
(37)	Al Lopez	185.00	75.00	45.00
(38)	Pepper Martin	110.00	45.00	25.00
(39)	"Johnny" Mize	185.00	75.00	45.00
(40)	Van L. Mungo	100.00	40.00	25.00
(41)	Bud Parmelee	90.00	35.00	20.00
(42)	Schoolboy Rowe	90.00	35.00	20.00
(43)	Chas. Ruffing	185.00	75.00	45.00
(44)	Eugene Schott	90.00	35.00	20.00
(45)	Casey Stengel	185.00	75.00	45.00
(46)	Bill Sullivan	90.00	35.00	20.00
(47)	Bill Swift	90.00	35.00	20.00
(48)	Floyd Vaughan, Hans Wagner	225.00	90.00	55.00
(49)	L. Waner, P. Waner, Big Jim Weaver	215.00	85.00	55.00
(50)	Ralph Winegarner	90.00	35.00	20.00

1936 R313

(See 1936 National Chicle "Fine Pens.")

1936 R314

(See 1936 Goudey "Wide Pen" Premiums.)

1929-1930 R315

Apparently issued over a period of at least two years, based on observed player/team combinations, the 58 cards in this set can be found in either black-and-white or yellow-and-black. The unnumbered, blank-backed cards measure a nominal 3-1/4" x 5-1/4" though original cutting variances abound. The cards feature either portraits or posed action photos. The set includes several different types of cards, depending on the caption. Cards can be found with the player's name and team inside a white box in a lower corner; other cards add the position and team in small type in the bottom border; a third type has the player's name in hand lettering near the bottom; and the final type includes the position and team printed in small type along the bottom border.

		NM	EX	VG
Complete Set (46):		6,000	2,400	1,200
Common Player:		45.00	20.00	10.00
(1)	Earl Averill	90.00	35.00	25.00
(2)	"Benny" Bengough	45.00	20.00	10.00
(3)	Laurence Benton (Lawrence)	45.00	20.00	10.00
(4)	"Max" Bishop	45.00	20.00	10.00
(5)	"Sunny Jim" Bottomley	90.00	35.00	20.00
(6)	Bill Cissell	45.00	20.00	10.00
(7)	Bud Clancey (Clancy)	45.00	20.00	10.00
(8)	"Freddy" Fitzsimmons	45.00	20.00	10.00
(9)	"Jimmy" Foxx	260.00	100.00	65.00
(10)	"Johnny" Fredericks (Frederick)	45.00	20.00	10.00
(11)	Frank Frisch	110.00	45.00	25.00
(12)	"Lou" Gehrig	1,500	600.00	375.00
(13)	"Goose" Goslin	90.00	35.00	20.00
(14)	Burleigh Grimes	90.00	35.00	20.00
(15)	"Lefty" Grove	110.00	45.00	25.00
(16)	"Mule" Haas	45.00	20.00	10.00
(17)	Harvey Hendricks (Hendrick)	45.00	20.00	10.00
(18)	"Babe" Herman	60.00	25.00	15.00
(19)	"Roger" Hornsby (Rogers)	135.00	55.00	35.00
(20)	Karl Hubbell (Carl)	90.00	35.00	20.00
(21)	"Stonewall" Jackson	90.00	35.00	20.00
(22)	Smead Jolley	45.00	20.00	10.00
(23)	"Chuck" Klein	90.00	35.00	20.00
(24)	Mark Koenig	45.00	20.00	10.00
(25)	"Tony" Lazerri (Lazzeri)	90.00	35.00	20.00
(26)	Fred Leach	45.00	20.00	10.00
(27)	"Freddy" Lindstrom	90.00	35.00	20.00
(28)	Fred Marberry	45.00	20.00	10.00
(29)	"Bing" Miller	45.00	20.00	10.00
(30)	"Bob" O'Farrell	45.00	20.00	10.00
(31)	Frank O'Doul	75.00	30.00	18.50
(32)	"Herbie" Pennock	90.00	35.00	20.00
(33)	George Pipgras	45.00	20.00	10.00
(34)	Andrew Reese	45.00	20.00	10.00
(35)	Carl Reynolds	45.00	20.00	10.00
(36)	"Babe" Ruth	1,600	640.00	400.00
(37)	"Bob" Shawkey	45.00	20.00	10.00
(38)	Art Shires	45.00	20.00	10.00
(39)	"Al" Simmons	90.00	35.00	20.00
(40)	"Riggs" Stephenson	45.00	20.00	10.00
(41)	"Bill" Terry	90.00	35.00	20.00
(42)	"Pie" Traynor	90.00	35.00	20.00
(43)	"Dazzy" Vance	90.00	35.00	20.00
(44)	Paul Waner	90.00	35.00	20.00
(45)	Hack Wilson	90.00	35.00	20.00
(46)	"Tom" Zachary	45.00	20.00	10.00

1929 R316

(See Kashin Publications.)

1929 R316 5x7 Photos

There is nothing concrete to connect this set of player photos with the Kashin Publications card set which carried the R316 designation in the American Card Catalog except that these 4-7/8" x 6-3/4" heavy-paper pictures use the same photos and graphics as the smaller cards. It is thought that the photos are the work of Charles M. Conlon and that the 5x7s may have some connection to the Spalding sporting goods company for whom he worked. Pictures feature white borders and facsimile autographs on front, along with the player's city and league on two lines of type at bottom. While the photos are all the same as seen on R316, the city/league designation on some of the photos is sometimes in black instead of white as on the card, or vice versa. Because almost every card from R316 is known in the 5x7 series, it is reasonable to expect that pictures of Frank Hogan and Jimmy Welsh may also exist. A number of players in the 5x7 set do not appear in the Kashin Publications set, and are noted here with an asterisk.

		NM	EX	VG
Complete Set (111):		7,000	3,500	2,100
Common Player:		50.00	25.00	15.00
(1)	Dale Alexander	50.00	25.00	15.00
(2)	Ethan N. Allen	50.00	25.00	15.00
(3)	Ray Benge (*)	50.00	25.00	15.00
(4)	Larry Benton	50.00	25.00	15.00
(5)	Moe Berg	65.00	32.50	20.00
(6)	Max Bishop	50.00	25.00	15.00
(7)	Del Bissonette	50.00	25.00	15.00
(8)	Lucerne A. Blue	50.00	25.00	15.00
(9)	James Bottomley	75.00	37.50	22.50
(10)	Raymond B. Bressler (*)	50.00	25.00	15.00
(11)	Fred Brickell (*)	50.00	25.00	15.00
(12)	Guy T. Bush	50.00	25.00	15.00
(13)	Harold G. Carlson	50.00	25.00	15.00
(14)	Owen Carroll	50.00	25.00	15.00
(15)	Chalmers W. Cissell (Chalmer)	50.00	25.00	15.00
(16)	Mickey Cochrane (*)	85.00	45.00	25.00
(17)	Earl (Earle) Combs	75.00	37.50	22.50
(18)	Hugh M. Critz	50.00	25.00	15.00
(19)	H.J. DeBerry	50.00	25.00	15.00
(20)	Pete Donohue	50.00	25.00	15.00
(21)	Taylor Douthit	50.00	25.00	15.00
(22)	Chas. W. Dressen	50.00	25.00	15.00
(23)	Clise Dudley (*)	50.00	25.00	15.00
(24)	Jimmy Dykes	50.00	25.00	15.00
(25)	Howard Ehmke	50.00	25.00	15.00
(26)	Elwood English	50.00	25.00	15.00
(27)	Urban Faber	75.00	37.50	22.50
(28)	Fred Fitzsimmons	50.00	25.00	15.00
(29)	Lewis A. Fonseca	50.00	25.00	15.00
(30)	Horace H. Ford	50.00	25.00	15.00
(31)	Jimmy Foxx	85.00	45.00	25.00
(32)	Frank Frisch	75.00	37.50	22.50
(33)	Lou Gehrig	335.00	165.00	100.00
(34)	Charles Gehringer	75.00	37.50	22.50
(35)	Walter Gilbert (*)	50.00	25.00	15.00
(36)	Leon Goslin	75.00	37.50	22.50
(37)	George Grantham	50.00	25.00	15.00
(38)	Burleigh Grimes	75.00	37.50	22.50
(39)	Robert Grove	85.00	45.00	25.00
(40)	Bump Hadley	50.00	25.00	15.00
(41)	Charlie Hafey	75.00	37.50	22.50
(42)	Jesse J. Haines	75.00	37.50	22.50
(43)	Harvey Hendrick	50.00	25.00	15.00
(44)	Floyd C. Herman	50.00	25.00	15.00
(45)	Andy High	50.00	25.00	15.00
(46)	Urban J. Hodapp	50.00	25.00	15.00
(47)	Frank Hogan (Existence not confirmed.)			
(48)	Rogers Hornsby	90.00	45.00	25.00
(49)	Waite Hoyt	75.00	37.50	22.50
(50)	Willis Hudlin	50.00	25.00	15.00
(51)	Frank O. Hurst	50.00	25.00	15.00
(52)	Charlie Jamieson	50.00	25.00	15.00
(53)	Roy C. Johnson	50.00	25.00	15.00
(54)	Percy Jones	50.00	25.00	15.00
(55)	Sam Jones	50.00	25.00	15.00
(56)	Joseph Judge	50.00	25.00	15.00
(57)	Willie Kamm	50.00	25.00	15.00
(58)	Charles Klein	75.00	37.50	22.50
(59)	Mark Koenig	50.00	25.00	15.00
(60)	Ralph Kress	50.00	25.00	15.00
(61)	Fred M. Leach	50.00	25.00	15.00
(62)	Carl Lind (*)	50.00	25.00	15.00
(63)	Fred Lindstrom	75.00	37.50	22.50
(64)	Ad Liska	50.00	25.00	15.00
(65)	Fred Lucas (Red)	50.00	25.00	15.00
(66)	Fred Maguire	50.00	25.00	15.00
(67)	Perce L. Malone	50.00	25.00	15.00
(68)	Harry Manush (Henry)	75.00	37.50	22.50
(69)	Walter Maranville	75.00	37.50	22.50
(70)	Earl McNeely (*)	50.00	25.00	15.00
(71)	Douglas McWeeney (McWeeny)	50.00	25.00	15.00
(72)	Oscar Melillo	50.00	25.00	15.00
(73)	Alex Metzler (*)	50.00	25.00	15.00
(74)	Ed "Bing" Miller	50.00	25.00	15.00
(75)	Clarence Mitchell (*)	50.00	25.00	15.00
(76)	Ed Morgan (*)	50.00	25.00	15.00
(77)	Chas. S. Myer (*)	50.00	25.00	15.00
(78)	Frank O'Doul	65.00	32.50	20.00
(79)	Melvin Ott	85.00	45.00	25.00
(80)	Herbert Pennock	75.00	37.50	22.50
(81)	William W. Regan	50.00	25.00	15.00
(82)	Harry F. Rice	50.00	25.00	15.00
(83)	Sam Rice	75.00	37.50	22.50
(84)	Lance Richbourgh (Richbourg)	50.00	25.00	15.00
(85)	Eddie Rommel	50.00	25.00	15.00
(86)	Chas. H. Root	50.00	25.00	15.00
(87)	Ed Roush	75.00	37.50	22.50
(88)	Harold Ruel (Herold)	50.00	25.00	15.00
(89)	Charles Ruffing	75.00	37.50	22.50
(90)	Jack Russell	50.00	25.00	15.00
(91)	Babe Ruth	425.00	210.00	125.00
(92)	Fred Schulte	50.00	25.00	15.00
(93)	Harry Seibold	50.00	25.00	15.00
(94)	Joe Sewell	75.00	37.50	22.50
(95)	Luke Sewell	50.00	25.00	15.00
(96)	Art Shires	50.00	25.00	15.00
(97)	Al Simmons	75.00	37.50	22.50
(98)	Bob Smith	50.00	25.00	15.00
(99)	Riggs Stephenson	50.00	25.00	15.00
(100)	Wm. H. Terry	75.00	37.50	22.50
(101)	Alphonse Thomas	50.00	25.00	15.00
(102)	Lafayette F. Thompson	50.00	25.00	15.00
(103)	Phil Todt	50.00	25.00	15.00
(104)	Harold J. Traynor	75.00	37.50	22.50
(105)	Dazzy Vance	75.00	37.50	22.50
(106)	Lloyd Waner	75.00	37.50	22.50
(107)	Paul Waner	75.00	37.50	22.50
(108)	Jimmy Welsh (Existence unconfirmed.)			
(109)	Earl Whitehill	50.00	25.00	15.00
(110)	A.C. Whitney	50.00	25.00	15.00
(111)	Claude Willoughby	50.00	25.00	15.00
(112)	Hack Wilson	75.00	37.50	22.50
(113)	Tom Zachary	50.00	25.00	15.00

1933 R337

(See 1933 Eclipse Import.)

1948 R346 Blue Tint

Issued circa 1948-49, the cards in this set derive their name from the distinctive blue coloring used to tint the black-and-white photos. The cards have blank backs and measure 2" x 2-5/8". The set has a high percentage of New York players and was originally issued in strips of six or eight cards each and therefore would have been more appropriately cataloged as a "W" strip card set. The set includes several variations of team desginations. It appears that all cards #25-48, along with possibly some of the team variations can also be found

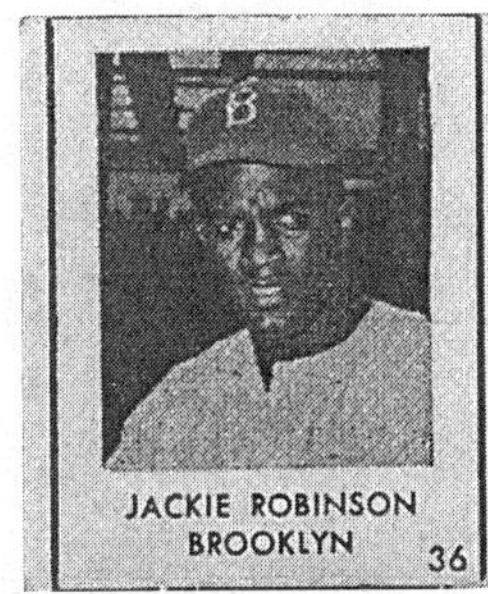

in black-and-white, rather than blue printing. The complete set price does not include the variations. Proof cards have been found with printing on the back indicating they were photographed by Al Weinstein of Brooklyn.

		NM	EX	VG
Complete Set (48):		1,300	650.00	375.00
Common Player:		15.00	7.50	4.50
Black-and-White: 1.5-3X				
1	Bill Johnson	15.00	7.50	4.50
2a	Leo Durocher (Brooklyn)	30.00	15.00	9.00
2b	Leo Durocher (New York)	30.00	15.00	9.00
3	Marty Marion	20.00	10.00	6.00
4	Ewell Blackwell	15.00	7.50	4.50
5	John Lindell	15.00	7.50	4.50
6	Larry Jansen	15.00	7.50	4.50
7	Ralph Kiner	30.00	15.00	9.00
8	Chuck Dressen	15.00	7.50	4.50
9	Bobby Brown	15.00	7.50	4.50
10	Luke Appling	30.00	15.00	9.00
11	Bill Nicholson	15.00	7.50	4.50
12	Phil Masi	15.00	7.50	4.50
13	Frank Shea	15.00	7.50	4.50
14	Bob Dillinger	15.00	7.50	4.50
15	Pete Suder	15.00	7.50	4.50
16	Joe DiMaggio	225.00	110.00	65.00
17	John Corriden	15.00	7.50	4.50
18a	Mel Ott (New York)	40.00	20.00	12.00
18b	Mel Ott (No team.)	40.00	20.00	12.00
19	Warren Rosar	15.00	7.50	4.50
20	Warren Spahn	35.00	17.50	10.00
21	Allie Reynolds	20.00	10.00	6.00
22	Lou Boudreau	30.00	15.00	9.00
23	Harry Majeski (Hank)(Photo actually Randy Gumpert.)	15.00	7.50	4.50
24	Frank Crosetti	15.00	7.50	4.50
25	Gus Niarhos	15.00	7.50	4.50
26	Bruce Edwards	15.00	7.50	4.50
27	Rudy York	15.00	7.50	4.50
28	Don Black	15.00	7.50	4.50
29	Lou Gehrig	225.00	110.00	65.00
30	Johnny Mize	30.00	15.00	9.00
31	Ed Stanky	15.00	7.50	4.50
32	Vic Raschi	20.00	10.00	6.00
33	Cliff Mapes	15.00	7.50	4.50
34	Enos Slaughter	30.00	15.00	9.00
35	Hank Greenberg	35.00	17.50	10.00
36	Jackie Robinson	125.00	65.00	40.00
37	Frank Hiller	15.00	7.50	4.50
38	Bob Elliot (Elliott)	15.00	7.50	4.50
39	Harry Walker	15.00	7.50	4.50
40	Ed Lopat	15.00	7.50	4.50
41	Bobby Thomson	20.00	10.00	6.00
42	Tommy Henrich	20.00	10.00	6.00
43	Bobby Feller	35.00	17.50	10.00
44	Ted Williams	100.00	50.00	30.00
45	Dixie Walker	15.00	7.50	4.50
46	Johnnie Vander Meer	20.00	10.00	6.00
47	Clint Hartung	15.00	7.50	4.50
(48)	Charlie Keller	20.00	10.00	6.00

1950 R423

These tiny (5/8" x 7/8") cards are numbered roughly in alphabetical order from 1 through 120. They were issued in 13-card perforated strips from vending machines. The black-and-white cards are printed on thin stock and include the player's name beneath his photo. The backs - most commonly printed in orange, but sometimes purple or green - display a rough drawing of a baseball infield with tiny figures at the various positions. It appears the cards were intended to be used to play a game of baseball. Many of the cards were printed on more than one strip, creating varying levels of scarcity not necessarily reflected in pricing.

		NM	EX	VG
Complete Set (119):		850.00	425.00	250.00
Common Player:		6.00	3.00	1.75
1	Richie Ashburn	12.50	6.25	3.75
2	Grover Alexander	10.00	5.00	3.00
3	Frank Baumholtz	6.00	3.00	1.75
4	Ralph Branca	6.00	3.00	1.75
5	Yogi Berra	15.00	7.50	4.50
6	Ewell Blackwell	7.50	3.75	2.25
7	Lou Boudreau	7.50	3.75	2.25
8	Harry Brecheen	6.00	3.00	1.75
9	Chico Carrasquel	6.00	3.00	1.75
10	Jerry Coleman	6.00	3.00	1.75
11	Walker Cooper	6.00	3.00	1.75
12	Roy Campanella	17.50	8.75	5.25
13	Phil Cavaretta (Cavarretta)	6.00	3.00	1.75
14a	Ty Cobb (W/ facsimile autograph.)	30.00	15.00	9.00
14b	Ty Cobb (No facsimile autograph.)	40.00	20.00	12.00
15	Mickey Cochrane	7.50	3.75	2.25
16	Ed Collins	7.50	3.75	2.25
17	Frank Crosetti	7.50	3.75	2.25
18	Larry Doby	7.50	3.75	2.25
19	Walter Dropo	6.00	3.00	1.75
20	Alvin Dark	6.00	3.00	1.75
21	Dizzy Dean	17.50	8.75	5.25
22	Bill Dickey	15.00	7.50	4.50
23	Murray Dickson (Murry)	6.00	3.00	1.75
24	Dom DiMaggio	7.50	3.75	2.25
25	Joe DiMaggio	50.00	25.00	15.00
26	Leo Durocher	7.50	3.75	2.25
27	Luke Easter	6.00	3.00	1.75
28	Bob Elliott	6.00	3.00	1.75
29	Del Ennis	6.00	3.00	1.75
30	Ferris Fain	6.00	3.00	1.75
31	Bob Feller	15.00	7.50	4.50
32	Frank Frisch	7.50	3.75	2.25
33	Billy Goodman	6.00	3.00	1.75
34	Lefty Gomez	7.50	3.75	2.25
35	Lou Gehrig	40.00	20.00	12.00
36	Joe Gordon	6.00	3.00	1.75
37	Sid Gordon	6.00	3.00	1.75
38	Hank Greenberg	15.00	7.50	4.50
39	Lefty Grove	10.00	5.00	3.00
40	Art Houtteman	6.00	3.00	1.75
41	Sid Hudson	6.00	3.00	1.75
42	Ken Heintzelman	6.00	3.00	1.75
43	Gene Hermanski	6.00	3.00	1.75
44	Jim Hearn	6.00	3.00	1.75
45	Gil Hodges	12.50	6.25	3.75
46	Harry Heilman (Heilmann)	7.50	3.75	2.25
47	Tommy Henrich	7.50	3.75	2.25
48	Roger Hornsby (Rogers)	10.00	5.00	3.00
49	Carl Hubbell	10.00	5.00	3.00
50	Edwin Joost	6.00	3.00	1.75
51	John Jorgensen	6.00	3.00	1.75
52	Larry Jansen	6.00	3.00	1.75
53	Nippy Jones	6.00	3.00	1.75
54	Walter Johnson	12.50	6.25	3.75
55	Ellis Kinder	6.00	3.00	1.75
56	Jim Konstanty	6.00	3.00	1.75
57	George Kell	7.50	3.75	2.25
58	Ralph Kiner	7.50	3.75	2.25
59	Bob Lemon	7.50	3.75	2.25
60	Whitey Lockman	6.00	3.00	1.75
61	Ed Lopat	7.50	3.75	2.25
62	Tony Lazzeri	7.50	3.75	2.25
63	Cass Michaels	6.00	3.00	1.75
64	Cliff Mapes	6.00	3.00	1.75
65	Willard Marshall	6.00	3.00	1.75
66	Clyde McCullough	6.00	3.00	1.75
67	Connie Mack	7.50	3.75	2.25
68	Christy Mathewson	17.50	8.75	5.25
69	Joe Medwick	7.50	3.75	2.25
70	Johnny Mize	7.50	3.75	2.25
71	Terry Moore	6.00	3.00	1.75
72	Stan Musial	20.00	10.00	6.00
73	Hal Newhouser	7.50	3.75	2.25
74	Don Newcombe	7.50	3.75	2.25
75	Lefty O'Doul	7.50	3.75	2.25
76	Mel Ott	10.00	5.00	3.00
77	Mel Parnell	6.00	3.00	1.75
78	Johnny Pesky	6.00	3.00	1.75
79	Gerald Priddy	6.00	3.00	1.75
80	Dave Philley	6.00	3.00	1.75
81	Bob Porterfield	6.00	3.00	1.75
82	Andy Pafko	6.00	3.00	1.75
83	Howie Pollet	6.00	3.00	1.75
84	Herb Pennock	7.50	3.75	2.25
85	Al Rosen	7.50	3.75	2.25
86	Pee Wee Reese	15.00	7.50	4.50
87	Del Rice	6.00	3.00	1.75
88	Vic Raschi	7.50	3.75	2.25
89	Allie Reynolds	7.50	3.75	2.25
90	Phil Rizzuto	15.00	7.50	4.50
91	Jackie Robinson	35.00	17.50	10.50
92	Babe Ruth	40.00	20.00	12.00
93	Casey Stengel	15.00	7.50	4.50
94	Vern Stephens	6.00	3.00	1.75
95	Duke Snider	15.00	7.50	4.50
96	Enos Slaughter	7.50	3.75	2.25
97	Al Schoendienst	7.50	3.75	2.25
98	Gerald Staley	6.00	3.00	1.75
99	Clyde Shoun	6.00	3.00	1.75
100	Unknown			
101	Hank Sauer	6.00	3.00	1.75
102	Al Simmons	7.50	3.75	2.25
103	George Sisler	7.50	3.75	2.25
104	Tris Speaker	12.50	6.25	3.75
105	Ed Stanky	6.00	3.00	1.75
106	Virgil Trucks	6.00	3.00	1.75
107	Henry Thompson	6.00	3.00	1.75
108	Bobby Thomson	7.50	3.75	2.25
109	Dazzy Vance	7.50	3.75	2.25
110	Lloyd Waner	7.50	3.75	2.25
111	Paul Waner	7.50	3.75	2.25
112	Gene Woodling	7.50	3.75	2.25
113	Ted Williams	35.00	17.50	10.50
114	Vic Wertz	6.00	3.00	1.75
115	Wes Westrom (Westrum)	6.00	3.00	1.75
116	Johnny Wyrostek	6.00	3.00	1.75
117	Eddie Yost	6.00	3.00	1.75
118	Allen Zarilla	6.00	3.00	1.75
119	Gus Zernial	6.00	3.00	1.75
120	Sam Zoldack (Zoldak)	6.00	3.00	1.75

1936 S and S Game

Small black-and-white player photos are featured on the fronts of this 52-card game set. Measuring about 2-1/4" x 3-1/2", with rounded corners, the cards feature plain green or cream-colored backs. Besides the player photo on front, there are a few biographical details and stats, and a pair of game scenarios. The cards are unnumbered and are checklisted here alphabetically. The complete game included a special scoreboard, at least two "directions" cards and a contest card.

		NM	EX	VG
Complete Set (52):		1,000	500.00	300.00
Complete Boxed Set:		1,250	625.00	375.00
Common Player:		12.50	6.25	3.75
(1)	Luke Appling	30.00	15.00	9.00
(2)	Earl Averill	30.00	15.00	9.00
(3)	Zeke Bonura	12.50	6.25	3.75
(4)	Dolph Camilli	12.50	6.25	3.75
(5)	Ben Cantwell	12.50	6.25	3.75
(6)	Phil Cavarretta (Cavarretta)	12.50	6.25	3.75
(7)	Rip Collins	12.50	6.25	3.75
(8)	Joe Cronin	30.00	15.00	9.00
(9)	Frank Crosetti	20.00	10.00	6.00
(10)	Kiki Cuyler	30.00	15.00	9.00
(11)	Virgil Davis	12.50	6.25	3.75
(12)	Frank Demaree	12.50	6.25	3.75
(13)	Paul Derringer	12.50	6.25	3.75
(14)	Bill Dickey	50.00	25.00	15.00
(15)	Woody English	12.50	6.25	3.75
(16)	Fred Fitzsimmons	12.50	6.25	3.75
(17)	Richard Ferrell	30.00	15.00	9.00
(18)	Pete Fox	12.50	6.25	3.75
(19)	Jimmy (Jimmie) Foxx	60.00	30.00	18.00
(20)	Larry French	12.50	6.25	3.75
(21)	Frank Frisch	30.00	15.00	9.00
(22)	August Galan	12.50	6.25	3.75
(23)	Chas. Gehringer	30.00	15.00	9.00
(24)	John Gill	12.50	6.25	3.75
(25)	Charles Grimm	12.50	6.25	3.75
(26)	Mule Haas	12.50	6.25	3.75
(27)	Stanley Hack	12.50	6.25	3.75
(28)	Bill Hallahan	12.50	6.25	3.75
(29)	Melvin Harder	12.50	6.25	3.75
(30)	Gabby Hartnett	30.00	15.00	9.00
(31)	Ray Hayworth	12.50	6.25	3.75
(32)	Ralston Hemsley	12.50	6.25	3.75
(33)	Bill Herman	30.00	15.00	9.00
(34)	Frank Higgins	12.50	6.25	3.75
(35)	Carl Hubbell	40.00	20.00	12.00
(36)	Bill Jurges	12.50	6.25	3.75
(37)	Vernon Kennedy	12.50	6.25	3.75
(38)	Chuck Klein	30.00	15.00	9.00
(39)	Mike Kreevich	12.50	6.25	3.75
(40)	Bill Lee	12.50	6.25	3.75
(41)	Jos. Medwick	30.00	15.00	9.00
(42)	Van Mungo	12.50	6.25	3.75
(43)	James O'Dea	12.50	6.25	3.75
(44)	Mel Ott	50.00	25.00	15.00
(45)	Rip Radcliff	12.50	6.25	3.75
(46)	Pie Traynor	30.00	15.00	9.00
(47)	Arky Vaughan (Vaughn)	30.00	15.00	9.00
(48)	Joe Vosmik	12.50	6.25	3.75
(49)	Lloyd Waner	30.00	15.00	9.00
(50)	Paul Waner	30.00	15.00	9.00
(51)	Lon Warneke	12.50	6.25	3.75
(52)	Floyd Young	12.50	6.25	3.75

1948-50 Safe-T-Card

The earliest known safety issue is this series sponsored by a children's television show which was in turn sponsored by a Washington, D.C. auto dealer. Player selection and team indications on the cards point to a three-year (1948-50) range of issue dates for the cards. Minor differences in typography and information printed on the front probably differentiate the years of issue. All cards are about 2-1/2" x 3-1/2" with rounded corners. Fronts feature rather crude black-and-white drawings of the players with a facsimile autograph superimposed. A safety message is at top and, on most cards, the player's position and team are printed at bottom. Backs are printed in one of several colors and have a picture of the TV host and an ad for the program and its sponsors. The set is checklisted here alphabetically, though it's possible other cards may be added

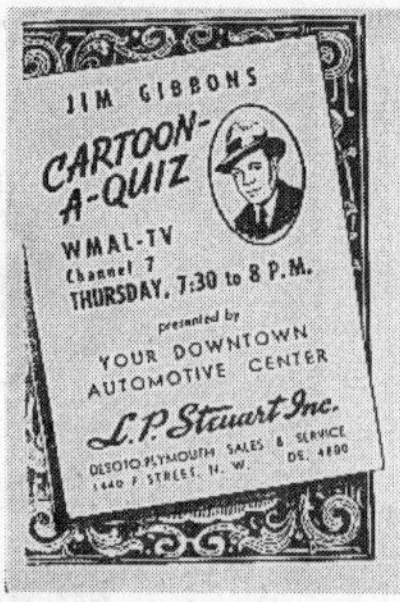

in the future. Only the baseball players from the set are listed here. Cards featuring football, basketball and other sports figures were also produced, along with cards for team executives, sports reporters and broadcasters.

		NM	EX	VG
Complete (Baseball) Set (21):		2,925	1,450	875.00
Common Player:		125.00	65.00	35.00
(1)	Ossie Bluege	125.00	65.00	35.00
(2)	Gil Coan	125.00	65.00	35.00
(3)	Sam Dente	125.00	65.00	35.00
(4)	Jake Early	125.00	65.00	35.00
(5)	Al Evans	125.00	65.00	35.00
(6)	Calvin Griffith	250.00	125.00	75.00
(7)	Clark Griffith	150.00	75.00	45.00
(8)	Bucky Harris	150.00	75.00	45.00
(9)	Sid Hudson	125.00	65.00	35.00
(10)	Joe Kuhel	125.00	65.00	35.00
(11)	Bob Lemon	150.00	75.00	45.00
(12)	Bill McGowan	400.00	200.00	120.00
(13)	George McQuinn	125.00	65.00	35.00
(14)	Don Newcombe	250.00	125.00	75.00
(15)	Joe Ostrowski	125.00	65.00	35.00
(16)	Sam Rice	150.00	75.00	45.00
(17)	Bert Shepard	150.00	75.00	45.00
(18)	Ray Scarborough	125.00	65.00	35.00
(19)	Mickey Vernon	125.00	65.00	35.00
(20)	Early Wynn	150.00	75.00	45.00
(21)	Eddie Yost	125.00	65.00	35.00

1976 Safelon Discs

One of several regional sponsors of player disc sets in 1976, Safelon, of New York, advertised its "Super Star Lunch Bags" in red and purple on the backs of its discs. The discs are 3-3/8" diameter with a black-and-white player portrait photo in the center of the baseball design. A line of red stars is above, while the left and right panels feature one of several bright colors. Produced by Michael Schechter Associates under license from the Major League Baseball Players Association, the player photos have had uniform and cap logos removed. The unnumbered checklist here is presented in alphabetical order.

		NM	EX	VG
Complete Set (70):		100.00	50.00	30.00
Common Player:		3.00	1.50	.90
(1)	Henry Aaron	20.00	10.00	6.00
(2)	Johnny Bench	8.00	4.00	2.50
(3)	Vida Blue	3.00	1.50	.90
(4)	Larry Bowa	3.00	1.50	.90
(5)	Lou Brock	6.00	3.00	1.75
(6)	Jeff Burroughs	3.00	1.50	.90
(7)	John Candelaria	3.00	1.50	.90
(8)	Jose Cardenal	3.00	1.50	.90
(9)	Rod Carew	6.00	3.00	1.75
(10)	Steve Carlton	6.00	3.00	1.75
(11)	Dave Cash	3.00	1.50	.90
(12)	Cesar Cedeno	3.00	1.50	.90
(13)	Ron Cey	3.00	1.50	.90
(14)	Carlton Fisk	6.00	3.00	1.75
(15)	Tito Fuentes	3.00	1.50	.90
(16)	Steve Garvey	4.00	2.00	1.25
(17)	Ken Griffey	3.00	1.50	.90
(18)	Don Gullett	3.00	1.50	.90
(19)	Willie Horton	3.00	1.50	.90
(20)	Al Hrabosky	3.00	1.50	.90
(21)	Catfish Hunter	6.00	3.00	1.75
(22)	Reggie Jackson (A's)	12.00	6.00	3.50
(23)	Randy Jones	3.00	1.50	.90
(24)	Jim Kaat	3.00	1.50	.90
(25)	Don Kessinger	3.00	1.50	.90
(26)	Dave Kingman	3.00	1.50	.90
(27)	Jerry Koosman	3.00	1.50	.90
(28)	Mickey Lolich	3.00	1.50	.90
(29)	Greg Luzinski	3.00	1.50	.90
(30)	Fred Lynn	3.00	1.50	.90
(31)	Bill Madlock	3.00	1.50	.90
(32)	Carlos May (White Sox)	3.00	1.50	.90
(33)	John Mayberry	3.00	1.50	.90
(34)	Bake McBride	3.00	1.50	.90
(35)	Doc Medich	3.00	1.50	.90
(36)	Andy Messersmith	3.00	1.50	.90
(37)	Rick Monday	3.00	1.50	.90
(38)	John Montefusco	3.00	1.50	.90
(39)	Jerry Morales	3.00	1.50	.90
(40)	Joe Morgan	6.00	3.00	1.75
(41)	Thurman Munson	5.00	2.50	1.50
(42)	Bobby Murcer	3.00	1.50	.90
(43)	Al Oliver	3.00	1.50	.90
(44)	Jim Palmer	6.00	3.00	1.75
(45)	Dave Parker	3.00	1.50	.90
(46)	Tony Perez	6.00	3.00	1.75
(47)	Jerry Reuss	3.00	1.50	.90
(48)	Brooks Robinson	9.00	4.50	2.75
(49)	Frank Robinson	9.00	4.50	2.75
(50)	Steve Rogers	3.00	1.50	.90
(51)	Pete Rose	15.00	7.50	4.50
(52)	Nolan Ryan	40.00	20.00	12.00
(53)	Manny Sanguillen	3.00	1.50	.90
(54)	Mike Schmidt	12.00	6.00	3.50
(55)	Tom Seaver	9.00	4.50	2.75
(56)	Ted Simmons	3.00	1.50	.90
(57)	Reggie Smith	3.00	1.50	.90
(58)	Willie Stargell	6.00	3.00	1.75
(59)	Rusty Staub	3.00	1.50	.90
(60)	Rennie Stennett	3.00	1.50	.90
(61)	Don Sutton	6.00	3.00	1.75
(62)	Andy Thornton (Cubs)	3.00	1.50	.90
(63)	Luis Tiant	3.00	1.50	.90
(64)	Joe Torre	3.00	1.50	.90
(65)	Mike Tyson	3.00	1.50	.90
(66)	Bob Watson	3.00	1.50	.90
(67)	Wilbur Wood	3.00	1.50	.90
(68)	Jimmy Wynn	3.00	1.50	.90
(69)	Carl Yastrzemski	9.00	4.50	2.75
(70)	Richie Zisk	3.00	1.50	.90

1977 Saga Discs

Virtually identical in format to the several locally sponsored disc sets of the previous year, these 3-3/8" diameter player discs were given away with the purchase of school lunches in the Philadelphia area. They are the scarcest of the 1977 disc sets. Discs once again feature black-and-white player portrait photos in the center of a baseball design. The left and right panels are in one of several bright colors. Licensed by the Players Association through Mike Schechter Associates, the player photos carry no uniform logos. Backs are printed in orange with background art of a sunrise over the mountains. The unnumbered discs are checklisted here alphabetically.

		NM	EX	VG
Complete Set (70):		850.00	425.00	250.00
Common Player:		12.50	6.25	3.75
(1)	Sal Bando	12.50	6.25	3.75
(2)	Buddy Bell	12.50	6.25	3.75
(3)	Johnny Bench	40.00	20.00	12.00
(4)	Larry Bowa	12.50	6.25	3.75
(5)	Steve Braun	12.50	6.25	3.75
(6)	George Brett	125.00	62.00	37.00
(7)	Lou Brock	35.00	17.50	10.50
(8)	Jeff Burroughs	12.50	6.25	3.75
(9)	Bert Campaneris	12.50	6.25	3.75
(10)	John Candelaria	12.50	6.25	3.75
(11)	Jose Cardenal	12.50	6.25	3.75
(12)	Rod Carew	35.00	17.50	10.50
(13)	Steve Carlton	35.00	17.50	10.50
(14)	Dave Cash	12.50	6.25	3.75
(15)	Cesar Cedeno	12.50	6.25	3.75
(16)	Ron Cey	12.50	6.25	3.75
(17)	Dave Concepcion	12.50	6.25	3.75
(18)	Dennis Eckersley	35.00	17.50	10.50
(19)	Mark Fidrych	17.50	8.75	5.25
(20)	Rollie Fingers	35.00	17.50	10.50
(21)	Carlton Fisk	35.00	17.50	10.50
(22)	George Foster	12.50	6.25	3.75
(23)	Wayne Garland	12.50	6.25	3.75
(24)	Ralph Garr	12.50	6.25	3.75
(25)	Steve Garvey	25.00	12.50	7.50
(26)	Cesar Geronimo	12.50	6.25	3.75
(27)	Bobby Grich	12.50	6.25	3.75
(28)	Ken Griffey Sr.	12.50	6.25	3.75
(29)	Don Gullett	12.50	6.25	3.75
(30)	Mike Hargrove	12.50	6.25	3.75
(31)	Al Hrabosky	12.50	6.25	3.75
(32)	Jim Hunter	35.00	17.50	10.50
(33)	Reggie Jackson	50.00	25.00	15.00
(34)	Randy Jones	12.50	6.25	3.75
(35)	Dave Kingman	15.00	7.50	4.50
(36)	Jerry Koosman	12.50	6.25	3.75
(37)	Dave LaRoche	12.50	6.25	3.75
(38)	Greg Luzinski	12.50	6.25	3.75
(39)	Fred Lynn	12.50	6.25	3.75
(40)	Bill Madlock	12.50	6.25	3.75
(41)	Rick Manning	12.50	6.25	3.75
(42)	Jon Matlock	12.50	6.25	3.75
(43)	John Mayberry	12.50	6.25	3.75
(44)	Hal McRae	12.50	6.25	3.75
(45)	Andy Messersmith	12.50	6.25	3.75
(46)	Rick Monday	12.50	6.25	3.75
(47)	John Montefusco	12.50	6.25	3.75
(48)	Joe Morgan	35.00	17.50	10.50
(49)	Thurman Munson	30.00	15.00	9.00
(50)	Bobby Murcer	12.50	6.25	3.75
(51)	Bill North	12.50	6.25	3.75
(52)	Jim Palmer	35.00	17.50	10.50
(53)	Tony Perez	35.00	17.50	10.50
(54)	Jerry Reuss	12.50	6.25	3.75
(55)	Brooks Robinson	40.00	20.00	12.00
(56)	Pete Rose	110.00	55.00	33.00
(57)	Joe Rudi	12.50	6.25	3.75
(58)	Nolan Ryan	135.00	67.00	40.00
(59)	Manny Sanguillen	12.50	6.25	3.75
(60)	Mike Schmidt	75.00	37.00	22.00
(61)	Tom Seaver	40.00	20.00	12.00
(62)	Bill Singer	12.50	6.25	3.75
(63)	Willie Stargell	35.00	17.50	10.50
(64)	Rusty Staub	15.00	7.50	4.50
(65)	Luis Tiant	12.50	6.25	3.75
(66)	Bob Watson	12.50	6.25	3.75
(67)	Butch Wynegar	12.50	6.25	3.75
(68)	Carl Yastrzemski	40.00	20.00	12.00
(69)	Robin Yount	35.00	17.50	10.50
(70)	Richie Zisk	12.50	6.25	3.75

1978 Saga Discs

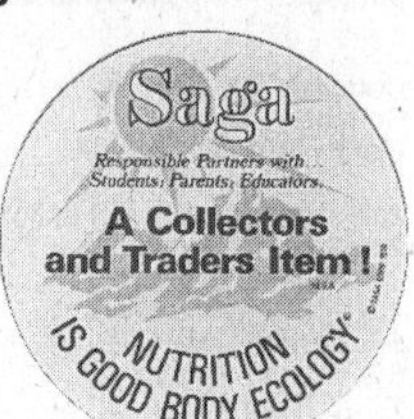

One player from each major league team was selected for inclusion in this disc set distributed by Saga, a provider of school lunches; discs were given one per lunch purchase at selected schools. The 3-3/8" diameter discs have a sepia-toned player portrait photo at center within a white diamond and surrounded by a brightly colored border with four colored stars at top. Licensed by the Players Association through Michael Schechter Associates, the photos have had uniform logos removed. Backs are nearly identical to the previous year, but printed in red. The unnumbered Saga discs are checklisted here according to the numbers found on the Big T/Tastee Freeze versions.

		NM	EX	VG
Complete Set (26):		130.00	65.00	40.00
Common Player:		6.00	3.00	1.75
(1)	Buddy Bell	6.00	3.00	1.75
(2)	Jim Palmer	12.50	6.25	3.75
(3)	Steve Garvey	7.50	3.75	2.25
(4)	Jeff Burroughs	6.00	3.00	1.75
(5)	Greg Luzinski	6.00	3.00	1.75
(6)	Lou Brock	12.50	6.25	3.75
(7)	Thurman Munson	10.00	5.00	3.00
(8)	Rod Carew	12.50	6.25	3.75
(9)	George Brett	50.00	25.00	15.00
(10)	Tom Seaver	15.00	7.50	4.50
(11)	Willie Stargell	12.50	6.25	3.75
(12)	Jerry Koosman	6.00	3.00	1.75
(13)	Bill North	6.00	3.00	1.75
(14)	Richie Zisk	6.00	3.00	1.75
(15)	Bill Madlock	6.00	3.00	1.75
(16)	Carl Yastrzemski	15.00	7.50	4.50
(17)	Dave Cash	6.00	3.00	1.75
(18)	Bob Watson	6.00	3.00	1.75
(19)	Dave Kingman	6.50	3.25	2.00
(20)	Gene Tenance (Tenace)	6.00	3.00	1.75
(21)	Ralph Garr	6.00	3.00	1.75
(22)	Mark Fidrych	6.50	3.25	2.00
(23)	Frank Tanana	6.00	3.00	1.75
(24)	Larry Hisle	6.00	3.00	1.75
(25)	Bruce Bochte	6.00	3.00	1.75
(26)	Bob Bailor	6.00	3.00	1.75

1962 John Sain Spinner Promotional Postcard

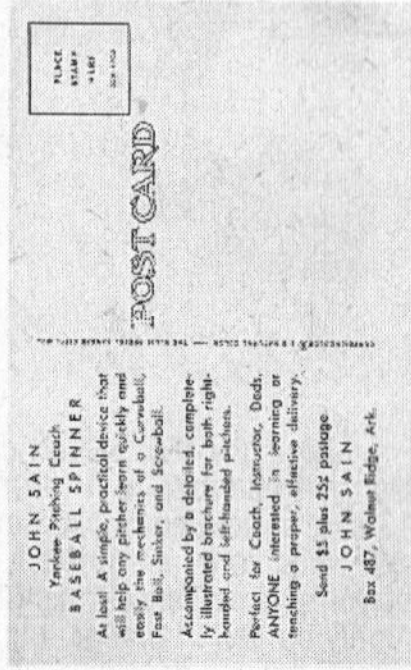

The attributed date of issue is approximate. This 3-7/16" x 5-7/16" color postcard was issued to promote the John Sain Spinner, a device to teach pitching mechanics. The front pictures the Yankees pitching coach in four views demonstrating the device, which is itself pictured at top. Black-and-white back is in traditional postcard divided-back format with information on the spinner and ordering information.

	NM	EX	VG
John Sain	15.00	7.50	4.50

1962 Salada-Junket Coins

These 1-3/8" diameter plastic coins were issued in packages of Salada Tea and Junket Pudding mix. There are 221 different players available, with variations bringing the total of different coins to 265. Each coin has a paper color photo inserted in the front which contains the player's name and position plus the coin number. The plastic rims come in six different colors, coded by team. Production began with 180 coins, but the addition of the New York Mets and Houston Colt .45's to the National League allowed the company to expand the set's size. Twenty expansion players were added along with 21 other players. Several players' coins were dropped after the initial 180 run, causing some scarcities. Embossed green plastic shields into which 10 coins could be placed were available via a mail-in offer. About 9" x 10-1/2", the shields have a banner near the top with the team name. Many of the players in the 180 series can be found with variations in the placement of the front typography relative to the colored portrait. Though these variations seem to affect a tiny percentage of some players' 180 coins, they are in most cases too difficult to distinguish except by direct comparison between specimens and are of interest only to the most dedicated Salada collectors.

		NM	EX	VG
	Complete Set, no variations (221):	3,000	1,500	900.00
	Complete Set, w/ variations (265):	6,500	3,250	2,000
	Complete Boxed Presentation Set (180):	1,900	950.00	575.00
	Complete Boxed Presentation Set (200):	2,600	1,300	800.00
	Uncut Sheet (180):	1,800	900.00	550.00
	Common Player (1-180):	4.00	2.00	1.25
	Common Player (181-221):	10.00	5.00	3.00
	Team Shield (Empty):	60.00	30.00	18.00
1	Jim Gentile	5.00	2.50	1.50
2	Bill Pierce	65.00	32.50	20.00
3a	Chico Fernandez (Light blue jersey piping.)	4.00	2.00	1.25
3b	Chico Fernandez (Dark blue jersey piping.)	12.00	6.00	3.50
4	Tom Brewer	15.00	7.50	4.50
5	Woody Held	4.00	2.00	1.25
6	Ray Herbert	22.50	11.00	7.00
7a	Ken Aspromonte (Angels)	10.00	5.00	3.00
7b	Ken Aspromonte (Indians)	10.00	5.00	3.00
8	Whitey Ford	20.00	10.00	6.00
9	Jim Lemon	4.00	2.00	1.25
10	Billy Klaus	4.00	2.00	1.25
11	Steve Barber	27.50	13.50	8.25
12	Nellie Fox	17.50	8.75	5.25
13	Jim Bunning	15.00	7.50	4.50
14	Frank Malzone	5.00	2.50	1.50
15	Tito Francona	4.00	2.00	1.25
16	Bobby Del Greco	4.00	2.00	1.25
17a	Steve Bilko (Red shirt buttons.)	9.00	4.50	2.75
17b	Steve Bilko (White shirt buttons.)	9.00	4.50	2.75
18	Tony Kubek	35.00	17.50	10.00
19	Earl Battey	4.00	2.00	1.25
20	Chuck Cottier	4.00	2.00	1.25
21	Willie Tasby	4.00	2.00	1.25
22	Bob Allison	6.00	3.00	1.75
23	Roger Maris	25.00	12.50	7.50
24a	Earl Averill (Red shirt buttons.)	9.00	4.50	2.75
24b	Earl Averill (White shirt buttons.)	5.00	2.50	1.50
25	Jerry Lumpe	4.00	2.00	1.25
26	Jim Grant	17.50	8.75	5.25
27	Carl Yastrzemski	30.00	15.00	9.00
28a	Rocky Colavito (Light blue jersey piping.)	20.00	10.00	6.00
28b	Rocky Colavito (Dark blue jersey piping.)	12.50	6.25	3.75
29	Al Smith	4.00	2.00	1.25
30	Jim Busby	30.00	15.00	9.00
31	Dick Howser	4.00	2.00	1.25
32	Jim Perry	4.00	2.00	1.25
33	Yogi Berra	25.00	12.50	7.50
34a	Ken Hamlin (Red shirt buttons.)	7.00	3.50	2.00
34b	Ken Hamlin (White shirt buttons.)	4.00	2.00	1.25
35	Dale Long	4.00	2.00	1.25
36	Harmon Killebrew	20.00	10.00	6.00
37a	Dick Brown (Light blue jersey piping.)	12.00	6.00	3.50
37b	Dick Brown (Dark blue jersey piping.)	4.00	2.00	1.25
38	Gary Geiger	4.00	2.00	1.25
39a	Minnie Minoso (White Sox)	20.00	10.00	6.00
39b	Minnie Minoso (Cardinals)	9.00	4.50	2.75
40	Brooks Robinson	20.00	10.00	6.00
41	Mickey Mantle	70.00	35.00	20.00
42	Bennie Daniels	4.00	2.00	1.25
43	Billy Martin	12.00	6.00	3.50
44	Vic Power	5.00	2.50	1.50
45	Joe Pignatano	4.00	2.00	1.25
46a	Ryne Duren (Red shirt buttons.)	9.00	4.50	2.75
46b	Ryne Duren (White shirt buttons.)	8.00	4.00	2.50
47a	Pete Runnels (2B)	12.00	6.00	3.50
47b	Pete Runnels (1B)	7.50	3.75	2.25
48a	Dick Williams (Name on right.)	1,800	900.00	550.00
48b	Dick Williams (Name on left.)	4.00	2.00	1.25
49	Jim Landis	4.00	2.00	1.25
50	Steve Boros	4.00	2.00	1.25
51a	Zoilo Versalles (Red shirt buttons.)	7.00	3.50	2.00
51b	Zoilo Versalles (White shirt buttons.)	7.00	3.50	2.00
52a	Johnny Temple (Indians)	12.50	6.25	3.75
52b	Johnny Temple (Orioles)	5.00	2.50	1.50
53a	Jackie Brandt (Oriole)	15.00	7.50	4.50
53b	Jackie Brandt (Orioles)	1,600	800.00	475.00
54	Joe McClain	4.00	2.00	1.25
55	Sherman Lollar	5.00	2.50	1.50
56	Gene Stephens	4.00	2.00	1.25
57a	Leon Wagner (Red shirt buttons.)	7.00	3.50	2.00
57b	Leon Wagner (White shirt buttons.)	5.00	2.50	1.50
58	Frank Lary	6.00	3.00	1.75
59	Bill Skowron	10.00	5.00	3.00
60	Vic Wertz	20.00	10.00	6.00
61	Willie Kirkland	4.00	2.00	1.25
62	Leo Posada	4.00	2.00	1.25
63a	Albie Pearson (Red shirt buttons.)	9.00	4.50	2.75
63b	Albie Pearson (White shirt buttons.)	8.00	4.00	2.50
64	Bobby Richardson	15.00	7.50	4.50
65a	Marv Breeding (SS)	9.00	4.50	2.75
65b	Marv Breeding (2B)	12.00	6.00	3.50
66	Roy Sievers	70.00	35.00	20.00
67	Al Kaline	25.00	12.50	7.50
68a	Don Buddin (Red Sox)	15.00	7.50	4.50
68b	Don Buddin (Colts)	5.00	2.50	1.50
69a	Lenny Green (Red shirt buttons.)	8.00	4.00	2.50
69b	Lenny Green (White shirt buttons.)	6.00	3.00	1.75
70	Gene Green	40.00	20.00	12.00
71	Luis Aparicio	12.00	6.00	3.50
72	Norm Cash	16.00	8.00	4.75
73	Jackie Jensen	20.00	10.00	6.00
74	Bubba Phillips	6.00	3.00	1.75
75	Jim Archer	4.00	2.00	1.25
76a	Ken Hunt (Red shirt buttons.)	9.00	4.50	2.75
76b	Ken Hunt (White shirt buttons.)	4.00	2.00	1.25
77	Ralph Terry	4.00	2.00	1.25
78	Camilo Pascual	4.00	2.00	1.25
79	Marty Keough	27.50	13.50	8.25
80	Cletis Boyer	10.00	5.00	3.00
81	Jim Pagliaroni	4.00	2.00	1.25
82a	Gene Leek (Red shirt buttons.)	9.00	4.50	2.75
82b	Gene Leek (White shirt buttons.)	4.00	2.00	1.25
83	Jake Wood	5.00	2.50	1.50
84	Coot Veal	25.00	12.50	7.50
85	Norm Siebern	5.00	2.50	1.50
86a	Andy Carey (White Sox)	25.00	12.50	7.50
86b	Andy Carey (Phillies)	9.00	4.50	2.75
87a	Bill Tuttle (Red shirt buttons.)	9.00	4.50	2.75
87b	Bill Tuttle (White shirt buttons.)	25.00	12.50	7.50
88a	Jimmy Piersall (Indians)	20.00	10.00	6.00
88b	Jimmy Piersall (Senators)	20.00	10.00	6.00
89	Ron Hansen	25.00	12.50	7.50
90a	Chuck Stobbs (Red shirt buttons.)	8.00	4.00	2.50
90b	Chuck Stobbs (White shirt buttons.)	4.00	2.00	1.25
91a	Ken McBride (Red shirt buttons.)	9.00	4.50	2.75
91b	Ken McBride (White shirt buttons.)	7.50	3.75	2.25
92	Bill Bruton	4.00	2.00	1.25
93	Gus Triandos	4.00	2.00	1.25
94	John Romano	4.00	2.00	1.25
95	Elston Howard	10.00	5.00	3.00
96	Gene Woodling	6.00	3.00	1.75
97a	Early Wynn (Pitching pose.)	45.00	22.00	13.50
97b	Early Wynn (Portrait)	15.00	7.50	4.50
98	Milt Pappas	4.00	2.00	1.25
99	Bill Monbouquette	4.00	2.00	1.25
100	Wayne Causey	4.00	2.00	1.25
101	Don Elston	4.00	2.00	1.25
102a	Charlie Neal (Dodgers)	12.00	6.00	3.50
102b	Charlie Neal (Mets)	4.00	2.00	1.25
103	Don Blasingame	4.00	2.00	1.25
104	Frank Thomas	30.00	15.00	9.00
105	Wes Covington	4.00	2.00	1.25
106	Chuck Hiller	5.00	2.50	1.50
107	Don Hoak	4.00	2.00	1.25
108a	Bob Lillis (Cardinals)	27.50	13.50	8.25
108b	Bob Lillis (Colts)	4.00	2.00	1.25
109	Sandy Koufax	30.00	15.00	9.00
110	Gordy Coleman	4.00	2.00	1.25
111	Ed Matthews (Mathews)	20.00	10.00	6.00
112	Art Mahaffey	4.00	2.00	1.25
113a	Ed Bailey (Partial left shoulder; "C" level w/ear.)	1,400	700.00	425.00
113b	Ed Bailey (Full left shoulder; second button red.)	10.00	5.00	3.00
113c	Ed Bailey (Full left shoulder; second button white.)	4.00	2.00	1.25
114	Smoky Burgess	7.00	3.50	2.00
115	Bill White	6.00	.3.00	1.75
116	Ed Bouchee	25.00	12.50	7.50
117	Bob Buhl	8.00	4.00	2.50
118	Vada Pinson	4.00	2.00	1.25
119	Carl Sawatski	4.00	2.00	1.25
120	Dick Stuart	6.00	3.00	1.75
121	Harvey Kuenn	40.00	20.00	12.00
122	Pancho Herrera	4.00	2.00	1.25
123a	Don Zimmer (Cubs)	12.50	6.25	3.75
123b	Don Zimmer (Mets)	5.00	2.50	1.50
124	Wally Moon	6.00	3.00	1.75
125	Joe Adcock	9.00	4.50	2.75
126	Joey Jay	4.00	2.00	1.25
127a	Maury Wills (Blue "3" on shirt.)	10.00	5.00	3.00
127b	Maury Wills (Red "3" on shirt.)	10.00	5.00	3.00
128	George Altman	4.00	2.00	1.25
129a	John Buzhardt (Phillies)	30.00	15.00	9.00
129b	John Buzhardt (White Sox)	10.00	5.00	3.00
130	Felipe Alou	4.00	2.00	1.25
131	Bill Mazeroski	15.00	7.50	4.50
132	Ernie Broglio	4.00	2.00	1.25
133	John Roseboro	4.00	2.00	1.25
134	Mike McCormick	4.00	2.00	1.25
135a	Chuck Smith (Phillies)	15.00	7.50	4.50
135b	Chuck Smith (White Sox)	10.00	5.00	3.00
136	Ron Santo	12.00	6.00	3.50
137	Gene Freese	4.00	2.00	1.25
138	Dick Groat	5.00	2.50	1.50
139	Curt Flood	4.00	2.00	1.25
140	Frank Bolling	4.00	2.00	1.25
141	Clay Dalrymple	4.00	2.00	1.25
142	Willie McCovey	16.00	8.00	4.75
143	Bob Skinner	4.00	2.00	1.25
144	Lindy McDaniel	4.00	2.00	1.25
145	Glen Hobbie	4.00	2.00	1.25
146a	Gil Hodges (Dodgers)	30.00	15.00	9.00
146b	Gil Hodges (Mets)	22.50	11.00	6.75
147	Eddie Kasko	4.00	2.00	1.25
148	Gino Cimoli	25.00	12.50	7.50
149	Willie Mays	30.00	15.00	9.00
150	Roberto Clemente	55.00	27.50	16.50
151	Red Schoendienst	15.00	7.50	4.50
152	Joe Torre	5.00	2.50	1.50
153	Bob Purkey	4.00	2.00	1.25
154a	Tommy Davis (3B)	7.50	3.75	2.25
154b	Tommy Davis (OF)	12.00	6.00	3.50
155a	Andre Rogers (Incorrect spelling, 1B.)	7.50	3.75	2.25
155b	Andre Rodgers (Correct spelling, SS.)	12.00	6.00	3.50
156	Tony Taylor	4.00	2.00	1.25
157	Bob Friend	4.00	2.00	1.25
158a	Gus Bell (Redlegs)	20.00	10.00	6.00
158b	Gus Bell (Mets)	4.00	2.00	1.25
159	Roy McMillan	4.00	2.00	1.25
160	Carl Warwick	4.00	2.00	1.25
161	Willie Davis	4.00	2.00	1.25
162	Sam Jones	60.00	30.00	18.00
163	Ruben Amaro	6.00	3.00	1.75
164	Sam Taylor	4.00	2.00	1.25
165	Frank Robinson	15.00	7.50	4.50
166	Lou Burdette	5.00	2.50	1.50
167	Ken Boyer	13.50	6.75	4.00
168	Bill Virdon	4.00	2.00	1.25
169	Jim Davenport	4.00	2.00	1.25
170	Don Demeter	4.00	2.00	1.25
171	Richie Ashburn	40.00	20.00	12.00
172	John Podres	8.00	4.00	2.50
173a	Joe Cunningham (Cardinals)	30.00	15.00	9.00
173b	Joe Cunningham (White Sox)	12.50	6.25	3.75
174	ElRoy Face	5.00	2.50	1.50
175	Orlando Cepeda	12.00	6.00	3.50
176a	Bobby Gene Smith (Phillies)	15.00	7.50	4.50
176b	Bobby Gene Smith (Mets)	6.00	3.00	1.75
177a	Ernie Banks (OF)	25.00	12.50	7.50
177b	Ernie Banks (SS)	20.00	10.00	6.00
178a	Daryl Spencer (3B)	20.00	10.00	6.00
178b	Daryl Spencer (1B)	12.00	6.00	3.50
179	Bob Schmidt	25.00	12.50	7.50
180	Hank Aaron	35.00	17.50	10.50
181	Hobie Landrith	10.00	5.00	3.00
182a	Ed Broussard (Bressoud)	400.00	200.00	120.00
182b	Ed Bressoud	25.00	12.50	7.50
183	Felix Mantilla	10.00	5.00	3.00
184	Dick Farrell	10.00	5.00	3.00
185	Bob Miller	10.00	5.00	3.00
186	Don Taussig	15.00	7.50	4.50
187	Pumpsie Green	10.00	5.00	3.00
188	Bobby Shantz	10.00	5.00	3.00
189	Roger Craig	10.00	5.00	3.00
190	Hal Smith	10.00	5.00	3.00
191	John Edwards	10.00	5.00	3.00
192	John DeMerit	10.00	5.00	3.00
193	Joe Amalfitano	10.00	5.00	3.00
194	Norm Larker	10.00	5.00	3.00
195	Al Heist	10.00	5.00	3.00
196	Al Spangler	10.00	5.00	3.00
197	Alex Grammas	10.00	5.00	3.00
198	Gerry Lynch	10.00	5.00	3.00
199	Jim McKnight	15.00	7.50	4.50
200	Jose Pagen (Pagan)	10.00	5.00	3.00
201	Junior Gilliam	20.00	10.00	6.00
202	Art Ditmar	10.00	5.00	3.00
203	Pete Daley	10.00	5.00	3.00
204	Johnny Callison	20.00	10.00	6.00
205	Stu Miller	10.00	5.00	3.00
206	Russ Snyder	10.00	5.00	3.00
207	Billy Williams	25.00	12.50	7.50
208	Walter Bond	10.00	5.00	3.00
209	Joe Koppe	10.00	5.00	3.00
210	Don Schwall	16.00	8.00	4.75
211	Billy Gardner	15.00	7.50	4.50
212	Chuck Estrada	10.00	5.00	3.00
213	Gary Bell	15.00	7.50	4.50
214	Floyd Robinson	10.00	5.00	3.00
215	Duke Snider	25.00	12.50	7.50
216	Lee Maye	10.00	5.00	3.00
217	Howie Bedell	10.00	5.00	3.00
218	Bob Will	10.00	5.00	3.00
219	Dallas Green	15.00	7.50	4.50
220	Carroll Hardy	15.00	7.50	4.50
221	Danny O'Connell	10.00	5.00	3.00

1962 Salada-Junket Coins - Clip Back

A very rare version of the Salada Tea/Junket Dessert plastic coins exists in a clip-back format. An extruded tab at back center would allow the coin to be slid onto a cap bill or shirt flap as a decoration. With the exception of Averill (Angels), all clip-back Saladas confirmed thus far depict Boston Red Sox players. It has been reported that the clip-back coins were created for use in Opening Day stadium promotions by the Red Sox, Yankees and Mets.

		NM	EX	VG
Common Player:		450.00	225.00	135.00
14	Frank Malzone	450.00	225.00	135.00
24	Earl Averill	450.00	225.00	135.00
27	Carl Yastrzemski	600.00	300.00	180.00
38	Gary Geiger	450.00	225.00	135.00
47	Pete Runnels	450.00	225.00	135.00
73	Jackie Jensen	450.00	225.00	135.00
81	Jim Pagliaroni	450.00	225.00	135.00
99	Bill Monbouquette	450.00	225.00	135.00
182	Ed Broussard (Bressoud)	450.00	225.00	135.00
187	Pumpsie Green	450.00	225.00	135.00
210	Don Schwall	450.00	225.00	135.00
220	Carroll Hardy	450.00	225.00	135.00

1963 Salada-Junket Coins

A much smaller set of baseball coins was issued by Salada/Junket in 1963. The 63 coins issued were called "All-Star Baseball Coins" and included most of the top players of the day. Unlike 1962, the coins were made of metal and measured a slightly larger 1-1/2" diameter. American League players have blue rims on their coins, while National Leaguers are rimmed in red. Coin fronts contain no printing on the full-color player photos, while backs list coin number, player name, team and position, along with brief statistics and the sponsors' logos.

		NM	EX	VG
Complete Set (63):		650.00	325.00	200.00
Common Player:		6.00	3.00	1.75
1	Don Drysdale	12.50	6.25	3.75
2	Dick Farrell	6.00	3.00	1.75
3	Bob Gibson	12.50	6.25	3.75
4	Sandy Koufax	35.00	17.50	10.00
5a	Juan Marichal (No buttons.)	12.50	6.25	3.75
5b	Juan Marichal (Jersey buttons.)	10.00	5.00	3.00
6	Bob Purkey	6.00	3.00	1.75
7	Bob Shaw	6.00	3.00	1.75
8	Warren Spahn	12.50	6.25	3.75
9	Johnny Podres	7.50	3.75	2.25
10	Art Mahaffey	6.00	3.00	1.75
11	Del Crandall	6.00	3.00	1.75
12	John Roseboro	6.00	3.00	1.75
13	Orlando Cepeda	10.00	5.00	3.00
14	Bill Mazeroski	10.00	5.00	3.00
15	Ken Boyer	7.50	3.75	2.25
16	Dick Groat	6.00	3.00	1.75
17	Ernie Banks	15.00	7.50	4.50
18	Frank Bolling	6.00	3.00	1.75
19	Jim Davenport	6.00	3.00	1.75
20	Maury Wills	7.50	3.75	2.25
21	Tommy Davis	6.00	3.00	1.75
22	Willie Mays	35.00	17.50	10.00
23	Roberto Clemente	45.00	22.50	13.50
24	Henry Aaron	30.00	15.00	9.00
25	Felipe Alou	7.50	3.75	2.25
26	Johnny Callison	6.00	3.00	1.75
27	Richie Ashburn	12.50	6.25	3.75
28	Eddie Mathews	12.50	6.25	3.75
29	Frank Robinson	10.00	5.00	3.00
30	Billy Williams	10.00	5.00	3.00
31	George Altman	6.00	3.00	1.75
32	Hank Aguirre	6.00	3.00	1.75
33	Jim Bunning	10.00	5.00	3.00
34	Dick Donovan	6.00	3.00	1.75
35	Bill Monbouquette	6.00	3.00	1.75
36	Camilo Pascual	6.00	3.00	1.75
37	David Stenhouse	6.00	3.00	1.75
38	Ralph Terry	6.00	3.00	1.75
39	Hoyt Wilhelm	10.00	5.00	3.00
40	Jim Kaat	7.50	3.75	2.25
41	Ken McBride	6.00	3.00	1.75
42	Ray Herbert	6.00	3.00	1.75
43	Milt Pappas	6.00	3.00	1.75
44	Earl Battey	6.00	3.00	1.75
45	Elston Howard	7.50	3.75	2.25
46	John Romano	6.00	3.00	1.75
47	Jim Gentile	6.00	3.00	1.75
48	Billy Moran	6.00	3.00	1.75
49	Rich Rollins	6.00	3.00	1.75
50	Luis Aparicio	10.00	5.00	3.00
51	Norm Siebern	6.00	3.00	1.75
52	Bobby Richardson	7.50	3.75	2.25
53	Brooks Robinson	15.00	7.50	4.50
54	Tom Tresh	7.50	3.75	2.25
55	Leon Wagner	6.00	3.00	1.75
56	Mickey Mantle	85.00	45.00	25.00
57	Roger Maris	25.00	12.50	7.50
58	Rocky Colavito	20.00	10.00	6.00
59	Lee Thomas	6.00	3.00	1.75
60	Jim Landis	6.00	3.00	1.75
61	Pete Runnels	6.00	3.00	1.75
62	Yogi Berra	22.50	11.00	6.75
63	Al Kaline	15.00	7.50	4.50

1961 Sam's Family Restaurants Roger Maris

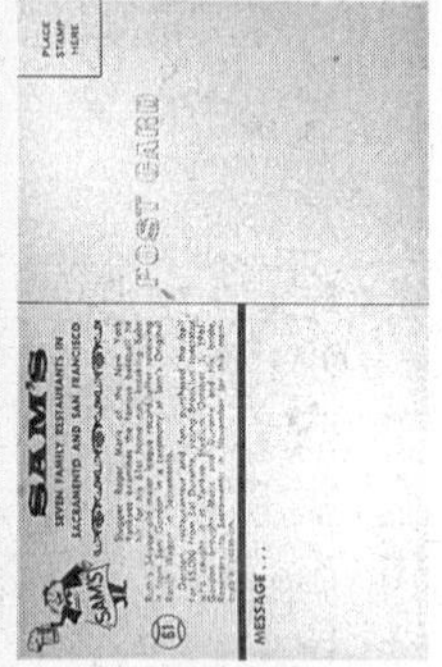

This postcard was issued to commemorate the presentation of Roger Maris' historic 61st home run ball back to the slugger. Pictured with Maris on this color 3-1/2" x 5-1/2" postcard is Sam Gordon, owner of a chain of family restaurants in northern California. Gordon purchased the ball from the fan who caught it, Sal Durante, and flew Durante and his wife, and Maris to Sacramento where he paid $5,000 for the ball and presented it to Maris, who later donated it to the Hall of Fame. On front is a borderless color photo of the presentation. Back has the historical details and the traditional postcard indicia.

		NM	EX	VG
61	Roger Maris, Sam Gordon	50.00	25.00	15.00

1886 W.H. Sanders New York Baseball Club (H812)

This rare 19th Century baseball issue can be classified under the general category of "trade" cards, a popular advertising vehicle of the period. The cards measure 3" x 4-3/4" and feature blue line-drawing portraits of members of the "New York Base Ball Club," which is printed along the top. As was common with this type of trade card, the bottom was left blank to accomodate various messages. The known examples of this set carry ads for local tobacco merchants and other businesses. The portraits are all based on the photographs used in the 1886 Old Judge set. The cards, which have been assigned an ACC designation of H812, are printed on thin paper rather than cardboard.

(See 1889 New York Baseball Club for checklist and values.)

1969 San Diego Padres Premium Pictures

Unlike most of the contemporary large-format (8-1/2" x 11") premium pictures, this issue carries no advertising and appears to have been a team-issue in the Padres inaugural

year. Fronts feature large portraits and smaller action pictures of the player against a dark background with a facsimile autograph at the bottom and the player's name printed in the white bottom border. The signature of the artist appears in the lower-left corner. The artwork was done by Nicholas Volpe, who produced many similar items for teams in all sports in the '60s, '70s and '80s. Backs have a large team logo at center and a sketch of the artist at bottom. There is evidence to suggest that the picture of Cito Gaston is scarcer than the other seven.

		NM	EX	VG
Complete Set (8):		60.00	30.00	18.00
Common Player:		7.50	3.75	2.25
(1)	Ollie Brown	7.50	3.75	2.25
(2)	Tommy Dean	7.50	3.75	2.25
(3)	Al Ferrara	7.50	3.75	2.25
(4)	Clarence Gaston	10.00	5.00	3.00
(5)	Preston Gomez	7.50	3.75	2.25
(6)	Johnny Podres	9.00	4.50	2.75
(7)	Al Santorini	7.50	3.75	2.25
(8)	Ed Spiezio	7.50	3.75	2.25

1977 San Diego Padres Schedule Cards

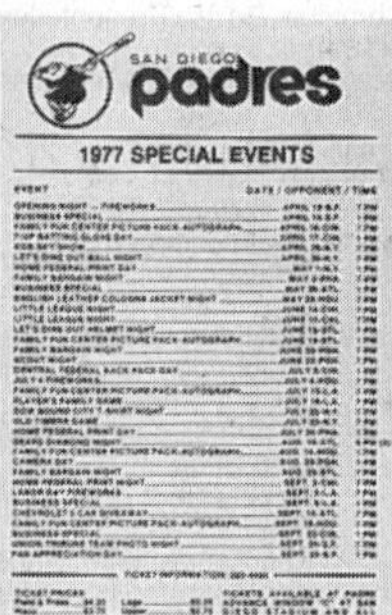

Members of the 1977 San Diego Padres, players and management, are featured in this set. The 2-1/4" x 3-3/8" cards are printed in brown on thin white stock. Fronts have a player photo with a pinstripe around and the team and player name at bottom. Backs have the team logo at top, a list of promotional dates in the center and ticket information at bottom. While some card backs state "One in a Series of 40 Player Photos," more than 80 variations are known, including some poses with blank backs. The unnumbered cards are checklisted here in alphabetical order, within three types differentiated by back printing.

		NM	EX	VG
Complete Set (89):		60.00	30.00	18.00
Common Player:		1.00	.50	.30
Type 1 - "Series of 40"				
(1)	Bill Almon	1.00	.50	.30
(2)	Joe Amalfitano	1.00	.50	.30
(3)	Buzzy Bavasi (General Manager)	1.00	.50	.30
(4)	Vic Bernal	1.00	.50	.30
(5)	Mike Champion	1.00	.50	.30
(6)	Billy Champion, Bill Almon	1.00	.50	.30
(7)	Roger Craig	1.00	.50	.30
(8)	John D'Acquisto	1.00	.50	.30
(9)	Bob Davis	1.00	.50	.30
(10)	Rollie Fingers	3.00	1.50	.90
(11)	Dave Freisleben	1.00	.50	.30
(12)	Tom Griffin	1.00	.50	.30
(13)	George Hendrick	1.00	.50	.30
(14)	Enzo Hernandez	1.00	.50	.30
(15)	Mike Ivie	1.00	.50	.30
(16)	Randy Jones (Follow-through.)	1.00	.50	.30
(17)	Randy Jones (Cy Young Award)	1.00	.50	.30
(18)	John McNamara	1.00	.50	.30
(19)	Luis Melendez	1.00	.50	.30
(20)	Butch Metzger	1.00	.50	.30
(21)	Bob Owchinko	1.00	.50	.30
(22)	Doug Rader	1.00	.50	.30
(23)	Merv Rettenmund	1.00	.50	.30
(24)	Gene Richards	1.00	.50	.30
(25)	Dave Roberts	1.00	.50	.30
(26)	Rick Sawyer	1.00	.50	.30
(27)	Bob Shirley	1.00	.50	.30

#	Player	NM	EX	VG
(28)	Bob Skinner	1.00	.50	.30
(29)	Dan Spillner	1.00	.50	.30
(30)	Brent Strom	1.00	.50	.30
(31)	Gary Sutherland	1.00	.50	.30
(32)	Gene Tenace	1.00	.50	.30
(33)	Dave Tomlin	1.00	.50	.30
(34)	Jerry Turner	1.00	.50	.30
(35)	Bobby Valentine	1.00	.50	.30
(36)	Dan Wehrmeister	1.00	.50	.30
(37)	Whitey Wietelmann	1.00	.50	.30
(38)	Don Williams	1.00	.50	.30
(39)	Dave Winfield (One bat.)	10.00	5.00	3.00
(40)	Dave Winfield (Two bats.)	5.00	2.50	1.50

Type 2 - No "Series of 40"

#	Player	NM	EX	VG
(1)	Bill Almon	1.00	.50	.30
(2)	Matty Alou	1.00	.50	.30
(3)	Steve Arlin (Glove to chest.)	1.00	.50	.30
(4)	Steve Arlin (Follow-through.)	1.00	.50	.30
(5)	Bob Barton	1.00	.50	.30
(6)	Glenn Beckert	1.50	.75	.45
(7)	Ollie Brown	1.00	.50	.30
(8)	Dave Campbell (Bat on shoulder.)	1.00	.50	.30
(9)	Dave Campbell/Kneeling	1.00	.50	.30
(10)	Enzo Hernandez, Nate Colbert	1.00	.50	.30
(11)	Nate Colbert	1.00	.50	.30
(12)	Colbert and Friend (With child.)	1.00	.50	.30
(13)	Jerry Coleman (Announcer)	1.00	.50	.30
(14)	Willie Davis	1.00	.50	.30
(15)	Jim Eakle ("TUBA MAN")	1.00	.50	.30
(16)	Rollie Fingers	3.00	1.50	.90
(17)	Cito Gaston (Bare hands.)	1.00	.50	.30
(18)	Cito Gaston (Batting gloves.)	1.00	.50	.30
(19)	Johnny Grubb	1.00	.50	.30
(20)	George Hendrick	1.00	.50	.30
(21)	Mike Ivie	1.00	.50	.30
(22)	Fred Kendall/Btg	1.00	.50	.30
(23)	Fred Kendall (Holding ball.)	1.00	.50	.30
(24)	Clay Kirby (Follow-through.)	1.00	.50	.30
(25)	Clay Kirby (Glove to chest.)	1.00	.50	.30
(26)	Dave Marshall	1.00	.50	.30
(27)	Willie McCovey (Moustache)	5.00	2.50	1.50
(28)	John McNamara	1.00	.50	.30
(29)	Bob Miller	1.00	.50	.30
(30)	Fred Norman (Arms above head.)	1.00	.50	.30
(31)	Fred Norman/Kneeling	1.00	.50	.30
(32)	Gene Richards	1.00	.50	.30
(33)	Ballard Smith (General Manager)	1.00	.50	.30
(34)	Ed Spiezio	1.00	.50	.30
(35)	Derrell (Darrel) Thomas (Glasses)	1.00	.50	.30
(36)	Derrel Thomas (No glasses.)	1.00	.50	.30
(37)	Bobby Tolan/Btg	1.00	.50	.30
(38)	Bobby Tolan/Kneeling	1.00	.50	.30
(39)	Jerry Turner	1.00	.50	.30
(40)	Dave Winfield	5.00	2.50	1.50

Type 3 - Blank back

#	Player	NM	EX	VG
(1)	Nate Colbert	1.00	.50	.30
(2)	Dave Freisleben	1.00	.50	.30
(3)	Mike Ivie	1.00	.50	.30
(4)	Randy Jones and Bowie Kuhn	1.00	.50	.30
(5)	Mike Kilkenny	1.00	.50	.30
(6)	Ray Kroc (Owner)	1.00	.50	.30
(7)	Willie McCovey	5.00	2.50	1.50
(8)	John McNamara (Facing his right.)	1.00	.50	.30
(9)	Dave Winfield	7.50	3.75	2.25

1932 Sanella Margarine

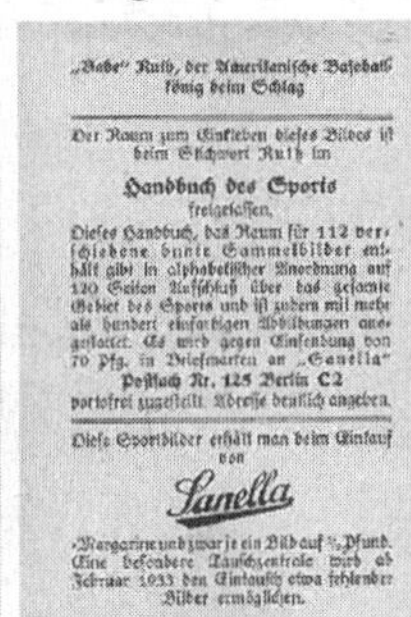

„Babe" Ruth, der Amerikanische Baseball-
könig beim Schlag

Der Raum zum Einkleben dieses Bildes ist
beim Stichwort Ruth im

Handbuch des Sports

freigelassen.

Dieses Handbuch, das Raum für 112 verschiedene bunte Sammelbilder enthält gibt in alphabetischer Anordnung auf 120 Seiten Aufschluß über das gesamte Gebiet des Sports und ist zudem mit mehr als hundert einfarbigen Abbildungen ausgestattet. Es wird gegen Einsendung von 70 Pfg. in Briefmarken an „Sanella"

Postfach Nr. 125 Berlin C2

portofrei zugestellt. Adresse deutlich angeben.

Diese Sportbilder erhält man beim Einkauf
von

Sanella

-Margarine und zwar je ein Bild auf ½ Pfund. Eine besondere Tauschzentrale wird ab Februar 1933 den Eintausch etwa fehlender Bilder ermöglichen.

One of several "foreign" Babe Ruth cards issued during his prime was included in a 112-card set produced as premiums for Sanella margarine in Germany. Ruth is the only major league ballplayer in the issue. Cards are in full color, measuring 2-3/4" x 4-1/8". Backs of the unnumbered cards are printed in German. Four types of backs can be found on the Ruth card. Type 1 has the Sanella name nearly centered. The Type 2 back has the brand name printed closer to the bottom of the card, with only four lines of type under it. Type 3 is a variation of Type 2 on which the appropriate page number (83) of the accompanying album is mentioned on the line immediately above "Handbuch des Sports" near the top. Type 4 cards also mention the page number and have the brand name near the center. One card was given with the purchase of each 1/2 pound of margarine and the album could be ordered by mail. See also Astra Margarine.

	NM	EX	VG
Type 1Babe Ruth (Centered w/83.)	200.00	100.00	60.00
Type 2Babe Ruth (At bottom.)	140.00	70.00	42.00
Type 3Babe Ruth (At bottom w/83.)	200.00	100.00	60.00

1958 San Francisco Call-Bulletin Giants

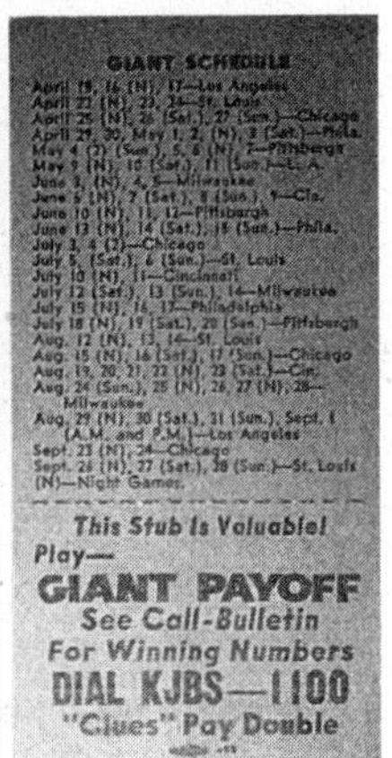

These unnumbered cards, picturing members of the San Francisco Giants, were inserted in copies of the San Francisco Call-Bulletin newspaper as part of a promotional contest. The 25 cards in the set measure 2" x 4" and were printed on orange paper. The top of the card contains a black and white player photo, while the bottom contains a perforated stub with a serial number used to win prizes. (Cards without the stub intact are approximately 50 percent of the prices listed.) The contest name, "Giant Payoff," appears prominently on both sides of the stub. The back of the card contains a 1958 Giants schedule.

#	Player	NM	EX	VG
	Complete Set (25):	1,800	900.00	550.00
	Common Player:	25.00	12.50	7.50
(1)	Johnny Antonelli	25.00	12.50	7.50
(2)	Curt Barclay	25.00	12.50	7.50
(3)	Tom Bowers/SP	400.00	200.00	120.00
(4)	Ed Bressoud/SP	150.00	75.00	45.00
(5)	Orlando Cepeda	250.00	125.00	75.00
(6)	Ray Crone	25.00	12.50	7.50
(7)	Jim Davenport	25.00	12.50	7.50
(8)	Paul Giel	25.00	12.50	7.50
(9)	Ruben Gomez	25.00	12.50	7.50
(10)	Marv Grissom	25.00	12.50	7.50
(11)	Ray Jablonski/SP	150.00	75.00	45.00
(12)	Willie Kirkland/SP	150.00	75.00	45.00
(13)	Whitey Lockman	25.00	12.50	7.50
(14)	Willie Mays	250.00	125.00	75.00
(15)	Mike McCormick	25.00	12.50	7.50
(16)	Stu Miller	25.00	12.50	7.50
(17)	Ramon Monzant	25.00	12.50	7.50
(18)	Danny O'Connell	25.00	12.50	7.50
(19)	Bill Rigney	25.00	12.50	7.50
(20)	Hank Sauer	25.00	12.50	7.50
(21)	Bob Schmidt	25.00	12.50	7.50
(22)	Daryl Spencer	25.00	12.50	7.50
(23)	Valmy Thomas	25.00	12.50	7.50
(24)	Bobby Thomson	45.00	22.50	13.50
(25)	Allan Worthington	25.00	12.50	7.50

1971-1982 San Francisco Giants Autograph Cards

For more than 10 years the Giants issued a number of different types of cards bearing facsimile autographs that the players could use to respond to fan mail. The cards vary in size from 3" x 5" to 3" x 6" and have a black-and-white photo (usually a portrait). The cards are blank-backed. Besides the cards with pre-printed autographs, a number of special cards in similar format were issued without facsimile signature. The listings are presented here in two major styles, those with player name in all-capital letters and those with names in upper and lower case.

#	Player	NM	EX	VG
	Common Player:	6.00	3.00	1.75

NAME IN ALL-CAPITAL LETTERS

TYPE 1 - Name only, letters 1/8" wide.

#	Player	NM	EX	VG
(1)	Doyle Alexander	6.00	3.00	1.75
(2)	Gary Alexander	6.00	3.00	1.75
(3)	Joe Altobelli	6.00	3.00	1.75
(4)	Rob Andrews/Portrait	6.00	3.00	1.75
(5)	Rob Andrews/Fldg	6.00	3.00	1.75
(6)	Jim Barr/Pitching	6.00	3.00	1.75
(7)	Dave Bergman	6.00	3.00	1.75
(8)	Vida Blue/Portrait	8.00	4.00	2.50
(9)	Vida Blue/Pitching	8.00	4.00	2.50
(10)	Bill Bordley	6.00	3.00	1.75
(11)	Fred Breining	6.00	3.00	1.75
(12)	Dave Bristol	6.00	3.00	1.75
(13)	Enos Cabell	6.00	3.00	1.75
(14)	Jack Clark (Ready to bat.)	8.00	4.00	2.50
(15)	Jack Clark (Swinging bat.)	8.00	4.00	2.50
(16)	Terry Cornutt	6.00	3.00	1.75
(17)	Heity Cruz	6.00	3.00	1.75
(18)	John Curtis	6.00	3.00	1.75
(19)	Jim Dwyer	6.00	3.00	1.75
(20)	Randy Elliott	6.00	3.00	1.75
(21)	Darrell Evans/Portrait	8.00	4.00	2.50
(22)	Darrell Evans/Btg	8.00	4.00	2.50
(23)	Tim Foli/Fldg	6.00	3.00	1.75
(24)	Tom Griffin	6.00	3.00	1.75
(25)	Ed Halicki/Portrait	6.00	3.00	1.75
(26)	Ed Halicki/Pitching	6.00	3.00	1.75
(27)	Vic Harris	6.00	3.00	1.75
(28)	Dave Heaverlo/Action	6.00	3.00	1.75
(29)	Tom Heintzelman	6.00	3.00	1.75
(30)	Larry Herndon	6.00	3.00	1.75
(31)	Marc Hill	6.00	3.00	1.75
(32)	Al Holland	6.00	3.00	1.75
(33)	Mike Ivie (Looks to side.)	6.00	3.00	1.75
(34)	Mike Ivie (Looks to front.)	6.00	3.00	1.75
(35)	Skip James	6.00	3.00	1.75
(36)	Bob Knepper	6.00	3.00	1.75
(37)	Gary Lavelle/Portrait	6.00	3.00	1.75
(38)	Gary Lavelle/Pitching	6.00	3.00	1.75
(39)	Johnnie Lemaster/Fldg	6.00	3.00	1.75
(40)	Dennis Littlejohn	6.00	3.00	1.75
(41)	Bill Madlock (Picture reversed.)	8.00	4.00	2.50
(42)	Bill Madlock (Corrected)	8.00	4.00	2.50
(43)	Jerry Martin	6.00	3.00	1.75
(44)	Milt May	6.00	3.00	1.75
(45)	Willie McCovey/Portrait	15.00	7.50	4.50
(46)	Willie McCovey/Btg	15.00	7.50	4.50
(47)	Lynn McGlothen/Pitching	6.00	3.00	1.75
(48)	Roger Metzger	6.00	3.00	1.75
(49)	Greg Minton	6.00	3.00	1.75
(50)	Randy Moffitt/Portrait	6.00	3.00	1.75
(51)	Randy Moffitt/Pitching	6.00	3.00	1.75
(52)	John Montefusco (To neck.)	6.00	3.00	1.75
(53)	John Montefusco (To letters.)	6.00	3.00	1.75
(54)	Joe Morgan	15.00	7.50	4.50
(55)	Rich Murray	6.00	3.00	1.75
(56)	Phil Nastu	6.00	3.00	1.75
(57)	Bill North	6.00	3.00	1.75
(58)	Joe Pettini	6.00	3.00	1.75
(59)	Allen Ripley	6.00	3.00	1.75
(60)	Dave Roberts	6.00	3.00	1.75
(61)	Frank Robinson	20.00	10.00	6.00
(62)	Mike Sadek (To neck.)	6.00	3.00	1.75
(63)	Mike Sadek (To letters.)	6.00	3.00	1.75
(64)	Billy Smith	6.00	3.00	1.75
(65)	Rennie Stennett	6.00	3.00	1.75
(66)	Joe Strain	6.00	3.00	1.75
(67)	John Tamargo	6.00	3.00	1.75
(68)	Derrel Thomas/Throwing	6.00	3.00	1.75
(69)	Gary Thomasson	6.00	3.00	1.75
(70)	Max Venable	6.00	3.00	1.75
(71)	Terry Whitfield	6.00	3.00	1.75
(72)	Ed Whitson	6.00	3.00	1.75
(73)	Charlie Williams	6.00	3.00	1.75
(74)	Jim Wohlford	6.00	3.00	1.75

TYPE 2 - Name only, letters 1/16" wide.

#	Player	NM	EX	VG
(1)	Jim Barr (Mouth closed.)	6.00	3.00	1.75
(2)	Jim Barr (Mouth open, fence.)	6.00	3.00	1.75
(3)	Jim Barr (Mouth open, no fence.)	6.00	3.00	1.75
(4)	Bobby Bonds	9.00	4.50	2.75
(5)	Tom Bradley	6.00	3.00	1.75
(6)	Ron Bryant	6.00	3.00	1.75
(7)	Don Carrithers (To neck.)	6.00	3.00	1.75
(8)	Don Carrithers (To letters.)	6.00	3.00	1.75
(9)	Pete Falcone	6.00	3.00	1.75
(10)	Charlie Fox	6.00	3.00	1.75
(11)	Tito Fuentes (To neck.)	6.00	3.00	1.75
(12)	Tito Fuentes (To letters.)	6.00	3.00	1.75
(13)	Alan Gallagher	6.00	3.00	1.75
(14)	Russ Gibson	6.00	3.00	1.75
(15)	Ed Goodson	6.00	3.00	1.75
(16)	Ed Halicki/Pitching	6.00	3.00	1.75
(17)	Marc Hill	6.00	3.00	1.75
(18)	Jim Howarth	6.00	3.00	1.75
(19)	Jerry Johnson	6.00	3.00	1.75
(20)	Von Joshua	6.00	3.00	1.75
(21)	Gary Lavelle/Pitching	6.00	3.00	1.75
(22)	Garry Maddox	6.00	3.00	1.75
(23)	Juan Marichal	15.00	7.50	4.50
(24)	Gary Matthews	8.00	4.00	2.50
(25)	Randy Moffitt	6.00	3.00	1.75
(26)	Willie McCovey	15.00	7.50	4.50
(27)	Willie Montanez	6.00	3.00	1.75
(28)	John Montefusco/Pitching	6.00	3.00	1.75
(29)	Bobby Murcer/Btg	8.00	4.00	2.50
(30)	Dave Rader	6.00	3.00	1.75
(31)	Ken Reitz/Btg	6.00	3.00	1.75
(32)	Bill Rigney	6.00	3.00	1.75
(33)	Mike Sadek	6.00	3.00	1.75
(34)	Elias Sosa	6.00	3.00	1.75
(35)	Chris Speier (To neck.)	6.00	3.00	1.75
(36)	Chris Speier (To shoulders.)	6.00	3.00	1.75

(37)	Steve Stone	8.00	4.00	2.50
(38)	Derrel Thomas	6.00	3.00	1.75
(39)	Gary Thomasson	6.00	3.00	1.75
(40)	Jim Willoughby	6.00	3.00	1.75
	TYPE 3 - 25th Anniversary Logo			
(1)	Jim Barr	6.00	3.00	1.75
(2)	Bob Brenly	6.00	3.00	1.75
(3)	Don Buford (1-1/2" autograph)	6.00	3.00	1.75
(4)	Don Buford (2-1/2" autograph)	6.00	3.00	1.75
(5)	Jim Davenport	6.00	3.00	1.75
(6)	Chili Davis	8.00	4.00	2.50
(7)	Alan Fowlkes	6.00	3.00	1.75
(8)	Rich Gale	6.00	3.00	1.75
(9)	Atlee Hammaker	6.00	3.00	1.75
(10)	Al Holland	6.00	3.00	1.75
(11)	Duane Kuiper	6.00	3.00	1.75
(12)	Bill Laskey	6.00	3.00	1.75
(13)	Jim Lefebvre	6.00	3.00	1.75
(14)	Johnnie Lemaster	6.00	3.00	1.75
(15)	Jeff Leonard (Chain in background.)	8.00	4.00	2.50
(16)	Jeff Leonard (No chain.)	8.00	4.00	2.50
(17)	Renie Martin	6.00	3.00	1.75
(18)	Willie McCovey	15.00	7.50	4.50
(19)	Don McMahon (2-3/8" autograph)	6.00	3.00	1.75
(20)	Don McMahon (2-5/8" autograph)	6.00	3.00	1.75
(21)	Greg Minton	6.00	3.00	1.75
(22)	Joe Morgan	15.00	7.50	4.50
(23)	Tom O'Malley	6.00	3.00	1.75
(24)	Frank Robinson	20.00	10.00	6.00
(25)	Mike Sadek	6.00	3.00	1.75
(26)	Reggie Smith	6.00	3.00	1.75
(27)	Guy Sularz	6.00	3.00	1.75
(28)	Champ Summers	6.00	3.00	1.75
(29)	John Van Ornum (2" autograph)	6.00	3.00	1.75
(30)	John Van Ornum (2-1/4" autograph)	6.00	3.00	1.75
(31)	Jim Wohlford	6.00	3.00	1.75
	TYPE 4 - Position after name, no autograph			
(1)	Chris Speier	6.00	3.00	1.75
	TYPE 5 - Courtesy Chevrolet, no autograph			
(1)	Bobby Bonds	9.00	4.50	2.75
(2)	Dick Dietz	6.00	3.00	1.75
(3)	Tito Fuentes	6.00	3.00	1.75
(4)	Ken Henderson	6.00	3.00	1.75
	TYPE 6 - West Valley Bicycles, no autograph			
(1)	Alan Gallagher	6.00	3.00	1.75
	TYPE 7 - Best Chevrolet, no autograph			
(1)	Tito Fuentes	6.00	3.00	1.75
(2)	Chris Speier	6.00	3.00	1.75
	TYPE 8 - Redwood City Tribune, no autograph			
(1)	Jim Barr	6.00	3.00	1.75
	NAME IN UPPER- AND LOWER CASE LETTERS			
	TYPE A - Name only			
(1)	John D'Acquisto	6.00	3.00	1.75
(2)	Mike Caldwell	6.00	3.00	1.75
(3)	Ed Goodson	6.00	3.00	1.75
(4)	Dave Kingman	8.00	4.00	2.50
(5)	Steve Ontiveros	6.00	3.00	1.75
(6)	Mike Phillips	6.00	3.00	1.75
(7)	"Wes" Westrum	6.00	3.00	1.75
(8)	Charlie Williams	6.00	3.00	1.75
	TYPE B - Team after name, no autograph			
(1)	Rich Robertson	6.00	3.00	1.75
	TYPE C - Courtesy Chevrolet, no autograph			
(1)	Rich Robertson	6.00	3.00	1.75
	TYPE D - Position after name			
(1)	Garry Maddox	6.00	3.00	1.75
	TYPE E - Redwood City Tribune, no logo, no autograph			
(1)	Chris Arnold	6.00	3.00	1.75
(2)	Jim Barr	6.00	3.00	1.75
(3)	Jim Howarth	6.00	3.00	1.75
(4)	Garry Maddox	6.00	3.00	1.75
(5)	Dave Rader	6.00	3.00	1.75
(6)	Chris Speier	6.00	3.00	1.75
	TYPE F - Redwood City Tribune, with newspaper logo, no autograph			
(1)	Chris Arnold	6.00	3.00	1.75
(2)	Jim Barr	6.00	3.00	1.75
(3)	Ed Goodson	6.00	3.00	1.75
	TYPE G - Name only, old Giants logo			
(1)	Dave Kingman	8.00	4.00	2.50
(2)	Juan Marichal	15.00	7.50	4.50

1977 San Francisco Giants Team Issue

These 3-1/2" x 5" blank-back cards feature black-and-white player photos surrounded by an orange frame with black borders. The manager, coaches and instructors are featured along with players in the issue. The unnumbered cards are checklisted here in alphabetical order.

		NM	EX	VG
	Complete Set (25):	15.00	7.50	4.50
	Common Player:	1.50	.75	.45
(1)	Joe Altobelli	1.50	.75	.45
(2)	Jim Barr	1.50	.75	.45
(3)	Jack Clark	2.50	1.25	.70
(4)	Terry Cornutt	1.50	.75	.45
(5)	Rob Dressler	1.50	.75	.45
(6)	Darrell Evans	2.50	1.25	.70
(7)	Frank Funk	1.50	.75	.45
(8)	Ed Halicki	1.50	.75	.45
(9)	Tom Haller	1.50	.75	.45
(10)	Marc Hill	1.50	.75	.45
(11)	Skip James	1.50	.75	.45
(12)	Bob Knepper	1.50	.75	.45
(13)	Gary Lavelle	1.50	.75	.45
(14)	Bill Madlock	1.75	.90	.50
(15)	Willie McCovey	6.00	3.00	1.75
(16)	Randy Moffitt	1.50	.75	.45
(17)	John Montefusco	1.50	.75	.45
(18)	Marty Perez	1.50	.75	.45
(19)	Frank Riccelli	1.50	.75	.45
(20)	Mike Sadek	1.50	.75	.45
(21)	Hank Sauer	1.50	.75	.45
(22)	Chris Speier	1.50	.75	.45
(23)	Gary Thomasson	1.50	.75	.45
(24)	Tommy Toms	1.50	.75	.45
(25)	Bobby Winkles	1.50	.75	.45

1979 San Francisco Giants Police

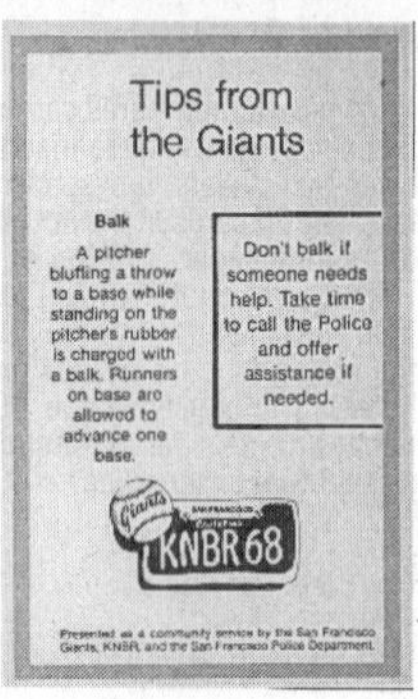

Each of the full-color cards measures 2-5/8" x 4-1/8" and is numbered by player uniform number. The set includes players and coaches. The player's name, position and facsimile autograph are on front, along with the Giants logo. Backs have a "Tip from the Giants" and sponsor logos for the Giants and radio station KNBR, all printed in orange and black. Half of the set was distributed as a ballpark promotion, while the other cards were available from police agencies in several San Francisco Bay area counties.

		NM	EX	VG
	Complete Set (29):	10.00	5.00	3.00
	Common Player:	.50	.25	.15
1	Dave Bristol	.50	.25	.15
2	Marc Hill	.50	.25	.15
3	Mike Sadek	.50	.25	.15
5	Tom Haller	.50	.25	.15
6	Joe Altobelli	.50	.25	.15
8	Larry Shepard	.50	.25	.15
9	Heity Cruz	.50	.25	.15
10	Johnnie LeMaster	.50	.25	.15
12	Jim Davenport	.50	.25	.15
14	Vida Blue	.75	.40	.25
15	Mike Ivie	.50	.25	.15
16	Roger Metzger	.50	.25	.15
17	Randy Moffitt	.50	.25	.15
18	Bill Madlock	.60	.30	.20
21	Rob Andrews	.50	.25	.15
22	Jack Clark	.75	.40	.25
25	Dave Roberts	.50	.25	.15
26	John Montefusco	.50	.25	.15
28	Ed Halicki	.50	.25	.15
30	John Tamargo	.50	.25	.15
31	Larry Herndon	.50	.25	.15
36	Bill North	.50	.25	.15
39	Bob Knepper	.50	.25	.15
40	John Curtis	.50	.25	.15
41	Darrell Evans	.75	.40	.25
43	Tom Griffin	.50	.25	.15
44	Willie McCovey	5.00	2.50	1.50
46	Gary Lavelle	.50	.25	.15
49	Max Venable	.50	.25	.15

1980 San Francisco Giants Police

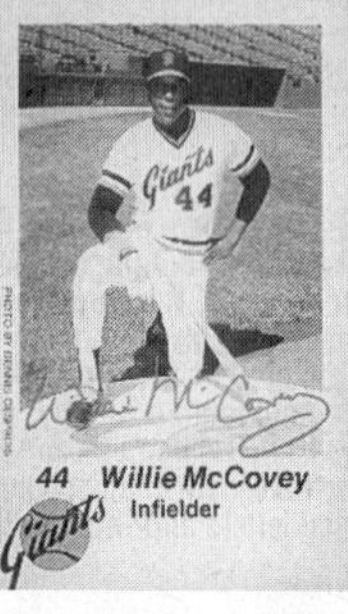

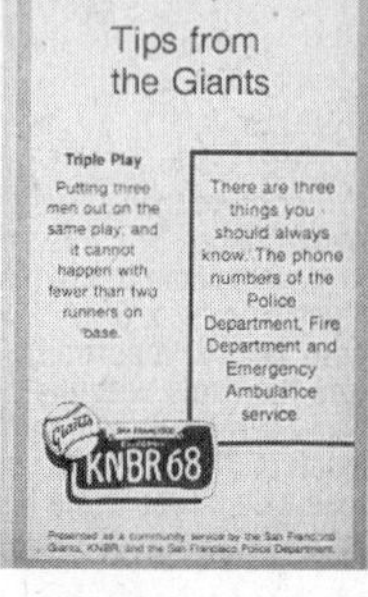

The 1980 Giants police set is virtually identical in format to its 1979 forerunner, with radio station KNBR and the San Francisco Police Department once again co-sponsors. The 2-5/8" x 4-1/8" cards feature full-color photos and facsimile autographs. Backs are in the team's orange and black colors. The set includes players and coaches, with each card numbered by uniform number. As in 1979, half the cards were distributed as a stadium promotion, with the remainder available only from police officers.

		NM	EX	VG
	Complete Set (31):	9.00	4.50	2.75
	Common Player:	.50	.25	.15
1	Dave Bristol	.50	.25	.15
2	Marc Hill	.50	.25	.15
3	Mike Sadek	.50	.25	.15
5	Jim Lefebvre	.50	.25	.15
6	Rennie Stennett	.50	.25	.15
7	Milt May	.50	.25	.15
8	Vern Benson	.50	.25	.15
9	Jim Wohlford	.50	.25	.15
10	Johnnie LeMaster	.50	.25	.15
12	Jim Davenport	.50	.25	.15
14	Vida Blue	.75	.40	.25
15	Mike Ivie	.50	.25	.15
16	Roger Metzger	.50	.25	.15
17	Randy Moffitt	.50	.25	.15
19	Al Holland	.50	.25	.15
20	Joe Strain	.50	.25	.15
22	Jack Clark	.50	.25	.15
26	John Montefusco	.50	.25	.15
28	Ed Halicki	.50	.25	.15
31	Larry Herndon	.50	.25	.15
32	Ed Whitson	.50	.25	.15
36	Bill North	.50	.25	.15
38	Greg Minton	.50	.25	.15
39	Bob Knepper	.50	.25	.15
41	Darrell Evans	.60	.30	.20
42	John Van Ornum	.50	.25	.15
43	Tom Griffin	.50	.25	.15
44	Willie McCovey	4.00	2.00	1.25
45	Terry Whitfield	.50	.25	.15
46	Gary Lavelle	.50	.25	.15
47	Don McMahon	.50	.25	.15

1940s Sarra Trade Cards

While the cards are undated, one of the uniforms shown places its issue between 1940-1950. These ad cards are about 3-1/2" x 5-3/8" and printed in sepia on thick cream-colored paper stock. The backs picture examples of the company's personal care products, including cologne, available in sizes up to one quart!

	NM	EX	VG
Ralph Kiner	250.00	125.00	75.00
Stan Musial	350.00	175.00	100.00
Babe Ruth	550.00	275.00	165.00

1938 Sawyer Biscuit Cubs/White Sox

In the late 1930s, a local baker ran a promotion by which fans could redeem a coupon found in its product along with a dime for a matted black-and-white portrait photo of a favorite Chicago ballplayer. The photo was delivered in a thick textured maroon frame about 4-3/4" x 5-3/4" in size that had a punch-out stand on back. The Sawyer company name is not found on the actual photo, but is seen on the envelope and cover letter which are sometimes found with the pictures. It is unknown whether the list presented here is complete.

	NM	EX	VG
Common Player:	600.00	300.00	180.00

	CHICAGO CUBS			
(1)	Jim Asbell	600.00	300.00	180.00
(2)	Clay Bryant	600.00	300.00	180.00
(3)	Tex Carleton	600.00	300.00	180.00
(4)	Phil Cavarretta	600.00	300.00	180.00
(5)	Rip Collins	600.00	300.00	180.00
(6)	Jerome "Dizzy" Dean	1,200	600.00	360.00
(7)	Frank Demaree	600.00	300.00	180.00
(8)	Al Epperly	600.00	300.00	180.00
(9)	Larry French	600.00	300.00	180.00
(10)	Augie Galan	600.00	300.00	180.00
(11)	Bob Garbark	600.00	300.00	180.00
(12)	Charlie Grimm	600.00	300.00	180.00
(13)	Stan Hack	650.00	325.00	195.00
(14)	Gabby Hartnett	750.00	375.00	225.00
(15)	Billy Herman	750.00	375.00	225.00
(16)	Bill Jurges	600.00	300.00	180.00
(17)	Tony Lazzeri	750.00	375.00	225.00
(18)	Bill Lee	600.00	300.00	180.00
(19)	Bob Logan	600.00	300.00	180.00
(20)	Joe Marty	600.00	300.00	180.00
(21)	Ken O'Dea	600.00	300.00	180.00
(22)	Carl Reynolds	600.00	300.00	180.00
(23)	Charlie Root	600.00	300.00	180.00
(24)	Jack Russell	600.00	300.00	180.00
	CHICAGO WHITE SOX			
(1)	Luke Appling	750.00	375.00	225.00
(2)	Boze Berger	600.00	300.00	180.00
(3)	Clint Brown	600.00	300.00	180.00
(4)	Frog Dietrich	600.00	300.00	180.00
(5)	Jimmie Dykes	600.00	300.00	180.00
(6)	Frank Gabler	600.00	300.00	180.00
(7)	Jackie Hayes	600.00	300.00	180.00
(8)	Jack Knott	600.00	300.00	180.00
(9)	Mike Kreevich	600.00	300.00	180.00
(10)	Joe Kuhel	600.00	300.00	180.00
(11)	Thornton Lee	600.00	300.00	180.00
(12)	Ted Lyons	750.00	375.00	225.00
(13)	Marv Owen	600.00	300.00	180.00
(14)	Tony Rensa	600.00	300.00	180.00
(15)	Dunc Rigney	600.00	300.00	180.00
(16)	Larry Rosenthal	600.00	300.00	180.00
(17)	Norm Schlueter	600.00	300.00	180.00
(18)	Luke Sewell	600.00	300.00	180.00
(19)	Henk Steinbacher	600.00	300.00	180.00
(20)	Monty Stratton	625.00	310.00	185.00
(21)	Gee Gee Walker	600.00	300.00	180.00
(22)	Porkshops Whitehead	600.00	300.00	180.00
	BROADCASTER			
	Bob Elson	600.00	300.00	180.00

1921-22 Schapira Bros. Big Show Candy

The players known, with the teams on which they are pictured, can pinpoint the issue date no closer than 1921-22. Nominally about 1-3/4" or 1-7/8" x 2-3/8" (size varies because the cards were printed without borders in sheet form, and are often found crudely cut), the cards were one of several types of insert cards and toys found in boxes of Schapira's "Big Show" candy. The cards have black-and-white borderless photos on which the player name is (usually) printed diagonally in script at lower right. Most cards have an Underwood & Underwood credit line on front, as well. Backs are blank. The unnumbered cards are listed here alphabetically, though the checklist may not be complete. Most cards are found with a horizontal crease at center, possibly to get them into the tight-fitting candy box.

		NM	EX	VG
Common Player:		200.00	100.00	60.00
(1)	George J. Burns	200.00	80.00	40.00
(2)	Ty Cobb	1,800	725.00	350.00
(3)	Stan Coveleski	250.00	100.00	50.00
(4)	(Jake) Daubert	200.00	80.00	40.00
(5)	Joe Dugan	200.00	80.00	40.00
(6)	Jimmy Dykes	200.00	80.00	40.00
(7)	Walter Holke	200.00	80.00	40.00
(8)	Walter Johnson	600.00	240.00	120.00
(9)	Joe Judge	200.00	80.00	40.00
(10)	Dick Kerr	200.00	80.00	40.00
(11)	Rabbit Maranville	250.00	100.00	50.00
(12)	Bob Meusel	200.00	80.00	40.00
(13)	Hy Meyers (Myers)	200.00	80.00	40.00
(14)	O'Neil (Mickey?)	200.00	80.00	40.00
(15)	Roger Peckinpaugh	200.00	80.00	40.00
(16)	Edd Rousch (Roush)	250.00	100.00	50.00
(17)	Ray Schalk	200.00	80.00	40.00
(18)	Everett Scott	200.00	80.00	40.00
(19)	Aaron Ward	200.00	80.00	40.00

1921 Schapira Bros. Candy Babe Ruth

The date assigned to this rare candy issue is a best guess based on the uniform in which the Babe is shown on the various cards. The blank-back cards measure between 1-5/8" and 1-3/4" in width, and are 2-1/2" tall. Printed in red, white and blue the cards were printed on a candy box and come in two types. Apparently each box contained a portrait card of Ruth which offered "a base ball autographed by Babe Ruth" for 250 of the pictures, plus one of five action photos. The portrait card would thus be much more common than any particular action pose, unless great numbers of them were redeemed. The cards illustrated here are not front and back, but show a typical action card and the portrait card. The unnumbered cards are checklisted here in alphabetical order based on the card's caption.

		NM	EX	VG
Complete Set (6):		5,500	2,200	1,100
(1)	Cleared the Bags (Babe Ruth)	1,000	400.00	200.00
(2)	Home Run (Babe Ruth)	1,000	400.00	200.00
(3)	Over the Fence (Babe Ruth)	1,000	400.00	200.00
(4)	They Passed Him (Babe Ruth)	1,000	400.00	200.00
(5)	Waiting for a High One (Babe Ruth)	1,000	400.00	200.00
(6a)	Babe Ruth/Portrait (Arrows point to top of ball.)	900.00	360.00	180.00
(6b)	Babe Ruth (No arrows.)	900.00	360.00	180.00

1975 Michael Schechter Associates Test Discs

Prior to rolling out its 70-disc set in 1976, Michael Schecter Associates issued this sample set of discs the previous year. Slightly larger, at 3-9/16" diameter, than the '76 issues, the '75 sample discs share a similar format. Fronts have a black-and-white player photo from which uniform logo details have been removed due to lack of licensing by Major League Baseball. Backs are blank. The Seaver and Bench discs are considerably scarcer than the other four players in the set.

		NM	EX	VG
Complete Set (6):		175.00	90.00	55.00
Common Player:		6.00	3.00	1.75
(1)	Hank Aaron	15.00	7.50	4.50
(2)	Johnny Bench	60.00	30.00	18.00
(3)	Catfish Hunter	6.00	3.00	1.75
(4)	Fred Lynn	6.00	3.00	1.75
(5)	Pete Rose	10.00	5.00	3.00
(6)	Tom Seaver	100.00	50.00	30.00

1976 Michael Schechter Associates Discs

Following its test issue of 1975, Michael Schechter Associates ran out its baseball player disc issues on a large scale in 1976. While most were sold with specific sponsor advertising on back, they were also made available with blank backs. The discs are 3-3/8" diameter with a black-and-white player portrait photo in the center of the baseball design. A line of red stars is above, while the left and right panels feature one of several bright colors. Produced by MSA under license from the Major League Players Association, the player photos have had uniform and cap logos removed. The unnumbered discs are presented in alphabetical order.

		NM	EX	VG
Complete Set (70):		60.00	30.00	18.00
Common Player:		.50	.25	.15
(1)	Henry Aaron	12.50	6.25	3.75
(2)	Johnny Bench	6.00	3.00	1.75
(3)	Vida Blue	.50	.25	.15
(4)	Larry Bowa	.50	.25	.15
(5)	Lou Brock	4.50	2.25	1.25
(6)	Jeff Burroughs	.50	.25	.15
(7)	John Candelaria	.50	.25	.15
(8)	Jose Cardenal	.50	.25	.15
(9)	Rod Carew	6.00	3.00	1.75
(10)	Steve Carlton	4.50	2.25	1.25
(11)	Dave Cash	.50	.25	.15
(12)	Cesar Cedeno	.50	.25	.15
(13)	Ron Cey	.50	.25	.15
(14)	Carlton Fisk	4.50	2.25	1.25
(15)	Tito Fuentes	.50	.25	.15
(16)	Steve Garvey	3.00	1.50	.90
(17)	Ken Griffey	.50	.25	.15
(18)	Don Gullett	.50	.25	.15
(19)	Willie Horton	.50	.25	.15
(20)	Al Hrabosky	.50	.25	.15
(21)	Catfish Hunter	4.50	2.25	1.25
(22)	Reggie Jackson (A's)	9.00	4.50	2.75
(23)	Randy Jones	.50	.25	.15
(24)	Jim Kaat	.50	.25	.15
(25)	Don Kessinger	.50	.25	.15
(26)	Dave Kingman	.50	.25	.15
(27)	Jerry Koosman	.50	.25	.15
(28)	Mickey Lolich	.60	.30	.20
(29)	Greg Luzinski	.50	.25	.15
(30)	Fred Lynn	.50	.25	.15
(31)	Bill Madlock	.50	.25	.15
(32)	Carlos May (White Sox)	.50	.25	.15
(33)	John Mayberry	.50	.25	.15
(34)	Bake McBride	.50	.25	.15
(35)	Doc Medich	.50	.25	.15
(36)	Andy Messersmith	.50	.25	.15
(37)	Rick Monday	.50	.25	.15
(38)	John Montefusco	.50	.25	.15
(39)	Jerry Morales	.50	.25	.15
(40)	Joe Morgan	4.50	2.25	1.25
(41)	Thurman Munson	4.50	2.25	1.25
(42)	Bobby Murcer	.50	.25	.15
(43)	Al Oliver	.50	.25	.15
(44)	Jim Palmer	4.50	2.25	1.25
(45)	Dave Parker	.50	.25	.15
(46)	Tony Perez	4.50	2.25	1.25
(47)	Jerry Reuss	.50	.25	.15
(48)	Brooks Robinson	6.00	3.00	1.75
(49)	Frank Robinson	6.00	3.00	1.75
(50)	Steve Rogers	.50	.25	.15
(51)	Pete Rose	10.00	5.00	3.00
(52)	Nolan Ryan	15.00	7.50	4.50
(53)	Manny Sanguillen	.50	.25	.15
(54)	Mike Schmidt	10.00	5.00	3.00
(55)	Tom Seaver	6.00	3.00	1.75
(56)	Ted Simmons	.50	.25	.15
(57)	Reggie Smith	.50	.25	.15
(58)	Willie Stargell	4.50	2.25	1.25
(59)	Rusty Staub	.75	.40	.25
(60)	Rennie Stennett	.50	.25	.15
(61)	Don Sutton	4.50	2.25	1.25
(62)	Andy Thornton	.50	.25	.15
(63)	Luis Tiant	.50	.25	.15
(64)	Joe Torre	.50	.25	.15
(65)	Mike Tyson	.50	.25	.15
(66)	Bob Watson	.50	.25	.15
(67)	Wilbur Wood	.50	.25	.15
(68)	Jimmy Wynn	.50	.25	.15
(69)	Carl Yastrzemski	6.00	3.00	1.75
(70)	Richie Zisk	.50	.25	.15

1977 Michael Schechter Associates Cup Lids

One of MSA's early baseball novelty issues was a set of drink-cup lids. The 3-1/2" diameter pieces are made of pressed and waxed cardboard. They are 3/16" thick and have a 3/8" die-cut hole for inserting a straw. Design is similar to other MSA issues of the era, with a black-and-white player portrait photo at center of a simulated baseball design. Personal data is printed in colored panels at left and right, and there is a row of colored stars above the photo. Player caps do not show team insignia because the issue was licensed only by the players' union, and not the owners. The unnumbered lids are checklisted here in alphabetical order.

	NM	EX	VG
Complete Set (49):	700.00	350.00	225.00
Common Player:	10.00	5.00	3.00
(1) Sal Bando	10.00	5.00	3.00
(2) Johnny Bench	30.00	15.00	9.00
(3) Larry Bowa	10.00	5.00	3.00
(4) Steve Braun	10.00	5.00	3.00
(5) George Brett	100.00	50.00	30.00
(6) Lou Brock	30.00	15.00	9.00
(7) Bert Campaneris	10.00	5.00	3.00
(8) Bill Campbell	10.00	5.00	3.00
(9) Jose Cardenal	10.00	5.00	3.00
(10) Rod Carew	30.00	15.00	9.00
(11) Dave Cash	10.00	5.00	3.00
(12) Cesar Cedeno	10.00	5.00	3.00
(13) Chris Chambliss	10.00	5.00	3.00
(14) Dave Concepcion	10.00	5.00	3.00
(15) Mark Fidrych	10.00	5.00	3.00
(16) Rollie Fingers	20.00	10.00	6.00
(17) George Foster	10.00	5.00	3.00
(18) Wayne Garland	10.00	5.00	3.00
(19) Steve Garvey	20.00	10.00	6.00
(20) Cesar Geronimo	10.00	5.00	3.00
(21) Bobby Grich	10.00	5.00	3.00
(22) Don Gullett	10.00	5.00	3.00
(23) Mike Hargrove	10.00	5.00	3.00
(24) Catfish Hunter	20.00	10.00	6.00
(25) Randy Jones	10.00	5.00	3.00
(26) Dave Kingman	15.00	7.50	4.50
(27) Dave LaRoche	10.00	5.00	3.00
(28) Greg Luzinski	10.00	5.00	3.00
(29) Fred Lynn	10.00	5.00	3.00
(30) Jon Matlack	10.00	5.00	3.00
(31) Bake McBride	10.00	5.00	3.00
(32) Joe Morgan	25.00	12.50	7.50
(33) Phil Niekro	20.00	10.00	6.00
(34) Jim Palmer	25.00	12.50	7.50
(35) Dave Parker	10.00	5.00	3.00
(36) Fred Patek	10.00	5.00	3.00
(37) Mickey Rivers	10.00	5.00	3.00
(38) Brooks Robinson	30.00	15.00	9.00
(39) Pete Rose	75.00	37.00	22.00
(40) Nolan Ryan	100.00	50.00	30.00
(41) Tom Seaver (1976)	60.00	30.00	18.00
(42) Mike Schmidt	50.00	25.00	15.00
(43) Bill Singer	10.00	5.00	3.00
(44) Chris Speier	10.00	5.00	3.00
(45) Willie Stargell	25.00	12.50	7.50
(46) Luis Tiant	12.50	6.25	3.75
(47) Butch Wynegar	10.00	5.00	3.00
(48) Robin Yount	20.00	10.00	6.00
(49) Richie Zisk	10.00	5.00	3.00

1977 Mike Schechter Associates Customized Sports Discs

Virtually identical in format to the several locally sponsored disc sets of the previous year, these 3-3/8" diameter player discs once again feature black-and-white player portrait photos in the center of a baseball design. The left and right panels are in one of several bright colors. Licensed by the Players' Association, the photos carry no uniform logos. Backs of the discs are printed in dark blue and carry an ad from MSA for "Customized Sports Discs" and novelties for which Schechter held the licenses. The unnumbered discs are checklisted here alphabetically.

	NM	EX	VG
Complete Set (70):	350.00	175.00	100.00
Common Player:	3.00	1.50	.90
(1) Sal Bando	3.00	1.50	.90
(2) Buddy Bell	3.00	1.50	.90
(3) Johnny Bench	20.00	10.00	6.00
(4) Larry Bowa	3.00	1.50	.90
(5) Steve Braun	3.00	1.50	.90
(6) George Brett	125.00	62.00	37.00
(7) Lou Brock	15.00	7.50	4.50
(8) Jeff Burroughs	3.00	1.50	.90
(9) Bert Campaneris	3.00	1.50	.90
(10) John Candelaria	3.00	1.50	.90
(11) Jose Cardenal	3.00	1.50	.90
(12) Rod Carew	20.00	10.00	6.00
(13) Steve Carlton	20.00	10.00	6.00
(14) Dave Cash	3.00	1.50	.90
(15) Cesar Cedeno	3.00	1.50	.90
(16) Ron Cey	3.00	1.50	.90
(17) Dave Concepcion	3.00	1.50	.90
(18) Dennis Eckersley	15.00	7.50	4.50
(19) Mark Fidrych	6.00	3.00	1.75
(20) Rollie Fingers	15.00	7.50	4.50
(21) Carlton Fisk	15.00	7.50	4.50
(22) George Foster	3.00	1.50	.90
(23) Wayne Garland	3.00	1.50	.90
(24) Ralph Garr	3.00	1.50	.90
(25) Steve Garvey	12.50	6.25	3.75
(26) Cesar Geronimo	3.00	1.50	.90
(27) Bobby Grich	3.00	1.50	.90
(28) Ken Griffey Sr.	3.00	1.50	.90
(29) Don Gullett	3.00	1.50	.90
(30) Mike Hargrove	3.00	1.50	.90
(31) Al Hrabosky	3.00	1.50	.90
(32) Jim Hunter	15.00	7.50	4.50
(33) Reggie Jackson	30.00	15.00	9.00
(34) Randy Jones	3.00	1.50	.90
(35) Dave Kingman	5.00	2.50	1.50
(36) Jerry Koosman	3.00	1.50	.90
(37) Dave LaRoche	3.00	1.50	.90
(38) Greg Luzinski	3.00	1.50	.90
(39) Fred Lynn	3.00	1.50	.90
(40) Bill Madlock	3.00	1.50	.90
(41) Rick Manning	3.00	1.50	.90
(42) Jon Matlock	3.00	1.50	.90
(43) John Mayberry	3.00	1.50	.90
(44) Hal McRae	3.00	1.50	.90
(45) Andy Messersmith	3.00	1.50	.90
(46) Rick Monday	3.00	1.50	.90
(47) John Montefusco	3.00	1.50	.90
(48) Joe Morgan	15.00	7.50	4.50
(49) Thurman Munson	12.50	6.25	3.75
(50) Bobby Murcer	3.00	1.50	.90
(51) Bill North	3.00	1.50	.90
(52) Jim Palmer	15.00	7.50	4.50
(53) Tony Perez	15.00	7.50	4.50
(54) Jerry Reuss	3.00	1.50	.90
(55) Brooks Robinson	20.00	10.00	6.00
(56) Pete Rose	75.00	37.00	22.00
(57) Joe Rudi	3.00	1.50	.90
(58) Nolan Ryan	125.00	62.00	37.00
(59) Manny Sanguillen	3.00	1.50	.90
(60) Mike Schmidt	100.00	50.00	30.00
(61) Tom Seaver	20.00	10.00	6.00
(62) Bill Singer	3.00	1.50	.90
(63) Willie Stargell	15.00	7.50	4.50
(64) Rusty Staub	5.00	2.50	1.50
(65) Luis Tiant	3.00	1.50	.90
(66) Bob Watson	3.00	1.50	.90
(67) Butch Wynegar	3.00	1.50	.90
(68) Carl Yastrzemski	20.00	10.00	6.00
(69) Robin Yount	15.00	7.50	4.50
(70) Richie Zisk	3.00	1.50	.90

1915 Schmelzer's Sporting Goods Pins

The date of issue attributed is speculative, based on the limited checklist currently available. These pin-back celluloid buttons measure about 1-1/4" in diameter. A color lithographed figure of a generic ballplayer shares the front with a smaller inset black-and-white photo of an actual player and a fancy script position designation. The player's last name appears at the bottom of the photo. Issuer identification is on back. It is presumed at least one pinback was issued for each of the nine positions.

		NM	EX	VG
Common Player:		350.00	175.00	105.00
RF	"Ty" Cobb	26,250	13,125	7,500
3B	Charlie Deal	5,625	2,813	1,688
C	Hank Gowdy	5,625	2,813	1,688
LF	Hoffman	5,625	2,813	1,688
CF	Joe Jackson	12,000	6,000	3,600
P	Christy Mathewson	6,750	3,375	2,025
SS	Rabbit Maranville	5,625	2,813	1,688
1B	Butch Schmidt	5,625	2,813	1,688

1921 C. Shulz Baseball Card Game

While this catalog generally does not attempt to list game cards which do not depict actual ballplayers, this set is considered exceptional due to its format similarity to the popularly collected 1922 American Caramel issue known as E120. Backs of the game cards are printed in blue on white and reproduce the border design of the National League cards of E120. The unnamed photo of Heinie Groh on back is identical to that on E120, except uniform lettering has been airbrushed away on the game card. Backs are printed in red with a ball-game situation. The credit line on back reads, "Instructions Copyrighted 1921 by C. Schulz." The game cards measure about 2-1/2" x 3-1/2".

	NM	EX	VG
Common Card:	35.00	17.50	10.00

1949 Schumacher Service Station

Because some of these cards have been found with the advertising of Schumacher Service Station (location unknown) printed in red on the back, the issue is so designated for cataloging purposes. Given that the (living) players from this set were with their respective teams in 1949-1950, the issue date could be either year. Measuring 2-5/8" x 3-9/16", the cards are black-and-white on the front. It is unknown whether other players were issued in this series.

	NM	EX	VG
Complete Set (9):	2,200	1,100	650.00
Common Player:	200.00	100.00	60.00
(1) Joe Garagiola	250.00	125.00	75.00
(2) Marty Marion	225.00	110.00	65.00
(3) Les Moss	200.00	100.00	60.00
(4) George (Red) Munger	200.00	100.00	60.00
(5) Don Newcomb (Newcombe)	250.00	125.00	75.00
(6) Howard Pollet	200.00	100.00	60.00
(7) George Herman (Babe) Ruth	600.00	300.00	180.00
(8) Red Schoendienst	250.00	125.00	75.00
(9) Vernon Stephens	200.00	100.00	60.00

1935 Schutter-Johnson (R332)

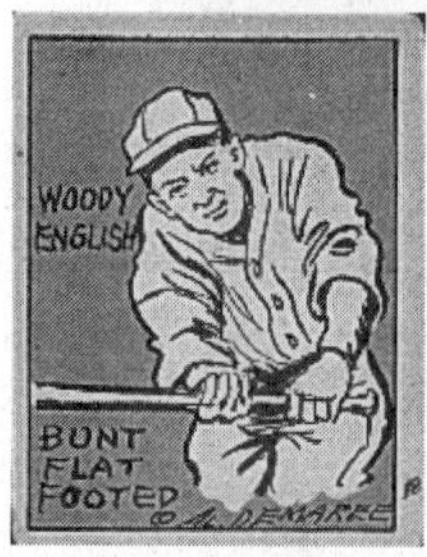

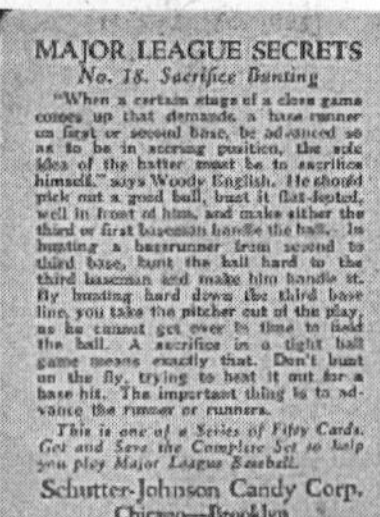
MAJOR LEAGUE SECRETS
No. 18. Sacrifice Bunting

"When a certain stage of a close game comes up that demands a base runner on first or second base, be advanced so as to be in scoring position, the sole idea of the batter must be to sacrifice himself," says Woody English. He should pick out a good ball, bunt it flat-footed, well in front of him, and make either the third or first baseman handle the ball. In bunting a baserunner from second to third base, bunt the ball hard to the third baseman and make him handle it. By bunting hard down the third base line, you take the pitcher out of the play, as he cannot get over in time to field the ball. A sacrifice in a tight ball game means exactly that. Don't bunt on the fly, trying to beat it out for a base hit. The important thing is to advance the runner or runners.

This is one of a Series of Fifty Cards. Get and Save the Complete Set to help you play Major League Baseball.

Schutter-Johnson Candy Corp.
Chicago—Brooklyn

This 50-card set was issued by the Schutter- Johnson Candy Corp. of Chicago and Brooklyn circa 1930 and features drawings of major league players offering baseball playing tips. The cards measure 2-1/4" x 2-7/8". The drawings on the front are set against a red background while the backs are titled "Major League Secrets" and give the player's advice on some aspect of the game. The Scutter-Johnson name appears at the bottom.

	NM	EX	VG
Complete Set (50):	17,500	7,000	3,500
Common Player:	200.00	100.00	50.00
1 Al Simmons	350.00	140.00	70.00
2 Lloyd Waner	275.00	110.00	55.00
3 Kiki Cuyler	275.00	110.00	55.00
4 Frank Frisch	275.00	110.00	55.00
5 Chick Hafey	275.00	110.00	55.00
6 Bill Klem (Umpire)	450.00	180.00	90.00
7 Rogers Hornsby	300.00	120.00	60.00
8 Carl Mays	200.00	100.00	50.00
9 Chas. Wrigley (Umpire)	275.00	110.00	55.00
10 Christy Mathewson	900.00	360.00	180.00
11 Bill Dickey	275.00	110.00	55.00
12 Walter Berger	200.00	100.00	50.00
13 George Earnshaw	200.00	100.00	50.00
14 Hack Wilson	275.00	110.00	55.00
15 Charley Grimm	200.00	100.00	50.00
16 Lloyd Waner, Paul Waner	275.00	110.00	55.00
17 Chuck Klein	275.00	110.00	55.00
18 Woody English	200.00	100.00	50.00
19 Grover Alexander	300.00	120.00	60.00
20 Lou Gehrig	2,000	800.00	400.00
21 Wes Ferrell	200.00	100.00	50.00
22 Carl Hubbell	300.00	120.00	60.00
23 Pie Traynor	275.00	110.00	55.00
24 Gus Mancuso	200.00	100.00	50.00
25 Ben Cantwell	200.00	100.00	50.00
26 Babe Ruth	2,350	940.00	470.00
27 "Goose" Goslin	275.00	110.00	55.00
28 Earle Combs	275.00	110.00	55.00
29 "Kiki" Cuyler	275.00	110.00	55.00
30 Jimmy Wilson	200.00	100.00	50.00

31	Dizzy Dean	450.00	180.00	90.00
32	Mickey Cochrane	275.00	110.00	55.00
33	Ted Lyons	275.00	110.00	55.00
34	Si Johnson	200.00	100.00	50.00
35	Dizzy Dean	450.00	180.00	90.00
36	Pepper Martin	225.00	90.00	45.00
37	Joe Cronin	275.00	110.00	55.00
38	Gabby Hartnett	275.00	110.00	55.00
39	Oscar Melillo	200.00	100.00	50.00
40	Ben Chapman	200.00	100.00	50.00
41	John McGraw	275.00	110.00	55.00
42	Babe Ruth	2,350	940.00	470.00
43	"Red" Lucas	200.00	100.00	50.00
44	Charley Root	200.00	100.00	50.00
45	Dazzy Vance	275.00	110.00	55.00
46	Hugh Critz	200.00	100.00	50.00
47	"Firpo" Marberry	200.00	100.00	50.00
48	Grover Alexander	300.00	120.00	60.00
49	Lefty Grove	325.00	130.00	65.00
50	Heinie Meine	200.00	100.00	50.00

1888 "Scrapps Tobacco" Die-Cuts

The origin of these die-cut, embossed player busts is not known, but they were apparently part of a book of "punch-outs" issued in the late 1880s. When out of their original album, they apparently resembled scraps of paper, presumably leading to their unusual name. An earlier theory that they were issued by "Scrapps Tobacco" has since been discounted after research indicated there never was such a company. The die-cuts include 18 different players - nine members of the American Association St. Louis Browns and nine from the National League Detroit Wolverines. Although they vary slightly in size, the player busts are generally about 2" wide and 3" high. The drawings for the St. Louis player busts were taken from the Old Judge "Brown's Champions" set. The player's name appears along the bottom.

		NM	EX	VG
Complete Set (18):		35,000	14,000	7,000
Common Player:		1,800	725.00	360.00
(1)	C.W. Bennett	1,800	725.00	360.00
(2)	D. Brouthers	2,400	960.00	480.00
(3)	A.J. Bushong	1,800	725.00	360.00
(4)	Robert L. Caruthers	1,800	725.00	360.00
(5)	Charles Comiskey	2,400	960.00	480.00
(6)	F. Dunlap	1,800	725.00	360.00
(7)	David L. Foutz	1,800	725.00	360.00
(8)	C.H. Getzen (Getzien)	1,800	725.00	360.00
(9)	Wm. Gleason	1,800	725.00	360.00
(10)	E. Hanlon	2,400	960.00	480.00
(11)	Walter A. Latham	1,800	725.00	360.00
(12)	James O'Neill	1,800	725.00	360.00
(13)	H. Richardson	1,800	725.00	360.00
(14)	Wm. Robinson	2,400	960.00	480.00
(15)	J.C. Rowe	1,800	725.00	360.00
(16)	S. Thompson	2,400	960.00	480.00
(17)	Curtis Welch	1,800	725.00	360.00
(18)	J.L. White	1,800	725.00	360.00

1949 Sealtest Phillies Stickers

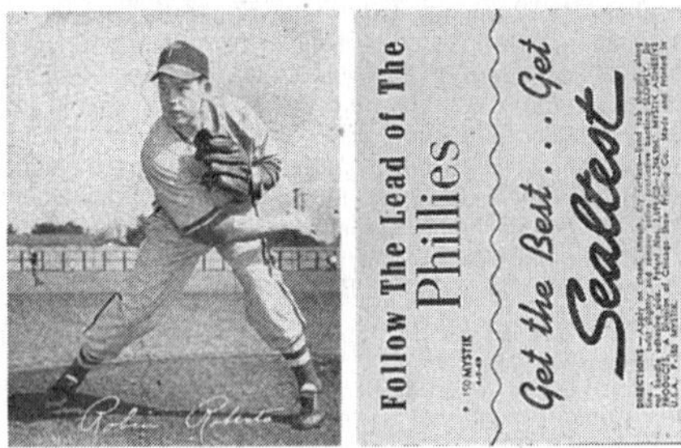

This regional Phillies set was issued in the Philadelphia area in 1949 by Sealtest Dairy. It consisted of 12 large (3-1/2" by 4-1/4") sticker cards with peel-off backs. The front of the unnumbered cards featured an action photo with facsimilie autograph, while the back has an advertisement for Sealtest products. The same format, photos and checklist were also used for the Lummis Peanut Butter card set issued in Philadelphia the same year.

		NM	EX	VG
Complete Set (12):		2,800	1,400	850.00
Common Player:		250.00	125.00	75.00
(1)	Rich Ashburn	700.00	350.00	210.00
(2)	Hank Borowy	250.00	125.00	75.00
(3)	Del Ennis	260.00	130.00	78.00
(4)	Granny Hamner	250.00	125.00	75.00
(5)	Puddinhead Jones	250.00	125.00	75.00
(6)	Russ Meyer	250.00	125.00	75.00
(7)	Bill Nicholson	250.00	125.00	75.00
(8)	Robin Roberts	700.00	350.00	210.00
(9)	"Schoolboy" Rowe	250.00	125.00	75.00
(10)	Andy Seminick	250.00	125.00	75.00
(11)	Curt Simmons	300.00	150.00	90.00
(12)	Eddie Waitkus	250.00	125.00	75.00

1946 Sears St. Louis Browns/ Cardinals Postcards

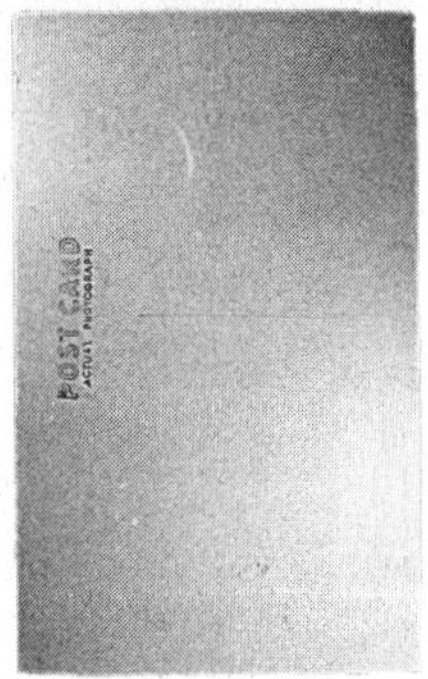

One of the more popular issues of the immediate post-war period are the black-and-white postcards of St. Louis Browns and Cardinals players issued by Sears in East St. Louis. The 3-1/2" x 5-3/8" postcards have posed player portraits on front with the player's name and Sears "Compliments of" line in the white border beneath. Backs are stamped "POST CARD / ACTUAL PHOTOGRAPH." The cards were reported to have been issued in groups of five on a bi-weekly basis, sold both at the Sears store and through the mail. The unnumbered cards are checklisted here alphabetically within team.

		NM	EX	VG
Complete Set (69):		8,000	4,000	2,400
Common Player:		100.00	50.00	30.00
	St. Louis Browns Set (33):	3,000	1,500	900.00
(1)	John Berardino	200.00	100.00	60.00
(2)	Frank Biscan	100.00	50.00	30.00
(3)	Mark Christman	100.00	50.00	30.00
(4)	Babe Dahlgren	100.00	50.00	30.00
(5)	Bob Dillinger	100.00	50.00	30.00
(6)	Stanley Ferens	100.00	50.00	30.00
(7)	Denny Galehouse	100.00	50.00	30.00
(8)	Joe Grace	100.00	50.00	30.00
(9)	Jeff Heath	100.00	50.00	30.00
(10)	Henry Helf	100.00	50.00	30.00
(11)	Fred Hoffman	100.00	50.00	30.00
(12)	Walt Judnich	100.00	50.00	30.00
(13)	Ellis Kinder	100.00	50.00	30.00
(14)	Jack Kramer	100.00	50.00	30.00
(15)	Chet Laabs	100.00	50.00	30.00
(16)	Al LaMacchia	125.00	65.00	35.00
(17)	John Lucadello	100.00	50.00	30.00
(18)	Frank Mancuso	100.00	50.00	30.00
(19)	Glenn McQuillen	100.00	50.00	30.00
(20)	John Miller	100.00	50.00	30.00
(21)	Al Milnar	150.00	75.00	45.00
(22)	Bob Muncrief	100.00	50.00	30.00
(23)	Nelson Potter	100.00	50.00	30.00
(24)	Ken Sears	100.00	50.00	30.00
(25)	Len Schulte	100.00	50.00	30.00
(26)	Luke Sewell	100.00	50.00	30.00
(27)	Joe Schultz	100.00	50.00	30.00
(28)	Tex Shirley	100.00	50.00	30.00
(29)	Vern Stephens	100.00	50.00	30.00
(30)	Chuck Stevens	100.00	50.00	30.00
(31)	Zack Taylor	100.00	50.00	30.00
(32)	Al Zarilla	100.00	50.00	30.00
(33)	Sam Zoldak	100.00	50.00	30.00
	St. Louis Cardinals Set (36):	5,000	2,500	1,500
(1)	Buster Adams	100.00	50.00	30.00
(2)	Red Barrett	100.00	50.00	30.00
(3)	Johnny Beazley	100.00	50.00	30.00
(4)	Al Brazle	100.00	50.00	30.00
(5)	Harry Brecheen	100.00	50.00	30.00
(6)	Ken Burkhart	100.00	50.00	30.00
(7)	Joffre Cross	100.00	50.00	30.00
(8)	Murray Dickson	100.00	50.00	30.00
(9)	George Dockins	100.00	50.00	30.00
(10)	Blix Donnelly	150.00	75.00	45.00
(11)	Erv Dusak	100.00	50.00	30.00
(12)	Eddie Dyer	100.00	50.00	30.00
(13)	Bill Endicott	100.00	50.00	30.00
(14)	Joe Garagiola	400.00	200.00	120.00
(15)	Mike Gonzales (Gonzalez)	125.00	65.00	35.00
(16)	Lou Klein	100.00	50.00	30.00
(17)	Clyde Kluttz	100.00	50.00	30.00
(18)	Howard Krist	100.00	50.00	30.00
(19)	George Kurowski	100.00	50.00	30.00
(20)	Danny Litwhiler	100.00	50.00	30.00
(21)	Marty Marion	150.00	75.00	45.00
(22)	Fred Martin	100.00	50.00	30.00
(23)	Terry Moore	125.00	65.00	35.00
(24)	Stan Musial	1,000	500.00	300.00
(25)	Ken O'Dea	100.00	50.00	30.00
(26)	Howard Pollet	100.00	50.00	30.00
(27)	Del Rice	100.00	50.00	30.00
(28)	Red Schoendienst	300.00	150.00	90.00
(29)	Walt Sessi	100.00	50.00	30.00
(30)	Dick Sisler	100.00	50.00	30.00
(31)	Enos Slaughter	300.00	150.00	90.00
(32)	Max Surkont	100.00	50.00	30.00
(33)	Harry Walker	100.00	50.00	30.00
(34)	Buzzy Wares	100.00	50.00	30.00
(35)	Ernie White	100.00	50.00	30.00
(36)	Ted Wilks	100.00	50.00	30.00

1969 Seattle Pilots Premium Pictures

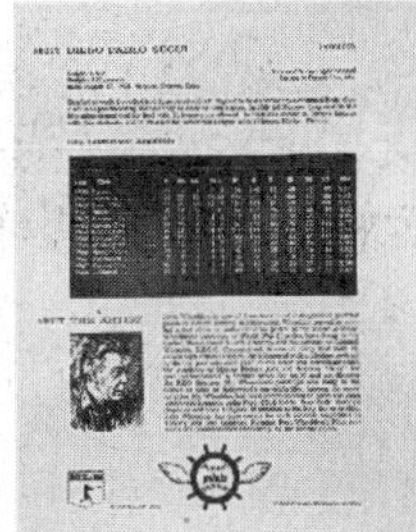

This set of 8-1/2" x 11" premium pictures is based on the artwork of John Wheeldon, who did contemporary issues for the Mets, Twins and Red Sox, as well. The pastels feature large portraits and smaller action pictures with a large facsimile autograph at bottom. Backs are in black-and-white and feature biographical data, comprehensive career summary and complete minor and major league stats. There is a self-portrait and biographical sketch of the artist on back, as well. The premiums were given away at selected Pilots home games during their lone season in Seattle. They were later sold for 25 cents each in the concession stand. The unnumbered pictures are checklisted here in alphabetical order.

		NM	EX	VG
Complete Set (8):		75.00	37.00	22.00
Common Player:		8.00	4.00	2.50
(1)	Wayne Comer	8.00	4.00	2.50
(2)	Tommy Harper	10.00	5.00	3.00
(3)	Mike Hegan	8.00	4.00	2.50
(4)	Jerry McNertney	8.00	4.00	2.50
(5)	Don Mincher	8.00	4.00	2.50
(6)	Ray Oyler	8.00	4.00	2.50
(7)	Marty Pattin	8.00	4.00	2.50
(8)	Diego Segui	8.00	4.00	2.50

1963 Mickey Sego S.F. Giants

These self-framing picutres feature the artwork of Mickey Sego, but the method of their distribution is unknown. Measuring 7" x 8-1/2", the pieces have a dark frame around a large black-and-white portrait and smaller cartoon drawing of the player. There are also a few words about the player's career. A simulated plaque at the bottom of the frame bears a facsimile autograph. Each picture has a hole at top for hanging.

		NM	EX	VG
Common Player:		15.00	7.50	4.50
(1)	Chuck Hiller	15.00	7.50	4.50
(2)	Harvey Kuenn	20.00	10.00	6.00
(3)	Willie Mays	85.00	42.00	25.00
(4)	Billy Pierce	17.50	8.75	5.25

1914 Lawrence Semon Postcards

Seven players are currently known in this series, but it's possible others remain to be reported. The approximately 3-1/2" x 5-1/2" postcards feature on their fronts either portrait or action drawings of star players by Lawrence Semon. A few biographical and career details are printed at bottom, which have allowed the assignment of 1914 as the year of issue. Backs are standard postcard style. The unnumbered cards are checklisted here alphabetically.

	NM	EX	VG
Common Player:	250.00	125.00	75.00
(1) George Burns	250.00	125.00	75.00
(2) Frank Chance	500.00	250.00	150.00
(3) Ty Cobb	2,500	1,250	750.00
(4) Walter Johnson	2,250	1,125	675.00
(5) Cornelius McGillicuddy (Connie Mack)	400.00	200.00	120.00
(6) Richard (Rube) Marquard	400.00	200.00	120.00
(7) John J. McGraw	400.00	200.00	120.00

1946-1947 Sensacion Premiums

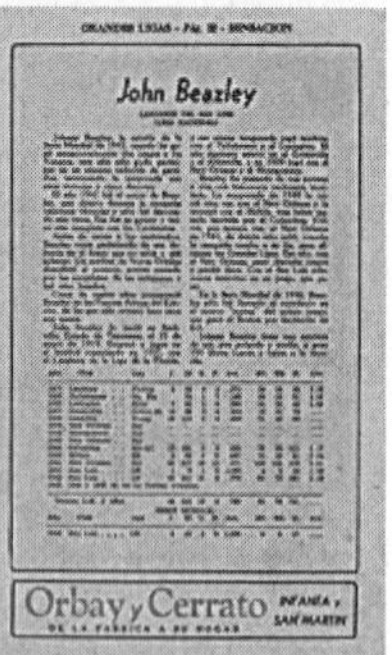

Two types of baseball premium pictures were issued by the magazine "Sensacion" during the winter league season of 1946-47. One series of 27 features Cuban stars (some of whom played in the Major Leagues), while a series of 11 Major League stars was also issued. Printed in color on newspaper stock, the pictures measure about 7-3/4" x 11". Fronts have large portraits or posed action photos with the player name in a fancy bottom border. Backs have lengthy career summaries and full stats, along with a small ad. The premiums were issued in magazines as well as in a complete album of each type. They are numbered according to the apparent order of their appearance.

	NM	EX	VG
Complete Set, Cubans (27):	1,500	750.00	450.00
Complete Set, Major Leaguers (11):	600.00	300.00	175.00
Common Cuban Player:	30.00	15.00	9.00
Common Major Leaguer:	45.00	22.50	13.50
Estrellas del Base Ball Cubano			
(1) Napoleon Reyes	45.00	22.50	13.50
(2) Fermin Guerra	30.00	15.00	9.00
(3) Gilberto Torres	30.00	15.00	9.00
(4) Martin Dihigo	750.00	375.00	225.00
(5) Lazaro Salazar	100.00	50.00	30.00
(6) Silvio Garcia	100.00	50.00	30.00
(7) Pollo Rodriguez	30.00	15.00	9.00
(8) Herberto Blanco	30.00	15.00	9.00
(9) Andres Fleitas	30.00	15.00	9.00
(10) Jorge J. Torres	30.00	15.00	9.00
(11) Salvador Hernandez	30.00	15.00	9.00
(12) Agapito Mayor	30.00	15.00	9.00
(13) Tomas de la Cruz	30.00	15.00	9.00
(14) Gilberto Valdivia	30.00	15.00	9.00
(15) Julio Moreno	30.00	15.00	9.00
(16) Regino Otero	30.00	15.00	9.00
(17) Claro Duany	50.00	25.00	15.00
(18) Pedro Jimenez	30.00	15.00	9.00
(19) Tony Castanos	30.00	15.00	9.00
(20) Alberto Hernandez	30.00	15.00	9.00
(21) Hector Rodriguez	40.00	20.00	12.00
(22) Carlos Blanco	30.00	15.00	9.00
(23) Roberto Ortiz	50.00	25.00	15.00
(24) Rene Monteagudo	30.00	15.00	9.00
(25) Pedro Pages	30.00	15.00	9.00
(26) Conrado Marrero	40.00	20.00	12.00
(27) Chino Hidalgo	30.00	15.00	9.00
Estrellas de las Grandes Ligas			
(1) Stan Musial	150.00	75.00	45.00
(2) Jim (Mickey) Vernon	50.00	25.00	15.00
(3) Dave Ferris	45.00	22.50	13.50
(4) Johnny Pesky	45.00	22.50	13.50
(5) Howie Pollett	45.00	22.50	13.50
(6) Ted Williams	200.00	100.00	60.00
(7) Johnny Hopp	45.00	22.50	13.50
(8) Dom DiMaggio	75.00	37.00	22.00
(9) Tex Hughson	45.00	22.50	13.50
(10) Johnny Beazley	45.00	22.00	13.50
(11) Tommy Holmes	45.00	22.50	13.50

1977 Sertoma Stars

This collectors' issue was produced by an Indianapolis service club. The 3" x 4" cards are printed in black on a textured yellow stock. Fronts have borderless player poses, many of which were lifted from earlier-issued cards. Backs have the Sertoma logo, set name and player name at top. Beneath a squiggly line is a business-card size ad for different members of the organization.

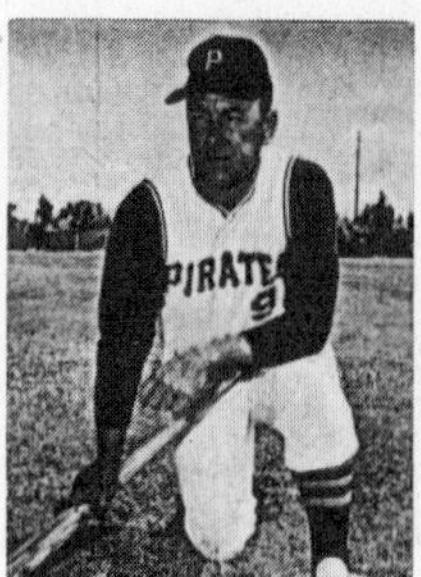

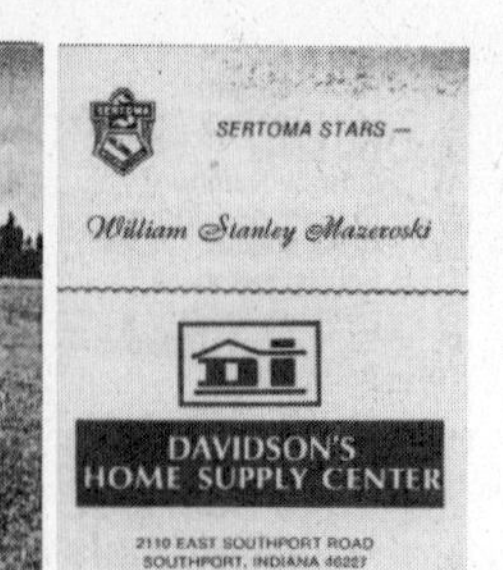

	NM	EX	VG
Complete Set (24):	45.00	22.50	13.50
Common Player:	2.00	1.00	.60
(1) Hank Aaron	10.00	5.00	3.00
(2) Bob Allison	2.00	.75	.60
(3) Clete Boyer	2.00	.75	.60
(4) Don Buford	2.00	.75	.60
(5) Rod Carew	3.00	1.50	.90
(6) Rico Carty	2.00	.75	.60
(7) Roberto Clemente	15.00	7.50	4.50
(8) Jim Ray Hart	2.00	.75	.60
(9) Dave Johnson	2.00	.75	.60
(10) Harmon Killebrew	3.00	1.50	.90
(11) Mickey Mantle	20.00	10.00	6.00
(12) Juan Marichal	3.00	1.50	.90
(13) Bill Mazeroski	3.00	1.50	.90
(14) Joe Morgan	3.00	1.50	.90
(15) Phil Niekro	2.50	1.25	.70
(16) Tony Oliva	2.00	1.00	.60
(17) Gaylord Perry	2.50	1.25	.70
(18) Boog Powell	2.00	1.00	.60
(19) Brooks Robinson	3.50	1.75	1.00
(20) Frank Robinson	3.50	1.75	1.00
(21) John Roseboro	2.00	.75	.60
(22) Rusty Staub	2.00	.75	.60
(23) Joe Torre	2.00	1.00	.60
(24) Jim Wynn	2.00	.75	.60

1977 Sertoma Stars - Puzzle Backs

This collectors set was issued in conjunction with the Indianapolis Sports Collectors Convention in 1977. The set was sold for $3 with proceeds benefiting the local Sertoma (Service to Mankind) Club's charity works. Cards measure 2-3/4" x 4-1/8". A 2-1/2" black circle at center contains a black-and-white player photo. The background on front is yellow, with red and black printing. Backs are borderless and form an old Pittsburgh Pirates team photo puzzle. Sets were originally sold for $3.50.

	NM	EX	VG
Complete Set (25):	75.00	37.50	22.50
Common Player:	2.00	1.00	.60
(1) Bernie Allen	2.00	1.00	.60
(2) Home Run Baker	2.00	1.00	.60
(3) Ted Beard	2.00	1.00	.60
(4) Don Buford	2.00	1.00	.60
(5) Eddie Cicotte	4.00	2.00	1.25
(6) Roberto Clemente	20.00	10.00	6.00
(7) Dom Dallessandro	2.00	1.00	.60
(8) Carl Erskine	2.00	1.00	.60
(9) Nellie Fox	6.00	3.00	1.75
(10) Lou Gehrig	20.00	10.00	6.00
(11) Joe Jackson	20.00	10.00	6.00
(12) Len Johnston	2.00	1.00	.60
(13) Benny Kauff	2.00	1.00	.60
(14) Dick Kenworthy	2.00	1.00	.60
(15) Harmon Killebrew	6.00	3.00	1.75
(16) "Lefty Bob" Logan	2.00	1.00	.60
(17) Willie Mays	15.00	7.50	4.50
(18) Satchel Paige	9.00	4.50	2.75
(19) Edd Roush	2.00	1.00	.60
(20) Chico Ruiz	2.00	1.00	.60
(21) Babe Ruth	20.00	10.00	6.00
(22) Herb Score	2.00	1.00	.60
(23) George Sisler	2.00	1.00	.60
(24) Buck Weaver	5.00	2.50	1.50
(25) Early Wynn	2.00	1.00	.60

1961 7-11

The first of 7-11's baseball card issues was a crude attempt which was abruptly halted. The checklist for the 30-card set indicated that it was the first of planned series to be issued two weeks apart. No follow-up to the first series was ever distributed.

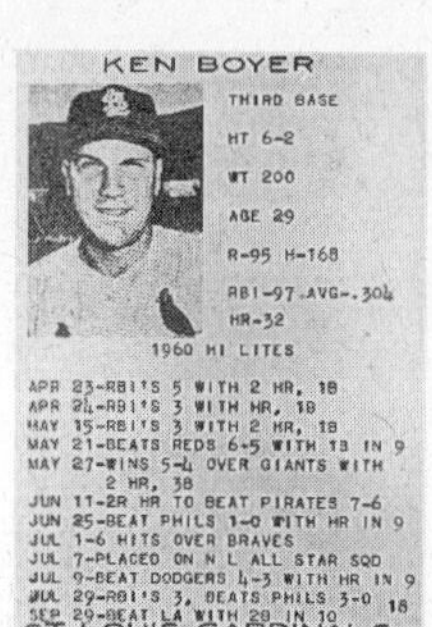

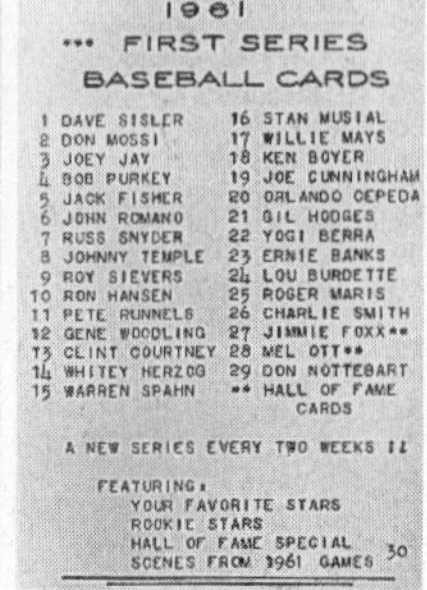

The 2-7/16" x 3-3/8" cards are printed on pink cardboard stock, with blank backs. Small black-and-white player portraits appear in the upper-left, with the player name at top, team name at bottom and card number in the lower-right corner. There are a few biographical bits and stats to the right of the photo, and several lines of 1960 season highlights below. The cards were sold seven for a nickel in vending machines.

	NM	EX	VG
Complete Set (30):	2,400	1,200	725.00
Common Player:	50.00	25.00	15.00
1 Dave Sisler	50.00	25.00	15.00
2 Don Mossi	50.00	25.00	15.00
3 Joey Jay	50.00	25.00	15.00
4 Bob Purkey	50.00	25.00	15.00
5 Jack Fisher	50.00	25.00	15.00
6 John Romano	50.00	25.00	15.00
7 Russ Snyder	50.00	25.00	15.00
8 Johnny Temple	50.00	25.00	15.00
9 Roy Sievers	50.00	25.00	15.00
10 Ron Hansen	50.00	25.00	15.00
11 Pete Runnels	50.00	25.00	15.00
12 Gene Woodling	50.00	25.00	15.00
13 Clint Courtney	50.00	25.00	15.00
14 Whitey Herzog	50.00	25.00	15.00
15 Warren Spahn	120.00	60.00	35.00
16 Stan Musial	250.00	125.00	75.00
17 Willie Mays	400.00	200.00	120.00
18 Ken Boyer	60.00	30.00	18.00
19 Joe Cunningham	50.00	25.00	15.00
20 Orlando Cepeda	90.00	45.00	27.00
21 Gil Hodges	125.00	65.00	35.00
22 Yogi Berra	150.00	75.00	45.00
23 Ernie Banks	200.00	100.00	60.00
24 Lou Burdette	50.00	25.00	15.00
25 Roger Maris	250.00	125.00	75.00
26 Charlie Smith	50.00	25.00	15.00
27 Jimmie Foxx	50.00	25.00	15.00
28 Mel Ott	50.00	25.00	15.00
29 Don Nottebart	50.00	25.00	15.00
---- Checklist	50.00	25.00	15.00

1975 Shakey's Pizza West Coast Greats

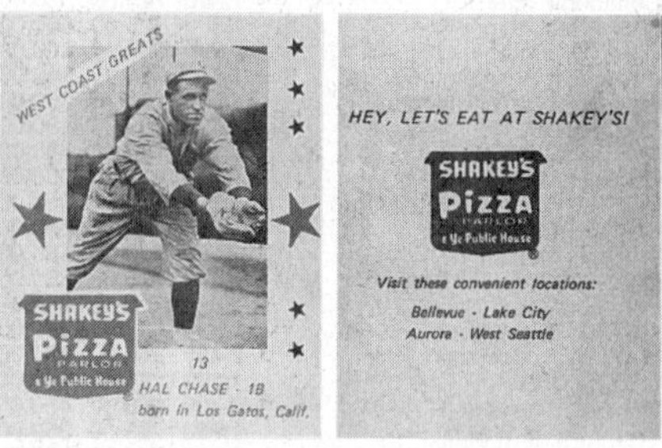

This collectors' issue was sponsored by Seattle area Shakey's Pizza restaurants in conjunction with the 1975 convention of the Washington State Sports Collectors Assn. Two thousand sets were produced featuring players who were born and/or played on the West Coast. The first 1,000 attendees at the convention were given a free sample of card #1, DiMaggio. Cards are 2-3/4" x about 3-5/8". Fronts have a black-and-white photo at center with black and red graphics. A large Shakey's logo is at lower-left. The card number, player name, position and connection to the West Coast are printed at lower-right. Backs are in red and white with the pizza chain's logo and a list of four Seattle-area locations.

	NM	EX	VG
Complete Set (18):	30.00	15.00	9.00
Common Player:	4.00	2.00	1.25
1 Joe DiMaggio	15.00	7.50	4.50
2 Paul Waner	4.00	2.00	1.25
3 Lefty Gomez	4.00	2.00	1.25
4 Earl Averill	4.00	2.00	1.25
5 Ernie Lombardi	4.00	2.00	1.25
6 Joe Cronin	4.00	2.00	1.25
7 George Burns	4.00	2.00	1.25
8 Casey Stengel	5.00	2.50	1.50
9 Wahoo Sam Crawford	4.00	2.00	1.25
10 Ted Williams	12.50	6.25	3.75
11 Fred Hutchinson	4.00	2.00	1.25
12 Duke Snider	7.50	3.75	2.25
13 Hal Chase	4.00	2.00	1.25
14 Bobby Doerr	4.00	2.00	1.25
15 Arky Vaughan	4.00	2.00	1.25

16	Tony Lazzeri	4.00	2.00	1.25
17	Lefty O'Doul	4.00	2.00	1.25
18	Stan Hack	4.00	2.00	1.25

1976 Shakey's Pizza Hall of Fame

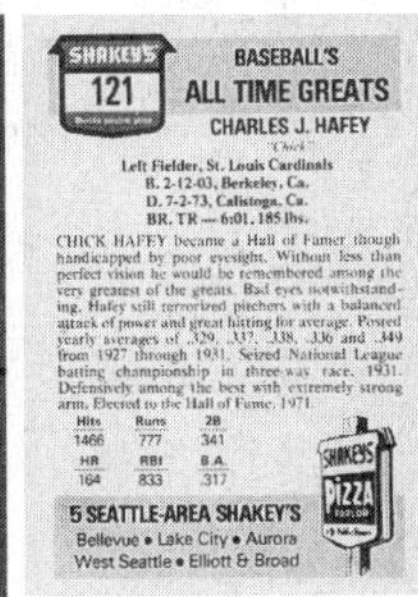

Between 1975-77 the Washington State Sports Collectors Assn. worked with the Shakey's pizza chain in the Seattle area to produce and distribute several sets of "old timers" cards. Generally one card from the set was given away to hobbyists attending the club's annual convention, with other cards available at the pizza places. Complete sets were also widely sold within the hobby. Interpretation of whether these are "legitimate" cards or a collector issue is up to each collector. The 1976 cards were issued in four series: Hall of Fame, Greatest Players, Immortals and All-Time Greats. The format was identical, with the (approximately) 2-1/2" x 3-1/2" cards featuring black-and-white player photos on front, surrounded by a red frame and bright blue border. Backs are in red, black and white with large Shakey ads at top and bottom. Also on back are player biographies and career stats. The cards were issued in order of the players' induction into the Hall of Fame. All four series are skip-numbered. Cards of Sam Thompson and Robin Roberts were re-issued in Series 2 to correct errors.

		NM	EX	VG
	Complete Set (160):	100.00	50.00	30.00
	Complete Set, no coupons (158):	75.00	37.50	22.00
	Common Player:	2.00	1.00	.60
	Series 1 - Baseball's Hall of Fame	35.00	17.50	10.50
A	Earl Averill ($1 off pizza coupon on back; card show giveaway)	4.00	2.00	1.25
1	Ty Cobb	7.50	3.75	2.25
3	Walter Johnson	3.00	1.50	.90
12	Connie Mack	2.00	1.00	.60
18	Lou Gehrig	9.00	4.50	2.75
20	George Sisler	2.00	1.00	.60
21	Cap Anson	2.00	1.00	.60
36	Mike "King" Kelly	2.00	1.00	.60
41	Jack Chesbro	2.00	1.00	.60
50	Mickey Cochrane	2.00	1.00	.60
52	Lefty Grove	2.00	1.00	.60
54	Herb Pennock	2.00	1.00	.60
55	Pie Traynor	2.00	1.00	.60
56	Charlie Gehringer	2.00	1.00	.60
57	Three-Finger Brown	2.00	1.00	.60
58	Kid Nichols	2.00	1.00	.60
59	Jimmie Foxx	2.00	1.00	.60
64	Al Simmons	2.00	1.00	.60
72	Rabbit Maranville	2.00	1.00	.60
73	Bill Terry	2.00	1.00	.60
80	Joe Cronin	2.00	1.00	.60
83	Joe McCarthy	2.00	1.00	.60
86	Bill Hamilton	2.00	1.00	.60
88	Jackie Robinson	7.50	3.75	2.25
89	Bill McKechnie	2.00	1.00	.60
93	Sam Rice	2.00	1.00	.60
95	Luke Appling	2.00	1.00	.60
103	Ted Williams	7.50	3.75	2.25
104	Casey Stengel	2.00	1.00	.60
107	Lloyd Waner	2.00	1.00	.60
108	Joe Medwick	2.00	1.00	.60
115	Lou Boudreau	2.00	1.00	.60
122	Harry Hooper	2.00	1.00	.60
127	Yogi Berra	3.00	1.50	.90
129	Lefty Gomez	2.00	1.00	.60
131	Sandy Koufax	7.50	3.75	2.25
143	Jocko Conlan	2.00	1.00	.60
144	Whitey Ford	2.00	1.00	.60
146	Sam Thompson	2.00	1.00	.60
147	Earl Averill	2.00	1.00	.60
149	Billy Herman	2.00	1.00	.60
154	Cal Hubbard	2.00	1.00	.60
156	Fred Lindstrom	2.00	1.00	.60
157	Robin Roberts	2.00	1.00	.60
	Series 2 - Baseball's Greatest Players	35.00	17.50	10.50
A	Earl Averill (Card show giveaway, coupon on back.)	2.00	1.00	.60
4	Christy Mathewson	3.00	1.50	.90
6	Nap Lajoie	2.00	1.00	.60
7	Tris Speaker	2.00	1.00	.60
9	Morgan Bulkeley	2.00	1.00	.60
10	Ban Johnson	2.00	1.00	.60
11	John McGraw	2.00	1.00	.60
14	Grover Alexander	2.00	1.00	.60
17	Eddie Collins	2.00	1.00	.60
19	Willie Keeler	2.00	1.00	.60
22	Charles Comiskey	2.00	1.00	.60
24	Buck Ewing	2.00	1.00	.60
31	Fred Clarke	2.00	1.00	.60
32	Jimmy Collins	2.00	1.00	.60
34	Hugh Duffy	2.00	1.00	.60
35	Hugh Jennings	2.00	1.00	.60
38	Wilbert Robinson	2.00	1.00	.60
40	Frank Chance	2.00	1.00	.60
42	John Evers	2.00	1.00	.60
43	Clark Griffith	2.00	1.00	.60
47	Joe Tinker	2.00	1.00	.60
51	Frank Frisch	2.00	1.00	.60
53	Carl Hubbell	2.00	1.00	.60
65	Ed Barrow	2.00	1.00	.60
66	Chief Bender	2.00	1.00	.60
67	Tommy Connolly	2.00	1.00	.60
74	Joe DiMaggio	12.50	6.25	3.75
75	Gabby Hartnett	2.00	1.00	.60
78	Home Run Baker	2.00	1.00	.60
81	Hank Greenberg	3.00	1.50	.90
87	Bob Feller	2.00	1.00	.60
90	Edd Roush	2.00	1.00	.60
109	Kiki Cuyler	2.00	1.00	.60
111	Roy Campanella	4.00	2.00	1.25
113	Stan Coveleski	2.00	1.00	.60
116	Earle Combs	2.00	1.00	.60
120	Jake Beckley	2.00	1.00	.60
125	Satchel Paige	4.00	2.00	1.25
128	Josh Gibson	3.00	1.50	.90
135	Roberto Clemente	10.00	5.00	3.00
141	Cool Papa Bell	2.00	1.00	.60
142	Jim Bottomley	2.00	1.00	.60
146	Sam Thompson	2.00	1.00	.60
150	Judy Johnson	2.00	1.00	.60
152	Oscar Charleston	2.00	1.00	.60
158	Robin Roberts	2.00	1.00	.60
	Series 3 - Baseball's Immortals	25.00	12.50	7.50
5	Honus Wagner	3.50	1.75	1.00
13	George Wright	2.00	1.00	.60
15	Alexander Cartwright	2.00	1.00	.60
16	Henry Chadwick	2.00	1.00	.60
23	Candy Cummings	2.00	1.00	.60
25	Old Hoss Radbourne	2.00	1.00	.60
26	Al Spalding	2.00	1.00	.60
28	Judge Landis	2.00	1.00	.60
29	Roger Bresnahan	2.00	1.00	.60
30	Dan Brouthers	2.00	1.00	.60
33	Ed Delahanty	2.00	1.00	.60
37	Jim O'Rourke	2.00	1.00	.60
39	Jesse Burkett	2.00	1.00	.60
44	Tommy McCarthy	2.00	1.00	.60
45	Joe McGinnity	2.00	1.00	.60
46	Eddie Plank	2.00	1.00	.60
49	Ed Walsh	2.00	1.00	.60
61	Harry Heilmann	2.00	1.00	.60
68	Bill Klem	2.00	1.00	.60
70	Harry Wright	2.00	1.00	.60
85	Max Carey	2.00	1.00	.60
91	John Clarkson	2.00	1.00	.60
92	Elmer Flick	2.00	1.00	.60
96	Red Faber	2.00	1.00	.60
97	Burleigh Grimes	2.00	1.00	.60
98	Miller Huggins	2.00	1.00	.60
99	Tim Keefe	2.00	1.00	.60
101	Monte Ward	2.00	1.00	.60
102	Pud Galvin	2.00	1.00	.60
110	Goose Goslin	2.00	1.00	.60
114	Waite Hoyt	2.00	1.00	.60
117	Ford Frick	2.00	1.00	.60
118	Jesse Haines	2.00	1.00	.60
126	George Weiss	2.00	1.00	.60
130	William Harridge	2.00	1.00	.60
132	Buck Leonard	2.00	1.00	.60
133	Early Wynn	2.00	1.00	.60
136	Billy Evans	2.00	1.00	.60
137	Monte Irvin	2.00	1.00	.60
138	George Kelly	2.00	1.00	.60
140	Mickey Welch	2.00	1.00	.60
148	Bucky Harris	2.00	1.00	.60
151	Ralph Kiner	2.00	1.00	.60
153	Roger Connor	2.00	1.00	.60
	Series 4 - Ball's All-Time Greats	20.00	10.00	6.00
2	Babe Ruth	12.50	6.25	3.75
8	Cy Young	2.50	1.25	.70
27	Rogers Hornsby	2.00	1.00	.60
48	Rube Waddell	2.00	1.00	.60
62	Paul Waner	2.00	1.00	.60
63	Dizzy Dean	2.50	1.25	.70
69	Bobby Wallace	2.00	1.00	.60
71	Bill Dickey	2.00	1.00	.60
77	Dazzy Vance	2.00	1.00	.60
79	Ray Schalk	2.00	1.00	.60
82	Sam Crawford	2.00	1.00	.60
84	Zack Wheat	2.00	1.00	.60
94	Eppa Rixey	2.00	1.00	.60
100	Heinie Manush	2.00	1.00	.60
105	Red Ruffing	2.00	1.00	.60
106	Branch Rickey	2.00	1.00	.60
112	Stan Musial	5.00	2.50	1.50
119	Dave Bancroft	2.00	1.00	.60
121	Chick Hafey	2.00	1.00	.60
123	Joe Kelley	2.00	1.00	.60
124	Rube Marquard	2.00	1.00	.60
134	Ross Youngs	2.00	1.00	.60
139	Warren Spahn	2.00	1.00	.60
145	Mickey Mantle	16.00	8.00	4.75
155	Bob Lemon	2.00	1.00	.60

1977 Shakey's All-Time Superstars

This set of baseball's all-time greatest (at least through the 1950s) was the final production of the Washington State Sports Collectors Assn. and local Shakey's restaurants. About 2-3/8" x 3", the cards feature black-and-white player photos at center with a red border around. A facsimile autograph appears in blue on the photo. Backs are similar to earlier Shakey's issues, with large logos for the pizza chain, player information and "Seasonal Bests" stats, all printed in red and black on white. Several special cards were produced for distribution at the 1977 annual convention and other venues.

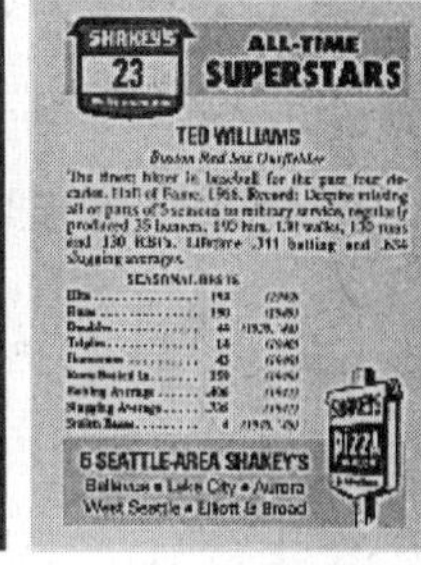

		NM	EX	VG
	Complete Set (28):	35.00	17.50	10.00
	Complete Set (25):	25.00	12.50	7.50
	Common Player:	2.00	1.00	.60
	Welcome to WSSCA Show Card (collectibles collage)	3.00	1.50	.90
A	Earl Averill	3.00	1.50	.90
B	John Mize ($1 coupon on back)	3.00	1.50	.90
C	Robert Lee Johnson	3.00	1.50	.90
1	Connie Mack	2.00	1.00	.60
2	John J. McGraw	2.00	1.00	.60
3	Denton T. (Cy) Young	4.00	2.00	1.25
4	Walter Johnson	4.00	2.00	1.25
5	G.C. Alexander	2.00	1.00	.60
6	Christy Mathewson	4.00	2.00	1.25
7	Lefty Grove	2.00	1.00	.60
8	Mickey Cochrane	2.00	1.00	.60
9	Bill Dickey	2.00	1.00	.60
10	Lou Gehrig	7.50	3.75	2.25
11	George Sisler	2.00	1.00	.60
12	Cap Anson	2.00	1.00	.60
13	Jimmie Foxx	2.00	1.00	.60
14	Rogers Hornsby	2.00	1.00	.60
15	Nap Lajoie	2.00	1.00	.60
16	Eddie Collins	2.00	1.00	.60
17	Pie Traynor	2.00	1.00	.60
18	Honus Wagner	4.00	2.00	1.25
19	Ty Cobb	7.50	3.75	2.25
20	Babe Ruth	10.00	5.00	3.00
21	Joe Jackson	10.00	5.00	3.00
22	Tris Speaker	2.00	1.00	.60
23	Ted Williams	6.00	3.00	1.75
24	Joe DiMaggio	7.50	3.75	2.25
25	Stan Musial	5.00	2.50	1.50
---	WSSCA Club Information Card	4.00	2.00	1.25

1952 Shelby Bicycles

The year of issue stated is conjectural, based on the familiar picture of Berra used for this promotional photo. The photo shows Yogi kneeling in full catcher's gear, except mask, ready to throw the ball; it is seen on his '50 Bowman card, among others. The blank-back, black-and-white photos are 5" x 7" with a white border all around. Scripted at bottom is, "Ride Shelby / The Winner's Bike / Sincerely / Yogi Berra."

	NM	EX	VG
Yogi Berra	150.00	75.00	45.00

1958-1959 Shillito's Boys' Shop Cincinnati Reds

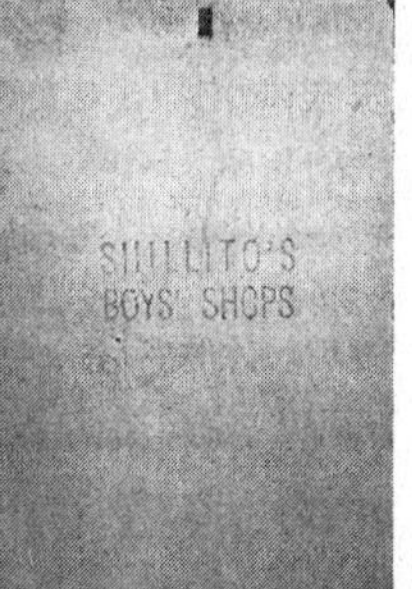

This rare regional set was issued by a Cincinnati-area chain department store. The 2-1/2" x 3-1/2" black-and-white glossy cards are essentially a version of contemporary team-issued photos except for the presence (usually) on the otherwise blank back of a purple "SHILLITO'S / BOYS' SHOPS" rubber-stamp. Some cards have been seen wuthout the ad on back. The unnumbered pictures are listed here in alphabetical order.

		NM	EX	VG
Complete Set (23):		3,500	1,750	1,050
Common Player:		200.00	100.00	60.00
(1)	Tom Acker	200.00	100.00	60.00
(2)	Ed Bailey	200.00	100.00	60.00
(3)	Gus Bell	200.00	100.00	60.00
(4)	John "Dutch" Dotterer	200.00	100.00	60.00
(5)	Walt Dropo	200.00	100.00	60.00
(6)	Del Ennis	200.00	100.00	60.00
(7)	Jay Hook	200.00	100.00	60.00
(8)	Hal Jeffcoat	200.00	100.00	60.00
(9)	Eddie Kasko	200.00	100.00	60.00
(10)	Brooks Lawrence	200.00	100.00	60.00
(11)	Jerry Lynch	200.00	100.00	60.00
(12)	Roy McMillan	200.00	100.00	60.00
(13)	Eddie Miksis	200.00	100.00	60.00
(14)	Don Newcombe	230.00	115.00	69.00
(15)	Joe Nuxhall	250.00	125.00	75.00
(16)	Jim O'Toole	200.00	100.00	60.00
(17)	Vada Pinson	250.00	125.00	75.00
(18)	Bob Purkey	200.00	100.00	60.00
(19)	Frank Robinson	500.00	250.00	150.00
(20)	Frank Thomas	200.00	100.00	60.00
(21)	Johnny Temple	200.00	100.00	60.00
(22)	Bob Thurman	200.00	100.00	60.00
(23)	Pete Whisenant	200.00	100.00	60.00

1974 Shillito's Pete Rose

Probably issued in conjunction with an autograph-signing appearance at the Cincinnati department store, this picture could have been issued in either 1974 or 1975. The glossy black-and-white, blank-back photo measures 5-1/2" x 8". The autograph on the example shown is genuine, the photo does not have a facsimile signature.

	NM	EX	VG
Pete Rose	150.00	75.00	45.00

1976 Shillito's Kahn's Reds Clubhouse

Though the format for each photo differs, this series of Reds player photos was issued under the sponsorship of the Shillito's department store and Kahn's meats. In about 5" x 7-3/16" format, the blank-back photos are black-and-white with at least one (Bench) having red highlights. The pictures were given out at player autograph appearances at various Shillito's locations between June 21 and August 13. Youngsters enrolled in the club received a membership card, probably entitling them to an autograph at each event. With five dates specifically mentioned, it is likely at least one more photo exists in this series.

		NM	EX	VG
Common Player:				
(1)	Johnny Bench (Kenwood Plaza)	100.00	50.00	30.00
(2)	Dave Concepcion (Kahn's - WLW Radio)	30.00	15.00	9.00
(3)	Doug Flynn (No sponsor.)	12.00	6.00	3.50
(4)	George Foster (Four sponsors listed.)	15.00	7.50	4.50
(5)	Pete Rose (Shillito's)	100.00	50.00	30.00
---	Membership Card	10.00	5.00	3.00

1962 Shirriff Coins

This is a Canadian version of the better-known Salada-Junket plastic player coins issued in the U.S. Backs specify an issue of 200; 21 of the players from the Salada set were not issued by Shirriff. Because the Canadian coins were produced after the U.S. version they are not found with all the variations known in Salada, nor the differing levels of scarcity. Shirriff coins were packed in bags of potato chips, with each coin sealed in a clear cellophane wrapper. Although the Canadian coins are much scarcer than the U.S., significantly less demand keeps prices lower, as well.

		NM	EX	VG
Complete Set (200):		1,600	800.00	525.00
Common Player:		6.00	3.00	1.75
1	Jim Gentile	7.00	3.50	2.00
2	NOT ISSUED (Bill Pierce)			
3	Chico Fernandez (Light blue piping.)	6.00	3.00	1.75
4	NOT ISSUED (Tom Brewer)			
5	Woody Held	6.00	3.00	1.75
6	NOT ISSUED (Ray Herbert)			
7	Ken Aspromonte (Indians)	6.00	3.00	1.75
8	Whitey Ford	40.00	20.00	12.00
9	Jim Lemon	6.00	3.00	1.75
10	Billy Klaus	6.00	3.00	1.75
11	NOT ISSUED (Steve Barber)			
12	Nellie Fox	25.00	12.50	7.50
13	Jim Bunning	25.00	12.50	7.50
14	Frank Malzone	6.00	3.00	1.75
15	Tito Francona	6.00	3.00	1.75
16	Bobby Del Greco	6.00	3.00	1.75
17	Steve Bilko	6.00	3.00	1.75
18	NOT ISSUED (Tony Kubek)			
19	Earl Battey	6.00	3.00	1.75
20	Chuck Cottier	6.00	3.00	1.75
21	Willie Tasby	6.00	3.00	1.75
22	Bob Allison	7.00	3.50	2.00
23	Roger Maris	40.00	20.00	12.00
24	Earl Averill	6.00	3.00	1.75
25	Jerry Lumpe	6.00	3.00	1.75
26	NOT ISSUED (Jim Grant)			
27	Carl Yastrzemski	50.00	25.00	15.00
28	Rocky Colavito (Blue piping.)	20.00	10.00	6.00
29	Al Smith	6.00	3.00	1.75
30	NOT ISSUED (Jim Busby)			
31	Dick Howser	6.00	3.00	1.75
32	Jim Perry	6.00	3.00	1.75
33	Yogi Berra	50.00	25.00	15.00
34	Ken Hamlin	6.00	3.00	1.75
35	Dale Long	6.00	3.00	1.75
36	Harmon Killebrew	35.00	17.50	10.50
37	Dick Brown	6.00	3.00	1.75
38	Gary Geiger	6.00	3.00	1.75
39	Minnie Minoso (Cardinals)	9.00	4.50	2.75
40	Brooks Robinson	35.00	17.50	10.50
41	Mickey Mantle	180.00	90.00	54.00
42	Bennie Daniels	6.00	3.00	1.75
43	Billy Martin	15.00	7.50	4.50
44	Vic Power	7.00	3.50	2.00
45	Joe Pignatano	6.00	3.00	1.75
46	Ryne Duren	7.00	3.50	2.00
47	Pete Runnels (1B)	6.00	3.00	1.75
48	Dick Williams	6.00	3.00	1.75
49	Jim Landis	6.00	3.00	1.75
50	Steve Boros	6.00	3.00	1.75
51	Zoilo Versalles	7.00	3.50	2.00
52	Johnny Temple (Orioles)	6.00	3.00	1.75
53	Jackie Brandt	6.00	3.00	1.75
54	Joe McClain	6.00	3.00	1.75
55	Sherman Lollar	6.00	3.00	1.75
56	Gene Stephens	6.00	3.00	1.75
57	Leon Wagner	6.00	3.00	1.75
58	Frank Lary	6.00	3.00	1.75
59	Bill Skowron	12.00	6.00	3.50
60	NOT ISSUED (Vic Wertz)			
61	Willie Kirkland	6.00	3.00	1.75
62	Leo Posada	6.00	3.00	1.75
63	Albie Pearson	7.00	3.50	2.00
64	Bobby Richardson	15.00	7.50	4.50
65	Marv Breeding (SS)	6.00	3.00	1.75
66	NOT ISSUED (Roy Sievers)			
67	Al Kaline	35.00	17.50	10.50
68	Don Buddin (Colts)	6.00	3.00	1.75
69	Lenny Green (White top button.)	6.00	3.00	1.75
70	NOT ISSUED (Gene Green)			
71	Luis Aparicio	25.00	12.50	7.50
72	Norm Cash	12.00	6.00	3.50
73	NOT ISSUED (Jackie Jensen)			
74	Bubba Phillips	6.00	3.00	1.75
75	Jim Archer	6.00	3.00	1.75
76	Ken Hunt	6.00	3.00	1.75
77	Ralph Terry	6.00	3.00	1.75
78	Camilo Pascual	6.00	3.00	1.75
79	NOT ISSUED (Marty Keough)			
80	Cletis Boyer	9.00	4.50	2.75
81	Jim Pagliaroni	6.00	3.00	1.75
82	Gene Leek	6.00	3.00	1.75
83	Jake Wood	6.00	3.00	1.75
84	NOT ISSUED (Coot Veal)			
85	Norm Siebern	6.00	3.00	1.75
86	Andy Carey (Phillies)	6.00	3.00	1.75
87	Bill Tuttle (White top button.)	6.00	3.00	1.75
88	Jimmy Piersall	6.00	3.00	1.75
89	NOT ISSUED (Ron Hansen)			
90	Chuck Stobbs	6.00	3.00	1.75
91	Ken McBride	6.00	3.00	1.75
92	Bill Bruton	6.00	3.00	1.75
93	Gus Triandos	6.00	3.00	1.75
94	John Romano	6.00	3.00	1.75
95	Elston Howard	12.00	6.00	3.50
96	Gene Woodling	6.00	3.00	1.75
97	Early Wynn (Portrait)	20.00	10.00	6.00
98	Milt Pappas	6.00	3.00	1.75
99	Bill Monbouquette	6.00	3.00	1.75
100	Wayne Causey	6.00	3.00	1.75
101	Don Elston	6.00	3.00	1.75
102	Charlie Neal	6.00	3.00	1.75
103	Don Blasingame	6.00	3.00	1.75
104	NOT ISSUED (Frank Thomas)			
105	Wes Covington	6.00	3.00	1.75
106	Chuck Hiller	6.00	3.00	1.75
107	Don Hoak	6.00	3.00	1.75
108	Bob Lillis (Colts)	6.00	3.00	1.75
109	Sandy Koufax	65.00	32.00	19.50
110	Gordy Coleman	6.00	3.00	1.75
111	Ed Matthews (Mathews)	30.00	15.00	9.00
112	Art Mahaffey	6.00	3.00	1.75
113	Ed Bailey (Name above ear.)	6.00	3.00	1.75
114	Smoky Burgess	7.00	3.50	2.00
115	Bill White	7.00	3.50	2.00
116	NOT ISSUED (Ed Bouchee)			
117	Bob Buhl	6.00	3.00	1.75
118	Vada Pinson	7.00	3.50	2.00
119	Carl Sawatski	6.00	3.00	1.75
120	Dick Stuart	7.00	3.50	2.00
121	NOT ISSUED (Harvey Kuenn)			
122	Pancho Herrera	6.00	3.00	1.75
123	Don Zimmer	7.00	3.50	2.00
124	Wally Moon	7.00	3.50	2.00
125	Joe Adcock	6.00	3.00	1.75
126	Joey Jay	6.00	3.00	1.75
127	Maury Wills (Red 3 on uniform.)	12.00	6.00	3.50
128	George Altman	6.00	3.00	1.75
129	John Buzhardt	6.00	3.00	1.75
130	Felipe Alou	7.00	3.50	2.00
131	Bill Mazeroski	25.00	12.50	7.50
132	Ernie Broglio	6.00	3.00	1.75
133	John Roseboro	7.00	3.50	2.00
134	Mike McCormick	6.00	3.00	1.75
135	Chuck Smith (White Sox)	6.00	3.00	1.75
136	Ron Santo	12.00	6.00	3.50
137	Gene Freese	6.00	3.00	1.75
138	Dick Groat	7.00	3.50	2.00
139	Curt Flood	7.00	3.50	2.00
140	Frank Bolling	6.00	3.00	1.75
141	Clay Dalrymple	6.00	3.00	1.75
142	Willie McCovey	30.00	15.00	9.00
143	Bob Skinner	6.00	3.00	1.75
144	Lindy McDaniel	6.00	3.00	1.75
145	Glen Hobbie	6.00	3.00	1.75
146	Gil Hodges	20.00	10.00	6.00
147	Eddie Kasko	6.00	3.00	1.75
148	NOT ISSUED (Gino Cimoli)			
149	Willie Mays	75.00	37.00	22.00
150	Roberto Clemente	90.00	45.00	27.00
151	Red Schoendienst	25.00	12.50	7.50
152	Joe Torre	9.00	4.50	2.75
153	Bob Purkey	6.00	3.00	1.75
154	Tommy Davis (3B)	7.50	3.75	2.25
155	Andre Rogers (Rodgers)	6.00	3.00	1.75
156	Tony Taylor	6.00	3.00	1.75
157	Bob Friend	6.00	3.00	1.75
158	Gus Bell	6.00	3.00	1.75
159	Roy McMillan	6.00	3.00	1.75
160	Carl Warwick	6.00	3.00	1.75
161	Willie Davis	6.00	3.00	1.75
162	NOT ISSUED (Sam Jones)			
163	Ruben Amaro	6.00	3.00	1.75
164	Sam Taylor	6.00	3.00	1.75
165	Frank Robinson	35.00	17.50	10.50
166	Lou Burdette	6.00	3.00	1.75
167	Ken Boyer	10.00	5.00	3.00
168	Bill Virdon	6.00	3.00	1.75
169	Jim Davenport	6.00	3.00	1.75
170	Don Demeter	6.00	3.00	1.75
171	NOT ISSUED (Richie Ashburn)			
172	John Podres	7.50	3.75	2.25
173	Joe Cunningham (White Sox)	6.00	3.00	1.75
174	ElRoy Face	6.00	3.00	1.75
175	Orlando Cepeda	25.00	12.50	7.50
176	Bobby Gene Smith	6.00	3.00	1.75
177	Ernie Banks (SS)	50.00	25.00	15.00
178	Daryl Spencer (1B)	6.00	3.00	1.75
179	NOT ISSUED (Bob Schmidt)			
180	Hank Aaron	75.00	37.00	22.00
181	Hobie Landrith	6.00	3.00	1.75
182	Ed Bressoud	6.00	3.00	1.75
183	Felix Mantilla	6.00	3.00	1.75
184	Dick Farrell	6.00	3.00	1.75
185	Bob Miller	6.00	3.00	1.75
186	Don Taussig	6.00	3.00	1.75
187	Pumpsie Green	6.00	3.00	1.75
188	Bobby Shantz	7.50	3.75	2.25
189	Roger Craig	6.00	3.00	1.75
190	Hal Smith	6.00	3.00	1.75
191	John Edwards	6.00	3.00	1.75
192	John DeMerit	6.00	3.00	1.75
193	Joe Amalfitano	6.00	3.00	1.75
194	Norm Larker	6.00	3.00	1.75

195	Al Heist	6.00	3.00	1.75
196	Al Spangler	6.00	3.00	1.75
197	Alex Grammas	6.00	3.00	1.75
198	Gerry Lynch	6.00	3.00	1.75
199	Jim McKnight	6.00	3.00	1.75
200	Jose Pagen (Pagan)	6.00	3.00	1.75
201	Junior Gilliam	7.50	3.75	2.25
202	Art Ditmar	6.00	3.00	1.75
203	Pete Daley	6.00	3.00	1.75
204	Johnny Callison	6.00	3.00	1.75
205	Stu Miller	6.00	3.00	1.75
206	Russ Snyder	6.00	3.00	1.75
207	Billy Williams	25.00	12.50	7.50
208	Walter Bond	6.00	3.00	1.75
209	Joe Koppe	6.00	3.00	1.75
210	Don Schwall	6.00	3.00	1.75
211	Billy Gardner	6.00	3.00	1.75
212	Chuck Estrada	6.00	3.00	1.75
213	Gary Bell	6.00	3.00	1.75
214	Floyd Robinson	6.00	3.00	1.75
215	Duke Snider	35.00	17.50	10.50
216	Lee Maye	6.00	3.00	1.75
217	Howie Bedell	6.00	3.00	1.75
218	Bob Will	6.00	3.00	1.75
219	Dallas Green	7.50	3.75	2.25
220	Carroll Hardy	6.00	3.00	1.75
221	Danny O'Connell	6.00	3.00	1.75

1928 Shonen Kulubu Babe Ruth Postcard

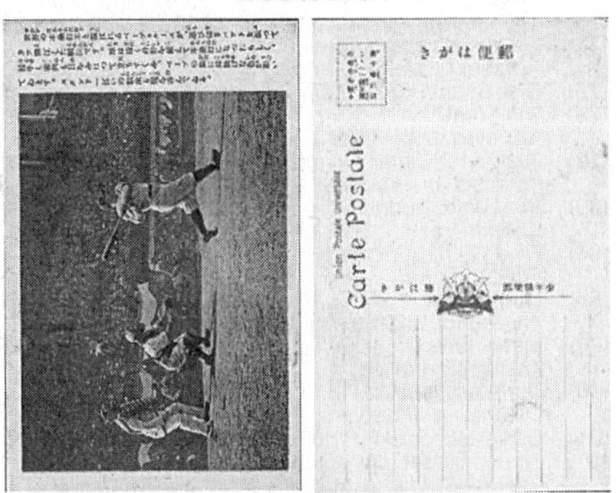

This card, which the Japanese inscription describes as picturing Babe Ruth hitting his first home run of 1926, was part of a multi-sport premium issue by the Japanese magazine Shonen Kubulu ("Youth Club"). The front has a colorized black-and-white photo, with blue inscriptions at right. Back is in blue with standard international postcard indicia.

	NM	EX	VG
Babe Ruth	500.00	250.00	150.00

1889 G. Waldon Smith Boston Beaneaters Cabinets

Whether the scope of this issue encompassed a greater portion of the 1889 Boston National Leaguers or just the four currently known players is presently unknown. Boston photographer G. Waldon Smith immortalized the players in a series of 4-1/4" x 6-1/2" cabinet cards. Each card features a capless, chest-up portrait of a mustachioed ballplayer. The studio's name and location are printed in red at bottom. The players are not identified on the pieces. The 1889 pictures can be differentiated from the 1890 issue by the ornateness of the studio address; the earlier is in plain type, the later is more ornate and includes the state abbreviation.

		NM	EX	VG
	Common Player:	3,600	1,800	1,080
(1)	Tom Brown	3,600	1,800	1,080
(2)	Harry Ganzel	3,600	1,800	1,080
(3)	Billy Nash	3,600	1,800	1,080
(4)	Pop Smith	3,600	1,800	1,080
(6)	The Boston Base Ball Club (Team photo, 21" x 18".)	18,000	9,000	5,400

1890 G. Waldon Smith Cabinets

As little as is known about the 1889 Smith baseball cabinets, the 1890 issue is even less well documented. Only a single player is currently recorded, Tom Brown, who also appears in the 1889 issue. In 1890, Brown was a member of the Boston Players League team; whether or not his teammates or those of the Boston National League club can be found in this issue remains unknown. Like the 1889 cabinets, size is about 4-1/4" x 6-1/2" and no player identification is presented. The 1890 cabinets can be differentiated from the 1889s by the more elaborate presentation of the studio address at bottom-right, including the state abbreviation.

	NM	EX	VG
Tom Brown	3,000	1,500	900.00
Boston Base Ball Club / Players' League (Team photo, 22" x 18".)	20,000	10,000	6,000

1904 G. Waldon Smith Cabinets

Following a move down Tremont St. to No. 164A, this Boston photographer was still producing baseball player cabinet photos. Like his earlier photos, the circa 1904 pieces have black-and-white photographs mounted on stiff 4-1/4" x 6-1/2" cardboard backings. The only currently known picture in this series is a full-length portrait of Kip Selbach. Others almost certainly exist.

	NM	EX	VG
Kip Selbach	2,500	1,250	750.00

1909 W.W. Smith Postcards

Only two subjects are known in this series of postcards issued contemporary with the 1909 World Series between the Tigers and Pirates, though it is possible a card of Ty Cobb might have also been issued. The 3-1/2" x 5-1/2" black-and-white cards have pencil portraits by W.W. Smith. Backs have standard postcard markings.

		NM	EX	VG
	Complete Set (2):	1,000	500.00	300.00
(1)	The Mighty Honus (Honus Wagner)	750.00	375.00	225.00
(2)	Two of a Kind (Ty Cobb, Honus Wagner)	3,000	1,500	900.00

1957 Sohio Gas Indians/Reds

In 1957 Sohio (Standard Oil of Ohio) gas stations in Ohio issued sets of Cleveland Indians and Cincinnati Reds photo-cards and team albums. The blank-backed cards are 5" x 7" and printed in black-and-white with one perforated edge. The cards have a facsimile autograph as the only identification. The unnumbered cards are checklisted here alphabetically within team.

		NM	EX	VG
	Complete Set (36):	650.00	325.00	195.00
	Common Player:	10.00	5.00	3.00
	CLEVELAND INDIANS			
	Complete Set (18):	300.00	150.00	90.00
(1)	Bob Avila	10.00	5.00	3.00
(2)	Jim Busby	10.00	5.00	3.00
(3)	Chico Carrasquel	10.00	5.00	3.00
(4)	Rocky Colavito	75.00	37.00	22.00
(5)	Mike Garcia	10.00	5.00	3.00
(6)	Jim Hegan	10.00	5.00	3.00
(7)	Bob Lemon	20.00	10.00	6.00
(8)	Roger Maris	150.00	75.00	45.00
(9)	Don Mossi	10.00	5.00	3.00
(10)	Ray Narleski	10.00	5.00	3.00
(11)	Russ Nixon	10.00	5.00	3.00
(12)	Herb Score	15.00	7.50	4.50
(13)	Al Smith	10.00	5.00	3.00
(14)	George Strickland	10.00	5.00	3.00
(15)	Bob Usher	10.00	5.00	3.00
(16)	Vic Wertz	10.00	5.00	3.00
(17)	Gene Woodling	10.00	5.00	3.00
(18)	Early Wynn	20.00	10.00	6.00
----	Cleveland Indians Album	60.00	30.00	18.00
	CINCINNATI REDS			
	Complete Set (18):	325.00	160.00	97.00
(1)	Ed Bailey	10.00	5.00	3.00
(2)	Gus Bell	10.00	5.00	3.00
(3)	Rocky Bridges	10.00	5.00	3.00
(4)	Smoky Burgess	10.00	5.00	3.00
(5)	Hersh Freeman	10.00	5.00	3.00
(6)	Alex Grammas	10.00	5.00	3.00
(7)	Don Gross	10.00	5.00	3.00
(8)	Warren Hacker	10.00	5.00	3.00
(9)	Don Hoak	10.00	5.00	3.00
(10)	Hal Jeffcoat	10.00	5.00	3.00
(11)	Johnny Klippstein	10.00	5.00	3.00
(12)	Ted Kluszewski	60.00	30.00	18.00
(13)	Brooks Lawrence	10.00	5.00	3.00
(14)	Roy McMillan	10.00	5.00	3.00
(15)	Joe Nuxhall	12.50	6.25	3.75
(16)	Wally Post	10.00	5.00	3.00
(17)	Frank Robinson	150.00	75.00	45.00
(18)	Johnny Temple	10.00	5.00	3.00
----	Cincinnati Redlegs Album	60.00	30.00	18.00

1969 Solon Kansas City Royals

This collectors' issue is believed to have originated with Illinois hobbyist Bob Solon. The black-and-white, blank-back cards feature members of the expansion Royals. The border beneath the posed photos features a team logo and player identification at bottom. Cards measure 2-1/8" x 3-5/8". The checklist here is arranged alphabetically, as the cards are unnumbered.

		NM	EX	VG
	Complete Set (15):	16.00	8.00	4.75
	Common Player:	2.00	1.00	.60
(1)	Jerry Adair	2.00	1.00	.60
(2)	Wally Bunker	2.00	1.00	.60
(3)	Moe Drabowsky	3.00	1.50	.90
(4)	Dick Drago	2.00	1.00	.60
(5)	Joe Foy	2.00	1.00	.60
(6)	Joe Gordon	2.00	1.00	.60
(7)	Chuck Harrison	2.00	1.00	.60
(8)	Mike Hedlund	2.00	1.00	.60
(9)	Jack Hernandez	2.00	1.00	.60
(10)	Pat Kelly	2.00	1.00	.60
(11)	Roger Nelson	2.00	1.00	.60
(12)	Bob Oliver	2.00	1.00	.60
(13)	Lou Piniella	6.00	3.00	1.75
(14)	Ellie Rodriguez	2.00	1.00	.60
(15)	Dave Wickersham	2.00	1.00	.60

1905 Souvenir Post Card Shop of Cleveland

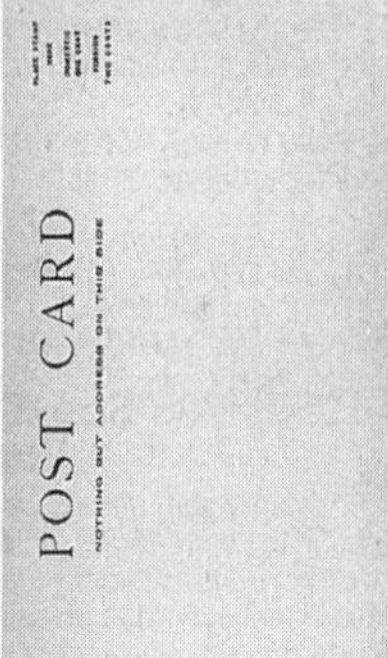

Formal portraits of the 1905 Cleveland Naps are featured in this set of black-and-white postcards. The 3-1/4" x 5-1/2" cards have a wide white border at bottom which carries the legend, "SOUVENIR POST CARD SHOP OF CLEVELAND." The player name is in white at the bottom of the photo. Backs have postage rate information and a notice, "NOTHING BUT ADDRESS ON THIS SIDE."

		NM	EX	VG
Complete Set (19):		16,500	8,250	5,000
Common Player:		950.00	475.00	285.00
(1)	Harry Bay	950.00	475.00	285.00
(2)	Harry Bemis	950.00	475.00	285.00
(3)	Bill Bernhard	950.00	475.00	285.00
(4)	Bill Bradley	950.00	475.00	285.00
(5)	Fred Buelow	950.00	475.00	285.00
(6)	Charles C. Carr	950.00	475.00	285.00
(7)	Frank Donahue	950.00	475.00	285.00
(8)	Elmer Flick	1,425	710.00	425.00
(9)	Otto Hess	950.00	475.00	285.00
(10)	Jay Jackson	950.00	475.00	285.00
(11)	Addie Joss	2,750	1,375	825.00
(12)	Nick Kahl	950.00	475.00	285.00
(13)	Napoleon Lajoie	2,000	1,000	600.00
(14)	Earl Moore	950.00	475.00	285.00
(15)	Robert Rhoads	950.00	475.00	285.00
(16)	George Stovall	950.00	475.00	285.00
(17)	Terry Turner	950.00	475.00	285.00
(18)	Ernest Vinson	950.00	475.00	285.00
(19)	Team Portraits Composite	1,500	750.00	450.00

1909-11 Sovereign Cigarettes

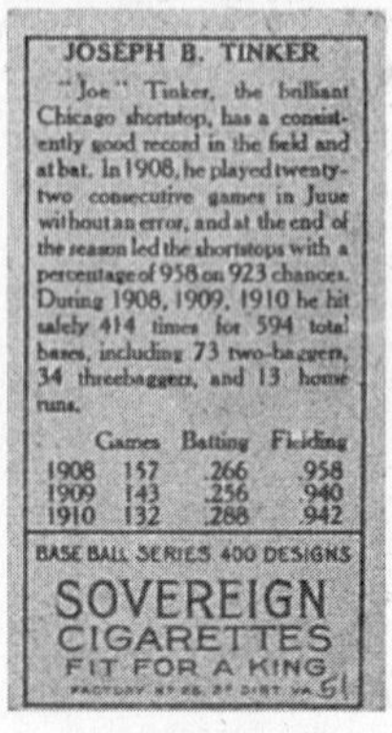

Premiums shown are for common-player cards. Hall of Famers or other high-demand cards generally realize little or no premium with Sovereign back. On T205s, the backs are printed in green.

PREMIUMS
T205: 1.25X
T206 150 Subjects: 1X
T206 350 Subjects: 1.5X
T206 460 Subjects: 1.5X
(See T205, T206 for checklists and base card values.)

1949 Spalding Joe DiMaggio Glove Premium Photos

The attributed date is only approximate. Lucky youngsters who received a Spalding Joe DiMaggio fielder's glove also got a pair of 8" x 10" black-and-white posed action photos of the Yankee Clipper. Each blank-back, borderless photo has a facsimile autograph.

		NM	EX	VG
(1)	Joe DiMaggio (No ball in photo.)	125.00	65.00	40.00
(2)	Joe DiMaggio (Ball in photo.)	125.00	65.00	40.00

1950s-70s Spalding Advisory Staff Photos

Advisory staff photos were a promtional item which debuted in the early 1950s, flourished in the 1960s and died in the early 1970s. Generally 8" x 10" (sometimes a little larger), these black-and-white (a few later were color) glossy photos picture players who had contracted with a major baseball

equipment company to endorse and use their product. Usually the product - most often a glove - was prominently displayed in the photo. The pictures were often displayed in the windows of sporting goods stores or the walls of sports departments and were sometimes made available to customers. Because the companies tended to stick with players over the years, some photos were reissued, sometimes with and sometimes without a change of team, pose or typography. Spalding staff photos of the era are checklisted here in alphabetical order. Team designation and pose description is given for each known picture. The photos are checklisted here in alphabetical order. It is unlikely this list is complete. Several arrangements of typography in the bottom border are seen for Spalding advisory staff pictures.

		NM	EX	VG
Common Player:		12.00	6.00	3.50
(1)	Richie Allen (Phillies, batting helmet.)	20.00	10.00	6.00
(2)	Gene Alley (Pirates, upper body.)	12.00	6.00	3.50
(3)	Mike Andrews (Red Sox, upper body.)	12.00	6.00	3.50
(4)	Bob Aspromonte (Dodgers, upper body.)	12.00	6.00	3.50
(5)	Sal Bando (A's, upper body.)	12.00	6.00	3.50
(7)	Steve Barber (Orioles, chest-to-cap.)	12.00	6.00	3.50
(8)	John Bateman (Colt .45s, upper body.)	12.00	6.00	3.50
(9)	Yogi Berra/Btg (Yankees)	30.00	15.00	9.00
(10)	Yogi Berra (Mets, upper body.)	30.00	15.00	9.00
(11)	Don Bessent (Brooklyn, follow-through.)	20.00	10.00	6.00
(12a)	Frank Bolling/Fldg (Tigers)	15.00	7.50	4.50
(12b)	Frank Bolling (Braves, chest up.)	15.00	7.50	4.50
(13)	Jim Bouton (Yankees, upper body.)	15.00	7.50	4.50
(14)	Jim Bunning (Phillies, upper body.)	20.00	10.00	6.00
(16)	John Callison (Phillies, batson shoulder.)	12.00	6.00	3.50
(17)	Rocky Colavito/Btg (Tigers)	25.00	12.50	7.50
(18)	Roger Craig (Brooklyn, follow-through.)	15.00	7.50	4.50
(19)	Clay Dalrymple (Phillies, upper body.)	12.00	6.00	3.50
(20)	Alvin Dark (Cardinals, batting follow-through.)	20.00	10.00	6.00
(21)	Don Drysdale (Dodgers, pitching follow-through.)	25.00	12.50	7.50
(22)	Sam Esposito (White Sox, hands on knees.)	12.00	6.00	3.50
(23)	Ron Fairly (Dodgers, upper body.)	12.00	6.00	3.50
(24)	Dick Farrell (Phillies, follow-through.)	25.00	12.50	7.50
(25)	Whitey Ford (Yankees, hands over head.)	30.00	15.00	9.00
(26)	Jim Fregosi (L.A. Angels, upper body.)	15.00	7.50	4.50
(27)	Jim Fregosi (California Angels, upper body, looking front.)	15.00	7.50	4.50
(28)	Jim Fregosi (California Angels, upper body, looking right.)	15.00	7.50	4.50
(29)	Jim Fregosi (Angels, green borders, b/w portrait.)	15.00	7.50	4.50
(30)	Bob Gibson (Color, stretch position.)	25.00	12.50	7.50
(33)	Tom Haller (Giants, catching crouch.)	12.00	6.00	3.50
(34)	Richie Hebner (Pirates, full-length.)	12.00	6.00	3.50
(35)	Mike Hegan (Brewers, upper body.)	12.00	6.00	3.50
(36)	Jim Hickman (Mets, upper body.)	12.00	6.00	3.50
(37)	Ken Hunt (Reds, follow-through.)	20.00	10.00	6.00
(38)	Jerry Koosman (Mets, ready to pitch.)	15.00	7.50	4.50
(39)	Jerry Koosman (Mets, upper body.)	15.00	7.50	4.50
(40)	Don Larsen (Yankees, follow-through.)	25.00	12.50	7.50
(41)	Charlie Lau (Braves, upper body.)	15.00	7.50	4.50
(42)	Mickey Lolich (Tigers, upper body, ready to pitch.)	15.00	7.50	4.50
(43)	Jerry Lumpe (Tigers, belt-up.)	12.00	6.00	3.50
(45)	Roger Maris/Btg (Yankees)	30.00	15.00	9.00
(46)	Roger Maris (Yankees, full-length.)	30.00	15.00	9.00
(47)	Roger Maris (Cardinals, "picture-frame," b/w photo.)	30.00	15.00	9.00
(49)	Dick McAuliffe/Portrait (Tigers)	12.00	6.00	3.50
(50)	Bill Monbouquette (Red Sox, wind-up.)	12.00	6.00	3.50
(51)	Bobby Murcer (Yankees, upper body.)	12.00	6.00	3.50
(53)	Jim Northrup/Btg (Tigers)	12.00	6.00	3.50
(56)	Jim Pagliaroni/Btg (Pirates)	12.00	6.00	3.50
(58)	Jim Palmer (Upper body.)	25.00	12.50	7.50
(60)	Joe Pepitone/Btg (Yankees)	15.00	7.50	4.50
(61)	Gary Peters (White Sox, green borders, b/w portrait.)	12.00	6.00	3.50
(62)	Rico Petrocelli (Red Sox, upper body.)	12.00	6.00	3.50
(64)	Joe Pignatano (A's, hands on hips.)	12.00	6.00	3.50
(66)	Bob Rodgers/Portrait (Angels)	12.00	6.00	3.50
(67)	Rich Rollins (Twins, arms crossed.)	12.00	6.00	3.50
(69)	Nolan Ryan (Angels, color, pitching.)	75.00	37.00	22.00
(72)	Tom Seaver (Mets, waist-to-cap.)	30.00	15.00	9.00
(73)	Tom Seaver/Pitching (Mets, color)	30.00	15.00	9.00
(75)	Mel Stottlemyre (Yankees, rust borders, b/w pitching pose .)	12.00	6.00	3.50
(76)	Dick Stuart/Btg (Pirates)	15.00	7.50	4.50
(78)	Joe Torre (Braves, upper body.)	15.00	7.50	4.50
(79)	Joe Torre (Cardinals, red borders, b/w portrait.)	15.00	7.50	4.50
(85)	Pete Ward/Portrait (White Sox)	12.00	6.00	3.50
(86)	Fred Whitfield/Portrait (Indians)	12.00	6.00	3.50
(87)	Maury Wills (Dodgers, chest-to-cap.)	15.00	7.50	4.50
(88)	Maury Wills (No team, full-length batting.)	12.00	6.00	3.50
(90)	Carl Yastrzemski (Kneeling w/ bats.)	30.00	15.00	9.00
(91)	Carl Yastrzemski (Picture-frame border, b/w portrait.)	30.00	15.00	9.00

1969 Spare-Time Products Minnesota Twins Discs

The intended use and manner of distribution of these 8" uniface color discs is unknown. The hard composition discs have a baseball design on which is centered a player portrait. A facsimile autograph is at bottom and there is a hole at top for hanging. Copyright information appears at lower-right.

		NM	EX	VG
Complete Set (8):		400.00	200.00	125.00
Common Player:		30.00	15.00	9.00
(1)	Dave Boswell	30.00	22.00	9.00
(2)	Leo Cardenas	30.00	15.00	9.00
(3)	Dean Chance	30.00	15.00	9.00
(4)	Jim Kaat	45.00	22.00	13.50
(5)	Tony Oliva/SP	150.00	75.00	45.00
(6)	Ron Perranoski	30.00	22.00	9.00
(7)	Jim Perry	30.00	15.00	9.00
(8)	John Roseboro	30.00	15.00	9.00

1948 Speedway 79 Tiger of the Week Photos

This set of blank-back, black-and-white 8" x 10" photos was issued by one of the Tigers radio sponsors. One photo, bearing a facsimile autograph on front, was given away each week to honor the outstanding Tigers performer. The photos have no markings identifying the issuer and they are unnumbered. They are checklisted here alphabetically.

	NM	EX	VG
Complete Set (14):	350.00	175.00	100.00
Common Player:	30.00	15.00	9.00
(1) Neil Berry	30.00	15.00	9.00
(2) "Hoot" Evers	30.00	15.00	9.00
(3) Ted Gray	30.00	15.00	9.00
(4) Art Houtteman	30.00	15.00	9.00
(5) Fred Hutchinson	30.00	15.00	9.00
(6) George Kell	50.00	25.00	15.00
(7) Eddie Lake	30.00	15.00	9.00
(8) Johnny Lipon	30.00	15.00	9.00
(9) Hal Newhouser	50.00	25.00	15.00
(10) Dizzy Trout	30.00	15.00	9.00
(11) Virgil Trucks	30.00	15.00	9.00
(12) George Vico	30.00	15.00	9.00
(13) Dick Wakefield	30.00	15.00	9.00
(14) Bill Wertz	30.00	15.00	9.00

1936 Spencer Shoes Jimmie Foxx Premium Photo

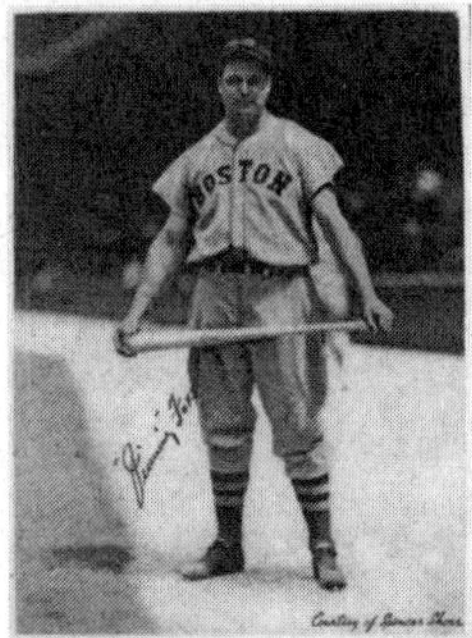

The attributed date is speculative, based on the uniform in which the player is pictured on this 7" x 9", blank-back, black-and-white premium photo. The picture has a facsimile autograph at left. At bottom-right in script is, "Courtesy of Spencer Shoes."

	NM	EX	VG
Jimmie Foxx	350.00	175.00	105.00

1953-55 Spic and Span Braves

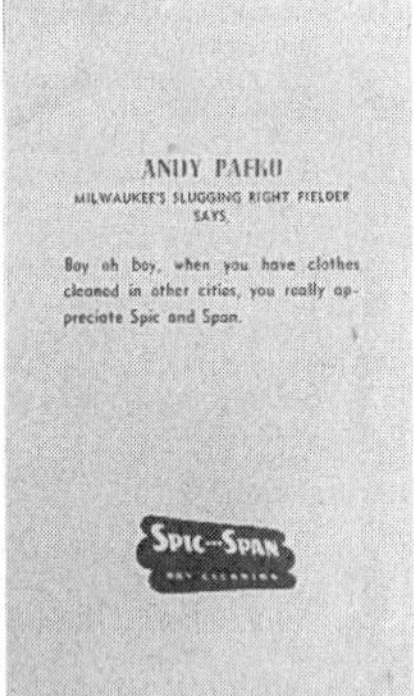

The first of several regional issues from a Milwaukee dry cleaner, the 1953-55 Spic and Span Braves set consists of black-and-white cards, 3-1/4" x 5-1/2". The fronts of the card have a facsimile autograph beneath the player photo. Cards are found with blank backs or with a Spic and Span advertising message on the back. Blank-backed cards are believed to have been issued by Wisco gas stations.

	NM	EX	VG
Complete Set (29):	1,800	900.00	540.00
Common Player:	50.00	25.00	15.00
(1) Hank Aaron	600.00	300.00	180.00
(2) Joe Adcock	50.00	25.00	15.00
(3) John Antonelli	50.00	25.00	15.00
(4) Vern Bickford	50.00	25.00	15.00
(5) Bill Bruton	50.00	25.00	15.00
(6) Bob Buhl	50.00	25.00	15.00
(7) Lew Burdette	50.00	25.00	15.00
(8) Dick Cole	50.00	25.00	15.00
(9) Walker Cooper	50.00	25.00	15.00
(10) Del Crandall	50.00	25.00	15.00
(11) George Crowe	50.00	25.00	15.00
(12) Jack Dittmer	50.00	25.00	15.00
(13) Sid Gordon	50.00	25.00	15.00
(14) Ernie Johnson	50.00	25.00	15.00
(15) Dave Jolly	50.00	25.00	15.00
(16) Don Liddle	50.00	25.00	15.00
(17) John Logan	50.00	25.00	15.00
(18) Ed Mathews	200.00	100.00	60.00
(19) Chet Nichols	50.00	25.00	15.00
(20) Dan O'Connell	50.00	25.00	15.00
(21) Andy Pafko	50.00	25.00	15.00
(22) Jim Pendleton	50.00	25.00	15.00
(23) Ebba St. Claire	50.00	25.00	15.00
(24) Warren Spahn	200.00	100.00	60.00
(25) Max Surkont	50.00	25.00	15.00
(26) Bob Thomson	75.00	37.50	22.00
(27) Bob Thorpe	50.00	25.00	15.00
(28) Roberto Vargas	50.00	25.00	15.00
(29) Jim Wilson	50.00	25.00	15.00

1953-57 Spic and Span Braves 7x10 Photos

This regional set was issued by Spic and Span Dry Cleaners of Milwaukee over a four-year period and consists of large (7" x 10") photos of Braves players. Of all the various Spic and Span sets, this one seems to be the easiest to find. The fronts feature a player photo with a facsimile autograph below. The Spic and Span logo also appears on the fronts, while the backs are blank. A header card picturing Milwaukee County Stadium also exists.

	NM	EX	VG
Complete Set (14):	335.00	165.00	100.00
Common Player:	25.00	12.50	7.50
(1) Joe Adcock	25.00	12.50	7.50
(2) William H. Bruton	25.00	12.50	7.50
(3) Robert Buhl	25.00	12.50	7.50
(4) Lou Burdette	25.00	12.50	7.50
(5) Del Crandall	25.00	12.50	7.50
(6) Jack Dittmer	25.00	12.50	7.50
(7) Johnny Logan	25.00	12.50	7.50
(8) Edwin L. Mathews, Jr.	75.00	37.50	22.00
(9) Chet Nichols	25.00	12.50	7.50
(10) Danny O'Connell	25.00	12.50	7.50
(11) Andy Pafko	25.00	12.50	7.50
(12) Warren E. Spahn	75.00	37.50	22.00
(13) Bob Thomson	35.00	17.50	10.00
(14) Milwaukee County Stadium	35.00	17.50	10.00

1954 Spic and Span Braves

Player selection points to 1954 as the date of this issue, making it contemporary with several other card sets produced by the chain of Wisconsin dry cleaners. These cards are printed in blue on 5-1/2" x 8-1/2" yellow cardstock. Fronts have player portraits by an artist signed as "Warmuth," facsimile autographs, a promotional quote from the player and the sponsor's logo. Backs are blank. It is not known whether the set is complete at 13.

	NM	EX	VG
Complete Set (13):	1,200	600.00	350.00
Common Player:	75.00	37.50	22.50
(1) Joe Adcock	90.00	45.00	27.50
(2) William H. Bruton	75.00	37.50	22.50
(3) Robert Buhl	75.00	37.50	22.50
(4) Lou Burdette	75.00	37.50	22.50
(5) Del Crandall	75.00	37.50	22.50
(6) Jack Dittmer	75.00	37.50	22.50
(7) Johnny Logan	75.00	37.50	22.50
(8) Edwin L. Mathews Jr.	225.00	110.00	70.00
(9) Chet Nichols	75.00	37.50	22.50
(10) Danny O'Connell	75.00	37.50	22.50
(11) Andy Pafko	75.00	37.50	22.50
(12) Warren E. Spahn	225.00	110.00	70.00
(13) Bob Thomson	90.00	45.00	27.50

1954-56 Spic and Span Braves

Issued during the three-year period from 1954-1956, this Spic and Span set consists of 18 postcard-size (4" x 6") cards. The front of the cards include a facsimile autograph printed in white and the Spic and Span logo.

	NM	EX	VG
Complete Set (18):	1,350	675.00	400.00
Common Player:	35.00	17.50	10.00
(1) Hank Aaron	400.00	200.00	120.00
(2) Joe Adcock	35.00	17.50	10.00
(3) William H. Bruton	35.00	17.50	10.00
(4) Robert Buhl	35.00	17.50	10.00
(5) Lou Burdette	35.00	17.50	10.00
(6) Gene Conley	35.00	17.50	10.00
(7) Del Crandall	35.00	17.50	10.00
(8) Ray Crone	35.00	17.50	10.00
(9) Jack Dittmer	35.00	17.50	10.00
(10) Ernie Johnson	35.00	17.50	10.00
(11) Dave Jolly	35.00	17.50	10.00
(12) Johnny Logan	35.00	17.50	10.00
(13) Edwin L. Mathews, Jr.	225.00	110.00	70.00
(14) Chet Nichols	35.00	17.50	10.00
(15) Danny O'Connell	35.00	17.50	10.00
(16) Andy Pafko	35.00	17.50	10.00
(17) Warren E. Spahn	220.00	110.00	70.00
(18) Bob Thomson	60.00	30.00	18.00

1955 Spic and Span Braves Die-cuts

This 17-card, die-cut set is the rarest of all the Spic and Span issues. The stand-ups, which measure approximately 7-1/2" x 7", picture the players in action poses and were designed to be punched out, allowing them to stand up. Most cards were used in this fashion, making better-condition cards very rare today. The front of the card includes a facsimile autograph and the Spic and Span logo.

	NM	EX	VG
Complete Set (18):	4,400	2,200	1,250
Common Player:	175.00	90.00	55.00
(1) Hank Aaron	900.00	450.00	275.00
(2) Joe Adcock	175.00	90.00	55.00
(3) Bill Bruton	175.00	90.00	55.00
(4) Bob Buhl	175.00	90.00	55.00
(5) Lew Burdette	175.00	90.00	55.00
(6) Gene Conley	175.00	90.00	55.00
(7) Del Crandall	175.00	90.00	55.00
(8) Jack Dittmer	175.00	90.00	55.00
(9) Ernie Johnson	175.00	90.00	55.00
(10) Dave Jolly	175.00	90.00	55.00
(11) John Logan	175.00	90.00	55.00
(12) Ed Mathews	450.00	225.00	135.00
(13) Chet Nichols	175.00	90.00	55.00
(14) Dan O'Connell	175.00	90.00	55.00
(15) Andy Pafko	175.00	90.00	55.00
(16) Warren Spahn	450.00	225.00	135.00
(17) Bob Thomson	225.00	110.00	65.00
(18) Jim Wilson	175.00	90.00	55.00

1957 Spic and Span Braves

This 20-card set was issued in 1957, the year the Braves were World Champions and is a highly desirable set. The cards measure 4" x 5" and have a wide white border surrounding the player photo. A blue Spic and Span logo appears in the lower-right corner and the card includes a salutation and facsimile autograph, also in blue.

	NM	EX	VG
Complete Set (20):	1,250	625.00	375.00
Common Player:	25.00	12.50	7.50
(1) Hank Aaron	400.00	200.00	120.00
(2) Joe Adcock	25.00	12.50	7.50
(3) Bill Bruton	25.00	12.50	7.50
(4) Bob Buhl	25.00	12.50	7.50
(5) Lew Burdette	25.00	12.50	7.50
(6) Gene Conley	25.00	12.50	7.50
(7) Wes Covington/SP	50.00	25.00	15.00
(8) Del Crandall	25.00	12.50	7.50
(9) Ray Crone	25.00	12.50	7.50
(10) Fred Haney	25.00	12.50	7.50
(11) Ernie Johnson	25.00	12.50	7.50
(12) John Logan	25.00	12.50	7.50
(13) Felix Mantilla/SP	50.00	25.00	15.00
(14) Ed Mathews	85.00	45.00	25.00
(15) Dan O'Connell	25.00	12.50	7.50
(16) Andy Pafko	25.00	12.50	7.50
(17) Red Schoendienst/SP	110.00	55.00	35.00
(18) Warren Spahn	85.00	45.00	25.00
(19) Bob Thomson	45.00	22.50	13.50
(20) Bob Trowbridge/SP	50.00	25.00	15.00

1960 Spic and Span Braves

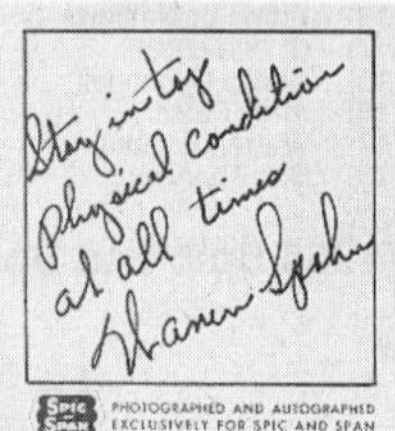

Spic and Span's final Milwaukee Braves issue consists of 26 cards, each measuring 2-3/4" x 3-1/8". The fronts contain a white-bordered photo with no printing, while the backs include a facsimile autograph and the words "Photographed and Autographed Exclusively for Spic and Span." The 1960 set includes the only known variation in the Spic and Span sets; a "flopped" negative error showing catcher Del Crandall batting left-handed was later corrected.

	NM	EX	VG
Complete Set (26):	1,650	825.00	500.00
Common Player:	35.00	17.50	10.00
(1) Hank Aaron	650.00	325.00	200.00
(2) Joe Adcock	35.00	17.50	10.00
(3) Bill Bruton	35.00	17.50	10.00
(4) Bob Buhl	35.00	17.50	10.00
(5) Lew Burdette	35.00	17.50	10.00
(6) Chuck Cottier	35.00	17.50	10.00
(7a) Del Crandall (Photo reversed.)	60.00	30.00	18.00
(7b) Del Crandall (Correct photo.)	35.00	17.50	10.00
(8) Chuck Dressen	35.00	17.50	10.00
(9) Joey Jay	35.00	17.50	10.00
(10) John Logan	35.00	17.50	10.00
(11) Felix Mantilla	35.00	17.50	10.00
(12) Ed Mathews	125.00	65.00	35.00
(13) Lee Maye	35.00	17.50	10.00
(14) Don McMahon	35.00	17.50	10.00
(15) George Myatt	35.00	17.50	10.00
(16) Andy Pafko	35.00	17.50	10.00
(17) Juan Pizarro	35.00	17.50	10.00
(18) Mel Roach	35.00	17.50	10.00
(19) Bob Rush	35.00	17.50	10.00
(20) Bob Scheffing	35.00	17.50	10.00
(21) Red Schoendienst	90.00	45.00	27.50
(22) Warren Spahn	125.00	65.00	35.00
(23) Al Spangler	35.00	17.50	10.00
(24) Frank Torre	35.00	17.50	10.00
(25) Carl Willey	35.00	17.50	10.00
(26) Whit Wyatt	35.00	17.50	10.00

1964-67 Sport Hobbyist Famous Card Series

These very early collectors issues were produced over a period of several years in the mid-1960s during Frank Nagy's ownership of the "Sport Hobbyist" magazine. The 2-1/4" x 3-3/4" black-and-white cards picture on their fronts reproductions of rare and famous baseball cards from Nagy's unequaled collection, including eight of the very rare Tarzan Bread issue of the mid-1930s which few collectors even today have seen. Backs have identification of the pictured card, utilizing the then-standard "American Card Catalog" set designations.

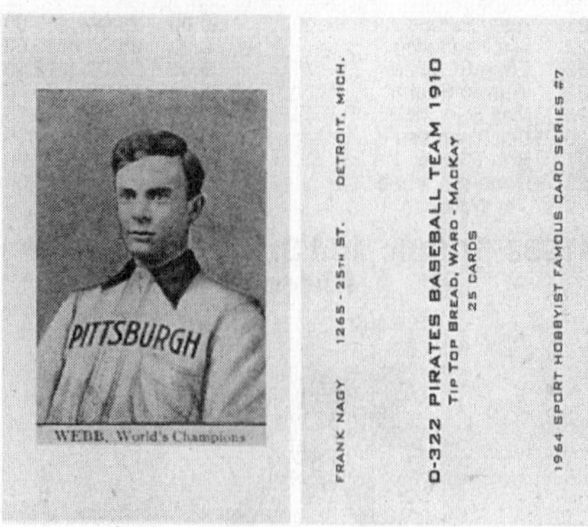

	NM	EX	VG
Complete Set (30):	90.00	45.00	27.50
Common Player:	5.00	2.50	1.50
1 T206 Honus Wagner	12.50	6.25	3.75
2 T212 Henley	5.00	2.50	1.50
3 C46 Simmons	5.00	2.50	1.50
4 M116 Christy Mathewson	5.00	2.50	1.50
5 M101-5 Jack Barry	5.00	2.50	1.50
6 T204 Mordecai Brown	5.00	2.50	1.50
7 D322 Tip Top Bread Webb	5.00	2.50	1.50
8 S74 Lou Criger	5.00	2.50	1.50
9 R333 DeLong Kiki Cuyler	5.00	2.50	1.50
10 R319 Nap Lajoie	7.50	3.75	2.25
11 T205 John McGraw	5.00	2.50	1.50
12 E107 Addie Joss	5.00	2.50	1.50
13 W502 George Sisler	5.00	2.50	1.50
14 Allen & Ginter N29 Buck Ewing	5.00	2.50	1.50
15 E90 Chief Bender	5.00	2.50	1.50
16 E104 George Mullin	5.00	2.50	1.50
17 E95 Fred Merkle	5.00	2.50	1.50
18 E121 Walter Schang	5.00	2.50	1.50
19 Allen & Ginter N28 Tim Keefe	5.00	2.50	1.50
20 E120 Harold (Muddy) Ruel	5.00	2.50	1.50
21 D382 Irving (Jack) Burns	5.00	2.50	1.50
22 D382 George Connally	5.00	2.50	1.50
23 D382 Myril Hoag	5.00	2.50	1.50
24 D382 Willie Kamm	5.00	2.50	1.50
25 D382 Dutch Leonard	5.00	2.50	1.50
26 D382 Clyde Manion	5.00	2.50	1.50
27 D382 Johnny Vergez	5.00	2.50	1.50
28 D382 Tom Zachary	5.00	2.50	1.50
29 E145 Ty Cobb	7.50	3.75	2.25
30 Playing Card, Richardson	5.00	2.50	1.50

1971 Sport Hobbyist Famous Card Series

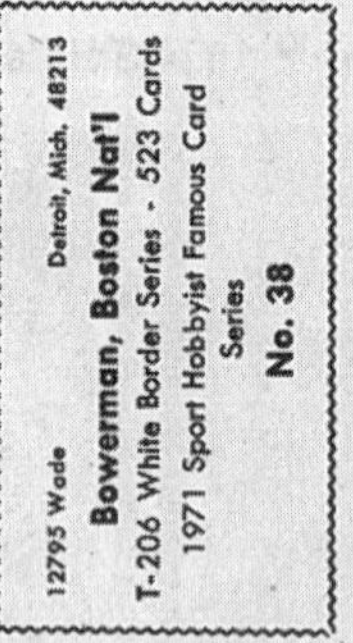

A new series of collector cards, designed as the first-ever attempt to reproduce the T206 tobacco set, was begun under the hobby paper's new ownership but quickly abandoned. The 2" x 3" cards have a black-and-white picture of a card at center, surrounded by a red frame (except Bescher, which has a black frame). Backs identify the card and include a card number.

	NM	EX	VG
Complete Set (21):	90.00	45.00	27.50
Common Card:	5.00	2.50	1.50
31 T206 Abbaticchio	5.00	2.50	1.50
32 T206 Barbeau	5.00	2.50	1.50
33 T206 Burch	5.00	2.50	1.50
34 T206 M. Brown	5.00	2.50	1.50
35 T206 Chase	5.00	2.50	1.50
36 T206 Ball	5.00	2.50	1.50
37 T206 Abstein	5.00	2.50	1.50
38 T206 Bowerman	5.00	2.50	1.50
39 T206 Chase	5.00	2.50	1.50
40 T206 Criss	5.00	2.50	1.50
41 T206 Beck	5.00	2.50	1.50
42 T206 Bresnahan	5.00	2.50	1.50
43 T206 Bradley	5.00	2.50	1.50
44 T206 Berger	5.00	2.50	1.50
45 T206 Bransfield	5.00	2.50	1.50
46 T206 Bescher	5.00	2.50	1.50
47 T206 Bell	5.00	2.50	1.50
48 T206 Bergen	5.00	2.50	1.50
49 T206 Bender	5.00	2.50	1.50
50 T206 Bush	5.00	2.50	1.50
51 T206 Chesbro	5.00	2.50	1.50

1975 Sport Hobbyist

This was one of several series of collectors issues produced in the 1960s and 1970s by the Sport Hobbyist, one of the card hobby's earliest periodicals. This series features the past greats of the game in postcard size (3-1/2" x 5-1/2"). Cards are found either blank-backed or with an ad offering various new-card products. Fronts of cards numbered through 115 have watercolor portraits in an oval frame. A box below offers a career summary. Higher number cards feature photos and/or artwork, sometimes with a caption, and sometimes with no identification. Cards are numbered with an SH prefix. Each series of 18 were originally sold for $1.50.

	NM	EX	VG
Complete Set (48):	150.00	75.00	45.00
Common Player:	5.00	2.50	1.50
98 Lou Gehrig	15.00	7.50	4.50
99 Ty Cobb	12.50	6.25	3.75
100 Joe DiMaggio	15.00	7.50	4.50
101 Mel Ott	5.00	2.50	1.50
102 Carl Hubbell	5.00	2.50	1.50
103 Babe Ruth	20.00	10.00	6.00
104 Rogers Hornsby	7.50	3.75	2.25
105 Tris Speaker	7.50	3.75	2.25
106 Hank Greenberg	7.50	3.75	2.25
107 Jimmy (Jimmie) Foxx	7.50	3.75	2.25
108 Ted Williams	15.00	7.50	4.50
109 Mickey Cochrane	5.00	2.50	1.50
110 Bob Feller	7.50	3.75	2.25
111 Cy Young	9.00	4.50	2.75
112 George Sissler (Sisler)	5.00	2.50	1.50
113 Honus Wagner	9.00	4.50	2.75
114 Lefty Grove	5.00	2.50	1.50
115 Dizzy Dean	7.50	3.75	2.25
116 Babe Ruth (Farewell address.)	9.00	4.50	2.75
117 Jackie Robinson	7.50	3.75	2.25
118 Mike Kelly (Woodcut)	5.00	2.50	1.50
119 Honus Wagner (Portrait and action.)	5.00	2.50	1.50
120 Babe Ruth (W/mascot Ray Kelly.)	9.00	4.50	2.75
121 Babe Ruth (Photos/artwork.)	5.00	2.50	1.50
122 John M. Ward (Newsboy cabinet.)	5.00	2.50	1.50
123 Babe Ruth (Photos/artwork.)	5.00	2.50	1.50
124 Babe Ruth (Artwork)	5.00	2.50	1.50
125 Hall of Fame Dedication, 1939	5.00	2.50	1.50
126 Babe Ruth (At microphone.)	5.00	2.50	1.50
127 Babe Ruth, Jacob Ruppert	7.50	3.75	2.25
128 Stan Musial	7.50	3.75	2.25
129 Babe Ruth (W/others.)	5.00	2.50	1.50
130 George Kell	5.00	2.50	1.50
131 Luke Appling	5.00	2.50	1.50
132 Cecil Travis	5.00	2.50	1.50
133 Larry "Yogi" Berra	7.50	3.75	2.25
134 Harry Heilman (Heilmann)	5.00	2.50	1.50
135 Johnny Mize	5.00	2.50	1.50
136 Christy Mathewson	7.50	3.75	2.25
137 Ralph Kiner	5.00	2.50	1.50
138 Bill Dickey	5.00	2.50	1.50
139 Hank Sauer	5.00	2.50	1.50
140 Hank Greenberg	7.50	3.75	2.25
141 Charlie Gehringer	5.00	2.50	1.50
142 Walter Evers	5.00	2.50	1.50
143 John Pepper Martin	5.00	2.50	1.50
144 Vern Stephens	5.00	2.50	1.50
145 Bobbie (Bobby) Doerr	5.00	2.50	1.50

1975 Sport Hobbyist Team Composites

This was one of several series of collectors issues produced in the 1960s and 1970s by the Sport Hobbyist, one of the card hobby's earliest periodicals. This series features black-and-white postcard size (about 3-1/2" x 5-1/4") reproductions of team composite photos from the 1931 Spalding Guide. Cards are blank-backed. Most of the cards are numbered, with an SH prefix, though some are not.

		NM	EX	VG
Common Card:		6.00	3.00	1.80
70	Chicago Cubs	6.00	3.00	1.80
71	Philadelphia Athletics	6.00	3.00	1.80
72	N.Y. Giants	6.00	3.00	1.80
73				
74	Pittsburgh Pirates	6.00	3.00	1.80
75	Chicago Cubs	6.00	3.00	1.80
76				
77	Boston Braves	6.00	3.00	1.80
78	Cincinnati Reds	6.00	3.00	1.80
79	Brooklyn Dodgers	6.00	3.00	1.80
80				
81	Philadelphia A's	6.00	3.00	1.80
82	Cleveland Indians	6.00	3.00	1.80
83	Detroit Tigers	6.00	3.00	1.80
84	Chicago White Sox	6.00	3.00	1.80
85	Chicago White Sox	6.00	3.00	1.80
86	Boston Red Sox	6.00	3.00	1.80
87	Boston Red Sox	6.00	3.00	1.80
88	N.Y. Yankees	10.00	5.00	3.00
89	Cleveland Indians	6.00	3.00	1.80
90	St. Louis Browns	6.00	3.00	1.80
91	Washington Senators	6.00	3.00	1.80
92	Boston Braves	6.00	3.00	1.80
93	St. Louis Browns	6.00	3.00	1.80
94	Washington Senators	6.00	3.00	1.80
95	Philadelphia Phillies	6.00	3.00	1.80
96	Cincinnati Reds	6.00	3.00	1.80
97	Philadelphia Phillies	6.00	3.00	1.80
	UNNUMBERED			
---	Brooklyn Dodgers	6.00	3.00	1.80
---	Detroit Tigers	6.00	3.00	1.80
---	N.Y. Yankees	10.00	5.00	3.00
---	Pittsburgh Pirates	6.00	3.00	1.80

1888-1889 Sporting Extra World Tour Imperial Cabinets

These large-format (about 9-3/4" x 6-1/2") imperial cabinet cards were issued in conjunction with "Spalding's World Base Ball Tour" of 1888-1889, though their method of distribution is unknown. The cards feature team portraits on a heavy cardboard, gilt-edge mount. At top is the name of the sponsoring cigarette brand, at bottom is the team name, printed in red. Backs are blank. Each of the cards that appeared in a 12/05 auction is believed unique.

(1) THE ALL AMERICA B.B. TOURISTS
(2) THE CHICAGO B.B. TOURISTS
Pair sold in 12/05 auction for $27,709.

1902-11 Sporting Life Cabinets (W600)

From 1902 through 1911, Sporting Life, a weekly newspaper published in Philadelphia, produced and sold a lengthy run of 5" x 7-1/2" "Cabinet Phototypes of Well-known Base-ball Players." They were collectively given the catalog number of W600 in "The American Card Catalog." Because many players were issued with different team designations as they moved about over the years, and because there are new discoveries from this issue being made even today, it is likely this checklist will remain in flux for some time to come. For that reason, gaps in the assigned card numbers in this checklist have been left to accommodate additions. Several different styles and colors of mattes were used over the years, with many players issued in more than one of them. Many of the earliest cabinets picture the players in suit-and-tie, while later issues show them in uniform. Where verified, cabinets showing players in street clothes are noted. The black-and-white player portraits are mounted on heavy cardboard mattes. The player's name, position, team and league are printed beneath the photo. Backs are blank. Each cabinet was issued in a transparent envelope. They were originally given away for three two-cents stamps and a coupon found in the paper; later they were offered for sale for 10 cents apiece; 12 for a dollar. The checklist here is presented in alphabetical order. Most of the names are as presented in contemporary ads from the newspaper; rife with misspellings and misidentifications, and may or may not represent the actual spelling shown on the cards. The year shown in parentheses indicates the first year the player was issued with that team. Because these cards were sold individually upon fan request, this is an issue in which the superstars of the day are more common than the benchwarmers. It is also likely that some of the cards on this list were never issued or do not survive.

		NM	EX	VG
Common Player:		2,400	1,200	720.00
(1)	Edward Abbatichio (Abbaticchio) (Boston NL, 1903.)	3,600	1,800	1,100
(2)	Edward Abbaticchio (Pittsburg, 1907.)	2,400	1,200	720.00
(3)	William Abstein (St. Louis AL, 1910.)	2,400	1,200	720.00
(4)	Charles B. Adams (Pittsburg, 1909.)	2,400	1,200	720.00
(5)	C.A. Alperman (Brooklyn, 1906.)	2,400	1,200	720.00
(6)	David Altizer (Washington, 1907.)	2,400	1,200	720.00
(7)	Nick Altrock (Chicago AL, 1903.)	4,300	2,150	1,300
(8)	Leon Ames (New York, NL, 1904.)	2,400	1,200	720.00
(9)	John Anderson (St. Louis AL, 1902, street.)	3,600	1,800	1,100
(10)	John Anderson (New York AL, 1904.)	2,400	1,200	720.00
(11)	John Anderson (Washington, 1905.)	2,400	1,200	720.00
(12)	Frank Arelanes (Arellanes) (Boston AL, 1910.)	2,400	1,200	720.00
(13)	Charles Armbruster (Boston AL, 1906.)	2,400	1,200	720.00
(14)	William R. Armour (Detroit, 1906.)	2,400	1,200	720.00
(15)	Harry Arndt (St. Louis NL, 1906.)	2,400	1,200	720.00
(16)	Harry J. Aubrey (Boston NL, 1903.)	3,600	1,800	1,100
(17)	James Austin (New York AL, 1910.)	2,400	1,200	720.00
(18)	Charles Babb (New York NL, 1903.)	3,600	1,800	1,100
(19)	Charles Babb (Brooklyn, 1904.)	2,400	1,200	720.00
(20)	William Bailey (St. Louis AL, 1910.)	2,400	1,200	720.00
(21)	Frank Baker (Philadelphia AL, 1910.)	6,500	3,250	1,950
(22)	J. Barbeau (Cleveland, 1906.)	2,400	1,200	720.00
(23)	G.O. Barclay (Boston NL, 1904.)	2,400	1,200	720.00
(24)	Edward Barger (First name Eros.) (Brooklyn, 1910.))	2,400	1,200	720.00
(25)	James Barrett (Detroit, 1902, street.)	3,600	1,800	1,100
(26)	James Barrett (Boston AL, 1906.)	2,400	1,200	720.00
(27)	John C. Barry (Philadelphia NL, 1902.)	3,600	1,800	1,100
(28)	John C. Barry (Chicago NL, 1904.)	2,400	1,200	720.00
(29)	John C. Barry (Cincinnati, 1905.)	2,400	1,200	720.00
(30)	John C. Barry (St. Louis NL, 1906.)	2,400	1,200	720.00
(31)	John J. Barry (Philadelphia AL, 1910.)	2,400	1,200	720.00
(32)	Harry L. Barton (Philadelphia AL, 1905.)	2,400	1,200	720.00
(33)	Henry Batch (Brooklyn, 1906.)	2,400	1,200	720.00
(34)	Joseph Bates (Johnny) (Boston NL, 1907.)	2,400	1,200	720.00
(35)	Harry Bay (Cleveland, 1903.)	3,600	1,800	1,100
(36)	Clarence H. Beaumont (Pittsburg, 1902, street.)	3,600	1,800	1,100
(37)	Clarence H. Beaumont (Pittsburg, 1902, uniform.)	3,600	1,800	1,100
(38)	Clarence H. Beaumont (Boston NL, 1907.)	2,400	1,200	720.00
(39)	Fred Beck (Boston NL, 1910.)	2,400	1,200	720.00
(40)	Harry Beckendorf (Detroit, 1910.)	2,400	1,200	720.00
(41)	Jacob Beckley (Cincinnati, 1902.)	7,900	4,000	2,375
(42)	Jacob Beckley (St. Louis NL, 1904.)	6,500	3,250	1,950
(43)	Fred L. Beebe (St. Louis NL, 1906.)	2,400	1,200	720.00
(44)	George C. Bell (Brooklyn, 1910.)	2,400	1,200	720.00
(45)	Harry Bemis (Cleveland, 1903.)	3,600	1,800	1,100
(46)	Charles Bender (Philadelphia AL, 1903, street.)	7,900	4,000	2,375
(47)	Charles Bender (Philadelphia AL, 1903, uniform.)	7,900	4,000	2,375
(48)	Justin J. Bennett (St. Louis NL, 1907.)	2,400	1,200	720.00
(49)	William Bergen (Brooklyn, 1904.)	2,400	1,200	720.00
(50)	Charles Berger (Cleveland, 1907.)	2,400	1,200	720.00
(51)	William Bernhardt (Bernhard) (Cleveland, 1902, street.)	3,600	1,800	1,100
(52)	Robert Bescher (Cincinnati, 1910.)	2,400	1,200	720.00
(53)	Walter Beville (Henry "Monte") (New York, AL 1903.))	3,600	1,800	1,100
(54)	Walter Beville (Henry "Monte") (Detroit, 1904.)	2,400	1,200	720.00
(55)	Russell Blackburne (Chicago AL, 1910.)	2,400	1,200	720.00
(56)	Elmer Bliss (St. Louis NL, 1910.)	2,400	1,200	720.00
(57)	Frank Bowerman (New York NL, 1903.)	3,600	1,800	1,100
(58)	Frank (William J.) Bradley (Cleveland, 1903.)	3,600	1,800	1,100
(59)	William J. Bradley (Cleveland, 1903.)	3,600	1,800	1,100
(60)	David L. Brain (St. Louis NL, 1903.)	3,600	1,800	1,100
(61)	David L. Brain (Pittsburg, 1905.)	2,400	1,200	720.00
(62)	David L. Brain (Boston NL, 1906.)	2,400	1,200	720.00
(63)	William Bransfield (Pittsburg, 1902, street.)	3,600	1,800	1,100
(64)	William Bransfield (Pittsburg, 1902, uniform.)	3,600	1,800	1,100
(65)	William Bransfield (Philadelphia NL, 1905.)	2,400	1,200	720.00
(66)	Roger Bresnahan (New York NL, 1903.)	7,900	4,000	2,375
(67)	Roger Bresnahan (St. Louis NL, 1909.)	6,500	3,250	1,950
(68)	Albert Bridwell (Boston NL, 1906.)	2,400	1,200	720.00
(69)	Herbert Briggs (Chicago NL, 1905.)	2,400	1,200	720.00
(70)	Herbert Briggs (Brooklyn, 1906.)	2,400	1,200	720.00
(71)	Charles E. Brown (St. Louis NL, 1906.)	2,400	1,200	720.00
(72)	Charles E. Brown (Philadelphia NL, 1907.)	2,400	1,200	720.00
(73)	Mordecai Brown (Chicago NL, 1904.)	6,500	3,250	1,950
(74)	Samuel Brown (Boston NL, 1907.)	2,400	1,200	720.00
(75)	George Browne (New York NL, 1903.)	3,600	1,800	1,100
(76)	Fred Buelow (Detroit, 1903.)	3,600	1,800	1,100
(77)	Fred Buelow (Cleveland, 1904.)	2,400	1,200	720.00
(78)	James T. Burke (St. Louis NL, 1903.)	3,600	1,800	1,100
(79)	James T. Burke (Philadelphia AL, 1906.)	2,400	1,200	720.00
(80)	Jesse Burkett (St. Louis AL, 1903.)	43,200	21,600	12,960
(81)	Jesse Burkett (Boston AL, 1905.)	6,500	3,250	1,950
(82)	James J. Callahan (Chicago AL, 1903.)	3,600	1,800	1,100
(83)	Howard Camnitz (Pittsburg, 1910.)	2,400	1,200	720.00
(84)	Wirt V. Cannell (Virgin Wirt) (Boston NL, 1903.)	3,600	1,800	1,100
(85)	Joseph Cantillion (Washington, 1907.)	2,400	1,200	720.00
(86)	George Carey (Washington, 1903.)	3,600	1,800	1,100
(87)	P.J. Carney (Boston NL, 1903.)	3,600	1,800	1,100
(88)	Charles C. Carr (Cleveland, 1904.)	2,400	1,200	720.00
(89)	Charles C. Carr (Cincinnati, 1906.)	2,400	1,200	720.00
(90)	William Carrigan (Boston AL, 1910.)	2,400	1,200	720.00
(91)	James P. Casey (Chicago NL, 1902, street.)	3,600	1,800	1,100
(92)	James P. Casey (Brooklyn, 1906.)	2,400	1,200	720.00
(93)	Joseph Cassidy (Washington, 1904.)	2,400	1,200	720.00
(94)	Luis Castro (Philadelphia AL, 1902, street.)	2,400	1,200	720.00
(95)	Frank Chance (Chicago NL, 1902, street.)	7,900	4,000	2,375
(96)	Frank Chance (Chicago NL, 1902, uniform.)	7,900	4,000	2,375
(97)	Harold Chase (New York AL, 1906.)	5,000	2,600	1,400
(98)	John Chesbro (Pittsburg, 1902, street.)	7,900	4,000	2,375
(99)	John Chesbro (New York AL, 1903, uniform.)	7,900	4,000	2,375
(100)	Edw. V. Cicotte (Boston AL, 1910.)	6,500	3,250	1,950
(101)	William Clark (Clarke) (Washington, 1903.)	3,600	1,800	1,100
(102)	William Clark (Clarke) (New York NL, 1905.)	2,400	1,200	720.00
(103)	Fred Clarke (Pittsburg, 1902, street.)	7,900	4,000	2,375
(104)	Fred Clarke (Pittsburg, 1902, uniform.)	7,900	4,000	2,375
(104)	Justin J. Clarke (Cleveland, 1906.)	2,400	1,200	720.00
(105)	Thomas Clarke (Cincinnati, 1910.)	2,400	1,200	720.00
(106)	Walter Clarkson (New York AL, 1906.)	2,400	1,200	720.00
(107)	Walter Clarkson (Cleveland, 1907.)	2,400	1,200	720.00
(108)	Otis Clymer (Pittsburg, 1905.)	2,400	1,200	720.00
(109)	Otis Clymer (Washington, 1907.)	2,400	1,200	720.00
(110)	Andrew Coakley (Philadelphia AL, 1905.)	2,400	1,200	720.00
(111)	Andrew Coakley (Cincinnati, 1907.)	2,400	1,200	720.00
(112)	Tyrus R. Cobb (Detroit, 1907.)	21,600	10,800	6,500
(115)	Edward Collins (Philadelphia AL, 1907.)	6,500	3,250	1,950
(116)	James Collins (Boston AL, 1902, uniform.)	7,200	3,600	2,150
(117)	W.M. Congalton (Cleveland, 1906.)	2,400	1,200	720.00

(118) W.A. Congalton (Boston AL, 1907.) 2,400 1,200 720.00
(119) William Conroy (New York AL, 1903.) 3,600 1,800 1,100
(120) Richard Cooley (Boston NL, 1902, street.) 3,600 1,800 1,100
(121) Richard Cooley (Detroit, 1905.) 2,400 1,200 720.00
(122) John W. Coombs (Philadelphia AL, 1910.) 2,400 1,200 720.00
(123) T.W. Corcoran (Cincinnati, 1904.) 2,400 1,200 720.00
(124) T.W. Corcoran (New York NL, 1907.) 2,400 1,200 720.00
(125) Frank J. Corridon (Philadelphia NL, 1907.) 2,400 1,200 720.00
(126) William Coughlin (Washington, 1903.) 3,600 1,800 1,100
(127) William Coughlin (Detroit, 1904.) 2,400 1,200 720.00
(128) Ernest Courtney (Philadelphia NL, 1905.) 2,400 1,200 720.00
(129) Otis Crandall (New York NL, 1910.) 2,400 1,200 720.00
(130) Samuel Crawford (Cincinnati, 1902, street.) 7,900 4,000 2,375
(131) Samuel Crawford (Detroit, 1903.) 7,900 4,000 2,375
(132) Burde Cree (Birdie) (New York AL, 1911.)) 2,400 1,200 720.00
(134) Louis Criger (Boston AL, 1903.) 3,600 1,800 1,100
(135) Dode Criss (St. Louis AL, 1910.) 2,400 1,200 720.00
(136) John Cronin (New York NL, 1903.) 3,600 1,800 1,100
(137) John Cronin (Brooklyn, 1904.) 2,400 1,200 720.00
(138) Lafayette Cross (Philadelphia AL, 1902, street.) 3,600 1,800 1,100
(139) Lafayette Cross (Washington, 1906.) 2,400 1,200 720.00
(140) Monte Cross (Philadelphia AL, 1902.) 3,600 1,800 1,100
(142) Clarence Currie (St. Louis NL, 1903.) 3,600 1,800 1,100
(143) Clarence Currie (Chicago NL, 1903.) 3,600 1,800 1,100
(145) William Dahlen (Brooklyn, 1902, street.) 4,300 2,150 1,300
(146) William Dahlen (New York NL, 1904.) 2,400 1,200 720.00
(147) Thomas Daly (Chicago AL, 1903, street.) 3,600 1,800 1,100
(148) Thomas Daly (Cincinnati, 1903.) 3,600 1,800 1,100
(148) George Davis (Chicago AL, 1902.) 7,900 4,000 2,375
(150) Harry Davis (Philadelphia AL, 1902, street.) 3,600 1,800 1,100
(152) Edward J. Delahanty (Washington, 1902, street.) 19,400 9,700 5,825
(153) James Delahanty (Boston NL, 1904.) 2,400 1,200 720.00
(154) James Delahanty (Cincinnati, 1906.) 2,400 1,200 720.00
(155) James Delahanty (St. Louis AL, 1907.) 2,400 1,200 720.00
(156) James Delahanty (Washington, 1907.) 2,400 1,200 720.00
(158) Arthur Devlin (New York NL, 1905.) 2,400 1,200 720.00
(159) Joshua Devore (New York NL, 1911.) 2,400 1,200 720.00
(160) Charles Dexter (Boston NL, 1903.) 3,600 1,800 1,100
(161) Frank Dillon (Brooklyn, 1903.) 3,600 1,800 1,100
(162) William Dinneen (Boston AL, 1903.) 3,600 1,800 1,100
(163) William Dineen (St. Louis AL, 1907.) 2,400 1,200 720.00
(164) John Dobbs (Brooklyn, 1903.) 3,600 1,800 1,100
(164) Edward Doheny (Pittsburg, 1903.) 3,600 1,800 1,100
(165) Harry Dolan (Patrick Henry "Cozy")(Cincinnati, 1904.)) 2,400 1,200 720.00
(166) Harry Dolan (Patrick Henry "Cozy")(Boston NL, 1905.)) 2,400 1,200 720.00
(167) Frank Donahue (St. Louis AL, 1903.) 3,600 1,800 1,100
(168) Frank Donahue (Cleveland, 1903.) 3,600 1,800 1,100
(169) Frank Donahue (Detroit, 1906.) 2,400 1,200 720.00
(170) J. "Jiggs" Donahue (Chicago AL, 1903.) 3,600 1,800 1,100
(171) Michael Donlin (Cincinnati, 1902, street.) 3,600 1,800 1,100
(172) Michael Donlin (New York NL, 1904.) 2,400 1,200 720.00
(173) P.J. (Patrick) Donovan (St. Louis NL, 1902, street.) 3,600 1,800 1,100
(174) Patrick J. Donovan (Washington, 1904.) 2,400 1,200 720.00
(175) Patrick J. Donovan (Brooklyn, 1906, street.) 2,400 1,200 720.00
(176) William Donovan (Detroit, 1903.) 3,600 1,800 1,100
(177) Charles Dooin (Philadelphia NL, 1903.) 3,600 1,800 1,100
(178) Michael Doolin (Doolan) (Philadelphia NL, 1906.) 2,400 1,200 720.00
(180) Thomas Doran (Boston AL, 1904.) 2,400 1,200 720.00
(181) Thomas Doran (Detroit, 1905.) 2,400 1,200 720.00
(182) August Dorner (Boston NL, 1907.) 2,400 1,200 720.00
(183) Patrick Dougherty (Boston AL, 1903.) 3,600 1,800 1,100
(184) Patrick Dougherty (New York AL, 1904.) 2,400 1,200 720.00
(185) Patrick Dougherty (Chicago AL, 1906.) 2,400 1,200 720.00
(186) William Douglas (Douglass) (Philadelphia NL, 1902.) 3,600 1,800 1,100
(187) Thomas Downey (Cincinnati, 1910.) 2,400 1,200 720.00
(188) J.W. Downs (Detroit, 1907.) 2,400 1,200 720.00
(189) Joe Doyle (New York AL, 1907.) 2,400 1,200 720.00
(190) John Doyle (Brooklyn, 1903.) 3,600 1,800 1,100
(191) John Doyle (Philadelphia NL, 1904.) 2,400 1,200 720.00
(192) Larry J. Doyle (New York NL, 1908.) 2,400 1,200 720.00
(194) Louis Drill (Washington, 1903.) 3,600 1,800 1,100
(195) Louis Drill (Detroit, 1904.) 2,400 1,200 720.00
(196) Hugh Duffy (Philadelphia NL, 1905.) 6,500 3,250 1,950
(197) William Duggleby (Philadelphia NL, 1903.) 3,600 1,800 1,100
(198) William Duggleby (Pittsburg, 1907.) 2,400 1,200 720.00
(199) August Dundon (Chicago AL, 1904.) 2,400 1,200 720.00
(200) Edward Dunkle (Washington, 1903.) 3,600 1,800 1,100
(201) James Dunleavy (John) (St. Louis NL, 1904.) 2,400 1,200 720.00
(202) John Dunn (New York NL, 1903.) 3,600 1,800 1,100
(203) James H. Dygert (Philadelphia AL, 1905.) 2,400 1,200 720.00
(204) Malcolm Eason (Brooklyn, 1906.) 2,400 1,200 720.00
(205) Harry Eells (Cleveland, 1906.) 2,400 1,200 720.00
(206) Richard J. Egan (Cincinnati, 1910.) 2,400 1,200 720.00
(207) Norman Elberfeld (Detroit, 1903.) 3,600 1,800 1,100
(208) Norman Elberfeld (New York AL, 1903.) 3,600 1,800 1,100
(209) Claude Elliott (New York NL, 1904.) 2,400 1,200 720.00
(210) George W. Ellis (St. Louis NL, 1910.) 2,400 1,200 720.00
(212) John Eubank (Detroit, 1906.) 2,400 1,200 720.00
(213) John Evers (Chicago NL, 1903.) 7,900 4,000 2,375
(214) Robert Ewing (George L.) (Cincinnati, 1904.) 2,400 1,200 720.00
(216) Fred Falkenberg (Washington, 1906.) 2,400 1,200 720.00
(217) Charles Farrell (Brooklyn, 1902, street.) 3,600 1,800 1,100
(218) Charles Farrell (Boston AL, 1903.) 3,600 1,800 1,100
(219) John S. Farrell (St. Louis NL, 1903.) 3,600 1,800 1,100
(220) Cecil Ferguson (George) (New York NL, 1906.) 2,400 1,200 720.00
(221) Hobe Ferris (Boston AL, 1903.) 3,600 1,800 1,100
(222) Thomas S. Fisher (Middle initial C.) (Boston NL, 1904.) 2,400 1,200 720.00
(223) Patrick Flaherty (Chicago AL, 1903.) 3,600 1,800 1,100
(224) Patrick Flaherty (Pittsburg, 1904.) 2,400 1,200 720.00
(225) Patrick Flaherty (Boston NL, 1907.) 2,400 1,200 720.00
(226) Elmer Flick (Cleveland, 1903.) 7,900 4,000 2,375
(227) John Flynn (Pittsburg, 1910.) 2,400 1,200 720.00
(229) William Foxen (Chicago NL, 1910.) 2,400 1,200 720.00
(231) Charles Fraser (Philadelphia NL, 1903, street.) 3,600 1,800 1,100
(232) Charles Fraser (Boston NL, 1905.) 2,400 1,200 720.00
(233) Charles Fraser (Chicago NL, 1907.) 2,400 1,200 720.00
(234) John ("Buck") Freeman (Boston AL, 1902.) 4,300 2,150 1,300
(235) William Friel (St. Louis AL, 1903.) 3,600 1,800 1,100
(236) Arthur Fromme (Cincinnati, 1910.) 2,400 1,200 720.00
(237) David L. Fultz (Philadelphia AL, 1902, street.) 3,600 1,800 1,100
(238) David L. Fultz (New York AL, 1903.) 3,600 1,800 1,100
(240) Robert S. Ganley (Pittsburg, 1906.) 2,400 1,200 720.00
(241) Robert S. Ganley (Washington, 1907.) 2,400 1,200 720.00
(242) John Ganzell (Ganzel) (New York AL, 1903.) 3,600 1,800 1,100
(243) John Ganzel (Ganzell) (Cincinnati, 1907.) 2,400 1,200 720.00
(244) Virgil Garvin (Brooklyn, 1903.) 3,600 1,800 1,100
(245) Harry L. Gaspar (Cincinnati, 1910.) 2,400 1,200 720.00
(246) Philip Geier (Boston NL, 1904.) 2,400 1,200 720.00
(247) Harry Gessler (Brooklyn, 1903.) 3,600 1,800 1,100
(248) Harry Gessler (Chicago NL, 1906.) 2,400 1,200 720.00
(250) George Gibson (Pittsburg, 1905.) 2,400 1,200 720.00
(251) Norwood Gibson (Boston AL, 1903.) 3,600 1,800 1,100
(252) William Gilbert (New York NL, 1903.) 3,600 1,800 1,100
(253) Frederick Glade (St. Louis AL, 1904.) 2,400 1,200 720.00
(254) Harry Gleason (Boston AL, 1903.) 3,600 1,800 1,100
(255) Harry Gleason (St. Louis AL, 1904.) 2,400 1,200 720.00
(256) William Gleason (Philadelphia NL, 1903.) 3,600 1,800 1,100
(258) William Gochnauer (John Gochnaur) (Cleveland, 1903.) 3,600 1,800 1,100
(259) Michael Grady (St. Louis NL, 1904.) 2,400 1,200 720.00
(260) Edward L. Grant (Philadelphia NL, 1910.) 3,450 1,725 1,050
(262) Daniel Green (Chicago AL, 1903.) 3,600 1,800 1,100
(263) E.W. Greminger (Boston NL, 1903.) 3,600 1,800 1,100
(264) E.W. Greminger (Detroit, 1904.) 2,400 1,200 720.00
(265) Clarke Griffith (Clark) (Chicago AL, 1902.) 7,900 4,000 2,375
(266) Clarke Griffith (Clark) (New York AL, 1903.) 7,900 4,000 2,375
(267) Myron Grimshaw (Boston AL, 1906.) 2,400 1,200 720.00
(269) James Hackett (St. Louis NL, 1903.) 3,600 1,800 1,100
(270) Edgar Hahn (Chicago AL, 1906.) 2,400 1,200 720.00
(271) Frank Hahn (Cincinnati, 1902, street.) 2,400 1,200 720.00
(272) Frank Hahn (New York AL, 1905.) 2,400 1,200 720.00
(273) Charles Hall (Cincinnati, 1907.) 2,400 1,200 720.00
(274) William H. Hallman (Philadelphia NL, 1903.) 3,600 1,800 1,100
(275) William H. Hallman (Pittsburg, 1906.) 2,400 1,200 720.00
(276) Edward Hanlon (Brooklyn, 1905, street.) 6,500 3,250 1,950
(277) Edward Hanlon (Cincinnati, 1906.) 6,500 3,250 1,950
(278) Richard Harley (Chicago NL, 1903.) 3,600 1,800 1,100
(279) Robert Harmon (St. Louis NL, 1910.) 2,400 1,200 720.00
(280) Charles Harper (Cincinnati, 1903.) 3,600 1,800 1,100
(281) Charles Harper (Chicago NL, 1906.) 2,400 1,200 720.00
(282) Joseph Harris (Boston AL, 1906.) 2,400 1,200 720.00
(283) Harry Hart (Chicago AL, 1906.) 2,400 1,200 720.00
(284) Frederick L. Hartzell (Hartsel) (Philadelphia AL, 1902.) 3,600 1,800 1,100
(285) Roy A. Hartzell (St. Louis AL, 1906.) 2,400 1,200 720.00
(287) J.E. Heidrick (St. Louis AL, 1903.) 3,600 1,800 1,100
(288) Charles Hemphill (St. Louis AL, 1903.) 3,600 1,800 1,100
(289) Weldon Henley (Philadelphia AL, 1903, street.) 3,600 1,800 1,100
(290) Otto Hess (Cleveland, 1904.) 2,400 1,200 720.00
(291) Edward Heydon (Mike) (Washington, 1906.) 2,400 1,200 720.00
(292) Charles Hickman (Cleveland, 1903.) 3,600 1,800 1,100
(293) Charles Hickman (Detroit, 1904.) 2,400 1,200 720.00
(294) Charles Hickman (Washington, 1905.) 2,400 1,200 720.00
(295) Charles Hickman (Chicago AL, 1907.) 2,400 1,200 720.00
(296) Hunter Hill (St. Louis AL, 1903.) 3,600 1,800 1,100
(297) Hunter Hill (Washington, 1904.) 2,400 1,200 720.00
(298) Homer Hillebrand (Pittsburg, 1905.) 2,400 1,200 720.00
(299) Harry Hinchman (Cleveland, 1907.) 2,400 1,200 720.00
(300) William Hinchman (Cleveland, 1907.) 2,400 1,200 720.00
(303) R. C. Hoblitzel (Cincinnati, 1910.) 2,400 1,200 720.00
(304) Daniel Hoffman (Philadelphia AL, 1903.) 3,600 1,800 1,100
(305) Daniel Hoffman (New York AL, 1906.) 2,400 1,200 720.00
(306) Arthur Hofman (Chicago NL, 1906.) 2,400 1,200 720.00
(307) William Hogg (New York AL, 1906.) 2,400 1,200 720.00
(308) A. Holesketter (St. Louis NL, 1907.) 2,400 1,200 720.00
(309) William Holmes (James Wm. "Ducky") (Chicago AL, 1903.) 3,600 1,800 1,100
(310) George Howard (Pittsburg, 1905.) 2,400 1,200 720.00
(311) George Howard (Boston NL, 1906.) 2,400 1,200 720.00
(312) Harry Howell (Baltimore, 1902, street.) 3,600 1,800 1,100
(313) Harry Howell (New York AL, 1903, street.) 3,600 1,800 1,100
(314) Harry Howell (St. Louis AL, 1904.) 2,400 1,200 720.00
(315) Miller Huggins (Cincinnati, 1906.) 6,500 3,250 1,950
(316) James Hughes (Brooklyn, 1902, street.) 3,600 1,800 1,100
(317) Thomas Hughes (Boston AL, 1902.) 3,600 1,800 1,100
(318) Thomas Hughes (New York AL, 1904.) 2,400 1,200 720.00

(319) Thomas Hughes (Washington, 1904.)	2,400	1,200	720.00
(320) John Hulseman (Frank Huelsman) (Washington, 1904.)	2,400	1,200	720.00
(321) Rudolph Hulswitt (Philadelphia NL, 1903.)	3,600	1,800	1,100
(322) John Hummell (Hummel) (Brooklyn, 1906.))	2,400	1,200	720.00
(323) Berthold J. Husting (Philadelphia AL, 1902, street.)	3,600	1,800	1,100
(324) Hamilton Hyatt (Pittsburg, 1909.)	2,400	1,200	720.00
(325) Frank Isbell (Chicago AL, 1903.)	3,600	1,800	1,100
(326) Fred Jacklitsch (Brooklyn, 1903, street.)	3,600	1,800	1,100
(327) Fred Jacklitsch (Philadelphia NL, 1907.)	2,400	1,200	720.00
(328) James Jackson (Cleveland, 1906.)	2,400	1,200	720.00
(329) Harry Jacobson (Albert "Beany") (Washington, 1904.)	2,400	1,200	720.00
(330) Harry Jacobson (Albert "Beany") (St. Louis AL, 1906.)	2,400	1,200	720.00
(331) Harry Jacobson (Albert "Beany") (Boston AL, 1907.)	2,400	1,200	720.00
(333) Hugh Jennings (Philadelphia NL, 1902.)	7,900	4,000	2,375
(334) Hugh Jennings (Detroit, 1907.)	6,500	3,250	1,950
(335) Charles Jones (Washington, 1905.)	2,400	1,200	720.00
(336) David Jones (Chicago NL, 1904.)	2,400	1,200	720.00
(337) David Jones (Detroit, 1906.)	2,400	1,200	720.00
(338) Fielder Jones (Chicago AL, 1902.)	3,600	1,800	1,100
(339) Oscar Jones (Brooklyn, 1903.)	3,600	1,800	1,100
(340) Thomas Jones (St. Louis AL, 1904.)	2,400	1,200	720.00
(341) Otto Jordan ("Dutch") (Brooklyn, 1903.)	3,600	1,800	1,100
(342) Otto Jordan ("Dutch") (Cleveland, 1905.)	2,400	1,200	720.00
(343) Tim Jordan (Brooklyn, 1906.)	2,400	1,200	720.00
(344) Adrian Joss (Cleveland, 1903.)	8,600	4,300	2,600
(345) Michael Kahoe (St. Louis AL, 1903.)	3,600	1,800	1,100
(346) Michael Kahoe (Philadelphia NL, 1905.)	2,400	1,200	720.00
(347) Michael Kahoe (Chicago NL, 1907.)	2,400	1,200	720.00
(348) Michael Kahoe (Washington, 1907.)	2,400	1,200	720.00
(349) Edward Karger (Edwin) (Boston AL, 1910.)	2,400	1,200	720.00
(350) Robert Keefe (New York AL, 1906.)	2,400	1,200	720.00
(351) William Keeler (Brooklyn, 1902, street.)	7,900	4,000	2,375
(352) William Keeler (New York, AL 1903, street.)	7,900	4,000	2,375
(353) William Keister (Philadelphia NL, 1903.)	3,600	1,800	1,100
(355) Joseph J. Kelley (Cincinnati, 1902, street.)	13,000	6,500	3,900
(356) William Kennedy (Pittsburg, 1903, street.)	3,600	1,800	1,100
(357) Edward Killian (Detroit, 1904.)	2,400	1,200	720.00
(358) James Kissinger (Chas. "Rube" Kisinger) (Detroit, 1903.)	3,600	1,800	1,100
(359) Frank Kitson (Brooklyn, 1902, street.)	3,600	1,800	1,100
(360) Frank Kitson (Detroit, 1903.)	3,600	1,800	1,100
(361) Frank Kitson (Washington, 1906.)	2,400	1,200	720.00
(362) Frank Kitson (New York AL, 1907.)	2,400	1,200	720.00
(363) Malachi Kittridge (Washington, 1903.)	3,600	1,800	1,100
(365) John Kleinow (New York AL, 1905, street.)	2,400	1,200	720.00
(366) John Kleinow (New York AL, 1905, uniform.)	2,400	1,200	720.00
(367) John Kling (Chicago NL, 1903.)	3,600	1,800	1,100
(368) F. Otto Knabe (Philadelphia NL, 1910.)	2,400	1,200	720.00
(369) John Knight (Philadelphia AL, 1905.)	2,400	1,200	720.00
(370) John Knight (Boston AL, 1907.)	2,400	1,200	720.00
(371) Bernard Koehler (St. Louis AL, 1906.)	2,400	1,200	720.00
(372) Edward Konetchy (St. Louis NL, 1907.)	2,400	1,200	720.00
(373) Harry Krause (Philadelphia AL, 1910.)	2,400	1,200	720.00
(374) Otto Krueger (Pittsburg, 1903.)	3,600	1,800	1,100
(375) Otto Krueger (Philadelphia NL, 1905.)	2,400	1,200	720.00
(376) George LaChance (Boston AL, 1903.)	3,600	1,800	1,100
(377) Napoleon Lajoie (Cleveland, 1902, street.)	7,900	4,000	2,375
(378) Napoleon Lajoie (Cleveland, 1902, uniform.)	7,900	4,000	2,375
(379) Joseph Lake (St. Louis AL, 1910.)	2,400	1,200	720.00
(380) Frank Laporte (LaPorte) (New York AL, 1906.)	2,400	1,200	720.00
(381) Louis Laroy (LeRoy)	2,400	1,200	720.00
(382) William Lauder (New York NL, 1903.)	3,600	1,800	1,100
(383) Thomas Leach (Pittsburg, 1902.)	3,600	1,800	1,100
(384) Wyatt Lee (Washington, 1903.)	3,600	1,800	1,100
(385) Wyatt Lee (Pittsburg, 1904.)	2,400	1,200	720.00
(386) Samuel Leever (Pittsburg, 1902, street.)	3,600	1,800	1,100
(387) Samuel Leever (Pittsburg, 1902, uniform.)	2,400	1,200	720.00
(388) Philip Lewis (Brooklyn, 1908.)	2,400	1,200	720.00
(389) Vive A. Lindaman (Boston NL, 1906.)	2,400	1,200	720.00
(390) Paddy Livingstone (Livingston) (Philadelphia AL, 1910.)	2,400	1,200	720.00
(391) John Lobert (Cincinnati, 1907.)	2,400	1,200	720.00
(392) Herman Long (Boston NL, 1902.)	3,600	1,800	1,100
(393) Herman Long (Detroit, 1903.)	3,600	1,800	1,100
(394) Herman Long (New York AL, 1903.)	3,600	1,800	1,100
(395) Briscoe Lord (Philadelphia AL, 1905.)	2,400	1,200	720.00
(396) Harry D. Lord (Chicago AL, 1910.)	2,400	1,200	720.00
(397) Robert H. Lowe (Detroit, 1907.)	2,400	1,200	720.00
(398) Harry Lumley (Brooklyn, 1904.)	2,400	1,200	720.00
(399) Carl Lundgren (Chicago NL, 1903.)	3,600	1,800	1,100
(400) John Lush	2,400	1,200	720.00
(401) William L. Lush (Detroit, 1903.)	3,600	1,800	1,100
(402) William L. Lush (Cleveland, 1904.)	2,400	1,200	720.00
(403) Michael M. Lynch (Pittsburg, 1906.)	2,400	1,200	720.00
(404) Michael M. Lynch (New York NL, 1907.)	2,400	1,200	720.00
(405) Connie Mack (Philadelphia AL, 1902, street.)	7,900	4,000	2,375
(406) Nick Maddox (Pittsburg, 1909.)	2,400	1,200	720.00
(407) Sherwood Magee (Philadelphia NL, 1905.)	2,400	1,200	720.00
(408) George H. Magoon (Chicago AL, 1903.)	3,600	1,800	1,100
(409) John Malarkey (Boston NL, 1903.)	3,600	1,800	1,100
(410) William Maloney (Chicago NL, 1905.)	2,400	1,200	720.00
(411) William Maloney (Brooklyn, 1906.)	2,400	1,200	720.00
(412) William R. Marshall (New York NL, 1905.)	2,400	1,200	720.00
(413) William R. Marshall (St. Louis NL, 1906.)	2,400	1,200	720.00
(414) William R. Marshall (Brooklyn, 1909.)	2,400	1,200	720.00
(415) Christopher Matthewson (Mathewson) (New York NL, 1902, street.)	21,600	10,800	6,500
(416a) Christopher Matthewson (Mathewson) (New York NL, 1902, uniform.)	19,400	9,700	5,825
(416b) Christopher Mathewson (New York, NL, uniform, corrected.)	17,280	8,600	5,200
(417) James A. McAleer (St. Louis AL, 1906.)	2,400	1,200	720.00
(418) Louis McAllister (Lewis) (Detroit, 1903.)	3,600	1,800	1,100
(419) John McCarthy (Cleveland, 1903.)	3,600	1,800	1,100
(420) John McCarthy (Chicago NL, 1903.)	3,600	1,800	1,100
(421) John McCarthy (Brooklyn, 1906.)	2,400	1,200	720.00
(422) John J. McCloskey (St. Louis NL, 1906.)	2,400	1,200	720.00
(423) Ambrose McConnell (Boston AL, 1910.)	2,400	1,200	720.00
(424) George W. McQuillan (Philadelphia NL, 1907.)	2,400	1,200	720.00
(425) Barry McCormick (St. Louis AL, 1903.)	3,600	1,800	1,100
(426) Barry McCormick (Washington, 1903.)	3,600	1,800	1,100
(427) Michael McCormick (Brooklyn, 1904.)	2,400	1,200	720.00
(428) Charles McFarland (St. Louis NL, 1903.)	3,600	1,800	1,100
(429) Charles McFarland (Pittsburg, 1906.)	2,400	1,200	720.00
(430) Edward McFarland (Chicago AL, 1902, street.)	3,600	1,800	1,100
(431) Herm McFarland (Hermas) (New York AL, 1903.)	3,600	1,800	1,100
(432) John McFetridge (Philadelphia NL, 1903.)	3,600	1,800	1,100
(433) Dan McGann (New York NL, 1903.)	3,600	1,800	1,100
(434) Joseph McGinnity (New York NL, 1902, street.)	7,900	4,000	2,375
(435) Joseph McGinnity (New York NL, 1902, uniform.)	7,900	4,000	2,375
(436) John J. McGraw (Infielder, New York NL, 1902, street.)	7,900	4,000	2,375
(437) John J. McGraw (Manager, New York NL, 1902, street.)	7,900	4,000	2,375
(438) James McGuire (Detroit, 1903.)	2,400	1,200	720.00
(439) James McGuire (New York AL, 1904.)	2,400	1,200	720.00
(440) James McGuire (Boston AL, 1907.)	2,400	1,200	720.00
(441) Harry McIntyre (McIntire) (Brooklyn, 1905.)	2,400	1,200	720.00
(442) Matty McIntyre (Detroit, 1904, street.)	2,400	1,200	720.00
(443) John B. McLean (Cincinnati, 1910.)	2,400	1,200	720.00
(444) John Menefee (Chicago NL, 1903.)	3,600	1,800	1,100
(445) Fred Merkle (New York NL, 1908.)	2,400	1,200	720.00
(446) Samuel Mertes (New York NL, 1903.)	3,600	1,800	1,100
(447) Samuel Mertes (St. Louis NL, 1906.)	2,400	1,200	720.00
(448) Samuel Mertes (Boston NL, 1907.)	2,400	1,200	720.00
(451) Clyde Milan (Washington, 1910.)	2,400	1,200	720.00
(452) John B. Miller (Pittsburg, 1909.)	2,400	1,200	720.00
(453) Roscoe Miller (New York NL, 1903.)	3,600	1,800	1,100
(454) Roscoe Miller (Pittsburg, 1903.)	3,600	1,800	1,100
(455) William Milligan (New York NL, 1904.)	2,400	1,200	720.00
(456) Frederick Mitchell (Philadelphia NL, 1903, street.)	3,600	1,800	1,100
(457) Frederick Mitchell (Brooklyn, 1904.)	2,400	1,200	720.00
(458) M.F. Mitchell (Cincinnati, 1910.)	2,400	1,200	720.00
(461) Earl Moore (Cleveland, 1903.)	3,600	1,800	1,100
(462) Earl Moore (New York AL, 1907.)	2,400	1,200	720.00
(463) Charles P. Moran (Middle initial V.) (Washington, 1904.)	2,400	1,200	720.00
(464) Charles P. Moran (Middle initial V.) (St. Louis AL, 1904.)	2,400	1,200	720.00
(465) Patrick J. Moran (Boston NL, 1902, street.)	3,600	1,800	1,100
(466) Patrick J. Moran (Chicago NL, 1906.)	2,400	1,200	720.00
(467) Lewis Moren (Philadelphia NL, 1910.)	2,400	1,200	720.00
(468) Harry R. Morgan (Philadelphia AL, 1910.)	2,400	1,200	720.00
(469) Eugene Moriarty (George)(New York AL, 1906.)	2,400	1,200	720.00
(470) John Morrissey (Cincinnati, 1903.)	3,600	1,800	1,100
(471) Michael Mowery (Cincinnati, 1907.)	2,400	1,200	720.00
(472) George Mullin (Detroit, 1903.)	3,600	1,800	1,100
(473) Daniel Murphy (Philadelphia AL, 1902, street.)	3,600	1,800	1,100
(474) John J. Murray (St. Louis NL, 1907.)	2,400	1,200	720.00
(475) William Murray (Boston NL, 1907.)	2,400	1,200	720.00
(477) Joseph Nealon (Jim) (Pittsburg, 1906.)	2,400	1,200	720.00
(478) Daniel Needham (Thomas) (Boston NL, 1904.)	2,400	1,200	720.00
(479) Eustace J. Newton (New York AL, 1906.)	2,400	1,200	720.00
(481) Simon Nicholls (Philadelphia AL, 1907.)	2,400	1,200	720.00
(482) Harry Niles (St. Louis AL, 1906.)	2,400	1,200	720.00
(483) George Nill (Washington, 1906.)	2,400	1,200	720.00
(484) George Nill (Cleveland, 1907.)	2,400	1,200	720.00
(485) Pete Noonan (St. Louis NL, 1906.)	2,400	1,200	720.00
(486) John O'Brien (Boston AL, 1903.)	3,600	1,800	1,100
(487) Peter O'Brien (St. Louis AL, 1906.)	2,400	1,200	720.00
(488) Peter O'Brien (Cleveland, 1907.)	2,400	1,200	720.00
(489) Peter O'Brien (Washington, 1907.)	2,400	1,200	720.00
(490) John O'Connor (Pittsburg, 1902.)	3,600	1,800	1,100
(491) John O'Connor (New York AL, 1903.)	3,600	1,800	1,100
(492) John O'Connor (St. Louis AL, 1904.)	2,400	1,200	720.00
(493) Reuben Oldring (Philadelphia AL, 1906.)	2,400	1,200	720.00
(494) Charles O'Leary (Detroit, 1904.)	2,400	1,200	720.00
(495) John J. O'Neil (O'Neill) (St. Louis NL, 1903.))	3,000	1,500	900.00
(496) John J. O'Neil (O'Neill) (Chicago NL, 1904.)	2,400	1,200	720.00
(497) John O'Neil (O'Neill) (Boston NL, 1906.)	2,400	1,200	720.00
(498) Michael J. O'Neil (O'Neill) (St. Louis NL, 1903.)	3,600	1,800	1,100
(499) Michael J. O'Neil (O'Neill) (Brooklyn, 1906.)	2,400	1,200	720.00
(500) Albert Orth (Washington, 1903.)	3,600	1,800	1,100
(501) Albert Orth (New York AL, 1904.)	2,400	1,200	720.00
(502) Orville Overall (Orval) (Chicago NL, 1906.)	2,400	1,200	720.00
(503) Frank Owen (Chicago AL, 1903.)	3,600	1,800	1,100
(504) Richard Padden (St. Louis AL, 1903.)	3,600	1,800	1,100
(505) Frederick Parent (Boston AL, 1902.)	3,600	1,800	1,100

(506) Frederick Parent (Chicago AL, 1908.) 2,400 1,200 720.00
(508) George Paskert (Cincinnati, 1910.) 2,400 1,200 720.00
(509) James Pastorious (Brooklyn, 1906.) 2,400 1,200 720.00
(510) Case Patten (Washington, 1903.) 3,600 1,800 1,100
(511) Roy Patterson (Chicago AL, 1903.) 3,600 1,800 1,100
(512) Frederick Payne (Detroit, 1906.) 2,400 1,200 720.00
(513) Henry Peitz (Cincinnati, 1904.) 2,400 1,200 720.00
(514) Henry Peitz (Pittsburg, 1905.) 2,400 1,200 720.00
(515) Barney Pelty (St. Louis AL, 1904.) 2,400 1,200 720.00
(516) Frank Pfeiffer ("Big Jeff" Pfeffer)(Chicago NL, 1905.) 2,400 1,200 720.00
(517) Frank Pfeiffer ("Big Jeff" Pfeffer)(Boston NL, 1906.) 2,400 1,200 720.00
(518) John Pfiester (Chicago NL, 1907.) 2,400 1,200 720.00
(519) Edward Phelps (Pittsburg, 1903.) 3,600 1,800 1,100
(520) Edward Phelps (Cincinnati, 1905.) 2,400 1,200 720.00
(521) Charles Phillippe (Pittsburg, 1903.) 3,600 1,800 1,100
(522) William Phillips (Cincinnati, 1902, street.) 3,600 1,800 1,100
(523) Wiley Piatt (Boston NL, 1903.) 3,600 1,800 1,100
(524) Oliver Pickering (Philadelphia AL, 1903.) 3,600 1,800 1,100
(525) Oliver Pickering (St. Louis AL, 1906.) 2,400 1,200 720.00
(526) Charles Pittinger (Boston NL, 1903.) 3,600 1,800 1,100
(527) Charles Pittinger (Philadelphia NL, 1905.) 2,400 1,200 720.00
(528) Edward S. Plank (Philadelphia AL, 1902 street.) 7,900 4,000 2,375
(529) Edward S. Plank (Philadelphia AL, 1902, uniform.) 7,900 4,000 2,375
(530) Edward Poole (Cincinnati, 1903.) 3,600 1,800 1,100
(531) Edward Poole (Brooklyn, 1904.) 2,400 1,200 720.00
(532) John Powell (St. Louis AL, 1903.) 3,600 1,800 1,100
(533) John Powell (New York AL, 1904.) 2,400 1,200 720.00
(534) Maurice R. Powers (Michael) (Philadelphia AL, 1902, street.) 3,600 1,800 1,100
(535) William Purtell (Boston AL, 1910.) 2,400 1,200 720.00
(536) Ambrose Puttmann (New York AL, 1905.) 2,400 1,200 720.00
(539) Thomas Raub (Chicago NL, 1903.) 3,600 1,800 1,100
(540) Frederick Raymer (Boston NL, 1904.) 2,400 1,200 720.00
(541) William Reidy (Brooklyn, 1903.) 3,600 1,800 1,100
(542) Ed Reulbach (Chicago NL, 1907.) 2,400 1,200 720.00
(543) R.B. Rhoades (Rhoads) (Cleveland, 1903.) 3,600 1,800 1,100
(544) Lewis Richie (Chicago NL, 1910.) 2,400 1,200 720.00
(545) Branch Rickey (New York AL, 1907.) 6,500 3,250 1,950
(546) Claude Ritchey (Pittsburg, 1902, street.) 3,600 1,800 1,100
(547) Claude Ritchey (Boston NL, 1907.) 2,400 1,200 720.00
(548) Louis Ritter (Lewis) (Brooklyn, 1903.) 3,600 1,800 1,100
(549) Clyde Robinson (Detroit, 1904.) 2,400 1,200 720.00
(550) George Rohe (Chicago AL, 1906.) 2,400 1,200 720.00
(553) Claude Rossman (Cleveland, 1906.) 2,400 1,200 720.00
(554) Claude Rossman (Detroit, 1907.) 2,400 1,200 720.00
(555) Frank Roth (Philadelphia NL, 1903.) 3,600 1,800 1,100
(556) Frank Roth (St. Louis AL, 1905.) 2,400 1,200 720.00
(557) Frank Roth (Chicago AL, 1906.) 2,400 1,200 720.00
(558) John A. Rowan (Cincinnati, 1910.) 2,400 1,200 720.00
(559) James Ryan (Washington, 1902, street.) 3,600 1,800 1,100
(562) Harry Sallee (St. Louis NL, 1910.) 2,400 1,200 720.00
(563) Herman Schaefer (Detroit, 1907.) 2,400 1,200 720.00
(564) George Schlei (Cincinnati, 1906.) 2,400 1,200 720.00
(565) Charles Schmidt (Detroit, 1906.) 2,400 1,200 720.00
(566) Harry Schmidt (Henry) (Brooklyn, 1903.) 3,600 1,800 1,100
(567) Osee F. Schreckengost (Ossee)(Philadelphia AL, 1902, street.)) 3,600 1,800 1,100
(568) Osee F. Schreckengost (Ossee)(Philadelphia AL, 1902, uniform.) 3,600 1,800 1,100
(569) Frank Schulte (Chicago NL, 1905.) 2,400 1,200 720.00
(570) Al Schweitzer (St. Louis AL, 1910.) 2,400 1,200 720.00
(571) James Sebring (Pittsburg, 1903.) 3,600 1,800 1,100
(572) James Sebring (Cincinnati, 1904.) 2,400 1,200 720.00
(573) James Sebring (Chicago NL, 1905.) 2,400 1,200 720.00
(575) Albert Selbach (Washington, 1903.) 3,600 1,800 1,100
(576) Albert Selbach (Boston AL, 1904.) 2,400 1,200 720.00
(577) Ralph O. "Socks" Seybold (Philadelphia AL, 1902, street.) 3,600 1,800 1,100
(578) J. Bentley Seymour (Cincinnati, 1903.) 3,600 1,800 1,100
(579) J. Bentley Seymour (New York NL, 1906.) 2,400 1,200 720.00
(580) Arthur Shafer (New York NL, 1910.) 2,400 1,200 720.00
(581) W.P. Shannon (St. Louis NL, 1904.) 2,400 1,200 720.00
(582) W.P. Shannon (New York NL, 1906.) 2,400 1,200 720.00
(583) Daniel Shay (St. Louis NL, 1904.) 2,400 1,200 720.00
(586) David Shean (Boston NL, 1910.) 2,400 1,200 720.00
(587) James Sheckard (Brooklyn, 1902, street.) 3,600 1,800 1,100
(588) James Sheckard (Chicago NL, 1906.) 2,400 1,200 720.00
(589) Edward Siever (Detroit, 1903.) 3,600 1,800 1,100
(590) Edward Siever (St. Louis AL, 1903.) 3,600 1,800 1,100
(591) James Slagle (Chicago NL, 1903.) 3,600 1,800 1,100
(592) John Slattery (Chicago AL, 1903.) 3,600 1,800 1,100
(593) Alexander Smith ("Broadway Aleck")(Boston AL, 1903.)) 3,600 1,800 1,100
(594) Alexander Smith ("Broadway Aleck")(Chicago NL, 1904.) 2,400 1,200 720.00
(595) Alexander Smith ("Broadway Aleck") (New York NL, 1906.) 2,400 1,200 720.00
(596) Charles Smith (Boston AL, 1910.) 2,400 1,200 720.00
(597) Edward Smith (St. Louis AL, 1906.) 2,400 1,200 720.00
(598) Frank Smith (Chicago AL, 1904.) 2,400 1,200 720.00
(599) Harry Smith (Pittsburg, 1902, street.) 3,600 1,800 1,100
(600) Heinie Smith (Detroit, 1903, street.) 3,600 1,800 1,100
(602) Homer Smoot (St. Louis NL, 1903.) 3,600 1,800 1,100
(603) Homer Smoot (Cincinnati, 1906.) 2,400 1,200 720.00
(604) Frank Sparks (T. Frank "Tully") (Philadelphia, NL, 1903 .) 3,600 1,800 1,100
(605) Charles ("Chic") Stahl (Boston AL, 1902.) 4,000 1,950 1,200
(606) Jacob G. Stahl (Washington, 1904.) 2,400 1,200 720.00
(607) Jacob G. Stahl (Washington) 2,400 1,200 720.00
(609) J.B. Stanley (Boston NL, 1903.) 3,600 1,800 1,100
(610) J.B. Stanley (Washington, 1905.) 2,400 1,200 720.00
(611) Harry Steinfeldt (Cincinnati, 1902, street.) 3,600 1,800 1,100
(612) Harry Steinfeldt (Chicago NL, 1905.) 2,400 1,200 720.00
(615) James Stephens (St. Louis AL, 1910.) 2,400 1,200 720.00
(616) George Stone (St. Louis AL, 1905.) 2,400 1,200 720.00
(617) George Stovall (Cleveland, 1904.) 2,400 1,200 720.00
(618) Jesse Stovall (Detroit, 1904.) 2,400 1,200 720.00
(619) Samuel Strang (Brooklyn, 1903.) 3,600 1,800 1,100
(620) Samuel Strang (New York NL, 1905.) 2,400 1,200 720.00
(621) Elmer Stricklett (Brooklyn, 1906.) 2,400 1,200 720.00
(622) Willie Sudhoff (St. Louis AL, 1903.) 3,600 1,800 1,100
(623) Willie Sudhoff (Washington, 1906.) 2,400 1,200 720.00
(624) Joseph Sugden (St. Louis AL, 1903.) 3,600 1,800 1,100
(625) George Suggs (Cincinnati, 1910.) 2,400 1,200 720.00
(628) William D. Sullivan (Middle initial J.) (Chicago AL, 1902.) 3,600 1,800 1,100
(629) Edgar Summers (Detroit, 1909.) 2,400 1,200 720.00
(630) William J. Sweeney (Boston NL, 1910.) 2,400 1,200 720.00
(632) Jesse Tannehill (New York AL, 1903.) 3,600 1,800 1,100
(633) Jesse Tannehill (Boston AL, 1904.) 2,400 1,200 720.00
(634) Lee Tannehill (Chicago AL, 1903.) 3,600 1,800 1,100
(636) John Taylor (Chicago NL, 1902.) 3,600 1,800 1,100
(637) John Taylor (St. Louis NL, 1904.) 2,400 1,200 720.00
(638) Luther H. Taylor (New York NL, 1903.) 7,900 4,000 2,375
(639) Fred Tenney (Boston NL, 1903.) 3,600 1,800 1,100
(640) Ira Thomas (New York AL, 1906.) 2,400 1,200 720.00
(641) Roy Thomas (Philadelphia NL, 1903.) 3,600 1,800 1,100
(642) John Thoney (Cleveland, 1903.) 3,600 1,800 1,100
(643) John Thoney (Washington, 1904.) 2,400 1,200 720.00
(644) John Thoney (New York AL, 1904.) 2,400 1,200 720.00
(645) Joseph B. Tinker (Chicago NL, 1903.) 7,900 4,000 2,375
(646) John Townsend (Washington, 1903.) 3,600 1,800 1,100
(647) John Townsend (Cleveland, 1906.) 2,400 1,200 720.00
(648) Terrence Turner (Cleveland, 1904.) 2,400 1,200 720.00
(650) Robert Unglaub (Boston AL, 1905.) 2,400 1,200 720.00
(652) George Van Haltren (New York NL, 1902, street.) 4,300 2,150 1,300
(653) George Van Haltren (New York NL, 1902, uniform.) 4,300 2,150 1,300
(654) Fred Veil (Pittsburg, 1903.) 3,600 1,800 1,100
(655) Ernest Vinson (Cleveland, 1905.) 2,400 1,200 720.00
(656) Ernest Vinson (Chicago AL, 1905.) 2,400 1,200 720.00
(660) George Edward "Rube" Waddell (Philadelphia AL, 1902, street.) 7,900 4,000 2,375
(661) George Edward Waddell (St. Louis AL, 1908.) 6,500 3,250 1,950
(663) Charles Wagner (Boston AL, 1910.) 2,400 1,200 720.00
(664) John ("Hans") Wagner (Pittsburg, 1902, street.) 19,400 9,700 5,825
(665) John ("Hans") Wagner (Pittsburg, 1905, uniform.) 11,520 5,750 3,450
(666) Robert Wallace (St. Louis AL, 1902.) 7,900 4,000 2,375
(668) Edward A. Walsh (Chicago AL, 1904.) 6,500 3,250 1,950
(670) John Warner (New York NL, 1903.) 3,600 1,800 1,100
(671) John Warner (St. Louis NL, 1905.) 2,400 1,200 720.00
(672) John Warner (Detroit, 1905.) 2,400 1,200 720.00
(673) John Warner (Washington, 1906.) 2,400 1,200 720.00
(674) Arthur Weaver (Pittsburg, 1903.) 3,600 1,800 1,100
(675) Arthur Weaver (St. Louis AL, 1905.) 2,400 1,200 720.00
(676) Jacob Weimer (Chicago NL, 1903.) 3,600 1,800 1,100
(677) Jacob Weimer (Cincinnati, 1906.) 2,400 1,200 720.00
(678) G. Harry White (G. Harris "Doc")(Chicago AL, 1903.) 3,600 1,800 1,100
(679) Robert Wicker (Chicago NL, 1903.) 3,600 1,800 1,100
(680) Robert Wicker (Cincinnati, 1906.) 2,400 1,200 720.00
(681) Fredrick Wilhelm (Irvin "Kaiser")(Pittsburg, 1903.) 3,600 1,800 1,100
(682) Fredrick Wilhelm (Irvin "Kaiser") (Boston NL, 1904.) 2,400 1,200 720.00
(683) Edgar Willett (Detroit, 1907.) 2,400 1,200 720.00
(684) James Williams (Baltimore, 1902, street.) 3,600 1,800 1,100
(685) James Williams (New York AL, 1903, street.) 3,600 1,800 1,100
(686) James Williams (New York AL, 1903, uniform.) 3,600 1,800 1,100
(687) Otto G. Williams (Chicago NL, 1904.) 2,400 1,200 720.00
(688) Otto G. Williams (Philadelphia AL, 1905.) 2,400 1,200 720.00
(689) Otto G. Williams (Washington, 1906.) 2,400 1,200 720.00
(692) Victor J. Willis (Boston NL, 1903.) 7,900 4,000 2,375
(693) Victor J. Willis (Pittsburg, 1906.) 6,500 2,350 1,950
(694) Howard P. Wilson (Philadelphia AL, 1902, street.) 3,600 1,800 1,100
(695) Howard P. Wilson (Washington, 1903.) 3,600 1,800 1,100
(696) Howard P. Wilson (Cleveland, 1906.) 2,400 1,200 720.00
(698) J. Owen Wilson (Pittsburg, 1910.) 2,400 1,200 720.00
(699) George Wiltse (New York NL, 1904.) 2,400 1,200 720.00
(700) Louis Wiltse (Lewis) (Baltimore, 1902.) 3,600 1,800 1,100
(701) Louis Wiltse (Lewis) (New York AL, 1903.)) 3,600 1,800 1,100
(702) George Winters (Winter) (Boston AL, 1902, street.) 3,600 1,800 1,100
(705) William Wolfe (Wilbert) (Washington, 1904.) 2,400 1,200 720.00
(706) Harry Wolverton (Philadelphia NL, 1902, street.) 3,600 1,800 1,100
(707) Harry Wolverton (Boston NL, 1905.) 2,400 1,200 720.00
(708) Robert Wood (Detroit, 1904.) 2,400 1,200 720.00
(710) Eugene Wright (Clarence Eugene) (Cleveland, 1903.)) 3,600 1,800 1,100
(711) Eugene Wright (Clarence Eugene)(St. Louis AL, 1903.) 3,600 1,800 1,100
(712) Joseph Yeager (Detroit, 1902, street.) 3,600 1,800 1,100
(713) Joseph Yeager (New York AL, 1905.) 2,400 1,200 720.00

		NM	EX	VG
(714)	Joseph Yeager (St. Louis AL, 1907.)	2,400	1,200	720.00
(715)	Denton ("Cy") Young (Boston AL, 1902.)	19,400	9,700	5,825
(716)	Irving Young (Boston NL, 1905.)	2,400	1,200	720.00
(717)	David Zearfoss (St. Louis NL, 1904.)	2,400	1,200	720.00
(718)	Charles Zimmer (Pittsburg, 1902.)	3,600	1,800	1,100
(719)	Charles Zimmer (Philadelphia NL, 1903.)	3,600	1,800	1,100
(720)	H. Zimmerman (Chicago NL, 1910.)	2,400	1,200	720.00
	TRAP SHOOTERS			
(T1)	Neas Apgar	950.00	500.00	300.00
(T2)	Chas. W. Budd	950.00	500.00	300.00
(T3)	W.R. Crosby	950.00	500.00	300.00
(T4)	J.A.R. Elliott	950.00	500.00	300.00
(T5)	J.S. Fanning	950.00	500.00	300.00
(T6)	Fred Gilbert	950.00	500.00	300.00
(T7)	Rolla O. Heikes	950.00	500.00	300.00
(T8)	H.C. Hirschy	950.00	500.00	300.00
(T9)	Tom A. Marshall	950.00	500.00	300.00
(T10)	Harvey McMurchy	950.00	500.00	300.00
(T11)	Ralph Trimble	950.00	500.00	300.00

1902 Sporting Life Team Composites (W601)

Printed on heavy 13" x 14" paper and featuring a composite of player photos arranged around that of the manager and a notice of league championship status, these prints were offered to readers of the weekly sports paper for six cents in postage stamps or 50 cents per dozen. The art was often found on the covers of "Sporting Life." While the prints were issued in 1902, they specify the teams as champions "for 1903." The Buck Weaver shown on the Butte composite is not the future Black Sox shortstop.

		NM	EX	VG
Complete Set:		4,500	2,200	1,350
Common Team:		300.00	150.00	90.00
(1)	Philadelphia, American League	500.00	250.00	150.00
(2)	Pittsburg, National League	500.00	250.00	150.00
(3)	Albany, New York State League	300.00	150.00	90.00
(4)	Butte, Pacific Northwest League	400.00	200.00	120.00
(5)	Indianapolis, American Assoc.	400.00	200.00	120.00
(6)	Kansas City, Western League	400.00	200.00	120.00
(7)	Manchester, New England League	300.00	150.00	90.00
(8)	Nashville, Southern League	350.00	175.00	105.00
(9)	New Haven, Connecticut League	300.00	150.00	90.00
(10)	Rockford, Illinois-Indiana-Iowa League	300.00	150.00	90.00
(11)	Toronto, Eastern League	400.00	200.00	120.00

1903 Sporting Life Team Composites (W601)

Portraits of the individual players, usually identified by name and position, surround the manager's portrait in this series of team composites sold by Sporting Life newspaper. The 1903 series is the first in which all major league team composites were available. The 13" x 14" pictures are printed on heavy enamel paper and were sold for six cents in postage stamps, 50 cents per dozen. In some years bound portfolio complete sets were also offered, as were some of the more popular minor league teams. Notations of league and World Championships were incorporated into the design where appropriate. While issued in 1903, the pictures of league championship teams carry the notation "For 1904."

		NM	EX	VG
Complete Set (25):		5,550	2,700	1,650
Common (Major League) Team:		400.00	200.00	120.00
(1)	Boston, National League	400.00	200.00	120.00
(2)	Brooklyn, National League	400.00	200.00	120.00
(3)	Chicago, National League	600.00	300.00	180.00
(4)	Cincinnati, National League	400.00	200.00	120.00
(5)	New York, National League	500.00	250.00	150.00
(6)	Philadelphia, National League	400.00	200.00	120.00
(7)	Pittsburgh, National League	500.00	250.00	150.00
(8)	St. Louis, National League	400.00	200.00	120.00
(9)	Boston, American League	450.00	225.00	135.00
(10)	Chicago, American League	400.00	200.00	120.00
(11)	Cleveland, American League	400.00	200.00	120.00
(12)	Detroit, American League	400.00	200.00	120.00
(13)	New York, American League	450.00	225.00	135.00
(14)	Philadelphia, American League	450.00	225.00	135.00
(15)	St. Louis, American League	400.00	200.00	120.00
(16)	Washington, American League	400.00	200.00	120.00
(17)	Ft. Wayne, Central League	250.00	125.00	75.00
(18)	Holyoke, Connecticut League	250.00	125.00	75.00
(19)	Jersey City, Eastern League	300.00	150.00	90.00
(20)	Los Angeles, Pacific Coast League	300.00	150.00	90.00
(21)	Lowell, New England League	250.00	125.00	75.00
(22)	Memphis, Southern League	250.00	125.00	75.00
(23)	Schenectady, New York State League	250.00	125.00	75.00
(24)	Sedalia, Missouri Valley League	250.00	125.00	75.00
(25)	St. Paul, American Assoc.	300.00	150.00	90.00

1904 Sporting Life Team Composites (W601)

Portraits of the individual players, usually identified by name and position, surround the manager's portrait in this series of team composites sold by Sporting Life newspaper. The 13" x 14" pictures are printed on heavy enamel paper and were sold for a dime apiece postpaid. In some years bound portfolio complete sets were also offered, as were some of the more popular minor league teams. Notations of league and World Championships were incorporated into the design where appropriate.

		NM	EX	VG
Complete Set (24):		5,550	2,700	1,650
Common (Major League) Team:		400.00	200.00	120.00
(1)	Boston, National League	400.00	200.00	120.00
(2)	Brooklyn, National League	400.00	200.00	120.00
(3)	Chicago, National League	600.00	300.00	180.00
(4)	Cincinnati, National League	400.00	200.00	120.00
(5)	New York, National League	500.00	250.00	150.00
(6)	Philadelphia, National League	400.00	200.00	120.00
(7)	Pittsburgh, National League	550.00	275.00	165.00
(8)	St. Louis, National League	400.00	200.00	120.00
(9)	Boston, American League	450.00	225.00	135.00
(10)	Chicago, American League	400.00	200.00	120.00
(11)	Cleveland, American League	400.00	200.00	120.00
(12)	Detroit, American League	400.00	200.00	120.00
(13)	New York, American League	450.00	225.00	135.00
(14)	Philadelphia, American League	450.00	225.00	135.00
(15)	St. Louis, American League	400.00	200.00	120.00
(16)	Washington, American League	400.00	200.00	120.00
(17)	Buffalo, Eastern League	300.00	150.00	90.00
(18)	Ft. Wayne, Central League	200.00	100.00	60.00
(19)	Haverhill, New England League	200.00	100.00	60.00
(20)	Macon, South Atlantic League	200.00	100.00	60.00
(21)	Memphis, Southern League	200.00	100.00	60.00
(22)	Springfield, Indiana-Illinois-Iowa League	200.00	100.00	60.00
(23)	St. Paul, American Association	250.00	125.00	75.00
(24)	Syracuse, New York League (1903 Indiana-Illinois-Iowa League Champs)	200.00	100.00	60.00

1905 Sporting Life Team Composites (W601)

Portraits of the individual players, usually identified by name and position, surround the manager's portrait in this series of team composites sold by Sporting Life newspaper. The 13" x 14" pictures are printed on heavy enamel paper and were sold for a dime apiece postpaid. In some years bound portfolio complete sets were also offered, as were some of the more popular minor league teams. Notations of league and World Championships were incorporated into the design where appropriate.

		NM	EX	VG
Complete Set (23):		5,500	2,700	1,650
Common (Major League) Team:		400.00	200.00	120.00
(1)	Boston, National League	400.00	200.00	120.00
(2)	Brooklyn, National League	400.00	200.00	120.00
(3)	Chicago, National League	600.00	300.00	180.00
(4)	Cincinnati, National League	400.00	200.00	120.00
(5)	New York, National League	450.00	225.00	135.00
(6)	Philadelphia, National League	400.00	200.00	120.00
(7)	Pittsburgh, National League	750.00	375.00	225.00
(8)	St. Louis, National League	400.00	200.00	120.00
(9)	Boston, American League	400.00	200.00	120.00
(10)	Chicago, American League	400.00	200.00	120.00
(11)	Cleveland, American League	400.00	200.00	120.00
(12)	Detroit, American League	400.00	200.00	120.00
(13)	New York, American League	600.00	300.00	180.00
(14)	Philadelphia, American League	600.00	300.00	180.00
(15)	St. Louis, American League	400.00	200.00	120.00
(16)	Washington, American League	400.00	200.00	120.00
(17)	A., J. & G., New York League	200.00	100.00	60.00
(18)	Columbus, American Assoc.	250.00	125.00	75.00
(19)	Concord, New England League	200.00	100.00	60.00
(20)	Des Moines, Western League	200.00	100.00	60.00
(21)	Macon, South Atlantic League	200.00	100.00	60.00
(22)	New Orleans, Southern League	250.00	125.00	75.00
(23)	Providence, Eastern League	250.00	125.00	75.00

1906-07 Sporting Life Team Composite Postcards

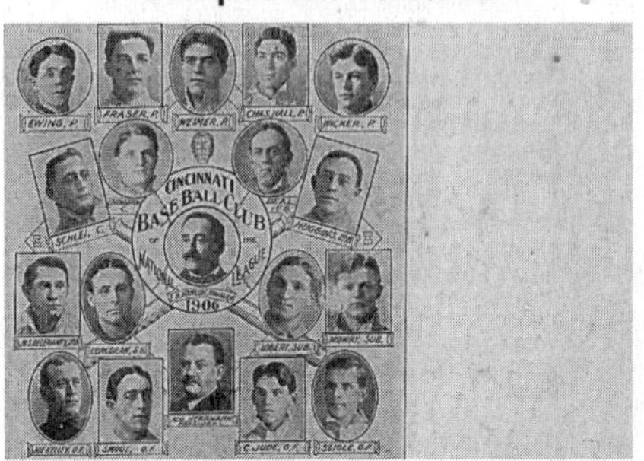

A miniature version of the Sporting Life's team composite lithographs was utilized to create a postcard set. In 3-5/8" x 5-7/16" format, the postcards have a composite of player portraits surrounding that of the manager, with a wide white right margin. Backs have standard postcard indicia. Some cards have been found with backs containing an ad offering either league's set for 10 cents in stamps.

		NM	EX	VG
Complete Set (16):		13,500	6,750	4,150
Common Team:		675.00	335.00	200.00
(1)	Boston, National League	675.00	335.00	200.00
(2)	Brooklyn, National League	900.00	450.00	270.00
(3)	Chicago, National League	900.00	450.00	270.00
(4)	Cincinnati, National League	850.00	425.00	255.00
(5)	New York, National League	850.00	425.00	255.00
(6)	Philadelphia, National League	675.00	335.00	200.00
(7)	Pittsburg, National League	1,000	500.00	300.00
(8)	St. Louis, National League	675.00	335.00	200.00
(9)	Boston, American League	700.00	350.00	210.00
(10)	Chicago, American League	750.00	375.00	225.00
(11)	Cleveland, American League	1,100	550.00	330.00
(12)	Detroit, American League	1,200	600.00	360.00
(13)	New York, American League	1,100	550.00	330.00
(14)	Philadelphia, American League	900.00	450.00	270.00
(15)	St. Louis, American League	900.00	450.00	270.00
(16)	Washington, American League	800.00	400.00	240.00

1906 Sporting Life Team Composites (W601)

Originally sold as a string-bound "Premier Art Portfolio" containing 24 major and minor league team composite pictures, single pieces from this premium issue are not uncommonly found as they were later offered individually for 10

cents apiece. The individual pieces measure 13" x 14" and are printed in black-and-white on heavy enameled paper. Individual player pictures are arranged around a baseball containing the manager's picture. Each player is identified beneath his photo by name and position. By 1906 the year printed on the pictures corresponds to the year of issue.

		NM	EX	VG
	Complete Set (24):	12,000	6,000	3,500
	Common Major League Team:	550.00	275.00	165.00
	Common Minor League Team:	300.00	150.00	90.00
(1)	Boston, National League	750.00	375.00	225.00
(2)	Brooklyn, National League	550.00	275.00	165.00
(3)	Chicago, National League	800.00	400.00	240.00
(4)	Cincinnati, National League	550.00	275.00	165.00
(5)	New York, National League	650.00	325.00	195.00
(6)	Philadelphia, National League	675.00	335.00	200.00
(7)	Pittsburg, National League	650.00	325.00	195.00
(8)	St. Louis, National League	550.00	275.00	165.00
(9)	Boston, American League	800.00	400.00	240.00
(10)	Chicago, American League	650.00	325.00	195.00
(11)	Cleveland, American League	1,200	600.00	360.00
(12)	Detroit, American League	1,200	600.00	360.00
(13)	New York, American League	800.00	400.00	240.00
(14)	Philadelphia, American League	800.00	400.00	240.00
(15)	St. Louis, American League	550.00	275.00	165.00
(16)	Washington, American League	550.00	275.00	165.00
(17)	National League president, managers	600.00	300.00	180.00
(18)	American League president, managers	600.00	300.00	180.00
(19)	Birmingham, Southern League	300.00	150.00	90.00
(20)	Buffalo, Eastern League	300.00	150.00	90.00
(21)	Columbus, American Assoc.	300.00	150.00	90.00
(22)	Grand Rapids, Central League	300.00	150.00	90.00
(23)	Norwich, Connecticut League	300.00	150.00	90.00
(24)	Scranton, New York League	300.00	150.00	90.00

1907 Sporting Life Team Composites (W601)

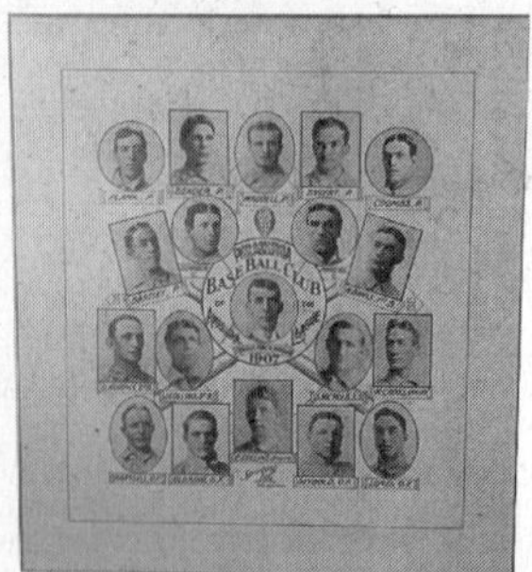

Portraits of the individual players, usually identified by name and position, surround the manager's portrait in this series of team composites sold by Sporting Life newspaper. The 13" x 14" pictures are printed on heavy enamel paper and were sold for a dime apiece postpaid. In some years bound portfolio complete sets were also offered, as were some of the more popular minor league teams. Notations of league and World Championships were incorporated into the design where appropriate.

		NM	EX	VG
	Complete Set (23):	5,500	2,700	1,600
	Common (Major League) Team:	400.00	200.00	120.00
(1)	Boston, National League	400.00	200.00	120.00
(2)	Brooklyn, National League	400.00	200.00	120.00
(3)	Chicago, National League	500.00	250.00	150.00
(4)	Cincinnati, National League	400.00	200.00	120.00
(5)	New York, National League	500.00	250.00	150.00
(6)	Philadelphia, National League	400.00	200.00	120.00
(7)	Pittsburgh, National League	450.00	225.00	135.00
(8)	St. Louis, National League	400.00	200.00	120.00
(9)	Boston, American League	400.00	200.00	120.00
(10)	Chicago, American League	400.00	200.00	120.00
(11)	Cleveland, American League	400.00	200.00	120.00
(12)	Detroit, American League	600.00	300.00	180.00
(13)	New York, American League	450.00	225.00	135.00
(14)	Philadelphia, American League	400.00	200.00	120.00
(15)	St. Louis, American League	400.00	200.00	120.00
(16)	Washington, American League	500.00	250.00	150.00
(17)	Toronto, Eastern League	300.00	150.00	90.00
(18)	Columbus, American Assoc.	300.00	150.00	90.00
(19)	Williamsport, Tri-State League	200.00	100.00	60.00
(20)	Albany, New York League	200.00	100.00	60.00
(21)	Atlanta, Southern League	200.00	100.00	60.00
(22)	Holyoke, Connecticut League	200.00	100.00	60.00
(23)	Norfolk, Virginia League	200.00	100.00	60.00

1908 Sporting Life Team Composites (W601)

Portraits of the individual players, usually identified by name and position, surround the manager's portrait in this series of team composites sold by Sporting Life newspaper. The 13" x 14" pictures are printed on heavy enamel paper and were sold for a dime apiece postpaid. In some years bound portfolio complete sets were also offered, as were some of the more popular minor league teams. Notations of league and World Championships were incorporated into the design where appropriate.

		NM	EX	VG
	Complete Set (16):	4,500	2,250	1,350
	Common Team:	400.00	200.00	120.00
(1)	Boston, National League	400.00	200.00	120.00
(2)	Brooklyn, National League	400.00	200.00	120.00
(3)	Chicago, National League	500.00	250.00	150.00
(4)	Cincinnati, National League	400.00	200.00	120.00
(5)	New York, National League	425.00	210.00	125.00
(6)	Philadelphia, National League	400.00	200.00	120.00
(7)	Pittsburgh, National League	450.00	225.00	135.00
(8)	St. Louis, National League	400.00	200.00	120.00
(9)	Boston, American League	400.00	200.00	120.00
(10)	Chicago, American League	400.00	200.00	120.00
(11)	Cleveland, American League	400.00	200.00	120.00
(12)	Detroit, American League	600.00	300.00	180.00
(13)	New York, American League	450.00	225.00	135.00
(14)	Philadelphia, American League	400.00	200.00	120.00
(15)	St. Louis, American League	400.00	200.00	120.00
(16)	Washington, American League	450.00	225.00	135.00

1909 Sporting Life Team Composites (W601)

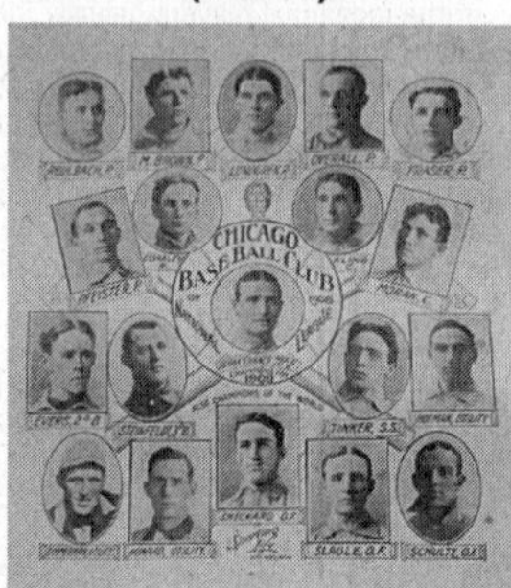

Portraits of the individual players, usually identified by name and position, surround the manager's portrait in this series of team composites sold by Sporting Life newspaper. The 13" x 14" pictures are printed on heavy enamel paper and were sold for a dime apiece postpaid. In some years bound portfolio complete sets were also offered, as were some of the more popular minor league teams. Notations of league and World Championships were incorporated into the design where appropriate.

		NM	EX	VG
	Complete Set (16):	6,500	3,250	1,850
	Common Team:	600.00	300.00	180.00
(1)	Boston, National League	600.00	300.00	180.00
(2)	Brooklyn, National League	600.00	300.00	180.00
(3)	Chicago, National League	750.00	375.00	225.00
(4)	Cincinnati, National League	600.00	300.00	180.00
(5)	New York, National League	675.00	335.00	200.00
(6)	Philadelphia, National League	600.00	300.00	180.00
(7)	Pittsburgh, National League	1,125	560.00	335.00
(8)	St. Louis, National League	1,000	500.00	300.00
(9)	Boston, American League	600.00	300.00	180.00
(10)	Chicago, American League	600.00	300.00	180.00
(11)	Cleveland, American League	600.00	300.00	180.00
(12)	Detroit, American League	900.00	450.00	270.00
(13)	New York, American League	675.00	335.00	200.00
(14)	Philadelphia, American League	600.00	300.00	180.00
(15)	St. Louis, American League	600.00	300.00	180.00
(16)	Washington, American League	675.00	335.00	200.00

The Mint-Mint examples of vintage cards carry a significant premium over the Near Mint values shown here. This premium reflects limited availability of the highest-grade cards as well as demand for particular cards or sets in the best possible condition.

1910 Sporting Life Team Composites (W601)

After several years of issuing composite team photos for all major league teams (and some minor league teams), Sporting Life in 1910 began issuing them only for the league and World's Champions. Like the others, they are 13" x 14", printed on heavy enamel paper with individual player portrait photos surrounding the manager at center.

		NM	EX	VG
	Complete Set (2):	1,200	600.00	350.00
	Common Team:	300.00	150.00	90.00
(1)	Chicago Cubs (N.L. Champs)	450.00	225.00	135.00
(2)	Philadelphia Athletics (World's Champions)	750.00	375.00	225.00

1910-11 Sporting Life (M116)

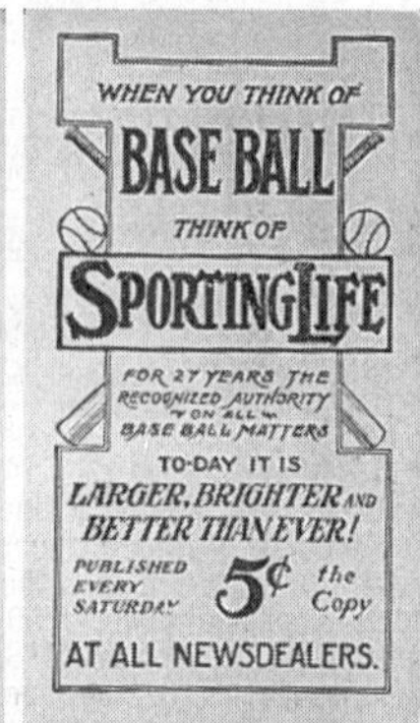

This set of nominally 1-1/2" x 2-5/8" (individual card sizes vary even moreso than typically found on early 20th Century cards, notably with the "high numbers" often found somewhat larger) cards was offered to subscribers to "Sporting Life," a major competitor of "The Sporting News" in the early part of the century. The cards were issued in 24 series of 12 cards each, sold by mail for four cents per series. Card fronts feature color-tinted black-and-white portrait photos with the name and team printed below. Backs have various ads for the weekly paper. The last three 24-card series are scarcer than the earlier cards. These 72 cards have "Over 300 subjects" printed on back. Values in this checklist are adjusted according to that scarcity. The scarce blue-background cards appear to have been a second printing of the first two 12-card series which no doubt sold out quickly in the original pastel-background version due to the popularity of the players included. The 12 players in the Third Series can be found in an original printing with the ad on back printed in black, and a later version with a blue back. Each of the Third Series cards also exhibits on front subtle differences in the size and coloring of the player portrait. The complete set price does not include variations.

		NM	EX	VG
	Common Player:	360.00	180.00	110.00
(1)	Ed Abbaticchio	360.00	180.00	110.00
(2a)	Babe Adams (Black back.)	520.00	260.00	155.00
(2b)	Babe Adams (Blue back.)	360.00	180.00	110.00
(3)	Red Ames	1,000	500.00	300.00
(4)	Jimmy Archer	1,000	500.00	300.00
(5)	Frank Arrelanes (Arellanes)	360.00	180.00	110.00
(6)	Tommy Atkins	1,000	500.00	300.00
(7)	Jimmy Austin	1,000	500.00	300.00
(8)	Les Bachman (Backman)	360.00	180.00	110.00
(9)	Bill Bailey	360.00	180.00	110.00
(10a)	Home Run Baker (Black back.)	2,400	1,200	720.00
(10b)	Home Run Baker (Blue back.)	1,600	800.00	480.00
(11)	Cy Barger	360.00	180.00	110.00
(12)	Jack Barry	360.00	180.00	110.00
(13a)	Johnny Bates (Philadelphia)	360.00	180.00	110.00
(13b)	Johnny Bates (Cincinnati) (A G-VG example sold at auction 4/06 for $22,987.)			
(14)	Ginger Beaumont	360.00	180.00	110.00
(15)	Fred Beck	360.00	180.00	110.00
(16)	Heinie Beckendorf	360.00	180.00	110.00
(17)	Fred Beebe	360.00	180.00	110.00
(18)	George Bell	360.00	180.00	110.00
(19)	Harry Bemis	360.00	180.00	110.00
(20a)	Chief Bender (Blue background.)	2,400	1,200	720.00
(20b)	Chief Bender (Pastel background.)	1,600	800.00	480.00
(21)	Bill Bergen	360.00	180.00	110.00

(22)	Heinie Berger	360.00	180.00	110.00
(23)	Bob Bescher	360.00	180.00	110.00
(24)	Joe Birmingham	360.00	180.00	110.00
(25)	Lena Blackburn (Blackburne)	360.00	180.00	110.00
(26)	John Bliss	1,000	500.00	300.00
(27)	Bruno Block	1,000	500.00	300.00
(28)	Bill Bradley	360.00	180.00	110.00
(29)	Kitty Bransfield	360.00	180.00	110.00
(30a)	Roger Bresnahan (Blue)	2,400	1,200	720.00
(30b)	Roger Bresnahan (Pastel)	1,600	800.00	480.00
(31)	Al Bridwell	360.00	180.00	110.00
(32)	Buster Brown (Boston)	360.00	180.00	110.00
(33a)	Mordecai Brown (Blue, Chicago.)	2,400	1,200	720.00
(33b)	Mordecai Brown (Pastel, Chicago.)	1,600	800.00	480.00
(34)	Al Burch	360.00	180.00	110.00
(35)	Donie Bush	360.00	180.00	110.00
(36)	Bobby Byrne	360.00	180.00	110.00
(37)	Howie Camnitz	360.00	180.00	110.00
(38)	Vin Campbell	1,000	500.00	300.00
(39)	Bill Carrigan	360.00	180.00	110.00
(40a)	Frank Chance (Blue)	2,400	1,200	720.00
(40b)	Frank Chance (Pastel)	1,600	800.00	480.00
(41)	Chappy Charles	360.00	180.00	110.00
(42a)	Hal Chase (Blue)	1,600	800.00	480.00
(42b)	Hal Chase (Pastel)	1,100	550.00	330.00
(43)	Ed Cicotte	1,800	900.00	540.00
(44a)	Fred Clarke (Pittsburgh, black back.)	2,400	1,200	720.00
(44b)	Fred Clarke (Pittsburgh, blue back.)	1,600	800.00	480.00
(45)	Nig Clarke (Cleveland)	360.00	180.00	110.00
(46)	Tommy Clarke (Cincinnati)	1,000	500.00	300.00
(47a)	Ty Cobb (Blue)	6,000	3,000	1,800
(47b)	Ty Cobb (Pastel)	18,000	9,000	5,400
(48a)	Eddie Collins (Blue)	2,400	1,200	720.00
(48b)	Eddie Collins (Pastel)	1,600	800.00	480.00
(49)	Ray Collins	1,000	500.00	300.00
(50)	Wid Conroy	360.00	180.00	110.00
(51)	Jack Coombs	360.00	180.00	110.00
(52)	Frank Corridon	360.00	180.00	110.00
(53)	Harry Coveleskie (Coveleski)	2,000	1,000	600.00
(54)	Doc Crandall	360.00	180.00	110.00
(55a)	Sam Crawford (Blue)	2,400	1,200	720.00
(55b)	Sam Crawford (Pastel)	1,600	800.00	480.00
(56)	Birdie Cree	360.00	180.00	110.00
(57)	Lou Criger	360.00	180.00	110.00
(58)	Dode Criss	1,000	500.00	300.00
(59)	Cliff Curtis	1,000	500.00	300.00
(60)	Bill Dahlen	360.00	180.00	110.00
(62)	Bill Davidson	1,000	500.00	300.00
(62a)	Harry Davis (Blue)	1,000	500.00	300.00
(62b)	Harry Davis (Pastel)	360.00	180.00	110.00
(63)	Jim Delehanty (Delahanty)	360.00	180.00	110.00
(64)	Ray Demmitt	1,000	500.00	300.00
(65)	Rube Dessau	1,000	500.00	300.00
(66a)	Art Devlin (Black back.)	520.00	260.00	155.00
(66b)	Art Devlin (Blue back.)	360.00	180.00	110.00
(67)	Josh Devore	1,000	500.00	300.00
(68)	Pat Donahue	360.00	180.00	110.00
(69)	Patsy Donovan	1,000	500.00	300.00
(70a)	Wild Bill Donovan (Blue)	1,000	500.00	300.00
(70b)	Wild Bill Donovan (Pastel)	360.00	180.00	110.00
(71a)	Red Dooin (Blue)	1,000	500.00	300.00
(71b)	Red Dooin (Pastel)	360.00	180.00	110.00
(72)	Mickey Doolan	360.00	180.00	110.00
(73)	Patsy Dougherty	360.00	180.00	110.00
(74)	Tom Downey	360.00	180.00	110.00
(75)	Jim Doyle	360.00	180.00	110.00
(76a)	Larry Doyle (Blue)	1,000	500.00	300.00
(76b)	Larry Doyle (Pastel)	360.00	180.00	110.00
(77)	Hugh Duffy	1,600	800.00	480.00
(78)	Jimmy Dygert	360.00	180.00	110.00
(79)	Dick Eagan (Egan)	360.00	180.00	110.00
(80)	Kid Elberfeld	360.00	180.00	110.00
(81)	Rube Ellis	360.00	180.00	110.00
(82)	Clyde Engle	360.00	180.00	110.00
(83)	Tex Erwin	1,000	500.00	300.00
(84)	Steve Evans	1,000	500.00	300.00
(85a)	Johnny Evers (Black back.)	2,400	1,200	720.00
(85b)	Johnny Evers (Blue back.)	1,600	800.00	480.00
(86)	Bob Ewing	360.00	180.00	110.00
(87)	Cy Falkenberg	360.00	180.00	110.00
(88)	George Ferguson	360.00	180.00	110.00
(89)	Art Fletcher	1,000	500.00	300.00
(90)	Elmer Flick	1,600	800.00	480.00
(91)	John Flynn	1,000	500.00	300.00
(92)	Russ Ford	1,000	500.00	300.00
(93)	Eddie Foster	1,000	500.00	300.00
(94)	Bill Foxen	360.00	180.00	110.00
(95)	John Frill	1,000	500.00	300.00
(96)	Sam Frock	1,000	500.00	300.00
(97)	Art Fromme	360.00	180.00	110.00
(98)	Earl Gardner (New York)	1,000	500.00	300.00
(99)	Larry Gardner (Boston)	1,000	500.00	300.00
(100)	Harry Gaspar	1,000	500.00	300.00
(101)	Doc Gessler	360.00	180.00	110.00
(102a)	George Gibson (Blue)	1,000	500.00	300.00
(102b)	George Gibson (Pastel)	360.00	180.00	110.00
(103)	Bill Graham (St. Louis)	360.00	180.00	110.00
(104)	Peaches Graham (Boston)	360.00	180.00	110.00
(105)	Eddie Grant	360.00	180.00	110.00
(106)	Clark Griffith	1,600	800.00	480.00
(107)	Ed Hahn	360.00	180.00	110.00
(108)	Charley Hall	360.00	180.00	110.00
(109)	Bob Harmon	1,000	500.00	300.00
(110)	Topsy Hartsel	360.00	180.00	110.00
(111)	Roy Hartzell	360.00	180.00	110.00
(112)	Heinie Heitmuller	360.00	180.00	110.00
(113)	Buck Herzog	360.00	180.00	110.00
(114)	Dick Hoblitzel (Hoblitzell)	360.00	180.00	110.00
(115)	Danny Hoffman	360.00	180.00	110.00
(116)	Solly Hofman	360.00	180.00	110.00
(117)	Harry Hooper	1,600	800.00	480.00
(118)	Harry Howell	360.00	180.00	110.00
(119)	Miller Huggins	1,600	800.00	480.00
(120)	Long Tom Hughes	1,000	500.00	300.00
(121)	Rudy Hulswitt	360.00	180.00	110.00
(122)	John Hummel	360.00	180.00	110.00
(123)	George Hunter	360.00	180.00	110.00
(124)	Ham Hyatt	360.00	180.00	110.00
(125)	Fred Jacklitsch	360.00	180.00	110.00
(126a)	Hughie Jennings (Blue)	2,400	1,200	720.00
(126b)	Hughie Jennings (Pastel)	1,600	800.00	480.00
(127)	Walter Johnson	7,000	3,500	2,100
(128a)	Davy Jones (Blue)	1,000	500.00	300.00
(128b)	Davy Jones (Pastel)	360.00	180.00	110.00
(129)	Tom Jones	360.00	180.00	110.00
(130a)	Tim Jordan (Blue)	1,000	500.00	300.00
(130b)	Tim Jordan (Pastel)	360.00	180.00	110.00
(131)	Addie Joss	1,800	900.00	540.00
(132)	Johnny Kane	360.00	180.00	110.00
(133)	Ed Karger	360.00	180.00	110.00
(134)	Red Killifer (Killefer)	1,000	500.00	300.00
(135)	Johnny Kling	360.00	180.00	110.00
(136)	Otto Knabe	360.00	180.00	110.00
(137)	John Knight	1,000	500.00	300.00
(138)	Ed Konetchy	360.00	180.00	110.00
(139)	Harry Krause	360.00	180.00	110.00
(140)	Rube Kroh	360.00	180.00	110.00
(141)	Art Krueger	1,600	800.00	480.00
(142a)	Nap Lajoie (Blue)	2,400	1,200	720.00
(142b)	Nap Lajoie (Pastel)	1,600	800.00	480.00
(143)	Fred Lake (Boston)	360.00	180.00	110.00
(144)	Joe Lake (St. Louis)	1,000	500.00	300.00
(145)	Frank LaPorte	360.00	180.00	110.00
(146)	Jack Lapp	1,000	500.00	300.00
(147)	Chick Lathers	1,000	500.00	300.00
(148a)	Tommy Leach (Blue)	1,000	500.00	300.00
(148b)	Tommy Leach (Pastel)	360.00	180.00	110.00
(149)	Sam Leever	360.00	180.00	110.00
(150)	Lefty Leifeld	360.00	180.00	110.00
(151)	Ed Lennox	360.00	180.00	110.00
(152)	Fred Linke (Link)	1,000	500.00	300.00
(153)	Paddy Livingstone (Livingston)	360.00	180.00	110.00
(154)	Hans Lobert	360.00	180.00	110.00
(155)	Bris Lord	360.00	180.00	110.00
(156a)	Harry Lord (Blue)	1,000	500.00	300.00
(156b)	Harry Lord (Pastel)	360.00	180.00	110.00
(157)	Johnny Lush	360.00	180.00	110.00
(158)	Connie Mack	1,600	800.00	480.00
(159)	Tom Madden	1,000	500.00	300.00
(160)	Nick Maddox	360.00	180.00	110.00
(161)	Sherry Magee	360.00	180.00	110.00
(162a)	Christy Mathewson (Blue)	10,000	5,000	3,000
(162b)	Christy Mathewson (Pastel)	5,400	2,700	1,625
(163)	Al Mattern	360.00	180.00	110.00
(164)	Jimmy McAleer	360.00	180.00	110.00
(165)	George McBride	1,000	500.00	300.00
(166a)	Amby McConnell (Boston)	360.00	180.00	110.00
(166b)	Amby McConnell (Chicago)	10,000	5,000	3,000
(167)	Pryor McElveen	360.00	180.00	110.00
(168)	John McGraw	1,600	800.00	480.00
(169)	Deacon McGuire	360.00	180.00	110.00
(170)	Stuffy McInnes (McInnis)	1,000	500.00	300.00
(171)	Harry McIntire (McIntyre)	360.00	180.00	110.00
(172)	Matty McIntyre	360.00	180.00	110.00
(173)	Larry McLean	360.00	180.00	110.00
(174)	Tommy McMillan	360.00	180.00	110.00
(175a)	George McQuillan (Blue, Philadelphia.)	1,000	500.00	300.00
(175b)	George McQuillan (Pastel, Philadelphia.)	360.00	180.00	110.00
(175c)	George McQuillan (Cincinnati)	5,000	2,500	1,500
(176)	Paul Meloan	1,000	500.00	300.00
(177)	Fred Merkle	360.00	180.00	110.00
(178)	Clyde Milan	360.00	180.00	110.00
(179)	Dots Miller (Pittsburgh)	360.00	180.00	110.00
(180)	Warren Miller (Washington)	1,000	500.00	300.00
(181)	Fred Mitchell	1,000	500.00	300.00
(182)	Mike Mitchell	360.00	180.00	110.00
(183)	Earl Moore	360.00	180.00	110.00
(184)	Pat Moran	360.00	180.00	110.00
(185a)	Lew Moren (Black back.)	520.00	260.00	155.00
(185b)	Lew Moren (Blue back.)	360.00	180.00	110.00
(186)	Cy Morgan	360.00	180.00	110.00
(187)	George Moriarty	360.00	180.00	110.00
(188)	Mike Mowery (Mowrey)	1,000	500.00	300.00
(189a)	George Mullin (Black back.)	520.00	260.00	155.00
(189b)	George Mullin (Blue back.)	360.00	180.00	110.00
(190)	Danny Murphy	360.00	180.00	110.00
(191)	Red Murray	360.00	180.00	110.00
(192)	Chief Myers (Meyers)	1,000	500.00	300.00
(193)	Tom Needham	360.00	180.00	110.00
(194)	Harry Niles	360.00	180.00	110.00
(195)	Rebel Oakes	1,000	500.00	300.00
(196)	Jack O'Connor	360.00	180.00	110.00
(197)	Paddy O'Connor	360.00	180.00	110.00
(198)	Bill O'Hara	1,000	500.00	300.00
(199)	Rube Oldring	360.00	180.00	110.00
(200)	Charley O'Leary	360.00	180.00	110.00
(201)	Orval Overall	360.00	180.00	110.00
(202)	Freddy Parent	360.00	180.00	110.00
(203)	Dode Paskert	1,000	500.00	300.00
(204)	Fred Payne	1,000	500.00	300.00
(205)	Barney Pelty	360.00	180.00	110.00
(206)	Hub Pernoll	1,000	500.00	300.00
(207)	George Perring	1,000	500.00	300.00
(208)	Big Jeff Pfeffer	1,000	500.00	300.00
(209)	Jack Pfiester	360.00	180.00	110.00
(210)	Art Phelan	1,000	500.00	300.00
(211)	Ed Phelps	360.00	180.00	110.00
(212)	Deacon Phillippe	360.00	180.00	110.00
(213)	Eddie Plank	4,800	2,400	1,450
(214)	Jack Powell	360.00	180.00	110.00
(215)	Billy Purtell	360.00	180.00	110.00
(216)	Farmer Ray	1,000	500.00	300.00
(217)	Bugs Raymond	360.00	180.00	110.00
(218)	Doc Reisling	360.00	180.00	110.00
(219)	Ed Reulbach	360.00	180.00	110.00
(220)	Lew Richie	360.00	180.00	110.00
(221)	Jack Rowan	360.00	180.00	110.00
(222a)	Nap Rucker (Black back.)	520.00	260.00	155.00
(222b)	Nap Rucker (Blue back.)	360.00	180.00	110.00
(223)	Slim Sallee	360.00	180.00	110.00
(224)	Doc Scanlon	360.00	180.00	110.00
(225)	Germany Schaefer	360.00	180.00	110.00
(226)	Lou Schettler	1,000	500.00	300.00
(227)	Admiral Schlei	360.00	180.00	110.00
(228)	Boss Schmidt	360.00	180.00	110.00
(229)	Wildfire Schulte	360.00	180.00	110.00
(230)	Al Schweitzer	360.00	180.00	110.00
(231)	Jim Scott	1,000	500.00	300.00
(232a)	Cy Seymour (N.Y.)	360.00	180.00	110.00
(232b)	Cy Seymour (Baltimore) (Two known; 4/04 auction $18,000+ Fair-Good.)			
(233)	Tillie Shafer	360.00	180.00	110.00
(234)	Bud Sharpe	1,000	500.00	300.00
(235)	Dave Shean	1,000	500.00	300.00
(236)	Jimmy Sheckard	360.00	180.00	110.00
(237)	Mike Simon	1,000	500.00	300.00
(238)	Charlie Smith (Boston)	1,000	500.00	300.00
(239)	Frank Smith (Chicago)	360.00	180.00	110.00
(240)	Harry Smith (Boston)	360.00	180.00	110.00
(241)	Fred Snodgrass	360.00	180.00	110.00
(242)	Bob Spade	360.00	180.00	110.00
(243)	Tully Sparks	360.00	180.00	110.00
(244)	Tris Speaker	3,000	1,500	900.00
(245)	Jake Stahl	360.00	180.00	110.00
(246)	George Stallings	360.00	180.00	110.00
(247)	Oscar Stanage	360.00	180.00	110.00
(248)	Harry Steinfeldt	360.00	180.00	110.00
(249)	Jim Stephens	360.00	180.00	110.00
(250)	George Stone	360.00	180.00	110.00
(251)	George Stovall	360.00	180.00	110.00
(252)	Gabby Street	360.00	180.00	110.00
(253)	Sailor Stroud	1,000	500.00	300.00
(254)	Amos Strunk	1,000	500.00	300.00
(255)	George Suggs	360.00	180.00	110.00
(256)	Billy Sullivan	360.00	180.00	110.00
(257a)	Ed Summers (Black back.)	520.00	260.00	155.00
(257b)	Ed Summers (Blue back.)	360.00	180.00	110.00
(258)	Bill Sweeney (Boston)	360.00	180.00	110.00
(259)	Jeff Sweeney (New York)	1,000	500.00	300.00
(260)	Lee Tannehill	360.00	180.00	110.00
(261a)	Fred Tenney (Blue)	1,000	500.00	300.00
(261b)	Fred Tenney (Pastel)	360.00	180.00	110.00
(262a)	Ira Thomas (Blue)	1,000	500.00	300.00
(262b)	Ira Thomas (Pastel)	360.00	180.00	110.00
(263)	Jack Thoney	360.00	180.00	110.00
(264a)	Joe Tinker (Black back.)	2,400	1,200	720.00
(264b)	Joe Tinker (Blue back.)	1,600	800.00	480.00
(265)	John Titus	1,000	500.00	300.00
(266)	Terry Turner	360.00	180.00	110.00
(267)	Bob Unglaub	360.00	180.00	110.00
(268a)	Rube Waddell (Black back.)	2,400	1,200	720.00
(268b)	Rube Waddell (Blue back.)	1,600	800.00	480.00
(269a)	Hans Wagner (Pittsburgh, blue.)	22,000	11,000	6,600
(269b)	Hans Wagner (Pittsburgh, pastel.)	4,000	2,000	1,200
(270)	Heinie Wagner (Boston)	360.00	180.00	110.00
(271)	Bobby Wallace	1,600	800.00	480.00
(272)	Ed Walsh (Chicago)	1,600	800.00	480.00
(273a)	Jimmy Walsh (Gray background, Philadelphia.)	1,400	700.00	420.00
(273b)	Jimmy Walsh (White background, Philadelphia.)	1,400	700.00	420.00
(274)	Doc White	360.00	180.00	110.00
(275)	Kaiser Wilhelm	360.00	180.00	110.00
(276)	Ed Willett	360.00	180.00	110.00
(277)	Vic Willis	1,600	800.00	480.00
(278)	Art Wilson (New York)	1,000	500.00	300.00
(279)	Owen Wilson (Pittsburgh)	360.00	180.00	110.00
(280)	Hooks Wiltse	360.00	180.00	110.00
(281)	Harry Wolter	360.00	180.00	110.00
(282)	Smokey Joe Wood	2,700	1,350	810.00
(283)	Ralph Works	360.00	180.00	110.00
(284a)	Cy Young (Black back.)	4,800	2,400	1,450
(284b)	Cy Young (Blue back.)	3,600	1,800	1,075
(285)	Irv Young	360.00	180.00	110.00
(286)	Heinie Zimmerman	1,000	500.00	300.00
(287)	Dutch Zwilling	360.00	180.00	110.00

1911 Sporting Life Cabinets (M110)

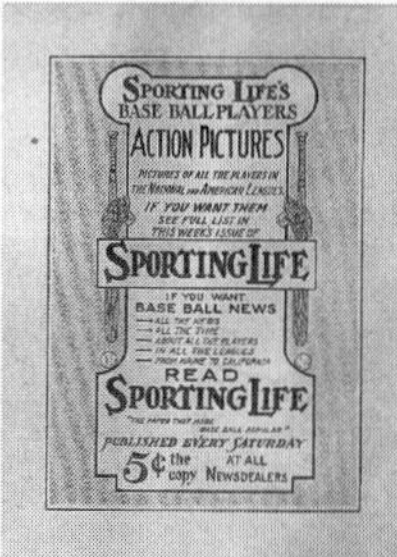

This set of 5-5/8" x 7-1/2" premium photos is similar to, but much scarcer than, the contemporary T3 Turkey Red cabinets. Like those, the Sporting Life cabinets feature a pastel player picture surrounded by a gray frame with a "gold" nameplate at bottom. Backs have advertising for the weekly sports paper printed in blue.

		NM	EX	VG
Complete Set (6):		90,000	35,000	17,500
Common Player:		5,500	2,200	1,325
(1)	Frank Chance	10,000	4,000	2,000
(2)	Hal Chase	8,000	3,200	1,600
(3)	Ty Cobb	25,000	10,000	5,000
(4)	Napoleon Lajoie	10,000	4,000	2,000
(5)	Christy Mathewson	20,000	8,000	4,000
(6)	Honus Wagner	35,000	17,500	8,750

1911 Sporting Life Team Composites (W601)

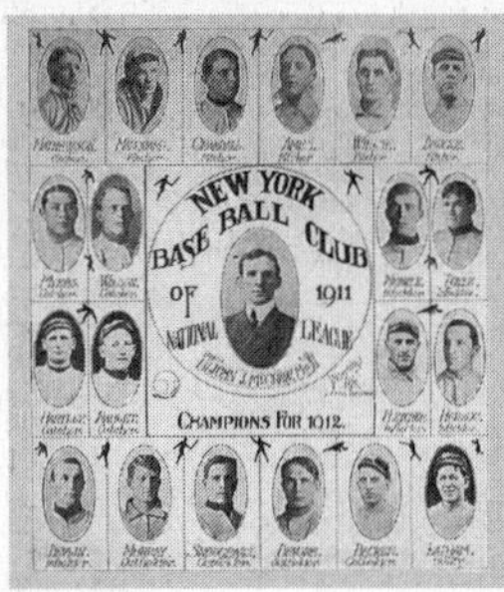

After several years of issuing composite team photos for all major league teams (and some minor league teams), Sporting Life in 1910 began issuing them only for the league and World's Champions. Like the others, they are 13" x 14", printed on heavy enamel paper with individual player portrait photos surrounding the manager at center.

		NM	EX	VG
Complete Set (2):		1,200	600.00	350.00
Common Team:		300.00	150.00	90.00
(1)	New York Giants (N.L. Champs)	600.00	300.00	180.00
(2)	Philadelphia Athletics (World's Champions)	750.00	375.00	225.00

1899-1900 Sporting News Supplements (M101-1)

For much of 1899 and 1900, the weekly issues of The Sporting News included a baseball player portrait supplement. About 8-3/4" x 11", the pictures offered vignetted photos of the era's stars on a glossy paper stock. Virtually all pictures were formal head-and-shoulders portraits; some in uniform, some in civilian clothes. A handful of players are depicted in full-length poses. The pictures were produced for the sports paper by National Copper Plate Co., (which issued its own set of prints listed elsewhere in this catalog). The TSN supplements have a logotype above the photo and the date in which it was included in the paper. Full player name and team/year are printed at bottom. Backs have a small box offering career information. Besides offering the pictures with weekly issues, portfolios of 50 could be had by starting or renewing a subscription for $2 a year.

		NM	EX	VG
Complete Set (62):		90,000	36,000	18,000
Common Player:		1,125	450.00	225.00
	1899	.00	.00	.00
(1)	William Lange (Apr. 22)	1,125	450.00	225.00
(2)	Hugh Duffy (Apr. 29)	1,875	750.00	375.00
(3)	Charles A. Nichols (May 6)	1,875	750.00	375.00
(4)	Martin Bergen (May 13)	1,125	450.00	225.00
(5)	Michael Griffin (May 20)	1,125	450.00	225.00
(6)	Wilbert Robinson (May 27)	1,875	750.00	375.00
(7)	Clark C. Griffith (June 3)	1,875	750.00	375.00
(8)	John J. Doyle (June 10)	1,125	450.00	225.00
(9)	R.J. Wallace (June 17)	1,875	750.00	375.00
(10)	John O'Connor (June 24)	1,125	450.00	225.00
(11)	Louis Criger (July 1)	1,125	450.00	225.00
(12)	Jerry H. Nops (July 8)	1,125	450.00	225.00
(13)	William Kennedy (July 15)	1,125	450.00	225.00
(14)	P.J. Donovan (July 22)	1,125	450.00	225.00
(15)	William H. Keeler (July 29)	1,875	750.00	375.00
(16)	John J. McGraw (Aug. 5)	1,875	750.00	375.00
(17)	James Hughes (Aug. 12)	1,125	450.00	225.00
(18)	John Wagner (Aug. 19)	11,250	4,500	2,250
(19)	Victor G. Willis (Aug. 26)	1,875	750.00	375.00
(20)	James J. Collins (Sept. 2)	1,875	750.00	375.00
(21)	Eugene DeMontreville (Sept. 9)	1,125	450.00	225.00
(22)	Joseph J. Kelley (Sept. 16)	1,875	750.00	375.00
(23)	Frank L. Donahue (Francis R. "Red")(Sept. 23)	1,125	450.00	225.00
(24)	Edward J. Delehanty (Delahanty)(Sept. 30)	1,125	450.00	225.00
(25)	Fred C. Clark (Clarke)(Oct. 7)	1,875	750.00	375.00
(26)	Napoleon Lajoie (Oct. 14)	1,875	750.00	375.00
(27)	Edward Hanlon (Oct. 21)	1,875	750.00	375.00
(28)	Charles Stahl (Oct. 28)	1,125	450.00	225.00
(29)	Lave N. Cross (Nov. 4)	1,125	450.00	225.00
(30)	Elmer H. Flick (Nov. 11)	1,875	750.00	375.00
(31)	Frank LeRoy Chance (Nov. 18)	1,875	750.00	375.00
(32)	George S. Davis (Nov. 25)	1,875	750.00	375.00
(33)	Hugh J. Jennings (Dec. 2)	1,875	750.00	375.00
(34)	Denton T. Young (Dec. 9)	3,750	1,500	750.00
	1900	.00	.00	.00
(35)	George E. Waddell (Apr. 14)	1,875	750.00	375.00
(36)	John Dunn (Apr. 21)	1,125	450.00	225.00
(37)	Clarence Beaumont (Apr. 28)	1,125	450.00	225.00
(38)	James T. McGuire (May 5)	1,125	450.00	225.00
(39)	William H. Dineen (May 12)	1,125	450.00	225.00
(40)	James T. Williams (May 19)	1,125	450.00	225.00
(41)	Thomas W. Corcoran (May 26)	1,125	450.00	225.00
(42)	John Freeman (June 2)	1,125	450.00	225.00
(43)	Henry Peitz (June 9)	1,125	450.00	225.00
(44)	Charles Phillippe (June 16)	1,125	450.00	225.00
(45)	Frank Hahn (June 23)	1,125	450.00	225.00
(46)	J. Emmet Heidrick (June 30)	1,125	450.00	225.00
(47)	Joseph McGinnity (July 7)	1,875	750.00	375.00
(48)	John D. Chesbro (July 14)	1,875	750.00	375.00
(49)	William R. Hamilton (July 21)	1,125	450.00	225.00
(50)	Samuel Leever (July 28)	1,125	450.00	225.00
(51)	Mike Donlin (Aug. 4)	1,125	450.00	225.00
(52)	William F. Dahlen (Aug. 11)	1,125	450.00	225.00
(53)	Frederick Tenney (Aug. 18)	1,125	450.00	225.00
(54)	Edward P. Scott (Aug. 25)	1,125	450.00	225.00
(55)	Edward M. Lewis (Sept. 1)	1,125	450.00	225.00
(56)	Theodore Breitenstein (Sept. 8)	1,125	450.00	225.00
(57)	Herman C. Long (Sept. 15)	1,125	450.00	225.00
(58)	Jesse Tannehill (Sept. 22)	1,125	450.00	225.00
(59)	Burt E. Jones (Sept. 29)	1,125	450.00	225.00
(60)	J. Callahan (Nixey)(Oct. 6)	1,125	450.00	225.00
(61)	Claude Ritchey (Oct. 13)	1,125	450.00	225.00
(62)	Roy Thomas (Oct. 20)	1,125	450.00	225.00

1909-1913 Sporting News Supplements (M101-2)

Among the finest large-format baseball collectibles published in the early part of the 20th Century was the 100-piece series of sepia-toned supplements issued by The Sporting News. Initially issued in a size of about 7-1/2" x 10", by late 1909 the size evolved to about 8-1/2" x 10" with the team photos issued in a 16" x 10" format. The series was begun with the insertion of a supplement in the July 22, 1909, issue of TSN. One supplement was issued with each week's paper through April 7, 1910. There were several gaps over the course of the next several years, until the final piece was issued with the TSN dated Dec. 11, 1913. Most of the supplements feature full-length poses of the players. Each is labeled "Supplement to The Sporting News" with the issue date at top. At bottom is a box with the player's name and team. Backs are usually blank, but some supplements are found with colored advertising on back for various other collectibles from the newspaper. The TSN supplements were printed on heavy paper and are usually found with corner creases or other signs of wear.

		NM	EX	VG
Complete Set (100):		25,000	12,500	7,500
Common Player:		80.00	40.00	25.00
Ad backs: 3X				
	1909			
(1)	Roger Bresnahan (7/22)	600.00	300.00	180.00
(2)	Denton Young, Louis Criger (7/29)	450.00	225.00	135.00
(3)	Christopher Mathewson (8/5)	1,000	500.00	300.00
(4)	Tyrus R. Cobb (8/12)	1,200	600.00	360.00
(5)	Napoleon Lajoie (8/19)	550.00	275.00	165.00
(6)	Sherwood N. Magee (8/26)	80.00	40.00	25.00
(7)	Frank L. Chance (9/2)	500.00	250.00	150.00
(8)	Edward Walsh (9/9)	500.00	250.00	150.00
(9)	Nap Rucker (9/16)	80.00	40.00	25.00
(10)	Honus Wagner (9/23)	1,000	500.00	300.00
(11)	Hugh Jennings (9/30)	550.00	275.00	165.00
(12)	Fred C. Clarke (10/7)	550.00	275.00	165.00
(13)	Byron Bancroft Johnson (10/14)	550.00	275.00	165.00
(14)	Charles A. Comiskey (10/21)	550.00	275.00	165.00
(15)	Edward Collins (10/28)	550.00	275.00	165.00
(16)	James A. McAleer (11/4)	160.00	80.00	50.00
(17)	Pittsburgh Team (11/11)	350.00	175.00	100.00
(18)	Detroit Team (11/18)	350.00	175.00	100.00
(19)	George Bell (11/25)	160.00	80.00	50.00
(20)	Tris Speaker (12/2)	650.00	325.00	195.00
(21)	Mordecai Brown (12/9)	550.00	275.00	165.00
(22)	Hal Chase (12/16)	550.00	275.00	165.00
(23)	Thomas W. Leach (12/23)	160.00	80.00	50.00
(24)	Owen Bush (12/30)	160.00	80.00	50.00
	1910			
(25)	John J. Evers (1/6)	400.00	200.00	120.00
(26)	Harry Krause (1/13)	80.00	40.00	25.00
(27)	Chas. B. Adams (1/20)	80.00	40.00	25.00
(28)	Addie Joss (1/27)	400.00	200.00	120.00
(29)	Orval Overall (2/3)	80.00	40.00	25.00
(30)	Samuel E. Crawford (2/10)	400.00	200.00	120.00
(31)	Fred Merkle (2/17)	90.00	45.00	25.00
(32)	George Mullin (2/24)	80.00	40.00	25.00
(33)	Edward Konetchy (3/3)	80.00	40.00	25.00
(34)	George Gibson, Arthur Raymond (3/10)	80.00	40.00	25.00
(35)	Ty Cobb, Hans Wagner (3/17)	2,000	1,000	600.00
(36)	Connie Mack (3/24)	400.00	200.00	120.00
(37)	Wm. Evans, "Silk" O'Loughlin, William Klem, Wm. Johnston (3/31)	550.00	275.00	165.00
(38)	Edward Plank (4/7)	325.00	160.00	95.00
(39)	Walter Johnson, Charles E. Street (9/1)	500.00	250.00	150.00
(40)	John C. Kling (9/8)	80.00	40.00	25.00
(41)	Frank Baker (9/15)	400.00	200.00	120.00
(42)	Charles S. Dooin (9/22)	80.00	40.00	25.00
(43)	Wm. F. Carrigan (9/29)	80.00	40.00	25.00
(44)	John B. McLean (10/6)	80.00	40.00	25.00
(45)	John W. Coombs (10/13)	80.00	40.00	25.00
(46)	Jos. B. Tinker (10/20)	350.00	175.00	100.00
(47)	John I. Taylor (10/27)	80.00	40.00	25.00
(48)	Russell Ford (11/3)	80.00	40.00	25.00
(49)	Leonard L. Cole (11/10)	80.00	40.00	25.00
(50)	Harry Lord (11/17)	80.00	40.00	25.00
(51)	Philadelphia-A Team (11/24)	130.00	65.00	40.00
(52)	Chicago-N Team (12/1)	130.00	65.00	40.00
(53)	Charles A. Bender (12/8)	400.00	200.00	120.00
(54)	Arthur Hofman (12/15)	80.00	40.00	25.00
(55)	Bobby Wallace (12/21)	325.00	160.00	95.00
(56)	Jno. J. McGraw (12/28)	325.00	160.00	95.00
	1911			
(57)	Harry H. Davis (1/5)	80.00	40.00	25.00
(58)	James P. Archer (1/12)	80.00	40.00	25.00
(59)	Ira Thomas (1/19)	80.00	40.00	25.00
(60)	Robert Byrnes (1/26)	80.00	40.00	25.00
(61)	Clyde Milan (2/2)	80.00	40.00	25.00
(62)	John T. Meyer (2/9)(Meyers)	80.00	40.00	25.00
(63)	Robert Bescher (2/16)	80.00	40.00	25.00
(64)	John J. Barry (2/23)	80.00	40.00	25.00
(65)	Frank Schulte (3/2)	80.00	40.00	25.00
(66)	C. Harris White (3/9)	80.00	40.00	25.00
(67)	Lawrence Doyle (3/16)	80.00	40.00	25.00
(68)	Joe Jackson (3/23)	2,500	1,250	750.00
(69)	Martin O'Toole, William Kelly (10/26)	80.00	40.00	25.00
(70)	Vean Gregg (11/2)	80.00	40.00	25.00
(71)	Richard W. Marquard (11/9)	325.00	160.00	95.00
(72)	John E. McInnis (11/16)	80.00	40.00	25.00
(73)	Grover C. Alexander (11/23)	350.00	175.00	100.00
(74)	Del Gainor (11/30)	80.00	40.00	25.00
(75)	Fred Snodgrass (12/7)	80.00	40.00	25.00
(76)	James J. Callahan (12/14)	80.00	40.00	25.00
(77)	Robert Harmon (12/21)	80.00	40.00	25.00
(78)	George Stovall (12/28)	80.00	40.00	25.00
	1912			
(79)	Zack D. Wheat (1/4)	325.00	160.00	95.00
(80)	Frank "Ping" Bodie (1/11)	80.00	40.00	25.00
(81)	Boston-A Team (10/10)	130.00	65.00	40.00
(82)	New York-N Team (10/17)	130.00	65.00	40.00
(83)	Jake Stahl (10/24)	80.00	40.00	25.00
(84)	Joe Wood (10/31)	275.00	135.00	80.00
(85)	Charles Wagner (11/7)	80.00	40.00	25.00
(86)	Lew Ritchie (11/14)	80.00	40.00	25.00
(87)	Clark Griffith (11/21)	325.00	160.00	95.00
(88)	Arnold Hauser (11/28)	80.00	40.00	25.00
(89)	Charles Herzog (12/5)	80.00	40.00	25.00
(90)	James Lavender (12/12)	80.00	40.00	25.00
(91)	Jeff Tesreau (12/19)	80.00	40.00	25.00
(92)	August Herrmann (12/26)	110.00	55.00	30.00
	1913			
(93)	Jake Daubert (10/23)	80.00	40.00	25.00
(94)	Heinie Zimmerman (10/30)	80.00	40.00	25.00
(95)	Ray Schalk (11/6)	325.00	160.00	95.00
(96)	Hans Lobert (11/13)	80.00	40.00	25.00
(97)	Albert W. Demaree (11/20)	80.00	40.00	25.00
(98)	Arthur Fletcher (11/27)	80.00	40.00	25.00
(99)	Charles A. Somers (12/4)	80.00	40.00	25.00
(100)	Joe Birmingham (12/11)	80.00	40.00	25.00

1913 Sporting News Postcards (M101-3)

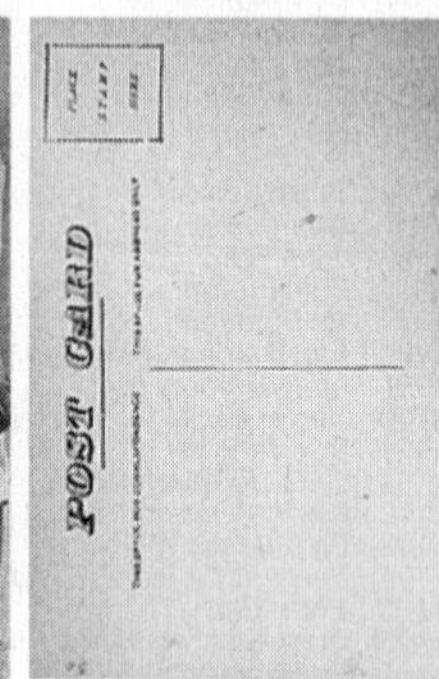

This six-card set was issued as a premium by the weekly sports newspaper. The 3-1/2" x 5-1/2" cards have borderless front photos printed in duotone color. Along with the player and team names at bottom is a "Published by The Sporting News" tag line. Postcard-format backs are in black-and-white. The unnumbered cards are checklisted here alphabetically.

		NM	EX	VG
Complete Set (6):		4,250	2,125	1,275
Common Player:		275.00	135.00	80.00
(1)	Roger Bresnahan	450.00	225.00	135.00

(2)	Ty Cobb	2,000	1,000	600.00
(3)	Eddie Collins	450.00	225.00	135.00
(4)	Vean Gregg	275.00	135.00	80.00
(5)	Walter Johnson, Gabby Street	750.00	375.00	225.00
(6)	Rube Marquard	450.00	225.00	135.00

1916 The Sporting News (M101-5)

(Though listed in catalogs for more than 25 years, it is now believed M101-5 cards with Sporting News backs do not exist.)

1916 The Sporting News (M101-4)

THE SPORTING NEWS
"THE BASEBALL PAPER of the WORLD"
FIVE CENTS THE COPY
PUBLISHED WEEKLY the YEAR 'ROUND
SAMPLE COPY FREE ON REQUEST
C. C. SPINK & SON : ST. LOUIS, MO.

The "update" version of the promotional premium issued by The Sporting News is nearly identical to the earlier cards. The 200 black-and-white cards once again are printed with player photo, name, position, team and card number on front and advertising on the backs. The set checklist, and, generally, values are the same for sets issued by several other businesses around the country. Most of the players included on the 1-5/8" x 3" cards also appear in the prior edition. Despite being labeled in the American Card Catalog as M101-4, this version was issued after the M101-5 version, with the first advertising appearing in August 1916. Cards could be ordered in series of 20 for a dime, or the complete set was free with a $2 subscription. The complete set price does not include variations.

		NM	EX	VG
Complete Set (200):		60,000	30,000	18,000
Common Player:		95.00	50.00	30.00
1	Babe Adams	110.00	50.00	30.00
2	Sam Agnew	95.00	50.00	30.00
3	Eddie Ainsmith	95.00	50.00	30.00
4	Grover Alexander	600.00	300.00	180.00
5	Leon Ames	95.00	50.00	30.00
6	Jimmy Archer	95.00	50.00	30.00
7	Jimmy Austin	95.00	50.00	30.00
8	H.D. Baird	95.00	50.00	30.00
9	J. Franklin Baker	390.00	190.00	115.00
10	Dave Bancroft	390.00	190.00	115.00
11	Jack Barry	95.00	50.00	30.00
12	Zinn Beck	95.00	50.00	30.00
13	"Chief" Bender	390.00	190.00	115.00
14	Joe Benz	95.00	50.00	30.00
15	Bob Bescher	95.00	50.00	30.00
16	Al Betzel	95.00	50.00	30.00
17	Mordecai Brown	390.00	190.00	115.00
18	Eddie Burns	95.00	50.00	30.00
19	George Burns	95.00	50.00	30.00
20	Geo. J. Burns	95.00	50.00	30.00
21	Joe Bush	95.00	50.00	30.00
22	"Donie" Bush	95.00	50.00	30.00
23	Art Butler	95.00	50.00	30.00
24	Bobbie Byrne	95.00	50.00	30.00
25	Forrest Cady	95.00	50.00	30.00
26	Jimmy Callahan	95.00	50.00	30.00
27	Ray Caldwell	95.00	50.00	30.00
28	Max Carey	390.00	190.00	115.00
29	George Chalmers	95.00	50.00	30.00
30	Ray Chapman	95.00	50.00	30.00
31	Larry Cheney	95.00	50.00	30.00
32	Eddie Cicotte	390.00	190.00	115.00
33	Tom Clarke	95.00	50.00	30.00
34	Eddie Collins	390.00	190.00	155.00
35	"Shauno" Collins	95.00	50.00	30.00
36	Charles Comiskey	390.00	190.00	115.00
37	Joe Connolly	95.00	50.00	30.00
38	Ty Cobb	4,800	2,400	1,440
39	Harry Coveleskie (Coveleski)	95.00	50.00	30.00
40	Gavvy Cravath	95.00	50.00	30.00
41	Sam Crawford	390.00	190.00	115.00
42	Jean Dale	95.00	50.00	30.00
43	Jake Daubert	95.00	50.00	30.00
44	Charles Deal	95.00	50.00	30.00
45	Al Demaree	95.00	50.00	30.00
46	Josh Devore	95.00	50.00	30.00
47	William Doak	95.00	50.00	30.00
48	Bill Donovan	95.00	50.00	30.00
49	Charles Dooin	95.00	50.00	30.00
50	Mike Doolan	95.00	50.00	30.00
51	Larry Doyle	95.00	50.00	30.00
52	Jean Dubuc	95.00	50.00	30.00
53	Oscar Dugey	95.00	50.00	30.00
54	Johnny Evers	390.00	190.00	115.00
55	Urban Faber	390.00	190.00	115.00
56	"Hap" Felsch	1,000	285.00	170.00
57	Bill Fischer	95.00	50.00	30.00
58	Ray Fisher	95.00	50.00	30.00
59	Max Flack	95.00	50.00	30.00
60	Art Fletcher	95.00	50.00	30.00
61	Eddie Foster	95.00	50.00	30.00
62	Jacques Fournier	95.00	50.00	30.00
63	Del Gainer (Gainor)	95.00	50.00	30.00
64	"Chic" Gandil	1,000	190.00	115.00
65	Larry Gardner	95.00	50.00	30.00
66	Joe Gedeon	95.00	50.00	30.00
67	Gus Getz	95.00	50.00	30.00
68	Geo. Gibson	95.00	50.00	30.00
69	Wilbur Good	95.00	50.00	30.00
70	Hank Gowdy	95.00	50.00	30.00
71	John Graney	95.00	50.00	30.00
72	Clark Griffith	390.00	190.00	115.00
73	Tom Griffith	95.00	50.00	30.00
74	Heinie Groh	95.00	50.00	30.00
75	Earl Hamilton	95.00	50.00	30.00
76	Bob Harmon	95.00	50.00	30.00
77	Roy Hartzell	95.00	50.00	30.00
78	Claude Hendrix	95.00	50.00	30.00
79	Olaf Henriksen	95.00	50.00	30.00
80	John Henry	95.00	50.00	30.00
81	"Buck" Herzog	95.00	50.00	30.00
82	Hugh High	95.00	50.00	30.00
83	Dick Hoblitzell	95.00	50.00	30.00
84	Harry Hooper	390.00	190.00	115.00
85	Ivan Howard	95.00	50.00	30.00
86	Miller Huggins	390.00	190.00	115.00
87	Joe Jackson	15,000	5,400	3,240
88	William James	95.00	50.00	30.00
89	Harold Janvrin	95.00	50.00	30.00
90	Hugh Jennings	390.00	190.00	115.00
91	Walter Johnson	1,140	570.00	345.00
92	Fielder Jones	95.00	50.00	30.00
93	Joe Judge	95.00	50.00	30.00
94	Bennie Kauff	95.00	50.00	30.00
95	Wm. Killefer Jr.	95.00	50.00	30.00
96	Ed. Konetchy	95.00	50.00	30.00
97	Napoleon Lajoie	390.00	190.00	115.00
98	Jack Lapp	95.00	50.00	30.00
99	John Lavan	95.00	50.00	30.00
100	Jimmy Lavender	95.00	50.00	30.00
101	"Nemo" Leibold	95.00	50.00	30.00
102	H.B. Leonard	95.00	50.00	30.00
103	Duffy Lewis	95.00	50.00	30.00
104	Hans Lobert	95.00	50.00	30.00
105	Tom Long	95.00	50.00	30.00
106	Fred Luderus	95.00	50.00	30.00
107	Connie Mack	390.00	190.00	115.00
108	Lee Magee	95.00	50.00	30.00
109	Sherwood Magee	95.00	50.00	30.00
110	Al. Mamaux	95.00	50.00	30.00
111	Leslie Mann	95.00	50.00	30.00
112	"Rabbit" Maranville	390.00	190.00	115.00
113	Rube Marquard	390.00	190.00	115.00
114	J. Erskine Mayer	150.00	80.00	45.00
115	George McBride	95.00	50.00	30.00
116	John J. McGraw	390.00	190.00	115.00
117	Jack McInnis	95.00	50.00	30.00
118	Fred Merkle	95.00	50.00	30.00
119	Chief Meyers	95.00	50.00	30.00
120	Clyde Milan	95.00	50.00	30.00
121	John Miller	95.00	50.00	30.00
122	Otto Miller	95.00	50.00	30.00
123	Willie Mitchell	95.00	50.00	30.00
124	Fred Mollwitz	95.00	50.00	30.00
125	Pat Moran	95.00	50.00	30.00
126	Ray Morgan	95.00	50.00	30.00
127	Geo. Moriarty	95.00	50.00	30.00
128	Guy Morton	95.00	50.00	30.00
129	Mike Mowrey	95.00	50.00	30.00
130	Ed. Murphy	95.00	50.00	30.00
131	"Hy" Myers	95.00	50.00	30.00
132	J.A. Niehoff	95.00	50.00	30.00
133	Rube Oldring	95.00	50.00	30.00
134	Oliver O'Mara	95.00	50.00	30.00
135	Steve O'Neill	95.00	50.00	30.00
136	"Dode" Paskert	95.00	50.00	30.00
137	Roger Peckinpaugh	95.00	50.00	30.00
138	Walter Pipp	95.00	50.00	30.00
139	Derril Pratt (Derrill)	95.00	50.00	30.00
140	Pat Ragan	95.00	50.00	30.00
141	Bill Rariden	95.00	50.00	30.00
142	Eppa Rixey	390.00	190.00	115.00
143	Davey Robertson	95.00	50.00	30.00
144	Wilbert Robinson	390.00	190.00	115.00
145	Bob Roth	95.00	50.00	30.00
146	Ed. Roush	390.00	190.00	115.00
147	Clarence Rowland	95.00	50.00	30.00
148	"Nap" Rucker	95.00	50.00	30.00
149	Dick Rudolph	95.00	50.00	30.00
150	Reb Russell	95.00	50.00	30.00
151	Babe Ruth	30,000	15,000	9,000
152	Vic Saier	95.00	50.00	30.00
153	"Slim" Sallee	95.00	50.00	30.00
154	Ray Schalk	390.00	190.00	115.00
155	Walter Schang	95.00	50.00	30.00
156	Frank Schulte	95.00	50.00	30.00
157	Everett Scott	95.00	50.00	30.00
158	Jim Scott	95.00	50.00	30.00
159	Tom Seaton	95.00	50.00	30.00
160	Howard Shanks	95.00	50.00	30.00
161	Bob Shawkey	95.00	50.00	30.00
162	Ernie Shore	95.00	50.00	30.00
163	Burt Shotton	95.00	50.00	30.00
164	Geo. Sisler	390.00	190.00	115.00
165	J. Carlisle Smith	95.00	50.00	30.00
166	Fred Snodgrass	95.00	50.00	30.00
167	Geo. Stallings	95.00	50.00	30.00
168a	Oscar Stanage/Catching	95.00	50.00	30.00
168b	Oscar Stanage (Portrait to thighs.)	900.00	450.00	270.00
169	Charles Stengel	390.00	190.00	115.00
170	Milton Stock	95.00	50.00	30.00
171	Amos Strunk	95.00	50.00	30.00
172	Billy Sullivan	95.00	50.00	30.00
173	"Jeff" Tesreau	95.00	50.00	30.00
174	Joe Tinker	390.00	190.00	115.00
175	Fred Toney	95.00	50.00	30.00
176	Terry Turner	95.00	50.00	30.00
177	George Tyler	95.00	50.00	30.00
178	Jim Vaughn	95.00	50.00	30.00
179	Bob Veach	95.00	50.00	30.00
180	James Viox	95.00	50.00	30.00
181	Oscar Vitt	95.00	50.00	30.00
182	Hans Wagner	2,500	660.00	395.00
183	Clarence Walker	95.00	50.00	30.00
184	Ed. Walsh	390.00	190.00	115.00
185	W. Wambsganss (Photo actually Fritz Coumbe.)	95.00	50.00	30.00
186	Buck Weaver	1,000	285.00	170.00
187	Carl Weilman	95.00	50.00	30.00
188	Zach Wheat	390.00	190.00	115.00
189	Geo. Whitted	95.00	50.00	30.00
190	Fred Williams	95.00	50.00	30.00
191	Art Wilson	95.00	50.00	30.00
192	J. Owen Wilson	95.00	50.00	30.00
193	Ivy Wingo	95.00	50.00	30.00
194	"Mel" Wolfgang	95.00	50.00	30.00
195	Joe Wood	500.00	120.00	75.00
196	Steve Yerkes	95.00	50.00	30.00
197	"Pep" Young	95.00	50.00	30.00
198	Rollie Zeider	95.00	50.00	30.00
199	Heiny Zimmerman	95.00	50.00	30.00
200	Ed. Zwilling	95.00	50.00	30.00

1919 Sporting News (M101-6)

(The issue listed in previous editions as 1919 Sporting News Supplements (M101-6) is now listed as 1917-1920 Felix Mendelsohn.)

1926 Sporting News Supplements (M101-7)

This set of 11 player photos was issued as a post-World Series weekly supplement by The Sporting News in 1926. Sepia-toned portrait or posed photos are featured on the 7" x 10" supplements. The player's name and team are printed at the bottom, while a line indentifying The Sporting News and the date appear in the upper left corner. The unnumbered set includes a half-dozen Hall of Famers. Large-format (10" x 14-1/4") team photos of the 1926 Yankees (October 28) and Cardinals were also issued in the weeks preceding the start of issue for the weekly player supplements.

		NM	EX	VG
Complete Set (13):		2,000	800.00	400.00
Common Player:		40.00	16.00	8.00
(1)	Hazen "Kiki" Cuyler	100.00	40.00	20.00
(2)	Rogers Hornsby	125.00	50.00	25.00
(3)	Tony Lazzeri	100.00	40.00	20.00
(4)	Harry E. Manush (Henry)	100.00	40.00	20.00
(5)	John Mostil	40.00	16.00	8.00
(6)	Harry Rice	40.00	16.00	8.00
(7)	George Herman "Babe" Ruth	1,200	480.00	240.00
(8)	Al Simmons	100.00	40.00	20.00
(9)	Harold "Pie" Traynor	100.00	40.00	20.00
(10)	George Uhle	40.00	16.00	8.00
(11)	Glenn Wright	40.00	16.00	8.00
(12)	1926 Cardinals Team Photo	100.00	40.00	20.00
(13)	1926 Yankees Team Photo	200.00	80.00	40.00

1927-1928 Sporting News Ad-Back Supplements (M101-7)

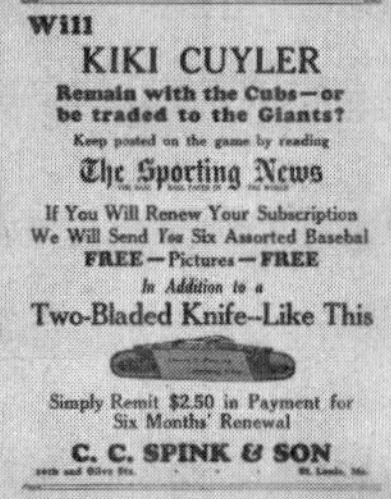

Evidently faced with a surplus of player supplements from its 1926 issue, The Sporting News recycled at least some of them in subsequent years as subscription sales advertising. Fronts of the supplements differ in that the sports paper's logo and the original issue date from 1926 have been removed from the upper-left border. Instead of blank backs, however, the re-

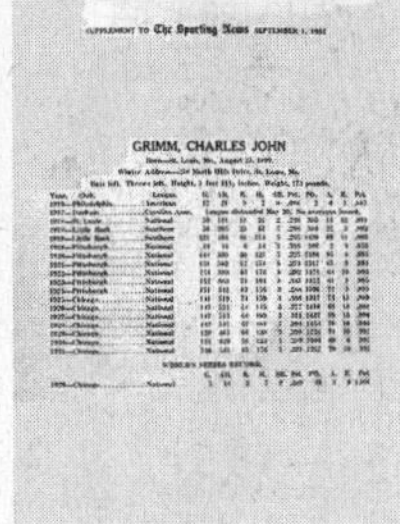
GRIMM, CHARLES JOHN

issues have color (blue or red seen to date) advertising on back. Respond-by dates in 1927 have been seen rubber-stamped on the back of some pieces, while that of Kiki Cuyler mentions his team as being the Cubs, who he joined in 1928.

	NM	EX	VG
Kiki Cuyler	300.00	125.00	65.00
Babe Ruth	1,500	600.00	300.00

1932 Sporting News Supplements (M101-8)

This issue of player-picture supplements from TSN is unusual not only in its brevity - only four were issued - but also in that the pictures have printed matter on back, consisting of player personal data and complete major/minor league stats. Only the Grimm piece has an issue date: Sept. 1, 1932. The pictures are on thin card stock in an 8-1/4" x 10-1/2" format. Fronts have a black-and-white photo with the player named in the wide bottom border.

		NM	EX	VG
Complete Set (4):		2,000	1,000	600.00
Common Player:		240.00	120.00	72.00
(1)	Jerome H. (Dizzy) Dean	900.00	450.00	270.00
(2)	Vernon Gomez	600.00	300.00	180.00
(3)	Charles John Grimm	250.00	125.00	75.00
(4)	Lonnie Warneke	250.00	125.00	75.00

1939 Sporting News Supplements (M101-9)

These dated supplements feature a trio of team photos and two star players as individuals. The team pictures are about 15" x 10-1/2" and comprise double-page spreads; the single players are 7-1/2" x 10".

		NM	EX	VG
Complete Set (5):		800.00	400.00	240.00
Common:		150.00	75.00	45.00
(1)	Joseph DiMaggio (Oct. 26)	200.00	100.00	60.00
(2)	Robert Feller (Nov. 9)	150.00	75.00	45.00
(3)	Cincinnati Reds Team (Nov. 2)	150.00	75.00	45.00
(4)	N.Y. Yankees Team (Oct. 19)	200.00	100.00	60.00
(5)	St. Louis Cardinals Team (Nov. 16)	150.00	75.00	45.00

1888 Sporting Times (M117)

Examples of these cards, issued in 1888 and 1889 by the Sporting Times weekly newspaper, are very rare. The complete set price includes all variations. The cabinet-size cards (7-1/4" x 4-1/2") feature line drawings of players in action poses on soft cardboard stock. The cards came in a variety of pastel colors surrounded by a 1/4" white border. The player's last name is printed on each drawing, as are the words "Courtesy Sporting Times New York." A pair of crossed bats and a baseball appear along the bottom of the card. Twenty-seven different players are known to exist. The drawing of Cap Anson is the same one used in the N28 Allen & Ginter series, and some of the other drawings are based on photos used in the popular Old Judge series.

		NM	EX	VG
Common Player:		15,000	10,000	6,000
(1)	Cap Anson	35,000	17,500	10,000
(2)	Jersey Bakely	15,000	10,000	6,000
(3)	Dan Brouthers	25,000	12,500	7,500
(4)	Doc Bushong	15,000	10,000	6,000
(5)	Jack Clements	15,000	10,000	6,000
(6)	Charlie Comiskey	25,000	12,500	7,500
(7)	Jerry Denny	15,000	10,000	6,000
(8)	Buck Ewing	25,000	12,500	7,500
(9)	Dude Esterbrook	15,000	10,000	6,000
(10)	Jay Faatz	15,000	10,000	6,000
(11)	Pud Galvin	25,000	12,500	7,500
(12)	Jack Glasscock	15,000	10,000	6,000
(13)	Tim Keefe	25,000	12,500	7,500
(14)	King Kelly	30,000	15,000	9,000
(15)	Matt Kilroy	15,000	10,000	6,000
(16)	Arlie Latham	15,000	10,000	6,000
(17)	Doggie Miller	15,000	10,000	6,000
(18)	Hank O'Day	15,000	10,000	6,000
(19)	Fred Pfeffer	15,000	10,000	6,000
(20)	Henry Porter	15,000	10,000	6,000
(21)	Toad Ramsey	15,000	10,000	6,000
(22)	Long John Reilly	15,000	10,000	6,000
(23)	Mike Smith	15,000	10,000	6,000
(24)	Harry Stovey	15,000	10,000	6,000
(25)	Sam Thompson	25,000	12,500	7,500
(26)	John Ward	25,000	12,500	7,500
(27)	Mickey Welch	25,000	12,500	7,500

1933 Sport Kings (R338)

This 48-card set features athletes at the top of several sports such as boxing, football, skiing, dogsled racing and swimming as well as three hall-of-fame baseball players. The cards measure 2-3/8" x 2-7/8" and feature waist-up portrait artwork.

		NM	EX	VG
Complete Set (48):		30,000	15,000	9,000
Common Player (1-24):		200.00	100.00	60.00
Common Player (25-48):		250.00	125.00	75.00
Advertising Poster:		7,500	4,000	2,400
1	Ty Cobb	6,000	3,000	1,800
2	Babe Ruth	7,000	3,500	2,100
3	Nat Holman	200.00	100.00	60.00
4	Harold "Red" Grange	1,000	500.00	300.00
5	Ed Wachter	200.00	100.00	60.00
6	Jim Thorpe	1,000	500.00	300.00
7	Bobby Walthour, Jr.	200.00	100.00	60.00
8	Walter Hagen	500.00	250.00	150.00
9	Ed Blood	200.00	100.00	60.00
10	Anton Lekang	200.00	100.00	60.00
11	Charles Jewtraw	200.00	100.00	60.00
12	Bobby McLean	200.00	100.00	60.00
13	LaVerne Fatour	200.00	100.00	60.00
14	Jim Londos	200.00	100.00	60.00
15	Reggie McNamara	200.00	100.00	60.00
16	William Tilden	200.00	100.00	60.00
17	Jack Dempsey	500.00	250.00	150.00
18	Gene Tunney	200.00	100.00	60.00
19	Eddie Shore	500.00	250.00	150.00
20	Duke Kahanamoku	200.00	100.00	60.00
21	Johnny Weissmuller	500.00	250.00	150.00
22	Gene Sarazen	500.00	250.00	150.00
23	Vincent Richards	200.00	100.00	60.00
24	Howie Morenz	500.00	250.00	150.00
25	Ralph Snoddy	250.00	125.00	75.00
26	James R. Wedell	250.00	125.00	75.00
27	Roscoe Turner	250.00	125.00	75.00
28	Jimmy Doolittle	250.00	125.00	75.00
29	Ace Bailey	250.00	125.00	75.00
30	Ching Johnson	250.00	125.00	75.00
31	Bobby Walthour, Jr.	250.00	125.00	75.00
32	Joe Lopchick	250.00	125.00	75.00
33	Eddie Burke	250.00	125.00	75.00
34	Irving Jaffee	250.00	125.00	75.00
35	Knute Rockne	1,000	500.00	300.00
36	Willie Hoppe	250.00	125.00	75.00
37	Helene Madison	250.00	125.00	75.00
38	Bobby Jones	3,000	1,500	900.00
39	Jack Westrope	250.00	125.00	75.00
40	Don George	250.00	125.00	75.00
41	Jim Browning	250.00	125.00	75.00
42	Carl Hubbell	500.00	250.00	150.00
43	Primo Carnera	250.00	125.00	75.00
44	Max Baer	250.00	125.00	75.00
45	Babe Didrickson	500.00	250.00	150.00
46	Ellsworth Vines	250.00	125.00	75.00
47	J. Hubert Stevens	250.00	125.00	75.00
48	Leonhard Seppala	250.00	125.00	75.00

1947 Sport Magazine Premium

This 8-1/2" x 11", blank-back, paper-stock picture appears to have been a premium issued in conjunction with Sport magazine's premiere issue in March 1947, perhaps as a send-away offer. The picture has a black-and-white portrait photo on a bright orange background, surrounded with a white border. In the lower-left corner is "March '47." "15 Sport" appears at lower-right.

		NM	EX	VG
15	Joe DiMaggio	35.00	17.50	10.50

1953 Sport Magazine All-Star Portfolio

This set of 5-3/8" x 7" glossy color pictures was used by Sport Magazine as a subscription premium. Featuring the outstanding photography of Ozzie Sweet, all but the Bob Mathias pictures are portraits, surrounded with a white border and the player name at bottom. Backs are blank. The heavy cardboard mailing envelope contains short athlete biographies.

		NM	EX	VG
Complete Set (10):		175.00	85.00	50.00
Common Player:		20.00	10.00	6.00
(1)	Joe Black	25.00	12.50	7.50
(2)	Robert Cousy (Basketball)	20.00	10.00	6.00
(3)	Elroy Hirsch (Football)	20.00	10.00	6.00
(4)	Rocky Marciano (Boxing)	30.00	15.00	9.00
(5)	Robert Bruce Mathias (Track and field.)	20.00	10.00	6.00
(6)	Stanley Frank Musial	45.00	22.50	13.50
(7)	John Olszewski (Football)	20.00	10.00	6.00
(8)	Allie Pierce Reynolds	20.00	10.00	6.00
(9)	Robin Evan Roberts	30.00	15.00	9.00
(10)	Robert Clayton Shantz	20.00	10.00	6.00

1968-69 Sports Cards for Collectors

These Myron Aronstein-drawn 3-1/2" x 4-1/4" postcards feature 78 pre-1950 players. Cards 1-36 feature blank backs, and 37-78 have brief biographical and statistical data. The last four are checklists.

		NM	EX	VG
Complete Set (82):		100.00	50.00	30.00
Common Player:		2.00	1.00	.60
1	Babe Ruth	15.00	7.50	5.00
2	Rube Marquard	2.00	1.00	.60
3	Zack Wheat	2.00	1.00	.60
4	John Clarkson	2.00	1.00	.60
5	Honus Wagner	2.00	1.00	.60
6	Johnny Evers	2.00	1.00	.60
7	Bill Dickey	2.00	1.00	.60
8	Elmer Smith	2.00	1.00	.60
9	Ty Cobb	10.00	5.00	3.00
10	Jack Chesbro	2.00	1.00	.60
11	George Gibson	2.00	1.00	.60
12	Bullet Joe Bush	2.00	1.00	.60
13	George Mullin	2.00	1.00	.60
14	Buddy Meyer	2.00	1.00	.60
15	Jimmy Collins	2.00	1.00	.60
16	Bill Wambsganss	2.00	1.00	.60
17	Jack Barry	2.00	1.00	.60

18	Dickie Kerr	2.00	1.00	.60
19	Connie Mack	2.00	1.00	.60
20	Rabbit Maranville	2.00	1.00	.60
21	Roger Peckinpaugh	2.00	1.00	.60
22	Mickey Cochrane	2.00	1.00	.60
23	George Kelly	2.00	1.00	.60
24	Frank "Home Rune" Baker	2.00	1.00	.60
25	Wally Schang	2.00	1.00	.60
26	Eddie Plank	2.00	1.00	.60
27	Bill Donovan	2.00	1.00	.60
28	Red Faber	2.00	1.00	.60
29	Hack Wilson	2.00	1.00	.60
30	Mordecai "3 Finger" Brown	2.00	1.00	.60
31	Fred Merkle	2.00	1.00	.60
32	Heinie Groh	2.00	1.00	.60
33	Stuffy McInnis	2.00	1.00	.60
34	Hal Chase	2.00	1.00	.60
35	Judge Kenesaw Mountain Landis	2.00	1.00	.60
36	Chief Bender	2.00	1.00	.60
37	Fred Snodgrass	2.00	1.00	.60
38	Tony Lazzeri	2.00	1.00	.60
39	John McGraw	2.00	1.00	.60
40	Mel Ott	10.00	5.00	3.00
41	Grover Alexander	2.00	1.00	.60
42	Rube Waddell	2.00	1.00	.60
43	Wilbert Robinson	2.00	1.00	.60
44	Cap Anson	2.00	1.00	.60
45	Eddie Cicotte	2.00	1.00	.60
46	Hank Gowdy	2.00	1.00	.60
47	Frankie Frisch	2.00	1.00	.60
48	Charles Comiskey	2.00	1.00	.60
49	Clyde Milan	2.00	1.00	.60
50	Jimmy Wilson	2.00	1.00	.60
51	Christy Mathewson	10.00	5.00	3.00
52	Tim Keefe	2.00	1.00	.60
53	Abner Doubleday	2.00	1.00	.60
54	Ed Walsh	2.00	1.00	.60
55	Jim Thorpe	10.00	5.00	3.00
56	Roger Bresnahan	2.00	1.00	.60
57	Frank Chance	2.00	1.00	.60
58	Heinie Manush	2.00	1.00	.60
59	Max Carey	2.00	1.00	.60
60	Joe Tinker	2.00	1.00	.60
61	Benny Kauff	2.00	1.00	.60
62	Fred Clarke	2.00	1.00	.60
63	Smokey Joe Wood	2.00	1.00	.60
64	George Burns	2.00	1.00	.60
65	Walter Johnson	10.00	5.00	3.00
66	Ferdie Schupp	2.00	1.00	.60
67	Jimmy McAleer	2.00	1.00	.60
68	Larry Gardner	2.00	1.00	.60
69	Buck Ewing	2.00	1.00	.60
70	George Sisler	2.00	1.00	.60
71	Charley Robertson	2.00	1.00	.60
72	Bill Dineen	2.00	1.00	.60
73	Kid Gleason	2.00	1.00	.60
74	Jim Bottomley	2.00	1.00	.60
75	Sam Crawford	2.00	1.00	.60
76	Kid Nichols	2.00	1.00	.60
77	Dick Rudolph	2.00	1.00	.60
78	Bill Klem	2.00	1.00	.60
79	Checklist			
80	Checklist			
81	Checklist			
82	Checklist			

1970 Sports Cards for Collectors Old Timer Postcards

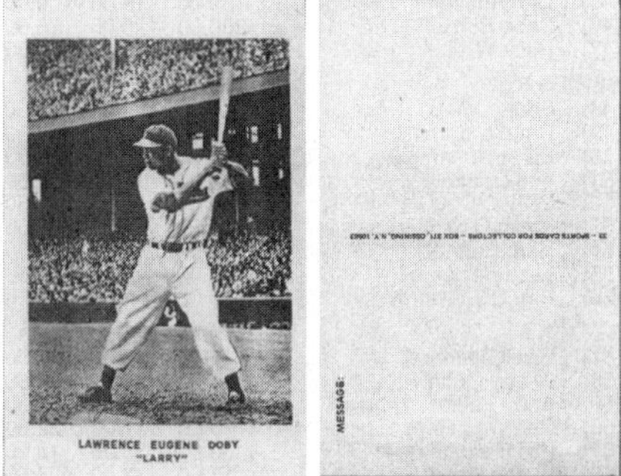

The date of issue given here is approximate. This collectors issue "Old Timer Postcard Series" features black-and-white photos bordered in white in a 3-1/2" x 5-1/2" format. Player identification in the bottom border usually offers his complete name on one line and his nickname below. Backs are divided by a card number and the name and address of the issuer. At left is a space for "MESSAGE:."

		NM	EX	VG
Complete Set (32):		75.00	37.50	22.00
Common Player:		4.00	2.00	1.25
1	Babe Ruth, Lou Gehrig	12.00	6.00	3.50
2	Larry Doby	6.00	3.00	1.75
3	Mike Garcia	4.00	2.00	1.25
4	Bob Feller	10.00	5.00	3.00
5	Early Wynn	4.00	2.00	1.25
6	Burleigh Grimes	4.00	2.00	1.25
7	Rabbit Maranville	4.00	2.00	1.25
8	Babe Ruth	15.00	7.50	4.50
9	Lou Gehrig	12.00	6.00	3.50
10	Joe DiMaggio	12.00	6.00	3.50
11	Ty Cobb	10.00	5.00	3.00
12	Lou Boudreau	4.00	2.00	1.25
13	Jimmie Foxx	4.00	2.00	1.25
14	Casey Stengel	6.00	3.00	1.75
15	Kenesaw M. Landis	4.00	2.00	1.25
16	Max Carey	4.00	2.00	1.25
17	Wilbert Robinson	4.00	2.00	1.25
18	Paul Richards	4.00	2.00	1.25
19	Zack Wheat	4.00	2.00	1.25
20	Rube Marquard	4.00	2.00	1.25
21	Dave Bancroft	4.00	2.00	1.25
22	Bobby Thomson	4.00	2.00	1.25
23	Mel Ott	4.00	2.00	1.25
24	Bobo Newsom	4.00	2.00	1.25
25	Johnny Mize	4.00	2.00	1.25
26	Walker Cooper	4.00	2.00	1.25
27	Fred "Dixie" Walker	4.00	2.00	1.25
28	Augie Galan	4.00	2.00	1.25
29	"Snuffy" Sturnweiss (Stirnweiss)	4.00	2.00	1.25
30	Floyd Caves "Babe" Herman	4.00	2.00	1.25
31	Babe Ruth	15.00	7.50	4.50
32	Babe Ruth	15.00	7.50	4.50

1970 Sports Cards for Collectors Sports Stuff

This set includes 10 Myron Aronsten-drawn 3-1/2" x 4-1/4" postcards depicting pre-1920 baseball luminaries, trivia, and legends.

		NM	EX	VG
Complete Set (10):		20.00	10.00	6.00
Common Player:		2.00	1.00	.60
1	Manager Trivia	2.00	1.00	.60
2	1914 Miracle Braves	2.00	1.00	.60
3	1919 Black Sox	2.00	1.00	.60
4	Eddie Plank, Fred Clarke, Roger Bresnahan, Babe Ruth	5.00	2.50	1.50
5	Bobby Lowe	2.00	1.00	.60
6	$100,000 Athletics Infield	2.00	1.00	.60
7	Joe Bush, Eddie Plank, Chief Bender	2.00	1.00	.60
8	Joe Tinker, Johnny Evers, Frank Chance	2.00	1.00	.60
9	Wilbert Robinson, John McGraw, Roger Peckinpaugh	2.00	1.00	.60
10	Ty Cobb	5.00	2.50	1.50

1977-79 Sportscaster

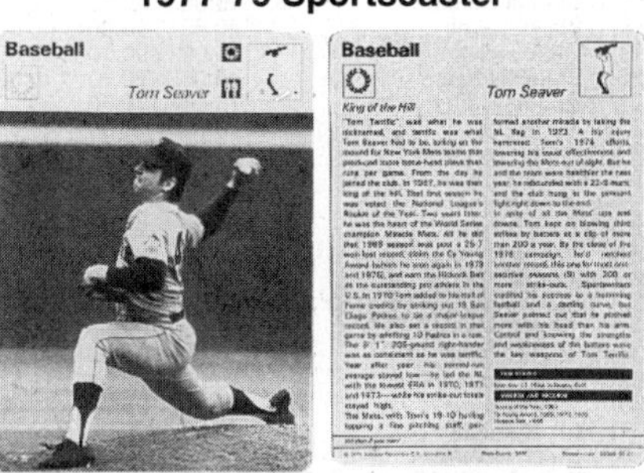

This massive set of full-color cards includes players from dozens of different sports - some of them very obscure - among more than 2,000 different subjects, making it one of the biggest sets of trading cards ever issued. Available by mail subscription from 1977 through 1979, the Sportscaster cards are large, measuring 4-3/4" x 6-1/4". Subscribers were mailed one series of 24 cards for $1.89 plus postage every month or so. The set has an international flavor to it, including such sports as rugby, soccer, lawn bowling, fencing, karate, bicycling, curling, skiing, bullfighting, auto racing, mountain climbing, hang gliding, yachting, sailing, badminton, bobsledding, etc. Each card has a series of icons in the upper-right corner to assist collectors in the various methods of sorting. Most popular among American collectors are the baseball, football and basketball stars in the set, which includes the 140 baseball subjects listed here. The checklist includes many Hall of Famers. Backs contain detailed write-ups of the player featured. Because the set was issued in series, and many collectors dropped out of the program before the end, cards in the higher series are especially scarce. This accounts for prices on some of the superstar cards, issued in early series, being lower than for some of the lesser-known players. The cards of Aaron and Bench are quite common because they were mailed to large numbers of persons as samples to introduce the program. The cards were also sold in several European countries and can be found with backs printed in French, Swedish and other languages.

		NM	EX	VG
Complete (Baseball) Set (140):		350.00	175.00	100.00
Common Player:		1.00	.50	.30
(1)	Henry Aaron	4.00	2.00	1.25
(2)	Danny Ainge	30.00	15.00	9.00
(3)	Emmett Ashford (Umpire)	2.50	1.25	.70
(4)	Ernie Banks	2.75	1.50	.80
(5)	Johnny Bench	7.50	3.75	2.25
(6)	Vida Blue	1.75	.90	.50
(7)	Bert Blyleven	1.25	.60	.40
(8)	Bobby Bonds	3.25	1.75	1.00
(9)	Lyman Bostock	1.25	.60	.40
(10)	George Brett	5.00	2.50	1.50
(11)	Lou Brock	3.25	1.75	1.00
(12)	Jeff Burroughs	1.25	.60	.40
(13)	Roy Campanella	8.00	4.00	2.50
(14)	John Candelaria	1.25	.60	.40
(15)	Rod Carew	3.25	1.75	1.00
(16)	Steve Carlton	4.00	2.00	1.25
(17)	Ron Cey	1.00	.50	.30
(18)	Roberto Clemente	10.00	5.00	3.00
(19)	Steve Dembowski	2.25	1.25	.70
(20)	Joe DiMaggio	5.00	2.50	1.50
(21)	Dennis Eckersley	4.00	2.00	1.25
(22)	Mark Fidrych	1.75	.90	.50
(23)	Carlton Fisk	6.00	3.00	1.75
(24)	Mike Flanagan	3.00	1.50	.90
(25)	Steve Garvey	5.00	2.50	1.50
(26)	Ron Guidry	3.00	1.50	.90
(27)	Gil Hodges	4.00	2.00	1.25
(28)	Catfish Hunter	4.00	2.00	1.25
(29)	Tommy John	1.25	.60	.40
(30)	Randy Jones	1.00	.50	.30
(31)	Dave Kingman	1.75	.90	.50
(32)	Sandy Koufax	6.00	3.00	1.75
(33)	Tommy Lasorda	6.50	3.25	2.00
(34)	Ron LeFlore	1.25	.60	.40
(35)	Greg Luzinski	1.00	.50	.30
(36)	Billy Martin	3.25	1.75	1.00
(37)	Willie Mays	4.00	2.00	1.25
(38)	Lee Mazzilli	5.00	2.50	1.50
(39)	Willie McCovey	3.75	2.00	1.25
(40)	Joe Morgan	2.75	1.50	.80
(41)	Thurman Munson	4.00	2.00	1.25
(42)	Stan Musial	5.00	2.50	1.50
(43)	Phil Niekro	4.00	2.00	1.25
(44)	Jim Palmer	3.00	1.50	.90
(45)	Dave Parker	1.75	.90	.50
(46)	Freddie Patek	1.25	.60	.40
(47)	Gaylord Perry	2.25	1.25	.70
(48)	Jim Piersall	2.75	1.50	.80
(49)	Vada Pinson	1.25	.60	.40
(50)	Rick Reuschel	1.25	.60	.40
(51)	Jim Rice	6.00	3.00	1.75
(52)	J.R. Richard	2.25	1.25	.70
(53)	Brooks Robinson	3.75	2.00	1.25
(54)	Frank Robinson	5.00	2.50	1.50
(55)	Jackie Robinson	5.00	2.50	1.50
(56)	Pete Rose	6.00	3.00	1.75
(57)	Joe Rudi	1.00	.50	.30
(58)	Babe Ruth	6.00	3.00	1.75
(59)	Nolan Ryan	7.00	3.50	2.00
(60)	Tom Seaver	3.75	2.00	1.25
(61)	Warren Spahn	3.75	2.00	1.25
(62)	Monty Stratton	2.25	1.25	.70
(63)	Craig Swan	1.75	.90	.50
(64)	Frank Tanana	1.00	.50	.30
(65)	Ron Taylor	2.25	1.25	.70
(66)	Garry Templeton	1.00	.50	.30
(67)	Gene Tenace	1.00	.50	.30
(68)	Bobby Thomson	1.75	.90	.50
(69)	Andre Thornton	1.25	.60	.40
(70)	Johnny VanderMeer	1.75	.90	.50
(71)	Ted Williams	7.00	3.50	2.00
(72)	Maury Wills	1.00	.50	.30
(73)	Hack Wilson	3.25	1.75	1.00
(74)	Dave Winfield/Htg	8.00	4.00	2.50
(75)	Dave Winfield/Portrait	4.00	2.00	1.25
(76)	Cy Young	2.75	1.50	.80
(77)	The 1927 Yankees	2.75	1.50	.80
(78)	1969 Mets	6.50	3.25	2.00
(79)	All-Star Game (Steve Garvey, Joe Morgan)	2.75	1.50	.80
(80)	Amateur Draft (Rick Monday)	1.25	.60	.40
(81)	At-A-Glance Reference (Tom Seaver)	5.00	2.50	1.50
(82)	Babe Ruth Baseball (Ed Figueroa)	6.50	3.25	2.00
(83)	Baltimore Memorial Stadium	3.00	1.50	.90
(84)	Boston's Fenway Park	5.00	2.50	1.50
(85)	Brother vs. Brother (Joe Niekro)	2.75	1.50	.80
(86)	Busch Memorial Stadium	2.50	1.25	.70
(87)	Candlestick Park	2.00	1.00	.60
(88)	Cape Cod League (Jim Beattie)	6.00	3.00	1.75
(89)	A Century and a Half of Baseball (Johnny Bench)	1.75	.90	.50
(90)	Cy Young Award (Tom Seaver)	2.75	1.50	.80
(91)	The Dean Brothers (Dizzy Dean, Paul Dean)	5.00	2.50	1.50
(92)	Designated Hitter (Rusty Staub)	2.25	1.25	.70
(93)	Dodger Stadium	2.75	1.50	.80
(94)	Perfect Game (Don Larsen)	3.25	1.75	1.00
(95)	The Double Steal (Davey Lopes)	5.00	2.50	1.50
(96)	Fenway Park	4.00	2.00	1.25
(97)	The Firemen (Goose Gossage)	4.00	2.00	1.25
(98)	Forever Blowing Bubbles (Davey Lopes)	2.00	1.00	.60
(99)	The Forsch Brothers (Bob Forsch, Ken Forsch)	5.00	2.50	1.50
(100)	Four Home Runs In A Game (Mike Schmidt)	6.50	3.25	2.00
(101)	400-Homer Club (Duke Snider)	5.00	2.50	1.50
(102)	Great Moments (Bob Gibson)	3.25	1.75	1.00
(103)	Great Moments (Ferguson Jenkins)	2.25	1.25	.70
(104)	Great Moments (Mickey Lolich)	1.75	.90	.50
(105)	Great Moments (Carl Yastrzemski)	3.25	1.75	1.00
(106)	Hidden Ball Trick (Carl Yastrzemski)	2.75	1.50	.80
(107)	Hit And Run (George Foster)	1.25	.60	.40
(108)	Hitting The Cutoff Man	1.00	.50	.30
(109)	Hitting Pitchers (Don Drysdale)	3.25	1.75	1.00
(110)	Infield Fly Rule (Bobby Grich)	1.25	.60	.40
(111)	Instruction (Rod Carew)	2.75	1.50	.80
(112)	Interference (Johnny Bench)	2.75	1.50	.80
(113)	Iron Mike (Pitching Machine)	2.75	1.50	.80

		NM	EX	VG
(114)	Keeping Score	1.75	.90	.50
(115)	Like Father, Like Son (Roy Smalley)	3.75	2.00	1.25
(116)	Lingo I (Gary Carter)	1.75	.90	.50
(117)	Lingo II (Earl Weaver)	2.75	1.50	.80
(118)	Little Leagues To Big Leagues (Hector Torres)	1.75	.90	.50
(119)	Maris and Mantle (Mickey Mantle, Roger Maris)	4.00	2.00	1.25
(120)	Measurements (Memorial Stadium)	1.00	.50	.30
(121)	The Money Game (Dennis Eckersley)	6.00	3.00	1.75
(122)	NCAA Tournament (Aggies-Longhorns)	1.75	.90	.50
(123)	The Oakland A's, 1971-75	3.00	1.50	.90
(124)	The Perfect Game (Sandy Koufax)	3.50	1.75	1.00
(125)	Pickoff (Luis Tiant)	1.25	.60	.40
(126)	The Presidential Ball (William Howard Taft)	1.75	.90	.50
(127)	Relief Pitching (Mike Marshall)	1.25	.60	.40
(128)	The Rules (Hank Aaron)	2.75	1.50	.80
(129)	Rundown (Mets vs. Astros)	1.75	.90	.50
(130)	7th Game of the World Series (Bert Campaneris)	2.25	1.25	.70
(131)	Shea Stadium	2.50	1.25	.70
(132)	The 3000 Hit Club (Roberto Clemente)	8.00	4.00	2.50
(133)	Training Camps (Orioles)	2.75	1.50	.80
(134)	Triple Crown (Carl Yastrzemski)	16.00	8.00	4.75
(135)	Triple Play (Rick Burleson)	2.75	1.50	.80
(136)	Triple Play (Bill Wambsganss)	1.75	.90	.50
(137)	Umpires Strike	1.75	.90	.50
(138)	Veterans Stadium	2.50	1.25	.70
(139)	Wrigley Marathon (Mike Schmidt)	8.00	4.00	2.50
(140)	Yankee Stadium	1.00	.50	.30

Beyond Sports (Baseball) Set: (6):

		NM	EX	VG
(1)	Clemente Award (Andre Thornton)	5.00	2.50	1.50
(2)	Clowns (Al Schact, Nick Altrock)	4.00	2.00	1.25
(3)	Fellowship of Christian Athletes (Don Kessinger)	4.00	2.00	1.25
(4)	High School Record Book (David Clyde)	2.50	1.25	.70
(5)	Hutchinson Award (Al Kaline)	40.00	20.00	12.00
(6)	Walkie-Talkie (Yogi Berra)	5.00	2.50	1.50

1977 Sports Challenge Records

Taped highlights and an interview with the player are featured on this series of 33-1/3 RPM records. The 6" diameter records have a centerhole to be punched out to play the record. Fronts have a stylized picture of the player, his name and a title. Backs describe the highlight and give other career details.

		NM	EX	VG
Complete Set (12):		250.00	125.00	75.00
Common Player:		20.00	10.00	6.00
(1)	Henry Aaron (Hits 715th Homer)	45.00	22.50	13.50
(2)	Johnny Bench (Beats Pirates in '72 Playoff)	30.00	15.00	9.00
(3)	Jerry Koosman, Donn Clendenon (1969 Miracle Mets)	20.00	10.00	6.00
(4)	Don Larsen ('56 World Series Perfect Game)	20.00	10.00	6.00
(5)	Fred Lynn (Has Incredible Day in Detroit)	20.00	10.00	6.00
(6)	Willie Mays (Hits 1st Met Homer)	35.00	17.50	10.50
(7)	Bill Mazeroski (Wins 1960 World Series)	25.00	12.50	7.50
(8)	Frank Robinson (Homers 1st Time as Indian)	20.00	10.00	6.00
(9)	Nolan Ryan (4th No Hitter)	45.00	22.50	13.50
(10)	Tom Seaver (Cubs Ruin Perfect Game)	25.00	12.50	7.50
(11)	Bobby Thomson (Shot Heard 'Round the World)	20.00	10.00	6.00
(12)	Ted Williams (Last Time at Bat in Boston)	35.00	17.50	10.50

1926 Sports Co. of America Champions

Little was known of these small (1-1/2" x 2-1/4") black-and-white cards until an original store display was discovered in the late 1980s. Carrying a copyright date of November 1926, from Sports Co. of America, a San Francisco publishing firm, these cards were produced for A. G. Spalding & Bros., the sporting goods firm. Each card was issued in a wax paper baggie with a like-sized red, white and blue "Sport-Scrip" which was serial numbered for use in a candy prize drawing at the store or could be redeemed for 10 cents on Spalding equipment. The cards themselves feature ornately framed photos at center, with "CHAMPIONS" in a cartouche at top

and the player's name and sport in a second ornate frame at bottom. Most backs have biographical data and career notes, but some are seen with advertising offering an album for the pieces. Nearly 50 baseball players are known from a list of over 175 male and female athletes from sports as diverse as fishing, chess and balloon racing. The unnumbered baseball players from the set are checklisted here in alphabetical order.

		NM	EX	VG
Common Baseball Player:		45.00	20.00	10.00
Ad Back: 2X				
(1)	"Babe" Adams	45.00	20.00	10.00
(2)	Grover Alexander	275.00	110.00	55.00
(3)	Nick Altrock	45.00	20.00	10.00
(4)	Dave Bancroft	220.00	90.00	45.00
(5)	Jesse Barnes	45.00	20.00	10.00
(6)	Oswald Bluege	45.00	20.00	10.00
(7)	Jim Bottomley	220.00	90.00	45.00
(8)	Max Carey	220.00	90.00	45.00
(9)	Ty Cobb	825.00	330.00	165.00
(10)	Mickey Cochrane	220.00	90.00	45.00
(11)	Eddie Collins	220.00	90.00	45.00
(12)	Stan Coveleskie (Coveleski)	220.00	90.00	45.00
(13)	Kiki Cuyler	220.00	90.00	45.00
(14)	Hank DeBerry	45.00	20.00	10.00
(15)	Jack Fournier	45.00	20.00	10.00
(16)	Goose Goslin	220.00	90.00	45.00
(17)	Charlie Grimm	45.00	20.00	10.00
(18)	Bucky Harris	220.00	90.00	45.00
(19)	Gabby Hartnett	220.00	90.00	45.00
(20)	Fred Hofmann	45.00	20.00	10.00
(21)	Rogers Hornsby	275.00	110.00	55.00
(22)	Waite Hoyt	220.00	90.00	45.00
(23)	Walter Johnson	715.00	290.00	145.00
(24)	Joe Judge	45.00	20.00	10.00
(25)	Willie Kamm	45.00	20.00	10.00
(26)	Tony Lazzeri	220.00	90.00	45.00
(27)	Rabbit Maranville	220.00	90.00	45.00
(28)	Fred Marberry	45.00	20.00	10.00
(29)	Rube Marquard	220.00	90.00	45.00
(30)	"Stuffy" McInnis	45.00	20.00	10.00
(31)	"Babe" Pinelli	45.00	20.00	10.00
(32)	Wally Pipp	45.00	20.00	10.00
(33)	Sam Rice	220.00	90.00	45.00
(34)	Emory Rigney	45.00	20.00	10.00
(35)	Dutch Ruether	45.00	20.00	10.00
(36a)	Babe Ruth (1926 copyright)	2,000	705.00	350.00
(36b)	Babe Ruth (1927 copyright)	4,000	1,320	660.00
(37)	Ray Schalk	220.00	90.00	45.00
(38)	Joey Sewell	220.00	90.00	45.00
(39)	Urban Shocker	45.00	20.00	10.00
(40)	Al Simmons	220.00	90.00	45.00
(41)	George Sisler	220.00	90.00	45.00
(42)	Tris Speaker	275.00	110.00	55.00
(43)	Pie Traynor	220.00	90.00	45.00
(44)	George Uhle	45.00	20.00	10.00
(45)	Paul Waner	220.00	90.00	45.00
(46)	Aaron L. Ward	45.00	20.00	10.00
(47)	Ken Williams	45.00	20.00	10.00
(48)	Glenn Wright	45.00	20.00	10.00
(49)	Emil Yde	45.00	20.00	10.00

1946-49 Sports Exchange All-Star Picture File

Produced and sold (originally at 50 cents per series) by "The Trading Post," one of the first card collectors' publications, over a period which spanned several years in the late 1940s, this 113-card set was issued in 12 series. Most of the series were nine cards each, printed in black-and-white, unnumbered and blank-backed in a 7" x 10" format. The first 27 cards carry no series designation but were advertised as Series 1A and 1B and Series 2. Series 3 features 11 cards and is printed in sepia tones rather than black-and-white. The fourth series is also unmarked. The final two series consist of 12 cards each, printed two per sheet in smaller format. The photos are labeled as originating with the International News Service. Most of the same players and photos appearing in this set are also found in the Sports Exchange Baseball Miniatures set. Because this was one of the first baseball card sets issued after World War II, it contains cards of several players not found in other issues. The set carries a W603 designation in the "American Card Catalog." Cards are listed alphabetically within series in the checklist which follows.

		NM	EX	VG
Complete Set (113):		2,750	1,350	825.00
Common Card:		15.00	7.50	4.50
SERIES 1A				
(1)	Phil Cavaretta	15.00	7.50	4.50
(2)	Walker Cooper	15.00	7.50	4.50
(3)	Dave Ferriss	15.00	7.50	4.50
(4)	Les Fleming	15.00	7.50	4.50
(5)	Whitey Kurowski	15.00	7.50	4.50
(6)	Marty Marion	20.00	10.00	6.00
(7)	Rip Sewell	15.00	7.50	4.50
(8)	Eddie Stanky	20.00	10.00	6.00
(9)	Dixie Walker	15.00	7.50	4.50
SERIES 1B				
(10)	Bill Dickey	40.00	20.00	12.00
(11)	Bobby Doerr	30.00	15.00	9.00
(12)	Bob Feller	40.00	20.00	12.00
(13)	Hank Greenberg	75.00	37.00	22.00
(14)	George McQuinn	15.00	7.50	4.50
(15)	Ray Mueller	15.00	7.50	4.50
(16)	Hal Newhouser	30.00	15.00	9.00
(17)	Dick Wakefield	15.00	7.50	4.50
(18)	Ted Williams	150.00	75.00	45.00
SERIES 2				
(19)	Al Benton	15.00	7.50	4.50
(20)	Lou Boudreau	30.00	15.00	9.00
(21)	Spud Chandler	15.00	7.50	4.50
(22)	Jeff Heath	15.00	7.50	4.50
(23)	Kirby Higbe	15.00	7.50	4.50
(24)	Tex Hughson	15.00	7.50	4.50
(25)	Stan Musial	175.00	90.00	55.00
(26)	Howie Pollet	15.00	7.50	4.50
(27)	Enos Slaughter	40.00	20.00	12.00
SERIES 3				
(28)	Harry Brecheen	15.00	7.50	4.50
(29)	Dom DiMaggio	30.00	15.00	9.00
(30)	Del Ennis	15.00	7.50	4.50
(31)	Al Evans	15.00	7.50	4.50
(32)	Johnny Lindell	15.00	7.50	4.50
(33)	Johnny Mize	35.00	17.50	10.50
(34)	Johnny Pesky	15.00	7.50	4.50
(35)	Pete Reiser	15.00	7.50	4.50
(36a)	Aaron Robinson (Throwing)	15.00	7.50	4.50
(36b)	Aaron Robinson (Fielding)	15.00	7.50	4.50
(37)	1946 Boston Red Sox Team	30.00	15.00	9.00
(38)	1946 St. Louis Cardinals Team	30.00	15.00	9.00
SERIES 4				
(39)	Jimmie Foxx	45.00	22.00	13.50
(40)	Frank Frisch	30.00	15.00	9.00
(41)	Lou Gehrig	150.00	75.00	45.00
(42)	Lefty Grove	35.00	17.50	10.50
(43)	Bill Hallahan	15.00	7.50	4.50
(44)	Rogers "Rajah" Hornsby	45.00	22.00	13.50
(45)	Carl Hubbell	30.00	15.00	9.00
(46)	Babe Ruth	250.00	125.00	75.00
(47)	Hack Wilson	30.00	15.00	9.00
SERIES 5				
(48)	Eddie Dyer	15.00	7.50	4.50
(49)	Charlie Grimm	15.00	7.50	4.50
(50)	Billy Herman	30.00	15.00	9.00
(51)	Ted Lyons	30.00	15.00	9.00
(52)	Lefty O'Doul	25.00	12.50	7.50
(53)	Steve O'Neill	15.00	7.50	4.50
(54)	Herb Pennock	30.00	15.00	9.00
(55)	Luke Sewell	15.00	7.50	4.50
(56)	Billy Southworth	15.00	7.50	4.50
SERIES 6				
(57)	Ewell Blackwell	25.00	12.50	7.50
(58)	Jimmy Outlaw	15.00	7.50	4.50
(59)	Andy Pafko	15.00	7.50	4.50
(60)	Pee Wee Reese	75.00	37.00	22.00
(61)	Phil Rizzuto	60.00	30.00	18.00
(62)	Buddy Rosar	15.00	7.50	4.50
(63)	Johnny Sain	25.00	12.50	7.50
(64)	Dizzy Trout	15.00	7.50	4.50
(65)	Harry Walker	15.00	7.50	4.50
SERIES 7				
(66)	Floyd Bevens	15.00	7.50	4.50
(67)	Hugh Casey	15.00	7.50	4.50
(68)	Sam Chapman	15.00	7.50	4.50
(69)	Joe DiMaggio	150.00	75.00	45.00
(70)	Tommy Henrich	25.00	12.50	7.50
(71)	Ralph Kiner	30.00	15.00	9.00
(72)	Cookie Lavagetto	15.00	7.50	4.50
(73)	Vic Lombardi	15.00	7.50	4.50
(74)	Cecil Travis	15.00	7.50	4.50
SERIES 8				
(75)	Nick Altrock	20.00	10.00	6.00
(76)	Mark Christman	15.00	7.50	4.50
(77)	Earle Combs	30.00	15.00	9.00
(78)	Travis Jackson	30.00	15.00	9.00
(79)	Bob Muncrief	15.00	7.50	4.50
(80)	Earl Neale	25.00	12.50	7.50
(81)	Joe Page	15.00	7.50	4.50
(82)	Honus Wagner	75.00	37.00	22.00
(83)	Mickey Witek	15.00	7.50	4.50
SERIES 9				
(84)	George Case	15.00	7.50	4.50

(85)	Jake Early	15.00	7.50	4.50
(86)	Carl Furillo	30.00	15.00	9.00
(87)	Augie Galan	15.00	7.50	4.50
(88)	Bert Haas	15.00	7.50	4.50
(89)	Johnny Hopp	15.00	7.50	4.50
(90)	Ray Lamanno	15.00	7.50	4.50
(91)	Buddy Lewis	15.00	7.50	4.50
(92)	Warren Spahn	40.00	20.00	12.00
SERIES 10				
(93)	Lu Blue	15.00	7.50	4.50
q94)	Bruce Edwards	15.00	7.50	4.50
(95)	Elbie Fletcher	15.00	7.50	4.50
(96)	Joe Gordon	15.00	7.50	4.50
(97)	Tommy Holmes	15.00	7.50	4.50
(98)	Billy Johnson	15.00	7.50	4.50
(99)	Phil Masi	15.00	7.50	4.50
(100)	Red Munger	15.00	7.50	4.50
(101)	Vern Stephens	15.00	7.50	4.50
SERIES 11				
(102)	Ralph Branca, Ken Keltner	20.00	10.00	6.00
(103)	Mickey Cochrane, Bob Dillinger	40.00	20.00	12.00
(104)	Dizzy Dean, Eddie Joost	80.00	40.00	24.00
(105)	Joe Jackson, Wally Westlake	400.00	200.00	120.00
(106)	Larry Jansen, Yogi Berra	80.00	40.00	24.00
(107)	Peanuts Lowrey, Heinie Manush	40.00	20.00	12.00
SERIES 12				
(108)	Gene Bearden, Dale Mitchell	45.00	22.00	13.50
(109)	Steve Gromek, Earl Torgeson	45.00	22.00	13.50
(110)	Jim Hegan, Mickey Vernon	45.00	22.00	13.50
(111)	Bob Lemon, Red Rolfe	100.00	50.00	30.00
(112)	Billy Meyer, Ben Chapman	45.00	22.00	13.50
(113)	Sibbi Sisti, Zach Taylor	45.00	22.00	13.50

1947 Sports Exchange Baseball Miniatures

Produced and sold (originally at $1 per series) by one of the hobby's first periodicals, "The Trading Post," this 108-card set was released in three series, designated by red, green and gold borders. The blank-back, unnumbered cards are printed in black-and-white and were sold in sheets of six. When cut from the sheets, individual cards in the red- and green-bordered series measure 2-1/2" x 3", while the gold-bordered cards measure 2-1/2" x 3-1/8". The set is checklisted here alphabetically within series. The set carries an American Card Catalog designation of W602.

		NM	EX	VG
Complete Set (108):		4,750	2,400	1,400
Common Player:		15.00	7.50	4.50
GREEN BORDER SERIES				
(1)	Nick Altrock	20.00	10.00	6.00
(2)	Floyd Bevens	15.00	7.50	4.50
(3)	Ewell Blackwell	20.00	10.00	6.00
(4)	Lou Boudreau	35.00	17.50	10.50
(5)	Harry Brecheen	15.00	7.50	4.50
(6)	Hugh Casey	15.00	7.50	4.50
(7)	Phil Cavaretta	15.00	7.50	4.50
(8)	Sam Chapman	15.00	7.50	4.50
(9)	Mark Christman	15.00	7.50	4.50
(10)	Bill Dickey	40.00	20.00	12.00
(11)	Dom DiMaggio	25.00	12.50	7.50
(12)	Joe DiMaggio	400.00	200.00	120.00
(13)	Eddie Dyer	15.00	7.50	4.50
(14)	Frank Frisch	40.00	20.00	12.00
(15)	Lou Gehrig	275.00	135.00	82.00
(16)	Charlie Grimm	15.00	7.50	4.50
(17)	Lefty Grove	40.00	20.00	12.00
(18)	Tommy Henrich	20.00	10.00	6.00
(19)	Ralph Kiner	35.00	17.50	10.50
(20)	Cookie Lavagetto	15.00	7.50	4.50
(21)	Vic Lombardi	15.00	7.50	4.50
(22)	Ted Lyons	35.00	17.50	10.50
(23)	Bob Muncrief	15.00	7.50	4.50
(24)	Stan Musial	160.00	80.00	48.00
(25)	Steve O'Neill	15.00	7.50	4.50
(26)	Jimmy Outlaw	15.00	7.50	4.50
(27)	Joe Page	15.00	7.50	4.50
(28)	Pee Wee Reese	65.00	32.00	19.50
(29)	Phil Rizzuto	65.00	32.00	19.50
(30)	Buddy Rosar	15.00	7.50	4.50
(31)	Johnny Sain	20.00	10.00	6.00
(32)	Billy Southworth	15.00	7.50	4.50
(33)	Cecil Travis	15.00	7.50	4.50
(34)	Honus Wagner	90.00	45.00	27.00
(35)	Harry Walker	15.00	7.50	4.50
(36)	Mickey Witek	15.00	7.50	4.50
RED BORDER SERIES				
(37)	Yogi Berra	80.00	40.00	24.00
(38)	Lu Blue	15.00	7.50	4.50
(39)	Ben Chapman	15.00	7.50	4.50
(40)	Mickey Cochrane	35.00	17.50	10.50
(41)	Earle Combs	35.00	17.50	10.50
(42)	Dizzy Dean	95.00	47.00	28.00
(43)	Bob Dillinger	15.00	7.50	4.50
(44)	Bobby Doerr	35.00	17.50	10.50
(45)	Al Evans	15.00	7.50	4.50
(46)	Jimmy (Jimmie) Foxx	50.00	25.00	15.00
(47)	Joe Gordon	15.00	7.50	4.50
(48)	Bill Hallahan	15.00	7.50	4.50
(49)	Tommy Holmes	15.00	7.50	4.50
(50)	Rogers Hornsby	50.00	25.00	15.00
(51)	Carl Hubbell	45.00	22.00	13.50
(52)	Travis Jackson	35.00	17.50	10.50
(53)	Bill Johnson	15.00	7.50	4.50
(54)	Ken Keltner	15.00	7.50	4.50
(55)	Whitey Kurowski	15.00	7.50	4.50
(56)	Ray Lamanno	15.00	7.50	4.50
(57)	Johnny Lindell	15.00	7.50	4.50
(58)	Peanuts Lowrey	15.00	7.50	4.50
(59)	Phil Masi	15.00	7.50	4.50
(60)	Earl Neale	20.00	10.00	6.00
(61)	Hal Newhouser	35.00	17.50	10.50
(62)	Lefty O'Doul	25.00	12.50	7.50
(63)	Herb Pennock	35.00	17.50	10.50
(64)	Red Rolfe	35.00	17.50	10.50
(65)	Babe Ruth	450.00	225.00	135.00
(66)	Luke Sewell	15.00	7.50	4.50
(67)	Rip Sewell	15.00	7.50	4.50
(68)	Warren Spahn	60.00	30.00	18.00
(69)	Vern Stephens	15.00	7.50	4.50
(70)	Dizzy Trout	15.00	7.50	4.50
(71)	Wally Westlake	15.00	7.50	4.50
(72)	Hack Wilson	50.00	25.00	15.00
GOLD BORDER SERIES				
(73)	Al Benton	30.00	15.00	9.00
(74)	Ralph Branca	25.00	12.50	7.50
(75)	George Case	30.00	15.00	9.00
(76)	Spud Chandler	30.00	15.00	9.00
(77)	Jake Early	30.00	15.00	9.00
(78)	Bruce Edwards	30.00	15.00	9.00
(79)	Del Ennis	30.00	15.00	9.00
(80)	Bob Feller	80.00	40.00	24.00
(81)	Dave Ferriss	30.00	15.00	9.00
(82)	Les Fleming	30.00	15.00	9.00
(83)	Carl Furillo	150.00	75.00	45.00
(84)	Augie Galan	30.00	15.00	9.00
(85)	Hank Greenberg	100.00	50.00	30.00
(86)	Bert Haas	30.00	15.00	9.00
(87)	Jeff Heath	30.00	15.00	9.00
(88)	Billy Herman	60.00	30.00	18.00
(89)	Kirby Higbe	30.00	15.00	9.00
(90)	Tex Hughson	30.00	15.00	9.00
(91)	Johnny Hopp	30.00	15.00	9.00
(92)	Joe Jackson	650.00	325.00	195.00
(93)	Larry Jansen	30.00	15.00	9.00
(94)	Eddie Joost	30.00	15.00	9.00
(95)	Buddy Lewis	30.00	15.00	9.00
(96)	Heinie Manush	60.00	30.00	18.00
(97)	Marty Marion	30.00	15.00	9.00
(98)	George McQuinn	30.00	15.00	9.00
(99)	Johnny Mize	60.00	30.00	18.00
(100)	Red Munger	30.00	15.00	9.00
(101)	Andy Pafko	30.00	15.00	9.00
(102)	Johnny Pesky	30.00	15.00	9.00
(103)	Howie Pollet	30.00	15.00	9.00
(104)	Pete Reiser	30.00	15.00	9.00
(105)	Aaron Robinson	30.00	15.00	9.00
(106)	Enos Slaughter	60.00	30.00	18.00
(107)	Dixie Walker	30.00	15.00	9.00
(108)	Ted Williams (Photo actually Bobby Doerr.)	200.00	100.00	60.00

1963 Sports "Hall of Fame" Busts

Licensed by the National Baseball Hall of Fame, this set of 20 plastic player busts was produced by Sports "Hall of Fame," Inc., of New York. Each six-inch statue has a white player figure atop a wood-look pedestal with a plaque providing career details. The busts were sold in a red, white and gold display box with photos of the players on the back. Though the box back promised "Many More," only the 20 players pictured were ever issued. Retail price at issue was $1-1.25. The first 12 busts are more common than the final eight, with Foxx and Greenberg especially scarce. Values quoted are for busts alone, add $25 for accompanying box and $50 or more for unopened box with cellophane.

		NM	EX	VG
Complete Set (20):		3,000	1,500	900.00
Common Player:		75.00	35.00	20.00
(1)	Babe Ruth	110.00	55.00	30.00
(2)	Ty Cobb	90.00	45.00	25.00
(3)	Joe DiMaggio	110.00	55.00	30.00
(4)	Rogers Hornsby	80.00	40.00	24.00
(5)	Lou Gehrig	100.00	50.00	30.00
(6)	Pie Traynor	75.00	35.00	20.00
(7)	Honus Wagner	150.00	75.00	45.00
(8)	Bill Dickey	110.00	55.00	30.00
(9)	Walter Johnson	135.00	65.00	40.00
(10)	Christy Mathewson	110.00	55.00	30.00
(11)	Jimmie Foxx	335.00	165.00	100.00
(12)	Tris Speaker	75.00	35.00	20.00
(13)	Joe Cronin	180.00	90.00	50.00
(14)	Paul Waner	165.00	80.00	45.00
(15)	Bobby Feller	225.00	110.00	65.00
(16)	Hank Greenberg	275.00	135.00	80.00
(17)	Jackie Robinson	260.00	130.00	75.00
(18)	George Sisler	200.00	100.00	60.00
(19)	John McGraw	200.00	100.00	60.00
(20)	Mickey Cochrane	200.00	100.00	60.00

1954 Sports Illustrated Topps Foldouts

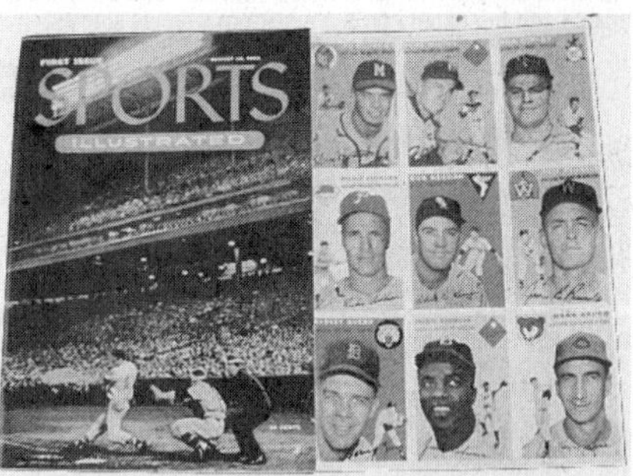

To illustrate a feature about baseball card collecting in its very first issue, Sports Illustrated included a three-page foldout featuring 27 contemporary Topps cards. Printed on glossy paper stock in full color, the paper cards are exact front and back reproductions of the real thing. The foldout panel is found in the Aug. 16, 1954, issue of SI which features on its cover a photo of Eddie Mathews at bat during a night game. The magazine's second issue also contains a 27-card foldout of New York Yankees. The insert reproduces all of Topps' 1954 Yankees cards in full color, and supplements them with black-and-white "cards" in the general style of '54 Topps for those Yankees who appeared only on Bowman cards or on no cards in 1954. The August 23 issue of SI features a stand of golf clubs on its cover. Survivng examples of SI issue #2 are actually scarcer than the debut issue. Singles of the paper cards are rarely encountered. In 2001, SI reprinted 50,000 copies of issue #1 as a subscription premium. These copies are unmarked as reprints and difficult to distinguish from the originals. Many surviving original copies have a mail-in subscription offer card which the reprint does not.

		NM	EX	VG
	Aug. 16, 1954 Issue (Original)	250.00	125.00	75.00
	Aug. 16, 1954 Issue (2001 Reprint)	30.00	15.00	9.00
1	Ted Williams			
2	Gus Zernial			
4	Hank Sauer			
6	Pete Runnels			
7	Ted Kluszewski			
9	Harvey Haddix			
10	Jackie Robinson			
15	Al Rosen			
24	Granny Hamner			
25	Harvey Kuenn			
26	Ray Jablonski			
27	Ferris Fain			
29	Jim Hegan			
30	Ed Mathews			
32	Duke Snider			
34	Jim Rivera			
40	Mel Parnell			
45	Richie Ashburn			
70	Larry Doby			
77	Ray Boone			
85	Bob Turley			
90	Willie Mays			
100	Bob Keegan			
102	Gil Hodges			
119	Johnny Antonelli			
137	Wally Moon			
235	Vern Law			
	Aug. 23, 1954 Issue	350.00	175.00	100.00
5	Ed Lopat			
17	Phil Rizzuto			
37	Whitey Ford			
50	Yogi Berra			
56	Willie Miranda			
62	Eddie Robinson			
83	Joe Collins			
96	Charlie Silvera			
101	Gene Woodling			
105	Andy Carey			
130	Hank Bauer			
175	Frank Leja			
205	Johnny Sain			
230	Bob Kuzava			
239	Bill Skowron			
	Harry Byrd			

Bob Cerv
Jerry Coleman
Tom Gorman
Bob Grim
Mickey Mantle
Jim McDonald
Gil McDougald
Tom Morgan
Irv Noren
Allie Reynolds
Enos Slaughter

1955 Sports Illustrated Topps Foldouts

SI kicked off the 1955 baseball season by including a page of 1955 Topps card reproductions in its April 11 and April 18 issues. Unlike the tri-fold panels of 1954, the 1955 issues contain only eight reproductions per magazine. Printed in full size in full color on glossy magazine paper, the pages are exact front and back replicas of regular-issue 1955 Topps cards. The April 11 issue features on its cover Willie Mays, Leo Durocher and Lorraine Day (Mrs. D.); the April 18 issue has Al Rosen at bat. Surviving examples of these 1955 SI issues are scarce and the paper cards are seldom seen as singles.

		NM	EX	VG
	April 11, 1955 Issue	200.00	100.00	60.00
1	Dusty Rhodes			
26	Dick Groat			
28	Ernie Banks			
31	Warren Spahn			
56	Ray Jablonski			
67	Wally Moon			
79	Danny Schell			
90	Karl Spooner			
	April 18, 1955 Issue	60.00	30.00	18.00
8	Hal Smith			
10	Bob Keegan			
11	Ferris Fain			
16	Roy Sievers			
38	Bob Turley			
70	Al Rosen			
77	Arnie Portocarrero			
106	Frank Sullivan			

1968-70 Sports Illustrated Posters

Between 1968-70, Sports Illustrated issued a series of baseball player posters. The 2' x 3' blank-back posters have borderless color action or posed photos. In an upper corner are the player identification, copyright, poster number, etc., in small type. Values for the posters issued in 1969 and 1970 are higher than those produced in 1968. Current market values reflect the fact that many superstars' posters were sold in larger quantities than those of journeyman players and survive in greater numbers. The posters are listed here alphabetically within year of issue. Original selling price of the posters was $1.50 each, plus postage.

		NM	EX	VG
Complete Set (86):		2,500	1,250	750.00
Common Player:		10.00	5.00	3.00
	1968			
(1)	Hank Aaron	45.00	22.50	13.50
(2)	Rich Allen	30.00	15.00	9.00
(3)	Gene Alley	15.00	7.50	4.50
(4)	Felipe Alou	15.00	7.50	4.50
(5)	Max Alvis	10.00	5.00	3.00
(6)	Bob Aspromonte	10.00	5.00	3.00
(7)	Ernie Banks (Photo actually Billy Williams.)	35.00	17.50	10.50
(8)	Clete Boyer	12.50	6.25	3.75
(9)	Lou Brock	15.00	7.50	4.50
(10)	John Callison	15.00	7.50	4.50
(11)	Campy Campaneris	12.50	6.25	3.75
(12)	Leo Cardenas	12.50	6.25	3.75
(13)	Paul Casanova	17.50	8.75	5.25
(14)	Orlando Cepeda	17.50	8.75	5.25
(15)	Roberto Clemente	185.00	95.00	55.00
(16)	Tony Conigliaro	20.00	10.00	6.00
(17)	Willie Davis	15.00	7.50	4.50
(18)	Don Drysdale	17.50	8.75	5.25
(19)	Al Ferrara	12.50	6.25	3.75
(20)	Curt Flood	15.00	7.50	4.50
(21)	Bill Freehan	30.00	15.00	9.00
(22)	Jim Fregosi	10.00	5.00	3.00
(23)	Bob Gibson	15.00	7.50	4.50
(24)	Bud Harrelson (Photo actually Ken Harrelson.)	20.00	10.00	6.00
(25)	Joe Horlen	10.00	5.00	3.00
(26)	Tony Horton	15.00	7.50	4.50
(27)	Tommy John	12.50	6.25	3.75
(28)	Al Kaline	40.00	20.00	12.00
(29)	Harmon Killebrew	17.50	8.75	5.25
(30)	Jim Lonborg	17.50	8.75	5.25
(31)	Jim Maloney	12.50	6.25	3.75
(32)	Mickey Mantle	185.00	92.00	55.00
(33)	Juan Marichal	17.50	8.75	5.25
(34)	Willie Mays	110.00	55.00	35.00
(35)	Bill Mazeroski	25.00	12.50	7.50
(36)	Tim McCarver	17.50	8.75	5.25
(37)	Mike McCormick	15.00	7.50	4.50
(38)	Willie McCovey	45.00	22.50	13.50
(39a)	Don Mincher (Angels)	15.00	7.50	4.50
(39b)	Don Mincher (Pilots)	20.00	10.00	6.00
(40)	Rick Monday	12.50	6.25	3.75
(41)	Tony Oliva	15.00	7.50	4.50
(42)	Rick Reichardt	10.00	5.00	3.00
(43)	Brooks Robinson	175.00	90.00	50.00
(44)	Frank Robinson	75.00	37.50	22.00
(45)	Pete Rose	100.00	50.00	30.00
(46)	Ron Santo	17.50	8.75	5.25
(47)	Tom Seaver	130.00	65.00	39.00
(48)	Chris Short	15.00	7.50	4.50
(49)	Reggie Smith	12.50	6.25	3.75
(50)	Rusty Staub	17.50	8.75	5.25
(51)	Mel Stottlemyre	20.00	10.00	6.00
(52)	Ron Swoboda	25.00	12.50	7.50
(53)	Cesar Tovar	15.00	7.50	4.50
(54)	Earl Wilson	17.50	8.75	5.25
(55)	Jim Wynn	10.00	5.00	3.00
(56)	Carl Yastrzemski	25.00	12.50	7.50
	1969			
(1)	Tommie Agee	17.50	8.75	5.25
(2)	Mike Andrews	12.50	6.25	3.75
(3)	Ernie Banks (Batting)	15.00	7.50	4.50
(4a)	Gary Bell (Indians)	20.00	10.00	6.00
(4b)	Gary Bell (Pilots)	20.00	10.00	6.00
(5a)	Tommy Davis (White Sox)	17.50	8.75	5.25
(5b)	Tommy Davis (Pilots)	20.00	10.00	6.00
(6)	Frank Howard	20.00	10.00	6.00
(7)	Reggie Jackson	95.00	47.00	28.00
(8)	Fergie Jenkins	45.00	22.00	13.50
(9)	Let's Go Mets (Tommie Agee, Jerry Grote, Cleon Jones, Jerry Koosman, Ed Kranepool, Tom Seaver, Ron Swoboda)	20.00	10.00	6.00
(10)	Denny McLain	15.00	7.50	4.50
(11)	Bobby Murcer	45.00	22.00	13.50
(12)	John Odom	17.50	8.75	5.25
(13)	Rico Petrocelli	17.50	8.75	5.25
(14)	Boog Powell	20.00	10.00	6.00
(15)	Roy White	25.00	12.50	7.50
	1970			
(1)	Glenn Beckert	17.50	8.75	5.25
(2)	Bobby Bonds	20.00	10.00	6.00
(3)	Rod Carew	17.50	8.75	5.25
(4)	Mike Cuellar	17.50	8.75	5.25
(5)	Mike Epstein	15.00	7.50	4.50
(6)	Ken Holtzman	15.00	7.50	4.50
(7)	Cleon Jones	15.00	7.50	4.50
(8)	Mickey Lolich	15.00	7.50	4.50
(9)	Sam McDowell	20.00	10.00	6.00
(10)	Phil Niekro	35.00	17.50	10.50
(11)	Wes Parker	17.50	8.75	5.25
(12)	Tony Perez	25.00	12.50	7.50
(13)	Bill Singer	10.00	5.00	3.00
(14)	Walt Williams	20.00	10.00	6.00

1968 Sports Memorabilia All Time Baseball Team

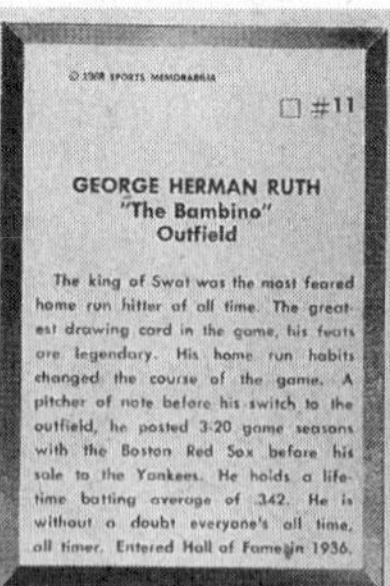

This is one of the earliest collectors' issue baseball card sets created for distribution solely within the hobby. The 2-1/2" x 3-1/2" cards feature the artwork of Art Oulette done in sepia tones on a white background and surrounded by a yellow border. Backs have career information, copyright and player identification. Issue price was $2.50.

		NM	EX	VG
Complete Set (15):		35.00	17.50	10.00
Common Player:		2.00	1.00	.60
1	Checklist	.50	.25	.15
2	"Connie" Mack	2.00	1.00	.60
3	Walter Johnson	4.00	2.00	1.25
4	Warren Spahn	2.00	1.00	.60
5	Christy Mathewson	4.00	2.00	1.25
6	Lefty Grove	2.00	1.00	.60
7	Mickey Cochrane	2.00	1.00	.60
8	Bill Dickey	2.00	1.00	.60
9	"Tris" Speaker	2.50	1.25	.75
10	"Ty" Cobb	6.00	3.00	2.00
11	"Babe" Ruth	10.00	5.00	3.00
12	"Lou" Gehrig	7.50	3.75	2.25
13	Rogers Hornsby	2.50	1.25	.75
14	"Honus" Wagner	5.00	2.50	1.50
15	"Pie" Traynor	2.00	1.00	.60

1960 Sports Novelties Inc. Genuine Baseball Photos

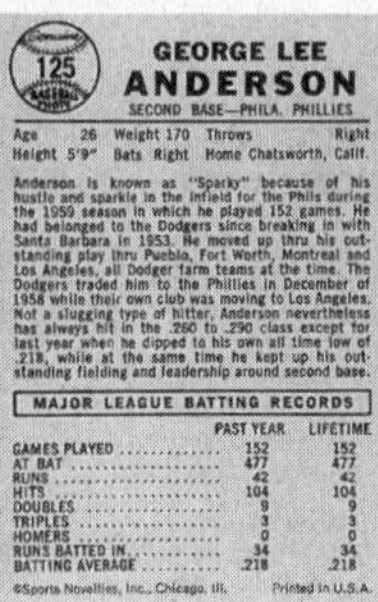

(See 1960 Leaf for checklist and price guide.)

1960s Sports Pix Premiums

These black-and-white blank-back pictures were distributed as a premium for Sports Pix magazine in the early 1960s. Two sizes are known: A smaller (about 8" x 10") style was issued in the early 1960s, while a larger (about 8-1/2" x 10-1/2") format was produced after 1963. Both styles have the photo bordered in white, with the player name centered at bottom. In the bottom-right corner is a three-line credit to the magazine and its Washington, D.C. address. Gaps have been left in the assigned numbering to accommodate future additions.

		NM	EX	VG
Common Player:		10.00	5.00	3.00
(1)	Ty Cobb (Large)	7.50	3.75	2.25
(2)	Mickey Cochrane (Large)	3.00	1.50	.90
(3)	Rocky Colavito (Large)	5.00	2.50	1.50
(3)	Joe Cronin (Large)	3.00	1.50	.90
(4)	Bill Dickey (Large)	3.00	2.00	1.00
(5)	Joe DiMaggio (Large, glossy, w/caption.)	7.50	3.75	2.25
(7)	Bob Feller (Large)	3.00	2.00	1.00
(8)	Lou Gehrig (Large)	7.50	3.75	2.25
(9)	Charlie Gehringer (Large)	3.00	2.00	1.00
(11)	"Lefty" Grove (Large)		2.00	1.00
(12)	Rogers Hornsby (Large)	3.00	2.00	1.00
(13)	Walter Johnson (Large)	5.00	2.50	1.50
(14)	Sandy Koufax (Small)	5.00	2.50	1.50
(15)	Sandy Koufax (Large)	5.00	2.50	1.50
(16)	Mickey Mantle (Large)	15.00	7.50	4.50
(17)	Mickey Mantle (Small)	15.00	7.50	4.50
(18)	Roger Maris (Large)	4.50	2.25	1.25
(19)	Willie Mays (Large)	7.50	3.75	2.25
(20)	Willie Mays (Small)	7.50	3.75	2.25
(21)	John McGraw (Large)	3.00	2.00	1.00
(22)	Stan Musial (Large)	5.00	2.50	1.50
(24)	Babe Ruth (Large)	7.50	3.75	2.25
(25)	George Sisler (Large)	3.00	2.00	1.00
(26)	Warren Spahn (Large)	3.00	2.00	1.00
(27)	"Casey" Stengel (Large)	3.00	2.00	1.00
(28)	"Pie" Traynor (Large)	3.00	2.00	1.00
(30)	"Honus" Wagner (Large)	4.50	2.25	1.25
(32)	Ted Williams (Large)	7.50	3.75	2.25

1979 Sports Reading Series

This set of large-format (about 8-1/2" x 14") was designed to encourage youthful readers. The black-and-white cards have one or more photos and lengthy text describing the player and/or action depicted.

		NM	EX	VG
Complete Set (50):		250.00	125.00	75.00
Common Player:		5.00	2.50	1.50
1	Carlos May	5.00	2.50	1.50
2	Babe Ruth	10.00	5.00	3.00
3	Eddie Gaedel	6.00	3.00	1.75
4	Cesar Gutierrez	5.00	2.50	1.50
5	Ted Williams	7.50	3.75	2.25
6	Pete Gray	6.00	3.00	1.75
7	Hank Aaron	7.50	3.75	2.25
8	Lou Brock	5.00	2.50	1.50
9	Virgil Trucks	5.00	2.50	1.50
10	Cesar Tovar	5.00	2.50	1.50
11	Wrigley Field	5.00	2.50	1.50
12	Ron Guidry	5.00	2.50	1.50
13	Bill Davis	5.00	2.50	1.50
14	Jimmy Piersall	5.00	2.50	1.50
15	Eddie Gaedel	6.00	3.00	1.75
16	Reggie Jackson	7.50	3.75	2.25

17	Mark Fidrych	5.00	2.50	1.50
18	Sandy Koufax	7.50	3.75	2.25
19	Dale Long	5.00	2.50	1.50
20	Herb Score	5.00	2.50	1.50
21	Dizzy Dean, Daffy Dean	5.00	2.50	1.50
22	Stan Musial	7.50	3.75	2.25
23	1903 N.Y. Giants	5.00	2.50	1.50
24	Pete Rose	7.50	3.75	2.25
25	Cy Young	5.00	2.50	1.50
26	Ferguson Jenkins	5.00	2.50	1.50
27	Minnie Minoso	5.00	2.50	1.50
28	Mort Cooper, Walker Cooper	5.00	2.50	1.50
29	Jim Thorpe	7.50	3.75	2.25
30	Lefty Grove	5.00	2.50	1.50
31	Roberto Clemente	9.00	4.50	2.75
32	Pres. Coolidge Throws Out First Ball	5.00	2.50	1.50
33	Lou Gehrig	7.50	3.75	2.25
34	Nolan Ryan	10.00	5.00	3.00
35	1969 N.Y. Mets	5.00	2.50	1.50
36	Yankee Stadium	5.00	2.50	1.50
37	Jackie Robinson	7.50	3.75	2.25
38	Carl Hubbell	5.00	2.50	1.50
39	Willie Mays	7.50	3.75	2.25
40	Mike Schmidt	6.00	3.00	1.75
41	Harvey Haddix	5.00	2.50	1.50
42	Pete Reiser	5.00	2.50	1.50
43	Gary Cooper (Pride of the Yankees)	5.00	2.50	1.50
44	Jackie Robinson	7.50	3.75	2.25
45	Walter Johnson	5.00	2.50	1.50
46	Hall of Fame	5.00	2.50	1.50
47	Jose Morales	5.00	2.50	1.50
48	Rod Carew	5.00	2.50	1.50
49	Lou Boudreau	5.00	2.50	1.50
50	Hank Greenberg	5.00	2.50	1.50

1950 Sport Stars Luckee Key Charms

This series of 1-3/8" square, diamond-format aluminum tags depicts on front an action picture of a player along with his facsimile autograph. A good luck and sportsmanship message appears on back. The charms are holed at the top to accomodate a beaded chain. While the charms themselves are not so marked, they were produced by Ralpat Co., of Cleveland, and sold on an approximately 3" x 5" cardboard backing card which has a line-art portrait of the player, his name, "Sport Stars" and "Luckee Key Charm." Values shown are for complete card/charm combinations. The metal charms themselves would be valued at about 35-50 percent.

		NM	EX	VG
Complete Set (5):		150.00	75.00	45.00
Common Player:		15.00	7.50	4.50
(1)	Ewell Blackwell	15.00	7.50	4.50
(2)	Bob Feller	30.00	15.00	9.00
(3)	Ralph Kiner	20.00	10.00	6.00
(4)	Hal Newhouser	17.50	8.75	5.25
(5)	Ted Williams	100.00	50.00	30.00

1976 Sportstix

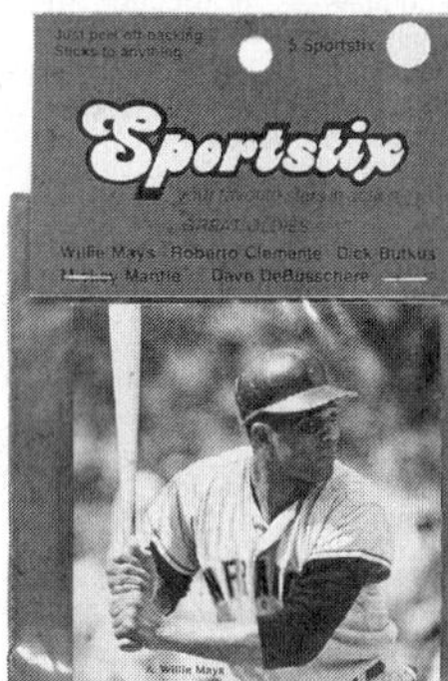

These peel-off player stickers were sold in five-piece plastic packs, with specific contents noted on the header. Stickers are found in three formats: 3-1/2" square, 3-1/2" square with clipped corners and 3" diameter round. The set includes 10 numbered current players and three retired baseball superstars identified as A, B and D. Stickers have full-color player pictures on front with no border. The player's name and sticker number are printed in black. Backs are blank. Besides the baseball players, there were stickers for football and basketball players, in a total issue of 30.

		NM	EX	VG
Complete Baseball Set (13):		40.00	20.00	12.00
Common Player:		1.00	.50	.30
A	Willie Mays	10.00	5.00	3.00
C	Roberto Clemente	12.50	6.25	3.75
D	Mickey Mantle	15.00	7.50	4.50
1	Dave Kingman	1.00	.50	.30
2	Steve Busby	1.00	.50	.30
3	Bill Madlock	1.00	.50	.30
4	Jeff Burroughs	1.00	.50	.30
5	Ted Simmons	1.00	.50	.30
6	Randy Jones	1.00	.50	.30
7	Buddy Bell	1.00	.50	.30
8	Dave Cash	1.00	.50	.30
9	Jerry Grote	1.00	.50	.30
10	Davey Lopes	1.00	.50	.30

1975 SSPC Promo Cards

1976
BASEBALL CARDS

Complete Set of 630 Cards
$12.99 + $1.00 Postage

You get the complete set of 630 cards in full color.
In depth biography and uniform number on the back of every card.

NOT AVAILABLE IN STORES

All the players on your favorite team - $1.00 + 50¢ postage.

SPORTS STARS PUBLISHING CO.
P. O. BOX #132 DEPT JG
Valley Cottage, N. Y. 10989

The six players in this sample set can each be found with three different backs. Some backs are similar to the cards issued in 1976, with player data and career summary. Some cards will have an ad message on back offering the complete 1976 SSPC set and team sets. Still others have blank backs. All cards are in 2-1/2" x 3-1/2" format with color photos on front surrounded by a white border and no extraneous graphics. Blank-back versions are worth 2-4X the values quoted here.

		NM	EX	VG
Complete Set (6):		15.00	7.50	4.50
Common Player:		1.50	.75	.45
(1)	Hank Aaron	4.00	2.00	1.25
(2)	Catfish Hunter	2.00	1.00	.60
(3)	Dave Kingman	1.50	.75	.45
(4)	Mickey Mantle	7.50	3.75	2.25
(5)	Willie Mays	4.00	2.00	1.25
(6)	Tom Seaver	3.00	1.50	.90

1975 SSPC Sample Cards

NEW YORK 41 METS

GEORGE THOMAS SEAVER
Pitcher Mets
6'1", 195 lbs. Bn. 11/17/44 BR-TR
His early '75 form indicated he has returned to the level that had won him 2 Cy Young Awards and three times won him 20 or more games. Moved into Mets' starting rotation after only one pro season, and has since compiled a 146-87 mark and a remarkable lifetime ERA of 2.47. Slumped to 11-11 with a 3.20 ERA last year, thanks to a hip injury, but still managed to strike out 201 men to become the first N.L. pitcher to K 200 or more 7 straight years.
©SSPC 1975

The Winter 1975 issue of "Collector's Quarterly" magazine (an advertising vehicle for Mike Aronstein, SSPC's principal) contained a two-page cardboard insert previewing the 1976 SSPC set. The cards could be cut apart into singles and represented something of a traded set, as each player or manager changed teams between the end of the 1975 season and the start of 1976. The cards have the players pictured on front in their old uniforms, with their new teams identified on back. Backs of the 2-1/2" x 3-1/2" cards are printed in red and black with a player biography and uniform number. "SAMPLE CARD 1975" is printed around the uniform number. A card number is in the lower-left corner, with 1975 copyright at bottom-right.

		NM	EX	VG
Complete Set, Uncut Sheet:		25.00	12.50	7.50
Complete Set, Singles (18):		20.00	10.00	6.00
Common Card:		1.50	.75	.45
1	Harry Parker	1.50	.75	.45
2	Jim Bibby	1.50	.75	.45
3	Mike Wallace	1.50	.75	.45
4	Tony Muser	1.50	.75	.45
5	Yogi Berra	7.50	3.75	2.25
6	Preston Gomez	1.50	.75	.45
7	Jack McKeon	1.50	.75	.45
8	Sam McDowell	1.50	.70	.45
9	Gaylord Perry	4.00	2.00	1.25
10	Fred Stanley	1.50	.75	.45
11	Willie Davis	1.50	.70	.45
12	Don Hopkins	1.50	.75	.45
13	Whitey Herzog	1.50	.70	.45
14	Ray Sadecki	1.50	.75	.45
15	Stan Bahnsen	1.50	.75	.45
16	Bob Oliver	1.50	.75	.45
17	Denny Doyle	1.50	.75	.45
18	Deron Johnson	1.50	.70	.45

1975 SSPC

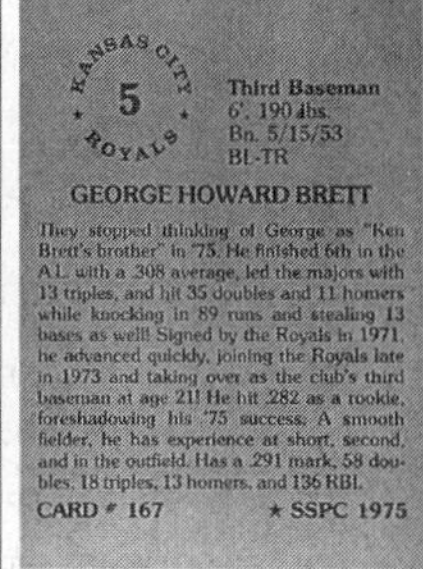

This set, produced by the Sport Star Publishing Company in 1975 as a collectors' issue (though not actually issued until 1976), was withdrawn from the market because of legal entanglements. Because SSPC agreed never to reprint the issue, some collectors feel it has an air of legitimacy. The complete set contains 630 full-color cards, each 2-1/2" x 3-1/2" in size. The cards look similar to 1953 Bowmans, with only the player picture (no identification) on the fronts. Card backs are in a vertical format, with personal stats, brief biographies, uniform and card numbers printed in a variety of colors. Sets originally sold for $9.99.

		NM	EX	VG
Complete Set (630):		60.00	30.00	18.00
Common Player:		.10	.05	.03
1	Lee William (Buzz) Capra	.10	.05	.03
2	Thomas Ross House	.10	.05	.03
3	Maximino Leon	.10	.05	.03
4	Carl Wendle Morton	.10	.05	.03
5	Philip Henry Niekro	1.50	.70	.45
6	Michael Wayne Thompson	.10	.05	.03
7	Elias Sosa (Martinez)	.10	.05	.03
8	Larvell Blanks	.10	.05	.03
9	Darrell Wayne Evans	.10	.05	.03
10	Rodney Joe Gilbreath	.10	.05	.03
11	Michael Ken-Wai Lum	.10	.05	.03
12	Craig George Robinson	.10	.05	.03
13	Earl Craig Williams, Jr.	.10	.05	.03
14	Victor Crosby Correll	.10	.05	.03
15	Biff Pocoroba	.10	.05	.03
16	Johnny B. (Dusty) Baker, Jr.	.35	.20	.11
17	Ralph Allen Garr	.10	.05	.03
18	Clarence Edward (Cito) Gaston	.10	.05	.03
19	David LaFrance May	.10	.05	.03
20	Rowland Johnnie Office	.10	.05	.03
21	Robert Brooks Beall	.10	.05	.03
22	George Lee (Sparky) Anderson	1.00	.50	.30
23	John Eugene Billingham	.10	.05	.03
24	Pedro Rodriguez Borbon	.10	.05	.03
25	Clay Palmer Carroll	.10	.05	.03
26	Patrick Leonard Darcy	.10	.05	.03
27	Donald Edward Gullett	.10	.05	.03
28	Clayton Laws Kirby	.10	.05	.03
29	Gary Lynn Nolan	.10	.05	.03
30	Fredie Hubert Norman	.10	.05	.03
31	Johnny Lee Bench	2.50	1.25	.70
32	William Francis Plummer	.10	.05	.03
33	Darrel Lee Chaney	.10	.05	.03
34	David Ismael Concepcion	.10	.05	.03
35	Terrence Michael Crowley	.10	.05	.03
36	Daniel Driessen	.10	.05	.03
37	Robert Douglas Flynn, Jr.	.10	.05	.03
38	Joe Leonard Morgan	2.00	1.00	.60
39	Atanasio Rigal (Tony) Perez	1.50	.70	.45
40	George Kenneth (Ken) Griffey	.35	.20	.11
41	Peter Edward Rose	5.00	2.50	1.50
42	Edison Rosanda Armbrister	.10	.05	.03
43	John Christopher Vukovich	.10	.05	.03
44	George Arthur Foster	.10	.05	.03
45	Cesar Francisco Geronimo	.10	.05	.03
46	Mervin Weldon Rettenmund	.10	.05	.03
47	James Frederick Crawford	.10	.05	.03
48	Kenneth Roth Forsch	.10	.05	.03
49	Douglas James Konieczny	.10	.05	.03
50	Joseph Franklin Niekro	.10	.05	.03
51	Clifford Johnson	.10	.05	.03
52	Alfred Henry (Skip) Jutze	.10	.05	.03
53	Milton Scott May	.10	.05	.03
54	Robert Patrick Andrews	.10	.05	.03
55	Kenneth George Boswell	.10	.05	.03
56	Tommy Vann Helms	.10	.05	.03
57	Roger Henry Metzger	.10	.05	.03
58	Lawrence William Milbourne	.10	.05	.03
59	Douglas Lee Rader	.10	.05	.03
60	Robert Jose Watson	.10	.05	.03
61	Enos Milton Cabell, Jr.	.10	.05	.03
62	Jose Delan Cruz	.10	.05	.03
63	Cesar Cedeno	.10	.05	.03
64	Gregory Eugene Gross	.10	.05	.03
65	Wilbur Leon Howard	.10	.05	.03
66	Alphonso Erwin Downing	.10	.05	.03
67	Burt Carlton Hooton	.10	.05	.03
68	Charles Oliver Hough	.10	.05	.03

69	Thomas Edward John	.25	.13	.08
70	John Alexander Messersmith	.10	.05	.03
71	Douglas James Rau	.10	.05	.03
72	Richard Alan Rhoden	.10	.05	.03
73	Donald Howard Sutton	1.50	.70	.45
74	Frederick Steven Auerbach	.10	.05	.03
75	Ronald Charles Cey	.10	.05	.03
76	Ivan De Jesus	.10	.05	.03
77	Steven Patrick Garvey	1.00	.50	.30
78	Leonadus Lacy	.10	.05	.03
79	David Earl Lopes	.10	.05	.03
80	Kenneth Lee McMullen	.10	.05	.03
81	Joseph Vance Ferguson	.10	.05	.03
82	Paul Ray Powell	.10	.05	.03
83	Stephen Wayne Yeager	.10	.05	.03
84	Willie Murphy Crawford	.10	.05	.03
85	Henry Cruz	.10	.05	.03
86	Charles Fuqua Manuel	.10	.05	.03
87	Manuel Mota	.10	.05	.03
88	Thomas Marian Paciorek	.10	.05	.03
89	James Sherman Wynn	.10	.05	.03
90	Walter Emmons Alston	1.00	.50	.30
91	William Joseph Buckner	.10	.05	.03
92	James Leland Barr	.10	.05	.03
93	Ralph Michael (Mike) Caldwell	.10	.05	.03
94	John Francis D'Acquisto	.10	.05	.03
95	David Wallace Heaverlo	.10	.05	.03
96	Gary Robert Lavelle	.10	.05	.03
97	John Joseph Montefusco, Jr.	.10	.05	.03
98	Charles Prosek Williams	.10	.05	.03
99	Christopher Paul Arnold	.10	.05	.03
100	Mark Kevin Hill (Marc)	.10	.05	.03
101	David Martin Rader	.10	.05	.03
102	Charles Bruce Miller	.10	.05	.03
103	Guillermo Naranjo (Willie) Montanez	.10	.05	.03
104	Steven Robert Ontiveros	.10	.05	.03
105	Chris Edward Speier	.10	.05	.03
106	Derrel Osbon Thomas	.10	.05	.03
107	Gary Leah Thomasson	.10	.05	.03
108	Glenn Charles Adams	.10	.05	.03
109	Von Everett Joshua	.10	.05	.03
110	Gary Nathaniel Matthews	.10	.05	.03
111	Bobby Ray Murcer	.10	.05	.03
112	Horace Arthur Speed III	.10	.05	.03
113	Wesley Noreen Westrum	.10	.05	.03
114	Richard Nevin Folkers	.10	.05	.03
115	Alan Benton Foster	.10	.05	.03
116	David James Freisleben	.10	.05	.03
117	Daniel Vincent Frisella	.10	.05	.03
118	Randall Leo Jones	.10	.05	.03
119	Daniel Ray Spillner	.10	.05	.03
120	Howard Lawrence (Larry) Hardy	.10	.05	.03
121	Cecil Randolph (Randy) Hundley	.10	.05	.03
122	Fred Lyn Kendall	.10	.05	.03
123	John Francis McNamara	.10	.05	.03
124	Rigoberto (Tito) Fuentes	.10	.05	.03
125	Enzo Octavio Hernandez	.10	.05	.03
126	Stephen Michael Huntz	.10	.05	.03
127	Michael Wilson Ivie	.10	.05	.03
128	Hector Epitacio Torres	.10	.05	.03
129	Theodore Rodger Kubiak	.10	.05	.03
130	John Maywood Grubb, Jr.	.10	.05	.03
131	John Henry Scott	.10	.05	.03
132	Robert Tolan	.10	.05	.03
133	David Mark Winfield	2.50	1.25	.70
134	William Joseph Gogolewski	.10	.05	.03
135	Danny L. Osborn	.10	.05	.03
136	James Lee Kaat	.25	.13	.08
137	Claude Wilson Osteen	.10	.05	.03
138	Cecil Lee Upshaw, Jr.	.10	.05	.03
139	Wilbur Forrester Wood, Jr.	.10	.05	.03
140	Lloyd Cecil Allen	.10	.05	.03
141	Brian Jay Downing	.10	.05	.03
142	James Sarkis Essian, Jr.	.10	.05	.03
143	Russell Earl (Bucky) Dent	.50	.25	.15
144	Jorge Orta	.10	.05	.03
145	Lee Edward Richard	.10	.05	.03
146	William Allen Stein	.10	.05	.03
147	Kenneth Joseph Henderson	.10	.05	.03
148	Carlos May	.10	.05	.03
149	Nyls Wallace Rex Nyman	.10	.05	.03
150	Robert Pasquali Coluccio, Jr.	.10	.05	.03
151	Charles William Tanner, Jr.	.10	.05	.03
152	Harold Patrick (Pat) Kelly	.10	.05	.03
153	Jerry Wayne Hairston Sr.	.10	.05	.03
154	Richard Fred (Pete) Varney, Jr.	.10	.05	.03
155	William Edwin Melton	.10	.05	.03
156	Richard Michael Gossage	.50	.25	.15
157	Terry Jay Forster	.10	.05	.03
158	Richard Michael Hinton	.10	.05	.03
159	Nelson Kelley Briles	.10	.05	.03
160	Alan James Fitzmorris	.10	.05	.03
161	Stephen Bernard Mingori	.10	.05	.03
162	Martin William Pattin	.10	.05	.03
163	Paul William Splittorff, Jr.	.10	.05	.03
164	Dennis Patrick Leonard	.10	.05	.03
165	John Albert (Buck) Martinez	.10	.05	.03
166	Gorrell Robert (Bob) Stinson III	.10	.05	.03
167	George Howard Brett	7.50	3.75	2.25
168	Harmon Clayton Killebrew, Jr.	2.50	1.25	.70
169	John Claiborn Mayberry	.10	.05	.03
170	Freddie Joe Patek	.10	.05	.03
171	Octavio (Cookie) Rojas	.10	.05	.03
172	Rodney Darrell Scott	.10	.05	.03
173	Tolia (Tony) Solaita	.10	.05	.03
174	Frank White, Jr.	.10	.05	.03
175	Alfred Edward Cowens, Jr.	.10	.05	.03
176	Harold Abraham McRae	.10	.05	.03
177	Amos Joseph Otis	.10	.05	.03
178	Vada Edward Pinson, Jr.	.50	.25	.15
179	James Eugene Wohlford	.10	.05	.03
180	James Douglas Bird	.10	.05	.03
181	Mark Alan Littell	.10	.05	.03
182	Robert McClure	.10	.05	.03
183	Steven Lee Busby	.10	.05	.03
184	Francis Xavier Healy	.10	.05	.03
185	Dorrel Norman Elvert (Whitey) Herzog	.10	.05	.03
186	Andrew Earl Hassler	.10	.05	.03
187	Lynn Nolan Ryan, Jr.	7.50	3.75	2.25
188	William Robert Singer	.10	.05	.03
189	Frank Daryl Tanana	.10	.05	.03
190	Eduardo Figueroa	.10	.05	.03
191	David S. Collins	.10	.05	.03
192	Richard Hirshfeld Williams	.10	.05	.03
193	Eliseo Rodriguez	.10	.05	.03
194	David Lee Chalk	.10	.05	.03
195	Winston Enriquillo Llenas	.10	.05	.03
196	Rudolph Bart Meoli	.10	.05	.03
197	Orlando Ramirez	.10	.05	.03
198	Gerald Peter Remy	.10	.05	.03
199	Billy Edward Smith	.10	.05	.03
200	Bruce Anton Bochte	.10	.05	.03
201	Joseph Michael Lahoud, Jr.	.10	.05	.03
202	Morris Nettles, Jr.	.10	.05	.03
203	John Milton (Mickey) Rivers	.10	.05	.03
204	Leroy Bobby Stanton	.10	.05	.03
205	Victor Albury	.10	.05	.03
206	Thomas Henry Burgmeier	.10	.05	.03
207	William Franklin Butler	.10	.05	.03
208	William Richard Campbell	.10	.05	.03
209	Alton Ray Corbin	.10	.05	.03
210	George Henry (Joe) Decker, Jr.	.10	.05	.03
211	James Michael Hughes	.10	.05	.03
212	Edward Norman Bane (photo actually Mike Pazik)	.10	.05	.03
213	Glenn Dennis Borgmann	.10	.05	.03
214	Rodney Cline Carew	2.50	1.25	.70
215	Stephen Robert Brye	.10	.05	.03
216	Darnell Glenn (Dan) Ford	.10	.05	.03
217	Antonio Oliva	.35	.20	.11
218	David Allan Goltz	.10	.05	.03
219	Rikalbert Blyleven	.25	.13	.08
220	Larry Eugene Hisle	.10	.05	.03
221	Stephen Russell Braun, III	.10	.05	.03
222	Jerry Wayne Terrell	.10	.05	.03
223	Eric Thane Soderholm	.10	.05	.03
224	Philip Anthony Roof	.10	.05	.03
225	Danny Leon Thompson	.10	.05	.03
226	James William Colborn	.10	.05	.03
227	Thomas Andrew Murphy	.10	.05	.03
228	Eduardo Rodriguez	.10	.05	.03
229	James Michael Slaton	.10	.05	.03
230	Edward Nelson Sprague	.10	.05	.03
231	Charles William Moore, Jr.	.10	.05	.03
232	Darrell Ray Porter	.10	.05	.03
233	Kurt Anthony Bevacqua	.10	.05	.03
234	Pedro Garcia	.10	.05	.03
235	James Michael (Mike) Hegan	.10	.05	.03
236	Donald Wayne Money	.10	.05	.03
237	George C. Scott, Jr.	.10	.05	.03
238	Robin R. Yount	5.00	2.50	1.50
239	Henry Louis Aaron	5.00	2.50	1.50
240	Robert Walker Ellis	.10	.05	.03
241	Sixto Lezcano	.10	.05	.03
242	Robert Vance Mitchell	.10	.05	.03
243	James Gorman Thomas, III	.10	.05	.03
244	William Edward Travers	.10	.05	.03
245	Peter Sven Broberg	.10	.05	.03
246	William Howard Sharp	.10	.05	.03
247	Arthur Bobby Lee Darwin	.10	.05	.03
248	Rick Gerald Austin (Photo actually Larry Anderson.)	.10	.05	.03
249	Lawrence Dennis Anderson (Photo actually Rick Austin.)	.10	.05	.03
250	Thomas Antony Bianco	.10	.05	.03
251	DeLancy LaFayette Currence	.10	.05	.03
252	Steven Raymond Foucault	.10	.05	.03
253	William Alfred Hands, Jr.	.10	.05	.03
254	Steven Lowell Hargan	.10	.05	.03
255	Ferguson Arthur Jenkins	1.50	.70	.45
256	Bob Mitchell Sheldon	.10	.05	.03
257	James Umbarger	.10	.05	.03
258	Clyde Wright	.10	.05	.03
259	William Roger Fahey	.10	.05	.03
260	James Howard Sundberg	.10	.05	.03
261	Leonardo Alfonso Cardenas	.10	.05	.03
262	James Louis Fregosi	.10	.05	.03
263	Dudley Michael (Mike) Hargrove	.10	.05	.03
264	Colbert Dale (Toby) Harrah	.10	.05	.03
265	Roy Lee Howell	.10	.05	.03
266	Leonard Shenoff Randle	.10	.05	.03
267	Roy Frederick Smalley III	.10	.05	.03
268	James Lloyd Spencer	.10	.05	.03
269	Jeffrey Alan Burroughs	.10	.05	.03
270	Thomas Alan Grieve	.10	.05	.03
271	Joseph Lovitto, Jr.	.10	.05	.03
272	Frank Joseph Lucchesi	.10	.05	.03
273	David Earl Nelson	.10	.05	.03
274	Ted Lyle Simmons	.10	.05	.03
275	Louis Clark Brock	2.00	1.00	.60
276	Ronald Ray Fairly	.10	.05	.03
277	Arnold Ray (Bake) McBride	.10	.05	.03
278	Carl Reginald (Reggie) Smith	.10	.05	.03
279	William Henry Davis	.10	.05	.03
280	Kenneth John Reitz	.10	.05	.03
281	Charles William (Buddy) Bradford	.10	.05	.03
282	Luis Antonio Melendez	.10	.05	.03
283	Michael Ray Tyson	.10	.05	.03
284	Ted Crawford Sizemore	.10	.05	.03
285	Mario Miguel Guerrero	.10	.05	.03
286	Larry Lintz	.10	.05	.03
287	Kenneth Victor Rudolph	.10	.05	.03
288	Richard Arlin Billings	.10	.05	.03
289	Jerry Wayne Mumphrey	.10	.05	.03
290	Michael Sherman Wallace	.10	.05	.03
291	Alan Thomas Hrabosky	.10	.05	.03
292	Kenneth Lee Reynolds	.10	.05	.03
293	Michael Douglas Garman	.10	.05	.03
294	Robert Herbert Forsch	.10	.05	.03
295	John Allen Denny	.10	.05	.03
296	Harold R. Rasmussen	.10	.05	.03
297	Lynn Everratt McGlothen (Everett)	.10	.05	.03
298	Michael Roswell Barlow	.10	.05	.03
299	Gregory John Terlecky	.10	.05	.03
300	Albert Fred (Red) Schoendienst	1.00	.50	.30
301	Ricky Eugene Reuschel	.10	.05	.03
302	Steven Michael Stone	.10	.05	.03
303	William Gordon Bonham	.10	.05	.03
304	Oscar Joseph Zamora	.10	.05	.03
305	Kenneth Douglas Frailing	.10	.05	.03
306	Milton Edward Wilcox	.10	.05	.03
307	Darold Duane Knowles	.10	.05	.03
308	Rufus James (Jim) Marshall	.10	.05	.03
309	Bill Madlock, Jr.	.10	.05	.03
310	Jose Domec Cardenal	.10	.05	.03
311	Robert James (Rick) Monday, Jr.	.10	.05	.03
312	Julio Ruben (Jerry) Morales	.10	.05	.03
313	Timothy Kenneth Hosley	.10	.05	.03
314	Gene Taylor Hiser	.10	.05	.03
315	Donald Eulon Kessinger	.10	.05	.03
316	Jesus Manuel (Manny) Trillo	.10	.05	.03
317	Ralph Pierre (Pete) LaCock, Jr.	.10	.05	.03
318	George Eugene Mitterwald	.10	.05	.03
319	Steven Eugene Swisher	.10	.05	.03
320	Robert Walter Sperring	.10	.05	.03
321	Victor Lanier Harris	.10	.05	.03
322	Ronald Ray Dunn	.10	.05	.03
323	Jose Manuel Morales	.10	.05	.03
324	Peter MacKanin, Jr.	.10	.05	.03
325	James Charles Cox	.10	.05	.03
326	Larry Alton Parrish	.10	.05	.03
327	Michael Jorgensen	.10	.05	.03
328	Timothy John Foli	.10	.05	.03
329	Harold Noel Breeden	.10	.05	.03
330	Nathan Colbert, Jr.	.10	.05	.03
331	Jesus Maria (Pepe) Frias	.10	.05	.03
332	James Patrick (Pat) Scanlon	.10	.05	.03
333	Robert Sherwood Bailey	.10	.05	.03
334	Gary Edmund Carter	2.00	1.00	.60
335	Jose Mauel (Pepe) Mangual	.10	.05	.03
336	Lawrence David Biittner	.10	.05	.03
337	James Lawrence Lyttle, Jr.	.10	.05	.03
338	Gary Roenicke	.10	.05	.03
339	Anthony Scott	.10	.05	.03
340	Jerome Cardell White	.10	.05	.03
341	James Edward Dwyer	.10	.05	.03
342	Ellis Clarence Valentine	.10	.05	.03
343	Frederick John Scherman, Jr.	.10	.05	.03
344	Dennis Herman Blair	.10	.05	.03
345	Woodrow Thompson Fryman	.10	.05	.03
346	Charles Gilbert Taylor	.10	.05	.03
347	Daniel Dean Warthen	.10	.05	.03
348	Donald George Carrithers	.10	.05	.03
349	Stephen Douglas Rogers	.10	.05	.03
350	Dale Albert Murray	.10	.05	.03
351	Edwin Donald (Duke) Snider	3.00	1.50	.90
352	Ralph George Houk	.10	.05	.03
353	John Frederick Hiller	.10	.05	.03
354	Michael Stephen Lolich	.10	.05	.03
355	David Lawrence Lemancyzk	.10	.05	.03
356	Lerrin Harris LaGrow	.10	.05	.03
357	Fred Arroyo	.10	.05	.03
358	Joseph Howard Coleman	.10	.05	.03
359	Benjamin A. Oglivie	.10	.05	.03
360	Willie Wattison Horton	.10	.05	.03
361	John Clinton Knox	.10	.05	.03
362	Leon Kauffman Roberts	.10	.05	.03
363	Ronald LeFlore	.10	.05	.03
364	Gary Lynn Sutherland	.10	.05	.03
365	Daniel Thomas Meyer	.10	.05	.03
366	Aurelio Rodriguez	.10	.05	.03
367	Thomas Martin Veryzer	.10	.05	.03
368	Lavern Jack Pierce	.10	.05	.03
369	Eugene Richard Michael	.10	.05	.03
370	Robert (Billy) Baldwin	.10	.05	.03
371	William James Gates Brown	.10	.05	.03
372	Mitchell Jack (Mickey) Stanley	.10	.05	.03
373	Terryal Gene Humphrey	.10	.05	.03
374	Doyle Lafayette Alexander	.10	.05	.03
375	Miguel Angel (Mike) Cuellar	.10	.05	.03
376	Marcus Wayne Garland	.10	.05	.03
377	Ross Albert Grimsley III	.10	.05	.03
378	Grant Dwight Jackson	.10	.05	.03
379	Dyar K. Miller	.10	.05	.03
380	James Alvin Palmer	2.00	1.00	.60
381	Michael Augustine Torrez	.10	.05	.03
382	Michael Henry Willis	.10	.05	.03
383	David Edwin Duncan	.10	.05	.03
384	Elrod Jerome Hendricks	.10	.05	.03
385	James Neamon Hutto Jr.	.10	.05	.03
386	Robert Michael Bailor	.10	.05	.03
387	Douglas Vernon DeCinces	.10	.05	.03
388	Robert Anthony Grich	.10	.05	.03
389	Lee Andrew May	.10	.05	.03
390	Anthony Joseph Muser	.10	.05	.03
391	Timothy C. Nordbrook	.10	.05	.03
392	Brooks Calbert Robinson, Jr.	2.50	1.25	.70
393	Royle Stillman	.10	.05	.03
394	Don Edward Baylor	.10	.05	.03
395	Paul L.D. Blair	.10	.05	.03
396	Alonza Benjamin Bumbry	.10	.05	.03
397	Larry Duane Harlow	.10	.05	.03
398	Herman Thomas (Tommy) Davis, Jr.	.10	.05	.03
399	James Thomas Northrup	.10	.05	.03
400	Kenneth Wayne Singleton	.10	.05	.03
401	Thomas Michael Shopay	.10	.05	.03
402	Fredrick Michael Lynn	.75	.40	.25
403	Carlton Ernest Fisk	2.00	1.00	.60
404	Cecil Celester Cooper	.10	.05	.03

405	James Edward Rice	1.00	.50	.30
406	Juan Jose Beniquez	.10	.05	.03
407	Robert Dennis Doyle	.10	.05	.03
408	Dwight Michael Evans	.10	.05	.03
409	Carl Michael Yastrzemski	3.00	1.50	.90
410	Richard Paul Burleson	.10	.05	.03
411	Bernardo Carbo	.10	.05	.03
412	Douglas Lee Griffin, Jr.	.10	.05	.03
413	Americo P. Petrocelli	.10	.05	.03
414	Robert Edward Montgomery	.10	.05	.03
415	Timothy P. Blackwell	.10	.05	.03
416	Richard Alan Miller	.10	.05	.03
417	Darrell Dean Johnson	.10	.05	.03
418	Jim Scott Burton	.10	.05	.03
419	James Arthur Willoughby	.10	.05	.03
420	Rogelio (Roger) Moret	.10	.05	.03
421	William Francis Lee, III	.10	.05	.03
422	Richard Anthony Drago	.10	.05	.03
423	Diego Pablo Segui	.10	.05	.03
424	Luis Clemente Tiant	.10	.05	.03
425	James Augustus (Catfish) Hunter	1.50	.70	.45
426	Richard Clyde Sawyer	.10	.05	.03
427	Rudolph May Jr.	.10	.05	.03
428	Richard William Tidrow	.10	.05	.03
429	Albert Walter (Sparky) Lyle	.10	.05	.03
430	George Francis (Doc) Medich	.10	.05	.03
431	Patrick Edward Dobson, Jr.	.10	.05	.03
432	David Percy Pagan	.10	.05	.03
433	Thurman Lee Munson	2.00	1.00	.60
434	Carroll Christopher Chambliss	.10	.05	.03
435	Roy Hilton White	.10	.05	.03
436	Walter Allen Williams	.10	.05	.03
437	Graig Nettles	.10	.05	.03
438	John Rikard (Rick) Dempsey	.10	.05	.03
439	Bobby Lee Bonds	.25	.13	.08
440	Edward Martin Hermann (Herrmann)	.10	.05	.03
441	Santos Alomar	.10	.05	.03
442	Frederick Blair Stanley	.10	.05	.03
443	Terry Bertland Whitfield	.10	.05	.03
444	Richard Alan Bladt	.10	.05	.03
445	Louis Victor Piniella	.50	.25	.15
446	Richard Allen Coggins	.10	.05	.03
447	Edwin Albert Brinkman	.10	.05	.03
448	James Percy Mason	.10	.05	.03
449	Larry Murray	.10	.05	.03
450	Ronald Mark Blomberg	.10	.05	.03
451	Elliott Maddox	.10	.05	.03
452	Kerry Dineen	.10	.05	.03
453	Alfred Manuel (Billy) Martin	.50	.25	.15
454	Dave Bergman	.10	.05	.03
455	Otoniel Velez	.10	.05	.03
456	Joseph Walter Hoerner	.10	.05	.03
457	Frank Edwin (Tug) McGraw, Jr.	.10	.05	.03
458	Henry Eugene (Gene) Garber	.10	.05	.03
459	Steven Norman Carlton	2.00	1.00	.60
460	Larry Richard Christenson	.10	.05	.03
461	Thomas Gerald Underwood	.10	.05	.03
462	James Reynold Lonborg	.10	.05	.03
463	John William (Jay) Johnstone, Jr.	.10	.05	.03
464	Lawrence Robert Bowa	.10	.05	.03
465	David Cash, Jr.	.10	.05	.03
466	Ollie Lee Brown	.10	.05	.03
467	Gregory Michael Luzinski	.10	.05	.03
468	Johnny Lane Oates	.10	.05	.03
469	Michael Allen Anderson	.10	.05	.03
470	Michael Jack Schmidt	4.00	2.00	1.25
471	Robert Raymond Boone	.10	.05	.03
472	Thomas George Hutton	.10	.05	.03
473	Richard Anthony Allen	.50	.25	.15
474	Antonio Taylor	.10	.05	.03
475	Jerry Lindsey Martin	.10	.05	.03
476	Daniel Leonard Ozark	.10	.05	.03
477	Richard David Ruthven	.10	.05	.03
478	James Richard Todd, Jr.	.10	.05	.03
479	Paul Aaron Lindblad	.10	.05	.03
480	Roland Glen Fingers	1.50	.70	.45
481	Vida Blue, Jr.	.10	.05	.03
482	Kenneth Dale Holtzman	.10	.05	.03
483	Richard Allen Bosman	.10	.05	.03
484	Wilfred Charles (Sonny) Siebert	.10	.05	.03
485	William Glenn Abbott	.10	.05	.03
486	Stanley Raymond Bahnsen	.10	.05	.03
487	Michael Norris	.10	.05	.03
488	Alvin Ralph Dark	.10	.05	.03
489	Claudell Washington	.10	.05	.03
490	Joseph Oden Rudi	.10	.05	.03
491	William Alex North	.10	.05	.03
492	Dagoberto Blanco (Bert) Campaneris	.10	.05	.03
493	Fury Gene Tenace	.10	.05	.03
494	Reginald Martinez Jackson	4.00	2.00	1.25
495	Philip Mason Garner	.10	.05	.03
496	Billy Leo Williams	2.00	1.00	.60
497	Salvatore Leonard Bando	.10	.05	.03
498	James William Holt	.10	.05	.03
499	Teodoro Noel Martinez	.10	.05	.03
500	Raymond Earl Fosse	.10	.05	.03
501	Matthew Alexander	.10	.05	.03
502	Wallace Larry Haney	.10	.05	.03
503	Angel Luis Mangual	.10	.05	.03
504	Fred Ray Beene	.10	.05	.03
505	Thomas William Buskey	.10	.05	.03
506	Dennis Lee Eckersley	2.00	1.00	.60
507	Roric Edward Harrison	.10	.05	.03
508	Donald Harris Hood	.10	.05	.03
509	James Lester Kern	.10	.05	.03
510	David Eugene LaRoche	.10	.05	.03
511	Fred Ingels (Fritz) Peterson	.10	.05	.03
512	James Michael Strickland	.10	.05	.03
513	Michael Richard (Rick) Waits	.10	.05	.03
514	Alan Dean Ashby	.10	.05	.03
515	John Charles Ellis	.10	.05	.03
516	Rick Cerone	.10	.05	.03
517	David Gus (Buddy) Bell	.10	.05	.03
518	John Anthony Brohamer, Jr.	.10	.05	.03
519	Ricardo Adolfo Jacobo Carty	.10	.05	.03
520	Edward Carlton Crosby	.10	.05	.03
521	Frank Thomas Duffy	.10	.05	.03
522	Duane Eugene Kuiper (Photo actually Rick Manning.)	.10	.05	.03
523	Joseph Anthony Lis	.10	.05	.03
524	John Wesley (Boog) Powell	.50	.25	.15
525	Frank Robinson	2.50	1.25	.70
526	Oscar Charles Gamble	.10	.05	.03
527	George Andrew Hendrick	.10	.05	.03
528	John Lee Lowenstein	.10	.05	.03
529	Richard Eugene Manning (Photo actually Duane Kuiper.)	.10	.05	.03
530	Tommy Alexander Smith	.10	.05	.03
531	Leslie Charles (Charlie) Spikes	.10	.05	.03
532	Steve Jack Kline	.10	.05	.03
533	Edward Emil Kranepool	.10	.05	.03
534	Michael Vail	.10	.05	.03
535	Delbert Bernard Unser	.10	.05	.03
536	Felix Bernardo Martinez Millan	.10	.05	.03
537	Daniel Joseph (Rusty) Staub	.25	.13	.08
538	Jesus Maria Rojas Alou	.10	.05	.03
539	Ronald Wayne Garrett	.10	.05	.03
540	Michael Dwaine Phillips	.10	.05	.03
541	Joseph Paul Torre	.10	.05	.03
542	David Arthur Kingman	.10	.05	.03
543	Eugene Anthony Clines	.10	.05	.03
544	Jack Seale Heidemann	.10	.05	.03
545	Derrel McKinley (Bud) Harrelson	.10	.05	.03
546	John Hardin Stearns	.10	.05	.03
547	John David Milner	.10	.05	.03
548	Robert John Apodaca	.10	.05	.03
549	Claude Edward (Skip) Lockwood Jr.	.10	.05	.03
550	Kenneth George Sanders	.10	.05	.03
551	George Thomas (Tom) Seaver	3.00	1.50	.90
552	Ricky Alan Baldwin	.10	.05	.03
553	Jonathan Trumpbour Matlack	.10	.05	.03
554	Henry Gaylon Webb	.10	.05	.03
555	Randall Lee Tate	.10	.05	.03
556	Tom Edward Hall	.10	.05	.03
557	George Heard Stone Jr.	.10	.05	.03
558	Craig Steven Swan	.10	.05	.03
559	Gerald Allen Cram	.10	.05	.03
560	Roy J. Staiger	.10	.05	.03
561	Kenton C. Tekulve	.10	.05	.03
562	Jerry Reuss	.10	.05	.03
563	John R. Candelaria	.10	.05	.03
564	Lawrence C. Demery	.10	.05	.03
565	David John Giusti Jr.	.10	.05	.03
566	James Phillip Rooker	.10	.05	.03
567	Ramon Gonzalez Hernandez	.10	.05	.03
568	Bruce Eugene Kison	.10	.05	.03
569	Kenneth Alven Brett (Alvin)	.10	.05	.03
570	Robert Ralph Moose Jr.	.10	.05	.03
571	Manuel Jesus Sanguillen	.10	.05	.03
572	David Gene Parker	.10	.05	.03
573	Wilver Dornel Stargell	2.00	1.00	.60
574	Richard Walter Zisk	.10	.05	.03
575	Renaldo Antonio Stennett	.10	.05	.03
576	Albert Oliver Jr.	.25	.13	.08
577	William Henry Robinson Jr.	.10	.05	.03
578	Robert Eugene Robertson	.10	.05	.03
579	Richard Joseph Hebner	.10	.05	.03
580	Edgar Leon Kirkpatrick	.10	.05	.03
581	Don Robert (Duffy) Dyer	.10	.05	.03
582	Craig Reynolds	.10	.05	.03
583	Franklin Fabian Taveras	.10	.05	.03
584	William Larry Randolph	.10	.05	.03
585	Arthur H. Howe	.10	.05	.03
586	Daniel Edward Murtaugh	.10	.05	.03
587	Charles Richard (Rich) McKinney	.10	.05	.03
588	James Edward Goodson	.10	.05	.03
589	George Brett, Al Cowans/Checklist	1.50	.70	.45
590	Keith Hernandez, Lou Brock/Checklist	.15	.08	.05
591	Jerry Koosman, Duke Snider/Checklist	.25	.13	.08
592	John Knox, Maury Wills/Checklist	.10	.05	.03
593a	Catfish Hunter, Noland Ryan/Checklist	4.00	2.00	1.25
593b	Catfish Hunter, Nolan Ryan/Checklist	3.00	1.50	.90
594	Pee Wee Reese, Ralph Branca, Carl Erskine	1.00	.50	.30
595	Willie Mays, Herb Score/Checklist	1.00	.50	.30
596	Larry Eugene Cox	.10	.05	.03
597	Eugene William Mauch	.10	.05	.03
598	William Frederick (Whitey) Wietelmann	.10	.05	.03
599	Wayne Kirby Simpson	.10	.05	.03
600	Melvin Erskine Thomason	.10	.05	.03
601	Issac Bernard (Ike) Hampton	.10	.05	.03
602	Kenneth S. Crosby	.10	.05	.03
603	Ralph Emanuel Rowe	.10	.05	.03
604	James Vernon Tyrone	.10	.05	.03
605	Michael Dennis Kelleher	.10	.05	.03
606	Mario Mendoza	.10	.05	.03
607	Michael George Rogodzinski	.10	.05	.03
608	Robert Collins Gallagher	.10	.05	.03
609	Jerry Martin Koosman	.10	.05	.03
610	Joseph Filmore Frazier	.10	.05	.03
611	Karl Kuehl	.10	.05	.03
612	Frank J. LaCorte	.10	.05	.03
613	Raymond Douglas Bare	.10	.05	.03
614	Billy Arnold Muffett	.10	.05	.03
615	William Harry Laxton	.10	.05	.03
616	Willie Howard Mays	5.00	2.50	1.50
617	Philip Joseph Cavaretta (Cavarretta)	.10	.05	.03
618	Theodore Bernard Kluszewski	.50	.25	.15
619	Elston Gene Howard	.10	.05	.03
620	Alexander Peter Grammas	.10	.05	.03
621	James Barton (Mickey) Vernon	.10	.05	.03
622	Richard Allan Sisler	.10	.05	.03
623	Harvey Haddix, Jr.	.10	.05	.03
624	Bobby Brooks Winkles	.10	.05	.03
625	John Michael Pesky	.10	.05	.03
626	James Houston Davenport	.10	.05	.03
627	David Allen Tomlin	.10	.05	.03
628	Roger Lee Craig	.10	.05	.03
629	John Joseph Amalfitano	.10	.05	.03
630	James Harrison Reese	.25	.13	.08

1975 SSPC Mets/Yankees

Team sets of the New York clubs were issued by SSPC bearing a 1975 copyright date and in the same "pure card" format as most of the company's other issues. The 2-1/2" x 3-1/2" cards have a posed color photo on front with a thin white border and no extraneous graphics - not even the player's name. Backs are printed in red and blue with personal data and a career summary, along with the player's full formal name. The checklist lists the player as he is best known. Issue price was $1.25 per team set.

		NM	EX	VG
Complete Set (45):		15.00	7.50	4.50
Common Player:		.25	.13	.08
	New York Mets Team Set:	9.00	4.50	2.75
1	John Milner	.25	.13	.08
2	Henry Webb	.25	.13	.08
3	Tom Hall	.25	.13	.08
4	Del Unser	.25	.13	.08
5	Wayne Garrett	.25	.13	.08
6	Jesus Alou	.25	.13	.08
7	Rusty Staub	.40	.20	.12
8	John Stearns	.25	.13	.08
9	Dave Kingman	.75	.40	.25
10	Ed Kranepool	.35	.20	.11
11	Cleon Jones	.40	.20	.12
12	Tom Seaver	4.00	2.00	1.25
13	George Stone	.25	.13	.08
14	Jerry Koosman	.35	.20	.11
15	Bob Apodaca	.25	.13	.08
16	Felix Millan	.25	.13	.08
17	Gene Clines	.25	.13	.08
18	Mike Phillips	.25	.13	.08
19	Yogi Berra	3.00	1.50	.90
20	Joe Torre	1.50	.70	.45
21	Jon Matlack	.25	.13	.08
22	Ricky Baldwin	.25	.13	.08
	New York Yankees Team Set:	9.00	4.50	2.75
1	Catfish Hunter	1.00	.50	.30
2	Bobby Bonds	.35	.20	.11
3	Ed Brinkman	.25	.13	.08
4	Ron Blomberg	.25	.13	.08
5	Thurman Munson	3.50	1.75	1.00
6	Roy White	.35	.20	.11
7	Larry Gura	.25	.13	.08
8	Ed Hermann	.25	.13	.08
9	Bill Virdon	.25	.13	.08
10	Elliott Maddox	.25	.13	.08
11	Lou Piniella	.50	.25	.15
12	Rick Dempsey	.25	.13	.08
13	Fred Stanley	.25	.13	.08
14	Chris Chambliss	.25	.13	.08
15	Doc Medich	.25	.13	.08
16	Pat Dobson	.25	.13	.08
17	Alex Johnson	.25	.13	.08
18	Jim Mason	.25	.13	.08
19	Sandy Alomar	.25	.13	.08
20	Graig Nettles	.50	.25	.15
21	Walt Williams	.25	.13	.08
22	Sparky Lyle	.35	.20	.11
23	Dick Tidrow	.25	.13	.08

1975 SSPC Puzzle Backs

A large black-and-white puzzle picture of Nolan Ryan and Catfish Hunter can be assembled with the backs of these cards. Fronts of the 3-9/16" x 4-1/4" cards have a color player pose with a white border. The player's name, position and team are printed at bottom. Fronts have a glossy surface. The SSPC identification only appears around the border of the puzzle. The unnumbered cards are checklisted here alphabetically. Issue price was $2.

Checklists showing are card numbers in parentheses ( ) indicates the numbers do not appear on the cards.

		NM	EX	VG
Complete Set, Uncut Sheet:		40.00	20.00	12.00
Complete Set (24):		20.00	10.00	6.00
Common Player:		.30	.15	.09
(1)	Hank Aaron	4.00	2.00	1.25
(2)	Johnny Bench	1.75	.90	.50
(3)	Bobby Bonds	.35	.20	.11
(4)	Jeff Burroughs	.30	.15	.09
(5)	Rod Carew	1.75	.90	.50
(6)	Dave Cash	.30	.15	.09
(7)	Cesar Cedeno	.30	.15	.09
(8)	Bucky Dent	.30	.15	.09
(9)	Rollie Fingers	1.25	.60	.40
(10)	Steve Garvey	1.00	.50	.30
(11)	John Grubb	.30	.15	.09
(12)	Reggie Jackson	2.00	1.00	.60
(13)	Jim Kaat	.30	.15	.09
(14)	Greg Luzinski	.30	.15	.09
(15)	Fred Lynn	.50	.25	.15
(16)	Bill Madlock	.30	.15	.09
(17)	Andy Messersmith	.30	.15	.09
(18)	Thurman Munson	1.50	.70	.45
(19)	Jim Palmer	1.25	.60	.40
(20)	Dave Parker	.30	.15	.09
(21)	Jim Rice	.50	.25	.15
(22)	Pete Rose	4.00	2.00	1.25
(23)	Tom Seaver	1.75	.90	.50
(24)	Chris Speier	.30	.15	.09

1975 SSPC Superstars

Nearly four dozen of the game's contemporary and former stars are featured in this set. Like other SSPC issues of 1975, fronts of the 2-1/2" x 3-1/2" cards have posed color photos with a white border. There are no other graphics, not even the player's name. The horizontal backs feature the player's full formal name (checklist here uses popular name) along with personal data, career summary and stats. Issue price was $4.

		NM	EX	VG
Complete Set (42):		25.00	12.50	7.50
Common Player:		.25	.13	.08
1	Wilbur Wood	.25	.13	.08
2	Johnny Sain	.25	.13	.08
3	Bill Melton	.25	.13	.08
4	Dick Allen	.50	.25	.15
5	Jim Palmer	1.00	.50	.30
6	Brooks Robinson	1.50	.70	.45
7	Tommy Davis	.25	.13	.08
8	Frank Robinson	1.50	.70	.45
9	Vada Pinson (Nolan Ryan in background of photo.)	1.00	.50	.30
10	Nolan Ryan	4.00	2.00	1.25
11	Reggie Jackson	3.00	1.50	.90
12	Vida Blue	.25	.13	.08
13	Sal Bando	.25	.13	.08
14	Bert Campaneris	.25	.13	.08
15	Tom Seaver	2.00	1.00	.60
16	Bud Harrelson	.25	.13	.08
17	Jerry Koosman	.25	.13	.08
18	Dave Nelson	.25	.13	.08
19	Ted Williams	3.50	1.75	1.00
20	Tony Oliva	.35	.20	.11
21	Mickey Lolich	.25	.13	.08
22	Amos Otis	.25	.13	.08
23	Carl Yastrzemski	2.00	1.00	.60
24	Mike Cuellar	.25	.13	.08
25	Doc Medich	.25	.13	.08
26	Cesar Cedeno	.25	.13	.08
27	Jeff Burroughs	.25	.13	.08
28	Ted Williams, Sparky Lyle	.75	.40	.25
29	Johnny Bench	2.00	1.00	.60
30	Gaylord Perry	1.00	.50	.30
31	John Mayberry	.25	.13	.08
32	Rod Carew	1.00	.50	.30
33	Whitey Ford	2.00	1.00	.60
34	Al Kaline	2.00	1.00	.60
35	Willie Mays	3.50	1.75	1.00
36	Warren Spahn	1.00	.50	.30
37	Mickey Mantle	5.00	2.50	1.50
38	Norm Cash	.35	.20	.11
39	Steve Busby	.25	.13	.08
40	Yogi Berra	2.00	1.00	.60
41	Harvey Kuenn	.25	.13	.08
42	Felipe Alou, Jesus Alou, Matty Alou	.60	.30	.20

1976 SSPC Yankees Old Timers Day

The Spring 1976 edition of "Collectors Quarterly" magazine contained a nine-card sheet of players who had appeared at an old timers' games in Yankees Stadium. The sheet could be cut into individual 2-1/2" x 3-1/2" cards with a color player photo and name on front. Backs form a black-and-white puzzle picture of Joe DiMaggio, Mickey Mantle, Whitey Ford, and Billy Martin. Cards are checklisted here alphabetically.

		NM	EX	VG
Complete Magazine:		25.00	12.50	7.50
Complete Set, Singles:		15.00	7.50	4.50
Common Player:		.35	.20	.11
(1)	Earl Averill	.35	.20	.11
(2)	Joe DiMaggio	6.00	3.00	1.75
(3)	Tommy Henrich	.35	.20	.11
(4)	Billy Herman	.35	.20	.11
(5)	Monte Irvin	.35	.20	.11
(6)	Jim Konstanty	.35	.20	.11
(7)	Mickey Mantle	7.50	3.75	2.25
(8)	Pee Wee Reese	3.00	1.50	.90
(9)	Bobby Thompson (Thomson)	.50	.25	.15

1976 SSPC 1887 World Series

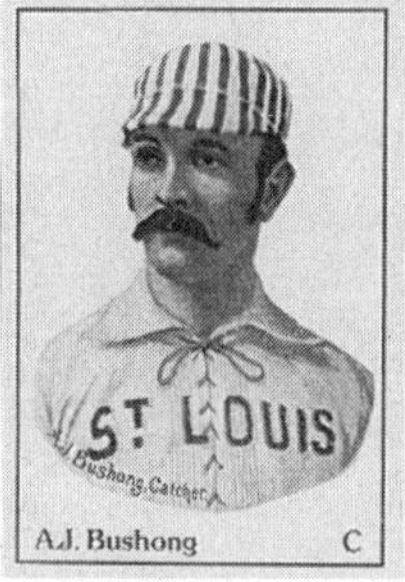

The history of the 1887 "World Series" between the Detroit Wolverines of the National League and the St. Louis Browns of the American Association is told on the backs of this collector's issue. The 2-1/2" x 3-1/2" cards were printed on a pair of uncut sheets inserted in the Fall 1976 issue of "Collectors Quarterly" magazine. Fronts of the cards reproduce in full color the Scrapps tobacco die-cut cards originally issued in 1888. Backs recount the individual players' performances in the series as well as giving a career summary; they are printed in red and black. Detroit won the Series, a best-of-15 contest.

		NM	EX	VG
Complete Magazine:		15.00	7.50	4.50
Complete Set, Singles:		12.00	6.00	3.50
Common Player:		.75	.40	.25
1	Bob Caruthers	.75	.40	.25
2	David Foutz	.75	.40	.25
3	W.A. Latham	.75	.40	.25
4	Charles H. Getzin (Getzien)	.75	.40	.25
5	J.C. Rowe	.75	.40	.25
6	Fred Dunlap	.75	.40	.25
7	James O'Neill	.75	.40	.25
8	Curtis Welch	.75	.40	.25
9	William Gleason	.75	.40	.25
10	Sam Thompson	.75	.40	.25
11	Ned Hanlon	.75	.40	.25
12	Dan Brothers (Brouthers)	.75	.40	.25
13	Albert Bushong	.75	.40	.25
14	Charles Comiskey	.75	.40	.25
15	Wm. Robinson	.75	.40	.25
16	Charles Bennett	.75	.40	.25
17	Hardy Richardson	.75	.40	.25
18	Deacon White	.75	.40	.25

1976 SSPC 1963 New York Mets

Issued in the Summer 1976 issue of "Collectors Quarterly" magazine as a two-page uncut sheet, this 18-card issue features the 1963 Mets. Like contemporary collectors' issues from SSPC, the cards feature white-bordered color photos on front with no other graphics or player identification. Backs are printed in black-and-white, contain player biographical data, a career summary and uniform number, by which the checklist is arranged. Size is standard 2-1/2" x 3-1/2".

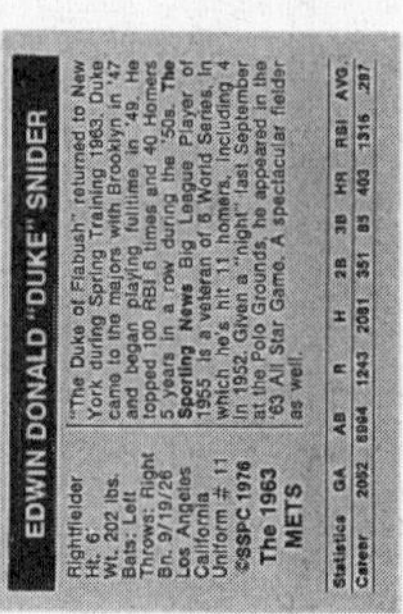

		NM	EX	VG
Complete Magazine:		25.00	12.50	7.50
Complete Set, Singles (18):		15.00	7.50	4.50
Common Player:		1.00	.50	.30
1	Duke Carmel	1.00	.50	.30
5	Norman Burt Sherry	1.00	.50	.30
7	Casey Stengel	5.00	2.50	1.50
9	Jim Hickman	1.00	.50	.30
10	Rod Kanehl	1.00	.50	.30
11	Duke Snider	7.50	3.75	2.25
12	Jesse Gonder	1.00	.50	.30
16	Dick Smith	1.00	.50	.30
17	Clarence Coleman	1.00	.50	.30
18	Pumpsie Green	1.00	.50	.30
23	Joe Christopher	1.00	.50	.30
36	Tracy Stallard	1.00	.50	.30
39	Steve Dillon	1.00	.50	.30
40	Rich Moran	1.00	.50	.30
41	Grover Powell	1.00	.50	.30
43	Ted Schreiber	1.00	.50	.30
53	Ernest White	1.00	.50	.30
56	Ed Bauta	1.00	.50	.30

1978 SSPC All Star Gallery

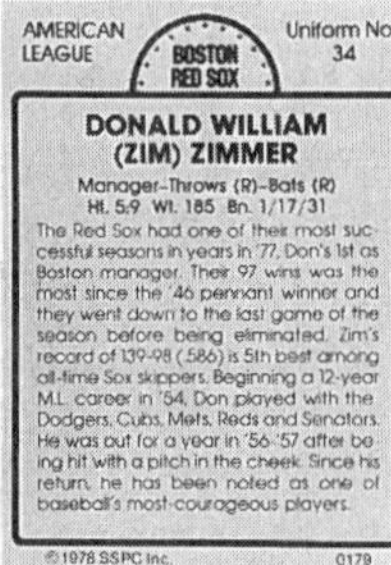

A series of team "Photo Fact Cards" was produced by Sports Stars Publishing Co., for insertion into its 48-page "All Star Gallery" magazine, sold for $2. Fully licensed by MLB and the Players Union, the 27 cards in each team set are printed on a triple-fold 24" x 10-7/8" cardboard sheet stapled into the center of the magazine. Cards are not perforated, though the back of each nine-card panel has dotted lines to guide the cutting of 2-1/2" x 3-1/2" single cards from the sheet. Fronts are full-color poses with no extraneous graphics. Backs are in black-and-white with a few vital data, a career summary, uniform number and a card number from within the overall issue of 270. Only eight teams are represented in the All-Star Gallery magazine series. The Yankees (#001-027) and Phillies cards (#028-054) issued with other magazines that year may be considered part of the All-Star Gallery issue.

		NM	EX	VG
Complete Set, Magazines (8):		135.00	65.00	40.00
Complete Set, Singles (216):		125.00	60.00	35.00
Common Player:		.50	.25	.15
	Los Angeles Dodgers Magazine:	15.00	7.50	4.50
0055	Burt Hooton	.50	.25	.15
0056	Bill Russell	.50	.25	.15
0057	Dusty Baker	.60	.30	.20
0058	Reggie Smith	.50	.25	.15
0059	Dick Rhoden	.50	.25	.15
0060	Jerry Grote	.50	.25	.15
0061	Bill Butler	.50	.25	.15
0062	Ron Cey	.50	.25	.15
0063	Ron Cey	.50	.25	.15
0064	Ted Martinez	.50	.25	.15
0065	Ed Goodson	.50	.25	.15
0066	Vic Davalillo	.50	.25	.15
0067	Davey Lopes	.50	.25	.15
0068	Terry Forster	.50	.25	.15
0069	Lee Lacy	.50	.25	.15
0070	Mike Garman	.50	.25	.15
0071	Steve Garvey	1.50	.70	.45
0072	Johnny Oates	.50	.25	.15
0073	Steve Yaeger	.50	.25	.15
0074	Rafael Landestoy	.50	.25	.15
0075	Tommy John	.60	.30	.20
0076	Glenn Burke	.50	.25	.15
0077	Rick Monday	.50	.25	.15
0078	Doug Rau	.50	.25	.15
0079	Manny Mota	.50	.25	.15
0080	Don Sutton	2.00	1.00	.60
0081	Charlie Hough	.50	.25	.15
	Texas Rangers Magazine:	12.50	6.25	3.75
0082	Mike Hargrove	.50	.25	.15

0083	Jim Sundberg	.50	.25	.15
0084	Fergie Jenkins	2.00	1.00	.60
0085	Paul Lindblad	.50	.25	.15
0086	Sandy Alomar	.50	.25	.15
0087	John Lowenstein	.50	.25	.15
0088	Claudell Washington	.50	.25	.15
0089	Toby Harrah	.50	.25	.15
0090	Jim Umbarger	.50	.25	.15
0091	Len Barker	.50	.25	.15
0092	Dave May	.50	.25	.15
0093	Kurt Bevacqua	.50	.25	.15
0094	Jim Mason	.50	.25	.15
0095	Bump Wills	.50	.25	.15
0096	Dock Ellis	.50	.25	.15
0097	Bill Fahey	.50	.25	.15
0098	Richie Zisk	.50	.25	.15
0099	Jon Matlack	.50	.25	.15
0100	John Ellis	.50	.25	.15
0101	Bert Campaneris	.50	.25	.15
0102	Doc Medich	.50	.25	.15
0103	Juan Beniquez	.50	.25	.15
0104	Bill Hunter	.50	.25	.15
0105	Doyle Alexander	.50	.25	.15
0106	Roger Moret	.50	.25	.15
0107	Mike Jorgensen	.50	.25	.15
0108	Al Oliver	.60	.30	.20
	Cincinnati Reds Magazine:	15.00	7.50	4.50
0109	Fred Norman	.50	.25	.15
0110	Ray Knight	.50	.25	.15
0111	Pedro Borbon	.50	.25	.15
0112	Bill Bonham	.50	.25	.15
0113	George Foster	.60	.30	.20
0114	Doug Bair	.50	.25	.15
0115	Cesar Geronimo	.50	.25	.15
0116	Tom Seaver	3.50	1.75	1.00
0117	Mario Soto	.50	.25	.15
0118	Ken Griffey	.50	.25	.15
0119	Mike Lum	.50	.25	.15
0120	Tom Hume	.50	.25	.15
0121	Joe Morgan	2.50	1.25	.70
0122	Manny Sarmiento	.50	.25	.15
0123	Dan Driessen	.50	.25	.15
0124	Ed Armbrister	.50	.25	.15
0125	John Summers	.50	.25	.15
0126	Fred Auerbach	.50	.25	.15
0127	Doug Capilla	.50	.25	.15
0128	Johnny Bench	3.50	1.75	1.00
0129	Sparky Anderson	1.50	.70	.45
0130	Raul Ferreyra	.50	.25	.15
0131	Dale Murray	.50	.25	.15
0132	Pete Rose	7.50	3.75	2.25
0133	Dave Concepcion	.50	.25	.15
0134	Junior Kennedy	.50	.25	.15
0135	Dave Collins	.50	.25	.15
	Chicago White Sox Magazine:	12.50	6.25	3.75
0136	Mike Eden	.50	.25	.15
0137	Lamar Johnson	.50	.25	.15
0138	Ron Schueler	.50	.25	.15
0139	Bob Lemon	.75	.40	.25
0140	Thad Bosley	.50	.25	.15
0141	Bobby Bonds	.60	.30	.20
0142	Wilbur Wood	.50	.25	.15
0143	Jorge Orta	.50	.25	.15
0144	Francisco Barrios	.50	.25	.15
0145	Greg Pryor	.50	.25	.15
0146	Chet Lemon	.50	.25	.15
0147	Mike Squires	.50	.25	.15
0148	Eric Soderholm	.50	.25	.15
0149	Reggie Sanders	.50	.25	.15
0150	Kevin Bell	.50	.25	.15
0151	Alan Bannister	.50	.25	.15
0152	Henry Cruz	.50	.25	.15
0153	Larry Doby	2.00	1.00	.60
0154	Don Kessinger	.50	.25	.15
0155	Ralph Garr	.50	.25	.15
0156	Bill Nahorodny	.50	.25	.15
0157	Ron Blomberg	.50	.25	.15
0158	Bob Molinaro	.50	.25	.15
0159	Junior Moore	.50	.25	.15
0160	Minnie Minoso	1.50	.70	.45
0161	Lerrin LaGrow	.50	.25	.15
0162	Wayne Nordhagen	.50	.25	.15
	Boston Red Sox Magazine:	20.00	10.00	6.00
0163	Ramon Aviles	.50	.25	.15
0164	Bob Stanley	.50	.25	.15
0165	Reggie Cleveland	.50	.25	.15
0166	John Brohamer	.50	.25	.15
0167	Bill Lee	.50	.25	.15
0168	Jim Burton	.50	.25	.15
0169	Bill Campbell	.50	.25	.15
0170	Mike Torrez	.50	.25	.15
0171	Dick Drago	.50	.25	.15
0172	Butch Hobson	.50	.25	.15
0173	Bob Bailey	.50	.25	.15
0174	Fred Lynn	.50	.25	.15
0175	Rick Burleson	.50	.25	.15
0176	Luis Tiant	.50	.25	.15
0177	Ted Williams	6.00	3.00	1.75
0178	Dennis Eckersley	2.00	1.00	.60
0179	Don Zimmer	.50	.25	.15
0180	Carlton Fisk	2.50	1.25	.70
0181	Dwight Evans	.50	.25	.15
0182	Fred Kendall	.50	.25	.15
0183	George Scott	.50	.25	.15
0184	Frank Duffy	.50	.25	.15
0185	Bernie Carbo	.50	.25	.15
0186	Jerry Remy	.50	.25	.15
0187	Carl Yastrzemski	4.00	2.00	1.25
0188	Allen Ripley	.50	.25	.15
0189	Jim Rice	.90	.45	.25
	California Angels Magazine:	20.00	10.00	6.00
0190	Ken Landreaux	.50	.25	.15
0191	Paul Hartzell	.50	.25	.15
0192	Ken Brett	.50	.25	.15
0193	Dave Garcia	.50	.25	.15
0194	Bobby Grich	.50	.25	.15
0195	Lyman Bostock	.50	.25	.15
0196	Isaac Hampton	.50	.25	.15
0197	Dave LaRoche	.50	.25	.15
0198	Dave Chalk	.50	.25	.15
0199	Rick Miller	.50	.25	.15
0200	Floyd Rayford	.50	.25	.15
0201	Willie Aikens	.50	.25	.15
0202	Balor Moore	.50	.25	.15
0203	Nolan Ryan	10.00	5.00	3.00
0204	Dan Goodwin	.50	.25	.15
0205	Ron Fairly	.50	.25	.15
0206	Dyar Miller	.50	.25	.15
0207	Carney Lansford	.50	.25	.15
0208	Don Baylor	.60	.30	.20
0209	Gil Flores	.50	.25	.15
0210	Terry Humphrey	.50	.25	.15
0211	Frank Tanana	.50	.25	.15
0212	Chris Knapp	.50	.25	.15
0213	Ron Jackson	.50	.25	.15
0214	Joe Rudi	.50	.25	.15
0215	Tony Solaita	.50	.25	.15
0216	Steve Mulliniks	.50	.25	.15
	Kansas City Royals Magazine:	20.00	10.00	6.00
0217	George Brett	6.00	3.00	1.75
0218	Doug Bird	.50	.25	.15
0219	Hal McRae	.50	.25	.15
0220	Dennis Leonard	.50	.25	.15
0221	Darrell Porter	.50	.25	.15
0222	Randy McGilberry	.50	.25	.15
0223	Pete LaCock	.50	.25	.15
0224	Whitey Herzog	.50	.25	.15
0225	Andy Hassler	.50	.25	.15
0226	Joe Lahoud	.50	.25	.15
0227	Amos Otis	.50	.25	.15
0228	Al Hrabosky	.50	.25	.15
0229	Clint Hurdle	.50	.25	.15
0230	Paul Splittorff	.50	.25	.15
0231	Marty Pattin	.50	.25	.15
0232	Frank White	.50	.25	.15
0233	John Wathan	.50	.25	.15
0234	Freddie Patek	.50	.25	.15
0235	Rich Gale	.50	.25	.15
0236	U.L. Washington	.50	.25	.15
0237	Larry Gura	.50	.25	.15
0238	Jim Colburn	.50	.25	.15
0239	Tom Poquette	.50	.25	.15
0240	Al Cowens	.50	.25	.15
0241	Willie Wilson	.50	.25	.15
0242	Steve Mingori	.50	.25	.15
0243	Jerry Terrell	.50	.25	.15
	Chicago Cubs Magazine:	12.50	6.25	3.75
0244	Larry Biittner	.50	.25	.15
0245	Rick Reuschel	.50	.25	.15
0246	Dave Rader	.50	.25	.15
0247	Paul Reuschel	.50	.25	.15
0248	Hector Cruz	.50	.25	.15
0249	Woody Fryman	.50	.25	.15
0250	Steve Ontiveros	.50	.25	.15
0251	Mike Gordon	.50	.25	.15
0252	Dave Kingman	.50	.25	.15
0253	Gene Clines	.50	.25	.15
0254	Bruce Sutter	2.00	1.00	.60
0255	Guillermo Hernandez	.50	.25	.15
0256	Ivan DeJesus	.50	.25	.15
0257	Greg Gross	.50	.25	.15
0258	Larry Cox	.50	.25	.15
0259	Joe Wallis	.50	.25	.15
0260	Dennis Lamp	.50	.25	.15
0261	Ray Burris	.50	.25	.15
0262	Bill Caudill	.50	.25	.15
0263	Donnie Moore	.50	.25	.15
0264	Bill Buckner	.60	.30	.20
0265	Bobby Murcer	.60	.30	.20
0266	Dave Roberts	.50	.25	.15
0267	Mike Krukow	.50	.25	.15
0268	Herman Franks	.50	.25	.15
0269	Mike Kelleher	.50	.25	.15
0270	Rudy Meoli	.50	.25	.15

1978 SSPC Baseball the Phillies Way

Road to the Majors

ROBERT RAYMOND (BOB) BOONE
Catcher

The son of former major leaguer Ray Boone, Bob was an infielder and pitcher during his amateur career. He was signed by the Phillies as a third baseman and wasn't shifted to catcher until his second minor-league season. Ironically, his dad began as a catcher and switched to the infield. At San Diego's Crawford High School Bob lettered in baseball, basketball and football. In his senior year he batted .386 with 27 RBI and also owned an incredible 15-0 pitching mark with an ERA of 0.71. Bob moved on to Stanford University where he co-captained the baseball team his senior year. His biggest thrill in college ball was beating Southern California, 3-2 in 1969, by pitching a four-hitter and hitting a game-winning homer. The Phillies signed Bob in 1969 and he was named to the Carolina League All-Star team his first season in pro ball. In 1976 Bob was a member of the National League All-star team.

© 1978 SSPC Inc. 0033

This team set was produced on a tri-fold insert in an SSPC magazine titled, "Baseball the Phillies Way." The magazine offered playing tips. Cards are in the contemporary SSPC format of a posed front photo with a white border and no other graphics. Backs are printed in red, white and black with player ID, career data and card numbers between 0028-0054, continuing the sequence begun with the Yankees yearbook team set which continues with the All-Star Gallery set. Cards could be cut from the sheets into 2-1/2" x 3-1/2" singles.

		NM	EX	VG
	Complete Magazine:	15.00	7.50	4.50
	Complete Set, Singles (27):	12.00	6.00	3.50
	Common Player:	.50	.25	.15
0028	Garry Maddox	.50	.25	.15
0029	Steve Carlton	2.50	1.25	.70
0030	Ron Reed	.50	.25	.15
0031	Greg Luzinski	.50	.25	.15
0032	Bobby Wine	.50	.25	.15
0033	Bob Boone	1.50	.70	.45
0034	Carroll Beringer	.50	.25	.15
0035	Dick Hebner	.50	.25	.15
0036	Ray Ripplemeyer	.50	.25	.15
0037	Terry Harmon	.50	.25	.15
0038	Gene Garber	.50	.25	.15
0039	Ted Sizemore	.50	.25	.15
0040	Barry Foote	.50	.25	.15
0041	Tony Taylor	.50	.25	.15
0042	Tug McGraw	.75	.40	.25
0043	Jay Johnstone	.65	.35	.20
0044	Randy Lerch	.50	.25	.15
0045	Billy DeMars	.50	.25	.15
0046	Mike Schmidt	5.00	2.50	1.50
0047	Larry Christenson	.50	.25	.15
0048	Tim McCarver	1.00	.50	.30
0049	Larry Bowa	.65	.35	.20
0050	Danny Ozark	.50	.25	.15
0051	Jerry Martin	.50	.25	.15
0052	Jim Lonborg	.50	.25	.15
0053	Bake McBride	.50	.25	.15
0054	Warren Brusstar	.50	.25	.15

1978 SSPC Yankees Yearbook

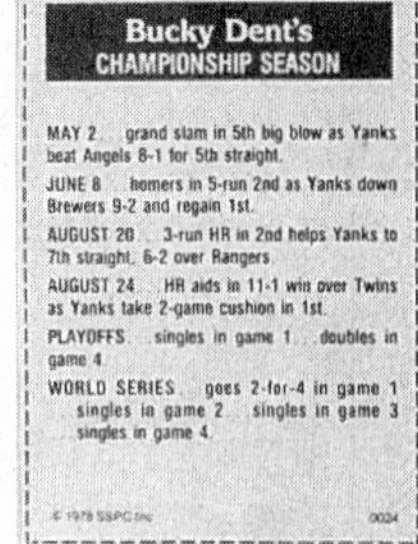

Bucky Dent's
CHAMPIONSHIP SEASON

MAY 2 ... grand slam in 5th big blow as Yanks beat Angels 8-1 for 5th straight.

JUNE 8 ... homers in 5-run 2nd as Yanks down Brewers 9-2 and regain 1st.

AUGUST 20 ... 3-run HR in 2nd helps Yanks to 7th straight, 6-2 over Rangers.

AUGUST 24 ... HR aids in 11-1 win over Twins as Yanks take 2-game cushion in 1st.

PLAYOFFS ... singles in game 1 ... doubles in game 4.

WORLD SERIES ... goes 2-for-4 in game 1 ... singles in game 2 ... singles in game 3 ... singles in game 4.

© 1978 SSPC Inc. 0024

This team set was printed on a tri-fold insert found both in the 1978 Yankees yearbook and a magazine titled "Diary of a Champion Yankee," produced by SSPC. The nine cards on each sheet could be cut apart into 2-1/2" x 3-1/2" singles. Cards follow the basic SSPC format of a posed color photo on front with a white border and no graphic elements. Backs have player identification, career summary and "CHAMPIONSHIP SEASON" highlights, printed in black and blue on white. Cards are numbered from 0001-0027, and may be considered part of the larger All-Star Gallery issue.

		NM	EX	VG
	Complete Magazine:	12.50	6.25	3.75
	Complete Set, Singles (27):	10.00	5.00	3.00
	Common Player:	.50	.25	.15
0001	Thurman Munson	3.00	1.50	.90
0002	Cliff Johnson	.50	.25	.15
0003	Lou Piniella	.75	.40	.25
0004	Dell Alston	.50	.25	.15
0005	Yankee Stadium	1.00	.50	.30
0006	Ken Holtzman	.50	.25	.15
0007	Chris Chambliss	.50	.25	.15
0008	Roy White	.60	.30	.20
0009	Ed Figueroa	.50	.25	.15
0010	Dick Tidrow	.50	.25	.15
0011	Sparky Lyle	.60	.30	.20
0012	Fred Stanley	.50	.25	.15
0013	Mickey Rivers	.50	.25	.15
0014	Billy Martin	.75	.40	.25
0015	George Zeber	.50	.25	.15
0016	Ken Clay	.50	.25	.15
0017	Ron Guidry	.75	.40	.25
0018	Don Gullett	.50	.25	.15
0019	Fran Healy	.50	.25	.15
0020	Paul Blair	.50	.25	.15
0021	Mickey Klutts	.50	.25	.15
0022	Yankee team	.50	.25	.15
0023	Catfish Hunter	1.50	.70	.45
0024	Bucky Dent	.75	.40	.25
0025	Graig Nettles	.75	.40	.25
0026	Reggie Jackson	3.00	1.50	.90
0027	Willie Randolph	.60	.30	.20

1889 "The Stage" Stars of the Diamond

Titled "Stars of the Diamond" and issued weekly between May 25-Aug. 31, 1889, these numbered supplements were printed in "The Stage" newspaper, a Philadelphia-based publication. Two types of supplements are found, those picturing New York players in uniforms (from Joseph Hall photos), and those picturing members of the Philadelphia National League and American Association teams in street clothes. The black-and-white portraits are printed in a 9" x 12" format on newsprint, making surviving examples very rare today.

		NM	EX	VG
	Common Player:	250.00	125.00	75.00
1	Charles Buffington	250.00	125.00	75.00
2	John Clements	250.00	125.00	75.00
3	Harry D. Stovey	250.00	125.00	75.00
4	"Gus" Weyhing	250.00	125.00	75.00
5	L.M. Cross	250.00	125.00	75.00
6	Edward Seward	250.00	125.00	75.00
7	Wm. Robinson (Wilbert)	375.00	185.00	110.00
8	Denny Lyons	375.00	185.00	110.00
9	A.B. Sanders	250.00	125.00	75.00
10	William Schriver	250.00	125.00	75.00

11	Daniel M. Casey	250.00	125.00	75.00
12	"Tim" Keefe	375.00	185.00	110.00
13	"Buck" Ewing	375.00	185.00	110.00
14	John Ward	375.00	185.00	110.00

1953 Stahl-Meyer Franks

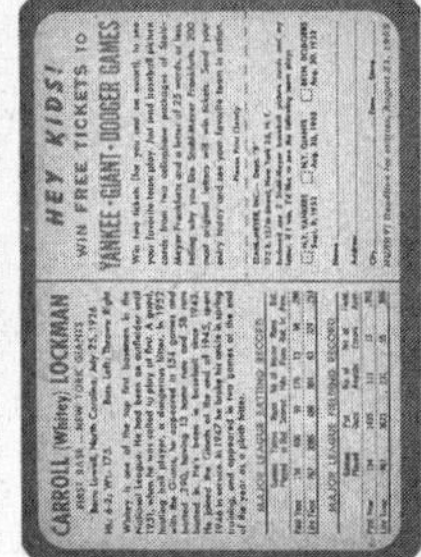

These nine cards, issued in packages of hot dogs by a New York area meat company, feature three players from each of the New York teams of the day - Dodgers Giants and Yankees. Cards in the set measure 3-1/4" x 4-1/2". The card fronts in this unnumbered set feature color photos with player name and facsimile autograph. The backs list both biographical and statistical information on half the card and a ticket offer promotion on the other half. The card corners are cut diagonally, although some cards (apparantly cut from sheets) with square corners have been seen. Cards are white-bordered.

		NM	EX	VG
Complete Set (9):		20,000	9,000	4,000
Common Player:		500.00	225.00	100.00
(1)	Hank Bauer	550.00	245.00	110.00
(2)	Roy Campanella	2,000	900.00	400.00
(3)	Gil Hodges	1,250	560.00	250.00
(4)	Monte Irvin	750.00	335.00	150.00
(5)	Whitey Lockman	500.00	225.00	100.00
(6)	Mickey Mantle	13,500	6,100	2,750
(7)	Phil Rizzuto	1,250	560.00	250.00
(8)	Duke Snider	2,000	900.00	400.00
(9)	Bobby Thomson	650.00	290.00	130.00

1954 Stahl-Meyer Franks

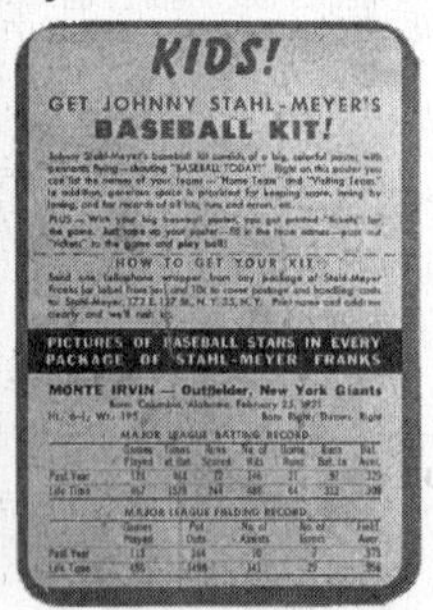

The 1954 set of Stahl-Meyer Franks was increased to 12 cards which retained the 3-1/4" x 4-1/2" size. The most prominent addition to the '54 set was New York Giants slugger Willie Mays. The card fronts are identical in format to the previous year's set. However, the backs are different as they are designed on a vertical format. The backs also contain an advertisement for a "Johnny Stahl-Meyer Baseball Kit." The cards in the set are unnumbered.

		NM	EX	VG
Complete Set (12):		30,000	13,500	6,000
Common Player:		650.00	290.00	130.00
(1)	Hank Bauer	750.00	335.00	150.00
(2)	Carl Erskine	750.00	335.00	150.00
(3)	Gil Hodges	2,000	900.00	400.00
(4)	Monte Irvin	1,000	450.00	200.00
(5)	Whitey Lockman	650.00	290.00	130.00
(6)	Gil McDougald	750.00	335.00	150.00
(7)	Mickey Mantle	12,000	5,400	2,400
(8)	Willie Mays	8,500	3,825	1,700
(9)	Don Mueller	650.00	290.00	130.00
(10)	Don Newcombe	750.00	335.00	150.00
(11)	Phil Rizzuto	2,000	900.00	400.00
(12)	Duke Snider	2,000	900.00	400.00

1955 Stahl-Meyer Franks

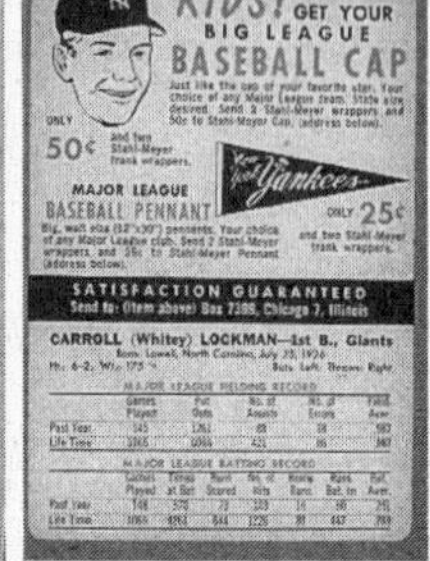

Eleven of the 12 players in the 1955 set are the same as those featured in 1954. The exception is the New York Giants Dusty Rhodes, who replaced Willie Mays on the 3-1/4" x 4-1/2" cards. The card fronts are again full-color photos bordered in yellow with diagonal corners, and four players from each of the three New York teams are featured. The backs offer a new promotion, with a drawing of Mickey Mantle and advertisements selling pennants and caps. Player statistics are still included on the vertical card backs. The cards in the set are unnumbered.

		NM	EX	VG
Complete Set (12):		20,000	9,000	4,000
Common Player:		500.00	225.00	100.00
(1)	Hank Bauer	600.00	275.00	125.00
(2)	Carl Erskine	600.00	275.00	125.00
(3)	Gil Hodges	1,500	675.00	300.00
(4)	Monte Irvin	800.00	360.00	160.00
(5)	Whitey Lockman	500.00	225.00	100.00
(6)	Mickey Mantle	12,000	5,400	2,400
(7)	Gil McDougald	600.00	275.00	125.00
(8)	Don Mueller	500.00	225.00	100.00
(9)	Don Newcombe	600.00	275.00	125.00
(10)	Jim Rhodes	500.00	225.00	100.00
(11)	Phil Rizzuto	1,500	675.00	300.00
(12)	Duke Snider	1,500	675.00	300.00

1916 Standard Biscuit (D350-1)

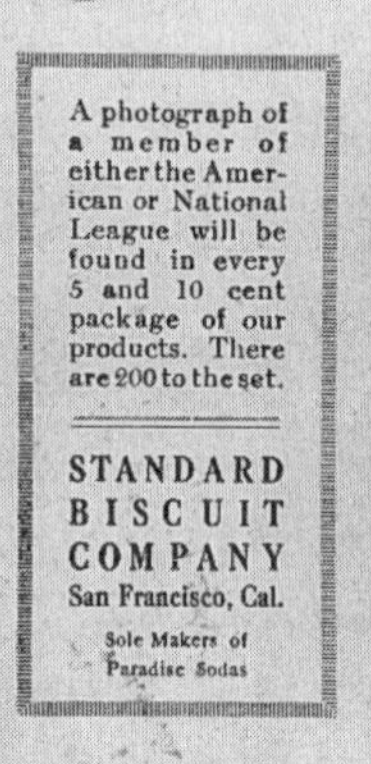

The range of cards in this issue is uncertain as examples can be found corresponding to the checklists of both of the 1916 sets known as M101-5 and M101-4 Blank Backs. Standard Biscuit cards in this format are also known that correspond to neither M101-5 nor M101-4. The approximately 1-5/8" x 3" black-and-white cards usually command a modest premium from collectors seeking to enhance a type collection or superstar collection. A trial checklist is begun herewith.

		NM	EX	VG
Common Player:		90.00	45.00	30.00
1	Babe Adams	90.00	45.00	30.00
3	Ed Ainsmith	90.00	45.00	30.00
6	Jimmy Archer	90.00	45.00	30.00
12	Beals Becker	90.00	45.00	30.00
13	Joe Benz	90.00	45.00	30.00
14	Bob Bescher	90.00	45.00	30.00
15	Al Betzel	90.00	45.00	30.00
18	Eddie Burns	90.00	45.00	30.00
27	George Chalmers	90.00	45.00	30.00
37	Joe Connolly	90.00	45.00	30.00
39	Harry Coveleskie (Coveleski)	90.00	45.00	30.00
42	Sam Crawford	400.00	200.00	130.00
48	William Doak	90.00	45.00	30.00
50	Charles Dooin	90.00	45.00	30.00
60	Max Flack	90.00	45.00	30.00
61	Art Fletcher	90.00	45.00	30.00
63	Jacques Fournier	90.00	45.00	30.00
64	"Chic" Gandil	900.00	450.00	300.00
66	Joe Gedeon	90.00	45.00	30.00
68	George Gibson	90.00	45.00	30.00
69	Wilbur Good	90.00	45.00	30.00
71	John Graney	90.00	45.00	30.00
72	Tom Griffith	90.00	45.00	30.00
73	Heinie Groh	90.00	45.00	30.00
75	Bob Harmon	90.00	45.00	30.00
77	Claude Hendrix	90.00	45.00	30.00
79	John Henry	90.00	45.00	30.00
80	Buck Herzog	90.00	45.00	30.00
82	Dick Hoblitzell	90.00	45.00	30.00
84	Ivan Howard	90.00	45.00	30.00
87	Joe Jackson	10,000	5,000	3,300
89	Hugh Jennings	400.00	200.00	130.00
131	Les Nunamaker	90.00	45.00	30.00
137	E.J. Pfeffer	90.00	45.00	30.00
164	Ernie Shore	90.00	45.00	30.00
172a	Milton Stock	90.00	45.00	30.00
172b	Billy Sullivan	90.00	45.00	30.00
176	Jim Thorpe	17,500	8,750	5,775
184	Honus Wagner	2,700	1,350	510.00
186	Bobby Wallace	600.00	300.00	200.00
191	Fred Williams	90.00	45.00	30.00
195	Joe Wood	350.00	175.00	115.00
196	Joe Wood	350.00	175.00	115.00
199	Heiny Zimmerman	90.00	45.00	30.00

1917 Standard Biscuit (D350-2)

The 200 cards in this set are more commonly found with the advertising of Collins-McCarthy Candy Co. on the back. The cards measure about 2" x 3-1/4" and are printed in black-

and-white. Though the Standard Biscuit cards are scarcer than the Collins-McCarthy version, collectors do not attach much premium to them.

		NM	EX	VG
Complete Set (200):		70,000	35,000	21,000
Common Player:		150.00	75.00	45.00
1	Sam Agnew	150.00	75.00	45.00
2	Grover Alexander	600.00	300.00	180.00
3	W.S. Alexander (W.E.)	150.00	75.00	45.00
4	Leon Ames	150.00	75.00	45.00
5	Fred Anderson	150.00	75.00	45.00
6	Ed Appleton	150.00	75.00	45.00
7	Jimmy Archer	150.00	75.00	45.00
8	Jimmy Austin	150.00	75.00	45.00
9	Jim Bagby	150.00	75.00	45.00
10	H.D. Baird	150.00	75.00	45.00
11	J. Franklin Baker	350.00	175.00	100.00
12	Dave Bancroft	350.00	175.00	100.00
13	Jack Barry	150.00	75.00	45.00
14	Joe Benz	150.00	75.00	45.00
15	Al Betzel	150.00	75.00	45.00
16	Ping Bodie	150.00	75.00	45.00
17	Joe Boehling	150.00	75.00	45.00
18	Eddie Burns	150.00	75.00	45.00
19	George Burns	150.00	75.00	45.00
20	Geo. J. Burns	150.00	75.00	45.00
21	Joe Bush	150.00	75.00	45.00
22	Owen Bush	150.00	75.00	45.00
23	Bobby Byrne	150.00	75.00	45.00
24	Forrest Cady	150.00	75.00	45.00
25	Max Carey	350.00	175.00	100.00
26	Ray Chapman	200.00	100.00	60.00
27	Larry Cheney	150.00	75.00	45.00
28	Eddie Cicotte	450.00	225.00	135.00
29	Tom Clarke	150.00	75.00	45.00
30	Ty Cobb	4,500	2,250	1,350
31	Eddie Collins	350.00	175.00	100.00
32	"Shauno" Collins (Shano)	150.00	75.00	45.00
33	Fred Coumbe	150.00	75.00	45.00
34	Harry Coveleskie (Coveleski)	150.00	75.00	45.00
35	Gavvy Cravath	150.00	75.00	45.00
36	Sam Crawford	350.00	175.00	100.00
37	Geo. Cutshaw	150.00	75.00	45.00
38	Jake Daubert	150.00	75.00	45.00
39	Geo. Dauss	150.00	75.00	45.00
40	Charles Deal	150.00	75.00	45.00
41	"Wheezer" Dell	150.00	75.00	45.00
42	William Doak	150.00	75.00	45.00
43	Bill Donovan	150.00	75.00	45.00
44	Larry Doyle	150.00	75.00	45.00
45	Johnny Evers	350.00	175.00	100.00
46	Urban Faber	350.00	175.00	100.00
47	"Hap" Felsch	750.00	375.00	225.00
48	Bill Fischer	150.00	75.00	45.00
49	Ray Fisher	150.00	75.00	45.00
50	Art Fletcher	150.00	75.00	45.00
51	Eddie Foster	150.00	75.00	45.00
52	Jacques Fournier	150.00	75.00	45.00
53	Del Gainer (Gainor)	150.00	75.00	45.00
54	Bert Gallia	150.00	75.00	45.00
55	"Chic" Gandil (Chick)	450.00	225.00	135.00
56	Larry Gardner	150.00	75.00	45.00
57	Joe Gedeon	150.00	75.00	45.00
58	Gus Getz	150.00	75.00	45.00
59	Frank Gilhooley	150.00	75.00	45.00
60	Wm. Gleason	150.00	75.00	45.00
61	M.A. Gonzales (Gonzalez)	165.00	80.00	50.00
62	Hank Gowdy	150.00	75.00	45.00
63	John Graney	150.00	75.00	45.00
64	Tom Griffith	150.00	75.00	45.00
65	Heinie Groh	150.00	75.00	45.00
66	Bob Groom	150.00	75.00	45.00
67	Louis Guisto	150.00	75.00	45.00
68	Earl Hamilton	150.00	75.00	45.00
69	Harry Harper	150.00	75.00	45.00
70	Grover Hartley	150.00	75.00	45.00
71	Harry Heilmann	350.00	175.00	100.00
72	Claude Hendrix	150.00	75.00	45.00
73	Olaf Henriksen	150.00	75.00	45.00
74	John Henry	150.00	75.00	45.00
75	"Buck" Herzog	150.00	75.00	45.00
76	Hugh High	150.00	75.00	45.00
77	Dick Hoblitzell	150.00	75.00	45.00
78	Walter Holke	150.00	75.00	45.00
79	Harry Hooper	350.00	175.00	100.00
80	Rogers Hornsby	650.00	325.00	195.00
81	Ivan Howard	150.00	75.00	45.00
82	Joe Jackson	15,000	7,500	4,500
83	Harold Janvrin	150.00	75.00	45.00
84	William James	150.00	75.00	45.00
85	C. Jamieson	150.00	75.00	45.00
86	Hugh Jennings	350.00	175.00	100.00
87	Walter Johnson	750.00	375.00	225.00
88	James Johnston	150.00	75.00	45.00

		NM	EX	VG
89	Fielder Jones	150.00	75.00	45.00
90	Joe Judge	150.00	75.00	45.00
91	Hans Lobert	150.00	75.00	45.00
92	Benny Kauff	150.00	75.00	45.00
93	Wm. Killefer Jr.	150.00	75.00	45.00
94	Ed. Konetchy	150.00	75.00	45.00
95	John Lavan	150.00	75.00	45.00
96	Jimmy Lavender	150.00	75.00	45.00
97	"Nemo" Leibold	150.00	75.00	45.00
98	H.B. Leonard	150.00	75.00	45.00
99	Duffy Lewis	150.00	75.00	45.00
100	Tom Long	150.00	75.00	45.00
101	Wm. Louden	150.00	75.00	45.00
102	Fred Luderus	150.00	75.00	45.00
103	Lee Magee	150.00	75.00	45.00
104	Sherwood Magee	150.00	75.00	45.00
105	Al Mamaux	150.00	75.00	45.00
106	Leslie Mann	150.00	75.00	45.00
107	"Rabbit" Maranville	350.00	175.00	100.00
108	Rube Marquard	350.00	175.00	100.00
109	Armando Marsans	165.00	85.00	50.00
110	J. Erskine Mayer	175.00	85.00	50.00
111	George McBride	150.00	75.00	45.00
112	Lew McCarty	150.00	75.00	45.00
113	John J. McGraw	350.00	175.00	100.00
114	Jack McInnis	150.00	75.00	45.00
115	Lee Meadows	150.00	75.00	45.00
116	Fred Merkle	150.00	75.00	45.00
117	"Chief" Meyers	150.00	75.00	45.00
118	Clyde Milan	150.00	75.00	45.00
119	Otto Miller	150.00	75.00	45.00
120	Clarence Mitchell	150.00	75.00	45.00
121	Ray Morgan	150.00	75.00	45.00
122	Guy Morton	150.00	75.00	45.00
123	"Mike" Mowrey	150.00	75.00	45.00
124	Elmer Myers	150.00	75.00	45.00
125	"Hy" Myers	150.00	75.00	45.00
126	A.E. Neale	175.00	85.00	50.00
127	Arthur Nehf	150.00	75.00	45.00
128	J.A. Niehoff	150.00	75.00	45.00
129	Steve O'Neill	150.00	75.00	45.00
130	"Dode" Paskert	150.00	75.00	45.00
131	Roger Peckinpaugh	150.00	75.00	45.00
132	"Pol" Perritt	150.00	75.00	45.00
133	"Jeff" Pfeffer	150.00	75.00	45.00
134	Walter Pipp	150.00	75.00	45.00
135	Derril Pratt (Derrill)	150.00	75.00	45.00
136	Bill Rariden	150.00	75.00	45.00
137	E.C. Rice	350.00	175.00	100.00
138	Wm. A. Ritter (Wm. H.)	150.00	75.00	45.00
139	Eppa Rixey	350.00	175.00	100.00
140	Davey Robertson	150.00	75.00	45.00
141	"Bob" Roth	150.00	75.00	45.00
142	Ed. Roush	350.00	175.00	100.00
143	Clarence Rowland	150.00	75.00	45.00
144	Dick Rudolph	150.00	75.00	45.00
145	William Rumler	150.00	75.00	45.00
146	Reb Russell	150.00	75.00	45.00
147	"Babe" Ruth	12,500	6,250	3,750
148	Vic Saier	150.00	75.00	45.00
149	"Slim" Sallee	150.00	75.00	45.00
150	Ray Schalk	350.00	175.00	100.00
151	Walter Schang	150.00	75.00	45.00
152	Frank Schulte	150.00	75.00	45.00
153	Ferd Schupp	150.00	75.00	45.00
154	Everett Scott	150.00	75.00	45.00
155	Hank Severeid	150.00	75.00	45.00
156	Howard Shanks	150.00	75.00	45.00
157	Bob Shawkey	150.00	75.00	45.00
158	Jas. Sheckard	150.00	75.00	45.00
159	Ernie Shore	150.00	75.00	45.00
160	C.H. Shorten	150.00	75.00	45.00
161	Burt Shotton	150.00	75.00	45.00
162	Geo. Sisler	350.00	175.00	100.00
163	Elmer Smith	150.00	75.00	45.00
164	J. Carlisle Smith	150.00	75.00	45.00
165	Fred Snodgrass	150.00	75.00	45.00
166	Tris Speaker	650.00	325.00	195.00
167	Oscar Stanage	150.00	75.00	45.00
168	Charles Stengel	350.00	175.00	100.00
169	Milton Stock	150.00	75.00	45.00
170	Amos Strunk	150.00	75.00	45.00
171	"Zeb" Terry	150.00	75.00	45.00
172	"Jeff" Tesreau	150.00	75.00	45.00
173	Chester Thomas	150.00	75.00	45.00
174	Fred Toney	150.00	75.00	45.00
175	Terry Turner	150.00	75.00	45.00
176	George Tyler	150.00	75.00	45.00
177	Jim Vaughn	150.00	75.00	45.00
178	Bob Veach	150.00	75.00	45.00
179	Oscar Vitt	150.00	75.00	45.00
180	Hans Wagner	3,500	1,750	1,050
181	Clarence Walker	150.00	75.00	45.00
182	Jim Walsh	150.00	75.00	45.00
183	Al Walters	150.00	75.00	45.00
184	W. Wambsganss	150.00	75.00	45.00
185	Buck Weaver	1,000	500.00	300.00
186	Carl Weilman	150.00	75.00	45.00
187	Zack Wheat	350.00	175.00	100.00
188	Geo. Whitted	150.00	75.00	45.00
189	Joe Wilhoit	150.00	75.00	45.00
190	Claude Williams	750.00	375.00	225.00
191	Fred Williams	150.00	75.00	45.00
192	Art Wilson	150.00	75.00	45.00
193	Lawton Witt	150.00	75.00	45.00
194	Joe Wood	150.00	75.00	45.00
195	William Wortman	150.00	75.00	45.00
196	Steve Yerkes	150.00	75.00	45.00
197	Earl Yingling	150.00	75.00	45.00
198	"Pep" (Ralph) Young	150.00	75.00	45.00
199	Rollie Zeider	150.00	75.00	45.00
200	Henry Zimmerman	150.00	75.00	45.00

1921 Standard Biscuit (D350-3)

It is unknown to what extent this scarcest of the three Standard Biscuit advertising issues actually parallels the E121 Series of 80, on which American Caramel Co. backs are more commonly found. This uncertainty contributes to the relatively low premium value (about 2X) attached to the Standard Biscuit versions. Backs have been seen in two styles; one mentions "80 to the set," the other mentions "contains 80 photographs." Cards are printed in black-and-white in a size of about 2" x 3-1/4". A checklist has been started here in an effort to better understand the issue.

PREMIUM: 2X

(3)	Jim Bagby
(4a)	J. Franklin Baker
(12)	Max Carey (Hands at hips.)
(14)	Ty Cobb (Throwing, looking front.)
(15b)	Ty Cobb (Throwing, looking right, manager on front.)
(16)	Eddie Collins
(19)	Dave Davenport
(37)	Tom Griffith
(40)	John Henry
(41)	Clarence Hodge
(52)	James Johnston
(61)	Al Mamaux
(62)	"Rabbit" Maranville
(83)	Eppa Rixey, Jr.
(86)	Babe Ruth
(90)	Ray Schalk
(103)	Chester Thomas
(109)	Jim Vaughn (Dark cap.)
(113)	Oscar Vitt
(116)	Zach Wheat
(120)	Joe Wood

1910 Standard Caramel Co. (E93)

BASE BALL STARS
This card is one of a set of 30 stars from original photographs
1. AMES, New York National
2. BENDER, Phila. American
3. BROWN, Chicago National
4. COLLINS, Phila. American
5. CHANCE, Chicago National
6. COVELESKIE, Cincinnati Nat'l
7. CHASE, New York American
8. COBB, Detroit American
9. CLARKE, Pittsburg National
10. DELEHANTY, Detroit American
11. DONOVAN, Detroit American
12. DOOIN, Philadelphia National
13. EVERS, Chicago National
14. GIBSON, Pittsburg National
15. GRIFFITH, Cincinnati National
16. JENNINGS, Detroit American
17. JONES, Detroit American
18. JOSS, Cleveland American
19. LAJOIE, Cleveland American
20. LEACH, Pittsburg National
21. MATHEWSON, N. Y. National
22. McGRAW, New York National
23. PHILLIPPI, Pittsburg National
24. PLANK, Philadelphia American
25. PASTORIUS, Brooklyn Nat'l
26. TINKER, Chicago National
27. WADDELL, St. Louis American
28. WAGNER, Pittsburg National
29. WILTSE, New York National
30. CY. YOUNG, Cleveland Amer.
Manufactured only by Standard Caramel Co., Lancaster, Pa.

This 30-card set issued in 1910 by Standard Caramel Co. of Lancaster, Pa., is closely related to several other candy sets from this period which share the same format and, in many cases, the same player poses. The cards measure 1-1/2" x 2-3/4" and utilize tinted black-and-white player photos. The back of each card contains an alphabetical checklist of the set plus a line indicating it was manufactured by Standard Caramel Co., Lancaster, Pa. The set carries the ACC designation of E93.

		NM	EX	VG
Complete Set (30):		100,000	40,000	20,000
Common Player:		1,500	600.00	300.00
(1)	Red Ames	1,500	600.00	300.00
(2)	Chief Bender	3,000	1,200	600.00
(3)	Mordecai Brown	3,000	1,200	600.00
(4)	Frank Chance	3,000	1,200	600.00
(5)	Hal Chase	2,200	880.00	440.00
(6)	Fred Clarke	3,000	1,200	600.00
(7)	Ty Cobb	15,000	6,000	3,000
(8)	Eddie Collins	3,000	1,200	600.00
(9)	Harry Coveleskie (Coveleski)	1,500	600.00	300.00
(10)	Jim Delehanty	2,000	1,000	500.00
(11)	Wild Bill Donovan	1,500	600.00	300.00
(12)	Red Dooin	1,500	600.00	300.00
(13)	Johnny Evers	3,000	1,200	600.00
(14)	George Gibson	1,500	600.00	300.00
(15)	Clark Griffith	3,000	1,200	600.00
(16)	Hugh Jennings	3,000	1,200	600.00
(17)	Davy Jones	1,500	600.00	300.00
(18)	Addie Joss	3,300	1,320	660.00
(19)	Nap Lajoie	3,000	120.00	600.00
(20)	Tommy Leach	1,500	600.00	300.00
(21)	Christy Mathewson	8,000	3,200	1,600
(22)	John McGraw	3,000	1,200	600.00
(23)	Jim Pastorious	1,500	600.00	300.00
(24)	Deacon Phillippi (Phillippe)	1,500	600.00	300.00
(25)	Eddie Plank	5,000	2,000	1,000
(26)	Joe Tinker	3,000	1,200	600.00
(27)	Rube Waddell	3,000	1,200	600.00
(28)	Honus Wagner	12,000	4,800	2,400
(29)	Hooks Wiltse	1,500	600.00	300.00
(30)	Cy Young	8,000	3,500	1,750

1960-70s Stan Musial & Biggie's Restaurant

These black-and-white photocards were prepared for Musial's use while glad-handing patrons at his St. Louis eatery. The pictures have a facsimile autograph. A "Compliments of . . ." message is printed in the bottom border. Backs are blank.

		NM	EX	VG
(1)	Stan Musial (Batting pose, 5" x 7".)	10.00	5.00	3.00
(2)	Stan Musial (Batting pose, 3-1/2" x 5-1/2".)	10.00	5.00	3.00
(3)	Stan Musial (Standing w/glove, 5" x 7".)	10.00	5.00	3.00

1952 Star-Cal Decals Type 1

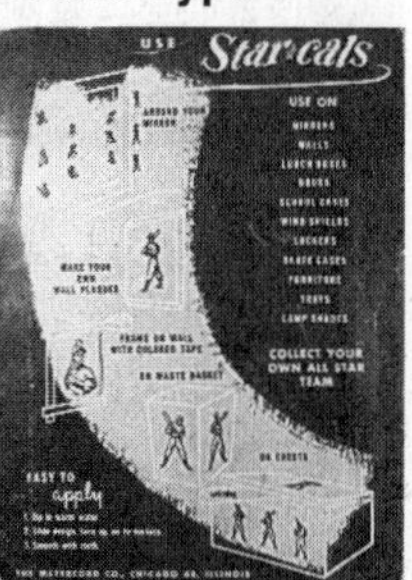

The Meyercord Co., of Chicago issued two sets of baseball player decals in 1952. The Type I Star-Cal Decal set consists of 68 different major leaguers, each pictured on a large (4-1/8" x 6-1/8") decal. The player's name and facsimile autograph appear on the decal, along with the decal number listed on the checklist here. Values shown are for decals complete with outer directions envelope.

		NM	EX	VG
Complete Set (68):		7,500	3,750	2,250
Common Player:		45.00	22.50	13.50
70A	Allie Reynolds	50.00	25.00	15.00
70B	Ed Lopat	50.00	25.00	15.00
70C	Yogi Berra	200.00	100.00	60.00
70D	Vic Raschi	50.00	25.00	15.00
70E	Jerry Coleman	45.00	22.50	13.50
70F	Phil Rizzuto	110.00	55.00	35.00
70G	Mickey Mantle	1,750	875.00	525.00
71A	Mel Parnell	45.00	22.50	13.50
71B	Ted Williams	400.00	200.00	120.00
71C	Ted Williams	400.00	200.00	120.00
71D	Vern Stephens	45.00	22.50	13.50
71E	Billy Goodman	45.00	22.50	13.50
71F	Dom DiMaggio	50.00	25.00	15.00
71G	Dick Gernert	45.00	22.50	13.50
71H	Hoot Evers	45.00	22.50	13.50
72A	George Kell	50.00	25.00	15.00
72B	Hal Newhouser	50.00	25.00	15.00
72C	Hoot Evers	45.00	22.50	13.50
72D	Vic Wertz	45.00	22.50	13.50
72E	Fred Hutchinson	45.00	22.50	13.50
72F	Johnny Groth	45.00	22.50	13.50
73A	Al Zarilla	45.00	22.50	13.50
73B	Billy Pierce	45.00	22.50	13.50
73C	Eddie Robinson	45.00	22.50	13.50
73D	Chico Carrasquel	50.00	25.00	15.00
73E	Minnie Minoso	50.00	25.00	15.00
73F	Jim Busby	45.00	22.50	13.50
73G	Nellie Fox	55.00	27.50	16.50
73H	Sam Mele	45.00	22.50	13.50
74A	Larry Doby	55.00	27.50	16.50
74B	Al Rosen	50.00	25.00	15.00
74C	Bob Lemon	55.00	27.00	16.50
74D	Jim Hegan	45.00	22.50	13.50
74E	Bob Feller	90.00	45.00	27.00
74F	Dale Mitchell	45.00	22.50	13.50
75A	Ned Garver	45.00	22.50	13.50
76A	Gus Zernial	45.00	22.50	13.50
76B	Ferris Fain	45.00	22.50	13.50

76C	Bobby Shantz	45.00	22.50	13.50
77A	Richie Ashburn	60.00	30.00	18.00
77B	Ralph Kiner	55.00	27.50	16.50
77C	Curt Simmons	45.00	22.50	13.50
78A	Bobby Thomson	55.00	27.50	16.50
78B	Alvin Dark	45.00	22.50	13.50
78C	Sal Maglie	45.00	22.50	13.50
78D	Larry Jansen	45.00	22.50	13.50
78E	Willie Mays	425.00	210.00	125.00
78F	Monte Irvin	55.00	27.50	16.50
78G	Whitey Lockman	45.00	22.50	13.50
79A	Gil Hodges	90.00	45.00	27.00
79B	Pee Wee Reese	110.00	55.00	35.00
79C	Roy Campanella	110.00	55.00	35.00
79D	Don Newcombe	55.00	27.50	16.50
79E	Duke Snider	110.00	55.00	35.00
79F	Preacher Roe	50.00	25.00	15.00
79G	Jackie Robinson	350.00	175.00	105.00
80A	Eddie Miksis	45.00	22.50	13.50
80B	Dutch Leonard	45.00	22.50	13.50
80C	Randy Jackson	45.00	22.50	13.50
80D	Bob Rush	45.00	22.50	13.50
80E	Hank Sauer	45.00	22.50	13.50
80F	Phil Cavarretta	45.00	22.50	13.50
80G	Warren Hacker	45.00	22.50	13.50
81A	Red Schoendienst	55.00	27.50	16.50
81B	Wally Westlake	45.00	22.50	13.50
81C	Cliff Chambers	45.00	22.50	13.50
81D	Enos Slaughter	55.00	27.50	16.50
81E	Stan Musial	275.00	135.00	85.00
81F	Stan Musial	275.00	135.00	85.00
81G	Jerry Staley	45.00	22.50	13.50

1952 Star-Cal Decals Type 2

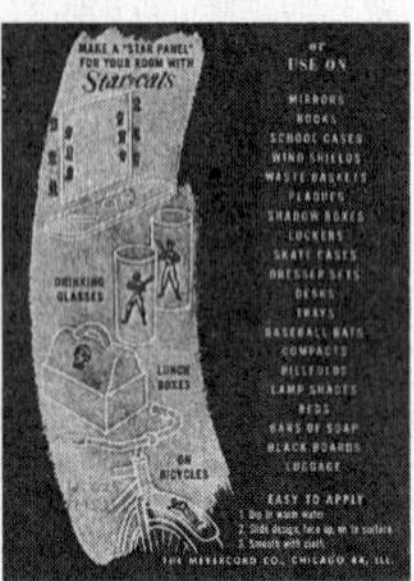

Also produced by Chicago's Meyercord Co. in 1952, these Star-Cal Decals are similar to the Type I variety, except the decal sheets are smaller, measuring 4-1/8" x 3-1/16", and each sheet features two players instead of one.

		NM	EX	VG
Complete Set (32):		3,000	1,500	900.00
Common Player:		45.00	22.50	13.50
84A	Vic Raschi, Allie Reynolds	80.00	40.00	25.00
84B	Yogi Berra, Ed Lopat	165.00	80.00	50.00
84C	Jerry Coleman, Phil Rizzuto	135.00	65.00	40.00
85A	Ted Williams, Ted Williams	450.00	225.00	135.00
85B	Dom DiMaggio, Mel Parnell	60.00	30.00	18.00
85C	Billy Goodman, Vern Stephens	45.00	22.50	13.50
86A	George Kell, Hal Newhouser	80.00	40.00	25.00
86B	Hoot Evers, Vic Wertz	45.00	22.50	13.50
86C	Johnny Groth, Fred Hutchinson	45.00	22.50	13.50
87A	Eddie Robinson, Eddie Robinson	45.00	22.50	13.50
87B	Chico Carrasquel, Minnie Minoso	60.00	30.00	18.00
87C	Nellie Fox, Billy Pierce	65.00	32.50	20.00
87D	Jim Busby, Al Zarilla	45.00	22.50	13.50
88A	Jim Hegan, Bob Lemon	65.00	32.50	20.00
88B	Larry Doby, Bob Feller	165.00	80.00	50.00
88C	Dale Mitchell, Al Rosen	45.00	22.50	13.50
89A	Ned Garver, Ned Garver	45.00	22.50	13.50
89B	Ferris Fain, Gus Zernial	45.00	22.50	13.50
89C	Richie Ashburn, Richie Ashburn	75.00	37.50	22.00
89D	Ralph Kiner, Ralph Kiner	75.00	37.50	22.00
90A	Monty Irvin, Willie Mays (Monte)	300.00	150.00	90.00
90B	Larry Jansen, Sal Maglie	45.00	22.50	13.50
90C	Al Dark, Bobby Thomson	55.00	27.50	16.50
91A	Gil Hodges, Pee Wee Reese	225.00	110.00	65.00
91B	Roy Campanella, Jackie Robinson	300.00	150.00	90.00
91C	Preacher Roe, Duke Snider	200.00	100.00	60.00
92A	Phil Cavarretta, Dutch Leonard	45.00	22.50	13.50
92B	Randy Jackson, Eddie Miksis	45.00	22.50	13.50
92C	Bob Rush, Hank Sauer	45.00	22.50	13.50
93A	Stan Musial, Stan Musial	350.00	175.00	105.00
93B	Red Schoendienst, Enos Slaughter	90.00	45.00	27.00
93C	Cliff Chambers, Wally Westlake	45.00	22.50	13.50

1976 Star Market Red Sox

Only Red Sox are featured in this set issued by the Star Market chain in the Boston area. Players are photographed hatless in jerseys which feature the Massachusetts Bicentennial logo. Pictures measure 5-7/8" x 9" and have a 3/16" white border all around. A facsimile autograph is printed on the front in black. Backs are blank. The unnumbered pictures are checklisted here alphabetically.

		NM	EX	VG
Complete Set (16):		35.00	17.50	10.00
Common Player:		1.50	.75	.45
(1)	Rick Burleson	1.50	.75	.45
(2)	Reggie Cleveland	1.50	.75	.45
(3)	Cecil Cooper	2.50	1.25	.70
(4)	Denny Doyle	1.50	.75	.45
(5)	Dwight Evans	2.50	1.25	.70
(6)	Carlton Fisk	5.00	2.50	1.50
(7)	Tom House	1.50	.75	.45
(8)	Fergie Jenkins	4.00	2.00	1.25
(9)	Bill Lee	1.50	.75	.45
(10)	Fred Lynn	2.50	1.25	.70
(11)	Rick Miller	1.50	.75	.45
(12)	Rico Petrocelli	2.50	1.25	.70
(13)	Jim Rice	3.50	1.75	1.00
(14)	Luis Tiant	2.50	1.25	.70
(15)	Rick Wise	1.50	.75	.45
(16)	Carl Yastrzemski	10.00	5.00	3.00

1928 Star Player Candy

Little is known about the origin of this set. The producer is not identified, but experienced collectors generally refer to it as the Star Player Candy set, possibly because it was distributed with a product of that name. The cards measure 1-7/8" x 2-7/8", are sepia-toned, blank-backed and printed on thin paper. The player's name (but no team designation) appears in the border below the photo in brown capital letters. To date the checklist of baseball players numbers 73, but more may exist, and cards of football players have also been found.

		NM	EX	VG
Common Player:		900.00	360.00	180.00
(1)	Dave Bancroft	2,000	800.00	400.00
(2)	Emile Barnes	900.00	360.00	180.00
(3)	L.A. Blue	900.00	360.00	180.00
(4)	Garland Buckeye	900.00	360.00	180.00
(5)	George Burns	900.00	360.00	180.00
(6)	Guy T. Bush	900.00	360.00	180.00
(7)	Owen T. Carroll	900.00	360.00	180.00
(8)	Chalmer Cissell	900.00	360.00	180.00
(9)	Ty Cobb	20,000	8,000	4,000
(10)	Gordon Cochrane	2,000	800.00	400.00
(11)	Richard Coffman	900.00	360.00	180.00
(12)	Eddie Collins	2,000	800.00	400.00
(13)	Stanley Coveleskie (Coveleski)	2,000	800.00	400.00
(14)	Hugh Critz	900.00	360.00	180.00
(15)	Hazen Cuyler	2,000	800.00	400.00
(16)	Charles Dressen	900.00	360.00	180.00
(17)	Joe Dugan	900.00	360.00	180.00
(18)	Elwood English	900.00	360.00	180.00
(19)	Bib Falk (Bibb)	900.00	360.00	180.00
(20)	Ira Flagstead	900.00	360.00	180.00
(21)	Bob Fothergill	900.00	360.00	180.00
(22)	Frank T. Frisch	2,000	800.00	400.00
(23)	Foster Ganzel	900.00	360.00	180.00
(24)	Lou Gehrig	22,500	9,000	4,500
(25)	Chas. Gihringer (Gehringer)	2,000	800.00	400.00
(26)	George Gerken	900.00	360.00	180.00
(27)	Grant Gillis	900.00	360.00	180.00
(28)	Miguel Gonzales (Gonzalez)	900.00	360.00	180.00
(29)	Sam Gray	900.00	360.00	180.00
(30)	Chas. J. Grimm	900.00	360.00	180.00
(31)	Robert M. Grove	2,250	900.00	450.00
(32)	Chas. J. Hafey	2,000	800.00	400.00
(33)	Jesse Haines	2,000	800.00	400.00
(34)	Chas. L. Hartnett	2,000	800.00	400.00
(35)	Clifton Heathcote	900.00	360.00	180.00
(36)	Harry Heilmann	2,000	800.00	400.00
(37)	John Heving	900.00	360.00	180.00
(38)	Waite Hoyt	2,000	800.00	400.00
(39)	Chas. Jamieson	900.00	360.00	180.00
(40)	Joe Judge	900.00	360.00	180.00
(41)	Willie Kamm	900.00	360.00	180.00
(42)	George Kelly	2,000	800.00	400.00
(43)	Tony Lazzeri	2,000	800.00	400.00
(44)	Adolfo Luque	900.00	360.00	180.00
(45)	Ted Lyons	2,000	800.00	400.00
(46)	Hugh McMullen	900.00	360.00	180.00
(47)	Bob Meusel	900.00	360.00	180.00
(48)	Wilcey Moore (Wilcy)	900.00	360.00	180.00
(49)	Ed C. Morgan	900.00	360.00	180.00
(50)	Buddy Myer	900.00	360.00	180.00
(51)	Herb Pennock	2,000	800.00	400.00
(52)	Everett Purdy	900.00	360.00	180.00
(53)	William Regan	900.00	360.00	180.00
(54)	Eppa Rixey	2,000	800.00	400.00
(55)	Charles Root	900.00	360.00	180.00
(56)	Jack Rothrock	900.00	360.00	180.00
(57)	Harold Ruel (Herold)	900.00	360.00	180.00
(58)	Babe Ruth	32,500	13,000	6,500
(59)	Wally Schang	900.00	360.00	180.00
(60)	Joe Sewell	2,000	800.00	400.00
(61)	Luke Sewell	900.00	360.00	180.00
(62)	Joe Shaute	900.00	360.00	180.00
(63)	George Sisler	2,000	800.00	400.00
(64)	Tris Speaker	2,500	1,000	500.00
(65)	Riggs Stephenson	900.00	360.00	180.00
(66)	Jack Tavener	900.00	360.00	180.00
(67)	Al Thomas	900.00	360.00	180.00
(68)	Harold J. Traynor	2,000	800.00	400.00
(69)	George Uhle	900.00	360.00	180.00
(70)	Dazzy Vance	2,000	800.00	400.00
(71)	Cy Williams	900.00	360.00	180.00
(72)	Ken Williams	900.00	360.00	180.00
(73)	Lewis R. Wilson	2,000	800.00	400.00

1929 Star Player Candy

The actual year of issue can only be approximated from the write-ups on the cards' backs. Only two players can be checklisted thus far, though the numbers on the backs would seem to indicate an issue of at least 32. The 1-7/8" x 2-7/8" cards are printed in sepia with wide borders on front and player name below the photo. Unlike the 1928 Star Candy issue, this series has printed and numbered backs.

		NM	EX	VG
21	Babe Ruth	20,000	10,000	6,000
32	Lou Gehrig	22,500	11,250	6,750

1892 J.U. Stead Studio Cabinets

Only members of the N.Y. Giants are thus far known in this series of cabinet cards from New York City photographer J.U. Stead. About standard cabinet size (4-1/2" x 6-1/2") the cards have black-and-white portraits. On the thick cardboard mount's bottom border is the name and address of the studio. Backs repeat that information and have three lines of type at bottom extolling "Instantaneous Photographs." Unless the player name was pencilled on the card by a previous owner, the players are not otherwise identified. Fortunately, the plethora of contemporary issues from other sources makes matching names and photos fairly easy. The issue date attributed is speculative.

	NM	EX	VG
Common Player:	3,000	1,500	900.00
Roger Connor	6,000	2,000	1,200
Willie Keeler	10,000	3,750	2,250
Mike Tiernan	3,000	1,500	900.00

1909-16 Max Stein Postcards (PC758)

Issued over a period of several years these sepia-toned photo postcards depict most of the stars of the day. In standard 3-1/2" x 5-1/2" format they have typical postcard indicia on the back. Some cards have been seen with a "United States Pub." legend on the back. Most of the subjects played in Stein's Chicago location. Besides the baseball players listed here, the series also included "Statesmen, etc., Aeroplanes and Flyers, Fighters, etc.," and, "Dancing Girls," according to advertising found on the back of some cards. Wholesale prices when issued were 35 cents per hundred, $2.75 per thousand.

		NM	EX	VG
	Common Player:	200.00	80.00	40.00
	Advertising Back: 1.5X			
(1)	Ping Bodie	200.00	80.00	40.00
(2)	Frank Chance	400.00	160.00	80.00
(3)	Ty Cobb	2,250	900.00	450.00
(4)	Johnny Evers	400.00	160.00	80.00
(5)	Rube Marquard	400.00	160.00	80.00
(6)	Christy Mathewson	1,200	480.00	240.00
(7)	John McGraw	400.00	160.00	80.00
(8)	Chief Meyers	200.00	80.00	40.00
(9)	Marty O'Toole	200.00	80.00	40.00
(10)	Wildfire Schulte	200.00	80.00	40.00
(11)	Tris Speaker	450.00	180.00	90.00
(12)	Jake Stahl	200.00	80.00	40.00
(13)	Jim Thorpe	2,500	1,000	500.00
(14)	Joe Tinker	400.00	160.00	80.00
(15)	Honus Wagner	1,500	600.00	300.00
(16)	Ed Walsh	400.00	160.00	80.00
(17)	Buck Weaver	1,750	700.00	350.00
(18)	Joe Wood	200.00	80.00	40.00
(19)	Heinie Zimmerman	200.00	80.00	40.00
(20)	Chicago Cubs (Jimmy Archer, Roger Bresnahan, Johnny Evers, Mike Hechinger, Tom Needham)	200.00	80.00	40.00
(21)	Chicago Cubs (Bill Clymer, Wilbur Good, Ward Miller, Mike Mitchell, Wildfire Schulte)	200.00	80.00	40.00
(22)	Boston Americans Team Photo	200.00	80.00	40.00
(23)	1916 Chicago Cubs Team Photo	300.00	120.00	60.00
(24)	1916 Cincinnati Reds Team Photo	200.00	80.00	40.00
(25)	New York Nationals Team Photo	200.00	80.00	40.00
(26)	Johnny Coulon, Jess Willard (Boxers)	200.00	80.00	40.00

1904 Stenzel's Rooter Buttons

The extent of the checklist for this rare Cincinnati 1-1/4" pinback celluloid button issue is unknown. According to a paper label found in the back of well-preserved examples, the buttons are the issue of "Jake Stenzel B.B. Exchange located opposite Ball Park." Fronts have "STENZEL'S ROOTER BUTTON" at top and a player portrait photo at center with last name and position below.

		NM	EX	VG
(1)	Mike Donlin	750.00	375.00	225.00
(2)	Bob Ewing	600.00	300.00	180.00
(3)	Jack Harper	600.00	300.00	180.00
(4)	Joe Kelley	1,750	875.00	525.00
(5)	Win Kellum	600.00	300.00	180.00
(6)	Peaches O'Neil (O'Neill)	900.00	450.00	275.00
(7)	Heinie Pietz (Peitz)	600.00	300.00	180.00
(8)	Admiral Schlei	600.00	300.00	180.00
(9)	Cy Seymour	600.00	300.00	180.00
(10)	Jack Sutthoff	600.00	300.00	180.00
(11)	Sam Woodruff	600.00	300.00	180.00

1911 Stevens Firearms Philadelphia Athletics

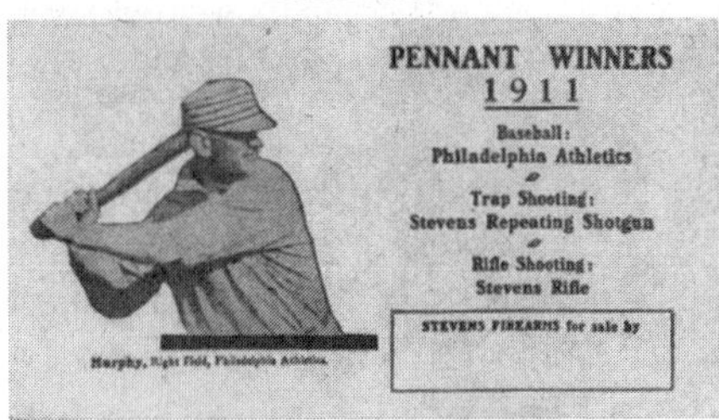

Riding on the coattails of the A's American League pennant (and eventual World Series) win, Stevens Firearms created this set of cards to promote its rifles and shotguns. About 6-3/16" x 3-7/16", the blank-back, medium-weight cards have a black-and-white posed action photo at left with the player identified by name, position and team. At top right is advertising, at bottom-right is a box where local retailers' addresses could be stamped or printed. Cards have been seen printed on several different colors of stock. In actuality, these are really ink blotters from the old fountain pen days as opposed to "cards." Other players are likely to have been issued.

		NM	EX	VG
	Common Player:	1,000	500.00	300.00
(1)	Frank Baker	1,500	750.00	450.00
(2)	Chief Bender	1,500	750.00	450.00
(3)	Bris Lord	1,000	500.00	300.00
(4)	Connie Mack	1,500	750.00	450.00
(5)	Danny Murphy	1,000	500.00	300.00
(6)	Rube Oldring	1,000	500.00	300.00
(7)	Harry Davis	1,000	500.00	300.00
(8)	Ira Thomas	1,000	500.00	300.00

1888-1889 Stevens Studio Australian Tour Cabinets

After the 1888 season, Albert Spalding toured to Australia with a group of major league players to increase interest in baseball Down Under (as well as to increase demand for the baseball equipment his firm sold). Prior to departure, many of the players gathered at Stevens Studio in Chicago for portrait photos to be made into cabinet cards, presumably for sale as souvenirs on the junket. Vignetted portraits present the players in their Sunday best. Below a decorative dividing line is "Spalding's Australian Base Ball Tour / Stevens 1888-89 Chicago." Back has a large ornate ad for the photographer. The full extent of the checklist is unknown.

	NM	EX	VG
Common Player:	3,500	1,750	1,000
Cap Anson	10,000	5,000	3,000
Jim Donnelly	3,500	1,750	1,000
Jim Fogarty	3,500	1,750	1,000
Ned Williamson	3,500	1,750	1,000

1890 Stevens Studio Chicago Pirates Cabinets

The single-season players' revolution that spawned the Players League is marked with this issue of cabinet cards from the Stevens studio of Chicago. Only members of the Chicago Pirates P.L. team have been seen in this issue, all in street clothes and identified by a name penned on the front. A composite-photo card is also known, providing reasonable expectations that more individual player cabinets will be discovered. The studio advertising on back is ornately printed in maroon.

		NM	EX	VG
	Common Player:	1,800	900.00	550.00
(1)	Charles Comiskey	3,850	1,925	1,100
(2)	Hugh Duffy	3,850	1,925	1,100
(3)	Silver Flint	1,800	900.00	550.00
(4)	Jimmy Ryan	1,800	900.00	550.00
(5)	Team Composite	10,000	5,000	3,000

1890 Stevens Studio Chicago White Stockings Cabinets

Cabinet cards in the standard 4-1/4" x 6-1/2" format of at least three of the 1890 Chicago National Leaguers, as well as a team composite picture are known to have been produced by the Stevens Art Studio. Fronts have vignetted portraits of the players in dress clothes. Backs have an ornate ad for the photographer, which includes the note, "DUPLICATES OF THIS PICTURE CAN BE HAD AT ANY TIME, AT REDUCED RATES." Player names are often found penned on the cards, as the photos are otherwise unidentified. At least two styles of cardboard mounts are seen with the White Stockings cabinets. The extent of the checklist is also unknown.

		NM	EX	VG
	Common Player:	1,800	900.00	550.00
(1)	Cap Anson	8,250	4,125	2,475
(2)	Mike Sullivan	1,800	900.00	550.00
(3)	Pat Wright	1,800	900.00	550.00
(4)	1890 Chicago White Stockings	4,400	2,200	1,325

1941 St. Louis Browns Team Issue (W753)

Measuring 2-1/8" x 2-5/8", this unnumbered boxed set of cards features the St. Louis Browns in black-and-white portrait photos on front. Backs have player name, position and personal and statistical information. There are also cards for coaches and one of the the club's two managers that season (Luke Sewell). As the Browns weren't much of a team in 1941 (or in most seasons for that matter) there are no major stars in the set. The issue was cataloged as W753 in the ACC.

		NM	EX	VG
	Complete Set (30):	850.00	425.00	250.00
	Common Player:	35.00	17.50	10.00
	Box:	75.00	35.00	25.00
(1)	Johnny Allen	35.00	17.50	10.00
(2)	Elden Auker (Eldon)	35.00	17.50	10.00
(3)	Donald L Barnes	35.00	17.50	10.00
(4)	Johnny Berardino	50.00	25.00	15.00
(5)	George Caster	35.00	17.50	10.00
(6)	Harlond Benton (Darky) Clift	35.00	17.50	10.00
(7)	Roy J. Cullenbine	35.00	17.50	10.00
(8)	William O. DeWitt (Vice-President)	35.00	17.50	10.00
(9)	Roberto Estalella	35.00	17.50	10.00
(10)	Richard Benjamin (Rick) Ferrell	60.00	30.00	18.00
(11)	Dennis W. Galehouse	35.00	17.50	10.00
(12)	Joseph L. Grace	35.00	17.50	10.00
(13)	Frank Grube	35.00	17.50	10.00
(14)	Robert A. Harris	35.00	17.50	10.00
(15)	Donald Henry Heffner	35.00	17.50	10.00
(16)	Fred Hofmann	35.00	17.50	10.00
(17)	Walter Franklin Judnich	35.00	17.50	10.00
(18)	John Henry (Jack) Kramer	35.00	17.50	10.00
(19)	Chester (Chet) Laabs	35.00	17.50	10.00
(20)	John Lucadello	35.00	17.50	10.00
(21)	George Hartley McQuinn	35.00	17.50	10.00
(22)	Robert Cleveland Muncrief, Jr.	35.00	17.50	10.00
(23)	John Niggeling	35.00	17.50	10.00
(24)	Fred Raymond (Fritz) Ostermueller	35.00	17.50	10.00
(25)	James Luther (Luke) Sewell	35.00	17.50	10.00
(26)	Alan Cochran Strange (Cochrane)	35.00	17.50	10.00
(27)	Robert Virgil (Bob) Swift	35.00	17.50	10.00
(28)	James W. (Zack) Taylor	35.00	17.50	10.00
(29)	William Felix (Bill) Trotter	35.00	17.50	10.00
(30)	Presentation Card/Order Form	10.00	5.00	3.00

1952 St. Louis Browns Postcards

This series of player postcards features black-and-white glossy photos on front with a white border. The cards bear no player identification and were evidently intended for use in honoring fan requests for autographs. The 1952 issue can be differentiated from that of 1953 by the absence of a stamp box on back. The unnumbered cards are checklisted here alphabetically, though the list may be incomplete. Multiple player names indicate known different poses.

	NM	EX	VG
Common Player:	50.00	25.00	15.00
(1) Tommy Byrne	50.00	25.00	15.00
(2) Bob Cain	50.00	25.00	15.00
(3) Bob Cain	50.00	25.00	15.00
(4) Clint Courtney	50.00	25.00	15.00
(5) Jim Delsing	50.00	25.00	15.00
(6) Jim Dyck	50.00	25.00	15.00
(7) Jim Dyck	50.00	25.00	15.00
(8) Ned Garver	50.00	25.00	15.00
(9) Marty Marion	60.00	30.00	18.00
(10) Cass Michaels	50.00	25.00	15.00
(11) Bob Nieman	50.00	25.00	15.00
(12) Satchel Paige	200.00	100.00	60.00
(13) Duane Pillette	50.00	25.00	15.00
(14) Jim Rivera	50.00	25.00	15.00
(15) Bill Veeck	75.00	37.00	22.00
(16) Bobby Young	50.00	25.00	15.00

1953 St. Louis Browns Postcards

This series of player postcards from the team's final year in St. Louis features black-and-white glossy photos on front with a white border. The cards bear no player identification and were evidently intended for use in honoring fan requests for autographs. The 1953 issue can be differentiated from that of 1952 by the presence of a stamp box on back identifying the issuer as Deorite Peerless. The unnumbered cards are checklisted here alphabetically though the list is likely incomplete.

	NM	EX	VG
Common Player:	50.00	25.00	15.00
(1) Connie Berry	50.00	25.00	15.00
(2) Mike Blyzka	50.00	25.00	15.00
(3) Harry Brecheen	50.00	25.00	15.00
(4) Bob Cain	50.00	25.00	15.00
(5) Clint Courtney	50.00	25.00	15.00
(6) Jim Dyck	50.00	25.00	15.00
(7) Hank Edwards	50.00	25.00	15.00
(8) Ned Garver	50.00	25.00	15.00
(9) Johnny Groth	50.00	25.00	15.00
(11) Bobo Holloman	50.00	25.00	15.00
(12) Billy Hunter	50.00	25.00	15.00
(13) Dick Kokos	50.00	25.00	15.00
(14) Dick Kryhoski	50.00	25.00	15.00
(15) Max Lanier	50.00	25.00	15.00
(16) Don Larsen	75.00	37.50	22.00
(17) Don Lenhardt	50.00	25.00	15.00
(18) Dick Littlefield	50.00	25.00	15.00
(19) Marty Marion	60.00	30.00	18.00
(21) Babe Martin	50.00	25.00	15.00
(22) Willy Miranda	50.00	25.00	15.00
(23) Les Moss	50.00	25.00	15.00
(24) Bill Norman	50.00	25.00	15.00
(25) Satchel Paigea/Kneeling	200.00	100.00	60.00
(26) Satchel Paige/Pitching	200.00	100.00	60.00
(27) Duane Pillette	50.00	25.00	15.00
(28) Bob Scheffing	50.00	25.00	15.00
(29) Roy Sievers	60.00	30.00	18.00
(31) Marlin Stuart	50.00	25.00	15.00
(32) Virgil Trucks	65.00	32.00	19.50
(33) Bill Veeck	75.00	37.00	22.00
(34) Vic Wertz	50.00	25.00	15.00
(35) Bobby Young	50.00	25.00	12.00

1941 St. Louis Cardinals Team Issue (W754)

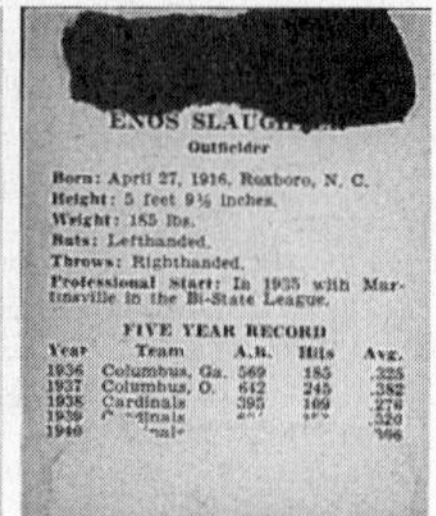

ENOS SLAUGHTER
Outfielder
Born: April 27, 1916, Roxboro, N. C.
Height: 5 feet 9½ inches.
Weight: 185 lbs.
Bats: Lefthanded.
Throws: Righthanded.
Professional Start: In 1935 with Martinsville in the Bi-State League.
FIVE YEAR RECORD

Year	Team	A.B.	Hits	Avg.
1936	Columbus, Ga.	569	185	.325
1937	Columbus, O.	612	245	.382
1938	Cardinals	395	109	.276

A companion set to W753, this time featuring the National League team in St. Louis. Cards measure 2-1/8" x 2-5/8" and are unnumbered. Like the Browns set, this issue features black-and-white portrait photos on front and the individual's name, position and personal and statistical information on back. One interesting addition to the set is a card of Branch Rickey which, coupled with cards of Enos Slaughter and Johnny Mize, gives the set a bit more appeal than the Browns set. ACC designation is W754.

	NM	EX	VG
Complete Set (30):	1,000	500.00	300.00
Common Player:	35.00	17.50	10.00
Box:	75.00	35.00	25.00
(1) Sam Breadon	35.00	17.50	10.00
(2) James Brown	35.00	17.50	10.00
(3) Morton Cooper	35.00	17.50	10.00
(4) William Walker Cooper	35.00	17.50	10.00
(5) Estel Crabtree	35.00	17.50	10.00
(6) Frank Crespi	35.00	17.50	10.00
(7) William Crouch	35.00	17.50	10.00
(8) Miguel Mike Gonzalez	50.00	25.00	15.00
(9) Harry Gumbert	35.00	17.50	10.00
(10) John Hopp	35.00	17.50	10.00
(11) Ira Hutchinson	35.00	17.50	10.00
(12) Howard Krist	35.00	17.50	10.00
(13) Edward E. Lake	35.00	17.50	10.00
(14) Hubert Max Lanier	35.00	17.50	10.00
(15) Gus Mancuso	35.00	17.50	10.00
(16) Martin Marion	55.00	27.50	16.50
(17) Steve Mesner	35.00	17.50	10.00
(18) John Mize	100.00	50.00	30.00
(19) Capt. Terry Moore	50.00	25.00	15.00
(20) Sam Nahem	35.00	17.50	10.00
(21) Don Padgett	35.00	17.50	10.00
(22) Branch Rickey (Vice-President)	60.00	30.00	18.00
(23) Clyde Shoun	35.00	17.50	10.00
(24) Enos Slaughter	100.00	50.00	30.00
(25) William H. (Billy) Southworth	35.00	17.50	10.00
(26) Herman Coaker Triplett	35.00	17.50	10.00
(27) Clyde Buzzy Wares	35.00	17.50	10.00
(28) Lon Warneke	35.00	17.50	10.00
(29) Ernest White	35.00	17.50	10.00
(30) Presentation Card/Order Form	10.00	5.00	3.00

1966 St. Louis Cardinals Busch Stadium Immortals Coins

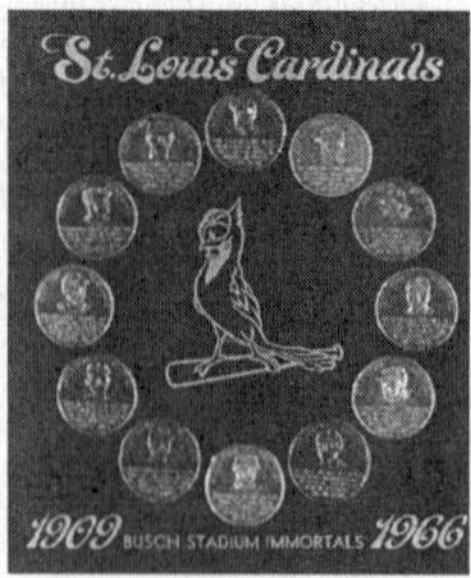

A dozen all-time great Cardinals are included in this set of commemorative medallions. Each 1-1/2" bright bronze "coin" has a portrait and career summary. The coins were issued in a 9" x 10-1/2" cardinal-red cardboard holder with gold logo and graphics.

	NM	EX	VG
Complete Board/Coin Set:	75.00	37.50	22.50
Common Player:	7.50	3.75	2.25
(1) Dizzy Dean	10.00	5.00	3.00
(2) Frank Frisch	7.50	3.75	2.25
(3) Chick Hafey	7.50	3.75	2.25
(4) Jesse Haines	7.50	3.75	2.25
(5) Marty Marion	7.50	3.75	2.25
(6) Joe Medwick	7.50	3.75	2.25
(7) Johnny Mize	7.50	3.75	2.25
(8) Terry Moore	7.50	3.75	2.25
(9) Stan Musial	15.00	7.50	4.50
(10) Red Schoendienst	7.50	3.75	2.25
(11) George Sisler	7.50	3.75	2.25
(12) Enos Slaughter	7.50	3.75	2.25

1953 Stop & Shop Boston Red Sox

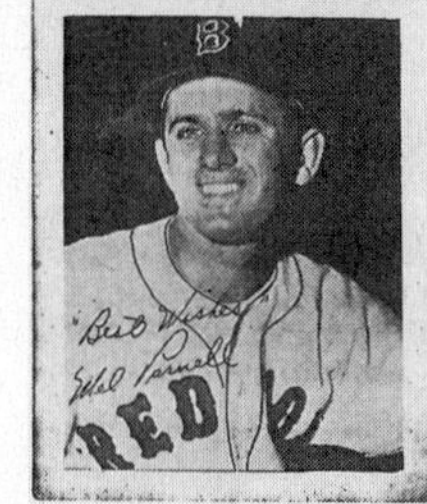

Four of the early 1950s Red Sox appear in this series issued by a Boston grocery chain. The cards may have been distributed in conjunction with players' in-store appearances. The cards measure 3-3/4" x 5" and are printed in black-and-white. A facsimile autograph appears on the front. Backs have the sponsor's advertising. The unnumbered cards are checklisted here alphabetically. See also 1953 First National Super Market Boston Red Sox.

	NM	EX	VG
Complete Set (4):	3,000	1,500	900.00
Common Player:	750.00	375.00	225.00
(1) Billy Goodman	750.00	375.00	225.00
(2) Ellis Kinder	750.00	375.00	225.00
(3) Mel Parnell	750.00	375.00	225.00
(4) Sammy White	750.00	375.00	225.00

1888 Sub Rosa Cigarettes Girl Baseball Players (N508)

(See 1888 Allen & Ginter Girl Baseball Players.)

1916 Successful Farming

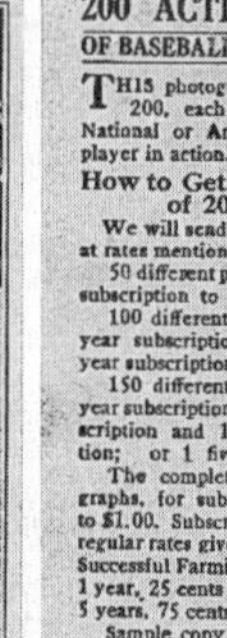

200 ACTION PHOTOS OF BASEBALL STARS FREE

This photograph is one of a set of 200, each showing a famous National or American League star player in action.

How to Get a Complete Set of 200 Photos

We will send photo sets postpaid, at rates mentioned below.

50 different players, for 1 one-year subscription to Successful Farming.

100 different players, for 2 one-year subscriptions; or for 1 three-year subscription.

150 different players, for 3 one-year subscriptions; or 1 one-year subscription and 1 three-year subscription; or 1 five-year subscription.

The complete set of 200 photographs, for subscriptions amounting to $1.00. Subscriptions to be taken at regular rates given below.

Successful Farming subscription rates: 1 year, 25 cents : 3 years, 50 cents 5 years, 75 cents : 7 years, $1.00

Sample copy of Successful Farming sent free on request.

Baseball Photo Dept.
SUCCESSFUL FARMING
DES MOINES : : IOWA

Best known for its use as a promotional medium for The Sporting News (M101-5), this 200-card set can be found with ads on the back for several local and regional businesses. Among them is Successful Farming magazine of Des Moines, Iowa. Type card collectors and superstar collectors can expect to pay a modest premium for individual cards with the magazine's advertising. Cards measure about 1-5/8" x 3" and are printed in black-and-white.

PREMIUM: 2-3X

(See 1916 Sporting News M101-5 for checklist and base card values.)

1976 Sugar Daddy Sports World

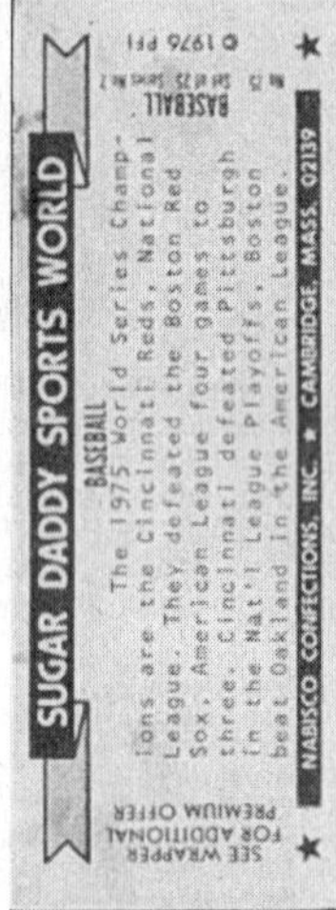

Two baseball related cards were issued as part of this multi-sport candy insert set. Each card is titled "BASEBALL" and they detail the 1974 and 1975 World Series and depict a player - though not naming him - in action. The cards are 1" x 2-3/4" and have a white-bordered color photo on front. Backs include various advertising details.

		NM	EX	VG
Complete Set (25):		60.00	30.00	18.00
12	Pete Rose (Series 1, 1974 World Series)	25.00	12.50	7.50
25	Bobby Murcer (Series 2, 1975 World Series)	17.50	9.00	5.00

1962 Sugardale Weiners

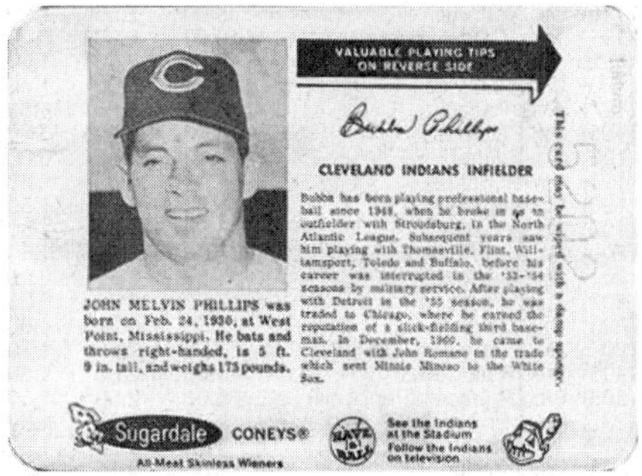

The Sugardale Meats set of black and white cards measure 5-1/8" x 3-3/4". The 22-card set includes 18 Cleveland Indians and four Pittsburgh Pirates players. The Indians cards are numbered from 1-19 with card number 6 not issued. The Pirates cards are lettered from A to D. The card fronts contain a relatively small player photo, with biographical information and Sugardale logo. The backs are printed in red and offer playing tips and another company logo. Card number 10 (Bob Nieman) is considerably more scarce than other cards in the set.

		NM	EX	VG
Complete Set (22):		10,000	4,000	2,000
Common Player:		325.00	130.00	65.00
A	Dick Groat	325.00	130.00	65.00
B	Roberto Clemente	3,250	1,300	650.00
C	Don Hoak	325.00	130.00	65.00
D	Dick Stuart	325.00	130.00	65.00
1	Barry Latman	325.00	130.00	65.00
2	Gary Bell	325.00	130.00	65.00
3	Dick Donovan	325.00	130.00	65.00
4	Frank Funk	325.00	130.00	65.00
5	Jim Perry	325.00	130.00	65.00
6	Not issued			
7	Johnny Romano	325.00	130.00	65.00
8	Ty Cline	325.00	130.00	65.00
9	Tito Francona	325.00	130.00	65.00
10	Bob Nieman/SP	1,200	480.00	240.00
11	Willie Kirkland	325.00	130.00	65.00
12	Woodie Held	325.00	130.00	65.00
13	Jerry Kindall	325.00	130.00	65.00
14	Bubba Phillips	325.00	130.00	65.00
15	Mel Harder	325.00	130.00	65.00
16	Salty Parker	325.00	130.00	65.00
17	Ray Katt	325.00	130.00	65.00
18	Mel McGaha	325.00	130.00	65.00
19	Pedro Ramos	325.00	130.00	65.00

1963 Sugardale Weiners

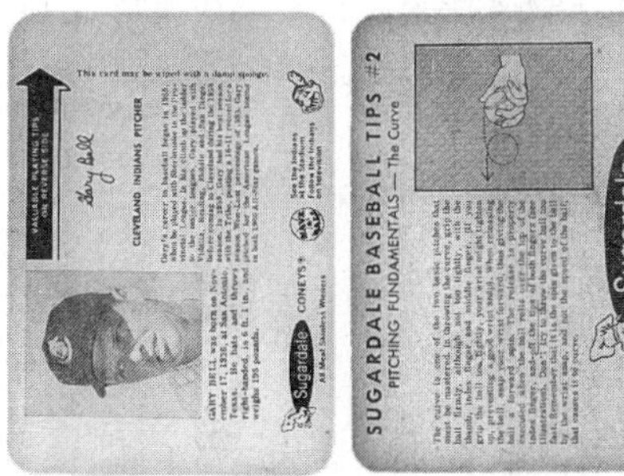

Sugardale Meats again featured Cleveland and Pittsburgh players in its 1963 set, which grew to 31 cards. The black and white cards again measure 5-1/8" x 3-3/4", and consist of 28 Indians and five Pirates players. Card formats are virtually identical to the 1962 cards, with the only real difference being the information included in the player biographies. The cards are numbered 1-38, with numbers 6, 21, 22 and 29-32 not issued. Cards for Bob Skinner (#35) and Jim Perry (#5) are scarce as these two players were traded during the season and their cards withdrawn from distribution. The red card backs again offer playing tips.

		NM	EX	VG
Complete Set (31):		10,000	4,000	2,000
Common Player:		325.00	130.00	65.00
A	Don Cardwell	325.00	130.00	65.00
B	Robert R. Skinner/SP	600.00	240.00	120.00
C	Donald B. Schwall	325.00	130.00	65.00
D	Jim Pagliaroni	325.00	130.00	65.00
E	Dick Schofield	325.00	130.00	65.00
1	Barry Latman	325.00	130.00	65.00
2	Gary Bell	325.00	130.00	65.00
3	Dick Donovan	325.00	130.00	65.00
4	Joe Adcock	400.00	160.00	80.00
5	Jim Perry/SP	600.00	240.00	120.00
6	Not Issued			
7	Johnny Romano	325.00	130.00	65.00
8	Mike de la Hoz	325.00	130.00	65.00
9	Tito Francona	325.00	130.00	65.00
10	Gene Green	325.00	130.00	65.00
11	Willie Kirkland	325.00	130.00	65.00
12	Woodie Held	325.00	130.00	65.00
13	Jerry Kindall	325.00	130.00	65.00
14	Max Alvis	325.00	130.00	65.00
15	Mel Harder	325.00	130.00	65.00
16	George Strickland	325.00	130.00	65.00
17	Elmer Valo	325.00	130.00	65.00
18	Birdie Tebbetts	325.00	130.00	65.00
19	Pedro Ramos	325.00	130.00	65.00
20	Al Luplow	325.00	130.00	65.00
21	Not Issued			
22	Not Issued			
23	Jim Grant	325.00	130.00	65.00
24	Victor Davalillo	325.00	130.00	65.00
25	Jerry Walker	325.00	130.00	65.00
26	Sam McDowell	400.00	160.00	80.00
27	Fred Whitfield	325.00	130.00	65.00
28	Jack Kralick	325.00	130.00	65.00
29	Not Issued			
30	Not Issued			
31	Not Issued			
32	Not Issued			
33	Bob Allen	325.00	130.00	65.00

1933 Sulima Cigarettes

This is one of several early 1930s German cigarette cards to picture Babe Ruth. In this case he is pictured on the 1-5/8" x 2-3/8" black-and-white card with American comedic actor Harold Lloyd. The card is part of a numbered set of 272 movie star cards. Backs are printed in German. The card is identical in format to the Josetti cigarette cards.

		NM	EX	VG
151	Babe Ruth, Harold Lloyd	1,100	550.00	330.00

1936 Sunday Advertiser Sport Stamps

(See 1936 Boston American Sport Stamps.)

1974 Sun-Glo Pop Al Kaline

This 2-1/4" x 4-1/2" card was issued as an attachment to bottles of soda pop. The blank-back card features a modishly dressed portrait of the former Tigers great and his endorsement for the soda. Cards are printed in black on various brightly colored backgrounds.

	NM	EX	VG
Al Kaline	6.00	3.00	1.75

1969 Sunoco Cubs/Brewers Pins

Fans in Southern Wisconsin and Northern Illinois could acquire 1-1/8" lithographed steel baseball player pins of the Cubs and Brewers at participating Sunoco gas stations. The blue-and-white (Cubs) or red-and-white (Brewers) pins have black-and-white player portrait photos at center on which cap logos have been removed. The Brewers pins are somewhat scarcer than those of the Cubs.

		NM	EX	VG
Complete Set (18):		100.00	50.00	30.00
Common Player:		4.00	2.00	1.25
	Chicago Cubs Team Set:	65.00	32.50	20.00
(1)	Ernie Banks	25.00	12.50	7.50
(2)	Glenn Beckert	4.00	2.00	1.25
(3)	Jim Hickman	4.00	2.00	1.25
(4)	Randy Hundley	4.00	2.00	1.25
(5)	Ferguson Jenkins	7.50	3.75	2.25
(6)	Don Kessinger	6.00	3.00	1.75
(7)	Joe Pepitone	6.00	3.00	1.75
(8)	Ron Santo	10.00	5.00	3.00
(9)	Billy Williams	12.50	6.25	3.75
	Milwaukee Brewers Team Set:	50.00	25.00	15.00
(1)	Tommy Harper	6.00	3.00	1.75
(2)	Mike Hegan	6.00	3.00	1.75
(3)	Lew Krausse	6.00	3.00	1.75
(4)	Ted Kubiak	6.00	3.00	1.75
(5)	Marty Pattin	6.00	3.00	1.75
(6)	Phil Roof	6.00	3.00	1.75
(7)	Ken Sanders	6.00	3.00	1.75
(8)	Ted Savage	6.00	3.00	1.75
(9)	Danny Walton	6.00	3.00	1.75

1931 Sun Pictures Photo Kits

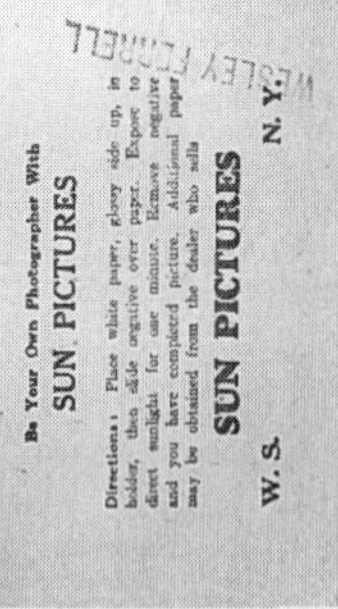

One of several contemporary kits for do-it-yourself production of photos, this issue was produced in New York City by a firm identified only as "W.S." A complete outfit consists of a 4-1/4" x 2-1/2" pink or kraft paper envelope with the name of the subject inside rubber-stamped on one end, a film negative, a piece of photo paper and a stand for producing/displaying the photo. The negative and resulting print measure 2-5/16" x 3-1/4". The set is listed in the American Card Catalog as W626. Prices shown are for complete kits; individual pieces would be prorated, with the negative the most valuable component. Because individual prints can be easily made even today, they have little collectible value. Only the baseball players are listed here.

		NM	EX	VG
Common Player Kit:		125.00	62.00	37.50
(1)	George Earnshaw	125.00	62.00	38.00
(2)	Wesley Ferrell	125.00	62.00	37.00
(3)	Lefty Grove	250.00	125.00	75.00
(4)	Leo Hartnett	225.00	112.00	67.00
(5)	Tony Lazzeri	250.00	125.00	75.00
(6)	Herb Pennock	225.00	112.00	67.00
(7)	Babe Ruth	2,400	1,200	725.00
(8)	Al Simmons	225.00	112.00	67.00
(9)	Dazzy Vance	225.00	112.00	67.00
(10)	Hack Wilson	250.00	125.00	75.00

1960s Sunny Ayr Farms Johnny Callison

In the absence of other player cardsm, it is impossible to date this issue any more precisely than Callison's tenure

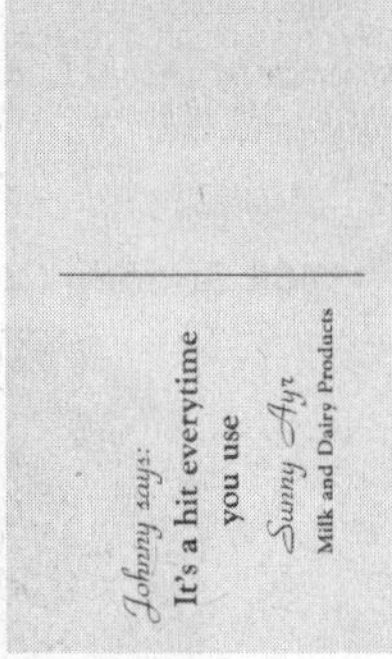

with the Phillies which encompassed the 1960s. The 3-1/2" x 5-1/2" black-and-white card had a facsimile autograph on front. The divided back is printed in red.

	NM	EX	VG
Johnny Callison	100.00	50.00	30.00

1970 Superballs

Manufactured by Chemtoy (though not credited on the balls), these high-bouncing hard rubber balls are composed of see-through material in which is imbedded a disc with a baseball player's portrait and identification. About 1-1/8" in diameter, the balls identify the player by name, team and position and include a four-digit number. In this checklist, the balls are listed alphabetically for lack of access to a complete list of the actual numbers. It is also possible the checklist in incomplete.

		NM	EX	VG
Complete Set (286):		1,650	825.00	500.00
Common Player:		5.00	2.50	1.50
(1)	Hank Aaron	40.00	20.00	12.00
(2)	Jerry Adair	5.00	2.50	1.50
(3)	Tommie Agee	5.00	2.50	1.50
(4)	Bernie Allen	5.00	2.50	1.50
(5)	Lloyd Allen	5.00	2.50	1.50
(6)	Gene Alley	5.00	2.50	1.50
(7)	Bob Allison	5.00	2.50	1.50
(8)	Sandy Alomar	5.00	2.50	1.50
(9)	Jesus Alou	5.00	2.50	1.50
(10)	Matty Alou	5.00	2.50	1.50
(11)	Max Alvis	5.00	2.50	1.50
(12)	Mike Andrews	5.00	2.50	1.50
(13)	Luis Aparicio	17.50	8.75	5.25
(14)	Jose Arcia	5.00	2.50	1.50
(15)	Bob Aspromonte	5.00	2.50	1.50
(16)	Jose Azcue	5.00	2.50	1.50
(17)	Bob Bailey	5.00	2.50	1.50
(18)	Jack Baldschun	5.00	2.50	1.50
(19)	Sal Bando	5.00	2.50	1.50
(20)	Ernie Banks	25.00	12.50	7.50
(21)	John Bateman	5.00	2.50	1.50
(22)	Glenn Beckert	5.00	2.50	1.50
(23)	Mark Belanger	5.00	2.50	1.50
(24)	Ken Berry	5.00	2.50	1.50
(25)	Paul Blair	5.00	2.50	1.50
(26)	Curt Blefary	5.00	2.50	1.50
(27)	John Boccabella	5.00	2.50	1.50
(28)	Bobby Bonds	5.00	2.50	1.50
(29)	John Boozer	5.00	2.50	1.50
(30)	Ken Boswell	5.00	2.50	1.50
(31)	Clete Boyer	5.00	2.50	1.50
(32)	Gene Brabender	5.00	2.50	1.50
(33)	Ron Brand	5.00	2.50	1.50
(34)	Jim Brewer	5.00	2.50	1.50
(35)	Johnny Briggs	5.00	2.50	1.50
(36)	Nelson Briles	5.00	2.50	1.50
(37)	Ed Brinkman	5.00	2.50	1.50
(38)	Lou Brock	17.50	8.75	5.25
(39)	Don Buford	5.00	2.50	1.50
(40)	Tom Burgmeier	5.00	2.50	1.50
(41)	Bill Butler	5.00	2.50	1.50
(42)	Johnny Callison	5.00	2.50	1.50
(43)	Bert Campaneris	5.00	2.50	1.50
(44)	Jim Campanis	5.00	2.50	1.50
(45)	Chris Cannizzaro	5.00	2.50	1.50
(46)	Jose Cardenal	5.00	2.50	1.50
(47)	Leo Cardenas	5.00	2.50	1.50
(48)	Rod Carew	20.00	10.00	6.00
(49)	Clay Carroll	5.00	2.50	1.50
(50)	Rico Carty	5.00	2.50	1.50
(51)	Paul Casanova	5.00	2.50	1.50
(52)	Norm Cash	10.00	5.00	3.00
(53)	Orlando Cepeda	17.50	8.75	5.25
(54)	Billy Champion	5.00	2.50	1.50
(55)	Dean Chance	5.00	2.50	1.50
(56a)	Roberto Clemente (Red insert.)	60.00	30.00	18.00
(56b)	Roberto Clemente (Blue insert.)	50.00	25.00	15.00
(57)	Tony Cloninger	5.00	2.50	1.50
(58)	Nate Colbert	5.00	2.50	1.50
(59)	Joe Coleman	5.00	2.50	1.50
(60)	Kevin Collins	5.00	2.50	1.50
(61)	Wayne Comer	5.00	2.50	1.50
(62)	Tony Conigliaro	10.00	5.00	3.00
(63)	Billy Cowan	5.00	2.50	1.50
(64)	Casey Cox	5.00	2.50	1.50
(65)	Willie Crawford	5.00	2.50	1.50
(66)	Mike Cuellar	5.00	2.50	1.50
(67)	Al Dark	5.00	2.50	1.50
(68)	Vic Davalillo	5.00	2.50	1.50
(69)	Jim Davenport	5.00	2.50	1.50
(70)	Willie Davis	5.00	2.50	1.50
(71)	Tommy Dean	5.00	2.50	1.50
(72)	Larry Dierker	5.00	2.50	1.50
(73)	Dick Dietz	5.00	2.50	1.50
(74)	Moe Drabowsky	5.00	2.50	1.50
(75)	Leo Durocher	13.50	6.75	4.00
(76)	Johnny Edwards	5.00	2.50	1.50
(77)	Dock Ellis	5.00	2.50	1.50
(78)	Dick Ellsworth	5.00	2.50	1.50
(79)	Mike Epstein	5.00	2.50	1.50
(80)	Andy Etchebarren	5.00	2.50	1.50
(81)	Ron Fairly	5.00	2.50	1.50
(82)	Al Ferrera	5.00	2.50	1.50
(83)	Rollie Fingers	13.50	6.75	4.00
(84)	Mike Fiore	5.00	2.50	1.50
(85)	Eddie Fisher	5.00	2.50	1.50
(86)	Jack Fisher	5.00	2.50	1.50
(87)	Ray Fosse	5.00	2.50	1.50
(88)	Bill Freehan	5.00	2.50	1.50
(89)	Jim Fregosi	5.00	2.50	1.50
(90)	Tito Fuentes	5.00	2.50	1.50
(91)	Vern Fuller	5.00	2.50	1.50
(92)	Woody Fryman	5.00	2.50	1.50
(93)	Len Gabrielson	5.00	2.50	1.50
(94)	Gary Gentry	5.00	2.50	1.50
(95)	Jake Gibbs	5.00	2.50	1.50
(96)	Russ Gibson	5.00	2.50	1.50
(97)	Billy Grabarkewitz	5.00	2.50	1.50
(98)	Dick Green	5.00	2.50	1.50
(99)	Tom Griffin	5.00	2.50	1.50
(100)	Jerry Grote	5.00	2.50	1.50
(101)	Tom Haller	5.00	2.50	1.50
(102)	Steve Hamilton	5.00	2.50	1.50
(103)	Ron Hansen	5.00	2.50	1.50
(104)	Tommy Harmon	5.00	2.50	1.50
(105)	Tommy Harper	5.00	2.50	1.50
(106)	Bud Harrelson	5.00	2.50	1.50
(107)	Jim Ray Hart	5.00	2.50	1.50
(108)	Richie Hebner	5.00	2.50	1.50
(109)	Mike Hedlund	5.00	2.50	1.50
(110)	Mike Hegan	5.00	2.50	1.50
(111)	Tommy Helms	5.00	2.50	1.50
(112)	Angel Hermoso	5.00	2.50	1.50
(113)	Ed Herrmann	5.00	2.50	1.50
(114)	Mike Hershberger	5.00	2.50	1.50
(115)	Jim Hickman	5.00	2.50	1.50
(116)	Jim Hicks	5.00	2.50	1.50
(117)	Chuck Hinton	5.00	2.50	1.50
(118)	Larry Hisle	5.00	2.50	1.50
(119)	Gil Hodges	13.50	6.75	4.00
(120)	Ken Holtzman	5.00	2.50	1.50
(121)	Joel Horlen	5.00	2.50	1.50
(122)	Willie Horton	5.00	2.50	1.50
(123)	Ralph Houk	5.00	2.50	1.50
(124)	Frank Howard	7.50	3.75	2.25
(125)	Randy Hundley	5.00	2.50	1.50
(126)	Ron Hunt	5.00	2.50	1.50
(127)	Jim Hunter	13.50	6.75	4.00
(128)	Steve Huntz	5.00	2.50	1.50
(129)	Al Jackson	5.00	2.50	1.50
(130)	Reggie Jackson	35.00	17.50	10.50
(131)	Pat Jarvis	5.00	2.50	1.50
(132)	Julian Javier	5.00	2.50	1.50
(133)	Tommy John	10.00	5.00	3.00
(134)	Dave Johnson	5.00	2.50	1.50
(135)	Jerry Johnson	5.00	2.50	1.50
(136)	Jay Johnstone	5.00	2.50	1.50
(137)	Cleon Jones	5.00	2.50	1.50
(138)	Dalton Jones	5.00	2.50	1.50
(139)	Jim Kaat	7.50	3.75	2.25
(140)	Al Kaline	20.00	10.00	6.00
(141)	Dick Kelley	5.00	2.50	1.50
(142)	Pat Kelly	5.00	2.50	1.50
(143)	John Kennedy	5.00	2.50	1.50
(144)	Joe Keough	5.00	2.50	1.50
(145)	Don Kessinger	5.00	2.50	1.50
(146)	Harmon Killebrew	20.00	10.00	6.00
(147)	Clay Kirby	5.00	2.50	1.50
(148)	Darold Knowles	5.00	2.50	1.50
(149)	Jerry Koosman	5.00	2.50	1.50
(150)	Andy Kosco	5.00	2.50	1.50
(151)	Ed Kranepool	5.00	2.50	1.50
(152)	Lew Krausse	5.00	2.50	1.50
(153)	Coco Laboy	5.00	2.50	1.50
(154)	Hal Lanier	5.00	2.50	1.50
(155)	George Lauzerique	5.00	2.50	1.50
(156)	Denny Lemaster	5.00	2.50	1.50
(157)	Bob Locker	5.00	2.50	1.50
(158)	Mickey Lolich	5.00	2.50	1.50
(159)	Jim Lonborg	5.00	2.50	1.50
(160)	Mike Lum	5.00	2.50	1.50
(161)	Jim Maloney	5.00	2.50	1.50
(162)	Juan Marichal	13.50	6.75	4.00
(163)	Dal Maxvill	5.00	2.50	1.50
(164)	Carlos May	5.00	2.50	1.50
(165)	Lee May	5.00	2.50	1.50
(166)	Willie Mays	40.00	20.00	12.00
(167)	Bill Mazeroski	17.50	8.75	5.25
(168)	Dick McAuliffe	5.00	2.50	1.50
(169)	Mike McCormick	5.00	2.50	1.50
(170)	Willie McCovey	20.00	10.00	6.00
(171)	Denny McLain	5.00	2.50	1.50
(172)	Jerry McNertney	5.00	2.50	1.50
(173)	Bill Melton	5.00	2.50	1.50
(174)	Denis Menke	5.00	2.50	1.50
(175)	Jim Merritt	5.00	2.50	1.50
(176)	Gene Michael	5.00	2.50	1.50
(177)	Pete Mikkelsen	5.00	2.50	1.50
(178)	Felix Millan	5.00	2.50	1.50
(179)	Norm Miller	5.00	2.50	1.50
(180)	Don Mincher	5.00	2.50	1.50
(181)	George Mitterwald	5.00	2.50	1.50
(182)	Rick Monday	5.00	2.50	1.50
(183)	Don Money	5.00	2.50	1.50
(184)	Bob Moose	5.00	2.50	1.50
(185)	Dave Morehead	5.00	2.50	1.50
(186)	Joe Morgan	20.00	10.00	6.00
(187)	Bobby Mercer (Murcer)	7.50	3.75	2.25
(188)	Ivan Murrell	5.00	2.50	1.50
(189)	Phil Niekro	13.50	6.75	4.00
(190)	Jim Northrup	5.00	2.50	1.50
(191)	Tony Oliva	10.00	5.00	3.00
(192)	Al Oliver	5.00	2.50	1.50
(193)	Claude Osteen	5.00	2.50	1.50
(194)	Jose Pagan	5.00	2.50	1.50
(195)	Jim Pagliaroni	5.00	2.50	1.50
(196)	Jim Palmer	20.00	10.00	6.00
(197)	Lowell Palmer	5.00	2.50	1.50
(198)	Milt Pappas	5.00	2.50	1.50
(199)	Marty Pattin	5.00	2.50	1.50
(200)	Roberto Pena	5.00	2.50	1.50
(201)	Joe Pepitone	7.50	3.75	2.25
(202)	Tony Perez	17.50	8.75	5.25
(203)	Gaylord Perry	13.50	6.75	4.00
(204)	Jim Perry	5.00	2.50	1.50
(205)	Fritz Peterson	5.00	2.50	1.50
(206)	Rico Petroceli (Petrocelli)	5.00	2.50	1.50
(207)	Lefty Phillips	5.00	2.50	1.50
(208)	Tom Phoebus	5.00	2.50	1.50
(209)	Lou Piniella	7.50	3.75	2.25
(210)	Vada Pinson	7.50	3.75	2.25
(211)	Boog Powell	10.00	5.00	3.00
(212)	Frank Quillici	5.00	2.50	1.50
(213)	Doug Rader	5.00	2.50	1.50
(214)	Ron Reed	5.00	2.50	1.50
(215)	Rich Reese	5.00	2.50	1.50
(216)	Rick Reichardt	5.00	2.50	1.50
(217)	Phil Regan	5.00	2.50	1.50
(218)	Roger Repoz	5.00	2.50	1.50
(219)	Juan Rios	5.00	2.50	1.50
(220)	Brooks Robinson	20.00	10.00	6.00
(221)	Frank Robinson	20.00	10.00	6.00
(222)	Cookie Rojas	5.00	2.50	1.50
(223)	Rich Rollins	5.00	2.50	1.50
(224)	Pete Rose	40.00	20.00	12.00
(225)	Gary Ross	5.00	2.50	1.50
(226)	Joe Rudi	5.00	2.50	1.50
(227)	Manny Sanguillen	5.00	2.50	1.50
(228)	Jose Santiago	5.00	2.50	1.50
(229)	Ron Santo	10.00	5.00	3.00
(230)	Tom Satriano	5.00	2.50	1.50
(231)	Richie Scheinblum	5.00	2.50	1.50
(232)	Red Schoendienst	13.50	6.75	4.00
(233)	George Scott	5.00	2.50	1.50
(234)	Tom Seaver	20.00	10.00	6.00
(235)	Norm Siebern	5.00	2.50	1.50
(236)	Sonny Siebert	5.00	2.50	1.50
(237)	Duke Sims	5.00	2.50	1.50
(238)	Tommie Sisk	5.00	2.50	1.50
(239)	Ted Sizemore	5.00	2.50	1.50
(240)	Mayo Smith	5.00	2.50	1.50
(241)	Reggie Smith	5.00	2.50	1.50
(242)	Willie Smith	5.00	2.50	1.50
(243)	Russ Snyder	5.00	2.50	1.50
(244)	Joe Sparma	5.00	2.50	1.50
(245)	Lee Stange	5.00	2.50	1.50
(246)	Mickey Stanley	5.00	2.50	1.50
(247)	Willie Stargell	17.50	8.75	5.25
(248)	Rusty Staub	7.50	3.75	2.25
(249)	Ron Stone	5.00	2.50	1.50
(250)	Bill Stoneman	5.00	2.50	1.50
(251)	Mel Stottlemyre	5.00	2.50	1.50
(252)	Ed Stroud	5.00	2.50	1.50
(253)	Bill Sudakis	5.00	2.50	1.50
(254)	Gary Sutherland	5.00	2.50	1.50
(255)	Ron Swoboda	5.00	2.50	1.50
(256)	Carl Taylor	5.00	2.50	1.50
(257)	Tony Taylor	5.00	2.50	1.50
(258)	Bob Tillman	5.00	2.50	1.50
(259)	Bobby Tolan	5.00	2.50	1.50
(260)	Cesar Tovar	5.00	2.50	1.50
(261)	Jeff Torborg	5.00	2.50	1.50
(262)	Joe Torre	10.00	5.00	3.00
(263)	Hector Torres	5.00	2.50	1.50
(264)	Tom Tresh	7.50	3.75	2.25
(265)	Ted Uhlaender	5.00	2.50	1.50
(266)	Del Unser	5.00	2.50	1.50
(267)	Bob Veale	5.00	2.50	1.50
(268)	Zoilo Versalles	5.00	2.50	1.50
(269)	Bill Voss	5.00	2.50	1.50
(270)	Pete Ward	5.00	2.50	1.50
(271)	Greg Washburn	5.00	2.50	1.50
(272)	Eddie Watt	5.00	2.50	1.50
(273)	Ramon Webster	5.00	2.50	1.50
(274)	Al Weis	5.00	2.50	1.50
(275)	Roy White	5.00	2.50	1.50
(276)	Billy Williams	17.50	8.75	5.25
(277)	Ted Williams	30.00	15.00	9.00
(278)	Walt Williams	5.00	2.50	1.50
(279)	Billy Wilson	5.00	2.50	1.50
(280)	Don Wilson	5.00	2.50	1.50
(281)	Earl Wilson	5.00	2.50	1.50
(282)	Rick Wise	5.00	2.50	1.50
(283)	Bobby Wine	5.00	2.50	1.50
(284)	Wilbur Wood	5.00	2.50	1.50
(285)	Woody Woodward	5.00	2.50	1.50
(286)	Billy Wynne	5.00	2.50	1.50

1980 Superstar

This collectors' issue, probably produced by Card Collectors Closet in Springfield, Mass., included up to five cards

each of the most famous former players. The 2-1/2" x 3-1/2" cards have black-and-white photos on front, with yellow, white and blue graphics. Backs are in black-and-white with career narrative. The set sold originally for $3.50.

		NM	EX	VG
Complete Set (45):		20.00	10.00	6.00
Common Player:		.75	.35	.20
1	Babe Ruth	1.25	.60	.40
2	Roberto Clemente	1.00	.50	.30
3	Roberto Clemente	1.00	.50	.30
4	Roberto Clemente	1.00	.50	.30
5	Lou Gehrig, Joe DiMaggio	.75	.35	.20
6	Mickey Mantle, Roger Maris	1.75	.90	.50
7	Roger Maris, Yogi Berra, Mickey Mantle	1.25	.60	.40
8	Whitey Ford, Sandy Koufax	.75	.35	.20
9	Babe Ruth	1.25	.60	.40
10	Roger Maris, Mickey Mantle	1.75	.90	.50
11	Ted Williams, Stan Musial, Willie Mays	.75	.35	.20
12	Mickey Mantle, Hank Aaron	1.25	.60	.40
13	Sandy Koufax	.75	.35	.20
14	Sandy Koufax	.75	.35	.20
15	Thurman Munson	.75	.35	.20
16	Sandy Koufax	.75	.35	.20
17	Sandy Koufax	.75	.35	.20
18	Willie Mays	.75	.35	.20
19	Willie Mays	.75	.35	.20
20	Willie Mays	.75	.35	.20
21	Willie Mays	.75	.35	.20
22	Ted Williams	.75	.35	.20
23	Ted Williams	.75	.35	.20
24	Ted Williams	.75	.35	.20
25	Ted Williams	.75	.35	.20
26	Lou Gehrig	.75	.35	.20
27	Lou Gehrig	.75	.35	.20
28	Lou Gehrig	.75	.35	.20
29	Lou Gehrig	.75	.35	.20
30	Mickey Mantle	2.00	1.00	.60
31	Mickey Mantle	2.00	1.00	.60
32	Mickey Mantle	2.00	1.00	.60
33	Mickey Mantle	2.00	1.00	.60
34	Hank Aaron	.75	.35	.20
35	Joe DiMaggio	.75	.35	.20
36	Joe DiMaggio	.75	.35	.20
37	Joe DiMaggio	.75	.35	.20
38	Joe DiMaggio	.75	.35	.20
39	Roberto Clemente	1.00	.50	.30
40	Babe Ruth	1.25	.60	.40
41	Babe Ruth	1.25	.60	.40
42	Babe Ruth	1.25	.60	.40
43	Hank Aaron	.75	.35	.20
44	Hank Aaron	.75	.35	.20
45	Hank Aaron	.75	.35	.20

1970 Super Valu Minnesota Twins

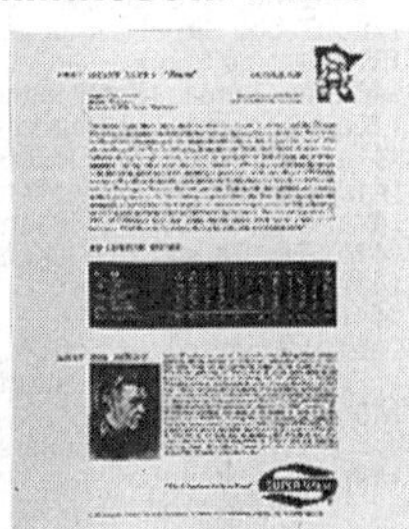

One of many Minnesota Twins regional issues from the team's first decade, this set of player portraits was painted by noted celebrity artist John Wheeldon. Individual player pictures were given away at Super Valu grocery stores. The premiums feature large portraits and smaller action pictures, painted in pastels, against a pastel background. A facsimile autograph is printed below the pictures and the player's name is printed in the bottom border. At 7-3/4" x 9-3/8", the Twins portraits are somewhat smaller than similar contemporary issues. Backs are printed in black-and-white and include a self-portrait and biography of the artist. Player information includes biographical bits, a lengthy career summary and complete major and minor league stats. Team and sponsor logo are also included on the unnumbered card backs. The set is checklisted here alphabetically.

		NM	EX	VG
Complete Set (12):		90.00	45.00	27.50
Common Player:		6.00	3.00	1.75
(1)	Brant Alyea	6.00	3.00	1.75
(2)	Leo Cardenas	6.00	3.00	1.75
(3)	Rod Carew	20.00	10.00	6.00
(4)	Jim Kaat	9.00	4.50	2.75
(5)	Harmon Killebrew	20.00	10.00	6.00
(6)	George Mitterwald	6.00	3.00	1.75
(7)	Tony Oliva	9.00	4.50	2.75
(8)	Ron Perranoski	6.00	3.00	1.75
(9)	Jim Perry	6.00	3.00	1.75
(10)	Rich Reese	6.00	3.00	1.75
(11)	Luis Tiant	7.50	3.75	2.25
(12)	Cesar Tovar	6.00	3.00	1.75

1874 Suppards & Fennemore Cabinets

Only members of the hometown 1874 Athletics (National Association) have been reported in this issue of cabinet cards from the Philadelphia studio. The 4-1/4" x 6-1/2" cards have full-length poses on front. Backs carry an ornate ad for the photographer. The players are not identified on the cards, unless an earlier owner has written the name. Thus far the team's most famous player, Cap Anson, has not been reported.

		NM	EX	VG
Common Player:		3,750	1,875	1,125
(1)	Joe Battin (Bat on shoulder.)	3,750	1,875	1,125
(2)	John Clapp (Cap on floor to his right.)	3,750	1,875	1,125
(3)	Wes Fisler (Bat at right side, no cap on floor.)	3,750	1,875	1,125
(4)	Dick McBride (Ball in hands at waist.)	3,750	1,875	1,125
(5)	Mike McGeary (Bat in crook of arm.)	3,750	1,875	1,125
(6)	John McMullin (Bat at his left, cap on floor at left.)	3,750	1,875	1,125
(7)	Tim Murnane (Bat at his right, cap on floor at left.)	4,050	2,025	1,200

1966 Swap-N-Save Album

While this 4" x 9" album pictures 1965 and 1966 Topps cards in full color on front and back, it is not connected with Topps. The album's interior pages feature die-cuts which allow the central panel to be removed so both front and back of each card can be viewed. Informational pages include team rosters.

	NM	EX	VG
Album:	80.00	40.00	20.00

1909-11 Sweet Caporal

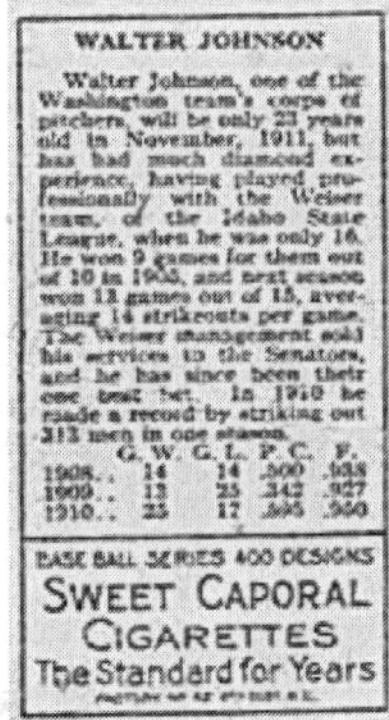

Among the most common of the American Tobacco Co. brands advertising on the backs of 1909-11 T206 and 1911 T205 is Sweet Caporal. T206s can be found with factory designations of No. 25, No. 30, No. 42 (overprinted), No. 649 and No. 649 (overprinted). In T205, Sweet Cap backs can be found printed in red (no factory number, or No. 42) or black, No. 25, No. 42.

(See T205, T206.)

1909-12 Sweet Caporal Domino Discs (PX7)

Domino Discs, distributed by Sweet Caporal Cigarettes from 1909 to 1912, are among the more obscure 20th Century tobacco issues. Although the disc set contains many of the same players - some even pictured in the same poses - as the later Sweet Caporal pin set, the discs have always lagged behind the pins in collector appeal. The Domino Discs, so called because each disc has a large, white domino printed on the back, measure approximately 1-1/8" in diameter and are made of thin cardboard surrounded by a metal rim. The fronts of the discs contain a player portrait set against a background of either red, green or blue. The words "Sweet Caporal Cigarettes" appear on the front along with the player's last name and team. There are 129 different major leaguers featured in the set. Each player can be found with two picture variations involving uniform or cap details, or just the size of the portrait. Also known to exist as part of the set is a disc which pictures a generic player and contains the words "Home Team" against a red background on one side and "Visiting Team" with a green background on the reverse. Because each of the players can theoretically be found in two pictures, with three different background colors and with varying numbers of dots on the dominoes, there is almost an impossible number of variations available. Collectors, however, generally collect the discs without regard to background color or domino arrangement. The Domino Disc set was assigned the designation PX7 in the American Card Catalog.

		NM	EX	VG
Complete Set (129):		10,000	5,000	3,000
Common Player:		60.00	30.00	18.00
(1)	Red Ames	60.00	30.00	18.00
(2)	Jimmy Archer	60.00	30.00	18.00
(3)	Jimmy Austin	60.00	30.00	18.00
(4)	Home Run Baker	130.00	65.00	40.00
(5)	Neal Ball	60.00	30.00	18.00
(6)	Cy Barger	60.00	30.00	18.00
(7)	Jack Barry	60.00	30.00	18.00
(8)	Johnny Bates	60.00	30.00	18.00
(9)	Beals Becker	60.00	30.00	18.00
(10)	George Bell	60.00	30.00	18.00
(11)	Chief Bender	130.00	65.00	40.00
(12)	Bill Bergen	60.00	30.00	18.00
(13)	Bob Bescher	60.00	30.00	18.00
(14)	Joe Birmingham	60.00	30.00	18.00
(15)	Roger Bresnahan	130.00	65.00	40.00
(16)	Al Bridwell	60.00	30.00	18.00
(17)	Mordecai Brown	130.00	65.00	40.00
(18)	Bobby Byrne	60.00	30.00	18.00
(19)	Nixey Callahan	60.00	30.00	18.00
(20)	Howie Camnitz	60.00	30.00	18.00
(21)	Bill Carrigan	60.00	30.00	18.00
(22)	Frank Chance	130.00	65.00	40.00
(23)	Hal Chase	60.00	30.00	18.00
(24)	Ed Cicotte	60.00	30.00	18.00
(25)	Fred Clarke	130.00	65.00	40.00
(26a)	Ty Cobb ("D" on cap.)	600.00	300.00	180.00
(26b)	Ty Cobb (No "D" on cap.)	600.00	300.00	180.00
(27)	Eddie Collins	130.00	65.00	40.00
(28)	Doc Crandall	60.00	30.00	18.00
(29)	Birdie Cree	60.00	30.00	18.00
(30)	Bill Dahlen	60.00	30.00	18.00
(31)	Jim Delahanty	60.00	30.00	18.00
(32)	Art Devlin	60.00	30.00	18.00
(33)	Josh Devore	60.00	30.00	18.00
(34)	Red Dooin	60.00	30.00	18.00
(35)	Mickey Doolan	60.00	30.00	18.00
(36)	Patsy Dougherty	60.00	30.00	18.00
(37)	Tom Downey	60.00	30.00	18.00
(38)	Larry Doyle	60.00	30.00	18.00
(39)	Louis Drucke	60.00	30.00	18.00
(40)	Clyde Engle	60.00	30.00	18.00
(41)	Tex Erwin	60.00	30.00	18.00
(42)	Steve Evans	60.00	30.00	18.00
(43)	Johnny Evers	130.00	65.00	40.00
(44)	Cecil Ferguson	60.00	30.00	18.00
(45)	Russ Ford	60.00	30.00	18.00
(46)	Art Fromme	60.00	30.00	18.00
(47)	Harry Gaspar	60.00	30.00	18.00
(48)	George Gibson	60.00	30.00	18.00
(49)	Eddie Grant	65.00	32.50	20.00
(50)	Clark Griffith	130.00	65.00	40.00
(51)	Bob Groom	60.00	30.00	18.00
(52)	Bob Harmon	60.00	30.00	18.00
(53)	Topsy Hartsel	60.00	30.00	18.00
(54)	Arnold Hauser	60.00	30.00	18.00
(55)	Dick Hoblitzell	60.00	30.00	18.00
(56)	Danny Hoffman	60.00	30.00	18.00
(57)	Miller Huggins	130.00	65.00	40.00
(58)	John Hummel	60.00	30.00	18.00
(59)	Hugh Jennings	130.00	65.00	40.00
(60)	Walter Johnson	350.00	175.00	100.00
(61)	Ed Karger	60.00	30.00	18.00
(62a)	Jack Knight (Yankees)	60.00	30.00	18.00
(62b)	Jack Knight (Senators)	60.00	30.00	18.00
(63)	Ed Konetchy	60.00	30.00	18.00
(64)	Harry Krause	60.00	30.00	18.00
(65)	Frank LaPorte	60.00	30.00	18.00
(66)	Nap Lajoie	130.00	65.00	40.00
(67)	Tommy Leach	60.00	30.00	18.00
(68)	Sam Leever	60.00	30.00	18.00
(69)	Lefty Leifield	60.00	30.00	18.00

(70)	Paddy Livingston	60.00	30.00	18.00
(71)	Hans Lobert	60.00	30.00	18.00
(72)	Harry Lord	60.00	30.00	18.00
(73)	Nick Maddox	60.00	30.00	18.00
(74)	Sherry Magee	60.00	30.00	18.00
(75)	Rube Marquard	130.00	65.00	40.00
(76)	Christy Mathewson	400.00	200.00	120.00
(77)	Al Mattern	60.00	30.00	18.00
(78)	George McBride	60.00	30.00	18.00
(79)	John McGraw	130.00	65.00	40.00
(80)	Harry McIntire	60.00	30.00	18.00
(81)	Matty McIntyre	60.00	30.00	18.00
(82)	Larry McLean	60.00	30.00	18.00
(83)	Fred Merkle	60.00	30.00	18.00
(84)	Chief Meyers	60.00	30.00	18.00
(85)	Clyde Milan	60.00	30.00	18.00
(86)	Dots Miller	60.00	30.00	18.00
(87)	Mike Mitchell	60.00	30.00	18.00
(88a)	Pat Moran (Cubs)	60.00	30.00	18.00
(88b)	Pat Moran (Phillies)	60.00	30.00	18.00
(89)	George Mullen (Mullin)	60.00	30.00	18.00
(90)	Danny Murphy	60.00	30.00	18.00
(91)	Red Murray	60.00	30.00	18.00
(92)	Tom Needham	60.00	30.00	18.00
(93)	Rebel Oakes	60.00	30.00	18.00
(94)	Rube Oldring	60.00	30.00	18.00
(95)	Fred Parent	60.00	30.00	18.00
(96)	Dode Paskert	60.00	30.00	18.00
(97)	Barney Pelty	60.00	30.00	18.00
(98)	Eddie Phelps	60.00	30.00	18.00
(99)	Deacon Phillippe	60.00	30.00	18.00
(100)	Jack Quinn	60.00	30.00	18.00
(101)	Ed Reulbach	60.00	30.00	18.00
(102)	Lew Richie	60.00	30.00	18.00
(103)	Jack Rowan	60.00	30.00	18.00
(104)	Nap Rucker	60.00	30.00	18.00
(105a)	Doc Scanlon (Scanlan) (Superbas)	60.00	30.00	18.00
(105b)	Doc Scanlon (Scanlan) (Phillies)	60.00	30.00	18.00
(106)	Germany Schaefer	60.00	30.00	18.00
(107)	Boss Schmidt	60.00	30.00	18.00
(108)	Wildfire Schulte	60.00	30.00	18.00
(109)	Jimmy Sheckard	60.00	30.00	18.00
(110)	Hap Smith	60.00	30.00	18.00
(111)	Tris Speaker	150.00	75.00	45.00
(112)	Harry Stovall	60.00	30.00	18.00
(113a)	Gabby Street (Senators)	60.00	30.00	18.00
(113b)	Gabby Street (Yankees)	60.00	30.00	18.00
(114)	George Suggs	60.00	30.00	18.00
(115)	Ira Thomas	60.00	30.00	18.00
(116)	Joe Tinker	130.00	65.00	40.00
(117)	John Titus	60.00	30.00	18.00
(118)	Terry Turner	60.00	30.00	18.00
(119)	Heinie Wagner	60.00	30.00	18.00
(120)	Bobby Wallace	130.00	65.00	40.00
(121)	Ed Walsh	130.00	65.00	40.00
(122)	Jack Warhop	60.00	30.00	18.00
(123)	Zach Wheat	130.00	65.00	40.00
(124)	Doc White	60.00	30.00	18.00
(125a)	Art Wilson (Dark cap, Pirates.)	60.00	30.00	18.00
(125b)	Art Wilson (Dark cap, Giants.)	60.00	30.00	18.00
(126a)	Owen Wilson (White cap, Giants.)	60.00	30.00	18.00
(126b)	Owen Wilson (White cap, Pirates.)	60.00	30.00	18.00
(127)	Hooks Wiltse	60.00	30.00	18.00
(128)	Harry Wolter	60.00	30.00	18.00
(129)	Cy Young	400.00	200.00	120.00

1910-12 Sweet Caporal Pins (P2)

Expanding its premiums to include more than just trading cards, the American Tobacco Co. issued a series of baseball pins circa 1910-12. The sepia-colored pins measure 7/8" in diameter. The set includes 152 different players, but because of numerous "large letter" and "small letter" variations, collectors generally consider the set complete at 205 different pins. Fifty of the players are pictured on a second pin that usually displays the same photo but has the player's name and team designation printed in larger letters. Three players (Bresnahan, Mullin and Wallace) have three pins each. It is now generally accepted that there are 153 pins with "small letters" and another 52 "large letter" variations in a complete set. Research among advanced collectors has shown that 19 of the pins, including six of the "large letter" variations, are considered more difficult to find. The back of each pin has a variously colored paper insert advertising Sweet Caporal Cigarettes. The red backings are generally less common. The Sweet Caporal pins are closely related to the popular T205 Gold Border tobacco cards, also issued by the American Tobacco Co. about the same time. All but nine of the players featured in the pin set were also pictured on T205 cards, and in nearly all cases the photos are identical. The Sweet Caporal pins are designated as P2 in the American Card Catalog. The complete set price includes all variations.

		NM	EX	VG
	Complete Set (204):	10,000	5,000	3,000
	Common Player:	30.00	15.00	9.00
(1)	Ed Abbaticchio	30.00	15.00	9.00
(2)	Red Ames	30.00	15.00	9.00
(3a)	Jimmy Archer (Small letters.)	30.00	15.00	9.00
(3b)	Jimmy Archer (Large letters.)	35.00	17.50	10.00
(4a)	Jimmy Austin (Small letters.)	30.00	15.00	9.00
(4b)	Jimmy Austin (Large letters.)	35.00	17.50	10.00
(5)	Home Run Baker	90.00	45.00	27.00
(6)	Neal Ball	30.00	15.00	9.00
(7)	Cy Barger	30.00	15.00	9.00
(8)	Jack Barry	30.00	15.00	9.00
(9)	Johnny Bates	30.00	15.00	9.00
(10)	Beals Becker	30.00	15.00	9.00
(11)	Fred Beebe	30.00	15.00	9.00
(12a)	George Bell (Small letters.)	30.00	15.00	9.00
(12b)	George Bell (Large letters.)	35.00	17.50	10.00
(13a)	"Chief" Bender (Small letters.)	90.00	45.00	27.00
(13b)	"Chief" Bender (Large letters.)	100.00	50.00	30.00
(14)	Bill Bergen	30.00	15.00	9.00
(15)	Bob Bescher	30.00	15.00	9.00
(16)	Joe Birmingham	30.00	15.00	9.00
(17)	Kitty Bransfield	65.00	32.50	20.00
(18a)	Roger Bresnahan (Mouth closed, small letters.)	90.00	45.00	27.00
(18b)	Roger Bresnahan (Mouth closed, large letters.)	100.00	50.00	30.00
(19)	Roger Bresnahan (Mouth open.)	90.00	45.00	27.00
(20)	Al Bridwell	30.00	15.00	9.00
(21a)	Mordecai Brown (Small letters.)	90.00	45.00	27.00
(21b)	Mordecai Brown (Large letters.)	100.00	50.00	30.00
(22)	Bobby Byrne	30.00	15.00	9.00
(23)	Nixey Callahan	30.00	15.00	9.00
(24a)	Howie Camnitz (Small letters.)	30.00	15.00	9.00
(24b)	Howie Camnitz (Large letters.)	35.00	17.50	10.00
(25a)	Bill Carrigan (Small letters.)	30.00	15.00	9.00
(25b)	Bill Carrigan (Large letters.)	35.00	17.50	10.00
(26a)	Frank Chance (Small letters.)	90.00	45.00	27.00
(26b)	Frank Chance (Large letters.)	100.00	50.00	30.00
(27)	Hal Chase (Small letters.)	50.00	25.00	15.00
(28)	Hal Chase (Large letters.)	90.00	45.00	27.00
(29)	Ed Cicotte	90.00	45.00	27.00
(30a)	Fred Clarke (Small letters.)	90.00	45.00	27.00
(30b)	Fred Clarke (Large letters.)	100.00	50.00	30.00
(31a)	Ty Cobb (Small letters, "D" on cap.)	600.00	300.00	180.00
(31b)	Ty Cobb (Large letters, no "D" on cap.)	675.00	335.00	200.00
(32a)	Eddie Collins (Small letters.)	90.00	45.00	27.00
(32b)	Eddie Collins (Large letters.)	100.00	50.00	30.00
(33)	Doc Crandall	30.00	15.00	9.00
(34)	Birdie Cree	65.00	32.50	20.00
(35)	Bill Dahlen	30.00	15.00	9.00
(36)	Jim Delahanty	30.00	15.00	9.00
(37)	Art Devlin	30.00	15.00	9.00
(38)	Josh Devore	30.00	15.00	9.00
(39)	Wild Bill Donovan	65.00	32.50	20.00
(40a)	Red Dooin (Small letters.)	30.00	15.00	9.00
(40b)	Red Dooin (Large letters.)	35.00	17.50	10.00
(41a)	Mickey Doolan (Small letters.)	30.00	15.00	9.00
(41b)	Mickey Doolan (Large letters.)	35.00	17.50	10.00
(42)	Patsy Dougherty	30.00	15.00	9.00
(43a)	Tom Downey (Small letters.)	30.00	15.00	9.00
(43b)	Tom Downey (Large letters.)	35.00	17.50	10.00
(44a)	Larry Doyle (Small letters.)	30.00	15.00	9.00
(44b)	Larry Doyle (Large letters.)	35.00	17.50	10.00
(45)	Louis Drucke	30.00	15.00	9.00
(46a)	Hugh Duffy (Small letters.)	90.00	45.00	27.00
(46b)	Hugh Duffy (Large letters.)	100.00	50.00	30.00
(47)	Jimmy Dygert	30.00	15.00	9.00
(48a)	Kid Elberfeld (Small letters.)	30.00	15.00	9.00
(48b)	Kid Elberfeld (Large letters.)	35.00	17.50	10.00
(49a)	Clyde Engle (Small letters.)	30.00	15.00	9.00
(49b)	Clyde Engle (Large letters.)	35.00	17.50	10.00
(50)	Tex Erwin	30.00	15.00	9.00
(51)	Steve Evans	30.00	15.00	9.00
(52)	Johnny Evers	90.00	45.00	27.00
(53)	Cecil Ferguson	30.00	15.00	9.00
(54)	John Flynn	30.00	15.00	9.00
(55a)	Russ Ford (Small letters.)	30.00	15.00	9.00
(55b)	Russ Ford (Large letters.)	35.00	17.50	10.00
(56)	Art Fromme	30.00	15.00	9.00
(57)	Harry Gaspar	30.00	15.00	9.00
(58a)	George Gibson (Small letters.)	30.00	15.00	9.00
(58b)	George Gibson (Large letters.)	35.00	17.50	10.00
(59)	Eddie Grant	65.00	32.50	20.00
(60)	Dolly Gray	30.00	15.00	9.00
(61a)	Clark Griffith (Small letters.)	90.00	45.00	27.00
(61b)	Clark Griffith (Large letters.)	100.00	50.00	30.00
(62)	Bob Groom	30.00	15.00	9.00
(63)	Bob Harmon	30.00	15.00	9.00
(64)	Topsy Hartsel	30.00	15.00	9.00
(65)	Arnold Hauser	65.00	32.50	20.00
(66)	Ira Hemphill	30.00	15.00	9.00
(67a)	Buck Herzog (Small letters.)	30.00	15.00	9.00
(67b)	Buck Herzog (Large letters.)	35.00	17.50	10.00
(68)	Dick Hoblitzell	30.00	15.00	9.00
(69)	Danny Hoffman	30.00	15.00	9.00
(70)	Harry Hooper	90.00	45.00	27.00
(71a)	Miller Huggins (Small letters.)	90.00	45.00	27.00
(71b)	Miller Huggins (Large letters.)	100.00	50.00	30.00
(72)	John Hummel	30.00	15.00	9.00
(73)	Hugh Jennings (Small letters.)	90.00	45.00	27.00
(74)	Hugh Jennings (Large letters.)	100.00	50.00	30.00
(75a)	Walter Johnson (Small letters.)	225.00	110.00	65.00
(75b)	Walter Johnson (Large letters.)	275.00	135.00	85.00
(76)	Tom Jones	65.00	32.50	20.00
(77)	Ed Karger	30.00	15.00	9.00
(78)	Ed Killian	65.00	32.50	20.00
(79a)	Jack Knight (Small letters.)	30.00	15.00	9.00
(79b)	Jack Knight (Large letters.)	35.00	17.50	10.00
(80)	Ed Konetchy	30.00	15.00	9.00
(81)	Harry Krause	30.00	15.00	9.00
(82)	Rube Kroh	30.00	15.00	9.00
(83)	Nap Lajoie	90.00	45.00	27.00
(84a)	Frank LaPorte (Small letters.)	30.00	15.00	9.00
(84b)	Frank LaPorte (Large letters.)	35.00	17.50	10.00
(85)	Arlie Latham	30.00	15.00	9.00
(86a)	Tommy Leach (Small letters.)	30.00	15.00	9.00
(86b)	Tommy Leach (Large letters.)	35.00	17.50	10.00
(87)	Sam Leever	30.00	15.00	9.00
(88)	Lefty Leifield	30.00	15.00	9.00
(89)	Hans Lobert	30.00	15.00	9.00
(90a)	Harry Lord (Small letters.)	30.00	15.00	9.00
(90b)	Harry Lord (Large letters.)	35.00	17.50	10.00
(91)	Paddy Livingston	30.00	15.00	9.00
(92)	Nick Maddox	30.00	15.00	9.00
(93)	Sherry Magee	30.00	15.00	9.00
(94)	Rube Marquard	90.00	45.00	27.00
(95a)	Christy Mathewson (Small letters.)	225.00	110.00	65.00
(95b)	Christy Mathewson (Large letters.)	275.00	135.00	80.00
(96a)	Al Mattern (Small letters.)	30.00	15.00	9.00
(96b)	Al Mattern (Large letters.)	35.00	17.50	10.00
(97)	George McBride	30.00	15.00	9.00
(98a)	John McGraw (Small letters.)	90.00	45.00	27.00
(98b)	John McGraw (Large letters.)	100.00	50.00	30.00
(99)	Harry McIntire (Cubs)	30.00	15.00	9.00
(100a)	Matty McIntyre (White Sox, small letters.)	30.00	15.00	9.00
(100b)	Matty McIntyre (White Sox, large letters.)	35.00	17.50	10.00
(101a)	John McLean (Small letters.)	30.00	15.00	9.00
(101b)	John McLean (Large letters.)	35.00	17.50	10.00
(102)	Fred Merkle	30.00	15.00	9.00
(103)	Chief Meyers	30.00	15.00	9.00
(104)	Clyde Milan	30.00	15.00	9.00
(105)	Dots Miller	30.00	15.00	9.00
(106)	Mike Mitchell	30.00	15.00	9.00
(107)	Pat Moran	30.00	15.00	9.00
(108a)	George Mullen (Mullin) (Small letters.)	30.00	15.00	9.00
(108b)	George Mullin (Large letters, white cap.)	90.00	45.00	27.00
(109)	Danny Murphy	30.00	15.00	9.00
(110a)	Red Murray (Small letters.)	35.00	17.50	10.00
(110b)	Red Murray (Large letters.)	30.00	15.00	9.00
(111)	Tom Needham	65.00	32.50	20.00
(112a)	Rebel Oakes (Small letters.)	30.00	15.00	9.00
(112b)	Rebel Oakes (Large letters.)	35.00	17.50	10.00
(113)	Rube Oldring	30.00	15.00	9.00
(114)	Charley O'Leary	30.00	15.00	9.00
(115)	Orval Overall	65.00	32.50	20.00
(116)	Fred Parent	30.00	15.00	9.00
(117a)	Dode Paskert (Small letters.)	30.00	15.00	9.00
(117b)	Dode Paskert (Large letters.)	35.00	17.50	10.00
(118)	Barney Pelty	30.00	15.00	9.00
(119)	Jake Pfeister	30.00	15.00	9.00
(120)	Eddie Phelps	30.00	15.00	9.00
(121)	Deacon Phillippe	30.00	15.00	9.00
(122)	Jack Quinn	30.00	15.00	9.00
(123)	Ed Reulbach	30.00	15.00	9.00
(124)	Lew Richie	30.00	15.00	9.00
(125)	Jack Rowan	30.00	15.00	9.00
(126a)	Nap Rucker (Small letters.)	30.00	15.00	9.00
(126b)	Nap Rucker (Large letters.)	35.00	17.50	10.00
(127)	Doc Scanlon (Scanlan)	65.00	32.50	20.00
(128)	Germany Schaefer	30.00	15.00	9.00
(129)	Jimmy Scheckard (Sheckard)	30.00	15.00	9.00
(130a)	Boss Schmidt (Small letters.)	30.00	15.00	9.00
(130b)	Boss Schmidt (Large letters.)	35.00	17.50	10.00
(131)	Wildfire Schulte	30.00	15.00	9.00
(132)	Hap Smith	30.00	15.00	9.00
(133a)	Tris Speaker (Small letters.)	150.00	75.00	45.00
(133b)	Tris Speaker (Large letters.)	175.00	85.00	50.00
(134)	Oscar Stanage	30.00	15.00	9.00
(135)	Harry Steinfeldt	30.00	15.00	9.00
(136)	George Stone	30.00	15.00	9.00
(137a)	George Stoval (Stovall) (Small letters.)	30.00	15.00	9.00
(137b)	George Stoval (Stovall) (Large letters.)	35.00	17.50	10.00
(138a)	Gabby Street (Small letters.)	30.00	15.00	9.00
(138b)	Gabby Street (Large letters.)	35.00	17.50	10.00
(139)	George Suggs	30.00	15.00	9.00
(140a)	Ira Thomas (Small letters.)	30.00	15.00	9.00
(140b)	Ira Thomas (Large letters.)	35.00	17.50	10.00
(141a)	Joe Tinker (Small letters.)	90.00	45.00	27.00
(141b)	Joe Tinker (Large letters.)	100.00	50.00	30.00
(142a)	John Titus (Small letters.)	30.00	15.00	9.00
(142b)	John Titus (Large letters.)	35.00	17.50	10.00
(143)	Terry Turner	30.00	15.00	9.00
(144)	Heinie Wagner	30.00	15.00	9.00
(145a)	Bobby Wallace (With cap, small letters.)	90.00	45.00	27.00
(145b)	Bobby Wallace (With cap, large letters.)	100.00	50.00	30.00
(146)	Bobby Wallace (Without cap.)	90.00	45.00	27.00
(147)	Ed Walsh	90.00	45.00	27.00
(148)	Jack Warhop	30.00	15.00	9.00
(149a)	Zach Wheat (Small letters.)	90.00	45.00	27.00
(149b)	Zach Wheat (Large letters.)	100.00	50.00	30.00
(150)	Doc White	30.00	15.00	9.00
(151)	Art Wilson (Giants)	30.00	15.00	9.00
(152)	Owen Wilson (Pirates)	30.00	15.00	9.00
(153)	Hooks Wiltse	30.00	15.00	9.00
(154)	Harry Wolter	30.00	15.00	9.00
(155a)	"Cy" Young ("C" on cap.)	200.00	100.00	60.00
(155b)	Old Cy Young (Plain cap.)	225.00	110.00	65.00

1928 Sweetman

The cards of this St. Louis firm share the format - about 1-3/8" x 2-1/2", black-and-white with card number in parentheses to the left of player name on front - and checklist with the 1928 York Caramels Type 2 issue, but are less frequently encountered. Backs of the Sweetman cards offer an album for 15 cents in stamps. The type of business is which Sweetman Co., Inc., was engaged is unknown.

This set consists of 60 of the most prominent Baseball players in the big Leagues. We have made up an album which will hold the complete set. On receipt of 15 cents in stamps we will send a blank album to any address in the United States.
Manufactured only by the
SWEETMAN CO. INC.
1611 Cass Ave. St. Louis, Mo.

		NM	EX	VG
Complete Set (60):		25,000	12,500	7,500
Common Player:		250.00	125.00	75.00
1	Burleigh Grimes	400.00	200.00	120.00
2	Walter Reuther (Ruether)	250.00	125.00	75.00
3	Joe Dugan	250.00	125.00	75.00
4	Red Faber	400.00	200.00	120.00
5	Gabby Hartnett	400.00	200.00	120.00
6	Babe Ruth	6,000	3,000	1,800
7	Bob Meusel	250.00	125.00	75.00
8	Herb Pennock	400.00	200.00	120.00
9	George Burns	250.00	125.00	75.00
10	Joe Sewell	400.00	200.00	120.00
11	George Uhle	250.00	125.00	75.00
12	Bob O'Farrell	250.00	125.00	75.00
13	Rogers Hornsby	500.00	250.00	150.00
14	"Pie" Traynor	400.00	200.00	120.00
15	Clarence Mitchell	250.00	125.00	75.00
16	Eppa Jepha Rixey	400.00	200.00	120.00
17	Carl Mays	300.00	150.00	90.00
18	Adolfo Luque	250.00	125.00	75.00
19	Dave Bancroft	400.00	200.00	120.00
20	George Kelly	400.00	200.00	120.00
21	Earl (Earle) Combs	400.00	200.00	120.00
22	Harry Heilmann	400.00	200.00	120.00
23	Ray W. Schalk	400.00	200.00	120.00
24	Johnny Mostil	250.00	125.00	75.00
25	Hack Wilson	400.00	200.00	120.00
26	Lou Gehrig	4,000	2,000	1,200
27	Ty Cobb	4,000	2,000	1,200
28	Tris Speaker	500.00	250.00	150.00
29	Tony Lazzeri	400.00	200.00	120.00
30	Waite Hoyt	400.00	200.00	120.00
31	Sherwood Smith	250.00	125.00	75.00
32	Max Carey	400.00	200.00	120.00
33	Eugene Hargrave	250.00	125.00	75.00
34	Miguel L. Gonzales (Miguel A. Gonzalez)	250.00	125.00	75.00
35	Joe Judge	250.00	125.00	75.00
36	E.C. (Sam) Rice	400.00	200.00	120.00
37	Earl Sheely	250.00	125.00	75.00
38	Sam Jones	250.00	125.00	75.00
39	Bib (Bibb) A. Falk	250.00	125.00	75.00
40	Willie Kamm	250.00	125.00	75.00
41	Stanley Harris	400.00	200.00	120.00
42	John J. McGraw	400.00	200.00	120.00
43	Artie Nehf	250.00	125.00	75.00
44	Grover Alexander	500.00	250.00	150.00
45	Paul Waner	400.00	200.00	120.00
46	William H. Terry	400.00	200.00	120.00
47	Glenn Wright	250.00	125.00	75.00
48	Earl Smith	250.00	125.00	75.00
49	Leon (Goose) Goslin	400.00	200.00	120.00
50	Frank Frisch	400.00	200.00	120.00
51	Joe Harris	250.00	125.00	75.00
52	Fred (Cy) Williams	250.00	125.00	75.00
53	Eddie Roush	400.00	200.00	120.00
54	George Sisler	400.00	200.00	120.00
55	Ed. Rommel	250.00	125.00	75.00
56	Rogers Peckinpaugh (Roger)	250.00	125.00	75.00
57	Stanley Coveleskie (Coveleski)	400.00	200.00	120.00
58	Lester Bell	250.00	125.00	75.00
59	Clyde Barnhart	250.00	125.00	75.00
60	John P. McInnis	250.00	125.00	75.00

1948 Swell Babe Ruth Story

No. 1
"THE BABE RUTH STORY"
IN THE MAKING

Babe Ruth gives William Bendix some fine pointers in the art of hitting home runs.
Bendix enacts the part of the Bambino in the film's glorification of Ruth's dramatic life, an Allied Artists picture produced by Roy Del Ruth.
At bat boy for the Yankees Ruth was Bendix's idol years ago. Little did he think that more than 20 years later he would be selected to play the Sultan of Swat in the motion picture "The Babe Ruth Story".

Send us 5 Swell Bubble Gum wrappers and 5c for a large autographed picture of William Bendix, starring as Babe Ruth.

SWELL BUBBLE GUM
Philadelphia Chewing Gum Corporation
Havertown, Pa.

The Philadelphia Gum Co., in 1948, created a card set about the movie "The Babe Ruth Story," which starred William Bendix and Claire Trevor. The set, whose American Card Catalog designation is R421, contains 28 black and white, numbered cards which measure 2" x 2-1/2". The Babe Ruth Story set was originally intended to consist of sixteen cards. Twelve additional cards (#'s 17-28) were added when Ruth died before the release of the film. The card backs include an offer for an autographed photo of William Bendix, starring as the Babe, for five Swell Bubble Gum wrappers and five cents.

		NM	EX	VG
Complete Set (28):		2,750	1,100	550.00
Common Card (1-16):		45.00	20.00	10.00
Common Card (17-28):		125.00	55.00	30.00
1	"The Babe Ruth Story" in the Making	150.00	65.00	35.00
2	Batboy Becomes the Babe (William Bendix)	45.00	20.00	10.00
3	Claire Hodgson (Claire Trevor)	45.00	20.00	10.00
4	Babe Ruth and Claire Hodgson	45.00	20.00	10.00
5	Brother Mathias (Charles Bickford)	45.00	20.00	10.00
6	Phil Conrad (Sam Levene)	45.00	20.00	10.00
7	Nightclub Singer (Gertrude Niesen)	45.00	20.00	10.00
8	Baseball's Famous Deal, Jack Dunn (William Frawley)	45.00	20.00	10.00
9	Mr. and Mrs. Babe Ruth	45.00	20.00	10.00
10	Babe Ruth, Claire Ruth and Brother Mathias	45.00	20.00	10.00
11	Babe Ruth and Miller Huggins (Fred Lightner)	45.00	20.00	10.00
12	Babe at Bed of Ill Boy Johnny Sylvester (Gregory Marshall)	45.00	20.00	10.00
13	Sylvester Family Listening to Game	45.00	20.00	10.00
14	"When a Feller Needs a Friend" (With dog at police station)	45.00	20.00	10.00
15	Dramatic Home Run	45.00	20.00	10.00
16	The Homer That Set the Record - #60 (#60)	75.00	34.00	18.50
17	"The Slap That Started Baseball's Famous Career"	125.00	55.00	30.00
18	The Babe Plays Santa Claus	125.00	55.00	30.00
19	Meeting of Owner and Manager	125.00	55.00	30.00
20	"Broken Window Paid Off"	125.00	55.00	30.00
21	Babe in a Crowd of Autograph Collectors	200.00	90.00	50.00
22	Charley Grimm, William Bendix	125.00	55.00	30.00
23	Ted Lyons, William Bendix	125.00	55.00	30.00
24	Lefty Gomez, William Bendix, Bucky Harris	150.00	65.00	35.00
25	Babe Ruth, William Bendix	400.00	180.00	100.00
26	Babe Ruth, William Bendix	400.00	180.00	100.00
27	Babe Ruth, Claire Trevor	400.00	180.00	100.00
28	William Bendix, Babe Ruth, Claire Trevor	400.00	180.00	100.00

1948 Swell Sport Thrills

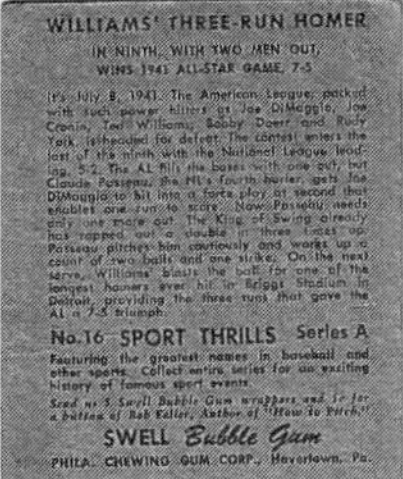

This is a set of black-and-white cards which depicts memorable events in baseball history. The cards measure 2-1/2" x 3" and have a picture frame border and event title on the card fronts. The card backs describe the event in detail. Twenty cards were produced in this set by the Swell Gum Co. of Philadelphia. Each card is numbered, and card numbers 9, 11, 16 and 20 are considered more difficult to obtain.

		NM	EX	VG
Complete Set (20):		1,500	675.00	375.00
Common Player:		30.00	13.50	7.00
1	Greatest Single Inning (Mickey Cochrane, Jimmy (Jimmie) Foxx, George Haas, Bing Miller, Al Simmons)	85.00	37.50	20.00
2	Amazing Record (Pete Reiser)	30.00	13.50	7.00
3	Dramatic Debut (Jackie Robinson)	175.00	80.00	45.00
4	Greatest Pitcher (Walter Johnson)	75.00	35.00	17.50
5	Three Strikes Not Out! (Tommy Henrich, Mickey Owen)	30.00	13.50	7.00
6	Home Run Wins Series (Bill Dickey)	35.00	16.00	9.00
7	Never Say Die Pitcher (Hal Schumacher)	30.00	13.50	7.00
8	Five Strikeouts! (Carl Hubbell)	40.00	18.00	10.00
9	Greatest Catch! (Al Gionfriddo)	55.00	25.00	13.50
10	No Hits! No Runs! (Johnny VanderMeer)	30.00	13.50	7.00
11	Bases Loaded! (Tony Lazzeri, Bob O'Farrell)	35.00	16.00	9.00
12	Most Dramatic Home Run (Lou Gehrig, Babe Ruth)	200.00	90.00	50.00
13	Winning Run (Tommy Bridges, Mickey Cochrane, Goose Goslin)	30.00	13.50	7.00
14	Great Slugging (Lou Gehrig)	225.00	100.00	55.00
15	Four Men to Stop Him! (Jim Bagby, Al Smith)	50.00	22.50	12.50
16	Three Run Homer in Ninth! (Joe DiMaggio, Joe Gordon, Ted Williams)	200.00	90.00	50.00
17	Football Block! (Whitey Kurowski, Johnny Lindell)	30.00	13.50	7.00
18	Home Run to Fame (Pee Wee Reese)	85.00	37.50	20.00
19	Strikout Record! (Bob Feller)	50.00	22.50	12.50
20	Rifle Arm! (Carl Furillo)	50.00	22.50	12.50

1957 Swift Meats

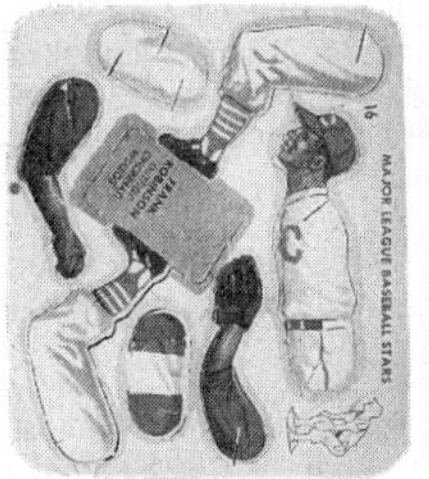

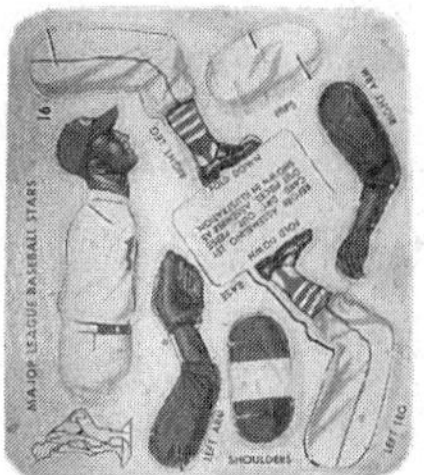

One of the really different baseball card issues of the 50s was the set of 18 3-D baseball player figures which could be punched out and assembled from cards included in packages of hot dogs. The unpunched cards measure approximately 3-1/2" x 4". Prices below are for unpunched cards. Values for assembled figures are problematical.

		NM	EX	VG
Complete Set, Singles (18):		1,500	750.00	450.00
Complete Set w/ Mailer, Playing Board:		2,650	1,300	775.00
Common Player:		60.00	30.00	18.00
1	John Podres	75.00	37.50	22.50
2	Gus Triandos	60.00	30.00	18.00
3	Dale Long	60.00	30.00	18.00
4	Billy Pierce	60.00	30.00	18.00
5	Ed Bailey	60.00	30.00	18.00
6	Vic Wertz	60.00	30.00	18.00
7	Nelson Fox	130.00	65.00	40.00
8	Ken Boyer	75.00	37.50	22.50
9	Gil McDougald	75.00	37.50	22.50
10	Junior Gilliam	75.00	37.50	22.50
11	Eddie Yost	60.00	30.00	18.00
12	Johnny Logan	60.00	30.00	18.00
13	Hank Aaron	200.00	100.00	60.00
14	Bill Tuttle	60.00	30.00	18.00
15	Jackie Jensen	60.00	30.00	18.00
16	Frank Robinson	200.00	100.00	60.00
17	Richie Ashburn	130.00	65.00	40.00
18	Rocky Colavito	200.00	100.00	60.00

1951 Sylvania Leo Durocher Postcard

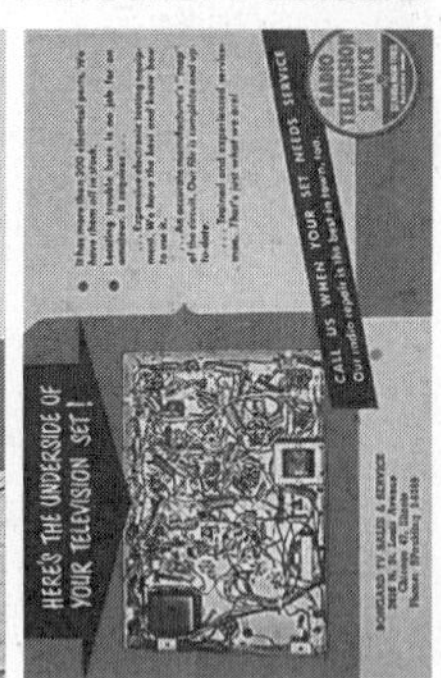

The N.Y. Giants manager endorses Sylvania radio/television service on this large-format (8-1/2" x 5-1/2") postcard. Color artwork features Durocher with a quotation endorsing Sylvania parts and service.

	NM	EX	VG
Leo Durocher	50.00	25.00	15.00

1910-11 S74 Silks - White

BASEBALL-ACTRESS SERIES ON SATIN
Useful in making pillow covers and other fancy articles for home decoration.
To remove satin from this paper back, loosen at corner and pull gently—moistening if necessary.
OLD MILL CIGARETTES.

Designated as S74 in the "American Card Catalog," these delicate fabric collectibles are popular with advanced collectors. The silks were issued as premiums with several different brands of cigarettes: Turkey Red, Old Mill, Red Sun, and, rarely, Helmar. The satin-like silks can be found in two different styles, either "white" or "colored." The white silks measure 1-7/8" x 3" and were originally issued with a brown paper backing that carried an advertisement for one of the cigarette brands. The backing also advised that the silks were "useful in making pillow covers and other fancy articles for home decoration." Many undoubtedly were used for such purposes, making silks with the paper backing still intact more difficult to find. White silks must have the backing intact to command top values shown here. Ninety-two subjects are known in the "white" silks. The silks feature the player pictures found in the popular T205 Gold Border tobacco card set.

		NM	EX	VG
Complete Set (92):		16,000	6,400	4,150
Common Player:		135.00	55.00	35.00
No Paper Backing: 50 Percent				
(1)	Home Run Baker	300.00	120.00	75.00
(2)	Cy Barger	135.00	55.00	35.00
(3)	Jack Barry	135.00	55.00	35.00
(4)	Johnny Bates	135.00	55.00	35.00
(5)	Fred Beck	135.00	55.00	35.00
(6)	Beals Becker	135.00	55.00	35.00
(7)	George Bell	135.00	55.00	35.00
(8)	Chief Bender	300.00	120.00	75.00
(9)	Roger Bresnahan	300.00	120.00	75.00
(10)	Al Bridwell	135.00	55.00	35.00
(11)	Mordecai Brown	300.00	120.00	75.00
(12)	Bobby Byrne	135.00	55.00	35.00
(13)	Howie Camnitz	135.00	55.00	35.00
(14)	Bill Carrigan	135.00	55.00	35.00
(15)	Frank Chance	300.00	120.00	75.00
(16)	Hal Chase	250.00	100.00	60.00
(17)	Fred Clarke	300.00	120.00	75.00
(18)	Ty Cobb	1,350	550.00	350.00
(19)	Eddie Collins	300.00	120.00	75.00
(20)	Doc Crandall	135.00	55.00	35.00
(21)	Lou Criger	135.00	55.00	35.00
(22)	Jim Delahanty	135.00	55.00	35.00
(23)	Art Devlin	135.00	55.00	35.00
(24)	Red Dooin	135.00	55.00	35.00
(25)	Mickey Doolan	135.00	55.00	35.00
(26)	Larry Doyle	135.00	55.00	35.00
(27)	Jimmy Dygert	135.00	55.00	35.00
(28)	Kid Elberfield (Elberfeld)	135.00	55.00	35.00
(29)	Steve Evans	135.00	55.00	35.00
(30)	Johnny Evers	300.00	120.00	75.00
(31)	Bob Ewing	135.00	55.00	35.00
(32)	Art Fletcher	135.00	55.00	35.00
(33)	John Flynn	135.00	55.00	35.00
(34)	Bill Foxen	135.00	55.00	35.00
(35)	George Gibson	135.00	55.00	35.00
(36)	Peaches Graham (Cubs)	135.00	55.00	35.00
(37)	Peaches Graham (Rustlers)	135.00	55.00	35.00
(38)	Clark Griffith	300.00	120.00	75.00
(39)	Topsy Hartsel	135.00	55.00	35.00
(40)	Arnold Hauser	135.00	55.00	35.00
(41)	Charlie Hemphill	135.00	55.00	35.00
(42)	Davy Jones	135.00	55.00	35.00
(43)	Jack Knight	135.00	55.00	35.00
(44)	Ed Konetchy	135.00	55.00	35.00
(45)	Harry Krause	135.00	55.00	35.00
(46)	Tommy Leach	135.00	55.00	35.00
(47)	Rube Marquard	300.00	120.00	75.00
(48)	Christy Mathewson	650.00	260.00	160.00
(49)	Al Mattern	135.00	55.00	35.00
(50)	Amby McConnell	135.00	55.00	35.00
(51)	John McGraw	300.00	120.00	75.00
(52)	Harry McIntire (McIntyre)	135.00	55.00	35.00
(53)	Fred Merkle	135.00	55.00	35.00
(54)	Chief Meyers	135.00	55.00	35.00
(55)	Dots Miller	135.00	55.00	35.00
(56)	Danny Murphy	135.00	55.00	35.00
(57)	Red Murray	135.00	55.00	35.00
(58)	Tom Needham	135.00	55.00	35.00
(59)	Rebel Oakes	135.00	55.00	35.00
(60)	Rube Oldring	135.00	55.00	35.00
(61)	Orval Overall	135.00	55.00	35.00
(62)	Fred Parent	135.00	55.00	35.00
(63)	Fred Payne	135.00	55.00	35.00
(64)	Barney Pelty	135.00	55.00	35.00
(65)	Deacon Phillippe	135.00	55.00	35.00
(66)	Jack Quinn	135.00	55.00	35.00
(67)	Bugs Raymond	135.00	55.00	35.00
(68)	Ed Reulbach	135.00	55.00	35.00
(69)	Doc Scanlon (Scanlan)	135.00	55.00	35.00
(70)	Germany Schaefer	135.00	55.00	35.00
(71)	Geo. Schlei	135.00	55.00	35.00
(72)	Wildfire Schulte	135.00	55.00	35.00
(73)	Dave Shean	135.00	55.00	35.00
(74)	Jimmy Sheckard	135.00	55.00	35.00
(75)	Tony Smith (Superbas)	135.00	55.00	35.00
(76)	Harry Smith (Rustlers)	500.00	200.00	125.00
(77)	Fred Snodgrass	135.00	55.00	35.00
(78)	Tris Speaker	350.00	140.00	87.00
(79)	Harry Steinfeldt (Cubs)	135.00	55.00	35.00
(80)	Harry Steinfeldt (Rustlers)	135.00	55.00	35.00
(81)	George Stone	135.00	55.00	35.00
(82)	Gabby Street	135.00	55.00	35.00
(83)	Ed Summers	135.00	55.00	35.00
(84)	Lee Tannehill	135.00	55.00	35.00
(85)	Joe Tinker	300.00	120.00	75.00
(86)	John Titus	135.00	55.00	35.00
(87)	Terry Turner	135.00	55.00	35.00
(88)	Bobby Wallace	300.00	120.00	75.00
(89)	Doc White	135.00	55.00	35.00
(90)	Ed Willett	135.00	55.00	35.00
(91)	Art Wilson	135.00	55.00	35.00
(92)	Harry Wolter	135.00	55.00	35.00

1911 S74 Silks - Colored

Factory No. 7, 3rd Dist. N. Y.
TIGERS
Ty Cobb
OF THE DETROIT AM.
TURKEY RED CIGARETTES

Designated as S74 in the "American Card Catalog," these delicate fabric collectibles are popular with advanced collectors. The silks were issued as premiums with several different brands of cigarettes: Turkey Red, Old Mill, Helmar, and, rarely, Red Sun. The satin-like silks can be found in two different styles, either "white" or "colored." The S74 "colored" silks, as their name indicates, were issued in a variety of colors. They are slightly larger than the white version, measuring 1-7/8" x 3-1/2", and were issued without a paper backing, carrying the cigarette brand name on the lower front of the fabric. (No color silks advertising the Helmar brand are known to exist.) In the colored silks, 120 subjects are known. The silks feature the same player pictures found in the popular T205 Gold Border tobacco card set.

		NM	EX	VG
Complete Set (120):		20,000	8,000	5,000
Common Player:		150.00	60.00	35.00
(1)	Red Ames	150.00	60.00	35.00
(2)	Jimmy Archer	150.00	60.00	35.00
(3)	Home Run Baker	300.00	120.00	70.00
(4)	Cy Barger	150.00	60.00	35.00
(5)	Jack Barry	150.00	60.00	35.00
(6)	Johnny Bates	150.00	60.00	35.00
(7)	Beals Becker	150.00	60.00	35.00
(8)	George Bell	150.00	60.00	35.00
(9)	Chief Bender	300.00	120.00	70.00
(10)	Bill Bergen	150.00	60.00	35.00
(11)	Bob Bescher	150.00	60.00	35.00
(12)	Roger Bresnahan (Mouth closed.)	300.00	120.00	70.00
(13)	Roger Bresnahan (Mouth open.)	300.00	120.00	70.00
(14)	Al Bridwell	150.00	60.00	35.00
(15)	Mordecai Brown	300.00	120.00	70.00
(16)	Bobby Byrne	150.00	60.00	35.00
(17)	Howie Camnitz	150.00	60.00	35.00
(18)	Bill Carrigan	150.00	60.00	35.00
(19)	Frank Chance	300.00	120.00	70.00
(20)	Hal Chase	225.00	90.00	55.00
(21)	Ed Cicotte	300.00	120.00	70.00
(22)	Fred Clarke	300.00	120.00	70.00
(23)	Ty Cobb	1,200	480.00	290.00
(24)	Eddie Collins	300.00	120.00	70.00
(25)	Doc Crandall	150.00	60.00	35.00
(26)	Bill Dahlen	150.00	60.00	35.00
(27)	Jake Daubert	150.00	60.00	35.00
(28)	Jim Delahanty	150.00	60.00	35.00
(29)	Art Devlin	150.00	60.00	35.00
(30)	Josh Devore	150.00	60.00	35.00
(31)	Red Dooin	150.00	60.00	35.00
(32)	Mickey Doolan	150.00	60.00	35.00
(33)	Tom Downey	150.00	60.00	35.00
(34)	Larry Doyle	150.00	60.00	35.00
(35)	Hugh Duffy	300.00	120.00	70.00
(36)	Jimmy Dygert	150.00	60.00	35.00
(37)	Kid Elberfield (Elberfeld)	150.00	60.00	35.00
(38)	Steve Evans	150.00	60.00	35.00
(39)	Johnny Evers	300.00	120.00	70.00
(40)	Bob Ewing	150.00	60.00	35.00
(41)	Art Fletcher	150.00	60.00	35.00
(42)	John Flynn	150.00	60.00	35.00
(43)	Russ Ford	150.00	60.00	35.00
(44)	Bill Foxen	150.00	60.00	35.00
(45)	Art Fromme	150.00	60.00	35.00
(46)	George Gibson	150.00	60.00	35.00
(47)	Peaches Graham	150.00	60.00	35.00
(48)	Eddie Grant	150.00	60.00	35.00
(49)	Clark Griffith	300.00	120.00	70.00
(50)	Topsy Hartsel	150.00	60.00	35.00
(51)	Arnold Hauser	150.00	60.00	35.00
(52)	Charlie Hemphill	150.00	60.00	35.00
(53)	Dick Hoblitzell	150.00	60.00	35.00
(54)	Miller Huggins	300.00	120.00	70.00
(55)	John Hummel	150.00	60.00	35.00
(56)	Walter Johnson	600.00	240.00	145.00
(57)	Davy Jones	150.00	60.00	35.00
(58)	Johnny Kling	150.00	60.00	35.00
(59)	Jack Knight	150.00	60.00	35.00
(60)	Ed Konetchy	150.00	60.00	35.00
(61)	Harry Krause	150.00	60.00	35.00
(62)	Tommy Leach	150.00	60.00	35.00
(63)	Lefty Leifield	150.00	60.00	35.00
(64)	Hans Lobert	150.00	60.00	35.00
(65)	Rube Marquard	300.00	120.00	70.00
(66)	Christy Mathewson	750.00	300.00	180.00
(67)	Al Mattern	150.00	60.00	35.00
(68)	Amby McConnell	150.00	60.00	35.00
(69)	John McGraw	300.00	120.00	70.00
(70)	Harry McIntire (McIntyre)	150.00	60.00	35.00
(71)	Fred Merkle	150.00	60.00	35.00
(72)	Chief Meyers	150.00	60.00	35.00
(73)	Dots Miller	150.00	60.00	35.00
(74)	Mike Mitchell	150.00	60.00	35.00
(75)	Pat Moran	150.00	60.00	35.00
(76)	George Moriarty	150.00	60.00	35.00
(77)	George Mullin	150.00	60.00	35.00
(78)	Danny Murphy	150.00	60.00	35.00
(79)	Red Murray	150.00	60.00	35.00
(80)	Tom Needham	150.00	60.00	35.00
(81)	Rebel Oakes	150.00	60.00	35.00
(82)	Rube Oldring	150.00	60.00	35.00
(83)	Orval Overall	150.00	60.00	35.00
(84)	Fred Parent	150.00	60.00	35.00
(85)	Dode Paskert	150.00	60.00	35.00
(86)	Fred Payne	150.00	60.00	35.00
(87)	Barney Pelty	150.00	60.00	35.00
(88)	Deacon Phillippe	150.00	60.00	35.00
(89)	Jack Quinn	150.00	60.00	35.00
(90)	Bugs Raymond	150.00	60.00	35.00
(91)	Ed Reulbach	150.00	60.00	35.00
(92)	Jack Rowan	150.00	60.00	35.00
(93)	Nap Rucker	150.00	60.00	35.00
(94)	Doc Scanlon (Scanlan)	150.00	60.00	35.00
(95)	Germany Schaefer	150.00	60.00	35.00
(96)	Geo. Schlei	150.00	60.00	35.00
(97)	Wildfire Schulte	150.00	60.00	35.00
(98)	Dave Shean	150.00	60.00	35.00
(99)	Jimmy Sheckard	150.00	60.00	35.00
(100)	Happy Smith	150.00	60.00	35.00
(101)	Fred Snodgrass	150.00	60.00	35.00
(102)	Tris Speaker	400.00	160.00	95.00
(103)	Jake Stahl	150.00	60.00	35.00
(104)	Harry Steinfeldt	150.00	60.00	35.00
(105)	George Stone	150.00	60.00	35.00
(106)	Gabby Street	150.00	60.00	35.00
(107)	Ed Summers	150.00	60.00	35.00
(108)	Lee Tannehill	150.00	60.00	35.00
(109)	Joe Tinker	300.00	120.00	70.00
(110)	John Titus	150.00	60.00	35.00
(111)	Terry Turner	150.00	60.00	35.00
(112)	Bobby Wallace	300.00	120.00	70.00
(113)	Zack Wheat	300.00	120.00	70.00
(114)	Doc White (White Sox)	150.00	60.00	35.00
(115)	Kirby White (Pirates)	150.00	60.00	35.00
(116)	Ed Willett	150.00	60.00	35.00
(117)	Owen Wilson	150.00	60.00	35.00
(118)	Hooks Wiltse	150.00	60.00	35.00
(119)	Harry Wolter	150.00	60.00	35.00
(120)	Cy Young	750.00	300.00	180.00

1912 S81 Silks

The 1912 S81 "Silks," so-called because they featured pictures of baseball players on a satin-like fabric rather than paper or cardboard, are closely related to the better-known T3 Turkey Red cabinet cards of the same era. The silks, which featured 25 of the day's top baseball players among its other various subjects, were available as a premium with Helmar "Turkish Trophies" cigarettes. According to an advertising sheet, one silk could be obtained for 25 Helmar coupons. The silks measure about 6-3/4" x 8-3/4" and, with a few exceptions, used the same pictures featured on the popular Turkey Red cards. Five players (Rube Marquard, Rube Benton, Marty O'Toole, Grover Alexander and Russ Ford) appear in the "Silks" set that were not included in the T3 set. In addition, an error involving the Frank Baker card was corrected for the "Silks" set. (In the T3 set, Baker's card actually pictured Jack Barry.) Several years ago a pair of New England collectors found a small stack of Christy Mathewson "Silks," making his, by far, the most common. Otherwise, the "Silks" are generally so rare that it is difficult to determine the relative scarcity of the others. Baseball enthusiasts are usually only attracted to the 25 baseball players in the "Silks" premium set, but it is interesting to note that the promotion also offered dozens of other subjects, including "beautiful women in bathing and athletic costumes, charming dancers in gorgeous attire, natiional flags and generals on horseback."

		NM	EX	VG
Complete Set (25):		145,000	50,000	27,500
Common Player:		3,000	1,000	575.00
86	Rube Marquard	6,500	2,275	1,225
87	Marty O'Toole	3,000	1,000	575.00
88	Rube Benton	3,000	1,000	575.00
89	Grover Alexander	9,000	3,150	1,700
90	Russ Ford	3,000	1,000	575.00
91	John McGraw	6,500	2,275	1,225

		NM	EX	VG
92	Nap Rucker	3,000	1,000	575.00
93	Mike Mitchell	3,000	1,000	575.00
94	Chief Bender	6,500	2,275	1,225
95	Home Run Baker	6,500	2,275	1,225
96	Nap Lajoie	6,500	2,275	1,225
97	Joe Tinker	6,500	2,275	1,225
98	Sherry Magee	3,000	1,000	575.00
99	Howie Camnitz	3,000	1,000	575.00
100	Eddie Collins	6,500	2,275	1,225
101	Red Dooin	3,000	1,000	575.00
102	Ty Cobb	15,000	5,250	2,850
103	Hugh Jennings	6,500	2,275	1,225
104	Roger Bresnahan	6,500	2,275	1,225
105	Jake Stahl	3,000	1,000	575.00
106	Tris Speaker	8,000	2,800	1,525
107	Ed Walsh	6,500	2,275	1,225
108	Christy Mathewson	6,000	2,100	1,150
109	Johnny Evers	6,500	2,275	1,225
110	Walter Johnson	12,000	4,200	2,275

1912 S110 Baseball Player Silks Pillow Case

Closely related to the S81 silks, and issued as a premuim for 100 coupons, this approximately 23" x 23" pillow case shares the same designs as the individual silks of the players thereon. Cross-stich borders for the player images on the cloth pillow case would indicate the silks were meant to be sewn on as they were acquired. Besides the baseball players pillow cases, similar premiums are known for the other Turkey Red/Helmar silks -- Indians, generals, etc.

		NM	EX	VG
(1)	Home Run Baker, Ty Cobb, Walter Johnson, Christy Mathewson, Tris Speaker	8,500	4,250	2,550
(2)	Home Run Baker, Ty Cobb, Christy Mathewson, Marty O'Toole, Tris Speaker	8,000	4,000	2,400

T

1928 Tabacalera la Morena

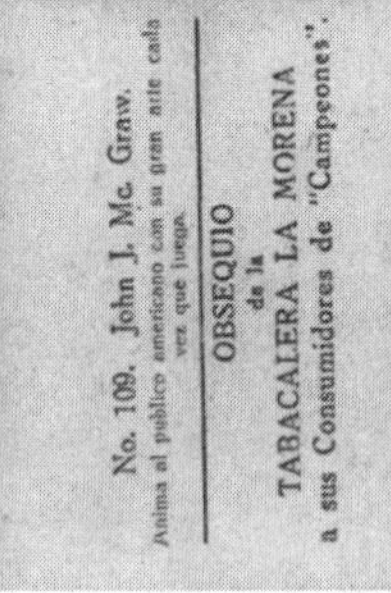

Believed to have been issued in El Salvador in the late 1920s, the extent of this card issue is not yet known. It is possible other American baseball players are included in the issue. Approximately 1-7/8" x 2-5/8", the cards are printed in black-and-white with some color tints added. The borderless front that includes the card number at bottom. Backs are printed in Spanish and repeat the card number along with player identification and a few words about the pictured players. An ad at bottom attributes the card (roughly): "Courtesy of Rich Brown Tobacco, the Champion among Consumers."

		NM	EX	VG
96	St. Louis Cardinals Team	100.00	50.00	30.00
97	Everett Scott	50.00	25.00	15.00
98	Babe Ruth	900.00	450.00	270.00
100	Lou Gehrig, Babe Ruth	500.00	250.00	150.00
101	George Kelly	100.00	50.00	30.00
103	Earl Webb	50.00	25.00	15.00
105	Ty Cobb, Babe Ruth	300.00	150.00	90.00
106	Jim Bottomley	100.00	50.00	30.00
107	Christy Mathewson, John McGraw	150.00	75.00	45.00
109	John J. Mc. Graw	100.00	50.00	30.00
110	Ullmann	50.00	25.00	15.00

111	Lee Todd, P Todd	50.00	25.00	15.00
114	St. Louis Cardinals/Brooklyn Robins	50.00	25.00	15.00
120	St. Louis Cardinals/Brooklyn Robins	50.00	25.00	15.00

1916 Tango Eggs

Chase, 1b. Cincinnati Nat'l.

Ask your grocer for
"TANGO BRAND EGGS"
Every one guaranteed
to be of
"FINEST QUALITY"
Packed only by
L. FRANK & COMPANY
NEW ORLEANS, LA.

Unknown until the discovery of a hoard of "fewer than 500" cards in 1991, this 20-card set was produced for L. Frank & Co. of New Orleans to be distributed in an as-yet unknown manner in connection with its Tango brand eggs. Similar in size (1-7/16" x 2-3/4") and format to contemporary caramel cards, the Tango set features familiar player pictures from those issues. In fact, several of the Tango cards have player designations which differ from the same pictures used in the E106 American Caramel issue of 1915. The Tango cards feature a glossy front surface, and are brightly colored. The hoard varied greatly in the number of each player's card. Some were found in quantities as low as one, while some were represented by more than 50 specimens. Because several of the cards exist in only a single specimen, no price for a complete set is quoted.

		NM	EX	VG
	Common Player:	240.00	95.00	50.00
(1)	Bob Bescher	240.00	95.00	50.00
(2)	Roger Bresnahan (Four known.)	2,400	960.00	480.00
(3)	Al Bridwell (Fewer than 10 known.)	870.00	350.00	175.00
(4)	Hal Chase	1,080	430.00	215.00
(5)	Ty Cobb (One known, VG, value undetermined.)			
(6)	Eddie Collins	1,920	770.00	385.00
(7)	Sam Crawford (Fewer than five known.)	2,400	960.00	480.00
(8)	Red Dooin	430.00	175.00	85.00
(9)	Johnny Evers (One known, G/VG, value undetermined.)			
(10)	Happy Felsch (Picture actually Ray Demmitt.) (2-3 known)	2,880	1,150	575.00
(11)	Hughie Jennings (20 known)	660.00	265.00	135.00
(12)	George McQuillen	510.00	205.00	100.00
(13)	Billy Meyer (Picture actually Fred Jacklitsch.)	450.00	180.00	90.00
(14)	Ray Morgan (Picture actually Mike Doolan.) (2-3 known))	1,920	770.00	385.00
(15)	Danny Murphy	270.00	110.00	55.00
(16)	Germany Schaefer (1-2 known)	2,400	960.00	480.00
(17)	Joe Tinker (Unconfirmed)	2,880	1,150	575.00
(18)	Honus Wagner (None confirmed.)			
(19)	Buck Weaver (Picture actually Joe Tinker.)	1,500	600.00	300.00
(20)	Heinie Zimmerman (Fewer than 10 known.)	870.00	350.00	175.00

1934 Tarzan Bread (D382)

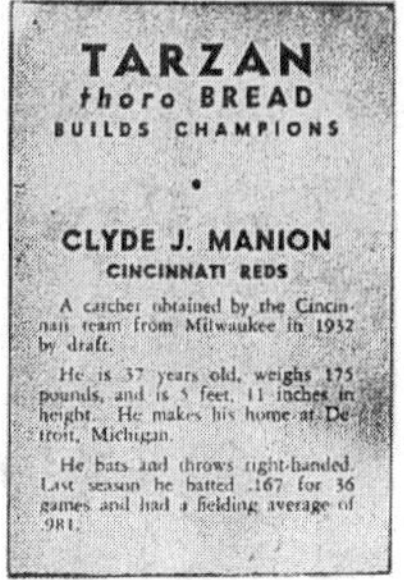

TARZAN
thoro BREAD
BUILDS CHAMPIONS
CLYDE J. MANION
CINCINNATI REDS
A catcher obtained by the Cincinnati team from Milwaukee in 1932 by draft.
He is 37 years old, weighs 175 pounds, and is 5 feet, 11 inches in height. He makes his home at Detroit, Michigan.
He bats and throws right-handed. Last season he batted .167 for 36 games and had a fielding average of .981.

Among the rarest issues of the 1930s is this set sponsored by an unusually named brand of bread from a bakery whose location is unknown. The cards are printed in black-and-white in 2-1/4" x 3-1/4" format. Borderless front photos have the player name in capital letters. Backs have the sponsor's name and a short career summary. The checklist here, almost certainly incomplete, is arranged alphabetically; the cards are unnumbered.

		NM	EX	VG
	Common Player:	2,200	1,100	650.00
(1)	Sparky Adams	2,200	1,100	650.00
(2)	Walter Betts	2,200	1,100	650.00
(3)	Ed Brandt	2,200	1,100	650.00
(4)	Tommy Bridges	2,200	1,100	650.00
(5)	Irving "Jack" Burns	2,200	1,100	650.00
(6)	Bruce Campbell	2,200	1,100	650.00
(7)	Tex Carleton	2,200	1,100	650.00
(8)	Dick Coffman	2,200	1,100	650.00
(9)	George Connally	2,200	1,100	650.00
(10)	Tony Cuccinello	2,200	1,100	650.00
(11)	Debs Garms	2,200	1,100	650.00
(12)	Milt Gaston	2,200	1,100	650.00
(13)	Bill Hallahan	2,200	1,100	650.00
(14)	Myril Hoag	2,200	1,100	650.00
(15)	Chief Hogsett	2,200	1,100	650.00
(16)	Arndt Jorgens	2,200	1,100	650.00
(17)	Willie Kamm	2,200	1,100	650.00
(18)	Dutch Leonard	2,200	1,100	650.00
(19)	Clyde Manion	2,200	1,100	650.00
(20)	Eric McNair	2,200	1,100	650.00
(21)	Oscar Melillo	2,200	1,100	650.00
(22)	Bob O'Farrell	2,200	1,100	650.00
(23)	Gus Suhr	2,200	1,100	650.00
(24)	Evar Swanson	2,200	1,100	650.00
(25)	Billy Urbanski	2,200	1,100	650.00
(26)	Johnny Vergez	2,200	1,100	650.00
(27)	Robert Worthington	2,200	1,100	650.00
(28)	Tom Zachary	2,200	1,100	650.00

1969 Tasco All-Star Collection Caricatures

This set of large - 11-1/2" x 16" - player posters features colorful caricatures with an emphasis on Tigers players, befitting the Detroit address of the publisher. Licensed by MLB-PA, the pictures are listed here alphabetically. They were originally sold for less than $1 apiece.

		NM	EX	VG
	Complete Set (46):	450.00	225.00	135.00
	Common Player:	7.50	3.75	2.25
(1)	Hank Aaron	35.00	17.50	10.50
(2)	Richie Allen	12.50	6.25	3.75
(3)	Luis Aparicio	17.50	8.75	5.25
(4)	Ernie Banks	25.00	12.50	7.50
(5)	Glenn Beckert	7.50	3.75	2.25
(6)	Johnny Bench	20.00	10.00	6.00
(7)	Norm Cash	10.00	5.00	3.00
(8)	Danny Cater	7.50	3.75	2.25
(9)	Pat Dobson	7.50	3.75	2.25
(10)	Don Drysdale	17.50	8.75	5.25
(11)	Bill Freehan	7.50	3.75	2.25
(12)	Jim Fregosi	7.50	3.75	2.25
(13)	Bob Gibson	17.50	8.75	5.25
(14)	Bill Hands	7.50	3.75	2.25
(15)	Ken Holtzman	7.50	3.75	2.25
(16)	Willie Horton	7.50	3.75	2.25
(17)	Frank Howard	9.00	4.50	2.75
(18)	Randy Hundley	7.50	3.75	2.25
(19)	Ferguson Jenkins	17.50	8.75	5.25
(20)	Al Kaline	25.00	12.50	7.50
(21)	Don Kessinger	7.50	3.75	2.25
(22)	Jerry Koosman	7.50	3.75	2.25
(23)	Mickey Lolich	7.50	3.75	2.25
(24)	Juan Marichal	17.50	8.75	5.25
(25)	Willie Mays	35.00	17.50	10.50
(26)	Bill Mazeroski	17.50	8.75	5.25
(27)	Dick McAuliffe	7.50	3.75	2.25
(28)	Denny McLain	7.50	3.75	2.25
(29)	Dave McNally	7.50	3.75	2.25
(30)	Jim Northrup	7.50	3.75	2.25
(31)	Tony Oliva	9.00	4.50	2.75
(32)	Adolfo Phillips	7.50	3.75	2.25
(33)	Jim Price	7.50	3.75	2.25
(34)	Brooks Robinson	20.00	10.00	6.00
(35)	Pete Rose	35.00	17.50	10.50
(36)	Ron Santo	15.00	7.50	4.50
(37)	Joe Sparma	7.50	3.75	2.25
(38)	Mickey Stanley	7.50	3.75	2.25
(39)	Mel Stottlemyre	7.50	3.75	2.25
(40)	Luis Tiant	7.50	3.75	2.25
(41)	Joe Torre	9.00	4.50	2.75
(42)	Dick Tracewski	7.50	3.75	2.25
(43)	Don Wert	7.50	3.75	2.25
(44)	Billy Williams	17.50	8.75	5.25
(45)	Earl Wilson	7.50	3.75	2.25
(46)	Carl Yastrzemski	25.00	12.50	7.50

1970 Tasco Caricatures

This group of colorful player caricatures was sold in a four-pack featuring two each baseball and football players. The 8-1/2" x 10-7/8" blank-back pictures have central images surrounded by colorful borders.

	NM	EX	VG
Complete Set (4):	150.00	75.00	45.00
Common Player:	40.00	20.00	12.00
(1) Jim "Catfish" Hunter	40.00	20.00	12.00
(2) Al Kaline	50.00	25.00	15.00
(3) Joe Namath	75.00	37.00	22.00
(4) O.J. Simpson	50.00	25.00	15.00

1933 Tattoo Orbit (R305)

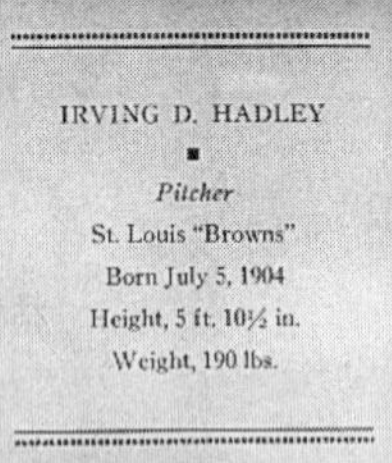
IRVING D. HADLEY

Pitcher

St. Louis "Browns"

Born July 5, 1904

Height, 5 ft. 10½ in.

Weight, 190 lbs.

Found in 1¢ packages of Tattoo gum, these 2" x 2-1/4" cards were produced by the Orbit Gum Co., of Chicago, a subsidiary of Wrigley's. Fronts feature a black-and-white photo which is tinted to give the skin some color. Stylized ballpark backgrounds are separated from the photograph by a black line. The rest of the background is printed in vivid red, yellow and green. Backs have player identification and vitals. Cards of Bump Hadley and George Blaeholder are the most elusive, followed by those of Ivy Andrews and Rogers Hornsby.

	NM	EX	VG
Complete Set (60):	20,000	8,000	4,000
Common Player:	250.00	100.00	60.00
(1) Dale Alexander	250.00	100.00	60.00
(2) Ivy Paul Andrews	900.00	360.00	225.00
(3) Earl Averill	400.00	160.00	100.00
(4) Richard Bartell	250.00	100.00	60.00
(5) Walter Berger	250.00	100.00	60.00
(6) George F. Blaeholder	1,000	400.00	250.00
(7) Irving J. Burns	250.00	100.00	60.00
(8) Guy T. Bush	250.00	100.00	60.00
(9) Bruce D. Campbell	250.00	100.00	60.00
(10) William Cissell	250.00	100.00	60.00
(11) Lefty Clark	250.00	100.00	60.00
(12) Mickey Cochrane	400.00	160.00	100.00
(13) Phil Collins	250.00	100.00	60.00
(14) Hazen Kiki Cuyler	400.00	160.00	100.00
(15) Dizzy Dean	575.00	230.00	145.00
(16) Jimmy Dykes	250.00	100.00	60.00
(17) George L. Earnshaw	250.00	100.00	60.00
(18) Woody English	250.00	100.00	60.00
(19) Lewis A. Fonseca	250.00	100.00	60.00
(20) Jimmy Foxx	750.00	300.00	185.00
(21) Burleigh A. Grimes	400.00	160.00	100.00
(22) Charles John Grimm	250.00	100.00	60.00
(23) Robert M. Grove	500.00	200.00	125.00
(24) Frank Grube	250.00	100.00	60.00
(25) George W. Haas	250.00	100.00	60.00
(26) Irving D. Hadley	1,000	400.00	250.00
(27) Chick Hafey	400.00	160.00	100.00
(28) Jesse Joseph Haines	400.00	160.00	100.00
(29) William Hallahan	250.00	100.00	60.00
(30) Melvin Harder	250.00	100.00	60.00
(31) Gabby Hartnett	400.00	160.00	100.00
(32) Babe Herman	250.00	100.00	60.00
(33) William Herman	400.00	160.00	100.00
(34) Rogers Hornsby	1,200	480.00	300.00
(35) Roy C. Johnson	250.00	100.00	60.00
(36) J. Smead Jolley	250.00	100.00	60.00
(37) William Jurges	250.00	100.00	60.00
(38) William Kamm	250.00	100.00	60.00
(39) Mark A. Koenig	250.00	100.00	60.00
(40) James J. Levey	450.00	180.00	110.00
(41) Ernie Lombardi	400.00	160.00	100.00
(42) Red Lucas	250.00	100.00	60.00
(43) Ted Lyons	400.00	160.00	100.00
(44) Connie Mack	400.00	160.00	100.00
(45) Pat Malone	250.00	100.00	60.00
(46) Pepper Martin	300.00	125.00	75.00
(47) Marty McManus	250.00	100.00	60.00
(48) Frank J. O'Doul	350.00	140.00	87.00
(49) Richard Porter	250.00	100.00	60.00
(50) Carl N. Reynolds	250.00	100.00	60.00
(51) Charles Henry Root	250.00	100.00	60.00
(52) Robert Seeds	250.00	100.00	60.00
(53) Al H. Simmons	400.00	160.00	100.00
(54) Jackson Riggs Stephenson	250.00	100.00	60.00
(55) Bud Tinning	250.00	100.00	60.00
(56) Joe Vosmik	250.00	100.00	60.00
(57) Rube Walberg	250.00	100.00	60.00
(58) Paul Waner	400.00	160.00	100.00
(59) Lonnie Warneke	250.00	100.00	60.00
(60) Arthur C. Whitney	250.00	100.00	60.00

1933 Tattoo Orbit (R308)

This obscure set of cards, issued with Tattoo Orbit gum, is numbered from 151 through 207, with a few of the numbers still unknown. Most surviving examples measure 1-7/8" x 1-1/4," but larger pieces (2-1/2" x 3-7/8") are also known with the same players and numbers. The player pictures on the cards "developed" when moistened and rubbed with a piece of blotting paper. Besides the baseball players, there were also pictures of movie stars and other celebrities.

	NM	EX	VG
Common Player:	200.00	90.00	50.00
Large-Format: 4X			
151 Vernon Gomez	500.00	225.00	125.00
152 Kiki Cuyler	500.00	225.00	125.00
153 Jimmy Foxx	850.00	380.00	210.00
154 Al Simmons	500.00	225.00	125.00
155 Chas. J. Grimm	200.00	90.00	50.00
156 William Jurges	200.00	90.00	50.00
157 Chuck Klein	500.00	225.00	125.00
158 Richard Bartell	200.00	90.00	50.00
159 Pepper Martin	275.00	125.00	69.00
160 Earl Averill	500.00	225.00	125.00
161 William Dickey	500.00	225.00	125.00
162 Wesley Ferrell	200.00	90.00	50.00
163 Oral Hildebrand	200.00	90.00	50.00
164 Wm. Kamm	200.00	90.00	50.00
165 Earl Whitehill	200.00	90.00	50.00
166 Charles Fullis	200.00	90.00	50.00
167 Jimmy Dykes	200.00	90.00	50.00
168 Ben Cantwell	200.00	90.00	50.00
169 George Earnshaw	200.00	90.00	50.00
170 Jackson Stephenson	200.00	90.00	50.00
171 Randolph Moore	200.00	90.00	50.00
172 Ted Lyons	500.00	225.00	125.00
173 Goose Goslin	500.00	225.00	125.00
174 E. Swanson	200.00	90.00	50.00
175 Lee Roy Mahaffey	200.00	90.00	50.00
176 Joe Cronin	500.00	225.00	125.00
177 Tom Bridges	200.00	90.00	50.00
178 Henry Manush	500.00	225.00	125.00
179 Walter Stewart	200.00	90.00	50.00
180 Frank Pytlak	200.00	90.00	50.00
181 Dale Alexander	200.00	90.00	50.00
182 Robert Grove	600.00	270.00	150.00
183 Charles Gehringer	500.00	225.00	125.00
184 Lewis Fonseca	200.00	90.00	50.00
185 Alvin Crowder	200.00	90.00	50.00
186 Mickey Cochrane	500.00	225.00	125.00
187 Max Bishop	200.00	90.00	50.00
188 Connie Mack	500.00	225.00	125.00
189 Guy Bush	200.00	90.00	50.00
190 Charlie Root	200.00	90.00	50.00
191a Burleigh Grimes	500.00	225.00	125.00
191b Gabby Hartnett	500.00	225.00	125.00
192 Pat Malone	200.00	90.00	50.00
193 Woody English	200.00	90.00	50.00
194 Lonnie Warneke	200.00	90.00	50.00
195 Babe Herman	275.00	125.00	69.00
196 Unknown			
197 Unknown			
198 Unknown			
199 Unknown			
200 Gabby Hartnett	500.00	225.00	125.00
201 Paul Waner	500.00	225.00	125.00
202 Dizzy Dean	750.00	335.00	185.00
203 Unknown			
204 Unknown			
205 Jim Bottomley	500.00	225.00	125.00
206 Unknown			
207 Charles Hafey	500.00	225.00	125.00
208 Unknown			
209 Unknown			
210 Unknown			

1907-09 H.M. Taylor Detroit Tigers Postcards

Various players and groups of players are featured in this issue of hometown heroes from H. M. Taylor in Detroit. The 5-1/2" x 3-1/2" black-and-white cards have white borders on front. Undivided backs have a gothic "Post Card" at top, a one-cent stamp box and, at bottom-left, "Rights reserved by H. M. Taylor, Detroit."

	NM	EX	VG
Complete Set (7):	5,000	2,500	1,500
Common Card:	525.00	260.00	150.00
(1) Tyrus Cobb (At bat.)	1,800	900.00	550.00
(2) Bill Coughlin/Btg	525.00	260.00	150.00
(3) Sam Crawford (Ready for the Ball.)	750.00	375.00	225.00
(4) Detroit Club (Team photo.)	850.00	425.00	250.00
(5) Wild Bill Donovan (Floral horseshoe presented at Philadelphia.)	525.00	260.00	150.00
(6) Hughie Jennings ("WEE'AH")	525.00	260.00	150.00
(7) Hughie Jennings, Wild Bill Donovan, Frank Chance (In dugout.)	525.00	260.00	150.00

1972 TCMA The 1930's

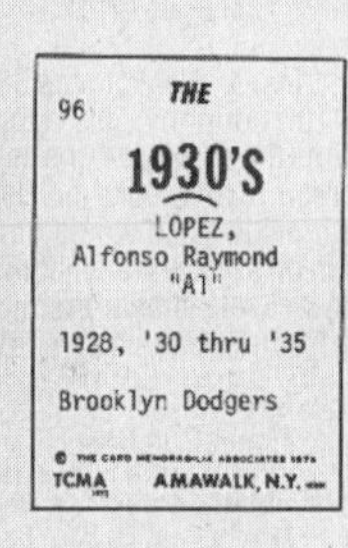
96

THE

1930'S

LOPEZ,

Alfonso Raymond

"Al"

1928, '30 thru '35

Brooklyn Dodgers

TCMA AMAWALK, N.Y.

Extending to over 500 cards, this was one of TCMA's first ventures into the business of creating collectors' edition card sets of former players. Over the length of the series there were a number of style differences. The set was issued in 21 series of 24 cards each. All cards were printed in black-and-white (except for Series 18-19 printed in blue) and feature player photos on usually borderless fronts. Dimensions were about 2" x 2-3/4" for most series, with Series 15-16 in a 2-1/2" x 3-1/2" format. Except for a TCMA copyright line on some of the earlier cards, there is no other printing on front. Backs have player identification, team affiliations, TCMA copyright and, after #72, a card number. Production is reported as 1,000 sets. Blank-bank versions and uncut panels of 12 exist.

	NM	EX	VG
Complete Set (504):	400.00	200.00	120.00
Common Player:	3.00	1.50	.90
(1) Roy Bell	3.00	1.50	.90
(2) Max Bishop	3.00	1.50	.90
(3) Bob Boken	3.00	1.50	.90
(4) Cliff Bolton	3.00	1.50	.90
(5) John Broaca	3.00	1.50	.90
(6) Bill Brubaker	3.00	1.50	.90
(7) Slick Castleman	3.00	1.50	.90
(8) Dick Coffman	3.00	1.50	.90
(9) Phil Collins	3.00	1.50	.90
(10) Earle Combs	3.00	1.50	.90
(11) Doc Cramer	3.00	1.50	.90
(12) Joe Cronin	3.00	1.50	.90
(13) Jack Crouch	3.00	1.50	.90
(14) Tony Cuccinello	3.00	1.50	.90
(15) Babe Dahlgren	3.00	1.50	.90
(16) Spud Davis	3.00	1.50	.90
(17) Dizzy Dean	6.00	3.00	1.75
(18) Paul Dean	3.00	1.50	.90
(19) Bill Dickey	3.00	1.50	.90
(20) Joe DiMaggio	10.00	5.00	3.00
(21) George Earnshaw	3.00	1.50	.90
(22) Woody English	3.00	1.50	.90
(23) Woody English	3.00	1.50	.90
(24) Hal Finney	3.00	1.50	.90
(25) Freddie Fitzsimmons, Bump Hadley	3.00	1.50	.90
(26) Tony Freitas	3.00	1.50	.90
(27) Frank Frisch	3.00	1.50	.90
(28) Milt Gaston	3.00	1.50	.90
(29) Sid Gautreaux	3.00	1.50	.90
(30) Charlie Gehringer	3.00	1.50	.90
(31) Charley Gelbert	3.00	1.50	.90
(32) Lefty Gomez	3.00	1.50	.90
(33) Lefty Grove	5.00	2.50	1.50
(34) Chick Hafey	3.00	1.50	.90
(35) Jesse Haines	3.00	1.50	.90
(36) Bill Hallahan	3.00	1.50	.90
(37) Bucky Harris	3.00	1.50	.90
(38) Ed Heusser	3.00	1.50	.90

No.	Player			
(39)	Carl Hubbell	3.00	1.50	.90
(40)	Carl Hubbell	3.00	1.50	.90
(41)	Jimmy Jordan	3.00	1.50	.90
(42)	Joe Judge	3.00	1.50	.90
(43)	Len Koenecke	3.00	1.50	.90
(44)	Mark Koenig	3.00	1.50	.90
(45)	Cookie Lavagetto	3.00	1.50	.90
(46)	Roxie Lawson	3.00	1.50	.90
(47)	Tony Lazzeri	3.00	1.50	.90
(48)	Gus Mancuso	3.00	1.50	.90
(49)	John McCarthy	3.00	1.50	.90
(50)	Joe Medwick	3.00	1.50	.90
(51)	Cliff Melton	3.00	1.50	.90
(52)	Terry Moore	3.00	1.50	.90
(53)	John Murphy	3.00	1.50	.90
(54)	Ken O'Dea	3.00	1.50	.90
(55)	Bob O'Farrell	3.00	1.50	.90
(56)	Manuel Onis	3.00	1.50	.90
(57)	Monte Pearson	3.00	1.50	.90
(58)	Paul Richards	3.00	1.50	.90
(59)	Max Rosenfeld	6.00	3.00	1.75
(60)	Red Ruffing	3.00	1.50	.90
(61)	Red Ruffing	3.00	1.50	.90
(62)	Hal Schumacher	3.00	1.50	.90
(63)	George Selkirk	3.00	1.50	.90
(64)	Joe Shaute	3.00	1.50	.90
(65)	Gordon Slade	3.00	1.50	.90
(66)	Lindo Storti	3.00	1.50	.90
(67)	Smokey Sundra	3.00	1.50	.90
(68)	Bill Terry	3.00	1.50	.90
(69)	Jack Tising	3.00	1.50	.90
(70)	Sandy Vance	3.00	1.50	.90
(71)	Rube Walberg	3.00	1.50	.90
(72)	Sammy West	3.00	1.50	.90
73	Vito Tamulis	3.00	1.50	.90
74	Kemp Wicker	3.00	1.50	.90
75	Bob Seeds	3.00	1.50	.90
76	Jack Saltzgaver	3.00	1.50	.90
77	Walter Brown	3.00	1.50	.90
78	Spud Chandler	3.00	1.50	.90
79	Myril Hoag	3.00	1.50	.90
80	Joe Glenn	3.00	1.50	.90
81	Lefty Gomez	3.00	1.50	.90
82	Arndt Jorgens	3.00	1.50	.90
83	Jesse Hill	3.00	1.50	.90
84	Red Rolfe	3.00	1.50	.90
85	Wes Ferrell	3.00	1.50	.90
86	Joe Morrissey	3.00	1.50	.90
87	Tony Piet	3.00	1.50	.90
88	Fred Walker	3.00	1.50	.90
89	Bill Dietrich	3.00	1.50	.90
90	Lyn Lary	3.00	1.50	.90
91	Lyn Lary	3.00	1.50	.90
92	Lyn Lary	3.00	1.50	.90
93	Lyn Lary	3.00	1.50	.90
94	Buzz Boyle	3.00	1.50	.90
95	Tony Malinosky	3.00	1.50	.90
96	Al Lopez	3.00	1.50	.90
97	Linus Frey	3.00	1.50	.90
98	Tony Malinosky	3.00	1.50	.90
99	Owen Carroll	3.00	1.50	.90
100	Buddy Hassett	3.00	1.50	.90
101	Gib Brack	3.00	1.50	.90
102	Sam Leslie	3.00	1.50	.90
103	Fred Heimach	3.00	1.50	.90
104	Burleigh Grimes	3.00	1.50	.90
105	Ray Benge	3.00	1.50	.90
106	Joe Stripp	3.00	1.50	.90
107	Joe Becker	3.00	1.50	.90
108	Oscar Melillo	3.00	1.50	.90
109	Charley O'Leary, Rogers Hornsby	3.00	1.50	.90
110	Luke Appling	3.00	1.50	.90
111	Stan Hack	3.00	1.50	.90
112	Ray Hayworth	3.00	1.50	.90
113	Charles Wilson	3.00	1.50	.90
114	Hal Trosky	3.00	1.50	.90
115	Wes Ferrell	3.00	1.50	.90
116	Lyn Lary	3.00	1.50	.90
117	Milt Gaston	3.00	1.50	.90
118	Eldon Auker	3.00	1.50	.90
119	Heinie Manush	3.00	1.50	.90
120	Jimmie Foxx	6.00	3.00	1.75
121	Don Heffner	3.00	1.50	.90
122	George Pipgras	3.00	1.50	.90
123	Bump Hadley	3.00	1.50	.90
124	Tommy Henrich	3.00	1.50	.90
125	Joe McCarthy	3.00	1.50	.90
126	Joe Sewell	3.00	1.50	.90
127	Frank Crosetti	3.00	1.50	.90
128	Fred Walker	3.00	1.50	.90
129	Ted Kleinhans	3.00	1.50	.90
130	Jake Powell	3.00	1.50	.90
131	Ben Chapman	3.00	1.50	.90
132	John Murphy	3.00	1.50	.90
133	Lon Warneke	3.00	1.50	.90
134	Augie Galan	3.00	1.50	.90
135	Gene Lillard	3.00	1.50	.90
136	Stan Hack	3.00	1.50	.90
137	Frank Demaree	3.00	1.50	.90
138	Tony Piet	3.00	1.50	.90
139	Tony Piet	3.00	1.50	.90
140	Don Brennan	3.00	1.50	.90
141	Hal Schumacher, Lefty Gomez	3.00	1.50	.90
142	Bump Hadley	3.00	1.50	.90
143	Ollie Bejma	3.00	1.50	.90
144	Jim Bottomley	3.00	1.50	.90
145	Clay Bryant	3.00	1.50	.90
146	Charlie Grimm	3.00	1.50	.90
147	Flea Clifton	3.00	1.50	.90
148	Rollie Stiles	3.00	1.50	.90
149	Al Simmons	3.00	1.50	.90
150	Al Simmons	3.00	1.50	.90
151	Lyn Lary	3.00	1.50	.90
152	Roy Weatherly	3.00	1.50	.90
153	Whit Wyatt	3.00	1.50	.90
154	Oscar Vitt	3.00	1.50	.90
155	Jack Kroner	3.00	1.50	.90
156	Ted Lyons	3.00	1.50	.90
157	Joe Malay	3.00	1.50	.90
158	John McCarthy	3.00	1.50	.90
159	Hy Vandenberg	3.00	1.50	.90
160	Hank Leiber	3.00	1.50	.90
161	Joe Moore	3.00	1.50	.90
162	Cliff Melton	3.00	1.50	.90
163	Harry Danning	3.00	1.50	.90
164	Ray Harrell	3.00	1.50	.90
165	Bruce Ogrodowski	3.00	1.50	.90
166	Leo Durocher	3.00	1.50	.90
167	Leo Durocher	3.00	1.50	.90
168	William Walker	3.00	1.50	.90
169	Alvin Crowder	3.00	1.50	.90
170	Gus Suhr	3.00	1.50	.90
171	Monty Stratton	4.50	2.25	1.25
172	Boze Berger	3.00	1.50	.90
173	John Whitehead	3.00	1.50	.90
174	Joe Heving	3.00	1.50	.90
175	Merv Shea	3.00	1.50	.90
176	Ed Durham	3.00	1.50	.90
177	Buddy Myer	3.00	1.50	.90
178	Earl Whitehill	3.00	1.50	.90
179	Joe Cronin	3.00	1.50	.90
180	Zeke Bonura	3.00	1.50	.90
181	John Knott	3.00	1.50	.90
182	John Allen	3.00	1.50	.90
183	William Knickerbocker	3.00	1.50	.90
184	Earl Averill	3.00	1.50	.90
185	Bob Feller	4.50	2.25	1.25
186	Steve O'Neill	3.00	1.50	.90
187	Bruce Campbell	3.00	1.50	.90
188	Ivy Andrews	3.00	1.50	.90
189	Ivy Andrews	3.00	1.50	.90
190	Muddy Ruel	3.00	1.50	.90
191	Art Scharein	3.00	1.50	.90
192	Merv Shea	3.00	1.50	.90
193	George Myatt	3.00	1.50	.90
194	Bill Werber	3.00	1.50	.90
195	Red Lucas	3.00	1.50	.90
196	Hugh Luby	3.00	1.50	.90
197	Vic Sorrell	3.00	1.50	.90
198	Mickey Cochrane	3.00	1.50	.90
199	Rudy York	3.00	1.50	.90
200	Ray Mack	3.00	1.50	.90
201	Vince DiMaggio	4.50	2.25	1.25
202	Mel Ott	4.50	2.25	1.25
203	John Lucadello	3.00	1.50	.90
204	Debs Garms	3.00	1.50	.90
205	John Murphy, Pat Malone, Bump Hadley, Kemp Wicker, John Broaca	3.00	1.50	.90
206	Stan Sperry	3.00	1.50	.90
207	Hal Schumacher	3.00	1.50	.90
208	Blondy Ryan	3.00	1.50	.90
209	Bob Seeds	3.00	1.50	.90
210	Danny MacFayden	3.00	1.50	.90
211	Fran Healy	3.00	1.50	.90
212	Al Spohrer	3.00	1.50	.90
213	Ed Linke	3.00	1.50	.90
214	Joe Schultz	3.00	1.50	.90
215	Casey Stengel	3.00	1.50	.90
216	Casey Stengel	3.00	1.50	.90
217	Phil Hensick	3.00	1.50	.90
218	Rollie Hemsley	3.00	1.50	.90
219	Ace Parker	4.50	2.25	1.25
220	Henry Helf	3.00	1.50	.90
221	Bill Schuster	3.00	1.50	.90
222	Heinie Schuble	3.00	1.50	.90
223	John Salveson	3.00	1.50	.90
224	Robert Grace	3.00	1.50	.90
225	Sig Gryska	3.00	1.50	.90
226	Mickey Haslin	3.00	1.50	.90
227	Randy Gumpert	3.00	1.50	.90
228	Frank Gustine	3.00	1.50	.90
229	Marv Gudat	3.00	1.50	.90
230	Bob Logan	3.00	1.50	.90
231	Marvin Owen	3.00	1.50	.90
232	Bucky Walters	3.00	1.50	.90
233	Marty Hopkins	3.00	1.50	.90
234	Jimmy Dykes	3.00	1.50	.90
235	Lefty O'Doul	3.00	1.50	.90
236	Larry Rosenthal	3.00	1.50	.90
237	Mickey Haslin	3.00	1.50	.90
238	Eugene Schott	3.00	1.50	.90
239	Sad Sam Jones	3.00	1.50	.90
240	Edwin Rommel	3.00	1.50	.90
241	Rip Collins	3.00	1.50	.90
242	Rosy Ryan	3.00	1.50	.90
243	James Bucher	3.00	1.50	.90
244	Ethan Allen	3.00	1.50	.90
245	Dick Bartell	3.00	1.50	.90
246	Henry Leiber	3.00	1.50	.90
247	Lou Chiozza	3.00	1.50	.90
248	Babe Herman	3.00	1.50	.90
249	Tommy Henrich	3.00	1.50	.90
250	Thornton Lee	3.00	1.50	.90
251	Joe Kuhel	3.00	1.50	.90
252	George Pipgras	3.00	1.50	.90
253	Luke Sewell	3.00	1.50	.90
254	Tony Lazzeri	3.00	1.50	.90
255	Ival Goodman	3.00	1.50	.90
256	George Rensa	3.00	1.50	.90
257	Hal Newhouser	3.00	1.50	.90
258	Rogers Hornsby	5.00	2.50	1.50
259	Tuck Stainback	3.00	1.50	.90
260	Vance Page	3.00	1.50	.90
261	Art Scharein	3.00	1.50	.90
262	Mike Ryba	3.00	1.50	.90
263	James Lindsey	3.00	1.50	.90
264	Ed Parsons	3.00	1.50	.90
265	Elon Hogsett	3.00	1.50	.90
266	Bud Hafey	3.00	1.50	.90
267	John Gill	3.00	1.50	.90
268	Owen Bush	3.00	1.50	.90
269	Ethan Allen	3.00	1.50	.90
270	Jim Bagby	3.00	1.50	.90
271	Bill Atwood	3.00	1.50	.90
272	Phil Cavarretta	3.00	1.50	.90
273	Travis Jackson	3.00	1.50	.90
274	Ted Olson	3.00	1.50	.90
275	Boze Berger	3.00	1.50	.90
276	Norb Kleinke	3.00	1.50	.90
277	Rip Radcliff	3.00	1.50	.90
278	Mule Haas	3.00	1.50	.90
279	Julius Solters	3.00	1.50	.90
280	Ivey Shiver	3.00	1.50	.90
281	Wes Schulmerich	3.00	1.50	.90
282	Ray Kolp	3.00	1.50	.90
283	Si Johnson	3.00	1.50	.90
284	Al Hollingsworth	3.00	1.50	.90
285	D'Arcy Flowers	3.00	1.50	.90
286	Adam Comorosky	3.00	1.50	.90
287	Allen Cooke	3.00	1.50	.90
288	Clyde Kimsey	3.00	1.50	.90
289	Fred Ostermueller	3.00	1.50	.90
290	Angelo Giuliani	3.00	1.50	.90
291	John Wilson	3.00	1.50	.90
292	George Dickman	3.00	1.50	.90
293	Jim DeShong	3.00	1.50	.90
294	Red Evans	3.00	1.50	.90
295	Curtis Davis	3.00	1.50	.90
296	Charlie Berry	3.00	1.50	.90
297	George Gibson	3.00	1.50	.90
298	Fern Bell	3.00	1.50	.90
299	Irv Bartling	3.00	1.50	.90
300	Babe Barna	3.00	1.50	.90
301	Henry Johnson	3.00	1.50	.90
302	Harlond Clift	3.00	1.50	.90
303	Lu Blue	3.00	1.50	.90
304	George Hockette	3.00	1.50	.90
305	Walt Bashore	3.00	1.50	.90
306	Walter Beck	3.00	1.50	.90
307	Jewel Ens	3.00	1.50	.90
308	Doc Prothro	3.00	1.50	.90
309	Morrie Arnovich	3.00	1.50	.90
310	Bill Killefer	3.00	1.50	.90
311	Pete Appleton	3.00	1.50	.90
312	Fred Archer	3.00	1.50	.90
313	Bill Lohrman	3.00	1.50	.90
314	Fred Haney	3.00	1.50	.90
315	Jimmy Ripple	3.00	1.50	.90
316	Johnny Kerr	3.00	1.50	.90
317	Harry Gumbert	3.00	1.50	.90
318	Samuel Derringer	3.00	1.50	.90
319	Firpo Marberry	3.00	1.50	.90
320	Waite Hoyt	3.00	1.50	.90
321	Rick Ferrell	3.00	1.50	.90
322	Hank Greenberg	6.00	3.00	1.75
323	Carl Reynolds	3.00	1.50	.90
324	Roy Johnson	3.00	1.50	.90
325	Gil English	3.00	1.50	.90
326	Al Smith	3.00	1.50	.90
327	Dolph Camilli	3.00	1.50	.90
328	Oscar Grimes	3.00	1.50	.90
329	Ray Berres	3.00	1.50	.90
330	Norm Schlueter	3.00	1.50	.90
331	Joe Vosmik	3.00	1.50	.90
332	Jimmy Dykes	3.00	1.50	.90
333	Vern Washington	3.00	1.50	.90
334	"Bad News" Hale	3.00	1.50	.90
335	Lew Fonseca	3.00	1.50	.90
336	Mike Kreevich	3.00	1.50	.90
337	Bob Johnson	3.00	1.50	.90
338	"Jeep" Handley	3.00	1.50	.90
339	Gabby Hartnett	3.00	1.50	.90
340	Freddie Lindstrom	3.00	1.50	.90
341	Bert Haas	3.00	1.50	.90
342	Elbie Fletcher	3.00	1.50	.90
343	Tom Hafey	3.00	1.50	.90
344	Rip Collins	3.00	1.50	.90
345	John Babich	3.00	1.50	.90
346	Joe Beggs	3.00	1.50	.90
347	Bobo Newsom	3.00	1.50	.90
348	Wally Berger	3.00	1.50	.90
349	Bud Thomas	3.00	1.50	.90
350	Tom Heath	3.00	1.50	.90
351	Cecil Travis	3.00	1.50	.90
352	Jack Redmond	3.00	1.50	.90
353	Fred Schulte	3.00	1.50	.90
354	Pat Malone	3.00	1.50	.90
355	Hugh Critz	3.00	1.50	.90
356	Frank Pytlak	3.00	1.50	.90
357	Glenn Liebhardt	3.00	1.50	.90
358	Al Milnar	3.00	1.50	.90
359	Al Benton	3.00	1.50	.90
360	Moe Berg	6.00	3.00	1.75
361	Al Brancato	3.00	1.50	.90
362	Mark Christman	3.00	1.50	.90
363	Fabian Gaffke	3.00	1.50	.90
364	George Gill	3.00	1.50	.90
365	Oral Hildebrand	3.00	1.50	.90
366	Lou Fette	3.00	1.50	.90
367	Tex Carleton	3.00	1.50	.90
368	Don Gutteridge	3.00	1.50	.90
369	Pete Fox	3.00	1.50	.90
370	George Blaeholder	3.00	1.50	.90
371	George Caster	3.00	1.50	.90
372	Joe Cascarella	3.00	1.50	.90
373	Jimmy Hitchcock	3.00	1.50	.90
374	Frank Croucher	3.00	1.50	.90
375	LeRoy Parmelee	3.00	1.50	.90
376	Joe Mulligan	3.00	1.50	.90
377	John Welch	3.00	1.50	.90
378	Donald McNair	3.00	1.50	.90
379	Frenchy Bordagaray	3.00	1.50	.90
380	Denny Galehouse	3.00	1.50	.90
381	Robert Harris	3.00	1.50	.90
382	Max Butcher	3.00	1.50	.90
383	Sam Byrd	3.00	1.50	.90
384	Pete Coscarart	3.00	1.50	.90
385	George Case	3.00	1.50	.90
386	John Hudson	3.00	1.50	.90
387	Frank Crespi	3.00	1.50	.90
388	Gene Desautels	3.00	1.50	.90
389	Bill Cissell	3.00	1.50	.90

390	John Burns	3.00	1.50	.90
391	Larry Benton	3.00	1.50	.90
392	James Holbrook	3.00	1.50	.90
393	Ernie Koy	3.00	1.50	.90
394	Bobby Doerr	3.00	1.50	.90
395	Harry Boyles	3.00	1.50	.90
396	Pinky Higgins	3.00	1.50	.90
397	Mel Almada	3.00	1.50	.90
398	Carl Fischer	3.00	1.50	.90
399	Rabbit Maranville, Johnny Evers, Hank Gowdy	3.00	1.50	.90
400	Lou Gehrig	10.00	5.00	3.00
401	Lincoln Blakely	3.00	1.50	.90
402	James Henry	3.00	1.50	.90
403	Ed Holley	3.00	1.50	.90
404	Elmer Hodgin	3.00	1.50	.90
405	Bob Garbark	3.00	1.50	.90
406	John Burnett	3.00	1.50	.90
407	David Harris	3.00	1.50	.90
408	Johnny Dickshot	3.00	1.50	.90
409	Ray Mueller	3.00	1.50	.90
410	John Welaj	3.00	1.50	.90
411	Les McCrabb	3.00	1.50	.90
412	George Uhle	3.00	1.50	.90
413	Leo Mangum	3.00	1.50	.90
414	Howard Maple	3.00	1.50	.90
415	Syl Johnson	3.00	1.50	.90
416	Hershel Martin	3.00	1.50	.90
417	Joe Martin	3.00	1.50	.90
418	Phil Masi	3.00	1.50	.90
419	Bobby Mattick	3.00	1.50	.90
420	Marshall Mauldin	3.00	1.50	.90
421	Frank May	3.00	1.50	.90
422	Merrill May	3.00	1.50	.90
423	Bill McAfee	3.00	1.50	.90
424	Benny McCoy	3.00	1.50	.90
425	Charlie George	3.00	1.50	.90
426	Roy Hughes	3.00	1.50	.90
427	Bill Kerksieck	3.00	1.50	.90
428	Wes Kingdon	3.00	1.50	.90
429	Lynn King	3.00	1.50	.90
430	Harry Kinzy	3.00	1.50	.90
431	Harry Kimberlin	3.00	1.50	.90
432	Bob Klinger	3.00	1.50	.90
433	Wilfred Knothe	3.00	1.50	.90
434	Lou Finney	3.00	1.50	.90
435	Roy Johnson	3.00	1.50	.90
436	Woody Jensen	3.00	1.50	.90
437	George Jeffcoat	3.00	1.50	.90
438	Roy Joiner	3.00	1.50	.90
439	Baxter Jordan	3.00	1.50	.90
440	Edwin Joost	3.00	1.50	.90
441	Bubber Jonnard	3.00	1.50	.90
442	Bucky Jacobs	3.00	1.50	.90
443	Art Jacobs	3.00	1.50	.90
444	Orville Jorgens	3.00	1.50	.90
445	Hal Kelleher	3.00	1.50	.90
446	Harry Kelley	3.00	1.50	.90
447	Ken Keltner	3.00	1.50	.90
448	Paul Kardon	3.00	1.50	.90
449	Alex Kampouris	3.00	1.50	.90
450	Willie Kamm	3.00	1.50	.90
451	Bob Kahle	3.00	1.50	.90
452	Billy Jurges	3.00	1.50	.90
453	Ken Jungles	3.00	1.50	.90
454	John Juelich	3.00	1.50	.90
455	John Marcum	3.00	1.50	.90
456	Walt Masterson	3.00	1.50	.90
457	Clint Brown	3.00	1.50	.90
458	Buddy Lewis	3.00	1.50	.90
459	Watty Clark	3.00	1.50	.90
460	Johnny Cooney	3.00	1.50	.90
461	Mel Harder	3.00	1.50	.90
462	Justin McLaughlin	3.00	1.50	.90
463	Frank Grube	3.00	1.50	.90
464	Jeff Heath	3.00	1.50	.90
465	Cliff Heathcote	3.00	1.50	.90
466	Harvey Hendrick	3.00	1.50	.90
467	Johnny Hodapp	3.00	1.50	.90
468	Bob Holland	3.00	1.50	.90
469	Otto Huber	3.00	1.50	.90
470	Rudy Hulswitt	3.00	1.50	.90
471	Roy Johnson	3.00	1.50	.90
472	Smead Jolley	3.00	1.50	.90
473	Rollie Hemsley, Bob Smith, John Moore	3.00	1.50	.90
474	John Jones	3.00	1.50	.90
475	Harry Kelley	3.00	1.50	.90
476	George Kelly	3.00	1.50	.90
477	Chuck Klein	3.00	1.50	.90
478	Joe Krakauskas	3.00	1.50	.90
479	Mike Kreevich	3.00	1.50	.90
480	Dick Lanahan	3.00	1.50	.90
481	Emil "Dutch" Leonard	3.00	1.50	.90
482	Harl Maggert	3.00	1.50	.90
483	Cyrus Malis	3.00	1.50	.90
484	Dario Lodigiani	3.00	1.50	.90
485	Walt Masterson	3.00	1.50	.90
486	Rabbit Maranville	3.00	1.50	.90
487	Ed Marshall	3.00	1.50	.90
488	Tim McKeithan	3.00	1.50	.90
489	Patrick McLaughlin	3.00	1.50	.90
490	Bob McNamara	3.00	1.50	.90
491	Steve Mesner	3.00	1.50	.90
492	Clarence Mitchell	3.00	1.50	.90
493	Mal Moss	3.00	1.50	.90
494	Joe Murray	3.00	1.50	.90
495	Pete Naktenis	3.00	1.50	.90
496	Bill Nicholson	3.00	1.50	.90
497	John Rigney	3.00	1.50	.90
498	Clyde Sukeforth	3.00	1.50	.90
499	Evar Swanson	3.00	1.50	.90
500	Dan Taylor	3.00	1.50	.90
501	Sloppy Thurston	3.00	1.50	.90
502	Forrest Wright	3.00	1.50	.90
503	Ray Lucas	3.00	1.50	.90
504	Nig Lipscomb	3.00	1.50	.90

1973-80 TCMA All-Time Greats Postcards

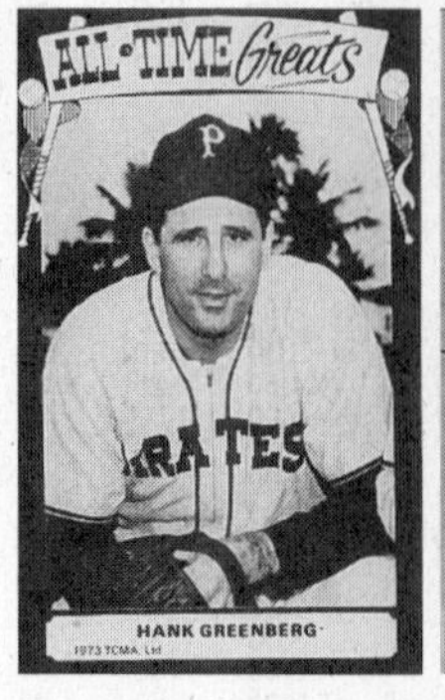

One of the longest collectors' series issued by TCMA in the 1970s was this set of player postcards. Measuring 3-1/2" x 5-1/2" the black-and-white cards have large photos on front, bordered in black and highlighted with banners and baseball equipment. Backs have postcard markings. Six series of cards were issued between 1973-80 and the unnumbered cards are checklisted here in alphabetical order within series.

		NM	EX	VG
	Complete Set (156):	150.00	75.00	45.00
	Common Player:	3.00	1.50	.90
	SERIES 1			
(1)	Luke Appling	3.00	1.50	.90
(2)	Mickey Cochrane	3.00	1.50	.90
(3)	Eddie Collins	3.00	1.50	.90
(4)	Kiki Cuyler	3.00	1.50	.90
(5)	Bill Dickey	3.00	1.50	.90
(6)	Joe DiMaggio	7.50	3.75	2.25
(7)	Bob Feller	3.00	1.50	.90
(8)	Frank Frisch	3.00	1.50	.90
(9)	Lou Gehrig	7.50	3.75	2.25
(10)	Goose Goslin	3.00	1.50	.90
(11)	Chick Hafey	3.00	1.50	.90
(12)	Gabby Hartnett	3.00	1.50	.90
(13)	Rogers Hornsby	4.00	2.00	1.25
(14)	Ted Lyons	3.00	1.50	.90
(15)	Connie Mack	3.00	1.50	.90
(16)	Heinie Manush	3.00	1.50	.90
(17)	Rabbit Maranville	3.00	1.50	.90
(18)	Ducky Medwick	3.00	1.50	.90
(19)	Al Simmons	3.00	1.50	.90
(20)	Bill Terry	3.00	1.50	.90
(21)	Pie Traynor	3.00	1.50	.90
(22)	Dazzy Vance	3.00	1.50	.90
(23)	Cy Young	5.00	2.50	1.50
(24)	Gabby Hartnett, Babe Ruth	6.00	3.00	1.75
	SERIES 2			
(1)	Roger Bresnahan	3.00	1.50	.90
(2)	Dizzy Dean	4.00	2.00	1.25
(3)	Buck Ewing & mascot	3.00	1.50	.90
(4)	Jimmie Foxx	4.50	2.25	1.25
(5)	Hank Greenberg	4.50	2.25	1.25
(6)	Burleigh Grimes	3.00	1.50	.90
(7)	Harry Heilmann	3.00	1.50	.90
(8)	Waite Hoyt	3.00	1.50	.90
(9)	Walter Johnson	5.00	2.50	1.50
(10)	George Kelly	3.00	1.50	.90
(11)	Christy Mathewson	5.00	2.50	1.50
(12)	John McGraw	3.00	1.50	.90
(13)	Stan Musial	4.00	2.00	1.25
(14)	Mel Ott	3.00	1.50	.90
(15)	Satchel Paige	6.00	3.00	1.75
(16)	Sam Rice	3.00	1.50	.90
(17)	Edd Roush	3.00	1.50	.90
(18)	Red Ruffing	3.00	1.50	.90
(19)	Casey Stengel	3.00	1.50	.90
(20)	Honus Wagner	6.00	3.00	1.75
(21)	Lloyd Waner	3.00	1.50	.90
(22)	Paul Waner	3.00	1.50	.90
(23)	Harry Wright	3.00	1.50	.90
(24)	Ross Youngs	3.00	1.50	.90
	SERIES 3			
(1)	Home Run Baker	3.00	1.50	.90
(2)	Chief Bender	3.00	1.50	.90
(3)	Jim Bottomley	3.00	1.50	.90
(4)	Lou Boudreau	3.00	1.50	.90
(5)	Mordecai Brown	3.00	1.50	.90
(6)	Roy Campanella	3.50	1.75	1.00
(7)	Max Carey	3.00	1.50	.90
(8)	Ty Cobb	7.50	3.75	2.25
(9)	Earle Combs	3.00	1.50	.90
(10)	Jocko Conlan	3.00	1.50	.90
(11)	Hugh Duffy	3.00	1.50	.90
(12)	Red Faber	3.00	1.50	.90
(13)	Lefty Grove	3.00	1.50	.90
(14)	Judge K.M. Landis	3.00	1.50	.90
(15)	Eddie Plank	3.00	1.50	.90
(16)	Hoss Radbourne	3.00	1.50	.90
(17)	Eppa Rixey	3.00	1.50	.90
(18)	Jackie Robinson	6.00	3.00	1.75
(19)	Babe Ruth	7.50	3.75	2.25
(20)	George Sisler	3.00	1.50	.90
(21)	Zack Wheat	3.00	1.50	.90
(22)	Ted Williams	6.00	3.00	1.75
(23)	Mel Ott, Babe Ruth	6.00	3.00	1.75
(24)	Tris Speaker, Wilbert Robinson	3.00	1.50	.90
	SERIES 4			
(1)	Grover C. Alexander	3.50	1.75	1.00
(2)	Cap Anson	3.00	1.50	.90
(3)	Earl Averill	3.00	1.50	.90
(4)	Ed Barrow	3.00	1.50	.90
(5)	Yogi Berra	3.50	1.75	1.00
(6)	Roberto Clemente	6.00	3.00	1.75
(7)	Jimmy Collins	3.00	1.50	.90
(8)	Whitey Ford	3.50	1.75	1.00
(9)	Ford Frick	3.00	1.50	.90
(10)	Vernon Gomez	3.00	1.50	.90
(11)	Bucky Harris	3.00	1.50	.90
(12)	Billy Herman	3.00	1.50	.90
(13)	Carl Hubbell	3.00	1.50	.90
(14)	Miller Huggins	3.00	1.50	.90
(15)	Monte Irvin	3.00	1.50	.90
(16)	Ralph Kiner	3.00	1.50	.90
(17)	Bill Klem	3.00	1.50	.90
(18)	Sandy Koufax	6.00	3.00	1.75
(19)	Napoleon Lajoie	3.00	1.50	.90
(20)	Bob Lemon	3.00	1.50	.90
(21)	Mickey Mantle	7.50	3.75	2.25
(22)	Rube Marquard	3.00	1.50	.90
(23)	Joe McCarthy	3.00	1.50	.90
(24)	Bill McKechnie	3.00	1.50	.90
(25)	Herb Pennock	3.00	1.50	.90
(26)	Warren Spahn	3.00	1.50	.90
(27)	Joe Tinker	3.00	1.50	.90
(28)	Early Wynn	3.00	1.50	.90
(29)	Joe Cronin, Honus Wagner, Bill Terry	3.00	1.50	.90
(30)	Jimmie Foxx, Lou Gehrig	6.00	3.00	1.75
(31)	Hank Greenberg, Ralph Kiner	3.00	1.50	.90
(32)	Walter Johnson, Connie Mack	3.00	1.50	.90
(33)	Connie Mack, Bob Feller	3.00	1.50	.90
(34)	Mel Ott, Lou Gehrig	6.00	3.00	1.75
(35)	Al Simmons, Tris Speaker, Ty Cobb	3.00	1.50	.90
(36)	Ted Williams, Lou Boudreau	3.00	1.50	.90
	SERIES 5			
(1)	Dave Bancroft	3.00	1.50	.90
(2)	Ernie Banks	3.50	1.75	1.00
(3)	Frank Chance	3.00	1.50	.90
(4)	Stan Coveleski	3.00	1.50	.90
(5)	Billy Evans	3.00	1.50	.90
(6)	Clark Griffith	3.00	1.50	.90
(7)	Jesse Haines	3.00	1.50	.90
(8)	Will Harridge	3.00	1.50	.90
(9)	Harry Hooper	3.00	1.50	.90
(10)	Cal Hubbard	3.00	1.50	.90
(11)	Hugh Jennings	3.00	1.50	.90
(12)	Wee Willie Keeler	3.00	1.50	.90
(13)	Fred Lindstrom	3.00	1.50	.90
(14)	Pop Lloyd	3.00	1.50	.90
(15)	Al Lopez	3.00	1.50	.90
(16)	Robin Roberts	3.00	1.50	.90
(17)	Amos Rusie	3.00	1.50	.90
(18)	Ray Schalk	3.00	1.50	.90
(19)	Joe Sewell	3.00	1.50	.90
(20)	Rube Waddell	3.00	1.50	.90
(21)	George Weiss	3.00	1.50	.90
(22)	Dizzy Dean, Gabby Hartnett	3.00	1.50	.90
(23)	Joe DiMaggio, Mickey Mantle	7.50	3.75	2.25
(24)	Ted Williams, Joe DiMaggio	6.00	3.00	1.75
	SERIES 6			
(1)	Jack Chesbro	3.00	1.50	.90
(2)	Tom Connolly	3.00	1.50	.90
(3)	Sam Crawford	3.00	1.50	.90
(4)	Elmer Flick	3.00	1.50	.90
(5)	Charlie Gehringer	3.00	1.50	.90
(6)	Warren Giles	3.00	1.50	.90
(7)	Ban Johnson	3.00	1.50	.90
(8)	Addie Joss	3.00	1.50	.90
(9)	Al Kaline	3.00	1.50	.90
(10)	Willie Mays	6.00	3.00	1.75
(11)	Joe McGinnity	3.00	1.50	.90
(12)	Larry McPhail (MacPhail)	3.00	1.50	.90
(13)	Branch Rickey	3.00	1.50	.90
(14)	Wilbert Robinson	3.00	1.50	.90
(15)	Duke Snider	3.00	1.50	.90
(16)	Tris Speaker	4.00	2.00	1.25
(17)	Bobby Wallace	3.00	1.50	.90
(18)	Hack Wilson	.45	.25	.14
(19)	Yogi Berra, Casey Stengel	4.00	2.00	1.25
(20)	Warren Giles, Roberto Clemente	4.50	2.25	1.25
(21)	Mickey Mantle, Willie Mays	6.00	3.00	1.75
(22)	John McGraw, Babe Ruth	6.00	3.00	1.75
(23)	Satchel Paige, Bob Feller	5.00	2.50	1.50
(24)	Paul Waner, Lloyd Waner	4.00	2.00	1.25

1973 TCMA All Time New York Yankees Team

Outfield-Mickey Mantle

Printed in black-and-white in 3-1/2" x 5-1/2" format, these cards have borderless photos on front with a white strip at bottom in which the player's position and name appear. Backs list the all-time roster but are not numbered or dated. Production was 1,000 sets.

		NM	EX	VG
Complete Set (12):		25.00	12.50	7.50
Common Player:		3.50	1.75	1.00
(1)	Bill Dickey	3.50	1.75	1.00
(2)	Joe DiMaggio	10.00	5.00	3.00
(3)	Whitey Ford	5.00	2.50	1.50
(4)	Lou Gehrig	10.00	5.00	3.00
(5)	Tony Lazzeri	3.50	1.75	1.00
(6)	Mickey Mantle	15.00	7.50	4.50
(7)	Johnny Murphy	3.50	1.75	1.00
(8)	Phil Rizzuto	5.00	2.50	1.50
(9)	Red Rolfe	3.50	1.75	1.00
(10)	Red Ruffing	3.50	1.75	1.00
(11)	Babe Ruth	10.00	5.00	3.00
(12)	Casey Stengel	3.50	1.75	1.00

1973 TCMA Autographs & Drawings Postcards

These black-and-white postcards feature drawings of the players, along with facsimile autographs.

		NM	EX	VG
Complete Set (12):		50.00	25.00	15.00
Common Player:		5.00	2.50	1.50
1	Mickey Cockran (Cochrane)	5.00	2.50	1.50
2	Christy Mathewson	5.00	2.50	1.50
3	Roberto Clemente	10.00	5.00	3.00
4	Rogers Hornsby	5.00	2.50	1.50
5	Pie Traynor	5.00	2.50	1.50
6	Frankie Frisch	5.00	2.50	1.50
7	Ty Cobb	7.50	3.75	2.25
8	Connie Mack	5.00	2.50	1.50
9	Babe Ruth	10.00	5.00	3.00
10	Lou Gehrig	8.00	4.00	2.50
11	Gil Hodges	5.00	2.50	1.50
12	Jackie Robinson	8.00	4.00	2.50

1973-1974 TCMA Autograph Series

These postcard-size black-and-white cards have borderless front photos with a wide white strip at bottom to accomodate an autograph. They are blank-backed.

		NM	EX	VG
Complete Set (36):		125.00	65.00	35.00
Common Player:		4.00	2.00	1.20
1	Satchel Paige	7.50	3.75	2.25
2	Phil Rizzuto	6.00	3.00	1.75
3	Sid Gordon	4.00	2.00	1.20
4	Ernie Lombardi	4.00	2.00	1.20
5	Jesse Haines	4.00	2.00	1.20
6	Joe Gordon	4.00	2.00	1.20
7	Bill Terry	4.00	2.00	1.20
8	Bill Dickey	6.00	3.00	1.75
9	Joe DiMaggio	12.00	6.00	3.50
10	Carl Hubbell	5.00	2.50	1.50
11	Fred Lindstrom	4.00	2.00	1.20
12	Ted Lyons	4.00	2.00	1.20
13	Red Ruffing	4.00	2.00	1.20
14	Joe Gordon	4.00	2.00	1.20
15	Bob Feller	6.00	3.00	1.75
16	Yogi Berra	7.50	3.75	2.25
17	Ford Frick, Whitey Ford	5.00	2.50	1.50
18	Sandy Koufax	12.00	6.00	3.50
19	Ted Williams	10.00	5.00	3.00
20	Warren Spahn	5.00	2.50	1.50
21	Al Rosen	4.00	2.00	1.20
22	Luke Appling	4.00	2.00	1.20
23	Joe Bush	4.00	2.00	1.20
24	Joe Medwick	4.00	2.00	1.20
25	Lou Boudreau	4.00	2.00	1.20
26	Ralph Kiner	4.00	2.00	1.20
27	Lloyd Waner	4.00	2.00	1.20
28	Pee Wee Reese	7.50	3.75	2.25
29	Duke Snider	7.50	3.75	2.25
30	Sal Maglie	4.00	2.00	1.20
31	Monte Irvin	4.00	2.00	1.20
32	Lefty Gomez	4.00	2.00	1.20
33	George Kelly	4.00	2.00	1.20
34	Joe Adcock	4.00	2.00	1.20
35	Max Carey	4.00	2.00	1.20
36	Rube Marquard	4.00	2.00	1.20

1973 TCMA "Bobo"

The major league travels of Bobo Newsom are chronicled in this set of 3-1/2" x 5-1/2" black-and-white cards depicting the pitcher in the uniforms of the nine teams for whom he played between 1929-53.

		NM	EX	VG
Complete Set (10):		25.00	12.50	7.50
Common Card:		4.00	2.00	1.25
(1)	Bobo Newsom (A's)	4.00	2.00	1.25
(2)	Bobo Newsom (A's, with Bobby Shantz)	4.00	2.00	1.25
(3)	Bobo Newsom (Browns)	4.00	2.00	1.25
(4)	Bobo Newsom (Cubs)	4.00	2.00	1.25
(5)	Bobo Newsom (Dodgers, with Leo Durocher)	4.00	2.00	1.25
(6)	Bobo Newsom (Giants)	4.00	2.00	1.25
(7)	Bobo Newsom (Red Sox)	4.00	2.00	1.25
(8)	Bobo Newsom (Senators, with Ossie Bluege)	4.00	2.00	1.25
(9)	Bobo Newsom (Tigers, with Paul Derringer)	4.00	2.00	1.25
(10)	Bobo Newsom (Yankees, with Vic Rashi, Bucky Harris)	4.00	2.00	1.25

1973 TCMA Giants 1886

		NM	EX	VG
Complete Set (15):		40.00	20.00	12.00
Common Player:		2.00	1.00	.60
1	Roger Connor	2.00	1.00	.60
2	Larry Corcoran	2.00	1.00	.60
3	Tom Deasley	2.00	1.00	.60
4	Mike Dorgan	2.00	1.00	.60
5	Dude Esterbrook	2.00	1.00	.60
6	Buck Ewing	2.00	1.00	.60
7	Joe Gerhardt	2.00	1.00	.60
8	Pete Gillespie	2.00	1.00	.60
9	Tim Keefe	2.00	1.00	.60
10	Jim Mutrie	2.00	1.00	.60
11	Jim O'Rourke	2.00	1.00	.60
12	Daniel Richardson	2.00	1.00	.60
13	John M. Ward	2.00	1.00	.60
14	Mickey Welch	2.00	1.00	.60
15	Bat Boy	2.00	1.00	.60

1973 TCMA Pudge Gautreaux

This custom-published postcard of the Brooklyn Dodgers catcher (1936-37) was printed in black-and-white in a 3-1/2" x 6" format. The issue date is approximate.

	NM	EX	VG
Sid "Pudge" Gautreaux	4.00	2.00	1.25

1973-78 TCMA League Leaders

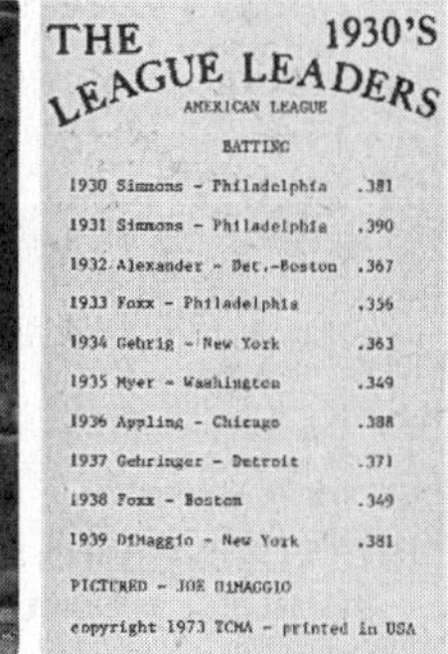

One of TCMA's earliest major series of collectors cards was this run of postcard-size (3-1/2" x 5-1/2") black-and-whites honoring various statistical leaders in each league from the 1920s through the 1950s. Backs have a list of the leaders by year within decade, with one of them pictured on the front. The unnumbered cards are checklisted here in alphabetical order within decade, as they were issued.

		NM	EX	VG
Complete Set (96):		190.00	95.00	55.00
Common Player:		5.00	2.50	1.50
	Complete Set, The 1920s	50.00	25.00	15.00
(1)	Grover C. Alexander	5.00	2.50	1.50
(2)	Jim Bagby, Sr.	5.00	2.50	1.50
(3)	Jim Bottomley	5.00	2.50	1.50
(4)	Eddie Collins	5.00	2.50	1.50
(5)	Earle Combs	5.00	2.50	1.50
(6)	Kiki Cuyler	5.00	2.50	1.50
(7)	Urban "Red" Faber	5.00	2.50	1.50
(8)	Johnny Frederick	5.00	2.50	1.50
(9)	Charlie Gehringer	5.00	2.50	1.50
(10)	Goose Goslin	5.00	2.50	1.50
(11)	Rogers Hornsby	5.00	2.50	1.50
(12)	Walter Johnson	6.00	3.00	1.75
(13)	Freddie Lindstrom	5.00	2.50	1.50
(14)	Bob Meusel	5.00	2.50	1.50
(15)	Charlie Root	5.00	2.50	1.50
(16)	Babe Ruth, Rogers Hornsby	7.50	3.75	2.25
(17)	Al Simmons, Babe Ruth	7.50	3.75	2.25
(18)	Tris Speaker	5.00	2.50	1.50
(19)	Dazzy Vance	5.00	2.50	1.50
(20)	Lloyd Waner	5.00	2.50	1.50
(21)	Cy Williams	5.00	2.50	1.50
(22)	Ken Williams	5.00	2.50	1.50
(23)	Hack Wilson	5.00	2.50	1.50
(24)	Ross Youngs	5.00	2.50	1.50
	Complete Set, The 1930s	50.00	25.00	15.00
(1)	Johnny Allen	5.00	2.50	1.50
(2)	Beau Bell	5.00	2.50	1.50
(3)	Cy Blanton	5.00	2.50	1.50
(4)	Ben Chapman	5.00	2.50	1.50
(5)	Joe Cronin	5.00	2.50	1.50
(6)	Dizzy Dean	6.50	3.25	2.00
(7)	Joe DiMaggio	20.00	10.00	6.00
(8)	Jimmie Foxx	5.00	2.50	1.50
(9)	Lou Gehrig	15.00	7.50	4.50
(10)	Charlie Gehringer	5.00	2.50	1.50
(11)	Lefty Gomez	5.00	2.50	1.50
(12)	Ival Goodman	5.00	2.50	1.50
(13)	Lefty Grove	5.00	2.50	1.50
(14)	Billy Herman	5.00	2.50	1.50
(15)	Ernie Lombardi	5.00	2.50	1.50
(16)	Chuck Klein	5.00	2.50	1.50
(17)	Heinie Manush	5.00	2.50	1.50
(18)	Pepper Martin	5.00	2.50	1.50
(19)	Joe Medwick	5.00	2.50	1.50
(20)	Van Mungo	5.00	2.50	1.50
(21)	Mel Ott	5.00	2.50	1.50
(22)	Bill Terry	5.00	2.50	1.50
(23)	Hal Trosky	5.00	2.50	1.50
(24)	Arky Vaughan	5.00	2.50	1.50
	Complete Set, The 1940s	50.00	25.00	15.00
(1)	Gene Bearden	5.00	2.50	1.50
(2)	Lou Boudreau	5.00	2.50	1.50
(3)	George Case	5.00	2.50	1.50
(4)	Phil Cavarretta	5.00	2.50	1.50
(5)	Bob Feller	6.00	3.00	1.75
(6)	Boo Ferriss	5.00	2.50	1.50
(7)	Hank Greenberg	9.00	4.50	2.75
(8)	Jeff Heath	5.00	2.50	1.50
(9)	Tommy Holmes	5.00	2.50	1.50
(10)	Larry Jansen	5.00	2.50	1.50
(11)	George Kell	5.00	2.50	1.50
(12)	Ralph Kiner	5.00	2.50	1.50
(13)	Marty Marion	5.00	2.50	1.50
(14)	Johnny Mize	5.00	2.50	1.50
(15)	Stan Musial	10.00	5.00	3.00
(16)	Bill Nicholson	5.00	2.50	1.50
(17)	Johnny Pesky	5.00	2.50	1.50
(18)	Jackie Robinson	10.00	5.00	3.00
(19)	Enos Slaughter	5.00	2.50	1.50
(20)	Snuffy Stirnweiss	5.00	2.50	1.50
(21)	Bill Voiselle	5.00	2.50	1.50
(22)	Bucky Walters	5.00	2.50	1.50
(23)	Ted Williams	10.00	5.00	3.00

		NM	EX	VG
(24)	Ted Williams, Joe DiMaggio	10.00	5.00	3.00
	Complete Set, The 1950s	50.00	25.00	15.00
(1)	Luis Aparicio	5.00	2.50	1.50
(2)	Ernie Banks	5.00	2.50	1.50
(3)	Bill Bruton	5.00	2.50	1.50
(4)	Lew Burdette	5.00	2.50	1.50
(5)	Rocky Colavito	5.00	2.50	1.50
(6)	Dom DiMaggio	5.00	2.50	1.50
(7)	Ferris Fain	5.00	2.50	1.50
(8)	Whitey Ford	5.00	2.50	1.50
(9)	Don Hoak	5.00	2.50	1.50
(10)	Sam Jethroe	5.00	2.50	1.50
(11)	Ted Kluszewski	5.00	2.50	1.50
(12)	Harvey Kuenn	5.00	2.50	1.50
(13)	Bob Lemon	5.00	2.50	1.50
(14)	Mickey Mantle	30.00	15.00	9.00
(15)	Willie Mays	15.00	7.50	4.50
(16)	Willie Mays, Bobby Avila	5.00	2.50	1.50
(17)	Minnie Minoso	5.00	2.50	1.50
(18)	Don Newcombe	5.00	2.50	1.50
(19)	Robin Roberts	5.00	2.50	1.50
(20)	Hank Sauer	5.00	2.50	1.50
(21)	Bobby Shantz	5.00	2.50	1.50
(22)	Roy Sievers	5.00	2.50	1.50
(23)	Duke Snider	6.00	3.00	1.75
(24)	Mickey Vernon	5.00	2.50	1.50

1973 TCMA Sports Scoop Hall of Fame

This set of large-format (3-1/2" x 5-1/2") black-and-white cards was produced by TCMA for the collectors' magazine Sports Scoop, which was promoting the players to be inducted into the Hall of Fame. Backs have information about the player's career and HoF credentials.

		NM	EX	VG
	Complete Set (12):	20.00	10.00	6.00
	Common Player:	2.00	1.00	.60
(1)	Earl Averill	2.50	1.25	.70
(2)	Ben Chapman	2.00	1.00	.60
(3)	Doc Cramer	2.00	1.00	.60
(4)	Spud Davis	2.00	1.00	.60
(5)	Babe Herman	2.00	1.00	.60
(6)	Billy Herman	2.50	1.25	.70
(7)	Chuck Klein	2.50	1.25	.70
(8)	Bob Meusel	2.00	1.00	.60
(9)	Johnny Mize	3.00	1.50	.90
(10)	Joe Sewell	2.50	1.25	.70
(11)	Enos Slaughter	3.00	1.50	.90
(12)	Hal Trosky	2.00	1.00	.60

1973 TCMA 1874 Philadelphia Athletics

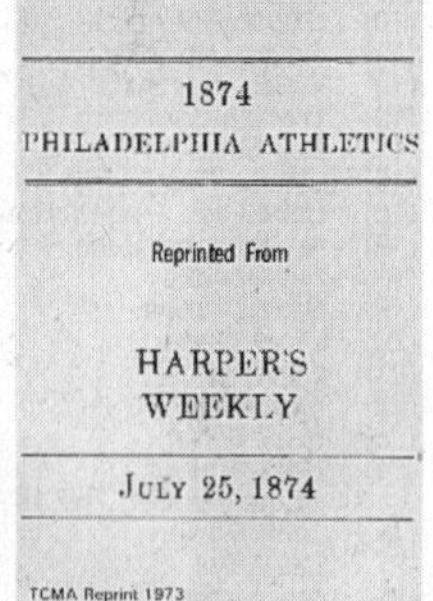

This early collectors' issue reproduces woodcuts of the A's as they appeared in the July 25, 1874, edition of Harper's Weekly. The 3-1/16" x 4-1/2" cards are printed in black-and-white with the player name and position in the white border at bottom. Identical backs credit the pictures' original source and state "TCMA Reprint 1973." The unnumbered cards are checklisted here alphabetically.

		NM	EX	VG
	Complete Set (9):	25.00	12.50	7.50
	Common Player:	3.00	1.50	.90
(1)	Cap Anson	10.00	5.00	3.00
(2)	Joseph Battin	3.00	1.50	.90
(3)	John Clapp	3.00	1.50	.90
(4)	Wes Fisler	3.00	1.50	.90
(5)	Count Gedney	3.00	1.50	.90
(6)	Dick McBride	3.00	1.50	.90
(7)	Mike McGeary	3.00	1.50	.90
(8)	J.F. McMullen	3.00	1.50	.90
(9)	Ezra Sutton	3.00	1.50	.90

1973 TCMA 1890 Base-ball Season

1890
BASE-BALL SEASON
HARPER'S
WEEKLY
MAY 3, 1890.
TCMA Reprint 1973

This set commemorates the baseball "war" of 1890 when many National League players - stars and journeymen alike - defected to a new player-owned league called, appropriately enough, the Players League. Fronts of these 3-1/8" x 4-1/2" black-and-white cards feature reproductions of woodcuts originally printed in Harper's Weekly. Backs have information about the teams in each league. The unnumbered cards are checklisted here in alphabetical order. Original issue price of the set was $3.

		NM	EX	VG
	Complete Set (30):	48.00	24.00	14.50
	Common Player:	2.00	1.00	.60
(1)	Cap Anson	2.00	1.00	.60
(2)	Dan Brouthers	2.00	1.00	.60
(3)	Thomas E. Burns	2.00	1.00	.60
(4)	John Clarkson	2.00	1.00	.60
(5)	C.A. Comiskey	2.00	1.00	.60
(6)	Roger Connor	2.00	1.00	.60
(7)	E.N. Crane	2.00	1.00	.60
(8)	Jeremiah Denny	2.00	1.00	.60
(9)	William B. Ewing	2.00	1.00	.60
(10)	D.L. Foutz	2.00	1.00	.60
(11)	John W. Glasscock	2.00	1.00	.60
(12)	W. Hallman	2.00	1.00	.60
(13)	Edward Hanlon	2.00	1.00	.60
(14)	Timothy J. Keefe	2.00	1.00	.60
(15)	M.J. Kelly	2.00	1.00	.60
(16)	M. Kilroy	2.00	1.00	.60
(17)	W.A. Latham	2.00	1.00	.60
(18)	J.A. McPhee	2.00	1.00	.60
(19)	Joseph Mulvey	2.00	1.00	.60
(20)	W.D. O'Brien	2.00	1.00	.60
(21)	David Orr	2.00	1.00	.60
(22)	John G. Reilly	2.00	1.00	.60
(23)	S.L. Thompson	2.00	1.00	.60
(24)	M. Tiernan	2.00	1.00	.60
(25)	John M. Ward	2.00	1.00	.60
(26)	M. Welsh (Welch)	2.00	1.00	.60
(27)	A. Weyhing	2.00	1.00	.60
(28)	Charles Zimmer	2.00	1.00	.60
(29)	A dive for second base	1.00	.50	.30
(30)	Brotherhood Players Header Card	1.00	.50	.30

1973 TCMA 1930's No Hit Pitchers and 6 for 6 Hitters

These large-format (3-1/2" x 5-1/2") cards feature the no-hit pitchers and 6-for-6 hitters of the 1930s. Borderless front photos are in black-and-white. On back of the pitchers' cards is a list of the decade's no-hitters, the date, score and opposing team. A similar list of the 6-for-6 hitters is on the back of their cards. The cards are unnumbered.

		NM	EX	VG
	Complete Set (12):	40.00	20.00	12.00
	Common Player:	4.00	2.00	1.25
	PITCHERS			
(1)	Paul Dean	6.00	3.00	1.75
(2)	Bill Dietrich	4.00	2.00	1.25
(3)	Vern Kennedy	4.00	2.00	1.25
(4)	Monte Pearson	4.00	2.00	1.25
(5)	Johnny Vander Meer	5.00	2.50	1.50
	HITTERS			
(6)	Jim Bottomley	6.00	3.00	1.75
(7)	Bruce Campbell	4.00	2.00	1.25
(8)	Doc Cramer	4.00	2.00	1.25
(9)	Myril Hoag	4.00	2.00	1.25
(10)	Cookie Lavagetto	4.00	2.00	1.25
(11)	Terry Moore	5.00	2.50	1.50
(12)	Henry Steinbacher	4.00	2.00	1.25

1973 TCMA 1941 Brooklyn Dodgers

These 3-3/8" x 2-1/2" cards are printed in blue-and-white. The unnumbered cards do not have player names on front.

		NM	EX	VG
	Complete Set (32):	50.00	25.00	15.00
	Common Player	2.00	1.00	.60
(1)	Title Card	1.00	.50	.30
(2)	John Allen	2.00	1.00	.60
(3)	Mace Brown	2.00	1.00	.60
(4)	Dolph Camilli	2.00	1.00	.60
(5)	Hugh Casey	2.00	1.00	.60
(6)	Curt Davis	2.00	1.00	.60
(7)	Tom Drake	2.00	1.00	.60
(8)	Leo Durocher	4.00	2.00	1.25
(9)	Fred Fitzsimmons	2.00	1.00	.60
(10)	Herman Franks	2.00	1.00	.60
(11)	Augie Galan	2.00	1.00	.60
(12)	Tony Giuliani	2.00	1.00	.60
(13)	Luke Hamlin	2.00	1.00	.60
(14)	Billy Herman	4.00	2.00	1.25
(15)	Kirby Higbe	2.00	1.00	.60
(16)	Alex Kampouris	2.00	1.00	.60
(17)	Newt Kimball	2.00	1.00	.60
(18)	Cookie Lavagetto	2.00	1.00	.60
(19)	Ducky Medwick	4.00	2.00	1.25
(20)	Van Mungo	2.00	1.00	.60
(21)	Mickey Owen	2.00	1.00	.60
(22)	Babe Phelps	2.00	1.00	.60
(23)	Pee Wee Reese	8.00	4.00	2.50
(24)	Pete Reiser	2.00	1.00	.60
(25)	Lew Riggs	2.00	1.00	.60
(26)	Bill Swift	2.00	1.00	.60
(27)	Vito Tamulis	2.00	1.00	.60
(28)	Joe Vosmik	2.00	1.00	.60
(29)	Dixie Walker	2.00	1.00	.60
(30)	Paul Waner	4.00	2.00	1.25
(31)	Jimmy Wasdell	2.00	1.00	.60
(32)	Whit Wyatt	2.00	1.00	.60

1973 TCMA Stan Martucci Postcards

This set of postcards was custom-produced by TCMA for card dealer Stan Martucci who apparently used them as "ride alongs" when filling orders. Approximately 3-1/2" x 5-1/2", the fronts have borderless, unidentified black-and-white photos of popular former stars. The back is in standard postcard format and had the player identified at top-left and a note from Martucci in the message area.

		NM	EX	VG
	Complete Set (16):	15.00	7.50	4.50
	Common Player:	1.00	.50	.30
(1)	Joe Cronin	1.00	.50	.30
(2)	Dizzy Dean	2.00	1.00	.60
(3)	Joe DiMaggio	5.00	2.50	1.50
(4)	Jimmie Foxx	2.00	1.00	.60
(5)	Lou Gehrig	5.00	2.50	1.50
(6)	Charlie Gehringer	1.00	.50	.30
(7)	Lefty Gomez	1.00	.50	.30
(8)	Lefty Grove	1.00	.50	.30
(9)	Carl Hubbell	1.00	.50	.30
(10)	Ted Lyons	1.00	.50	.30
(11)	Heinie Manush	1.00	.50	.30
(12)	Joe Medwick	1.00	.50	.30
(13)	Mel Ott	1.00	.50	.30
(14)	Red Ruffing	1.00	.50	.30
(15)	Bill Terry	1.00	.50	.30
(16)	Paul Waner	1.00	.50	.30

1974 TCMA Nicknames

Nicknames of notable ballplayers of the 1930s-40s are featured in this early collectors' set. Fronts of the 2-5/16" x 3-1/2" cards have a black-and-white photo with the player's nickname in the bottom border and "Nicknames" in the top border, both printed in red. Backs have a card number, the player's full name, position and the teams and years he played in the major leagues. The set originally sold for $3.

		NM	EX	VG
	Complete Set (28):	40.00	20.00	12.00
	Common Player:	3.00	1.50	.90
1	Rapid Robert Feller	4.50	2.25	1.25
2	Babe Dahlgren	3.00	1.50	.90
3	Spud Chandler	3.00	1.50	.90
4	Ducky Medwick	3.00	1.50	.90
5	Silent Cal Benge	3.00	1.50	.90
6	Goose Goslin	3.00	1.50	.90
7	Mule Haas	3.00	1.50	.90
8	Dizzy Dean	6.00	3.00	1.75
9	Cowboy Harrell	3.00	1.50	.90
10	Buzz Boyle	3.00	1.50	.90
11	Coonskin Davis	3.00	1.50	.90
12	Moose Solters	3.00	1.50	.90
13	Sad Sam Jones	3.00	1.50	.90
14	Bad News Hale	3.00	1.50	.90
15	Bucky Harris	3.00	1.50	.90
16	Lord Jim Jordan	3.00	1.50	.90
17	Zeke Bonura	3.00	1.50	.90
18	Heave-o Hafey	3.00	1.50	.90
19	Spud Davis	3.00	1.50	.90
20	Bing Miller	3.00	1.50	.90
21	Preacher Roe	3.00	1.50	.90
22	Wild Bill Hallahan	3.00	1.50	.90
23	Indian Bob Johnson	3.00	1.50	.90
24	Flash Gordon	3.00	1.50	.90
25	Tot Pressnell	3.00	1.50	.90
26	Hot Potato Hamlin	3.00	1.50	.90
27	Old Reliable Henrich	3.00	1.50	.90
28	Tom Hafey	3.00	1.50	.90

1974 TCMA Sports Nostalgia Store Postcards

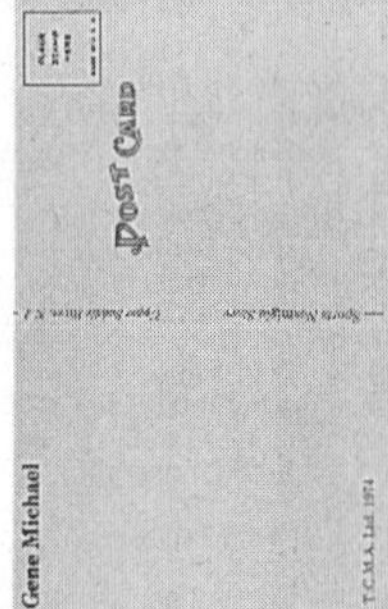

To celebrate the opening of one of the first, if not the first, sports collectors' retail stores, TCMA issued a set of four 3-1/2" x 5-1/2" black-and-white postcards. The set includes one current N.Y. Yankees player and three former boxers. The set was issued in an editon of 1,000.

	NM	EX	VG
Complete Set (4):	20.00	10.00	6.00
Common Card:	5.00	2.50	1.50
(1) Gene Michael	7.50	3.75	2.25
(2) Emile Griffith	5.00	2.50	1.50
(3) Floyd Patterson	5.00	2.50	1.50
(4) Willie Pep	5.00	2.50	1.50

1974 TCMA Stadium Postcards

These 5" x 3-1/2" black-and-white postcards are not numbered and are listed here alphabetically.

	NM	EX	VG
Complete Set (12):	35.00	17.50	10.50
Common Card:	4.00	2.00	1.20
(1) Baltimore Stadium	4.00	2.00	1.20
(2) Boston Braves Field	4.00	2.00	1.20
(3) Crosley Field	4.00	2.00	1.20
(4) Ebbett's (Ebbets) Field	6.00	3.00	1.75
(5) Forbes Field	4.00	2.00	1.20
(6) Griffith Field	4.00	2.00	1.20
(7) Milwaukee County Stadium	4.00	2.00	1.20
(8) Narvin (Navin) Field	4.00	2.00	1.20
(9) Polo Grounds	4.00	2.00	1.20
(10) Shea Stadium	4.00	2.00	1.20
(11) Wrigley Field	5.00	2.50	1.50
(12) Yankee Stadium	7.50	3.75	2.25

1974-75 TCMA St. Louis Browns

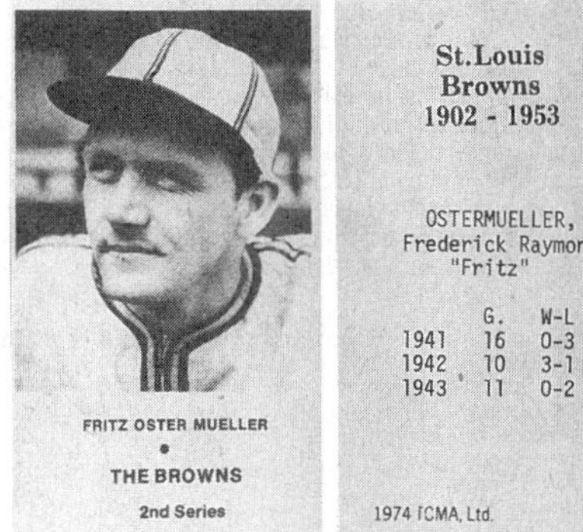

FRITZ OSTER MUELLER
THE BROWNS
2nd Series
St.Louis
Browns
1902 - 1953
OSTERMUELLER,
Frederick Raymond
"Fritz"
G. W-L
1941 16 0-3
1942 10 3-1
1943 11 0-2
1974 TCMA, Ltd.

Some of baseball's most loveable losers from about the 1930s through the team's flight to Baltimore in 1953 are presented in this multi-series collectors' issue. Cards are printed in a 2-1/4" x 3-7/8" format, with brown ink used on front and on back of Series 1 and 2; Series 3 cards have black ink on back. Some cards have player identification on front, some only on back. All cards have a TCMA copyright date line and a few player stats for his years with the Brownies. The unnumbered cards are checklisted here alphabetically by series.

	NM	EX	VG
Complete Set (108):	80.00	40.00	20.00
Common Player:	1.50	.75	.45
Series 1 - 1974	25.00	12.50	7.50
(1) Ethan Allen	1.50	.75	.45
(2) Mel Almada	2.00	1.00	.60
(3) Ed Baecht	1.50	.75	.45
(4) John Berardino	4.00	2.00	1.25
(5) Emil Bildilli	1.50	.75	.45
(6) John Blake	1.50	.75	.45
(7) Julio Bonetti	1.50	.75	.45
(8) Earl Caldwell	1.50	.75	.45
(9) Scoops Carey	1.50	.75	.45
(10) Stinky Davis	1.50	.75	.45
(11) Fred Haney	1.50	.75	.45
(12) Jeff Heath	1.50	.75	.45
(13) Don Heffner	1.50	.75	.45
(14) Rollie Hemsley	1.50	.75	.45
(15) Oral Hildebrand	1.50	.75	.45
(16) Elon Hogsett	1.50	.75	.45
(17) Ben Huffman	1.50	.75	.45
(18) Sig Jakucki	1.50	.75	.45
(19) Billy Knickerbocker	1.50	.75	.45
(20) John Knott	1.50	.75	.45
(21) Jack Kramer	1.50	.75	.45
(22) Red Kress	1.50	.75	.45
(23) Chet Laabs	1.50	.75	.45
(24) Gerard "Nig" Lipscomb	1.50	.75	.45
(25) John Lucadello	1.50	.75	.45
(26) Mel Mazzera	1.50	.75	.45
(27) Red McQuillen	1.50	.75	.45
(28) George McQuinn	1.50	.75	.45
(29) Oscar Melillo	1.50	.75	.45
(30) Howard Mills	1.50	.75	.45
(31) Bob Muncrief	1.50	.75	.45
(32) Hank Thompson	1.50	.75	.45
(33) Russell "Sheriff" Van Atta	1.50	.75	.45
(34) Joe Vosmik	1.50	.75	.45
(35) Jim Walkup	1.50	.75	.45
(36) Sam West	1.50	.75	.45
Series 2 - 1974	30.00	15.00	9.00
(37) Floyd Baker	1.50	.75	.45
(38) John Bassler	1.50	.75	.45
(39) Ollie Bejma	1.50	.75	.45
(40) Jim Bottomley	2.00	1.00	.60
(41) Willard Brown	4.50	2.25	1.25
(42) Bob Dillinger	1.50	.75	.45
(43) Owen Red" Friend	1.50	.75	.45
(44) Eddie Gaedel	5.00	2.50	1.50
(45) Dennis Galehouse	1.50	.75	.45
(46) Joseph Gallagher	1.50	.75	.45
(47) Ned Garver	1.50	.75	.45
(48) Robert Harris	1.50	.75	.45
(49) Al Hollingsworth	1.50	.75	.45
(50) Walter Judnich	1.50	.75	.45
(51) William "Lefty" Kennedy	1.50	.75	.45
(52) Lou Kretlow	1.50	.75	.45
(53) Martin Marion	1.50	.70	.45
(54) Les Moss	1.50	.75	.45
(55) Louis "Bobo" Newsom	1.50	.75	.45
(56) Fritz Ostermueller	1.50	.75	.45
(57) Joe Ostrowski	1.50	.75	.45
(58) Edward Pellagrini	1.50	.75	.45
(59) Duane Pillette	1.50	.75	.45
(60) Nelson Potter	1.50	.75	.45
(61) Raymond "Rip" Radcliff	1.50	.75	.45
(62) Harry Rice	1.50	.75	.45
(63) Jim Rivera	1.50	.75	.45
(64) John "Fred" Sanford	1.50	.75	.45
(65) Luke Sewell	1.50	.75	.45
(66) Al Shirley	1.50	.75	.45
(67) Junior Stephens	1.50	.75	.45
(68) Thomas Turner	1.50	.75	.45
(69) Ken Wood	1.50	.75	.45
(70) Allen "Zeke" Zarilla	1.50	.75	.45
(71) Samuel "Sad Sam" Zoldak	1.50	.75	.45
(72) 1944 Infield	1.50	.75	.45
Series 3 - 1975	30.00	15.00	9.00
(73) Bow-Wow Arft	1.50	.75	.45
(74) Matthew Batts	1.50	.75	.45
(75) Tommy Byrne	1.50	.75	.45
(76) Skippy Byrnes	1.50	.75	.45
(77) Raymond Coleman	1.50	.75	.45
(78) Scrap Iron Courtney	1.50	.75	.45
(79) James Delsing	1.50	.75	.45
(80) William "Kid" DeMars	1.50	.75	.45
(81) Clifford "Mule" Fannin	1.50	.75	.45
(82) Tom Fine	1.50	.75	.45
(83) Pete Gray	5.00	2.50	1.50
(84) Red Hayworth	1.50	.75	.45
(85) Procopio Herrera	1.50	.70	.45
(86) Fred Hoffman	1.50	.75	.45
(87) Walter "Union Man" Holke	1.50	.75	.45
(88) Hal Hudson	1.50	.70	.45
(89) Richard Kokos	1.50	.75	.45
(90) Michael Kreevich	1.50	.75	.45
(91) Richard Kryhoski	1.50	.75	.45
(92) Paul "Peanuts" Lehner	1.50	.75	.45
(93) Footsie Lenhardt	1.50	.75	.45
(94) Joe Lutz	1.50	.75	.45
(95) Robert Mahoney	1.50	.75	.45
(96) Frank Mancuso	1.50	.75	.45
(97) Clifford Mapes	1.50	.75	.45
(98) Cass Michaels	1.50	.75	.45
(99) Frank "Stubby" Overmire	1.50	.75	.45
(100) Satchel Paige	5.00	2.50	1.50
(101) Roy Sievers	1.50	.75	.45
(102) Louis Sleator	1.50	.75	.45
(103) Richard Starr	1.50	.75	.45
(104) Thomas "Muscles" Upton	1.50	.75	.45
(105) Jerome Witte	1.50	.75	.45
(106) Robert Young	1.50	.75	.45
(107) 1951 Browns	1.50	.75	.45
(108) 1952 Browns	1.50	.75	.45

1974 TCMA The Babe Postcards

This set of black-and-white postcards features photos of Ruth with contemporary players and managers. Cards measure 5-1/2" x 3-1/2" and have standard postcard indicia on the backs.

	NM	EX	VG
Complete Set (6):	20.00	10.00	6.00
Common Card:	5.00	2.50	1.50
1 Babe Ruth, Bill Terry	5.00	2.50	1.50
2 Babe Ruth, Walter Johnson	5.00	2.50	1.50
3 Babe Ruth, Lou Gehrig, Joe McCarthy	5.00	2.50	1.50
4 Babe Ruth, Miller Huggins	5.00	2.50	1.50
5 Babe Ruth, Tony Lazzeri	5.00	2.50	1.50
6 Babe Ruth and 1934 All-Stars	5.00	2.50	1.50

1974 TCMA 1890 Brooklyn Club

The National League champion Brooklyn Bridegrooms are featured in this collectors issue. Fronts of the 3-1/2" x 3-3/4" black-and-white cards picture the players in dress suits with ornate designs around the border. The design was copied from an 1890 Brooklyn scorecard/yearbook. Backs have biographical information and career highlights, also copied from the earlier publication. The back also includes a 1974 TCMA reprint notice. The unnumbered cards are checklisted here in alphabetical order.

	NM	EX	VG
Complete Set (16):	30.00	15.00	9.00
Common Player:	3.00	1.50	.90
(1) Thomas P. Burns	3.00	1.50	.90
(2) Albert J. Bushong	3.00	1.50	.90
(3) Robert Lee Caruthers	3.00	1.50	.90
(4) Robert H. Clark	3.00	1.50	.90
(5) Hubbert Collins	3.00	1.50	.90
(6) John S. Oorkhill	3.00	1.50	.90
(7) Thomas P. Daly	3.00	1.50	.90
(8) D.L. Foutz	3.00	1.50	.90
(9) Michael F. Hughes	3.00	1.50	.90
(10) Thomas J. Lovett	3.00	1.50	.90
(11) W.H. McGunnigle	3.00	1.50	.90
(12) Wm. D. O'Brien	3.00	1.50	.90
(13) George Burton Pinkney	3.00	1.50	.90
(14) George J. Smith	3.00	1.50	.90
(15) George T. Stallings	3.00	1.50	.90
(16) Wm. H. Terry	3.00	1.50	.90

1974 TCMA 1910-14 Philadelphia Athletics Postcards

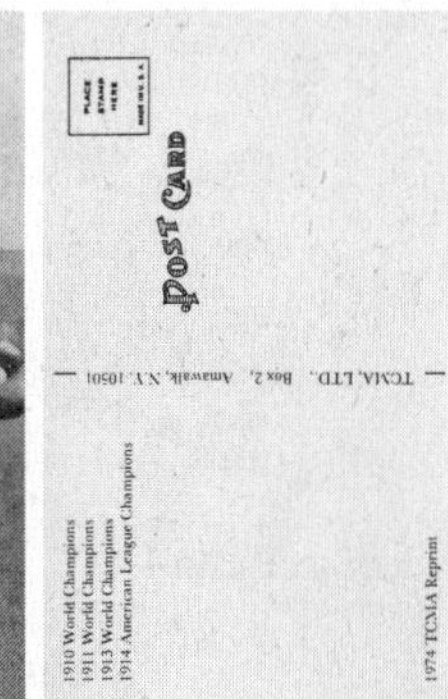

This series of collectors' issue postcards (about 3-1/2" x 5-3/4") was issued in two forms; printed front and back in black-and-white or in blue-and-white. While numbered between 501 and 518, only 12 cards were issued. The cards are reproductions of the images from the 1911 Pinkerton cabinets (T5). The postcard-format backs have a "1974 TCMA Reprint" notice along with the list of the dynasty's league and world championships.

	NM	EX	VG
Complete Set (12):	10.00	5.00	3.00
Common Player:	1.00	.50	.30
501 Chas. Bender	1.50	.70	.45
502 John Coombs	1.00	.50	.30
503 Eddie Plank	1.50	.70	.45
504 Amos Strunk	1.00	.50	.30
506 Ira Thomas	1.00	.50	.30
508 Stuffy McInnis	1.00	.50	.30
510 Rube Oldring	1.00	.50	.30
511 Eddie Collins	1.50	.70	.45
512 Frank Baker	1.50	.70	.45
515 Jack Barry	1.00	.50	.30
516 Jack Lapp	1.00	.50	.30
518 Danny Murphy	1.00	.50	.30

1974 TCMA 1929-31 Athletics

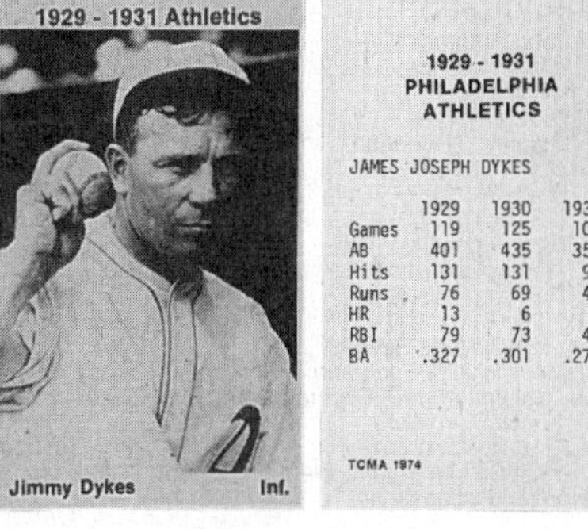

1929 - 1931 Athletics
Jimmy Dykes Inf.
1929 - 1931
PHILADELPHIA
ATHLETICS
JAMES JOSEPH DYKES
1929 1930 1931
Games 119 125 101
AB 401 435 355
Hits 131 131 97
Runs 76 69 48
HR 13 6 3
RBI 79 73 46
BA .327 .301 .273
TCMA 1974

Stars of the Philadelphia A's dynasty which won two World Series and an A.L. pennant from 1929-31 are featured in this collectors issue. The 2-5/8" x 4" cards have black-and-white player photos at center. Printed in green in the white border at top is "1929-31 Athletics." At bottom, printed in black, is the player's name and position. Backs are in black-and-white with stats for 1929, 1930 and 1931, as appropriate. The unnumbered cards are checklisted here in alphabetical order.

	NM	EX	VG
Complete Set (29):	30.00	15.00	9.00
Common Player:	2.00	1.00	.60
(1) Max Bishop	2.00	1.00	.60
(2) Joe Boley	2.00	1.00	.60
(3) George Burns	2.00	1.00	.60
(4) Mickey Cochrane	3.00	1.50	.90
(5) Eddie Collins, Lew Krausse	2.00	1.00	.60
(6) "Doc" Cramer	2.00	1.00	.60
(7) Jimmy Dykes	2.00	1.00	.60
(8) George Earnshaw	2.00	1.00	.60
(9) Howard Ehmke	2.00	1.00	.60
(10) Lou Finney, John Heving	2.00	1.00	.60
(11) Jimmie Foxx	4.00	2.00	1.25
(12) Walt French, Waite Hoyt	2.00	1.00	.60
(13) "Lefty" Grove	3.00	1.50	.90
(14) "Mule" Haas	2.00	1.00	.60
(15) Sammy Hale	2.00	1.00	.60
(16) "Pinky" Higgins, Phil Todt	2.00	1.00	.60
(17) Earle Mack, Connie Mack	2.00	1.00	.60
(18) Roy Mahaffey	2.00	1.00	.60
(19) Eric McNair	2.00	1.00	.60
(20) Bing Miller	2.00	1.00	.60
(21) Jim Moore, Jim Peterson	2.00	1.00	.60
(22) Jack Quinn	2.00	1.00	.60
(23) Eddie Rommel	2.00	1.00	.60
(24) Wally Schang	2.50	1.25	.70
(25) Al Simmons	2.50	1.25	.70
(26) Homer Summa	2.00	1.00	.60
(27) Rube Walberg	2.00	1.00	.60
(28) "Dib" Williams	2.00	1.00	.60
(29) Team Photo Card (10" x 5")	10.00	5.00	3.00

1974 TCMA 1934 St. Louis Cardinals

The "Gas House Gang" (as some of these cards are designated) is featured in this collectors' issue. Cards are 2-1/4" x 3-5/8" (#27-31 are 4-1/2" x 3-3/4") and feature black-and-white photos on front with red typography. Backs have a few stats in black-and-white. Some cards have a title at top front reading "1934 Cardinals." The unnumbered cards are checklisted here in alphabetical order.

	NM	EX	VG
Complete Set (31):	50.00	25.00	15.00
Common Player:	2.00	1.00	.60
(1) "Tex" Carleton	2.00	1.00	.60
(2) "Ripper" Collins	2.00	1.00	.60
(3) "Pat" Crawford	2.00	1.00	.60
(4) "Spud" Davis	2.00	1.00	.60
(5) "Daffy" Dean	2.50	1.25	.70
(6) "Dizzy" Dean	4.00	2.00	1.25
(7) Bill DeLancey	2.00	1.00	.60
(8) Leo Durocher	2.50	1.25	.70
(9) Frank Frisch	2.50	1.25	.70
(10) "Chick" Fullis	2.00	1.00	.60
(11) "Mike" Gonzalez	2.50	1.25	.70
(12) "Pop" Haines	2.50	1.25	.70
(13) Bill Hallahan	2.00	1.00	.60
(14) Francis Healey (Healy)	2.00	1.00	.60
(15) Jim Lindsey	2.00	1.00	.60
(16) "Pepper" Martin	2.50	1.25	.70
(17) "Ducky" Medwick	2.50	1.25	.70
(18) Jim Mooney	2.00	1.00	.60
(19) Ernie Orsatti	2.00	1.00	.60
(20) Flint Rhem	2.00	1.00	.60
(21) John Rothrock	2.00	1.00	.60
(22) "Dazzy" Vance	2.50	1.25	.70
(23) Bill Walker	2.00	1.00	.60
(24) "Buzzy" Wares	2.00	1.00	.60
(25) "Whitey" Whitehead	2.00	1.00	.60
(26) Jim Winford	2.00	1.00	.60
(27) "Daffy" & "Dizzy" (Daffy Dean, Dizzy Dean)	6.00	3.00	1.75
(28) Dizzy & Leo Celebrate (Dizzy Dean, Leo Durocher)	4.00	2.00	1.25
(29) Durocher Scores (Leo Durocher) (1934 World Series)	4.00	2.00	1.25
(30) Medwick Out Cochrane Catcher (Mickey Cochrane, Ducky Medwick) (1934 World Series)	4.00	2.00	1.25
(31) 1934 St. Louis Cardinals World Champions	4.00	2.00	1.25

1974 TCMA 1934-5 Detroit Tigers

Members of the 1934 A.L. Champion and 1935 World's Champion teams are featured in this collectors issue team set. Except for a pair of large-format (4-1/4" x 3-3/4") cards, the cards measure about 2-1/8" x 3-5/8". Fronts have black-and-white photos. Above and below the photo are white stripes with the set title, player name and position. Backs are in black-and-white with 1934 and/or 1935 stats. The unnumbered cards are checklisted here alphabetically.

	NM	EX	VG
Complete Set (36):	35.00	17.50	10.00
Common Player:	2.00	1.00	.60
(1) Eldon Auker	2.00	1.00	.60
(2) Del Baker	2.00	1.00	.60
(3) Tommy Bridges	2.00	1.00	.60
(4) "Flea" Clifton	2.00	1.00	.60
(5) Mickey Cochrane	4.00	2.00	1.25
(6) "General" Crowder	2.00	1.00	.60
(7) Frank Doljack	2.00	1.00	.60
(8) Carl Fischer	2.00	1.00	.60
(9) Pete Fox	2.00	1.00	.60
(10) Vic Frasier	2.00	1.00	.60
(11) Charlie Gehringer	4.00	2.00	1.25
(12) Goose Goslin	2.00	1.00	.60
(13) Hank Greenberg	5.00	2.50	1.50
(14) Luke Hamlin	2.00	1.00	.60
(15) Clyde Hatter	2.00	1.00	.60
(16) Ray Hayworth	2.00	1.00	.60
(17) "Chief" Hogsett	2.00	1.00	.60
(18) Roxie Lawson	2.00	1.00	.60
(19) "Firpo" Marberry	2.00	1.00	.60
(20) Chet Morgan	2.00	1.00	.60
(21) Marv Owen	2.00	1.00	.60
(22) "Cy" Perkins	2.00	1.00	.60
(23) "Red" Phillips	2.00	1.00	.60
(24) Frank Reiber	2.00	1.00	.60
(25) Billy Rogell	2.00	1.00	.60
(26) "Schoolboy" Rowe	2.00	1.00	.60
(27) "Heinie" Schuble	2.00	1.00	.60
(28) Hugh Shelley	2.00	1.00	.60
(29) Vic Sorrell	2.00	1.00	.60
(30) Joe Sullivan	2.00	1.00	.60
(31) "Gee" Walker	2.00	1.00	.60
(32) "Hub" Walker	2.00	1.00	.60
(33) "Jo-Jo" White	2.00	1.00	.60
(34) Rudy York	2.00	1.00	.60
(35) 1934 Pitchers (Eldon Auker, Firpo Marberry, Tommy Bridges, Schoolboy Rowe) (4-1/4" x 3-3/4")	5.00	2.50	1.50
(36) 1935 Outfield (Goose Goslin, Jo-Jo White, Pete Fox) (4-1/4" x 3-3/4")	5.00	2.50	1.50

1974 TCMA 1936-37 New York Giants

This is the rarest of the TCMA Great Teams sets. Fewer than half of the 1,000 sets got into the hands of customers before legal action by Dick Bartell forced the company to halt sales and destroy more than 500 sets. The 2-5/8" x 3-3/8" cards are printed in black-and-orange. They are unnumbered and checklisted here in alphabetical order.

	NM	EX	VG
Complete Set (36):	90.00	45.00	27.50
Common Player:	2.50	1.25	.75
(1) Title card	1.00	.50	.30
(2) Tom Baker	2.50	1.25	.75
(3) Dick Bartell	2.50	1.25	.75
(4) Wally Berger	2.50	1.25	.75
(5) Don Brennan	2.50	1.25	.75
(6) Walter Brown	2.50	1.25	.75
(7) Clyde Castleman	2.50	1.25	.75
(8) Lou Chiozza	2.50	1.25	.70
(9) Dick Coffman	2.50	1.25	.75
(10) Harry Danning	2.50	1.25	.75
(11) George Davis	2.50	1.25	.75
(12) Charlie English	2.50	1.25	.75
(13) Freddie Fitzsimmons	2.50	1.25	.75
(14) Frank Gabler	2.50	1.25	.75
(15) Harry Gumbert	2.50	1.25	.75
(16) Mickey Haslin	2.50	1.25	.75
(17) Carl Hubbell	6.00	3.00	1.75
(18) Travis Jackson	4.00	2.00	1.25
(19) Mark Koenig	2.50	1.25	.75
(20) Hank Leiber	2.50	1.25	.75
(21) Sam Leslie	2.50	1.25	.75
(22) Bill Lohrman	2.50	1.25	.75
(23) Eddie Mayo	2.50	1.25	.75
(24) John McCarthy	2.50	1.25	.75
(25) Cliff Melton	2.50	1.25	.75
(26) Jo Jo Moore	2.50	1.25	.75
(27) Mel Ott	6.00	3.00	1.75
(28) Jimmy Ripple	2.50	1.25	.75
(29) Hal Schumacher	2.50	1.25	.75
(30) Al Smith	2.50	1.25	.75
(31) Roy Spencer	2.50	1.25	.75
(32) Bill Terry	5.00	2.50	1.50
(33) Hy Vandenberg	2.50	1.25	.75
(34) Phil Weintraub	2.50	1.25	.75
(35) Burgess Whitehead	2.50	1.25	.75
(36) Babe Young	2.50	1.25	.75

1974 TCMA 1936-1939 Yankee Dynasty

Many of the players who participated in one or more of the Yankees' four consecutive World Champion seasons in the late 1930s are included in this collectors' edition. Cards are 2-3/4" x 4" and feature black-and-white photos on front. In the white borders at top and bottom, the set name and player identification are printed in blue. Backs have stats for each season and are printed in black-and-white on a white background. A virtual reprint of this set was made circa 1983 with two player cards added and a brown background on back. The unnumbered cards are checklisted here alphabetically.

	NM	EX	VG
Complete Set (56):	75.00	37.50	22.50
Complete Set (51):	45.00	22.50	13.50
Common Player:	2.00	1.00	.60
(1) "Poison Ivy" Andrews	2.00	1.00	.60
(2) Joe Beggs	2.00	1.00	.60
(3) Marv Breuer	2.00	1.00	.60
(4) Johnny Broaca	2.00	1.00	.60
(5) "Jumbo" Brown	2.00	1.00	.60
(6) "Spud" Chandler	2.00	1.00	.60
(7) Ben Chapman	2.00	1.00	.60
(8) Earle Combs	2.00	1.00	.60
(9) Frankie Crosetti	2.00	1.00	.60
(10) "Babe" Dahlgren	2.00	1.00	.60
(11) Bill Dickey	2.50	1.25	.70
(12) Joe DiMaggio	10.00	5.00	3.00
(13) Atley Donald	2.00	1.00	.60
(14) Wes Ferrell	2.00	1.00	.60
(15) Artie Fletcher	2.00	1.00	.60
(16) Joe Gallagher	2.00	1.00	.60
(17) Lou Gehrig	10.00	5.00	3.00
(18) Joe Glenn	2.00	1.00	.60
(19) "Lefty" Gomez	2.00	1.00	.60
(20) Joe Gordon	2.00	1.00	.60
(21) "Bump" Hadley	2.00	1.00	.60
(22) Don Heffner	2.00	1.00	.60
(23) Tommy Henrich	2.00	1.00	.60
(24) Oral Hildebrand	2.00	1.00	.60
(25) Myril Hoag	2.00	1.00	.60
(26) Roy Johnson	2.00	1.00	.60
(27) Arndt Jorgens	2.00	1.00	.60
(28) Charlie Keller	2.00	1.00	.60
(29) Ted Kleinhans	2.00	1.00	.60
(30) Billy Knickerbocker	2.00	1.00	.60
(31) Tony Lazzeri	2.50	1.25	.70
(32) Frank Makosky	2.00	1.00	.60
(33) "Pat" Malone	2.00	1.00	.60
(34) Johnny Murphy	2.00	1.00	.60
(35) "Monty" Pearson	2.00	1.00	.60
(36) "Jake" Powell	2.00	1.00	.60
(37) "Red" Rolfe	2.00	1.00	.60
(38) "Buddy" Rosar	2.00	1.00	.60
(39) "Red" Ruffing	2.50	1.25	.70
(40) Marius Russo	2.00	1.00	.60
(41) "Jack" Saltzgaver	2.00	1.00	.60
(42) Paul Schreiber	2.00	1.00	.60
(43) Johnny Schulte	2.00	1.00	.60
(44) Bob Seeds	2.00	1.00	.60
(45) "Twinkletoes" Selkirk	2.00	1.00	.60
(46) Lee Stine	2.00	1.00	.60
(47) Steve Sundra	2.00	1.00	.60
(48) "Sandy" Vance	2.00	1.00	.60
(49) Dixie Walker	2.00	1.00	.60
(50) Kemp Wicker	2.00	1.00	.60
(51) Joe McCarthy, Jacob Ruppert	2.00	1.00	.60
5-1/2" x 4" FEATURE CARDS			
(52) Joe DiMaggio, Frank Crosetti, Tony Lazzeri, Bill Dickey, Lou Gehrig, Jake Powell, George Selkirk	5.00	2.50	1.50
(53) Lou Gehrig, Joe DiMaggio	7.50	3.75	2.25
(54) Gehrig Hits Another	6.00	3.00	1.75
(55) Red Rolfe, Tony Lazzeri, Lou Gehrig, Frank Crosetti	5.00	2.50	1.50
(56) World Champions - 1936	6.00	3.00	1.75

1974 TCMA 1952 Brooklyn Dodgers

1952
BROOKLYN
DODGERS

ALBERT BLUFORD WALKER

Catcher #10

Games 46
AB 139
Hits 36
Runs 9
HR 1
RBI 19
BA .259

T.C.M.A. 1974

The National League champion '52 Dodgers are featured in this collectors issue. Nominally 2-3/4" x 3-3/8", the cards are often found with minor variations in size. Fronts are printed in red and blue with a white border. The only identification on front is the player's first name or nickname. Backs are in black-and-white with the player's full name, position, uniform number, 1952 stats and TCMA copyright. Cards are checklisted here in alphabetical order.

	NM	EX	VG
Complete Set (40):	25.00	15.00	7.50
Common Player:	2.00	1.00	.60
(1) Header/Team History Card (Jackie Robinson, Gil Hodges, Roy Campanella, Billy Cox, Pee Wee Reese)	2.00	1.00	.60
(2) Cal Abrams	2.00	1.00	.60
(3) Sandy Amoros	2.00	1.00	.60
(4) Joe Black	2.00	1.00	.60
(5) Ralph Branca	2.00	1.00	.60
(6) Rocky Bridges	2.00	1.00	.60
(7) Roy Campanella	4.00	2.00	1.25
(8) Billy Cox	2.00	1.00	.60
(9) Chuck Dressen	2.00	1.00	.60
(10) Carl Erskine	2.00	1.00	.60
(11) Carl Furillo	3.00	1.50	.90
(12) Billy Herman	2.00	1.00	.60
(13) Gil Hodges	4.00	2.00	1.25
(14) Tommy Holmes	2.00	1.00	.60
(15) Jim Hughes	2.00	1.00	.60
(16) Clyde King	2.00	1.00	.60
(17) Clem Labine	2.00	1.00	.60
(18) Joe Landrum	2.00	1.00	.60
(19) Cookie Lavagetto	2.00	1.00	.60
(20) Ken Lehman	2.00	1.00	.60
(21) Steve Lembo	2.00	1.00	.60
(22) Billy Loes	2.00	1.00	.60
(23) Ray Moore	2.00	1.00	.60
(24) Bobby Morgan	2.00	1.00	.60
(25) Ron Negray	2.00	1.00	.60
(26) Rocky Nelson	2.00	1.00	.60
(27) Andy Pafko	2.00	1.00	.60
(28) Jake Pitler	2.00	1.00	.60
(29) Bud Podbielan	2.00	1.00	.60
(30) Pee Wee Reese	4.00	2.00	1.25
(31) Jackie Robinson	7.50	3.75	2.25
(32) Preacher Roe	2.00	1.00	.60
(33) Johnny Rutherford	2.00	1.00	.60
(34) Johnny Schmitz	2.00	1.00	.60
(35) George Shuba	2.00	1.00	.60
(36) Duke Snider	4.00	2.00	1.25
(37) Chris Van Cuyk	2.00	1.00	.60
(38) Ben Wade	2.00	1.00	.60
(39) Rube Walker	2.00	1.00	.60
(40) Dick Williams	2.00	1.00	.60

1975 TCMA All Time Brooklyn/Los Angeles Dodgers

ALL TIME
BROOKLYN/LOS ANGELES
DODGERS

1b	Gil Hodges
2b	Jackie Robinson
ss	Pee Wee Reese
3b	Junior Gilliam
OF	Duke Snider
OF	Dixie Walker
OF	Zack Wheat
C	Roy Campanella
RHP	Don Drysdale
LHP	Sandy Koufax
RP	Hugh Casey
Mgr	Walter Alston

T.C.M.A. Ltd. 1975

A picked team of former Dodgers stars is featured in this collectors issue team set. Cards are in black-and-white in the standard 2-1/2" x 3-1/2" format. Fronts have player identification in the border beneath the photo. Backs have a checklist by position and a TCMA copyright line. The unnumbered cards are checklisted here in the order presented on back.

	NM	EX	VG
Complete Set (12):	36.00	18.00	11.00
Common Player:	2.25	1.25	.70
(1) Gil Hodges	3.00	1.50	.90
(2) Jackie Robinson	10.00	5.00	3.00
(3) Pee Wee Reese	3.00	1.50	.90
(4) Junior Gilliam	2.25	1.25	.70
(5) Duke Snider	3.00	1.50	.90
(6) Dixie Walker	2.25	1.25	.70
(7) Zack Wheat	2.25	1.25	.70
(8) Roy Campanella	4.00	2.00	1.25
(9) Don Drysdale	3.00	1.50	.90
(10) Sandy Koufax	8.00	4.00	2.50
(11) Hugh Casey	2.25	1.25	.70
(12) Walter Alston	2.25	1.25	.70

1975 TCMA All-Time Greats

LOUIS BOUDREAU

Shortstop

Indians Red Sox
1938 - 1952

Games 1646
At Bats 6030
Hits 1779
Home Runs 68
Batting Ave. .295

Hall of Fame 1970

This is a smaller - both in size and number - version of TCMA's Hall of Famer postcard set issued between 1973-80. These collectors' edition cards measure 2-3/8" x 3-3/4" and were issued in strips of six. Two printings were done, the first with blue-and-white fronts and red backs, the second in black-and-white, blank-backed. Surrounding the photo on front is a blue or black border with baseball equipment ornamentation. The unnumbered cards are checklisted here in alphabetical order.

	NM	EX	VG
Complete Set (39):	40.00	20.00	12.00
Common Player:	2.00	1.00	.60
(1) "Luke" Appling	2.00	1.00	.60
(2) Roger Bresnahan	2.00	1.00	.60
(3) Ty Cobb	8.00	4.00	2.50
(4) Mickey Cochrane	2.00	1.00	.60
(5) Eddie Collins	2.00	1.00	.60
(6) Kiki Cuyler	2.00	1.00	.60
(7) Dizzy Dean	4.00	2.00	1.25
(8) Bill Dickey	2.00	1.00	.60
(9) Joe DiMaggio	8.00	4.00	2.50
(10) Bob Feller	2.00	1.00	.60
(11) Elmer Flick	2.00	1.00	.60
(12) Frank Frisch	2.00	1.00	.60
(13) Lou Gehrig	8.00	4.00	2.50
(14) Hank Greenberg	4.00	2.00	1.25
(15) Goose Goslin	2.00	1.00	.60
(16) Chick Hafey	2.00	1.00	.60
(17) Gabby Hartnett	2.00	1.00	.60
(18) Harry Heilmann	2.00	1.00	.60
(19) Rogers Hornsby	2.00	1.00	.60
(20) Waite Hoyt	2.00	1.00	.60
(21) Walter Johnson	4.00	2.00	1.25
(22) George Kelly	2.00	1.00	.60
(23) Ted Lyons	2.00	1.00	.60
(24) Connie Mack	2.00	1.00	.60
(25) Mickey Mantle	10.00	5.00	3.00
(26) Rabbit Maranville	2.00	1.00	.60
(27) Mel Ott	2.00	1.00	.60
(28) Edd Roush	2.00	1.00	.60
(29) Red Ruffing	2.00	1.00	.60
(30) Babe Ruth	10.00	5.00	3.00
(31) Al Simmons	2.00	1.00	.60
(32) Casey Stengel	2.00	1.00	.60
(33) Pie Traynor	2.00	1.00	.60
(34) Dazzy Vance	2.00	1.00	.60
(35) Honus Wagner	4.00	2.00	1.25
(36) Lloyd Waner	2.00	1.00	.60
(37) Paul Waner	2.00	1.00	.60
(38) Ted Williams	6.00	3.00	1.75
(39) Harry Wright	2.00	1.00	.60

1975 TCMA All Time New York Giants

ALL TIME
NEW YORK GIANTS

1b	Bill Terry
2b	Frankie Frisch
ss	Alvin Dark
3b	Fred Lindstrom
LF	Bobby Thomson
CF	Willie Mays
RF	Mel Ott
C	Wes Westrum
LHP	Carl Hubbell
RHP	Christy Mathewson
RP	Hoyt Wilhelm
Mgr	John McGraw

TCMA Ltd. 1975

An all-time line-up of Giants is presented in this collector issue. Fronts of the 2-1/2" x 3-1/2" cards have black-and-white player photos with the player's name and position printed in red in the white bottom border. Backs are in black-and-white and present the all-time roster. The unnumbered cards are checklisted here alphabetically.

	NM	EX	VG
Complete Set (12):	30.00	15.00	9.00
Common Player:	2.00	1.00	.60
(1) Alvin Dark	2.00	1.00	.60
(2) Frankie Frisch	2.00	1.00	.60
(3) Carl Hubbell	2.00	1.00	.60
(4) Freddie Lindstrom	2.00	1.00	.60
(5) Christy Mathewson	4.00	2.00	1.25
(6) Willie Mays	15.00	7.50	4.50
(7) John McGraw	2.00	1.00	.60
(8) Mel Ott	2.00	1.00	.60
(9) Bill Terry	2.00	1.00	.60
(10) Bobby Thomson	2.00	1.00	.60
(11) Wes Westrum	2.00	1.00	.60
(12) Hoyt Wilhelm	2.00	1.00	.60

1975 TCMA All Time New York Yankees

ALL TIME
NEW YORK
YANKEE TEAM

1B	Lou Gehrig
2B	Tony Lazzeri
3B	Red Rolfe
SS	Phil Rizzuto
OF	Babe Ruth
OF	Mickey Mantle
OF	Joe DiMaggio
C	Bill Dickey
P	Red Ruffing
P	Whitey Ford
RP	Johnny Murphy
Mgr	Casey Stengel

T.C.M.A. LTD 1975

The best players on the best team in baseball history are featured in this collectors' edition. Cards measure 2-1/2" x 3-3/4" and feature black-and-white photos on front, with white borders. Player name and position are printed in a white strip toward the bottom of the picture. Backs have a list of the all-time team. The unnumbered cards are listed here in that order.

	NM	EX	VG
Complete Set (12):	15.00	7.50	4.50
Common Player:	2.00	1.00	.60
(1) Lou Gehrig	4.00	2.00	1.25
(2) Tony Lazzeri	2.00	1.00	.60
(3) Red Rolfe	2.00	1.00	.60
(4) Phil Rizzuto	2.50	1.25	.70
(5) Babe Ruth	5.00	2.50	1.50
(6) Mickey Mantle	6.00	3.00	1.75
(7) Joe DiMaggio	4.00	2.00	1.25
(8) Bill Dickey	2.00	1.00	.60
(9) Red Ruffing	2.00	1.00	.60
(10) Whitey Ford	2.50	1.25	.70
(11) Johnny Murphy	2.00	1.00	.60
(12) Casey Stengel	2.00	1.00	.60

1975 TCMA Larry French Postcards

The career of National League pitcher Larry French is recounted in this set of 3-1/2" x 5-1/2" black-and-white postcard-size cards. Fronts have photos of him with the Pirates, Cubs and Dodgers. Backs have a continuing biography.

	NM	EX	VG
Complete Set (6):	15.00	7.50	4.50
Common Card:	3.00	1.50	.90
1 Larry French (Pittsburgh Pirates)	3.00	1.50	.90
2 Larry French (Chicago Cubs)	3.00	1.50	.90
3 Larry French (W/Bill Lee, Charlie Root, Tuck Stainback.)	3.00	1.50	.90
4 Larry French (W/Charlie Grimm, Fred Lindstrom.)	3.00	1.50	.90
5 Larry French (Brooklyn Dodgers)	3.00	1.50	.90
6 Larry French (W/Mickey Owen.)	3.00	1.50	.90

1975 TCMA Guam WW2

This set of 3-1/2" x 5-1/2" black-and-white cards details the connection between Major League Baseball and the Pacific island of Guam during WWII. Some cards picture players in the their military uniforms, others shown them in baseball uniforms. Backs contain a narrative of the series.

	NM	EX	VG
Complete Set (18):	25.00	12.50	7.50
Common Card:	1.00	.50	.30
1 Phil Rizzuto, Terry Moore	5.00	2.50	1.50
2 Gab Gab Guam 1945	1.00	.50	.30
3 Team Photo	1.00	.50	.30
4 Merrill May, Pee Wee Reese, Johnny Vander Meer	2.50	1.25	.70

		NM	EX	VG
5	Team Photo	1.00	.50	.30
6	Team Photo	1.00	.50	.30
7	Del Ennis	2.00	1.00	.60
8	Mace Brown	2.00	1.00	.60
9	Pee Wee Reese, Joe Gordon, Bill Dickey	3.50	1.75	1.00
10	Glenn McQuillen	2.00	1.00	.60
11	Mike Budnick	2.00	1.00	.60
12	Team Photo	1.00	.50	.30
13	"Skeets" Dickey	2.00	1.00	.60
14	Connie Ryan	2.00	1.00	.60
15	Hal White	2.00	1.00	.60
16	Mickey Cochrane	7.50	3.75	2.25
17	Barney McCosky	2.00	1.00	.60
18	Ben Huffman	2.00	1.00	.60

1975 TCMA 1913 Philadelphia Athletics

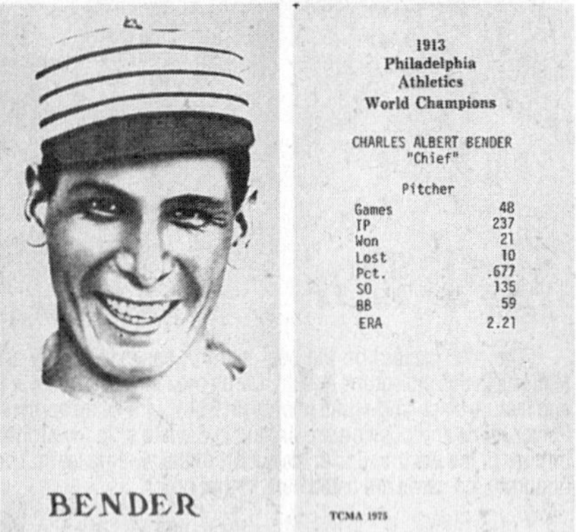

Members of the World Champion A's of 1913 are featured in this collectors' edition card set. In an unusual 3-1/8" x 5-11/16" format, the cards have black-and-white photos on front, with white borders and player identification at bottom. Backs feature season statistics. The unnumbered cards are checklisted here alphabetically.

		NM	EX	VG
Complete Set (16):		20.00	10.00	6.00
Common Player:		3.00	1.50	.90
(1)	Home Run Baker	3.00	1.50	.90
(2)	Jack Barry	3.00	1.50	.90
(3)	Chief Bender	3.00	1.50	.90
(4)	Joe Bush	3.00	1.50	.90
(5)	Eddie Collins	3.00	1.50	.90
(6)	Jack Coombs	3.00	1.50	.90
(7)	Jack Lapp	3.00	1.50	.90
(8)	Connie Mack	3.00	1.50	.90
(9)	Stuffy McInnis	3.00	1.50	.90
(10)	Dan Murphy	3.00	1.50	.90
(11)	Eddie Murphy	3.00	1.50	.90
(12)	Rube Oldring	3.00	1.50	.90
(13)	William Orr	3.00	1.50	.90
(14)	Ed Plank	3.00	1.50	.90
(15)	Walter Schang	3.00	1.50	.90
(16)	Amos Strunk	3.00	1.50	.90

1975 TCMA 1919 Chicago White Sox

The infamous Black Sox who threw the 1919 World Series, and their teammates, are featured in this collectors' edition. The 2-1/2" x 3-1/2" cards are printed in black-and-white. Fronts have player photos with identification in the white border at bottom. Backs have 1919 season stats. The unnumbered cards are checklisted here alphabetically.

		NM	EX	VG
Complete Set (28):		35.00	17.50	10.00
Common Player:		1.00	.50	.30
(1)	Joe Benz	1.00	.50	.30
(2)	Eddie Cicotte	3.50	1.75	1.00
(3)	Eddie Collins	2.50	1.25	.70
(4)	Shano Collins	1.00	.50	.30
(5)	Dave Danforth	1.00	.50	.30
(6)	Red Faber	1.00	.40	.25
(7)	Happy Felsch	3.50	1.75	1.00
(8)	Chick Gandil	5.00	2.50	1.50
(9)	Kid Gleason	1.00	.50	.30
(10)	Joe Jackson	10.00	5.00	3.00
(11)	Bill James	1.00	.50	.30
(12)	Dickie Kerr	1.00	.50	.30
(13)	Nemo Leibold	1.00	.50	.30
(14)	Byrd Lynn	1.00	.50	.30
(15)	Erskine Mayer	2.00	1.00	.60
(16)	Harvey McClellan	1.00	.50	.30
(17)	Fred McMullin	4.00	2.00	1.25
(18)	Eddie Murphy	1.00	.50	.30
(19)	Pat Ragan	1.00	.50	.30
(20)	Swede Risberg	4.00	2.00	1.25
(21)	Charlie Robertson	1.00	.50	.30
(22)	Reb Russell	1.00	.50	.30
(23)	Ray Schalk	1.00	.40	.25
(24)	Buck Weaver	6.00	3.00	1.75
(25)	Roy Wilkinson	1.00	.50	.30
(26)	Lefty Williams	4.00	2.00	1.25
(27)	Frank Shellenback, Grover Lowdermilk, Joe Jenkins, Dickie Kerr, Ray Schalk	1.00	.50	.30
(28)	Team Photo (4-3/4" x 3-1/2")	7.50	3.75	2.25

1975 TCMA 1924-1925 Washington Senators

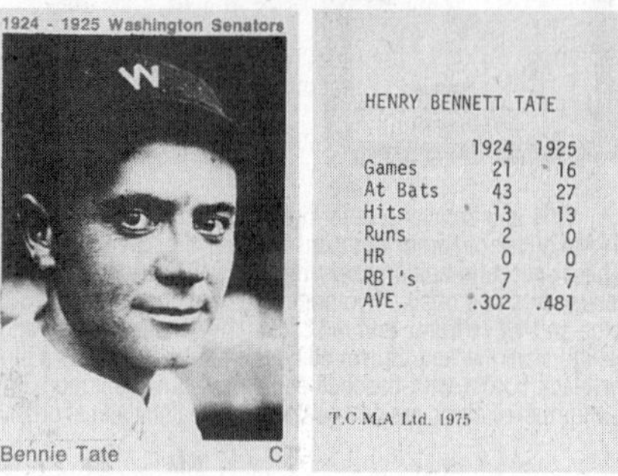

The back-to-back American League champion Senators of 1924-25 are featured in this collectors' edition card set. Cards measure 2-3/8" x 3-7/16". Fronts have black-and-white photos with blue captions and white borders. Backs have player stats for the two seasons. The unnmubered cards are checklisted here in alphabetical order.

		NM	EX	VG
Complete Set (42):		30.00	15.00	9.00
Common Player:		1.50	.75	.45
(1)	Spencer Adams	1.50	.75	.45
(2)	Nick Altrock	1.50	.75	.45
(3)	Ossie Bluege	1.50	.75	.45
(4)	Stan Coveleski	1.50	.75	.45
(5)	Alex Ferguson	1.50	.75	.45
(6)	Showboat Fisher	1.50	.75	.45
(7)	Goose Goslin	1.50	.75	.45
(8)	Bart Griffith	1.50	.75	.45
(9)	Pinky Hargrave	1.50	.75	.45
(10)	Bucky Harris	1.50	.75	.45
(11)	Joe Harris	1.50	.75	.45
(12)	Tex Jeanes	1.50	.75	.45
(13)	Walter Johnson	4.00	2.00	1.25
(14)	Joe Judge	1.50	.75	.45
(15)	Wade Lefler	1.50	.75	.45
(16)	Nemo Leibold	1.50	.75	.45
(17)	Firpo Marberry	1.50	.75	.45
(18)	Joe Martina	1.50	.75	.45
(19)	Wid Matthews	1.50	.75	.45
(20)	Mike McNally	1.50	.75	.45
(21)	Earl McNeely	1.50	.75	.45
(22)	Ralph Miller	1.50	.75	.45
(23)	George Mogridge	1.50	.75	.45
(24)	Buddy Myer	1.50	.75	.45
(25)	Curly Ogden	1.50	.75	.45
(26)	Roger Peckinpaugh	1.50	.75	.45
(27)	Spencer Pumpelly	1.50	.75	.45
(28)	Sam Rice	1.50	.75	.45
(29)	Muddy Ruel	1.50	.75	.45
(30)	Dutch Ruether	1.50	.75	.45
(31)	Allen Russell	1.50	.75	.45
(32)	Everett Scott	1.50	.75	.45
(33)	Hank Severeid	1.50	.75	.45
(34)	Mule Shirley	1.50	.75	.45
(35)	Byron Speece	1.50	.75	.45
(36)	Benny Tate	1.50	.75	.45
(37)	Bobby Veach	1.50	.75	.45
(38)	Tom Zachary	1.50	.75	.45
(39)	Paul Zahniser	1.50	.75	.45
	5" x 3-1/2" FEATURE CARDS	1.50	.75	.45
(40)	Bucky Harris, Bill McKechnie	2.00	1.00	.60
(41)	Ossie Bluege, Roger Peckinpaugh, Bucky Harris, Joe Judge	2.00	1.00	.60
(42)	Tom Zachary, Firpo Marberry, Alex Ferguson, Walter Johnson	2.50	1.25	.70

1975 TCMA 1927 New York Yankees

One of the greatest teams in baseball history is featured in this set of collectors' cards. The 2-1/2" x 3-1/2" cards have black-and-white photos with a white border. At top is the team identification, at bottom is player name and position. The back has the player's 1927 season stats. The unnumbered cards are checklisted here alphabetically.

Checklists showing are card numbers in parentheses ( ) indicates the numbers do not appear on the cards.

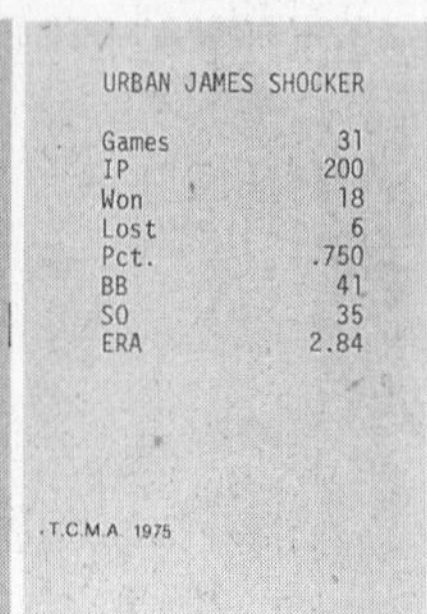

		NM	EX	VG
Complete Set (30):		40.00	20.00	12.00
Common Player:		2.00	1.00	.60
(1)	Walter Beall	2.00	1.00	.60
(2)	Benny Bengough	2.00	1.00	.60
(3)	Pat Collins	2.00	1.00	.60
(4)	Earle Combs	2.00	1.00	.60
(5)	Joe Dugan	2.00	1.00	.60
(6)	Cedric Durst	2.00	1.00	.60
(7)	Mike Gazella	2.00	1.00	.60
(8)	Lou Gehrig	7.50	3.75	2.25
(9)	Joe Giard	2.00	1.00	.60
(10)	Johnny Grabowski	2.00	1.00	.60
(11)	Waite Hoyt	2.00	1.00	.60
(12)	Miller Huggins	2.00	1.00	.60
(13)	Mark Koenig	2.00	1.00	.60
(14)	Tony Lazzeri	2.00	1.00	.60
(15)	Bob Meusel	2.00	1.00	.60
(16)	Wilcy Moore	2.00	1.00	.60
(17)	Ray Morehart	2.00	1.00	.60
(18)	Ben Paschal	2.00	1.00	.60
(19)	Herb Pennock	2.00	1.00	.60
(20)	George Pipgras	2.00	1.00	.60
(21)	Dutch Ruether	2.00	1.00	.60
(22)	Jacob Ruppert	2.00	1.00	.60
(23)	Babe Ruth	12.00	6.00	3.50
(24)	Bob Shawkey	2.00	1.00	.60
(25)	Urban Shocker	2.00	1.00	.60
(26)	Myles Thomas	2.00	1.00	.60
(27)	Julie Wera	2.00	1.00	.60
(28)	Yankee Coaches and Manager (Charlie O'Leary, Miller Huggins, Artie Fletcher)	2.00	1.00	.60
(29)	Yankee Stadium	3.00	1.50	.90
(30)	Yankees infield (Lou Gehrig, Tony Lazzeri, Mark Koenig, Joe Dugan) (5" x 3-5/8")	9.00	4.50	2.75

1975 TCMA 1942-46 St. Louis Cardinals

This collectors' issue set features players and staff from the Cards' war-years dynasty. In 2-1/2" x 3-5/8" format, the cards have black-and-white photos with red printing on front. The unnumbered cards have statistics on back.

		NM	EX	VG
Complete Set (66):		40.00	20.00	12.00
Common Player:		1.00	.50	.30
(1)	Buster Adams	1.00	.50	.30
(2)	Red Barrett	1.00	.50	.30
(3)	John Beazley	1.00	.50	.30
(4)	Al Brazle	1.00	.50	.30
(5)	Harry Brecheen	1.00	.50	.30
(6)	Jimmy Brown	1.00	.50	.30
(7)	Ken Burkhart	1.00	.50	.30
(8)	Bud Byerly	1.00	.50	.30
(9)	Mort Cooper	1.00	.50	.30
(10)	Walker Cooper	1.00	.50	.30
(11)	Estel Crabtree	1.00	.50	.30
(12)	Creepy Crespi	1.00	.50	.30
(13)	Jeff Cross	1.00	.50	.30
(14)	Frank Demaree	1.00	.50	.30
(15)	Murrey Dickson (Murry)	1.00	.50	.30
(16)	Blix Donnelly	1.00	.50	.30
(17)	Erv Dusak	1.00	.50	.30
(18)	Eddie Dyer	1.00	.50	.30
(19)	Bill Endicott	1.00	.50	.30
(20)	George Fallon	1.00	.50	.30
(21)	Joe Garagiola	3.00	1.50	.90
(22)	Debs Garms	1.00	.50	.30
(23)	Mike Gonzalez	1.25	.60	.40
(24)	Johnny Grodzicki	1.00	.50	.30
(25)	Harry Gumbert	1.00	.50	.30
(26)	Johnny Hopp	1.00	.50	.30

(27)	Nippy Jones	1.00	.50	.30
(28)	Lou Klein	1.00	.50	.30
(29)	Clyde Kluttz	1.00	.50	.30
(30)	Howie Krist	1.00	.50	.30
(31)	Whitey Kurowski	1.00	.50	.30
(32)	Max Lanier	1.00	.50	.30
(33)	Danny Litwhiler	1.00	.50	.30
(34)	Bill Lohrman	1.00	.50	.30
(35)	Marty Marion	1.50	.70	.45
(36)	Freddie Martin	1.00	.50	.30
(37)	Pepper Martin	2.00	1.00	.60
(38)	Terry Moore	1.00	.50	.30
(39)	Red Munger	1.00	.50	.30
(40)	Stan Musial	5.00	2.50	1.50
(41)	Sam Narron	1.00	.50	.30
(42)	Ken O'Dea	1.00	.50	.30
(43)	Howie Pollet	1.00	.50	.30
(44)	Del Rice	1.00	.50	.30
(45)	Ray Sanders	1.00	.50	.30
(46)	Fred Schmidt	1.00	.50	.30
(47)	Red Schoendienst	3.00	1.50	.90
(48)	Walt Sessi	1.00	.50	.30
(49)	Clyde Shoun	1.00	.50	.30
(50)	Dick Sisler	1.00	.50	.30
(51)	Enos Slaughter	3.00	1.50	.90
(52)	Billy Southworth	1.00	.50	.30
(53)	Coaker Triplett	1.00	.50	.30
(54)	Emil Verban	1.00	.50	.30
(55)	Harry Walker	1.00	.50	.30
(56)	Buzzy Wares	1.00	.50	.30
(57)	Lon Warneke	1.00	.50	.30
(58)	Ernie White	1.00	.50	.30
(59)	Del Wilber	1.00	.50	.30
(60)	Ted Wilks	1.00	.50	.30
(61)	Leo Durocher, Eddie Dyer	1.00	.50	.30
(62)	Stan Musial, Billy Southworth, Johnny Hopp	1.00	.50	.30
(63)	Stan Musial, Billy Southworth, Ray Sanders	1.00	.50	.30
(64)	Red Ruffing, Johnny Beazley	1.00	.50	.30
(65)	1942 St. Louis Cardinals (5" x 3-1/2")	3.00	1.50	.90
(66)	Sportsman's Park (5" x 3-1/2")	2.50	1.25	.70

1975 TCMA 1946 Boston Red Sox

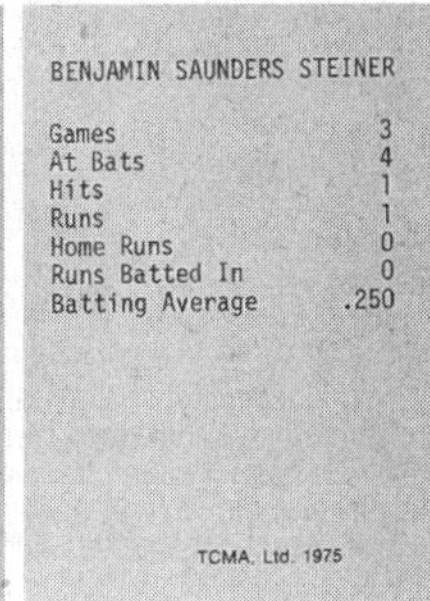

BENJAMIN SAUNDERS STEINER
Games 3
At Bats 4
Hits 1
Runs 1
Home Runs 0
Runs Batted In 0
Batting Average .250
TCMA, Ltd. 1975

The Red Sox American League champions of 1946 are featured in this collectors' issue. Blue-and-white player photos appear on front, with the player's name and position in black below. At bottom-front is the team name in red. Backs of the 2-1/2" x 3-1/2" cards have the player's 1946 stats. The unnumbered cards are checklisted here in alphabetical order.

		NM	EX	VG
	Complete Set (43):	45.00	22.50	13.50
	Common Player:	1.50	.75	.45
(1)	Jim Bagby	1.50	.75	.45
(2)	Del Baker	1.50	.75	.45
(3)	Mace Brown	1.50	.75	.45
(4)	Bill Butland	1.50	.75	.45
(5)	Paul Campbell	1.50	.75	.45
(6)	Tom Carey	1.50	.75	.45
(7)	Joe Cronin	2.00	1.00	.60
(8)	Leon Culberson	1.50	.75	.45
(9)	Tom Daly	1.50	.75	.45
(10)	Dom DiMaggio	2.50	1.25	.70
(11)	Joe Dobson	1.50	.75	.45
(12)	Bobby Doerr	1.50	.75	.45
(13)	Clem Dreisewerd	1.50	.75	.45
(14)	"Boo" Ferriss	1.50	.75	.45
(15)	Andy Gilbert	1.50	.75	.45
(16)	Don Gutteridge	1.50	.75	.45
(17)	Mickey Harris	1.50	.75	.45
(18)	Randy Heflin	1.50	.75	.45
(19)	"Pinky" Higgins	1.50	.75	.45
(20)	"Tex" Hughson	1.50	.75	.45
(21)	Earl Johnson	1.50	.75	.45
(22)	Bob Klinger	1.50	.75	.45
(23)	Johnny Lazor	1.50	.75	.45
(24)	Tom McBride	1.50	.75	.45
(25)	Ed McGah	1.50	.75	.45
(26)	"Catfish" Metkovich	1.50	.75	.45
(27)	Wally Moses	1.50	.75	.45
(28)	Roy Partee	1.50	.75	.45
(29)	Eddie Pellagrini	1.50	.75	.45
(30)	Johnny Pesky	1.50	.75	.45
(31)	Frank Pytlak	1.50	.75	.45
(32)	"Rip" Russell	1.50	.75	.45
(33)	Mike Ryba	1.50	.75	.45
(34)	Ben Steiner	1.50	.70	.45
(35)	Charlie Wagner	1.50	.75	.45
(36)	Hal Wagner	1.50	.75	.45
(37)	Ted Williams	7.50	3.75	2.25
(38)	Larry Woodall	1.50	.75	.45
(39)	Rudy York	1.50	.75	.45
(40)	Bill Zuber	1.50	.75	.45
(41)	Team Photo	2.00	1.00	.60
(42)	Larry Woodall, Hal Wagner, Del Baker	1.50	.75	.45
(43)	Rudy York, Wally Moses, Dom DiMaggio, Bobby Doerr, Charlie Wagner (5" x 3-1/2")	4.00	2.00	1.25

1975 TCMA 1950 Philadelphia Phillies/Whiz Kids

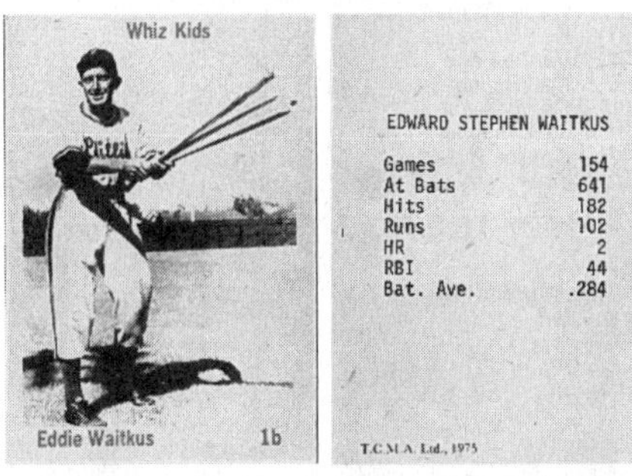

Whiz Kids
Eddie Waitkus 1b
EDWARD STEPHEN WAITKUS
Games 154
At Bats 641
Hits 182
Runs 102
HR 2
RBI 44
Bat. Ave. .284
T.C.M.A. Ltd., 1975

The National League Champion "Whiz Kids" are featured in this collectors' issue. The 2-1/2" x 3-1/2" cards have black-and-white photos on front with the player's name and position in red at bottom and either "Whiz Kids" or "1950 Philadelphia Phillies" in red at top. Black-and-white backs have 1950 season stats. The unnumbered cards are checklisted here alphabetically. The large-format multiple-player card was issued coincidentally with the set.

		NM	EX	VG
	Complete Set (32):	45.00	22.50	13.50
	Common Player:	2.00	1.00	.60
(1)	Richie Ashburn	11.00	5.50	3.25
(2)	Benny Bengough	2.00	1.00	.60
(3)	Jimmy Bloodworth	2.00	1.00	.60
(4)	Hank Borowy	2.00	1.00	.60
(5)	"Putsy" Caballero	2.00	1.00	.60
(6)	"Bubba" Church	2.00	1.00	.60
(7)	Dusty Cooke	2.00	1.00	.60
(8)	Blix Donnelly	2.00	1.00	.60
(9)	Del Ennis	2.00	1.00	.60
(10)	Mike Goliat	2.00	1.00	.60
(11)	Granny Hamner	2.00	1.00	.60
(12)	Ken Heintzelman	2.00	1.00	.60
(13)	Stan Hollmig	2.00	1.00	.60
(14)	Ken Johnson	2.00	1.00	.60
(15)	"Puddin-Head" Jones	2.00	1.00	.60
(16)	Jim Konstanty	2.00	1.00	.60
(17)	Stan Lopata	2.00	1.00	.60
(18)	Jackie Mayo	2.00	1.00	.60
(19)	Russ Meyer	2.00	1.00	.60
(20)	Bob Miller	2.00	1.00	.60
(21)	Bill Nicholson	2.00	1.00	.60
(22)	Cy Perkins	2.00	1.00	.60
(23)	Robin Roberts	11.00	5.50	3.25
(24)	Eddie Sawyer	2.00	1.00	.60
(25)	Andy Seminick	2.00	1.00	.60
(26)	Ken Silvestri	2.00	1.00	.60
(27)	Curt Simmons	2.00	1.00	.60
(28)	Dick Sisler	2.00	1.00	.60
(29)	"Jocko" Thompson	2.00	1.00	.60
(30)	Eddie Waitkus	2.00	1.00	.60
(31)	Dick Whitman	2.00	1.00	.60
(32)	Russ Meyer, Hank Borowy, Bill Nicholson, Willie Jones (4-7/8" x 3-1/2")	15.00	7.50	4.50

1975 TCMA 1951 New York Giants

Artie Wilson OF
1951 NEW YORK GIANTS
ARTHUR LEE WILSON
Infielder
Games 19
At Bats 44
Hits 4
Runs 2
HR 0
RBI 1
Bat Ave. .182
TCMA, Ltd. 1975

The National League Champion Giants of 1951 are honored in this collectors' issue card set. The 2-1/2" x 3-1/2" cards have black-and-white photos on front, with player name, team and position in the bottom border in red-orange ink. Backs are black-and-white with 1951 stats. The unnumbered cards are listed here in alphabetical order.

		NM	EX	VG
	Complete Set (34):	35.00	17.50	10.00
	Common Player:	1.50	.75	.45
(1)	George Bamberger	1.50	.75	.45
(2)	Roger Bowman	1.50	.75	.45
(3)	Al Corwin	1.50	.75	.45
(4)	Alvin Dark	2.00	1.00	.60
(5)	Allen Gettel	1.50	.75	.45
(6)	Clint Hartung	1.50	.75	.45
(7)	Jim Hearn	1.50	.75	.45
(8)	Monte Irvin	2.00	1.00	.60
(9)	Larry Jansen	1.50	.75	.45
(10)	Sheldon Jones	1.50	.75	.45
(11)	"Spider" Jorgensen	1.50	.75	.45
(12)	Monte Kennedy	1.50	.75	.45
(13)	Alex Konikowski	1.50	.70	.45
(14)	Dave Koslo	1.50	.75	.45
(15)	Jack Kramer	1.50	.75	.45
(16)	Whitey Lockman	1.50	.75	.45
(17)	"Lucky" Lohrke	1.50	.75	.45
(18)	Sal Maglie	1.50	.70	.45
(19)	Jack Maguire	1.50	.70	.45
(20)	Willie Mays	10.00	5.00	3.00
(21)	Don Mueller	1.50	.75	.45
(22)	Ray Noble	1.50	.75	.45
(23)	Earl Rapp	1.50	.75	.45
(24)	Bill Rigney	1.50	.75	.45
(25)	George Spencer	1.50	.75	.45
(26)	Eddie Stanky	1.50	.70	.45
(27)	Hank Thompson	1.50	.75	.45
(28)	Bobby Thomson	2.50	1.20	.70
(29)	Wes Westrum	1.50	.75	.45
(30)	Davey Williams	1.50	.75	.45
(31)	Artie Wilson	1.50	.75	.45
(32)	Sal Yvars	1.50	.75	.45
(33)	Leo Durocher, Willie Mays (3-5/8" x 5")	7.00	3.50	2.00
(34)	Durocher and coaches (3-5/8" x 5")	3.00	1.50	.90

1975 TCMA 1954 Cleveland Indians

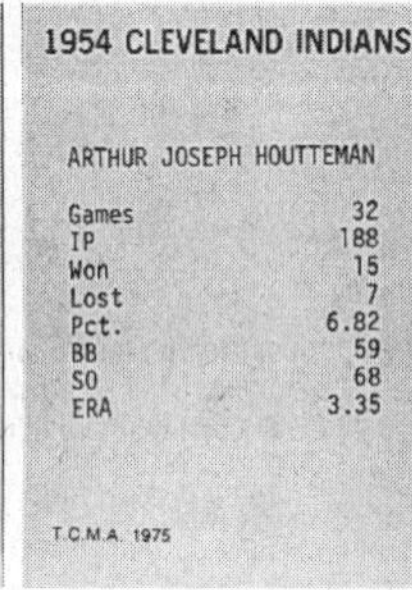

1954 CLEVELAND INDIANS
ARTHUR JOSEPH HOUTTEMAN
Games 32
IP 188
Won 15
Lost 7
Pct. 6.82
BB 59
SO 68
ERA 3.35
T.C.M.A. 1975

The American League Champions of 1954 are featured in this collectors issue. Individual player cards are 2-1/2" x 3-1/2" printed in black-and-white. Backs have 1954 season stats. Three large-format (3-3/4" x 5-1/8") multi-player cards were issued with the complete set. The unnumbered cards are checklisted here alphabetically.

		NM	EX	VG
	Complete Set (39):	35.00	17.50	10.00
	Common Player:	1.50	.75	.45
(1)	Bobby Avila	2.00	1.00	.60
(2)	Bob Chakales	1.50	.75	.45
(3)	Tony Cuccinello	1.50	.75	.45
(4)	Sam Dente	1.50	.75	.45
(5)	Larry Doby	3.50	1.75	1.00
(6)	Luke Easter	2.00	1.00	.60
(7)	Bob Feller	5.00	2.50	1.50
(8)	Mike Garcia	2.00	1.00	.60
(9)	Joe Ginsberg	1.50	.75	.45
(10)	Bill Glynn	1.50	.75	.45
(11)	Mickey Grasso	1.50	.75	.45
(12)	Mel Harder	1.50	.75	.45
(13)	Jim Hegan	1.50	.75	.45
(14)	Bob Hooper	1.50	.75	.45
(15)	Dave Hoskins	1.50	.75	.45
(16)	Art Houtteman	1.50	.75	.45
(17)	Bob Kennedy	1.50	.75	.45
(18)	Bob Lemon	2.50	1.25	.70
(19)	Al Lopez	2.50	1.25	.70
(20)	Hank Majeski	1.50	.75	.45
(21)	Dale Mitchell	1.50	.75	.45
(22)	Don Mossi	1.50	.75	.45
(23)	Hal Naragon	1.50	.75	.45
(24)	Ray Narleski	1.50	.75	.45
(25)	Rocky Nelson	1.50	.75	.45
(26)	Hal Newhouser	2.50	1.25	.70
(27)	Dave Philley	1.50	.75	.45
(28)	Dave Pope	1.50	.75	.45
(29)	Rudy Regaldo	1.50	.75	.45
(30)	Al Rosen	2.00	1.00	.60
(31)	Jose Santiago	1.50	.75	.45
(32)	Al Smith	1.50	.75	.45
(33)	George Strickland	1.50	.75	.45
(34)	Vic Wertz	1.50	.75	.45
(35)	Wally Westlake	1.50	.75	.45
(36)	Early Wynn	2.50	1.25	.70
	Large Format Cards	1.50	.75	.45
(37)	Al Lopez and Coaches	5.00	2.50	1.50
(38)	Al Lopez and Pitchers	5.00	2.50	1.50
(39)	Indians Outfielders	5.00	2.50	1.50

1975 TCMA/ASCCA Ad Card

To promote the American Sports Card Collectors Association Show in New York City, this 3-1/2" x 5-1/2" black-and-white card done in the format of the All-Time Greats postcards was issued. The front pictures two of the game's greatest pitchers and offers a discount on show admission. The back provides a detailed description of the show.

	NM	EX	VG
Dizzy Dean, Lefty Grove	6.00	3.00	1.80

1976 TCMA DiMaggio Brothers Postcard

This black-and-white postcard was issued singly circa the mid-1970s. It measures approximately 3-1/2" x 5-1/2".

	NM	EX	VG
Dom DiMaggio, Joe DiMaggio, Vince DiMaggio	12.00	6.00	3.50

1976 TCMA Larry Rosenthal

This custom-published card of the long-time American League outfielder (1936-1945) was printed in red, black and white in a 2-5/8" x 4-5/8" format. The issue date is approximate.

	NM	EX	VG
Larry Rosenthal	6.00	3.00	2.00

1976 TCMA Umpires

Eight of the better-known umpires of the era apparently commissioned TCMA to produce cards for them. The cards are black-and-white in the standard 2-1/2" x 3-1/2" format.

		NM	EX	VG
Complete Set (8):		25.00	12.50	7.50
Common Card:		4.00	2.00	1.25
(1)	Larry Barnett	4.00	2.00	1.25
(2)	Al Clark	4.00	2.00	1.25
(3)	Nick Colosi	4.00	2.00	1.25
(4)	Don Denkinger	4.00	2.00	1.25
(5)	Art Frantz	4.00	2.00	1.25
(6)	Marty Springstead	4.00	2.00	1.25
(7)	Ed Sudol	4.00	2.00	1.25
(8)	Bill Williams	4.00	2.00	1.25

1976 TCMA 1911 N.Y. Highlanders Postcard

This black-and-white postcard was issued singly circa the mid-1970s. It measures approximately 6" x 3-1/2".

	NM	EX	VG
1911 N.Y. Highlanders Team Photo	12.00	6.00	3.50

1976 TCMA 1938 Chicago Cubs

Augie Galan
OF
AUGUST JOHN GALAN
Games 110
At Bats 395
Hits 113
Runs 52
Home Runs 6
RBI 69
Bat. Ave. .286
1938 CHICAGO CUBS
NATIONAL LEAGUE CHAMPIONS

The National League Champion Chicago Cubs of 1938 are featured in this collectors issue. The 2-1/2" x 3-1/2" cards have black-and-white player photos on front with the player's name and position in blue at bottom. Backs are in black-and-white with season stats. The unnumbered cards are checklisted here alphabetically.

		NM	EX	VG
Complete Set (33):		40.00	20.00	12.00
Common Player:		2.00	1.00	.60
(1)	Jim Asbell	2.00	1.00	.60
(2)	Clay Bryant	2.00	1.00	.60
(3)	Tex Carleton	2.00	1.00	.60
(4)	Phil Cavarretta	2.00	1.00	.60
(5)	Ripper Collins	2.00	1.00	.60
(6)	"Red" Corriden	2.00	1.00	.60
(7)	Dizzy Dean	7.50	3.75	2.25
(8)	Frank Demaree	2.00	1.00	.60
(9)	Al Epperly	2.00	1.00	.60
(10)	Larry French	2.00	1.00	.60
(11)	Augie Galan	2.00	1.00	.60
(12)	Bob Garbark	2.00	1.00	.60
(13)	Charlie Grimm	2.00	1.00	.60
(14)	Stan Hack	2.00	1.00	.60
(15)	Gabby Hartnett	3.00	1.50	.90
(16)	Billy Herman	3.00	1.50	.90
(17)	Kirby Higbe	2.00	1.00	.60
(18)	Hardrock Johnson	2.00	1.00	.60
(19)	Billy Jurges	2.00	1.00	.60
(20)	Newt Kimball	2.00	1.00	.60
(21)	Tony Lazzeri	3.00	1.50	.90
(22)	Bill Lee	2.00	1.00	.60
(23)	Bob Logan	2.00	1.00	.60
(24)	Joe Marty	2.00	1.00	.60
(25)	Bobby Mattick	2.00	1.00	.60
(26)	Steve Mesner	2.00	1.00	.60
(27)	Ken O'Dea	2.00	1.00	.60
(28)	Vance Page	2.00	1.00	.60
(29)	Carl Reynolds	2.00	1.00	.60
(30)	Charlie Root	2.00	1.00	.60
(31)	Jack Russell	2.00	1.00	.60
(32)	Coaker Triplett	2.00	1.00	.60
(33)	Team History Card	.70	.35	.20

1977 TCMA All-Time White Sox

Ray Schalk
C
All-Time
Chicago White Sox
Eddie Robinson 1B
Eddie Collins 2B
Willie Kamm 3B
Luke Appling SS
Ray Schalk C
Al Simmons LF
Johnny Mostil CF
Harry Hooper RF
Ted Lyons RHP
Billy Pierce LHP
Gerry Staley RP
Al Lopez Mgr

Because this is one of the few early TCMA issues not to have a date printed on the back, the quoted year of issue is approximate. Fronts of the 2-1/2" x 3-1/2" cards have black-and-white player photos with name and position printed in red in the bottom border. Black-and-white backs have an all-time team roster of position players, pitchers and manager. The unnumbered cards are checklisted here in alphabetical order.

		NM	EX	VG
Complete Set (12):		24.00	12.00	7.25
Common Player:		2.00	1.00	.60
(1)	Luke Appling	2.50	1.25	.70
(2)	Eddie Collins	2.50	1.25	.70
(3)	Harry Hooper	2.00	1.00	.60
(4)	Willie Kamm	2.00	1.00	.60
(5)	Al Lopez	2.00	1.00	.60
(6)	Ted Lyons	2.00	1.00	.60
(7)	Johnny Mostil	2.00	1.00	.60
(8)	Billy Pierce	2.00	1.00	.60
(9)	Eddie Robinson	2.00	1.00	.60
(10)	Ray Schalk	2.00	1.00	.60
(11)	Al Simmons	2.00	1.00	.60
(12)	Gerry Staley	2.00	1.00	.60

1977 TCMA Chicago Cubs All Time Team

Chicago Cubs
ALL TIME TEAM
RF - Kiki Cuyler
Chicago Cubs
All Time Team
1B - Charlie Grimm
2B - Rogers Hornsby
SS - Ernie Banks
3B - Ron Santo
C - Gabby Hartnett
LF - Billy Williams
RF - Kiki Cuyler
CF - Hack Wilson
RHP - Charlie Root
LHR - Larry French
RP - Emil Kush
MGR - Charlie Grimm
INF - Billy Herman

The best of the Cubs are presented in this collectors issue. An all-time great at each position is featured on the 2-1/2" x 3-1/2" card. Fronts have black-and-white photos with orange graphics. Backs are in black-and-white and list the team by position. The unnumbered cards are checklisted here in that order.

		NM	EX	VG
Complete Set (12):		30.00	15.00	9.00
Common Player:		3.00	1.50	.90
(1)	Charlie Grimm	3.00	1.50	.90
(2)	Rogers Hornsby	4.00	2.00	1.25
(3)	Ernie Banks	4.00	2.00	1.25
(4)	Ron Santo	3.00	1.50	.90
(5)	Gabby Hartnett	3.00	1.50	.90
(6)	Billy Williams	3.00	1.50	.90
(7)	Kiki Cuyler	3.00	1.50	.90
(8)	Hack Wilson	4.00	2.00	1.25
(9)	Charlie Root	3.00	1.50	.90
(10)	Larry French	3.00	1.50	.90
(11)	Emil Kush	3.00	1.50	.90
(12)	Billy Herman	3.00	1.50	.90

1977 TCMA Stars of the Twenties

Six players are featured on this 22" x 11" triple-folder which was glued into issues of the Summer, 1977, "Baseball Quarterly" magazine from TCMA. The pictures feature art-

work by John Anderson in sepia tones on heavy cream-colored textured paper stock. The pictures are back-to-back in pairs as listed here, with individual pictures varying in width from 7-1/4" to 7-1/2".

		NM	EX	VG
Complete Foldout:		10.00	5.00	3.00
Common Pair:		3.00	1.50	.90
(1/2)	Joe Bush, Gabby Hartnett	3.00	1.50	.90
(3/4)	Jim Bottomley, "Mule" Haas	3.00	1.50	.90
(5/6)	Sam Rice, Buddy Myer	3.00	1.50	.90

1977-80 TCMA The War Years

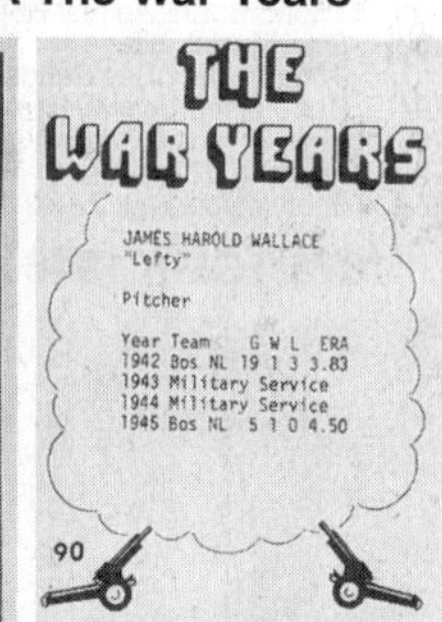

THE WAR YEARS
JAMES HAROLD WALLACE
"Lefty"
Pitcher
Year Team G W L ERA
1942 Bos. NL 19 1 3 3.83
1943 Military Service
1944 Military Service
1945 Bos. NL 5 1 0 4.50
90

The decimated major league rosters circa 1942-46 are reflected in this collectors' card set. The 2-1/2" x 3-1/2" cards have black-and-white player photos on front, with a white border around. There is no typography on front. Backs have player identification, stats and the set title. Series 1, cards #1-45 was issued in 1977 and is much scarcer than Series 2, #46-90, which was issued in 1980.

		NM	EX	VG
Complete Set (90):		140.00	70.00	42.50
Common Player:		2.00	1.00	.60
1	Samuel Narron	3.00	1.50	.90
2	Raymond Mack	3.00	1.50	.90
3	Arnold (Mickey) Owen	3.00	1.50	.90
4	John Peacock	3.00	1.50	.90
5	Paul (Dizzy) Trout	3.00	1.50	.90
6	George (Birdie) Tebbetts	3.00	1.50	.90
7	Alfred Todd	3.00	1.50	.90
8	Harlond Clift	3.00	1.50	.90
9	Don G.N. (Gil) Torres	3.00	1.50	.90
10	Alfonso Lopez	4.00	2.00	1.25
11	Ulysses (Tony) Lupien	3.00	1.50	.90
12	Lucius Appling	4.00	2.00	1.25
13	James (Pat) Seery	3.00	1.50	.90
14	Phil Masi	3.00	1.50	.90
15	Thomas Turner	3.00	1.50	.90
16	Nicholas Piccuito	3.00	1.50	.90
17	Mel Ott	7.50	3.75	2.25
18	Thadford Treadway	3.00	1.50	.90
19	Sam Naham (Neham)	3.00	1.50	.90
20	Truett (Rip) Sewell	3.00	1.50	.90
21	Roy Partee	3.00	1.50	.90
22	Richard Siebert	3.00	1.50	.90
23	Francis (Red) Barrett	3.00	1.50	.90
24	Paul O'Dea	3.00	1.50	.90
25	Lou Parisse	3.00	1.50	.90
26	Martin Marion	4.00	2.00	1.25
27	Eugene Moore	3.00	1.50	.90
28	Walter Beck	3.00	1.50	.90
29	Donald Manno	3.00	1.50	.90
30	Harold Newhouser	4.00	2.00	1.25
31	August Mancuso	3.00	1.50	.90
32	Merrill May	3.00	1.50	.90
33	Gerald Priddy	3.00	1.50	.90
34	Herman Besse	3.00	1.50	.90
35	Luis Olmo	3.00	1.50	.90
36	Robert O'Neill	3.00	1.50	.90
37	John Barrett	3.00	1.50	.90
38	Gordon Maltzberger	3.00	1.50	.90
39	William Nicholson	3.00	1.50	.90
40	Ron Northey	3.00	1.50	.90
41	Howard Pollet	3.00	1.50	.90
42	Aloysius Piechota	3.00	1.50	.90
43	Albert Shepard	7.50	3.75	2.25
44	Alfred Anderson	3.00	1.50	.90
45	Damon Phillips	3.00	1.50	.90
46	Herman Franks	2.00	1.00	.60
47	Aldon Wilke	2.00	1.00	.60
48	Max Macon	2.00	1.00	.60

#	Player	NM	EX	VG
49	Lester Webber	2.00	1.00	.60
50	Robert Swift	2.00	1.00	.60
51	Philip Weintraub	2.00	1.00	.60
52	Nicholas Strincevich	2.00	1.00	.60
53	Michael Tresh	2.00	1.00	.60
54	William Trotter	2.00	1.00	.60
55	1943 Yankees (Spud Chandler, Frank Crosetti, Bill Dickey, Nick Etten, Joe Gordon, Billy Johnson, Charlie Keller, John Lindell, Bud Metheny)	4.00	2.00	1.25
56	John Sturm	2.00	1.00	.60
57	Silas Johnson	2.00	1.00	.60
58	Donald Kolloway	2.00	1.00	.60
59	Cecil Vaughn (Vaughan)	2.00	1.00	.60
60	St. Louis Browns Bombers (Harlond Clift, Walt Judnich, Chet Laabs)	3.00	1.50	.90
61	Harold Wagner	2.00	1.00	.60
62	Alva Javery	2.00	1.00	.60
63	1941 Boston Bees Pitchers (George Barnicle, Ed Carnett, Art Johnson, Frank LaManna, Casey Stengel, Bob Williams)	3.00	1.50	.90
64	Adolph Camilli	2.00	1.00	.60
65	Myron McCormick	2.00	1.00	.60
66	Richard Wakefield	2.00	1.00	.60
67	James (Mickey) Vernon	3.00	1.50	.90
68	John Vander Meer	3.00	1.50	.90
69	James McDonnell	4.00	2.00	1.25
70	Thomas Jordan	2.00	1.00	.60
71	Maurice Van Robays	2.00	1.00	.60
72	Charles Stanceau	2.00	1.00	.60
73	Samuel Zoldak	2.00	1.00	.60
74	Raymond Starr	2.00	1.00	.60
75	Roger Wolff	2.00	1.00	.60
76	Cecil Travis	2.00	1.00	.60
77	Arthur Johnson	2.00	1.00	.60
78	Louis (Lewis) Riggs	2.00	1.00	.60
79	Peter Suder	2.00	1.00	.60
80	Thomas Warren	2.00	1.00	.60
81	John Welaj	2.00	1.00	.60
82	Gerald Walker	2.00	1.00	.60
83	Dewey Williams	2.00	1.00	.60
84	Leonard Merullo	2.00	1.00	.60
85	John Johnson	2.00	1.00	.60
86	Eugene Thompson	2.00	1.00	.60
87	William Zuber	2.00	1.00	.60
88	Earl Johnson	2.00	1.00	.60
89	Norman Young	2.00	1.00	.60
90	James Wallace	2.00	1.00	.60

1977 TCMA 1920 Cleveland Indians

The World Champion Indians are pictured on this collectors' issue team set. In standard 2-1/2" x 3-1/2" size with black-and-white photos, the cards are unnumbered. Some of the players are pictured in their 1921 uniforms with the "World Champions" lettering.

		NM	EX	VG
Complete Set (22):		25.00	12.50	7.50
Common Player:		2.00	1.00	.60
(1)	Jim Bagby	2.00	1.00	.60
(2)	George Burns	2.00	1.00	.60
(3)	Ray Caldwell	2.00	1.00	.60
(4)	Ray Chapman	3.00	1.50	.90
(5)	Stan Coveleski	2.50	1.25	.70
(6)	Joe Evans	2.00	1.00	.60
(7)	Larry Gardner	2.00	1.00	.60
(8)	Jack Graney	2.00	1.00	.60
(9)	Charlie Jamieson	2.00	1.00	.60
(10)	Doc Johnston	2.00	1.00	.60
(11)	Harry Lunte	2.00	1.00	.60
(12)	Duster Mails	2.00	1.00	.60
(13)	Guy Morton	2.00	1.00	.60
(14)	Les Nunamaker	2.00	1.00	.60
(15)	Steve O'Neill	2.00	1.00	.60
(16)	Joe Sewell	2.50	1.25	.70
(17)	Elmer Smith	2.00	1.00	.60
(18)	Tris Speaker	4.00	2.00	1.25
(19)	George Uhle	2.00	1.00	.60
(20)	Bill Wambsganss	2.50	1.25	.70
(21)	Joe Wood	2.50	1.25	.70
(22)	World Series Foes (Wilbert Robinson, Tris Speaker) (5-1/2" x 3")	4.00	2.00	1.25

1977 TCMA 1927 Yankees 50th Anniversary

As an insert in its inaugural issue of "Baseball Quarterly" magazine dated Winter, 1977, TCMA included a 16-3/4" x 11" cardboard panel with 18 black-and-white cards featuring members of the 1927 N.Y. Yankees. Measuring about 2-1/2" x 3-3/8" if cut apart, the individual cards have unadorned photos on front framed in black with a white border. Backs have player identification, a 50th anniversary logo, career summary and 1927 and career stats. The unnumbered cards are listed here in alphabetical order.

		NM	EX	VG
Complete Panel:		35.00	17.50	10.50
Complete Set (18):		25.00	12.50	7.50
Common Player:		2.00	1.00	.60
(1)	Bernard Oliver Bengough	2.00	1.00	.60
(2)	Tharon Patrick Collins	2.00	1.00	.60
(3)	Earle Bryan Combs	2.00	1.00	.60
(4)	Joseph Anthony Dugan	2.00	1.00	.60
(5)	Henry Louis Gehrig	6.00	3.00	1.75
(6)	John Patrick Grabowski	2.00	1.00	.60
(7)	Waite Charles Hoyt	2.00	1.00	.60
(8)	Miller James Huggins	2.00	1.00	.60
(9)	Mark Anthony Koenig	2.00	1.00	.60
(10)	Anthony Michael Lazzeri	2.00	1.00	.60
(11)	Robert Williams Meusel	2.00	1.00	.60
(12)	William Wilcy Moore	2.00	1.00	.60
(13)	Herbert Jeffries Pennock	2.00	1.00	.60
(14)	George William Pipgras	2.00	1.00	.60
(15)	Walter Henry Ruether	2.00	1.00	.60
(16)	George Herman Ruth	8.00	4.00	2.50
(17)	James Robert Shawkey	2.00	1.00	.60
(18)	Urban James Shocker	2.00	1.00	.60

1977 TCMA 1939-40 Cincinnati Reds

The National League Champion Reds of 1939 and the World's Champion team of 1940 are featured in this collectors' issue. The 2-1/2" x 3-1/2" cards have black-and-white photos on front surrounded by red borders. Backs, also in black-and white, have 1939 and/or 1940 season stats.

		NM	EX	VG
Complete Set (45):		35.00	17.50	10.00
Common Player:		1.50	.75	.45
1	Vince DiMaggio	2.50	1.25	.70
2	Wally Berger	1.50	.75	.45
3	Nolan Richardson (Nolen)	1.50	.75	.45
4	Ernie Lombardi	2.50	1.25	.70
5	Ival Goodman	1.50	.75	.45
6	Jim Turner	1.50	.75	.45
7	Bucky Walters	1.50	.75	.45
8	Jimmy Ripple	1.50	.75	.45
9	Hank Johnson	1.50	.75	.45
10	Bill Baker	1.50	.75	.45
11	Al Simmons	2.00	1.00	.60
12	Johnny Hutchings	1.50	.75	.45
13	Peaches Davis	1.50	.75	.45
14	Willard Hershberger	2.50	1.25	.70
15	Bill Werber	1.50	.75	.45
16	Harry Craft	1.50	.75	.45
17	Milt Galatzer	1.50	.75	.45
18	Dick West	1.50	.75	.45
19	Art Jacobs	1.50	.75	.45
20	Joe Beggs	1.50	.75	.45
21	Frenchy Bordagaray	1.50	.75	.45
22	Lee Gamble	1.50	.75	.45
23	Lee Grissom	1.50	.75	.45
24	Eddie Joost	1.50	.75	.45
25	Milt Shofner	1.50	.75	.45
26	Morrie Arnovich	1.50	.75	.45
27	Pete Naktenis	1.50	.75	.45
28	Jim Weaver	1.50	.75	.45
29	Mike McCormick	1.50	.75	.45
30	John Niggeling	1.50	.75	.45
31	Les Scarsella	1.50	.75	.45
32	Lonny Frey	1.50	.75	.45
33	Bill Myers	1.50	.75	.45
34	Frank McCormick	1.50	.75	.45
35	Lew Riggs	1.50	.75	.45
36	Nino Bongiovanni	1.50	.75	.45
37	Johnny Rizzo	1.50	.75	.45
38	Wes Livengood	1.50	.75	.45
39	Junior Thompson	1.50	.75	.45
40	Mike Dejan	1.50	.75	.45
41	Jimmy Wilson	1.50	.75	.45
42	Paul Derringer	1.50	.75	.45
43	Johnny Vander Meer	2.00	1.00	.60
44	Whitey Moore	1.50	.75	.45
45	Bill McKechnie	2.00	1.00	.60

1977 TCMA 1960 Pittsburgh Pirates

The World's Champions Pirates are featured on this collector issue. The 2-1/2" x 3-1/2" cards have black-and-white photos on front surrounded by orange borders. Backs, also in black-and-white, have a card number, player name and position at top and season stats.

		NM	EX	VG
Complete Set (42):		100.00	50.00	30.00
Common Player:		3.00	1.50	.90
1	Danny Murtaugh	3.00	1.50	.90
2	Dick Stuart	4.00	2.00	1.25
3	Bill Mazeroski	10.00	5.00	3.00
4	Dick Groat	4.00	2.00	1.25
5	Don Hoak	3.00	1.50	.90
6	Roberto Clemente	20.00	10.00	6.00
7	Bill Virdon	3.00	1.50	.90
8	Bob Skinner	3.00	1.50	.90
9	Smoky Burgess	3.00	1.50	.90
10	Gino Cimoli	3.00	1.50	.90
11	Rocky Nelson	3.00	1.50	.90
12	Hal Smith	3.00	1.50	.90
13	Dick Schofield	3.00	1.50	.90
14	Joe Christopher	3.00	1.50	.90
15	Gene Baker	3.00	1.50	.90
16	Bob Oldis	3.00	1.50	.90
17	Vern Law	3.00	1.50	.90
18	Bob Friend	3.00	1.50	.90
19	Wilmer Mizell	3.00	1.50	.90
20	Harvey Haddix	3.00	1.50	.90
21	Roy Face	3.00	1.50	.90
22	Fred Green	3.00	1.50	.90
23	Joe Gibbon	3.00	1.50	.90
24	Clem Labine	3.00	1.50	.90
25	Paul Giel	3.00	1.50	.90
26	Tom Cheney	3.00	1.50	.90
27	Earl Francis	3.00	1.50	.90
28	Jim Umbricht	3.00	1.50	.90
29	George Witt	3.00	1.50	.90
30	Bennie Daniels	3.00	1.50	.90
31	Don Gross	3.00	1.50	.90
32	Diomedes Olivo	4.00	2.00	1.25
33	Roman Mejias	3.00	1.50	.90
34	R.C. Stevens	3.00	1.50	.90
35	Mickey Vernon	3.00	1.50	.90
36	Danny Kravitz	3.00	1.50	.90
37	Harry Bright	3.00	1.50	.90
38	Dick Barone	3.00	1.50	.90
39	Bill Burwell	3.00	1.50	.90
40	Lenny Levy	4.00	2.00	1.25
41	Sam Narron	3.00	1.50	.90
42	Team Card (Bob Friend)	3.00	1.50	.90

1977 TCMA/ASCCA Ad Card

To promote the American Sports Card Collectors Association Show in New York City, this 2-1/2" x 3-1/2" black-and-white, gold highlighted card was issued. The front pictures Babe Ruth and offers a 25-cent discount on show admission. The back provides a detailed description of the show.

	NM	EX	VG
Babe Ruth	6.00	3.00	1.80

1977-84 TCMA/Renata Galasso

This issue of six 45-card series is in similar format but with different players, checklists and copyright dates produced by TCMA and marketed by Renata Galasso. In 2-1/2" x 3-1/2" format the cards have black-and-white photos on front. Backs are printed in red and blue and include a career summary, large Galasso ad and TCMA dateline.

		NM	EX	VG
Complete Set (270):		50.00	25.00	15.00
Common Player:		.25	.13	.08
	SERIES 1 - 1977	12.50	6.25	3.75
1	Joe DiMaggio	4.00	2.00	1.25
2	Ralph Kiner	.25	.13	.08
3	Don Larsen	.25	.13	.08
4	Robin Roberts	.25	.13	.08
5	Roy Campanella	.50	.25	.15
6	Smoky Burgess	.25	.13	.08
7	Mickey Mantle	6.00	3.00	1.75

8	Willie Mays	3.00	1.50	.90
9	George Kell	.25	.13	.08
10	Ted Williams	3.00	1.50	.90
11	Carl Furillo	.25	.13	.08
12	Bob Feller	.25	.13	.08
13	Casey Stengel	.25	.13	.08
14	Richie Ashburn	.25	.13	.08
15	Gil Hodges	.25	.13	.08
16	Stan Musial	.75	.40	.25
17	Don Newcombe	.25	.13	.08
18	Jackie Jensen	.25	.13	.08
19	Lou Boudreau	.25	.13	.08
20	Jackie Robinson	2.00	1.00	.60
21	Billy Goodman	.25	.13	.08
22	Satchel Paige	1.00	.50	.30
23	Hoyt Wilhelm	.25	.13	.08
24	Duke Snider	.25	.13	.08
25	Whitey Ford	.25	.13	.08
26	Monte Irvin	.25	.13	.08
27	Hank Sauer	.25	.13	.08
28	Sal Maglie	.25	.13	.08
29	Ernie Banks	.25	.13	.08
30	Billy Pierce	.25	.13	.08
31	Pee Wee Reese	.25	.13	.08
32	Al Lopez	.25	.13	.08
33	Allie Reynolds	.25	.13	.08
34	Eddie Mathews	.25	.13	.08
35	Al Rosen	.25	.13	.08
36	Early Wynn	.25	.13	.08
37	Phil Rizzuto	.25	.13	.08
38	Warren Spahn	.25	.13	.08
39	Bobby Thomson	.25	.13	.08
40	Enos Slaughter	.25	.13	.08
41	Roberto Clemente	4.00	2.00	1.25
42	Luis Aparicio	.25	.13	.08
43	Roy Sievers	.25	.13	.08
44	Hank Aaron	4.00	2.00	1.25
45	Mickey Vernon	.25	.13	.08
	SERIES 2 - 1979	10.00	5.00	3.00
46	Lou Gehrig	3.00	1.50	.90
47	Lefty O'Doul	.25	.13	.08
48	Chuck Klein	.25	.13	.08
49	Paul Waner	.25	.13	.08
50	Mel Ott	.25	.13	.08
51	Riggs Stephenson	.25	.13	.08
52	Dizzy Dean	.50	.25	.15
53	Frankie Frisch	.25	.13	.08
54	Red Ruffing	.25	.13	.08
55	Lefty Grove	.25	.13	.08
56	Heinie Manush	.25	.13	.08
57	Jimmie Foxx	.25	.13	.08
58	Al Simmons	.25	.13	.08
59	Charlie Root	.25	.13	.08
60	Goose Goslin	.25	.13	.08
61	Mickey Cochrane	.25	.13	.08
62	Gabby Hartnett	.25	.13	.08
63	Ducky Medwick	.25	.13	.08
64	Ernie Lombardi	.25	.13	.08
65	Joe Cronin	.25	.13	.08
66	Pepper Martin	.25	.13	.08
67	Jim Bottomley	.25	.13	.08
68	Bill Dickey	.25	.13	.08
69	Babe Ruth	5.00	2.50	1.50
70	Joe McCarthy	.25	.13	.08
71	Doc Cramer	.25	.13	.08
72	Kiki Cuyler	.25	.13	.08
73	Johnny Vander Meer	.25	.13	.08
74	Paul Derringer	.25	.13	.08
75	Freddie Fitzsimmons	.25	.13	.08
76	Lefty Gomez	.25	.13	.08
77	Arky Vaughan	.25	.13	.08
78	Stan Hack	.25	.13	.08
79	Earl Averill	.25	.13	.08
80	Luke Appling	.25	.13	.08
81	Mel Harder	.25	.13	.08
82	Hank Greenberg	.25	.13	.08
83	Schoolboy Rowe	.25	.13	.08
84	Billy Herman	.25	.13	.08
85	Gabby Street	.25	.13	.08
86	Lloyd Waner	.25	.13	.08
87	Jocko Conlan	.25	.13	.08
88	Carl Hubbell	.25	.13	.08
89	Series 1 checklist	.25	.13	.08
90	Series 2 checklist	.25	.13	.08
	SERIES 3 - 1980	7.50	3.75	2.25
91	Babe Ruth	3.00	1.50	.90
92	Rogers Hornsby	.25	.13	.08
93	Edd Roush	.25	.13	.08
94	George Sisler	.25	.13	.08
95	Harry Heilmann	.25	.13	.08
96	Tris Speaker	.25	.13	.08
97	Burleigh Grimes	.25	.13	.08
98	John McGraw	.25	.13	.08
99	Eppa Rixey	.25	.13	.08
100	Ty Cobb	1.00	.50	.30
101	Zack Wheat	.25	.13	.08
102	Pie Traynor	.25	.13	.08
103	Max Carey	.25	.13	.08
104	Dazzy Vance	.25	.13	.08
105	Walter Johnson	.50	.25	.15
106	Herb Pennock	.25	.13	.08
107	Joe Sewell	.25	.13	.08
108	Sam Rice	.25	.13	.08
109	Earle Combs	.25	.13	.08
110	Ted Lyons	.25	.13	.08
111	Eddie Collins	.25	.13	.08
112	Bill Terry	.25	.13	.08
113	Hack Wilson	.25	.13	.08
114	Rabbit Maranville	.25	.13	.08
115	Charlie Grimm	.25	.13	.08
116	Tony Lazzeri	.25	.13	.08
117	Waite Hoyt	.25	.13	.08
118	Stan Coveleski	.25	.13	.08
119	George Kelly	.25	.13	.08
120	Jimmy Dykes	.25	.13	.08
121	Red Faber	.25	.13	.08
122	Dave Bancroft	.25	.13	.08
123	Judge Landis	.25	.13	.08
124	Branch Rickey	.25	.13	.08
125	Jesse Haines	.25	.13	.08
126	Carl Mays	.25	.13	.08
127	Fred Lindstrom	.25	.13	.08
128	Miller Huggins	.25	.13	.08
129	Sad Sam Jones	.25	.13	.08
130	Joe Judge	.25	.13	.08
131	Ross Young (Youngs)	.25	.13	.08
132	Bucky Harris	.25	.13	.08
133	Bob Meusel	.25	.13	.08
134	Billy Evans	.25	.13	.08
135	1927 N.Y. Yankees Team Photo/Checklist	.50	.25	.15
	SERIES 4 - 1981	7.50	3.75	2.25
136	Ty Cobb	1.00	.50	.30
137	Nap Lajoie	.25	.13	.08
138	Tris Speaker	.25	.13	.08
139	Heinie Groh	.25	.13	.08
140	Sam Crawford	.25	.13	.08
141	Clyde Milan	.25	.13	.08
142	Chief Bender	.25	.13	.08
143	Big Ed Walsh	.25	.13	.08
144	Walter Johnson	.50	.25	.15
145	Connie Mack	.25	.13	.08
146	Hal Chase	.25	.13	.08
147	Hugh Duffy	.25	.13	.08
148	Honus Wagner	.50	.25	.15
149	Tom Connolly	.25	.13	.08
150	Clark Griffith	.25	.13	.08
151	Zack Wheat	.25	.13	.08
152	Christy Mathewson	.50	.25	.15
153	Grover C. Alexander	.25	.13	.08
154	Joe Jackson	3.00	1.50	.90
155	Home Run Baker	.25	.13	.08
156	Ed Plank	.25	.13	.08
157	Larry Doyle	.25	.13	.08
158	Rube Marquard	.25	.13	.08
159	Johnny Evers	.25	.13	.08
160	Joe Tinker	.25	.13	.08
161	Frank Chance	.25	.13	.08
162	Wilbert Robinson	.25	.13	.08
163	Roger Peckinpaugh	.25	.13	.08
164	Fred Clarke	.25	.13	.08
165	Babe Ruth	3.00	1.50	.90
166	Wilbur Cooper	.25	.13	.08
167	Germany Schaefer	.25	.13	.08
168	Addie Joss	.25	.13	.08
169	Cy Young	.50	.25	.15
170	Ban Johnson	.25	.13	.08
171	Joe Judge	.25	.13	.08
172	Harry Hooper	.25	.13	.08
173	Bill Klem	.25	.13	.08
174	Ed Barrow	.25	.13	.08
175	Ed Cicotte	.25	.13	.08
176	Hughie Jennings	.25	.13	.08
177	Ray Schalk	.25	.13	.08
178	Nick Altrock	.25	.13	.08
179	Roger Bresnahan	.25	.13	.08
180	$100,000 Infield	.25	.13	.08
	SERIES 5 - 1983	7.50	3.75	2.25
181	Lou Gehrig	3.00	1.50	.90
182	Eddie Collins	.25	.13	.08
183	Art Fletcher	.25	.13	.08
184	Jimmie Foxx	.25	.13	.08
185	Lefty Gomez	.25	.13	.08
186	Oral Hildebrand	.25	.13	.08
187	General Crowder	.25	.13	.08
188	Bill Dickey	.25	.13	.08
189	Wes Ferrell	.25	.13	.08
190	Al Simmons	.25	.13	.08
191	Tony Lazzeri	.25	.13	.08
192	Sam West	.25	.13	.08
193	Babe Ruth	3.00	1.50	.90
194	Connie Mack	.25	.13	.08
195	Lefty Grove	.25	.13	.08
196	Eddie Rommel	.25	.13	.08
197	Ben Chapman	.25	.13	.08
198	Joe Cronin	.25	.13	.08
199	Rich Ferrell (Rick)	.25	.13	.08
200	Charlie Gehringer	.25	.13	.08
201	Jimmy Dykes	.25	.13	.08
202	Earl Averill	.25	.13	.08
203	Pepper Martin	.25	.13	.08
204	Bill Terry	.25	.13	.08
205	Pie Traynor	.25	.13	.08
206	Gabby Hartnett	.25	.13	.08
207	Frank Frisch	.25	.13	.08
208	Carl Hubbell	.25	.13	.08
209	Paul Waner	.25	.13	.08
210	Woody English	.25	.13	.08
211	Bill Hallahan	.25	.13	.08
212	Dick Bartell	.25	.13	.08
213	Bill McKechnie	.25	.13	.08
214	Max Carey	.25	.13	.08
215	John McGraw	.25	.13	.08
216	Jimmie Wilson	.25	.13	.08
217	Chick Hafey	.25	.13	.08
218	Chuck Klein	.25	.13	.08
219	Lefty O'Doul	.25	.13	.08
220	Wally Berger	.25	.13	.08
221	Hal Schumacher	.25	.13	.08
222	Lon Warneke	.25	.13	.08
223	Tony Cuccinello	.25	.13	.08
(224)	1933 A.L. All-Stars	.50	.25	.15
(225)	1933 N.L. All-Stars	.50	.25	.15
	SERIES 6 - 1984	15.00	7.50	4.50
226	Roger Maris	.75	.40	.25
227	Babe Ruth	3.00	1.50	.90
228	Jackie Robinson	2.00	1.00	.60
229	Pete Gray	.75	.40	.25
230	Ted Williams	3.00	1.50	.90
231	Hank Aaron	3.00	1.50	.90
232	Mickey Mantle	5.00	2.50	1.50
233	Gil Hodges	.25	.13	.08
234	Walter Johnson	.50	.25	.15
235	Joe DiMaggio	3.00	1.50	.90
236	Lou Gehrig	3.00	1.50	.90
237	Stan Musial	.75	.40	.25
238	Mickey Cochrane	.25	.13	.08
239	Denny McLain	.25	.13	.08
240	Carl Hubbell	.25	.13	.08
241	Harvey Haddix	.25	.13	.08
242	Christy Mathewson	.50	.25	.15
243	Johnny VanderMeer	.25	.13	.08
244	Sandy Koufax	3.00	1.50	.90
245	Willie Mays	3.00	1.50	.90
246	Don Drysdale	.25	.13	.08
247	Bobby Richardson	.25	.13	.08
248	Hoyt Wilhelm	.25	.13	.08
249	Yankee Stadium	.25	.13	.08
250	Bill Terry	.25	.13	.08
251	Roy Campanella	.50	.25	.15
252	Roberto Clemente	3.00	1.50	.90
253	Casey Stengel	.25	.13	.08
254	Ernie Banks	.50	.25	.15
255	Bobby Thomson	.25	.13	.08
256	Mel Ott	.25	.13	.08
257	Tony Oliva	.25	.13	.08
258	Satchel Paige	1.00	.50	.30
259	Joe Jackson	3.00	1.50	.90
260	Larry Lajoie	.25	.13	.08
261	Bill Mazeroski	.25	.13	.08
262	Bill Wambsganss	.25	.13	.08
263	Willie McCovey	.25	.13	.08
264	Warren Spahn	.25	.13	.08
265	Lefty Gomez	.25	.13	.08
266	Dazzy Vance	.25	.13	.08
267	Sam Crawford	.25	.13	.08
268	Tris Speaker	.25	.13	.08
269	Lou Brock	.25	.13	.08
270	Cy Young	.25	.13	.08

1978 TCMA Baseball Nostalgia Postcard

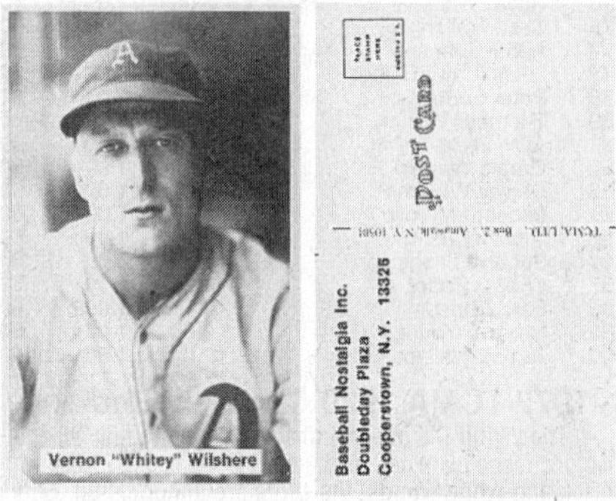

TCMA produced this card for Baseball Nostalgia, Inc., a Cooperstown, N.Y., hobby shop, in an edition of 500. The card pictures a Cooperstown resident who taught at the local high school following a short (1934-36) major league pitching career. The 3-1/2" x 5-1/2" black-and-white card has standard postcard markings on back.

	NM	EX	VG
Vernon "Whitey" Wilshere	6.00	3.00	1.80

1978 TCMA The 1960's

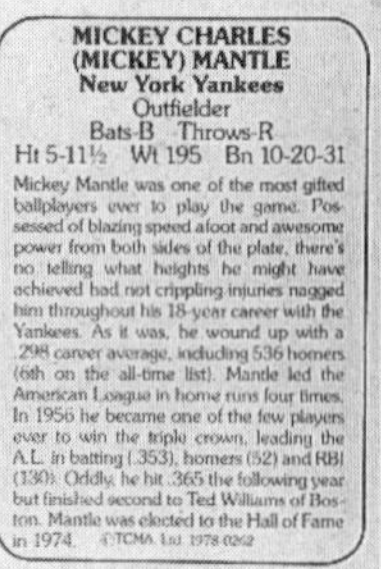

MICKEY CHARLES (MICKEY) MANTLE
New York Yankees
Outfielder
Bats-B Throws-R
Ht 5-11½ Wt 195 Bn 10-20-31

Mickey Mantle was one of the most gifted ballplayers ever to play the game. Possessed of blazing speed afoot and awesome power from both sides of the plate, there's no telling what heights he might have achieved had not crippling injuries nagged him throughout his 18-year career with the Yankees. As it was, he wound up with a .298 career average, including 536 homers (6th on the all-time list). Mantle led the American League in home runs four times. In 1956 he became one of the few players ever to win the triple crown, leading the A.L. in batting (.353), homers (52) and RBI (130). Oddly, he hit .365 the following year but finished second to Ted Williams of Boston. Mantle was elected to the Hall of Fame in 1974. ©TCMA Ltd. 1978 0262

Nearly 300 players of the 1960s are featured in this collectors issue. Fronts of the 2-1/2" x 3-1/2" cards have a color photo with a black frameline and white border. There are no other graphics. Backs are printed in green and include a lengthy career summary. On some cards the set's title, "The 1960's" is printed at top. Several mistakes in card numbering are noted in the accompanying checklist.

		NM	EX	VG
	Complete Set (293):	40.00	20.00	12.00
	Common Player:	.25	.13	.08
1	Smoky Burgess	.25	.13	.08
2	Juan Marichal	1.00	.50	.30
3	Don Drysdale	1.00	.50	.30
4	Jim Gentile	.25	.13	.08
5	Roy Face	.25	.13	.08
6	Joe Pepitone	.25	.13	.08
7	Joe Christopher	.25	.13	.08
8	Wayne Causey	.25	.13	.08
9	Frank Bolling	.25	.13	.08
10	Jim Maloney	.25	.13	.08
11	Roger Maris	2.50	1.25	.70
12	Bill White	.25	.13	.08
13	Roberto Clemente	7.50	3.75	2.25
14	Bob Saverine	.25	.13	.08

15	Barney Schultz	.25	.13	.08
16	Albie Pearson	.25	.13	.08
17	Denny Lemaster	.25	.13	.08
18	Ernie Broglio	.25	.13	.08
19	Bobby Klaus	.25	.13	.08
20	Tony Cloninger	.25	.13	.08
21	Whitey Ford	1.50	.70	.45
22	Ron Santo	.60	.30	.20
23	Jim Duckworth	.25	.13	.08
24	Willie Davis	.25	.13	.08
25	Ed Charles	.25	.13	.08
26	Bob Allison	.25	.13	.08
27	Fritz Ackley	.25	.13	.08
28	Ruben Amaro	.25	.13	.08
29	Johnny Callison	.25	.13	.08
30	Greg Bollo	.25	.13	.08
31	Felix Millan	.25	.13	.08
32	Camilo Pascual	.25	.13	.08
33	Jackie Brandt	.25	.13	.08
34	Don Lock	.25	.13	.08
35	Chico Ruiz	.25	.13	.08
36	Joe Azcue	.25	.13	.08
37	Ed Bailey	.25	.13	.08
38	Pete Ramos	.25	.13	.08
39	Eddie Bressoud	.25	.13	.08
40	Al Kaline	1.50	.70	.45
41	Ron Brand	.25	.13	.08
42	Bob Lillis	.25	.13	.08
43	Not Issued (See #125.)	.25	.13	.08
44	Buster Narum	.25	.13	.08
45	Jim Gilliam	.25	.13	.08
46	Claude Raymond	.25	.13	.08
47	Billy Bryan	.25	.13	.08
48	Marshall Bridges	.25	.13	.08
49	Norm Cash	.45	.25	.14
50	Orlando Cepeda	1.00	.50	.30
51	Lee Maye	.25	.13	.08
52	Andre Rodgers	.25	.13	.08
53	Ken Berry	.25	.13	.08
54	Don Mincher	.25	.13	.08
55	Jerry Lumpe	.25	.13	.08
56	Milt Pappas	.25	.13	.08
57	Steve Barber	.25	.13	.08
58	Denis Menke	.25	.13	.08
59	Larry Maxie	.25	.13	.08
60	Bob Gibson	1.00	.50	.30
61	Larry Bearnarth	.25	.13	.08
62	Bill Mazeroski	1.00	.50	.30
63	Bob Rodgers	.25	.13	.08
64	Jerry Arrigo	.25	.13	.08
65	Joe Nuxhall	.25	.13	.08
66	Dean Chance	.25	.13	.08
67	Ken Boyer	.60	.30	.20
68	John Odom	.25	.13	.08
69	Chico Cardenas	.25	.13	.08
70	Maury Wills	.35	.20	.11
71	Tony Oliva	.45	.25	.14
72	Don Nottebart	.25	.13	.08
73	Joe Adcock	.25	.13	.08
74	Felipe Alou	.25	.13	.08
75	Matty Alou	.25	.13	.08
76	Dick Radatz	.25	.13	.08
77	Jim Bouton	.25	.13	.08
78	John Blanchard	.25	.13	.08
79	Juan Pizarro	.25	.13	.08
80	Boog Powell	.45	.25	.14
81	Earl Robinson	.25	.13	.08
82	Bob Chance	.25	.13	.08
83	Max Alvis	.25	.13	.08
84	Don Blasingame	.25	.13	.08
85	Tom Cheney	.25	.13	.08
86	Jerry Arrigo	.25	.13	.08
87	Tommy Davis	.25	.13	.08
88	Steve Boros	.25	.13	.08
89	Don Cardwell	.25	.13	.08
90	Harmon Killebrew	1.50	.70	.45
91	Jim Pagliaroni	.25	.13	.08
92	Jim O'Toole	.25	.13	.08
93	Dennis Bennett	.25	.13	.08
94	Dick McAuliffe	.25	.13	.08
95	Dick Brown	.25	.13	.08
96	Joe Amalfitano	.25	.13	.08
97	Phil Linz	.25	.13	.08
98	Not Issued (See #165.)	.25	.13	.08
99	Dave Nicholson	.25	.13	.08
100	Hoyt Wilhelm	1.00	.50	.30
101	Don Leppert	.25	.13	.08
102	Jose Pagan	.25	.13	.08
103	Sam McDowell	.25	.13	.08
104	Jack Baldschun	.25	.13	.08
105	Jim Perry	.25	.13	.08
106	Hal Reniff	.25	.13	.08
107	Lee Maye	.25	.13	.08
108	Joe Adcock	.25	.13	.08
109	Bob Bolin	.25	.13	.08
110	Don Leppert	.25	.13	.08
111	Bill Monbouquette	.25	.13	.08
112	Bobby Richardson	.45	.25	.14
113	Earl Battey	.25	.13	.08
114	Bob Veale	.25	.13	.08
115	Lou Jackson	.25	.13	.08
116	Frank Kreutzer	.25	.13	.08
117	Jerry Zimmerman	.25	.13	.08
118	Don Schwall	.25	.13	.08
119	Rich Rollins	.25	.13	.08
120	Pete Ward	.25	.13	.08
121	Moe Drabowsky	.25	.13	.08
122	Jesse Gonder	.25	.13	.08
123	Hal Woodeshick	.25	.13	.08
124	John Herrnstein	.25	.13	.08
125a	Gary Peters (Should be #43.)	.25	.13	.08
125b	Leon Wagner	.25	.13	.08
126	Dwight Siebler	.25	.13	.08
027	Gary Kroll	.25	.13	.08
128	Tony Horton	.25	.13	.08
129	John DeMerit	.25	.13	.08
130	Sandy Koufax	6.00	3.00	1.75
131	Jim Davenport	.25	.13	.08
132	Wes Covington	.25	.13	.08
133	Tony Taylor	.25	.13	.08
134	Jack Kralick	.25	.13	.08
135	Bill Pleis	.25	.13	.08
136	Russ Snyder	.25	.13	.08
137	Joe Torre	.75	.40	.25
138	Ted Wills	.25	.13	.08
139	Wes Stock	.25	.13	.08
140	Frank Robinson	1.50	.70	.45
141	Dave Stenhouse	.25	.13	.08
142	Ron Hansen	.25	.13	.08
143	Don Elston	.25	.13	.08
144	Del Crandall	.25	.13	.08
145	Bennie Daniels	.25	.13	.08
146	Vada Pinson	.45	.25	.14
147	Bill Spanswick	.25	.13	.08
148	Earl Wilson	.25	.13	.08
149	Ty Cline	.25	.13	.08
150	Dick Groat	.25	.13	.08
151	Jim Duckworth	.25	.13	.08
152	Jimmie Schaffer	.25	.13	.08
153	George Thomas	.25	.13	.08
154	Wes Stock	.25	.13	.08
155	Mike White	.25	.13	.08
156	John Podres	.25	.13	.08
157	Willie Crawford	.25	.13	.08
158	Fred Gladding	.25	.13	.08
159	John Wyatt	.25	.13	.08
160	Bob Friend	.25	.13	.08
161	Ted Uhlaender	.25	.13	.08
162	Dick Stigman	.25	.13	.08
163	Don Wert	.25	.13	.08
164	Eddie Bressoud	.25	.13	.08
165a	Ed Roebuck (Should be #98.)	.25	.13	.08
165b	Leon Wagner	.25	.13	.08
166	Al Spangler	.25	.13	.08
167	Bob Sadowski	.25	.13	.08
168	Ralph Terry	.25	.13	.08
169	Jimmie Schaffer	.25	.13	.08
170a	Jim Fregosi (Should be #180.)	.25	.13	.08
170b	Dick Hall	.25	.13	.08
171	Al Spangler	.25	.13	.08
172	Bob Tillman	.25	.13	.08
173	Ed Bailey	.25	.13	.08
174	Cesar Tovar	.25	.13	.08
175	Morrie Stevens	.25	.13	.08
176	Floyd Weaver	.25	.13	.08
177	Frank Malzone	.25	.13	.08
178	Norm Siebern	.25	.13	.08
179	Dick Phillips	.25	.13	.08
180	Not Issued (See #170.)	.25	.13	.08
181	Bobby Wine	.25	.13	.08
182	Masanori Murakami	.75	.40	.25
183	Chuck Schilling	.25	.13	.08
184	Jimmie Schaffer	.25	.13	.08
185	John Roseboro	.25	.13	.08
186	Jake Wood	.25	.13	.08
187	Dallas Green	.25	.13	.08
188	Tom Haller	.25	.13	.08
189	Chuck Cottier	.25	.13	.08
190	Brooks Robinson	1.50	.70	.45
191	Ty Cline	.25	.13	.08
192	Bubba Phillips	.25	.13	.08
193	Al Jackson	.25	.13	.08
194	Herm Starrette	.25	.13	.08
195	Dave Wickersham	.25	.13	.08
196	Vic Power	.25	.13	.08
197	Ray Culp	.25	.13	.08
198	Don Demeter	.25	.13	.08
199	Dick Schofield	.25	.13	.08
200	Stephen Grant	.25	.13	.08
201	Roger Craig	.25	.13	.08
202	Dick Farrell	.25	.13	.08
203	Clay Dalrymple	.25	.13	.08
204	Jim Duffalo	.25	.13	.08
205	Tito Francona	.25	.13	.08
206	Tony Conigliaro	.45	.25	.14
207	Jim King	.25	.13	.08
208	Joe Gibbon	.25	.13	.08
209	Arnold Earley	.25	.13	.08
210	Denny McLain	.25	.13	.08
211	Don Larsen	.25	.13	.08
212	Ron Hunt	.25	.13	.08
213	Deron Johnson	.25	.13	.08
214	Harry Bright	.25	.13	.08
215	Ernie Fazio	.25	.13	.08
216	Joey Jay	.25	.13	.08
217	Jim Coates	.25	.13	.08
218	Jerry Kindall	.25	.13	.08
219	Joe Gibbon	.25	.13	.08
220	Frank Howard	.35	.20	.11
221	Howie Koplitz	.25	.13	.08
222	Larry Jackson	.25	.13	.08
223	Dale Long	.25	.13	.08
224	Jimmy Dykes	.25	.13	.08
225	Hank Aguirre	.25	.13	.08
226	Earl Francis	.25	.13	.08
227	Vic Wertz	.25	.13	.08
228	Larry Haney	.25	.13	.08
229	Tony LaRussa	.45	.25	.14
230	Moose Skowron	.35	.20	.11
231a	Tito Francona (Should be #235.)	.25	.13	.08
231b	Lee Thomas	.25	.13	.08
232	Ken Johnson	.25	.13	.08
233	Dick Howser	.25	.13	.08
234	Bobby Knoop	.25	.13	.08
235	Not Issued (See #231.)	.25	.13	.08
236	Elston Howard	.35	.20	.11
237	Donn Clendenon	.25	.13	.08
238	Jesse Gonder	.25	.13	.08
239	Vern Law	.25	.13	.08
240	Curt Flood	.25	.13	.08
241	Dal Maxvill	.25	.13	.08
242	Roy Sievers	.25	.13	.08
243	Jim Brewer	.25	.13	.08
244	Harry Craft	.25	.13	.08
245	Dave Eilers	.25	.13	.08
246	Dave DeBusschere	.25	.13	.08
247	Ken Harrelson	.25	.13	.08
248	Not Issued (See #249.)	.25	.13	.08
249a	Jim Duffalo	.25	.13	.08
249b	Eddie Kasko (Should be #248.)	.25	.13	.08
250	Luis Aparicio	1.00	.50	.30
251	Ron Kline	.25	.13	.08
252	Chuck Hinton	.25	.13	.08
253	Frank Lary	.25	.13	.08
254	Stu Miller	.25	.13	.08
255	Ernie Banks	2.00	1.00	.60
256	Dick Farrell	.25	.13	.08
257	Bud Daley	.25	.13	.08
258	Luis Arroyo	.25	.13	.08
259	Bob Del Greco	.25	.13	.08
260	Ted Williams	6.00	3.00	1.75
261	Mike Epstein	.25	.13	.08
262	Mickey Mantle	10.00	5.00	3.00
263	Jim LeFebvre	.25	.13	.08
264	Pat Jarvis	.25	.13	.08
265	Chuck Hinton	.25	.13	.08
266	Don Larsen	.25	.13	.08
267	Jim Coates	.25	.13	.08
268	Gary Kolb	.25	.13	.08
269	Jim Ray Hart	.25	.13	.08
270	Dave McNally	.25	.13	.08
271	Jerry Kindall	.25	.13	.08
272	Hector Lopez	.25	.13	.08
273	Claude Osteen	.25	.13	.08
274	Jack Aker	.25	.13	.08
275	Mike Shannon	.25	.13	.08
276	Lew Burdette	.25	.13	.08
277	Mack Jones	.25	.13	.08
278	Art Shamsky	.25	.13	.08
279	Bob Johnson	.25	.13	.08
280	Willie Mays	6.00	3.00	1.75
281	Rich Nye	.25	.13	.08
282	Bill Cowan	.25	.13	.08
283	Gary Kolb	.25	.13	.08
284	Woody Held	.25	.13	.08
285	Bill Freehan	.25	.13	.08
286	Larry Jackson	.25	.13	.08
287	Mike Hershberger	.25	.13	.08
288	Julian Javier	.25	.13	.08
289	Charley Smith	.25	.13	.08
290	Hank Aaron	6.00	3.00	1.75
291	John Boccabella	.25	.13	.08
292	Charley James	.25	.13	.08
293	Sammy Ellis	.25	.13	.08

1978 TCMA 1941 Brooklyn Dodgers

Freddie Fitzsimmons • Pitcher

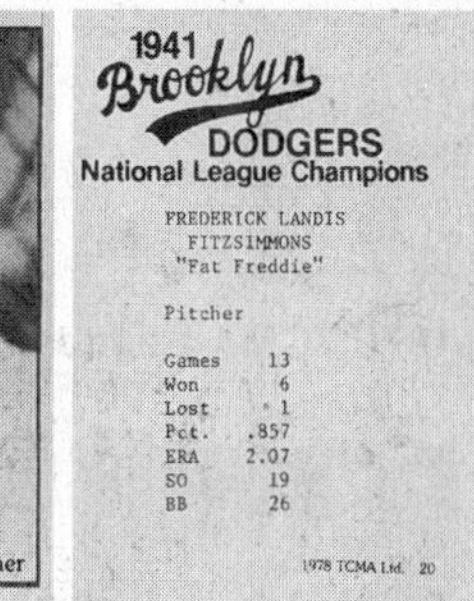

The National League Champion Brooklyn Dodgers are featured in the collectors' edition card set. Measuring 2-1/2" x 3-1/2", the cards have blue duotone player photos on front with the name and position overprinted in black at bottom. A white border surrounds the photo. Backs are in black-and-white with a large championship logo and a few stats from the 1941 season.

		NM	EX	VG
Complete Set (43):		25.00	12.50	7.50
Common Player:		1.50	.75	.45
1	Mickey Owen	2.50	1.25	.70
2	Pee Wee Reese	7.50	3.75	2.25
3	Hugh Casey	1.50	.75	.45
4	Larry French	1.50	.75	.45
5	Tom Drake	1.50	.75	.45
6	Ed Albosta	1.50	.75	.45
7	Tommy Tatum	1.50	.75	.45
8	Paul Waner	3.50	1.75	1.00
9	Van Lingle Mungo	2.50	1.25	.70
10	Bill Swift	1.50	.75	.45
11	Dolph Camilli	2.50	1.25	.70
12	Pete Coscarart	1.50	.75	.45
13	Vito Tamulis	1.50	.75	.45
14	John Allen	1.50	.75	.45
15	Lee Grissom	1.50	.75	.45
16	Billy Herman	2.50	1.25	.70
17	Joe Vosmik	1.50	.75	.45
18	Babe Phelps	1.50	.75	.45
19	Mace Brown	1.50	.75	.45
20	Freddie Fitzsimmons	1.50	.75	.45
21	Angelo Guiliani	1.50	.75	.45
22	Lewis Riggs	1.50	.75	.45
23	Jimmy Wasdell	1.50	.75	.45
24	Herman Franks	1.50	.75	.45
25	Alex Kampouris	1.50	.75	.45
26	Kirby Higbe	1.50	.75	.45
27	Joe Medwick	2.50	1.25	.70
28	Newt Kimball	1.50	.75	.45
29	Curt Davis	1.50	.75	.45
30	Augie Galan	1.50	.75	.45
31	Luke Hamlin	1.50	.75	.45
32	Cookie Lavagetto	1.50	.75	.45
33	Joe Gallagher	1.50	.75	.45

34	Whitlow Wyatt	1.50	.75	.45
35	Dixie Walker	1.50	.75	.45
36	Pete Reiser	1.50	.75	.45
37	Leo Durocher	2.50	1.25	.70
38	Pee Wee Reese, Joe Medwick (3" x 5")	4.50	2.25	1.25
39	Dixie Walker, Joe Medwick, Dolph Camilli, Pete Reiser (3" x 5")	4.50	2.25	1.25
40	Team photo	3.00	1.50	.90
41	Kemp Wicker	1.50	.75	.45
42	George Pfister	2.00	1.00	.60
43	Chuck Dressen	1.50	.75	.45

1979 TCMA All Time Tigers

ALL TIME DETROIT TIGER TEAM

Hank Greenberg	1B
Charlie Gehringer	2B
George Kell	3B
Billy Rogell	SS
Ty Cobb	OF
Harry Heilmann	OF
Al Kaline	OF
Mickey Cochrane	C
Denny McLain	RHP
Hal Newhouser	LHP
Terry Fox	RP
Steve O'Neil	Mgr

T.C.M.A. Ltd., 1979

Utilizing a format similar to its several minor league team sets of the same year, this collectors' issue from TCMA features an "All Time" Tigers team selection of position players, pitchers and manager. The 2-1/2" x 3-1/2" cards have black-and-white photos on front with the player's name and position in an orange "wave" at bottom; the whole is surrounded by a white border. Backs are in black-and-white and detail the all-time line-up. The unnumbered cards are checklisted here alphabetically.

		NM	EX	VG
Complete Set (12):		20.00	10.00	6.00
Common Player:		1.50	.70	.45
(1)	Ty Cobb	6.00	3.00	1.75
(2)	Mickey Cochrane	1.50	.70	.45
(3)	Terry Fox	1.50	.70	.45
(4)	Charlie Gehringer	2.50	1.25	.70
(5)	Hank Greenberg	5.00	2.50	1.50
(6)	Harry Heilmann	1.50	.70	.45
(7)	Al Kaline	5.00	2.50	1.50
(8)	George Kell	1.50	.70	.45
(9)	Denny McLain	1.50	.70	.45
(10)	Hal Newhouser	1.50	.70	.45
(11)	Steve O'Neil (O'Neill)	1.50	.70	.45
(12)	Billy Rogell	1.50	.70	.45

1979 TCMA Baseball History Series: The Fifties

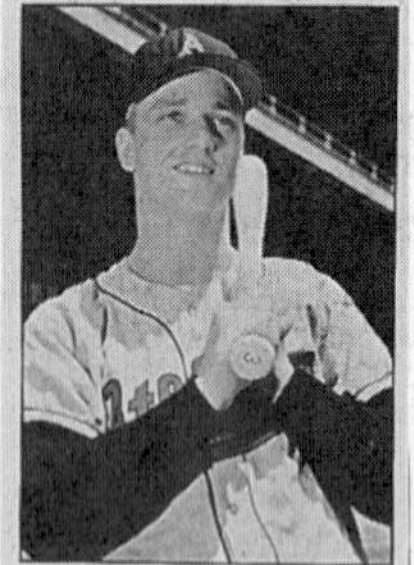

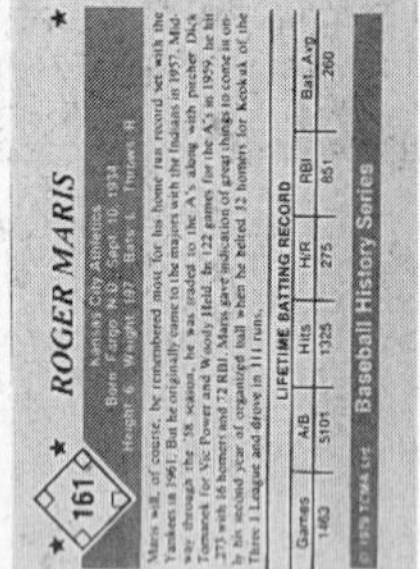

The "pure" format of the 1953 Bowman set was borrowed in this collectors' issue featuring the stars and journeymen of baseball in the 1950s. The 2-1/2" x 3-1/2" cards have color photos on front with white borders. Backs are in red and black with personal data and career summary and stats. Each set originally sold by TCMA came with two large-format (5" x 3-1/2") team-photo cards.

		NM	EX	VG
Complete Set (291):		35.00	17.50	10.00
Common Player:		.25	.13	.08
1	Joe DiMaggio	7.50	3.75	2.25
2	Yogi Berra	1.50	.70	.45
3	Warren Spahn	.75	.40	.25
4	Robin Roberts	.60	.30	.20
5	Ernie Banks	1.50	.70	.45
6	Willie Mays	5.00	2.50	1.50
7	Mickey Mantle	10.00	5.00	3.00
8	Roy Campanella	1.50	.70	.45
9	Stan Musial	4.00	2.00	1.25
10	Ted Williams	5.00	2.50	1.50
11	Ed Bailey	.25	.13	.08
12	Ted Kluszewski	.60	.30	.20
13	Ralph Kiner	.60	.30	.20
14	Dick Littlefield	.25	.13	.08
15	Nellie Fox	.60	.30	.20
16	Billy Pierce	.25	.13	.08
17	Richie Ashburn	.60	.30	.20
18	Del Ennis	.25	.13	.08
19	Bob Lemon	.50	.25	.15
20	Early Wynn	.50	.25	.15
21	Joe Collins	.25	.13	.08
22	Hank Bauer	.25	.13	.08
23	Roberto Clemente	6.00	3.00	1.75
24	Frank Thomas	.25	.13	.08
25	Alvin Dark	.25	.13	.08
26	Whitey Lockman	.25	.13	.08
27	Larry Doby	.60	.30	.20
28	Bob Feller	.75	.40	.25
29	Willie Jones	.25	.13	.08
30	Granny Hamner	.25	.13	.08
31	Clem Labine	.25	.13	.08
32	Ralph Branca	.25	.13	.08
33	Jack Harshman	.25	.13	.08
34	Dick Donovan	.25	.13	.08
35	Tommy Henrich	.25	.13	.08
36	Jerry Coleman	.25	.13	.08
37	Billy Hoeft	.25	.13	.08
38	Johnny Groth	.25	.13	.08
39	Harvey Haddix	.25	.13	.08
40	Gerry Staley	.25	.13	.08
41	Dale Long	.25	.13	.08
42	Vern Law	.25	.13	.08
43	Dodger Power	1.50	.70	.45
44	Sam Jethroe	.25	.13	.08
45	Vic Wertz	.25	.13	.08
46	Wes Westrum	.25	.13	.08
47	Dee Fondy	.25	.13	.08
48	Gene Baker	.25	.13	.08
49	Sandy Koufax	5.00	2.50	1.50
50	Billy Loes	.25	.13	.08
51	Chuck Diering	.25	.13	.08
52	Joe Ginsberg	.25	.13	.08
53	Jim Konstanty	.25	.13	.08
54	Curt Simmons	.25	.13	.08
55	Alex Kellner	.25	.13	.08
56	Charlie Dressen	.25	.13	.08
57	Frank Sullivan	.25	.13	.08
58	Mel Parnell	.25	.13	.08
59	Bobby Hofman	.25	.13	.08
60	Bill Connelly	.25	.13	.08
61	Charlie Valentine	.25	.13	.08
62	Johnny Klippstein	.25	.13	.08
63	Chuck Tanner	.25	.13	.08
64	Dick Drott	.25	.13	.08
65	Dean Stone	.25	.13	.08
66	Jim Busby	.25	.13	.08
67	Sid Gordon	.25	.13	.08
68	Del Crandall	.25	.13	.08
69	Walker Cooper	.25	.13	.08
70	Hank Sauer	.25	.13	.08
71	Gil Hodges	.75	.40	.25
72	Duke Snider	1.00	.50	.30
73	Sherman Lollar	.25	.13	.08
74	Chico Carrasquel	.25	.13	.08
75	Gus Triandos	.25	.13	.08
76	Bob Harrison	.25	.13	.08
77	Eddie Waitkus	.25	.13	.08
78	Ken Heintzelman	.25	.13	.08
79	Harry Simpson	.25	.13	.08
80	Luke Easter	.25	.13	.08
81	Ed Dick	.25	.13	.08
82	Jim DePaola	.25	.13	.08
83	Billy Cox	.25	.13	.08
84	Pee Wee Reese	1.00	.50	.30
85	Virgil Trucks	.25	.13	.08
86	George Kell	.50	.25	.15
87	Mickey Vernon	.25	.13	.08
88	Eddie Yost	.25	.13	.08
89	Gus Bell	.25	.13	.08
90	Wally Post	.25	.13	.08
91	Ed Lopat	.25	.13	.08
92	Dick Wakefield	.25	.13	.08
93	Solly Hemus	.25	.13	.08
94	Al "Red" Schoendienst	.60	.30	.20
95	Sammy White	.25	.13	.08
96	Billy Goodman	.25	.13	.08
97	Jim Hearn	.25	.13	.08
98	Ruben Gomez	.25	.13	.08
99	Marty Marion	.25	.13	.08
100	Bill Virdon	.25	.13	.08
101	Chuck Stobbs	.25	.13	.08
102	Ron Samford	.25	.13	.08
103	Bill Tuttle	.25	.13	.08
104	Harvey Kuenn	.25	.13	.08
105	Joe Cunningham	.25	.13	.08
106	Bill Sarni	.25	.13	.08
107	Jack Kramer	.25	.13	.08
108	Eddie Stanky	.25	.13	.08
109	Carmen Mauro	.25	.13	.08
110	Wayne Belardi	.25	.13	.08
111	Preston Ward	.25	.13	.08
112	Jack Shepard	.25	.13	.08
113	Buddy Kerr	.25	.13	.08
114	Vern Bickford	.25	.13	.08
115	Ellis Kinder	.25	.13	.08
116	Walt Dropo	.25	.13	.08
117	Duke Maas	.25	.13	.08
118	Billy Hunter	.25	.13	.08
119	Ewell Blackwell	.25	.13	.08
120	Hershell Freeman	.25	.13	.08
121	Freddie Martin	.25	.13	.08
122	Erv Dusak	.25	.13	.08
123	Roy Hartsfield	.25	.13	.08
124	Willard Marshall	.25	.13	.08
125	Jack Sanford	.25	.13	.08
126	Herm Wehmeier	.25	.13	.08
127	Hal Smith	.25	.13	.08
128	Jim Finigan	.25	.13	.08
129	Bob Hale	.25	.13	.08
130	Jim Wilson	.25	.13	.08
131	Bill Wight	.25	.13	.08
132	Mike Fornieles	.25	.13	.08
133	Steve Gromek	.25	.13	.08
134	Herb Score	.35	.20	.11
135	Ryne Duren	.25	.13	.08
136	Bob Turley	.25	.13	.08
137	Wally Moon	.25	.13	.08
138	Fred Hutchinson	.25	.13	.08
139	Jim Hegan	.25	.13	.08
140	Dale Mitchell	.25	.13	.08
141	Walt Moryn	.25	.13	.08
142	Cal Neeman	.25	.13	.08
143	Billy Martin	.50	.25	.15
144	Phil Rizzuto	1.00	.50	.30
145	Preacher Roe	.25	.13	.08
146	Carl Erskine	.25	.13	.08
147	Vic Power	.25	.13	.08
148	Elmer Valo	.25	.13	.08
149	Don Mueller	.25	.13	.08
150	Hank Thompson	.25	.13	.08
151	Stan Lopata	.25	.13	.08
152	Dick Sisler	.25	.13	.08
153	Willard Schmidt	.25	.13	.08
154	Roy McMillan	.25	.13	.08
155	Gil McDougald	.25	.13	.08
156	Gene Woodling	.25	.13	.08
157	Eddie Mathews	.75	.40	.25
158	Johnny Logan	.25	.13	.08
159	Dan Bankhead	.25	.13	.08
160	Joe Black	.25	.13	.08
161	Roger Maris	1.50	.70	.45
162	Bob Cerv	.25	.13	.08
163	Paul Minner	.25	.13	.08
164	Bob Rush	.25	.13	.08
165	Gene Hermanski	.25	.13	.08
166	Harry Brecheen	.25	.13	.08
167	Davey Williams	.25	.13	.08
168	Monte Irvin	.60	.30	.20
169	Clint Courtney	.25	.13	.08
170	Sandy Consuegra	.25	.13	.08
171	Bobby Shantz	.25	.13	.08
172	Harry Byrd	.25	.13	.08
173	Marv Throneberry	.25	.13	.08
174	Woody Held	.25	.13	.08
175	Al Rosen	.25	.13	.08
176	Rance Pless	.25	.13	.08
177	Steve Bilko	.25	.13	.08
178	Joe Presko	.25	.13	.08
179	Ray Boone	.25	.13	.08
180	Jim Lemon	.25	.13	.08
181	Andy Pafko	.25	.13	.08
182	Don Newcombe	.35	.20	.11
183	Frank Lary	.25	.13	.08
184	Al Kaline	.75	.40	.25
185	Allie Reynolds	.25	.13	.08
186	Vic Raschi	.25	.13	.08
187	Dodger Braintrust	.50	.25	.15
188	Jim Piersall	.25	.13	.08
189	George Wilson	.25	.13	.08
190	Jim "Dusty" Rhodes	.25	.13	.08
191	Duane Pillette	.25	.13	.08
192	Dave Philley	.25	.13	.08
193	Bobby Morgan	.25	.13	.08
194	Russ Meyer	.25	.13	.08
195	Hector Lopez	.25	.13	.08
196	Arnie Portocarrero	.25	.13	.08
197	Joe Page	.25	.13	.08
198	Tommy Byrne	.25	.13	.08
199	Ray Monzant	.25	.13	.08
200	John "Windy" McCall	.25	.13	.08
201	Leo Durocher	.50	.25	.15
202	Bobby Thomson	.35	.20	.11
203	Jack Banta	.25	.13	.08
204	Joe Pignatano	.25	.13	.08
205	Carlos Paula	.25	.13	.08
206	Roy Sievers	.25	.13	.08
207	Mickey McDermott	.25	.13	.08
208	Ray Scarborough	.25	.13	.08
209	Bill Miller	.25	.13	.08
210	Bill Skowron	.25	.13	.08
211	Bob Nieman	.25	.13	.08
212	Al Pilarcik	.25	.13	.08
213	Jerry Priddy	.25	.13	.08
214	Frank House	.25	.13	.08
215	Don Mossi	.25	.13	.08
216	Rocky Colavito	.60	.30	.20
217	Brooks Lawrence	.25	.13	.08
218	Ted Wilks	.25	.13	.08
219	Zack Monroe	.25	.13	.08
220	Art Ditmar	.25	.13	.08
221	Cal McLish	.25	.13	.08
222	Gene Bearden	.25	.13	.08
223	Norm Siebern	.25	.13	.08
224	Bob Wiesler	.25	.13	.08
225	Foster Castleman	.25	.13	.08
226	Daryl Spencer	.25	.13	.08
227	Dick Williams	.25	.13	.08
228	Don Zimmer	.25	.13	.08
229	Jackie Jensen	.25	.13	.08
230	Billy Johnson	.25	.13	.08
231	Dave Koslo	.25	.13	.08
232	Al Corwin	.25	.13	.08
233	Erv Palica	.25	.13	.08
234	Bob Milliken	.25	.13	.08
235	Ray Katt	.25	.13	.08
236	Sammy Calderone	.25	.13	.08
237	Don Demeter	.25	.13	.08
238	Karl Spooner	.25	.13	.08
239	The Veteran and The Rookie	.50	.25	.15
240	Enos Slaughter	.50	.25	.15
241	Dick Kryhoski	.25	.13	.08
242	Art Houtteman	.25	.13	.08
243	Andy Carey	.25	.13	.08
244	Tony Kubek	.35	.20	.11
245	Mike McCormick	.25	.13	.08
246	Bob Schmidt	.25	.13	.08
247	Nelson King	.25	.13	.08
248	Bob Skinner	.25	.13	.08
249	Dick Bokelmann	.25	.13	.08
250	Eddie Kazak	.25	.13	.08
251	Billy Klaus	.25	.13	.08
252	Norm Zauchin	.25	.13	.08
253	Art Schult	.25	.13	.08
254	Bob Martyn	.25	.13	.08
255	Larry Jansen	.25	.13	.08
256	Sal Maglie	.25	.13	.08

257	Bob Darnell	.25	.13	.08
258	Ken Lehman	.25	.13	.08
259	Jim Blackburn	.25	.13	.08
260	Bob Purkey	.25	.13	.08
261	Harry Walker	.25	.13	.08
262	Joe Garagiola	.35	.20	.11
263	Gus Zernial	.25	.13	.08
264	Walter "Hoot" Evers	.25	.13	.08
265	Mark Freeman	.25	.13	.08
266	Charlie Silvera	.25	.13	.08
267	Johnny Podres	.25	.13	.08
268	Jim Hughes	.25	.13	.08
269	Al Worthington	.25	.13	.08
270	Hoyt Wilhelm	.50	.25	.15
271	Elston Howard	.25	.13	.08
272	Don Larsen	.40	.20	.12
273	Don Hoak	.25	.13	.08
274	Chico Fernandez	.25	.13	.08
275	Gail Harris	.25	.13	.08
276	Valmy Thomas	.25	.13	.08
277	George Shuba	.25	.13	.08
278	Al "Rube" Walker	.25	.13	.08
279	Willard Ramsdell	.25	.13	.08
280	Lindy McDaniel	.25	.13	.08
281	Bob Wilson	.25	.13	.08
282	Chuck Templeton	.25	.13	.08
283	Eddie Robinson	.25	.13	.08
284	Bob Porterfield	.25	.13	.08
285	Larry Miggins	.25	.13	.08
286	Minnie Minoso	.25	.13	.08
287	Lou Boudreau	.50	.25	.15
288	Jim Davenport	.25	.13	.08
289	Bob Miller	.25	.13	.08
290	Jim Gilliam	.25	.13	.08
291	Jackie Robinson	4.00	2.00	1.25
Bonus 1	1955 Brooklyn Dodgers Team Card	10.00	5.00	3.00
Bonus 2	1957 Milwaukee Braves Team	10.00	5.00	3.00

1979 TCMA Japan Pro Baseball

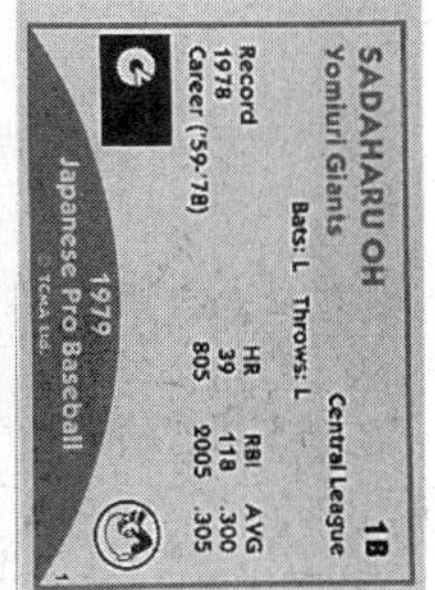

Stars of Japan's Pacific and Central "major" leagues are featured in this collectors' issue. More than a dozen Americans playing or managing in Japan at the time are included in the set, as well as several Japanese Hall of Famers including home-run king Sadaharu Oh. Cards feature a color posed portrait with a light blue semi-circle at bottom containing the team and player name in royal blue. Backs are printed in red and black on white and have a few personal data, 1978 and career stats, plus league and team logos and TCMA copyright. Cards are nominally standard 2-1/2" x 3-1/2" in size, but actual size varies a bit due to cutting discrepancies.

		NM	EX	VG
	Complete Set (90):	50.00	25.00	15.00
	Common Player:	.50	.25	.15
1	Sadaharu Oh	15.00	7.50	4.50
2	Jinten Haku	.50	.25	.15
3	Toshizo Sakamoto	.50	.25	.15
4	Tony Muser	1.00	.50	.30
5	Makoto Matsubara	.50	.25	.15
6	Masayuki Nakaysuka	.50	.25	.15
7	Daisuke Yamashita	.50	.25	.15
8	Koji Yamamoto	.50	.25	.15
9	Sachio Kinugasa	4.00	2.00	1.25
10	Bernie Williams	.60	.30	.20
11	Bobby Marcano	.60	.30	.20
12	Koichi Tabuchi	.50	.25	.15
13	Katsuya Nomura	3.00	1.50	.90
14	Jack Maloof	.60	.30	.20
15	Masahiro Doi	.50	.25	.15
16	Hiroyuki Yamazaki	.50	.25	.15
17	Vernon Law	2.00	1.00	.60
18	Dave Hilton	.60	.30	.20
19	Katsuo Osugi	.50	.25	.15
20	Tsutomu Wakamatsu	.50	.25	.15
21	John Scott	.60	.30	.20
22	Toru Sugiura	.50	.25	.15
23	Akihiko Kondo	.50	.25	.15
24	Shintaro Mizutani	.50	.25	.15
25	Tatsuro Hirooka	.50	.25	.15
26	Kojiro Ikegaya	.50	.25	.15
27	Yutaka Enatsu	1.50	.70	.45
28	Tomehiro Kaneda	.50	.25	.15
29	Yoshihiko Takahashi	.50	.25	.15
30	Jitsuo Mizutani	.50	.25	.15
31	Adrian Garrett	.60	.30	.20
32	Jim Lyttle	.60	.30	.20
33	Takeshi Koba	.50	.25	.15
34	Sam Ewing	.60	.30	.20
35	Kazumi Takahashi	.50	.25	.15
36	Kazushi Saeki	.50	.25	.15
37	Masanori Murakami	7.50	3.75	2.25
38	Toshiro Kato	.50	.25	.15
39	Junichi Kashiwabara	.50	.25	.15
40	Masaru Tomita	.50	.25	.15
41	Bobby Mitchell	.60	.30	.20
42	Mikio Sendoh	.50	.25	.15
43	Chris Arnold	.60	.30	.20
44	Charlie Manuel	.60	.30	.20
45	Keiji Suzuki	.50	.25	.15
46	Toru Ogawa	.50	.25	.15
47	Shigeru Ishiwata	.50	.25	.15
48	Kyosuke Sasaki	.50	.25	.15
49	Iwao Ikebe	.50	.25	.15
50	Kaoru Betto	.50	.25	.15
51	Gene Martin	.60	.30	.20
52	Felix Millan	1.00	.50	.30
53	Mitsuo Motoi	.50	.25	.15
54	Tomio Tashiro	.50	.25	.15
55	Shigeo Nagashima	7.50	3.75	2.25
56	Yoshikazu Takagi	.50	.25	.15
57	Keiichi Nagasaki	.50	.25	.15
58	Rick Krueger	.60	.30	.20
59	John Sipin	.60	.30	.20
60	Osao Shibata	.50	.25	.15
61	Isao Harimoto	.50	.25	.15
62	Shigeru Takada	.50	.25	.15
63	Michiyo Arito	.50	.25	.15
64	Hisao Niura	.50	.25	.15
65	Teruhide Sakurai	.50	.25	.15
66	Yoshito Oda	.50	.25	.15
67	Leron Lee	.60	.30	.20
68	Carlos May	.60	.30	.20
69	Frank Ortenzio	.60	.30	.20
70	Leon Lee	.60	.30	.20
71	Mitsuru Fujiwara	.50	.25	.15
72	Senichi Hoshino	.50	.25	.15
73	Tatsuhiko Kimata	.50	.25	.15
74	Morimichi Takagi	.50	.25	.15
75	Yasunori Oshima	.50	.25	.15
76	Yasushi Tao	.50	.25	.15
77	Wayne Garrett	.60	.30	.20
78	Bob Jones	.60	.30	.20
79	Toshiro Naka	.50	.25	.15
80	Don Blasingame	3.00	1.50	.90
81	Mike Reinbach	.60	.30	.20
82	Masashi Takenouchi	.50	.25	.15
83	Masayuki Kakefu	.50	.25	.15
84	Katsuhiro Nakamura	.50	.25	.15
85	Shigeru Kobayashi	.50	.25	.15
86	Lee Stanton	.60	.30	.20
87	Takenori Emoto	.50	.25	.15
88	Sohachi Aniya	.50	.25	.15
89	Wally Yonamine	4.00	2.00	1.25
90	Kazuhiro Yamauchi	.50	.25	.15

1979 TCMA 1927 New York Yankees

1927 NEW YORK YANKEES
ARTHUR FLETCHER
COACH
Ht. 5-10 Wt. 170 Ba. R Th. R
Bn. 1/5/85 Dd. 2/6/50

Art coached for the Yankees from '27 to '45 and managed the team for the last 11 games in '29 when Miller Huggins died. Prior to his coaching career with the Yankees, he was a shortstop for the New York Giants and Philadelphia Phillies in a 13-year big league career, '09-'22. He was the Giants' regular shortstop from '12 to '20 when he was shipped to the Phillies and became their regular shortstop for two seasons. Art was a .277 lifetime hitter and played in four World Series, all with the Giants. He also managed the Phillies from '23 to '26, but finished no higher than sixth place.

© TCMA 1979 7

Perhaps the finest baseball team of all time is featured in this collectors' set. The sepia oval photos at center are surrounded by black-and-white graphics of baseball equipment and other ornamentation. Player name and position are in a strip beneath the photo. Backs have personal data and a career summary. The cards are in standard 2-1/2" x 3-1/2".

		NM	EX	VG
	Complete Set (32):	20.00	10.00	6.00
	Common Player:	1.00	.50	.30
1	Babe Ruth	6.00	3.00	1.75
2	Lou Gehrig	4.00	2.00	1.25
3	Tony Lazzeri	1.00	.50	.30
4	Mark Koenig	1.00	.50	.30
5	Julie Wera	1.00	.50	.30
6	Ray Morehart	1.00	.50	.30
7	Art Fletcher	1.00	.50	.30
8	Joe Dugan	1.00	.50	.30
9	Charley O'Leary	1.00	.50	.30
10	Bob Meusel	1.00	.50	.30
11	Earle Combs	1.00	.50	.30
12	Cedric Durst	1.00	.50	.30
13	Johnny Grabowski	1.00	.50	.30
14	Mike Gazella	1.00	.50	.30
15	Pat Collins	1.00	.50	.30
16	Waite Hoyt	1.00	.50	.30
17	Myles Thomas	1.00	.50	.30
18	Benny Bengough	1.00	.50	.30
19	Herb Pennock	1.00	.50	.30
20	Wilcy Moore	1.00	.50	.30
21	Urban Shocker	1.00	.50	.30
22	Dutch Ruether	1.00	.50	.30
23	George Pipgras	1.00	.50	.30
24	Jacob Ruppert	1.00	.50	.30
25	Eddie Bennett	1.00	.50	.30
26	Ed Barrow	1.00	.50	.30
27	Ben Paschal	1.00	.50	.30
28	Miller Huggins	1.00	.50	.30
29	Joe Giard	1.00	.50	.30
30	Bob Shawkey	1.00	.50	.30
31	Walter Beall	1.00	.50	.30
32	Don Miller	1.00	.50	.30

1980 TCMA All-Time Teams

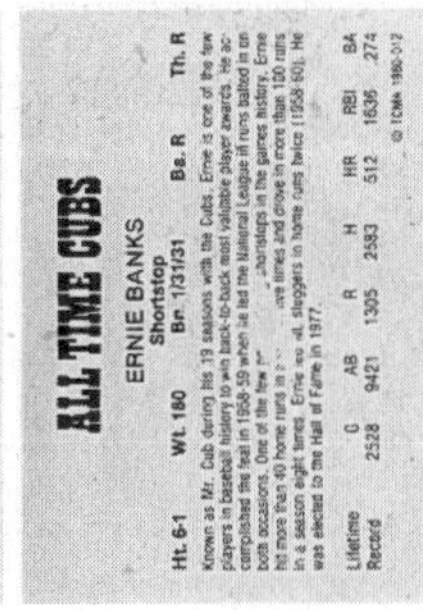

In 1980, TCMA began a new series of sets featuring 11 all-time great players and a manager from several of the 26 teams. In standard 2-1/2" x 3-1/2" format, most of the cards utilize black-and-white player photos, though some more recent stars are pictured in color. Several decorative borders, varying by team, surround the front photos. On most team sets there is an "All Time" designation at top, with the player name and (usually) position at bottom. Backs are fairly uniform, printed in blue or black, and offering a few biographical details and career highlights or a checklist. Besides hobby sales, these old-timers' sets were also sold in several major retail chains.

(Team sets listed individually.)

1980 TCMA All Time Brooklyn Dodgers

		NM	EX	VG
	Complete Set (12):	6.00	3.00	1.80
	Common Player:	.50	.25	.15
1	Gil Hodges	1.00	.50	.30
2	Jim Gilliam	.50	.25	.15
3	Pee Wee Reese	1.00	.50	.30
4	Jackie Robinson	3.00	1.50	.90
5	Sandy Koufax	3.00	1.50	.90
6	Zach Wheat	.50	.25	.15
7	Dixie Walker	.50	.25	.15
8	Hugh Casey	.50	.25	.15
9	Dazzy Vance	.50	.25	.15
10	Duke Snider	1.00	.50	.30
11	Roy Campanella	1.50	.70	.45
12	Walter Alston	.50	.25	.15

1980 TCMA All Time Cubs

		NM	EX	VG
	Complete Set (12):	6.00	3.00	1.80
	Common Player:	.50	.25	.15
1	Billy Williams	1.50	.70	.45
2	Charlie Root	.50	.25	.15
3	Ron Santo	1.50	.70	.45
4	Larry French	.50	.25	.15
5	Gabby Hartnett	.50	.25	.15
6	Emil Kush	.50	.25	.15
7	Charlie Grimm	.50	.25	.15
8	Kiki Cuyler	.50	.25	.15
9	Billy Herman	.50	.25	.15
10	Hack Wilson	1.00	.50	.30
11	Rogers Hornsby	1.00	.50	.30
12	Ernie Banks	4.00	2.00	1.25

1980 TCMA All Time N.Y. Giants

ALL TIME N.Y. GIANTS
BILL TERRY

Bill Terry, nicknamed "Memphis Bill" was one of the greatest hitters in baseball history. Over his fourteen year career he maintained a .341 batting average. Although he was not known as a slugger, he knocked home one hundred or more runs in six consecutive years. Terry is best remembered as the last .400 hitter in the National League, as he batted .401 in 1930. Terry, a Hall of Fame selection in 1954, also succeeded John McGraw as the Giant's manager. He led them to three pennants over a ten year period.

©TCMA Ltd 1980-0007

		NM	EX	VG
Complete Set (12):		6.00	3.00	1.80
Common Player:		.50	.25	.15
1	Willie Mays	4.00	2.00	1.25
2	Wes Westrum	.50	.25	.15
3	Carl Hubbell	.50	.25	.15
4	Hoyt Wilhelm	.50	.25	.15
5	Bobby Thomson	1.00	.50	.30
6	Frankie Frisch	.50	.25	.15
7	Bill Terry	.50	.25	.15
8	Alvin Dark	.50	.25	.15
9	Mel Ott	1.00	.50	.30
10	Christy Mathewson	2.50	1.25	.70
11	Freddie Lindstrom	.50	.25	.15
12	John McGraw	.50	.25	.15

1980 TCMA All Time Tigers

ALL TIME TIGERS
JOHN HILLER
Relief Pitcher

Sets printed with blue or red borders.

		NM	EX	VG
Complete Set (12):		6.00	3.00	1.80
Common Player:		.50	.25	.15
1	George Kell	.50	.25	.15
2	Billy Rogell	.50	.25	.15
3	Ty Cobb	4.00	2.00	1.25
4	Hank Greenberg	2.50	1.25	.70
5	Al Kaline	1.50	.70	.45
6	Charlie Gehringer	.75	.40	.25
7	Harry Heilmann	.50	.25	.15
8	Hal Newhouser	.50	.25	.15
9	Steve O'Neill	.50	.25	.15
10	Denny McLain	.50	.25	.15
11	Mickey Cochrane	.50	.25	.15
12	John Hiller	.50	.25	.15

1980 TCMA All Time White Sox

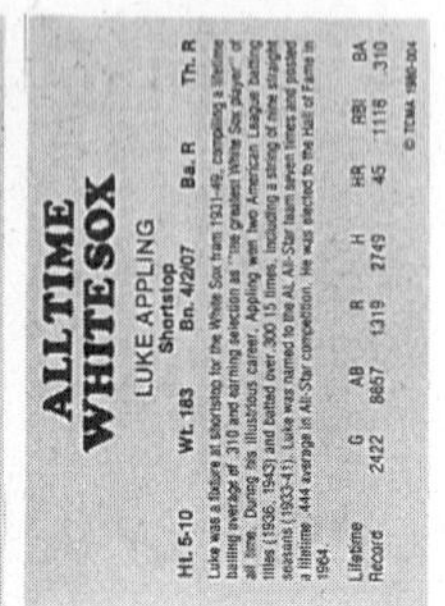

		NM	EX	VG
Complete Set (12):		6.00	3.00	1.80
Common Player:		.50	.25	.15
1	Ted Lyons	.50	.25	.15
2	Eddie Collins	2.00	1.00	.60
3	Al Lopez	.75	.40	.25
4	Luke Appling	2.00	1.00	.60
5	Billy Pierce	.75	.40	.25
6	Willie Kamm	.50	.25	.15
7	Johnny Mostil	.50	.25	.15
8	Al Simmons	.75	.40	.25
9	Ray Schalk	.50	.25	.15
10	Gerry Staley	.50	.25	.15
11	Harry Hooper	.50	.25	.15
12	Eddie Robinson	.50	.25	.15

1980 TCMA All Time Yankees

ALL TIME N.Y. YANKEES

1B Lou Gehrig
2B Tony Lazzeri
3B Red Rolfe
SS Phil Rizzuto
OF Babe Ruth
OF Mickey Mantle
OF Joe DiMaggio
C Bill Dickey
P Red Ruffing
P Whitey Ford
RP Johnny Murphy
Mgr Casey Stengel

		NM	EX	VG
Complete Set (12):		16.00	8.00	4.75
Common Player:		.50	.25	.15
1	Lou Gehrig	4.00	2.00	1.25
2	Tony Lazzeri	.50	.25	.15
3	Red Rolfe	.50	.25	.15
4	Phil Rizzuto	1.00	.50	.30
5	Babe Ruth	4.00	2.00	1.25
6	Mickey Mantle	5.00	2.50	1.50
7	Joe DiMaggio	4.00	2.00	1.25
8	Bill Dickey	.75	.40	.25
9	Red Ruffing	.50	.25	.15
10	Whitey Ford	1.00	.50	.30
11	Johnny Murphy	.50	.25	.15
12	Casey Stengel	.75	.40	.25

1980 TCMA 1914 Miracle (Boston) Braves

The 1914 Boston Braves team which went from dead last in the National League in mid-July to winning the pennant by 10-1/2 games and sweeping the Philadelphia A's in the World Series is featured on this collectors' issue. In standard 2-1/2" x 3-1/2" format, the cards feature sepia photos in fancy borders. Backs have details of the person's contribution to the "Miracle," along with stats and biographical data.

		NM	EX	VG
Complete Set (32):		30.00	15.00	9.00
Common Player:		1.00	.50	.30
1	Joe Connolly	1.00	.50	.30
2	Lefty Tyler	1.00	.50	.30
3	Tom Hughes	1.00	.50	.30
4	Hank Gowdy	1.00	.50	.30
5	Gene Cochreham (Cocreham)	1.25	.60	.40
6	Larry Gilbert	1.00	.50	.30
7	George Davis	1.00	.50	.30
8	Hub Perdue	1.00	.50	.30
9	Otto Hess	1.00	.50	.30
10	Clarence Kraft	1.25	.60	.40
11	Tommy Griffith	1.00	.50	.30
12	1914 World Series	1.00	.50	.30
13	Oscar Dugey	1.00	.50	.30
14	Josh Devore	1.00	.50	.30
15	George Stallings	1.00	.50	.30
16	Rabbit Maranville	1.50	.70	.45
17	Paul Strand	1.00	.50	.30
18	Charlie Deal	1.00	.50	.30
19	Dick Rudolph	1.00	.50	.30
20	Butch Schmidt	1.00	.50	.30
21	Johnny Evers	2.00	1.00	.60
22	Dick Crutcher	1.25	.60	.40
23	Possum Whitted	1.00	.50	.30
24	Fred Mitchell	1.00	.50	.30
25	Herbie Moran	1.00	.50	.30
26	Bill James	1.00	.50	.30
27	Ted Cather	1.00	.50	.30
28	Red Smith	1.00	.50	.30
29	Les Mann	1.00	.50	.30
30	Herbie Moran, Wally Schrang (Schang)	1.00	.50	.30
31	NOT ISSUED			
32	Johnny Evers (1914 MVP)	1.00	.50	.30
33	Jim Gaffney	1.25	.60	.40

1980 TCMA 1950 Philadelphia Phillies/Whiz Kids

1950 PHILADELPHIA PHILLIES
JOHN LEWIS MAYO
Outfielder

The National League Champions of 1950 are featured in this collectors' issue team-set. The 2-1/2" x 3-1/2" cards have black-and-white player photo surrounded by red borders. Backs are in black-and-white with player personal data, career summary and 1950 and lifetime stats.

		NM	EX	VG
Complete Set (31):		20.00	10.00	6.00
Common Player:		.60	.30	.20
1	Ken Silvestri	.50	.25	.15
2	Hank Borowy	.50	.25	.15
3	Bob Miller	.50	.25	.15
4	Jocko Thompson	.50	.25	.15
5	Curt Simmons	.50	.25	.15
6	Dick Sisler	.50	.25	.15
7	Eddie Waitkus	.50	.25	.15
8	Dick Whitman	.50	.25	.15
9	Andy Seminick	.50	.25	.15
10	Richie Ashburn	5.00	2.50	1.50
11	Bubba Church	.50	.25	.15
12	Jackie Mayo	.50	.25	.15
13	Eddie Sawyer	.50	.25	.15
14	Benny Bengough	.50	.25	.15
15	Jim Konstanty	.50	.25	.15
16	Robin Roberts	5.00	2.50	1.50
17	Del Ennis	.50	.25	.15
18	Dusty Cooke	.50	.25	.15
19	Mike Goliat	.50	.25	.15
20	Russ Meyer	.50	.25	.15
21	Granny Hamner	.50	.25	.15
22	Stan Lopata	.50	.25	.15
23	Willie Jones	.50	.25	.15
24	Stan Hollmig	.50	.25	.15
25	Jimmy Bloodworth	.50	.25	.15
26	Ken Johnson	.50	.25	.15
27	Bill Nicholson	.50	.25	.15
28	Ken Heintzelman	.50	.25	.15
29	Blix Donnelly	.50	.25	.15
30	Putsy Caballero	.50	.25	.15
31	Cy Perkins	.50	.25	.15

1980 TCMA 1957 Milwaukee Braves

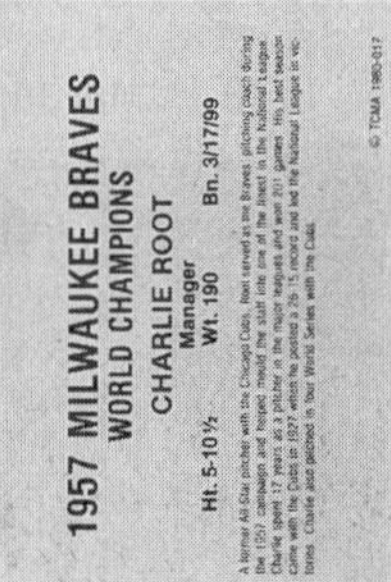

The World Champion Milwaukee Braves are featured in this collectors' issue. The 2-1/2" x 3-1/2" cards have blue-and-white player photos with white borders, blue typography and red graphics. Backs are in blue-and-white with a few bits of player data, career information and stats, along with a TCMA copyright line.

		NM	EX	VG
Complete Set (42):		30.00	15.00	9.00
Common Player:		.50	.25	.15
1	Don McMahon	.50	.25	.15
2	Joey Jay	.75	.40	.25
3	Phil Paine	.50	.25	.15
4	Bob Trowbridge	.50	.25	.15
5	Bob Buhl	.50	.25	.15
6	Lew Burdette	.75	.40	.25
7	Ernie Johnson	.50	.25	.15
8	Ray Crone	.50	.25	.15
9	Taylor Phillips	.50	.25	.15
10	Johnny Logan	.50	.25	.15
11	Frank Torre	.50	.25	.15
12	John DeMerit	.50	.25	.15
13	Red Murff	.50	.25	.15
14	Nippy Jones	.50	.25	.15
15	Bobby Thomson	.75	.40	.25
16	Chuck Tanner	.50	.25	.15
17	Charlie Root	.50	.25	.15
18	Juan Pizarro	.50	.25	.15
19	Hawk Taylor	.50	.25	.15
20	Mel Roach	.50	.25	.15
21	Bob Hazle	.75	.40	.25
22	Del Rice	.50	.25	.15
23	Felix Mantilla	.50	.25	.15
24	Andy Pafko	.50	.25	.15
25	Del Crandall	.75	.40	.25
26	Wes Covington	.50	.25	.15
27	Eddie Mathews	5.00	2.50	1.50
28	Joe Adcock	.75	.40	.25
29	Dick Cole	.50	.25	.15
30	Carl Sawatski	.50	.25	.15
31	Warren Spahn	5.00	2.50	1.50
32	Hank Aaron	10.00	5.00	3.00
33	Bob Keely	.50	.25	.15
34	Johnny Riddle	.50	.25	.15
35	Connie Ryan	.50	.25	.15
36	Harry Hanebrink	.50	.25	.15
37	Danny O'Connell	.50	.25	.15
38	Fred Haney	.50	.25	.15
39	Dave Jolly	.50	.25	.15
40	Red Schoendienst	3.50	1.75	1.00
41	Gene Conley	.50	.25	.15
42	Bill Bruton	.50	.25	.15

1980 TCMA 1959 L.A. Dodgers

This collectors' issue features the members of the 1959 World Champion L.A. Dodgers. The 2-1/2" x 3-1/2" cards can be found printed in either black-and-white or blue-and-white on front and back. Fronts have player photos with white bor-

ders. Backs have personal data, 1959 and career stats and a few sentences about the player's performance in the championship season.

	NM	EX	VG
Complete Set (40):	40.00	20.00	12.00
Common Player:	1.00	.50	.30
1 Joe Pignatano	1.00	.50	.30
2 Carl Furillo	1.50	.70	.45
3 Bob Lillis	1.00	.50	.30
4 Chuck Essegian	1.00	.50	.30
5 Dick Gray	1.00	.50	.30
6 Rip Repulski	1.00	.50	.30
7 Jim Baxes	1.00	.50	.30
8 Frank Howard	2.50	1.25	.70
9 Solly Drake	1.00	.50	.30
10 Sandy Amoros	1.50	.70	.45
11 Norm Sherry	1.50	.70	.45
12 Tommy Davis	1.50	.70	.45
13 Jim Gilliam	1.50	.70	.45
14 Duke Snider	5.00	2.50	1.50
15 Maury Wills	2.50	1.25	.70
16 Don Demeter	1.00	.50	.30
17 Wally Moon	1.50	.70	.45
18 John Roseboro	1.50	.70	.45
19 Ron Fairly	1.50	.70	.45
20 Norm Larker	1.50	.70	.45
21 Charlie Neal	1.50	.70	.45
22 Don Zimmer	1.50	.70	.45
23 Chuck Dressen	1.00	.50	.30
24 Gil Hodges	4.00	2.00	1.25
25 Joe Becker	1.00	.50	.30
26 Walter Alston	1.50	.70	.45
27 Greg Mulleavy	1.00	.50	.30
28 Don Drysdale	4.00	2.00	1.25
29 Johnny Podres	1.50	.70	.45
30 Sandy Koufax	7.50	3.75	2.25
31 Roger Craig	1.50	.70	.45
32 Danny McDevitt	1.00	.50	.30
33 Bill Harris	1.00	.50	.30
34 Larry Sherry	1.00	.50	.30
35 Stan Williams	1.50	.70	.45
36 Clem Labine	1.50	.70	.45
37 Chuck Churn	1.00	.50	.30
38 Johnny Klippstein	1.00	.50	.30
39 Carl Erskine	1.50	.70	.45
40 Fred Kipp	1.00	.50	.30

1980 TCMA 1960 Pittsburgh Pirates

The World Champion 1960 Pirates are featured in this collectors issue team-set. Black-and-white player photos are bordered in gold on the fronts of the 2-1/2" x 3-1/2" cards. Backs are in black-and-white with personal data, career summary and stats for the 1960 season and career. The Cimoli error card #39 was pulled from distribution and replaced with the unnumbered corrected version.

	NM	EX	VG
Complete Set (41): (No #39 Cimoli error.)	30.00	15.00	9.00
Common Player:	.50	.25	.15
1 Clem Labine	.50	.25	.15
2 Bob Friend	.75	.40	.25
3 Roy Face	.75	.40	.25
4 Vern Law	.75	.40	.25
5 Harvey Haddix	.75	.40	.25
6 Vinegar Bend Mizell	.50	.25	.15
7 Bill Burwell	.50	.25	.15
8 Diomedes Olivo	.50	.25	.15
9 Don Gross	.50	.25	.15
10 Fred Green	.50	.25	.15
11 Jim Umbricht	.50	.25	.15
12 George Witt	.50	.25	.15
13 Tom Cheney	.50	.25	.15
14 Bennie Daniels	.50	.25	.15
15 Earl Francis	.50	.25	.15
16 Joe Gibbon	.50	.25	.15
17 Paul Giel	.50	.25	.15
18 Danny Kravitz	.50	.25	.15
19 R.C. Stevens	.50	.25	.15
20 Roman Mejias	.50	.25	.15
21 Dick Barone	.50	.25	.15
22 Sam Narron	.50	.25	.15
23 Harry Bright	.50	.25	.15
24 Mickey Vernon	.50	.25	.15
25 Bob Skinner	.60	.30	.20
26 Smoky Burgess	.60	.30	.20
27 Bill Virdon	.60	.30	.20
28 NOT ISSUED			
29 Don Hoak	.60	.30	.20
30 Bill Mazeroski	6.00	3.00	1.75
31 Dick Stuart	1.50	.70	.45
32 Dick Groat	1.50	.70	.45
33 Bob Oldis	.50	.25	.15
34 Gene Baker	.50	.25	.15
35 Joe Christopher	.50	.25	.15
36 Dick Schofield	.60	.30	.20
37 Hal Smith	.50	.25	.15
38 Rocky Nelson	.50	.25	.15
39 Gino Cimoli (Photo actually Dick Schofield.)	6.00	3.00	1.75
40 Danny Murtaugh	.50	.25	.15
41 Lenny Levy	.50	.25	.15
--- Gino Cimoli	.50	.25	.15
--- Roberto Clemente	12.00	6.00	3.50

1980 TCMA 1961 Cincinnati Reds

Virtually every member of the World Champion Cincinnati Reds team of 1961 is included in this collectors issue. Fronts of the 2-1/2" x 3-1/2" cards feature black-and-white player poses with red graphics. Backs are in black-and-white with personal data, 1961 and career stats and a short career summary.

	NM	EX	VG
Complete Set (41):	30.00	15.00	9.00
Common Player:	1.00	.50	.30
1 Eddie Kasko	1.00	.50	.30
2 Wally Post	1.00	.50	.30
3 Vada Pinson	2.50	1.25	.70
4 Frank Robinson	7.50	3.75	2.25
5 Pete Whisenant	1.00	.50	.30
6 Reggie Otero	1.00	.50	.30
7 Dick Sisler	1.00	.50	.30
8 Jim Turner	1.00	.50	.30
9 Fred Hutchinson	1.00	.50	.30
10 Gene Freese	1.00	.50	.30
11 Gordy Coleman	1.00	.50	.30
12 Don Blasingame	1.00	.50	.30
13 Gus Bell	1.00	.50	.30
14 Leo Cardenas	1.00	.50	.30
15 Elio Chacon	1.00	.50	.30
16 Dick Gernert	1.00	.50	.30
17 Jim Baumer	1.00	.50	.30
18 Willie Jones	1.00	.50	.30
19 Joe Gaines	1.00	.50	.30
20 Cliff Cook	1.00	.50	.30
21 Harry Anderson	1.00	.50	.30
22 Jerry Zimmerman	1.00	.50	.30
23 Johnny Edwards	1.00	.50	.30
24 Bob Schmidt	1.00	.50	.30
25 Darrell Johnson	1.00	.50	.30
26 Ed Bailey	1.00	.50	.30
27 Joey Jay	1.00	.50	.30
28 Jim O'Toole	1.00	.50	.30
29 Bob Purkey	1.00	.50	.30
30 Jim Brosnan	1.00	.50	.30
31 Ken Hunt	1.00	.50	.30
32 Ken Johnson	1.00	.50	.30
33 Jim Mahoney	1.00	.50	.30
34 Bill Henry	1.00	.50	.30
35 Jerry Lynch	1.00	.50	.30
36 Hal Bevan	1.00	.50	.30
37 Howie Nunn	1.00	.50	.30
38 Sherman Jones	1.00	.50	.30
39 Jay Hook	1.00	.50	.30
40 Claude Osteen	1.00	.50	.30
41 Marshall Bridges	1.00	.50	.30

1980 TCMA/Sports Nostalgia Store Babe Ruth

The same photo on the Babe Ruth card which appeared in TCMA's 1927 N.Y. Yankees set from 1979 was utilized by Sports Nostalgia as an advertising medium. On the back of the ad card is store information and an offer to redeem the card there for a free picture of Ruth. Production was 500 cards.

	NM	EX	VG
Babe Ruth	7.50	3.75	2.25

1978 Allen P. Terach Immortals of Baseball

These souvenir cards were issued as the first of what was intended to be a series honoring baseball's greatest players. No succeeding issues were forthcoming. The images on the 9" x 6-1/2" blank-back cards are printed in black-and-white and sepia. Fine print at the bottom states the card is part of an edition of 3,500. Issue price was just under $5 apiece.

	NM	EX	VG
Souvenir Card:			
1 Babe Ruth, Joe DiMaggio	9.00	4.50	2.75
2 Ty Cobb, Stan Musial	6.00	3.00	1.75

1914 Texas Tommy Type 1 (E224)

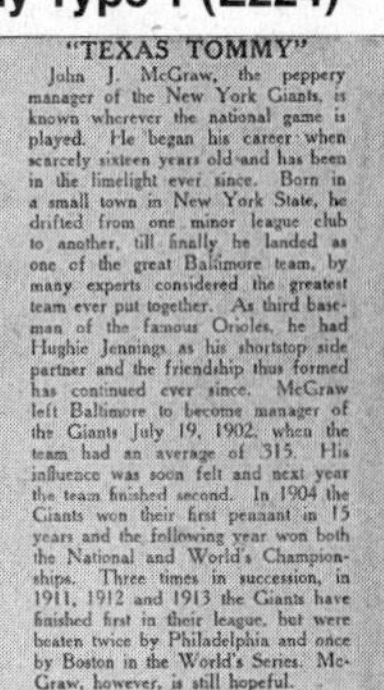

"TEXAS TOMMY"

John J. McGraw, the peppery manager of the New York Giants, is known wherever the national game is played. He began his career when scarcely sixteen years old and has been in the limelight ever since. Born in a small town in New York State, he drifted from one minor league club to another, till finally he landed as one of the great Baltimore team, by many experts considered the greatest team ever put together. As third baseman of the famous Orioles, he had Hughie Jennings as his shortstop side partner and the friendship thus formed has continued ever since. McGraw left Baltimore to become manager of the Giants July 19, 1902, when the team had an average of 315. His influence was soon felt and next year the team finished second. In 1904 the Giants won their first pennant in 15 years and the following year won both the National and World's Championships. Three times in succession, in 1911, 1912 and 1913 the Giants have finished first in their league, but were beaten twice by Philadelphia and once by Boston in the World's Series. McGraw, however, is still hopeful.

Designated as E224 in the American Card Catalog these cards measure about 2-3/8" x 3-1/2". Fronts feature sepia-toned action photos with the player's name in capital letters and his team below in parenthesis. The back carries a lengthy player biography and most cards, although not all, include year-by-year statistics at the bottom. The words "Texas Tommy" appear at the top. Texas Tommy was a candy bar brand from the Cardinet Candy Co., Oakland, Calif. The candy bar took its name from a popular dance of the era. Most examples of this set have been found in northern California. There is also a second variety of the set, smaller in size (1-7/8" x 3"), which have borderless pictures and a glossy finish. Gaps have been left in the assigned numbers on this checklist to accomodate future additions.

	NM	EX	VG
Common Player:	5,850	2,925	1,755
(1) Jimmy Archer	5,850	2,925	1,755
(2) Jimmy Austin	5,850	2,925	1,755
(3) Home Run Baker	9,750	4,875	2,925
(4) Chief Bender	9,750	4,875	2,925
(5) Bob Bescher	5,850	2,925	1,755
(6) Ping Bodie	5,850	2,925	1,755
(7) Donie Bush	5,850	2,925	1,755
(8) Bobby Byrne	5,850	2,925	1,755
(9) Nixey Callanan (Callahan)	5,850	2,925	1,755
(10) Howie Camnitz	5,850	2,925	1,755
(11) Frank Chance	9,750	4,875	2,925
(12) Hal Chase	8,450	4,225	2,535
(13) Ty Cobb	45,500	22,750	13,000
(14) Jack Coombs	5,850	2,925	1,755
(15) Sam Crawford	9,750	4,875	2,925
(16) Birdie Cree	5,850	2,925	1,755
(17) Al Demaree	5,850	2,925	1,755
(18) Red Dooin	5,850	2,925	1,755
(19) Larry Doyle	5,850	2,925	1,755
(20) Johnny Evers	9,750	4,875	2,925
(21) Vean Gregg	5,850	2,925	1,755
(22) Bob Harmon	5,850	2,925	1,755
(23) Joe Jackson	58,500	29,250	17,550
(24) Walter Johnson	19,500	9,750	5,850
(25) Otto Knabe	5,850	2,925	1,755
(26) Nap Lajoie	9,750	4,875	2,925
(27) Harry Lord	5,850	2,925	1,755
(28) Connie Mack	9,750	4,875	2,925
(29) Armando Marsans	5,850	2,925	1,755
(30) Christy Mathewson	9,750	4,875	2,925
(31) George McBride	5,850	2,925	1,755
(32) John McGraw	9,750	4,875	2,925
(33) Stuffy McInnis	5,850	2,925	1,755
(34) Chief Meyers	5,850	2,925	1,755
(35) Earl Moore	5,850	2,925	1,755
(36) Mike Mowrey	5,850	2,925	1,755
(37) Rebel Oakes	5,850	2,925	1,755
(38) Marty O'Toole	5,850	2,925	1,755

		NM	EX	VG
(39)	Eddie Plank	13,000	6,500	3,900
(41)	Bud Ryan	5,850	2,925	1,755
(42)	Tris Speaker	16,250	8,125	4,875
(43)	Jake Stahl	5,850	2,925	1,755
(44)	Oscar Strange (Stanage)	5,850	2,925	1,755
(45)	Bill Sweeney	5,850	2,925	1,755
(46)	Honus Wagner	39,000	19,500	11,700
(47)	Ed Walsh	9,750	4,875	2,925
(48)	Zach Wheat	9,750	4,875	2,925
(49)	Harry Wolter	5,850	2,925	1,755
(50)	Joe Wood	7,150	3,575	2,145
(51)	Steve Yerkes	5,850	2,925	1,755
(52)	Heinie Zimmerman	5,850	2,925	1,755

1914 Texas Tommy Type 2 (E224)

Type 2 Texas Tommy cards are smaller in size, at about 1-7/8" x 3" to 3-1/16", have a glossy front surface and are blank-backed. Their only real link to the Type 1 Texas Tommy cards is the shared front on those players who appear in both checklists.

		NM	EX	VG
Common Player:		6,000	3,000	1,800
(1)	Ping Bodie	6,000	3,000	1,800
(2)	Larry Doyle	6,000	3,000	1,800
(3)	Vean Gregg	6,000	3,000	1,800
(4)	Harry Hooper	7,800	3,900	2,340
(5)	Walter Johnson	12,000	6,000	3,600
(6)	Connie Mack	7,800	3,900	2,340
(7)	Rube Marquard	7,800	3,900	2,340
(8)	Christy Mathewson	14,400	7,200	4,320
(9)	John McGraw	7,800	3,900	2,340
(10)	Chief Meyers	6,000	3,000	1,800
(11)	Fred Snodgrass	6,000	3,000	1,800
(12)	Jake Stahl	6,000	3,000	1,800
(13)	Honus Wagner	16,200	8,100	4,860
(14)	Joe Wood	6,600	3,300	1,980
(15)	Steve Yerkes	6,000	3,000	1,800

1928 Tharp's Ice Cream

SAVE THESE PICTURES
One ice cream bar will be given free for each picture of Babe Ruth.
ALSO
One gallon of Tharp's ice cream will be delivered free to the holder of a complete set of sixty different Baseball Stars, upon surrender of same to any Tharp dealer.

Sharing the same format and checklist with several other contemporary ice cream sets this 60-card set includes all of the top stars of the day. Cards are printed in black-and-white on a 1-3/8" x 2-1/2" format. There appears to have been two different types issued, but the extent of each version is unknown. The variations are found in the player's name and card number which can appear either in a strip within the frame of the photo, or printed in the border beneath the photo. Card backs have a redemption offer that includes an ice cream bar in exchange for a Babe Ruth card, or a gallon of ice cream for a complete set of 60.

		NM	EX	VG
Complete Set (60):		20,000	8,000	4,000
Common Player:		115.00	45.00	20.00
1	Burleigh Grimes	225.00	90.00	45.00
2	Walter Reuther (Ruether)	115.00	45.00	20.00
3	Joe Dugan	115.00	45.00	20.00
4	Red Faber	225.00	90.00	45.00
5	Gabby Hartnett	225.00	90.00	45.00
6a	Babe Ruth (Portrait)	7,500	3,000	1,500
6b	Babe Ruth/Throwing	7,500	3,000	1,500
7	Bob Meusel	115.00	45.00	20.00
8	Herb Pennock	225.00	90.00	45.00
9	George Burns	115.00	45.00	20.00
10	Joe Sewell	225.00	90.00	45.00
11	George Uhle	115.00	45.00	20.00
12	Bob O'Farrell	115.00	45.00	20.00
13	Rogers Hornsby	350.00	140.00	70.00
14	"Pie" Traynor	225.00	90.00	45.00
15	Clarence Mitchell	115.00	45.00	20.00
16a	Eppa Jepha Rixey	225.00	90.00	45.00
16b	Eppa Rixey	225.00	90.00	45.00
17	Carl Mays	115.00	45.00	20.00
18	Adolfo Luque	125.00	50.00	25.00
19	Dave Bancroft	225.00	90.00	45.00
20	George Kelly	225.00	90.00	45.00
21	Earl (Earle) Combs	225.00	90.00	45.00
22	Harry Heilmann	225.00	90.00	45.00
23a	Ray W. Schalk	225.00	90.00	45.00
23b	Ray Schalk	225.00	90.00	45.00
24	Johnny Mostil	115.00	45.00	20.00
25	Hack Wilson	225.00	90.00	45.00
26	Lou Gehrig	2,500	1,000	500.00
27	Ty Cobb	1,500	600.00	300.00
28	Tris Speaker	350.00	140.00	70.00
29	Tony Lazzeri	225.00	90.00	45.00
30	Waite Hoyt	225.00	90.00	45.00
31	Sherwood Smith	115.00	45.00	20.00
32	Max Carey	225.00	90.00	45.00
33	Eugene Hargrave	115.00	45.00	20.00
34	Miguel L. Gonzalez (Middle initial A.)	125.00	50.00	25.00
35	Joe Judge	115.00	45.00	20.00
36	E.C. (Sam) Rice	225.00	90.00	45.00
37	Earl Sheely	115.00	45.00	20.00
38	Sam Jones	115.00	45.00	20.00
39	Bib (Bibb) A. Falk	115.00	45.00	20.00
40	Willie Kamm	115.00	45.00	20.00
41	Stanley Harris	225.00	90.00	45.00
42	John J. McGraw	225.00	90.00	45.00
43	Artie Nehf	115.00	45.00	20.00
44	Grover Alexander	700.00	280.00	140.00
45	Paul Waner	225.00	90.00	45.00
46	William H. Terry (Photo actually Zeb Terry.)	225.00	90.00	45.00
47	Glenn Wright	115.00	45.00	20.00
48	Earl Smith	115.00	45.00	20.00
49	Leon (Goose) Goslin	225.00	90.00	45.00
50	Frank Frisch	225.00	90.00	45.00
51	Joe Harris	115.00	45.00	20.00
52	Fred (Cy) Williams	115.00	45.00	20.00
53	Eddie Roush	225.00	90.00	45.00
54	George Sisler	225.00	90.00	45.00
55	Ed. Rommel	115.00	45.00	20.00
56	Rogers Peckinpaugh (Roger)	115.00	45.00	20.00
57	Stanley Coveleskie (Coveleski)	225.00	90.00	45.00
58	Lester Bell	115.00	45.00	20.00
59	L. Waner	225.00	90.00	45.00
60	John P. McInnis	115.00	45.00	20.00

1978 The Card Coach Milwaukee Braves Greats

Stars of the Milwaukee Braves from the early 1950s through the early 1960s are featured in this collectors' issue. The 2-1/2" x 3-1/2" cards have black-and-white player photos on front with the player name in the white border at bottom. Backs are also in black-and-white with personal data, career summary and stats. Cards are numbered by uniform number.

		NM	EX	VG
Complete Set (15):		10.00	5.00	3.00
Common Player:		2.00	1.00	.60
1	Del Crandall	2.00	1.00	.60
4	Red Schoendienst	2.00	1.00	.60
8	Bob Uecker	2.50	1.25	.70
9	Joe Adcock	2.00	1.00	.60
10	Bob Buhl	2.00	1.00	.60
15	Joe Torre	2.50	1.25	.70
16	Carlton Willey	2.00	1.00	.60
21	Warren Spahn	3.00	1.50	.90
22	Johnny Logan	2.00	1.00	.60
33	Lew Burdette	2.00	1.00	.60
34	Billy Bruton	2.00	1.00	.60
41	Eddie Mathews	3.00	1.50	.90
43	Wes Covington	2.00	1.00	.60
44	Hank Aaron	7.50	3.75	2.25
48	Andy Pafko (Checklist)	2.00	1.00	.60

1971 Ticketron L.A. Dodgers/S.F. Giants

Essentially large team schedule cards with promotional dates noted and an ad for the ticket service, the Ticketron Dodgers/Giants cards of 1971 are similar in format. Each has a color photo on front with facsimile autograph. The

Dodgers cards are 4" x 6" with no borders on fronts; the 3-3/4" x 5-3/4" Giants cards have a white border. Backs are white with red and blue printing. The unnumbered cards are checklisted here alphabetically within team.

		NM	EX	VG
Complete Dodgers Set (20):		75.00	37.00	22.00
Complete Giants Set (10):		150.00	75.00	45.00
Common Dodger Player:		3.00	1.50	.90
Common Giant Player:		6.00	3.00	1.75
	LOS ANGELES DODGERS			
(1)	Richie Allen	15.00	7.50	4.50
(2)	Walter Alston	6.00	3.00	1.75
(3)	Jim Brewer	3.00	1.50	.90
(4)	Willie Crawford	3.00	1.50	.90
(5)	Willie Davis	4.50	2.25	1.25
(6)	Steve Garvey	20.00	10.00	6.00
(7)	Bill Grabarkewitz	3.00	1.50	.90
(8)	Jim Lefebvre	3.00	1.50	.90
(9)	Pete Mikkelsen	3.00	1.50	.90
(10)	Joe Moeller	3.00	1.50	.90
(11)	Manny Mota	4.50	2.25	1.25
(12)	Claude Osteen	3.00	1.50	.90
(13)	Wes Parker	3.00	1.50	.90
(14)	Bill Russell	4.50	2.25	1.25
(15)	Duke Sims	3.00	1.50	.90
(16)	Bill Singer	3.00	1.50	.90
(17)	Bill Sudakis	3.00	1.50	.90
(18)	Don Sutton	20.00	10.00	6.00
(19)	Maury Wills	7.50	3.75	2.25
(20)	Jerry Doggett, Vin Scully	3.00	1.50	.90
	SAN FRANSICO GIANTS			
(1)	Bobby Bonds	9.00	4.50	2.75
(2)	Dick Dietz	6.00	3.00	1.75
(3)	Charles Fox	6.00	3.00	1.75
(4)	Tito Fuentes	6.00	3.00	1.75
(5)	Ken Henderson	6.00	3.00	1.75
(6)	Juan Marichal	20.00	10.00	6.00
(7)	Willie Mays	60.00	30.00	18.00
(8)	Willie McCovey	25.00	12.50	7.50
(9)	Don McMahon	3.00	1.50	.90
(10)	Gaylord Perry	15.00	7.50	4.50

1972 Ticketron Phillies

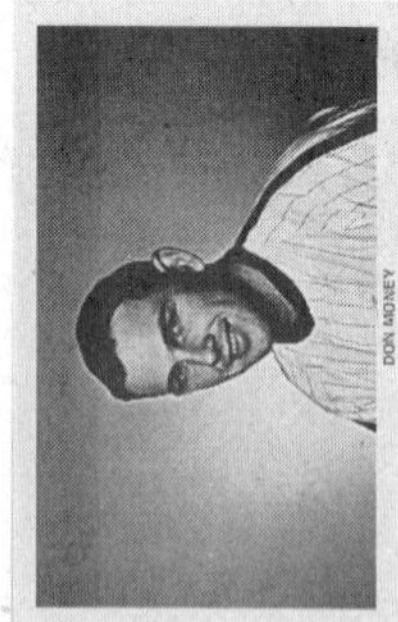

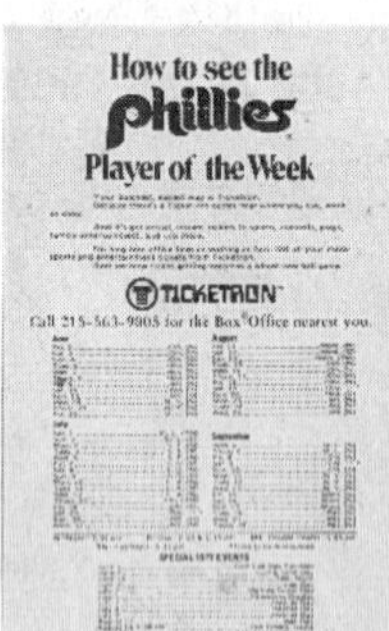

The Phillies' main off-site ticket outlet produced this set of schedule cards. Fronts are in horizontal 6" x 3-7/8" format with a color player photo at center. Backs are in black-and-white and include a Phillies home schedule and sponsor advertising. Because he was traded to the Expos in mid-season, the card of Tim McCarver is scarcer than the others.

		NM	EX	VG
Complete Set (10):		95.00	47.00	28.00
Common Player:		8.00	4.00	2.50
(1)	Mike Anderson	8.00	4.00	2.50
(2)	Larry Bowa	8.00	4.00	2.50
(3)	Steve Carlton	15.00	7.50	4.50
(4)	Deron Johnson	8.00	4.00	2.50
(5)	Frank Lucchesi	8.00	4.00	2.50
(6)	Greg Luzinski	10.00	5.00	3.00
(7)	Tim McCarver	35.00	17.50	10.50
(8)	Don Money	8.00	4.00	2.50
(9)	Willie Montanez	8.00	4.00	2.50
(10)	Dick Selma	8.00	4.00	2.50

1959 Ticoa Tires Frank Malzone

This black-and-white J.D. McCarthy postcard of the former Red Sox infielder was issued in conjunction with Malzone's endorsement of the Boston area tire store chain. The card measures 3-1/4" x 5-1/2" and has a blue facsimile autograph on front. A similar promotional postcard is listed under Molinari's Restaurant.

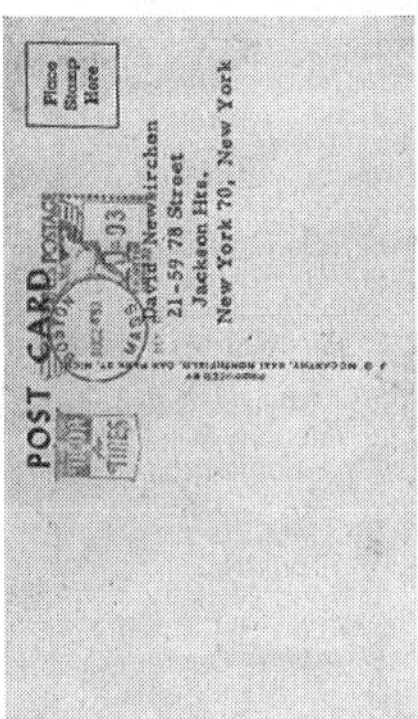

	NM	EX	VG
Frank Malzone	25.00	12.50	7.50

1910 Tip-Top Bread Pittsburgh Pirates (D322)

WAGNER, World's Champions

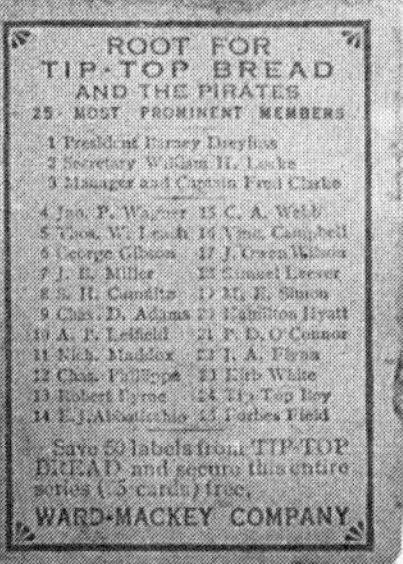

The previous season's World Champion Pittsburgh Pirates are featured in this issue. The cards have an unusual - for the era - nearly square (1-13/16" x 2-3/8") format. Fronts have pastel paintings of the subjects with identification in the white border below as "World's Champions." Backs have a checklist, ad for the bakery and offer to send the complete set of cards for 50 bread labels.

		NM	EX	VG
Complete Set (25):		90,000	45,000	27,000
Common Player:		2,300	1,150	700.00
1	Barney Dreyfuss (President)	8,000	4,500	3,000
2	William H. Locke (Secretary)	2,300	1,150	700.00
3	Fred Clarke	8,000	4,500	3,000
4	Honus Wagner	50,000	30,000	15,000
5	Tom Leach	2,300	1,150	700.00
6	George Gibson	2,300	1,150	700.00
7	Dots Miller	2,300	1,150	700.00
8	Howie Camnitz	2,300	1,150	700.00
9	Babe Adams	2,300	1,150	700.00
10	Lefty Leifield	2,300	1,150	700.00
11	Nick Maddox	2,300	1,150	700.00
12	Deacon Philippe	2,300	1,150	700.00
13	Bobby Byrne	2,300	1,150	700.00
14	Ed Abbaticchio	2,300	1,150	700.00
15	Lefty Webb	2,300	1,150	700.00
16	Vin Campbell	2,300	1,150	700.00
17	Owen Wilson	2,300	1,150	700.00
18	Sam Leever	2,300	1,150	700.00
19	Mike Simon	2,300	1,150	700.00
20	Ham Hyatt	2,300	1,150	700.00
21	Paddy O'Connor	2,300	1,150	700.00
22	John Flynn	2,350	1,150	700.00
23	Kirby White	2,300	1,150	700.00
24	Tip Top Boy Mascot	6,000	3,000	2,000
25	Forbes Field	5,000	2,500	1,750

1939 Tip-Top Bread Joe DiMaggio Pin

This 1-1/4" black-and-white photo portrati pin has a white background and printed endorsement for the Ward's brand. Similar pins were issued of boxer Billy Conn and hockey star Eddie Shore.

	NM	EX	VG
Joe DiMaggio	600.00	300.00	180.00

1947 Tip Top Bread

ENOS SLAUGHTER
Outfield, St. Louis, N.L.

This 163-card set actually consists of a group of regional issues, some of which are scarcer than others. The 2-1/4" x 3" cards are borderless at top and sides, with a black-and-white player photo below which is a white strip containing the player identification. Backs carry an illustrated advertisement. The set is known for a quantity of obscure players, many of whom played during the talent-lean World War II seasons.

		NM	EX	VG
Complete Set (163):		16,000	6,400	3,200
Common Player:		60.00	25.00	12.50
(1)	Bill Ayers	60.00	25.00	12.50
(2)	Floyd Baker	100.00	40.00	20.00
(3)	Charles Barrett	100.00	40.00	20.00
(4)	Eddie Basinski	60.00	25.00	12.50
(5)	John Berardino	100.00	40.00	20.00
(6)	Larry Berra	500.00	200.00	100.00
(7)	Bill Bevens	100.00	40.00	20.00
(8)	Robert Blattner	60.00	25.00	12.50
(9)	Ernie Bonham	60.00	25.00	12.50
(10)	Bob Bragan	80.00	32.00	16.00
(11)	Ralph Branca	125.00	50.00	25.00
(12)	Alpha Brazle	60.00	25.00	12.50
(13)	Bobbie Brown (Bobby)	100.00	40.00	20.00
(14)	Mike Budnick	60.00	25.00	12.50
(15)	Ken Burkhart	60.00	25.00	12.50
(16)	Thomas Byrne	100.00	40.00	20.00
(17)	Earl Caldwell	100.00	40.00	20.00
(18)	"Hank" Camelli	100.00	40.00	20.00
(19)	Hugh Casey	80.00	32.00	16.00
(20)	Phil Cavarretta	100.00	40.00	20.00
(21)	Bob Chipman	100.00	40.00	20.00
(22)	Lloyd Christopher	100.00	40.00	20.00
(23)	Bill Cox	60.00	25.00	12.50
(24)	Bernard Creger	60.00	25.00	12.50
(25)	Frank Crosetti	100.00	40.00	20.00
(26)	Joffre Cross	60.00	25.00	12.50
(27)	Leon Culberson	100.00	40.00	20.00
(28)	Dick Culler	100.00	40.00	20.00
(29)	Dom DiMaggio	200.00	80.00	40.00
(30)	George Dickey	100.00	40.00	20.00
(31)	Chas. E. Diering	60.00	25.00	12.50
(32)	Joseph Dobson	100.00	40.00	20.00
(33)	Bob Doerr	260.00	105.00	52.00
(34)	Ervin Dusak	60.00	25.00	12.50
(35)	Bruce Edwards	60.00	24.00	12.00
(36)	Walter "Hoot" Evers	130.00	52.00	26.00
(37)	Clifford Fannin	60.00	25.00	12.50
(38)	"Nanny" Fernandez	100.00	40.00	20.00
(39)	Dave "Boo" Ferriss	100.00	40.00	20.00
(40)	Elbie Fletcher	60.00	25.00	12.50
(41)	Dennis Galehouse	60.00	25.00	12.50
(42)	Joe Garagiola	225.00	90.00	45.00
(43)	Sid Gordon	60.00	25.00	12.50
(44)	John Gorsica	100.00	40.00	20.00
(45)	Hal Gregg	60.00	24.00	12.00
(46)	Frank Gustine	60.00	25.00	12.50
(47)	Stanley Hack	100.00	40.00	20.00
(48)	Mickey Harris	100.00	40.00	20.00
(49)	Clinton Hartung	60.00	25.00	12.50
(50)	Joe Hatten	60.00	24.00	12.00
(51)	Frank Hayes	100.00	40.00	20.00
(52)	"Jeff" Heath	60.00	25.00	12.50
(53)	Tom Henrich	130.00	52.00	26.00
(54)	Gene Hermanski	60.00	24.00	12.00
(55)	Kirby Higbe	60.00	25.00	12.50
(56)	Ralph Hodgin	100.00	40.00	20.00
(57)	Tex Hughson	100.00	40.00	20.00
(58)	Fred Hutchinson	150.00	60.00	30.00
(59)	LeRoy Jarvis	60.00	25.00	12.50
(60)	"Si" Johnson	100.00	40.00	20.00
(61)	Don Johnson	100.00	40.00	20.00
(62)	Earl Johnson	80.00	32.00	16.00
(63)	John Jorgensen	60.00	24.00	12.00
(64)	Walter Judnick (Judnich)	60.00	25.00	12.50
(65)	Tony Kaufmann	60.00	25.00	12.50
(66)	George Kell	260.00	105.00	52.00
(67)	Charlie Keller	100.00	40.00	20.00
(68)	Bob Kennedy	100.00	40.00	20.00
(69)	Montia Kennedy	60.00	25.00	12.50
(70)	Ralph Kiner	140.00	56.00	28.00
(71)	Dave Koslo	60.00	25.00	12.50
(72)	Jack Kramer	60.00	25.00	12.50
(73)	Joe Kuhel	100.00	40.00	20.00
(74)	George Kurowski	60.00	25.00	12.50
(75)	Emil Kush	100.00	40.00	20.00
(76)	"Eddie" Lake	100.00	40.00	20.00
(77)	Harry Lavagetto	80.00	32.00	16.00
(78)	Bill Lee	100.00	40.00	20.00
(79)	Thornton Lee	100.00	40.00	20.00
(80)	Paul Lehner	60.00	25.00	12.50
(81)	John Lindell	100.00	40.00	20.00
(82)	Danny Litwhiler	100.00	40.00	20.00
(83)	"Mickey" Livingston	100.00	40.00	20.00
(84)	Carroll Lockman	60.00	25.00	12.50
(85)	Jack Lohrke	60.00	25.00	12.50
(86)	Ernie Lombardi	140.00	56.00	28.00
(87)	Vic Lombardi	60.00	24.00	12.00
(88)	Edmund Lopat	130.00	52.00	26.00
(89)	Harry Lowrey	100.00	40.00	20.00
(90)	Marty Marion	80.00	32.00	16.00
(91)	Willard Marshall	60.00	25.00	12.50
(92)	Phil Masi	100.00	40.00	20.00
(93)	Edward J. Mayo	100.00	40.00	20.00
(94)	Clyde McCullough	100.00	40.00	20.00
(95)	Frank Melton	100.00	40.00	20.00
(96)	Cass Michaels	100.00	40.00	20.00
(97)	Ed Miksis	100.00	40.00	20.00
(98)	Arthur Mills	100.00	40.00	20.00
(99)	Johnny Mize	140.00	56.00	28.00
(100)	Lester Moss	60.00	25.00	12.50
(101)	"Pat" Mullin	100.00	40.00	20.00
(102)	"Bob" Muncrief	60.00	25.00	12.50
(103)	George Munger	60.00	25.00	12.50
(104)	Fritz Ostermueller	60.00	25.00	12.50
(105)	James P. Outlaw	100.00	40.00	20.00
(106)	Frank "Stub" Overmire	100.00	40.00	20.00
(107)	Andy Pafko	100.00	40.00	20.00
(108)	Joe Page	100.00	40.00	20.00
(109)	Roy Partee	100.00	40.00	20.00
(110)	Johnny Pesky	100.00	40.00	20.00
(111)	Nelson Potter	60.00	25.00	12.50
(112)	Mel Queen	100.00	40.00	20.00
(113)	Marion Rackley	60.00	24.00	12.00
(114)	Al Reynolds	125.00	50.00	25.00
(115)	Del Rice	60.00	25.00	12.50
(116)	Marv Rickert	100.00	40.00	20.00
(117)	John Rigney	100.00	40.00	20.00
(118)	Phil Rizzuto	375.00	150.00	75.00
(119)	Aaron Robinson	100.00	40.00	20.00
(120)	"Preacher" Roe	80.00	32.00	16.00
(121)	Carvel Rowell	100.00	40.00	20.00
(122)	Jim Russell	60.00	25.00	12.50
(123)	Rip Russell	100.00	40.00	20.00
(124)	Connie Ryan	100.00	40.00	20.00
(125)	John Sain	100.00	40.00	20.00
(126)	Ray Sanders	100.00	40.00	20.00
(127)	Fred Sanford	60.00	25.00	12.50
(128)	Johnny Schmitz	100.00	40.00	20.00
(129)	Joe Schultz	60.00	25.00	12.50
(130)	"Rip" Sewell	60.00	25.00	12.50
(131)	Dick Sisler	60.00	25.00	12.50
(132)	"Sibby" Sisti	100.00	40.00	20.00
(133)	Enos Slaughter	130.00	52.00	26.00
(134)	"Billy" Southworth	100.00	40.00	20.00
(135)	Warren Spahn	475.00	190.00	95.00
(136)	Verne Stephens (Vern)	60.00	25.00	12.50
(137)	George Sternweiss (Stirnweiss)	100.00	40.00	20.00
(138)	Ed Stevens	60.00	24.00	12.00
(139)	Nick Strincevich	60.00	25.00	12.50
(140)	"Bobby" Sturgeon	100.00	40.00	20.00
(141)	Robt. "Bob" Swift	100.00	40.00	20.00
(142)	Geo. "Birdie" Tibbetts (Tebbetts)	100.00	40.00	20.00
(143)	"Mike" Tresh	100.00	40.00	20.00
(144)	Ken Trinkle	60.00	25.00	12.50
(145)	Paul "Diz" Trout	100.00	40.00	20.00
(146)	Virgil "Fire" Trucks	100.00	40.00	20.00
(147)	Thurman Tucker	100.00	40.00	20.00
(148)	Bill Voiselle	60.00	25.00	12.50
(149)	Hal Wagner	100.00	40.00	20.00
(150)	Honus Wagner	475.00	190.00	95.00
(151)	Eddy Waitkus	100.00	40.00	20.00
(152)	Richard "Dick" Wakefield	100.00	40.00	20.00
(153)	Jack Wallaesa	100.00	40.00	20.00
(154)	Charles Wensloff	100.00	40.00	20.00
(155)	Ted Wilks	60.00	25.00	12.50
(156)	Mickey Witek	60.00	25.00	12.50
(157)	"Jerry" Witte	60.00	25.00	12.50
(158)	Ed Wright	100.00	40.00	20.00
(159)	Taft Wright	100.00	40.00	20.00
(160)	Henry Wyse	100.00	40.00	20.00
(161)	"Rudy" York	100.00	40.00	20.00
(162)	Al Zarilla	60.00	25.00	12.50
(163)	Bill Zuber	125.00	50.00	25.00

1952 Tip Top Bread Labels

This unnumbered set of bread end-labels consists of 48 different labels, including two of Phil Rizzuto. The player's photo, name and team appear inside a star, with the words "Tip Top" printed above. The labels measure approximately 2-1/2" x 2-3/4". An advertising message appears in red on back. A large fold-out sheet to collect and display the labels was also issued. Each space is labeled with a player name and basic information, and is die-cut to allow the label to be slid in.

		NM	EX	VG
Complete Set (48):		20,000	9,000	4,500
Common Player:		400.00	180.00	100.00
Display Sheet:		250.00	125.00	75.00
(1)	Hank Bauer	450.00	200.00	110.00
(2)	Yogi Berra	700.00	315.00	175.00
(3)	Ralph Branca	450.00	200.00	110.00
(4)	Lou Brissie	400.00	180.00	100.00
(5)	Roy Campanella	700.00	315.00	175.00
(6)	Phil Cavarreta (Cavarretta)	400.00	180.00	100.00
(7)	Murray Dickson (Murry)	400.00	180.00	100.00
(8)	Ferris Fain	400.00	180.00	100.00
(9)	Carl Furillo	450.00	200.00	110.00
(10)	Ned Garver	400.00	180.00	100.00
(11)	Sid Gordon	400.00	180.00	100.00
(12)	John Groth	400.00	180.00	100.00
(13)	Gran Hamner	400.00	180.00	100.00
(14)	Jim Hearn	400.00	180.00	100.00
(15)	Gene Hermanski	400.00	180.00	100.00
(16)	Gil Hodges	550.00	245.00	135.00
(17)	Larry Jansen	400.00	180.00	100.00
(18)	Eddie Joost	400.00	180.00	100.00
(19)	George Kell	500.00	225.00	125.00
(20)	Dutch Leonard	400.00	180.00	100.00
(21)	Whitey Lockman	400.00	180.00	100.00
(22)	Ed Lopat	450.00	200.00	110.00
(23)	Sal Maglie	400.00	180.00	100.00
(24)	Mickey Mantle	4,500	2,000	1,125
(25)	Gil McDougald	450.00	200.00	110.00
(26)	Dale Mitchell	400.00	180.00	100.00
(27)	Don Mueller	400.00	180.00	100.00
(28)	Andy Pafko	400.00	180.00	100.00
(29)	Bob Porterfield	400.00	180.00	100.00
(30)	Ken Raffensberger	400.00	180.00	100.00
(31)	Allie Reynolds	450.00	200.00	110.00
(32a)	Phil Rizutto (Rizzuto) ("NY" shows on shirt.)	600.00	275.00	150.00
(32b)	Phil Rizutto (Rizzuto) (No "NY" visible on shirt.)	600.00	275.00	150.00
(33)	Robin Roberts	550.00	245.00	135.00
(34)	Saul Rogovin	400.00	180.00	100.00
(35)	Ray Scarborough	400.00	180.00	100.00
(36)	Red Schoendienst	500.00	225.00	125.00
(37)	Dick Sisler	400.00	180.00	100.00
(38)	Enos Slaughter	500.00	225.00	125.00
(39)	Duke Snider	600.00	275.00	150.00
(40)	Warren Spahn	600.00	275.00	150.00
(41)	Vern Stephens	400.00	180.00	100.00
(42)	Earl Torgeson	400.00	180.00	100.00
(43)	Mickey Vernon	400.00	180.00	100.00
(44)	Ed Waitkus	400.00	180.00	100.00
(45)	Wes Westrum	400.00	180.00	100.00
(46)	Eddie Yost	400.00	180.00	100.00
(47)	Al Zarilla	400.00	180.00	100.00

1887 Tobin Lithographs Color

The Tobin lithographs, measuring about 3" x 4-1/2", are typical of the "trade" cards that were popular advertising vehicles in the late 19th Century. Found in both black-and-white and color, the lithos include 10 cards depicting caricature action drawings of popular baseball players of the era. Each cartoon-like drawing is accompanied by a colorful caption along with the player's name in parenthesis below. The team affiliation is printed in the upper-left corner, while a large space in the upper-right corner was left blank to accomodate advertising messages. As a result, Tobin cards can be found with ads for various products and services or left blank. Similarly the backs of the cards are also found either blank or with advertising. The set takes its name from the manufacturer, whose name ("Tobin N.Y.") appears in the lower-right corner of each card.

		NM	EX	VG
Complete Set (10):		6,650	2,650	1,325
Common Player:		675.00	275.00	135.00
(1)	"Go It Old Boy" (Ed Andrews)	675.00	275.00	135.00
(2)	"Oh, Come Off!" (Cap Anson)	1,325	525.00	275.00
(3)	"Watch Me Soak it" (Dan Brouthers)	800.00	325.00	160.00
(4)	"Not Onto It" (Charlie Ferguson)	675.00	275.00	135.00
(5)	"Struck By A Cyclone" (Pebbly Jack Glasscock)	675.00	275.00	135.00
(6)	"An Anxious Moment" (Paul Hines)	675.00	275.00	135.00
(7)	"Where'l You Have It?" (Tim Keefe)	800.00	325.00	160.00
(8)	"The Flower Of The Flock" (Our Own Kelly)	1,000	400.00	200.00
(9)	"A Slide For Home" (Jim M'Cormick) (McCormick)	675.00	275.00	135.00
(10)	"Ain't It A Daisy?" (Smiling Mickey Welch)	800.00	325.00	160.00

1887 Tobin Lithographs B/W

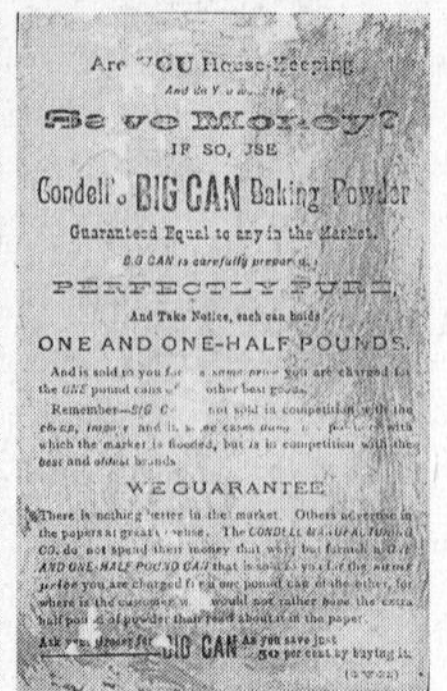

The black-and-white Tobin Lithographs were likely created to offer 19th Century advertisers a lower-cost venue than the lavishly colored version of the same cards. It appears, however, that most advertisers opted for the color type and/or that the color cards were saved more often because the black-and-white cards are today many times scarcer than their color counterparts. Despite the disparity in rarity, the black-and-whites carry only a modest premium value over the color, again probably attributable to the grander overall appearance of the colored cards.

		NM	EX	VG
Complete Set (10):		12,500	5,000	2,500
Common Player:		1,250	500.00	250.00
(1)	"Go It Old Boy" (Ed Andrews)	1,250	500.00	250.00
(2)	"Oh, Come Off!" (Cap Anson)	2,500	1,000	500.00
(3)	"Watch Me Soak it" (Dan Brouthers)	1,500	600.00	300.00
(4)	"Not Onto It" (Charlie Ferguson)	1,250	500.00	250.00
(5)	"Struck By A Cyclone" (Pebbly Jack Glasscock)	1,250	500.00	250.00
(6)	"An Anxious Moment" (Paul Hines)	1,250	500.00	250.00
(7)	"Where'l You Have It?" (Tim Keefe)	1,500	600.00	300.00
(8)	"The Flower Of The Flock" (Our Own Kelly)	1,900	760.00	380.00
(9)	"A Slide For Home" (Jim M'Cormick) (McCormick)	1,250	500.00	250.00
(10)	"Ain't It A Daisy?" (Smiling Mickey Welch)	1,500	600.00	300.00

1948-1949 Toleteros

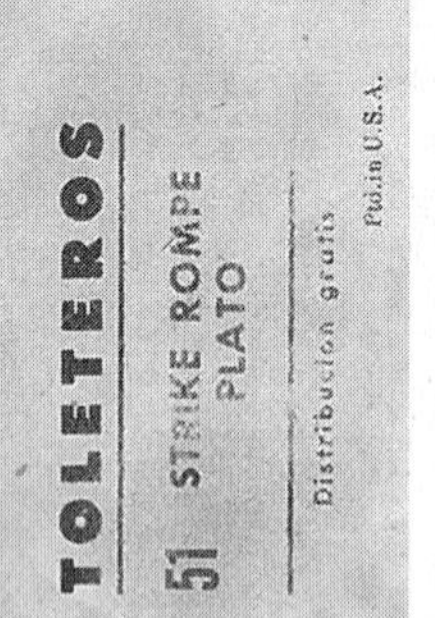

This was the first of three annual issues during the Puerto Rican League winter seasons. Cards are about 1-1/2" x 2-1/4", printed in sepia on thin cardboard. Backs are printed in black-and-white and have a "play" designation for use in a card game. They are numbered, but the numbers are not unique to specific players. Several of the cards were issued in photographic format, rather than printed. It is believed these are scarcer than the regular cards and may account for most of the seven cards which are not currently checklisted. They are designated here with a (P) notation. This checklist is presented alphabetically. An album was issued with the set, and like most contemporary Caribbean issues, cards are usually found in well-used condition with evidence of past mounting. Toleteros is roughly translated as "sluggers."

		NM	EX	VG
Complete Set (168): Value Undetermined				
Common Player:		150.00	75.00	45.00
Album:				
(1)	Yuyo Acosta	150.00	75.00	45.00
(2)	Hector Agosto	150.00	75.00	45.00
(3)	Alberto Alberdeston	150.00	75.00	45.00
(4)	Alberto Alicea	150.00	75.00	45.00
(5)	Jaime Almendro	150.00	75.00	45.00
(6)	Guinea Alomar	150.00	75.00	45.00
(7)	Pedro Alomar	150.00	75.00	45.00
(8)	Alfredo Alonso	150.00	75.00	45.00
(9)	Yiyo Alonso	150.00	75.00	45.00
(10)	Pablo Andino	150.00	75.00	45.00
(11)	Jueyito Andrade	150.00	75.00	45.00
(12)	Paday Anglero	150.00	75.00	45.00
(13)	Luis Arroyo	200.00	100.00	60.00
(14)	Pedro J. Arroyo	150.00	75.00	45.00
(15)	Joe Atkins (P)	300.00	150.00	90.00
(16)	Eugene Baker	300.00	150.00	90.00
(17)	Dan Bankhead	300.00	150.00	90.00
(18)	Bennett	150.00	75.00	45.00
(19)	Carlos Bernier	200.00	100.00	60.00
(20)	Hiram Bithorn	250.00	125.00	75.00
(21)	Efrain Blasini	150.00	75.00	45.00
(22)	Oswaldo Brau	150.00	75.00	45.00
(23)	Johnny Britton	150.00	75.00	45.00
(25)	George Brown	150.00	75.00	45.00
(26)	Willard Brown	4,500	2,250	1,350
(27)	Jose Burgos	150.00	75.00	45.00
(28)	Tommy Butts	1,200	600.00	360.00
(29)	Joe Buzas	150.00	75.00	45.00
(30)	Luis R. Cabrera	150.00	75.00	45.00
(31)	Marzo Cabrera	150.00	75.00	45.00
(32)	Eugenio Camara	150.00	75.00	45.00
(33)	Juan Carrero	150.00	75.00	45.00
(34)	Medina Chapman	150.00	75.00	45.00
(35)	Fernando Clara	150.00	75.00	45.00
(36)	Buster Clarkson (P)	800.00	400.00	240.00
(37)	Francisco Coimbre	1,000	500.00	300.00
(38)	Eugene Collins	400.00	200.00	120.00
(39)	Cefo Conde	150.00	75.00	45.00
(40)	Johnny Cox	150.00	75.00	45.00
(41)	Vitin Cruz	150.00	75.00	45.00
(42)	Johnny Davis	500.00	250.00	150.00
(43)	Piper Davis	500.00	250.00	150.00
(44)	Felle Delgado	150.00	75.00	45.00
(45)	Luke Easter	500.00	250.00	150.00
(46)	Howard Easterling	600.00	300.00	180.00
(47)	Saturnino Escalera	150.00	75.00	45.00
(49)	Teggy Espinosa	150.00	75.00	45.00
(50)	Coco Ferrer	150.00	75.00	45.00
(51)	Wilmer Fields	400.00	200.00	120.00
(52)	Tite Figueroa	150.00	75.00	45.00
(53)	Oscar Mir Flores	150.00	75.00	45.00
(54)	Jesus M. Freyre	150.00	75.00	45.00
(55)	Cinque Garcia	150.00	75.00	45.00
(56)	Alfonso Gerard	150.00	75.00	45.00
(57)	Jim Gilliam (P)	800.00	400.00	240.00
(58)	Charlie Glock	150.00	75.00	45.00
(59)	Ruben Gomez	250.00	125.00	75.00
(60)	David Gonzalez	150.00	75.00	45.00
(61)	Gely Goyco	150.00	75.00	45.00
(62)	Jack Graham	150.00	75.00	45.00
(63)	Roberto Griffith	600.00	300.00	180.00
(64)	Jesus Guilbe	150.00	75.00	45.00
(65)	Juan Guilbe	150.00	75.00	45.00
(66)	Hector Haddock	150.00	75.00	45.00
(67)	Sam Hairston	200.00	100.00	60.00
(68)	Van Harrington	150.00	75.00	45.00
(69)	Luman Harris	150.00	75.00	45.00
(70)	Manuel Hernandez	150.00	75.00	45.00
(71)	Efrain Hidalgo	150.00	75.00	45.00
(73)	Dixie Howell	150.00	75.00	45.00
(74)	Jim Lamarque (P)	800.00	400.00	240.00
(75)	Carlos Lanauze	150.00	75.00	45.00
(76)	Ramon Lasa	150.00	75.00	45.00
(77)	Lee Layton	150.00	75.00	45.00
(78)	Liebould	150.00	75.00	45.00
(79)	Royce Lint	150.00	75.00	45.00
(80)	Radames Lopez	150.00	75.00	45.00
(81)	Louis Louden	250.00	125.00	75.00
(82)	Robert Lynn	150.00	75.00	45.00
(83)	Caro Maldonado	150.00	75.00	45.00
(84)	Canena Marquez	500.00	250.00	150.00
(85)	Antonio Marrero	150.00	75.00	45.00
(86)	Gilberto Marrero	150.00	75.00	45.00
(87)	Humberto Marti	150.00	75.00	45.00
(88)	Millito Martinez	150.00	75.00	45.00
(89)	Jose E. Montalvo	150.00	75.00	45.00
(90)	Luis Morales	150.00	75.00	45.00
(91)	Willie Morales	150.00	75.00	45.00
(92)	Howard Moss	150.00	75.00	45.00
(93)	Chaguin Muratti	150.00	75.00	45.00
(94)	Domingo Navarro	150.00	75.00	45.00
(95)	Millito Navarro	200.00	100.00	60.00
(97)	Alfredo Olivencia	150.00	75.00	45.00
(98)	Guayubin Olivo	200.00	100.00	60.00
(99)	Noel Oquendo	150.00	75.00	45.00
(100)	Otoniel Ortiz	150.00	75.00	45.00
(101)	Rafaelito Ortiz	150.00	75.00	45.00
(102)	Alberto Padilla	150.00	75.00	45.00
(103)	Fernando Diaz Pedroso	200.00	100.00	60.00
(104)	Victor Pellot (Power)	250.00	125.00	75.00
(105)	Pedro Pena	150.00	75.00	45.00
(106)	Pepin Pereira	150.00	75.00	45.00
(107)	Ismael Perez	150.00	75.00	45.00
(108)	Juan Perez	150.00	75.00	45.00
(109)	Palomo Perez	150.00	75.00	45.00
(110)	Villodas Perez	150.00	75.00	45.00
(111)	Alonso Perry	500.00	250.00	150.00
(112)	Jose Polanco	150.00	75.00	45.00
(113)	Bill Powell	200.00	100.00	60.00
(114)	Tomas Quinones	200.00	100.00	60.00
(115)	R. Cuebas Quintana	150.00	75.00	45.00
(116)	Milton Ralat	150.00	75.00	45.00
(117)	Otto Ralat	150.00	75.00	45.00
(118)	Fernando Ramos	150.00	75.00	45.00
(119)	Xavier Rescigno	150.00	75.00	45.00
(121)	Miguel L. Rivera	150.00	75.00	45.00
(122)	Charlie Rivero	150.00	75.00	45.00
(123)	Bienvenido Rodriguez	150.00	75.00	45.00
(124)	Pedro Rodriguez	150.00	75.00	45.00
(125)	Anastasio Rosario	150.00	75.00	45.00
(126)	Jorge Rosas	150.00	75.00	45.00
(127)	Cafe Salaberrios	150.00	75.00	45.00
(128)	Wilfredo Salas	150.00	75.00	45.00
(129)	Juan Sanchez	150.00	75.00	45.00
(130)	Carlos M. Santiago	150.00	75.00	45.00
(131)	Jose G. Santiago (P)	400.00	200.00	120.00
(132)	Ed Sauer	150.00	75.00	45.00

(133)	George Scales	1,200	600.00	360.00
(134)	Kermit Schmidt	150.00	75.00	45.00
(135)	Ken Sears (P)	400.00	200.00	120.00
(136)	Herbert Sewell (Souell)	250.00	125.00	75.00
(137)	Dwain Sloat	150.00	75.00	45.00
(138)	Eugene Smith	200.00	100.00	60.00
(139)	Hilton Smith	20,000	10,000	6,000
(140)	John Ford Smith	400.00	200.00	120.00
(141)	Fernando Sola	150.00	75.00	45.00
(142)	Ismael Solla	150.00	75.00	45.00
(143)	Francisco Sostre	150.00	75.00	45.00
(144)	Earl Taborn	200.00	100.00	60.00
(145)	Freddie Thon	150.00	75.00	45.00
(146)	Bob Thurman	400.00	200.00	120.00
(147)	Griffin Tirado	150.00	75.00	45.00
(148)	Leon Tirado	150.00	75.00	45.00
(149)	Pedro J. Toro	150.00	75.00	45.00
(150)	Bin Torres	150.00	75.00	45.00
(151)	Carmelo Torres	150.00	75.00	45.00
(152)	Onofre Torres	150.00	75.00	45.00
(153)	Penpen Torres	150.00	75.00	45.00
(154)	Quincy Trouppe	1,000	500.00	300.00
(155)	Foca Valentin	150.00	75.00	45.00
(156)	Roberto Vargas	150.00	75.00	45.00
(157)	Tetelo Vargas	1,000	500.00	300.00
(158)	Rafael Vasquez	150.00	75.00	45.00
(159)	Guillermo Vega	150.00	75.00	45.00
(160)	Jose L. Velazquez	150.00	75.00	45.00
(161)	Laru Velazquez	150.00	75.00	45.00
(162)	Vicente Villafane	150.00	75.00	45.00
(165)	Luis Villodas	200.00	100.00	60.00
(166)	Jesse Williams	200.00	100.00	60.00
(167)	Artie Wilson	500.00	250.00	150.00
(168)	Rogelio Wiscovich	150.00	75.00	45.00

1949-1950 Toleteros

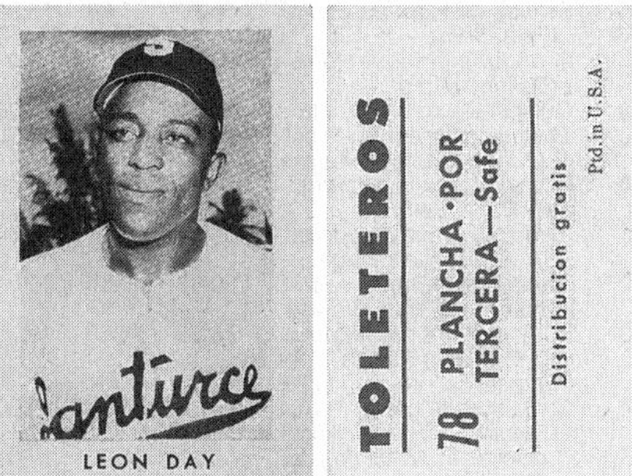

The second of three annual issues during the Puerto Rican League winter seasons, these cards are similar in format to the previous year's set. Front photos are printed in black-and-white, and the backs are printed in red. Cards are about 1-1/2" x 2-1/4", printed on thin cardboard with a light gloss. Backs have a "play" designation for use in a card game and are numbered, though the numbers are not unique to specific players. This checklist is presented alphabetically. Some players can be found in two different poses. Where the variations are known, they are described parenthetically; where the poses are not known, an asterisk is shown. Players with a (P) designation were produced on photographic, rather than printed stock and are scarcer than the regular cards. An album was issued with the set, and like most contemporary Caribbean issues, cards are usually found in well-used condition with evidence of past mounting. Toleteros is roughly translated as "sluggers."

		NM	EX	VG
Complete Set (216): Value Undetermined				
Common Player:		100.00	50.00	30.00
Album:		600.00	300.00	180.00
(1)	Hector Agosto	100.00	50.00	30.00
(2)	Alberto Alberdeston	100.00	50.00	30.00
(3)	Alberto Alicea	100.00	50.00	30.00
(4)	Jaime Almendro (*)	100.00	50.00	30.00
(5)	Guinea Alomar	100.00	50.00	30.00
(6)	Pedro Alomar	100.00	50.00	30.00
(7)	Alfredo Alonso	100.00	50.00	30.00
(8)	Yiyo Alonso	100.00	50.00	30.00
(9)	Ismael Alvarado	100.00	50.00	30.00
(10)	Manuel Alvarez (*)	100.00	50.00	30.00
(11)	Pablo Andino	100.00	50.00	30.00
(12)	Jueyito Andrade	100.00	50.00	30.00
(13)	Paday Anglero	100.00	50.00	30.00
(14)	Luis Arroyo (*)	125.00	65.00	40.00
(15)	Pedro J. Arroyo	100.00	50.00	30.00
(16)	Eugene Baker	150.00	75.00	45.00
(17)	Dan Bankhead	150.00	75.00	45.00
(18)	Sammy Bankhead	300.00	150.00	90.00
(19)	Ramon Bayron	100.00	50.00	30.00
(20)	Carlos Bernier	125.00	65.00	40.00
(21)	Hiram Bithorn	200.00	100.00	60.00
(22)	Efrain Blasini	100.00	50.00	30.00
(23)	Anil Bonilla (*)	100.00	50.00	30.00
(24)	Stan Bread (Breard)	100.00	50.00	30.00
(25)	Chester Brewer	1,000	500.00	300.00
(26)	Johnny Britton	100.00	50.00	30.00
(27)	George Brown	100.00	50.00	30.00
(28)	Willard Brown (*)	3,600	1,800	1,075
(29)	J.A. Burgos (*)	100.00	50.00	30.00
(30)	Tommy Butts	300.00	150.00	90.00
(31)	Joe Buzas	100.00	50.00	30.00
(32)	Rafael Cabezudo	100.00	50.00	30.00
(33)	Luis R. Cabrera	100.00	50.00	30.00
(34)	Marzo Cabrera	100.00	50.00	30.00
(35)	Manolete Caceres (*)	100.00	50.00	30.00
(36)	Eugenio Camara	100.00	50.00	30.00
(37)	Maximo Casals	100.00	50.00	30.00
(38)	Rafael Casanovas	100.00	50.00	30.00
(39)	Nino Zurdo Castro	100.00	50.00	30.00
(40)	Perucho Cepeda (*)	500.00	250.00	150.00
(41)	Medina Chapman	100.00	50.00	30.00
(42)	T. Gomez Checo	100.00	50.00	30.00
(43)	Buster Clarkson	300.00	150.00	90.00
(44)	Francisco Coimbre	400.00	200.00	120.00
(45a)	Eugene Collins (Chest-up.)	200.00	100.00	60.00
(45b)	Eugene Collins (Waist-up.)	200.00	100.00	60.00
(46)	Luis Colmenero	100.00	50.00	30.00
(47)	Luis Colon	100.00	50.00	30.00
(48)	Monchile Concepcion (*)	125.00	65.00	40.00
(49)	Cefo Conde	100.00	50.00	30.00
(50)	Omar Cordero	100.00	50.00	30.00
(51)	Johnny Cox	100.00	50.00	30.00
(52)	Vitin Cruz	100.00	50.00	30.00
(53)	Johnny Davis	400.00	200.00	120.00
(54)	Lomax Davis	125.00	65.00	40.00
(55)	Piper Davis	200.00	100.00	60.00
(56)	Leon Day	12,000	6,000	3,600
(57)	Felle Delgado	100.00	50.00	30.00
(58)	Carmelo Delpin	100.00	50.00	30.00
(59)	Ruben Diaz	100.00	50.00	30.00
(60)	Lucius Easter	300.00	150.00	90.00
(61)	Howard Easterling	200.00	100.00	60.00
(62)	Saturnino Escalera	100.00	50.00	30.00
(63)	Teggy Espinosa	100.00	50.00	30.00
(64)	George Fallon	100.00	50.00	30.00
(65)	Coco Ferrer (*)	100.00	50.00	30.00
(66)	Walter Fialla (Fiala)	100.00	50.00	30.00
(67)	Wilmer Fields (*)	300.00	150.00	90.00
(68)	Tite Figueroa	100.00	50.00	30.00
(69)	Oscar Mir Flores	100.00	50.00	30.00
(70)	Jesus M. Freyre	100.00	50.00	30.00
(71)	Les Fusselmann (Fusselman)	100.00	50.00	30.00
(72)	Cinque Garcia	100.00	50.00	30.00
(73)	Alfonso Gerard	100.00	50.00	30.00
(74)	Alban Glossopp (Glossop)	100.00	50.00	30.00
(75)	Ruben Gomez (*)	150.00	75.00	45.00
(76)	Faelo Gonzalez (P)	200.00	100.00	60.00
(77)	Rafael Gonzalez	100.00	50.00	30.00
(78)	Gely Goyco	100.00	50.00	30.00
(79)	Jack Graham	100.00	50.00	30.00
(80)	Bill Greason	125.00	65.00	40.00
(81)	Felo Guilbe	100.00	50.00	30.00
(82)	Jesus Guilbe	100.00	50.00	30.00
(83)	Juan Guilbe	100.00	50.00	30.00
(84)	Hector Haddock	100.00	50.00	30.00
(85)	Sam Hairston	150.00	75.00	45.00
(86)	Luman Harris	100.00	50.00	30.00
(87a)	Vic Harris (Black background.)	1,000	500.00	300.00
(87b)	Vic Harris (Outdoors background.)	1,000	500.00	300.00
(88)	Angel Hernaiz (P)	200.00	100.00	60.00
(89)	Manuel Hernandez	100.00	50.00	30.00
(90)	Efrain Hidalgo	100.00	50.00	30.00
(91)	Dixie Howell	100.00	50.00	30.00
(92)	Roy Hughes (*)	100.00	50.00	30.00
(93)	Natalio Irizarry	100.00	50.00	30.00
(94)	Walter James	100.00	50.00	30.00
(95)	Cecyl Kayser (P)	300.00	150.00	90.00
(96)	Jack Krauss	100.00	50.00	30.00
(97)	Jim Lamarque	200.00	100.00	60.00
(98)	Carlos Lanauze	100.00	50.00	30.00
(99)	Ramon Lasa	100.00	50.00	30.00
(100)	Rafael Lastra	100.00	50.00	30.00
(101)	Lee Layton	100.00	50.00	30.00
(102)	Lettish	100.00	50.00	30.00
(103)	Johnny Logan	100.00	50.00	30.00
(104)	Radames Lopez	100.00	50.00	30.00
(105)	Louis Louden	150.00	75.00	45.00
(106)	Robert Lynn	100.00	50.00	30.00
(107)	Al Lyons	100.00	50.00	30.00
(108)	Cirico Machuca	100.00	50.00	30.00
(109)	Caro Maldonado	100.00	50.00	30.00
(110)	Clifford Mapes	100.00	50.00	30.00
(111)	Jim Markland (P)	200.00	100.00	60.00
(112)	Canena Marquez	200.00	100.00	60.00
(113)	Leo Marquez	100.00	50.00	30.00
(114)	Antonio Marrero (*)	100.00	50.00	30.00
(115)	Gilberto Marrero	100.00	50.00	30.00
(116)	Humberto Marti	100.00	50.00	30.00
(117)	Achin Matos	100.00	50.00	30.00
(118)	Booker McDaniels	150.00	75.00	45.00
(119)	George McQuillen	100.00	50.00	30.00
(120)	Agustin Medina	100.00	50.00	30.00
(121)	John Medina	100.00	50.00	30.00
(122)	Vicente Medina	100.00	50.00	30.00
(123)	Henry Miller (P)	300.00	150.00	90.00
(124)	Jose E. Montalvo	100.00	50.00	30.00
(125)	Luis A. Morales (*)	100.00	50.00	30.00
(126)	Pedroso Morales	100.00	50.00	30.00
(127)	Willie Morales	100.00	50.00	30.00
(128)	Howard Moss	100.00	50.00	30.00
(129)	Gallego Munoz	100.00	50.00	30.00
(130)	Digno Navarro	100.00	50.00	30.00
(131)	Domingo Navarro	100.00	50.00	30.00
(132)	Millito Navarro	125.00	65.00	40.00
(133)	Earl Naylor (P)	200.00	100.00	60.00
(134)	Alfredo Olivencia	100.00	50.00	30.00
(135)	Guayubin Olivo	125.00	65.00	40.00
(136)	Noel Oquendo	100.00	50.00	30.00
(137)	Otoniel Ortiz	100.00	50.00	30.00
(138)	Rafaelito Ortiz	100.00	50.00	30.00
(139)	Alberto Padilla	100.00	50.00	30.00
(140)	Miguel Payano (P)	200.00	100.00	60.00
(141)	Fernando Diaz Pedroso (*)	125.00	65.00	40.00
(142)	Victor Pellot (Power)	150.00	75.00	45.00
(143)	Pedro Pena	100.00	50.00	30.00
(144)	Pepin Pereira (*)	100.00	50.00	30.00
(145)	Ismael Perez	100.00	50.00	30.00
(146)	Juan Perez	100.00	50.00	30.00
(147)	Palomo Perez	100.00	50.00	30.00
(148)	Rogelio Perez	100.00	50.00	30.00
(149)	Villodas Perez	100.00	50.00	30.00
(150)	Alonso Perry	200.00	100.00	60.00
(151)	Russ Peters	100.00	50.00	30.00
(152)	Jose Polanco	100.00	50.00	30.00
(153)	Bill Powell	100.00	50.00	30.00
(154)	Thomas Quinones (*)	125.00	65.00	40.00
(155)	Milton Ralat	100.00	50.00	30.00
(156)	Otto Ralat	100.00	50.00	30.00
(157)	Fernando Ramos	100.00	50.00	30.00
(158)	Lionel Richards	100.00	50.00	30.00
(159)	Enrique Reinoso	100.00	50.00	30.00
(160)	Xavier Rescigno	100.00	50.00	30.00
(161)	Miguel L. Rivera	100.00	50.00	30.00
(162)	Bienvenido Rodriguez	100.00	50.00	30.00
(163)	Pedro Rodriguez	100.00	50.00	30.00
(164)	Jose M. Roque	100.00	50.00	30.00
(165)	Fachy Rosado	100.00	50.00	30.00
(166)	Jorge Rosas	100.00	50.00	30.00
(167)	Ramon Salgado (*)	100.00	50.00	30.00
(168)	Juan Sanchez	100.00	50.00	30.00
(169)	Carlos M. Santiago	100.00	50.00	30.00
(170)	Jose G. Santiago	100.00	50.00	30.00
(171)	Ed Sauer (*)	100.00	50.00	30.00
(172)	George Scales	800.00	400.00	240.00
(173)	Kermit Schmidt (*)	100.00	50.00	30.00
(174)	Ken Sears	100.00	50.00	30.00
(175)	Dick Seay	700.00	350.00	210.00
(176)	Jose Seda	100.00	50.00	30.00
(177)	Barney Serrell	200.00	100.00	60.00
(178)	McDuffie Sevilla (*)	100.00	50.00	30.00
(179)	Dwain Sloat	100.00	50.00	30.00
(180)	Eugene Smith	125.00	65.00	40.00
(181)	Hilton Smith	12,000	6,000	3,600
(182)	John Ford Smith	150.00	75.00	45.00
(183)	Jerome Snider	100.00	50.00	30.00
(184)	Ismael Solla	100.00	50.00	30.00
(185)	Francisco Sostre	100.00	50.00	30.00
(186)	Herb Souell	100.00	50.00	30.00
(187)	Luis St. Clair	100.00	50.00	30.00
(188)	Tetelo Sterling	100.00	50.00	30.00
(189)	Lonnie Summers	125.00	65.00	40.00
(190)	Jim Tabor (*)	100.00	50.00	30.00
(191)	Earl Taborn	100.00	50.00	30.00
(192)	Israel Ten (*)	100.00	50.00	30.00
(193)	Leo Thomas	100.00	50.00	30.00
(194)	Freddie Thon	100.00	50.00	30.00
(195)	Bob Thurman (*)	200.00	100.00	60.00
(196)	Griffin Tirado (*)	100.00	50.00	30.00
(197)	Leon Tirado	100.00	50.00	30.00
(198)	Bin Torres	100.00	50.00	30.00
(199)	Carmelo Torres	100.00	50.00	30.00
(200)	Indian Torres	100.00	50.00	30.00
(201)	Quincy Trouppe	700.00	350.00	210.00
(202)	Hector Trussa	100.00	50.00	30.00
(203)	Foca Valentin	100.00	50.00	30.00
(204)	Roberto Vargas	100.00	50.00	30.00
(205)	Tetelo Vargas	300.00	150.00	90.00
(206)	Rafael Vazquez	100.00	50.00	30.00
(207)	Guillermo Vega	100.00	50.00	30.00
(208)	Jose L. Velazquez	100.00	50.00	30.00
(209)	Vicente Villafane (*)	100.00	50.00	30.00
(210)	Luis Villodas	100.00	50.00	30.00
(211)	Curley Williams (P)	300.00	150.00	90.00
(212)	Marvin Williams (P)	300.00	150.00	90.00
(213)	Artie Wilson	300.00	150.00	90.00
(214)	Robert Wilson (*)	100.00	50.00	30.00
(215)	Rogelio Wiscovich	100.00	50.00	30.00
(216)	Rafael Zavala	100.00	50.00	30.00

1950-1951 Toleteros

The last of three annual issues during the Puerto Rican League winter seasons, these cards are similar in format to the previous years' sets, with the principal difference being that the approximately 1-3/4" x 2-1/2" cards are printed in color rather than black-and-white. Most are printed on thin cardboard, but some are produced on photographic stock and believed to be scarcer than the others. Those are designated with a (P) in the checklist. Unlike the previous years' issues, backs are blank. This checklist is presented alphabetically. An album was issued with the set, and like most contemporary Caribbean issues, cards are usually found in well-used condition with evidence of past mounting. Toleteros is roughly translated as "sluggers."

		NM	EX	VG
Complete Set (192): Value Undetermined				
Common Player:		60.00	30.00	18.00
Album:		300.00	150.00	90.00
(1)	Hector Agosto	60.00	30.00	18.00
(2)	Robert Alexander	60.00	30.00	18.00
(3)	Alberto Alicea	60.00	30.00	18.00
(4)	Jaime Almendro (Blue Senadores.)	60.00	30.00	18.00

(5) Jaime Almendro (Red Senadores.) 60.00 30.00 18.00
(6) Pedro Alomar 60.00 30.00 18.00
(7) Ismael Alvarado (Ponce) 60.00 30.00 18.00
(8) Ismael Alvarado (Aguadilla) 60.00 30.00 18.00
(9) Jueyito Andrade 60.00 30.00 18.00
(10) Nick Andromidas 60.00 30.00 18.00
(11) Pacay Anglero 60.00 30.00 18.00
(12) Luis (Tite) Arroyo 75.00 37.50 22.50
(13) Pedro J. Arroyo 60.00 30.00 18.00
(14) Dan Bankhead 100.00 50.00 30.00
(15) Babe Barna 60.00 30.00 18.00
(16) Carlos Bernier 75.00 37.50 22.50
(17) John Bero 60.00 30.00 18.00
(18) Wayne Blackburn 60.00 30.00 18.00
(19) Efrain Blasini 60.00 30.00 18.00
(20) Bill Boyd 75.00 37.50 22.50
(21) Stan Breard 60.00 30.00 18.00
(22) Willard Brown 4,000 2,000 1,200
(23) Lou Burdette (P) 125.00 65.00 35.00
(24) Jose A. Burgos 60.00 30.00 18.00
(25) Rafael Cabezudo 60.00 30.00 18.00
(26) Luis R. Cabrera 60.00 30.00 18.00
(27) Marzo Cabrera 60.00 30.00 18.00
(28) Manolete Caceres 60.00 30.00 18.00
(29) Rafael Casanova 60.00 30.00 18.00
(30) Medina Chapman 60.00 30.00 18.00
(31) Al Cihosky (P) 125.00 65.00 35.00
(32) Mike Clark 60.00 30.00 18.00
(33) Buster Clarkson (Santurce) 250.00 125.00 75.00
(34) Buster Clarkson (Ponce) 250.00 125.00 75.00
(35) Francisco Coimbre 300.00 150.00 90.00
(36) Rafael Colmenero 60.00 30.00 18.00
(37) Luis Colon 60.00 30.00 18.00
(38) Monchile Concepcion 75.00 37.50 22.50
(39) Cefo Conde 60.00 30.00 18.00
(40) Omar Cordero 60.00 30.00 18.00
(41) William Costa 60.00 30.00 18.00
(42) Clinton Courtney 75.00 37.50 22.50
(43) George Crowe 75.00 37.50 22.50
(44) Johnny Davis (Mayaguez) 150.00 75.00 45.00
(45) Johnny Davis (San Juan) 150.00 75.00 45.00
(46) Piper Davis 200.00 100.00 60.00
(47) Ellis Deal 75.00 37.50 22.50
(48) Felle Delgado 60.00 30.00 18.00
(49) Luke Easter 175.00 85.00 50.00
(50) Jaime A. Escalera 60.00 30.00 18.00
(51) Saturnino Escalera 60.00 30.00 18.00
(52) Luis Ferbe 60.00 30.00 18.00
(53) L.E. Fernandez 60.00 30.00 18.00
(54) Coco Ferrer 60.00 30.00 18.00
(55) Walter Fialla (Fiala) 60.00 30.00 18.00
(56) Wilmer Fields 150.00 75.00 45.00
(57) Jose A. Figueroa 75.00 37.50 22.50
(58) Oscar Mir Flores 60.00 30.00 18.00
(59) Jesus M. Freyre 60.00 30.00 18.00
(60) Dominic Galata 60.00 30.00 18.00
(61) Felipe Garcia 60.00 30.00 18.00
(62) Alfonso Gerard 60.00 30.00 18.00
(63) Al Gerheauser (P) 125.00 60.00 35.00
(64) Joshua Gibson 75,000 37,500 20,000
(65) Jim Gilliam 150.00 75.00 45.00
(66) Ruben Gomez 75.00 37.50 22.50
(67) Rafael Gonzalez 60.00 30.00 18.00
(68) Felo Guilbe (Ponce) 60.00 30.00 18.00
(69) Felo Guilbe (San Juan) 60.00 30.00 18.00
(70) Juan Guilbe 60.00 30.00 18.00
(71) Hector Haddock 60.00 30.00 18.00
(72) Red Hardy (P) 125.00 60.00 35.00
(73) Van Harrington (P) 125.00 60.00 35.00
(74) Ray Hathaway 60.00 30.00 18.00
(75) Ralston Hemsley 75.00 37.50 22.50
(76) Angel Hernaiz 60.00 30.00 18.00
(77) Rudy Hernandez 60.00 30.00 18.00
(78) Don Hoak 100.00 50.00 30.00
(79) Rogers Hornsby 500.00 250.00 150.00
(80) Dixie Howell 60.00 30.00 18.00
(81) Natalio Irizarry (P) 125.00 60.00 35.00
(82) Walter James 60.00 30.00 18.00
(83) Stan Karpinsky (P) 125.00 60.00 35.00
(84) Cecyl Kayser 100.00 50.00 30.00
(85) Carlos Lanauze 60.00 30.00 18.00
(86) Rafael Lastra 60.00 30.00 18.00
(87) Quique Leon 60.00 30.00 18.00
(88) George Lerchen (P) 125.00 60.00 35.00
(89) Lou Limmer 60.00 30.00 18.00
(90) Royce Lint 60.00 30.00 18.00
(91) Al Lyons 60.00 30.00 18.00
(92) Glenn MacQuillen 60.00 30.00 18.00
(93) Jim Markland 60.00 30.00 18.00
(94) Luis A. Marquez 225.00 110.00 65.00
(95) Bob Marquis 60.00 30.00 18.00
(96) Antonio Marrero 60.00 30.00 18.00
(97) Humberto Marti 60.00 30.00 18.00
(98) Vicente Medina 60.00 30.00 18.00
(99) M. Monserrate Jr. 60.00 30.00 18.00
(100) Jose E. Montalvo (Blue Senadores.) 60.00 30.00 18.00
(101) Jose E. Montalvo (Red Senadores.) 60.00 30.00 18.00
(102) Luis Morales 60.00 30.00 18.00
(103) Pedroso Morales 60.00 30.00 18.00
(104) Willie Morales 60.00 30.00 18.00
(105) Luis M. Munoz (Blue Senadores.) 60.00 30.00 18.00
(106) Luis M. Munoz (Red Senadores.) 60.00 30.00 18.00
(107) Napier 60.00 30.00 18.00
(108) Digno Navarro 60.00 30.00 18.00
(109) Ernest Nevel 60.00 30.00 18.00
(110) Alfredo Olivencia 60.00 30.00 18.00
(111) L. Rodriguez Olmo 75.00 37.50 22.50
(112) Noel Oquendo 60.00 30.00 18.00
(113) Otoniel Ortiz 60.00 30.00 18.00
(114) Rafaelito Ortiz 60.00 30.00 18.00
(115) Roy Partlow 175.00 85.00 50.00
(116) Miguel Payano (Red Senadores.) 60.00 30.00 18.00
(117) Miguel Payano (Mayaguez) 60.00 30.00 18.00
(118) Fernando Pedroso 75.00 37.50 22.50
(119) Victor Pellot (Power) 100.00 50.00 30.00
(120) Pedro Pena 60.00 30.00 18.00
(121) Jose Pereira 60.00 30.00 18.00
(122) Ismael Perez 60.00 30.00 18.00
(123) Juan Perez 60.00 30.00 18.00
(124) Villodas Perez 60.00 30.00 18.00
(125) Alonso Perry 225.00 110.00 65.00
(126) Alonso Perry 225.00 110.00 65.00
(127) Jose D. Polanco 60.00 30.00 18.00
(128) A. Portocarrero 60.00 30.00 18.00
(129) Bill Powell 75.00 37.50 22.50
(130) Tomas Quinones 75.00 37.50 22.50
(131) Milton Ralat 60.00 30.00 18.00
(132) Fernando Ramos 60.00 30.00 18.00
(133) Henry Rementeria 60.00 30.00 18.00
(134) Luis Renta 60.00 30.00 18.00
(135) Herminio Reyes 60.00 30.00 18.00
(136) Lionel Richards 60.00 30.00 18.00
(137) Gene Richardson 75.00 37.50 22.50
(138) Jim Rivera 60.00 30.00 18.00
(139) Miguel A. Rivera 60.00 30.00 18.00
(140) Roberto Rivera 60.00 30.00 18.00
(141) Jack Robinson 60.00 30.00 18.00
(142) Ministro Rodriguez 60.00 30.00 18.00
(143) Pedro Rodriguez 60.00 30.00 18.00
(144) Jorge Rosas 60.00 30.00 18.00
(145) Miguel Ruiz 60.00 30.00 18.00
(146) Ramon Salgado 60.00 30.00 18.00
(147) Juan Sanchez 60.00 30.00 18.00
(148) Carlos M. Santiago 60.00 30.00 18.00
(149) Jose G. Santiago 60.00 30.00 18.00
(150) George Scales 600.00 300.00 180.00
(151) Scarpatte 60.00 30.00 18.00
(152) Kermit Schmidt (Ponce) 60.00 30.00 18.00
(153) Kermit Schmidt (Red Senadores.) 60.00 30.00 18.00
(154) Ken Sears 60.00 30.00 18.00
(155) Dick Seay 300.00 150.00 90.00
(156) Pedro Seda 60.00 30.00 18.00
(157) McDuffie Sevilla 60.00 30.00 18.00
(158) Vincent Shuppe 60.00 30.00 18.00
(159) William Skowron 150.00 75.00 45.00
(160) Dwain Sloat 60.00 30.00 18.00
(161) John Ford Smith 175.00 85.00 50.00
(162) Francisco Sostre 60.00 30.00 18.00
(163) Jose St. Clair (Looking forward.) 60.00 30.00 18.00
(164) Jose St. Clair (Looking left.) 60.00 30.00 18.00
(165) Luis St. Clair 60.00 30.00 18.00
(166) Jimmy Starks 75.00 37.50 22.50
(167) Israel Ten 60.00 30.00 18.00
(168) Leo Thomas 60.00 30.00 18.00
(169) Valmy Thomas (P) 150.00 75.00 45.00
(170) Freddie Thon 60.00 30.00 18.00
(171) Bob Thurman 175.00 85.00 50.00
(172) Miguel A. Tineo 60.00 30.00 18.00
(173) Griffin Tirado (Blue background.) 60.00 30.00 18.00
(174) Griffin Tirado (Trees in background.) 60.00 30.00 18.00
(175) Bin Torres 60.00 30.00 18.00
(176) Clarkson Torres 60.00 30.00 18.00
(177) Manuel Traboux 60.00 30.00 18.00
(178) Gilberto Valentin 60.00 30.00 18.00
(179) Roberto Vargas 60.00 30.00 18.00
(180) Tetelo Vargas 350.00 175.00 100.00
(181) Rafael Vazquez 60.00 30.00 18.00
(182) Guillermo Vega 60.00 30.00 18.00
(183) Jose L. Velazquez 60.00 30.00 18.00
(184) Vicente Villafane 60.00 30.00 18.00
(185) Luis Villodas 75.00 37.50 22.50
(186) Curley Williams (P) 150.00 75.00 45.00
(187) Artie Wilson 225.00 110.00 65.00
(188) Robert Wilson (P) 150.00 75.00 45.00
(189) Jerry Witte (P) 125.00 60.00 35.00
(190) Pete Wojey 60.00 30.00 18.00
(191) Andres Zabala 60.00 30.00 18.00
(192) Rafael Zavala 60.00 30.00 18.00

1950-1951 Toleteros In Action

90. Piper intenta sacar a Tetelo- SAFE

		NM	EX	VG
Complete Set (178):		6,500	3,250	2,000
Common Card:		50.00	25.00	15.00
1	Pellot fildea con elegencia. (Victor Pellot (Power))	60.00	30.00	18.00
2	Burgos conecta hit de piernas. (Jose Burgos)	50.00	25.00	15.00
3	OUT por medio paso.	50.00	25.00	15.00
4	Te gusta el mamabo, Canena? (Canena Marquez)	65.00	32.50	20.00
5	OUT!!	50.00	25.00	15.00
6	Lanauze se eleva tras la bola. (Carlos Lanauze)	50.00	25.00	15.00
7	Simpson se escurre en tercera. . .	50.00	25.00	15.00
8	Si no se la cae la bola. . .	50.00	25.00	15.00
9	Escalera realiza brillante cogida. (Saturnino Escalera)	50.00	25.00	15.00
10	Lucha Grecoromana?	50.00	25.00	15.00
11	Gallego a punto deslizarse. . . (Gallego Munoz)	50.00	25.00	15.00
12	Parece. . .pero no lo empuja. . .	50.00	25.00	15.00
13	Ramos da out a Felo en primera. (Fernando Ramos)	50.00	25.00	15.00
14	El Chiquitin y El Magnifico.	50.00	25.00	15.00
15	Limmer llege de pie tras triple. (Lou Limmer)	50.00	25.00	15.00
16	Arroyo toca a Costa. . .OUT. (Luis Arroyo)	50.00	25.00	15.00
17	Thon a salvo en tercera. (Freddie Thon)	50.00	25.00	15.00
18	Thurman hacia home Scales lo felicita. (Bob Thurman, George Scales)	65.00	32.50	20.00
19	NOT ISSUED			
20	NOT ISSUED			
21	Coca trata de escurrirse - OUT. (Coco Ferrer)	50.00	25.00	15.00
22	Thurman out a manos de Lanauze (Bob Thurman, Carlos Lanauzue)	65.00	32.50	20.00
23	Santiago felicita a Atkins (Carlos M. Santiago, Joe Atkins)	50.00	25.00	15.00
24	Griffin captura a Miller en home. (Griffin Tirado, Henry Miller)	50.00	25.00	15.00
25	"Detente Villodas": Escalera. (Luis Villodas, Saturnino Escalera)	50.00	25.00	15.00
26	Felo se desliza. . .SAFE. (Felo Guilbe)	50.00	25.00	15.00
27	Gallego llega safe a Home. (Gallego Munoz)	50.00	25.00	15.00
28	Que pena! Se cayo la bola. . .	50.00	25.00	15.00
29	Easterling esperando la bola - OUT. (Howard Easterling)	50.00	25.00	15.00
30	Pitcher McDuffie anotando. (McDuffie Sevilla)	50.00	25.00	15.00
31	El raudo Roberto se desliza - SAFE. (Roberto Vargas)	50.00	25.00	15.00
32	Harris felicita Brown tras homerun (Willard Brown)	200.00	100.00	60.00
33	Burgos intenta sacar Easter - SAFE. (Jose Burgos, Luke Easter)	65.00	32.50	20.00
34	Los Leones felicitan a Clarkson. (Buster Clarkson)	65.00	32.50	20.00
35	Otoniel realiza dificil cogida. . . (Otoniel Ortiz)	50.00	25.00	15.00
36	Thurman safe en tercera. . . (Bob Thurman)	65.00	32.50	20.00
37	Bernier safe en home. (Carlos Bernier)	50.00	25.00	15.00
38	Chifflan Clark se va de homerun. (Chifflan Clark)	50.00	25.00	15.00
39	El gran Easter llega tras homerun. (Luke Easter)	65.00	32.50	20.00
40	Se cae bola a Fields; Graham safe. (Wilmer Fields, Jack Graham)	60.00	30.00	18.00
41	Otoniel trata sacar Taborn - SAFE. (Otoniel Ortiz, Earl Taborn)	50.00	25.00	15.00
42	McQuillen se desliza tercera - SAFE. (George McQuillen)	50.00	25.00	15.00
43	Uno, dos y tres. . .Y anota Coimbre (Francisco Coimbre)	90.00	45.00	27.50
44	Carlos Manuel llega trade. . .OUT. (Carlos M. Santiago)	50.00	25.00	15.00
45	Aprieta el paso, Griffin. . . (Griffin Tirado)	50.00	25.00	15.00
46	Pepe Lucas saca out a Resbaloso. (Pepe Lucas)	50.00	25.00	15.00
47	"No hay quien pase", dice Howell (Dixie Howell)	50.00	25.00	15.00
48	Y que dice el Umpiere?	50.00	25.00	15.00
49	Pedroso intenta robo home - OUT. (Fernando Pedroso)	50.00	25.00	15.00
50	Se formo el nudo. . .	50.00	25.00	15.00
51	Cogelo con calma, Leo. . . (Leo Thomas)	50.00	25.00	15.00
52	Tetelo galopando hacia primera. . . (Tetelo Vargas)	90.00	45.00	27.50
53	Haciendose burla?	50.00	25.00	15.00
54	Los tiburones felicitan. . .	50.00	25.00	15.00
55	La No. 29 de Bernier. (Carlos Bernier)	50.00	25.00	15.00
56	Jockey entra facilmente a primera.	50.00	25.00	15.00
57	Buzas felicita a Collins. (Joe Buzas, Eugene Collins)	50.00	25.00	15.00
58	Ya es tarde, Jose Enrique. . .	50.00	25.00	15.00
59	Lomax Davis entra tras homerun (Lomax Davis)	50.00	25.00	15.00
60	Haddock no puede sacar Villafane. (Hector Haddock)	50.00	25.00	15.00
61	Otoniel Ortiz se va de hom,erun. . . (Otoniel Ortiz)	50.00	25.00	15.00
62	Otra mas para Bernier (Carlos Bernier)	50.00	25.00	15.00
63	Montalvo se desliza en tercera (?) (Jose E. Montalvo)	50.00	25.00	15.00
64	Willie es todo ojos. . . (Willie Morales)	50.00	25.00	15.00
65	La Mucura esta llegando. . . (Johnny Davis)	60.00	30.00	18.00
66	Chapman da out espectacular. (Medina Chapman)	50.00	25.00	15.00

67	McQuilen pisa plato tras homerun (George McQuillen)	50.00	25.00	15.00
68	"Coimbre, Safe." . .dice el Umpire. (Francisco Coimbre)	90.00	45.00	27.50
69	Llega Perry despues de Homerun. . . (Alonso Perry)	65.00	32.50	20.00
70	Griffin, ya es tuyo. . . (Griffin Tirado)	50.00	25.00	15.00
71	Fields pisa plato tras Homerun. . . (Wilmer Fields)	50.00	25.00	15.00
72	EL HOMBRE ESE. . . (Willard Brown)	200.00	100.00	60.00
73	Jockey se desliza violentamente. . .	50.00	25.00	15.00
74	Montalvo esperando a Tite - OUT. (Jose E. Montalvo)	50.00	25.00	15.00
75	Perry anota transqueando. . . (Alonso Perry)	65.00	32.50	20.00
76	Fields pivotea para double-play. (Wilmer Fields)	60.00	30.00	18.00
77	Andando en la cuerda, Piper? (Piper Davis)	65.00	32.50	20.00
78	Montalvo en pie de combate. . . (Jose E. Montalvo)	50.00	25.00	15.00
79	EN GRAN EXPECTATIVA. . .	50.00	25.00	15.00
80	Indios reciben Gachito tras homer	50.00	25.00	15.00
81	Butts esquiva la bola - SAFE. (Pee Wee Butts)	50.00	25.00	15.00
82	Otro para el Gaucho Davis. . . (Johnny Davis)	60.00	30.00	18.00
83	Los leones se alborotan. . . (Piper Davis)	60.00	30.00	18.00
84	Lanauze safe en home. . . (Carlos Lanauze)	50.00	25.00	15.00
85	Lanauze se alarga - OUT. (Carlos Lanauze)	50.00	25.00	15.00
86	Thurman llega tras homerun. (Bob Thurman)	65.00	32.50	20.00
87	Sauer roba home especta-cularmente (Ed Sauer)	50.00	25.00	15.00
88	PERRY SE ESTIRA. . .OUT. (Alonso Perry)	65.00	32.50	20.00
89	Clarkson conecta otro homerun. (Buster Clarkson)	65.00	32.50	20.00
90	Piper intenta sacar a Tetelo - SAFE (Tetelo Vargas, Piper Davis)	90.00	45.00	27.50
91	QUE QUE USTED DICE. . .?	50.00	25.00	15.00
92	Bernier se roba el home. . . (Carlos Bernier)	50.00	25.00	15.00
93	UNA ESCENA DE RUTINA. . . (Willard Brown)	200.00	100.00	60.00
94	Taborn trata de esquvarse - OUT. (Earl Taborn)	50.00	25.00	15.00
95	Pita Marti safe en tercera. (Humberto Marti)	50.00	25.00	15.00
96	PIE CONTRA PIE. . .(?)	50.00	25.00	15.00
97	NO QUIERE NI VERLO. . .	50.00	25.00	15.00
98	SUDOR Y ARENA. . .	50.00	25.00	15.00
99	Jueyito safe en primera. (Jueyito Andrade)	50.00	25.00	15.00
100	QUIEN LLEGO PRIMERO?	50.00	25.00	15.00
101	LLEGO TARDE EL TIRO..SAFE.	50.00	25.00	15.00
102	Escalera se estira. . .pero es SAFE. (Saturnino Escalera)	50.00	25.00	15.00
103	Howell aspera. . .Almendro observa. (Dixie Howell)	50.00	25.00	15.00
104	A todo vapor hacia tercera. . .	50.00	25.00	15.00
105	Buena cogida, pero es SAFE.	50.00	25.00	15.00
106	El arbitro observa. . .SAFE.	50.00	25.00	15.00
107	SAFE EN HOME.	50.00	25.00	15.00
108	Regreso a tiempo. . .SAFE.	50.00	25.00	15.00
109	Canena es felicitados tras Homer. (Canena Marquez)	65.00	32.50	20.00
110	"COC SAFE", canta el umpiere. (Coco Ferrer)	50.00	25.00	15.00
111	Taft Wright jonronen. . . (Taft Wright)	50.00	25.00	15.00
112	Esta solo. . .pero siempre gana.	50.00	25.00	15.00
113	????????, CANTE!	50.00	25.00	15.00
114	Casanovas quieto en tercera. . . (Rafael Casanovas)	50.00	25.00	15.00
115	Wilson espera pero no llega. . .SAFE. (Artie Wilson)	65.00	32.50	20.00
116	FELLE FELICITA MONTALVO (Felle Delgado, Jose E. Montalvo)	50.00	25.00	15.00
117	El tigre tambien se desliza. . .Safe.	50.00	25.00	15.00
118	Limmer se adelanta. . .Montalvo out. (Lou Limmer, Jose E. Montalvo)	50.00	25.00	15.00
119	TIRO MALO. . .BUTTS SAFE. (Pee Wee Butts)	50.00	25.00	15.00
120	SAFE EN TERCERA.	50.00	25.00	15.00
121	EL JIBARO CONECTA HIT. . .	50.00	25.00	15.00
122	Chapman no puede alcanzarla. . . (Medina Chapman)	50.00	25.00	15.00
123	Guinea Alomar da OUT en Home. (Guinea Alomar)	50.00	25.00	15.00
124	INDIO ANOTA EN SLIDE. . .	50.00	25.00	15.00
125	Miller saca a Serrel en primera. (Henry Miller, Barney Serrell)	50.00	25.00	15.00
126	El gran COIMBRE llega SAFE. (Francisco Coimbre)	90.00	45.00	27.50
127	El arbitro tome impulsa. . .OUT!	50.00	25.00	15.00
128	TROUPPE DA OUT EN HOME. (Quincy Trouppe)	90.00	45.00	27.50
129	BANKHEAD OUT EN PRIMERA. (Bankhead)	60.00	30.00	18.00
130	Tiene que pensarlo bien. . .	50.00	25.00	15.00
131	Escalera a salvo en tercera. . . (Saturnino Escalera)	50.00	25.00	15.00
132	DOS MANOS QUE BUSCAN. . .	50.00	25.00	15.00
133	FIGUEROA SE DESLIZA - SAFE (Tite Figueroa)	50.00	25.00	15.00
134	VIENE LA BOLA. . .OUT.	50.00	25.00	15.00
135	Esperando el tiro. . .OUT.	50.00	25.00	15.00
136	KAYSER SAFE EN PRIMERA. (Cecyl Kayser)	50.00	25.00	15.00
137	COCO FERRER DA OUT. (Coco Ferrer)	50.00	25.00	15.00
138	Lo atajaron a tiempo... .OUT.	50.00	25.00	15.00
139	Limmer da su primer homer. (Lou Limmer)	50.00	25.00	15.00
140	Starks y Blasini alegan. . . (Jimmy Starks, Efrain Blasini)	50.00	25.00	15.00
141	BARNA SE VA DE HOMERUN. (Babe Barna)	50.00	25.00	15.00
142	"La antesala del gran choque. . . (George Scales)	60.00	30.00	18.00
143	"QUIETO." DICE EL UMPIRE.	50.00	25.00	15.00
144	LO SACARON POR UN PELO. . .	50.00	25.00	15.00
145	Un recibimiento poco agradable.	50.00	25.00	15.00
146	Montalvo se desliza. . .OUT. (Jose E. Montalvo)	50.00	25.00	15.00
147	ALOMAR OUT EN HOME. . . (Alomar)	50.00	25.00	15.00
148	EASTER SAFE EN HOME. . . (Luke Easter)	65.00	32.50	20.00
149	Grillo se anota hit de piernas. . .	50.00	25.00	15.00
150	BARNA SAFE EN TERCERA. (Babe Barna)	50.00	25.00	15.00
151	Esta en la base pero es OUT.	50.00	25.00	15.00
152	TYBOR DA OUT A TABORN. (Jim Tabor, Earl Taborn)	50.00	25.00	15.00
153	BUTTS OUT EN PRIMERA. (Pee Wee Butts)	50.00	25.00	15.00
154	Viene la bola. . .Hernaiz SAFE. (Angel Hernaiz)	50.00	25.00	15.00
155	VILLODAS LO ESPERA. . .OUT. (Luis Villodas)	50.00	25.00	15.00
156	TYBOR SACA A COCA FERRER. (Jim Tabor, Coco Ferrer)	50.00	25.00	15.00
157	LO FUSILAN EN TERCERA.	50.00	25.00	15.00
158	B L O Q U E A D O. . .	50.00	25.00	15.00
159	"Estoy firme en base", dice Coco. (Coco Ferrer)	50.00	25.00	15.00
160	Ruben Gomez se tira slide. . .SAFE. (Ruben Gomez)	50.00	25.00	15.00
161	HOWELL OUT EN PRIMERA. (Dixie Howell)	50.00	25.00	15.00
162	SAFE EN HOME.	50.00	25.00	15.00
163	PERRY ES ESCURRE. . .SAFE. (Alonso Perry)	65.00	32.50	20.00
164	PEDROSO SE LESIONA. (Fernando Pedroso)	50.00	25.00	15.00
165	LA APOTEOSIS DEL TRIUNFO.	50.00	25.00	15.00
166	Ruben jonroneo ganar su juego. (Ruben Gomez)	50.00	25.00	15.00
167	Primer homerun CANENA 1950-51 (Canena Marquez)	65.00	32.50	20.00
168	GOLPE DE IZQUIRDA? SAFE.	50.00	25.00	15.00
169	PELLOT OUT EN HOME. (Victor Pellot (Power))	65.00	32.50	20.00
170	Muchos ojos tras Scales y Mullens. (George Scales)	60.00	30.00	18.00
171	Nube de polvo en el Castillo. . .	50.00	25.00	15.00
172	Bero participa carnaval jonrones. (John Bero)	50.00	25.00	15.00
173	Lanauze completa out a Butts. (Carlos Lanauze, Pee Wee Butts)	50.00	25.00	15.00
174	SE LE ESCAPO LA PILDORA.	50.00	25.00	15.00
175	EL UMPIRE DECIDIRA. . .	50.00	25.00	15.00
176	Llego tarde el HOMBRE ESE. (Willard Brown)	200.00	100.00	60.00
177	THON SE DESLIZA. . .SAFE. (Freddie Thon)	50.00	25.00	15.00
178	AL REVES, PERO SAFE. . .	50.00	25.00	15.00
179	Hughes no puede sacar al corredor. (Roy Hughes)	50.00	25.00	15.00
180	"Chiflan Safe." . .dice el Umpiere. (Chiflan Clark)	50.00	25.00	15.00

1909-11 Tolstoi Cigarettes

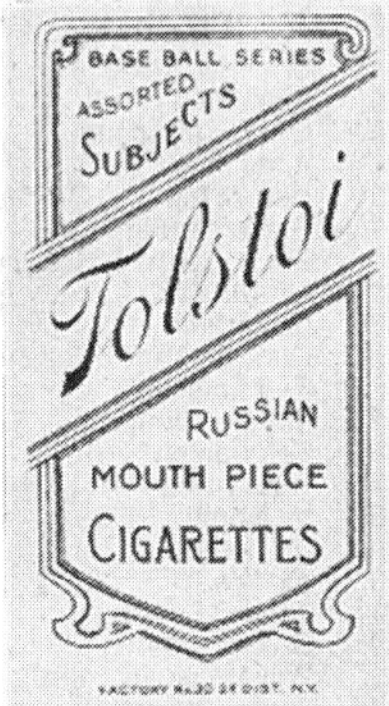

PREMIUMS:
Commons: 1.5-2X
Hall of Famers: 1-2X
(See T206 for checklist and base values.)

1887 Tomlinson Studios Cabinets

The extent to which this Detroit photographer promulgated individual player cabinet cards of the 1887 Wolverines is unknown. However, since the portrait on the known Bennett card is the same as that found on a team-composite cabinet card, it is not unreasonable to expect that each of the other 13 players pictured on the team card may have been issued individually. The cabinet is in the typical 4-1/4" x 6-1/2" format, with blank back.

	NM	EX	VG
C.W. Bennett/Portrait	5,000	2,500	1,500
C.W. Bennett/Btg	5,000	2,500	1,500
Jimmy Manning	5,000	2,500	1,500

1909 Topping & Co. Detroit Tigers Postcards

This set of postcards features the members of the 1909 American League Champion Detroit Tigers. About 3-1/2" x 5-1/2" in size, vertically formatted fronts have black-and-white player portraits at center within a yellow six-pointed star. "Tiger Stars" appears in script in a yellow stripe at top, while the player name and position are in a similar strip at bottom. Black trim surrounds the design elements. Backs are black-and-white with standard postcard markings and a credit line for Topping and Publishers Co., Detroit. The unnumbered cards are listed here alphabetically.

		NM	EX	VG
Complete Set (21):		12,000	6,000	3,500
Common Player:		400.00	200.00	120.00
(1)	Henry Beckendorf	400.00	200.00	120.00
(2)	Donie Bush	400.00	200.00	120.00
(3)	Ty Cobb	3,500	1,750	1,000
(4)	Sam Crawford	1,000	500.00	300.00
(5)	Jim Delehanty	400.00	200.00	120.00
(6)	Bill Donovan	400.00	200.00	120.00
(7)	Hughie Jennings	400.00	200.00	120.00
(8)	Davy Jones	400.00	200.00	120.00
(9)	Tom Jones	400.00	200.00	120.00
(10)	Ed Killian	400.00	200.00	120.00
(11)	Matty McIntyre	400.00	200.00	120.00
(12)	George Moriarty	400.00	200.00	120.00
(13)	George Mullin	400.00	200.00	120.00
(14)	Charley O'Leary	400.00	200.00	120.00
(15)	Germany Schaefer	400.00	200.00	120.00
(16)	Charlie Schmidt	400.00	200.00	120.00
(17)	George Speer	400.00	200.00	120.00
(18)	Oscar Stanage	400.00	200.00	120.00
(19)	Eddie Summers	400.00	200.00	120.00
(20)	Ed Willett	400.00	200.00	120.00
(21)	Ralph Works	400.00	200.00	120.00

1948 Topps Magic Photos

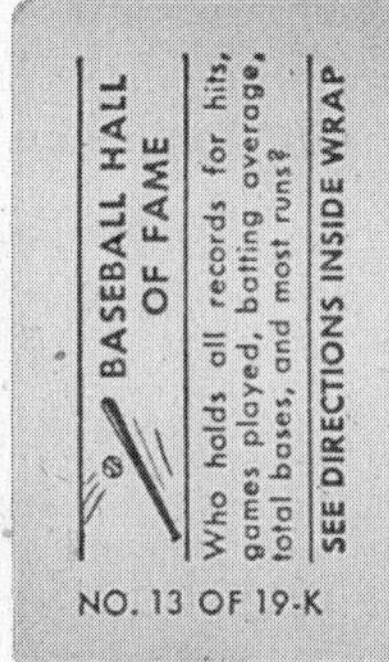

The first Topps baseball cards appeared as a subset of 19 cards from an issue of 252 "Magic Photos." The set takes its name from the self-developing nature of the cards. The cards were blank on the front when first taken from the wrapper. By spitting on the wrapper and holding it to the card while exposing it to light the black-and-white photo appeared. Measuring 7/8" x 1-1/2", the cards are very similar to Topps 1955 and 1956 "Hocus Focus" issues.

		NM	EX	VG
Complete Set (19):		2,400	1,200	725.00
Common Card:		60.00	30.00	18.00
1	Lou Boudreau	75.00	37.50	22.50
2	Cleveland Indians	60.00	30.00	18.00
3	Bob Elliott	75.00	37.50	22.50
4	Cleveland Indians 4-3	60.00	30.00	18.00
5	Cleveland Indians 4-1	60.00	30.00	18.00
6	Babe Ruth	450.00	225.00	135.00
7	Tris Speaker	90.00	45.00	27.50
8	Rogers Hornsby	90.00	45.00	27.50
9	Connie Mack	75.00	37.50	22.50
10	Christy Mathewson	150.00	75.00	45.00
11	Hans Wagner	100.00	50.00	30.00
12	Grover Alexander	90.00	45.00	27.50
13	Ty Cobb	275.00	135.00	80.00
14	Lou Gehrig	275.00	135.00	80.00
15	Walter Johnson	125.00	65.00	35.00
16	Cy Young	125.00	65.00	35.00
17	George Sisler	75.00	37.50	22.50
18	Tinker and Evers	125.00	65.00	35.00
19	Third Base Cleveland Indians	75.00	37.50	22.50

1951 Topps Red Backs

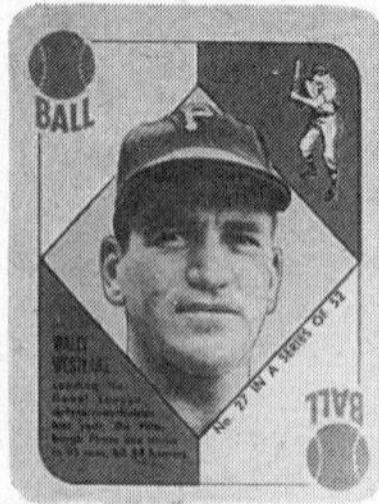

Like the Blue Backs, the Topps Red Backs which were sold at the same time came two to a package for 1¢. Their black-and-white photographs appear on a red, white, blue and yellow background. The back printing is red on white. Their 2" x 2-5/8" size is the same as Blue Backs. Also identical is the set size (52 cards) and the game situations to be found on the fronts of the cards, for use in playing a card game of baseball. Red Backs are more common than the Blue Backs by virtue of a 1980s discovery of a large hoard of unopened boxes. Red Backs are also known to have been sold in a plastic-bagged set along with a foldout paper game board for 29 cents.

		NM	EX	VG
Complete Set (52):		900.00	450.00	275.00
Common Player:		12.00	6.00	3.50
Wax Pack (2):		75.00		
1	Larry (Yogi) Berra	75.00	37.50	22.00
2	Sid Gordon	12.00	6.00	3.50
3	Ferris Fain	12.00	6.00	3.50
4	Verne Stephens	12.00	6.00	3.50
5	Phil Rizzuto	40.00	20.00	12.00
6	Allie Reynolds	20.00	10.00	6.00
7	Howie Pollet	12.00	6.00	3.50
8	Early Wynn	25.00	12.50	7.50
9	Roy Sievers	12.00	6.00	3.50
10	Mel Parnell	12.00	6.00	3.50
11	Gene Hermanski	12.00	6.00	3.50
12	Jim Hegan	12.00	6.00	3.50
13	Dale Mitchell	12.00	6.00	3.50
14	Wayne Terwilliger	12.00	6.00	3.50
15	Ralph Kiner	25.00	12.50	7.50
16	Preacher Roe	20.00	10.00	6.00
17	Dave Bell	12.00	6.00	3.50
18	Gerry Coleman	15.00	7.50	4.50
19	Dick Kokos	12.00	6.00	3.50
20	Dominick DiMaggio	20.00	10.00	6.00
21	Larry Jansen	12.00	6.00	3.50
22	Bob Feller	45.00	22.50	13.50
23	Ray Boone	12.00	6.00	3.50
24	Hank Bauer	15.00	7.50	4.50
25	Cliff Chambers	12.00	6.00	3.50
26	Luke Easter	15.00	7.50	4.50
27	Wally Westlake	12.00	6.00	3.50
28	Elmer Valo	12.00	6.00	3.50
29	Bob Kennedy	12.00	6.00	3.50
30	Warren Spahn	45.00	22.00	13.50
31	Gil Hodges	35.00	17.50	10.50
32	Henry Thompson	12.00	6.00	3.50
33	William Werle	12.00	6.00	3.50
34	Grady Hatton	12.00	6.00	3.50
35	Al Rosen	15.00	7.50	4.50
36a	Gus Zernial (Chicago in bio.)	50.00	25.00	15.00
36b	Gus Zernial (Philadelphia in bio.)	22.50	11.00	6.75
37	Wes Westrum	12.00	6.00	3.50
38	Ed (Duke) Snider	50.00	25.00	15.00
39	Ted Kluszewski	20.00	10.00	6.00
40	Mike Garcia	12.00	6.00	3.50
41	Whitey Lockman	12.00	6.00	3.50
42	Ray Scarborough	12.00	6.00	3.50
43	Maurice McDermott	12.00	6.00	3.50
44	Sid Hudson	12.00	6.00	3.50
45	Andy Seminick	12.00	6.00	3.50
46	Billy Goodman	12.00	6.00	3.50
47	Tommy Glaviano	12.00	6.00	3.50
48	Eddie Stanky	12.00	6.00	3.50
49	Al Zarilla	12.00	6.00	3.50
50	Monte Irvin	25.00	12.50	7.50
51	Eddie Robinson	12.00	6.00	3.50
52a	Tommy Holmes (Boston in bio.)	50.00	25.00	15.00
52b	Tommy Holmes (Hartford in bio.)	22.50	11.00	6.75

1951 Topps Blue Backs

Sold two cards in a package with a piece of candy for 1¢, the Topps Blue Backs are considerably scarcer than their Red Back counterparts. The 2" x 2-5/8" cards carry a black-and-white player photograph on a red, white, yellow and green background along with the player's name and other information including their 1950 record on the front. The back is printed in blue on a white background. The 52-card set has varied baseball situations on them, making the playing of a rather elementary game of baseball possible. Although scarce, Blue Backs were printed on thick cardboard and have survived quite well over the years. There are, however, few stars in the set.

		NM	EX	VG
Complete Set (52):		1,900	950.00	575.00
Common Player:		25.00	12.50	7.50
Wax Pack (2):		175.00		
1	Eddie Yost	35.00	12.50	7.50
2	Henry (Hank) Majeski	25.00	12.50	7.50
3	Richie Ashburn	225.00	110.00	65.00
4	Del Ennis	25.00	12.50	7.50
5	Johnny Pesky	25.00	12.50	7.50
6	Albert (Red) Schoendienst	125.00	65.00	35.00
7	Gerald Staley	25.00	12.50	7.50
8	Dick Sisler	25.00	12.50	7.50
9	Johnny Sain	35.00	17.50	10.00
10	Joe Page	25.00	12.50	7.50
11	Johnny Groth	25.00	12.50	7.50
12	Sam Jethroe	25.00	12.50	7.50
13	James (Mickey) Vernon	25.00	12.50	7.50
14	George Munger	25.00	12.50	7.50
15	Eddie Joost	25.00	12.50	7.50
16	Murry Dickson	25.00	12.50	7.50
17	Roy Smalley	25.00	12.50	7.50
18	Ned Garver	25.00	12.50	7.50
19	Phil Masi	25.00	12.50	7.50
20	Ralph Branca	35.00	17.50	10.00
21	Billy Johnson	25.00	12.50	7.50
22	Bob Kuzava	25.00	12.50	7.50
23	Paul (Dizzy) Trout	25.00	12.50	7.50
24	Sherman Lollar	25.00	12.50	7.50
25	Sam Mele	25.00	12.50	7.50
26	Chico Carrasquel	25.00	12.50	7.50
27	Andy Pafko	25.00	12.50	7.50
28	Harry (The Cat) Brecheen	25.00	12.50	7.50
29	Granville Hamner	25.00	12.50	7.50
30	Enos (Country) Slaughter	125.00	65.00	35.00
31	Lou Brissie	25.00	12.50	7.50
32	Bob Elliott	25.00	12.50	7.50
33	Don Lenhardt	25.00	12.50	7.50
34	Earl Torgeson	25.00	12.50	7.50
35	Tommy Byrne	25.00	12.50	7.50
36	Cliff Fannin	25.00	12.50	7.50
37	Bobby Doerr	125.00	65.00	35.00
38	Irv Noren	25.00	12.50	7.50
39	Ed Lopat	35.00	17.50	10.00
40	Vic Wertz	25.00	12.50	7.50
41	Johnny Schmitz	25.00	12.50	7.50
42	Bruce Edwards	25.00	12.50	7.50
43	Willie (Puddin' Head) Jones	25.00	12.50	7.50
44	Johnny Wyrostek	25.00	12.50	7.50
45	Bill Pierce	25.00	12.50	7.50
46	Gerry Priddy	25.00	12.50	7.50
47	Herman Wehmeier	25.00	12.50	7.50
48	Billy Cox	25.00	12.50	7.50
49	Henry (Hank) Sauer	25.00	12.50	7.50
50	Johnny Mize	125.00	62.00	37.00
51	Eddie Waitkus	25.00	12.50	7.50
52	Sam Chapman	25.00	12.50	7.50

1951 Topps Connie Mack's All-Stars

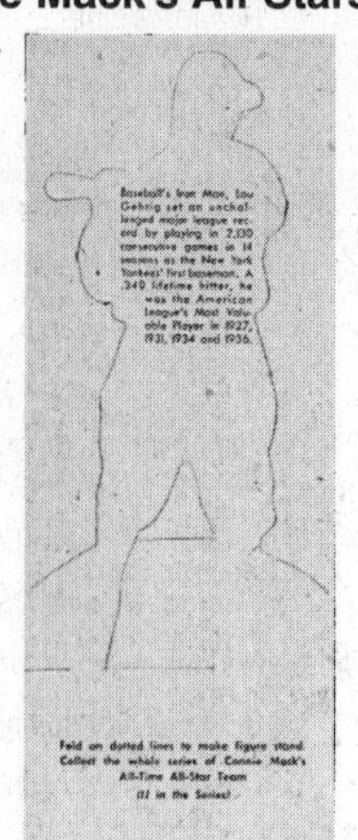

A set of die-cut, 2-1/16" x 5-1/4" cards, all 11 players are Hall of Famers. The cards feature a black-and-white action player photograph printed on a red background with a colored name plaque underneath. Like the "Current All-Stars," with which they were issued, the background could be folded, making it possible for the card to stand up. This practice, however, resulted in the card's mutilation and lowers its condition in the eyes of today's collectors. Connie Mack All-Stars are scarce today and, despite being relatively expensive, retain a certain popularity as one of Topps first issues.

		NM	EX	VG
Complete Set (11):		16,000	8,000	4,750
Common Player:		525.00	260.00	155.00
(1)	Grover Cleveland Alexander	900.00	450.00	275.00
(2)	Gordon Stanley Cochrane	600.00	300.00	180.00
(3)	Edward Trowbridge Collins	600.00	300.00	180.00
(4)	James J. Collins	600.00	300.00	180.00
(5)	Lou Gehrig	4,500	2,250	1,350
(6)	Walter Johnson	1,000	500.00	300.00
(7)	Connie Mack	600.00	300.00	180.00
(8)	Christopher Mathewson	1,125	560.00	335.00
(9)	George Herman Ruth	5,500	2,750	1,650
(10)	Tris Speaker	600.00	300.00	180.00
(11)	Honus Wagner	1,250	625.00	375.00

1951 Topps Major League All-Stars

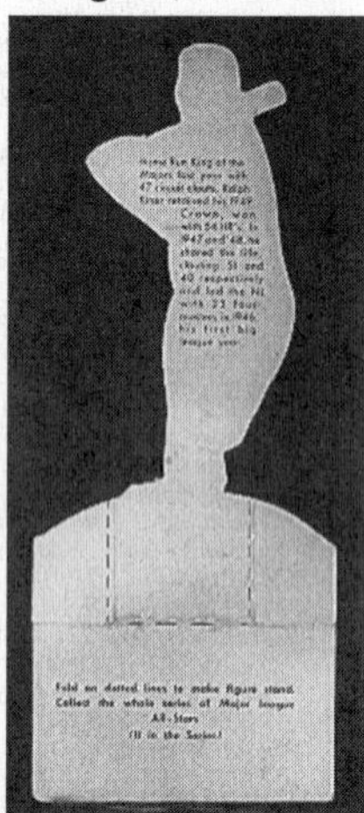

The Topps Major League All-Stars are very similar to the Connie Mack All-Stars of the same year. The 2-1/16" x 5-1/4" cards have a black-and-white photograph on a red die-cut background. Most of the background could be folded over so that the card would stand up. A plaque at the base carries brief biographical information. The set was to contain 11 cards, but only eight were actually issued in gum packs. Those of Konstanty, Roberts and Stanky were not issued and are very rare, with only a handful of each known. A big problem with the set is that if the card was used as it was intended it was folded and, thus, damaged from a collector's viewpoint. That makes top quality examples of any players difficult to find and quite expensive.

		NM	EX	VG
Complete Set (11):		14,000	7,000	4,200
Common Player:		1,025	510.00	305.00
(1)	Yogi Berra	3,000	1,500	900.00
(2)	Larry Doby	1,900	950.00	575.00

(3)	Walt Dropo	900.00	450.00	270.00
(4)	"Hoot" Evers	900.00	450.00	270.00
(5)	George Clyde Kell	1,600	800.00	480.00
(6)	Ralph Kiner	1,600	800.00	480.00
(7)	Jim Konstanty	30,000	15,000	9,000
(8)	Bob Lemon	1,600	800.00	480.00
(9)	Phil Rizzuto	2,750	1,375	825.00
(10)	Robin Roberts	35,000	17,500	10,500
(11)	Ed Stanky	30,000	15,000	9,000

1951 Topps Teams

An innovative issue for 1951, the Topps team cards were a nine-card set, 5-1/4" x 2-1/16", which carry a black-and-white picture of a major league team surrounded by a yellow border on the front. The back identifies team members with red printing on white cardboard. There are two versions of each card, with and without the date "1950" in the banner that carries the team name. Undated versions are valued slightly higher than the cards with dates. Strangely only nine teams were issued. Scarcity varies, with the Cardinals and Red Sox being the most difficult to obtain.

		NM	EX	VG
(1a)	Boston Red Sox/1950	475.00	235.00	140.00
(1b)	Boston Red Sox (Undated)	500.00	250.00	150.00
(2a)	Brooklyn Dodgers/1950	375.00	185.00	110.00
(2b)	Brooklyn Dodgers (Undated)	400.00	200.00	120.00
(3a)	Chicago White Sox/1950	275.00	135.00	80.00
(3b)	Chicago White Sox (Undated)	250.00	125.00	75.00
(4a)	Cincinnati Reds/1950	300.00	150.00	90.00
(4b)	Cincinnati Reds (Undated)	325.00	160.00	95.00
(5a)	New York Giants/1950	300.00	150.00	90.00
(5b)	New York Giants (Undated)	325.00	160.00	95.00
(6a)	Philadelphia Athletics/1950	225.00	110.00	65.00
(6b)	Philadelphia Athletics (Undated)	250.00	125.00	75.00
(7a)	Philadelphia Phillies/1950	225.00	110.00	65.00
(7b)	Philadelphia Phillies (Undated)	400.00	200.00	120.00
(8a)	St. Louis Cardinals/1950	400.00	200.00	120.00
(8b)	St. Louis Cardinals (Undated)	425.00	210.00	125.00
(9a)	Washington Senators/1950	250.00	125.00	75.00
(9b)	Washington Senators (Undated)	300.00	150.00	90.00

1952 Topps

At 407 cards, the 1952 Topps set was the largest set of its day, both in number of cards and physical dimensions of the cards. Cards are 2-5/8" x 3-3/4" with a colorized black-and-white photo on front. Major baseball card innovations presented in the set include the first-ever use of color team logos as part of the design, and the inclusion of stats for the previous season and career on the backs. The first 80 cards in the set can be found with backs printed entirely in black or black and red. While "Black Backs" used to command a significant premium over the "Red Back" version, that differential has diminished in recent years to the point of insignificance. Several cards in the #1-80 range can be found with noticeable color differences on front depending on whether they are Red Back or Black Back. Cards #311-407, known as the "high numbers," were distributed in limited areas and are extremely rare.

	NM	EX	VG
Complete Set (407):	90,000	42,500	24,000
Common Player (1-250):	45.00	22.50	13.50
Common Player (251-310):	60.00	30.00	18.00
Common Player (311-407):	275.00	135.00	80.00

1	Andy Pafko	3,500	375.00	190.00
2	***James E. Runnels***	400.00	40.00	20.00
3	Hank Thompson	45.00	22.50	13.50
4	Don Lenhardt	45.00	22.50	13.50
5	Larry Jansen	45.00	22.50	13.50
6	Grady Hatton	45.00	22.50	13.50
7	Wayne Terwilliger	55.00	27.50	16.50
8	Fred Marsh	45.00	22.50	13.50
9	Bobby Hogue	55.00	27.50	16.50
10	Al Rosen	160.00	80.00	45.00
11	Phil Rizzuto	375.00	185.00	110.00
12	Monty Basgall	45.00	22.50	13.50
13	Johnny Wyrostek	45.00	22.50	13.50
14	Bob Elliott	45.00	22.50	13.50
15	Johnny Pesky	45.00	22.50	13.50
16	Gene Hermanski	45.00	22.50	13.50
17	Jim Hegan	45.00	22.50	13.50
18	Merrill Combs	45.00	22.50	13.50
19	Johnny Bucha	45.00	22.50	13.50
20	***Billy Loes***	225.00	110.00	65.00
21	Ferris Fain	60.00	30.00	18.00
22	Dom DiMaggio	145.00	75.00	45.00
23	Billy Goodman	45.00	22.50	13.50
24	Luke Easter	60.00	30.00	18.00
25	Johnny Groth	45.00	22.50	13.50
26	Monty Irvin	125.00	65.00	35.00
27	Sam Jethroe	45.00	22.50	13.50
28	Jerry Priddy	45.00	22.50	13.50
29	Ted Kluszewski	225.00	110.00	65.00
30	Mel Parnell	45.00	22.50	13.50
31	Gus Zernial	125.00	65.00	35.00
32	Eddie Robinson	45.00	22.50	13.50
33	Warren Spahn	225.00	110.00	65.00
34	Elmer Valo	45.00	22.50	13.50
35	Hank Sauer	45.00	22.50	13.50
36	Gil Hodges	225.00	110.00	65.00
37	Duke Snider	350.00	175.00	100.00
38	Wally Westlake	45.00	22.50	13.50
39	"Dizzy" Trout	45.00	22.50	13.50
40	Irv Noren	45.00	22.50	13.50
41	Bob Wellman	45.00	22.50	13.50
42	Lou Kretlow	45.00	22.50	13.50
43	Ray Scarborough	45.00	22.50	13.50
44	Con Dempsey	45.00	22.50	13.50
45	Eddie Joost	45.00	22.50	13.50
46	Gordon Goldsberry	45.00	22.50	13.50
47	Willie Jones	45.00	22.50	13.50
48a	Joe Page (Wrong (Sain) back.)	850.00	425.00	255.00
48b	Joe Page (Correct back.)	165.00	80.00	50.00
49a	Johnny Sain (Wrong (Page) back.)	900.00	450.00	275.00
49b	Johnny Sain (Correct back.)	175.00	85.00	50.00
50	Marv Rickert	45.00	22.50	13.50
51	Jim Russell	55.00	27.50	16.50
52	Don Mueller	45.00	22.50	13.50
53	Chris Van Cuyk	55.00	27.50	16.50
54	Leo Kiely	45.00	22.50	13.50
55	Ray Boone	45.00	22.50	13.50
56	Tommy Glaviano	45.00	22.50	13.50
57	Ed Lopat	90.00	45.00	25.00
58	Bob Mahoney	45.00	22.50	13.50
59	Robin Roberts	200.00	100.00	60.00
60	Sid Hudson	45.00	22.50	13.50
61	"Tookie" Gilbert	45.00	22.50	13.50
62	Chuck Stobbs	45.00	22.50	13.50
63	Howie Pollet	45.00	22.50	13.50
64	Roy Sievers	45.00	22.50	13.50
65	Enos Slaughter	130.00	65.00	40.00
66	"Preacher" Roe	115.00	55.00	35.00
67	Allie Reynolds	120.00	60.00	35.00
68	Cliff Chambers	45.00	22.50	13.50
69	Virgil Stallcup	45.00	22.50	13.50
70	Al Zarilla	45.00	22.50	13.50
71	Tom Upton	45.00	22.50	13.50
72	Karl Olson	45.00	22.50	13.50
73	William Werle	45.00	22.50	13.50
74	Andy Hansen	45.00	22.50	13.50
75	Wes Westrum	45.00	22.50	13.50
76	Eddie Stanky	45.00	22.50	13.50
77	Bob Kennedy	45.00	22.50	13.50
78	Ellis Kinder	45.00	22.50	13.50
79	Gerald Staley	45.00	22.50	13.50
80	Herman Wehmeier	45.00	22.50	13.50
81	Vernon Law	45.00	22.50	13.50
82	Duane Pillette	45.00	22.50	13.50
83	Billy Johnson	45.00	22.50	13.50
84	Vern Stephens	45.00	22.50	13.50
85	Bob Kuzava	55.00	27.50	16.50
86	Ted Gray	45.00	22.50	13.50
87	Dale Coogan	45.00	22.50	13.50
88	Bob Feller	190.00	95.00	60.00
89	Johnny Lipon	45.00	22.50	13.50
90	Mickey Grasso	45.00	22.50	13.50
91	Al Schoendienst	135.00	65.00	40.00
92	Dale Mitchell	45.00	22.50	13.50
93	Al Sima	45.00	22.50	13.50
94	Sam Mele	45.00	22.50	13.50
95	Ken Holcombe	45.00	22.50	13.50
96	Willard Marshall	45.00	22.50	13.50
97	Earl Torgeson	45.00	22.50	13.50
98	Bill Pierce	55.00	27.50	16.50
99	Gene Woodling	80.00	40.00	24.00
100	Del Rice	45.00	22.50	13.50
101	Max Lanier	45.00	22.50	13.50
102	Bill Kennedy	45.00	22.50	13.50
103	Cliff Mapes	45.00	22.50	13.50
104	Don Kolloway	45.00	22.50	13.50
105	John Pramesa	45.00	22.50	13.50
106	Mickey Vernon	45.00	22.50	13.50
107	Connie Ryan	45.00	22.50	13.50
108	Jim Konstanty	45.00	22.50	13.50
109	Ted Wilks	45.00	22.50	13.50
110	Dutch Leonard	45.00	22.50	13.50
111	Harry Lowrey	45.00	22.50	13.50
112	Henry Majeski	45.00	22.50	13.50
113	Dick Sisler	45.00	22.50	13.50
114	Willard Ramsdell	45.00	22.50	13.50
115	George Munger	45.00	22.50	13.50
116	Carl Scheib	45.00	22.50	13.50
117	Sherman Lollar	45.00	22.50	13.50
118	Ken Raffensberger	45.00	22.50	13.50
119	Maurice McDermott	45.00	22.50	13.50
120	Bob Chakales	45.00	22.50	13.50
121	Gus Niarhos	45.00	22.50	13.50
122	Jack Jensen	100.00	50.00	30.00
123	Eddie Yost	45.00	22.50	13.50
124	Monte Kennedy	45.00	22.50	13.50
125	Bill Rigney	45.00	22.50	13.50
126	Fred Hutchinson	45.00	22.50	13.50
127	Paul Minner	45.00	22.50	13.50
128	Don Bollweg	55.00	27.50	16.50
129	Johnny Mize	200.00	100.00	60.00
130	Sheldon Jones	45.00	22.50	13.50
131	Morrie Martin	45.00	22.50	13.50
132	Clyde Kluttz	45.00	22.50	13.50
133	Al Widmar	45.00	22.50	13.50
134	Joe Tipton	45.00	22.50	13.50
135	Dixie Howell	45.00	22.50	13.50
136	Johnny Schmitz	45.00	22.50	13.50
137	***Roy McMillan***	50.00	25.00	15.00
138	Bill MacDonald	45.00	22.50	13.50
139	Ken Wood	45.00	22.50	13.50
140	John Antonelli	45.00	22.50	13.50
141	Clint Hartung	45.00	22.50	13.50
142	Harry Perkowski	45.00	22.50	13.50
143	Les Moss	45.00	22.50	13.50
144	Ed Blake	45.00	22.50	13.50
145	Joe Haynes	45.00	22.50	13.50
146	Frank House	45.00	22.50	13.50
147	Bob Young	45.00	22.50	13.50
148	Johnny Klippstein	45.00	22.50	13.50
149	Dick Kryhoski	45.00	22.50	13.50
150	Ted Beard	45.00	22.50	13.50
151	***Wally Post***	55.00	27.50	16.50
152	Al Evans	45.00	22.50	13.50
153	Bob Rush	45.00	22.50	13.50
154	Joe Muir	45.00	22.50	13.50
155	Frank Overmire	55.00	27.50	16.50
156	Frank Hiller	45.00	22.50	13.50
157	Bob Usher	45.00	22.50	13.50
158	Eddie Waitkus	45.00	22.50	13.50
159	Saul Rogovin	45.00	22.50	13.50
160	Owen Friend	45.00	22.50	13.50
161	Bud Byerly	45.00	22.50	13.50
162	Del Crandall	45.00	22.50	13.50
163	Stan Rojek	45.00	22.50	13.50
164	Walt Dubiel	45.00	22.50	13.50
165	Eddie Kazak	45.00	22.50	13.50
166	Paul LaPalme	45.00	22.50	13.50
167	Bill Howerton	45.00	22.50	13.50
168	***Charlie Silvera***	75.00	37.50	22.50
169	Howie Judson	45.00	22.50	13.50
170	Gus Bell	65.00	32.50	20.00
171	Ed Erautt	45.00	22.50	13.50
172	Eddie Miksis	45.00	22.50	13.50
173	Roy Smalley	45.00	22.50	13.50
174	Clarence Marshall	45.00	22.50	13.50
175	***Billy Martin***	375.00	185.00	110.00
176	Hank Edwards	45.00	22.50	13.50
177	Bill Wight	45.00	22.50	13.50
178	Cass Michaels	45.00	22.50	13.50
179	Frank Smith	45.00	22.50	13.50
180	***Charley Maxwell***	60.00	30.00	18.00
181	Bob Swift	45.00	22.50	13.50
182	Billy Hitchcock	45.00	22.50	13.50
183	Erv Dusak	45.00	22.50	13.50
184	Bob Ramazzotti	45.00	22.50	13.50
185	Bill Nicholson	45.00	22.50	13.50
186	Walt Masterson	45.00	22.50	13.50
187	Bob Miller	45.00	22.50	13.50
188	Clarence Podbielan	45.00	22.50	13.50
189	Pete Reiser	45.00	22.50	13.50
190	Don Johnson	45.00	22.50	13.50
191	Yogi Berra	750.00	375.00	225.00
192	Myron Ginsberg	45.00	22.50	13.50
193	Harry Simpson	45.00	22.50	13.50
194	Joe Hatten	45.00	22.50	13.50
195	***Orestes Minoso***	135.00	65.00	40.00
196	Solly Hemus	45.00	22.50	13.50
197	George Strickland	45.00	22.50	13.50
198	Phil Haugstad	50.00	25.00	15.00
199	George Zuverink	45.00	22.50	13.50
200	Ralph Houk	100.00	50.00	30.00
201	Alex Kellner	45.00	22.50	13.50
202	Joe Collins	60.00	30.00	18.00
203	Curt Simmons	45.00	22.50	13.50
204	Ron Northey	45.00	22.50	13.50
205	Clyde King	45.00	22.50	13.50
206	Joe Ostrowski	55.00	27.50	16.50
207	Mickey Harris	45.00	22.50	13.50
208	Marlin Stuart	45.00	22.50	13.50
209	Howie Fox	45.00	22.50	13.50
210	Dick Fowler	45.00	22.50	13.50
211	Ray Coleman	45.00	22.50	13.50
212	Ned Garver	45.00	22.50	13.50
213	Nippy Jones	45.00	22.50	13.50
214	Johnny Hopp	55.00	27.50	16.50
215	Hank Bauer	95.00	45.00	25.00
216	Richie Ashburn	185.00	90.00	55.00
217	George Stirnweiss	45.00	22.50	13.50
218	Clyde McCullough	45.00	22.50	13.50
219	Bobby Shantz	55.00	27.50	16.50
220	Joe Presko	45.00	22.50	13.50
221	Granny Hamner	45.00	22.50	13.50
222	"Hoot" Evers	45.00	22.50	13.50
223	Del Ennis	45.00	22.50	13.50
224	Bruce Edwards	45.00	22.50	13.50
225	Frank Baumholtz	45.00	22.50	13.50
226	Dave Philley	45.00	22.50	13.50
227	Joe Garagiola	110.00	55.00	35.00
228	Al Brazle	45.00	22.50	13.50
229	Gene Bearden	45.00	22.50	13.50
230	Matt Batts	45.00	22.50	13.50
231	Sam Zoldak	45.00	22.50	13.50
232	Billy Cox	90.00	45.00	25.00
233	***Bob Friend***	75.00	37.50	22.50

#	Player	NM	EX	VG
234	Steve Souchock	45.00	22.50	13.50
235	Walt Dropo	45.00	22.50	13.50
236	Ed Fitz Gerald	45.00	22.50	13.50
237	Jerry Coleman	60.00	30.00	18.00
238	Art Houtteman	45.00	22.50	13.50
239	***Rocky Bridges***	45.00	22.50	13.50
240	Jack Phillips	45.00	22.50	13.50
241	Tommy Byrne	45.00	22.50	13.50
242	Tom Poholsky	45.00	22.50	13.50
243	Larry Doby	150.00	75.00	45.00
244	Vic Wertz	45.00	22.50	13.50
245	Sherry Robertson	45.00	22.50	13.50
246	George Kell	110.00	55.00	35.00
247	Randy Gumpert	45.00	22.50	13.50
248	Frank Shea	45.00	22.50	13.50
249	Bobby Adams	45.00	22.50	13.50
250	Carl Erskine	120.00	60.00	35.00
251	Chico Carrasquel	95.00	47.50	27.50
252	Vern Bickford	60.00	30.00	18.00
253	Johnny Berardino	75.00	37.50	22.50
254	Joe Dobson	60.00	30.00	18.00
255	Clyde Vollmer	60.00	30.00	18.00
256	Pete Suder	60.00	30.00	18.00
257	Bobby Avila	60.00	30.00	18.00
258	Steve Gromek	60.00	30.00	18.00
259	Bob Addis	60.00	30.00	18.00
260	Pete Castiglione	60.00	30.00	18.00
261	Willie Mays	1,750	750.00	375.00
262	Virgil Trucks	60.00	30.00	18.00
263	Harry Brecheen	60.00	30.00	18.00
264	Roy Hartsfield	60.00	30.00	18.00
265	Chuck Diering	60.00	30.00	18.00
266	Murry Dickson	60.00	30.00	18.00
267	Sid Gordon	60.00	30.00	18.00
268	Bob Lemon	135.00	65.00	40.00
269	Willard Nixon	60.00	30.00	18.00
270	Lou Brissie	60.00	30.00	18.00
271	Jim Delsing	60.00	30.00	18.00
272	Mike Garcia	60.00	30.00	18.00
273	Erv Palica	70.00	35.00	20.00
274	Ralph Branca	160.00	80.00	45.00
275	Pat Mullin	60.00	30.00	18.00
276	Jim Wilson	60.00	30.00	18.00
277	Early Wynn	175.00	85.00	50.00
278	Al Clark	60.00	30.00	18.00
279	Ed Stewart	60.00	30.00	18.00
280	Cloyd Boyer	60.00	30.00	18.00
281	Tommy Brown	60.00	30.00	18.00
282	Birdie Tebbetts	60.00	30.00	18.00
283	Phil Masi	60.00	30.00	18.00
284	Hank Arft	60.00	30.00	18.00
285	Cliff Fannin	60.00	30.00	18.00
286	Joe De Maestri	60.00	30.00	18.00
287	Steve Bilko	60.00	30.00	18.00
288	Chet Nichols	60.00	30.00	18.00
289	Tommy Holmes	60.00	30.00	18.00
290	Joe Astroth	60.00	30.00	18.00
291	Gil Coan	60.00	30.00	18.00
292	Floyd Baker	60.00	30.00	18.00
293	Sibby Sisti	60.00	30.00	18.00
294	Walker Cooper	60.00	30.00	18.00
295	Phil Cavarretta	60.00	30.00	18.00
296	"Red" Rolfe	60.00	30.00	18.00
297	Andy Seminick	60.00	30.00	18.00
298	Bob Ross	60.00	30.00	18.00
299	Ray Murray	60.00	30.00	18.00
300	Barney McCosky	60.00	30.00	18.00
301	Bob Porterfield	60.00	30.00	18.00
302	Max Surkont	60.00	30.00	18.00
303	Harry Dorish	60.00	30.00	18.00
304	Sam Dente	60.00	30.00	18.00
305	Paul Richards	60.00	30.00	18.00
306	Lou Sleator	60.00	30.00	18.00
307a	Frank Campos (Black star on back to right of "TOPPS BASEBALL.") (Graded "Good" example auctioned 4/06 for $4,640.)			
307b	Frank Campos (Red star on back to right of "TOPPS BASEBALL.")	60.00	30.00	18.00
308	Luis Aloma	60.00	30.00	18.00
309	Jim Busby	60.00	30.00	18.00
310	George Metkovich	125.00	30.00	18.00
311	Mickey Mantle/DP	27,500	13,750	8,000
312	Jackie Robinson/DP	1,700	895.00	350.00
313	Bobby Thomson/DP	275.00	135.00	80.00
314	Roy Campanella	1,350	675.00	400.00
315	Leo Durocher	475.00	235.00	140.00
316	Davey Williams	275.00	135.00	80.00
317	Connie Marrero	275.00	135.00	80.00
318	Hal Gregg	275.00	135.00	80.00
319	Al Walker	300.00	150.00	90.00
320	John Rutherford	300.00	150.00	90.00
321	***Joe Black***	600.00	300.00	180.00
322	Randy Jackson	275.00	135.00	80.00
323	Bubba Church	275.00	135.00	80.00
324	Warren Hacker	275.00	135.00	80.00
325	Bill Serena	275.00	135.00	80.00
326	George Shuba	325.00	160.00	95.00
327	Archie Wilson	275.00	135.00	80.00
328	Bob Borkowski	275.00	135.00	80.00
329	Ivan Delock	275.00	135.00	80.00
330	Turk Lown	275.00	135.00	80.00
331	Tom Morgan	275.00	135.00	80.00
332	Tony Bartirome	275.00	135.00	80.00
333	Pee Wee Reese	1,200	600.00	360.00
334	Wilmer Mizell	275.00	135.00	80.00
335	Ted Lepcio	275.00	135.00	80.00
336	Dave Koslo	275.00	135.00	80.00
337	Jim Hearn	275.00	135.00	80.00
338	Sal Yvars	275.00	135.00	80.00
339	Russ Meyer	275.00	135.00	80.00
340	Bob Hooper	275.00	135.00	80.00
341	Hal Jeffcoat	275.00	135.00	80.00
342	***Clem Labine***	750.00	375.00	225.00
343	Dick Gernert	275.00	135.00	80.00
344	Ewell Blackwell	275.00	135.00	80.00
345	Sam White	275.00	135.00	80.00
346	George Spencer	275.00	135.00	80.00
347	Joe Adcock	350.00	175.00	100.00
348	Bob Kelly	275.00	135.00	80.00
349	Bob Cain	275.00	135.00	80.00
350	Cal Abrams	275.00	135.00	80.00
351	Al Dark	300.00	150.00	90.00
352	Karl Drews	275.00	135.00	80.00
353	Bob Del Greco	275.00	135.00	80.00
354	Fred Hatfield	275.00	135.00	80.00
355	Bobby Morgan	300.00	150.00	90.00
356	Toby Atwell	275.00	135.00	80.00
357	Smoky Burgess	350.00	175.00	100.00
358	John Kucab	275.00	135.00	80.00
359	Dee Fondy	275.00	135.00	80.00
360	George Crowe	275.00	135.00	80.00
361	Bill Posedel	275.00	135.00	80.00
362	Ken Heintzelman	275.00	135.00	80.00
363	Dick Rozek	275.00	135.00	80.00
364	Clyde Sukeforth	275.00	135.00	80.00
365	"Cookie" Lavagetto	275.00	135.00	80.00
366	Dave Madison	275.00	135.00	80.00
367	Bob Thorpe	275.00	135.00	80.00
368	Ed Wright	275.00	135.00	80.00
369	***Dick Groat***	400.00	200.00	120.00
370	Billy Hoeft	275.00	135.00	80.00
371	Bob Hofman	275.00	135.00	80.00
372	***Gil McDougald***	500.00	250.00	150.00
373	Jim Turner	300.00	150.00	90.00
374	Al Benton	275.00	135.00	80.00
375	Jack Merson	275.00	135.00	80.00
376	Faye Throneberry	275.00	135.00	80.00
377	Chuck Dressen	275.00	135.00	80.00
378	Les Fusselman	275.00	135.00	80.00
379	Joe Rossi	275.00	135.00	80.00
380	Clem Koshorek	275.00	135.00	80.00
381	Milton Stock	275.00	135.00	80.00
382	Sam Jones	275.00	135.00	80.00
383	Del Wilber	275.00	135.00	80.00
384	Frank Crosetti	400.00	200.00	120.00
385	Herman Franks	275.00	135.00	80.00
386	Eddie Yuhas	275.00	135.00	80.00
387	Billy Meyer	275.00	135.00	80.00
388	Bob Chipman	275.00	135.00	80.00
389	Ben Wade	300.00	150.00	90.00
390	Glenn Nelson	300.00	150.00	90.00
391	Ben Chapman (Photo actually Sam Chapman.)	275.00	135.00	80.00
392	***Hoyt Wilhelm***	750.00	375.00	225.00
393	Ebba St. Claire	275.00	135.00	80.00
394	Billy Herman	400.00	200.00	120.00
395	Jake Pitler	300.00	150.00	90.00
396	***Dick Williams***	400.00	200.00	120.00
397	Forrest Main	275.00	135.00	80.00
398	Hal Rice	275.00	135.00	80.00
399	Jim Fridley	275.00	135.00	80.00
400	Bill Dickey	800.00	400.00	240.00
401	Bob Schultz	275.00	135.00	80.00
402	Earl Harrist	275.00	135.00	80.00
403	Bill Miller	300.00	150.00	90.00
404	Dick Brodowski	275.00	135.00	80.00
405	Eddie Pellagrini	275.00	135.00	80.00
406	***Joe Nuxhall***	600.00	300.00	180.00
407	***Eddie Mathews***	10,000	3,600	1,525

1952 Topps "Canadian"

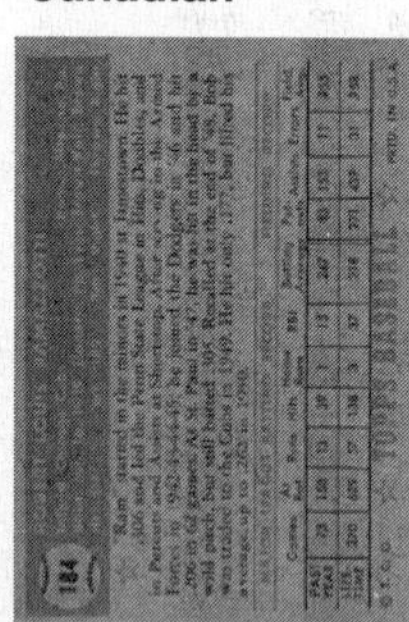

Perhaps because the "gray back" 1954 Topps cards have long been known as the "Canadian" issue, there is growing hobby support for the belief that a similar abbreviated set was printed in Canada for distribution there. The cards differ from the regular 1952 Topps of the same numerical range in that they are printed on a gray-backed cardboard stock, distinctly different from the cream-colored stock found on most '52 Topps #131-190. Additionally, the fronts of most, but not all, of the "Canadian" cards have colors which are subjectively darker or more muted than the the "U.S.A." versions. The market is just beginning to differentiate values between the two types, though the gray-backs are considered scarcer.

		NM	EX	VG
Complete Set (60):		5,000	2,500	1,500
Common Player:		80.00	40.00	24.00
131	Morrie Martin	80.00	40.00	24.00
132	Clyde Kluttz	80.00	40.00	24.00
133	Al Widmar	80.00	40.00	24.00
134	Joe Tipton	80.00	40.00	24.00
135	Dixie Howell	80.00	40.00	24.00
136	Johnny Schmitz	85.00	42.50	25.00
137	Roy McMillan	80.00	40.00	24.00
138	Bill MacDonald	80.00	40.00	24.00
139	Ken Wood	80.00	40.00	24.00
140	John Antonelli	80.00	40.00	24.00
141	Clint Hartung	80.00	40.00	24.00
142	Harry Perkowski	80.00	40.00	24.00
143	Les Moss	80.00	40.00	24.00
144	Ed Blake	80.00	40.00	24.00
145	Joe Haynes	80.00	40.00	24.00
146	Frank House	80.00	40.00	24.00
147	Bob Young	80.00	40.00	24.00
148	Johnny Klippstein	80.00	40.00	24.00
149	Dick Kryhoski	80.00	40.00	24.00
150	Ted Beard	80.00	40.00	24.00
151	Wally Post	80.00	40.00	24.00
152	Al Evans	80.00	40.00	24.00
153	Bob Rush	80.00	40.00	24.00
154	Joe Muir	80.00	40.00	24.00
155	Frank Overmire	85.00	42.50	25.00
156	Frank Hiller	80.00	40.00	24.00
157	Bob Usher	80.00	40.00	24.00
158	Eddie Waitkus	80.00	40.00	24.00
159	Saul Rogovin	80.00	40.00	24.00
160	Owen Friend	80.00	40.00	24.00
161	Bud Byerly	80.00	40.00	24.00
162	Del Crandall	80.00	40.00	24.00
163	Stan Rojek	80.00	40.00	24.00
164	Walt Dubiel	80.00	40.00	24.00
165	Eddie Kazak	80.00	40.00	24.00
166	Paul LaPalme	80.00	40.00	24.00
167	Bill Howerton	80.00	40.00	24.00
168	Charlie Silvera	100.00	50.00	30.00
169	Howie Judson	80.00	40.00	24.00
170	Gus Bell	100.00	50.00	30.00
171	Ed Erautt	80.00	40.00	24.00
172	Eddie Miksis	80.00	40.00	24.00
173	Roy Smalley	80.00	40.00	24.00
174	Clarence Marshall	80.00	40.00	24.00
175	Billy Martin	500.00	250.00	150.00
176	Hank Edwards	80.00	40.00	24.00
177	Bill Wight	80.00	40.00	24.00
178	Cass Michaels	80.00	40.00	24.00
179	Frank Smith	80.00	40.00	24.00
180	Charley Maxwell	80.00	40.00	24.00
181	Bob Swift	80.00	40.00	24.00
182	Billy Hitchcock	80.00	40.00	24.00
183	Erv Dusak	80.00	40.00	24.00
184	Bob Ramazzotti	80.00	40.00	24.00
185	Bill Nicholson	80.00	40.00	24.00
186	Walt Masterson	80.00	40.00	24.00
187	Bob Miller	80.00	40.00	24.00
188	Clarence Podbielan	80.00	40.00	24.00
189	Pete Reiser	80.00	40.00	24.00
190	Don Johnson	80.00	40.00	24.00

1953 Topps

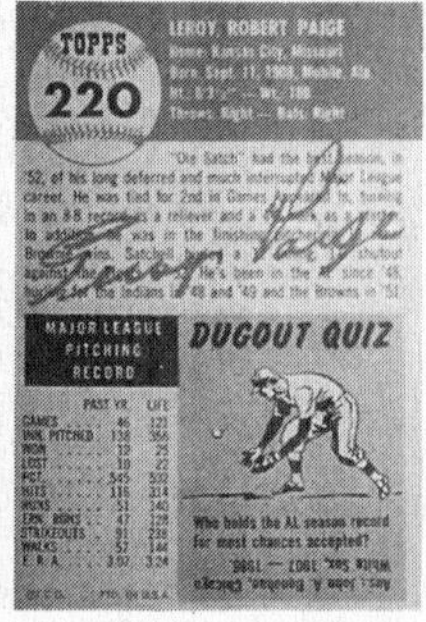

The 1953 Topps set reflects the company's continuing legal battles with Bowman. The set, originally intended to consist of 280 cards, is lacking six numbers (253, 261, 267, 268, 271 and 275) that represent players whose contracts were lost to the competition. The 2-5/8" x 3-3/4" cards feature painted player pictures. A color team logo appears at a bottom panel (red for American League and black for National). Card backs contain the first baseball-card trivia questions along with brief statistics and player biographies. In the red panel at the top, which lists the player's personal data, cards from the 2nd Series (#86-165 plus 10, 44, 61, 72 and 81) can be found with that data printed in either black or white, black being the marginally scarcer variety. Eighty-five cards between #1-165 were printed in noticeably larger quantities than the others, and are indicated in these listings with a double-print (DP) notation. Cards #221-280, the high numbers, were printed late in the season, in smaller quantities than the earlier series. Among the high numbers, even scarcer short-printed (SP) cards are interspersed in the series.

		NM	EX	VG
Complete Set (274):		20,000	9,250	5,250
Common Player (1-165):		30.00	15.00	9.00
Common Player (166-220):		35.00	17.50	10.00
Common Player (221-280):		60.00	30.00	18.00
Short-print Player (221-280):		90.00	45.00	27.50
1	Jackie Robinson/DP	900.00	200.00	100.00
2	Luke Easter/DP	40.00	20.00	12.00
3	George Crowe	40.00	20.00	12.00
4	Ben Wade	45.00	22.50	13.50
5	Joe Dobson	40.00	20.00	12.00
6	Sam Jones	40.00	20.00	12.00
7	Bob Borkowski/DP	30.00	15.00	9.00
8	Clem Koshorek/DP	30.00	15.00	9.00
9	Joe Collins	45.00	22.50	13.50
10	Smoky Burgess/SP	70.00	35.00	20.00
11	Sal Yvars	40.00	20.00	12.00
12	Howie Judson/DP	30.00	15.00	9.00
13	Connie Marrero/DP	30.00	15.00	9.00
14	Clem Labine/DP	60.00	30.00	18.00
15	Bobo Newsom/DP	30.00	15.00	9.00
16	Harry Lowrey/DP	30.00	15.00	9.00
17	Billy Hitchcock	40.00	20.00	12.00
18	Ted Lepcio/DP	30.00	15.00	9.00

#	Player	NM	EX	VG
19	Mel Parnell/DP	30.00	15.00	9.00
20	Hank Thompson	40.00	20.00	12.00
21	Billy Johnson	40.00	20.00	12.00
22	Howie Fox	40.00	20.00	12.00
23	Toby Atwell/DP	30.00	15.00	9.00
24	Ferris Fain	40.00	20.00	12.00
25	Ray Boone	40.00	20.00	12.00
26	Dale Mitchell/DP	30.00	15.00	9.00
27	Roy Campanella/DP	180.00	90.00	55.00
28	Eddie Pellagrini	40.00	20.00	12.00
29	Hal Jeffcoat	40.00	20.00	12.00
30	Willard Nixon	40.00	20.00	12.00
31	Ewell Blackwell	55.00	27.50	16.50
32	Clyde Vollmer	40.00	20.00	12.00
33	Bob Kennedy/DP	30.00	15.00	9.00
34	George Shuba	60.00	30.00	18.00
35	Irv Noren/DP	35.00	17.50	10.00
36	Johnny Groth/DP	30.00	15.00	9.00
37	Ed Mathews/DP	135.00	65.00	40.00
38	Jim Hearn/DP	30.00	15.00	9.00
39	Eddie Miksis	40.00	20.00	12.00
40	John Lipon	40.00	20.00	12.00
41	Enos Slaughter	80.00	40.00	24.00
42	Gus Zernial/DP	30.00	15.00	9.00
43	Gil McDougald	75.00	37.50	22.50
44	Ellis Kinder/SP	75.00	37.50	22.50
45	Grady Hatton/DP	30.00	15.00	9.00
46	Johnny Klippstein/DP	30.00	15.00	9.00
47	Bubba Church/DP	30.00	15.00	9.00
48	Bob Del Greco/DP	30.00	15.00	9.00
49	Faye Throneberry/DP	30.00	15.00	9.00
50	Chuck Dressen/DP	40.00	20.00	12.00
51	Frank Campos/DP	30.00	15.00	9.00
52	Ted Gray/DP	30.00	15.00	9.00
53	Sherman Lollar/DP	30.00	15.00	9.00
54	Bob Feller/DP	160.00	80.00	50.00
55	Maurice McDermott/DP	30.00	15.00	9.00
56	Gerald Staley/DP	30.00	15.00	9.00
57	Carl Scheib	40.00	20.00	12.00
58	George Metkovich	40.00	20.00	12.00
59	Karl Drews/DP	30.00	15.00	9.00
60	Cloyd Boyer/DP	30.00	15.00	9.00
61	Early Wynn/SP	90.00	45.00	27.50
62	Monte Irvin/DP	100.00	50.00	30.00
63	Gus Niarhos/DP	30.00	15.00	9.00
64	Dave Philley	40.00	20.00	12.00
65	Earl Harrist	40.00	20.00	12.00
66	Orestes Minoso	70.00	35.00	20.00
67	Roy Sievers/DP	30.00	15.00	9.00
68	Del Rice	40.00	20.00	12.00
69	Dick Brodowski	40.00	20.00	12.00
70	Ed Yuhas	40.00	20.00	12.00
71	Tony Bartirome	40.00	20.00	12.00
72	Fred Hutchinson/SP	75.00	37.50	22.50
73	Eddie Robinson	40.00	20.00	12.00
74	Joe Rossi	40.00	20.00	12.00
75	Mike Garcia	40.00	20.00	12.00
76	Pee Wee Reese	180.00	90.00	55.00
77	Johnny Mize/DP	75.00	37.50	22.50
78	Al Schoendienst	100.00	50.00	30.00
79	Johnny Wyrostek	40.00	20.00	12.00
80	Jim Hegan	40.00	20.00	12.00
81	Joe Black/SP	120.00	60.00	35.00
82	Mickey Mantle	2,600	1,000	475.00
83	Howie Pollet	40.00	20.00	12.00
84	Bob Hooper/DP	30.00	15.00	9.00
85	Bobby Morgan/DP	35.00	17.50	10.00
86	Billy Martin	140.00	70.00	40.00
87	Ed Lopat	60.00	30.00	18.00
88	Willie Jones/DP	30.00	15.00	9.00
89	Chuck Stobbs/DP	30.00	15.00	9.00
90	Hank Edwards/DP	30.00	15.00	9.00
91	Ebba St. Claire/DP	30.00	15.00	9.00
92	Paul Minner/DP	30.00	15.00	9.00
93	Hal Rice/DP	30.00	15.00	9.00
94	William Kennedy/DP	30.00	15.00	9.00
95	Willard Marshall/DP	30.00	15.00	9.00
96	Virgil Trucks	40.00	20.00	12.00
97	Don Kolloway/DP	30.00	15.00	9.00
98	Cal Abrams/DP	30.00	15.00	9.00
99	Dave Madison	40.00	20.00	12.00
100	Bill Miller	40.00	20.00	12.00
101	Ted Wilks	40.00	20.00	12.00
102	Connie Ryan/DP	30.00	15.00	9.00
103	Joe Astroth/DP	30.00	15.00	9.00
104	Yogi Berra	260.00	130.00	75.00
105	Joe Nuxhall/DP	35.00	17.50	10.00
106	John Antonelli	40.00	20.00	12.00
107	Danny O'Connell/DP	30.00	15.00	9.00
108	Bob Porterfield/DP	30.00	15.00	9.00
109	Alvin Dark	40.00	20.00	12.00
110	Herman Wehmeier/DP	30.00	15.00	9.00
111	Hank Sauer/DP	30.00	15.00	9.00
112	Ned Garver/DP	30.00	15.00	9.00
113	Jerry Priddy	40.00	20.00	12.00
114	Phil Rizzuto	160.00	80.00	45.00
115	George Spencer	40.00	20.00	12.00
116	Frank Smith/DP	30.00	15.00	9.00
117	Sid Gordon/DP	30.00	15.00	9.00
118	Gus Bell/DP	30.00	15.00	9.00
119	John Sain	75.00	37.50	22.50
120	Davey Williams	40.00	20.00	12.00
121	Walt Dropo	40.00	20.00	12.00
122	Elmer Valo	40.00	20.00	12.00
123	Tommy Byrne/DP	30.00	15.00	9.00
124	Sibby Sisti/DP	30.00	15.00	9.00
125	Dick Williams/DP	35.00	17.50	10.00
126	Bill Connelly/DP	30.00	15.00	9.00
127	Clint Courtney/DP	30.00	15.00	9.00
128	Wilmer Mizell/DP	30.00	15.00	9.00
129	Keith Thomas	40.00	20.00	12.00
130	Turk Lown/DP	30.00	15.00	9.00
131	Harry Byrd/DP	30.00	15.00	9.00
132	Tom Morgan	45.00	22.50	13.50
133	Gil Coan	40.00	20.00	12.00
134	Rube Walker	45.00	22.50	13.50
135	Al Rosen/DP	45.00	22.50	13.50
136	Ken Heintzelman/DP	30.00	15.00	9.00
137	John Rutherford/DP	35.00	17.50	10.00
138	George Kell	55.00	27.50	16.50
139	Sammy White	40.00	20.00	12.00
140	Tommy Glaviano	40.00	20.00	12.00
141	Allie Reynolds/DP	75.00	37.50	22.50
142	Vic Wertz	40.00	20.00	12.00
143	Billy Pierce	40.00	20.00	12.00
144	Bob Schultz/DP	30.00	15.00	9.00
145	Harry Dorish/DP	30.00	15.00	9.00
146	Granville Hamner	40.00	20.00	12.00
147	Warren Spahn	165.00	85.00	50.00
148	Mickey Grasso	40.00	20.00	12.00
149	Dom DiMaggio/DP	65.00	32.50	20.00
150	Harry Simpson/DP	30.00	15.00	9.00
151	Hoyt Wilhelm	80.00	40.00	24.00
152	Bob Adams/DP	30.00	15.00	9.00
153	Andy Seminick/DP	30.00	15.00	9.00
154	Dick Groat	40.00	20.00	12.00
155	Dutch Leonard	40.00	20.00	12.00
156	Jim Rivera/DP	30.00	15.00	9.00
157	Bob Addis/DP	30.00	15.00	9.00
158	***John Logan***	40.00	20.00	12.00
159	Wayne Terwilliger/DP	30.00	15.00	9.00
160	Bob Young	40.00	20.00	12.00
161	Vern Bickford/DP	30.00	15.00	9.00
162	Ted Kluszewski	80.00	40.00	24.00
163	Fred Hatfield/DP	30.00	15.00	9.00
164	Frank Shea/DP	30.00	15.00	9.00
165	Billy Hoeft	40.00	20.00	12.00
166	Bill Hunter	35.00	17.50	10.00
167	Art Schult	35.00	17.50	10.00
168	Willard Schmidt	35.00	17.50	10.00
169	Dizzy Trout	35.00	17.50	10.00
170	Bill Werle	35.00	17.50	10.00
171	Bill Glynn	35.00	17.50	10.00
172	Rip Repulski	35.00	17.50	10.00
173	Preston Ward	35.00	17.50	10.00
174	Billy Loes	45.00	22.50	13.50
175	Ron Kline	35.00	17.50	10.00
176	***Don Hoak***	40.00	20.00	12.00
177	Jim Dyck	35.00	17.50	10.00
178	Jim Waugh	35.00	17.50	10.00
179	Gene Hermanski	35.00	17.50	10.00
180	Virgil Stallcup	35.00	17.50	10.00
181	Al Zarilla	35.00	17.50	10.00
182	Bob Hofman	35.00	17.50	10.00
183	***Stu Miller***	35.00	17.50	10.00
184	***Hal Brown***	35.00	17.50	10.00
185	***Jim Pendleton***	35.00	17.50	10.00
186	Charlie Bishop	35.00	17.50	10.00
187	Jim Fridley	35.00	17.50	10.00
188	***Andy Carey***	60.00	30.00	18.00
189	Ray Jablonski	35.00	17.50	10.00
190	Dixie Walker	35.00	17.50	10.00
191	Ralph Kiner	90.00	45.00	27.50
192	Wally Westlake	35.00	17.50	10.00
193	Mike Clark	35.00	17.50	10.00
194	Eddie Kazak	35.00	17.50	10.00
195	Ed McGhee	35.00	17.50	10.00
196	Bob Keegan	35.00	17.50	10.00
197	Del Crandall	35.00	17.50	10.00
198	Forrest Main	35.00	17.50	10.00
199	Marion Fricano	35.00	17.50	10.00
200	Gordon Goldsberry	35.00	17.50	10.00
201	Paul La Palme	35.00	17.50	10.00
202	Carl Sawatski	35.00	17.50	10.00
203	Cliff Fannin	35.00	17.50	10.00
204	Dick Bokelmann	35.00	17.50	10.00
205	Vern Benson	35.00	17.50	10.00
206	***Ed Bailey***	35.00	17.50	10.00
207	Whitey Ford	210.00	100.00	65.00
208	Jim Wilson	35.00	17.50	10.00
209	Jim Greengrass	35.00	17.50	10.00
210	***Bob Cerv***	45.00	22.20	13.50
211	J.W. Porter	35.00	17.50	10.00
212	Jack Dittmer	35.00	17.50	10.00
213	Ray Scarborough	35.00	17.50	10.00
214	***Bill Bruton***	35.00	17.50	10.00
215	***Gene Conley***	35.00	17.50	10.00
216	Jim Hughes	40.00	20.00	12.00
217	Murray Wall	35.00	17.50	10.00
218	Les Fusselman	35.00	17.50	10.00
219	Pete Runnels (Picture actually Don Johnson.)	35.00	17.50	10.00
220	Satchell Paige	500.00	200.00	110.00
221	Bob Milliken/SP	100.00	50.00	30.00
222	Vic Janowicz	100.00	50.00	30.00
223	John O'Brien	60.00	30.00	18.00
224	Lou Sleater	60.00	30.00	18.00
225	Bobby Shantz/SP	90.00	45.00	27.50
226	Ed Erautt/SP	90.00	45.00	27.50
227	Morris Martin/SP	90.00	45.00	27.50
228	Hal Newhouser/SP	140.00	70.00	45.00
229	Rocky Krsnich/SP	90.00	45.00	27.50
230	Johnny Lindell	60.00	30.00	18.00
231	Solly Hemus	60.00	30.00	18.00
232	Dick Kokos/SP	90.00	45.00	27.50
233	Al Aber/SP	90.00	45.00	27.50
234	Ray Murray	60.00	30.00	18.00
235	John Hetki	60.00	30.00	18.00
236	Harry Perkowski	60.00	30.00	18.00
237	Clarence Podbielan	60.00	30.00	18.00
238	Cal Hogue	60.00	30.00	18.00
239	Jim Delsing/SP	90.00	45.00	27.50
240	Freddie Marsh/SP	90.00	45.00	27.50
241	Al Sima	60.00	30.00	18.00
242	Charlie Silvera/SP	100.00	50.00	30.00
243	Carlos Bernier	60.00	30.00	18.00
244	Willie Mays/SP	2,600	650.00	300.00
245	Bill Norman	90.00	45.00	27.50
246	***Roy Face***	75.00	37.50	22.50
247	Mike Sandlock	60.00	30.00	18.00
248	Gene Stephens	60.00	30.00	18.00
249	Ed O'Brien/SP	90.00	45.00	27.50
250	Bob Wilson/SP	90.00	45.00	27.50
251	Sid Hudson/SP	90.00	45.00	27.50
252	Henry Foiles/SP	90.00	45.00	27.50
253	Not Issued			
254	Preacher Roe	125.00	65.00	35.00
255	Dixie Howell/SP	100.00	50.00	30.00
256	Les Peden/SP	90.00	45.00	27.50
257	Bob Boyd/SP	90.00	45.00	27.50
258	***Jim Gilliam/SP***	265.00	130.00	80.00
259	Roy McMillan	60.00	30.00	18.00
260	Sam Calderone/SP	90.00	45.00	27.50
261	Not Issued			
262	Bob Oldis/SP	90.00	45.00	27.50
263	***Johnny Podres***/SP	275.00	135.00	85.00
264	Gene Woodling	95.00	47.50	27.50
265	Jackie Jensen/SP	100.00	50.00	30.00
266	Bob Cain/SP	90.00	45.00	27.50
267	Not Issued			
268	Not Issued			
269	Duane Pillette/SP	90.00	45.00	27.50
270	Vern Stephens/SP	90.00	45.00	27.50
271	Not Issued			
272	Bill Antonello/SP	100.00	50.00	30.00
273	***Harvey Haddix/SP***	160.00	80.00	47.50
274	John Riddle/SP	90.00	45.00	27.50
275	Not Issued			
276	Ken Raffensberger/SP	90.00	45.00	27.50
277	Don Lund/SP	90.00	45.00	27.50
278	Willie Miranda/SP	90.00	45.00	27.50
279	Joe Coleman	60.00	30.00	18.00
280	***Milt Bolling***/SP	400.00	115.00	45.00

1954 Topps

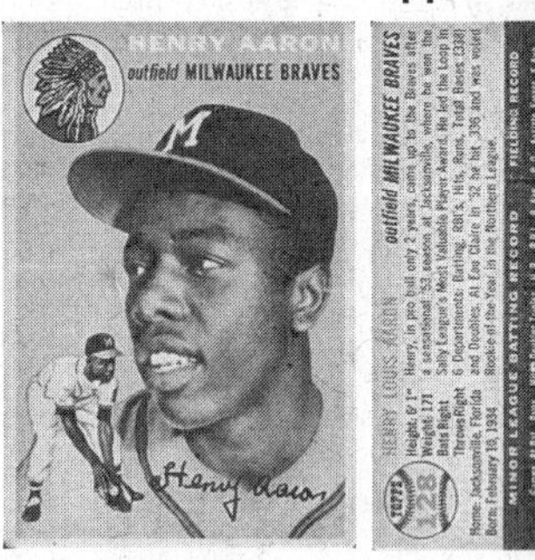

The first issue to use two player pictures on the front, the 1954 Topps set remains popular today. Solid color backgrounds frame both color portraits and black-and-white action pictures of the player. The player's name, position, team and team logo appear at the top. Backs include an "Inside Baseball" cartoon regarding the player as well as statistics and biography. The 250-card, 2-5/8" x 3-3/4", set includes manager and coaches cards. A gray-back version of cards #1-50 is known, distinguished by the use of dark gray cardboard on back. These are often attributed to Canadian issue and carry a modest premium.

		NM	EX	VG
Complete Set (250):		9,250	4,000	2,400
Common Player (1-50):		20.00	10.00	6.00
Common Player (51-75):		35.00	17.50	10.00
Common Player (76-250):		20.00	10.00	6.00
1	Ted Williams	675.00	175.00	80.00
2	Gus Zernial	35.00	10.00	6.00
3	Monte Irvin	60.00	30.00	18.00
4	Hank Sauer	20.00	10.00	6.00
5	Ed Lopat	25.00	12.50	7.50
6	Pete Runnels	20.00	10.00	6.00
7	Ted Kluszewski	35.00	17.50	10.00
8	Bobby Young	20.00	10.00	6.00
9	Harvey Haddix	20.00	10.00	6.00
10	Jackie Robinson	235.00	115.00	70.00
11	Paul Smith	20.00	10.00	6.00
12	Del Crandall	20.00	10.00	6.00
13	Billy Martin	75.00	37.50	22.00
14	Preacher Roe	35.00	17.50	10.00
15	Al Rosen	30.00	15.00	9.00
16	Vic Janowicz	25.00	12.50	7.50
17	Phil Rizzuto	85.00	42.50	25.00
18	Walt Dropo	20.00	10.00	6.00
19	Johnny Lipon	20.00	10.00	6.00
20	Warren Spahn	85.00	42.50	25.00
21	Bobby Shantz	20.00	10.00	6.00
22	Jim Greengrass	20.00	10.00	6.00
23	Luke Easter	25.00	12.50	7.50
24	Granny Hamner	20.00	10.00	6.00
25	***Harvey Kuenn***	35.00	17.50	10.00
26	Ray Jablonski	20.00	10.00	6.00
27	Ferris Fain	20.00	10.00	6.00
28	Paul Minner	20.00	10.00	6.00
29	Jim Hegan	20.00	10.00	6.00
30	Ed Mathews	70.00	35.00	20.00
31	Johnny Klippstein	20.00	10.00	6.00
32	Duke Snider	130.00	65.00	40.00
33	Johnny Schmitz	20.00	10.00	6.00
34	Jim Rivera	20.00	10.00	6.00
35	Junior Gilliam	35.00	17.50	10.00
36	Hoyt Wilhelm	40.00	20.00	12.00
37	Whitey Ford	100.00	50.00	30.00
38	Eddie Stanky	20.00	10.00	6.00
39	Sherm Lollar	20.00	10.00	6.00
40	Mel Parnell	20.00	10.00	6.00
41	Willie Jones	20.00	10.00	6.00
42	Don Mueller	20.00	10.00	6.00
43	Dick Groat	20.00	10.00	6.00
44	Ned Garver	20.00	10.00	6.00
45	Richie Ashburn	60.00	30.00	18.00
46	Ken Raffensberger	20.00	10.00	6.00
47	Ellis Kinder	20.00	10.00	6.00
48	Billy Hunter	20.00	10.00	6.00
49	Ray Murray	20.00	10.00	6.00

50	Yogi Berra	165.00	80.00	50.00
51	Johnny Lindell	35.00	17.50	10.00
52	***Vic Power***	40.00	20.00	12.00
53	Jack Dittmer	35.00	17.50	10.00
54	Vern Stephens	35.00	17.50	10.00
55	Phil Cavarretta	35.00	17.50	10.00
56	Willie Miranda	35.00	17.50	10.00
57	Luis Aloma	35.00	17.50	10.00
58	Bob Wilson	35.00	17.50	10.00
59	Gene Conley	35.00	17.50	10.00
60	Frank Baumholtz	35.00	17.50	10.00
61	Bob Cain	35.00	17.50	10.00
62	Eddie Robinson	40.00	20.00	12.00
63	Johnny Pesky	35.00	17.50	10.00
64	Hank Thompson	35.00	17.50	10.00
65	Bob Swift	35.00	17.50	10.00
66	Ted Lepcio	35.00	17.50	10.00
67	Jim Willis	35.00	17.50	10.00
68	Sammy Calderone	35.00	17.50	10.00
69	Bud Podbielan	35.00	17.50	10.00
70	Larry Doby	85.00	42.50	25.00
71	Frank Smith	35.00	17.50	10.00
72	Preston Ward	35.00	17.50	10.00
73	Wayne Terwilliger	35.00	17.50	10.00
74	Bill Taylor	35.00	17.50	10.00
75	Fred Haney	35.00	17.50	10.00
76	Bob Scheffing	20.00	10.00	6.00
77	Ray Boone	20.00	10.00	6.00
78	Ted Kazanski	20.00	10.00	6.00
79	Andy Pafko	20.00	10.00	6.00
80	Jackie Jensen	30.00	15.00	9.00
81	Dave Hoskins	20.00	10.00	6.00
82	Milt Bolling	20.00	10.00	6.00
83	Joe Collins	25.00	12.50	7.50
84	Dick Cole	20.00	10.00	6.00
85	***Bob Turley***	35.00	17.50	10.00
86	Billy Herman	45.00	22.50	13.50
87	Roy Face	20.00	10.00	6.00
88	Matt Batts	20.00	10.00	6.00
89	Howie Pollet	20.00	10.00	6.00
90	Willie Mays	375.00	185.00	110.00
91	Bob Oldis	20.00	10.00	6.00
92	Wally Westlake	20.00	10.00	6.00
93	Sid Hudson	20.00	10.00	6.00
94	***Ernie Banks***	850.00	300.00	180.00
95	Hal Rice	20.00	10.00	6.00
96	Charlie Silvera	25.00	12.50	7.50
97	Jerry Lane	20.00	10.00	6.00
98	Joe Black	55.00	27.50	16.50
99	Bob Hofman	20.00	10.00	6.00
100	Bob Keegan	20.00	10.00	6.00
101	Gene Woodling	50.00	25.00	15.00
102	Gil Hodges	95.00	47.50	27.00
103	***Jim Lemon***	25.00	12.50	7.50
104	Mike Sandlock	20.00	10.00	6.00
105	Andy Carey	25.00	12.50	7.50
106	Dick Kokos	20.00	10.00	6.00
107	Duane Pillette	20.00	10.00	6.00
108	Thornton Kipper	20.00	10.00	6.00
109	Bill Bruton	20.00	10.00	6.00
110	Harry Dorish	20.00	10.00	6.00
111	Jim Delsing	20.00	10.00	6.00
112	Bill Renna	20.00	10.00	6.00
113	Bob Boyd	20.00	10.00	6.00
114	Dean Stone	20.00	10.00	6.00
115	"Rip" Repulski	20.00	10.00	6.00
116	Steve Bilko	20.00	10.00	6.00
117	Solly Hemus	20.00	10.00	6.00
118	Carl Scheib	20.00	10.00	6.00
119	Johnny Antonelli	20.00	10.00	6.00
120	Roy McMillan	20.00	10.00	6.00
121	Clem Labine	45.00	22.50	13.50
122	Johnny Logan	20.00	10.00	6.00
123	Bobby Adams	20.00	10.00	6.00
124	Marion Fricano	20.00	10.00	6.00
125	Harry Perkowski	20.00	10.00	6.00
126	Ben Wade	25.00	12.50	7.50
127	Steve O'Neill	20.00	10.00	6.00
128	***Hank Aaron***	1,400	500.00	275.00
129	Forrest Jacobs	20.00	10.00	6.00
130	Hank Bauer	45.00	22.50	13.50
131	Reno Bertoia	20.00	10.00	6.00
132	***Tom Lasorda***	135.00	65.00	40.00
133	Del Baker	20.00	10.00	6.00
134	Cal Hogue	20.00	10.00	6.00
135	Joe Presko	20.00	10.00	6.00
136	Connie Ryan	20.00	10.00	6.00
137	***Wally Moon***	35.00	17.50	10.00
138	Bob Borkowski	20.00	10.00	6.00
139	Ed O'Brien, Johnny O'Brien	75.00	37.50	22.50
140	Tom Wright	20.00	10.00	6.00
141	***Joe Jay***	40.00	20.00	12.00
142	Tom Poholsky	20.00	10.00	6.00
143	Rollie Hemsley	20.00	10.00	6.00
144	Bill Werle	20.00	10.00	6.00
145	Elmer Valo	20.00	10.00	6.00
146	Don Johnson	20.00	10.00	6.00
147	John Riddle	20.00	10.00	6.00
148	Bob Trice	20.00	10.00	6.00
149	Jim Robertson	20.00	10.00	6.00
150	Dick Kryhoski	20.00	10.00	6.00
151	Alex Grammas	20.00	10.00	6.00
152	Mike Blyzka	20.00	10.00	6.00
153	Rube Walker	25.00	12.50	7.50
154	Mike Fornieles	20.00	10.00	6.00
155	Bob Kennedy	20.00	10.00	6.00
156	Joe Coleman	20.00	10.00	6.00
157	Don Lenhardt	20.00	10.00	6.00
158	"Peanuts" Lowrey	20.00	10.00	6.00
159	Dave Philley	20.00	10.00	6.00
160	"Red" Kress	20.00	10.00	6.00
161	John Hetki	20.00	10.00	6.00
162	Herman Wehmeier	20.00	10.00	6.00
163	Frank House	20.00	10.00	6.00
164	Stu Miller	20.00	10.00	6.00
165	Jim Pendleton	20.00	10.00	6.00
166	Johnny Podres	45.00	22.50	13.50
167	Don Lund	20.00	10.00	6.00
168	Morrie Martin	20.00	10.00	6.00
169	Jim Hughes	25.00	12.50	7.50
170	***Jim Rhodes***	40.00	20.00	12.00
171	Leo Kiely	20.00	10.00	6.00
172	Hal Brown	20.00	10.00	6.00
173	Jack Harshman	20.00	10.00	6.00
174	Tom Qualters	20.00	10.00	6.00
175	***Frank Leja***	25.00	12.50	7.50
176	Bob Keely	20.00	10.00	6.00
177	Bob Milliken	25.00	12.50	7.50
178	Bill Gylnn (Glynn)	20.00	10.00	6.00
179	Gair Allie	20.00	10.00	6.00
180	Wes Westrum	20.00	10.00	6.00
181	Mel Roach	20.00	10.00	6.00
182	Chuck Harmon	20.00	10.00	6.00
183	Earle Combs	25.00	12.50	7.50
184	Ed Bailey	20.00	10.00	6.00
185	Chuck Stobbs	20.00	10.00	6.00
186	Karl Olson	20.00	10.00	6.00
187	"Heinie" Manush	25.00	12.50	7.50
188	Dave Jolly	20.00	10.00	6.00
189	Bob Ross	20.00	10.00	6.00
190	Ray Herbert	20.00	10.00	6.00
191	***Dick Schofield***	25.00	12.50	7.50
192	"Cot" Deal	20.00	10.00	6.00
193	Johnny Hopp	20.00	10.00	6.00
194	Bill Sarni	20.00	10.00	6.00
195	Bill Consolo	20.00	10.00	6.00
196	Stan Jok	20.00	10.00	6.00
197	"Schoolboy" Rowe	20.00	10.00	6.00
198	Carl Sawatski	20.00	10.00	6.00
199	"Rocky" Nelson	20.00	10.00	6.00
200	Larry Jansen	20.00	10.00	6.00
201	***Al Kaline***	425.00	200.00	100.00
202	***Bob Purkey***	20.00	10.00	6.00
203	Harry Brecheen	20.00	10.00	6.00
204	Angel Scull	20.00	10.00	6.00
205	Johnny Sain	30.00	15.00	9.00
206	Ray Crone	20.00	10.00	6.00
207	Tom Oliver	20.00	10.00	6.00
208	Grady Hatton	20.00	10.00	6.00
209	Charlie Thompson	25.00	12.50	7.50
210	***Bob Buhl***	20.00	10.00	6.00
211	Don Hoak	25.00	12.50	7.50
212	Mickey Micelotta	20.00	10.00	6.00
213	John Fitzpatrick	20.00	10.00	6.00
214	Arnold Portocarrero	20.00	10.00	6.00
215	Ed McGhee	20.00	10.00	6.00
216	Al Sima	20.00	10.00	6.00
217	Paul Schreiber	20.00	10.00	6.00
218	Fred Marsh	20.00	10.00	6.00
219	Charlie Kress	20.00	10.00	6.00
220	Ruben Gomez	20.00	10.00	6.00
221	Dick Brodowski	20.00	10.00	6.00
222	Bill Wilson	20.00	10.00	6.00
223	Joe Haynes	20.00	10.00	6.00
224	Dick Weik	20.00	10.00	6.00
225	Don Liddle	20.00	10.00	6.00
226	Jehosie Heard	20.00	10.00	6.00
227	Buster Mills	20.00	10.00	6.00
228	Gene Hermanski	20.00	10.00	6.00
229	Bob Talbot	20.00	10.00	6.00
230	Bob Kuzava	25.00	12.50	7.50
231	Roy Smalley	20.00	10.00	6.00
232	Lou Limmer	20.00	10.00	6.00
233	Augie Galan	20.00	10.00	6.00
234	***Jerry Lynch***	20.00	10.00	6.00
235	Vern Law	20.00	10.00	6.00
236	Paul Penson	20.00	10.00	6.00
237	Mike Ryba	20.00	10.00	6.00
238	Al Aber	20.00	10.00	6.00
239	***Bill Skowron***	85.00	42.50	25.00
240	Sam Mele	20.00	10.00	6.00
241	Bob Miller	20.00	10.00	6.00
242	Curt Roberts	20.00	10.00	6.00
243	Ray Blades	20.00	10.00	6.00
244	Leroy Wheat	20.00	10.00	6.00
245	Roy Sievers	20.00	10.00	6.00
246	Howie Fox	20.00	10.00	6.00
247	Eddie Mayo	20.00	10.00	6.00
248	***Al Smith***	20.00	10.00	6.00
249	Wilmer Mizell	20.00	10.00	6.00
250	Ted Williams	600.00	190.00	100.00

1954 Topps "Canadian"

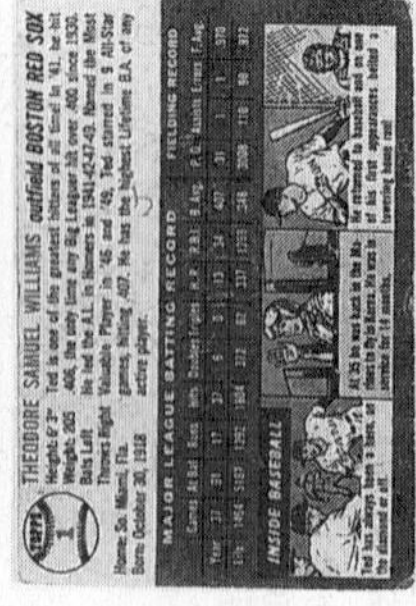

This version of the first 50 cards from 1954 Topps has long been known as the "Canadian" issue. It is widely believed that the abbreviated set was intended solely for Canadian distribution. The cards differ from the regular 1954 Topps in that they are printed on a gray-backed cardboard stock, distinctly different from the white stock found on most '54 Topps. Later series white-back Topps cards were sold in Canada in O-Pee-Chee marked wrappers at four for a nickel as opposed to six for five cents in the U.S.

		NM	EX	VG
Complete Set (50):		5,500	2,750	1,750
Common Player:		40.00	20.00	12.00
1	Ted Williams	1,500	700.00	450.00
2	Gus Zernial	60.00	20.00	12.00
3	Monte Irvin	115.00	55.00	35.00
4	Hank Sauer	40.00	20.00	12.00
5	Ed Lopat	50.00	25.00	15.00
6	Pete Runnels	40.00	20.00	12.00
7	Ted Kluszewski	75.00	35.00	22.50
8	Bobby Young	40.00	20.00	12.00
9	Harvey Haddix	40.00	20.00	12.00
10	Jackie Robinson	525.00	250.00	150.00
11	Paul Smith	40.00	20.00	12.00
12	Del Crandall	40.00	20.00	12.00
13	Billy Martin	225.00	100.00	65.00
14	Preacher Roe	75.00	35.00	22.50
15	Al Rosen	85.00	40.00	25.00
16	Vic Janowicz	45.00	22.00	13.50
17	Phil Rizzuto	225.00	110.00	65.00
18	Walt Dropo	40.00	20.00	12.00
19	Johnny Lipon	40.00	20.00	12.00
20	Warren Spahn	215.00	100.00	60.00
21	Bobby Shantz	45.00	22.50	13.50
22	Jim Greengrass	40.00	20.00	12.00
23	Luke Easter	40.00	20.00	12.00
24	Granny Hamner	40.00	20.00	12.00
25	Harvey Kuenn	75.00	35.00	22.50
26	Ray Jablonski	40.00	20.00	12.00
27	Ferris Fain	40.00	20.00	12.00
28	Paul Minner	40.00	20.00	12.00
29	Jim Hegan	40.00	20.00	12.00
30	Ed Mathews	165.00	80.00	47.50
31	Johnny Klippstein	40.00	20.00	12.00
32	Duke Snider	315.00	150.00	90.00
33	Johnny Schmitz	40.00	20.00	12.00
34	Jim Rivera	40.00	20.00	12.00
35	Junior Gilliam	85.00	40.00	25.00
36	Hoyt Wilhelm	115.00	55.00	32.50
37	Whitey Ford	215.00	100.00	60.00
38	Eddie Stanky	45.00	22.50	13.50
39	Sherm Lollar	40.00	20.00	12.00
40	Mel Parnell	40.00	20.00	12.00
41	Willie Jones	40.00	20.00	12.00
42	Don Mueller	40.00	20.00	12.00
43	Dick Groat	40.00	20.00	12.00
44	Ned Garver	40.00	20.00	12.00
45	Richie Ashburn	140.00	70.00	40.00
46	Ken Raffensberger	40.00	20.00	12.00
47	Ellis Kinder	40.00	20.00	12.00
48	Billy Hunter	40.00	20.00	12.00
49	Ray Murray	40.00	20.00	12.00
50	Yogi Berra	365.00	175.00	100.00

1954 Topps Look 'N See

Among the 135 historical figures in this set is only one baseball player - Babe Ruth. These 2-1/16" x 2-15/16" cards feature colorful portrait paintings on the front and biographies on the back. The answer to a trivia question on back can be discovered by laying a piece of red cellophane over the question box.

		NM	EX	VG
Complete Set (135):		3,000	1,500	900.00
Common Card:		4.00	2.00	1.25
15	Babe Ruth	150.00	75.00	45.00

1954 Topps Scoops

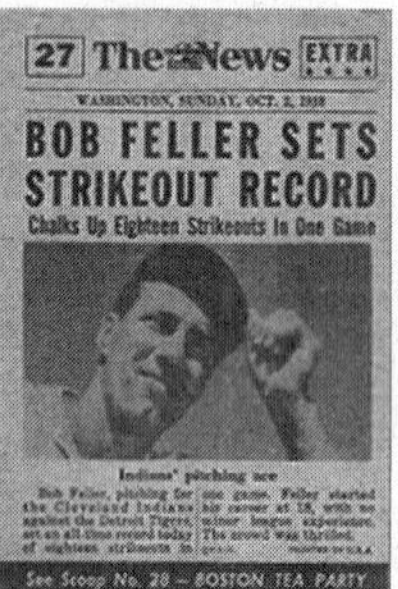

World - and sports - history from the mid-18th Century through October 1953, is chronicled in this 156-card set. Four baseball subjects are presented in the set. Cards are 2-1/16" x 2-15/16" and feature on the front a color painting with a dated caption box at bottom. Originally a black scratch-off ink covered the caption box (cards with the black ink removed can still be considered Mint as those with the ink currently command little premium value). Backs feature a simulated newspaper front page with banner headline and picture, along with a description of the event.

		NM	EX	VG
Complete Set (156):		1,750	875.00	525.00
Common Card:		6.00	3.00	1.75
27	Bob Feller Strikeout King, Oct. 2, 1938 (Bob Feller)	60.00	30.00	18.00
41	Babe Ruth Sets Record, Sept. 30, 1927 (Babe Ruth)	250.00	125.00	75.00
130	Braves Go to Milwaukee	40.00	20.00	12.00
154	26-Inning Tie Game May 1, 1920	60.00	30.00	18.00

1955 Topps

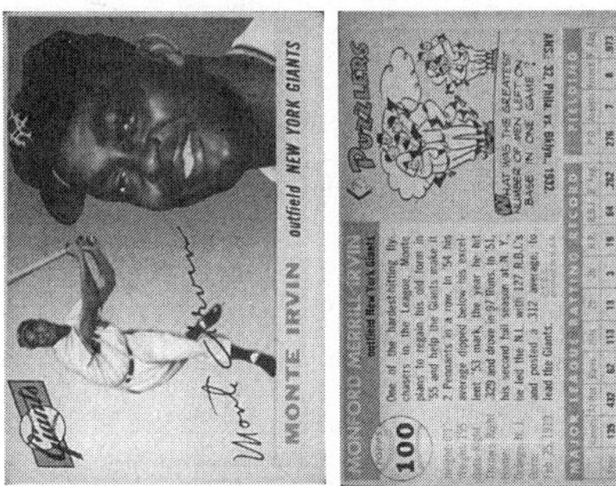

The 1955 Topps set is numerically the smallest of the regular annual issues. The 3-3/4" x 2-5/8" cards mark the first time that Topps used a horizontal format for the entire set. While that format was new, the design was not; they are very similar to the 1954 cards to the point many pictures appeared in both years. Although it was slated for a 210-card set, the 1955 Topps set turned out to be only 206 cards with numbers 175, 186, 203 and 209 never being released. The scarce high numbers in this set begin with #161.

		NM	EX	VG
Complete Set (206):		8,000	3,750	2,250
Common Player (1-150):		20.00	10.00	6.00
Common Player (151-160):		25.00	12.50	7.50
Common Player (161-210):		45.00	22.50	13.50
1	"Dusty" Rhodes	85.00	20.00	6.00
2	Ted Williams	400.00	175.00	90.00
3	Art Fowler	20.00	10.00	6.00
4	Al Kaline	150.00	75.00	45.00
5	Jim Gilliam	40.00	20.00	12.00
6	Stan Hack	25.00	12.50	7.50
7	Jim Hegan	20.00	10.00	6.00
8	Hal Smith	20.00	10.00	6.00
9	Bob Miller	20.00	10.00	6.00
10	Bob Keegan	20.00	10.00	6.00
11	Ferris Fain	20.00	10.00	6.00
12	"Jake" Thies	20.00	10.00	6.00
13	Fred Marsh	20.00	10.00	6.00
14	Jim Finigan	20.00	10.00	6.00
15	Jim Pendleton	20.00	10.00	6.00
16	Roy Sievers	20.00	10.00	6.00
17	Bobby Hofman	20.00	10.00	6.00
18	Russ Kemmerer	20.00	10.00	6.00
19	Billy Herman	45.00	22.50	13.50
20	Andy Carey	25.00	12.50	7.50
21	Alex Grammas	20.00	10.00	6.00
22	Bill Skowron	35.00	17.50	10.00
23	Jack Parks	20.00	10.00	6.00
24	Hal Newhouser	50.00	25.00	15.00
25	Johnny Podres	40.00	20.00	12.00
26	Dick Groat	20.00	10.00	6.00
27	***Billy Gardner***	20.00	10.00	6.00
28	Ernie Banks	135.00	65.00	40.00
29	Herman Wehmeier	20.00	10.00	6.00
30	Vic Power	20.00	10.00	6.00
31	Warren Spahn	90.00	45.00	27.50
32	Ed McGhee	20.00	10.00	6.00
33	Tom Qualters	20.00	10.00	6.00
34	Wayne Terwilliger	20.00	10.00	6.00
35	Dave Jolly	20.00	10.00	6.00
36	Leo Kiely	20.00	10.00	6.00
37	***Joe Cunningham***	20.00	10.00	6.00
38	Bob Turley	27.50	13.50	8.25
39	Bill Glynn	20.00	10.00	6.00
40	Don Hoak	25.00	12.50	7.50
41	Chuck Stobbs	20.00	10.00	6.00
42	"Windy" McCall	20.00	10.00	6.00
43	Harvey Haddix	20.00	10.00	6.00
44	"Corky" Valentine	20.00	10.00	6.00
45	Hank Sauer	20.00	10.00	6.00
46	Ted Kazanski	20.00	10.00	6.00
47	Hank Aaron	265.00	130.00	80.00
48	Bob Kennedy	20.00	10.00	6.00
49	J.W. Porter	20.00	10.00	6.00
50	Jackie Robinson	260.00	130.00	80.00
51	Jim Hughes	25.00	12.50	7.50
52	Bill Tremel	20.00	10.00	6.00
53	Bill Taylor	20.00	10.00	6.00
54	Lou Limmer	20.00	10.00	6.00
55	"Rip" Repulski	20.00	10.00	6.00
56	Ray Jablonski	20.00	10.00	6.00
57	***Billy O'Dell***	20.00	10.00	6.00
58	Jim Rivera	20.00	10.00	6.00
59	Gair Allie	20.00	10.00	6.00
60	Dean Stone	20.00	10.00	6.00
61	"Spook" Jacobs	20.00	10.00	6.00
62	Thornton Kipper	20.00	10.00	6.00
63	Joe Collins	25.00	12.50	7.50
64	***Gus Triandos***	25.00	12.50	7.50
65	Ray Boone	20.00	10.00	6.00
66	Ron Jackson	20.00	10.00	6.00
67	Wally Moon	20.00	10.00	6.00
68	Jim Davis	20.00	10.00	6.00
69	Ed Bailey	20.00	10.00	6.00
70	Al Rosen	40.00	20.00	12.00
71	Ruben Gomez	20.00	10.00	6.00
72	Karl Olson	20.00	10.00	6.00
73	Jack Shepard	20.00	10.00	6.00
74	Bob Borkowski	20.00	10.00	6.00
75	***Sandy Amoros***	45.00	22.50	13.50
76	Howie Pollet	20.00	10.00	6.00
77	Arnold Portocarrero	20.00	10.00	6.00
78	Gordon Jones	20.00	10.00	6.00
79	Danny Schell	20.00	10.00	6.00
80	Bob Grim	25.00	12.50	7.50
81	Gene Conley	20.00	10.00	6.00
82	Chuck Harmon	20.00	10.00	6.00
83	Tom Brewer	20.00	10.00	6.00
84	***Camilo Pascual***	35.00	17.50	10.00
85	***Don Mossi***	35.00	17.50	10.00
86	Bill Wilson	20.00	10.00	6.00
87	Frank House	20.00	10.00	6.00
88	***Bob Skinner***	20.00	10.00	6.00
89	***Joe Frazier***	20.00	10.00	6.00
90	***Karl Spooner***	25.00	12.50	7.50
91	Milt Bolling	20.00	10.00	6.00
92	***Don Zimmer***	90.00	45.00	27.50
93	Steve Bilko	20.00	10.00	6.00
94	Reno Bertoia	20.00	10.00	6.00
95	Preston Ward	20.00	10.00	6.00
96	Charlie Bishop	20.00	10.00	6.00
97	Carlos Paula	20.00	10.00	6.00
98	Johnny Riddle	20.00	10.00	6.00
99	Frank Leja	25.00	12.50	7.50
100	Monte Irvin	40.00	20.00	12.00
101	Johnny Gray	20.00	10.00	6.00
102	Wally Westlake	20.00	10.00	6.00
103	Charlie White	20.00	10.00	6.00
104	Jack Harshman	20.00	10.00	6.00
105	Chuck Diering	20.00	10.00	6.00
106	***Frank Sullivan*** (Several variations exist in the size, shape and density of the dot over the "i" in the facsimile autograph.)	20.00	10.00	6.00
107	Curt Roberts	20.00	10.00	6.00
108	"Rube" Walker	25.00	12.50	7.50
109	Ed Lopat	30.00	15.00	9.00
110	Gus Zernial	20.00	10.00	6.00
111	Bob Milliken	25.00	12.50	7.50
112	Nelson King	20.00	10.00	6.00
113	Harry Brecheen	20.00	10.00	6.00
114	Lou Ortiz	20.00	10.00	6.00
115	Ellis Kinder	20.00	10.00	6.00
116	Tom Hurd	20.00	10.00	6.00
117	Mel Roach	20.00	10.00	6.00
118	Bob Purkey	20.00	10.00	6.00
119	Bob Lennon	20.00	10.00	6.00
120	Ted Kluszewski	45.00	22.50	13.50
121	Bill Renna	20.00	10.00	6.00
122	Carl Sawatski	20.00	10.00	6.00
123	***"Sandy" Koufax***	575.00	250.00	160.00
124	***Harmon Killebrew***	200.00	80.00	35.00
125	***Ken Boyer***	80.00	40.00	24.00
126	***Dick Hall***	20.00	10.00	6.00
127	***Dale Long***	20.00	10.00	6.00
128	Ted Lepcio	20.00	10.00	6.00
129	Elvin Tappe	20.00	10.00	6.00
130	Mayo Smith	20.00	10.00	6.00
131	Grady Hatton	20.00	10.00	6.00
132	Bob Trice	20.00	10.00	6.00
133	Dave Hoskins	20.00	10.00	6.00
134	Joe Jay	20.00	10.00	6.00
135	Johnny O'Brien	20.00	10.00	6.00
136	"Bunky" Stewart	20.00	10.00	6.00
137a	Harry Elliott (Last line in bio is, "the Cards in '53.")	20.00	10.00	6.00
137b	Harry Elliott (Last line in bio ends, "the Cards in (crescent mark).")	20.00	10.00	6.00
137c	Harry Elliott (Last line in bio ends, "the Cards in.")	20.00	10.00	6.00
138	Ray Herbert	20.00	10.00	6.00
139	Steve Kraly	25.00	12.50	7.50
140	Mel Parnell	20.00	10.00	6.00
141	Tom Wright	20.00	10.00	6.00
142	Jerry Lynch	20.00	10.00	6.00
143	Dick Schofield	20.00	10.00	6.00
144	***Joe Amalfitano***	20.00	10.00	6.00
145	Elmer Valo	20.00	10.00	6.00
146	***Dick Donovan***	20.00	10.00	6.00
147	Laurin Pepper	20.00	10.00	6.00
148	Hal Brown	20.00	10.00	6.00
149	Ray Crone	20.00	10.00	6.00
150	Mike Higgins	20.00	10.00	6.00
151	"Red" Kress	25.00	12.50	7.50
152	***Harry Agganis***	135.00	65.00	40.00
153	"Bud" Podbielan	25.00	12.50	7.50
154	Willie Miranda	25.00	12.50	7.50
155	Ed Mathews	110.00	55.00	35.00
156	Joe Black	60.00	30.00	18.00
157	Bob Miller	25.00	12.50	7.50
158	Tom Carroll	35.00	17.50	10.50
159	Johnny Schmitz	25.00	12.50	7.50
160	Ray Narleski	25.00	12.50	7.50
161	***Chuck Tanner***	50.00	25.00	15.00
162	Joe Coleman	45.00	22.50	13.50
163	Faye Throneberry	45.00	22.50	13.50
164	***Roberto Clemente***	1,400	575.00	350.00
165	Don Johnson	45.00	22.50	13.50
166	Hank Bauer	60.00	30.00	18.00
167	Tom Casagrande	45.00	22.50	13.50
168	Duane Pillette	45.00	22.50	13.50
169	Bob Oldis	45.00	22.50	13.50
170	Jim Pearce	45.00	22.50	13.50
171	Dick Brodowski	45.00	22.50	13.50
172	Frank Baumholtz	45.00	22.50	13.50
173	Bob Kline	45.00	22.50	13.50
174	Rudy Minarcin	45.00	22.50	13.50
175	Not Issued			
176	Norm Zauchin	45.00	22.50	13.50
177	Jim Robertson	45.00	22.50	13.50
178	Bobby Adams	45.00	22.50	13.50
179	Jim Bolger	45.00	22.50	13.50
180	Clem Labine	60.00	30.00	18.00
181	Roy McMillan	45.00	22.50	13.50
182	Humberto Robinson	45.00	22.50	13.50
183	Tony Jacobs	45.00	22.50	13.50
184	Harry Perkowski	45.00	22.50	13.50
185	Don Ferrarese	45.00	22.50	13.50
186	Not Issued			
187	Gil Hodges	140.00	70.00	40.00
188	Charlie Silvera	50.00	25.00	15.00
189	Phil Rizzuto	160.00	80.00	50.00
190	Gene Woodling	50.00	25.00	15.00
191	Ed Stanky	45.00	22.50	13.50
192	Jim Delsing	45.00	22.50	13.50
193	Johnny Sain	55.00	27.50	16.50
194	Willie Mays	475.00	175.00	100.00
195	Ed Roebuck	50.00	25.00	15.00
196	Gale Wade	45.00	22.50	13.50
197	Al Smith	45.00	22.50	13.50
198	Yogi Berra	250.00	125.00	75.00
199	Bert Hamric	50.00	25.00	15.00
200	Jack Jensen	60.00	30.00	18.00
201	Sherm Lollar	45.00	22.50	13.50
202	Jim Owens	45.00	22.50	13.50
203	Not Issued			
204	Frank Smith	45.00	22.50	13.50
205	Gene Freese	45.00	22.50	13.50
206	Pete Daley	45.00	22.50	13.50
207	Bill Consolo	45.00	22.50	13.50
208	Ray Moore	45.00	22.50	13.50
209	Not Issued			
210	Duke Snider	600.00	130.00	80.00

1955 Topps Doubleheaders

This set is a throwback to the 1911 T201 Mecca Double Folders. The cards are perforated through the middle, allowing them to be folded. Open, there is a color painting of a player set against a stadium background. When folded, a different player and stadium appears; both players share the same lower legs and feet. Backs have abbreviated career histories and stats. Placed side by side in reverse numerical order, the backgrounds form a continuous stadium scene. When open the cards measure 2-1/16" x 4-7/8". The 66 cards in the set mean 132 total players, all of whom also appeared in the lower numbers of the regular 1955 Topps set.

		NM	EX	VG
Complete Set (66):		4,000	2,000	1,200
Common Card:		45.00	22.50	13.50
Wax Pack:		240.00		
1-2	Al Rosen, Chuck Diering	60.00	25.00	15.00
3-4	Monte Irvin, Russ Kemmerer	60.00	30.00	18.00
5-6	Ted Kazanski, Gordon Jones	45.00	22.50	13.50
7-8	Bill Taylor, Billy O'Dell	45.00	22.50	13.50
9-10	J.W. Porter, Thornton Kipper	45.00	22.50	13.50
11-12	Curt Roberts, Arnie Portocarrero	45.00	22.50	13.50
13-14	Wally Westlake, Frank House	45.00	22.50	13.50
15-16	Rube Walker, Lou Limmer	45.00	22.50	13.50
17-18	Dean Stone, Charlie White	45.00	22.50	13.50
19-20	Karl Spooner, Jim Hughes	50.00	25.00	15.00
21-22	Bill Skowron, Frank Sullivan	60.00	30.00	18.00
23-24	Jack Shepard, Stan Hack	45.00	22.50	13.50
25-26	Jackie Robinson, Don Hoak	325.00	160.00	100.00
27-28	Dusty Rhodes, Jim Davis	45.00	22.50	13.50
29-30	Vic Power, Ed Bailey	45.00	22.50	13.50
31-32	Howie Pollet, Ernie Banks	200.00	100.00	60.00
33-34	Jim Pendleton, Gene Conley	45.00	22.50	13.50
35-36	Karl Olson, Andy Carey	45.00	22.50	13.50
37-38	Wally Moon, Joe Cunningham	45.00	22.50	13.50
39-40	Fred Marsh, "Jake" Thies	45.00	22.50	13.50
41-42	Ed Lopat, Harvey Haddix	45.00	22.50	13.50
43-44	Leo Kiely, Chuck Stobbs	45.00	22.50	13.50
45-46	Al Kaline, "Corky" Valentine	225.00	110.00	65.00
47-48	"Spook" Jacobs, Johnny Gray	45.00	22.50	13.50
49-50	Ron Jackson, Jim Finigan	45.00	22.50	13.50
51-52	Ray Jablonski, Bob Keegan	45.00	22.50	13.50
53-54	Billy Herman, Sandy Amoros	60.00	30.00	18.00
55-56	Chuck Harmon, Bob Skinner	45.00	22.50	13.50
57-58	Dick Hall, Bob Grim	45.00	22.50	13.50
59-60	Bill Glynn, Bob Miller	45.00	22.50	13.50

		NM	EX	VG
61-62	Billy Gardner, John Hetki	45.00	22.50	13.50
63-64	Bob Borkowski, Bob Turley	45.00	22.50	13.50
65-66	Joe Collins, Jack Harshman	45.00	22.50	13.50
67-68	Jim Hegan, Jack Parks	45.00	22.50	13.50
69-70	Ted Williams, Hal Smith	425.00	210.00	125.00
71-72	Gair Allie, Grady Hatton	45.00	22.50	13.50
73-74	Jerry Lynch, Harry Brecheen	45.00	22.50	13.50
75-76	Tom Wright, "Bunky" Stewart	45.00	22.50	13.50
77-78	Dave Hoskins, Ed McGhee	45.00	22.50	13.50
79-80	Roy Sievers, Art Fowler	45.00	22.50	13.50
81-82	Danny Schell, Gus Triandos	45.00	22.50	13.50
83-84	Joe Frazier, Don Mossi	45.00	22.50	13.50
85-86	Elmer Valo, Hal Brown	45.00	22.50	13.50
87-88	Bob Kennedy, "Windy" McCall	45.00	22.50	13.50
89-90	Ruben Gomez, Jim Rivera	45.00	22.50	13.50
91-92	Lou Ortiz, Milt Bolling	45.00	22.50	13.50
93-94	Carl Sawatski, Elvin Tappe	45.00	22.50	13.50
95-96	Dave Jolly, Bobby Hofman	45.00	22.50	13.50
97-98	Preston Ward, Don Zimmer	45.00	22.50	13.50
99-100	Bill Renna, Dick Groat	45.00	22.50	13.50
101-102	Bill Wilson, Bill Tremel	45.00	22.50	13.50
103-104	Hank Sauer, Camilo Pascual	45.00	22.50	13.50
105-106	Hank Aaron, Ray Herbert	400.00	200.00	120.00
107-108	Alex Grammas, Tom Qualters	45.00	22.50	13.50
109-110	Hal Newhouser, Charlie Bishop	60.00	30.00	18.00
111-112	Harmon Killebrew, John Podres	225.00	110.00	65.00
113-114	Ray Boone, Bob Purkey	45.00	22.50	13.50
115-116	Dale Long, Ferris Fain	45.00	22.50	13.50
117-118	Steve Bilko, Bob Milliken	45.00	22.50	13.50
119-120	Mel Parnell, Tom Hurd	45.00	22.50	13.50
121-122	Ted Kluszewski, Jim Owens	60.00	30.00	18.00
123-124	Gus Zernial, Bob Trice	45.00	22.50	13.50
125-126	"Rip" Repulski, Ted Lepcio	45.00	22.50	13.50
127-128	Warren Spahn, Tom Brewer	150.00	75.00	45.00
129-130	Jim Gilliam, Ellis Kinder	60.00	30.00	18.00
131-132	Herm Wehmeier, Wayne Terwilliger	45.00	22.50	13.50

1955 Topps Hocus Focus

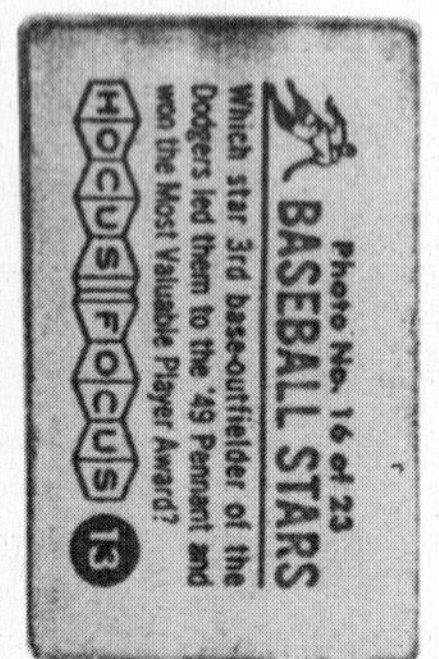

This set is a direct descendant of the 1948 "Topps Magic Photo" issue. Again, the baseball players were part of a larger overall series covering several topical areas. The cards, 7/8" x 1-3/8", state on the back that they are a series of 23, though only 14 are known. The photos on these cards were developed by wetting the card's surface and exposing to light. Prices below are for cards with well- developed pictures. Cards with poorly developed photos are worth significantly less.

		NM	EX	VG
	Common Player:	255.00	125.00	76.00
1	Babe Ruth	3,500	1,750	1,000
2	Lou Gehrig	3,500	1,750	1,000
3	Dick Groat	275.00	135.00	80.00
4	Ed Lopat	400.00	200.00	120.00
5	Hank Sauer	250.00	125.00	75.00
6	"Dusty" Rhodes	250.00	125.00	75.00
7	Ted Williams	1,950	975.00	585.00
8	Harvey Haddix	250.00	125.00	75.00
9	Ray Boone	250.00	125.00	75.00
10	Al Rosen	450.00	225.00	135.00
11	Unknown			
12	Warren Spahn	600.00	300.00	180.00
13	Jim Rivera	250.00	125.00	75.00
14	Ted Kluszewski	600.00	300.00	180.00
15	Gus Zernial	250.00	125.00	75.00
16	Jackie Robinson	1,750	875.00	525.00
17	Unknown			
18	Johnny Schmitz	250.00	125.00	75.00
19	Unknown			
20	Karl Spooner	275.00	135.00	80.00
21	Ed Mathews	600.00	300.00	180.00
22	Unknown			
23	Unknown			

1955 Topps Stamps

An extremely rare and enigmatic test issue, these stamps are the same size as Topps' 1955 card issue and have a blank, gummed back. Most of the specimens currently known are imperforate along one of the sides. All of the known examples have counterparts in the regular set which range from card #6 through 108. The unnumbered stamps are checklisted here alphabetically, with gaps left in the numbering to accommodate future discoveries.

		NM	EX	VG
	Common Player:	750.00	375.00	225.00
(1)	Ray Boone	750.00	375.00	225.00
(2)	Joe Cunningham	750.00	375.00	225.00
(3)	Jim Davis	750.00	375.00	225.00
(4)	Chuck Diering	750.00	375.00	225.00
(5)	Ruben Gomez	750.00	375.00	225.00
(6)	Alex Grammas	750.00	375.00	225.00
(7)	Stan Hack	750.00	375.00	225.00
(8)	Harvey Haddix	750.00	375.00	225.00
(9)	Bobby Hofman	750.00	375.00	225.00
(11)	Ray Jablonski	750.00	375.00	225.00
(12)	Dave Jolly	750.00	375.00	225.00
(13)	Ted Kazanski	750.00	375.00	225.00
(14)	Don Mossi	775.00	385.00	230.00
(15)	Jim Pendleton	750.00	375.00	225.00
(16)	Howie Pollet	750.00	375.00	225.00
(17)	Jack Shepard	750.00	375.00	225.00
(18)	Bob Skinner	750.00	375.00	225.00
(19)	Bill Skowron	975.00	485.00	290.00
(20)	Karl Spooner	775.00	385.00	230.00
(21)	Bill Tremel	750.00	375.00	225.00
(22)	Corky Valentine	750.00	375.00	225.00
(23)	Rube Walker	775.00	385.00	230.00
(24)	Charlie White	750.00	375.00	225.00

1956 Topps

This set is similar in format to the 1955 Topps set, again using both a portrait and an "action" picture. Some portraits are the same as those used in 1955 (and even 1954). Innovations found in the 1956 Topps set of 2-5/8" x 3-3/4" cards include team cards introduced as part of a regular set. Additionally, there are two unnumbered checklist cards (the complete set price quoted below does not include the checklist cards). Finally, there are cards of the two league presidents, William Harridge and Warren Giles. On the backs, a three-panel cartoon depicts big moments from the player's career while biographical information appears above the cartoon and the statistics below. Card backs for numbers 1-180 can be found with either white or gray cardboard. Some hobbyists feel a premium is warranted for gray backs between #1-100 and white backs from #101-180.

		NM	EX	VG
	Complete Set (340):	9,000	4,250	2,550
	Common Player (1-180):	15.00	7.50	4.50
	Common Player (181-340):	20.00	10.00	6.00
1	William Harridge	125.00	25.00	15.00
2	Warren Giles	65.00	12.00	6.00
3	Elmer Valo	15.00	7.50	4.50
4	Carlos Paula	15.00	7.50	4.50
5	Ted Williams	375.00	130.00	70.00
6	Ray Boone	15.00	7.50	4.50
7	Ron Negray	15.00	7.50	4.50
8	Walter Alston	45.00	22.50	13.50
9	Ruben Gomez	15.00	7.50	4.50
10	Warren Spahn	75.00	37.50	22.50
11a	Chicago Cubs/1955	125.00	65.00	35.00
11b	Chicago Cubs (No date, name centered.)	60.00	30.00	18.00
11c	Chicago Cubs (No date, name at left.)	70.00	35.00	20.00
12	Andy Carey	20.00	10.00	6.00
13	Roy Face	15.00	7.50	4.50
14	Ken Boyer	25.00	12.50	7.50
15	Ernie Banks	100.00	50.00	30.00
16	***Hector Lopez***	20.00	10.00	6.00
17	Gene Conley	15.00	7.50	4.50
18	Dick Donovan	15.00	7.50	4.50
19	Chuck Diering	15.00	7.50	4.50
20	Al Kaline	75.00	37.50	22.50
21	Joe Collins	20.00	10.00	6.00
22	Jim Finigan	15.00	7.50	4.50
23	Freddie Marsh	20.00	10.00	6.00
24	Dick Groat	20.00	10.00	6.00
25	Ted Kluszewski	35.00	17.50	10.00
26	Grady Hatton	15.00	7.50	4.50
27	Nelson Burbrink	15.00	7.50	4.50
28	Bobby Hofman	15.00	7.50	4.50
29	Jack Harshman	15.00	7.50	4.50
30	Jackie Robinson	165.00	85.00	50.00
31	Hank Aaron	225.00	110.00	65.00
32	Frank House	15.00	7.50	4.50
33	Roberto Clemente	250.00	125.00	75.00
34	Tom Brewer	15.00	7.50	4.50
35	Al Rosen	20.00	10.00	6.00
36	Rudy Minarcin	15.00	7.50	4.50
37	Alex Grammas	15.00	7.50	4.50
38	Bob Kennedy	15.00	7.50	4.50
39	Don Mossi	15.00	7.50	4.50
40	Bob Turley	25.00	12.50	7.50
41	Hank Sauer	15.00	7.50	4.50
42	Sandy Amoros	25.00	12.50	7.50
43	Ray Moore	15.00	7.50	4.50
44	"Windy" McCall	15.00	7.50	4.50
45	Gus Zernial	15.00	7.50	4.50
46	Gene Freese	15.00	7.50	4.50
47	Art Fowler	15.00	7.50	4.50
48	Jim Hegan	15.00	7.50	4.50
49	***Pedro Ramos***	20.00	10.00	6.00
50	"Dusty" Rhodes	15.00	7.50	4.50
51	Ernie Oravetz	15.00	7.50	4.50
52	Bob Grim	20.00	10.00	6.00
53	Arnold Portocarrero	15.00	7.50	4.50
54	Bob Keegan	15.00	7.50	4.50
55	Wally Moon	15.00	7.50	4.50
56	Dale Long	15.00	7.50	4.50
57	"Duke" Maas	15.00	7.50	4.50
58	Ed Roebuck	20.00	10.00	6.00
59	Jose Santiago	15.00	7.50	4.50
60	Mayo Smith	15.00	7.50	4.50
61	Bill Skowron	35.00	17.50	10.00
62	Hal Smith	15.00	7.50	4.50
63	***Roger Craig***	27.50	13.50	8.00
64	Luis Arroyo	15.00	7.50	4.50
65	Johnny O'Brien	15.00	7.50	4.50
66	Bob Speake	15.00	7.50	4.50
67	Vic Power	15.00	7.50	4.50
68	Chuck Stobbs	15.00	7.50	4.50
69	Chuck Tanner	15.00	7.50	4.50
70	Jim Rivera	15.00	7.50	4.50
71	Frank Sullivan	15.00	7.50	4.50
72a	Philadelphia Phillies - 1955	80.00	40.00	24.00
72b	Philadelphia Phillies (No date, name centered.)	40.00	20.00	12.00
72c	Philadelphia Phillies (No date, name at left.)	60.00	30.00	18.00
73	Wayne Terwilliger	15.00	7.50	4.50
74	Jim King	15.00	7.50	4.50
75	Roy Sievers	15.00	7.50	4.50
76	Ray Crone	15.00	7.50	4.50
77	Harvey Haddix	15.00	7.50	4.50
78	Herman Wehmeier	15.00	7.50	4.50
79	Sandy Koufax	185.00	90.00	50.00
80	Gus Triandos	15.00	7.50	4.50
81	Wally Westlake	15.00	7.50	4.50
82	Bill Renna	15.00	7.50	4.50
83	Karl Spooner	20.00	10.00	6.00
84	"Babe" Birrer	15.00	7.50	4.50
85a	Cleveland Indians - 1955	85.00	42.50	25.00
85b	Cleveland Indians (No date, name centered.)	50.00	25.00	15.00
85c	Cleveland Indians (No date, name at left.)	60.00	30.00	18.00
86	Ray Jablonski	15.00	7.50	4.50
87	Dean Stone	15.00	7.50	4.50
88	Johnny Kucks	20.00	10.00	6.00
89	Norm Zauchin	15.00	7.50	4.50
90a	Cincinnati Redlegs - 1955	100.00	50.00	30.00
90b	Cincinnati Redlegs (No date, name centered.)	45.00	22.50	13.50
90c	Cincinnati Redlegs (No date, name at left.)	90.00	45.00	27.50
91	Gail Harris	15.00	7.50	4.50
92	"Red" Wilson	15.00	7.50	4.50
93	George Susce, Jr.	15.00	7.50	4.50
94	Ronnie Kline	15.00	7.50	4.50
95a	Milwaukee Braves - 1955	160.00	80.00	50.00
95b	Milwaukee Braves (No date, name centered.)	60.00	30.00	18.00
95c	Milwaukee Braves (No date, name at left.)	55.00	27.50	16.50
96	Bill Tremel	15.00	7.50	4.50
97	Jerry Lynch	15.00	7.50	4.50
98	Camilo Pascual	15.00	7.50	4.50
99	Don Zimmer	30.00	15.00	9.00
100a	Baltimore Orioles - 1955	160.00	80.00	45.00
100b	Baltimore Orioles (No date, name centered.)	110.00	55.00	35.00
100c	Baltimore Orioles (No date, name at left.)	110.00	55.00	35.00
101	Roy Campanella	100.00	50.00	30.00
102	Jim Davis	15.00	7.50	4.50
103	Willie Miranda	15.00	7.50	4.50
104	Bob Lennon	15.00	7.50	4.50
105	Al Smith	15.00	7.50	4.50
106	Joe Astroth	15.00	7.50	4.50
107	Ed Mathews	70.00	35.00	20.00
108	Laurin Pepper	15.00	7.50	4.50
109	Enos Slaughter	32.50	16.00	10.00
110	Yogi Berra	115.00	55.00	35.00
111	Boston Red Sox	35.00	17.50	10.00
112	Dee Fondy	15.00	7.50	4.50
113	Phil Rizzuto	95.00	47.50	27.50
114	Jim Owens	15.00	7.50	4.50
115	Jackie Jensen	20.00	10.00	6.00
116	Eddie O'Brien	15.00	7.50	4.50
117	Virgil Trucks	15.00	7.50	4.50
118	"Nellie" Fox	50.00	25.00	15.00
119	***Larry Jackson***	15.00	7.50	4.50
120	Richie Ashburn	50.00	25.00	15.00
121	Pittsburgh Pirates	65.00	32.50	20.00
122	Willard Nixon	15.00	7.50	4.50
123	Roy McMillan	15.00	7.50	4.50
124	Don Kaiser	15.00	7.50	4.50
125	"Minnie" Minoso	30.00	15.00	9.00
126	Jim Brady	15.00	7.50	4.50
127	Willie Jones	15.00	7.50	4.50
128	Eddie Yost	15.00	7.50	4.50
129	"Jake" Martin	15.00	7.50	4.50
130	Willie Mays	225.00	110.00	65.00
131	Bob Roselli	15.00	7.50	4.50

132	Bobby Avila	15.00	7.50	4.50
133	Ray Narleski	15.00	7.50	4.50
134	St. Louis Cardinals	25.00	12.50	7.50
135	Mickey Mantle	875.00	400.00	215.00
136	Johnny Logan	15.00	7.50	4.50
137	Al Silvera	15.00	7.50	4.50
138	Johnny Antonelli	15.00	7.50	4.50
139	Tommy Carroll	20.00	10.00	6.00
140	***Herb Score***	35.00	17.50	10.00
141	Joe Frazier	15.00	7.50	4.50
142	Gene Baker	15.00	7.50	4.50
143	Jim Piersall	20.00	10.00	6.00
144	Leroy Powell	15.00	7.50	4.50
145	Gil Hodges	55.00	27.50	16.50
146	Washington Nationals	40.00	20.00	12.00
147	Earl Torgeson	15.00	7.50	4.50
148	Alvin Dark	15.00	7.50	4.50
149	"Dixie" Howell	15.00	7.50	4.50
150	"Duke" Snider	95.00	47.50	27.50
151	"Spook" Jacobs	15.00	7.50	4.50
152	Billy Hoeft	15.00	7.50	4.50
153	Frank Thomas	15.00	7.50	4.50
154	Dave Pope	15.00	7.50	4.50
155	Harvey Kuenn	15.00	7.50	4.50
156	Wes Westrum	15.00	7.50	4.50
157	Dick Brodowski	15.00	7.50	4.50
158	Wally Post	15.00	7.50	4.50
159	Clint Courtney	15.00	7.50	4.50
160	Billy Pierce	15.00	7.50	4.50
161	Joe De Maestri	15.00	7.50	4.50
162	"Gus" Bell	15.00	7.50	4.50
163	Gene Woodling	15.00	7.50	4.50
164	Harmon Killebrew	100.00	50.00	30.00
165	"Red" Schoendienst	35.00	17.50	10.00
166	Brooklyn Dodgers	135.00	65.00	40.00
167	Harry Dorish	15.00	7.50	4.50
168	Sammy White	15.00	7.50	4.50
169	Bob Nelson	15.00	7.50	4.50
170	Bill Virdon	15.00	7.50	4.50
171	Jim Wilson	15.00	7.50	4.50
172	***Frank Torre***	20.00	10.00	6.00
173	Johnny Podres	30.00	15.00	9.00
174	Glen Gorbous	15.00	7.50	4.50
175	Del Crandall	15.00	7.50	4.50
176	Alex Kellner	15.00	7.50	4.50
177	Hank Bauer	30.00	15.00	9.00
178	Joe Black	20.00	10.00	6.00
179	Harry Chiti	15.00	7.50	4.50
180	Robin Roberts	40.00	20.00	12.00
181	Billy Martin	50.00	25.00	15.00
182	Paul Minner	20.00	10.00	6.00
183	Stan Lopata	20.00	10.00	6.00
184	Don Bessent	25.00	12.50	7.50
185	Bill Bruton	20.00	10.00	6.00
186	Ron Jackson	20.00	10.00	6.00
187	Early Wynn	55.00	27.50	16.50
188	Chicago White Sox	75.00	37.50	22.50
189	Ned Garver	20.00	10.00	6.00
190	Carl Furillo	45.00	22.50	13.50
191	Frank Lary	20.00	10.00	6.00
192	"Smoky" Burgess	20.00	10.00	6.00
193	Wilmer Mizell	20.00	10.00	6.00
194	Monte Irvin	55.00	27.50	16.50
195	George Kell	45.00	22.50	13.50
196	Tom Poholsky	20.00	10.00	6.00
197	Granny Hamner	20.00	10.00	6.00
198	Ed Fitzgerald	20.00	10.00	6.00
199	Hank Thompson	20.00	10.00	6.00
200	Bob Feller	100.00	50.00	30.00
201	"Rip" Repulski	20.00	10.00	6.00
202	Jim Hearn	20.00	10.00	6.00
203	Bill Tuttle	20.00	10.00	6.00
204	Art Swanson	20.00	10.00	6.00
205	"Whitey" Lockman	20.00	10.00	6.00
206	Erv Palica	20.00	10.00	6.00
207	Jim Small	20.00	10.00	6.00
208	Elston Howard	45.00	22.50	13.50
209	Max Surkont	20.00	10.00	6.00
210	Mike Garcia	20.00	10.00	6.00
211	Murry Dickson	20.00	10.00	6.00
212	Johnny Temple	20.00	10.00	6.00
213	Detroit Tigers	60.00	30.00	18.00
214	Bob Rush	20.00	10.00	6.00
215	Tommy Byrne	25.00	12.50	7.50
216	Jerry Schoonmaker	20.00	10.00	6.00
217	Billy Klaus	20.00	10.00	6.00
218	Joe Nuxall (Nuxhall)	25.00	12.50	7.50
219	Lew Burdette	20.00	10.00	6.00
220	Del Ennis	20.00	10.00	6.00
221	Bob Friend	20.00	10.00	6.00
222	Dave Philley	20.00	10.00	6.00
223	Randy Jackson	25.00	12.50	7.50
224	"Bud" Podbielan	20.00	10.00	6.00
225	Gil McDougald	35.00	17.50	10.00
226	New York Giants	50.00	25.00	15.00
227	Russ Meyer	20.00	10.00	6.00
228	"Mickey" Vernon	20.00	10.00	6.00
229	Harry Brecheen	20.00	10.00	6.00
230	"Chico" Carrasquel	20.00	10.00	6.00
231	Bob Hale	20.00	10.00	6.00
232	"Toby" Atwell	20.00	10.00	6.00
233	Carl Erskine	30.00	15.00	9.00
234	"Pete" Runnels	20.00	10.00	6.00
235	Don Newcombe	55.00	27.50	16.50
236	Kansas City Athletics	35.00	17.50	10.00
237	Jose Valdivielso	20.00	10.00	6.00
238	Walt Dropo	20.00	10.00	6.00
239	Harry Simpson	20.00	10.00	6.00
240	"Whitey" Ford	90.00	45.00	27.50
241	Don Mueller	20.00	10.00	6.00
242	Hershell Freeman	20.00	10.00	6.00
243	Sherm Lollar	20.00	10.00	6.00
244	Bob Buhl	20.00	10.00	6.00
245	Billy Goodman	20.00	10.00	6.00
246	Tom Gorman	20.00	10.00	6.00
247	Bill Sarni	20.00	10.00	6.00
248	Bob Porterfield	20.00	10.00	6.00
249	Johnny Klippstein	20.00	10.00	6.00
250	Larry Doby	45.00	22.50	13.50
251	New York Yankees	250.00	125.00	75.00
252	Vernon Law	20.00	10.00	6.00
253	Irv Noren	25.00	12.50	7.50
254	George Crowe	20.00	10.00	6.00
255	Bob Lemon	35.00	17.50	10.00
256	Tom Hurd	20.00	10.00	6.00
257	Bobby Thomson	25.00	12.50	7.50
258	Art Ditmar	20.00	10.00	6.00
259	Sam Jones	20.00	10.00	6.00
260	"Pee Wee" Reese	120.00	60.00	35.00
261	Bobby Shantz	20.00	10.00	6.00
262	Howie Pollet	20.00	10.00	6.00
263	Bob Miller	20.00	10.00	6.00
264	Ray Monzant	20.00	10.00	6.00
265	Sandy Consuegra	20.00	10.00	6.00
266	Don Ferrarese	20.00	10.00	6.00
267	Bob Nieman	20.00	10.00	6.00
268	Dale Mitchell	20.00	10.00	6.00
269	Jack Meyer	20.00	10.00	6.00
270	Billy Loes	25.00	12.50	7.50
271	Foster Castleman	20.00	10.00	6.00
272	Danny O'Connell	20.00	10.00	6.00
273	Walker Cooper	20.00	10.00	6.00
274	Frank Baumholtz	20.00	10.00	6.00
275	Jim Greengrass	20.00	10.00	6.00
276	George Zuverink	20.00	10.00	6.00
277	Daryl Spencer	20.00	10.00	6.00
278	Chet Nichols	20.00	10.00	6.00
279	Johnny Groth	20.00	10.00	6.00
280	Jim Gilliam	45.00	22.50	13.50
281	Art Houtteman	20.00	10.00	6.00
282	Warren Hacker	20.00	10.00	6.00
283	Hal Smith	20.00	10.00	6.00
284	Ike Delock	20.00	10.00	6.00
285	Eddie Miksis	20.00	10.00	6.00
286	Bill Wight	20.00	10.00	6.00
287	Bobby Adams	20.00	10.00	6.00
288	Bob Cerv/SP	45.00	22.50	13.50
289	Hal Jeffcoat	20.00	10.00	6.00
290	Curt Simmons	20.00	10.00	6.00
291	Frank Kellert	20.00	10.00	6.00
292	***Luis Aparicio***	100.00	50.00	30.00
293	Stu Miller	20.00	10.00	6.00
294	Ernie Johnson	20.00	10.00	6.00
295	Clem Labine	30.00	15.00	9.00
296	Andy Seminick	20.00	10.00	6.00
297	Bob Skinner	20.00	10.00	6.00
298	Johnny Schmitz	20.00	10.00	6.00
299	Charley Neal/SP	35.00	17.50	10.00
300	Vic Wertz	20.00	10.00	6.00
301	Marv Grissom	20.00	10.00	6.00
302	Eddie Robinson	25.00	12.50	7.50
303	Jim Dyck	20.00	10.00	6.00
304	Frank Malzone	20.00	10.00	6.00
305	Brooks Lawrence	20.00	10.00	6.00
306	Curt Roberts	20.00	10.00	6.00
307	Hoyt Wilhelm	40.00	20.00	12.00
308	"Chuck" Harmon	20.00	10.00	6.00
309	***Don Blasingame***	25.00	12.50	7.50
310	Steve Gromek	20.00	10.00	6.00
311	Hal Naragon	20.00	10.00	6.00
312	Andy Pafko	20.00	10.00	6.00
313	Gene Stephens	20.00	10.00	6.00
314	Hobie Landrith	20.00	10.00	6.00
315	Milt Bolling	20.00	10.00	6.00
316	Jerry Coleman	25.00	12.50	7.50
317	Al Aber	20.00	10.00	6.00
318	Fred Hatfield	20.00	10.00	6.00
319	Jack Crimian	20.00	10.00	6.00
320	Joe Adcock	20.00	10.00	6.00
321	Jim Konstanty	25.00	12.50	7.50
322	Karl Olson	20.00	10.00	6.00
323	Willard Schmidt	20.00	10.00	6.00
324	"Rocky" Bridges	20.00	10.00	6.00
325	Don Liddle	20.00	10.00	6.00
326	Connie Johnson	20.00	10.00	6.00
327	Bob Wiesler	20.00	10.00	6.00
328	Preston Ward	20.00	10.00	6.00
329	Lou Berberet	20.00	10.00	6.00
330	Jim Busby	20.00	10.00	6.00
331	Dick Hall	20.00	10.00	6.00
332	Don Larsen	55.00	27.50	16.50
333	"Rube" Walker	25.00	12.50	7.50
334	Bob Miller	20.00	10.00	6.00
335	Don Hoak	20.00	10.00	6.00
336	Ellis Kinder	20.00	10.00	6.00
337	Bobby Morgan	20.00	10.00	6.00
338	Jim Delsing	20.00	10.00	6.00
339	Rance Pless	20.00	10.00	6.00
340	Mickey McDermott	45.00	15.00	8.00
----	Checklist 1/3	150.00	45.00	30.00
----	Checklist 2/4	190.00	60.00	35.00

1956 Topps Hocus Focus

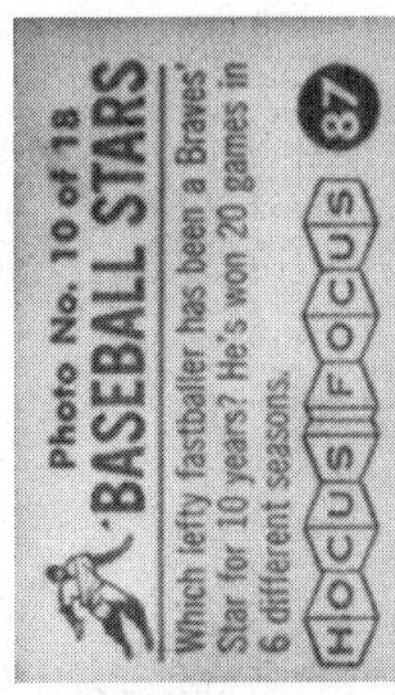

Following its 1955 issue with a somewhat larger format (1" x 1-5/8") the following year, the baseball players in this set are part of a larger overall series covering several topical areas. Cards backs specify an issue of 18 baseball stars. The black-and-white photos on these cards were developed by wetting the card's surface and exposing to light. Prices below are for cards with well-developed pictures. Cards with poorly developed photos are worth significantly less.

		NM	EX	VG
Complete Set (18):		7,000	3,500	2,100
Common Player:		220.00	110.00	66.00
1	Dick Groat	225.00	110.00	65.00
2	Ed Lopat	425.00	210.00	125.00
3	Hank Sauer	225.00	110.00	65.00
4	"Dusty" Rhodes	225.00	110.00	65.00
5	Ted Williams	1,600	800.00	480.00
6	Harvey Haddix	225.00	110.00	65.00
7	Ray Boone	225.00	110.00	65.00
8	Al Rosen	250.00	125.00	75.00
9	Mayo Smith	225.00	110.00	65.00
10	Warren Spahn	550.00	275.00	165.00
11	Jim Rivera	225.00	110.00	65.00
12	Ted Kluszewski	450.00	225.00	135.00
13	Gus Zernial	225.00	110.00	65.00
14	Jackie Robinson	1,350	675.00	400.00
15	Hal Smith	225.00	110.00	65.00
16	Johnny Schmitz	225.00	110.00	65.00
17	"Spook" Jacobs	225.00	110.00	65.00
18	Mel Parnell	225.00	110.00	65.00

1956 Topps Pins

One of Topps first specialty issues, the 60-pin set of ballplayers issued in 1956 contains a high percentage of big-name stars which, combined with the scarcity of the pins, makes collecting a complete set extremely challenging. Compounding the situation is the fact that some pins are seen far less often than others, though the reason is unknown. Chuck Stobbs, Hector Lopez and Chuck Diering are unaccountably scarce. Measuring 1-1/8" in diameter, the pins utilize the same portraits found on 1956 Topps baseball cards. The photos are set against a solid color background. The pins were sold in a box picturing the Ted Williams pin, with a piece of bubblegum for five cents.

		NM	EX	VG
Complete Set (60):		3,600	1,800	1,100
Common Player:		40.00	20.00	12.00
Box:		500.00	250.00	150.00
(1)	Hank Aaron	200.00	100.00	60.00
(2)	Sandy Amoros	50.00	25.00	15.00
(3)	Luis Arroyo	40.00	20.00	12.00
(4)	Ernie Banks	150.00	75.00	45.00
(5)	Yogi Berra	150.00	75.00	45.00
(6)	Joe Black	60.00	30.00	18.00
(7)	Ray Boone	40.00	20.00	12.00
(8)	Ken Boyer	45.00	22.50	13.50
(9)	Joe Collins	45.00	22.50	13.50
(10)	Gene Conley	40.00	20.00	12.00
(11)	Chuck Diering	275.00	135.00	85.00
(12)	Dick Donovan	40.00	20.00	12.00
(13)	Jim Finigan	40.00	20.00	12.00
(14)	Art Fowler	40.00	20.00	12.00
(15)	Ruben Gomez	40.00	20.00	12.00
(16)	Dick Groat	40.00	20.00	12.00
(17)	Harvey Haddix	40.00	20.00	12.00
(18)	Jack Harshman	40.00	20.00	12.00
(19)	Grady Hatton	40.00	20.00	12.00
(20)	Jim Hegan	40.00	20.00	12.00
(21)	Gil Hodges	100.00	50.00	30.00
(22)	Bobby Hofman	40.00	20.00	12.00
(23)	Frank House	40.00	20.00	12.00
(24)	Jackie Jensen	45.00	22.50	13.50
(25)	Al Kaline	100.00	50.00	30.00
(26)	Bob Kennedy	40.00	20.00	12.00
(27)	Ted Kluszewski	85.00	42.50	25.00
(28)	Dale Long	40.00	20.00	12.00
(29)	Hector Lopez	400.00	200.00	120.00
(30)	Ed Mathews	100.00	50.00	30.00
(31)	Willie Mays	200.00	100.00	60.00
(32)	Roy McMillan	40.00	20.00	12.00
(33)	Willie Miranda	40.00	20.00	12.00
(34)	Wally Moon	40.00	20.00	12.00
(35)	Don Mossi	40.00	20.00	12.00
(36)	Ron Negray	40.00	20.00	12.00
(37)	Johnny O'Brien	40.00	20.00	12.00
(38)	Carlos Paula	40.00	20.00	12.00
(39)	Vic Power	40.00	20.00	12.00
(40)	Jim Rivera	40.00	20.00	12.00
(41)	Phil Rizzuto	150.00	75.00	45.00
(42)	Jackie Robinson	180.00	90.00	55.00
(43)	Al Rosen	45.00	22.50	13.50
(44)	Hank Sauer	40.00	20.00	12.00
(45)	Roy Sievers	40.00	20.00	12.00
(46)	Bill Skowron	45.00	22.50	13.50
(47)	Al Smith	40.00	20.00	12.00
(48)	Hal Smith	40.00	20.00	12.00

#	Player	NM	EX	VG
(49)	Mayo Smith	40.00	20.00	12.00
(50)	Duke Snider	125.00	65.00	35.00
(51)	Warren Spahn	100.00	50.00	30.00
(52)	Karl Spooner	45.00	22.50	13.50
(53)	Chuck Stobbs	225.00	110.00	65.00
(54)	Frank Sullivan	40.00	20.00	12.00
(55)	Bill Tremel	40.00	20.00	12.00
(56)	Gus Triandos	40.00	20.00	12.00
(57)	Bob Turley	50.00	25.00	15.00
(58)	Herman Wehmeier	40.00	20.00	12.00
(59)	Ted Williams	225.00	110.00	65.00
(60)	Gus Zernial	40.00	20.00	12.00

1957 Topps

For 1957, Topps reduced the size of its cards to the now-standard 2-1/2" x 3-1/2". Set size was increased to 407 cards. Another change came in the form of the use of real color photographs as opposed to the hand-colored black and whites of previous years. For the first time since 1954, there were also cards with more than one player. The two, "Dodger Sluggers" and "Yankees' Power Hitters" began a trend toward the increased use of multiple-player cards. Another first-time innovation, found on the backs, is complete players statistics. The scarce cards in the set are not the highest numbers, but rather numbers 265-352. Four unnumbered checklist cards were issued along with the set. They are quite expensive and are not included in the complete set prices quoted below.

#	Player	NM	EX	VG
	Complete Set (407):	10,000	5,000	3,000
	Common Player (1-264):	12.00	6.00	3.50
	Common Player (265-352):	25.00	12.50	7.50
	Common Player (353-407):	12.00	6.00	3.50
1	Ted Williams	375.00	135.00	65.00
2	Yogi Berra	120.00	60.00	35.00
3	Dale Long	12.00	6.00	3.50
4	Johnny Logan	12.00	6.00	3.50
5	Sal Maglie	20.00	10.00	6.00
6	Hector Lopez	12.00	6.00	3.50
7	Luis Aparicio	40.00	20.00	12.00
8	Don Mossi	12.00	6.00	3.50
9	Johnny Temple	12.00	6.00	3.50
10	Willie Mays	215.00	100.00	65.00
11	George Zuverink	12.00	6.00	3.50
12	Dick Groat	12.00	6.00	3.50
13	Wally Burnette	12.00	6.00	3.50
14	Bob Nieman	12.00	6.00	3.50
15	Robin Roberts	50.00	25.00	15.00
16	Walt Moryn	12.00	6.00	3.50
17	Billy Gardner	12.00	6.00	3.50
18	***Don Drysdale***	165.00	80.00	50.00
19	Bob Wilson	12.00	6.00	3.50
20	Hank Aaron (Photo reversed.)	200.00	100.00	60.00
21	Frank Sullivan	12.00	6.00	3.50
22	Jerry Snyder (Photo actually Ed Fitz Gerald.)	12.00	6.00	3.50
23	Sherman Lollar	12.00	6.00	3.50
24	***Bill Mazeroski***	75.00	37.50	22.50
25	Whitey Ford	90.00	45.00	27.50
26	Bob Boyd	12.00	6.00	3.50
27	Ted Kazanski	12.00	6.00	3.50
28	Gene Conley	12.00	6.00	3.50
29	***Whitey Herzog***	15.00	7.50	4.50
30	Pee Wee Reese	75.00	37.50	22.50
31	Ron Northey	12.00	6.00	3.50
32	Hersh Freeman	12.00	6.00	3.50
33	Jim Small	12.00	6.00	3.50
34	Tom Sturdivant	15.00	7.50	4.50
35	***Frank Robinson***	180.00	75.00	35.00
36	Bob Grim	15.00	7.50	4.50
37	Frank Torre	12.00	6.00	3.50
38	Nellie Fox	40.00	20.00	12.00
39	Al Worthington	12.00	6.00	3.50
40	Early Wynn	30.00	15.00	9.00
41	Hal Smith	12.00	6.00	3.50
42	Dee Fondy	12.00	6.00	3.50
43	Connie Johnson	12.00	6.00	3.50
44	Joe DeMaestri	12.00	6.00	3.50
45	Carl Furillo	40.00	20.00	12.00
46	Bob Miller	12.00	6.00	3.50
47	Don Blasingame	12.00	6.00	3.50
48	Bill Bruton	12.00	6.00	3.50
49	Daryl Spencer	12.00	6.00	3.50
50	Herb Score	25.00	12.50	7.50
51	Clint Courtney	12.00	6.00	3.50
52	Lee Walls	12.00	6.00	3.50
53	Clem Labine	20.00	10.00	6.00
54	Elmer Valo	12.00	6.00	3.50
55	Ernie Banks	85.00	42.50	25.00
56	Dave Sisler	12.00	6.00	3.50
57	Jim Lemon	12.00	6.00	3.50
58	Ruben Gomez	12.00	6.00	3.50
59	Dick Williams	12.00	6.00	3.50
60	Billy Hoeft	12.00	6.00	3.50
61	Dusty Rhodes	12.00	6.00	3.50
62	Billy Martin	40.00	20.00	12.00
63	Ike Delock	12.00	6.00	3.50
64	Pete Runnels	12.00	6.00	3.50
65	Wally Moon	12.00	6.00	3.50
66	Brooks Lawrence	12.00	6.00	3.50
67	Chico Carrasquel	12.00	6.00	3.50
68	Ray Crone	12.00	6.00	3.50
69	Roy McMillan	12.00	6.00	3.50
70	Richie Ashburn	45.00	22.50	13.50
71	Murry Dickson	12.00	6.00	3.50
72	Bill Tuttle	12.00	6.00	3.50
73	George Crowe	12.00	6.00	3.50
74	Vito Valentinetti	12.00	6.00	3.50
75	Jim Piersall	15.00	7.50	4.50
76	Bob Clemente	175.00	90.00	45.00
77	Paul Foytack	12.00	6.00	3.50
78	Vic Wertz	12.00	6.00	3.50
79	***Lindy McDaniel***	15.00	7.50	4.50
80	Gil Hodges	45.00	22.50	13.50
81	Herm Wehmeier	12.00	6.00	3.50
82	Elston Howard	30.00	15.00	9.00
83	Lou Skizas	12.00	6.00	3.50
84	Moe Drabowsky	12.00	6.00	3.50
85	Larry Doby	40.00	20.00	12.00
86	Bill Sarni	12.00	6.00	3.50
87	Tom Gorman	12.00	6.00	3.50
88	Harvey Kuenn	12.00	6.00	3.50
89	Roy Sievers	12.00	6.00	3.50
90	Warren Spahn	60.00	30.00	18.00
91	Mack Burk	12.00	6.00	3.50
92	Mickey Vernon	12.00	6.00	3.50
93	Hal Jeffcoat	12.00	6.00	3.50
94	Bobby Del Greco	12.00	6.00	3.50
95	Mickey Mantle	650.00	275.00	180.00
96	***Hank Aguirre***	12.00	6.00	3.50
97	New York Yankees Team	65.00	32.50	20.00
98	Al Dark	12.00	6.00	3.50
99	Bob Keegan	12.00	6.00	3.50
100	League Presidents (Warren Giles, William Harridge)	60.00	30.00	18.00
101	Chuck Stobbs	12.00	6.00	3.50
102	Ray Boone	12.00	6.00	3.50
103	Joe Nuxhall	12.00	6.00	3.50
104	Hank Foiles	12.00	6.00	3.50
105	Johnny Antonelli	12.00	6.00	3.50
106	Ray Moore	12.00	6.00	3.50
107	Jim Rivera	12.00	6.00	3.50
108	Tommy Byrne	15.00	7.50	4.50
109	Hank Thompson	12.00	6.00	3.50
110	Bill Virdon	12.00	6.00	3.50
111	Hal Smith	12.00	6.00	3.50
112	Tom Brewer	12.00	6.00	3.50
113	Wilmer Mizell	12.00	6.00	3.50
114	Milwaukee Braves Team	30.00	15.00	9.00
115	Jim Gilliam	27.50	13.50	8.25
116	Mike Fornieles	12.00	6.00	3.50
117	Joe Adcock	12.00	6.00	3.50
118	Bob Porterfield	12.00	6.00	3.50
119	Stan Lopata	12.00	6.00	3.50
120	Bob Lemon	35.00	17.50	10.00
121	***Cletis Boyer***	30.00	15.00	9.00
122	Ken Boyer	20.00	10.00	6.00
123	Steve Ridzik	12.00	6.00	3.50
124	Dave Philley	12.00	6.00	3.50
125	Al Kaline	75.00	37.50	22.50
126	Bob Wiesler	12.00	6.00	3.50
127	Bob Buhl	12.00	6.00	3.50
128	Ed Bailey	12.00	6.00	3.50
129	Saul Rogovin	12.00	6.00	3.50
130	Don Newcombe	25.00	12.50	7.50
131	Milt Bolling	12.00	6.00	3.50
132	Art Ditmar	12.00	6.00	3.50
133	Del Crandall	12.00	6.00	3.50
134	Don Kaiser	12.00	6.00	3.50
135	Bill Skowron	30.00	15.00	9.00
136	Jim Hegan	12.00	6.00	3.50
137	Bob Rush	12.00	6.00	3.50
138	Minnie Minoso	25.00	12.50	7.50
139	Lou Kretlow	12.00	6.00	3.50
140	Frank Thomas	12.00	6.00	3.50
141	Al Aber	12.00	6.00	3.50
142	Charley Thompson	12.00	6.00	3.50
143	Andy Pafko	12.00	6.00	3.50
144	Ray Narleski	12.00	6.00	3.50
145	Al Smith	12.00	6.00	3.50
146	Don Ferrarese	12.00	6.00	3.50
147	Al Walker	15.00	7.50	4.50
148	Don Mueller	12.00	6.00	3.50
149	Bob Kennedy	12.00	6.00	3.50
150	Bob Friend	12.00	6.00	3.50
151	Willie Miranda	12.00	6.00	3.50
152	Jack Harshman	12.00	6.00	3.50
153	Karl Olson	12.00	6.00	3.50
154	Red Schoendienst	30.00	15.00	9.00
155	Jim Brosnan	12.00	6.00	3.50
156	Gus Triandos	12.00	6.00	3.50
157	Wally Post	12.00	6.00	3.50
158	Curt Simmons	12.00	6.00	3.50
159	Solly Drake	12.00	6.00	3.50
160	Billy Pierce	12.00	6.00	3.50
161	Pitsburgh Pirates Team	20.00	10.00	6.00
162	Jack Meyer	12.00	6.00	3.50
163	Sammy White	12.00	6.00	3.50
164	Tommy Carroll	15.00	7.50	4.50
165	Ted Kluszewski	65.00	32.50	20.00
166	Roy Face	12.00	6.00	3.50
167	Vic Power	12.00	6.00	3.50
168	Frank Lary	12.00	6.00	3.50
169	Herb Plews	12.00	6.00	3.50
170	Duke Snider	95.00	47.50	27.50
171	Boston Red Sox Team	32.50	16.00	10.00
172	Gene Woodling	12.00	6.00	3.50
173	Roger Craig	15.00	7.50	4.50
174	Willie Jones	12.00	6.00	3.50
175	Don Larsen	35.00	17.50	10.00
176a	Gene Baker	12.00	6.00	3.50
176b	Gene Baker (Error on back, "EUGENF W. BAKEP.")	650.00	360.00	215.00
177	Eddie Yost	12.00	6.00	3.50
178	Don Bessent	15.00	7.50	4.50
179	Ernie Oravetz	12.00	6.00	3.50
180	Gus Bell	12.00	6.00	3.50
181	Dick Donovan	12.00	6.00	3.50
182	Hobie Landrith	12.00	6.00	3.50
183	Chicago Cubs Team	25.00	12.50	7.50
184	***Tito Francona***	12.00	6.00	3.50
185	Johnny Kucks	15.00	7.50	4.50
186	Jim King	12.00	6.00	3.50
187	Virgil Trucks	12.00	6.00	3.50
188	Felix Mantilla	12.00	6.00	3.50
189	Willard Nixon	12.00	6.00	3.50
190	Randy Jackson	15.00	7.50	4.50
191	Joe Margoneri	12.00	6.00	3.50
192	Jerry Coleman	15.00	7.50	4.50
193	Del Rice	12.00	6.00	3.50
194	Hal Brown	12.00	6.00	3.50
195	Bobby Avila	12.00	6.00	3.50
196	Larry Jackson	12.00	6.00	3.50
197	Hank Sauer	12.00	6.00	3.50
198	Detroit Tigers Team	20.00	10.00	6.00
199	Vernon Law	12.00	6.00	3.50
200	Gil McDougald	25.00	12.50	7.50
201	Sandy Amoros	25.00	12.50	7.50
202	Dick Gernert	12.00	6.00	3.50
203	Hoyt Wilhelm	25.00	12.50	7.50
204	Kansas City A's Team	20.00	10.00	6.00
205	Charley Maxwell	12.00	6.00	3.50
206	Willard Schmidt	12.00	6.00	3.50
207	Billy Hunter	12.00	6.00	3.50
208	Lew Burdette	12.00	6.00	3.50
209	Bob Skinner	12.00	6.00	3.50
210	Roy Campanella	95.00	47.50	27.50
211	Camilo Pascual	12.00	6.00	3.50
212	***Rocky Colavito***	70.00	35.00	20.00
213	Les Moss	12.00	6.00	3.50
214	Philadelphia Phillies Team	25.00	12.50	7.50
215	Enos Slaughter	35.00	17.50	10.00
216	Marv Grissom	12.00	6.00	3.50
217	Gene Stephens	12.00	6.00	3.50
218	Ray Jablonski	12.00	6.00	3.50
219	Tom Acker	12.00	6.00	3.50
220	Jackie Jensen	17.50	8.75	5.25
221	Dixie Howell	12.00	6.00	3.50
222	Alex Grammas	12.00	6.00	3.50
223	Frank House	12.00	6.00	3.50
224	Marv Blaylock	12.00	6.00	3.50
225	Harry Simpson	12.00	6.00	3.50
226	Preston Ward	12.00	6.00	3.50
227	Jerry Staley	12.00	6.00	3.50
228	Smoky Burgess	12.00	6.00	3.50
229	George Susce	12.00	6.00	3.50
230	George Kell	25.00	12.50	7.50
231	Solly Hemus	12.00	6.00	3.50
232	Whitey Lockman	12.00	6.00	3.50
233	Art Fowler	12.00	6.00	3.50
234	Dick Cole	12.00	6.00	3.50
235	Tom Poholsky	12.00	6.00	3.50
236	Joe Ginsberg	12.00	6.00	3.50
237	Foster Castleman	12.00	6.00	3.50
238	Eddie Robinson	12.00	6.00	3.50
239	Tom Morgan	12.00	6.00	3.50
240	Hank Bauer	30.00	15.00	9.00
241	Joe Lonnett	12.00	6.00	3.50
242	Charley Neal	15.00	7.50	4.50
243	St. Louis Cardinals Team	20.00	10.00	6.00
244	Billy Loes	12.00	6.00	3.50
245	Rip Repulski	12.00	6.00	3.50
246	Jose Valdivielso	12.00	6.00	3.50
247	Turk Lown	12.00	6.00	3.50
248	Jim Finigan	12.00	6.00	3.50
249	Dave Pope	12.00	6.00	3.50
250	Ed Mathews	55.00	27.50	16.50
251	Baltimore Orioles Team	20.00	10.00	6.00
252	Carl Erskine	20.00	10.00	6.00
253	Gus Zernial	12.00	6.00	3.50
254	Ron Negray	12.00	6.00	3.50
255	Charlie Silvera	12.00	6.00	3.50
256	Ronnie Kline	12.00	6.00	3.50
257	Walt Dropo	12.00	6.00	3.50
258	Steve Gromek	12.00	6.00	3.50
259	Eddie O'Brien	12.00	6.00	3.50
260	Del Ennis	12.00	6.00	3.50
261	Bob Chakales	12.00	6.00	3.50
262	Bobby Thomson	15.00	7.50	4.50
263	George Strickland	12.00	6.00	3.50
264	Bob Turley	25.00	12.50	7.50
265	Harvey Haddix	25.00	12.50	7.50
266	Ken Kuhn	25.00	12.50	7.50
267	Danny Kravitz	25.00	12.50	7.50
268	Jackie Collum	25.00	12.50	7.50
269	Bob Cerv	25.00	12.50	7.50
270	Washington Senators Team	45.00	22.50	13.50
271	Danny O'Connell	25.00	12.50	7.50
272	Bobby Shantz	40.00	20.00	12.00
273	Jim Davis	25.00	12.50	7.50
274	Don Hoak	25.00	12.50	7.50
275	Cleveland Indians Team	40.00	20.00	12.00
276	Jim Pyburn	25.00	12.50	7.50
277	Johnny Podres	40.00	20.00	12.00
278	Fred Hatfield	25.00	12.50	7.50
279	Bob Thurman	25.00	12.50	7.50
280	Alex Kellner	25.00	12.50	7.50
281	Gail Harris	25.00	12.50	7.50
282	Jack Dittmer	25.00	12.50	7.50
283	***Wes Covington***	25.00	12.50	7.50
284	Don Zimmer	40.00	20.00	12.00
285	Ned Garver	25.00	12.50	7.50
286	***Bobby Richardson***	100.00	50.00	30.00
287	Sam Jones	25.00	12.50	7.50
288	Ted Lepcio	25.00	12.50	7.50
289	Jim Bolger	25.00	12.50	7.50
290	Andy Carey	35.00	17.50	10.00
291	Windy McCall	20.00	10.00	6.00
292	Billy Klaus	25.00	12.50	7.50

293	Ted Abernathy	25.00	12.50	7.50
294	Rocky Bridges	25.00	12.50	7.50
295	Joe Collins	35.00	17.50	10.50
296	Johnny Klippstein	25.00	12.50	7.50
297	Jack Crimian	25.00	12.50	7.50
298	Irv Noren	25.00	12.50	7.50
299	Chuck Harmon	25.00	12.50	7.50
300	Mike Garcia	25.00	12.50	7.50
301	Sam Esposito	25.00	12.50	7.50
302	Sandy Koufax	225.00	110.00	65.00
303	Billy Goodman	25.00	12.50	7.50
304	Joe Cunningham	25.00	12.50	7.50
305	Chico Fernandez	25.00	12.50	7.50
306	***Darrell Johnson***	35.00	17.50	10.00
307	Jack Phillips	25.00	12.50	7.50
308	Dick Hall	25.00	12.50	7.50
309	Jim Busby	25.00	12.50	7.50
310	Max Surkont	25.00	12.50	7.50
311	Al Pilarcik	25.00	12.50	7.50
312	***Tony Kubek***	70.00	35.00	20.00
313	Mel Parnell	25.00	12.50	7.50
314	Ed Bouchee	25.00	12.50	7.50
315	Lou Berberet	25.00	12.50	7.50
316	Billy O'Dell	25.00	12.50	7.50
317	New York Giants Team	40.00	20.00	12.00
318	Mickey McDermott	25.00	12.50	7.50
319	***Gino Cimoli***	30.00	15.00	9.00
320	Neil Chrisley	25.00	12.50	7.50
321	Red Murff	25.00	12.50	7.50
322	Cincinnati Redlegs Team	45.00	22.50	13.50
323	Wes Westrum	25.00	12.50	7.50
324	Brooklyn Dodgers Team	100.00	50.00	30.00
325	Frank Bolling	25.00	12.50	7.50
326	Pedro Ramos	25.00	12.50	7.50
327	Jim Pendleton	25.00	12.50	7.50
328	***Brooks Robinson***	245.00	130.00	65.00
329	Chicago White Sox Team	45.00	22.50	13.50
330	Jim Wilson	25.00	12.50	7.50
331	Ray Katt	25.00	12.50	7.50
332	Bob Bowman	25.00	12.50	7.50
333	Ernie Johnson	25.00	12.50	7.50
334	Jerry Schoonmaker	25.00	12.50	7.50
335	Granny Hamner	25.00	12.50	7.50
336	***Haywood Sullivan***	25.00	12.50	7.50
337	Rene Valdes (Valdez)	30.00	15.00	9.00
338	***Jim Bunning***	85.00	42.50	25.00
339	Bob Speake	25.00	12.50	7.50
340	Bill Wight	25.00	12.50	7.50
341	Don Gross	25.00	12.50	7.50
342	Gene Mauch	25.00	12.50	7.50
343	Taylor Phillips	25.00	12.50	7.50
344	Paul LaPalme	25.00	12.50	7.50
345	Paul Smith	25.00	12.50	7.50
346	Dick Littlefield	25.00	12.50	7.50
347	Hal Naragon	25.00	12.50	7.50
348	Jim Hearn	25.00	12.50	7.50
349	Nelson King	25.00	12.50	7.50
350	Eddie Miksis	25.00	12.50	7.50
351	Dave Hillman	25.00	12.50	7.50
352	Ellis Kinder	25.00	12.50	7.50
353	Cal Neeman	12.00	6.00	3.50
354	Rip Coleman	12.00	6.00	3.50
355	Frank Malzone	12.00	6.00	3.50
356	Faye Throneberry	12.00	6.00	3.50
357	Earl Torgeson	12.00	6.00	3.50
358	Jerry Lynch	12.00	6.00	3.50
359	Tom Cheney	12.00	6.00	3.50
360	Johnny Groth	12.00	6.00	3.50
361	Curt Barclay	12.00	6.00	3.50
362	Roman Mejias	12.00	6.00	3.50
363	Eddie Kasko	12.00	6.00	3.50
364	***Cal McLish***	12.00	6.00	3.50
365	Ossie Virgil	12.00	6.00	3.50
366	Ken Lehman	15.00	7.50	4.50
367	Ed FitzGerald	12.00	6.00	3.50
368	Bob Purkey	12.00	6.00	3.50
369	Milt Graff	12.00	6.00	3.50
370	Warren Hacker	12.00	6.00	3.50
371	Bob Lennon	12.00	6.00	3.50
372	Norm Zauchin	12.00	6.00	3.50
373	Pete Whisenant	12.00	6.00	3.50
374	Don Cardwell	12.00	6.00	3.50
375	***Jim Landis***	12.00	6.00	3.50
376	Don Elston	15.00	7.50	4.50
377	Andre Rodgers	12.00	6.00	3.50
378	Elmer Singleton	12.00	6.00	3.50
379	Don Lee	12.00	6.00	3.50
380	Walker Cooper	12.00	6.00	3.50
381	Dean Stone	12.00	6.00	3.50
382	Jim Brideweser	12.00	6.00	3.50
383	***Juan Pizarro***	12.00	6.00	3.50
384	Bobby Gene Smith	12.00	6.00	3.50
385	Art Houtteman	12.00	6.00	3.50
386	Lyle Luttrell	12.00	6.00	3.50
387	***Jack Sanford***	12.00	6.00	3.50
388	Pete Daley	12.00	6.00	3.50
389	Dave Jolly	12.00	6.00	3.50
390	Reno Bertoia	12.00	6.00	3.50
391	***Ralph Terry***	15.00	7.50	4.50
392	Chuck Tanner	12.00	6.00	3.50
393	Raul Sanchez	12.00	6.00	3.50
394	Luis Arroyo	12.00	6.00	3.50
395	Bubba Phillips	12.00	6.00	3.50
396	Casey Wise	12.00	6.00	3.50
397	Roy Smalley	12.00	6.00	3.50
398	Al Cicotte	15.00	7.50	4.50
399	Billy Consolo	12.00	6.00	3.50
400	Dodgers' Sluggers (Roy Campanella, Carl Furillo, Gil Hodges, Duke Snider)	150.00	75.00	45.00
401	***Earl Battey***	15.00	7.50	4.50
402	Jim Pisoni	12.00	6.00	3.50
403	Dick Hyde	12.00	6.00	3.50
404	Harry Anderson	12.00	6.00	3.50
405	Duke Maas	12.00	6.00	3.50
406	Bob Hale	12.00	6.00	3.50
407	Yankees' Power Hitters (Mickey Mantle, Yogi Berra)	325.00	140.00	65.00
----	Checklist Series 1-2 (Big Blony ad on back)	300.00	140.00	90.00
----	Checklist Series 1-2 (Bazooka ad on back)	300.00	140.00	90.00
----	Checklist Series 2-3 (Big Blony)	350.00	200.00	130.00
----	Checklist Series 2-3 (Bazooka)	350.00	200.00	130.00
----	Checklist Series 3-4 (Twin Blony)	800.00	300.00	195.00
----	Checklist Series 3-4 (Bazooka)	800.00	300.00	195.00
----	Checklist Series 4-5 (Twin Blony)	1,150	575.00	345.00
----	Checklist Series 4-5 (Bazooka)	1,150	575.00	345.00
----	Contest May 4	120.00	60.00	35.00
----	Contest May 25	135.00	65.00	40.00
----	Contest June 22	145.00	75.00	45.00
----	Contest July 19	200.00	100.00	60.00
----	Lucky Penny insert card	300.00	150.00	90.00

1958 Topps

Topps continued to expand its set size in 1958 with the release of a 494-card set. One card (#145) was not issued after Ed Bouchee was suspended from baseball. Cards retained the 2-1/2" x 3-1/2" size. There are a number of variations, including player or team names found in either yellow or white lettering on 33 cards between numbers 2-108 (higher priced yellow-letter variations checklisted below are not included in the complete set prices). The number of multiple-player cards was increased. A major innovation is the addition of 20 "All-Star" cards. For the first time, checklists were incorporated into the numbered series, on the backs of team cards.

		NM	EX	VG
	Complete Set (494):	8,500	4,250	2,500
	Common Player (1-495):	9.00	4.50	2.57
1	Ted Williams	360.00	115.00	55.00
2a	Bob Lemon (Yellow team.)	80.00	40.00	24.00
2b	Bob Lemon (White team.)	30.00	15.00	9.00
3	Alex Kellner	9.00	4.50	2.57
4	Hank Foiles	9.00	4.50	2.57
5	Willie Mays	190.00	95.00	55.00
6	George Zuverink	9.00	4.50	2.57
7	Dale Long	9.00	4.50	2.57
8a	Eddie Kasko (Yellow name.)	60.00	30.00	18.00
8b	Eddie Kasko (White name.)	9.00	4.50	2.57
9	Hank Bauer	20.00	10.00	6.00
10	Lou Burdette	9.00	4.50	2.57
11a	Jim Rivera (Yellow team.)	60.00	30.00	18.00
11b	Jim Rivera (White team.)	9.00	4.50	2.57
12	George Crowe	9.00	4.50	2.57
13a	Billy Hoeft (Yellow name.)	60.00	30.00	18.00
13b	Billy Hoeft (White name, orange triangle by foot.)	9.00	4.50	2.57
13c	Billy Hoeft (White name, red triangle by foot.)	9.00	4.50	2.57
14	Rip Repulski	9.00	4.50	2.57
15	Jim Lemon	9.00	4.50	2.57
16	Charley Neal	9.00	4.50	2.57
17	Felix Mantilla	9.00	4.50	2.57
18	Frank Sullivan	9.00	4.50	2.57
19	1957 Giants Team	40.00	20.00	12.00
20a	Gil McDougald (Yellow name.)	75.00	37.50	22.00
20b	Gil McDougald (White name.)	20.00	10.00	6.00
21	Curt Barclay	9.00	4.50	2.57
22	Hal Naragon	9.00	4.50	2.57
23a	Bill Tuttle (Yellow name.)	60.00	30.00	18.00
23b	Bill Tuttle (White name.)	9.00	4.50	2.57
24a	Hobie Landrith (Yellow name.)	60.00	30.00	18.00
24b	Hobie Landrith (White name.)	9.00	4.50	2.57
25	Don Drysdale	45.00	22.50	13.50
26	Ron Jackson	9.00	4.50	2.57
27	Bud Freeman	9.00	4.50	2.57
28	Jim Busby	9.00	4.50	2.57
29	Ted Lepcio	9.00	4.50	2.57
30a	Hank Aaron (Yellow name.)	380.00	165.00	95.00
30b	Hank Aaron (White name.)	165.00	80.00	45.00
31	Tex Clevenger	9.00	4.50	2.57
32a	J.W. Porter (Yellow name.)	60.00	30.00	18.00
32b	J.W. Porter (White name.)	9.00	4.50	2.57
33a	Cal Neeman (Yellow team.)	60.00	30.00	18.00
33b	Cal Neeman (White team.)	9.00	4.50	2.57
34	Bob Thurman	9.00	4.50	2.57
35a	Don Mossi (Yellow team.)	60.00	30.00	18.00
35b	Don Mossi (White team.)	9.00	4.50	2.57
36	Ted Kazanski	9.00	4.50	2.57
37	***Mike McCormick*** (Photo actually Ray Monzant.)	9.00	4.50	2.57
38	Dick Gernert	9.00	4.50	2.57
39	Bob Martyn	9.00	4.50	2.57
40	George Kell	20.00	10.00	6.00
41	Dave Hillman	9.00	4.50	2.57
42	***John Roseboro***	25.00	12.50	7.50
43	Sal Maglie	12.50	6.25	3.75
44	Wash. Senators Team	20.00	10.00	6.00
45	Dick Groat	9.00	4.50	2.57
46a	Lou Sleater (Yellow name.)	60.00	30.00	18.00
46b	Lou Sleater (White name.)	9.00	4.50	2.57
47	***Roger Maris***	285.00	140.00	85.00
48	Chuck Harmon	9.00	4.50	2.57
49	Smoky Burgess	9.00	4.50	2.57
50a	Billy Pierce (Yellow team.)	60.00	30.00	18.00
50b	Billy Pierce (White team.)	9.00	4.50	2.57
51	Del Rice	9.00	4.50	2.57
52a	Bob Clemente (Yellow team.)	425.00	210.00	125.00
52b	Bob Clemente (White team.)	200.00	100.00	60.00
53a	Morrie Martin (Yellow name.)	60.00	30.00	18.00
53b	Morrie Martin (White name.)	9.00	4.50	2.57
54	***Norm Siebern***	12.50	6.25	3.75
55	Chico Carrasquel	9.00	4.50	2.57
56	Bill Fischer	9.00	4.50	2.57
57a	Tim Thompson (Yellow name.)	60.00	30.00	18.00
57b	Tim Thompson (White name.)	9.00	4.50	2.57
58a	Art Schult (Yellow team.)	60.00	30.00	18.00
58b	Art Schult (White team.)	9.00	4.50	2.57
59	Dave Sisler	9.00	4.50	2.57
60a	Del Ennis (Yellow name.)	60.00	30.00	18.00
60b	Del Ennis (White name.)	9.00	4.50	2.57
61a	Darrell Johnson (Yellow name.)	100.00	50.00	30.00
61b	Darrell Johnson (White name.)	15.00	7.50	4.50
62	Joe DeMaestri	9.00	4.50	2.57
63	Joe Nuxhall	9.00	4.50	2.57
64	Joe Lonnett	9.00	4.50	2.57
65a	Von McDaniel (Yellow name.)	60.00	30.00	18.00
65b	Von McDaniel (White name.)	9.00	4.50	2.57
66	Lee Walls	9.00	4.50	2.57
67	Joe Ginsberg	9.00	4.50	2.57
68	Daryl Spencer	9.00	4.50	2.57
69	Wally Burnette	9.00	4.50	2.57
70a	Al Kaline (Yellow name.)	225.00	110.00	65.00
70b	Al Kaline (White name.)	65.00	32.50	20.00
71	1957 Dodgers Team	60.00	30.00	18.00
72	Bud Byerly (Photo actually Hal Griggs.)	9.00	4.50	2.57
73	Pete Daley	9.00	4.50	2.57
74	Roy Face	9.00	4.50	2.57
75	Gus Bell	9.00	4.50	2.57
76a	Dick Farrell (Yellow team.)	60.00	30.00	18.00
76b	Dick Farrell (White team.)	9.00	4.50	2.57
77a	Don Zimmer (Yellow team.)	80.00	40.00	24.00
77b	Don Zimmer (White team.)	15.00	7.50	4.50
78a	Ernie Johnson (Yellow name.)	60.00	30.00	18.00
78b	Ernie Johnson (White name.)	9.00	4.50	2.57
79a	Dick Williams (Yellow team.)	60.00	30.00	18.00
79b	Dick Williams (White team.)	9.00	4.50	2.57
80	Dick Drott	9.00	4.50	2.57
81a	***Steve Boros*** (Yellow team.)	60.00	30.00	18.00
81b	***Steve Boros*** (White team.)	9.00	4.50	2.57
82	Ronnie Kline	9.00	4.50	2.57
83	***Bob Hazle***	9.00	4.50	2.57
84	Billy O'Dell	9.00	4.50	2.57
85a	Luis Aparicio (Yellow team.)	140.00	70.00	40.00
85b	Luis Aparicio (White team.)	30.00	15.00	9.00
86	Valmy Thomas	9.00	4.50	2.57
87	Johnny Kucks	10.00	5.00	3.00
88	Duke Snider	45.00	22.50	13.50
89	Billy Klaus	9.00	4.50	2.57
90	Robin Roberts	30.00	15.00	9.00
91	Chuck Tanner	9.00	4.50	2.57
92a	Clint Courtney (Yellow name.)	60.00	30.00	18.00
92b	Clint Courtney (White name.)	9.00	4.50	2.57
93	Sandy Amoros	12.00	6.00	3.50
94	Bob Skinner	9.00	4.50	2.57
95	Frank Bolling	9.00	4.50	2.57
96	Joe Durham	9.00	4.50	2.57
97a	Larry Jackson (Yellow name.)	60.00	30.00	18.00
97b	Larry Jackson (White name.)	9.00	4.50	2.57
98a	Billy Hunter (Yellow name.)	60.00	30.00	18.00
98b	Billy Hunter (White name.)	9.00	4.50	2.57
99	Bobby Adams	9.00	4.50	2.57
100a	Early Wynn (Yellow team.)	90.00	45.00	27.50
100b	Early Wynn (White team.)	20.00	10.00	6.00
101a	Bobby Richardson (Yellow name.)	100.00	50.00	30.00
101b	Bobby Richardson (White name.)	30.00	15.00	9.00
102	George Strickland	9.00	4.50	2.57
103	Jerry Lynch	9.00	4.50	2.57
104	Jim Pendleton	9.00	4.50	2.57
105	Billy Gardner	9.00	4.50	2.57
106	Dick Schofield	9.00	4.50	2.57
107	Ossie Virgil	9.00	4.50	2.57
108a	Jim Landis (Yellow team.)	60.00	30.00	18.00
108b	Jim Landis (White team.)	9.00	4.50	2.57
109	Herb Plews	9.00	4.50	2.57
110	Johnny Logan	9.00	4.50	2.57
111	Stu Miller	9.00	4.50	2.57
112	Gus Zernial	9.00	4.50	2.57
113	Jerry Walker	9.00	4.50	2.57
114	Irv Noren	9.00	4.50	2.57
115	Jim Bunning	20.00	10.00	6.00
116	Dave Philley	9.00	4.50	2.57
117	Frank Torre	9.00	4.50	2.57
118	Harvey Haddix	9.00	4.50	2.57
119	Harry Chiti	9.00	4.50	2.57
120	Johnny Podres	12.00	6.00	3.50
121	Eddie Miksis	9.00	4.50	2.57
122	Walt Moryn	9.00	4.50	2.57
123	Dick Tomanek	9.00	4.50	2.57
124	Bobby Usher	9.00	4.50	2.57
125	Al Dark	9.00	4.50	2.57
126	Stan Palys	9.00	4.50	2.57
127	Tom Sturdivant	10.00	5.00	3.00
128	***Willie Kirkland***	9.00	4.50	2.57
129	Jim Derrington	9.00	4.50	2.57
130	Jackie Jensen	10.00	5.00	3.00
131	Bob Henrich	9.00	4.50	2.57
132	Vernon Law	9.00	4.50	2.57
133	Russ Nixon	9.00	4.50	2.57
134	Phila. Phillies Team	16.00	8.00	4.75

135	Mike Drabowsky	9.00	4.50	2.57
136	Jim Finingan	9.00	4.50	2.57
137	Russ Kemmerer	9.00	4.50	2.57
138	Earl Torgeson	9.00	4.50	2.57
139	George Brunet	9.00	4.50	2.57
140	Wes Covington	9.00	4.50	2.57
141	Ken Lehman	9.00	4.50	2.57
142	Enos Slaughter	25.00	12.50	7.50
143	Billy Muffett	9.00	4.50	2.57
144	Bobby Morgan	9.00	4.50	2.57
145	Not Issued			
146	Dick Gray	9.00	4.50	2.57
147	***Don McMahon***	9.00	4.50	2.57
148	Billy Consolo	9.00	4.50	2.57
149	Tom Acker	9.00	4.50	2.57
150	Mickey Mantle	615.00	250.00	135.00
151	Buddy Pritchard	9.00	4.50	2.57
152	Johnny Antonelli	9.00	4.50	2.57
153	Les Moss	9.00	4.50	2.57
154	Harry Byrd	9.00	4.50	2.57
155	Hector Lopez	9.00	4.50	2.57
156	Dick Hyde	9.00	4.50	2.57
157	Dee Fondy	9.00	4.50	2.57
158	Cleve. Indians Team	25.00	12.50	7.50
159	Taylor Phillips	9.00	4.50	2.57
160	Don Hoak	9.00	4.50	2.57
161	Don Larsen	25.00	12.50	7.50
162	Gil Hodges	30.00	15.00	9.00
163	Jim Wilson	9.00	4.50	2.57
164	Bob Taylor	9.00	4.50	2.57
165	Bob Nieman	9.00	4.50	2.57
166	Danny O'Connell	9.00	4.50	2.57
167	Frank Baumann	9.00	4.50	2.57
168	Joe Cunningham	9.00	4.50	2.57
169	Ralph Terry	9.00	4.50	2.57
170	Vic Wertz	9.00	4.50	2.57
171	Harry Anderson	9.00	4.50	2.57
172	Don Gross	9.00	4.50	2.57
173	Eddie Yost	9.00	4.50	2.57
174	K.C. Athletics Team	20.00	10.00	6.00
175	***Marv Throneberry***	25.00	12.50	7.50
176	Bob Buhl	9.00	4.50	2.57
177	Al Smith	9.00	4.50	2.57
178	Ted Kluszewski	20.00	10.00	6.00
179	Willy Miranda	9.00	4.50	2.57
180	Lindy McDaniel	9.00	4.50	2.57
181	Willie Jones	9.00	4.50	2.57
182	Joe Caffie	9.00	4.50	2.57
183	Dave Jolly	9.00	4.50	2.57
184	Elvin Tappe	9.00	4.50	2.57
185	Ray Boone	9.00	4.50	2.57
186	Jack Meyer	9.00	4.50	2.57
187	Sandy Koufax	160.00	80.00	45.00
188	Milt Bolling (Photo actually Lou Berberet.)	9.00	4.50	2.57
189	George Susce	9.00	4.50	2.57
190	Red Schoendienst	20.00	10.00	6.00
191	Art Ceccarelli	9.00	4.50	2.57
192	Milt Graff	9.00	4.50	2.57
193	***Jerry Lumpe***	12.50	6.25	3.75
194	Roger Craig	9.00	4.50	2.57
195	Whitey Lockman	9.00	4.50	2.57
196	Mike Garcia	9.00	4.50	2.57
197	Haywood Sullivan	9.00	4.50	2.57
198	Bill Virdon	9.00	4.50	2.57
199	Don Blasingame	9.00	4.50	2.57
200	Bob Keegan	9.00	4.50	2.57
201	Jim Bolger	9.00	4.50	2.57
202	***Woody Held***	9.00	4.50	2.57
203	Al Walker	9.00	4.50	2.57
204	Leo Kiely	9.00	4.50	2.57
205	Johnny Temple	9.00	4.50	2.57
206	Bob Shaw	9.00	4.50	2.57
207	Solly Hemus	9.00	4.50	2.57
208	Cal McLish	9.00	4.50	2.57
209	Bob Anderson	9.00	4.50	2.57
210	Wally Moon	9.00	4.50	2.57
211	Pete Burnside	9.00	4.50	2.57
212	Bubba Phillips	9.00	4.50	2.57
213	Red Wilson	9.00	4.50	2.57
214	Willard Schmidt	9.00	4.50	2.57
215	Jim Gilliam	12.50	6.25	3.75
216	St. Louis Cards Team	25.00	12.50	7.50
217	Jack Harshman	9.00	4.50	2.57
218	Dick Rand	9.00	4.50	2.57
219	Camilo Pascual	9.00	4.50	2.57
220	Tom Brewer	9.00	4.50	2.57
221	Jerry Kindall	9.00	4.50	2.57
222	Bud Daley	9.00	4.50	2.57
223	Andy Pafko	9.00	4.50	2.57
224	Bob Grim	10.00	5.00	3.00
225	Billy Goodman	9.00	4.50	2.57
226	Bob Smith (Photo actually Bobby Gene Smith.)	9.00	4.50	2.57
227	Gene Stephens	9.00	4.50	2.57
228	Duke Maas	9.00	4.50	2.57
229	Frank Zupo	9.00	4.50	2.57
230	Richie Ashburn	30.00	15.00	9.00
231	Lloyd Merritt	9.00	4.50	2.57
232	Reno Bertoia	9.00	4.50	2.57
233	Mickey Vernon	9.00	4.50	2.57
234	Carl Sawatski	9.00	4.50	2.57
235	Tom Gorman	9.00	4.50	2.57
236	Ed FitzGerald	9.00	4.50	2.57
237	Bill Wight	9.00	4.50	2.57
238	Bill Mazeroski	30.00	15.00	9.00
239	Chuck Stobbs	9.00	4.50	2.57
240	Moose Skowron	20.00	10.00	6.00
241	Dick Littlefield	9.00	4.50	2.57
242	Johnny Klippstein	9.00	4.50	2.57
243	Larry Raines	9.00	4.50	2.57
244	***Don Demeter***	9.00	4.50	2.57
245	***Frank Lary***	9.00	4.50	2.57
246	New York Yankees Team	75.00	37.50	22.50
247	Casey Wise	9.00	4.50	2.57
248	Herm Wehmeier	9.00	4.50	2.57
249	Ray Moore	9.00	4.50	2.57
250	Roy Sievers	9.00	4.50	2.57
251	Warren Hacker	9.00	4.50	2.57
252	Bob Trowbridge	9.00	4.50	2.57
253	Don Mueller	9.00	4.50	2.57
254	Alex Grammas	9.00	4.50	2.57
255	Bob Turley	25.00	12.50	7.50
256	Chicago White Sox Team	20.00	10.00	6.00
257	Hal Smith	9.00	4.50	2.57
258	Carl Erskine	17.50	8.75	5.25
259	Al Pilarcik	9.00	4.50	2.57
260	Frank Malzone	9.00	4.50	2.57
261	Turk Lown	9.00	4.50	2.57
262	Johnny Groth	9.00	4.50	2.57
263	Eddie Bressoud	9.00	4.50	2.57
264	Jack Sanford	9.00	4.50	2.57
265	Pete Runnels	9.00	4.50	2.57
266	Connie Johnson	9.00	4.50	2.57
267	Sherm Lollar	9.00	4.50	2.57
268	Granny Hamner	9.00	4.50	2.57
269	Paul Smith	9.00	4.50	2.57
270	Warren Spahn	50.00	25.00	15.00
271	Billy Martin	20.00	10.00	6.00
272	Ray Crone	9.00	4.50	2.57
273	Hal Smith	9.00	4.50	2.57
274	Rocky Bridges	9.00	4.50	2.57
275	Elston Howard	20.00	10.00	6.00
276	Bobby Avila	9.00	4.50	2.57
277	Virgil Trucks	9.00	4.50	2.57
278	Mack Burk	9.00	4.50	2.57
279	Bob Boyd	9.00	4.50	2.57
280	Jim Piersall	9.00	4.50	2.57
281	Sam Taylor	9.00	4.50	2.57
282	Paul Foytack	9.00	4.50	2.57
283	Ray Shearer	9.00	4.50	2.57
284	Ray Katt	9.00	4.50	2.57
285	Frank Robinson	60.00	30.00	18.00
286	Gino Cimoli	9.00	4.50	2.57
287	Sam Jones	9.00	4.50	2.57
288	Harmon Killebrew	60.00	30.00	18.00
289	Series Hurling Rivals (Lou Burdette, Bobby Shantz)	25.00	12.50	7.50
290	Dick Donovan	9.00	4.50	2.57
291	Don Landrum	9.00	4.50	2.57
292	Ned Garver	9.00	4.50	2.57
293	Gene Freese	9.00	4.50	2.57
294	Hal Jeffcoat	9.00	4.50	2.57
295	Minnie Minoso	20.00	10.00	6.00
296	***Ryne Duren***	50.00	25.00	15.00
297	Don Buddin	9.00	4.50	2.57
298	Jim Hearn	9.00	4.50	2.57
299	Harry Simpson	9.00	4.50	2.57
300	League Presidents (Warren Giles, William Harridge)	35.00	17.50	10.00
301	Randy Jackson	9.00	4.50	2.57
302	Mike Baxes	9.00	4.50	2.57
303	Neil Chrisley	9.00	4.50	2.57
304	Tigers' Big Bats (Al Kaline, Harvey Kuenn)	35.00	17.50	10.00
305	Clem Labine	12.50	6.25	3.75
306	Whammy Douglas	9.00	4.50	2.57
307	Brooks Robinson	75.00	37.50	22.00
308	Paul Giel	9.00	4.50	2.57
309	Gail Harris	9.00	4.50	2.57
310	Ernie Banks	75.00	37.50	22.50
311	Bob Purkey	9.00	4.50	2.57
312	Boston Red Sox Team	25.00	12.50	7.50
313	Bob Rush	9.00	4.50	2.57
314	Dodgers' Boss & Power (Duke Snider, Walter Alston)	35.00	17.50	10.00
315	Bob Friend	9.00	4.50	2.57
316	Tito Francona	9.00	4.50	2.57
317	***Albie Pearson***	10.00	5.00	3.00
318	Frank House	9.00	4.50	2.57
319	Lou Skizas	9.00	4.50	2.57
320	Whitey Ford	60.00	30.00	18.00
321	Sluggers Supreme (Ted Kluszewski, Ted Williams)	65.00	32.50	20.00
322	Harding Peterson	9.00	4.50	2.57
323	Elmer Valo	9.00	4.50	2.57
324	Hoyt Wilhelm	20.00	10.00	6.00
325	Joe Adcock	9.00	4.50	2.57
326	Bob Miller	9.00	4.50	2.57
327	Chicago Cubs Team	20.00	10.00	6.00
328	Ike Delock	9.00	4.50	2.57
329	Bob Cerv	9.00	4.50	2.57
330	Ed Bailey	9.00	4.50	2.57
331	Pedro Ramos	9.00	4.50	2.57
332	Jim King	9.00	4.50	2.57
333	Andy Carey	10.00	5.00	3.00
334	Mound Aces (Bob Friend, Billy Pierce)	12.00	6.00	3.50
335	Ruben Gomez	9.00	4.50	2.57
336	Bert Hamric	9.00	4.50	2.57
337	Hank Aguirre	9.00	4.50	2.57
338	Walt Dropo	9.00	4.50	2.57
339	Fred Hatfield	9.00	4.50	2.57
340	Don Newcombe	25.00	12.50	7.50
341	Pittsburgh Pirates Team	30.00	15.00	9.00
342	Jim Brosnan	9.00	4.50	2.57
343	***Orlando Cepeda***	70.00	35.00	20.00
344	Bob Porterfield	9.00	4.50	2.57
345	Jim Hegan	9.00	4.50	2.57
346	Steve Bilko	9.00	4.50	2.57
347	Don Rudolph	9.00	4.50	2.57
348	Chico Fernandez	9.00	4.50	2.57
349	Murry Dickson	9.00	4.50	2.57
350	Ken Boyer	12.50	6.25	3.75
351	Braves' Fence Busters (Hank Aaron, Joe Adcock, Del Crandall, Eddie Mathews)	60.00	30.00	18.00
352	Herb Score	12.50	6.25	3.75
353	Stan Lopata	9.00	4.50	2.57
354	Art Ditmar	10.00	5.00	3.00
355	Bill Bruton	9.00	4.50	2.57
356	Bob Malkmus	9.00	4.50	2.57
357	Danny McDevitt	9.00	4.50	2.57
358	Gene Baker	9.00	4.50	2.57
359	Billy Loes	9.00	4.50	2.57
360	Roy McMillan	9.00	4.50	2.57
361	Mike Fornieles	9.00	4.50	2.57
362	Ray Jablonski	9.00	4.50	2.57
363	Don Elston	9.00	4.50	2.57
364	Earl Battey	9.00	4.50	2.57
365	Tom Morgan	9.00	4.50	2.57
366	Gene Green	9.00	4.50	2.57
367	Jack Urban	9.00	4.50	2.57
368	Rocky Colavito	50.00	25.00	15.00
369	Ralph Lumenti	9.00	4.50	2.57
370	Yogi Berra	80.00	40.00	25.00
371	Marty Keough	9.00	4.50	2.57
372	Don Cardwell	9.00	4.50	2.57
373	Joe Pignatano	9.00	4.50	2.57
374	Brooks Lawrence	9.00	4.50	2.57
375	Pee Wee Reese	45.00	22.50	13.50
376	Charley Rabe	9.00	4.50	2.57
377a	Milwaukee Braves Team (Alphabetical checklist.)	20.00	10.00	6.00
377b	Milwaukee Braves Team (Numerical checklist.)	140.00	70.00	40.00
378	Hank Sauer	9.00	4.50	2.57
379	Ray Herbert	9.00	4.50	2.57
380	Charley Maxwell	9.00	4.50	2.57
381	Hal Brown	9.00	4.50	2.57
382	Al Cicotte	10.00	5.00	3.00
383	Lou Berberet	9.00	4.50	2.57
384	John Goryl	9.00	4.50	2.57
385	Wilmer Mizell	9.00	4.50	2.57
386	Birdie's Young Sluggers (Ed Bailey, Frank Robinson, Birdie Tebbetts)	20.00	10.00	6.00
387	Wally Post	9.00	4.50	2.57
388	Billy Moran	9.00	4.50	2.57
389	Bill Taylor	9.00	4.50	2.57
390	Del Crandall	9.00	4.50	2.57
391	Dave Melton	9.00	4.50	2.57
392	Bennie Daniels	9.00	4.50	2.57
393	Tony Kubek	20.00	10.00	6.00
394	***Jim Grant***	10.00	5.00	3.00
395	Willard Nixon	9.00	4.50	2.57
396	Dutch Dotterer	9.00	4.50	2.57
397a	Detroit Tigers Team (Alphabetical checklist.)	15.00	7.50	4.50
397b	Detroit Tigers Team (Numerical checklist.)	125.00	65.00	35.00
398	Gene Woodling	9.00	4.50	2.57
399	Marv Grissom	9.00	4.50	2.57
400	Nellie Fox	25.00	12.50	7.50
401	Don Bessent	9.00	4.50	2.57
402	Bobby Gene Smith	9.00	4.50	2.57
403	Steve Korcheck	9.00	4.50	2.57
404	Curt Simmons	9.00	4.50	2.57
405	Ken Aspromonte	9.00	4.50	2.57
406	Vic Power	9.00	4.50	2.57
407	Carlton Willey	9.00	4.50	2.57
408a	Baltimore Orioles Team (Alphabetical checklist.)	15.00	7.50	4.50
408b	Baltimore Orioles Team (Numerical checklist.)	125.00	65.00	35.00
409	Frank Thomas	9.00	4.50	2.57
410	Murray Wall	9.00	4.50	2.57
411	***Tony Taylor***	9.00	4.50	2.57
412	Jerry Staley	9.00	4.50	2.57
413	***Jim Davenport***	9.00	4.50	2.57
414	Sammy White	9.00	4.50	2.57
415	Bob Bowman	9.00	4.50	2.57
416	Foster Castleman	9.00	4.50	2.57
417	Carl Furillo	15.00	7.50	4.50
418	World Series Foes (Hank Aaron, Mickey Mantle)	215.00	105.00	65.00
419	Bobby Shantz	15.00	7.50	4.50
420	***Vada Pinson***	20.00	10.00	6.00
421	Dixie Howell	9.00	4.50	2.57
422	Norm Zauchin	9.00	4.50	2.57
423	Phil Clark	9.00	4.50	2.57
424	Larry Doby	20.00	10.00	6.00
425	Sam Esposito	9.00	4.50	2.57
426	Johnny O'Brien	9.00	4.50	2.57
427	Al Worthington	9.00	4.50	2.57
428a	Cincinnati Redlegs Team (Alphabetical checklist.)	15.00	7.50	4.50
428b	Cincinnati Redlegs Team (Numerical checklist.)	125.00	65.00	35.00
429	Gus Triandos	9.00	4.50	2.57
430	Bobby Thomson	12.00	6.00	3.50
431	Gene Conley	9.00	4.50	2.57
432	John Powers	9.00	4.50	2.57
433	Pancho Herrera	9.00	4.50	2.57
433a	Pancho Herrera (Printing error, no "a" in Herrera.)	4,000	2,000	1,200
434	Harvey Kuenn	9.00	4.50	2.57
435	Ed Roebuck	9.00	4.50	2.57
436	Rival Fence Busters (Willie Mays, Duke Snider)	75.00	37.50	22.50
437	Bob Speake	9.00	4.50	2.57
438	Whitey Herzog	9.00	4.50	2.57
439	Ray Narleski	9.00	4.50	2.57
440	Ed Mathews	65.00	32.50	20.00
441	Jim Marshall	9.00	4.50	2.57
442	Phil Paine	9.00	4.50	2.57
443	Billy Harrell/SP	15.00	7.50	4.50
444	Danny Kravitz	9.00	4.50	2.57
445	Bob Smith	9.00	4.50	2.57
446	Carroll Hardy/SP	15.00	7.50	4.50
447	Ray Monzant	9.00	4.50	2.57
448	***Charlie Lau***	13.50	7.00	4.00
449	Gene Fodge	9.00	4.50	2.57
450	Preston Ward/SP	15.00	7.50	4.50
451	Joe Taylor	9.00	4.50	2.57
452	Roman Mejias	9.00	4.50	2.57
453	Tom Qualters	9.00	4.50	2.57
454	Harry Hanebrink	9.00	4.50	2.57
455	Hal Griggs (Photo actually Bud Byerly.)	9.00	4.50	2.57
456	Dick Brown	9.00	4.50	2.57
457	***Milt Pappas***	10.00	5.00	3.00
458	Julio Becquer	9.00	4.50	2.57

459	Ron Blackburn	9.00	4.50	2.57
460	Chuck Essegian	9.00	4.50	2.57
461	Ed Mayer	9.00	4.50	2.57
462	Gary Geiger/SP	15.00	7.50	4.50
463	Vito Valentinetti	9.00	4.50	2.57
464	***Curt Flood***	30.00	15.00	9.00
465	Arnie Portocarrero	9.00	4.50	2.57
466	Pete Whisenant	9.00	4.50	2.57
467	Glen Hobbie	9.00	4.50	2.57
468	Bob Schmidt	9.00	4.50	2.57
469	Don Ferrarese	9.00	4.50	2.57
470	R.C. Stevens	9.00	4.50	2.57
471	Lenny Green	9.00	4.50	2.57
472	Joe Jay	9.00	4.50	2.57
473	Bill Renna	9.00	4.50	2.57
474	Roman Semproch	9.00	4.50	2.57
475	All-Star Managers (Fred Haney, Casey Stengel)	30.00	15.00	9.00
476	Stan Musial/AS	35.00	17.50	10.00
477	Bill Skowron/AS	15.00	7.50	4.50
478	Johnny Temple/AS	10.00	5.00	3.00
479	Nellie Fox/AS	15.00	7.50	4.50
480	Eddie Mathews/AS	25.00	12.50	7.50
481	Frank Malzone/AS	10.00	5.00	3.00
482	Ernie Banks/AS	30.00	15.00	9.00
483	Luis Aparicio/AS	20.00	10.00	6.00
484	Frank Robinson/AS	30.00	15.00	9.00
485	Ted Williams/AS	75.00	37.50	22.00
486	Willie Mays/AS	55.00	27.50	16.50
487	Mickey Mantle/AS (Triple Print)	110.00	55.00	35.00
488	Hank Aaron/AS	55.00	27.50	16.50
489	Jackie Jensen/AS	12.00	6.00	3.50
490	Ed Bailey/AS	10.00	5.00	3.00
491	Sherman Lollar/AS	10.00	5.00	3.00
492	Bob Friend/AS	10.00	5.00	3.00
493	Bob Turley/AS	15.00	7.50	4.50
494	Warren Spahn/AS	25.00	12.50	7.50
495	Herb Score/AS	15.00	7.50	4.50
----	Contest Card (All-Star Game, July 8)	70.00	35.00	20.00
----	Felt Emblems Insert Card	45.00	22.50	13.50

1959 Topps

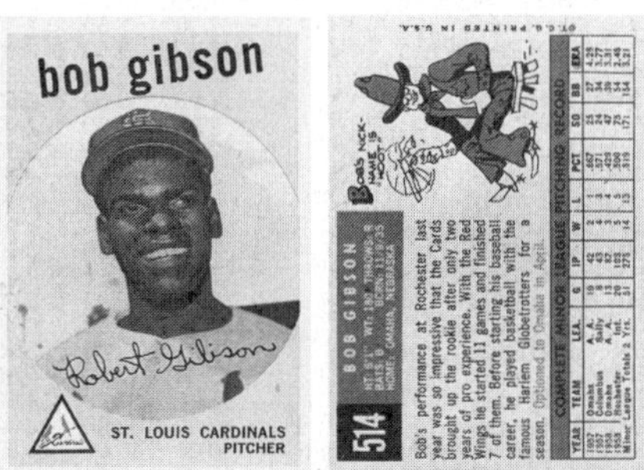

These 2-1/2" x 3-1/2" cards have a round photograph on front with a solid-color background above and below and a white border. A facsimile autograph is found across the photo. The 572-card set marks the largest set issued to that time. Card numbers below 507 have red and green printing on back with the card number in white in a green box. On high number cards beginning with #507, the printing is black and red and the card number is in a black box. Specialty cards include multiple-player cards, team cards with checklists on back, "All-Star" cards, "Baseball Thrills," and 31 "Rookie Stars." There is also a card of the commissioner, Ford Frick, and one of Roy Campanella in a wheelchair. A handful of cards can be found with and without lines added to the biographies on back indicating trades or demotions; those without the added lines are scarcer and more valuable and are not included in the complete set price. Card numbers 199-286 can be found with either white or gray backs, with the gray stock being the less common.

		NM	EX	VG
Complete Set (572):		6,500	3,250	1,900
Common Player (1-506):		7.00	3.50	2.00
Common Player (507-572):		15.00	7.50	4.50
1	Ford Frick	100.00	25.00	4.00
2	Eddie Yost	12.00	3.50	2.00
3	Don McMahon	7.00	3.50	2.00
4	Albie Pearson	7.00	3.50	2.00
5	Dick Donovan	7.00	3.50	2.00
6	Alex Grammas	7.00	3.50	2.00
7	Al Pilarcik	7.00	3.50	2.00
8	Philadelphia Phillies Team/SP	90.00	45.00	27.50
9	Paul Giel	7.00	3.50	2.00
10	Mickey Mantle	515.00	225.00	125.00
11	Billy Hunter	7.00	3.50	2.00
12	Vern Law	7.00	3.50	2.00
13	Dick Gernert	7.00	3.50	2.00
14	Pete Whisenant	7.00	3.50	2.00
15	Dick Drott	7.00	3.50	2.00
16	Joe Pignatano	7.00	3.50	2.00
17	Danny's All-Stars (Ted Kluszewski, Danny Murtaugh, Frank J. Thomas)	13.50	7.00	4.00
18	Jack Urban	7.00	3.50	2.00
19	Ed Bressoud	7.00	3.50	2.00
20	Duke Snider	40.00	20.00	12.00
21	Connie Johnson	7.00	3.50	2.00
22	Al Smith	7.00	3.50	2.00
23	Murry Dickson	7.00	3.50	2.00
24	Red Wilson	7.00	3.50	2.00
25	Don Hoak	7.00	3.50	2.00
26	Chuck Stobbs	7.00	3.50	2.00
27	Andy Pafko	7.00	3.50	2.00
28	Red Worthington	7.00	3.50	2.00
29	Jim Bolger	7.00	3.50	2.00
30	Nellie Fox	30.00	15.00	9.00
31	Ken Lehman	7.00	3.50	2.00
32	Don Buddin	7.00	3.50	2.00
33	Ed Fitz Gerald	7.00	3.50	2.00
34	Pitchers Beware (Al Kaline, Charlie Maxwell)	25.00	12.50	7.50
35	Ted Kluszewski	17.50	8.75	5.25
36	Hank Aguirre	7.00	3.50	2.00
37	Gene Green	7.00	3.50	2.00
38	Morrie Martin	7.00	3.50	2.00
39	Ed Bouchee	7.00	3.50	2.00
40a	Warren Spahn (Born 1931.)	85.00	42.50	25.00
40b	Warren Spahn (Born 1931, "3" partially obscured.)	75.00	37.50	22.50
40c	Warren Spahn (Born 1921.)	65.00	32.50	20.00
41	Bob Martyn	7.00	3.50	2.00
42	Murray Wall	7.00	3.50	2.00
43	Steve Bilko	7.00	3.50	2.00
44	Vito Valentinetti	7.00	3.50	2.00
45	Andy Carey	9.00	4.50	2.75
46	Bill Henry	7.00	3.50	2.00
47	Jim Finigan	7.00	3.50	2.00
48	Baltimore Orioles Team	17.50	8.75	5.25
49	Bill Hall	7.00	3.50	2.00
50	Willie Mays	115.00	55.00	35.00
51	Rip Coleman	7.00	3.50	2.00
52	Coot Veal	7.00	3.50	2.00
53	*Stan Williams*	20.00	10.00	6.00
54	Mel Roach	7.00	3.50	2.00
55	Tom Brewer	7.00	3.50	2.00
56	Carl Sawatski	7.00	3.50	2.00
57	Al Cicotte	7.00	3.50	2.00
58	Eddie Miksis	7.00	3.50	2.00
59	Irv Noren	7.00	3.50	2.00
60	Bob Turley	15.00	7.50	4.50
61	Dick Brown	7.00	3.50	2.00
62	Tony Taylor	7.00	3.50	2.00
63	Jim Hearn	7.00	3.50	2.00
64	Joe DeMaestri	7.00	3.50	2.00
65	Frank Torre	7.00	3.50	2.00
66	Joe Ginsberg	7.00	3.50	2.00
67	Brooks Lawrence	7.00	3.50	2.00
68	Dick Schofield	7.00	3.50	2.00
69	San Francisco Giants Team	17.50	8.75	5.25
70	Harvey Kuenn	7.00	3.50	2.00
71	Don Bessent	7.00	3.50	2.00
72	Bill Renna	7.00	3.50	2.00
73	Ron Jackson	7.00	3.50	2.00
74	Directing the Power (Cookie Lavagetto, Jim Lemon, Roy Sievers)	9.00	4.50	2.75
75	Sam Jones	7.00	3.50	2.00
76	Bobby Richardson	25.00	12.50	7.50
77	John Goryl	7.00	3.50	2.00
78	Pedro Ramos	7.00	3.50	2.00
79	Harry Chiti	7.00	3.50	2.00
80	Minnie Minoso	15.00	7.50	4.50
81	Hal Jeffcoat	7.00	3.50	2.00
82	Bob Boyd	7.00	3.50	2.00
83	Bob Smith	7.00	3.50	2.00
84	Reno Bertoia	7.00	3.50	2.00
85	Harry Anderson	7.00	3.50	2.00
86	Bob Keegan	7.00	3.50	2.00
87	Danny O'Connell	7.00	3.50	2.00
88	Herb Score	15.00	7.50	4.50
89	Billy Gardner	7.00	3.50	2.00
90	Bill Skowron/SP	60.00	30.00	18.00
91	Herb Moford	7.00	3.50	2.00
92	Dave Philley	7.00	3.50	2.00
93	Julio Becquer	7.00	3.50	2.00
94	Chicago White Sox Team	17.50	8.75	5.25
95	Carl Willey	7.00	3.50	2.00
96	Lou Berberet	7.00	3.50	2.00
97	Jerry Lynch	7.00	3.50	2.00
98	Arnie Portocarrero	7.00	3.50	2.00
99	Ted Kazanski	7.00	3.50	2.00
100	Bob Cerv	7.00	3.50	2.00
101	Alex Kellner	7.00	3.50	2.00
102	*Felipe Alou*	25.00	12.50	7.50
103	Billy Goodman	7.00	3.50	2.00
104	Del Rice	7.00	3.50	2.00
105	Lee Walls	7.00	3.50	2.00
106	Hal Woodeshick	7.00	3.50	2.00
107	*Norm Larker*	10.00	5.00	3.00
108	Zack Monroe	9.00	4.50	2.75
109	Bob Schmidt	7.00	3.50	2.00
110	George Witt	7.00	3.50	2.00
111	Cincinnati Red Legs Team	16.00	8.00	4.75
112	Billy Consolo	7.00	3.50	2.00
113	Taylor Phillips	7.00	3.50	2.00
114	Earl Battey	7.00	3.50	2.00
115	Mickey Vernon	7.00	3.50	2.00
116	*Bob Allison*	13.50	7.00	4.00
117	*John Blanchard*	15.00	7.50	4.50
118	John Buzhardt	7.00	3.50	2.00
119	*John Callison*	12.50	6.25	3.75
120	Chuck Coles	7.00	3.50	2.00
121	Bob Conley	7.00	3.50	2.00
122	Bennie Daniels	7.00	3.50	2.00
123	Don Dillard	7.00	3.50	2.00
124	Dan Dobbek	7.00	3.50	2.00
125	*Ron Fairly*	13.50	6.75	4.00
126	Eddie Haas	7.00	3.50	2.00
127	Kent Hadley	7.00	3.50	2.00
128	Bob Hartman	7.00	3.50	2.00
129	Frank Herrera	7.00	3.50	2.00
130	Lou Jackson	7.00	3.50	2.00
131	*Deron Johnson*	10.00	5.00	3.00
132	Don Lee	7.00	3.50	2.00
133	*Bob Lillis*	7.00	3.50	2.00
134	Jim McDaniel	7.00	3.50	2.00
135	Gene Oliver	7.00	3.50	2.00
136	*Jim O'Toole*	7.50	3.75	2.25
137	Dick Ricketts	7.00	3.50	2.00
138	John Romano	7.00	3.50	2.00
139	Ed Sadowski	7.00	3.50	2.00
140	Charlie Secrest	7.00	3.50	2.00
141	Joe Shipley	7.00	3.50	2.00
142	Dick Stigman	7.00	3.50	2.00
143	Willie Tasby	7.00	3.50	2.00
144	Jerry Walker	7.00	3.50	2.00
145	Dom Zanni	7.00	3.50	2.00
146	Jerry Zimmerman	7.00	3.50	2.00
147	Cubs' Clubbers (Ernie Banks, Dale Long, Walt Moryn)	20.00	10.00	6.00
148	Mike McCormick	7.00	3.50	2.00
149	Jim Bunning	20.00	10.00	6.00
150	Stan Musial	80.00	40.00	24.00
151	Bob Malkmus	7.00	3.50	2.00
152	Johnny Klippstein	7.00	3.50	2.00
153	Jim Marshall	7.00	3.50	2.00
154	Ray Herbert	7.00	3.50	2.00
155	Enos Slaughter	20.00	10.00	6.00
156	Ace Hurlers (Billy Pierce, Robin Roberts)	12.50	6.25	3.75
157	Felix Mantilla	7.00	3.50	2.00
158	Walt Dropo	7.00	3.50	2.00
159	Bob Shaw	7.00	3.50	2.00
160	Dick Groat	7.00	3.50	2.00
161	Frank Baumann	7.00	3.50	2.00
162	Bobby G. Smith	7.00	3.50	2.00
163	Sandy Koufax	130.00	65.00	40.00
164	Johnny Groth	7.00	3.50	2.00
165	Bill Bruton	7.00	3.50	2.00
166	Destruction Crew (Rocky Colavito, Larry Doby, Minnie Minoso)	20.00	10.00	6.00
167	Duke Maas	7.00	3.50	2.00
168	Carroll Hardy	7.00	3.50	2.00
169	Ted Abernathy	7.00	3.50	2.00
170	Gene Woodling	7.00	3.50	2.00
171	Willard Schmidt	7.00	3.50	2.00
172	Kansas City Athletics Team	16.00	8.00	4.75
173	*Bill Monbouquette*	7.00	3.50	2.00
174	Jim Pendleton	7.00	3.50	2.00
175	Dick Farrell	7.00	3.50	2.00
176	Preston Ward	7.00	3.50	2.00
177	Johnny Briggs	7.00	3.50	2.00
178	Ruben Amaro	7.00	3.50	2.00
179	Don Rudolph	7.00	3.50	2.00
180	Yogi Berra	65.00	32.50	20.00
181	Bob Porterfield	7.00	3.50	2.00
182	Milt Graff	7.00	3.50	2.00
183	Stu Miller	7.00	3.50	2.00
184	Harvey Haddix	7.00	3.50	2.00
185	Jim Busby	7.00	3.50	2.00
186	Mudcat Grant	7.00	3.50	2.00
187	Bubba Phillips	7.00	3.50	2.00
188	Juan Pizarro	7.00	3.50	2.00
189	Neil Chrisley	7.00	3.50	2.00
190	Bill Virdon	7.00	3.50	2.00
191	Russ Kemmerer	7.00	3.50	2.00
192	Charley Beamon	7.00	3.50	2.00
193	Sammy Taylor	7.00	3.50	2.00
194	Jim Brosnan	7.00	3.50	2.00
195	Rip Repulski	7.00	3.50	2.00
196	Billy Moran	7.00	3.50	2.00
197	Ray Semproch	7.00	3.50	2.00
198	Jim Davenport	7.00	3.50	2.00
199	Leo Kiely	7.00	3.50	2.00
200	Warren Giles	20.00	10.00	6.00
201	Tom Acker	7.00	3.50	2.00
202	Roger Maris	85.00	42.50	25.00
203	Ozzie Virgil	7.00	3.50	2.00
204	Casey Wise	7.00	3.50	2.00
205	Don Larsen	17.50	8.75	5.25
206	Carl Furillo	17.50	8.75	5.25
207	George Strickland	7.00	3.50	2.00
208	Willie Jones	7.00	3.50	2.00
209	Lenny Green	7.00	3.50	2.00
210	Ed Bailey	7.00	3.50	2.00
211	Bob Blaylock	7.00	3.50	2.00
212	Fence Busters (Hank Aaron, Eddie Mathews)	50.00	25.00	15.00
213	Jim Rivera	7.00	3.50	2.00
214	Marcelino Solis	7.00	3.50	2.00
215	Jim Lemon	7.00	3.50	2.00
216	Andre Rodgers	7.00	3.50	2.00
217	Carl Erskine	12.50	6.25	3.75
218	Roman Mejias	7.00	3.50	2.00
219	George Zuverink	7.00	3.50	2.00
220	Frank Malzone	7.00	3.50	2.00
221	Bob Bowman	7.00	3.50	2.00
222	Bobby Shantz	15.00	7.50	4.50
223	St. Louis Cardinals Team	20.00	10.00	6.00
224	*Claude Osteen*	7.50	3.75	2.25
225	Johnny Logan	7.00	3.50	2.00
226	Art Ceccarelli	7.00	3.50	2.00
227	Hal Smith	7.00	3.50	2.00
228	Don Gross	7.00	3.50	2.00
229	Vic Power	7.00	3.50	2.00
230	Bill Fischer	7.00	3.50	2.00
231	Ellis Burton	7.00	3.50	2.00
232	Eddie Kasko	7.00	3.50	2.00
233	Paul Foytack	7.00	3.50	2.00
234	Chuck Tanner	7.00	3.50	2.00
235	Valmy Thomas	7.00	3.50	2.00
236	Ted Bowsfield	7.00	3.50	2.00
237	Run Preventers (Gil McDougald, Bobby Richardson, Bob Turley)	20.00	10.00	6.00
238	Gene Baker	7.00	3.50	2.00
239	Bob Trowbridge	7.00	3.50	2.00
240	Hank Bauer	13.50	7.00	4.00
241	Billy Muffett	7.00	3.50	2.00
242	Ron Samford	7.00	3.50	2.00
243	Marv Grissom	7.00	3.50	2.00
244	Dick Gray	7.00	3.50	2.00
245	Ned Garver	7.00	3.50	2.00
246	J.W. Porter	7.00	3.50	2.00
247	Don Ferrarese	7.00	3.50	2.00
248	Boston Red Sox Team	16.00	8.00	4.75
249	Bobby Adams	7.00	3.50	2.00
250	Billy O'Dell	7.00	3.50	2.00
251	Cletis Boyer	15.00	7.50	4.50
252	Ray Boone	7.00	3.50	2.00

253	Seth Morehead	7.00	3.50	2.00
254	Zeke Bella	7.00	3.50	2.00
255	Del Ennis	7.00	3.50	2.00
256	Jerry Davie	7.00	3.50	2.00
257	*Leon Wagner*	9.00	4.50	2.75
258	Fred Kipp	7.00	3.50	2.00
259	Jim Pisoni	7.00	3.50	2.00
260	Early Wynn	20.00	10.00	6.00
261	Gene Stephens	7.00	3.50	2.00
262	Hitters' Foes (Don Drysdale, Clem Labine, Johnny Podres)	20.00	10.00	6.00
263	Buddy Daley	7.00	3.50	2.00
264	Chico Carrasquel	7.00	3.50	2.00
265	Ron Kline	7.00	3.50	2.00
266	Woody Held	7.00	3.50	2.00
267	John Romonosky	7.00	3.50	2.00
268	Tito Francona	7.00	3.50	2.00
269	Jack Meyer	7.00	3.50	2.00
270	Gil Hodges	20.00	10.00	6.00
271	*Orlando Pena*	7.00	3.50	2.00
272	Jerry Lumpe	9.00	4.50	2.75
273	Joe Jay	7.00	3.50	2.00
274	Jerry Kindall	7.00	3.50	2.00
275	Jack Sanford	7.00	3.50	2.00
276	Pete Daley	7.00	3.50	2.00
277	Turk Lown	7.00	3.50	2.00
278	Chuck Essegian	7.00	3.50	2.00
279	Ernie Johnson	7.00	3.50	2.00
280	Frank Bolling	7.00	3.50	2.00
281	Walt Craddock	7.00	3.50	2.00
282	R.C. Stevens	7.00	3.50	2.00
283	Russ Heman	7.00	3.50	2.00
284	Steve Korcheck	7.00	3.50	2.00
285	Joe Cunningham	7.00	3.50	2.00
286	Dean Stone	7.00	3.50	2.00
287	Don Zimmer	12.50	6.25	3.75
288	Dutch Dotterer	7.00	3.50	2.00
289	Johnny Kucks	9.00	4.50	2.75
290	Wes Covington	7.00	3.50	2.00
291	Pitching Partners (Camilo Pascual, Pedro Ramos)	9.00	4.50	2.75
292	Dick Williams	7.00	3.50	2.00
293	Ray Moore	7.00	3.50	2.00
294	Hank Foiles	7.00	3.50	2.00
295	Billy Martin	17.50	8.75	5.25
296	*Ernie Broglio*	7.00	3.50	2.00
297	*Jackie Brandt*	7.00	3.50	2.00
298	Tex Clevenger	7.00	3.50	2.00
299	Billy Klaus	7.00	3.50	2.00
300	Richie Ashburn	25.00	12.50	7.50
301	Earl Averill	7.00	3.50	2.00
302	Don Mossi	7.00	3.50	2.00
303	Marty Keough	7.00	3.50	2.00
304	Chicago Cubs Team	16.00	8.00	4.75
305	Curt Raydon	7.00	3.50	2.00
306	Jim Gilliam	12.00	6.00	3.50
307	Curt Barclay	7.00	3.50	2.00
308	Norm Siebern	9.00	4.50	2.75
309	Sal Maglie	7.00	3.50	2.00
310	Luis Aparicio	25.00	12.50	7.50
311	Norm Zauchin	7.00	3.50	2.00
312	Don Newcombe	9.00	4.50	2.75
313	Frank House	7.00	3.50	2.00
314	Don Cardwell	7.00	3.50	2.00
315	Joe Adcock	7.00	3.50	2.00
316a	Ralph Lumenti (No optioned statement.)	75.00	37.50	22.50
316b	Ralph Lumenti (Optioned statement.)	7.00	3.50	2.00
317	N.L. Hitting Kings (Richie Ashburn, Willie Mays)	45.00	22.50	13.50
318	Rocky Bridges	7.00	3.50	2.00
319	Dave Hillman	7.00	3.50	2.00
320	Bob Skinner	7.00	3.50	2.00
321a	Bob Giallombardo (No optioned statement.)	75.00	37.50	22.50
321b	Bob Giallombardo (Optioned statement.)	7.00	3.50	2.00
322a	Harry Hanebrink (No trade statement.)	90.00	45.00	27.50
322b	Harry Hanebrink (Trade statement.)	7.00	3.50	2.00
323	Frank Sullivan	7.00	3.50	2.00
324	Don Demeter	7.00	3.50	2.00
325	Ken Boyer	13.50	7.00	4.00
326	Marv Throneberry	10.00	5.00	3.00
327	*Gary Bell*	7.00	3.50	2.00
328	Lou Skizas	7.00	3.50	2.00
329	Detroit Tigers Team	17.50	8.75	5.25
330	Gus Triandos	7.00	3.50	2.00
331	Steve Boros	7.00	3.50	2.00
332	Ray Monzant	7.00	3.50	2.00
333	Harry Simpson	7.00	3.50	2.00
334	Glen Hobbie	7.00	3.50	2.00
335	Johnny Temple	7.00	3.50	2.00
336a	Billy Loes (No trade statement.)	75.00	37.50	22.50
336b	Billy Loes (Trade statement.)	7.00	3.50	2.00
337	George Crowe	7.00	3.50	2.00
338	*George Anderson* (Sparky)	30.00	15.00	9.00
339	Roy Face	7.00	3.50	2.00
340	Roy Sievers	7.00	3.50	2.00
341	Tom Qualters	7.00	3.50	2.00
342	Ray Jablonski	7.00	3.50	2.00
343	Billy Hoeft	7.00	3.50	2.00
344	Russ Nixon	7.00	3.50	2.00
345	Gil McDougald	12.50	6.25	3.75
346	Batter Bafflers (Tom Brewer, Dave Sisler)	9.00	4.50	2.75
347	Bob Buhl	7.00	3.50	2.00
348	Ted Lepcio	7.00	3.50	2.00
349	Hoyt Wilhelm	15.00	7.50	4.50
350	Ernie Banks	50.00	25.00	15.00
351	Earl Torgeson	7.00	3.50	2.00
352	Robin Roberts	20.00	10.00	6.00
353	Curt Flood	12.00	6.00	3.50
354	Pete Burnside	7.00	3.50	2.00
355	Jim Piersall	9.00	4.50	2.75
356	Bob Mabe	7.00	3.50	2.00
357	*Dick Stuart*	10.00	5.00	3.00
358	Ralph Terry	7.00	3.50	2.00
359	*Bill White*	12.50	6.25	3.75
360	Al Kaline	35.00	17.50	10.00
361	Willard Nixon	7.00	3.50	2.00
362a	Dolan Nichols (No optioned statement.)	80.00	40.00	24.00
362b	Dolan Nichols (Optioned statement.)	7.00	3.50	2.00
363	Bobby Avila	7.00	3.50	2.00
364	Danny McDevitt	7.00	3.50	2.00
365	Gus Bell	7.00	3.50	2.00
366	Humberto Robinson	7.00	3.50	2.00
367	Cal Neeman	7.00	3.50	2.00
368	Don Mueller	7.00	3.50	2.00
369	Dick Tomanek	7.00	3.50	2.00
370	Pete Runnels	7.00	3.50	2.00
371	Dick Brodowski	7.00	3.50	2.00
372	Jim Hegan	7.00	3.50	2.00
373	Herb Plews	7.00	3.50	2.00
374	Art Ditmar	9.00	4.50	2.75
375	Bob Nieman	7.00	3.50	2.00
376	Hal Naragon	7.00	3.50	2.00
377	Johnny Antonelli	7.00	3.50	2.00
378	Gail Harris	7.00	3.50	2.00
379	Bob Miller	7.00	3.50	2.00
380	Hank Aaron	110.00	55.00	35.00
381	Mike Baxes	7.00	3.50	2.00
382	Curt Simmons	7.00	3.50	2.00
383	Words of Wisdom (Don Larsen, Casey Stengel)	16.00	8.00	4.75
384	Dave Sisler	7.00	3.50	2.00
385	Sherm Lollar	7.00	3.50	2.00
386	Jim Delsing	7.00	3.50	2.00
387	Don Drysdale	25.00	12.50	7.50
388	Bob Will	7.00	3.50	2.00
389	Joe Nuxhall	7.00	3.50	2.00
390	Orlando Cepeda	25.00	12.50	7.50
391	Milt Pappas	7.00	3.50	2.00
392	Whitey Herzog	7.00	3.50	2.00
393	Frank Lary	7.00	3.50	2.00
394	Randy Jackson	7.00	3.50	2.00
395	Elston Howard	15.00	7.50	4.50
396	Bob Rush	7.00	3.50	2.00
397	Washington Senators Team	16.00	8.00	4.75
398	Wally Post	7.00	3.50	2.00
399	Larry Jackson	7.00	3.50	2.00
400	Jackie Jensen	10.00	5.00	3.00
401	Ron Blackburn	7.00	3.50	2.00
402	Hector Lopez	7.00	3.50	2.00
403	Clem Labine	12.50	6.25	3.75
404	Hank Sauer	7.00	3.50	2.00
405	Roy McMillan	7.00	3.50	2.00
406	Solly Drake	7.00	3.50	2.00
407	Moe Drabowsky	7.00	3.50	2.00
408	Keystone Combo (Luis Aparicio, Nellie Fox)	20.00	10.00	6.00
409	Gus Zernial	7.00	3.50	2.00
410	Billy Pierce	7.00	3.50	2.00
411	Whitey Lockman	7.00	3.50	2.00
412	Stan Lopata	7.00	3.50	2.00
413	Camillo (Camilo) Pascual	7.00	3.50	2.00
414	Dale Long	7.00	3.50	2.00
415	Bill Mazeroski	20.00	10.00	6.00
416a	Haywood Sullivan (No circle around copyright symbol, no period after "A" in "U.S.A.")	15.00	7.50	4.50
416b	Haywood Sullivan (No circle around copyright symbol, period added after "A" in "U.S.A.")	7.00	3.50	2.00
416c	Haywood Sullivan (Circle around copyright symbol, period after "A" in "U.S.A.")	7.00	3.50	2.00
417	Virgil Trucks	7.00	3.50	2.00
418	Gino Cimoli	7.00	3.50	2.00
419	Milwaukee Braves Team	16.00	8.00	4.75
420	Rocky Colavito	20.00	10.00	6.00
421	Herm Wehmeier	7.00	3.50	2.00
422	Hobie Landrith	7.00	3.50	2.00
423	Bob Grim	7.00	3.50	2.00
424	Ken Aspromonte	7.00	3.50	2.00
425	Del Crandall	7.00	3.50	2.00
426	Jerry Staley	7.00	3.50	2.00
427	Charlie Neal	7.00	3.50	2.00
428	Buc Hill Aces (Roy Face, Bob Friend, Ron Kline, Vern Law)	9.00	4.50	2.75
429	Bobby Thomson	9.00	4.50	2.75
430	Whitey Ford	40.00	20.00	12.00
431	Whammy Douglas	7.00	3.50	2.00
432	Smoky Burgess	7.00	3.50	2.00
433	Billy Harrell	7.00	3.50	2.00
434	Hal Griggs	7.00	3.50	2.00
435	Frank Robinson	30.00	15.00	9.00
436	Granny Hamner	7.00	3.50	2.00
437	Ike Delock	7.00	3.50	2.00
438	Sam Esposito	7.00	3.50	2.00
439	Brooks Robinson	30.00	15.00	9.00
440	Lou Burdette	7.00	3.50	2.00
441	John Roseboro	7.00	3.50	2.00
442	Ray Narleski	7.00	3.50	2.00
443	Daryl Spencer	7.00	3.50	2.00
444	*Ronnie Hansen*	7.00	3.50	2.00
445	Cal McLish	7.00	3.50	2.00
446	Rocky Nelson	7.00	3.50	2.00
447	Bob Anderson	7.00	3.50	2.00
448	Vada Pinson	7.00	3.50	2.00
449	Tom Gorman	7.00	3.50	2.00
450	Ed Mathews	45.00	22.50	13.50
451	Jimmy Constable	7.00	3.50	2.00
452	Chico Fernandez	7.00	3.50	2.00
453	Les Moss	7.00	3.50	2.00
454	Phil Clark	7.00	3.50	2.00
455	Larry Doby	15.00	7.50	4.50
456	Jerry Casale	7.00	3.50	2.00
457	Los Angeles Dodgers Team	20.00	10.00	6.00
458	Gordon Jones	7.00	3.50	2.00
459	Bill Tuttle	7.00	3.50	2.00
460	Bob Friend	7.00	3.50	2.00
461	Mantle Hits 42nd Homer For Crown (Mickey Mantle)	70.00	35.00	20.00
462	Colavito's Great Catch Saves Game (Rocky Colavito)	12.50	6.25	3.75
463	Kaline Becomes Youngest Batting Champ (Al Kaline)	15.00	7.50	4.50
464	Mays' Catch Makes Series History (Willie Mays)	35.00	17.50	10.00
465	Sievers Sets Homer Mark (Roy Sievers)	7.00	3.50	2.00
466	Pierce All-Star Starter (Billy Pierce)	7.00	3.50	2.00
467	Aaron Clubs World Series Homer (Hank Aaron)	25.00	12.50	7.50
468	Snider's Play Brings L.A. Victory (Duke Snider)	15.00	7.50	4.50
469	Hustler Banks Wins M.V.P. Award (Ernie Banks)	16.00	8.00	5.00
470	Musial Raps Out 3,000th Hit (Stan Musial)	25.00	12.50	7.50
471	Tom Sturdivant	9.00	4.50	2.75
472	Gene Freese	7.00	3.50	2.00
473	Mike Fornieles	7.00	3.50	2.00
474	Moe Thacker	7.00	3.50	2.00
475	Jack Harshman	7.00	3.50	2.00
476	Cleveland Indians Team	16.00	8.00	4.75
477	Barry Latman	7.00	3.50	2.00
478	Bob Clemente	110.00	55.00	35.00
479	Lindy McDaniel	7.00	3.50	2.00
480	Red Schoendienst	20.00	10.00	6.00
481	Charley Maxwell	7.00	3.50	2.00
482	Russ Meyer	7.00	3.50	2.00
483	Clint Courtney	7.00	3.50	2.00
484	Willie Kirkland	7.00	3.50	2.00
485	Ryne Duren	10.00	5.00	3.00
486	Sammy White	7.00	3.50	2.00
487	Hal Brown	7.00	3.50	2.00
488	Walt Moryn	7.00	3.50	2.00
489	John C. Powers	7.00	3.50	2.00
490	Frank Thomas	7.00	3.50	2.00
491	Don Blasingame	7.00	3.50	2.00
492	Gene Conley	7.00	3.50	2.00
493	Jim Landis	7.00	3.50	2.00
494	Don Pavletich	7.00	3.50	2.00
495	Johnny Podres	11.00	5.50	3.25
496	Wayne Terwilliger	7.00	3.50	2.00
497	Hal R. Smith	7.00	3.50	2.00
498	Dick Hyde	7.00	3.50	2.00
499	Johnny O'Brien	7.00	3.50	2.00
500	Vic Wertz	7.00	3.50	2.00
501	Bobby Tiefenauer	7.00	3.50	2.00
502	Al Dark	7.00	3.50	2.00
503	Jim Owens	7.00	3.50	2.00
504	Ossie Alvarez	7.00	3.50	2.00
505	Tony Kubek	20.00	10.00	6.00
506	Bob Purkey	7.00	3.50	2.00
507	Bob Hale	15.00	7.50	4.50
508	Art Fowler	15.00	7.50	4.50
509	*Norm Cash*	60.00	30.00	18.00
510	New York Yankees Team	80.00	40.00	24.00
511	George Susce	15.00	7.50	4.50
512	George Altman	15.00	7.50	4.50
513	Tom Carroll	15.00	7.50	4.50
514	*Bob Gibson*	200.00	90.00	55.00
515	Harmon Killebrew	95.00	47.50	27.50
516	Mike Garcia	15.00	7.50	4.50
517	Joe Koppe	15.00	7.50	4.50
518	*Mike Cuellar*	20.00	10.00	6.00
519	Infield Power (Dick Gernert, Frank Malzone, Pete Runnels)	17.50	8.75	5.25
520	Don Elston	15.00	7.50	4.50
521	Gary Geiger	15.00	7.50	4.50
522	Gene Snyder	15.00	7.50	4.50
523	Harry Bright	15.00	7.50	4.50
524	Larry Osborne	15.00	7.50	4.50
525	Jim Coates	17.50	8.75	5.25
526	Bob Speake	15.00	7.50	4.50
527	Solly Hemus	15.00	7.50	4.50
528	Pittsburgh Pirates Team	40.00	20.00	12.00
529	*George Bamberger*	15.00	7.50	4.50
530	Wally Moon	15.00	7.50	4.50
531	Ray Webster	15.00	7.50	4.50
532	Mark Freeman	15.00	7.50	4.50
533	Darrell Johnson	17.50	8.75	5.25
534	Faye Throneberry	15.00	7.50	4.50
535	Ruben Gomez	15.00	7.50	4.50
536	Dan Kravitz	15.00	7.50	4.50
537	Rodolfo Arias	15.00	7.50	4.50
538	Chick King	15.00	7.50	4.50
539	Gary Blaylock	15.00	7.50	4.50
540	Willy Miranda	15.00	7.50	4.50
541	Bob Thurman	15.00	7.50	4.50
542	*Jim Perry*	30.00	15.00	9.00
543	Corsair Outfield Trio (Roberto Clemente, Bob Skinner, Bill Virdon)	60.00	30.00	18.00
544	Lee Tate	15.00	7.50	4.50
545	Tom Morgan	15.00	7.50	4.50
546	Al Schroll	15.00	7.50	4.50
547	Jim Baxes	15.00	7.50	4.50
548	Elmer Singleton	15.00	7.50	4.50
549	Howie Nunn	15.00	7.50	4.50
550	Roy Campanella (Symbol of Courage)	90.00	45.00	27.50
551	Fred Haney/AS	15.00	7.50	4.50
552	Casey Stengel/AS	25.00	12.50	7.50
553	Orlando Cepeda/AS	25.00	12.50	7.50
554	Bill Skowron/AS	22.50	11.00	6.75
555	Bill Mazeroski/AS	25.00	12.50	7.50
556	Nellie Fox/AS	27.50	13.50	8.25
557	Ken Boyer/AS	20.00	10.00	6.00
558	Frank Malzone/AS	15.00	7.50	4.50
559	Ernie Banks/AS	45.00	22.50	13.50
560	Luis Aparicio/AS	20.00	10.00	6.00
561	Hank Aaron/AS	75.00	37.50	22.50

562	Al Kaline/AS	30.00	15.00	9.00
563	Willie Mays/AS	70.00	35.00	20.00
564	Mickey Mantle/AS	250.00	125.00	60.00
565	Wes Covington/AS	15.00	7.50	4.50
566	Roy Sievers/AS	15.00	7.50	4.50
567	Del Crandall/AS	15.00	7.50	4.50
568	Gus Triandos/AS	15.00	7.50	4.50
569	Bob Friend/AS	15.00	7.50	4.50
570	Bob Turley/AS	17.50	8.75	5.25
571	Warren Spahn/AS	27.50	13.50	8.25
572	Billy Pierce/AS	150.00	10.00	6.00
----	Elect Your Favorite Rookie Insert (Paper stock, September 29 date on back.)	200.00	100.00	60.00
----	Felt Pennants Insert (paper stock)	30.00	15.00	9.00

1960 Topps

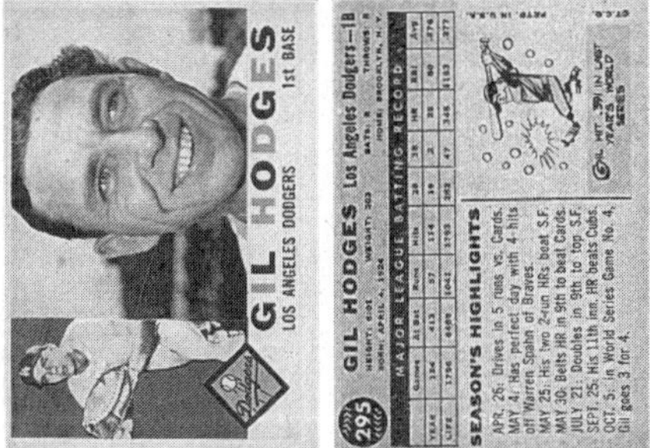

In 1960, Topps opted for a horizontal format in standard 3-1/2" x 2-1/2" size. Basic fronts have a large color portrait or pose at right and black-and-white action photograph at left. After a one-year hiatus, backs returned to the use of lifetime statistics along with a cartoon and short career summary or previous season highlights. Specialty cards in the 572-card set are multi-player cards, managers and coaches cards, and highlights of the 1959 World Series. Two groups of rookie cards are included. The first are numbers 117-148, which are the Sport Magazine rookies. The second group is called "Topps All-Star Rookies." Finally, there is a run of All-Star cards to close out the set in the scarcer high numbers. Cards #375-440 can be found with backs printed on either white or grey cardboard, with the white stock being the less common. Team cards have checklists on the back.

		NM	EX	VG
Complete Set (572):		6,500	3,250	2,000
Common Player (1-440):		6.00	3.00	1.75
Common Player (441-506):		9.00	4.50	2.75
Common Player (507-572):		15.00	7.50	4.50
1	Early Wynn	40.00	10.00	6.00
2	Roman Mejias	20.00	4.00	1.75
3	Joe Adcock	6.00	3.00	1.75
4	Bob Purkey	6.00	3.00	1.75
5	Wally Moon	6.00	3.00	1.75
6	Lou Berberet	6.00	3.00	1.75
7	Master and Mentor (Willie Mays, Bill Rigney)	20.00	10.00	6.00
8	Bud Daley	6.00	3.00	1.75
9	Faye Throneberry	6.00	3.00	1.75
10	Ernie Banks	50.00	25.00	15.00
11	Norm Siebern	6.00	3.00	1.75
12	Milt Pappas	6.00	3.00	1.75
13	Wally Post	6.00	3.00	1.75
14	Jim Grant	6.00	3.00	1.75
15	Pete Runnels	6.00	3.00	1.75
16	Ernie Broglio	6.00	3.00	1.75
17	Johnny Callison	6.00	3.00	1.75
18	Los Angeles Dodgers Team	35.00	17.50	10.00
19	Felix Mantilla	6.00	3.00	1.75
20	Roy Face	6.00	3.00	1.75
21	Dutch Dotterer	6.00	3.00	1.75
22	Rocky Bridges	6.00	3.00	1.75
23	Eddie Fisher	6.00	3.00	1.75
24	Dick Gray	6.00	3.00	1.75
25	Roy Sievers	6.00	3.00	1.75
26	Wayne Terwilliger	6.00	3.00	1.75
27	Dick Drott	6.00	3.00	1.75
28	Brooks Robinson	40.00	20.00	12.00
29	Clem Labine	8.00	4.00	2.50
30	Tito Francona	6.00	3.00	1.75
31	Sammy Esposito	6.00	3.00	1.75
32	Sophomore Stalwarts (Jim O'Toole, Vada Pinson)	9.00	4.50	2.75
33	Tom Morgan	6.00	3.00	1.75
34	George Anderson (Sparky)	20.00	10.00	6.00
35	Whitey Ford	35.00	17.50	10.00
36	Russ Nixon	6.00	3.00	1.75
37	Bill Bruton	6.00	3.00	1.75
38	Jerry Casale	6.00	3.00	1.75
39	Earl Averill	6.00	3.00	1.75
40	Joe Cunningham	6.00	3.00	1.75
41	Barry Latman	6.00	3.00	1.75
42	Hobie Landrith	6.00	3.00	1.75
43	Washington Senators Team	15.00	7.50	4.50
44	Bobby Locke	6.00	3.00	1.75
45	Roy McMillan	6.00	3.00	1.75
46	Jack Fisher	6.00	3.00	1.75
47	Don Zimmer	12.00	6.00	3.50
48	Hal Smith	6.00	3.00	1.75
49	Curt Raydon	6.00	3.00	1.75
50	Al Kaline	35.00	17.50	10.00
51	Jim Coates	6.00	3.00	1.75
52	Dave Philley	6.00	3.00	1.75
53	Jackie Brandt	6.00	3.00	1.75
54	Mike Fornieles	6.00	3.00	1.75
55	Bill Mazeroski	20.00	10.00	6.00
56	Steve Korcheck	6.00	3.00	1.75
57	Win-Savers (Turk Lown, Gerry Staley)	6.00	3.00	1.75
58	Gino Cimoli	6.00	3.00	1.75
59	Juan Pizarro	6.00	3.00	1.75
60	Gus Triandos	6.00	3.00	1.75
61	Eddie Kasko	6.00	3.00	1.75
62	Roger Craig	6.00	3.00	1.75
63	George Strickland	6.00	3.00	1.75
64	Jack Meyer	6.00	3.00	1.75
65	Elston Howard	15.00	7.50	4.50
66	Bob Trowbridge	6.00	3.00	1.75
67	***Jose Pagan***	6.00	3.00	1.75
68	Dave Hillman	6.00	3.00	1.75
69	Billy Goodman	6.00	3.00	1.75
70	Lou Burdette	6.00	3.00	1.75
71	Marty Keough	6.00	3.00	1.75
72	Detroit Tigers Team	15.00	7.50	4.50
73	Bob Gibson	50.00	25.00	15.00
74	Walt Moryn	6.00	3.00	1.75
75	Vic Power	6.00	3.00	1.75
76	Bill Fischer	6.00	3.00	1.75
77	Hank Foiles	6.00	3.00	1.75
78	Bob Grim	6.00	3.00	1.75
79	Walt Dropo	6.00	3.00	1.75
80	Johnny Antonelli	6.00	3.00	1.75
81	Russ Snyder	6.00	3.00	1.75
82	Ruben Gomez	6.00	3.00	1.75
83	Tony Kubek	25.00	12.50	7.50
84	Hal Smith	6.00	3.00	1.75
85	Frank Lary	6.00	3.00	1.75
86	Dick Gernert	6.00	3.00	1.75
87	John Romonosky	6.00	3.00	1.75
88	John Roseboro	6.00	3.00	1.75
89	Hal Brown	6.00	3.00	1.75
90	Bobby Avila	6.00	3.00	1.75
91	Bennie Daniels	6.00	3.00	1.75
92	Whitey Herzog	6.00	3.00	1.75
93	Art Schult	6.00	3.00	1.75
94	Leo Kiely	6.00	3.00	1.75
95	Frank Thomas	6.00	3.00	1.75
96	Ralph Terry	7.50	3.75	2.25
97	Ted Lepcio	6.00	3.00	1.75
98	Gordon Jones	6.00	3.00	1.75
99	Lenny Green	6.00	3.00	1.75
100	Nellie Fox	20.00	10.00	6.00
101	Bob Miller	6.00	3.00	1.75
102	Kent Hadley	6.00	3.00	1.75
103	Dick Farrell	6.00	3.00	1.75
104	Dick Schofield	6.00	3.00	1.75
105	***Larry Sherry***	12.00	6.00	3.50
106	Billy Gardner	6.00	3.00	1.75
107	Carl Willey	6.00	3.00	1.75
108	Pete Daley	6.00	3.00	1.75
109	Cletis Boyer	13.50	6.75	4.00
110	Cal McLish	6.00	3.00	1.75
111	Vic Wertz	6.00	3.00	1.75
112	Jack Harshman	6.00	3.00	1.75
113	Bob Skinner	6.00	3.00	1.75
114	Ken Aspromonte	6.00	3.00	1.75
115	Fork and Knuckler (Roy Face, Hoyt Wilhelm)	9.00	4.50	2.75
116	Jim Rivera	6.00	3.00	1.75
117	Tom Borland	6.00	3.00	1.75
118	Bob Bruce	6.00	3.00	1.75
119	***Chico Cardenas***	6.00	3.00	1.75
120	Duke Carmel	6.00	3.00	1.75
121	Camilo Carreon	6.00	3.00	1.75
122	Don Dillard	6.00	3.00	1.75
123	Dan Dobbek	6.00	3.00	1.75
124	Jim Donohue	6.00	3.00	1.75
125	***Dick Ellsworth***	6.00	3.00	1.75
126	***Chuck Estrada***	6.00	3.00	1.75
127	Ronnie Hansen	6.00	3.00	1.75
128	Bill Harris	6.00	3.00	1.75
129	Bob Hartman	6.00	3.00	1.75
130	Frank Herrera	6.00	3.00	1.75
131	Ed Hobaugh	6.00	3.00	1.75
132	***Frank Howard***	20.00	10.00	6.00
133	***Manuel Javier***	6.00	3.00	1.75
134	Deron Johnson	7.50	3.75	2.25
135	Ken Johnson	6.00	3.00	1.75
136	***Jim Kaat***	20.00	10.00	6.00
137	Lou Klimchock	6.00	3.00	1.75
138	***Art Mahaffey***	6.00	3.00	1.75
139	Carl Mathias	6.00	3.00	1.75
140	Julio Navarro	6.00	3.00	1.75
141	Jim Proctor	6.00	3.00	1.75
142	Bill Short	6.00	3.00	1.75
143	Al Spangler	6.00	3.00	1.75
144	Al Stieglitz	6.00	3.00	1.75
145	Jim Umbricht	6.00	3.00	1.75
146	Ted Wieand	6.00	3.00	1.75
147	Bob Will	6.00	3.00	1.75
148	***Carl Yastrzemski***	130.00	65.00	35.00
149	Bob Nieman	6.00	3.00	1.75
150	Billy Pierce	6.00	3.00	1.75
151	San Francisco Giants Team	15.00	7.50	4.50
152	Gail Harris	6.00	3.00	1.75
153	Bobby Thomson	7.50	3.75	2.25
154	Jim Davenport	6.00	3.00	1.75
155	Charlie Neal	6.00	3.00	1.75
156	Art Ceccarelli	6.00	3.00	1.75
157	Rocky Nelson	6.00	3.00	1.75
158	Wes Covington	6.00	3.00	1.75
159	Jim Piersall	8.00	4.00	2.50
160	Rival All-Stars (Ken Boyer, Mickey Mantle)	60.00	30.00	18.00
161	Ray Narleski	6.00	3.00	1.75
162	Sammy Taylor	6.00	3.00	1.75
163	Hector Lopez	6.00	3.00	1.75
164	Cincinnati Reds Team	15.00	7.50	4.50
165	Jack Sanford	6.00	3.00	1.75
166	Chuck Essegian	6.00	3.00	1.75
167	Valmy Thomas	6.00	3.00	1.75
168	Alex Grammas	6.00	3.00	1.75
169	Jake Striker	6.00	3.00	1.75
170	Del Crandall	6.00	3.00	1.75
171	Johnny Groth	6.00	3.00	1.75
172	Willie Kirkland	6.00	3.00	1.75
173	Billy Martin	10.00	5.00	3.00
174	Cleveland Indians Team	15.00	7.50	4.50
175	Pedro Ramos	6.00	3.00	1.75
176	Vada Pinson	10.00	5.00	3.00
177	Johnny Kucks	6.00	3.00	1.75
178	Woody Held	6.00	3.00	1.75
179	Rip Coleman	6.00	3.00	1.75
180	Harry Simpson	6.00	3.00	1.75
181	Billy Loes	6.00	3.00	1.75
182	Glen Hobbie	6.00	3.00	1.75
183	Eli Grba	6.00	3.00	1.75
184	Gary Geiger	6.00	3.00	1.75
185	Jim Owens	6.00	3.00	1.75
186	Dave Sisler	6.00	3.00	1.75
187	Jay Hook	6.00	3.00	1.75
188	Dick Williams	6.00	3.00	1.75
189	Don McMahon	6.00	3.00	1.75
190	Gene Woodling	6.00	3.00	1.75
191	Johnny Klippstein	6.00	3.00	1.75
192	Danny O'Connell	6.00	3.00	1.75
193	Dick Hyde	6.00	3.00	1.75
194	Bobby Gene Smith	6.00	3.00	1.75
195	Lindy McDaniel	6.00	3.00	1.75
196	Andy Carey	6.00	3.00	1.75
197	Ron Kline	6.00	3.00	1.75
198	Jerry Lynch	6.00	3.00	1.75
199	Dick Donovan	6.00	3.00	1.75
200	Willie Mays	90.00	45.00	27.50
201	Larry Osborne	6.00	3.00	1.75
202	Fred Kipp	6.00	3.00	1.75
203	Sammy White	6.00	3.00	1.75
204	Ryne Duren	7.50	3.75	2.25
205	Johnny Logan	6.00	3.00	1.75
206	Claude Osteen	6.00	3.00	1.75
207	Bob Boyd	6.00	3.00	1.75
208	Chicago White Sox Team	15.00	7.50	4.50
209	Ron Blackburn	6.00	3.00	1.75
210	Harmon Killebrew	30.00	15.00	9.00
211	Taylor Phillips	6.00	3.00	1.75
212	Walt Alston	12.00	6.00	3.50
213	Chuck Dressen	6.00	3.00	1.75
214	Jimmie Dykes	6.00	3.00	1.75
215	Bob Elliott	6.00	3.00	1.75
216	Joe Gordon	6.00	3.00	1.75
217	Charley Grimm	6.00	3.00	1.75
218	Solly Hemus	6.00	3.00	1.75
219	Fred Hutchinson	6.00	3.00	1.75
220	Billy Jurges	6.00	3.00	1.75
221	Cookie Lavagetto	6.00	3.00	1.75
222	Al Lopez	10.00	5.00	3.00
223	Danny Murtaugh	6.00	3.00	1.75
224	Paul Richards	6.00	3.00	1.75
225	Bill Rigney	6.00	3.00	1.75
226	Eddie Sawyer	6.00	3.00	1.75
227	Casey Stengel	17.50	8.75	5.25
228	Ernie Johnson	6.00	3.00	1.75
229	Joe Morgan	6.00	3.00	1.75
230	Mound Magicians (Bob Buhl, Lou Burdette, Warren Spahn)	17.50	8.75	5.25
231	Hal Naragon	6.00	3.00	1.75
232	Jim Busby	6.00	3.00	1.75
233	Don Elston	6.00	3.00	1.75
234	Don Demeter	6.00	3.00	1.75
235	Gus Bell	6.00	3.00	1.75
236	Dick Ricketts	6.00	3.00	1.75
237	Elmer Valo	6.00	3.00	1.75
238	Danny Kravitz	6.00	3.00	1.75
239	Joe Shipley	6.00	3.00	1.75
240	Luis Aparicio	17.50	8.75	5.25
241	Albie Pearson	6.00	3.00	1.75
242	St. Louis Cardinals Team	15.00	7.50	4.50
243	Bubba Phillips	6.00	3.00	1.75
244	Hal Griggs	6.00	3.00	1.75
245	Eddie Yost	6.00	3.00	1.75
246	Lee Maye	6.00	3.00	1.75
247	Gil McDougald	12.00	6.00	3.50
248	Del Rice	6.00	3.00	1.75
249	***Earl Wilson***	6.00	3.00	1.75
250	Stan Musial	65.00	32.50	20.00
251	Bobby Malkmus	6.00	3.00	1.75
252	Ray Herbert	6.00	3.00	1.75
253	Eddie Bressoud	6.00	3.00	1.75
254	Arnie Portocarrero	6.00	3.00	1.75
255	Jim Gilliam	10.00	5.00	3.00
256	Dick Brown	6.00	3.00	1.75
257	Gordy Coleman	6.00	3.00	1.75
258	Dick Groat	6.00	3.00	1.75
259	George Altman	6.00	3.00	1.75
260	Power Plus (Rocky Colavito, Tito Francona)	11.00	5.50	3.25
261	Pete Burnside	6.00	3.00	1.75
262	Hank Bauer	7.50	3.75	2.25
263	Darrell Johnson	6.00	3.00	1.75
264	Robin Roberts	12.50	6.25	3.75
265	Rip Repulski	6.00	3.00	1.75
266	Joe Jay	6.00	3.00	1.75
267	Jim Marshall	6.00	3.00	1.75
268	Al Worthington	6.00	3.00	1.75
269	Gene Green	6.00	3.00	1.75
270	Bob Turley	10.00	5.00	3.00
271	Julio Becquer	6.00	3.00	1.75
272	Fred Green	6.00	3.00	1.75
273	Neil Chrisley	6.00	3.00	1.75
274	Tom Acker	6.00	3.00	1.75
275	Curt Flood	9.00	4.50	2.75
276	Ken McBride	6.00	3.00	1.75
277	Harry Bright	6.00	3.00	1.75
278	Stan Williams	6.00	3.00	1.75
279	Chuck Tanner	6.00	3.00	1.75
280	Frank Sullivan	6.00	3.00	1.75
281	Ray Boone	6.00	3.00	1.75
282	Joe Nuxhall	6.00	3.00	1.75
283	John Blanchard	7.50	3.75	2.25
284	Don Gross	6.00	3.00	1.75

285 Harry Anderson 6.00 3.00 1.75
286 Ray Semproch 6.00 3.00 1.75
287 Felipe Alou 7.50 3.75 2.25
288 Bob Mabe 6.00 3.00 1.75
289 Willie Jones 6.00 3.00 1.75
290 Jerry Lumpe 6.00 3.00 1.75
291 Bob Keegan 6.00 3.00 1.75
292 Dodger Backstops (Joe Pignatano, John Roseboro) 7.50 3.75 2.25
293 Gene Conley 6.00 3.00 1.75
294 Tony Taylor 6.00 3.00 1.75
295 Gil Hodges 15.00 7.50 4.50
296 Nelson Chittum 6.00 3.00 1.75
297 Reno Bertoia 6.00 3.00 1.75
298 George Witt 6.00 3.00 1.75
299 Earl Torgeson 6.00 3.00 1.75
300 Hank Aaron 115.00 55.00 35.00
301 Jerry Davie 6.00 3.00 1.75
302 Philadelphia Phillies Team 15.00 7.50 4.50
303 Billy O'Dell 6.00 3.00 1.75
304 Joe Ginsberg 6.00 3.00 1.75
305 Richie Ashburn 15.00 7.50 4.50
306 Frank Baumann 6.00 3.00 1.75
307 Gene Oliver 6.00 3.00 1.75
308 Dick Hall 6.00 3.00 1.75
309 Bob Hale 6.00 3.00 1.75
310 Frank Malzone 6.00 3.00 1.75
311 Raul Sanchez 6.00 3.00 1.75
312 Charlie Lau 6.00 3.00 1.75
313 Turk Lown 6.00 3.00 1.75
314 Chico Fernandez 6.00 3.00 1.75
315 Bobby Shantz 11.00 5.50 3.25
316 ***Willie McCovey*** 90.00 45.00 27.50
317 Pumpsie Green 7.50 3.75 2.25
318 Jim Baxes 6.00 3.00 1.75
319 Joe Koppe 6.00 3.00 1.75
320 Bob Allison 6.00 3.00 1.75
321 Ron Fairly 6.00 3.00 1.75
322 Willie Tasby 6.00 3.00 1.75
323 Johnny Romano 6.00 3.00 1.75
324 Jim Perry 7.50 3.75 2.25
325 Jim O'Toole 6.00 3.00 1.75
326 Bob Clemente 95.00 47.50 27.50
327 ***Ray Sadecki*** 6.00 3.00 1.75
328 Earl Battey 6.00 3.00 1.75
329 Zack Monroe 6.00 3.00 1.75
330 Harvey Kuenn 6.00 3.00 1.75
331 Henry Mason 6.00 3.00 1.75
332 New York Yankees Team 37.50 18.50 11.00
333 Danny McDevitt 6.00 3.00 1.75
334 Ted Abernathy 6.00 3.00 1.75
335 Red Schoendienst 12.50 6.25 3.75
336 Ike Delock 6.00 3.00 1.75
337 Cal Neeman 6.00 3.00 1.75
338 Ray Monzant 6.00 3.00 1.75
339 Harry Chiti 6.00 3.00 1.75
340 Harvey Haddix 6.00 3.00 1.75
341 Carroll Hardy 6.00 3.00 1.75
342 Casey Wise 6.00 3.00 1.75
343 Sandy Koufax 85.00 42.50 25.00
344 Clint Courtney 6.00 3.00 1.75
345 Don Newcombe 7.50 3.75 2.25
346 J.C. Martin (Photo actually Gary Peters.) 6.00 3.00 1.75
347 Ed Bouchee 6.00 3.00 1.75
348 Barry Shetrone 6.00 3.00 1.75
349 Moe Drabowsky 6.00 3.00 1.75
350 Mickey Mantle 350.00 160.00 95.00
351 Don Nottebart 6.00 3.00 1.75
352 Cincy Clouters (Gus Bell, Jerry Lynch, Frank Robinson) 12.00 6.00 3.50
353 Don Larsen 8.00 4.00 2.50
354 Bob Lillis 6.00 3.00 1.75
355 Bill White 6.00 3.00 1.75
356 Joe Amalfitano 6.00 3.00 1.75
357 Al Schroll 6.00 3.00 1.75
358 Joe De Maestri 6.00 3.00 1.75
359 Buddy Gilbert 6.00 3.00 1.75
360 Herb Score 7.50 3.75 2.25
361 Bob Oldis 6.00 3.00 1.75
362 Russ Kemmerer 6.00 3.00 1.75
363 Gene Stephens 6.00 3.00 1.75
364 Paul Foytack 6.00 3.00 1.75
365 Minnie Minoso 12.50 6.25 3.75
366 ***Dallas Green*** 9.00 4.50 2.75
367 Bill Tuttle 6.00 3.00 1.75
368 Daryl Spencer 6.00 3.00 1.75
369 Billy Hoeft 6.00 3.00 1.75
370 Bill Skowron 17.50 8.75 5.25
371 Bud Byerly 6.00 3.00 1.75
372 Frank House 6.00 3.00 1.75
373 Don Hoak 6.00 3.00 1.75
374 Bob Buhl 6.00 3.00 1.75
375 Dale Long 6.00 3.00 1.75
376 Johnny Briggs 6.00 3.00 1.75
377 Roger Maris 80.00 40.00 24.00
378 Stu Miller 6.00 3.00 1.75
379 Red Wilson 6.00 3.00 1.75
380 Bob Shaw 6.00 3.00 1.75
381 Milwaukee Braves Team 16.00 8.00 4.75
382 Ted Bowsfield 6.00 3.00 1.75
383 Leon Wagner 6.00 3.00 1.75
384 Don Cardwell 6.00 3.00 1.75
385 World Series Game 1 (Neal Steals Second) 10.00 5.00 3.00
386 World Series Game 2 (Neal Belts 2nd Homer) 10.00 5.00 3.00
387 World Series Game 3 (Furillo Breaks Up Game) 10.00 5.00 3.00
388 World Series Game 4 (Hodges' Winning Homer) 10.00 5.00 3.00
389 World Series Game 5 (Luis Swipes Base) 12.00 6.00 3.50
390 World Series Game 6 (Scrambling After Ball) 10.00 5.00 3.00
391 World Series Summary (The Champs Celebrate) 10.00 5.00 3.00
392 Tex Clevenger 6.00 3.00 1.75
393 Smoky Burgess 6.00 3.00 1.75
394 Norm Larker 6.00 3.00 1.75
395 Hoyt Wilhelm 13.50 6.75 4.00
396 Steve Bilko 6.00 3.00 1.75
397 Don Blasingame 6.00 3.00 1.75
398 Mike Cuellar 6.00 3.00 1.75
399 Young Hill Stars (Jack Fisher, Milt Pappas, Jerry Walker) 6.00 3.00 1.75
400 Rocky Colavito 20.00 10.00 6.00
401 Bob Duliba 6.00 3.00 1.75
402 Dick Stuart 6.00 3.00 1.75
403 Ed Sadowski 6.00 3.00 1.75
404 Bob Rush 6.00 3.00 1.75
405 Bobby Richardson 25.00 12.50 7.50
406 Billy Klaus 6.00 3.00 1.75
407 ***Gary Peters*** (Photo actually J.C. Martin.) 6.00 3.00 1.75
408 Carl Furillo 11.00 5.50 3.25
409 Ron Samford 6.00 3.00 1.75
410 Sam Jones 6.00 3.00 1.75
411 Ed Bailey 6.00 3.00 1.75
412 Bob Anderson 6.00 3.00 1.75
413 Kansas City Athletics Team 15.00 7.50 4.50
414 Don Williams 6.00 3.00 1.75
415 Bob Cerv 6.00 3.00 1.75
416 Humberto Robinson 6.00 3.00 1.75
417 Chuck Cottier 6.00 3.00 1.75
418 Don Mossi 6.00 3.00 1.75
419 George Crowe 6.00 3.00 1.75
420 Ed Mathews 25.00 12.50 7.50
421 Duke Maas 6.00 3.00 1.75
422 Johnny Powers 6.00 3.00 1.75
423 Ed Fitz Gerald 6.00 3.00 1.75
424 Pete Whisenant 6.00 3.00 1.75
425 Johnny Podres 10.00 5.00 3.00
426 Ron Jackson 6.00 3.00 1.75
427 Al Grunwald 6.00 3.00 1.75
428 Al Smith 6.00 3.00 1.75
429 American League Kings (Nellie Fox, Harvey Kuenn) 12.50 6.25 3.75
430 Art Ditmar 6.00 3.00 1.75
431 Andre Rodgers 6.00 3.00 1.75
432 Chuck Stobbs 6.00 3.00 1.75
433 Irv Noren 6.00 3.00 1.75
434 Brooks Lawrence 6.00 3.00 1.75
435 Gene Freese 6.00 3.00 1.75
436 Marv Throneberry 6.00 3.00 1.75
437 Bob Friend 6.00 3.00 1.75
438 Jim Coker 6.00 3.00 1.75
439 Tom Brewer 6.00 3.00 1.75
440 Jim Lemon 6.00 3.00 1.75
441 Gary Bell 9.00 4.50 2.75
442 Joe Pignatano 9.00 4.50 2.75
443 Charlie Maxwell 9.00 4.50 2.75
444 Jerry Kindall 9.00 4.50 2.75
445 Warren Spahn 35.00 17.50 10.00
446 Ellis Burton 9.00 4.50 2.75
447 Ray Moore 9.00 4.50 2.75
448 ***Jim Gentile*** 15.00 7.50 4.50
449 Jim Brosnan 9.00 4.50 2.75
450 Orlando Cepeda 30.00 15.00 9.00
451 Curt Simmons 9.00 4.50 2.75
452 Ray Webster 9.00 4.50 2.75
453 Vern Law 9.00 4.50 2.75
454 Hal Woodeshick 9.00 4.50 2.75
455 Baltimomre Orioles Coaches (Harry Brecheen, Lum Harris, Eddie Robinson) 9.00 4.50 2.75
456 Boston Red Sox Coaches (Del Baker, Billy Herman, Sal Maglie, Rudy York) 15.00 7.50 4.50
457 Chicago Cubs Coaches (Lou Klein, Charlie Root, Elvin Tappe) 9.00 4.50 2.75
458 Chicago White Sox Coaches (Ray Berres, Johnny Cooney, Tony Cuccinello, Don Gutteridge) 9.00 4.50 2.75
459 Cincinnati Reds Coaches (Cot Deal, Wally Moses, Reggie Otero) 9.00 4.50 2.75
460 Cleveland Indians Coaches (Mel Harder, Red Kress, Bob Lemon, Jo-Jo White) 10.00 5.00 3.00
461 Detroit Tigers Coaches (Luke Appling, Tom Ferrick, Billy Hitchcock) 10.00 5.00 3.00
462 Kansas City A's Coaches (Walker Cooper, Fred Fitzsimmons, Don Heffner) 9.00 4.50 2.75
463 L.A. Dodgers Coaches (Joe Becker, Bobby Bragan, Greg Mulleavy, Pete Reiser) 9.00 4.50 2.75
464 Milwaukee Braves Coaches (George Myatt, Andy Pafko, Bob Scheffing, Whitlow Wyatt) 9.00 4.50 2.75
465 N.Y. Yankees Coaches (Frank Crosetti, Bill Dickey, Ralph Houk, Ed Lopat) 20.00 10.00 6.00
466 Phila. Phillies Coaches (Dick Carter, Andy Cohen, Ken Silvestri) 9.00 4.50 2.75
467 Pitts. Pirates Coaches (Bill Burwell, Sam Narron, Frank Oceak, Mickey Vernon) 9.00 4.50 2.75
468 St. Louis Cards Coaches (Ray Katt, Johnny Keane, Howie Pollet, Harry Walker) 9.00 4.50 2.75
469 San Fran. Giants Coaches (Salty Parker, Bill Posedel, Wes Westrum) 9.00 4.50 2.75
470 Wash. Senators Coaches (Ellis Clary, Sam Mele, Bob Swift) 9.00 4.50 2.75
471 Ned Garver 9.00 4.50 2.75
472 Al Dark 9.00 4.50 2.75
473 Al Cicotte 9.00 4.50 2.75
474 Haywood Sullivan 9.00 4.50 2.75
475 Don Drysdale 35.00 17.50 10.00
476 Lou Johnson 9.00 4.50 2.75
477 Don Ferrarese 9.00 4.50 2.75
478 Frank Torre 9.00 4.50 2.75
479 Georges Maranda 9.00 4.50 2.75
480 Yogi Berra 65.00 32.50 20.00
481 Wes Stock 9.00 4.50 2.75
482 Frank Bolling 9.00 4.50 2.75
483 Camilo Pascual 9.00 4.50 2.75
484 Pittsburgh Pirates Team 25.00 12.50 7.50
485 Ken Boyer 15.00 7.50 4.50
486 Bobby Del Greco 9.00 4.50 2.75
487 Tom Sturdivant 9.00 4.50 2.75
488 Norm Cash 15.00 7.50 4.50
489 Steve Ridzik 9.00 4.50 2.75
490 Frank Robinson 40.00 20.00 12.00
491 Mel Roach 9.00 4.50 2.75
492 Larry Jackson 9.00 4.50 2.75
493 Duke Snider 40.00 20.00 12.00
494 Baltimore Orioles Team 20.00 10.00 6.00
495 Sherm Lollar 9.00 4.50 2.75
496 Bill Virdon 9.00 4.50 2.75
497 John Tsitouris 9.00 4.50 2.75
498 Al Pilarcik 9.00 4.50 2.75
499 Johnny James 9.00 4.50 2.75
500 Johnny Temple 9.00 4.50 2.75
501 Bob Schmidt 9.00 4.50 2.75
502 Jim Bunning 20.00 10.00 6.00
503 Don Lee 9.00 4.50 2.75
504 Seth Morehead 9.00 4.50 2.75
505 Ted Kluszewski 15.00 7.50 4.50
506 Lee Walls 9.00 4.50 2.75
507 Dick Stigman 15.00 7.50 4.50
508 Billy Consolo 15.00 7.50 4.50
509 ***Tommy Davis*** 20.00 10.00 6.00
510 Jerry Staley 15.00 7.50 4.50
511 Ken Walters 15.00 7.50 4.50
512 Joe Gibbon 15.00 7.50 4.50
513 Chicago Cubs Team 20.00 10.00 6.00
514 ***Steve Barber*** 17.50 8.75 5.25
515 Stan Lopata 15.00 7.50 4.50
516 Marty Kutyna 15.00 7.50 4.50
517 Charley James 15.00 7.50 4.50
518 ***Tony Gonzalez*** 15.00 7.50 4.50
519 Ed Roebuck 15.00 7.50 4.50
520 Don Buddin 15.00 7.50 4.50
521 Mike Lee 15.00 7.50 4.50
522 Ken Hunt 15.00 7.50 4.50
523 ***Clay Dalrymple*** 15.00 7.50 4.50
524 Bill Henry 15.00 7.50 4.50
525 Marv Breeding 15.00 7.50 4.50
526 Paul Giel 15.00 7.50 4.50
527 Jose Valdivielso 15.00 7.50 4.50
528 Ben Johnson 15.00 7.50 4.50
529 Norm Sherry 17.50 8.75 5.25
530 Mike McCormick 15.00 7.50 4.50
531 Sandy Amoros 15.00 7.50 4.50
532 Mike Garcia 15.00 7.50 4.50
533 Lu Clinton 15.00 7.50 4.50
534 Ken MacKenzie 15.00 7.50 4.50
535 Whitey Lockman 15.00 7.50 4.50
536 Wynn Hawkins 15.00 7.50 4.50
537 Boston Red Sox Team 25.00 12.50 7.50
538 Frank Barnes 15.00 7.50 4.50
539 Gene Baker 15.00 7.50 4.50
540 Jerry Walker 15.00 7.50 4.50
541 Tony Curry 15.00 7.50 4.50
542 Ken Hamlin 15.00 7.50 4.50
543 Elio Chacon 15.00 7.50 4.50
544 Bill Monbouquette 15.00 7.50 4.50
545 Carl Sawatski 15.00 7.50 4.50
546 Hank Aguirre 15.00 7.50 4.50
547 ***Bob Aspromonte*** 17.50 8.75 5.25
548 ***Don Mincher*** 15.00 7.50 4.50
549 John Buzhardt 15.00 7.50 4.50
550 Jim Landis 15.00 7.50 4.50
551 Ed Rakow 15.00 7.50 4.50
552 Walt Bond 15.00 7.50 4.50
553 Bill Skowron/AS 20.00 10.00 6.00
554 Willie McCovey/AS 35.00 17.50 10.00
555 Nellie Fox/AS 20.00 10.00 6.00
556 Charlie Neal/AS 17.50 8.75 5.25
557 Frank Malzone/AS 17.50 8.75 5.25
558 Eddie Mathews/AS 25.00 12.50 7.50
559 Luis Aparicio/AS 20.00 10.00 6.00
560 Ernie Banks/AS 35.00 17.50 10.00
561 Al Kaline/AS 30.00 15.00 9.00
562 Joe Cunningham/AS 17.50 8.75 5.25
563 Mickey Mantle/AS 150.00 75.00 45.00
564 Willie Mays/AS 60.00 30.00 18.00
565 Roger Maris/AS 70.00 35.00 20.00
566 Hank Aaron/AS 65.00 32.50 20.00
567 Sherm Lollar/AS 17.50 8.75 5.25
568 Del Crandall/AS 17.50 8.75 5.25
569 Camilo Pascual/AS 17.50 8.75 5.25
570 Don Drysdale/AS 25.00 12.50 7.50
571 Billy Pierce/AS 17.50 8.75 5.25
572 Johnny Antonelli/AS 25.00 9.00 5.25
---- Elect Your Favorite Rookie Insert (Paper stock, no date on back.) 30.00 15.00 9.00
---- Hot Iron Transfer Insert (Paper stock.) 30.00 15.00 9.00

1960 Topps Proofs

Subsequent to a pair of December 1959 trades, the 1960 Topps cards of three players were significantly changed. Whether the change occurred prior to regular production printing and packaging or while the cards were still in the proofing stage is unknown. The changes affect the cards of Gino Cimoli, Kent Hadley and, reportedly, Marv Throneberry. In the very rare versions each player's card has at bottom left the logo of his team prior to the trade. The common

regular-issue version has the new team logo. The front of Hadley's rare card names his team as the Yankees, while Cimoli's rare version says Cardinals.

		NM	EX	VG
58	Gino Cimoli (Cardinals logo.) (No recent sales.)			
102	Kent Hadley (A's logo.) (Nov., 1999 auction record.)	13,500		
436	Marv Throneberry (Yankees logo.) (Existence not confirmed.)			

1960 Topps Tattoos

Probably the least popular of all Topps products among parents and teachers, the Tattoos were printed on the reverse of the wrappers of Topps "Tattoo Bubble Gum." The entire wrapper was 1-9/16" x 3-1/2". The owner moistened their skin and applied the back of the wrapper to the wet spot, producing a colorful "tattoo" (although often blurred by running colors). The set offered 96 tattoo possibilities of which 55 were players, 16 teams, 15 action pictures and 10 autographed balls. Because the packaged gum slides easily in and out of the "sealed" wrapper, allowing the tattoo to be easily seen, unopened packs command little premium.

		NM	EX	VG
Complete Set (96):		2,750	1,350	825.00
Common Player:		20.00	10.00	6.00
Common Non-player:		12.00	6.00	3.50
(1)	Hank Aaron	150.00	75.00	45.00
(2)	Bob Allison	20.00	10.00	6.00
(3)	John Antonelli	20.00	10.00	6.00
(4)	Richie Ashburn	40.00	20.00	12.00
(5)	Ernie Banks	65.00	32.00	19.50
(6)	Yogi Berra	60.00	30.00	18.00
(7)	Lew Burdette	20.00	10.00	6.00
(8)	Orlando Cepeda	35.00	17.50	10.50
(9)	Rocky Colavito	35.00	17.50	10.50
(10)	Joe Cunningham	20.00	10.00	6.00
(11)	Buddy Daley	20.00	10.00	6.00
(12)	Don Drysdale	40.00	20.00	12.00
(13)	Ryne Duren	20.00	10.00	6.00
(14)	Roy Face	20.00	10.00	6.00
(15)	Whitey Ford	60.00	30.00	18.00
(16)	Nellie Fox	35.00	17.50	10.50
(17)	Tito Francona	20.00	10.00	6.00
(18)	Gene Freese	20.00	10.00	6.00
(19)	Jim Gilliam	20.00	10.00	6.00
(20)	Dick Groat	20.00	10.00	6.00
(21)	Ray Herbert	20.00	10.00	6.00
(22)	Glen Hobbie	20.00	10.00	6.00
(23)	Jackie Jensen	20.00	10.00	6.00
(24)	Sam Jones	20.00	10.00	6.00
(25)	Al Kaline	60.00	30.00	18.00
(26)	Harmon Killebrew	40.00	20.00	12.00
(27)	Harvey Kuenn	20.00	10.00	6.00
(28)	Frank Lary	20.00	10.00	6.00
(29)	Vernon Law	20.00	10.00	6.00
(30)	Frank Malzone	20.00	10.00	6.00
(31)	Mickey Mantle	300.00	150.00	90.00
(32)	Roger Maris	75.00	37.00	22.00
(33)	Ed Mathews	40.00	20.00	12.00
(34)	Willie Mays	150.00	75.00	45.00
(35)	Cal Mclish	20.00	10.00	6.00
(36)	Wally Moon	20.00	10.00	6.00
(37)	Walt Moryn	20.00	10.00	6.00
(38)	Don Mossi	20.00	10.00	6.00
(39)	Stan Musial	100.00	50.00	30.00
(40)	Charlie Neal	20.00	10.00	6.00
(41)	Don Newcombe	20.00	10.00	6.00
(42)	Milt Pappas	20.00	10.00	6.00
(43)	Camilo Pascual	20.00	10.00	6.00
(44)	Billie (Billy) Pierce	20.00	10.00	6.00
(45)	Robin Roberts	35.00	17.50	10.50
(46)	Frank Robinson	40.00	20.00	12.00
(47)	Pete Runnels	20.00	10.00	6.00
(48)	Herb Score	20.00	10.00	6.00
(49)	Warren Spahn	35.00	17.50	10.50
(50)	Johnny Temple	20.00	10.00	6.00
(51)	Gus Triandos	20.00	10.00	6.00
(52)	Jerry Walker	20.00	10.00	6.00
(53)	Bill White	20.00	10.00	6.00
(54)	Gene Woodling	20.00	10.00	6.00
(55)	Early Wynn	35.00	17.50	10.50
(56)	Chicago Cubs Logo	15.00	7.50	4.50
(57)	Cincinnati Reds Logo	15.00	7.50	4.50
(58)	Los Angeles Dodgers Logo	15.00	7.50	4.50
(59)	Milwaukee Braves Logo	15.00	7.50	4.50
(60)	Philadelphia Phillies Logo	15.00	7.50	4.50
(61)	Pittsburgh Pirates Logo	20.00	10.00	6.00
(62)	San Francisco Giants Logo	15.00	7.50	4.50
(63)	St. Louis Cardinals Logo	15.00	7.50	4.50
(64)	Baltimore Orioles Logo	15.00	7.50	4.50
(65)	Boston Red Sox Logo	15.00	7.50	4.50
(66)	Chicago White Sox Logo	15.00	7.50	4.50
(67)	Cleveland Indians Logo	15.00	7.50	4.50
(68)	Detroit Tigers Logo	15.00	7.50	4.50
(69)	Kansas City Athletics Logo	15.00	7.50	4.50
(70)	New York Yankees Logo	20.00	10.00	6.00
(71)	Washington Senators Logo	15.00	7.50	4.50
(72)	Autograph (Richie Ashburn)	20.00	10.00	6.00
(73)	Autograph (Rocky Colavito)	25.00	12.50	7.50
(74)	Autograph (Roy Face)	15.00	7.50	4.50
(75)	Autograph (Jackie Jensen)	15.00	7.50	4.50
(76)	Autograph (Harmon Killebrew)	25.00	12.50	7.50
(77)	Autograph (Mickey Mantle)	100.00	50.00	30.00
(78)	Autograph (Willie Mays)	50.00	25.00	15.00
(79)	Autograph (Stan Musial)	50.00	25.00	15.00
(80)	Autograph (Billy Pierce)	15.00	7.50	4.50
(81)	Autograph (Jerry Walker)	15.00	7.50	4.50
(82)	Run-Down	12.00	6.00	3.50
(83)	Out At First	12.00	6.00	3.50
(84)	The Final Word	12.00	6.00	3.50
(85)	Twisting Foul	12.00	6.00	3.50
(86)	Out At Home	12.00	6.00	3.50
(87)	Circus Catch	12.00	6.00	3.50
(88)	Great Catch	12.00	6.00	3.50
(89)	Stolen Base	12.00	6.00	3.50
(90)	Grand Slam Homer	12.00	6.00	3.50
(91)	Double Play	12.00	6.00	3.50
(92)	Right-Handed Follow Thru	12.00	6.00	3.50
(93)	Right-Handed High Leg Kick	12.00	6.00	3.50
(94)	Left-handed pitcher	12.00	6.00	3.50
(95)	Right-handed batter	12.00	6.00	3.50
(96)	Left-handed batter	12.00	6.00	3.50

1950s-60s Topps "PROMOTIONAL SAMPLES"

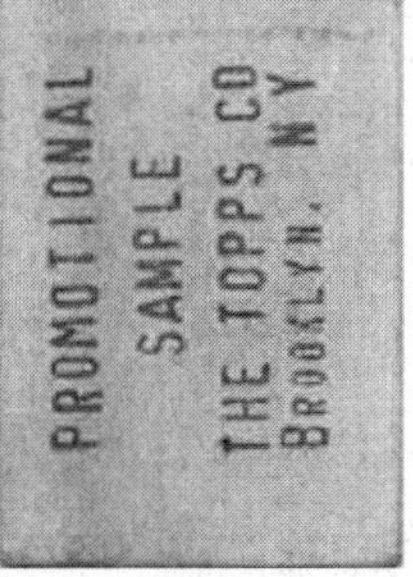

These mini sample cards are fantasy items created in the late 1990s to defraud collectors. Often sold grouped in an older frame or otherwise made to look old, they are pictures which have been cut out of the "Topps Baseball Cards" books or the team-issued Surf books which reproduced Topps cards in about 1-1/4" x 1-3/4" format. The color glossy pictures were then glued to a cardboard back which has been rubber-stamped "PROMOTIONAL / SAMPLE / THE TOPPS CO / BROOKLYN, N Y." There were no legitimate miniature Topps promotional or sample cards produced.

(No Collectible Value.)

1961 Topps

Except for some of the specialty cards, Topps returned to a vertical format with their 1961 cards. The set is numbered through 598, however, only 587 cards were printed. No numbers 426, 587 and 588 were issued. Two cards numbered 463 exist (one a Braves team card and one a player card of Jack Fisher). Actually, the Braves team card is checklisted as #426. Designs for 1961 are basically large color portraits; the backs return to extensive statistics. A three-panel cartoon highlighting the player's career appears on the card backs. Innovations include numbered checklists, cards for statistical leaders, and 10 "Baseball Thrills" cards. The scarce high numbers are card numbers 523-589.

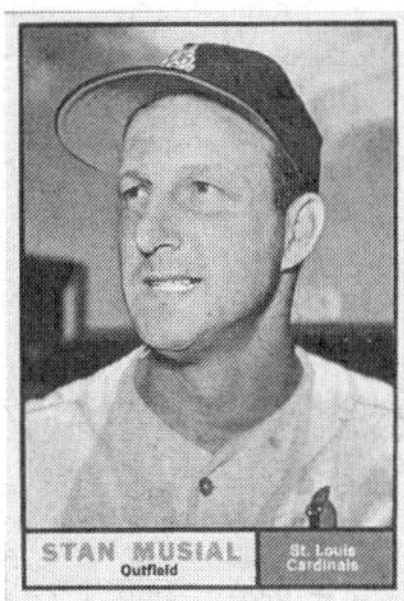

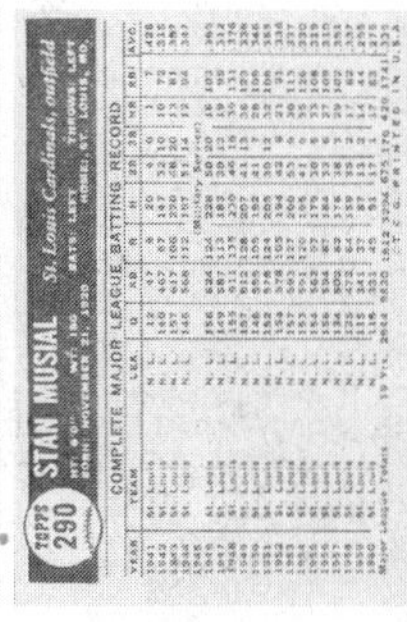

		NM	EX	VG
Complete Set (587):		7,500	3,750	2,250
Common Player (1-522):		6.00	3.00	1.75
Common Player (523-589):		20.00	10.00	6.00
1	Dick Groat	25.00	6.00	2.00
2	Roger Maris	145.00	50.00	30.00
3	John Buzhardt	6.00	3.00	1.75
4	Lenny Green	6.00	3.00	1.75
5	Johnny Romano	6.00	3.00	1.75
6	Ed Roebuck	6.00	3.00	1.75
7	Chicago White Sox Team	10.00	5.00	3.00
8	Dick Williams	6.00	3.00	1.75
9	Bob Purkey	6.00	3.00	1.75
10	Brooks Robinson	30.00	15.00	9.00
11	Curt Simmons	6.00	3.00	1.75
12	Moe Thacker	6.00	3.00	1.75
13	Chuck Cottier	6.00	3.00	1.75
14	Don Mossi	6.00	3.00	1.75
15	Willie Kirkland	6.00	3.00	1.75
16	Billy Muffett	6.00	3.00	1.75
17	1st Series Checklist (1-88)	12.00	6.00	3.50
18	Jim Grant	6.00	3.00	1.75
19	Cletis Boyer	10.00	5.00	3.00
20	Robin Roberts	15.00	7.50	4.50
21	***Zoilo Versalles***	12.50	6.25	3.75
22	Clem Labine	6.00	3.00	1.75
23	Don Demeter	6.00	3.00	1.75
24	Ken Johnson	6.00	3.00	1.75
25	Reds' Heavy Artillery (Gus Bell, Vada Pinson, Frank Robinson)	15.00	7.50	4.50
26	Wes Stock	6.00	3.00	1.75
27	Jerry Kindall	6.00	3.00	1.75
28	Hector Lopez	6.00	3.00	1.75
29	Don Nottebart	6.00	3.00	1.75
30	Nellie Fox	20.00	10.00	6.00
31	Bob Schmidt	6.00	3.00	1.75
32	Ray Sadecki	6.00	3.00	1.75
33	Gary Geiger	6.00	3.00	1.75
34	Wynn Hawkins	6.00	3.00	1.75
35	***Ron Santo***	35.00	17.50	10.00
36	Jack Kralick	6.00	3.00	1.75
37	Charlie Maxwell	6.00	3.00	1.75
38	Bob Lillis	6.00	3.00	1.75
39	Leo Posada	6.00	3.00	1.75
40	Bob Turley	10.00	5.00	3.00
41	N.L. Batting Leaders (Roberto Clemente, Dick Groat, Norm Larker, Willie Mays)	20.00	10.00	6.00
42	A.L. Batting Leaders (Minnie Minoso, Pete Runnels, Bill Skowron, Al Smith)	9.00	4.50	2.75
43	N.L. Home Run Leaders (Hank Aaron, Ernie Banks, Ken Boyer, Eddie Mathews)	17.50	8.75	5.25
44	A.L. Home Run Leaders (Rocky Colavito, Jim Lemon, Mickey Mantle, Roger Maris)	45.00	22.00	13.50
45	N.L. E.R.A. Leaders (Ernie Broglio, Don Drysdale, Bob Friend, Mike McCormick, Stan Williams)	7.00	3.50	2.00
46	A.L. E.R.A. Leaders (Frank Baumann, Hal Brown, Jim Bunning, Art Ditmar)	9.00	4.50	2.75
47a	N.L. Pitching Leaders (Ernie Broglio, Lou Burdette, Vern Law, Warren Spahn) (Vertical black bar in Burdette's box to right of 19.)	12.00	6.00	3.50
47b	N.L. Pitching Leaders (Ernie Broglio, Lew Burdette, Vern Law, Warren Spahn) (No black bar.)	12.00	6.00	3.50
48	A.L. Pitching Leaders (Bud Daley, Art Ditmar, Chuck Estrada, Frank Lary, Milt Pappas, Jim Perry)	7.00	3.50	2.00
49	N.L. Strikeout Leaders (Ernie Broglio, Don Drysdale, Sam Jones, Sandy Koufax)	16.00	8.00	4.75
50	A.L. Strikeout Leaders (Jim Bunning, Frank Lary, Pedro Ramos, Early Wynn)	12.00	6.00	3.50
51	Detroit Tigers Team	10.00	5.00	3.00
52	George Crowe	6.00	3.00	1.75
53	Russ Nixon	6.00	3.00	1.75
54	Earl Francis	6.00	3.00	1.75
55	Jim Davenport	6.00	3.00	1.75
56	Russ Kemmerer	6.00	3.00	1.75
57	Marv Throneberry	6.00	3.00	1.75
58	Joe Schaffernoth	6.00	3.00	1.75
59	Jim Woods	6.00	3.00	1.75
60	Woodie Held	6.00	3.00	1.75
61	Ron Piche	6.00	3.00	1.75

62	Al Pilarcik	6.00	3.00	1.75
63	Jim Kaat	9.00	4.50	2.75
64	Alex Grammas	6.00	3.00	1.75
65	Ted Kluszewski	10.00	5.00	3.00
66	Bill Henry	6.00	3.00	1.75
67	Ossie Virgil	6.00	3.00	1.75
68	Deron Johnson	6.00	3.00	1.75
69	Earl Wilson	6.00	3.00	1.75
70	Bill Virdon	6.00	3.00	1.75
71	Jerry Adair	6.00	3.00	1.75
72	Stu Miller	6.00	3.00	1.75
73	Al Spangler	6.00	3.00	1.75
74	Joe Pignatano	6.00	3.00	1.75
75	Lindy Shows Larry (Larry Jackson, Lindy McDaniel)	6.00	3.00	1.75
76	Harry Anderson	6.00	3.00	1.75
77	Dick Stigman	6.00	3.00	1.75
78	Lee Walls	6.00	3.00	1.75
79	Joe Ginsberg	6.00	3.00	1.75
80	Harmon Killebrew	25.00	12.50	7.50
81	Tracy Stallard	6.00	3.00	1.75
82	Joe Christopher	6.00	3.00	1.75
83	Bob Bruce	6.00	3.00	1.75
84	Lee Maye	6.00	3.00	1.75
85	Jerry Walker	6.00	3.00	1.75
86	Los Angeles Dodgers Team	11.00	5.50	3.25
87	Joe Amalfitano	6.00	3.00	1.75
88	Richie Ashburn	15.00	7.50	4.50
89	Billy Martin	9.00	4.50	2.75
90	Jerry Staley	6.00	3.00	1.75
91	Walt Moryn	6.00	3.00	1.75
92	Hal Naragon	6.00	3.00	1.75
93	Tony Gonzalez	6.00	3.00	1.75
94	Johnny Kucks	6.00	3.00	1.75
95	Norm Cash	12.50	6.25	3.75
96	Billy O'Dell	6.00	3.00	1.75
97	Jerry Lynch	6.00	3.00	1.75
98a	2nd Series Checklist (9-176) ("Checklist" in red on front.)	12.00	6.00	3.50
98b	2nd Series Checklist (89-176) ("Checklist" in yellow, 98 on back in black.)	12.00	6.00	3.50
98c	2nd Series Checklist (89-176) ("Checklist" in yellow, 98 on back in white.)	12.00	6.00	3.50
99	Don Buddin	6.00	3.00	1.75
100	Harvey Haddix	6.00	3.00	1.75
101	Bubba Phillips	6.00	3.00	1.75
102	Gene Stephens	6.00	3.00	1.75
103	Ruben Amaro	6.00	3.00	1.75
104	John Blanchard	7.50	3.75	2.25
105	Carl Willey	6.00	3.00	1.75
106	Whitey Herzog	6.00	3.00	1.75
107	Seth Morehead	6.00	3.00	1.75
108	Dan Dobbek	6.00	3.00	1.75
109	Johnny Podres	7.50	3.75	2.25
110	Vada Pinson	9.00	4.50	2.75
111	Jack Meyer	6.00	3.00	1.75
112	Chico Fernandez	6.00	3.00	1.75
113	Mike Fornieles	6.00	3.00	1.75
114	Hobie Landrith	6.00	3.00	1.75
115	Johnny Antonelli	6.00	3.00	1.75
116	Joe DeMaestri	6.00	3.00	1.75
117	Dale Long	6.00	3.00	1.75
118	Chris Cannizzaro	6.00	3.00	1.75
119	A's Big Armor (Hank Bauer, Jerry Lumpe, Norm Siebern)	9.00	4.50	2.75
120	Ed Mathews	20.00	10.00	6.00
121	Eli Grba	6.00	3.00	1.75
122	Chicago Cubs Team	10.00	5.00	3.00
123	Billy Gardner	6.00	3.00	1.75
124	J.C. Martin	6.00	3.00	1.75
125	Steve Barber	6.00	3.00	1.75
126	Dick Stuart	6.00	3.00	1.75
127	Ron Kline	6.00	3.00	1.75
128	Rip Repulski	6.00	3.00	1.75
129	Ed Hobaugh	6.00	3.00	1.75
130	Norm Larker	6.00	3.00	1.75
131	Paul Richards	6.00	3.00	1.75
132	Al Lopez	12.50	6.25	3.75
133	Ralph Houk	25.00	12.50	7.50
134	Mickey Vernon	6.00	3.00	1.75
135	Fred Hutchinson	6.00	3.00	1.75
136	Walt Alston	12.50	6.25	3.75
137	Chuck Dressen	6.00	3.00	1.75
138	Danny Murtaugh	6.00	3.00	1.75
139	Solly Hemus	6.00	3.00	1.75
140	Gus Triandos	6.00	3.00	1.75
141	***Billy Williams***	35.00	17.50	10.00
142	Luis Arroyo	6.00	3.00	1.75
143	Russ Snyder	6.00	3.00	1.75
144	Jim Coker	6.00	3.00	1.75
145	Bob Buhl	6.00	3.00	1.75
146	Marty Keough	6.00	3.00	1.75
147	Ed Rakow	6.00	3.00	1.75
148	Julian Javier	6.00	3.00	1.75
149	Bob Oldis	6.00	3.00	1.75
150	Willie Mays	60.00	30.00	18.00
151	Jim Donohue	6.00	3.00	1.75
152	Earl Torgeson	6.00	3.00	1.75
153	Don Lee	6.00	3.00	1.75
154	Bobby Del Greco	6.00	3.00	1.75
155	Johnny Temple	6.00	3.00	1.75
156	Ken Hunt	6.00	3.00	1.75
157	Cal McLish	6.00	3.00	1.75
158	Pete Daley	6.00	3.00	1.75
159	Baltimore Orioles Team	10.00	5.00	3.00
160	Whitey Ford	30.00	15.00	9.00
161	Sherman Jones	6.00	3.00	1.75
162	Jay Hook	6.00	3.00	1.75
163	Ed Sadowski	6.00	3.00	1.75
164	Felix Mantilla	6.00	3.00	1.75
165	Gino Cimoli	6.00	3.00	1.75
166	Danny Kravitz	6.00	3.00	1.75
167	San Francisco Giants Team	10.00	5.00	3.00
168	Tommy Davis	6.00	3.00	1.75
169	Don Elston	6.00	3.00	1.75
170	Al Smith	6.00	3.00	1.75
171	Paul Foytack	6.00	3.00	1.75
172	Don Dillard	6.00	3.00	1.75
173	Beantown Bombers (Jackie Jensen, Frank Malzone, Vic Wertz)	9.00	4.50	2.75
174	Ray Semproch	6.00	3.00	1.75
175	Gene Freese	6.00	3.00	1.75
176	Ken Aspromonte	6.00	3.00	1.75
177	Don Larsen	7.50	3.75	2.25
178	Bob Nieman	6.00	3.00	1.75
179	Joe Koppe	6.00	3.00	1.75
180	Bobby Richardson	15.00	7.50	4.50
181	Fred Green	6.00	3.00	1.75
182	***Dave Nicholson***	6.00	3.00	1.75
183	Andre Rodgers	6.00	3.00	1.75
184	Steve Bilko	6.00	3.00	1.75
185	Herb Score	6.00	3.00	1.75
186	Elmer Valo	6.00	3.00	1.75
187	Billy Klaus	6.00	3.00	1.75
188	Jim Marshall	6.00	3.00	1.75
189a	3rd Series Checklist (177-264) (No "4" on player at left.)	10.00	5.00	3.00
189b	3rd Series Checklist (177-264) ("4" shows on player on left)	10.00	5.00	3.00
190	Stan Williams	6.00	3.00	1.75
191	Mike de la Hoz	6.00	3.00	1.75
192	Dick Brown	6.00	3.00	1.75
193	Gene Conley	6.00	3.00	1.75
194	Gordy Coleman	6.00	3.00	1.75
195	Jerry Casale	6.00	3.00	1.75
196	Ed Bouchee	6.00	3.00	1.75
197	Dick Hall	6.00	3.00	1.75
198	Carl Sawatski	6.00	3.00	1.75
199	Bob Boyd	6.00	3.00	1.75
200	Warren Spahn	25.00	12.50	7.50
201	Pete Whisenant	6.00	3.00	1.75
202	Al Neiger	6.00	3.00	1.75
203	Eddie Bressoud	6.00	3.00	1.75
204	Bob Skinner	6.00	3.00	1.75
205	Bill Pierce	6.00	3.00	1.75
206	Gene Green	6.00	3.00	1.75
207	Dodger Southpaws (Sandy Koufax, Johnny Podres)	20.00	10.00	6.00
208	Larry Osborne	6.00	3.00	1.75
209	Ken McBride	6.00	3.00	1.75
210	Pete Runnels	6.00	3.00	1.75
211	Bob Gibson	25.00	12.50	7.50
212	Haywood Sullivan	6.00	3.00	1.75
213	***Bill Stafford***	6.00	3.00	1.75
214	Danny Murphy	6.00	3.00	1.75
215	Gus Bell	6.00	3.00	1.75
216	Ted Bowsfield	6.00	3.00	1.75
217	Mel Roach	6.00	3.00	1.75
218	Hal Brown	6.00	3.00	1.75
219	Gene Mauch	6.00	3.00	1.75
220	Al Dark	6.00	3.00	1.75
221	Mike Higgins	6.00	3.00	1.75
222	Jimmie Dykes	6.00	3.00	1.75
223	Bob Scheffing	6.00	3.00	1.75
224	Joe Gordon	6.00	3.00	1.75
225	Bill Rigney	6.00	3.00	1.75
226	Harry Lavagetto	6.00	3.00	1.75
227	Juan Pizarro	6.00	3.00	1.75
228	New York Yankees Team	40.00	20.00	12.00
229	Rudy Hernandez	6.00	3.00	1.75
230	Don Hoak	6.00	3.00	1.75
231	Dick Drott	6.00	3.00	1.75
232	Bill White	6.00	3.00	1.75
233	Joe Jay	6.00	3.00	1.75
234	Ted Lepcio	6.00	3.00	1.75
235	Camilo Pascual	6.00	3.00	1.75
236	Don Gile	6.00	3.00	1.75
237	Billy Loes	6.00	3.00	1.75
238	Jim Gilliam	7.50	3.75	2.25
239	Dave Sisler	6.00	3.00	1.75
240	Ron Hansen	6.00	3.00	1.75
241	Al Cicotte	6.00	3.00	1.75
242	Hal W. Smith	6.00	3.00	1.75
243	Frank Lary	6.00	3.00	1.75
244	Chico Cardenas	6.00	3.00	1.75
245	Joe Adcock	6.00	3.00	1.75
246	Bob Davis	6.00	3.00	1.75
247	Billy Goodman	6.00	3.00	1.75
248	Ed Keegan	6.00	3.00	1.75
249	Cincinnati Reds Team	10.00	5.00	3.00
250	Buc Hill Aces (Roy Face, Vern Law)	9.00	4.50	2.75
251	Bill Bruton	6.00	3.00	1.75
252	Bill Short	6.00	3.00	1.75
253	Sammy Taylor	6.00	3.00	1.75
254	Ted Sadowski	6.00	3.00	1.75
255	Vic Power	6.00	3.00	1.75
256	Billy Hoeft	6.00	3.00	1.75
257	Carroll Hardy	6.00	3.00	1.75
258	Jack Sanford	6.00	3.00	1.75
259	John Schaive	6.00	3.00	1.75
260	Don Drysdale	25.00	12.50	7.50
261	Charlie Lau	6.00	3.00	1.75
262	Tony Curry	6.00	3.00	1.75
263	Ken Hamlin	6.00	3.00	1.75
264	Glen Hobbie	6.00	3.00	1.75
265	Tony Kubek	15.00	7.50	4.50
266	Lindy McDaniel	6.00	3.00	1.75
267	Norm Siebern	6.00	3.00	1.75
268	Ike DeLock (Delock)	6.00	3.00	1.75
269	Harry Chiti	6.00	3.00	1.75
270	Bob Friend	6.00	3.00	1.75
271	Jim Landis	6.00	3.00	1.75
272	Tom Morgan	6.00	3.00	1.75
273a	4th Series Checklist (265-352) (Copyright ends opposite fifth name.)	12.00	6.00	3.50
273b	4th Series Checklist (265-352) (Copyright ends opposite top name.)	12.00	6.00	3.50
274	Gary Bell	6.00	3.00	1.75
275	Gene Woodling	6.00	3.00	1.75
276	Ray Rippelmeyer	6.00	3.00	1.75
277	Hank Foiles	6.00	3.00	1.75
278	Don McMahon	6.00	3.00	1.75
279	Jose Pagan	6.00	3.00	1.75
280	Frank Howard	9.00	4.50	2.75
281	Frank Sullivan	6.00	3.00	1.75
282	Faye Throneberry	6.00	3.00	1.75
283	Bob Anderson	6.00	3.00	1.75
284	Dick Gernert	6.00	3.00	1.75
285	Sherm Lollar	6.00	3.00	1.75
286	George Witt	6.00	3.00	1.75
287	Carl Yastrzemski	45.00	22.50	13.50
288	Albie Pearson	6.00	3.00	1.75
289	Ray Moore	6.00	3.00	1.75
290	Stan Musial	50.00	25.00	15.00
291	Tex Clevenger	6.00	3.00	1.75
292	Jim Baumer	6.00	3.00	1.75
293	Tom Sturdivant	6.00	3.00	1.75
294	Don Blasingame	6.00	3.00	1.75
295	Milt Pappas	6.00	3.00	1.75
296	Wes Covington	6.00	3.00	1.75
297	Kansas City Athletics Team	10.00	5.00	3.00
298	Jim Golden	6.00	3.00	1.75
299	Clay Dalrymple	6.00	3.00	1.75
300	Mickey Mantle	325.00	135.00	85.00
301	Chet Nichols	6.00	3.00	1.75
302	Al Heist	6.00	3.00	1.75
303	Gary Peters	6.00	3.00	1.75
304	Rocky Nelson	6.00	3.00	1.75
305	Mike McCormick	6.00	3.00	1.75
306	World Series Game 1 (Virdon Saves Game)	9.00	4.50	2.75
307	World Series Game 2 (Mantle Slams 2 Homers)	45.00	22.50	13.50
308	World Series Game 3 (Richardson Is Hero)	20.00	10.00	6.00
309	World Series Game 4 (Cimoli Safe In Crucial Play)	9.00	4.50	2.75
310	World Series Game 5 (Face Saves The Day)	10.00	5.00	3.00
311	World Series Game 6 (Ford Pitches Second Shutout)	15.00	7.50	4.50
312	World Series Game 7 (Mazeroski's Homer Wins It!)	25.00	12.50	7.50
313	World Series (The Winners Celebrate)	12.50	6.25	3.75
314	Bob Miller	6.00	3.00	1.75
315	Earl Battey	6.00	3.00	1.75
316	Bobby Gene Smith	6.00	3.00	1.75
317	***Jim Brewer***	6.00	3.00	1.75
318	Danny O'Connell	6.00	3.00	1.75
319	Valmy Thomas	6.00	3.00	1.75
320	Lou Burdette	6.00	3.00	1.75
321	Marv Breeding	6.00	3.00	1.75
322	Bill Kunkel	6.00	3.00	1.75
323	Sammy Esposito	6.00	3.00	1.75
324	Hank Aguirre	6.00	3.00	1.75
325	Wally Moon	6.00	3.00	1.75
326	Dave Hillman	6.00	3.00	1.75
327	***Matty Alou***	12.50	6.25	3.75
328	Jim O'Toole	6.00	3.00	1.75
329	Julio Becquer	6.00	3.00	1.75
330	Rocky Colavito	15.00	7.50	4.50
331	Ned Garver	6.00	3.00	1.75
332	Dutch Dotterer (Photo actually Tommy Dotterer.)	6.00	3.00	1.75
333	Fritz Brickell	6.00	3.00	1.75
334	Walt Bond	6.00	3.00	1.75
335	Frank Bolling	6.00	3.00	1.75
336	Don Mincher	6.00	3.00	1.75
337	Al's Aces (Al Lopez, Herb Score, Early Wynn)	9.00	4.50	2.75
338	Don Landrum	6.00	3.00	1.75
339	Gene Baker	6.00	3.00	1.75
340	Vic Wertz	6.00	3.00	1.75
341	Jim Owens	6.00	3.00	1.75
342	Clint Courtney	6.00	3.00	1.75
343	Earl Robinson	6.00	3.00	1.75
344	Sandy Koufax	60.00	30.00	18.00
345	Jim Piersall	7.50	3.75	2.25
346	Howie Nunn	6.00	3.00	1.75
347	St. Louis Cardinals Team	10.00	5.00	3.00
348	Steve Boros	6.00	3.00	1.75
349	Danny McDevitt	6.00	3.00	1.75
350	Ernie Banks	30.00	15.00	9.00
351	Jim King	6.00	3.00	1.75
352	Bob Shaw	6.00	3.00	1.75
353	Howie Bedell	6.00	3.00	1.75
354	Billy Harrell	6.00	3.00	1.75
355	Bob Allison	6.00	3.00	1.75
356	Ryne Duren	7.50	3.75	2.25
357	Daryl Spencer	6.00	3.00	1.75
358	Earl Averill	6.00	3.00	1.75
359	Dallas Green	7.50	3.75	2.25
360	Frank Robinson	25.00	12.50	7.50
361a	5th Series Checklist (353-429) ("Topps Baseball" in black on front.)	10.00	5.00	3.00
361b	5th Series Checklist (353-429) ("Topps Baseball" in yellow.)	12.00	6.00	3.50
362	Frank Funk	6.00	3.00	1.75
363	John Roseboro	6.00	3.00	1.75
364	Moe Drabowsky	6.00	3.00	1.75
365	Jerry Lumpe	6.00	3.00	1.75
366	Eddie Fisher	6.00	3.00	1.75
367	Jim Rivera	6.00	3.00	1.75
368	Bennie Daniels	6.00	3.00	1.75
369	Dave Philley	6.00	3.00	1.75
370	Roy Face	6.00	3.00	1.75
371	Bill Skowron/SP	40.00	20.00	12.00
372	Bob Hendley	6.00	3.00	1.75
373	Boston Red Sox Team	10.00	5.00	3.00
374	Paul Giel	6.00	3.00	1.75
375	Ken Boyer	13.50	6.75	4.00
376	Mike Roarke	6.00	3.00	1.75
377	Ruben Gomez	6.00	3.00	1.75

378	Wally Post	6.00	3.00	1.75
379	Bobby Shantz	6.00	3.00	1.75
380	Minnie Minoso	9.00	4.50	2.75
381	Dave Wickersham	6.00	3.00	1.75
382	Frank Thomas	6.00	3.00	1.75
383	Frisco First Liners (Mike McCormick, Billy O'Dell, Jack Sanford)	7.50	3.75	2.25
384	Chuck Essegian	6.00	3.00	1.75
385	Jim Perry	6.00	3.00	1.75
386	Joe Hicks	6.00	3.00	1.75
387	Duke Maas	6.00	3.00	1.75
388	Bob Clemente	70.00	35.00	20.00
389	Ralph Terry	6.00	3.00	1.75
390	Del Crandall	6.00	3.00	1.75
391	Winston Brown	6.00	3.00	1.75
392	Reno Bertoia	6.00	3.00	1.75
393	Batter Bafflers (Don Cardwell, Glen Hobbie)	7.50	3.75	2.25
394	Ken Walters	6.00	3.00	1.75
395	Chuck Estrada	6.00	3.00	1.75
396	Bob Aspromonte	6.00	3.00	1.75
397	Hal Woodeshick	6.00	3.00	1.75
398	Hank Bauer	7.50	3.75	2.25
399	Cliff Cook	6.00	3.00	1.75
400	Vern Law	6.00	3.00	1.75
401	Babe Ruth Hits 60th Homer	50.00	25.00	15.00
402	Larsen Pitches Perfect Game/SP	25.00	12.50	7.50
403	Brooklyn-Boston Play 26-Inning Tie	6.00	3.00	1.75
404	Hornsby Tops N.L. with .424 Average	9.00	4.50	2.75
405	Gehrig Benched After 2,130 Games	35.00	17.50	10.00
406	Mantle Blasts 565 ft. Home Run	45.00	22.50	13.50
407	Jack Chesbro Wins 41st Game	6.00	3.00	1.75
408	Mathewson Strikes Out 267 Batters/SP	17.50	8.75	5.25
409	Johnson Hurls 3rd Shutout In 4 Days	9.00	4.50	2.75
410	Haddix Pitches 12 Perfect Innings	7.50	3.75	2.25
411	Tony Taylor	6.00	3.00	1.75
412	Larry Sherry	6.00	3.00	1.75
413	Eddie Yost	6.00	3.00	1.75
414	Dick Donovan	6.00	3.00	1.75
415	Hank Aaron	85.00	42.50	25.00
416	***Dick Howser***/SP	12.50	6.25	3.75
417	***Juan Marichal***	60.00	30.00	18.00
418	Ed Bailey	6.00	3.00	1.75
419	Tom Borland	6.00	3.00	1.75
420	Ernie Broglio	6.00	3.00	1.75
421	Ty Cline/SP	12.50	6.25	3.75
422	Bud Daley	6.00	3.00	1.75
423	Charlie Neal/SP	12.50	6.25	3.75
424	Turk Lown	6.00	3.00	1.75
425	Yogi Berra	50.00	25.00	15.00
426	Not Issued (See #463.)			
427	Dick Ellsworth	6.00	3.00	1.75
428	Ray Barker/SP	12.50	6.25	3.75
429	Al Kaline	30.00	15.00	9.00
430	Bill Mazeroski/SP	35.00	17.50	10.00
431	Chuck Stobbs	6.00	3.00	1.75
432	Coot Veal	6.00	3.00	1.75
433	Art Mahaffey	6.00	3.00	1.75
434	Tom Brewer	6.00	3.00	1.75
435	Orlando Cepeda	15.00	7.50	4.50
436	***Jim Maloney/SP***	20.00	10.00	6.00
437a	6th Series Checklist (430-506) (#440 is Louis Aparicio)	12.00	6.00	3.50
437b	6th Series Checklist (430-506) (#440 is Luis Aparicio)	10.00	5.00	3.00
438	Curt Flood	7.50	3.75	2.25
439	***Phil Regan***	6.00	3.00	1.75
440	Luis Aparicio	15.00	7.50	4.50
441	Dick Bertell	6.00	3.00	1.75
442	Gordon Jones	6.00	3.00	1.75
443	Duke Snider	30.00	15.00	9.00
444	Joe Nuxhall	6.00	3.00	1.75
445	Frank Malzone	6.00	3.00	1.75
446	Bob "Hawk" Taylor	6.00	3.00	1.75
447	Harry Bright	6.00	3.00	1.75
448	Del Rice	6.00	3.00	1.75
449	***Bobby Bolin***	6.00	3.00	1.75
450	Jim Lemon	6.00	3.00	1.75
451	Power For Ernie (Ernie Broglio, Daryl Spencer, Bill White)	7.50	3.75	2.25
452	Bob Allen	6.00	3.00	1.75
453	Dick Schofield	6.00	3.00	1.75
454	Pumpsie Green	6.00	3.00	1.75
455	Early Wynn	12.50	6.25	3.75
456	Hal Bevan	6.00	3.00	1.75
457	Johnny James	6.00	3.00	1.75
458	Willie Tasby	6.00	3.00	1.75
459	Terry Fox	6.00	3.00	1.75
460	Gil Hodges	12.50	6.25	3.75
461	Smoky Burgess	6.00	3.00	1.75
462	Lou Klimchock	6.00	3.00	1.75
463a	Milwaukee Braves Team (Should be card #426.)	10.00	5.00	3.00
463b	Jack Fisher	6.00	3.00	1.75
464	***Leroy Thomas***	6.00	3.00	1.75
465	Roy McMillan	6.00	3.00	1.75
466	Ron Moeller	6.00	3.00	1.75
467	Cleveland Indians Team	10.00	5.00	3.00
468	Johnny Callison	6.00	3.00	1.75
469	Ralph Lumenti	6.00	3.00	1.75
470	Roy Sievers	6.00	3.00	1.75
471	Phil Rizzuto (MVP)	25.00	12.50	7.50
472	Yogi Berra (MVP)	45.00	22.50	13.50
473	Bobby Shantz (MVP)	7.50	3.75	2.25
474	Al Rosen (MVP)	7.50	3.75	2.25
475	Mickey Mantle (MVP)	120.00	60.00	36.00
476	Jackie Jensen (MVP)	7.50	3.75	2.25
477	Nellie Fox (MVP)	17.50	8.75	5.25
478	Roger Maris (MVP)	40.00	20.00	12.00
479	Jim Konstanty (MVP)	6.00	3.00	1.75
480	Roy Campanella (MVP)	25.00	12.50	7.50
481	Hank Sauer (MVP)	6.00	3.00	1.75
482	Willie Mays (MVP)	40.00	20.00	12.00
483	Don Newcombe (MVP)	7.50	3.75	2.25
484	Hank Aaron (MVP)	35.00	17.50	10.00
485	Ernie Banks (MVP)	20.00	10.00	6.00
486	Dick Groat (MVP)	7.50	3.75	2.25
487	Gene Oliver	6.00	3.00	1.75
488	Joe McClain	6.00	3.00	1.75
489	Walt Dropo	6.00	3.00	1.75
490	Jim Bunning	12.50	6.25	3.75
491	Philadelphia Phillies Team	10.00	5.00	3.00
492	Ron Fairly	6.00	3.00	1.75
493	Don Zimmer	7.50	3.75	2.25
494	Tom Cheney	6.00	3.00	1.75
495	Elston Howard	15.00	7.50	4.50
496	Ken MacKenzie	6.00	3.00	1.75
497	Willie Jones	6.00	3.00	1.75
498	Ray Herbert	6.00	3.00	1.75
499	***Chuck Schilling***	6.00	3.00	1.75
500	Harvey Kuenn	6.00	3.00	1.75
501	John DeMerit	6.00	3.00	1.75
502	Clarence Coleman	6.00	3.00	1.75
503	Tito Francona	6.00	3.00	1.75
504	Billy Consolo	6.00	3.00	1.75
505	Red Schoendienst	12.50	6.25	3.75
506	***Willie Davis***	13.50	6.75	4.00
507	Pete Burnside	6.00	3.00	1.75
508	Rocky Bridges	6.00	3.00	1.75
509	Camilo Carreon	6.00	3.00	1.75
510	Art Ditmar	6.00	3.00	1.75
511	Joe Morgan	6.00	3.00	1.75
512	Bob Will	6.00	3.00	1.75
513	Jim Brosnan	6.00	3.00	1.75
514	Jake Wood	6.00	3.00	1.75
515	Jackie Brandt	6.00	3.00	1.75
516a	7th Series Checklist (507-587) (Second "C" of "CHECK" above #13's cap.)	12.00	6.00	3.50
516b	7th Series Checklist (506-587) (Second "C" of "CHECK" covers top of #13's cap.)	12.00	6.00	3.50
517	Willie McCovey	25.00	12.50	7.50
518	Andy Carey	6.00	3.00	1.75
519	Jim Pagliaroni	6.00	3.00	1.75
520	Joe Cunningham	6.00	3.00	1.75
521	Brother Battery (Larry Sherry, Norm Sherry)	10.00	5.00	3.00
522	Dick Farrell	6.00	3.00	1.75
523	Joe Gibbon	20.00	10.00	6.00
524	Johnny Logan	20.00	10.00	6.00
525	***Ron Perranoski***	25.00	12.50	7.50
526	R.C. Stevens	20.00	10.00	6.00
527	Gene Leek	20.00	10.00	6.00
528	Pedro Ramos	20.00	10.00	6.00
529	Bob Roselli	20.00	10.00	6.00
530	Bobby Malkmus	20.00	10.00	6.00
531	Jim Coates	20.00	10.00	6.00
532	Bob Hale	20.00	10.00	6.00
533	Jack Curtis	20.00	10.00	6.00
534	Eddie Kasko	20.00	10.00	6.00
535	Larry Jackson	20.00	10.00	6.00
536	Bill Tuttle	20.00	10.00	6.00
537	Bobby Locke	20.00	10.00	6.00
538	Chuck Hiller	20.00	10.00	6.00
539	Johnny Klippstein	20.00	10.00	6.00
540	Jackie Jensen	22.50	11.00	7.00
541	Roland Sheldon	20.00	10.00	6.00
542	Minnesota Twins Team	35.00	17.50	10.00
543	Roger Craig	20.00	10.00	6.00
544	George Thomas	20.00	10.00	6.00
545	Hoyt Wilhelm	32.50	16.00	10.00
546	Marty Kutyna	20.00	10.00	6.00
547	Leon Wagner	20.00	10.00	6.00
548	Ted Wills	20.00	10.00	6.00
549	Hal R. Smith	20.00	10.00	6.00
550	Frank Baumann	20.00	10.00	6.00
551	George Altman	20.00	10.00	6.00
552	Jim Archer	20.00	10.00	6.00
553	Bill Fischer	20.00	10.00	6.00
554	Pittsburgh Pirates Team	45.00	22.50	13.50
555	Sam Jones	20.00	10.00	6.00
556	Ken R. Hunt	20.00	10.00	6.00
557	Jose Valdivielso	20.00	10.00	6.00
558	Don Ferrarese	20.00	10.00	6.00
559	Jim Gentile	75.00	37.50	22.50
560	Barry Latman	20.00	10.00	6.00
561	Charley James	20.00	10.00	6.00
562	Bill Monbouquette	20.00	10.00	6.00
563	Bob Cerv	20.00	10.00	6.00
564	Don Cardwell	20.00	10.00	6.00
565	Felipe Alou	30.00	15.00	9.00
566	Paul Richards/AS	20.00	10.00	6.00
567	Danny Murtaugh/AS	20.00	10.00	6.00
568	Bill Skowron/AS	25.00	12.50	7.50
569	Frank Herrera/AS	20.00	10.00	6.00
570	Nellie Fox/AS	30.00	15.00	9.00
571	Bill Mazeroski/AS	32.50	16.00	10.00
572	Brooks Robinson/AS	50.00	25.00	15.00
573	Ken Boyer/AS	22.50	11.00	6.75
574	Luis Aparicio/AS	30.00	15.00	9.00
575	Ernie Banks/AS	60.00	30.00	18.00
576	Roger Maris/AS	100.00	50.00	30.00
577	Hank Aaron/AS	100.00	50.00	30.00
578	Mickey Mantle/AS	285.00	140.00	85.00
579	Willie Mays/AS	90.00	45.00	27.00
580	Al Kaline/AS	50.00	25.00	15.00
581	Frank Robinson/AS	50.00	25.00	15.00
582	Earl Battey/AS	20.00	10.00	6.00
583	Del Crandall/AS	20.00	10.00	6.00
584	Jim Perry/AS	20.00	10.00	6.00
585	Bob Friend/AS	20.00	10.00	6.00
586	Whitey Ford/AS	60.00	30.00	18.00
587	Not Issued			
588	Not Issued			
589	Warren Spahn/AS	60.00	30.00	18.00

1961 Topps Dice Game

One of the more obscure Topps test issues that may have never actually been issued is the 1961 Topps Dice Game. Eighteen black and white cards, each measuring 2-1/2" x 3-1/2" in size, comprise the set. Interestingly, there are no identifying marks, such as copyrights or trademarks, to indicate the set was produced by Topps. The card backs contain various baseball plays that occur when a certain pitch is called and a specific number of the dice is rolled.

		NM	EX	VG
Common Player:		1,850	925.00	550.00
(1)	Earl Battey	1,850	925.00	550.00
(2)	Del Crandall	1,850	925.00	550.00
(3)	Jim Davenport	1,850	925.00	550.00
(4)	Don Drysdale	4,500	2,250	1,350
(5)	Dick Groat	1,850	925.00	550.00
(6)	Al Kaline	7,500	3,750	2,250
(7)	Tony Kubek	3,250	1,625	975.00
(8)	Mickey Mantle	45,000	22,500	13,500
(9)	Willie Mays	20,000	8,500	5,100
(10)	Bill Mazeroski	4,500	2,250	1,350
(11)	Stan Musial	20,000	10,000	6,000
(12)	Camilo Pascual	1,850	925.00	550.00
(13)	Bobby Richardson	3,500	1,750	1,050
(14)	Brooks Robinson	7,500	3,750	2,250
(15)	Frank Robinson	7,500	3,750	2,250
(16)	Norm Siebern	1,850	925.00	550.00
(17)	Leon Wagner	1,850	925.00	550.00
(18)	Bill White	1,850	925.00	550.00

1961 Topps Magic Rub-Offs

Not too different in concept from the tattoos of the previous year, the Topps Magic Rub-Off was designed to leave impressions of team themes or individual players when properly applied. Measuring 2-1/16" x 3-1/16", the Magic Rub-Off was not designed specifically for application to the owner's skin. The set features team themes that are a far cry from official logos, and the players (one per team) seem to have been included for their nicknames.

		NM	EX	VG
Complete Set (36):		200.00	100.00	60.00
Common Player:		6.00	3.00	1.75
(1)	Baltimore Orioles Pennant	6.00	3.00	1.75
(2)	Ernie "Bingo" Banks	15.00	7.50	4.50
(3)	Yogi Berra	15.00	7.50	4.50
(4)	Boston Red Sox Pennant	6.00	3.00	1.75
(5)	Jackie "Ozark" Brandt	6.00	3.00	1.75
(6)	Jim "Professor" Brosnan	6.00	3.00	1.75
(7)	Chicago Cubs Pennant	6.00	3.00	1.75
(8)	Chicago White Sox Pennant	6.00	3.00	1.75
(9)	Cincinnati Red Legs Pennant	6.00	3.00	1.75
(10)	Cleveland Indians Pennant	6.00	3.00	1.75
(11)	Detroit Tigers Pennant	6.00	3.00	1.75
(12)	Henry "Dutch" Dotterer	6.00	3.00	1.75
(13)	Joe "Flash" Gordon	6.00	3.00	1.75
(14)	Harvey "The Kitten" Haddix	6.00	3.00	1.75
(15)	Frank "Pancho" Hererra	6.00	3.00	1.75
(16)	Frank "Tower" Howard	7.50	3.75	2.25
(17)	"Sad" Sam Jones	6.00	3.00	1.75
(18)	Kansas City Athletics Pennant	6.00	3.00	1.75
(19)	Los Angeles Angels Pennant	7.50	3.75	2.25
(20)	Los Angeles Dodgers Pennant	7.50	3.75	2.25
(21)	Omar "Turk" Lown	6.00	3.00	1.75
(22)	Billy "The Kid" Martin	7.50	3.75	2.25
(23)	Duane "Duke" Mass (Maas)	6.00	3.00	1.75
(24)	Charlie "Paw Paw" Maxwell	6.00	3.00	1.75

(25)	Milwaukee Braves Pennant	6.00	3.00	1.75
(26)	Minnesota Twins Pennant	7.50	3.75	2.25
(27)	"Farmer" Ray Moore	6.00	3.00	1.75
(28)	Walt "Moose" Moryn	6.00	3.00	1.75
(29)	New York Yankees Pennant	9.00	4.50	2.75
(30)	Philadelphia Phillies Pennant	6.00	3.00	1.75
(31)	Pittsburgh Pirates Pennant	6.00	3.00	1.75
(32)	John "Honey" Romano	6.00	3.00	1.75
(33)	"Pistol Pete" Runnels	6.00	3.00	1.75
(34)	St. Louis Cardinals Pennant	6.00	3.00	1.75
(35)	San Francisco Giants Pennant	6.00	3.00	1.75
(36)	Washington Senators Pennant	9.00	4.50	2.75

1961 Topps Stamps

Issued as an added insert to 1961 Topps wax packs these 1-3/8" x 1-3/16" stamps were desigend to be collected and placed in an album which could be bought for an additional 10¢. Packs of cards contained two stamps. There are 208 stamps in a complete set which depict 207 different players (Al Kaline appears twice). There are 104 players on brown stamps and 104 on green. While there are many Hall of Famers on the stamps, prices remain low because there is relatively little interest in what is a non-card set.

		NM	EX	VG
Complete Set (208):		750.00	375.00	225.00
Common Player:		2.00	1.00	.60
Stamp Album (Green):		65.00	30.00	20.00
(1)	Hank Aaron	20.00	10.00	6.00
(2)	Joe Adcock	2.00	1.00	.60
(3)	Hank Aguirre	2.00	1.00	.60
(4)	Bob Allison	2.00	1.00	.60
(5)	George Altman	2.00	1.00	.60
(6)	Bob Anderson	2.00	1.00	.60
(7)	Johnny Antonelli	2.00	1.00	.60
(8)	Luis Aparicio	12.00	6.00	3.50
(9)	Luis Arroyo	2.00	1.00	.60
(10)	Richie Ashburn	13.50	6.75	4.00
(11)	Ken Aspromonte	2.00	1.00	.60
(12)	Ed Bailey	2.00	1.00	.60
(13)	Ernie Banks	13.50	6.75	4.00
(14)	Steve Barber	2.00	1.00	.60
(15)	Earl Battey	2.00	1.00	.60
(16)	Hank Bauer	2.00	1.00	.60
(17)	Gus Bell	2.00	1.00	.60
(18)	Yogi Berra	13.50	6.75	4.00
(19)	Reno Bertoia	2.00	1.00	.60
(20)	John Blanchard	2.00	1.00	.60
(21)	Don Blasingame	2.00	1.00	.60
(22)	Frank Bolling	2.00	1.00	.60
(23)	Steve Boros	2.00	1.00	.60
(24)	Ed Bouchee	2.00	1.00	.60
(25)	Bob Boyd	2.00	1.00	.60
(26)	Cletis Boyer	2.00	1.00	.60
(27)	Ken Boyer	3.00	1.50	.90
(28)	Jackie Brandt	2.00	1.00	.60
(29)	Marv Breeding	2.00	1.00	.60
(30)	Eddie Bressoud	2.00	1.00	.60
(31)	Jim Brewer	2.00	1.00	.60
(32)	Tom Brewer	2.00	1.00	.60
(33)	Jim Brosnan	2.00	1.00	.60
(34)	Bill Bruton	2.00	1.00	.60
(35)	Bob Buhl	2.00	1.00	.60
(36)	Jim Bunning	10.00	5.00	3.00
(37)	Smoky Burgess	2.00	1.00	.60
(38)	John Buzhardt	2.00	1.00	.60
(39)	Johnny Callison	2.00	1.00	.60
(40)	Chico Cardenas	2.00	1.00	.60
(41)	Andy Carey	2.00	1.00	.60
(42)	Jerry Casale	2.00	1.00	.60
(43)	Norm Cash	4.00	2.00	1.25
(44)	Orlando Cepeda	10.00	5.00	3.00
(45)	Bob Cerv	2.00	1.00	.60
(46)	Harry Chiti	2.00	1.00	.60
(47)	Gene Conley	2.00	1.00	.60
(48)	Wes Covington	2.00	1.00	.60
(49)	Del Crandall	2.00	1.00	.60
(50)	Tony Curry	2.00	1.00	.60
(51)	Bud Daley	2.00	1.00	.60
(52)	Pete Daley	2.00	1.00	.60
(53)	Clay Dalrymple	2.00	1.00	.60
(54)	Jim Davenport	2.00	1.00	.60
(55)	Tommy Davis	2.00	1.00	.60
(56)	Bobby Del Greco	2.00	1.00	.60
(57)	Ike Delock	2.00	1.00	.60
(58)	Art Ditmar	2.00	1.00	.60
(59)	Dick Donovan	2.00	1.00	.60
(60)	Don Drysdale	13.50	6.75	4.00
(61)	Dick Ellsworth	2.00	1.00	.60
(62)	Don Elston	2.00	1.00	.60
(63)	Chuck Estrada	2.00	1.00	.60
(64)	Roy Face	2.00	1.00	.60
(65)	Dick Farrell	2.00	1.00	.60
(66)	Chico Fernandez	2.00	1.00	.60
(67)	Curt Flood	2.00	1.00	.60
(68)	Whitey Ford	13.50	6.75	4.00
(69)	Tito Francona	2.00	1.00	.60
(70)	Gene Freese	2.00	1.00	.60
(71)	Bob Friend	2.00	1.00	.60
(72)	Billy Gardner	2.00	1.00	.60
(73)	Ned Garver	2.00	1.00	.60
(74)	Gary Geiger	2.00	1.00	.60
(75)	Jim Gentile	2.00	1.00	.60
(76)	Dick Gernert	2.00	1.00	.60
(77)	Tony Gonzalez	2.00	1.00	.60
(78)	Alex Grammas	2.00	1.00	.60
(79)	Jim Grant	2.00	1.00	.60
(80)	Dick Groat	2.00	1.00	.60
(81)	Dick Hall	2.00	1.00	.60
(82)	Ron Hansen	2.00	1.00	.60
(83)	Bob Hartman	2.00	1.00	.60
(84)	Woodie Held	2.00	1.00	.60
(85)	Ray Herbert	2.00	1.00	.60
(86)	Frank Herrera	2.00	1.00	.60
(87)	Whitey Herzog	2.00	1.00	.60
(88)	Don Hoak	2.00	1.00	.60
(89)	Elston Howard	5.00	2.50	1.50
(90)	Frank Howard	4.00	2.00	1.25
(91)	Ken Hunt	2.00	1.00	.60
(92)	Larry Jackson	2.00	1.00	.60
(93)	Julian Javier	2.00	1.00	.60
(94)	Joe Jay	2.00	1.00	.60
(95)	Jackie Jensen	2.00	1.00	.60
(96)	Jim Kaat	2.50	1.25	.70
(97a)	Al Kaline (Green)	25.00	12.50	7.50
(97b)	Al Kaline (Brown)	15.00	7.50	4.50
(98)	Eddie Kasko	2.00	1.00	.60
(99)	Russ Kemmerer	2.00	1.00	.60
(100)	Harmon Killebrew	13.50	6.75	4.00
(101)	Billy Klaus	2.00	1.00	.60
(102)	Ron Kline	2.00	1.00	.60
(103)	Johnny Klippstein	2.00	1.00	.60
(104)	Ted Kluszewski	10.00	5.00	3.00
(105)	Tony Kubek	5.00	2.50	1.50
(106)	Harvey Kuenn	2.00	1.00	.60
(107)	Jim Landis	2.00	1.00	.60
(108)	Hobie Landrith	2.00	1.00	.60
(109)	Norm Larker	2.00	1.00	.60
(110)	Frank Lary	2.00	1.00	.60
(111)	Barry Latman	2.00	1.00	.60
(112)	Vern Law	2.00	1.00	.60
(113)	Jim Lemon	2.00	1.00	.60
(114)	Sherman Lollar	2.00	1.00	.60
(115)	Dale Long	2.00	1.00	.60
(116)	Jerry Lumpe	2.00	1.00	.60
(117)	Jerry Lynch	2.00	1.00	.60
(118)	Art Mahaffey	2.00	1.00	.60
(119)	Frank Malzone	2.00	1.00	.60
(120)	Felix Mantilla	2.00	1.00	.60
(121)	Mickey Mantle	60.00	30.00	18.00
(122)	Juan Marichal	13.50	6.75	4.00
(123)	Roger Maris	25.00	12.50	7.50
(124)	Billy Martin	5.00	2.50	1.50
(125)	J.C. Martin	2.00	1.00	.60
(126)	Ed Mathews	13.50	6.75	4.00
(127)	Charlie Maxwell	2.00	1.00	.60
(128)	Willie Mays	20.00	10.00	6.00
(129)	Bill Mazeroski	12.00	6.00	3.50
(130)	Mike McCormick	2.00	1.00	.60
(131)	Willie McCovey	13.50	6.75	4.00
(132)	Lindy McDaniel	2.00	1.00	.60
(133)	Roy McMillan	2.00	1.00	.60
(134)	Minnie Minoso	3.00	1.50	.90
(135)	Bill Monbouquette	2.00	1.00	.60
(136)	Wally Moon	2.00	1.00	.60
(137)	Stan Musial	20.00	10.00	6.00
(138)	Charlie Neal	2.00	1.00	.60
(139)	Rocky Nelson	2.00	1.00	.60
(140)	Russ Nixon	2.00	1.00	.60
(141)	Billy O'Dell	2.00	1.00	.60
(142)	Jim O'Toole	2.00	1.00	.60
(143)	Milt Pappas	2.00	1.00	.60
(144)	Camilo Pascual	2.00	1.00	.60
(145)	Jim Perry	2.00	1.00	.60
(146)	Bubba Phillips	2.00	1.00	.60
(147)	Bill Pierce	2.00	1.00	.60
(148)	Jim Piersall	2.00	1.00	.60
(149)	Vada Pinson	3.00	1.50	.90
(150)	Johnny Podres	2.50	1.25	.70
(151)	Wally Post	2.00	1.00	.60
(152)	Vic Powers (Power)	2.00	1.00	.60
(153)	Pedro Ramos	2.00	1.00	.60
(154)	Robin Roberts	10.00	5.00	3.00
(155)	Brooks Robinson	13.50	6.75	4.00
(156)	Frank Robinson	13.50	6.75	4.00
(157)	Ed Roebuck	2.00	1.00	.60
(158)	John Romano	2.00	1.00	.60
(159)	John Roseboro	2.00	1.00	.60
(160)	Pete Runnels	2.00	1.00	.60
(161)	Ed Sadowski	2.00	1.00	.60
(162)	Jack Sanford	2.00	1.00	.60
(163)	Ron Santo	3.00	1.50	.90
(164)	Ray Semproch	2.00	1.00	.60
(165)	Bobby Shantz	2.00	1.00	.60
(166)	Bob Shaw	2.00	1.00	.60
(167)	Larry Sherry	2.00	1.00	.60
(168)	Norm Siebern	2.00	1.00	.60
(169)	Roy Sievers	2.00	1.00	.60
(170)	Curt Simmons	2.00	1.00	.60
(171)	Dave Sisler	2.00	1.00	.60
(172)	Bob Skinner	2.00	1.00	.60
(173)	Al Smith	2.00	1.00	.60
(174)	Hal Smith	2.00	1.00	.60
(175)	Hal Smith	2.00	1.00	.60
(176)	Duke Snider	13.50	6.75	4.00
(177)	Warren Spahn	13.50	6.75	4.00
(178)	Daryl Spencer	2.00	1.00	.60
(179)	Bill Stafford	2.00	1.00	.60
(180)	Jerry Staley	2.00	1.00	.60
(181)	Gene Stephens	2.00	1.00	.60
(182)	Chuck Stobbs	2.00	1.00	.60
(183)	Dick Stuart	2.00	1.00	.60
(184)	Willie Tasby	2.00	1.00	.60
(185)	Sammy Taylor	2.00	1.00	.60
(186)	Tony Taylor	2.00	1.00	.60
(187)	Johnny Temple	2.00	1.00	.60
(188)	Marv Throneberry	2.00	1.00	.60
(189)	Gus Triandos	2.00	1.00	.60
(190)	Bob Turley	2.00	1.00	.60
(191)	Bill Tuttle	2.00	1.00	.60
(192)	Zoilo Versalles	2.00	1.00	.60
(193)	Bill Virdon	2.00	1.00	.60
(194)	Lee Walls	2.00	1.00	.60
(195)	Vic Wertz	2.00	1.00	.60
(196)	Pete Whisenant	2.00	1.00	.60
(197)	Bill White	2.00	1.00	.60
(198)	Hoyt Wilhelm	10.00	5.00	3.00
(199)	Bob Will	2.00	1.00	.60
(200)	Carl Willey	2.00	1.00	.60
(201)	Billy Williams	12.00	6.00	3.50
(202)	Dick Williams	2.00	1.00	.60
(203)	Stan Williams	2.00	1.00	.60
(204)	Gene Woodling	2.00	1.00	.60
(205)	Early Wynn	10.00	5.00	3.00
(206)	Carl Yastrzemski	13.50	6.75	4.00
(207)	Eddie Yost	2.00	1.00	.60

1961 Topps Stamps Panels

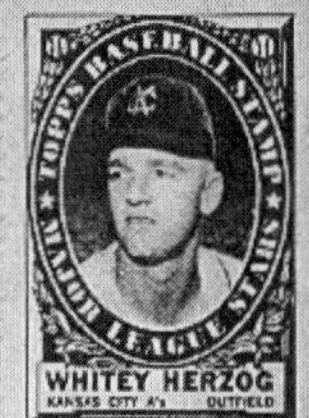

Some advanced collectors pursue the 1961 Topps stamps in the form of the two-stamp panels in which they were issued. The 208 different stamps which make up the issue can be found on 182 different two-stamp panels. The unnumbered stamps are listed here alphabetically according to the name of the player which appears on the left end of the panel. Values shown are for complete panels of two players stamps plus the attached tab at left.

		NM	EX	VG
Complete Panel Set (182):		3,000	1,500	900.00
Common Panel:		9.00	4.50	2.75
(1)	Hank Aguirre/Bob Boyd	9.00	4.50	2.75
(2)	Bob Allison/Orlando Cepeda	20.00	10.00	6.00
(3)	Bob Allison/Early Wynn	20.00	10.00	6.00
(4)	George Altman/Andy Carey	9.00	4.50	2.75
(5)	George Altman/ Lindy McDaniel	9.00	4.50	2.75
(6)	Johnny Antonelli/Ken Hunt	9.00	4.50	2.75
(7)	Richie Ashburn/Don Drysdale	30.00	15.00	9.00
(8)	Richie Ashburn/Joe Jay	25.00	12.50	7.50
(9)	Ken Aspromonte/ Chuck Estrada	9.00	4.50	2.75
(10)	Ken Aspromonte/Jerry Lynch	9.00	4.50	2.75
(11)	Ed Bailey/Marv Breeding	9.00	4.50	2.75
(12)	Ed Bailey/Smoky Burgess	9.00	4.50	2.75
(13)	Ernie Banks/Chico Fernandez	30.00	15.00	9.00
(14)	Ernie Banks/Pedro Ramos	30.00	15.00	9.00
(15)	Steve Barber/Eddie Kasko	9.00	4.50	2.75
(16)	Steve Barber/Roy Sievers	9.00	4.50	2.75
(17)	Earl Battey/Art Ditmar	9.00	4.50	2.75
(18)	Earl Battey/Bill White	9.00	4.50	2.75
(19)	Gus Bell/Gary Geiger	9.00	4.50	2.75
(20)	Gus Bell/Early Wynn	20.00	10.00	6.00
(21)	John Blanchard/Dick Donovan	9.00	4.50	2.75
(22)	John Blanchard/ Ray Semproch	9.00	4.50	2.75
(23)	Don Blasingame/ Elston Howard	12.00	6.00	3.50
(24)	Don Blasingame/ Charlie Maxwell	9.00	4.50	2.75
(25)	Frank Bolling/Luis Aparicio	20.00	10.00	6.00
(26)	Frank Bolling/Whitey Herzog	9.00	4.50	2.75
(27)	Steve Boros/Ike Delock	9.00	4.50	2.75
(28)	Steve Boros/Russ Nixon	9.00	4.50	2.75
(29)	Ed Bouchee/Larry Sherry	9.00	4.50	2.75
(30)	Ed Bouchee/Willie Tasby	9.00	4.50	2.75
(31)	Cletis Boyer/Johnny Klippstein	9.00	4.50	2.75
(32)	Jim Brewer/Vern Law	9.00	4.50	2.75
(33)	Jim Brewer/Camilo Pascual	9.00	4.50	2.75
(34)	Tom Brewer/Tommy Davis	9.00	4.50	2.75
(35)	Tom Brewer/Larry Sherry	9.00	4.50	2.75
(36)	Jim Brosnan/Roy McMillan	9.00	4.50	2.75
(37)	Jim Brosnan/Calr Willey	9.00	4.50	2.75
(38)	Bill Bruton/Ken Boyer	12.00	6.00	3.50
(39)	Bill Bruton/Mickey Mantle	200.00	100.00	60.00
(40)	Bob Buhl/Willie Mays	60.00	30.00	18.00
(41)	Bob Buhl/Roy Sievers	9.00	4.50	2.75
(42)	Jim Bunning/Bob Boyd	20.00	10.00	6.00
(43)	Jim Bunning/Ron Hansen	20.00	10.00	6.00
(44)	John Buzhardt/ Brooks Robinson	30.00	15.00	9.00
(45)	John Buzhardt/Dick Williams	9.00	4.50	2.75
(46)	Johnny Callison/Jim Landis	9.00	4.50	2.75
(47)	Johnny Callison/Ed Roebuck	9.00	4.50	2.75
(48)	Harry Chiti/Jackie Brandt	9.00	4.50	2.75
(49)	Harry Chiti/Gene Conley	9.00	4.50	2.75
(50)	Del Crandall/Billy Gardner	9.00	4.50	2.75
(51)	Bud Daley/Al Kaline	30.00	15.00	9.00
(52)	Bud Daley/Dave Sisler	9.00	4.50	2.75
(53)	Pete Daley/Dick Ellsworth	9.00	4.50	2.75
(54)	Pete Daley/Hal (R.) Smith	9.00	4.50	2.75
(55)	Clay Dalrymple/Norm Larker	9.00	4.50	2.75

(56)	CLay Dalrymple/Stan Williams	9.00	4.50	2.75
(57)	Jim Davenport/Reno Bertoia	9.00	4.50	2.75
(58)	Jim Davenport/Jerry Lynch	9.00	4.50	2.75
(59)	Bobby Del Greco/Roy Face	9.00	4.50	2.75
(60)	Bobby Del Greco/ Frank Howard	12.00	6.00	3.50
(61)	Gene Freese/Wes Covington	9.00	4.50	2.75
(62)	Gene Freese/Vada Pinson	9.00	4.50	2.75
(63)	Bob Friend/Hank Aaron	60.00	30.00	18.00
(64)	Bob Friend/Lee Walls	9.00	4.50	2.75
(65)	Jim Gentile/Chuck Estrada	9.00	4.50	2.75
(66)	Jim Gentile/Billy O'Dell	9.00	4.50	2.75
(67)	Dick Gernert/Russ Nixon	9.00	4.50	2.75
(68)	Alex Grammas/ Eddie Bressoud	9.00	4.50	2.75
(69)	Frank Herrera/Joe Jay	9.00	4.50	2.75
(70)	Frank Herrera/Jim Landis	9.00	4.50	2.75
(71)	Julian Javier/Eddie Kasko	9.00	4.50	2.75
(72)	Jackie Jensen/Hank Bauer	15.00	7.50	4.50
(73)	Jackie Jensen/Mickey Mantle	200.00	100.00	60.00
(74)	Al Kaline/Dick Hall	30.00	15.00	9.00
(75)	Al Kaline/Ray Herbert	30.00	15.00	9.00
(76)	Russ Kemmerer/Ed Sadowski	9.00	4.50	2.75
(77)	Harmon Killebrew/Bill Stafford	30.00	15.00	9.00
(78)	Harmon Killebrew/Bill White	30.00	15.00	9.00
(79)	Billy Klaus/Bob Anderson	9.00	4.50	2.75
(80)	Ron Kline/Juan Marichal	20.00	10.00	6.00
(81)	Ron Kline/Curt Simmons	9.00	4.50	2.75
(82)	Tony Kubek/Reno Bertoia	12.00	6.00	3.50
(83)	Frank Lary/Andy Carey	9.00	4.50	2.75
(84)	Barry Latman/Hank Bauer	9.00	4.50	2.75
(85)	Jim Lemon/Tony Curry	9.00	4.50	2.75
(86)	Jim Lemon/Dick Williams	9.00	4.50	2.75
(87)	Sherm Lollar/Willie Mays	60.00	30.00	18.00
(88)	Sherm Lollar/Duke Snider	30.00	15.00	9.00
(89)	Dale Long/Bob Anderson	9.00	4.50	2.75
(90)	Dale Long/Don Elston	9.00	4.50	2.75
(91)	Art Mahaffey/Vada Pinson	9.00	4.50	2.75
(92)	Art Mahaffey/Robin Roberts	20.00	10.00	6.00
(93)	Frank Malzone/Dick Hall	9.00	4.50	2.75
(94)	Frank Malzone/Bob Hartman	9.00	4.50	2.75
(95)	Felix Mantilla/Billy Gardner	9.00	4.50	2.75
(96)	Felix Mantilla/Gary Geiger	9.00	4.50	2.75
(97)	Roger Maris/Johnny Klippstein	45.00	22.00	13.50
(98)	Roger Maris/Ray Semproch	45.00	22.00	13.50
(99)	Billy Martin/Hank Aaron	60.00	30.00	18.00
(100)	Billy Martin/Whitey Herzog	15.00	7.50	4.50
(101)	J.C. Martin/Bob Cerv	9.00	4.50	2.75
(102)	J.C. Martin/Eddie Yost	9.00	4.50	2.75
(103)	Ed Mathews/Chico Cardenas	30.00	15.00	9.00
(104)	Bill Mazeroski/Joe Adcock	20.00	10.00	6.00
(105)	Bill Mazeroski/Elston Howard	20.00	10.00	6.00
(106)	Mike McCormick/ Rocky Nelson	9.00	4.50	2.75
(107)	Mike McCormick/ Curt Simmons	9.00	4.50	2.75
(108)	Wille McCovey/ Smoky Burgess	30.00	15.00	9.00
(109)	Minnie Minoso/ Ted Kluszewski	15.00	7.50	4.50
(110)	Minnie Minoso/Eddie Yost	12.00	6.00	3.50
(111)	Bikll Monbouquette/ Tony Curry	9.00	4.50	2.75
(112)	Bill Monbouquette/ Sammy Taylor	9.00	4.50	2.75
(113)	Wally Moon/Roy Face	9.00	4.50	2.75
(114)	Stan Musial/Rocky Nelson	60.00	30.00	18.00
(115)	Charlie Neal/Marv Breeding	9.00	4.50	2.75
(116)	Charlie Neal/Jim Grant	9.00	4.50	2.75
(117)	Jim O'Toole/Chico Cardenas	9.00	4.50	2.75
(118)	Jim O'Toole/Roy McMillan	9.00	4.50	2.75
(119)	Milt Pappas/Tito Francona	9.00	4.50	2.75
(120)	Milt Pappas/Jim Piersall	9.00	4.50	2.75
(121)	Jim Perry/Bob Cerv	9.00	4.50	2.75
(122)	Jim Perry/Ken Hunt	9.00	4.50	2.75
(123)	Bubba Phillips/Art Ditmar	9.00	4.50	2.75
(124)	Bubba Phillips/Jim Kaat	15.00	7.50	4.50
(125)	Johnny Podres/Dick Farrell	9.00	4.50	2.75
(126)	Wally Post/Dick Farrell	9.00	4.50	2.75
(127)	Wally Post/Robin Roberts	20.00	10.00	6.00
(128)	Frank Robinson/Jim Grant	30.00	15.00	9.00
(129)	Frank Robinson/Don Hoak	30.00	15.00	9.00
(130)	John Romano/Al Kaline	30.00	15.00	9.00
(131)	John Roseboro/Dick Groat	9.00	4.50	2.75
(132)	Pete Runnels/Larry Jackson	9.00	4.50	2.75
(133)	Jack Sanford/Whitey Ford	30.00	15.00	9.00
(134)	Jack Sanford/Pedro Ramos	9.00	4.50	2.75
(135)	Ron Santo/Harvey Kuenn	15.00	7.50	4.50
(136)	Ron Santo/Vern Law	15.00	7.50	4.50
(137)	Bobby Shantz/Joe Adcock	9.00	4.50	2.75
(138)	Bobby Shantz/Dick Groat	9.00	4.50	2.75
(139)	Bob Shaw/Jerry Casale	9.00	4.50	2.75
(140)	Bob Shaw/Ned Garver	9.00	4.50	2.75
(141)	Norm Siebern/ Tony Gonzalez	9.00	4.50	2.75
(142)	Norm Siebern/Woodie Held	9.00	4.50	2.75
(143)	Bob Skinner/Hobie Landrith	9.00	4.50	2.75
(144)	Bob Skinner/Juan Marichal	20.00	10.00	6.00
(145)	Al Smith/Don Drysdale	25.00	12.50	7.50
(146)	Hal (W.) Smith/ Eddie Bressoud	9.00	4.50	2.75
(147)	Hal (W.) Smith/Harvey Kuenn	9.00	4.50	2.75
(148)	Daryl Spencer/Norm Cash	9.00	4.50	2.75
(149)	Daryl Spencer/Vic Powers (Power)	9.00	4.50	2.75
(150)	Jerry Staley/Ned Garver	9.00	4.50	2.75
(151)	Jerry Staley/Ed Sadowski	9.00	4.50	2.75
(152)	Gene Stephens/Gene Conley	9.00	4.50	2.75
(153)	Gene Stephens/Ike Delock	9.00	4.50	2.75
(154)	Chuck Stobbs/Ken Boyer	12.00	6.00	3.50
(155)	Chuck Stobbs/Curt Flood	9.00	4.50	2.75
(156)	Dick Stuart/Whitey Ford	30.00	15.00	9.00
(157)	Dick Stuart/Larry Jackson	9.00	4.50	2.75
(158)	Tony Taylor/Frank Howard	12.00	6.00	3.50
(159)	Tony Taylor/Norm Larker	9.00	4.50	2.75
(160)	Johnny Temple/Norm Cash	9.00	4.50	2.75
(161)	Johnny Temple/Dave Sisler	9.00	4.50	2.75
(162)	Marv Throneberry/Yogi Berra	45.00	22.00	13.50
(163)	Marv Throneberry/ Tommy Davis	9.00	4.50	2.75
(164)	Gus Triandos/Sammy Taylor	9.00	4.50	2.75
(165)	Bob Turley/Luis Aparicio	20.00	10.00	6.00
(166)	Bill Tuttle/Jerry Casale	9.00	4.50	2.75
(167)	Bill Tuttle/Bill Pierce	9.00	4.50	2.75
(168)	Zoilo Versalles/Bill Stafford	9.00	4.50	2.75
(169)	Bill Virdon/Yogi Berra	30.00	15.00	9.00
(170)	Vic Wertz/Bob Hartman	9.00	4.50	2.75
(171)	Vic Wertz/Jerry Lumpe	9.00	4.50	2.75
(172)	Pete Whisenant/Luis Arroyo	9.00	4.50	2.75
(173)	Pete Whisenant/Dick Donovan	9.00	4.50	2.75
(174)	Hoyt Wilhelm/Ron Hansen	20.00	10.00	6.00
(175)	Hoyt Wilhelm/Jim Piersall	20.00	10.00	6.00
(176)	Bob Will/Tony Gonzalez	9.00	4.50	2.75
(177)	Bob Will/Lindy McDaniel	9.00	4.50	2.75
(178)	Billy Williams/Warren Spahn	30.00	15.00	9.00
(179)	Billy Williams/Carl Willey	25.00	12.50	7.50
(180)	Gene Woodling/Don Elston	9.00	4.50	2.75
(181)	Gene Woodling/Hal (R.) Smith	9.00	4.50	2.75
(182)	Carl Yastrzemski/Jerry Lumpe	60.00	30.00	18.00

1962 Topps

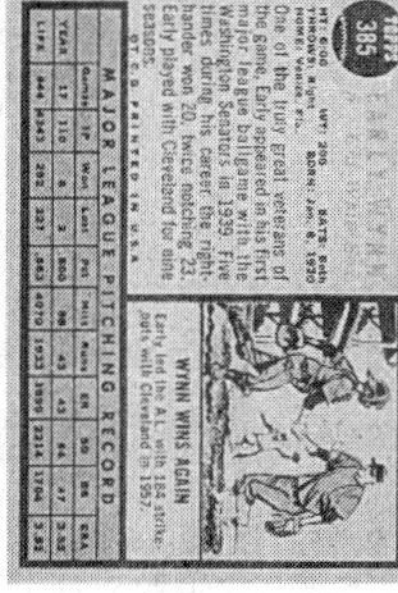

The 1962 Topps set established another plateau for set size with 598 cards. The 2-1/2" x 3-1/2" cards feature a photograph set against a woodgrain background. The lower-right corner has been made to look like it is curling away. Many established specialty cards dot the set including statistical leaders, multi-player cards, team cards, checklists, World Series cards and All-Stars. Of note is that 1962 was the first year of the multi-player rookie card. There is a nine-card "In Action" subset and a 10-card run of special Babe Ruth cards. Photo variations of several cards in the 2nd Series (#110-196) exist. All cards in the 2nd Series can be found with two distinct printing variations, an early printing with the cards containing a very noticeable greenish tint, having been corrected to clear photos in subsequent print runs. The complete set price in the checklist that follows does not include the higher-priced variations. Among the high numbers (#523-598) certain cards were "short-printed," produced in lesser quantities. These cards carry a higher value and are indicated in the checklist by the notation (SP) after the player name.

		NM	EX	VG
Complete Set (598):		5,500	2,750	1,650
Common Player (1-446):		4.00	2.00	1.25
Common Player (447-522):		7.00	3.50	2.00
Common Player (523-598):		10.00	5.00	3.00
1	Roger Maris	270.00	70.00	40.00
2	Jim Brosnan	4.00	2.00	1.25
3	Pete Runnels	4.00	2.00	1.25
4	John DeMerit	4.00	2.00	1.25
5	Sandy Koufax	100.00	50.00	30.00
6	Marv Breeding	4.00	2.00	1.25
7	Frank Thomas	4.00	2.00	1.25
8	Ray Herbert	4.00	2.00	1.25
9	Jim Davenport	4.00	2.00	1.25
10	Bob Clemente	95.00	47.50	27.50
11	Tom Morgan	4.00	2.00	1.25
12	Harry Craft	4.00	2.00	1.25
13	Dick Howser	4.00	2.00	1.25
14	Bill White	4.00	2.00	1.25
15	Dick Donovan	4.00	2.00	1.25
16	Darrell Johnson	4.00	2.00	1.25
17	Johnny Callison	4.00	2.00	1.25
18	Managers' Dream (Mickey Mantle, Willie Mays)	120.00	60.00	35.00
19	***Ray Washburn***	4.00	2.00	1.25
20	Rocky Colavito	15.00	7.50	4.50
21	Jim Kaat	6.00	3.00	1.75
22a	1st Series Checklist (1-88) (Numbers 121-176 on back.)	6.00	3.00	1.75
22b	1st Series Checklist (1-88) (Numbers 33-88 on back.)	9.00	4.50	2.75
23	Norm Larker	4.00	2.00	1.25
24	Detroit Tigers Team	7.00	3.50	2.00
25	Ernie Banks	40.00	20.00	12.00
26	Chris Cannizzaro	4.00	2.00	1.25
27	Chuck Cottier	4.00	2.00	1.25
28	Minnie Minoso	9.00	4.50	2.75
29	Casey Stengel	13.50	6.75	4.00
30	Ed Mathews	25.00	12.50	7.50
31	***Tom Tresh***	13.50	6.75	4.00
32	John Roseboro	4.00	2.00	1.25
33	Don Larsen	4.00	2.00	1.25
34	Johnny Temple	4.00	2.00	1.25
35	***Don Schwall***	4.00	2.00	1.25
36	Don Leppert	4.00	2.00	1.25
37	Tribe Hill Trio (Barry Latman, Jim Perry, Dick Stigman)	6.00	3.00	1.75
38	Gene Stephens	4.00	2.00	1.25
39	Joe Koppe	4.00	2.00	1.25
40	Orlando Cepeda	16.00	8.00	4.75
41	Cliff Cook	4.00	2.00	1.25
42	Jim King	4.00	2.00	1.25
43	Los Angeles Dodgers Team	10.00	5.00	3.00
44	Don Taussig	4.00	2.00	1.25
45	Brooks Robinson	25.00	12.50	7.50
46	***Jack Baldschun***	4.00	2.00	1.25
47	Bob Will	4.00	2.00	1.25
48	Ralph Terry	4.00	2.00	1.25
49	Hal Jones	4.00	2.00	1.25
50	Stan Musial	50.00	25.00	15.00
51	A.L. Batting Leaders (Norm Cash, Elston Howard, Al Kaline, Jim Piersall)	12.50	6.25	3.75
52	N.L. Batting Leaders (Ken Boyer, Roberto Clemente, Wally Moon, Vada Pinson)	15.00	7.50	4.50
53	A.L. Home Run Leaders (Jim Gentile, Harmon Killebrew, Mickey Mantle, Roger Maris)	55.00	27.50	16.50
54	N.L. Home Run Leaders (Orlando Cepeda, Willie Mays, Frank Robinson)	12.50	6.25	3.75
55	A.L. E.R.A. Leaders (Dick Donovan, Don Mossi, Milt Pappas, Bill Stafford)	6.00	3.00	1.75
56	N.L. E.R.A. Leaders (Mike McCormick, Jim O'Toole, Curt Simmons, Warren Spahn)	7.00	3.50	2.00
57	A.L. Win Leaders (Steve Barber, Jim Bunning, Whitey Ford, Frank Lary)	10.00	5.00	3.00
58	N.L. Win Leaders (Joe Jay, Jim O'Toole, Warren Spahn)	7.00	3.50	2.00
59	A.L. Strikeout Leaders (Jim Bunning, Whitey Ford, Camilo Pascual, Juan Pizzaro)	7.50	3.75	2.25
60	N.L. Strikeout Leaders (Don Drysdale, Sandy Koufax, Jim O'Toole, Stan Williams)	16.00	8.00	4.75
61	St. Louis Cardinals Team	7.00	3.50	2.00
62	Steve Boros	4.00	2.00	1.25
63	***Tony Cloninger***	7.00	3.50	2.00
64	Russ Snyder	4.00	2.00	1.25
65	Bobby Richardson	15.00	7.50	4.50
66	Cuno Barragon (Barragan)	4.00	2.00	1.25
67	Harvey Haddix	4.00	2.00	1.25
68	Ken L. Hunt	4.00	2.00	1.25
69	Phil Ortega	4.00	2.00	1.25
70	Harmon Killebrew	25.00	12.50	7.50
71	Dick LeMay	4.00	2.00	1.25
72	Bob's Pupils (Steve Boros, Bob Scheffing, Jake Wood)	4.50	2.25	1.25
73	Nellie Fox	16.00	8.00	4.75
74	Bob Lillis	4.00	2.00	1.25
75	Milt Pappas	4.00	2.00	1.25
76	Howie Bedell	4.00	2.00	1.25
77	Tony Taylor	4.00	2.00	1.25
78	Gene Green	4.00	2.00	1.25
79	Ed Hobaugh	4.00	2.00	1.25
80	Vada Pinson	7.00	3.50	2.00
81	Jim Pagliaroni	4.00	2.00	1.25
82	Deron Johnson	4.00	2.00	1.25
83	Larry Jackson	4.00	2.00	1.25
84	Lenny Green	4.00	2.00	1.25
85	Gil Hodges	15.00	7.50	4.50
86	***Donn Clendenon***	6.00	3.00	1.75
87	Mike Roarke	4.00	2.00	1.25
88	Ralph Houk	10.00	5.00	3.00
89	Barney Schultz	4.00	2.00	1.25
90	Jim Piersall	6.00	3.00	1.75
91	J.C. Martin	4.00	2.00	1.25
92	Sam Jones	4.00	2.00	1.25
93	John Blanchard	5.00	2.50	1.50
94	Jay Hook	4.00	2.00	1.25
95	Don Hoak	4.00	2.00	1.25
96	Eli Grba	4.00	2.00	1.25
97	Tito Francona	4.00	2.00	1.25
98	2nd Series Checklist (89-176)	6.00	3.00	1.75
99	***John Powell*** (Boog)	20.00	10.00	6.00
100	Warren Spahn	30.00	15.00	9.00
101	Carroll Hardy	4.00	2.00	1.25
102	Al Schroll	4.00	2.00	1.25
103	Don Blasingame	4.00	2.00	1.25
104	Ted Savage	4.00	2.00	1.25
105	Don Mossi	4.00	2.00	1.25
106	Carl Sawatski	4.00	2.00	1.25
107	Mike McCormick	4.00	2.00	1.25
108	Willie Davis	5.00	2.50	1.50
109	Bob Shaw	4.00	2.00	1.25
110	Bill Skowron	22.50	11.00	7.00
111	Dallas Green	4.00	2.00	1.25
112	Hank Foiles	4.00	2.00	1.25
113	Chicago White Sox Team	7.00	3.50	2.00
114	Howie Koplitz	4.00	2.00	1.25
115	Bob Skinner	4.00	2.00	1.25
116	Herb Score	4.00	2.00	1.25
117	Gary Geiger	4.00	2.00	1.25
118	Julian Javier	4.00	2.00	1.25
119	Danny Murphy	4.00	2.00	1.25
120	Bob Purkey	4.00	2.00	1.25
121	Billy Hitchcock	4.00	2.00	1.25
122	Norm Bass	4.00	2.00	1.25
123	Mike de la Hoz	4.00	2.00	1.25
124	Bill Pleis	4.00	2.00	1.25
125	Gene Woodling	4.00	2.00	1.25
126	Al Cicotte	4.00	2.00	1.25
127	Pride of the A's (Hank Bauer, Jerry Lumpe, Norm Siebern)	4.50	2.25	1.25
128	Art Fowler	4.00	2.00	1.25
129a	Lee Walls (Pinstriped jersey.)	20.00	10.00	6.00
129b	Lee Walls (Plain jersey.)	6.00	3.00	1.75
130	Frank Bolling	4.00	2.00	1.25
131	***Pete Richert***	4.00	2.00	1.25
132a	Los Angeles Angels Team (With inset photos.)	13.50	6.75	4.00
132b	Los Angeles Angels Team (No inset photos.)	7.00	3.50	2.00

133	Felipe Alou	9.00	4.50	2.75
134a	Billy Hoeft (Green sky.)	15.00	7.50	4.50
134b	Billy Hoeft (Blue sky.)	12.00	6.00	3.50
135	Babe as a Boy (Babe Ruth)	20.00	10.00	6.00
136	Babe Joins Yanks (Babe Ruth)	20.00	10.00	6.00
137	Babe and Mgr. Huggins (Babe Ruth)	20.00	10.00	6.00
138	The Famous Slugger (Babe Ruth)	20.00	10.00	6.00
139a	Hal Reniff /Pitching	40.00	20.00	12.00
139b	Hal Reniff/Portrait	15.00	7.50	4.50
139c	Babe Hits 60 (Babe Ruth) (Pole in background at left.)	35.00	17.50	10.00
139d	Babe Hits 60 (Babe Ruth) (No pole.)	35.00	17.50	10.00
140	Gehrig and Ruth (Babe Ruth)	35.00	17.50	10.00
141	Twilight Years (Babe Ruth)	20.00	10.00	6.00
142	Coaching for the Dodgers (Babe Ruth)	20.00	10.00	6.00
143	Greatest Sports Hero (Babe Ruth)	20.00	10.00	6.00
144	Farewell Speech (Babe Ruth)	20.00	10.00	6.00
145	Barry Latman	4.00	2.00	1.25
146	Don Demeter	4.00	2.00	1.25
147a	Bill Kunkel (Ball in hand.)	17.50	8.75	5.25
147b	Bill Kunkel/Portrait	12.00	6.00	3.50
148	Wally Post	4.00	2.00	1.25
149	Bob Duliba	4.00	2.00	1.25
150	Al Kaline	30.00	15.00	9.00
151	Johnny Klippstein	4.00	2.00	1.25
152	Mickey Vernon	4.00	2.00	1.25
153	Pumpsie Green	4.00	2.00	1.25
154	Lee Thomas	4.00	2.00	1.25
155	Stu Miller	4.00	2.00	1.25
156	Merritt Ranew	4.00	2.00	1.25
157	Wes Covington	4.00	2.00	1.25
158	Milwaukee Braves Team	7.00	3.50	2.00
159	Hal Reniff	4.00	2.00	1.25
160	Dick Stuart	4.00	2.00	1.25
161	Frank Baumann	4.00	2.00	1.25
162	Sammy Drake	4.00	2.00	1.25
163	Hot Corner Guardians (Cletis Boyer, Billy Gardner)	10.00	5.00	3.00
164	Hal Naragon	4.00	2.00	1.25
165	Jackie Brandt	4.00	2.00	1.25
166	Don Lee	4.00	2.00	1.25
167	***Tim McCarver***	17.50	8.75	5.25
168	Leo Posada	4.00	2.00	1.25
169	Bob Cerv	4.00	2.00	1.25
170	Ron Santo	12.50	6.25	3.75
171	Dave Sisler	4.00	2.00	1.25
172	Fred Hutchinson	4.00	2.00	1.25
173	Chico Fernandez	4.00	2.00	1.25
174a	Carl Willey (With cap.)	15.00	7.50	4.50
174b	Carl Willey (No cap.)	8.00	4.00	2.50
175	Frank Howard	5.00	2.50	1.50
176a	Eddie Yost/Btg	15.00	7.50	4.50
176b	Eddie Yost/Portrait	4.00	2.00	1.25
177	Bobby Shantz	4.00	2.00	1.25
178	Camilo Carreon	4.00	2.00	1.25
179	Tom Sturdivant	4.00	2.00	1.25
180	Bob Allison	4.00	2.00	1.25
181	Paul Brown	4.00	2.00	1.25
182	Bob Nieman	4.00	2.00	1.25
183	Roger Craig	4.00	2.00	1.25
184	Haywood Sullivan	4.00	2.00	1.25
185	Roland Sheldon	4.00	2.00	1.25
186	***Mack Jones***	4.00	2.00	1.25
187	Gene Conley	4.00	2.00	1.25
188	Chuck Hiller	4.00	2.00	1.25
189	Dick Hall	4.00	2.00	1.25
190a	Wally Moon (With cap.)	20.00	10.00	6.00
190b	Wally Moon (No cap.)	6.00	3.00	1.75
191	Jim Brewer	4.00	2.00	1.25
192a	3rd Series Checklist (177-264) (192 is Check List, 3)	7.00	3.50	2.00
192b	3rd Series Checklist (177-264) (192 is Check List 3)	8.00	4.00	2.50
193	Eddie Kasko	4.00	2.00	1.25
194	***Dean Chance***	12.50	6.25	3.75
195	Joe Cunningham	4.00	2.00	1.25
196	Terry Fox	4.00	2.00	1.25
197	Daryl Spencer	4.00	2.00	1.25
198	Johnny Keane	4.00	2.00	1.25
199	***Gaylord Perry***	55.00	27.50	16.50
200	Mickey Mantle	410.00	145.00	65.00
201	Ike Delock	4.00	2.00	1.25
202	Carl Warwick	4.00	2.00	1.25
203	Jack Fisher	4.00	2.00	1.25
204	Johnny Weekly	4.00	2.00	1.25
205	Gene Freese	4.00	2.00	1.25
206	Washington Senators Team	7.00	3.50	2.00
207	Pete Burnside	4.00	2.00	1.25
208	Billy Martin	12.00	6.00	3.50
209	***Jim Fregosi***	15.00	7.50	4.50
210	Roy Face	4.00	2.00	1.25
211	Midway Masters (Frank Bolling, Roy McMillan)	4.50	2.25	1.25
212	Jim Owens	4.00	2.00	1.25
213	Richie Ashburn	20.00	10.00	6.00
214	Dom Zanni	4.00	2.00	1.25
215	Woody Held	4.00	2.00	1.25
216	Ron Kline	4.00	2.00	1.25
217	Walt Alston	10.00	5.00	3.00
218	***Joe Torre***	55.00	27.50	16.50
219	***Al Downing***	12.00	6.00	3.50
220	Roy Sievers	4.00	2.00	1.25
221	Bill Short	4.00	2.00	1.25
222	Jerry Zimmerman	4.00	2.00	1.25
223	Alex Grammas	4.00	2.00	1.25
224	Don Rudolph	4.00	2.00	1.25
225	Frank Malzone	4.00	2.00	1.25
226	San Francisco Giants Team	7.00	3.50	2.00
227	Bobby Tiefenauer	4.00	2.00	1.25
228	Dale Long	4.00	2.00	1.25
229	Jesus McFarlane	4.00	2.00	1.25
230	Camlio Pascual	4.00	2.00	1.25
231	Ernie Bowman	4.00	2.00	1.25
232	World Series Game 1 (Yanks Win Opener)	8.00	4.00	2.50
233	World Series Game 2 (Jay Ties It Up)	10.00	5.00	3.00
234	World Series Game 3 (Maris Wins It In the 9th)	22.50	11.00	7.00
235	World Series Game 4 (Ford Sets New Mark)	17.50	8.75	5.25
236	World Series Game 5 (Yanks Crush Reds in Finale)	7.00	3.50	2.00
237	World Series (The Winners Celebrate)	10.00	5.00	3.00
238	Norm Sherry	4.00	2.00	1.25
239	Cecil Butler	4.00	2.00	1.25
240	George Altman	4.00	2.00	1.25
241	Johnny Kucks	4.00	2.00	1.25
242	Mel McGaha	4.00	2.00	1.25
243	Robin Roberts	15.00	7.50	4.50
244	Don Gile	4.00	2.00	1.25
245	Ron Hansen	4.00	2.00	1.25
246	Art Ditmar	4.00	2.00	1.25
247	Joe Pignatano	4.00	2.00	1.25
248	Bob Aspromonte	4.00	2.00	1.25
249	Ed Keegan	4.00	2.00	1.25
250	Norm Cash	12.00	6.00	3.50
251	New York Yankees Team	32.50	16.00	10.00
252	Earl Francis	4.00	2.00	1.25
253	Harry Chiti	4.00	2.00	1.25
254	Gordon Windhorn	4.00	2.00	1.25
255	Juan Pizarro	4.00	2.00	1.25
256	Elio Chacon	4.00	2.00	1.25
257	Jack Spring	4.00	2.00	1.25
258	Marty Keough	4.00	2.00	1.25
259	Lou Klimchock	4.00	2.00	1.25
260	Bill Pierce	4.00	2.00	1.25
261	George Alusik	4.00	2.00	1.25
262	Bob Schmidt	4.00	2.00	1.25
263	The Right Pitch (Joe Jay, Bob Purkey, Jim Turner)	4.50	2.25	1.25
264	Dick Ellsworth	4.00	2.00	1.25
265	Joe Adcock	4.00	2.00	1.25
266	John Anderson	4.00	2.00	1.25
267	Dan Dobbek	4.00	2.00	1.25
268	Ken McBride	4.00	2.00	1.25
269	Bob Oldis	4.00	2.00	1.25
270	Dick Groat	4.00	2.00	1.25
271	Ray Rippelmeyer	4.00	2.00	1.25
272	Earl Robinson	4.00	2.00	1.25
273	Gary Bell	4.00	2.00	1.25
274	Sammy Taylor	4.00	2.00	1.25
275	Norm Siebern	4.00	2.00	1.25
276	Hal Kostad	4.00	2.00	1.25
277	4th Series Checklist (265-352)	7.00	3.50	2.00
278	Ken Johnson	4.00	2.00	1.25
279	Hobie Landrith	4.00	2.00	1.25
280	Johnny Podres	7.50	3.75	2.25
281	***Jake Gibbs***	7.50	3.75	2.25
282	Dave Hillman	4.00	2.00	1.25
283	Charlie Smith	4.00	2.00	1.25
284	Ruben Amaro	4.00	2.00	1.25
285	Curt Simmons	4.00	2.00	1.25
286	Al Lopez	9.00	4.50	2.75
287	George Witt	4.00	2.00	1.25
288	Billy Williams	25.00	12.50	7.50
289	Mike Krsnich	4.00	2.00	1.25
290	Jim Gentile	6.00	3.00	1.75
291	Hal Stowe	4.00	2.00	1.25
292	Jerry Kindall	4.00	2.00	1.25
293	Bob Miller	4.00	2.00	1.25
294	Philadelphia Phillies Team	7.50	3.75	2.25
295	Vern Law	4.00	2.00	1.25
296	Ken Hamlin	4.00	2.00	1.25
297	Ron Perranoski	4.00	2.00	1.25
298	Bill Tuttle	4.00	2.00	1.25
299	***Don Wert***	4.00	2.00	1.25
300	Willie Mays	150.00	75.00	45.00
301	Galen Cisco	4.00	2.00	1.25
302	***John Edwards***	4.00	2.00	1.25
303	Frank Torre	4.00	2.00	1.25
304	Dick Farrell	4.00	2.00	1.25
305	Jerry Lumpe	4.00	2.00	1.25
306	Redbird Rippers (Larry Jackson, Lindy McDaniel)	5.00	2.50	1.50
307	Jim Grant	4.00	2.00	1.25
308	Neil Chrisley	4.00	2.00	1.25
309	Moe Morhardt	4.00	2.00	1.25
310	Whitey Ford	32.50	16.00	10.00
311	Kubek Makes The Double Play (Tony Kubek)	12.00	6.00	3.50
312	Spahn Shows No-Hit Form (Warren Spahn)	15.00	7.50	4.50
313	Maris Blasts 61st (Roger Maris)	40.00	20.00	12.00
314	Colavito's Power (Rocky Colavito)	11.00	5.50	3.25
315	Ford Tosses a Curve (Whitey Ford)	20.00	10.00	6.00
316	Killebrew Sends One into Orbit (Harmon Killebrew)	20.00	10.00	6.00
317	Musial Plays 21st Season (Stan Musial)	17.50	8.75	5.25
318	The Switch Hitter Connects (Mickey Mantle)	90.00	45.00	25.00
319	McCormick Shows His Stuff (Mike McCormick)	6.00	3.00	1.75
320	Hank Aaron	100.00	50.00	30.00
321	Lee Stange	4.00	2.00	1.25
322	Al Dark	4.00	2.00	1.25
323	Don Landrum	4.00	2.00	1.25
324	Joe McClain	4.00	2.00	1.25
325	Luis Aparicio	15.00	7.50	4.50
326	Tom Parsons	4.00	2.00	1.25
327	Ozzie Virgil	4.00	2.00	1.25
328	Ken Walters	4.00	2.00	1.25
329	Bob Bolin	4.00	2.00	1.25
330	Johnny Romano	4.00	2.00	1.25
331	Moe Drabowsky	4.00	2.00	1.25
332	Don Buddin	4.00	2.00	1.25
333	Frank Cipriani	4.00	2.00	1.25
334	Boston Red Sox Team	9.00	4.50	2.75
335	Bill Bruton	4.00	2.00	1.25
336	Billy Muffett	4.00	2.00	1.25
337	Jim Marshall	4.00	2.00	1.25
338	Billy Gardner	4.00	2.00	1.25
339	Jose Valdivielso	4.00	2.00	1.25
340	Don Drysdale	30.00	15.00	9.00
341	Mike Hershberger	4.00	2.00	1.25
342	Ed Rakow	4.00	2.00	1.25
343	Albie Pearson	4.00	2.00	1.25
344	Ed Bauta	4.00	2.00	1.25
345	Chuck Schilling	4.00	2.00	1.25
346	Jack Kralick	4.00	2.00	1.25
347	Chuck Hinton	4.00	2.00	1.25
348	Larry Burright	4.00	2.00	1.25
349	Paul Foytack	4.00	2.00	1.25
350	Frank Robinson	40.00	20.00	12.00
351	Braves' Backstops (Del Crandall, Joe Torre)	12.00	6.00	3.50
352	Frank Sullivan	4.00	2.00	1.25
353	Bill Mazeroski	20.00	10.00	6.00
354	Roman Mejias	4.00	2.00	1.25
355	Steve Barber	4.00	2.00	1.25
356	Tom Haller	4.00	2.00	1.25
357	Jerry Walker	4.00	2.00	1.25
358	Tommy Davis	4.00	2.00	1.25
359	Bobby Locke	4.00	2.00	1.25
360	Yogi Berra	50.00	25.00	15.00
361	Bob Hendley	4.00	2.00	1.25
362	Ty Cline	4.00	2.00	1.25
363	Bob Roselli	4.00	2.00	1.25
364	Ken Hunt	4.00	2.00	1.25
365	Charley Neal	4.00	2.00	1.25
366	Phil Regan	4.00	2.00	1.25
367	5th Checklist (353-429)	8.00	4.00	2.50
368	Bob Tillman	4.00	2.00	1.25
369	Ted Bowsfield	4.00	2.00	1.25
370	Ken Boyer	7.50	3.75	2.25
371	Earl Battey	4.00	2.00	1.25
372	Jack Curtis	4.00	2.00	1.25
373	Al Heist	4.00	2.00	1.25
374	Gene Mauch	4.00	2.00	1.25
375	Ron Fairly	4.00	2.00	1.25
376	Bud Daley	4.00	2.00	1.25
377	Johnny Orsino	4.00	2.00	1.25
378	Bennie Daniels	4.00	2.00	1.25
379	Chuck Essegian	4.00	2.00	1.25
380	Lou Burdette	4.00	2.00	1.25
381	Chico Cardenas	4.00	2.00	1.25
382	Dick Williams	4.00	2.00	1.25
383	Ray Sadecki	4.00	2.00	1.25
384	Kansas City Athletics Team	8.00	4.00	2.50
385	Early Wynn	12.00	6.00	3.50
386	Don Mincher	4.00	2.00	1.25
387	***Lou Brock***	95.00	45.00	25.00
388	Ryne Duren	4.00	2.00	1.25
389	Smoky Burgess	4.00	2.00	1.25
390	Orlando Cepeda/AS	10.00	5.00	3.00
391	Bill Mazeroski/AS	12.00	6.00	3.50
392	Ken Boyer/AS	7.00	3.50	2.00
393	Roy McMillan/AS	4.00	2.00	1.25
394	Hank Aaron/AS	32.50	16.00	10.00
395	Willie Mays/AS	32.50	16.00	10.00
396	Frank Robinson/AS	13.50	6.75	4.00
397	John Roseboro/AS	4.00	2.00	1.25
398	Don Drysdale/AS	13.50	6.75	4.00
399	Warren Spahn/AS	13.50	6.75	4.00
400	Elston Howard	15.00	7.50	4.50
401	AL & NL Homer Kings (Roger Maris, Orlando Cepeda)	45.00	22.50	13.50
402	Gino Cimoli	4.00	2.00	1.25
403	Chet Nichols	4.00	2.00	1.25
404	Tim Harkness	4.00	2.00	1.25
405	Jim Perry	4.00	2.00	1.25
406	Bob Taylor	4.00	2.00	1.25
407	Hank Aguirre	4.00	2.00	1.25
408	Gus Bell	4.00	2.00	1.25
409	Pittsburgh Pirates Team	11.00	5.50	3.25
410	Al Smith	4.00	2.00	1.25
411	Danny O'Connell	4.00	2.00	1.25
412	Charlie James	4.00	2.00	1.25
413	Matty Alou	4.00	2.00	1.25
414	Joe Gaines	4.00	2.00	1.25
415	Bill Virdon	4.00	2.00	1.25
416	Bob Scheffing	4.00	2.00	1.25
417	Joe Azcue	4.00	2.00	1.25
418	Andy Carey	4.00	2.00	1.25
419	Bob Bruce	4.00	2.00	1.25
420	Gus Triandos	4.00	2.00	1.25
421	Ken MacKenzie	4.00	2.00	1.25
422	Steve Bilko	4.00	2.00	1.25
423	Rival League Relief Aces (Roy Face, Hoyt Wilhelm)	9.00	4.50	2.75
424	Al McBean	4.00	2.00	1.25
425	Carl Yastrzemski	75.00	37.50	22.00
426	Bob Farley	4.00	2.00	1.25
427	Jake Wood	4.00	2.00	1.25
428	Joe Hicks	4.00	2.00	1.25
429	Bill O'Dell	4.00	2.00	1.25
430	Tony Kubek	15.00	7.50	4.50
431	***Bob Rodgers***	4.00	2.00	1.25
432	Jim Pendleton	4.00	2.00	1.25
433	Jim Archer	4.00	2.00	1.25
434	Clay Dalrymple	4.00	2.00	1.25
435	Larry Sherry	4.00	2.00	1.25
436	Felix Mantilla	4.00	2.00	1.25
437	Ray Moore	4.00	2.00	1.25
438	Dick Brown	4.00	2.00	1.25
439	Jerry Buchek	4.00	2.00	1.25
440	Joe Jay	4.00	2.00	1.25
441a	6th Series Checklist (430-506) (Large "CHECKLIST.")	9.00	4.50	2.75
441b	6th Series Checklist (430-506) (Small "CHECKLIST.")	9.00	4.50	2.75
442	Wes Stock	4.00	2.00	1.25
443	Del Crandall	4.00	2.00	1.25
444	Ted Wills	4.00	2.00	1.25

445	Vic Power	4.00	2.00	1.25
446	Don Elston	4.00	2.00	1.25
447	Willie Kirkland	7.00	3.50	2.00
448	Joe Gibbon	7.00	3.50	2.00
449	Jerry Adair	7.00	3.50	2.00
450	Jim O'Toole	7.00	3.50	2.00
451	***Jose Tartabull***	7.00	3.50	2.00
452	Earl Averill	7.00	3.50	2.00
453	Cal McLish	7.00	3.50	2.00
454	Floyd Robinson	7.00	3.50	2.00
455	Luis Arroyo	7.00	3.50	2.00
456	Joe Amalfitano	7.00	3.50	2.00
457	Lou Clinton	7.00	3.50	2.00
458a	Bob Buhl ("M" on cap)	17.50	8.75	5.25
458b	Bob Buhl (Plain cap.)	15.00	7.50	4.50
459	Ed Bailey	7.00	3.50	2.00
460	Jim Bunning	20.00	10.00	6.00
461	***Ken Hubbs***	15.00	7.50	4.50
462a	Willie Tasby ("W" on cap)	17.50	8.75	5.25
462b	Willie Tasby (Plain cap.)	16.00	8.00	4.75
463	Hank Bauer	9.00	4.50	2.75
464	***Al Jackson***	7.00	3.50	2.00
465	Cincinnati Reds Team	11.00	5.50	3.25
466	Norm Cash/AS	13.50	6.75	4.00
467	Chuck Schilling/AS	7.00	3.50	2.00
468	Brooks Robinson/AS	15.00	7.50	4.50
469	Luis Aparicio/AS	11.00	5.50	3.25
470	Al Kaline/AS	20.00	10.00	6.00
471	Mickey Mantle/AS	125.00	60.00	35.00
472	Rocky Colavito/AS	12.00	6.00	3.50
473	Elston Howard/AS	10.00	5.00	3.00
474	Frank Lary/AS	7.00	3.50	2.00
475	Whitey Ford/AS	15.00	7.50	4.50
476	Baltimore Orioles Team	12.50	6.25	3.75
477	Andre Rodgers	7.00	3.50	2.00
478	Don Zimmer	12.50	6.25	3.75
479	***Joel Horlen***	7.00	3.50	2.00
480	Harvey Kuenn	7.00	3.50	2.00
481	Vic Wertz	7.00	3.50	2.00
482	Sam Mele	7.00	3.50	2.00
483	Don McMahon	7.00	3.50	2.00
484	Dick Schofield	7.00	3.50	2.00
485	Pedro Ramos	7.00	3.50	2.00
486	Jim Gilliam	12.00	6.00	3.50
487	Jerry Lynch	7.00	3.50	2.00
488	Hal Brown	7.00	3.50	2.00
489	Julio Gotay	7.00	3.50	2.00
490	Clete Boyer	13.50	6.75	4.00
491	Leon Wagner	7.00	3.50	2.00
492	Hal Smith	7.00	3.50	2.00
493	Danny McDevitt	7.00	3.50	2.00
494	Sammy White	7.00	3.50	2.00
495	Don Cardwell	7.00	3.50	2.00
496	Wayne Causey	7.00	3.50	2.00
497	Ed Bouchee	7.00	3.50	2.00
498	Jim Donohue	7.00	3.50	2.00
499	Zoilo Versalles	7.00	3.50	2.00
500	Duke Snider	40.00	20.00	12.00
501	Claude Osteen	7.00	3.50	2.00
502	Hector Lopez	7.00	3.50	2.00
503	Danny Murtaugh	7.00	3.50	2.00
504	Eddie Bressoud	7.00	3.50	2.00
505	Juan Marichal	30.00	15.00	9.00
506	Charley Maxwell	7.00	3.50	2.00
507	Ernie Broglio	7.00	3.50	2.00
508	Gordy Coleman	7.00	3.50	2.00
509	***Dave Giusti***	7.00	3.50	2.00
510	Jim Lemon	7.00	3.50	2.00
511	Bubba Phillips	7.00	3.50	2.00
512	Mike Fornieles	7.00	3.50	2.00
513	Whitey Herzog	7.00	3.50	2.00
514	Sherm Lollar	7.00	3.50	2.00
515	Stan Williams	7.00	3.50	2.00
516a	7th Series Checklist (507-598) (Boxes are yellow.)	9.00	4.50	2.75
516b	7th Series Checklist (507-598) (Boxes are white.)	9.00	4.50	2.75
517	Dave Wickersham	7.00	3.50	2.00
518	Lee Maye	7.00	3.50	2.00
519	Bob Johnson	7.00	3.50	2.00
520	Bob Friend	7.00	3.50	2.00
521	Jacke Davis	7.00	3.50	2.00
522	Lindy McDaniel	7.00	3.50	2.00
523	Russ Nixon/SP	15.00	7.50	4.50
524	Howie Nunn/SP	15.00	7.50	4.50
525	George Thomas	10.00	5.00	3.00
526	Hal Woodeshick/SP	15.00	7.50	4.50
527	***Dick McAuliffe***	10.00	5.00	3.00
528	Turk Lown	10.00	5.00	3.00
529	John Schaive/SP	15.00	7.50	4.50
530	Bob Gibson/SP	85.00	42.50	25.00
531	Bobby G. Smith	10.00	5.00	3.00
532	Dick Stigman	10.00	5.00	3.00
533	Charley Lau/SP	15.00	7.50	4.50
534	Tony Gonzalez/SP	15.00	7.50	4.50
535	Ed Roebuck	10.00	5.00	3.00
536	Dick Gernert	10.00	5.00	3.00
537	Cleveland Indians Team	20.00	10.00	6.00
538	Jack Sanford	10.00	5.00	3.00
539	Billy Moran	10.00	5.00	3.00
540	Jim Landis/SP	15.00	7.50	4.50
541	Don Nottebart/SP	15.00	7.50	4.50
542	Dave Philley	10.00	5.00	3.00
543	Bob Allen/SP	15.00	7.50	4.50
544	Willie McCovey/SP	70.00	35.00	20.00
545	Hoyt Wilhelm/SP	40.00	20.00	12.00
546	Moe Thacker/SP	15.00	7.50	4.50
547	Don Ferrarese	10.00	5.00	3.00
548	Bobby Del Greco	10.00	5.00	3.00
549	Bill Rigney/SP	15.00	7.50	4.50
550	Art Mahaffey/SP	15.00	7.50	4.50
551	Harry Bright	10.00	5.00	3.00
552	Chicago Cubs Team/SP	35.00	17.50	10.00
553	Jim Coates	10.00	5.00	3.00
554	Bubba Morton/SP	15.00	7.50	4.50
555	John Buzhardt/SP	15.00	7.50	4.50
556	Al Spangler	10.00	5.00	3.00
557	Bob Anderson/SP	15.00	7.50	4.50
558	John Goryl	10.00	5.00	3.00
559	Mike Higgins	10.00	5.00	3.00
560	Chuck Estrada/SP	15.00	7.50	4.50
561	Gene Oliver/SP	15.00	7.50	4.50
562	Bill Henry	10.00	5.00	3.00
563	Ken Aspromonte	10.00	5.00	3.00
564	Bob Grim	10.00	5.00	3.00
565	Jose Pagan	10.00	5.00	3.00
566	Marty Kutyna/SP	15.00	7.50	4.50
567	Tracy Stallard/SP	15.00	7.50	4.50
568	Jim Golden	10.00	5.00	3.00
569	Ed Sadowski/SP	15.00	7.50	4.50
570	Bill Stafford	10.00	5.00	3.00
571	Billy Klaus/SP	15.00	7.50	4.50
572	Bob Miller/SP	15.00	7.50	4.50
573	Johnny Logan	10.00	5.00	3.00
574	Dean Stone	10.00	5.00	3.00
575	Red Schoendienst	25.00	12.50	7.50
576	Russ Kemmerer/SP	15.00	7.50	4.50
577	Dave Nicholson/SP	15.00	7.50	4.50
578	Jim Duffalo	10.00	5.00	3.00
579	Jim Schaffer/SP	15.00	7.50	4.50
580	Bill Monbouquette	10.00	5.00	3.00
581	Mel Roach	10.00	5.00	3.00
582	Ron Piche	10.00	5.00	3.00
583	Larry Osborne	10.00	5.00	3.00
584	Minnesota Twins Team/SP	40.00	20.00	12.00
585	Glen Hobbie/SP	15.00	7.50	4.50
586	Sammy Esposito/SP	15.00	7.50	4.50
587	Frank Funk/SP	15.00	7.50	4.50
588	Birdie Tebbetts	10.00	5.00	3.00
589	Bob Turley	17.50	8.75	5.25
590	Curt Flood	17.50	8.75	5.25
591	Rookie Parade Pitchers ***(Sam McDowell, Ron Nischwitz, Art Quirk, Dick Radatz, Ron Taylor)***	40.00	20.00	12.00
592	Rookie Parade Pitchers **(Bo Belinsky, Joe Bonikowski, Jim Bouton, Dan Pfister, Dave Stenhouse)**	45.00	22.50	13.50
593	Rookie Parade Pitchers ***(Craig Anderson, Jack Hamilton, Jack Lamabe, Bob Moorhead, Bob Veale)***	40.00	20.00	12.00
594	Rookie Parade Catchers ***(Doug Camilli, Doc Edwards, Don Pavletich, Ken Retzer, Bob Uecker)***	65.00	32.50	20.00
595	Rookie Parade Infielders **(Ed Charles, Marlin Coughtry, Bob Sadowski, Felix Torres)**	25.00	12.50	7.50
596	Rookie Parade Infielders ***(Bernie Allen, Phil Linz, Joe Pepitone, Rich Rollins)***	55.00	27.50	16.50
597	Rookie Parade Infielders **(Rod Kanehl, Jim McKnight, Denis Menke, Amado Samuel)**	40.00	20.00	12.00
598	Rookie Parade Outfielders ***(Howie Goss, Jim Hickman, Manny Jimenez, Al Luplow, Ed Olivares)***	70.00	20.00	12.00

1962 Topps Baseball Bucks

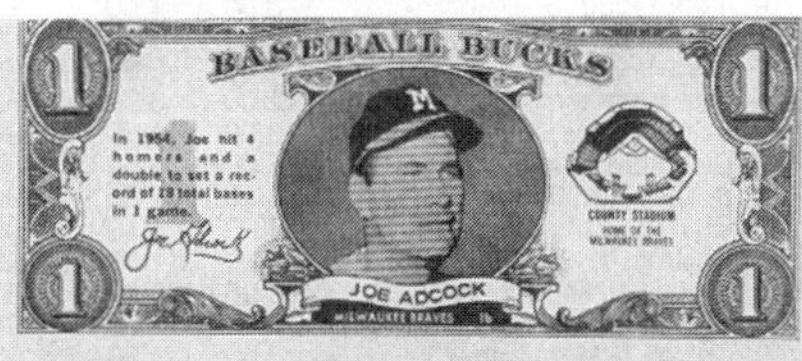

Issued in their own one-cent package, "Baseball Bucks" measure 4-1/8" x 1-3/4", were printed in black on green paper and designed to resemble dollar bills. The center player portrait has a banner underneath with the player's name. His home park is shown on the right and there is some biographical information at left. The back features a large denomination, with the player's league and team logo on either side. Poorly centered examples of this issue are the rule, rather than the exception. Sixty-two of the players appear on facsimile $1 notes. There are 24 $5 stars and 10 $10 superstars. Baseball Bucks are graded without regard to the vertical fold with which they were issued.

		NM	EX	VG
Complete Set (96):		2,000	1,000	600.00
Common Player:		7.50	3.75	2.25
Wax Pack:		175.00		
(1)	Hank Aaron ($5)	50.00	25.00	15.00
(2)	Joe Adcock	7.50	3.75	2.25
(3)	George Altman	7.50	3.75	2.25
(4)	Jim Archer	7.50	3.75	2.25
(5)	Richie Ashburn ($5)	40.00	20.00	12.00
(6)	Ernie Banks ($10)	45.00	22.00	13.50
(7)	Earl Battey	7.50	3.75	2.25
(8)	Gus Bell	7.50	3.75	2.25
(9)	Yogi Berra ($5)	40.00	20.00	12.00
(10)	Ken Boyer ($10)	15.00	7.50	4.50
(11)	Jackie Brandt	7.50	3.75	2.25
(12)	Jim Bunning	15.00	7.50	4.50
(13)	Lou Burdette ($5)	7.50	3.75	2.25
(14)	Don Cardwell	7.50	3.75	2.25
(15)	Norm Cash ($5)	15.00	7.50	4.50
(16)	Orlando Cepeda ($5)	30.00	15.00	9.00
(17)	Roberto Clemente ($5)	200.00	100.00	60.00
(18)	Rocky Colavito ($5)	25.00	12.50	7.50
(19)	Chuck Cottier	7.50	3.75	2.25
(20)	Roger Craig	7.50	3.75	2.25
(21)	Bennie Daniels	7.50	3.75	2.25
(22)	Don Demeter	7.50	3.75	2.25
(23)	Don Drysdale	30.00	15.00	9.00
(24)	Chuck Estrada	7.50	3.75	2.25
(25)	Dick Farrell	7.50	3.75	2.25
(26)	Whitey Ford ($10)	40.00	20.00	12.00
(27)	Nellie Fox ($5)	30.00	15.00	9.00
(28)	Tito Francona	7.50	3.75	2.25
(29)	Bob Friend	7.50	3.75	2.25
(30)	Jim Gentile ($5)	7.50	3.75	2.25
(31)	Dick Gernert	7.50	3.75	2.25
(32)	Lenny Green	7.50	3.75	2.25
(33)	Dick Groat	7.50	3.75	2.25
(34)	Woody Held	7.50	3.75	2.25
(35)	Don Hoak	7.50	3.75	2.25
(36)	Gil Hodges ($5)	25.00	12.50	7.50
(37)	Frank Howard	10.00	5.00	3.00
(38)	Elston Howard	10.00	5.00	3.00
(39)	Dick Howser	7.50	3.75	2.25
(40)	Ken Hunt	7.50	3.75	2.25
(41)	Larry Jackson	7.50	3.75	2.25
(42)	Joe Jay	7.50	3.75	2.25
(43)	Al Kaline	30.00	15.00	9.00
(44)	Harmon Killebrew ($5)	40.00	20.00	12.00
(45)	Sandy Koufax ($5)	75.00	37.00	22.00
(46)	Harvey Kuenn	7.50	3.75	2.25
(47)	Jim Landis	7.50	3.75	2.25
(48)	Norm Larker	7.50	3.75	2.25
(49)	Frank Lary ($5)	7.50	3.75	2.25
(50)	Jerry Lumpe	7.50	3.75	2.25
(51)	Art Mahaffey	7.50	3.75	2.25
(52)	Frank Malzone	7.50	3.75	2.25
(53)	Felix Mantilla	7.50	3.75	2.25
(54)	Mickey Mantle ($10)	350.00	175.00	105.00
(55)	Roger Maris ($10)	45.00	22.00	13.50
(56)	Ed Mathews ($10)	35.00	17.50	10.50
(57)	Willie Mays ($10)	65.00	32.00	19.50
(58)	Ken McBride	7.50	3.75	2.25
(59)	Mike McCormick	7.50	3.75	2.25
(60)	Stu Miller	7.50	3.75	2.25
(61)	Minnie Minoso	10.00	5.00	3.00
(62)	Wally Moon ($5)	7.50	3.75	2.25
(63)	Stan Musial ($10)	60.00	30.00	18.00
(64)	Danny O'Connell	7.50	3.75	2.25
(65)	Jim O'Toole	7.50	3.75	2.25
(66)	Camilo Pascual ($5)	7.50	3.75	2.25
(67)	Jim Perry	7.50	3.75	2.25
(68)	Jimmy Piersall ($5)	12.00	6.00	3.50
(69)	Vada Pinson ($5)	12.00	6.00	3.50
(70)	Juan Pizarro	7.50	3.75	2.25
(71)	Johnny Podres	10.00	5.00	3.00
(72)	Vic Power ($5)	7.50	3.75	2.25
(73)	Bob Purkey	7.50	3.75	2.25
(74)	Pedro Ramos	7.50	3.75	2.25
(75)	Brooks Robinson ($5)	30.00	15.00	9.00
(76)	Floyd Robinson	7.50	3.75	2.25
(77)	Frank Robinson ($10)	35.00	17.50	10.50
(78)	Johnny Romano	7.50	3.75	2.25
(79)	Pete Runnels ($5)	7.50	3.75	2.25
(80)	Don Schwall	7.50	3.75	2.25
(81)	Bobby Shantz ($5)	7.50	3.75	2.25
(82)	Norm Siebern	7.50	3.75	2.25
(83)	Roy Sievers ($5)	7.50	3.75	2.25
(84)	Hal (W.) Smith	7.50	3.75	2.25
(85)	Warren Spahn ($10)	40.00	20.00	12.00
(86)	Dick Stuart	7.50	3.75	2.25
(87)	Tony Taylor	7.50	3.75	2.25
(88)	Lee Thomas	7.50	3.75	2.25
(89)	Gus Triandos	7.50	3.75	2.25
(90)	Leon Wagner	7.50	3.75	2.25
(91)	Jerry Walker	7.50	3.75	2.25
(92)	Bill White	7.50	3.75	2.25
(93)	Billy Williams	15.00	7.50	4.50
(94)	Gene Woodling	7.50	3.75	2.25
(95)	Early Wynn ($5)	15.00	7.50	4.50
(96)	Carl Yastrzemski	40.00	20.00	12.00

1962 Topps Stamps

An artistic improvement over the somewhat drab Topps stamps of the previous year, the 1962 stamps, 1-3/8" x 1-7/8", had color player photographs set on red or yellow backgrounds. As in 1961, they were issued in two-stamp panels as insert with Topps baseball cards. A change from 1961 was the inclusion of team emblems in the set. A complete set consists of 201 stamps; Roy Sievers was originally portrayed on the wrong team - Athletics - and was later corrected to the Phillies.

	NM	EX	VG
Complete Set (200):	800.00	400.00	240.00
Common Player:	3.00	1.50	.90
Stamp Album (Red):	60.00	30.00	18.00
(1) Hank Aaron	15.00	7.50	4.50
(2) Jerry Adair	3.00	1.50	.90
(3) Joe Adcock	3.00	1.50	.90
(4) Bob Allison	3.00	1.50	.90
(5) Felipe Alou	4.00	2.00	1.25
(6) George Altman	3.00	1.50	.90
(7) Joe Amalfitano	3.00	1.50	.90
(8) Ruben Amaro	3.00	1.50	.90
(9) Luis Aparicio	6.00	3.00	1.75
(10) Jim Archer	3.00	1.50	.90
(11) Bob Aspromonte	3.00	1.50	.90
(12) Ed Bailey	3.00	1.50	.90
(13) Jack Baldschun	3.00	1.50	.90
(14) Ernie Banks	9.00	4.50	2.75
(15) Earl Battey	3.00	1.50	.90
(16) Gus Bell	3.00	1.50	.90
(17) Yogi Berra	12.00	6.00	3.50
(18) Dick Bertell	3.00	1.50	.90
(19) Steve Bilko	3.00	1.50	.90
(20) Frank Bolling	3.00	1.50	.90
(21) Steve Boros	3.00	1.50	.90
(22) Ted Bowsfield	3.00	1.50	.90
(23) Clete Boyer	3.00	1.50	.90
(24) Ken Boyer	4.00	2.00	1.25
(25) Jackie Brandt	3.00	1.50	.90
(26) Bill Bruton	3.00	1.50	.90
(27) Jim Bunning	6.00	3.00	1.75
(28) Lou Burdette	3.00	1.50	.90
(29) Smoky Burgess	3.00	1.50	.90
(30) Johnny Callizon (Callison)	3.00	1.50	.90
(31) Don Cardwell	3.00	1.50	.90
(32) Camilo Carreon	3.00	1.50	.90
(33) Norm Cash	4.00	2.00	1.25
(34) Orlando Cepeda	6.00	3.00	1.75
(35) Roberto Clemente	20.00	10.00	6.00
(36) Ty Cline	3.00	1.50	.90
(37) Rocky Colavito	6.00	3.00	1.75
(38) Gordon Coleman	3.00	1.50	.90
(39) Chuck Cottier	3.00	1.50	.90
(40) Roger Craig	3.00	1.50	.90
(41) Del Crandall	3.00	1.50	.90
(42) Pete Daley	3.00	1.50	.90
(43) Clay Dalrymple	3.00	1.50	.90
(44) Bennie Daniels	3.00	1.50	.90
(45) Jim Davenport	3.00	1.50	.90
(46) Don Demeter	3.00	1.50	.90
(47) Dick Donovan	3.00	1.50	.90
(48) Don Drysdale	10.00	5.00	3.00
(49) John Edwards	3.00	1.50	.90
(50) Dick Ellsworth	3.00	1.50	.90
(51) Chuck Estrada	3.00	1.50	.90
(52) Roy Face	3.00	1.50	.90
(53) Ron Fairly	3.00	1.50	.90
(54) Dick Farrell	3.00	1.50	.90
(55) Whitey Ford	12.00	6.00	3.50
(56) Mike Fornieles	3.00	1.50	.90
(57) Nellie Fox	7.00	3.50	2.00
(58) Tito Francona	3.00	1.50	.90
(59) Gene Freese	3.00	1.50	.90
(60) Bob Friend	3.00	1.50	.90
(61) Gary Geiger	3.00	1.50	.90
(62) Jim Gentile	3.00	1.50	.90
(63) Tony Gonzalez	3.00	1.50	.90
(64) Lenny Green	3.00	1.50	.90
(65) Dick Groat	3.00	1.50	.90
(66) Ron Hansen	3.00	1.50	.90
(67) Al Heist	3.00	1.50	.90
(68) Woody Held	3.00	1.50	.90
(69) Ray Herbert	3.00	1.50	.90
(70) Chuck Hinton	3.00	1.50	.90
(71) Don Hoak	3.00	1.50	.90
(72) Glen Hobbie	3.00	1.50	.90
(73) Gil Hodges	6.00	3.00	1.75
(74) Jay Hook	3.00	1.50	.90
(75) Elston Howard	4.00	2.00	1.25
(76) Frank Howard	3.00	1.50	.90
(77) Dick Howser	3.00	1.50	.90
(78) Ken Hunt	3.00	1.50	.90
(79) Larry Jackson	3.00	1.50	.90
(80) Julian Javier	3.00	1.50	.90
(81) Joe Jay	3.00	1.50	.90
(82) Bob Johnson	3.00	1.50	.90
(83) Sam Jones	3.00	1.50	.90
(84) Al Kaline	9.00	4.50	2.75
(85) Eddie Kasko	3.00	1.50	.90
(86) Harmon Killebrew	10.00	5.00	3.00
(87) Sandy Koufax	15.00	7.50	4.50
(88) Jack Kralick	3.00	1.50	.90
(89) Tony Kubek	4.00	2.00	1.25
(90) Harvey Kuenn	3.00	1.50	.90
(91) Jim Landis	3.00	1.50	.90
(92) Hobie Landrith	3.00	1.50	.90
(93) Frank Lary	3.00	1.50	.90
(94) Barry Latman	3.00	1.50	.90
(95) Jerry Lumpe	3.00	1.50	.90
(96) Art Mahaffey	3.00	1.50	.90
(97) Frank Malzone	3.00	1.50	.90
(98) Felix Mantilla	3.00	1.50	.90
(99) Mickey Mantle	50.00	25.00	15.00
(100) Juan Marichal	6.00	3.00	1.75
(101) Roger Maris	13.50	6.75	4.00
(102) J.C. Martin	3.00	1.50	.90
(103) Ed Mathews	9.00	4.50	2.75
(104) Willie Mays	15.00	7.50	4.50
(105) Bill Mazeroski	6.00	3.00	1.75
(106) Ken McBride	3.00	1.50	.90
(107) Tim McCarver	3.00	1.50	.90
(108) Joe McClain	3.00	1.50	.90
(109) Mike McCormick	3.00	1.50	.90
(110) Lindy McDaniel	3.00	1.50	.90
(111) Roy McMillan	3.00	1.50	.90
(112) Bob L. Miller	3.00	1.50	.90
(113) Stu Miller	3.00	1.50	.90
(114) Minnie Minoso	6.00	3.00	1.75
(115) Bill Monbouquette	3.00	1.50	.90
(116) Wally Moon	3.00	1.50	.90
(117) Don Mossi	3.00	1.50	.90
(118) Stan Musial	15.00	7.50	4.50
(119) Russ Nixon	3.00	1.50	.90
(120) Danny O'Connell	3.00	1.50	.90
(121) Jim O'Toole	3.00	1.50	.90
(122) Milt Pappas	3.00	1.50	.90
(123) Camilo Pascual	3.00	1.50	.90
(124) Albie Pearson	3.00	1.50	.90
(125) Jim Perry	3.00	1.50	.90
(126) Bubba Phillips	3.00	1.50	.90
(127) Jimmy Piersall	3.00	1.50	.90
(128) Vada Pinson	3.00	1.50	.90
(129) Juan Pizarro	3.00	1.50	.90
(130) Johnny Podres	3.00	1.50	.90
(131) Leo Posada	3.00	1.50	.90
(132) Vic Power	3.00	1.50	.90
(133) Bob Purkey	3.00	1.50	.90
(134) Pedro Ramos	3.00	1.50	.90
(135) Bobby Richardson	3.00	1.50	.90
(136) Brooks Robinson	10.00	5.00	3.00
(137) Floyd Robinson	3.00	1.50	.90
(138) Frank Robinson	10.00	5.00	3.00
(139) Bob Rodgers	3.00	1.50	.90
(140) Johnny Romano	3.00	1.50	.90
(141) John Roseboro	3.00	1.50	.90
(142) Pete Runnels	3.00	1.50	.90
(143) Ray Sadecki	3.00	1.50	.90
(144) Ron Santo	3.00	1.50	.90
(145) Chuck Schilling	3.00	1.50	.90
(146) Barney Schultz	3.00	1.50	.90
(147) Don Schwall	3.00	1.50	.90
(148) Bobby Shantz	3.00	1.50	.90
(149) Bob Shaw	3.00	1.50	.90
(150) Norm Siebern	3.00	1.50	.90
(151a) Roy Sievers (Kansas City)	3.00	1.50	.90
(151b) Roy Sievers (Philadelphia)	3.00	1.50	.90
(152) Bill Skowron	4.00	2.00	1.25
(153) Hal (W.) Smith	3.00	1.50	.90
(154) Duke Snider	12.00	6.00	3.50
(155) Warren Spahn	9.00	4.50	2.75
(156) Al Spangler	3.00	1.50	.90
(157) Daryl Spencer	3.00	1.50	.90
(158) Gene Stephens	3.00	1.50	.90
(159) Dick Stuart	3.00	1.50	.90
(160) Haywood Sullivan	3.00	1.50	.90
(161) Tony Taylor	3.00	1.50	.90
(162) George Thomas	3.00	1.50	.90
(163) Lee Thomas	3.00	1.50	.90
(164) Bob Tiefenauer	3.00	1.50	.90
(165) Joe Torre	6.00	3.00	1.75
(166) Gus Triandos	3.00	1.50	.90
(167) Bill Tuttle	3.00	1.50	.90
(168) Zoilo Versalles	3.00	1.50	.90
(169) Bill Virdon	3.00	1.50	.90
(170) Leon Wagner	3.00	1.50	.90
(171) Jerry Walker	3.00	1.50	.90
(172) Lee Walls	3.00	1.50	.90
(173) Bill White	3.00	1.50	.90
(174) Hoyt Wilhelm	4.00	2.00	1.25
(175) Billy Williams	6.00	3.00	1.75
(176) Jake Wood	3.00	1.50	.90
(177) Gene Woodling	3.00	1.50	.90
(178) Early Wynn	4.00	2.00	1.25
(179) Carl Yastrzemski	12.00	6.00	3.50
(180) Don Zimmer	3.00	1.50	.90
(181) Baltimore Orioles Logo	3.00	1.50	.90
(182) Boston Red Sox Logo	3.00	1.50	.90
(183) Chicago Cubs Logo	3.00	1.50	.90
(184) Chicago White Sox Logo	3.00	1.50	.90
(185) Cincinnati Reds Logo	3.00	1.50	.90
(186) Cleveland Indians Logo	3.00	1.50	.90
(187) Detroit Tigers Logo	3.00	1.50	.90
(188) Houston Colts Logo	3.00	1.50	.90
(189) Kansas City Athletics Logo	3.00	1.50	.90
(190) Los Angeles Angels Logo	3.00	1.50	.90
(191) Los Angeles Dodgers Logo	3.00	1.50	.90
(192) Milwaukee Braves Logo	3.00	1.50	.90
(193) Minnesota Twins Logo	3.00	1.50	.90
(194) New York Mets Logo	3.00	1.50	.90
(195) New York Yankees Logo	6.00	3.00	1.75
(196) Philadelphia Phillies Logo	3.00	1.50	.90
(197) Pittsburgh Pirates Logo	3.00	1.50	.90
(198) St. Louis Cardinals Logo	3.00	1.50	.90
(199) San Francisco Giants Logo	3.00	1.50	.90
(200) Washington Senators Logo	3.00	1.50	.90

1962 Topps Stamps Panels

Some advanced collectors pursue the 1962 Topps stamps in the form of the two-stamp panels in which they were issued. The 200 different stamps which make up the issue can be found on 245 different two-stamp panels, flanked at left by a smaller tab advertising the accompanying album. The unnumbered stamps are listed here alphabetically according to the name of the player or team which apears on the left end of the panel. Values shown are for full three-piece panels.

	NM	EX	VG
Complete Panel Set (245):	2,750	1,375	825.00
Common Panel:	4.00	2.00	1.25
(1) Hank Aaron/Ted Bowsfield	35.00	17.50	10.50
(2) Jerry Adair/Tony Gonzalez	8.00	4.00	2.50
(3) Joe Adcock/George Thomas	8.00	4.00	2.50
(4) Bob Allison/Jim Davenport	8.00	4.00	2.50
(5) Felipe Alou/Mickey Mantle	100.00	50.00	30.00
(6) Felipe Alou/Chuck Schilling	9.00	4.50	2.75
(7) George Altman/ Rocky Colavito	10.00	5.00	3.00
(8) George Altman/Don Schwall	8.00	4.00	2.50
(9) Joe Amalfitano/Jim Gentile	8.00	4.00	2.50
(10) Joe Amalfitano/Vic Power	8.00	4.00	2.50
(11) Ruben Amaro/ Carl Yastrzemski	30.00	15.00	9.00
(12) Luis Aparicio/Dick Farrell	10.00	5.00	3.00
(13) Luis Aparicio/Al Heist	10.00	5.00	3.00
(14) Bob Aspromonte/Al Kaline	15.00	7.50	4.50
(15) Ed Bailey/Jim Piersall	8.00	4.00	2.50
(16) Ernie Banks/Milt Pappas	20.00	10.00	6.00
(17) Earl Battey/Bob Clemente	35.00	17.50	10.50
(18) Earl Battey/Ed Mathews	12.00	6.00	3.50
(19) Gus Bell/Steve Boros	8.00	4.00	2.50
(20) Gus Bell/Ty Cline	8.00	4.00	2.50
(21) Yogi Berra/Roy Face	20.00	10.00	6.00
(22) Yogi Berra/Jack Kralick	15.00	7.50	4.50
(23) Dick Bertell/Hoyt Wilhelm	10.00	5.00	3.00
(24) Dick Bertell/Don Zimmer	9.00	4.50	2.75
(25) Steve Bilko/Ruben Amaro	8.00	4.00	2.50
(26) Steve Bilko/Roy Sievers	8.00	4.00	2.50
(27) Frank Bolling/Nellie Fox	10.00	5.00	3.00
(28) Steve Boros/Art Mahaffey	8.00	4.00	2.50
(29) Clete Boyer/Chuck Cottier	9.00	4.50	2.75
(30) Ken Boyer/Bob Friend	9.00	4.50	2.75
(31) Jackie Brandt /Frank Robinson	15.00	7.50	4.50
(32) Bill Bruton/Ernie Banks	20.00	10.00	6.00
(33) Bill Bruton/Jay Hook	8.00	4.00	2.50
(34) Jim Bunning/Bob Miller	10.00	5.00	3.00
(35) Jim Bunning/Jim O'Toole	10.00	5.00	3.00
(36) Jim Bunning/Daryl Spencer	10.00	5.00	3.00
(37) Lou Burdette/Ed Mathews	12.00	6.00	3.50
(38) Lou Burdette/Willie Mays	35.00	17.50	10.50
(39) Smoky Burgess/ Bobby Richardson	9.00	4.50	2.75
(40) Johnny Callizon (Callison)/Barry Latman	9.00	4.50	2.75
(41) Johnny Callizon (Callison)/ Frank Malzone	9.00	4.50	2.75
(42) Johnny Callizon (Callison)/ Willie Mays	35.00	17.50	10.50
(43) Don Cardwell/Hoyt Wilhelm	10.00	5.00	3.00
(44) Norm Cash/Dick Bertell	9.00	4.50	2.75
(45) Norm Cash/Don Cardwell	9.00	4.50	2.75
(46) Norm Cash/Dick Howser	9.00	4.50	2.75
(47) Ty Cline/Art Mahaffey	8.00	4.00	2.50
(48) Rocky Colavito/Sam Jones	10.00	5.00	3.00
(49) Gordon Coleman/Pete Daley	8.00	4.00	2.50
(50) Gordon Coleman/ Danny O'Connell	8.00	4.00	2.50
(51) Roger Craig/Ted Bowsfield	8.00	4.00	2.50
(52) Roger Craig/Minnie Minoso	9.00	4.50	2.75
(53) Del Crandall/Clete Boyer	9.00	4.50	2.75
(54) Del Crandall/Ray Sadecki	8.00	4.00	2.50
(55) Pete Daley/Bob Friend	8.00	4.00	2.50
(56) Pete Daley/Mike McCormick	8.00	4.00	2.50
(57) Clay Dalrymple/Woody Held	8.00	4.00	2.50
(58) Clay Dalrymple/Pedro Ramos	8.00	4.00	2.50
(59) Bennie Daniels/Jerry Walker	8.00	4.00	2.50
(60) Jim Davenport/ Harmon Killebrew	15.00	7.50	4.50
(61) Don Demeter/ Haywood Sullivan	8.00	4.00	2.50
(62) Don Demeter/Gus Triandos	8.00	4.00	2.50
(63) Don Demeter/Lee Walls	8.00	4.00	2.50
(64) Dick Donovan/Jerry Adair	8.00	4.00	2.50
(65) Dick Donovan/Jim Perry	8.00	4.00	2.50
(66) Dick Donovan/Vada Pinson	9.00	4.50	2.75
(67) John Edwards/Jerry Walker	8.00	4.00	2.50
(68) Dick Ellsworth/Glen Hobbie	8.00	4.00	2.50
(69) Dick Ellsworth/Pete Runnels	8.00	4.00	2.50
(70) Chuck Estrada/Don Drysdale	12.00	6.00	3.50
(71) Chuck Estrada/Al Kaline	15.00	7.50	4.50
(72) Roy Face/Minnie Minoso	9.00	4.50	2.75
(73) Ron Fairly/Jim Landis	8.00	4.00	2.50
(74) Dick Farrell/Frank Lary	8.00	4.00	2.50
(75) Whitey Ford/Joe Torre	15.00	7.50	4.50
(76) Nellie Fox/Willie Mays	35.00	17.50	10.50
(77) Tito Francona/Ken Boyer	9.00	4.50	2.75
(78) Tito Francona/Bob Johnson	8.00	4.00	2.50
(79) Gene Freese/Bob Allison	8.00	4.00	2.50
(80) Gene Freese/Ernie Banks	15.00	7.50	4.50
(81) Gary Geiger/ Bobby Richardson	9.00	4.50	2.75
(82) Jim Gentile/Hal W. Smith	8.00	4.00	2.50
(83) Dick Groat/Joe McClain	8.00	4.00	2.50
(84) Al Heist/Frank Lary	8.00	4.00	2.50
(85) Woody Held/Orlando Cepeda	10.00	5.00	3.00
(86) Ray Herbert/Frank Bolling	8.00	4.00	2.50
(87) Ray Herbert/Eddie Kasko	8.00	4.00	2.50
(88) Chuck Hinton/Dick Groat	8.00	4.00	2.50
(89) Chuck Hinton/Stu Miller	8.00	4.00	2.50
(90) Don Hoak/Bob Allison	8.00	4.00	2.50
(91) Gil Hodges/Bennie Daniels	10.00	5.00	3.00
(92) Gil Hodges/John Edwards	10.00	5.00	3.00
(93) Elston Howard/Bob Clemente	35.00	17.50	10.50
(94) Dick Howser/Don Zimmer	9.00	4.50	2.75
(95) Ken Hunt/Lenny Green	8.00	4.00	2.50
(96) Larry Jackson/Smoky Burgess	8.00	4.00	2.50
(97) Larry Jackson/Gary Geiger	8.00	4.00	2.50

(98)	Joe Jay/Johnny Romano	8.00	4.00	2.50
(99)	Bob Johnson/Bob Friend	8.00	4.00	2.50
(100)	Al Kaline/Don Hoak	15.00	7.50	4.50
(101)	Eddie Kasko/Nellie Fox	10.00	5.00	3.00
(102)	Sandy Koufax/Joe Adcock	30.00	15.00	9.00
(103)	Sandy Koufax/Hobie Landrith	30.00	15.00	9.00
(104)	Sandy Koufax/Bob Shaw	30.00	15.00	9.00
(105)	Jack Kralick/Minnie Minoso	9.00	4.50	2.75
(106)	Harvey Kuenn/Ken Hunt	8.00	4.00	2.50
(107)	Havey Kuenn/Gene Woodling	8.00	4.00	2.50
(108)	Hobie Landrith/Mike Fornieles	8.00	4.00	2.50
(109)	Barry Latman/Tony Kubek	9.00	4.50	2.75
(110)	Barry Latman/Johnny Podres	8.00	4.00	2.50
(111)	Frank Malzone/Johnny Podres	8.00	4.00	2.50
(112)	Frank Malzone/Duke Snider	15.00	7.50	4.50
(113)	Felix Mantilla/Camilo Carreon	8.00	4.00	2.50
(114)	Mickey Mantle/Hank Aaron	125.00	62.00	37.00
(115)	Mickey Mantle/Dick Stuart	110.00	55.00	33.00
(116)	Juan Marichal/Bill Bruton	12.00	6.00	3.50
(117)	Juan Marichal/Gene Freese	12.00	6.00	3.50
(118)	Juan Marichal/Don Hoak	12.00	6.00	3.50
(119)	Roger Maris/Lou Burdette	20.00	10.00	6.00
(120)	Roger Maris/Nellie Fox	20.00	10.00	6.00
(121)	Roger Maris/Lee Thomas	20.00	10.00	6.00
(122)	J.C. Martin/Felix Mantilla	8.00	4.00	2.50
(123)	J.C. Martin/Barney Schultz	8.00	4.00	2.50
(124)	Willie Mays/Tony Kubek	35.00	17.50	10.50
(125)	Bill Mazeroski/Earl Battey	10.00	5.00	3.00
(126)	Bill Mazeroski/Elston Howard	10.00	5.00	3.00
(127)	Bill Mazeroski/Early Wynn	12.00	6.00	3.50
(128)	Ken McBride/Joe Torre	9.00	4.50	2.75
(129)	Tim McCarver/Bill Tuttle	9.00	4.50	2.75
(130)	Lindy McDaniel/Jim Piersall	8.00	4.00	2.50
(131)	Roy McMillan/Bob Allison	8.00	4.00	2.50
(132)	Roy McMillan/Albie Pearson	8.00	4.00	2.50
(133)	Roy McMillan/Leon Wagner	8.00	4.00	2.50
(134)	Bob Miller/Ron Hansen	8.00	4.00	2.50
(135)	Stu Miller/Joe McCain	8.00	4.00	2.50
(136)	Bill Monbouquette/Don Hoak	8.00	4.00	2.50
(137)	Bill Monbouquette/Joe Torre	9.00	4.50	2.75
(138)	Wally Moon/Frank Malzone	8.00	4.00	2.50
(139)	Wally Moon/Juan Pizarro	8.00	4.00	2.50
(140)	Wally Moon/Brooks Robinson	20.00	10.00	6.00
(141)	Don Mossi/Bill Bruton	8.00	4.00	2.50
(142)	Don Mossi/Johnny Podres	8.00	4.00	2.50
(143)	Don Mossi/Al Spangler	8.00	4.00	2.50
(144)	Stan Musial/Whitey Ford	30.00	15.00	9.00
(145)	Stan Musial/Joe Torre	30.00	15.00	9.00
(146)	Russ Nixon/Ed Bailey	8.00	4.00	2.50
(147)	Russ Nixon/Lindy McDaniel	8.00	4.00	2.50
(148)	Danny O'Connell/ Mike McCormick	8.00	4.00	2.50
(149)	Jim O'Toole/Ron Hansen	8.00	4.00	2.50
(150)	Jim O'Toole/Gene Stephens	8.00	4.00	2.50
(151)	Camilo Pascual/Pete Daley	8.00	4.00	2.50
(152)	Camilo Pascual/Tim McCarver	9.00	4.50	2.75
(153)	Camilo Pascual/Bill Virdon	8.00	4.00	2.50
(154)	Albie Pearson/Julian Javier	8.00	4.00	2.50
(155)	Jim Perry/Frank Howard	8.00	4.00	2.50
(156)	Bubba Phillips/Don Drysdale	12.00	6.00	3.50
(157)	Vada Pinson/Tony Gonzalez	9.00	4.50	2.75
(158)	Vada Pinson/Frank Howard	9.00	4.50	2.75
(159)	Juan Pizarro/Jack Baldschun	8.00	4.00	2.50
(160)	Johnny Podres/Jim Archer	8.00	4.00	2.50
(161)	Leo Posada/Milt Pappas	8.00	4.00	2.50
(162)	Leo Posada/Johnny Romano	8.00	4.00	2.50
(163)	Vic Power/Hal W. Smith	8.00	4.00	2.50
(164)	Bob Purkey/Harmon Killebrew	15.00	7.50	4.50
(165)	Pedro Ramos/ Orlando Cepeda	10.00	5.00	3.00
(166)	Brooks Robinson/ Jack Baldschun	15.00	7.50	4.50
(167)	Brooks Robinson/Duke Snider	20.00	10.00	6.00
(168)	Floyd Robinson/Ron Fairly	8.00	4.00	2.50
(169)	Floyd Robinson/Tony Taylor	8.00	4.00	2.50
(170)	Bob Rodgers/Hank Aaron	35.00	17.50	10.50
(171)	Bob Rodgers/Roger Craig	8.00	4.00	2.50
(172)	Bob Rodgers/Johnny Romano	8.00	4.00	2.50
(173)	Johnny Romano/ Minnie Minoso	9.00	4.50	2.75
(174)	John Roseboro/ Bob Aspromonte	8.00	4.00	2.50
(175)	John Roseboro/ Chuck Estrada	8.00	4.00	2.50
(176)	John Roseboro/Bubba Phillips	8.00	4.00	2.50
(177)	Ray Sadecki/Chuck Cottier	8.00	4.00	2.50
(178)	Ron Santo/Ernie Banks	20.00	10.00	6.00
(179)	Ron Santo/Joe Jay	9.00	4.50	2.75
(180)	Ron Santo/Leo Posada	9.00	4.50	2.75
(181)	Chuck Schilling/Hank Aaron	35.00	17.50	10.50
(182)	Chuck Schilling/Dick Stuart	8.00	4.00	2.50
(183)	Barney Schultz/ Camilo Carreon	8.00	4.00	2.50
(184)	Don Schwall/Sam Jones	8.00	4.00	2.50
(185)	Bobby Shantz/Pete Runnels	8.00	4.00	2.50
(186)	Bob Shaw/Mike Fornieles	8.00	4.00	2.50
(187)	Bob Shaw/George Thomas	8.00	4.00	2.50
(188)	Norm Siebern/Dick Ellsworth	8.00	4.00	2.50
(189)	Norm Siebern/Bobby Shantz	8.00	4.00	2.50
(190)	Norm Siebern/Early Wynn	10.00	5.00	3.00
(191)	Roy Sievers/Carl Yastrzemski	30.00	15.00	9.00
(192)	Bill Skowron/Jim Davenport	9.00	4.50	2.75
(193)	Bill Skowron/Bob Purkey	9.00	4.50	2.75
(194)	Warren Spahn/Whitey Ford	20.00	10.00	6.00
(195)	Al Spangler/Jim Archer	8.00	4.00	2.50
(196)	Al Spangler/Jay Hook	8.00	4.00	2.50
(197)	Daryl Spencer/Gene Stephens	8.00	4.00	2.50
(198)	Haywood Sullivan/ Jerry Lumpe	8.00	4.00	2.50
(199)	Haywood Sullivan/ Billy Williams	10.00	5.00	3.00
(200)	Tony Taylor/Jim Landis	8.00	4.00	2.50
(201)	Lee Thomas/Ed Mathews	12.00	6.00	3.50
(202)	Bob Tiefenauer/Jackie Brandt	8.00	4.00	2.50
(203)	Bob Tiefenauer/Jake Wood	8.00	4.00	2.50
(204)	Gus Triandos/Billy Williams	10.00	5.00	3.00
(205)	Zoilo Versalles/Whitey Ford	12.50	6.25	3.75
(206)	Zoilo Versalles/Stan Musial	30.00	15.00	9.00
(207)	Zoilo Veraalles/Warren Spahn	12.00	6.00	3.50
(208)	Bill Virdon/Bob Friend	8.00	4.00	2.50
(209)	Bill Virdon/Bill Tuttle	8.00	4.00	2.50
(210)	Leon Wagner/Jim Davenport	8.00	4.00	2.50
(211)	Leon Wagner/Julian Javier	8.00	4.00	2.50
(212)	Lee Walls/Jerry Lumpe	8.00	4.00	2.50
(213)	Bill White/Al Kaline	15.00	7.50	4.50
(214)	Bill White/Ken McBride	8.00	4.00	2.50
(215)	Bill White/Bill Monbouquette	8.00	4.00	2.50
(216)	Jake Wood/Frank Robinson	12.00	6.00	3.50
(217)	Gene Woodling/Lenny Green	8.00	4.00	2.50
(218)	Early Wynn/Glen Hobbie	10.00	5.00	3.00
(219)	Early Wynn/Ed Mathews	15.00	7.50	4.50
(220)	Angels/Athletics	8.00	4.00	2.50
(221)	Angels/Colts	9.00	4.50	2.75
(222)	Angels/Orioles	8.00	4.00	2.50
(223)	Athletics/Mets	10.00	5.00	3.00
(224)	Athletics/Pirates	9.00	4.50	2.75
(225)	Cardinals/Indians	9.00	4.50	2.75
(226)	Colts/Mets	12.00	6.00	3.50
(227)	Colts/Twins	9.00	4.50	2.75
(228)	Cubs/Senators	9.00	4.50	2.75
(229)	Giants/Red Sox	9.00	4.50	2.75
(230)	Giants/Tigers	9.00	4.50	2.75
(231)	Giants/White Sox	12.00	6.00	3.50
(232)	Indians/Reds	9.00	4.50	2.75
(233)	Mets/Dodgers	10.00	5.00	3.00
(234)	Orioles/Pirates	9.00	4.50	2.75
(235)	Phillies/Senators	9.00	4.50	2.75
(236)	Red Sox/Braves	9.00	4.50	2.75
(237)	Red Sox/Phillies	9.00	4.50	2.75
(238)	Reds/Indians	9.00	4.50	2.75
(239)	Reds/Yankees	12.50	6.25	3.75
(240)	Tigers/Braves	9.00	4.50	2.75
(241)	Twins/Dodgers	12.50	6.25	3.75
(242)	White Sox/Cubs	10.00	5.00	3.00
(243)	White Sox/Phillies	10.00	5.00	3.00
(244)	Yankees/Cardinals	12.50	6.25	3.75
(245)	Yankees/Reds	12.50	6.25	3.75

1963 Topps

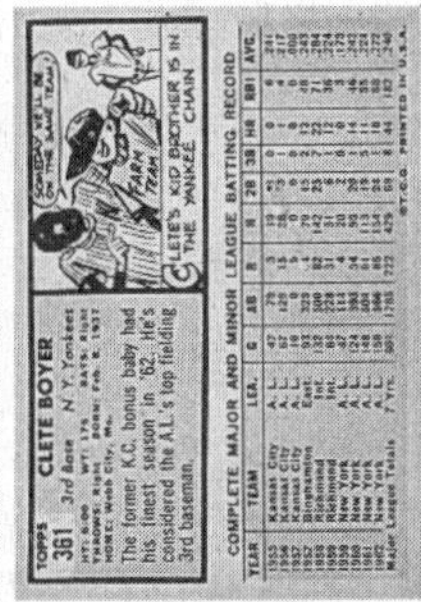

Although the number of cards dropped to 576, the 1963 Topps set is among the most popular of the 1960s. A color photo dominates the 2-1/2" x 3-1/2" card, but a colored circle at the bottom carries a black and white portrait as well. A colored band gives the player's name, team and position. The backs again feature career statistics and a cartoon, career summary and brief biographical details. The set is somewhat unlike those immediately preceding it in that there are fewer specialty cards. The major groupings are statistical leaders, World Series highlights and rookies. It is one rookie which makes the set special - Pete Rose. As one of most avidly sought cards in history and a high-numbered card at that, the Rose rookie card accounts for much of the value of a complete set.

		NM	EX	VG
Complete Set (576):		5,250	2,600	1,550
Common Player (1-446):		4.00	2.00	1.25
Common Player (447-576):		9.00	4.50	2.75
1	N.L. Batting Leaders (Hank Aaron, Bill White, Frank Robinson, Tommy Davis, Stan Musial)	60.00	15.00	9.00
2	A.L. Batting Leaders (Chuck Hinton, Mickey Mantle, Floyd Robinson, Pete Runnels, Norm Siebern)	30.00	15.00	9.00
3	N.L. Home Run Leaders (Hank Aaron, Ernie Banks, Orlando Cepeda, Willie Mays, Frank Robinson)	40.00	20.00	12.00
4	A.L. Home Run Leaders (Norm Cash, Rocky Colavito, Jim Gentile, Harmon Killebrew, Roger Maris, Leon Wagner)	20.00	10.00	6.00
5	N.L. E.R.A. Leaders (Don Drysdale, Bob Gibson, Sandy Koufax, Bob Shaw, Bob Purkey)	17.50	8.75	5.25
6	A.L. E.R.A. Leaders (Hank Aguirre, Dean Chance, Eddie Fisher, Whitey Ford, Robin Roberts)	10.00	5.00	3.00
7	N.L. Pitching Leaders (Don Drysdale, Joe Jay, Art Mahaffey, Billy O'Dell, Bob Purkey, Jack Sanford)	12.00	6.00	3.50
8	A.L. Pitching Leaders (Jim Bunning, Dick Donovan, Ray Herbert, Camilo Pascual, Ralph Terry)	10.00	5.00	3.00
9	N.L. Strikeout Leaders (Don Drysdale, Dick Farrell, Bob Gibson, Sandy Koufax, Billy O'Dell)	20.00	10.00	6.00
10	A.L. Strikeout Leaders (Jim Bunning, Jim Kaat, Camilo Pascual, Juan Pizarro, Ralph Terry)	9.00	4.50	2.75
11	Lee Walls	4.00	2.00	1.25
12	Steve Barber	4.00	2.00	1.25
13	Philadelphia Phillies Team	7.00	3.50	2.00
14	Pedro Ramos	4.00	2.00	1.25
15	Ken Hubbs	10.00	5.00	3.00
16	Al Smith	4.00	2.00	1.25
17	Ryne Duren	4.00	2.00	1.25
18	Buc Blasters (Smoky Burgess, Roberto Clemente, Bob Skinner, Dick Stuart)	40.00	20.00	12.00
19	Pete Burnside	4.00	2.00	1.25
20	Tony Kubek	12.50	6.25	3.75
21	Marty Keough	4.00	2.00	1.25
22	Curt Simmons	4.00	2.00	1.25
23	Ed Lopat	4.00	2.00	1.25
24	Bob Bruce	4.00	2.00	1.25
25	Al Kaline	35.00	17.50	10.00
26	Ray Moore	4.00	2.00	1.25
27	Choo Choo Coleman	4.00	2.00	1.25
28	Mike Fornieles	4.00	2.00	1.25
29a	1962 Rookie Stars (**Sammy Ellis, Ray Culp, John Boozer, Jesse Gonder**)	6.00	3.00	1.75
29b	1963 Rookie Stars (**Sammy Ellis, Ray Culp, John Boozer, Jesse Gonder**)	4.00	2.00	1.25
30	Harvey Kuenn	4.00	2.00	1.25
31	Cal Koonce	4.00	2.00	1.25
32	Tony Gonzalez	4.00	2.00	1.25
33	Bo Belinsky	4.00	2.00	1.25
34	Dick Schofield	4.00	2.00	1.25
35	John Buzhardt	4.00	2.00	1.25
36	Jerry Kindall	4.00	2.00	1.25
37	Jerry Lynch	4.00	2.00	1.25
38	Bud Daley	4.00	2.00	1.25
39	Los Angeles Angels Team	7.00	3.50	2.00
40	Vic Power	4.00	2.00	1.25
41	Charlie Lau	4.00	2.00	1.25
42	Stan Williams	4.00	2.00	1.25
43	Veteran Masters (Casey Stengel, Gene Woodling)	7.50	3.75	2.25
44	Terry Fox	4.00	2.00	1.25
45	Bob Aspromonte	4.00	2.00	1.25
46	***Tommie Aaron***	5.00	2.50	1.50
47	Don Lock	4.00	2.00	1.25
48	Birdie Tebbetts	4.00	2.00	1.25
49	***Dal Maxvill***	4.00	2.00	1.25
50	Bill Pierce	4.00	2.00	1.25
51	George Alusik	4.00	2.00	1.25
52	Chuck Schilling	4.00	2.00	1.25
53	Joe Moeller	4.00	2.00	1.25
54a	1962 Rookie Stars (***Nelson Mathews, Harry Fanok, Jack Cullen, Dave DeBusschere***)	10.00	5.00	3.00
54b	1963 Rookie Stars (***Jack Cullen, Dave DeBusschere, Harry Fanok, Nelson Mathews***)	8.00	4.00	2.50
55	Bill Virdon	4.00	2.00	1.25
56	Dennis Bennett	4.00	2.00	1.25
57	Billy Moran	4.00	2.00	1.25
58	Bob Will	4.00	2.00	1.25
59	Craig Anderson	4.00	2.00	1.25
60	Elston Howard	9.00	4.50	2.75
61	Ernie Bowman	4.00	2.00	1.25
62	Bob Hendley	4.00	2.00	1.25
63	Cincinnati Reds Team	7.00	3.50	2.00
64	Dick McAuliffe	4.00	2.00	1.25
65	Jackie Brandt	4.00	2.00	1.25
66	Mike Joyce	4.00	2.00	1.25
67	Ed Charles	4.00	2.00	1.25
68	Friendly Foes (Gil Hodges, Duke Snider)	15.00	7.50	4.50
69	Bud Zipfel	4.00	2.00	1.25
70	Jim O'Toole	4.00	2.00	1.25
71	***Bobby Wine***	4.00	2.00	1.25
72	Johnny Romano	4.00	2.00	1.25
73	Bobby Bragan	4.00	2.00	1.25
74	***Denver Lemaster***	4.00	2.00	1.25
75	Bob Allison	4.00	2.00	1.25
76	Earl Wilson	4.00	2.00	1.25
77	Al Spangler	4.00	2.00	1.25
78	Marv Throneberry	4.00	2.00	1.25
79	1st Series Checklist (1-88)	6.00	3.00	1.75
80	Jim Gilliam	6.00	3.00	1.75
81	Jimmie Schaffer	4.00	2.00	1.25
82	Ed Rakow	4.00	2.00	1.25
83	Charley James	4.00	2.00	1.25
84	Ron Kline	4.00	2.00	1.25
85	Tom Haller	4.00	2.00	1.25
86	Charley Maxwell	4.00	2.00	1.25
87	Bob Veale	4.00	2.00	1.25
88	Ron Hansen	4.00	2.00	1.25
89	Dick Stigman	4.00	2.00	1.25
90	Gordy Coleman	4.00	2.00	1.25
91	Dallas Green	4.00	2.00	1.25
92	Hector Lopez	4.00	2.00	1.25
93	Galen Cisco	4.00	2.00	1.25
94	Bob Schmidt	4.00	2.00	1.25
95	Larry Jackson	4.00	2.00	1.25
96	Lou Clinton	4.00	2.00	1.25
97	Bob Duliba	4.00	2.00	1.25
98	George Thomas	4.00	2.00	1.25
99	Jim Umbricht	4.00	2.00	1.25
100	Joe Cunningham	4.00	2.00	1.25
101	Joe Gibbon	4.00	2.00	1.25
102a	2nd Series Checklist (89-176) ("Checklist" in red on yellow.)	6.00	3.00	1.75

102b	2nd Series Checklist (89-176) ("Checklist" in white on red.)	10.00	5.00	3.00
103	Chuck Essegian	4.00	2.00	1.25
104	Lew Krausse	4.00	2.00	1.25
105	Ron Fairly	4.00	2.00	1.25
106	Bob Bolin	4.00	2.00	1.25
107	Jim Hickman	4.00	2.00	1.25
108	Hoyt Wilhelm	15.00	7.50	4.50
109	Lee Maye	4.00	2.00	1.25
110	Rich Rollins	4.00	2.00	1.25
111	Al Jackson	4.00	2.00	1.25
112	Dick Brown	4.00	2.00	1.25
113	Don Landrum (Photo actally Ron Santo.)	4.00	2.00	1.25
114	Dan Osinski	4.00	2.00	1.25
115	Carl Yastrzemski	40.00	20.00	12.00
116	Jim Brosnan	4.00	2.00	1.25
117	Jacke Davis	4.00	2.00	1.25
118	Sherm Lollar	4.00	2.00	1.25
119	Bob Lillis	4.00	2.00	1.25
120	Roger Maris	60.00	30.00	18.00
121	Jim Hannan	4.00	2.00	1.25
122	Julio Gotay	4.00	2.00	1.25
123	Frank Howard	4.00	2.00	1.25
124	Dick Howser	4.00	2.00	1.25
125	Robin Roberts	15.00	7.50	4.50
126	Bob Uecker	17.50	8.75	5.25
127	Bill Tuttle	4.00	2.00	1.25
128	Matty Alou	4.00	2.00	1.25
129	Gary Bell	4.00	2.00	1.25
130	Dick Groat	4.00	2.00	1.25
131	Washington Senators Team	7.00	3.50	2.00
132	Jack Hamilton	4.00	2.00	1.25
133	Gene Freese	4.00	2.00	1.25
134	Bob Scheffing	4.00	2.00	1.25
135	Richie Ashburn	15.00	7.50	4.50
136	Ike Delock	4.00	2.00	1.25
137	Mack Jones	4.00	2.00	1.25
138	Pride of N.L. (Willie Mays, Stan Musial)	40.00	20.00	12.00
139	Earl Averill	4.00	2.00	1.25
140	Frank Lary	4.00	2.00	1.25
141	***Manny Mota***	6.00	3.00	1.75
142	World Series Game 1 (Yanks' Ford Wins Series Opener)	11.00	5.50	3.25
143	World Series Game 2 (Sanford Flashes Shutout Magic)	5.00	2.50	1.50
144	World Series Game 3 (Maris Sparks Yankee Rally)	12.00	6.00	3.50
145	World Series Game 4 (Hiller Blasts Grand Slammer)	5.00	2.50	1.50
146	World Series Game 5 (Tresh's Homer Defeats Giants)	6.00	3.00	1.75
147	World Series Game 6 (Pierce Stars in 3-Hit Victory)	6.00	3.00	1.75
148	World Series Game 7 (Yanks Celebrate as Terry Wins)	7.00	3.50	2.00
149	Marv Breeding	4.00	2.00	1.25
150	Johnny Podres	6.00	3.00	1.75
151	Pittsburgh Pirates Team	10.00	5.00	3.00
152	Ron Nischwitz	4.00	2.00	1.25
153	Hal Smith	4.00	2.00	1.25
154	Walt Alston	7.50	3.75	2.25
155	Bill Stafford	4.00	2.00	1.25
156	Roy McMillan	4.00	2.00	1.25
157	***Diego Segui***	4.00	2.00	1.25
158	1963 Rookie Stars **(Rogelio Alvarez, Tommy Harper, Dave Roberts, Bob Saverine)**	6.00	3.00	1.75
159	Jim Pagliaroni	4.00	2.00	1.25
160	Juan Pizarro	4.00	2.00	1.25
161	Frank Torre	4.00	2.00	1.25
162	Minnesota Twins Team	7.00	3.50	2.00
163	Don Larsen	4.00	2.00	1.25
164	Bubba Morton	4.00	2.00	1.25
165	Jim Kaat	5.00	2.50	1.50
166	Johnny Keane	4.00	2.00	1.25
167	Jim Fregosi	4.00	2.00	1.25
168	Russ Nixon	4.00	2.00	1.25
169	1963 Rookie Stars ***(Dick Egan, Julio Navarro, Gaylord Perry, Tommie Sisk)***	17.50	8.75	5.25
170	Joe Adcock	4.00	2.00	1.25
171	Steve Hamilton	4.00	2.00	1.25
172	Gene Oliver	4.00	2.00	1.25
173	Bombers' Best (Tom Tresh, Mickey Mantle, Bobby Richardson)	75.00	37.50	22.00
174	Larry Burright	4.00	2.00	1.25
175	Bob Buhl	4.00	2.00	1.25
176	Jim King	4.00	2.00	1.25
177	Bubba Phillips	4.00	2.00	1.25
178	Johnny Edwards	4.00	2.00	1.25
179	Ron Piche	4.00	2.00	1.25
180	Bill Skowron	10.00	5.00	3.00
181	Sammy Esposito	4.00	2.00	1.25
182	Albie Pearson	4.00	2.00	1.25
183	Joe Pepitone	10.00	5.00	3.00
184	Vern Law	4.00	2.00	1.25
185	Chuck Hiller	4.00	2.00	1.25
186	Jerry Zimmerman	4.00	2.00	1.25
187	Willie Kirkland	4.00	2.00	1.25
188	Eddie Bressoud	4.00	2.00	1.25
189	Dave Giusti	4.00	2.00	1.25
190	Minnie Minoso	6.00	3.00	1.75
191	3rd Series Checklist (177-264)	8.00	4.00	2.50
192	Clay Dalrymple	4.00	2.00	1.25
193	Andre Rodgers	4.00	2.00	1.25
194	Joe Nuxhall	4.00	2.00	1.25
195	Manny Jimenez	4.00	2.00	1.25
196	Doug Camilli	4.00	2.00	1.25
197	Roger Craig	4.00	2.00	1.25
198	Lenny Green	4.00	2.00	1.25
199	Joe Amalfitano	4.00	2.00	1.25
200	Mickey Mantle	300.00	150.00	90.00
201	Cecil Butler	4.00	2.00	1.25

202	Boston Red Sox Team	7.00	3.50	2.00
203	Chico Cardenas	4.00	2.00	1.25
204	Don Nottebart	4.00	2.00	1.25
205	Luis Aparicio	15.00	7.50	4.50
206	Ray Washburn	4.00	2.00	1.25
207	Ken Hunt	4.00	2.00	1.25
208	1963 Rookie Stars **(Ron Herbel, John Miller, Ron Taylor, Wally Wolf)**	4.00	2.00	1.25
209	Hobie Landrith	4.00	2.00	1.25
210	Sandy Koufax	125.00	60.00	35.00
211	Fred Whitfield	4.00	2.00	1.25
212	Glen Hobbie	4.00	2.00	1.25
213	Billy Hitchcock	4.00	2.00	1.25
214	Orlando Pena	4.00	2.00	1.25
215	Bob Skinner	4.00	2.00	1.25
216	Gene Conley	4.00	2.00	1.25
217	Joe Christopher	4.00	2.00	1.25
218	Tiger Twirlers (Jim Bunning, Frank Lary, Don Mossi)	7.50	3.75	2.25
219	Chuck Cottier	4.00	2.00	1.25
220	Camilo Pascual	4.00	2.00	1.25
221	*Cookie Rojas*	4.00	2.00	1.25
222	Chicago Cubs Team	7.00	3.50	2.00
223	Eddie Fisher	4.00	2.00	1.25
224	Mike Roarke	4.00	2.00	1.25
225	Joe Jay	4.00	2.00	1.25
226	Julian Javier	4.00	2.00	1.25
227	Jim Grant	4.00	2.00	1.25
228	1963 Rookie Stars ***(Max Alvis, Bob Bailey, Ed Kranepool, Tony Oliva)***	40.00	20.00	12.00
229	Willie Davis	4.00	2.00	1.25
230	Pete Runnels	4.00	2.00	1.25
231	Eli Grba (Photo actually Ryne Duren.)	4.00	2.00	1.25
232	Frank Malzone	4.00	2.00	1.25
233	Casey Stengel	15.00	7.50	4.50
234	Dave Nicholson	4.00	2.00	1.25
235	Billy O'Dell	4.00	2.00	1.25
236	Bill Bryan	4.00	2.00	1.25
237	Jim Coates	4.00	2.00	1.25
238	Lou Johnson	4.00	2.00	1.25
239	Harvey Haddix	4.00	2.00	1.25
240	Rocky Colavito	17.50	8.75	5.25
241	Billy Smith	4.00	2.00	1.25
242	Power Plus (Hank Aaron, Ernie Banks)	50.00	25.00	15.00
243	Don Leppert	4.00	2.00	1.25
244	John Tsitouris	4.00	2.00	1.25
245	Gil Hodges	12.50	6.25	3.75
246	Lee Stange	4.00	2.00	1.25
247	New York Yankees Team	30.00	15.00	9.00
248	Tito Francona	4.00	2.00	1.25
249	Leo Burke	4.00	2.00	1.25
250	Stan Musial	65.00	32.50	20.00
251	Jack Lamabe	4.00	2.00	1.25
252	Ron Santo	13.50	6.75	4.00
253	1963 Rookie Stars **(Len Gabrielson, Pete Jernigan, Deacon Jones, John Wojcik)**	4.00	2.00	1.25
254	Mike Hershberger	4.00	2.00	1.25
255	Bob Shaw	4.00	2.00	1.25
256	Jerry Lumpe	4.00	2.00	1.25
257	Hank Aguirre	4.00	2.00	1.25
258	Alvin Dark	4.00	2.00	1.25
259	Johnny Logan	4.00	2.00	1.25
260	Jim Gentile	4.00	2.00	1.25
261	Bob Miller	4.00	2.00	1.25
262	Ellis Burton	4.00	2.00	1.25
263	Dave Stenhouse	4.00	2.00	1.25
264	Phil Linz	4.00	2.00	1.25
265	Vada Pinson	7.00	3.50	2.00
266	Bob Allen	4.00	2.00	1.25
267	Carl Sawatski	4.00	2.00	1.25
268	Don Demeter	4.00	2.00	1.25
269	Don Mincher	4.00	2.00	1.25
270	Felipe Alou	5.00	2.50	1.50
271	Dean Stone	4.00	2.00	1.25
272	Danny Murphy	4.00	2.00	1.25
273	Sammy Taylor	4.00	2.00	1.25
274	6th Series Checklist (265-352)	8.00	4.00	2.50
275	Ed Mathews	25.00	12.50	7.50
276	Barry Shetrone	4.00	2.00	1.25
277	Dick Farrell	4.00	2.00	1.25
278	Chico Fernandez	4.00	2.00	1.25
279	Wally Moon	4.00	2.00	1.25
280	Bob Rodgers	4.00	2.00	1.25
281	Tom Sturdivant	4.00	2.00	1.25
282	Bob Del Greco	4.00	2.00	1.25
283	Roy Sievers	4.00	2.00	1.25
284	Dave Sisler	4.00	2.00	1.25
285	Dick Stuart	4.00	2.00	1.25
286	Stu Miller	4.00	2.00	1.25
287	Dick Bertell	4.00	2.00	1.25
288	Chicago White Sox Team	8.00	4.00	2.50
289	Hal Brown	4.00	2.00	1.25
290	Bill White	4.00	2.00	1.25
291	Don Rudolph	4.00	2.00	1.25
292	Pumpsie Green	4.00	2.00	1.25
293	Bill Pleis	4.00	2.00	1.25
294	Bill Rigney	4.00	2.00	1.25
295	Ed Roebuck	4.00	2.00	1.25
296	Doc Edwards	4.00	2.00	1.25
297	Jim Golden	4.00	2.00	1.25
298	Don Dillard	4.00	2.00	1.25
299	1963 Rookie Stars **(Tom Butters, Bob Dustal, Dave Morehead, Dan Schneider)**	4.00	2.00	1.25
300	Willie Mays	110.00	55.00	35.00
301	Bill Fischer	4.00	2.00	1.25
302	Whitey Herzog	4.00	2.00	1.25
303	Earl Francis	4.00	2.00	1.25
304	Harry Bright	4.00	2.00	1.25
305	Don Hoak	4.00	2.00	1.25
306	Star Receivers (Earl Battey, Elston Howard)	5.00	2.50	1.50

307	Chet Nichols	4.00	2.00	1.25
308	Camilo Carreon	4.00	2.00	1.25
309	Jim Brewer	4.00	2.00	1.25
310	Tommy Davis	6.00	3.00	1.75
311	Joe McClain	4.00	2.00	1.25
312	Houston Colt .45s Team	13.50	6.75	4.00
313	Ernie Broglio	4.00	2.00	1.25
314	John Goryl	4.00	2.00	1.25
315	Ralph Terry	4.00	2.00	1.25
316	Norm Sherry	4.00	2.00	1.25
317	Sam McDowell	5.00	2.50	1.50
318	Gene Mauch	4.00	2.00	1.25
319	Joe Gaines	4.00	2.00	1.25
320	Warren Spahn	40.00	20.00	12.00
321	Gino Cimoli	4.00	2.00	1.25
322	Bob Turley	4.00	2.00	1.25
323	Bill Mazeroski	20.00	10.00	6.00
324	1963 Rookie Stars **(Vic Davalillo, Phil Roof, Pete Ward, George Williams)**	6.00	3.00	1.75
325	Jack Sanford	4.00	2.00	1.25
326	Hank Foiles	4.00	2.00	1.25
327	Paul Foytack	4.00	2.00	1.25
328	Dick Williams	4.00	2.00	1.25
329	Lindy McDaniel	4.00	2.00	1.25
330	Chuck Hinton	4.00	2.00	1.25
331	Series Foes (Bill Pierce, Bill Stafford)	7.00	3.50	2.00
332	Joel Horlen	4.00	2.00	1.25
333	Carl Warwick	4.00	2.00	1.25
334	Wynn Hawkins	4.00	2.00	1.25
335	Leon Wagner	4.00	2.00	1.25
336	Ed Bauta	4.00	2.00	1.25
337	Los Angeles Dodgers Team	15.00	7.50	4.50
338	Russ Kemmerer	4.00	2.00	1.25
339	Ted Bowsfield	4.00	2.00	1.25
340	Yogi Berra	70.00	35.00	20.00
341a	Jack Baldschun (White slash across body in inset photo.)	8.00	4.00	2.50
341b	Jack Baldschun (Slash repaired with red/mottling.)	4.00	2.00	1.25
342	Gene Woodling	4.00	2.00	1.25
343	Johnny Pesky	4.00	2.00	1.25
344	Don Schwall	4.00	2.00	1.25
345	Brooks Robinson	40.00	20.00	12.00
346	Billy Hoeft	4.00	2.00	1.25
347	Joe Torre	17.50	8.75	5.25
348	Vic Wertz	4.00	2.00	1.25
349	Zoilo Versalles	4.00	2.00	1.25
350	Bob Purkey	4.00	2.00	1.25
351	Al Luplow	4.00	2.00	1.25
352	Ken Johnson	4.00	2.00	1.25
353	Billy Williams	20.00	10.00	6.00
354	Dom Zanni	4.00	2.00	1.25
355	Dean Chance	4.00	2.00	1.25
356	John Schaive	4.00	2.00	1.25
357	George Altman	4.00	2.00	1.25
358	Milt Pappas	4.00	2.00	1.25
359	Haywood Sullivan	4.00	2.00	1.25
360	Don Drysdale	40.00	20.00	12.00
361	Clete Boyer	9.00	4.50	2.75
362	5th Series Checklist (353-429)	9.00	4.50	2.75
363	Dick Radatz	4.00	2.00	1.25
364	Howie Goss	4.00	2.00	1.25
365	Jim Bunning	13.50	6.75	4.00
366	Tony Taylor	4.00	2.00	1.25
367	Tony Cloninger	4.00	2.00	1.25
368	Ed Bailey	4.00	2.00	1.25
369	Jim Lemon	4.00	2.00	1.25
370	Dick Donovan	4.00	2.00	1.25
371	Rod Kanehl	4.00	2.00	1.25
372	Don Lee	4.00	2.00	1.25
373	Jim Campbell	4.00	2.00	1.25
374	Claude Osteen	4.00	2.00	1.25
375	Ken Boyer	10.00	5.00	3.00
376	Johnnie Wyatt	4.00	2.00	1.25
377	Baltimore Orioles Team	9.00	4.50	2.75
378	Bill Henry	4.00	2.00	1.25
379	Bob Anderson	4.00	2.00	1.25
380	Ernie Banks	65.00	32.50	20.00
381	Frank Baumann	4.00	2.00	1.25
382	Ralph Houk	6.00	3.00	1.75
383	Pete Richert	4.00	2.00	1.25
384	Bob Tillman	4.00	2.00	1.25
385	Art Mahaffey	4.00	2.00	1.25
386	1963 Rookie Stars **(John Bateman, Larry Bearnarth, Ed Kirkpatrick, Garry Roggenburk)**	5.00	2.50	1.50
387	Al McBean	4.00	2.00	1.25
388	Jim Davenport	4.00	2.00	1.25
389	Frank Sullivan	4.00	2.00	1.25
390	Hank Aaron	110.00	55.00	35.00
391	Bill Dailey	4.00	2.00	1.25
392	Tribe Thumpers (Tito Francona, Johnny Romano)	4.50	2.25	1.25
393	Ken MacKenzie	4.00	2.00	1.25
394	Tim McCarver	9.00	4.50	2.75
395	Don McMahon	4.00	2.00	1.25
396	Joe Koppe	4.00	2.00	1.25
397	Kansas City Athletics Team	9.00	4.50	2.75
398	Boog Powell	12.50	6.25	3.75
399	Dick Ellsworth	4.00	2.00	1.25
400	Frank Robinson	45.00	22.50	13.50
401	Jim Bouton	12.00	6.00	3.50
402	Mickey Vernon	4.00	2.00	1.25
403	Ron Perranoski	4.00	2.00	1.25
404	Bob Oldis	4.00	2.00	1.25
405	Floyd Robinson	4.00	2.00	1.25
406	Howie Koplitz	4.00	2.00	1.25
407	1963 Rookie Stars **(Larry Elliot, Frank Kostro, Chico Ruiz, Dick Simpson)**	4.00	2.00	1.25
408	Billy Gardner	4.00	2.00	1.25
409	Roy Face	4.00	2.00	1.25
410	Earl Battey	4.00	2.00	1.25
411	Jim Constable	4.00	2.00	1.25

412	Dodgers' Big Three (Johnny Podres, Don Drysdale, Sandy Koufax)	75.00	37.50	22.50
413	Jerry Walker	4.00	2.00	1.25
414	Ty Cline	4.00	2.00	1.25
415	Bob Gibson	45.00	22.50	13.50
416	Alex Grammas	4.00	2.00	1.25
417	San Francisco Giants Team	9.00	4.50	2.75
418	Johnny Orsino	4.00	2.00	1.25
419	Tracy Stallard	4.00	2.00	1.25
420	Bobby Richardson	12.50	6.25	3.75
421	Tom Morgan	4.00	2.00	1.25
422	Fred Hutchinson	4.00	2.00	1.25
423	Ed Hobaugh	4.00	2.00	1.25
424	Charley Smith	4.00	2.00	1.25
425	Smoky Burgess	4.00	2.00	1.25
426	Barry Latman	4.00	2.00	1.25
427	Bernie Allen	4.00	2.00	1.25
428	Carl Boles	4.00	2.00	1.25
429	Lou Burdette	4.00	2.00	1.25
430	Norm Siebern	4.00	2.00	1.25
431a	6th Series Checklist (430-506) ("Checklist" in black on front.)	8.00	4.00	2.50
431b	6th Series Checklist (430-506) ("Checklist" in white.)	20.00	10.00	6.00
432	Roman Mejias	4.00	2.00	1.25
433	Denis Menke	4.00	2.00	1.25
434	Johnny Callison	4.00	2.00	1.25
435	Woody Held	4.00	2.00	1.25
436	Tim Harkness	4.00	2.00	1.25
437	Bill Bruton	4.00	2.00	1.25
438	Wes Stock	4.00	2.00	1.25
439	Don Zimmer	6.00	3.00	1.75
440	Juan Marichal	25.00	12.50	7.50
441	Lee Thomas	4.00	2.00	1.25
442	J.C. Hartman	4.00	2.00	1.25
443	Jim Piersall	7.00	3.50	2.00
444	Jim Maloney	4.00	2.00	1.25
445	Norm Cash	9.00	4.50	2.75
446	Whitey Ford	40.00	20.00	12.00
447	Felix Mantilla	9.00	4.50	2.75
448	Jack Kralick	9.00	4.50	2.75
449	Jose Tartabull	9.00	4.50	2.75
450	Bob Friend	9.00	4.50	2.75
451	Cleveland Indians Team	20.00	10.00	6.00
452	Barney Schultz	9.00	4.50	2.75
453	Jake Wood	9.00	4.50	2.75
454a	Art Fowler (Card # on orange background.)	9.00	4.50	2.75
454b	Art Fowler (Card # on white background.)	30.00	15.00	9.00
455	Ruben Amaro	9.00	4.50	2.75
456	Jim Coker	9.00	4.50	2.75
457	Tex Clevenger	9.00	4.50	2.75
458	Al Lopez	20.00	10.00	6.00
459	Dick LeMay	9.00	4.50	2.75
460	Del Crandall	9.00	4.50	2.75
461	Norm Bass	9.00	4.50	2.75
462	Wally Post	9.00	4.50	2.75
463	Joe Schaffernoth	9.00	4.50	2.75
464	Ken Aspromonte	9.00	4.50	2.75
465	Chuck Estrada	9.00	4.50	2.75
466	1963 Rookie Stars **(Bill Freehan, Tony Martinez, Nate Oliver, Jerry Robinson)**	32.50	16.00	10.00
467	Phil Ortega	9.00	4.50	2.75
468	Carroll Hardy	9.00	4.50	2.75
469	Jay Hook	9.00	4.50	2.75
470	Tom Tresh/SP	35.00	17.50	10.00
471	Ken Retzer	9.00	4.50	2.75
472	Lou Brock	65.00	32.50	20.00
473	New York Mets Team	40.00	20.00	12.00
474	Jack Fisher	9.00	4.50	2.75
475	Gus Triandos	9.00	4.50	2.75
476	Frank Funk	9.00	4.50	2.75
477	Donn Clendenon	9.00	4.50	2.75
478	Paul Brown	9.00	4.50	2.75
479	***Ed Brinkman***	9.00	4.50	2.75
480	Bill Monbouquette	9.00	4.50	2.75
481	Bob Taylor	9.00	4.50	2.75
482	Felix Torres	9.00	4.50	2.75
483	Jim Owens	9.00	4.50	2.75
484	Dale Long/SP	15.00	7.50	4.50
485	Jim Landis	9.00	4.50	2.75
486	Ray Sadecki	9.00	4.50	2.75
487	John Roseboro	9.00	4.50	2.75
488	Jerry Adair	9.00	4.50	2.75
489	Paul Toth	9.00	4.50	2.75
490	Willie McCovey	60.00	30.00	18.00
491	Harry Craft	9.00	4.50	2.75
492	Dave Wickersham	9.00	4.50	2.75
493	Walt Bond	9.00	4.50	2.75
494	Phil Regan	9.00	4.50	2.75
495	Frank Thomas/SP	15.00	7.50	4.50
496	1963 Rookie Stars **(Carl Bouldin, Steve Dalkowski, Fred Newman, Jack Smith)**	20.00	10.00	6.00
497	Bennie Daniels	9.00	4.50	2.75
498	Eddie Kasko	9.00	4.50	2.75
499	J.C. Martin	9.00	4.50	2.75
500	Harmon Killebrew/SP	80.00	40.00	24.00
501	Joe Azcue	9.00	4.50	2.75
502	Daryl Spencer	9.00	4.50	2.75
503	Milwaukee Braves Team	15.00	7.50	4.50
504	Bob Johnson	9.00	4.50	2.75
505	Curt Flood	15.00	7.50	4.50
506	Gene Green	9.00	4.50	2.75
507	Roland Sheldon	9.00	4.50	2.75
508	Ted Savage	9.00	4.50	2.75
509a	7th Series Checklist (507-576) (Copyright centered.)	17.50	8.75	5.25
509b	7th Series Checklist (509-576) (Copyright to right.)	17.50	8.75	5.25
510	Ken McBride	9.00	4.50	2.75
511	Charlie Neal	9.00	4.50	2.75
512	Cal McLish	9.00	4.50	2.75
513	Gary Geiger	9.00	4.50	2.75
514	Larry Osborne	9.00	4.50	2.75
515	Don Elston	9.00	4.50	2.75
516	Purnal Goldy	9.00	4.50	2.75
517	Hal Woodeshick	9.00	4.50	2.75
518	Don Blasingame	9.00	4.50	2.75
519	Claude Raymond	9.00	4.50	2.75
520	Orlando Cepeda	30.00	15.00	9.00
521	Dan Pfister	9.00	4.50	2.75
522	1963 Rookie Stars **(Mel Nelson, Gary Peters, Art Quirk, Jim Roland)**	9.00	4.50	2.75
523	Bill Kunkel	9.00	4.50	2.75
524	St. Louis Cardinals Team	20.00	10.00	6.00
525	Nellie Fox	30.00	15.00	9.00
526	Dick Hall	9.00	4.50	2.75
527	Ed Sadowski	9.00	4.50	2.75
528	Carl Willey	9.00	4.50	2.75
529	Wes Covington	9.00	4.50	2.75
530	Don Mossi	9.00	4.50	2.75
531	Sam Mele	9.00	4.50	2.75
532	Steve Boros	9.00	4.50	2.75
533	Bobby Shantz	9.00	4.50	2.75
534	Ken Walters	9.00	4.50	2.75
535	Jim Perry	9.00	4.50	2.75
536	Norm Larker	9.00	4.50	2.75
537	1963 Rookie Stars ***(Pedro Gonzalez, Ken McMullen, Pete Rose, Al Weis)***	800.00	400.00	240.00
538	George Brunet	9.00	4.50	2.75
539	Wayne Causey	9.00	4.50	2.75
540	Bob Clemente	150.00	75.00	45.00
541	Ron Moeller	9.00	4.50	2.75
542	Lou Klimchock	9.00	4.50	2.75
543	Russ Snyder	9.00	4.50	2.75
544	1963 Rookie Stars ***(Duke Carmel, Bill Haas, Dick Phillips, Rusty Staub)***	30.00	15.00	9.00
545	Jose Pagan	9.00	4.50	2.75
546	Hal Reniff	9.00	4.50	2.75
547	Gus Bell	9.00	4.50	2.75
548	Tom Satriano	9.00	4.50	2.75
549	1963 Rookie Stars **(Marcelino Lopez, Pete Lovrich, Elmo Plaskett, Paul Ratliff)**	11.00	5.50	3.25
550	Duke Snider	45.00	22.50	13.50
551	Billy Klaus	9.00	4.50	2.75
552	Detroit Tigers Team	25.00	12.50	7.50
553	1963 Rookie Stars ***(Brock Davis, Jim Gosger, John Herrnstein, Willie Stargell)***	80.00	40.00	24.00
554	Hank Fischer	9.00	4.50	2.75
555	John Blanchard	12.00	6.00	3.50
556	Al Worthington	9.00	4.50	2.75
557	Cuno Barragan	9.00	4.50	2.75
558	1963 Rookie Stars ***(Bill Faul, Ron Hunt, Bob Lipski, Al Moran)***	11.00	5.50	3.25
559	Danny Murtaugh	9.00	4.50	2.75
560	Ray Herbert	9.00	4.50	2.75
561	Mike de la Hoz	9.00	4.50	2.75
562	1963 Rookie Stars ***(Randy Cardinal, Dave McNally, Don Rowe, Ken Rowe)***	25.00	12.50	7.50
563	Mike McCormick	9.00	4.50	2.75
564	George Banks	9.00	4.50	2.75
565	Larry Sherry	9.00	4.50	2.75
566	Cliff Cook	9.00	4.50	2.75
567	Jim Duffalo	9.00	4.50	2.75
568	Bob Sadowski	9.00	4.50	2.75
569	Luis Arroyo	9.00	4.50	2.75
570	Frank Bolling	9.00	4.50	2.75
571	Johnny Klippstein	9.00	4.50	2.75
572	Jack Spring	9.00	4.50	2.75
573	Coot Veal	9.00	4.50	2.75
574	Hal Kolstad	9.00	4.50	2.75
575	Don Cardwell	9.00	4.50	2.75
576	Johnny Temple	13.50	5.00	3.00

1963 Topps Famous Americans Stamps

Actually marketed as "Stamp Gum," this obscure test issue features 80 perforated stamps depicting great Americans from all walks of life, including two baseball players. The 2-9/16" x 1-3/8" stamps are printed in black, blue and yellow and combine a photographic portrait with a cartoon drawing. Centering is often a problem with these pieces. Only the baseball players are listed here.

		NM	EX	VG
50	Babe Ruth	300.00	150.00	90.00
60	Lou Gehrig	250.00	125.00	75.00

1963 Topps Mickey Mantle Plaque

Advertised as a "mask" on high-number 1963 Topps wax wrappers, this is actually a plastic plaque. About 6" x 8", the plaque features a color picture of Mantle in embossed plastic with a faux wood frame, also embossed plastic, around it. A holed tab at top allows hanging.

	NM	EX	VG
Mickey Mantle	900.00	450.00	270.00

1963 Topps Peel-Offs

Measuring 1-1/4" x 2-3/4", Topps Peel-Offs were an insert with 1963 Topps baseball cards. There are 46 players in the unnumbered set, each pictured in a color photo inside an oval with the player's name, team and position in a band below. The back of the Peel-Off is removable, leaving a sticky surface that made the Peel-Off a popular decorative item among youngsters of the day. Naturally, that makes them quite scarce today. The stickers can be found both blank-backed (much scarcer) and with instructions printed on the peel-off backing.

		NM	EX	VG
Complete Set (46):		525.00	275.00	160.00
Common Player:		4.00	2.00	1.25
(1)	Hank Aaron	35.00	17.50	10.00
(2)	Luis Aparicio	12.50	6.25	3.75
(3)	Richie Ashburn	17.50	8.75	5.25
(4)	Bob Aspromonte	4.00	2.00	1.25
(5)	Ernie Banks	22.50	11.00	6.75
(6)	Ken Boyer	7.50	3.75	2.25
(7)	Jim Bunning	10.00	5.00	3.00
(8)	Johnny Callison	4.00	2.00	1.25
(9)	Orlando Cepeda	10.00	5.00	3.00
(10)	Roberto Clemente	40.00	20.00	12.00
(11)	Rocky Colavito	9.00	4.50	2.75
(12)	Tommy Davis	4.00	2.00	1.25
(13)	Dick Donovan	4.00	2.00	1.25
(14)	Don Drysdale	15.00	7.50	4.50
(15)	Dick Farrell	4.00	2.00	1.25
(16)	Jim Gentile	4.00	2.00	1.25
(17)	Ray Herbert	4.00	2.00	1.25
(18)	Chuck Hinton	4.00	2.00	1.25
(19)	Ken Hubbs	7.50	3.75	2.25
(20)	Al Jackson	4.00	2.00	1.25
(21)	Al Kaline	17.50	8.75	5.25
(22)	Harmon Killebrew	17.50	8.75	5.25
(23)	Sandy Koufax	40.00	20.00	12.00
(24)	Jerry Lumpe	4.00	2.00	1.25
(25)	Art Mahaffey	4.00	2.00	1.25
(26)	Mickey Mantle	100.00	50.00	30.00
(27)	Willie Mays	35.00	17.50	10.00
(28)	Bill Mazeroski	12.50	6.25	3.75
(29)	Bill Monbouquette	4.00	2.00	1.25
(30)	Stan Musial	35.00	17.50	10.00
(31)	Camilo Pascual	4.00	2.00	1.25
(32)	Bob Purkey	4.00	2.00	1.25
(33)	Bobby Richardson	9.00	4.50	2.75
(34)	Brooks Robinson	17.50	8.75	5.25
(35)	Floyd Robinson	4.00	2.00	1.25
(36)	Frank Robinson	17.50	8.75	5.25
(37)	Bob Rodgers	4.00	2.00	1.25
(38)	Johnny Romano	4.00	2.00	1.25
(39)	Jack Sanford	4.00	2.00	1.25
(40)	Norm Siebern	4.00	2.00	1.25
(41)	Warren Spahn	17.50	8.75	5.25
(42)	Dave Stenhouse	4.00	2.00	1.25
(43)	Ralph Terry	4.00	2.00	1.25
(44)	Lee Thomas	4.00	2.00	1.25
(45)	Bill White	4.00	2.00	1.25
(46)	Carl Yastrzemski	20.00	10.00	6.00

1963 Topps Valentine Foldees

Featuring the artwork of 1960s cartoonist Jack Davis, this set of specialty cards had the left and right panels of the 4-1/2" x 2-3/8" pieces slit to allow either the top or the bottom

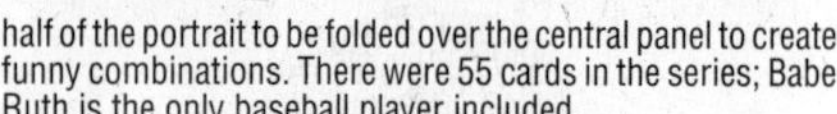

half of the portrait to be folded over the central panel to create funny combinations. There were 55 cards in the series; Babe Ruth is the only baseball player included.

		NM	EX	VG
Complete Set (55):		150.00	75.00	45.00
6	Babe Ruth	25.00	12.50	7.50

1964 Topps

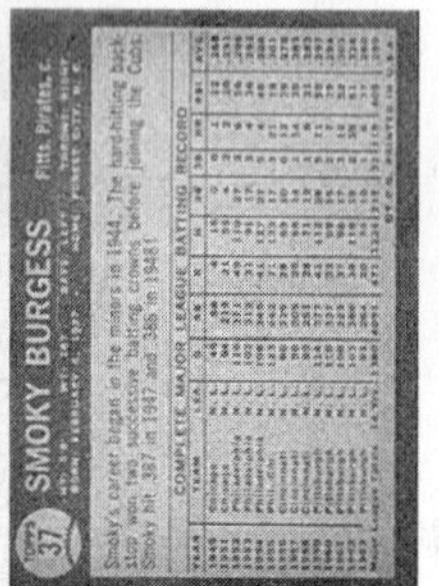

The 1964 Topps set is a 587-card issue of 2-1/2" x 3-1/2" cards which is considered by many as being among the company's best efforts. Card fronts feature a large color photo which blends into a top panel which contains the team name, while a panel below the picture carries the player's name and position. An interesting innovation on the back is a baseball quiz question which required the rubbing of a white panel to reveal the answer. As in 1963, specialty cards remained modest in number with a 12-card set of statistical leaders, a few multi-player cards, rookies and World Series highlights. An interesting card is an "In Memoriam" card for Ken Hubbs who was killed in an airplane crash.

		NM	EX	VG
Complete Set (587):		4,250	2,125	1,250
Common Player (1-370):		3.50	1.75	1.00
Common Player (371-522):		6.00	3.00	1.75
Common Player (523-587):		9.00	4.50	2.75
1	N.L. E.R.A. Leaders (Dick Ellsworth, Bob Friend, Sandy Koufax)	20.00	10.00	6.00
2	A.L. E.R.A. Leaders (Camilo Pascual, Gary Peters, Juan Pizarro)	12.00	3.00	2.00
3	N.L. Pitching Leaders (Sandy Koufax, Jim Maloney, Juan Marichal, Warren Spahn)	20.00	10.00	6.00
4a	A.L. Pitching Leaders (Jim Bouton, Whitey Ford, Camilo Pascual) (Apostrophe after "Pitching" on back.)	17.50	8.75	5.25
4b	A.L. Pitching Leaders (Jim Bouton, Whitey Ford, Camilo Pascual) (No apostrophe.)	17.50	8.75	5.25
5	N.L. Strikeout Leaders (Don Drysdale, Sandy Koufax, Jim Maloney)	20.00	10.00	6.00
6	A.L. Strikeout Leaders (Jim Bunning, Camilo Pascual, Dick Stigman)	12.50	6.25	3.75
7	N.L. Batting Leaders (Hank Aaron, Roberto Clemente, Tommy Davis, Dick Groat)	16.00	8.00	4.75
8	A.L. Batting Leaders (Al Kaline, Rich Rollins, Carl Yastrzemski)	12.50	6.25	3.75
9	N.L. Home Run Leaders (Hank Aaron, Orlando Cepeda, Willie Mays, Willie McCovey)	20.00	10.00	6.00
10	A.L. Home Run Leaders (Bob Allison, Harmon Killebrew, Dick Stuart)	12.00	6.00	3.50
11	N.L. R.B.I. Leaders (Hank Aaron, Ken Boyer, Bill White)	12.50	6.25	3.75
12	A.L. R.B.I. Leaders (Al Kaline, Harmon Killebrew, Dick Stuart)	13.50	6.75	4.00
13	Hoyt Wilhelm	15.00	7.50	4.50
14	Dodgers Rookies **(Dick Nen, Nick Willhite)**	3.50	1.75	1.00
15	Zoilo Versalles	3.50	1.75	1.00
16	John Boozer	3.50	1.75	1.00
17	Willie Kirkland	3.50	1.75	1.00
18	Billy O'Dell	3.50	1.75	1.00
19	Don Wart	3.50	1.75	1.00
20	Bob Friend	3.50	1.75	1.00
21	Yogi Berra	35.00	17.50	10.00
22	Jerry Adair	3.50	1.75	1.00
23	Chris Zachary	3.50	1.75	1.00
24	Carl Sawatski	3.50	1.75	1.00
25	Bill Monbouquette	3.50	1.75	1.00
26	Gino Cimoli	3.50	1.75	1.00
27	New York Mets Team	7.50	3.75	2.25
28	Claude Osteen	3.50	1.75	1.00
29	Lou Brock	24.00	12.00	7.25
30	Ron Perranoski	3.50	1.75	1.00
31	Dave Nicholson	3.50	1.75	1.00
32	Dean Chance	3.50	1.75	1.00
33	Reds Rookies **(Sammy Ellis, Mel Queen)**	3.50	1.75	1.00
34	Jim Perry	3.50	1.75	1.00
35	Ed Mathews	20.00	10.00	6.00
36	Hal Reniff	3.50	1.75	1.00
37	Smoky Burgess	3.50	1.75	1.00
38	***Jim Wynn***	5.00	2.50	1.50
39	Hank Aguirre	3.50	1.75	1.00
40	Dick Groat	3.50	1.75	1.00
41	Friendly Foes (Willie McCovey, Leon Wagner)	10.00	5.00	3.00
42	Moe Drabowsky	3.50	1.75	1.00
43	Roy Sievers	3.50	1.75	1.00
44	Duke Carmel	3.50	1.75	1.00
45	Milt Pappas	3.50	1.75	1.00
46	Ed Brinkman	3.50	1.75	1.00
47	Giants Rookies **(Jesus Alou, Ron Herbel)**	5.00	2.50	1.75
48	Bob Perry	3.50	1.75	1.00
49	Bill Henry	3.50	1.75	1.00
50	Mickey Mantle	225.00	100.00	65.00
51	Pete Richert	3.50	1.75	1.00
52	Chuck Hinton	3.50	1.75	1.00
53	Denis Menke	3.50	1.75	1.00
54	Sam Mele	3.50	1.75	1.00
55	Ernie Banks	35.00	17.50	10.00
56	Hal Brown	3.50	1.75	1.00
57	Tim Harkness	3.50	1.75	1.00
58	Don Demeter	3.50	1.75	1.00
59	Ernie Broglio	3.50	1.75	1.00
60	Frank Malzone	3.50	1.75	1.00
61	Angel Backstops (Bob Rodgers, Ed Sadowski)	3.50	1.75	1.00
62	Ted Savage	3.50	1.75	1.00
63	Johnny Orsino	3.50	1.75	1.00
64	Ted Abernathy	3.50	1.75	1.00
65	Felipe Alou	4.50	2.25	1.25
66	Eddie Fisher	3.50	1.75	1.00
67	Detroit Tigers Team	6.00	3.00	1.75
68	Willie Davis	3.50	1.75	1.00
69	Clete Boyer	10.00	5.00	3.00
70	Joe Torre	12.00	6.00	3.50
71	Jack Spring	3.50	1.75	1.00
72	Chico Cardenas	3.50	1.75	1.00
73	***Jimmie Hall***	3.50	1.75	1.00
74	Pirates Rookies **(Tom Butters, Bob Priddy)**	3.50	1.75	1.00
75	Wayne Causey	3.50	1.75	1.00
76	1st Series Checklist (1-88)	5.00	2.50	1.50
77	Jerry Walker	3.50	1.75	1.00
78	Merritt Ranew	3.50	1.75	1.00
79	Bob Heffner	3.50	1.75	1.00
80	Vada Pinson	9.00	4.50	2.75
81	All-Star Vets (Nellie Fox, Harmon Killebrew)	12.50	6.25	3.75
82	Jim Davenport	3.50	1.75	1.00
83	Gus Triandos	3.50	1.75	1.00
84	Carl Willey	3.50	1.75	1.00
85	Pete Ward	3.50	1.75	1.00
86	Al Downing	3.50	1.75	1.00
87	St. Louis Cardinals Team	6.00	3.00	1.75
88	John Roseboro	3.50	1.75	1.00
89	Boog Powell	7.50	3.75	2.25
90	Earl Battey	3.50	1.75	1.00
91	Bob Bailey	3.50	1.75	1.00
92	Steve Ridzik	3.50	1.75	1.00
93	Gary Geiger	3.50	1.75	1.00
94	Braves Rookies (Jim Britton, Larry Maxie)	3.50	1.75	1.00
95	George Altman	3.50	1.75	1.00
96	Bob Buhl	3.50	1.75	1.00
97	Jim Fregosi	3.50	1.75	1.00
98	Bill Bruton	3.50	1.75	1.00
99	Al Stanek	3.50	1.75	1.00
100	Elston Howard	12.50	6.25	3.75
101	Walt Alston	6.00	3.00	1.75
102	2nd Series Checklist (89-176)	6.00	3.00	1.75
103	Curt Flood	5.00	2.50	1.50
104	Art Mahaffey	3.50	1.75	1.00
105	Woody Held	3.50	1.75	1.00
106	Joe Nuxhall	3.50	1.75	1.00
107	White Sox Rookies **(Bruce Howard, Frank Kreutzer)**	3.50	1.75	1.00
108	John Wyatt	3.50	1.75	1.00
109	Rusty Staub	10.00	5.00	3.00
110	Albie Pearson	3.50	1.75	1.00
111	Don Elston	3.50	1.75	1.00
112	Bob Tillman	3.50	1.75	1.00
113	Grover Powell	3.50	1.75	1.00
114	Don Lock	3.50	1.75	1.00
115	Frank Bolling	3.50	1.75	1.00
116	Twins Rookies **(Tony Oliva, Jay Ward)**	9.00	4.50	2.75
117	Earl Francis	3.50	1.75	1.00
118	John Blanchard	5.00	2.50	1.50
119	Gary Kolb	3.50	1.75	1.00
120	Don Drysdale	17.50	8.75	5.25
121	Pete Runnels	3.50	1.75	1.00
122	Don McMahon	3.50	1.75	1.00
123	Jose Pagan	3.50	1.75	1.00
124	Orlando Pena	3.50	1.75	1.00
125	Pete Rose	140.00	70.00	40.00
126	Russ Snyder	3.50	1.75	1.00
127	Angels Rookies **(Aubrey Gatewood, Dick Simpson)**	3.50	1.75	1.00
128	***Mickey Lolich***	12.50	6.25	3.75
129	Amado Samuel	3.50	1.75	1.00
130	Gary Peters	3.50	1.75	1.00
131	Steve Boros	3.50	1.75	1.00
132	Milwaukee Braves Team	6.00	3.00	1.75
133	Jim Grant	3.50	1.75	1.00
134	Don Zimmer	5.00	2.50	1.50
135	Johnny Callison	3.50	1.75	1.00
136	World Series Game 1 (Koufax Strikes Out 15)	30.00	15.00	9.00
137	World Series Game 2 (Davis Sparks Rally)	9.00	4.50	2.75
138	World Series Game 3 (L.A. Takes 3rd Straight)	9.00	4.50	2.75
139	World Series Game 4 (Sealing Yanks' Doom)	7.00	3.50	2.00
140	World Series (The Dodgers Celebrate)	7.00	3.50	2.00
141	Danny Murtaugh	3.50	1.75	1.00
142	John Bateman	3.50	1.75	1.00
143	Bubba Phillips	3.50	1.75	1.00
144	Al Worthington	3.50	1.75	1.00
145	Norm Siebern	3.50	1.75	1.00
146	Indians Rookies **(Bob Chance, Tommy John)**	17.50	8.75	5.25
147	Ray Sadecki	3.50	1.75	1.00
148	J.C. Martin	3.50	1.75	1.00
149	Paul Foytack	3.50	1.75	1.00
150	Willie Mays	90.00	45.00	27.50
151	K.C. Athletics Team	6.00	3.00	1.75
152	Denver Lemaster	3.50	1.75	1.00
153	Dick Williams	3.50	1.75	1.00
154	Dick Tracewski	3.50	1.75	1.00
155	Duke Snider	15.00	7.50	4.50
156	Bill Dailey	3.50	1.75	1.00
157	Gene Mauch	3.50	1.75	1.00
158	Ken Johnson	3.50	1.75	1.00
159	Charlie Dees	3.50	1.75	1.00
160	Ken Boyer	8.00	4.00	2.50
161	Dave McNally	3.50	1.75	1.00
162	Hitting Area (Vada Pinson, Dick Sisler)	5.00	2.50	1.50
163	Donn Clendenon	3.50	1.75	1.00
164	Bud Daley	3.50	1.75	1.00
165	Jerry Lumpe	3.50	1.75	1.00
166	Marty Keough	3.50	1.75	1.00
167	Senators Rookies **(*Mike Brumley, Lou Piniella*)**	27.50	13.50	8.25
168	Al Weis	3.50	1.75	1.00
169	Del Crandall	3.50	1.75	1.00
170	Dick Radatz	3.50	1.75	1.00
171	Ty Cline	3.50	1.75	1.00
172	Cleveland Indians Team	6.00	3.00	1.75
173	Ryne Duren	3.50	1.75	1.00
174	Doc Edwards	3.50	1.75	1.00
175	Billy Williams	17.50	8.75	5.25
176	Tracy Stallard	3.50	1.75	1.00
177	Harmon Killebrew	22.50	11.00	7.00
178	Hank Bauer	4.50	2.25	1.25
179	Carl Warwick	3.50	1.75	1.00
180	Tommy Davis	3.50	1.75	1.00
181	Dave Wickersham	3.50	1.75	1.00
182	Sox Sockers (Chuck Schilling, Carl Yastrzemski)	17.50	8.75	5.25
183	Ron Taylor	3.50	1.75	1.00
184	Al Luplow	3.50	1.75	1.00
185	Jim O'Toole	3.50	1.75	1.00
186	Roman Mejias	3.50	1.75	1.00
187	Ed Roebuck	3.50	1.75	1.00
188	3rd Series Checklist (177-264)	5.00	2.50	1.50
189	Bob Hendley	3.50	1.75	1.00
190	Bobby Richardson	12.50	6.25	3.75
191	Clay Dalrymple	3.50	1.75	1.00
192	Cubs Rookies **(John Boccabella, Billy Cowan)**	3.50	1.75	1.00
193	Jerry Lynch	3.50	1.75	1.00
194	John Goryl	3.50	1.75	1.00
195	Floyd Robinson	3.50	1.75	1.00
196	Jim Gentile	3.50	1.75	1.00
197	Frank Lary	3.50	1.75	1.00
198	Len Gabrielson	3.50	1.75	1.00
199	Joe Azcue	3.50	1.75	1.00
200	Sandy Koufax	70.00	35.00	20.00
201	Orioles Rookies **(*Sam Bowens, Wally Bunker*)**	3.50	1.75	1.00
202	Galen Cisco	3.50	1.75	1.00
203	John Kennedy	3.50	1.75	1.00
204	Matty Alou	3.50	1.75	1.00
205	Nellie Fox	12.50	6.25	3.75
206	Steve Hamilton	3.50	1.75	1.00
207	Fred Hutchinson	3.50	1.75	1.00
208	Wes Covington	3.50	1.75	1.00
209	Bob Allen	3.50	1.75	1.00
210	Carl Yastrzemski	35.00	17.50	10.00
211	Jim Coker	3.50	1.75	1.00
212	Pete Lovrich	3.50	1.75	1.00
213	Los Angeles Angels Team	6.00	3.00	1.75
214	Ken McMullen	3.50	1.75	1.00
215	Ray Herbert	3.50	1.75	1.00
216	Mike de la Hoz	3.50	1.75	1.00
217	Jim King	3.50	1.75	1.00
218	Hank Fischer	3.50	1.75	1.00
219	Young Aces (Jim Bouton, Al Downing)	8.00	4.00	2.50

220	Dick Ellsworth	3.50	1.75	1.00
221	Bob Saverine	3.50	1.75	1.00
222	Bill Pierce	3.50	1.75	1.00
223	George Banks	3.50	1.75	1.00
224	Tommie Sisk	3.50	1.75	1.00
225	Roger Maris	55.00	27.50	16.50
226	Colts Rookies **(Gerald Grote, Larry Yellen)**	5.00	2.50	1.50
227	Barry Latman	3.50	1.75	1.00
228	Felix Mantilla	3.50	1.75	1.00
229	Charley Lau	3.50	1.75	1.00
230	Brooks Robinson	22.50	11.00	6.75
231	Dick Calmus	3.50	1.75	1.00
232	Al Lopez	6.00	3.00	1.75
233	Hal Smith	3.50	1.75	1.00
234	Gary Bell	3.50	1.75	1.00
235	Ron Hunt	3.50	1.75	1.00
236	Bill Faul	3.50	1.75	1.00
237	Chicago Cubs Team	6.50	3.25	2.00
238	Roy McMillan	3.50	1.75	1.00
239	Herm Starrette	3.50	1.75	1.00
240	Bill White	3.50	1.75	1.00
241	Jim Owens	3.50	1.75	1.00
242	Harvey Kuenn	3.50	1.75	1.00
243	Phillies Rookies **(Richie Allen, John Herrnstein)**	17.50	8.75	5.25
244	***Tony LaRussa***	17.50	8.75	5.25
245	Dick Stigman	3.50	1.75	1.00
246	Manny Mota	3.50	1.75	1.00
247	Dave DeBusschere	5.00	2.50	1.50
248	Johnny Pesky	3.50	1.75	1.00
249	Doug Camilli	3.50	1.75	1.00
250	Al Kaline	22.50	11.00	7.00
251	Choo Choo Coleman	3.50	1.75	1.00
252	Ken Aspromonte	3.50	1.75	1.00
253	Wally Post	3.50	1.75	1.00
254	Don Hoak	3.50	1.75	1.00
255	Lee Thomas	3.50	1.75	1.00
256	Johnny Weekly	3.50	1.75	1.00
257	San Francisco Giants Team	6.00	3.00	1.75
258	Garry Roggenburk	3.50	1.75	1.00
259	Harry Bright	3.50	1.75	1.00
260	Frank Robinson	22.50	11.00	7.00
261	Jim Hannan	3.50	1.75	1.00
262	Cardinals Rookies **(*Harry Fanok, Mike Shannon*)**	9.00	4.50	2.75
263	Chuck Estrada	3.50	1.75	1.00
264	Jim Landis	3.50	1.75	1.00
265	Jim Bunning	12.50	6.25	3.75
266	Gene Freese	3.50	1.75	1.00
267	*Wilbur Wood*	5.00	2.50	1.50
268	Bill's Got It (Danny Murtaugh, Bill Virdon)	3.50	1.75	1.00
269	Ellis Burton	3.50	1.75	1.00
270	Rich Rollins	3.50	1.75	1.00
271	Bob Sadowski	3.50	1.75	1.00
272	Jake Wood	3.50	1.75	1.00
273	Mel Nelson	3.50	1.75	1.00
274	4th Series Checklist (265-352)	6.00	3.00	1.75
275	John Tsitouris	3.50	1.75	1.00
276	Jose Tartabull	3.50	1.75	1.00
277	Ken Retzer	3.50	1.75	1.00
278	Bobby Shantz	3.50	1.75	1.00
279	Joe Koppe	3.50	1.75	1.00
280	Juan Marichal	12.50	6.25	3.75
281	Yankees Rookies **(Jake Gibbs, Tom Metcalf)**	5.00	2.50	1.50
282	Bob Bruce	3.50	1.75	1.00
283	***Tommy McCraw***	3.50	1.75	1.00
284	Dick Schofield	3.50	1.75	1.00
285	Robin Roberts	12.50	6.25	3.75
286	Don Landrum	3.50	1.75	1.00
287	Red Sox Rookies **(Tony Conigliaro, Bill Spanswick)**	35.00	17.50	10.00
288	Al Moran	3.50	1.75	1.00
289	Frank Funk	3.50	1.75	1.00
290	Bob Allison	3.50	1.75	1.00
291	Phil Ortega	3.50	1.75	1.00
292	Mike Roarke	3.50	1.75	1.00
293	Phillies Team	6.00	3.00	1.75
294	Ken Hunt	3.50	1.75	1.00
295	Roger Craig	3.50	1.75	1.00
296	Ed Kirkpatrick	3.50	1.75	1.00
297	Ken MacKenzie	3.50	1.75	1.00
298	Harry Craft	3.50	1.75	1.00
299	Bill Stafford	3.50	1.75	1.00
300	Hank Aaron	70.00	35.00	20.00
301	Larry Brown	3.50	1.75	1.00
302	Dan Pfister	3.50	1.75	1.00
303	Jim Campbell	3.50	1.75	1.00
304	Bob Johnson	3.50	1.75	1.00
305	Jack Lamabe	3.50	1.75	1.00
306	Giant Gunners (Orlando Cepeda, Willie Mays)	25.00	12.50	7.50
307	Joe Gibbon	3.50	1.75	1.00
308	Gene Stephens	3.50	1.75	1.00
309	Paul Toth	3.50	1.75	1.00
310	Jim Gilliam	5.00	2.50	1.50
311	Tom Brown	3.50	1.75	1.00
312	Tigers Rookies **(Fritz Fisher, Fred Gladding)**	3.50	1.75	1.00
313	Chuck Hiller	3.50	1.75	1.00
314	Jerry Buchek	3.50	1.75	1.00
315	Bo Belinsky	3.50	1.75	1.00
316	Gene Oliver	3.50	1.75	1.00
317	Al Smith	3.50	1.75	1.00
318	Twins Team	6.00	3.00	1.75
319	Paul Brown	3.50	1.75	1.00
320	Rocky Colavito	12.50	6.25	3.75
321	Bob Lillis	3.50	1.75	1.00
322	George Brunet	3.50	1.75	1.00
323	John Buzhardt	3.50	1.75	1.00
324	Casey Stengel	12.50	6.25	3.75
325	Hector Lopez	3.50	1.75	1.00
326	Ron Brand	3.50	1.75	1.00
327	Don Blasingame	3.50	1.75	1.00
328	Bob Shaw	3.50	1.75	1.00
329	Russ Nixon	3.50	1.75	1.00
330	Tommy Harper	3.50	1.75	1.00
331	A.L. Bombers (Norm Cash, Al Kaline, Mickey Mantle, Roger Maris)	100.00	50.00	30.00
332	Ray Washburn	3.50	1.75	1.00
333	Billy Moran	3.50	1.75	1.00
334	Lew Krausse	3.50	1.75	1.00
335	Don Mossi	3.50	1.75	1.00
336	Andre Rodgers	3.50	1.75	1.00
337	Dodgers Rookies ***(Al Ferrara, Jeff Torborg)***	6.00	3.00	1.75
338	Jack Kralick	3.50	1.75	1.00
339	Walt Bond	3.50	1.75	1.00
340	Joe Cunningham	3.50	1.75	1.00
341	Jim Roland	3.50	1.75	1.00
342	Willie Stargell	25.00	12.50	7.50
343	Senators Team	6.00	3.00	1.75
344	Phil Linz	3.50	1.75	1.00
345	Frank Thomas	3.50	1.75	1.00
346	Joe Jay	3.50	1.75	1.00
347	Bobby Wine	3.50	1.75	1.00
348	Ed Lopat	3.50	1.75	1.00
349	Art Fowler	3.50	1.75	1.00
350	Willie McCovey	20.00	10.00	6.00
351	Dan Schneider	3.50	1.75	1.00
352	Eddie Bressoud	3.50	1.75	1.00
353	Wally Moon	3.50	1.75	1.00
354	Dave Giusti	3.50	1.75	1.00
355	Vic Power	3.50	1.75	1.00
356	Reds Rookies **(Bill McCool, Chico Ruiz)**	3.50	1.75	1.00
357	Charley James	3.50	1.75	1.00
358	Ron Kline	3.50	1.75	1.00
359	Jim Schaffer	3.50	1.75	1.00
360	Joe Pepitone	4.50	2.25	1.25
361	Jay Hook	3.50	1.75	1.00
362	5th Series Checklist (353-429)	6.00	3.00	1.75
363	Dick McAuliffe	3.50	1.75	1.00
364	Joe Gaines	3.50	1.75	1.00
365	Cal McLish	3.50	1.75	1.00
366	Nelson Mathews	3.50	1.75	1.00
367	Fred Whitfield	3.50	1.75	1.00
368	White Sox Rookies ***(Fritz Ackley, Don Buford)***	5.50	2.75	1.75
369	Jerry Zimmerman	3.50	1.75	1.00
370	Hal Woodeshick	3.50	1.75	1.00
371	Frank Howard	7.50	3.75	2.25
372	Howie Koplitz	6.00	3.00	1.75
373	Pittsburgh Pirates Team	11.00	5.50	3.25
374	Bobby Bolin	6.00	3.00	1.75
375	Ron Santo	20.00	10.00	6.00
376	Dave Morehead	6.00	3.00	1.75
377	Bob Skinner	6.00	3.00	1.75
378	Braves Rookies **(*Jack Smith, Woody Woodward*)**	6.00	3.00	1.75
379	Tony Gonzalez	6.00	3.00	1.75
380	Whitey Ford	30.00	15.00	9.00
381	Bob Taylor	6.00	3.00	1.75
382	Wes Stock	6.00	3.00	1.75
383	Bill Rigney	6.00	3.00	1.75
384	Ron Hansen	6.00	3.00	1.75
385	Curt Simmons	6.00	3.00	1.75
386	Lenny Green	6.00	3.00	1.75
387	Terry Fox	6.00	3.00	1.75
388	Athletics Rookies **(John O'Donoghue, George Williams)**	6.00	3.00	1.75
389	Jim Umbricht	6.00	3.00	1.75
390	Orlando Cepeda	17.50	8.75	5.25
391	Sam McDowell	6.00	3.00	1.75
392	Jim Pagliaroni	6.00	3.00	1.75
393	Casey Teaches (Ed Kranepool, Casey Stengel)	12.50	6.25	3.75
394	Bob Miller	6.00	3.00	1.75
395	Tom Tresh	13.50	6.75	4.00
396	Dennis Bennett	6.00	3.00	1.75
397	Chuck Cottier	6.00	3.00	1.75
398	Mets Rookies **(Bill Haas, Dick Smith)**	6.00	3.00	1.75
399	Jackie Brandt	6.00	3.00	1.75
400	Warren Spahn	30.00	15.00	9.00
401	Charlie Maxwell	6.00	3.00	1.75
402	Tom Sturdivant	6.00	3.00	1.75
403	Cincinnati Reds Team	10.00	5.00	3.00
404	Tony Martinez	6.00	3.00	1.75
405	Ken McBride	6.00	3.00	1.75
406	Al Spangler	6.00	3.00	1.75
407	Bill Freehan	6.00	3.00	1.75
408	Cubs Rookies **(Fred Burdette, Jim Stewart)**	6.00	3.00	1.75
409	Bill Fischer	6.00	3.00	1.75
410	Dick Stuart	6.00	3.00	1.75
411	Lee Walls	6.00	3.00	1.75
412	Ray Culp	6.00	3.00	1.75
413	Johnny Keane	6.00	3.00	1.75
414	Jack Sanford	6.00	3.00	1.75
415	Tony Kubek	12.50	6.25	3.75
416	Lee Maye	6.00	3.00	1.75
417	Don Cardwell	6.00	3.00	1.75
418	Orioles Rookies **(Darold Knowles, Les Narum)**	6.00	3.00	1.75
419	***Ken Harrelson***	9.00	4.50	2.75
420	Jim Maloney	6.00	3.00	1.75
421	Camilo Carreon	6.00	3.00	1.75
422	Jack Fisher	6.00	3.00	1.75
423	Tops in N.L. (Hank Aaron, Willie Mays)	85.00	42.50	25.00
424	Dick Bertell	6.00	3.00	1.75
425	Norm Cash	12.00	6.00	3.50
426	Bob Rodgers	6.00	3.00	1.75
427	Don Rudolph	6.00	3.00	1.75
428	Red Sox Rookies **(Archie Skeen, Pete Smith)**	6.00	3.00	1.75
429	Tim McCarver	12.50	6.25	3.75
430	Juan Pizarro	6.00	3.00	1.75
431	George Alusik	6.00	3.00	1.75
432	Ruben Amaro	6.00	3.00	1.75
433	New York Yankees Team	20.00	10.00	6.00
434	Don Nottebart	6.00	3.00	1.75
435	Vic Davalillo	6.00	3.00	1.75
436	Charlie Neal	6.00	3.00	1.75
437	Ed Bailey	6.00	3.00	1.75
438	6th Series Checklist (430-506)	11.00	5.50	3.25
439	Harvey Haddix	6.00	3.00	1.75
440	Bob Clemente	145.00	75.00	45.00
441	Bob Duliba	6.00	3.00	1.75
442	Pumpsie Green	6.00	3.00	1.75
443	Chuck Dressen	6.00	3.00	1.75
444	Larry Jackson	6.00	3.00	1.75
445	Bill Skowron	9.00	4.50	2.75
446	Julian Javier	6.00	3.00	1.75
447	Ted Bowsfield	6.00	3.00	1.75
448	Cookie Rojas	6.00	3.00	1.75
449	Deron Johnson	6.00	3.00	1.75
450	Steve Barber	6.00	3.00	1.75
451	Joe Amalfitano	6.00	3.00	1.75
452	Giants Rookies ***(Gil Garrido, Jim Hart)***	7.50	3.75	2.25
453	Frank Baumann	6.00	3.00	1.75
454	Tommie Aaron	6.00	3.00	1.75
455	Bernie Allen	6.00	3.00	1.75
456	Dodgers Rookies **(Wes Parker, John Werhas)**	6.00	3.00	1.75
457	Jesse Gonder	6.00	3.00	1.75
458	Ralph Terry	6.00	3.00	1.75
459	Red Sox Rookies **(Pete Charton, Dalton Jones)**	6.00	3.00	1.75
460	Bob Gibson	25.00	12.50	7.50
461	George Thomas	6.00	3.00	1.75
462	Birdie Tebbetts	6.00	3.00	1.75
463	Don Leppert	6.00	3.00	1.75
464	Dallas Green	6.00	3.00	1.75
465	Mike Hershberger	6.00	3.00	1.75
466	Athletics Rookies **(Dick Green, Aurelio Monteagudo)**	6.00	3.00	1.75
467	Bob Aspromonte	6.00	3.00	1.75
468	Gaylord Perry	20.00	10.00	6.00
469	Cubs Rookies **(Fred Norman, Sterling Slaughter)**	6.00	3.00	1.75
470	Jim Bouton	10.00	5.00	3.00
471	***Gates Brown***	6.50	3.25	2.00
472	Vern Law	6.00	3.00	1.75
473	Baltimore Orioles Team	9.00	4.50	3.75
474	Larry Sherry	6.00	3.00	1.75
475	Ed Charles	6.00	3.00	1.75
476	Braves Rookies **(Rico Carty, Dick Kelley)**	9.00	4.50	2.75
477	Mike Joyce	6.00	3.00	1.75
478	Dick Howser	6.00	3.00	1.75
479	Cardinals Rookies **(Dave Bakenhaster, Johnny Lewis)**	6.00	3.00	1.75
480	Bob Purkey	6.00	3.00	1.75
481	Chuck Schilling	6.00	3.00	1.75
482	Phillies Rookies **(*John Briggs, Danny Cater*)**	6.00	3.00	1.75
483	Fred Valentine	6.00	3.00	1.75
484	Bill Pleis	6.00	3.00	1.75
485	Tom Haller	6.00	3.00	1.75
486	Bob Kennedy	6.00	3.00	1.75
487	Mike McCormick	6.00	3.00	1.75
488	Yankees Rookies **(Bob Meyer, Pete Mikkelsen)**	6.00	3.00	1.75
489	Julio Navarro	6.00	3.00	1.75
490	Ron Fairly	6.00	3.00	1.75
491	Ed Rakow	6.00	3.00	1.75
492	Colts Rookies **(Jim Beauchamp, Mike White)**	6.00	3.00	1.75
493	Don Lee	6.00	3.00	1.75
494	Al Jackson	6.00	3.00	1.75
495	Bill Virdon	6.00	3.00	1.75
496	Chicago White Sox Team	9.00	4.50	2.75
497	Jeoff Long	6.00	3.00	1.75
498	Dave Stenhouse	6.00	3.00	1.75
499	Indians Rookies **(Chico Salmon, Gordon Seyfried)**	6.00	3.00	1.75
500	Camilo Pascual	6.00	3.00	1.75
501	Bob Veale	6.00	3.00	1.75
502	Angels Rookies **(Bobby Knoop, Bob Lee)**	6.00	3.00	1.75
503	Earl Wilson	6.00	3.00	1.75
504	Claude Raymond	6.00	3.00	1.75
505	Stan Williams	6.00	3.00	1.75
506	Bobby Bragan	6.00	3.00	1.75
507	John Edwards	6.00	3.00	1.75
508	Diego Segui	6.00	3.00	1.75
509	Pirates Rookies **(Gene Alley, Orlando McFarlane)**	6.00	3.00	1.75
510	Lindy McDaniel	6.00	3.00	1.75
511	Lou Jackson	6.00	3.00	1.75
512	Tigers Rookies **(*Willie Horton, Joe Sparma*)**	22.50	11.00	6.75
513	Don Larsen	6.00	3.00	1.75
514	Jim Hickman	6.00	3.00	1.75
515	Johnny Romano	6.00	3.00	1.75
516	Twins Rookies **(Jerry Arrigo, Dwight Siebler)**	6.00	3.00	1.75
517a	7th Series Checklist (507-587) (Wrong numbering on back.)	15.00	7.50	4.50
517b	7th Series Checklist (507-587) (Correct numbering on back.)	11.00	5.50	3.25
518	Carl Bouldin	6.00	3.00	1.75
519	Charlie Smith	6.00	3.00	1.75
520	Jack Baldschun	6.00	3.00	1.75
521	Tom Satriano	6.00	3.00	1.75
522	Bobby Tiefenauer	6.00	3.00	1.75
523	Lou Burdette	9.00	4.50	2.75
524	Reds Rookies **(Jim Dickson, Bobby Klaus)**	9.00	4.50	2.75
525	Al McBean	9.00	4.50	2.75
526	Lou Clinton	9.00	4.50	2.75
527	Larry Bearnarth	9.00	4.50	2.75
528	Athletics Rookies **(Dave Duncan, Tom Reynolds)**	9.00	4.50	2.75
529	Al Dark	9.00	4.50	2.75

#	Player	NM	EX	VG
530	Leon Wagner	9.00	4.50	2.75
531	L.A. Dodgers Team	17.50	8.75	5.25
532	Twins Rookies **(Bud Bloomfield, Joe Nossek)**	9.00	4.50	2.75
533	Johnny Klippstein	9.00	4.50	2.75
534	Gus Bell	9.00	4.50	2.75
535	Phil Regan	9.00	4.50	2.75
536	Mets Rookies **(Larry Elliot, John Stephenson)**	9.00	4.50	2.75
537	Dan Osinski	9.00	4.50	2.75
538	Minnie Minoso	13.50	6.75	4.00
539	Roy Face	9.00	4.50	2.75
540	Luis Aparicio	35.00	17.50	10.00
541	Braves Rookies **(Phil Niekro, Phil Roof)**	50.00	25.00	15.00
542	Don Mincher	9.00	4.50	2.75
543	Bob Uecker	30.00	15.00	9.00
544	Colts Rookies **(Steve Hertz, Joe Hoerner)**	9.00	4.50	2.75
545	Max Alvis	9.00	4.50	2.75
546	Joe Christopher	9.00	4.50	2.75
547	Gil Hodges	15.00	7.50	4.50
548	N.L. Rookies **(Wayne Schurr, Paul Speckenbach)**	9.00	4.50	2.75
549	Joe Moeller	9.00	4.50	2.75
550	Ken Hubbs - In Memoriam	20.00	10.00	6.00
551	Billy Hoeft	9.00	4.50	2.75
552	Indians Rookies ***(Tom Kelley, Sonny Siebert)***	11.00	5.50	3.25
553	Jim Brewer	9.00	4.50	2.75
554	Hank Foiles	9.00	4.50	2.75
555	Lee Stange	9.00	4.50	2.75
556	Mets Rookies **(Steve Dillon, Ron Locke)**	9.00	4.50	2.75
557	Leo Burke	9.00	4.50	2.75
558	Don Schwall	9.00	4.50	2.75
559	Dick Phillips	9.00	4.50	2.75
560	Dick Farrell	9.00	4.50	2.75
561	Phillies Rookies ***(Dave Bennett, Rick Wise)***	11.00	5.50	3.25
562	Pedro Ramos	9.00	4.50	2.75
563	Dal Maxvill	9.00	4.50	2.75
564	A.L. Rookies **(Joe McCabe, Jerry McNertney)**	9.00	4.50	2.75
565	Stu Miller	9.00	4.50	2.75
566	Ed Kranepool	9.00	4.50	2.75
567	Jim Kaat	12.50	6.25	3.75
568	N.L. Rookies **(Phil Gagliano, Cap Peterson)**	9.00	4.50	2.75
569	Fred Newman	9.00	4.50	2.75
570	Bill Mazeroski	25.00	12.50	7.50
571	Gene Conley	9.00	4.50	2.75
572	A.L. Rookies **(Dick Egan, Dave Gray)**	9.00	4.50	2.75
573	Jim Duffalo	9.00	4.50	2.75
574	Manny Jimenez	9.00	4.50	2.75
575	Tony Cloninger	9.00	4.50	2.75
576	Mets Rookies **(Jerry Hinsley, Bill Wakefield)**	9.00	4.50	2.75
577	Gordy Coleman	9.00	4.50	2.75
578	Glen Hobbie	9.00	4.50	2.75
579	Boston Red Sox Team	17.50	8.75	5.25
580	Johnny Podres	11.00	5.50	3.25
581	Yankees Rookies **(Pedro Gonzalez, Archie Moore)**	9.00	4.50	2.75
582	Rod Kanehl	9.00	4.50	2.75
583	Tito Francona	9.00	4.50	2.75
584	Joel Horlen	9.00	4.50	2.75
585	Tony Taylor	9.00	4.50	2.75
586	Jim Piersall	10.00	5.00	3.00
587	Bennie Daniels	12.00	6.00	3.50

1964 Topps Coins

The 164 metal coins in this set were issued by Topps as inserts in the company's baseball card wax packs. The series is divided into two principal types, 120 "regular" coins and 44 All-Star coins. The 1-1/2" diameter coins feature a full-color background for the player photos in the "regular" series, while the players in the All-Star series are featured against plain red or blue backgrounds. There are two variations each of the Mantle, Causey and Hinton coins among the All-Star subset.

#	Player	NM	EX	VG
	Complete Set (164):	1,125	550.00	325.00
	Common Player:	6.00	3.00	1.75
1	Don Zimmer	6.00	3.00	1.75
2	Jim Wynn	6.00	3.00	1.75
3	Johnny Orsino	6.00	3.00	1.75
4	Jim Bouton	7.50	3.75	2.25
5	Dick Groat	6.00	3.00	1.75
6	Leon Wagner	6.00	3.00	1.75
7	Frank Malzone	6.00	3.00	1.75
8	Steve Barber	6.00	3.00	1.75
9	Johnny Romano	6.00	3.00	1.75
10	Tom Tresh	7.50	3.75	2.25
11	Felipe Alou	6.00	3.00	1.75
12	Dick Stuart	6.00	3.00	1.75
13	Claude Osteen	6.00	3.00	1.75
14	Juan Pizarro	6.00	3.00	1.75
15	Donn Clendenon	6.00	3.00	1.75
16	Jimmie Hall	6.00	3.00	1.75
17	Larry Jackson	6.00	3.00	1.75
18	Brooks Robinson	15.00	7.50	4.50
19	Bob Allison	6.00	3.00	1.75
20	Ed Roebuck	6.00	3.00	1.75
21	Pete Ward	6.00	3.00	1.75
22	Willie McCovey	12.50	6.25	3.75
23	Elston Howard	7.00	3.50	2.00
24	Diego Segui	6.00	3.00	1.75
25	Ken Boyer	7.00	3.50	2.00
26	Carl Yastrzemski	20.00	10.00	6.00
27	Bill Mazeroski	12.50	6.25	3.75
28	Jerry Lumpe	6.00	3.00	1.75
29	Woody Held	6.00	3.00	1.75
30	Dick Radatz	6.00	3.00	1.75
31	Luis Aparicio	10.00	5.00	3.00
32	Dave Nicholson	6.00	3.00	1.75
33	Ed Mathews	15.00	7.50	4.50
34	Don Drysdale	15.00	7.50	4.50
35	Ray Culp	6.00	3.00	1.75
36	Juan Marichal	10.00	5.00	3.00
37	Frank Robinson	15.00	7.50	4.50
38	Chuck Hinton	6.00	3.00	1.75
39	Floyd Robinson	6.00	3.00	1.75
40	Tommy Harper	6.00	3.00	1.75
41	Ron Hansen	6.00	3.00	1.75
42	Ernie Banks	20.00	10.00	6.00
43	Jesse Gonder	6.00	3.00	1.75
44	Billy Williams	10.00	5.00	3.00
45	Vada Pinson	7.00	3.50	2.00
46	Rocky Colavito	9.00	4.50	2.75
47	Bill Monbouquette	6.00	3.00	1.75
48	Max Alvis	6.00	3.00	1.75
49	Norm Siebern	6.00	3.00	1.75
50	John Callison	6.00	3.00	1.75
51	Rich Rollins	6.00	3.00	1.75
52	Ken McBride	6.00	3.00	1.75
53	Don Lock	6.00	3.00	1.75
54	Ron Fairly	6.00	3.00	1.75
55	Roberto Clemente	30.00	15.00	9.00
56	Dick Ellsworth	6.00	3.00	1.75
57	Tommy Davis	6.00	3.00	1.75
58	Tony Gonzalez	6.00	3.00	1.75
59	Bob Gibson	15.00	7.50	4.50
60	Jim Maloney	6.00	3.00	1.75
61	Frank Howard	7.00	3.50	2.00
62	Jim Pagliaroni	6.00	3.00	1.75
63	Orlando Cepeda	10.00	5.00	3.00
64	Ron Perranoski	6.00	3.00	1.75
65	Curt Flood	6.00	3.00	1.75
66	Al McBean	6.00	3.00	1.75
67	Dean Chance	6.00	3.00	1.75
68	Ron Santo	7.50	3.75	2.25
69	Jack Baldschun	6.00	3.00	1.75
70	Milt Pappas	6.00	3.00	1.75
71	Gary Peters	6.00	3.00	1.75
72	Bobby Richardson	7.50	3.75	2.25
73	Lee Thomas	6.00	3.00	1.75
74	Hank Aguirre	6.00	3.00	1.75
75	Carl Willey	6.00	3.00	1.75
76	Camilo Pascual	6.00	3.00	1.75
77	Bob Friend	6.00	3.00	1.75
78	Bill White	6.00	3.00	1.75
79	Norm Cash	7.50	3.75	2.25
80	Willie Mays	30.00	15.00	9.00
81	Duke Carmel	6.00	3.00	1.75
82	Pete Rose	35.00	17.50	10.50
83	Hank Aaron	30.00	15.00	9.00
84	Bob Aspromonte	6.00	3.00	1.75
85	Jim O'Toole	6.00	3.00	1.75
86	Vic Davalillo	6.00	3.00	1.75
87	Bill Freehan	6.00	3.00	1.75
88	Warren Spahn	15.00	7.50	4.50
89	Ron Hunt	6.00	3.00	1.75
90	Denis Menke	6.00	3.00	1.75
91	Turk Farrell	6.00	3.00	1.75
92	Jim Hickman	6.00	3.00	1.75
93	Jim Bunning	9.00	4.50	2.75
94	Bob Hendley	6.00	3.00	1.75
95	Ernie Broglio	6.00	3.00	1.75
96	Rusty Staub	7.00	3.50	2.00
97	Lou Brock	10.00	5.00	3.00
98	Jim Fregosi	6.00	3.00	1.75
99	Jim Grant	6.00	3.00	1.75
100	Al Kaline	15.00	7.50	4.50
101	Earl Battey	6.00	3.00	1.75
102	Wayne Causey	6.00	3.00	1.75
103	Chuck Schilling	6.00	3.00	1.75
104	Boog Powell	7.50	3.75	2.25
105	Dave Wickersham	6.00	3.00	1.75
106	Sandy Koufax	30.00	15.00	9.00
107	John Bateman	6.00	3.00	1.75
108	Ed Brinkman	6.00	3.00	1.75
109	Al Downing	6.00	3.00	1.75
110	Joe Azcue	6.00	3.00	1.75
111	Albie Pearson	6.00	3.00	1.75
112	Harmon Killebrew	15.00	7.50	4.50
113	Tony Taylor	6.00	3.00	1.75
114	Alvin Jackson	6.00	3.00	1.75
115	Billy O'Dell	6.00	3.00	1.75
116	Don Demeter	6.00	3.00	1.75
117	Ed Charles	6.00	3.00	1.75
118	Joe Torre	7.50	3.75	2.25
119	Don Nottebart	6.00	3.00	1.75
120	Mickey Mantle	65.00	32.00	19.50
121	Joe Pepitone/AS	7.50	3.75	2.25
122	Dick Stuart/AS	6.00	3.00	1.75
123	Bobby Richardson/AS	7.50	3.75	2.25
124	Jerry Lumpe/AS	6.00	3.00	1.75
125	Brooks Robinson/AS	12.50	6.25	3.75
126	Frank Malzone/AS	6.00	3.00	1.75
127	Luis Aparicio/AS	9.00	4.50	2.75
128	Jim Fregosi/AS	6.00	3.00	1.75
129	Al Kaline/AS	12.50	6.25	3.75
130	Leon Wagner/AS	6.00	3.00	1.75
131a	Mickey Mantle/AS (Lefthanded)	45.00	22.00	13.50
131b	Mickey Mantle/AS (Righthanded)	50.00	25.00	15.00
132	Albie Pearson/AS	6.00	3.00	1.75
133	Harmon Killebrew/AS	12.50	6.25	3.75
134	Carl Yastrzemski/AS	17.50	8.75	5.25
135	Elston Howard/AS	7.00	3.50	2.00
136	Earl Battey/AS	6.00	3.00	1.75
137	Camilo Pascual/AS	6.00	3.00	1.75
138	Jim Bouton/AS	7.00	3.50	2.00
139	Whitey Ford/AS	15.00	7.50	4.50
140	Gary Peters/AS	6.00	3.00	1.75
141	Bill White/AS	6.00	3.00	1.75
142	Orlando Cepeda/AS	9.00	4.50	2.75
143	Bill Mazeroski/AS	10.00	5.00	3.00
144	Tony Taylor/AS	6.00	3.00	1.75
145	Ken Boyer/AS	7.00	3.50	2.00
146	Ron Santo/AS	7.50	3.75	2.25
147	Dick Groat/AS	6.00	3.00	1.75
148	Roy McMillan/AS	6.00	3.00	1.75
149	Hank Aaron/AS	27.50	13.50	8.25
150	Roberto Clemente/AS	27.50	13.50	8.25
151	Willie Mays/AS	27.50	13.50	8.25
152	Vada Pinson/AS	7.00	3.50	2.00
153	Tommy Davis/AS	6.00	3.00	1.75
154	Frank Robinson/AS	12.50	6.25	3.75
155	Joe Torre/AS	7.50	3.75	2.25
156	Tim McCarver/AS	6.00	3.00	1.75
157	Juan Marichal/AS	10.00	5.00	3.00
158	Jim Maloney/AS	6.00	3.00	1.75
159	Sandy Koufax/AS	27.50	13.50	8.25
160	Warren Spahn/AS	12.50	6.25	3.75
161a	Wayne Causey/AS (N.L. on back.)	20.00	10.00	6.00
161b	Wayne Causey/AS (A.L. on back.)	6.00	3.00	1.75
162a	Chuck Hinton/AS (N.L. on back.)	20.00	10.00	6.00
162b	Chuck Hinton/AS (A.L. on back.)	6.00	3.00	1.75
163	Bob Aspromonte/AS	6.00	3.00	1.75
164	Ron Hunt/AS	6.00	3.00	1.75

1964 Topps Giants

Measuring 3-1/8" x 5-1/4" the Topps Giants were the company's first postcard-size issue. The cards feature large color photographs surrounded by white borders with a white baseball containing the player's name, position and team. Card backs carry another photo of the player surrounded by a newspaper-style explanation of the depicted career highlight. The 60-card set contains primarily stars which means it's an excellent place to find inexpensive cards of Hall of Famers. The '64 Giants were not printed in equal quantity and seven of the cards, including Sandy Koufax and Willie Mays, are significantly scarcer than the remainder of the set.

#	Player	NM	EX	VG
	Complete Set (60):	265.00	135.00	80.00
	Common Player:	3.00	1.50	.90
1	Gary Peters	3.00	1.50	.90
2	Ken Johnson	3.00	1.50	.90
3	Sandy Koufax/SP	35.00	17.50	10.00
4	Bob Bailey	3.00	1.50	.90
5	Milt Pappas	3.00	1.50	.90
6	Ron Hunt	3.00	1.50	.90
7	Whitey Ford	10.00	5.00	3.00
8	Roy McMillan	3.00	1.50	.90
9	Rocky Colavito	6.00	3.00	1.75
10	Jim Bunning	6.00	3.00	1.75
11	Roberto Clemente	17.50	8.75	5.25
12	Al Kaline	9.00	4.50	2.75
13	Nellie Fox	7.00	3.50	2.00
14	Tony Gonzalez	3.00	1.50	.90
15	Jim Gentile	3.00	1.50	.90
16	Dean Chance	3.00	1.50	.90
17	Dick Ellsworth	3.00	1.50	.90
18	Jim Fregosi	3.00	1.50	.90
19	Dick Groat	3.00	1.50	.90
20	Chuck Hinton	3.00	1.50	.90
21	Elston Howard	4.50	2.25	1.25
22	Dick Farrell	3.00	1.50	.90
23	Albie Pearson	3.00	1.50	.90
24	Frank Howard	4.00	2.00	1.25
25	Mickey Mantle	35.00	17.50	10.00
26	Joe Torre	5.00	2.50	1.50
27	Ed Brinkman	3.00	1.50	.90
28	Bob Friend/SP	12.50	6.25	3.75
29	Frank Robinson	8.00	4.00	2.50
30	Bill Freehan	3.00	1.50	.90
31	Warren Spahn	8.00	4.00	2.50
32	Camilo Pascual	3.00	1.50	.90
33	Pete Ward	3.00	1.50	.90
34	Jim Maloney	3.00	1.50	.90
35	Dave Wickersham	3.00	1.50	.90
36	Johnny Callison	3.00	1.50	.90

37	Juan Marichal	7.00	3.50	2.00
38	Harmon Killebrew	9.00	4.50	2.75
39	Luis Aparicio	7.00	3.50	2.00
40	Dick Radatz	3.00	1.50	.90
41	Bob Gibson	7.00	3.50	2.00
42	Dick Stuart/SP	15.00	7.50	4.50
43	Tommy Davis	3.00	1.50	.90
44	Tony Oliva	3.50	1.75	1.00
45	Wayne Causey/SP	15.00	7.50	4.50
46	Max Alvis	3.00	1.50	.90
47	Galen Cisco/SP	13.50	6.75	4.00
48	Carl Yastrzemski	9.00	4.50	2.75
49	Hank Aaron	17.50	8.75	5.25
50	Brooks Robinson	9.00	4.50	2.75
51	Willie Mays/SP	35.00	17.50	10.00
52	Billy Williams	8.00	4.00	2.50
53	Juan Pizarro	3.00	1.50	.90
54	Leon Wagner	3.00	1.50	.90
55	Orlando Cepeda	7.00	3.50	2.00
56	Vada Pinson	3.50	1.75	1.00
57	Ken Boyer	3.50	1.75	1.00
58	Ron Santo	5.00	2.50	1.50
59	John Romano	3.00	1.50	.90
60	Bill Skowron/SP	16.00	8.00	4.75

1964 Topps Photo Tatoos

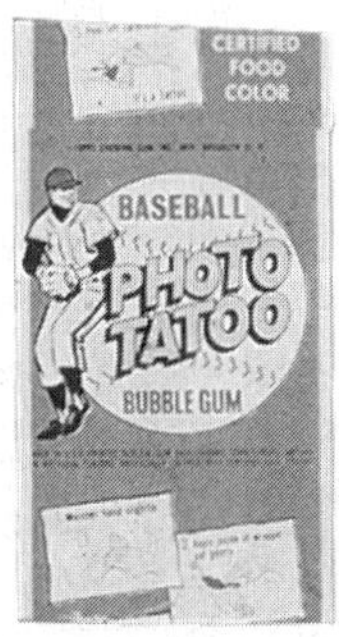

Apparently not content to leave the skin of American children without adornment, Topps jumped back into the tattoo field in 1964 with the release of a new series, measuring 1-9/16" x 3-1/2". The picture side for the 20 team tattoos gives the team logo and name.

	NM	EX	VG
Complete Set (79):	3,000	1,500	900.00
Common Player:	15.00	7.50	4.50
Unopened Pack:	160.00		
(1) Hank Aaron	135.00	65.00	40.00
(2) Hank Aguirre	15.00	7.50	4.50
(3) Max Alvis	15.00	7.50	4.50
(4) Ernie Banks	80.00	40.00	24.00
(5) Steve Barber	15.00	7.50	4.50
(6) Ken Boyer	20.00	10.00	6.00
(7) Johnny Callison	15.00	7.50	4.50
(8) Norm Cash	20.00	10.00	6.00
(9) Wayne Causey	15.00	7.50	4.50
(10) Orlando Cepeda	50.00	25.00	15.00
(11) Rocky Colavito	50.00	25.00	15.00
(12) Ray Culp	15.00	7.50	4.50
(13) Vic Davalillo	15.00	7.50	4.50
(14) Moe Drabowsky	15.00	7.50	4.50
(15) Dick Ellsworth	15.00	7.50	4.50
(16) Curt Flood	15.00	7.50	4.50
(17) Bill Freehan	15.00	7.50	4.50
(18) Jim Fregosi	15.00	7.50	4.50
(19) Bob Friend	15.00	7.50	4.50
(20) Dick Groat	15.00	7.50	4.50
(21) Woody Held	15.00	7.50	4.50
(22) Frank Howard	20.00	10.00	6.00
(23) Al Jackson	15.00	7.50	4.50
(24) Larry Jackson	15.00	7.50	4.50
(25) Ken Johnson	15.00	7.50	4.50
(26) Al Kaline	60.00	30.00	18.00
(27) Harmon Killebrew (Green background.)	60.00	30.00	18.00
(28) Harmon Killebrew (Red background.)	60.00	30.00	18.00
(29) Sandy Koufax (Horizontal band.)	135.00	65.00	40.00
(30) Sandy Koufax (Diagonal band.)	145.00	75.00	45.00
(31) Don Lock	15.00	7.50	4.50
(32) Frank Malzone	15.00	7.50	4.50
(33) Mickey Mantle (Diagonal yellow band.)	325.00	160.00	100.00
(34) Mickey Mantle (Red triangle.)	325.00	160.00	100.00
(35) Eddie Mathews	60.00	30.00	18.00
(36) Willie Mays (Yellow background encompasses head.)	135.00	65.00	40.00
(37) Willie Mays (Yellow background ears-to-chin.)	135.00	65.00	40.00
(38) Bill Mazeroski	60.00	30.00	18.00
(39) Ken McBride	15.00	7.50	4.50
(40) Bill Monbouquette	15.00	7.50	4.50
(41) Dave Nicholson	15.00	7.50	4.50
(42) Claude Osteen	15.00	7.50	4.50
(43) Milt Pappas	15.00	7.50	4.50
(44) Camilio Pascual	15.00	7.50	4.50
(45) Albie Pearson	15.00	7.50	4.50
(46) Ron Perranoski	15.00	7.50	4.50
(47) Gary Peters	15.00	7.50	4.50
(48) Boog Powell	20.00	10.00	6.00
(49) Frank Robinson	60.00	30.00	18.00
(50) John Romano	15.00	7.50	4.50
(51) Norm Siebern	15.00	7.50	4.50
(52) Warren Spahn	60.00	30.00	18.00
(53) Dick Stuart	15.00	7.50	4.50
(54) Lee Thomas	15.00	7.50	4.50
(55) Joe Torre	25.00	12.50	7.50
(56) Pete Ward	15.00	7.50	4.50
(57) Carlton Willey	15.00	7.50	4.50
(58) Billy Williams	60.00	30.00	18.00
(59) Carl Yastrzemski	75.00	37.50	22.50
(60) Baltimore Orioles Logo	20.00	10.00	6.00
(61) Boston Red Sox Logo	20.00	10.00	6.00
(62) Chicago Cubs Logo	20.00	10.00	6.00
(63) Chicago White Sox Logo	20.00	10.00	6.00
(64) Cincinnati Reds Logo	20.00	10.00	6.00
(65) Cleveland Indians Logo	20.00	10.00	6.00
(66) Detroit Tigers Logo	20.00	10.00	6.00
(67) Houston Colts Logo	25.00	12.50	7.50
(68) Kansas City Athletics Logo	20.00	10.00	6.00
(69) Los Angeles Angels Logo	20.00	10.00	6.00
(70) Los Angeles Dodgers Logo	20.00	10.00	6.00
(71) Milwaukee Braves Logo	20.00	10.00	6.00
(72) Minnesota Twins Logo	20.00	10.00	6.00
(73) New York Mets Logo	25.00	12.50	7.50
(74) New York Yankees Logo	25.00	12.50	7.50
(75) Philadelphia Phillies Logo	20.00	10.00	6.00
(76) Pittsburgh Pirates Logo	20.00	10.00	6.00
(77) St. Louis Cardinals Logo	20.00	10.00	6.00
(78) San Francisco Giants Logo	20.00	10.00	6.00
(79) Washington Senators Logo	20.00	10.00	6.00

1964 Topps Rookie All-Star Banquet

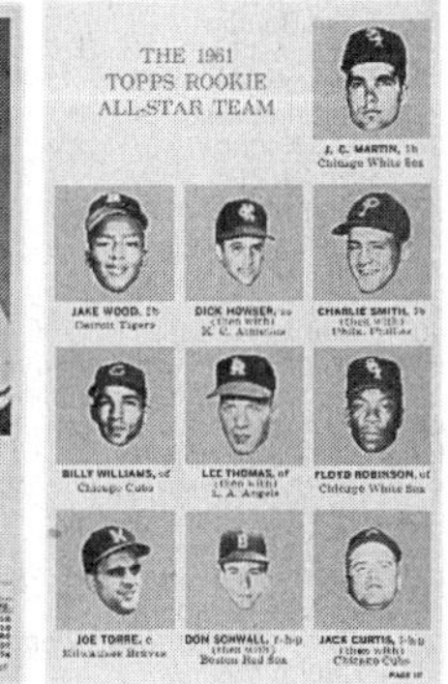

Since 1959, Topss has sponsored a formal post-season banquet to honor its annual Rookie All-Star team. In 1964, the gum company deviated from the tradition dinner program by issuing a 36-card boxed set. Each of the cards is printed in black-and-white, with red or light blue graphic highlights. The first seven cards in the set feature Topps staff and baseball dignitaries involved in the selection of the rookie team. Cards #8-12 are composite photos of the 1959-63 Rookie All-Star team. Cards #13-34A showcase the '64 honorees. Each player's card is matched with a card from the team's public relations officer extolling the rookie's virtues. Each card in this unique dinner program measures 3" x 5-1/4" and is numbered as a "PAGE" in the lower-right corner.

		NM	EX	VG
	Complete Boxed Set (36):	2,800	1,400	850.00
	Common Player:	17.50	8.75	5.25
1	"6th Annual Topps Rookie All-Star Team Awards" Header Card	17.50	8.75	5.25
2	The Baseball World Votes (Tommy Davis, Jeff Torborg, Ron Santo, Billy Williams)	17.50	8.75	5.25
3	The Baseball World Votes (Six more clubhouse scenes.)	17.50	8.75	5.25
4	Topps Rookie All-Star Team Honorary Election Committee (Photos of media and Hall of Famers Hank Greenberg and Fran Frisch.)	55.00	27.00	16.50
5	Topps Rookie All-Star Team Honorary Election Committee (Photos of five media, Topps' VP Joel Shorin and Jackie Robinson.)	120.00	60.00	35.00
6	Executive Director of the Committee and His Associates (Topps' Cy Berger, three others.)	17.50	8.75	5.25
7	Topps Salutes Joe Garagiola (Joe Garagiola)	95.00	45.00	25.00
8	The 1959 Topps Rookie All-Star Team (Willie McCovey, Pumpsie Green, Joe Koppe, Jim Baxes, Bobby Allison, Ron Fairly, Willie Tasby, John Romano, Jim Perry, Jim O'Toole)	225.00	110.00	65.00
9	The 1960 Topps Rookie All-Star Team (Jim Gentile, Julian Javier, Ron Hansen, Ron Santo, Tommy Davis, Frank Howard, Tony Curry, Jimmie Coker, Chuck Estrada, Dick Stigman)	225.00	110.00	65.00
10	The 1961 Topps Rookie All-Star Team (J.C. Martin, Jake Wood, Dick Howser, Charlie Smith, Billy Williams, Lee Thomas, Floyd Robinson, Joe Torre, Don Schwall, Jack Curtis)	185.00	90.00	55.00
11	The 1962 Topps Rookie All-Star Team (Fred Whitfield, Bernie Allen, Tom Tresh, Ed Charles, Manny Jiminez, Al Luplow, Boog Powell, Buck Rodgers, Dean Chance, Al Jackson)	185.00	90.00	55.00
12	The 1963 Topps Rookie All-Star Team (Pete Rose, Rusty Staub, Al Weis, Pete Ward, Jimmie Hall, Vic Davalillo, Tommy Harper, Jesse Gonder, Ray Culp, Gary Peters)	1,400	700.00	425.00
13	1964 Topps Rookie All-Star Team Header Card	17.50	8.75	5.25
14	Ed Uhas, Cleveland Indians PR	17.50	8.75	5.25
15	Bob Chance	135.00	65.00	40.00
16	Garry Schumacher, S.F. Giants PR	17.50	8.75	5.25
17	Hal Lanier	135.00	65.00	40.00
18	Larry Shenk, Phillies PR	17.50	8.75	5.25
19	Richie Allen	300.00	150.00	90.00
20	Jim Schaaf, Athletics PR	17.50	8.75	5.25
21	Bert Campaneris	160.00	80.00	45.00
22	Ernie Johnson, Braves PR	17.50	8.75	5.25
23	Rico Carty	160.00	80.00	45.00
24	Bill Crowley, Red Sox PR	17.50	8.75	5.25
25	Tony Conigliaro	345.00	175.00	100.00
26	Tom Mee, Twins PR	17.50	8.75	5.25
27	Tony Oliva	210.00	100.00	60.00
28	Burt Hawkins, Senators PR	17.50	8.75	5.25
29	Mike Brumley	135.00	65.00	40.00
30	Hank Zureick, Reds PR	17.50	8.75	5.25
31	Bill McCool	135.00	65.00	40.00
32	Rob Brown, Orioles PR	17.50	8.75	5.25
33	Wally Bunker	135.00	65.00	40.00
34	"5th Annual Topps Minor League Player of the Year" Header Card	17.50	8.75	5.25
34A	Luis Tiant (Minor League Player of the Year)	160.00	80.00	45.00
35	Rookie All-Star Trophy	17.50	8.75	5.25

1964 Topps Stand-Ups

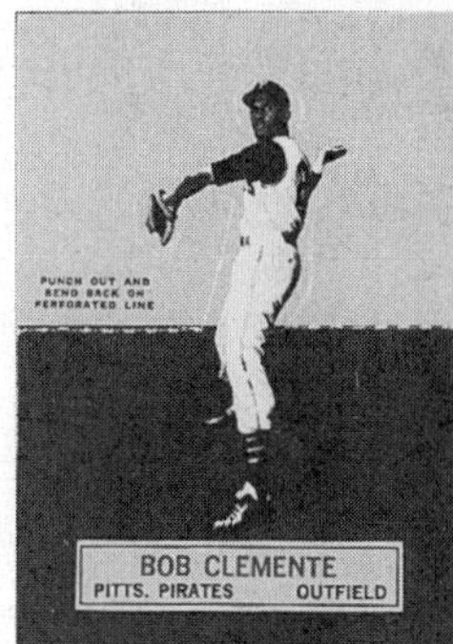

These 2-1/2" x 3-1/2" cards were the first since the All-Star sets of 1951 to be die-cut. This made it possible for a folded card to stand on display. The 77-cards in the set feature color photographs of the player with yellow and green backgrounds. Directions for folding are on the yellow top background, and when folded only the green background remains. Of the 77 cards, 55 were double-printed while 22 were single-printed, making them twice as scarce.

	NM	EX	VG
Complete Set (77):	2,250	1,125	650.00
Common Player:	12.00	6.00	3.50
Wax Pack (1):	600.00		
(1) Hank Aaron	90.00	45.00	27.50
(2) Hank Aguirre	12.00	6.00	3.50
(3) George Altman	12.00	6.00	3.50
(4) Max Alvis	12.00	6.00	3.50
(5) Bob Aspromonte	12.00	6.00	3.50
(6) Jack Baldschun/SP	20.00	10.00	6.00
(7) Ernie Banks	55.00	27.50	16.50
(8) Steve Barber	12.00	6.00	3.50
(9) Earl Battey	12.00	6.00	3.50
(10) Ken Boyer	20.00	10.00	6.00
(11) Ernie Broglio	12.00	6.00	3.50
(12) Johnny Callison	12.00	6.00	3.50
(13) Norm Cash/SP	50.00	25.00	15.00
(14) Wayne Causey	12.00	6.00	3.50
(15) Orlando Cepeda	27.50	13.50	8.25
(16) Ed Charles	12.00	6.00	3.50
(17) Roberto Clemente	150.00	75.00	45.00
(18) Donn Clendenon/SP	20.00	10.00	6.00
(19) Rocky Colavito	25.00	12.50	7.50
(20) Ray Culp/SP	20.00	10.00	6.00
(21) Tommy Davis	12.00	6.00	3.50
(22) Don Drysdale/SP	55.00	27.50	16.50
(23) Dick Ellsworth	12.00	6.00	3.50
(24) Dick Farrell	12.00	6.00	3.50
(25) Jim Fregosi	12.00	6.00	3.50
(26) Bob Friend	12.00	6.00	3.50
(27) Jim Gentile	12.00	6.00	3.50

(28)	Jesse Gonder/SP	20.00	10.00	6.00
(29)	Tony Gonzalez/SP	20.00	10.00	6.00
(30)	Dick Groat	12.50	6.25	3.75
(31)	Woody Held	12.00	6.00	3.50
(32)	Chuck Hinton	12.00	6.00	3.50
(33)	Elston Howard	20.00	10.00	6.00
(34)	Frank Howard/SP	27.50	13.50	8.25
(35)	Ron Hunt	12.00	6.00	3.50
(36)	Al Jackson	12.00	6.00	3.50
(37)	Ken Johnson	12.00	6.00	3.50
(38)	Al Kaline	40.00	20.00	12.00
(39)	Harmon Killebrew	50.00	25.00	15.00
(40)	Sandy Koufax	100.00	50.00	30.00
(41)	Don Lock/SP	20.00	10.00	6.00
(42)	Jerry Lumpe/SP	20.00	10.00	6.00
(43)	Jim Maloney	12.00	6.00	3.50
(44)	Frank Malzone	12.00	6.00	3.50
(45)	Mickey Mantle	465.00	230.00	140.00
(46)	Juan Marichal/SP	50.00	25.00	15.00
(47)	Ed Mathews/SP	60.00	30.00	18.00
(48)	Willie Mays	135.00	65.00	40.00
(49)	Bill Mazeroski	22.50	11.00	7.00
(50)	Ken McBride	12.00	6.00	3.50
(51)	Willie McCovey/SP	50.00	25.00	15.00
(52)	Claude Osteen	12.00	6.00	3.50
(53)	Jim O'Toole	12.00	6.00	3.50
(54)	Camilo Pascual	12.00	6.00	3.50
(55)	Albie Pearson/SP	20.00	10.00	6.00
(56)	Gary Peters	12.00	6.00	3.50
(57)	Vada Pinson	15.00	7.50	4.50
(58)	Juan Pizarro	12.00	6.00	3.50
(59)	Boog Powell	20.00	10.00	6.00
(60)	Bobby Richardson	20.00	10.00	6.00
(61)	Brooks Robinson	60.00	30.00	18.00
(62)	Floyd Robinson	12.00	6.00	3.50
(63)	Frank Robinson	50.00	25.00	15.00
(64)	Ed Roebuck/SP	20.00	10.00	6.00
(65)	Rich Rollins	12.00	6.00	3.50
(66)	Johnny Romano	12.00	6.00	3.50
(67)	Ron Santo/SP	35.00	17.50	10.00
(68)	Norm Siebern	12.00	6.00	3.50
(69)	Warren Spahn/SP	60.00	30.00	18.00
(70)	Dick Stuart/SP	20.00	10.00	6.00
(71)	Lee Thomas	12.00	6.00	3.50
(72)	Joe Torre	30.00	15.00	9.00
(73)	Pete Ward	12.00	6.00	3.50
(74)	Bill White/SP	25.00	12.50	7.50
(75)	Billy Williams/SP	45.00	22.50	13.50
(76)	Hal Woodeshick/SP	20.00	10.00	6.00
(77)	Carl Yastrzemski/SP	225.00	110.00	65.00

1965 Topps

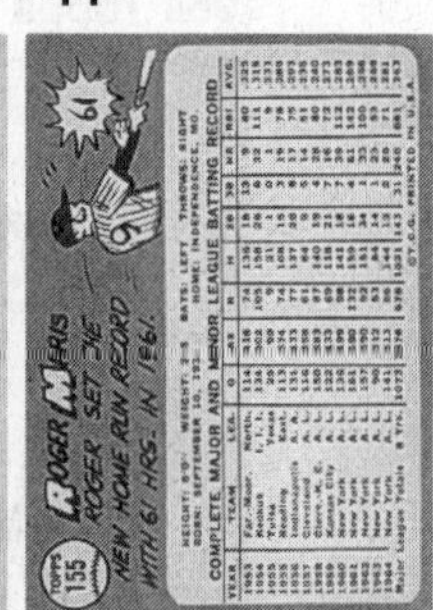

The 1965 Topps set features a large color photograph of the player surrounded by a colored, round-cornered frame and a white border. The bottom of the 2-1/2" x 3-1/2" cards includes a pennant with a color team logo and name over the left side of a rectangle which features the player's name and position. Backs feature statistics and, if space allowed, a cartoon and headline about the player. There are no multi-player cards in the 1965 set other than the usual team cards and World Series highlights. Rookie cards include team, as well as league groupings from two to four players per card. Also present in the 598-card set are statistical leaders. Certain cards in the high-number series (#523-598) were produced in lesser quantities than the rest of the series. Known as "short-prints," and valued somewhat higher than the other high numbers, they are indicated in the checklist by an (SP) after the player name.

		NM	EX	VG
Complete Set (598):		4,000	2,000	1,200
Common Player (1-370):		3.00	1.50	.90
Common Player (371-598):		6.00	3.00	1.75
1	A.L. Batting Leaders (Elston Howard, Tony Oliva, Brooks Robinson)	17.50	8.75	5.25
2	N.L. Batting Leaders (Hank Aaron, Rico Carty, Roberto Clemente)	25.00	12.50	7.50
3	A.L. Home Run Leaders (Harmon Killebrew, Mickey Mantle, Boog Powell)	35.00	17.50	10.00
4	N.L. Home Run Leaders (Johnny Callison, Orlando Cepeda, Jim Hart, Willie Mays, Billy Williams)	20.00	10.00	6.00
5	A.L. RBI Leaders (Harmon Killebrew, Mickey Mantle, Brooks Robinson, Dick Stuart)	35.00	17.50	10.00
6	N.L. RBI Leaders (Ken Boyer, Willie Mays, Ron Santo)	13.50	6.75	4.00
7	A.L. ERA Leaders (Dean Chance, Joel Horlen)	3.50	1.75	1.00
8	N.L. ERA Leaders (Don Drysdale, Sandy Koufax)	25.00	12.50	7.50
9	A.L. Pitching Leaders (Wally Bunker, Dean Chance, Gary Peters, Juan Pizarro, Dave Wickersham)	3.50	1.75	1.00
10	N.L. Pitching Leaders (Larry Jackson, Juan Marichal, Ray Sadecki)	4.50	2.25	1.25
11	A.L. Strikeout Leaders (Dean Chance, Al Downing, Camilo Pascual)	3.50	1.75	1.00
12	N.L. Strikeout Leaders (Don Drysdale, Bob Gibson, Bob Veale)	12.00	6.00	3.50
13	Pedro Ramos	3.00	1.50	.90
14	Len Gabrielson	3.00	1.50	.90
15	Robin Roberts	12.50	6.25	3.75
16	Astros Rookies **(Sonny Jackson, Joe Morgan)**	50.00	25.00	15.00
17	Johnny Romano	3.00	1.50	.90
18	Bill McCool	3.00	1.50	.90
19	Gates Brown	3.00	1.50	.90
20	Jim Bunning	10.00	5.00	3.00
21	Don Blasingame	3.00	1.50	.90
22	Charlie Smith	3.00	1.50	.90
23	Bob Tiefenauer	3.00	1.50	.90
24	Twins Team	7.50	3.75	2.25
25	Al McBean	3.00	1.50	.90
26	Bobby Knoop	3.00	1.50	.90
27	Dick Bertell	3.00	1.50	.90
28	Barney Schultz	3.00	1.50	.90
29	Felix Mantilla	3.00	1.50	.90
30	Jim Bouton	4.50	2.25	1.25
31	Mike White	3.00	1.50	.90
32	Herman Franks	3.00	1.50	.90
33	Jackie Brandt	3.00	1.50	.90
34	Cal Koonce	3.00	1.50	.90
35	Ed Charles	3.00	1.50	.90
36	Bobby Wine	3.00	1.50	.90
37	Fred Gladding	3.00	1.50	.90
38	Jim King	3.00	1.50	.90
39	Gerry Arrigo	3.00	1.50	.90
40	Frank Howard	4.50	2.25	1.25
41	White Sox Rookies **(Bruce Howard, Marv Staehle)**	3.00	1.50	.90
42	Earl Wilson	3.00	1.50	.90
43	Mike Shannon	3.00	1.50	.90
44	Wade Blasingame	3.00	1.50	.90
45	Roy McMillan	3.00	1.50	.90
46	Bob Lee	3.00	1.50	.90
47	Tommy Harper	3.00	1.50	.90
48	Claude Raymond	3.00	1.50	.90
49	Orioles Rookies **(Curt Blefary, John Miller)**	3.00	1.50	.90
50	Juan Marichal	13.50	6.75	4.00
51	Billy Bryan	3.00	1.50	.90
52	Ed Roebuck	3.00	1.50	.90
53	Dick McAuliffe	3.00	1.50	.90
54	Joe Gibbon	3.00	1.50	.90
55	Tony Conigliaro	12.00	6.00	3.50
56	Ron Kline	3.00	1.50	.90
57	Cards Team	7.50	3.75	2.25
58	Fred Talbot	3.00	1.50	.90
59	Nate Oliver	3.00	1.50	.90
60	Jim O'Toole	3.00	1.50	.90
61	Chris Cannizzaro	3.00	1.50	.90
62	Jim Katt (Kaat)	3.50	1.75	1.00
63	Ty Cline	3.00	1.50	.90
64	Lou Burdette	3.00	1.50	.90
65	Tony Kubek	11.00	5.50	3.25
66	Bill Rigney	3.00	1.50	.90
67	Harvey Haddix	3.00	1.50	.90
68	Del Crandall	3.00	1.50	.90
69	Bill Virdon	3.00	1.50	.90
70	Bill Skowron	3.50	1.75	1.00
71	John O'Donoghue	3.00	1.50	.90
72	Tony Gonzalez	3.00	1.50	.90
73	Dennis Ribant	3.00	1.50	.90
74	Red Sox Rookies **(Rico Petrocelli, Jerry Stephenson)**	13.50	6.75	4.00
75	Deron Johnson	3.00	1.50	.90
76	Sam McDowell	3.00	1.50	.90
77	Doug Camilli	3.00	1.50	.90
78	Dal Maxvill	3.00	1.50	.90
79a	1st Series Checklist (1-88) (61 is C. Cannizzaro)	3.50	1.75	1.00
79b	1st Series Checklist (1-88) (61 is Cannizzaro)	7.00	3.50	2.00
80	Turk Farrell	3.00	1.50	.90
81	Don Buford	3.00	1.50	.90
82	Braves Rookies **(Santos Alomar, John Braun)**	4.50	2.25	1.25
83	George Thomas	3.00	1.50	.90
84	Ron Herbel	3.00	1.50	.90
85	Willie Smith	3.00	1.50	.90
86	Les Narum	3.00	1.50	.90
87	Nelson Mathews	3.00	1.50	.90
88	Jack Lamabe	3.00	1.50	.90
89	Mike Hershberger	3.00	1.50	.90
90	Rich Rollins	3.00	1.50	.90
91	Cubs Team	7.50	3.75	2.25
92	Dick Howser	3.00	1.50	.90
93	Jack Fisher	3.00	1.50	.90
94	Charlie Lau	3.00	1.50	.90
95	Bill Mazeroski	12.50	6.25	3.75
96	Sonny Siebert	3.00	1.50	.90
97	Pedro Gonzalez	3.00	1.50	.90
98	Bob Miller	3.00	1.50	.90
99	Gil Hodges	9.00	4.50	2.75
100	Ken Boyer	4.50	2.25	1.25
101	Fred Newman	3.00	1.50	.90
102	Steve Boros	3.00	1.50	.90
103	Harvey Kuenn	3.00	1.50	.90
104	2nd Series Checklist (89-176)	4.00	2.00	1.25
105	Chico Salmon	3.00	1.50	.90
106	Gene Oliver	3.00	1.50	.90
107	Phillies Rookies **(Pat Corrales, Costen Shockley)**	4.00	2.00	1.25
108	Don Mincher	3.00	1.50	.90
109	Walt Bond	3.00	1.50	.90
110	Ron Santo	12.00	6.00	3.50
111	Lee Thomas	3.00	1.50	.90
112	Derrell Griffith	3.00	1.50	.90
113	Steve Barber	3.00	1.50	.90
114	Jim Hickman	3.00	1.50	.90
115	Bobby Richardson	12.00	6.00	3.50
116	Cardinals Rookies ***(Dave Dowling, Bob Tolan)***	3.00	1.50	.90
117	Wes Stock	3.00	1.50	.90
118	***Hal Lanier***	3.00	1.50	.90
119	John Kennedy	3.00	1.50	.90
120	Frank Robinson	20.00	10.00	6.00
121	Gene Alley	3.00	1.50	.90
122	Bill Pleis	3.00	1.50	.90
123	Frank Thomas	3.00	1.50	.90
124	Tom Satriano	3.00	1.50	.90
125	Juan Pizarro	3.00	1.50	.90
126	Dodgers Team	7.50	3.75	2.25
127	Frank Lary	3.00	1.50	.90
128	Vic Davalillo	3.00	1.50	.90
129	Bennie Daniels	3.00	1.50	.90
130	Al Kaline	20.00	10.00	6.00
131	Johnny Keane	4.00	2.00	1.25
132	World Series Game 1 (Cards Take Opener)	10.00	5.00	3.00
133	World Series Game 2 (Stottlemyre Wins)	12.50	6.25	3.75
134	World Series Game 3 (Mantle's Clutch HR)	40.00	20.00	12.00
135	World Series Game 4 (Boyer's Grand-Slam)	10.00	5.00	3.00
136	World Series Game 5 (10th Inning Triumph)	7.00	3.50	2.00
137	World Series Game 6 (Bouton Wins Again)	10.00	5.00	3.00
138	World Series Game 7 (Gibson Wins Finale)	15.00	7.50	4.50
139	World Series (The Cards Celebrate)	9.00	4.50	2.75
140	Dean Chance	3.00	1.50	.90
141	Charlie James	3.00	1.50	.90
142	Bill Monbouquette	3.00	1.50	.90
143	Pirates Rookies **(John Gelnar, Jerry May)**	3.00	1.50	.90
144	Ed Kranepool	3.00	1.50	.90
145	***Luis Tiant***	12.00	6.00	3.50
146	Ron Hansen	3.00	1.50	.90
147	Dennis Bennett	3.00	1.50	.90
148	Willie Kirkland	3.00	1.50	.90
149	Wayne Schurr	3.00	1.50	.90
150	Brooks Robinson	20.00	10.00	6.00
151	Athletics Team	7.50	3.75	2.25
152	Phil Ortega	3.00	1.50	.90
153	Norm Cash	9.00	4.50	2.75
154	Bob Humphreys	3.00	1.50	.90
155	Roger Maris	50.00	25.00	15.00
156	Bob Sadowski	3.00	1.50	.90
157	Zoilo Versalles	3.00	1.50	.90
158	Dick Sisler	3.00	1.50	.90
159	Jim Duffalo	3.00	1.50	.90
160	Bob Clemente	95.00	47.50	27.50
161	Frank Baumann	3.00	1.50	.90
162	Russ Nixon	3.00	1.50	.90
163	John Briggs	3.00	1.50	.90
164	Al Spangler	3.00	1.50	.90
165	Dick Ellsworth	3.00	1.50	.90
166	Indians Rookies **(Tommie Agee, George Culver)**	9.00	4.50	2.75
167	Bill Wakefield	3.00	1.50	.90
168	Dick Green	3.00	1.50	.90
169	Dave Vineyard	3.00	1.50	.90
170	Hank Aaron	80.00	40.00	24.00
171	Jim Roland	3.00	1.50	.90
172	Jim Piersall	6.00	3.00	1.75
173	Tigers Team	8.00	4.00	2.50
174	Joe Jay	3.00	1.50	.90
175	Bob Aspromonte	3.00	1.50	.90
176	Willie McCovey	17.50	8.75	5.25
177	Pete Mikkelsen	3.00	1.50	.90
178	Dalton Jones	3.00	1.50	.90
179	Hal Woodeshick	3.00	1.50	.90
180	Bob Allison	3.00	1.50	.90
181	Senators Rookies **(Don Loun, Joe McCabe)**	3.00	1.50	.90
182	Mike de la Hoz	3.00	1.50	.90
183	Dave Nicholson	3.00	1.50	.90
184	John Boozer	3.00	1.50	.90
185	Max Alvis	3.00	1.50	.90
186	Billy Cowan	3.00	1.50	.90
187	Casey Stengel	12.50	6.25	3.75
188	Sam Bowens	3.00	1.50	.90
189	3rd Series Checklist (177-264)	6.50	3.25	2.00
190	Bill White	3.00	1.50	.90
191	Phil Regan	3.00	1.50	.90
192	Jim Coker	3.00	1.50	.90
193	Gaylord Perry	12.00	6.00	3.50
194	Angels Rookies ***(Bill Kelso, Rick Reichardt)***	3.00	1.50	.90
195	Bob Veale	3.00	1.50	.90
196	Ron Fairly	3.00	1.50	.90
197	Diego Segui	3.00	1.50	.90
198	Smoky Burgess	3.00	1.50	.90
199	Bob Heffner	3.00	1.50	.90
200	Joe Torre	12.00	6.00	3.50
201	Twins Rookies **(Cesar Tovar, Sandy Valdespino)**	3.00	1.50	.90
202	Leo Burke	3.00	1.50	.90
203	Dallas Green	3.00	1.50	.90
204	Russ Snyder	3.00	1.50	.90
205	Warren Spahn	20.00	10.00	6.00
206	Willie Horton	3.00	1.50	.90
207	Pete Rose	100.00	50.00	30.00

208 Tommy John 6.00 3.00 1.75
209 Pirates Team 7.50 3.75 2.25
210 Jim Fregosi 3.00 1.50 .90
211 Steve Ridzik 3.00 1.50 .90
212 Ron Brand 3.00 1.50 .90
213 Jim Davenport 3.00 1.50 .90
214 Bob Purkey 3.00 1.50 .90
215 Pete Ward 3.00 1.50 .90
216 Al Worthington 3.00 1.50 .90
217 Walt Alston 9.00 4.50 2.75
218 Dick Schofield 3.00 1.50 .90
219 Bob Meyer 3.00 1.50 .90
220 Billy Williams 25.00 12.50 7.50
221 John Tsitouris 3.00 1.50 .90
222 Bob Tillman 3.00 1.50 .90
223 Dan Osinski 3.00 1.50 .90
224 Bob Chance 3.00 1.50 .90
225 Bo Belinsky 3.00 1.50 .90
226 Yankees Rookies **(Jake Gibbs, Elvio Jimenez)** 9.00 4.50 2.75
227 Bobby Klaus 3.00 1.50 .90
228 Jack Sanford 3.00 1.50 .90
229 Lou Clinton 3.00 1.50 .90
230 Ray Sadecki 3.00 1.50 .90
231 Jerry Adair 3.00 1.50 .90
232 ***Steve Blass*** 3.00 1.50 .90
233 Don Zimmer 6.00 3.00 1.75
234 White Sox Team 7.50 3.75 2.25
235 Chuck Hinton 3.00 1.50 .90
236 ***Dennis McLain*** 15.00 7.50 4.50
237 Bernie Allen 3.00 1.50 .90
238 Joe Moeller 3.00 1.50 .90
239 Doc Edwards 3.00 1.50 .90
240 Bob Bruce 3.00 1.50 .90
241 Mack Jones 3.00 1.50 .90
242 George Brunet 3.00 1.50 .90
243 Reds Rookies **(*Ted Davidson, Tommy Helms*)** 3.00 1.50 .90
244 Lindy McDaniel 3.00 1.50 .90
245 Joe Pepitone 10.00 5.00 3.00
246 Tom Butters 3.00 1.50 .90
247 Wally Moon 3.00 1.50 .90
248 Gus Triandos 3.00 1.50 .90
249 Dave McNally 3.00 1.50 .90
250 Willie Mays 85.00 42.50 25.00
251 Billy Herman 7.50 3.75 2.25
252 Pete Richert 3.00 1.50 .90
253 Danny Cater 3.00 1.50 .90
254 Roland Sheldon 3.00 1.50 .90
255 Camilo Pascual 3.00 1.50 .90
256 Tito Francona 3.00 1.50 .90
257 Jim Wynn 3.00 1.50 .90
258 Larry Bearnarth 3.00 1.50 .90
259 Tigers Rookies **(*Jim Northrup, Ray Oyler*)** 4.00 2.00 1.25
260 Don Drysdale 20.00 10.00 6.00
261 Duke Carmel 3.00 1.50 .90
262 Bud Daley 3.00 1.50 .90
263 Marty Keough 3.00 1.50 .90
264 Bob Buhl 3.00 1.50 .90
265 Jim Pagliaroni 3.00 1.50 .90
266 ***Bert Campaneris*** 15.00 7.50 4.50
267 Senators Team 7.50 3.75 2.25
268 Ken McBride 3.00 1.50 .90
269 Frank Bolling 3.00 1.50 .90
270 Milt Pappas 3.00 1.50 .90
271 Don Wert 3.00 1.50 .90
272 Chuck Schilling 3.00 1.50 .90
273 4th Series Checklist (265-352) 7.50 3.75 2.25
274 Lum Harris 3.00 1.50 .90
275 Dick Groat 3.00 1.50 .90
276 Hoyt Wilhelm 12.50 6.25 3.75
277 Johnny Lewis 3.00 1.50 .90
278 Ken Retzer 3.00 1.50 .90
279 Dick Tracewski 3.00 1.50 .90
280 Dick Stuart 3.00 1.50 .90
281 Bill Stafford 3.00 1.50 .90
282 Giants Rookies **(*Dick Estelle, Masanori Murakami*)** 20.00 10.00 6.00
283 Fred Whitfield 3.00 1.50 .90
284 Nick Willhite 3.00 1.50 .90
285 Ron Hunt 3.00 1.50 .90
286 Athletic Rookies **(Jim Dickson, Aurelio Monteagudo)** 3.00 1.50 .90
287 Gary Kolb 3.00 1.50 .90
288 Jack Hamilton 3.00 1.50 .90
289 Gordy Coleman 3.00 1.50 .90
290 Wally Bunker 3.00 1.50 .90
291 Jerry Lynch 3.00 1.50 .90
292 Larry Yellen 3.00 1.50 .90
293 Angels Team 7.50 3.75 2.25
294 Tim McCarver 8.00 4.00 2.50
295 Dick Radatz 3.00 1.50 .90
296 Tony Taylor 3.00 1.50 .90
297 Dave DeBusschere 4.00 2.00 1.25
298 Jim Stewart 3.00 1.50 .90
299 Jerry Zimmerman 3.00 1.50 .90
300 Sandy Koufax 95.00 47.50 27.50
301 Birdie Tebbetts 3.00 1.50 .90
302 Al Stanek 3.00 1.50 .90
303 Johnny Orsino 3.00 1.50 .90
304 Dave Stenhouse 3.00 1.50 .90
305 Rico Carty 3.00 1.50 .90
306 Bubba Phillips 3.00 1.50 .90
307 Barry Latman 3.00 1.50 .90
308 Mets Rookies **(Cleon Jones, Tom Parsons)** 8.00 4.00 2.50
309 Steve Hamilton 3.00 1.50 .90
310 Johnny Callison 3.00 1.50 .90
311 Orlando Pena 3.00 1.50 .90
312 Joe Nuxhall 3.00 1.50 .90
313 Jimmie Schaffer 3.00 1.50 .90
314 Sterling Slaughter 3.00 1.50 .90
315 Frank Malzone 3.00 1.50 .90
316 Reds Team 7.00 3.50 2.00
317 Don McMahon 3.00 1.50 .90
318 Matty Alou 3.00 1.50 .90
319 Ken McMullen 3.00 1.50 .90
320 Bob Gibson 25.00 12.50 7.50
321 Rusty Staub 7.50 3.75 2.25
322 Rick Wise 3.00 1.50 .90
323 Hank Bauer 3.00 1.50 .90
324 Bobby Locke 3.00 1.50 .90
325 Donn Clendenon 3.00 1.50 .90
326 Dwight Siebler 3.00 1.50 .90
327 Denis Menke 3.00 1.50 .90
328 Eddie Fisher 3.00 1.50 .90
329 Hawk Taylor 3.00 1.50 .90
330 Whitey Ford 25.00 12.50 7.50
331 Dodgers Rookies **(Al Ferrara, John Purdin)** 3.00 1.50 .90
332 Ted Abernathy 3.00 1.50 .90
333 Tommie Reynolds 3.00 1.50 .90
334 Vic Roznovsky 3.00 1.50 .90
335 Mickey Lolich 6.00 3.00 1.75
336 Woody Held 3.00 1.50 .90
337 Mike Cuellar 3.00 1.50 .90
338 Phillies Team 7.50 3.75 2.25
339 Ryne Duren 3.00 1.50 .90
340 Tony Oliva 15.00 7.50 4.50
341 Bobby Bolin 3.00 1.50 .90
342 Bob Rodgers 3.00 1.50 .90
343 Mike McCormick 3.00 1.50 .90
344 Wes Parker 3.00 1.50 .90
345 Floyd Robinson 3.00 1.50 .90
346 Bobby Bragan 3.00 1.50 .90
347 Roy Face 3.00 1.50 .90
348 George Banks 3.00 1.50 .90
349 Larry Miller 3.00 1.50 .90
350 Mickey Mantle 325.00 155.00 95.00
351 Jim Perry 3.00 1.50 .90
352 ***Alex Johnson*** 3.50 1.75 1.00
353 Jerry Lumpe 3.00 1.50 .90
354 Cubs Rookies **(Billy Ott, Jack Warner)** 3.00 1.50 .90
355 Vada Pinson 8.00 4.00 2.50
356 Bill Spanswick 3.00 1.50 .90
357 Carl Warwick 3.00 1.50 .90
358 Albie Pearson 3.00 1.50 .90
359 Ken Johnson 3.00 1.50 .90
360 Orlando Cepeda 20.00 10.00 6.00
361 5th Series Checklist (353-429) 9.00 4.50 2.75
362 Don Schwall 3.00 1.50 .90
363 Bob Johnson 3.00 1.50 .90
364 Galen Cisco 3.00 1.50 .90
365 Jim Gentile 3.00 1.50 .90
366 Dan Schneider 3.00 1.50 .90
367 Leon Wagner 3.00 1.50 .90
368 White Sox Rookies **(Ken Berry, Joel Gibson)** 3.00 1.50 .90
369 Phil Linz 3.00 1.50 .90
370 Tommy Davis 3.00 1.50 .90
371 Frank Kreutzer 7.50 3.75 2.25
372 Clay Dalrymple 7.50 3.75 2.25
373 Curt Simmons 7.50 3.75 2.25
374 Angels Rookies **(Jose Cardenal, Dick Simpson)** 9.00 4.50 2.75
375 Dave Wickersham 7.50 3.75 2.25
376 Jim Landis 7.50 3.75 2.25
377 Willie Stargell 20.00 10.00 6.00
378 Chuck Estrada 7.50 3.75 2.25
379 Giants Team 10.00 5.00 3.00
380 Rocky Colavito 12.00 6.00 3.50
381 Al Jackson 7.50 3.75 2.25
382 J.C. Martin 7.50 3.75 2.25
383 Felipe Alou 9.00 4.50 2.75
384 Johnny Klippstein 7.50 3.75 2.25
385 Carl Yastrzemski 35.00 17.50 10.00
386 Cubs Rookies **(Paul Jaeckel, Fred Norman)** 7.50 3.75 2.25
387 Johnny Podres 9.00 4.50 2.75
388 John Blanchard 7.50 3.75 2.25
389 Don Larsen 7.50 3.75 2.25
390 Bill Freehan 7.50 3.75 2.25
391 Mel McGaha 7.50 3.75 2.25
392 Bob Friend 7.50 3.75 2.25
393 Ed Kirkpatrick 7.50 3.75 2.25
394 Jim Hannan 7.50 3.75 2.25
395 Jim Hart 7.50 3.75 2.25
396 Frank Bertaina 7.50 3.75 2.25
397 Jerry Buchek 7.50 3.75 2.25
398 Reds Rookies **(*Dan Neville, Art Shamsky*)** 7.50 3.75 2.25
399 Ray Herbert 7.50 3.75 2.25
400 Harmon Killebrew 35.00 17.50 10.00
401 Carl Willey 7.50 3.75 2.25
402 Joe Amalfitano 7.50 3.75 2.25
403 Red Sox Team 10.00 5.00 3.00
404 Stan Williams 7.50 3.75 2.25
405 John Roseboro 7.50 3.75 2.25
406 Ralph Terry 7.50 3.75 2.25
407 Lee Maye 7.50 3.75 2.25
408 Larry Sherry 7.50 3.75 2.25
409 Astros Rookies **(*Jim Beauchamp, Larry Dierker*)** 9.00 4.50 2.75
410 Luis Aparicio 17.50 8.75 5.25
411 Roger Craig 7.50 3.75 2.25
412 Bob Bailey 7.50 3.75 2.25
413 Hal Reniff 7.50 3.75 2.25
414 Al Lopez 12.50 6.25 3.75
415 Curt Flood 12.50 6.25 3.75
416 Jim Brewer 7.50 3.75 2.25
417 Ed Brinkman 7.50 3.75 2.25
418 Johnny Edwards 7.50 3.75 2.25
419 Ruben Amaro 7.50 3.75 2.25
420 Larry Jackson 7.50 3.75 2.25
421 Twins Rookies **(Gary Dotter, Jay Ward)** 7.50 3.75 2.25
422 Aubrey Gatewood 7.50 3.75 2.25
423 Jesse Gonder 7.50 3.75 2.25
424 Gary Bell 7.50 3.75 2.25
425 Wayne Causey 7.50 3.75 2.25
426 Braves Team 10.00 5.00 3.00
427 Bob Saverine 7.50 3.75 2.25
428 Bob Shaw 7.50 3.75 2.25
429 Don Demeter 7.50 3.75 2.25
430 Gary Peters 7.50 3.75 2.25
431 Cardinals Rookies **(Nelson Briles, Wayne Spiezio)** 9.00 4.50 2.75
432 Jim Grant 7.50 3.75 2.25
433 John Bateman 7.50 3.75 2.25
434 Dave Morehead 7.50 3.75 2.25
435 Willie Davis 7.50 3.75 2.25
436 Don Elston 7.50 3.75 2.25
437 Chico Cardenas 7.50 3.75 2.25
438 Harry Walker 7.50 3.75 2.25
439 Moe Drabowsky 7.50 3.75 2.25
440 Tom Tresh 12.50 6.25 3.75
441 Denver Lemaster 7.50 3.75 2.25
442 Vic Power 7.50 3.75 2.25
443 6th Series Checklist (430-506) 9.00 4.50 2.75
444 Bob Hendley 7.50 3.75 2.25
445 Don Lock 7.50 3.75 2.25
446 Art Mahaffey 7.50 3.75 2.25
447 Julian Javier 7.50 3.75 2.25
448 Lee Stange 7.50 3.75 2.25
449 Mets Rookies **(Jerry Hinsley, Gary Kroll)** 7.50 3.75 2.25
450 Elston Howard 12.00 6.00 3.50
451 Jim Owens 7.50 3.75 2.25
452 Gary Geiger 7.50 3.75 2.25
453 Dodgers Rookies **(Willie Crawford, John Werhas)** 7.50 3.75 2.25
454 Ed Rakow 7.50 3.75 2.25
455 Norm Siebern 7.50 3.75 2.25
456 Bill Henry 7.50 3.75 2.25
457 Bob Kennedy 7.50 3.75 2.25
458 John Buzhardt 7.50 3.75 2.25
459 Frank Kostro 7.50 3.75 2.25
460 Richie Allen 20.00 10.00 6.00
461 Braves Rookies **(Clay Carroll, Phil Niekro)** 25.00 12.50 7.50
462 Lew Krausse (Photo actually Pete Lovrich.) 7.50 3.75 2.25
463 Manny Mota 7.50 3.75 2.25
464 Ron Piche 7.50 3.75 2.25
465 Tom Haller 7.50 3.75 2.25
466 Senators Rookies **(Pete Craig, Dick Nen)** 7.50 3.75 2.25
467 Ray Washburn 7.50 3.75 2.25
468 Larry Brown 7.50 3.75 2.25
469 Don Nottebart 7.50 3.75 2.25
470 Yogi Berra 32.50 16.00 10.00
471 Billy Hoeft 7.50 3.75 2.25
472 Don Pavletich 7.50 3.75 2.25
473 Orioles Rookies **(*Paul Blair, Dave Johnson*)** 12.50 6.25 3.75
474 Cookie Rojas 7.50 3.75 2.25
475 Clete Boyer 10.00 5.00 3.00
476 Billy O'Dell 7.50 3.75 2.25
477 Cardinals Rookies **(*Fritz Ackley, Steve Carlton*)** 90.00 45.00 27.50
478 Wilbur Wood 7.50 3.75 2.25
479 Ken Harrelson 7.50 3.75 2.25
480 Joel Horlen 7.50 3.75 2.25
481 Indians Team 10.00 5.00 3.00
482 Bob Priddy 7.50 3.75 2.25
483 George Smith 7.50 3.75 2.25
484 Ron Perranoski 7.50 3.75 2.25
485 Nellie Fox 15.00 7.50 4.50
486 Angels Rookies **(Tom Egan, Pat Rogan)** 7.50 3.75 2.25
487 Woody Woodward 7.50 3.75 2.25
488 Ted Wills 7.50 3.75 2.25
489 Gene Mauch 7.50 3.75 2.25
490 Earl Battey 7.50 3.75 2.25
491 Tracy Stallard 7.50 3.75 2.25
492 Gene Freese 7.50 3.75 2.25
493 Tigers Rookies **(Bruce Brubaker, Bill Roman)** 7.50 3.75 2.25
494 Jay Ritchie 7.50 3.75 2.25
495 Joe Christopher 7.50 3.75 2.25
496 Joe Cunningham 7.50 3.75 2.25
497 Giants Rookies **(Ken Henderson, Jack Hiatt)** 7.50 3.75 2.25
498 Gene Stephens 7.50 3.75 2.25
499 Stu Miller 7.50 3.75 2.25
500 Ed Mathews 27.50 13.50 8.25
501 Indians Rookies **(Ralph Gagliano, Jim Rittwage)** 7.50 3.75 2.25
502 Don Cardwell 7.50 3.75 2.25
503 Phil Gagliano 7.50 3.75 2.25
504 Jerry Grote 7.50 3.75 2.25
505 Ray Culp 7.50 3.75 2.25
506 Sam Mele 7.50 3.75 2.25
507 Sammy Ellis 7.50 3.75 2.25
508a 7th Series Checklist (507-598) (Large print on front.) 9.00 4.50 2.75
508b 7th Series Checklist (507-598) (Small print on front.) 9.00 4.50 2.75
509 Red Sox Rookies (Bob Guindon, Gerry Vezendy) 7.50 3.75 2.25
510 Ernie Banks 45.00 22.50 13.50
511 Ron Locke 7.50 3.75 2.25
512 Cap Peterson 7.50 3.75 2.25
513 Yankees Team 20.00 10.00 6.00
514 Joe Azcue 7.50 3.75 2.25
515 Vern Law 7.50 3.75 2.25
516 Al Weis 7.50 3.75 2.25
517 Angels Rookies **(Paul Schaal, Jack Warner)** 7.50 3.75 2.25
518 Ken Rowe 7.50 3.75 2.25
519 Bob Uecker 30.00 15.00 9.00
520 Tony Cloninger 7.50 3.75 2.25
521 Phillies Rookies **(Dave Bennett, Morrie Stevens)** 7.50 3.75 2.25
522 Hank Aguirre 7.50 3.75 2.25
523 Mike Brumley/SP 9.00 4.50 2.75
524 Dave Giusti/SP 9.00 4.50 2.75
525 Eddie Bressoud 7.50 3.75 2.25

526	Athletics Rookies (*Catfish Hunter, Rene Lachemann, Skip Lockwood, Johnny Odom*)/SP	50.00	25.00	15.00
527	Jeff Torborg/SP	9.00	4.50	2.75
528	George Altman	7.50	3.75	2.25
529	Jerry Fosnow/SP	9.00	4.50	2.75
530	Jim Maloney	7.50	3.75	2.25
531	Chuck Hiller	7.50	3.75	2.25
532	Hector Lopez	9.00	4.50	2.75
533	Mets Rookies (***Jim Bethke, Tug McGraw, Dan Napolean, Ron Swoboda***)/SP	17.50	8.75	5.25
534	John Herrnstein	7.50	3.75	2.25
535	Jack Kralick/SP	9.00	4.50	2.75
536	Andre Rodgers/SP	9.00	4.50	2.75
537	Angels Rookies (**Marcelino Lopez, Rudy May, Phil Roof**)	9.00	4.50	2.75
538	Chuck Dressen/SP	9.00	4.50	2.75
539	Herm Starrette	7.50	3.75	2.25
540	Lou Brock/SP	35.00	17.50	10.00
541	White Sox Rookies **Greg Bollo, Bob Locker)**	7.50	3.75	2.25
542	Lou Klimchock	7.50	3.75	2.25
543	Ed Connolly/SP	9.00	4.50	2.75
544	Howie Reed	7.50	3.75	2.25
545	Jesus Alou/SP	9.00	4.50	2.75
546	Indians Rookies (**Ray Barker, Bill Davis, Mike Hedlund, Floyd Weaver**)	7.50	3.75	2.25
547	Jake Wood/SP	9.00	4.50	2.75
548	Dick Stigman	7.50	3.75	2.25
549	Cubs Rookies (**Glenn Beckert, Roberto Pena**)/SP	12.00	6.00	3.50
550	***Mel Stottlemyre***/SP	20.00	10.00	6.00
551	Mets Team/SP	16.00	8.00	4.75
552	Julio Gotay	7.50	3.75	2.25
553	Houston Rookies (**Dan Coombs, Jack McClure, Gene Ratliff**)	7.50	3.75	2.25
554	Chico Ruiz/SP	9.00	4.50	2.75
555	Jack Baldschun/SP	9.00	4.50	2.75
556	Red Schoendienst/SP	12.50	6.25	3.75
557	Jose Santiago	7.50	3.75	2.25
558	Tommie Sisk	7.50	3.75	2.25
559	Ed Bailey/SP	9.00	4.50	2.75
560	Boog Powell/SP	10.00	5.00	3.00
561	Dodgers Rookies (**Dennis Daboll, Mike Kekich, Jim Lefebvre, Hector Valle**)	12.00	6.00	3.50
562	Billy Moran	7.50	3.75	2.25
563	Julio Navarro	7.50	3.75	2.25
564	Mel Nelson	7.50	3.75	2.25
565	Ernie Broglio/SP	9.00	4.50	2.75
566	Yankees Rookies (**Gil Blanco, Art Lopez, Ross Moschitto**)/SP	10.00	5.00	3.00
567	Tommie Aaron	7.50	3.75	2.25
568	Ron Taylor/SP	9.00	4.50	2.75
569	Gino Cimoli/SP	9.00	4.50	2.75
570	Claude Osteen/SP	9.00	4.50	2.75
571	Ossie Virgil/SP	9.00	4.50	2.75
572	Orioles team/SP	15.00	7.50	4.50
573	Red Sox Rookies (**Jim Lonborg, Gerry Moses, Mike Ryan, Bill Schlesinger**)/SP	13.50	6.75	4.00
574	Roy Sievers	7.50	3.75	2.25
575	Jose Pagan	7.50	3.75	2.25
576	Terry Fox/SP	9.00	4.50	2.75
577	A.L. Rookies (**Jim Buschhorn, Darold Knowles, Richie Scheinblum**)/SP	9.00	4.50	2.75
578	Camilo Carreon/SP	9.00	4.50	2.75
579	Dick Smith/SP	9.00	4.50	2.75
580	Jimmie Hall/SP	9.00	4.50	2.75
581	N.L. Rookies (**Kevin Collins, Tony Perez, Dave Ricketts**)/SP	60.00	30.00	18.00
582	Bob Schmidt/SP	9.00	4.50	2.75
583	Wes Covington/SP	9.00	4.50	2.75
584	Harry Bright	7.50	3.75	2.25
585	Hank Fischer	7.50	3.75	2.25
586	Tommy McCraw/SP	9.00	4.50	2.75
587	Joe Sparma	7.50	3.75	2.25
588	Lenny Green	7.50	3.75	2.25
589	Giants Rookies (**Frank Linzy, Bob Schroder**)/SP	9.00	4.50	2.75
590	Johnnie Wyatt	7.50	3.75	2.25
591	Bob Skinner/SP	9.00	4.50	2.75
592	Frank Bork/SP	9.00	4.50	2.75
593	Tigers Rookies (**Jackie Moore, John Sullivan**)/SP	9.00	4.50	2.75
594	Joe Gaines	7.50	3.75	2.25
595	Don Lee	7.50	3.75	2.25
596	Don Landrum/SP	9.00	4.50	2.75
597	Twins Rookies (**Joe Nossek, Dick Reese, John Sevcik**)	7.00	3.50	2.00
598	Al Downing/SP	25.00	6.00	3.00

1965 Topps Embossed

Inserted in regular packs, the 2-1/8" x 3-1/2" Topps Embossed cards feature a 3-D profile portrait on gold foil-like cardboard (some collectors report finding the cards with silver cardboard). The player's name, team and position are below the portrait - which is good, because most of the embossed portraits are otherwise unrecognizeable. There is a gold border with American League players framed in blue and National Leaguers in red.

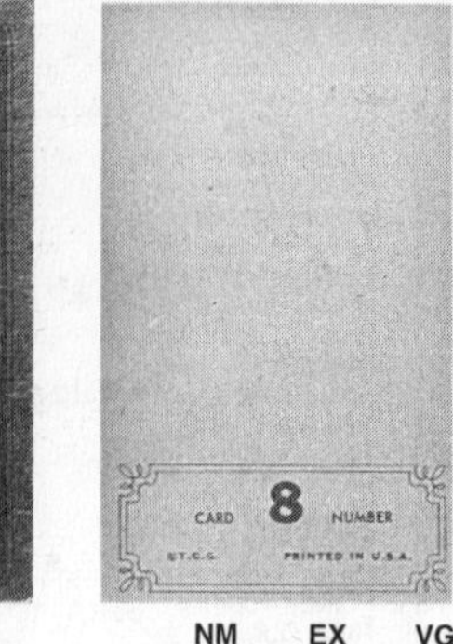

		NM	EX	VG
Complete Set (72):		400.00	140.00	60.00
Common Player:		4.00	1.50	.60
1	Carl Yastrzemski	15.00	5.25	2.25
2	Ron Fairly	4.00	1.50	.60
3	Max Alvis	4.00	1.50	.60
4	Jim Ray Hart	4.00	1.50	.60
5	Bill Skowron	5.00	1.75	.70
6	Ed Kranepool	4.00	1.50	.60
7	Tim McCarver	5.00	1.75	.70
8	Sandy Koufax	25.00	9.00	4.00
9	Donn Clendenon	4.00	1.50	.60
10	John Romano	4.00	1.50	.60
11	Mickey Mantle	60.00	20.00	9.00
12	Joe Torre	6.00	2.00	.90
13	Al Kaline	15.00	5.25	2.25
14	Al McBean	4.00	1.50	.60
15	Don Drysdale	10.00	3.50	1.50
16	Brooks Robinson	12.50	4.50	2.00
17	Jim Bunning	9.00	3.25	1.25
18	Gary Peters	4.00	1.50	.60
19	Roberto Clemente	40.00	14.00	6.00
20	Milt Pappas	4.00	1.50	.60
21	Wayne Causey	4.00	1.50	.60
22	Frank Robinson	12.50	4.50	2.00
23	Bill Mazeroski	9.00	3.25	1.25
24	Diego Segui	4.00	1.50	.60
25	Jim Bouton	4.00	1.50	.60
26	Ed Mathews	10.00	3.50	1.50
27	Willie Mays	25.00	9.00	4.00
28	Ron Santo	6.00	2.00	.90
29	Boog Powell	6.00	2.00	.90
30	Ken McBride	4.00	1.50	.60
31	Leon Wagner	4.00	1.50	.60
32	John Callison	4.00	1.50	.60
33	Zoilo Versalles	4.00	1.50	.60
34	Jack Baldschun	4.00	1.50	.60
35	Ron Hunt	4.00	1.50	.60
36	Richie Allen	6.00	2.00	.90
37	Frank Malzone	4.00	1.50	.60
38	Bob Allison	4.00	1.50	.60
39	Jim Fregosi	4.00	1.50	.60
40	Billy Williams	9.00	3.25	1.25
41	Bill Freehan	4.00	1.50	.60
42	Vada Pinson	5.00	1.75	.70
43	Bill White	4.00	1.50	.60
44	Roy McMillan	4.00	1.50	.60
45	Orlando Cepeda	9.00	3.25	1.25
46	Rocky Colavito	7.50	2.75	1.25
47	Ken Boyer	5.00	1.75	.70
48	Dick Radatz	4.00	1.50	.60
49	Tommy Davis	4.00	1.50	.60
50	Walt Bond	4.00	1.50	.60
51	John Orsino	4.00	1.50	.60
52	Joe Christopher	4.00	1.50	.60
53	Al Spangler	4.00	1.50	.60
54	Jim King	4.00	1.50	.60
55	Mickey Lolich	4.00	1.50	.60
56	Harmon Killebrew	10.00	3.50	1.50
57	Bob Shaw	4.00	1.50	.60
58	Ernie Banks	15.00	5.25	2.25
59	Hank Aaron	25.00	9.00	4.00
60	Chuck Hinton	4.00	1.50	.60
61	Bob Aspromonte	4.00	1.50	.60
62	Lee Maye	4.00	1.50	.60
63	Joe Cunningham	4.00	1.50	.60
64	Pete Ward	4.00	1.50	.60
65	Bobby Richardson	6.00	2.00	.90
66	Dean Chance	4.00	1.50	.60
67	Dick Ellsworth	4.00	1.50	.60
68	Jim Maloney	4.00	1.50	.60
69	Bob Gibson	9.00	3.25	1.25
70	Earl Battey	4.00	1.50	.60
71	Tony Kubek	5.00	1.75	.70
72	Jack Kralick	4.00	1.50	.60

1965 Topps Push-Pull

Part of a 36-card set combining sports and non-sport subjects, the Push-Pull novelties have a louvered shutter attached to a tab at the bottom. When the tab is moved, from position to position, each of the underlying photos is revealed in turn. The cards measure 2-1/2" x 4-11/16". Backs are printed in black-and-white and contain biographical data. Three of the cards in the set feature baseball players.

		NM	EX	VG
Complete Set (36):		3,650	1,800	1,050
(1)	Lou Gehrig, Babe Ruth	500.00	250.00	150.00
(2)	Casey Stengel Wins/Loses	75.00	37.00	22.00
(3)	Yogi Berra, Mickey Mantle	950.00	475.00	285.00

1965 Topps Transfers

Issued as strips of three players each as inserts in 1965, the Topps Transfers were 2" x 3" portraits of players. The transfers have blue or red bands at the top and bottom with the team name and position in the top band and the player's name in the bottom. As is so often the case, the superstars in the transfer set can be quite expensive, but like many of Topps non-card products, the common transfers are neither terribly expensive or popular today.

		NM	EX	VG
Complete Set (72):		750.00	375.00	225.00
Common Player:		6.00	3.00	1.75
(1)	Hank Aaron	50.00	25.00	15.00
(2)	Richie Allen	12.00	6.00	3.50
(3)	Bob Allison	6.00	3.00	1.75
(4)	Max Alvis	6.00	3.00	1.75
(5)	Luis Aparicio	17.50	8.75	5.25
(6)	Bob Aspromonte	6.00	3.00	1.75
(7)	Walt Bond	6.00	3.00	1.75
(8)	Jim Bouton	9.00	4.50	2.75
(9)	Ken Boyer	10.00	5.00	3.00
(10)	Jim Bunning	17.50	8.75	5.25
(11)	John Callison	6.00	3.00	1.75
(12)	Rico Carty	6.00	3.00	1.75
(13)	Wayne Causey	6.00	3.00	1.75
(14)	Orlando Cepeda	17.50	8.75	5.25
(15)	Bob Chance	6.00	3.00	1.75
(16)	Dean Chance	6.00	3.00	1.75
(17)	Joe Christopher	6.00	3.00	1.75
(18)	Roberto Clemente	60.00	30.00	18.00
(19)	Rocky Colavito	15.00	7.50	4.50
(20)	Tony Conigliaro	10.00	5.00	3.00
(21)	Tommy Davis	6.00	3.00	1.75
(22)	Don Drysdale	17.50	8.75	5.25
(23)	Bill Freehan	6.00	3.00	1.75
(24)	Jim Fregosi	6.00	3.00	1.75
(25)	Bob Gibson	17.50	8.75	5.25
(26)	Dick Groat	6.00	3.00	1.75
(27)	Tom Haller	6.00	3.00	1.75
(28)	Chuck Hinton	6.00	3.00	1.75
(29)	Elston Howard	9.00	4.50	2.75
(30)	Ron Hunt	6.00	3.00	1.75
(31)	Al Jackson	6.00	3.00	1.75
(32)	Al Kaline	25.00	12.50	7.50
(33)	Harmon Killebrew	20.00	10.00	6.00
(34)	Jim King	6.00	3.00	1.75
(35)	Ron Kline	6.00	3.00	1.75
(36)	Bobby Knoop	6.00	3.00	1.75
(37)	Sandy Koufax	45.00	22.00	13.50
(38)	Ed Kranepool	6.00	3.00	1.75
(39)	Jim Maloney	6.00	3.00	1.75
(40)	Mickey Mantle	90.00	45.00	27.00
(41)	Juan Marichal	17.50	8.75	5.25
(42)	Lee Maye	6.00	3.00	1.75
(43)	Willie Mays	50.00	25.00	15.00
(44)	Bill Mazeroski	17.50	8.75	5.25
(45)	Tony Oliva	7.50	3.75	2.25
(46)	Jim O'Toole	6.00	3.00	1.75
(47)	Milt Pappas	6.00	3.00	1.75
(48)	Camilo Pascual	6.00	3.00	1.75
(49)	Gary Peters	6.00	3.00	1.75
(50)	Vada Pinson	6.00	3.00	1.75
(51)	Juan Pizarro	6.00	3.00	1.75
(52)	Boog Powell	10.00	5.00	3.00
(53)	Dick Radatz	6.00	3.00	1.75
(54)	Bobby Richardson	10.00	5.00	3.00
(55)	Brooks Robinson	20.00	10.00	6.00
(56)	Frank Robinson	20.00	10.00	6.00
(57)	Bob Rodgers	6.00	3.00	1.75
(58)	John Roseboro	6.00	3.00	1.75
(59)	Ron Santo	12.00	6.00	3.50
(60)	Diego Segui	6.00	3.00	1.75
(61)	Bill Skowron	9.00	4.50	2.75
(62)	Al Spangler	6.00	3.00	1.75
(63)	Dick Stuart	6.00	3.00	1.75
(64)	Luis Tiant	6.00	3.00	1.75
(65)	Joe Torre	12.00	6.00	3.50

No.	Player	NM	EX	VG
(66)	Bob Veale	6.00	3.00	1.75
(67)	Leon Wagner	6.00	3.00	1.75
(68)	Pete Ward	6.00	3.00	1.75
(69)	Bill White	6.00	3.00	1.75
(70)	Dave Wickersham	6.00	3.00	1.75
(71)	Billy Williams	17.50	8.75	5.25
(72)	Carl Yastrzemski	25.00	12.50	7.50

1966 Topps

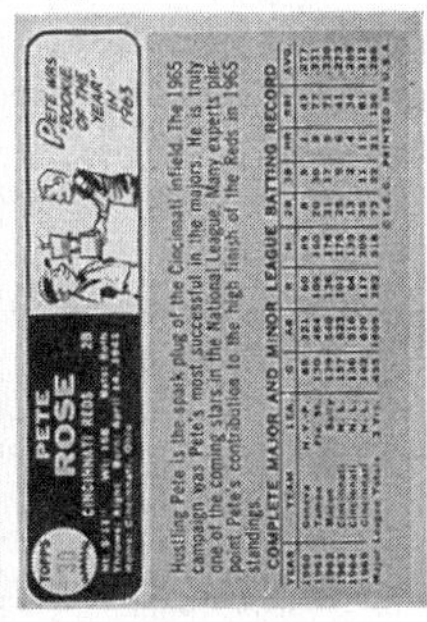

In 1966, Topps produced another 598-card set. The 2-1/2" x 3-1/2" cards feature the traditional color photograph with a diagonal strip in the upper left-hand corner carrying the team name. A band at the bottom carries the player's name and position. Multi-player cards returned in 1966 after a year's hiatus. The statistical leader cards feature the categorical leader and two runners-up. Most team managers have cards as well. The 1966 set features a handful of cards found with or without a notice of the player's sale or trade to another team. Cards without the notice bring higher prices and are not included in the complete set prices. Some cards in the high series (#523-598) were short-printed - produced in lesser quantities than the rest of the series. They are valued somewhat higher than the others and are indicated in the checklist by an (SP) notation following the player name.

No.	Player	NM	EX	VG
	Complete Set (598):	4,600	2,300	1,375
	Common Player (1-370):	4.00	2.00	1.25
	Common Player (371-446):	7.50	3.75	2.25
	Common Player (447-522):	9.00	4.50	2.75
	Common Player (523-598):	12.50	6.25	3.75
1	Willie Mays	200.00	50.00	30.00
2	Ted Abernathy	4.00	2.00	1.25
3	Sam Mele	4.00	2.00	1.25
4	Ray Culp	4.00	2.00	1.25
5	Jim Fregosi	4.00	2.00	1.25
6	Chuck Schilling	4.00	2.00	1.25
7	Tracy Stallard	4.00	2.00	1.25
8	Floyd Robinson	4.00	2.00	1.25
9	Clete Boyer	8.00	4.00	2.50
10	Tony Cloninger	4.00	2.00	1.25
11	Senators Rookies **(Brant Alyea, Pete Craig)**	4.00	2.00	1.25
12	John Tsitouris	4.00	2.00	1.25
13	Lou Johnson	4.00	2.00	1.25
14	Norm Siebern	4.00	2.00	1.25
15	Vern Law	4.00	2.00	1.25
16	Larry Brown	4.00	2.00	1.25
17	Johnny Stephenson	4.00	2.00	1.25
18	Roland Sheldon	4.00	2.00	1.25
19	Giants Team	7.50	3.75	2.25
20	Willie Horton	4.00	2.00	1.25
21	Don Nottebart	4.00	2.00	1.25
22	Joe Nossek	4.00	2.00	1.25
23	Jack Sanford	4.00	2.00	1.25
24	***Don Kessinger***	7.50	3.75	2.25
25	Pete Ward	4.00	2.00	1.25
26	Ray Sadecki	4.00	2.00	1.25
27	Orioles Rookies **(Andy Etchebarren, Darold Knowles)**	6.00	3.00	1.75
28	Phil Niekro	15.00	7.50	4.50
29	Mike Brumley	4.00	2.00	1.25
30	Pete Rose	60.00	30.00	18.00
31	Jack Cullen	4.00	2.00	1.25
32	Adolfo Phillips	4.00	2.00	1.25
33	Jim Pagliaroni	4.00	2.00	1.25
34	1st Series Checklist (1-88)	7.50	3.75	2.25
35	Ron Swoboda	4.00	2.00	1.25
36	Jim Hunter	15.00	7.50	4.50
37	Billy Herman	6.00	3.00	1.75
38	Ron Nischwitz	4.00	2.00	1.25
39	Ken Henderson	4.00	2.00	1.25
40	Jim Grant	4.00	2.00	1.25
41	Don LeJohn	4.00	2.00	1.25
42	Aubrey Gatewood	4.00	2.00	1.25
43a	Don Landrum (No button on pants.)	4.00	2.00	1.25
43b	Don Landrum (Partial button on pants.)	6.00	3.00	1.75
43c	Don Landrum (Full button on pants.)	6.00	3.00	1.75
44	Indians Rookies **(Bill Davis, Tom Kelley)**	4.00	2.00	1.25
45	Jim Gentile	4.00	2.00	1.25
46	Howie Koplitz	4.00	2.00	1.25
47	J.C. Martin	4.00	2.00	1.25
48	Paul Blair	4.00	2.00	1.25
49	Woody Woodward	4.00	2.00	1.25
50	Mickey Mantle	180.00	90.00	55.00
51	Gordon Richardson	4.00	2.00	1.25
52	Power Plus (Johnny Callison, Wes Covington)	4.00	2.00	1.25
53	Bob Duliba	4.00	2.00	1.25
54	Jose Pagan	4.00	2.00	1.25
55	Ken Harrelson	4.00	2.00	1.25
56	Sandy Valdespino	4.00	2.00	1.25
57	Jim Lefebvre	4.00	2.00	1.25
58	Dave Wickersham	4.00	2.00	1.25
59	Reds Team	7.00	3.50	2.00
60	Curt Flood	4.00	2.00	1.25
61	Bob Bolin	4.00	2.00	1.25
62a	Merritt Ranew (No sold statement.)	20.00	10.00	6.00
62b	Merritt Ranew (With sold statement.)	4.00	2.00	1.25
63	Jim Stewart	4.00	2.00	1.25
64	Bob Bruce	4.00	2.00	1.25
65	Leon Wagner	4.00	2.00	1.25
66	Al Weis	4.00	2.00	1.25
67	Mets Rookies **(Cleon Jones, Dick Selma)**	4.00	2.00	1.25
68	Hal Reniff	4.00	2.00	1.25
69	Ken Hamlin	4.00	2.00	1.25
70	Carl Yastrzemski	30.00	15.00	9.00
71	Frank Carpin	4.00	2.00	1.25
72	Tony Perez	22.50	11.00	7.00
73	Jerry Zimmerman	4.00	2.00	1.25
74	Don Mossi	4.00	2.00	1.25
75	Tommy Davis	4.00	2.00	1.25
76	Red Schoendienst	7.50	3.75	2.25
77	Johnny Orsino	4.00	2.00	1.25
78	Frank Linzy	4.00	2.00	1.25
79	Joe Pepitone	8.00	4.00	2.50
80	Richie Allen	6.00	3.00	1.75
81	Ray Oyler	4.00	2.00	1.25
82	Bob Hendley	4.00	2.00	1.25
83	Albie Pearson	4.00	2.00	1.25
84	Braves Rookies **(Jim Beauchamp, Dick Kelley)**	4.00	2.00	1.25
85	Eddie Fisher	4.00	2.00	1.25
86	John Bateman	4.00	2.00	1.25
87	Dan Napoleon	4.00	2.00	1.25
88	Fred Whitfield	4.00	2.00	1.25
89	Ted Davidson	4.00	2.00	1.25
90	Luis Aparicio	15.00	7.50	4.50
91a	Bob Uecker (No trade statement.)	60.00	30.00	18.00
91b	Bob Uecker (With trade statement.)	20.00	10.00	6.00
92	Yankees Team	15.00	7.50	4.50
93	Jim Lonborg	4.00	2.00	1.25
94	Matty Alou	4.00	2.00	1.25
95	Pete Richert	4.00	2.00	1.25
96	Felipe Alou	6.00	3.00	1.75
97	Jim Merritt	4.00	2.00	1.25
98	Don Demeter	4.00	2.00	1.25
99	Buc Belters (Donn Clendenon, Willie Stargell)	8.00	4.00	2.50
100	Sandy Koufax	65.00	32.50	20.00
101a	2nd Series Checklist (89-176) (115 is Spahn)	12.50	6.25	3.75
101b	2nd Series Checklist (89-176) (115 is Henry)	7.50	3.75	2.25
102	Ed Kirkpatrick	4.00	2.00	1.25
103a	Dick Groat (No trade statement.)	20.00	10.00	6.00
103b	Dick Groat (With trade statement.)	4.00	2.00	1.25
104a	Alex Johnson (No trade statement.)	20.00	10.00	6.00
104b	Alex Johnson (With trade statement.)	4.00	2.00	1.25
105	Milt Pappas	4.00	2.00	1.25
106	Rusty Staub	6.00	3.00	1.75
107	Athletics Rookies **(Larry Stahl, Ron Tompkins)**	4.00	2.00	1.25
108	Bobby Klaus	4.00	2.00	1.25
109	Ralph Terry	4.00	2.00	1.25
110	Ernie Banks	30.00	15.00	9.00
111	Gary Peters	4.00	2.00	1.25
112	Manny Mota	4.00	2.00	1.25
113	Hank Aguirre	4.00	2.00	1.25
114	Jim Gosger	4.00	2.00	1.25
115	Bill Henry	4.00	2.00	1.25
116	Walt Alston	6.00	3.00	1.75
117	Jake Gibbs	4.00	2.00	1.25
118	Mike McCormick	4.00	2.00	1.25
119	Art Shamsky	4.00	2.00	1.25
120	Harmon Killebrew	20.00	10.00	6.00
121	Ray Herbert	4.00	2.00	1.25
122	Joe Gaines	4.00	2.00	1.25
123	Pirates Rookies **(Frank Bork, Jerry May)**	4.00	2.00	1.25
124	Tug McGraw	4.00	2.00	1.25
125	Lou Brock	20.00	10.00	6.00
126	***Jim Palmer***	55.00	27.50	16.50
127	Ken Berry	4.00	2.00	1.25
128	Jim Landis	4.00	2.00	1.25
129	Jack Kralick	4.00	2.00	1.25
130	Joe Torre	6.00	3.00	1.75
131	Angels Team	7.50	3.75	2.25
132	Orlando Cepeda	15.00	7.50	4.50
133	Don McMahon	4.00	2.00	1.25
134	Wes Parker	4.00	2.00	1.25
135	Dave Morehead	4.00	2.00	1.25
136	Woody Held	4.00	2.00	1.25
137	Pat Corrales	4.00	2.00	1.25
138	Roger Repoz	4.00	2.00	1.25
139	Cubs Rookies **(Byron Browne, Don Young)**	4.00	2.00	1.25
140	Jim Maloney	4.00	2.00	1.25
141	Tom McCraw	4.00	2.00	1.25
142	Don Dennis	4.00	2.00	1.25
143	Jose Tartabull	4.00	2.00	1.25
144	Don Schwall	4.00	2.00	1.25
145	Bill Freehan	4.00	2.00	1.25
146	George Altman	4.00	2.00	1.25
147	Lum Harris	4.00	2.00	1.25
148	Bob Johnson	4.00	2.00	1.25
149	Dick Nen	4.00	2.00	1.25
150	Rocky Colavito	12.00	6.00	3.50
151	Gary Wagner	4.00	2.00	1.25
152	Frank Malzone	4.00	2.00	1.25
153	Rico Carty	4.00	2.00	1.25
154	Chuck Hiller	4.00	2.00	1.25
155	Marcelino Lopez	4.00	2.00	1.25
156	D P Combo (Hal Lanier, Dick Schofield)	4.00	2.00	1.25
157	Rene Lachemann	4.00	2.00	1.25
158	Jim Brewer	4.00	2.00	1.25
159	Chico Ruiz	4.00	2.00	1.25
160	Whitey Ford	25.00	12.50	7.50
161	Jerry Lumpe	4.00	2.00	1.25
162	Lee Maye	4.00	2.00	1.25
163	Tito Francona	4.00	2.00	1.25
164	White Sox Rookies **(Tommie Agee, Marv Staehle)**	4.00	2.00	1.25
165	Don Lock	4.00	2.00	1.25
166	Chris Krug	4.00	2.00	1.25
167	Boog Powell	6.00	3.00	1.75
168	Dan Osinski	4.00	2.00	1.25
169	Duke Sims	4.00	2.00	1.25
170	Cookie Rojas	4.00	2.00	1.25
171	Nick Willhite	4.00	2.00	1.25
172	Mets Team	6.00	3.00	1.75
173	Al Spangler	4.00	2.00	1.25
174	Ron Taylor	4.00	2.00	1.25
175	Bert Campaneris	4.00	2.00	1.25
176	Jim Davenport	4.00	2.00	1.25
177	Hector Lopez	4.00	2.00	1.25
178	Bob Tillman	4.00	2.00	1.25
179	Cardinals Rookies **(Dennis Aust, Bob Tolan)**	4.00	2.00	1.25
180	Vada Pinson	7.50	3.75	2.25
181	Al Worthington	4.00	2.00	1.25
182	Jerry Lynch	4.00	2.00	1.25
183a	3rd Series Checklist (177-264) (Large print on front.)	7.50	3.75	2.25
183b	3rd Series Checklist (177-264) (Small print on front.)	9.00	4.50	2.75
184	Denis Menke	4.00	2.00	1.25
185	Bob Buhl	4.00	2.00	1.25
186	Ruben Amaro	4.00	2.00	1.25
187	Chuck Dressen	4.00	2.00	1.25
188	Al Luplow	4.00	2.00	1.25
189	John Roseboro	4.00	2.00	1.25
190	Jimmie Hall	4.00	2.00	1.25
191	Darrell Sutherland	4.00	2.00	1.25
192	Vic Power	4.00	2.00	1.25
193	Dave McNally	4.00	2.00	1.25
194	Senators Team	6.00	3.00	1.75
195	Joe Morgan	25.00	12.50	7.50
196	Don Pavletich	4.00	2.00	1.25
197	Sonny Siebert	4.00	2.00	1.25
198	***Mickey Stanley***	6.00	3.00	1.75
199	Chisox Clubbers (Floyd Robinson, Johnny Romano, Bill Skowron)	6.00	3.00	1.75
200	Ed Mathews	20.00	10.00	6.00
201	Jim Dickson	4.00	2.00	1.25
202	Clay Dalrymple	4.00	2.00	1.25
203	Jose Santiago	4.00	2.00	1.25
204	Cubs Team	7.50	3.75	2.25
205	Tom Tresh	9.00	4.50	2.75
206	Alvin Jackson	4.00	2.00	1.25
207	Frank Quilici	4.00	2.00	1.25
208	Bob Miller	4.00	2.00	1.25
209	Tigers Rookies **(Fritz Fisher, *John Hiller*)**	4.00	2.00	1.25
210	Bill Mazeroski	17.50	8.75	5.25
211	Frank Kreutzer	4.00	2.00	1.25
212	Ed Kranepool	4.00	2.00	1.25
213	Fred Newman	4.00	2.00	1.25
214	Tommy Harper	4.00	2.00	1.25
215	N.L. Batting Leaders (Hank Aaron, Roberto Clemente, Willie Mays)	40.00	20.00	12.00
216	A.L. Batting Leaders (Vic Davalillo, Tony Oliva, Carl Yastrzemski)	16.00	8.00	4.75
217	N.L. Home Run Leaders (Willie Mays, Willie McCovey, Billy Williams)	25.00	12.50	7.50
218	A.L. Home Run Leaders (Norm Cash, Tony Conigliaro, Willie Horton)	12.50	6.25	3.75
219	N.L. RBI Leaders (Deron Johnson, Willie Mays, Frank Robinson)	20.00	10.00	6.00
220	A.L. RBI Leaders (Rocky Colavito, Willie Horton, Tony Oliva)	12.00	6.00	3.50
221	N.L. ERA Leaders (Sandy Koufax, Vern Law, Juan Marichal)	15.00	7.50	4.50
222	A.L. ERA Leaders (Eddie Fisher, Sam McDowell, Sonny Siebert)	6.00	3.00	1.75
223	N.L. Pitching Leaders (Tony Cloninger, Don Drysdale, Sandy Koufax)	16.00	8.00	4.75
224	A.L. Pitching Leaders (Jim Grant, Jim Kaat, Mel Stottlemyre)	9.00	4.50	2.75
225	N.L. Strikeout Leaders (Bob Gibson, Sandy Koufax, Bob Veale)	15.00	7.50	4.50
226	A.L. Strikeout Leaders (Mickey Lolich, Sam McDowell, Denny McLain, Sonny Siebert)	10.00	5.00	3.00
227	Russ Nixon	4.00	2.00	1.25
228	Larry Dierker	4.00	2.00	1.25
229	Hank Bauer	4.50	2.25	1.25
230	Johnny Callison	4.00	2.00	1.25
231	Floyd Weaver	4.00	2.00	1.25
232	Glenn Beckert	4.00	2.00	1.25
233	Dom Zanni	4.00	2.00	1.25
234	Yankees Rookies ***(Rich Beck, Roy White)***	15.00	7.50	4.50

235	Don Cardwell	4.00	2.00	1.25
236	Mike Hershberger	4.00	2.00	1.25
237	Billy O'Dell	4.00	2.00	1.25
238	Dodgers Team	9.00	4.50	2.75
239	Orlando Pena	4.00	2.00	1.25
240	Earl Battey	4.00	2.00	1.25
241	Dennis Ribant	4.00	2.00	1.25
242	Jesus Alou	4.00	2.00	1.25
243	Nelson Briles	4.00	2.00	1.25
244	Astros Rookies **(Chuck Harrison, Sonny Jackson)**	4.00	2.00	1.25
245	John Buzhardt	4.00	2.00	1.25
246	Ed Bailey	4.00	2.00	1.25
247	Carl Warwick	4.00	2.00	1.25
248	Pete Mikkelsen	4.00	2.00	1.25
249	Bill Rigney	4.00	2.00	1.25
250	Sam Ellis	4.00	2.00	1.25
251	Ed Brinkman	4.00	2.00	1.25
252	Denver Lemaster	4.00	2.00	1.25
253	Don Wert	4.00	2.00	1.25
254	Phillies Rookies **(Fergie Jenkins, Bill Sorrell)**	45.00	22.50	13.50
255	Willie Stargell	20.00	10.00	6.00
256	Lew Krausse	4.00	2.00	1.25
257	Jeff Torborg	4.00	2.00	1.25
258	Dave Giusti	4.00	2.00	1.25
259	Red Sox Team	7.50	3.75	2.25
260	Bob Shaw	4.00	2.00	1.25
261	Ron Hansen	4.00	2.00	1.25
262	Jack Hamilton	4.00	2.00	1.25
263	Tom Egan	4.00	2.00	1.25
264	Twins Rookies **(Andy Kosco, Ted Uhlaender)**	4.00	2.00	1.25
265	Stu Miller	4.00	2.00	1.25
266	Pedro Gonzalez	4.00	2.00	1.25
267	Joe Sparma	4.00	2.00	1.25
268	John Blanchard	4.00	2.00	1.25
269	Don Heffner	4.00	2.00	1.25
270	Claude Osteen	4.00	2.00	1.25
271	Hal Lanier	4.00	2.00	1.25
272	Jack Baldschun	4.00	2.00	1.25
273	Astro Aces (Bob Aspromonte, Rusty Staub)	6.00	3.00	1.75
274	Buster Narum	4.00	2.00	1.25
275	Tim McCarver	7.50	3.75	2.25
276	Jim Bouton	6.00	3.00	1.75
277	George Thomas	4.00	2.00	1.25
278	Calvin Koonce	4.00	2.00	1.25
279a	4th Series Checklist (265-352) (Player's cap black.)	7.00	3.50	2.00
279b	4th Series Checklist (265-352) (Player's cap red.)	7.50	3.75	2.25
280	Bobby Knoop	4.00	2.00	1.25
281	Bruce Howard	4.00	2.00	1.25
282	Johnny Lewis	4.00	2.00	1.25
283	Jim Perry	4.00	2.00	1.25
284	Bobby Wine	4.00	2.00	1.25
285	Luis Tiant	4.00	2.00	1.25
286	Gary Geiger	4.00	2.00	1.25
287	Jack Aker	4.00	2.00	1.25
288	Dodgers Rookies (***Bill Singer, Don Sutton***)	40.00	20.00	12.00
289	Larry Sherry	4.00	2.00	1.25
290	Ron Santo	12.50	6.25	3.75
291	Moe Drabowsky	4.00	2.00	1.25
292	Jim Coker	4.00	2.00	1.25
293	Mike Shannon	4.00	2.00	1.25
294	Steve Ridzik	4.00	2.00	1.25
295	Jim Hart	4.00	2.00	1.25
296	Johnny Keane	4.00	2.00	1.25
297	Jim Owens	4.00	2.00	1.25
298	Rico Petrocelli	6.00	3.00	1.75
299	Lou Burdette	4.00	2.00	1.25
300	Bob Clemente	100.00	50.00	30.00
301	Greg Bollo	4.00	2.00	1.25
302	Ernie Bowman	4.00	2.00	1.25
303a	Indians Team (Dot between "PLACE" and "AMERICAN.")	6.00	3.00	1.75
303b	Indians Team (No dot.)	6.00	3.00	1.75
304	John Herrnstein	4.00	2.00	1.25
305	Camilo Pascual	4.00	2.00	1.25
306	Ty Cline	4.00	2.00	1.25
307	Clay Carroll	4.00	2.00	1.25
308	Tom Haller	4.00	2.00	1.25
309	Diego Segui	4.00	2.00	1.25
310	Frank Robinson	35.00	17.50	10.00
311	Reds Rookies **(Tommy Helms, Dick Simpson)**	4.00	2.00	1.25
312	Bob Saverine	4.00	2.00	1.25
313	Chris Zachary	4.00	2.00	1.25
314	Hector Valle	4.00	2.00	1.25
315	Norm Cash	11.00	5.50	3.25
316	Jack Fisher	4.00	2.00	1.25
317	Dalton Jones	4.00	2.00	1.25
318	Harry Walker	4.00	2.00	1.25
319	Gene Freese	4.00	2.00	1.25
320	Bob Gibson	30.00	15.00	9.00
321	Rick Reichardt	4.00	2.00	1.25
322	Bill Faul	4.00	2.00	1.25
323	Ray Barker	4.00	2.00	1.25
324	John Boozer	4.00	2.00	1.25
325	Vic Davalillo	4.00	2.00	1.25
326a	Braves Team (Dot between "PLACE" and "NATIONAL.")	7.50	3.75	2.25
326b	Braves Team (No dot.)	7.50	3.75	2.25
327	Bernie Allen	4.00	2.00	1.25
328	Jerry Grote	4.00	2.00	1.25
329	Pete Charton	4.00	2.00	1.25
330	Ron Fairly	4.00	2.00	1.25
331	Ron Herbel	4.00	2.00	1.25
332	Billy Bryan	4.00	2.00	1.25
333	Senators Rookies **(Joe Coleman, Jim French)**	4.00	2.00	1.25
334	Marty Keough	4.00	2.00	1.25
335	Juan Pizarro	4.00	2.00	1.25
336	Gene Alley	4.00	2.00	1.25
337	Fred Gladding	4.00	2.00	1.25
338	Dal Maxvill	4.00	2.00	1.25
339	Del Crandall	4.00	2.00	1.25
340	Dean Chance	4.00	2.00	1.25
341	Wes Westrum	4.00	2.00	1.25
342	Bob Humphreys	4.00	2.00	1.25
343	Joe Christopher	4.00	2.00	1.25
344	Steve Blass	4.00	2.00	1.25
345	Bob Allison	4.00	2.00	1.25
346	Mike de la Hoz	4.00	2.00	1.25
347	Phil Regan	4.00	2.00	1.25
348	Orioles Team	8.00	4.00	2.50
349	Cap Peterson	4.00	2.00	1.25
350	Mel Stottlemyre	6.00	3.00	1.75
351	Fred Valentine	4.00	2.00	1.25
352	Bob Aspromonte	4.00	2.00	1.25
353	Al McBean	4.00	2.00	1.25
354	Smoky Burgess	4.00	2.00	1.25
355	Wade Blasingame	4.00	2.00	1.25
356	Red Sox Rookies **(Owen Johnson, Ken Sanders)**	4.00	2.00	1.25
357	Gerry Arrigo	4.00	2.00	1.25
358	Charlie Smith	4.00	2.00	1.25
359	Johnny Briggs	4.00	2.00	1.25
360	Ron Hunt	4.00	2.00	1.25
361	Tom Satriano	4.00	2.00	1.25
362	Gates Brown	4.00	2.00	1.25
363	5th Series Checklist (353-429)	9.00	4.50	2.75
364	Nate Oliver	4.00	2.00	1.25
365	Roger Maris	45.00	22.50	13.50
366	Wayne Causey	4.00	2.00	1.25
367	Mel Nelson	4.00	2.00	1.25
368	Charlie Lau	4.00	2.00	1.25
369	Jim King	4.00	2.00	1.25
370	Chico Cardenas	4.00	2.00	1.25
371	Lee Stange	7.50	3.75	2.25
372	Harvey Kuenn	7.50	3.75	2.25
373	Giants Rookies **(Dick Estelle, Jack Hiatt)**	7.50	3.75	2.25
374	Bob Locker	7.50	3.75	2.25
375	Donn Clendenon	7.50	3.75	2.25
376	Paul Schaal	7.50	3.75	2.25
377	Turk Farrell	7.50	3.75	2.25
378	Dick Tracewski	7.50	3.75	2.25
379	Cards Team	10.00	5.00	3.00
380	Tony Conigliaro	12.50	6.25	3.75
381	Hank Fischer	7.50	3.75	2.25
382	Phil Roof	7.50	3.75	2.25
383	Jackie Brandt	7.50	3.75	2.25
384	Al Downing	7.50	3.75	2.25
385	Ken Boyer	10.00	5.00	3.00
386	Gil Hodges	11.00	5.50	3.25
387	Howie Reed	7.50	3.75	2.25
388	Don Mincher	7.50	3.75	2.25
389	Jim O'Toole	7.50	3.75	2.25
390	Brooks Robinson	35.00	17.50	10.00
391	Chuck Hinton	7.50	3.75	2.25
392	Cubs Rookies (***Bill Hands, Randy Hundley***)	12.00	6.00	3.50
393	George Brunet	7.50	3.75	2.25
394	Ron Brand	7.50	3.75	2.25
395	Len Gabrielson	7.50	3.75	2.25
396	Jerry Stephenson	7.50	3.75	2.25
397	Bill White	7.50	3.75	2.25
398	Danny Cater	7.50	3.75	2.25
399	Ray Washburn	7.50	3.75	2.25
400	Zoilo Versalles	7.50	3.75	2.25
401	Ken McMullen	7.50	3.75	2.25
402	Jim Hickman	7.50	3.75	2.25
403	Fred Talbot	7.50	3.75	2.25
404a	Pirates Team (Dot between "PLACE" and "NATIONAL.")	12.50	6.25	3.75
404b	Pirates Team (No dot.)	12.50	6.25	3.75
405	Elston Howard	9.00	4.50	2.75
406	Joe Jay	7.50	3.75	2.25
407	John Kennedy	7.50	3.75	2.25
408	Lee Thomas	7.50	3.75	2.25
409	Billy Hoeft	7.50	3.75	2.25
410	Al Kaline	35.00	17.50	10.00
411	Gene Mauch	7.50	3.75	2.25
412	Sam Bowens	7.50	3.75	2.25
413	John Romano	7.50	3.75	2.25
414	Dan Coombs	7.50	3.75	2.25
415	Max Alvis	7.50	3.75	2.25
416	Phil Ortega	7.50	3.75	2.25
417	Angels Rookies **(Jim McGlothlin, Ed Sukla)**	7.50	3.75	2.25
418	Phil Gagliano	7.50	3.75	2.25
419	Mike Ryan	7.50	3.75	2.25
420	Juan Marichal	20.00	10.00	6.00
421	Roy McMillan	7.50	3.75	2.25
422	Ed Charles	7.50	3.75	2.25
423	Ernie Broglio	7.50	3.75	2.25
424	Reds Rookies **(Lee May, Darrell Osteen)**	10.00	5.00	3.00
425	Bob Veale	7.50	3.75	2.25
426	White Sox Team	10.00	5.00	3.00
427	John Miller	7.50	3.75	2.25
428	Sandy Alomar	7.50	3.75	2.25
429	Bill Monbouquette	7.50	3.75	2.25
430	Don Drysdale	20.00	10.00	6.00
431	Walt Bond	7.50	3.75	2.25
432	Bob Heffner	7.50	3.75	2.25
433	Alvin Dark	7.50	3.75	2.25
434	Willie Kirkland	7.50	3.75	2.25
435	Jim Bunning	15.00	7.50	4.50
436	Julian Javier	7.50	3.75	2.25
437	Al Stanek	7.50	3.75	2.25
438	Willie Smith	7.50	3.75	2.25
439	Pedro Ramos	7.50	3.75	2.25
440	Deron Johnson	7.50	3.75	2.25
441	Tommie Sisk	7.50	3.75	2.25
442	Orioles Rookies **(Ed Barnowski, Eddie Watt)**	7.50	3.75	2.25
443	Bill Wakefield	7.50	3.75	2.25
444a	6th Series Checklist(430-506) (456 is R. Sox Rookies)	7.50	3.75	2.25
444b	6th Series Checklist (430-506) (456 is Red Sox Rookies)	9.00	4.50	2.75
445	Jim Kaat	9.00	4.50	2.75
446	Mack Jones	7.50	3.75	2.25
447	Dick Ellsworth (Photo actually Ken Hubbs.)	12.50	6.25	3.75
448	Eddie Stanky	9.00	4.50	2.75
449	Joe Moeller	9.00	4.50	2.75
450	Tony Oliva	15.00	7.50	4.50
451	Barry Latman	9.00	4.50	2.75
452	Joe Azcue	9.00	4.50	2.75
453	Ron Kline	9.00	4.50	2.75
454	Jerry Buchek	9.00	4.50	2.75
455	Mickey Lolich	9.00	4.50	2.75
456	Red Sox Rookies **(Darrell Brandon, Joe Foy)**	9.00	4.50	2.75
457	Joe Gibbon	9.00	4.50	2.75
458	Manny Jiminez (Jimenez)	9.00	4.50	2.75
459	Bill McCool	9.00	4.50	2.75
460	Curt Blefary	9.00	4.50	2.75
461	Roy Face	9.00	4.50	2.75
462	Bob Rodgers	9.00	4.50	2.75
463	Phillies Team	12.00	6.00	3.50
464	Larry Bearnarth	9.00	4.50	2.75
465	Don Buford	9.00	4.50	2.75
466	Ken Johnson	9.00	4.50	2.75
467	Vic Roznovsky	9.00	4.50	2.75
468	Johnny Podres	9.00	4.50	2.75
469	Yankees Rookies **(Bobby Murcer, Dooley Womack)**	22.50	11.00	6.75
470	Sam McDowell	9.00	4.50	2.75
471	Bob Skinner	9.00	4.50	2.75
472	Terry Fox	9.00	4.50	2.75
473	Rich Rollins	9.00	4.50	2.75
474	Dick Schofield	9.00	4.50	2.75
475	Dick Radatz	9.00	4.50	2.75
476	Bobby Bragan	9.00	4.50	2.75
477	Steve Barber	9.00	4.50	2.75
478	Tony Gonzalez	9.00	4.50	2.75
479	Jim Hannan	9.00	4.50	2.75
480	Dick Stuart	9.00	4.50	2.75
481	Bob Lee	9.00	4.50	2.75
482	Cubs Rookies **(John Boccabella, Dave Dowling)**	9.00	4.50	2.75
483	Joe Nuxhall	9.00	4.50	2.75
484	Wes Covington	9.00	4.50	2.75
485	Bob Bailey	9.00	4.50	2.75
486	Tommy John	9.00	4.50	2.75
487	Al Ferrara	9.00	4.50	2.75
488	George Banks	9.00	4.50	2.75
489	Curt Simmons	9.00	4.50	2.75
490	Bobby Richardson	15.00	7.50	4.50
491	Dennis Bennett	9.00	4.50	2.75
492	Athletics Team	12.00	6.00	3.50
493	Johnny Klippstein	9.00	4.50	2.75
494	Gordon Coleman	9.00	4.50	2.75
495	Dick McAuliffe	9.00	4.50	2.75
496	Lindy McDaniel	9.00	4.50	2.75
497	Chris Cannizzaro	9.00	4.50	2.75
498	Pirates Rookies **(Woody Fryman, Luke Walker)**	9.00	4.50	2.75
499	Wally Bunker	9.00	4.50	2.75
500	Hank Aaron	100.00	50.00	30.00
501	John O'Donoghue	9.00	4.50	2.75
502	Lenny Green	9.00	4.50	2.75
503	Steve Hamilton	9.00	4.50	2.75
504	Grady Hatton	9.00	4.50	2.75
505	Jose Cardenal	9.00	4.50	2.75
506	Bo Belinsky	9.00	4.50	2.75
507	John Edwards	9.00	4.50	2.75
508	***Steve Hargan***	9.00	4.50	2.75
509	Jake Wood	9.00	4.50	2.75
510	Hoyt Wilhelm	16.00	8.00	4.75
511	Giants Rookies (***Bob Barton, Tito Fuentes***)	9.00	4.50	2.75
512	Dick Stigman	9.00	4.50	2.75
513	Camilo Carreon	9.00	4.50	2.75
514	Hal Woodeshick	9.00	4.50	2.75
515	Frank Howard	9.00	4.50	2.75
516	Eddie Bressoud	9.00	4.50	2.75
517a	7th Series Checklist (507-598) (529 is W. Sox Rookies)	11.00	5.50	3.25
517b	7th Series Checklist (507-598) (529 is White Sox Rookies)	13.50	6.75	4.00
518	Braves Rookies (Herb Hippauf, Arnie Umbach)	9.00	4.50	2.75
519	Bob Friend	9.00	4.50	2.75
520	Jim Wynn	9.00	4.50	2.75
521	John Wyatt	9.00	4.50	2.75
522	Phil Linz	9.00	4.50	2.75
523	Bob Sadowski	12.50	6.25	3.75
524	Giants Rookies **(Ollie Brown, Don Mason)**/SP	16.00	8.00	4.75
525	Gary Bell/SP	16.00	8.00	4.75
526	Twins Team/SP	60.00	30.00	18.00
527	Julio Navarro	12.50	6.25	3.75
528	Jesse Gonder/SP	16.00	8.00	4.75
529	White Sox Rookies **(Lee Elia, Dennis Higgins, Bill Voss)**	12.50	6.25	3.75
530	Robin Roberts	25.00	12.50	7.50
531	Joe Cunningham	12.50	6.25	3.75
532	Aurelio Monteagudo/SP	16.00	8.00	4.75
533	Jerry Adair/SP	16.00	8.00	4.75
534	Mets Rookies **(Dave Eilers, Rob Gardner)**	12.50	6.25	3.75
535	Willie Davis/SP	16.00	8.00	4.75
536	Dick Egan	12.50	6.25	3.75
537	Herman Franks	12.50	6.25	3.75
538	Bob Allen/SP	16.00	8.00	4.75
539	Astros Rookies **(Bill Heath, Carroll Sembera)**	12.50	6.25	3.75
540	Denny McLain/SP	50.00	25.00	15.00
541	Gene Oliver/SP	16.00	8.00	4.75
542	George Smith	12.50	6.25	3.75
543	Roger Craig/SP	16.00	8.00	4.75
544	Cardinals Rookies **(Joe Hoerner, George Kernek, Jimmy Williams)/SP**	16.00	8.00	4.75
545	Dick Green/SP	16.00	8.00	4.75
546	Dwight Siebler	12.50	6.25	3.75

547	***Horace Clarke*/SP**	60.00	30.00	18.00
548	Gary Kroll/SP	16.00	8.00	4.75
549	Senators Rookies **(Al Closter, Casey Cox)**	12.50	6.25	3.75
550	Willie McCovey/SP	60.00	30.00	18.00
551	Bob Purkey/SP	16.00	8.00	4.75
552	Birdie Tebbetts/SP	16.00	8.00	4.75
553	Major League Rookies **(Pat Garrett, Jackie Warner)**	12.50	6.25	3.75
554	Jim Northrup/SP	16.00	8.00	4.75
555	Ron Perranoski/SP	16.00	8.00	4.75
556	Mel Queen/SP	16.00	8.00	4.75
557	Felix Mantilla/SP	16.00	8.00	4.75
558	Red Sox Rookies **(*Guido Grilli, Pete Magrini, George Scott*)**	20.00	10.00	6.00
559	Roberto Pena/SP	16.00	8.00	4.75
560	Joel Horlen	12.50	6.25	3.75
561	Choo Choo Coleman/SP	30.00	15.00	9.00
562	Russ Snyder	12.50	6.25	3.75
563	Twins Rookies **(Pete Cimino, Cesar Tovar)**	12.50	6.25	3.75
564	Bob Chance/SP	16.00	8.00	4.75
565	Jimmy Piersall/SP	17.50	8.75	5.25
566	Mike Cuellar/SP	16.00	8.00	4.75
567	Dick Howser/SP	16.00	8.00	4.75
568	Athletics Rookies **(Paul Lindblad, Ron Stone)**	12.50	6.25	3.75
569	Orlando McFarlane/SP	16.00	8.00	4.75
570	Art Mahaffey/SP	16.00	8.00	4.75
571	Dave Roberts/SP	16.00	8.00	4.75
572	Bob Priddy	12.50	6.25	3.75
573	Derrell Griffith	12.50	6.25	3.75
574	Mets Rookies **(Bill Hepler, Bill Murphy)**	12.50	6.25	3.75
575	Earl Wilson	12.50	6.25	3.75
576	Dave Nicholson/SP	16.00	8.00	4.75
577	Jack Lamabe/SP	16.00	8.00	4.75
578	Chi Chi Olivo/SP	16.00	8.00	4.75
579	Orioles Rookies **(Frank Bertaina, Gene Brabender, Dave Johnson)**	17.50	8.75	5.25
580	Billy Williams/SP	45.00	22.50	13.50
581	Tony Martinez	12.50	6.25	3.75
582	Garry Roggenburk	12.50	6.25	3.75
583	Tigers Team/SP	75.00	37.50	22.50
584	Yankees Rookies **(*Frank Fernandez, Fritz Peterson*)**	15.00	7.50	4.50
585	Tony Taylor	12.50	6.25	3.75
586	Claude Raymond/SP	16.00	8.00	4.75
587	Dick Bertell	12.50	6.25	3.75
588	Athletics Rookies **(Chuck Dobson, Ken Suarez)**	12.50	6.25	3.75
589	Lou Klimchock/SP	16.00	8.00	4.75
590	Bill Skowron/SP	25.00	12.50	7.50
591	N.L. Rookies **(Grant Jackson, Bart Shirley)/SP**	16.00	8.00	4.75
592	Andre Rodgers	12.50	6.25	3.75
593	Doug Camilli/SP	16.00	8.00	4.75
594	Chico Salmon	12.50	6.25	3.75
595	Larry Jackson	12.50	6.25	3.75
596	Astros Rookies **(Nate Colbert, Greg Sims)/SP**	20.00	10.00	6.00
597	John Sullivan	12.50	6.25	3.75
598	Gaylord Perry/SP	100.00	30.00	15.00

1966 Topps Comic Book Foldees

Comic book heroes and other fictional characters were the focus of this set of 44 "foldees." The pictures on the left and right ends of the 4-1/2" x 2-3/8" cards were cut through the middle to allow them to be folded over the central picture and each other to create funny combinations. Babe Ruth, in a rather generic drawing, is the only baseball player represented in the issue. A version of the set exists which carries a "T.G.C. PRINTED IN CANADA" copyright line; it is valued similarly.

	NM	EX	VG
Complete Set (44):	100.00	50.00	30.00
12 Babe Ruth	20.00	10.00	7.25

1966 Topps Punch-Outs

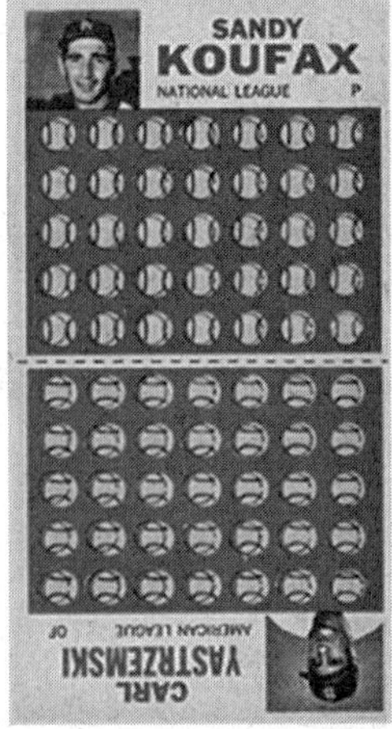

Only a handful of surviving examples of this issue are known. It is believed they represent a prototype for the 1967 Topps Punch-Outs which were themselves issued only on a test basis. The cards are blank-backed, measuring about 2-1/2" x 4-5/8" and perforated at center to allow the American League and National League to be separated for game play. A team captain is pictured in black-and-white on each half of the card. The A.L. side has a red background with 35 yellow baseballs to be punched out to determine game action. Background on the N.L. side is blue. Because of their rarity and lack of recent sales records, valuations for most pieces are not provided. This checklist is likely incomplete.

		NM	EX	VG
(1)	Ernie Banks, Mel Stottlemyre			
(2)	Johnny Callison/Jim Grant			
(3)	Donn Clendenon, Al Kaline			
(4)	Curt Flood, Bill Skowron			
(5)	Jim Ray Hart, Mickey Mantle			
(6)	Juan Marichal, Rich Rollins			
(7)	Sandy Koufax, Carl Yastrzemski (12/04 auction)	6,700		
(8)	John Roseboro, Bobby Richardson			
(9)	Willie Stargell, Felix Mantilla			

1966 Topps Rub-Offs

Returning to a concept last tried in 1961, Topps tried an expanded version of Rub-Offs in 1966. Measuring 2-1/16" x 3", the Rub-Offs are in vertical format for the 100 players and horizontal for the 20 team pennants. The player Rub-Offs feature a color photo. Cutting procedures left well-centered examples in the distinct minority.

		NM	EX	VG
Complete Set (120):		800.00	265.00	120.00
Common Player:		5.00	1.50	.75
(1)	Hank Aaron	30.00	11.00	5.00
(2)	Jerry Adair	5.00	1.50	.75
(3)	Richie Allen	6.00	2.00	.90
(4)	Jesus Alou	5.00	1.50	.75
(5)	Max Alvis	5.00	1.50	.75
(6)	Bob Aspromonte	5.00	1.50	.75
(7)	Ernie Banks	15.00	5.00	2.50
(8)	Earl Battey	5.00	1.50	.75
(9)	Curt Blefary	5.00	1.50	.75
(10)	Ken Boyer	6.00	2.00	.90
(11)	Bob Bruce	5.00	1.50	.75
(12)	Jim Bunning	10.00	3.50	1.50
(13)	Johnny Callison	5.00	1.50	.75
(14)	Bert Campaneris	5.00	1.50	.75
(15)	Jose Cardenal	5.00	1.50	.75
(16)	Dean Chance	5.00	1.50	.75
(17)	Ed Charles	5.00	1.50	.75
(18)	Bob Clemente	35.00	12.00	5.00
(19)	Tony Cloninger	5.00	1.50	.75
(20)	Rocky Colavito	6.00	2.00	.90
(21)	Tony Conigliaro	6.50	2.25	1.00
(22)	Vic Davalillo	5.00	1.50	.75
(23)	Willie Davis	5.00	1.50	.75
(24)	Don Drysdale	10.00	3.50	1.50
(25)	Sammy Ellis	5.00	1.50	.75
(26)	Dick Ellsworth	5.00	1.50	.75
(27)	Ron Fairly	5.00	1.50	.75
(28)	Dick Farrell	5.00	1.50	.75
(29)	Eddie Fisher	5.00	1.50	.75
(30)	Jack Fisher	5.00	1.50	.75
(31)	Curt Flood	5.00	1.50	.75
(32)	Whitey Ford	15.00	5.25	2.25
(33)	Bill Freehan	5.00	1.50	.75
(34)	Jim Fregosi	5.00	1.50	.75
(35)	Bob Gibson	10.00	3.50	1.50
(36)	Jim Grant	5.00	1.50	.75
(37)	Jimmie Hall	5.00	1.50	.75
(38)	Ken Harrelson	5.00	1.50	.75
(39)	Jim Hart	5.00	1.50	.75
(40)	Joel Horlen	5.00	1.50	.75
(41)	Willie Horton	5.00	1.50	.75
(42)	Frank Howard	6.00	2.00	.90
(43)	Deron Johnson	5.00	1.50	.75
(44)	Al Kaline	12.50	4.50	2.00
(45)	Harmon Killebrew	10.00	3.50	1.50
(46)	Bobby Knoop	5.00	1.50	.75
(47)	Sandy Koufax	30.00	10.00	5.00
(48)	Ed Kranepool	5.00	1.50	.75
(49)	Gary Kroll	5.00	1.50	.75
(50)	Don Landrum	5.00	1.50	.75
(51)	Vernon Law	5.00	1.50	.75
(52)	Johnny Lewis	5.00	1.50	.75
(53)	Don Lock	5.00	1.50	.75
(54)	Mickey Lolich	5.00	1.50	.75
(55)	Jim Maloney	5.00	1.50	.75
(56)	Felix Mantilla	5.00	1.50	.75
(57)	Mickey Mantle	55.00	20.00	8.00
(58)	Juan Marichal	10.00	3.50	1.50
(59)	Ed Mathews	10.00	3.50	1.50
(60)	Willie Mays	30.00	10.00	5.00
(61)	Bill Mazeroski	10.00	3.50	1.50
(62)	Dick McAuliffe	5.00	1.50	.75
(63)	Tim McCarver	6.00	2.00	.90
(64)	Willie McCovey	10.00	3.50	1.50
(65)	Sammy McDowell	5.00	1.50	.75
(66)	Ken McMullen	5.00	1.50	.75
(67)	Denis Menke	5.00	1.50	.75
(68)	Bill Monbouquette	5.00	1.50	.75
(69)	Joe Morgan	10.00	3.50	1.50
(70)	Fred Newman	5.00	1.50	.75
(71)	John O'Donoghue	5.00	1.50	.75
(72)	Tony Oliva	6.00	2.00	.90
(73)	Johnny Orsino	5.00	1.50	.75
(74)	Phil Ortega	5.00	1.50	.75
(75)	Milt Pappas	5.00	1.50	.75
(76)	Dick Radatz	5.00	1.50	.75
(77)	Bobby Richardson	6.50	2.25	1.00
(78)	Pete Richert	5.00	1.50	.75
(79)	Brooks Robinson	12.50	4.50	2.00
(80)	Floyd Robinson	5.00	1.50	.75
(81)	Frank Robinson	12.50	4.50	2.00
(82)	Cookie Rojas	5.00	1.50	.75
(83)	Pete Rose	25.00	9.00	4.00
(84)	John Roseboro	5.00	1.50	.75
(85)	Ron Santo	6.50	2.25	1.00
(86)	Bill Skowron	5.00	1.75	.70
(87)	Willie Stargell	10.00	3.50	1.50
(88)	Mel Stottlemyre	5.00	1.50	.75
(89)	Dick Stuart	5.00	1.50	.75
(90)	Ron Swoboda	5.00	1.50	.75
(91)	Fred Talbot	5.00	1.50	.75
(92)	Ralph Terry	5.00	1.50	.75
(93)	Joe Torre	6.50	2.25	1.00
(94)	Tom Tresh	5.00	1.50	.75
(95)	Bob Veale	5.00	1.50	.75
(96)	Pete Ward	5.00	1.50	.75
(97)	Bill White	5.00	1.50	.75
(98)	Billy Williams	10.00	3.50	1.50
(99)	Jim Wynn	5.00	1.50	.75
(100)	Carl Yastrzemski	15.00	5.25	2.25
(101)	Angels Pennant	7.00	2.50	1.00
(102)	Astros Pennant	7.00	2.50	1.00
(103)	Athletics Pennant	7.00	2.50	1.00
(104)	Braves Pennant	7.00	2.50	1.00
(105)	Cards Pennant	7.00	2.50	1.00
(106)	Cubs Pennant	7.00	2.50	1.00
(107)	Dodgers Pennant	7.00	2.50	1.00
(108)	Giants Pennant	7.00	2.50	1.00
(109)	Indians Pennant	7.00	2.50	1.00
(110)	Mets Pennant	7.00	2.50	1.00
(111)	Orioles Pennant	7.00	2.50	1.00
(112)	Phillies Pennant	7.00	2.50	1.00
(113)	Pirates Pennant	7.00	2.50	1.00
(114)	Red Sox Pennant	7.00	2.50	1.00
(115)	Reds Pennant	7.00	2.50	1.00
(116)	Senators Pennant	7.00	2.50	1.00
(117)	Tigers Pennant	7.00	2.50	1.00
(118)	Twins Pennant	7.00	2.50	1.00
(119)	White Sox Pennant	7.00	2.50	1.00
(120)	Yankees Pennant	9.00	3.25	1.25

1967 Topps

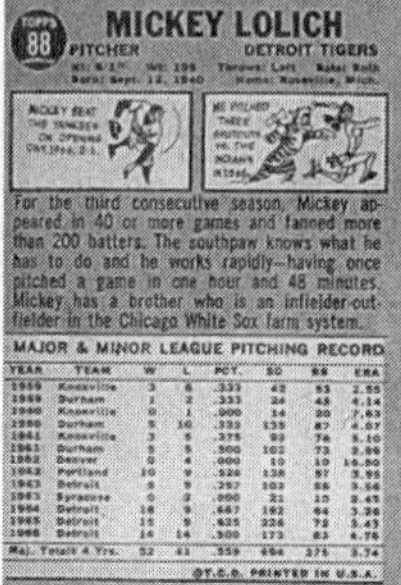

This 609-card set of 2-1/2" x 3-1/2" cards marked the largest set up to that time for Topps. Card fronts feature large color photographs bordered by white. The player's name and position are printed at the top with the team at the bottom. Across the front of the card with the exception of #254 (Milt Pappas) there is a facsimile autograph. The backs were the first to be done vertically, although they continued to carry familiar statistical and biographical information. The only subsets are statistical leaders and World Series highlights. Rookie cards are done by team or league with two players per card. The high numbers (#534-609) in '67 are quite scarce, and while it is known that some are even scarcer, by virtue of having been short-printed in relation to the rest of the series, there is no general agreement on which cards are involved. Cards in the high series which are generally believed to have been double-printed - and thus worth somewhat less than the other cards in the series - are indicated in the checklist by a/DP notation following the player name.

		NM	EX	VG
	Complete Set (609):	4,500	2,250	1,350
	Common Player (1-370):	2.00	1.00	.60
	Common Player (371-457):	4.00	2.00	1.25
	Common Player (458-533):	7.00	3.50	2.00
	Common Player (534-609):	12.00	6.00	3.50
1	The Champs (Hank Bauer, Brooks Robinson, Frank Robinson)	20.00	9.00	5.00
2	Jack Hamilton	2.00	1.00	.60
3	Duke Sims	2.00	1.00	.60
4	Hal Lanier	2.00	1.00	.60
5	Whitey Ford	25.00	12.50	7.50
6	Dick Simpson	2.00	1.00	.60
7	Don McMahon	2.00	1.00	.60
8	Chuck Harrison	2.00	1.00	.60
9	Ron Hansen	2.00	1.00	.60
10	Matty Alou	2.00	1.00	.60
11	Barry Moore	2.00	1.00	.60
12	Dodgers Rookies **(Jimmy Campanis, Bill Singer)**	2.00	1.00	.60
13	Joe Sparma	2.00	1.00	.60
14	Phil Linz	2.00	1.00	.60
15	Earl Battey	2.00	1.00	.60
16	Bill Hands	2.00	1.00	.60
17	Jim Gosger	2.00	1.00	.60
18	Gene Oliver	2.00	1.00	.60
19	Jim McGlothlin	2.00	1.00	.60
20	Orlando Cepeda	15.00	7.50	4.50
21	Dave Bristol	2.00	1.00	.60
22	Gene Brabender	2.00	1.00	.60
23	Larry Elliot	2.00	1.00	.60
24	Bob Allen	2.00	1.00	.60
25	Elston Howard	7.00	3.50	2.00
26a	Bob Priddy (No trade statement.)	30.00	15.00	9.00
26b	Bob Priddy (With trade statement.)	2.00	1.00	.60
27	Bob Saverine	2.00	1.00	.60
28	Barry Latman	2.00	1.00	.60
29	Tommy McCraw	2.00	1.00	.60
30	Al Kaline	20.00	10.00	6.00
31	Jim Brewer	2.00	1.00	.60
32	Bob Bailey	2.00	1.00	.60
33	Athletics Rookies **(Sal Bando, Randy Schwartz)**	4.00	2.00	1.25
34	Pete Cimino	2.00	1.00	.60
35	Rico Carty	2.00	1.00	.60
36	Bob Tillman	2.00	1.00	.60
37	Rick Wise	2.00	1.00	.60
38	Bob Johnson	2.00	1.00	.60
39	Curt Simmons	2.00	1.00	.60
40	Rick Reichardt	2.00	1.00	.60
41	Joe Hoerner	2.00	1.00	.60
42	Mets Team	8.00	4.00	2.50
43	Chico Salmon	2.00	1.00	.60
44	Joe Nuxhall	2.00	1.00	.60
45a	Roger Maris (Cards on front.)	35.00	17.50	10.00
45b	Roger Maris (Yankees on front, blank-back proof.)	2,250	1,125	635.00
46	Lindy McDaniel	2.00	1.00	.60
47	Ken McMullen	2.00	1.00	.60
48	Bill Freehan	2.00	1.00	.60
49	Roy Face	2.00	1.00	.60
50	Tony Oliva	6.00	3.00	1.75
51	Astros Rookies **(Dave Adlesh, Wes Bales)**	2.00	1.00	.60
52	Dennis Higgins	2.00	1.00	.60
53	Clay Dalrymple	2.00	1.00	.60
54	Dick Green	2.00	1.00	.60
55	Don Drysdale	20.00	10.00	6.00
56	Jose Tartabull	2.00	1.00	.60
57	***Pat Jarvis***	2.00	1.00	.60
58a	Paul Schaal (Bat green above name.)	15.00	7.50	4.50
58b	Paul Schaal (Bat natural above name.)	2.00	1.00	.60
59	Ralph Terry	2.00	1.00	.60
60	Luis Aparicio	15.00	7.50	4.50
61	Gordy Coleman	2.00	1.00	.60
62a	1st Series Check List (1-109) (Frank Robinson) (Copyright symbol beneath T of Tribe.)	7.00	3.50	2.00
62b	1st Series Check List (1-109) (Frank Robinson) (Copyright symbol beneath r of Tribe.)	7.00	3.50	2.00
63	Cards Clubbers (Lou Brock, Curt Flood)	12.00	6.00	3.50
64	Fred Valentine	2.00	1.00	.60
65	Tom Haller	2.00	1.00	.60
66	Manny Mota	2.00	1.00	.60
67	Ken Berry	2.00	1.00	.60
68	Bob Buhl	2.00	1.00	.60
69	Vic Davalillo	2.00	1.00	.60
70	Ron Santo	6.00	3.00	1.75
71	Camilo Pascual	2.00	1.00	.60
72	Tigers Rookies **(George Korince, John Matchick)** (Korince photo actually James M. Brown.)	2.00	1.00	.60
73	Rusty Staub	3.00	1.50	.90
74	Wes Stock	2.00	1.00	.60
75	George Scott	2.00	1.00	.60
76	Jim Barbieri	2.00	1.00	.60
77	Dooley Womack	2.00	1.00	.60
78	Pat Corrales	2.00	1.00	.60
79	Bubba Morton	2.00	1.00	.60
80	Jim Maloney	2.00	1.00	.60
81	Eddie Stanky	2.00	1.00	.60
82	Steve Barber	2.00	1.00	.60
83	Ollie Brown	2.00	1.00	.60
84	Tommie Sisk	2.00	1.00	.60
85	Johnny Callison	2.00	1.00	.60
86a	Mike McCormick (No trade statement.)	30.00	15.00	9.00
86b	Mike McCormick (With trade statement.)	2.00	1.00	.60
87	George Altman	2.00	1.00	.60
88	Mickey Lolich	2.00	1.00	.60
89	***Felix Millan***	2.00	1.00	.60
90	Jim Nash	2.00	1.00	.60
91	Johnny Lewis	2.00	1.00	.60
92	Ray Washburn	2.00	1.00	.60
93	Yankees Rookies **(*Stan Bahnsen, Bobby Murcer*)**	12.00	6.00	3.50
94	Ron Fairly	2.00	1.00	.60
95	Sonny Siebert	2.00	1.00	.60
96	Art Shamsky	2.00	1.00	.60
97	Mike Cuellar	2.00	1.00	.60
98	Rich Rollins	2.00	1.00	.60
99	Lee Stange	2.00	1.00	.60
100	Frank Robinson	20.00	10.00	6.00
101	Ken Johnson	2.00	1.00	.60
102	Phillies Team	3.50	1.75	1.00
103a	2nd Series Check List (110-196) (Mickey Mantle) (170 is D McAuliffe)	25.00	12.50	7.50
103b	2nd Series Check List (110-196) (Mickey Mantle) (170 is D. McAuliffe)	25.00	12.50	7.50
104	Minnie Rojas	2.00	1.00	.60
105	Ken Boyer	5.00	2.50	1.50
106	Randy Hundley	2.00	1.00	.60
107	Joel Horlen	2.00	1.00	.60
108	Alex Johnson	2.00	1.00	.60
109	Tribe Thumpers (Rocky Colavito, Leon Wagner)	9.00	4.50	2.75
110	Jack Aker	2.00	1.00	.60
111	John Kennedy	2.00	1.00	.60
112	Dave Wickersham	2.00	1.00	.60
113	Dave Nicholson	2.00	1.00	.60
114	Jack Baldschun	2.00	1.00	.60
115	Paul Casanova	2.00	1.00	.60
116	Herman Franks	2.00	1.00	.60
117	Darrell Brandon	2.00	1.00	.60
118	Bernie Allen	2.00	1.00	.60
119	Wade Blasingame	2.00	1.00	.60
120	Floyd Robinson	2.00	1.00	.60
121	Ed Bressoud	2.00	1.00	.60
122	George Brunet	2.00	1.00	.60
123	Pirates Rookies **(Jim Price, Luke Walker)**	2.00	1.00	.60
124	Jim Stewart	2.00	1.00	.60
125	Moe Drabowsky	2.00	1.00	.60
126	Tony Taylor	2.00	1.00	.60
127	John O'Donoghue	2.00	1.00	.60
128a	Ed Spiezio (Most of "SPIE" missing at top.)	75.00	37.50	22.50
128b	Ed Spiezio (Lettering all there.)	2.00	1.00	.60
129	Phil Roof	2.00	1.00	.60
130	Phil Regan	2.00	1.00	.60
131	Yankees Team	9.00	4.50	2.75
132	Ozzie Virgil	2.00	1.00	.60
133	Ron Kline	2.00	1.00	.60
134	Gates Brown	2.00	1.00	.60
135	Deron Johnson	2.00	1.00	.60
136	Carroll Sembera	2.00	1.00	.60
137	Twins Rookies **(Ron Clark, Jim Ollom)**	2.00	1.00	.60
138	Dick Kelley	2.00	1.00	.60
139	Dalton Jones	2.00	1.00	.60
140	Willie Stargell	20.00	10.00	6.00
141	John Miller	2.00	1.00	.60
142	Jackie Brandt	2.00	1.00	.60
143	Sox Sockers (Don Buford, Pete Ward)	2.00	1.00	.60
144	Bill Hepler	2.00	1.00	.60
145	Larry Brown	2.00	1.00	.60
146	Steve Carlton	27.50	13.50	8.25
147	Tom Egan	2.00	1.00	.60
148	Adolfo Phillips	2.00	1.00	.60
149a	Joe Moeller (White streak between "M" and cap.)	30.00	15.00	9.00
149b	Joe Moeller (No white streak.)	2.00	1.00	.60
150	Mickey Mantle	180.00	90.00	55.00
151	World Series Game 1 (Moe Mows Down 11)	6.00	3.00	1.75
152	World Series Game 2 (Palmer Blanks Dodgers)	11.00	5.50	3.25
153	World Series Game 3 (Blair's Homer Defeats L.A.)	6.00	3.00	1.75
154	World Series Game 4 (Orioles Win 4th Straight)	6.00	3.00	1.75
155	World Series (The Winners Celebrate)	7.50	3.75	2.25
156	Ron Herbel	2.00	1.00	.60
157	Danny Cater	2.00	1.00	.60
158	Jimmy Coker	2.00	1.00	.60
159	Bruce Howard	2.00	1.00	.60
160	Willie Davis	2.00	1.00	.60
161	Dick Williams	2.00	1.00	.60
162	Billy O'Dell	2.00	1.00	.60
163	Vic Roznovsky	2.00	1.00	.60
164	Dwight Siebler	2.00	1.00	.60
165	Cleon Jones	2.00	1.00	.60
166	Ed Mathews	20.00	10.00	6.00
167	Senators Rookies **(Joe Coleman, Tim Cullen)**	2.00	1.00	.60
168	Ray Culp	2.00	1.00	.60
169	Horace Clarke	2.00	1.00	.60
170	Dick McAuliffe	2.00	1.00	.60
171	Calvin Koonce	2.00	1.00	.60
172	Bill Heath	2.00	1.00	.60
173	Cards Team	5.00	2.50	1.50
174	Dick Radatz	2.00	1.00	.60
175	Bobby Knoop	2.00	1.00	.60
176	Sammy Ellis	2.00	1.00	.60
177	Tito Fuentes	2.00	1.00	.60
178	John Buzhardt	2.00	1.00	.60
179	Braves Rookies **(Cecil Upshaw, Chas. Vaughan)**	2.00	1.00	.60
180	Curt Blefary	2.00	1.00	.60
181	Terry Fox	2.00	1.00	.60
182	Ed Charles	2.00	1.00	.60
183	Jim Pagliaroni	2.00	1.00	.60
184	George Thomas	2.00	1.00	.60
185	***Ken Holtzman***	4.00	2.00	1.25
186	Mets Maulers (Ed Kranepool, Ron Swoboda)	3.50	1.75	1.00
187	Pedro Ramos	2.00	1.00	.60
188	Ken Harrelson	2.00	1.00	.60
189	Chuck Hinton	2.00	1.00	.60
190	Turk Farrell	2.00	1.00	.60
191a	3rd Series Check List (197-283) (Willie Mays) (214 is Dick Kelley)	9.00	4.50	2.75
191b	3rd Series Check List (197-283) (Willie Mays) (214 is Tom Kelley)	12.00	6.00	3.50
192	Fred Gladding	2.00	1.00	.60
193	Jose Cardenal	2.00	1.00	.60
194	Bob Allison	2.00	1.00	.60
195	Al Jackson	2.00	1.00	.60
196	Johnny Romano	2.00	1.00	.60
197	Ron Perranoski	2.00	1.00	.60
198	Chuck Hiller	2.00	1.00	.60
199	Billy Hitchcock	2.00	1.00	.60
200	Willie Mays	65.00	32.50	20.00
201	Hal Reniff	2.00	1.00	.60
202	Johnny Edwards	2.00	1.00	.60
203	Al McBean	2.00	1.00	.60
204	Orioles Rookies **(Mike Epstein, Tom Phoebus)**	2.00	1.00	.60
205	Dick Groat	2.00	1.00	.60
206	Dennis Bennett	2.00	1.00	.60
207	John Orsino	2.00	1.00	.60
208	Jack Lamabe	2.00	1.00	.60
209	Joe Nossek	2.00	1.00	.60
210	Bob Gibson	20.00	10.00	6.00
211	Twins Team	6.00	3.00	1.75
212	Chris Zachary	2.00	1.00	.60
213	***Jay Johnstone***	4.00	2.00	1.25
214	Tom Kelley	2.00	1.00	.60
215	Ernie Banks	25.00	12.50	7.50
216	Bengal Belters (Norm Cash, Al Kaline)	15.00	7.50	4.50
217	Rob Gardner	2.00	1.00	.60
218	Wes Parker	2.00	1.00	.60
219	Clay Carroll	2.00	1.00	.60
220	Jim Hart	2.00	1.00	.60
221	Woody Fryman	2.00	1.00	.60
222	Reds Rookies **(Lee May, Darrell Osteen)**	2.00	1.00	.60
223	Mike Ryan	2.00	1.00	.60
224	Walt Bond	2.00	1.00	.60
225	Mel Stottlemyre	4.00	2.00	1.25
226	Julian Javier	2.00	1.00	.60
227	Paul Lindblad	2.00	1.00	.60
228	Gil Hodges	9.00	4.50	2.75
229	Larry Jackson	2.00	1.00	.60
230	Boog Powell	6.00	3.00	1.75
231	John Bateman	2.00	1.00	.60
232	Don Buford	2.00	1.00	.60
233	A.L. ERA Leaders (Steve Hargan, Joel Horlen, Gary Peters)	3.00	1.50	.90
234	N.L. ERA Leaders (Mike Cuellar, Sandy Koufax, Juan Marichal)	12.00	6.00	3.50
235	A.L. Pitching Leaders (Jim Kaat, Denny McLain, Earl Wilson)	3.50	1.75	1.00
236	N.L. Pitching Leaders (Bob Gibson, Sandy Koufax, Juan Marichal, Gaylord Perry)	16.00	8.00	4.75
237	A.L. Strikeout Leaders (Jim Kaat, Sam McDowell, Earl Wilson)	3.50	1.75	1.00
238	N.L. Strikeout Leaders (Jim Bunning, Sandy Koufax, Bob Veale)	12.00	6.00	3.50
239	A.L. Batting Leaders (Al Kaline, Tony Oliva, Frank Robinson)	16.00	8.00	4.75
240	N.L. Batting Leaders (Felipe Alou, Matty Alou, Rico Carty)	11.00	5.50	3.25
241	A.L. RBI Leaders (Harmon Killebrew, Boog Powell, Frank Robinson)	11.00	5.50	3.25
242	N.L. RBI Leaders (Hank Aaron, Richie Allen, Bob Clemente)	17.50	8.75	5.25
243	A.L. Home Run Leaders (Harmon Killebrew, Boog Powell, Frank Robinson)	11.00	5.50	3.25
244	N.L. Home Run Leaders (Hank Aaron, Richie Allen, Willie Mays)	15.00	7.50	4.50
245	Curt Flood	5.00	2.50	1.50
246	Jim Perry	2.00	1.00	.60
247	Jerry Lumpe	2.00	1.00	.60

248	Gene Mauch	2.00	1.00	.60
249	Nick Willhite	2.00	1.00	.60
250	Hank Aaron	65.00	32.50	20.00
251	Woody Held	2.00	1.00	.60
252a	Bob Bolin (White streak between Bob and Bolin.)	60.00	30.00	18.00
252b	Bob Bolin (No white streak.)	2.00	1.00	.60
253	Indians Rookies **(Bill Davis, Gus Gil)**	2.00	1.00	.60
254	Milt Pappas	2.00	1.00	.60
255	Frank Howard	2.50	1.25	.70
256	Bob Hendley	2.00	1.00	.60
257	Charley Smith	2.00	1.00	.60
258	Lee Maye	2.00	1.00	.60
259	Don Dennis	2.00	1.00	.60
260	Jim Lefebvre	2.00	1.00	.60
261	John Wyatt	2.00	1.00	.60
262	Athletics Team	6.00	3.00	1.75
263	Hank Aguirre	2.00	1.00	.60
264	Ron Swoboda	2.00	1.00	.60
265	Lou Burdette	2.00	1.00	.60
266	Pitt Power (Donn Clendenon, Willie Stargell)	12.00	6.00	3.50
267	Don Schwall	2.00	1.00	.60
268	John Briggs	2.00	1.00	.60
269	Don Nottebart	2.00	1.00	.60
270	Zoilo Versalles	2.00	1.00	.60
271	Eddie Watt	2.00	1.00	.60
272	Cubs Rookies **(Bill Connors, Dave Dowling)**	2.00	1.00	.60
273	Dick Lines	2.00	1.00	.60
274	Bob Aspromonte	2.00	1.00	.60
275	Fred Whitfield	2.00	1.00	.60
276	Bruce Brubaker	2.00	1.00	.60
277	Steve Whitaker	2.00	1.00	.60
278	4th Series Check List (284-370) (Jim Kaat)	7.00	3.50	2.00
279	Frank Linzy	2.00	1.00	.60
280	Tony Conigliaro	9.00	4.50	2.75
281	Bob Rodgers	2.00	1.00	.60
282	Johnny Odom	2.00	1.00	.60
283	Gene Alley	2.00	1.00	.60
284	Johnny Podres	3.00	1.50	.90
285	Lou Brock	17.50	8.75	5.25
286	Wayne Causey	2.00	1.00	.60
287	Mets Rookies **(Greg Goossen, Bart Shirley)**	2.00	1.00	.60
288	Denver Lemaster	2.00	1.00	.60
289	Tom Tresh	6.00	3.00	1.75
290	Bill White	2.00	1.00	.60
291	Jim Hannan	2.00	1.00	.60
292	Don Pavletich	2.00	1.00	.60
293	Ed Kirkpatrick	2.00	1.00	.60
294	Walt Alston	7.00	3.50	2.00
295	Sam McDowell	2.00	.70	.60
296	Glenn Beckert	2.00	1.00	.60
297	Dave Morehead	2.00	1.00	.60
298	Ron Davis	2.00	1.00	.60
299	Norm Siebern	2.00	1.00	.60
300	Jim Kaat	4.00	2.00	1.25
301	Jesse Gonder	2.00	1.00	.60
302	Orioles Team	6.00	3.00	1.75
303	Gil Blanco	2.00	1.00	.60
304	Phil Gagliano	2.00	1.00	.60
305	Earl Wilson	2.00	1.00	.60
306	***Bud Harrelson***	7.00	3.50	2.00
307	Jim Beauchamp	2.00	1.00	.60
308	Al Downing	2.00	1.00	.60
309	Hurlers Beware (Richie Allen, Johnny Callison)	6.00	3.00	1.75
310	Gary Peters	2.00	1.00	.60
311	Ed Brinkman	2.00	1.00	.60
312	Don Mincher	2.00	1.00	.60
313	Bob Lee	2.00	1.00	.60
314	Red Sox Rookies (***Mike Andrews, Reggie Smith***)	12.00	6.00	3.50
315	Billy Williams	17.50	8.75	5.25
316	Jack Kralick	2.00	1.00	.60
317	Cesar Tovar	2.00	1.00	.60
318	Dave Giusti	2.00	1.00	.60
319	Paul Blair	2.00	1.00	.60
320	Gaylord Perry	15.00	7.50	4.50
321	Mayo Smith	2.00	1.00	.60
322	Jose Pagan	2.00	1.00	.60
323	Mike Hershberger	2.00	1.00	.60
324	Hal Woodeshick	2.00	1.00	.60
325	Chico Cardenas	2.00	1.00	.60
326	Bob Uecker	12.00	6.00	3.50
327	Angels Team	6.00	3.00	1.75
328	Clete Boyer	4.00	2.00	1.25
329	Charlie Lau	2.00	1.00	.60
330	Claude Osteen	2.00	1.00	.60
331	Joe Foy	2.00	1.00	.60
332	Jesus Alou	2.00	1.00	.60
333	Fergie Jenkins	16.00	8.00	4.75
334	Twin Terrors (Bob Allison, Harmon Killebrew)	15.00	7.50	4.50
335	Bob Veale	2.00	1.00	.60
336	Joe Azcue	2.00	1.00	.60
337	Joe Morgan	17.50	8.75	5.25
338	Bob Locker	2.00	1.00	.60
339	Chico Ruiz	2.00	1.00	.60
340	Joe Pepitone	4.00	2.00	1.25
341	Giants Rookies **(Dick Dietz, Bill Sorrell)**	2.00	1.00	.60
342	Hank Fischer	2.00	1.00	.60
343	Tom Satriano	2.00	1.00	.60
344	Ossie Chavarria	2.00	1.00	.60
345	Stu Miller	2.00	1.00	.60
346	Jim Hickman	2.00	1.00	.60
347	Grady Hatton	2.00	1.00	.60
348	Tug McGraw	3.00	1.50	.90
349	Bob Chance	2.00	1.00	.60
350	Joe Torre	7.00	3.50	2.00
351	Vern Law	2.00	1.00	.60
352	Ray Oyler	2.00	1.00	.60
353	Bill McCool	2.00	1.00	.60
354	Cubs Team	6.00	3.00	1.75
355	Carl Yastrzemski	45.00	22.50	13.50
356	Larry Jaster	2.00	1.00	.60
357	Bill Skowron	5.00	2.50	1.50
358	Ruben Amaro	2.00	1.00	.60
359	Dick Ellsworth	2.00	1.00	.60
360	Leon Wagner	2.00	1.00	.60
361	5th Series Check List (371-457) (Roberto Clemente)	9.00	4.50	2.75
362	Darold Knowles	2.00	1.00	.60
363	Dave Johnson	2.00	1.00	.60
364	Claude Raymond	2.00	1.00	.60
365	John Roseboro	2.00	1.00	.60
366	Andy Kosco	2.00	1.00	.60
367	Angels Rookies **(Bill Kelso, Don Wallace)**	2.00	1.00	.60
368	Jack Hiatt	2.00	1.00	.60
369	Jim Hunter	15.00	7.50	4.50
370	Tommy Davis	2.00	1.00	.60
371	Jim Lonborg	4.00	2.00	1.25
372	Mike de la Hoz	4.00	2.00	1.25
373	White Sox Rookies **(Duane Josephson, Fred Klages)**	4.00	2.00	1.25
374a	Mel Queen (Rule under stats totals nearly gone.)	4.00	2.00	1.25
374b	Mel Queen (Full rule.)	4.00	2.00	1.25
375	Jake Gibbs	4.00	2.00	1.25
376	Don Lock	4.00	2.00	1.25
377	Luis Tiant	4.00	2.00	1.25
378	Tigers Team	7.00	3.50	2.00
379	Jerry May	4.00	2.00	1.25
380	Dean Chance	4.00	2.00	1.25
381	Dick Schofield	4.00	2.00	1.25
382	Dave McNally	4.00	2.00	1.25
383	Ken Henderson	4.00	2.00	1.25
384	Cards Rookies **(Jim Cosman, Dick Hughes)**	4.00	2.00	1.25
385	Jim Fregosi	4.00	2.00	1.25
386	Dick Selma	4.00	2.00	1.25
387	Cap Peterson	4.00	2.00	1.25
388	Arnold Earley	4.00	2.00	1.25
389	Al Dark	4.00	2.00	1.25
390	Jim Wynn	4.00	2.00	1.25
391	Wilbur Wood	4.00	2.00	1.25
392	Tommy Harper	4.00	2.00	1.25
393	Jim Bouton	7.00	3.50	2.00
394	Jake Wood	4.00	2.00	1.25
395	Chris Short	4.00	2.00	1.25
396	Atlanta Aces (Tony Cloninger, Denis Menke)	7.00	3.50	2.00
397	Willie Smith	4.00	2.00	1.25
398	Jeff Torborg	4.00	2.00	1.25
399	Al Worthington	4.00	2.00	1.25
400	Roberto Clemente	80.00	40.00	24.00
401	Jim Coates	4.00	2.00	1.25
402a	Phillies Rookies **(Grant Jackson, Billy Wilson)** (Incomplete line under Wilson's stats.)	6.50	3.25	2.00
402b	Grant Jackson, Billy Wilson (Complete line.)	4.00	2.00	1.25
403	Dick Nen	4.00	2.00	1.25
404	Nelson Briles	4.00	2.00	1.25
405	Russ Snyder	4.00	2.00	1.25
406	Lee Elia	4.00	2.00	1.25
407	Reds Team	7.00	3.50	2.00
408	Jim Northrup	4.00	2.00	1.25
409	Ray Sadecki	4.00	2.00	1.25
410	Lou Johnson	4.00	2.00	1.25
411	Dick Howser	4.00	2.00	1.25
412	Astros Rookies (***Norm Miller, Doug Rader***)	5.00	2.50	1.50
413	Jerry Grote	4.00	2.00	1.25
414	Casey Cox	4.00	2.00	1.25
415	Sonny Jackson	4.00	2.00	1.25
416	Roger Repoz	4.00	2.00	1.25
417a	Bob Bruce (RBAVES on back.)	30.00	15.00	9.00
417b	Bob Bruce (Corrected)	4.00	2.00	1.25
418	Sam Mele	4.00	2.00	1.25
419	Don Kessinger	4.00	2.00	1.25
420	Denny McLain	7.00	3.50	2.00
421	Dal Maxvill	4.00	2.00	1.25
422	Hoyt Wilhelm	15.00	7.50	4.50
423	Fence Busters (Willie Mays, Willie McCovey)	25.00	12.50	7.50
424	Pedro Gonzalez	4.00	2.00	1.25
425	Pete Mikkelsen	4.00	2.00	1.25
426	Lou Clinton	4.00	2.00	1.25
427a	Ruben Gomez (Stats totals line nearly gone.)	12.00	6.00	3.50
427b	Ruben Gomez (Full stats totals line.)	4.00	2.00	1.25
428	Dodgers Rookies (***Tom Hutton, Gene Michael***)	6.00	3.00	1.75
429	Garry Roggenburk	4.00	2.00	1.25
430	Pete Rose	65.00	32.50	20.00
431	Ted Uhlaender	4.00	2.00	1.25
432	Jimmie Hall	4.00	2.00	1.25
433	Al Luplow	4.00	2.00	1.25
434	Eddie Fisher	4.00	2.00	1.25
435	Mack Jones	4.00	2.00	1.25
436	Pete Ward	4.00	2.00	1.25
437	Senators Team	7.00	3.50	2.00
438	Chuck Dobson	4.00	2.00	1.25
439	Byron Browne	4.00	2.00	1.25
440	Steve Hargan	4.00	2.00	1.25
441	Jim Davenport	4.00	2.00	1.25
442	Yankees Rookies **(Bill Robinson, Joe Verbanic)**	6.00	3.00	1.75
443	Tito Francona	4.00	2.00	1.25
444	George Smith	4.00	2.00	1.25
445	Don Sutton	15.00	7.50	4.50
446	Russ Nixon	4.00	2.00	1.25
447a	Bo Belinsky (1966 S.D. stats nearly gone)	6.00	3.00	1.75
447b	Bo Belinsky (Full 1966 S.D. stats line.)	4.00	2.00	1.25
448	Harry Walker	4.00	2.00	1.25
449	Orlando Pena	4.00	2.00	1.25
450	Richie Allen	12.00	6.00	3.50
451	Fred Newman	4.00	2.00	1.25
452	Ed Kranepool	4.00	2.00	1.25
453	Aurelio Monteagudo	4.00	2.00	1.25
454a	6th Series Check List (458-533) (Juan Marichal) (Left ear shows.)	9.00	4.50	2.75
454b	6th Series Check List (458-533) (Juan Marichal) (No left ear.)	12.00	6.00	3.50
455	Tommie Agee	4.00	2.00	1.25
456	Phil Niekro	15.00	7.50	4.50
457	Andy Etchebarren	4.00	2.00	1.25
458	Lee Thomas	7.00	3.50	2.00
459	Senators Rookies **(Dick Bosman, Pete Craig)**	7.00	3.50	2.00
460	Harmon Killebrew	35.00	17.50	10.00
461	Bob Miller	7.00	3.50	2.00
462	Bob Barton	7.00	3.50	2.00
463	Hill Aces (Sam McDowell, Sonny Siebert)	11.00	5.50	3.25
464	Dan Coombs	7.00	3.50	2.00
465	Willie Horton	7.00	3.50	2.00
466	Bobby Wine	7.00	3.50	2.00
467	Jim O'Toole	7.00	3.50	2.00
468	Ralph Houk	7.00	3.50	2.00
469	Len Gabrielson	7.00	3.50	2.00
470	Bob Shaw	7.00	3.50	2.00
471	Rene Lachemann	7.00	3.50	2.00
472	Pirates Rookies **(John Gelnar, George Spriggs)**	7.00	3.50	2.00
473	Jose Santiago	7.00	3.50	2.00
474	Bob Tolan	7.00	3.50	2.00
475	Jim Palmer	35.00	17.50	10.00
476	Tony Perez/SP	40.00	20.00	12.00
477	Braves Team	11.00	5.50	3.25
478	Bob Humphreys	7.00	3.50	2.00
479	Gary Bell	7.00	3.50	2.00
480	Willie McCovey	35.00	17.50	10.00
481	Leo Durocher	12.00	6.00	3.50
482	Bill Monbouquette	7.00	3.50	2.00
483	Jim Landis	7.00	3.50	2.00
484	Jerry Adair	7.00	3.50	2.00
485	Tim McCarver	17.50	8.75	5.25
486	Twins Rookies **(Rich Reese, Bill Whitby)**	7.00	3.50	2.00
487	Tom Reynolds	7.00	3.50	2.00
488	Gerry Arrigo	7.00	3.50	2.00
489	Doug Clemens	7.00	3.50	2.00
490	Tony Cloninger	7.00	3.50	2.00
491	Sam Bowens	7.00	3.50	2.00
492	Pirates Team	16.00	8.00	4.75
493	Phil Ortega	7.00	3.50	2.00
494	Bill Rigney	7.00	3.50	2.00
495	Fritz Peterson	7.00	3.50	2.00
496	Orlando McFarlane	7.00	3.50	2.00
497	Ron Campbell	7.00	3.50	2.00
498	Larry Dierker	7.00	3.50	2.00
499	Indians Rookies **(George Culver, Jose Vidal)**	7.00	3.50	2.00
500	Juan Marichal	25.00	12.50	7.50
501	Jerry Zimmerman	7.00	3.50	2.00
502	Derrell Griffith	7.00	3.50	2.00
503	Dodgers Team	16.00	8.00	4.75
504	Orlando Martinez	7.00	3.50	2.00
505	Tommy Helms	7.00	3.50	2.00
506	Smoky Burgess	7.00	3.50	2.00
507	Orioles Rookies **(Ed Barnowski, Larry Haney)**	7.00	3.50	2.00
508	Dick Hall	7.00	3.50	2.00
509	Jim King	7.00	3.50	2.00
510	Bill Mazeroski	20.00	10.00	6.00
511	Don Wert	7.00	3.50	2.00
512	Red Schoendienst	15.00	7.50	4.50
513	Marcelino Lopez	7.00	3.50	2.00
514	John Werhas	7.00	3.50	2.00
515	Bert Campaneris	7.00	3.50	2.00
516	Giants Team	17.50	8.75	5.25
517	Fred Talbot	7.00	3.50	2.00
518	Denis Menke	7.00	3.50	2.00
519	Ted Davidson	7.00	3.50	2.00
520	Max Alvis	7.00	3.50	2.00
521	Bird Bombers (Curt Blefary, Boog Powell)	7.50	3.75	2.25
522	John Stephenson	7.00	3.50	2.00
523	Jim Merritt	7.00	3.50	2.00
524	Felix Mantilla	7.00	3.50	2.00
525	Ron Hunt	7.00	3.50	2.00
526	Tigers Rookies **(Pat Dobson, George Korince)**	11.00	5.50	3.25
527	Dennis Ribant	7.00	3.50	2.00
528	Rico Petrocelli	12.50	6.25	3.75
529	Gary Wagner	7.00	3.50	2.00
530	Felipe Alou	12.00	6.00	3.50
531	7th Series Check List (534-609) (Brooks Robinson)	12.00	6.00	3.50
532	Jim Hicks	7.00	3.50	2.00
533	Jack Fisher	7.00	3.50	2.00
534	Hank Bauer/DP	8.00	4.00	2.50
535	Donn Clendenon	12.00	6.00	3.50
536	Cubs Rookies **(Joe Niekro, Paul Popovich)**	32.50	16.00	10.00
537	Chuck Estrada/DP	8.00	4.00	2.50
538	J.C. Martin	12.00	6.00	3.50
539	Dick Egan/DP	8.00	4.00	2.50
540	Norm Cash	45.00	22.50	13.50
541	Joe Gibbon	12.00	6.00	3.50
542	Athletics Rookies (**Rick Monday, Tony Pierce**)/DP	12.50	6.25	3.75
543	Dan Schneider	12.00	6.00	3.50
544	Indians Team	40.00	20.00	12.00
545	Jim Grant	12.00	6.00	3.50
546	Woody Woodward	12.00	6.00	3.50
547	Red Sox Rookies (**Russ Gibson, Bill Rohr**)/DP	8.00	4.00	2.50
548	Tony Gonzalez/DP	8.00	4.00	2.50
549	Jack Sanford	12.00	6.00	3.50

550	Vada Pinson/DP	12.00	6.00	3.50
551	Doug Camilli/DP	8.00	4.00	2.50
552	Ted Savage	12.00	6.00	3.50
553	Yankees Rookies **(Mike Hegan, Thad Tillotson)**	25.00	12.50	7.50
554	Andre Rodgers/DP	8.00	4.00	2.50
555	Don Cardwell	12.00	6.00	3.50
556	Al Weis/DP	8.00	4.00	2.50
557	Al Ferrara	12.00	6.00	3.50
558	Orioles Rookies **(Mark Belanger, Bill Dillman)**	45.00	22.50	13.50
559	Dick Tracewski/DP	8.00	4.00	2.50
560	Jim Bunning	50.00	25.00	15.00
561	Sandy Alomar	12.00	6.00	3.50
562	Steve Blass/DP	8.00	4.00	2.50
563	Joe Adcock	15.00	7.50	4.50
564	Astros Rookies **(Alonzo Harris, Aaron Pointer)**/DP	8.00	4.00	2.50
565	Lew Krausse	12.00	6.00	3.50
566	Gary Geiger/DP	8.00	4.00	2.50
567	Steve Hamilton	12.00	6.00	3.50
568	John Sullivan	12.00	6.00	3.50
569	A.L. Rookies **(*Hank Allen, Rod Carew*)/DP**	165.00	80.00	50.00
570	Maury Wills	70.00	35.00	20.00
571	Larry Sherry	12.00	6.00	3.50
572	Don Demeter	12.00	6.00	3.50
573	White Sox Team (Indians team stats on back)	25.00	12.50	7.50
574	Jerry Buchek	12.00	6.00	3.50
575	***Dave Boswell***	12.00	6.00	3.50
576	N.L. Rookies **(Norm Gigon, Ramon Hernandez)**	12.00	6.00	3.50
577	Bill Short	12.00	6.00	3.50
578	John Boccabella	12.00	6.00	3.50
579	Bill Henry	12.00	6.00	3.50
580	Rocky Colavito	70.00	35.00	20.00
581	Mets Rookies **(*Bill Denehy, Tom Seaver*)**	340.00	170.00	100.00
582	Jim Owens/DP	8.00	4.00	2.50
583	Ray Barker	12.00	6.00	3.50
584	Jim Piersall	20.00	10.00	6.00
585	Wally Bunker	12.00	6.00	3.50
586	Manny Jimenez	12.00	6.00	3.50
587	N.L. Rookies **(Don Shaw, Gary Sutherland)**	12.00	6.00	3.50
588	Johnny Klippstein/DP	8.00	4.00	2.50
589	Dave Ricketts/DP	8.00	4.00	2.50
590	Pete Richert	12.00	6.00	3.50
591	Ty Cline	12.00	6.00	3.50
592	N.L. Rookies **(Jim Shellenback, Ron Willis)**	12.00	6.00	3.50
593	Wes Westrum	12.00	6.00	3.50
594	Dan Osinski	12.00	6.00	3.50
595	Cookie Rojas	12.00	6.00	3.50
596	Galen Cisco/DP	8.00	4.00	2.50
597	Ted Abernathy	12.00	6.00	3.50
598	White Sox Rookies **(Ed Stroud, Walt Williams)**	12.00	6.00	3.50
599	Bob Duliba/DP	8.00	4.00	2.50
600	Brooks Robinson/SP	155.00	75.00	45.00
601	Bill Bryan/DP	8.00	4.00	2.50
602	Juan Pizarro	12.00	6.00	3.50
603	Athletics Rookies **(Tim Talton, Ramon Webster)**	12.00	6.00	3.50
604	Red Sox Team	85.00	42.50	25.00
605	Mike Shannon	45.00	22.50	13.50
606	Ron Taylor	12.00	6.00	3.50
607	Mickey Stanley	25.00	12.50	7.50
608	Cubs Rookies **(Rich Nye, John Upham)/DP**	8.00	4.00	2.50
609	Tommy John	60.00	20.00	12.00

1967 Topps Discs

Similar to the more common 28-piece set of 1968, this set of all-stars is known only in proof form, evidently intended to be pressed onto a pin-back button issue which never materialized. Printed on blank-backed silver foil about 2-3/8" square, the pieces have a 2-1/4" diameter center with color player portrait with name and position printed in black across the chest. Some pieces have a team name to the left and right of the player's picture. "JAPAN" is printed in tiny black letters at top-left, apparently intended to be folded under the rim of the button. The unnumbered discs are checklisted here alphabetically.

		NM	EX	VG
Complete Set (24):		12,500	6,250	3,750
Common Player:		185.00	90.00	55.00
(1)	Hank Aaron	1,400	700.00	420.00
(2)	Johnny Callison	185.00	90.00	55.00
(3)	Bert Campaneris	185.00	90.00	55.00
(4)	Leo Cardenas	185.00	90.00	55.00
(5)	Orlando Cepeda	600.00	300.00	180.00
(6)	Roberto Clemente	1,850	925.00	555.00
(7)	Frank Howard	210.00	105.00	63.00
(8)	Cleon Jones	185.00	90.00	55.00
(9)	Bobby Knoop	185.00	90.00	55.00
(10)	Sandy Koufax	1,150	575.00	345.00
(11)	Mickey Mantle	2,800	1,400	840.00
(12)	Juan Marichal	600.00	300.00	180.00
(13)	Willie Mays	1,400	700.00	420.00
(14)	Sam McDowell	185.00	90.00	55.00
(15)	Denny McLain	210.00	105.00	63.00
(16)	Joe Morgan	600.00	300.00	180.00
(17)	Tony Oliva	185.00	90.00	55.00
(18)	Boog Powell	225.00	110.00	67.00
(19)	Brooks Robinson	750.00	375.00	225.00
(20)	Frank Robinson	750.00	375.00	225.00
(21)	Johnny Romano	185.00	90.00	55.00
(22)	Ron Santo	210.00	105.00	63.00
(23)	Joe Torre	450.00	225.00	135.00
(24)	Carl Yastrzemski	750.00	375.00	225.00

1967 Topps S.F. Giants Discs

One of several prototypes for pinback button sets which were never issued. Generally found in the form of a silver-foil cardboard square, about 2-3/8" a side, the 2-1/4" round center features color player photos or team booster slogans. The player's name and position are printed across his chest, the team name at top. At top-left is a tiny black "JAPAN." The unnumbered discs are checklisted here alphabetically.

		NM	EX	VG
Complete Set (24):		8,000	4,000	2,400
Common Player:		185.00	92.00	55.00
(1)	Jesus Alou	185.00	92.00	55.00
(2)	Bob Bolin	185.00	92.00	55.00
(3)	Ollie Brown	185.00	92.00	55.00
(4)	Jim Davenport	185.00	92.00	55.00
(5)	Herman Franks	185.00	92.00	55.00
(6)	Len Gabrielson	185.00	92.00	55.00
(7)	Joe Gibbon	185.00	92.00	55.00
(8)	Tom Haller	185.00	92.00	55.00
(9)	Jim Ray Hart	185.00	92.00	55.00
(10)	Ron Herbel	185.00	92.00	55.00
(11)	Hal Lanier	185.00	92.00	55.00
(12)	Frank Linzy	185.00	92.00	55.00
(13)	Juan Marichal	925.00	460.00	275.00
(14)	Willie Mays	1,625	810.00	485.00
(15)	Willie McCovey	925.00	460.00	275.00
(16)	Lindy McDaniel	185.00	92.00	55.00
(17)	Gaylord Perry	825.00	410.00	245.00
(18)	Cap Peterson	185.00	92.00	55.00
(19)	Bob Priddy	185.00	92.00	55.00
(20)	Happiness is a Giant Win	115.00	57.00	34.00
(21)	I Love the Giants	115.00	57.00	34.00
(22)	Let's Go Giants	115.00	57.00	34.00
(23)	Willie Mays for Mayor (Willie Mays)	700.00	350.00	210.00
(24)	S.F. Giants Logo	115.00	57.00	34.00

1967 Topps Pin-Ups

The 5" x 7" "All Star Pin-ups" were wax pack inserts. They feature a full color picture with the player's name, position and team in a circle in one of the lower corners on the front. The numbered set consists of 32 players (generally big names). Because the large paper pin-ups had to be folded several times to fit into the wax packs, the factory-created folds are not considered when grading unless paper separations have developed along the seams. At least one of the pin-ups (Clemente) has been seen in an unnumbered version printed on better-quality sticker stock and not having fold lines.

		NM	EX	VG
Complete Set (32):		150.00	65.00	35.00
Common Player:		2.00	.70	.30
1	Boog Powell	2.50	.90	.40
2	Bert Campaneris	2.00	.70	.30
3	Brooks Robinson	9.00	3.25	1.25
4	Tommie Agee	2.00	.70	.30
5	Carl Yastrzemski	9.00	3.25	1.25
6	Mickey Mantle	40.00	14.00	6.00
7	Frank Howard	2.50	.90	.40
8	Sam McDowell	2.00	.70	.30
9	Orlando Cepeda	6.00	2.00	.90
10	Chico Cardenas	2.00	.70	.30
11	Roberto Clemente	20.00	7.00	3.00
12	Willie Mays	15.00	5.25	2.25
13	Cleon Jones	2.00	.70	.30
14	John Callison	2.00	.70	.30
15	Hank Aaron	15.00	5.25	2.25
16	Don Drysdale	7.50	2.75	1.25
17	Bobby Knoop	2.00	.70	.30
18	Tony Oliva	2.50	.90	.40
19	Frank Robinson	9.00	3.25	1.25
20	Denny McLain	2.50	.90	.40
21	Al Kaline	9.00	3.25	1.25
22	Joe Pepitone	3.00	1.00	.45
23	Harmon Killebrew	7.50	2.75	1.25
24	Leon Wagner	2.00	.70	.30
25	Joe Morgan	7.50	2.75	1.25
26	Ron Santo	3.00	1.00	.45
27	Joe Torre	4.50	1.50	.70
28	Juan Marichal	6.00	2.00	.90
29	Matty Alou	2.00	.70	.30
30	Felipe Alou	2.00	.70	.30
31	Ron Hunt	2.00	.70	.30
32	Willie McCovey	7.50	2.75	1.25

1967 Topps Punch-Outs

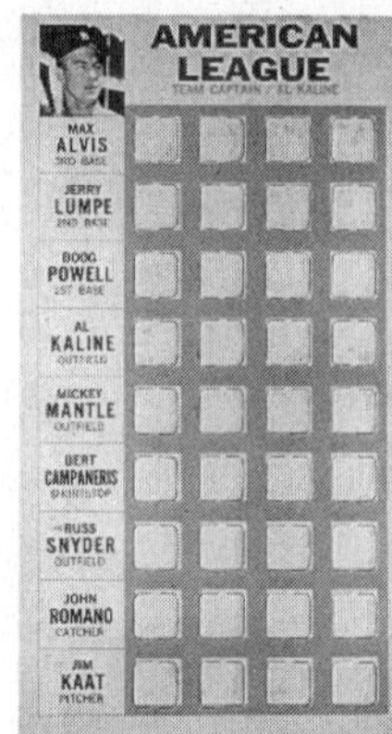

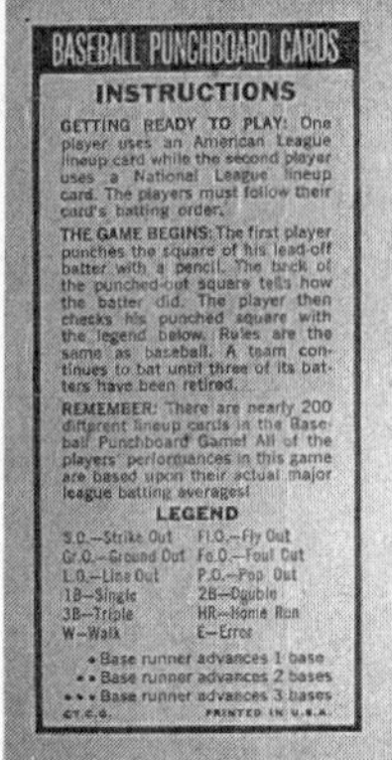

This test issue was reportedly released around Maryland in cello packs containing two perforated strips of three game cards each. Cards are printed in black, white and red and measure 2-1/2" x 4-2/3". Backs have instructions on how to play a baseball game by punching out the small squares. Only the "Team Captain" is pictured on the card; each captain can be found with at least two different lineups on his team, creating a large number of collectible variations. Variations in some player photos have also been noted. The unnumbered issue is checklisted here in alphabetical order. Note, punch-outs of the following players are now believed not to exist: Campaneris, Gibson, Grote, McMillan, and Brooks Robinson.

		NM	EX	VG
Complete Set (91):		19,000	9,500	5,750
Common Player:		80.00	40.00	24.00
(1)	Hank Aaron	1,500	750.00	450.00
(2)	Richie Allen	150.00	75.00	45.00
(3)	Gene Alley	80.00	40.00	24.00
(4)	Felipe Alou	90.00	45.00	27.00
(5)	Matty Alou	80.00	40.00	24.00
(6)	Max Alvis	80.00	40.00	24.00
(7)	Luis Aparicio	200.00	100.00	60.00
(8)	Steve Barber	80.00	40.00	24.00
(9)	Earl Battey	80.00	40.00	24.00
(10)	Clete Boyer	80.00	40.00	24.00
(11)	Ken Boyer	100.00	50.00	30.00
(12)	Lou Brock	200.00	100.00	60.00
(13)	Jim Bunning	175.00	87.00	52.00
(14)	Johnny Callison	80.00	40.00	24.00
(15)	Bert Campaneris (Believed not to exist.	80.00	40.00	24.00
(16)	Leo Cardenas	80.00	40.00	24.00
(17)	Rico Carty	80.00	40.00	24.00
(18)	Norm Cash	90.00	45.00	27.00
(19)	Orlando Cepeda	175.00	87.00	52.00
(20)	Ed Charles	80.00	40.00	24.00
(21a)	Roberto Clemente (Plain background photo.)	1,500	750.00	450.00
(21b)	Roberto Clemente (Stadium background photo.)	2,000	1,000	600.00
(22)	Donn Clendenon	80.00	40.00	24.00
(23)	Rocky Colavito	150.00	75.00	45.00
(24)	Tony Conigliaro	90.00	45.00	27.00
(25)	Willie Davis	80.00	40.00	24.00
(26)	Johnny Edwards	80.00	40.00	24.00
(27)	Andy Etchebarren	80.00	40.00	24.00
(28)	Curt Flood	80.00	40.00	24.00
(29)	Bill Freehan	80.00	40.00	24.00
(30)	Jim Fregosi	80.00	40.00	24.00
(31)	Bob Gibson (Believed not to exist.)	300.00	150.00	90.00
(32)	Dick Green	80.00	40.00	24.00
(33)	Dick Groat	80.00	40.00	24.00
(34)	Jerry Grote (Believed not to exist.)	80.00	40.00	24.00
(35)	Tom Haller	80.00	40.00	24.00

(36)	Jim Ray Hart	80.00	40.00	24.00
(37)	Mike Hershberger	80.00	40.00	24.00
(38)	Elston Howard	100.00	50.00	30.00
(39)	Frank Howard	90.00	45.00	27.00
(40)	Ron Hunt	80.00	40.00	24.00
(41)	Sonny Jackson	80.00	40.00	24.00
(42)	Cleon Jones	80.00	40.00	24.00
(43)	Jim Kaat	100.00	50.00	30.00
(44)	Al Kaline	400.00	200.00	120.00
(45)	Harmon Killebrew	300.00	150.00	90.00
(46)	Bobby Knoop	80.00	40.00	24.00
(47)	Sandy Koufax	1,500	750.00	450.00
(48)	Ed Kranepool	80.00	40.00	24.00
(49)	Jim Lefebvre	80.00	40.00	24.00
(50)	Don Lock	80.00	40.00	24.00
(51)	Jerry Lumpe	80.00	40.00	24.00
(52)	Mickey Mantle	2,400	1,200	720.00
(53)	Juan Marichal	175.00	87.00	52.00
(54)	Willie Mays	1,500	750.00	450.00
(55)	Bill Mazeroski	175.00	87.00	52.00
(56)	Dick McAuliffe	80.00	40.00	24.00
(57)	Tim McCarver	90.00	45.00	27.00
(58)	Willie McCovey	200.00	100.00	60.00
(59)	Denny McLain	90.00	45.00	27.00
(60)	Roy McMillan (Believed not to exist.)	80.00	40.00	24.00
(61)	Denis Menke	80.00	40.00	24.00
(62)	Joe Morgan	200.00	100.00	60.00
(63)	Tony Oliva	90.00	45.00	27.00
(64)	Joe Pepitone	100.00	50.00	30.00
(65)	Gaylord Perry	175.00	87.00	52.00
(66)	Vada Pinson	90.00	45.00	27.00
(67)	Boog Powell	100.00	50.00	30.00
(68)	Rick Reichardt	80.00	40.00	24.00
(69)	Brooks Robinson (Believed not to exist.)	400.00	200.00	120.00
(70)	Floyd Robinson	80.00	40.00	24.00
(71)	Frank Robinson	400.00	200.00	120.00
(72)	Johnny Romano	80.00	40.00	24.00
(73)	Pete Rose	1,250	625.00	375.00
(74)	John Roseboro	80.00	40.00	24.00
(75)	Ron Santo	100.00	50.00	30.00
(76)	Chico Salmon	80.00	40.00	24.00
(77)	George Scott	80.00	40.00	24.00
(78)	Sonny Siebert	80.00	40.00	24.00
(79)	Russ Snyder	80.00	40.00	24.00
(80)	Willie Stargell	200.00	100.00	60.00
(81)	Mel Stottlemyre	80.00	40.00	24.00
(82)	Joe Torre	120.00	60.00	36.00
(83)	Cesar Tovar	80.00	40.00	24.00
(84)	Tom Tresh	90.00	45.00	27.00
(85)	Zoilo Versalles	80.00	40.00	24.00
(86)	Leon Wagner	80.00	40.00	24.00
(87)	Bill White	80.00	40.00	24.00
(88)	Fred Whitfield	80.00	40.00	24.00
(89)	Billy Williams	175.00	87.00	52.00
(90)	Jimmy Wynn	80.00	40.00	24.00
(91)	Carl Yastrzemski	450.00	225.00	135.00

1967 Topps Stand-Ups

Never actually issued, no more than a handful of each of these rare test issues have made their way into the hobby market. Designed so that the color photo of the player's head could be popped out of the black background and placed into a punch-out base to create a stand-up display, examples of these 3-1/8" x 5-1/4" cards can be found either on thick stock, die-cut around the portrait and with a die-cut stand, or as thin-stock proofs without the die-cutting. Blank-backed, there are 24 cards in the set, numbered on the front at bottom left.

		NM	EX	VG
Complete Set, Thick (24):		75,000	37,500	22,500
Complete Set, Thin (24):		60,000	30,000	18,000
Common Player, Thick:		1,250	625.00	375.00
Common Player, Thin:		1,000	500.00	300.00
	THICK STOCK, DIE-CUT			
1	Pete Rose	4,750	2,375	1,425
2	Gary Peters	1,250	625.00	375.00
3	Frank Robinson	2,400	1,200	720.00
4	Jim Lonborg	1,250	625.00	375.00
5	Ron Swoboda	1,250	625.00	375.00
6	Harmon Killebrew	2,100	1,050	630.00
7	Roberto Clemente	8,500	4,250	2,550
8	Mickey Mantle	12,500	6,250	3,750
9	Jim Fregosi	1,250	625.00	375.00
10	Al Kaline	3,000	1,500	900.00
11	Don Drysdale	2,500	1,250	750.00
12	Dean Chance	1,250	625.00	375.00
13	Orlando Cepeda	1,750	875.00	525.00
14	Tim McCarver	1,400	700.00	420.00
15	Frank Howard	1,400	700.00	420.00
16	Max Alvis	1,250	625.00	375.00
17	Rusty Staub	1,400	700.00	420.00
18	Richie Allen	1,400	700.00	420.00
19	Willie Mays	8,500	4,250	2,550
20	Hank Aaron	8,500	4,250	2,550
21	Carl Yastrzemski	7,000	3,500	2,100
22	Ron Santo	1,400	700.00	420.00
23	Catfish Hunter	1,750	875.00	525.00
24	Jim Wynn	1,250	625.00	375.00
	THIN STOCK, PROOFS			
1	Pete Rose	3,750	1,875	1,125
2	Gary Peters	1,000	500.00	300.00
3	Frank Robinson	1,900	950.00	570.00
4	Jim Lonborg	1,000	500.00	300.00
5	Ron Swoboda	1,000	500.00	300.00
6	Harmon Killebrew	1,650	825.00	495.00
7	Roberto Clemente	6,500	3,250	1,950
8	Mickey Mantle	10,000	5,000	3,000
9	Jim Fregosi	1,000	500.00	300.00
10	Al Kaline	2,500	1,250	750.00
11	Don Drysdale	2,000	1,000	600.00
12	Dean Chance	1,000	500.00	300.00
13	Orlando Cepeda	1,400	700.00	420.00
14	Tim McCarver	1,100	550.00	330.00
15	Frank Howard	1,100	550.00	330.00
16	Max Alvis	1,000	500.00	300.00
17	Rusty Staub	1,100	550.00	330.00
18	Richie Allen	1,100	550.00	330.00
19	Willie Mays	7,000	3,500	2,100
20	Hank Aaron	7,000	3,500	2,100
21	Carl Yastrzemski	5,500	2,750	1,650
22	Ron Santo	1,100	550.00	330.00
23	Catfish Hunter	1,400	700.00	420.00
24	Jim Wynn	1,000	500.00	300.00

1967 Topps Pirates Stickers

Considered a "test" issue, this 33-sticker set of 2-1/2" x 3-1/2" stickers is very similar to the Red Sox stickers which were produced the same year. Player stickers have a color picture (often just the player's head) and the player's name in large "comic book" letters. Besides the players, there are other topics such as "I Love the Pirates," "Bob Clemente for Mayor," and a number of similar sentiments. The stickers have blank backs and are rather scarce.

		NM	EX	VG
Complete Set (33):		750.00	375.00	225.00
Common Player:		15.00	7.50	4.50
1	Gene Alley	15.00	7.50	4.50
2	Matty Alou	15.00	7.50	4.50
3	Dennis Ribant	15.00	7.50	4.50
4	Steve Blass	15.00	7.50	4.50
5	Juan Pizarro	15.00	7.50	4.50
6	Bob Clemente	175.00	85.00	50.00
7	Donn Clendenon	15.00	7.50	4.50
8	Roy Face	15.00	7.50	4.50
9	Woody Fryman	15.00	7.50	4.50
10	Jesse Gonder	15.00	7.50	4.50
11	Vern Law	15.00	7.50	4.50
12	Al McBean	15.00	7.50	4.50
13	Jerry May	15.00	7.50	4.50
14	Bill Mazeroski	35.00	17.50	10.00
15	Pete Mikkelsen	15.00	7.50	4.50
16	Manny Mota	15.00	7.50	4.50
17	Billy O'Dell	15.00	7.50	4.50
18	Jose Pagan	15.00	7.50	4.50
19	Jim Pagliaroni	15.00	7.50	4.50
20	Johnny Pesky	15.00	7.50	4.50
21	Tommie Sisk	15.00	7.50	4.50
22	Willie Stargell	60.00	30.00	18.00
23	Bob Veale	15.00	7.50	4.50
24	Harry Walker	15.00	7.50	4.50
25	I Love The Pirates	20.00	10.00	6.00
26	Let's Go Pirates	20.00	10.00	6.00
27	Bob Clemente For Mayor	100.00	50.00	30.00
28	National League Batting Champion (Matty Alou)	15.00	7.50	4.50
29	Happiness Is A Pirate Win	20.00	10.00	6.00
30	Donn Clendenon Is My Hero	15.00	7.50	4.50
31	Pirates' Home Run Champion (Willie Stargell)	30.00	15.00	9.00
32	Pirates Logo	20.00	10.00	6.00
33	Pirates Pennant	25.00	12.50	7.50

1967 Topps Red Sox Stickers

Like the 1967 Pirates Stickers, the Red Sox Stickers were part of the same test procedure. The Red Sox Stickers have the same 2-1/2" x 3-1/2" dimensions, color picture and large

player's name on the front. A set is complete at 33 stickers. The majority are players, but themes such as "Let's Go Red Sox" are also included.

		NM	EX	VG
Complete Set (33):		500.00	250.00	150.00
Common Player:		10.00	5.00	3.00
1	Dennis Bennett	10.00	5.00	3.00
2	Darrell Brandon	10.00	5.00	3.00
3	Tony Conigliaro	35.00	17.50	10.00
4	Don Demeter	10.00	5.00	3.00
5	Hank Fischer	10.00	5.00	3.00
6	Joe Foy	10.00	5.00	3.00
7	Mike Andrews	10.00	5.00	3.00
8	Dalton Jones	10.00	5.00	3.00
9	Jim Lonborg	10.00	5.00	3.00
10	Don McMahon	10.00	5.00	3.00
11	Dave Morehead	10.00	5.00	3.00
12	George Smith	10.00	5.00	3.00
13	Rico Petrocelli	15.00	7.50	4.50
14	Mike Ryan	10.00	5.00	3.00
15	Jose Santiago	10.00	5.00	3.00
16	George Scott	10.00	5.00	3.00
17	Sal Maglie	10.00	5.00	3.00
18	Reggie Smith	10.00	5.00	3.00
19	Lee Stange	10.00	5.00	3.00
20	Jerry Stephenson	10.00	5.00	3.00
21	Jose Tartabull	10.00	5.00	3.00
22	George Thomas	10.00	5.00	3.00
23	Bob Tillman	10.00	5.00	3.00
24	Johnnie Wyatt	10.00	5.00	3.00
25	Carl Yastrzemski	90.00	45.00	27.50
26	Dick Williams	10.00	5.00	3.00
27	I Love The Red Sox	12.50	6.25	3.75
28	Let's Go Red Sox	12.50	6.25	3.75
29	Carl Yastrzemski For Mayor	50.00	25.00	15.00
30	Tony Conigliaro Is My Hero	27.50	13.50	8.25
31	Happiness Is A Boston Win	12.50	6.25	3.75
32	Red Sox Logo	15.00	7.50	4.50
33	Red Sox Pennant	20.00	10.00	6.00

1967 Topps Who Am I?

A cartoon caption and goofy facial features were printed on the front of these 2-1/2" x 3-1/2" cards and were designed to be scratched off to reveal the portrait, name and claim to fame of the person beneath. This 44-card set includes all manner of U.S. and international historical figures, including four baseball players. Backs are printed in red and have a large question mark with several hints printed thereon. Unscratched cards are much rarer than scratched cards, though they carry only about a 50 percent premium.

		NM	EX	VG
Complete Set (44):		850.00	425.00	250.00
Wax Pack:		350.00		
12	Babe Ruth	100.00	50.00	30.00
22	Mickey Mantle	225.00	110.00	65.00
33	Willie Mays	100.00	50.00	30.00
41	Sandy Koufax	100.00	50.00	30.00

1968 Topps

In 1968, Topps returned to a 598-card set of 2-1/2" x 3-1/2" cards. It is not, however, more of the same by way of appearance as the cards feature a color photograph on a background of what appears to be a burlap fabric. The player's name is below the photo but on the unusual background. A colored circle on the lower right carries the team and position. Backs were also changed, while retaining the vertical format introduced the previous year, with stats in the middle and cartoon at the bottom. The set features many of the old favorite subsets, including statistical leaders, World Series highlights, multi-player cards,

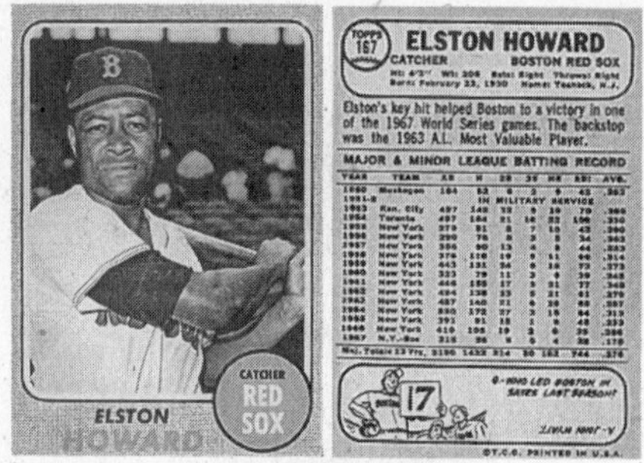

checklists, rookie cards and the return of All-Star cards. Most checklist cards are double-printed, once in the series preceding the series it lists and once within the series it lists; subtle variations between the pairs are listed where known.

		NM	EX	VG
	Complete Set (598):	3,000	1,500	900.00
	Common Player (1-457):	2.00	1.00	.60
	Common Player (458-598):	5.00	2.50	1.50
1	N.L. Batting Leaders (Matty Alou, Roberto Clemente, Tony Gonzalez)	12.50	6.25	3.75
2	A.L. Batting Leaders (Al Kaline, Frank Robinson, Carl Yastrzemski)	20.00	10.00	6.00
3	N.L. RBI Leaders (Hank Aaron, Orlando Cepeda, Roberto Clemente)	22.50	11.00	6.75
4	A.L. RBI Leaders (Harmon Killebrew, Frank Robinson, Carl Yastrzemski)	12.00	6.00	3.50
5	N.L. Home Run Leaders (Hank Aaron, Willie McCovey, Ron Santo, Jim Wynn)	20.00	10.00	6.00
6	A.L. Home Run Leaders (Frank Howard, Harmon Killebrew, Carl Yastrzemski)	12.00	6.00	3.50
7	N.L. ERA Leaders (Jim Bunning, Phil Niekro, Chris Short)	7.00	3.50	2.00
8	A.L. ERA Leaders (Joe Horlen, Gary Peters, Sonny Siebert)	2.00	1.00	.60
9	N.L. Pitching Leaders (Jim Bunning, Fergie Jenkins, Mike McCormick, Claude Osteen)	7.00	3.50	2.00
10a	A.L. Pitching Leaders (Dean Chance, Jim Lonborg, Earl Wilson) ("Lonberg" on back.)	9.00	4.50	2.75
10b	A.L. Pitching Leaders (Dean Chance, Jim Lonborg, Earl Wilson) ("Lonborg" on back.)	7.00	3.50	2.00
11	N.L. Strikeout Leaders (Jim Bunning, Fergie Jenkins, Gaylord Perry)	7.00	3.50	2.00
12	A.L. Strikeout Leaders (Dean Chance, Jim Lonborg, Sam McDowell)	7.00	3.50	2.00
13	Chuck Hartenstein	2.00	1.00	.60
14	Jerry McNertney	2.00	1.00	.60
15	Ron Hunt	2.00	1.00	.60
16	Indians Rookies **(Lou Piniella, Richie Scheinblum)**	5.00	2.50	1.50
17	Dick Hall	2.00	1.00	.60
18	Mike Hershberger	2.00	1.00	.60
19	Juan Pizarro	2.00	1.00	.60
20	Brooks Robinson	15.00	7.50	4.50
21	Ron Davis	2.00	1.00	.60
22	Pat Dobson	2.00	1.00	.60
23	Chico Cardenas	2.00	1.00	.60
24	Bobby Locke	2.00	1.00	.60
25	Julian Javier	2.00	1.00	.60
26	Darrell Brandon	2.00	1.00	.60
27	Gil Hodges	7.50	3.75	2.25
28	Ted Uhlaender	2.00	1.00	.60
29	Joe Verbanic	2.00	1.00	.60
30	Joe Torre	8.00	4.00	2.50
31	Ed Stroud	2.00	1.00	.60
32	Joe Gibbon	2.00	1.00	.60
33	Pete Ward	2.00	1.00	.60
34	Al Ferrara	2.00	1.00	.60
35	Steve Hargan	2.00	1.00	.60
36	Pirates Rookies ***(Bob Moose, Bob Robertson)***	2.00	1.00	.60
37	Billy Williams	13.50	6.75	4.00
38	Tony Pierce	2.00	1.00	.60
39	Cookie Rojas	2.00	1.00	.60
40	Denny McLain	6.00	3.00	1.75
41	Julio Gotay	2.00	1.00	.60
42	Larry Haney	2.00	1.00	.60
43	Gary Bell	2.00	1.00	.60
44	Frank Kostro	2.00	1.00	.60
45	Tom Seaver	30.00	15.00	9.00
46	Dave Ricketts	2.00	1.00	.60
47	Ralph Houk	2.50	1.25	.70
48	Ted Davidson	2.00	1.00	.60
49a	Ed Brinkman (Yellow team.)	120.00	60.00	36.00
49b	Ed Brinkman (White team.)	2.00	1.00	.60
50	Willie Mays	50.00	25.00	15.00
51	Bob Locker	2.00	1.00	.60
52	Hawk Taylor	2.00	1.00	.60
53	Gene Alley	2.00	1.00	.60
54	Stan Williams	2.00	1.00	.60
55	Felipe Alou	5.00	2.50	1.50
56	Orioles Rookies **(Dave Leonhard, Dave May)**	2.00	1.00	.60
57	Dan Schneider	2.00	1.00	.60
58	Ed Mathews	13.50	6.75	4.00
59	Don Lock	2.00	1.00	.60
60	Ken Holtzman	2.00	1.00	.60
61	Reggie Smith	2.00	1.00	.60
62	Chuck Dobson	2.00	1.00	.60
63	Dick Kenworthy	2.00	1.00	.60
64	Jim Merritt	2.00	1.00	.60
65	John Roseboro	2.00	1.00	.60
66a	Casey Cox (Yellow team.)	120.00	60.00	36.00
66b	Casey Cox (White team.)	2.00	1.00	.60
67	1st Series Check List (1-109) (Jim Kaat)	5.00	2.50	1.50
68	Ron Willis	2.00	1.00	.60
69	Tom Tresh	6.00	3.00	1.75
70	Bob Veale	2.00	1.00	.60
71	Vern Fuller	2.00	1.00	.60
72	Tommy John	5.00	2.50	1.50
73	Jim Hart	2.00	1.00	.60
74	Milt Pappas	2.00	1.00	.60
75	Don Mincher	2.00	1.00	.60
76	Braves Rookies ***(Jim Britton, Ron Reed)***	2.00	1.00	.60
77	***Don Wilson***	2.00	1.00	.60
78	Jim Northrup	2.00	1.00	.60
79	Ted Kubiak	2.00	1.00	.60
80	Rod Carew	17.50	8.75	5.25
81	Larry Jackson	2.00	1.00	.60
82	Sam Bowens	2.00	1.00	.60
83	John Stephenson	2.00	1.00	.60
84	Bob Tolan	2.00	1.00	.60
85	Gaylord Perry	9.00	4.50	2.75
86	Willie Stargell	12.00	6.00	3.50
87	Dick Williams	2.00	1.00	.60
88	Phil Regan	2.00	1.00	.60
89	Jake Gibbs	2.00	1.00	.60
90	Vada Pinson	5.00	2.50	1.50
91	Jim Ollom	2.00	1.00	.60
92	Ed Kranepool	2.00	1.00	.60
93	Tony Cloninger	2.00	1.00	.60
94	Lee Maye	2.00	1.00	.60
95	Bob Aspromonte	2.00	1.00	.60
96	Senators Rookies **(Frank Coggins, Dick Nold)**	2.00	1.00	.60
97	Tom Phoebus	2.00	1.00	.60
98	Gary Sutherland	2.00	1.00	.60
99	Rocky Colavito	7.00	3.50	2.00
100	Bob Gibson	17.50	8.75	5.25
101	Glenn Beckert	2.00	1.00	.60
102	Jose Cardenal	2.00	1.00	.60
103	Don Sutton	9.00	4.50	2.75
104	Dick Dietz	2.00	1.00	.60
105	Al Downing	2.00	1.00	.60
106	Dalton Jones	2.00	1.00	.60
107	2nd Series Check List (110-196) (Juan Marichal)	5.00	2.50	1.50
108	Don Pavletich	2.00	1.00	.60
109	Bert Campaneris	2.00	1.00	.60
110	Hank Aaron	45.00	22.50	13.50
111	Rich Reese	2.00	1.00	.60
112	Woody Fryman	2.00	1.00	.60
113	Tigers Rookies **(Tom Matchick, Daryl Patterson)**	2.00	1.00	.60
114	Ron Swoboda	2.00	1.00	.60
115	Sam McDowell	2.00	1.00	.60
116	Ken McMullen	2.00	1.00	.60
117	Larry Jaster	2.00	1.00	.60
118	Mark Belanger	2.00	1.00	.60
119	Ted Savage	2.00	1.00	.60
120	Mel Stottlemyre	5.00	2.50	1.50
121	Jimmie Hall	2.00	1.00	.60
122	Gene Mauch	2.00	1.00	.60
123	Jose Santiago	2.00	1.00	.60
124	Nate Oliver	2.00	1.00	.60
125	Joe Horlen	2.00	1.00	.60
126	Bobby Etheridge	2.00	1.00	.60
127	Paul Lindblad	2.00	1.00	.60
128	Astros Rookies **(Tom Dukes, Alonzo Harris)**	2.00	1.00	.60
129	Mickey Stanley	2.00	1.00	.60
130	Tony Perez	10.00	5.00	3.00
131	Frank Bertaina	2.00	1.00	.60
132	Bud Harrelson	2.00	1.00	.60
133	Fred Whitfield	2.00	1.00	.60
134	Pat Jarvis	2.00	1.00	.60
135	Paul Blair	2.00	1.00	.60
136	Randy Hundley	2.00	1.00	.60
137	Twins Team	5.00	2.50	1.50
138	Ruben Amaro	2.00	1.00	.60
139	Chris Short	2.00	1.00	.60
140	Tony Conigliaro	5.00	2.50	1.50
141	Dal Maxvill	2.00	1.00	.60
142	White Sox Rookies **(Buddy Bradford, Bill Voss)**	2.00	1.00	.60
143	Pete Cimino	2.00	1.00	.60
144	Joe Morgan	12.00	6.00	3.50
145	Don Drysdale	15.00	7.50	4.50
146	Sal Bando	2.00	1.00	.60
147	Frank Linzy	2.00	1.00	.60
148	Dave Bristol	2.00	1.00	.60
149	Bob Saverine	2.00	1.00	.60
150	Roberto Clemente	50.00	25.00	15.00
151	World Series Game 1 (Brock Socks 4 Hits in Opener)	6.00	3.00	1.75
152	World Series Game 2 (Yaz Smashes Two Homers)	10.00	5.00	3.00
153	World Series Game 3 (Briles Cools Off Boston)	3.00	1.50	.90
154	World Series Game 4 (Gibson Hurls Shutout)	9.00	4.50	2.75
155	World Series Game 5 (Lonborg Wins Again)	6.00	3.00	1.75
156	World Series Game 6 (Petrocelli Socks Two Homers)	6.00	3.00	1.75
157	World Series Game 7 (St. Louis Wins It)	6.00	3.00	1.75
158	1967 World Series (The Cardinals Celebrate)	5.00	2.50	1.50
159	Don Kessinger	2.00	1.00	.60
160	Earl Wilson	2.00	1.00	.60
161	Norm Miller	2.00	1.00	.60
162	Cards Rookies ***(Hal Gilson, Mike Torrez)***	2.00	1.00	.60
163	Gene Brabender	2.00	1.00	.60
164	Ramon Webster	2.00	1.00	.60
165	Tony Oliva	5.00	2.50	1.50
166	Claude Raymond	2.00	1.00	.60
167	Elston Howard	5.00	2.50	1.50
168	Dodgers Team	5.00	2.50	1.50
169	Bob Bolin	2.00	1.00	.60
170	Jim Fregosi	2.00	1.00	.60
171	Don Nottebart	2.00	1.00	.60
172	Walt Williams	2.00	1.00	.60
173	John Boozer	2.00	1.00	.60
174	Bob Tillman	2.00	1.00	.60
175	Maury Wills	2.00	1.00	.60
176	Bob Allen	2.00	1.00	.60
177	Mets Rookies ***(Jerry Koosman, Nolan Ryan)***	375.00	175.00	85.00
178	Don Wert	2.00	1.00	.60
179	Bill Stoneman	2.00	1.00	.60
180	Curt Flood	3.00	1.50	.90
181	Jerry Zimmerman	2.00	1.00	.60
182	Dave Giusti	2.00	1.00	.60
183	Bob Kennedy	2.00	1.00	.60
184	Lou Johnson	2.00	1.00	.60
185	Tom Haller	2.00	1.00	.60
186	Eddie Watt	2.00	1.00	.60
187	Sonny Jackson	2.00	1.00	.60
188	Cap Peterson	2.00	1.00	.60
189	Bill Landis	2.00	1.00	.60
190	Bill White	2.00	1.00	.60
191	Dan Frisella	2.00	1.00	.60
192a	3rd Series Check List (197-283) (Carl Yastrzemski) ("To increase the..." on back.)	6.00	3.00	1.75
192b	3rd Series Check List (197-283) (Carl Yastrzemski) ("To increase your..." on back.)	6.00	3.00	1.75
193	Jack Hamilton	2.00	1.00	.60
194	Don Buford	2.00	1.00	.60
195	Joe Pepitone	5.00	2.50	1.50
196	Gary Nolan	2.00	1.00	.60
197	Larry Brown	2.00	1.00	.60
198	Roy Face	2.00	1.00	.60
199	A's Rookies **(Darrell Osteen, Roberto Rodriguez)**	2.00	1.00	.60
200	Orlando Cepeda	11.00	5.50	3.25
201	***Mike Marshall***	3.00	1.50	.90
202	Adolfo Phillips	2.00	1.00	.60
203	Dick Kelley	2.00	1.00	.60
204	Andy Etchebarren	2.00	1.00	.60
205	Juan Marichal	9.00	4.50	2.75
206	Cal Ermer	2.00	1.00	.60
207	Carroll Sembera	2.00	1.00	.60
208	Willie Davis	2.00	1.00	.60
209	Tim Cullen	2.00	1.00	.60
210	Gary Peters	2.00	1.00	.60
211	J.C. Martin	2.00	1.00	.60
212	Dave Morehead	2.00	1.00	.60
213	Chico Ruiz	2.00	1.00	.60
214	Yankees Rookies **(Stan Bahnsen, Frank Fernandez)**	2.00	1.00	.60
215	Jim Bunning	9.00	4.50	2.75
216	Bubba Morton	2.00	1.00	.60
217	Turk Farrell	2.00	1.00	.60
218	Ken Suarez	2.00	1.00	.60
219	Rob Gardner	2.00	1.00	.60
220	Harmon Killebrew	17.50	8.75	5.25
221	Braves Team	5.00	2.50	1.50
222	Jim Hardin	2.00	1.00	.60
223	Ollie Brown	2.00	1.00	.60
224	Jack Aker	2.00	1.00	.60
225	Richie Allen	6.00	3.00	1.75
226	Jimmie Price	2.00	1.00	.60
227	Joe Hoerner	2.00	1.00	.60
228	Dodgers Rookies **(Jack Billingham, Jim Fairey)**	2.00	1.00	.60
229	Fred Klages	2.00	1.00	.60
230	Pete Rose	45.00	22.50	13.50
231	Dave Baldwin	2.00	1.00	.60
232	Denis Menke	2.00	1.00	.60
233	George Scott	2.00	1.00	.60
234	Bill Monbouquette	2.00	1.00	.60
235	Ron Santo	6.00	3.00	1.75
236	Tug McGraw	2.00	1.00	.60
237	Alvin Dark	2.00	1.00	.60
238	Tom Satriano	2.00	1.00	.60
239	Bill Henry	2.00	1.00	.60
240	Al Kaline	20.00	10.00	6.00
241	Felix Millan	2.00	1.00	.60
242	Moe Drabowsky	2.00	1.00	.60
243	Rich Rollins	2.00	1.00	.60
244	John Donaldson	2.00	1.00	.60
245	Tony Gonzalez	2.00	1.00	.60
246	Fritz Peterson	2.00	1.00	.60
247	Reds Rookies **(Johnny Bench, Ron Tompkins)**	85.00	40.00	25.00
248	Fred Valentine	2.00	1.00	.60
249	Bill Singer	2.00	1.00	.60
250	Carl Yastrzemski	20.00	10.00	6.00
251	***Manny Sanguillen***	4.50	2.25	1.25
252	Angels Team	5.00	2.50	1.50
253	Dick Hughes	2.00	1.00	.60
254	Cleon Jones	2.00	1.00	.60
255	Dean Chance	2.00	1.00	.60
256	Norm Cash	7.00	3.50	2.00
257	Phil Niekro	9.00	4.50	2.75
258	Cubs Rookies **(Jose Arcia, Bill Schlesinger)**	2.00	1.00	.60
259	Ken Boyer	5.00	2.50	1.50

260	Jim Wynn	2.00	1.00	.60
261	Dave Duncan	2.00	1.00	.60
262	Rick Wise	2.00	1.00	.60
263	Horace Clarke	2.00	1.00	.60
264	Ted Abernathy	2.00	1.00	.60
265	Tommy Davis	2.00	1.00	.60
266	Paul Popovich	2.00	1.00	.60
267	Herman Franks	2.00	1.00	.60
268	Bob Humphreys	2.00	1.00	.60
269	Bob Tiefenauer	2.00	1.00	.60
270	Matty Alou	2.00	1.00	.60
271	Bobby Knoop	2.00	1.00	.60
272	Ray Culp	2.00	1.00	.60
273	Dave Johnson	2.00	1.00	.60
274	Mike Cuellar	2.00	1.00	.60
275	Tim McCarver	5.00	2.50	1.50
276	Jim Roland	2.00	1.00	.60
277	Jerry Buchek	2.00	1.00	.60
278a	4th Series Check List (284-370) (Orlando Cepeda) (Copyright at right.)	5.00	2.50	1.50
278b	4th Series Check List (284-370) (Orlando Cepeda) (Copyright at left.)	5.50	2.75	1.75
279	Bill Hands	2.00	1.00	.60
280	Mickey Mantle	155.00	75.00	45.00
281	Jim Campanis	2.00	1.00	.60
282	Rick Monday	2.00	1.00	.60
283	Mel Queen	2.00	1.00	.60
284	John Briggs	2.00	1.00	.60
285	Dick McAuliffe	2.00	1.00	.60
286	Cecil Upshaw	2.00	1.00	.60
287	White Sox Rookies **(Mickey Abarbanel, Cisco Carlos)**	2.00	1.00	.60
288	Dave Wickersham	2.00	1.00	.60
289	Woody Held	2.00	1.00	.60
290	Willie McCovey	17.50	8.75	5.25
291	Dick Lines	2.00	1.00	.60
292	Art Shamsky	2.00	1.00	.60
293	Bruce Howard	2.00	1.00	.60
294	Red Schoendienst	7.00	3.50	2.00
295	Sonny Siebert	2.00	1.00	.60
296	Byron Browne	2.00	1.00	.60
297	Russ Gibson	2.00	1.00	.60
298	Jim Brewer	2.00	1.00	.60
299	Gene Michael	2.00	1.00	.60
300	Rusty Staub	2.50	1.25	.70
301	Twins Rookies **(George Mitterwald, Rick Renick)**	2.00	1.00	.60
302	Gerry Arrigo	2.00	1.00	.60
303	Dick Green	2.00	1.00	.60
304	Sandy Valdespino	2.00	1.00	.60
305	Minnie Rojas	2.00	1.00	.60
306	Mike Ryan	2.00	1.00	.60
307	John Hiller	2.00	1.00	.60
308	Pirates Team	6.00	3.00	1.75
309	Ken Henderson	2.00	1.00	.60
310	Luis Aparicio	11.00	5.50	3.25
311	Jack Lamabe	2.00	1.00	.60
312	Curt Blefary	2.00	1.00	.60
313	Al Weis	2.00	1.00	.60
314	Red Sox Rookies **(Bill Rohr, George Spriggs)**	2.00	1.00	.60
315	Zoilo Versalles	2.00	1.00	.60
316	Steve Barber	2.00	1.00	.60
317	Ron Brand	2.00	1.00	.60
318	Chico Salmon	2.00	1.00	.60
319	George Culver	2.00	1.00	.60
320	Frank Howard	2.50	1.25	.70
321	Leo Durocher	6.00	3.00	1.75
322	Dave Boswell	2.00	1.00	.60
323	Deron Johnson	2.00	1.00	.60
324	Jim Nash	2.00	1.00	.60
325	Manny Mota	2.00	1.00	.60
326	Dennis Ribant	2.00	1.00	.60
327	Tony Taylor	2.00	1.00	.60
328	Angels Rookies **(Chuck Vinson, Jim Weaver)**	2.00	1.00	.60
329	Duane Josephson	2.00	1.00	.60
330	Roger Maris	30.00	15.00	9.00
331	Dan Osinski	2.00	1.00	.60
332	Doug Rader	2.00	1.00	.60
333	Ron Herbel	2.00	1.00	.60
334	Orioles Team	5.00	2.50	1.50
335	Bob Allison	2.00	1.00	.60
336	John Purdin	2.00	1.00	.60
337	Bill Robinson	2.00	1.00	.60
338	Bob Johnson	2.00	1.00	.60
339	Rich Nye	2.00	1.00	.60
340	Max Alvis	2.00	1.00	.60
341	Jim Lemon	2.00	1.00	.60
342	Ken Johnson	2.00	1.00	.60
343	Jim Gosger	2.00	1.00	.60
344	Donn Clendenon	2.00	1.00	.60
345	Bob Hendley	2.00	1.00	.60
346	Jerry Adair	2.00	1.00	.60
347	George Brunet	2.00	1.00	.60
348	Phillies Rookies **(Larry Colton, Dick Thoenen)**	2.00	1.00	.60
349	Ed Spiezio	2.00	1.00	.60
350	Hoyt Wilhelm	9.00	4.50	2.75
351	Bob Barton	2.00	1.00	.60
352	Jackie Hernandez	2.00	1.00	.60
353	Mack Jones	2.00	1.00	.60
354	Pete Richert	2.00	1.00	.60
355	Ernie Banks	20.00	10.00	6.00
356a	5th Series Check List (371-457) (Ken Holtzman) (Top of cap away from black circle.)	5.00	2.50	1.50
356b	5th Series Check List (371-457) (Ken Holtzman) (Top of cap near black circle.)	5.00	2.50	1.50
357	Len Gabrielson	2.00	1.00	.60
358	Mike Epstein	2.00	1.00	.60
359	Joe Moeller	2.00	1.00	.60
360	Willie Horton	2.00	1.00	.60
361	Harmon Killebrew/AS	7.50	3.75	2.25
362	Orlando Cepeda/AS	5.00	2.50	1.50
363	Rod Carew/AS	6.50	3.25	2.00
364	Joe Morgan/AS	6.00	3.00	1.75
365	Brooks Robinson/AS	7.50	3.75	2.25
366	Ron Santo/AS	5.00	2.50	1.50
367	Jim Fregosi/AS	2.00	1.00	.60
368	Gene Alley/AS	2.00	1.00	.60
369	Carl Yastrzemski/AS	7.50	3.75	2.25
370	Hank Aaron/AS	16.00	8.00	4.75
371	Tony Oliva/AS	2.50	1.25	.70
372	Lou Brock/AS	6.00	3.00	1.75
373	Frank Robinson/AS	7.50	3.75	2.25
374	Roberto Clemente/AS	20.00	10.00	6.00
375	Bill Freehan/AS	2.00	1.00	.60
376	Tim McCarver/AS	3.00	1.50	.90
377	Joe Horlen/AS	2.00	1.00	.60
378	Bob Gibson/AS	7.00	3.50	2.00
379	Gary Peters/AS	2.00	1.00	.60
380	Ken Holtzman/AS	2.00	1.00	.60
381	Boog Powell	3.00	1.50	.90
382	Ramon Hernandez	2.00	1.00	.60
383	Steve Whitaker	2.00	1.00	.60
384	Red Rookies ***(Bill Henry, Hal McRae)***	6.00	3.00	1.75
385	Jim Hunter	10.00	5.00	3.00
386	Greg Goossen	2.00	1.00	.60
387	Joe Foy	2.00	1.00	.60
388	Ray Washburn	2.00	1.00	.60
389	Jay Johnstone	2.00	1.00	.60
390	Bill Mazeroski	10.00	5.00	3.00
391	Bob Priddy	2.00	1.00	.60
392	Grady Hatton	2.00	1.00	.60
393	Jim Perry	2.00	1.00	.60
394	Tommie Aaron	2.00	1.00	.60
395	Camilo Pascual	2.00	1.00	.60
396	Bobby Wine	2.00	1.00	.60
397	Vic Davalillo	2.00	1.00	.60
398	Jim Grant	2.00	1.00	.60
399	Ray Oyler	2.00	1.00	.60
400a	Mike McCormick (White team.)	450.00	225.00	135.00
400b	Mike McCormick (Yellow team.)	2.00	1.00	.60
401	Mets Team	5.00	2.50	1.50
402	Mike Hegan	2.00	1.00	.60
403	John Buzhardt	2.00	1.00	.60
404	Floyd Robinson	2.00	1.00	.60
405	Tommy Helms	2.00	1.00	.60
406	Dick Ellsworth	2.00	1.00	.60
407	Gary Kolb	2.00	1.00	.60
408	Steve Carlton	15.00	7.50	4.50
409	Orioles Rookies **(Frank Peters, Ron Stone)**	2.00	1.00	.60
410	Fergie Jenkins	10.00	5.00	3.00
411	Ron Hansen	2.00	1.00	.60
412	Clay Carroll	2.00	1.00	.60
413	Tommy McCraw	2.00	1.00	.60
414	Mickey Lolich	2.00	1.00	.60
415	Johnny Callison	2.00	1.00	.60
416	Bill Rigney	2.00	1.00	.60
417	Willie Crawford	2.00	1.00	.60
418	Eddie Fisher	2.00	1.00	.60
419	Jack Hiatt	2.00	1.00	.60
420	Cesar Tovar	2.00	1.00	.60
421	Ron Taylor	2.00	1.00	.60
422	Rene Lachemann	2.00	1.00	.60
423	Fred Gladding	2.00	1.00	.60
424	White Sox Team	5.00	2.50	1.50
425	Jim Maloney	2.00	1.00	.60
426	Hank Allen	2.00	1.00	.60
427	Dick Calmus	2.00	1.00	.60
428	Vic Roznovsky	2.00	1.00	.60
429	Tommie Sisk	2.00	1.00	.60
430	Rico Petrocelli	2.00	1.00	.60
431	Dooley Womack	2.00	1.00	.60
432	Indians Rookies **(Bill Davis, Jose Vidal)**	2.00	1.00	.60
433	Bob Rodgers	2.00	1.00	.60
434	Ricardo Joseph	2.00	1.00	.60
435	Ron Perranoski	2.00	1.00	.60
436	Hal Lanier	2.00	1.00	.60
437	Don Cardwell	2.00	1.00	.60
438	Lee Thomas	2.00	1.00	.60
439	Luman Harris	2.00	1.00	.60
440	Claude Osteen	2.00	1.00	.60
441	Alex Johnson	2.00	1.00	.60
442	Dick Bosman	2.00	1.00	.60
443	Joe Azcue	2.00	1.00	.60
444	Jack Fisher	2.00	1.00	.60
445	Mike Shannon	2.00	1.00	.60
446	Ron Kline	2.00	1.00	.60
447	Tigers Rookies **(George Korince, Fred Lasher)**	2.00	1.00	.60
448	Gary Wagner	2.00	1.00	.60
449	Gene Oliver	2.00	1.00	.60
450	Jim Kaat	2.50	1.25	.70
451	Al Spangler	2.00	1.00	.60
452	Jesus Alou	2.00	1.00	.60
453	Sammy Ellis	2.00	1.00	.60
454a	6th Series Check List (458-533) (Frank Robinson) (Neck chain shows.)	6.00	3.00	1.75
454b	6th Series Check List (458-533) (Frank Robinson) (No neck chain.)	6.00	3.00	1.75
455	Rico Carty	2.00	1.00	.60
456	John O'Donoghue	2.00	1.00	.60
457	Jim Lefebvre	2.00	1.00	.60
458	Lew Krausse	5.00	2.50	1.50
459	Dick Simpson	5.00	2.50	1.50
460	Jim Lonborg	5.00	2.50	1.50
461	Chuck Hiller	5.00	2.50	1.50
462	Barry Moore	5.00	2.50	1.50
463	Jimmie Schaffer	5.00	2.50	1.50
464	Don McMahon	5.00	2.50	1.50
465	Tommie Agee	5.00	2.50	1.50
466	Bill Dillman	5.00	2.50	1.50
467	Dick Howser	5.00	2.50	1.50
468	Larry Sherry	5.00	2.50	1.50
469	Ty Cline	5.00	2.50	1.50
470	Bill Freehan	5.00	2.50	1.50
471	Orlando Pena	5.00	2.50	1.50
472	Walt Alston	8.00	4.00	2.50
473	Al Worthington	5.00	2.50	1.50
474	Paul Schaal	5.00	2.50	1.50
475	Joe Niekro	5.00	2.50	1.50
476	Woody Woodward	5.00	2.50	1.50
477	Phillies Team	6.00	3.00	1.75
478	Dave McNally	5.00	2.50	1.50
479	Phil Gagliano	5.00	2.50	1.50
480	Manager's Dream (Chico Cardenas, Roberto Clemente, Tony Oliva)	40.00	20.00	12.00
481	John Wyatt	5.00	2.50	1.50
482	Jose Pagan	5.00	2.50	1.50
483	Darold Knowles	5.00	2.50	1.50
484	Phil Roof	5.00	2.50	1.50
485	Ken Berry	5.00	2.50	1.50
486	Cal Koonce	5.00	2.50	1.50
487	Lee May	5.00	2.50	1.50
488	Dick Tracewski	5.00	2.50	1.50
489	Wally Bunker	5.00	2.50	1.50
490	Super Stars (Harmon Killebrew, Mickey Mantle, Willie Mays)	110.00	55.00	35.00
491	Denny Lemaster	5.00	2.50	1.50
492	Jeff Torborg	5.00	2.50	1.50
493	Jim McGlothlin	5.00	2.50	1.50
494	Ray Sadecki	5.00	2.50	1.50
495	Leon Wagner	5.00	2.50	1.50
496	Steve Hamilton	5.00	2.50	1.50
497	Cards Team	6.00	3.00	1.75
498	Bill Bryan	5.00	2.50	1.50
499	Steve Blass	5.00	2.50	1.50
500	Frank Robinson	25.00	12.50	7.50
501	John Odom	5.00	2.50	1.50
502	Mike Andrews	5.00	2.50	1.50
503	Al Jackson	5.00	2.50	1.50
504	Russ Snyder	5.00	2.50	1.50
505	Joe Sparma	5.00	2.50	1.50
506	Clarence Jones	5.00	2.50	1.50
507	Wade Blasingame	5.00	2.50	1.50
508	Duke Sims	5.00	2.50	1.50
509	Dennis Higgins	5.00	2.50	1.50
510	Ron Fairly	5.00	2.50	1.50
511	Bill Kelso	5.00	2.50	1.50
512	Grant Jackson	5.00	2.50	1.50
513	Hank Bauer	5.00	2.50	1.50
514	Al McBean	5.00	2.50	1.50
515	Russ Nixon	5.00	2.50	1.50
516	Pete Mikkelsen	5.00	2.50	1.50
517	Diego Segui	5.00	2.50	1.50
518a	7th Series Check List (534-598) (Clete Boyer) (539 is Maj. L. Rookies)	6.00	3.00	1.75
518b	7th Series Check List (534-598) (Clete Boyer) (539 is Amer. L. Rookies)	10.00	5.00	3.00
519	Jerry Stephenson	5.00	2.50	1.50
520	Lou Brock	20.00	10.00	6.00
521	Don Shaw	5.00	2.50	1.50
522	Wayne Causey	5.00	2.50	1.50
523	John Tsitouris	5.00	2.50	1.50
524	Andy Kosco	5.00	2.50	1.50
525	Jim Davenport	5.00	2.50	1.50
526	Bill Denehy	5.00	2.50	1.50
527	Tito Francona	5.00	2.50	1.50
528	Tigers Team	30.00	15.00	9.00
529	Bruce Von Hoff	5.00	2.50	1.50
530	Bird Belters (Brooks Robinson, Frank Robinson)	27.50	13.50	8.25
531	Chuck Hinton	5.00	2.50	1.50
532	Luis Tiant	5.00	2.50	1.50
533	Wes Parker	5.00	2.50	1.50
534	Bob Miller	5.00	2.50	1.50
535	Danny Cater	5.00	2.50	1.50
536	Bill Short	5.00	2.50	1.50
537	Norm Siebern	5.00	2.50	1.50
538	Manny Jimenez	5.00	2.50	1.50
539	Major League Rookies **(Mike Ferraro, Jim Ray)**	5.00	2.50	1.50
540	Nelson Briles	5.00	2.50	1.50
541	Sandy Alomar	5.00	2.50	1.50
542	John Boccabella	5.00	2.50	1.50
543	Bob Lee	5.00	2.50	1.50
544	Mayo Smith	5.00	2.50	1.50
545	Lindy McDaniel	5.00	2.50	1.50
546	Roy White	4.50	2.25	1.25
547	Dan Coombs	5.00	2.50	1.50
548	Bernie Allen	5.00	2.50	1.50
549	Orioles Rookies **(Curt Motton, Roger Nelson)**	5.00	2.50	1.50
550	Clete Boyer	5.00	2.50	1.50
551	Darrell Sutherland	5.00	2.50	1.50
552	Ed Kirkpatrick	5.00	2.50	1.50
553	Hank Aguirre	5.00	2.50	1.50
554	A's Team	6.00	3.00	1.75
555	Jose Tartabull	5.00	2.50	1.50
556	Dick Selma	5.00	2.50	1.50
557	Frank Quilici	5.00	2.50	1.50
558	John Edwards	5.00	2.50	1.50
559	Pirates Rookies **(Carl Taylor, Luke Walker)**	5.00	2.50	1.50
560	Paul Casanova	5.00	2.50	1.50
561	Lee Elia	5.00	2.50	1.50
562	Jim Bouton	6.00	3.00	1.75
563	Ed Charles	5.00	2.50	1.50
564	Eddie Stanky	5.00	2.50	1.50
565	Larry Dierker	5.00	2.50	1.50
566	Ken Harrelson	5.00	2.50	1.50
567	Clay Dalrymple	5.00	2.50	1.50
568	Willie Smith	5.00	2.50	1.50
569	N.L. Rookies **(Ivan Murrell, Les Rohr)**	5.00	2.50	1.50
570	Rick Reichardt	5.00	2.50	1.50
571	Tony LaRussa	6.00	3.00	1.75
572	Don Bosch	5.00	2.50	1.50

		NM	EX	VG
573	Joe Coleman	5.00	2.50	1.50
574	Reds Team	7.50	3.75	2.25
575	Jim Palmer	20.00	10.00	6.00
576	Dave Adlesh	5.00	2.50	1.50
577	Fred Talbot	5.00	2.50	1.50
578	Orlando Martinez	5.00	2.50	1.50
579	N.L. Rookies (***Larry Hisle, Mike Lum***)	5.00	2.50	1.50
580	Bob Bailey	5.00	2.50	1.50
581	Garry Roggenburk	5.00	2.50	1.50
582	Jerry Grote	5.00	2.50	1.50
583	Gates Brown	6.00	3.00	1.75
584	Larry Shepard	5.00	2.50	1.50
585	Wilbur Wood	5.00	2.50	1.50
586	Jim Pagliaroni	5.00	2.50	1.50
587	Roger Repoz	5.00	2.50	1.50
588	Dick Schofield	5.00	2.50	1.50
589	Twins Rookies (**Ron Clark, Moe Ogier**)	5.00	2.50	1.50
590	Tommy Harper	5.00	2.50	1.50
591	Dick Nen	5.00	2.50	1.50
592	John Bateman	5.00	2.50	1.50
593	Lee Stange	5.00	2.50	1.50
594	Phil Linz	5.00	2.50	1.50
595	Phil Ortega	5.00	2.50	1.50
596	Charlie Smith	5.00	2.50	1.50
597	Bill McCool	5.00	2.50	1.50
598	Jerry May	11.00	2.00	1.25

1968 Topps Action All-Star Stickers

Another of the many Topps test issues of the late 1960s, Action All-Star stickers were sold in a strip of three, with bubblegum, for 10 cents. The strip is comprised of three 3-1/4" x 5-1/4" panels, perforated at the joints for separation. The numbered central panel contains a large photo of a star player. The top and bottom panels each contain smaller pictures of three players. While there are 16 numbered center panels, only 12 of them are different; panels 13-16 are double-prints. Similarly, the triple-player panels at top and bottom of stickers 13-16 repeat panels from #1-4. Prices below are for stickers which have all three panels still joined. Individual panels are priced signicantly lower.

		NM	EX	VG
	Complete Set (16):	3,850	1,900	1,150
	Common Panel:	100.00	50.00	30.00
1	Orlando Cepeda, Joe Horlen, Al Kaline, Bill Mazeroski, Claude Osteen, Mel Stottlemyre, Carl Yastrzemski	300.00	150.00	90.00
2	Don Drysdale, Harmon Killebrew, Mike McCormick, Tom Phoebus, George Scott, Ron Swoboda, Pete Ward	125.00	65.00	35.00
3	Hank Aaron, Paul Casanova, Jim Maloney, Joe Pepitone, Rick Reichardt, Frank Robinson, Tom Seaver	115.00	55.00	35.00
4	Bob Aspromonte, Johnny Callison, Dean Chance, Jim Lefebvre, Jim Lonborg, Frank Robinson, Ron Santo	150.00	75.00	45.00
5	Bert Campaneris, Al Downing, Willie Horton, Ed Kranepool, Willie Mays, Pete Rose, Ron Santo	375.00	185.00	110.00
6	Max Alvis, Ernie Banks, Al Kaline, Tim McCarver, Rusty Staub, Walt Williams, Carl Yastrzemski	300.00	150.00	90.00
7	Rod Carew, Tony Gonzalez, Steve Hargan, Mickey Mantle, Willie McCovey, Rick Monday, Billy Williams	500.00	250.00	150.00
8	Clete Boyer, Jim Bunning, Tony Conigliaro, Mike Cuellar, Joe Horlen, Ken McMullen, Don Mincher	100.00	50.00	30.00
9	Orlando Cepeda, Bob Clemente, Jim Fregosi, Harmon Killebrew, Willie Mays, Chris Short, Earl Wilson	300.00	150.00	90.00
10	Hank Aaron, Bob Gibson, Bud Harrelson, Jim Hunter, Mickey Mantle, Gary Peters, Vada Pinson	375.00	185.00	110.00
11	Don Drysdale, Bill Freehan, Frank Howard, Ferguson Jenkins, Tony Oliva, Bob Veale, Jim Wynn	235.00	115.00	70.00
12	Richie Allen, Bob Clemente, Sam McDowell, Jim McGlothlin, Tony Perez, Brooks Robinson, Joe Torre	850.00	425.00	255.00
13	Dean Chance, Don Drysdale, Jim Lefebvre, Tom Phoebus, Frank Robinson, George Scott, Carl Yastrzemski	300.00	150.00	90.00
14	Paul Casanova, Orlando Cepeda, Joe Horlen, Harmon Killebrew, Bill Mazeroski, Rick Reichardt, Tom Seaver	175.00	85.00	50.00
15	Bob Aspromonte, Johnny Callison, Jim Lonborg, Mike McCormick, Frank Robinson, Ron Swoboda, Pete Ward	125.00	62.00	37.00
16	Hank Aaron, Al Kaline, Jim Maloney, Claude Osteen, Joe Pepitone, Ron Santo, Mel Stottlemyre	225.00	110.00	65.00

1968 Topps "Batter Up" Game

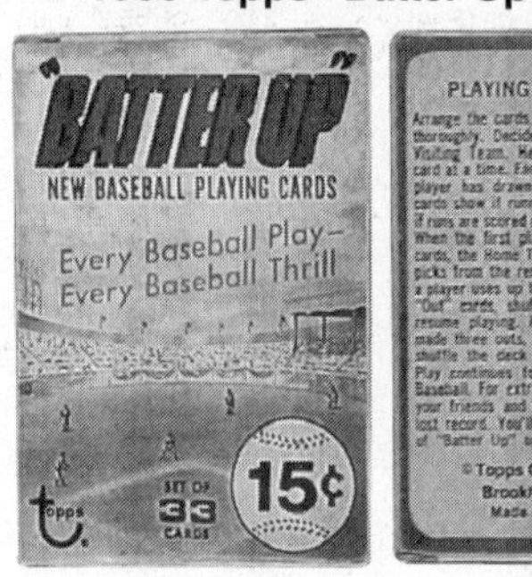

The same cards which were issued as pack inserts in 1968 Topps were sold in a much scarcer boxed-set form. Packaged in a colorful cardboard box with game rules on back, the set is labeled "Batter Up" and can be found in versions with 10 or 15 original retail price.

	NM	EX	VG
Complete Boxed Set:	275.00	85.00	45.00

(See 1968 Topps Game for individual card checklist and values.)

1968 Topps Deckle Edge Proofs

While most Topps proofs are so rare as to preclude their listing in this catalog, the 1968 Deckle Edge test set is an exception. Usually found in the form of a 7-3/4" x 11" uncut sheet of nine black-and-white cards, single cards are sometimes encountered. The blank-backed sheet and cards can be found with the players' facsimile autographs printed in red, black or blue. Unnumbered cards are checklisted here alphabetically.

		NM	EX	VG
	Complete Set, Singles (9):	700.00	350.00	225.00
	Uncut Sheet:	700.00	350.00	225.00
	Common Player:	50.00	25.00	15.00
(1)	Dave Adlesh	50.00	25.00	15.00
(2)	Hank Aguire	50.00	25.00	15.00
(3)	Sandy Alomar	50.00	25.00	15.00
(4)	Sonny Jackson	50.00	25.00	15.00
(5)	Bob Johnson	50.00	25.00	15.00
(6)	Claude Osteen	50.00	25.00	15.00
(7)	Juan Pizarro	50.00	25.00	15.00
(8)	Hal Woodeshick	50.00	25.00	15.00
(9)	Carl Yastrzemski	400.00	200.00	120.00

1968 Topps Discs

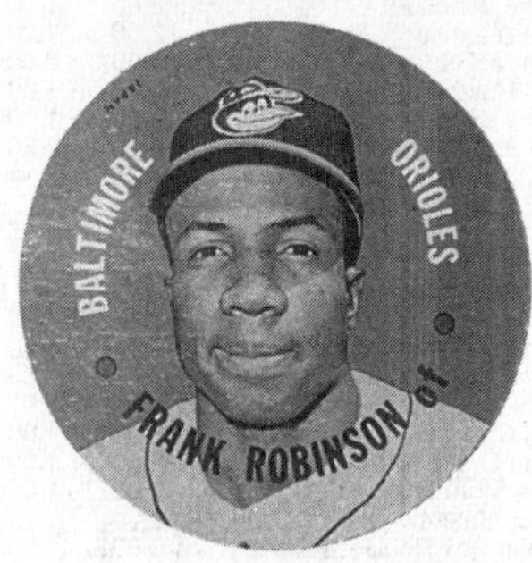

One of the scarcer Topps baseball collectibles, this set was apparently a never-completed test issue. These full-color, cardboard discs, which measure approximately 2-1/4" in diameter, were probably intended to be made into a pin set but production was never completed and no actual pins are known to exist. Uncut sheets of the player discs have been found. The discs include a player portrait photo with the name beneath and (usually) the city and team nickname along the sides.

		NM	EX	VG
	Complete Set (28):	8,000	4,000	2,400
	Common Player:	125.00	65.00	35.00
(1)	Hank Aaron	625.00	310.00	185.00
(2)	Richie Allen	140.00	75.00	40.00
(3)	Gene Alley	125.00	65.00	35.00
(4)	Rod Carew	350.00	175.00	100.00
(5)	Orlando Cepeda	300.00	150.00	90.00
(6)	Dean Chance	125.00	65.00	35.00
(7)	Roberto Clemente	850.00	425.00	255.00
(8)	Tommy Davis	125.00	65.00	35.00
(9)	Bill Freehan	125.00	65.00	35.00
(10)	Jim Fregosi	125.00	65.00	35.00
(11)	Steve Hargan	125.00	65.00	35.00
(12)	Frank Howard	125.00	65.00	35.00
(13)	Al Kaline	350.00	175.00	100.00
(14)	Harmon Killebrew	350.00	175.00	100.00
(15)	Mickey Mantle	1,750	875.00	525.00
(16)	Willie Mays	625.00	310.00	185.00
(17)	Mike McCormick	125.00	65.00	35.00
(18)	Rick Monday	125.00	65.00	35.00
(19)	Claude Osteen	125.00	65.00	35.00
(20)	Gary Peters	125.00	65.00	35.00
(21)	Brooks Robinson	350.00	175.00	100.00
(22)	Frank Robinson	350.00	175.00	100.00
(23)	Pete Rose	550.00	275.00	165.00
(24)	Ron Santo	150.00	75.00	45.00
(25)	Rusty Staub	135.00	70.00	40.00
(26)	Joe Torre	125.00	65.00	35.00
(27)	Bob Veale	125.00	65.00	35.00
(28)	Carl Yastrzemski	350.00	175.00	100.00

1968 Topps Game

A throwback to the Red and Blue Back sets of 1951, the 33-cards in the 1968 Topps Game set, inserted into packs of regular '68 Topps cards or purchases as a complete boxed set, enable the owner to play a game of baseball based on the game situations on each card. Also on the 2-1/4" x 3-1/4" cards were a color photograph of a player and his facsimile autograph. One redeeming social value of the set (assuming you're not mesmerized by the game) is that it affords an inexpensive way to get big-name cards as the set is loaded with stars, but not at all popular with collectors.

		NM	EX	VG
	Complete Set (33):	115.00	55.00	35.00
	Common Player:	2.00	1.00	.60
1	Mateo Alou	2.00	1.00	.60
2	Mickey Mantle	30.00	15.00	9.00
3	Carl Yastrzemski	10.00	5.00	3.00
4	Henry Aaron	12.00	6.00	3.50
5	Harmon Killebrew	9.00	4.50	2.75
6	Roberto Clemente	15.00	7.50	4.50
7	Frank Robinson	9.00	4.50	2.75

8	Willie Mays	12.00	6.00	3.50
9	Brooks Robinson	9.00	4.50	2.75
10	Tommy Davis	2.00	1.00	.60
11	Bill Freehan	2.00	1.00	.60
12	Claude Osteen	2.00	1.00	.60
13	Gary Peters	2.00	1.00	.60
14	Jim Lonborg	2.00	1.00	.60
15	Steve Hargan	2.00	1.00	.60
16	Dean Chance	2.00	1.00	.60
17	Mike McCormick	2.00	1.00	.60
18	Tim McCarver	3.00	1.50	.90
19	Ron Santo	6.00	3.00	1.75
20	Tony Gonzalez	2.00	1.00	.60
21	Frank Howard	3.00	1.50	.90
22	George Scott	2.00	1.00	.60
23	Rich Allen	6.00	3.00	1.75
24	Jim Wynn	2.00	1.00	.60
25	Gene Alley	2.00	1.00	.60
26	Rick Monday	2.00	1.00	.60
27	Al Kaline	9.00	4.50	2.75
28	Rusty Staub	3.00	1.50	.90
29	Rod Carew	9.00	4.50	2.75
30	Pete Rose	12.00	6.00	3.50
31	Joe Torre	6.00	3.00	1.75
32	Orlando Cepeda	6.00	3.00	1.75
33	Jim Fregosi	2.00	1.00	.60

1968 Topps Plaks

Among the scarcest Topps test issues of the late 1960s, the "All Star Baseball Plaks" were plastic busts of two dozen stars of the era which came packaged like model airplane parts. The busts had to be snapped off a sprue and could be inserted into a base which carried the player's name. Packed with the plastic plaks was one of two checklist cards which featured six color photos per side. The 2-1/8" x 4" checklist cards are popular with superstar collectors and are considerably easier to find today than the actual plaks. Wax packs of three plaks and two sticks of bubblegum were sold for a dime.

		NM	EX	VG
Complete Set (24):		9,000	4,500	2,750
Common Player:		100.00	50.00	30.00
1	Max Alvis	100.00	50.00	30.00
2	Dean Chance	100.00	50.00	30.00
3	Jim Fregosi	100.00	50.00	30.00
4	Frank Howard	125.00	62.00	37.00
5	Jim Hunter	250.00	125.00	75.00
6	Al Kaline	400.00	200.00	120.00
7	Harmon Killebrew	400.00	200.00	120.00
8	Jim Lonborg	100.00	50.00	30.00
9	Mickey Mantle	1,850	925.00	555.00
10	Gary Peters	100.00	50.00	30.00
11	Frank Robinson	400.00	200.00	120.00
12	Carl Yastrzemski	450.00	225.00	135.00
13	Hank Aaron	750.00	375.00	225.00
14	Richie Allen	125.00	62.00	37.00
15	Orlando Cepeda	300.00	150.00	90.00
16	Roberto Clemente	1,350	675.00	400.00
17	Tommy Davis	100.00	50.00	30.00
18	Don Drysdale	400.00	200.00	120.00
19	Willie Mays	750.00	375.00	225.00
20	Tim McCarver	125.00	62.00	37.00
21	Ron Santo	125.00	62.00	37.00
22	Rusty Staub	125.00	62.00	37.00
23	Pete Rose	650.00	325.00	195.00
24	Jim Wynn	100.00	50.00	30.00
---	Checklist Card 1-12	1,000	500.00	300.00
---	Checklist Card 13-24	1,500	750.00	450.00

1968 Topps Posters

Yet another innovation from the creative minds at Topps appeared in 1968; a set of color player posters. Measuring 9-3/4" x 18-1/8", each poster was sold separately with its own piece of gum, rather than as an insert. The posters feature a large color photograph with a star at the bottom containing the player's name, position and team. There are 24 different posters which were folded numerous times to fit into the package they were sold in. Unless the paper has split at the folds, they are not considered in grading.

		NM	EX	VG
Complete Set (24):		650.00	325.00	200.00
Common Player:		15.00	7.50	4.50
Unopened Pack:		175.00		
1	Dean Chance	15.00	7.50	4.50
2	Max Alvis	15.00	7.50	4.50
3	Frank Howard	17.50	8.75	5.25
4	Jim Fregosi	15.00	7.50	4.50
5	Catfish Hunter	20.00	10.00	6.00
6	Roberto Clemente	60.00	30.00	18.00
7	Don Drysdale	25.00	12.50	7.50
8	Jim Wynn	15.00	7.50	4.50
9	Al Kaline	25.00	12.50	7.50
10	Harmon Killebrew	25.00	12.50	7.50
11	Jim Lonborg	15.00	7.50	4.50
12	Orlando Cepeda	20.00	10.00	6.00
13	Gary Peters	15.00	7.50	4.50
14	Hank Aaron	50.00	25.00	15.00
15	Richie Allen	17.50	8.75	5.25
16	Carl Yastrzemski	30.00	15.00	9.00
17	Ron Swoboda	15.00	7.50	4.50
18	Mickey Mantle	80.00	40.00	24.00
19	Tim McCarver	15.00	7.50	4.50
20	Willie Mays	50.00	25.00	15.00
21	Ron Santo	17.50	8.75	5.25
22	Rusty Staub	17.50	8.75	5.25
23	Pete Rose	50.00	25.00	15.00
24	Frank Robinson	25.00	12.50	7.50

1968 Tipps From Topps Book

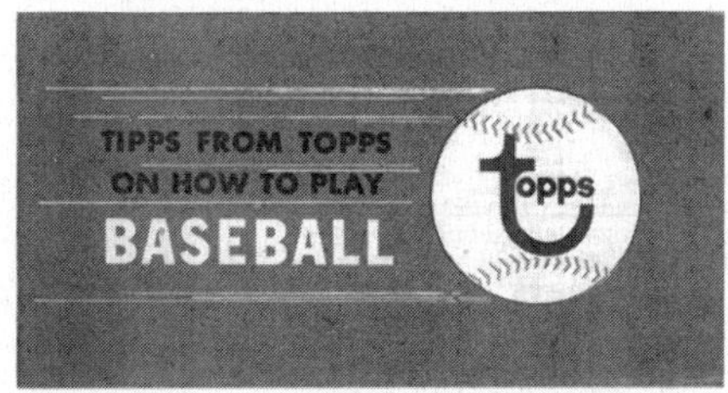

While the Bazooka brand is not referenced in this booklet, it presents the baseball playing tips that appeared on box backs of Bazooka gum. The player photo and cartoon tips are printed in blue in the interior pages of the 5-7/8" x 3" book. The front and back covers are black, white and green. The manner of distribution for this premium is not known.

	NM	EX	VG
Tipps From Topps Book	150.00	75.00	45.00

1968 Topps 3-D Prototype

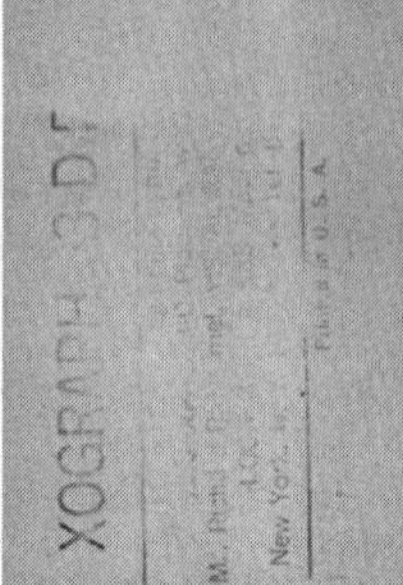

Apparently produced as a prototype for the 3-D cards which Topps issued as a test in 1968, this prototype card is 2-1/4" x 3-1/4" with square corners. The team name is in red block letters at top. The back carries a rubber-stamped notice which identifies the card as a "Xograph 3-D" product from New York City.

	NM	EX	VG
Brooks Robinson	20,000	10,000	6,000

1968 Topps 3-D

These very rare test-issue cards measure 2-1/4" x 3-1/2" with rounded corners and blank backs. They simulate a three-dimensional effect with backgrounds purposely blurred, in front of which is a sharp color player photograph. The outer layer is a thin coating of ribbed plastic. The special process gives the picture the illusion of depth when the card is moved or tilted. As this was done two years before Kellogg's began its 3-D cards, this test issue really was breaking new ground. Production and distribution were limited, making the cards very tough to find. Some cards, said to have been the first produced, are stamped on back with a notice from Visual Panographics of New York. "This is an experimental XOGRAPH card produced as a limited edition. Not for public circulation or distribution. Not for resale. To be returned to:".

		NM	EX	VG
Complete Set (12):		17,500	8,750	5,250
Common Player:		500.00	250.00	150.00
Wrapper:		900.00	450.00	275.00
(1)	Bob Clemente	12,000	6,000	3,600
(2)	Willie Davis	500.00	250.00	150.00
(3)	Ron Fairly	500.00	250.00	150.00
(4)	Curt Flood	650.00	325.00	200.00
(5)	Jim Lonborg	500.00	250.00	150.00
(6)	Jim Maloney	500.00	250.00	150.00
(7)	Tony Perez	1,000	500.00	300.00
(8)	Boog Powell	750.00	375.00	225.00
(9)	Bill Robinson	500.00	250.00	150.00
(10)	Rusty Staub	750.00	375.00	225.00
(11)	Mel Stottlemyre	500.00	250.00	150.00
(12)	Ron Swoboda	500.00	250.00	150.00

1968 Topps/Milton Bradley

As part of a Win-A-Card trading card board game, Milton Bradley contracted with Topps to print 132 special versions of its 1968 baseball cards, 1967 football cards and hot rod cards. The baseball cards can be differentiated from regular-issue 1968 Topps in that the yellow ink on back is much lighter and brighter than the dark yellow/gold ink usually found on back. Also, some of the card fronts will show evidence of the white-bordered football and hot rod cards at one or more edges. Collectors currently will pay only a small premium for the MB version, but that gap is likely to widen in the future.

		NM	EX	VG
Complete (Baseball) Set (76):				
Common Player:				
7	N.L. ERA Leaders (Jim Bunning, Phil Niekro, Chris Short)	7.00	3.50	2.00
8	A.L. ERA Leaders (Joe Horlen, Gary Peters, Sonny Siebert)	2.00	1.00	.60
10	A.L. Pitching Leaders (Dean Chance, Jim Lonborg, Earl Wilson)	9.00	4.50	2.75
13	Chuck Hartenstein	2.00	1.00	.60
16	Indians Rookies (Lou Piniella, Richie Scheinblum)	4.00	2.00	1.25
17	Dick Hall	2.00	1.00	.60
18	Mike Hershberger	2.00	1.00	.60
19	Juan Pizarro	2.00	1.00	.60
20	Brooks Robinson	15.00	7.50	4.50
24	Bobby Locke	2.00	1.00	.60
26	Darrell Brandon	2.00	1.00	.60
34	Al Ferrara	2.00	1.00	.60
36	Pirates Rookies (***Bob Moose, Bob Robertson***)	2.00	1.00	.60
38	Tony Pierce	2.00	1.00	.60
43	Gary Bell	2.00	1.00	.60
44	Frank Kostro	2.00	1.00	.60
45	Tom Seaver	30.00	15.00	9.00
48	Ted Davidson	2.00	1.00	.60
49	Ed Brinkman (Yellow team.)	50.00	25.00	15.00
53	Gene Alley	2.00	1.00	.60
57	Dan Schneider	2.00	1.00	.60
58	Ed Mathews	13.50	6.75	4.00
60	Ken Holtzman	2.00	1.00	.60
61	Reggie Smith	2.00	1.00	.60
62	Chuck Dobson	2.00	1.00	.60
64	Jim Merritt	2.00	1.00	.60
66	Casey Cox (Yellow team.)	50.00	25.00	15.00
68	Ron Willis	2.00	1.00	.60
72	Tommy John	4.00	2.00	1.25
74	Milt Pappas	2.00	1.00	.60
77	***Don Wilson***	2.00	1.00	.60
78	Jim Northrup	2.00	1.00	.60

No.	Player	NM	EX	VG
80	Rod Carew	17.50	8.75	5.25
81	Larry Jackson	2.00	1.00	.60
85	Gaylord Perry	9.00	4.50	2.75
89	Jake Gibbs	2.00	1.00	.60
94	Lee Maye	2.00	1.00	.60
98	Gary Sutherland	2.00	1.00	.60
99	Rocky Colavito	7.00	3.50	2.00
100	Bob Gibson	17.50	8.75	5.25
105	Al Downing	2.00	1.00	.60
106	Dalton Jones	2.00	1.00	.60
107	2nd Series Check List (110-196) (Juan Marichal)	4.00	2.00	1.25
108	Don Pavletich	2.00	1.00	.60
110	Hank Aaron	40.00	20.00	12.00
112	Woody Fryman	2.00	1.00	.60
113	Tigers Rookies **(Tom Matchick, Daryl Patterson)**	2.00	1.00	.60
117	Larry Jaster	2.00	1.00	.60
118	Mark Belanger	2.00	1.00	.60
119	Ted Savage	2.00	1.00	.60
120	Mel Stottlemyre	4.00	2.00	1.25
121	Jimmie Hall	2.00	1.00	.60
124	Nate Oliver	2.00	1.00	.60
127	Paul Lindblad	2.00	1.00	.60
128	Astros Rookies **(Tom Dukes, Alonzo Harris)**	2.00	1.00	.60
129	Mickey Stanley	2.00	1.00	.60
136	Randy Hundley	2.00	1.00	.60
139	Chris Short	2.00	1.00	.60
143	Pete Cimino	2.00	1.00	.60
146	Sal Bando	2.00	1.00	.60
149	Bob Saverine	2.00	1.00	.60
155	World Series Game 5 (Lonborg Wins Again)	6.00	3.00	1.75
156	World Series Game 6 (Petrocelli Socks Two Homers)	6.00	3.00	1.75
165	Tony Oliva	4.00	2.00	1.25
168	Dodgers Team	5.00	2.50	1.50
172	Walt Williams	2.00	1.00	.60
175	Maury Wills	2.00	1.00	.60
176	Bob Allen	2.00	1.00	.60
177	Mets Rookies ***(Jerry Koosman, Nolan Ryan)***	335.00	190.00	95.00
179	Bill Stoneman	2.00	1.00	.60
180	Curt Flood	3.00	1.50	.90
185	Tom Haller	2.00	1.00	.60
189	Bill Landis	2.00	1.00	.60
191	Dan Frisella	2.00	1.00	.60
193	Jack Hamilton	2.00	1.00	.60
195	Joe Pepitone	4.00	2.00	1.25

1969 Topps

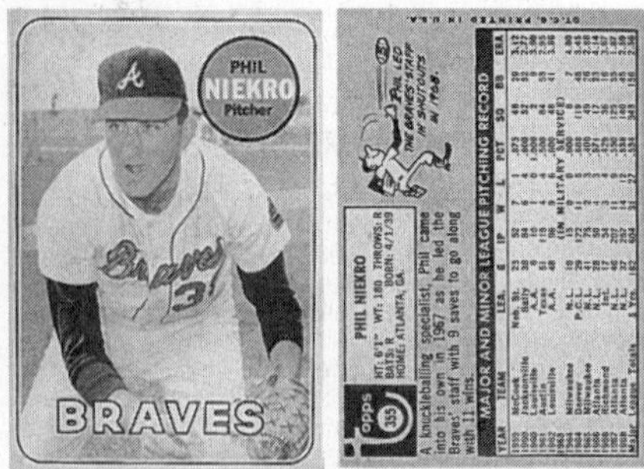

The 1969 Topps set broke yet another record for quantity as the issue is officially a whopping 664 cards. With substantial numbers of variations, the number of possible cards runs closer to 700. The design of the 2-1/2" x 3-1/2" cards in the set feature a color photo with the team name printed in block letters underneath. A circle contains the player's name and position. Card backs returned to a horizontal format. Despite the size of the set, it contains no team cards. It does, however, have multi-player cards, All-Stars, statistical leaders, and World Series highlights. Most significant among the varieties are white and yellow letter cards from the run of #'s 440-511. The complete set prices below do not include the scarcer and more expensive "white letter" variations.

	NM	EX	VG
Complete Set (664):	3,150	1,550	925.00
Common Player (1-588):	2.00	1.00	.60
Common Player (589-664):	3.00	1.50	.90

No.	Player	NM	EX	VG
1	A.L. Batting Leaders (Danny Cater, Tony Oliva, Carl Yastrzemski)	11.00	5.50	3.25
2	N.L. Batting Leaders (Felipe Alou, Matty Alou, Pete Rose)	15.00	7.50	4.50
3	A.L. RBI Leaders (Ken Harrelson, Frank Howard, Jim Northrup)	2.50	1.25	.75
4	N.L. RBI Leaders (Willie McCovey, Ron Santo, Billy Williams)	9.00	4.50	2.75
5	A.L. Home Run Leaders (Ken Harrelson, Willie Horton, Frank Howard)	6.00	3.00	1.75
6	N.L. Home Run Leaders (Richie Allen, Ernie Banks, Willie McCovey)	8.00	4.00	2.50
7	A.L. ERA Leaders (Sam McDowell, Dave McNally, Luis Tiant)	3.00	1.50	.90
8	N.L. ERA Leaders (Bobby Bolin, Bob Gibson, Bob Veale)	4.00	2.00	1.25
9	A.L. Pitching Leaders (Denny McLain, Dave McNally, Mel Stottlemyre, Luis Tiant)	4.00	2.00	1.25
10	N.L. Pitching Leaders (Bob Gibson, Fergie Jenkins, Juan Marichal)	5.00	2.50	1.50
11	A.L. Strikeout Leaders (Sam McDowell, Denny McLain, Luis Tiant)	3.00	1.50	.90
12	N.L. Strikeout Leaders (Bob Gibson, Fergie Jenkins, Bill Singer)	5.00	2.50	1.50
13	Mickey Stanley	2.00	1.00	.60
14	Al McBean	2.00	1.00	.60
15	Boog Powell	3.00	1.50	.90
16	Giants Rookies **(Cesar Gutierrez, Rich Robertson)**	2.00	1.00	.60
17	Mike Marshall	2.00	1.00	.60
18	Dick Schofield	2.00	1.00	.60
19	Ken Suarez	2.00	1.00	.60
20	Ernie Banks	25.00	12.50	7.50
21	Jose Santiago	2.00	1.00	.60
22	Jesus Alou	2.00	1.00	.60
23	Lew Krausse	2.00	1.00	.60
24	Walt Alston	4.00	2.00	1.25
25	Roy White	2.00	1.00	.60
26	Clay Carroll	2.00	1.00	.60
27	Bernie Allen	2.00	1.00	.60
28	Mike Ryan	2.00	1.00	.60
29	Dave Morehead	2.00	1.00	.60
30	Bob Allison	2.00	1.00	.60
31	Mets Rookies ***(Gary Gentry, Amos Otis)***	3.00	1.50	.90
32	Sammy Ellis	2.00	1.00	.60
33	Wayne Causey	2.00	1.00	.60
34	Gary Peters	2.00	1.00	.60
35	Joe Morgan	10.00	5.00	3.00
36	Luke Walker	2.00	1.00	.60
37	Curt Motton	2.00	1.00	.60
38	Zoilo Versalles	2.00	1.00	.60
39	Dick Hughes	2.00	1.00	.60
40	Mayo Smith	2.00	1.00	.60
41	Bob Barton	2.00	1.00	.60
42	Tommy Harper	2.00	1.00	.60
43	Joe Niekro	2.00	1.00	.60
44	Danny Cater	2.00	1.00	.60
45	Maury Wills	2.00	1.00	.60
46	Fritz Peterson	2.00	1.00	.60
47a	Paul Popovich (Emblem visible thru airbrush.)	15.00	7.50	4.50
47b	Paul Popovich (Helmet emblem completely airbrushed.)	2.00	1.00	.60
48	Brant Alyea	2.00	1.00	.60
49a	Royals Rookies **(Steve Jones, Eliseo Rodriquez)** (Rodriquez on front.)	15.00	7.50	4.50
49b	Royals Rookies **(Steve Jones, Eliseo Rodriguez)** (Rodriguez on front.)	2.00	1.00	.60
50	Roberto Clemente	40.00	20.00	12.00
51	Woody Fryman	2.00	1.00	.60
52	Mike Andrews	2.00	1.00	.60
53	Sonny Jackson	2.00	1.00	.60
54	Cisco Carlos	2.00	1.00	.60
55	Jerry Grote	2.00	1.00	.60
56	Rich Reese	2.00	1.00	.60
57	1st Series Check List (1-109) (Denny McLain)	4.00	2.00	1.25
58	Fred Gladding	2.00	1.00	.60
59	Jay Johnstone	2.00	1.00	.60
60	Nelson Briles	2.00	1.00	.60
61	Jimmie Hall	2.00	1.00	.60
62	Chico Salmon	2.00	1.00	.60
63	Jim Hickman	2.00	1.00	.60
64	Bill Monbouquette	2.00	1.00	.60
65	Willie Davis	2.00	1.00	.60
66	Orioles Rookies ***(Mike Adamson, Merv Rettenmund)***	2.00	1.00	.60
67	Bill Stoneman	2.00	1.00	.60
68	Dave Duncan	2.00	1.00	.60
69	Steve Hamilton	2.00	1.00	.60
70	Tommy Helms	2.00	1.00	.60
71	Steve Whitaker	2.00	1.00	.60
72	Ron Taylor	2.00	1.00	.60
73	Johnny Briggs	2.00	1.00	.60
74	Preston Gomez	2.00	1.00	.60
75	Luis Aparicio	9.00	4.50	2.75
76	Norm Miller	2.00	1.00	.60
77a	Ron Perranoski (LA visible thru airbrush.)	25.00	12.50	7.50
77b	Ron Perranoski (Cap emblem completely airbrushed.)	2.00	1.00	.60
78	Tom Satriano	2.00	1.00	.60
79	Milt Pappas	2.00	1.00	.60
80	Norm Cash	6.00	3.00	1.75
81	Mel Queen	2.00	1.00	.60
82	Pirates Rookies ***(Rich Hebner, Al Oliver)***	10.00	5.00	3.00
83	Mike Ferraro	2.00	1.00	.60
84	Bob Humphreys	2.00	1.00	.60
85	Lou Brock	20.00	10.00	6.00
86	Pete Richert	2.00	1.00	.60
87	Horace Clarke	2.00	1.00	.60
88	Rich Nye	2.00	1.00	.60
89	Russ Gibson	2.00	1.00	.60
90	Jerry Koosman	2.00	1.00	.60
91	Al Dark	2.00	1.00	.60
92	Jack Billingham	2.00	1.00	.60
93	Joe Foy	2.00	1.00	.60
94	Hank Aguirre	2.00	1.00	.60
95	Johnny Bench	50.00	25.00	15.00
96	Denver Lemaster	2.00	1.00	.60
97	Buddy Bradford	2.00	1.00	.60
98	Dave Giusti	2.00	1.00	.60
99a	Twins Rookies **(Danny *Morris, Graig Nettles*)** (Black loop above "Twins.")	13.50	6.75	4.00
99b	Twins Rookies **(Danny *Morris, Graig Nettles*)** (No black loop.)	12.50	6.25	3.75
100	Hank Aaron	50.00	25.00	15.00
101	Daryl Patterson	2.00	1.00	.60
102	Jim Davenport	2.00	1.00	.60
103	Roger Repoz	2.00	1.00	.60
104	Steve Blass	2.00	1.00	.60
105	Rick Monday	2.00	1.00	.60
106	Jim Hannan	2.00	1.00	.60
107a	2nd Series Check List (110-218) (Bob Gibson) (161 is Jim Purdin)	4.00	2.00	1.25
107b	2nd Series Check List (110-218) (Bob Gibson) (161 is John Purdin)	6.00	3.00	1.75
108	Tony Taylor	2.00	1.00	.60
109	Jim Lonborg	2.00	1.00	.60
110	Mike Shannon	2.00	1.00	.60
111	Johnny Morris	2.00	1.00	.60
112	J.C. Martin	2.00	1.00	.60
113	Dave May	2.00	1.00	.60
114	Yankees Rookies **(Alan Closter, John Cumberland)**	2.00	1.00	.60
115	Bill Hands	2.00	1.00	.60
116	Chuck Harrison	2.00	1.00	.60
117	Jim Fairey	2.00	1.00	.60
118	Stan Williams	2.00	1.00	.60
119	Doug Rader	2.00	1.00	.60
120	Pete Rose	35.00	17.50	10.00
121	Joe Grzenda	2.00	1.00	.60
122	Ron Fairly	2.00	1.00	.60
123	Wilbur Wood	2.00	1.00	.60
124	Hank Bauer	2.00	1.00	.60
125	Ray Sadecki	2.00	1.00	.60
126	Dick Tracewski	2.00	1.00	.60
127	Kevin Collins	2.00	1.00	.60
128	Tommie Aaron	2.00	1.00	.60
129	Bill McCool	2.00	1.00	.60
130	Carl Yastrzemski	25.00	12.50	7.50
131	Chris Cannizzaro	2.00	1.00	.60
132	Dave Baldwin	2.00	1.00	.60
133	Johnny Callison	2.00	1.00	.60
134	Jim Weaver	2.00	1.00	.60
135	Tommy Davis	2.00	1.00	.60
136	Cards Rookies **(Steve Huntz, Mike Torrez)**	2.00	1.00	.60
137	Wally Bunker	2.00	1.00	.60
138	John Bateman	2.00	1.00	.60
139	Andy Kosco	2.00	1.00	.60
140	Jim Lefebvre	2.00	1.00	.60
141	Bill Dillman	2.00	1.00	.60
142	Woody Woodward	2.00	1.00	.60
143	Joe Nossek	2.00	1.00	.60
144	Bob Hendley	2.00	1.00	.60
145	Max Alvis	2.00	1.00	.60
146	Jim Perry	2.00	1.00	.60
147	Leo Durocher	5.00	2.50	1.50
148	Lee Stange	2.00	1.00	.60
149	Ollie Brown	2.00	1.00	.60
150	Denny McLain	5.00	2.50	1.50
151a	Clay Dalrymple (Phillies)	22.50	11.00	6.75
151b	Clay Dalrymple (Orioles)	2.00	1.00	.60
152	Tommie Sisk	2.00	1.00	.60
153	Ed Brinkman	2.00	1.00	.60
154	Jim Britton	2.00	1.00	.60
155	Pete Ward	2.00	1.00	.60
156	Astros Rookies **(Hal Gilson, Leon McFadden)**	2.00	1.00	.60
157	Bob Rodgers	2.00	1.00	.60
158	Joe Gibbon	2.00	1.00	.60
159	Jerry Adair	2.00	1.00	.60
160	Vada Pinson	3.00	1.50	.90
161	John Purdin	2.00	1.00	.60
162	World Series Game 1 (Gibson Fans 17; Sets New Record)	15.00	7.50	4.50
163	World Series Game 2 (Tiger Homers Deck The Cards)	6.00	3.00	1.75
164	World Series Game 3 (McCarver's Homer Puts St. Louis Ahead)	7.00	3.50	2.00
165	World Series Game 4 (Brock's Lead-Off HR Starts Cards' Romp)	7.00	3.50	2.00
166	World Series Game 5 (Kaline's Key Hit Sparks Tiger Rally)	7.00	3.50	2.00
167	World Series Game 6 (Tiger 10-Run Inning Ties Mark)	6.00	3.00	1.75
168	World Series Game 7 (Lolich Series Hero Outduels Gibson)	9.00	4.50	2.75
169	World Series (Tigers Celebrate Their Victory)	12.00	6.00	3.50
170	Frank Howard	3.00	1.50	.90
171	Glenn Beckert	2.00	1.00	.60
172	Jerry Stephenson	2.00	1.00	.60
173	White Sox Rookies **(Bob Christian, Gerry Nyman)**	2.00	1.00	.60
174	Grant Jackson	2.00	1.00	.60
175	Jim Bunning	8.00	4.00	2.50
176	Joe Azcue	2.00	1.00	.60
177	Ron Reed	2.00	1.00	.60
178	Ray Oyler	2.00	1.00	.60
179	Don Pavletich	2.00	1.00	.60
180	Willie Horton	2.00	1.00	.60
181	Mel Nelson	2.00	1.00	.60
182	Bill Rigney	2.00	1.00	.60
183	Don Shaw	2.00	1.00	.60
184	Roberto Pena	2.00	1.00	.60
185	Tom Phoebus	2.00	1.00	.60
186	John Edwards	2.00	1.00	.60
187	Leon Wagner	2.00	1.00	.60

188 Rick Wise 2.00 1.00 .60
189 Red Sox Rookies **(Joe Lahoud, John Thibdeau)** 2.00 1.00 .60
190 Willie Mays 55.00 27.50 16.50
191 Lindy McDaniel 2.00 1.00 .60
192 Jose Pagan 2.00 1.00 .60
193 Don Cardwell 2.00 1.00 .60
194 Ted Uhlaender 2.00 1.00 .60
195 John Odom 2.00 1.00 .60
196 Lum Harris 2.00 1.00 .60
197 Dick Selma 2.00 1.00 .60
198 Willie Smith 2.00 1.00 .60
199 Jim French 2.00 1.00 .60
200 Bob Gibson 15.00 7.50 4.50
201 Russ Snyder 2.00 1.00 .60
202 Don Wilson 2.00 1.00 .60
203 Dave Johnson 2.00 1.00 .60
204 Jack Hiatt 2.00 1.00 .60
205 Rick Reichardt 2.00 1.00 .60
206 Phillies Rookies **(Larry Hisle, Barry Lersch)** 2.00 1.00 .60
207 Roy Face 2.00 1.00 .60
208a Donn Clendenon (Expos) 25.00 12.50 7.50
208b Donn Clendenon (Houston) 2.00 1.00 .60
209 Larry Haney (Photo reversed.) 2.00 1.00 .60
210 Felix Millan 2.00 1.00 .60
211 Galen Cisco 2.00 1.00 .60
212 Tom Tresh 6.00 3.00 1.75
213 Gerry Arrigo 2.00 1.00 .60
214 3rd Series Check List (219-327) 4.00 2.00 1.25
215 Rico Petrocelli 2.00 1.00 .60
216 Don Sutton 8.00 4.00 2.50
217 John Donaldson 2.00 1.00 .60
218 John Roseboro 2.00 1.00 .60
219 *Freddie Patek* 2.00 1.00 .60
220 Sam McDowell 2.00 1.00 .60
221 Art Shamsky 2.00 1.00 .60
222 Duane Josephson 2.00 1.00 .60
223 Tom Dukes 2.00 1.00 .60
224 Angels Rookies **(Bill Harrelson, Steve Kealey)** 2.00 1.00 .60
225 Don Kessinger 2.00 1.00 .60
226 Bruce Howard 2.00 1.00 .60
227 Frank Johnson 2.00 1.00 .60
228 Dave Leonhard 2.00 1.00 .60
229 Don Lock 2.00 1.00 .60
230 Rusty Staub 3.00 1.50 .90
231 Pat Dobson 2.00 1.00 .60
232 Dave Ricketts 2.00 1.00 .60
233 Steve Barber 2.00 1.00 .60
234 Dave Bristol 2.00 1.00 .60
235 Jim Hunter 9.00 4.50 2.75
236 Manny Mota 2.00 1.00 .60
237 ***Bobby Cox*** 12.00 6.00 3.50
238 Ken Johnson 2.00 1.00 .60
239 Bob Taylor 2.00 1.00 .60
240 Ken Harrelson 2.00 1.00 .60
241 Jim Brewer 2.00 1.00 .60
242 Frank Kostro 2.00 1.00 .60
243 Ron Kline 2.00 1.00 .60
244 Indians Rookies **(Ray Fosse, George Woodson)** 3.50 1.75 1.00
245 Ed Charles 2.00 1.00 .60
246 Joe Coleman 2.00 1.00 .60
247 Gene Oliver 2.00 1.00 .60
248 Bob Priddy 2.00 1.00 .60
249 Ed Spiezio 2.00 1.00 .60
250 Frank Robinson 25.00 12.50 7.50
251 Ron Herbel 2.00 1.00 .60
252 Chuck Cottier 2.00 1.00 .60
253 Jerry Johnson 2.00 1.00 .60
254 Joe Schultz 2.00 1.00 .60
255 Steve Carlton 15.00 7.50 4.50
256 Gates Brown 2.00 1.00 .60
257 Jim Ray 2.00 1.00 .60
258 Jackie Hernandez 2.00 1.00 .60
259 Bill Short 2.00 1.00 .60
260 ***Reggie Jackson*** 170.00 60.00 40.00
261 Bob Johnson 2.00 1.00 .60
262 Mike Kekich 2.00 1.00 .60
263 Jerry May 2.00 1.00 .60
264 Bill Landis 2.00 1.00 .60
265 Chico Cardenas 2.00 1.00 .60
266 Dodgers Rookies **(Alan Foster, Tom Hutton)** 2.00 1.00 .60
267 Vicente Romo 2.00 1.00 .60
268 Al Spangler 2.00 1.00 .60
269 Al Weis 2.00 1.00 .60
270 Mickey Lolich 2.00 1.00 .60
271 Larry Stahl 2.00 1.00 .60
272 Ed Stroud 2.00 1.00 .60
273 Ron Willis 2.00 1.00 .60
274 Clyde King 2.00 1.00 .60
275 Vic Davalillo 2.00 1.00 .60
276 Gary Wagner 2.00 1.00 .60
277 ***Rod Hendricks*** 2.00 1.00 .60
278 Gary Geiger 2.00 1.00 .60
279 Roger Nelson 2.00 1.00 .60
280 Alex Johnson 2.00 1.00 .60
281 Ted Kubiak 2.00 1.00 .60
282 Pat Jarvis 2.00 1.00 .60
283 Sandy Alomar 2.00 1.00 .60
284 Expos Rookies **(Jerry Robertson; Mike Wegener)** 2.00 1.00 .60
285 Don Mincher 2.00 1.00 .60
286 ***Dock Ellis*** 3.00 1.50 .90
287 Jose Tartabull 2.00 1.00 .60
288 Ken Holtzman 2.00 1.00 .60
289 Bart Shirley 2.00 1.00 .60
290 Jim Kaat 3.00 1.50 .90
291 Vern Fuller 2.00 1.00 .60
292 Al Downing 2.00 1.00 .60
293 Dick Dietz 2.00 1.00 .60
294 Jim Lemon 2.00 1.00 .60
295 Tony Perez 10.00 5.00 3.00
296 ***Andy Messersmith*** 3.00 1.50 .90
297 Deron Johnson 2.00 1.00 .60
298 Dave Nicholson 2.00 1.00 .60
299 Mark Belanger 2.00 1.00 .60
300 Felipe Alou 4.00 2.00 1.25
301 Darrell Brandon 2.00 1.00 .60
302 Jim Pagliaroni 2.00 1.00 .60
303 Cal Koonce 2.00 1.00 .60
304 Padres Rookies ***(Bill Davis, Clarence Gaston)*** 4.00 2.00 1.25
305 Dick McAuliffe 2.00 1.00 .60
306 Jim Grant 2.00 1.00 .60
307 Gary Kolb 2.00 1.00 .60
308 Wade Blasingame 2.00 1.00 .60
309 Walt Williams 2.00 1.00 .60
310 Tom Haller 2.00 1.00 .60
311 ***Sparky Lyle*** 6.00 3.00 1.75
312 Lee Elia 2.00 1.00 .60
313 Bill Robinson 2.00 1.00 .60
314 4th Series Check List (328-425) (Don Drysdale) 5.00 2.50 1.50
315 Eddie Fisher 2.00 1.00 .60
316 Hal Lanier 2.00 1.00 .60
317 Bruce Look 2.00 1.00 .60
318 Jack Fisher 2.00 1.00 .60
319 Ken McMullen 2.00 1.00 .60
320 Dal Maxvill 2.00 1.00 .60
321 Jim McAndrew 2.00 1.00 .60
322 Jose Vidal 2.00 1.00 .60
323 Larry Miller 2.00 1.00 .60
324 Tigers Rookies **(Les Cain, Dave Campbell)** 2.00 1.00 .60
325 Jose Cardenal 2.00 1.00 .60
326 Gary Sutherland 2.00 1.00 .60
327 Willie Crawford 2.00 1.00 .60
328 Joe Horlen 2.00 1.00 .60
329 Rick Joseph 2.00 1.00 .60
330 Tony Conigliaro 6.00 3.00 1.75
331 Braves Rookies ***(Gil Garrido, Tom House)*** 2.00 1.00 .60
332 Fred Talbot 2.00 1.00 .60
333 Ivan Murrell 2.00 1.00 .60
334 Phil Roof 2.00 1.00 .60
335 Bill Mazeroski 10.00 5.00 3.00
336 Jim Roland 2.00 1.00 .60
337 Marty Martinez 2.00 1.00 .60
338 ***Del Unser*** 2.00 1.00 .60
339 Reds Rookies **(Steve Mingori, Jose Pena)** 2.00 1.00 .60
340 Dave McNally 2.00 1.00 .60
341 Dave Adlesh 2.00 1.00 .60
342 Bubba Morton 2.00 1.00 .60
343 Dan Frisella 2.00 1.00 .60
344 Tom Matchick 2.00 1.00 .60
345 Frank Linzy 2.00 1.00 .60
346 Wayne Comer 2.00 1.00 .60
347 Randy Hundley 2.00 1.00 .60
348 Steve Hargan 2.00 1.00 .60
349 Dick Williams 2.00 1.00 .60
350 Richie Allen 4.00 2.00 1.25
351 Carroll Sembera 2.00 1.00 .60
352 Paul Schaal 2.00 1.00 .60
353 Jeff Torborg 2.00 1.00 .60
354 Nate Oliver 2.00 1.00 .60
355 Phil Niekro 8.00 4.00 2.50
356 Frank Quilici 2.00 1.00 .60
357 Carl Taylor 2.00 1.00 .60
358 Athletics Rookies **(George Lauzerique, Roberto Rodriguez)** 2.00 1.00 .60
359 Dick Kelley 2.00 1.00 .60
360 Jim Wynn 2.00 1.00 .60
361 Gary Holman 2.00 1.00 .60
362 Jim Maloney 2.00 1.00 .60
363 Russ Nixon 2.00 1.00 .60
364 Tommie Agee 2.00 1.00 .60
365 Jim Fregosi 2.00 1.00 .60
366 Bo Belinsky 2.00 1.00 .60
367 Lou Johnson 2.00 1.00 .60
368 Vic Roznovsky 2.00 1.00 .60
369 Bob Skinner 2.00 1.00 .60
370 Juan Marichal 8.00 4.00 2.50
371 Sal Bando 2.00 1.00 .60
372 Adolfo Phillips 2.00 1.00 .60
373 Fred Lasher 2.00 1.00 .60
374 Bob Tillman 2.00 1.00 .60
375 Harmon Killebrew 20.00 10.00 6.00
376 Royals Rookies ***(Mike Fiore, Jim Rooker)*** 2.00 1.00 .60
377 Gary Bell 2.00 1.00 .60
378 Jose Herrera 2.00 1.00 .60
379 Ken Boyer 2.00 1.00 .60
380 Stan Bahnsen 2.00 1.00 .60
381 Ed Kranepool 2.00 1.00 .60
382 Pat Corrales 2.00 1.00 .60
383 Casey Cox 2.00 1.00 .60
384 Larry Shepard 2.00 1.00 .60
385 Orlando Cepeda 10.00 5.00 3.00
386 Jim McGlothlin 2.00 1.00 .60
387 Bobby Klaus 2.00 1.00 .60
388 Tom McCraw 2.00 1.00 .60
389 Dan Coombs 2.00 1.00 .60
390 Bill Freehan 2.00 1.00 .60
391 Ray Culp 2.00 1.00 .60
392 Bob Burda 2.00 1.00 .60
393 Gene Brabender 2.00 1.00 .60
394 Pilots Rookies **(Lou Piniella, Marv Staehle)** 4.00 2.00 1.25
395 Chris Short 2.00 1.00 .60
396 Jim Campanis 2.00 1.00 .60
397 Chuck Dobson 2.00 1.00 .60
398 Tito Francona 2.00 1.00 .60
399 Bob Bailey 2.00 1.00 .60
400 Don Drysdale 15.00 7.50 4.50
401 Jake Gibbs 2.00 1.00 .60
402 Ken Boswell 2.00 1.00 .60
403 Bob Miller 2.00 1.00 .60
404 Cubs Rookies **(Vic LaRose, Gary Ross)** 2.00 1.00 .60
405 Lee May 2.00 1.00 .60
406 Phil Ortega 2.00 1.00 .60
407 Tom Egan 2.00 1.00 .60
408 Nate Colbert 2.00 1.00 .60
409 Bob Moose 2.00 1.00 .60
410 Al Kaline 20.00 10.00 6.00
411 Larry Dierker 2.00 1.00 .60
412 5th Series Check List (426-512) (Mickey Mantle) 17.50 8.75 5.25
413 Roland Sheldon 2.00 1.00 .60
414 Duke Sims 2.00 1.00 .60
415 Ray Washburn 2.00 1.00 .60
416 Willie McCovey/AS 7.00 3.50 2.00
417 Ken Harrelson/AS 2.00 1.00 .60
418 Tommy Helms/AS 2.00 1.00 .60
419 Rod Carew/AS 8.00 4.00 2.50
420 Ron Santo/AS 4.00 2.00 1.25
421 Brooks Robinson/AS 9.00 4.50 2.75
422 Don Kessinger/AS 2.00 1.00 .60
423 Bert Campaneris/AS 2.00 1.00 .60
424 Pete Rose/AS 20.00 10.00 6.00
425 Carl Yastrzemski/AS 13.50 6.75 4.00
426 Curt Flood/AS 3.00 1.50 .90
427 Tony Oliva/AS 3.00 1.50 .90
428 Lou Brock/AS 7.00 3.50 2.00
429 Willie Horton/AS 2.00 1.00 .60
430 Johnny Bench/AS 12.50 6.25 3.75
431 Bill Freehan/AS 2.00 1.00 .60
432 Bob Gibson/AS 8.00 4.00 2.50
433 Denny McLain/AS 3.00 1.50 .90
434 Jerry Koosman/AS 2.00 1.00 .60
435 Sam McDowell/AS 2.00 1.00 .60
436 Gene Alley 2.00 1.00 .60
437 Luis Alcaraz 2.00 1.00 .60
438 Gary Waslewski 2.00 1.00 .60
439 White Sox Rookies **(Ed Herrmann, Dan Lazar)** 2.00 1.00 .60
440a Willie McCovey (Last name in white.) 150.00 75.00 45.00
440b Willie McCovey (Last name in yellow.) 13.50 6.75 4.00
441a Dennis Higgins (Last name in white.) 60.00 30.00 18.00
441b Dennis Higgins (Last name in yellow.) 2.00 1.00 .60
442 Ty Cline 2.00 1.00 .60
443 Don Wert 2.00 1.00 .60
444a Joe Moeller (Last name in white.) 60.00 30.00 18.00
444b Joe Moeller (Last name in yellow.) 2.00 1.00 .60
445 Bobby Knoop 2.00 1.00 .60
446 Claude Raymond 2.00 1.00 .60
447a Ralph Houk (Last name in white.) 80.00 40.00 24.00
447b Ralph Houk (Last name in yellow.) 5.00 2.50 1.50
448 Bob Tolan 2.00 1.00 .60
449 Paul Lindblad 2.00 1.00 .60
450 Billy Williams 13.50 6.75 4.00
451a Rich Rollins (First name in white.) 60.00 30.00 18.00
451b Rich Rollins (First name in yellow.) 2.00 1.00 .60
452a Al Ferrara (First name in white.) 60.00 30.00 18.00
452b Al Ferrara (First name in yellow.) 2.00 1.00 .60
453 Mike Cuellar 2.00 1.00 .60
454a Phillies Rookies ***(Larry Colton, Don Money)*** (Names in white.) 60.00 30.00 18.00
454b Phillies Rookies ***(Larry Colton, Don Money)*** (Names in yellow.) 2.00 1.00 .60
455 Sonny Siebert 2.00 1.00 .60
456 Bud Harrelson 2.00 1.00 .60
457 Dalton Jones 2.00 1.00 .60
458 Curt Blefary 2.00 1.00 .60
459 Dave Boswell 2.00 1.00 .60
460 Joe Torre 5.00 2.50 1.50
461a Mike Epstein (Last name in white.) 60.00 30.00 18.00
461b Mike Epstein (Last name in yellow.) 2.00 1.00 .60
462 Red Schoendienst 7.00 3.50 2.00
463 Dennis Ribant 2.00 1.00 .60
464a Dave Marshall (Last name in white.) 60.00 30.00 18.00
464b Dave Marshall (Last name in yellow.) 2.00 1.00 .60
465 Tommy John 4.00 2.00 1.25
466 John Boccabella 2.00 1.00 .60
467 Tom Reynolds 2.00 1.00 .60
468a Pirates Rookies **(Bruce Dal Canton, Bob Robertson)** (Names in white.) 60.00 30.00 18.00
468b Pirates Rookies **(Bruce Dal Canton, Bob Robertson)** (Names in yellow.) 2.00 1.00 .60
469 Chico Ruiz 2.00 1.00 .60
470a Mel Stottlemyre (Last name in white.) 60.00 30.00 18.00
470b Mel Stottlemyre (Last name in yellow.) 3.00 1.50 .90
471a Ted Savage (Last name in white.) 60.00 30.00 18.00
471b Ted Savage (Last name in yellow.) 2.00 1.00 .60
472 Jim Price 2.00 1.00 .60
473a Jose Arcia (First name in white.) 60.00 30.00 18.00
473b Jose Arcia (First name in yellow.) 2.00 1.00 .60
474 Tom Murphy 2.00 1.00 .60
475 Tim McCarver 3.00 1.50 .90
476a Red Sox Rookies **(Ken Brett, Gerry Moses)** (Names in white.) 60.00 30.00 18.00

No.	Player	NM	EX	VG
476b	Red Sox Rookies **(Ken Brett, Gerry Moses)** (Names in yellow.)	3.00	1.50	.90
477	Jeff James	2.00	1.00	.60
478	Don Buford	2.00	1.00	.60
479	Richie Scheinblum	2.00	1.00	.60
480	Tom Seaver	30.00	15.00	9.00
481	***Bill Melton***	2.00	1.00	.60
482a	Jim Gosger (First name in white.)	60.00	30.00	18.00
482b	Jim Gosger (First name in yellow.)	2.00	1.00	.60
483	Ted Abernathy	2.00	1.00	.60
484	Joe Gordon	2.00	1.00	.60
485a	Gaylord Perry (Last name in white.)	90.00	45.00	27.50
485b	Gaylord Perry (Last name in yellow.)	8.00	4.00	2.50
486a	Paul Casanova (Last name in white.)	60.00	30.00	18.00
486b	Paul Casanova (Last name in yellow.)	2.00	1.00	.60
487	Denis Menke	2.00	1.00	.60
488	Joe Sparma	2.00	1.00	.60
489	Clete Boyer	3.00	1.50	.90
490	Matty Alou	2.00	1.00	.60
491a	Twins Rookies **(Jerry Crider, George Mitterwald)** (Names in white.)	60.00	30.00	18.00
491b	Twins Rookies **(Jerry Crider, George Mitterwald)** (Names in yellow.)	2.00	1.00	.60
492	Tony Cloninger	2.00	1.00	.60
493a	Wes Parker (Last name in white.)	60.00	30.00	18.00
493b	Wes Parker (Last name in yellow.)	2.00	1.00	.60
494	Ken Berry	2.00	1.00	.60
495	Bert Campaneris	2.00	1.00	.60
496	Larry Jaster	2.00	1.00	.60
497	Julian Javier	2.00	1.00	.60
498	Juan Pizarro	2.00	1.00	.60
499	Astros Rookies **(Don Bryant, Steve Shea)**	2.00	1.00	.60
500a	Mickey Mantle (Last name in white.)	1,750	600.00	375.00
500b	Mickey Mantle (Last name in yellow.)	200.00	90.00	55.00
501a	Tony Gonzalez (First name in white.)	60.00	30.00	18.00
501b	Tony Gonzalez (First name in yellow.)	2.00	1.00	.60
502	Minnie Rojas	2.00	1.00	.60
503	Larry Brown	2.00	1.00	.60
504	6th Series Check List (513-588) (Brooks Robinson)	7.00	3.50	2.00
505a	Bobby Bolin (Last name in white.)	60.00	30.00	18.00
505b	Bobby Bolin (Last name in yellow.)	2.00	1.00	.60
506	Paul Blair	2.00	1.00	.60
507	Cookie Rojas	2.00	1.00	.60
508	Moe Drabowsky	2.00	1.00	.60
509	Manny Sanguillen	2.00	1.00	.60
510	Rod Carew	20.00	10.00	6.00
511a	Diego Segui (First name in white.)	60.00	30.00	18.00
511b	Diego Segui (First name in yellow.)	2.00	1.00	.60
512	Cleon Jones	2.00	1.00	.60
513	Camilo Pascual	2.00	1.00	.60
514	Mike Lum	2.00	1.00	.60
515	Dick Green	2.00	1.00	.60
516	Earl Weaver	9.00	4.50	2,75
517	Mike McCormick	2.00	1.00	.60
518	Fred Whitfield	2.00	1.00	.60
519	Yankees Rookies **(Len Boehmer, Gerry Kenney)**	2.00	1.00	.60
520	Bob Veale	2.00	1.00	.60
521	George Thomas	2.00	1.00	.60
522	Joe Hoerner	2.00	1.00	.60
523	Bob Chance	2.00	1.00	.60
524	Expos Rookies **(Jose Laboy, Floyd Wicker)**	2.00	1.00	.60
525	Earl Wilson	2.00	1.00	.60
526	Hector Torres	2.00	1.00	.60
527	Al Lopez	6.00	3.00	1.75
528	Claude Osteen	2.00	1.00	.60
529	Ed Kirkpatrick	2.00	1.00	.60
530	Cesar Tovar	2.00	1.00	.60
531	Dick Farrell	2.00	1.00	.60
532	Bird Hill Aces (Mike Cuellar, Jim Hardin, Dave McNally, Tom Phoebus)	3.50	1.75	1.00
533	Nolan Ryan	135.00	50.00	30.00
534	Jerry McNertney	2.00	1.00	.60
535	Phil Regan	2.00	1.00	.60
536	Padres Rookies ***(Danny Breeden, Dave Roberts)***	2.00	1.00	.60
537	Mike Paul	2.00	1.00	.60
538	Charlie Smith	2.00	1.00	.60
539	Ted Shows How (Mike Epstein, Ted Williams)	13.50	6.75	4.00
540	Curt Flood	3.00	1.50	.90
541	Joe Verbanic	2.00	1.00	.60
542	Bob Aspromonte	2.00	1.00	.60
543	Fred Newman	2.00	1.00	.60
544	Tigers Rookies **(Mike Kilkenny, Ron Woods)**	2.00	1.00	.60
545	Willie Stargell	15.00	7.50	4.50
546	Jim Nash	2.00	1.00	.60
547	Billy Martin	6.00	3.00	1.75
548	Bob Locker	2.00	1.00	.60
549	Ron Brand	2.00	1.00	.60
550	Brooks Robinson	25.00	12.50	7.50
551	Wayne Granger	2.00	1.00	.60
552	Dodgers Rookies ***(Ted Sizemore, Bill Sudakis)***	3.00	1.50	.90
553	Ron Davis	2.00	1.00	.60
554	Frank Bertaina	2.00	1.00	.60
555	Jim Hart	2.00	1.00	.60
556	A's Stars (Sal Bando, Bert Campaneris, Danny Cater)	3.00	1.50	.90
557	Frank Fernandez	2.00	1.00	.60
558	***Tom Burgmeier***	2.00	1.00	.60
559	Cards Rookies **(Joe Hague, Jim Hicks)**	2.00	1.00	.60
560	Luis Tiant	2.00	1.00	.60
561	Ron Clark	2.00	1.00	.60
562	***Bob Watson***	4.00	2.00	1.25
563	Marty Pattin	2.00	1.00	.60
564	Gil Hodges	7.00	3.50	2.00
565	Hoyt Wilhelm	8.00	4.00	2.50
566	Ron Hansen	2.00	1.00	.60
567a	Pirates Rookies **(Elvio Jimenez, Jim Shellenback)** (No black outline around title letters.)	45.00	22.50	13.50
567b	Pirates Rookies **(Elvio Jiminez, Jim Shellenback)** (Title letters outlined in black.)	2.00	1.00	.60
568	Cecil Upshaw	2.00	1.00	.60
569	Billy Harris	2.00	1.00	.60
570	Ron Santo	10.00	5.00	3.00
571	Cap Peterson	2.00	1.00	.60
572	Giants Heroes (Juan Marichal, Willie McCovey)	9.00	4.50	2.75
573	Jim Palmer	13.50	6.75	4.00
574	George Scott	2.00	1.00	.60
575	Bill Singer	2.00	1.00	.60
576	Phillies Rookies **(Ron Stone, Bill Wilson)**	2.00	1.00	.60
577	Mike Hegan	2.00	1.00	.60
578	Don Bosch	2.00	1.00	.60
579	***Dave Nelson***	2.00	1.00	.60
580	Jim Northrup	2.00	1.00	.60
581	Gary Nolan	2.00	1.00	.60
582a	7th Series Check List (589-664) (Tony Oliva) (Red circle on back.)	4.50	2.25	1.25
582b	7th Series Check List (589-664) (Tony Oliva) (White circle on back.)	3.00	1.50	.90
583	***Clyde Wright***	2.00	1.00	.60
584	Don Mason	2.00	1.00	.60
585	Ron Swoboda	2.00	1.00	.60
586	Tim Cullen	2.00	1.00	.60
587	***Joe Rudi***	5.00	2.50	1.50
588	Bill White	3.00	1.50	.90
589	Joe Pepitone	6.00	3.00	1.75
590	Rico Carty	3.00	1.50	.90
591	Mike Hedlund	3.00	1.50	.90
592	Padres Rookies **(Rafael Robles, Al Santorini)**	3.00	1.50	.90
593	Don Nottebart	3.00	1.50	.90
594	Dooley Womack	3.00	1.50	.90
595	Lee Maye	3.00	1.50	.90
596	Chuck Hartenstein	3.00	1.50	.90
597	A.L. Rookies **(Larry Burchart, Rollie Fingers, Bob Floyd)**	25.00	12.50	7.50
598	Ruben Amaro	3.00	1.50	.90
599	John Boozer	3.00	1.50	.90
600	Tony Oliva	6.00	3.00	1.75
601	Tug McGraw	4.00	2.00	1.25
602	Cubs Rookies **(Alec Distaso, Jim Qualls, Don Young)**	3.00	1.50	.90
603	Joe Keough	3.00	1.50	.90
604	Bobby Etheridge	3.00	1.50	.90
605	Dick Ellsworth	3.00	1.50	.90
606	Gene Mauch	3.00	1.50	.90
607	Dick Bosman	3.00	1.50	.90
608	Dick Simpson	3.00	1.50	.90
609	Phil Gagliano	3.00	1.50	.90
610	Jim Hardin	3.00	1.50	.90
611	Braves Rookies **(Bob Didier, Walt Hriniak, Gary Neibauer)**	3.00	1.50	.90
612	Jack Aker	3.00	1.50	.90
613	Jim Beauchamp	3.00	1.50	.90
614	Astros Rookies **(Tom Griffin, Skip Guinn)**	3.00	1.50	.90
615	Len Gabrielson	3.00	1.50	.90
616	Don McMahon	3.00	1.50	.90
617	Jesse Gonder	3.00	1.50	.90
618	Ramon Webster	3.00	1.50	.90
619	Royals Rookies **(Bill Butler, Pat Kelly, Juan Rios)**	3.00	1.50	.90
620	Dean Chance	3.00	1.50	.90
621	Bill Voss	3.00	1.50	.90
622	Dan Osinski	3.00	1.50	.90
623	Hank Allen	3.00	1.50	.90
624	N.L. Rookies **(Darrel Chaney, Duffy Dyer, Terry Harmon)**	3.00	1.50	.90
625	Mack Jones	3.00	1.50	.90
626	Gene Michael	3.00	1.50	.90
627	George Stone	3.00	1.50	.90
628	Red Sox Rookies **(Bill Conigliaro, Syd O'Brien, Fred Wenz)**	4.00	2.00	1.25
629	Jack Hamilton	3.00	1.50	.90
630	***Bobby Bonds***	25.00	12.50	7.50
631	John Kennedy	3.00	1.50	.90
632	Jon Warden	3.00	1.50	.90
633	Harry Walker	3.00	1.50	.90
634	Andy Etchebarren	3.00	1.50	.90
635	George Culver	3.00	1.50	.90
636	Woodie Held	3.00	1.50	.90
637	Padres Rookies **(Jerry DaVanon, Clay Kirby, Frank Reberger)**	3.00	1.50	.90
638	Ed Sprague	3.00	1.50	.90
639	Barry Moore	3.00	1.50	.90
640	Fergie Jenkins	12.50	6.25	3.75
641	N.L. Rookies **(Bobby Darwin, Tommy Dean, John Miller)**	3.00	1.50	.90
642	John Hiller	3.00	1.50	.90
643	Billy Cowan	3.00	1.50	.90
644	Chuck Hinton	3.00	1.50	.90
645	George Brunet	3.00	1.50	.90
646	Expos Rookies ***(Dan McGinn, Carl Morton)***	3.00	1.50	.90
647	Dave Wickersham	3.00	1.50	.90
648	Bobby Wine	3.00	1.50	.90
649	Al Jackson	3.00	1.50	.90
650	Ted Williams	20.00	10.00	6.00
651	Gus Gil	3.00	1.50	.90
652	Eddie Watt	3.00	1.50	.90
653	***Aurelio Rodriguez*** (Photo actually batboy Leonard Garcia.)	6.00	3.00	1.75
654	White Sox Rookies **(Carlos May, Rich Morales, Don Secrist)**	3.50	1.75	1.00
655	Mike Hershberger	3.00	1.50	.90
656	Dan Schneider	3.00	1.50	.90
657	Bobby Murcer	6.00	3.00	1.75
658	A.L. Rookies **(Bill Burbach, Tom Hall, Jim Miles)**	3.00	1.50	.90
659	Johnny Podres	3.00	1.50	.90
660	Reggie Smith	3.00	1.50	.90
661	Jim Merritt	3.00	1.50	.90
662	Royals Rookies **(Dick Drago, Bob Oliver, George Spriggs)**	3.00	1.50	.90
663	Dick Radatz	4.50	2.25	1.25
664	Ron Hunt	13.50	3.00	1.00

1969 Topps Decals

Designed as an insert for 1969 regular issue card packs, these decals are virtually identical in format to the '69 cards. The 48 decals in the set measure 1" x 2-1/2", although they are mounted on white paper backing which measures 1-3/4" x 2-1/8". In March 2001, a hoard consisting of two original 10,000-piece rolls - 833 each of half the players in the set - was sold at auction. The players represented in that find are indicated in these listings with an asterisk.

		NM	EX	VG
Complete Set (48):		350.00	175.00	100.00
Common Player:		4.00	2.00	1.25
(1)	Hank Aaron	25.00	12.50	7.50
(2)	Richie Allen	7.00	3.50	2.00
(3)	Felipe Alou	5.00	2.50	1.50
(4)	Matty Alou	4.00	2.00	1.25
(5)	Luis Aparicio	9.00	4.50	2.75
(6)	Bob Clemente	30.00	15.00	9.00
(7)	Donn Clendenon	4.00	2.00	1.25
(8)	Tommy Davis (*)	4.00	2.00	1.25
(9)	Don Drysdale (*)	10.00	5.00	3.00
(10)	Joe Foy (*)	4.00	2.00	1.25
(11)	Jim Fregosi	4.00	2.00	1.25
(12)	Bob Gibson (*)	10.00	5.00	3.00
(13)	Tony Gonzalez	4.00	2.00	1.25
(14)	Tom Haller	4.00	2.00	1.25
(15)	Ken Harrelson	4.00	2.00	1.25
(16)	Tommy Helms	4.00	2.00	1.25
(17)	Willie Horton (*)	4.00	2.00	1.25
(18)	Frank Howard	4.50	2.25	1.25
(19)	Reggie Jackson (*)	20.00	10.00	6.00
(20)	Fergie Jenkins	9.00	4.50	2.75
(21)	Harmon Killebrew (*)	10.00	5.00	3.00
(22)	Jerry Koosman (*)	4.00	2.00	1.25
(23)	Mickey Mantle	40.00	20.00	12.00
(24)	Willie Mays (*)	20.00	10.00	6.00
(25)	Tim McCarver	4.50	2.25	1.25
(26)	Willie McCovey	10.00	5.00	3.00
(27)	Sam McDowell (*)	4.00	2.00	1.25
(28)	Denny McLain (*)	4.00	2.00	1.25
(29)	Dave McNally (*)	4.00	2.00	1.25
(30)	Don Mincher	4.00	2.00	1.25
(31)	Rick Monday	4.00	2.00	1.25
(32)	Tony Oliva (*)	4.50	2.25	1.25
(33)	Camilo Pascual	4.00	2.00	1.25
(34)	Rick Reichardt (*)	4.00	2.00	1.25
(35)	Frank Robinson (*)	10.00	5.00	3.00
(36)	Pete Rose (*)	20.00	10.00	6.00
(37)	Ron Santo (*)	5.00	2.50	1.50
(38)	Tom Seaver (*)	12.00	6.00	3.50
(39)	Dick Selma (*)	4.00	2.00	1.25
(40)	Chris Short (*)	4.00	2.00	1.25
(41)	Rusty Staub	4.00	2.00	1.25
(42)	Mel Stottlemyre	4.00	2.00	1.25
(43)	Luis Tiant (*)	4.00	2.00	1.25
(44)	Pete Ward	4.00	2.00	1.25
(45)	Hoyt Wilhelm (*)	7.50	3.75	2.25
(46)	Maury Wills (*)	4.00	2.00	1.25

		NM	EX	VG
(47)	Jim Wynn	4.00	2.00	1.25
(48)	Carl Yastrzemski (*)	12.00	6.00	3.50

1969 Topps Deckle Edge

These 2-1/4" x 3-1/4" cards take their name from their borders which have a scalloped effect. Fronts have a black-and-white player photo along with a blue facsimile autograph. Backs have the player's name and the card number in light blue ink in a small box at the bottom of the card. While there are only 33 numbered cards, there are actually 35 possible players; both Jim Wynn and Hoyt Wilhelm cards are found as #11 while cards of Joe Foy and Rusty Staub as #22. Straight-edged proof cards are sometimes found but these were never formally issued; they carry a premium.

		NM	EX	VG
Complete Set (33):		80.00	40.00	25.00
Common Player:		1.00	.50	.30
Proofs: 6-8X				
1	Brooks Robinson	9.00	4.50	2.75
2	Boog Powell	1.50	.70	.45
3	Ken Harrelson	1.00	.50	.30
4	Carl Yastrzemski	9.00	4.50	2.75
5	Jim Fregosi	1.00	.50	.30
6	Luis Aparicio	7.50	3.75	2.25
7	Luis Tiant	1.00	.50	.30
8	Denny McLain	1.00	.50	.30
9	Willie Horton	1.00	.50	.30
10	Bill Freehan	1.00	.50	.30
11a	Hoyt Wilhelm	6.00	3.00	1.75
11b	Jim Wynn	12.00	6.00	3.50
12	Rod Carew	7.50	3.75	2.25
13	Mel Stottlemyre	1.00	.50	.30
14	Rick Monday	1.00	.50	.30
15	Tommy Davis	1.00	.50	.30
16	Frank Howard	1.50	.70	.45
17	Felipe Alou	1.00	.50	.30
18	Don Kessinger	1.00	.50	.30
19	Ron Santo	2.00	1.00	.60
20	Tommy Helms	1.00	.50	.30
21	Pete Rose	15.00	7.50	4.50
22a	Rusty Staub	2.00	1.00	.60
22b	Joe Foy	9.00	4.50	2.75
23	Tom Haller	1.00	.50	.30
24	Maury Wills	1.00	.50	.30
25	Jerry Koosman	1.00	.50	.30
26	Richie Allen	3.00	1.50	.90
27	Roberto Clemente	20.00	10.00	6.00
28	Curt Flood	1.00	.50	.30
29	Bob Gibson	7.50	3.75	2.25
30	Al Ferrara	1.00	.50	.30
31	Willie McCovey	7.50	3.75	2.25
32	Juan Marichal	6.00	3.00	1.75
33	Willie Mays	15.00	7.50	4.50

1969 Topps Stamps

Topps continued to refine its efforts at baseball stamps in 1969 with the release of 240 player stamps, each measuring 1" x 1-7/16". Each stamp has a color photo along with the player's name, position and team. Unlike prior stamp issues, the 1969 stamps have 24 separate albums (one per team). The stamps were issued in strips of 12, many players appearing on two different strips.

	NM	EX	VG
Complete Sheet Set (24):	200.00	100.00	60.00
Common Sheet:	5.00	2.50	1.50
Complete Stamp Album Set (24):	80.00	40.00	20.00
Single Stamp Album:	3.00	1.50	.90
Unopened Pack:	50.00		

		NM	EX	VG
(1)	Tommie Agee, Sandy Alomar, Jose Cardenal, Dean Chance, Joe Foy, Jim Grant, Don Kessinger, Mickey Mantle, Jerry May, Bob Rodgers, Cookie Rojas, Gary Sutherland	55.00	27.50	16.50
(2)	Jesus Alou, Mike Andrews, Larry Brown, Moe Drabowsky, Alex Johnson, Lew Krausse, Jim Lefebvre, Dal Maxvill, John Odom, Claude Osteen, Rick Reichardt, Luis Tiant	5.00	2.50	1.50
(3)	Hank Aaron, Matty Alou, Max Alvis, Nelson Briles, Eddie Fisher, Bud Harrelson, Willie Horton, Randy Hundley, Larry Jaster, Jim Kaat, Gary Peters, Pete Ward	20.00	10.00	6.00
(4)	Don Buford, John Callison, Tommy Davis, Jackie Hernandez, Fergie Jenkins, Lee May, Denny McLain, Bob Oliver, Roberto Pena, Tony Perez, Joe Torre, Tom Tresh	7.50	3.75	2.25
(5)	Jim Bunning, Dean Chance, Joe Foy, Sonny Jackson, Don Kessinger, Rick Monday, Gaylord Perry, Roger Repoz, Cookie Rojas, Mel Stottlemyre, Leon Wagner, Jim Wynn	7.50	3.75	2.25
(6)	Felipe Alou, Gerry Arrigo, Bob Aspromonte, Gary Bell, Clay Dalrymple, Jim Fregosi, Tony Gonzalez, Duane Josephson, Dick McAuliffe, Tony Oliva, Brooks Robinson, Willie Stargell	20.00	10.00	6.00
(7)	Steve Barber, Donn Clendenon, Joe Coleman, Vic Davalillo, Russ Gibson, Jerry Grote, Tom Haller, Andy Kosco, Willie McCovey, Don Mincher, Joe Morgan, Don Wilson	7.50	3.75	2.25
(8)	George Brunet, Don Buford, John Callison, Danny Cater, Tommy Davis, Willie Davis, John Edwards, Jim Hart, Mickey Lolich, Willie Mays, Roberto Pena, Mickey Stanley	25.00	12.50	7.50
(9)	Ernie Banks, Glenn Beckert, Ken Berry, Horace Clarke, Roberto Clemente, Larry Dierker, Len Gabrielson, Jake Gibbs, Jerry Koosman, Sam McDowell, Tom Satriano, Bill Singer	25.00	12.50	7.50
(10)	Gene Alley, Lou Brock, Larry Brown, Moe Drabowsky, Frank Howard, Tommie John, Roger Nelson, Claude Osteen, Phil Regan, Rick Reichardt, Tony Taylor, Roy White	7.50	3.75	2.25
(11)	Bob Allison, John Bateman, Don Drysdale, Dave Johnson, Harmon Killebrew, Jim Maloney, Bill Mazeroski, Gerry McNertney, Ron Perranoski, Rico Petrocelli, Pete Rose, Billy Williams	35.00	17.50	10.50
(12)	Bernie Allen (Senators), Jose Arcia, Stan Bahnsen, Sal Bando, Jim Davenport, Tito Francona, Dick Green, Ron Hunt, Mack Jones, Vada Pinson, George Scott, Don Wert	5.00	2.50	1.50
(13)	Gerry Arrigo, Bob Aspromonte, Joe Azcue, Curt Blefary, Orlando Cepeda, Bill Freehan, Jim Fregosi, Dave Giusti, Duane Josephson, Tim McCarver, Jose Santiago, Bob Tolan	7.50	3.75	2.25
(14)	Jerry Adair, Johnny Bench, Clete Boyer, John Briggs, Bert Campaneris, Woody Fryman, Ron Kline, Bobby Knoop, Ken McMullen, Adolfo Phillips, John Roseboro, Tom Seaver	20.00	10.00	6.00
(15)	Norm Cash, Ron Fairly, Bob Gibson, Bill Hands, Cleon Jones, Al Kaline, Paul Schaal, Mike Shannon, Duke Sims, Reggie Smith, Steve Whitaker, Carl Yastrzemski	15.00	7.50	4.50
(16)	Steve Barber, Paul Casanova, Dick Dietz, Russ Gibson, Jerry Grote, Tom Haller, Ed Kranepool, Juan Marichal, Denis Menke, Jim Nash, Bill Robinson, Frank Robinson	15.00	7.50	4.50
(17)	Bobby Bolin, Ollie Brown, Rod Carew, Mike Epstein, Bud Harrelson, Larry Jaster, Dave McNally, Willie Norton, Milt Pappas, Gary Peters, Paul Popovich, Stan Williams	7.50	3.75	2.25
(18)	Ted Abernathy, Bob Allison, Ed Brinkman, Don Drysdale, Jim Hardin, Julian Javier, Hal Lanier, Jim McGlothlin, Ron Perranoski, Rich Rollins, Ron Santo, Billy Williams	15.00	7.50	4.50
(19)	Richie Allen, Luis Aparicio, Wally Bunker, Curt Flood, Ken Harrelson, Jim Hunter, Denver Lemaster, Felix Millan, Jim Northrop (Northrup), Art Shamsky, Larry Stahl, Ted Uhlaender	7.50	3.75	2.25
(20)	Bob Bailey, Johnny Bench, Woody Fryman, Jim Hannan, Ron Kline, Al McBean, Camilo Pascual, Joe Pepitone, Doug Rader, Ron Reed, John Roseboro, Sonny Siebert	7.50	3.75	2.25
(21)	Jack Aker, Tommy Harper, Tommy Helms, Dennis Higgins, Jim Hunter, Don Lock, Lee Maye, Felix Millan, Jim Northrop (Northrup), Larry Stahl, Don Sutton, Zoilo Versalles	7.50	3.75	2.25
(22)	Norm Cash, Ed Charles, Joe Horlen, Pat Jarvis, Jim Lonborg, Manny Mota, Boog Powell, Dick Selma, Mike Shannon, Duke Sims, Steve Whitaker, Hoyt Wilhelm	7.50	3.75	2.25
(23)	Bernie Allen (Senator), Ray Culp, Al Ferrara, Tito Francona, Dick Green, Ron Hunt, Ray Oyler, Tom Phoebus, Rusty Staub, Bob Veale, Maury Wills, Wilbur Wood	5.00	2.50	1.50
(24)	Ernie Banks, Mark Belanger, Steve Blass, Horace Clarke, Bob Clemente, Larry Dierker, Dave Duncan, Chico Salmon, Chris Short, Ron Swoboda, Cesar Tovar, Rick Wise	20.00	10.00	6.00

1969 Topps Super

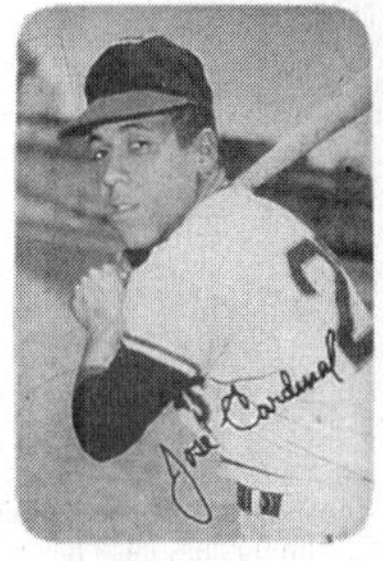

These 2-1/4" x 3-1/4" cards are not the bigger "Super" cards which would be seen in following years. Rather, what enabled Topps to dub them "Super Baseball Cards" is their high-gloss finish which enhances the bright color photograph used on their fronts. The only other design element on the front is a facsimile autograph. The backs contain a box at the the bottom which carries the player's name, team, position, a copyright line and the card number. Another unusual feature is that the cards have rounded corners, although square-cornered proof cards are also known, completely printed on front and back.

		NM	EX	VG
Complete Set (66):		6,000	3,000	1,800
Common Player:		20.00	10.00	6.00
Proofs: 2-3X				
1	Dave McNally	20.00	10.00	6.00
2	Frank Robinson	175.00	85.00	50.00
3	Brooks Robinson	175.00	85.00	50.00
4	Ken Harrelson	20.00	10.00	6.00
5	Carl Yastrzemski	250.00	125.00	75.00
6	Ray Culp	20.00	10.00	6.00
7	James Fregosi	20.00	10.00	6.00
8	Rick Reichardt	20.00	10.00	6.00
9	Vic Davalillo	20.00	10.00	6.00
10	Luis Aparicio	100.00	50.00	30.00
11	Pete Ward	20.00	10.00	6.00
12	Joe Horlen	20.00	10.00	6.00
13	Luis Tiant	20.00	10.00	6.00
14	Sam McDowell	20.00	10.00	6.00
15	Jose Cardenal	20.00	10.00	6.00
16	Willie Horton	20.00	10.00	6.00
17	Denny McLain	20.00	10.00	6.00
18	Bill Freehan	20.00	10.00	6.00
19	Harmon Killebrew	175.00	85.00	50.00
20	Tony Oliva	20.00	10.00	6.00
21	Dean Chance	20.00	10.00	6.00
22	Joe Foy	20.00	10.00	6.00
23	Roger Nelson	20.00	10.00	6.00
24	Mickey Mantle	1,100	550.00	350.00
25	Mel Stottlemyre	20.00	10.00	6.00
26	Roy White	20.00	10.00	6.00
27	Rick Monday	20.00	10.00	6.00
28	Reggie Jackson	400.00	200.00	120.00
29	Bert Campaneris	20.00	10.00	6.00
30	Frank Howard	20.00	10.00	6.00

31	Camilo Pascual	20.00	10.00	6.00
32	Tommy Davis	20.00	10.00	6.00
33	Don Mincher	20.00	10.00	6.00
34	Henry Aaron	400.00	200.00	120.00
35	Felipe Alou	20.00	10.00	6.00
36	Joe Torre	50.00	25.00	15.00
37	Fergie Jenkins	100.00	50.00	30.00
38	Ronald Santo	35.00	17.50	10.00
39	Billy Williams	100.00	50.00	30.00
40	Tommy Helms	20.00	10.00	6.00
41	Pete Rose	400.00	200.00	120.00
42	Joe Morgan	100.00	50.00	30.00
43	Jim Wynn	20.00	10.00	6.00
44	Curt Blefary	20.00	10.00	6.00
45	Willie Davis	20.00	10.00	6.00
46	Don Drysdale	135.00	65.00	40.00
47	Tom Haller	20.00	10.00	6.00
48	Rusty Staub	35.00	17.50	10.00
49	Maurice Wills	20.00	10.00	6.00
50	Cleon Jones	20.00	10.00	6.00
51	Jerry Koosman	20.00	10.00	6.00
52	Tom Seaver	175.00	87.00	52.00
53	Rich Allen	45.00	22.50	13.50
54	Chris Short	20.00	10.00	6.00
55	Cookie Rojas	20.00	10.00	6.00
56	Mateo Alou	20.00	10.00	6.00
57	Steve Blass	20.00	10.00	6.00
58	Roberto Clemente	500.00	250.00	150.00
59	Curt Flood	20.00	10.00	6.00
60	Bob Gibson	125.00	65.00	35.00
61	Tim McCarver	35.00	17.50	10.00
62	Dick Selma	20.00	10.00	6.00
63	Ollie Brown	20.00	10.00	6.00
64	Juan Marichal	100.00	50.00	30.00
65	Willie Mays	400.00	200.00	120.00
66	Willie McCovey	120.00	60.00	36.00

1969 Topps Team Posters

Picking up where the 1968 posters left off, the 1969 poster is larger at about 12" x 20". The posters each have a team focus with a large pennant carrying the team name, along with nine or 10 photos of players. Each of the photos has a facsimile autograph. The size of posters meant they had to be folded to fit in their packages. These original folds are not considered when grading, unless the paper has split on those seams.

		NM	EX	VG
Complete Set (24):		2,250	1,125	675.00
Common Poster:		55.00	27.50	16.00
Unopened Pack:		190.00		
1	Detroit Tigers (Norm Cash, Bill Freehan, Willie Horton, Al Kaline, Mickey Lolich, Dick McAuliffe, Denny McLain, Jim Northrup, Mickey Stanley, Don Wert, Earl Wilson)	125.00	65.00	35.00
2	Atlanta Braves (Hank Aaron, Felipe Alou, Clete Boyer, Rico Carty, Tito Francona, Sonny Jackson, Pat Jarvis, Felix Millan, Phil Niekro, Milt Pappas, Joe Torre)	90.00	45.00	27.00
3	Boston Red Sox (Mike Andrews, Tony Conigliaro, Ray Culp, Russ Gibson, Ken Harrelson, Jim Lonborg, Rico Petrocelli, Jose Santiago, George Scott, Reggie Smith, Carl Yastrzemski)	100.00	50.00	30.00
4	Chicago Cubs (Ernie Banks, Glenn Beckert, Bill Hands, Jim Hickman, Ken Holtzman, Randy Hundley, Fergie Jenkins, Don Kessinger, Adolfo Phillips, Ron Santo, Billy Williams)	90.00	45.00	27.00
5	Baltimore Orioles (Mark Belanger, Paul Blair, Don Buford, Andy Etchebarren, Jim Hardin, Dave Johnson, Dave McNally, Tom Phoebus, Boog Powell, Brooks Robinson, Frank Robinson)	80.00	40.00	24.00
6	Houston Astros (Curt Blefary, Donn Clendenon, Larry Dierker, John Edwards, Denny Lemaster, Denis Menke, Norm Miller, Joe Morgan, Doug Rader, Don Wilson, Jim Wynn)	55.00	27.50	16.00
7	Kansas City Royals (Jerry Adair, Wally Bunker, Mike Fiore, Joe Foy, Jackie Hernandez, Pat Kelly, Dave Morehead, Roger Nelson, Dave Nicholson, Eliseo Rodriguez, Steve Whitaker)	55.00	27.50	16.00
8	Philadelphia Phillies (Richie Allen, Johnny Callison, Woody Fryman, Larry Hisle, Don Money, Cookie Rojas, Mike Ryan, Chris Short, Tony Taylor, Bill White, Rick Wise)	60.00	30.00	18.00
9	Seattle Pilots (Jack Aker, Steve Barber, Gary Bell, Tommy Davis, Jim Gosger, Tommy Harper, Gerry McNertney, Don Mincher, Ray Oyler, Rich Rollins, Chico Salmon)	150.00	75.00	45.00
10	Montreal Expos (Bob Bailey, John Bateman, Jack Billingham, Jim Grant, Larry Jaster, Mack Jones, Manny Mota, Rusty Staub, Gary Sutherland, Jim Williams, Maury Wills)	50.00	25.00	15.00
11	Chicago White Sox (Sandy Alomar, Luis Aparicio, Ken Berry, Buddy Bradford, Joe Horlen, Tommy John, Duane Josephson, Tom McCraw, Bill Melton, Pete Ward, Wilbur Wood)	55.00	27.50	16.00
12	San Diego Padres (Jose Arcia, Danny Breeden, Ollie Brown, Bill Davis, Ron Davis, Tony Gonzalez, Dick Kelley, Al McBean, Roberto Pena, Dick Selma, Ed Spiezio)	55.00	27.50	16.00
13	Cleveland Indians (Max Alvis, Joe Azcue, Jose Cardenal, Vern Fuller, Lou Johnson, Sam McDowell, Sonny Siebert, Duke Sims, Russ Snyder, Luis Tiant, Zoilo Versalles)	75.00	37.00	22.00
14	San Francisco Giants (Bobby Bolin, Jim Davenport, Dick Dietz, Jim Hart, Ron Hunt, Hal Lanier, Juan Marichal, Willie Mays, Willie McCovey, Gaylord Perry, Charlie Smith)	125.00	65.00	35.00
15	Minnesota Twins (Bob Allison, Chico Cardenas, Rod Carew, Dean Chance, Jim Kaat, Harmon Killebrew, Tony Oliva, Jim Perry, John Roseboro, Cesar Tovar, Ted Uhlaender)	100.00	50.00	30.00
16	Pittsburgh Pirates (Gene Alley, Matty Alou, Steve Blass, Jim Bunning, Bob Clemente, Rich Hebner, Jerry May, Bill Mazeroski, Bob Robertson, Willie Stargell, Bob Veale)	135.00	65.00	40.00
17	California Angels (Ruben Amaro, George Brunet, Bob Chance, Vic Davalillo, Jim Fregosi, Bobby Knoop, Jim McGlothlin, Rick Reichardt, Roger Repoz, Bob Rodgers, Hoyt Wilhelm)	60.00	30.00	18.00
18	St. Louis Cardinals (Nelson Briles, Lou Brock, Orlando Cepeda, Curt Flood, Bob Gibson, Julian Javier, Dal Maxvill, Tim McCarver, Vada Pinson, Mike Shannon, Ray Washburn)	75.00	37.50	22.00
19	New York Yankees (Stan Bahnsen, Horace Clarke, Bobby Cox, Jake Gibbs, Mickey Mantle, Joe Pepitone, Fritz Peterson, Bill Robinson, Mel Stottlemyre, Tom Tresh, Roy White)	165.00	82.00	49.00
20	Cincinnati Reds (Gerry Arrigo, Johnny Bench, Tommy Helms, Alex Johnson, Jim Maloney, Lee May, Gary Nolan, Tony Perez, Pete Rose, Bob Tolan, Woody Woodward)	110.00	55.00	33.00
21	Oakland Athletics (Sal Bando, Bert Campaneris, Danny Cater, Dick Green, Mike Hershberger, Jim Hunter, Reggie Jackson, Rick Monday, Jim Nash, John Odom, Jim Pagliaroni)	100.00	50.00	30.00
22	Los Angeles Dodgers (Willie Crawford, Willie Davis, Don Drysdale, Ron Fairly, Tom Haller, Andy Kosco, Jim Lefebvre, Claude Osteen, Paul Popovich, Bill Singer, Bill Sudakis)	80.00	40.00	24.00
23	Washington Senators (Bernie Allen, Brant Alyea, Ed Brinkman, Paul Casanova, Joe Coleman, Mike Epstein, Jim Hannan, Frank Howard, Ken McMullen, Camilo Pascual, Del Unser)	80.00	40.00	24.00
24	New York Mets (Tommie Agee, Ken Boswell, Ed Charles, Jerry Grote, Bud Harrelson, Cleon Jones, Jerry Koosman, Ed Kranepool, Jim McAndrew, Tom Seaver, Ron Swoboda)	150.00	75.00	45.00

1969 Topps 4-On-1 Mini Stickers

Another in the long line of Topps test issues, the 4-on-1s are 2-1/2" x 3-1/2" cards with blank backs featuring a quartet of miniature stickers in the design of the same cards from the 1969 Topps regular set. There are 25 different cards, for a total of 100 different stickers. As they are not common, Mint cards bring fairly strong prices on today's market. As the set was drawn from the 3rd Series of the regular cards, it includes some rookie stickers and World Series highlight stickers.

		NM	EX	VG
Complete Set (25):		2,250	1,125	675.00
Common 4-in-1:		50.00	25.00	15.00
Unopened Pack:		375.00		
(1)	Jerry Adair, Willie Mays, Johnny Morris, Don Wilson	400.00	200.00	120.00
(2)	Tommie Aaron, Jim Britton, Donn Clendenon, Woody Woodward	50.00	25.00	15.00
(3)	Tommy Davis, Don Pavletich, Vada Pinson, World Series Game 4 (Lou Brock)	75.00	37.50	22.00
(4)	Max Alvis, Glenn Beckert, Ron Fairly, Rick Wise	50.00	25.00	15.00
(5)	Johnny Callison, Jim French, Lum Harris, Dick Selma	50.00	25.00	15.00
(6)	Bob Gibson, Larry Haney, Rick Reichardt, World Series Game 3 (Tim McCarver)	125.00	65.00	35.00
(7)	Wally Bunker, Don Cardwell, Joe Gibbon, Astros Rookies (Gilsen, McFadden)	50.00	25.00	15.00
(8)	Ollie Brown, Jim Bunning, Andy Kosco, Ron Reed	50.00	25.00	15.00
(9)	Bill Dillman, Jim Lefebvre, John Purdin, John Roseboro	50.00	25.00	15.00
(10)	Bill Hands, Chuck Harrison, Lindy McDaniel, Felix Millan	50.00	25.00	15.00
(11)	Jack Hiatt, Dave Johnson, Mel Nelson, Tommie Sisk	50.00	25.00	15.00
(12)	Clay Dalrymple, Leo Durocher, John Odom, Wilbur Wood	50.00	25.00	15.00
(13)	Hank Bauer, Kevin Collins, Ray Oyler, Russ Snyder	50.00	25.00	15.00
(14)	Gerry Arrigo, Jim Perry, Red Sox Rookies (Lahoud, Thibdeau), World Series Game 7 (Mickey Lolich)	50.00	25.00	15.00
(15)	Bill McCool, Roberto Pena, Doug Rader, World Series Game 2 (Willie Horton)	75.00	37.50	22.00
(16)	Ed Brinkman, Roy Face, Willie Horton, Bob Rodgers	50.00	25.00	15.00
(17)	Dave Baldwin, J.C. Martin, Dave May, Ray Sadecki	50.00	25.00	15.00
(18)	Jose Pagan, Tom Phoebus, Mike Shannon, World Series Game 1 (Bob Gibson)	50.00	25.00	15.00
(19)	Pete Rose, Lee Stange, Don Sutton, Ted Uhlaender	500.00	250.00	150.00
(20)	Joe Grzenda, Frank Howard, Dick Tracewski, Jim Weaver	50.00	25.00	15.00
(21)	Joe Azcue, Grant Jackson, Denny McLain, White Sox Rookies (Christman, Nyman)	50.00	25.00	15.00
(22)	John Edwards, Jim Fairey, Phillies Rookies, Stan Williams	50.00	25.00	15.00
(23)	John Bateman, Willie Smith, Leon Wagner, World Series Summary	50.00	25.00	15.00

(24)	Chris Cannizzaro, Bob Hendley, World Series Game 5 (Al Kaline), Yankees Rookies (Closter, Cumberland)	50.00	25.00	15.00
(25)	Joe Nossek, Rico Petrocelli, Carl Yastrzemski, Cardinals Rookies (Huntz, Torrez)	350.00	175.00	105.00

1969 Topps Bowie Kuhn

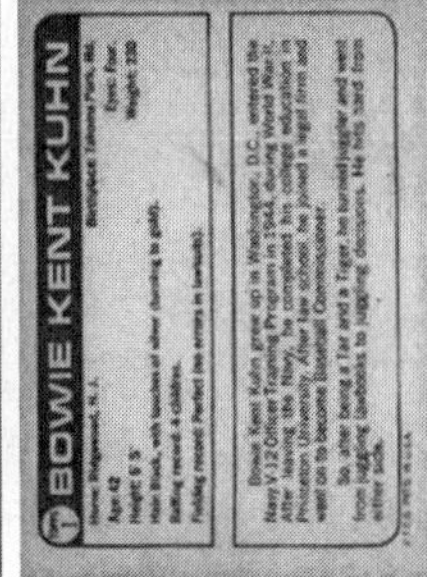

Following Kuhn's election as Commissioner in February 1969, Topps produced this special card, presumably for his personal use. In standard 2-1/2" x 3-1/2" format, but printed on thinner than usual card stock, the front has a photo of Kuhn's face composited with the drawing of a crowned baseball player sitting on top of the world. The horizontal back has a few personal data and a career summary.

		NM	EX	VG
1	Bowie Kuhn	90.00	45.00	27.50

1970 Topps

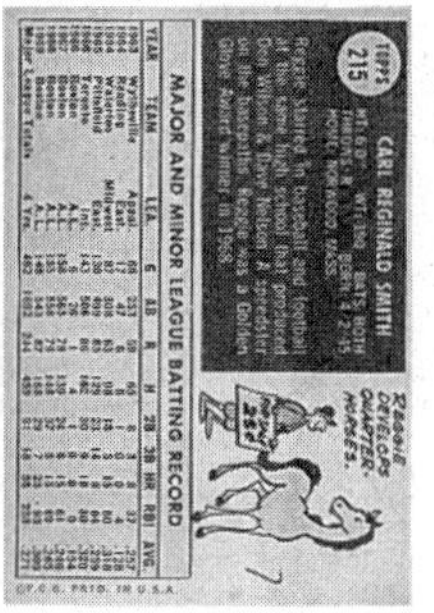

Topps established another set size record by coming out with 720 cards in 1970. The 2-1/2" x 3-1/2" cards have a color photo with a thin white frame. The photos have the player's team overprinted at the top, while the player's name in script and his position are at the bottom. A gray border surrounds the front. Card backs follow the normal design pattern, although they are more readable than some issues of the past. Team cards returned and were joined with many of the usual specialty cards. The World Series highlights were joined by cards with playoff highlights. Statistical leaders and All-Stars are also included in the set. High-numbered cards provide the most expensive cards in the set.

		NM	EX	VG
Complete Set (720):		2,400	1,200	725.00
Common Player (1-546):		1.50	.75	.45
Common Player (547-633):		4.00	2.00	1.00
Common Player (634-720):		8.00	4.00	2.25
1	World Champions (Mets Team)	25.00	12.50	7.50
2	Diego Segui	1.50	.75	.45
3	Darrel Chaney	1.50	.75	.45
4	Tom Egan	1.50	.75	.45
5	Wes Parker	1.50	.75	.45
6	Grant Jackson	1.50	.75	.45
7	Indians Rookies **(Gary Boyd, Russ Nagelson)**	1.50	.75	.45
8	Jose Martinez	1.50	.75	.45
9	1st Series Check List (1-132)	8.00	4.00	2.50
10	Carl Yastrzemski	25.00	12.50	7.50
11	Nate Colbert	1.50	.75	.45
12	John Hiller	1.50	.75	.45
13	Jack Hiatt	1.50	.75	.45
14	Hank Allen	1.50	.75	.45
15	Larry Dierker	1.50	.75	.45
16	Charlie Metro	1.50	.75	.45
17	Hoyt Wilhelm	6.00	3.00	1.75
18	Carlos May	1.50	.75	.45
19	John Boccabella	1.50	.75	.45
20	Dave McNally	1.50	.75	.45
21	Athletics Rookies ***(Vida Blue, Gene Tenace)***	8.00	4.00	2.50
22	Ray Washburn	1.50	.75	.45
23	Bill Robinson	1.50	.75	.45
24	Dick Selma	1.50	.75	.45
25	Cesar Tovar	1.50	.75	.45
26	Tug McGraw	1.50	.75	.45
27	Chuck Hinton	1.50	.75	.45
28	Billy Wilson	1.50	.75	.45
29	Sandy Alomar	1.50	.75	.45
30	Matty Alou	1.50	.75	.45
31	Marty Pattin	1.50	.75	.45
32	Harry Walker	1.50	.75	.45
33	Don Wert	1.50	.75	.45
34	Willie Crawford	1.50	.75	.45
35	Joe Horlen	1.50	.75	.45
36	Reds Rookies ***(Danny Breeden, Bernie Carbo)***	1.50	.75	.45
37	Dick Drago	1.50	.75	.45
38	Mack Jones	1.50	.75	.45
39	Mike Nagy	1.50	.75	.45
40	Rich Allen	3.00	1.50	.90
41	George Lauzerique	1.50	.75	.45
42	Tito Fuentes	1.50	.75	.45
43	Jack Aker	1.50	.75	.45
44	Roberto Pena	1.50	.75	.45
45	Dave Johnson	1.50	.75	.45
46	Ken Rudolph	1.50	.75	.45
47	Bob Miller	1.50	.75	.45
48	Gill Garrido (Gil)	1.50	.75	.45
49	Tim Cullen	1.50	.75	.45
50	Tommie Agee	1.50	.75	.45
51	Bob Christian	1.50	.75	.45
52	Bruce Dal Canton	1.50	.75	.45
53	John Kennedy	1.50	.75	.45
54	Jeff Torborg	1.50	.75	.45
55	John Odom	1.50	.75	.45
56	Phillies Rookies **(Joe Lis, Scott Reid)**	1.50	.75	.45
57	Pat Kelly	1.50	.75	.45
58	Dave Marshall	1.50	.75	.45
59	Dick Ellsworth	1.50	.75	.45
60	Jim Wynn	1.50	.75	.45
61	N.L. Batting Leaders (Roberto Clemente, Cleon Jones, Pete Rose)	20.00	10.00	6.00
62	A.L. Batting Leaders (Rod Carew, Tony Oliva, Reggie Smith)	6.00	3.00	1.75
63	N.L. RBI Leaders (Willie McCovey, Tony Perez, Ron Santo)	5.00	2.50	1.50
64	A.L. RBI Leaders (Reggie Jackson, Harmon Killebrew, Boog Powell)	10.00	5.00	3.00
65	N.L. Home Run Leaders (Hank Aaron, Lee May, Willie McCovey)	10.00	5.00	3.00
66	A.L. Home Run Leaders (Frank Howard, Reggie Jackson, Harmon Killebrew)	8.00	4.00	2.50
67	N.L. ERA Leaders (Steve Carlton, Bob Gibson, Juan Marichal)	8.00	4.00	2.50
68	A.L. ERA Leaders (Dick Bosman, Mike Cuellar, Jim Palmer)	4.00	2.00	1.25
69	N.L. Pitching Leaders (Fergie Jenkins, Juan Marichal, Phil Niekro, Tom Seaver)	10.00	5.00	3.00
70	A.L. Pitching Leaders (Dave Boswell, Mike Cuellar, Dennis McLain, Dave McNally, Jim Perry, Mel Stottlemyre)	4.00	2.00	1.25
71	N.L. Strikeout Leaders (Bob Gibson, Fergie Jenkins, Bill Singer)	6.00	3.00	1.75
72	A.L. Strikeout Leaders (Mickey Lolich, Sam McDowell, Andy Messersmith)	4.00	2.00	1.25
73	Wayne Granger	1.50	.75	.45
74	Angels Rookies **(Greg Washburn, Wally Wolf)**	1.50	.75	.45
75	Jim Kaat	1.50	.75	.45
76	Carl Taylor	1.50	.75	.45
77	Frank Linzy	1.50	.75	.45
78	Joe Lahoud	1.50	.75	.45
79	Clay Kirby	1.50	.75	.45
80	Don Kessinger	1.50	.75	.45
81	Dave May	1.50	.75	.45
82	Frank Fernandez	1.50	.75	.45
83	Don Cardwell	1.50	.75	.45
84	Paul Casanova	1.50	.75	.45
85	Max Alvis	1.50	.75	.45
86	Lum Harris	1.50	.75	.45
87	Steve Renko	1.50	.75	.45
88	Pilots Rookies **(Dick Baney, Miguel Fuentes)**	1.50	.75	.45
89	Juan Rios	1.50	.75	.45
90	Tim McCarver	3.00	1.50	.90
91	Rich Morales	1.50	.75	.45
92	George Culver	1.50	.75	.45
93	Rick Renick	1.50	.75	.45
94	Fred Patek	1.50	.75	.45
95	Earl Wilson	1.50	.75	.45
96	Cards Rookies ***(Leron Lee, Jerry Reuss)***	3.00	1.50	.90
97	Joe Moeller	1.50	.75	.45
98	Gates Brown	1.50	.75	.45
99	Bobby Pfeil	1.50	.75	.45
100	Mel Stottlemyre	1.50	.75	.45
101	Bobby Floyd	1.50	.75	.45
102	Joe Rudi	1.50	.75	.45
103	Frank Reberger	1.50	.75	.45
104	Gerry Moses	1.50	.75	.45
105	Tony Gonzalez	1.50	.75	.45
106	Darold Knowles	1.50	.75	.45
107	Bobby Etheridge	1.50	.75	.45
108	Tom Burgmeier	1.50	.75	.45
109	Expos Rookies **(Garry Jestadt, Carl Morton)**	1.50	.75	.45
110	Bob Moose	1.50	.75	.45
111	Mike Hegan	1.50	.75	.45
112	Dave Nelson	1.50	.75	.45
113	Jim Ray	1.50	.75	.45
114	Gene Michael	1.50	.75	.45
115	Alex Johnson	1.50	.75	.45
116	Sparky Lyle	1.50	.75	.45
117	Don Young	1.50	.75	.45
118	George Mitterwald	1.50	.75	.45
119	Chuck Taylor	1.50	.75	.45
120	Sal Bando	1.50	.75	.45
121	Orioles Rookies ***(Fred Beene, Terry Crowley)***	1.50	.75	.45
122	George Stone	1.50	.75	.45
123	Don Gutteridge	1.50	.75	.45
124	Larry Jaster	1.50	.75	.45
125	Deron Johnson	1.50	.75	.45
126	Marty Martinez	1.50	.75	.45
127	Joe Coleman	1.50	.75	.45
128a	2nd Series Check List (133-263) (226 is R Perranoski)	5.00	2.50	1.50
128b	2nd Series Check List (133-263) (226 is R. Perranoski)	5.00	2.50	1.50
129	Jimmie Price	1.50	.75	.45
130	Ollie Brown	1.50	.75	.45
131	Dodgers Rookies **(Ray Lamb, Bob Stinson)**	1.50	.75	.45
132	Jim McGlothlin	1.50	.75	.45
133	Clay Carroll	1.50	.75	.45
134	Danny Walton	1.50	.75	.45
135	Dick Dietz	1.50	.75	.45
136	Steve Hargan	1.50	.75	.45
137	Art Shamsky	1.50	.75	.45
138	Joe Foy	1.50	.75	.45
139	Rich Nye	1.50	.75	.45
140	Reggie Jackson	40.00	20.00	12.00
141	Pirates Rookies **(Dave Cash, Johnny Jeter)**	1.50	.75	.45
142	Fritz Peterson	1.50	.75	.45
143	Phil Gagliano	1.50	.75	.45
144	Ray Culp	1.50	.75	.45
145	Rico Carty	1.50	.75	.45
146	Danny Murphy	1.50	.75	.45
147	Angel Hermoso	1.50	.75	.45
148	Earl Weaver	4.00	2.00	1.25
149	Billy Champion	1.50	.75	.45
150	Harmon Killebrew	10.00	5.00	3.00
151	Dave Roberts	1.50	.75	.45
152	Ike Brown	1.50	.75	.45
153	Gary Gentry	1.50	.75	.45
154	Senators Rookies **(Jan Dukes, Jim Miles)**	1.50	.75	.45
155	Denis Menke	1.50	.75	.45
156	Eddie Fisher	1.50	.75	.45
157	Manny Mota	1.50	.75	.45
158	Jerry McNertney	1.50	.75	.45
159	Tommy Helms	1.50	.75	.45
160	Phil Niekro	6.00	3.00	1.75
161	Richie Scheinblum	1.50	.75	.45
162	Jerry Johnson	1.50	.75	.45
163	Syd O'Brien	1.50	.75	.45
164	Ty Cline	1.50	.75	.45
165	Ed Kirkpatrick	1.50	.75	.45
166	Al Oliver	2.00	1.00	.60
167	Bill Burbach	1.50	.75	.45
168	Dave Watkins	1.50	.75	.45
169	Tom Hall	1.50	.75	.45
170	Billy Williams	8.00	4.00	2.50
171	Jim Nash	1.50	.75	.45
172	Braves Rookies **(Ralph Garr, Garry Hill)**	2.00	1.00	.60
173	Jim Hicks	1.50	.75	.45
174	Ted Sizemore	1.50	.75	.45
175	Dick Bosman	1.50	.75	.45
176	Jim Hart	1.50	.75	.45
177	Jim Northrup	1.50	.75	.45
178	Denny Lemaster	1.50	.75	.45
179	Ivan Murrell	1.50	.75	.45
180	Tommy John	2.00	1.00	.60
181	Sparky Anderson	6.00	3.00	1.75
182	Dick Hall	1.50	.75	.45
183	Jerry Grote	1.50	.75	.45
184	Ray Fosse	1.50	.75	.45
185	Don Mincher	1.50	.75	.45
186	Rick Joseph	1.50	.75	.45
187	Mike Hedlund	1.50	.75	.45
188	Manny Sanguillen	1.50	.75	.45
189	Yankees Rookies ***(Dave McDonald, Thurman Munson)***	75.00	37.00	22.00
190	Joe Torre	6.00	3.00	1.75
191	Vicente Romo	1.50	.75	.45
192	Jim Qualls	1.50	.75	.45
193	Mike Wegener	1.50	.75	.45
194	Chuck Manuel	1.50	.75	.45
195	N.L.C.S. Game 1 (Seaver Wins Opener!)	10.00	5.00	3.00
196	N.L.C.S. Game 2 (Mets Show Muscle!)	6.00	3.00	1.75
197	N.L.C.S. Game 3 (Ryan Saves the Day!)	20.00	10.00	6.00
198	Mets Celebrate (We're Number One!)(Nolan Ryan)	15.00	7.50	4.50
199	A.L.C.S. Game 1 (Orioles Win A Squeeker!)	4.00	2.00	1.25
200	A.L.C.S. Game 2 (Powell Scores Winning Run!)	4.00	2.00	1.25
201	A.L.C.S. Game 3 (Birds Wrap It Up!)	3.00	1.50	.90
202	Oriole Celebrate (Sweep Twins In Three!)	3.00	1.50	.90
203	Rudy May	1.50	.75	.45
204	Len Gabrielson	1.50	.75	.45
205	Bert Campaneris	1.50	.75	.45
206	Clete Boyer	1.50	.75	.45
207	Tigers Rookies **(Norman McRae, Bob Reed)**	1.50	.75	.45
208	Fred Gladding	1.50	.75	.45
209	Ken Suarez	1.50	.75	.45
210	Juan Marichal	6.00	3.00	1.75
211	Ted Williams	15.00	7.50	4.50
212	Al Santorini	1.50	.75	.45
213	Andy Etchebarren	1.50	.75	.45
214	Ken Boswell	1.50	.75	.45
215	Reggie Smith	1.50	.75	.45

216 Chuck Hartenstein 1.50 .75 .45
217 Ron Hansen 1.50 .75 .45
218 Ron Stone 1.50 .75 .45
219 Jerry Kenney 1.50 .75 .45
220 Steve Carlton 10.00 5.00 3.00
221 Ron Brand 1.50 .75 .45
222 Jim Rooker 1.50 .75 .45
223 Nate Oliver 1.50 .75 .45
224 Steve Barber 1.50 .75 .45
225 Lee May 1.50 .75 .45
226 Ron Perranoski 1.50 .75 .45
227 Astros Rookies **(John Mayberry, Bob Watkins)** 1.50 .75 .45
228 Aurelio Rodriguez 1.50 .75 .45
229 Rich Robertson 1.50 .75 .45
230 Brooks Robinson 20.00 10.00 6.00
231 Luis Tiant 1.50 .75 .45
232 Bob Didier 1.50 .75 .45
233 Lew Krausse 1.50 .75 .45
234 Tommy Dean 1.50 .75 .45
235 Mike Epstein 1.50 .75 .45
236 Bob Veale 1.50 .75 .45
237 Russ Gibson 1.50 .75 .45
238 Jose Laboy 1.50 .75 .45
239 Ken Berry 1.50 .75 .45
240 Fergie Jenkins 6.00 3.00 1.75
241 Royals Rookies **(Al Fitzmorris, Scott Northey)** 1.50 .75 .45
242 Walter Alston 4.00 2.00 1.25
243 Joe Sparma 1.50 .75 .45
244a 3rd Series Check List (264-372) (Red bat on front.) 6.00 3.00 1.75
244b 3rd Series Check List (264-372) (Brown bat on front.) 6.00 3.00 1.75
245 Leo Cardenas 1.50 .75 .45
246 Jim McAndrew 1.50 .75 .45
247 Lou Klimchock 1.50 .75 .45
248 Jesus Alou 1.50 .75 .45
249 Bob Locker 1.50 .75 .45
250 Willie McCovey 10.00 5.00 3.00
251 Dick Schofield 1.50 .75 .45
252 Lowell Palmer 1.50 .75 .45
253 Ron Woods 1.50 .75 .45
254 Camilo Pascual 1.50 .75 .45
255 ***Jim Spencer*** 1.50 .75 .45
256 Vic Davalillo 1.50 .75 .45
257 Dennis Higgins 1.50 .75 .45
258 Paul Popovich 1.50 .75 .45
259 Tommie Reynolds 1.50 .75 .45
260 Claude Osteen 1.50 .75 .45
261 Curt Motton 1.50 .75 .45
262 Padres Rookies **(Jerry Morales, Jim Williams)** 1.50 .75 .45
263 Duane Josephson 1.50 .75 .45
264 Rich Hebner 1.50 .75 .45
265 Randy Hundley 1.50 .75 .45
266 Wally Bunker 1.50 .75 .45
267 Twins Rookies **(Herman Hill, Paul Ratliff)** 1.50 .75 .45
268 Claude Raymond 1.50 .75 .45
269 Cesar Gutierrez 1.50 .75 .45
270 Chris Short 1.50 .75 .45
271 Greg Goossen 1.50 .75 .45
272 Hector Torres 1.50 .75 .45
273 Ralph Houk 4.00 2.00 1.25
274 Gerry Arrigo 1.50 .75 .45
275 Duke Sims 1.50 .75 .45
276 Ron Hunt 1.50 .75 .45
277 Paul Doyle 1.50 .75 .45
278 Tommie Aaron 1.50 .75 .45
279 ***Bill Lee*** 1.50 .75 .45
280 Donn Clendenon 1.50 .75 .45
281 Casey Cox 1.50 .75 .45
282 Steve Huntz 1.50 .75 .45
283 Angel Bravo 1.50 .75 .45
284 Jack Baldschun 1.50 .75 .45
285 Paul Blair 1.50 .75 .45
286 Dodgers Rookies **(Bill Buckner, Jack Jenkins)** 6.00 3.00 1.75
287 Fred Talbot 1.50 .75 .45
288 Larry Hisle 1.50 .75 .45
289 Gene Brabender 1.50 .75 .45
290 Rod Carew 10.00 5.00 3.00
291 Leo Durocher 4.00 2.00 1.25
292 Eddie Leon 1.50 .75 .45
293 Bob Bailey 1.50 .75 .45
294 Jose Azcue 1.50 .75 .45
295 Cecil Upshaw 1.50 .75 .45
296 Woody Woodward 1.50 .75 .45
297 Curt Blefary 1.50 .75 .45
298 Ken Henderson 1.50 .75 .45
299 Buddy Bradford 1.50 .75 .45
300 Tom Seaver 25.00 12.50 7.50
301 Chico Salmon 1.50 .75 .45
302 Jeff James 1.50 .75 .45
303 Brant Alyea 1.50 .75 .45
304 ***Bill Russell*** 4.00 2.00 1.25
305 World Series Game 1 (Buford Belts Leadoff Homer!) 4.00 2.00 1.25
306 World Series Game 2 (Clendenon's HR Breaks Ice!) 4.00 2.00 1.25
307 World Series Game 3 (Agee's Catch Saves The Day!) 4.00 2.00 1.25
308 World Series Game 4 (Martin's Bunt Ends Deadlock!) 4.00 2.00 1.25
309 World Series Game 5 (Koosman Shuts The Door!) 4.00 2.00 1.25
310 World Series Celebration (Mets Whoop It Up!) 8.00 4.00 2.50
311 Dick Green 1.50 .75 .45
312 Mike Torrez 1.50 .75 .45
313 Mayo Smith 1.50 .75 .45
314 Bill McCool 1.50 .75 .45
315 Luis Aparicio 8.00 4.00 2.50
316 Skip Guinn 1.50 .75 .45
317 Red Sox Rookies **(Luis Alvarado, Billy Conigliaro)** 1.50 .75 .45
318 Willie Smith 1.50 .75 .45
319 Clayton Dalrymple 1.50 .75 .45
320 Jim Maloney 1.50 .75 .45
321 Lou Piniella 3.00 1.50 .90
322 Luke Walker 1.50 .75 .45
323 Wayne Comer 1.50 .75 .45
324 Tony Taylor 1.50 .75 .45
325 Dave Boswell 1.50 .75 .45
326 Bill Voss 1.50 .75 .45
327 Hal King 1.50 .75 .45
328 George Brunet 1.50 .75 .45
329 Chris Cannizzaro 1.50 .75 .45
330 Lou Brock 10.00 5.00 3.00
331 Chuck Dobson 1.50 .75 .45
332 Bobby Wine 1.50 .75 .45
333 Bobby Murcer 3.00 1.50 .90
334 Phil Regan 1.50 .75 .45
335 Bill Freehan 1.50 .75 .45
336 Del Unser 1.50 .75 .45
337 Mike McCormick 1.50 .75 .45
338 Paul Schaal 1.50 .75 .45
339 Johnny Edwards 1.50 .75 .45
340 Tony Conigliaro 4.00 2.00 1.25
341 Bill Sudakis 1.50 .75 .45
342 Wilbur Wood 1.50 .75 .45
343a 4th Series Check List (373-459) (Red bat on front.) 5.00 2.50 1.50
343b 4th Series Check List (373-459) (Brown bat on front.) 5.00 2.50 1.50
344 Marcelino Lopez 1.50 .75 .45
345 Al Ferrara 1.50 .75 .45
346 Red Schoendienst 4.00 2.00 1.25
347 Russ Snyder 1.50 .75 .45
348 Mets Rookies **(Jesse Hudson, Mike Jorgensen)** 1.50 .75 .45
349 Steve Hamilton 1.50 .75 .45
350 Roberto Clemente 50.00 25.00 15.00
351 Tom Murphy 1.50 .75 .45
352 Bob Barton 1.50 .75 .45
353 Stan Williams 1.50 .75 .45
354 Amos Otis 1.50 .75 .45
355 Doug Rader 1.50 .75 .45
356 Fred Lasher 1.50 .75 .45
357 Bob Burda 1.50 .75 .45
358 ***Pedro Borbon*** 1.50 .75 .45
359 Phil Roof 1.50 .75 .45
360 Curt Flood 2.00 1.00 .60
361 Ray Jarvis 1.50 .75 .45
362 Joe Hague 1.50 .75 .45
363 Tom Shopay 1.50 .75 .45
364 Dan McGinn 1.50 .75 .45
365 Zoilo Versalles 1.50 .75 .45
366 Barry Moore 1.50 .75 .45
367 Mike Lum 1.50 .75 .45
368 Ed Herrmann 1.50 .75 .45
369 Alan Foster 1.50 .75 .45
370 Tommy Harper 1.50 .75 .45
371 Rod Gaspar 1.50 .75 .45
372 Dave Giusti 1.50 .75 .45
373 Roy White 2.50 1.25 .75
374 Tommie Sisk 1.50 .75 .45
375 Johnny Callison 1.50 .75 .45
376 Lefty Phillips 1.50 .75 .45
377 Bill Butler 1.50 .75 .45
378 Jim Davenport 1.50 .75 .45
379 Tom Tischinski 1.50 .75 .45
380 Tony Perez 8.00 4.00 2.50
381 Athletics Rookies **(Bobby Brooks, Mike Olivo)** 1.50 .75 .45
382 Jack DiLauro 1.50 .75 .45
383 Mickey Stanley 1.50 .75 .45
384 Gary Neibauer 1.50 .75 .45
385 George Scott 1.50 .75 .45
386 Bill Dillman 1.50 .75 .45
387 Baltimore Orioles Team 3.00 1.50 .90
388 Byron Browne 1.50 .75 .45
389 Jim Shellenback 1.50 .75 .45
390 Willie Davis 1.50 .75 .45
391 Larry Brown 1.50 .75 .45
392 Walt Hriniak 1.50 .75 .45
393 John Gelnar 1.50 .75 .45
394 Gil Hodges 6.00 3.00 1.75
395 Walt Williams 1.50 .75 .45
396 Steve Blass 1.50 .75 .45
397 Roger Repoz 1.50 .75 .45
398 Bill Stoneman 1.50 .75 .45
399 New York Yankees Team 8.00 4.00 2.50
400 Denny McLain 1.50 .70 .45
401 Giants Rookies **(John Harrell, Bernie Williams)** 1.50 .75 .45
402 Ellie Rodriguez 1.50 .75 .45
403 Jim Bunning 6.00 3.00 1.75
404 Rich Reese 1.50 .75 .45
405 Bill Hands 1.50 .75 .45
406 Mike Andrews 1.50 .75 .45
407 Bob Watson 1.50 .75 .45
408 Paul Lindblad 1.50 .75 .45
409 Bob Tolan 1.50 .75 .45
410 Boog Powell 5.00 2.50 1.50
411 Los Angeles Dodgers Team 6.00 3.00 1.75
412 Larry Burchart 1.50 .75 .45
413 Sonny Jackson 1.50 .75 .45
414 Paul Edmondson 1.50 .75 .45
415 Julian Javier 1.50 .75 .45
416 Joe Verbanic 1.50 .75 .45
417 John Bateman 1.50 .75 .45
418 John Donaldson 1.50 .75 .45
419 Ron Taylor 1.50 .75 .45
420 Ken McMullen 1.50 .75 .45
421 Pat Dobson 1.50 .75 .45
422 Kansas City Royals Team 3.00 1.50 .90
423 Jerry May 1.50 .75 .45
424 Mike Kilkenny 1.50 .75 .45
425 Bobby Bonds 3.00 1.50 .90
426 Bill Rigney 1.50 .75 .45
427 Fred Norman 1.50 .75 .45
428 Don Buford 1.50 .75 .45
429 Cubs Rookies **(Randy Bobb, Jim Cosman)** 1.50 .75 .45
430 A. Messersmith 1.50 .75 .45
431 Ron Swoboda 1.50 .75 .45
432a 5th Series Check List (460-546) ("Baseball" on front in yellow.) 4.00 2.00 1.25
432b 5th Series Check List (460-546) ("Baseball" on front in white.) 4.00 2.00 1.25
433 Ron Bryant 1.50 .75 .45
434 Felipe Alou 2.50 1.25 .75
435 Nelson Briles 1.50 .75 .45
436 Philadelphia Phillies Team 3.00 1.50 .90
437 Danny Cater 1.50 .75 .45
438 Pat Jarvis 1.50 .75 .45
439 Lee Maye 1.50 .75 .45
440 Bill Mazeroski 8.00 4.00 2.50
441 John O'Donoghue 1.50 .75 .45
442 Gene Mauch 1.50 .75 .45
443 Al Jackson 1.50 .75 .45
444 White Sox Rookies **(Bill Farmer, John Matias)** 1.50 .75 .45
445 Vada Pinson 2.00 1.00 .60
446 ***Billy Grabarkewitz*** 1.50 .75 .45
447 Lee Stange 1.50 .75 .45
448 Houston Astros Team 3.00 1.50 .90
449 Jim Palmer 8.00 4.00 2.50
450 Willie McCovey/AS 6.00 3.00 1.75
451 Boog Powell/AS 2.00 1.00 .60
452 Felix Millan/AS 1.50 .75 .45
453 Rod Carew/AS 6.00 3.00 1.75
454 Ron Santo/AS 3.00 1.50 .90
455 Brooks Robinson/AS 6.00 3.00 1.75
456 Don Kessinger/AS 1.50 .75 .45
457 Rico Petrocelli/AS 1.50 .75 .45
458 Pete Rose/AS 20.00 10.00 6.00
459 Reggie Jackson/AS 10.00 5.00 3.00
460 Matty Alou/AS 1.50 .75 .45
461 Carl Yastrzemski/AS 10.00 5.00 3.00
462 Hank Aaron/AS 25.00 12.50 7.50
463 Frank Robinson/AS 8.00 4.00 2.50
464 Johnny Bench/AS 10.00 5.00 3.00
465 Bill Freehan/AS 1.50 .75 .45
466 Juan Marichal/AS 6.00 3.00 1.75
467 Denny McLain/AS 1.50 .70 .45
468 Jerry Koosman/AS 1.50 .75 .45
469 Sam McDowell/AS 1.50 .75 .45
470 Willie Stargell 10.00 5.00 3.00
471 Chris Zachary 1.50 .75 .45
472 Atlanta Braves Team 3.00 1.50 .90
473 Don Bryant 1.50 .75 .45
474 Dick Kelley 1.50 .75 .45
475 Dick McAuliffe 1.50 .75 .45
476 Don Shaw 1.50 .75 .45
477 Orioles Rookies **(Roger Freed, Al Severinsen)** 1.50 .75 .45
478 Bob Heise 1.50 .75 .45
479 Dick Woodson 1.50 .75 .45
480 Glenn Beckert 1.50 .75 .45
481 Jose Tartabull 1.50 .75 .45
482 Tom Hilgendorf 1.50 .75 .45
483 Gail Hopkins 1.50 .75 .45
484 Gary Nolan 1.50 .75 .45
485 Jay Johnstone 1.50 .75 .45
486 Terry Harmon 1.50 .75 .45
487 Cisco Carlos 1.50 .75 .45
488 J.C. Martin 1.50 .75 .45
489 Eddie Kasko 1.50 .75 .45
490 Bill Singer 1.50 .75 .45
491 Graig Nettles 3.00 2.00 .90
492 Astros Rookies **(Keith Lampard, Scipio Spinks)** 1.50 .75 .45
493 Lindy McDaniel 1.50 .75 .45
494 Larry Stahl 1.50 .75 .45
495 Dave Morehead 1.50 .75 .45
496 Steve Whitaker 1.50 .75 .45
497 Eddie Watt 1.50 .75 .45
498 Al Weis 1.50 .75 .45
499 Skip Lockwood 1.50 .75 .45
500 Hank Aaron 40.00 20.00 12.00
501 Chicago White Sox Team 3.00 1.50 .90
502 Rollie Fingers 8.00 4.00 2.50
503 Dal Maxvill 1.50 .75 .45
504 Don Pavletich 1.50 .75 .45
505 Ken Holtzman 1.50 .75 .45
506 Ed Stroud 1.50 .75 .45
507 Pat Corrales 1.50 .75 .45
508 Joe Niekro 1.50 .75 .45
509 Montreal Expos Team 3.00 1.50 .90
510 Tony Oliva 3.50 1.75 1.00
511 Joe Hoerner 1.50 .75 .45
512 Billy Harris 1.50 .75 .45
513 Preston Gomez 1.50 .75 .45
514 Steve Hovley 1.50 .75 .45
515 Don Wilson 1.50 .75 .45
516 Yankees Rookies **(John Ellis, Jim Lyttle)** 1.50 .75 .45
517 Joe Gibbon 1.50 .75 .45
518 Bill Melton 1.50 .75 .45
519 Don McMahon 1.50 .75 .45
520 Willie Horton 1.50 .75 .45
521 Cal Koonce 1.50 .75 .45
522 California Angels Team 3.00 1.50 .90
523 Jose Pena 1.50 .75 .45
524 Alvin Dark 1.50 .75 .45
525 Jerry Adair 1.50 .75 .45
526 Ron Herbel 1.50 .75 .45
527 Don Bosch 1.50 .75 .45
528 Elrod Hendricks 1.50 .75 .45
529 Bob Aspromonte 1.50 .75 .45
530 Bob Gibson 12.00 6.00 3.50
531 Ron Clark 1.50 .75 .45
532 Danny Murtaugh 1.50 .75 .45
533 Buzz Stephen 1.50 .75 .45
534 Minnesota Twins Team 3.00 1.50 .90
535 Andy Kosco 1.50 .75 .45

536	Mike Kekich	1.50	.75	.45
537	Joe Morgan	10.00	5.00	3.00
538	Bob Humphreys	1.50	.75	.45
539	Phillies Rookies **(Larry Bowa, Dennis Doyle)**	6.00	3.00	1.75
540	Gary Peters	1.50	.75	.45
541	Bill Heath	1.50	.75	.45
542a	6th Series Check List (547-633) (Gray bat on front.)	5.00	2.50	1.50
542b	6th Series Check List (547-633) (Brown bat on front.)	5.00	2.50	1.50
543	Clyde Wright	1.50	.75	.45
544	Cincinnati Reds Team	5.00	2.50	1.50
545	Ken Harrelson	1.50	.75	.45
546	Ron Reed	1.50	.75	.45
547	Rick Monday	4.00	2.00	1.25
548	Howie Reed	3.00	1.50	.90
549	St. Louis Cardinals Team	6.00	3.00	1.75
550	Frank Howard	5.00	2.50	1.50
551	Dock Ellis	4.00	2.00	1.25
552	Royals Rookies **(Don O'Riley, Dennis Paepke, Fred Rico)**	4.00	2.00	1.25
553	Jim Lefebvre	4.00	2.00	1.25
554	Tom Timmermann	4.00	2.00	1.25
555	Orlando Cepeda	12.00	6.00	3.50
556	Dave Bristol	4.00	2.00	1.25
557	Ed Kranepool	4.00	2.00	1.25
558	Vern Fuller	4.00	2.00	1.25
559	Tommy Davis	4.00	2.00	1.25
560	Gaylord Perry	8.00	4.00	2.50
561	Tom McCraw	4.00	2.00	1.25
562	Ted Abernathy	4.00	2.00	1.25
563	Boston Red Sox Team	8.00	4.00	2.50
564	Johnny Briggs	4.00	2.00	1.25
565	Jim Hunter	8.00	4.00	2.50
566	Gene Alley	4.00	2.00	1.25
567	Bob Oliver	4.00	2.00	1.25
568	Stan Bahnsen	4.00	2.00	1.25
569	Cookie Rojas	4.00	2.00	1.25
570	Jim Fregosi	5.00	2.50	1.50
571	Jim Brewer	4.00	2.00	1.25
572	Frank Quilici	4.00	2.00	1.25
573	Padres Rookies **(Mike Corkins, Rafael Robles, Ron Slocum)**	4.00	2.00	1.25
574	Bobby Bolin	4.00	2.00	1.25
575	Cleon Jones	4.00	2.00	1.25
576	Milt Pappas	4.00	2.00	1.25
577	Bernie Allen	4.00	2.00	1.25
578	Tom Griffin	4.00	2.00	1.25
579	Detroit Tigers Team	8.00	4.00	2.50
580	Pete Rose	50.00	25.00	15.00
581	Tom Satriano	4.00	2.00	1.25
582	Mike Paul	4.00	2.00	1.25
583	Hal Lanier	4.00	2.00	1.25
584	Al Downing	5.00	2.50	1.50
585	Rusty Staub	6.00	3.00	1.75
586	Rickey Clark	4.00	2.00	1.25
587	Jose Arcia	4.00	2.00	1.25
588a	7th Series Check List (634-720) (666 is Adolpho Phillips)	6.00	3.00	1.75
588b	7th Series Check List (634-720) (666 is Adolfo Phillips)	6.00	3.00	1.75
589	Joe Keough	4.00	2.00	1.25
590	Mike Cuellar	4.00	2.00	1.25
591	Mike Ryan	4.00	2.00	1.25
592	Daryl Patterson	4.00	2.00	1.25
593	Chicago Cubs Team	8.00	4.00	2.50
594	Jake Gibbs	4.00	2.00	1.25
595	Maury Wills	4.00	2.00	1.25
596	Mike Hershberger	4.00	2.00	1.25
597	Sonny Siebert	4.00	2.00	1.25
598	Joe Pepitone	5.00	2.50	1.50
599	Senators Rookies **(Gene Martin, Dick Stelmaszek, Dick Such)**	4.00	2.00	1.25
600	Willie Mays	60.00	30.00	18.00
601	Pete Richert	4.00	2.00	1.25
602	Ted Savage	4.00	2.00	1.25
603	Ray Oyler	4.00	2.00	1.25
604	Clarence Gaston	6.00	3.00	1.75
605	Rick Wise	4.00	2.00	1.25
606	Chico Ruiz	4.00	2.00	1.25
607	Gary Waslewski	4.00	2.00	1.25
608	Pittsburgh Pirates Team	8.00	4.00	2.50
609	***Buck Martinez***	6.00	3.00	1.75
610	Jerry Koosman	6.00	3.00	1.75
611	Norm Cash	6.00	3.00	1.75
612	Jim Hickman	4.00	2.00	1.25
613	Dave Baldwin	4.00	2.00	1.25
614	Mike Shannon	4.00	2.00	1.25
615	Mark Belanger	4.00	2.00	1.25
616	Jim Merritt	4.00	2.00	1.25
617	Jim French	4.00	2.00	1.25
618	Billy Wynne	4.00	2.00	1.25
619	Norm Miller	4.00	2.00	1.25
620	Jim Perry	4.00	2.00	1.25
621	Braves Rookies **(Darrell Evans, Rick Kester, Mike McQueen)**	10.00	5.00	3.00
622	Don Sutton	8.00	4.00	2.50
623	Horace Clarke	4.00	2.00	1.25
624	Clyde King	4.00	2.00	1.25
625	Dean Chance	4.00	2.00	1.25
626	Dave Ricketts	4.00	2.00	1.25
627	Gary Wagner	4.00	2.00	1.25
628	Wayne Garrett	4.00	2.00	1.25
629	Merv Rettenmund	4.00	2.00	1.25
630	Ernie Banks	40.00	20.00	12.00
631	Oakland Athletics Team	8.00	4.00	2.50
632	Gary Sutherland	4.00	2.00	1.25
633	Roger Nelson	4.00	2.00	1.25
634	Bud Harrelson	8.00	4.00	2.50
635	Bob Allison	8.00	4.00	2.50
636	Jim Stewart	8.00	4.00	2.50
637	Cleveland Indians Team	12.00	6.00	3.50
638	Frank Bertaina	8.00	4.00	2.50
639	Dave Campbell	8.00	4.00	2.50
640	Al Kaline	40.00	20.00	12.00
641	Al McBean	8.00	4.00	2.50
642	Angels Rookies **(Greg Garrett, Gordon Lund, Jarvis Tatum)**	8.00	4.00	2.50
643	Jose Pagan	8.00	4.00	2.50
644	Gerry Nyman	8.00	4.00	2.50
645	Don Money	8.00	4.00	2.50
646	Jim Britton	8.00	4.00	2.50
647	Tom Matchick	8.00	4.00	2.50
648	Larry Haney	8.00	4.00	2.50
649	Jimmie Hall	8.00	4.00	2.50
650	Sam McDowell	10.00	5.00	3.00
651	Jim Gosger	8.00	4.00	2.50
652	Rich Rollins	10.00	5.00	3.00
653	Moe Drabowsky	8.00	4.00	2.50
654	N.L. Rookies **(Boots Day, Oscar Gamble, Angel Mangual)**	10.00	5.00	3.00
655	John Roseboro	8.00	4.00	2.50
656	Jim Hardin	8.00	4.00	2.50
657	San Diego Padres Team	15.00	7.50	4.50
658	Ken Tatum	8.00	4.00	2.50
659	Pete Ward	8.00	4.00	2.50
660	Johnny Bench	60.00	30.00	18.00
661	Jerry Robertson	8.00	4.00	2.50
662	Frank Lucchesi	8.00	4.00	2.50
663	Tito Francona	8.00	4.00	2.50
664	Bob Robertson	8.00	4.00	2.50
665	Jim Lonborg	8.00	4.00	2.50
666	Adolfo Phillips	8.00	4.00	2.50
667	Bob Meyer	8.00	4.00	2.50
668	Bob Tillman	8.00	4.00	2.50
669	White Sox Rookies **(Bart Johnson, Dan Lazar, Mickey Scott)**	8.00	4.00	2.50
670	Ron Santo	15.00	7.50	4.50
671	Jim Campanis	10.00	5.00	3.00
672	Leon McFadden	8.00	4.00	2.50
673	Ted Uhlaender	8.00	4.00	2.50
674	Dave Leonhard	8.00	4.00	2.50
675	Jose Cardenal	10.00	5.00	3.00
676	Washington Senators Team	15.00	7.50	4.50
677	Woodie Fryman	8.00	4.00	2.50
678	Dave Duncan	15.00	7.50	4.50
679	Ray Sadecki	8.00	4.00	2.50
680	Rico Petrocelli	10.00	5.00	3.00
681	Bob Garibaldi	8.00	4.00	2.50
682	Dalton Jones	8.00	4.00	2.50
683	Reds Rookies **(Vern Geishert, Hal McRae, Wayne Simpson)**	10.00	5.00	3.00
684	Jack Fisher	8.00	4.00	2.50
685	Tom Haller	8.00	4.00	2.50
686	Jackie Hernandez	8.00	4.00	2.50
687	Bob Priddy	8.00	4.00	2.50
688	Ted Kubiak	8.00	4.00	2.50
689	Frank Tepedino	8.00	4.00	2.50
690	Ron Fairly	8.00	4.00	2.50
691	Joe Grzenda	8.00	4.00	2.50
692	Duffy Dyer	8.00	4.00	2.50
693	Bob Johnson	8.00	4.00	2.50
694	Gary Ross	8.00	4.00	2.50
695	Bobby Knoop	8.00	4.00	2.50
696	San Francisco Giants Team	15.00	7.50	4.50
697	Jim Hannan	8.00	4.00	2.50
698	Tom Tresh	10.00	5.00	3.00
699	Hank Aguirre	8.00	4.00	2.50
700	Frank Robinson	40.00	20.00	12.00
701	Jack Billingham	8.00	4.00	2.50
702	A.L. Rookies **(Bob Johnson, Ron Klimkowski, Bill Zepp)**	8.00	4.00	2.50
703	Lou Marone	8.00	4.00	2.50
704	Frank Baker	8.00	4.00	2.50
705	Tony Cloninger	8.00	4.00	2.50
706	John McNamara	8.00	4.00	2.50
707	Kevin Collins	8.00	4.00	2.50
708	Jose Santiago	8.00	4.00	2.50
709	Mike Fiore	8.00	4.00	2.50
710	Felix Millan	8.00	4.00	2.50
711	Ed Brinkman	8.00	4.00	2.50
712	Nolan Ryan	180.00	90.00	54.00
713	Seattle Pilots Team	20.00	10.00	6.00
714	Al Spangler	8.00	4.00	2.50
715	Mickey Lolich	8.00	4.00	2.50
716	Cards Rookies **(Sal Campisi, Reggie Cleveland, Santiago Guzman)**	10.00	5.00	3.00
717	Tom Phoebus	8.00	4.00	2.50
718	Ed Spiezio	8.00	4.00	2.50
719	Jim Roland	8.00	4.00	2.50
720	Rick Reichardt	12.00	5.00	2.50

1970 Topps Candy Lids

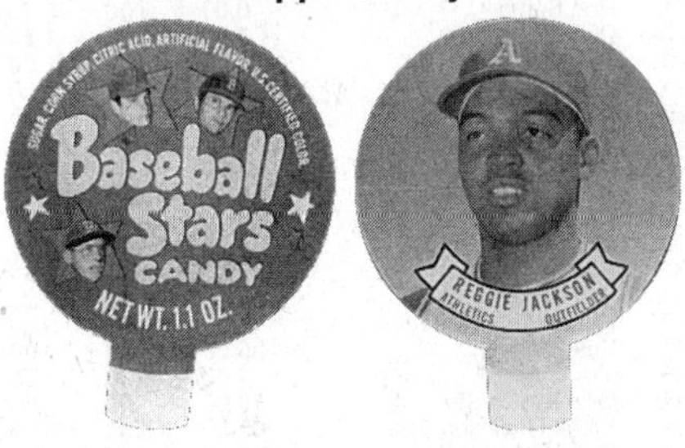

The 1970 Topps Candy Lids are a test issue that was utilized again in 1973. The set is made up of 24 lids that measure 1-7/8" in diameter and were the tops of small 1.1 oz. tubs of "Baseball Stars Candy." Unlike the 1973 versions, the 1970 lids have no border surrounding the full-color photos. Frank Howard, Tom Seaver and Carl Yastrzemski photos are found on the top (outside) of the candy lid.

		NM	EX	VG
Complete Set (24):		2,800	1,400	840.00
Common Player:		40.00	20.00	12.00
(1)	Hank Aaron	350.00	175.00	105.00
(2)	Rich Allen	75.00	37.00	22.00
(3)	Luis Aparicio	140.00	70.00	42.00
(4)	Johnny Bench	225.00	110.00	67.00
(5)	Ollie Brown	40.00	20.00	12.00
(6)	Willie Davis	40.00	20.00	12.00
(7)	Jim Fregosi	40.00	20.00	12.00
(8)	Mike Hegan	40.00	20.00	12.00
(9)	Frank Howard	60.00	30.00	18.00
(10)	Reggie Jackson	275.00	135.00	82.00
(11)	Fergie Jenkins	130.00	65.00	39.00
(12)	Harmon Killebrew	175.00	87.00	52.00
(13)	Juan Marichal	140.00	70.00	42.00
(14)	Bill Mazeroski	140.00	70.00	42.00
(15)	Tim McCarver	60.00	30.00	18.00
(16)	Sam McDowell	40.00	20.00	12.00
(17)	Denny McLain	60.00	30.00	18.00
(18)	Lou Piniella	45.00	22.00	13.50
(19)	Frank Robinson	175.00	87.00	52.00
(20)	Tom Seaver	200.00	100.00	60.00
(21)	Rusty Staub	60.00	30.00	18.00
(22)	Mel Stottlemyre	40.00	20.00	12.00
(23)	Jim Wynn	40.00	20.00	12.00
(24)	Carl Yastrzemski	225.00	110.00	67.00

1970 Topps Cloth Stickers

The earliest and rarest of the Topps cloth sticker test issues, only 15 subjects are known, and only a single specimen apiece is known for many of them. In the same 2-1/2" x 3-1/2" size, and with the same design as the 1970 Topps baseball cards, the stickers are blank-backed. The stickers of Denny Lemaster, Dennis Higgins and Rich Nye use photos that are different from their '70 Topps cards. It is quite likely that the checklist presented here is incomplete. The stickers are unnumbered and are checklisted alphabetically.

		NM	EX	VG
Common Player:		1,750	875.00	525.00
(1)	A.L. Playoff Game 2 (Boog Powell)	1,900	950.00	570.00
(2)	Bill Burbach	1,750	875.00	525.00
(3)	Gary Gentry	1,750	875.00	525.00
(4)	Tom Hall	1,750	875.00	525.00
(5)	Chuck Hartenstein	1,750	875.00	525.00
(6)	Dennis Higgins	1,750	875.00	525.00
(7)	Jose Laboy	1,750	875.00	525.00
(8)	Denny Lemaster	1,750	875.00	525.00
(9)	Juan Marichal	2,200	1,100	660.00
(10)	Jerry McNertney	1,750	875.00	525.00
(11)	Curt Motton	1,750	875.00	525.00
(12)	Ivan Murrell	1,750	875.00	525.00
(13)	N.L. Playoff Game 1 (Tom Seaver)	1,750	875.00	525.00
(14)	N.L. Playoff Game 3 (Nolan Ryan)	3,000	1,500	900.00
(15)	Phil Niekro	2,100	1,050	630.00
(16)	Jim Northrup	1,750	875.00	525.00
(17)	Rich Nye	1,750	875.00	525.00
(18)	Ron Perranoski	1,750	875.00	525.00
(19)	Al Santorini	1,750	875.00	525.00

1970 Topps Posters

Helping to ease a price increase, Topps included extremely fragile 8-11/16" x 9-5/8" posters in packs of regular cards. The posters feature color portraits and a smaller black and white "action" pose as well as the player's name, team and position at the top. Although there are Hall of Famers in the 24-poster set, all the top names are not represented. Folds from original packaging are not considered in grading unless they split the paper.

		NM	EX	VG
Complete Set (24):		60.00	30.00	18.00
Common Player:		3.00	1.50	.90
1	Joe Horlen	3.00	1.50	.90
2	Phil Niekro	6.00	3.00	1.75
3	Willie Davis	3.00	1.50	.90
4	Lou Brock	7.00	3.50	2.00
5	Ron Santo	4.00	2.00	1.25
6	Ken Harrelson	3.00	1.50	.90
7	Willie McCovey	7.00	3.50	2.00
8	Rick Wise	3.00	1.50	.90
9	Andy Messersmith	3.00	1.50	.90
10	Ron Fairly	3.00	1.50	.90
11	Johnny Bench	10.00	5.00	3.00
12	Frank Robinson	10.00	5.00	3.00
13	Tommie Agee	3.00	1.50	.90
14	Roy White	3.00	1.50	.90
15	Larry Dierker	3.00	1.50	.90
16	Rod Carew	9.00	4.50	2.75
17	Don Mincher	3.00	1.50	.90
18	Ollie Brown	3.00	1.50	.90
19	Ed Kirkpatrick	3.00	1.50	.90
20	Reggie Smith	3.00	1.50	.90
21	Roberto Clemente	25.00	12.50	7.50
22	Frank Howard	3.00	1.50	.90
23	Bert Campaneris	3.00	1.50	.90
24	Denny McLain	3.00	1.50	.90

1970 Topps Scratch-Offs

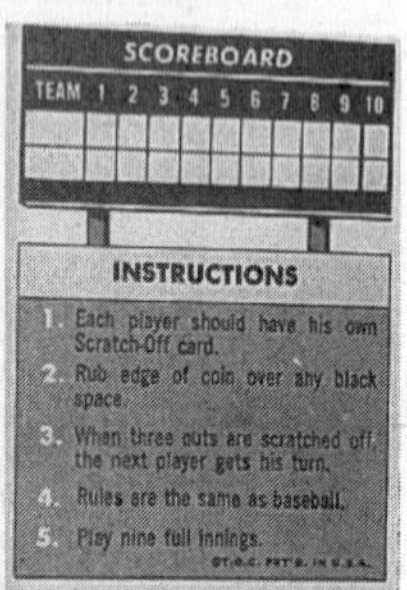

Not having given up on the idea of a game which could be played with baseball cards, Topps provided a new game - the baseball scratch-off - in 1970. Unfolded, cards measure 3-3/8" x 5", and reveal a baseball game played by rubbing the black ink off playing squares to determine the "action." Fronts have a player picture as "captain," while backs have instructions and a scoreboard. Inserts with white centers are from 1970 while those with red centers are from 1971.

		NM	EX	VG
Complete Set (24):		60.00	30.00	18.00
Common Player:		1.50	.75	.45
(1)	Hank Aaron	12.00	6.00	3.50
(2)	Rich Allen	2.50	1.25	.70
(3)	Luis Aparicio	3.50	1.75	1.00
(4)	Sal Bando	1.50	.75	.45
(5)	Glenn Beckert	1.50	.75	.45
(6)	Dick Bosman	1.50	.75	.45
(7)	Nate Colbert	1.50	.75	.45
(8)	Mike Hegan	1.50	.75	.45
(9)	Mack Jones	1.50	.75	.45
(10)	Al Kaline	4.50	2.25	1.25
(11)	Harmon Killebrew	4.50	2.25	1.25
(12)	Juan Marichal	3.50	1.75	1.00
(13)	Tim McCarver	2.50	1.25	.70
(14)	Sam McDowell	1.50	.75	.45
(15)	Claude Osteen	1.50	.75	.45
(16)	Tony Perez	3.50	1.75	1.00
(17)	Lou Piniella	1.50	.75	.45
(18)	Boog Powell	2.50	1.25	.70
(19)	Tom Seaver	4.50	2.25	1.25
(20)	Jim Spencer	1.50	.75	.45
(21)	Willie Stargell	3.50	1.75	1.00
(22)	Mel Stottlemyre	1.50	.75	.45
(23)	Jim Wynn	1.50	.75	.45
(24)	Carl Yastrzemski	6.00	3.00	1.75

1970 Topps Story Booklets

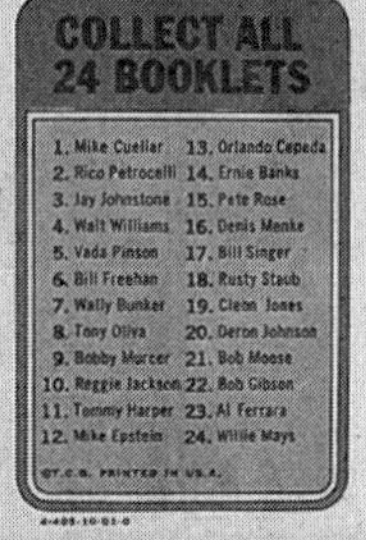

Measuring 2-1/2" x 3-7/16", the Topps Story Booklet was a 1970 regular pack insert. The booklet feature a photo, title and booklet number on the "cover." Inside are six pages of comic book story. The backs give a checklist of other available booklets. Not every star had a booklet as the set is only 24 in number.

		NM	EX	VG
Complete Set (24):		65.00	32.50	20.00
Common Player:		1.50	.75	.45
1	Mike Cuellar	1.50	.75	.45
2	Rico Petrocelli	1.50	.75	.45
3	Jay Johnstone	1.50	.75	.45
4	Walt Williams	1.50	.75	.45
5	Vada Pinson	2.25	1.25	.70
6	Bill Freehan	1.50	.75	.45
7	Wally Bunker	1.50	.75	.45
8	Tony Oliva	2.25	1.25	.70
9	Bobby Murcer	2.00	1.00	.60
10	Reggie Jackson	9.00	4.50	2.75
11	Tommy Harper	1.50	.75	.45
12	Mike Epstein	1.50	.75	.45
13	Orlando Cepeda	4.00	2.00	1.25
14	Ernie Banks	7.00	3.50	2.00
15	Pete Rose	10.00	5.00	3.00
16	Denis Menke	1.50	.75	.45
17	Bill Singer	1.50	.75	.45
18	Rusty Staub	2.00	1.00	.60
19	Cleon Jones	1.50	.75	.45
20	Deron Johnson	1.50	.75	.45
21	Bob Moose	1.50	.75	.45
22	Bob Gibson	5.00	2.50	1.50
23	Al Ferrara	1.50	.75	.45
24	Willie Mays	10.00	5.00	3.00

1970 Topps Super

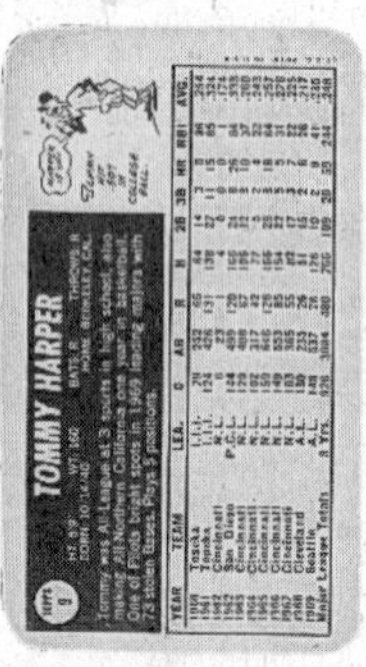

Representing a refinement of the concept begun in 1969, the 1970 Topps Supers had a new 3-1/8" x 5-1/4" size. Printed on thick stock with rounded corners, card fronts feature a borderless color photograph and facsimile autograph. Backs are an enlarged version of the player's regular 1970 Topps card. Probably due to the press sheet configuration, eight of the 42 cards were short-printed. The most elusive is card #38 (Boog Powell). The set was more widely produced than was the case in 1969. Square-cornered proofs, either with blank or printed backs, are known, valued from 1X-2X the regular-card price.

		NM	EX	VG
Complete Set (42):		250.00	125.00	75.00
Common Player:		4.00	2.00	1.25
Unopened Pack:		95.00		
Proofs: 1-2X				
1	Claude Osteen/SP	10.00	5.00	3.00
2	Sal Bando/SP	10.00	5.00	3.00
3	Luis Aparicio	9.00	4.50	2.75
4	Harmon Killebrew	15.00	7.50	4.50
5	Tom Seaver/SP	25.00	12.50	7.50
6	Larry Dierker	4.00	2.00	1.25
7	Bill Freehan	4.00	2.00	1.25
8	Johnny Bench	20.00	10.00	6.00
9	Tommy Harper	4.00	2.00	1.25
10	Sam McDowell	4.00	2.00	1.25
11	Lou Brock	12.00	6.00	3.50
12	Roberto Clemente	40.00	20.00	12.00
13	Willie McCovey	12.00	6.00	3.50
14	Rico Petrocelli	4.00	2.00	1.25
15	Phil Niekro	9.00	4.50	2.75
16	Frank Howard	4.00	2.00	1.25
17	Denny McLain	4.00	2.00	1.25
18	Willie Mays	35.00	17.50	10.00
19	Willie Stargell	12.00	6.00	3.50
20	Joe Horlen	4.00	2.00	1.25
21	Ron Santo	6.00	3.00	1.75
22	Dick Bosman	4.00	2.00	1.25
23	Tim McCarver	5.00	2.50	1.50
24	Henry Aaron	35.00	17.50	10.00
25	Andy Messersmith	4.00	2.00	1.25
26	Tony Oliva	5.00	2.50	1.50
27	Mel Stottlemyre	4.00	2.00	1.25
28	Reggie Jackson	30.00	15.00	9.00
29	Carl Yastrzemski	20.00	10.00	6.00
30	James Fregosi	4.00	2.00	1.25
31	Vada Pinson	5.00	2.50	1.50
32	Lou Piniella	4.00	2.00	1.25
33	Robert Gibson	10.00	5.00	3.00
34	Pete Rose	35.00	17.50	10.00
35	Jim Wynn	4.00	2.00	1.25
36	Ollie Brown/SP	10.00	5.00	3.00
37	Frank Robinson/SP	35.00	17.50	10.00
38	Boog Powell/SP	60.00	30.00	18.00
39	Willie Davis/SP	10.00	5.00	3.00
40	Billy Williams/SP	20.00	10.00	6.00
41	Rusty Staub	5.00	2.50	1.50
42	Tommie Agee	4.00	2.00	1.25

1971 Topps

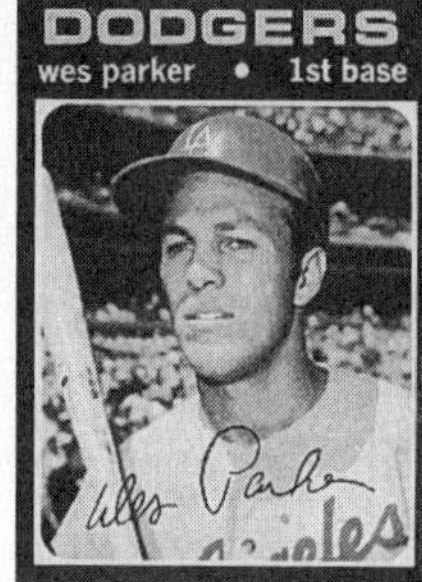

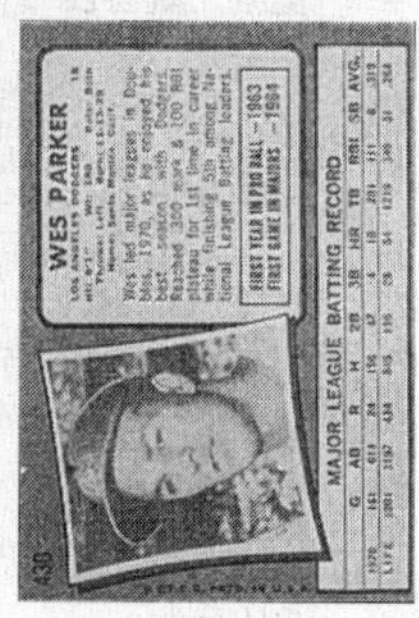

In 1971, Topps again increased the size of its set to 752 cards. These 2-1/2" x 3-1/2" cards feature a large color photo with a thin white frame. Above the picture, in the card's overall black border, is the player's name, team and position. A facsimile autograph completes the front. Backs feature a major change as a black-and-white "snapshot" of the player appears. Abbreviated statistics, a line giving the player's first pro and major league games and a short biography complete the back. Specialty cards in this issue are limited. There are statistical leaders as well as World Series and playoff highlights. High-number cards #644-752 are scarce, with about half of the cards being short-printed.

		NM	EX	VG
Complete Set (752):		3,000	1,500	900.00
Common Player (1-523):		2.00	1.00	.60
Common Player (524-643):		4.00	2.00	1.00
Common Player (644-752):		6.00	3.00	1.75
1	World Champions (Orioles Team)	20.00	10.00	6.00
2	Dock Ellis	2.00	1.00	.60
3	Dick McAuliffe	2.00	1.00	.60
4	Vic Davalillo	2.00	1.00	.60
5	Thurman Munson	120.00	60.00	36.00
6	Ed Spiezio	2.00	1.00	.60
7	Jim Holt	2.00	1.00	.60
8	Mike McQueen	2.00	1.00	.60
9	George Scott	2.00	1.00	.60
10	Claude Osteen	2.00	1.00	.60
11	***Elliott Maddox***	2.00	1.00	.60
12	Johnny Callison	2.00	1.00	.60
13	White Sox Rookies **(Charlie Brinkman, Dick Moloney)**	2.00	1.00	.60
14	***Dave Concepcion***	15.00	7.50	4.50
15	Andy Messersmith	2.00	1.00	.60
16	***Ken Singleton***	4.00	2.00	1.25
17	Billy Sorrell	2.00	1.00	.60
18	Norm Miller	2.00	1.00	.60
19	Skip Pitlock	2.00	1.00	.60
20	Reggie Jackson	50.00	25.00	15.00
21	Dan McGinn	2.00	1.00	.60
22	Phil Roof	2.00	1.00	.60
23	Oscar Gamble	2.00	1.00	.60
24	Rich Hand	2.00	1.00	.60
25	Clarence Gaston	2.00	1.00	.60
26	***Bert Blyleven***	20.00	10.00	6.00
27	Pirates Rookies **(Fred Cambria, Gene Clines)**	2.00	1.00	.60
28	Ron Klimkowski	2.00	1.00	.60
29	Don Buford	2.00	1.00	.60
30	Phil Niekro	8.00	4.00	2.50
31	Eddie Kasko	2.00	1.00	.60
32	Jerry DaVanon	2.00	1.00	.60
33	Del Unser	2.00	1.00	.60
34	Sandy Vance	2.00	1.00	.60
35	Lou Piniella	4.00	2.00	1.25
36	Dean Chance	2.00	1.00	.60
37	Rich McKinney	2.00	1.00	.60
38	***Jim Colborn***	2.00	1.00	.60
39	Tigers Rookies ***(Gene Lamont, Lerrin LaGrow)***	2.00	1.00	.60
40	Lee May	2.00	1.00	.60
41	Rick Austin	2.00	1.00	.60
42a	Boots Day (Stadium lights behind ear.)	8.00	4.00	2.50
42b	Boots Day (No stadium lights.)	8.00	4.00	2.50
43	Steve Kealey	2.00	1.00	.60
44	Johnny Edwards	2.00	1.00	.60
45	Jim Hunter	8.00	4.00	2.50
46	Dave Campbell	2.00	1.00	.60
47	Johnny Jeter	2.00	1.00	.60
48	Dave Baldwin	2.00	1.00	.60
49	Don Money	2.00	1.00	.60
50	Willie McCovey	10.00	5.00	3.00
51	Steve Kline	2.00	1.00	.60
52	Braves Rookies ***(Oscar Brown, Earl Williams)***	2.00	1.00	.60
53	Paul Blair	2.00	1.00	.60
54	1st Series Checklist (1-132)	5.00	2.50	1.50
55	Steve Carlton	20.00	10.00	6.00
56	Duane Josephson	2.00	1.00	.60
57	Von Joshua	2.00	1.00	.60
58	Bill Lee	2.00	1.00	.60
59	Gene Mauch	2.00	1.00	.60
60	Dick Bosman	2.00	1.00	.60
61	A.L. Batting Leaders (Alex Johnson, Tony Oliva, Carl Yastrzemski)	8.00	4.00	2.50
62	N.L. Batting Leaders (Rico Carty, Manny Sanguillen, Joe Torre)	6.00	3.00	1.75

63	A.L. RBI Leaders (Tony Conigliaro, Frank Howard, Boog Powell)	6.00	3.00	1.75
64	N.L. RBI Leaders (Johnny Bench, Tony Perez, Billy Williams)	8.00	4.00	2.50
65	A.L. Home Run Leaders (Frank Howard, Harmon Killebrew, Carl Yastrzemski)	8.00	4.00	2.50
66	N.L. Home Run Leaders (Johnny Bench, Tony Perez, Billy Williams)	10.00	5.00	3.00
67	A.L. ERA Leaders (Jim Palmer, Diego Segui, Clyde Wright)	6.00	3.00	1.75
68	N.L. ERA Leaders (Tom Seaver, Wayne Simpson, Luke Walker)	6.00	3.00	1.75
69	A.L. Pitching Leaders (Mike Cuellar, Dave McNally, Jim Perry)	3.00	1.50	.90
70	N.L. Pitching Leaders (Bob Gibson, Fergie Jenkins, Gaylord Perry)	8.00	4.00	2.50
71	A.L. Strikeout Leaders (Bob Johnson, Mickey Lolich, Sam McDowell)	3.00	1.50	.90
72	N.L. Strikeout Leaders (Bob Gibson, Fergie Jenkins, Tom Seaver)	8.00	4.00	2.50
73	George Brunet	2.00	1.00	.60
74	Twins Rookies **(Pete Hamm, Jim Nettles)**	2.00	1.00	.60
75	Gary Nolan	2.00	1.00	.60
76	Ted Savage	2.00	1.00	.60
77	Mike Compton	2.00	1.00	.60
78	Jim Spencer	2.00	1.00	.60
79	Wade Blasingame	2.00	1.00	.60
80	Bill Melton	2.00	1.00	.60
81	Felix Millan	2.00	1.00	.60
82	Casey Cox	2.00	1.00	.60
83	Mets Rookies **(*Randy Bobb, Tim Foli*)**	2.00	1.00	.60
84	Marcel Lachemann	2.00	1.00	.60
85	Billy Grabarkewitz	2.00	1.00	.60
86	Mike Kilkenny	2.00	1.00	.60
87	Jack Heidemann	2.00	1.00	.60
88	Hal King	2.00	1.00	.60
89	Ken Brett	2.00	1.00	.60
90	Joe Pepitone	2.00	1.00	.60
91	Bob Lemon	4.00	2.00	1.25
92	Fred Wenz	2.00	1.00	.60
93	Senators Rookies **(Norm McRae, Denny Riddleberger)**	2.00	1.00	.60
94	Don Hahn	2.00	1.00	.60
95	Luis Tiant	2.00	1.00	.60
96	Joe Hague	2.00	1.00	.60
97	Floyd Wicker	2.00	1.00	.60
98	Joe Decker	2.00	1.00	.60
99	Mark Belanger	2.00	1.00	.60
100	Pete Rose	85.00	42.00	25.00
101	Les Cain	2.00	1.00	.60
102	Astros Rookies **(Ken Forsch, Larry Howard)**	2.00	1.00	.60
103	Rich Severson	2.00	1.00	.60
104	Dan Frisella	2.00	1.00	.60
105	Tony Conigliaro	6.00	3.00	1.75
106	Tom Dukes	2.00	1.00	.60
107	Roy Foster	2.00	1.00	.60
108	John Cumberland	2.00	1.00	.60
109	Steve Hovley	2.00	1.00	.60
110	Bill Mazeroski	10.00	5.00	3.00
111	Yankees Rookies **(Loyd Colson, Bobby Mitchell)**	2.00	1.00	.60
112	Manny Mota	2.00	1.00	.60
113	Jerry Crider	2.00	1.00	.60
114	Billy Conigliaro	2.00	1.00	.60
115	Donn Clendenon	2.00	1.00	.60
116	Ken Sanders	2.00	1.00	.60
117	***Ted Simmons***	8.00	4.00	2.50
118	Cookie Rojas	2.00	1.00	.60
119	Frank Lucchesi	2.00	1.00	.60
120	Willie Horton	2.00	1.00	.60
121	Cubs Rookies **(Jim Dunegan, Roe Skidmore)**	2.00	1.00	.60
122	Eddie Watt	2.00	1.00	.60
123a	2nd Series Checklist (133-263) (Card # on right, orange helmet.)	5.00	2.50	1.50
123b	2nd Series Checklist (133-263) (Card # on right, red helmet.)	5.00	2.50	1.50
123c	2nd Series Checklist (133-263) (Card # centered.)	5.00	2.50	1.50
124	***Don Gullett***	2.00	1.00	.60
125	Ray Fosse	2.00	1.00	.60
126	Danny Coombs	2.00	1.00	.60
127	***Danny Thompson***	2.00	1.00	.60
128	Frank Johnson	2.00	1.00	.60
129	Aurelio Monteagudo	2.00	1.00	.60
130	Denis Menke	2.00	1.00	.60
131	Curt Blefary	2.00	1.00	.60
132	Jose Laboy	2.00	1.00	.60
133	Mickey Lolich	2.00	1.00	.60
134	Jose Arcia	2.00	1.00	.60
135	Rick Monday	2.00	1.00	.60
136	Duffy Dyer	2.00	1.00	.60
137	Marcelino Lopez	2.00	1.00	.60
138	Phillies Rookies **(*Joe Lis, Willie Montanez*)**	2.00	1.00	.60
139	Paul Casanova	2.00	1.00	.60
140	Gaylord Perry	8.00	4.00	2.50
141	Frank Quilici	2.00	1.00	.60
142	Mack Jones	2.00	1.00	.60
143	Steve Blass	2.00	1.00	.60
144	Jackie Hernandez	2.00	1.00	.60
145	Bill Singer	2.00	1.00	.60
146	Ralph Houk	2.00	1.00	.60
147	Bob Priddy	2.00	1.00	.60
148	John Mayberry	2.00	1.00	.60
149	Mike Hershberger	2.00	1.00	.60
150	Sam McDowell	2.00	1.00	.60
151	Tommy Davis	2.00	1.00	.60
152	Angels Rookies **(Lloyd Allen, Winston Llenas)**	2.00	1.00	.60
153	Gary Ross	2.00	1.00	.60
154	Cesar Gutierrez	2.00	1.00	.60
155	Ken Henderson	2.00	1.00	.60
156	Bart Johnson	2.00	1.00	.60
157	Bob Bailey	2.00	1.00	.60
158	Jerry Reuss	2.00	1.00	.60
159	Jarvis Tatum	2.00	1.00	.60
160	Tom Seaver	25.00	12.50	7.50
161	Coins Checklist	4.00	2.00	1.25
162	Jack Billingham	2.00	1.00	.60
163	Buck Martinez	2.00	1.00	.60
164	Reds Rookies **(*Frank Duffy, Milt Wilcox*)**	2.00	1.00	.60
165	Cesar Tovar	2.00	1.00	.60
166	Joe Hoerner	2.00	1.00	.60
167	Tom Grieve	2.00	1.00	.60
168	Bruce Dal Canton	2.00	1.00	.60
169	Ed Herrmann	2.00	1.00	.60
170	Mike Cuellar	2.00	1.00	.60
171	Bobby Wine	2.00	1.00	.60
172	Duke Sims	2.00	1.00	.60
173	Gil Garrido	2.00	1.00	.60
174	***Dave LaRoche***	2.00	1.00	.60
175	Jim Hickman	2.00	1.00	.60
176	Red Sox Rookies **(Doug Griffin, Bob Montgomery)**	2.00	1.00	.60
177	Hal McRae	2.00	1.00	.60
178	Dave Duncan	2.00	1.00	.60
179	Mike Corkins	2.00	1.00	.60
180	Al Kaline	20.00	10.00	6.00
181	Hal Lanier	2.00	1.00	.60
182	Al Downing	2.00	1.00	.60
183	Gil Hodges	10.00	5.00	3.00
184	Stan Bahnsen	2.00	1.00	.60
185	Julian Javier	2.00	1.00	.60
186	Bob Spence	2.00	1.00	.60
187	Ted Abernathy	2.00	1.00	.60
188	Dodgers Rookies **(*Mike Strahler, Bob Valentine*)**	4.00	2.00	1.25
189	George Mitterwald	2.00	1.00	.60
190	Bob Tolan	2.00	1.00	.60
191	Mike Andrews	2.00	1.00	.60
192	Billy Wilson	2.00	1.00	.60
193	***Bob Grich***	5.00	2.50	1.50
194	Mike Lum	2.00	1.00	.60
195	A.L. Playoff Game 1 (Powell Muscles Twins!)	5.00	2.50	1.50
196	A.L. Playoff Game 2 (McNally Makes It Two Straight!)	3.00	1.50	.90
197	A.L. Playoff Game 3 (Palmer Mows 'Em Down!)	6.00	3.00	1.75
198	Orioles Celebrate! (A Team Effort!)	3.00	1.50	.90
199	N.L. Playoff Game 1 (Cline Pinch-Triple Decides It!)	3.00	1.50	.90
200	N.L. Playoff Game 2 (Tolan Scores For Third Time!)	3.00	1.50	.90
201	N.L. Playoff Game 3 (Cline Scores Winning Run!)	3.00	1.50	.90
202	Reds Celebrate! (World Series Bound!)	3.00	1.50	.90
203	***Larry Gura***	2.00	1.00	.60
204	Brewers Rookies **(George Kopacz, Bernie Smith)**	2.00	1.00	.60
205	Gerry Moses	2.00	1.00	.60
206a	3rd Series Checklist (264-393) (Orange helmet.)	6.00	3.00	1.75
206b	3rd Series Checklist (264-393) (Red helmet.)	6.00	3.00	1.75
207	Alan Foster	2.00	1.00	.60
208	Billy Martin	8.00	4.00	2.50
209	Steve Renko	2.00	1.00	.60
210	Rod Carew	15.00	7.50	4.50
211	Phil Hennigan	2.00	1.00	.60
212	Rich Hebner	2.00	1.00	.60
213	Frank Baker	2.00	1.00	.60
214	Al Ferrara	2.00	1.00	.60
215	Diego Segui	2.00	1.00	.60
216	Cards Rookies **(Reggie Cleveland, Luis Melendez)**	2.00	1.00	.60
217	Ed Stroud	2.00	1.00	.60
218	Tony Cloninger	2.00	1.00	.60
219	Elrod Hendricks	2.00	1.00	.60
220	Ron Santo	8.00	4.00	2.50
221	Dave Morehead	2.00	1.00	.60
222	Bob Watson	2.00	1.00	.60
223	Cecil Upshaw	2.00	1.00	.60
224	Alan Gallagher	2.00	1.00	.60
225	Gary Peters	2.00	1.00	.60
226	Bill Russell	2.00	1.00	.60
227	Floyd Weaver	2.00	1.00	.60
228	Wayne Garrett	2.00	1.00	.60
229	Jim Hannan	2.00	1.00	.60
230	Willie Stargell	15.00	7.50	4.50
231	Indians Rookies **(*Vince Colbert, John Lowenstein*)**	2.00	1.00	.60
232	John Strohmayer	2.00	1.00	.60
233	Larry Bowa	2.00	1.00	.60
234	Jim Lyttle	2.00	1.00	.60
235	Nate Colbert	2.00	1.00	.60
236	Bob Humphreys	2.00	1.00	.60
237	***Cesar Cedeno***	6.00	3.00	1.75
238	Chuck Dobson	2.00	1.00	.60
239	Red Schoendienst	6.00	3.00	1.75
240	Clyde Wright	2.00	1.00	.60
241	Dave Nelson	2.00	1.00	.60
242	Jim Ray	2.00	1.00	.60
243	Carlos May	2.00	1.00	.60
244	Bob Tillman	2.00	1.00	.60
245	Jim Kaat	3.00	1.50	.90
246	Tony Taylor	2.00	1.00	.60
247	Royals Rookies **(*Jerry Cram, Paul Splittorff*)**	2.00	1.00	.60
248	Hoyt Wilhelm	8.00	4.00	2.50
249	Chico Salmon	2.00	1.00	.60
250	Johnny Bench	60.00	30.00	18.00
251	Frank Reberger	2.00	1.00	.60
252	Eddie Leon	2.00	1.00	.60
253	Bill Sudakis	2.00	1.00	.60
254	Cal Koonce	2.00	1.00	.60
255	Bob Robertson	2.00	1.00	.60
256	Tony Gonzalez	2.00	1.00	.60
257	Nelson Briles	2.00	1.00	.60
258	Dick Green	2.00	1.00	.60
259	Dave Marshall	2.00	1.00	.60
260	Tommy Harper	2.00	1.00	.60
261	Darold Knowles	2.00	1.00	.60
262	Padres Rookies **(Dave Robinson, Jim Williams)**	2.00	1.00	.60
263	John Ellis	2.00	1.00	.60
264	Joe Morgan	12.00	6.00	3.50
265a	Jim Northrup (Black "dot" at right of photo.)	2.00	1.00	.60
265b	Jim Northrup (Black "blob" at right of photo.)	2.00	1.00	.60
266	Bill Stoneman	2.00	1.00	.60
267	Rich Morales	2.00	1.00	.60
268	Phillies Team	4.00	2.00	1.25
269	Gail Hopkins	2.00	1.00	.60
270	Rico Carty	2.00	1.00	.60
271	Bill Zepp	2.00	1.00	.60
272	Tommy Helms	2.00	1.00	.60
273	Pete Richert	2.00	1.00	.60
274	Ron Slocum	2.00	1.00	.60
275	Vada Pinson	5.00	2.50	1.50
276	Giants Rookies **(*Mike Davison, George Foster*)**	15.00	7.50	4.50
277	Gary Waslewski	2.00	1.00	.60
278	Jerry Grote	2.00	1.00	.60
279	Lefty Phillips	2.00	1.00	.60
280	Fergie Jenkins	10.00	5.00	3.00
281	Danny Walton	2.00	1.00	.60
282	Jose Pagan	2.00	1.00	.60
283	Dick Such	2.00	1.00	.60
284	Jim Gosger	2.00	1.00	.60
285	Sal Bando	2.00	1.00	.60
286	Jerry McNertney	2.00	1.00	.60
287	Mike Fiore	2.00	1.00	.60
288	Joe Moeller	2.00	1.00	.60
289	White Sox Team	4.00	2.00	1.25
290	Tony Oliva	4.00	2.00	1.25
291	George Culver	2.00	1.00	.60
292	Jay Johnstone	2.00	1.00	.60
293	Pat Corrales	2.00	1.00	.60
294	Steve Dunning	2.00	1.00	.60
295	Bobby Bonds	4.00	2.00	1.25
296	Tom Timmermann	2.00	1.00	.60
297	Johnny Briggs	2.00	1.00	.60
298	Jim Nelson	2.00	1.00	.60
299	Ed Kirkpatrick	2.00	1.00	.60
300	Brooks Robinson	20.00	10.00	6.00
301	Earl Wilson	2.00	1.00	.60
302	Phil Gagliano	2.00	1.00	.60
303	Lindy McDaniel	2.00	1.00	.60
304	Ron Brand	2.00	1.00	.60
305	Reggie Smith	2.00	1.00	.60
306a	Jim Nash (Black blob, left center.)	4.00	2.00	1.25
306b	Jim Nash (Blob airbrushed away.)	2.00	1.00	.60
307	Don Wert	2.00	1.00	.60
308	Cards Team	3.00	1.50	.90
309	Dick Ellsworth	2.00	1.00	.60
310	Tommie Agee	2.00	1.00	.60
311	Lee Stange	2.00	1.00	.60
312	Harry Walker	2.00	1.00	.60
313	Tom Hall	2.00	1.00	.60
314	Jeff Torborg	2.00	1.00	.60
315	Ron Fairly	2.00	1.00	.60
316	Fred Scherman	2.00	1.00	.60
317	Athletics Rookies **(Jim Driscoll, Angel Mangual)**	2.00	1.00	.60
318	Rudy May	2.00	1.00	.60
319	Ty Cline	2.00	1.00	.60
320	Dave McNally	2.00	1.00	.60
321	Tom Matchick	2.00	1.00	.60
322	Jim Beauchamp	2.00	1.00	.60
323	Billy Champion	2.00	1.00	.60
324	Graig Nettles	4.00	2.00	1.25
325	Juan Marichal	8.00	4.00	2.50
326	Richie Scheinblum	2.00	1.00	.60
327	World Series Game 1 (Powell Homers To Opposite Field!)	3.00	1.50	.90
328	World Series Game 2 (Buford Goes 2-For-4!)	2.00	1.00	.60
329	World Series Game 3 (F. Robinson Shows Muscle!)	6.00	3.00	1.75
330	World Series Game 4 (Reds Stay Alive!)	2.00	1.00	.60
331	World Series Game 5 (B. Robinson Commits Robbery!)	8.00	4.00	2.50
332	World Series Celebration! (Convincing Performance!)	5.00	2.50	1.50
333	Clay Kirby	2.00	1.00	.60
334	Roberto Pena	2.00	1.00	.60
335	Jerry Koosman	2.00	1.00	.60
336	Tigers Team	4.00	2.00	1.25
337	Jesus Alou	2.00	1.00	.60
338	Gene Tenace	2.00	1.00	.60
339	Wayne Simpson	2.00	1.00	.60
340	Rico Petrocelli	2.00	1.00	.60
341	***Steve Garvey***	30.00	15.00	9.00
342	Frank Tepedino	2.00	1.00	.60

343 Pirates Rookies (***Ed Acosta, Milt May***) 2.00 1.00 .60
344 Ellie Rodriguez 2.00 1.00 .60
345 Joe Horlen 2.00 1.00 .60
346 Lum Harris 2.00 1.00 .60
347 Ted Uhlaender 2.00 1.00 .60
348 Fred Norman 2.00 1.00 .60
349 Rich Reese 2.00 1.00 .60
350 Billy Williams 12.00 6.00 3.50
351 Jim Shellenback 2.00 1.00 .60
352 Denny Doyle 2.00 1.00 .60
353 Carl Taylor 2.00 1.00 .60
354 Don McMahon 2.00 1.00 .60
355 Bud Harrelson 2.00 1.00 .60
356 Bob Locker 2.00 1.00 .60
357 Reds Team 4.00 2.00 1.25
358 Danny Cater 2.00 1.00 .60
359 Ron Reed 2.00 1.00 .60
360 Jim Fregosi 2.00 1.00 .60
361 Don Sutton 8.00 4.00 2.50
362 Orioles Rookies **(Mike Adamson, Roger Freed)** 2.00 1.00 .60
363 Mike Nagy 2.00 1.00 .60
364 Tommy Dean 2.00 1.00 .60
365 Bob Johnson 2.00 1.00 .60
366 Ron Stone 2.00 1.00 .60
367 Dalton Jones 2.00 1.00 .60
368 Bob Veale 2.00 1.00 .60
369a 4th Series Checklist (394-523) (Orange helmet.) 5.00 2.50 1.50
369b 4th Series Checklist (394-523) (Red helmet, black line above ear.) 6.00 3.00 1.75
369c 4th Series Checklist (394-523) (Red helmet, no line.) 6.00 3.00 1.75
370 Joe Torre 6.00 3.00 1.75
371 Jack Hiatt 2.00 1.00 .60
372 Lew Krausse 2.00 1.00 .60
373 Tom McCraw 2.00 1.00 .60
374 Clete Boyer 2.00 1.00 .60
375 Steve Hargan 2.00 1.00 .60
376 Expos Rookies **(Clyde Mashore, Ernie McAnally)** 2.00 1.00 .60
377 Greg Garrett 2.00 1.00 .60
378 Tito Fuentes 2.00 1.00 .60
379 Wayne Granger 2.00 1.00 .60
380 Ted Williams 12.00 6.00 3.50
381 Fred Gladding 2.00 1.00 .60
382 Jake Gibbs 2.00 1.00 .60
383 Rod Gaspar 2.00 1.00 .60
384 Rollie Fingers 8.00 4.00 2.50
385 Maury Wills 4.00 2.00 1.25
386 Red Sox Team 4.00 2.00 1.25
387 Ron Herbel 2.00 1.00 .60
388 Al Oliver 2.00 1.00 .60
389 Ed Brinkman 2.00 1.00 .60
390 Glenn Beckert 2.00 1.00 .60
391 Twins Rookies **(Steve Brye, Cotton Nash)** 2.00 1.00 .60
392 Grant Jackson 2.00 1.00 .60
393 Merv Rettenmund 2.00 1.00 .60
394 Clay Carroll 2.00 1.00 .60
395 Roy White 2.00 1.00 .60
396 Dick Schofield 2.00 1.00 .60
397 Alvin Dark 2.00 1.00 .60
398 Howie Reed 2.00 1.00 .60
399 Jim French 2.00 1.00 .60
400 Hank Aaron 70.00 35.00 21.00
401 Tom Murphy 2.00 1.00 .60
402 Dodgers Team 4.00 2.00 1.25
403 Joe Coleman 2.00 1.00 .60
404 Astros Rookies **(Buddy Harris, Roger Metzger)** 2.00 1.00 .60
405 Leo Cardenas 2.00 1.00 .60
406 Ray Sadecki 2.00 1.00 .60
407 Joe Rudi 2.00 1.00 .60
408 Rafael Robles 2.00 1.00 .60
409 Don Pavletich 2.00 1.00 .60
410 Ken Holtzman 2.00 1.00 .60
411 George Spriggs 2.00 1.00 .60
412 Jerry Johnson 2.00 1.00 .60
413 Pat Kelly 2.00 1.00 .60
414 Woodie Fryman 2.00 1.00 .60
415 Mike Hegan 2.00 1.00 .60
416 Gene Alley 2.00 1.00 .60
417 Dick Hall 2.00 1.00 .60
418 Adolfo Phillips 2.00 1.00 .60
419 Ron Hansen 2.00 1.00 .60
420 Jim Merritt 2.00 1.00 .60
421 John Stephenson 2.00 1.00 .60
422 Frank Bertaina 2.00 1.00 .60
423 Tigers Rookies **(Tim Marting, Dennis Saunders)** 2.00 1.00 .60
424 Roberto Rodriquez (Rodriguez) 2.00 1.00 .60
425 Doug Rader 2.00 1.00 .60
426 Chris Cannizzaro 2.00 1.00 .60
427 Bernie Allen 2.00 1.00 .60
428 Jim McAndrew 2.00 1.00 .60
429 Chuck Hinton 2.00 1.00 .60
430 Wes Parker 2.00 1.00 .60
431 Tom Burgmeier 2.00 1.00 .60
432 Bob Didier 2.00 1.00 .60
433 Skip Lockwood 2.00 1.00 .60
434 Gary Sutherland 2.00 1.00 .60
435 Jose Cardenal 2.00 1.00 .60
436 Wilbur Wood 2.00 1.00 .60
437 Danny Murtaugh 2.00 1.00 .60
438 Mike McCormick 2.00 1.00 .60
439 Phillies Rookies **(Greg Luzinski, Scott Reid)** 5.00 2.50 1.50
440 Bert Campaneris 2.00 1.00 .60
441 Milt Pappas 2.00 1.00 .60
442 Angels Team 4.00 2.00 1.25
443 Rich Robertson 2.00 1.00 .60
444 Jimmie Price 2.00 1.00 .60
445 Art Shamsky 2.00 1.00 .60
446 Bobby Bolin 2.00 1.00 .60
447 ***Cesar Geronimo*** 3.00 1.50 .90
448 Dave Roberts 2.00 1.00 .60
449 Brant Alyea 2.00 1.00 .60
450 Bob Gibson 15.00 7.50 4.50
451 Joe Keough 2.00 1.00 .60
452 John Boccabella 2.00 1.00 .60
453 Terry Crowley 2.00 1.00 .60
454 Mike Paul 2.00 1.00 .60
455 Don Kessinger 2.00 1.00 .60
456 Bob Meyer 2.00 1.00 .60
457 Willie Smith 2.00 1.00 .60
458 White Sox Rookies **(Dave Lemonds, Ron Lolich)** 2.00 1.00 .60
459 Jim Lefebvre 2.00 1.00 .60
460 Fritz Peterson 2.00 1.00 .60
461 Jim Hart 2.00 1.00 .60
462 Senators Team 5.00 2.50 1.50
463 Tom Kelley 2.00 1.00 .60
464 Aurelio Rodriguez 2.00 1.00 .60
465 Tim McCarver 6.00 3.00 1.75
466 Ken Berry 2.00 1.00 .60
467 Al Santorini 2.00 1.00 .60
468 Frank Fernandez 2.00 1.00 .60
469 Bob Aspromonte 2.00 1.00 .60
470 Bob Oliver 2.00 1.00 .60
471 Tom Griffin 2.00 1.00 .60
472 Ken Rudolph 2.00 1.00 .60
473 Gary Wagner 2.00 1.00 .60
474 Jim Fairey 2.00 1.00 .60
475 Ron Perranoski 2.00 1.00 .60
476 Dal Maxvill 2.00 1.00 .60
477 Earl Weaver 5.00 2.50 1.50
478 Bernie Carbo 2.00 1.00 .60
479 Dennis Higgins 2.00 1.00 .60
480 Manny Sanguillen 2.00 1.00 .60
481 Daryl Patterson 2.00 1.00 .60
482 Padres Team 5.00 2.50 1.50
483 Gene Michael 2.00 1.00 .60
484 Don Wilson 2.00 1.00 .60
485 Ken McMullen 2.00 1.00 .60
486 Steve Huntz 2.00 1.00 .60
487 Paul Schaal 2.00 1.00 .60
488 Jerry Stephenson 2.00 1.00 .60
489 Luis Alvarado 2.00 1.00 .60
490 Deron Johnson 2.00 1.00 .60
491 Jim Hardin 2.00 1.00 .60
492 Ken Boswell 2.00 1.00 .60
493 Dave May 2.00 1.00 .60
494 Braves Rookies **(Ralph Garr, Rick Kester)** 2.00 1.00 .60
495 Felipe Alou 3.00 1.50 .90
496 Woody Woodward 2.00 1.00 .60
497 Horacio Pina 2.00 1.00 .60
498 John Kennedy 2.00 1.00 .60
499 5th Series Checklist (524-643) 6.00 3.00 1.75
500 Jim Perry 2.00 1.00 .60
501 Andy Etchebarren 2.00 1.00 .60
502 Cubs Team 5.00 2.50 1.50
503 Gates Brown 2.00 1.00 .60
504 Ken Wright 2.00 1.00 .60
505 Ollie Brown 2.00 1.00 .60
506 Bobby Knoop 2.00 1.00 .60
507 George Stone 2.00 1.00 .60
508 Roger Repoz 2.00 1.00 .60
509 Jim Grant 2.00 1.00 .60
510 Ken Harrelson 2.00 1.00 .60
511 Chris Short 2.00 1.00 .60
512 Red Sox Rookies **(Mike Garman, Dick Mills)** 2.00 1.00 .60
513 Nolan Ryan 140.00 70.00 42.00
514 Ron Woods 2.00 1.00 .60
515 Carl Morton 2.00 1.00 .60
516 Ted Kubiak 2.00 1.00 .60
517 Charlie Fox 2.00 1.00 .60
518 Joe Grzenda 2.00 1.00 .60
519 Willie Crawford 2.00 1.00 .60
520 Tommy John 5.00 2.50 1.50
521 Leron Lee 2.00 1.00 .60
522 Twins Team 4.00 2.00 1.25
523 John Odom 2.00 1.00 .60
524 Mickey Stanley 4.00 2.00 1.25
525 Ernie Banks 40.00 20.00 12.00
526 Ray Jarvis 4.00 2.00 1.25
527 Cleon Jones 4.00 2.00 1.25
528 Wally Bunker 4.00 2.00 1.25
529 N.L. Rookies **(Bill Buckner, Enzo Hernandez, Marty Perez)** 6.00 3.00 1.75
530 Carl Yastrzemski 25.00 12.50 7.50
531 Mike Torrez 4.00 2.00 1.25
532 Bill Rigney 4.00 2.00 1.25
533 Mike Ryan 4.00 2.00 1.25
534 Luke Walker 4.00 2.00 1.25
535 Curt Flood 5.00 2.50 1.50
536 Claude Raymond 4.00 2.00 1.25
537 Tom Egan 4.00 2.00 1.25
538 Angel Bravo 4.00 2.00 1.25
539 Larry Brown 4.00 2.00 1.25
540 Larry Dierker 4.00 2.00 1.25
541 Bob Burda 4.00 2.00 1.25
542 Bob Miller 4.00 2.00 1.25
543 Yankees Team 8.00 4.00 2.50
544 Vida Blue 5.00 2.50 1.50
545 Dick Dietz 4.00 2.00 1.25
546 John Matias 4.00 2.00 1.25
547 Pat Dobson 4.00 2.00 1.25
548 Don Mason 4.00 2.00 1.25
549 Jim Brewer 4.00 2.00 1.25
550 Harmon Killebrew 25.00 12.50 7.50
551 Frank Linzy 4.00 2.00 1.25
552 Buddy Bradford 4.00 2.00 1.25
553 Kevin Collins 4.00 2.00 1.25
554 Lowell Palmer 4.00 2.00 1.25
555 Walt Williams 4.00 2.00 1.25
556 Jim McGlothlin 4.00 2.00 1.25
557 Tom Satriano 4.00 2.00 1.25
558 Hector Torres 4.00 2.00 1.25
559 A.L. Rookies **(Terry Cox, Bill Gogolewski, Gary Jones)** 4.00 2.00 1.25
560 Rusty Staub 5.00 2.50 1.50
561 Syd O'Brien 4.00 2.00 1.25
562 Dave Giusti 4.00 2.00 1.25
563 Giants Team 10.00 5.00 3.00
564 Al Fitzmorris 4.00 2.00 1.25
565 Jim Wynn 4.00 2.00 1.25
566 Tim Cullen 4.00 2.00 1.25
567 Walt Alston 6.00 3.00 1.75
568 Sal Campisi 4.00 2.00 1.25
569 Ivan Murrell 4.00 2.00 1.25
570 Jim Palmer 25.00 12.50 7.50
571 Ted Sizemore 4.00 2.00 1.25
572 Jerry Kenney 4.00 2.00 1.25
573 Ed Kranepool 4.00 2.00 1.25
574 Jim Bunning 8.00 4.00 2.50
575 Bill Freehan 4.00 2.00 1.25
576 Cubs Rookies **(Brock Davis, Adrian Garrett, Garry Jestadt)** 4.00 2.00 1.25
577 Jim Lonborg 4.00 2.00 1.25
578 Ron Hunt 4.00 2.00 1.25
579 Marty Pattin 4.00 2.00 1.25
580 Tony Perez 20.00 10.00 6.00
581 Roger Nelson 4.00 2.00 1.25
582 Dave Cash 4.00 2.00 1.25
583 Ron Cook 4.00 2.00 1.25
584 Indians Team 10.00 5.00 3.00
585 Willie Davis 4.00 2.00 1.25
586 Dick Woodson 4.00 2.00 1.25
587 Sonny Jackson 4.00 2.00 1.25
588 Tom Bradley 4.00 2.00 1.25
589 Bob Barton 4.00 2.00 1.25
590 Alex Johnson 4.00 2.00 1.25
591 Jackie Brown 4.00 2.00 1.25
592 Randy Hundley 4.00 2.00 1.25
593 Jack Aker 4.00 2.00 1.25
594 Cards Rookies **(Bob Chlupsa, Al Hrabosky, Bob Stinson)** 6.00 3.00 1.75
595 Dave Johnson 4.00 2.00 1.25
596 Mike Jorgensen 4.00 2.00 1.25
597 Ken Suarez 4.00 2.00 1.25
598 Rick Wise 4.00 2.00 1.25
599 Norm Cash 6.00 3.00 1.75
600 Willie Mays 100.00 50.00 30.00
601 Ken Tatum 4.00 2.00 1.25
602 Marty Martinez 4.00 2.00 1.25
603 Pirates Team 8.00 4.00 2.50
604 John Gelnar 4.00 2.00 1.25
605 Orlando Cepeda 15.00 7.50 4.50
606 Chuck Taylor 4.00 2.00 1.25
607 Paul Ratliff 4.00 2.00 1.25
608 Mike Wegener 4.00 2.00 1.25
609 Leo Durocher 8.00 4.00 2.50
610 Amos Otis 4.00 2.00 1.25
611 Tom Phoebus 4.00 2.00 1.25
612 Indians Rookies **(Lou Camilli, Ted Ford, Steve Mingori)** 4.00 2.00 1.25
613 Pedro Borbon 4.00 2.00 1.25
614 Billy Cowan 4.00 2.00 1.25
615 Mel Stottlemyre 6.00 3.00 1.75
616 Larry Hisle 4.00 2.00 1.25
617 Clay Dalrymple 4.00 2.00 1.25
618 Tug McGraw 4.00 2.00 1.25
619a 6th Series Checklist (644-752) (No copyright on back.) 5.00 2.50 1.50
619b 6th Series Checklist (644-752) (With copyright, no wavy line on helmet brim.) 4.00 2.00 1.25
619c 6th Series Checklist (644-752) (With copyright, wavy line on helmet brim.) 4.00 2.00 1.25
620 Frank Howard 5.00 2.50 1.50
621 Ron Bryant 4.00 2.00 1.25
622 Joe Lahoud 4.00 2.00 1.25
623 Pat Jarvis 4.00 2.00 1.25
624 Athletics Team 10.00 5.00 3.00
625 Lou Brock 25.00 12.50 7.50
626 Freddie Patek 4.00 2.00 1.25
627 Steve Hamilton 4.00 2.00 1.25
628 John Bateman 4.00 2.00 1.25
629 John Hiller 4.00 2.00 1.25
630 Roberto Clemente 140.00 70.00 42.00
631 Eddie Fisher 4.00 2.00 1.25
632 Darrel Chaney 4.00 2.00 1.25
633 A.L. Rookies **(Bobby Brooks, Pete Koegel, Scott Northey)** 4.00 2.00 1.25
634 Phil Regan 4.00 2.00 1.25
635 Bobby Murcer 15.00 7.50 4.50
636 Denny Lemaster 4.00 2.00 1.25
637 Dave Bristol 4.00 2.00 1.25
638 Stan Williams 4.00 2.00 1.25
639 Tom Haller 4.00 2.00 1.25
640 Frank Robinson 40.00 20.00 12.00
641 Mets Team 10.00 5.00 3.00
642 Jim Roland 4.00 2.00 1.25
643 Rick Reichardt 4.00 2.00 1.25
644 Jim Stewart/SP 8.00 4.00 2.50
645 Jim Maloney/SP 8.00 4.00 2.50
646 Bobby Floyd/SP 8.00 4.00 2.50
647 Juan Pizarro 6.00 3.00 1.75
648 Mets Rookies **(*Rich Folkers, Ted Martinez, Jon Matlack*)**/SP 20.00 10.00 6.00
649 Sparky Lyle/SP 10.00 5.00 3.00
650 Rich Allen/SP 30.00 15.00 9.00
651 Jerry Robertson/SP 8.00 4.00 2.50
652 Braves Team 10.00 5.00 3.00
653 Russ Snyder/SP 8.00 4.00 2.50
654 Don Shaw/SP 8.00 4.00 2.50
655 Mike Epstein/SP 8.00 4.00 2.50

656	Gerry Nyman/SP	8.00	4.00	2.50
657	Jose Azcue	6.00	3.00	1.75
658	Paul Lindblad/SP	8.00	4.00	2.50
659	Byron Browne/SP	8.00	4.00	2.50
660	Ray Culp	6.00	3.00	1.75
661	Chuck Tanner/SP	8.00	4.00	2.50
662	Mike Hedlund/SP	8.00	4.00	2.50
663	Marv Staehle	6.00	3.00	1.75
664	Major League Rookies **(Archie Reynolds, Bob Reynolds, Ken Reynolds)/SP**	8.00	4.00	2.50
665	Ron Swoboda/SP	8.00	4.00	2.50
666	Gene Brabender/SP	8.00	4.00	2.50
667	Pete Ward	6.00	3.00	1.75
668	Gary Neibauer	6.00	3.00	1.75
669	Ike Brown/SP	8.00	4.00	2.50
670	Bill Hands	6.00	3.00	1.75
671	Bill Voss/SP	8.00	4.00	2.50
672	Ed Crosby/SP	8.00	4.00	2.50
673	Gerry Janeski/SP	8.00	4.00	2.50
674	Expos Team	12.00	6.00	3.50
675	Dave Boswell	6.00	3.00	1.75
676	Tommie Reynolds	6.00	3.00	1.75
677	Jack DiLauro/SP	8.00	4.00	2.50
678	George Thomas	6.00	3.00	1.75
679	Don O'Riley	6.00	3.00	1.75
680	Don Mincher/SP	8.00	4.00	2.50
681	Bill Butler	6.00	3.00	1.75
682	Terry Harmon	6.00	3.00	1.75
683	Bill Burbach/SP	8.00	4.00	2.50
684	Curt Motton	6.00	3.00	1.75
685	Moe Drabowsky	6.00	3.00	1.75
686	Chico Ruiz/SP	8.00	4.00	2.50
687	Ron Taylor/SP	8.00	4.00	2.50
688	Sparky Anderson/SP	25.00	12.50	7.50
689	Frank Baker	6.00	3.00	1.75
690	Bob Moose	6.00	3.00	1.75
691	Bob Heise	6.00	3.00	1.75
692	A.L. Rookies **(Hal Haydel, Rogelio Moret, Wayne Twitchell)/SP**	8.00	4.00	2.50
693	Jose Pena/SP	8.00	4.00	2.50
694	Rick Renick/SP	8.00	4.00	2.50
695	Joe Niekro	6.00	3.00	1.75
696	Jerry Morales	6.00	3.00	1.75
697	Rickey Clark/SP	8.00	4.00	2.50
698	Brewers Team/SP	20.00	10.00	6.00
699	Jim Britton	6.00	3.00	1.75
700	Boog Powell/SP	20.00	10.00	6.00
701	Bob Garibaldi	6.00	3.00	1.75
702	Milt Ramirez	6.00	3.00	1.75
703	Mike Kekich	6.00	3.00	1.75
704	J.C. Martin/SP	8.00	4.00	2.50
705	Dick Selma/SP	8.00	4.00	2.50
706	Joe Foy/SP	8.00	4.00	2.50
707	Fred Lasher	6.00	3.00	1.75
708	Russ Nagelson/SP	8.00	4.00	2.50
709	Major League Rookies ***(Dusty Baker, Don Baylor, Tom Paciorek)*/SP**	60.00	30.00	18.00
710	Sonny Siebert	6.00	3.00	1.75
711	Larry Stahl/SP	8.00	4.00	2.50
712	Jose Martinez	6.00	3.00	1.75
713	Mike Marshall/SP	8.00	4.00	2.50
714	Dick Williams/SP	8.00	4.00	2.50
715	Horace Clarke/SP	8.00	4.00	2.50
716	Dave Leonhard	6.00	3.00	1.75
717	Tommie Aaron/SP	8.00	4.00	2.50
718	Billy Wynne	6.00	3.00	1.75
719	Jerry May/SP	8.00	4.00	2.50
720	Matty Alou	6.00	3.00	1.75
721	John Morris	6.00	3.00	1.75
722	Astros Team/SP	15.00	7.50	4.50
723	Vicente Romo/SP	8.00	4.00	2.50
724	Tom Tischinski/SP	8.00	4.00	2.50
725	Gary Gentry/SP	8.00	4.00	2.50
726	Paul Popovich	6.00	3.00	1.75
727	Ray Lamb/SP	8.00	4.00	2.50
728	N.L. Rookies **(Keith Lampard, Wayne Redmond, Bernie Williams)**	6.00	3.00	1.75
729	Dick Billings	6.00	3.00	1.75
730	Jim Rooker	6.00	3.00	1.75
731	Jim Qualls/SP	8.00	4.00	2.50
732	Bob Reed	6.00	3.00	1.75
733	Lee Maye/SP	8.00	4.00	2.50
734	Rob Gardner/SP	8.00	4.00	2.50
735	Mike Shannon/SP	8.00	4.00	2.50
736	Mel Queen/SP	8.00	4.00	2.50
737	Preston Gomez/SP	8.00	4.00	2.50
738	Russ Gibson/SP	8.00	4.00	2.50
739	Barry Lersch/SP	8.00	4.00	2.50
740	Luis Aparicio/SP	25.00	12.50	7.50
741	Skip Guinn	6.00	3.00	1.75
742	Royals Team	10.00	5.00	3.00
743	John O'Donoghue/SP	8.00	4.00	2.50
744	Chuck Manuel/SP	8.00	4.00	2.50
745	Sandy Alomar/SP	8.00	4.00	2.50
746	Andy Kosco	6.00	3.00	1.75
747	N.L. Rookies **(Balor Moore, Al Severinsen, Scipio Spinks)**	6.00	3.00	1.75
748	John Purdin/SP	8.00	4.00	2.50
749	Ken Szotkiewicz	6.00	3.00	1.75
750	Denny McLain/SP	20.00	10.00	6.00
751	Al Weis/SP	6.00	3.00	1.75
752	Dick Drago	10.00	5.00	3.00

1971 Topps All-Star Rookies Artist's Proofs

There exists only one set of these artist's proofs for a proposed set of All-Star Rookie cards. The standard-size card fronts are pasted onto 9-1/2" x 6-1/2" cardboard backing. It may have been intended that these be issued in card form for Topps' annual banquet. There is a player for each position on the 1970 All-Rookie Team, plus right- and left-handed pitchers. Players are listed here in alphabetical order.

		NM	EX	VG
Complete Set (10):		1,500	750.00	450.00
Common Player:		200.00	100.00	60.00
(1)	Larry Bowa	350.00	175.00	105.00
(2)	Les Cain	200.00	100.00	60.00
(3)	Bernie Carbo	200.00	100.00	60.00
(4)	Dave Cash	200.00	100.00	60.00
(5)	Billy Conigliaro	200.00	100.00	60.00
(6)	John Ellis	200.00	100.00	60.00
(7)	Roy Foster	200.00	100.00	60.00
(8)	Alan Gallagher	200.00	100.00	60.00
(9)	Carl Morton	200.00	100.00	60.00
(10)	Thurman Munson	750.00	375.00	225.00

1971 Topps Coins

Measuring 1-1/2" in diameter, the latest edition of the Topps coins was a 153-piece set. The coins feature a color photograph surrounded by a colored band on the front. The band carries the player's name, team, position and several stars. Backs have a short biography, the coin number and encouragement to collect the entire set. Back colors differ, with #s 1-51 having a brass back, #s 52-102 chrome backs, and the rest have blue backs. Most of the stars of the period are included in the set.

		NM	EX	VG
Complete Set (153):		500.00	250.00	150.00
Common Player:		2.00	1.00	.60
1	Cito Gaston	2.00	1.00	.60
2	Dave Johnson	2.00	1.00	.60
3	Jim Bunning	8.00	4.00	2.50
4	Jim Spencer	2.00	1.00	.60
5	Felix Millan	2.00	1.00	.60
6	Gerry Moses	2.00	1.00	.60
7	Fergie Jenkins	8.00	4.00	2.50
8	Felipe Alou	2.50	1.25	.70
9	Jim McGlothlin	2.00	1.00	.60
10	Dick McAuliffe	2.00	1.00	.60
11	Joe Torre	5.00	2.50	1.50
12	Jim Perry	2.00	1.00	.60
13	Bobby Bonds	2.00	1.00	.60
14	Danny Cater	2.00	1.00	.60
15	Bill Mazeroski	8.00	4.00	2.50
16	Luis Aparicio	8.00	4.00	2.50
17	Doug Rader	2.00	1.00	.60
18	Vada Pinson	3.00	1.50	.90
19	John Bateman	2.00	1.00	.60
20	Lew Krausse	2.00	1.00	.60
21	Billy Grabarkewitz	2.00	1.00	.60
22	Frank Howard	2.00	1.00	.60
23	Jerry Koosman	2.00	1.00	.60
24	Rod Carew	10.00	5.00	3.00
25	Al Ferrara	2.00	1.00	.60
26	Dave McNally	2.00	1.00	.60
27	Jim Hickman	2.00	1.00	.60
28	Sandy Alomar	2.00	1.00	.60
29	Lee May	2.00	1.00	.60
30	Rico Petrocelli	2.00	1.00	.60
31	Don Money	2.00	1.00	.60
32	Jim Rooker	2.00	1.00	.60
33	Dick Dietz	2.00	1.00	.60
34	Roy White	2.00	1.00	.60
35	Carl Morton	2.00	1.00	.60
36	Walt Williams	2.00	1.00	.60
37	Phil Niekro	8.00	4.00	2.50
38	Bill Freehan	2.00	1.00	.60
39	Julian Javier	2.00	1.00	.60
40	Rick Monday	2.00	1.00	.60
41	Don Wilson	2.00	1.00	.60
42	Ray Fosse	2.00	1.00	.60
43	Art Shamsky	2.00	1.00	.60
44	Ted Savage	2.00	1.00	.60
45	Claude Osteen	2.00	1.00	.60
46	Ed Brinkman	2.00	1.00	.60
47	Matty Alou	2.00	1.00	.60
48	Bob Oliver	2.00	1.00	.60
49	Danny Coombs	2.00	1.00	.60
50	Frank Robinson	10.00	5.00	3.00
51	Randy Hundley	2.00	1.00	.60
52	Cesar Tovar	2.00	1.00	.60
53	Wayne Simpson	2.00	1.00	.60
54	Bobby Murcer	2.00	1.00	.60
55	Tony Taylor	2.00	1.00	.60
56	Tommy John	3.00	1.50	.90
57	Willie McCovey	9.00	4.50	2.75
58	Carl Yastrzemski	13.50	6.75	4.00
59	Bob Bailey	2.00	1.00	.60
60	Clyde Wright	2.00	1.00	.60
61	Orlando Cepeda	8.00	4.00	2.50
62	Al Kaline	10.00	5.00	3.00
63	Bob Gibson	9.00	4.50	2.75
64	Bert Campaneris	2.00	1.00	.60
65	Ted Sizemore	2.00	1.00	.60
66	Duke Sims	2.00	1.00	.60
67	Bud Harrelson	2.00	1.00	.60
68	Jerry McNertney	2.00	1.00	.60
69	Jim Wynn	2.00	1.00	.60
70	Dick Bosman	2.00	1.00	.60
71	Roberto Clemente	30.00	15.00	9.00
72	Rich Reese	2.00	1.00	.60
73	Gaylord Perry	8.00	4.00	2.50
74	Boog Powell	3.00	1.50	.90
75	Billy Williams	9.00	4.50	2.75
76	Bill Melton	2.00	1.00	.60
77	Nate Colbert	2.00	1.00	.60
78	Reggie Smith	2.00	1.00	.60
79	Deron Johnson	2.00	1.00	.60
80	Catfish Hunter	8.00	4.00	2.50
81	Bob Tolan	2.00	1.00	.60
82	Jim Northrup	2.00	1.00	.60
83	Ron Fairly	2.00	1.00	.60
84	Alex Johnson	2.00	1.00	.60
85	Pat Jarvis	2.00	1.00	.60
86	Sam McDowell	2.00	1.00	.60
87	Lou Brock	9.00	4.50	2.75
88	Danny Walton	2.00	1.00	.60
89	Denis Menke	2.00	1.00	.60
90	Jim Palmer	9.00	4.50	2.75
91	Tommie Agee	2.00	1.00	.60
92	Duane Josephson	2.00	1.00	.60
93	Willie Davis	2.00	1.00	.60
94	Mel Stottlemyre	2.00	1.00	.60
95	Ron Santo	5.00	2.50	1.50
96	Amos Otis	2.00	1.00	.60
97	Ken Henderson	2.00	1.00	.60
98	George Scott	2.00	1.00	.60
99	Dock Ellis	2.00	1.00	.60
100	Harmon Killebrew	10.00	5.00	3.00
101	Pete Rose	20.00	10.00	6.00
102	Rick Reichardt	2.00	1.00	.60
103	Cleon Jones	2.00	1.00	.60
104	Ron Perranoski	2.00	1.00	.60
105	Tony Perez	9.00	4.50	2.75
106	Mickey Lolich	2.00	1.00	.60
107	Tim McCarver	3.00	1.50	.90
108	Reggie Jackson	15.00	7.50	4.50
109	Chris Cannizzaro	2.00	1.00	.60
110	Steve Hargan	2.00	1.00	.60
111	Rusty Staub	3.00	1.50	.90
112	Andy Messersmith	2.00	1.00	.60
113	Rico Carty	2.00	1.00	.60
114	Brooks Robinson	10.00	5.00	3.00
115	Steve Carlton	9.00	4.50	2.75
116	Mike Hegan	2.00	1.00	.60
117	Joe Morgan	9.00	4.50	2.75
118	Thurman Munson	8.00	4.00	2.50
119	Don Kessinger	2.00	1.00	.60
120	Joe Horlen	2.00	1.00	.60
121	Wes Parker	2.00	1.00	.60
122	Sonny Siebert	2.00	1.00	.60
123	Willie Stargell	9.00	4.50	2.75
124	Ellie Rodriguez	2.00	1.00	.60
125	Juan Marichal	8.00	4.00	2.50
126	Mike Epstein	2.00	1.00	.60
127	Tom Seaver	10.00	5.00	3.00
128	Tony Oliva	3.00	1.50	.90
129	Jim Merritt	2.00	1.00	.60
130	Willie Horton	2.00	1.00	.60
131	Rick Wise	2.00	1.00	.60
132	Sal Bando	2.00	1.00	.60
133	Ollie Brown	2.00	1.00	.60
134	Ken Harrelson	2.00	1.00	.60
135	Mack Jones	2.00	1.00	.60
136	Jim Fregosi	2.00	1.00	.60
137	Hank Aaron	25.00	12.50	7.50
138	Fritz Peterson	2.00	1.00	.60
139	Joe Hague	2.00	1.00	.60
140	Tommy Harper	2.00	1.00	.60
141	Larry Dierker	2.00	1.00	.60
142	Tony Conigliaro	4.00	2.00	1.25
143	Glenn Beckert	2.00	1.00	.60
144	Carlos May	2.00	1.00	.60
145	Don Sutton	8.00	4.00	2.50
146	Paul Casanova	2.00	1.00	.60
147	Bob Moose	2.00	1.00	.60
148	Leo Cardenas	2.00	1.00	.60
149	Johnny Bench	10.00	5.00	3.00
150	Mike Cuellar	2.00	1.00	.60
151	Donn Clendenon	2.00	1.00	.60
152	Lou Piniella	3.00	1.50	.90
153	Willie Mays	25.00	12.50	7.50

1971 Topps Greatest Moments

This 55-card set features highlights from the careers of top players of the day. The front of the 2-1/2" x 4-3/4" cards features a portrait photo of the player at left and deckle-edge action photo at right. There is a small headline on the white border of the action photo. The player's name and "One of Baseball's Greatest Moments" along with a black border complete the front. The back features a detail from the front photo and the story of the event. The newspaper style presentation

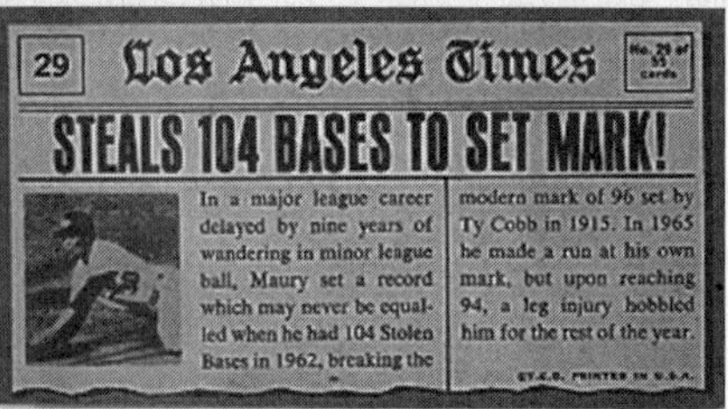

includes the name of real newspapers. Relatively scarce, virtually every card in this set is a star or at least an above-average player. Because of their unusual size, 22 of the cards were double-printed, as indicated in the checklist here. Because of endemic centering problems there is a greater than usual value difference between NM and lower-grade cards.

		NM	EX	VG
Complete Set (55):		4,500	2,250	1,350
Common Player:		20.00	10.00	6.00
1	Thurman Munson/DP	300.00	150.00	90.00
2	Hoyt Wilhelm	75.00	37.50	22.50
3	Rico Carty	65.00	32.50	20.00
4	Carl Morton/DP	20.00	10.00	6.00
5	Sal Bando/DP	20.00	10.00	6.00
6	Bert Campaneris/DP	20.00	10.00	6.00
7	Jim Kaat	70.00	35.00	20.00
8	Harmon Killebrew	225.00	110.00	65.00
9	Brooks Robinson	250.00	125.00	75.00
10	Jim Perry	45.00	22.50	13.50
11	Tony Oliva	125.00	62.50	37.50
12	Vada Pinson	125.00	62.50	37.50
13	Johnny Bench	300.00	150.00	90.00
14	Tony Perez	100.00	50.00	30.00
15	Pete Rose/DP	145.00	75.00	45.00
16	Jim Fregosi/DP	20.00	10.00	6.00
17	Alex Johnson/DP	20.00	10.00	6.00
18	Clyde Wright/DP	20.00	10.00	6.00
19	Al Kaline/DP	100.00	50.00	30.00
20	Denny McLain	50.00	25.00	15.00
21	Jim Northrup	45.00	22.50	13.50
22	Bill Freehan	50.00	25.00	15.00
23	Mickey Lolich	60.00	30.00	18.00
24	Bob Gibson/DP	75.00	37.50	22.50
25	Tim McCarver/DP	35.00	17.50	10.00
26	Orlando Cepeda/DP	45.00	22.50	13.50
27	Lou Brock/DP	60.00	30.00	18.00
28	Nate Colbert/DP	20.00	10.00	6.00
29	Maury Wills	50.00	25.00	15.00
30	Wes Parker	65.00	32.50	20.00
31	Jim Wynn	55.00	27.50	16.50
32	Larry Dierker	60.00	30.00	18.00
33	Bill Melton	60.00	30.00	18.00
34	Joe Morgan	75.00	37.50	22.50
35	Rusty Staub	65.00	32.50	20.00
36	Ernie Banks/DP	95.00	47.50	27.50
37	Billy Williams	75.00	37.50	22.50
38	Lou Piniella	80.00	40.00	24.00
39	Rico Petrocelli/DP	35.00	17.50	10.00
40	Carl Yastrzemski/DP	95.00	47.50	27.50
41	Willie Mays/DP	175.00	85.00	55.00
42	Tommy Harper	45.00	22.50	13.50
43	Jim Bunning/DP	25.00	12.50	7.50
44	Fritz Peterson	60.00	30.00	18.00
45	Roy White	75.00	37.50	22.50
46	Bobby Murcer	165.00	80.00	50.00
47	Reggie Jackson	600.00	300.00	180.00
48	Frank Howard	60.00	30.00	18.00
49	Dick Bosman	50.00	25.00	15.00
50	Sam McDowell/DP	25.00	12.50	7.50
51	Luis Aparicio/DP	45.00	22.50	13.50
52	Willie McCovey/DP	65.00	32.50	20.00
53	Joe Pepitone	65.00	32.50	20.00
54	Jerry Grote	45.00	22.50	13.50
55	Bud Harrelson	90.00	45.00	27.50

1971 Topps Scratch-Offs

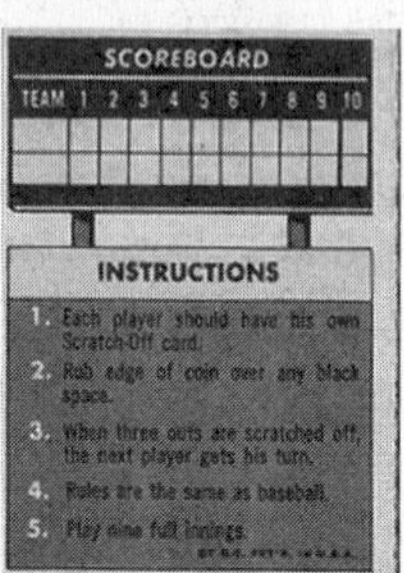

For a second year in 1971, Topps continued its scratch-off baseball card game with the same checklist of 24 players from the previous year. Unfolded, cards measure 3-3/8" x 5", and reveal a baseball game played by rubbing the black ink off squares to determine the "action." Fronts of the cards have a player picture as "captain," while backs have instructions and a scoreboard. Inserts with white centers are from 1970 while those with red centers are from 1971.

		NM	EX	VG
Complete Set (24):		65.00	32.50	20.00
Common Player:		1.50	.75	.45
(1)	Hank Aaron	7.50	3.75	2.25
(2)	Rich Allen	2.00	1.00	.60
(3)	Luis Aparicio	3.50	1.75	1.00
(4)	Sal Bando	1.50	.75	.45
(5)	Glenn Beckert	1.50	.75	.45
(6)	Dick Bosman	1.50	.75	.45
(7)	Nate Colbert	1.50	.75	.45
(8)	Mike Hegan	1.50	.75	.45
(9)	Mack Jones	1.50	.75	.45
(10)	Al Kaline	5.00	2.50	1.50
(11)	Harmon Killebrew	5.00	2.50	1.50
(12)	Juan Marichal	3.50	1.75	1.00
(13)	Tim McCarver	2.00	1.00	.60
(14)	Sam McDowell	1.50	.75	.45
(15)	Claude Osteen	1.50	.75	.45
(16)	Tony Perez	3.50	1.75	1.00
(17)	Lou Piniella	1.50	.75	.45
(18)	Boog Powell	2.00	1.00	.60
(19)	Tom Seaver	5.00	2.50	1.50
(20)	Jim Spencer	1.50	.75	.45
(21)	Willie Stargell	3.50	1.75	1.00
(22)	Mel Stottlemyre	1.50	.75	.45
(23)	Jim Wynn	1.50	.75	.45
(24)	Carl Yastrzemski	5.00	2.50	1.50

1971 Topps Super

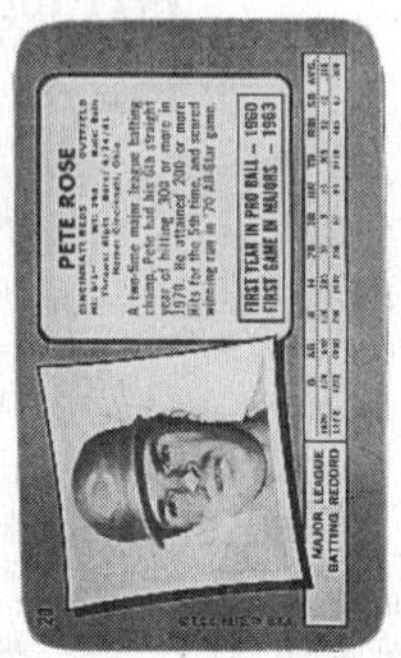

Topps continued to produce its special oversized cards in 1971. Measuring 3-1/8" x 5-1/4" with rounded corners, they feature a borderless color photograph with a facsimile autograph on front. Backs are basically enlargements of the player's regular Topps card. The set size was enlarged to 63 cards in 1971, so there are no short-printed cards as in 1970. Proof cards with square corners and blank backs, measuring about 3-3/8" x 5-1/2", are known.

		NM	EX	VG
Complete Set (63):		300.00	150.00	90.00
Common Player:		3.00	1.50	.90
Wax Pack (3):		50.00		
Proofs: 1-2X				
1	Reggie Smith	3.00	1.50	.90
2	Gaylord Perry	7.50	3.75	2.25
3	Ted Savage	3.00	1.50	.90
4	Donn Clendenon	3.00	1.50	.90
5	Boog Powell	4.50	2.25	1.25
6	Tony Perez	7.50	3.75	2.25
7	Dick Bosman	3.00	1.50	.90
8	Alex Johnson	3.00	1.50	.90
9	Rusty Staub	3.50	1.75	1.00
10	Mel Stottlemyre	3.00	1.50	.90
11	Tony Oliva	4.00	2.00	1.25
12	Bill Freehan	3.00	1.50	.90
13	Fritz Peterson	3.00	1.50	.90
14	Wes Parker	3.00	1.50	.90
15	Cesar Cedeno	3.00	1.50	.90
16	Sam McDowell	3.00	1.50	.90
17	Frank Howard	3.00	1.50	.90
18	Dave McNally	3.00	1.50	.90
19	Rico Petrocelli	3.00	1.50	.90
20	Pete Rose	25.00	12.50	7.50
21	Luke Walker	3.00	1.50	.90
22	Nate Colbert	3.00	1.50	.90
23	Luis Aparicio	7.50	3.75	2.25
24	Jim Perry	3.00	1.50	.90
25	Louis Brock	9.00	4.50	2.75
26	Roy White	3.00	1.50	.90
27	Claude Osteen	3.00	1.50	.90
28	Carl W. Morton	3.00	1.50	.90
29	Rico Carty	3.00	1.50	.90
30	Larry Dierker	3.00	1.50	.90
31	Bert Campaneris	3.00	1.50	.90
32	Johnny Bench	10.00	5.00	3.00
33	Felix Millan	3.00	1.50	.90
34	Tim McCarver	3.50	1.75	1.00
35	Ronald Santo	6.00	3.00	1.75
36	Tommie Agee	3.00	1.50	.90
37	Roberto Clemente	40.00	20.00	12.00
38	Reggie Jackson	20.00	10.00	6.00
39	Clyde Wright	3.00	1.50	.90
40	Rich Allen	4.50	2.25	1.25
41	Curt Flood	3.50	1.75	1.00
42	Fergie Jenkins	7.50	3.75	2.25
43	Willie Stargell	9.00	4.50	2.75
44	Henry Aaron	25.00	12.50	7.50
45	Amos Otis	3.00	1.50	.90
46	Willie McCovey	9.00	4.50	2.75
47	William Melton	3.00	1.50	.90
48	Bob Gibson	9.00	4.50	2.75
49	Carl Yastrzemski	12.00	6.00	3.50
50	Glenn Beckert	3.00	1.50	.90
51	Ray Fosse	3.00	1.50	.90
52	Clarence Gaston	3.00	1.50	.90
53	Tom Seaver	10.00	5.00	3.00
54	Al Kaline	10.00	5.00	3.00
55	Jim Northrup	3.00	1.50	.90
56	Willie Mays	25.00	12.50	7.50
57	Sal Bando	3.00	1.50	.90
58	Deron Johnson	3.00	1.50	.90
59	Brooks Robinson	10.00	5.00	3.00
60	Harmon Killebrew	9.00	4.50	2.75
61	Joseph Torre	4.50	2.25	1.25
62	Lou Piniella	4.50	2.25	1.25
63	Tommy Harper	3.00	1.50	.90

1971 Topps Tattoos

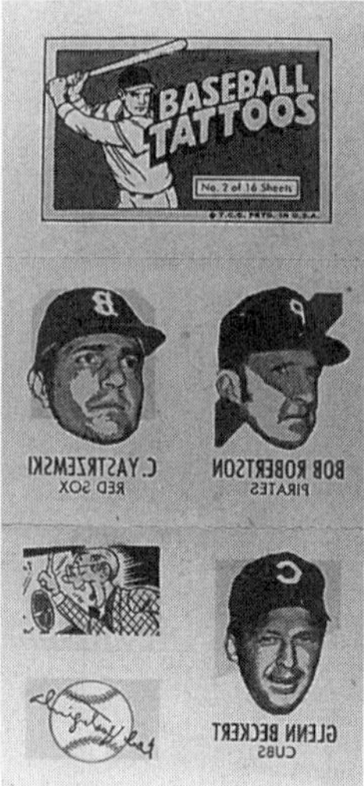

Topps once again produced baseball tattoos in 1971. This time, the tattoos came in a variety of sizes, shapes and themes. The sheets of tattoos measure 3-1/2" x 14-1/4". Each sheet contains an assortment of tattoos in two sizes, 1-3/4" x 2-3/8", or 1-3/16" x 1-3/4". There are players, facsimile autographed baseballs, team pennants and assorted baseball cartoon figures carried on the 16 different sheets. Listings below are for complete sheets; with the exception of the biggest-name stars, individual tattoos have little or no collector value.

		NM	EX	VG
Complete Sheet Set (16):		350.00	175.00	100.00
Common Sheet:		10.00	5.00	3.00
Unopened Pack:		25.00		
1	Brooks Robinson Autograph Montreal Expos Pennant San Francisco Giants Pennant (Sal Bando, Dick Bosman, Nate Colbert, Cleon Jones, Juan Marichal)	25.00	12.50	7.50
2	Red Sox Pennant Carl Yastrzemski Autograph New York Mets Pennant (Glenn Beckert, Tommy Harper, Ken Henderson, Fritz Peterson, Bob Robertson, Carl Yastrzemski)	35.00	17.50	10.00
3	Jim Fregosi Autograph New York Yankees Pennant Philadelphia Phillies Pennant (Orlando Cepeda, Jim Fregosi, Randy Hundley, Reggie Jackson, Jerry Koosman, Jim Palmer)	35.00	17.50	10.00
4	Kansas City Royals Pennant Oakland Athletics Pennant Sam McDowell Autograph (Dick Dietz, Cito Gaston, Dave Johnson, Sam McDowell, Gary Nolan, Amos Otis)	10.00	5.00	3.00
5	Al Kaline Autograph Braves Pennant L.A. Dodgers Pennant (Bill Grabarkewitz, Al Kaline, Lee May, Tom Murphy, Vada Pinson, Manny Sanguillen)	20.00	10.00	6.00
6	Chicago Cubs Pennant Cincinnati Reds Pennant Harmon Kilebrew Autograph (Luis Aparicio, Paul Blair, Chris Cannizzaro, Donn Clendenon, Larry Dieker, Harmon Killebrew)	25.00	12.50	7.50

7	Boog Powell Autograph Cleveland Indians Pennant Milwaukee Brewers Pennant (Rich Allen, Bert Campaneris, Don Money, Boog Powell, Ted Savage, Rusty Staub)	15.00	7.50	4.50
8	Chicago White Sox Pennant Frank Howard Autograph San Diego Padres Pennant (Leo Cardenas, Bill Hands, Frank Howard, Wes Parker, Reggie Smith, Willie Stargell)	10.00	5.00	3.00
9	Detroit Tigers Pennant Henry Aaron Autograph (Hank Aaron, Tommy Agee, Jim Hunter, Dick McAuliffe, Tony Perez, Lou Piniella)	35.00	17.50	10.00
10	Baltimore Orioles Pennant Fergie Jenkins Autograph (Roberto Clemente, Tony Conigliaro, Fergie Jenkins, Thurman Munson, Gary Peters, Joe Torre)	50.00	25.00	15.00
11	Johnny Bench Autograph Washington Senators Pennant (Johnny Bench, Rico Carty, Bill Mazeroski, Bob Oliver, Rico Petrocelli, Frank Robinson)	35.00	17.50	10.00
12	Billy Williams Autograph Houston Astros Pennant (Bill Freehan, Dave McNally, Felix Millan, Mel Stottlemyre, Bob Tolan, Billy Williams)	15.00	7.50	4.50
13	Pittsburgh Pirates Pennant Willie McCovey Autograph (Ray Culp, Bud Harrelson, Mickey Lolich, Willie McCovey, Ron Santo, Roy White)	20.00	10.00	6.00
14	Minnesota Twins Pennant Tom Seaver Autograph (Bill Melton, Jim Perry, Pete Rose, Tom Seaver, Maury Wills, Clyde Wright)	45.00	22.00	13.50
15	Robert Gibson Autograph St. Louis Cardinals Pennant (Rod Carew, Bob Gibson, Alex Johnson, Don Kessinger, Jim Merritt, Rick Monday)	20.00	10.00	6.00
16	Angels Pennant Willie Mays Autograph (Larry Bowa, Mike Cuellar, Ray Fosse, Willie Mays, Carl Morton, Tony Oliva)	25.00	12.50	7.50

1972 Topps

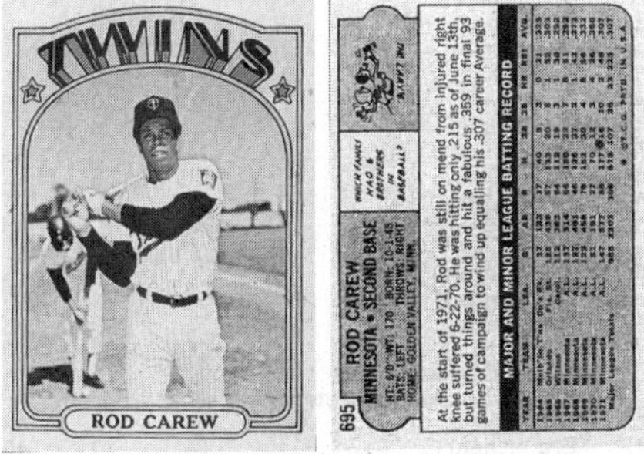

The largest Topps issue of its time appeared in 1972, with the set size reaching the 787 mark. The 2-1/2" x 3-1/2" cards are something special as well. Their fronts have a color photo which is shaped into an arch and surrounded by two different color borders, all of which is inside the overall white border. The player's name is in a white panel below the picture while the team name is above the picture in what might best be described as "superhero" type in a variety of colors. No mention of the player's position appears on the front. Cards backs are tame by comparison, featuring statistics and a trivia question. The set features a record number of specialty cards including more than six dozen "In Action" (shown as "IA" in checklists below) cards featuring action shots of popular players. There are the usual statistical leaders, playoff and World Series highlights. Other innovations are 16 "Boyhood Photo" cards which depict scrapbook black and white photos of 1972's top players, and a group of cards depicting the trophies which comprise baseball's major awards. Finally, a group of seven "Traded" cards was included which feature a large "Traded" across the front of the card.

		NM	EX	VG
	Complete Set (787):	1,600	800.00	475.00
	Common Player (1-525):	1.50	.70	.45
	Common Player (526-656):	3.00	1.50	.90
	Common Player (657-787):	10.00	5.00	3.00
1	Pirates Team (World Champions)	8.00	4.00	2.50
2	Ray Culp	1.50	.70	.45
3	Bob Tolan	1.50	.70	.45
4	1st Series Checklist (1-132)	4.00	2.00	1.25
5	John Bateman	1.50	.70	.45
6	Fred Scherman	1.50	.70	.45
7	Enzo Hernandez	1.50	.70	.45
8	Ron Swoboda	1.50	.70	.45
9	Stan Williams	1.50	.70	.45
10	Amos Otis	1.50	.70	.45
11	Bobby Valentine	1.50	.70	.45
12	Jose Cardenal	1.50	.70	.45
13	Joe Grzenda	1.50	.70	.45
14	Phillies Rookies **(Mike Anderson, Pete Koegel, Wayne Twitchell)**	1.50	.70	.45
15	Walt Williams	1.50	.70	.45
16	Mike Jorgensen	1.50	.70	.45
17	Dave Duncan	1.50	.70	.45
18a	Juan Pizarro (Green under "C" and "S.")	7.50	3.75	2.25
18b	Juan Pizarro (Yellow under "C" and "S.")	1.50	.70	.45
19	Billy Cowan	1.50	.70	.45
20	Don Wilson	1.50	.70	.45
21	Braves Team	3.00	1.50	.90
22	Rob Gardner	1.50	.70	.45
23	Ted Kubiak	1.50	.70	.45
24	Ted Ford	1.50	.70	.45
25	Bill Singer	1.50	.70	.45
26	Andy Etchebarren	1.50	.70	.45
27	Bob Johnson	1.50	.70	.45
28	Twins Rookies **(Steve Brye, Bob Gebhard, Hal Haydel)**	1.50	.70	.45
29a	Bill Bonham (Green under "C" and "S.")	7.50	3.75	2.25
29b	Bill Bonham (Yellow under "C" and "S.")	1.50	.70	.45
30	Rico Petrocelli	1.50	.70	.45
31	Cleon Jones	1.50	.70	.45
32	Cleon Jones/IA	1.50	.70	.45
33	Billy Martin	6.00	3.00	1.75
34	Billy Martin/IA	2.00	1.00	.60
35	Jerry Johnson	1.50	.70	.45
36	Jerry Johnson/IA	1.50	.70	.45
37	Carl Yastrzemski	8.00	4.00	2.50
38	Carl Yastrzemski/IA	5.00	2.50	1.50
39	Bob Barton	1.50	.70	.45
40	Bob Barton/IA	1.50	.70	.45
41	Tommy Davis	1.50	.70	.45
42	Tommy Davis/IA	1.50	.70	.45
43	Rick Wise	1.50	.70	.45
44	Rick Wise/IA	1.50	.70	.45
45a	Glenn Beckert (Green under "C" and "S.")	7.50	3.75	2.25
45b	Glenn Beckert (Yellow under "C" and "S.")	1.50	.70	.45
46	Glenn Beckert/IA	1.50	.70	.45
47	John Ellis	1.50	.70	.45
48	John Ellis/IA	1.50	.70	.45
49	Willie Mays	40.00	20.00	12.00
50	Willie Mays/IA	20.00	10.00	6.00
51	Harmon Killebrew	8.00	4.00	2.50
52	Harmon Killebrew/IA	5.00	2.50	1.50
53	Bud Harrelson	1.50	.70	.45
54	Bud Harrelson/IA	1.50	.70	.45
55	Clyde Wright	1.50	.70	.45
56	Rich Chiles	1.50	.70	.45
57	Bob Oliver	1.50	.70	.45
58	Ernie McAnally	1.50	.70	.45
59	***Fred Stanley***	1.50	.70	.45
60	Manny Sanguillen	1.50	.70	.45
61	Cubs Rookies **(Gene Hiser, Burt Hooton, Earl Stephenson)**	1.50	.70	.45
62	Angel Mangual	1.50	.70	.45
63	Duke Sims	1.50	.70	.45
64	Pete Broberg	1.50	.70	.45
65	Cesar Cedeno	1.50	.70	.45
66	Ray Corbin	1.50	.70	.45
67	Red Schoendienst	4.00	2.00	1.25
68	Jim York	1.50	.70	.45
69	Roger Freed	1.50	.70	.45
70	Mike Cuellar	1.50	.70	.45
71	Angels Team	3.00	1.50	.90
72	***Bruce Kison***	1.50	.70	.45
73	Steve Huntz	1.50	.70	.45
74	Cecil Upshaw	1.50	.70	.45
75	Bert Campaneris	1.50	.70	.45
76	Don Carrithers	1.50	.70	.45
77	Ron Theobald	1.50	.70	.45
78	Steve Arlin	1.50	.70	.45
79	Red Sox Rookies **(Cecil Cooper, Carlton Fisk, Mike Garman)**	40.00	20.00	12.00
80	Tony Perez	6.00	3.00	1.75
81	Mike Hedlund	1.50	.70	.45
82	Ron Woods	1.50	.70	.45
83	Dalton Jones	1.50	.70	.45
84	Vince Colbert	1.50	.70	.45
85	N.L. Batting Leaders (Glenn Beckert, Ralph Garr, Joe Torre)	4.00	2.00	1.25
86	A.L. Batting Leaders (Bobby Murcer, Tony Oliva, Merv Rettenmund)	3.00	1.50	.90
87	N.L. R.B.I. Leaders (Hank Aaron, Willie Stargell, Joe Torre)	6.00	3.00	1.75
88	A.L. R.B.I. Leaders (Harmon Killebrew, Frank Robinson, Reggie Smith)	3.00	1.50	.90
89	N.L. Home Run Leaders (Hank Aaron, Lee May, Willie Stargell)	6.00	3.00	1.75
90	A.L. Home Run Leaders (Norm Cash, Reggie Jackson, Bill Melton)	4.00	2.00	1.25
91	N.L. E.R.A. Leaders (Dave Roberts (Picture is Denny Coombs), Tom Seaver, Don Wilson)	2.50	1.25	.70
92	A.L. E.R.A. Leaders (Vida Blue, Jim Palmer, Wilbur Wood)	2.00	1.00	.60
93	N.L. Pitching Leaders (Steve Carlton, Al Downing, Fergie Jenkins, Tom Seaver)	4.00	2.00	1.25
94	A.L. Pitching Leaders (Vida Blue, Mickey Lolich, Wilbur Wood)	1.50	.70	.45
95	N.L. Strikeout Leaders (Fergie Jenkins, Tom Seaver, Bill Stoneman)	4.00	2.00	1.25
96	A.L. Strikeout Leaders (Vida Blue, Joe Coleman, Mickey Lolich)	1.50	.70	.45
97	Tom Kelley	1.50	.70	.45
98	Chuck Tanner	1.50	.70	.45
99	***Ross Grimsley***	1.50	.70	.45
100	Frank Robinson	8.00	4.00	2.50
101	Astros Rookies ***(Ray Busse, Bill Grief, J.R. Richard)***	4.00	2.00	1.25
102	Lloyd Allen	1.50	.70	.45
103	2nd Series Checklist (133-263)	2.00	1.00	.60
104	***Toby Harrah***	1.50	.70	.45
105	Gary Gentry	1.50	.70	.45
106	Brewers Team	3.00	1.50	.90
107	***Jose Cruz***	3.00	1.50	.90
108	Gary Waslewski	1.50	.70	.45
109	Jerry May	1.50	.70	.45
110	Ron Hunt	1.50	.70	.45
111	Jim Grant	1.50	.70	.45
112	Greg Luzinski	1.50	.70	.45
113	Rogelio Moret	1.50	.70	.45
114	Bill Buckner	1.50	.70	.45
115	Jim Fregosi	1.50	.70	.45
116	***Ed Farmer***	1.50	.70	.45
117a	Cleo James (Green under "C" and "S.")	7.50	3.75	2.25
117b	Cleo James (Yellow under "C" and "S.")	1.50	.70	.45
118	Skip Lockwood	1.50	.70	.45
119	Marty Perez	1.50	.70	.45
120	Bill Freehan	1.50	.70	.45
121	Ed Sprague	1.50	.70	.45
122	Larry Biittner	1.50	.70	.45
123	Ed Acosta	1.50	.70	.45
124	Yankees Rookies **(Alan Closter, Roger Hambright, Rusty Torres)**	1.50	.70	.45
125	Dave Cash	1.50	.70	.45
126	Bart Johnson	1.50	.70	.45
127	Duffy Dyer	1.50	.70	.45
128	Eddie Watt	1.50	.70	.45
129	Charlie Fox	1.50	.70	.45
130	Bob Gibson	8.00	4.00	2.50
131	Jim Nettles	1.50	.70	.45
132	Joe Morgan	8.00	4.00	2.50
133	Joe Keough	1.50	.70	.45
134	Carl Morton	1.50	.70	.45
135	Vada Pinson	2.50	1.25	.70
136	Darrel Chaney	1.50	.70	.45
137	Dick Williams	1.50	.70	.45
138	Mike Kekich	1.50	.70	.45
139	Tim McCarver	3.00	1.50	.90
140	Pat Dobson	1.50	.70	.45
141	Mets Rookies **(Buzz Capra, Jon Matlack, Leroy Stanton)**	1.50	.70	.45
142	***Chris Chambliss***	3.00	1.50	.90
143	Garry Jestadt	1.50	.70	.45
144	Marty Pattin	1.50	.70	.45
145	Don Kessinger	1.50	.70	.45
146	Steve Kealey	1.50	.70	.45
147	***Dave Kingman***	6.00	3.00	1.75
148	Dick Billings	1.50	.70	.45
149	Gary Neibauer	1.50	.70	.45
150	Norm Cash	2.50	1.25	.70
151	Jim Brewer	1.50	.70	.45
152	Gene Clines	1.50	.70	.45
153	Rick Auerbach	1.50	.70	.45
154	Ted Simmons	4.00	2.00	1.25
155	Larry Dierker	1.50	.70	.45
156	Twins Team	3.00	1.50	.90
157	Don Gullett	1.50	.70	.45
158	Jerry Kenney	1.50	.70	.45
159	John Boccabella	1.50	.70	.45
160	Andy Messersmith	1.50	.70	.45
161	Brock Davis	1.50	.70	.45
162	Brewers Rookies **(Jerry Bell, Darrell Porter, Bob Reynolds)** (Bell and Porter photos transposed.)	1.50	.70	.45
163	Tug McGraw	1.50	.70	.45
164	Tug McGraw/IA	1.50	.70	.45
165	***Chris Speier***	1.50	.70	.45
166	Chris Speier/IA	1.50	.70	.45
167	Deron Johnson	1.50	.70	.45
168	Deron Johnson/IA	1.50	.70	.45
169	Vida Blue	4.00	2.00	1.25
170	Vida Blue/IA	2.00	1.00	.60
171	Darrell Evans	3.00	1.50	.90
172	Darrell Evans/IA	2.00	1.00	.60
173	Clay Kirby	1.50	.70	.45
174	Clay Kirby/IA	1.50	.70	.45
175	Tom Haller	1.50	.70	.45
176	Tom Haller/IA	1.50	.70	.45
177	Paul Schaal	1.50	.70	.45
178	Paul Schaal/IA	1.50	.70	.45
179	Dock Ellis	1.50	.70	.45
180	Dock Ellis/IA	1.50	.70	.45
181	Ed Kranepool	1.50	.70	.45
182	Ed Kranepool/IA	1.50	.70	.45
183	Bill Melton	1.50	.70	.45
184	Bill Melton/IA	1.50	.70	.45
185	Ron Bryant	1.50	.70	.45
186	Ron Bryant/IA	1.50	.70	.45
187	Gates Brown	1.50	.70	.45
188	Frank Lucchesi	1.50	.70	.45
189	Gene Tenace	1.50	.70	.45
190	Dave Giusti	1.50	.70	.45

191 ***Jeff Burroughs*** 3.00 1.50 .90
192 Cubs Team 4.00 2.00 1.25
193 ***Kurt Bevacqua*** 1.50 .70 .45
194 Fred Norman 1.50 .70 .45
195 Orlando Cepeda 6.00 3.00 1.75
196 Mel Queen 1.50 .70 .45
197 Johnny Briggs 1.50 .70 .45
198 Dodgers Rookies **(Charlie Hough, Bob O'Brien, Mike Strahler)** 5.00 2.50 1.50
199 Mike Fiore 1.50 .70 .45
200 Lou Brock 8.00 4.00 2.50
201 Phil Roof 1.50 .70 .45
202 Scipio Spinks 1.50 .70 .45
203 ***Ron Blomberg*** 2.50 1.25 .70
204 Tommy Helms 1.50 .70 .45
205 Dick Drago 1.50 .70 .45
206 Dal Maxvill 1.50 .70 .45
207 Tom Egan 1.50 .70 .45
208 Milt Pappas 1.50 .70 .45
209 Joe Rudi 1.50 .70 .45
210 Denny McLain 3.00 1.50 .90
211 Gary Sutherland 1.50 .70 .45
212 Grant Jackson 1.50 .70 .45
213 Angels Rookies **(Art Kusnyer, Billy Parker, Tom Silverio)** 1.50 .70 .45
214 Mike McQueen 1.50 .70 .45
215 Alex Johnson 1.50 .70 .45
216 Joe Niekro 1.50 .70 .45
217 Roger Metzger 1.50 .70 .45
218 Eddie Kasko 1.50 .70 .45
219 ***Rennie Stennett*** 1.50 .70 .45
220 Jim Perry 1.50 .70 .45
221 N.L. Playoffs (Bucs Champs) 4.00 2.00 1.25
222 A.L. Playoffs (Orioles Champs) 5.00 2.50 1.50
223 World Series Game 1 4.00 2.00 1.25
224 World Series Game 2 4.00 2.00 1.25
225 World Series Game 3 4.00 2.00 1.25
226 World Series Game 4 (Roberto Clemente) 10.00 5.00 3.00
227 World Series Game 5 4.00 2.00 1.25
228 World Series Game 6 4.00 2.00 1.25
229 World Series Game 7 4.00 2.00 1.25
230 Series Celebration (On Top of the World) 4.00 2.00 1.25
231 Casey Cox 1.50 .70 .45
232 Giants Rookies **(Chris Arnold, Jim Barr, Dave Rader)** 1.50 .70 .45
233 Jay Johnstone 1.50 .70 .45
234 Ron Taylor 1.50 .70 .45
235 Merv Rettenmund 1.50 .70 .45
236 Jim McGlothlin 1.50 .70 .45
237 Yankees Team 4.00 2.00 1.25
238 Leron Lee 1.50 .70 .45
239 Tom Timmermann 1.50 .70 .45
240 Rich Allen 3.00 1.50 .90
241 Rollie Fingers 6.00 3.00 1.75
242 Don Mincher 1.50 .70 .45
243 Frank Linzy 1.50 .70 .45
244 Steve Braun 1.50 .70 .45
245 Tommie Agee 1.50 .70 .45
246 Tom Burgmeier 1.50 .70 .45
247 Milt May 1.50 .70 .45
248 Tom Bradley 1.50 .70 .45
249 Harry Walker 1.50 .70 .45
250 Boog Powell 2.00 1.00 .60
251a 3rd Series Checklist (264-394) (Small print on front.) 3.00 1.50 .90
251b 3rd Series Checklist (264-394) (Large print on front.) 3.00 1.50 .90
252 Ken Reynolds 1.50 .70 .45
253 Sandy Alomar 1.50 .70 .45
254 Boots Day 1.50 .70 .45
255 Jim Lonborg 1.50 .70 .45
256 George Foster 2.50 1.25 .70
257 Tigers Rookies **(Jim Foor, Tim Hosley, Paul Jata)** 1.50 .70 .45
258 Randy Hundley 1.50 .70 .45
259 Sparky Lyle 1.50 .70 .45
260 Ralph Garr 1.50 .70 .45
261 Steve Mingori 1.50 .70 .45
262 Padres Team 3.00 1.50 .90
263 Felipe Alou 2.00 1.00 .60
264 Tommy John 2.00 1.00 .60
265 Wes Parker 1.50 .70 .45
266 Bobby Bolin 1.50 .70 .45
267 Dave Concepcion 2.00 1.00 .60
268 A's Rookies **(Dwain Anderson, Chris Floethe)** 1.50 .70 .45
269 Don Hahn 1.50 .70 .45
270 Jim Palmer 8.00 4.00 2.50
271 Ken Rudolph 1.50 .70 .45
272 ***Mickey Rivers*** 2.00 1.00 .60
273 Bobby Floyd 1.50 .70 .45
274 Al Severinsen 1.50 .70 .45
275 Cesar Tovar 1.50 .70 .45
276 Gene Mauch 1.50 .70 .45
277 Elliott Maddox 1.50 .70 .45
278 Dennis Higgins 1.50 .70 .45
279 Larry Brown 1.50 .70 .45
280 Willie McCovey 8.00 4.00 2.50
281 Bill Parsons 1.50 .70 .45
282 Astros Team 4.00 2.00 1.25
283 Darrell Brandon 1.50 .70 .45
284 Ike Brown 1.50 .70 .45
285 Gaylord Perry 6.00 3.00 1.75
286 Gene Alley 1.50 .70 .45
287 Jim Hardin 1.50 .70 .45
288 Johnny Jeter 1.50 .70 .45
289 Syd O'Brien 1.50 .70 .45
290 Sonny Siebert 1.50 .70 .45
291 Hal McRae 2.50 1.25 .70
292 Hal McRae/IA 1.50 .70 .45
293 Danny Frisella 1.50 .70 .45
294 Danny Frisella/IA 1.50 .70 .45
295 Dick Dietz 1.50 .70 .45
296 Dick Dietz/IA 1.50 .70 .45
297 Claude Osteen 1.50 .70 .45
298 Claude Osteen/IA 1.50 .70 .45
299 Hank Aaron 40.00 20.00 12.00
300 Hank Aaron/IA 25.00 12.50 7.50
301 George Mitterwald 1.50 .70 .45
302 George Mitterwald/IA 1.50 .70 .45
303 Joe Pepitone 2.00 1.00 .60
304 Joe Pepitone/IA 1.50 .70 .45
305 Ken Boswell 1.50 .70 .45
306 Ken Boswell/IA 1.50 .70 .45
307 Steve Renko 1.50 .70 .45
308 Steve Renko/IA 1.50 .70 .45
309 Roberto Clemente 50.00 25.00 15.00
310 Roberto Clemente/IA 30.00 15.00 9.00
311 Clay Carroll 1.50 .70 .45
312 Clay Carroll/IA 1.50 .70 .45
313 Luis Aparicio 6.00 3.00 1.75
314 Luis Aparicio/IA 4.00 2.00 1.25
315 Paul Splittorff 1.50 .70 .45
316 Cardinals Rookies **(Jim Bibby, Santiago Guzman, Jorge Roque)** 1.50 .70 .45
317 Rich Hand 1.50 .70 .45
318 Sonny Jackson 1.50 .70 .45
319 Aurelio Rodriguez 1.50 .70 .45
320 Steve Blass 1.50 .70 .45
321 Joe Lahoud 1.50 .70 .45
322 Jose Pena 1.50 .70 .45
323 Earl Weaver 5.00 2.50 1.50
324 Mike Ryan 1.50 .70 .45
325 Mel Stottlemyre 1.50 .70 .45
326 Pat Kelly 1.50 .70 .45
327 ***Steve Stone*** 3.00 1.50 .90
328 Red Sox Team 5.00 2.50 1.50
329 Roy Foster 1.50 .70 .45
330 Jim Hunter 6.00 3.00 1.75
331 Stan Swanson 1.50 .70 .45
332 Buck Martinez 1.50 .70 .45
333 Steve Barber 1.50 .70 .45
334 Rangers Rookies **(Bill Fahey, Jim Mason, Tom Ragland)** 1.50 .70 .45
335 Bill Hands 1.50 .70 .45
336 Marty Martinez 1.50 .70 .45
337 Mike Kilkenny 1.50 .70 .45
338 Bob Grich 1.50 .70 .45
339 Ron Cook 1.50 .70 .45
340 Roy White 1.50 .70 .45
341 Joe Torre (Boyhood Photo) 2.50 1.25 .70
342 Wilbur Wood (Boyhood Photo) 1.50 .70 .45
343 Willie Stargell (Boyhood Photo) 2.00 1.00 .60
344 Dave McNally (Boyhood Photo) 1.50 .70 .45
345 Rick Wise (Boyhood Photo) 1.50 .70 .45
346 Jim Fregosi (Boyhood Photo) 1.50 .70 .45
347 Tom Seaver (Boyhood Photo) 3.00 1.50 .90
348 Sal Bando (Boyhood Photo) 1.50 .70 .45
349 Al Fitzmorris 1.50 .70 .45
350 Frank Howard 2.00 1.00 .60
351 Braves Rookies **(Jimmy Britton, Tom House, Rick Kester)** 1.50 .70 .45
352 Dave LaRoche 1.50 .70 .45
353 Art Shamsky 1.50 .70 .45
354 Tom Murphy 1.50 .70 .45
355 Bob Watson 1.50 .70 .45
356 Gerry Moses 1.50 .70 .45
357 Woodie Fryman 1.50 .70 .45
358 Sparky Anderson 4.00 2.00 1.25
359 Don Pavletich 1.50 .70 .45
360 Dave Roberts 1.50 .70 .45
361 Mike Andrews 1.50 .70 .45
362 Mets Team 4.00 2.00 1.25
363 Ron Klimkowski 1.50 .70 .45
364 Johnny Callison 1.50 .70 .45
365 Dick Bosman 1.50 .70 .45
366 Jimmy Rosario 1.50 .70 .45
367 Ron Perranoski 1.50 .70 .45
368 Danny Thompson 1.50 .70 .45
369 Jim Lefebvre 1.50 .70 .45
370 Don Buford 1.50 .70 .45
371 Denny Lemaster 1.50 .70 .45
372 Royals Rookies **(Lance Clemons, Monty Montgomery)** 1.50 .70 .45
373 John Mayberry 1.50 .70 .45
374 Jack Heidemann 1.50 .70 .45
375 Reggie Cleveland 1.50 .70 .45
376 Andy Kosco 1.50 .70 .45
377 Terry Harmon 1.50 .70 .45
378 4th Series Checklist (395-525) 3.00 1.50 .90
379 Ken Berry 1.50 .70 .45
380 Earl Williams 1.50 .70 .45
381 White Sox Team 3.00 1.50 .90
382 Joe Gibbon 1.50 .70 .45
383 Brant Alyea 1.50 .70 .45
384 Dave Campbell 1.50 .70 .45
385 Mickey Stanley 1.50 .70 .45
386 Jim Colborn 1.50 .70 .45
387 Horace Clarke 1.50 .70 .45
388 Charlie Williams 1.50 .70 .45
389 Bill Rigney 1.50 .70 .45
390 Willie Davis 1.50 .70 .45
391 Ken Sanders 1.50 .70 .45
392 Pirates Rookies ***(Fred Cambria, Richie Zisk)*** 2.00 1.00 .60
393 Curt Motton 1.50 .70 .45
394 Ken Forsch 1.50 .70 .45
395 Matty Alou 1.50 .70 .45
396 Paul Lindblad 1.50 .70 .45
397 Phillies Team 4.00 2.00 1.25
398 Larry Hisle 2.00 1.00 .60
399 Milt Wilcox 1.50 .70 .45
400 Tony Oliva 3.00 1.50 .90
401 Jim Nash 1.50 .70 .45
402 Bobby Heise 1.50 .70 .45
403 John Cumberland 1.50 .70 .45
404 Jeff Torborg 1.50 .70 .45
405 Ron Fairly 1.50 .70 .45
406 ***George Hendrick*** 2.00 1.00 .60
407 Chuck Taylor 1.50 .70 .45
408 Jim Northrup 1.50 .70 .45
409 Frank Baker 1.50 .70 .45
410 Fergie Jenkins 6.00 3.00 1.75
411 Bob Montgomery 1.50 .70 .45
412 Dick Kelley 1.50 .70 .45
413 White Sox Rookies **(Don Eddy, Dave Lemonds)** 1.50 .70 .45
414 Bob Miller 1.50 .70 .45
415 Cookie Rojas 1.50 .70 .45
416 Johnny Edwards 1.50 .70 .45
417 Tom Hall 1.50 .70 .45
418 Tom Shopay 1.50 .70 .45
419 Jim Spencer 1.50 .70 .45
420 Steve Carlton 15.00 7.50 4.50
421 Ellie Rodriguez 1.50 .70 .45
422 Ray Lamb 1.50 .70 .45
423 Oscar Gamble 1.50 .70 .45
424 Bill Gogolewski 1.50 .70 .45
425 Ken Singleton 1.50 .70 .45
426 Ken Singleton/IA 1.50 .70 .45
427 Tito Fuentes 1.50 .70 .45
428 Tito Fuentes/IA 1.50 .70 .45
429 Bob Robertson 1.50 .70 .45
430 Bob Robertson/IA 1.50 .70 .45
431 Clarence Gaston 1.50 .70 .45
432 Clarence Gaston/IA 1.50 .70 .45
433 Johnny Bench 20.00 10.00 6.00
434 Johnny Bench/IA 10.00 5.00 3.00
435 Reggie Jackson 25.00 12.50 7.50
436 Reggie Jackson /IA 12.00 6.00 3.50
437 Maury Wills 1.50 .70 .45
438 Maury Wills/IA 1.50 .70 .45
439 Billy Williams 8.00 4.00 2.50
440 Billy Williams/IA 5.00 2.50 1.50
441 Thurman Munson 15.00 7.50 4.50
442 Thurman Munson/IA 10.00 5.00 3.00
443 Ken Henderson 1.50 .70 .45
444 Ken Henderson/IA 1.50 .70 .45
445 Tom Seaver 25.00 12.50 7.50
446 Tom Seaver/IA 15.00 7.50 4.50
447 Willie Stargell 8.00 4.00 2.50
448 Willie Stargell/IA 5.00 2.50 1.50
449 Bob Lemon 4.00 2.00 1.25
450 Mickey Lolich 1.50 .70 .45
451 Tony LaRussa 2.50 1.25 .70
452 Ed Herrmann 1.50 .70 .45
453 Barry Lersch 1.50 .70 .45
454 A's Team 4.00 2.00 1.25
455 Tommy Harper 1.50 .70 .45
456 Mark Belanger 1.50 .70 .45
457 Padres Rookies ***(Darcy Fast, Mike Ivie, Derrel Thomas)*** 1.50 .70 .45
458 Aurelio Monteagudo 1.50 .70 .45
459 Rick Renick 1.50 .70 .45
460 Al Downing 1.50 .70 .45
461 Tim Cullen 1.50 .70 .45
462 Rickey Clark 1.50 .70 .45
463 Bernie Carbo 1.50 .70 .45
464 Jim Roland 1.50 .70 .45
465 Gil Hodges 4.00 2.00 1.25
466 Norm Miller 1.50 .70 .45
467 Steve Kline 1.50 .70 .45
468 Richie Scheinblum 1.50 .70 .45
469 Ron Herbel 1.50 .70 .45
470 Ray Fosse 1.50 .70 .45
471 Luke Walker 1.50 .70 .45
472 Phil Gagliano 1.50 .70 .45
473 Dan McGinn 1.50 .70 .45
474 Orioles Rookies ***(Don Baylor, Roric Harrison, Johnny Oates)*** 10.00 5.00 3.00
475 Gary Nolan 1.50 .70 .45
476 Lee Richard 1.50 .70 .45
477 Tom Phoebus 1.50 .70 .45
478a 5th Series Checklist (526-656) (Small print on front.) 2.50 1.25 .70
478b 5th Series Checklist (526-656) (Large printing on front.) 2.50 1.25 .70
479 Don Shaw 1.50 .70 .45
480 Lee May 1.50 .70 .45
481 Billy Conigliaro 1.50 .70 .45
482 Joe Hoerner 1.50 .70 .45
483 Ken Suarez 1.50 .70 .45
484 Lum Harris 1.50 .70 .45
485 Phil Regan 1.50 .70 .45
486 John Lowenstein 1.50 .70 .45
487 Tigers Team 5.00 2.50 1.50
488 Mike Nagy 1.50 .70 .45
489 Expos Rookies **(Terry Humphrey, Keith Lampard)** 1.50 .70 .45
490 Dave McNally 1.50 .70 .45
491 Lou Piniella (Boyhood Photo) 1.50 .70 .45
492 Mel Stottlemyre (Boyhood Photo) 1.50 .70 .45
493 Bob Bailey (Boyhood Photo) 1.50 .70 .45
494 Willie Horton (Boyhood Photo) 1.50 .70 .45
495 Bill Melton (Boyhood Photo) 1.50 .70 .45
496 Bud Harrelson (Boyhood Photo) 1.50 .70 .45
497 Jim Perry (Boyhood Photo) 1.50 .70 .45
498 Brooks Robinson (Boyhood Photo) 4.00 2.00 1.25
499 Vicente Romo 1.50 .70 .45
500 Joe Torre 5.00 2.50 1.50
501 Pete Hamm 1.50 .70 .45
502 Jackie Hernandez 1.50 .70 .45
503 Gary Peters 1.50 .70 .45
504 Ed Spiezio 1.50 .70 .45
505 Mike Marshall 1.50 .70 .45

506	Indians Rookies (***Terry Ley, Jim Moyer, Dick Tidrow***)	1.50	.70	.45
507	Fred Gladding	1.50	.70	.45
508	Ellie Hendricks	1.50	.70	.45
509	Don McMahon	1.50	.70	.45
510	Ted Williams	10.00	5.00	3.00
511	Tony Taylor	1.50	.70	.45
512	Paul Popovich	1.50	.70	.45
513	Lindy McDaniel	1.50	.70	.45
514	Ted Sizemore	1.50	.70	.45
515	Bert Blyleven	3.00	1.50	.90
516	Oscar Brown	1.50	.70	.45
517	Ken Brett	1.50	.70	.45
518	Wayne Garrett	1.50	.70	.45
519	Ted Abernathy	1.50	.70	.45
520	Larry Bowa	1.50	.70	.45
521	Alan Foster	1.50	.70	.45
522	Dodgers Team	4.00	2.00	1.25
523	Chuck Dobson	1.50	.70	.45
524	Reds Rookies (**Ed Armbrister, Mel Behney**)	1.50	.70	.45
525	Carlos May	1.50	.70	.45
526	Bob Bailey	3.00	1.50	.90
527	Dave Leonhard	3.00	1.50	.90
528	Ron Stone	3.00	1.50	.90
529	Dave Nelson	3.00	1.50	.90
530	Don Sutton	10.00	5.00	3.00
531	Freddie Patek	4.00	2.00	1.25
532	Fred Kendall	3.00	1.50	.90
533	Ralph Houk	6.00	3.00	1.75
534	Jim Hickman	3.00	1.50	.90
535	Ed Brinkman	3.00	1.50	.90
536	Doug Rader	3.00	1.50	.90
537	Bob Locker	3.00	1.50	.90
538	Charlie Sands	3.00	1.50	.90
539	***Terry Forster***	4.00	2.00	1.25
540	Felix Millan	3.00	1.50	.90
541	Roger Repoz	3.00	1.50	.90
542	Jack Billingham	3.00	1.50	.90
543	Duane Josephson	3.00	1.50	.90
544	Ted Martinez	3.00	1.50	.90
545	Wayne Granger	3.00	1.50	.90
546	Joe Hague	3.00	1.50	.90
547	Indians Team	6.00	3.00	1.75
548	Frank Reberger	3.00	1.50	.90
549	Dave May	3.00	1.50	.90
550	Brooks Robinson	25.00	12.50	7.50
551	Ollie Brown	3.00	1.50	.90
552	Ollie Brown/IA	3.00	1.50	.90
553	Wilbur Wood	3.00	1.50	.90
554	Wilbur Wood/IA	3.00	1.50	.90
555	Ron Santo	8.00	4.00	2.50
556	Ron Santo/IA	4.00	2.00	1.25
557	John Odom	3.00	1.50	.90
558	John Odom/IA	3.00	1.50	.90
559	Pete Rose	50.00	25.00	15.00
560	Pete Rose/IA	30.00	15.00	9.00
561	Leo Cardenas	3.00	1.50	.90
562	Leo Cardenas/IA	3.00	1.50	.90
563	Ray Sadecki	3.00	1.50	.90
564	Ray Sadecki/IA	3.00	1.50	.90
565	Reggie Smith	3.00	1.50	.90
566	Reggie Smith/IA	3.00	1.50	.90
567	Juan Marichal	10.00	5.00	3.00
568	Juan Marichal/IA	5.00	2.50	1.50
569	Ed Kirkpatrick	3.00	1.50	.90
570	Ed Kirkpatrick/IA	3.00	1.50	.90
571	Nate Colbert	3.00	1.50	.90
572	Nate Colbert/IA	3.00	1.50	.90
573	Fritz Peterson	3.00	1.50	.90
574	Fritz Peterson/IA	3.00	1.50	.90
575	Al Oliver	4.00	2.00	1.25
576	Leo Durocher	5.00	2.50	1.50
577	Mike Paul	3.00	1.50	.90
578	Billy Grabarkewitz	3.00	1.50	.90
579	***Doyle Alexander***	4.00	2.00	1.25
580	Lou Piniella	5.00	2.50	1.50
581	Wade Blasingame	3.00	1.50	.90
582	Expos Team	6.00	3.00	1.75
583	Darold Knowles	3.00	1.50	.90
584	Jerry McNertney	3.00	1.50	.90
585	George Scott	3.00	1.50	.90
586	Denis Menke	3.00	1.50	.90
587	Billy Wilson	3.00	1.50	.90
588	Jim Holt	3.00	1.50	.90
589	Hal Lanier	3.00	1.50	.90
590	Graig Nettles	3.00	1.50	.90
591	Paul Casanova	3.00	1.50	.90
592	Lew Krausse	3.00	1.50	.90
593	Rich Morales	3.00	1.50	.90
594	Jim Beauchamp	3.00	1.50	.90
595	Nolan Ryan	100.00	50.00	30.00
596	Manny Mota	3.00	1.50	.90
597	Jim Magnuson	3.00	1.50	.90
598	Hal King	3.00	1.50	.90
599	Billy Champion	3.00	1.50	.90
600	Al Kaline	25.00	12.50	7.50
601	George Stone	3.00	1.50	.90
602	Dave Bristol	3.00	1.50	.90
603	Jim Ray	3.00	1.50	.90
604a	6th Series Checklist (657-787) (Copyright on right.)	6.00	3.00	1.75
604b	6th Series Checklist (657-787) (Copyright on left.)	6.00	3.00	1.75
605	Nelson Briles	3.00	1.50	.90
606	Luis Melendez	3.00	1.50	.90
607	Frank Duffy	3.00	1.50	.90
608	Mike Corkins	3.00	1.50	.90
609	Tom Grieve	3.00	1.50	.90
610	Bill Stoneman	3.00	1.50	.90
611	Rich Reese	3.00	1.50	.90
612	Joe Decker	3.00	1.50	.90
613	Mike Ferraro	3.00	1.50	.90
614	Ted Uhlaender	3.00	1.50	.90
615	Steve Hargan	3.00	1.50	.90
616	***Joe Ferguson***	3.00	1.50	.90
617	Royals Team	6.00	3.00	1.75
618	Rich Robertson	3.00	1.50	.90
619	Rich McKinney	3.00	1.50	.90
620	Phil Niekro	10.00	5.00	3.00
621	Commissioners Award	3.00	1.50	.90
622	Most Valuable Player Award	3.00	1.50	.90
623	Cy Young Award	3.00	1.50	.90
624	Minor League Player Of The Year Award	3.00	1.50	.90
625	Rookie of the Year Award	3.00	1.50	.90
626	Babe Ruth Award	3.00	1.50	.90
627	Moe Drabowsky	3.00	1.50	.90
628	Terry Crowley	3.00	1.50	.90
629	Paul Doyle	3.00	1.50	.90
630	Rich Hebner	3.00	1.50	.90
631	John Strohmayer	3.00	1.50	.90
632	Mike Hegan	3.00	1.50	.90
633	Jack Hiatt	3.00	1.50	.90
634	Dick Woodson	3.00	1.50	.90
635	Don Money	3.00	1.50	.90
636	Bill Lee	3.00	1.50	.90
637	Preston Gomez	3.00	1.50	.90
638	Ken Wright	3.00	1.50	.90
639	J.C. Martin	3.00	1.50	.90
640	Joe Coleman	3.00	1.50	.90
641	Mike Lum	3.00	1.50	.90
642	Denny Riddleberger	3.00	1.50	.90
643	Russ Gibson	3.00	1.50	.90
644	Bernie Allen	3.00	1.50	.90
645	Jim Maloney	3.00	1.50	.90
646	Chico Salmon	3.00	1.50	.90
647	Bob Moose	3.00	1.50	.90
648	Jim Lyttle	3.00	1.50	.90
649	Pete Richert	3.00	1.50	.90
650	Sal Bando	3.00	1.50	.90
651	Reds Team	8.00	4.00	2.50
652	Marcelino Lopez	3.00	1.50	.90
653	Jim Fairey	3.00	1.50	.90
654	Horacio Pina	3.00	1.50	.90
655	Jerry Grote	3.00	1.50	.90
656	Rudy May	3.00	1.50	.90
657	Bobby Wine	10.00	5.00	3.00
658	Steve Dunning	10.00	5.00	3.00
659	Bob Aspromonte	10.00	5.00	3.00
660	Paul Blair	10.00	5.00	3.00
661	Bill Virdon	10.00	5.00	3.00
662	Stan Bahnsen	10.00	5.00	3.00
663	Fran Healy	10.00	5.00	3.00
664	Bobby Knoop	10.00	5.00	3.00
665	Chris Short	10.00	5.00	3.00
666	Hector Torres	10.00	5.00	3.00
667	Ray Newman	10.00	5.00	3.00
668	Rangers Team	20.00	10.00	6.00
669	Willie Crawford	10.00	5.00	3.00
670	Ken Holtzman	10.00	5.00	3.00
671	Donn Clendenon	10.00	5.00	3.00
672	Archie Reynolds	10.00	5.00	3.00
673	Dave Marshall	10.00	5.00	3.00
674	John Kennedy	10.00	5.00	3.00
675	Pat Jarvis	10.00	5.00	3.00
676	Danny Cater	10.00	5.00	3.00
677	Ivan Murrell	10.00	5.00	3.00
678	Steve Luebber	10.00	5.00	3.00
679	Astros Rookies (**Bob Fenwick, Bob Stinson**)	10.00	5.00	3.00
680	Dave Johnson	10.00	5.00	3.00
681	Bobby Pfeil	10.00	5.00	3.00
682	Mike McCormick	10.00	5.00	3.00
683	Steve Hovley	10.00	5.00	3.00
684	Hal Breeden	10.00	5.00	3.00
685	Joe Horlen	10.00	5.00	3.00
686	Steve Garvey	25.00	12.50	7.50
687	Del Unser	10.00	5.00	3.00
688	Cardinals Team	20.00	10.00	6.00
689	Eddie Fisher	10.00	5.00	3.00
690	Willie Montanez	10.00	5.00	3.00
691	Curt Blefary	10.00	5.00	3.00
692	Curt Blefary/IA	10.00	5.00	3.00
693	Alan Gallagher	10.00	5.00	3.00
694	Alan Gallagher/IA	10.00	5.00	3.00
695	Rod Carew	50.00	25.00	15.00
696	Rod Carew/IA	25.00	12.50	7.50
697	Jerry Koosman	15.00	7.50	4.50
698	Jerry Koosman/IA	10.00	5.00	3.00
699	Bobby Murcer	12.00	6.00	3.50
700	Bobby Murcer/IA	10.00	5.00	3.00
701	Jose Pagan	10.00	5.00	3.00
702	Jose Pagan/IA	10.00	5.00	3.00
703	Doug Griffin	10.00	5.00	3.00
704	Doug Griffin/IA	10.00	5.00	3.00
705	Pat Corrales	10.00	5.00	3.00
706	Pat Corrales/IA	10.00	5.00	3.00
707	Tim Foli	10.00	5.00	3.00
708	Tim Foli/IA	10.00	5.00	3.00
709	Jim Kaat	15.00	7.50	4.50
710	Jim Kaat/IA	10.00	5.00	3.00
711	Bobby Bonds	15.00	7.50	4.50
712	Bobby Bonds/IA	10.00	5.00	3.00
713	Gene Michael	10.00	5.00	3.00
714	Gene Michael/IA	10.00	5.00	3.00
715	Mike Epstein	10.00	5.00	3.00
716	Jesus Alou	10.00	5.00	3.00
717	Bruce Dal Canton	10.00	5.00	3.00
718	Del Rice	10.00	5.00	3.00
719	Cesar Geronimo	10.00	5.00	3.00
720	Sam McDowell	10.00	5.00	3.00
721	Eddie Leon	10.00	5.00	3.00
722	Bill Sudakis	10.00	5.00	3.00
723	Al Santorini	10.00	5.00	3.00
724	A.L. Rookies (**John Curtis, Rich Hinton, Mickey Scott**)	10.00	5.00	3.00
725	Dick McAuliffe	10.00	5.00	3.00
726	Dick Selma	10.00	5.00	3.00
727	Jose Laboy	10.00	5.00	3.00
728	Gail Hopkins	10.00	5.00	3.00
729	Bob Veale	10.00	5.00	3.00
730	Rick Monday	10.00	5.00	3.00
731	Orioles Team	15.00	7.50	4.50
732	George Culver	10.00	5.00	3.00
733	Jim Hart	10.00	5.00	3.00
734	Bob Burda	10.00	5.00	3.00
735	Diego Segui	10.00	5.00	3.00
736	Bill Russell	10.00	5.00	3.00
737	***Lenny Randle***	10.00	5.00	3.00
738	Jim Merritt	10.00	5.00	3.00
739	Don Mason	10.00	5.00	3.00
740	Rico Carty	10.00	5.00	3.00
741	Major League Rookies (***Tom Hutton, Rick Miller, John Milner***)	10.00	5.00	3.00
742	Jim Rooker	10.00	5.00	3.00
743	Cesar Gutierrez	10.00	5.00	3.00
744	***Jim Slaton***	10.00	5.00	3.00
745	Julian Javier	10.00	5.00	3.00
746	Lowell Palmer	10.00	5.00	3.00
747	Jim Stewart	10.00	5.00	3.00
748	Phil Hennigan	10.00	5.00	3.00
749	Walter Alston	15.00	7.50	4.50
750	Willie Horton	10.00	5.00	3.00
751	Steve Carlton (Traded)	30.00	15.00	9.00
752	Joe Morgan (Traded)	30.00	15.00	9.00
753	Denny McLain (Traded)	15.00	7.50	4.50
754	Frank Robinson (Traded)	40.00	20.00	12.00
755	Jim Fregosi (Traded)	15.00	7.50	4.50
756	Rick Wise (Traded)	10.00	5.00	3.00
757	Jose Cardenal (Traded)	10.00	5.00	3.00
758	Gil Garrido	10.00	5.00	3.00
759	Chris Cannizzaro	10.00	5.00	3.00
760	Bill Mazeroski	20.00	10.00	6.00
761	A.L.-N.L. Rookies (**Ron Cey, Ben Oglivie, Bernie Williams**)	20.00	10.00	6.00
762	Wayne Simpson	10.00	5.00	3.00
763	Ron Hansen	10.00	5.00	3.00
764	Dusty Baker	15.00	7.50	4.50
765	Ken McMullen	10.00	5.00	3.00
766	Steve Hamilton	10.00	5.00	3.00
767	Tom McCraw	10.00	5.00	3.00
768	Denny Doyle	10.00	5.00	3.00
769	Jack Aker	10.00	5.00	3.00
770	Jim Wynn	10.00	5.00	3.00
771	Giants Team	20.00	10.00	6.00
772	Ken Tatum	10.00	5.00	3.00
773	Ron Brand	10.00	5.00	3.00
774	Luis Alvarado	10.00	5.00	3.00
775	Jerry Reuss	10.00	5.00	3.00
776	Bill Voss	10.00	5.00	3.00
777	Hoyt Wilhelm	25.00	12.50	7.50
778	Twins Rookies (**Vic Albury, Rick Dempsey, Jim Strickland**)	20.00	10.00	6.00
779	Tony Cloninger	10.00	5.00	3.00
780	Dick Green	10.00	5.00	3.00
781	Jim McAndrew	10.00	5.00	3.00
782	Larry Stahl	10.00	5.00	3.00
783	Les Cain	10.00	5.00	3.00
784	Ken Aspromonte	10.00	5.00	3.00
785	Vic Davalillo	10.00	5.00	3.00
786	Chuck Brinkman	10.00	5.00	3.00
787	Ron Reed	12.00	5.00	3.00

1972 Topps Candy Lid Test Issue

Between the production of its regular-issue candy lid sets of 1970 and 1973, Topps was working on another issue that survives today in proof form, either as uncropped squares or cut to the 1-7/8" diameter tabbed lid form meant to cover a plastic bucket of bubblegum nuggets. The 1972 proofs are very close to the 1973 issue in format; the principal difference is the player portrait does not have a solid-color border as on the 1973s, and that the pictures of Seaver and Yaz on the front are set against green, rather than orange, stars. The extent of the checklist is unknown.

		NM	EX	VG
Common Player:		100.00	50.00	30.00
(1)	Hank Aaron	900.00	450.00	275.00
(2)	Dick Allen	150.00	75.00	45.00
(3)	Dusty Baker	100.00	50.00	35.00
(4)	Sal Bando	100.00	50.00	30.00
(5)	Johnny Bench	450.00	225.00	135.00
(6)	Bobby Bonds	100.00	50.00	30.00
(7)	Dick Bosman	100.00	50.00	30.00
(8)	Lou Brock	250.00	125.00	75.00
(9)	Rod Carew	300.00	150.00	90.00
(10)	Steve Carlton	300.00	150.00	90.00
(11)	Nate Colbert	100.00	50.00	30.00
(12)	Willie Davis	100.00	50.00	30.00
(13)	Larry Dierker	100.00	50.00	30.00
(14)	Mike Epstein	100.00	50.00	30.00
(15)	Carlton Fisk	300.00	150.00	90.00
(16)	Tim Foli	100.00	50.00	30.00
(17)	Ray Fosse	100.00	50.00	30.00
(18)	Bill Freehan	100.00	50.00	30.00
(19)	Bob Gibson	300.00	150.00	90.00
(20)	Bud Harrelson	100.00	50.00	30.00
(21)	Catfish Hunter	250.00	125.00	75.00
(22)	Reggie Jackson	650.00	325.00	195.00

(23)	Fergie Jenkins	250.00	125.00	75.00
(24)	Al Kaline	350.00	175.00	100.00
(25)	Harmon Killebrew	350.00	175.00	100.00
(26)	Clay Kirby	100.00	50.00	30.00
(27)	Mickey Lolich	100.00	50.00	30.00
(28)	Greg Luzinski	100.00	50.00	30.00
(29)	Mike Marshall	100.00	50.00	30.00
(30)	Lee May	100.00	50.00	30.00
(31)	John Mayberry	100.00	50.00	30.00
(32)	Willie Mays	900.00	450.00	275.00
(33)	Willie McCovey	250.00	125.00	75.00
(34)	Thurman Munson	300.00	150.00	90.00
(35)	Bobby Murcer	150.00	75.00	45.00
(36)	Gary Nolan	100.00	50.00	30.00
(37)	Amos Otis	100.00	50.00	30.00
(38)	Jim Palmer	250.00	125.00	75.00
(39)	Gaylord Perry	250.00	125.00	75.00
(40)	Lou Piniella	150.00	75.00	45.00
(41)	Brooks Robinson	350.00	175.00	100.00
(42)	Frank Robinson	350.00	175.00	100.00
(43)	Ellie Rodriguez	100.00	50.00	30.00
(44)	Pete Rose	900.00	450.00	275.00
(45)	Nolan Ryan	2,500	1,250	750.00
(46)	Manny Sanguillen	100.00	50.00	30.00
(47)	George Scott	100.00	50.00	30.00
(48)	Tom Seaver	350.00	175.00	100.00
(49)	Chris Speier	100.00	50.00	30.00
(50)	Willie Stargell	250.00	125.00	75.00
(51)	Don Sutton	250.00	125.00	75.00
(52)	Joe Torre	150.00	75.00	45.00
(53)	Billy Williams	250.00	125.00	75.00
(54)	Wilbur Wood	100.00	50.00	30.00
(55)	Carl Yastrzemski	450.00	225.00	135.00

1972 Topps Cloth Stickers

Despite the fact they were never actually issued, examples of this test issue can readily be found within the hobby. The set of 33 contains stickers with designs identical to cards found in three contiguous rows of a regular Topps card sheet that year; thus the inclusion of a meaningless checklist card. Sometimes found in complete 33-sticker strips, or 132-piece sheets, individual stickers nominally measure 2-1/2" x 3-1/2", though dimensions vary according to the care with which they were cut. Stickers are unnumbered and blank-backed; most are found without the original paper backing as the glue used did not hold up well over the years. Eleven of the stickers are prone to miscutting and are identified with an (SP) in the checklist.

		NM	EX	VG
Complete Set (33):		1,300	650.00	390.00
Common Player:		20.00	10.00	6.00
(1)	Hank Aaron	200.00	100.00	60.00
(2)	Luis Aparicio/IA/SP	60.00	30.00	18.00
(3)	Ike Brown	20.00	10.00	6.00
(4)	Johnny Callison	20.00	10.00	6.00
(5)	Checklist 264-319	10.00	5.00	3.00
(6)	Roberto Clemente/IA	300.00	150.00	90.00
(7)	Dave Concepcion/SP	40.00	20.00	12.00
(8)	Ron Cook	20.00	10.00	6.00
(9)	Willie Davis	20.00	10.00	6.00
(10)	Al Fitzmorris	20.00	10.00	6.00
(11)	Bobby Floyd	20.00	10.00	6.00
(12)	Roy Foster	20.00	10.00	6.00
(13)	Jim Fregosi (Boyhood Photo)	20.00	10.00	6.00
(14)	Danny Frisella/IA	20.00	10.00	6.00
(15)	Woody Fryman/SP	25.00	12.50	7.50
(16)	Terry Harmon	20.00	10.00	6.00
(17)	Frank Howard/SP	40.00	20.00	12.00
(18)	Ron Klimkowski	20.00	10.00	6.00
(19)	Joe Lahoud	20.00	10.00	6.00
(20)	Jim Lefebvre	20.00	10.00	6.00
(21)	Elliott Maddox	20.00	10.00	6.00
(22)	Marty Martinez	20.00	10.00	6.00
(23)	Willie McCovey/SP	100.00	50.00	30.00
(24)	Hal McRae/SP	30.00	15.00	9.00
(25)	Syd O'Brien/SP	25.00	12.50	7.50
(26)	Red Sox team	25.00	12.50	7.50
(27)	Aurelio Rodriguez	20.00	10.00	6.00
(28)	Al Severinsen	20.00	10.00	6.00
(29)	Art Shamsky/SP	25.00	12.50	7.50
(30)	Steve Stone/SP	30.00	15.00	9.00
(31)	Stan Swanson/SP	25.00	12.50	7.50
(32)	Bob Watson	20.00	10.00	6.00
(33)	Roy White/SP	30.00	15.00	9.00

1972 Topps Posters

Issued as a separate set, rather than as a wax pack insert, these 9-7/16" x 18" posters feature a borderless full-color picture on the front with the player's name, team and position. Printed on very thin paper, the posters were folded for packaging, causing large creases that cannot be removed. Grading of these posters is done without regard to those packaging folds.

		NM	EX	VG
Complete Set (24):		700.00	350.00	200.00
Common Player:		12.00	6.00	3.50
Wax Pack:		50.00		
1	Dave McNally	12.00	6.00	3.50
2	Carl Yastrzemski	45.00	22.50	13.50
3	Bill Melton	12.00	6.00	3.50
4	Ray Fosse	12.00	6.00	3.50
5	Mickey Lolich	12.00	6.00	3.50
6	Amos Otis	12.00	6.00	3.50
7	Tony Oliva	15.00	7.50	4.50
8	Vida Blue	12.00	6.00	3.50
9	Hank Aaron	75.00	37.50	22.00
10	Fergie Jenkins	30.00	15.00	9.00
11	Pete Rose	75.00	37.50	22.00
12	Willie Davis	12.00	6.00	3.50
13	Tom Seaver	40.00	20.00	12.00
14	Rick Wise	12.00	6.00	3.50
15	Willie Stargell	30.00	15.00	9.00
16	Joe Torre	17.50	8.75	5.25
17	Willie Mays	75.00	37.50	22.00
18	Andy Messersmith	12.00	6.00	3.50
19	Wilbur Wood	12.00	6.00	3.50
20	Harmon Killebrew	35.00	17.50	10.00
21	Billy Williams	30.00	15.00	9.00
22	Bud Harrelson	12.00	6.00	3.50
23	Roberto Clemente	125.00	65.00	35.00
24	Willie McCovey	30.00	15.00	9.00

1973 Topps

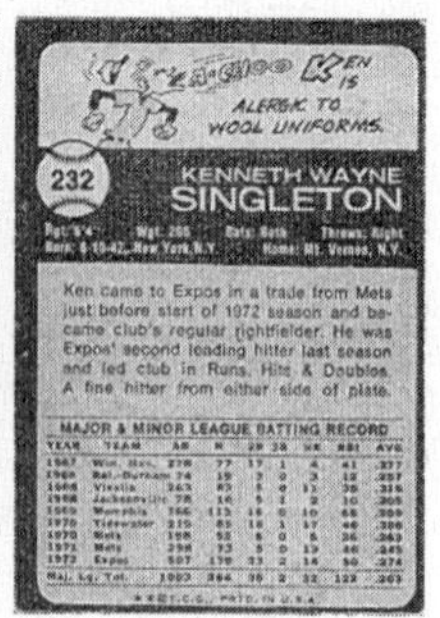

Topps cut back to 660 cards in 1973. The set is interesting for it marks the last time cards were issued by series, a procedure which had produced many a scarce high number card over the years. These 2-1/2" x 3-1/2" cards have a color photo, accented by a silhouette of a player on the front, indicative of his position. Card backs are vertical for the first time since 1968, with the usual statistical and biographical information. Specialty cards begin with card number 1, which depicted Ruth, Mays and Aaron as the all-time home run leaders. It was followed by statistical leaders, although there also were additional all-time leader cards. Also present are playoff and World Series highlights. From the age-and-youth department, the 1973 Topps set has coaches and managers as well as more "Boyhood Photos."

		NM	EX	VG
Complete Set (660):		650.00	325.00	195.00
Common Player (1-396):		.75	.40	.25
Common Player (397-528):		1.00	.50	.30
Common Player (529-660):		2.00	1.00	.60
Series 1/2/3 Wax Pack (10):		80.00		
Series 4 Wax Pack (10):		165.00		
Series 5 Wax Pack (10+1):		215.00		
1	All Time Home Run Leaders (Hank Aaron, Willie Mays, Babe Ruth)	40.00	20.00	12.00
2	Rich Hebner	.75	.40	.25
3	Jim Lonborg	.75	.40	.25
4	John Milner	.75	.40	.25
5	Ed Brinkman	.75	.40	.25
6	Mac Scarce	.75	.40	.25
7	Texas Rangers Team	1.00	.50	.30
8	Tom Hall	.75	.40	.25
9	Johnny Oates	.75	.40	.25
10	Don Sutton	3.00	1.50	.90
11	Chris Chambliss	.75	.40	.25
12a	Padres Mgr./Coaches (Dave Garcia, Johnny Podres, Bob Skinner, Whitey Wietelmann, Don Zimmer) (Coaches background brown.)	1.00	.50	.30
12b	Padres Mgr./Coaches (Dave Garcia, Johnny Podres, Bob Skinner, Whitey Wietelmann, Don Zimmer) (Coaches background orange.)	1.00	.50	.30
13	George Hendrick	.75	.40	.25
14	Sonny Siebert	.75	.40	.25
15	Ralph Garr	.75	.40	.25
16	Steve Braun	.75	.40	.25
17	Fred Gladding	.75	.40	.25
18	Leroy Stanton	.75	.40	.25
19	Tim Foli	.75	.40	.25
20a	Stan Bahnsen (Small gap in left border.)	1.00	.50	.30
20b	Stan Bahnsen (No gap.)	.75	.40	.25
21	Randy Hundley	.75	.40	.25
22	Ted Abernathy	.75	.40	.25
23	Dave Kingman	1.00	.50	.30
24	Al Santorini	.75	.40	.25
25	Roy White	.75	.40	.25
26	Pittsburgh Pirates Team	2.00	1.00	.60
27	Bill Gogolewski	.75	.40	.25
28	Hal McRae	.75	.40	.25
29	Tony Taylor	.75	.40	.25
30	Tug McGraw	.75	.40	.25
31a	***Buddy Bell*** (Small gap in right border.)	6.00	3.00	1.75
31b	***Buddy Bell*** (No gap.)	6.00	3.00	1.75
32	Fred Norman	.75	.40	.25
33	Jim Breazeale	.75	.40	.25
34	Pat Dobson	.75	.40	.25
35	Willie Davis	.75	.40	.25
36	Steve Barber	.75	.40	.25
37	Bill Robinson	.75	.40	.25
38	Mike Epstein	.75	.40	.25
39	Dave Roberts	.75	.40	.25
40	Reggie Smith	.75	.40	.25
41	Tom Walker	.75	.40	.25
42	Mike Andrews	.75	.40	.25
43	***Randy Moffitt***	.75	.40	.25
44	Rick Monday	.75	.40	.25
45	Ellie Rodriguez (Photo actually Paul Ratliff.)	.75	.40	.25
46	Lindy McDaniel	.75	.40	.25
47	Luis Melendez	.75	.40	.25
48	Paul Splittorff	.75	.40	.25
49a	Twins Mgr./Coaches (Vern Morgan, Frank Quilici, Bob Rodgers, Ralph Rowe, Al Worthington) (Coaches background brown.)	.75	.40	.25
49b	Twins Mgr./Coaches (Vern Morgan, Frank Quilici, Bob Rodgers, Ralph Rowe, Al Worthington) (Coaches background orange.)	.75	.40	.25
50	Roberto Clemente	40.00	20.00	12.00
51	Chuck Seelbach	.75	.40	.25
52	Denis Menke	.75	.40	.25
53	Steve Dunning	.75	.40	.25
54	Checklist 1-132	1.00	.50	.30
55	Jon Matlack	.75	.40	.25
56	Merv Rettenmund	.75	.40	.25
57	Derrel Thomas	.75	.40	.25
58	Mike Paul	.75	.40	.25
59	***Steve Yeager***	.75	.40	.25
60	Ken Holtzman	.75	.40	.25
61	Batting Leaders (Rod Carew, Billy Williams)	1.00	.50	.30
62	Home Run Leaders (Dick Allen, Johnny Bench)	1.00	.50	.30
63	Runs Batted In Leaders (Dick Allen, Johnny Bench)	1.00	.50	.30
64	Stolen Base Leaders (Lou Brock, Bert Campaneris)	1.00	.50	.30
65	Earned Run Average Leaders (Steve Carlton, Luis Tiant)	1.00	.50	.30
66	Victory Leaders (Steve Carlton, Gaylord Perry, Wilbur Wood)	1.00	.50	.30
67	Strikeout Leaders (Steve Carlton, Nolan Ryan)	20.00	10.00	6.00
68	Leading Firemen (Clay Carroll, Sparky Lyle)	.75	.40	.25
69	Phil Gagliano	.75	.40	.25
70	Milt Pappas	.75	.40	.25
71	Johnny Briggs	.75	.40	.25
72	Ron Reed	.75	.40	.25
73	Ed Herrmann	.75	.40	.25
74	Billy Champion	.75	.40	.25
75	Vada Pinson	1.00	.50	.30
76	Doug Rader	.75	.40	.25
77	Mike Torrez	.75	.40	.25
78	Richie Scheinblum	.75	.40	.25
79	Jim Willoughby	.75	.40	.25

80	Tony Oliva ("MINNSEOTA" on front is uncorrected error.)	1.00	.50	.30
81a	Cubs Mgr./Coaches (Hank Aguirre, Ernie Banks, Larry Jansen, Whitey Lockman, Pete Reiser) (Trees in coaches background.)	1.25	.60	.40
81b	Cubs Mgr./Coaches (Hank Aguirre, Ernie Banks, Larry Jansen, Whitey Lockman, Pete Reiser) (Solid orange background.)	1.25	.60	.40
82	Fritz Peterson	.75	.40	.25
83	Leron Lee	.75	.40	.25
84	Rollie Fingers	3.00	1.50	.90
85	Ted Simmons	.75	.40	.25
86	Tom McCraw	.75	.40	.25
87	Ken Boswell	.75	.40	.25
88	Mickey Stanley	.75	.40	.25
89	Jack Billingham	.75	.40	.25
90	Brooks Robinson	8.00	4.00	2.50
91	Los Angeles Dodgers Team	2.00	1.00	.60
92	Jerry Bell	.75	.40	.25
93	Jesus Alou	.75	.40	.25
94	Dick Billings	.75	.40	.25
95	Steve Blass	.75	.40	.25
96	Doug Griffin	.75	.40	.25
97	Willie Montanez	.75	.40	.25
98	Dick Woodson	.75	.40	.25
99	Carl Taylor	.75	.40	.25
100	Hank Aaron	40.00	20.00	12.00
101	Ken Henderson	.75	.40	.25
102	Rudy May	.75	.40	.25
103	Celerino Sanchez	.75	.40	.25
104	Reggie Cleveland	.75	.40	.25
105	Carlos May	.75	.40	.25
106	Terry Humphrey	.75	.40	.25
107	Phil Hennigan	.75	.40	.25
108	Bill Russell	1.00	.50	.30
109	Doyle Alexander	.75	.40	.25
110	Bob Watson	.75	.40	.25
111	Dave Nelson	.75	.40	.25
112	Gary Ross	.75	.40	.25
113	Jerry Grote	.75	.40	.25
114	Lynn McGlothen	.75	.40	.25
115	Ron Santo	2.00	1.00	.60
116a	Yankees Mgr./Coaches (Jim Hegan, Ralph Houk, Elston Howard, Dick Howser, Jim Turner) (Coaches background brown.)	2.00	1.00	.60
116b	Yankees Mgr./Coaches (Jim Hegan, Ralph Houk, Elston Howard, Dick Howser, Jim Turner) (Coaches background orange.)	2.00	1.00	.60
117	Ramon Hernandez	.75	.40	.25
118	John Mayberry	.75	.40	.25
119	Larry Bowa	1.50	.70	.45
120	Joe Coleman	.75	.40	.25
121	Dave Rader	.75	.40	.25
122	Jim Strickland	.75	.40	.25
123	Sandy Alomar	.75	.40	.25
124	Jim Hardin	.75	.40	.25
125	Ron Fairly	.75	.40	.25
126	Jim Brewer	.75	.40	.25
127	Milwaukee Brewers Team	2.00	1.00	.60
128	Ted Sizemore	.75	.40	.25
129	Terry Forster	.75	.40	.25
130	Pete Rose	30.00	15.00	9.00
131a	Red Sox Mgr./Coaches (Doug Camilli, Eddie Kasko, Don Lenhardt, Eddie Popowski, Lee Stange) (Coaches background brown.)	.75	.40	.25
131b	Red Sox Mgr./Coaches (Doug Camilli, Eddie Kasko, Don Lenhardt, Eddie Popowski, Lee Stange) (Coaches background orange.)	.75	.40	.25
132	Matty Alou	.75	.40	.25
133	Dave Roberts	.75	.40	.25
134	Milt Wilcox	.75	.40	.25
135	Lee May	.75	.40	.25
136a	Orioles Mgr./Coaches (George Bamberger, Jim Frey, Billy Hunter, George Staller, Earl Weaver) (Coaches background brown.)	2.00	1.00	.60
136b	Orioles Mgr./Coaches (George Bamberger, Jim Frey, Billy Hunter, George Staller, Earl Weaver) (Coaches background orange.)	2.00	1.00	.60
137	Jim Beauchamp	.75	.40	.25
138	Horacio Pina	.75	.40	.25
139	Carmen Fanzone	.75	.40	.25
140	Lou Piniella	2.00	1.00	.60
141	Bruce Kison	.75	.40	.25
142	Thurman Munson	10.00	5.00	3.00
143	John Curtis	.75	.40	.25
144	Marty Perez	.75	.40	.25
145	Bobby Bonds	2.00	1.00	.60
146	Woodie Fryman	.75	.40	.25
147	Mike Anderson	.75	.40	.25
148	***Dave Goltz***	.75	.40	.25
149	Ron Hunt	.75	.40	.25
150	Wilbur Wood	1.50	.70	.45
151	Wes Parker	.75	.40	.25
152	Dave May	.75	.40	.25
153	Al Hrabosky	1.50	.70	.45
154	Jeff Torborg	.75	.40	.25
155	Sal Bando	.75	.40	.25
156	Cesar Geronimo	.75	.40	.25
157	Denny Riddleberger	.75	.40	.25
158	Houston Astros Team	2.00	1.00	.60
159	Clarence Gaston	.75	.40	.25
160	Jim Palmer	6.00	3.00	1.75
161	Ted Martinez	.75	.40	.25
162	Pete Broberg	.75	.40	.25
163	Vic Davalillo	.75	.40	.25
164	Monty Montgomery	.75	.40	.25
165	Luis Aparicio	4.00	2.00	1.25
166	Terry Harmon	.75	.40	.25
167	Steve Stone	1.00	.50	.30
168	Jim Northrup	.75	.40	.25
169	Ron Schueler	.75	.40	.25
170	Harmon Killebrew	6.00	3.00	1.75
171	Bernie Carbo	.75	.40	.25
172	Steve Kline	.75	.40	.25
173	Hal Breeden	.75	.40	.25
174	***Rich Gossage***	12.00	6.00	3.50
175	Frank Robinson	8.00	4.00	2.50
176	Chuck Taylor	.75	.40	.25
177	Bill Plummer	.75	.40	.25
178	Don Rose	.75	.40	.25
179a	A's Mgr./Coaches (Jerry Adair, Vern Hoscheit, Irv Noren, Wes Stock, Dick Williams) (Coaches background brown.)	1.00	.50	.30
179b	A's Mgr./Coaches (Jerry Adair, Vern Hoscheit, Irv Noren, Wes Stock, Dick Williams) (Coaches background orange.)	1.00	.50	.30
180	Fergie Jenkins	4.00	2.00	1.25
181	Jack Brohamer	.75	.40	.25
182	***Mike Caldwell***	.75	.40	.25
183	Don Buford	.75	.40	.25
184	Jerry Koosman	1.00	.50	.30
185	Jim Wynn	.75	.40	.25
186	Bill Fahey	.75	.40	.25
187	Luke Walker	.75	.40	.25
188	Cookie Rojas	.75	.40	.25
189	Greg Luzinski	1.50	.70	.45
190	Bob Gibson	6.00	3.00	1.75
191	Detroit Tigers Team	2.00	1.00	.60
192	Pat Jarvis	.75	.40	.25
193	Carlton Fisk	8.00	4.00	2.50
194	***Jorge Orta***	.75	.40	.25
195	Clay Carroll	.75	.40	.25
196	Ken McMullen	.75	.40	.25
197	Ed Goodson	.75	.40	.25
198	Horace Clarke	.75	.40	.25
199	Bert Blyleven	1.50	.70	.45
200	Billy Williams	5.00	2.50	1.50
201	A.L. Playoffs (Hendrick Scores Winning Run.)	1.00	.50	.30
202	N.L. Playoffs (Foster's Run Decides It.)	1.00	.50	.30
203	World Series Game 1 (Tenace The Menace.)	1.00	.50	.30
204	World Series Game 2 (A's Make It Two Straight.)	1.00	.50	.30
205	World Series Game 3 (Reds Win Squeeker.)	1.00	.50	.30
206	World Series Game 4 (Tenace Singles In Ninth.)	1.00	.50	.30
207	World Series Game 5 (Odom Out At Plate.)	1.00	.50	.30
208	World Series Game 6 (Reds' Slugging Ties Series.)	4.00	2.00	1.25
209	World Series Game 7 (Campy Starts Winning Rally.)	1.00	.50	.30
210	A's Win! (World Champions.)	1.50	.70	.45
211	Balor Moore	.75	.40	.25
212	Joe Lahoud	.75	.40	.25
213	Steve Garvey	3.00	1.50	.90
214	Dave Hamilton	.75	.40	.25
215	Dusty Baker	1.00	.50	.30
216	Toby Harrah	.75	.40	.25
217	Don Wilson	.75	.40	.25
218	Aurelio Rodriguez	.75	.40	.25
219	St. Louis Cardinals Team	2.00	1.00	.60
220	Nolan Ryan	50.00	25.00	15.00
221	Fred Kendall	.75	.40	.25
222	Rob Gardner	.75	.40	.25
223	Bud Harrelson	.75	.40	.25
224	Bill Lee	.75	.40	.25
225	Al Oliver	1.00	.50	.30
226	Ray Fosse	.75	.40	.25
227	Wayne Twitchell	.75	.40	.25
228	Bobby Darwin	.75	.40	.25
229	Roric Harrison	.75	.40	.25
230	Joe Morgan	6.00	3.00	1.75
231	Bill Parsons	.75	.40	.25
232	Ken Singleton	.75	.40	.25
233	Ed Kirkpatrick	.75	.40	.25
234	***Bill North***	.75	.40	.25
235	Jim Hunter	3.00	1.50	.90
236	Tito Fuentes	.75	.40	.25
237a	Braves Mgr./Coaches (Lew Burdette, Jim Busby, Roy Hartsfield, Eddie Mathews, Ken Silvestri) (Coaches background brown.)	1.00	.50	.30
237b	Braves Mgr./Coaches (Lew Burdette, Jim Busby, Roy Hartsfield, Eddie Mathews, Ken Silvestri) (Coaches background orange.)	1.00	.50	.30
238	Tony Muser	.75	.40	.25
239	Pete Richert	.75	.40	.25
240	Bobby Murcer	1.00	.50	.30
241	Dwain Anderson	.75	.40	.25
242	George Culver	.75	.40	.25
243	California Angels Team	2.00	1.00	.60
244	Ed Acosta	.75	.40	.25
245	Carl Yastrzemski	10.00	5.00	3.00
246	Ken Sanders	.75	.40	.25
247	Del Unser	.75	.40	.25
248	Jerry Johnson	.75	.40	.25
249	Larry Biittner	.75	.40	.25
250	Manny Sanguillen	.75	.40	.25
251	Roger Nelson	.75	.40	.25
252a	Giants Mgr./Coaches (Joe Amalfitano, Charlie Fox, Andy Gilbert, Don McMahon, John McNamara) (Coaches background brown.)	.75	.40	.25
252b	Giants Mgr./Coaches (Joe Amalfitano, Charlie Fox, Andy Gilbert, Don McMahon, John McNamara) (Coaches background orange.)	.75	.40	.25
253	Mark Belanger	.75	.40	.25
254	Bill Stoneman	.75	.40	.25
255	Reggie Jackson	12.00	6.00	3.50
256	Chris Zachary	.75	.40	.25
257a	Mets Mgr./Coaches (Yogi Berra, Roy McMillan, Joe Pignatano, Rube Walker, Eddie Yost) (Coaches background brown.)	2.00	1.00	.60
257b	Mets Mgr./Coaches (Yogi Berra, Roy McMillan, Joe Pignatano, Rube Walker, Eddie Yost) (Coaches background orange.)	2.00	1.00	.60
258	Tommy John	1.00	.50	.30
259	Jim Holt	.75	.40	.25
260	Gary Nolan	.75	.40	.25
261	Pat Kelly	.75	.40	.25
262	Jack Aker	.75	.40	.25
263	George Scott	.75	.40	.25
264	Checklist 133-264	1.00	.50	.30
265	Gene Michael	.75	.40	.25
266	Mike Lum	.75	.40	.25
267	Lloyd Allen	.75	.40	.25
268	Jerry Morales	.75	.40	.25
269	Tim McCarver	1.50	.70	.45
270	Luis Tiant	.75	.40	.25
271	Tom Hutton	.75	.40	.25
272	Ed Farmer	.75	.40	.25
273	Chris Speier	.75	.40	.25
274	Darold Knowles	.75	.40	.25
275	Tony Perez	5.00	2.50	1.50
276	Joe Lovitto	.75	.40	.25
277	Bob Miller	.75	.40	.25
278	Baltimore Orioles Team	3.00	1.50	.90
279	Mike Strahler	.75	.40	.25
280	Al Kaline	8.00	4.00	2.50
281	Mike Jorgensen	.75	.40	.25
282	Steve Hovley	.75	.40	.25
283	Ray Sadecki	.75	.40	.25
284	Glenn Borgmann	.75	.40	.25
285	Don Kessinger	.75	.40	.25
286	Frank Linzy	.75	.40	.25
287	Eddie Leon	.75	.40	.25
288	Gary Gentry	.75	.40	.25
289	Bob Oliver	.75	.40	.25
290	Cesar Cedeno	.75	.40	.25
291	Rogelio Moret	.75	.40	.25
292	Jose Cruz	.75	.40	.25
293	Bernie Allen	.75	.40	.25
294	Steve Arlin	.75	.40	.25
295	Bert Campaneris	.75	.40	.25
296	Reds Mgr./Coaches (Sparky Anderson, Alex Grammas, Ted Kluszewski, George Scherger, Larry Shepard)	2.50	1.25	.70
297	Walt Williams	.75	.40	.25
298	Ron Bryant	.75	.40	.25
299	Ted Ford	.75	.40	.25
300	Steve Carlton	8.00	4.00	2.50
301	Billy Grabarkewitz	.75	.40	.25
302	Terry Crowley	.75	.40	.25
303	Nelson Briles	.75	.40	.25
304	Duke Sims	.75	.40	.25
305	Willie Mays	40.00	20.00	12.00
306	Tom Burgmeier	.75	.40	.25
307	Boots Day	.75	.40	.25
308	Skip Lockwood	.75	.40	.25
309	Paul Popovich	.75	.40	.25
310	Dick Allen	1.50	.70	.45
311	Joe Decker	.75	.40	.25
312	Oscar Brown	.75	.40	.25
313	Jim Ray	.75	.40	.25
314	Ron Swoboda	.75	.40	.25
315	John Odom	.75	.40	.25
316	San Diego Padres Team	2.00	1.00	.60
317	Danny Cater	.75	.40	.25
318	Jim McGlothlin	.75	.40	.25
319	Jim Spencer	.75	.40	.25
320	Lou Brock	6.00	3.00	1.75
321	Rich Hinton	.75	.40	.25
322	***Garry Maddox***	1.00	.50	.30
323	Tigers Mgr./Coaches (Art Fowler, Billy Martin, Joe Schultz, Charlie Silvera, Dick Tracewski)	1.00	.50	.30
324	Al Downing	.75	.40	.25
325	Boog Powell	1.00	.50	.30
326	Darrell Brandon	.75	.40	.25
327	John Lowenstein	.75	.40	.25
328	Bill Bonham	.75	.40	.25
329	Ed Kranepool	.75	.40	.25
330	Rod Carew	6.00	3.00	1.75
331	Carl Morton	.75	.40	.25
332	***John Felske***	.75	.40	.25
333	Gene Clines	.75	.40	.25
334	Freddie Patek	.75	.40	.25
335	Bob Tolan	.75	.40	.25
336	Tom Bradley	.75	.40	.25
337	Dave Duncan	1.00	.50	.30

338	Checklist 265-396	1.00	.50	.30
339	Dick Tidrow	.75	.40	.25
340	Nate Colbert	.75	.40	.25
341	Jim Palmer (Boyhood Photo)	1.50	.70	.45
342	Sam McDowell (Boyhood Photo)	.75	.40	.25
343	Bobby Murcer (Boyhood Photo)	.75	.40	.25
344	Jim Hunter (Boyhood Photo)	1.50	.70	.45
345	Chris Speier (Boyhood Photo)	.75	.40	.25
346	Gaylord Perry (Boyhood Photo)	1.50	.70	.45
347	Kansas City Royals Team	2.00	1.00	.60
348	Rennie Stennett	.75	.40	.25
349	Dick McAuliffe	.75	.40	.25
350	Tom Seaver	10.00	5.00	3.00
351	Jimmy Stewart	.75	.40	.25
352	***Don Stanhouse***	.75	.40	.25
353	Steve Brye	.75	.40	.25
354	Billy Parker	.75	.40	.25
355	Mike Marshall	.75	.40	.25
356	White Sox Mgr./Coaches (Joe Lonnett, Jim Mahoney, Al Monchak, Johnny Sain, Chuck Tanner)	.75	.40	.25
357	Ross Grimsley	.75	.40	.25
358	Jim Nettles	.75	.40	.25
359	Cecil Upshaw	.75	.40	.25
360	Joe Rudi (Photo actually Gene Tenace.)	.75	.40	.25
361	Fran Healy	.75	.40	.25
362	Eddie Watt	.75	.40	.25
363	Jackie Hernandez	.75	.40	.25
364	Rick Wise	.75	.40	.25
365	Rico Petrocelli	.75	.40	.25
366	Brock Davis	.75	.40	.25
367	Burt Hooton	.75	.40	.25
368	Bill Buckner	1.00	.50	.30
369	Lerrin LaGrow	.75	.40	.25
370	Willie Stargell	6.00	3.00	1.75
371	Mike Kekich	.75	.40	.25
372	Oscar Gamble	.75	.40	.25
373	Clyde Wright	.75	.40	.25
374	Darrell Evans	1.00	.50	.30
375	Larry Dierker	.75	.40	.25
376	Frank Duffy	.75	.40	.25
377	Expos Mgr./Coaches (Dave Bristol, Larry Doby, Gene Mauch, Cal McLish, Jerry Zimmerman)	1.00	.50	.30
378	Lenny Randle	.75	.40	.25
379	Cy Acosta	.75	.40	.25
380	Johnny Bench	10.00	5.00	3.00
381	Vicente Romo	.75	.40	.25
382	Mike Hegan	.75	.40	.25
383	Diego Segui	.75	.40	.25
384	Don Baylor	3.00	1.50	.90
385	Jim Perry	.75	.40	.25
386	Don Money	.75	.40	.25
387	Jim Barr	.75	.40	.25
388	Ben Oglivie	.75	.40	.25
389	New York Mets Team	4.00	2.00	1.25
390	Mickey Lolich	.75	.40	.25
391	***Lee Lacy***	.75	.40	.25
392	Dick Drago	.75	.40	.25
393	Jose Cardenal	.75	.40	.25
394	Sparky Lyle	.75	.40	.25
395	Roger Metzger	.75	.40	.25
396	Grant Jackson	.75	.40	.25
397	Dave Cash	1.00	.50	.30
398	Rich Hand	1.00	.50	.30
399	George Foster	1.00	.50	.30
400	Gaylord Perry	5.00	2.50	1.50
401	Clyde Mashore	1.00	.50	.30
402	Jack Hiatt	1.00	.50	.30
403	Sonny Jackson	1.00	.50	.30
404	Chuck Brinkman	1.00	.50	.30
405	Cesar Tovar	1.00	.50	.30
406	Paul Lindblad	1.00	.50	.30
407	Felix Millan	1.00	.50	.30
408	Jim Colborn	1.00	.50	.30
409	Ivan Murrell	1.00	.50	.30
410	Willie McCovey	8.00	4.00	2.50
411	Ray Corbin	1.00	.50	.30
412	Manny Mota	1.00	.50	.30
413	Tom Timmermann	1.00	.50	.30
414	Ken Rudolph	1.00	.50	.30
415	Marty Pattin	1.00	.50	.30
416	Paul Schaal	1.00	.50	.30
417	Scipio Spinks	1.00	.50	.30
418	Bobby Grich	1.00	.50	.30
419	Casey Cox	1.00	.50	.30
420	Tommie Agee	1.00	.50	.30
421	Angels Mgr./Coaches (Tom Morgan, Salty Parker, Jimmie Reese, John Roseboro, Bobby Winkles)	1.50	.70	.45
422	Bob Robertson	1.00	.50	.30
423	Johnny Jeter	1.00	.50	.30
424	Denny Doyle	1.00	.50	.30
425	Alex Johnson	1.00	.50	.30
426	Dave LaRoche	1.00	.50	.30
427	Rick Auerbach	1.00	.50	.30
428	Wayne Simpson	1.00	.50	.30
429	Jim Fairey	1.00	.50	.30
430	Vida Blue	1.50	.70	.45
431	Gerry Moses	1.00	.50	.30
432	Dan Frisella	1.00	.50	.30
433	Willie Horton	1.00	.50	.30
434	San Francisco Giants Team	3.00	1.50	.90
435	Rico Carty	1.00	.50	.30
436	Jim McAndrew	1.00	.50	.30
437	John Kennedy	1.00	.50	.30
438	Enzo Hernandez	1.00	.50	.30
439	Eddie Fisher	1.00	.50	.30
440	Glenn Beckert	1.00	.50	.30
441	Gail Hopkins	1.00	.50	.30
442	Dick Dietz	1.00	.50	.30
443	Danny Thompson	1.00	.50	.30
444	Ken Brett	1.00	.50	.30
445	Ken Berry	1.00	.50	.30
446	Jerry Reuss	1.00	.50	.30
447	Joe Hague	1.00	.50	.30
448	John Hiller	1.00	.50	.30
449a	Indians Mgr./Coaches (Ken Aspromonte, Rocky Colavito, Joe Lutz, Warren Spahn) (Spahn's ear pointed.)	1.50	.70	.45
449b	Indians Mgr./Coaches (Ken Aspromonte, Rocky Colavito, Joe Lutz, Warren Spahn) (Spahn's ear round.)	2.00	1.00	.60
450	Joe Torre	3.00	1.50	.90
451	John Vukovich	1.00	.50	.30
452	Paul Casanova	1.00	.50	.30
453	Checklist 397-528	1.25	.60	.40
454	Tom Haller	1.00	.50	.30
455	Bill Melton	1.00	.50	.30
456	Dick Green	1.00	.50	.30
457	John Strohmayer	1.00	.50	.30
458	Jim Mason	1.00	.50	.30
459	Jimmy Howarth	1.00	.50	.30
460	Bill Freehan	1.00	.50	.30
461	Mike Corkins	1.00	.50	.30
462	Ron Blomberg	1.00	.50	.30
463	Ken Tatum	1.00	.50	.30
464	Chicago Cubs Team	4.00	2.00	1.25
465	Dave Giusti	1.00	.50	.30
466	Jose Arcia	1.00	.50	.30
467	Mike Ryan	1.00	.50	.30
468	Tom Griffin	1.00	.50	.30
469	Dan Monzon	1.00	.50	.30
470	Mike Cuellar	1.00	.50	.30
471	All-Time Hit Leader (Ty Cobb)	10.00	5.00	3.00
472	All-Time Grand Slam Leader (Lou Gehrig)	12.00	6.00	3.50
473	All-Time Total Base Leader (Hank Aaron)	10.00	5.00	3.00
474	All-Time RBI Leader (Babe Ruth)	20.00	10.00	6.00
475	All-Time Batting Leader (Ty Cobb)	8.00	4.00	2.50
476	All-Time Shutout Leader (Walter Johnson)	3.00	1.50	.90
477	All-Time Victory Leader (Cy Young)	3.00	1.50	.90
478	All-Time Strikeout Leader (Walter Johnson)	3.00	1.50	.90
479	Hal Lanier	1.00	.50	.30
480	Juan Marichal	6.00	3.00	1.75
481	Chicago White Sox Team	3.00	1.50	.90
482	***Rick Reuschel***	2.00	1.00	.60
483	Dal Maxvill	1.00	.50	.30
484	Ernie McAnally	1.00	.50	.30
485	Norm Cash	1.50	.70	.45
486a	Phillies Mgr./Coaches (Carroll Berringer, Billy DeMars, Danny Ozark, Ray Rippelmeyer, Bobby Wine) (Coaches background brown-red.)	1.00	.50	.30
486b	Phillies Mgr./Coaches (Carroll Beringer, Billy DeMars, Danny Ozark, Ray Rippelmeyer, Bobby Wine) (Coaches background orange.)	1.00	.50	.30
487	Bruce Dal Canton	1.00	.50	.30
488	Dave Campbell	1.00	.50	.30
489	Jeff Burroughs	1.00	.50	.30
490	Claude Osteen	1.00	.50	.30
491	Bob Montgomery	1.00	.50	.30
492	Pedro Borbon	1.00	.50	.30
493	Duffy Dyer	1.00	.50	.30
494	Rich Morales	1.00	.50	.30
495	Tommy Helms	1.00	.50	.30
496	Ray Lamb	1.00	.50	.30
497	Cardinals Mgr./Coaches (Vern Benson, George Kissell, Red Schoendienst, Barney Schultz)	1.50	.70	.45
498	Graig Nettles	1.50	.70	.45
499	Bob Moose	1.00	.50	.30
500	Oakland A's Team	4.00	2.00	1.25
501	Larry Gura	1.00	.50	.30
502	Bobby Valentine	1.00	.50	.30
503	Phil Niekro	5.00	2.50	1.50
504a	Earl Williams (Small gap in each side border.)	1.25	.60	.40
504b	Earl Williams (No gaps in border.)	1.00	.50	.30
505	Bob Bailey	1.00	.50	.30
506	Bart Johnson	1.00	.50	.30
507	Darrel Chaney	1.00	.50	.30
508	Gates Brown	1.00	.50	.30
509	Jim Nash	1.00	.50	.30
510	Amos Otis	1.00	.50	.30
511	Sam McDowell	1.00	.50	.30
512	Dalton Jones	1.00	.50	.30
513	Dave Marshall	1.00	.50	.30
514	Jerry Kenney	1.00	.50	.30
515	Andy Messersmith	1.00	.50	.30
516	Danny Walton	1.00	.50	.30
517a	Pirates Mgr./Coaches (Don Leppert, Bill Mazeroski, Dave Ricketts, Bill Virdon, Mel Wright) (Coaches background brown.)	1.50	.70	.45
517b	Pirates Mgr./Coaches (Don Leppert, Bill Mazeroski, Dave Ricketts, Bill Virdon, Mel Wright) (Coaches background orange.)	1.50	.70	.45
518	Bob Veale	1.00	.50	.30
519	John Edwards	1.00	.50	.30
520	Mel Stottlemyre	1.25	.60	.40
521	Atlanta Braves Team	4.00	2.00	1.25
522	Leo Cardenas	1.00	.50	.30
523	Wayne Granger	1.00	.50	.30
524	Gene Tenace	1.00	.50	.30
525	Jim Fregosi	1.00	.50	.30
526	Ollie Brown	1.00	.50	.30
527	Dan McGinn	1.00	.50	.30
528	Paul Blair	1.00	.50	.30
529	Milt May	2.00	1.00	.60
530	Jim Kaat	4.00	2.00	1.25
531	Ron Woods	2.00	1.00	.60
532	Steve Mingori	2.00	1.00	.60
533	Larry Stahl	2.00	1.00	.60
534	Dave Lemonds	2.00	1.00	.60
535	John Callison	2.00	1.00	.60
536	Philadelphia Phillies Team	6.00	3.00	1.75
537	Bill Slayback	2.00	1.00	.60
538	Jim Hart	2.00	1.00	.60
539	Tom Murphy	2.00	1.00	.60
540	Cleon Jones	2.00	1.00	.60
541	Bob Bolin	2.00	1.00	.60
542	Pat Corrales	2.00	1.00	.60
543	Alan Foster	2.00	1.00	.60
544	Von Joshua	2.00	1.00	.60
545	Orlando Cepeda	10.00	5.00	3.00
546	Jim York	2.00	1.00	.60
547	Bobby Heise	2.00	1.00	.60
548	Don Durham	2.00	1.00	.60
549	Rangers Mgr./Coaches (Chuck Estrada, Whitey Herzog, Chuck Hiller, Jackie Moore)	2.00	1.00	.60
550	Dave Johnson	2.00	1.00	.60
551	Mike Kilkenny	2.00	1.00	.60
552	J.C. Martin	2.00	1.00	.60
553	Mickey Scott	2.00	1.00	.60
554	Dave Concepcion	2.00	1.00	.60
555	Bill Hands	2.00	1.00	.60
556	New York Yankees Team	10.00	5.00	3.00
557	Bernie Williams	2.00	1.00	.60
558	Jerry May	2.00	1.00	.60
559	Barry Lersch	2.00	1.00	.60
560	Frank Howard	3.00	1.50	.90
561	Jim Geddes	2.00	1.00	.60
562	Wayne Garrett	2.00	1.00	.60
563	Larry Haney	2.00	1.00	.60
564	Mike Thompson	2.00	1.00	.60
565	Jim Hickman	2.00	1.00	.60
566	Lew Krausse	2.00	1.00	.60
567	Bob Fenwick	2.00	1.00	.60
568	Ray Newman	2.00	1.00	.60
569	Dodgers Mgr./Coaches (Red Adams, Walt Alston, Monty Basgall, Jim Gilliam, Tom Lasorda)	5.00	2.50	1.50
570	Bill Singer	2.00	1.00	.60
571	Rusty Torres	2.00	1.00	.60
572	Gary Sutherland	2.00	1.00	.60
573	Fred Beene	2.00	1.00	.60
574	Bob Didier	2.00	1.00	.60
575	Dock Ellis	2.00	1.00	.60
576	Montreal Expos Team	5.00	2.50	1.50
577	***Eric Soderholm***	2.00	1.00	.60
578	Ken Wright	2.00	1.00	.60
579	Tom Grieve	2.00	1.00	.60
580	Joe Pepitone	2.00	1.00	.60
581	Steve Kealey	2.00	1.00	.60
582	Darrell Porter	2.00	1.00	.60
583	Bill Greif	2.00	1.00	.60
584	Chris Arnold	2.00	1.00	.60
585	Joe Niekro	2.00	1.00	.60
586	Bill Sudakis	2.00	1.00	.60
587	Rich McKinney	2.00	1.00	.60
588	Checklist 529-660	15.00	7.50	4.50
589	Ken Forsch	2.00	1.00	.60
590	Deron Johnson	2.00	1.00	.60
591	Mike Hedlund	2.00	1.00	.60
592	John Boccabella	2.00	1.00	.60
593	Royals Mgr./Coaches (Galen Cisco, Harry Dunlop, Charlie Lau, Jack McKeon)	2.00	1.00	.60
594	Vic Harris	2.00	1.00	.60
595	Don Gullett	2.00	1.00	.60
596	Boston Red Sox Team	5.00	2.50	1.50
597	Mickey Rivers	2.00	1.00	.60
598	Phil Roof	2.00	1.00	.60
599	Ed Crosby	2.00	1.00	.60
600	Dave McNally	2.00	1.00	.60
601	Rookie Catchers (**George Pena, Sergio Robles, Rick Stelmaszek**)	3.00	1.50	.90
602	Rookie Pitchers (***Mel Behney, Ralph Garcia, Doug Rau***)	3.00	1.50	.90
603	Rookie Third Basemen (***Terry Hughes, Bill McNulty, Ken Reitz***)	3.00	1.50	.90
604	Rookie Pitchers (**Jesse Jefferson, Dennis O'Toole, Bob Strampe**)	3.00	1.50	.90
605	Rookie First Basemen (**Pat Bourque, Enos Cabell, Gonzalo Marquez**)	3.00	1.50	.90
606	Rookie Outfielders (**Gary Matthews, Tom Paciorek, Jorge Roque**)	4.00	2.00	1.25
607	Rookie Shortstops (**Ray Busse, Pepe Frias, Mario Guerrero**)	3.00	1.50	.90

608	Rookie Pitchers (***Steve Busby, Dick Colpaert, George Medich***)	3.00	1.50	.90
609	Rookie Second Basemen (***Larvell Blanks, Pedro Garcia, Dave Lopes***)	5.00	2.50	1.50
610	Rookie Pitchers (**Jimmy Freeman, Charlie Hough, Hank Webb**)	4.00	2.00	1.25
611	Rookie Outfielders (**Rich Coggins, Jim Wohlford, Richie Zisk**)	3.00	1.50	.90
612	Rookie Pitchers (**Steve Lawson, Bob Reynolds, Brent Strom**)	3.00	1.50	.90
613	Rookie Catchers (**Bob Boone, Mike Ivie, Skip Jutze**)	15.00	7.50	4.50
614	Rookie Outfielders (**Al Bumbry, Dwight Evans, Charlie Spikes**)	20.00	10.00	6.00
615	Rookie Third Basemen (***Ron Cey, John Hilton, Mike Schmidt***)	150.00	75.00	45.00
616	Rookie Pitchers (**Norm Angelini, Steve Blateric, Mike Garman**)	3.00	1.50	.90
617	Rich Chiles	2.00	1.00	.60
618	Andy Etchebarren	2.00	1.00	.60
619	Billy Wilson	2.00	1.00	.60
620	Tommy Harper	2.00	1.00	.60
621	Joe Ferguson	2.00	1.00	.60
622	Larry Hisle	2.00	1.00	.60
623	Steve Renko	2.00	1.00	.60
624	Astros Mgr./Coaches (Leo Durocher, Preston Gomez, Grady Hatton, Hub Kittle, Jim Owens)	3.00	1.50	.90
625	Angel Mangual	2.00	1.00	.60
626	Bob Barton	2.00	1.00	.60
627	Luis Alvarado	2.00	1.00	.60
628	Jim Slaton	2.00	1.00	.60
629	Cleveland Indians Team	5.00	2.50	1.50
630	Denny McLain	6.00	3.00	1.75
631	Tom Matchick	2.00	1.00	.60
632	Dick Selma	2.00	1.00	.60
633	Ike Brown	2.00	1.00	.60
634	Alan Closter	2.00	1.00	.60
635	Gene Alley	2.00	1.00	.60
636	Rick Clark	2.00	1.00	.60
637	Norm Miller	2.00	1.00	.60
638	Ken Reynolds	2.00	1.00	.60
639	Willie Crawford	2.00	1.00	.60
640	Dick Bosman	2.00	1.00	.60
641	Cincinnati Reds Team	6.00	3.00	1.75
642	Jose Laboy	2.00	1.00	.60
643	Al Fitzmorris	2.00	1.00	.60
644	Jack Heidemann	2.00	1.00	.60
645	Bob Locker	2.00	1.00	.60
646	Brewers Mgr./Coaches (Del Crandall, Harvey Kuenn, Joe Nossek, Bob Shaw, Jim Walton)	2.00	1.00	.60
647	George Stone	2.00	1.00	.60
648	Tom Egan	2.00	1.00	.60
649	Rich Folkers	2.00	1.00	.60
650	Felipe Alou	4.00	2.00	1.25
651	Don Carrithers	2.00	1.00	.60
652	Ted Kubiak	2.00	1.00	.60
653	Joe Hoerner	2.00	1.00	.60
654	Minnesota Twins Team	4.00	2.00	1.25
655	Clay Kirby	2.00	1.00	.60
656	John Ellis	2.00	1.00	.60
657	Bob Johnson	2.00	1.00	.60
658	Elliott Maddox	2.00	1.00	.60
659	Jose Pagan	2.00	1.00	.60
660	Fred Scherman	2.00	1.00	.60

1973 Topps Candy Lids

A bit out of the ordinary, the Topps Candy Lids were the top of a product called "Baseball Stars Bubble Gum." The bottom (inside) of the lids carry a color photo of a player with a ribbon containing the name, position and team. The lids are 1-7/8" in diameter. A total of 55 different lids were made, featuring most of the stars of the day.

		NM	EX	VG
Complete Set (55):		750.00	375.00	225.00
Common Player:		6.00	3.00	1.75
Unopened Tub:		135.00		
(1)	Hank Aaron	60.00	30.00	18.00
(2)	Dick Allen	7.50	3.75	2.25
(3)	Dusty Baker	6.00	3.00	1.75
(4)	Sal Bando	6.00	3.00	1.75
(5)	Johnny Bench	30.00	15.00	9.00
(6)	Bobby Bonds	6.00	3.00	1.75
(7)	Dick Bosman	6.00	3.00	1.75
(8)	Lou Brock	15.00	7.50	4.50
(9)	Rod Carew	25.00	12.50	7.50
(10)	Steve Carlton	25.00	12.50	7.50
(11)	Nate Colbert	6.00	3.00	1.75
(12)	Willie Davis	6.00	3.00	1.75
(13)	Larry Dierker	6.00	3.00	1.75
(14)	Mike Epstein	6.00	3.00	1.75
(15)	Carlton Fisk	15.00	7.50	4.50
(16)	Tim Foli	6.00	3.00	1.75
(17)	Ray Fosse	6.00	3.00	1.75
(18)	Bill Freehan	6.00	3.00	1.75
(19)	Bob Gibson	25.00	12.50	7.50
(20)	Bud Harrelson	6.00	3.00	1.75
(21)	Catfish Hunter	15.00	7.50	4.50
(22)	Reggie Jackson	40.00	20.00	12.00
(23)	Fergie Jenkins	15.00	7.50	4.50
(24)	Al Kaline	30.00	15.00	9.00
(25)	Harmon Killebrew	30.00	15.00	9.00
(26)	Clay Kirby	6.00	3.00	1.75
(27)	Mickey Lolich	6.00	3.00	1.75
(28)	Greg Luzinski	6.00	3.00	1.75
(29)	Mike Marshall	6.00	3.00	1.75
(30)	Lee May	6.00	3.00	1.75
(31)	John Mayberry	6.00	3.00	1.75
(32)	Willie Mays	60.00	30.00	18.00
(33)	Willie McCovey	15.00	7.50	4.50
(34)	Thurman Munson	25.00	12.50	7.50
(35)	Bobby Murcer	12.50	6.25	3.75
(36)	Gary Nolan	6.00	3.00	1.75
(37)	Amos Otis	6.00	3.00	1.75
(38)	Jim Palmer	15.00	7.50	4.50
(39)	Gaylord Perry	15.00	7.50	4.50
(40)	Lou Piniella	7.50	3.75	2.25
(41)	Brooks Robinson	30.00	15.00	9.00
(42)	Frank Robinson	30.00	15.00	9.00
(43)	Ellie Rodriguez	6.00	3.00	1.75
(44)	Pete Rose	50.00	25.00	15.00
(45)	Nolan Ryan	200.00	100.00	60.00
(46)	Manny Sanguillen	6.00	3.00	1.75
(47)	George Scott	6.00	3.00	1.75
(48)	Tom Seaver	25.00	12.50	7.50
(49)	Chris Speier	6.00	3.00	1.75
(50)	Willie Stargell	15.00	7.50	4.50
(51)	Don Sutton	15.00	7.50	4.50
(52)	Joe Torre	7.50	3.75	2.25
(53)	Billy Williams	15.00	7.50	4.50
(54)	Wilbur Wood	6.00	3.00	1.75
(55)	Carl Yastrzemski	35.00	17.50	10.50

1973 Topps Comics

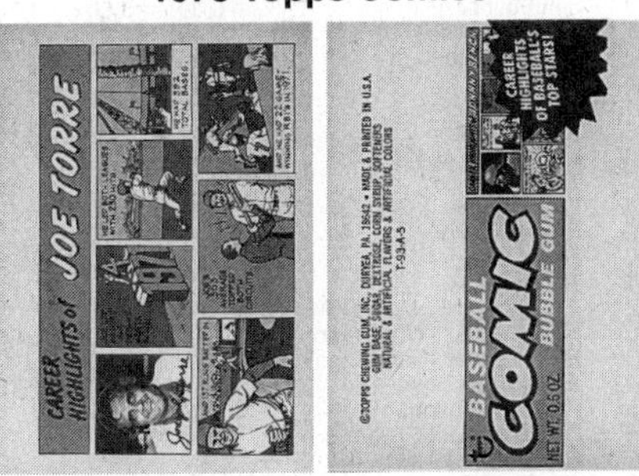

Strictly a test issue, if ever publicly distributed at all (most are found without any folding which would have occurred had they actually been used to wrap a piece of bubblegum), the 24 players in the 1973 Topps Comics issue appear on 4-5/8" x 3-7/16" waxed paper wrappers. The inside of the wrapper combines a color photo and facsimile autograph with a comic-style presentation of the player's career highlights. The Comics share a checklist with the 1973 Topps Pin-Ups, virtually all star players.

		NM	EX	VG
Complete Set (24):		15,000	7,500	4,500
Common Player:		200.00	100.00	60.00
(1)	Hank Aaron	1,100	550.00	330.00
(2)	Dick Allen	375.00	185.00	110.00
(3)	Johnny Bench	675.00	335.00	200.00
(4)	Steve Carlton	550.00	275.00	165.00
(5)	Nate Colbert	200.00	100.00	60.00
(6)	Willie Davis	200.00	100.00	60.00
(7)	Mike Epstein	200.00	100.00	60.00
(8)	Reggie Jackson	1,100	550.00	330.00
(9)	Harmon Killebrew	550.00	275.00	165.00
(10)	Mickey Lolich	200.00	100.00	60.00
(11)	Mike Marshall	200.00	100.00	60.00
(12)	Lee May	200.00	100.00	60.00
(13)	Willie McCovey	550.00	275.00	165.00
(14)	Bobby Murcer	300.00	150.00	90.00
(15)	Gaylord Perry	525.00	260.00	155.00
(16)	Lou Piniella	300.00	150.00	90.00
(17)	Brooks Robinson	900.00	450.00	270.00
(18)	Nolan Ryan	3,500	1,750	1,000
(19)	George Scott	200.00	100.00	60.00
(20)	Tom Seaver	750.00	375.00	225.00
(21)	Willie Stargell	550.00	275.00	165.00
(22)	Joe Torre	300.00	150.00	90.00
(23)	Billy Williams	525.00	260.00	155.00
(24)	Carl Yastrzemski	1,100	550.00	330.00

The Mint-Mint examples of vintage cards carry a significant premium over the Near Mint values shown here. This premium reflects limited availability of the highest-grade cards as well as demand for particular cards or sets in the best possible condition.

1973 Topps Pin-Ups

Another test issue of 1973, the 24 Topps Pin-Ups include the same basic format and the same checklist of star-caliber players as the Comics test issue of the same year. The 3-7/16" x 4-5/8" Pin-Ups are actually the inside of a wrapper for a piece of bubblegum. The color player photo features a decorative lozenge inserted at bottom with the player's name, team and position. There is also a facsimile autograph. Curiously, neither the Pin-Ups nor the Comics of 1973 bear team logos on the players' caps.

		NM	EX	VG
Complete Set (24):		9,000	4,500	2,750
Common Player:		250.00	125.00	75.00
(1)	Hank Aaron	800.00	400.00	240.00
(2)	Dick Allen	300.00	150.00	90.00
(3)	Johnny Bench	600.00	300.00	180.00
(4)	Steve Carlton	500.00	250.00	150.00
(5)	Nate Colbert	250.00	125.00	75.00
(6)	Willie Davis	250.00	125.00	75.00
(7)	Mike Epstein	265.00	130.00	80.00
(8)	Reggie Jackson	800.00	400.00	240.00
(9)	Harmon Killebrew	550.00	275.00	165.00
(10)	Mickey Lolich	265.00	130.00	80.00
(11)	Mike Marshall	250.00	125.00	75.00
(12)	Lee May	250.00	125.00	75.00
(13)	Willie McCovey	550.00	275.00	165.00
(14)	Bobby Murcer	300.00	150.00	90.00
(15)	Gaylord Perry	500.00	250.00	150.00
(16)	Lou Piniella	300.00	150.00	90.00
(17)	Brooks Robinson	600.00	300.00	180.00
(18)	Nolan Ryan	900.00	450.00	270.00
(19)	George Scott	250.00	125.00	75.00
(20)	Tom Seaver	600.00	300.00	180.00
(21)	Willie Stargell	550.00	275.00	165.00
(22)	Joe Torre	275.00	135.00	82.00
(23)	Billy Williams	550.00	275.00	165.00
(24)	Carl Yastrzemski	650.00	325.00	195.00

1973 Topps Team Checklists

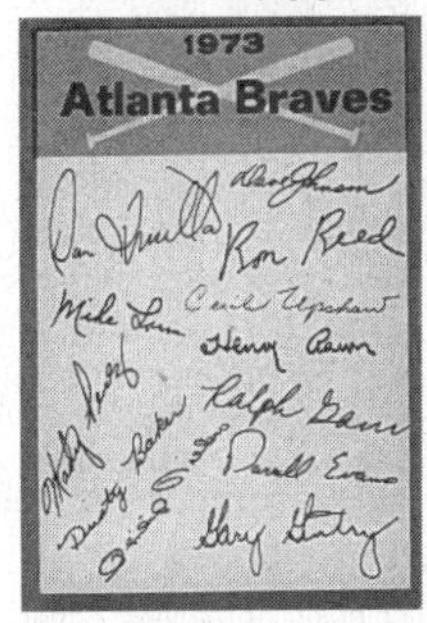

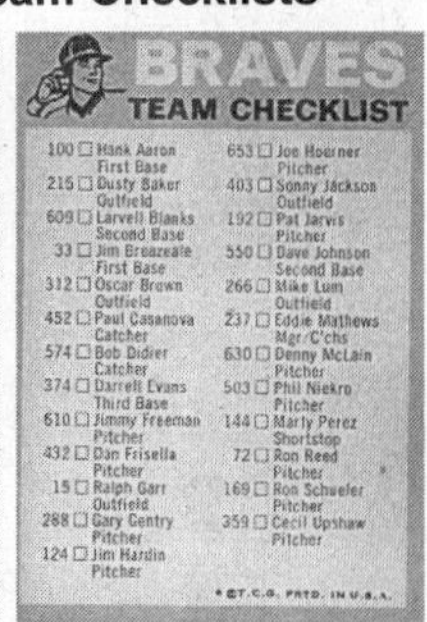

This is a 24-card unnumbered set of 2-1/2" x 3-1/2" cards that is generally believed to have been included with the high-numbered series in 1973, while also being made available in a mail-in offer. The front of the cards have the team name at the top and a white panel with various facsimile autographs takes up the rest of the space except for a blue border. Backs feature the team name and checklist. Relatively scarce, these somewhat mysterious cards are not included by many in their collections despite their obvious relationship to the regular set.

		NM	EX	VG
Complete Set (24):		100.00	50.00	30.00
Common Checklist:		3.50	1.75	1.00
(1)	Atlanta Braves	3.50	1.75	1.00
(2)	Baltimore Orioles	3.50	1.75	1.00
(3)	Boston Red Sox	5.00	2.50	1.50
(4)	California Angels	3.50	1.75	1.00
(5)	Chicago Cubs	3.50	1.75	1.00
(6)	Chicago White Sox	3.50	1.75	1.00
(7)	Cincinnati Reds	5.00	2.50	1.50
(8)	Cleveland Indians	3.50	1.75	1.00
(9)	Detroit Tigers	6.00	3.00	1.75
(10)	Houston Astros	3.50	1.75	1.00
(11)	Kansas City Royals	3.50	1.75	1.00
(12)	Los Angeles Dodgers	3.50	1.75	1.00
(13)	Milwaukee Brewers	3.50	1.75	1.00
(14)	Minnesota Twins	3.50	1.75	1.00
(15)	Montreal Expos	3.50	1.75	1.00
(16)	New York Mets	6.00	3.00	1.75
(17)	New York Yankees	6.00	3.00	1.75
(18)	Oakland A's	6.00	3.00	1.75

(19)	Philadelphia Phillies	3.50	1.75	1.00
(20)	Pittsburgh Pirates	3.50	1.75	1.00
(21)	St. Louis Cardinals	3.50	1.75	1.00
(22)	San Diego Padres	3.50	1.75	1.00
(23)	San Francisco Giants	3.50	1.75	1.00
(24)	Texas Rangers	3.50	1.75	1.00

1973 Topps 1953 Reprints

Long before Topps reprinted virtually the entire 1953 set in its "Archives" program in 1991, selected cards from the '53 set had been reprinted in a rare eight-card issue. Some sources say the cards were produced as table favors at a Topps banquet, while at least one contemporary hobby periodical said they were sold on a test-issue basis in Brooklyn. It was said only 300 of the sets were made. Unlike the original cards in 2-5/8" x 3-3/4" format, the test issue cards are modern standard 2-1/2" x 3-1/2". Three of the players in the issue were misidentified. Card backs feature a career summary written as though in 1953; the backs are formatted differently than original 1953 Topps cards and are printed in black-and-white.

		NM	EX	VG
Complete Set (8):		750.00	375.00	225.00
Common Player:		35.00	17.50	10.00
1	Satchell Paige	225.00	110.00	65.00
2	Jackie Robinson	300.00	150.00	90.00
3	Carl Furillo (Picture actually Bill Antonello.)	50.00	25.00	15.00
4	Al Rosen (Picture actually Jim Fridley.)	35.00	17.50	10.00
5	Hal Newhouser	40.00	20.00	12.00
6	Clyde McCullough (Picture actually Vic Janowicz.)	35.00	17.50	10.00
7	"Peanuts" Lowrey	35.00	17.50	10.00
8	Johnny Mize	85.00	42.50	25.00

1974 Topps

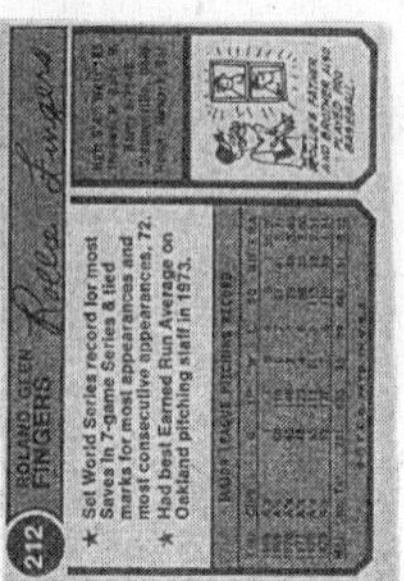

Issued all at once at the beginning of the year, rather than by series throughout the baseball season as had been done since 1952, this 660-card '74 Topps set features a famous group of error cards. At the time the cards were printed, it was uncertain whether the San Diego Padres would move to Washington, D.C., and by the time a decision was made some Padres cards had appeared with a "Washington, Nat'l League" designation on the front. A total of 15 cards were affected, and those with the Washington designation bring prices well in excess of regular cards of the same players (the Washington variations are not included in the complete set prices quoted below). The 2-1/2" x 3-1/2" cards feature color photos (frequently game-action shots) along with the player's name, team and position. Specialty cards abound, starting with a Hank Aaron tribute and running through the usual managers, statistical leaders, playoff and World Series highlights, multi-player rookie cards and All-Stars.

		NM	EX	VG
Unopened Factory Set (704):		600.00		
Complete Set (660):		350.00	175.00	100.00
Common Player:		.40	.20	.10
Wax Pack (2):		9.00		
Wax Pack (8+1 - B.T.C.):		40.00		
Wax Box (36):		1,600		
Wax Pack (12+1 - B.T.C.):		45.00		
Wax Box (24):		1,700		
Cello Pack: (22):		125.00		
Rack Pack: (42):		325.00		
Vending Box (500):		925.00		
1	Hank Aaron (All-Time Home Run King)	50.00	25.00	15.00
2	Hank Aaron (Aaron Special 1954-57)	10.00	5.00	3.00
3	Hank Aaron (Aaron Special 1958-61)	10.00	5.00	3.00
4	Hank Aaron (Aaron Special 1962-65)	10.00	5.00	3.00
5	Hank Aaron (Aaron Special 1966-69)	10.00	5.00	3.00
6	Hank Aaron (Aaron Special 1970-73)	10.00	5.00	3.00
7	Jim Hunter	4.00	2.00	1.25
8	George Theodore	.40	.20	.10
9	Mickey Lolich	.40	.20	.09
10	Johnny Bench	15.00	7.50	4.50
11	Jim Bibby	.40	.20	.10
12	Dave May	.40	.20	.10
13	Tom Hilgendorf	.40	.20	.10
14	Paul Popovich	.40	.20	.10
15	Joe Torre	2.00	1.00	.60
16	Baltimore Orioles Team	2.00	1.00	.60
17	Doug Bird	.40	.20	.10
18	Gary Thomasson	.40	.20	.10
19	Gerry Moses	.40	.20	.10
20	Nolan Ryan	40.00	20.00	12.00
21	Bob Gallagher	.40	.20	.10
22	Cy Acosta	.40	.20	.10
23	Craig Robinson	.40	.20	.10
24	John Hiller	.40	.20	.10
25	Ken Singleton	.40	.20	.10
26	***Bill Campbell***	.40	.20	.10
27	George Scott	.40	.20	.10
28	Manny Sanguillen	.40	.20	.10
29	Phil Niekro	4.00	2.00	1.25
30	Bobby Bonds	.40	.20	.09
31	Astros Mgr./Coaches (Roger Craig, Preston Gomez, Grady Hatton, Hub Kittle, Bob Lillis)	.40	.20	.09
32a	John Grubb (Washington)	3.00	1.50	.90
32b	John Grubb (San Diego)	.40	.20	.10
33	Don Newhauser	.40	.20	.10
34	Andy Kosco	.40	.20	.10
35	Gaylord Perry	4.00	2.00	1.25
36	St. Louis Cardinals Team	2.00	1.00	.60
37	Dave Sells	.40	.20	.10
38	Don Kessinger	.40	.20	.10
39	Ken Suarez	.40	.20	.10
40	Jim Palmer	6.00	3.00	1.75
41	Bobby Floyd	.40	.20	.10
42	Claude Osteen	.40	.20	.10
43	Jim Wynn	.40	.20	.10
44	Mel Stottlemyre	.75	.40	.25
45	Dave Johnson	.40	.20	.10
46	Pat Kelly	.40	.20	.10
47	***Dick Ruthven***	.40	.20	.10
48	Dick Sharon	.40	.20	.10
49	Steve Renko	.40	.20	.10
50	Rod Carew	6.00	3.00	1.75
51	Bobby Heise	.40	.20	.10
52	Al Oliver	.50	.25	.15
53a	Fred Kendall (Washington)	3.00	1.50	.90
53b	Fred Kendall (San Diego)	.40	.20	.10
54	***Elias Sosa***	.40	.20	.10
55	Frank Robinson	6.00	3.00	1.75
56	New York Mets Team	1.50	.70	.45
57	Darold Knowles	.40	.20	.10
58	Charlie Spikes	.40	.20	.10
59	Ross Grimsley	.40	.20	.10
60	Lou Brock	5.00	2.50	1.50
61	Luis Aparicio	4.00	2.00	1.25
62	Bob Locker	.40	.20	.10
63	Bill Sudakis	.40	.20	.10
64	Doug Rau	.40	.20	.10
65	Amos Otis	.40	.20	.10
66	Sparky Lyle	.40	.20	.10
67	Tommy Helms	.40	.20	.10
68	Grant Jackson	.40	.20	.10
69	Del Unser	.40	.20	.10
70	Dick Allen	.75	.40	.25
71	Danny Frisella	.40	.20	.10
72	Aurelio Rodriguez	.40	.20	.10
73	Mike Marshall	.40	.20	.10
74	Minnesota Twins Team	1.00	.50	.30
75	Jim Colborn	.40	.20	.10
76	Mickey Rivers	.40	.20	.10
77a	Rich Troedson (Washington)	3.00	1.50	.90
77b	Rich Troedson (San Diego)	.40	.20	.10
78	Giants Mgr./Coaches (Joe Amalfitano, Charlie Fox, Andy Gilbert, Don McMahon, John McNamara)	.40	.20	.10
79	Gene Tenace	.40	.20	.10
80	Tom Seaver	10.00	5.00	3.00
81	Frank Duffy	.40	.20	.10
82	Dave Giusti	.40	.20	.10
83	Orlando Cepeda	4.00	2.00	1.25
84	Rick Wise	.40	.20	.10
85	Joe Morgan	6.00	3.00	1.75
86	Joe Ferguson	.40	.20	.10
87	Fergie Jenkins	4.00	2.00	1.25
88	Freddie Patek	.40	.20	.10
89	Jackie Brown	.40	.20	.10
90	Bobby Murcer	.50	.25	.15
91	Ken Forsch	.40	.20	.10
92	Paul Blair	.40	.20	.10
93	Rod Gilbreath	.40	.20	.10
94	Detroit Tigers Team	1.00	.50	.30
95	Steve Carlton	6.00	3.00	1.75
96	***Jerry Hairston Sr.***	.40	.20	.10
97	Bob Bailey	.40	.20	.10
98	Bert Blyleven	.75	.40	.25
99	Brewers Mgr./Coaches (Del Crandall, Harvey Kuenn, Joe Nossek, Jim Walton, Al Widmar)	.40	.20	.10
100	Willie Stargell	5.00	2.50	1.50
101	Bobby Valentine	.40	.20	.10
102a	Bill Greif (Washington)	3.00	1.50	.90
102b	Bill Greif (San Diego)	.40	.20	.10
103	Sal Bando	.40	.20	.10
104	Ron Bryant	.40	.20	.10
105	Carlton Fisk	10.00	5.00	3.00
106	Harry Parker	.40	.20	.10
107	Alex Johnson	.40	.20	.10
108	Al Hrabosky	.40	.20	.10
109	Bob Grich	.40	.20	.10
110	Billy Williams	5.00	2.50	1.50
111	Clay Carroll	.40	.20	.10
112	Dave Lopes	.40	.20	.10
113	Dick Drago	.40	.20	.10
114	California Angels Team	1.00	.50	.30
115	Willie Horton	.40	.20	.10
116	Jerry Reuss	.40	.20	.10
117	Ron Blomberg	.40	.20	.10
118	Bill Lee	.40	.20	.10
119	Phillies Mgr./Coaches (Carroll Beringer, Bill DeMars, Danny Ozark, Ray Ripplemeyer, Bobby Wine)	.40	.20	.10
120	Wilbur Wood	.40	.20	.10
121	Larry Lintz	.40	.20	.10
122	Jim Holt	.40	.20	.10
123	Nelson Briles	.40	.20	.10
124	Bob Coluccio	.40	.20	.10
125a	Nate Colbert (Washington)	3.00	1.50	.90
125b	Nate Colbert (San Diego)	.40	.20	.10
126	Checklist 1-132	.75	.40	.25
127	Tom Paciorek	.40	.20	.10
128	John Ellis	.40	.20	.10
129	Chris Speier	.40	.20	.10
130	Reggie Jackson	15.00	7.50	4.50
131	Bob Boone	1.50	.70	.45
132	Felix Millan	.40	.20	.10
133	***David Clyde***	.40	.20	.10
134	Denis Menke	.40	.20	.10
135	Roy White	.40	.20	.10
136	Rick Reuschel	.40	.20	.10
137	Al Bumbry	.40	.20	.10
138	Ed Brinkman	.40	.20	.10
139	Aurelio Monteagudo	.40	.20	.10
140	Darrell Evans	.75	.40	.25
141	Pat Bourque	.40	.20	.10
142	Pedro Garcia	.40	.20	.10
143	Dick Woodson	.40	.20	.10
144	Dodgers Mgr./Coaches (Red Adams, Walter Alston, Monty Basgall, Jim Gilliam, Tom Lasorda)	1.00	.50	.30
145	Dock Ellis	.40	.20	.10
146	Ron Fairly	.40	.20	.10
147	Bart Johnson	.40	.20	.10
148a	Dave Hilton (Washington)	3.00	1.50	.90
148b	Dave Hilton (San Diego)	.40	.20	.10
149	Mac Scarce	.40	.20	.10
150	John Mayberry	.40	.20	.10
151	Diego Segui	.40	.20	.10
152	Oscar Gamble	.40	.20	.10
153	Jon Matlack	.40	.20	.10
154	Houston Astros Team	1.50	.70	.45
155	Bert Campaneris	.40	.20	.10
156	Randy Moffitt	.40	.20	.10
157	Vic Harris	.40	.20	.10
158	Jack Billingham	.40	.20	.10
159	Jim Ray Hart	.40	.20	.10
160	Brooks Robinson	6.00	3.00	1.75
161	***Ray Burris***	.40	.20	.10
162	Bill Freehan	.40	.20	.10
163	Ken Berry	.40	.20	.10
164	Tom House	.40	.20	.10
165	Willie Davis	.40	.20	.10
166	Royals Mgr./Coaches (Galen Cisco, Harry Dunlop, Charlie Lau, Jack McKeon)	.40	.20	.10
167	Luis Tiant	1.00	.50	.30
168	Danny Thompson	.40	.20	.10
169	***Steve Rogers***	.40	.20	.10
170	Bill Melton	.40	.20	.10
171	Eduardo Rodriguez	.40	.20	.10
172	Gene Clines	.40	.20	.10
173a	***Randy Jones*** (Washington)	3.00	1.50	.90
173b	***Randy Jones*** (San Diego)	.40	.20	.10
174	Bill Robinson	.40	.20	.10
175	Reggie Cleveland	.40	.20	.10
176	John Lowenstein	.40	.20	.10
177	Dave Roberts	.40	.20	.10
178	Garry Maddox	.40	.20	.10
179	Mets Mgr./Coaches (Yogi Berra, Roy McMillan, Joe Pignatano, Rube Walker, Eddie Yost)	1.50	.70	.45
180	Ken Holtzman	.40	.20	.10
181	Cesar Geronimo	.40	.20	.10
182	Lindy McDaniel	.40	.20	.10
183	Johnny Oates	.40	.20	.10
184	Texas Rangers Team	1.00	.50	.30
185	Jose Cardenal	.40	.20	.10
186	Fred Scherman	.40	.20	.10
187	Don Baylor	1.00	.50	.30
188	Rudy Meoli	.40	.20	.10
189	Jim Brewer	.40	.20	.10
190	Tony Oliva	1.50	.70	.45
191	Al Fitzmorris	.40	.20	.10
192	Mario Guerrero	.40	.20	.10
193	Tom Walker	.40	.20	.10
194	Darrell Porter	.40	.20	.10
195	Carlos May	.40	.20	.10
196	Jim Fregosi	.75	.40	.25
197a	Vicente Romo (Washington)	3.00	1.50	.90
197b	Vicente Romo (San Diego)	.40	.20	.10
198	Dave Cash	.40	.20	.10
199	Mike Kekich	.40	.20	.10
200	Cesar Cedeno	.40	.20	.10
201	Batting Leaders (Rod Carew, Pete Rose)	6.00	3.00	1.75

202	Home Run Leaders (Reggie Jackson, Willie Stargell)	4.00	2.00	1.25
203	RBI Leaders (Reggie Jackson, Willie Stargell)	4.00	2.00	1.25
204	Stolen Base Leaders (Lou Brock, Tommy Harper)	1.50	.70	.45
205	Victory Leaders (Ron Bryant, Wilbur Wood)	1.00	.50	.30
206	Earned Run Average Leaders (Jim Palmer, Tom Seaver)	2.00	1.00	.60
207	Strikeout Leaders (Nolan Ryan, Tom Seaver)	10.00	5.00	3.00
208	Leading Firemen (John Hiller, Mike Marshall)	1.00	.50	.30
209	Ted Sizemore	.40	.20	.10
210	Bill Singer	.40	.20	.10
211	Chicago Cubs Team	1.00	.50	.30
212	Rollie Fingers	4.00	2.00	1.25
213	Dave Rader	.40	.20	.10
214	Billy Grabarkewitz	.40	.20	.10
215	Al Kaline	10.00	5.00	3.00
216	Ray Sadecki	.40	.20	.10
217	Tim Foli	.40	.20	.10
218	Johnny Briggs	.40	.20	.10
219	Doug Griffin	.40	.20	.10
220	Don Sutton	4.00	2.00	1.25
221	White Sox Mgr./Coaches (Joe Lonnett, Jim Mahoney, Alex Monchak, Johnny Sain, Chuck Tanner)	.40	.20	.10
222	Ramon Hernandez	.40	.20	.10
223	Jeff Burroughs	.40	.20	.10
224	Roger Metzger	.40	.20	.10
225	Paul Splittorff	.40	.20	.10
226a	Washington Nat'l. Team	8.00	4.00	2.50
226b	San Diego Padres Team	2.00	1.00	.60
227	Mike Lum	.40	.20	.10
228	Ted Kubiak	.40	.20	.10
229	Fritz Peterson	.40	.20	.10
230	Tony Perez	4.00	2.00	1.25
231	Dick Tidrow	.40	.20	.10
232	Steve Brye	.40	.20	.10
233	Jim Barr	.40	.20	.10
234	John Milner	.40	.20	.10
235	Dave McNally	.40	.20	.10
236	Cardinals Mgr./Coaches (Vern Benson, George Kissell, Johnny Lewis, Red Schoendienst, Barney Schultz)	.75	.40	.25
237	Ken Brett	.40	.20	.10
238	Fran Healy	.40	.20	.10
239	Bill Russell	.40	.20	.10
240	Joe Coleman	.40	.20	.10
241a	Glenn Beckert (Washington)	3.00	1.50	.90
241b	Glenn Beckert (San Diego)	.40	.20	.10
242	Bill Gogolewski	.40	.20	.10
243	Bob Oliver	.40	.20	.10
244	Carl Morton	.40	.20	.10
245	Cleon Jones	.40	.20	.10
246	Oakland A's Team	2.00	1.00	.60
247	Rick Miller	.40	.20	.10
248	Tom Hall	.40	.20	.10
249	George Mitterwald	.40	.20	.10
250a	Willie McCovey (Washington)	20.00	10.00	6.00
250b	Willie McCovey (San Diego)	6.00	3.00	1.75
251	Graig Nettles	1.50	.70	.45
252	***Dave Parker***	8.00	4.00	2.50
253	John Boccabella	.40	.20	.10
254	Stan Bahnsen	.40	.20	.10
255	Larry Bowa	1.00	.50	.30
256	Tom Griffin	.40	.20	.10
257	Buddy Bell	.40	.20	.10
258	Jerry Morales	.40	.20	.10
259	Bob Reynolds	.40	.20	.10
260	Ted Simmons	.75	.40	.25
261	Jerry Bell	.40	.20	.10
262	Ed Kirkpatrick	.40	.20	.10
263	Checklist 133-264	1.00	.50	.30
264	Joe Rudi	.40	.20	.10
265	Tug McGraw	.40	.20	.10
266	Jim Northrup	.40	.20	.10
267	Andy Messersmith	.40	.20	.10
268	Tom Grieve	.40	.20	.10
269	Bob Johnson	.40	.20	.10
270	Ron Santo	3.00	1.50	.90
271	Bill Hands	.40	.20	.10
272	Paul Casanova	.40	.20	.10
273	Checklist 265-396	.75	.40	.25
274	Fred Beene	.40	.20	.10
275	Ron Hunt	.40	.20	.10
276	Angels Mgr./Coaches (Tom Morgan, Salty Parker, Jimmie Reese, John Roseboro, Bobby Winkles)	.40	.20	.10
277	Gary Nolan	.40	.20	.10
278	Cookie Rojas	.40	.20	.10
279	Jim Crawford	.40	.20	.10
280	Carl Yastrzemski	10.00	5.00	3.00
281	San Francisco Giants Team	1.00	.50	.30
282	Doyle Alexander	.40	.20	.10
283	Mike Schmidt	20.00	10.00	6.00
284	Dave Duncan	.40	.20	.10
285	Reggie Smith	.40	.20	.10
286	Tony Muser	.40	.20	.10
287	Clay Kirby	.40	.20	.10
288	***Gorman Thomas***	2.00	1.00	.60
289	Rick Auerbach	.40	.20	.10
290	Vida Blue	1.00	.50	.30
291	Don Hahn	.40	.20	.10
292	Chuck Seelbach	.40	.20	.10
293	Milt May	.40	.20	.10
294	Steve Foucault	.40	.20	.10
295	Rick Monday	.40	.20	.10
296	Ray Corbin	.40	.20	.10
297	Hal Breeden	.40	.20	.10

298	Roric Harrison	.40	.20	.10
299	Gene Michael	.40	.20	.10
300	Pete Rose	25.00	12.50	7.50
301	Bob Montgomery	.40	.20	.10
302	Rudy May	.40	.20	.10
303	George Hendrick	.40	.20	.10
304	Don Wilson	.40	.20	.10
305	Tito Fuentes	.40	.20	.10
306	Orioles Mgr./Coaches (George Bamberger, Jim Frey, Billy Hunter, George Staller, Earl Weaver)	2.00	1.00	.60
307	Luis Melendez	.40	.20	.10
308	Bruce Dal Canton	.40	.20	.10
309a	Dave Roberts (Washington)	3.00	1.50	.90
309b	Dave Roberts (San Diego)	.40	.20	.10
310	Terry Forster	.40	.20	.10
311	Jerry Grote	.40	.20	.10
312	Deron Johnson	.40	.20	.10
313	Berry Lersch	.40	.20	.10
314	Milwaukee Brewers Team	1.00	.50	.30
315	Ron Cey	.50	.25	.15
316	Jim Perry	.40	.20	.10
317	Richie Zisk	.40	.20	.10
318	Jim Merritt	.40	.20	.10
319	Randy Hundley	.40	.20	.10
320	Dusty Baker	1.00	.50	.30
321	Steve Braun	.40	.20	.10
322	Ernie McAnally	.40	.20	.10
323	Richie Scheinblum	.40	.20	.10
324	Steve Kline	.40	.20	.10
325	Tommy Harper	.40	.20	.10
326	Reds Mgr./Coaches (Sparky Anderson, Alex Grammas, Ted Kluszewski, George Scherger, Larry Shepard)	2.00	1.00	.60
327	Tom Timmermann	.40	.20	.10
328	Skip Jutze	.40	.20	.10
329	Mark Belanger	.40	.20	.10
330	Juan Marichal	4.00	2.00	1.25
331	All-Star Catchers (Johnny Bench, Carlton Fisk)	4.00	2.00	1.25
332	All-Star First Basemen (Hank Aaron, Dick Allen)	6.00	3.00	1.75
333	All-Star Second Basemen (Rod Carew, Joe Morgan)	3.00	1.50	.90
334	All-Star Third Basemen (Brooks Robinson, Ron Santo)	2.00	1.00	.60
335	All-Star Shortstops (Bert Campaneris, Chris Speier)	1.00	.50	.30
336	All-Star Left Fielders (Bobby Murcer, Pete Rose)	5.00	2.50	1.50
337	All-Star Center Fielders (Cesar Cedeno, Amos Otis)	.75	.40	.25
338	All-Star Right Fielders (Reggie Jackson, Billy Williams)	4.00	2.00	1.25
339	All-Star Pitchers (Jim Hunter, Rick Wise)	2.00	1.00	.60
340	Thurman Munson	8.00	4.00	2.50
341	***Dan Driessen***	.40	.20	.10
342	Jim Lonborg	.40	.20	.10
343	Kansas City Royals Team	1.00	.50	.30
344	Mike Caldwell	.40	.20	.10
345	Bill North	.40	.20	.10
346	Ron Reed	.40	.20	.10
347	Sandy Alomar	.40	.20	.10
348	Pete Richert	.40	.20	.10
349	John Vukovich	.40	.20	.10
350	Bob Gibson	6.00	3.00	1.75
351	Dwight Evans	1.00	.50	.30
352	Bill Stoneman	.40	.20	.10
353	Rich Coggins	.40	.20	.10
354	Cubs Mgr./Coaches (Hank Aguirre, Whitey Lockman, Jim Marshall, J.C. Martin, Al Spangler)	.40	.20	.10
355	Dave Nelson	.40	.20	.10
356	Jerry Koosman	.40	.20	.10
357	Buddy Bradford	.40	.20	.10
358	Dal Maxvill	.40	.20	.10
359	Brent Strom	.40	.20	.10
360	Greg Luzinski	1.00	.50	.30
361	Don Carrithers	.40	.20	.10
362	Hal King	.40	.20	.10
363	New York Yankees Team	2.00	1.00	.60
364a	Clarence Gaston (Washington)	3.00	1.50	.90
364b	Clarence Gaston (San Diego)	.40	.20	.10
365	Steve Busby	.40	.20	.10
366	Larry Hisle	.40	.20	.10
367	Norm Cash	1.00	.50	.30
368	Manny Mota	.40	.20	.10
369	Paul Lindblad	.40	.20	.10
370	Bob Watson	.40	.20	.10
371	Jim Slaton	.40	.20	.10
372	Ken Reitz	.40	.20	.10
373	John Curtis	.40	.20	.10
374	Marty Perez	.40	.20	.10
375	Earl Williams	.40	.20	.10
376	Jorge Orta	.40	.20	.10
377	Ron Woods	.40	.20	.10
378	Burt Hooton	.40	.20	.10
379	Rangers Mgr./Coaches (Art Fowler, Frank Lucchesi, Billy Martin, Jackie Moore, Charlie Silvera)	.45	.25	.15
380	Bud Harrelson	.40	.20	.10
381	Charlie Sands	.40	.20	.10
382	Bob Moose	.40	.20	.10
383	Philadelphia Phillies Team	1.00	.50	.30
384	Chris Chambliss	.75	.40	.25
385	Don Gullett	.40	.20	.10
386	Gary Matthews	.40	.20	.10
387a	Rich Morales (Washington)	3.00	1.50	.90
387b	Rich Morales (San Diego)	.40	.20	.10

388	Phil Roof	.40	.20	.10
389	Gates Brown	.40	.20	.10
390	Lou Piniella	2.00	1.00	.60
391	Billy Champion	.40	.20	.10
392	Dick Green	.40	.20	.10
393	Orlando Pena	.40	.20	.10
394	Ken Henderson	.40	.20	.10
395	Doug Rader	.40	.20	.10
396	Tommy Davis	.40	.20	.10
397	George Stone	.40	.20	.10
398	Duke Sims	.40	.20	.10
399	Mike Paul	.40	.20	.10
400	Harmon Killebrew	5.00	2.50	1.50
401	Elliott Maddox	.40	.20	.10
402	Jim Rooker	.40	.20	.10
403	Red Sox Mgr./Coaches (Don Bryant, Darrell Johnson, Eddie Popowski, Lee Stange, Don Zimmer)	.40	.20	.10
404	Jim Howarth	.40	.20	.10
405	Ellie Rodriguez	.40	.20	.10
406	Steve Arlin	.40	.20	.10
407	Jim Wohlford	.40	.20	.10
408	Charlie Hough	1.00	.50	.30
409	Ike Brown	.40	.20	.10
410	Pedro Borbon	.40	.20	.10
411	Frank Baker	.40	.20	.10
412	Chuck Taylor	.40	.20	.10
413	Don Money	.40	.20	.10
414	Checklist 397-528	2.00	1.00	.60
415	Gary Gentry	.40	.20	.10
416	Chicago White Sox Team	1.00	.50	.30
417	Rich Folkers	.40	.20	.10
418	Walt Williams	.40	.20	.10
419	Wayne Twitchell	.40	.20	.10
420	Ray Fosse	.40	.20	.10
421	Dan Fife	.40	.20	.10
422	Gonzalo Marquez	.40	.20	.10
423	Fred Stanley	.40	.20	.10
424	Jim Beauchamp	.40	.20	.10
425	Pete Broberg	.40	.20	.10
426	Rennie Stennett	.40	.20	.10
427	Bobby Bolin	.40	.20	.10
428	Gary Sutherland	.40	.20	.10
429	Dick Lange	.40	.20	.10
430	Matty Alou	.40	.20	.10
431	***Gene Garber***	.40	.20	.10
432	Chris Arnold	.40	.20	.10
433	Lerrin LaGrow	.40	.20	.10
434	Ken McMullen	.40	.20	.10
435	Dave Concepcion	1.00	.50	.30
436	Don Hood	.40	.20	.10
437	Jim Lyttle	.40	.20	.10
438	Ed Herrmann	.40	.20	.10
439	Norm Miller	.40	.20	.10
440	Jim Kaat	1.50	.70	.45
441	Tom Ragland	.40	.20	.10
442	Alan Foster	.40	.20	.10
443	Tom Hutton	.40	.20	.10
444	Vic Davalillo	.40	.20	.10
445	George Medich	.40	.20	.10
446	Len Randle	.40	.20	.10
447	Twins Mgr./Coaches (Vern Morgan, Frank Quilici, Bob Rodgers, Ralph Rowe)	.40	.20	.10
448	Ron Hodges	.40	.20	.10
449	Tom McCraw	.40	.20	.10
450	Rich Hebner	.40	.20	.10
451	Tommy John	1.00	.50	.30
452	Gene Hiser	.40	.20	.10
453	Balor Moore	.40	.20	.10
454	Kurt Bevacqua	.40	.20	.10
455	Tom Bradley	.40	.20	.10
456	***Dave Winfield***	50.00	25.00	15.00
457	Chuck Goggin	.40	.20	.10
458	Jim Ray	.40	.20	.10
459	Cincinnati Reds Team	1.50	.70	.45
460	Boog Powell	1.00	.50	.30
461	John Odom	.40	.20	.10
462	Luis Alvarado	.40	.20	.10
463	Pat Dobson	.40	.20	.10
464	Jose Cruz	.40	.20	.10
465	Dick Bosman	.40	.20	.10
466	Dick Billings	.40	.20	.10
467	Winston Llenas	.40	.20	.10
468	Pepe Frias	.40	.20	.10
469	Joe Decker	.40	.20	.10
470	A.L. Playoffs (Reggie Jackson)	4.00	2.00	1.25
471	N.L. Playoffs (Jon Matlack)	.50	.25	.15
472	World Series Game 1 (Darold Knowles)	.50	.25	.15
473	World Series Game 2 (Willie Mays)	6.00	3.00	1.75
474	World Series Game 3	1.00	.50	.30
475	World Series Game 4	1.00	.50	.30
476	World Series Game 5	1.00	.50	.30
477	World Series Game 6 (Reggie Jackson)	4.00	2.00	1.25
478	World Series Game 7	1.50	.75	.45
479	A's Celebrate (Win 2nd Consecutive Championship!)	1.00	.50	.30
480	Willie Crawford	.40	.20	.10
481	Jerry Terrell	.40	.20	.10
482	Bob Didier	.40	.20	.10
483	Atlanta Braves Team	1.00	.50	.30
484	Carmen Fanzone	.40	.20	.10
485	Felipe Alou	.50	.25	.15
486	Steve Stone	.40	.20	.10
487	Ted Martinez	.40	.20	.10
488	Andy Etchebarren	.40	.20	.10
489	Pirates Mgr./Coaches (Don Leppert, Bill Mazeroski, Danny Murtaugh, Don Osborn, Bob Skinner)	.75	.40	.25
490	Vada Pinson	1.00	.50	.30
491	Roger Nelson	.40	.20	.10

No.	Player	NM	EX	VG
492	Mike Rogodzinski	.40	.20	.10
493	Joe Hoerner	.40	.20	.10
494	Ed Goodson	.40	.20	.10
495	Dick McAuliffe	.40	.20	.10
496	Tom Murphy	.40	.20	.10
497	Bobby Mitchell	.40	.20	.10
498	Pat Corrales	.40	.20	.10
499	Rusty Torres	.40	.20	.10
500	Lee May	.75	.40	.25
501	Eddie Leon	.40	.20	.10
502	Dave LaRoche	.40	.20	.10
503	Eric Soderholm	.40	.20	.10
504	Joe Niekro	.75	.40	.25
505	Bill Buckner	.75	.40	.25
506	Ed Farmer	.40	.20	.10
507	Larry Stahl	.40	.20	.10
508	Montreal Expos Team	1.00	.50	.30
509	Jesse Jefferson	.40	.20	.10
510	Wayne Garrett	.40	.20	.10
511	Toby Harrah	.40	.20	.10
512	Joe Lahoud	.40	.20	.10
513	Jim Campanis	.40	.20	.10
514	Paul Schaal	.40	.20	.10
515	Willie Montanez	.40	.20	.10
516	Horacio Pina	.40	.20	.10
517	Mike Hegan	.40	.20	.10
518	Derrel Thomas	.40	.20	.10
519	Bill Sharp	.40	.20	.10
520	Tim McCarver	1.50	.70	.45
521	Indians Mgr./Coaches (Ken Aspromonte, Clay Bryant, Tony Pacheco)	.40	.20	.10
522	J.R. Richard	1.00	.50	.30
523	Cecil Cooper	1.00	.50	.30
524	Bill Plummer	.40	.20	.10
525	Clyde Wright	.40	.20	.10
526	Frank Tepedino	.40	.20	.10
527	Bobby Darwin	.40	.20	.10
528	Bill Bonham	.40	.20	.10
529	Horace Clarke	.40	.20	.10
530	Mickey Stanley	.40	.20	.10
531	Expos Mgr./Coaches (Dave Bristol, Larry Doby, Gene Mauch, Cal McLish, Jerry Zimmerman)	.40	.20	.10
532	Skip Lockwood	.40	.20	.10
533	Mike Phillips	.40	.20	.10
534	Eddie Watt	.40	.20	.10
535	Bob Tolan	.40	.20	.10
536	Duffy Dyer	.40	.20	.10
537	Steve Mingori	.40	.20	.10
538	Cesar Tovar	.40	.20	.10
539	Lloyd Allen	.40	.20	.10
540	Bob Robertson	.40	.20	.10
541	Cleveland Indians Team	1.00	.50	.30
542	Rich Gossage	4.00	2.00	1.25
543	Danny Cater	.40	.20	.10
544	Ron Schueler	.40	.20	.10
545	Billy Conigliaro	.40	.20	.10
546	Mike Corkins	.40	.20	.10
547	Glenn Borgmann	.40	.20	.10
548	Sonny Siebert	.40	.20	.10
549	Mike Jorgensen	.40	.20	.10
550	Sam McDowell	.40	.20	.10
551	Von Joshua	.40	.20	.10
552	Denny Doyle	.40	.20	.10
553	Jim Willoughby	.40	.20	.10
554	Tim Johnson	.40	.20	.10
555	Woodie Fryman	.40	.20	.10
556	Dave Campbell	.40	.20	.10
557	Jim McGlothlin	.40	.20	.10
558	Bill Fahey	.40	.20	.10
559	Darrel Chaney	.40	.20	.10
560	Mike Cuellar	.40	.20	.10
561	Ed Kranepool	.40	.20	.10
562	Jack Aker	.40	.20	.10
563	Hal McRae	.75	.40	.25
564	Mike Ryan	.40	.20	.10
565	Milt Wilcox	.40	.20	.10
566	Jackie Hernandez	.40	.20	.10
567	Boston Red Sox Team	1.50	.75	.45
568	Mike Torrez	.40	.20	.10
569	Rick Dempsey	.40	.20	.10
570	Ralph Garr	.40	.20	.10
571	Rich Hand	.40	.20	.10
572	Enzo Hernandez	.40	.20	.10
573	Mike Adams	.40	.20	.10
574	Bill Parsons	.40	.20	.10
575	Steve Garvey	2.00	1.00	.60
576	Scipio Spinks	.40	.20	.10
577	Mike Sadek	.40	.20	.10
578	Ralph Houk	.75	.40	.25
579	Cecil Upshaw	.40	.20	.10
580	Jim Spencer	.40	.20	.10
581	Fred Norman	.40	.20	.10
582	***Bucky Dent***	2.00	1.00	.60
583	Marty Pattin	.40	.20	.10
584	Ken Rudolph	.40	.20	.10
585	Merv Rettenmund	.40	.20	.10
586	Jack Brohamer	.40	.20	.10
587	***Larry Christenson***	.40	.20	.10
588	Hal Lanier	.40	.20	.10
589	Boots Day	.40	.20	.10
590	Rogelio Moret	.40	.20	.10
591	Sonny Jackson	.40	.20	.10
592	Ed Bane	.40	.20	.10
593	Steve Yeager	.40	.20	.10
594	Leroy Stanton	.40	.20	.10
595	Steve Blass	.40	.20	.10
596	Rookie Pitchers **(Wayne Garland, Fred Holdsworth, Mark Littell, Dick Pole)**	.40	.20	.10
597	Rookie Shortstops ***(Dave Chalk, John Gamble, Pete Mackanin, Manny Trillo)***	1.00	.50	.30
598	Rookie Outfielders ***(Dave Augustine, Ken Griffey, Steve Ontiveros, Jim Tyrone)***	10.00	5.00	3.00
599a	Rookie Pitchers **(Ron Diorio, Dave Freisleben, Frank Riccelli, Greg Shanahan)** (Freisleben- Washington)	1.00	.50	.30
599b	Rookie Pitchers **(Ron Diorio, Dave Freisleben, Frank Riccelli, Greg Shanahan)** (Freisleben- San Diego large print.)	3.00	1.50	.90
599c	Rookie Pitchers **(Ron Diorio, Dave Freisleben, Frank Riccelli, Greg Shanahan)** (Freisleben- San Diego small print.)	5.00	2.50	1.50
600	Rookie Infielders ***(Ron Cash, Jim Cox, Bill Madlock, Reggie Sanders)***	5.00	2.50	1.50
601	Rookie Outfielders ***(Ed Armbrister, Rich Bladt, Brian Downing, Bake McBride)***	2.00	1.00	.60
602	Rookie Pitchers **(Glenn Abbott, Rick Henninger, Craig Swan, Dan Vossler)**	.75	.40	.25
603	Rookie Catchers **(Barry Foote, Tom Lundstedt, Charlie Moore, Sergio Robles)**	.75	.40	.25
604	Rookie Infielders ***(Terry Hughes, John Knox, Andy Thornton, Frank White)***	4.00	2.00	1.25
605	Rookie Pitchers ***(Vic Albury, Ken Frailing, Kevin Kobel, Frank Tanana)***	3.00	1.50	.90
606	Rookie Outfielders **(Jim Fuller, Wilbur Howard, Tommy Smith, Otto Velez)**	.75	.40	.25
607	Rookie Shortstops ***(Leo Foster, Tom Heintzelman, Dave Rosello, Frank Taveras)***	.75	.40	.25
608a	Rookie Pitchers **(Bob Apodaco, Dick Baney, John D'Acquisto, Mike Wallace)** (Apodaca incorrect)	1.50	.75	.45
608b	Rookie Pitchers **(Bob Apodaca, Dick Baney, John D'Acquisto, Mike Wallace)** (Corrected)	.75	.40	.25
609	Rico Petrocelli	1.00	.50	.30
610	Dave Kingman	.75	.40	.25
611	Rick Stelmaszek	.40	.20	.10
612	Luke Walker	.40	.20	.10
613	Dan Monzon	.40	.20	.10
614	Adrian Devine	.40	.20	.10
615	Johnny Jeter	.40	.20	.10
616	Larry Gura	.40	.20	.10
617	Ted Ford	.40	.20	.10
618	Jim Mason	.40	.20	.10
619	Mike Anderson	.40	.20	.10
620	Al Downing	.40	.20	.10
621	Bernie Carbo	.40	.20	.10
622	Phil Gagliano	.40	.20	.10
623	Celerino Sanchez	.40	.20	.10
624	Bob Miller	.40	.20	.10
625	Ollie Brown	.40	.20	.10
626	Pittsburgh Pirates Team	1.00	.50	.30
627	Carl Taylor	.40	.20	.10
628	Ivan Murrell	.40	.20	.10
629	Rusty Staub	.75	.40	.25
630	Tommie Agee	.40	.20	.10
631	Steve Barber	.40	.20	.10
632	George Culver	.40	.20	.10
633	Dave Hamilton	.40	.20	.10
634	Braves Mgr./Coaches (Jim Busby, Eddie Mathews, Connie Ryan, Ken Silvestri, Herm Starrette)	2.00	1.00	.60
635	John Edwards	.40	.20	.10
636	Dave Goltz	.40	.20	.10
637	Checklist 529-660	1.00	.50	.30
638	Ken Sanders	.40	.20	.10
639	Joe Lovitto	.40	.20	.10
640	Milt Pappas	.40	.20	.10
641	Chuck Brinkman	.40	.20	.10
642	Terry Harmon	.40	.20	.10
643	Los Angeles Dodgers Team	2.50	1.25	.75
644	Wayne Granger	.40	.20	.10
645	Ken Boswell	.40	.20	.10
646	George Foster	.75	.40	.25
647	***Juan Beniquez***	.40	.20	.10
648	Terry Crowley	.40	.20	.10
649	Fernando Gonzalez	.40	.20	.10
650	Mike Epstein	.40	.20	.10
651	Leron Lee	.40	.20	.10
652	Gail Hopkins	.40	.20	.10
653	Bob Stinson	.40	.20	.10
654a	Jesus Alou (No position.)	4.00	2.00	1.25
654b	Jesus Alou ("Outfield")	.40	.20	.10
655	Mike Tyson	.40	.20	.10
656	Adrian Garrett	.40	.20	.10
657	Jim Shellenback	.40	.20	.10
658	Lee Lacy	.40	.20	.10
659	Joe Lis	.40	.20	.10
660	Larry Dierker	1.50	.70	.45

1974 Topps Traded

Appearing late in the season, these 2-1/2" x 3-1/2" cards share the format of the regular-issue Topps cards. The major change is a large yellow panel with the word "Traded" in red, added below the player photo. Backs feature a "Baseball News" design that contains the details of the trade. Card numbers correspond to the player's regular card number in 1974 except that the suffix "T" is added. The set consists of 43 player cards and a checklist. In most cases, Topps did not obtain pictures of the players in their new uniforms. Instead, the Topps artists simply provided the needed changes to existing photos.

No.	Player	NM	EX	VG
	Complete Set (44):	25.00	12.50	7.50
	Common Player:	.50	.25	.15
23T	Craig Robinson	.50	.25	.15
42T	Claude Osteen	.50	.25	.15
43T	Jim Wynn	.50	.25	.15
51T	Bobby Heise	.50	.25	.15
59T	Ross Grimsley	.50	.25	.15
62T	Bob Locker	.50	.25	.15
63T	Bill Sudakis	.50	.25	.15
73T	Mike Marshall	.50	.25	.15
123T	Nelson Briles	.50	.25	.15
139T	Aurelio Monteagudo	.50	.25	.15
151T	Diego Segui	.50	.25	.15
165T	Willie Davis	.50	.25	.15
175T	Reggie Cleveland	.50	.25	.15
182T	Lindy McDaniel	.50	.25	.15
186T	Fred Scherman	.50	.25	.15
249T	George Mitterwald	.50	.25	.15
262T	Ed Kirkpatrick	.50	.25	.15
269T	Bob Johnson	.50	.25	.15
270T	Ron Santo	3.00	1.50	.90
313T	Barry Lersch	.50	.25	.15
319T	Randy Hundley	.50	.25	.15
330T	Juan Marichal	4.00	2.00	1.25
348T	Pete Richert	.50	.25	.15
373T	John Curtis	.50	.25	.15
390T	Lou Piniella	2.00	1.00	.60
428T	Gary Sutherland	.50	.25	.15
454T	Kurt Bevacqua	.50	.25	.15
458T	Jim Ray	.50	.25	.15
485T	Felipe Alou	.75	.40	.25
486T	Steve Stone	.75	.40	.25
496T	Tom Murphy	.50	.25	.15
516T	Horacio Pina	.50	.25	.15
534T	Eddie Watt	.50	.25	.15
538T	Cesar Tovar	.50	.25	.15
544T	Ron Schueler	.50	.25	.15
579T	Cecil Upshaw	.50	.25	.15
585T	Merv Rettenmund	.50	.25	.15
612T	Luke Walker	.50	.25	.15
616T	Larry Gura	.50	.25	.15
618T	Jim Mason	.50	.25	.15
630T	Tommie Agee	.50	.25	.15
648T	Terry Crowley	.50	.25	.15
649T	Fernando Gonzalez	.50	.25	.15
----	Traded Checklist	.50	.25	.15

1974 Topps Action Emblem Cloth Stickers

This enigmatic Topps test issue has never found favor with collectors because no actual ballplayers are pictured.

In fact, official team logos are not used either, negating the necessity of licensing from either Major League Baseball or the Players Association. The 2-1/2" x 3-1/2" cloth stickers were sold with a rub-off baseball game card in a Topps white test wrapper with a sticker describing them as "Topps Baseball Action Emblems Cloth Stickers." Each sticker features a generic ballplayer on front with a city (not team) name. At bottom is a pennant with another major league city named and a generic baseball symbol at its left. Backs are blank. This issue can be found in either a cloth sticker version or cardboard version. The cardboard pieces are worth about 4X the cloth type.

		NM	EX	VG
Complete Set (24):		900.00	450.00	275.00
Common Sticker:		40.00	20.00	12.00
Wax Pack:		75.00		
Cardboard: 4X				
(1)	Atlanta/Baltimore	40.00	20.00	12.00
(2)	Baltimore/Montreal	40.00	20.00	12.00
(3)	Boston/Oakland	40.00	20.00	12.00
(4)	California/St. Louis	40.00	20.00	12.00
(5)	Chicago/Houston	40.00	20.00	12.00
(6)	Chicago/Pittsburgh	40.00	20.00	12.00
(7)	Cincinnati/Minnesota	40.00	20.00	12.00
(8)	Cleveland/San Diego	40.00	20.00	12.00
(9)	Detroit/New York	40.00	20.00	12.00
(10)	Houston/Chicago	40.00	20.00	12.00
(11)	Kansas City/Philadelphia	40.00	20.00	12.00
(12)	Los Angeles/Milwaukee	40.00	20.00	12.00
(13)	Milwaukee/New York	40.00	20.00	12.00
(14)	Minnesota/California	40.00	20.00	12.00
(15)	Montreal/San Francisco	40.00	20.00	12.00
(16)	New York/Cincinnati	40.00	20.00	12.00
(17)	New York/Texas	40.00	20.00	12.00
(18)	Oakland/Boston	40.00	20.00	12.00
(19)	Philadelphia/Los Angeles	40.00	20.00	12.00
(20)	Pittsburgh/Cleveland	40.00	20.00	12.00
(21)	St. Louis/Kansas City	40.00	20.00	12.00
(22)	San Diego/Detroit	40.00	20.00	12.00
(23)	San Francisco/Chicago	40.00	20.00	12.00
(24)	Texas/Atlanta	40.00	20.00	12.00

1974 Topps Deckle Edge

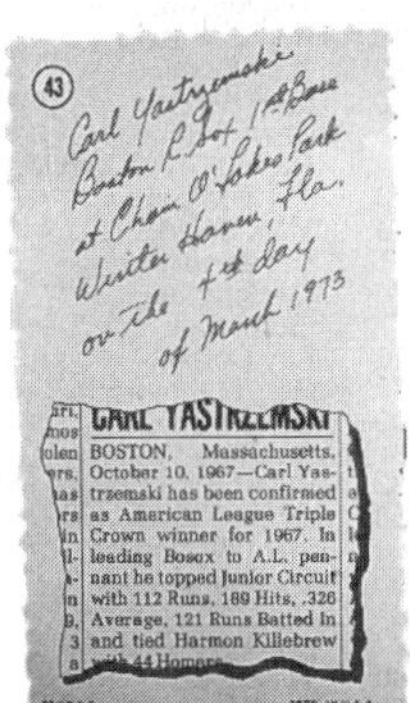

These borderless 2-7/8" x 5" cards feature a black-and-white photograph with a blue facsimile autograph on the front. The backs have in handwritten script the player's name, team, position and the date and location of the picture. Below is a mock newspaper clipping providing a detail from the player's career. Backs can be found in either gray or white (somewhat scarcer). The cards take their names from their specially cut edges which give them a scalloped appearance. The 72-card set was a test issue and received rather limited distribution around Massachusetts. The cards were sold three per pack for five cents with a piece of gum, or in two-card pack with no gum. Proof versions with straight edges and white or gray backs are known; they are slightly larger, at about 3-1/8" x 5-1/4".

		NM	EX	VG
Complete Set (72):		5,000	2,500	1,500
Common Player:		20.00	10.00	6.00
White Backs: 1.5X				
Proofs: .75-1X				
Wax Pack (5):		375.00		
1	Amos Otis	20.00	10.00	6.00
2	Darrell Evans	20.00	10.00	6.00
3	Bob Gibson	135.00	65.00	40.00
4	David Nelson	20.00	10.00	6.00
5	Steve Carlton	135.00	65.00	40.00
6	Catfish Hunter	90.00	45.00	27.50
7	Thurman Munson	135.00	65.00	40.00
8	Bob Grich	20.00	10.00	6.00
9	Tom Seaver	150.00	75.00	45.00
10	Ted Simmons	20.00	10.00	6.00
11	Bobby Valentine	20.00	10.00	6.00
12	Don Sutton	90.00	45.00	27.50
13	Wilbur Wood	20.00	10.00	6.00
14	Doug Rader	20.00	10.00	6.00
15	Chris Chambliss	20.00	10.00	6.00
16	Pete Rose	275.00	135.00	80.00
17	John Hiller	20.00	10.00	6.00
18	Burt Hooton	20.00	10.00	6.00
19	Tim Foli	20.00	10.00	6.00
20	Lou Brock	100.00	50.00	30.00
21	Ron Bryant	20.00	10.00	6.00
22	Manuel Sanguillen	20.00	10.00	6.00
23	Bobby Tolan	20.00	10.00	6.00
24	Greg Luzinski	20.00	10.00	6.00
25	Brooks Robinson	150.00	75.00	45.00
26	Felix Millan	20.00	10.00	6.00
27	Luis Tiant	20.00	10.00	6.00
28	Willie McCovey	100.00	50.00	30.00
29	Chris Speier	20.00	10.00	6.00
30	George Scott	20.00	10.00	6.00
31	Willie Stargell	100.00	50.00	30.00
32	Rod Carew	135.00	65.00	40.00
33	Charlie Spikes	20.00	10.00	6.00
34	Nate Colbert	20.00	10.00	6.00
35	Richie Hebner	20.00	10.00	6.00
36	Bobby Bonds	20.00	10.00	6.00
37	Buddy Bell	20.00	10.00	6.00
38	Claude Osteen	20.00	10.00	6.00
39	Rich Allen	55.00	27.50	16.50
40	Bill Russell	20.00	10.00	6.00
41	Nolan Ryan	900.00	450.00	275.00
42	Willie Davis	20.00	10.00	6.00
43	Carl Yastrzemski	160.00	80.00	45.00
44	Jon Matlack	20.00	10.00	6.00
45	Jim Palmer	135.00	65.00	40.00
46	Bert Campaneris	20.00	10.00	6.00
47	Bert Blyleven	20.00	10.00	6.00
48	Jeff Burroughs	20.00	10.00	6.00
49	Jim Colborn	20.00	10.00	6.00
50	Dave Johnson	20.00	10.00	6.00
51	John Mayberry	20.00	10.00	6.00
52	Don Kessinger	20.00	10.00	6.00
53	Joe Coleman	20.00	10.00	6.00
54	Tony Perez	90.00	45.00	27.50
55	Jose Cardenal	20.00	10.00	6.00
56	Paul Splittorff	20.00	10.00	6.00
57	Henry Aaron	275.00	135.00	80.00
58	David May	20.00	10.00	6.00
59	Fergie Jenkins	90.00	45.00	27.50
60	Ron Blomberg	20.00	10.00	6.00
61	Reggie Jackson	175.00	85.00	50.00
62	Tony Oliva	40.00	20.00	12.00
63	Bobby Murcer	45.00	22.50	13.50
64	Carlton Fisk	100.00	50.00	30.00
65	Steve Rogers	20.00	10.00	6.00
66	Frank Robinson	150.00	75.00	45.00
67	Joe Ferguson	20.00	10.00	6.00
68	Bill Melton	20.00	10.00	6.00
69	Bob Watson	20.00	10.00	6.00
70	Larry Bowa	20.00	10.00	6.00
71	Johnny Bench	150.00	75.00	45.00
72	Willie Horton	20.00	10.00	6.00

1974 Topps Puzzles

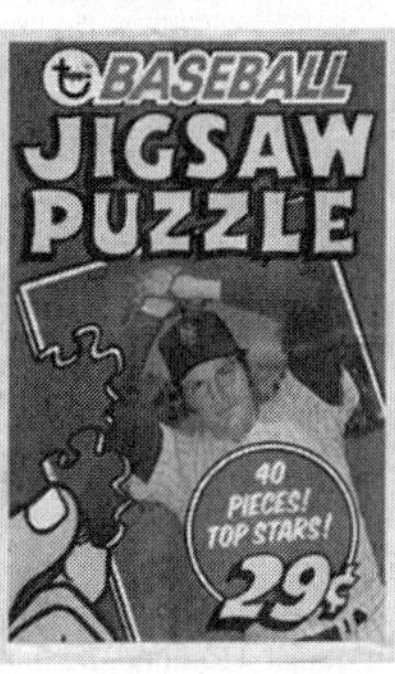

One of many test issues by Topps in the mid-1970s, the 12-player jigsaw puzzle set was an innovation which never caught on with collectors. The 40-piece puzzles (4-3/4" x 7-1/2") feature color photos with a decorative lozenge at bottom naming the player, team and position. The 25-cent or 29-cent puzzles came in individual wrappers picturing Tom Seaver. Centering, particularly of the Ryan puzzle, is a plague with the puzzles, accounting for the greater than usual spread betwerrn NM and lower- grade values.

		NM	EX	VG
Complete Set (12):		2,000	700.00	300.00
Common Player:		65.00	32.50	20.00
Wax Pack:		225.00		
Wrapper:		20.00		
(1)	Hank Aaron	250.00	90.00	35.00
(2)	Dick Allen	75.00	30.00	15.00
(3)	Johnny Bench	125.00	44.00	18.50
(4)	Bobby Bonds	65.00	25.00	10.00
(5)	Bob Gibson	125.00	44.00	18.50
(6)	Reggie Jackson	200.00	70.00	30.00
(7)	Bobby Murcer	65.00	25.00	10.00
(8)	Jim Palmer	100.00	35.00	15.00
(9)	Nolan Ryan	650.00	225.00	100.00
(10)	Tom Seaver	125.00	44.00	18.50
(11)	Willie Stargell	100.00	35.00	15.00
(12)	Carl Yastrzemski	250.00	87.00	37.00

The Mint-Mint examples of vintage cards carry a significant premium over the Near Mint values shown here. This premium reflects limited availability of the highest-grade cards as well as demand for particular cards or sets in the best possible condition.

1974 Topps Stamps

Topps continued to market baseball stamps in 1974 through the release of 240 unnumbered stamps featuring color player portraits. The player's name, team and position are found in an oval at the bottom of the 1" x 1-1/2" stamps. The stamps, sold separately rather than issued as an insert, came in panels of 12. Two dozen team albums designed to hold 10 stamps were also issued.

		NM	EX	VG
Complete Sheet Set (24):		90.00	45.00	25.00
Common Sheet:		2.00	1.00	.60
Complete Stamp Album Set (24):		300.00	150.00	90.00
Single Stamp Album:		5.00	2.50	1.50
(1)	Hank Aaron, Luis Aparicio, Bob Bailey, Johnny Bench, Ron Blomberg, Bob Boone, Lou Brock, Bud Harrelson, Randy Jones, Dave Rader, Nolan Ryan, Joe Torre	15.00	7.50	4.50
(2)	Buddy Bell, Steve Braun, Jerry Grote, Tommy Helms, Bill Lee, Mike Lum, Dave May, Brooks Robinson, Bill Russell, Del Unser, Wilbur Wood, Carl Yastrzemski	9.00	4.50	2.75
(3)	Jerry Bell, Jim Colborn, Toby Harrah, Ken Henderson, John Hiller, Randy Hundley, Don Kessinger, Jerry Koosman, Dave Lopes, Felix Millan, Thurman Munson, Ted Simmons	6.00	3.00	1.75
(4)	Jerry Bell, Bill Buckner, Jim Colborn, Ken Henderson, Don Kessinger, Felix Millan, George Mitterwald, Dave Roberts, Ted Simmons, Jim Slaton, Charlie Spikes, Paul Splittorff	2.00	1.00	.60
(5)	Glenn Beckert, Jim Bibby, Bill Buckner, Jim Lonborg, George Mitterwald, Dave Parker, Dave Roberts, Jim Slaton, Reggie Smith, Charlie Spikes, Paul Splittorff, Bob Watson	2.00	1.00	.60
(6)	Paul Blair, Bobby Bonds, Ed Brinkman, Norm Cash, Mike Epstein, Tommy Harper, Mike Marshall, Phil Niekro, Cookie Rojas, George Scott, Mel Stottlemyre, Jim Wynn	2.00	1.00	.60
(7)	Jack Billingham, Reggie Cleveland, Bobby Darwin, Dave Duncan, Tim Foli, Ed Goodson, Cleon Jones, Mickey Lolich, George Medich, John Milner, Rick Monday, Bobby Murcer	2.00	1.00	.60
(8)	Steve Carlton, Orlando Cepeda, Joe Decker, Reggie Jackson, Dave Johnson, John Mayberry, Bill Melton, Roger Metzger, Dave Nelson, Jerry Reuss, Jim Spencer, Bobby Valentine	10.00	5.00	3.00
(9)	Dan Driessen, Pedro Garcia, Grant Jackson, Al Kaline, Clay Kirby, Carlos May, Willie Montanez, Rogelio Moret, Jim Palmer, Doug Rader, J. R. Richard, Frank Robinson	7.50	3.75	2.25
(10)	Pedro Garcia, Ralph Garr, Wayne Garrett, Ron Hunt, Al Kaline, Fred Kendall, Carlos May, Jim Palmer, Doug Rader, Frank Robinson, Rick Wise, Richie Zisk	7.50	3.75	2.25

(11)	Dusty Baker, Larry Bowa, Steve Busby, Chris Chambliss, Dock Ellis, Cesar Geronimo, Fran Healy, Deron Johnson, Jorge Orta, Joe Rudi, Mickey Stanley, Rennie Stennett	2.00	1.00	.60
(12)	Bob Coluccio, Ray Corbin, John Ellis, Oscar Gamble, Dave Giusti, Bill Greif, Alex Johnson, Mike Jorgensen, Andy Messersmith, Bill Robinson, Elias Sosa, Willie Stargell	2.00	1.00	.60
(13)	Ron Bryant, Nate Colbert, Jose Cruz, Dan Driessen, Billy Grabarkewitz, Don Gullett, Willie Horton, Grant Jackson, Clay Kirby, Willie Montanez, Rogelio Moret, J. R. Richard	2.00	1.00	.60
(14)	Carlton Fisk, Bill Freehan, Bobby Grich, Vic Harris, George Hendrick, Ed Herrmann, Jim Holt, Ken Holtzman, Fergie Jenkins, Lou Piniella, Steve Rogers, Ken Singleton	5.00	2.50	1.50
(15)	Stan Bahnsen, Sal Bando, Mark Belanger, David Clyde, Willie Crawford, Burt Hooton, Jon Matlack, Tim McCarver, Joe Morgan, Gene Tenace, Dick Tidrow, Dave Winfield	7.50	3.75	2.25
(16)	Hank Aaron, Stan Bahnsen, Bob Bailey, Johnny Bench, Bob Boone, Jon Matlack, Tim McCarver, Joe Morgan, Dave Rader, Gene Tenace, Dick Tidrow, Joe Torre	10.00	5.00	3.00
(17)	John Boccabella, Frank Duffy, Darrell Evans, Sparky Lyle, Lee May, Don Money, Bill North, Ted Sizemore, Chris Speier, Wayne Twitchell, Billy Williams, Earl Williams	2.00	1.00	.60
(18)	John Boccabella, Bobby Darwin, Frank Duffy, Dave Duncan, Tim Foli, Cleon Jones, Mickey Lolich, Sparky Lyle, Lee May, Rick Monday, Bill North, Billy Williams	2.00	1.00	.60
(19)	Tom Bradley, Jose Cardenal, Ron Cey, Greg Luzinski, Johnny Oates, Tony Oliva, Al Oliver, Tony Perez, Darrell Porter, Roy White, Don Baylor, Vida Blue	3.00	1.50	.90
(20)	Pedro Borbon, Rod Carew, Roric Harrison, Jim Hunter, Ed Kirkpatrick, Garry Maddox, Gene Michael, Rick Miller, Claude Osteen, Amos Otis, Rich Reuschel, Mike Tyson	5.00	2.50	1.50
(21)	Sandy Alomar, Bert Campaneris, Dave Concepcion, Tommy Davis, Joe Ferguson, Tito Fuentes, Jerry Morales, Carl Morton, Gaylord Perry, Vada Pinson, Dave Roberts, Ellie Rodriguez	2.00	1.00	.60
(22)	Dick Allen, Jeff Burroughs, Joe Coleman, Terry Forster, Bob Gibson, Harmon Killebrew, Tug McGraw, Bob Oliver, Steve Renko, Pete Rose, Luis Tiant, Otto Velez	12.00	6.00	3.50
(23)	Johnny Briggs, Willie Davis, Jim Fregosi, Rich Hebner, Pat Kelly, Dave Kingman, Willie McCovey, Graig Nettles, Freddie Patek, Marty Pattin, Manny Sanguillen, Richie Scheinblum	5.00	2.50	1.50
(24)	Bert Blyleven, Nelson Briles, Cesar Cedeno, Ron Fairly, Johnny Grubb, Dave McNally, Aurelio Rodriguez, Ron Santo, Tom Seaver, Bill Singer, Bill Sudakis, Don Sutton	6.00	3.00	1.75

1974 Topps Team Checklists

This set is a repeat of the 1973 set in the form of 24 unnumbered 2-1/2" x 3-1/2" checklist cards. Cards feature a team name on the front at the top with a white panel and a number of facsimile autographs below. Backs feature the team name and a checklist. The big difference between the 1973 and 1974 checklists is that the 1973s have blue borders while the 1974s have red borders. The 1974s were inserted into packages of the regular issue Topps cards and were also available in uncut sheet form as a wrapper redemption.

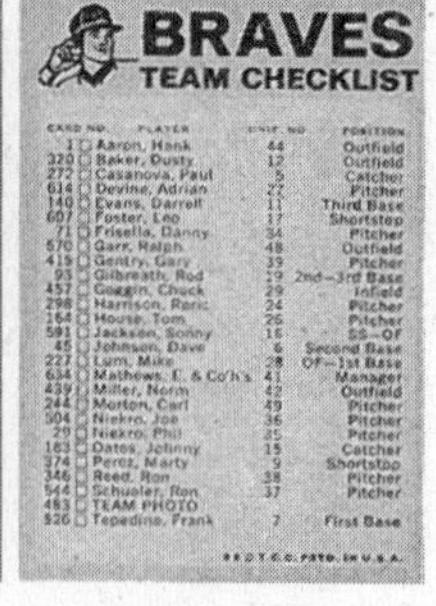

		NM	EX	VG
Complete Set (24):		25.00	12.50	7.50
Common Checklist:		1.50	.75	.45
Uncut Sheet:		25.00	12.50	7.50
(1)	Atlanta Braves	1.50	.75	.45
(2)	Baltimore Orioles	1.50	.75	.45
(3)	Boston Red Sox	1.50	.75	.45
(4)	California Angels	1.50	.75	.45
(5)	Chicago Cubs	1.50	.75	.45
(6)	Chicago White Sox	1.50	.75	.45
(7)	Cincinnati Reds	1.50	.75	.45
(8)	Cleveland Indians	1.50	.75	.45
(9)	Detroit Tigers	1.50	.75	.45
(10)	Houston Astros	1.50	.75	.45
(11)	Kansas City Royals	1.50	.75	.45
(12)	Los Angeles Dodgers	1.50	.75	.45
(13)	Milwaukee Brewers	1.50	.75	.45
(14)	Minnesota Twins	1.50	.75	.45
(15)	Montreal Expos	1.50	.75	.45
(16)	New York Mets	1.50	.75	.45
(17)	New York Yankees	1.50	.75	.45
(18)	Oakland A's	1.50	.75	.45
(19)	Philadelphia Phillies	1.50	.75	.45
(20)	Pittsburgh Pirates	1.50	.75	.45
(21)	St. Louis Cardinals	1.50	.75	.45
(22)	San Diego Padres	1.50	.75	.45
(23)	San Francisco Giants	1.50	.75	.45
(24)	Texas Rangers	1.50	.75	.45

1975 Topps

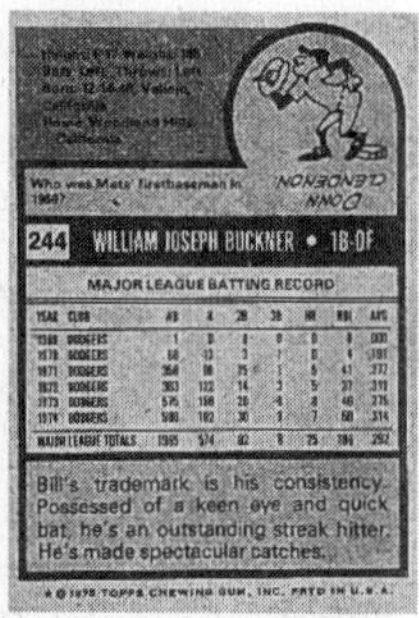

What was once seen as the strongest rookie card crop of any modern card set made this a collector favorite from the outset. Featuring the most colorful designs since 1972, cards feature large front photos with facsimile autographs. Red-and-green backs include a cartoon trivia fact and complete stats. A subset of 1951-74 MVP cards which reproduces or creates contemporary cards of past stars is one of several special features of the set, as are a group of four-on-one rookie cards. While the cards were all issued at one time, the first 132 cards have been discovered to have been printed in somewhat lesser quantities than the rest of the issue. This scarcity is not noted among the mini-version of the set which was produced as a test issue. Team/manager cards are sometimes found on thinner, white cardboard stock; these are a special version produced for a mail-in offer.

		NM	EX	VG
Complete Set (660):		450.00	225.00	135.00
Common Player:		.40	.20	.10
Mini Stars/Rookies: 1-1.5X				
Wax Pack (10):		50.00		
Wax Box (36):		1,200		
Cello Pack (18):		80.00		
Rack Pack (42):		175.00		
Vending Box (500):				
1	Hank Aaron ('74 Highlights)	30.00	15.00	9.00
2	Lou Brock ('74 Highlights)	2.00	1.00	.60
3	Bob Gibson ('74 Highlights)	2.00	1.00	.60
4	Al Kaline ('74 Highlights)	4.00	2.00	1.25
5	Nolan Ryan ('74 Highlights)	12.00	6.00	3.50
6	Mike Marshall ('74 Highlights)	.40	.20	.10
7	Dick Bosman, Steve Busby, Nolan Ryan ('74 Highlights)	8.00	4.00	2.50
8	Rogelio Moret	.40	.20	.10
9	Frank Tepedino	.40	.20	.10
10	Willie Davis	.40	.20	.10
11	Bill Melton	.40	.20	.10
12	David Clyde	.40	.20	.10
13	Gene Locklear	.40	.20	.10
14	Milt Wilcox	.40	.20	.10
15	Jose Cardenal	.40	.20	.10
16	Frank Tanana	.40	.20	.10
17	Dave Concepcion	.40	.20	.10
18	Tigers team (Ralph Houk)	1.50	.70	.45
19	Jerry Koosman	.40	.20	.10
20	Thurman Munson	8.00	4.00	2.50
21	Rollie Fingers	3.00	1.50	.90
22	Dave Cash	.40	.20	.10
23	Bill Russell	.75	.40	.25
24	Al Fitzmorris	.40	.20	.10
25	Lee May	.75	.40	.25
26	Dave McNally	.40	.20	.10
27	Ken Reitz	.40	.20	.10
28	Tom Murphy	.40	.20	.10
29	Dave Parker	1.50	.70	.45
30	Bert Blyleven	1.50	.70	.45
31	Dave Rader	.40	.20	.10
32	Reggie Cleveland	.40	.20	.10
33	Dusty Baker	1.50	.70	.45
34	Steve Renko	.40	.20	.10
35	Ron Santo	2.00	1.00	.60
36	Joe Lovitto	.40	.20	.10
37	Dave Freisleben	.40	.20	.10
38	Buddy Bell	.75	.40	.25
39	Andy Thornton	.75	.40	.25
40	Bill Singer	.40	.20	.10
41	Cesar Geronimo	.40	.20	.10
42	Joe Coleman	.40	.20	.10
43	Cleon Jones	.40	.20	.10
44	Pat Dobson	.40	.20	.10
45	Joe Rudi	.40	.20	.10
46	Phillies Team (Danny Ozark)	1.50	.70	.45
47	Tommy John	1.50	.70	.45
48	Freddie Patek	.40	.20	.10
49	Larry Dierker	.75	.40	.25
50	Brooks Robinson	8.00	4.00	2.50
51	***Bob Forsch***	.75	.40	.25
52	Darrell Porter	.75	.40	.25
53	Dave Giusti	.40	.20	.10
54	Eric Soderholm	.40	.20	.10
55	Bobby Bonds	1.50	.70	.45
56	Rick Wise	.40	.20	.10
57	Dave Johnson	.75	.40	.25
58	Chuck Taylor	.40	.20	.10
59	Ken Henderson	.40	.20	.10
60	Fergie Jenkins	3.00	1.50	.90
61	Dave Winfield	12.00	6.00	3.50
62	Fritz Peterson	.40	.20	.10
63	Steve Swisher	.40	.20	.10
64	Dave Chalk	.40	.20	.10
65	Don Gullett	.40	.20	.10
66	Willie Horton	.40	.20	.10
67	Tug McGraw	.40	.20	.10
68	Ron Blomberg	.40	.20	.10
69	John Odom	.40	.20	.10
70	Mike Schmidt	20.00	10.00	6.00
71	Charlie Hough	.75	.40	.25
72	Royals Team (Jack McKeon)	1.00	.50	.30
73	J.R. Richard	.40	.20	.10
74	Mark Belanger	.40	.20	.10
75	Ted Simmons	1.00	.50	.30
76	Ed Sprague	.40	.20	.10
77	Richie Zisk	.40	.20	.10
78	Ray Corbin	.40	.20	.10
79	Gary Matthews	.40	.20	.10
80	Carlton Fisk	6.00	3.00	1.75
81	Ron Reed	.40	.20	.10
82	Pat Kelly	.40	.20	.10
83	Jim Merritt	.40	.20	.10
84	Enzo Hernandez	.40	.20	.10
85	Bill Bonham	.40	.20	.10
86	Joe Lis	.40	.20	.10
87	George Foster	1.00	.50	.30
88	Tom Egan	.40	.20	.10
89	Jim Ray	.40	.20	.10
90	Rusty Staub	1.00	.50	.30
91	Dick Green	.40	.20	.10
92	Cecil Upshaw	.40	.20	.10
93	Dave Lopes	1.00	.50	.30
94	Jim Lonborg	.75	.40	.25
95	John Mayberry	.75	.40	.25
96	Mike Cosgrove	.40	.20	.10
97	Earl Williams	.40	.20	.10
98	Rich Folkers	.40	.20	.10
99	Mike Hegan	.40	.20	.10
100	Willie Stargell	4.00	2.00	1.25
101	Expos Team (Gene Mauch)	1.00	.50	.30
102	Joe Decker	.40	.20	.10
103	Rick Miller	.40	.20	.10
104	Bill Madlock	.75	.40	.25
105	Buzz Capra	.40	.20	.10
106	***Mike Hargrove***	2.00	1.00	.60
107	Jim Barr	.40	.20	.10
108	Tom Hall	.40	.20	.10
109	George Hendrick	.40	.20	.10
110	Wilbur Wood	.40	.20	.10
111	Wayne Garrett	.40	.20	.10
112	Larry Hardy	.40	.20	.10
113	Elliott Maddox	.40	.20	.10
114	Dick Lange	.40	.20	.10
115	Joe Ferguson	.40	.20	.10
116	Lerrin LaGrow	.40	.20	.10
117	Orioles Team (Earl Weaver)	3.00	1.50	.90
118	Mike Anderson	.40	.20	.10
119	Tommy Helms	.40	.20	.10
120	Steve Busby (Photo actually Fran Healy.)	.40	.20	.10
121	Bill North	.40	.20	.10
122	Al Hrabosky	.75	.40	.25
123	Johnny Briggs	.40	.20	.10
124	Jerry Reuss	.75	.40	.25
125	Ken Singleton	.75	.40	.25
126	Checklist 1-132	2.00	1.00	.60
127	Glen Borgmann	.40	.20	.10
128	Bill Lee	.40	.20	.10
129	Rick Monday	.40	.20	.10
130	Phil Niekro	3.00	1.50	.90
131	Toby Harrah	.40	.20	.10
132	Randy Moffitt	.40	.20	.10
133	Dan Driessen	.40	.20	.10
134	Ron Hodges	.40	.20	.10
135	Charlie Spikes	.40	.20	.10
136	Jim Mason	.40	.20	.10

137	Terry Forster	.40	.20	.10
138	Del Unser	.40	.20	.10
139	Horacio Pina	.40	.20	.10
140	Steve Garvey	2.00	1.00	.60
141	Mickey Stanley	.40	.20	.10
142	Bob Reynolds	.40	.20	.10
143	***Cliff Johnson***	.40	.20	.10
144	Jim Wohlford	.40	.20	.10
145	Ken Holtzman	.40	.20	.10
146	Padres Team (John McNamara)	1.00	.50	.30
147	Pedro Garcia	.40	.20	.10
148	Jim Rooker	.40	.20	.10
149	Tim Foli	.40	.20	.10
150	Bob Gibson	5.00	2.50	1.50
151	Steve Brye	.40	.20	.10
152	Mario Guerrero	.40	.20	.10
153	Rick Reuschel	.40	.20	.10
154	Mike Lum	.40	.20	.10
155	Jim Bibby	.40	.20	.10
156	Dave Kingman	1.00	.50	.30
157	Pedro Borbon	.40	.20	.10
158	Jerry Grote	.40	.20	.10
159	Steve Arlin	.40	.20	.10
160	Graig Nettles	1.00	.50	.30
161	Stan Bahnsen	.40	.20	.10
162	Willie Montanez	.40	.20	.10
163	Jim Brewer	.40	.20	.10
164	Mickey Rivers	.40	.20	.10
165	Doug Rader	.40	.20	.10
166	Woodie Fryman	.40	.20	.10
167	Rich Coggins	.40	.20	.10
168	Bill Greif	.40	.20	.10
169	Cookie Rojas	.40	.20	.10
170	Bert Campaneris	.40	.20	.10
171	Ed Kirkpatrick	.40	.20	.10
172	Red Sox Team (Darrell Johnson)	1.50	.70	.45
173	Steve Rogers	.40	.20	.10
174	Bake McBride	.40	.20	.10
175	Don Money	.40	.20	.10
176	Burt Hooton	.40	.20	.10
177	Vic Correll	.40	.20	.10
178	Cesar Tovar	.40	.20	.10
179	Tom Bradley	.40	.20	.10
180	Joe Morgan	5.00	2.50	1.50
181	Fred Beene	.40	.20	.10
182	Don Hahn	.40	.20	.10
183	Mel Stottlemyre	.40	.20	.10
184	Jorge Orta	.40	.20	.10
185	Steve Carlton	5.00	2.50	1.50
186	Willie Crawford	.40	.20	.10
187	Denny Doyle	.40	.20	.10
188	Tom Griffin	.40	.20	.10
189	1951-MVPs (Yogi Berra, Roy Campanella)	3.00	1.50	.90
190	1952-MVPs (Hank Sauer, Bobby Shantz)	1.00	.50	.30
191	1953-MVPs (Roy Campanella, Al Rosen)	1.50	.70	.45
192	1954-MVPs (Yogi Berra, Willie Mays)	4.00	2.00	1.25
193	1955-MVPs (Yogi Berra, Roy Campanella)	3.00	1.50	.90
194	1956-MVPs (Mickey Mantle, Don Newcombe)	10.00	5.00	3.00
195	1957-MVPs (Hank Aaron, Mickey Mantle)	12.00	6.00	3.50
196	1958-MVPs (Ernie Banks, Jackie Jensen)	2.50	1.25	.70
197	1959-MVPs (Ernie Banks, Nellie Fox)	2.00	1.00	.60
198	1960-MVPs (Dick Groat, Roger Maris)	1.50	.70	.45
199	1961-MVPs (Roger Maris, Frank Robinson)	2.00	1.00	.60
200	1962-MVPs (Mickey Mantle, Maury Wills)	10.00	5.00	3.00
201	1963-MVPs (Elston Howard, Sandy Koufax)	2.50	1.25	.70
202	1964-MVPs (Ken Boyer, Brooks Robinson)	1.00	.50	.30
203	1965-MVPs (Willie Mays, Zoilo Versalles)	2.00	1.00	.60
204	1966-MVPs (Roberto Clemente, Frank Robinson)	5.00	2.50	1.50
205	1967-MVPs (Orlando Cepeda, Carl Yastrzemski)	1.50	.70	.45
206	1968-MVPs (Bob Gibson, Denny McLain)	1.50	.70	.45
207	1969-MVPs (Harmon Killebrew, Willie McCovey)	2.00	1.00	.60
208	1970-MVPs (Johnny Bench, Boog Powell)	2.00	1.00	.60
209	1971-MVPs (Vida Blue, Joe Torre)	1.00	.50	.30
210	1972-MVPs (Rich Allen, Johnny Bench)	2.00	1.00	.60
211	1973-MVPs (Reggie Jackson, Pete Rose)	4.00	2.00	1.25
212	1974-MVPs (Jeff Burroughs, Steve Garvey)	1.00	.50	.30
213	Oscar Gamble	.40	.20	.10
214	Harry Parker	.40	.20	.10
215	Bobby Valentine	.40	.20	.10
216	Giants Team (Wes Westrum)	1.00	.50	.30
217	Lou Piniella	1.50	.70	.45
218	Jerry Johnson	.40	.20	.10
219	Ed Herrmann	.40	.20	.10
220	Don Sutton	3.00	1.50	.90
221	Aurelio Rodriquez (Rodriguez)	.40	.20	.10
222	Dan Spillner	.40	.20	.10
223	***Robin Yount***	50.00	25.00	15.00
224	Ramon Hernandez	.40	.20	.10
225	Bob Grich	.75	.40	.25
226	Bill Campbell	.40	.20	.10
227	Bob Watson	.40	.20	.10
228	***George Brett***	70.00	35.00	21.00

229	Barry Foote	.40	.20	.10
230	Jim Hunter	3.00	1.50	.90
231	Mike Tyson	.40	.20	.10
232	Diego Segui	.40	.20	.10
233	Billy Grabarkewitz	.40	.20	.10
234	Tom Grieve	.40	.20	.10
235	Jack Billingham	.40	.20	.10
236	Angels Team (Dick Williams)	1.00	.50	.30
237	Carl Morton	.40	.20	.10
238	Dave Duncan	.75	.40	.25
239	George Stone	.40	.20	.10
240	Garry Maddox	.40	.20	.10
241	Dick Tidrow	.40	.20	.10
242	Jay Johnstone	.40	.20	.10
243	Jim Kaat	1.50	.70	.45
244	Bill Buckner	.75	.40	.25
245	Mickey Lolich	1.00	.50	.30
246	Cardinals Team (Red Schoendienst)	1.00	.50	.30
247	Enos Cabell	.40	.20	.10
248	Randy Jones	.40	.20	.10
249	Danny Thompson	.40	.20	.10
250	Ken Brett	.40	.20	.10
251	Fran Healy	.40	.20	.10
252	Fred Scherman	.40	.20	.10
253	Jesus Alou	.40	.20	.10
254	Mike Torrez	.40	.20	.10
255	Dwight Evans	1.00	.50	.30
256	Billy Champion	.40	.20	.10
257	Checklist 133-264	2.00	1.00	.60
258	Dave LaRoche	.40	.20	.10
259	Len Randle	.40	.20	.10
260	Johnny Bench	15.00	7.50	4.50
261	Andy Hassler	.40	.20	.10
262	Rowland Office	.40	.20	.10
263	Jim Perry	.40	.20	.10
264	John Milner	.40	.20	.10
265	Ron Bryant	.40	.20	.10
266	Sandy Alomar	.40	.20	.10
267	Dick Ruthven	.40	.20	.10
268	Hal McRae	.75	.40	.25
269	Doug Rau	.40	.20	.10
270	Ron Fairly	.40	.20	.10
271	Jerry Moses	.40	.20	.10
272	Lynn McGlothen	.40	.20	.10
273	Steve Braun	.40	.20	.10
274	Vicente Romo	.40	.20	.10
275	Paul Blair	.40	.20	.10
276	White Sox Team (Chuck Tanner)	1.00	.50	.30
277	Frank Taveras	.40	.20	.10
278	Paul Lindblad	.40	.20	.10
279	Milt May	.40	.20	.10
280	Carl Yastrzemski	10.00	5.00	3.00
281	Jim Slaton	.40	.20	.10
282	Jerry Morales	.40	.20	.10
283	Steve Foucault	.40	.20	.10
284	Ken Griffey	2.00	1.00	.60
285	Ellie Rodriguez	.40	.20	.10
286	Mike Jorgensen	.40	.20	.10
287	Roric Harrison	.40	.20	.10
288	Bruce Ellingsen	.40	.20	.10
289	Ken Rudolph	.40	.20	.10
290	Jon Matlack	.40	.20	.10
291	Bill Sudakis	.40	.20	.10
292	Ron Schueler	.40	.20	.10
293	Dick Sharon	.40	.20	.10
294	***Geoff Zahn***	.40	.20	.10
295	Vada Pinson	1.50	.70	.45
296	Alan Foster	.40	.20	.10
297	Craig Kusick	.40	.20	.10
298	Johnny Grubb	.40	.20	.10
299	Bucky Dent	1.00	.50	.30
300	Reggie Jackson	12.00	6.00	3.50
301	Dave Roberts	.40	.20	.10
302	***Rick Burleson***	.75	.40	.25
303	Grant Jackson	.40	.20	.10
304	Pirates Team (Danny Murtaugh)	1.50	.70	.45
305	Jim Colborn	.40	.20	.10
306	Batting Leaders (Rod Carew, Ralph Garr)	1.50	.70	.45
307	Home Run Leaders (Dick Allen, Mike Schmidt)	3.00	1.50	.90
308	Runs Batted In Leaders (Johnny Bench, Jeff Burroughs)	1.50	.70	.45
309	Stolen Base Leaders (Lou Brock, Bill North)	1.50	.70	.45
310	Victory Leaders (Jim Hunter, Fergie Jenkins, Andy Messersmith, Phil Niekro)	1.50	.70	.45
311	Earned Run Average Leaders (Buzz Capra, Jim Hunter)	1.50	.70	.45
312	Strikeout Leaders (Steve Carlton, Nolan Ryan)	10.00	5.00	3.00
313	Leading Firemen (Terry Forster, Mike Marshall)	1.00	.50	.30
314	Buck Martinez	.40	.20	.10
315	Don Kessinger	.40	.20	.10
316	Jackie Brown	.40	.20	.10
317	Joe Lahoud	.40	.20	.10
318	Ernie McAnally	.40	.20	.10
319	Johnny Oates	.40	.20	.10
320	Pete Rose	25.00	12.50	7.50
321	Rudy May	.40	.20	.10
322	Ed Goodson	.40	.20	.10
323	Fred Holdsworth	.40	.20	.10
324	Ed Kranepool	.40	.20	.10
325	Tony Oliva	1.50	.70	.45
326	Wayne Twitchell	.40	.20	.10
327	Jerry Hairston Sr.	.40	.20	.10
328	Sonny Siebert	.40	.20	.10
329	Ted Kubiak	.40	.20	.10
330	Mike Marshall	.40	.20	.10
331	Indians Team (Frank Robinson)	1.50	.75	.45

332	Fred Kendall	.40	.20	.10
333	Dick Drago	.40	.20	.10
334	***Greg Gross***	.40	.20	.10
335	Jim Palmer	4.00	2.00	1.25
336	Rennie Stennett	.40	.20	.10
337	Kevin Kobel	.40	.20	.10
338	Rick Stelmaszek	.40	.20	.10
339	Jim Fregosi	1.00	.50	.30
340	Paul Splittorff	.40	.20	.10
341	Hal Breeden	.40	.20	.10
342	Leroy Stanton	.40	.20	.10
343	Danny Frisella	.40	.20	.10
344	Ben Oglivie	1.00	.50	.30
345	Clay Carroll	.40	.20	.10
346	Bobby Darwin	.40	.20	.10
347	Mike Caldwell	.40	.20	.10
348	Tony Muser	.40	.20	.10
349	Ray Sadecki	.40	.20	.10
350	Bobby Murcer	.75	.40	.25
351	Bob Boone	1.50	.70	.45
352	Darold Knowles	.40	.20	.10
353	Luis Melendez	.40	.20	.10
354	Dick Bosman	.40	.20	.10
355	Chris Cannizzaro	.40	.20	.10
356	Rico Petrocelli	.75	.40	.25
357	Ken Forsch	.40	.20	.10
358	Al Bumbry	.40	.20	.10
359	Paul Popovich	.40	.20	.10
360	George Scott	.40	.20	.10
361	Dodgers Team (Walter Alston)	1.50	.75	.45
362	Steve Hargan	.40	.20	.10
363	Carmen Fanzone	.40	.20	.10
364	Doug Bird	.40	.20	.10
365	Bob Bailey	.40	.20	.10
366	Ken Sanders	.40	.20	.10
367	Craig Robinson	.40	.20	.10
368	Vic Albury	.40	.20	.10
369	Merv Rettenmund	.40	.20	.10
370	Tom Seaver	10.00	5.00	3.00
371	Gates Brown	.40	.20	.10
372	John D'Acquisto	.40	.20	.10
373	Bill Sharp	.40	.20	.10
374	Eddie Watt	.40	.20	.10
375	Roy White	.45	.25	.15
376	Steve Yeager	.40	.20	.10
377	Tom Hilgendorf	.40	.20	.10
378	Derrel Thomas	.40	.20	.10
379	Bernie Carbo	.40	.20	.10
380	Sal Bando	.40	.20	.10
381	John Curtis	.40	.20	.10
382	Don Baylor	1.50	.70	.45
383	Jim York	.40	.20	.10
384	Brewers Team (Del Crandall)	1.50	.70	.45
385	Dock Ellis	.40	.20	.10
386	Checklist 265-396	2.00	1.00	.60
387	Jim Spencer	.40	.20	.10
388	Steve Stone	.75	.40	.25
389	Tony Solaita	.40	.20	.10
390	Ron Cey	1.00	.50	.30
391	Don DeMola	.40	.20	.10
392	Bruce Bochte	.40	.20	.10
393	Gary Gentry	.40	.20	.10
394	Larvell Blanks	.40	.20	.10
395	Bud Harrelson	.40	.20	.10
396	Fred Norman	.40	.20	.10
397	Bill Freehan	.75	.40	.25
398	Elias Sosa	.40	.20	.10
399	Terry Harmon	.40	.20	.10
400	Dick Allen	1.00	.50	.30
401	Mike Wallace	.40	.20	.10
402	Bob Tolan	.40	.20	.10
403	Tom Buskey	.40	.20	.10
404	Ted Sizemore	.40	.20	.10
405	John Montague	.40	.20	.10
406	Bob Gallagher	.40	.20	.10
407	***Herb Washington***	1.00	.50	.30
408	Clyde Wright	.40	.20	.10
409	Bob Robertson	.40	.20	.10
410	Mike Cueller (Cuellar)	.40	.20	.10
411	George Mitterwald	.40	.20	.10
412	Bill Hands	.40	.20	.10
413	Marty Pattin	.40	.20	.10
414	Manny Mota	.40	.20	.10
415	John Hiller	.40	.20	.10
416	Larry Lintz	.40	.20	.10
417	Skip Lockwood	.40	.20	.10
418	Leo Foster	.40	.20	.10
419	Dave Goltz	.40	.20	.10
420	Larry Bowa	1.50	.70	.45
421	Mets Team (Yogi Berra)	2.50	1.25	.70
422	Brian Downing	.40	.20	.10
423	Clay Kirby	.40	.20	.10
424	John Lowenstein	.40	.20	.10
425	Tito Fuentes	.40	.20	.10
426	George Medich	.40	.20	.10
427	Clarence Gaston	.40	.20	.10
428	Dave Hamilton	.40	.20	.10
429	***Jim Dwyer***	.40	.20	.10
430	Luis Tiant	1.00	.50	.30
431	Rod Gilbreath	.40	.20	.10
432	Ken Berry	.40	.20	.10
433	Larry Demery	.40	.20	.10
434	Bob Locker	.40	.20	.10
435	Dave Nelson	.40	.20	.10
436	Ken Frailing	.40	.20	.10
437	***Al Cowens***	.40	.20	.10
438	Don Carrithers	.40	.20	.10
439	Ed Brinkman	.40	.20	.10
440	Andy Messersmith	.40	.20	.10
441	Bobby Heise	.40	.20	.10
442	Maximino Leon	.40	.20	.10
443	Twins Team (Frank Quilici)	1.00	.50	.30
444	Gene Garber	.40	.20	.10
445	Felix Millan	.40	.20	.10
446	Bart Johnson	.40	.20	.10
447	Terry Crowley	.40	.20	.10
448	Frank Duffy	.40	.20	.10
449	Charlie Williams	.40	.20	.10

450	Willie McCovey	5.00	2.50	1.50
451	Rick Dempsey	.40	.20	.10
452	Angel Mangual	.40	.20	.10
453	Claude Osteen	.40	.20	.10
454	Doug Griffin	.40	.20	.10
455	Don Wilson	.40	.20	.10
456	Bob Coluccio	.40	.20	.10
457	Mario Mendoza	.40	.20	.10
458	Ross Grimsley	.40	.20	.10
459	A.L. Championships (Brooks Robinson)	1.00	.50	.30
460	N.L. Championships (Steve Garvey)	1.00	.50	.30
461	World Series Game 1 (Reggie Jackson)	2.00	1.00	.60
462	World Series Game 2 (Joe Ferguson)	.75	.40	.25
463	World Series Game 3 (Rollie Fingers)	1.50	.70	.45
464	World Series Game 4	.75	.40	.25
465	World Series Game 5	.75	.40	.25
466	A's Do It Again! (Win 3rd Straight World Series!)	1.50	.70	.45
467	Ed Halicki	.40	.20	.10
468	Bobby Mitchell	.40	.20	.10
469	Tom Dettore	.40	.20	.10
470	Jeff Burroughs	.40	.20	.10
471	Bob Stinson	.40	.20	.10
472	Bruce Dal Canton	.40	.20	.10
473	Ken McMullen	.40	.20	.10
474	Luke Walker	.40	.20	.10
475	Darrell Evans	1.00	.50	.30
476	***Ed Figueroa***	.40	.20	.10
477	Tom Hutton	.40	.20	.10
478	Tom Burgmeier	.40	.20	.10
479	Ken Boswell	.40	.20	.10
480	Carlos May	.40	.20	.10
481	***Will McEnaney***	.40	.20	.10
482	Tom McCraw	.40	.20	.10
483	Steve Ontiveros	.40	.20	.10
484	Glenn Beckert	.40	.20	.10
485	Sparky Lyle	.40	.20	.10
486	Ray Fosse	.40	.20	.10
487	Astros Team (Preston Gomez)	1.00	.50	.30
488	Bill Travers	.40	.20	.10
489	Cecil Cooper	1.00	.50	.30
490	Reggie Smith	.75	.40	.25
491	Doyle Alexander	.40	.20	.10
492	Rich Hebner	.40	.20	.10
493	Don Stanhouse	.40	.20	.10
494	***Pete LaCock***	.40	.20	.10
495	Nelson Briles	.40	.20	.10
496	Pepe Frias	.40	.20	.10
497	Jim Nettles	.40	.20	.10
498	Al Downing	.40	.20	.10
499	Marty Perez	.40	.20	.10
500	Nolan Ryan	50.00	25.00	15.00
501	Bill Robinson	.40	.20	.10
502	Pat Bourque	.40	.20	.10
503	Fred Stanley	.40	.20	.10
504	Buddy Bradford	.40	.20	.10
505	Chris Speier	.40	.20	.10
506	Leron Lee	.40	.20	.10
507	Tom Carroll	.40	.20	.10
508	Bob Hansen	.40	.20	.10
509	Dave Hilton	.40	.20	.10
510	Vida Blue	.75	.40	.25
511	Rangers Team (Billy Martin)	1.50	.75	.45
512	Larry Milbourne	.40	.20	.10
513	Dick Pole	.40	.20	.10
514	Jose Cruz	.40	.20	.10
515	Manny Sanguillen	.40	.20	.10
516	Don Hood	.40	.20	.10
517	Checklist 397-528	2.00	1.00	.60
518	Leo Cardenas	.40	.20	.10
519	Jim Todd	.40	.20	.10
520	Amos Otis	.40	.20	.10
521	Dennis Blair	.40	.20	.10
522	Gary Sutherland	.40	.20	.10
523	Tom Paciorek	.40	.20	.10
524	John Doherty	.40	.20	.10
525	Tom House	.40	.20	.10
526	Larry Hisle	.40	.20	.10
527	Mac Scarce	.40	.20	.10
528	Eddie Leon	.40	.20	.10
529	Gary Thomasson	.40	.20	.10
530	Gaylord Perry	3.00	1.50	.90
531	Reds Team (Sparky Anderson)	5.00	2.50	1.50
532	Gorman Thomas	.40	.20	.10
533	Rudy Meoli	.40	.20	.10
534	Alex Johnson	.40	.20	.10
535	Gene Tenace	.40	.20	.10
536	Bob Moose	.40	.20	.10
537	Tommy Harper	.40	.20	.10
538	Duffy Dyer	.40	.20	.10
539	Jesse Jefferson	.40	.20	.10
540	Lou Brock	5.00	2.50	1.50
541	Roger Metzger	.40	.20	.10
542	Pete Broberg	.40	.20	.10
543	Larry Biittner	.40	.20	.10
544	Steve Mingori	.40	.20	.10
545	Billy Williams	5.00	2.50	1.50
546	John Knox	.40	.20	.10
547	Von Joshua	.40	.20	.10
548	Charlie Sands	.40	.20	.10
549	Bill Butler	.40	.20	.10
550	Ralph Garr	.40	.20	.10
551	Larry Christenson	.40	.20	.10
552	Jack Brohamer	.40	.20	.10
553	John Boccabella	.40	.20	.10
554	Rich Gossage	1.50	.70	.45
555	Al Oliver	1.00	.50	.30
556	Tim Johnson	.40	.20	.10
557	Larry Gura	.40	.20	.10
558	Dave Roberts	.40	.20	.10
559	Bob Montgomery	.40	.20	.10
560	Tony Perez	4.00	2.00	1.25
561	A's Team (Alvin Dark)	1.00	.50	.30
562	Gary Nolan	.40	.20	.10
563	Wilbur Howard	.40	.20	.10
564	Tommy Davis	.40	.20	.10
565	Joe Torre	2.00	1.00	.60
566	Ray Burris	.40	.20	.10
567	***Jim Sundberg***	1.00	.50	.30
568	Dale Murray	.40	.20	.10
569	Frank White	.40	.20	.10
570	Jim Wynn	.40	.20	.10
571	Dave Lemanczyk	.40	.20	.10
572	Roger Nelson	.40	.20	.10
573	Orlando Pena	.40	.20	.10
574	Tony Taylor	.40	.20	.10
575	Gene Clines	.40	.20	.10
576	Phil Roof	.40	.20	.10
577	John Morris	.40	.20	.10
578	Dave Tomlin	.40	.20	.10
579	Skip Pitlock	.40	.20	.10
580	Frank Robinson	6.00	3.00	1.75
581	Darrel Chaney	.40	.20	.10
582	Eduardo Rodriguez	.40	.20	.10
583	Andy Etchebarren	.40	.20	.10
584	Mike Garman	.40	.20	.10
585	Chris Chambliss	.75	.40	.25
586	Tim McCarver	1.00	.50	.30
587	Chris Ward	.40	.20	.10
588	Rick Auerbach	.40	.20	.10
589	Braves Team (Clyde King)	1.00	.50	.30
590	Cesar Cedeno	.40	.20	.10
591	Glenn Abbott	.40	.20	.10
592	Balor Moore	.40	.20	.10
593	Gene Lamont	.40	.20	.10
594	Jim Fuller	.40	.20	.10
595	Joe Niekro	.40	.20	.10
596	Ollie Brown	.40	.20	.10
597	Winston Llenas	.40	.20	.10
598	Bruce Kison	.40	.20	.10
599	Nate Colbert	.40	.20	.10
600	Rod Carew	6.00	3.00	1.75
601	Juan Beniquez	.40	.20	.10
602	John Vukovich	.40	.20	.10
603	Lew Krausse	.40	.20	.10
604	Oscar Zamora	.40	.20	.10
605	John Ellis	.40	.20	.10
606	Bruce Miller	.40	.20	.10
607	Jim Holt	.40	.20	.10
608	Gene Michael	.40	.20	.10
609	Ellie Hendricks	.40	.20	.10
610	Ron Hunt	.40	.20	.10
611	Yankees Team (Bill Virdon)	2.00	1.00	.60
612	Terry Hughes	.40	.20	.10
613	Bill Parsons	.40	.20	.10
614	Rookie Pitchers (**Jack Kucek, Dyar Miller, Vern Ruhle, Paul Siebert**)	.40	.20	.10
615	Rookie Pitchers (**Pat Darcy, Dennis Leonard, Tom Underwood, Hank Webb**)	.40	.20	.10
616	Rookie Outfielders (***Dave Augustine, Pepe Mangual, Jim Rice, John Scott***)	20.00	10.00	6.00
617	Rookie Infielders (**Mike Cubbage, Doug DeCinces, Reggie Sanders, Manny Trillo**)	1.50	.70	.45
618	Rookie Pitchers (***Jamie Easterly, Tom Johnson, Scott McGregor, Rick Rhoden***)	2.00	1.00	.60
619	Rookie Outfielders (**Benny Ayala, Nyls Nyman, Tommy Smith, Jerry Turner**)	.40	.20	.10
620	Rookie Catchers-Outfielders (***Gary Carter, Marc Hill, Danny Meyer, Leon Roberts***)	15.00	7.50	4.50
621	Rookie Pitchers (**John Denny, Rawly Eastwick, Jim Kern, Juan Veintidos**)	.50	.25	.15
622	Rookie Outfielders (***Ed Armbrister, Fred Lynn, Tom Poquette, Terry Whitfield***)	8.00	4.00	2.50
623	Rookie Infielders (***Phil Garner, Keith Hernandez, Bob Sheldon, Tom Veryzer***)	8.00	4.00	2.50
624	Rookie Pitchers (**Doug Konieczny, Gary Lavelle, Jim Otten, Eddie Solomon**)	.40	.20	.10
625	Boog Powell	1.00	.50	.30
626	Larry Haney	.40	.20	.10
627	Tom Walker	.40	.20	.10
628	***Ron LeFlore***	.75	.40	.25
629	Joe Hoerner	.40	.20	.10
630	Greg Luzinski	1.00	.50	.30
631	Lee Lacy	.40	.20	.10
632	Morris Nettles	.40	.20	.10
633	Paul Casanova	.40	.20	.10
634	Cy Acosta	.40	.20	.10
635	Chuck Dobson	.40	.20	.10
636	Charlie Moore	.40	.20	.10
637	Ted Martinez	.40	.20	.10
638	Cubs Team (Jim Marshall)	1.50	.70	.45
639	Steve Kline	.40	.20	.10
640	Harmon Killebrew	6.00	3.00	1.75
641	Jim Northrup	.40	.20	.10
642	Mike Phillips	.40	.20	.10
643	Brent Strom	.40	.20	.10
644	Bill Fahey	.40	.20	.10
645	Danny Cater	.40	.20	.10
646	Checklist 529-660	1.00	.50	.30
647	***Claudell Washington***	.75	.40	.25
648	Dave Pagan	.40	.20	.10
649	Jack Heidemann	.40	.20	.10
650	Dave May	.40	.20	.10
651	John Morlan	.40	.20	.10
652	Lindy McDaniel	.40	.20	.10
653	Lee Richards	.40	.20	.10
654	Jerry Terrell	.40	.20	.10
655	Rico Carty	.40	.20	.10
656	Bill Plummer	.40	.20	.10
657	Bob Oliver	.40	.20	.10
658	Vic Harris	.40	.20	.10
659	Bob Apodaca	.40	.20	.10
660	Hank Aaron	30.00	15.00	9.00

1975 Topps Mini

This popular set was actually a test issue to see how collectors would react to cards which were 20 percent smaller than the standard 2-1/2" x 3-1/2". Other than their 2-1/4" x 3-1/8" size, they are exactly the same front and back as the regular-issue '75 Topps. The experimental cards were sold in Michigan and on the West Coast, where they were quickly gobbled up by collectors, dealers and speculators. While the minis for many years enjoyed a 2X premium over regular 1975 Topps values, that differential has shrunk in recent years.

	NM	EX	VG
Complete Set (660):	425.00	210.00	125.00
Common Player:	.50	.25	.15
Wax Pack (10):	40.00		
Wax Box (36):	1,600		
Cello Pack (18):	100.00		
Rack Pack (42):	200.00		

(Stars and rookies valued 1X to 1.5X regular 1975 Topps.)

1975 Topps Team Checklist Sheet

Via a mail-in wrapper redemption, collectors could receive an uncut sheet of the 24 team photo/checklist cards from the 1975 Topps baseball set. Measuring about 10-1/2" x 20-1/8", the sheet could be cut into individual team cards of standard size. The sheet-cut cards differ from issued versions in that they have white backs and are printed on thinner stock than the pack-issued versions.

	NM	EX	VG
Complete Sheet:	50.00	25.00	15.00

1976 Topps

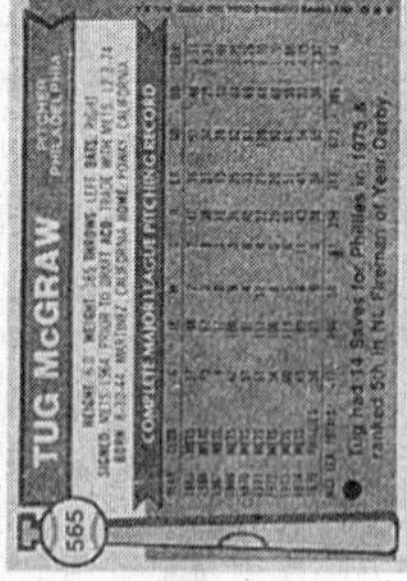

These 2-1/2" x 3-1/2" cards begin a design trend for Topps. The focus was more on the photo quality than in past years with a corresponding trend toward simplicity in the borders. The front of the cards has the player's name and team in two strips while his position is in the lower-left corner under a drawing of a player representing that position. The backs have a bat and ball with the card number on the left; statistics and personal information and career highlights on the right. The 660-card set features a number of specialty sets including record-setting performances, statistical leaders, playoff and World Series highlights, the Sporting News All-Time All-Stars and father and son combinations.

	NM	EX	VG
Complete Set (660):	250.00	125.00	75.00
Common Player:	.40	.20	.10
Wax Pack (6):	40.00		
Wax Box (36 six-card):	1,350		
Wax Pack (10):	65.00		
Wax Box (36 10-card):	2,400		
Cello Pack (18):	75.00		
Cello Box (24):	1,950		
Rack Pack (42):	135.00		
Vending Box (500):	550.00		
1 Hank Aaron (Record Breaker)	12.00	6.00	3.50
2 Bobby Bonds (Record Breaker)	1.50	.70	.45

3	Mickey Lolich (Record Breaker)	.40	.20	.10
4	Dave Lopes (Record Breaker)	.40	.20	.10
5	Tom Seaver (Record Breaker)	3.00	1.50	.90
6	Rennie Stennett (Record Breaker)	.40	.20	.10
7	Jim Umbarger	.40	.20	.10
8	Tito Fuentes	.40	.20	.10
9	Paul Lindblad	.40	.20	.10
10	Lou Brock	5.00	2.50	1.50
11	Jim Hughes	.40	.20	.10
12	Richie Zisk	.40	.20	.10
13	Johnny Wockenfuss	.40	.20	.10
14	Gene Garber	.40	.20	.10
15	George Scott	.40	.20	.10
16	Bob Apodaca	.40	.20	.10
17	New York Yankees Team (Billy Martin)	1.50	.70	.45
18	Dale Murray	.40	.20	.10
19	George Brett	25.00	12.50	7.50
20	Bob Watson	.40	.20	.10
21	Dave LaRoche	.40	.20	.10
22	Bill Russell	1.00	.50	.30
23	Brian Downing	.40	.20	.10
24	Cesar Geronimo	.40	.20	.10
25	Mike Torrez	.40	.20	.10
26	Andy Thornton	.75	.40	.25
27	Ed Figueroa	.40	.20	.10
28	Dusty Baker	1.50	.70	.45
29	Rick Burleson	.40	.20	.10
30	***John Montefusco***	.40	.20	.10
31	Len Randle	.40	.20	.10
32	Danny Frisella	.40	.20	.10
33	Bill North	.40	.20	.10
34	Mike Garman	.40	.20	.10
35	Tony Oliva	1.00	.50	.30
36	Frank Taveras	.40	.20	.10
37	John Hiller	.40	.20	.10
38	Garry Maddox	.40	.20	.10
39	Pete Broberg	.40	.20	.10
40	Dave Kingman	.75	.40	.25
41	***Tippy Martinez***	.75	.40	.25
42	Barry Foote	.40	.20	.10
43	Paul Splittorff	.40	.20	.10
44	Doug Rader	.40	.20	.10
45	Boog Powell	.75	.40	.25
46	Los Angeles Dodgers Team (Walter Alston)	1.00	.50	.30
47	Jesse Jefferson	.40	.20	.10
48	Dave Concepcion	.40	.20	.10
49	Dave Duncan	.40	.20	.10
50	Fred Lynn	.75	.40	.25
51	Ray Burris	.40	.20	.10
52	Dave Chalk	.40	.20	.10
53	Mike Beard	.40	.20	.10
54	Dave Rader	.40	.20	.10
55	Gaylord Perry	3.00	1.50	.90
56	Bob Tolan	.40	.20	.10
57	Phil Garner	.40	.20	.10
58	Ron Reed	.40	.20	.10
59	Larry Hisle	.40	.20	.10
60	Jerry Reuss	.40	.20	.10
61	Ron LeFlore	.40	.20	.10
62	Johnny Oates	.40	.20	.10
63	Bobby Darwin	.40	.20	.10
64	Jerry Koosman	.40	.20	.10
65	Chris Chambliss	.40	.20	.10
66	Father & Son (Buddy Bell, Gus Bell)	.40	.20	.10
67	Father & Son (Bob Boone, Ray Boone)	.40	.20	.12
68	Father & Son (Joe Coleman, Joe Coleman, Jr.)	.40	.20	.10
69	Father & Son (Jim Hegan, Mike Hegan)	.40	.20	.10
70	Father & Son (Roy Smalley, III, Roy Smalley, Jr.)	.40	.20	.10
71	Steve Rogers	.40	.20	.10
72	Hal McRae	.40	.20	.10
73	Baltimore Orioles Team (Earl Weaver)	1.00	.50	.30
74	Oscar Gamble	.40	.20	.10
75	Larry Dierker	.40	.20	.10
76	Willie Crawford	.40	.20	.10
77	Pedro Borbon	.40	.20	.10
78	Cecil Cooper	.40	.20	.10
79	Jerry Morales	.40	.20	.10
80	Jim Kaat	.75	.40	.25
81	Darrell Evans	.75	.40	.25
82	Von Joshua	.40	.20	.10
83	Jim Spencer	.40	.20	.10
84	Brent Strom	.40	.20	.10
85	Mickey Rivers	.40	.20	.10
86	Mike Tyson	.40	.20	.10
87	Tom Burgmeier	.40	.20	.10
88	Duffy Dyer	.40	.20	.10
89	Vern Ruhle	.40	.20	.10
90	Sal Bando	.40	.20	.10
91	Tom Hutton	.40	.20	.10
92	Eduardo Rodriguez	.40	.20	.10
93	Mike Phillips	.40	.20	.10
94	Jim Dwyer	.40	.20	.10
95	Brooks Robinson	6.00	3.00	1.75
96	Doug Bird	.40	.20	.10
97	Wilbur Howard	.40	.20	.10
98	***Dennis Eckersley***	25.00	12.50	7.50
99	Lee Lacy	.40	.20	.10
100	Jim Hunter	3.00	1.50	.90
101	Pete LaCock	.40	.20	.10
102	Jim Willoughby	.40	.20	.10
103	Biff Pocoroba	.40	.20	.10
104	Cincinnati Reds Team (Sparky Anderson)	1.00	.50	.30
105	Gary Lavelle	.40	.20	.10
106	Tom Grieve	.40	.20	.10
107	Dave Roberts	.40	.20	.10
108	Don Kirkwood	.40	.20	.10
109	Larry Lintz	.40	.20	.10

110	Carlos May	.40	.20	.10
111	Danny Thompson	.40	.20	.10
112	***Kent Tekulve***	.75	.40	.25
113	Gary Sutherland	.40	.20	.10
114	Jay Johnstone	.40	.20	.10
115	Ken Holtzman	.40	.20	.10
116	Charlie Moore	.40	.20	.10
117	Mike Jorgensen	.40	.20	.10
118	Boston Red Sox Team (Darrell Johnson)	1.00	.50	.30
119	Checklist 1-132	1.00	.50	.30
120	Rusty Staub	.75	.40	.25
121	Tony Solaita	.40	.20	.10
122	Mike Cosgrove	.40	.20	.10
123	Walt Williams	.40	.20	.10
124	Doug Rau	.40	.20	.10
125	Don Baylor	1.50	.70	.45
126	Tom Dettore	.40	.20	.10
127	Larvell Blanks	.40	.20	.10
128	Ken Griffey	1.00	.50	.30
129	Andy Etchebarren	.40	.20	.10
130	Luis Tiant	1.00	.50	.30
131	Bill Stein	.40	.20	.10
132	Don Hood	.40	.20	.10
133	Gary Matthews	.40	.20	.10
134	Mike Ivie	.40	.20	.10
135	Bake McBride	.40	.20	.10
136	Dave Goltz	.40	.20	.10
137	Bill Robinson	.40	.20	.10
138	Lerrin LaGrow	.40	.20	.10
139	Gorman Thomas	.75	.40	.25
140	Vida Blue	1.00	.50	.30
141	***Larry Parrish***	1.00	.50	.30
142	Dick Drago	.40	.20	.10
143	Jerry Grote	.40	.20	.10
144	Al Fitzmorris	.40	.20	.10
145	Larry Bowa	1.00	.50	.30
146	George Medich	.40	.20	.10
147	Houston Astros Team (Bill Virdon)	1.00	.50	.30
148	Stan Thomas	.40	.20	.10
149	Tommy Davis	.40	.20	.10
150	Steve Garvey	2.00	1.00	.60
151	Bill Bonham	.40	.20	.10
152	Leroy Stanton	.40	.20	.10
153	Buzz Capra	.40	.20	.10
154	Bucky Dent	.40	.20	.10
155	Jack Billingham	.40	.20	.10
156	Rico Carty	.40	.20	.10
157	Mike Caldwell	.40	.20	.10
158	Ken Reitz	.40	.20	.10
159	Jerry Terrell	.40	.20	.10
160	Dave Winfield	8.00	4.00	2.50
161	Bruce Kison	.40	.20	.10
162	Jack Pierce	.40	.20	.10
163	Jim Slaton	.40	.20	.10
164	Pepe Mangual	.40	.20	.10
165	Gene Tenace	.40	.20	.10
166	Skip Lockwood	.40	.20	.10
167	Freddie Patek	.40	.20	.10
168	Tom Hilgendorf	.40	.20	.10
169	Graig Nettles	.75	.40	.25
170	Rick Wise	.40	.20	.10
171	Greg Gross	.40	.20	.10
172	Texas Rangers Team (Frank Lucchesi)	1.00	.50	.30
173	Steve Swisher	.40	.20	.10
174	Charlie Hough	.75	.40	.25
175	Ken Singleton	.40	.20	.10
176	Dick Lange	.40	.20	.10
177	Marty Perez	.40	.20	.10
178	Tom Buskey	.40	.20	.10
179	George Foster	.75	.40	.25
180	Rich Gossage	1.00	.50	.30
181	Willie Montanez	.40	.20	.10
182	Harry Rasmussen	.40	.20	.10
183	Steve Braun	.40	.20	.10
184	Bill Greif	.40	.20	.10
185	Dave Parker	1.00	.50	.30
186	Tom Walker	.40	.20	.10
187	Pedro Garcia	.40	.20	.10
188	Fred Scherman	.40	.20	.10
189	Claudell Washington	.40	.20	.10
190	Jon Matlack	.40	.20	.10
191	N.L. Batting Leaders (Bill Madlock, Manny Sanguillen, Ted Simmons)	.75	.40	.25
192	A.L. Batting Leaders (Rod Carew, Fred Lynn, Thurman Munson)	1.00	.50	.30
193	N.L. Home Run Leaders (Dave Kingman, Greg Luzinski, Mike Schmidt)	2.00	1.00	.60
194	A.L. Home Run Leaders (Reggie Jackson, John Mayberry, George Scott)	2.00	1.00	.60
195	N.L. RBI Leaders (Johnny Bench, Greg Luzinski, Tony Perez)	1.00	.50	.30
196	A.L. RBI Leaders (Fred Lynn, John Mayberry, George Scott)	.40	.20	.10
197	N.L. Stolen Base Leaders (Lou Brock, Dave Lopes, Joe Morgan)	1.50	.70	.45
198	A.L. Stolen Base Leaders (Amos Otis, Mickey Rivers, Claudell Washington)	.40	.20	.10
199	N.L. Victory Leaders (Randy Jones, Andy Messersmith, Tom Seaver)	2.00	1.00	.60
200	A.L. Victory Leaders (Vida Blue, Jim Hunter, Jim Palmer)	1.00	.50	.30
201	N.L. ERA Leaders (Randy Jones, Andy Messersmith, Tom Seaver)	1.00	.50	.30

202	A.L. ERA Leaders (Dennis Eckersley, Jim Hunter, Jim Palmer)	2.00	1.00	.60
203	N.L. Strikeout Leaders (Andy Messersmith, John Montefusco, Tom Seaver)	1.50	.70	.45
204	A.L. Strikeout Leaders (Bert Blyleven, Gaylord Perry, Frank Tanana)	1.00	.50	.30
205	Major League Leading Firemen (Rich Gossage, Al Hrabosky)	.75	.40	.25
206	Manny Trillo	.40	.20	.10
207	Andy Hassler	.40	.20	.10
208	Mike Lum	.40	.20	.10
209	Alan Ashby	.40	.20	.10
210	Lee May	.40	.20	.10
211	Clay Carroll	.40	.20	.10
212	Pat Kelly	.40	.20	.10
213	Dave Heaverlo	.40	.20	.10
214	Eric Soderholm	.40	.20	.10
215	Reggie Smith	.40	.20	.10
216	Montreal Expos Team (Karl Kuehl)	1.00	.50	.30
217	Dave Freisleben	.40	.20	.10
218	John Knox	.40	.20	.10
219	Tom Murphy	.40	.20	.10
220	Manny Sanguillen	.40	.20	.10
221	Jim Todd	.40	.20	.10
222	Wayne Garrett	.40	.20	.10
223	Ollie Brown	.40	.20	.10
224	Jim York	.40	.20	.10
225	Roy White	.40	.20	.10
226	Jim Sundberg	.40	.20	.10
227	Oscar Zamora	.40	.20	.10
228	John Hale	.40	.20	.10
229	***Jerry Remy***	.40	.20	.10
230	Carl Yastrzemski	10.00	5.00	3.00
231	Tom House	.40	.20	.10
232	Frank Duffy	.40	.20	.10
233	Grant Jackson	.40	.20	.10
234	Mike Sadek	.40	.20	.10
235	Bert Blyleven	1.00	.50	.30
236	Kansas City Royals Team (Whitey Herzog)	1.00	.50	.30
237	Dave Hamilton	.40	.20	.10
238	Larry Biittner	.40	.20	.10
239	John Curtis	.40	.20	.10
240	Pete Rose	25.00	12.50	7.50
241	Hector Torres	.40	.20	.10
242	Dan Meyer	.40	.20	.10
243	Jim Rooker	.40	.20	.10
244	Bill Sharp	.40	.20	.10
245	Felix Millan	.40	.20	.10
246	Cesar Tovar	.40	.20	.10
247	Terry Harmon	.40	.20	.10
248	Dick Tidrow	.40	.20	.10
249	Cliff Johnson	.40	.20	.10
250	Fergie Jenkins	3.00	1.50	.90
251	Rick Monday	.40	.20	.10
252	Tim Nordbrook	.40	.20	.10
253	Bill Buckner	.75	.40	.25
254	Rudy Meoli	.40	.20	.10
255	Fritz Peterson	.40	.20	.10
256	Rowland Office	.40	.20	.10
257	Ross Grimsley	.40	.20	.10
258	Nyls Nyman	.40	.20	.10
259	Darrel Chaney	.40	.20	.10
260	Steve Busby	.40	.20	.10
261	Gary Thomasson	.40	.20	.10
262	Checklist 133-264	1.00	.50	.30
263	***Lyman Bostock***	.75	.40	.25
264	Steve Renko	.40	.20	.10
265	Willie Davis	.40	.20	.10
266	Alan Foster	.40	.20	.10
267	Aurelio Rodriguez	.40	.20	.10
268	Del Unser	.40	.20	.10
269	Rick Austin	.40	.20	.10
270	Willie Stargell	4.00	2.00	1.25
271	Jim Lonborg	.40	.20	.10
272	Rick Dempsey	.40	.20	.10
273	Joe Niekro	.40	.20	.10
274	Tommy Harper	.40	.20	.10
275	***Rick Manning***	.75	.40	.25
276	Mickey Scott	.40	.20	.10
277	Chicago Cubs Team (Jim Marshall)	1.00	.50	.30
278	Bernie Carbo	.40	.20	.10
279	Roy Howell	.40	.20	.10
280	Burt Hooton	.40	.20	.10
281	Dave May	.40	.20	.10
282	Dan Osborn	.40	.20	.10
283	Merv Rettenmund	.40	.20	.10
284	Steve Ontiveros	.40	.20	.10
285	Mike Cuellar	.40	.20	.10
286	Jim Wohlford	.40	.20	.10
287	Pete Mackanin	.40	.20	.10
288	Bill Campbell	.40	.20	.10
289	Enzo Hernandez	.40	.20	.10
290	Ted Simmons	.40	.20	.10
291	Ken Sanders	.40	.20	.10
292	Leon Roberts	.40	.20	.10
293	Bill Castro	.40	.20	.10
294	Ed Kirkpatrick	.40	.20	.10
295	Dave Cash	.40	.20	.10
296	Pat Dobson	.40	.20	.10
297	Roger Metzger	.40	.20	.10
298	Dick Bosman	.40	.20	.10
299	Champ Summers	.40	.20	.10
300	Johnny Bench	10.00	5.00	3.00
301	Jackie Brown	.40	.20	.10
302	Rick Miller	.40	.20	.10
303	Steve Foucault	.40	.20	.10
304	California Angels Team (Dick Williams)	1.00	.50	.30
305	Andy Messersmith	.40	.20	.10
306	Rod Gilbreath	.40	.20	.10
307	Al Bumbry	.40	.20	.10

308	Jim Barr	.40	.20	.10
309	Bill Melton	.40	.20	.10
310	Randy Jones	.40	.20	.10
311	Cookie Rojas	.40	.20	.10
312	Don Carrithers	.40	.20	.10
313	***Dan Ford***	.40	.20	.10
314	Ed Kranepool	.40	.20	.10
315	Al Hrabosky	.40	.20	.10
316	Robin Yount	12.00	6.00	3.50
317	***John Candelaria***	1.00	.50	.30
318	Bob Boone	.75	.40	.25
319	Larry Gura	.40	.20	.10
320	Willie Horton	.40	.20	.10
321	Jose Cruz	.75	.40	.25
322	Glenn Abbott	.40	.20	.10
323	Rob Sperring	.40	.20	.10
324	Jim Bibby	.40	.20	.10
325	Tony Perez	4.00	2.00	1.25
326	Dick Pole	.40	.20	.10
327	Dave Moates	.40	.20	.10
328	Carl Morton	.40	.20	.10
329	Joe Ferguson	.40	.20	.10
330	Nolan Ryan	25.00	12.50	7.50
331	San Diego Padres Team (John McNamara)	1.00	.50	.30
332	Charlie Williams	.40	.20	.10
333	Bob Coluccio	.40	.20	.10
334	Dennis Leonard	.40	.20	.10
335	Bob Grich	.75	.40	.25
336	Vic Albury	.40	.20	.10
337	Bud Harrelson	.40	.20	.10
338	Bob Bailey	.40	.20	.10
339	John Denny	.40	.20	.10
340	Jim Rice	3.00	1.50	.90
341	Lou Gehrig (All Time 1B)	10.00	5.00	3.00
342	Rogers Hornsby (All Time 2B)	2.50	1.25	.70
343	Pie Traynor (All Time 3B)	1.00	.50	.30
344	Honus Wagner (All Time SS)	5.00	2.50	1.50
345	Babe Ruth (All Time OF)	15.00	7.50	4.50
346	Ty Cobb (All Time OF)	10.00	5.00	3.00
347	Ted Williams (All Time OF)	10.00	5.00	3.00
348	Mickey Cochrane (All Time C)	1.00	.50	.30
349	Walter Johnson (All Time RHP)	4.00	2.00	1.25
350	Lefty Grove (All Time LHP)	1.00	.50	.30
351	Randy Hundley	.40	.20	.10
352	Dave Giusti	.40	.20	.10
353	***Sixto Lezcano***	.75	.40	.25
354	Ron Blomberg	.40	.20	.10
355	Steve Carlton	4.00	2.00	1.25
356	Ted Martinez	.40	.20	.10
357	Ken Forsch	.40	.20	.10
358	Buddy Bell	.40	.20	.10
359	Rick Reuschel	.40	.20	.10
360	Jeff Burroughs	.40	.20	.10
361	Detroit Tigers Team (Ralph Houk)	1.00	.50	.30
362	Will McEnaney	.40	.20	.10
363	***Dave Collins***	.40	.20	.12
364	Elias Sosa	.40	.20	.10
365	Carlton Fisk	5.00	2.50	1.50
366	Bobby Valentine	.40	.20	.10
367	Bruce Miller	.40	.20	.10
368	Wilbur Wood	.40	.20	.10
369	Frank White	.75	.40	.25
370	Ron Cey	.75	.40	.25
371	Ellie Hendricks	.40	.20	.10
372	Rick Baldwin	.40	.20	.10
373	Johnny Briggs	.40	.20	.10
374	Dan Warthen	.40	.20	.10
375	Ron Fairly	.40	.20	.10
376	Rich Hebner	.40	.20	.10
377	Mike Hegan	.40	.20	.10
378	Steve Stone	.40	.20	.10
379	Ken Boswell	.40	.20	.10
380	Bobby Bonds	1.00	.50	.30
381	Denny Doyle	.40	.20	.10
382	Matt Alexander	.40	.20	.10
383	John Ellis	.40	.20	.10
384	Philadelphia Phillies Team (Danny Ozark)	1.00	.50	.30
385	Mickey Lolich	.75	.40	.25
386	Ed Goodson	.40	.20	.10
387	Mike Miley	.40	.20	.10
388	Stan Perzanowski	.40	.20	.10
389	Glenn Adams	.40	.20	.10
390	Don Gullett	.40	.20	.10
391	Jerry Hairston Sr.	.40	.20	.10
392	Checklist 265-396	1.00	.50	.30
393	Paul Mitchell	.40	.20	.10
394	Fran Healy	.40	.20	.10
395	Jim Wynn	.40	.20	.10
396	Bill Lee	.40	.20	.10
397	Tim Foli	.40	.20	.10
398	Dave Tomlin	.40	.20	.10
399	Luis Melendez	.40	.20	.10
400	Rod Carew	5.00	2.50	1.50
401	Ken Brett	.40	.20	.10
402	Don Money	.40	.20	.10
403	Geoff Zahn	.40	.20	.10
404	Enos Cabell	.40	.20	.10
405	Rollie Fingers	3.00	1.50	.90
406	Ed Herrmann	.40	.20	.10
407	Tom Underwood	.40	.20	.10
408	Charlie Spikes	.40	.20	.10
409	Dave Lemanczyk	.40	.20	.10
410	Ralph Garr	.40	.20	.10
411	Bill Singer	.40	.20	.10
412	Toby Harrah	.40	.20	.10
413	Pete Varney	.40	.20	.10
414	Wayne Garland	.40	.20	.10
415	Vada Pinson	1.00	.50	.30
416	Tommy John	1.00	.50	.30
417	Gene Clines	.40	.20	.10
418	Jose Morales	.40	.20	.10
419	Reggie Cleveland	.40	.20	.10
420	Joe Morgan	4.00	2.00	1.25
421	Oakland A's Team	1.00	.50	.30
422	Johnny Grubb	.40	.20	.10
423	Ed Halicki	.40	.20	.10
424	Phil Roof	.40	.20	.10
425	Rennie Stennett	.40	.20	.10
426	Bob Forsch	.40	.20	.10
427	Kurt Bevacqua	.40	.20	.10
428	Jim Crawford	.40	.20	.10
429	Fred Stanley	.40	.20	.10
430	Jose Cardenal	.40	.20	.10
431	Dick Ruthven	.40	.20	.10
432	Tom Veryzer	.40	.20	.10
433	Rick Waits	.40	.20	.10
434	Morris Nettles	.40	.20	.10
435	Phil Niekro	3.00	1.50	.90
436	Bill Fahey	.40	.20	.10
437	Terry Forster	.40	.20	.10
438	Doug DeCinces	.40	.20	.10
439	Rick Rhoden	.40	.20	.10
440	John Mayberry	.40	.20	.10
441	Gary Carter	6.00	3.00	1.75
442	Hank Webb	.40	.20	.10
443	San Francisco Giants Team	1.00	.50	.30
444	Gary Nolan	.40	.20	.10
445	Rico Petrocelli	.40	.20	.10
446	Larry Haney	.40	.20	.10
447	Gene Locklear	.40	.20	.10
448	Tom Johnson	.40	.20	.10
449	Bob Robertson	.40	.20	.10
450	Jim Palmer	4.00	2.00	1.25
451	Buddy Bradford	.40	.20	.10
452	Tom Hausman	.40	.20	.10
453	Lou Piniella	1.50	.70	.45
454	Tom Griffin	.40	.20	.10
455	Dick Allen	.75	.40	.25
456	Joe Coleman	.40	.20	.10
457	Ed Crosby	.40	.20	.10
458	Earl Williams	.40	.20	.10
459	Jim Brewer	.40	.20	.10
460	Cesar Cedeno	.40	.20	.10
461	NL & AL Championships	.75	.40	.25
462	1975 World Series	.75	.40	.25
463	Steve Hargan	.40	.20	.10
464	Ken Henderson	.40	.20	.10
465	Mike Marshall	.40	.20	.10
466	Bob Stinson	.40	.20	.10
467	Woodie Fryman	.40	.20	.10
468	Jesus Alou	.40	.20	.10
469	Rawly Eastwick	.40	.20	.10
470	Bobby Murcer	.75	.40	.25
471	Jim Burton	.40	.20	.10
472	Bob Davis	.40	.20	.10
473	Paul Blair	.40	.20	.10
474	Ray Corbin	.40	.20	.10
475	Joe Rudi	.40	.20	.10
476	Bob Moose	.40	.20	.10
477	Cleveland Indians Team (Frank Robinson)	1.50	.70	.45
478	Lynn McGlothen	.40	.20	.10
479	Bobby Mitchell	.40	.20	.10
480	Mike Schmidt	15.00	7.50	4.50
481	Rudy May	.40	.20	.10
482	Tim Hosley	.40	.20	.10
483	Mickey Stanley	.40	.20	.10
484	Eric Raich	.40	.20	.10
485	Mike Hargrove	.40	.20	.10
486	Bruce Dal Canton	.40	.20	.10
487	Leron Lee	.40	.20	.10
488	Claude Osteen	.40	.20	.10
489	Skip Jutze	.40	.20	.10
490	Frank Tanana	.40	.20	.10
491	Terry Crowley	.40	.20	.10
492	Marty Pattin	.40	.20	.10
493	Derrel Thomas	.40	.20	.10
494	Craig Swan	.40	.20	.10
495	Nate Colbert	.40	.20	.10
496	Juan Beniquez	.40	.20	.10
497	Joe McIntosh	.40	.20	.10
498	Glenn Borgmann	.40	.20	.10
499	Mario Guerrero	.40	.20	.10
500	Reggie Jackson	10.00	5.00	3.00
501	Billy Champion	.40	.20	.10
502	Tim McCarver	1.00	.50	.30
503	Elliott Maddox	.40	.20	.10
504	Pittsburgh Pirates Team (Danny Murtaugh)	1.00	.50	.30
505	Mark Belanger	.40	.20	.10
506	George Mitterwald	.40	.20	.10
507	Ray Bare	.40	.20	.10
508	***Duane Kuiper***	.40	.20	.10
509	Bill Hands	.40	.20	.10
510	Amos Otis	.40	.20	.10
511	Jamie Easterly	.40	.20	.10
512	Ellie Rodriguez	.40	.20	.10
513	Bart Johnson	.40	.20	.10
514	Dan Driessen	.40	.20	.10
515	Steve Yeager	.40	.20	.10
516	Wayne Granger	.40	.20	.10
517	John Milner	.40	.20	.10
518	***Doug Flynn***	.40	.20	.10
519	Steve Brye	.40	.20	.10
520	Willie McCovey	4.00	2.00	1.25
521	Jim Colborn	.40	.20	.10
522	Ted Sizemore	.40	.20	.10
523	Bob Montgomery	.40	.20	.10
524	Pete Falcone	.40	.20	.10
525	Billy Williams	4.00	2.00	1.25
526	Checklist 397-528	1.00	.50	.30
527	Mike Anderson	.40	.20	.10
528	Dock Ellis	.40	.20	.10
529	Deron Johnson	.40	.20	.10
530	Don Sutton	3.00	1.50	.90
531	New York Mets Team (Joe Frazier)	1.00	.50	.30
532	Milt May	.40	.20	.10
533	Lee Richard	.40	.20	.10
534	Stan Bahnsen	.40	.20	.10
535	Dave Nelson	.40	.20	.10
536	Mike Thompson	.40	.20	.10
537	Tony Muser	.40	.20	.10
538	Pat Darcy	.40	.20	.10
539	John Balaz	.40	.20	.10
540	Bill Freehan	.40	.20	.10
541	Steve Mingori	.40	.20	.10
542	Keith Hernandez	1.00	.50	.30
543	Wayne Twitchell	.40	.20	.10
544	Pepe Frias	.40	.20	.10
545	Sparky Lyle	.40	.20	.10
546	Dave Rosello	.40	.20	.10
547	Roric Harrison	.40	.20	.10
548	Manny Mota	.40	.20	.10
549	Randy Tate	.40	.20	.10
550	Hank Aaron	25.00	12.50	7.50
551	Jerry DaVanon	.40	.20	.10
552	Terry Humphrey	.40	.20	.10
553	Randy Moffitt	.40	.20	.10
554	Ray Fosse	.40	.20	.10
555	Dyar Miller	.40	.20	.10
556	Minnesota Twins Team (Gene Mauch)	1.00	.50	.30
557	Dan Spillner	.40	.20	.10
558	Clarence Gaston	.40	.20	.10
559	Clyde Wright	.40	.20	.10
560	Jorge Orta	.40	.20	.10
561	Tom Carroll	.40	.20	.10
562	Adrian Garrett	.40	.20	.10
563	Larry Demery	.40	.20	.10
564	Kurt Bevacqua (Bubble Gum Blowing Champ)	.40	.20	.10
565	Tug McGraw	.75	.40	.25
566	Ken McMullen	.40	.20	.10
567	George Stone	.40	.20	.10
568	Rob Andrews	.40	.20	.10
569	Nelson Briles	.40	.20	.10
570	George Hendrick	.40	.20	.10
571	Don DeMola	.40	.20	.10
572	Rich Coggins	.40	.20	.10
573	Bill Travers	.40	.20	.10
574	Don Kessinger	.40	.20	.10
575	Dwight Evans	.75	.40	.25
576	Maximino Leon	.40	.20	.10
577	Marc Hill	.40	.20	.10
578	Ted Kubiak	.40	.20	.10
579	Clay Kirby	.40	.20	.10
580	Bert Campaneris	.40	.20	.10
581	St. Louis Cardinals Team (Red Schoendienst)	1.50	.70	.45
582	Mike Kekich	.40	.20	.10
583	Tommy Helms	.40	.20	.10
584	Stan Wall	.40	.20	.10
585	Joe Torre	1.50	.70	.45
586	Ron Schueler	.40	.20	.10
587	Leo Cardenas	.40	.20	.10
588	Kevin Kobel	.40	.20	.10
589	Rookie Pitchers **(Santo Alcala, Mike Flanagan, Joe Pactwa, Pablo Torrealba)**	1.00	.50	.30
590	Rookie Outfielders **(Henry Cruz, Chet Lemon, Ellis Valentine, Terry Whitfield)**	.75	.40	.25
591	Rookie Pitchers **(Steve Grilli, Craig Mitchell, Jose Sosa, George Throop)**	.40	.20	.10
592	Rookie Infielders (***Dave McKay, Willie Randolph, Jerry Royster, Roy Staiger***)	6.00	3.00	1.75
593	Rookie Pitchers (***Larry Anderson, Ken Crosby, Mark Littell, Butch Metzger***)	.40	.20	.10
594	Rookie Catchers & Outfielders **(Andy Merchant, Ed Ott, Royle Stillman, Jerry White)**	.40	.20	.10
595	Rookie Pitchers **(Steve Barr, Art DeFilippis, Randy Lerch, Sid Monge)**	.40	.20	.10
596	Rookie Infielders (***Lamar Johnson, Johnny LeMaster, Jerry Manuel, Craig Reynolds***)	.40	.20	.10
597	Rookie Pitchers **(Don Aase, Jack Kucek, Frank LaCorte, Mike Pazik)**	.40	.20	.10
598	Rookie Outfielders **(Hector Cruz, Jamie Quirk, Jerry Turner, Joe Wallis)**	.40	.20	.10
599	Rookie Pitchers (***Rob Dressler, Ron Guidry, Bob McClure, Pat Zachry***)	8.00	4.00	2.50
600	Tom Seaver	8.00	4.00	2.50
601	Ken Rudolph	.40	.20	.10
602	Doug Konieczny	.40	.20	.10
603	Jim Holt	.40	.20	.10
604	Joe Lovitto	.40	.20	.10
605	Al Downing	.40	.20	.10
606	Milwaukee Brewers Team (Alex Grammas)	1.00	.50	.30
607	Rich Hinton	.40	.20	.10
608	Vic Correll	.40	.20	.10
609	Fred Norman	.40	.20	.10
610	Greg Luzinski	.75	.40	.25
611	Rich Folkers	.40	.20	.10
612	Joe Lahoud	.40	.20	.10
613	Tim Johnson	.40	.20	.10
614	Fernando Arroyo	.40	.20	.10
615	Mike Cubbage	.40	.20	.10
616	Buck Martinez	.40	.20	.10
617	Darold Knowles	.40	.20	.10
618	Jack Brohamer	.40	.20	.10
619	Bill Butler	.40	.20	.10
620	Al Oliver	.75	.40	.25
621	Tom Hall	.40	.20	.10
622	Rick Auerbach	.40	.20	.10
623	Bob Allietta	.40	.20	.10
624	Tony Taylor	.40	.20	.10

625	J.R. Richard	.40	.20	.10
626	Bob Sheldon	.40	.20	.10
627	Bill Plummer	.40	.20	.10
628	John D'Acquisto	.40	.20	.10
629	Sandy Alomar	.40	.20	.10
630	Chris Speier	.40	.20	.10
631	Atlanta Braves Team (Dave Bristol)	1.00	.50	.30
632	Rogelio Moret	.40	.20	.10
633	***John Stearns***	.40	.20	.10
634	Larry Christenson	.40	.20	.10
635	Jim Fregosi	.40	.20	.10
636	Joe Decker	.40	.20	.10
637	Bruce Bochte	.40	.20	.10
638	Doyle Alexander	.40	.20	.10
639	Fred Kendall	.40	.20	.10
640	Bill Madlock	.75	.40	.25
641	Tom Paciorek	.40	.20	.10
642	Dennis Blair	.40	.20	.10
643	Checklist 529-660	1.00	.50	.30
644	Tom Bradley	.40	.20	.10
645	Darrell Porter	.40	.20	.10
646	John Lowenstein	.40	.20	.10
647	Ramon Hernandez	.40	.20	.10
648	Al Cowens	.40	.20	.10
649	Dave Roberts	.40	.20	.10
650	Thurman Munson	6.00	3.00	1.75
651	John Odom	.40	.20	.10
652	Ed Armbrister	.40	.20	.10
653	***Mike Norris***	.40	.20	.10
654	Doug Griffin	.40	.20	.10
655	Mike Vail	.40	.20	.10
656	Chicago White Sox Team (Chuck Tanner)	1.00	.50	.30
657	***Roy Smalley***	.40	.20	.10
658	Jerry Johnson	.40	.20	.10
659	Ben Oglivie	.40	.20	.10
660	Dave Lopes	1.00	.50	.30

1976 Topps Traded

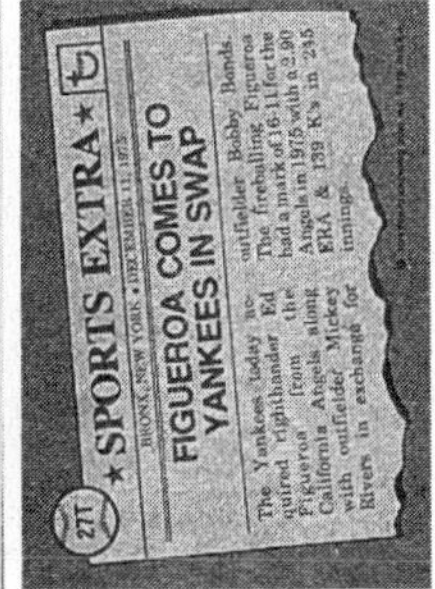

Similar to the Topps Traded set of 1974, the 2-1/2" x 3-1/2" cards feature photos of players traded after the printing deadline. The style of the cards is essentially the same as the regular issue, but with a large "Sports Extra" headline announcing the trade and its date. The backs continue in newspaper style to detail the specifics of the trade. There are 43 player cards and one checklist in the set. Numbers remain the same as the player's regular card, with the addition of a "T" suffix.

		NM	EX	VG
Complete Set (44):		20.00	10.00	6.00
Common Player:		.75	.35	.20
27T	Ed Figueroa	.75	.35	.20
28T	Dusty Baker	1.25	.60	.40
44T	Doug Rader	.75	.35	.20
58T	Ron Reed	.75	.35	.20
74T	Oscar Gamble	.75	.35	.20
80T	Jim Kaat	.75	.35	.20
83T	Jim Spencer	.75	.35	.20
85T	Mickey Rivers	.75	.35	.20
99T	Lee Lacy	.75	.35	.20
120T	Rusty Staub	.75	.35	.20
127T	Larvell Blanks	.75	.35	.20
146T	George Medich	.75	.35	.20
158T	Ken Reitz	.75	.35	.20
208T	Mike Lum	.75	.35	.20
211T	Clay Carroll	.75	.35	.20
231T	Tom House	.75	.35	.20
250T	Fergie Jenkins	3.00	1.50	.90
259T	Darrel Chaney	.75	.35	.20
292T	Leon Roberts	.75	.35	.20
296T	Pat Dobson	.75	.35	.20
309T	Bill Melton	.75	.35	.20
338T	Bob Bailey	.75	.35	.20
380T	Bobby Bonds	.75	.35	.20
383T	John Ellis	.75	.35	.20
385T	Mickey Lolich	.75	.35	.20
401T	Ken Brett	.75	.35	.20
410T	Ralph Garr	.75	.35	.20
411T	Bill Singer	.75	.35	.20
428T	Jim Crawford	.75	.35	.20
434T	Morris Nettles	.75	.35	.20
464T	Ken Henderson	.75	.35	.20
497T	Joe McIntosh	.75	.35	.20
524T	Pete Falcone	.75	.35	.20
527T	Mike Anderson	.75	.35	.20
528T	Dock Ellis	.75	.35	.20
532T	Milt May	.75	.35	.20
554T	Ray Fosse	.75	.35	.20
579T	Clay Kirby	.75	.35	.20
583T	Tommy Helms	.75	.35	.20
592T	Willie Randolph	.75	.35	.20
618T	Jack Brohamer	.75	.35	.20
632T	Rogelio Moret	.75	.35	.20
649T	Dave Roberts	.75	.35	.20
----	Traded Checklist	.75	.35	.20

1976 Topps Cloth Sticker Prototypes

Apparently produced to test different materials for the cloth sticker set which would be issued the following year, these prototypes were never issued. Each of the players can be found on four different types of material. The blank-backed stickers feature the card fronts as they appeared in the regular 1976 issue. It is unknown whether other players were produced for the test.

		NM	EX	VG
Common Player:		30.00	15.00	9.00
(1a)	Bob Apodaca (Silk)	30.00	15.00	9.00
(1b)	Bob Apodaca (Thin felt.)	30.00	15.00	9.00
(1c)	Bob Apodaca (Textured felt.)	60.00	30.00	18.00
(1d)	Bob Apodaca (Thick felt.)	30.00	15.00	9.00
(2a)	Duffy Dyer (Silk)	30.00	15.00	9.00
(2b)	Duffy Dyer (Thin felt.)	30.00	15.00	9.00
(2c)	Duffy Dyer (Textured felt.)	60.00	30.00	18.00
(2d)	Duffy Dyer (Thick felt.)	30.00	15.00	9.00

1976 Topps Team Checklist Sheet

Via a mail-in redemption (50¢ and a wrapper), collectors could receive an uncut sheet of the 24 team photo/checklist cards from the 1976 Topps baseball set. Measuring about 10-1/2" x 20-1/8", the sheet could be cut into individual team cards of standard size, though printed on stock that is lighter than pack-issued versions.

	NM	EX	VG
Complete Sheet:	35.00	17.50	10.00

1976 Topps Joe Garagiola

Topps produced this personal business card for long-time NBC announcer and former major leaguer Joe Garagiola. The front is in the format of a 1973 Topps card and has a color portrait. The back resembles the 1976 Topps card, is in black-and-white and provides contact information.

		NM	EX	VG
1	Joe Garagiola	20.00	10.00	6.00

1976 Topps/Dynamite Magazine Panels

In at least one issue of its "Dynamite" kids' magazine, Scholastic Book Club teamed with Topps to insert a six-card panel of its 1976 baseball issue. Values shown are for just the uncut panel; complete magazines would bear a small premium.

		NM	EX	VG
Complete Panel:		20.00	10.00	6.00
469	Rawly Eastwick			
471	Jim Burton			
474	Ray Corbin			
481	Rudy May			
482	Tim Hosley			
522	Ted Sizemore			

1977 Topps

The 1977 Topps Set is a 660-card effort featuring front designs dominated by a color photograph on which there is a facsimile autograph. Above the picture are the player's name, team and position. The backs of the 2-1/2" x 3-1/2" cards include personal and career statistics along with newspaper-style highlights and a cartoon. Specialty cards include statistical leaders, record performances, a new "Turn Back The Clock" feature which highlighted great past moments and a "Big League Brothers" feature.

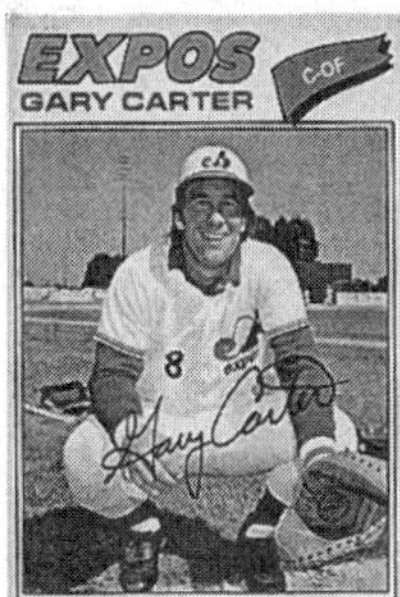

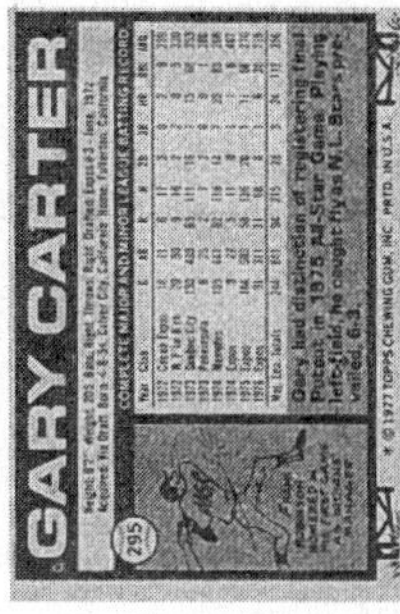

		NM	EX	VG
Complete Set (660):		200.00	95.00	55.00
Common Player:		.25	.10	.06
Wax Pack (10):		22.50		
Wax Box (36):		625.00		
Cello Pack (18):		50.00		
Cello Box (24):		1,200		
Rack Pack (39):		60.00		
Rack Box (24):		1,850		
Vending Box (500):		300.00		
1	Batting Leaders (George Brett, Bill Madlock)	6.00	3.00	1.75
2	Home Run Leaders (Graig Nettles, Mike Schmidt)	2.00	1.00	.60
3	RBI Leaders (George Foster, Lee May)	.75	.40	.25
4	Stolen Base Leaders (Dave Lopes, Bill North)	.50	.25	.15
5	Victory Leaders (Randy Jones, Jim Palmer)	1.00	.50	.30
6	Strikeout Leaders (Nolan Ryan, Tom Seaver)	10.00	5.00	3.00
7	ERA Leaders (John Denny, Mark Fidrych)	.50	.25	.15
8	Leading Firemen (Bill Campbell, Rawly Eastwick)	.25	.10	.06
9	Doug Rader	.25	.10	.06
10	Reggie Jackson	8.00	4.00	2.50
11	Rob Dressler	.25	.10	.06
12	Larry Haney	.25	.10	.06
13	Luis Gomez	.25	.10	.06
14	Tommy Smith	.25	.10	.06
15	Don Gullett	.25	.10	.06
16	Bob Jones	.25	.10	.06
17	Steve Stone	.25	.10	.06
18	Indians Team (Frank Robinson)	1.50	.70	.45
19	John D'Acquisto	.25	.10	.06
20	Graig Nettles	.75	.40	.25
21	Ken Forsch	.25	.10	.06
22	Bill Freehan	.25	.10	.06
23	Dan Driessen	.25	.10	.06
24	Carl Morton	.25	.10	.06
25	Dwight Evans	.75	.40	.25
26	Ray Sadecki	.25	.10	.06
27	Bill Buckner	.75	.40	.25
28	Woodie Fryman	.25	.10	.06
29	Bucky Dent	.50	.25	.15
30	Greg Luzinski	.50	.25	.15
31	Jim Todd	.25	.10	.06
32	Checklist 1-132	1.00	.50	.30
33	Wayne Garland	.25	.10	.06
34	Angels Team (Norm Sherry)	1.00	.50	.30
35	Rennie Stennett	.25	.10	.06
36	John Ellis	.25	.10	.06
37	Steve Hargan	.25	.10	.06
38	Craig Kusick	.25	.10	.06
39	Tom Griffin	.25	.10	.06
40	Bobby Murcer	.50	.25	.15
41	Jim Kern	.25	.10	.06
42	Jose Cruz	.25	.10	.06
43	Ray Bare	.25	.10	.06
44	Bud Harrelson	.25	.10	.06
45	Rawly Eastwick	.25	.10	.06
46	Buck Martinez	.25	.10	.06
47	Lynn McGlothen	.25	.10	.06
48	Tom Paciorek	.25	.10	.06
49	Grant Jackson	.25	.10	.06
50	Ron Cey	.50	.25	.15
51	Brewers Team (Alex Grammas)	1.00	.50	.30
52	Ellis Valentine	.25	.10	.06
53	Paul Mitchell	.25	.10	.06
54	Sandy Alomar	.25	.10	.06
55	Jeff Burroughs	.25	.10	.06
56	Rudy May	.25	.10	.06
57	Marc Hill	.25	.10	.06
58	Chet Lemon	.25	.10	.06
59	Larry Christenson	.25	.10	.06
60	Jim Rice	2.00	1.00	.60
61	Manny Sanguillen	.25	.10	.06
62	Eric Raich	.25	.10	.06
63	Tito Fuentes	.25	.10	.06
64	Larry Biittner	.25	.10	.06
65	Skip Lockwood	.25	.10	.06
66	Roy Smalley	.25	.10	.06
67	***Joaquin Andujar***	.50	.25	.15
68	Bruce Bochte	.25	.10	.06
69	Jim Crawford	.25	.10	.06
70	Johnny Bench	6.00	3.00	1.75
71	Dock Ellis	.25	.10	.06
72	Mike Anderson	.25	.10	.06
73	Charlie Williams	.25	.10	.06
74	A's Team (Jack McKeon)	1.00	.50	.30
75	Dennis Leonard	.25	.10	.06
76	Tim Foli	.25	.10	.06
77	Dyar Miller	.25	.10	.06
78	Bob Davis	.25	.10	.06

79	Don Money	.25	.10	.06
80	Andy Messersmith	.25	.10	.06
81	Juan Beniquez	.25	.10	.06
82	Jim Rooker	.25	.10	.06
83	Kevin Bell	.25	.10	.06
84	Ollie Brown	.25	.10	.06
85	Duane Kuiper	.25	.10	.06
86	Pat Zachry	.25	.10	.06
87	Glenn Borgmann	.25	.10	.06
88	Stan Wall	.25	.10	.06
89	***Butch Hobson***	.25	.10	.06
90	Cesar Cedeno	.25	.10	.06
91	John Verhoeven	.25	.10	.06
92	Dave Rosello	.25	.10	.06
93	Tom Poquette	.25	.10	.06
94	Craig Swan	.25	.10	.06
95	Keith Hernandez	.75	.40	.25
96	Lou Piniella	.75	.40	.25
97	Dave Heaverlo	.25	.10	.06
98	Milt May	.25	.10	.06
99	Tom Hausman	.25	.10	.06
100	Joe Morgan	3.00	1.50	.90
101	Dick Bosman	.25	.10	.06
102	Jose Morales	.25	.10	.06
103	Mike Bacsik	.25	.10	.06
104	***Omar Moreno***	.50	.25	.15
105	Steve Yeager	.50	.25	.15
106	Mike Flanagan	.50	.25	.15
107	Bill Melton	.25	.10	.06
108	Alan Foster	.25	.10	.06
109	Jorge Orta	.25	.10	.06
110	Steve Carlton	4.00	2.00	1.25
111	Rico Petrocelli	.50	.25	.15
112	Bill Greif	.25	.10	.06
113	Blue Jays Mgr./Coaches (Roy Hartsfield, Don Leppert, Bob Miller, Jackie Moore, Harry Warner)	.75	.40	.25
114	Bruce Dal Canton	.25	.10	.06
115	Rick Manning	.25	.10	.06
116	Joe Niekro	.25	.10	.06
117	Frank White	.25	.10	.06
118	Rick Jones	.25	.10	.06
119	John Stearns	.25	.10	.06
120	Rod Carew	3.00	1.50	.90
121	Gary Nolan	.25	.10	.06
122	Ben Oglivie	.25	.10	.06
123	Fred Stanley	.25	.10	.06
124	George Mitterwald	.25	.10	.06
125	Bill Travers	.25	.10	.06
126	Rod Gilbreath	.25	.10	.06
127	Ron Fairly	.25	.10	.06
128	Tommy John	.50	.25	.15
129	Mike Sadek	.25	.10	.06
130	Al Oliver	.75	.40	.25
131	Orlando Ramirez	.25	.10	.06
132	Chip Lang	.25	.10	.06
133	Ralph Garr	.25	.10	.06
134	Padres Team (John McNamara)	.75	.40	.25
135	Mark Belanger	.25	.10	.06
136	***Jerry Mumphrey***	.25	.10	.06
137	Jeff Terpko	.25	.10	.06
138	Bob Stinson	.25	.10	.06
139	Fred Norman	.25	.10	.06
140	Mike Schmidt	10.00	5.00	3.00
141	Mark Littell	.25	.10	.06
142	Steve Dillard	.25	.10	.06
143	Ed Herrmann	.25	.10	.06
144	***Bruce Sutter***	15.00	7.50	4.50
145	Tom Veryzer	.25	.10	.06
146	Dusty Baker	1.00	.50	.30
147	Jackie Brown	.25	.10	.06
148	Fran Healy	.25	.10	.06
149	Mike Cubbage	.25	.10	.06
150	Tom Seaver	6.00	3.00	1.75
151	Johnnie LeMaster	.25	.10	.06
152	Gaylord Perry	2.50	1.25	.70
153	Ron Jackson	.25	.10	.06
154	Dave Giusti	.25	.10	.06
155	Joe Rudi	.25	.10	.06
156	Pete Mackanin	.25	.10	.06
157	Ken Brett	.25	.10	.06
158	Ted Kubiak	.25	.10	.06
159	Bernie Carbo	.25	.10	.06
160	Will McEnaney	.25	.10	.06
161	***Garry Templeton***	1.00	.50	.30
162	Mike Cuellar	.25	.10	.06
163	Dave Hilton	.25	.10	.06
164	Tug McGraw	.25	.10	.06
165	Jim Wynn	.25	.10	.06
166	Bill Campbell	.25	.10	.06
167	Rich Hebner	.25	.10	.06
168	Charlie Spikes	.25	.10	.06
169	Darold Knowles	.25	.10	.06
170	Thurman Munson	6.00	3.00	1.75
171	Ken Sanders	.25	.10	.06
172	John Milner	.25	.10	.06
173	Chuck Scrivener	.25	.10	.06
174	Nelson Briles	.25	.10	.06
175	***Butch Wynegar***	.25	.10	.06
176	Bob Robertson	.25	.10	.06
177	Bart Johnson	.25	.10	.06
178	Bombo Rivera	.25	.10	.06
179	Paul Hartzell	.25	.10	.06
180	Dave Lopes	.50	.25	.15
181	Ken McMullen	.25	.10	.06
182	Dan Spillner	.25	.10	.06
183	Cardinals Team (Vern Rapp)	1.00	.50	.30
184	Bo McLaughlin	.25	.10	.06
185	Sixto Lezcano	.25	.10	.06
186	Doug Flynn	.25	.10	.06
187	Dick Pole	.25	.10	.06
188	Bob Tolan	.25	.10	.06
189	Rick Dempsey	.25	.10	.06
190	Ray Burris	.25	.10	.06
191	Doug Griffin	.25	.10	.06
192	Clarence Gaston	.25	.10	.06
193	Larry Gura	.25	.10	.06
194	Gary Matthews	.25	.10	.06
195	Ed Figueroa	.25	.10	.06
196	Len Randle	.25	.10	.06
197	Ed Ott	.25	.10	.06
198	Wilbur Wood	.25	.10	.06
199	Pepe Frias	.25	.10	.06
200	Frank Tanana	.25	.10	.06
201	Ed Kranepool	.25	.10	.06
202	Tom Johnson	.25	.10	.06
203	Ed Armbrister	.25	.10	.06
204	Jeff Newman	.25	.10	.06
205	Pete Falcone	.25	.10	.06
206	Boog Powell	.75	.40	.25
207	Glenn Abbott	.25	.10	.06
208	Checklist 133-264	.75	.40	.25
209	Rob Andrews	.25	.10	.06
210	Fred Lynn	.50	.25	.15
211	Giants Team (Joe Altobelli)	.75	.40	.25
212	Jim Mason	.25	.10	.06
213	Maximino Leon	.25	.10	.06
214	Darrell Porter	.25	.10	.06
215	Butch Metzger	.25	.10	.06
216	Doug DeCinces	.25	.10	.06
217	Tom Underwood	.25	.10	.06
218	***John Wathan***	.25	.10	.06
219	Joe Coleman	.25	.10	.06
220	Chris Chambliss	.50	.25	.15
221	Bob Bailey	.25	.10	.06
222	Francisco Barrios	.25	.10	.06
223	Earl Williams	.25	.10	.06
224	Rusty Torres	.25	.10	.06
225	Bob Apodaca	.25	.10	.06
226	Leroy Stanton	.25	.10	.06
227	***Joe Sambito***	.25	.10	.06
228	Twins Team (Gene Mauch)	1.00	.50	.30
229	Don Kessinger	.25	.10	.06
230	Vida Blue	.25	.10	.06
231	George Brett (Record Breaker)	5.00	2.50	1.50
232	Minnie Minoso (Record Breaker)	.50	.25	.15
233	Jose Morales (Record Breaker)	.50	.25	.15
234	Nolan Ryan (Record Breaker)	10.00	5.00	3.00
235	Cecil Cooper	.25	.10	.06
236	Tom Buskey	.25	.10	.06
237	Gene Clines	.25	.10	.06
238	Tippy Martinez	.25	.10	.06
239	Bill Plummer	.25	.10	.06
240	Ron LeFlore	.25	.10	.06
241	Dave Tomlin	.25	.10	.06
242	Ken Henderson	.25	.10	.06
243	Ron Reed	.25	.10	.06
244	John Mayberry	.25	.10	.06
245	Rick Rhoden	.25	.10	.06
246	Mike Vail	.25	.10	.06
247	Chris Knapp	.25	.10	.06
248	Wilbur Howard	.25	.10	.06
249	Pete Redfern	.25	.10	.06
250	Bill Madlock	.50	.25	.15
251	Tony Muser	.25	.10	.06
252	Dale Murray	.25	.10	.06
253	John Hale	.25	.10	.06
254	Doyle Alexander	.25	.10	.06
255	George Scott	.25	.10	.06
256	Joe Hoerner	.25	.10	.06
257	Mike Miley	.25	.10	.06
258	Luis Tiant	.50	.25	.15
259	Mets Team (Joe Frazier)	1.00	.50	.30
260	J.R. Richard	.25	.10	.06
261	Phil Garner	.50	.25	.15
262	Al Cowens	.25	.10	.06
263	Mike Marshall	.25	.10	.06
264	Tom Hutton	.25	.10	.06
265	***Mark Fidrych***	5.00	2.50	1.50
266	Derrel Thomas	.25	.10	.06
267	Ray Fosse	.25	.10	.06
268	Rick Sawyer	.25	.10	.06
269	Joe Lis	.25	.10	.06
270	Dave Parker	.50	.25	.15
271	Terry Forster	.25	.10	.06
272	Lee Lacy	.25	.10	.06
273	Eric Soderholm	.25	.10	.06
274	Don Stanhouse	.25	.10	.06
275	Mike Hargrove	.25	.10	.06
276	A.L. Championship (Chambliss' Dramatic Homer Decides It)	.25	.13	.08
277	N.L. Championship (Reds Sweep Phillies 3 In Row)	3.00	1.50	.90
278	Danny Frisella	.25	.10	.06
279	Joe Wallis	.25	.10	.06
280	Jim Hunter	2.50	1.25	.70
281	Roy Staiger	.25	.10	.06
282	Sid Monge	.25	.10	.06
283	Jerry DaVanon	.25	.10	.06
284	Mike Norris	.25	.10	.06
285	Brooks Robinson	4.00	2.00	1.25
286	Johnny Grubb	.25	.10	.06
287	Reds Team (Sparky Anderson)	1.00	.50	.30
288	Bob Montgomery	.25	.10	.06
289	Gene Garber	.25	.10	.06
290	Amos Otis	.25	.10	.06
291	***Jason Thompson***	.25	.10	.06
292	Rogelio Moret	.25	.10	.06
293	Jack Brohamer	.25	.10	.06
294	George Medich	.25	.10	.06
295	Gary Carter	3.00	1.50	.90
296	Don Hood	.25	.10	.06
297	Ken Reitz	.25	.10	.06
298	Charlie Hough	.25	.10	.06
299	Otto Velez	.25	.10	.06
300	Jerry Koosman	.25	.10	.06
301	Toby Harrah	.25	.10	.06
302	Mike Garman	.25	.10	.06
303	Gene Tenace	.25	.10	.06
304	Jim Hughes	.25	.10	.06
305	Mickey Rivers	.25	.10	.06
306	Rick Waits	.25	.10	.06
307	Gary Sutherland	.25	.10	.06
308	Gene Pentz	.25	.10	.06
309	Red Sox Team (Don Zimmer)	1.50	.70	.45
310	Larry Bowa	.50	.25	.15
311	Vern Ruhle	.25	.10	.06
312	Rob Belloir	.25	.10	.06
313	Paul Blair	.25	.10	.06
314	Steve Mingori	.25	.10	.06
315	Dave Chalk	.25	.10	.06
316	Steve Rogers	.25	.10	.06
317	Kurt Bevacqua	.25	.10	.06
318	Duffy Dyer	.25	.10	.06
319	Rich Gossage	.75	.40	.25
320	Ken Griffey	.75	.40	.25
321	Dave Goltz	.25	.10	.06
322	Bill Russell	.50	.25	.15
323	Larry Lintz	.25	.10	.06
324	John Curtis	.25	.10	.06
325	Mike Ivie	.25	.10	.06
326	Jesse Jefferson	.25	.10	.06
327	Astros Team (Bill Virdon)	.75	.40	.25
328	Tommy Boggs	.25	.10	.06
329	Ron Hodges	.25	.10	.06
330	George Hendrick	.25	.10	.06
331	Jim Colborn	.25	.10	.06
332	Elliott Maddox	.25	.10	.06
333	Paul Reuschel	.25	.10	.06
334	Bill Stein	.25	.10	.06
335	Bill Robinson	.25	.10	.06
336	Denny Doyle	.25	.10	.06
337	Ron Schueler	.25	.10	.06
338	Dave Duncan	.25	.10	.06
339	Adrian Devine	.25	.10	.06
340	Hal McRae	.50	.25	.15
341	Joe Kerrigan	.25	.10	.06
342	Jerry Remy	.25	.10	.06
343	Ed Halicki	.25	.10	.06
344	Brian Downing	.25	.10	.06
345	Reggie Smith	.25	.10	.06
346	Bill Singer	.25	.10	.06
347	George Foster	.25	.10	.06
348	Brent Strom	.25	.10	.06
349	Jim Holt	.25	.10	.06
350	Larry Dierker	.25	.10	.06
351	Jim Sundberg	.25	.10	.06
352	Mike Phillips	.25	.10	.06
353	Stan Thomas	.25	.10	.06
354	Pirates Team (Chuck Tanner)	.75	.40	.25
355	Lou Brock	3.00	1.50	.90
356	Checklist 265-396	.75	.40	.25
357	Tim McCarver	.75	.40	.25
358	Tom House	.25	.10	.06
359	Willie Randolph	.75	.40	.25
360	Rick Monday	.25	.10	.06
361	Eduardo Rodriguez	.25	.10	.06
362	Tommy Davis	.25	.10	.06
363	Dave Roberts	.25	.10	.06
364	Vic Correll	.25	.10	.06
365	Mike Torrez	.25	.10	.06
366	Ted Sizemore	.25	.10	.06
367	Dave Hamilton	.25	.10	.06
368	Mike Jorgensen	.25	.10	.06
369	Terry Humphrey	.25	.10	.06
370	John Montefusco	.25	.10	.06
371	Royals Team (Whitey Herzog)	1.00	.50	.30
372	Rich Folkers	.25	.10	.06
373	Bert Campaneris	.25	.10	.06
374	Kent Tekulve	.25	.10	.06
375	Larry Hisle	.25	.10	.06
376	Nino Espinosa	.25	.10	.06
377	Dave McKay	.25	.10	.06
378	Jim Umbarger	.25	.10	.06
379	Larry Cox	.25	.10	.06
380	Lee May	.25	.10	.06
381	Bob Forsch	.25	.10	.06
382	Charlie Moore	.25	.10	.06
383	Stan Bahnsen	.25	.10	.06
384	Darrel Chaney	.25	.10	.06
385	Dave LaRoche	.25	.10	.06
386	Manny Mota	.25	.10	.06
387	Yankees Team (Billy Martin)	2.00	1.00	.60
388	Terry Harmon	.25	.10	.06
389	Ken Kravec	.25	.10	.06
390	Dave Winfield	3.00	1.50	.90
391	Dan Warthen	.25	.10	.06
392	Phil Roof	.25	.10	.06
393	John Lowenstein	.25	.10	.06
394	Bill Laxton	.25	.10	.06
395	Manny Trillo	.25	.10	.06
396	Tom Murphy	.25	.10	.06
397	***Larry Herndon***	.25	.10	.06
398	Tom Burgmeier	.25	.10	.06
399	Bruce Boisclair	.25	.10	.06
400	Steve Garvey	2.00	1.00	.60
401	Mickey Scott	.25	.10	.06
402	Tommy Helms	.25	.10	.06
403	Tom Grieve	.25	.10	.06
404	Eric Rasmussen	.25	.10	.06
405	Claudell Washington	.25	.10	.06
406	Tim Johnson	.25	.10	.06
407	Dave Freisleben	.25	.10	.06
408	Cesar Tovar	.25	.10	.06
409	Pete Broberg	.25	.10	.06
410	Willie Montanez	.25	.10	.06
411	World Series Games 1 & 2 (Joe Morgan, Johnny Bench)	2.00	1.00	.60
412	World Series Games 3 & 4 (Johnny Bench)	2.00	1.00	.60
413	World Series Summary	.75	.40	.25
414	Tommy Harper	.25	.10	.06
415	Jay Johnstone	.25	.10	.06
416	Chuck Hartenstein	.25	.10	.06
417	Wayne Garrett	.25	.10	.06
418	White Sox Team (Bob Lemon)	1.00	.50	.30
419	Steve Swisher	.25	.10	.06

420	Rusty Staub	.50	.25	.15
421	Doug Rau	.25	.10	.06
422	Freddie Patek	.25	.10	.06
423	Gary Lavelle	.25	.10	.06
424	Steve Brye	.25	.10	.06
425	Joe Torre	1.00	.50	.30
426	Dick Drago	.25	.10	.06
427	Dave Rader	.25	.10	.06
428	Rangers Team (Frank Lucchesi)	.75	.40	.25
429	Ken Boswell	.25	.10	.06
430	Fergie Jenkins	2.50	1.25	.70
431	Dave Collins	.25	.10	.06
432	Buzz Capra	.25	.10	.06
433	Nate Colbert (Turn Back The Clock)	.25	.10	.06
434	Carl Yastrzemski (Turn Back The Clock)	1.50	.70	.45
435	Maury Wills (Turn Back The Clock)	.50	.25	.15
436	Bob Keegan (Turn Back The Clock)	.25	.10	.06
437	Ralph Kiner (Turn Back The Clock)	.75	.40	.25
438	Marty Perez	.25	.10	.06
439	Gorman Thomas	.25	.10	.06
440	Jon Matlack	.25	.10	.06
441	Larvell Blanks	.25	.10	.06
442	Braves Team (Dave Bristol)	1.00	.50	.30
443	Lamar Johnson	.25	.10	.06
444	Wayne Twitchell	.25	.10	.06
445	Ken Singleton	.25	.10	.06
446	Bill Bonham	.25	.10	.06
447	Jerry Turner	.25	.10	.06
448	Ellie Rodriguez	.25	.10	.06
449	Al Fitzmorris	.25	.10	.06
450	Pete Rose	15.00	7.50	4.50
451	Checklist 397-528	1.00	.50	.30
452	Mike Caldwell	.25	.10	.06
453	Pedro Garcia	.25	.10	.06
454	Andy Etchebarren	.25	.10	.06
455	Rick Wise	.25	.10	.06
456	Leon Roberts	.25	.10	.06
457	Steve Luebber	.25	.10	.06
458	Leo Foster	.25	.10	.06
459	Steve Foucault	.25	.10	.06
460	Willie Stargell	4.00	2.00	1.25
461	Dick Tidrow	.25	.10	.06
462	Don Baylor	.30	.15	.10
463	Jamie Quirk	.25	.10	.06
464	Randy Moffitt	.25	.10	.06
465	Rico Carty	.25	.10	.06
466	Fred Holdsworth	.25	.10	.06
467	Phillies Team (Danny Ozark)	.50	.25	.15
468	Ramon Hernandez	.25	.10	.06
469	Pat Kelly	.25	.10	.06
470	Ted Simmons	.50	.25	.15
471	Del Unser	.25	.10	.06
472	Rookie Pitchers (**Don Aase, Bob McClure, Gil Patterson** (Photo is Sheldon Gill.), Dave Wehrmeister)	.25	.10	.06
473	Rookie Outfielders (***Andre Dawson, Gene Richards, John Scott, Denny Walling***)	15.00	7.50	4.50
474	Rookie Shortstops (**Bob Bailor, Kiko Garcia, Craig Reynolds, Alex Taveras**)	.25	.10	.06
475	Rookie Pitchers (**Chris Batton, Rick Camp, Scott McGregor, Manny Sarmiento**)	.25	.10	.06
476	Rookie Catchers (***Gary Alexander, Rick Cerone, Dale Murphy, Kevin Pasley***)	12.00	6.00	3.50
477	Rookie Infielders (**Doug Ault, Rich Dauer, Orlando Gonzalez, Phil Mankowski**)	.25	.10	.06
478	Rookie Pitchers (**Jim Gideon, Leon Hooten, Dave Johnson, Mark Lemongello**)	.25	.10	.06
479	Rookie Outfielders (**Brian Asselstine, Wayne Gross, Sam Mejias, Alvis Woods**)	.25	.10	.06
480	Carl Yastrzemski	6.00	3.00	1.75
481	Roger Metzger	.25	.10	.06
482	Tony Solaita	.25	.10	.06
483	Richie Zisk	.25	.10	.06
484	Burt Hooton	.25	.10	.06
485	Roy White	.25	.10	.06
486	Ed Bane	.25	.10	.06
487	Rookie Pitchers (**Larry Anderson, Ed Glynn, Joe Henderson, Greg Terlecky**)	.25	.10	.06
488	Rookie Outfielders (***Jack Clark, Ruppert Jones, Lee Mazzilli, Dan Thomas***)	3.00	1.50	.90
489	Rookie Pitchers (**Len Barker, Randy Lerch, Greg Minton, Mike Overy**)	.75	.40	.25
490	Rookie Shortstops (**Billy Almon, Mickey Klutts, Tommy McMillan, Mark Wagner**)	.25	.10	.06
491	Rookie Pitchers (***Mike Dupree, Dennis Martinez, Craig Mitchell, Bob Sykes***)	3.00	1.50	.90
492	Rookie Outfielders (***Tony Armas, Steve Kemp, Carlos Lopez, Gary Woods***)	.75	.40	.25
493	Rookie Pitchers (**Mike Krukow, Jim Otten, Gary Wheelock, Mike Willis**)	.25	.10	.06
494	Rookie Infielders (***Juan Bernhardt, Mike Champion, Jim Gantner, Bump Wills***)	1.00	.50	.30
495	Al Hrabosky	.50	.25	.15
496	Gary Thomasson	.25	.10	.06
497	Clay Carroll	.25	.10	.06
498	Sal Bando	.25	.10	.06
499	Pablo Torrealba	.25	.10	.06
500	Dave Kingman	.75	.40	.25
501	Jim Bibby	.25	.10	.06
502	Randy Hundley	.25	.10	.06
503	Bill Lee	.25	.10	.06
504	Dodgers Team (Tom Lasorda)	1.50	.70	.45
505	Oscar Gamble	.50	.25	.15
506	Steve Grilli	.25	.10	.06
507	Mike Hegan	.25	.10	.06
508	Dave Pagan	.25	.10	.06
509	Cookie Rojas	.25	.10	.06
510	John Candelaria	.25	.10	.06
511	Bill Fahey	.25	.10	.06
512	Jack Billingham	.25	.10	.06
513	Jerry Terrell	.25	.10	.06
514	Cliff Johnson	.25	.10	.06
515	Chris Speier	.25	.10	.06
516	Bake McBride	.25	.10	.06
517	***Pete Vuckovich***	.50	.25	.15
518	Cubs Team (Herman Franks)	1.00	.50	.30
519	Don Kirkwood	.25	.10	.06
520	Garry Maddox	.50	.25	.15
521	Bob Grich	.25	.10	.06
522	Enzo Hernandez	.25	.10	.06
523	Rollie Fingers	2.50	1.25	.70
524	Rowland Office	.25	.10	.06
525	Dennis Eckersley	4.00	2.00	1.25
526	Larry Parrish	.25	.10	.06
527	Dan Meyer	.25	.10	.06
528	Bill Castro	.25	.10	.06
529	Jim Essian	.25	.10	.06
530	Rick Reuschel	.25	.10	.06
531	Lyman Bostock	.25	.10	.06
532	Jim Willoughby	.25	.10	.06
533	Mickey Stanley	.25	.10	.06
534	Paul Splittorff	.25	.10	.06
535	Cesar Geronimo	.25	.10	.06
536	Vic Albury	.25	.10	.06
537	Dave Roberts	.25	.10	.06
538	Frank Taveras	.25	.10	.06
539	Mike Wallace	.25	.10	.06
540	Bob Watson	.25	.10	.06
541	John Denny	.25	.10	.06
542	Frank Duffy	.25	.10	.06
543	Ron Blomberg	.25	.10	.06
544	Gary Ross	.25	.10	.06
545	Bob Boone	.25	.10	.06
546	Orioles Team (Earl Weaver)	1.50	.70	.45
547	Willie McCovey	3.00	1.50	.90
548	***Joel Youngblood***	.25	.10	.06
549	Jerry Royster	.25	.10	.06
550	Randy Jones	.25	.10	.06
551	Bill North	.25	.10	.06
552	Pepe Mangual	.25	.10	.06
553	Jack Heidemann	.25	.10	.06
554	Bruce Kimm	.25	.10	.06
555	Dan Ford	.25	.10	.06
556	Doug Bird	.25	.10	.06
557	Jerry White	.25	.10	.06
558	Elias Sosa	.25	.10	.06
559	Alan Bannister	.25	.10	.06
560	Dave Concepcion	.25	.10	.06
561	Pete LaCock	.25	.10	.06
562	Checklist 529-660	.75	.40	.25
563	Bruce Kison	.25	.10	.06
564	Alan Ashby	.25	.10	.06
565	Mickey Lolich	.50	.25	.15
566	Rick Miller	.25	.10	.06
567	Enos Cabell	.25	.10	.06
568	Carlos May	.25	.10	.06
569	Jim Lonborg	.25	.10	.06
570	Bobby Bonds	.75	.40	.25
571	Darrell Evans	.25	.10	.06
572	Ross Grimsley	.25	.10	.06
573	Joe Ferguson	.25	.10	.06
574	Aurelio Rodriguez	.25	.10	.06
575	Dick Ruthven	.25	.10	.06
576	Fred Kendall	.25	.10	.06
577	Jerry Augustine	.25	.10	.06
578	Bob Randall	.25	.10	.06
579	Don Carrithers	.25	.10	.06
580	George Brett	12.00	6.00	3.50
581	Pedro Borbon	.25	.10	.06
582	Ed Kirkpatrick	.25	.10	.06
583	Paul Lindblad	.25	.10	.06
584	Ed Goodson	.25	.10	.06
585	Rick Burleson	.25	.10	.06
586	Steve Renko	.25	.10	.06
587	Rick Baldwin	.25	.10	.06
588	Dave Moates	.25	.10	.06
589	Mike Cosgrove	.25	.10	.06
590	Buddy Bell	.25	.10	.06
591	Chris Arnold	.25	.10	.06
592	Dan Briggs	.25	.10	.06
593	Dennis Blair	.25	.10	.06
594	Biff Pocoroba	.25	.10	.06
595	John Hiller	.25	.10	.06
596	***Jerry Martin***	.25	.10	.06
597	Mariners Mgr./Coaches (Don Bryant, Jim Busby, Darrell Johnson, Vada Pinson, Wes Stock)	1.00	.50	.30
598	Sparky Lyle	.25	.10	.06
599	Mike Tyson	.25	.10	.06
600	Jim Palmer	3.00	1.50	.90
601	Mike Lum	.25	.10	.06
602	Andy Hassler	.25	.10	.06
603	Willie Davis	.25	.10	.06
604	Jim Slaton	.25	.10	.06
605	Felix Millan	.25	.10	.06
606	Steve Braun	.25	.10	.06
607	Larry Demery	.25	.10	.06
608	Roy Howell	.25	.10	.06
609	Jim Barr	.25	.10	.06
610	Jose Cardenal	.25	.10	.06
611	Dave Lemanczyk	.25	.10	.06
612	Barry Foote	.25	.10	.06
613	Reggie Cleveland	.25	.10	.06
614	Greg Gross	.25	.10	.06
615	Phil Niekro	2.50	1.25	.70
616	Tommy Sandt	.25	.10	.06
617	Bobby Darwin	.25	.10	.06
618	Pat Dobson	.25	.10	.06
619	Johnny Oates	.25	.10	.06
620	Don Sutton	2.50	1.25	.70
621	Tigers Team (Ralph Houk)	1.00	.50	.30
622	Jim Wohlford	.25	.10	.06
623	Jack Kucek	.25	.10	.06
624	Hector Cruz	.25	.10	.06
625	Ken Holtzman	.25	.10	.06
626	Al Bumbry	.25	.10	.06
627	Bob Myrick	.25	.10	.06
628	Mario Guerrero	.25	.10	.06
629	Bobby Valentine	.25	.10	.06
630	Bert Blyleven	.75	.40	.25
631	Big League Brothers (George Brett, Ken Brett)	5.00	2.50	1.50
632	Big League Brothers (Bob Forsch, Ken Forsch)	.25	.10	.06
633	Big League Brothers (Carlos May, Lee May)	.25	.10	.06
634	Big League Brothers (Paul Reuschel, Rick Reuschel) (Names switched.)	.25	.10	.06
635	Robin Yount	5.00	2.50	1.50
636	Santo Alcala	.25	.10	.06
637	Alex Johnson	.25	.10	.06
638	Jim Kaat	.50	.25	.15
639	Jerry Morales	.25	.10	.06
640	Carlton Fisk	4.00	2.00	1.25
641	Dan Larson	.25	.10	.06
642	Willie Crawford	.25	.10	.06
643	Mike Pazik	.25	.10	.06
644	Matt Alexander	.25	.10	.06
645	Jerry Reuss	.25	.10	.06
646	Andres Mora	.25	.10	.06
647	Expos Team (Dick Williams)	.75	.40	.25
648	Jim Spencer	.25	.10	.06
649	Dave Cash	.25	.10	.06
650	Nolan Ryan	25.00	12.50	7.50
651	Von Joshua	.25	.10	.06
652	Tom Walker	.25	.10	.06
653	Diego Segui	.25	.10	.06
654	Ron Pruitt	.25	.10	.06
655	Tony Perez	3.00	1.50	.90
656	Ron Guidry	1.00	.50	.30
657	Mick Kelleher	.25	.10	.06
658	Marty Pattin	.25	.10	.06
659	Merv Rettenmund	.25	.10	.06
660	Willie Horton	1.00	.50	.30

1977 Topps Proofs

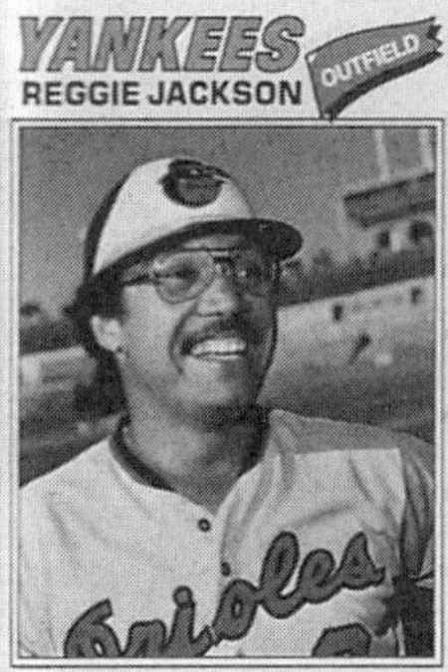

Perhaps the most sought-after Topps proof card is the 1977 blank-back featuring Reggie Jackson in an Orioles uniform but designating his team as the Yankees, with whom he signed as a free agent prior to the 1977 season. Less well-known are a group of other players' cards that have uniform/team variations from the regularly issued versions. All of the handful of known examples were hand-cut from sheets. Backs are blank.

	NM	EX	VG
Don Baylor	350.00	175.00	100.00
Rollie Fingers	900.00	450.00	275.00
Al Fitzmorris	300.00	150.00	90.00
Wayne Garland	300.00	150.00	90.00
Bill Greif	200.00	100.00	60.00
Reggie Jackson (5/04 auction)	6,000		
Pat Kelly	300.00	150.00	90.00
Gary Matthews	450.00	225.00	135.00
Dan Meyer	300.00	150.00	90.00
Bill Singer	200.00	100.00	60.00
Steve Stone	350.00	175.00	100.00
Gene Tenace	425.00	210.00	125.00

1977 Topps Team Checklist Sheet

A redemption offer on packs of 1977 Topps cards offered an uncut sheet of the 26 team/checklist cards by mail. Besides the perforated team cards, the 10-1/2" x 22-1/2" sheet has a card offering collectors a card locker. The cards on the sheet are identical to the single team/checklist cards issued in packs, except they are printed on thinner card stock.

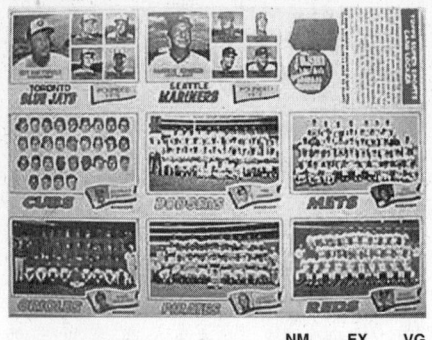

	NM	EX	VG
Uncut Sheet	35.00	17.50	10.50

1977 Topps/Dynamite Magazine Panels

In at least two issues of its "Dynamite" kids' magazine, Scholastic Book Club teamed with Topps to insert a six-card panel of its 1977 baseball issue. Values shown are for just the uncut panel; complete magazines would bear a small premium.

		NM	EX	VG
Complete Panel Set (2):		50.00	25.00	15.00
	PANEL 1	25.00	12.50	7.50
215	Butch Metzger			
335	Bill Robinson			
599	Mike Tyson			
625	Ken Holtzman			
630	Bert Blyleven			
641	Dan Larson			
	PANEL 2	30.00	15.00	9.00
242	Ken Henderson			
294	George Medich			
415	Jay Johnstone			
535	Cesar Geronimo			
580	George Brett			
626	Al Bumbry			

1977 Topps Cloth Stickers

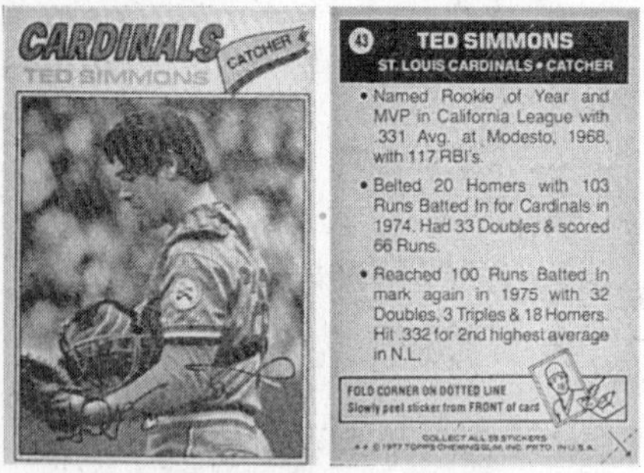

One of the few Topps specialty issues of the late 1970s, the 73-piece set of cloth stickers issued in 1977 includes 55 player stickers and 18 puzzle cards which could be joined to form a photo of the American League or National League All-Star teams. Issued as a separate issue, the 2-1/2" x 3-1/2" stickers have a paper backing which could be removed to allow the cloth to be adhered to a jacket, notebook, etc.

		NM	EX	VG
Complete Set (73):		75.00	37.70	22.50
Common Player:		1.00	.50	.30
Wax Pack:		12.50		
Wax Box (36):		325.00		
1	Alan Ashby	1.00	.50	.30
2	Buddy Bell	1.00	.50	.30
3	Johnny Bench	5.00	2.50	1.50
4	Vida Blue	1.00	.50	.30
5	Bert Blyleven	1.00	.50	.30
6	Steve Braun	1.00	.50	.30
7	George Brett	8.00	4.00	2.50
8	Lou Brock	4.00	2.00	1.25
9	Jose Cardenal	1.00	.50	.30
10	Rod Carew	5.00	2.50	1.50
11	Steve Carlton	4.00	2.00	1.25
12	Dave Cash	1.00	.50	.30
13	Cesar Cedeno	1.00	.50	.30
14	Ron Cey	1.00	.50	.30
15	Mark Fidrych	2.50	1.25	.70
16	Dan Ford	1.00	.50	.30
17	Wayne Garland	1.00	.50	.30
18	Ralph Garr	1.00	.50	.30
19	Steve Garvey	2.00	1.00	.60
20	Mike Hargrove	1.00	.50	.30
21	Catfish Hunter	3.00	1.50	.90
22	Reggie Jackson	8.00	4.00	2.50
23	Randy Jones	1.00	.50	.30
24	Dave Kingman	1.00	.50	.30
25	Bill Madlock	1.00	.50	.30
26	Lee May	1.00	.50	.30
27	John Mayberry	1.00	.50	.30
28	Andy Messersmith	1.00	.50	.30
29	Willie Montanez	1.00	.50	.30
30	John Montefusco	1.00	.50	.30
31	Joe Morgan	4.00	2.00	1.25
32	Thurman Munson	4.00	2.00	1.25
33	Bobby Murcer	1.00	.50	.30
34	Al Oliver	1.00	.50	.30
35	Dave Pagan	1.00	.50	.30
36	Jim Palmer	4.00	2.00	1.25
37	Tony Perez	3.00	1.50	.90
38	Pete Rose	10.00	5.00	3.00
39	Joe Rudi	1.00	.50	.30
40	Nolan Ryan	20.00	10.00	6.00
41	Mike Schmidt	8.00	4.00	2.50
42	Tom Seaver	5.00	2.50	1.50
43	Ted Simmons	1.00	.50	.30
44	Bill Singer	1.00	.50	.30
45	Willie Stargell	4.00	2.00	1.25
46	Rusty Staub	1.25	.60	.40
47	Don Sutton	3.00	1.50	.90
48	Luis Tiant	1.00	.50	.30
49	Bill Travers	1.00	.50	.30
50	Claudell Washington	1.00	.50	.30
51	Bob Watson	1.00	.50	.30
52	Dave Winfield	4.00	2.00	1.25
53	Carl Yastrzemski	7.00	3.50	2.00
54	Robin Yount	4.00	2.00	1.25
55	Richie Zisk	1.00	.50	.30
---	American League Nine-Piece Puzzle	6.00	3.00	1.75
---	National League Nine-Piece Puzzle	6.00	3.00	1.75

1978 Topps

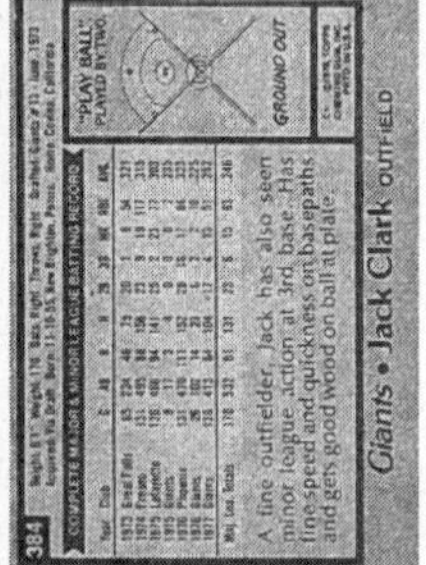

At 726 cards, this was the largest issue from Topps since 1972. In design, the color player photo is slightly larger than usual, with the player's name and team at the bottom. In the upper right-hand corner of the 2-1/2" x 3-1/2" cards, there is a small white baseball with the player's position. Most of the starting All-Stars from the previous year had a red, white and blue shield instead of the baseball. Backs feature statistics and a baseball situation which made a card game of baseball possible. Specialty cards include baseball records, statistical leaders and the World Series and playoffs. As one row of cards per sheet had to be double-printed to accommodate the 726-card set size, some cards are more common, yet that seems to have no serious impact on their prices.

		NM	EX	VG
Complete Set (726):		200.00	100.00	45.00
Common Player:		.20	.10	.06
Wax Pack (14):		15.00		
Wax Box (36):		480.00		
Cello Pack (21):		35.00		
Cello Box (24):		600.00		
Rack Pack (39):		45.00		
Rack Box (24):		925.00		
Vending Box (500):		210.00		
1	Lou Brock (Record Breaker)	1.00	.50	.30
2	Sparky Lyle (Record Breaker)	.20	.10	.06
3	Willie McCovey (Record Breaker)	.50	.25	.15
4	Brooks Robinson (Record Breaker)	2.00	1.00	.60
5	Pete Rose (Record Breaker)	4.50	2.25	1.25
6	Nolan Ryan (Record Breaker)	6.00	3.00	1.75
7	Reggie Jackson (Record Breaker)	4.00	2.00	1.25
8	Mike Sadek	.20	.10	.06
9	Doug DeCinces	.20	.10	.06
10	Phil Niekro	3.00	1.50	.90
11	Rick Manning	.20	.10	.06
12	Don Aase	.20	.10	.06
13	Art Howe	.20	.10	.06
14	Lerrin LaGrow	.20	.10	.06
15	Tony Perez	4.00	2.00	1.25
16	Roy White	.20	.10	.06
17	Mike Krukow	.20	.10	.06
18	Bob Grich	.20	.10	.06
19	Darrell Porter	.20	.10	.06
20	Pete Rose	6.00	3.00	1.75
21	Steve Kemp	.20	.10	.06
22	Charlie Hough	.20	.10	.06
23	Bump Wills	.20	.10	.06
24	Don Money	.20	.10	.06
25	Jon Matlack	.20	.10	.06
26	Rich Hebner	.20	.10	.06
27	Geoff Zahn	.20	.10	.06
28	Ed Ott	.20	.10	.06
29	Bob Lacey	.20	.10	.06
30	George Hendrick	.20	.10	.06
31	Glenn Abbott	.20	.10	.06
32	Garry Templeton	.20	.10	.06
33	Dave Lemanczyk	.20	.10	.06
34	Willie McCovey	4.00	2.00	1.25
35	Sparky Lyle	.20	.10	.06
36	***Eddie Murray***	17.50	8.75	5.25
37	Rick Waits	.20	.10	.06
38	Willie Montanez	.20	.10	.06
39	***Floyd Bannister***	.45	.25	.14
40	Carl Yastrzemski	5.00	2.50	1.50
41	Burt Hooton	.20	.10	.06
42	Jorge Orta	.20	.10	.06
43	Bill Atkinson	.20	.10	.06
44	Toby Harrah	.20	.10	.06
45	Mark Fidrych	.30	.15	.09
46	Al Cowens	.20	.10	.06
47	Jack Billingham	.20	.10	.06
48	Don Baylor	.25	.13	.08
49	Ed Kranepool	.20	.10	.06
50	Rick Reuschel	.20	.10	.06
51	Charlie Moore	.20	.10	.06
52	Jim Lonborg	.20	.10	.06
53	Phil Garner	.20	.10	.06
54	Tom Johnson	.20	.10	.06
55	Mitchell Page	.20	.10	.06
56	Randy Jones	.20	.10	.06
57	Dan Meyer	.20	.10	.06
58	Bob Forsch	.20	.10	.06
59	Otto Velez	.20	.10	.06
60	Thurman Munson	4.00	2.00	1.25
61	Larvell Blanks	.20	.10	.06
62	Jim Barr	.20	.10	.06
63	Don Zimmer	.20	.10	.06
64	Gene Pentz	.20	.10	.06
65	Ken Singleton	.20	.10	.06
66	White Sox Team	.30	.15	.09
67	Claudell Washington	.20	.10	.06
68	Steve Foucault	.20	.10	.06
69	Mike Vail	.20	.10	.06
70	Rich Gossage	.20	.10	.06
71	Terry Humphrey	.20	.10	.06
72	Andre Dawson	3.00	1.50	.90
73	Andy Hassler	.20	.10	.06
74	Checklist 1-121	.20	.10	.06
75	Dick Ruthven	.20	.10	.06
76	Steve Ontiveros	.20	.10	.06
77	Ed Kirkpatrick	.20	.10	.06
78	Pablo Torrealba	.20	.10	.06
79	Darrell Johnson/DP	.20	.10	.06
80	Ken Griffey	.20	.10	.06
81	Pete Redfern	.20	.10	.06
82	Giants team	.30	.15	.09
83	Bob Montgomery	.20	.10	.06
84	Kent Tekulve	.20	.10	.06
85	Ron Fairly	.20	.10	.06
86	Dave Tomlin	.20	.10	.06
87	John Lowenstein	.20	.10	.06
88	Mike Phillips	.20	.10	.06
89	Ken Clay	.20	.10	.06
90	Larry Bowa	.20	.10	.06
91	Oscar Zamora	.20	.10	.06
92	Adrian Devine	.20	.10	.06
93	Bobby Cox	.40	.20	.12
94	Chuck Scrivener	.20	.10	.06
95	Jamie Quirk	.20	.10	.06
96	Orioles Team	.30	.15	.09
97	Stan Bahnsen	.20	.10	.06
98	Jim Essian	.20	.10	.06
99	***Willie Hernandez***	.30	.15	.09
100	George Brett	6.00	3.00	1.75
101	Sid Monge	.20	.10	.06
102	Matt Alexander	.20	.10	.06
103	Tom Murphy	.20	.10	.06
104	Lee Lacy	.20	.10	.06
105	Reggie Cleveland	.20	.10	.06
106	Bill Plummer	.20	.10	.06
107	Ed Halicki	.20	.10	.06
108	Von Joshua	.20	.10	.06
109	Joe Torre	.55	.30	.15
110	Richie Zisk	.20	.10	.06
111	Mike Tyson	.20	.10	.06
112	Astros team	.30	.15	.09
113	Don Carrithers	.20	.10	.06
114	Paul Blair	.20	.10	.06
115	Gary Nolan	.20	.10	.06
116	Tucker Ashford	.20	.10	.06
117	John Montague	.20	.10	.06
118	Terry Harmon	.20	.10	.06
119	Denny Martinez	.20	.10	.06
120	Gary Carter	4.00	2.00	1.25
121	Alvis Woods	.20	.10	.06
122	Dennis Eckersley	4.00	2.00	1.25
123	Manny Trillo	.20	.10	.06
124	***Dave Rozema***	.20	.10	.06
125	George Scott	.20	.10	.06
126	Paul Moskau	.20	.10	.06
127	Chet Lemon	.20	.10	.06
128	Bill Russell	.20	.10	.06
129	Jim Colborn	.20	.10	.06
130	Jeff Burroughs	.20	.10	.06
131	Bert Blyleven	.20	.10	.06
132	Enos Cabell	.20	.10	.06
133	Jerry Augustine	.20	.10	.06
134	***Steve Henderson***	.20	.10	.06
135	Ron Guidry	.30	.15	.09
136	Ted Sizemore	.20	.10	.06
137	Craig Kusick	.20	.10	.06
138	Larry Demery	.20	.10	.06
139	Wayne Gross	.20	.10	.06
140	Rollie Fingers	3.00	1.50	.90
141	Ruppert Jones	.20	.10	.06
142	John Montefusco	.20	.10	.06
143	Keith Hernandez	.20	.10	.06
144	Jesse Jefferson	.20	.10	.06
145	Rick Monday	.20	.10	.06
146	Doyle Alexander	.20	.10	.06
147	Lee Mazzilli	.20	.10	.06
148	Andre Thornton	.20	.10	.06
149	Dale Murray	.20	.10	.06
150	Bobby Bonds	.20	.10	.06
151	Milt Wilcox	.20	.10	.06
152	***Ivan DeJesus***	.20	.10	.06
153	Steve Stone	.20	.10	.06
154	Cecil Cooper	.20	.10	.06
155	Butch Hobson	.20	.10	.06
156	Andy Messersmith	.20	.10	.06
157	Pete LaCock	.20	.10	.06
158	Joaquin Andujar	.20	.10	.06

159	Lou Piniella	.30	.15	.09
160	Jim Palmer	4.00	2.00	1.25
161	Bob Boone	.20	.10	.06
162	Paul Thormodsgard	.20	.10	.06
163	Bill North	.20	.10	.06
164	Bob Owchinko	.20	.10	.06
165	Rennie Stennett	.20	.10	.06
166	Carlos Lopez	.20	.10	.06
167	Tim Foli	.20	.10	.06
168	Reggie Smith	.20	.10	.06
169	Jerry Johnson	.20	.10	.06
170	Lou Brock	4.00	2.00	1.25
171	Pat Zachry	.20	.10	.06
172	Mike Hargrove	.20	.10	.06
173	Robin Yount	4.00	2.00	1.25
174	Wayne Garland	.20	.10	.06
175	Jerry Morales	.20	.10	.06
176	Milt May	.20	.10	.06
177	Gene Garber	.20	.10	.06
178	Dave Chalk	.20	.10	.06
179	Dick Tidrow	.20	.10	.06
180	Dave Concepcion	.20	.10	.06
181	Ken Forsch	.20	.10	.06
182	Jim Spencer	.20	.10	.06
183	Doug Bird	.20	.10	.06
184	Checklist 122-242	.20	.10	.06
185	Ellis Valentine	.20	.10	.06
186	***Bob Stanley***	.20	.10	.06
187	Jerry Royster	.20	.10	.06
188	Al Bumbry	.20	.10	.06
189	Tom Lasorda	.55	.30	.15
190	John Candelaria	.20	.10	.06
191	Rodney Scott	.20	.10	.06
192	Padres Team	.30	.15	.09
193	Rich Chiles	.20	.10	.06
194	Derrel Thomas	.20	.10	.06
195	Larry Dierker	.20	.10	.06
196	Bob Bailor	.20	.10	.06
197	Nino Espinosa	.20	.10	.06
198	Ron Pruitt	.20	.10	.06
199	Craig Reynolds	.20	.10	.06
200	Reggie Jackson	6.00	3.00	1.75
201	Batting Leaders (Rod Carew, Dave Parker)	.50	.25	.15
202	Home Run Leaders (George Foster, Jim Rice)	.25	.13	.08
203	RBI Leaders (George Foster, Larry Hisle)	.20	.10	.06
204	Stolen Base Leaders (Freddie Patek, Frank Taveras)	.20	.10	.06
205	Victory Leaders (Steve Carlton, Dave Goltz, Dennis Leonard, Jim Palmer)	.50	.25	.15
206	Strikeout Leaders (Phil Niekro, Nolan Ryan)	3.00	1.50	.90
207	ERA Leaders (John Candelaria, Frank Tanana)	.20	.10	.06
208	Leading Firemen (Bill Campbell, Rollie Fingers)	.25	.13	.08
209	Dock Ellis	.20	.10	.06
210	Jose Cardenal	.20	.10	.06
211	Earl Weaver (DP)	.50	.25	.15
212	Mike Caldwell	.20	.10	.06
213	Alan Bannister	.20	.10	.06
214	Angels Team	.30	.15	.09
215	Darrell Evans	.25	.13	.08
216	Mike Paxton	.20	.10	.06
217	Rod Gilbreath	.20	.10	.06
218	Marty Pattin	.20	.10	.06
219	Mike Cubbage	.20	.10	.06
220	Pedro Borbon	.20	.10	.06
221	Chris Speier	.20	.10	.06
222	Jerry Martin	.20	.10	.06
223	Bruce Kison	.20	.10	.06
224	Jerry Tabb	.20	.10	.06
225	Don Gullett	.20	.10	.06
226	Joe Ferguson	.20	.10	.06
227	Al Fitzmorris	.20	.10	.06
228	Manny Mota	.20	.10	.06
229	Leo Foster	.20	.10	.06
230	Al Hrabosky	.20	.10	.06
231	Wayne Nordhagen	.20	.10	.06
232	Mickey Stanley	.20	.10	.06
233	Dick Pole	.20	.10	.06
234	Herman Franks	.20	.10	.06
235	Tim McCarver	.30	.15	.09
236	Terry Whitfield	.20	.10	.06
237	Rich Dauer	.20	.10	.06
238	Juan Beniquez	.20	.10	.06
239	Dyar Miller	.20	.10	.06
240	Gene Tenace	.20	.10	.06
241	Pete Vuckovich	.20	.10	.06
242	Barry Bonnell	.20	.10	.06
243	Bob McClure	.20	.10	.06
244	Expos Team	.30	.15	.09
245	Rick Burleson	.20	.10	.06
246	Dan Driessen	.20	.10	.06
247	Larry Christenson	.20	.10	.06
248	Frank White	.20	.10	.06
249	Dave Goltz	.20	.10	.06
250	Graig Nettles	.25	.13	.08
251	Don Kirkwood	.20	.10	.06
252	Steve Swisher	.20	.10	.06
253	Jim Kern	.20	.10	.06
254	Dave Collins	.20	.10	.06
255	Jerry Reuss	.20	.10	.06
256	Joe Altobelli	.20	.10	.06
257	Hector Cruz	.20	.10	.06
258	John Hiller	.20	.10	.06
259	Dodgers Team	.50	.25	.15
260	Bert Campaneris	.20	.10	.06
261	Tim Hosley	.20	.10	.06
262	Rudy May	.20	.10	.06
263	Danny Walton	.20	.10	.06
264	Jamie Easterly	.20	.10	.06
265	Sal Bando	.20	.10	.06
266	***Bob Shirley***	.20	.10	.06
267	Doug Ault	.20	.10	.06
268	Gil Flores	.20	.10	.06
269	Wayne Twitchell	.20	.10	.06
270	Carlton Fisk	4.00	2.00	1.25
271	Randy Lerch	.20	.10	.06
272	Royle Stillman	.20	.10	.06
273	Fred Norman	.20	.10	.06
274	Freddie Patek	.20	.10	.06
275	Dan Ford	.20	.10	.06
276	Bill Bonham	.20	.10	.06
277	Bruce Boisclair	.20	.10	.06
278	Enrique Romo	.20	.10	.06
279	Bill Virdon	.20	.10	.06
280	Buddy Bell	.20	.10	.06
281	Eric Rasmussen	.20	.10	.06
282	Yankees Team	1.00	.50	.30
283	Omar Moreno	.20	.10	.06
284	Randy Moffitt	.20	.10	.06
285	Steve Yeager	.20	.10	.06
286	Ben Oglivie	.20	.10	.06
287	Kiko Garcia	.20	.10	.06
288	Dave Hamilton	.20	.10	.06
289	Checklist 243-363	.20	.10	.06
290	Willie Horton	.20	.10	.06
291	Gary Ross	.20	.10	.06
292	Gene Richard	.20	.10	.06
293	Mike Willis	.20	.10	.06
294	Larry Parrish	.20	.10	.06
295	Bill Lee	.20	.10	.06
296	Biff Pocoroba	.20	.10	.06
297	Warren Brusstar	.20	.10	.06
298	Tony Armas	.20	.10	.06
299	Whitey Herzog	.20	.10	.06
300	Joe Morgan	4.00	2.00	1.25
301	Buddy Schultz	.20	.10	.06
302	Cubs Team	.30	.15	.09
303	Sam Hinds	.20	.10	.06
304	John Milner	.20	.10	.06
305	Rico Carty	.20	.10	.06
306	Joe Niekro	.20	.10	.06
307	Glenn Borgmann	.20	.10	.06
308	Jim Rooker	.20	.10	.06
309	Cliff Johnson	.20	.10	.06
310	Don Sutton	3.00	1.50	.90
311	Jose Baez	.20	.10	.06
312	Greg Minton	.20	.10	.06
313	Andy Etchebarren	.20	.10	.06
314	Paul Lindblad	.20	.10	.06
315	Mark Belanger	.20	.10	.06
316	Henry Cruz	.20	.10	.06
317	Dave Johnson	.20	.10	.06
318	Tom Griffin	.20	.10	.06
319	Alan Ashby	.20	.10	.06
320	Fred Lynn	.20	.10	.06
321	Santo Alcala	.20	.10	.06
322	Tom Paciorek	.20	.10	.06
323	Jim Fregosi/DP	.20	.10	.06
324	Vern Rapp	.20	.10	.06
325	Bruce Sutter	3.00	1.50	.90
326	Mike Lum	.20	.10	.06
327	Rick Langford	.20	.10	.06
328	Brewers Team	.30	.15	.09
329	John Verhoeven	.20	.10	.06
330	Bob Watson	.20	.10	.06
331	Mark Littell	.20	.10	.06
332	Duane Kuiper	.20	.10	.06
333	Jim Todd	.20	.10	.06
334	John Stearns	.20	.10	.06
335	Bucky Dent	.20	.10	.06
336	Steve Busby	.20	.10	.06
337	Tom Grieve	.20	.10	.06
338	Dave Heaverlo	.20	.10	.06
339	Mario Guerrero	.20	.10	.06
340	Bake McBride	.20	.10	.06
341	Mike Flanagan	.20	.10	.06
342	Aurelio Rodriguez	.20	.10	.06
343	John Wathan/DP	.20	.10	.06
344	Sam Ewing	.20	.10	.06
345	Luis Tiant	.20	.10	.06
346	Larry Biittner	.20	.10	.06
347	Terry Forster	.20	.10	.06
348	Del Unser	.20	.10	.06
349	Rick Camp/DP	.20	.10	.06
350	Steve Garvey	2.00	1.00	.60
351	Jeff Torborg	.20	.10	.06
352	Tony Scott	.20	.10	.06
353	Doug Bair	.20	.10	.06
354	Cesar Geronimo	.20	.10	.06
355	Bill Travers	.20	.10	.06
356	Mets Team	.60	.30	.20
357	Tom Poquette	.20	.10	.06
358	Mark Lemongello	.20	.10	.06
359	Marc Hill	.20	.10	.06
360	Mike Schmidt	6.00	3.00	1.75
361	Chris Knapp	.20	.10	.06
362	Dave May	.20	.10	.06
363	Bob Randall	.20	.10	.06
364	Jerry Turner	.20	.10	.06
365	Ed Figueroa	.20	.10	.06
366	Larry Milbourne/DP	.20	.10	.06
367	Rick Dempsey	.20	.10	.06
368	Balor Moore	.20	.10	.06
369	Tim Nordbrook	.20	.10	.06
370	Rusty Staub	.25	.13	.08
371	Ray Burris	.20	.10	.06
372	Brian Asselstine	.20	.10	.06
373	Jim Willoughby	.20	.10	.06
374a	Jose Morales (Red stitching on position ball.)	.20	.10	.06
374b	Jose Morales (Black overprint on red stitching.)	.20	.10	.06
375	Tommy John	.30	.15	.09
376	Jim Wohlford	.20	.10	.06
377	Manny Sarmiento	.20	.10	.06
378	Bobby Winkles	.20	.10	.06
379	Skip Lockwood	.20	.10	.06
380	Ted Simmons	.20	.10	.06
381	Phillies Team	.35	.20	.11
382	Joe Lahoud	.20	.10	.06
383	Mario Mendoza	.20	.10	.06
384	Jack Clark	.30	.15	.09
385	Tito Fuentes	.20	.10	.06
386	Bob Gorinski	.20	.10	.06
387	Ken Holtzman	.20	.10	.06
388	Bill Fahey/DP	.20	.10	.06
389	Julio Gonzalez	.20	.10	.06
390	Oscar Gamble	.20	.10	.06
391	Larry Haney	.20	.10	.06
392	Billy Almon	.20	.10	.06
393	Tippy Martinez	.20	.10	.06
394	Roy Howell	.20	.10	.06
395	Jim Hughes	.20	.10	.06
396	Bob Stinson	.20	.10	.06
397	Greg Gross	.20	.10	.06
398	Don Hood	.20	.10	.06
399	Pete Mackanin	.20	.10	.06
400	Nolan Ryan	9.00	4.50	2.75
401	Sparky Anderson	.55	.30	.15
402	Dave Campbell	.20	.10	.06
403	Bud Harrelson	.20	.10	.06
404	Tigers Team	.30	.15	.09
405	Rawly Eastwick	.20	.10	.06
406	Mike Jorgensen	.20	.10	.06
407	Odell Jones	.20	.10	.06
408	Joe Zdeb	.20	.10	.06
409	Ron Schueler	.20	.10	.06
410	Bill Madlock	.20	.10	.06
411	A.L. Championships (Yankees Rally To Defeat Royals)	.50	.25	.15
412	N.L. Championships (Dodgers Overpower Phillies In Four)	.50	.25	.15
413	World Series (Reggie & Yankees Reign Supreme)	2.00	1.00	.60
414	Darold Knowles/DP	.20	.10	.06
415	Ray Fosse	.20	.10	.06
416	Jack Brohamer	.20	.10	.06
417	Mike Garman	.20	.10	.06
418	Tony Muser	.20	.10	.06
419	Jerry Garvin	.20	.10	.06
420	Greg Luzinski	.20	.10	.06
421	Junior Moore	.20	.10	.06
422	Steve Braun	.20	.10	.06
423	Dave Rosello	.20	.10	.06
424	Red Sox Team	.45	.25	.14
425	Steve Rogers	.20	.10	.06
426	Fred Kendall	.20	.10	.06
427	***Mario Soto***	.35	.20	.11
428	Joel Youngblood	.20	.10	.06
429	Mike Barlow	.20	.10	.06
430	Al Oliver	.30	.15	.09
431	Butch Metzger	.20	.10	.06
432	Terry Bulling	.20	.10	.06
433	Fernando Gonzalez	.20	.10	.06
434	Mike Norris	.20	.10	.06
435	Checklist 364-484	.20	.10	.06
436	Vic Harris/DP	.20	.10	.06
437	Bo McLaughlin	.20	.10	.06
438	John Ellis	.20	.10	.06
439	Ken Kravec	.20	.10	.06
440	Dave Lopes	.20	.10	.06
441	Larry Gura	.20	.10	.06
442	Elliott Maddox	.20	.10	.06
443	Darrel Chaney	.20	.10	.06
444	Roy Hartsfield	.20	.10	.06
445	Mike Ivie	.20	.10	.06
446	Tug McGraw	.20	.10	.06
447	Leroy Stanton	.20	.10	.06
448	Bill Castro	.20	.10	.06
449	Tim Blackwell	.20	.10	.06
450	Tom Seaver	5.00	2.50	1.50
451	Twins Team	.30	.15	.09
452	Jerry Mumphrey	.20	.10	.06
453	Doug Flynn	.20	.10	.06
454	Dave LaRoche	.20	.10	.06
455	Bill Robinson	.20	.10	.06
456	Vern Ruhle	.20	.10	.06
457	Bob Bailey	.20	.10	.06
458	Jeff Newman	.20	.10	.06
459	Charlie Spikes	.20	.10	.06
460	Jim Hunter	3.00	1.50	.90
461	Rob Andrews	.20	.10	.06
462	Rogelio Moret	.20	.10	.06
463	Kevin Bell	.20	.10	.06
464	Jerry Grote	.20	.10	.06
465	Hal McRae	.20	.10	.06
466	Dennis Blair	.20	.10	.06
467	Alvin Dark	.20	.10	.06
468	***Warren Cromartie***	.20	.10	.06
469	Rick Cerone	.20	.10	.06
470	J.R. Richard	.20	.10	.06
471	Roy Smalley	.20	.10	.06
472	Ron Reed	.20	.10	.06
473	Bill Buckner	.20	.10	.06
474	Jim Slaton	.20	.10	.06
475	Gary Matthews	.20	.10	.06
476	Bill Stein	.20	.10	.06
477	Doug Capilla	.20	.10	.06
478	Jerry Remy	.20	.10	.06
479	Cardinals Team	.30	.15	.09
480	Ron LeFlore	.20	.10	.06
481	Jackson Todd	.20	.10	.06
482	Rick Miller	.20	.10	.06
483	Ken Macha	.20	.10	.06
484	Jim Norris	.20	.10	.06
485	Chris Chambliss	.20	.10	.06
486	John Curtis	.20	.10	.06
487	Jim Tyrone	.20	.10	.06
488	Dan Spillner	.20	.10	.06
489	Rudy Meoli	.20	.10	.06
490	Amos Otis	.20	.10	.06
491	Scott McGregor	.20	.10	.06
492	Jim Sundberg	.20	.10	.06
493	Steve Renko	.20	.10	.06
494	Chuck Tanner	.20	.10	.06
495	Dave Cash	.20	.10	.06

496	***Jim Clancy***	.20	.10	.06
497	Glenn Adams	.20	.10	.06
498	Joe Sambito	.20	.10	.06
499	Mariners Team	.30	.15	.09
500	George Foster	.20	.10	.06
501	Dave Roberts	.20	.10	.06
502	Pat Rockett	.20	.10	.06
503	Ike Hampton	.20	.10	.06
504	Roger Freed	.20	.10	.06
505	Felix Millan	.20	.10	.06
506	Ron Blomberg	.20	.10	.06
507	Willie Crawford	.20	.10	.06
508	Johnny Oates	.20	.10	.06
509	Brent Strom	.20	.10	.06
510	Willie Stargell	4.00	2.00	1.25
511	Frank Duffy	.20	.10	.06
512	Larry Herndon	.20	.10	.06
513	Barry Foote	.20	.10	.06
514	Rob Sperring	.20	.10	.06
515	Tim Corcoran	.20	.10	.06
516	Gary Beare	.20	.10	.06
517	Andres Mora	.20	.10	.06
518	Tommy Boggs/DP	.20	.10	.06
519	Brian Downing	.20	.10	.06
520	Larry Hisle	.20	.10	.06
521	Steve Staggs	.20	.10	.06
522	Dick Williams	.20	.10	.06
523	***Donnie Moore***	.20	.10	.06
524	Bernie Carbo	.20	.10	.06
525	Jerry Terrell	.20	.10	.06
526	Reds Team	.45	.25	.14
527	Vic Correll	.20	.10	.06
528	Rob Picciolo	.20	.10	.06
529	Paul Hartzell	.20	.10	.06
530	Dave Winfield	4.00	2.00	1.25
531	Tom Underwood	.20	.10	.06
532	Skip Jutze	.20	.10	.06
533	Sandy Alomar	.20	.10	.06
534	Wilbur Howard	.20	.10	.06
535	Checklist 485-605	.20	.10	.06
536	Roric Harrison	.20	.10	.06
537	Bruce Bochte	.20	.10	.06
538	Johnnie LeMaster	.20	.10	.06
539	Vic Davalillo	.20	.10	.06
540	Steve Carlton	4.00	2.00	1.25
541	Larry Cox	.20	.10	.06
542	Tim Johnson	.20	.10	.06
543	Larry Harlow	.20	.10	.06
544	Len Randle	.20	.10	.06
545	Bill Campbell	.20	.10	.06
546	Ted Martinez	.20	.10	.06
547	John Scott	.20	.10	.06
548	Billy Hunter/DP	.20	.10	.06
549	Joe Kerrigan	.20	.10	.06
550	John Mayberry	.20	.10	.06
551	Braves Team	.30	.15	.09
552	Francisco Barrios	.20	.10	.06
553	***Terry Puhl***	.25	.13	.08
554	Joe Coleman	.20	.10	.06
555	Butch Wynegar	.20	.10	.06
556	Ed Armbrister	.20	.10	.06
557	Tony Solaita	.20	.10	.06
558	Paul Mitchell	.20	.10	.06
559	Phil Mankowski	.20	.10	.06
560	Dave Parker	.20	.10	.06
561	Charlie Williams	.20	.10	.06
562	Glenn Burke	.20	.10	.06
563	Dave Rader	.20	.10	.06
564	Mick Kelleher	.20	.10	.06
565	Jerry Koosman	.20	.10	.06
566	Merv Rettenmund	.20	.10	.06
567	Dick Drago	.20	.10	.06
568	Tom Hutton	.20	.10	.06
569	***Lary Sorensen***	.20	.10	.06
570	Dave Kingman	.20	.10	.06
571	Buck Martinez	.20	.10	.06
572	Rick Wise	.20	.10	.06
573	Luis Gomez	.20	.10	.06
574	Bob Lemon	.50	.25	.15
575	Pat Dobson	.20	.10	.06
576	Sam Mejias	.20	.10	.06
577	A's Team	.30	.15	.09
578	Buzz Capra	.20	.10	.06
579	***Rance Mulliniks***	.25	.13	.08
580	Rod Carew	4.00	2.00	1.25
581	Lynn McGlothen	.20	.10	.06
582	Fran Healy	.20	.10	.06
583	George Medich	.20	.10	.06
584	John Hale	.20	.10	.06
585	Woodie Fryman	.20	.10	.06
586	Ed Goodson	.20	.10	.06
587	John Urrea	.20	.10	.06
588	Jim Mason	.20	.10	.06
589	***Bob Knepper***	.20	.10	.06
590	Bobby Murcer	.20	.10	.06
591	George Zeber	.20	.10	.06
592	Bob Apodaca	.20	.10	.06
593	Dave Skaggs	.20	.10	.06
594	Dave Freisleben	.20	.10	.06
595	Sixto Lezcano	.20	.10	.06
596	Gary Wheelock	.20	.10	.06
597	Steve Dillard	.20	.10	.06
598	Eddie Solomon	.20	.10	.06
599	Gary Woods	.20	.10	.06
600	Frank Tanana	.20	.10	.06
601	Gene Mauch	.20	.10	.06
602	Eric Soderholm	.20	.10	.06
603	Will McEnaney	.20	.10	.06
604	Earl Williams	.20	.10	.06
605	Rick Rhoden	.20	.10	.06
606	Pirates team	.30	.15	.09
607	Fernando Arroyo	.20	.10	.06
608	Johnny Grubb	.20	.10	.06
609	John Denny	.20	.10	.06
610	Garry Maddox	.20	.10	.06
611	Pat Scanlon	.20	.10	.06
612	Ken Henderson	.20	.10	.06
613	Marty Perez	.20	.10	.06
614	Joe Wallis	.20	.10	.06
615	Clay Carroll	.20	.10	.06
616	Pat Kelly	.20	.10	.06
617	Joe Nolan	.20	.10	.06
618	Tommy Helms	.20	.10	.06
619	***Thad Bosley***	.20	.10	.06
620	Willie Randolph	.20	.10	.06
621	Craig Swan	.20	.10	.06
622	Champ Summers	.20	.10	.06
623	Eduardo Rodriguez	.20	.10	.06
624	Gary Alexander	.20	.10	.06
625	Jose Cruz	.20	.10	.06
626	Blue Jays team	.30	.15	.09
627	Dave Johnson	.20	.10	.06
628	Ralph Garr	.20	.10	.06
629	Don Stanhouse	.20	.10	.06
630	Ron Cey	.20	.10	.06
631	Danny Ozark	.20	.10	.06
632	Rowland Office	.20	.10	.06
633	Tom Veryzer	.20	.10	.06
634	Len Barker	.20	.10	.06
635	Joe Rudi	.20	.10	.06
636	Jim Bibby	.20	.10	.06
637	Duffy Dyer	.20	.10	.06
638	Paul Splittorff	.20	.10	.06
639	Gene Clines	.20	.10	.06
640	Lee May	.20	.10	.06
641	Doug Rau	.20	.10	.06
642	Denny Doyle	.20	.10	.06
643	Tom House	.20	.10	.06
644	Jim Dwyer	.20	.10	.06
645	Mike Torrez	.20	.10	.06
646	Rick Auerbach	.20	.10	.06
647	Steve Dunning	.20	.10	.06
648	Gary Thomasson	.20	.10	.06
649	***Moose Haas***	.20	.10	.06
650	Cesar Cedeno	.20	.10	.06
651	Doug Rader	.20	.10	.06
652	Checklist 606-726	.20	.10	.06
653	Ron Hodges	.20	.10	.06
654	Pepe Frias	.20	.10	.06
655	Lyman Bostock	.20	.10	.06
656	Dave Garcia	.20	.10	.06
657	Bombo Rivera	.20	.10	.06
658	Manny Sanguillen	.20	.10	.06
659	Rangers team	.30	.15	.09
660	Jason Thompson	.20	.10	.06
661	Grant Jackson	.20	.10	.06
662	Paul Dade	.20	.10	.06
663	Paul Reuschel	.20	.10	.06
664	Fred Stanley	.20	.10	.06
665	Dennis Leonard	.20	.10	.06
666	Billy Smith	.20	.10	.06
667	Jeff Byrd	.20	.10	.06
668	Dusty Baker	.35	.20	.11
669	Pete Falcone	.20	.10	.06
670	Jim Rice	.75	.40	.25
671	Gary Lavelle	.20	.10	.06
672	Don Kessinger	.20	.10	.06
673	Steve Brye	.20	.10	.06
674	***Ray Knight***	1.00	.50	.30
675	Jay Johnstone	.20	.10	.06
676	Bob Myrick	.20	.10	.06
677	Ed Herrmann	.20	.10	.06
678	Tom Burgmeier	.20	.10	.06
679	Wayne Garrett	.20	.10	.06
680	Vida Blue	.20	.10	.06
681	Rob Belloir	.20	.10	.06
682	Ken Brett	.20	.10	.06
683	Mike Champion	.20	.10	.06
684	Ralph Houk	.20	.10	.06
685	Frank Taveras	.20	.10	.06
686	Gaylord Perry	3.00	1.50	.90
687	***Julio Cruz***	.25	.13	.08
688	George Mitterwald	.20	.10	.06
689	Indians team	.30	.15	.09
690	Mickey Rivers	.20	.10	.06
691	Ross Grimsley	.20	.10	.06
692	Ken Reitz	.20	.10	.06
693	Lamar Johnson	.20	.10	.06
694	Elias Sosa	.20	.10	.06
695	Dwight Evans	.20	.10	.06
696	Steve Mingori	.20	.10	.06
697	Roger Metzger	.20	.10	.06
698	Juan Bernhardt	.20	.10	.06
699	Jackie Brown	.20	.10	.06
700	Johnny Bench	5.00	2.50	1.50
701	Rookie Pitchers (**Tom Hume, Larry Landreth, Steve McCatty, Bruce Taylor**)	.20	.10	.06
702	Rookie Catchers (**Bill Nahorodny, Kevin Pasley, Rick Sweet, Don Werner**)	.20	.10	.06
703	Rookie Pitchers (***Larry Andersen, Tim Jones, Mickey Mahler, Jack Morris***)	3.50	1.75	1.00
704	Rookie 2nd Basemen (***Garth Iorg, Dave Oliver, Sam Perlozzo, Lou Whitaker***)	4.50	2.25	1.25
705	Rookie Outfielders (**Dave Bergman, Miguel Dilone, Clint Hurdle, Willie Norwood**)	.20	.10	.06
706	Rookie 1st Basemen (***Wayne Cage, Ted Cox, Pat Putnam, Dave Revering***)	.20	.10	.06
707	Rookie Shortstops (***Mickey Klutts, Paul Molitor, Alan Trammell, U.L. Washington***)	17.50	8.75	5.25
708	Rookie Catchers (***Bo Diaz, Dale Murphy, Lance Parrish, Ernie Whitt***)	6.00	3.00	1.75
709	Rookie Pitchers (***Steve Burke, Matt Keough, Lance Rautzhan, Dan Schatzeder***)	.20	.10	.06
710	Rookie Outfielders (**Dell Alston, Rick Bosetti, Mike Easler, Keith Smith**)	.20	.10	.06
711	Rookie Pitchers (**Cardell Camper, Dennis Lamp, Craig Mitchell, Roy Thomas**)	.20	.10	.06
712	Bobby Valentine	.20	.10	.06
713	Bob Davis	.20	.10	.06
714	Mike Anderson	.20	.10	.06
715	Jim Kaat	.20	.10	.06
716	Clarence Gaston	.20	.10	.06
717	Nelson Briles	.20	.10	.06
718	Ron Jackson	.20	.10	.06
719	Randy Elliott	.20	.10	.06
720	Fergie Jenkins	3.00	1.50	.90
721	Billy Martin	.50	.25	.15
722	Pete Broberg	.20	.10	.06
723	Johnny Wockenfuss	.20	.10	.06
724	Royals team	.30	.15	.09
725	Kurt Bevacqua	.20	.10	.06
726	Wilbur Wood	.20	.10	.06

1978 Topps Team Checklist Sheet

A redemption offer on packs of 1978 Topps cards offered an uncut sheet of the 26 team/checklist cards by mail. Besides the team cards, the 10-1/2" x 22-1/2" sheet has a card offering collectors card boxes. The cards on the sheet are identical to the single team/checklist cards issued in packs.

	NM	EX	VG
Uncut Sheet	25.00	12.50	7.50

1978 Topps/Dynamite Magazine Panels

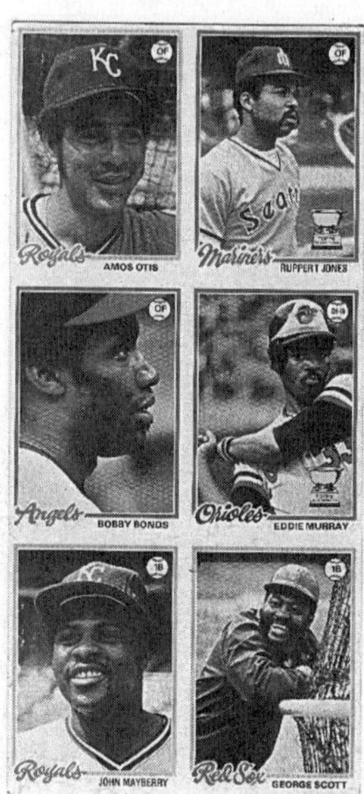

In issue No. 47 of its "Dynamite" kids' magazine, Scholastic Book Club teamed with Topps to insert a six-card panel of its 1978 baseball issue. Three such panels have been found thus far, one of which includes an Eddie Murray rookie. card. Values shown are for just the uncut panel; complete magazines would bear a small premium.

		NM	EX	VG
Complete Panel Set (3):		60.00	30.00	18.00
	PANEL 1	40.00	20.00	12.00
36	Eddie Murray			
125	George Scott			
141	Ruppert Jones			
150	Bobby Bonds			
490	Amos Otis			
550	John Mayberry			
	PANEL 2	10.00	5.00	3.00
21	Steve Kemp			
168	Reggie Smith			
200	Reggie Jackson			
245	Rick Burleson			
332	Duane Kuiper			
440	Davey Lopes			
	PANEL 3	15.00	7.50	4.50
44	Toby Harrah			
120	Gary Carter			
130	Jeff Burroughs			
320	Fred Lynn			
335	Bucky Dent			
670	Jim Rice			

1978 Topps/Zest Soap

Produced by Topps for a Zest Soap promotion, the five cards in this set are almost identical to the regular issue, except the backs are printed in both Spanish and English, the game feature on back has been replaced by MLB and MLBPA logos and the card numbers are different. The cards measure 2-1/2" x 3-1/2". Because of the player selection and

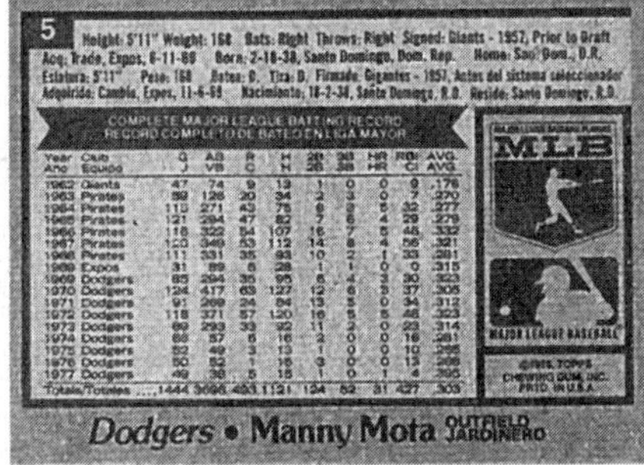

the bilingual backs, it seems obvious that this set was aimed at the Hispanic community. Cards were issued as complete sets in a cello package.

		NM	EX	VG
Complete Set (5):				
Common Player:				
1	Joaquin Andujar	2.00	1.00	.60
2	Bert Campaneris	4.50	2.25	1.25
3	Ed Figueroa	1.50	.70	.45
4	Willie Montanez	1.50	.70	.45
5	Manny Mota	4.50	2.25	1.25

1979 Topps

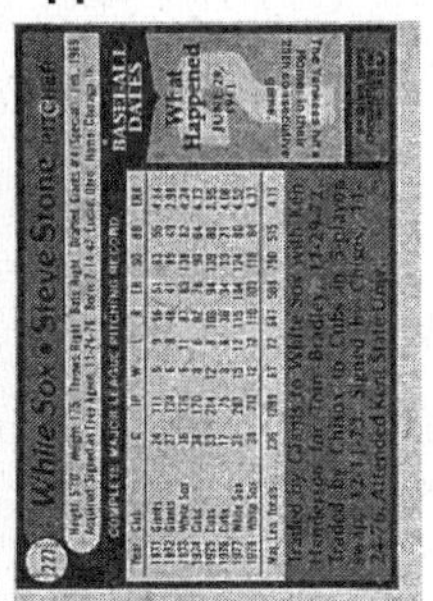

The size of this issue remained the same as in 1978 with 726 cards making their appearance. Actually, the 2-1/2" x 3-1/2" cards have a relatively minor design change from the previous year. The large color photo still dominates the front, with the player's name, team and position below it. The baseball with the player's position was moved to the lower left and the position replaced by a Topps logo. On the back, the printing color was changed and the game situation was replaced by a quiz called "Baseball Dates." Specialty cards include statistical leaders, major league records set during the season and eight cards devoted to career records. For the first time, rookies were arranged by teams under the heading of "Prospects." The key Ozzie Smith rookie card is usually seen with very poor centering.

		NM	EX	VG
Complete Set (726):		115.00	55.00	35.00
Common Player:		.15	.08	.05
Wax Pack (12):		12.00		
Wax Box (36):		295.00		
Cello Pack (18):		20.00		
Cello Box (24):		335.00		
Super Cello Pack (28):				
Super Cello Box (24):				
Rack Pack (39):		25.00		
Rack Box (24):		575.00		
Vending Box (500):		155.00		
1	Batting Leaders (Rod Carew, Dave Parker)	1.00	.50	.30
2	Home Run Leaders (George Foster, Jim Rice)	.15	.08	.05
3	RBI Leaders (George Foster, Jim Rice)	.15	.08	.05
4	Stolen Base Leaders (Ron LeFlore, Omar Moreno)	.15	.08	.05
5	Victory Leaders (Ron Guidry, Gaylord Perry)	.15	.08	.05
6	Strikeout Leaders (J.R. Richard, Nolan Ryan)	4.00	2.00	1.25
7	ERA Leaders (Ron Guidry, Craig Swan)	.15	.08	.05
8	Leading Firemen (Rollie Fingers, Rich Gossage)	.20	.10	.06
9	Dave Campbell	.15	.08	.05
10	Lee May	.15	.08	.05
11	Marc Hill	.15	.08	.05
12	Dick Drago	.15	.08	.05
13	Paul Dade	.15	.08	.05
14	Rafael Landestoy	.15	.08	.05
15	Ross Grimsley	.15	.08	.05
16	Fred Stanley	.15	.08	.05
17	Donnie Moore	.15	.08	.05
18	Tony Solaita	.15	.08	.05
19	Larry Gura	.15	.08	.05
20	Joe Morgan	3.00	1.50	.90
21	Kevin Kobel	.15	.08	.05
22	Mike Jorgensen	.15	.08	.05
23	Terry Forster	.15	.08	.05
24	Paul Molitor	6.00	3.00	1.75
25	Steve Carlton	3.00	1.50	.90
26	Jamie Quirk	.15	.08	.05
27	Dave Goltz	.15	.08	.05
28	Steve Brye	.15	.08	.05
29	Rick Langford	.15	.08	.05
30	Dave Winfield	3.00	1.50	.90
31	Tom House	.15	.08	.05
32	Jerry Mumphrey	.15	.08	.05
33	Dave Rozema	.15	.08	.05
34	Rob Andrews	.15	.08	.05
35	Ed Figueroa	.15	.08	.05
36	Alan Ashby	.15	.08	.05
37	Joe Kerrigan	.15	.08	.05
38	Bernie Carbo	.15	.08	.05
39	Dale Murphy	2.00	1.00	.60
40	Dennis Eckersley	2.50	1.25	.70
41	Twins Team (Gene Mauch)	.25	.13	.08
42	Ron Blomberg	.15	.08	.05
43	Wayne Twitchell	.15	.08	.05
44	Kurt Bevacqua	.15	.08	.05
45	Al Hrabosky	.15	.08	.05
46	Ron Hodges	.15	.08	.05
47	Fred Norman	.15	.08	.05
48	Merv Rettenmund	.15	.08	.05
49	Vern Ruhle	.15	.08	.05
50	Steve Garvey	1.50	.70	.45
51	Ray Fosse	.15	.08	.05
52	Randy Lerch	.15	.08	.05
53	Mick Kelleher	.15	.08	.05
54	Dell Alston	.15	.08	.05
55	Willie Stargell	3.00	1.50	.90
56	John Hale	.15	.08	.05
57	Eric Rasmussen	.15	.08	.05
58	Bob Randall	.15	.08	.05
59	John Denny	.15	.08	.05
60	Mickey Rivers	.15	.08	.05
61	Bo Diaz	.15	.08	.05
62	Randy Moffitt	.15	.08	.05
63	Jack Brohamer	.15	.08	.05
64	Tom Underwood	.15	.08	.05
65	Mark Belanger	.15	.08	.05
66	Tigers Team (Les Moss)	.25	.13	.08
67	Jim Mason	.15	.08	.05
68	Joe Niekro	.15	.08	.05
69	Elliott Maddox	.15	.08	.05
70	John Candelaria	.15	.08	.05
71	Brian Downing	.15	.08	.05
72	Steve Mingori	.15	.08	.05
73	Ken Henderson	.15	.08	.05
74	***Shane Rawley***	.15	.08	.05
75	Steve Yeager	.15	.08	.05
76	Warren Cromartie	.15	.08	.05
77	Dan Briggs	.15	.08	.05
78	Elias Sosa	.15	.08	.05
79	Ted Cox	.15	.08	.05
80	Jason Thompson	.15	.08	.05
81	Roger Erickson	.15	.08	.05
82	Mets Team (Joe Torre)	.75	.40	.25
83	Fred Kendall	.15	.08	.05
84	Greg Minton	.15	.08	.05
85	Gary Matthews	.15	.08	.05
86	Rodney Scott	.15	.08	.05
87	Pete Falcone	.15	.08	.05
88	Bob Molinaro	.15	.08	.05
89	Dick Tidrow	.15	.08	.05
90	Bob Boone	.15	.08	.05
91	Terry Crowley	.15	.08	.05
92	Jim Bibby	.15	.08	.05
93	Phil Mankowski	.15	.08	.05
94	Len Barker	.15	.08	.05
95	Robin Yount	3.00	1.50	.90
96	Indians Team (Jeff Torborg)	.25	.13	.08
97	Sam Mejias	.15	.08	.05
98	Ray Burris	.15	.08	.05
99	John Wathan	.15	.08	.05
100	Tom Seaver	3.50	1.75	1.00
101	Roy Howell	.15	.08	.05
102	Mike Anderson	.15	.08	.05
103	Jim Todd	.15	.08	.05
104	Johnny Oates	.15	.08	.05
105	Rick Camp	.15	.08	.05
106	Frank Duffy	.15	.08	.05
107	Jesus Alou	.15	.08	.05
108	Eduardo Rodriguez	.15	.08	.05
109	Joel Youngblood	.15	.08	.05
110	Vida Blue	.15	.08	.05
111	Roger Freed	.15	.08	.05
112	Phillies Team (Danny Ozark)	.25	.13	.08
113	Pete Redfern	.15	.08	.05
114	Cliff Johnson	.15	.08	.05
115	Nolan Ryan	6.00	3.00	1.75
116	***Ozzie Smith***	20.00	10.00	6.00
117	Grant Jackson	.15	.08	.05
118	Bud Harrelson	.15	.08	.05
119	Don Stanhouse	.15	.08	.05
120	Jim Sundberg	.15	.08	.05
121	Checklist 1-121	.15	.08	.05
122	Mike Paxton	.15	.08	.05
123	Lou Whitaker	1.00	.50	.30
124	Dan Schatzeder	.15	.08	.05
125	Rick Burleson	.15	.08	.05
126	Doug Bair	.15	.08	.05
127	Thad Bosley	.15	.08	.05
128	Ted Martinez	.15	.08	.05
129	Marty Pattin	.15	.08	.05
130	Bob Watson	.15	.08	.05
131	Jim Clancy	.15	.08	.05
132	Rowland Office	.15	.08	.05
133	Bill Castro	.15	.08	.05
134	Alan Bannister	.15	.08	.05
135	Bobby Murcer	.15	.08	.05
136	Jim Kaat	.15	.08	.05
137	Larry Wolfe	.15	.08	.05
138	Mark Lee	.15	.08	.05
139	Luis Pujols	.15	.08	.05
140	Don Gullett	.15	.08	.05
141	Tom Paciorek	.15	.08	.05
142	Charlie Williams	.15	.08	.05
143	Tony Scott	.15	.08	.05
144	Sandy Alomar	.15	.08	.05
145	Rick Rhoden	.15	.08	.05
146	Duane Kuiper	.15	.08	.05
147	Dave Hamilton	.15	.08	.05
148	Bruce Boisclair	.15	.08	.05
149	Manny Sarmiento	.15	.08	.05
150	Wayne Cage	.15	.08	.05
151	John Hiller	.15	.08	.05
152	Rick Cerone	.15	.08	.05
153	Dennis Lamp	.15	.08	.05
154	Jim Gantner	.15	.08	.05
155	Dwight Evans	.15	.08	.05
156	Buddy Solomon	.15	.08	.05
157	U.L. Washington	.15	.08	.05
158	Joe Sambito	.15	.08	.05
159	Roy White	.15	.08	.05
160	Mike Flanagan	.15	.08	.05
161	Barry Foote	.15	.08	.05
162	Tom Johnson	.15	.08	.05
163	Glenn Burke	.15	.08	.05
164	Mickey Lolich	.15	.08	.05
165	Frank Taveras	.15	.08	.05
166	Leon Roberts	.15	.08	.05
167a	Roger Metzger (Solid vertical black line between first and last names, through "A" of "GIANTS.")	.50	.25	.15
167b	Roger Metzger (Partial black line.)	.25	.13	.08
167c	Roger Metzger (No black line.)	.15	.08	.05
168	Dave Freisleben	.15	.08	.05
169	Bill Nahorodny	.15	.08	.05
170	Don Sutton	2.50	1.25	.70
171	Gene Clines	.15	.08	.05
172	Mike Bruhert	.15	.08	.05
173	John Lowenstein	.15	.08	.05
174	Rick Auerbach	.15	.08	.05
175	George Hendrick	.15	.08	.05
176	Aurelio Rodriguez	.15	.08	.05
177	Ron Reed	.15	.08	.05
178	Alvis Woods	.15	.08	.05
179	Jim Beattie	.15	.08	.05
180	Larry Hisle	.15	.08	.05
181	Mike Garman	.15	.08	.05
182	Tim Johnson	.15	.08	.05
183	Paul Splittorff	.15	.08	.05
184	Darrel Chaney	.15	.08	.05
185	Mike Torrez	.15	.08	.05
186	Eric Soderholm	.15	.08	.05
187	Mark Lemongello	.15	.08	.05
188	Pat Kelly	.15	.08	.05
189	***Eddie Whitson***	.25	.13	.08
190	Ron Cey	.15	.08	.05
191	Mike Norris	.15	.08	.05
192	Cardinals Team (Ken Boyer)	.25	.13	.08
193	Glenn Adams	.15	.08	.05
194	Randy Jones	.15	.08	.05
195	Bill Madlock	.15	.08	.05
196	Steve Kemp	.15	.08	.05
197	Bob Apodaca	.15	.08	.05
198	Johnny Grubb	.15	.08	.05
199	Larry Milbourne	.15	.08	.05
200	Johnny Bench	3.50	1.75	1.00
201	Mike Edwards (Record Breaker)	.15	.08	.05
202	Ron Guidry (Record Breaker)	.15	.08	.05
203	J.R. Richard (Record Breaker)	.15	.08	.05
204	Pete Rose (Record Breaker)	1.00	.50	.30
205	John Stearns (Record Breaker)	.15	.08	.05
206	Sammy Stewart (Record Breaker)	.15	.08	.05
207	Dave Lemanczyk	.15	.08	.05
208	Clarence Gaston	.15	.08	.05
209	Reggie Cleveland	.15	.08	.05
210	Larry Bowa	.15	.08	.05
211	Denny Martinez	.15	.08	.05
212	***Carney Lansford***	.60	.30	.20
213	Bill Travers	.15	.08	.05
214	Red Sox Team (Don Zimmer)	.25	.13	.08
215	Willie McCovey	3.00	1.50	.90
216	Wilbur Wood	.15	.08	.05
217	Steve Dillard	.15	.08	.05
218	Dennis Leonard	.15	.08	.05
219	Roy Smalley	.15	.08	.05
220	Cesar Geronimo	.15	.08	.05
221	Jesse Jefferson	.15	.08	.05
222	Bob Beall	.15	.08	.05
223	Kent Tekulve	.15	.08	.05
224	Dave Revering	.15	.08	.05
225	Rich Gossage	.25	.13	.08
226	Ron Pruitt	.15	.08	.05
227	Steve Stone	.15	.08	.05
228	Vic Davalillo	.15	.08	.05
229	Doug Flynn	.15	.08	.05
230	Bob Forsch	.15	.08	.05
231	Johnny Wockenfuss	.15	.08	.05
232	Jimmy Sexton	.15	.08	.05
233	Paul Mitchell	.15	.08	.05
234	Toby Harrah	.15	.08	.05
235	Steve Rogers	.15	.08	.05
236	Jim Dwyer	.15	.08	.05
237	Billy Smith	.15	.08	.05
238	Balor Moore	.15	.08	.05
239	Willie Horton	.15	.08	.05
240	Rick Reuschel	.15	.08	.05
241	Checklist 122-242	.15	.08	.05
242	Pablo Torrealba	.15	.08	.05
243	Buck Martinez	.15	.08	.05
244	Pirates Team (Chuck Tanner)	.25	.13	.08
245	Jeff Burroughs	.15	.08	.05
246	Darrell Jackson	.15	.08	.05
247	Tucker Ashford	.15	.08	.05
248	Pete LaCock	.15	.08	.05
249	Paul Thormodsgard	.15	.08	.05
250	Willie Randolph	.15	.08	.05
251	Jack Morris	.40	.20	.12

252	Bob Stinson	.15	.08	.05
253	Rick Wise	.15	.08	.05
254	Luis Gomez	.15	.08	.05
255	Tommy John	.30	.15	.09
256	Mike Sadek	.15	.08	.05
257	Adrian Devine	.15	.08	.05
258	Mike Phillips	.15	.08	.05
259	Reds Team (Sparky Anderson)	.75	.40	.25
260	Richie Zisk	.15	.08	.05
261	Mario Guerrero	.15	.08	.05
262	Nelson Briles	.15	.08	.05
263	Oscar Gamble	.15	.08	.05
264	***Don Robinson***	.15	.08	.05
265	Don Money	.15	.08	.05
266	Jim Willoughby	.15	.08	.05
267	Joe Rudi	.15	.08	.05
268	Julio Gonzalez	.15	.08	.05
269	Woodie Fryman	.15	.08	.05
270	Butch Hobson	.15	.08	.05
271	Rawly Eastwick	.15	.08	.05
272	Tim Corcoran	.15	.08	.05
273	Jerry Terrell	.15	.08	.05
274	Willie Norwood	.15	.08	.05
275	Junior Moore	.15	.08	.05
276	Jim Colborn	.15	.08	.05
277	Tom Grieve	.15	.08	.05
278	Andy Messersmith	.15	.08	.05
279	Jerry Grote	.15	.08	.05
280	Andre Thornton	.15	.08	.05
281	Vic Correll	.15	.08	.05
282	Blue Jays Team (Roy Hartsfield)	.25	.13	.08
283	Ken Kravec	.15	.08	.05
284	Johnnie LeMaster	.15	.08	.05
285	Bobby Bonds	.15	.08	.05
286	Duffy Dyer	.15	.08	.05
287	Andres Mora	.15	.08	.05
288	Milt Wilcox	.15	.08	.05
289	Jose Cruz	.15	.08	.05
290	Dave Lopes	.15	.08	.05
291	Tom Griffin	.15	.08	.05
292	Don Reynolds	.15	.08	.05
293	Jerry Garvin	.15	.08	.05
294	Pepe Frias	.15	.08	.05
295	Mitchell Page	.15	.08	.05
296	Preston Hanna	.15	.08	.05
297	Ted Sizemore	.15	.08	.05
298	Rich Gale	.15	.08	.05
299	Steve Ontiveros	.15	.08	.05
300	Rod Carew	3.00	1.50	.90
301	Tom Hume	.15	.08	.05
302	Braves Team (Bobby Cox)	.45	.25	.14
303	Lary Sorensen	.15	.08	.05
304	Steve Swisher	.15	.08	.05
305	Willie Montanez	.15	.08	.05
306	Floyd Bannister	.15	.08	.05
307	Larvell Blanks	.15	.08	.05
308	Bert Blyleven	.15	.08	.05
309	Ralph Garr	.15	.08	.05
310	Thurman Munson	5.00	2.50	1.50
311	Gary Lavelle	.15	.08	.05
312	Bob Robertson	.15	.08	.05
313	Dyar Miller	.15	.08	.05
314	Larry Harlow	.15	.08	.05
315	Jon Matlack	.15	.08	.05
316	Milt May	.15	.08	.05
317	Jose Cardenal	.15	.08	.05
318	***Bob Welch***	1.50	.70	.45
319	Wayne Garrett	.15	.08	.05
320	Carl Yastrzemski	3.50	1.75	1.00
321	Gaylord Perry	2.50	1.25	.70
322	Danny Goodwin	.15	.08	.05
323	Lynn McGlothen	.15	.08	.05
324	Mike Tyson	.15	.08	.05
325	Cecil Cooper	.15	.08	.05
326	Pedro Borbon	.15	.08	.05
327	Art Howe	.15	.08	.05
328	A's Team (Jack McKeon)	.25	.13	.08
329	Joe Coleman	.15	.08	.05
330	George Brett	6.00	3.00	1.75
331	Mickey Mahler	.15	.08	.05
332	Gary Alexander	.15	.08	.05
333	Chet Lemon	.15	.08	.05
334	Craig Swan	.15	.08	.05
335	Chris Chambliss	.15	.08	.05
336	Bobby Thompson	.15	.08	.05
337	John Montague	.15	.08	.05
338	Vic Harris	.15	.08	.05
339	Ron Jackson	.15	.08	.05
340	Jim Palmer	3.00	1.50	.90
341	***Willie Upshaw***	.20	.10	.06
342	Dave Roberts	.15	.08	.05
343	Ed Glynn	.15	.08	.05
344	Jerry Royster	.15	.08	.05
345	Tug McGraw	.15	.08	.05
346	Bill Buckner	.15	.08	.05
347	Doug Rau	.15	.08	.05
348	Andre Dawson	1.50	.70	.45
349	Jim Wright	.15	.08	.05
350	Garry Templeton	.15	.08	.05
351	Wayne Nordhagen	.15	.08	.05
352	Steve Renko	.15	.08	.05
353	Checklist 243-363	.15	.08	.05
354	Bill Bonham	.15	.08	.05
355	Lee Mazzilli	.15	.08	.05
356	Giants Team (Joe Altobelli)	.25	.13	.08
357	Jerry Augustine	.15	.08	.05
358	Alan Trammell	2.00	1.00	.60
359	Dan Spillner	.15	.08	.05
360	Amos Otis	.15	.08	.05
361	Tom Dixon	.15	.08	.05
362	Mike Cubbage	.15	.08	.05
363	Craig Skok	.15	.08	.05
364	Gene Richards	.15	.08	.05
365	Sparky Lyle	.15	.08	.05
366	Juan Bernhardt	.15	.08	.05
367	Dave Skaggs	.15	.08	.05
368	Don Aase	.15	.08	.05
369a	Bump Wills (Blue Jays)	2.00	1.00	.60
369b	Bump Wills (Rangers)	2.00	1.00	.60
370	Dave Kingman	.15	.08	.05
371	Jeff Holly	.15	.08	.05
372	Lamar Johnson	.15	.08	.05
373	Lance Rautzhan	.15	.08	.05
374	Ed Herrmann	.15	.08	.05
375	Bill Campbell	.15	.08	.05
376	Gorman Thomas	.15	.08	.05
377	Paul Moskau	.15	.08	.05
378	Rob Picciolo	.15	.08	.05
379	Dale Murray	.15	.08	.05
380	John Mayberry	.15	.08	.05
381	Astros Team (Bill Virdon)	.25	.13	.08
382	Jerry Martin	.15	.08	.05
383	Phil Garner	.15	.08	.05
384	Tommy Boggs	.15	.08	.05
385	Dan Ford	.15	.08	.05
386	Francisco Barrios	.15	.08	.05
387	Gary Thomasson	.15	.08	.05
388	Jack Billingham	.15	.08	.05
389	Joe Zdeb	.15	.08	.05
390	Rollie Fingers	2.50	1.25	.70
391	Al Oliver	.30	.15	.09
392	Doug Ault	.15	.08	.05
393	Scott McGregor	.15	.08	.05
394	Randy Stein	.15	.08	.05
395	Dave Cash	.15	.08	.05
396	Bill Plummer	.15	.08	.05
397	Sergio Ferrer	.15	.08	.05
398	Ivan DeJesus	.15	.08	.05
399	David Clyde	.15	.08	.05
400	Jim Rice	.50	.25	.15
401	Ray Knight	.15	.08	.05
402	Paul Hartzell	.15	.08	.05
403	Tim Foli	.15	.08	.05
404	White Sox Team (Don Kessinger)	.25	.13	.08
405	Butch Wynegar	.15	.08	.05
406	Joe Wallis	.15	.08	.05
407	Pete Vuckovich	.15	.08	.05
408	Charlie Moore	.15	.08	.05
409	***Willie Wilson***	2.00	1.00	.60
410	Darrell Evans	.15	.08	.05
411	All-Time Hits Leaders (Ty Cobb, George Sisler)	.50	.25	.15
412	All-Time RBI Leaders (Hank Aaron, Hack Wilson)	.50	.25	.15
413	All-Time Home Run Leaders (Hank Aaron, Roger Maris)	4.50	2.25	1.25
414	All-Time Batting Average Leaders (Ty Cobb, Roger Hornsby)	.50	.25	.15
415	All-Time Stolen Bases Leader (Lou Brock)	.30	.15	.09
416	All-Time Wins Leaders (Jack Chesbro, Cy Young)	.25	.13	.08
417	All-Time Strikeout Leaders (Walter Johnson, Nolan Ryan)	4.50	2.25	1.25
418	All-Time ERA Leaders (Walter Johnson, Dutch Leonard)	.20	.10	.06
419	Dick Ruthven	.15	.08	.05
420	Ken Griffey	.15	.08	.05
421	Doug DeCinces	.15	.08	.05
422	Ruppert Jones	.15	.08	.05
423	Bob Montgomery	.15	.08	.05
424	Angels Team (Jim Fregosi)	.25	.13	.08
425	Rick Manning	.15	.08	.05
426	Chris Speier	.15	.08	.05
427	Andy Replogle	.15	.08	.05
428	Bobby Valentine	.15	.08	.05
429	John Urrea	.15	.08	.05
430	Dave Parker	.15	.08	.05
431	Glenn Borgmann	.15	.08	.05
432	Dave Heaverlo	.15	.08	.05
433	Larry Biittner	.15	.08	.05
434	Ken Clay	.15	.08	.05
435	Gene Tenace	.15	.08	.05
436	Hector Cruz	.15	.08	.05
437	Rick Williams	.15	.08	.05
438	Horace Speed	.15	.08	.05
439	Frank White	.15	.08	.05
440	Rusty Staub	.15	.08	.05
441	Lee Lacy	.15	.08	.05
442	Doyle Alexander	.15	.08	.05
443	Bruce Bochte	.15	.08	.05
444	***Aurelio Lopez***	.15	.08	.05
445	Steve Henderson	.15	.08	.05
446	Jim Lonborg	.15	.08	.05
447	Manny Sanguillen	.15	.08	.05
448	Moose Haas	.15	.08	.05
449	Bombo Rivera	.15	.08	.05
450	Dave Concepcion	.15	.08	.05
451	Royals Team (Whitey Herzog)	.25	.13	.08
452	Jerry Morales	.15	.08	.05
453	Chris Knapp	.15	.08	.05
454	Len Randle	.15	.08	.05
455	Bill Lee	.15	.08	.05
456	Chuck Baker	.15	.08	.05
457	Bruce Sutter	2.50	1.25	.70
458	Jim Essian	.15	.08	.05
459	Sid Monge	.15	.08	.05
460	Graig Nettles	.15	.08	.05
461	Jim Barr	.15	.08	.05
462	Otto Velez	.15	.08	.05
463	Steve Comer	.15	.08	.05
464	Joe Nolan	.15	.08	.05
465	Reggie Smith	.15	.08	.05
466	Mark Littell	.15	.08	.05
467	Don Kessinger	.15	.08	.05
468	Stan Bahnsen	.15	.08	.05
469	Lance Parrish	.30	.15	.09
470	Garry Maddox	.15	.08	.05
471	Joaquin Andujar	.15	.08	.05
472	Craig Kusick	.15	.08	.05
473	Dave Roberts	.15	.08	.05
474	Dick Davis	.15	.08	.05
475	Dan Driessen	.15	.08	.05
476	Tom Poquette	.15	.08	.05
477	Bob Grich	.15	.08	.05
478	Juan Beniquez	.15	.08	.05
479	Padres Team (Roger Craig)	.25	.13	.08
480	Fred Lynn	.15	.08	.05
481	Skip Lockwood	.15	.08	.05
482	Craig Reynolds	.15	.08	.05
483	Checklist 364-484	.15	.08	.05
484	Rick Waits	.15	.08	.05
485	Bucky Dent	.15	.08	.05
486	Bob Knepper	.15	.08	.05
487	Miguel Dilone	.15	.08	.05
488	Bob Owchinko	.15	.08	.05
489	Larry Cox (Photo actually Dave Rader.)	.15	.08	.05
490	Al Cowens	.15	.08	.05
491	Tippy Martinez	.15	.08	.05
492	Bob Bailor	.15	.08	.05
493	Larry Christenson	.15	.08	.05
494	Jerry White	.15	.08	.05
495	Tony Perez	2.00	1.00	.60
496	Barry Bonnell	.15	.08	.05
497	Glenn Abbott	.15	.08	.05
498	Rich Chiles	.15	.08	.05
499	Rangers Team (Pat Corrales)	.25	.13	.08
500	Ron Guidry	.20	.10	.06
501	Junior Kennedy	.15	.08	.05
502	Steve Braun	.15	.08	.05
503	Terry Humphrey	.15	.08	.05
504	***Larry McWilliams***	.15	.08	.05
505	Ed Kranepool	.15	.08	.05
506	John D'Acquisto	.15	.08	.05
507	Tony Armas	.15	.08	.05
508	Charlie Hough	.15	.08	.05
509	Mario Mendoza	.15	.08	.05
510	Ted Simmons	.15	.08	.05
511	Paul Reuschel	.15	.08	.05
512	Jack Clark	.15	.08	.05
513	Dave Johnson	.15	.08	.05
514	Mike Proly	.15	.08	.05
515	Enos Cabell	.15	.08	.05
516	Champ Summers	.15	.08	.05
517	Al Bumbry	.15	.08	.05
518	Jim Umbarger	.15	.08	.05
519	Ben Oglivie	.15	.08	.05
520	Gary Carter	3.00	1.50	.90
521	Sam Ewing	.15	.08	.05
522	Ken Holtzman	.15	.08	.05
523	John Milner	.15	.08	.05
524	Tom Burgmeier	.15	.08	.05
525	Freddie Patek	.15	.08	.05
526	Dodgers Team (Tom Lasorda)	.60	.30	.20
527	Lerrin LaGrow	.15	.08	.05
528	Wayne Gross	.15	.08	.05
529	Brian Asselstine	.15	.08	.05
530	Frank Tanana	.15	.08	.05
531	Fernando Gonzalez	.15	.08	.05
532	Buddy Schultz	.15	.08	.05
533	Leroy Stanton	.15	.08	.05
534	Ken Forsch	.15	.08	.05
535	Ellis Valentine	.15	.08	.05
536	Jerry Reuss	.15	.08	.05
537	Tom Veryzer	.15	.08	.05
538	Mike Ivie	.15	.08	.05
539	John Ellis	.15	.08	.05
540	Greg Luzinski	.15	.08	.05
541	Jim Slaton	.15	.08	.05
542	Rick Bosetti	.15	.08	.05
543	Kiko Garcia	.15	.08	.05
544	Fergie Jenkins	2.00	1.00	.60
545	John Stearns	.15	.08	.05
546	Bill Russell	.15	.08	.05
547	Clint Hurdle	.15	.08	.05
548	Enrique Romo	.15	.08	.05
549	Bob Bailey	.15	.08	.05
550	Sal Bando	.15	.08	.05
551	Cubs Team (Herman Franks)	.25	.13	.08
552	Jose Morales	.15	.08	.05
553	Denny Walling	.15	.08	.05
554	Matt Keough	.15	.08	.05
555	Biff Pocoroba	.15	.08	.05
556	Mike Lum	.15	.08	.05
557	Ken Brett	.15	.08	.05
558	Jay Johnstone	.15	.08	.05
559	Greg Pryor	.15	.08	.05
560	John Montefusco	.15	.08	.05
561	Ed Ott	.15	.08	.05
562	Dusty Baker	.20	.10	.06
563	Roy Thomas	.15	.08	.05
564	Jerry Turner	.15	.08	.05
565	Rico Carty	.15	.08	.05
566	Nino Espinosa	.15	.08	.05
567	Rich Hebner	.15	.08	.05
568	Carlos Lopez	.15	.08	.05
569	Bob Sykes	.15	.08	.05
570	Cesar Cedeno	.15	.08	.05
571	Darrell Porter	.15	.08	.05
572	Rod Gilbreath	.15	.08	.05
573	Jim Kern	.15	.08	.05
574	Claudell Washington	.15	.08	.05
575	Luis Tiant	.15	.08	.05
576	Mike Parrott	.15	.08	.05
577	Brewers Team (George Bamberger)	.25	.13	.08
578	Pete Broberg	.15	.08	.05
579	Greg Gross	.15	.08	.05
580	Ron Fairly	.15	.08	.05
581	Darold Knowles	.15	.08	.05
582	Paul Blair	.15	.08	.05
583	Julio Cruz	.15	.08	.05
584	Jim Rooker	.15	.08	.05
585	Hal McRae	.15	.08	.05
586	***Bob Horner***	1.00	.50	.30
587	Ken Reitz	.15	.08	.05
588	Tom Murphy	.15	.08	.05

#	Player	NM	EX	VG
589	Terry Whitfield	.15	.08	.05
590	J.R. Richard	.15	.08	.05
591	Mike Hargrove	.15	.08	.05
592	Mike Krukow	.15	.08	.05
593	Rick Dempsey	.15	.08	.05
594	Bob Shirley	.15	.08	.05
595	Phil Niekro	2.00	1.00	.60
596	Jim Wohlford	.15	.08	.05
597	Bob Stanley	.15	.08	.05
598	Mark Wagner	.15	.08	.05
599	Jim Spencer	.15	.08	.05
600	George Foster	.15	.08	.05
601	Dave LaRoche	.15	.08	.05
602	Checklist 485-605	.15	.08	.05
603	Rudy May	.15	.08	.05
604	Jeff Newman	.15	.08	.05
605	Rick Monday	.15	.08	.05
606	Expos Team (Dick Williams)	.25	.13	.08
607	Omar Moreno	.15	.08	.05
608	Dave McKay	.15	.08	.05
609	Silvio Martinez	.15	.08	.05
610	Mike Schmidt	6.00	3.00	1.75
611	Jim Norris	.15	.08	.05
612	***Rick Honeycutt***	.25	.13	.08
613	Mike Edwards	.15	.08	.05
614	Willie Hernandez	.15	.08	.05
615	Ken Singleton	.15	.08	.05
616	Billy Almon	.15	.08	.05
617	Terry Puhl	.15	.08	.05
618	Jerry Remy	.15	.08	.05
619	***Ken Landreaux***	.15	.08	.05
620	Bert Campaneris	.15	.08	.05
621	Pat Zachry	.15	.08	.05
622	Dave Collins	.15	.08	.05
623	Bob McClure	.15	.08	.05
624	Larry Herndon	.15	.08	.05
625	Mark Fidrych	.20	.10	.06
626	Yankees Team (Bob Lemon)	.60	.30	.20
627	Gary Serum	.15	.08	.05
628	Del Unser	.15	.08	.05
629	Gene Garber	.15	.08	.05
630	Bake McBride	.15	.08	.05
631	Jorge Orta	.15	.08	.05
632	Don Kirkwood	.15	.08	.05
633	Rob Wilfong	.15	.08	.05
634	Paul Lindblad	.15	.08	.05
635	Don Baylor	.30	.15	.09
636	Wayne Garland	.15	.08	.05
637	Bill Robinson	.15	.08	.05
638	Al Fitzmorris	.15	.08	.05
639	Manny Trillo	.15	.08	.05
640	Eddie Murray	6.00	3.00	1.75
641	***Bobby Castillo***	.15	.08	.05
642	Wilbur Howard	.15	.08	.05
643	Tom Hausman	.15	.08	.05
644	Manny Mota	.15	.08	.05
645	George Scott	.15	.08	.05
646	Rick Sweet	.15	.08	.05
647	Bob Lacey	.15	.08	.05
648	Lou Piniella	.25	.13	.08
649	John Curtis	.15	.08	.05
650	Pete Rose	6.00	3.00	1.75
651	Mike Caldwell	.15	.08	.05
652	Stan Papi	.15	.08	.05
653	Warren Brusstar	.15	.08	.05
654	Rick Miller	.15	.08	.05
655	Jerry Koosman	.15	.08	.05
656	Hosken Powell	.15	.08	.05
657	George Medich	.15	.08	.05
658	Taylor Duncan	.15	.08	.05
659	Mariners Team (Darrell Johnson)	.25	.13	.08
660	Ron LeFlore	.15	.08	.05
661	Bruce Kison	.15	.08	.05
662	Kevin Bell	.15	.08	.05
663	Mike Vail	.15	.08	.05
664	Doug Bird	.15	.08	.05
665	Lou Brock	3.00	1.50	.90
666	Rich Dauer	.15	.08	.05
667	Don Hood	.15	.08	.05
668	Bill North	.15	.08	.05
669	Checklist 606-726	.15	.08	.05
670	Jim Hunter	3.00	1.50	.90
671	Joe Ferguson	.15	.08	.05
672	Ed Halicki	.15	.08	.05
673	Tom Hutton	.15	.08	.05
674	Dave Tomlin	.15	.08	.05
675	Tim McCarver	.25	.13	.08
676	Johnny Sutton	.15	.08	.05
677	Larry Parrish	.15	.08	.05
678	Geoff Zahn	.15	.08	.05
679	Derrel Thomas	.15	.08	.05
680	Carlton Fisk	3.00	1.50	.90
681	***John Henry Johnson***	.15	.08	.05
682	Dave Chalk	.15	.08	.05
683	Dan Meyer	.15	.08	.05
684	Jamie Easterly	.15	.08	.05
685	Sixto Lezcano	.15	.08	.05
686	Ron Schueler	.15	.08	.05
687	Rennie Stennett	.15	.08	.05
688	Mike Willis	.15	.08	.05
689	Orioles Team (Earl Weaver)	.60	.30	.20
690	Buddy Bell	.15	.08	.05
691	Dock Ellis	.15	.08	.05
692	Mickey Stanley	.15	.08	.05
693	Dave Rader	.15	.08	.05
694	Burt Hooton	.15	.08	.05
695	Keith Hernandez	.15	.08	.05
696	Andy Hassler	.15	.08	.05
697	Dave Bergman	.15	.08	.05
698	Bill Stein	.15	.08	.05
699	Hal Dues	.15	.08	.05
700	Reggie Jackson	4.00	2.00	1.25
701	Orioles Prospects ***(Mark Corey, John Flinn, Sammy Stewart)***	.15	.08	.05
702	Red Sox Prospects **(Joel Finch, Garry Hancock, Allen Ripley)**	.15	.08	.05
703	Angels Prospects **(Jim Anderson, Dave Frost, Bob Slater)**	.15	.08	.05
704	White Sox Prospects ***(Ross Baumgarten, Mike Colbern, Mike Squires)***	.15	.08	.05
705	Indians Prospects **(Alfredo Griffin, Tim Norrid, Dave Oliver)**	.25	.13	.08
706	Tigers Prospects **(Dave Stegman, Dave Tobik, Kip Young)**	.15	.08	.05
707	Royals Prospects **(Randy Bass, Jim Gaudet, Randy McGilberry)**	.15	.08	.05
708	Brewers Prospects **(Kevin Bass, Eddie Romero, Ned Yost)**	.25	.13	.08
709	Twins Prospects **(Sam Perlozzo, Rick Sofield, Kevin Stanfield)**	.15	.08	.05
710	Yankees Prospects **(Brian Doyle, Mike Heath, Dave Rajsich)**	.20	.10	.06
711	A's Prospects **(Dwayne Murphy, Bruce Robinson, Alan Wirth)**	.15	.08	.05
712	Mariners Prospects **(Bud Anderson, Greg Biercevicz, Byron McLaughlin)**	.15	.08	.05
713	Rangers Prospects ***(Danny Darwin, Pat Putnam, Billy Sample)***	.25	.13	.08
714	Blue Jays Prospects **(Victor Cruz, Pat Kelly, Ernie Whitt)**	.15	.08	.05
715	Braves Prospects **(Bruce Benedict, Glenn Hubbard, Larry Whisenton)**	.25	.13	.08
716	Cubs Prospects ***(Dave Geisel, Karl Pagel, Scot Thompson)***	.15	.08	.05
717	Reds Prospects ***(Mike LaCoss, Ron Oester, Harry Spilman)***	.15	.08	.05
718	Astros Prospects **(Bruce Bochy, Mike Fischlin, Don Pisker)**	.15	.08	.05
719	Dodgers Prospects (**Pedro Guerrero, Rudy Law, Joe Simpson)**	1.50	.70	.45
720	Expos Prospects ***(Jerry Fry, Jerry Pirtle, Scott Sanderson)***	.30	.15	.09
721	Mets Prospects **(Juan Berenguer, Dwight Bernard, Dan Norman)**	.15	.08	.05
722	Phillies Prospects ***(Jim Morrison, Lonnie Smith, Jim Wright)***	.50	.25	.15
723	Pirates Prospects **(Dale Berra, Eugenio Cotes, Ben Wiltbank)**	.15	.08	.05
724	Cardinals Prospects ***(Tom Bruno, George Frazier, Terry Kennedy)***	.20	.10	.06
725	Padres Prospects **(Jim Beswick, Steve Mura, Broderick Perkins)**	.15	.08	.05
726	Giants Prospects **(Greg Johnston, Joe Strain, John Tamargo)**	.15	.08	.05

1979 Topps Team Checklist Sheet

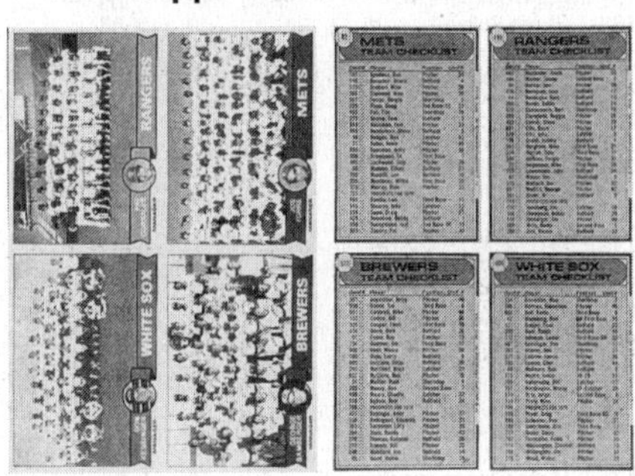

This uncut sheet of 26 team card/checklists was available via a mail-in offer. The sheet was mailed with two folds. The sheet cards are printed on lighter stock.

	NM	EX	VG
Uncut Sheet:	20.00	10.00	6.00

1979 Topps Comics

Issued as the 3" x 3-3/4" wax wrapper for a five-cent piece of bubblegum, this "test" issue was bought up in great quantities by speculators and remains rather common. It is also inexpensive, because the comic-style player representations were not popular with collectors. The set is complete at 33 pieces. Each wax box contains only 11 different players. Original packaging folds are not considered in grading.

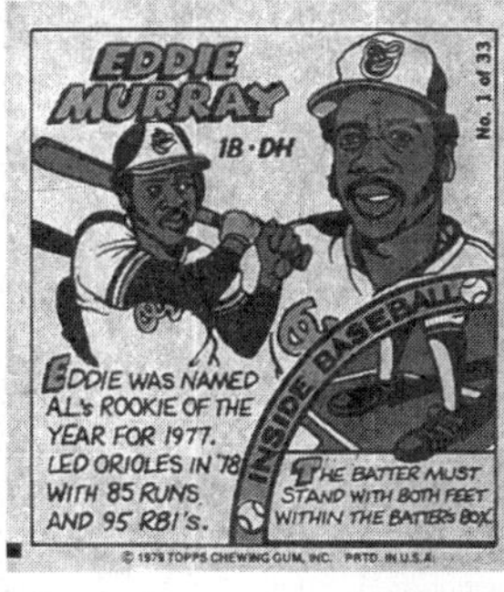

		NM	EX	VG
Complete Set (33):		15.00	7.50	4.50
Common Player:		.25	.13	.08
Wax Box (72):		55.00		
1	Eddie Murray	1.50	.70	.45
2	Jim Rice	.60	.30	.20
3	Carl Yastrzemski	1.50	.70	.45
4	Nolan Ryan	5.00	2.50	1.50
5	Chet Lemon	.25	.13	.08
6	Andre Thornton	.25	.13	.08
7	Rusty Staub	.25	.13	.08
8	Ron LeFlore	.25	.13	.08
9	George Brett	3.00	1.50	.90
10	Larry Hisle	.25	.13	.08
11	Rod Carew	1.50	.70	.45
12	Reggie Jackson	2.50	1.25	.70
13	Ron Guidry	.25	.13	.08
14	Mitchell Page	.25	.13	.08
15	Leon Roberts	.25	.13	.08
16	Al Oliver	.25	.13	.08
17	John Mayberry	.25	.13	.08
18	Bob Horner	.25	.13	.08
19	Phil Niekro	1.00	.50	.30
20	Dave Kingman	.25	.13	.08
21	John Bench	1.50	.70	.45
22	Tom Seaver	1.50	.70	.45
23	J.R. Richard	.25	.13	.08
24	Steve Garvey	.60	.30	.20
25	Reggie Smith	.25	.13	.08
26	Ross Grimsley	.25	.13	.08
27	Craig Swan	.25	.13	.08
28	Pete Rose	3.50	1.75	1.00
29	Dave Parker	.25	.13	.08
30	Ted Simmons	.25	.13	.08
31	Dave Winfield	1.50	.70	.45
32	Jack Clark	.25	.13	.08
33	Vida Blue	.25	.13	.08

1979 Topps/Dynamite Magazine Panels

In at least two issue of its "Dynamite" kids' magazine, Scholastic Book Club teamed with Topps to insert a six-card panel of its 1979 baseball issue. Complete magazines would bear a small premium.

		NM	EX	VG
	Complete Panel:	20.00	10.00	6.00
2	Home Run Leaders (Jim Rice, George Foster)			
5	Victory Leaders (Ron Guidry, Gaylord Perry)			
6	Strikeout Leaders (Nolan Ryan, J.R. Richard)			
201	Mike Edwards (Record Breaker)			
202	Ron Guidry (Record Breaker)			
203	J.R. Richard (Record Breaker)			
	Complete Panel:	15.00	7.50	4.50
232	Jimmy Sexton			
292	Don Reynolds			
336	Bobby Thompson			
432	Dave Heaverlo			
532	Buddy Schultz			
539	John Ellis			

1980 Topps

Again numbering 726 cards measuring 2-1/2" x 3-1/2", Topps did make some design changes in 1980. Fronts have the usual color picture with a facsimile autograph. The player's name appears above the picture, while his position is on a pennant at the upper left and his team on another pennant in the lower right. Backs no longer feature games, returning instead to statistics, personal information, a few headlines and a cartoon about the player. Specialty cards include statistical leaders, and previous season highlights. Many rookies again appear in team threesomes.

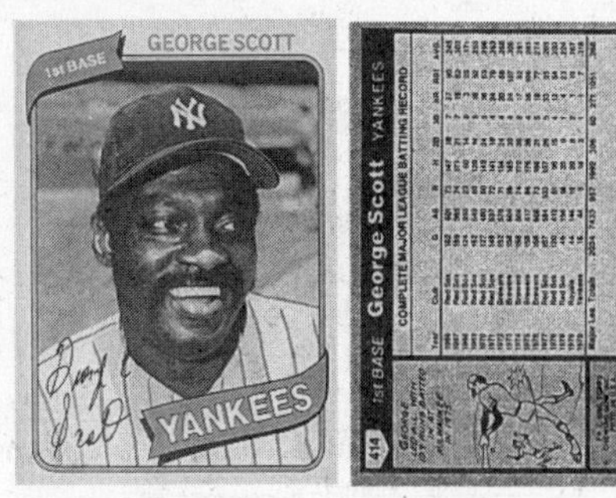

		NM	EX	VG
	Complete Set (726):	100.00	50.00	30.00
	Common Player:	.15	.08	.05
	Wax Pack (15):	10.00		
	Wax Box (36):	260.00		
	Cello Pack (25):	12.50		
	Cello Box (24):	265.00		
	Super Cello Pack (28):	16.00		
	Super Cello Box (24):	275.00		
	Rack Pack (42):	22.50		
	Rack Box (24):	450.00		
	Vending Box (500):	120.00		
1	Lou Brock, Carl Yastrzemski (Highlights)	1.00	.50	.30
2	Willie McCovey (Highlights)	.30	.15	.09
3	Manny Mota (Highlights)	.15	.08	.05
4	Pete Rose (Highlights)	2.00	1.00	.60
5	Garry Templeton (Highlights)	.15	.08	.05
6	Del Unser (Highlights)	.15	.08	.05
7	Mike Lum	.15	.08	.05
8	Craig Swan	.15	.08	.05
9a	Steve Braun (Name in yellow.)	200.00	100.00	60.00
9b	Steve Braun (Name in red.)	.15	.08	.05
10	Denny Martinez	.15	.08	.05
11	Jimmy Sexton	.15	.08	.05
12	John Curtis	.15	.08	.05
13	Ron Pruitt	.15	.08	.05
14	Dave Cash	.15	.08	.05
15	Bill Campbell	.15	.08	.05
16	Jerry Narron	.15	.08	.05
17	Bruce Sutter	2.00	1.00	.60
18	Ron Jackson	.15	.08	.05
19	Balor Moore	.15	.08	.05
20	Dan Ford	.15	.08	.05
21	Manny Sarmiento	.15	.08	.05
22	Pat Putnam	.15	.08	.05
23	Derrel Thomas	.15	.08	.05
24	Jim Slaton	.15	.08	.05
25	Lee Mazzilli	.15	.08	.05
26	Marty Pattin	.15	.08	.05
27	Del Unser	.15	.08	.05
28	Bruce Kison	.15	.08	.05
29	Mark Wagner	.15	.08	.05
30	Vida Blue	.15	.08	.05
31	Jay Johnstone	.15	.08	.05
32	Julio Cruz	.15	.08	.05
33	Tony Scott	.15	.08	.05
34	Jeff Newman	.15	.08	.05
35	Luis Tiant	.15	.08	.05
36	Rusty Torres	.15	.08	.05
37	Kiko Garcia	.15	.08	.05
38	Dan Spillner	.15	.08	.05
39	Rowland Office	.15	.08	.05
40	Carlton Fisk	2.50	1.25	.70
41	Rangers team (Pat Corrales)	.25	.13	.08
42	***Dave Palmer***	.15	.08	.05
43	Bombo Rivera	.15	.08	.05
44	Bill Fahey	.15	.08	.05
45	Frank White	.15	.08	.05
46	Rico Carty	.15	.08	.05
47	Bill Bonham	.15	.08	.05
48	Rick Miller	.15	.08	.05
49	Mario Guerrero	.15	.08	.05
50	J.R. Richard	.15	.08	.05
51	Joe Ferguson	.15	.08	.05
52	Warren Brusstar	.15	.08	.05
53	Ben Oglivie	.15	.08	.05
54	Dennis Lamp	.15	.08	.05
55	Bill Madlock	.15	.08	.05
56	Bobby Valentine	.15	.08	.05
57	Pete Vuckovich	.15	.08	.05
58	Doug Flynn	.15	.08	.05
59	Eddy Putman	.15	.08	.05
60	Bucky Dent	.20	.10	.06
61	Gary Serum	.15	.08	.05
62	Mike Ivie	.15	.08	.05
63	Bob Stanley	.15	.08	.05
64	Joe Nolan	.15	.08	.05
65	Al Bumbry	.15	.08	.05
66	Royals Team (Jim Frey)	.25	.13	.08
67	Doyle Alexander	.15	.08	.05
68	Larry Harlow	.15	.08	.05
69	Rick Williams	.15	.08	.05
70	Gary Carter	2.50	1.25	.70
71	John Milner	.15	.08	.05
72	Fred Howard	.15	.08	.05
73	Dave Collins	.15	.08	.05
74	Sid Monge	.15	.08	.05
75	Bill Russell	.15	.08	.05
76	John Stearns	.15	.08	.05
77	***Dave Stieb***	1.00	.50	.30
78	Ruppert Jones	.15	.08	.05
79	Bob Owchinko	.15	.08	.05
80	Ron LeFlore	.15	.08	.05
81	Ted Sizemore	.15	.08	.05
82	Astros Team (Bill Virdon)	.25	.13	.08
83	***Steve Trout***	.15	.08	.05
84	Gary Lavelle	.15	.08	.05
85	Ted Simmons	.15	.08	.05
86	Dave Hamilton	.15	.08	.05
87	Pepe Frias	.15	.08	.05
88	Ken Landreaux	.15	.08	.05
89	Don Hood	.15	.08	.05
90	Manny Trillo	.15	.08	.05
91	Rick Dempsey	.15	.08	.05
92	Rick Rhoden	.15	.08	.05
93	Dave Roberts	.15	.08	.05
94	***Neil Allen***	.15	.08	.05
95	Cecil Cooper	.15	.08	.05
96	A's Team (Jim Marshall)	.25	.13	.08
97	Bill Lee	.15	.08	.05
98	Jerry Terrell	.15	.08	.05
99	Victor Cruz	.15	.08	.05
100	Johnny Bench	3.00	1.50	.90
101	Aurelio Lopez	.15	.08	.05
102	Rich Dauer	.15	.08	.05
103	***Bill Caudill***	.15	.08	.05
104	Manny Mota	.15	.08	.05
105	Frank Tanana	.15	.08	.05
106	***Jeff Leonard***	.25	.13	.08
107	Francisco Barrios	.15	.08	.05
108	Bob Horner	.15	.08	.05
109	Bill Travers	.15	.08	.05
110	Fred Lynn	.15	.08	.05
111	Bob Knepper	.15	.08	.05
112	White Sox Team (Tony LaRussa)	.45	.25	.14
113	Geoff Zahn	.15	.08	.05
114	Juan Beniquez	.15	.08	.05
115	Sparky Lyle	.15	.08	.05
116	Larry Cox	.15	.08	.05
117	Dock Ellis	.15	.08	.05
118	Phil Garner	.15	.08	.05
119	Sammy Stewart	.15	.08	.05
120	Greg Luzinski	.15	.08	.05
121	Checklist 1-121	.15	.08	.05
122	Dave Rosello	.15	.08	.05
123	Lynn Jones	.15	.08	.05
124	Dave Lemanczyk	.15	.08	.05
125	Tony Perez	2.00	1.00	.60
126	Dave Tomlin	.15	.08	.05
127	Gary Thomasson	.15	.08	.05
128	Tom Burgmeier	.15	.08	.05
129	Craig Reynolds	.15	.08	.05
130	Amos Otis	.15	.08	.05
131	Paul Mitchell	.15	.08	.05
132	Biff Pocoroba	.15	.08	.05
133	Jerry Turner	.15	.08	.05
134	Matt Keough	.15	.08	.05
135	Bill Buckner	.15	.08	.05
136	Dick Ruthven	.15	.08	.05
137	***John Castino***	.15	.08	.05
138	Ross Baumgarten	.15	.08	.05
139	***Dane Iorg***	.15	.08	.05
140	Rich Gossage	.25	.13	.08
141	Gary Alexander	.15	.08	.05
142	Phil Huffman	.15	.08	.05
143	Bruce Bochte	.15	.08	.05
144	Steve Comer	.15	.08	.05
145	Darrell Evans	.15	.08	.05
146	Bob Welch	.15	.08	.05
147	Terry Puhl	.15	.08	.05
148	Manny Sanguillen	.15	.08	.05
149	Tom Hume	.15	.08	.05
150	Jason Thompson	.15	.08	.05
151	Tom Hausman	.15	.08	.05
152	John Fulgham	.15	.08	.05
153	Tim Blackwell	.15	.08	.05
154	Lary Sorensen	.15	.08	.05
155	Jerry Remy	.15	.08	.05
156	Tony Brizzolara	.15	.08	.05
157	Willie Wilson	.15	.08	.05
158	Rob Picciolo	.15	.08	.05
159	Ken Clay	.15	.08	.05
160	Eddie Murray	3.00	1.50	.90
161	Larry Christenson	.15	.08	.05
162	Bob Randall	.15	.08	.05
163	Steve Swisher	.15	.08	.05
164a	Greg Pryor (No name.)	200.00	100.00	60.00
164b	Greg Pryor (Name in blue.)	.15	.08	.05
165	Omar Moreno	.15	.08	.05
166	Glenn Abbott	.15	.08	.05
167	Jack Clark	.15	.08	.05
168	Rick Waits	.15	.08	.05
169	Luis Gomez	.15	.08	.05
170	Burt Hooton	.15	.08	.05
171	Fernando Gonzalez	.15	.08	.05
172	Ron Hodges	.15	.08	.05
173	John Henry Johnson	.15	.08	.05
174	Ray Knight	.15	.08	.05
175	Rick Reuschel	.15	.08	.05
176	Champ Summers	.15	.08	.05
177	Dave Heaverlo	.15	.08	.05
178	Tim McCarver	.15	.08	.05
179	***Ron Davis***	.25	.13	.08
180	Warren Cromartie	.15	.08	.05
181	Moose Haas	.15	.08	.05
182	Ken Reitz	.15	.08	.05
183	Jim Anderson	.15	.08	.05
184	Steve Renko	.15	.08	.05
185	Hal McRae	.15	.08	.05
186	Junior Moore	.15	.08	.05
187	Alan Ashby	.15	.08	.05
188	Terry Crowley	.15	.08	.05
189	Kevin Kobel	.15	.08	.05
190	Buddy Bell	.15	.08	.05
191	Ted Martinez	.15	.08	.05
192	Braves Team (Bobby Cox)	.45	.25	.14
193	Dave Goltz	.15	.08	.05
194	Mike Easler	.15	.08	.05
195	John Montefusco	.15	.08	.05
196	Lance Parrish	.15	.08	.05
197	Byron McLaughlin	.15	.08	.05
198	Dell Alston	.15	.08	.05
199	Mike LaCoss	.15	.08	.05
200	Jim Rice	.30	.15	.09
201	Batting Leaders (Keith Hernandez, Fred Lynn)	.15	.08	.05
202	Home Run Leaders (Dave Kingman, Gorman Thomas)	.15	.08	.05
203	Runs Batted In Leaders (Don Baylor, Dave Winfield)	.35	.20	.11
204	Stolen Base Leaders (Omar Moreno, Willie Wilson)	.15	.08	.05
205	Victory Leaders (Mike Flanagan, Joe Niekro, Phil Niekro)	.25	.13	.08
206	Strikeout Leaders (J.R. Richard, Nolan Ryan)	3.50	1.75	1.00
207	ERA Leaders (Ron Guidry, J.R. Richard)	.25	.13	.08
208	Wayne Cage	.15	.08	.05
209	Von Joshua	.15	.08	.05
210	Steve Carlton	2.50	1.25	.70
211	Dave Skaggs	.15	.08	.05
212	Dave Roberts	.15	.08	.05
213	Mike Jorgensen	.15	.08	.05
214	Angels Team (Jim Fregosi)	.25	.13	.08
215	Sixto Lezcano	.15	.08	.05
216	Phil Mankowski	.15	.08	.05
217	Ed Halicki	.15	.08	.05
218	Jose Morales	.15	.08	.05
219	Steve Mingori	.15	.08	.05
220	Dave Concepcion	.15	.08	.05
221	Joe Cannon	.15	.08	.05
222	***Ron Hassey***	.25	.13	.08
223	Bob Sykes	.15	.08	.05
224	Willie Montanez	.15	.08	.05
225	Lou Piniella	.25	.13	.08
226	Bill Stein	.15	.08	.05
227	Len Barker	.15	.08	.05
228	Johnny Oates	.15	.08	.05
229	Jim Bibby	.15	.08	.05
230	Dave Winfield	2.50	1.25	.70
231	Steve McCatty	.15	.08	.05
232	Alan Trammell	.60	.30	.20
233	LaRue Washington	.15	.08	.05
234	Vern Ruhle	.15	.08	.05
235	Andre Dawson	1.00	.50	.30
236	Marc Hill	.15	.08	.05
237	Scott McGregor	.15	.08	.05
238	Rob Wilfong	.15	.08	.05
239	Don Aase	.15	.08	.05
240	Dave Kingman	.15	.08	.05
241	Checklist 122-242	.15	.08	.05
242	Lamar Johnson	.15	.08	.05
243	Jerry Augustine	.15	.08	.05
244	Cardinals Team (Ken Boyer)	.25	.13	.08
245	Phil Niekro	2.00	1.00	.60
246	Tim Foli	.15	.08	.05
247	Frank Riccelli	.15	.08	.05
248	Jamie Quirk	.15	.08	.05
249	Jim Clancy	.15	.08	.05
250	Jim Kaat	.15	.08	.05
251	Kip Young	.15	.08	.05
252	Ted Cox	.15	.08	.05
253	John Montague	.15	.08	.05
254	Paul Dade	.15	.08	.05
255	Dusty Baker	.15	.08	.05
256	Roger Erickson	.15	.08	.05
257	Larry Herndon	.15	.08	.05
258	Paul Moskau	.15	.08	.05
259	Mets Team (Joe Torre)	.60	.30	.20
260	Al Oliver	.20	.10	.06
261	Dave Chalk	.15	.08	.05
262	Benny Ayala	.15	.08	.05
263	Dave LaRoche	.15	.08	.05
264	Bill Robinson	.15	.08	.05
265	Robin Yount	2.50	1.25	.70
266	Bernie Carbo	.15	.08	.05
267	Dan Schatzeder	.15	.08	.05
268	Rafael Landestoy	.15	.08	.05
269	Dave Tobik	.15	.08	.05
270	Mike Schmidt	4.50	2.25	1.25
271	Dick Drago	.15	.08	.05
272	Ralph Garr	.15	.08	.05
273	Eduardo Rodriguez	.15	.08	.05
274	Dale Murphy	1.50	.70	.45
275	Jerry Koosman	.15	.08	.05
276	Tom Veryzer	.15	.08	.05
277	Rick Bosetti	.15	.08	.05
278	Jim Spencer	.15	.08	.05
279	Rob Andrews	.15	.08	.05
280	Gaylord Perry	2.00	1.00	.60
281	Paul Blair	.15	.08	.05
282	Mariners Team (Darrell Johnson)	.25	.13	.08
283	John Ellis	.15	.08	.05
284	Larry Murray	.15	.08	.05
285	Don Baylor	.25	.13	.08
286	Darold Knowles	.15	.08	.05
287	John Lowenstein	.15	.08	.05
288	Dave Rozema	.15	.08	.05
289	Bruce Bochy	.15	.08	.05
290	Steve Garvey	1.00	.50	.30
291	Randy Scarbery	.15	.08	.05
292	Dale Berra	.15	.08	.05
293	Elias Sosa	.15	.08	.05
294	Charlie Spikes	.15	.08	.05
295	Larry Gura	.15	.08	.05
296	Dave Rader	.15	.08	.05
297	Tim Johnson	.15	.08	.05
298	Ken Holtzman	.15	.08	.05
299	Steve Henderson	.15	.08	.05
300	Ron Guidry	.25	.13	.08
301	Mike Edwards	.15	.08	.05
302	Dodgers Team (Tom Lasorda)	.60	.30	.20
303	Bill Castro	.15	.08	.05
304	Butch Wynegar	.15	.08	.05
305	Randy Jones	.15	.08	.05
306	Denny Walling	.15	.08	.05
307	Rick Honeycutt	.15	.08	.05
308	Mike Hargrove	.15	.08	.05

309	Larry McWilliams	.15	.08	.05
310	Dave Parker	.15	.08	.05
311	Roger Metzger	.15	.08	.05
312	Mike Barlow	.15	.08	.05
313	Johnny Grubb	.15	.08	.05
314	***Tim Stoddard***	.15	.08	.05
315	Steve Kemp	.15	.08	.05
316	Bob Lacey	.15	.08	.05
317	Mike Anderson	.15	.08	.05
318	Jerry Reuss	.15	.08	.05
319	Chris Speier	.15	.08	.05
320	Dennis Eckersley	2.00	1.00	.60
321	Keith Hernandez	.15	.08	.05
322	Claudell Washington	.15	.08	.05
323	Mick Kelleher	.15	.08	.05
324	Tom Underwood	.15	.08	.05
325	Dan Driessen	.15	.08	.05
326	Bo McLaughlin	.15	.08	.05
327	Ray Fosse	.15	.08	.05
328	Twins Team (Gene Mauch)	.25	.13	.08
329	Bert Roberge	.15	.08	.05
330	Al Cowens	.15	.08	.05
331	Rich Hebner	.15	.08	.05
332	Enrique Romo	.15	.08	.05
333	Jim Norris	.15	.08	.05
334	Jim Beattie	.15	.08	.05
335	Willie McCovey	2.50	1.25	.70
336	George Medich	.15	.08	.05
337	Carney Lansford	.15	.08	.05
338	Johnny Wockenfuss	.15	.08	.05
339	John D'Acquisto	.15	.08	.05
340	Ken Singleton	.15	.08	.05
341	Jim Essian	.15	.08	.05
342	Odell Jones	.15	.08	.05
343	Mike Vail	.15	.08	.05
344	Randy Lerch	.15	.08	.05
345	Larry Parrish	.15	.08	.05
346	Buddy Solomon	.15	.08	.05
347	***Harry Chappas***	.15	.08	.05
348	Checklist 243-363	.15	.08	.05
349	Jack Brohamer	.15	.08	.05
350	George Hendrick	.15	.08	.05
351	Bob Davis	.15	.08	.05
352	Dan Briggs	.15	.08	.05
353	Andy Hassler	.15	.08	.05
354	Rick Auerbach	.15	.08	.05
355	Gary Matthews	.15	.08	.05
356	Padres Team (Jerry Coleman)	.25	.13	.08
357	Bob McClure	.15	.08	.05
358	Lou Whitaker	.25	.13	.08
359	Randy Moffitt	.15	.08	.05
360	Darrell Porter	.15	.08	.05
361	Wayne Garland	.15	.08	.05
362	Danny Goodwin	.15	.08	.05
363	Wayne Gross	.15	.08	.05
364	Ray Burris	.15	.08	.05
365	Bobby Murcer	.25	.13	.08
366	Rob Dressler	.15	.08	.05
367	Billy Smith	.15	.08	.05
368	***Willie Aikens***	.20	.10	.06
369	Jim Kern	.15	.08	.05
370	Cesar Cedeno	.15	.08	.05
371	Jack Morris	.15	.08	.05
372	Joel Youngblood	.15	.08	.05
373	***Dan Petry***	.20	.10	.06
374	Jim Gantner	.15	.08	.05
375	Ross Grimsley	.15	.08	.05
376	Gary Allenson	.15	.08	.05
377	Junior Kennedy	.15	.08	.05
378	Jerry Mumphrey	.15	.08	.05
379	Kevin Bell	.15	.08	.05
380	Garry Maddox	.15	.08	.05
381	Cubs Team (Preston Gomez)	.25	.13	.08
382	Dave Freisleben	.15	.08	.05
383	Ed Ott	.15	.08	.05
384	Joey McLaughlin	.15	.08	.05
385	Enos Cabell	.15	.08	.05
386	Darrell Jackson	.15	.08	.05
387a	Fred Stanley (Name in yellow.)	260.00	130.00	78.00
387b	Fred Stanley (Name in red.)	.15	.08	.05
388	Mike Paxton	.15	.08	.05
389	Pete LaCock	.15	.08	.05
390	Fergie Jenkins	2.00	1.00	.60
391	Tony Armas	.15	.08	.05
392	Milt Wilcox	.15	.08	.05
393	Ozzie Smith	5.00	2.50	1.50
394	Reggie Cleveland	.15	.08	.05
395	Ellis Valentine	.15	.08	.05
396	Dan Meyer	.15	.08	.05
397	Roy Thomas	.15	.08	.05
398	Barry Foote	.15	.08	.05
399	Mike Proly	.15	.08	.05
400	George Foster	.15	.08	.05
401	Pete Falcone	.15	.08	.05
402	Merv Rettenmund	.15	.08	.05
403	Pete Redfern	.15	.08	.05
404	Orioles Team (Earl Weaver)	.60	.30	.20
405	Dwight Evans	.15	.08	.05
406	Paul Molitor	2.50	1.25	.70
407	Tony Solaita	.15	.08	.05
408	Bill North	.15	.08	.05
409	Paul Splittorff	.15	.08	.05
410	Bobby Bonds	.15	.08	.05
411	Frank LaCorte	.15	.08	.05
412	Thad Bosley	.15	.08	.05
413	Allen Ripley	.15	.08	.05
414	George Scott	.15	.08	.05
415	Bill Atkinson	.15	.08	.05
416	***Tom Brookens***	.15	.08	.05
417	Craig Chamberlain	.15	.08	.05
418	Roger Freed	.15	.08	.05
419	Vic Correll	.15	.08	.05
420	Butch Hobson	.15	.08	.05
421	Doug Bird	.15	.08	.05
422	Larry Milbourne	.15	.08	.05
423	Dave Frost	.15	.08	.05
424	Yankees Team (Dick Howser)	.45	.25	.14
425	Mark Belanger	.15	.08	.05
426	Grant Jackson	.15	.08	.05
427	Tom Hutton	.15	.08	.05
428	Pat Zachry	.15	.08	.05
429	Duane Kuiper	.15	.08	.05
430	Larry Hisle	.15	.08	.05
431	Mike Krukow	.15	.08	.05
432	Willie Norwood	.15	.08	.05
433	Rich Gale	.15	.08	.05
434	Johnnie LeMaster	.15	.08	.05
435	Don Gullett	.15	.08	.05
436	Billy Almon	.15	.08	.05
437	Joe Niekro	.15	.08	.05
438	Dave Revering	.15	.08	.05
439	Mike Phillips	.15	.08	.05
440	Don Sutton	2.00	1.00	.60
441	Eric Soderholm	.15	.08	.05
442	Jorge Orta	.15	.08	.05
443	Mike Parrott	.15	.08	.05
444	Alvis Woods	.15	.08	.05
445	Mark Fidrych	.25	.13	.08
446	Duffy Dyer	.15	.08	.05
447	Nino Espinosa	.15	.08	.05
448	Jim Wohlford	.15	.08	.05
449	Doug Bair	.15	.08	.05
450	George Brett	5.00	2.50	1.50
451	Indians Team (Dave Garcia)	.25	.13	.08
452	Steve Dillard	.15	.08	.05
453	Mike Bacsik	.15	.08	.05
454	Tom Donohue	.15	.08	.05
455	Mike Torrez	.15	.08	.05
456	Frank Taveras	.15	.08	.05
457	Bert Blyleven	.15	.08	.05
458	Billy Sample	.15	.08	.05
459	Mickey Lolich	.15	.08	.05
460	Willie Randolph	.15	.08	.05
461	Dwayne Murphy	.15	.08	.05
462	Mike Sadek	.15	.08	.05
463	Jerry Royster	.15	.08	.05
464	John Denny	.15	.08	.05
465	Rick Monday	.15	.08	.05
466	Mike Squires	.15	.08	.05
467	Jesse Jefferson	.15	.08	.05
468	Aurelio Rodriguez	.15	.08	.05
469	Randy Niemann	.15	.08	.05
470	Bob Boone	.20	.10	.06
471	Hosken Powell	.15	.08	.05
472	Willie Hernandez	.15	.08	.05
473	Bump Wills	.15	.08	.05
474	Steve Busby	.15	.08	.05
475	Cesar Geronimo	.15	.08	.05
476	Bob Shirley	.15	.08	.05
477	Buck Martinez	.15	.08	.05
478	Gil Flores	.15	.08	.05
479	Expos Team (Dick Williams)	.25	.13	.08
480	Bob Watson	.15	.08	.05
481	Tom Paciorek	.15	.08	.05
482	***Rickey Henderson***	20.00	10.00	6.00
483	Bo Diaz	.15	.08	.05
484	Checklist 364-484	.15	.08	.05
485	Mickey Rivers	.15	.08	.05
486	Mike Tyson	.15	.08	.05
487	Wayne Nordhagen	.15	.08	.05
488	Roy Howell	.15	.08	.05
489	Preston Hanna	.15	.08	.05
490	Lee May	.15	.08	.05
491	Steve Mura	.15	.08	.05
492	Todd Cruz	.15	.08	.05
493	Jerry Martin	.15	.08	.05
494	Craig Minetto	.15	.08	.05
495	Bake McBride	.15	.08	.05
496	Silvio Martinez	.15	.08	.05
497	Jim Mason	.15	.08	.05
498	Danny Darwin	.15	.08	.05
499	Giants Team (Dave Bristol)	.25	.13	.08
500	Tom Seaver	3.00	1.50	.90
501	Rennie Stennett	.15	.08	.05
502	Rich Wortham	.15	.08	.05
503	Mike Cubbage	.15	.08	.05
504	Gene Garber	.15	.08	.05
505	Bert Campaneris	.15	.08	.05
506	Tom Buskey	.15	.08	.05
507	Leon Roberts	.15	.08	.05
508	U.L. Washington	.15	.08	.05
509	Ed Glynn	.15	.08	.05
510	Ron Cey	.15	.08	.05
511	Eric Wilkins	.15	.08	.05
512	Jose Cardenal	.15	.08	.05
513	Tom Dixon	.15	.08	.05
514	Steve Ontiveros	.15	.08	.05
515	Mike Caldwell	.15	.08	.05
516	Hector Cruz	.15	.08	.05
517	Don Stanhouse	.15	.08	.05
518	Nelson Norman	.15	.08	.05
519	Steve Nicosia	.15	.08	.05
520	Steve Rogers	.15	.08	.05
521	Ken Brett	.15	.08	.05
522	Jim Morrison	.15	.08	.05
523	Ken Henderson	.15	.08	.05
524	Jim Wright	.15	.08	.05
525	Clint Hurdle	.15	.08	.05
526	Phillies Team (Dallas Green)	.60	.30	.20
527	Doug Rau	.15	.08	.05
528	Adrian Devine	.15	.08	.05
529	Jim Barr	.15	.08	.05
530	Jim Sundberg	.15	.08	.05
531	Eric Rasmussen	.15	.08	.05
532	Willie Horton	.15	.08	.05
533	Checklist 485-605	.15	.08	.05
534	Andre Thornton	.15	.08	.05
535	Bob Forsch	.15	.08	.05
536	Lee Lacy	.15	.08	.05
537	***Alex Trevino***	.15	.08	.05
538	Joe Strain	.15	.08	.05
539	Rudy May	.15	.08	.05
540	Pete Rose	5.00	2.50	1.50
541	Miguel Dilone	.15	.08	.05
542	Joe Coleman	.15	.08	.05
543	Pat Kelly	.15	.08	.05
544	***Rick Sutcliffe***	2.00	1.00	.60
545	Jeff Burroughs	.15	.08	.05
546	Rick Langford	.15	.08	.05
547a	John Wathan (Name in yellow.)	200.00	100.00	60.00
547b	John Wathan (Name in red.)	.15	.08	.05
548	Dave Rajsich	.15	.08	.05
549	Larry Wolfe	.15	.08	.05
550	Ken Griffey	.15	.08	.05
551	Pirates Team (Chuck Tanner)	.25	.13	.08
552	Bill Nahorodny	.15	.08	.05
553	Dick Davis	.15	.08	.05
554	Art Howe	.15	.08	.05
555	Ed Figueroa	.15	.08	.05
556	Joe Rudi	.15	.08	.05
557	Mark Lee	.15	.08	.05
558	Alfredo Griffin	.15	.08	.05
559	Dale Murray	.15	.08	.05
560	Dave Lopes	.15	.08	.05
561	Eddie Whitson	.15	.08	.05
562	Joe Wallis	.15	.08	.05
563	Will McEnaney	.15	.08	.05
564	Rick Manning	.15	.08	.05
565	Dennis Leonard	.15	.08	.05
566	Bud Harrelson	.15	.08	.05
567	Skip Lockwood	.15	.08	.05
568	***Gary Roenicke***	.15	.08	.05
569	Terry Kennedy	.15	.08	.05
570	Roy Smalley	.15	.08	.05
571	Joe Sambito	.15	.08	.05
572	Jerry Morales	.15	.08	.05
573	Kent Tekulve	.15	.08	.05
574	Scot Thompson	.15	.08	.05
575	Ken Kravec	.15	.08	.05
576	Jim Dwyer	.15	.08	.05
577	Blue Jays Team (Bobby Mattick)	.25	.13	.08
578	Scott Sanderson	.15	.08	.05
579	Charlie Moore	.15	.08	.05
580	Nolan Ryan	7.50	3.75	2.25
581	Bob Bailor	.15	.08	.05
582	Brian Doyle	.15	.08	.05
583	Bob Stinson	.15	.08	.05
584	Kurt Bevacqua	.15	.08	.05
585	Al Hrabosky	.15	.08	.05
586	Mitchell Page	.15	.08	.05
587	Garry Templeton	.15	.08	.05
588	Greg Minton	.15	.08	.05
589	Chet Lemon	.15	.08	.05
590	Jim Palmer	2.50	1.25	.70
591	Rick Cerone	.15	.08	.05
592	Jon Matlack	.15	.08	.05
593	Jesus Alou	.15	.08	.05
594	Dick Tidrow	.15	.08	.05
595	Don Money	.15	.08	.05
596	Rick Matula	.15	.08	.05
597a	Tom Poquette (Name in yellow.)	200.00	100.00	60.00
597b	Tom Poquette (Name in red.)	.15	.08	.05
598	Fred Kendall	.15	.08	.05
599	Mike Norris	.15	.08	.05
600	Reggie Jackson	4.00	2.00	1.25
601	Buddy Schultz	.15	.08	.05
602	Brian Downing	.15	.08	.05
603	Jack Billingham	.15	.08	.05
604	Glenn Adams	.15	.08	.05
605	Terry Forster	.15	.08	.05
606	Reds Team (John McNamara)	.25	.13	.08
607	Woodie Fryman	.15	.08	.05
608	Alan Bannister	.15	.08	.05
609	Ron Reed	.15	.08	.05
610	Willie Stargell	2.50	1.25	.70
611	Jerry Garvin	.15	.08	.05
612	Cliff Johnson	.15	.08	.05
613	Randy Stein	.15	.08	.05
614	John Hiller	.15	.08	.05
615	Doug DeCinces	.15	.08	.05
616	Gene Richards	.15	.08	.05
617	Joaquin Andujar	.15	.08	.05
618	Bob Montgomery	.15	.08	.05
619	Sergio Ferrer	.15	.08	.05
620	Richie Zisk	.15	.08	.05
621	Bob Grich	.15	.08	.05
622	Mario Soto	.15	.08	.05
623	Gorman Thomas	.15	.08	.05
624	Lerrin LaGrow	.15	.08	.05
625	Chris Chambliss	.15	.08	.05
626	Tigers Team (Sparky Anderson)	.75	.40	.25
627	Pedro Borbon	.15	.08	.05
628	Doug Capilla	.15	.08	.05
629	Jim Todd	.15	.08	.05
630	Larry Bowa	.15	.08	.05
631	Mark Littell	.15	.08	.05
632	Barry Bonnell	.15	.08	.05
633	Bob Apodaca	.15	.08	.05
634	Glenn Borgmann	.15	.08	.05
635	John Candelaria	.15	.08	.05
636	Toby Harrah	.15	.08	.05
637	Joe Simpson	.15	.08	.05
638	***Mark Clear***	.15	.08	.05
639	Larry Biittner	.15	.08	.05
640	Mike Flanagan	.15	.08	.05
641	Ed Kranepool	.15	.08	.05
642	Ken Forsch	.15	.08	.05
643	John Mayberry	.15	.08	.05
644	Charlie Hough	.15	.08	.05
645	Rick Burleson	.15	.08	.05
646	Checklist 606-726	.15	.08	.05
647	Milt May	.15	.08	.05
648	Roy White	.15	.08	.05
649	Tom Griffin	.15	.08	.05
650	Joe Morgan	2.50	1.25	.70
651	Rollie Fingers	2.00	1.00	.60
652	Mario Mendoza	.15	.08	.05
653	Stan Bahnsen	.15	.08	.05
654	Bruce Boisclair	.15	.08	.05
655	Tug McGraw	.15	.08	.05

656	Larvell Blanks	.15	.08	.05
657	Dave Edwards	.15	.08	.05
658	Chris Knapp	.15	.08	.05
659	Brewers Team (George Bamberger)	.25	.13	.08
660	Rusty Staub	.15	.08	.05
661	Orioles Future Stars **(Mark Corey, Dave Ford, Wayne Krenchicki)**	.15	.08	.05
662	Red Sox Future Stars **(Joel Finch, Mike O'Berry, Chuck Rainey)**	.15	.08	.05
663	Angels Future Stars ***(Ralph Botting, Bob Clark, Dickie Thon)***	.25	.13	.08
664	White Sox Future Stars **(Mike Colbern, Guy Hoffman, Dewey Robinson)**	.15	.08	.05
665	Indians Future Stars **(Larry Andersen, Bobby Cuellar, Sandy Wihtol)**	.15	.08	.05
666	Tigers Future Stars **(Mike Chris, Al Greene, Bruce Robbins)**	.15	.08	.05
667	Royals Future Stars ***(Renie Martin, Bill Paschall, Dan Quisenberry)***	1.00	.50	.30
668	Brewers Future Stars **(Danny Boitano, Willie Mueller, Lenn Sakata)**	.15	.08	.05
669	Twins Future Stars ***(Dan Graham, Rick Sofield, Gary Ward)***	.25	.13	.08
670	Yankees Future Stars **(Bobby Brown, Brad Gulden, Darryl Jones)**	.15	.08	.05
671	A's Future Stars ***(Derek Bryant, Brian Kingman, Mike Morgan)***	.50	.25	.15
672	Mariners Future Stars **(Charlie Beamon, Rodney Craig, Rafael Vasquez)**	.15	.08	.05
673	Rangers Future Stars **(Brian Allard, Jerry Don Gleaton, Greg Mahlberg)**	.15	.08	.05
674	Blue Jays Future Stars **(Butch Edge, Pat Kelly, Ted Wilborn)**	.15	.08	.05
675	Braves Future Stars **(Bruce Benedict, Larry Bradford, Eddie Miller)**	.15	.08	.05
676	Cubs Future Stars **(Dave Geisel, Steve Macko, Karl Pagel)**	.15	.08	.05
677	Reds Future Stars **(Art DeFreites, Frank Pastore, Harry Spilman)**	.15	.08	.05
678	Astros Future Stars ***(Reggie Baldwin, Alan Knicely, Pete Ladd)***	.15	.08	.05
679	Dodgers Future Stars **(Joe Beckwith, Mickey Hatcher, Dave Patterson)**	.25	.13	.08
680	Expos Future Stars **(Tony Bernazard, Randy Miller, John Tamargo)**	.15	.08	.05
681	Mets Future Stars ***(Dan Norman, Jesse Orosco, Mike Scott)***	1.00	.50	.30
682	Phillies Future Stars **(Ramon Aviles, Dickie Noles, Kevin Saucier)**	.15	.08	.05
683	Pirates Future Stars **(Dorian Boyland, Alberto Lois, Harry Saferight)**	.15	.08	.05
684	Cardinals Future Stars **(George Frazier, Tom Herr, Dan O'Brien)**	.30	.15	.09
685	Padres Future Stars **(Tim Flannery, Brian Greer, Jim Wilhelm)**	.15	.08	.05
686	Giants Future Stars **(Greg Johnston, Dennis Littlejohn, Phil Nastu)**	.15	.08	.05
687	Mike Heath	.15	.08	.05
688	Steve Stone	.15	.08	.05
689	Red Sox Team (Don Zimmer)	.25	.13	.08
690	Tommy John	.25	.13	.08
691	Ivan DeJesus	.15	.08	.05
692	Rawly Eastwick	.15	.08	.05
693	Craig Kusick	.15	.08	.05
694	Jim Rooker	.15	.08	.05
695	Reggie Smith	.15	.08	.05
696	Julio Gonzalez	.15	.08	.05
697	David Clyde	.15	.08	.05
698	Oscar Gamble	.15	.08	.05
699	Floyd Bannister	.15	.08	.05
700	Rod Carew	2.50	1.25	.70
701	***Ken Oberkfell***	.15	.08	.05
702	Ed Farmer	.15	.08	.05
703	Otto Velez	.15	.08	.05
704	Gene Tenace	.15	.08	.05
705	Freddie Patek	.15	.08	.05
706	Tippy Martinez	.15	.08	.05
707	Elliott Maddox	.15	.08	.05
708	Bob Tolan	.15	.08	.05
709	Pat Underwood	.15	.08	.05
710	Graig Nettles	.25	.13	.08
711	Bob Galasso	.15	.08	.05
712	Rodney Scott	.15	.08	.05
713	Terry Whitfield	.15	.08	.05
714	Fred Norman	.15	.08	.05
715	Sal Bando	.15	.08	.05
716	Lynn McGlothen	.15	.08	.05
717	Mickey Klutts	.15	.08	.05
718	Greg Gross	.15	.08	.05
719	Don Robinson	.15	.08	.05
720	Carl Yastrzemski	3.00	1.50	.90
721	Paul Hartzell	.15	.08	.05
722	Jose Cruz	.15	.08	.05
723	Shane Rawley	.15	.08	.05
724	Jerry White	.15	.08	.05
725	Rick Wise	.15	.08	.05
726	Steve Yeager	.15	.08	.05

1980 Topps Team Checklist Sheet

This uncut sheet of 26 1980 Topps team cards was available via a mail-in offer. The sheet was mailed with two folds and includes an offer to picture yourself on a baseball card. The sheet cards are printed on lighter card stock.

	NM	EX	VG
Uncut Sheet	15.00	7.50	4.50

1980 Topps N.Y. Yankees Proof

One of the most popular proof cards of the era is this N.Y. Yankees team photo card with an inset photo of manager Billy Martin, who was fired in October, 1979, after punching a marshmellow salesman. By the time the cards were issued, Martin's name and photo had been replaced by rookie manager Dick Howser. The card is blank-backed and usually shows evidence of having been handcut from a proof sheet.

	NM	EX	VG
N.Y. Yankees	200.00	100.00	60.00

1980 Topps Stickers Prototypes

These appear to be prototypes for a Topp sticker issue that never materialized. In 3-1/2" x 2-1/2" format, the pieces have player picture pairs stuck onto a cardboard backing. Backs are blank. It is unknown if the listed examples, all of which are unique, comprise the entirety of the samples.

		NM	EX	VG
Common Card:		125.00	60.00	35.00
(1)	Johnny Bench, Maury Wills	200.00	100.00	60.00
(2)	Nino Espinosa, Ron Cey	125.00	60.00	35.00
(3)	Dwight Evans, Carlton Fisk	150.00	75.00	45.00
(4)	Don (Ron) Guidry, Dave Parker	125.00	60.00	35.00
(5)	Reggie Jackson, J.R. Richard	200.00	100.00	60.00

1980 Topps Superstar 5x7 Photos

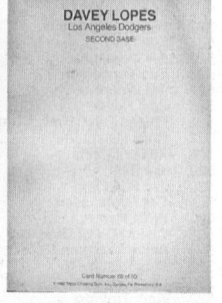

In actuality, these cards measure 4-7/8" x 6-7/8". These were another Topps "test" issue that was bought out almost entirely by speculators. The 60 cards have a color photo on the front and a blue ink facsimile autograph. Backs have the player's name, team, position and card number. The issue was printed on different cardboard stocks, with the first on thick cardboard with a white back and the second on thinner cardboard with a gray back. Prices below are for the more common gray backs; white backs are valued 2.5X-3X the figures shown, except for triple-print cards (indicated by "3P" in checklist), which are valued at about 7.5X the gray-back price in the white-back version. The white backs were test marketed in three-card cello packs in selected geographical areas.

		NM	EX	VG
Complete Set, Gray Backs (60):		10.00	5.00	3.00
Complete Set, White Backs (60):		20.00	10.00	6.00
Common Player, Gray Back:		.25	.13	.08
Common Player, White Back:		.75	.40	.25
Wax Box (48):		10.00		
1	Willie Stargell	1.00	.50	.30
2	Mike Schmidt (3P)	1.50	.70	.45
3	Johnny Bench	1.00	.50	.30
4	Jim Palmer	.75	.40	.25
5	Jim Rice	.50	.25	.15
6	Reggie Jackson (3P)	1.50	.70	.45
7	Ron Guidry	.45	.25	.14
8	Lee Mazzilli	.25	.13	.08
9	Don Baylor	.50	.25	.15
10	Fred Lynn	.25	.13	.08
11	Ken Singleton	.25	.13	.08
12	Rod Carew (3P)	.75	.40	.25
13	Steve Garvey (3P)	.50	.25	.15
14	George Brett (3P)	1.50	.70	.45
15	Tom Seaver	1.50	.70	.45
16	Dave Kingman	.25	.13	.08
17	Dave Parker (3P)	.25	.13	.08
18	Dave Winfield	1.00	.50	.30
19	Pete Rose	2.00	1.00	.60
20	Nolan Ryan	4.00	2.00	1.25
21	Graig Nettles	.25	.13	.08
22	Carl Yastrzemski	1.50	.70	.45
23	Tommy John	.40	.20	.12
24	George Foster	.25	.13	.08
25	J.R. Richard	.25	.13	.08
26	Keith Hernandez	.25	.13	.08
27	Bob Horner	.25	.13	.08
28	Eddie Murray	1.50	.70	.45
29	Steve Kemp	.25	.13	.08
30	Gorman Thomas	.25	.13	.08
31	Sixto Lezcano	.25	.13	.08
32	Bruce Sutter	1.00	.50	.30
33	Cecil Cooper	.25	.13	.08
34	Larry Bowa	.25	.13	.08
35	Al Oliver	.35	.20	.11
36	Ted Simmons	.25	.13	.08
37	Garry Templeton	.25	.13	.08
38	Jerry Koosman	.25	.13	.08
39	Darrell Porter	.25	.13	.08
40	Roy Smalley	.25	.13	.08
41	Craig Swan	.25	.13	.08
42	Jason Thompson	.25	.13	.08
43	Andre Thornton	.25	.13	.08
44	Rick Manning	.25	.13	.08
45	Kent Tekulve	.25	.13	.08
46	Phil Niekro	.75	.40	.25
47	Buddy Bell	.25	.13	.08
48	Randy Jones	.25	.13	.08
49	Brian Downing	.25	.13	.08
50	Amos Otis	.25	.13	.08
51	Rick Bosetti	.25	.13	.08
52	Gary Carter	.75	.40	.25
53	Larry Parrish	.25	.13	.08
54	Jack Clark	.25	.13	.08
55	Bruce Bochte	.25	.13	.08
56	Cesar Cedeno	.25	.13	.08
57	Chet Lemon	.25	.13	.08
58	Dave Revering	.25	.13	.08
59	Vida Blue	.25	.13	.08
60	Davey Lopes	.25	.13	.08

1980 Topps Test Coins

These silver-dollar size (1-3/8" diameter) metal coins appear to have been a Topps test issue. The coins have a player portrait at center on obverse. On reverse center is player personal data and a Topps copyright line. Coins have been seen in compositions resembling bronze, silver and gold. Some of the coins have a hole at top.

	NM	EX	VG
Rod Carew	150.00	75.00	45.00
Steve Garvey	150.00	75.00	45.00
Reggie Jackson	300.00	150.00	90.00

1953 Top Taste Bread Milwaukee Braves

This series of black-and-white mini-posters (8-1/2" x 11-1/4") depicts members of the 1953 Braves holding loaves of bread. They were probably intended for grocery store win-

dow or bakery aisle display. Backs are blank. It's unknown how many players are in the set. See also, Pictsweet Milwaukee Braves.

	NM	EX	VG
Common Player:	150.00	75.00	45.00
(1) Lew Burdette	150.00	75.00	45.00
(2) George Crowe	150.00	75.00	45.00
(3) Andy Pafko	150.00	75.00	45.00
(4) Bucky Walters	150.00	75.00	45.00

1976 Towne Club discs

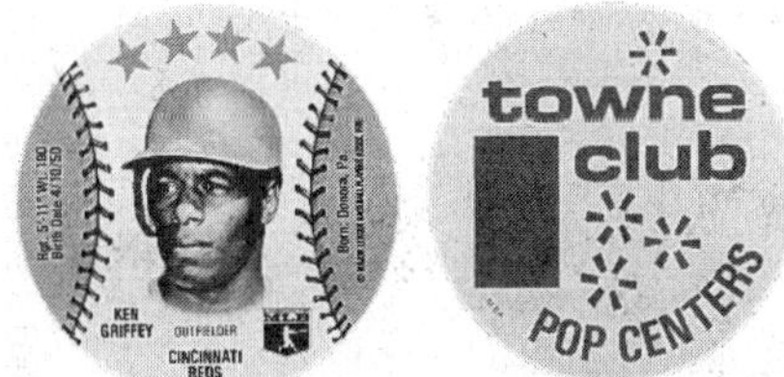

One of several regional sponsors of player disc sets in 1976 was the Towne Club Pop Centers chain. The discs are 3-3/8" diameter with a black-and-white player portrait photo in the center of the baseball design. A line of red stars is above, while the left and right panels feature one of several bright colors. Produced by Michael Schecter Associates under license from the Major League Baseball Players Association, the player photos have had uniform and cap logos removed. Backs are printed in red. The unnumbered checklist here is presented in alphabetical order.

	NM	EX	VG
Complete Set (70):	50.00	25.00	15.00
Common Player:	1.00	.50	.30
(1) Henry Aaron	10.00	5.00	3.00
(2) Johnny Bench	5.00	2.50	1.50
(3) Vida Blue	1.00	.50	.30
(4) Larry Bowa	1.00	.50	.30
(5) Lou Brock	4.00	2.00	1.25
(6) Jeff Burroughs	1.00	.50	.30
(7) John Candelaria	1.00	.50	.30
(8) Jose Cardenal	1.00	.50	.30
(9) Rod Carew	4.00	2.00	1.25
(10) Steve Carlton	4.00	2.00	1.25
(11) Dave Cash	1.00	.50	.30
(12) Cesar Cedeno	1.00	.50	.30
(13) Ron Cey	1.00	.50	.30
(14) Carlton Fisk	4.00	2.00	1.25
(15) Tito Fuentes	1.00	.50	.30
(16) Steve Garvey	3.00	1.50	.90
(17) Ken Griffey	1.00	.50	.30
(18) Don Gullett	1.00	.50	.30
(19) Willie Horton	1.00	.50	.30
(20) Al Hrabosky	1.00	.50	.30
(21) Catfish Hunter	4.00	2.00	1.25
(22) Reggie Jackson (A's)	7.50	3.75	2.25
(23) Randy Jones	1.00	.50	.30
(24) Jim Kaat	1.00	.50	.30
(25) Don Kessinger	1.00	.50	.30
(26) Dave Kingman	1.00	.50	.30
(27) Jerry Koosman	1.00	.50	.30
(28) Mickey Lolich	1.00	.50	.30
(29) Greg Luzinski	1.00	.50	.30
(30) Fred Lynn	1.00	.50	.30
(31) Bill Madlock	1.00	.50	.30
(32) Carlos May	1.00	.50	.30
(33) John Mayberry	1.00	.50	.30
(34) Bake McBride	1.00	.50	.30
(35) Doc Medich	1.00	.50	.30
(36) Andy Messersmith	1.00	.50	.30
(37) Rick Monday	1.00	.50	.30
(38) John Montefusco	1.00	.50	.30
(39) Jerry Morales	1.00	.50	.30
(40) Joe Morgan	4.00	2.00	1.25
(41) Thurman Munson	5.00	2.50	1.50
(42) Bobby Murcer	1.00	.50	.30
(43) Al Oliver	1.00	.50	.30
(44) Jim Palmer	4.00	2.00	1.25
(45) Dave Parker	1.00	.50	.30
(46) Tony Perez	4.00	2.00	1.25
(47) Jerry Reuss	1.00	.50	.30
(48) Brooks Robinson	5.00	2.50	1.50
(49) Frank Robinson	5.00	2.50	1.50
(50) Steve Rogers	1.00	.50	.30
(51) Pete Rose	10.00	5.00	3.00
(52) Nolan Ryan	20.00	10.00	6.00
(53) Manny Sanguillen	1.00	.50	.30
(54) Mike Schmidt	7.50	3.75	2.25
(55) Tom Seaver	5.00	2.50	1.50
(56) Ted Simmons	1.00	.50	.30
(57) Reggie Smith	1.00	.50	.30
(58) Willie Stargell	4.00	2.00	1.25
(59) Rusty Staub	1.50	.70	.45
(60) Rennie Stennett	1.00	.50	.30
(61) Don Sutton	4.00	2.00	1.25
(62) Andy Thornton	1.00	.50	.30
(63) Luis Tiant	1.00	.50	.30
(64) Joe Torre	2.50	1.25	.70
(65) Mike Tyson	1.00	.50	.30
(66) Bob Watson	1.00	.50	.30
(67) Wilbur Wood	1.00	.50	.30
(68) Jimmy Wynn	1.00	.50	.30
(69) Carl Yastrzemski	6.00	3.00	1.75
(70) Richie Zisk	1.00	.50	.30

1910 Toy Town Post Office

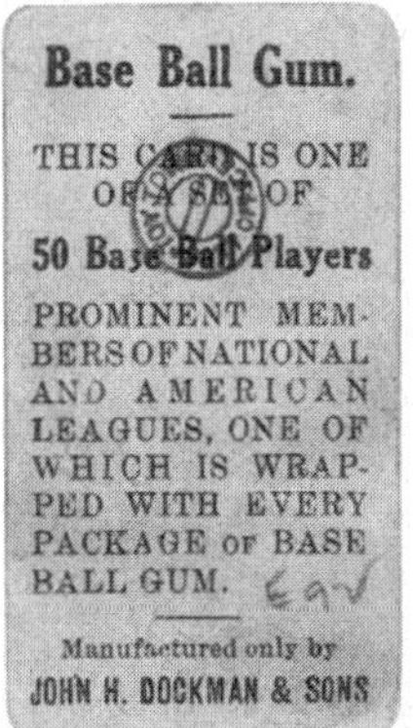
Base Ball Gum.
THIS CARD IS ONE OF A SET OF 50 Base Ball Players
PROMINENT MEMBERS OF NATIONAL AND AMERICAN LEAGUES, ONE OF WHICH IS WRAPPED WITH EVERY PACKAGE OF BASE BALL GUM.
Manufactured only by
JOHN H. DOCKMAN & SONS

Rather than a card issuer, this enigmatic rubber-stamp has been found on the backs of dozens of 1910-era baseball cards. Measuring 1/2" in diameter the seal is in purple ink. At center is a barred circle with "TOY TOWN" above and "POST OFFICE" below. The stamp was part of a Milton Bradley post office toy set and has been seen on different types of cards that eventually made their way into the hobby. On low-grade cards, the stamp neither greatly adds nor detracts from the value of the card on which it is placed.

(See individual card issuers for base values.)

1965 Trade Bloc Minnesota Twins

These cards were produced as part of a baseball game which was marketed at Metropolitan Stadium for $1. The blank-back cards measure 2-1/4" x 3-1/2" and are printed in either blue or sepia tones. Besides Twins players and staff, the set includes cards of various team souvenir items as well as old Met Stadium. Besides the player photo, cards include a facsimile autograph, stats and personal data. The unnumbered cards are checklisted here in alphabetical order.

	NM	EX	VG
Complete Set (52):	600.00	300.00	175.00
Common Player:	15.00	7.50	4.50
Common Non-player Card:	5.00	2.50	1.50
(1) Bernard Allen	15.00	7.50	4.50
(2) Bob Allison	20.00	10.00	6.00
(3) Earl Battey	15.00	7.50	4.50
(4) Dave Boswell	15.00	7.50	4.50
(5) Gerald Fosnow	15.00	7.50	4.50
(6) James Grant	15.00	7.50	4.50
(7) Calvin Griffith	20.00	10.00	6.00
(8) Jimmie Hall	15.00	7.50	4.50
(9) Jim Kaat	25.00	12.50	7.50
(10) Harmon Killebrew	60.00	30.00	18.00
(11) Jerry Kindall	15.00	7.50	4.50
(12) Johnny Klippstein	15.00	7.50	4.50
(13) Frank Kostro	15.00	7.50	4.50
(14) James Lemon	15.00	7.50	4.50
(15) George "Doc" Lentz	15.00	7.50	4.50
(16) Alfred Martin (Billy)	30.00	15.00	9.00
(17) Sam Mele	15.00	7.50	4.50
(18) Donald Mincher	15.00	7.50	4.50
(19) Harold Naragon	15.00	7.50	4.50
(20) Melvin Nelson	15.00	7.50	4.50
(21) Joseph Nossek	15.00	7.50	4.50
(22) Pedro Oliva (Tony)	40.00	20.00	12.00
(23) Camilo Pascual	20.00	10.00	6.00
(24) James Perry	15.00	7.50	4.50
(25) Bill Pleis	15.00	7.50	4.50
(26) Richard Rollins	15.00	7.50	4.50
(27) John Sain	15.00	7.50	4.50
(28) John Sevcik	15.00	7.50	4.50
(29) Richard Stigman	15.00	7.50	4.50
(30) Sandy Valdespino	15.00	7.50	4.50
(31) Zoilo Versalles	25.00	12.50	7.50
(32) Allan Worthington	15.00	7.50	4.50
(33) Gerald Zimmerman	15.00	7.50	4.50
(34) Metropolitan Stadium	10.00	5.00	3.00
(35) L.A. Angels Logo	5.00	2.50	1.50
(36) K.C. Athletics Logo	5.00	2.50	1.50
(37) Cleveland Indians Logo	5.00	2.50	1.50
(38) Baltimore Orioles Logo	5.00	2.50	1.50
(39) Boston Red Sox Logo	5.00	2.50	1.50
(40) Washington Senators Logo	5.00	2.50	1.50
(41) Detroit Tigers Logo	5.00	2.50	1.50
(42) Minnesota Twins Logo	5.00	2.50	1.50
(43) Chicago White Sox Logo	5.00	2.50	1.50
(44) N.Y. Yankees Logo	5.00	2.50	1.50
(45) Twins Autographed Ball	5.00	2.50	1.50
(46) Twins Autographed Bat	5.00	2.50	1.50
(47) Twins Bobbin' Head Doll	5.00	2.50	1.50
(48) Twins Cap	5.00	2.50	1.50
(49) Twins Pennant	5.00	2.50	1.50
(50) Twins Scorebook	5.00	2.50	1.50
(51) Twins Warmup Jacket	5.00	2.50	1.50
(52) Twins Yearbook	5.00	2.50	1.50

1964 Transfer-ette Chicago Cubs Iron-ons

This novelty item features artist-rendered portraits of Cubs players which were designed to be transferred to t-shirts, notebook covers or other items via an iron-on process. Each package contains three sheets of nine images; one each in blue, black and red. The sheets are about 8-3/8" x 10-3/4" with each player image about 2-1/2" x 2-3/4". According to the packaging, other teams were planned, along with larger two-color player portraits.

	NM	EX	VG
Complete Set:	50.00	25.00	15.00

BLACK SHEET
Ernie Banks
Dick Bertell
John Boccabella
Glen Hobbie
Calvin Koonce
Merritt Ranew
Andre Rodgers
Ron Santo
Jim Stewart
BLUE SHEET
Steve Boros
Lou Brock
Bob Buhl
Ellis Burton
Bill Cowan
Dick Ellsworth
Don Elston
Bob Kennedy
Jimmie Schaffer
RED SHEET
Tom Baker
Jim Brewer
Leo Burke
Larry Jackson
Don Landrum
Paul Toth
Jack Warner
Billy Williams
Chicago Cubs Logo

1964 Transfer-ette Chicago White Sox Iron-ons

This novelty item features artist-rendered portraits of White Sox players which were designed to be transferred to t-shirts, notebook covers or other items via an iron-on process. Each package contains three sheets of nine images; one each in blue, black and red. The sheets are about 8-3/8" x 10-3/4" with each player image about 2-1/2" x 2-3/4". According to the packaging, other teams were planned, along with larger two-color player portraits.

	NM	EX	VG
Complete Set:	40.00	20.00	12.00
BLACK SHEET			
Jim Brosnan			
Don Buford			
John Buzhardt			
Joe Cunningham			
Jim Golden			
Joel Horlen			
Charlie Maxwell			
Dave Nicholson			
Gene Stephens			
BLUE SHEET			
Fritz Ackley			
Frank Bauman (Baumann)			
Camilo Carreon			
Dave DeBusschere			
Ed Fisher			
Mike Joyce			
J.C. Martin			
Tom McCraw			
Hoyt Wilhelm			
RED SHEET			
Ron Hansen			
Ray Herbert			
Mike Hershberger			
Jim Landis			
Gary Peters			
Floyd Robinson			
Pete Ward			
Al Weis			
White Sox Logo			

1969 Transogram

These 2-1/2" x 3-1/2" cards were printed on the back of toy baseball player statue boxes. The cards feature a color photo of the player surrounded by a rounded white border. Below the photo is the player's name in red and his team and other personal details all printed in black. The overall background is yellow. The cards were designed to be cut off the box, but collectors prefer to find the box intact and, better still, with the statue inside. While the cards themselves are not numbered, there is a number on each box's end flap, which is the order in which the cards are checklisted here. Three-player boxes were also sold.

		NM	EX	VG
	CUT CARD OR STATUE			
(1)	Joe Azcue	12.50	6.25	3.75
(2)	Willie Horton	12.50	6.25	3.75
(3)	Luis Tiant	12.50	6.25	3.75
(4)	Denny McLain	12.50	6.25	3.75
(5)	Jose Cardenal	12.50	6.25	3.75
(6)	Al Kaline	30.00	15.00	9.00
(7)	Tony Oliva	15.00	7.50	4.50
(8)	Blue Moon Odom	12.50	6.25	3.75
(9)	Cesar Tovar	12.50	6.25	3.75
(10)	Rick Monday	12.50	6.25	3.75
(11)	Harmon Killebrew	25.00	12.50	7.50
(12)	Danny Cater	12.50	6.25	3.75
(13)	Brooks Robinson	35.00	17.50	10.00
(14)	Jim Fregosi	12.50	6.25	3.75
(15)	Dave McNally	12.50	6.25	3.75
(16)	Frank Robinson	35.00	17.50	10.00
(17)	Bobby Knoop	12.50	6.25	3.75
(18)	Rick Reichardt	12.50	6.25	3.75
(19)	Carl Yastrzemski	35.00	17.50	10.00
(20)	Pete Ward	12.50	6.25	3.75
(21)	Rico Petrocelli	12.50	6.25	3.75
(22)	Tommy John	15.00	7.50	4.50
(23)	Ken Harrelson	12.50	6.25	3.75
(24)	Luis Aparicio	25.00	12.50	7.50
(25)	Mike Epstein	12.50	6.25	3.75
(26)	Roy White	12.50	6.25	3.75
(27)	Camilo Pascual	12.50	6.25	3.75
(28)	Mel Stottlemyre	12.50	6.25	3.75
(29)	Frank Howard	15.00	7.50	4.50
(30)	Mickey Mantle	185.00	90.00	55.00
(31)	Lou Brock	25.00	12.50	7.50
(32)	Juan Marichal	25.00	12.50	7.50
(33)	Bob Gibson	25.00	12.50	7.50
(34)	Willie Mays	60.00	30.00	18.00
(35)	Tim McCarver	15.00	7.50	4.50
(36)	Willie McCovey	25.00	12.50	7.50
(37)	Don Wilson	12.50	6.25	3.75
(38)	Billy Williams	25.00	12.50	7.50
(39)	Dan Staub (Rusty)	15.00	7.50	4.50
(40)	Ernie Banks	45.00	22.50	13.50
(41)	Jim Wynn	12.50	6.25	3.75
(42)	Ron Santo	15.00	7.50	4.50
(43)	Tom Haller	12.50	6.25	3.75
(44)	Ron Swoboda	12.50	6.25	3.75
(45)	Willie Davis	12.50	6.25	3.75
(46)	Jerry Koosman	12.50	6.25	3.75
(47)	Jim Lefebvre	12.50	6.25	3.75
(48)	Tom Seaver	30.00	15.00	9.00
(49)	Joe Torre (Atlanta)	20.00	10.00	6.00
(50)	Tony Perez	25.00	12.50	7.50
(51)	Felipe Alou	12.50	6.25	3.75
(52)	Lee May	12.50	6.25	3.75
(53)	Hank Aaron	60.00	30.00	18.00
(54)	Pete Rose	60.00	30.00	18.00
(55)	Cookie Rojas	12.50	6.25	3.75
(56)	Roberto Clemente	60.00	30.00	18.00
(57)	Richie Allen	15.00	7.50	4.50
(58)	Matty Alou	12.50	6.25	3.75
(59)	Johnny Callison	12.50	6.25	3.75
(60)	Bill Mazeroski	25.00	12.50	7.50
	COMPLETE BOX W/STATUE			
(1)	Joe Azcue	85.00	42.50	25.00
(2)	Willie Horton	85.00	42.50	25.00
(3)	Luis Tiant	85.00	42.50	25.00
(4)	Denny McLain	85.00	42.50	25.00
(5)	Jose Cardenal	85.00	42.50	25.00
(6)	Al Kaline	175.00	85.00	50.00
(7)	Tony Oliva	100.00	50.00	30.00
(8)	Blue Moon Odom	85.00	42.50	25.00
(9)	Cesar Tovar	85.00	42.50	25.00
(10)	Rick Monday	85.00	42.50	25.00
(11)	Harmon Killebrew	200.00	100.00	60.00
(12)	Danny Cater	85.00	42.50	25.00
(13)	Brooks Robinson	250.00	125.00	76.00
(14)	Jim Fregosi	85.00	42.50	25.00
(15)	Dave McNally	85.00	42.50	25.00
(16)	Frank Robinson	250.00	125.00	75.00
(17)	Bobby Knoop	85.00	42.50	25.00
(18)	Rick Reichardt	85.00	42.50	25.00
(19)	Carl Yastrzemski	300.00	150.00	90.00
(20)	Pete Ward	85.00	42.50	25.00
(21)	Rico Petrocelli	85.00	42.50	25.00
(22)	Tommy John	120.00	60.00	36.00
(23)	Ken Harrelson	85.00	42.50	25.00
(24)	Luis Aparicio	175.00	85.00	50.00
(25)	Mike Epstein	85.00	42.50	25.00
(26)	Roy White	85.00	42.50	25.00
(27)	Camilo Pascual	85.00	42.50	25.00
(28)	Mel Stottlemyre	85.00	42.50	25.00
(29)	Frank Howard	100.00	50.00	30.00
(30)	Mickey Mantle	850.00	425.00	255.00
(31)	Lou Brock	175.00	85.00	50.00
(32)	Juan Marichal	175.00	85.00	50.00
(33)	Bob Gibson	175.00	85.00	50.00
(34)	Willie Mays	400.00	200.00	120.00
(35)	Tim McCarver	100.00	50.00	30.00
(36)	Willie McCovey	175.00	85.00	50.00
(37)	Don Wilson	85.00	42.50	25.00
(38)	Billy Williams	175.00	85.00	50.00
(39)	Dan Staub (Rusty)	120.00	60.00	36.00
(40)	Ernie Banks	350.00	175.00	100.00
(41)	Jim Wynn	85.00	42.50	25.00
(42)	Ron Santo	120.00	60.00	36.00
(43)	Tom Haller	85.00	42.50	25.00
(44)	Ron Swoboda	85.00	42.50	25.00
(45)	Willie Davis	85.00	42.50	25.00
(46)	Jerry Koosman	120.00	60.00	36.00
(47)	Jim Lefebvre	85.00	42.50	25.00
(48)	Tom Seaver	200.00	100.00	60.00
(49)	Joe Torre (Atlanta)	100.00	50.00	30.00
(50)	Tony Perez	175.00	85.00	50.00
(51)	Felipe Alou	100.00	50.00	30.00
(52)	Lee May	85.00	42.50	25.00
(53)	Hank Aaron	400.00	200.00	120.00
(54)	Pete Rose	400.00	200.00	120.00
(55)	Cookie Rojas	85.00	42.50	25.00
(56)	Roberto Clemente	450.00	225.00	135.00
(57)	Richie Allen	100.00	50.00	30.00
(58)	Matty Alou	85.00	42.50	25.00
(59)	Johnny Callison	85.00	42.50	25.00
(60)	Bill Mazeroski	175.00	85.00	50.00

1970 Transogram

The 1970 Transogram cards were found printed on boxes of three Transogram baseball player statues. The individual player cards are slightly larger than 1969's, at 2-9/16" x 3-1/2". The 30-card set has the same pictures as the 1969 set except for Joe Torre. All players in the '70 set were also in the '69 Transogram issue except for Reggie Jackson, Sam McDowell and Boog Powell. Each box contains a side panel with a series number and 1" x 1-1/4" portrait photos of the players in the series. Prices shown are for cards cut from the box.

		NM	EX	VG
Complete Set (30):		550.00	275.00	175.00
Complete Set, Boxes/Statues (10):		2,255	1,100	650.00
Common Player:		10.00	5.00	3.00
	Series 1 Boxed Set:	400.00	200.00	120.00
(1)	Pete Rose	50.00	25.00	15.00
(2)	Willie Mays	60.00	30.00	18.00
(3)	Cleon Jones	10.00	5.00	3.00
	Series 2 Boxed Set:	160.00	80.00	48.00
(4)	Ron Santo	15.00	7.50	4.50
(5)	Willie Davis	10.00	5.00	3.00
(6)	Willie McCovey	17.50	8.75	5.25
	Series 3 Boxed Set:	275.00	135.00	82.00
(7)	Juan Marichal	17.50	8.75	5.25
(8)	Joe Torre (St. Louis)	15.00	7.50	4.50
(9)	Ernie Banks	30.00	15.00	9.00
	Series 4 Boxed Set:	375.00	185.00	110.00
(10)	Hank Aaron	60.00	30.00	18.00
(11)	Jim Wynn	10.00	5.00	3.00
(12)	Tom Seaver	25.00	12.50	7.50
	Series 5 Boxed Set:	450.00	225.00	135.00
(13)	Bob Gibson	17.50	8.75	5.25
(14)	Roberto Clemente	100.00	50.00	30.00
(15)	Jerry Koosman	10.00	5.00	3.00
	Series 11 Boxed Set:	300.00	150.00	90.00
(16)	Denny McLain	12.50	6.25	3.75
(17)	Reggie Jackson	30.00	15.00	9.00
(18)	Boog Powell	15.00	7.50	4.50
	Series 12 Boxed Set:	175.00	87.00	52.00
(19)	Frank Robinson	25.00	12.50	7.50
(20)	Frank Howard	10.00	5.00	3.00
(21)	Rick Reichardt	10.00	5.00	3.00
	Series 13 Boxed Set:	225.00	110.00	67.00
(22)	Carl Yastrzemski	25.00	12.50	7.50
(23)	Tony Oliva	15.00	7.50	4.50
(24)	Mel Stottlemyre	10.00	5.00	3.00
	Series 14 Boxed Set:	180.00	90.00	54.00
(25)	Al Kaline	25.00	12.50	7.50
(26)	Jim Fregosi	10.00	5.00	3.00
(27)	Sam McDowell	10.00	5.00	3.00
	Series 15 Boxed Set:	180.00	90.00	54.00
(28)	Blue Moon Odom	10.00	5.00	3.00
(29)	Harmon Killebrew	25.00	12.50	7.50
(30)	Rico Petrocelli	10.00	5.00	3.00

1970 Transogram Mets

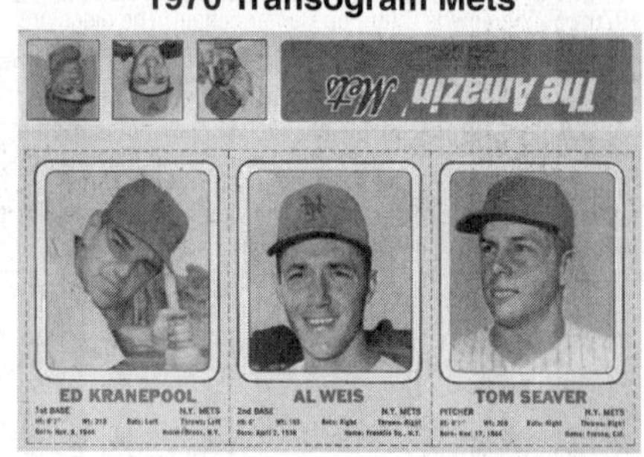

This Transogram set features members of the World Champion N.Y. Mets. Like the other 1970 Transograms, the issue was packaged in a three-statue cardboard box with cellophane front panel and cards printed on the back. Player cards are 2-9/16" x 3-1/2" and retain the basic format of Transogram cards of 1969-70: a color photo with player name in red and team, position and biographical details in black. Backs are blank. Values shown here are for cards cut from the box. Complete unopened boxes are worth 3-4X the figures shown.

		NM	EX	VG
Complete Boxed Set (5):		1,400	700.00	425.00
Complete Panel Set (5):		650.00	325.00	200.00
Complete Card Set (15):		350.00	175.00	100.00
Common Player:		12.50	6.25	3.75
	Series 21 Boxed Set	225.00	110.00	65.00
	Series 21 Uncut Box/Panel	125.00	65.00	35.00
(1)	Ed Kranepool	12.50	6.25	3.75
(2)	Al Weis	12.50	6.25	3.75
(3)	Tom Seaver	35.00	17.50	10.00
	Series 22 Boxed Set	125.00	65.00	35.00
	Series 22 Uncut Box/Panel	60.00	30.00	18.00
(4)	Ken Boswell	12.50	6.25	3.75
(5)	Jerry Koosman	12.50	6.25	3.75
(6)	Jerry Grote	12.50	6.25	3.75
	Series 23 Boxed Set	125.00	65.00	35.00
	Series 23 Uncut Box/Panel	60.00	30.00	18.00
(7)	Art Shamsky	12.50	6.25	3.75
(8)	Gary Gentry	12.50	6.25	3.75
(9)	Tommie Agee	12.50	6.25	3.75
	Series 24 Boxed Set	685.00	340.00	200.00
	Series 24 Uncut Box/Panel	350.00	175.00	100.00
(10)	Nolan Ryan	225.00	110.00	65.00
(11)	Tug McGraw	12.50	6.25	3.75
(12)	Cleon Jones	12.50	6.25	3.75
	Series 25 Boxed Set	150.00	75.00	45.00
	Series 25 Uncut Box/Panel	60.00	30.00	18.00
(13)	Ron Swoboda	12.50	6.25	3.75
(14)	Bud Harrelson	12.50	6.25	3.75
(15)	Donn Clendenon	12.50	6.25	3.75

1920s Otto Treulich & Son

This promotional photocard was issued, according to the blue rubber-stamped advertising on back, by Chicago clothier Otto Treulich & Son. Front of the approximately 2-3/4" x 3-1/2"

card has a black-and-white studio portrait of Cubs pitcher Grover Cleveland Alexander, dressed to the nines (presumably in the haberdashery of the sponsor), and bearing a facsimile autograph.

	NM	EX	VG
Grover Alexander	400.00	200.00	120.00

1909 T.T.T. Cigarettes (T204)

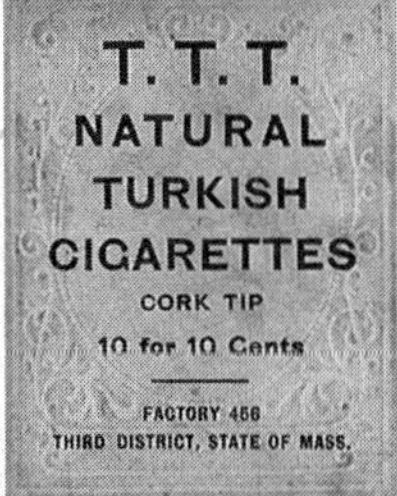

This is one of two brands of cigarette advertising found on the backs of the ornate, gold-trimmed T204 cards. The initials stand for T.T. Tinayens, the Boston firm which also produced Ramly cigarettes, more commonly found mentioned on the cards' backs. In recent years collectors have begun paying a premium as high as 4-5X for the T.T.T. versions.

Premium: 4-5X
(See checklist under Ramly Cigarettes listing.)

1888 Rafael Tuck & Sons Artistic Series Baseball

This series of die-cut color lithographed player figures does not represent actual players, but rather generic figures in late 19th Century uniforms labeled with the names of various major league teams of the era. The actual date of issue is unknown. The cardboard figures were issued in a sheet of 20 with duplicates. Individual figures vary in size with a typical piece about 1-1/2" wide and 2-3/4". Players are shown in batting, throwing and fielding poses. The set was lithographed in Germany and published in England by Rafael Tuck & Sons, a famous postcard publisher.

		NM	EX	VG
Complete Set (10):		3,000	1,500	900.00
Common Card:		325.00	160.00	95.00
(1)	Baltimore	325.00	160.00	95.00
(2)	Boston	325.00	160.00	95.00
(3)	Brooklyn	325.00	160.00	95.00
(4)	Chicago	325.00	160.00	95.00
(5)	Detroit	325.00	160.00	95.00
(6)	Indianapolis	325.00	160.00	95.00
(7)	New York	325.00	160.00	95.00
(8)	Philadelphia	325.00	160.00	95.00
(9)	Pittsburgh	325.00	160.00	95.00
(10)	St. Louis	325.00	160.00	95.00

1925 Turf Cigarettes

"Sports Records" is the name of a two-series, 50-card issue by Turf Cigarettes. The last card in the set depicts George Sisler (though not named) on the front in a color action scene. Black-and-white back of the card describes Sisler's batting prowess. Like other British tobacco cards of the era, size is 2-5/8" x 1-3/8".

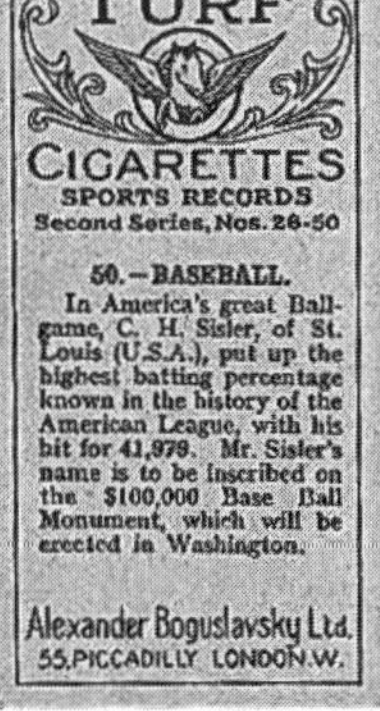

		NM	EX	VG
50	Baseball (George Sisler)	90.00	45.00	25.00

1909-11 Ty Cobb Tobacco (T206)

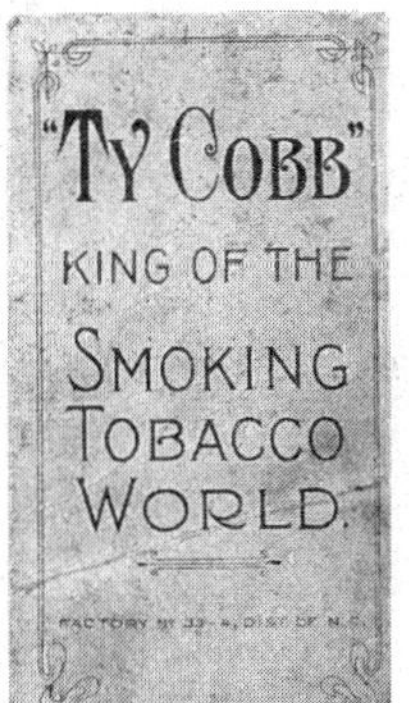

Much rarer than the famed Honus Wagner card from the related cigarette card series known collectively as T206, the Ty Cobb brand tobacco back was known in only about half a dozen collections until June 1997 when a find of five lower-grade specimens was auctioned. Because T206 was generally collected by front design, rather than back, through most of the hobby's history, it has only been in recent years that the value of the "Ty Cobb-back" T206 has begun to approach the other great rarities of the series. The only front known with a Cobb tobacco back is the red-background portrait. Some of the extant examples appear to have been hand-cut from a sheet. In April 2002 a PSA-graded Good example sold at an auction for $18,055. Most recently, an SGC-graded card sold at an auction for $25,000 in May 2005, and another sold at an auction for $24,655 in November 2005.

(See T206, #95b. Approximately 11 known.)

1910-1911 T3 Turkey Red Cabinets

Turkey Red cabinet cards were obtained by mailing in coupons found in Turkey Red, Fez and Old Mill brand cigarettes. Turkey Reds measure 5-3/4" x 8", and feature full-color lithograph fronts with wide gray frames. Backs are known in three styles: 1) checklist with no ordering information, 2) checklist with ordering information, and, 3) with an illustrated ad for Turkey Red cigarettes. The checklist backs are found with both low- and high-number cards, the ad backs are only on cards #77-126. The series consists of 25 boxers and 100 baseball players. Coupons issued in the cigarette boxes indicate the first 50 baseball player cards were produced for spring, 1910, delivery, with the 25 boxers produced later that year and the final 50 baseball players issued in 1911.

		NM	EX	VG
Complete (Baseball) Set (100):		160,000	80,000	48,000
Common Player:		1,200	600.00	360.00
Turkey Red Ad Back: 1.5-2X				
1	Mordecai Brown	3,000	1,500	900.00
2	Bill Bergen	1,200	600.00	360.00
3	Tommy Leach	1,200	600.00	360.00
4	Roger Bresnahan	2,400	1,200	720.00
5	Sam Crawford	2,400	1,200	720.00
6	Hal Chase	1,440	720.00	435.00
7	Howie Camnitz	1,200	600.00	360.00
8	Fred Clarke	2,400	1,200	720.00
9	Ty Cobb	35,000	15,000	9,000
10	Art Devlin	1,200	600.00	360.00
11	Bill Dahlen	1,200	600.00	360.00
12	Wild Bill Donovan	1,200	600.00	360.00
13	Larry Doyle	1,200	600.00	360.00
14	Red Dooin	1,200	600.00	360.00
15	Kid Elberfeld	1,200	600.00	360.00
16	Johnny Evers	2,400	1,200	720.00
17	Clark Griffith	2,400	1,200	720.00
18	Hughie Jennings	2,400	1,200	720.00
19	Addie Joss	3,600	1,800	1,080
20	Tim Jordan	1,200	600.00	360.00
21	Red Kleinow	1,200	600.00	360.00
22	Harry Krause	1,200	600.00	360.00
23	Nap Lajoie	4,000	1,500	900.00
24	Mike Mitchell	1,200	600.00	360.00
25	Matty McIntyre	1,200	600.00	360.00
26	John McGraw	5,000	2,500	1,500
27	Christy Mathewson	15,000	5,000	2,500
28a	Harry McIntyre (Brooklyn)	1,200	600.00	360.00
28b	Harry McIntyre (Brooklyn and Chicago)	1,200	600.00	360.00
29	Amby McConnell	2,000	1,000	600.00
30	George Mullin	1,200	600.00	360.00
31	Sherry Magee	1,200	600.00	360.00
32	Orval Overall	1,200	600.00	360.00
33	Jake Pfeister	1,200	600.00	360.00
34	Nap Rucker	1,200	600.00	360.00
35	Joe Tinker	2,400	1,200	720.00
36	Tris Speaker	6,000	3,000	1,800
37	Slim Sallee	1,200	600.00	360.00
38	Jake Stahl	1,200	600.00	360.00
39	Hube Waddell	2,400	1,200	720.00
40	Vic Willis	2,400	1,200	720.00
41	Hooks Wiltse	1,200	600.00	360.00
42	Cy Young	9,000	3,600	2,160
43	Out At Third	1,400	700.00	400.00
44	Trying To Catch Him Napping	1,400	700.00	400.00
45	Jordan & Herzog At First	1,400	700.00	400.00
46	Safe At Third	1,400	700.00	400.00
47	Frank Chance	2,800	1,400	800.00
48	Jack Murray	1,200	600.00	360.00
49	A Close Play At Second	1,400	700.00	400.00
50	Chief Myers	1,200	600.00	360.00
77	Red Ames	1,200	600.00	360.00
78	Home Run Baker	2,400	1,200	720.00
79	George Bell	1,200	600.00	360.00
80	Chief Bender	2,400	1,200	720.00
81	Bob Bescher	1,200	600.00	360.00
82	Kitty Bransfield	1,200	600.00	360.00
83	Al Bridwell	1,200	600.00	360.00
84	George Browne	1,200	600.00	360.00
85	Bill Burns	1,200	600.00	360.00
86	Bill Carrigan	1,200	600.00	360.00
87	Eddie Collins	2,400	1,200	720.00
88	Harry Coveleski	1,200	600.00	360.00
89	Lou Criger	1,200	600.00	360.00
90a	Mickey Doolin (Doolan)	1,320	660.00	395.00
90b	Mickey Doolan (Name correct.)	1,200	600.00	360.00
91	Tom Downey	1,200	600.00	360.00
92	Jimmy Dygert	1,200	600.00	360.00
93	Art Fromme	1,200	600.00	360.00
94	George Gibson	1,200	600.00	360.00
95	Peaches Graham	1,200	600.00	360.00
96	Bob Groom	1,200	600.00	360.00
97	Dick Hoblitzell	1,200	600.00	360.00
98	Solly Hofman	1,200	600.00	360.00
99	Walter Johnson	15,000	5,000	2,900
100	Davy Jones	1,200	600.00	360.00
101	Wee Willie Keeler	2,400	1,200	720.00
102	Johnny Kling	1,200	600.00	360.00
103	Ed Konetchy	1,200	600.00	360.00
104	Ed Lennox	1,200	600.00	360.00
105	Hans Lobert	1,200	600.00	360.00
106	Harry Lord	1,200	600.00	360.00
107	Rube Manning	2,000	1,000	600.00
108	Fred Merkle	1,200	600.00	360.00
109	Pat Moran	1,200	600.00	360.00
110	George McBride	1,200	600.00	360.00
111	Harry Niles	1,200	600.00	360.00
112a	Dode Paskert (Cincinnati)	1,200	600.00	360.00
112b	Dode Paskert (Cincinnati and Philadelphia)	1,200	600.00	360.00
113	Bugs Raymond	1,200	600.00	360.00
114	Bob Rhoades (Rhoads)	12,000	4,000	2,400
115	Admiral Schlei	1,200	600.00	360.00
116	Boss Schmidt	1,200	600.00	360.00
117	Wildfire Schulte	1,200	600.00	360.00
118	Frank Smith	1,200	600.00	360.00
119	George Stone	1,200	600.00	360.00
120	Gabby Street	1,200	600.00	360.00
121	Billy Sullivan	1,200	600.00	360.00
122a	Fred Tenney (New York)	1,200	600.00	360.00
122b	Fred Tenney (New York and Boston)	1,200	600.00	360.00
123	Ira Thomas	1,200	600.00	360.00
124	Bobby Wallace	2,400	1,200	720.00
125	Ed Walsh	2,400	1,200	720.00
126	Owen Wilson	1,200	600.00	360.00

1911 T5 Pinkerton Cabinets

Because they are photographs affixed to a cardboard backing, the cards in the 1911 Pinkerton set are considered "true" cabinet cards. The Pinkerton cabinets are a rather obscure issue, and because of their original method of distribution, it would be virtually impossible to assemble a complete set today. It remains uncertain how many subjects exist in the set. Pinkerton, the parent of Red Man and other tobacco products, offered the cabinets in exchange for coupons found in cigarette packages. According to an original advertising sheet, some 376 different photos were available. A consumer could exchange 10 coupons for the card of his choice. The photos available included players from the 16 major league teams plus teams from the minor league American Association, Southern Michigan Association, and, probably, others. Pinkertons vary in both size and type of mount. The most desirable combination is a 3-3/8" x 5-1/2" photograph affixed to a thick cardboard mount measuring approximately 4-3/4" x 7-3/4". But original Pinkerton cabinets have also been found in different sizes and with less substantial backings. The most attractive mounts are embossed around the picture, but some Pinkertons have a white border surrounding the photograph. Prices listed are for cards with cardboard mounts. Cards with paper mounts are worth about 50-75 percent of listed prices. Some of the Pinkerton photos were reproduced in postcard size printed issues in later years; some with postcard style backs, some with scorecard backs and others are blank-backed (See 1911 Pinkerton).

		NM	EX	VG
Common Player:		1,000	500.00	315.00
Checklist Brochure:		625.00	315.00	190.00
Redemption Coupon:		500.00	250.00	150.00
Blank-Back Card: 5-10 Percent				
Postcard-Back: 10-15 Percent				
101	Jim Stephens	1,000	500.00	315.00
102	Bobby Wallace	2,190	1,095	655.00
103	Joe Lake	1,000	500.00	315.00
104	George Stone	1,000	500.00	315.00
105	Jack O'Connor	1,000	500.00	315.00
106	Bill Abstein	1,000	500.00	315.00
107	Rube Waddell	2,190	1,095	655.00
108	Roy Hartzell	1,000	500.00	315.00
109	Danny Hoffman	1,000	500.00	315.00
110	Dode Cris	1,000	500.00	315.00
111	Al Schweitzer	1,000	500.00	315.00
112	Art Griggs	1,000	500.00	315.00
113	Bill Bailey	1,000	500.00	315.00
114	Pat Newman	1,000	500.00	315.00
115	Harry Howell	1,000	500.00	315.00
117	Hobe Ferris	1,000	500.00	315.00
118	John McAleese	1,000	500.00	315.00
119	Ray Demmitt	1,000	500.00	315.00
120	Red Fisher	1,000	500.00	315.00
121	Frank Truesdale	1,000	500.00	315.00
122	Barney Pelty	1,000	500.00	315.00
123	Ed Killifer (Killefer)	1,000	500.00	315.00
151	Matty McIntyre	1,000	500.00	315.00
152	Jim Delahanty	1,000	500.00	315.00
153	Hughey Jennings	2,190	1,095	655.00
154	Ralph Works	1,000	500.00	315.00
155	George Moriarity (Moriarty)	1,000	500.00	315.00
156	Sam Crawford	2,190	1,095	655.00
157	Boss Schmidt	1,000	500.00	315.00
158	Owen Bush	1,000	500.00	315.00
159	Ty Cobb	8,750	4,375	2,625
160	Bill Donovan	1,000	500.00	315.00
161	Oscar Stanage	1,000	500.00	315.00
162	George Mullen (Mullin)	1,000	500.00	315.00
163	Davy Jones	1,000	500.00	315.00
164	Charley O'Leary	1,000	500.00	315.00
165	Tom Jones	1,000	500.00	315.00
166	Joe Casey	1,000	500.00	315.00
167	Ed Willetts (Willett)	1,000	500.00	315.00
168	Ed Lafeite (Lafitte)	1,000	500.00	315.00
169	Ty Cobb	20,000	4,530	2,720
170	Ty Cobb	20,000	4,530	2,720
201	John Evers	2,190	1,095	655.00
202	Mordecai Brown	2,190	1,095	655.00
203	King Cole	1,000	500.00	315.00
204	Johnny Cane	1,000	500.00	315.00
205	Heinie Zimmerman	1,000	500.00	315.00
206	Wildfire Schulte	1,000	500.00	315.00
207	Frank Chance	2,190	1,095	655.00
208	Joe Tinker	2,190	1,095	655.00
209	Orvall Overall	1,000	500.00	315.00
210	Jimmy Archer	1,000	500.00	315.00
211	Johnny Kling	1,000	500.00	315.00
212	Jimmy Sheckard	1,000	500.00	315.00
213	Harry McIntyre	1,000	500.00	315.00
214	Lew Richie	1,000	500.00	315.00
215	Ed Ruelbach	1,000	500.00	315.00
216	Artie Hoffman (Hofman)	1,000	500.00	315.00
217	Jake Pfeister	1,000	500.00	315.00
218	Harry Steinfeldt	1,000	500.00	315.00
219	Tom Needham	1,000	500.00	315.00
220	Ginger Beaumont	1,000	500.00	315.00
251	Christy Mathewson	10,000	2,815	1,690
252	Fred Merkle	1,000	500.00	315.00
253	Hooks Wiltsie	1,000	500.00	315.00
254	Art Devlin	1,000	500.00	315.00
255	Fred Snodgrass	1,000	500.00	315.00
256	Josh Devore	1,000	500.00	315.00
257	Red Murray	1,000	500.00	315.00
258	Cy Seymour	1,000	500.00	315.00
259	Rube Marquard	2,190	1,095	655.00
260	Larry Doyle	1,000	500.00	315.00
261	Bugs Raymond	1,000	500.00	315.00
262	Doc Crandall	1,000	500.00	315.00
263	Admiral Schlei	1,000	500.00	315.00
264	Chief Myers (Meyers)	1,000	500.00	315.00
265	Bill Dahlen	1,000	500.00	315.00
266	Beals Becker	1,000	500.00	315.00
267	Louis Drucke	1,000	500.00	315.00
301	Fred Luderus	1,000	500.00	315.00
302	John Titus	1,000	500.00	315.00
303	Red Dooin	1,000	500.00	315.00
304	Eddie Stack	1,000	500.00	315.00
305	Kitty Bransfield	1,000	500.00	315.00
306	Sherry Magee	1,000	500.00	315.00
307	Otto Knabe	1,000	500.00	315.00
308	Jimmy "Runt" Walsh	1,000	500.00	315.00
309	Earl Moore	1,000	500.00	315.00
310	Mickey Doolan	1,000	500.00	315.00
311	Ad Brennan	1,000	500.00	315.00
312	Bob Ewing	1,000	500.00	315.00
313	Lou Schettler	1,000	500.00	315.00
351	Joe Willis	1,000	500.00	315.00
352	Rube Ellis	1,000	500.00	315.00
353	Steve Evans	1,000	500.00	315.00
354	Miller Huggins	2,190	1,095	655.00
355	Arnold Hauser	1,000	500.00	315.00
356	Frank Corridon	1,000	500.00	315.00
357	Roger Bresnahan	2,190	1,095	655.00
358	Slim Sallee	1,000	500.00	315.00
359	Mike Mowrey	1,000	500.00	315.00
360	Ed Konetchy	1,000	500.00	315.00
361	Beckman	1,000	500.00	315.00
362	Rebel Oakes	1,000	500.00	315.00
363	Johnny Lush	1,000	500.00	315.00
364	Eddie Phelps	1,000	500.00	315.00
365	Robert Harmon	1,000	500.00	315.00
401	Lou (Pat) Moran	1,000	500.00	315.00
402	George McQuillian (McQuillan)	1,000	500.00	315.00
403	Johnny Bates	1,000	500.00	315.00
404	Eddie Grant	1,000	500.00	315.00
405	Tommy McMillan	1,000	500.00	315.00
406	Tommy Clark (Clarke)	1,000	500.00	315.00
407	Jack Rowan	1,000	500.00	315.00
408	Bob Bescher	1,000	500.00	315.00
409	Fred Beebe	1,000	500.00	315.00
410	Tom Downey	1,000	500.00	315.00
411	George Suggs	1,000	500.00	315.00
412	Hans Lobert	1,000	500.00	315.00
413	Jimmy Phelan	1,000	500.00	315.00
414	Dode Paskert	1,000	500.00	315.00
415	Ward Miller	1,000	500.00	315.00
416	Richard J. Egan	1,000	500.00	315.00
417	Art Fromme	1,000	500.00	315.00
418	Bill Burns	1,000	500.00	315.00
419	Clark Griffith	2,190	1,095	655.00
420	Dick Hoblitzell	1,000	500.00	315.00
421	Harry Gasper	1,000	500.00	315.00
422	Dave Altizer	1,000	500.00	315.00
423	Larry McLean	1,000	500.00	315.00
424	Mike Mitchell	1,000	500.00	315.00
451	John Hummel	1,000	500.00	315.00
452	Tony Smith	1,000	500.00	315.00
453	Bill Davidson	1,000	500.00	315.00
454	Ed Lennox	1,000	500.00	315.00
455	Zach Wheat	2,190	1,095	655.00
457	Elmer Knetzer	1,000	500.00	315.00
458	Rube Dessau	1,000	500.00	315.00
459	George Bell	1,000	500.00	315.00
460	Jake Daubert	1,000	500.00	315.00
461	Doc Scanlan	1,000	500.00	315.00
462	Nap Rucker	1,000	500.00	315.00
463	Cy Barger	1,000	500.00	315.00
464	Kaiser Wilhelm	1,000	500.00	315.00
465	Bill Bergen	1,000	500.00	315.00
466	Tex Erwin	1,000	500.00	315.00
501	Chas. Bender	2,190	1,095	655.00
502	John Coombs	1,000	500.00	315.00
503	Ed Plank	4,000	1,565	935.00
504	Amos Strunk	1,000	500.00	315.00
505	Connie Mack	2,190	1,095	655.00
506	Ira Thomas	1,000	500.00	315.00
507	Biscoe Lord (Briscoe)	1,000	500.00	315.00
508	Stuffy McInnis	1,000	500.00	315.00
509	Jimmy Dygert	1,000	500.00	315.00
510	Rube Oldring	1,000	500.00	315.00
511	Eddie Collins	2,190	1,095	655.00
512	Home Run Baker	2,190	1,095	655.00
513	Harry Krause	1,000	500.00	315.00
514	Harry Davis	1,000	500.00	315.00
515	Jack Barry	1,000	500.00	315.00
516	Jack Lapp	1,000	500.00	315.00
517	Cy Morgan	1,000	500.00	315.00
518	Danny Murphy	1,000	500.00	315.00
519	Topsy Hartsell	1,000	500.00	315.00
520	Paddy Livingston	1,000	500.00	315.00
521	P. Adkins	1,000	500.00	315.00
522	Eddie Collins	2,190	1,095	655.00
523	Paddy Livingston	1,000	500.00	315.00
551	Doc Gessler	1,000	500.00	315.00
552	Bill Cunningham	1,000	500.00	315.00
554	John Henry	1,000	500.00	315.00
555	Jack Lelivelt	1,000	500.00	315.00
556	Bobby Groome	1,000	500.00	315.00
557	Doc Ralston	1,000	500.00	315.00
558	Kid Elberfelt (Elberfeld)	1,000	500.00	315.00
559	Doc Reisling	1,000	500.00	315.00
560	Herman Schaefer	1,000	500.00	315.00
561	Walter Johnson	6,000	2,500	1,500
562	Dolly Gray	1,000	500.00	315.00
563	Wid Conroy	1,000	500.00	315.00
564	Charley Street	1,000	500.00	315.00
565	Bob Unglaub	1,000	500.00	315.00
566	Clyde Milan	1,000	500.00	315.00
567	George Browne	1,000	500.00	315.00
568	George McBride	1,000	500.00	315.00
569	Red Killifer (Killefer)	1,000	500.00	315.00
601	Addie Joss	2,190	1,095	655.00
602	Addie Joss	2,190	1,095	655.00
603	Napoleon Lajoie	2,190	1,095	655.00
604	Nig Clark (Clarke)	1,000	500.00	315.00
605	Cy Falkenberg	1,000	500.00	315.00
606	Harry Bemis	1,000	500.00	315.00
607	George Stovall	1,000	500.00	315.00
608	Fred Blanding	1,000	500.00	315.00
609	Elmer Koestner	1,000	500.00	315.00
610	Ted Easterly	1,000	500.00	315.00
611	Willie Mitchell	1,000	500.00	315.00
612	Hornhorst	1,000	500.00	315.00
613	Elmer Flick	2,190	1,095	655.00
614	Speck Harkness	1,000	500.00	315.00
615	Tuck Turner	1,000	500.00	315.00
616	Joe Jackson	50,000	10,000	6,000
617	Grover Land	1,000	500.00	315.00
618	Gladstone Graney	1,000	500.00	315.00
619	Dave Callahan	1,000	500.00	315.00
620	Ben DeMott	1,000	500.00	315.00
621	Neill Ball (Neal)	1,000	500.00	315.00
622	Dode Birmingham	1,000	500.00	315.00
623	George Kaler (Kahler)	1,000	500.00	315.00
624	Sid Smith	1,000	500.00	315.00
625	Bert Adams	1,000	500.00	315.00
626	Bill Bradley	1,000	500.00	315.00
627	Napoleon Lajoie	2,190	1,095	655.00
651	Bill Corrigan (Carrigan)	1,000	500.00	315.00
652	Joe Woods (Wood)	1,000	500.00	315.00
653	Heinie Wagner	1,000	500.00	315.00
654	Billy Purtell	1,000	500.00	315.00
655	Frank Smith	1,000	500.00	315.00
656	Harry Lord	1,000	500.00	315.00
657	Patsy Donovan	1,000	500.00	315.00
658	Duffy Lewis	1,000	500.00	315.00
659	Jack Kleinow	1,000	500.00	315.00
660	Ed Karger	1,000	500.00	315.00
661	Clyde Engle	1,000	500.00	315.00
662	Ben Hunt	1,000	500.00	315.00
663	Charlie Smith	1,000	500.00	315.00
664	Tris Speaker	3,000	1,155	695.00
665	Tom Madden	1,000	500.00	315.00
666	Larry Gardner	1,000	500.00	315.00
667	Harry Hooper	2,190	1,095	655.00
668	Marty McHale	1,000	500.00	315.00
669	Ray Collins	1,000	500.00	315.00
670	Jake Stahl	1,000	500.00	315.00
701	Dave Shean	1,000	500.00	315.00
702	Roy Miller	1,000	500.00	315.00
703	Fred Beck	1,000	500.00	315.00
704	Bill Collings (Collins)	1,000	500.00	315.00
705	Bill Sweeney	1,000	500.00	315.00
706	Buck Herzog	1,000	500.00	315.00
707	Bud Sharp (Sharpe)	1,000	500.00	315.00
708	Cliff Curtis	1,000	500.00	315.00
709	Al Mattern	1,000	500.00	315.00
710	Buster Brown	1,000	500.00	315.00
711	Bill Rariden	1,000	500.00	315.00
712	Grant	1,000	500.00	315.00
713	Ed Abbaticchio	1,000	500.00	315.00
714	Cecil Ferguson	1,000	500.00	315.00
715	Billy Burke	1,000	500.00	315.00
716	Sam Frock	1,000	500.00	315.00
717	Wilbur Goode (Good)	1,000	500.00	315.00
751	Charlie French	1,000	500.00	315.00
752	Patsy Dougherty	1,000	500.00	315.00
753	Shano Collins	1,000	500.00	315.00
754	Fred Parent	1,000	500.00	315.00
755	Willis Cole	1,000	500.00	315.00
756	Billy Sullivan	1,000	500.00	315.00
757	Rube Sutor (Suter)	1,000	500.00	315.00
758	Chick Gandil	2,315	1,155	695.00
759	Jim Scott	1,000	500.00	315.00
760	Ed Walsh	2,190	1,095	655.00
761	Gavvy Cravath	1,000	500.00	315.00
762	Bobby Messenger	1,000	500.00	315.00
763	Doc White	1,000	500.00	315.00
764	Rollie Zeider	1,000	500.00	315.00
765	Fred Payne	1,000	500.00	315.00
766	Lee Tannehill	1,000	500.00	315.00
767	Eddie Hahn	1,000	500.00	315.00
768	Hugh Duffy	2,190	1,095	655.00
769	Fred Olmstead	1,000	500.00	315.00
770	Lena Blackbourne (Blackburne)	1,000	500.00	315.00
771	Young "Cy" Young	1,000	500.00	315.00
801	Lew Brockett	1,000	500.00	315.00
802	Frank Laporte (LaPorte)	1,000	500.00	315.00
803	Bert Daniels	1,000	500.00	315.00
804	Walter Blair	1,000	500.00	315.00
805	Jack Knight	1,000	500.00	315.00
806	Jimmy Austin	1,000	500.00	315.00
807	Hal Chase	1,190	595.00	355.00
808	Birdie Cree	1,000	500.00	315.00
809	Jack Quinn	1,000	500.00	315.00
810	Walter Manning	1,000	500.00	315.00
811	Jack Warhop	1,000	500.00	315.00
812	Jeff Sweeney	1,000	500.00	315.00
813	Charley Hemphill	1,000	500.00	315.00
814	Harry Wolters	1,000	500.00	315.00
815	Tom Hughes	1,000	500.00	315.00
816	Earl Gardiner (Gardner)	1,000	500.00	315.00
851	John Flynn	1,000	500.00	315.00
852	Bill Powell	1,000	500.00	315.00
853	Honus Wagner	15,000	3,750	2,250
854	Bill Powell	1,000	500.00	315.00
855	Fred Clarke	2,190	1,095	655.00
856	Owen Wilson	1,000	500.00	315.00
857	George Gibson	1,000	500.00	315.00
858	Mike Simon	1,000	500.00	315.00
859	Tommy Leach	1,000	500.00	315.00

860	Lefty Leifeld (Leifield)	1,000	500.00	315.00
861	Nick Maddox	1,000	500.00	315.00
862	Dots Miller	1,000	500.00	315.00
863	Howard Camnitz	1,000	500.00	315.00
864	Deacon Phillippi (Phillippe)	1,000	500.00	315.00
865	Babe Adams	1,000	500.00	315.00
866	Ed Abbaticchio	1,000	500.00	315.00
867	Paddy O'Connor	1,000	500.00	315.00
868	Bobby Byrne	1,000	500.00	315.00
869	Vin Campbell	1,000	500.00	315.00
870	Ham Hyatt	1,000	500.00	315.00
871	Sam Leever	1,000	500.00	315.00
872	Hans Wagner	15,000	3,750	2,250
873	Hans Wagner	15,000	3,750	2,250
874	Bill McKecknie (McKechnie)	2,190	1,095	655.00
875	Kirby White	1,000	500.00	315.00
901	Jimmie Burke	1,000	500.00	315.00
902	Charlie Carr	1,000	500.00	315.00
903	Larry Cheney	1,000	500.00	315.00
904	Chet Chadbourne	1,000	500.00	315.00
905	Dan Howley	1,000	500.00	315.00
906	Jimmie Burke	1,000	500.00	315.00
907	Ray Mowe	1,000	500.00	315.00
908	Billy Milligan	1,000	500.00	315.00
909	Frank Oberlin	1,000	500.00	315.00
910	Ralph Glaze	1,000	500.00	315.00
911	O'Day	1,000	500.00	315.00
912	Kerns	1,000	500.00	315.00
913	Jim Duggan	1,000	500.00	315.00
914	Simmy Murch	1,000	500.00	315.00
915	Frank Delehanty	1,000	500.00	315.00
916	Craig	1,000	500.00	315.00
917	Jack Coffee (Coffey)	1,000	500.00	315.00
918	Lefty George	1,000	500.00	315.00
919	Otto Williams	1,000	500.00	315.00
920	M. Hayden	1,000	500.00	315.00
951	Joe Cantillion	1,000	500.00	315.00
952	Smith	1,000	500.00	315.00
953	Claud Rossman (Claude)	1,000	500.00	315.00
1001	Tony James	1,000	500.00	315.00
1002	Jack Powell	1,000	500.00	315.00
1003	Wm. J. Harbeau	1,000	500.00	315.00
1004	Homer Smoot	1,000	500.00	315.00
1051	Bill Friel	1,000	500.00	315.00
1052	Bill Friel	1,000	500.00	315.00
1053	Fred Odwell	1,000	500.00	315.00
1054	Alex Reilley	1,000	500.00	315.00
1055	Eugene Packard	1,000	500.00	315.00
1056	Irve Wrattan	1,000	500.00	315.00
1057	"Red" Nelson	1,000	500.00	315.00
1058	George Perring	1,000	500.00	315.00
1059	Glen Liebhardt	1,000	500.00	315.00
1060	Jimmie O'Rourke	1,000	500.00	315.00
1061	Fred Cook	1,000	500.00	315.00
1062	Charles Arbogast	1,000	500.00	315.00
1063	Jerry Downs	1,000	500.00	315.00
1064	"Bunk" Congalton	1,000	500.00	315.00
1065	Fred Carisch	1,000	500.00	315.00
1066	"Red" Sitton	1,000	500.00	315.00
1067	George Kaler (Kahler)	1,000	500.00	315.00
1068	Arthur Kruger	1,000	500.00	315.00
1102	Earl Yingling	1,000	500.00	315.00
1103	Jerry Freeman	1,800	500.00	315.00
1104	Harry Hinchman	1,000	500.00	315.00
1105	Jim Baskette (Toledo)	1,000	500.00	315.00
1106	Denny Sullivan	1,000	500.00	315.00
1107	Carl Robinson	1,000	500.00	315.00
1108	Bill Rodgers	1,000	500.00	315.00
1109	Hi West	1,000	500.00	315.00
1110	Billy Hallman	1,000	500.00	315.00
1111	Wm. Elwert	1,000	500.00	315.00
1112	Piano Legs Hickman	1,000	500.00	315.00
1113	Joe McCarthy	2,190	1,095	655.00
1114	Fred Abbott	1,000	500.00	315.00
1115	Jack Guilligan (Gilligan)	1,000	500.00	315.00
1510	Musser	1,000	500.00	315.00
1613	C. Winger	1,000	500.00	315.00

1911 T201 Mecca Double Folders

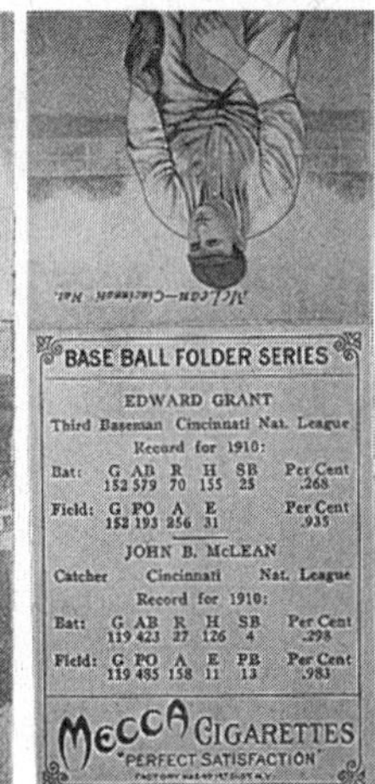

These cards found in packages of Mecca cigarettes feature one player when the card is open, and another when the card is folded; two players sharing the same pair of legs. Mecca Double Folders measure about 2-1/8" to 2-3/16" x 4-11/16". The pictures are color lithographs, the text is printed in black. The cards contain an innovation in the form of the first use of player statistics. The 50-card set contains 100 different players including a number of Hall of Famers. Examples authenticated and graded by major certification firms carry a much larger premium than most other cards of the era.

	NM	EX	VG
Complete Set (50):	25,000	7,000	2,650
Common Player:	385.00	85.00	30.00
(1) William Abstein, John Butler	385.00	85.00	30.00
(2) Frank Baker, Edward Collins	560.00	180.00	75.00
(3) Harry Baker, Thomas Downie (Downey)	385.00	85.00	30.00
(4) James Barrett, Grant McGlynn	385.00	85.00	30.00
(5) John Barry, John Lapp	385.00	85.00	30.00
(6) Charles Bender, Reuben Oldring	435.00	135.00	55.00
(7) William Bergen, Zack Wheat	400.00	130.00	50.00
(8) Walter Blair, Roy Hartzell	385.00	85.00	30.00
(9) Roger Bresnahan, Miller Huggins	650.00	200.00	80.00
(10) Albert Bridwell, Christy Matthewson (Mathewson)	1,200	375.00	150.00
(11) Mordecai Brown, Arthur Hofman	425.00	140.00	55.00
(12) Robert Byrne, Fred Clarke	400.00	115.00	45.00
(13) Frank Chance, John Evers	600.00	200.00	80.00
(14) Harold Chase, Edward Sweeney	400.00	100.00	40.00
(15) Edward Cicotte, John Thoney	625.00	140.00	55.00
(16) Thomas Clarke, Harry Gaspar	385.00	85.00	30.00
(17) Ty Cobb, Sam Crawford	3,000	1,000	400.00
(18) Leonard Cole, John Kling	385.00	85.00	30.00
(19) John Coombs, Ira Thomas	385.00	85.00	30.00
(20) Jake Daubert, Nap Rucker	385.00	85.00	30.00
(21) Bill Donovan, Ralph Stroud	385.00	85.00	30.00
(22) Charles Dooin, John Titus	385.00	85.00	30.00
(23) Patsy Dougherty, Harry Lord	500.00	165.00	65.00
(24) Jerry Downs, Fred Odwell	385.00	85.00	30.00
(25) Larry Doyle, Chief Meyers	385.00	85.00	30.00
(26) James Dygert, Cy Seymour	385.00	85.00	30.00
(27) Norman Elberfeld, George McBride	385.00	85.00	30.00
(28) Fred Falkenberg, Napoleon Lajoie	575.00	190.00	75.00
(29) Edward Fitzpatrick, Ed Killian	385.00	85.00	30.00
(30) Russell Ford, Otis Johnson	385.00	85.00	30.00
(31) Edward Foster, Joseph Ward	385.00	85.00	30.00
(32) Earl Gardner, Tris Speaker	600.00	200.00	80.00
(33) George Gibson, Thomas Leach	385.00	85.00	30.00
(34) George Graham, Al Mattern	385.00	85.00	30.00
(35) Edward Grant, John McLean	385.00	85.00	30.00
(36) Arnold Hauser, Ernest Lush	385.00	85.00	30.00
(37) Charles Herzog, Roy Miller	385.00	85.00	30.00
(38) Charles Hickman, Harry Hinchman	385.00	85.00	30.00
(39) Hugh Jennings, Edgar Summers	425.00	140.00	55.00
(40) Walter Johnson, Charles Street	1,200	400.00	160.00
(41) Frank LaPorte, James Stephens	385.00	85.00	30.00
(42) Joseph Lake, Robert Wallace	400.00	130.00	50.00
(43) Albert Leifield, Mike Simon	385.00	85.00	30.00
(44) John Lobert, Earl Moore	385.00	85.00	30.00
(45) Arthur McCabe, Charles Starr	385.00	85.00	30.00
(46) Lewis McCarty, Joseph McGinnity	400.00	130.00	60.00
(47) Fred Merkle, George Wiltse	385.00	85.00	30.00
(48) Frederick Payne, Edward Walsh	400.00	130.00	60.00
(49) George Stovall, Terrence Turner	385.00	85.00	30.00
(50) Otto Williams, Orville Woodruff	385.00	85.00	30.00

1912 T202 Hassan Triple Folders

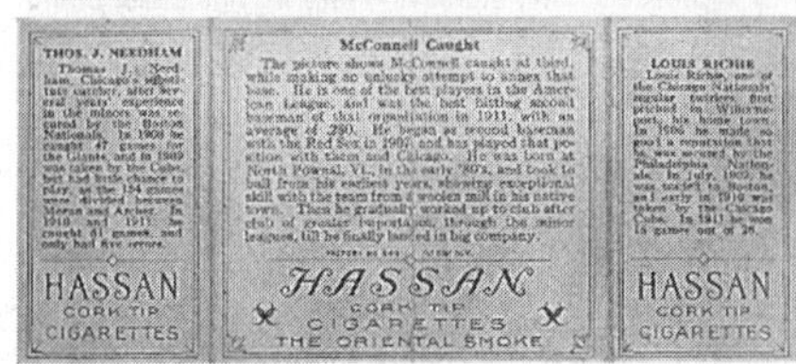

Measuring about 5-1/4" x 2-1/4", Hassan cigarette cards carried the concept of multiple-player cards even further than the double-fold Mecca set of the previous year. Scored so that the player pictures on each end - which are full-color and very close to exact duplicates of T205 "Gold Borders" cards - can fold over the black-and-white action-photo center panel, the Hassan Triple Folder appears like a booklet when closed. The individual player panels are not necessarily related to the action scene. The Hassan Triple Folders feature player biographies on the back of the two individual cards with a description of the action on the back of the center panel. Values depend on the player featured in the center panel, as well as the players featured on the end cards. Moreso than most contemporary cards, the value of NM or better T202s that have been graded by a major certification company well as the players featured on the end cards. Moreso than most contemporary issues, T202s that have been graded NM or better by a reputable certification company carry a larger premium over ungraded examples.

	NM	EX	VG
Complete Set (132):	175,000	45,000	20,000
Common Player:	700.00	200.00	70.00
(1) A Close Play At The Home Plate (LaPorte, Wallace)	700.00	200.00	70.00
(2) A Close Play At The Home Plate (Pelty, Wallace)	700.00	200.00	70.00
(3) A Desperate Slide For Third (Cobb, O'Leary)	5,400	1,850	475.00
(4) A Great Batsman (Barger, Bergen)	700.00	200.00	70.00
(5) A Great Batsman (Bergen, Rucker)	700.00	200.00	70.00
(6) Ambrose McConnell At Bat (Blair, Quinn)	700.00	200.00	70.00
(7) A Wide Throw Saves Crawford (Mullin, Stanage)	700.00	200.00	70.00
(8) Baker Gets His Man (Baker, Collins)	1,200	400.00	200.00
(9) Birmingham Gets To Third (Johnson, Street)	1,400	500.00	200.00
(10) Birmingham's Home Run (Birmingham, Turner)	700.00	200.00	70.00
(11) Bush Just Misses Austin (Magee, Moran)	700.00	200.00	70.00
(12) Carrigan Blocks His Man (Gaspar, McLean)	700.00	200.00	70.00
(13) Carrigan Blocks His Man (Carrigan, Wagner)	700.00	200.00	70.00
(14) Catching Him Napping (Bresnahan, Oakes)	700.00	200.00	70.00
(15) Caught Asleep Off First (Bresnahan, Harmon)	700.00	200.00	70.00
(16) Chance Beats Out A Hit (Chance, Foxen)	1,200	300.00	125.00
(17) Chance Beats Out A Hit (Archer, McIntyre)	700.00	200.00	70.00
(18) Chance Beats Out A Hit (Archer, Overall)	700.00	200.00	70.00
(19) Chance Beats Out A Hit (Archer, Rowan)	700.00	200.00	70.00
(20) Chance Beats Out A Hit (Chance, Shean)	1,500	400.00	200.00
(21) Chase Dives Into Third (Chase, Wolter)	700.00	200.00	70.00
(22) Chase Dives Into Third (Clarke, Gibson)	700.00	200.00	70.00
(23) Chase Dives Into Third (Gibson, Phillippe)	700.00	200.00	70.00
(24) Chase Gets Ball Too Late (Egan, Mitchell)	700.00	200.00	70.00
(25) Chase Gets Ball Too Late (Chase, Wolter)	700.00	200.00	70.00
(26) Chase Guarding First (Chase, Wolter)	700.00	200.00	70.00
(27) Chase Guarding First (Clarke, Gibson)	700.00	200.00	70.00
(28) Chase Guarding First (Gibson, Leifield)	700.00	200.00	70.00
(29) Chase Ready For The Squeeze Play (Magee, Paskert)	700.00	200.00	70.00
(30) Chase Safe At Third (Baker, Barry)	700.00	200.00	70.00
(31) Chief Bender Waiting For A Good One (Bender, Thomas)	700.00	200.00	70.00
(32) Clarke Hikes For Home (Bridwell, Kling)	700.00	200.00	70.00
(33) Close At First (Ball, Stovall)	700.00	200.00	70.00
(34) Close At The Plate (Payne, Walsh)	700.00	200.00	70.00
(35) Close At The Plate (Payne, White)	700.00	200.00	70.00
(36) Close At Third - Speaker (Speaker, Wood)	1,400	500.00	200.00
(37) Close At Third - Wagner (Carrigan, Wagner)	700.00	200.00	70.00
(38) Collins Easily Safe (Byrne, Clarke)	700.00	200.00	70.00
(39) Collins Easily Safe (Baker, Collins)	700.00	200.00	70.00
(40) Collins Easily Safe (Collins, Murphy)	700.00	200.00	70.00
(41) Crawford About To Smash One (Stanage, Summers)	700.00	200.00	70.00
(42) Cree Rolls Home (Daubert, Hummel)	700.00	200.00	70.00
(43) Davy Jones' Great Slide (Delahanty, Jones)	700.00	200.00	70.00
(44) Devlin Gets His Man (Devlin (Giants), Mathewson)	1,800	600.00	300.00
(45) Devlin Gets His Man (Devlin (Rustlers), Mathewson)	3,500	1,200	500.00
(46) Devlin Gets His Man (Fletcher, Mathewson)	1,900	700.00	300.00
(47) Devlin Gets His Man (Mathewson, Meyers)	2,000	700.00	300.00
(48) Donlin Out At First (Camnitz, Gibson)	700.00	200.00	70.00
(49) Donlin Out At First (Doyle, Merkle)	700.00	200.00	70.00
(50) Donlin Out At First (Leach, Wilson)	700.00	200.00	70.00
(51) Donlin Out At First (Dooin, Magee)	700.00	200.00	70.00
(52) Donlin Out At First (Gibson, Phillippe)	700.00	200.00	70.00
(53) Dooin Gets His Man (Dooin, Doolan)	700.00	200.00	70.00

(54)	Dooin Gets His Man (Dooin, Lobert)	700.00	200.00	70.00
(55)	Dooin Gets His Man (Dooin, Titus)	700.00	200.00	70.00
(56)	Easy For Larry (Doyle, Merkle)	700.00	200.00	70.00
(57)	Elberfeld Beats The Throw (Elberfeld, Milan)	700.00	200.00	70.00
(58)	Elberfeld Gets His Man (Elberfeld, Milan)	700.00	200.00	70.00
(59)	Engle In A Close Play (Engle, Speaker)	1,300	400.00	200.00
(60)	Evers Makes A Safe Slide (Archer, Evers)	700.00	200.00	70.00
(61)	Evers Makes A Safe Slide (Chance, Evers)	1,700	600.00	300.00
(62)	Evers Makes A Safe Slide (Archer, Overall)	700.00	200.00	70.00
(63)	Evers Makes A Safe Slide (Archer, Reulbach)	700.00	200.00	70.00
(64)	Evers Makes A Safe Slide (Chance, Tinker)	3,000	1,000	400.00
(65)	Fast Work At Third (Cobb, O'Leary)	4,000	1,200	675.00
(66)	Ford Putting Over A Spitter (Ford, Vaughn)	700.00	200.00	70.00
(67)	Ford Putting Over A Spitter (Sweeney, Ford)	700.00	200.00	70.00
(68)	Good Play At Third (Cobb, Moriarity (Moriarty))	4,500	1,600	800.00
(69)	Grant Gets His Man (Grant, Hoblitzell)	700.00	200.00	70.00
(70)	Hal Chase Too Late (McConnell, McIntyre)	700.00	200.00	70.00
(71)	Hal Chase Too Late (McLean, Suggs)	700.00	200.00	70.00
(72)	Harry Lord At Third (Lennox, Tinker)	700.00	200.00	70.00
(73)	Hartzell Covering Third (Dahlen, Scanlan)	700.00	200.00	70.00
(74)	Hartsel Strikes Out (Gray, Groom)	700.00	200.00	70.00
(75)	Held At Third (Lord, Tannehill)	700.00	200.00	70.00
(76)	Jake Stahl Guarding First (Cicotte, Stahl)	1,300	500.00	200.00
(77)	Jim Delahanty At Bat (Delahanty, Jones)	700.00	200.00	70.00
(78)	Just Before The Battle (Ames, Meyers)	700.00	200.00	70.00
(79)	Just Before The Battle (Bresnahan, McGraw)	700.00	200.00	70.00
(80)	Just Before The Battle (Crandall, Meyers)	700.00	200.00	70.00
(81)	Just Before The Battle (Becker, Devore)	700.00	200.00	70.00
(82)	Just Before The Battle (Fletcher, Mathewson)	1,900	700.00	300.00
(83)	Just Before The Battle (Marquard, Meyers)	700.00	200.00	70.00
(84)	Just Before The Battle (Jennings, McGraw)	700.00	200.00	70.00
(85)	Just Before The Battle (Mathewson, Meyers)	1,300	500.00	200.00
(86)	Just Before The Battle (Murray, Snodgrass)	700.00	200.00	70.00
(87)	Just Before The Battle (Meyers, Wiltse)	700.00	200.00	70.00
(88)	Knight Catches A Runner (Johnson, Knight)	1,300	500.00	200.00
(89)	Lobert Almost Caught (Bridwell, Kling)	700.00	200.00	70.00
(90)	Lobert Almost Caught (Kling, Young)	1,700	400.00	200.00
(91)	Lobert Almost Caught (Kling, Mattern)	700.00	200.00	70.00
(92)	Lobert Almost Caught (Kling, Steinfeldt)	700.00	200.00	70.00
(93)	Lobert Gets Tenney (Dooin, Lobert)	700.00	200.00	70.00
(94)	Lord Catches His Man (Lord, Tannehil)	700.00	200.00	70.00
(95)	McConnell Caught (Needham, Richie)	700.00	200.00	70.00
(96)	McIntyre At Bat (McConnell, McIntyre)	700.00	200.00	70.00
(97)	Moriarty Spiked (Stanage, Willett)	700.00	200.00	70.00
(98)	Nearly Caught (Bates, Bescher)	700.00	200.00	70.00
(99)	Oldring Almost Home (Lord, Oldring)	700.00	200.00	70.00
(100)	Schaefer On First (McBride, Milan)	700.00	200.00	70.00
(101)	Schaefer Steals Second (Griffith, McBride)	700.00	200.00	70.00
(102)	Scoring From Second (Lord, Oldring)	700.00	200.00	70.00
(103)	Scrambling Back To First (Barger, Bergen)	700.00	200.00	70.00
(104)	Scrambling Back To First (Chase, Wolter)	700.00	200.00	70.00
(105)	Speaker Almost Caught (Clarke, Miller)	1,300	500.00	200.00
(106)	Speaker Rounding Third (Speaker, Wood)	2,000	700.00	300.00
(107)	Speaker Scores (Engle, Speaker)	2,000	700.00	300.00
(108)	Stahl Safe (Austin, Stovall)	700.00	200.00	70.00
(109)	Stone About To Swing (Schulte, Sheckard)	700.00	200.00	70.00
(110)	Sullivan Puts Up A High One (Evans, Huggins)	700.00	200.00	70.00
(111)	Sullivan Puts Up A High One (Gray, Groom)	700.00	200.00	70.00
(112)	Sweeney Gets Stahl (Ford, Vaughn)	700.00	200.00	70.00
(113)	Sweeney Gets Stahl (Ford, Sweeney)	700.00	200.00	70.00
(114)	Tenney Lands Safely (Latham, Raymond)	700.00	200.00	70.00
(115)	The Athletic Infield (Baker, Barry)	700.00	200.00	70.00
(116)	The Athletic Infield (Brown, Graham)	700.00	200.00	70.00
(117)	The Athletic Infield (Hauser, Konetchy)	700.00	200.00	70.00
(118)	The Athletic Infield (Krause, Thomas)	700.00	200.00	70.00
(119)	The Pinch Hitter (Egan, Hoblitzell)	700.00	200.00	70.00
(120)	The Scissors Slide (Birmingham, Turner)	700.00	200.00	70.00
(121)	Tom Jones At Bat (Fromme, McLean)	700.00	200.00	70.00
(122)	Tom Jones At Bat (Gaspar, McLean)	700.00	200.00	70.00
(123)	Too Late For Devlin (Ames, Meyers)	700.00	200.00	70.00
(124)	Too Late For Devlin (Crandall, Meyers)	700.00	200.00	70.00
(125)	Too Late For Devlin (Devlin (Giants), Mathewson)	2,000	700.00	300.00
(126)	Too Late For Devlin (Devlin (Rustlers), Mathewson)	3,900	1,400	600.00
(127)	Too Late For Devlin (Marquard, Meyers)	700.00	200.00	70.00
(128)	Too Late For Devlin (Meyers, Wiltse)	700.00	200.00	70.00
(129)	Ty Cobb Steals Third (Cobb, Jennings)	7,400	2,600	1,100
(130)	Ty Cobb Steals Third (Cobb, Moriarty)	5,400	1,850	850.00
(131)	Ty Cobb Steals Third (Austin, Stovall)	3,000	1,100	500.00
(132)	Wheat Strikes Out (Dahlen, Wheat)	1,300	500.00	200.00

1909 T204

(See 1909 Ramly Cigarettes, 1909 T.T.T. Cigarettes.)

1911 T205 Gold Border

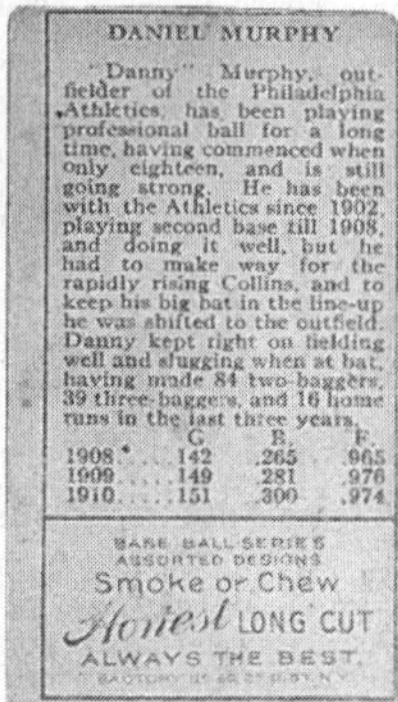

Featuring distinctive gold-leaf borders, these cards were issued in a number of different cigarette brands. The cards nominally measure 1-7/16" x 2-5/8" although many cards, even though untrimmed or unaltered, measure somewhat less than those dimensions in length and/or width. American League cards feature a color lithograph of the player inside a stylized baseball diamond. National League cards have head-and-shoulders portraits on a plain background, plus the first-ever use of a facsimile autograph in a major card set. The 12 minor league players in the set feature three-quarter length portraits or action pictures in an elaborate frame of columns and other devices. Card backs of the major leaguers carry the player's full name (another first) and statistics. Card backs of the minor leaguers lack the statistics. The complete set price does not include the scarcer of the letter-suffixed variations. Values shown are for cards with the most common cigarette advertising on back: Piedmont and Sweet Caporal. Cards of other brands may carry a premium (see listings under brand name). The condition of the fragile gold leaf on the borders is an important grading consideration.

		NM	EX	VG
	Common Player:	720.00	100.00	45.00
(1)	Edward J. Abbaticchio	720.00	100.00	45.00
(2)	Doc Adkins	1,620	240.00	95.00
(3)	Leon K. Ames	720.00	100.00	45.00
(4)	Jas. P. Archer	720.00	100.00	45.00
(5)	Jimmy Austin	720.00	100.00	45.00
(6)	Bill Bailey	720.00	100.00	45.00
(7)	Home Run Baker	2,340	350.00	140.00
(8)	Neal Ball	720.00	100.00	45.00
(9)	E.B. Barger (Full "B" on cap.)	1,500	220.00	90.00
(10)	E.B. Barger (Partial "B" on cap.)	2,400	360.00	145.00
(11)	Jack Barry	720.00	100.00	45.00
(12)	Emil Batch	1,620	240.00	95.00
(13)	John W. Bates	720.00	100.00	45.00
(14)	Fred Beck	720.00	100.00	45.00
(15)	B. Becker	720.00	100.00	45.00
(16)	George G. Bell	720.00	100.00	45.00
(17)	Chas. Bender	2,100	315.00	120.00
(18)	William Bergen	720.00	100.00	45.00
(19)	Bob Bescher	720.00	100.00	45.00
(20)	Joe Birmingham	720.00	100.00	45.00
(21)	Lena Blackburne	720.00	100.00	45.00
(22)	William E. Bransfield	720.00	100.00	45.00
(23)	Roger P. Bresnahan (Mouth closed.)	1,680	250.00	105.00
(24)	Roger P. Bresnahan (Mouth open.)	3,420	510.00	210.00
(25)	A.H. Bridwell	720.00	100.00	45.00
(26)	Mordecai Brown	1,980	295.00	120.00
(27)	Robert Byrne	720.00	100.00	45.00
(28)	Hick Cady	1,620	240.00	95.00
(29)	H. Camnitz	720.00	100.00	45.00
(30)	Bill Carrigan	720.00	100.00	45.00
(31)	Frank J. Chance	2,280	345.00	140.00
(32a)	Hal Chase (Both ears show, gold diamond frame extends below shoulders.)	1,080	165.00	65.00
(32b)	Hal Chase (Both ears show, gold diamond frame ends at shoulders.)	1,620	240.00	95.00
(33)	Hal Chase (Only left ear shows.)	3,240	480.00	195.00
(34)	Ed Cicotte	2,580	390.00	150.00
(35)	Fred C. Clarke	1,440	215.00	90.00
(36)	Ty Cobb	13,200	3,750	1,080
(37)	Eddie Collins (Mouth closed.)	2,100	315.00	120.00
(38)	Eddie Collins (Mouth open.)	4,680	700.00	285.00
(39)	Jimmy Collins	2,580	390.00	155.00
(40)	Frank J. Corridon	720.00	100.00	45.00
(41a)	Otis Crandall ("t" not crossed in name)	1,020	150.00	60.00
(41b)	Otis Crandall ("t" crossed in name)	1,320	200.00	80.00
(42)	Lou Criger	720.00	100.00	45.00
(43)	W.F. Dahlen	2,200	400.00	175.00
(44)	Jake Daubert	720.00	10.00	45.00
(45)	Jim Delahanty	720.00	100.00	45.00
(46)	Arthur Devlin	720.00	100.00	45.00
(47)	Josh Devore	720.00	100.00	45.00
(48)	W.R. Dickson	720.00	100.00	45.00
(49)	Jiggs Donohue (Donahue)	2,880	435.00	175.00
(50)	Chas. S. Dooin	720.00	100.00	45.00
(51)	Michael J. Doolan	720.00	100.00	45.00
(52a)	Patsy Dougherty (Red sock for team emblem.)	2,500	500.00	200.00
(52b)	Patsy Dougherty (White sock for team emblem.)	1,000	400.00	100.00
(53)	Thomas Downey	720.00	100.00	45.00
(54)	Larry Doyle	720.00	100.00	45.00
(55)	Hugh Duffy	2,820	420.00	170.00
(56)	Jack Dunn	2,640	395.00	155.00
(57)	Jimmy Dygert	720.00	100.00	45.00
(58)	R. Egan	720.00	100.00	45.00
(59)	Kid Elberfeld	720.00	100.00	45.00
(60)	Clyde Engle	720.00	100.00	45.00
(61)	Louis Evans	720.00	100.00	45.00
(62)	John J. Evers	3,300	495.00	200.00
(63)	Robert Ewing	720.00	100.00	45.00
(64)	G.C. Ferguson	720.00	100.00	45.00
(65)	Ray Fisher	2,940	440.00	175.00
(66)	Arthur Fletcher	720.00	100.00	45.00
(67)	John A. Flynn	720.00	100.00	45.00
(68)	Russ Ford (Black cap.)	700.00	100.00	50.00
(69)	Russ Ford (White cap.)	2,220	330.00	135.00
(70)	Wm. A. Foxen	720.00	100.00	45.00
(71)	Jimmy Frick	1,620	240.00	100.00
(72)	Arthur Fromme	720.00	100.00	45.00
(73)	Earl Gardner	700.00	100.00	50.00
(74)	H.L. Gaspar	720.00	100.00	45.00
(75)	George Gibson	720.00	100.00	45.00
(76)	Wilbur Goode	720.00	100.00	45.00
(77)	George F. Graham (Rustlers)	720.00	100.00	45.00
(78)	George F. Graham (Cubs)	1,680	255.00	105.00
(79)	Edward L. Grant	2,400	360.00	145.00
(80a)	Dolly Gray (No stats on back.)	1,000	200.00	50.00
(80b)	Dolly Gray (Stats on back.)	4,800	720.00	290.00
(81)	Clark Griffith	1,800	270.00	110.00
(82)	Bob Groom	720.00	100.00	55.00
(83)	Charlie Hanford	1,620	240.00	100.00
(84)	Bob Harmon (Both ears show.)	720.00	100.00	45.00
(85)	Bob Harmon (Only left ear shows.)	2,520	380.00	150.00
(86)	Topsy Hartsel	720.00	100.00	45.00
(87)	Arnold J. Hauser	720.00	100.00	45.00
(88)	Charlie Hemphill	720.00	100.00	45.00
(89)	C.L. Herzog	720.00	100.00	45.00
(90a)	R. Hoblitzell (No stats on back.) (A PSA-graded EX-MT example was auctioned for $33,000 in 2005.))		21,600	9,900
(90b)	R. Hoblitzell ("Cin." after 2nd 1908 in stats.)	1,560	235.00	100.00
(90c)	R. Hoblitzel (Name incorrect, no "Cin." after 1908 in stats.)	3,420	510.00	210.00
(90d)	R. Hoblitzell (Name correct, no "Cin." after 1908 in stats.)	8,400	1,200	510.00
(91)	Danny Hoffman	720.00	100.00	45.00
(92)	Miller J. Huggins	1,920	290.00	115.00
(93)	John E. Hummel	720.00	100.00	45.00
(94)	Fred Jacklitsch	720.00	100.00	45.00
(95)	Hughie Jennings	1,440	215.00	85.00
(96)	Walter Johnson	8,400	1,320	510.00
(97)	D. Jones	720.00	100.00	45.00
(98)	Tom Jones	720.00	100.00	45.00
(99)	Addie Joss	9,000	1,500	700.00
(100)	Ed Karger	1,600	300.00	100.00
(101)	Ed Killian	720.00	100.00	45.00
(102)	Red Kleinow	1,560	235.00	90.00
(103)	John G. Kling	720.00	100.00	45.00
(104)	Jack Knight	720.00	100.00	45.00
(105)	Ed Konetchy	720.00	100.00	45.00
(106)	Harry Krause	720.00	100.00	45.00
(107)	Floyd M. Kroh	720.00	100.00	45.00
(108)	Frank LaPorte	720.00	100.00	45.00
(109)	Frank Lang (Lange)	720.00	100.00	45.00
(110a)	A. Latham (A. Latham on back.)	700.00	100.00	50.00
(110b)	A. Latham (W.A. Latham on back.)	1,600	300.00	50.00
(111)	Thomas W. Leach	720.00	100.00	45.00
(112)	Watty Lee	1,620	240.00	100.00

(113)	Sam Leever	720.00	100.00	45.00
(114a)	A. Leifield (Initial "A." on front.)	700.00	100.00	50.00
(114b)	A.P. Leifield (Initials "A.P." on front.)	1,600	300.00	50.00
(115)	Edgar Lennox	720.00	100.00	45.00
(116)	Paddy Livingston	720.00	100.00	45.00
(117)	John B. Lobert	720.00	100.00	45.00
(118)	Bris Lord (Athletics)	720.00	100.00	45.00
(119)	Harry Lord (White Sox)	720.00	100.00	45.00
(120)	Jno. C. Lush	720.00	100.00	45.00
(121)	Nick Maddox	720.00	100.00	45.00
(122)	Sherwood R. Magee	870.00	135.00	50.00
(123)	R.W. Marquard	2,280	345.00	140.00
(124)	C. Mathewson	8,820	1,320	495.00
(125)	A.A. Mattern	720.00	100.00	45.00
(126)	Sport McAllister	1,620	240.00	100.00
(127)	George McBride	870.00	135.00	55.00
(128)	Amby McConnell	720.00	100.00	45.00
(129)	P.M. McElveen	720.00	100.00	45.00
(130)	J.J. McGraw	2,280	345.00	140.00
(131)	Harry McIntire (Cubs)	720.00	100.00	45.00
(132)	Matty McIntyre (White Sox)	720.00	100.00	45.00
(133)	M.A. McLean (Initials actually J.B.)	720.00	100.00	435.00
(134)	Fred Merkle	720.00	100.00	45.00
(135)	George Merritt	1,620	240.00	100.00
(136)	J.T. Meyers	720.00	100.00	45.00
(137)	Clyde Milan	720.00	100.00	45.00
(138)	J.D. Miller	720.00	100.00	45.00
(139)	M.F. Mitchell	720.00	100.00	45.00
(140a)	P.J. Moran (Stray line of type below stats.)	12,000	1,800	720.00
(140b)	P.J. Moran (No stray line.)	720.00	100.00	45.00
(141)	George Moriarty	720.00	100.00	45.00
(142)	George Mullin	720.00	100.00	45.00
(143)	Danny Murphy	720.00	100.00	45.00
(144)	Jack Murray	720.00	100.00	45.00
(145)	John Nee	1,620	240.00	100.00
(146)	Thomas J. Needham	720.00	100.00	45.00
(147)	Rebel Oakes	720.00	100.00	45.00
(148)	Rube Oldring	720.00	100.00	45.00
(149)	Charley O'Leary	720.00	100.00	45.00
(150)	Fred Olmstead	720.00	100.00	45.00
(151)	Orval Overall	720.00	100.00	45.00
(152)	Freddy Parent	720.00	100.00	45.00
(153)	George Paskert	720.00	100.00	45.00
(154)	Fred Payne	720.00	100.00	45.00
(155)	Barney Pelty	840.00	135.00	55.00
(156)	John Pfeister	720.00	100.00	45.00
(157)	Jimmy Phelan	1,620	240.00	100.00
(158)	E.J. Phelps	720.00	100.00	45.00
(159)	C. Phillippe	720.00	100.00	45.00
(160)	Jack Quinn	720.00	100.00	45.00
(161)	A.L. Raymond	1,600	400.00	200.00
(162)	E.M. Reulbach	720.00	100.00	45.00
(163)	Lewis Richie	720.00	100.00	45.00
(164)	John A. Rowan	3,000	500.00	200.00
(165)	George N. Rucker	720.00	100.00	45.00
(166)	W.D. Scanlan	2,940	440.00	175.00
(167)	Germany Schaefer	720.00	100.00	45.00
(168)	George Schlei	720.00	100.00	45.00
(169)	Boss Schmidt	720.00	100.00	45.00
(170)	F.M. Schulte	720.00	100.00	45.00
(171)	Jim Scott	720.00	100.00	45.00
(172)	B.H. Sharpe	720.00	100.00	45.00
(173)	David Shean (Rustlers)	720.00	100.00	45.00
(174)	David Shean (Cubs)	2,520	380.00	150.00
(175)	Jas. T. Sheckard	720.00	100.00	45.00
(176)	Hack Simmons	720.00	100.00	45.00
(177)	Tony Smith	720.00	100.00	45.00
(178)	Fred C. Snodgrass	720.00	100.00	45.00
(179)	Tris Speaker	5,190	780.00	315.00
(180)	Jake Stahl	1,140	170.00	75.00
(181)	Oscar Stanage	720.00	100.00	45.00
(182)	Harry Steinfeldt	720.00	100.00	45.00
(183)	George Stone	720.00	100.00	45.00
(184)	George Stovall	720.00	100.00	45.00
(185)	Gabby Street	720.00	100.00	45.00
(186)	George F. Suggs	3,000	500.00	200.00
(187)	Ed Summers	720.00	100.00	45.00
(188)	Jeff Sweeney	2,700	405.00	165.00
(189)	Lee Tannehill	720.00	100.00	45.00
(190)	Ira Thomas	720.00	100.00	45.00
(191)	Joe Tinker	2,160	330.00	135.00
(192)	John Titus	720.00	100.00	45.00
(193)	Terry Turner	2,640	395.00	155.00
(194)	James Vaughn	2,880	435.00	175.00
(195)	Charles Wagner	3,180	475.00	195.00
(196)	Bobby Wallace (With cap.)	1,770	270.00	110.00
(197a)	Bobby Wallace (No cap, one line of 1910 stats.)	18,000	2,700	1,080
(197b)	Bobby Wallace (No cap, two lines of 1910 stats.)	7,800	1,170	470.00
(198)	Ed Walsh	5,400	810.00	330.00
(199)	Z.D. Wheat	2,280	345.00	140.00
(200)	Doc White (White Sox)	720.00	100.00	45.00
(201)	Kirb. White (Pirates)	1,600	300.00	100.00
(202a)	Irvin K. Wilhelm ("suffered" in 18th line of bio)	4,500	700.00	300.00
(202b)	Irvin K. Wilhelm ("suffe ed" in 18th line of bio)	4,500	675.00	270.00
(203)	Ed Willett	720.00	100.00	45.00
(204)	J. Owen Wilson	720.00	100.00	45.00
(205)	George R. Wiltse (Both ears show.)	720.00	100.00	45.00
(206)	George R. Wiltse (Only right ear shows.)	2,580	390.00	155.00
(207)	Harry Wolter	720.00	100.00	45.00
(208)	Cy Young	11,100	1,650	665.00

1909-11 T206 White Border

SWEET
CAPORAL
CIGARETTES
The Standard
for Years
BASE BALL SERIES
150
SUBJECTS

The nearly 525 cards which make up the T206 set are the most popular of the early tobacco card issues. Players are depicted in color lithographs surrounded by a white border. The player's last name on the 1-7/16" x 2-5/8" cards appears at the bottom with the city and league, when a city had more than one team. Backs contain an ad for one of 16 brands of cigarettes. There are 389 major leaguer cards and 134 minor leaguer cards in the set, but with front/back varieties the number of potentially different cards runs into the thousands. The set features many expensive cards including a number of pose and/or team variations. Values shown are for cards with the most common advertising on back: Piedmont and Sweet Caporal. Other backs carry a premium depending on scarcity (see listings under brand names). Several popularly collected printing errors have been included in the listings.

		NM	EX	VG
	Common Player:	400.00	100.00	50.00
(1)	Ed Abbaticchio (Blue sleeves.)	400.00	100.00	50.00
(2)	Ed Abbaticchio (Brown sleeves.)	400.00	100.00	50.00
(3)	Fred Abbott	400.00	100.00	50.00
(4)	Bill Abstein	400.00	100.00	50.00
(5)	Doc Adkins	400.00	100.00	50.00
(6)	Whitey Alperman	400.00	100.00	50.00
(7)	Red Ames (Hands at chest.)	800.00	200.00	75.00
(8)	Red Ames (Hands above head.)	400.00	100.00	50.00
(9)	Red Ames (Portrait)	400.00	100.00	50.00
(10)	John Anderson	400.00	100.00	50.00
(11)	Frank Arellanes	400.00	100.00	50.00
(12)	Herman Armbruster	400.00	100.00	50.00
(13)	Harry Arndt	400.00	100.00	50.00
(14)	Jake Atz	400.00	100.00	50.00
(15)	Home Run Baker	1,700	350.00	175.00
(16)	Neal Ball (New York)	400.00	100.00	50.00
(17)	Neal Ball (Cleveland)	400.00	100.00	50.00
(18)	Jap Barbeau	400.00	100.00	50.00
(19)	Cy Barger	400.00	100.00	50.00
(20)	Jack Barry (Philadelphia)	400.00	100.00	50.00
(21)	Shad Barry (Milwaukee)	400.00	100.00	50.00
(22)	Jack Bastian	1,300	350.00	110.00
(23)	Emil Batch	400.00	100.00	50.00
(24)	Johnny Bates	400.00	100.00	50.00
(25)	Harry Bay	1,300	350.00	110.00
(26)	Ginger Beaumont	400.00	100.00	50.00
(27)	Fred Beck	400.00	100.00	50.00
(28)	Beals Becker	400.00	100.00	50.00
(29)	Jake Beckley	1,500	300.00	100.00
(30)	George Bell (Hands above head.)	400.00	100.00	50.00
(31)	George Bell (Pitching follow through.)	400.00	100.00	50.00
(32)	Chief Bender/Pitching (No trees in background.)	1,800	300.00	100.00
(33)	Chief Bender /Pitching (Trees in background.)	1,900	400.00	125.00
(34)	Chief Bender/Portrait	1,300	300.00	100.00
(35)	Bill Bergen/Btg	400.00	100.00	50.00
(36)	Bill Bergen/Catching	400.00	100.00	50.00
(37)	Heinie Berger	400.00	100.00	50.00
(38)	Bill Bernhard	1,300	400.00	110.00
(39)	Bob Bescher (Hands in air.)	400.00	100.00	50.00
(40)	Bob Bescher/Portrait	400.00	100.00	50.00
(41)	Joe Birmingham	900.00	200.00	100.00
(42)	Lena Blackburne	400.00	100.00	50.00
(43)	Jack Bliss	400.00	100.00	50.00
(44)	Frank Bowerman	400.00	100.00	50.00
(45)	Bill Bradley/Portrait	400.00	100.00	50.00
(46)	Bill Bradley (With bat.)	400.00	100.00	50.00
(47)	Dave Brain	400.00	100.00	50.00
(48)	Kitty Bransfield	400.00	100.00	50.00
(49)	Roy Brashear	400.00	100.00	50.00
(50)	Ted Breitenstein	1,300	400.00	110.00
(51)	Roger Bresnahan/Portrait	1,700	300.00	100.00
(52)	Roger Bresnahan (With bat.)	1,350	300.00	100.00
(53)	Al Bridwell/Portrait (No cap.)	400.00	100.00	50.00
(54)	Al Bridwell/Portrait (With cap.)	400.00	100.00	50.00
(55a)	George Brown (Browne) (Chicago)	400.00	100.00	50.00
(55b)	George Brown (Browne) (Washington)	2,100	400.00	200.00
(56)	Mordecai Brown (Chicago on shirt.)	1,600	300.00	100.00
(57)	Mordecai Brown (Cubs on shirt.)	3,600	700.00	300.00
(58)	Mordecai Brown/Portrait	1,500	300.00	100.00
(59)	Al Burch/Btg	1,000	200.00	100.00
(60)	Al Burch/Fldg	400.00	100.00	50.00
(61)	Fred Burchell	400.00	100.00	50.00
(62)	Jimmy Burke	400.00	100.00	50.00
(63)	Bill Burns	400.00	100.00	50.00
(64)	Donie Bush	400.00	100.00	50.00
(65)	John Butler	400.00	100.00	50.00
(66)	Bobby Byrne	400.00	100.00	50.00
(67)	Howie Camnitz (Arm at side.)	400.00	100.00	50.00
(68)	Howie Camnitz (Arms folded.)	400.00	100.00	50.00
(69)	Howie Camnitz (Hands above head.)	400.00	100.00	50.00
(70)	Billy Campbell	400.00	100.00	50.00
(71)	Scoops Carey	1,300	400.00	110.00
(72)	Charley Carr	400.00	100.00	50.00
(73)	Bill Carrigan	400.00	100.00	50.00
(74)	Doc Casey	400.00	100.00	50.00
(75)	Peter Cassidy	400.00	100.00	50.00
(76)	Frank Chance/Btg	1,800	300.00	100.00
(77)	Frank Chance/Portrait (Red background.)	1,900	400.00	100.00
(78)	Frank Chance/Portrait (Yellow background.)	1,400	300.00	100.00
(79)	Bill Chappelle	400.00	100.00	50.00
(80)	Chappie Charles	400.00	100.00	50.00
(81)	Hal Chase (Holding trophy.)	800.00	200.00	100.00
(82)	Hal Chase/Portrait (Blue background.)	900.00	200.00	100.00
(83)	Hal Chase/Portrait (Pink background.)	1,000	200.00	100.00
(84)	Hal Chase/Throwing (Dark cap.)	1,000	200.00	100.00
(85)	Hal Chase/Throwing (White cap.)	1,000	200.00	100.00
(86)	Jack Chesbro	1,900	300.00	125.00
(87)	Ed Cicotte	1,400	300.00	100.00
(88)	Bill Clancy (Clancey)	400.00	100.00	50.00
(89)	Josh Clark (Columbus) (Clarke)	400.00	100.00	50.00
(90)	Fred Clarke (Pittsburgh, holding bat.)	1,200	200.00	100.00
(91)	Fred Clarke/Portrait (Pittsburgh)	1,400	300.00	100.00
(92)	J.J. Clarke (Nig) (Cleveland)	400.00	100.00	50.00
(93)	Bill Clymer	400.00	100.00	50.00
(94)	Ty Cobb/Portrait (Green background.)	9,000	2,600	1,500
(95a)	Ty Cobb/Portrait (Red background.)	4,500	1,600	900.00
(95b)	Ty Cobb/Portrait (Red background, Ty Cobb brand back.)		120,000	72,000
(96)	Ty Cobb (Bat off shoulder.)	9,600	2,300	1,000
(97)	Ty Cobb (Bat on shoulder.)	9,300	1,900	1,000
(98)	Cad Coles	1,300	400.00	110.00
(99)	Eddie Collins (Philadelphia)	1,400	300.00	125.00
(100)	Jimmy Collins (Minneapolis)	1,300	200.00	100.00
(101)	Bunk Congalton	400.00	100.00	50.00
(102)	Wid Conroy/Fldg	400.00	100.00	50.00
(103)	Wid Conroy (With bat.)	400.00	100.00	50.00
(104)	Harry Covaleski (Coveleski)	400.00	100.00	50.00
(105)	Doc Crandall/Portrait (No cap.)	400.00	100.00	50.00
(106)	Doc Crandall/Portrait (With cap.)	400.00	100.00	50.00
(107)	Bill Cranston	1,300	400.00	110.00
(108)	Gavvy Cravath	400.00	100.00	50.00
(109)	Sam Crawford/Throwing	1,700	300.00	100.00
(110)	Sam Crawford (With bat.)	1,500	300.00	100.00
(111)	Birdie Cree	400.00	100.00	50.00
(112)	Lou Criger	400.00	100.00	50.00
(113)	Dode Criss	400.00	100.00	50.00
(114)	Monte Cross	400.00	100.00	50.00
(115a)	Bill Dahlen (Boston)	1,000	200.00	100.00
(115b)	Bill Dahlen (Brooklyn)	2,100	400.00	200.00
(116)	Paul Davidson	400.00	100.00	50.00
(117)	George Davis (Chicago)	1,600	300.00	100.00
(118)	Harry Davis (Philadelphia, Davis on front.)	400.00	100.00	50.00
(119)	Harry Davis (Philadelphia, H. Davis on front.)	400.00	100.00	50.00
(120)	Frank Delehanty (Delahanty) (Louisville)	400.00	100.00	50.00
(121)	Jim Delehanty (Delahanty) (Washington)	400.00	100.00	50.00
(122a)	Ray Demmitt (New York)	400.00	100.00	50.00
(122b)	Ray Demmitt (St. Louis)	42,000	8,000	3,800
(123)	Rube Dessau	400.00	100.00	50.00
(124)	Art Devlin	400.00	100.00	50.00
(125)	Josh Devore	400.00	100.00	50.00
(126)	Bill Dineen (Dinneen)	400.00	100.00	50.00
(127)	Mike Donlin/Fldg	800.00	200.00	100.00
(128)	Mike Donlin (Seated)	800.00	200.00	100.00
(129)	Mike Donlin (With bat.)	400.00	100.00	50.00
(130)	Jiggs Donohue (Donahue)	400.00	100.00	50.00
(131)	Wild Bill Donovan/Portrait	400.00	100.00	50.00
(132)	Wild Bill Donovan/Throwing	400.00	100.00	50.00
(133)	Red Dooin	400.00	100.00	50.00
(134)	Mickey Doolan/Btg	400.00	100.00	50.00
(135)	Mickey Doolan/Fldg	400.00	100.00	50.00
(136)	Mickey Doolin (Doolan)	400.00	100.00	50.00
(137)	Gus Dorner	400.00	100.00	50.00
(138)	Patsy Dougherty (Arm in air.)	400.00	100.00	50.00
(139)	Patsy Dougherty (Portrait)	400.00	100.00	50.00
(140)	Tom Downey (Batting)	400.00	100.00	50.00
(141)	Tom Downey/Fldg	400.00	100.00	50.00
(142)	Jerry Downs	400.00	100.00	50.00
(143a)	Joe Doyle (N.Y. Nat'l., hands above head.)			72,000
(143b)	Joe Doyle (N.Y., hands above head.)	2,200	500.00	100.00
(144)	Larry Doyle/Portrait (N.Y. Nat'l.)	400.00	100.00	50.00
(145)	Larry Doyle/Throwing (N.Y. Nat'l.)	400.00	100.00	50.00
(146)	Larry Doyle (N.Y. Nat'l., with bat.)	400.00	100.00	50.00
(147)	Jean Dubuc	400.00	100.00	50.00
(148)	Hugh Duffy	1,700	300.00	110.00
(149)	Jack Dunn (Baltimore)	400.00	100.00	50.00
(150)	Joe Dunn (Brooklyn)	400.00	100.00	50.00
(151)	Bull Durham	400.00	100.00	50.00
(152)	Jimmy Dygert	400.00	100.00	50.00
(153)	Ted Easterly	400.00	100.00	50.00
(154)	Dick Egan	400.00	100.00	50.00

(155a) Kid Elberfeld (New York) 400.00 100.00 50.00
(155b) Kid Elberfeld/Portrait (Washington) 6,600 1,200 500.00
(156) Kid Elberfeld/Fldg (Washington) 400.00 100.00 50.00
(157) Roy Ellam 1,300 400.00 110.00
(158) Clyde Engle 400.00 100.00 50.00
(159) Steve Evans 400.00 100.00 50.00
(160) Johnny Evers/Portrait 3,000 600.00 200.00
(161) Johnny Evers (With bat, Chicago on shirt.) 1,400 300.00 100.00
(162) Johnny Evers (With bat, Cubs on shirt.) 1,900 400.00 150.00
(163) Bob Ewing 400.00 100.00 50.00
(164) Cecil Ferguson 400.00 100.00 50.00
(165) Hobe Ferris 400.00 100.00 50.00
(166) Lou Fiene/Portrait 400.00 100.00 50.00
(167) Lou Fiene/Throwing 400.00 100.00 50.00
(168) Steamer Flanagan 400.00 100.00 50.00
(169) Art Fletcher 400.00 100.00 50.00
(170) Elmer Flick 2,000 400.00 100.00
(171) Russ Ford 400.00 100.00 50.00
(172) Ed Foster 1,300 400.00 110.00
(173) Jerry Freeman 400.00 100.00 50.00
(174) John Frill 400.00 100.00 50.00
(175) Charlie Fritz 1,300 400.00 110.00
(176) Art Fromme 400.00 100.00 50.00
(177) Chick Gandil 1,200 300.00 100.00
(178) Bob Ganley 400.00 100.00 50.00
(179) John Ganzel 400.00 100.00 50.00
(180) Harry Gasper 400.00 100.00 50.00
(181) Rube Geyer 400.00 100.00 50.00
(182) George Gibson 400.00 100.00 50.00
(183) Billy Gilbert 400.00 100.00 50.00
(184) Wilbur Goode (Good) 400.00 100.00 50.00
(185) Bill Graham (St. Louis) 400.00 100.00 50.00
(186) Peaches Graham (Boston) 400.00 100.00 50.00
(187) Dolly Gray 400.00 100.00 50.00
(188) Ed Greminger 1,300 400.00 110.00
(189) Clark Griffith/Btg 1,800 300.00 100.00
(190) Clark Griffith/Portrait 1,600 300.00 100.00
(191) Moose Grimshaw 400.00 100.00 50.00
(192) Bob Groom 400.00 100.00 50.00
(193) Tom Guiheen 1,300 400.00 110.00
(194) Ed Hahn 400.00 100.00 50.00
(195) Bob Hall 400.00 100.00 50.00
(196) Bill Hallman 400.00 100.00 50.00
(197) Jack Hannifan (Hannifin) 400.00 100.00 50.00
(198) Bill Hart (Little Rock) 1,300 400.00 110.00
(199) Jimmy Hart (Montgomery) 1,300 400.00 110.00
(200) Topsy Hartsel 400.00 100.00 50.00
(201) Jack Hayden 400.00 100.00 50.00
(202) J. Ross Helm 1,300 400.00 110.00
(203) Charlie Hemphill 400.00 100.00 50.00
(204) Buck Herzog (Boston) 800.00 200.00 100.00
(205) Buck Herzog (New York) 400.00 100.00 50.00
(206) Gordon Hickman 1,300 400.00 110.00
(207) Bill Hinchman (Cleveland) 400.00 100.00 50.00
(208) Harry Hinchman (Toledo) 400.00 100.00 50.00
(209) Dick Hoblitzell 400.00 100.00 50.00
(210) Danny Hoffman (St. Louis) 400.00 100.00 50.00
(211) Izzy Hoffman (Providence) 400.00 100.00 50.00
(212) Solly Hofman 400.00 100.00 50.00
(213) Bock Hooker 1,300 400.00 110.00
(214) Del Howard (Chicago) 400.00 100.00 50.00
(215) Ernie Howard (Savannah) 1,300 400.00 110.00
(216) Harry Howell (Hand at waist.) 400.00 100.00 50.00
(217) Harry Howell/Portrait 400.00 100.00 50.00
(218) Miller Huggins (Hands at mouth.) 1,400 300.00 100.00
(219) Miller Huggins/Portrait 1,200 200.00 100.00
(220) Rudy Hulswitt 400.00 100.00 50.00
(221) John Hummel 400.00 100.00 50.00
(222) George Hunter 400.00 100.00 50.00
(223) Frank Isbell 400.00 100.00 50.00
(224) Fred Jacklitsch 400.00 100.00 50.00
(225) Jimmy Jackson 400.00 100.00 50.00
(226) Hughie Jennings (One hand showing.) 1,300 200.00 100.00
(227) Hughie Jennings (Both hands showing.) 1,400 300.00 100.00
(228) Hughie Jennings/Portrait 1,300 200.00 125.00
(229) Walter Johnson (Hands at chest.) 5,400 1,000 400.00
(230) Walter Johnson/Portrait 4,800 1,400 700.00
(231) Fielder Jones (Chicago, hands at hips.) 400.00 100.00 50.00
(232) Fielder Jones/Portrait (Chicago) 400.00 100.00 50.00
(233) Davy Jones (Detroit) 400.00 100.00 50.00
(234) Tom Jones (St. Louis) 400.00 100.00 50.00
(235) Dutch Jordan (Atlanta) 1,300 400.00 110.00
(236) Tim Jordan/Btg (Brooklyn) 400.00 100.00 50.00
(237) Tim Jordan/Portrait (Brooklyn) 400.00 100.00 50.00
(238) Addie Joss/Pitching 1,800 300.00 100.00
(239) Addie Joss/Portrait 1,500 300.00 125.00
(240) Ed Karger 400.00 100.00 50.00
(241) Willie Keeler/Portrait 2,500 500.00 200.00
(242) Willie Keeler (W/bat.) 2,500 500.00 200.00
(243) Joe Kelley 1,300 200.00 100.00
(244) J.F. Kiernan 1,300 400.00 110.00
(245) Ed Killian/Pitching 400.00 100.00 50.00
(246) Ed Killian/Portrait 400.00 100.00 50.00
(247) Frank King 1,300 400.00 110.00
(248) Rube Kisinger 400.00 100.00 50.00
(249a) Red Kleinow (Boston) 2,100 400.00 200.00
(249b) Red Kleinow/Catching (New York) 400.00 100.00 50.00
(250) Red Kleinow (New York, with bat.) 400.00 100.00 50.00
(251) Johnny Kling 400.00 100.00 50.00
(252) Otto Knabe 400.00 100.00 50.00
(253) Jack Knight/Portrait 400.00 100.00 50.00
(254) Jack Knight (With bat.) 400.00 100.00 50.00
(255) Ed Konetchy (Glove above head.) 400.00 100.00 50.00
(256) Ed Konetchy (Glove near ground.) 400.00 100.00 50.00
(257) Harry Krause/Pitching 400.00 100.00 50.00
(258) Harry Krause/Portait 400.00 100.00 50.00
(259) Rube Kroh 400.00 100.00 50.00
(260) Otto Kruger (Krueger) 400.00 100.00 50.00
(261) James Lafitte 1,300 400.00 110.00
(262) Nap Lajoie/Portait 3,600 700.00 300.00
(263) Nap Lajoie/Throwing 2,900 500.00 200.00
(264) Nap Lajoie (With bat.) 3,600 800.00 200.00
(265) Joe Lake (New York) 400.00 100.00 50.00
(266) Joe Lake (St. Louis, ball in hand.) 400.00 100.00 50.00
(267) Joe Lake (St. Louis, no ball in hand.) 400.00 100.00 50.00
(268) Frank LaPorte 400.00 100.00 50.00
(269) Arlie Latham 400.00 100.00 50.00
(270) Bill Lattimore 400.00 100.00 50.00
(271) Jimmy Lavender 400.00 100.00 50.00
(272) Tommy Leach (Bending over.) 400.00 100.00 50.00
(273) Tommy Leach/Portait 400.00 100.00 50.00
(274) Lefty Leifield/Btg 400.00 100.00 50.00
(275) Lefty Leifield/Pitching 400.00 100.00 50.00
(276) Ed Lennox 400.00 100.00 50.00
(277) Harry Lentz (Sentz) 1,300 400.00 110.00
(278) Glenn Liebhardt 400.00 100.00 50.00
(279) Vive Lindaman 400.00 100.00 50.00
(280) Perry Lipe 1,300 400.00 110.00
(281) Paddy Livingstone (Livingston) 400.00 100.00 50.00
(282) Hans Lobert 400.00 100.00 50.00
(283) Harry Lord 400.00 100.00 50.00
(284) Harry Lumley 400.00 100.00 50.00
(285a) Carl Lundgren (Chicago) 3,800 800.00 300.00
(285b) Carl Lundgren (Kansas City) 400.00 100.00 50.00
(286) Nick Maddox 400.00 100.00 50.00
(287a) Sherry Magie (Magee)
Values shown represent recent auctions of examples graded by PSA, SGC or GAI. Purchase of ungraded specimens is not recommended.
VG-EX - 21,250 / 19,720
VG - 9,600
GOOD - 12,000
FAIR - 8,000
POOR - 4,500
(287b) Sherry Magee/Portait 800.00 100.00 60.00
(288) Sherry Magee (With bat.) 400.00 100.00 50.00
(289) Bill Malarkey 400.00 100.00 50.00
(290) Billy Maloney 400.00 100.00 50.00
(291) George Manion 1,300 400.00 110.00
(292) Rube Manning/Btg 400.00 100.00 50.00
(293) Rube Manning/Pitching 400.00 100.00 50.00
(294) Rube Marquard (Hands at thighs.) 1,600 300.00 100.00
(295) Rube Marquard (Follow-through.) 1,600 300.00 100.00
(296) Rube Marquard/Portait 1,800 300.00 100.00
(297) Doc Marshall 400.00 100.00 50.00
(298) Christy Mathewson (Dark cap.) 2,700 1,000 300.00
(299) Christy Mathewson/Portait 5,200 1,100 450.00
(300) Christy Mathewson (White cap.) 5,100 900.00 400.00
(301) Al Mattern 400.00 100.00 50.00
(302) John McAleese 400.00 100.00 50.00
(303) George McBride 400.00 100.00 50.00
(304) Pat McCauley 1,300 400.00 110.00
(305) Moose McCormick 400.00 100.00 50.00
(306) Pryor McElveen 400.00 100.00 50.00
(307) Dan McGann 400.00 100.00 50.00
(308) Jim McGinley 400.00 100.00 50.00
(309) Iron Man McGinnity 1,400 200.00 100.00
(310) Stoney McGlynn 400.00 100.00 50.00
(311) John McGraw (Finger in air.) 2,100 400.00 200.00
(312) John McGraw (Glove at hip.) 2,000 400.00 100.00
(313) John McGraw/Portait (No cap.) 1,700 300.00 100.00
(314) John McGraw/Portait (With cap.) 1,400 300.00 100.00
(315) Harry McIntyre (Brooklyn) 400.00 100.00 50.00
(316) Harry McIntyre (Brooklyn & Chicago) 400.00 100.00 50.00
(317) Matty McIntyre (Detroit) 400.00 100.00 50.00
(318) Larry McLean 400.00 100.00 50.00
(319) George McQuillan (Ball in hand.) 400.00 100.00 50.00
(320) George McQuillan (With bat.) 400.00 100.00 50.00
(321) Fred Merkle/Portait 400.00 100.00 60.00
(322) Fred Merkle/Throwing 400.00 100.00 50.00
(323) George Merritt 400.00 100.00 50.00
(324) Chief Meyers 400.00 100.00 50.00
(325) Clyde Milan 400.00 100.00 50.00
(326) Dots Miller (Pittsburgh) 400.00 100.00 50.00
(327) Molly Miller (Dallas) 1,300 400.00 110.00
(328) Bill Milligan 400.00 100.00 50.00
(329) Fred Mitchell (Toronto) 400.00 100.00 50.00
(330) Mike Mitchell (Cincinnati) 400.00 100.00 50.00
(331) Dan Moeller 400.00 100.00 50.00
(332) Carlton Molesworth 1,300 400.00 110.00
(333) Herbie Moran (Providence) 400.00 100.00 50.00
(334) Pat Moran (Chicago) 400.00 100.00 50.00
(335) George Moriarty 400.00 100.00 50.00
(336) Mike Mowrey 400.00 100.00 50.00
(337) Dom Mullaney 1,300 400.00 110.00
(338) George Mullen (Mullin) 400.00 100.00 50.00
(339) George Mullin/Throwing 900.00 200.00 100.00
(340) George Mullin (With bat.) 400.00 100.00 50.00
(341) Danny Murphy/Btg 400.00 100.00 50.00
(342) Danny Murphy/Throwing 900.00 200.00 100.00
(343) Red Murray/Btg 400.00 100.00 50.00
(344) Red Murray/Portait 400.00 100.00 50.00
(345) Chief Myers (Meyers)/Btg 400.00 100.00 50.00
(346) Chief Myers (Meyers)/Fldg 400.00 100.00 50.00
(347) Billy Nattress 400.00 100.00 50.00
(348) Tom Needham 400.00 100.00 50.00
(349) Simon Nicholls (Hands on knees.) 400.00 100.00 50.00
(350) Simon Nichols (Nicholls)/Btg 400.00 100.00 50.00
(351) Harry Niles 400.00 100.00 50.00
(352) Rebel Oakes 400.00 100.00 50.00
(353) Frank Oberlin 400.00 100.00 50.00
(354) Peter O'Brien 400.00 100.00 50.00
(355a) Bill O'Hara (New York) 400.00 100.00 50.00
(355b) Bill O'Hara (St. Louis) 42,000 10,000 4,000
(356) Rube Oldring/Btg 400.00 100.00 50.00
(357) Rube Oldring/Fldg 400.00 100.00 50.00
(358) Charley O'Leary (Hands on knees.) 400.00 100.00 50.00
(359) Charley O'Leary/Portait 400.00 100.00 50.00
(360) William J. O'Neil 400.00 100.00 50.00
(361) Al Orth 1,300 400.00 110.00
(362) William Otey 1,300 400.00 110.00
(363) Orval Overall (Hand face level.) 400.00 100.00 50.00
(364) Orval Overall (Hands waist level.) 400.00 100.00 50.00
(365) Orval Overall/Portait 400.00 100.00 50.00
(366) Frank Owen 400.00 100.00 50.00
(367) George Paige 1,300 400.00 110.00
(368) Fred Parent 400.00 100.00 50.00
(369) Dode Paskert 400.00 100.00 50.00
(370) Jim Pastorius 400.00 100.00 50.00
(371) Harry Pattee 900.00 200.00 100.00
(372) Fred Payne 400.00 100.00 50.00
(373) Barney Pelty (Horizontal photo.) 900.00 200.00 100.00
(374) Barney Pelty (Vertical photo.) 400.00 100.00 50.00
(375) Hub Perdue 1,300 400.00 110.00
(376) George Perring 400.00 100.00 50.00
(377) Arch Persons 1,300 400.00 110.00
(378) Francis (Big Jeff) Pfeffer 400.00 100.00 50.00
(379) Jake Pfeister (Pfiester)/Seated 400.00 100.00 50.00
(380) Jake Pfeister (Pfiester)/Throwing 400.00 100.00 50.00
(381) Jimmy Phelan 400.00 100.00 50.00
(382) Eddie Phelps 400.00 100.00 50.00
(383) Deacon Phillippe 400.00 100.00 50.00
(384) Ollie Pickering 400.00 100.00 50.00
(385) Eddie Plank
Values shown reflect recent auctions of examples graded by PSA, SGC or GAI. Purchase of ungraded specimens is not recommended.
EX - MT - 100,000
VG - 60,000
Good - 35,000
Poor - 20,000
(386) Phil Poland 400.00 100.00 50.00
(387) Jack Powell 900.00 200.00 100.00
(388) Mike Powers 400.00 100.00 50.00
(389) Billy Purtell 400.00 100.00 50.00
(390) Ambrose Puttman (Puttmann) 400.00 100.00 50.00
(391) Lee Quillen (Quillin) 400.00 100.00 50.00
(392) Jack Quinn 400.00 100.00 50.00
(393) Newt Randall 400.00 100.00 50.00
(394) Bugs Raymond 400.00 100.00 50.00
(395) Ed Reagan 1,300 400.00 110.00
(396) Ed Reulbach (Glove showing.) 900.00 200.00 100.00
(397) Ed Reulbach (No glove showing.) 400.00 100.00 50.00
(398) Dutch Revelle 1,300 400.00 110.00
(399) Bob Rhoades (Rhoads) (Hands at chest.) 400.00 100.00 50.00
(400) Bob Rhoades (Rhoads) (Right arm extended.) 900.00 200.00 60.00
(401) Charlie Rhodes 400.00 100.00 50.00
(402) Claude Ritchey 400.00 100.00 50.00
(403) Lou Ritter 400.00 100.00 50.00
(404) Ike Rockenfeld 1,300 400.00 110.00
(405) Claude Rossman 400.00 100.00 50.00
(406) Nap Rucker/Portait 400.00 100.00 50.00
(407) Nap Rucker/Throwing 400.00 100.00 50.00
(408) Dick Rudolph 400.00 100.00 50.00
(409) Ray Ryan 1,300 400.00 110.00
(410) Germany Schaefer (Detroit) 400.00 100.00 50.00
(411) Germany Schaefer (Washington) 400.00 100.00 50.00
(412) George Schirm 400.00 100.00 50.00
(413) Larry Schlafly 400.00 100.00 50.00
(414) Admiral Schlei/Btg 400.00 100.00 50.00
(415) Admiral Schlei/Catching 400.00 100.00 50.00
(416) Admiral Schlei/Portait 400.00 100.00 50.00
(417) Boss Schmidt/Portait 400.00 100.00 50.00
(418) Boss Schmidt/Throwing 400.00 100.00 50.00
(419) Ossee Schreck (Schreckengost) 780.00 140.00 55.00
(420) Wildfire Schulte (Front view.) 1,000 100.00 60.00
(421) Wildfire Schulte (Back view.) 400.00 100.00 50.00
(422) Jim Scott 400.00 100.00 50.00
(423) Charles Seitz 1,300 400.00 110.00
(424) Cy Seymour/Btg 400.00 100.00 50.00
(425) Cy Seymour/Portait 400.00 100.00 50.00
(426) Cy Seymour/Throwing 400.00 100.00 50.00
(427) Spike Shannon 400.00 100.00 50.00
(428) Bud Sharpe 400.00 100.00 50.00
(429) Shag Shaughnessy 1,300 400.00 110.00
(430) Al Shaw (St. Louis) 400.00 100.00 50.00
(431) Hunky Shaw (Providence) 400.00 100.00 50.00
(432) Jimmy Sheckard (Glove showing.) 400.00 100.00 50.00
(433) Jimmy Sheckard (No glove showing.) 400.00 100.00 50.00
(434) Bill Shipke 400.00 100.00 50.00
(435) Jimmy Slagle 400.00 100.00 50.00
(436) Carlos Smith (Shreveport) 1,300 400.00 110.00
(437) Frank Smith (Chicago, F. Smith on front.) 400.00 100.00 50.00

(438a)	Frank Smith (Chicago, white cap.)	400.00	100.00	50.00
(438b)	Frank Smith (Chicago & Boston)	1,700	300.00	125.00
(439)	Happy Smith (Brooklyn)	400.00	100.00	50.00
(440)	Heinie Smith (Buffalo)	400.00	100.00	50.00
(441)	Sid Smith (Atlanta)	1,300	400.00	110.00
(442)	Fred Snodgrass/Btg	400.00	100.00	50.00
(443)	Fred Snodgrass/Catching	400.00	100.00	50.00
(444)	Bob Spade	400.00	100.00	50.00
(445)	Tris Speaker	4,500	800.00	325.00
(446)	Tubby Spencer	400.00	100.00	50.00
(447)	Jake Stahl (Glove shows.)	400.00	100.00	50.00
(448)	Jake Stahl (No glove shows.)	400.00	100.00	50.00
(449)	Oscar Stanage	400.00	100.00	50.00
(450)	Dolly Stark	1,300	400.00	110.00
(451)	Charlie Starr	400.00	100.00	50.00
(452)	Harry Steinfeldt/Portait	400.00	100.00	50.00
(453)	Harry Steinfeldt (With bat.)	400.00	100.00	50.00
(454)	Jim Stephens	400.00	100.00	50.00
(455)	George Stone	400.00	100.00	50.00
(456)	George Stovall/Portait	400.00	100.00	50.00
(457)	George Stovall/Portait	400.00	100.00	50.00
(458)	Sam Strang	400.00	100.00	50.00
(459)	Gabby Street/Catching	400.00	100.00	50.00
(460)	Gabby Street/Portait	400.00	100.00	50.00
(461)	Billy Sullivan	400.00	100.00	50.00
(462)	Ed Summers	400.00	100.00	50.00
(463)	Bill Sweeney (Boston)	400.00	100.00	50.00
(464)	Jeff Sweeney (New York)	400.00	100.00	50.00
(465)	Jesse Tannehill (Washington)	400.00	100.00	50.00
(466)	Lee Tannehill (Chicago, L. Tannehill on front.)	400.00	100.00	50.00
(467)	Lee Tannehill (Chicago, Tannehill on front.)	400.00	100.00	50.00
(468)	Dummy Taylor	400.00	100.00	50.00
(469)	Fred Tonney	400.00	100.00	50.00
(470)	Tony Thebo	1,300	400.00	110.00
(471)	Jake Thielman	400.00	100.00	50.00
(472)	Ira Thomas	400.00	100.00	50.00
(473)	Woodie Thornton	1,300	400.00	110.00
(474)	Joe Tinker (Bat off shoulder.)	1,800	400.00	100.00
(475)	Joe Tinker (Bat on shoulder.)	1,700	300.00	100.00
(476)	Joe Tinker (Hands on knees.)	1,700	300.00	100.00
(477)	Joe Tinker/Portait	1,800	400.00	125.00
(478)	John Titus	400.00	100.00	50.00
(479)	Terry Turner	400.00	100.00	50.00
(480)	Bob Unglaub	400.00	100.00	50.00
(481)	Juan Violat (Viola)	1,300	400.00	110.00
(482)	Rube Waddell/Portait	1,800	300.00	100.00
(483)	Rube Waddell/Throwing	1,800	400.00	100.00
(484)	Heinie Wagner (Bat on left shoulder.)	400.00	100.00	50.00
(485)	Heinie Wagner (Bat on right shoulder.)	400.00	100.00	50.00
(486)	Honus Wagner Values shown refelct recent auctions of examples graded by PSA, SGC or GAI. Purchase of ungraded specimens is not recommended. NM-MT - \$2,800,000 VG+ - 456,000 VG - 400,000. GOOD - 350,000 FAIR - 300,000. POOR - 270,000.			
(487)	Bobby Wallace	1,500	300.00	100.00
(488)	Ed Walsh	2,300	400.00	200.00
(489)	Jack Warhop	400.00	100.00	50.00
(490)	Jake Weimer	400.00	100.00	50.00
(491)	James Westlake	1,300	400.00	110.00
(492)	Zack Wheat	1,500	300.00	110.00
(493)	Doc White/Pitching (Chicago)	400.00	100.00	50.00
(494)	Doc White/Portait (Chicago)	400.00	100.00	50.00
(495)	Foley White (Houston)	1,300	400.00	110.00
(496)	Jack White (Buffalo)	400.00	100.00	50.00
(497)	Kaiser Wilhelm (Hands at chest.)	400.00	100.00	50.00
(498)	Kaiser Wilhelm (With bat.)	400.00	100.00	50.00
(499)	Ed Willett	400.00	100.00	50.00
(500)	Ed Willetts (Willett)	400.00	100.00	50.00
(501)	Jimmy Williams	400.00	100.00	50.00
(502)	Vic Willis/Portait	1,700	400.00	100.00
(503)	Vic Willis/Throwing	1,700	300.00	100.00
(504)	Vic Willis (With bat.)	1,200	200.00	100.00
(505)	Owen Wilson	400.00	100.00	50.00
(506)	Hooks Wiltse/Pitching	400.00	100.00	50.00
(507)	Hooks Wiltse/Portait (No cap.)	400.00	100.00	50.00
(508)	Hooks Wiltse/Portait (With cap.)	400.00	100.00	50.00
(509)	Lucky Wright	400.00	100.00	50.00
(510)	Cy Young (Cleveland, glove shows.)	3,800	700.00	350.00
(511)	Cy Young (Cleveland, bare hand shows.)	4,400	800.00	350.00
(512)	Cy Young/Portait (Cleveland)	8,700	1,600	700.00
(513)	Irv Young (Minneapolis)	400.00	100.00	50.00
(514)	Heinie Zimmerman	400.00	100.00	50.00

1909-11 T206 Errors

Because of the complexity of the lithographic process by which T206 cards were printed, a number of significant printing errors - missing colors, broken or missing type, etc. - are known. Early in hobby history some of these errors were collected alongside such true design variations as the "Magie" misspelling and Joe Doyle "N.Y. Nat'l." Because of the continued popularity of T206, some of these errors remain in demand today and can command significant premium values. It should be noted, however, that not all similar errors within T206 bring such high prices; value seems dependent on the length of time the errors have been known

in the hobby. Because of the ease with which various typographic elements - "S" in Snodgrass, "o" in Toronto, can be erased, many fakes of this type of error are known; collectors should be wary and consider having the cards professionally authenticated.

		NM	EX	VG
(27)	Beck, no "B"s (Missing red ink.)	1,500	750.00	450.00
(28)	Becker, no "B" (Missing red ink.)	1,500	750.00	450.00
(95a)	Cobb, orange background (Missing red ink.)	4,000	1,500	900.00
(164)	Ferguson, no "B" (Missing red ink.)	2,300	1,150	700.00
(279)	Lindaman, no "B" (Missing red ink.)	1,500	750.00	450.00
(286)	Maddox, Pittsburg (No team, name, city.)	6,000	3,000	1,800
(297)	Marshall, no "B" (Missing blue ink.)	2,000	1,000	600.00
(329)	Mitchell, "TORONT" (No last "O.")	2,000	1,000	600.00
(343)	Murray (Yellow background.)	1,500	750.00	450.00
(344)	Murr'y (Broken "A" in name, Lenox, Tolstoi, and Old Mill Back."))	7,000	3,500	2,100
(428)	Shappe, Newark (Should be Sharpe.)	4,000	2,000	1,000
(442)	nodgrass - batting (Should be Snodgrass; most of initial "S" missing.)	4,000	2,000	1,000
(443)	nodgrass - catching (All known examples, even those in grading company holders, are altered specimens with no collectible value.)			
(463)	Sweeney, no "B" (Missing magenta ink.)	9,000	4,500	2,700
(484)	Wagner, no "B" (Bat on left shoulder, missing magenta.)	2,500	1,250	750.00
	Common Player (Missing one or more colors.)	500.00	250.00	150.00

1912 T207 Brown Background

Harry Lord

Harry Lord, the brilliant White Sox third baseman, came to Chicago in one of the queerest baseball deals ever recorded. Lord first achieved success in the New England League, where, in 1908, he was lifted to the Boston Americans. Although rated as a wonderful ball player, he fell out with the club management and was traded to Comiskey, who secured a star. Lord played wonderful ball in 1911 and is rated by many as the greatest third baseman now playing—a worthy successor to Bradley and Collins. Last season he batted .321, fielded .941 and led his club with stolen bases.

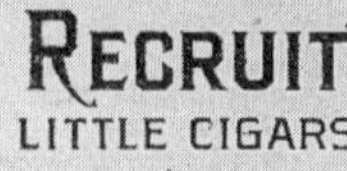

Less popular and even less understood than their T205 and T206 antecedents from American Tobacco, the T207 "Brown Background" series shares the same approximately 1-7/16" x 2-5/8" format with the earlier T-cards. A chocolate background frames the rather drab player drawings, which rely on occasional bit of color on the uniform to break up the predominant earth tones. The cards have beige borders. A white strip below the picture has the player's last name, city and league. Unlike most other cards of its time, T207 has a glossy coating on front which over the years tends to crack and/or "craze" exacerbating the appaearance of creases and other signs of wear. Card backs have the player's full name, career summary and (usually) an ad for one of several brands of cigarettes. Red Cross brand backs are virtually impossible to find, while red Cycle advertising is noticeably scarcer than more common Broadleaf or "anonymous" (no-advertising) versions. Cards with Recruit Little Cigars advertising on back are the most common. There are a number of unaccountably scarce cards in the set, including a higher than usual number of obscure players. The Davis card with blue "C" on cap carried in earlier catalogs has been removed for lack of evidence of its existence. The previously listed Carrigan-Wagner wrongbacks have also been de-listed due to their nature as wrong-back printing errors rather than true variations.

		NM	EX	VG
	Common Player:	220.00	75.00	45.00
(1)	John B. Adams	1,760	615.00	355.00
(2)	Edward Ainsmith	220.00	75.00	45.00
(3)	Rafael Almeida	1,250	625.00	300.00
(4a)	James Austin (Insignia on shirt.)	440.00	155.00	90.00
(4b)	James Austin (No insignia on shirt.)	220.00	75.00	45.00
(5)	Neal Ball	200.00	75.00	45.00
(6)	Eros Barger	220.00	75.00	45.00
(7)	Jack Barry	250.00	90.00	50.00
(8)	Charles Bauman ((Baumann))	1,250	625.00	300.00
(9)	Beals Becker	330.00	110.00	65.00
(10)	Chief (Albert) Bender	525.00	180.00	110.00
(11)	Joseph Benz	1,250	625.00	300.00
(12)	Robert Bescher	220.00	75.00	45.00
(13)	Joe Birmingham	1,250	625.00	300.00
(14)	Russell Blackburne	1,250	625.00	300.00
(15)	Fred Blanding	1,250	625.00	300.00
(16)	Jimmy Block	495.00	170.00	100.00
(17)	Ping Bodie	220.00	75.00	45.00
(18)	Hugh Bradley	220.00	75.00	45.00
(19)	Roger Bresnaham (Bresnahan)	495.00	170.00	100.00
(20)	J.F. Bushelman	1,250	625.00	300.00
(21)	Henry (Hank) Butcher	1,250	625.00	300.00
(22)	Robert M. Byrne	220.00	75.00	45.00
(23)	John James Callahan	220.00	75.00	45.00
(24)	Howard Camnitz	220.00	75.00	45.00
(25)	Max Carey	855.00	305.00	165.00
(26)	Bill Carrigan	220.00	75.00	45.00
(27)	George Chalmers	220.00	75.00	45.00
(28)	Frank Leroy Chance	715.00	250.00	145.00
(29)	Edward Cicotte	1,100	385.00	220.00
(30)	Tom Clarke	220.00	75.00	45.00
(31)	Leonard Cole	220.00	75.00	45.00
(32)	John Collins	305.00	105.00	60.00
(33)	Robert Coulson	220.00	75.00	45.00
(34)	Tex Covington	220.00	75.00	45.00
(35)	Otis Crandall	220.00	75.00	45.00
(36)	William Cunningham	1,250	625.00	300.00
(37)	Dave Danforth	250.00	95.00	50.00
(38)	Bert Daniels	440.00	155.00	90.00
(39)	John Daubert (Jake)	220.00	75.00	45.00
(40)	Harry Davis	250.00	90.00	50.00
(41)	Jim Delehanty	220.00	75.00	45.00
(42)	Claude Derrick	220.00	75.00	45.00
(43)	Arthur Devlin	250.00	95.00	50.00
(44)	Joshua Devore	220.00	75.00	45.00
(45)	Mike Donlin	2,000	1,250	500.00
(46)	Edward Donnelly	1,250	625.00	300.00
(47)	Charles Dooin	220.00	75.00	45.00
(48)	Tom Downey	880.00	310.00	175.00
(49)	Lawrence Doyle	440.00	155.00	90.00
(50)	Del Drake	385.00	135.00	75.00
(51)	Ted Easterly	220.00	75.00	45.00
(52)	George Ellis	660.00	230.00	135.00
(53)	Clyde Engle	360.00	125.00	70.00
(54)	R.E. Erwin	660.00	230.00	135.00
(55)	Louis Evans	220.00	75.00	45.00
(56)	John Ferry	220.00	75.00	45.00
(57a)	Ray Fisher (Blue cap.)	220.00	75.00	45.00
(57b)	Ray Fisher (White cap.)	300.00	150.00	75.00
(58)	Arthur Fletcher	220.00	75.00	45.00
(59)	Jacques Fournier	1,250	625.00	300.00
(60)	Arthur Fromme	250.00	90.00	50.00
(61)	Del Gainor	220.00	75.00	45.00
(62)	William Lawrence Gardner	330.00	110.00	65.00
(63)	Lefty George	300.00	150.00	75.00
(64)	Roy Golden	220.00	75.00	45.00
(65)	Harry Gowdy	220.00	75.00	45.00
(66)	George Graham	660.00	230.00	135.00
(67)	J.G. Graney	825.00	285.00	165.00
(68)	Vean Gregg	1,250	625.00	300.00
(69)	Casey Hageman	440.00	155.00	90.00
(70)	Charlie Hall	440.00	155.00	90.00
(71)	E.S. Hallinan	220.00	75.00	45.00
(72)	Earl Hamilton	220.00	75.00	45.00
(73)	Robert Harmon	220.00	75.00	45.00
(74)	Grover Hartley	440.00	155.00	90.00
(75)	Olaf Henriksen	230.00	110.00	60.00
(76)	John Henry	440.00	155.00	90.00
(77)	Charles Herzog	1,250	625.00	300.00
(78)	Robert Higgins	310.00	110.00	60.00
(79)	Chester Hoff	1,250	625.00	300.00
(80)	William Hogan	310.00	110.00	60.00
(81)	Harry Hooper	1,320	470.00	265.00
(82)	Ben Houser	1,250	625.00	300.00
(83)	Hamilton Hyatt	1,250	625.00	300.00
(84)	Walter Johnson	2,090	730.00	420.00
(85)	George Kaler	220.00	75.00	45.00
(86)	William Kelly	1,250	625.00	300.00
(87)	Jay Kirke	440.00	155.00	90.00
(88)	John Kling	715.00	250.00	145.00
(89)	Otto Knabe	220.00	75.00	45.00
(90)	Elmer Knetzer	220.00	75.00	45.00
(91)	Edward Konetchy	220.00	75.00	45.00
(92)	Harry Krause	220.00	75.00	45.00
(93)	"Red" Kuhn	1,250	625.00	300.00
(94)	Joseph Kutina	1,250	625.00	300.00
(95)	F.H. (Bill) Lange	1,250	625.00	300.00
(96)	Jack Lapp	220.00	75.00	45.00
(97)	W. Arlington Latham	220.00	75.00	45.00
(98)	Thomas W. Leach	220.00	75.00	45.00
(99)	Albert Leifield	220.00	75.00	45.00

(100)	Edgar Lennox	220.00	75.00	45.00
(101)	Duffy Lewis	495.00	170.00	100.00
(102a)	Irving Lewis (No emblem on sleeve.)	20,000	10,000	5,000
(102b)	Irving Lewis (Emblem on sleeve.)	10,450	5,000	3,000
(103)	Jack Lively	220.00	75.00	45.00
(104a)	Paddy Livingston ("A" on shirt.)	1,200	425.00	245.00
(104b)	Paddy Livingston (Big "C" on shirt.)	1,265	440.00	255.00
(104c)	Paddy Livingston (Small "C" on shirt.)	330.00	115.00	65.00
(105)	Briscoe Lord (Philadelphia)	440.00	155.00	90.00
(106)	Harry Lord (Chicago)	440.00	155.00	90.00
(107)	Louis Lowdermilk	10,450	3,660	2,090
(108)	Richard Marquard	605.00	210.00	120.00
(109)	Armando Marsans	770.00	270.00	155.00
(110)	George McBride	310.00	110.00	60.00
(111)	Alexander McCarthy	1,250	625.00	300.00
(112)	Edward McDonald	330.00	110.00	65.00
(113)	John J. McGraw	635.00	220.00	125.00
(114)	Harry McIntire	220.00	75.00	45.00
(115)	Matthew McIntyre	220.00	75.00	45.00
(116)	William McKechnie	2,000	1,000	500.00
(117)	Larry McLean	220.00	75.00	45.00
(118)	Clyde Milan	220.00	75.00	45.00
(119)	John B. Miller (Pittsburg)	220.00	75.00	45.00
(120)	Otto Miller (Brooklyn)	440.00	155.00	90.00
(121)	Roy Miller (Boston)	990.00	345.00	200.00
(122)	Ward Miller (Chicago)	8,000	4,000	2,000
(123)	Mike Mitchell (Cleveland, picture is Willie Mitchell.)	220.00	75.00	45.00
(124)	Mike Mitchell (Cincinnati)	330.00	110.00	65.00
(125)	Geo. Mogridge	1,500	750.00	375.00
(126)	Earl Moore	1,250	625.00	300.00
(127)	Patrick J. Moran	220.00	75.00	45.00
(128)	Cy Morgan (Philadelphia)	220.00	75.00	45.00
(129)	Ray Morgan (Washington)	220.00	75.00	45.00
(130)	George Moriarty	1,250	625.00	300.00
(131a)	George Mullin ("D" on cap.)	250.00	90.00	50.00
(131b)	George Mullin (No "D" on cap.)	745.00	260.00	150.00
(132)	Thomas Needham	330.00	110.00	65.00
(133)	Red Nelson	1,250	625.00	300.00
(134)	Herbert Northen (Hubbard)	310.00	110.00	60.00
(135)	Leslie Nunamaker	220.00	75.00	45.00
(136)	Rebel Oakes	220.00	75.00	45.00
(137)	Buck O'Brien	330.00	110.00	65.00
(138)	Rube Oldring	220.00	75.00	45.00
(139)	Ivan Olson	220.00	75.00	45.00
(140)	Martin J. O'Toole	220.00	75.00	45.00
(141)	George Paskart (Paskert)	220.00	75.00	45.00
(142)	Barney Pelty	2,000	1,250	500.00
(143)	Herbert Perdue	310.00	110.00	60.00
(144)	O.C. Peters	1,250	625.00	300.00
(145)	Arthur Phelan	1,250	625.00	300.00
(146)	Jack Quinn	440.00	155.00	90.00
(147)	Don Carlos Ragan	1,250	625.00	300.00
(148)	Arthur Rasmussen	1,250	625.00	300.00
(149)	Morris Rath	1,250	625.00	300.00
(150)	Edward Reulbach	330.00	115.00	65.00
(151)	Napoleon Rucker	440.00	155.00	90.00
(152)	J.B. Ryan	1,250	625.00	300.00
(153)	Victor Saier	2,300	810.00	470.00
(154)	William Scanlon	220.00	75.00	45.00
(155)	Germany Schaefer	220.00	75.00	45.00
(156)	Wilbur Schardt	220.00	75.00	45.00
(157)	Frank Schulte	220.00	75.00	45.00
(158)	Jim Scott	495.00	170.00	100.00
(159)	Henry Severoid (Severeid)	220.00	75.00	45.00
(160)	Mike Simon	220.00	75.00	45.00
(161)	Frank E. Smith (Cincinnati)	220.00	75.00	45.00
(162)	Wallace Smith (St. Louis)	220.00	75.00	45.00
(163)	Fred Snodgrass	220.00	75.00	45.00
(164)	Tristam Speaker	4,000	2,000	750.00
(165)	Harry Lee Spratt	220.00	75.00	45.00
(166)	Edward Stack	550.00	195.00	110.00
(167)	Oscar Stanage	220.00	75.00	45.00
(168)	William Steele	660.00	230.00	135.00
(169)	Harry Steinfeldt	440.00	155.00	90.00
(170)	George Stovall	220.00	75.00	45.00
(171)	Charles (Gabby) Street	250.00	90.00	50.00
(172)	Amos Strunk	220.00	75.00	45.00
(173)	William Sullivan	310.00	110.00	60.00
(174)	William J. Sweeney	1,250	625.00	300.00
(175)	Leeford Tannehill	220.00	75.00	45.00
(176)	C.D. Thomas	715.00	250.00	145.00
(177)	Joseph Tinker	880.00	310.00	175.00
(178)	Bert Tooley	220.00	75.00	45.00
(179)	Terence Turner (Terrence)	220.00	75.00	45.00
(180)	George Tyler	2,000	1,000	500.00
(181)	Jim Vaughn	385.00	135.00	75.00
(182)	Chas. (Heinie) Wagner	220.00	75.00	45.00
(183)	Ed (Dixie) Walker	220.00	75.00	45.00
(184)	Robert Wallace	1,250	625.00	300.00
(185)	John Warhop	220.00	75.00	45.00
(186)	George Weaver	5,225	1,815	1,045
(187)	Zach Wheat	880.00	310.00	175.00
(188)	G. Harris White	310.00	110.00	60.00
(189)	Ernest Wilie	275.00	95.00	55.00
(190)	Bob Williams	220.00	75.00	45.00
(191)	Arthur Wilson (New York)	250.00	90.00	50.00
(192)	Owen Wilson (Pittsburg)	1,250	625.00	300.00
(193)	George Wiltse	220.00	75.00	45.00
(194)	Ivey Wingo	385.00	135.00	75.00
(195)	Harry Wolverton	220.00	75.00	45.00
(196)	Joe Wood	2,640	925.00	530.00
(197)	Eugene Woodburn	880.00	310.00	175.00
(198)	Ralph Works	1,250	625.00	300.00
(199)	Stanley Yerkes	220.00	75.00	45.00
(200)	Rollie Zeider	330.00	110.00	65.00

1912 T227 Series Of Champions

The 1912 "Series of Champions" card set issued by the "Honest Long Cut" and "Miners Extra" tobacco brands features several baseball stars among its 25 famous athletes of

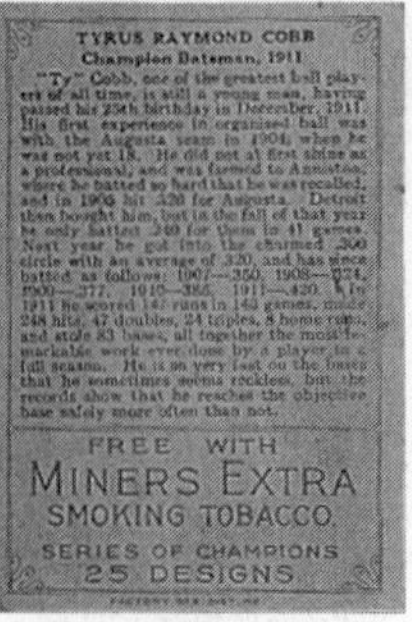

the day. Larger than a standard-size tobacco issue, each card in the "Champions" series measures 3-3/8" x 2-5/16". The back includes a relatively lengthy player biography, while the front features a lithograph of the player in action. Although the set includes only four baseball players, these attractive cards are popular among collectors because of the stature of the four players selected. The "Champions" series holds additional significance because it includes the only known baseball cards issued under the "Miners Extra" brand name. The set carries the American Card Catalog designation of T227.

		NM	EX	VG
	Complete Set (4):	22,500	10,000	5,500
	Common Player:	3,600	1,620	900.00
(1)	"Home Run" Baker	3,600	1,620	900.00
(2)	"Chief" Bender	3,600	1,620	900.00
(3)	Ty Cobb	16,200	7,200	4,200
(4)	Rube Marquard	3,600	1,620	900.00

U

1906 Ullman Postcards

The designation of Giants' players as "World's Champions" dates this issue to 1906. The 3-1/2" x 5-1/2" cards have a black-and-white photo surrounded by a greenish or reddish-brown tone wooden-look frame with a plaque printed in the bottom border. Backs are printed in brown with typical postcard markings and include mention of "Ullman's 'Art Frame' Series." This checklist is likely not complete. The card of "Harry" (name actually Henry) Mathewson is the only known baseball card appearance of Christy's kid brother.

		NM	EX	VG
	Common Player:	750.00	375.00	225.00
(1)	Leon Ames	750.00	375.00	225.00
(2)	Mike Donlin	750.00	375.00	225.00
(3)	George Ferguson	750.00	375.00	225.00
(4)	Matty Fitzgerald	750.00	375.00	225.00
(5)	Billy Gilbert	750.00	375.00	225.00
(6)	Christy Matthewson (Mathewson)	3,500	1,750	1,000
(7)	Harry (Henry) Mathewson	1,200	600.00	360.00
(8)	Dan McGann (McGann on 1st Base.)	750.00	375.00	225.00
(9)	"Iron Arm" McGinnity	1,000	500.00	300.00
(10)	Manager McGraw	1,500	750.00	450.00
(11)	Strang and Bowerman (Sammy Strang, Frank Bowerman)	900.00	450.00	250.00
(12)	Hooks Wiltse	750.00	375.00	225.00
(13)	1906 National League Champion Chicago, Cubs			

1933 Uncle Jacks Candy

One of the lesser-known candy issues of the early 1930s was this New England regional set from Uncle Jacks, Inc., of Springfield, Mass., and Newport, R.I. The 1-7/8" x 2-7/8" blank-backed cards can be found printed in blue, red, purple or green duotone, and were sold in a see-through wax paper wrapper with a piece of candy and a coupon which could be redeemed (in quantities of 100) for a "league baseball" and a chance at

a trip to the 1933 World Series. The set is among those listed in the American Card Catalog under the catchall number R317. The unnumbered cards are checklisted here alphabetically.

		NM	EX	VG
	Complete Set (30):	25,000	12,500	7,500
	Common Player:	400.00	200.00	120.00
(1)	Earl Averill	1,000	500.00	300.00
(2)	James L. Bottomley	1,000	500.00	300.00
(3)	Ed Brandt	400.00	200.00	120.00
(4)	Ben Chapman	400.00	200.00	120.00
(5)	Gordon Cochrane	1,000	500.00	300.00
(6)	Joe Cronin	1,000	500.00	300.00
(7)	Hazen Cuyler	1,000	500.00	300.00
(8)	George Earnshaw	400.00	200.00	120.00
(9)	Wesley Ferrell	400.00	200.00	120.00
(10)	Jimmie Foxx	1,500	750.00	450.00
(11)	Frank Frisch	1,000	500.00	300.00
(12)	Burleigh Grimes	1,000	500.00	300.00
(13)	"Lefty" Grove	1,250	625.00	375.00
(14)	"Wild Bill" Hallahan	400.00	200.00	120.00
(15)	Leo Hartnett	1,000	500.00	300.00
(16)	"Babe" Herman	400.00	200.00	120.00
(17)	Rogers Hornsby	1,200	600.00	360.00
(18)	Charles Klein	1,000	500.00	300.00
(19)	Tony Lazzeri	1,000	500.00	300.00
(20)	Fred Lindstrom	1,000	500.00	300.00
(21)	Ted Lyons	1,000	500.00	300.00
(22)	"Pepper" Martin	650.00	325.00	200.00
(23)	Herb Pennock	1,000	500.00	300.00
(24)	"Babe" Ruth ("King of Swat")	4,000	2,000	1,200
(25)	Al Simmons	1,000	500.00	300.00
(26)	"Bill" Terry	1,000	500.00	300.00
(27)	"Dazzy" Vance	1,000	500.00	300.00
(28)	Lloyd Waner	1,000	500.00	300.00
(29)	Paul Waner	1,000	500.00	300.00
(30)	Hack Wilson	1,000	500.00	300.00

1958 Union 76 Sports Club Booklets

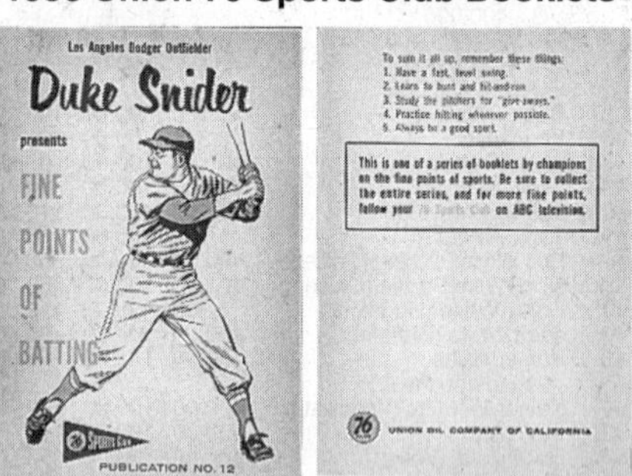

This series of sports instructional booklets was issued by Union Oil in conjunction with its Sports Club television program for youngsters. Besides seven baseball players, the series featured football, track, bowling, skiing, and other stars. The booklets are 12 pages and measure about 4" x 5-1/2". Fronts have a drawing of the player and are printed in Union Oil logo colors of orange and blue. The sports tips inside are well illustrated. Books are numbered on front.

		NM	EX	VG
	Complete (Baseball) Set (7):	160.00	80.00	45.00
	Common Player:	15.00	7.50	4.50
12	Duke Snider	35.00	17.50	10.50
14	Bob Lemon	20.00	10.00	6.00
15	Red Schoendienst	20.00	10.00	6.00
20	Bill Rigney	15.00	7.50	4.50
38	Jackie Jensen	15.00	7.50	4.50
39	Warren Spahn	25.00	12.50	7.50
41	Ernie Banks	35.00	17.50	10.50

1960 Union Oil Dodger Family Booklets

For its first major issue of Dodgers memorabilia, Union 76 gas stations in Southern California distributed a series of booklets profiling players and staff. Each 5-1/2" x 7-1/2" booklet has 16 black-and-white pages highlighted with red graphics. The covers have action poses with many other photos on the inside pages, along with a biography, personal information, career highlights, playing tips, etc. On back is

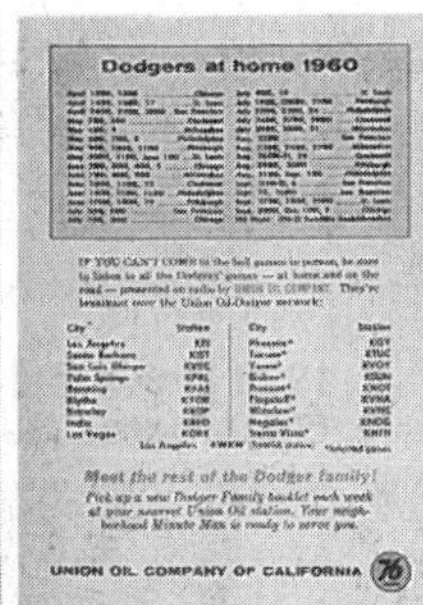

a Dodgers schedule and Union 76 ad. The booklets were distributed on a one-per-week basis. They are listed here in alphabetical order.

		NM	EX	VG
Complete Set (23):		150.00	75.00	45.00
Common Player:		6.00	3.00	1.75
(1)	Walter Alston	7.50	3.75	2.25
(2)	Roger Craig	6.00	3.00	1.75
(3)	Tom Davis	7.50	3.75	2.25
(4)	Don Demeter	6.00	3.00	1.75
(5)	Don Drysdale	15.00	7.50	4.50
(6)	Chuck Essegian	6.00	3.00	1.75
(7)	Jim Gilliam	7.50	3.75	2.25
(8)	Gil Hodges	12.00	6.00	3.50
(9)	Frank Howard	7.50	3.75	2.25
(10)	Sandy Koufax	40.00	20.00	12.00
(11)	Norm Larker	6.00	3.00	1.75
(12)	Wally Moon	6.00	3.00	1.75
(13)	Charlie Neal	6.00	3.00	1.75
(14)	Johnny Podres	6.00	3.00	1.75
(15)	Ed Roebuck	6.00	3.00	1.75
(16)	John Roseboro	6.00	3.00	1.75
(17)	Larry Sherry	6.00	3.00	1.75
(18)	Norm Sherry	6.00	3.00	1.75
(19)	Duke Snider	15.00	7.50	4.50
(20)	Stan Williams	6.00	3.00	1.75
(21)	Maury Wills	7.50	3.75	2.25
(22)	Coaches (Joe Becker, Bobby Bragan, Greg Mulleavy, Pete Reiser)	6.00	3.00	1.75
(23)	Jerry Doggett, Vin Scully/ Announcers	6.00	3.00	1.75

1961 Union Oil Dodger Family Booklets

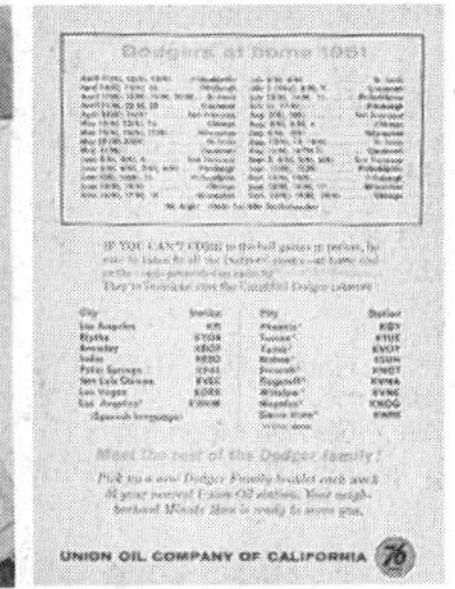

For a second consecutive year, Union 76 gas stations in Southern California distributed a series of booklets profiling team members and staff. The 5-1/2" x 7-1/2" booklets have 16 black-and-white pages highlighted with red graphics. The covers have large portraits while there are many photos on the inside pages, along with a biography, personal information, career highlights, playing tips, etc. On back is a Dodgers schedule and radio network information. The booklets were distributed on a one-per-week basis. They are listed here in alphabetical order.

		NM	EX	VG
Complete Set (24):		175.00	85.00	50.00
Common Player:		6.00	3.00	1.75
(1)	Walter Alston	7.50	3.75	2.25
(2)	Roger Craig	6.00	3.00	1.75
(3)	Tommy Davis	7.50	3.75	2.25
(4)	Willie Davis	7.50	3.75	2.25
(5)	Don Drysdale	15.00	7.50	4.50
(6)	Dick Farrell	6.00	3.00	1.75
(7)	Ron Fairly	6.00	3.00	1.75
(8)	Jim Gilliam	7.50	3.75	2.25
(9)	Gil Hodges	10.00	5.00	3.00
(10)	Frank Howard	7.50	3.75	2.25
(11)	Sandy Koufax	30.00	15.00	9.00
(12)	Norm Larker	6.00	3.00	1.75
(13)	Wally Moon	6.00	3.00	1.75
(14)	Charlie Neal	6.00	3.00	1.75
(15)	Ron Perranoski	6.00	3.00	1.75
(16)	Johnny Podres	6.00	3.00	1.75
(17)	John Roseboro	6.00	3.00	1.75
(18)	Larry Sherry	6.00	3.00	1.75
(19)	Norm Sherry	6.00	3.00	1.75
(20)	Duke Snider	15.00	7.50	4.50
(21)	Daryl Spencer	6.00	3.00	1.75
(22)	Stan Williams	6.00	3.00	1.75
(23)	Maury Wills	7.50	3.75	2.25
(24)	Jerry Doggett, Vin Scully/ Announcers	6.00	3.00	1.75

1962 Union Oil Dodgers Premium Pictures

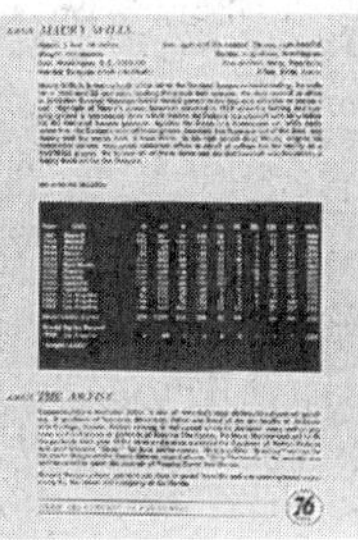

One of many premiums issued by Union Oil during the Dodgers' early years in Los Angeles, this set of player pictures is the most popular with collectors. The 8-1/2" x 11" pictures feature a large color pastel portrait of the player on front, along with a smaller action picture. The player's name is printed in the white border below. The artist's signature and a 1962 copyright are printed below the portrait. Backs are printed in black-and-white and include a career summary and complete minor and major league stats, a profile of sports artist Nicholas Volpe and an ad at bottom for Union Oil and its Union 76 brand of gasoline. The unnumbered pictures are checklisted here alphabetically. It was reported that 200,000 of each picture were produced.

		NM	EX	VG
Complete Set (24):		225.00	115.00	70.00
Common Player:		8.00	4.00	2.50
(1)	Larry Burright	8.00	4.00	2.50
(2)	Doug Camilli	8.00	4.00	2.50
(3)	Andy Carey	8.00	4.00	2.50
(4)	Tom Davis	10.00	5.00	3.00
(5)	Willie Davis	10.00	5.00	3.00
(6)	Don Drysdale	20.00	10.00	6.00
(7)	Ron Fairly	8.00	4.00	2.50
(8)	Jim Gilliam	10.00	5.00	3.00
(9)	Tim Harkness	8.00	4.00	2.50
(10)	Frank Howard	10.00	5.00	3.00
(11)	Sandy Koufax	40.00	20.00	12.00
(12)	Joe Moeller	8.00	4.00	2.50
(13)	Wally Moon	8.00	4.00	2.50
(14)	Ron Perranoski	8.00	4.00	2.50
(15)	Johnny Podres	8.00	4.00	2.50
(16)	Ed Roebuck	8.00	4.00	2.50
(17)	John Roseboro	8.00	4.00	2.50
(18)	Larry Sherry	8.00	4.00	2.50
(19)	Norm Sherry	8.00	4.00	2.50
(20)	Duke Snider	25.00	12.50	7.50
(21)	Daryl Spencer	8.00	4.00	2.50
(22)	Lee Walls	8.00	4.00	2.50
(23)	Stan Williams	8.00	4.00	2.50
(24)	Maury Wills	10.00	5.00	3.00

1964 Union Oil Dodgers Premium Pictures

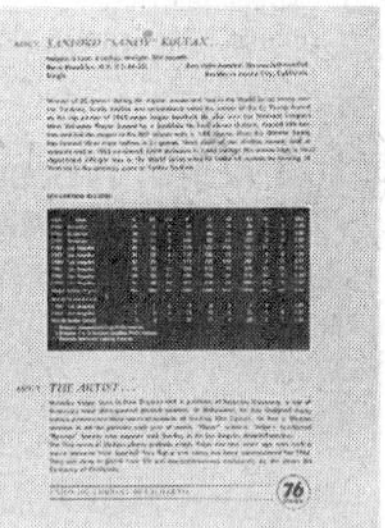

Paired pastel portraits, one in uniform and one in mufti, from sports artist Nicholas Volpe are featured on these large-format (8-1/2" x 11") premium pictures sponsored by Union Oil. The player's name is printed in the bottom border while the artist's signature is printed beneath the portraits. Backs are in black-and-white and feature personal data about the player and artist, complete minor and major league stats and Union Oil/Union 76 logos. The unnumbered pictures are checklisted here alphabetically.

		NM	EX	VG
Complete Set (18):		165.00	80.00	50.00
Common Player:		8.00	4.00	2.50
(1)	Tommy Davis	10.00	5.00	3.00
(2)	Willie Davis	10.00	5.00	3.00
(3)	Don Drysdale	20.00	10.00	6.00
(4)	Ron Fairly	8.00	4.00	2.50
(5)	Jim Gilliam	10.00	5.00	3.00
(6)	Frank Howard	10.00	5.00	3.00
(7)	Sandy Koufax	35.00	17.50	10.00
(8)	Bob Miller	8.00	4.00	2.50
(9)	Joe Moeller	8.00	4.00	2.50
(10)	Wally Moon	8.00	4.00	2.50
(11)	Phil Ortega	8.00	4.00	2.50
(12)	Wes Parker	8.00	4.00	2.50
(13)	Ron Perranoski	8.00	4.00	2.50
(14)	John Podres	8.00	4.00	2.50
(15)	John Roseboro	8.00	4.00	2.50
(16)	Dick Tracewski	8.00	4.00	2.50
(17)	Lee Walls	8.00	4.00	2.50
(18)	Maury Wills	10.00	5.00	3.00

1969 Union Oil Dodgers Premium Pictures

These 8-1/2" x 11" cards were given to fans attending week night "Player Portrait Night" promotional games. The premiums are similar in format to earlier and later sets sponsored by Union Oil and created by sports artist Nicholas Volpe. Fronts have pastel player portraits and action drawings against a black background. Backs are in black-and-white and have player biographies, stats and a career summary, along with a word about the artist and an ad for Union Oil/Union 76. The unnumbered pictures are checklisted here alphabetically.

		NM	EX	VG
Complete Set (13):		120.00	60.00	35.00
Common Player:		8.00	4.00	2.50
(1)	Walt Alston	10.00	5.00	3.00
(2)	Jim Brewer	8.00	4.00	2.50
(3)	Willie Davis	10.00	5.00	3.00
(4)	Don Drysdale	20.00	10.00	6.00
(5)	Ron Fairly	8.00	4.00	2.50
(6)	Tom Haller	8.00	4.00	2.50
(7)	Jim Lefebvre	8.00	4.00	2.50
(8)	Claude Osteen	8.00	4.00	2.50
(9)	Wes Parker	8.00	4.00	2.50
(10)	Paul Popovich	8.00	4.00	2.50
(11)	Bill Singer	8.00	4.00	2.50
(12)	Bill Sudakis	8.00	4.00	2.50
(13)	Don Sutton	13.50	6.75	4.00

1968 Uniroyal Keds Cincinnati Reds

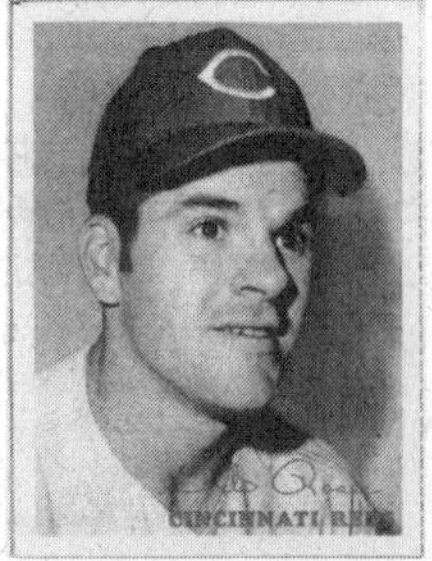

These 2-1/2" x 3-1/4" cards are printed in blue duotone on thin paper. Blank backed, they were intended to be put into an accompanying album. It is unknown whether this checklist is complete.

		NM	EX	VG
Common Player:		20.00	10.00	6.00
(1)	Dave Bristol	20.00	10.00	6.00
(2)	Bob Johnson	20.00	10.00	6.00
(3)	Bob Lee	20.00	10.00	6.00
(4)	Jim Maloney	20.00	10.00	6.00
(5)	Lee May	20.00	10.00	6.00
(6)	Vada Pinson	25.00	12.50	7.50
(7)	Pete Rose	150.00	75.00	45.00

1979 United Press International

SPORTS NOSTALGIA

THEODORE SAMUEL WILLIAMS (1918-)

"Ted" Williams was born in San Diego, California and during his career, he won six batting titles and hit 521 home runs. In 1946 he hit over .400, the last major league player to do so. He played for the Boston Red Sox (1939-42; 1946-60) and was elected to the Baseball Hall of Fame in 1966.

On September 28, 1960, Williams hit a 420-foot home run in the 8th inning during a game with Baltimore at Fenway Park. It was his 29th homer of the season and turned out to be Ted Williams' last 'at bat' in the majors before retiring.

Not widely circulated, and perhaps issued only as a prototype, these cards feature a tiny (2" x 2-1/4" clear vinyl record attached to the back. Overall, the card is 2-3/4" x 5" and has on front a black-and-white or color photo with a UPI credit line in the very wide white border at bottom. The back is headed either "Sports Nostalgia" or "Great Moments in Sports." Player identification and career highlights are printed on back. The vinyl mini-record could be played on an ancient electronic entertainment device known as a turntable. Similar card/records were produced for other sports and historical highlights.

		NM	EX	VG
Complete Set (9):		150.00	75.00	45.00
Common Player:		10.00	5.00	3.00
(1)	Hank Aaron (715th HR)	15.00	7.50	4.50
(2)	Joe DiMaggio (Hitting Streak Ends)	20.00	10.00	6.00
(3)	Lou Gehrig (Gehrig Day 7/4/39)	20.00	10.00	6.00
(4)	Mickey Mantle (Record HR)	25.00	12.50	7.50
(5)	Stan Musial (3,000th Hit)	15.00	7.50	4.50
(6)	Babe Ruth (Famous Home Run)	20.00	10.00	6.00
(7)	Gene Tenace (Record HR)	10.00	5.00	3.00
(8)	Bobby Thomson (Famous HR)	12.00	6.00	3.50
(9)	Ted Williams (Last At-Bat)	15.00	7.50	4.50

1932 Universal Pictures Babe Ruth Premium

This 8" x 10" black-and-white photo was issued to promote what was advertised as a series of Babe Ruth shorts. The front pictures the movie star in a generic uniform with a facsimile autograph. On back is advertising for the theater bill. It is likely the pictures were distributed blank-backed, allowing local theaters to have their advertising added.

	NM	EX	VG
Babe Ruth	750.00	375.00	225.00

1925 Universal Toy & Novelty Brooklyn Dodgers (W504)

Printed on cheap paper in blue ink and intended to be cut apart into a team photo and 16 individual player cards, this set was originally issued on a 5-1/2" x 13" sheet. Single cut cards measure about 1-3/8" x 2-3/8", with the team picture about 5-1/2" x 3-1/2". Cards are blank-back. Cards are numbered in roughly alphabetical order beneath the photo, where the name, team, position and birth year are also printed.

		NM	EX	VG
Complete Sheet:		1,800	900.00	540.00
Complete Set, Singles (17):		1,200	600.00	360.00
Common Player:		50.00	25.00	15.00
101	Edward W. Brown	50.00	25.00	15.00
102	John H. De Berry	50.00	25.00	15.00
103	William L. Doak	50.00	25.00	15.00
104	Wm. C. Ehrhardt (First name Welton.)	50.00	25.00	15.00
105	J.F. Fournier	50.00	25.00	15.00
106	T.H. Griffith	50.00	25.00	15.00
107	Burleigh A. Grimes	100.00	50.00	30.00
108	C.P. Hargreaves	50.00	25.00	15.00
109	Andrew A. High	50.00	25.00	15.00
110	Andy. H. Johnston (First name Jimmy.)	50.00	25.00	15.00
111	John Mitchell	50.00	25.00	15.00
112	"Tiny" Osborne	50.00	25.00	15.00
113	Milton Stock	50.00	25.00	15.00
114	James W. Taylor	50.00	25.00	15.00
115	"Dazzy" Vance	100.00	50.00	30.00
116	Zack D. Wheat	100.00	50.00	30.00
---	Brooklyn National League Team Photo	550.00	275.00	165.00

1925 Universal Toy & Novelty New York Giants (W504)

Printed on thick cardboard and intended to be cut apart into a team photo and 16 individual player cards, this set was originally issued on a 5-1/2" x 13" sheet. Single cut cards measure about 1-3/8" x 2-3/8", with the team picture about 5" x 3-1/2". Cards are blank-back. Player cards are numbered beneath the photo, where the name, team, position and birth year are also printed.

		NM	EX	VG
Complete Sheet:		3,500	1,750	1,000
Complete Set (17):		3,000	1,500	900.00
Common Player:		125.00	60.00	35.00
133	Virgil Barnes	125.00	60.00	35.00
134	John N. Bentley	125.00	60.00	35.00
135	Frank Frisch	225.00	110.00	65.00
136	Harry Gowdy	125.00	60.00	35.00
137	Henry Groh	125.00	60.00	35.00
138	Travis Jackson	200.00	100.00	60.00
139	George Kelly	200.00	100.00	60.00
140	Emil Meusel	125.00	60.00	35.00
141	Hugh McQuillan	125.00	60.00	35.00
142	Arthur Nehf	125.00	60.00	35.00
143	Wilfred D. Ryan	125.00	60.00	35.00
144	Frank Snyder	125.00	60.00	35.00
145	Lewis R. Wilson	225.00	110.00	65.00
146	Ross Youngs	200.00	100.00	60.00
147	Hugh Jennings	200.00	100.00	60.00
148	John J. McGraw	200.00	100.00	60.00
---	New York National League Team Photo	400.00	200.00	120.00

1925 Universal Toy & Novelty N.Y. Yankees (W504)

Printed on thick cardboard and intended to be cut apart into a team photo and 16 individual player cards, this set was originally issued on a 5-1/2" x 13" sheet. Single cut cards measure about 1-3/8" x 2-3/8", with the team picture about 5" x 3-1/2". Cards are blank-back. Player cards are numbered in alphabetical order beneath the photo, where the name, team, position and birth year are also printed.

		NM	EX	VG
Complete Sheet:		4,000	2,000	1,200
Complete Set (17):		3,500	1,750	1,000
Common Player:		125.00	60.00	35.00
117	Bernard Bengough	125.00	60.00	35.00
118	Joseph Dugan	125.00	60.00	35.00
119	Waite Hoyt	200.00	100.00	60.00
120	Sam Jones	125.00	60.00	35.00
121	Robert Meusel	125.00	60.00	35.00
122	Walter C. Pipp	125.00	60.00	35.00
123	G.H. "Babe" Ruth	1,200	600.00	360.00
124	Wal. H. Schang	125.00	60.00	35.00
125	Robert J. Shawkey	125.00	60.00	35.00
126	Everett Scott	125.00	60.00	35.00
127	Urban Shocker	125.00	60.00	35.00
128	Aaron L. Ward	125.00	60.00	35.00
129	Lawton Witt	125.00	60.00	35.00
130	Carl Mays	140.00	70.00	42.00
131	Miller Huggins	200.00	100.00	60.00
132	Benj. Paschal	125.00	60.00	35.00
----	New York American League Team Photo	800.00	400.00	240.00

1925 Universal Toy & Novelty Washington Senators (W504)

Printed on thick cardboard and intended to be cut apart into a team photo and 16 individual player cards, this set was originally issued on a 5-1/2" x 13" sheet. Single cut cards measure about 1-3/8" x 2-3/8", with the team picture about 5" x 3-1/2". Cards are blank-back. Player cards are numbered beneath the photo, where the name, team, position and birth year are also printed.

		NM	EX	VG
Complete Sheet:				
Complete Set (17):				
Common Player:		50.00	25.00	15.00
149	Joe Judge	50.00	25.00	15.00
150	Wm. Hargrave	50.00	25.00	15.00
151	R. Peckinpaugh	50.00	25.00	15.00
152	O.L. Bluege	50.00	25.00	15.00
153	M.J. McNally	50.00	25.00	15.00
154	Sam Rice	200.00	100.00	60.00
155				
156				
157				
158				
159	Wm. Hargrave	50.00	25.00	15.00
160				
161				
162	Harold (Herold) Ruel	50.00	25.00	15.00
163				
164	George Mogridge	50.00	25.00	15.00
---	Washinton American League Team Photo	400.00	200.00	120.00

1933 U.S. Caramel (R328)

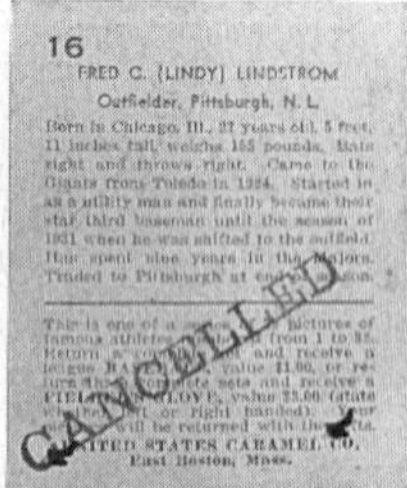

Produced by a Boston confectioner, this set is not limited to baseball, but is a set of 32 "Famous Athletes," of which 27 are baseball players. The 2-1/2" x 3" cards have a black-and-white picture on front with a red background and white border. Backs feature the player's name, position, team and league as well as a redemption ad and card number. The issue was among the last of the caramel card sets. The cards could be redeemed for a baseball and glove and were returned punch-cancelled and stamped. Card #16, short-printed to limit the number of prizes claimed, was first discovered in the late 1980s; only two examples are currently known.

		NM	EX	VG
Common Player:		600.00	275.00	150.00
1	Edward T. (Eddie) Collins	1,000	450.00	250.00
2	Paul (Big Poison) Waner	1,000	450.00	250.00
3	Robert T. (Bobby) Jones (Golfer)			
4	William (Bill) Terry	1,000	450.00	250.00
5	Earl B. Combs (Earle)	1,000	450.00	250.00
6	William (Bill) Dickey	1,000	450.00	250.00
7	Joseph (Joe) Cronin	1,000	450.00	250.00
8	Charles (Chick) Hafey	1,000	450.00	250.00

		NM	EX	VG
9	Gene Sarazen (Golfer)			
10	Walter (Rabbit) Maranville	1,000	450.00	250.00
11	Rogers (Rajah) Hornsby	1,750	785.00	435.00
12	Gordon (Mickey) Cochrane	1,000	450.00	250.00
13	Lloyd (Little Poison) Waner	1,000	450.00	250.00
14	Tyrus (Ty) Cobb	3,000	1,350	750.00
15	Eugene (Gene) Tunney (Boxer)			
16	Charles (Lindy) Lindstrom (2 known)			80,000
17	Al. Simmons	1,000	450.00	250.00
18	Anthony (Tony) Lazzeri	1,000	450.00	250.00
19	Walter (Wally) Berger	600.00	275.00	150.00
20	Charles (Large Charlie) Ruffing	1,000	450.00	250.00
21	Charles (Chuck) Klein	1,000	450.00	250.00
22	John (Jack) Dempsey (Boxer)			
23	James (Jimmy) Foxx	1,750	785.00	435.00
24	Frank J. (Lefty) O'Doul	750.00	335.00	185.00
25	Jack (Sailor Jack) Sharkey (Boxer)			
26	Henry (Lou) Gehrig	6,000	2,700	1,500
27	Robert (Lefty) Grove	1,200	540.00	300.00
28	Edward Brant (Brandt)	600.00	275.00	150.00
29	George Earnshaw	600.00	275.00	150.00
30	Frank (Frankie) Frisch	1,000	450.00	250.00
31	Vernon (Lefty) Gomez	1,000	450.00	250.00
32	George (Babe) Ruth	7,500	3,250	1,900

1973 U.S. Playing Card Ruth/Gehrig

These decks of playing cards were produced for sale by the Smithsonian Institution in Washington, D.C. The 2-1/4" x 3-1/2" cards were sold as a pair. Backs have colorized pictures of the Yankees greats; Ruth on an orange background and Gehrig on red.

	NM	EX	VG
Complete Set, Ruth (54):	25.00	12.50	7.50
Single Card, Ruth:	1.50	.75	.45
Complete Set, Gehrig (54):	15.00	7.50	4.50
Single Card, Gehrig:	.75	.40	.25

(A 50% premium attaches to a complete boxed pair of decks.)

1909-11 Uzit Cigarettes

Uzit is generally accepted as the second scarcest back advertiser (after Drum) found on T206. The typographic back is printed in light blue ink.

PREMIUMS
Commons: 35-45X
Hall of Famers: 6-8X
(See T206 for checklist.)

The Mint-Mint examples of vintage cards carry a significant premium over the Near Mint values shown here. This premium reflects limited availability of the highest-grade cards as well as demand for particular cards or sets in the best possible condition.

V

1938-39 Val Decker Packing Co. Cincinnati Reds Postcards

 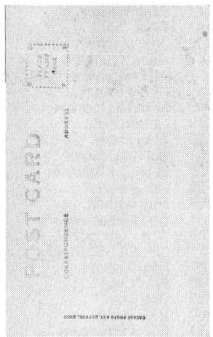

(See 1937-39 Orcajo Cincinnati Reds postcards for checklist and values.)

1950s-70s Van Heusen Advisory Staff Photos

Not a great deal is known about the distribution of these 8" x 10" black-and-white player photos. It is likely the checklist here is not complete. The photos are bordered in white with the player name at bottom. In one of the lower corners is the logo of the clothing manufacturer. This issue is differentiated from the Phillies photos because of the action poses and multi-team composition of the known examples.

		NM	EX	VG
	Common Player:	20.00	10.00	6.00
(1)	Paul Blair	20.00	10.00	6.00
(2)	Curt Blefary	20.00	10.00	6.00
(3)	Jerry Coleman/Throwing (Yankees)	25.00	12.50	7.50
(4)	Tommy Davis/Btg (Dodgers)	20.00	10.00	6.00
(5)	Dick Hall/Portrait (Phillies)	20.00	10.00	6.00
(6)	Bob Hendley (Braves, follow-through.)	20.00	10.00	6.00
(7)	Chuck Hinton	20.00	10.00	6.00
(8)	Don Lock (Phillies, upper body.)	20.00	10.00	6.00
(9)	Jim Piersall	25.00	12.50	7.50
(10)	Cookie Rojas (Phillies, bat on shoulder.)	20.00	10.00	6.00
(11)	Bill Skowron (Dodgers, full-length.)	25.00	12.50	7.50
(12)	Maury Wills/Btg (Dodgers)	25.00	12.50	7.50

1967 Van Heusen Phillies

Not a great deal is known about the distribution of these 8" x 10" black-and-white player portraits. It is possible the checklist here is not complete. The photos are bordered in white with the player name at bottom. At lower-right is the logo of the clothing manufacturer. This issue is differentiated from the Advisory Staff Photos because of the similitude of the portrait photos of the teammates.

		NM	EX	VG
	Common Player:	20.00	10.00	6.00
(1)	Bo Belinsky	20.00	10.00	6.00
(2)	Jim Bunning	35.00	17.50	10.50
(3)	Wes Covington	20.00	10.00	6.00
(4)	Dick Ellsworth	20.00	10.00	6.00
(5)	Dick Groat	20.00	10.00	6.00
(6)	Chris Short	20.00	10.00	6.00
(7)	Bill White	20.00	10.00	6.00

1912 Vassar Sweaters

TY COBB

Star players of the day are pictured wearing the sponsor's product over their uniforms in this issue of 4" x 6-3/4" black-and-white cards. Player names are in the white border at bottom. It is not known whether this checklist is complete.

		NM	EX	VG
	Common Player:	1,250	625.00	375.00
(1)	Ty Cobb	5,000	2,500	1,500
(2)	Sam Crawford	1,750	875.00	525.00
(3)	Walter Johnson	2,750	1,375	825.00
(4)	Napoleon Lajoie	1,750	875.00	525.00
(5)	Smokey Joe Wood	1,250	625.00	375.00

1959 Venezuelan Topps

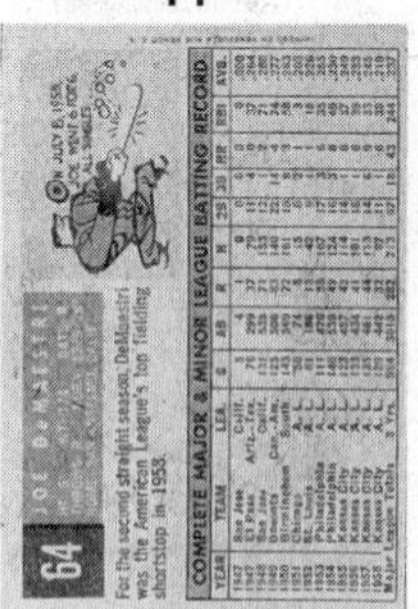

Beginning in 1959, Topps began marketing baseball cards in Venezuela, always a hotbed of baseball fandom. In most years, such as the debut set in 1959, the cards destined for the South American market represented a parallel of the first couple of series of Topps' regular U.S. issue. Print quality (usually lack of gloss on front) is the major difference between the two issues. Backs of some of the 1959 Venezuelan cards carry the credit line: "Impreso en Venezuela por Benco C.A." A reality of the Venezuelan cards is that they tend to survive in low-grade condition due to the local custom of gluing cards into albums and scrapbooks. After its 1959 issue, Topps produced Venezuelan cards only in the even-numbered years, except for 1967, until the last of the sets was issued in 1968.

		NM	EX	VG
	Complete Set (196):	10,000	4,000	2,400
	Common Player:	45.00	18.00	11.00
1	Ford Frick	60.00	24.00	14.50
2	Eddie Yost	45.00	18.00	11.00
3	Don McMahon	45.00	18.00	11.00
4	Albie Pearson	45.00	18.00	11.00
5	Dick Donovan	45.00	18.00	11.00
6	Alex Grammas	45.00	18.00	11.00
7	Al Pilarcik	45.00	18.00	11.00
8	Phillies Team	75.00	30.00	18.00
9	Paul Giel	45.00	18.00	11.00
10	Mickey Mantle	2,000	550.00	350.00
11	Billy Hunter	45.00	18.00	11.00
12	Vern Law	45.00	18.00	11.00
13	Dick Gernert	45.00	18.00	11.00
14	Pete Whisenant	45.00	18.00	11.00
15	Dick Drott	45.00	18.00	11.00
16	Joe Pignatano	45.00	18.00	11.00
17	Danny's All-Stars (Ted Kluszewski, Danny Murtaugh, Frank Thomas)	50.00	20.00	12.00

18	Jack Urban	45.00	18.00	11.00
19	Ed Bressoud	45.00	18.00	11.00
20	Duke Snider	200.00	80.00	48.00
21	Connie Johnson	45.00	18.00	11.00
22	Al Smith	45.00	18.00	11.00
23	Murry Dickson	45.00	18.00	11.00
24	Red Wilson	45.00	18.00	11.00
25	Don Hoak	45.00	18.00	11.00
26	Chuck Stobbs	45.00	18.00	11.00
27	Andy Pafko	45.00	18.00	11.00
28	Red Worthington	45.00	18.00	11.00
29	Jim Bolger	45.00	18.00	11.00
30	Nellie Fox	100.00	40.00	24.00
31	Ken Lehman	45.00	18.00	11.00
32	Don Buddin	45.00	18.00	11.00
33	Ed Fitz Gerald	45.00	18.00	11.00
34	Pitchers Beware (Al Kaline, Charlie Maxwell)	90.00	36.00	22.00
35	Ted Kluszewski	60.00	24.00	14.50
36	Hank Aguirre	45.00	18.00	11.00
37	Gene Green	45.00	18.00	11.00
38	Morrie Martin	45.00	18.00	11.00
39	Ed Bouchee	45.00	18.00	11.00
40	Warren Spahn	125.00	50.00	30.00
41	Bob Martyn	45.00	18.00	11.00
42	Murray Wall	45.00	18.00	11.00
43	Steve Bilko	45.00	18.00	11.00
44	Vito Valentinetti	45.00	18.00	11.00
45	Andy Carey	45.00	18.00	11.00
46	Bill Henry	45.00	18.00	11.00
47	Jim Finigan	45.00	18.00	11.00
48	Orioles Team/Checklist 1-88	75.00	30.00	18.00
49	Bill Hall	45.00	18.00	11.00
50	Willie Mays	450.00	180.00	108.00
51	Rip Coleman	45.00	18.00	11.00
52	Coot Veal	45.00	18.00	11.00
53	Stan Williams	45.00	18.00	11.00
54	Mel Roach	45.00	18.00	11.00
55	Tom Brewer	45.00	18.00	11.00
56	Carl Sawatski	45.00	18.00	11.00
57	Al Cicotte	45.00	18.00	11.00
58	Eddie Miksis	45.00	18.00	11.00
59	Irv Noren	45.00	18.00	11.00
60	Bob Turley	45.00	18.00	11.00
61	Dick Brown	45.00	18.00	11.00
62	Tony Taylor	45.00	18.00	11.00
63	Jim Hearn	45.00	18.00	11.00
64	Joe DeMaestri	45.00	18.00	11.00
65	Frank Torre	45.00	18.00	11.00
66	Joe Ginsberg	45.00	18.00	11.00
67	Brooks Lawrence	45.00	18.00	11.00
68	Dick Schofield	45.00	18.00	11.00
69	Giants Team/Checklist 89-176	75.00	30.00	18.00
70	Harvey Kuenn	50.00	20.00	12.00
71	Don Bessent	45.00	18.00	11.00
72	Bill Renna	45.00	18.00	11.00
73	Ron Jackson	45.00	18.00	11.00
74	Directing the Power (Cookie Lavagetto, Jim Lemon, Roy Sievers)	45.00	18.00	11.00
75	Sam Jones	45.00	18.00	11.00
76	Bobby Richardson	50.00	20.00	12.00
77	John Goryl	45.00	18.00	11.00
78	Pedro Ramos	45.00	18.00	11.00
79	Harry Chiti	45.00	18.00	11.00
80	Minnie Minoso	55.00	22.00	13.00
81	Hal Jeffcoat	45.00	18.00	11.00
82	Bob Boyd	45.00	18.00	11.00
83	Bob Smith	45.00	18.00	11.00
84	Reno Bertoia	45.00	18.00	11.00
85	Harry Anderson	45.00	18.00	11.00
86	Bob Keegan	45.00	18.00	11.00
87	Danny O'Connell	45.00	18.00	11.00
88	Herb Score	45.00	18.00	11.00
89	Billy Gardner	45.00	18.00	11.00
90	Bill Skowron	55.00	22.00	13.00
91	Herb Moford	45.00	18.00	11.00
92	Dave Philley	45.00	18.00	11.00
93	Julio Becquer	45.00	18.00	11.00
94	White Sox Team	100.00	40.00	24.00
95	Carl Willey	45.00	18.00	11.00
96	Lou Berberet	45.00	18.00	11.00
97	Jerry Lynch	45.00	18.00	11.00
98	Arnie Portocarrero	45.00	18.00	11.00
99	Ted Kazanski	45.00	18.00	11.00
100	Bob Cerv	45.00	18.00	11.00
101	Alex Kellner	45.00	18.00	11.00
102	Felipe Alou	60.00	24.00	14.50
103	Billy Goodman	45.00	18.00	11.00
104	Del Rice	45.00	18.00	11.00
105	Lee Walls	45.00	18.00	11.00
106	Hal Woodeshick	45.00	18.00	11.00
107	Norm Larker	45.00	18.00	11.00
108	Zack Monroe	45.00	18.00	11.00
109	Bob Schmidt	45.00	18.00	11.00
110	George Witt	45.00	18.00	11.00
111	Redlegs Team/ Checklist 89-176	75.00	30.00	18.00
112	Billy Consolo	45.00	18.00	11.00
113	Taylor Phillips	45.00	18.00	11.00
114	Earl Battey	45.00	18.00	11.00
115	Mickey Vernon	45.00	18.00	11.00
116	Bob Allison	45.00	18.00	11.00
117	John Blanchard	45.00	18.00	11.00
118	John Buzhardt	45.00	18.00	11.00
119	John Callison	45.00	18.00	11.00
120	Chuck Coles	45.00	18.00	11.00
121	Bob Conley	45.00	18.00	11.00
122	Bennie Daniels	45.00	18.00	11.00
123	Don Dillard	45.00	18.00	11.00
124	Dan Dobbek	45.00	18.00	11.00
125	Ron Fairly	45.00	18.00	11.00
126	Eddie Haas	45.00	18.00	11.00
127	Kent Hadley	45.00	18.00	11.00
128	Bob Hartman	45.00	18.00	11.00
129	Frank Herrera	45.00	18.00	11.00
130	Lou Jackson	45.00	18.00	11.00
131	Deron Johnson	50.00	20.00	12.00
132	Don Lee	45.00	18.00	11.00
133	Bob Lillis	45.00	18.00	11.00
134	Jim McDaniel	45.00	18.00	11.00
135	Gene Oliver	45.00	18.00	11.00
136	Jim O'Toole	45.00	18.00	11.00
137	Dick Ricketts	45.00	18.00	11.00
138	John Romano	45.00	18.00	11.00
139	Ed Sadowski	45.00	18.00	11.00
140	Charlie Secrest	45.00	18.00	11.00
141	Joe Shipley	45.00	18.00	11.00
142	Dick Stigman	45.00	18.00	11.00
143	Willie Tasby	45.00	18.00	11.00
144	Jerry Walker	45.00	18.00	11.00
145	Dom Zanni	45.00	18.00	11.00
146	Jerry Zimmerman	45.00	18.00	11.00
147	Cubs' Clubbers (Ernie Banks, Dale Long, Walt Moryn)	90.00	36.00	22.00
148	Mike McCormick	45.00	18.00	11.00
149	Jim Bunning	100.00	40.00	24.00
150	Stan Musial	400.00	160.00	100.00
151	Bob Malkmus	45.00	18.00	11.00
152	Johnny Klippstein	45.00	18.00	11.00
153	Jim Marshall	45.00	18.00	11.00
154	Ray Herbert	45.00	18.00	11.00
155	Enos Slaughter	90.00	36.00	22.00
156	Ace Hurlers (Billy Pierce, Robin Roberts)	65.00	26.00	15.50
157	Felix Mantilla	45.00	18.00	11.00
158	Walt Dropo	45.00	18.00	11.00
159	Bob Shaw	45.00	18.00	11.00
160	Dick Groat	45.00	18.00	11.00
161	Frank Baumann	45.00	18.00	11.00
162	Bobby G. Smith	45.00	18.00	11.00
163	Sandy Koufax	450.00	180.00	110.00
164	Johnny Groth	45.00	18.00	11.00
165	Bill Bruton	45.00	18.00	11.00
166	Destruction Crew (Rocky Colavito, Larry Doby, Minnie Minoso)	125.00	50.00	30.00
167	Duke Maas	45.00	18.00	11.00
168	Carroll Hardy	45.00	18.00	11.00
169	Ted Abernathy	45.00	18.00	11.00
170	Gene Woodling	45.00	18.00	11.00
171	Willard Schmidt	45.00	18.00	11.00
172	A's Team/Checklist 177-242	75.00	30.00	18.00
173	Bill Monbouquette	45.00	18.00	11.00
174	Jim Pendleton	45.00	18.00	11.00
175	Dick Farrell	45.00	18.00	11.00
176	Preston Ward	45.00	18.00	11.00
177	Johnny Briggs	45.00	18.00	11.00
178	Ruben Amaro	45.00	18.00	11.00
179	Don Rudolph	45.00	18.00	11.00
180	Yogi Berra	200.00	80.00	48.00
181	Bob Porterfield	45.00	18.00	11.00
182	Milt Graff	45.00	18.00	11.00
183	Stu Miller	45.00	18.00	11.00
184	Harvey Haddix	45.00	18.00	11.00
185	Jim Busby	45.00	18.00	11.00
186	Mudcat Grant	45.00	18.00	11.00
187	Bubba Phillips	45.00	18.00	11.00
188	Juan Pizarro	45.00	18.00	11.00
189	Neil Chrisley	45.00	18.00	11.00
190	Bill Virdon	45.00	18.00	11.00
191	Russ Kemmerer	45.00	18.00	11.00
192	Charley Beamon	45.00	18.00	11.00
193	Sammy Taylor	45.00	18.00	11.00
194	Jim Brosnan	45.00	18.00	11.00
195	Rip Repulski	45.00	18.00	11.00
196	Billy Moran	45.00	18.00	11.00

1960 Venezuelan Topps

Unlike its 1959 issue, which had a printed-in-Venezuela notice on the backs, Topps' 1960 issue for that South American market is virtually identical, front and back, to the company's U.S. product. The Venezuelan cards have less gloss on the front and the black ink on their backs is lighter. The Latin American version is a parallel of the first 198 cards from Topps' set. As usual with Latin American cards, low-grade examples are the norm due to the local collecting custom of pasting cards into albums and scrapbooks.

		NM	EX	VG
Complete Set (198):		7,900	3,150	1,900
Common Player:		40.00	16.00	9.50
1	Early Wynn	95.00	30.00	20.00
2	Roman Mejias	40.00	16.00	9.50
3	Joe Adcock	40.00	16.00	9.50
4	Bob Purkey	40.00	16.00	9.50
5	Wally Moon	40.00	16.00	9.50
6	Lou Berberet	40.00	16.00	9.50
7	Master and Mentor (Willie Mays, Bill Rigney)	125.00	50.00	30.00
8	Bud Daley	40.00	16.00	9.50
9	Faye Throneberry	40.00	16.00	9.50
10	Ernie Banks	150.00	60.00	36.00
11	Norm Siebern	40.00	16.00	9.50
12	Milt Pappas	40.00	16.00	9.50
13	Wally Post	40.00	16.00	9.50
14	Jim Grant	40.00	16.00	9.50
15	Pete Runnels	40.00	16.00	9.50
16	Ernie Broglio	40.00	16.00	9.50
17	Johnny Callison	40.00	16.00	9.50
18	Dodgers Team/ Checklist 1-88	100.00	40.00	24.00
19	Felix Mantilla	40.00	16.00	9.50
20	Roy Face	40.00	16.00	9.50
21	Dutch Dotterer	40.00	16.00	9.50
22	Rocky Bridges	40.00	16.00	9.50
23	Eddie Fisher	40.00	16.00	9.50
24	Dick Gray	40.00	16.00	9.50
25	Roy Sievers	40.00	16.00	9.50
26	Wayne Terwilliger	40.00	16.00	9.50
27	Dick Drott	40.00	16.00	9.50
28	Brooks Robinson	150.00	60.00	36.00
29	Clem Labine	40.00	16.00	9.50
30	Tito Francona	40.00	16.00	9.50
31	Sammy Esposito	40.00	16.00	9.50
32	Sophomore Stalwarts (Jim O'Toole, Vada Pinson)	40.00	16.00	9.50
33	Tom Morgan	40.00	16.00	9.50
34	Sparky Anderson	90.00	45.00	27.00
35	Whitey Ford	150.00	60.00	36.00
36	Russ Nixon	40.00	16.00	9.50
37	Bill Bruton	40.00	16.00	9.50
38	Jerry Casale	40.00	16.00	9.50
39	Earl Averill	40.00	16.00	9.50
40	Joe Cunningham	40.00	16.00	9.50
41	Barry Latman	40.00	16.00	9.50
42	Hobie Landrith	40.00	16.00	9.50
43	Senators Team/ Checklist 1-88	75.00	30.00	18.00
44	Bobby Locke	40.00	16.00	9.50
45	Roy McMillan	40.00	16.00	9.50
46	Jack Fisher	40.00	16.00	9.50
47	Don Zimmer	40.00	16.00	9.50
48	Hal Smith	40.00	16.00	9.50
49	Curt Raydon	40.00	16.00	9.50
50	Al Kaline	150.00	60.00	36.00
51	Jim Coates	40.00	16.00	9.50
52	Dave Philley	40.00	16.00	9.50
53	Jackie Brandt	40.00	16.00	9.50
54	Mike Fornieles	40.00	16.00	9.50
55	Bill Mazeroski	90.00	45.00	27.00
56	Steve Korcheck	40.00	16.00	9.50
57	Win-Savers (Turk Lown, Gerry Staley)	40.00	16.00	9.50
58	Gino Cimoli	40.00	16.00	9.50
59	Juan Pizarro	40.00	16.00	9.50
60	Gus Triandos	40.00	16.00	9.50
61	Eddie Kasko	40.00	16.00	9.50
62	Roger Craig	40.00	16.00	9.50
63	George Strickland	40.00	16.00	9.50
64	Jack Meyer	40.00	16.00	9.50
65	Elston Howard	45.00	18.00	11.00
66	Bob Trowbridge	40.00	16.00	9.50
67	Jose Pagan	40.00	16.00	9.50
68	Dave Hillman	40.00	16.00	9.50
69	Billy Goodman	40.00	16.00	9.50
70	Lou Burdette	40.00	16.00	9.50
71	Marty Keough	40.00	16.00	9.50
72	Tigers Team/ Checklist 89-176	75.00	30.00	18.00
73	Bob Gibson	100.00	40.00	24.00
74	Walt Moryn	40.00	16.00	9.50
75	Vic Power	40.00	16.00	9.50
76	Bill Fischer	40.00	16.00	9.50
77	Hank Foiles	40.00	16.00	9.50
78	Bob Grim	40.00	16.00	9.50
79	Walt Dropo	40.00	16.00	9.50
80	Johnny Antonelli	40.00	16.00	9.50
81	Russ Snyder	40.00	16.00	9.50
82	Ruben Gomez	40.00	16.00	9.50
83	Tony Kubek	40.00	16.00	9.50
84	Hal Smith	40.00	16.00	9.50
85	Frank Lary	40.00	16.00	9.50
86	Dick Gernert	40.00	16.00	9.50
87	John Romonosky	40.00	16.00	9.50
88	John Roseboro	40.00	16.00	9.50
89	Hal Brown	40.00	16.00	9.50
90	Bobby Avila	40.00	16.00	9.50
91	Bennie Daniels	40.00	16.00	9.50
92	Whitey Herzog	45.00	18.00	11.00
93	Art Schult	40.00	16.00	9.50
94	Leo Kiely	40.00	16.00	9.50
95	Frank Thomas	40.00	16.00	9.50
96	Ralph Terry	40.00	16.00	9.50
97	Ted Lepcio	40.00	16.00	9.50
98	Gordon Jones	40.00	16.00	9.50
99	Lenny Green	40.00	16.00	9.50
100	Nellie Fox	90.00	36.00	22.00
101	Bob Miller	40.00	16.00	9.50
102	Kent Hadley	40.00	16.00	9.50
103	Dick Farrell	40.00	16.00	9.50
104	Dick Schofield	40.00	16.00	9.50
105	Larry Sherry	40.00	16.00	9.50
106	Billy Gardner	40.00	16.00	9.50
107	Carl Willey	40.00	16.00	9.50
108	Pete Daley	40.00	16.00	9.50
109	Cletis Boyer	40.00	16.00	9.50
110	Cal McLish	40.00	16.00	9.50
111	Vic Wertz	40.00	16.00	9.50
112	Jack Harshman	40.00	16.00	9.50
113	Bob Skinner	40.00	16.00	9.50
114	Ken Aspromonte	40.00	16.00	9.50
115	Fork and Knuckler (Roy Face, Hoyt Wilhelm)	45.00	18.00	11.00
116	Jim Rivera	40.00	16.00	9.50
117	Tom Borland	40.00	16.00	9.50
118	Bob Bruce	40.00	16.00	9.50
119	Chico Cardenas	40.00	16.00	9.50
120	Duke Carmel	40.00	16.00	9.50
121	Camilo Carreon	40.00	16.00	9.50
122	Don Dillard	40.00	16.00	9.50
123	Dan Dobbek	40.00	16.00	9.50
124	Jim Donohue	40.00	16.00	9.50
125	Dick Ellsworth	40.00	16.00	9.50
126	Chuck Estrada	40.00	16.00	9.50
127	Ronnie Hansen	40.00	16.00	9.50
128	Bill Harris	40.00	16.00	9.50
129	Bob Hartman	40.00	16.00	9.50
130	Frank Herrera	40.00	16.00	9.50
131	Ed Hobaugh	40.00	16.00	9.50
132	Frank Howard	50.00	20.00	12.00
133	Manuel Javier	40.00	16.00	9.50
134	Deron Johnson	45.00	18.00	11.00
135	Ken Johnson	40.00	16.00	9.50
136	Jim Kaat	60.00	24.00	14.50
137	Lou Klimchock	40.00	16.00	9.50
138	Art Mahaffey	40.00	16.00	9.50
139	Carl Mathias	40.00	16.00	9.50
140	Julio Navarro	40.00	16.00	9.50
141	Jim Proctor	40.00	16.00	9.50
142	Bill Short	40.00	16.00	9.50

143	Al Spangler	40.00	16.00	9.50
144	Al Stieglitz	40.00	16.00	9.50
145	Jim Umbricht	40.00	16.00	9.50
146	Ted Wieand	40.00	16.00	9.50
147	Bob Will	40.00	16.00	9.50
148	Carl Yastrzemski	550.00	275.00	165.00
149	Bob Nieman	40.00	16.00	9.50
150	Billy Pierce	40.00	16.00	9.50
151	Giants Team/ Checklist 177-264	75.00	30.00	18.00
152	Gail Harris	40.00	16.00	9.50
153	Bobby Thomson	40.00	16.00	9.50
154	Jim Davenport	40.00	16.00	9.50
155	Charlie Neal	40.00	16.00	9.50
156	Art Ceccarelli	40.00	16.00	9.50
157	Rocky Nelson	40.00	16.00	9.50
158	Wes Covington	40.00	16.00	9.50
159	Jim Piersall	45.00	18.00	11.00
160	Rival All-Stars (Ken Boyer, Mickey Mantle)	600.00	250.00	150.00
161	Ray Narleski	40.00	16.00	9.50
162	Sammy Taylor	40.00	16.00	9.50
163	Hector Lopez	40.00	16.00	9.50
164	Reds Team/Checklist 89-176	75.00	30.00	18.00
165	Jack Sanford	40.00	16.00	9.50
166	Chuck Essegian	40.00	16.00	9.50
167	Valmy Thomas	40.00	16.00	9.50
168	Alex Grammas	40.00	16.00	9.50
169	Jake Striker	40.00	16.00	9.50
170	Del Crandall	40.00	16.00	9.50
171	Johnny Groth	40.00	16.00	9.50
172	Willie Kirkland	40.00	16.00	9.50
173	Billy Martin	45.00	18.00	11.00
174	Indians Team/ Checklist 89-176	75.00	30.00	18.00
175	Pedro Ramos	40.00	16.00	9.50
176	Vada Pinson	45.00	18.00	11.00
177	Johnny Kucks	40.00	16.00	9.50
178	Woody Held	40.00	16.00	9.50
179	Rip Coleman	40.00	16.00	9.50
180	Harry Simpson	40.00	16.00	9.50
181	Billy Loes	40.00	16.00	9.50
182	Glen Hobbie	40.00	16.00	9.50
183	Eli Grba	40.00	16.00	9.50
184	Gary Geiger	40.00	16.00	9.50
185	Jim Owens	40.00	16.00	9.50
186	Dave Sisler	40.00	16.00	9.50
187	Jay Hook	40.00	16.00	9.50
188	Dick Williams	40.00	16.00	9.50
189	Don McMahon	40.00	16.00	9.50
190	Gene Woodling	40.00	16.00	9.50
191	Johnny Klippstein	40.00	16.00	9.50
192	Danny O'Connell	40.00	16.00	9.50
193	Dick Hyde	40.00	16.00	9.50
194	Bobby Gene Smith	40.00	16.00	9.50
195	Lindy McDaniel	40.00	16.00	9.50
196	Andy Carey	40.00	16.00	9.50
197	Ron Kline	40.00	16.00	9.50
198	Jerry Lynch	40.00	16.00	9.50

1962 Venezuelan Topps

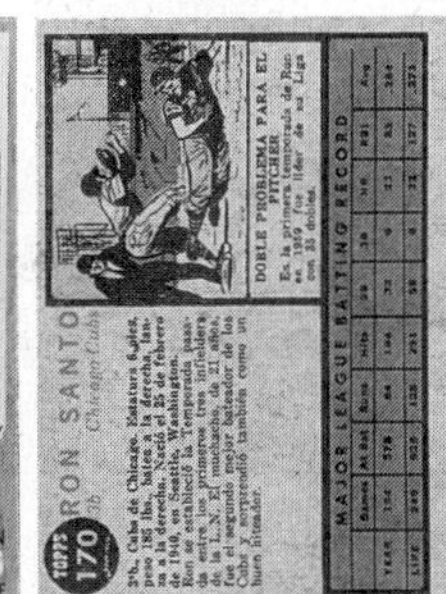

For the first time in its short history of producing baseball cards for the Venezuelan market, Topps in 1962 reprinted virtually the entire back of each card in Spanish (except the League Leaders cards #51-60). The player personal data, career summary and even the cartoon are En Espanol; only the stats are in English. There is no Topps credit or copyright line on the backs. Otherwise identical in format to the 1962 Topps North American issue, the Venezuelan set comprises the first 198 cards of the Topps issue, though cards #197 (Daryl Spencer) and 198 (Johnny Keane) have been replaced with two local Major Leaguers. Survivors of this issue tend to be in lower grades due to the common practice of gluing cards into albums or scrapbooks.

		NM	EX	VG
Complete Set (198):		8,000	3,200	2,000
Common Player:		30.00	12.00	7.50
1	Roger Maris	750.00	300.00	185.00
2	Jim Brosnan	30.00	12.00	7.50
3	Pete Runnels	30.00	12.00	7.50
4	John DeMerit	30.00	12.00	7.50
5	Sandy Koufax	400.00	160.00	100.00
6	Marv Breeding	30.00	12.00	7.50
7	Frank Thomas	30.00	12.00	7.50
8	Ray Herbert	30.00	12.00	7.50
9	Jim Davenport	30.00	12.00	7.50
10	Roberto Clemente	550.00	220.00	135.00
11	Tom Morgan	30.00	12.00	7.50
12	Harry Craft	30.00	12.00	7.50
13	Dick Howser	30.00	12.00	7.50
14	Bill White	30.00	12.00	7.50
15	Dick Donovan	30.00	12.00	7.50
16	Darrell Johnson	30.00	12.00	7.50
17	Johnny Callison	30.00	12.00	7.50
18	Managers' Dream (Mickey Mantle, Willie Mays)	1,500	600.00	375.00
19	Ray Washburn	30.00	12.00	7.50
20	Rocky Colavito	60.00	24.00	15.00
21	Jim Kaat	30.00	12.00	7.50
22	Checklist 1-88	30.00	12.00	7.50
23	Norm Larker	30.00	12.00	7.50
24	Tigers team	90.00	36.00	22.00
25	Ernie Banks	175.00	70.00	45.00
26	Chris Cannizzaro	30.00	12.00	7.50
27	Chuck Cottier	30.00	12.00	7.50
28	Minnie Minoso	45.00	18.00	11.00
29	Casey Stengel	125.00	50.00	30.00
30	Eddie Mathews	125.00	50.00	30.00
31	Tom Tresh	40.00	16.00	10.00
32	John Roseboro	30.00	12.00	7.50
33	Don Larsen	30.00	12.00	7.50
34	Johnny Temple	30.00	12.00	7.50
35	Don Schwall	30.00	12.00	7.50
36	Don Leppert	30.00	12.00	7.50
37	Tribe Hill Trio (Barry Latman, Jim Perry, Dick Stigman)	30.00	12.00	7.50
38	Gene Stephens	30.00	12.00	7.50
39	Joe Koppe	30.00	12.00	7.50
40	Orlando Cepeda	65.00	25.00	15.00
41	Cliff Cook	30.00	12.00	7.50
42	Jim King	30.00	12.00	7.50
43	Dodgers team	125.00	50.00	30.00
44	Don Taussig	30.00	12.00	7.50
45	Brooks Robinson	200.00	80.00	50.00
46	Jack Baldschun	30.00	12.00	7.50
47	Bob Will	30.00	12.00	7.50
48	Ralph Terry	30.00	12.00	7.50
49	Hal Jones	30.00	12.00	7.50
50	Stan Musial	250.00	100.00	60.00
51	A.L. Batting Leaders (Norm Cash, Elston Howard, Al Kaline, Jim Piersall)	80.00	32.00	20.00
52	N.L. Batting Leaders (Ken Boyer, Roberto Clemente, Wally Moon, Vada Pinson)	225.00	90.00	55.00
53	A.L. Home Run Leaders (Jim Gentile, Harmon Killebrew, Mickey Mantle, Roger Maris)	400.00	160.00	100.00
54	N.L. Home Run Leaders (Orlando Cepeda, Willie Mays, Frank Robinson)	125.00	50.00	30.00
55	A.L. E.R.A. Leaders (Dick Donovan, Don Mossi, Milt Pappas, Bill Stafford)	30.00	12.00	7.50
56	N.L. E.R.A. Leaders (Mike McCormick, Jim O'Toole, Curt Simmons, Warren Spahn)	35.00	14.00	8.75
57	A.L. Win Leaders (Steve Barber, Jim Bunning, Whitey Ford, Frank Lary)	45.00	18.00	11.00
58	N.L. Win Leaders (Joe Jay, Jim O'Toole, Warren Spahn)	35.00	14.00	8.75
59	A.L. Strikeout Leaders (Jim Bunning, Whitey Ford, Camilo Pascual, Juan Pizzaro)	45.00	18.00	11.00
60	N.L. Strikeout Leaders (Don Drysdale, Sandy Koufax, Jim O'Toole, Stan Williams)	100.00	40.00	25.00
61	Cardinals Team	90.00	36.00	22.00
62	Steve Boros	30.00	12.00	7.50
63	Tony Cloninger	30.00	12.00	7.50
64	Russ Snyder	30.00	12.00	7.50
65	Bobby Richardson	40.00	16.00	10.00
66	Cuno Barragon (Barragan)	30.00	12.00	7.50
67	Harvey Haddix	30.00	12.00	7.50
68	Ken Hunt	30.00	12.00	7.50
69	Phil Ortega	30.00	12.00	7.50
70	Harmon Killebrew	125.00	50.00	30.00
71	Dick LeMay	30.00	12.00	7.50
72	Bob's Pupils (Steve Boros, Bob Scheffing, Jake Wood)	30.00	12.00	7.50
73	Nellie Fox	125.00	50.00	30.00
74	Bob Lillis	30.00	12.00	7.50
75	Milt Pappas	30.00	12.00	7.50
76	Howie Bedell	30.00	12.00	7.50
77	Tony Taylor	30.00	12.00	7.50
78	Gene Green	30.00	12.00	7.50
79	Ed Hobaugh	30.00	12.00	7.50
80	Vada Pinson	35.00	14.00	8.75
81	Jim Pagliaroni	30.00	12.00	7.50
82	Deron Johnson	30.00	12.00	7.50
83	Larry Jackson	30.00	12.00	7.50
84	Lenny Green	30.00	12.00	7.50
85	Gil Hodges	80.00	32.00	20.00
86	Donn Clendenon	30.00	12.00	7.50
87	Mike Roarke	30.00	12.00	7.50
88	Ralph Houk	30.00	12.00	7.50
89	Barney Schultz	30.00	12.00	7.50
90	Jim Piersall	30.00	12.00	7.50
91	J.C. Martin	30.00	12.00	7.50
92	Sam Jones	30.00	12.00	7.50
93	John Blanchard	30.00	12.00	7.50
94	Jay Hook	30.00	12.00	7.50
95	Don Hoak	30.00	12.00	7.50
96	Eli Grba	30.00	12.00	7.50
97	Tito Francona	30.00	12.00	7.50
98	Checklist 89-176	30.00	12.00	7.50
99	Boog Powell	75.00	30.00	18.50
100	Warren Spahn	125.00	50.00	30.00
101	Carroll Hardy	30.00	12.00	7.50
102	Al Schroll	30.00	12.00	7.50
103	Don Blasingame	30.00	12.00	7.50
104	Ted Savage	30.00	12.00	7.50
105	Don Mossi	30.00	12.00	7.50
106	Carl Sawatski	30.00	12.00	7.50
107	Mike McCormick	30.00	12.00	7.50
108	Willie Davis	30.00	12.00	7.50
109	Bob Shaw	30.00	12.00	7.50
110	Bill Skowron	35.00	14.00	8.75
111	Dallas Green	30.00	12.00	7.50
112	Hank Foiles	30.00	12.00	7.50
113	White Sox team	90.00	36.00	22.00
114	Howie Koplitz	30.00	12.00	7.50
115	Bob Skinner	30.00	12.00	7.50
116	Herb Score	30.00	12.00	7.50
117	Gary Geiger	30.00	12.00	7.50
118	Julian Javier	30.00	12.00	7.50
119	Danny Murphy	30.00	12.00	7.50
120	Bob Purkey	30.00	12.00	7.50
121	Billy Hitchcock	30.00	12.00	7.50
122	Norm Bass	30.00	12.00	7.50
123	Mike de la Hoz	30.00	12.00	7.50
124	Bill Pleis	30.00	12.00	7.50
125	Gene Woodling	30.00	12.00	7.50
126	Al Cicotte	30.00	12.00	7.50
127	Pride of the A's (Hank Bauer, Jerry Lumpe, Norm Siebern)	30.00	12.00	7.50
128	Art Fowler	30.00	12.00	7.50
129	Lee Walls	30.00	12.00	7.50
130	Frank Bolling	30.00	12.00	7.50
131	Pete Richert	30.00	12.00	7.50
132	Angels Team	90.00	36.00	22.00
133	Felipe Alou	45.00	18.00	11.00
134	Billy Hoeft	30.00	12.00	7.50
135	Babe as a Boy (Babe Ruth)	165.00	65.00	40.00
136	Babe Joins Yanks (Babe Ruth)	200.00	80.00	50.00
137	Babe and Mgr. Huggins (Babe Ruth)	165.00	65.00	40.00
138	The Famous Slugger (Babe Ruth)	200.00	80.00	50.00
139	Babe Hits 60 (Babe Ruth)	300.00	120.00	75.00
140	Gehrig and Ruth (Babe Ruth)	225.00	90.00	55.00
141	Twilight Years (Babe Ruth)	165.00	65.00	40.00
142	Coaching for the Dodgers (Babe Ruth)	165.00	65.00	40.00
143	Greatest Sports Hero (Babe Ruth)	165.00	65.00	40.00
144	Farewell Speech (Babe Ruth)	165.00	65.00	40.00
145	Barry Latman	30.00	12.00	7.50
146	Don Demeter	30.00	12.00	7.50
147	Bill Kunkel	30.00	12.00	7.50
148	Wally Post	30.00	12.00	7.50
149	Bob Duliba	30.00	12.00	7.50
150	Al Kaline	135.00	55.00	35.00
151	Johnny Klippstein	30.00	12.00	7.50
152	Mickey Vernon	30.00	12.00	7.50
153	Pumpsie Green	30.00	12.00	7.50
154	Lee Thomas	30.00	12.00	7.50
155	Stu Miller	30.00	12.00	7.50
156	Merritt Ranew	30.00	12.00	7.50
157	Wes Covington	30.00	12.00	7.50
158	Braves Team	90.00	36.00	22.00
159	Hal Reniff	30.00	12.00	7.50
160	Dick Stuart	30.00	12.00	7.50
161	Frank Baumann	30.00	12.00	7.50
162	Sammy Drake	30.00	12.00	7.50
163	Hot Corner Guardians (Cletis Boyer, Billy Gardner)	30.00	12.00	7.50
164	Hal Naragon	30.00	12.00	7.50
165	Jackie Brandt	30.00	12.00	7.50
166	Don Lee	30.00	12.00	7.50
167	Tim McCarver	125.00	50.00	30.00
168	Leo Posada	30.00	12.00	7.50
169	Bob Cerv	30.00	12.00	7.50
170	Ron Santo	40.00	16.00	10.00
171	Dave Sisler	30.00	12.00	7.50
172	Fred Hutchinson	30.00	12.00	7.50
173	Chico Fernandez	30.00	12.00	7.50
174	Carl Willey	30.00	12.00	7.50
175	Frank Howard	30.00	12.00	7.50
176	Eddie Yost	30.00	12.00	7.50
177	Bobby Shantz	30.00	12.00	7.50
178	Camilo Carreon	30.00	12.00	7.50
179	Tom Sturdivant	30.00	12.00	7.50
180	Bob Allison	30.00	12.00	7.50
181	Paul Brown	30.00	12.00	7.50
182	Bob Nieman	30.00	12.00	7.50
183	Roger Craig	30.00	12.00	7.50
184	Haywood Sullivan	30.00	12.00	7.50
185	Roland Sheldon	30.00	12.00	7.50
186	Mack Jones	30.00	12.00	7.50
187	Gene Conley	30.00	12.00	7.50
188	Chuck Hiller	30.00	12.00	7.50
189	Dick Hall	30.00	12.00	7.50
190	Wally Moon	30.00	12.00	7.50
191	Jim Brewer	30.00	12.00	7.50
192	Checklist 177-264	30.00	12.00	7.50
193	Eddie Kasko	30.00	12.00	7.50
194	Dean Chance	30.00	12.00	7.50
195	Joe Cunningham	30.00	12.00	7.50
196	Terry Fox	30.00	12.00	7.50
199	Elio Chacon	60.00	24.00	15.00
200	Luis Aparicio	250.00	100.00	62.00

1964 Venezuelan Topps

The first 370 cards of Topps' baseball set were issued in a parallel version for sale in Venezuela. Printed on thin cardboard with no front gloss, the cards are differentiated from the U.S. version by the use of a black border on back. Survivors of the issue are usually in low grade because of the common Latin American practice of collectors gluing the cards into the album that was available. Venezuelan Topps cards were often cut up to 1/8" smaller than their U.S. counterparts.

		NM	EX	VG
Complete Set (370):		9,500	3,800	2,400
Common Player:		30.00	12.00	7.50
Album:		300.00	125.00	75.00
1	N.L. E.R.A. Leaders (Dick Ellsworth, Bob Friend, Sandy Koufax)	90.00	36.00	22.00
2	A.L. E.R.A. Leaders (Camilo Pascual, Gary Peters, Juan Pizarro)	30.00	12.00	7.50
3	N.L. Pitching Leaders (Sandy Koufax, Jim Maloney, Juan Marichal, Warren Spahn)	60.00	24.00	15.00
4	A.L. Pitching Leaders (Jim Bouton, Whitey Ford, Camilo Pascual)	45.00	18.00	11.00
5	N.L. Strikeout Leaders (Don Drysdale, Sandy Koufax, Jim Maloney)	60.00	24.00	15.00
6	A.L. Strikeout Leaders (Jim Bunning, Camilo Pascual, Dick Stigman)	35.00	14.00	8.75
7	N.L. Batting Leaders (Hank Aaron, Roberto Clemente, Tommy Davis, Dick Groat)	100.00	40.00	25.00
8	A.L. Batting Leaders (Al Kaline, Rich Rollins, Carl Yastrzemski)	50.00	20.00	12.50
9	N.L. Home Run Leaders (Hank Aaron, Orlando Cepeda, Willie Mays, Willie McCovey)	75.00	30.00	18.50
10	A.L. Home Run Leaders (Bob Allison, Harmon Killebrew, Dick Stuart)	45.00	18.00	11.00
11	N.L. R.B.I. Leaders (Hank Aaron, Ken Boyer, Bill White)	50.00	20.00	12.50
12	A.L. R.B.I. Leaders (Al Kaline, Harmon Killebrew, Dick Stuart)	45.00	18.00	11.00
13	Hoyt Wilhelm	50.00	20.00	12.50
14	Dodgers Rookies (Dick Nen, Nick Willhite)	30.00	12.00	7.50
15	Zoilo Versalles	30.00	12.00	7.50
16	John Boozer	30.00	12.00	7.50
17	Willie Kirkland	30.00	12.00	7.50
18	Billy O'Dell	30.00	12.00	7.50
19	Don Wart	30.00	12.00	7.50
20	Bob Friend	30.00	12.00	7.50
21	Yogi Berra	100.00	40.00	25.00
22	Jerry Adair	30.00	12.00	7.50
23	Chris Zachary	30.00	12.00	7.50
24	Carl Sawatski	30.00	12.00	7.50
25	Bill Monbouquette	30.00	12.00	7.50
26	Gino Cimoli	30.00	12.00	7.50
27	Mets Team	65.00	26.00	16.00
28	Claude Osteen	30.00	12.00	7.50
29	Lou Brock	75.00	30.00	18.50
30	Ron Perranoski	30.00	12.00	7.50
31	Dave Nicholson	30.00	12.00	7.50
32	Dean Chance	30.00	12.00	7.50
33	Reds Rookies (Sammy Ellis, Mel Queen)	30.00	12.00	7.50
34	Jim Perry	30.00	12.00	7.50
35	Eddie Mathews	75.00	30.00	18.50
36	Hal Reniff	30.00	12.00	7.50
37	Smoky Burgess	30.00	12.00	7.50
38	Jim Wynn	30.00	12.00	7.50
39	Hank Aguirre	30.00	12.00	7.50
40	Dick Groat	30.00	12.00	7.50
41	Friendly Foes (Willie McCovey, Leon Wagner)	35.00	14.00	8.75
42	Moe Drabowsky	30.00	12.00	7.50
43	Roy Sievers	30.00	12.00	7.50
44	Duke Carmel	30.00	12.00	7.50
45	Milt Pappas	30.00	12.00	7.50
46	Ed Brinkman	30.00	12.00	7.50
47	Giants Rookies (Jesus Alou, Ron Herbel)	30.00	12.00	7.50
48	Bob Perry	30.00	12.00	7.50
49	Bill Henry	30.00	12.00	7.50
50	Mickey Mantle	1,800	720.00	450.00
51	Pete Richert	30.00	12.00	7.50
52	Chuck Hinton	30.00	12.00	7.50
53	Denis Menke	30.00	12.00	7.50
54	Sam Mele	30.00	12.00	7.50
55	Ernie Banks	75.00	30.00	18.50
56	Hal Brown	30.00	12.00	7.50
57	Tim Harkness	30.00	12.00	7.50
58	Don Demeter	30.00	12.00	7.50
59	Ernie Broglio	30.00	12.00	7.50
60	Frank Malzone	30.00	12.00	7.50
61	Angel Backstops (Bob Rodgers, Ed Sadowski)	30.00	12.00	7.50
62	Ted Savage	30.00	12.00	7.50
63	Johnny Orsino	30.00	12.00	7.50
64	Ted Abernathy	30.00	12.00	7.50
65	Felipe Alou	35.00	14.00	8.75
66	Eddie Fisher	30.00	12.00	7.50
67	Tigers Team	50.00	20.00	12.50
68	Willie Davis	30.00	12.00	7.50
69	Clete Boyer	35.00	14.00	8.75
70	Joe Torre	45.00	18.00	11.00
71	Jack Spring	30.00	12.00	7.50
72	Chico Cardenas	30.00	12.00	7.50
73	Jimmie Hall	30.00	12.00	7.50
74	Pirates Rookies (Tom Butters, Bob Priddy)	30.00	12.00	7.50
75	Wayne Causey	30.00	12.00	7.50
76	Checklist 1-88	30.00	12.00	7.50
77	Jerry Walker	30.00	12.00	7.50
78	Merritt Ranew	30.00	12.00	7.50
79	Bob Heffner	30.00	12.00	7.50
80	Vada Pinson	45.00	18.00	11.00
81	All-Star Vets (Nellie Fox, Harmon Killebrew)	50.00	20.00	12.50
82	Jim Davenport	30.00	12.00	7.50
83	Gus Triandos	30.00	12.00	7.50
84	Carl Willey	30.00	12.00	7.50
85	Pete Ward	30.00	12.00	7.50
86	Al Downing	30.00	12.00	7.50
87	Cardinals Team	100.00	40.00	25.00
88	John Roseboro	30.00	12.00	7.50
89	Boog Powell	35.00	14.00	8.75
90	Earl Battey	30.00	12.00	7.50
91	Bob Bailey	30.00	12.00	7.50
92	Steve Ridzik	30.00	12.00	7.50
93	Gary Geiger	30.00	12.00	7.50
94	Braves Rookies (Jim Britton, Larry Maxie)	30.00	12.00	7.50
95	George Altman	30.00	12.00	7.50
96	Bob Buhl	30.00	12.00	7.50
97	Jim Fregosi	30.00	12.00	7.50
98	Bill Bruton	30.00	12.00	7.50
99	Al Stanek	30.00	12.00	7.50
100	Elston Howard	35.00	14.00	8.75
101	Walt Alston	50.00	20.00	12.50
102	Checklist 89-176	30.00	12.00	7.50
103	Curt Flood	35.00	14.00	8.75
104	Art Mahaffey	30.00	12.00	7.50
105	Woody Held	30.00	12.00	7.50
106	Joe Nuxhall	30.00	12.00	7.50
107	White Sox Rookies (Bruce Howard, Frank Kreutzer)	30.00	12.00	7.50
108	John Wyatt	30.00	12.00	7.50
109	Rusty Staub	35.00	14.00	8.75
110	Albie Pearson	30.00	12.00	7.50
111	Don Elston	30.00	12.00	7.50
112	Bob Tillman	30.00	12.00	7.50
113	Grover Powell	30.00	12.00	7.50
114	Don Lock	30.00	12.00	7.50
115	Frank Bolling	30.00	12.00	7.50
116	Twins Rookies (Tony Oliva, Jay Ward)	45.00	18.00	11.00
117	Earl Francis	30.00	12.00	7.50
118	John Blanchard	30.00	12.00	7.50
119	Gary Kolb	30.00	12.00	7.50
120	Don Drysdale	75.00	30.00	18.50
121	Pete Runnels	30.00	12.00	7.50
122	Don McMahon	30.00	12.00	7.50
123	Jose Pagan	30.00	12.00	7.50
124	Orlando Pena	30.00	12.00	7.50
125	Pete Rose	450.00	180.00	110.00
126	Russ Snyder	30.00	12.00	7.50
127	Angels Rookies (Aubrey Gatewood, Dick Simpson)	30.00	12.00	7.50
128	Mickey Lolich	35.00	14.00	8.75
129	Amado Samuel	30.00	12.00	7.50
130	Gary Peters	30.00	12.00	7.50
131	Steve Boros	30.00	12.00	7.50
132	Braves Team	50.00	20.00	12.50
133	Jim Grant	30.00	12.00	7.50
134	Don Zimmer	30.00	12.00	7.50
135	Johnny Callison	30.00	12.00	7.50
136	World Series Game 1 (Koufax Strikes Out 15)	30.00	12.00	7.50
137	World Series Game 2 (Davis Sparks Rally)	30.00	12.00	7.50
138	World Series Game 3 (L.A. Takes 3rd Straight)	30.00	12.00	7.50
139	World Series Game 4 (Sealing Yanks' Doom)	30.00	12.00	7.50
140	World Series Summary (The Dodgers Celebrate)	30.00	12.00	7.50
141	Danny Murtaugh	30.00	12.00	7.50
142	John Bateman	30.00	12.00	7.50
143	Bubba Phillips	30.00	12.00	7.50
144	Al Worthington	30.00	12.00	7.50
145	Norm Siebern	30.00	12.00	7.50
146	Indians Rookies (Bob Chance, Tommy John)	50.00	20.00	12.50
147	Ray Sadecki	30.00	12.00	7.50
148	J.C. Martin	30.00	12.00	7.50
149	Paul Foytack	30.00	12.00	7.50
150	Willie Mays	375.00	150.00	94.00
151	Athletics Team	50.00	20.00	12.50
152	Denver Lemaster	30.00	12.00	7.50
153	Dick Williams	30.00	12.00	7.50
154	Dick Tracewski	30.00	12.00	7.50
155	Duke Snider	100.00	40.00	25.00
156	Bill Dailey	30.00	12.00	7.50
157	Gene Mauch	30.00	12.00	7.50
158	Ken Johnson	30.00	12.00	7.50
159	Charlie Dees	30.00	12.00	7.50
160	Ken Boyer	35.00	14.00	8.75
161	Dave McNally	30.00	12.00	7.50
162	Hitting Area (Vada Pinson, Dick Sisler)	30.00	12.00	7.50
163	Donn Clendenon	30.00	12.00	7.50
164	Bud Daley	30.00	12.00	7.50
165	Jerry Lumpe	30.00	12.00	7.50
166	Marty Keough	30.00	12.00	7.50
167	Senators Rookies (Mike Brumley, Lou Piniella)	60.00	24.00	15.00
168	Al Weis	30.00	12.00	7.50
169	Del Crandall	30.00	12.00	7.50
170	Dick Radatz	30.00	12.00	7.50
171	Ty Cline	30.00	12.00	7.50
172	Indians Team	50.00	20.00	12.50
173	Ryne Duren	30.00	12.00	7.50
174	Doc Edwards	30.00	12.00	7.50
175	Billy Williams	50.00	20.00	12.50
176	Tracy Stallard	30.00	12.00	7.50
177	Harmon Killebrew	75.00	30.00	18.50
178	Hank Bauer	30.00	12.00	7.50
179	Carl Warwick	30.00	12.00	7.50
180	Tommy Davis	30.00	12.00	7.50
181	Dave Wickersham	30.00	12.00	7.50
182	Sox Sockers (Chuck Schilling, Carl Yastrzemski)	50.00	20.00	12.50
183	Ron Taylor	30.00	12.00	7.50
184	Al Luplow	30.00	12.00	7.50
185	Jim O'Toole	30.00	12.00	7.50
186	Roman Mejias	30.00	12.00	7.50
187	Ed Roebuck	30.00	12.00	7.50
188	Checklist 177-264	30.00	12.00	7.50
189	Bob Hendley	30.00	12.00	7.50
190	Bobby Richardson	35.00	14.00	8.75
191	Clay Dalrymple	30.00	12.00	7.50
192	Cubs Rookies (John Boccabella, Billy Cowan)	30.00	12.00	7.50
193	Jerry Lynch	30.00	12.00	7.50
194	John Goryl	30.00	12.00	7.50
195	Floyd Robinson	30.00	12.00	7.50
196	Jim Gentile	30.00	12.00	7.50
197	Frank Lary	30.00	12.00	7.50
198	Len Gabrielson	30.00	12.00	7.50
199	Joe Azcue	30.00	12.00	7.50
200	Sandy Koufax	300.00	120.00	75.00
201	Orioles Rookies (Sam Bowens, Wally Bunker)	30.00	12.00	7.50
202	Galen Cisco	30.00	12.00	7.50
203	John Kennedy	30.00	12.00	7.50
204	Matty Alou	30.00	12.00	7.50
205	Nellie Fox	65.00	26.00	16.00
206	Steve Hamilton	30.00	12.00	7.50
207	Fred Hutchinson	30.00	12.00	7.50
208	Wes Covington	30.00	12.00	7.50
209	Bob Allen	30.00	12.00	7.50
210	Carl Yastrzemski	100.00	40.00	25.00
211	Jim Coker	30.00	12.00	7.50
212	Pete Lovrich	30.00	12.00	7.50
213	Angels Team	50.00	20.00	12.50
214	Ken McMullen	30.00	12.00	7.50
215	Ray Herbert	30.00	12.00	7.50
216	Mike de la Hoz	30.00	12.00	7.50
217	Jim King	30.00	12.00	7.50
218	Hank Fischer	30.00	12.00	7.50
219	Young Aces (Jim Bouton, Al Downing)	35.00	14.00	8.75
220	Dick Ellsworth	30.00	12.00	7.50
221	Bob Saverine	30.00	12.00	7.50
222	Bill Pierce	30.00	12.00	7.50
223	George Banks	30.00	12.00	7.50
224	Tommie Sisk	30.00	12.00	7.50
225	Roger Maris	300.00	120.00	75.00
226	Colts Rookies (Gerald Grote, Larry Yellen)	30.00	12.00	7.50
227	Barry Latman	30.00	12.00	7.50
228	Felix Mantilla	30.00	12.00	7.50
229	Charley Lau	30.00	12.00	7.50
230	Brooks Robinson	110.00	45.00	25.00
231	Dick Calmus	30.00	12.00	7.50
232	Al Lopez	50.00	20.00	12.50
233	Hal Smith	30.00	12.00	7.50
234	Gary Bell	30.00	12.00	7.50
235	Ron Hunt	30.00	12.00	7.50
236	Bill Faul	30.00	12.00	7.50
237	Cubs Team	50.00	20.00	12.50
238	Roy McMillan	30.00	12.00	7.50
239	Herm Starrette	30.00	12.00	7.50
240	Bill White	30.00	12.00	7.50
241	Jim Owens	30.00	12.00	7.50
242	Harvey Kuenn	30.00	12.00	7.50
243	Phillies Rookies (Richie Allen, John Herrnstein)	50.00	20.00	12.50
244	Tony LaRussa	35.00	14.00	8.75
245	Dick Stigman	30.00	12.00	7.50
246	Manny Mota	30.00	12.00	7.50
247	Dave DeBusschere	30.00	12.00	7.50
248	Johnny Pesky	30.00	12.00	7.50
249	Doug Camilli	30.00	12.00	7.50
250	Al Kaline	110.00	45.00	25.00
251	Choo Choo Coleman	30.00	12.00	7.50
252	Ken Aspromonte	30.00	12.00	7.50
253	Wally Post	30.00	12.00	7.50
254	Don Hoak	30.00	12.00	7.50
255	Lee Thomas	30.00	12.00	7.50
256	Johnny Weekly	30.00	12.00	7.50
257	Giants Team	50.00	20.00	12.50
258	Garry Roggenburk	30.00	12.00	7.50
259	Harry Bright	30.00	12.00	7.50
260	Frank Robinson	100.00	40.00	25.00
261	Jim Hannan	30.00	12.00	7.50
262	Cardinals Rookies (Harry Fanok, Mike Shannon)	35.00	14.00	8.75
263	Chuck Estrada	30.00	12.00	7.50
264	Jim Landis	30.00	12.00	7.50
265	Jim Bunning	50.00	20.00	12.50
266	Gene Freese	30.00	12.00	7.50
267	Wilbur Wood	30.00	12.00	7.50
268	Bill's Got It (Danny Murtaugh, Bill Virdon)	30.00	12.00	7.50
269	Ellis Burton	30.00	12.00	7.50
270	Rich Rollins	30.00	12.00	7.50
271	Bob Sadowski	30.00	12.00	7.50
272	Jake Wood	30.00	12.00	7.50
273	Mel Nelson	30.00	12.00	7.50
274	Checklist 265-352	30.00	12.00	7.50
275	John Tsitouris	30.00	12.00	7.50
276	Jose Tartabull	30.00	12.00	7.50
277	Ken Retzer	30.00	12.00	7.50
278	Bobby Shantz	30.00	12.00	7.50
279	Joe Koppe	30.00	12.00	7.50
280	Juan Marichal	65.00	26.00	16.00
281	Yankees Rookies (Jake Gibbs, Tom Metcalf)	30.00	12.00	7.50
282	Bob Bruce	30.00	12.00	7.50
283	Tommy McCraw	30.00	12.00	7.50
284	Dick Schofield	30.00	12.00	7.50
285	Robin Roberts	65.00	26.00	16.00

286	Don Landrum	30.00	12.00	7.50
287	Red Sox Rookies (Tony Conigliaro, Bill Spanswick)	35.00	14.00	8.75
288	Al Moran	30.00	12.00	7.50
289	Frank Funk	30.00	12.00	7.50
290	Bob Allison	30.00	12.00	7.50
291	Phil Ortega	30.00	12.00	7.50
292	Mike Roarke	30.00	12.00	7.50
293	Phillies Team	50.00	20.00	12.50
294	Ken Hunt	30.00	12.00	7.50
295	Roger Craig	30.00	12.00	7.50
296	Ed Kirkpatrick	30.00	12.00	7.50
297	Ken MacKenzie	30.00	12.00	7.50
298	Harry Craft	30.00	12.00	7.50
299	Bill Stafford	30.00	12.00	7.50
300	Hank Aaron	375.00	150.00	94.00
301	Larry Brown	30.00	12.00	7.50
302	Dan Pfister	30.00	12.00	7.50
303	Jim Campbell	30.00	12.00	7.50
304	Bob Johnson	30.00	12.00	7.50
305	Jack Lamabe	30.00	12.00	7.50
306	Giant Gunners (Orlando Cepeda, Willie Mays)	50.00	20.00	12.50
307	Joe Gibbon	30.00	12.00	7.50
308	Gene Stephens	30.00	12.00	7.50
309	Paul Toth	30.00	12.00	7.50
310	Jim Gilliam	30.00	12.00	7.50
311	Tom Brown	30.00	12.00	7.50
312	Tigers Rookies (Fritz Fisher, Fred Gladding)	30.00	12.00	7.50
313	Chuck Hiller	30.00	12.00	7.50
314	Jerry Buchek	30.00	12.00	7.50
315	Bo Belinsky	30.00	12.00	7.50
316	Gene Oliver	30.00	12.00	7.50
317	Al Smith	30.00	12.00	7.50
318	Twins Team	50.00	20.00	12.50
319	Paul Brown	30.00	12.00	7.50
320	Rocky Colavito	50.00	20.00	12.50
321	Bob Lillis	30.00	12.00	7.50
322	George Brunet	30.00	12.00	7.50
323	John Buzhardt	30.00	12.00	7.50
324	Casey Stengel	50.00	20.00	12.50
325	Hector Lopez	30.00	12.00	7.50
326	Ron Brand	30.00	12.00	7.50
327	Don Blasingame	30.00	12.00	7.50
328	Bob Shaw	30.00	12.00	7.50
329	Russ Nixon	30.00	12.00	7.50
330	Tommy Harper	30.00	12.00	7.50
331	A.L. Bombers (Norm Cash, Al Kaline, Mickey Mantle, Roger Maris)	600.00	240.00	150.00
332	Ray Washburn	30.00	12.00	7.50
333	Billy Moran	30.00	12.00	7.50
334	Lew Krausse	30.00	12.00	7.50
335	Don Mossi	30.00	12.00	7.50
336	Andre Rodgers	30.00	12.00	7.50
337	Dodgers Rookies (Al Ferrara, Jeff Torborg)	30.00	12.00	7.50
338	Jack Kralick	30.00	12.00	7.50
339	Walt Bond	30.00	12.00	7.50
340	Joe Cunningham	30.00	12.00	7.50
341	Jim Roland	30.00	12.00	7.50
342	Willie Stargell	65.00	26.00	16.00
343	Senators Team	50.00	20.00	12.50
344	Phil Linz	30.00	12.00	7.50
345	Frank Thomas	30.00	12.00	7.50
346	Joe Jay	30.00	12.00	7.50
347	Bobby Wine	30.00	12.00	7.50
348	Ed Lopat	30.00	12.00	7.50
349	Art Fowler	30.00	12.00	7.50
350	Willie McCovey	75.00	30.00	18.50
351	Dan Schneider	30.00	12.00	7.50
352	Eddie Bressoud	30.00	12.00	7.50
353	Wally Moon	30.00	12.00	7.50
354	Dave Giusti	30.00	12.00	7.50
355	Vic Power	30.00	12.00	7.50
356	Reds Rookies (Bill McCool, Chico Ruiz)	30.00	12.00	7.50
357	Charley James	30.00	12.00	7.50
358	Ron Kline	30.00	12.00	7.50
359	Jim Schaffer	30.00	12.00	7.50
360	Joe Pepitone	30.00	12.00	7.50
361	Jay Hook	30.00	12.00	7.50
362	Checklist 353-429	30.00	12.00	7.50
363	Dick McAuliffe	30.00	12.00	7.50
364	Joe Gaines	30.00	12.00	7.50
365	Cal McLish	30.00	12.00	7.50
366	Nelson Mathews	30.00	12.00	7.50
367	Fred Whitfield	30.00	12.00	7.50
368	White Sox Rookies (Fritz Ackley, Don Buford)	30.00	12.00	7.50
369	Jerry Zimmerman	30.00	12.00	7.50
370	Hal Woodeshick	30.00	12.00	7.50

1966 Venezuelan Topps

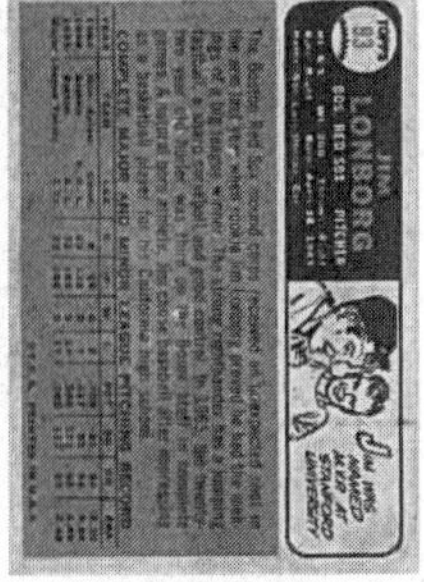

The first 370 cards on Topps' 1966 baseball set were reprinted for sale in the Venezuelan market. Identical in design to the Topps cards, they have no Spanish on them. The South American version is printed on darker cardboard that has virtually no gloss on front and bright orange-pink highlights on back. Low-grade cards are the norm for this and other Venezuelan issues as it is common collector practice south of the border to mount cards in scrapbooks and albums. The Venezuelan cards are often found up to 1/8" smaller than their U.S. counterparts.

		NM	EX	VG
Complete Set (370):		8,000	3,250	2,000
Common Player:		30.00	12.00	7.50
1	Willie Mays	400.00	160.00	100.00
2	Ted Abernathy	30.00	12.00	7.50
3	Sam Mele	30.00	12.00	7.50
4	Ray Culp	30.00	12.00	7.50
5	Jim Fregosi	30.00	12.00	7.50
6	Chuck Schilling	30.00	12.00	7.50
7	Tracy Stallard	30.00	12.00	7.50
8	Floyd Robinson	30.00	12.00	7.50
9	Clete Boyer	35.00	14.00	8.75
10	Tony Cloninger	30.00	12.00	7.50
11	Senators Rookies (Brant Alyea, Pete Craig)	30.00	12.00	7.50
12	John Tsitouris	30.00	12.00	7.50
13	Lou Johnson	30.00	12.00	7.50
14	Norm Siebern	30.00	12.00	7.50
15	Vern Law	30.00	12.00	7.50
16	Larry Brown	30.00	12.00	7.50
17	Johnny Stephenson	30.00	12.00	7.50
18	Roland Sheldon	30.00	12.00	7.50
19	Giants Team	75.00	30.00	18.50
20	Willie Horton	30.00	12.00	7.50
21	Don Nottebart	30.00	12.00	7.50
22	Joe Nossek	30.00	12.00	7.50
23	Jack Sanford	30.00	12.00	7.50
24	Don Kessinger	30.00	12.00	7.50
25	Pete Ward	30.00	12.00	7.50
26	Ray Sadecki	30.00	12.00	7.50
27	Orioles Rookies (Andy Etchebarren, Darold Knowles)	30.00	12.00	7.50
28	Phil Niekro	100.00	40.00	25.00
29	Mike Brumley	30.00	12.00	7.50
30	Pete Rose	375.00	150.00	94.00
31	Jack Cullen	30.00	12.00	7.50
32	Adolfo Phillips	30.00	12.00	7.50
33	Jim Pagliaroni	30.00	12.00	7.50
34	Checklist 1-88	30.00	12.00	7.50
35	Ron Swoboda	30.00	12.00	7.50
36	Catfish Hunter	100.00	40.00	25.00
37	Billy Herman	90.00	36.00	22.00
38	Ron Nischwitz	30.00	12.00	7.50
39	Ken Henderson	30.00	12.00	7.50
40	Jim Grant	30.00	12.00	7.50
41	Don LeJohn	30.00	12.00	7.50
42	Aubrey Gatewood	30.00	12.00	7.50
43	Don Landrum	30.00	12.00	7.50
44	Indians Rookies (Bill Davis, Tom Kelley)	30.00	12.00	7.50
45	Jim Gentile	30.00	12.00	7.50
46	Howie Koplitz	30.00	12.00	7.50
47	J.C. Martin	30.00	12.00	7.50
48	Paul Blair	30.00	12.00	7.50
49	Woody Woodward	30.00	12.00	7.50
50	Mickey Mantle	1,500	600.00	375.00
51	Gordon Richardson	30.00	12.00	7.50
52	Power Plus (Johnny Callison, Wes Covington)	30.00	12.00	7.50
53	Bob Duliba	30.00	12.00	7.50
54	Jose Pagan	30.00	12.00	7.50
55	Ken Harrelson	30.00	12.00	7.50
56	Sandy Valdespino	30.00	12.00	7.50
57	Jim Lefebvre	30.00	12.00	7.50
58	Dave Wickersham	30.00	12.00	7.50
59	Reds Team	75.00	30.00	18.50
60	Curt Flood	35.00	14.00	8.75
61	Bob Bolin	30.00	12.00	7.50
62	Merritt Ranew	30.00	12.00	7.50
63	Jim Stewart	30.00	12.00	7.50
64	Bob Bruce	30.00	12.00	7.50
65	Leon Wagner	30.00	12.00	7.50
66	Al Weis	30.00	12.00	7.50
67	Mets Rookies (Cleon Jones, Dick Selma)	35.00	14.00	8.75
68	Hal Reniff	30.00	12.00	7.50
69	Ken Hamlin	30.00	12.00	7.50
70	Carl Yastrzemski	150.00	60.00	37.00
71	Frank Carpin	30.00	12.00	7.50
72	Tony Perez	150.00	60.00	37.00
73	Jerry Zimmerman	30.00	12.00	7.50
74	Don Mossi	30.00	12.00	7.50
75	Tommy Davis	30.00	12.00	7.50
76	Red Schoendienst	90.00	36.00	22.00
77	Johnny Orsino	30.00	12.00	7.50
78	Frank Linzy	30.00	12.00	7.50
79	Joe Pepitone	30.00	12.00	7.50
80	Richie Allen	45.00	18.00	11.00
81	Ray Oyler	30.00	12.00	7.50
82	Bob Hendley	30.00	12.00	7.50
83	Albie Pearson	30.00	12.00	7.50
84	Braves Rookies (Jim Beauchamp, Dick Kelley)	30.00	12.00	7.50
85	Eddie Fisher	30.00	12.00	7.50
86	John Bateman	30.00	12.00	7.50
87	Dan Napoleon	30.00	12.00	7.50
88	Fred Whitfield	30.00	12.00	7.50
89	Ted Davidson	30.00	12.00	7.50
90	Luis Aparicio	250.00	100.00	62.00
91	Bob Uecker	45.00	18.00	11.00
92	Yankees Team	125.00	50.00	30.00
93	Jim Lonborg	30.00	12.00	7.50
94	Matty Alou	30.00	12.00	7.50
95	Pete Richert	30.00	12.00	7.50
96	Felipe Alou	45.00	18.00	11.00
97	Jim Merritt	30.00	12.00	7.50
98	Don Demeter	30.00	12.00	7.50
99	Buc Belters (Donn Clendenon, Willie Stargell)	60.00	24.00	15.00
100	Sandy Koufax	300.00	120.00	75.00
101	Checklist 89-176	30.00	12.00	7.50
102	Ed Kirkpatrick	30.00	12.00	7.50
103	Dick Groat	30.00	12.00	7.50
104	Alex Johnson	30.00	12.00	7.50
105	Milt Pappas	30.00	12.00	7.50
106	Rusty Staub	35.00	14.00	8.75
107	Athletics Rookies (Larry Stahl, Ron Tompkins)	30.00	12.00	7.50
108	Bobby Klaus	30.00	12.00	7.50
109	Ralph Terry	30.00	12.00	7.50
110	Ernie Banks	200.00	80.00	50.00
111	Gary Peters	30.00	12.00	7.50
112	Manny Mota	30.00	12.00	7.50
113	Hank Aguirre	30.00	12.00	7.50
114	Jim Gosger	30.00	12.00	7.50
115	Bill Henry	30.00	12.00	7.50
116	Walt Alston	90.00	36.00	22.00
117	Jake Gibbs	30.00	12.00	7.50
118	Mike McCormick	30.00	12.00	7.50
119	Art Shamsky	30.00	12.00	7.50
120	Harmon Killebrew	150.00	60.00	37.00
121	Ray Herbert	30.00	12.00	7.50
122	Joe Gaines	30.00	12.00	7.50
123	Pirates Rookies (Frank Bork, Jerry May)	30.00	12.00	7.50
124	Tug McGraw	30.00	12.00	7.50
125	Lou Brock	125.00	50.00	30.00
126	Jim Palmer	200.00	80.00	50.00
127	Ken Berry	30.00	12.00	7.50
128	Jim Landis	30.00	12.00	7.50
129	Jack Kralick	30.00	12.00	7.50
130	Joe Torre	45.00	18.00	11.00
131	Angels Team	75.00	30.00	18.50
132	Orlando Cepeda	100.00	40.00	25.00
133	Don McMahon	30.00	12.00	7.50
134	Wes Parker	30.00	12.00	7.50
135	Dave Morehead	30.00	12.00	7.50
136	Woody Held	30.00	12.00	7.50
137	Pat Corrales	30.00	12.00	7.50
138	Roger Repoz	30.00	12.00	7.50
139	Cubs Rookies (Byron Browne, Don Young)	30.00	12.00	7.50
140	Jim Maloney	30.00	12.00	7.50
141	Tom McCraw	30.00	12.00	7.50
142	Don Dennis	30.00	12.00	7.50
143	Jose Tartabull	30.00	12.00	7.50
144	Don Schwall	30.00	12.00	7.50
145	Bill Freehan	30.00	12.00	7.50
146	George Altman	30.00	12.00	7.50
147	Lum Harris	30.00	12.00	7.50
148	Bob Johnson	30.00	12.00	7.50
149	Dick Nen	30.00	12.00	7.50
150	Rocky Colavito	75.00	30.00	18.50
151	Gary Wagner	30.00	12.00	7.50
152	Frank Malzone	30.00	12.00	7.50
153	Rico Carty	30.00	12.00	7.50
154	Chuck Hiller	30.00	12.00	7.50
155	Marcelino Lopez	30.00	12.00	7.50
156	D P Combo (Hal Lanier, Dick Schofield)	30.00	12.00	7.50
157	Rene Lachemann	30.00	12.00	7.50
158	Jim Brewer	30.00	12.00	7.50
159	Chico Ruiz	30.00	12.00	7.50
160	Whitey Ford	150.00	60.00	37.00
161	Jerry Lumpe	30.00	12.00	7.50
162	Lee Maye	30.00	12.00	7.50
163	Tito Francona	30.00	12.00	7.50
164	White Sox Rookies (Tommie Agee, Marv Staehle)	30.00	12.00	7.50
165	Don Lock	30.00	12.00	7.50
166	Chris Krug	30.00	12.00	7.50
167	Boog Powell	45.00	18.00	11.00
168	Dan Osinski	30.00	12.00	7.50
169	Duke Sims	30.00	12.00	7.50
170	Cookie Rojas	30.00	12.00	7.50
171	Nick Willhite	30.00	12.00	7.50
172	Mets Team	150.00	60.00	37.00
173	Al Spangler	30.00	12.00	7.50
174	Ron Taylor	30.00	12.00	7.50
175	Bert Campaneris	45.00	18.00	11.00
176	Jim Davenport	30.00	12.00	7.50
177	Hector Lopez	30.00	12.00	7.50
178	Bob Tillman	30.00	12.00	7.50
179	Cardinals Rookies (Dennis Aust, Bob Tolan)	30.00	12.00	7.50
180	Vada Pinson	35.00	14.00	8.75
181	Al Worthington	30.00	12.00	7.50
182	Jerry Lynch	30.00	12.00	7.50
183	Checklist 177-264	30.00	12.00	7.50
184	Denis Menke	30.00	12.00	7.50
185	Bob Buhl	30.00	12.00	7.50
186	Ruben Amaro	30.00	12.00	7.50
187	Chuck Dressen	30.00	12.00	7.50
188	Al Luplow	30.00	12.00	7.50
189	John Roseboro	30.00	12.00	7.50
190	Jimmie Hall	30.00	12.00	7.50
191	Darrell Sutherland	30.00	12.00	7.50
192	Vic Power	30.00	12.00	7.50
193	Dave McNally	30.00	12.00	7.50
194	Senators Team	75.00	30.00	18.50
195	Joe Morgan	125.00	50.00	30.00
196	Don Pavletich	30.00	12.00	7.50
197	Sonny Siebert	30.00	12.00	7.50
198	Mickey Stanley	30.00	12.00	7.50
199	Chisox Clubbers (Floyd Robinson, Johnny Romano, Bill Skowron)	30.00	12.00	7.50
200	Eddie Mathews	125.00	50.00	30.00
201	Jim Dickson	30.00	12.00	7.50
202	Clay Dalrymple	30.00	12.00	7.50
203	Jose Santiago	30.00	12.00	7.50
204	Cubs Team	90.00	36.00	22.00
205	Tom Tresh	30.00	12.00	7.50
206	Alvin Jackson	30.00	12.00	7.50

207	Frank Quilici	30.00	12.00	7.50
208	Bob Miller	30.00	12.00	7.50
209	Tigers Rookies (Fritz Fisher, John Hiller)	30.00	12.00	7.50
210	Bill Mazeroski	75.00	30.00	18.50
211	Frank Kreutzer	30.00	12.00	7.50
212	Ed Kranepool	30.00	12.00	7.50
213	Fred Newman	30.00	12.00	7.50
214	Tommy Harper	30.00	12.00	7.50
215	N.L. Batting Leaders (Hank Aaron, Roberto Clemente, Willie Mays)	300.00	120.00	75.00
216	A.L. Batting Leaders (Vic Davalillo, Tony Oliva, Carl Yastrzemski)	150.00	60.00	37.00
217	N.L. Home Run Leaders (Willie Mays, Willie McCovey, Billy Williams)	150.00	60.00	37.00
218	A.L. Home Run Leaders (Norm Cash, Tony Conigliaro, Willie Horton)	60.00	24.00	15.00
219	N.L. RBI Leaders (Deron Johnson, Willie Mays, Frank Robinson)	90.00	36.00	22.00
220	A.L. RBI Leaders (Rocky Colavito, Willie Horton, Tony Oliva)	60.00	24.00	15.00
221	N.L. ERA Leaders (Sandy Koufax, Vern Law, Juan Marichal)	90.00	36.00	22.00
222	A.L. ERA Leaders (Eddie Fisher, Sam McDowell, Sonny Siebert)	35.00	14.00	8.75
223	N.L. Pitching Leaders (Tony Cloninger, Don Drysdale, Sandy Koufax)	90.00	36.00	22.00
224	A.L. Pitching Leaders (Jim Grant, Jim Kaat, Mel Stottlemyre)	30.00	12.00	7.50
225	N.L. Strikeout Leaders (Bob Gibson, Sandy Koufax, Bob Veale)	90.00	36.00	22.00
226	A.L. Strikeout Leaders (Mickey Lolich, Sam McDowell, Denny McLain, Sonny Siebert)	45.00	18.00	11.00
227	Russ Nixon	30.00	12.00	7.50
228	Larry Dierker	30.00	12.00	7.50
229	Hank Bauer	30.00	12.00	7.50
230	Johnny Callison	30.00	12.00	7.50
231	Floyd Weaver	30.00	12.00	7.50
232	Glenn Beckert	30.00	12.00	7.50
233	Dom Zanni	30.00	12.00	7.50
234	Yankees Rookies (Rich Beck, Roy White)	35.00	14.00	8.75
235	Don Cardwell	30.00	12.00	7.50
236	Mike Hershberger	30.00	12.00	7.50
237	Billy O'Dell	30.00	12.00	7.50
238	Dodgers Team	100.00	40.00	25.00
239	Orlando Pena	30.00	12.00	7.50
240	Earl Battey	30.00	12.00	7.50
241	Dennis Ribant	30.00	12.00	7.50
242	Jesus Alou	30.00	12.00	7.50
243	Nelson Briles	30.00	12.00	7.50
244	Astros Rookies (Chuck Harrison, Sonny Jackson)	30.00	12.00	7.50
245	John Buzhardt	30.00	12.00	7.50
246	Ed Bailey	30.00	12.00	7.50
247	Carl Warwick	30.00	12.00	7.50
248	Pete Mikkelsen	30.00	12.00	7.50
249	Bill Rigney	30.00	12.00	7.50
250	Sam Ellis	30.00	12.00	7.50
251	Ed Brinkman	30.00	12.00	7.50
252	Denver Lemaster	30.00	12.00	7.50
253	Don Wert	30.00	12.00	7.50
254	Phillies Rookies (Fergie Jenkins, Bill Sorrell)	100.00	40.00	25.00
255	Willie Stargell	125.00	50.00	30.00
256	Lew Krausse	30.00	12.00	7.50
257	Jeff Torborg	30.00	12.00	7.50
258	Dave Giusti	30.00	12.00	7.50
259	Red Sox Team	75.00	30.00	18.50
260	Bob Shaw	30.00	12.00	7.50
261	Ron Hansen	30.00	12.00	7.50
262	Jack Hamilton	30.00	12.00	7.50
263	Tom Egan	30.00	12.00	7.50
264	Twins Rookies (Andy Kosco, Ted Uhlaender)	30.00	12.00	7.50
265	Stu Miller	30.00	12.00	7.50
266	Pedro Gonzalez	30.00	12.00	7.50
267	Joe Sparma	30.00	12.00	7.50
268	John Blanchard	30.00	12.00	7.50
269	Don Heffner	30.00	12.00	7.50
270	Claude Osteen	30.00	12.00	7.50
271	Hal Lanier	30.00	12.00	7.50
272	Jack Baldschun	30.00	12.00	7.50
273	Astro Aces (Bob Aspromonte, Rusty Staub)	30.00	12.00	7.50
274	Buster Narum	30.00	12.00	7.50
275	Tim McCarver	35.00	14.00	8.75
276	Jim Bouton	35.00	14.00	8.75
277	George Thomas	30.00	12.00	7.50
278	Calvin Koonce	30.00	12.00	7.50
279	Checklist 265-352	30.00	12.00	7.50
280	Bobby Knoop	30.00	12.00	7.50
281	Bruce Howard	30.00	12.00	7.50
282	Johnny Lewis	30.00	12.00	7.50
283	Jim Perry	30.00	12.00	7.50
284	Bobby Wine	30.00	12.00	7.50
285	Luis Tiant	45.00	18.00	11.00
286	Gary Geiger	30.00	12.00	7.50
287	Jack Aker	30.00	12.00	7.50
288	Dodgers Rookies (Bill Singer, Don Sutton)	125.00	50.00	30.00
289	Larry Sherry	30.00	12.00	7.50
290	Ron Santo	45.00	18.00	11.00
291	Moe Drabowsky	30.00	12.00	7.50
292	Jim Coker	30.00	12.00	7.50
293	Mike Shannon	30.00	12.00	7.50
294	Steve Ridzik	30.00	12.00	7.50
295	Jim Hart	30.00	12.00	7.50
296	Johnny Keane	30.00	12.00	7.50
297	Jim Owens	30.00	12.00	7.50
298	Rico Petrocelli	30.00	12.00	7.50
299	Lou Burdette	30.00	12.00	7.50
300	Roberto Clemente	650.00	260.00	160.00
301	Greg Bollo	30.00	12.00	7.50
302	Ernie Bowman	30.00	12.00	7.50
303	Indians Team	75.00	30.00	18.50
304	John Herrnstein	30.00	12.00	7.50
305	Camilo Pascual	30.00	12.00	7.50
306	Ty Cline	30.00	12.00	7.50
307	Clay Carroll	30.00	12.00	7.50
308	Tom Haller	30.00	12.00	7.50
309	Diego Segui	30.00	12.00	7.50
310	Frank Robinson	125.00	50.00	30.00
311	Reds Rookies (Tommy Helms, Dick Simpson)	30.00	12.00	7.50
312	Bob Saverine	30.00	12.00	7.50
313	Chris Zachary	30.00	12.00	7.50
314	Hector Valle	30.00	12.00	7.50
315	Norm Cash	30.00	12.00	7.50
316	Jack Fisher	30.00	12.00	7.50
317	Dalton Jones	30.00	12.00	7.50
318	Harry Walker	30.00	12.00	7.50
319	Gene Freese	30.00	12.00	7.50
320	Bob Gibson	125.00	50.00	30.00
321	Rick Reichardt	30.00	12.00	7.50
322	Bill Faul	30.00	12.00	7.50
323	Ray Barker	30.00	12.00	7.50
324	John Boozer	30.00	12.00	7.50
325	Vic Davalillo	100.00	40.00	25.00
326	Braves Team	75.00	30.00	18.50
327	Bernie Allen	30.00	12.00	7.50
328	Jerry Grote	30.00	12.00	7.50
329	Pete Charton	30.00	12.00	7.50
330	Ron Fairly	30.00	12.00	7.50
331	Ron Herbel	30.00	12.00	7.50
332	Billy Bryan	30.00	12.00	7.50
333	Senators Rookies (Joe Coleman, Jim French)	30.00	12.00	7.50
334	Marty Keough	30.00	12.00	7.50
335	Juan Pizarro	30.00	12.00	7.50
336	Gene Alley	30.00	12.00	7.50
337	Fred Gladding	30.00	12.00	7.50
338	Dal Maxvill	30.00	12.00	7.50
339	Del Crandall	30.00	12.00	7.50
340	Dean Chance	30.00	12.00	7.50
341	Wes Westrum	30.00	12.00	7.50
342	Bob Humphreys	30.00	12.00	7.50
343	Joe Christopher	30.00	12.00	7.50
344	Steve Blass	30.00	12.00	7.50
345	Bob Allison	30.00	12.00	7.50
346	Mike de la Hoz	30.00	12.00	7.50
347	Phil Regan	30.00	12.00	7.50
348	Orioles Team	125.00	50.00	30.00
349	Cap Peterson	30.00	12.00	7.50
350	Mel Stottlemyre	30.00	12.00	7.50
351	Fred Valentine	30.00	12.00	7.50
352	Bob Aspromonte	30.00	12.00	7.50
353	Al McBean	30.00	12.00	7.50
354	Smoky Burgess	30.00	12.00	7.50
355	Wade Blasingame	30.00	12.00	7.50
356	Red Sox Rookies (Owen Johnson, Ken Sanders)	30.00	12.00	7.50
357	Gerry Arrigo	30.00	12.00	7.50
358	Charlie Smith	30.00	12.00	7.50
359	Johnny Briggs	30.00	12.00	7.50
360	Ron Hunt	30.00	12.00	7.50
361	Tom Satriano	30.00	12.00	7.50
362	Gates Brown	30.00	12.00	7.50
363	Checklist 353-429	30.00	12.00	7.50
364	Nate Oliver	30.00	12.00	7.50
365	Roger Maris	200.00	80.00	50.00
366	Wayne Causey	30.00	12.00	7.50
367	Mel Nelson	30.00	12.00	7.50
368	Charlie Lau	30.00	12.00	7.50
369	Jim King	30.00	12.00	7.50
370	Chico Cardenas	30.00	12.00	7.50

1967 Venezuelan League

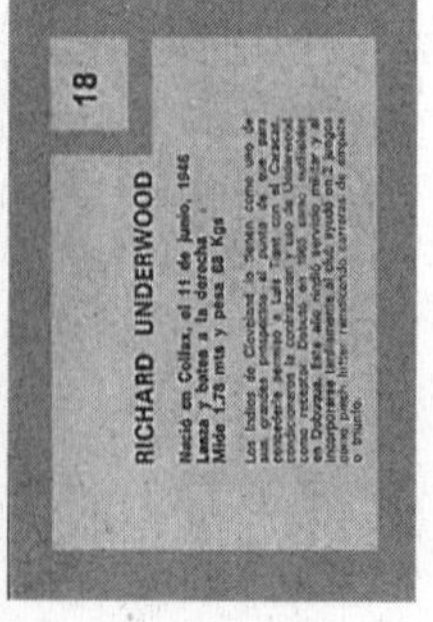

Three distinct series of baseball cards were issued in 1967 for sale in Venezuela, contiguously numbered. Cards #1-138 are players (including many future big leaguers) active in the country's Winter League. Cards are irregularly cut and somewhat smaller than the standard 2-1/2" x 3-1/2". Fronts have posed photos and a thin white border. The player name and position are at top in black, the team name is in large colored letters at bottom. Backs are printed horizontally in black on magenta with a few biographical bits and a one paragraph career summary. Like most of the Venezuelan cards of the era, these are crudely printed on cheap cardboard. Also like most Venezuelan cards, they are virtually impossible to find in any condition above Ex. Many are found with back damage due to having been glued into an album or scrapbook.

		NM	EX	VG
Complete Set (138):		3,500	1,750	1,000
Common Player:		20.00	10.00	6.00
1	Regino Otero	40.00	20.00	12.00
2	Alejandro Carrasquel	20.00	10.00	6.00
3	Pompeyo Davilillo	25.00	12.50	7.50
4	Gonzalo Marquez	20.00	10.00	6.00
5	Octavio (Cookie) Rojas	35.00	17.50	10.50
6	Teodoro Obregon	20.00	10.00	6.00
7	Paul Schaal	25.00	12.50	7.50
8	Juan Francia	20.00	10.00	6.00
9	Luis Tiant	60.00	30.00	18.00
10	Jose Tartabull	30.00	15.00	9.00
11	Vic Davalillo	25.00	12.50	7.50
12	Cesar Tovar	25.00	12.50	7.50
13	Ron Klimkowski	20.00	10.00	6.00
14	Diego Segui	35.00	17.50	10.50
15	Luis Penalver	20.00	10.00	6.00
16	Urbano Lugo	20.00	10.00	6.00
17	Aurelio Monteagudo	20.00	10.00	6.00
18	Richard Underwood	25.00	12.50	7.50
19	Nelson Castellanos	20.00	10.00	6.00
20	Manuel Mendible	20.00	10.00	6.00
21	Fidel Garcia	40.00	20.00	12.00
22	Luis Cordoba	20.00	10.00	6.00
23	Jesus Padron	20.00	10.00	6.00
24	Lorenzo Fernandez	20.00	10.00	6.00
25	Leopoldo Tovar	20.00	10.00	6.00
26	Carlos Loreto	20.00	10.00	6.00
27	Oswaldo Blanco	20.00	10.00	6.00
28	Sid (Syd) O'Brien	20.00	10.00	6.00
29	Cesar Gutierrez	20.00	10.00	6.00
30	Luis Garcia	20.00	10.00	6.00
31	Fred Klages	20.00	10.00	6.00
32	Isaias Chavez	20.00	10.00	6.00
33	Walter Williams	25.00	12.50	7.50
34	Jim Hicks	20.00	10.00	6.00
35	Gustavo Sposito	20.00	10.00	6.00
36	Cisco Carlos	20.00	10.00	6.00
37	Jim Mooring	20.00	10.00	6.00
38	Alonso Olivares	20.00	10.00	6.00
39	Graciliano Parra	20.00	10.00	6.00
40	Merritt Ranew	20.00	10.00	6.00
41	Everest Contramaestre	20.00	10.00	6.00
42	Orlando Reyes	20.00	10.00	6.00
43	Edicto Arteaga	20.00	10.00	6.00
44	Francisco Diaz	20.00	10.00	6.00
45	Victor Colina	20.00	10.00	6.00
46a	Ramon Diaz	20.00	10.00	6.00
46b	Francisco Diaz (Blue back.)	20.00	10.00	6.00
47	Luis E. Aparicio	185.00	90.00	55.00
48	Reynaldo Cordeiro	60.00	30.00	18.00
49	Luis Aparicio, Sr.	25.00	12.50	7.50
50	Ramon Webster	20.00	10.00	6.00
51	Remigio Hermoso	20.00	10.00	6.00
52	Miguel de la Hoz	20.00	10.00	6.00
53	Enzo Hernandez	20.00	10.00	6.00
54	Ed Watt	20.00	10.00	6.00
55	Angel Bravo	20.00	10.00	6.00
56	Marv (Merv) Rettenmund	25.00	12.50	7.50
57	Jose Herrera	20.00	10.00	6.00
58	Tom Fisher	20.00	10.00	6.00
59	Jim Weaver	20.00	10.00	6.00
60a	Juan Quintana	20.00	10.00	6.00
60b	Frank Fernandez (Blue back.)	20.00	10.00	6.00
61	Hector Urbano	20.00	10.00	6.00
62	Hector Brito (Blue back.)	20.00	10.00	6.00
63	Jesus Romero	20.00	10.00	6.00
64	Carlos A. Moreno	20.00	10.00	6.00
65	Nestor Mendible	20.00	10.00	6.00
66	Armando Ortiz	20.00	10.00	6.00
67	Graciano Ravelo	20.00	10.00	6.00
68	Paul Knechtges	20.00	10.00	6.00
69	Marcelino Lopez	25.00	12.50	7.50
70	Wilfredo Calvino	25.00	12.50	7.50
71	Jesus Avila	20.00	10.00	6.00
72	Carlos Pascual	45.00	22.00	13.50
73	Bob Burda	20.00	10.00	6.00
74	Elio Chacon	20.00	10.00	6.00
75	Jacinto Hernandez	20.00	10.00	6.00
76	Jose M. Tovar	20.00	10.00	6.00
77	Bill Whitby	20.00	10.00	6.00
78	Enrique Izquierdo	20.00	10.00	6.00
79	Hilario Valdespino	30.00	15.00	9.00
80	John Lewis	20.00	10.00	6.00
81	Hector Martinez	40.00	20.00	12.00
82	Rene Paredes	20.00	10.00	6.00
83	Danny Morris	20.00	10.00	6.00
84	Pedro Ramos	25.00	12.50	7.50
85	Jose Ramon Lopez	20.00	10.00	6.00
86	Jesus Rizales	20.00	10.00	6.00
87	Winston Acosta	20.00	10.00	6.00
88	Pablo Bello	20.00	10.00	6.00
89	David Concepcion	200.00	100.00	60.00
90	Manuel Garcia	20.00	10.00	6.00
91	Anibal Longa	20.00	10.00	6.00
92	Francisco Moscoso	20.00	10.00	6.00
93	Mel McGaha	20.00	10.00	6.00
94	Aquiles Gomez	20.00	10.00	6.00
95	Alfonso Carrasquel (Blue back.)	40.00	20.00	12.00
96	Tom Murray	20.00	10.00	6.00
97	Gustavo Gil	20.00	10.00	6.00
98	Damaso Blanco	20.00	10.00	6.00
99	Alberto Cambero	20.00	10.00	6.00
100	Don Bryant	20.00	10.00	6.00
101	George Culver	20.00	10.00	6.00
102	Teolindo Acosta	20.00	10.00	6.00
103	Aaron Pointer	20.00	10.00	6.00
104	Ed Kirkpatrick	20.00	10.00	6.00
105	Luis Rodriguez	20.00	10.00	6.00
106	Mike Daniel	20.00	10.00	6.00
107	Cecilio Prieto (Blue back.)	20.00	10.00	6.00

#	Player	NM	EX	VG
108	Juan Quiroz	20.00	10.00	6.00
108				6.00
109	Juan Campos	20.00	10.00	6.00
110	Freddy Rivero	20.00	10.00	6.00
111	Dick LeMay	20.00	10.00	6.00
112	Raul Ortega	20.00	10.00	6.00
113	Bruno Estaba	20.00	10.00	6.00
114	Evangelista Nunez	20.00	10.00	6.00
115a	Robert Munoz	20.00	10.00	6.00
115b	Alfonso Carrasquel (Red back.)	40.00	20.00	12.00
116	Tony Castanos	20.00	10.00	6.00
117	Domingo Barboza	20.00	10.00	6.00
118	Lucio Celis	20.00	10.00	6.00
119	Carlos Santeliz	20.00	10.00	6.00
120	Barton Shirley	25.00	12.50	7.50
121	Neudo Morales	20.00	10.00	6.00
122	Robert Cox	100.00	50.00	30.00
123	Cruz Amaya (Blue back.)	20.00	10.00	6.00
124	Jim Campanis	75.00	37.50	22.00
125	Dave Roberts	20.00	10.00	6.00
126	Gerry Crider	20.00	10.00	6.00
127	Domingo Carrasquel	20.00	10.00	6.00
128	Leo Marentette	20.00	10.00	6.00
129	Frank Kreutzer	20.00	10.00	6.00
130	Jim Dickson	20.00	10.00	6.00
131	Bob Oliver	20.00	10.00	6.00
132	Jose Bracho	20.00	10.00	6.00
133a	Pablo Torrealba	20.00	10.00	6.00
133b	Pablo Torrealba (Different picture.)	20.00	10.00	6.00
134	Iran Paz	20.00	10.00	6.00
135	Eliecer Bueno	20.00	10.00	6.00
136	Claudio Urdaneta	20.00	10.00	6.00
137	Faustino Zabala	20.00	10.00	6.00
138	Dario Chirinos	20.00	10.00	6.00

1967 Venezuelan Retirado

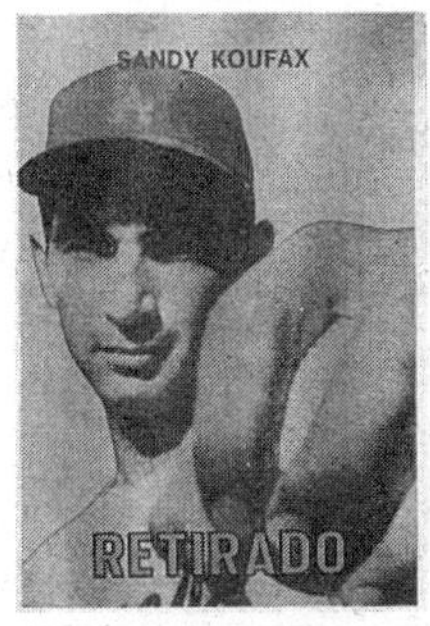

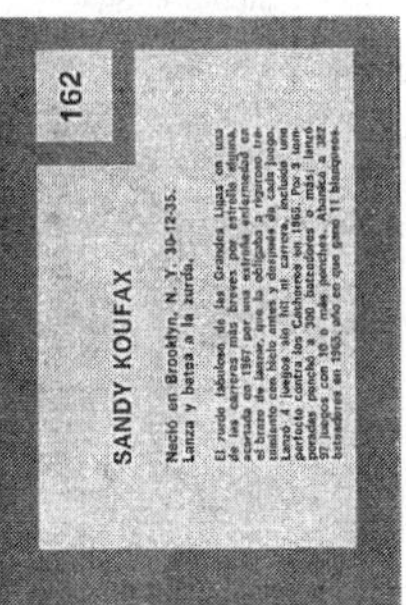

Three distinct series of baseball cards were issued in 1967 for sale in Venezuela, contiguously numbered. Cards #139-188 are former big league stars. The fronts of the roughly 2-1/2" x 3-1/2" Retirado cards have a blue background with the player's name in black at top and "RETIRADO" in red block letters at bottom. Player photos on the Retirado cards are sepia. Horizontal backs are printed in black on green with a bit of personal data and a career summary. Like most of the Venezuelan cards of the era, these are crudely printed on cheap cardboard. Also like most Venezuelan cards, they are virtually impossible to find in any condition above Ex. Many are found with back damage due to having been glued into an album or scrapbook.

#	Player	NM	EX	VG
	Complete Set (50):	12,000	4,800	1,800
	Common Player:	250.00	100.00	37.00
139	Walter Johnson	750.00	300.00	110.00
140	Bill Dickey	300.00	120.00	45.00
141	Lou Gehrig	1,750	700.00	260.00
142	Rogers Hornsby	300.00	120.00	45.00
143	Honus Wagner	650.00	260.00	100.00
144	Pie Traynor	250.00	100.00	35.00
145	Joe DiMaggio	1,850	740.00	275.00
146	Ty Cobb	1,350	540.00	200.00
147	Babe Ruth	2,400	960.00	360.00
148	Ted Williams	1,000	400.00	150.00
149	Mel Ott	250.00	100.00	35.00
150	Cy Young	370.00	150.00	55.00
151	Christy Mathewson	750.00	300.00	110.00
152	Warren Spahn	300.00	120.00	45.00
153	Mickey Cochrane	250.00	100.00	35.00
154	George Sisler	250.00	100.00	35.00
155	Jimmy Collins	250.00	100.00	35.00
156	Tris Speaker	300.00	120.00	45.00
157	Stan Musial	700.00	280.00	100.00
158	Luke Appling	250.00	100.00	35.00
159	Nap Lajoie	250.00	100.00	35.00
160	Bill Terry	250.00	100.00	35.00
161	Bob Feller	370.00	150.00	55.00
162	Sandy Koufax	800.00	320.00	120.00
163	Jimmie Foxx	300.00	120.00	45.00
164	Joe Cronin	250.00	100.00	35.00
165	Frankie Frisch	250.00	100.00	35.00
166	Paul Waner	250.00	100.00	35.00
167	Lloyd Waner	250.00	100.00	35.00
168	Lefty Grove	250.00	100.00	35.00
169	Bobby Doerr	250.00	100.00	35.00
170	Al Simmons	250.00	100.00	35.00
171	Grover Alexander	350.00	140.00	50.00
172	Carl Hubbell	250.00	100.00	35.00
173	Mordecai Brown	250.00	100.00	35.00
174	Ted Lyons	250.00	100.00	35.00
175	Johnny Vander Meer	250.00	100.00	35.00
176	Alex Carrasquel	300.00	120.00	45.00
177	Satchel Paige	600.00	240.00	90.00
178	Whitey Ford	500.00	200.00	75.00
179	Yogi Berra	500.00	200.00	75.00
180	Roy Campanella	450.00	180.00	65.00
181	Alfonso Carrasquel	370.00	150.00	55.00
182	Johnny Mize	250.00	100.00	35.00
183	Ted Kluszewski (Photo actually Gene Bearden.)	300.00	120.00	45.00
184	Jackie Robinson	750.00	300.00	110.00
185	Bobby Avila	250.00	100.00	35.00
186	Phil Rizzuto	300.00	120.00	45.00
187	Minnie Minoso	300.00	120.00	45.00
188	Connie Marrero	250.00	100.00	35.00

1967 Venezuelan Topps

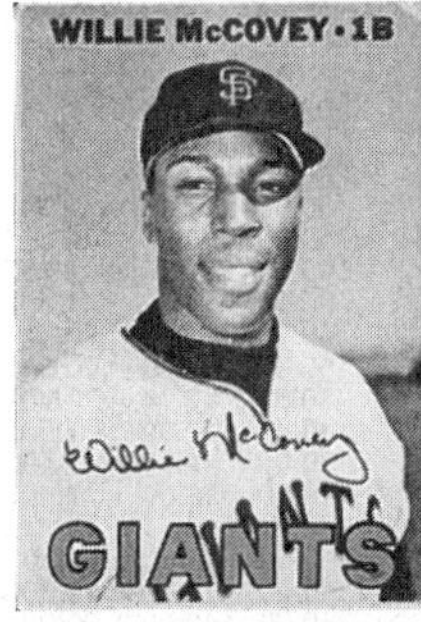

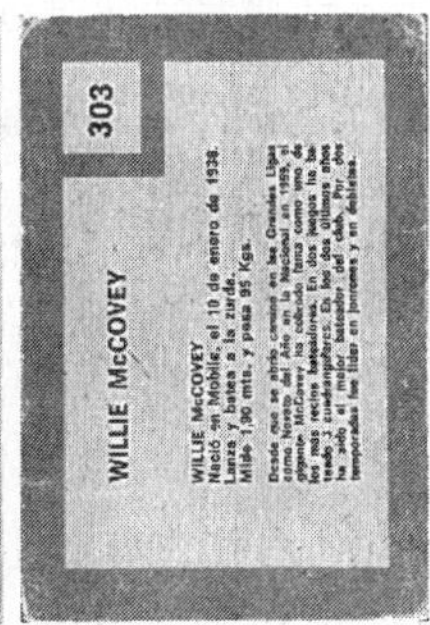

Cards numbered #189-338 in the 1967 Venezuelan issue feature then-current major leaguers. Card fronts are taken from Topps' 1967 baseball series, but are borderless, making them somewhat smaller than 2-1/2" x 3-1/2". Backs of the South American cards are horizontal and printed in black on blue and offer a few bits of personal data and a one-paragraph career summary. Like most Venezuelan cards of the era, these are crudely printed on cheap cardboard and seldom found in condition better than Ex. Many will show evidence on back of having been glued into an album or scrapbook.

#	Player	NM	EX	VG
	Complete Set (150):	8,000	2,000	750.00
	Common Player:	35.00	14.00	5.25
189	Luis Aparicio	150.00	60.00	22.00
190	Vic Davalillo	35.00	14.00	5.25
191	Cesar Tovar	35.00	14.00	5.25
192	Mickey Mantle	1,500	600.00	225.00
193	Carl Yastrzemski	100.00	40.00	15.00
194	Frank Robinson	100.00	40.00	15.00
195	Willie Horton	35.00	14.00	5.25
196	Gary Peters	35.00	14.00	5.25
197	Bert Campaneris	40.00	16.00	6.00
198	Norm Cash	35.00	14.00	5.25
199	Boog Powell	35.00	14.00	5.25
200	George Scott	35.00	14.00	5.25
201	Frank Howard	35.00	14.00	5.25
202	Rick Reichardt	35.00	14.00	5.25
203	Jose Cardenal	35.00	14.00	5.25
204	Rico Petrocelli	35.00	14.00	5.25
205	Lew Krausse	35.00	14.00	5.25
206	Harmon Killebrew	100.00	40.00	15.00
207	Leon Wagner	35.00	14.00	5.25
208	Joe Foy	35.00	14.00	5.25
209	Joe Pepitone	40.00	16.00	6.00
210	Al Kaline	100.00	40.00	15.00
211	Brooks Robinson	100.00	40.00	15.00
212	Bill Freehan	35.00	14.00	5.25
213	Jim Lonborg	35.00	14.00	5.25
214a	Ed Mathews	100.00	40.00	15.00
214b	Jim Bunning (Should be #174.)	90.00	36.00	13.50
215	Dick Green	35.00	14.00	5.25
216	Tom Tresh	40.00	16.00	6.00
217	Dean Chance	35.00	14.00	5.25
218	Paul Blair	35.00	14.00	5.25
219	Larry Brown	35.00	14.00	5.25
220	Fred Valentine	35.00	14.00	5.25
221	Al Downing	35.00	14.00	5.25
222	Earl Battey	35.00	14.00	5.25
223	Don Mincher	35.00	14.00	5.25
224	Tommie Agee	35.00	14.00	5.25
225	Jim McGlothlin	35.00	14.00	5.25
226	Zoilo Versalles	35.00	14.00	5.25
227	Curt Blefary	35.00	14.00	5.25
228	Joel Horlen	35.00	14.00	5.25
229	Stu Miller	35.00	14.00	5.25
230	Tony Oliva	40.00	16.00	6.00
231	Paul Casanova	35.00	14.00	5.25
232	Orlando Pena	35.00	14.00	5.25
233	Ron Hansen	35.00	14.00	5.25
234	Earl Wilson	35.00	14.00	5.25
235	Ken Boyer	40.00	16.00	6.00
236	Jim Kaat	35.00	14.00	5.25
237	Dalton Jones	35.00	14.00	5.25
238	Pete Ward	35.00	14.00	5.25
239	Mickey Lolich	35.00	14.00	5.25
240	Jose Santiago	35.00	14.00	5.25
241	Dick McAuliffe	35.00	14.00	5.25
242	Mel Stottlemyre	35.00	14.00	5.25
243	Camilo Pascual	35.00	14.00	5.25
244	Jim Fregosi	35.00	14.00	5.25
245	Tony Conigliaro	40.00	16.00	6.00
246	Sonny Siebert	35.00	14.00	5.25
247	Jim Perry	35.00	14.00	5.25
248	Dave McNally	35.00	14.00	5.25
249	Fred Whitfield	35.00	14.00	5.25
250	Ken Berry	35.00	14.00	5.25
251	Jim Grant	35.00	14.00	5.25
252	Hank Aguirre	35.00	14.00	5.25
253	Don Wert	35.00	14.00	5.25
254	Wally Bunker	35.00	14.00	5.25
255	Elston Howard	40.00	16.00	6.00
256	Dave Johnson	35.00	14.00	5.25
257	Hoyt Wilhelm	75.00	30.00	11.00
258	Don Buford	35.00	14.00	5.25
259	Sam McDowell	35.00	14.00	5.25
260	Bobby Knoop	35.00	14.00	5.25
261	Denny McLain	35.00	14.00	5.25
262	Steve Hargan	35.00	14.00	5.25
263	Jim Nash	35.00	14.00	5.25
264	Jerry Adair	35.00	14.00	5.25
265	Tony Gonzalez	35.00	14.00	5.25
266	Mike Shannon	35.00	14.00	5.25
267	Bob Gibson	90.00	36.00	13.50
268	John Roseboro	35.00	14.00	5.25
269	Bob Aspromonte	35.00	14.00	5.25
270	Pete Rose	250.00	100.00	37.00
271	Rico Carty	40.00	16.00	6.00
272	Juan Pizarro	35.00	14.00	5.25
273	Willie Mays	250.00	100.00	37.00
274	Jim Bunning	90.00	36.00	13.50
275	Ernie Banks	100.00	40.00	15.00
276	Curt Flood	40.00	16.00	6.00
277	Mack Jones	35.00	14.00	5.25
278	Roberto Clemente	450.00	180.00	67.00
279	Sammy Ellis	35.00	14.00	5.25
280	Willie Stargell	90.00	36.00	13.50
281	Felipe Alou	40.00	16.00	6.00
282	Ed Kranepool	35.00	14.00	5.25
283	Nelson Briles	35.00	14.00	5.25
284	Hank Aaron	250.00	100.00	37.00
285	Vada Pinson	40.00	16.00	6.00
286	Jim LeFebvre	35.00	14.00	5.25
287	Hal Lanier	35.00	14.00	5.25
288	Ron Swoboda	35.00	14.00	5.25
289	Mike McCormick	35.00	14.00	5.25
290	Lou Johnson	35.00	14.00	5.25
291	Orlando Cepeda	90.00	36.00	13.50
292	Rusty Staub	40.00	16.00	6.00
293	Manny Mota	35.00	14.00	5.25
294	Tommy Harper	35.00	14.00	5.25
295	Don Drysdale	90.00	36.00	13.50
296	Mel Queen	35.00	14.00	5.25
297	Red Schoendienst	75.00	30.00	11.00
298	Matty Alou	35.00	14.00	5.25
299	Johnny Callison	35.00	14.00	5.25
300	Juan Marichal	90.00	36.00	13.50
301	Al McBean	35.00	14.00	5.25
302	Claude Osteen	35.00	14.00	5.25
303	Willie McCovey	90.00	36.00	13.50
304	Jim Owens	35.00	14.00	5.25
305	Chico Ruiz	35.00	14.00	5.25
306	Ferguson Jenkins	90.00	36.00	13.50
307	Lou Brock	90.00	36.00	13.50
308	Joe Morgan	90.00	36.00	13.50
309	Ron Santo	50.00	20.00	7.50
310	Chico Cardenas	35.00	14.00	5.25
311	Richie Allen	45.00	18.00	6.75
312	Gaylord Perry	75.00	30.00	11.00
313	Bill Mazeroski	75.00	30.00	11.00
314	Tony Taylor	35.00	14.00	5.25
315	Tommy Helms	35.00	14.00	5.25
316	Jim Wynn	35.00	14.00	5.25
317	Don Sutton	75.00	30.00	11.00
318	Mike Cuellar	45.00	18.00	6.75
319	Willie Davis	35.00	14.00	5.25
320	Julian Javier	35.00	14.00	5.25
321	Maury Wills	35.00	14.00	5.25
322	Gene Alley	35.00	14.00	5.25
323	Ray Sadecki	35.00	14.00	5.25
324	Joe Torre	45.00	18.00	6.75
325	Jim Maloney	35.00	14.00	5.25
326	Jim Davenport	35.00	14.00	5.25
327	Tony Perez	90.00	36.00	13.50
328	Roger Maris	100.00	40.00	15.00
329	Chris Short	35.00	14.00	5.25
330	Jesus Alou	35.00	14.00	5.25
331	Darron Johnson	35.00	14.00	5.25
332	Tommy Davis	35.00	14.00	5.25
333	Bob Veale	35.00	14.00	5.25
334	Bill McCool	35.00	14.00	5.25
335	Jim Hart	35.00	14.00	5.25
336	Roy Face	35.00	14.00	5.25
337	Billy Williams	75.00	30.00	11.00
338	Dick Groat	35.00	14.00	5.25

1968 Venezuelan Topps

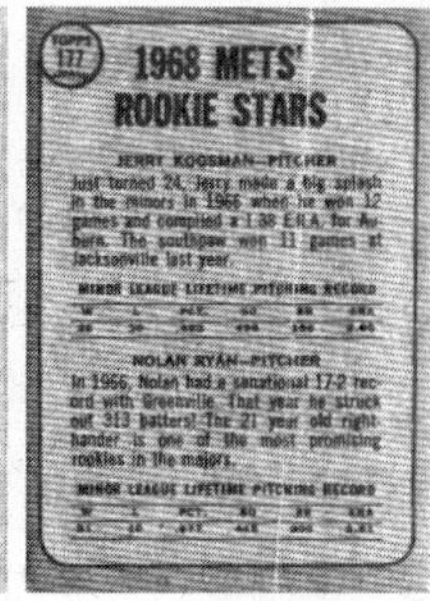

The first 370 cards of Topps' 1968 baseball card set were reproduced in South America for sale in Venezuela. Besides being rather crudely printed on cheaper, non-gloss cardboard, the cards are virtually identical to the Topps U.S. version. The only difference is a tiny line of yellow type on back which reads: "Hecho en Venezuela - C.A. Litoven." Like most 1960s Venezuelan issues, these cards are seldom found in condition better than Excellent, and often with evidence on back of having been glued into an album or scrapbook. Venezuelan Topps cards are often found cut slightly smaller than the U.S. version, up to 1/8".

		NM	EX	VG
	Complete Set (370):	25,000	10,000	6,250
	Common Player:	30.00	12.00	7.50
1	N.L. Batting Leaders (Matty Alou, Roberto Clemente, Tony Gonzalez)	80.00	32.00	20.00
2	A.L. Batting Leaders (Al Kaline, Frank Robinson, Carl Yastrzemski)	50.00	20.00	12.50
3	N.L. RBI Leaders (Hank Aaron, Orlando Cepeda, Roberto Clemente)	80.00	32.00	20.00
4	A.L. RBI Leaders (Harmon Killebrew, Frank Robinson, Carl Yastrzemski)	50.00	20.00	12.50
5	N.L. Home Run Leaders (Hank Aaron, Willie McCovey, Ron Santo, Jim Wynn)	60.00	24.00	15.00
6	A.L. Home Run Leaders (Frank Howard, Harmon Killebrew, Carl Yastrzemski)	50.00	20.00	12.50
7	N.L. ERA Leaders (Jim Bunning, Phil Niekro, Chris Short)	30.00	12.00	7.50
8	A.L. ERA Leaders (Joe Horlen, Gary Peters, Sonny Siebert)	30.00	12.00	7.50
9	N.L. Pitching Leaders (Jim Bunning, Fergie Jenkins, Mike McCormick, Claude Osteen)	30.00	12.00	7.50
10	A.L. Pitching Leaders (Dean Chance, Jim Lonborg, Earl Wilson)	30.00	12.00	7.50
11	N.L. Strikeout Leaders (Jim Bunning, Fergie Jenkins, Gaylord Perry)	30.00	12.00	7.50
12	A.L. Strikeout Leaders (Dean Chance, Jim Lonborg, Sam McDowell)	30.00	12.00	7.50
13	Chuck Hartenstein	30.00	12.00	7.50
14	Jerry McNertney	30.00	12.00	7.50
15	Ron Hunt	30.00	12.00	7.50
16	Indians Rookies **(Lou Piniella, Richie Scheinblum)**	40.00	16.00	10.00
17	Dick Hall	30.00	12.00	7.50
18	Mike Hershberger	30.00	12.00	7.50
19	Juan Pizarro	30.00	12.00	7.50
20	Brooks Robinson	120.00	48.00	30.00
21	Ron Davis	30.00	12.00	7.50
22	Pat Dobson	30.00	12.00	7.50
23	Chico Cardenas	30.00	12.00	7.50
24	Bobby Locke	30.00	12.00	7.50
25	Julian Javier	30.00	12.00	7.50
26	Darrell Brandon	30.00	12.00	7.50
27	Gil Hodges	50.00	20.00	12.50
28	Ted Uhlaender	30.00	12.00	7.50
29	Joe Verbanic	30.00	12.00	7.50
30	Joe Torre	40.00	16.00	10.00
31	Ed Stroud	30.00	12.00	7.50
32	Joe Gibbon	30.00	12.00	7.50
33	Pete Ward	30.00	12.00	7.50
34	Al Ferrara	30.00	12.00	7.50
35	Steve Hargan	30.00	12.00	7.50
36	Pirates Rookies **(Bob Moose, Bob Robertson)**	30.00	12.00	7.50
37	Billy Williams	80.00	32.00	20.00
38	Tony Pierce	30.00	12.00	7.50
39	Cookie Rojas	30.00	12.00	7.50
40	Denny McLain	40.00	16.00	10.00
41	Julio Gotay	30.00	12.00	7.50
42	Larry Haney	30.00	12.00	7.50
43	Gary Bell	30.00	12.00	7.50
44	Frank Kostro	30.00	12.00	7.50
45	Tom Seaver	120.00	48.00	30.00
46	Dave Ricketts	30.00	12.00	7.50
47	Ralph Houk	30.00	12.00	7.50
48	Ted Davidson	30.00	12.00	7.50
49	Ed Brinkman	30.00	12.00	7.50
50	Willie Mays	350.00	140.00	90.00
51	Bob Locker	30.00	12.00	7.50
52	Hawk Taylor	30.00	12.00	7.50
53	Gene Alley	30.00	12.00	7.50
54	Stan Williams	30.00	12.00	7.50
55	Felipe Alou	40.00	16.00	10.00
56	Orioles Rookies **(Dave Leonhard, Dave May)**	30.00	12.00	7.50
57	Dan Schneider	30.00	12.00	7.50
58	Eddie Mathews	120.00	48.00	30.00
59	Don Lock	30.00	12.00	7.50
60	Ken Holtzman	30.00	12.00	7.50
61	Reggie Smith	30.00	12.00	7.50
62	Chuck Dobson	30.00	12.00	7.50
63	Dick Kenworthy	30.00	12.00	7.50
64	Jim Merritt	30.00	12.00	7.50
65	John Roseboro	30.00	12.00	7.50
66	Casey Cox	30.00	12.00	7.50
67	Checklist 1-109 (Jim Kaat)	30.00	12.00	7.50
68	Ron Willis	30.00	12.00	7.50
69	Tom Tresh	30.00	12.00	7.50
70	Bob Veale	30.00	12.00	7.50
71	Vern Fuller	30.00	12.00	7.50
72	Tommy John	30.00	12.00	7.50
73	Jim Hart	30.00	12.00	7.50
74	Milt Pappas	30.00	12.00	7.50
75	Don Mincher	30.00	12.00	7.50
76	Braves Rookies **(Jim Britton, Ron Reed)**	30.00	12.00	7.50
77	Don Wilson	30.00	12.00	7.50
78	Jim Northrup	30.00	12.00	7.50
79	Ted Kubiak	30.00	12.00	7.50
80	Rod Carew	120.00	48.00	30.00
81	Larry Jackson	30.00	12.00	7.50
82	Sam Bowens	30.00	12.00	7.50
83	John Stephenson	30.00	12.00	7.50
84	Bob Tolan	30.00	12.00	7.50
85	Gaylord Perry	80.00	32.00	20.00
86	Willie Stargell	100.00	40.00	25.00
87	Dick Williams	30.00	12.00	7.50
88	Phil Regan	30.00	12.00	7.50
89	Jake Gibbs	30.00	12.00	7.50
90	Vada Pinson	40.00	16.00	10.00
91	Jim Ollom	30.00	12.00	7.50
92	Ed Kranepool	30.00	12.00	7.50
93	Tony Cloninger	30.00	12.00	7.50
94	Lee Maye	30.00	12.00	7.50
95	Bob Aspromonte	30.00	12.00	7.50
96	Senators Rookies **(Frank Coggins, Dick Nold)**	30.00	12.00	7.50
97	Tom Phoebus	30.00	12.00	7.50
98	Gary Sutherland	30.00	12.00	7.50
99	Rocky Colavito	50.00	20.00	12.50
100	Bob Gibson	90.00	36.00	22.00
101	Glenn Beckert	30.00	12.00	7.50
102	Jose Cardenal	30.00	12.00	7.50
103	Don Sutton	80.00	32.00	20.00
104	Dick Dietz	30.00	12.00	7.50
105	Al Downing	30.00	12.00	7.50
106	Dalton Jones	30.00	12.00	7.50
107	Checklist 110-196 (Juan Marichal)	30.00	12.00	7.50
108	Don Pavletich	30.00	12.00	7.50
109	Bert Campaneris	40.00	16.00	10.00
110	Hank Aaron	350.00	140.00	90.00
111	Rich Reese	30.00	12.00	7.50
112	Woody Fryman	30.00	12.00	7.50
113	Tigers Rookies **(Tom Matchick, Daryl Patterson)**	30.00	12.00	7.50
114	Ron Swoboda	30.00	12.00	7.50
115	Sam McDowell	30.00	12.00	7.50
116	Ken McMullen	30.00	12.00	7.50
117	Larry Jaster	30.00	12.00	7.50
118	Mark Belanger	30.00	12.00	7.50
119	Ted Savage	30.00	12.00	7.50
120	Mel Stottlemyre	30.00	12.00	7.50
121	Jimmie Hall	30.00	12.00	7.50
122	Gene Mauch	30.00	12.00	7.50
123	Jose Santiago	30.00	12.00	7.50
124	Nate Oliver	30.00	12.00	7.50
125	Joe Horlen	30.00	12.00	7.50
126	Bobby Etheridge	30.00	12.00	7.50
127	Paul Lindblad	30.00	12.00	7.50
128	Astros Rookies **(Tom Dukes, Alonzo Harris)**	30.00	12.00	7.50
129	Mickey Stanley	30.00	12.00	7.50
130	Tony Perez	90.00	36.00	22.00
131	Frank Bertaina	30.00	12.00	7.50
132	Bud Harrelson	30.00	12.00	7.50
133	Fred Whitfield	30.00	12.00	7.50
134	Pat Jarvis	30.00	12.00	7.50
135	Paul Blair	30.00	12.00	7.50
136	Randy Hundley	30.00	12.00	7.50
137	Twins Team	40.00	16.00	10.00
138	Ruben Amaro	30.00	12.00	7.50
139	Chris Short	30.00	12.00	7.50
140	Tony Conigliaro	40.00	16.00	10.00
141	Dal Maxvill	30.00	12.00	7.50
142	White Sox Rookies **(Buddy Bradford, Bill Voss)**	30.00	12.00	7.50
143	Pete Cimino	30.00	12.00	7.50
144	Joe Morgan	100.00	40.00	25.00
145	Don Drysdale	100.00	40.00	25.00
146	Sal Bando	30.00	12.00	7.50
147	Frank Linzy	30.00	12.00	7.50
148	Dave Bristol	30.00	12.00	7.50
149	Bob Saverine	30.00	12.00	7.50
150	Roberto Clemente	600.00	240.00	150.00
151	World Series Game 1 (Brock Socks 4 Hits in Opener)	30.00	12.00	7.50
152	World Series Game 2 (Yaz Smashes Two Homers)	40.00	16.00	10.00
153	World Series Game 3 (Briles Cools Off Boston)	30.00	12.00	7.50
154	World Series Game 4 (Gibson Hurls Shutout)	30.00	12.00	7.50
155	World Series Game 5 (Lonborg Wins Again)	30.00	12.00	7.50
156	World Series Game 6 (Petrocelli Socks Two Homers)	30.00	12.00	7.50
157	World Series Game 7 (St. Louis Wins It)	30.00	12.00	7.50
158	World Series Summary (The Cardinals Celebrate)	30.00	12.00	7.50
159	Don Kessinger	30.00	12.00	7.50
160	Earl Wilson	30.00	12.00	7.50
161	Norm Miller	30.00	12.00	7.50
162	Cardinals Rookies **(Hal Gilson, Mike Torrez)**	30.00	12.00	7.50
163	Gene Brabender	30.00	12.00	7.50
164	Ramon Webster	30.00	12.00	7.50
165	Tony Oliva	40.00	16.00	10.00
166	Claude Raymond	30.00	12.00	7.50
167	Elston Howard	30.00	12.00	7.50
168	Dodgers Team	50.00	20.00	12.50
169	Bob Bolin	30.00	12.00	7.50
170	Jim Fregosi	30.00	12.00	7.50
171	Don Nottebart	30.00	12.00	7.50
172	Walt Williams	30.00	12.00	7.50
173	John Boozer	30.00	12.00	7.50
174	Bob Tillman	30.00	12.00	7.50
175	Maury Wills	30.00	12.00	7.50
176	Bob Allen	30.00	12.00	7.50
177	Mets Rookies ***(Jerry Koosman, Nolan Ryan)***	12,000	4,800	3,000
178	Don Wert	30.00	12.00	7.50
179	Bill Stoneman	30.00	12.00	7.50
180	Curt Flood	30.00	12.00	7.50
181	Jerry Zimmerman	30.00	12.00	7.50
182	Dave Giusti	30.00	12.00	7.50
183	Bob Kennedy	30.00	12.00	7.50
184	Lou Johnson	30.00	12.00	7.50
185	Tom Haller	30.00	12.00	7.50
186	Eddie Watt	30.00	12.00	7.50
187	Sonny Jackson	30.00	12.00	7.50
188	Cap Peterson	30.00	12.00	7.50
189	Bill Landis	30.00	12.00	7.50
190	Bill White	30.00	12.00	7.50
191	Dan Frisella	30.00	12.00	7.50
192	Checklist 197-283 (Carl Yastrzemski)	40.00	16.00	10.00
193	Jack Hamilton	30.00	12.00	7.50
194	Don Buford	30.00	12.00	7.50
195	Joe Pepitone	30.00	12.00	7.50
196	Gary Nolan	30.00	12.00	7.50
197	Larry Brown	30.00	12.00	7.50
198	Roy Face	30.00	12.00	7.50
199	A's Rookies **(Darrell Osteen, Roberto Rodriguez)**	30.00	12.00	7.50
200	Orlando Cepeda	80.00	32.00	20.00
201	Mike Marshall	30.00	12.00	7.50
202	Adolfo Phillips	30.00	12.00	7.50
203	Dick Kelley	30.00	12.00	7.50
204	Andy Etchebarren	30.00	12.00	7.50
205	Juan Marichal	90.00	36.00	22.00
206	Cal Ermer	30.00	12.00	7.50
207	Carroll Sembera	30.00	12.00	7.50
208	Willie Davis	30.00	12.00	7.50
209	Tim Cullen	30.00	12.00	7.50
210	Gary Peters	30.00	12.00	7.50
211	J.C. Martin	30.00	12.00	7.50
212	Dave Morehead	30.00	12.00	7.50
213	Chico Ruiz	30.00	12.00	7.50
214	Yankees Rookies **(Stan Bahnsen, Frank Fernandez)**	30.00	12.00	7.50
215	Jim Bunning	90.00	36.00	22.00
216	Bubba Morton	30.00	12.00	7.50
217	Turk Farrell	30.00	12.00	7.50
218	Ken Suarez	30.00	12.00	7.50
219	Rob Gardner	30.00	12.00	7.50
220	Harmon Killebrew	120.00	48.00	30.00
221	Braves Team	40.00	16.00	10.00
222	Jim Hardin	30.00	12.00	7.50
223	Ollie Brown	30.00	12.00	7.50
224	Jack Aker	30.00	12.00	7.50
225	Richie Allen	40.00	16.00	10.00
226	Jimmie Price	30.00	12.00	7.50
227	Joe Hoerner	30.00	12.00	7.50
228	Dodgers Rookies **(Jack Billingham, Jim Fairey)**	30.00	12.00	7.50
229	Fred Klages	30.00	12.00	7.50
230	Pete Rose	350.00	140.00	90.00
231	Dave Baldwin	30.00	12.00	7.50
232	Denis Menke	30.00	12.00	7.50
233	George Scott	30.00	12.00	7.50
234	Bill Monbouquette	30.00	12.00	7.50
235	Ron Santo	50.00	20.00	12.50
236	Tug McGraw	30.00	12.00	7.50
237	Alvin Dark	30.00	12.00	7.50
238	Tom Satriano	30.00	12.00	7.50
239	Bill Henry	30.00	12.00	7.50
240	Al Kaline	120.00	48.00	30.00
241	Felix Millan	30.00	12.00	7.50
242	Moe Drabowsky	30.00	12.00	7.50
243	Rich Rollins	30.00	12.00	7.50
244	John Donaldson	30.00	12.00	7.50
245	Tony Gonzalez	30.00	12.00	7.50
246	Fritz Peterson	30.00	12.00	7.50
247	Reds Rookies **(Johnny Bench, Ron Tompkins)**	400.00	160.00	100.00
248	Fred Valentine	30.00	12.00	7.50
249	Bill Singer	30.00	12.00	7.50
250	Carl Yastrzemski	130.00	52.00	32.00
251	Manny Sanguillen	40.00	16.00	10.00
252	Angels Team	40.00	16.00	10.00
253	Dick Hughes	30.00	12.00	7.50
254	Cleon Jones	30.00	12.00	7.50
255	Dean Chance	30.00	12.00	7.50
256	Norm Cash	40.00	16.00	10.00
257	Phil Niekro	80.00	32.00	20.00
258	Cubs Rookies **(Jose Arcia, Bill Schlesinger)**	30.00	12.00	7.50
259	Ken Boyer	30.00	12.00	7.50
260	Jim Wynn	30.00	12.00	7.50
261	Dave Duncan	30.00	12.00	7.50
262	Rick Wise	30.00	12.00	7.50
263	Horace Clarke	30.00	12.00	7.50
264	Ted Abernathy	30.00	12.00	7.50
265	Tommy Davis	30.00	12.00	7.50
266	Paul Popovich	30.00	12.00	7.50
267	Herman Franks	30.00	12.00	7.50
268	Bob Humphreys	30.00	12.00	7.50
269	Bob Tiefenauer	30.00	12.00	7.50
270	Matty Alou	30.00	12.00	7.50
271	Bobby Knoop	30.00	12.00	7.50
272	Ray Culp	30.00	12.00	7.50
273	Dave Johnson	30.00	12.00	7.50
274	Mike Cuellar	30.00	12.00	7.50
275	Tim McCarver	30.00	12.00	7.50
276	Jim Roland	30.00	12.00	7.50
277	Jerry Buchek	30.00	12.00	7.50
278	Checklist 284-370 (Orlando Cepeda)	30.00	12.00	7.50
279	Bill Hands	30.00	12.00	7.50
280	Mickey Mantle	1,900	760.00	475.00
281	Jim Campanis	30.00	12.00	7.50
282	Rick Monday	30.00	12.00	7.50
283	Mel Queen	30.00	12.00	7.50
284	John Briggs	30.00	12.00	7.50
285	Dick McAuliffe	30.00	12.00	7.50
286	Cecil Upshaw	30.00	12.00	7.50
287	White Sox Rookies **(Mickey Abarbanel, Cisco Carlos)**	30.00	12.00	7.50

288	Dave Wickersham	30.00	12.00	7.50
289	Woody Held	30.00	12.00	7.50
290	Willie McCovey	120.00	48.00	30.00
291	Dick Lines	30.00	12.00	7.50
292	Art Shamsky	30.00	12.00	7.50
293	Bruce Howard	30.00	12.00	7.50
294	Red Schoendienst	80.00	32.00	20.00
295	Sonny Siebert	30.00	12.00	7.50
296	Byron Browne	30.00	12.00	7.50
297	Russ Gibson	30.00	12.00	7.50
298	Jim Brewer	30.00	12.00	7.50
299	Gene Michael	30.00	12.00	7.50
300	Rusty Staub	40.00	16.00	10.00
301	Twins Rookies **(George Mitterwald, Rick Renick)**	30.00	12.00	7.50
302	Gerry Arrigo	30.00	12.00	7.50
303	Dick Green	30.00	12.00	7.50
304	Sandy Valdespino	30.00	12.00	7.50
305	Minnie Rojas	30.00	12.00	7.50
306	Mike Ryan	30.00	12.00	7.50
307	John Hiller	30.00	12.00	7.50
308	Pirates Team	50.00	20.00	12.50
309	Ken Henderson	30.00	12.00	7.50
310	Luis Aparicio	150.00	60.00	37.00
311	Jack Lamabe	30.00	12.00	7.50
312	Curt Blefary	30.00	12.00	7.50
313	Al Weis	30.00	12.00	7.50
314	Red Sox Rookies **(Bill Rohr, George Spriggs)**	30.00	12.00	7.50
315	Zoilo Versalles	30.00	12.00	7.50
316	Steve Barber	30.00	12.00	7.50
317	Ron Brand	30.00	12.00	7.50
318	Chico Salmon	30.00	12.00	7.50
319	George Culver	30.00	12.00	7.50
320	Frank Howard	40.00	16.00	10.00
321	Leo Durocher	50.00	20.00	12.50
322	Dave Boswell	30.00	12.00	7.50
323	Deron Johnson	30.00	12.00	7.50
324	Jim Nash	30.00	12.00	7.50
325	Manny Mota	30.00	12.00	7.50
326	Dennis Ribant	30.00	12.00	7.50
327	Tony Taylor	30.00	12.00	7.50
328	Angels Rookies **(Chuck Vinson, Jim Weaver)**	30.00	12.00	7.50
329	Duane Josephson	30.00	12.00	7.50
330	Roger Maris	120.00	48.00	30.00
331	Dan Osinski	30.00	12.00	7.50
332	Doug Rader	30.00	12.00	7.50
333	Ron Herbel	30.00	12.00	7.50
334	Orioles Team	50.00	20.00	12.50
335	Bob Allison	30.00	12.00	7.50
336	John Purdin	30.00	12.00	7.50
337	Bill Robinson	30.00	12.00	7.50
338	Bob Johnson	30.00	12.00	7.50
339	Rich Nye	30.00	12.00	7.50
340	Max Alvis	30.00	12.00	7.50
341	Jim Lemon	30.00	12.00	7.50
342	Ken Johnson	30.00	12.00	7.50
343	Jim Gosger	30.00	12.00	7.50
344	Donn Clendenon	30.00	12.00	7.50
345	Bob Hendley	30.00	12.00	7.50
346	Jerry Adair	30.00	12.00	7.50
347	George Brunet	30.00	12.00	7.50
348	Phillies Rookies **(Larry Colton, Dick Thoenen)**	30.00	12.00	7.50
349	Ed Spiezio	30.00	12.00	7.50
350	Hoyt Wilhelm	80.00	32.00	20.00
351	Bob Barton	30.00	12.00	7.50
352	Jackie Hernandez	30.00	12.00	7.50
353	Mack Jones	30.00	12.00	7.50
354	Pete Richert	30.00	12.00	7.50
355	Ernie Banks	130.00	55.00	35.00
356	Checklist 371-457 (Ken Holtzman)	30.00	12.00	7.50
357	Len Gabrielson	30.00	12.00	7.50
358	Mike Epstein	30.00	12.00	7.50
359	Joe Moeller	30.00	12.00	7.50
360	Willie Horton	30.00	12.00	7.50
361	Harmon Killebrew/AS	50.00	20.00	12.50
362	Orlando Cepeda/AS	40.00	16.00	10.00
363	Rod Carew/AS	50.00	20.00	12.50
364	Joe Morgan/AS	40.00	16.00	10.00
365	Brooks Robinson/AS	50.00	20.00	12.50
366	Ron Santo/AS	40.00	16.00	10.00
367	Jim Fregosi/AS	30.00	12.00	7.50
368	Gene Alley/AS	30.00	12.00	7.50
369	Carl Yastrzemski/AS	50.00	20.00	12.50
370	Hank Aaron/AS	250.00	100.00	62.00

1970 Ovenca Venezuelan League

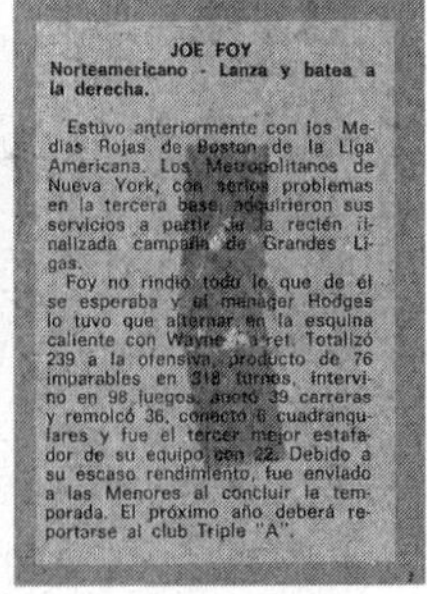

JOE FOY
Norteamericano - Lanza y batea a la derecha.

Estuvo anteriormente con los Medias Rojas de Boston de la Liga Americana. Los Metropolitanos de Nueva York, con serios problemas en la tercera base, adquirieron sus servicios a partir de la recién finalizada campaña de Grandes Ligas.

Foy no rindió todo lo que de él se esperaba y el manager Hodges lo tuvo que alternar en la esquina caliente con Wayne [illegible]ret. Totalizó 239 a la ofensiva, producto de 76 imparables en 318 turnos, intervino en 98 juegos, anotó 39 carreras y remolcó 36, conectó 6 cuadrangulares y fue el tercer mejor estafador de su equipo con 22. Debido a su escaso rendimiento, fue enviado a las Menores al concluir la temporada. El próximo año deberá reportarse al club Triple "A".

After partial parallels of Topps cards were produced off and on between 1959 and 1968, Venezuelan collectors and fans were offered a completely home-brewed baseball card issue for the 1970-71 winter league season. Similar in quality (i.e., less substantial card stock) to earlier sets, these were printed by Sport Grafico for Ovenca, though neither entity is mentioned on the cards. Slightly larger than 2-1/2" x 3-1/2", cards have large color photos with color stripes above and below bearing player and team name and card number. Backs are printed in black on blue with lengthy comments about the player and his career. Gaps in this checklist will be filled as information comes to light.

		NM	EX	VG
Complete Set (300):		2,250	1,100	650.00
Common Player:		20.00	10.00	6.00
Album:		200.00	100.00	60.00
1	Cesar Gutierrez	20.00	10.00	6.00
2	Elio Chacon	20.00	10.00	6.00
3	Luis Rodriguez	20.00	10.00	6.00
4	David Concepcion	75.00	37.50	22.00
5	Roberto Munoz	20.00	10.00	6.00
6	Jesus Rizales	20.00	10.00	6.00
7	Virgilio Mata	20.00	10.00	6.00
8	Manuel Garcia	30.00	15.00	9.00
9	Cesar Garrido	20.00	10.00	6.00
10	Alejandro Tovar	20.00	10.00	6.00
11	William Salazar	20.00	10.00	6.00
12	Jose Lopez	20.00	10.00	6.00
13	Romulo Castillo	20.00	10.00	6.00
14	Victor Jimenez	20.00	10.00	6.00
15	Jose Saiz	20.00	10.00	6.00
16	Wilfredo Calvino	20.00	10.00	6.00
17	Jesus Avila	20.00	10.00	6.00
18	Cruz Rodriguez	20.00	10.00	6.00
19	Julio Bracho	20.00	10.00	6.00
20	David Concepcion, Cesar Gutierrez	25.00	12.50	7.50
21	Double Play (David Concepcion)	25.00	12.50	7.50
22	Tigres de Aragua Logo	10.00	5.00	3.00
23	Orlando Tavares	20.00	10.00	6.00
24	David Concepcion/IA	30.00	15.00	9.00
25	Aragua Action	10.00	5.00	3.00
26	Aragua Action	10.00	5.00	3.00
27	Cesar Gutierrez	20.00	10.00	6.00
28	Play at Home	10.00	5.00	3.00
29	Joe Foy	20.00	10.00	6.00
30	Dennis Paepke	20.00	10.00	6.00
31	Fred Norman	20.00	10.00	6.00
32	John Purdin	20.00	10.00	6.00
33	Steve Huntz	20.00	10.00	6.00
34	Claide (Clyde) Mashore	20.00	10.00	6.00
35	Steve Mingori	20.00	10.00	6.00
36	Jim Breazeale	20.00	10.00	6.00
37	Charles Day	20.00	10.00	6.00
38	Bob Stinson	20.00	10.00	6.00
39	Phil Hennigan	20.00	10.00	6.00
40	Aragua Checklist (Wilfredo Calvino)	25.00	12.50	7.50
41	Faustino Zabala	20.00	10.00	6.00
42	Pablo Torrealba	20.00	10.00	6.00
43	Erasmo Diaz	20.00	10.00	6.00
44	Sebastian Martinez	20.00	10.00	6.00
45	Neudo Morales	20.00	10.00	6.00
46	Iran Paz	20.00	10.00	6.00
47	Franklyn Moreno	20.00	10.00	6.00
48	Claudio Urdaneta	20.00	10.00	6.00
49	Dario Chirinos	20.00	10.00	6.00
50	Domingo Carrasquel	20.00	10.00	6.00
51	Enrique Gonzalez	20.00	10.00	6.00
52	Ednio Gonzalez	20.00	10.00	6.00
53	Humberto Donquis	20.00	10.00	6.00
54	Antonio Ruiz	20.00	10.00	6.00
55	Efrain Urquiola	20.00	10.00	6.00
56	Tony Pacheco	20.00	10.00	6.00
57	Lucio Celis	20.00	10.00	6.00
58	Domingo Barboza	20.00	10.00	6.00
59	Faustino Zabala, Neudo Morales	15.00	7.50	4.50
60	Lara Action	10.00	5.00	3.00
61	Tony Pacheco, Lucio Celis, Domingo Barboza	15.00	7.50	4.50
62	Lara Team Logo	10.00	5.00	3.00
63	Alexis Corro	20.00	10.00	6.00
64	Lara Rookies in Action	10.00	5.00	3.00
65	Lara Play at First	10.00	5.00	3.00
66	Lara Play at Home	10.00	5.00	3.00
67	Lara Action	10.00	5.00	3.00
68	Jim Shellenback	20.00	10.00	6.00
69	Scipio Spinks	20.00	10.00	6.00
70	Ken Forsch	20.00	10.00	6.00
71	Oscar Zamora	20.00	10.00	6.00
72	Ronald Cook	20.00	10.00	6.00
73	Jackie Brown	20.00	10.00	6.00
74	Orlando Martinez	20.00	10.00	6.00
75	Bobby Watson	25.00	12.50	7.50
76	Jose Martinez	20.00	10.00	6.00
77	Roger Metzger	20.00	10.00	6.00
78	Tommy Reynolds	20.00	10.00	6.00
79	Cleo James	20.00	10.00	6.00
80	Lara Checkist (Tony Pacheco)	10.00	5.00	3.00
81	Gustavo Gil	20.00	10.00	6.00
82	Jesus Aristimuno	20.00	10.00	6.00
83	Armando Ortiz	20.00	10.00	6.00
84	Orlando Reyes	20.00	10.00	6.00
85	Damaso Blanco	20.00	10.00	6.00
86				
87	Victor Colina	20.00	10.00	6.00
88	Nelson Cana	20.00	10.00	6.00
89	Francisco Diaz	20.00	10.00	6.00
90	Edito Arteaga	20.00	10.00	6.00
91	Concepcion Escalona	20.00	10.00	6.00
92	Gilberto Marcano	20.00	10.00	6.00
93	Luis A. Serrano	20.00	10.00	6.00
94				
95	Raul Ortega	20.00	10.00	6.00
96	Carlos Patato Pascual	20.00	10.00	6.00
97	Leopold Tovar	20.00	10.00	6.00
98	Manuel Gonzalez	20.00	10.00	6.00
99	Magallanes Action	10.00	5.00	3.00
100	Comienza el Partido	20.00	10.00	6.00
101	Magallanes Rookies	15.00	7.50	4.50
102				
103	Marcano en la Lomita	15.00	7.50	4.50
104	Magallanes Fans	10.00	5.00	3.00
105	Magallanes Action	10.00	5.00	3.00
106				
107	Hal King, Jim Holt, Clarence Gaston, Herman Hill	15.00	7.50	4.50
108	Magallanes Caribbean Champions	10.00	5.00	3.00
109				
110	Herman Hill	20.00	10.00	6.00
111	Jim Holt	20.00	10.00	6.00
112	Orlando Pena	20.00	10.00	6.00
113	Magallanes Action	10.00	5.00	3.00
114	Hal King	20.00	10.00	6.00
115	Jorge Lauzerique	20.00	10.00	6.00
116	Rigoberto Mendoza	20.00	10.00	6.00
117	Allan (Alan) Closter	20.00	10.00	6.00
118	Clarence Gaston	25.00	12.50	7.50
119	John Morris	20.00	10.00	6.00
120	Patato Pascual, Unknown	15.00	7.50	4.50
121	Victor Davalillo	20.00	10.00	6.00
122	Cesar Tovar	20.00	10.00	6.00
123	Gonzalo Marquez	20.00	10.00	6.00
124	Luis Penalver	20.00	10.00	6.00
125	Alberto Cambero	20.00	10.00	6.00
126	Urbano Lugo	20.00	10.00	6.00
127	Juan Campos	20.00	10.00	6.00
128	William Castillo	20.00	10.00	6.00
129	Nelson Garcia	20.00	10.00	6.00
130	Ramon Guanchez	20.00	10.00	6.00
131	Jesus Marcano Trillo	40.00	20.00	12.00
132	Manuel Mendible	20.00	10.00	6.00
133	Teodoro Obregon	20.00	10.00	6.00
134	Jesus Padron	20.00	10.00	6.00
135	Ulises Urrieta	20.00	10.00	6.00
136	Antonio "Loco" Torres	20.00	10.00	6.00
137	Leopoldo Posada	20.00	10.00	6.00
138	Pompeyo Davalillo	20.00	10.00	6.00
139	Alonso Olivares	20.00	10.00	6.00
140	Cesar Tovar/IA	15.00	7.50	4.50
141	Caracas Rookies in Action	15.00	7.50	4.50
142				
143	Andres Barrios	20.00	10.00	6.00
144	Heriberto Morillo	20.00	10.00	6.00
145	Angel Cordova	20.00	10.00	6.00
146	Freddy Rivero	20.00	10.00	6.00
147	Rafael Velasquez	20.00	10.00	6.00
148	Camilo Pascual	30.00	15.00	9.00
149	Cesar Tovar, Vic Davalillo	20.00	10.00	6.00
150	Luis Tiant	30.00	15.00	9.00
151	Roberto Musulungo Hernandez	20.00	10.00	6.00
152	Kurt Devecqua (Bevacqua)	30.00	15.00	9.00
153	Cookie Rojas	30.00	15.00	9.00
154	Larry Howard	20.00	10.00	6.00
155	Rick Scheinblum	20.00	10.00	6.00
156	Diego Segui	25.00	12.50	7.50
157	Gregory Conger	20.00	10.00	6.00
158	Richard Falker (Falkner)	20.00	10.00	6.00
159	Ed Sprague	20.00	10.00	6.00
160	Zulia Checklist (Pompeyo Davilillo)	15.00	7.50	4.50
161	Luis Aparicio	75.00	37.00	22.00
162	Teolindo Acosta	20.00	10.00	6.00
163	Gustavo Sposito	20.00	10.00	6.00
164	Juan Francia	20.00	10.00	6.00
165	Graciliano Parra	20.00	10.00	6.00
166	Simon Salaya	20.00	10.00	6.00
167	Nelson Castellanos	20.00	10.00	6.00
168	Edgar Urbina	20.00	10.00	6.00
169	Luis Gonzalez	20.00	10.00	6.00
170	Olinto Rojas	20.00	10.00	6.00
171	Everest Contramaestre	20.00	10.00	6.00
172	Juan Quiroz	20.00	10.00	6.00
173	Juan Quintana	20.00	10.00	6.00
174	Hugo Bello	20.00	10.00	6.00
175	Jesus Llamozas	20.00	10.00	6.00
176	Luis Aparicio (Manager)	45.00	22.00	13.50
177	Luis Aparicio, Sr.	25.00	12.50	7.50
178	Antonio Brinez	20.00	10.00	6.00
179	Carlos Dickson Bell	20.00	10.00	6.00
180	Alfonso Carrasquel	30.00	15.00	9.00
181	Zulia Action	10.00	5.00	3.00
182	Zulia Eagles Team Logo	20.00	10.00	6.00
183	Nidio Sirit	20.00	10.00	6.00
184	Zulia Action	10.00	5.00	3.00
185	Zulia Eagles Team Photo	10.00	5.00	3.00
186	Bobby Cox/AS	20.00	10.00	6.00
187	Zulia Play at Home	10.00	5.00	3.00
188	Alfonso Carrasquel, Luis Aparicio	25.00	12.50	7.50
189	Teolindo Acosta, Gustavo Sposito	15.00	7.50	4.50
190	Leonardo Cardenas	20.00	10.00	6.00
191	Bart Johnson	20.00	10.00	6.00
192	Jerry Crider	20.00	10.00	6.00
193	Getty Janesky (Gerry Janeski)	20.00	10.00	6.00
194	John Matias	20.00	10.00	6.00
195	Walter Williams	25.00	12.50	7.50
196	Steve Hovley	20.00	10.00	6.00
197	Frank Fernandez	20.00	10.00	6.00
198	John Donaldson	20.00	10.00	6.00
199	Donald Eddy	20.00	10.00	6.00
200	Zulia Checklist (Luis Aparicio)	30.00	15.00	9.00
201	Jose Herrera	20.00	10.00	6.00
202	Aurelio Monteagudo	20.00	10.00	6.00
203	Remigio Hermoso	20.00	10.00	6.00
204	Angel Bravo	20.00	10.00	6.00
205	Enzo Hernandez	20.00	10.00	6.00
206	Oswaldo Blanco	20.00	10.00	6.00
207	Carlos Moreno	20.00	10.00	6.00
208	Adolfo Philips (Phillips)	20.00	10.00	6.00
209	Roberto Romero	20.00	10.00	6.00
210	Euclides Camejo	20.00	10.00	6.00
211	Oswaldo Troconis	20.00	10.00	6.00
212	Roberto Marcano	20.00	10.00	6.00

213	Victor Patino	20.00	10.00	6.00
214	Hector Urbano	20.00	10.00	6.00
215	Antonio Pipo Correa	20.00	10.00	6.00
216	Dave Garcia	25.00	12.50	7.50
217	Graciano Ravelo	20.00	10.00	6.00
218	Reinaldo Cordeiro	20.00	10.00	6.00
219	La Guaira Action	10.00	5.00	3.00
220	La Tropa Completa	20.00	10.00	6.00
221	Tomas Liscano Arias	20.00	10.00	6.00
222				
223	Jesus Romero	20.00	10.00	6.00
224	Julian Yanez	20.00	10.00	6.00
225	Enrique Gutierrez	20.00	10.00	6.00
226	Dionel Durand	20.00	10.00	6.00
227	Jose Gregorio Salas	20.00	10.00	6.00
228	Luis Camaleon Garcia	20.00	10.00	6.00
229	Alfredo Ortiz	20.00	10.00	6.00
230	Luis Contreras	20.00	10.00	6.00
231	Ed Spiezio	20.00	10.00	6.00
232	Paul Casanova	25.00	12.50	7.50
233	Mike Epstein	25.00	12.50	7.50
234	Casey Cox	20.00	10.00	6.00
235	Marcelino Lopez	20.00	10.00	6.00
236	Jerry Cram	20.00	10.00	6.00
237	Danny Coombs	20.00	10.00	6.00
238	Del Unser	20.00	10.00	6.00
239	Hector Brito	20.00	10.00	6.00
240	La Guaira Checklist	10.00	5.00	3.00
241	Larry Howard, Richie Scheinblum/IA	15.00	7.50	4.50
242	Ed Spiezio/IA	15.00	7.50	4.50
243	Clarence Gaston, Cesar Tovar/IA	15.00	7.50	4.50
244	Paul Casanova, Unknown	15.00	7.50	4.50
245	Vitico, Cesar Tovar	15.00	7.50	4.50
246	Pasion en el Juego	10.00	5.00	3.00
247	Luis Apariciov	35.00	17.50	10.50
248	Angel Bravo/IA	15.00	7.50	4.50
249	Bobby Watson/IA	20.00	10.00	6.00
250	Alejandro "Palon" Carrasquel (Immortal)	25.00	12.50	7.50
251	Enrique Fonseca (Veteran)	20.00	10.00	6.00
252	Manuel Pollo Malpica (Immortal)	20.00	10.00	6.00
253	Emilio Cueche	20.00	10.00	6.00
254				
255	Felix "Tirahuequito" Machado (Veteran)			
256	Herberto Leal (Veteran)	20.00	10.00	6.00
257	Chucho Ramos (Veteran)	20.00	10.00	6.00
258	Julian Ladera (Veteran)	20.00	10.00	6.00
259	Carlos Ascanio (Veteran)	20.00	10.00	6.00
260	Jose Perez Colmenare (Immortal)	20.00	10.00	6.00
261	Isaias "Latigo" Chaves (Immortal)	20.00	10.00	6.00
262	Victor Garcia (Veteran)	20.00	10.00	6.00
263	Valentin Arevalo (Immortal)	20.00	10.00	6.00
264	Adolfredo Gonzalez (Veteran)	20.00	10.00	6.00
265	Hector Benitez Redondo (Veteran)	20.00	10.00	6.00
266	Ramon Fernandez (Veteran)	20.00	10.00	6.00
267	Guillermo Vento (Veteran)	20.00	10.00	6.00
268	Rafael Garcia Cedeno (Veteran)	20.00	10.00	6.00
269	Luis Oliveros (Veteran)	20.00	10.00	6.00
270	Luis Mono Zuloaga (Veteran)	20.00	10.00	6.00
271	Carlos Santeliz (Veteran)	20.00	10.00	6.00
272	Aureliano Patino	20.00	10.00	6.00
273	Rafael Olivares (Veteran)	20.00	10.00	6.00
274	Tarzan Contreras (Veteran)	20.00	10.00	6.00
275	Daniel Canonico	20.00	10.00	6.00
276	Babbino Fuenmayor (Veteran)	20.00	10.00	6.00
277	Rafael Galiz Tello (Veteran)	20.00	10.00	6.00
278	Pantaleon Espinoza	20.00	10.00	6.00
279	Miguel Sanabria (Veteran)	20.00	10.00	6.00
280				
281	Alfonso Carrasquel (Veteran)	40.00	20.00	12.00
282	Luis "Camaleon" Garcia (Veteran)	20.00	10.00	6.00
283	Balbino Inojosa (Veteran)	20.00	10.00	6.00
284	Humberto Popita Leal (Veteran)	20.00	10.00	6.00
285	Manuel Carrasquel (Veteran)	20.00	10.00	6.00
286	Ignacio Florez (Veteran)	20.00	10.00	6.00
287	Oscar Buzo Solorzino (Veteran)	20.00	10.00	6.00
288	Pelayo Chacon (Veteran)	20.00	10.00	6.00
289				
290	Micolas Berbesia (Veteran)	20.00	10.00	6.00
291	Julio Bracho (Veteran)	20.00	10.00	6.00
292	Dionisio Acosta (Veteran)	20.00	10.00	6.00
293	Gualberto Acosta (Veteran)	20.00	10.00	6.00
294	Winston Acosta (Veteran)	20.00	10.00	6.00
295	Jose Manuel Tovar (Veteran)	20.00	10.00	6.00
296	Carrao Bracho (Veteran)	20.00	10.00	6.00
297	Luis Romero Petit (Veteran)	20.00	10.00	6.00
298	Dalmiro Finol (Veteran)	20.00	10.00	6.00
299	Cerveceria Caracas Team Photo	20.00	10.00	6.00
300	Magallanes Campeones Nacionales Team	20.00	10.00	6.00

1972 Venezuelan Baseball Stamps

Utilizing most of the same photos as the 1972 Topps baseball cards, the 242 player stamps in this set feature only Major Leaguers, though with an overrepresentation of Hispanics, rather than the usual mix of U.S. and local talent. Stamps measure 2" x 2-9/16" and feature tombstone-shaped color photos at center, surrounded by a green background. The only printing is the player name, team name (in Spanish) and stamp number, all in black. A white border surrounds the whole. Backs are blank as the stamps were meant to be mounted in an album. Because stamps are seldom seen in higher grade, only a VG price is presented here. Stamps in Good should be valued at 50 percent of the price shown, and stamps grading Fair at 25 percent.

		NM	EX	VG
	Complete Set (242):	4,900	1,950	980.00
	Common Player:	15.00	6.00	3.00
	Album:	150.00	75.00	45.00
1	Vic Davalillo	50.00	20.00	10.00
2	Doug Griffin	15.00	6.00	3.00
3	Rod Carew	150.00	60.00	30.00
4	Joel Horlen	15.00	6.00	3.00
5	Jim Fregosi	15.00	6.00	3.00
6	Rod Carew ("en acion" - In Action)	100.00	40.00	20.00
7	Billy Champion	15.00	6.00	3.00
8	Ron Hansen	15.00	6.00	3.00
9	Bobby Murcer	15.00	6.00	3.00
10	Nellie Briles	15.00	6.00	3.00
11	Fred Patek	15.00	6.00	3.00
12	Mike Epstein	15.00	6.00	3.00
13	Dave Marshall	15.00	6.00	3.00
14	Steve Hargan	15.00	6.00	3.00
15	Duane Josephson	15.00	6.00	3.00
16	Steve Garvey	22.50	9.00	4.50
17	Eddie Fisher	15.00	6.00	3.00
18	Jack Aker	15.00	6.00	3.00
19	Ron Brand	15.00	6.00	3.00
20	Del Rice	15.00	6.00	3.00
21	Ollie Brown	15.00	6.00	3.00
22	Jamie McAndrew	15.00	6.00	3.00
23	Willie Horton	15.00	6.00	3.00
24	Eddie Leon	15.00	6.00	3.00
25	Steve Hovley	15.00	6.00	3.00
26	Moe Drabowsky	15.00	6.00	3.00
27	Dick Selma	15.00	6.00	3.00
28	Jim Lyttle	15.00	6.00	3.00
29	Sal Bando	15.00	6.00	3.00
30	Bill Lee	15.00	6.00	3.00
31	Al Kaline	150.00	60.00	30.00
32	Mike Lum	15.00	6.00	3.00
33	Les Cain	15.00	6.00	3.00
34	Richie Hebner	15.00	6.00	3.00
35	Donn Clendenon	15.00	6.00	3.00
36	Ralph Houk	15.00	6.00	3.00
37	Luis Melendez	15.00	6.00	3.00
38	Jim Hickman	15.00	6.00	3.00
39	Manny Mota	15.00	6.00	3.00
40	Bob Locker	15.00	6.00	3.00
41	Ron Santo	20.00	8.00	4.00
42	Tony Cloninger	15.00	6.00	3.00
43	Joe Ferguson	15.00	6.00	3.00
44	Mike McCormick	15.00	6.00	3.00
45	Bobby Wine	15.00	6.00	3.00
46	Preston Gomez	15.00	6.00	3.00
47	Pat Corrales/IA	15.00	6.00	3.00
48	Hector Torres	15.00	6.00	3.00
49	Fritz Peterson	15.00	6.00	3.00
50	Jim Rooker	15.00	6.00	3.00
51	Chris Short	15.00	6.00	3.00
52	Juan Marichal/IA	22.50	9.00	4.50
53	Teddy Martinez	15.00	6.00	3.00
54	Ken Aspromonte	15.00	6.00	3.00
55	Bobby Bonds	15.00	6.00	3.00
56	Rich Robertson	15.00	6.00	3.00
57	Nate Colbert/IA	15.00	6.00	3.00
58	Jose Pagan/IA	15.00	6.00	3.00
59	Curt Blefary/IA	15.00	6.00	3.00
60	Bill Mazeroski	100.00	40.00	20.00
61	John Odom	15.00	6.00	3.00
62	George Stone	15.00	6.00	3.00
63	Lew Krausse	15.00	6.00	3.00
64	Bobby Knoop	15.00	6.00	3.00
65	Pete Rose/IA	225.00	90.00	45.00
66	Steve Luebber	15.00	6.00	3.00
67	Bill Voss	15.00	6.00	3.00
68	Chico Salmon	15.00	6.00	3.00
69	Ivan Murrell	15.00	6.00	3.00
70	Gil Garrido	15.00	6.00	3.00
71	Terry Crowley	15.00	6.00	3.00
72	Bill Russell	15.00	6.00	3.00
73	Steve Dunning	15.00	6.00	3.00
74	Ray Sadecki/IA	15.00	6.00	3.00
75	Al Gallagher/IA	15.00	6.00	3.00
76	Cesar Gutierrez	15.00	6.00	3.00
77	John Kennedy	15.00	6.00	3.00
78	Joe Hague	15.00	6.00	3.00
79	Bruce Del Canton	15.00	6.00	3.00
80	Ken Holtzman	15.00	6.00	3.00
81	Rico Carty	15.00	6.00	3.00
82	Roger Repoz	15.00	6.00	3.00
83	Fran Healy	15.00	6.00	3.00
84	Al Gallagher	15.00	6.00	3.00
85	Rich McKinney	15.00	6.00	3.00
86	Lowell Palmer	15.00	6.00	3.00
87	Jose Cardenal	15.00	6.00	3.00
88	Ed Kirkpatrick/IA	15.00	6.00	3.00
89	Steve Carlton	150.00	60.00	30.00
90	Gail Hopkins	15.00	6.00	3.00
91	Reggie Smith	15.00	6.00	3.00
92	Denny Riddleberger	15.00	6.00	3.00
93	Don Sutton	60.00	24.00	12.00
94	Bob Moose	15.00	6.00	3.00
95	Joe Decker	15.00	6.00	3.00
96	Bill Wilson	15.00	6.00	3.00
97	Mike Ferraro	15.00	6.00	3.00
98	Jack Hiatt	15.00	6.00	3.00
99	Bill Grabarkewitz	15.00	6.00	3.00
100	Larry Stahl	15.00	6.00	3.00
101	Jim Slaton	15.00	6.00	3.00
102	Jim Wynn	15.00	6.00	3.00
103	Phil Niekro	60.00	24.00	12.00
104	Danny Cater	15.00	6.00	3.00
105	Ray Sadecki	15.00	6.00	3.00
106	Jack Billingham	15.00	6.00	3.00
107	Dave Nelson	15.00	6.00	3.00
108	Rudy May	15.00	6.00	3.00
109	Don Money	15.00	6.00	3.00
110	Diego Segui	15.00	6.00	3.00
111	Jose Pagan	15.00	6.00	3.00
112	John Strohmayer	15.00	6.00	3.00
113	Wade Blasingame	15.00	6.00	3.00
114	Ken Wright	15.00	6.00	3.00
115	Ken Tatum	15.00	6.00	3.00
116	Mike Paul	15.00	6.00	3.00
117	Tom McCraw	15.00	6.00	3.00
118	Bob Gibson	125.00	50.00	25.00
119	Al Santorini	15.00	6.00	3.00
120	Leo Cardenas	15.00	6.00	3.00
121	Jimmy Stewart	15.00	6.00	3.00
122	Willie Crawford	15.00	6.00	3.00
123	Bob Aspromonte	15.00	6.00	3.00
124	Frank Duffy	15.00	6.00	3.00
125	Hal Lanier	15.00	6.00	3.00
126	Nate Colbert	15.00	6.00	3.00
127	Russ Gibson	15.00	6.00	3.00
128	Cesar Geronimo	15.00	6.00	3.00
129	Pat Kelly	15.00	6.00	3.00
130	Horacio Pina	15.00	6.00	3.00
131	Charlie Brinkman	15.00	6.00	3.00
132	Bill Virdon	15.00	6.00	3.00
133	Hal McRae	15.00	6.00	3.00
134	Tony Oliva/IA	25.00	10.00	5.00
135	Gonzalo Marquez	15.00	6.00	3.00
136	Willie Montanez	15.00	6.00	3.00
137	Dick Green	15.00	6.00	3.00
138	Jim Ray	15.00	6.00	3.00
139	Denis Menke	15.00	6.00	3.00
140	Fred Kendall	15.00	6.00	3.00
141	Vida Blue	15.00	6.00	3.00
142	Tom Grieve	15.00	6.00	3.00
143	Ed Kirkpatrick/IA	15.00	6.00	3.00
144	George Scott	15.00	6.00	3.00
145	Hal Breeden	15.00	6.00	3.00
146	Ken McMullen	15.00	6.00	3.00
147	Jim Perry/IA	15.00	6.00	3.00
148	Wayne Granger	15.00	6.00	3.00
149	Mike Hegan	15.00	6.00	3.00
150	Al Oliver	20.00	8.00	4.00
151	Frank Robinson/IA	100.00	40.00	20.00
152	Paul Blair	15.00	6.00	3.00
153	Phil Hennigan	15.00	6.00	3.00
154	Ron Stone	15.00	6.00	3.00
155	Gene Michael	15.00	6.00	3.00
156	Jerry McNertney	15.00	6.00	3.00
157	Marcelino Lopez	15.00	6.00	3.00
158	Dave May	15.00	6.00	3.00
159	Jim Hart	15.00	6.00	3.00
160	Joe Coleman	15.00	6.00	3.00
161	Rick Reichardt	15.00	6.00	3.00
162	Ed Brinkman	15.00	6.00	3.00
163	Dick McAuliffe	15.00	6.00	3.00
164	Paul Doyle	15.00	6.00	3.00
165	Terry Forster	15.00	6.00	3.00
166	Steve Hamilton	15.00	6.00	3.00
167	Mike Corkins	15.00	6.00	3.00
168	Dave Concepcion	75.00	30.00	15.00
169	Bill Sudakis	15.00	6.00	3.00
170	Juan Marichal	100.00	40.00	20.00
171	Harmon Killebrew	150.00	60.00	30.00
172	Luis Tiant	20.00	8.00	4.00
173	Ted Uhlaender	15.00	6.00	3.00
174	Tim Foli	15.00	6.00	3.00
175	Luis Aparicio/IA	200.00	80.00	40.00
176	Bert Campaneris	15.00	6.00	3.00
177	Charlie Sands	15.00	6.00	3.00
178	Darold Knowles	15.00	6.00	3.00
179	Jerry Koosman	15.00	6.00	3.00
180	Leo Cardenas/IA	15.00	6.00	3.00
181	Luis Alvarado	15.00	6.00	3.00
182	Graig Nettles	17.50	7.00	3.50
183	Walter Alston	20.00	8.00	4.00
184	Nolan Ryan	550.00	220.00	110.00
185	Ed Sprague	15.00	6.00	3.00
186	Rich Reese	15.00	6.00	3.00
187	Pete Rose	300.00	120.00	60.00
188	Bernie Allen	15.00	6.00	3.00
189	Lou Piniella	17.50	7.00	3.50
190	Jerry Reuss	15.00	6.00	3.00
191	Bob Pfeil	15.00	6.00	3.00
192	Bob Burda	15.00	6.00	3.00
193	Walt Williams	15.00	6.00	3.00
194	Dusty Baker	17.50	7.00	3.50
195	Rich Morales	15.00	6.00	3.00
196	Bill Stoneman	15.00	6.00	3.00
197	Hal King	15.00	6.00	3.00
198	Julian Javier	15.00	6.00	3.00
199	Dave Mason	15.00	6.00	3.00
200	Bob Veale	15.00	6.00	3.00
201	Jim Beauchamp	15.00	6.00	3.00
202	Ron Santo/IA	17.50	7.00	3.50
203	Tom Seaver	150.00	60.00	30.00
204	Jim Merritt	15.00	6.00	3.00
205	Jerry Koosman/IA	15.00	6.00	3.00
206	Dick Woodson	15.00	6.00	3.00

207	Wayne Simpson	15.00	6.00	3.00
208	Jose Laboy	15.00	6.00	3.00
209	Sam McDowell	15.00	6.00	3.00
210	Bob Bailey	15.00	6.00	3.00
211	Jim Fairey	15.00	6.00	3.00
212	Felipe Alou	25.00	10.00	5.00
213	Dave Concepcion/IA	50.00	20.00	10.00
214	Wilbur Wood/IA	15.00	6.00	3.00
215	Enzo Hernandez	15.00	6.00	3.00
216	Ron Reed	15.00	6.00	3.00
217	Stan Bahnsen	15.00	6.00	3.00
218	Ollie Brown/IA	15.00	6.00	3.00
219	Pat Jarvis	15.00	6.00	3.00
220	Tim Foli/IA	15.00	6.00	3.00
221	Denny McLain	15.00	6.00	3.00
222	Jerry Grote	15.00	6.00	3.00
223	Davey Johnson	15.00	6.00	3.00
224	John Odom/IA	15.00	6.00	3.00
225	Paul Casanova	15.00	6.00	3.00
226	George Culver	15.00	6.00	3.00
227	Pat Corrales	15.00	6.00	3.00
228	Jim Kaat	15.00	6.00	3.00
229	Archie Reynolds	15.00	6.00	3.00
230	Frank Reberger	15.00	6.00	3.00
231	Carl Yastrzemski	150.00	60.00	30.00
232	Jim Holt	15.00	6.00	3.00
233	Lenny Randle	15.00	6.00	3.00
234	Doug Griffin/IA	15.00	6.00	3.00
235	Doug Rader	15.00	6.00	3.00
236	Jesus Alou	15.00	6.00	3.00
237	Wilbur Wood/IA	15.00	6.00	3.00
238	Jim Kaat/IA	15.00	6.00	3.00
239	Fritz Peterson/IA	15.00	6.00	3.00
240	Dennis Leonard	15.00	6.00	3.00
241	Brooks Robinson	150.00	60.00	30.00
242	Felix Millan	15.00	6.00	3.00

1972 Venezuelan League Stickers

Issued in the winter league season of 1972-73, the Venezuelan League sticker set bears more than a passing similitude to the 1972 Topps baseball cards. The 2-1/2" x 3-1/2" stickers have tombstone-shaped photos framed in multi-colored borders with the team name at top and the player name in an oval cartouche at bottom. The sticker number is in a circle at top-right. Because they were intended to be mounted in an accompanying album, the backs are blank. Because so many of the stickers were once pasted into albums, and due to unfavorable climactic conditions, high-grade examples of Venezuelan stickers from the era are particularly scarce.

		NM	EX	VG
Complete Set (249):		1,500	750.00	450.00
Common Player:		20.00	10.00	6.00
Album:		75.00	40.00	20.00
1	Dave Concepcion	30.00	15.00	9.00
2	Luis Rodriguez	25.00	12.50	7.50
3	Roberto Munoz	25.00	12.50	7.50
4	William Castillo	25.00	12.50	7.50
5	Jose Lopez	25.00	12.50	7.50
6	Armando Chacon	25.00	12.50	7.50
7	Juan Francia	25.00	12.50	7.50
8	Roric Harrison	25.00	12.50	7.50
9	Dave Concepcion, Escalona	30.00	15.00	9.00
10	Enrique Gutierrez	25.00	12.50	7.50
11	Luis Gonzalez	25.00	12.50	7.50
12	Jose Torres	25.00	12.50	7.50
13	William Salazar	25.00	12.50	7.50
14	Everest Contramaestre	25.00	12.50	7.50
15	Jesus Rizales	25.00	12.50	7.50
16	Ramon Velasquez	25.00	12.50	7.50
17	Rafael J. Velasquez	25.00	12.50	7.50
18	Jesus Loreto	25.00	12.50	7.50
19	Orlando Galindo	25.00	12.50	7.50
20	Jose Torres	25.00	12.50	7.50
21	Victor Jimenez	25.00	12.50	7.50
22	Hernan Silva	25.00	12.50	7.50
23	Leroy Stanton	25.00	12.50	7.50
24	Jesus Yanez	25.00	12.50	7.50
25	Orlando Tavares	25.00	12.50	7.50
26	Eddie Baez	25.00	12.50	7.50
27	Jim Frey	30.00	15.00	9.00
28	Eddie Watt	25.00	12.50	7.50
29	Aragua Team Logo	10.00	5.00	3.00
30	Carlos Orea	25.00	12.50	7.50
31	Rod Carew	75.00	37.00	22.00
32	Rod Carew, Enos Cabell	35.00	17.50	10.50
33	George Mitterwald	25.00	12.50	7.50
34	Enos Cabell	25.00	12.50	7.50
35	Eddy Baez	25.00	12.50	7.50
36	Teolindo Acosta	25.00	12.50	7.50
37	Ron Theobald	25.00	12.50	7.50
38	Milt Wilcox	30.00	15.00	9.00
39	Cesar Gutierrez	25.00	12.50	7.50
40	Ed Farmer	25.00	12.50	7.50
41	Dario Chirinos	25.00	12.50	7.50
42	Alberto Cambero	25.00	12.50	7.50
43	Eddy Diaz	25.00	12.50	7.50
44	Graciliano Parra	25.00	12.50	7.50
45	Bob Lee	25.00	12.50	7.50
46	Joe Keough	25.00	12.50	7.50
47	Dario Chirinos, Pablo Torrealba	25.00	12.50	7.50
48	Rafael Alvarez	25.00	12.50	7.50
49	Lucio Celis	25.00	12.50	7.50
50	Jose Martinez	25.00	12.50	7.50
51	Faustino Zabala	25.00	12.50	7.50
52	Jose Herrera	25.00	12.50	7.50
53	Monty Montgomery	25.00	12.50	7.50
54	Al Cowens	25.00	12.50	7.50
55	Lara Team	10.00	5.00	3.00
56	Luis Aparicio	60.00	30.00	18.00
57	Virgilio Mata	25.00	12.50	7.50
58	Franklin Moreno	25.00	12.50	7.50
59	Fidel Garcia	25.00	12.50	7.50
60	Victor Montilla	25.00	12.50	7.50
61	Bobby Mitchell	25.00	12.50	7.50
62	Pablo Torrealba	25.00	12.50	7.50
63	Joe Keough	25.00	12.50	7.50
64	Al Cowens	25.00	12.50	7.50
65	Dwight Evans	35.00	17.50	10.50
66	Rick Henninger	25.00	12.50	7.50
67	Lew Krausse	25.00	12.50	7.50
68	George Manz	25.00	12.50	7.50
69	John Lowenstein	25.00	12.50	7.50
70	Juan Quiroz	25.00	12.50	7.50
71	Sebastian Martinez	25.00	12.50	7.50
72	Claudio Urdaneta	25.00	12.50	7.50
73	Barry Raziano	25.00	12.50	7.50
74	Luis Aparicio	60.00	30.00	18.00
75	Lara Team Logo	10.00	5.00	3.00
76	Bobby Mitchell	25.00	12.50	7.50
77	Harold Hunter	25.00	12.50	7.50
78	Dick Pole	25.00	12.50	7.50
79	Carlos Davila	25.00	12.50	7.50
80	Enrique Gonzalez	25.00	12.50	7.50
81	Carlos Pascual	25.00	12.50	7.50
82	Edito Arteaga	25.00	12.50	7.50
83	William Fahey	25.00	12.50	7.50
84	Tomas Gonzalez	25.00	12.50	7.50
85	Rigoberto Mendoza	25.00	12.50	7.50
86	Rafael Jimenez	25.00	12.50	7.50
87	Jesus Aristimuno	25.00	12.50	7.50
88	Armando Ortiz	25.00	12.50	7.50
89	Bill Butler	25.00	12.50	7.50
90	Charles Day	25.00	12.50	7.50
91	Miguel Motolongo	25.00	12.50	7.50
92	Kurt Bavacqua (Bevacqua)	25.00	12.50	7.50
93	Esteban Padron	25.00	12.50	7.50
94	Angel Baez	25.00	12.50	7.50
95	Oscar Zamora	25.00	12.50	7.50
96	Manny Sarmiento	25.00	12.50	7.50
97	Nelson Canas	25.00	12.50	7.50
98	Victor Colina	25.00	12.50	7.50
99	Jerry Pirtle	25.00	12.50	7.50
100	Charles Day	25.00	12.50	7.50
101	Miguel Motolongo	25.00	12.50	7.50
102	Magallanes Group Photo	10.00	5.00	3.00
103	Jim Holt	25.00	12.50	7.50
104	Bob Darwin	25.00	12.50	7.50
105	Magallanes Team Logo	10.00	5.00	3.00
106	Oscar Del Busto	25.00	12.50	7.50
107	Jerry Jones	25.00	12.50	7.50
108	Eddie Leon	25.00	12.50	7.50
109	Armando Ortiz	25.00	12.50	7.50
110	Magallanes Team Photo	10.00	5.00	3.00
111	Magallanes Team Photo	10.00	5.00	3.00
112	Bob Darwin (Puzzle)	10.00	5.00	3.00
113	Bob Darwin	25.00	12.50	7.50
114	Rafael Cariel	25.00	12.50	7.50
115	Bob Darwin (Puzzle)	10.00	5.00	3.00
116	Bob Darwin (Puzzle)	10.00	5.00	3.00
117	Orlando Reyes	25.00	12.50	7.50
118	Edito Arteaga	25.00	12.50	7.50
119	Magallanes Roster (Carlos Pascual)	10.00	5.00	3.00
120	National Anthem	10.00	5.00	3.00
121	Barry Lersch	25.00	12.50	7.50
122	Elias Lugo	25.00	12.50	7.50
123	Simon Barreto	25.00	12.50	7.50
124	Manny Trillo	25.00	12.50	7.50
125	Joe Ferguson	25.00	12.50	7.50
126	Wilibaldo Quintana	25.00	12.50	7.50
127	Edgar Urbina	25.00	12.50	7.50
128	Nelson Garcia	25.00	12.50	7.50
129	Arguilio Freites	25.00	12.50	7.50
130	Carlos Rodriguez	25.00	12.50	7.50
131	Ozzie Virgil	25.00	12.50	7.50
132	Caracas Lions Team Logo	10.00	5.00	3.00
133	Virgilio Velasquez	25.00	12.50	7.50
134	Ed Sprague	25.00	12.50	7.50
135	Nelson Garcia	25.00	12.50	7.50
136	Jose Caldera	25.00	12.50	7.50
137	Antonio Armas	30.00	15.00	9.00
138	Dick Lange	25.00	12.50	7.50
139	Luis Sanz	25.00	12.50	7.50
140	Dave Lopez	25.00	12.50	7.50
141	Ulises Urrieta	25.00	12.50	7.50
142	Urbano Lugo	25.00	12.50	7.50
143	Bo Diaz	25.00	12.50	7.50
144	Andres Barrios	25.00	12.50	7.50
145	Victor Boll	25.00	12.50	7.50
146	Antonio Torres	25.00	12.50	7.50
147	Bert Campaneris	30.00	15.00	9.00
148	Carlos Alfonzo	25.00	12.50	7.50
149	Teodoro Obregon	25.00	12.50	7.50
150	Luis Penalver	25.00	12.50	7.50
151	Jose Ramon Jimenez	25.00	12.50	7.50
152	Cesar Tovar	25.00	12.50	7.50
153	Gonzalo Marquez	25.00	12.50	7.50
154	Dick Baney	25.00	12.50	7.50
155	Ed Armbrister	25.00	12.50	7.50
156	Ramon Webster	25.00	12.50	7.50
157	Francisco Navas	25.00	12.50	7.50
158	Hal McRae	25.00	12.50	7.50
159	Victor Davilillo	25.00	12.50	7.50
160	Geoff Zahn	25.00	12.50	7.50
161	Jesus Camacaro	25.00	12.50	7.50
162	Ruiz, Parra	25.00	12.50	7.50
163	Posada, Dick Billings	25.00	12.50	7.50
164	Tom Grieve	25.00	12.50	7.50
165	Tom Grieve	25.00	12.50	7.50
166	Dick Billings	25.00	12.50	7.50
167	Peter Broberg	25.00	12.50	7.50
168	Victor Fainette	25.00	12.50	7.50
169	Cruz Rodriguez	25.00	12.50	7.50
170	Oscar Gamble	25.00	12.50	7.50
171	Olinto Rojas	25.00	12.50	7.50
172	Nelson Paiva	25.00	12.50	7.50
173	Jackie Brown	25.00	12.50	7.50
174	Gustavo Sposito	25.00	12.50	7.50
175	Levy Ochoa	25.00	12.50	7.50
176	Larry Bittner (Biittner)	25.00	12.50	7.50
177	William Kirkpatrick	25.00	12.50	7.50
178	Nevil Romero	25.00	12.50	7.50
179	Eduardo Benitez	25.00	12.50	7.50
180	Heriberto Lemus	25.00	12.50	7.50
181	Toby Harrah	25.00	12.50	7.50
182	Alfonzo Collazo	25.00	12.50	7.50
183	Jesus Reyes	25.00	12.50	7.50
184	Hely Boscan	25.00	12.50	7.50
185	Mike (Mickey) Scott	25.00	12.50	7.50
186	Roberto Bracho	25.00	12.50	7.50
187	Walter William (Williams)	25.00	12.50	7.50
188	Nevil Romero	25.00	12.50	7.50
189	Jose Alfaro	25.00	12.50	7.50
190	Leonel Carrion	25.00	12.50	7.50
191	Jesus Padron	25.00	12.50	7.50
192	Posada, Chico Carrasquel	25.00	12.50	7.50
193	Domingo Barboza	25.00	12.50	7.50
194	Eduardo Benitez	25.00	12.50	7.50
195	Nidio Sirit	25.00	12.50	7.50
196	Jose Carrao Bracho	25.00	12.50	7.50
197	Levi Ochoa	25.00	12.50	7.50
198	Hely Boscan	25.00	12.50	7.50
199	Victor Fainette, Leonel Carrion	25.00	12.50	7.50
200	Luis Rivas	25.00	12.50	7.50
201	Luis Tiant	25.00	12.50	7.50
202	Graciano Ravelo	25.00	12.50	7.50
203	Hector Artiles	25.00	12.50	7.50
204	Enzo Hernandez	25.00	12.50	7.50
205	Remigio Hermoso	25.00	12.50	7.50
206	Hector Brito	25.00	12.50	7.50
207	Victor Patino	25.00	12.50	7.50
208	Romualdo Blanco	25.00	12.50	7.50
209	Antonio Carrera	25.00	12.50	7.50
210	Euclides Camejo	25.00	12.50	7.50
211	Carlos Moreno	25.00	12.50	7.50
212	Oswaldo Blanco	25.00	12.50	7.50
213	Jorge Padron	25.00	12.50	7.50
214	Manuel Garcia	25.00	12.50	7.50
215	La Guaira Group Photo	10.00	5.00	3.00
216	La Guaira Group Photo	10.00	5.00	3.00
217	Jose Salas	25.00	12.50	7.50
218	Luis Sanchez	25.00	12.50	7.50
219	Raul Velarde	25.00	12.50	7.50
220	Al Bumbry	25.00	12.50	7.50
221	Group Photo	10.00	5.00	3.00
222	Ivan Murrell	25.00	12.50	7.50
223	Jose Cardenal	25.00	12.50	7.50
224	Group Photo	10.00	5.00	3.00
225	Group Photo	10.00	5.00	3.00
226	Angel Bravo	25.00	12.50	7.50
227	Tom Murphy	25.00	12.50	7.50
228	Hector Urbano	25.00	12.50	7.50
229	Camilo Pascual	25.00	12.50	7.50
230	Pat Kelly	25.00	12.50	7.50
231	Robert Marcano	25.00	12.50	7.50
232	Paul Casanova	25.00	12.50	7.50
233	Preston Gomez	25.00	12.50	7.50
234	La Guaira Team Logo	10.00	5.00	3.00
235	Ken Forsch	25.00	12.50	7.50
236	Luis Tiant (Puzzle)	10.00	5.00	3.00
237	Luis Tiant (Puzzle)	10.00	5.00	3.00
238	Dionel Durand	25.00	12.50	7.50
239	Luis Tiant (Puzzle)	10.00	5.00	3.00
240	Luis Tiant (Puzzle)	10.00	5.00	3.00
241	Jim Rooker (Puzzle)	10.00	5.00	3.00
242	Jim Rooker (Puzzle)	10.00	5.00	3.00
243	William Parker	25.00	12.50	7.50
244	Jim Rooker (Puzzle)	10.00	5.00	3.00
245	Jim Rooker (Puzzle)	10.00	5.00	3.00
246	Jose Herrera	25.00	12.50	7.50
247	Aurelio Monteagudo	25.00	12.50	7.50
248	Ivan Murrell	25.00	12.50	7.50
249	Roster (Preston Gomez)	10.00	5.00	3.00

1973 Venezuelan League Stickers

These stickers were made for collection in an album and as such are typically found in low grade and/or with evidence of once having been so mounted. Several gaps in the reported checklist require further research. Many former and future Major Leaguers are included in the issue. The basic player stickers have color photos surrounded by a multi-color border with the team name at top and the player name at bottom. Stickers are about 2-1/2" x 3-1/2" and numbered on front. A colorful album to house the set was also issued.

		NM	EX	VG
Common Player:		20.00	10.00	6.00
Album:		75.00	40.00	25.00
1	Orlando Galindo	20.00	10.00	6.00
2	William Castillo	20.00	10.00	6.00
3	Everest Contramaestre	20.00	10.00	6.00
4	Luis Gonzalez	20.00	10.00	6.00
5	Jose Lopez	20.00	10.00	6.00
6	Cesar Orea	20.00	10.00	6.00
7	Luis H. Silva	20.00	10.00	6.00
8	Victor Jimenez	20.00	10.00	6.00
9	David Torres	20.00	10.00	6.00
10	Jose Torres	20.00	10.00	6.00
11	Ramon Velasquez	20.00	10.00	6.00
12	Jesus Avila	20.00	10.00	6.00
13	Carlos Loreto	20.00	10.00	6.00
14	Jesus Padron	20.00	10.00	6.00
15	Don Osborne	20.00	10.00	6.00
16	John Glass	20.00	10.00	6.00
17	Teolindo Acosta	20.00	10.00	6.00
18	Jim Todd	20.00	10.00	6.00
19	Roberto Munoz	20.00	10.00	6.00
20	Pete Lakock (LaCock)	20.00	10.00	6.00
21	Francisco Leandro	20.00	10.00	6.00
22	Jesus Rizales	20.00	10.00	6.00
23	Enos Cabell	25.00	12.50	7.50
24	Adrian Garret (Garrett)	20.00	10.00	6.00
25	Kurt Bavaqua (Bevacqua)	20.00	10.00	6.00
26	Jerry Moses	20.00	10.00	6.00
27	Jim Wiloughby (Willoughby)	20.00	10.00	6.00
28	Joel Youngblood	20.00	10.00	6.00
29	Milt Wilcox	25.00	12.50	7.50
30	Cesar Gutierrez	20.00	10.00	6.00
31	Efrain Urquiola	20.00	10.00	6.00
32	Carlos Pascual	20.00	10.00	6.00
33	Julio Bracho	20.00	10.00	6.00
34	Rafael Velasquez	20.00	10.00	6.00
35	Eddy Baez	20.00	10.00	6.00
36	Daniel Dubuc	20.00	10.00	6.00
37	Angel Leon	20.00	10.00	6.00
38	Angel Vargas	20.00	10.00	6.00
39	Motis Romero	20.00	10.00	6.00
40	Graciliano Parra	20.00	10.00	6.00
41	John Lowenstein	20.00	10.00	6.00
42	Nelson Garcia	20.00	10.00	6.00
43	Richard Burleson	25.00	12.50	7.50
44	Doug DeCinces	35.00	17.50	10.50
45	Eugene Martin	20.00	10.00	6.00
46	Jim Cox	20.00	10.00	6.00
47	Mike Adams	20.00	10.00	6.00
48	Richard Henninger	20.00	10.00	6.00
49	Sebastian Martinez	20.00	10.00	6.00
50	Lucio Celis	20.00	10.00	6.00
51	Alberto Cambero	20.00	10.00	6.00
52	Claudio Urdaneta	20.00	10.00	6.00
53	Victor Montilla	20.00	10.00	6.00
54	Pastor Perez	20.00	10.00	6.00
55	Enrique Gonzalez	20.00	10.00	6.00
56	Andres Barrios	20.00	10.00	6.00
57	Diego Herrera	20.00	10.00	6.00
58	Luis Aparicio	60.00	30.00	18.00
59	Teodoro Obregon	20.00	10.00	6.00
60	Dave Johnson	25.00	12.50	7.50
61	Roger Polanco	20.00	10.00	6.00
62	Ray Miller	20.00	10.00	6.00
63	Craig Caskey	20.00	10.00	6.00
64	David Wallace	20.00	10.00	6.00
65	Lara Team Logo	10.00	5.00	3.00
66	Herbert Hutson	20.00	10.00	6.00
67	Edgar Carusi	20.00	10.00	6.00
68	Luis Aponte	20.00	10.00	6.00
69	Joel Alcala	20.00	10.00	6.00
70	Dario Chirinos	20.00	10.00	6.00
71	Arnaldo Alvarado	20.00	10.00	6.00
72	Jose Bekis	20.00	10.00	6.00
73	Bill Moran	20.00	10.00	6.00
74	Steve McCartney	20.00	10.00	6.00
75	Lara Action	10.00	5.00	3.00
76	Rafael Alvarez	20.00	10.00	6.00
77	Juan Quiroz	20.00	10.00	6.00
78	Jim Rice	125.00	62.00	37.00
79	Ivan Murrel (Murrell)	20.00	10.00	6.00
80	James McKee	20.00	10.00	6.00
81	Rafael Cariel	20.00	10.00	6.00
82	George Theodore	20.00	10.00	6.00
83	Esteban Padron	20.00	10.00	6.00
84	Manuel Gonzalez	20.00	10.00	6.00
85	Edito Arteaga	20.00	10.00	6.00
86	Gus Gil	20.00	10.00	6.00
87	Oswaldo Olivares	20.00	10.00	6.00
88	Nelson Canas	20.00	10.00	6.00
89	Jesus Aristimuno	20.00	10.00	6.00
90	Orlando Reyes	20.00	10.00	6.00
91	Armando Ortiz	20.00	10.00	6.00
92	Gregorio Machado	20.00	10.00	6.00
93	Victor Colina	20.00	10.00	6.00
94	Alexis Ramirez	20.00	10.00	6.00
95	Jose Rios-Chiripa	20.00	10.00	6.00
96	Ed Napoleon	20.00	10.00	6.00
97	Bob Bailor	25.00	12.50	7.50
98	Dave Agustine (Augustine)	20.00	10.00	6.00
99	Bob Darwin	20.00	10.00	6.00
100	Gilberto Marcano	20.00	10.00	6.00
101	Jim Frey	25.00	12.50	7.50
102	Steve Braun	20.00	10.00	6.00
103	Don Hood	20.00	10.00	6.00
104	Mike Reinbach	20.00	10.00	6.00
105	Thomas Dettore	20.00	10.00	6.00
106	Wayne Garland	20.00	10.00	6.00
107	Mark Weens	20.00	10.00	6.00
108	Nelson Paiva	20.00	10.00	6.00
109	Manuel Sarmiento	20.00	10.00	6.00
110	Miguel Motolongo	20.00	10.00	6.00
111	Miguel Navas	20.00	10.00	6.00
112	Angel Baez	20.00	10.00	6.00
113	Raul Ortega	20.00	10.00	6.00
114	Humberto Montero	20.00	10.00	6.00
115	Tomas Gonzalez	20.00	10.00	6.00
116	Ruben Cabrera	20.00	10.00	6.00
117	Flores Bolivar	20.00	10.00	6.00
118	Felix Rodriguez	20.00	10.00	6.00
119	Ali Arape	20.00	10.00	6.00
120	Alexis Heredia	20.00	10.00	6.00
121	Arguilio Freites	20.00	10.00	6.00
122	Alfredo Ortiz	20.00	10.00	6.00
123	Simon Barreto	20.00	10.00	6.00
124	Urbano Lugo	20.00	10.00	6.00
125	Bo Diaz	20.00	10.00	6.00
126	Victor Boll	20.00	10.00	6.00
127	Jose Vinay Caldera	20.00	10.00	6.00
128	Leopoldo Tovar	20.00	10.00	6.00
129	Wilibaldo Quintana	20.00	10.00	6.00
130	Edgar Urbina	20.00	10.00	6.00
131	Ulises Urrieta	20.00	10.00	6.00
132	Antonio Torres	20.00	10.00	6.00
133	Luis Penalver	20.00	10.00	6.00
134	Heriberto Morillo	20.00	10.00	6.00
135	Tony Pacheco	20.00	10.00	6.00
136	Victor Davalillo	20.00	10.00	6.00
137	Jose Martinez	20.00	10.00	6.00
138	Jacinto Betancourt	20.00	10.00	6.00
139	Antonio Armas	40.00	20.00	12.00
140	Cesar Tovar	20.00	10.00	6.00
141	Jerry Johnson	20.00	10.00	6.00
142	Mike Anderson	20.00	10.00	6.00
143	Gonzalo Marquez	20.00	10.00	6.00
144	Peter Koegel	20.00	10.00	6.00
145	Pat Dobson	20.00	10.00	6.00
146	Craig Robinson	20.00	10.00	6.00
147	Luis Saez	20.00	10.00	6.00
148	Francisco Navas	20.00	10.00	6.00
149	Elias Lugo	20.00	10.00	6.00
150	Pablo Torrealba	20.00	10.00	6.00
151	Tom Grieve	20.00	10.00	6.00
152	Manny Trillo	40.00	20.00	12.00
153	Ed Sprague	20.00	10.00	6.00
154	Virgilio Velasquez	20.00	10.00	6.00
155	Dave Hamilton	20.00	10.00	6.00
156	Rafael Jimenez	20.00	10.00	6.00
157	Ubaldo Heredia	20.00	10.00	6.00
158	Rich Dempsey	30.00	15.00	9.00
159	Bill Parson (Parsons)	20.00	10.00	6.00
160	Caracas Leones	10.00	5.00	3.00
161	Gene Garber	25.00	12.50	7.50
162	Frank White	35.00	17.50	10.50
163	John Buck Martinez	20.00	10.00	6.00
164	Manuel Garcia	20.00	10.00	6.00
165	Jesus Padron	20.00	10.00	6.00
166	Oscar Gamble	25.00	12.50	7.50
167	Nelson Castellanos	20.00	10.00	6.00
168	Leo Posada	20.00	10.00	6.00
169	Eduardo Benitez	20.00	10.00	6.00
170	Luis Rivas	20.00	10.00	6.00
171	Alfonso Collazo	20.00	10.00	6.00
172	Levy Ochoa	20.00	10.00	6.00
173	Heriberto Lemus	20.00	10.00	6.00
174	Domingo Barboza	20.00	10.00	6.00
175	Jesus Reyes Barrios	20.00	10.00	6.00
176	Inal Fainete	20.00	10.00	6.00
177	Nidio Sirit	20.00	10.00	6.00
178	Nelson Paiva	20.00	10.00	6.00
179	Alfonso Carrasquel	35.00	17.50	10.50
180	Heli Boscan	20.00	10.00	6.00
181	Leonel Carrion	20.00	10.00	6.00
182	Jose Bracho	20.00	10.00	6.00
183	Gustavo Sposito	20.00	10.00	6.00
184	Iran Paz	20.00	10.00	6.00
185	Rich Reese	20.00	10.00	6.00
186	Al Cowans (Cowens)	25.00	12.50	7.50
187	Zulio Group Photo	10.00	5.00	3.00
188	Leo Posada, Alfonso Carrasquel	15.00	7.50	4.50
189	Octavio Rojas	20.00	10.00	6.00
190	Orlando Reyes	20.00	10.00	6.00
191	Mickey Scott	20.00	10.00	6.00
192	Harold King	20.00	10.00	6.00
193	Eduardo Acosta	20.00	10.00	6.00
194	Carlos Alfonso	20.00	10.00	6.00
195	Jose Lopez	20.00	10.00	6.00
196	Jerry Martin	20.00	10.00	6.00
197	Craig Kusick	20.00	10.00	6.00
198	Charles Murray	20.00	10.00	6.00
199	Alexis Corro	20.00	10.00	6.00
200	Jose Luis Alfaro	20.00	10.00	6.00
201	Juan Fco. Monasterio	20.00	10.00	6.00
202	Oscar Zamora	20.00	10.00	6.00
203	Ramon Moreno	20.00	10.00	6.00
204	Carlos Castillo	20.00	10.00	6.00
205	Ken Forsch	20.00	10.00	6.00
206	Leroy Stanton	20.00	10.00	6.00
207	Nevil Romero	20.00	10.00	6.00
208	Romualdo Blanco	20.00	10.00	6.00
209	Remigio Hermoso	20.00	10.00	6.00
210	Paul Casanova	20.00	10.00	6.00
211	Oswaldo Blanco	20.00	10.00	6.00
212	Oswaldo Troconis	20.00	10.00	6.00
213	Antonio Pipo Correa	20.00	10.00	6.00
214	Euclides Camejo	20.00	10.00	6.00
215	Dionel Duran	20.00	10.00	6.00
216	Hector Brito	20.00	10.00	6.00
217	Reinaldo Cordeiro	20.00	10.00	6.00
218	Jose Herrera	20.00	10.00	6.00
219	Hector Urbano	20.00	10.00	6.00
220	Jose Salas	20.00	10.00	6.00
221	Robert Marcano	20.00	10.00	6.00
222	Enzo Hernandez	20.00	10.00	6.00
223	Angel Bravo	20.00	10.00	6.00
224	Tomas Liscano	20.00	10.00	6.00
225	James Granford	20.00	10.00	6.00
226	Luis Salazar	20.00	10.00	6.00
227	Carlos Moreno	20.00	10.00	6.00
228	Manuel Malave	20.00	10.00	6.00
229	Al Bumbry	25.00	12.50	7.50
230	Luis Sanchez	20.00	10.00	6.00
231	Graziano Ravelo	20.00	10.00	6.00
232	La Guaira Tiburones Logo	10.00	5.00	3.00
233	John Jetter (Jeter)	20.00	10.00	6.00
234	Unknown			
235	Orlando Martinez	20.00	10.00	6.00
236	Tom Griffin	20.00	10.00	6.00
237	Lee Pitlock	20.00	10.00	6.00
238	Ray Burry	20.00	10.00	6.00
239	Preston Gomez	20.00	10.00	6.00
240	Aurelio Monteagudo	20.00	10.00	6.00
241	Carvajal/Bat Boy	20.00	10.00	6.00
242-249	Unknown			
250	Eduardo Benitez (a-t)	20.00	10.00	6.00
251	Ted (Tom) Heintzelman (b-t)	20.00	10.00	6.00
252	Ossie Virgil (c-t)	25.00	12.50	7.50
253	Alan Closter (d-t)	20.00	10.00	6.00
254	Carlos Avila (e-t)	20.00	10.00	6.00
255	David Concepcion (g-t)	40.00	20.00	12.00
256	Enrique Colina (h-t)	20.00	10.00	6.00
257	Damaso Blanco (a-n)	20.00	10.00	6.00
258	George Manz (a-c)	20.00	10.00	6.00
259	Peter MacKanin (b-c)	20.00	10.00	6.00
260	Neldy Castillo (c-c)	20.00	10.00	6.00
261	Leovanny Baez (a-z)	20.00	10.00	6.00
262	Mike Easler (b-z)	25.00	12.50	7.50
263	Peter Broberg (c-z)	20.00	10.00	6.00
264	Reggie Cleveland (d-z)	20.00	10.00	6.00
265	Stan Perzanowky (Perzanowski) (e-z)	20.00	10.00	6.00
266	Jerry Terrel (Terrell) (f-z)	20.00	10.00	6.00
267	Toby Harrah (h-z)	30.00	15.00	9.00
268	Franklyn Moreno (y-z)	20.00	10.00	6.00
269-275	Unknown			

1974 Venezuelan League Stickers

The 1974-75 winter league set of Venezuelan League stickers is a dead ringer for the 1968 Topps baseball cards. About 2-3/8" x 3-3/16", the stickers have photos framed in orange-mottled borders. The team name and position are in a circle at bottom, along with the player name in two colors. Because they were intended to be mounted in an accompanying album, the backs are blank. Because so many of the stickers were once pasted into albums, and due to unfavorable climactic conditions, high-grade examples of Venezuelan stickers from the era are particularly scarce.

		NM	EX	VG
Complete Set (275):		1,500	750.00	450.00
Common Player:		20.00	10.00	6.00
Album:		75.00	40.00	25.00
1	Aragua Team Photo	10.00	5.00	3.00
2	Aragua Team Photo	10.00	5.00	3.00
3	Aragua Team Logo	10.00	5.00	3.00
4	Dave Concepcion	40.00	20.00	12.00
5	Ramon Velazquez	20.00	10.00	6.00
6	Carlos Orea	20.00	10.00	6.00
7	Francisco Leandro	20.00	10.00	6.00
8	Angel Hernandez	20.00	10.00	6.00
9	Armando Ortiz	20.00	10.00	6.00
10	Carlos Pascual	20.00	10.00	6.00
11	Argua Action	10.00	5.00	3.00
12	Milton Wilcox	25.00	12.50	7.50
13	Don Hood	20.00	10.00	6.00
14	Timothy Hosley	20.00	10.00	6.00
15	Teolindo Acosta	20.00	10.00	6.00
16	William Castillo	20.00	10.00	6.00
17	Aragua Action	10.00	5.00	3.00
18	Jesus Padron	20.00	10.00	6.00
19	Enos Cabell	25.00	12.50	7.50
20	Luis Silva	20.00	10.00	6.00
21	Aragua Action	10.00	5.00	3.00
22	Aragua Action	10.00	5.00	3.00
23	Joel Youngblood	25.00	12.50	7.50
24	Angel Vargas	20.00	10.00	6.00
25	Carlos Avila	20.00	10.00	6.00
26	Phil Gardner (Garner)	25.00	12.50	7.50
27	James Willoughby	20.00	10.00	6.00
28	Daniel Dubuc	20.00	10.00	6.00
29	Pancho	20.00	10.00	6.00
30	Aragua Action	10.00	5.00	3.00
31	Eastwick Rawlings (Rawly Eastwick)	25.00	12.50	7.50

32	David Torres	20.00	10.00	6.00
33	Robert Flynn	20.00	10.00	6.00
34	Duane Kuiper	25.00	12.50	7.50
35	Jesus Avila	20.00	10.00	6.00
36	Aragua Action	10.00	5.00	3.00
37	Aragua Action	10.00	5.00	3.00
38	Roberto Munoz	20.00	10.00	6.00
39	Eduardo Benitez	20.00	10.00	6.00
40	Aragua Action	10.00	5.00	3.00
41	Adrian Garret (Garrett)	20.00	10.00	6.00
42	Julio Bracho	20.00	10.00	6.00
43	Juan Quiroz	20.00	10.00	6.00
44	Angel Leon	20.00	10.00	6.00
45	Ossie Virgil	30.00	15.00	9.00
46	Lara Team Photo	10.00	5.00	3.00
47	Lara Team Photo	10.00	5.00	3.00
48	Lara Team Logo	10.00	5.00	3.00
49	Andres Barrios	20.00	10.00	6.00
50	Pastor Perez	20.00	10.00	6.00
51	Peter Koegel	20.00	10.00	6.00
52	Lara Action	10.00	5.00	3.00
53	Lowell Palmer	20.00	10.00	6.00
54	Alberto Cambero	20.00	10.00	6.00
55	Frank Snook	20.00	10.00	6.00
56	Steve McCartney	20.00	10.00	6.00
57	Lara Action	10.00	5.00	3.00
58	Dario Chirinos	20.00	10.00	6.00
59	Lara Action	10.00	5.00	3.00
60	Jim Cox	20.00	10.00	6.00
61	Terry Whitfield	20.00	10.00	6.00
62	Nelson Garcia	20.00	10.00	6.00
63	Lara Action	10.00	5.00	3.00
64	Sebastian Martinez	20.00	10.00	6.00
65	Lara Action	10.00	5.00	3.00
66	Rick Sawyer	20.00	10.00	6.00
67	Enrique Gonzalez	20.00	10.00	6.00
68	Tippy Martinez	30.00	15.00	9.00
69	Rafael Jimenez	20.00	10.00	6.00
70	Lara Action	10.00	5.00	3.00
71	Larvell Blanks	20.00	10.00	6.00
72	Franklin Tua	20.00	10.00	6.00
73	Craig Skok	20.00	10.00	6.00
74	Basilio Alvarado	20.00	10.00	6.00
75	Blas Arriechi	20.00	10.00	6.00
76	Dave Pagan	20.00	10.00	6.00
77	Roger Polanco	20.00	10.00	6.00
78	John Lowenstein	20.00	10.00	6.00
79	Francisco Leandro	20.00	10.00	6.00
80	Lucio Celis	20.00	10.00	6.00
81	Lara Action	10.00	5.00	3.00
82	Teodoro Obregon	20.00	10.00	6.00
83	Luis Aponte	20.00	10.00	6.00
84	Roberto Cox	40.00	20.00	12.00
85	Magallanes Team Photo	10.00	5.00	3.00
86	Magallanes Team Photo	10.00	5.00	3.00
87	Magallanes Team Logo	10.00	5.00	3.00
88	Oswaldo Olivares	20.00	10.00	6.00
89	Bob Bailor	25.00	12.50	7.50
90	Ali Arape	20.00	10.00	6.00
91	Jesus Aristimuno	20.00	10.00	6.00
92	Bob Andrews	20.00	10.00	6.00
93	Magallanes Action	10.00	5.00	3.00
94	Rick Stelmaszek	20.00	10.00	6.00
95	Damaso Blanco	20.00	10.00	6.00
96	Graciliano Parra	20.00	10.00	6.00
97	Merv Rettemund (Rettenmund)	25.00	12.50	7.50
98	Don Baylor	45.00	22.00	13.50
99	William Lister	20.00	10.00	6.00
100	Magallanes Action	10.00	5.00	3.00
101	Gregorio Machado	20.00	10.00	6.00
102	Doug Bair	20.00	10.00	6.00
103	Gilberto Marcano	20.00	10.00	6.00
104	Magallanes Action	10.00	5.00	3.00
105	Jim Sadowski	20.00	10.00	6.00
106	Miguel Nava	20.00	10.00	6.00
107	Ken (Kent) Tekulve	40.00	20.00	12.00
108	Wayne Garland	20.00	10.00	6.00
109	Magallanes Action	10.00	5.00	3.00
110	Alexis Ramirez	20.00	10.00	6.00
111	Dave Parker	60.00	30.00	18.00
112	Bob Veale	20.00	10.00	6.00
113	Manuel Sarmiento	20.00	10.00	6.00
114	Alberto Pedroza	20.00	10.00	6.00
115	Ruben Cabrera	20.00	10.00	6.00
116	Felix Rodriguez	20.00	10.00	6.00
117	Magallanes Action	10.00	5.00	3.00
118	Humberto Montero	20.00	10.00	6.00
119	Manuel Gonzalez	20.00	10.00	6.00
120	D. Flores	20.00	10.00	6.00
121	Jim Holt	20.00	10.00	6.00
122	Rafael Cariel	20.00	10.00	6.00
123	Magallanes Action	10.00	5.00	3.00
124	Deisi Bolivar	20.00	10.00	6.00
125	Edito Arteaga	20.00	10.00	6.00
126	Gustavo Gil	20.00	10.00	6.00
127	Larry Demeris (Demery)	20.00	10.00	6.00
128	Nelson Paiva	20.00	10.00	6.00
129	Steve Demeter	20.00	10.00	6.00
130	Caracas Leones Team Photo	10.00	5.00	3.00
131	Caracas Leones Team Photo	10.00	5.00	3.00
132	Caracas Leones Team Logo	10.00	5.00	3.00
133	Antonio Armas	40.00	20.00	12.00
134	Richard Dempsey	40.00	20.00	12.00
135	Toribio Garboza	20.00	10.00	6.00
136	Neldy Castillo	20.00	10.00	6.00
137	Ubaldo Heredia	20.00	10.00	6.00
138	Caracas Action	10.00	5.00	3.00
139	Jesus Marcano Trillo	40.00	20.00	12.00
140	Victor Albury	20.00	10.00	6.00
141	Uknown			
142	Peter Broberg	20.00	10.00	6.00
143	Alfredo Ortiz	20.00	10.00	6.00
144	Leopoldo Tovar	20.00	10.00	6.00
145	Caracas Action	10.00	5.00	3.00
146	Tom Buskey	20.00	10.00	6.00
147	Virgilio Velasquez	20.00	10.00	6.00
148	Cesar Tovar	20.00	10.00	6.00
149	Caracas Stadium	10.00	5.00	3.00
150	Don Stanhouse	20.00	10.00	6.00
151	Edgar Urbina	20.00	10.00	6.00
152	Pablo Torrealba	20.00	10.00	6.00
153	Jack Heidemann	20.00	10.00	6.00
154	Caracas Action	10.00	5.00	3.00
155	Luis Sanz	20.00	10.00	6.00
156	Gonzalo Marquez	20.00	10.00	6.00
157	Victor Davilillo	20.00	10.00	6.00
158	Bo Diaz	20.00	10.00	6.00
159	Caracas Action	10.00	5.00	3.00
160	Bill Butler	20.00	10.00	6.00
161	Elias Lugo	20.00	10.00	6.00
162	Tom Grieve	20.00	10.00	6.00
163	Caracas Action	10.00	5.00	3.00
164	Antonio Torres	20.00	10.00	6.00
165	Luis Penalver	20.00	10.00	6.00
166	Lenny Randle	20.00	10.00	6.00
167	Juan Gonzalez	20.00	10.00	6.00
168	Chuck Dobson	20.00	10.00	6.00
169	Urbano Lugo	20.00	10.00	6.00
170	Francisco Navas	20.00	10.00	6.00
171	Caracas Action	10.00	5.00	3.00
172	Jacinto Betancourt	20.00	10.00	6.00
173	Camilo Pascual	30.00	15.00	9.00
174	Frank White	30.00	15.00	9.00
175	Urbano Quintana	20.00	10.00	6.00
176	Jose Caldera	20.00	10.00	6.00
177	Caracas Action	10.00	5.00	3.00
178	Ulises Urrieta	20.00	10.00	6.00
179	Tomas Pacheco	20.00	10.00	6.00
180	La Guaira Tiburones Team Photo	10.00	5.00	3.00
181	La Guaira Tiburones Team Photo	10.00	5.00	3.00
182	La Guaira Tiburones Team Photo	10.00	5.00	3.00
183	Angel Bravo	20.00	10.00	6.00
184	Al Bumbry	25.00	12.50	7.50
185	Aurelio Monteagudo	20.00	10.00	6.00
186	Carlos Moreno	20.00	10.00	6.00
187	La Guaira Action	10.00	5.00	3.00
188	Hector Brito	20.00	10.00	6.00
189	Leroy Stanton	20.00	10.00	6.00
190	Romo Blanco	20.00	10.00	6.00
191	Marquina para Gorrias	10.00	5.00	3.00
192	Luis M. Sanchez	20.00	10.00	6.00
193	La Guaria Action	10.00	5.00	3.00
194	Jose Herrera	20.00	10.00	6.00
195	Victor Colina	20.00	10.00	6.00
196	Tiburones Team Bus	10.00	5.00	3.00
197	Jose Salas	20.00	10.00	6.00
198	La Guaira Action	10.00	5.00	3.00
199	Enzo Hernandez	20.00	10.00	6.00
200	Tomas Liscano	20.00	10.00	6.00
201	Paul Casanova	20.00	10.00	6.00
202	Machine	10.00	5.00	3.00
203	Graziano Ravelo	20.00	10.00	6.00
204	Ice Maker	10.00	5.00	3.00
205	Roland (Rowland) Office	20.00	10.00	6.00
206	Clubhouse	10.00	5.00	3.00
207	La Guaira Action	10.00	5.00	3.00
208	Dusty Baker	45.00	22.00	13.50
209	Replacements	10.00	5.00	3.00
210	Roric Harrison	20.00	10.00	6.00
211	Tom House	20.00	10.00	6.00
212	Jesus Aquino	20.00	10.00	6.00
213	Machine	10.00	5.00	3.00
214	La Guaira Action	10.00	5.00	3.00
215	Juan Monasterios	20.00	10.00	6.00
216	Angel Remigio Hermoso	20.00	10.00	6.00
217	Machine	10.00	5.00	3.00
218	Oswaldo Blanco	20.00	10.00	6.00
219	Infrared Light	10.00	5.00	3.00
220	Roberto Marcano	20.00	10.00	6.00
221	La Guaira Action	10.00	5.00	3.00
222	Jose Carvajal	20.00	10.00	6.00
223	Victor Patino	20.00	10.00	6.00
224	James Bird	20.00	10.00	6.00
225	La Guaira Action	10.00	5.00	3.00
226	Roland Sonny Jackson	25.00	12.50	7.50
227	Oscar Zamora	20.00	10.00	6.00
228	Antonio Pipo Correa	20.00	10.00	6.00
229	Manuel Malave	20.00	10.00	6.00
230	Nap Reyes	20.00	10.00	6.00
231	Zulia Aguilas Team Photo	10.00	5.00	3.00
232	Zluia Aguilas Team Photo	10.00	5.00	3.00
233	Zulia Aguilas Team Logo	10.00	5.00	3.00
234	Levy Ochoa	20.00	10.00	6.00
235	Billy Moran	20.00	10.00	6.00
236	Iran Paz	20.00	10.00	6.00
237	Alexis Corro	20.00	10.00	6.00
238	Zulia Action	10.00	5.00	3.00
239	Gus Sposito	20.00	10.00	6.00
240	Orlando Reyes	20.00	10.00	6.00
241	Carlos Alonso	20.00	10.00	6.00
242	Craig Kusick	20.00	10.00	6.00
243	Zulia Action	10.00	5.00	3.00
244	Domingo Barboza	20.00	10.00	6.00
245	Leonel Carrion	20.00	10.00	6.00
246	Jose Lopez	20.00	10.00	6.00
247	Bill Kirkpatrick	20.00	10.00	6.00
248	Alfonso Carrasquel	20.00	10.00	6.00
249	Richard Billings	20.00	10.00	6.00
250	Alfonzo Collazo	20.00	10.00	6.00
251	Orlando Ramirez	20.00	10.00	6.00
252	Ralph (Mickey) Scott	20.00	10.00	6.00
253	Luis Aparicio	60.00	30.00	18.00
254	Julio Bracho	20.00	10.00	6.00
255	Zulia Action	10.00	5.00	3.00
256	B. Jones	20.00	10.00	6.00
257	Heli Ramon Boscan	20.00	10.00	6.00
258	David Clyde	20.00	10.00	6.00
259	Cesar Gutierrez	20.00	10.00	6.00
260	Bob Randall	20.00	10.00	6.00
261	Jesus Reyes Barrios	20.00	10.00	6.00
262	Jose L. Alfaro	20.00	10.00	6.00
263	Claudio Urdaneta	20.00	10.00	6.00
264	Zulia Action	10.00	5.00	3.00
265	James Sundberg	30.00	15.00	9.00
266	Simon Barreto	20.00	10.00	6.00
267	Anthony Scott	20.00	10.00	6.00
268	Nidio Sirit	20.00	10.00	6.00
269	Zulia Action	10.00	5.00	3.00
270	Zulia Action	10.00	5.00	3.00
271	Leovanni Baez	20.00	10.00	6.00
272	Jefrey (Jeffrey) Terpko	20.00	10.00	6.00
273	Stan Perzanowski	20.00	10.00	6.00
274	Mike Easler	25.00	12.50	7.50
275	Jackie Moore	20.00	10.00	6.00

1976 Venezuelan League Stickers

The basic player stickers utizilize a design very similar to Topps' 1975 baseball cards, with player photos surrounded by a colorful border with the team name in large outline letters at top and the position is a baseball at bottom. Stickers are 2-3/8" x 3-3/16" and numbered on front. Like other Latin issues of the era, they are seldom available in high grade due to their intended useage and climactic conditions. Most of the stickers after #217 are specialty pieces with action photos, non-player subjects, multiple players, etc. A colorful album to house the set was also issued.

		NM	EX	VG
Complete Set (330):		2,000	1,000	600.00
Common Player:		20.00	10.00	6.00
Album:		75.00	40.00	25.00
1	Ossie Virgil	30.00	15.00	9.00
2	Patato Pascual	20.00	10.00	6.00
3	Jesus Avila	20.00	10.00	6.00
4	Raul Ortega	20.00	10.00	6.00
5	Dave Concepcion	40.00	20.00	12.00
6	Jesus Araujo	20.00	10.00	6.00
7	Preston Hanna	20.00	10.00	6.00
8	Victor Davilillo	20.00	10.00	6.00
9	Jesus Padron	20.00	10.00	6.00
10	Joseph Sdeb (Zdeb)	20.00	10.00	6.00
11	Alfredo Ortiz	20.00	10.00	6.00
12	Teolindo Acosta	20.00	10.00	6.00
13	Cesar Tovar	20.00	10.00	6.00
14	Craig Kusick	20.00	10.00	6.00
15	Angel Hernandez	20.00	10.00	6.00
16	Roberto Munoz	20.00	10.00	6.00
17	Fred Andrews	20.00	10.00	6.00
18	Rafael Alvarez	20.00	10.00	6.00
19	Luis Aparicio	50.00	25.00	15.00
20	Jeffrey Newman	20.00	10.00	6.00
21	Tommy Sant (Sandt)	20.00	10.00	6.00
22	Simon Barreto	20.00	10.00	6.00
23	Willie Norwood	20.00	10.00	6.00
24	Juan Quiroz	20.00	10.00	6.00
25	Douglas Capilla	20.00	10.00	6.00
26	William Butler	20.00	10.00	6.00
27	William Castillo	20.00	10.00	6.00
28	Robert Maneely	20.00	10.00	6.00
29	Peter Bromberg (Broberg)	20.00	10.00	6.00
30	Jesse Jefferson	20.00	10.00	6.00
31	Carlos Avila	20.00	10.00	6.00
32	Aragua Action	10.00	5.00	3.00
33	Aragua Action	10.00	5.00	3.00
34	Terry Whitfield	20.00	10.00	6.00
35	Aragua Action	10.00	5.00	3.00
36	Gary Lance	20.00	10.00	6.00
37	Robert Cox	40.00	20.00	12.00
38	Leo Posada	20.00	10.00	6.00
39	Lucio Celis	20.00	10.00	6.00
40	Enrique Gonzalez	20.00	10.00	6.00
41	Jose Musiu Lopez	20.00	10.00	6.00
42	Jose Sandoval	20.00	10.00	6.00
43	Victor Correll	20.00	10.00	6.00
44	Pedro Lobaton	20.00	10.00	6.00
45	Jim Norris	20.00	10.00	6.00
46	Luis Aponte	20.00	10.00	6.00
47	Orlando Gonzalez	20.00	10.00	6.00
48	Edguardo Benitez	20.00	10.00	6.00
49	George Zeber	20.00	10.00	6.00
50	Carlos Rodriguez	20.00	10.00	6.00
51	Graig (Craig) Robinson	20.00	10.00	6.00
52	Hernan Silva	20.00	10.00	6.00
53	Bob Oliver	20.00	10.00	6.00
54	Jose Herrera	20.00	10.00	6.00
55	Pete Mackanin	20.00	10.00	6.00
56	Roger Polanco	20.00	10.00	6.00
57	Lara Stadium	10.00	5.00	3.00
58	Arnaldo Alvarado	20.00	10.00	6.00
59	Ron Selak	20.00	10.00	6.00
60	Nelson Canas	20.00	10.00	6.00
61	John Sutton	20.00	10.00	6.00
62	Nelson Garcia	20.00	10.00	6.00
63	Victor Patino	20.00	10.00	6.00
64	Francisco Navas	20.00	10.00	6.00
65	Robert Polinsky	20.00	10.00	6.00

66	Franklin Tua	20.00	10.00	6.00
67	Oscar Zamora	20.00	10.00	6.00
68	David Torres	20.00	10.00	6.00
69	Eddie Baez	20.00	10.00	6.00
70	Walter Williams	25.00	12.50	7.50
71	Cloyd Boyer	25.00	12.50	7.50
72	Carl (Garth?) Iorg	20.00	10.00	6.00
73	Pat Corrales	20.00	10.00	6.00
74	Alfonso Carrasquel	20.00	10.00	6.00
75	Antonio Torres	20.00	10.00	6.00
76	Camilo Pascual	30.00	15.00	9.00
77	Antonio Armas	40.00	20.00	12.00
78	Baudilio Diaz	20.00	10.00	6.00
79	Gary Beare	20.00	10.00	6.00
80	Steve Barr	20.00	10.00	6.00
81	Toribio Garboza	20.00	10.00	6.00
82	Mike Bassik (Bacsik)	20.00	10.00	6.00
83	Diego Segui	20.00	10.00	6.00
84	Jack Bastable	20.00	10.00	6.00
85	Ubaldo Heredia	20.00	10.00	6.00
86	Warren Cromartie	25.00	12.50	7.50
87	Elias Lugo	20.00	10.00	6.00
88	Mike (Mick) Kelleher	20.00	10.00	6.00
89	Marcano Trillo	40.00	20.00	12.00
90	Lenny Randle	20.00	10.00	6.00
91	Gonzalo Marquez	20.00	10.00	6.00
92	Jim Sadowski	20.00	10.00	6.00
93	Len Barker	25.00	12.50	7.50
94	Willi Quintana	20.00	10.00	6.00
95	Pablo Torrealba	20.00	10.00	6.00
96	Jim Hughes	20.00	10.00	6.00
97	Jose V. Caldera	20.00	10.00	6.00
98	Angel Vargas	20.00	10.00	6.00
99	Juan Gonzalez	20.00	10.00	6.00
100	Ulises Urrieta	20.00	10.00	6.00
101	Flores Bolivar	20.00	10.00	6.00
102	Robert Bowling	20.00	10.00	6.00
103	Rick Bladt	20.00	10.00	6.00
104	Luis Turner	20.00	10.00	6.00
105	Neldy Castillo	20.00	10.00	6.00
106	Adrian Garret (Garrett)	20.00	10.00	6.00
107	Bob Davis	20.00	10.00	6.00
108	La Guaira Action	10.00	5.00	3.00
109	Pompeyo Davalillo	20.00	10.00	6.00
110	Graciano Ravelo	20.00	10.00	6.00
111	Luis Lunar	20.00	10.00	6.00
112	Lester Morales	20.00	10.00	6.00
113	Enzo Hernandez	20.00	10.00	6.00
114	Aurelio Monteagudo	20.00	10.00	6.00
115	Angel Bravo	20.00	10.00	6.00
116	Carlos Moreno	20.00	10.00	6.00
117	Jose Cardenal	25.00	12.50	7.50
118	Rupert (Ruppert) Jones	20.00	10.00	6.00
119	Romo Blanco	20.00	10.00	6.00
120	Milton Ramirez	20.00	10.00	6.00
121	Antonio Correa	20.00	10.00	6.00
122	Clarence Gaston	25.00	12.50	7.50
123	Steve Lubber (Luebber)	20.00	10.00	6.00
124	Edwin Verhelst	20.00	10.00	6.00
125	Robert Johnson	20.00	10.00	6.00
126	Earl Bass	20.00	10.00	6.00
127	Jose Salas	20.00	10.00	6.00
128	Oswaldo Blanco	20.00	10.00	6.00
129	Steve Staag (Staggs)	20.00	10.00	6.00
130	Steve Patchin	20.00	10.00	6.00
131	Mike Kekish (Kekich)	20.00	10.00	6.00
132	Oswaldo Troconis	20.00	10.00	6.00
133	Dave May	20.00	10.00	6.00
134	Luis Salazar	20.00	10.00	6.00
135	Larry Gura	20.00	10.00	6.00
136	Rich Dauer	20.00	10.00	6.00
137	Pastor Perez	20.00	10.00	6.00
138	Paul Siebert	20.00	10.00	6.00
139	Luis M. Sanchez	20.00	10.00	6.00
140	Victor Colina	20.00	10.00	6.00
141	Adrian Devine	20.00	10.00	6.00
142	Robert Marcano	20.00	10.00	6.00
143	Juan Berenger (Berenguer)	25.00	12.50	7.50
144	Juan Monasterio	20.00	10.00	6.00
145	Donald Leppert	20.00	10.00	6.00
146	Gregorio Machado	20.00	10.00	6.00
147	Manuel Gonzalez	20.00	10.00	6.00
148	Wayne Granger	20.00	10.00	6.00
149	Remigio Hermoso	20.00	10.00	6.00
150	Rafael Cariel	20.00	10.00	6.00
151	Steve Dillard	20.00	10.00	6.00
152	Mitchell Page	20.00	10.00	6.00
153	Alexis Ramirez, Felix Rodriguez	15.00	7.50	4.50
154	Gary Wood	20.00	10.00	6.00
155	Ali Arape	20.00	10.00	6.00
156	Chris Batton	20.00	10.00	6.00
157	Gustavo Gil	20.00	10.00	6.00
158	Craig Reynolds	20.00	10.00	6.00
159	Jesus Aristimuno	20.00	10.00	6.00
160	Miguel Barreto	20.00	10.00	6.00
161	Alfonso Collazo	20.00	10.00	6.00
162	Steve Nicosia	20.00	10.00	6.00
163	Oswaldo Olivares	20.00	10.00	6.00
164	Robert Galasso	20.00	10.00	6.00
165	Alexis Ramirez	20.00	10.00	6.00
166	Craig Mitchell	20.00	10.00	6.00
167	Nelson Paiva	20.00	10.00	6.00
168	Ken Macha	20.00	10.00	6.00
169	Ruben Cabrera	20.00	10.00	6.00
170	Paul Reuschell (Reuschel)	20.00	10.00	6.00
171	Edito Arteaga	20.00	10.00	6.00
172	Olinto Rojas	20.00	10.00	6.00
173	Magallanes Action	10.00	5.00	3.00
174	Manny Sarmiento	20.00	10.00	6.00
175	Billy Moran	20.00	10.00	6.00
176	Eddie Watt	20.00	10.00	6.00
177	Michael Willis	20.00	10.00	6.00
178	Felix Rodriguez	20.00	10.00	6.00
179	James Easterly	20.00	10.00	6.00
180	Dave Parker	40.00	20.00	12.00
181	Luis Aparicio	50.00	25.00	15.00
182	Teodoro Obregon	20.00	10.00	6.00
183	Domingo Barboza	20.00	10.00	6.00
184	Not Issued, See #190			
185	Gilberto Marcano	20.00	10.00	6.00
186	Jose Alfaro	20.00	10.00	6.00
187	Jesus Reyes	20.00	10.00	6.00
188	Mike (Mickey) Scott	20.00	10.00	6.00
189	Carl Frost	20.00	10.00	6.00
190a	Norman Shiera	20.00	10.00	6.00
190b	Orlando Pena (See #184.)	20.00	10.00	6.00
191	Orlando Reyes	20.00	10.00	6.00
192	Milt Wilcox	25.00	12.50	7.50
193	Andrew Dyes	20.00	10.00	6.00
194	J. Hernandez	20.00	10.00	6.00
195	Dario Chirinos	20.00	10.00	6.00
196	Greg Shanahan	20.00	10.00	6.00
197	Gustavo Sposito	20.00	10.00	6.00
198	Sebastian Martinez	20.00	10.00	6.00
199	Leonel Carrion	20.00	10.00	6.00
200	Dennis Lawallyn (Lewallyn)	20.00	10.00	6.00
201	Charky (Charlie) Moore	20.00	10.00	6.00
202	Steve Mallory	20.00	10.00	6.00
203	Gary Martz	20.00	10.00	6.00
204	Lamar Johnson	20.00	10.00	6.00
205	Tim Johnson	20.00	10.00	6.00
206	Levy Ochoa	20.00	10.00	6.00
207	Bill Dancy	20.00	10.00	6.00
208	Antonio Garcia	20.00	10.00	6.00
209	Nidio Sirit	20.00	10.00	6.00
210	Norman Shiera	20.00	10.00	6.00
211	Not Issued, See #221			
212	Jesus Alfaro	20.00	10.00	6.00
213	Bobby Darwin	20.00	10.00	6.00
214	Zulia Action	10.00	5.00	3.00
215	Mike Seoane	20.00	10.00	6.00
216	Jim Gatner (Gantner)	20.00	10.00	6.00
217	Caracas Action	10.00	5.00	3.00
218	Caracas Action	10.00	5.00	3.00
219	Caracas Action	10.00	5.00	3.00
220	Caracas Action	10.00	5.00	3.00
221a	Caracas Action	10.00	5.00	3.00
221b	Joe Chourio (See #211.)	20.00	10.00	6.00
222	Lara Action	10.00	5.00	3.00
223	Ulises Urrieta, Antonio Armas, Manny Trillo	20.00	10.00	6.00
224	Magallanes Dugout	10.00	5.00	3.00
225	Remigio Hermoso, Gustavo Gil	15.00	7.50	4.50
226	Caracas Action	10.00	5.00	3.00
227	Manny Trillo, Dave Concepcion	20.00	10.00	6.00
228	Zulia Action	10.00	5.00	3.00
229	Caracas Pizarra Scoreboard	10.00	5.00	3.00
230	La Guaira Action	10.00	5.00	3.00
231	Caracas Action	10.00	5.00	3.00
232	La Guaira Action	10.00	5.00	3.00
233	Zulia Action	10.00	5.00	3.00
234	Caracas Publico	10.00	5.00	3.00
235	Magallanes Action	10.00	5.00	3.00
236	Aragua Action	10.00	5.00	3.00
237	La Guaira Action	10.00	5.00	3.00
238	La Guaira Action	10.00	5.00	3.00
239	La Guaira Action	10.00	5.00	3.00
240	La Guaira Action	10.00	5.00	3.00
241	Manny Trillo, Jose Cardenal	20.00	10.00	6.00
242	Pompeyo Davilillo, Lacheman	15.00	7.50	4.50
243	La Guaira Action	10.00	5.00	3.00
244	La Guaira Action	10.00	5.00	3.00
245	Action	10.00	5.00	3.00
246	Zulia Action	10.00	5.00	3.00
247	Zulia Action	10.00	5.00	3.00
248	Tim Johnson	20.00	10.00	6.00
249	La Guaira Action	10.00	5.00	3.00
250	La Guaira Action	10.00	5.00	3.00
251	La Guaira Action	10.00	5.00	3.00
252	La Guaira Action	10.00	5.00	3.00
253	La Guaira Action	10.00	5.00	3.00
254	La Guaira Action	10.00	5.00	3.00
255	La Guaira Action	10.00	5.00	3.00
256	La Guaira Action	10.00	5.00	3.00
257	Caracas Action	10.00	5.00	3.00
258	La Guaira Action	10.00	5.00	3.00
259	Zulia Action	10.00	5.00	3.00
260	Caracas Action	10.00	5.00	3.00
261	Caracas Action	10.00	5.00	3.00
262	La Guaira Clubhouse	10.00	5.00	3.00
263	La Guaira Clubhouse	10.00	5.00	3.00
264	La Guaira Clubhouse	10.00	5.00	3.00
265	La Guaira Clubhouse	10.00	5.00	3.00
266	La Guaira Action	10.00	5.00	3.00
267	La Guaira Action	10.00	5.00	3.00
268	La Guaira Action	10.00	5.00	3.00
269	Panoramica	10.00	5.00	3.00
270	Zulia Action	10.00	5.00	3.00
271	Aragua Puzzle	10.00	5.00	3.00
272	Aragua Puzzle	10.00	5.00	3.00
273	Aragua Puzzle	10.00	5.00	3.00
274	Aragua Puzzle	10.00	5.00	3.00
275	Aragua Puzzle	10.00	5.00	3.00
276	Aragua Puzzle	10.00	5.00	3.00
277	Aragua Puzzle	10.00	5.00	3.00
278	Aragua Puzzle	10.00	5.00	3.00
279	Aragua Puzzle	10.00	5.00	3.00
280	Lara Puzzle	10.00	5.00	3.00
281	Lara Puzzle	10.00	5.00	3.00
282	Lara Puzzle	10.00	5.00	3.00
283	Lara Puzzle	10.00	5.00	3.00
284	Lara Puzzle	10.00	5.00	3.00
285	Lara Puzzle	10.00	5.00	3.00
286	Lara Puzzle	10.00	5.00	3.00
287	Lara Puzzle	10.00	5.00	3.00
288	Lara Puzzle	10.00	5.00	3.00
289	Caracas Puzzle	10.00	5.00	3.00
290	Caracas Puzzle	10.00	5.00	3.00
291	Caracas Puzzle	10.00	5.00	3.00
292	Caracas Puzzle	10.00	5.00	3.00
293	Caracas Puzzle	10.00	5.00	3.00
294	Caracas Puzzle	10.00	5.00	3.00
295	Caracas Puzzle	10.00	5.00	3.00
296	Caracas Puzzle	10.00	5.00	3.00
297	Caracas Puzzle	10.00	5.00	3.00
298	La Guaira Puzzle	10.00	5.00	3.00
299	La Guaira Puzzle	10.00	5.00	3.00
300	La Guaira Puzzle	10.00	5.00	3.00
301	La Guaira Puzzle	10.00	5.00	3.00
302	La Guaira Puzzle	10.00	5.00	3.00
303	La Guaira Puzzle	10.00	5.00	3.00
304	La Guaira Puzzle	10.00	5.00	3.00
305	La Guaira Puzzle	10.00	5.00	3.00
306	La Guaira Puzzle	10.00	5.00	3.00
307	Magallanes Puzzle	10.00	5.00	3.00
308	Magallanes Puzzle	10.00	5.00	3.00
309	Magallanes Puzzle	10.00	5.00	3.00
310	Magallanes Puzzle	10.00	5.00	3.00
311	Magallanes Puzzle	10.00	5.00	3.00
312	Magallanes Puzzle	10.00	5.00	3.00
313	Magallanes Puzzle	10.00	5.00	3.00
314	Magallanes Puzzle	10.00	5.00	3.00
315	Magallanes Puzzle	10.00	5.00	3.00
316	Zulia Puzzle	10.00	5.00	3.00
317	Zulia Puzzle	10.00	5.00	3.00
318	Zulia Puzzle	10.00	5.00	3.00
319	Zulia Puzzle	10.00	5.00	3.00
320	Zulia Puzzle	10.00	5.00	3.00
321	Zulia Puzzle	10.00	5.00	3.00
322	Zulia Puzzle	10.00	5.00	3.00
323	Zulia Puzzle	10.00	5.00	3.00
324	Zulia Puzzle	10.00	5.00	3.00
325	Magallanes Navagantes Logo	10.00	5.00	3.00
326	Aragua Tigres Logo	10.00	5.00	3.00
327	Caracas Leones Logo	10.00	5.00	3.00
328	Zulia Aguilas Logo	10.00	5.00	3.00
329	Lara Cardenales Logo	10.00	5.00	3.00
330	La Guaira Tiburones Logo	10.00	5.00	3.00

1977 Venezuelan Baseball Stickers

More than 400 pieces comprise this set of 2-3/8" x 3-1/8" blank-back stickers. The majority have color photos of winter league players with the team name, logo and position printed above, and the sticker number and name beneath the picture. There are many former and future Major League players in this group. A subset of some 50 stickers of American Major Leaguers is printed in reproduction of their 1977 Topps cards. Other stickers include group pictures, action photos, puzzle pieces, etc. The album issued to house the stickers has a player write-up in each space. Printed on very thin paper, and often removed from albums, these stickers are generally not found in condition above Very Good. For Good condition pieces, figure value at 50 percent of the prices shown here; stickers in Fair condition should be valued at 25 percent. Many of the stickers have player names misspelled.

		NM	EX	VG
Complete Set (402):		4,000	1,600	800.00
Common Player:		15.00	6.00	3.00
Album:		125.00	50.00	25.00
1	Aragua Tigers Logo	15.00	6.00	3.00
2	Ozzie Virgil Sr.	20.00	8.00	4.00
3	Jesus Avila	15.00	6.00	3.00
4	Raul Ortega	15.00	6.00	3.00
5	Simon Barreto	15.00	6.00	3.00
6	Gustavo Quiroz	15.00	6.00	3.00
7	Jerry Cram	15.00	6.00	3.00
8	Pat Cristelli	15.00	6.00	3.00
9	Preston Hanna	15.00	6.00	3.00
10	Angel Hernandez	15.00	6.00	3.00
11	John M'Callen	15.00	6.00	3.00
12	Randy Miller	15.00	6.00	3.00
13	Dale Murray	15.00	6.00	3.00
14	Mike Nagy	15.00	6.00	3.00
15	Stan Perzanowski	15.00	6.00	3.00
16	Juan Quiroz	15.00	6.00	3.00
17	Graciano Parra	15.00	6.00	3.00
18	Larry Cox	15.00	6.00	3.00
19	Lenn Sakata	15.00	6.00	3.00
20	Lester Straker	15.00	6.00	3.00
21	Nelson Torres	15.00	6.00	3.00
22	Carlos Avila	15.00	6.00	3.00
23	Orlando Galindo	15.00	6.00	3.00
24	Dave Wagner	15.00	6.00	3.00
25	Dave Concepcion	60.00	24.00	12.00
26	Alfredo Ortiz	15.00	6.00	3.00
27	Mike Lum, Dave Concepcion, Larry Parrish	15.00	6.00	3.00
28	Jesus Padron	15.00	6.00	3.00
29	Larry Parrish	15.00	6.00	3.00
30	Rob Picciolo	15.00	6.00	3.00
31	Luis Rivas	15.00	6.00	3.00
32	Bob Slater	15.00	6.00	3.00
33	Larry Murray	15.00	6.00	3.00
34	Dave Soderholm	15.00	6.00	3.00

35	Luis Benitez	15.00	6.00	3.00
36	Cesar Tovar, Victor Davalillo	20.00	8.00	4.00
37	Luis Bravo	15.00	6.00	3.00
38	William Castillo	15.00	6.00	3.00
39	Terry Whitfield	15.00	6.00	3.00
40	Victor Davalillo	30.00	12.00	6.00
41	Mike Lum	15.00	6.00	3.00
42	Willie Norwood	15.00	6.00	3.00
43	Cesar Tovar	15.00	6.00	3.00
44	Joe Zdeb	15.00	6.00	3.00
45	Focion, Ozzie Virgil Sr.	15.00	6.00	3.00
46	Caracas Lions Logo	15.00	6.00	3.00
47	Felipe Alou	20.00	8.00	4.00
48	Alfonso Carrasquel (Chico)	35.00	14.00	7.00
49	Antonio Torres	15.00	6.00	3.00
50	Len Barker	15.00	6.00	3.00
51	Gary Beare	15.00	6.00	3.00
52	Cardell Camper	15.00	6.00	3.00
53	Juan Gonzalez	15.00	6.00	3.00
54	Paul Mirabella	15.00	6.00	3.00
55	Carney Lansford	15.00	6.00	3.00
56	Ubaldo Heredia	15.00	6.00	3.00
57	Elias Lugo	15.00	6.00	3.00
58	Oswaldo Troconis	15.00	6.00	3.00
59	Diego Segui	15.00	6.00	3.00
60	Lary Sorensen	15.00	6.00	3.00
61	Pablo Torrealba	15.00	6.00	3.00
62	Gustavo Bastardo	15.00	6.00	3.00
63	Luis Sanz	15.00	6.00	3.00
64	Steve Bowling	15.00	6.00	3.00
65	Tim Corcoran	15.00	6.00	3.00
66	Antonio Armas (Tony)	35.00	14.00	7.00
67	Toribio Garboza	15.00	6.00	3.00
68	Bob Molinaro	15.00	6.00	3.00
69	Willibaldo Quintana	15.00	6.00	3.00
70	Luis Turnes	15.00	6.00	3.00
71	Chuck Baker	15.00	6.00	3.00
72	Rob Belloir	15.00	6.00	3.00
73	Tom Brookens	15.00	6.00	3.00
74	Ron Hassey	15.00	6.00	3.00
75	Gonzalo Marquez	15.00	6.00	3.00
76	Bob Clark	15.00	6.00	3.00
77	Marcano Trillo (Manny)	30.00	12.00	6.00
78	Angel Vargas	15.00	6.00	3.00
79	Flores Bolivar	15.00	6.00	3.00
80	Baudilo Diaz (Bo)	15.00	6.00	3.00
81	Camilo Pascual	15.00	6.00	3.00
82	La Guaira Sharks Logo	15.00	6.00	3.00
83	Pompeyo Davalillo	17.50	7.00	3.50
84	Jose Martinez	15.00	6.00	3.00
85	Jim Willoughby	15.00	6.00	3.00
86	Romo Blanco	15.00	6.00	3.00
87	Mark Daly	15.00	6.00	3.00
88	Tom House	15.00	6.00	3.00
89	Danny Osborne	15.00	6.00	3.00
90	David Clyde	15.00	6.00	3.00
91	Luis Lunar	15.00	6.00	3.00
92	Randy McGilberry	15.00	6.00	3.00
93	Greg Minton	15.00	6.00	3.00
94	Aurelio Monteagudo	15.00	6.00	3.00
95	Carlos Moreno	15.00	6.00	3.00
96	Luis M. Sanchez	15.00	6.00	3.00
97	George Throop	15.00	6.00	3.00
98	Victor Colina	15.00	6.00	3.00
99	Edwin Verheist	15.00	6.00	3.00
100	John Wathan	15.00	6.00	3.00
101	Ruben Alcala	15.00	6.00	3.00
102	Ossie Blanco	15.00	6.00	3.00
103	Dave Cripe	15.00	6.00	3.00
104	Bob Marcano	15.00	6.00	3.00
105	Rudy Meoli	15.00	6.00	3.00
106	Pastor Perez	15.00	6.00	3.00
107	Milton Ramirez	15.00	6.00	3.00
108	Luis Salazar	15.00	6.00	3.00
109	Angel Bravo	15.00	6.00	3.00
110	Gene Clines	15.00	6.00	3.00
111	Jose Cardenal	15.00	6.00	3.00
112	Gabriel Ferrerc	15.00	6.00	3.00
113	Clint Hurdle	15.00	6.00	3.00
114	Juan Monasterio	15.00	6.00	3.00
115	Lester Morales	15.00	6.00	3.00
116	Carlos Hernandez	15.00	6.00	3.00
117	Nelo Lira	15.00	6.00	3.00
118	Raul Perez	15.00	6.00	3.00
119	Marcos Lunar	15.00	6.00	3.00
120	Franklin Moreno	15.00	6.00	3.00
121	Jerry Manuel	15.00	6.00	3.00
122	Ossie Blanco, Raul Perez	15.00	6.00	3.00
123	Tom McMillan	15.00	6.00	3.00
124	Roric Harrison	15.00	6.00	3.00
125	Tom Griffin	15.00	6.00	3.00
126	Juan Berenguer	15.00	6.00	3.00
127	Puzzle Piece (Reggie Jackson)	15.00	6.00	3.00
128	Puzzle Piece (Reggie Jackson)	15.00	6.00	3.00
129	Puzzle Piece (Reggie Jackson)	15.00	6.00	3.00
130	Puzzle Piece (Reggie Jackson)	15.00	6.00	3.00
131	Puzzle Piece (Reggie Jackson)	15.00	6.00	3.00
132	Puzzle Piece (Reggie Jackson)	15.00	6.00	3.00
133	Puzzle Piece (Reggie Jackson)	15.00	6.00	3.00
134	Puzzle Piece (Reggie Jackson)	15.00	6.00	3.00
135	Puzzle Piece (Reggie Jackson)	15.00	6.00	3.00
136	Reggie Jackson	325.00	130.00	65.00
137	Rod Carew	175.00	70.00	35.00
138	Dave Concepcion	90.00	36.00	18.00
139	Joe Morgan	125.00	50.00	25.00
140	Dave Parker	15.00	6.00	3.00
141	Carlton Fisk	125.00	50.00	25.00
142	Garry Maddox	15.00	6.00	3.00
143	George Foster	15.00	6.00	3.00
144	Fred Lynn	15.00	6.00	3.00
145	Lou Piniella	17.50	7.00	3.50
146	Mark Fidrych	15.00	6.00	3.00
147	Lou Brock	125.00	50.00	25.00
148	Mitchell Page	15.00	6.00	3.00
149	Sparky Lyle	15.00	6.00	3.00
150	Manny Sanguillen	15.00	6.00	3.00
151	Steve Carlton	125.00	50.00	25.00
152	Al Oliver	17.50	7.00	3.50
153	Davey Lopes	15.00	6.00	3.00
154	Johnny Bench	175.00	70.00	35.00
155	Richie Hebner	15.00	6.00	3.00
156	Cesar Cedeno	15.00	6.00	3.00
157	Manny Trillo	15.00	6.00	3.00
158	Nolan Ryan	1,500	600.00	300.00
159	Tom Seaver	175.00	70.00	35.00
160	Jim Palmer	125.00	50.00	25.00
161	Randy Jones	15.00	6.00	3.00
162	George Brett	325.00	130.00	65.00
163	Bill Madlock	15.00	6.00	3.00
164	Cesar Geronimo	15.00	6.00	3.00
165	Vida Blue	15.00	6.00	3.00
166	Tony Armas	35.00	14.00	7.00
167	Bill Campbell	15.00	6.00	3.00
168	Graig Nettles	15.00	6.00	3.00
169	Mike Schmidt	325.00	130.00	65.00
170	Willie Stargell	125.00	50.00	25.00
171	Ron Cey	15.00	6.00	3.00
172	Victor Davalillo	25.00	10.00	5.00
173	Pete Rose	375.00	150.00	75.00
174	Steve Yaeger	15.00	6.00	3.00
175	Frank Tanana	15.00	6.00	3.00
176	Carl Yastrzemski	175.00	70.00	35.00
177	Willie McCovey	125.00	50.00	25.00
178	Thurman Munson	125.00	50.00	25.00
179	Chris Chambliss	15.00	6.00	3.00
180	Bill Russell	15.00	6.00	3.00
181	Lara Cardinals Logo	15.00	6.00	3.00
182	Leo Posada	15.00	6.00	3.00
183	Lucio Celis	15.00	6.00	3.00
184	Enrique Gonzalez	15.00	6.00	3.00
185	Brian Abraham	15.00	6.00	3.00
186	Luis Aponte	15.00	6.00	3.00
187	Jose Lopez	15.00	6.00	3.00
188	Bobby Ramos	15.00	6.00	3.00
189	Tom Dixon	15.00	6.00	3.00
190	Gary Melson	15.00	6.00	3.00
191	Mark Budaska	15.00	6.00	3.00
192	Mark Fischlin	15.00	6.00	3.00
193	Garth Iorg	15.00	6.00	3.00
194	Mike Rowland	15.00	6.00	3.00
195	Dennis DeBarr	15.00	6.00	3.00
196	Gary Wilson	15.00	6.00	3.00
197	Dave McKay	15.00	6.00	3.00
198	Roberto Munoz	15.00	6.00	3.00
199	Roger Polanco	15.00	6.00	3.00
200	Pat Kelly	15.00	6.00	3.00
201	Hernan Silva	15.00	6.00	3.00
202	Francisco Navas	15.00	6.00	3.00
203	Pedro Lobaton	15.00	6.00	3.00
204	Pete Mackanin	15.00	6.00	3.00
205	Jose Caldera	15.00	6.00	3.00
206	Carlos Rodriguez/IA	15.00	6.00	3.00
207	Eddy Baez	15.00	6.00	3.00
208	Gary Metzeger	15.00	6.00	3.00
209	Rafael Sandoval	15.00	6.00	3.00
210	Arturo Sanchez	15.00	6.00	3.00
211	Franklin Tua	15.00	6.00	3.00
212	Teolindo Acosta	15.00	6.00	3.00
213	Arnaldo Alvarado	15.00	6.00	3.00
214	Orlando Gonzalez	15.00	6.00	3.00
215	Nelson Garcia	15.00	6.00	3.00
216	Terry Puhl	15.00	6.00	3.00
217	David Torres	15.00	6.00	3.00
218	Teolindo Acosta, Roberto Munoz	15.00	6.00	3.00
219	Terry Puhl, Mark Budaska	15.00	6.00	3.00
220	Gary Gray	15.00	6.00	3.00
221	Gustavo Gil	15.00	6.00	3.00
222	Epi Guerrero	15.00	6.00	3.00
223	Bobby Ramos, Enrique Gonzalez	15.00	6.00	3.00
224	Rick Sawyer	15.00	6.00	3.00
225	S. Byre	15.00	6.00	3.00
226	Magallanes Navigators Logo	15.00	6.00	3.00
227	Alex Monchak	15.00	6.00	3.00
228	Manuel Gonzalez	15.00	6.00	3.00
229	Olinto Rojas	15.00	6.00	3.00
230	Gregorio Machado	15.00	6.00	3.00
231	Ali Arape	15.00	6.00	3.00
232	Miguel Barreto	15.00	6.00	3.00
233	Manny Sarmiento	15.00	6.00	3.00
234	Jesus Aristimuno, Alexis Ramirez, Felix Rodriguez	15.00	6.00	3.00
235	Ed Glynn	15.00	6.00	3.00
236	Luis Jiminez	15.00	6.00	3.00
237	Bob Adams	15.00	6.00	3.00
238	Edito Arteaga	15.00	6.00	3.00
239	Rafael Cariel	15.00	6.00	3.00
240	Eddie Solomon	15.00	6.00	3.00
241	Rick Williams	15.00	6.00	3.00
242	Miguel Nava	15.00	6.00	3.00
243	Rod Scurry	15.00	6.00	3.00
244	Mike Eduards (Edwards)	15.00	6.00	3.00
245	Earl Stephenson	15.00	6.00	3.00
246	Alfonso Collazo	15.00	6.00	3.00
247	Ruben Cabrera	15.00	6.00	3.00
248	Alfredo Torres	15.00	6.00	3.00
249	John Valle	15.00	6.00	3.00
250	Jesus Aristimuno	15.00	6.00	3.00
251	Joe Cannon	15.00	6.00	3.00
252	John Pacella	15.00	6.00	3.00
253	Oswaldo Olivares	15.00	6.00	3.00
254	Gary Hargis	15.00	6.00	3.00
255	Nelson Paiva	15.00	6.00	3.00
256	Bob Oliver	15.00	6.00	3.00
257	Alexis Ramirez	15.00	6.00	3.00
258	Larry Wolfe	15.00	6.00	3.00
259	Don Boyland (Doe)	15.00	6.00	3.00
260	Mark Wagner	15.00	6.00	3.00
261	Jim Wright	15.00	6.00	3.00
262	Mitchell Page	15.00	6.00	3.00
263	Felix Rodriguez	15.00	6.00	3.00
264	Willie Aaron	15.00	6.00	3.00
265	Justo Massaro	15.00	6.00	3.00
266	Norm Angelini	15.00	6.00	3.00
267	Fred Breining	15.00	6.00	3.00
268	Bill Sample	15.00	6.00	3.00
269	Than Smith	15.00	6.00	3.00
270	Harry Doris (Dorish)	15.00	6.00	3.00
271	Zulia Eagles Logo	15.00	6.00	3.00
272	Luis Aparicio	35.00	14.00	7.00
273	Toni Taylor (Tony)	15.00	6.00	3.00
274	Teodoro Obregon	15.00	6.00	3.00
275	Gilberto Marcano	15.00	6.00	3.00
276	Jose Alfaro	15.00	6.00	3.00
277	Danny Boitano	15.00	6.00	3.00
278	Jesus Reyes	15.00	6.00	3.00
279	Johel Chourio	15.00	6.00	3.00
280	Scott Sanderson	15.00	6.00	3.00
281	Charles Kiffin	15.00	6.00	3.00
282	Bill Dancy	15.00	6.00	3.00
283	Tim Johnson	15.00	6.00	3.00
284	Norman Shiera	15.00	6.00	3.00
285	Lonnie Smith	15.00	6.00	3.00
286	Manny Seoane	15.00	6.00	3.00
287	David Wallace	15.00	6.00	3.00
288	Lareu Whashington (LaRue Washington)	15.00	6.00	3.00
289	Danny Warthen	15.00	6.00	3.00
290	Sebastian Martinez	15.00	6.00	3.00
291	Warren Brusstar	15.00	6.00	3.00
292	Steven Waterburry (Waterbury)	15.00	6.00	3.00
293	Gustavo Sposito	15.00	6.00	3.00
294	Billy Connors	15.00	6.00	3.00
295	Bod Reece (Bob)	15.00	6.00	3.00
296	Al Velasquez	15.00	6.00	3.00
297	Jesus Alfaro	15.00	6.00	3.00
298	Todd Cruz	15.00	6.00	3.00
299	Efren Chourio	15.00	6.00	3.00
300	Tim Norrid	15.00	6.00	3.00
301	Leonel Carrion	15.00	6.00	3.00
302	Dario Chirinos	15.00	6.00	3.00
303	Bobby Darwin	15.00	6.00	3.00
304	Levy Ochoa	15.00	6.00	3.00
305	Orlando Reyez (Reyes)	15.00	6.00	3.00
306	Antonio Garcia	15.00	6.00	3.00
307	Fred Andrews	15.00	6.00	3.00
308	Domingo Barboza	15.00	6.00	3.00
309	Emilio Rodriguez	15.00	6.00	3.00
310	Roger Brown (Rogers "Bobby")	15.00	6.00	3.00
311	Nelson Munoz	15.00	6.00	3.00
312	Unknown	15.00	6.00	3.00
313	Greg Pryor	15.00	6.00	3.00
314	Early Espina	15.00	6.00	3.00
315	Leonel Carrion, Dario Chirinos	15.00	6.00	3.00
316	Luis Aparicio	25.00	10.00	5.00
317	Alfonso Carrasquel (Chico)	20.00	8.00	4.00
318	Dave Concepcion	20.00	8.00	4.00
319	Antonio Armas (Tony)	20.00	8.00	4.00
320	Marcano Trillo (Manny)	20.00	8.00	4.00
321	Pablo Torrealba	15.00	6.00	3.00
322	Manny Sarmiento	15.00	6.00	3.00
323	Baudilo Diaz (Bo)	15.00	6.00	3.00
324	Victor Davalillo	15.00	6.00	3.00
325	Puzzle Piece (Dave Parker)	15.00	6.00	3.00
326	Puzzle Piece (Dave Parker)	15.00	6.00	3.00
327	Puzzle Piece (Dave Parker)	15.00	6.00	3.00
328	Puzzle Piece (Dave Parker)	15.00	6.00	3.00
329	Puzzle Piece (Dave Parker)	15.00	6.00	3.00
330	Puzzle Piece (Dave Parker)	15.00	6.00	3.00
331	Puzzle Piece (Dave Parker)	15.00	6.00	3.00
332	Puzzle Piece (Dave Parker)	15.00	6.00	3.00
333	Puzzle Piece (Dave Parker)	15.00	6.00	3.00
334	Dave Parker	15.00	6.00	3.00
335	Steve Bowling	15.00	6.00	3.00
336	Jose Herrera	15.00	6.00	3.00
337	Mitchell Page	15.00	6.00	3.00
338	Enos Cabell	15.00	6.00	3.00
339	Orlando Reyes	15.00	6.00	3.00
340	Felix Rodriguez	15.00	6.00	3.00
341	Baudilo Diaz (Bo)	15.00	6.00	3.00
342	Gonzalo Marquez	15.00	6.00	3.00
343	Mike Kelleher	15.00	6.00	3.00
344	Juan Monasterio	15.00	6.00	3.00
345	Diego Segui	15.00	6.00	3.00
346	Steve Lueber (Luebber)	15.00	6.00	3.00
347	Mike Scott	15.00	6.00	3.00
348	Angel Bravo	15.00	6.00	3.00
349	Terry Whitfield	15.00	6.00	3.00
350	Bob Oliver	15.00	6.00	3.00
351	Tim Jonhson (Johnson)	15.00	6.00	3.00
352	Gustavo Sposito	15.00	6.00	3.00
353	Jim Norris	15.00	6.00	3.00
354	Marcano Trillo (Manny)	20.00	8.00	4.00
355	Gary Woods	15.00	6.00	3.00
356	Felix Rodriguez	15.00	6.00	3.00
357	Dave May	15.00	6.00	3.00
358	Don Lepper (Leppert)	15.00	6.00	3.00
359	Magallanes Team Photo	15.00	6.00	3.00
360	Magallanes Team Photo	15.00	6.00	3.00
361	Action Photo	15.00	6.00	3.00
362	Action Photo	15.00	6.00	3.00
363	Antonio Torres, Leo Posada	15.00	6.00	3.00
364	Action Photo	15.00	6.00	3.00
365	Action Photo	15.00	6.00	3.00
366	Action Photo	15.00	6.00	3.00
367	Action Photo	15.00	6.00	3.00
368	Action Photo	15.00	6.00	3.00
369	Action Photo	15.00	6.00	3.00
370	Action Photo	15.00	6.00	3.00
371	Action Photo	15.00	6.00	3.00
372	Action Photo	15.00	6.00	3.00

373	Action Photo	15.00	6.00	3.00
374	Action Photo	15.00	6.00	3.00
375	Action Photo	15.00	6.00	3.00
376	Action Photo	15.00	6.00	3.00
377	Action Photo	15.00	6.00	3.00
378	Action Photo	15.00	6.00	3.00
399	Action Photo (Misnumbered)	15.00	6.00	3.00
380	Action Photo	15.00	6.00	3.00
381	Action Photo	15.00	6.00	3.00
382	Action Photo	15.00	6.00	3.00
383	Action Photo	15.00	6.00	3.00
384	Action Photo	15.00	6.00	3.00
385	Action Photo	15.00	6.00	3.00
386	Action Photo	15.00	6.00	3.00
387	Action Photo	15.00	6.00	3.00
388	Action Photo	15.00	6.00	3.00
389	Antonio Torres, Franklin Parra	15.00	6.00	3.00
390	Action Photo	15.00	6.00	3.00
391	Angel Bravo, Luis Aparicio	20.00	8.00	4.00
392	Action Photo	15.00	6.00	3.00
393	Action Photo	15.00	6.00	3.00
394	Action Photo	15.00	6.00	3.00
395	Action Photo	15.00	6.00	3.00
396	Action Photo	15.00	6.00	3.00
397	Action Photo	15.00	6.00	3.00
398	Action Photo	15.00	6.00	3.00
399	Action Photo	15.00	6.00	3.00
400	Action Photo	15.00	6.00	3.00
401	Action Photo	15.00	6.00	3.00
402	Tony Armas, Manny Trillo, Gonzalo Marquez	15.00	6.00	3.00

1952 Victoria

Produced during the 1952-53 Winter League season, these paper cards were formatted in the popular Latin American manner to be pasted into a colorful accompanying album. It is possible a principal venue for the set was the ballpark at Havana, since each card urges attendance at games there. The cards are printed on paper in a 2-1/8" x 3-1/8" size. Fronts have colorized photos with white borders, but no player identification. Backs are, of course, in Spanish and include a card number player personal data, career summary and a copyright notice. Besides local players, and former, current and future major league players, the set includes league umpires and broadcasters, etc. Names as presented in this checklist may not correspond exactly with those printed on card backs and may not be correct spellings of player names.

		NM	EX	VG
Complete Set (168):		6,500	3,000	1,500
Common Player:		45.00	20.00	10.00
Album:		350.00	160.00	90.00
1	Amado Maestri (Umpire)	45.00	20.00	10.00
2	John Mullen (Umpire)	45.00	20.00	10.00
3	Havana Stadium	45.00	20.00	10.00
4	Bernardino Rodriguez (Umpire)	45.00	20.00	10.00
5	Raul Atan (Umpire)	45.00	20.00	10.00
6	Cuco Conde (Broadcaster)	45.00	20.00	10.00
7	Manolo de la Reguera (Broadcaster)	45.00	20.00	10.00
8	Rafael (Felo) Ramirez (Broadcaster)	60.00	30.00	20.00
9	Rafael Rubi (Broadcaster)	45.00	20.00	10.00
10	Gabino Delgado (Broadcaster)	45.00	20.00	10.00
11	Fernando Menendez (Broadcaster)	45.00	20.00	10.00
12	Buck Canel (Broadcaster)	50.00	25.00	15.00
13	Orlando Sanchez Diago (Broadcaster)	45.00	20.00	10.00
14	Pedro Galiana (Broadcaster)	45.00	20.00	10.00
15	Jess Losada (Broadcaster)	45.00	20.00	10.00
16	Juan Ealo (Broadcaster)	45.00	20.00	10.00
17	Rene Molina (Broadcaster)	45.00	20.00	10.00
18	Miguel A. Ruiz (Broadcaster)	45.00	20.00	10.00
19	Ruben Rodriguez (Broadcaster)	45.00	20.00	10.00
20	Havana Lions Pennant	30.00	15.00	9.00
21	Miguel Gonzalez	60.00	30.00	20.00
22	Tomas (Pipo) de la Noval	45.00	20.00	10.00
23	Salvador Hernandez	45.00	20.00	10.00
24	Manuel Garcia	45.00	20.00	10.00
25	Edilio Alfaro	45.00	20.00	10.00
26	Julio Navarro	45.00	20.00	10.00
27	Richard Rand	45.00	20.00	10.00
28	Andres Fleitas	45.00	20.00	10.00
29	Isaac Seoane	45.00	20.00	10.00
30	Jimmie Kerrigan	45.00	20.00	10.00
31	Robert Alexander	45.00	20.00	10.00
32	Charles Sipples	45.00	20.00	10.00
33	Adrian Zabala	45.00	20.00	10.00
34	Rogelio Martinez	45.00	20.00	10.00
35	Carlos Pascual	60.00	30.00	20.00
36	Mario Picone	45.00	20.00	10.00
37	Eusebio Perez (Silverio)	45.00	20.00	10.00
38	Julio Moreno	45.00	20.00	10.00
39	Gilberto Torres	45.00	20.00	10.00
40	Bert Haas	45.00	20.00	10.00
41	Johnny Jorgensen	45.00	20.00	10.00
42	Lou Klein	45.00	20.00	10.00
43	Damon Phillips	45.00	20.00	10.00
44	Orlando Varona	45.00	20.00	10.00
45	Jorge Lopez	45.00	20.00	10.00
46	Pedro Formenthal	60.00	30.00	20.00
47	Robert Usher	45.00	20.00	10.00
48	Edmundo (Sandy) Amoros	60.00	30.00	20.00
49	Alejandro Crespo	50.00	25.00	15.00
50	Oscar Sardinas	45.00	20.00	10.00
51	Almendares Pennant	30.00	15.00	9.00
52	Robert Bragan	50.00	25.00	15.00
53	Clemente (Sungo) Carreras	45.00	20.00	10.00
54	Rodolfo Fernandez	45.00	20.00	10.00
55	Manuel Fernandez	45.00	20.00	10.00
56	Orlando Echevarria	45.00	20.00	10.00
57	Charles Thompson	45.00	20.00	10.00
58	Oscar Fernandez	45.00	20.00	10.00
59	Hal Erickson	45.00	20.00	10.00
60	Conrado Marrero	50.00	25.00	15.00
61	Agapito Mayor	45.00	20.00	10.00
62	Octavio Rubert	45.00	20.00	10.00
63	Edward Roebuck	45.00	20.00	10.00
64	Duke Markell	50.00	20.00	10.00
65	Rene Massip	45.00	20.00	10.00
66	Pedro Naranjo	45.00	20.00	10.00
67	Roque Contreras	45.00	20.00	10.00
68	Wayne McLeland	45.00	20.00	10.00
69	Frank Kellert	45.00	20.00	10.00
70	Forrest Jacobs	50.00	25.00	15.00
71	Hector Rodriguez	50.00	25.00	15.00
72	Willy Miranda	50.00	25.00	15.00
73	Roberto Ortiz	50.00	25.00	15.00
74	Frank Carswell	45.00	20.00	10.00
75	Asdrubal Baro	45.00	20.00	10.00
76	Paul Smith	45.00	20.00	10.00
77	Antonio Napoles	45.00	20.00	10.00
78	Francisco Campos	45.00	20.00	10.00
79	Angel Scull	45.00	20.00	10.00
80	Raymond Coleman	45.00	20.00	10.00
81	Gino Cimolli (Cimoli)	50.00	25.00	15.00
82	Amado Ibanez	45.00	20.00	10.00
83	Avelino Canizarez	45.00	20.00	10.00
84	Conrado Perez	45.00	20.00	10.00
85	Marianao Pennant	30.00	15.00	9.00
86	Fermin Guerra	50.00	25.00	15.00
87	Jose Maria Fernandez	50.00	25.00	15.00
88	Jose (Joe) Olivares	45.00	20.00	10.00
89	Ramon Carneado	45.00	20.00	10.00
90	Alejandro (Baby) Fernandez	45.00	20.00	10.00
91	Emilio Cabrera	45.00	20.00	10.00
92	Sandalio Consuegra	50.00	25.00	15.00
93	Tomas Fine	45.00	20.00	10.00
94	Miguel Fornieles	50.00	25.00	15.00
95	Camilo Pascual	60.00	30.00	18.00
96	Miguel Lopez	45.00	20.00	10.00
97	Clarence Iott	50.00	25.00	15.00
98	Dale Matthewson	45.00	20.00	10.00
99	Hampton Coleman	50.00	25.00	15.00
100	Terris McDuffie	60.00	30.00	18.00
101	Raul Sanchez	45.00	20.00	10.00
102	Lorenzo Cabrera	45.00	20.00	10.00
103	Ray Dandridge	800.00	400.00	240.00
104	Silvio Garcia	45.00	20.00	10.00
105	Carlos De Souza	45.00	20.00	10.00
106	Oreste (Minnie) Minoso	100.00	50.00	30.00
107	Sebastian Basso	45.00	20.00	10.00
108	William Wilson	45.00	20.00	10.00
109	Hank Workman	50.00	25.00	15.00
110	Fernando Pedroso	45.00	20.00	10.00
111	Juan Antonio Vistuer	45.00	20.00	10.00
112	Hiram Gonzalez	45.00	20.00	10.00
113	Julio Becquer	45.00	20.00	10.00
114	Stan Rojek	45.00	20.00	10.00
115	Ramiro (Cuco) Vasquez	45.00	20.00	10.00
116	Juan Izaguirre	45.00	20.00	10.00
117	Cienfuegos Pennant	30.00	15.00	9.00
118	Billy Herman	110.00	55.00	35.00
119	Oscar Rodriguez	45.00	20.00	10.00
120	Julio Rojo	45.00	20.00	10.00
121	Pedro Pages	45.00	20.00	10.00
122	Felix Masud	45.00	20.00	10.00
123	Rafael Noble	50.00	25.00	15.00
124	Mario Diaz	45.00	20.00	10.00
125	Luis Aloma	45.00	20.00	10.00
126	Santiago Ulrich	45.00	20.00	10.00
127	Armando Roche	45.00	20.00	10.00
128	Raul Lopez	45.00	20.00	10.00
129	Armando Suarez	45.00	20.00	10.00
130	Vincente Lopez	45.00	20.00	10.00
131	Ernesto Morillas	45.00	20.00	10.00
132	Alfredo Ibanez	45.00	20.00	10.00
133	Allen J. Gettel	45.00	20.00	10.00
134	Ken Lehman	45.00	20.00	10.00
135	Pat Mc Clothin (McGlothin)	50.00	25.00	15.00
136	Rogenio Otero	45.00	20.00	10.00
137	Felipe Montemayor	45.00	20.00	10.00
138	Jack Cassini	50.00	25.00	15.00
139	Donald Zimmer	75.00	37.00	22.00
140	Robert Wilson	45.00	20.00	10.00
141	Humberto Fernandez	45.00	20.00	10.00
142	Pedro Ballester	45.00	20.00	10.00
143	Walt Morin (Moryn)	50.00	25.00	15.00
144	Roberto Fernandez	45.00	20.00	10.00
145	Claro Duany	60.00	30.00	18.00
146	Pablo Garcia	45.00	20.00	10.00
147	James Pendleton	50.00	25.00	15.00
148	Oscar Sierra	45.00	20.00	10.00
149	Adolfo Luque	80.00	40.00	25.00
150	Cando Lopez	45.00	20.00	10.00
151	Joe Black	100.00	50.00	30.00
152	Napoleon Reyes	60.00	30.00	18.00
153	Rafael (Villa) Cabrera	45.00	20.00	10.00
154	Charles (Red) Barrett	50.00	25.00	15.00
155	Fred Martin	45.00	20.00	10.00
156	Isidoro Leon	45.00	20.00	10.00
157	John Rutherford	50.00	20.00	10.00
158	Max Lanier	50.00	25.00	15.00
159	Julio Ramos	45.00	20.00	10.00
160	Manuel Hidalgo	45.00	20.00	10.00
161	Wilfredo Calvino	45.00	20.00	10.00
162	Joe Nakamura	60.00	30.00	20.00
163	Martiniano Garay	45.00	20.00	10.00
164	Fernando Rodriguez	45.00	20.00	10.00
165	Anibal Navarrette	45.00	20.00	10.00
166	Rafael Rivas	45.00	20.00	10.00
167	Wilfredo Salas	45.00	20.00	10.00
168	Jocko Thompson	45.00	20.00	10.00

1908 Victor Publishing Cy Young

Eschewing booze, women and gambling made Cy Young famous, according to this postcard issued by an Ohio company near the end of the pitcher's career. The 3-1/2" x 5-1/2" card has a large black-and-white photographic portrait at center with maroon and black illustrations emblematic of typical ballplayers' vices in the corners. The divided-back is printed in black with typical postcard markings.

	NM	EX	VG
Cy Young	450.00	225.00	135.00

1915 Victory Tobacco (T214)

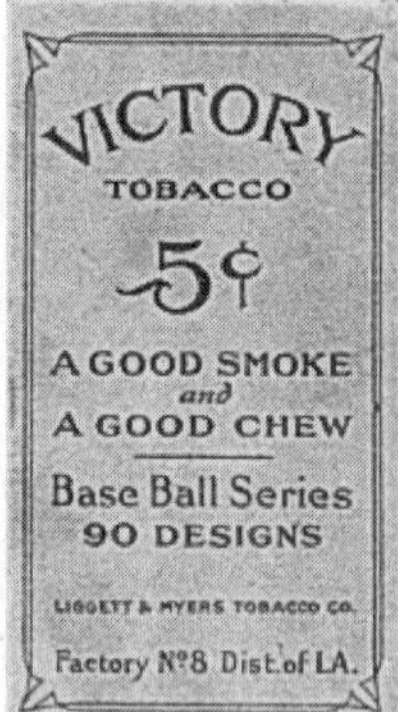

The T214 Victory set of 1915 is an obscure series of tobacco cards that is sometimes mistaken for the better-known T206 "White Border" set. The confusion is understandable because identical player poses were used for both sets. The Victory set can be easily identified, however, by the advertising for the Victory brand on the back of the cards. The set features players from the Federal League, both major leagues and at least one minor leaguer. While card backs advertise "90 Designs," fewer than 60 subjects have surfaced to date. The set had such limited distribution - apparently restricted to just the Louisiana area - and the cards are so rare that it may never be completely checklisted. Except for the advertising on the backs, the Victory cards are almost identical to the "Type 2" Coupon cards (T213), another obscure Louisiana tobacco set issued during the same period. Of the several tobacco sets issued in Louisana in the early part of the 20th Century, the T214 Victory cards are considered the most difficult to find. Gaps have been left in the numbering sequence to accommodate future additions.

		NM	EX	VG
Common Player:		3,600	1,620	750.00
(1)	Red Ames	7,200	2,880	1,440
(2)	Chief Bender	14,400	5,760	2,880
(3)	Roger Bresnahan	14,400	5,760	2,880
(4)	Al Bridwell	7,200	2,880	1,440
(5)	Howie Camnitz	7,200	2,880	1,440
(6)	Hal Chase/Portrait	10,200	4,080	2,040
(7)	Hal Chase/Throwing	10,200	4,080	2,040
(8)	Ty Cobb/Portrait (Red background.)	30,000	12,000	6,000
(9)	Doc Crandall	7,200	2,880	1,440
(10)	Birdie Cree	7,200	2,880	1,440
(11)	Josh Devore	7,200	2,880	1,440
(12)	Ray Demmitt	7,200	2,880	1,440

(13)	Mickey Doolan	7,200	2,880	1,440
(14)	Mike Donlin	7,200	2,880	1,440
(15)	Tom Downey	7,200	2,880	1,440
(16)	Larry Doyle	7,200	2,880	1,440
(17)	Kid Elberfeld	7,200	2,880	1,440
(18)	Johnny Evers	14,400	5,760	2,880
(19)	Russ Ford	7,200	2,880	1,440
(20)	Art Fromme	7,200	2,880	1,440
(21)	Chick Gandil	14,400	5,760	2,880
(22)	Rube Geyer	7,200	2,880	1,440
(23)	Clark Griffith	14,400	5,760	2,880
(24)	Bob Groom	7,200	2,880	1,440
(25)	Buck Herzog	7,200	2,880	1,440
(26)	Hughie Jennings	14,400	5,760	2,880
(27)	Walter Johnson (Hands at chest.)	18,000	7,200	3,600
(28)	Joe Kelley	14,400	5,760	2,880
(29)	Ed Konetchy	7,200	2,880	1,440
(30)	Nap Lajoie	14,400	5,760	2,880
(31)	Ed Lennox	7,200	2,880	1,440
(32)	Sherry Magee	7,200	2,880	1,440
(33)	Rube Marquard	14,400	5,760	2,880
(34)	John McGraw	14,400	5,760	2,880
(35)	George McQuillan	7,200	2,880	1,440
(36)	Chief Meyers/Catching	7,200	2,880	1,440
(37)	Chief Meyers/Portrait	7,200	2,880	1,440
(38)	George Mullin	7,200	2,880	1,440
(41)	Red Murray	7,200	2,880	1,440
(42)	Tom Needham	7,200	2,880	1,440
(43)	Rebel Oakes	7,200	2,880	1,440
(44)	Dode Paskert	7,200	2,880	1,440
(45)	Jack Quinn	7,200	2,880	1,440
(46)	Nap Rucker	7,200	2,880	1,440
(47)	Germany Schaefer	7,200	2,880	1,440
(48)	Wildfire Schulte	7,200	2,880	1,440
(49)	Frank Smith	7,200	2,880	1,440
(51)	Tris Speaker	16,200	6,480	3,240
(52)	George Stovall	7,200	2,880	1,440
(53)	Ed Summers	7,200	2,880	1,440
(54)	Bill Sweeney	7,200	2,880	1,440
(55)	Jeff Sweeney	7,200	2,880	1,440
(56)	Ira Thomas	7,200	2,880	1,440
(57)	Joe Tinker	14,400	5,760	2,880
(58)	Heinie Wagner	7,200	2,880	1,440
(59)	Zack Wheat	14,400	5,760	2,880
(60)	Kaiser Wilhelm	7,200	2,880	1,440
(61)	Hooks Wiltse	7,200	2,880	1,440

1886 Virginia Brights Black Stocking Nine (N48)

Issued during the late 1880s, though the attributed date is speculative, this series of cabinet-size (about 5" x 7-1/2") blank-back cards was available by sending in coupons found in Allen & Ginter's Virginia Brights brand cigarettes. Fronts have a sepia photo of Rubenesque women in baseball uniforms posed before a painted ballpark backdrop. In the bottom border is "BLACK STOCKING NINE. ALLEN & GINTER'S / Virginia Brights Cigarettes. / Crop of 1884 / HAND MADE CROP OF 1884." The beveled edges of the cabinet mount were originially gilt-trimmed.

	NM	EX	VG
Common Card:	1,200	600.00	350.00

1887 Virginia Brights Polka Dot Nine

Issued during the late 1880s, though the attributed date is speculative, this series of cabinet-size (about 5" x 7-1/2") blank-back cards was available by sending in coupons found in Allen & Ginter's Virginia Brights brand cigarettes. Fronts have a sepia photo of women in baseball uniforms and polka-dot bandanas posed before a backdrop. In the top border of the yellow cardboard mount, printed in gold leaf, is "Virginia Brights / Cigarettes / CROP OF 1884." In a cartouche beneath the photo is "POLKA DOT NINE." Below that is "THE FULL SET OF THIS SERIES COMPRISES NINE DIFFERENT SUBJECTS. / REPRESENTING THE VARIOUS POSITIONS IN BASE BALL."

	NM	EX	VG
Common Card:	1,100	540.00	330.00

1888 Virginia Brights Girl Baseball Players

(See 1888 Allen & Ginter Girl Baseball Players.)

1888 Virginia Brights Black Stocking Nine

Issued during the late 1880s, this series of cabinet-size (about 5" x 7-1/2") blank-back cards was available by sending in coupons found in Allen & Ginter's Virginia Brights brand cigarettes. Fronts have a sepia photo of Rubenesque women in a baseball uniform posed before a painted ballpark backdrop. The picture is framed by a fancy design. In the border above is "Virginia Brights / Cigarettes / Crop of 1884." Below the photo is the series title "Black Stocking Nine" and "The Full Set of this Series Comprises Nine Different / Subjects Representing the Various Positions in Base-Ball."

	NM	EX	VG
Common Card:	2,400	1,200	725.00

1911-16 Virginia Extra Cigarettes (T216)

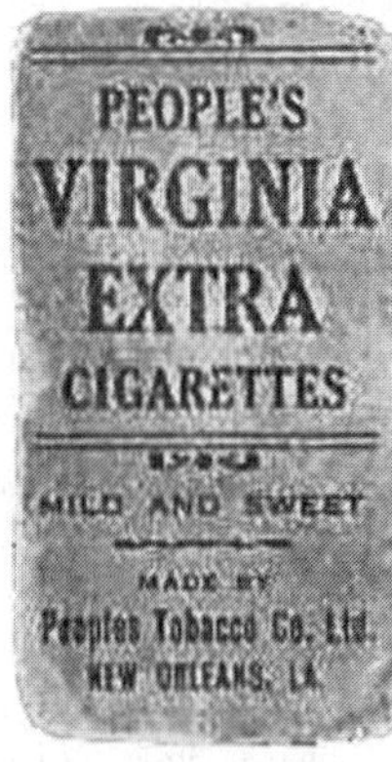

The T216 baseball card set, issued by several brands of the Peoples Tobacco Co., is the last of the Louisana cigarette sets and the most confusing. Apparently issued over a period of several years between 1911 and 1916, the set employs the same pictures as several contemporary caramel and bakery sets. Cards measure a nominal 1-1/2" x 2-5/8", thought reasonable allowance must be made in consideration of original cutting methodology. Positive identification can be made by the back of the cards. The Peoples Tobacco cards carry advertising for one of three brands of cigarettes: Kotton, Mino or Virginia Extra. The Kotton brand is the most common, while the Virginia Extra and Mino backs command a premium. T216 cards are found in two types; one has a glossy front finish, while a second scarcer type is printed on a thin paper. The thin paper cards command an additional 15 percent premium. The cards represent players from the American, National and Federal Leagues.

		NM	EX	VG
Common Player:		3,300	1,320	660.00
(1)	Jack Barry/Btg	3,300	1,320	660.00
(2)	Jack Barry/Fldg	3,300	1,320	660.00
(3)	Harry Bemis	3,300	1,320	660.00
(4a)	Chief Bender (Philadelphia, striped cap.)	8,800	3,520	1,760
(4b)	Chief Bender (Baltimore, striped cap.)	8,800	3,520	1,760
(5a)	Chief Bender (Philadelphia, white cap.)	8,800	3,520	1,760
(5b)	Chief Bender (Baltimore, white cap.)	8,800	3,520	1,760
(6)	Bill Bergen	3,300	1,320	660.00
(7a)	Bob Bescher (Cincinnati)	3,300	1,320	660.00
(7b)	Bob Bescher (St. Louis)	3,300	1,320	660.00
(8)	Roger Bresnahan	8,800	3,520	1,760
(9)	Al Bridwell/Btg	3,300	1,320	660.00
(10a)	Al Bridwell/Sliding (New York)	3,300	1,320	660.00
(10b)	Al Bridwell/Sliding (St. Louis)	3,300	1,320	660.00
(11)	Donie Bush	3,300	1,320	660.00
(12)	Doc Casey	3,300	1,320	660.00
(13)	Frank Chance	8,800	3,520	1,760
(14a)	Hal Chase/Fldg (New York)	3,300	1,320	660.00
(14b)	Hal Chase/Fldg (Buffalo)	3,300	1,320	660.00
(15)	Hal Chase/Portrait	3,300	1,320	660.00
(16a)	Ty Cobb/Standing (Detroit Am.)	35,750	14,300	7,150
(16b)	Ty Cobb/Standing (Detroit Americans)	33,000	13,200	6,600
(17)	Ty Cobb/Btg (Detroit Americans)	33,000	13,200	6,600
(18a)	Eddie Collins (Phila. Am.)	8,800	3,520	1,760
(18b)	Eddie Collins (Phila. Amer.)	8,800	3,520	1,760
(19)	Eddie Collins (Chicago)	8,800	3,520	1,760
(20a)	Sam Crawford (Small print.)	8,800	3,520	1,760
(20b)	Sam Crawford (Large print.)	8,800	3,520	1,760
(21)	Harry Davis	3,300	1,320	660.00
(22)	Ray Demmitt	3,300	1,320	660.00
(23)	Art Devlin	3,300	1,320	660.00
(24a)	Wild Bill Donovan (Detroit)	3,300	1,320	660.00
(24b)	Wild Bill Donovan (New York)	3,300	1,320	660.00
(25a)	Red Dooin (Philadelphia)	3,300	1,320	660.00
(25b)	Red Dooin (Cincinnati)	3,300	1,320	660.00
(26a)	Mickey Doolan (Philadelphia)	3,300	1,320	660.00
(26b)	Mickey Doolan (Baltimore)	3,300	1,320	660.00
(27)	Patsy Dougherty	3,300	1,320	660.00
(28a)	Larry Doyle, Larry Doyle/Btg (N.Y. Nat'l)	3,300	1,320	660.00
(28b)	Larry Doyle/Btg (New York Nat'l)	3,300	1,320	660.00
(29)	Larry Doyle/Throwing	3,300	1,320	660.00
(30)	Clyde Engle	3,300	1,320	660.00
(31a)	Johnny Evers (Chicago)	8,800	3,520	1,760
(31b)	Johnny Evers (Boston)	8,800	3,520	1,760
(32)	Art Fromme	3,300	1,320	660.00
(33a)	George Gibson (Pittsburg Nat'l, back view.)	3,300	1,320	660.00
(33b)	George Gibson (Pittsburgh Nat'l., back view.)	3,300	1,320	660.00
(34a)	George Gibson (Pittsburg Nat'l, front view.)	3,300	1,320	660.00
(34b)	George Gibson (Pittsburgh Nat'l., front view.)	3,300	1,320	660.00
(35a)	Topsy Hartsel (Phila. Am.)	3,300	1,320	660.00
(35b)	Topsy Hartsel (Phila. Amer.)	3,300	1,320	660.00
(36)	Roy Hartzell/Btg	3,300	1,320	660.00
(37)	Roy Hartzell/Catching	3,300	1,320	660.00
(38a)	Fred Jacklitsch (Philadelphia)	3,300	1,320	660.00
(38b)	Fred Jacklitsch (Baltimore)	3,300	1,320	660.00
(39a)	Hughie Jennings (Orange background.)	8,800	3,520	1,760
(39b)	Hughie Jennings (Red background.)	8,800	3,520	1,760
(40)	Red Kleinow	3,300	1,320	660.00
(41a)	Otto Knabe (Philadelphia)	3,300	1,320	660.00
(41b)	Otto Knabe (Baltimore)	3,300	1,320	660.00
(42)	Jack Knight	3,300	1,320	660.00
(43a)	Nap Lajoie/Fldg (Philadelphia)	13,750	5,500	2,750
(43b)	Nap Lajoie/Fldg (Cleveland)	13,750	5,500	2,750
(44)	Nap Lajoie/Portrait	13,750	5,500	2,750
(45a)	Hans Lobert (Cincinnati)	3,300	1,320	660.00
(45b)	Hans Lobert (New York)	3,300	1,320	660.00
(46)	Sherry Magee	3,300	1,320	660.00
(47)	Rube Marquard	8,800	3,520	1,760
(48a)	Christy Matthewson (Mathewson) (Large print.)	33,000	13,200	6,600
(48b)	Christy Matthewson (Mathewson) (Small print.)	33,000	13,200	6,600
(49a)	John McGraw (Large print.)	8,800	3,520	1,760
(49b)	John McGraw (Small print.)	8,800	3,520	1,760
(50)	Larry McLean	3,300	1,320	660.00
(51)	George McQuillan	3,300	1,320	660.00
(52)	Dots Miller/Btg	3,300	1,320	660.00
(53a)	Dots Miller/Fldg (Pittsburg)	3,300	1,320	660.00
(53b)	Dots Miller/Fldg (St. Louis)	3,300	1,320	660.00
(54a)	Danny Murphy (Philadelphia)	3,300	1,320	660.00
(54b)	Danny Murphy (Brooklyn)	3,300	1,320	660.00
(55)	Rebel Oakes	3,300	1,320	660.00
(56)	Bill O'Hara	3,300	1,320	660.00
(57)	Eddie Plank	8,800	3,520	1,760
(58a)	Germany Schaefer (Washington)	3,300	1,320	660.00
(58b)	Germany Schaefer (Newark)	3,300	1,320	660.00
(59)	Admiral Schlei	3,300	1,320	660.00
(60)	Boss Schmidt	3,300	1,320	660.00
(61)	Johnny Seigle	3,300	1,320	660.00
(62)	Dave Shean	3,300	1,320	660.00
(63)	Boss Smith (Schmidt)	3,300	1,320	660.00
(64)	Tris Speaker	16,500	6,600	3,300
(65)	Oscar Stanage	3,300	1,320	660.00
(66)	George Stovall	3,300	1,320	660.00
(67)	Jeff Sweeney	3,300	1,320	660.00
(68a)	Joe Tinker/Btg (Chicago Nat'l)	8,800	3,520	1,760
(68b)	Joe Tinker/Btg (Chicago Feds)	8,800	3,520	1,760
(69)	Joe Tinker/Portrait	8,800	3,520	1,760
(70a)	Honus Wagner/Btg (S.S.)	33,000	13,200	6,600
(70b)	Honus Wagner/Btg (2b.)	33,000	13,200	6,600

		NM	EX	VG
(71a)	Honus Wagner/Throwing (S.S.)	33,000	13,200	6,600
(71b)	Honus Wagner/Throwing (2b.)	33,000	13,200	6,600
(72)	Hooks Wiltse	3,300	1,320	660.00
(73)	Cy Young	22,000	8,800	4,400
(74a)	Heinie Zimmerman (2b.)	3,300	1,320	660.00
(74b)	Heinie Zimmerman (3b.)	3,300	1,320	660.00

1949 Vis-Ed Cleveland Indian Slide-cards

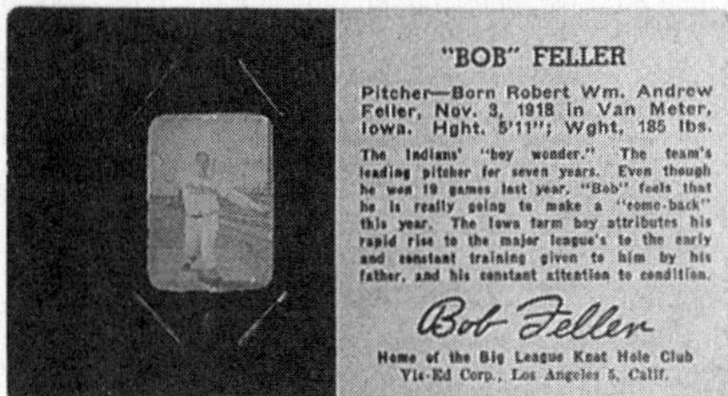

These unique novelties feature the members of the World Champion 1948 Cleveland Indians. The players are pictured on a single frame of 16mm film which has been inserted into slits cut on one end of the cardboard. The cardboard holders are dark blue and yellow, with blue printing. Fronts have player personal data, career highlights, the player's name in script and identification of the issuer. Backs have a list of "Magic Slides" which could be ordered for 33 cents each. It is likely that a slide-card exists for each of the players on that list, but only those which have been confirmed to date are checklisted here, in alphabetical order. Complete slide-cards measure 3-3/4" x 2". A plastic baseball-shaped viewer was sold with the slides.

		NM	EX	VG
Common Player:		75.00	37.00	22.00
(1)	Lou Boudreau	90.00	45.00	27.00
(2)	Larry Doby	100.00	50.00	30.00
(3)	Bob Feller	125.00	62.00	37.00
(4)	Joe Gordon	75.00	37.00	22.00
(5)	Jim Hegan	75.00	37.00	22.00
(6)	Ken Keltner	75.00	37.00	22.00

1949 Vis-Ed Cleveland Indian Magic Dials

Similar in concept to a Viewmaster, these hand-held "Magic Dial Big League Viewers" feature the members of the World Champion 1948 Cleveland Indians, plus Mickey Vernon, who joined the team in 1949, and, inexplicably, Pittsburgh Pirate Ralph Kiner. Each of the players is pictured on six single frames of 8 mm movie film (once in color, but now usually faded to sepia tones) mounted on a 2" cardboard circle within a red, white and blue 2-1/4" x 2" rectangular frame; the whole is held together by a metal rivet. The pictures can be viewed by turning the round cardboard dial. The dials came with a playing tips instructional pamphlet. Original price was 29 cents apiece.

		NM	EX	VG
Complete Set (15):		1,200	600.00	350.00
Common Player:		75.00	37.00	22.00
(1)	Gene Bearden	75.00	37.00	22.00
(2)	Lou Boudreau/Btg	125.00	62.00	37.00
(3)	Lou Boudreau (Double play.)	125.00	62.00	37.00
(4)	Lou Boudreau (Shortstop)	125.00	62.00	37.00
(5)	Larry Doby	125.00	62.00	37.00
(6)	Bob Feller	150.00	75.00	45.00
(7)	Joe Gordon (Double play.)	75.00	37.00	22.00
(8)	Joe Gordon (Second base.)	75.00	37.00	22.00
(9)	Jim Hegan	75.00	37.00	22.00
(10)	Ken Keltner	75.00	37.00	22.00
(11)	Ralph Kiner	125.00	62.00	37.00
(12)	Bob Lemon	125.00	62.00	37.00
(13)	Dale Mitchell	75.00	37.00	22.00
(14)	Satchel Paige	200.00	100.00	60.00
(15)	Mickey Vernon	75.00	37.00	22.00

1966 Volpe Tumblers

A number of teams co-operated in the production of baseball player 12-oz. thermal tumblers which were distributed at local gas stations for a small sum and/or a minimum

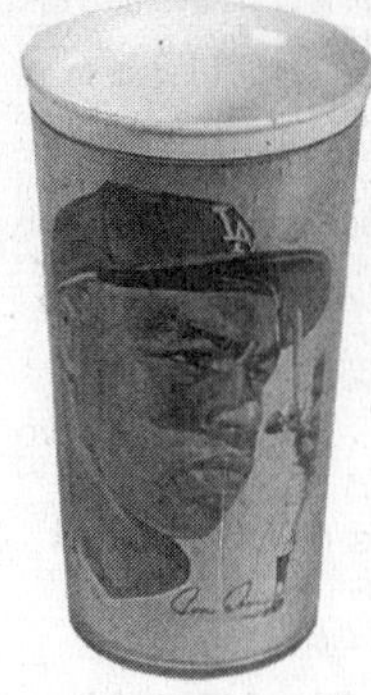

fuel purchase. The plastic tumblers have artwork portraits and smaller action pictures by Nicholas Volpe and facsimile autographs on colorful backgrounds. The glasses are 5-1/4" tall and 3" in diameter at the rim.

		NM	EX	VG
Common Player:		20.00	10.00	6.00
	CINCINNATI REDS			
(1)	Chico Cardenas	20.00	10.00	6.00
(2)	Gordy Coleman	20.00	10.00	6.00
(3)	John Edwards	20.00	10.00	6.00
(4)	Sammy Ellis	20.00	10.00	6.00
(5)	Tommy Harper	20.00	10.00	6.00
(6)	Deron Johnson	20.00	10.00	6.00
(7)	Jim Maloney	20.00	10.00	6.00
(8)	Billy McCool	20.00	10.00	6.00
(9)	Joe Nuxhall	20.00	10.00	6.00
(10)	Jim O'Toole	20.00	10.00	6.00
(11)	Vada Pinson	30.00	15.00	9.00
(12)	Pete Rose	75.00	37.00	22.00
	CLEVELAND INDIANS			
(1)	Max Alvis	20.00	10.00	6.00
(2)	Joe Azcue	20.00	10.00	6.00
(3)	Larry Brown	20.00	10.00	6.00
(4)	Rocky Colavito	50.00	25.00	15.00
(5)	Vic Davalillo	20.00	10.00	6.00
(6)	Chuck Hinton	20.00	10.00	6.00
(7)	Dick Howser	20.00	10.00	6.00
(8)	Sam McDowell	20.00	10.00	6.00
(9)	Don McMahon	20.00	10.00	6.00
(10)	Sonny Siebert	20.00	10.00	6.00
(11)	Leon Wagner	20.00	10.00	6.00
(12)	Fred Whitfield	20.00	10.00	6.00
	NEW YORK METS			
(1)	Larry Bearnarth	20.00	10.00	6.00
(2)	Yogi Berra	50.00	25.00	15.00
(3)	Jack Fisher	20.00	10.00	6.00
(4)	Rob Gardner	20.00	10.00	6.00
(5)	Jim Hickman	20.00	10.00	6.00
(6)	Ron Hunt	20.00	10.00	6.00
(7)	Ed Kranepool	20.00	10.00	6.00
(8)	Johnny Lewis	20.00	10.00	6.00
(9)	Tug McGraw	20.00	10.00	6.00
(10)	Roy McMillan	20.00	10.00	6.00
(11)	Dick Stuart	20.00	10.00	6.00
(12)	Ron Swoboda	20.00	10.00	6.00
	DETROIT TIGERS			
(1)	Hank Aguirre	20.00	10.00	6.00
(2)	Norm Cash	30.00	15.00	9.00
(3)	Don Demeter	20.00	10.00	6.00
(4)	Bill Freehan	20.00	10.00	6.00
(5)	Willie Horton	20.00	10.00	6.00
(6)	Al Kaline	50.00	25.00	15.00
(7)	Mickey Lolich	20.00	10.00	6.00
(8)	Dick McAuliffe	20.00	10.00	6.00
(9)	Denny McLain	20.00	10.00	6.00
(10)	Joe Sparma	20.00	10.00	6.00
(11)	Don Wert	20.00	10.00	6.00
(12)	Dave Wickersham	20.00	10.00	6.00
	LOS ANGELES DODGERS			
(1)	Tommy Davis	20.00	10.00	6.00
(2)	Willie Davis	20.00	10.00	6.00
(3)	Don Drysdale	40.00	20.00	12.00
(4)	Ron Fairly	20.00	10.00	6.00
(5)	John Kennedy	20.00	10.00	6.00
(6)	Jim Lefebvre	20.00	10.00	6.00
(7)	Sandy Koufax	60.00	30.00	18.00
(8)	Claude Osteen	20.00	10.00	6.00
(9)	Wes Parker	20.00	10.00	6.00
(10)	Ron Perranoski	20.00	10.00	6.00
(11)	Johnny Roseboro	20.00	10.00	6.00
(12)	Maury Wills	20.00	10.00	6.00

1913 Voskamp's Coffee Pittsburgh Pirates

The 1913 Pittsburgh Pirates are featured in this set of cards given away in packages of coffee and tea and redeemable for seats at Pirates games. The 2-1/4" x 3-5/8" cards have black-and-white player photos on a plain white background, along with ID and a "Photo by Johnston" credit line. The black-and-white back has a checklist of the set and details of the ticket redemption program. Pose variations of the Hofman and O'Toole cards are reported to exist. The checklist for the unnumbered cards is presented here alphabetically. Because the set was issued just after the great tobacco card era, several of the Pirates in this set are not found on any other cards.

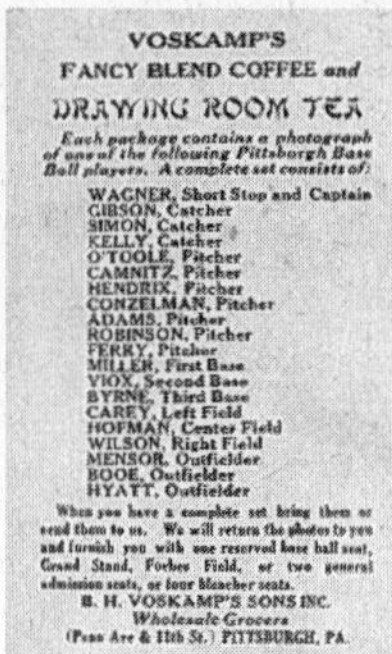
VOSKAMP'S
FANCY BLEND COFFEE *and*
DRAWING ROOM TEA

Each package contains a photograph of one of the following Pittsburgh Base Ball players. A complete set consists of:

WAGNER, Short Stop and Captain
GIBSON, Catcher
SIMON, Catcher
KELLY, Catcher
O'TOOLE, Pitcher
CAMNITZ, Pitcher
HENDRIX, Pitcher
CONZELMAN, Pitcher
ADAMS, Pitcher
ROBINSON, Pitcher
FERRY, Pitcher
MILLER, First Base
VIOX, Second Base
BYRNE, Third Base
CAREY, Left Field
HOFMAN, Center Field
WILSON, Right Field
MENSOR, Outfielder
BOOE, Outfielder
HYATT, Outfielder

When you have a complete set bring them or send them to us. We will return the photos to you and furnish you with one reserved base ball seat, Grand Stand, Forbes Field, or two general admission seats, or four bleacher seats.

B. H. VOSKAMP'S SONS INC.
Wholesale Grocers
(Penn Ave & 11th St.) PITTSBURGH, PA.

		NM	EX	VG
Complete Set (20):		60,000	30,000	18,000
Common Player:		2,025	1,015	600.00
(1)	Babe Adams	2,025	1,015	600.00
(2)	Everitt Booe	2,025	1,015	600.00
(3)	Bobby Byrne	2,025	1,015	600.00
(4)	Howie Camnitz	2,025	1,015	600.00
(5)	Max Carey	3,000	1,500	900.00
(6)	Joe Conzelman	2,025	1,015	600.00
(7)	Jack Ferry	2,025	1,015	600.00
(8)	George Gibson	2,025	1,015	600.00
(9)	Claude Hendrix	2,025	1,015	600.00
(10)	Solly Hofman	2,025	1,015	600.00
(11)	Ham Hyatt	2,025	1,015	600.00
(12)	Bill Kelly	2,025	1,015	600.00
(13)	Ed Mensor	2,025	1,015	600.00
(14)	Dots Miller	2,025	1,015	600.00
(15)	Marty O'Toole	2,025	1,015	600.00
(16)	Hank Robinson	2,025	1,015	600.00
(17)	Mike Simon	2,025	1,015	600.00
(18)	Jim Viox	2,025	1,015	600.00
(19)	Honus Wagner	22,500	11,250	6,750
(20)	Owen Wilson	2,025	1,015	600.00

1910 Hans Wagner Cigars

Circa 1910 the Freeman Cigar Co. apparently envisioned marketing a product named for the Pirates star shortstop. While it appears the cigar was never actually produced, various packaging elements have survived in proof examples. Most pieces are embossed and have a color lithograph which features a portrait of Wagner against a ballgame background. "HANS WAGNER" is in red and gold above. Usually found in the bottom border is "Title & Design Registered by Freeman Cigar Co." Collectors must be aware that various modern fantasy pieces purporting to be of the same genre exist in the market.

	NM	EX	VG
Hans Wagner (7-1/4" x 6-1/2" box label)	15,000	7,500	4,500
Hans Wagner (4-1/2" octagonal label)	12,000	6,000	3,500
Hans Wagner (4-1/4" oval label)	15,000	7,500	4,500
Hans Wagner (3" cigar band)	1,600	800.00	480.00
Hans Wagner (Typographic box-side label.)	1,500	750.00	450.00
Hans Wagner (Typographic box-top label.)	7,500	3,750	2,250

1880s John M. Ward Fan

The specific date of production for this ornate hand fan is unknown. Some examples show on their back an advertisement for "C. Philpot" of Springfield, Maine. The central portion of the fan is a round piece of heavy cardboard, about 7-3/4" in diameter, that features a color lithographic portrait of Ward on a baseball background. Around the picture is a peach-colored ribbon. A wooden handle is attached on back.

	NM	EX	VG
John M. Ward	7,800	4,200	2,700

1934 Ward's Sporties Pins

The date of issue can only be approximated for this issue pf 1-1/4" diameter celluloid pin-back buttons. Ward's Sporties was evidently some kind of food product; at the center of each button is a black-and-white or blue-and-white portrait photo of a player with his name above and "Eats" below the picture. Printed around the photo portion in white on a red background is: "Good Sports Enjoy / WARD'S SPORTIES." Ward's bakeries issue several type of baseball cards and collectibles over the years, such as the 1947 Tip-Top bread cards. The checklist is in alphabetical order, and may not yet be complete.

	NM	EX	VG
Complete Set (8):	4,500	2,250	1,350
Common Player:	325.00	160.00	100.00
(1) Dizzy Dean	1,000	500.00	300.00
(2) Jimmy Dykes	325.00	160.00	100.00
(3) Jimmie Foxx	1,000	500.00	300.00
(4) Frank Frisch	650.00	325.00	195.00
(5) Charlie Gehringer	650.00	325.00	195.00
(6) Charlie Grimm	325.00	160.00	100.00
(7) Schoolboy Rowe	325.00	160.00	100.00
(8) Jimmie Wilson	325.00	160.00	100.00

1916 Ware's

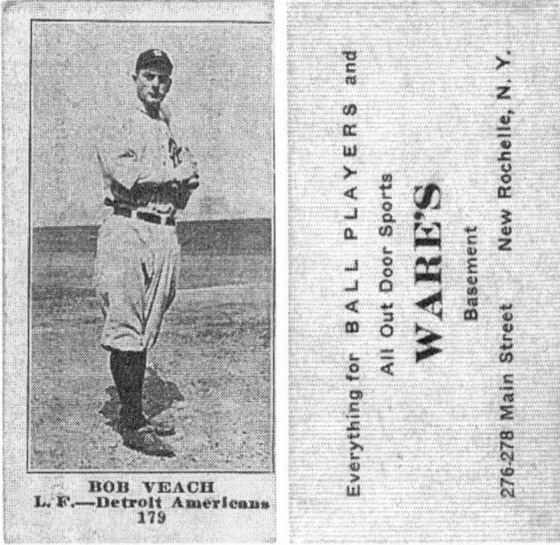

BOB VEACH
L. F.—Detroit Americans
179
Everything for BALL PLAYERS and
All Out Door Sports
WARE'S
Basement
276-278 Main Street New Rochelle, N. Y.

One of several regional advertisers to use this 200-card set as a promotional medium was this New Rochelle, N.Y., store's sporting goods department. The checklist and relative value information are listed under 1916 M101-4 Blank Backs. Collectors can expect to pay a significant premium for individual cards to enhance a type card or superstar card collection. The American Card Catalog listed these 1-5/8" x 3" black-and-white cards as H801-9.

PREMIUMS:
Common Players: 2-4X
Hall of Famers: 1.5-2.5X
(See 1916 Sporting News M101-4 for checklist and price guide.)

1872 Warren Studio Boston Red Stockings Cabinets

The champions from the premiere season of baseball's first professional league (some wearing their championship pins), are pictured on these cabinet cards. Members of the Boston Red Stockings were photographed in uniform at a local studio. The cards measure about 4-1/4" x 6-1/2" with sepia photos. In the bottom border is the name and address of the studio; information that is repeated on the otherwise blank back. Player identification is not found on the cards but can be deduced by studying contemporary team pictures.

	NM	EX	VG
Common Player:	6,500	2,750	1,650
(1) Ross Barnes	9,000	3,000	1,800
(2) Dave Birdsall	6,500	2,750	1,650
(3) Charles Gould	6,500	2,750	1,650
(4) Andy Leonard	6,500	2,750	1,650
(5) Cal McVey	9,000	3,000	1,800
(6) Fraley Rogers	6,500	2,750	1,650
(7) John Ryan	6,500	2,750	1,650
(8) Harry Schafer	6,500	2,750	1,650
(9) Albert Spalding	42,000	9,000	5,400
(10) George Wright	30,000	9,000	5,400
(11) Harry Wright	30,000	9,000	5,400

1872 Warren Studio Boston Red Stockings CDVs

The champions from the premiere season of baseball's first professional league (some wearing their championship pins), are pictured on these cartes de visites depict. Members of the Boston Red Stockings were photographed at a local studio, most of them being pictured in coat-and-tie with only Harry Wright in uniform. The cards measure about 2-1/2" x 4-1/4" with sepia photos bordered in white. In the bottom border is the name and address of the studio; information which is repeated on the otherwise blank back. Player identification is not found on the cards but can be deduced by studying contemporary team pictures.

	NM	EX	VG
Common Player:	3,500	1,750	1,000
(1) Ross Barnes	3,500	1,750	1,000
(2) Dave Birdsall	3,500	1,750	1,000
(3) Charlie Gould	3,500	1,750	1,000
(4) Andy Leonard	3,500	1,750	1,000
(5) Cal McVey	3,500	1,750	1,000
(6) Fraley Rogers	3,500	1,750	1,000
(7) John Ryan	3,500	1,750	1,000
(8) Harry Schafer	3,500	1,750	1,000
(9) Albert Spalding	15,000	7,500	3,750
(10) George Wright	10,000	5,000	3,000
(11) Harry Wright (street clothes)	10,000	5,000	3,000
(12) Harry Wright (uniform)	10,000	5,000	3,000

1874 Warren Studio Boston Red Stockings Cabinets

The champions from the National Association Boston Red Stockings were photographed in uniform at a local studio. The cards measure about 4-1/4" x 6-1/2" with sepia photos. In the bottom border is the name and address of the studio. Player identification is not found on the cards but can be deduced by studying contemporary team pictures.

	NM	EX	VG
Common Player:	5,500	2,750	1,650
(1) Ross Barnes	8,250	2,750	1,650
(2) Tommy Beals	6,600	2,750	1,650
(3) George Hall	6,600	2,750	1,650
(4) Andy Leonard	5,500	2,750	1,650
(5) Cal McVey	8,250	2,750	1,650
(6) Harry Schafer	6,600	2,750	1,650

1931 Washington Senators Picture Pack

This set of souvenir pictures offers player photos in a black-and-white, blank-back format of about 6-1/8" x 9-1/2". Each picture has a white border and a facsimile player autograph.

	NM	EX	VG
Complete Set (30):	800.00	400.00	240.00
Common Player:	25.00	12.50	7.50
(1) Nick Altrock	35.00	17.50	10.50
(2) Oswald Bluege	25.00	12.50	7.50
(3) Cliff Bolton	25.00	12.50	7.50
(4) Lloyd Brown	25.00	12.50	7.50
(5) Robert Burke	25.00	12.50	7.50
(6) Joe Cronin	50.00	25.00	15.00
(7) Alvin Crowder	25.00	12.50	7.50
(8) E.B. Eynon, Jr. (Secretary-Treasurer)	25.00	12.50	7.50
(9) Charles Fischer	25.00	12.50	7.50
(10) Edward Gharrity	25.00	12.50	7.50
(11) Clark Griffith	45.00	22.00	13.50
(12) Irving Hadley	25.00	12.50	7.50
(13) William Hargrave	25.00	12.50	7.50
(14) David Harris	25.00	12.50	7.50
(15) Jack Hayes	25.00	12.50	7.50
(16) Walter Johnson	125.00	62.00	37.00
(17) Sam Jones	25.00	12.50	7.50
(18) Baxter Jordan	25.00	12.50	7.50
(19) Joe Judge	25.00	12.50	7.50
(20) Joe Kuhel	25.00	12.50	7.50
(21) Henry Manush	50.00	25.00	15.00
(22) Fred Marberry	25.00	12.50	7.50
(23) Mike Martin	25.00	12.50	7.50
(24) Walter Masters	25.00	12.50	7.50
(25) Charles Myer	25.00	12.50	7.50
(26) Harry Rice	25.00	12.50	7.50
(27) Sam Rice	25.00	12.50	7.50
(28) Al Schacht	35.00	17.50	10.50
(29) Roy Spencer	25.00	12.50	7.50
(30) Sam West	25.00	12.50	7.50

1970 Washington Senators Traffic Safety

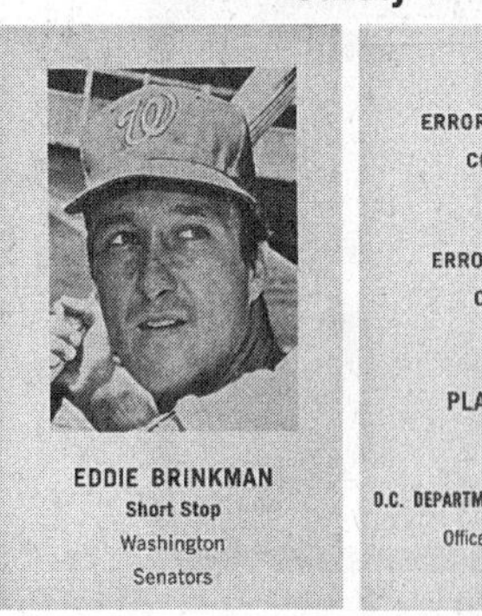

EDDIE BRINKMAN
Short Stop
Washington
Senators
ERRORS IN BASEBALL
COST GAMES
ERRORS IN TRAFFIC
COST LIVES
PLAY IT SAFE!
D.C. DEPARTMENT OF MOTOR VEHICLES
Office of Traffic Safety

Distributed in 1970 by the Washington, D.C. Department of Motor Vehicles, this issue promoting traffic safety was one of the first police sets. Featuring black-and-white player photos, the cards measure 2-1/2" x 3-7/8" and have large borders surrounding the pictures. The player's name and position are below; the team name appears in smaller type at the bottom. The set can be found on either pink card stock, used for the original print run, or on bright yellow stock, used for two subsequent printings. Aurelio Rodriguez, who joined the team after the season began, is known only in yellow; all other players can be found in both yellow and pink. The pink varieties carry a higher value. The backs of the cards offer traffic safety tips.

	NM	EX	VG
Complete Set, Pink (10):	150.00	75.00	45.00
Common Player, Pink:	3.50	1.75	1.00
Complete Set, Yellow (11):	25.00	12.50	7.50
Common Player, Yellow:	2.50	1.25	.70
(1a) Dick Bosman (Pink)	3.50	1.75	1.00
(1b) Dick Bosman (Yellow)	2.50	1.25	.70
(2a) Eddie Brinkman (Pink)	3.50	1.75	1.00
(2b) Eddie Brinkman (Yellow)	2.50	1.25	.70
(3a) Paul Casanova (Pink)	3.50	1.75	1.00
(3b) Paul Casanova (Yellow)	2.50	1.25	.70
(4a) Mike Epstein (Pink)	3.50	1.75	1.00
(4b) Mike Epstein (Yellow)	2.50	1.25	.70
(5a) Frank Howard (Pink)	10.00	5.00	3.00
(5b) Frank Howard (Yellow)	7.50	3.75	2.25
(6a) Darold Knowles (Pink)	3.50	1.75	1.00
(6b) Darold Knowles (Yellow)	2.50	1.25	.70
(7a) Lee Maye (Pink)	3.50	1.75	1.00
(7b) Lee Maye (Yellow)	2.50	1.25	.70
(8a) Dave Nelson/SP (Pink)	125.00	62.00	37.00
(8b) Dave Nelson (Yellow)	2.50	1.25	.70
(9) Aurelio Rodriguez/SP (Yellow)	5.00	2.50	1.50
(10a) John Roseboro (Pink)	3.50	1.75	1.00

(10b)	John Roseboro (Yellow)	2.50	1.25	.70
(11a)	Ed Stroud (Pink)	3.50	1.75	1.00
(11b)	Ed Stroud (Yellow)	2.50	1.25	.70

1971 Washington Senators Traffic Safety

The 1971 Senators safety set was again issued by the Washington, D.C., Department of Motor Vehicles and was similar in design and size (2-1/2" x 3-7/8") to the previous year, except that it was printed on a pale yellow stock. The set, which features several new players, contains no scarce cards. The backs contain traffic safety messages.

		NM	EX	VG
Complete Set (10):		12.50	6.25	3.75
Uncut Sheet:		12.50	6.25	3.75
Common Player:		1.00	.50	.30
(1)	Dick Bosman	1.00	.50	.30
(2)	Paul Casanova	1.00	.50	.30
(3)	Tim Cullen	1.00	.50	.30
(4)	Joe Foy	1.00	.50	.30
(5)	Toby Harrah	1.00	.50	.30
(6)	Frank Howard	2.50	1.25	.70
(7)	Elliott Maddox	1.00	.50	.30
(8)	Tom McCraw	1.00	.50	.30
(9)	Denny McLain	3.00	1.50	.90
(10)	Don Wert	.60	.30	.20

1910 Washington Times

Only American League players have so far been found in this issue by the Washington Times newspaper. The 2-9/16" x 3-9/16" cards have portrait or action photos of the players within a wide border. A white panel at bottom has the player name and team at left and "Washington Times Series" at right. All printing is in dark red. Backs are blank. The manner in which these cards were distributed is unknown, as is the extent of the checklist. The unnumbered cards are checklisted here in alphabetical order.

		NM	EX	VG
Common Player:		2,500	1,250	750.00
(1)	Ty Cobb	20,000	10,000	6,000
(2)	Eddie Collins	7,500	3,750	2,250
(3)	Wid Conroy	2,500	1,250	750.00
(4)	Sam Crawford	7,500	3,750	2,250
(5)	Harry Davis	2,500	1,250	750.00
(6)	Bob Groom	2,500	1,250	750.00
(7)	Nap Lajoie	7,500	3,750	2,250
(8)	George McBride	2,500	1,250	750.00
(9)	Clyde Milan	2,500	1,250	750.00
(10)	Frank Oberlin	2,500	1,250	750.00
(11)	Rube Oldring	2,500	1,250	750.00
(12)	Freddie Parent (Freddy)	2,500	1,250	750.00
(13)	Doc Reisling	2,500	1,250	750.00
(14)	Gabby Street	2,500	1,250	750.00
(15)	Lee Tannehill	2,500	1,250	750.00
(16)	Bob Unglaub	2,500	1,250	750.00
(17)	Dixie Walker	2,500	1,250	750.00
(18)	Ed. Walsh	7,500	3,750	2,250
(19)	Joe Wood	2,000	1,000	600.00
(20)	Cy Young	12,500	6,250	3,750

1951 WBKB "Lucky Fan" Chicago Cubs

This series of black-and-white player glossies appears to have been a promotional giveaway from WBKB radio or television station in conjunction with Ben Bey's "Lucky Fan"

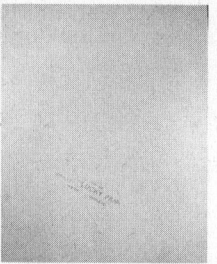

club or contest. The 8-1/8" x 10" photos have a facsimile autograph on front. On back is a three-line rubber-stamped "COURTESY OF / BEN BEY "LUCKY FAN" / WBKB - CHICAGO." The checklist is arranged alphabetically.

		NM	EX	VG
Complete Set (28):		900.00	450.00	270.00
Common Player:		40.00	20.00	12.00
(1)	Frank Baumholtz	40.00	20.00	12.00
(2)	Bob Borkowski	40.00	20.00	12.00
(3)	Smoky Burgess	50.00	25.00	15.00
(4)	Phil Cavarretta	40.00	20.00	12.00
(5)	Chuck Connors	100.00	50.00	30.00
(6)	Jack Cusick	40.00	20.00	12.00
(7)	Bruce Edwards	40.00	20.00	12.00
(8)	Dee Fondy	40.00	20.00	12.00
(9)	Joe Hatten	40.00	20.00	12.00
(10)	Gene Hermanski	40.00	20.00	12.00
(11)	Frank Hiller	40.00	20.00	12.00
(12)	Ransom Jackson	40.00	20.00	12.00
(13)	Hal Jeffcoat	40.00	20.00	12.00
(14)	Bob Kelly	40.00	20.00	12.00
(15)	Johnny Klippstein	40.00	20.00	12.00
(16)	Dutch Leonard	40.00	20.00	12.00
(17)	Turk Lown	40.00	20.00	12.00
(18)	Cal McLish	40.00	20.00	12.00
(19)	Eddie Miksis	40.00	20.00	12.00
(20)	Paul Minner	40.00	20.00	12.00
(21)	Mickey Owen	40.00	20.00	12.00
(22)	Andy Pafko	50.00	25.00	15.00
(23)	Bob Ramazotti	40.00	20.00	12.00
(24)	Bob Rush	40.00	20.00	12.00
(25)	Hank Sauer	40.00	20.00	12.00
(26)	Bob Schultz	40.00	20.00	12.00
(27)	Bill Serena	40.00	20.00	12.00
(28)	Roy Smalley	45.00	22.00	13.50

1911-14 Weber Bakery (D304)

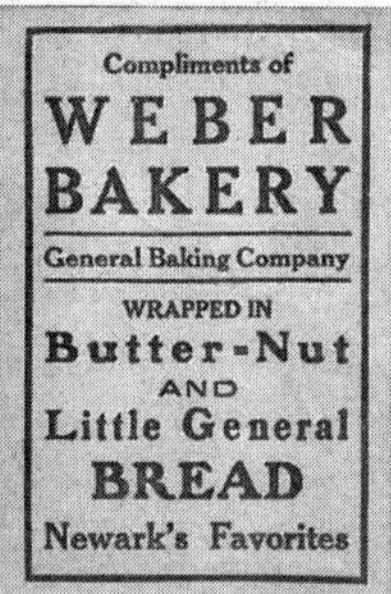

(See 1911-14 General Baking Co. for checklist and price information.)

1916 Weil Baking Co. (D329)

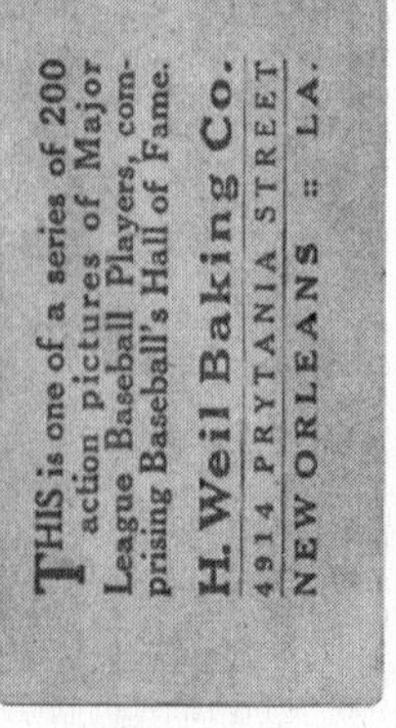

One of several issues by the New Orleans bakery, this 1-3/8" x 3" black-and-white set of 200 shares a checklist and relative values with the 1916 M101-4 Blank Backs set. Collectors can expect to pay a premium for a card with the Weil Baking ad on back to add to a type collection or superstar collection. The American Card Catalog lists this issue as D329.

		NM	EX	VG
Complete Set (200):		77,000	38,500	23,100
Common Player:		195.00	100.00	50.00
1	Babe Adams	195.00	100.00	50.00
2	Sam Agnew	195.00	100.00	50.00
3	Eddie Ainsmith	195.00	100.00	50.00
4	Grover Alexander	880.00	455.00	230.00
5	Leon Ames	195.00	100.00	50.00
6	Jimmy Archer	195.00	100.00	50.00
7	Jimmy Austin	195.00	100.00	50.00
8	H.D. Baird	195.00	100.00	50.00
9	J. Franklin Baker	715.00	375.00	190.00
10	Dave Bancroft	715.00	375.00	190.00
11	Jack Barry	195.00	100.00	50.00
12	Zinn Beck	195.00	100.00	50.00
13	"Chief" Bender	715.00	375.00	190.00
14	Joe Benz	195.00	100.00	50.00
15	Bob Bescher	195.00	100.00	50.00
16	Al Betzel	195.00	100.00	50.00
17	Mordecai Brown	715.00	375.00	190.00
18	Eddie Burns	195.00	100.00	50.00
19	George Burns	195.00	100.00	50.00
20	Geo. J. Burns	195.00	100.00	50.00
21	Joe Bush	195.00	100.00	50.00
22	"Donie" Bush	195.00	100.00	50.00
23	Art Butler	195.00	100.00	50.00
24	Bobbie Byrne	195.00	100.00	50.00
25	Forrest Cady	195.00	100.00	50.00
26	Jimmy Callahan	195.00	100.00	50.00
27	Ray Caldwell	195.00	100.00	50.00
28	Max Carey	715.00	375.00	190.00
29	George Chalmers	195.00	100.00	50.00
30	Ray Chapman	195.00	100.00	50.00
31	Larry Cheney	195.00	100.00	50.00
32	Eddie Cicotte	1,000	375.00	190.00
33	Tom Clarke	195.00	100.00	50.00
34	Eddie Collins	715.00	375.00	190.00
35	"Shauno" Collins	195.00	100.00	50.00
36	Charles Comiskey	715.00	375.00	190.00
37	Joe Connolly	195.00	100.00	50.00
38	Ty Cobb	5,500	2,860	1,430
39	Harry Coveleskie (Coveleski)	195.00	100.00	50.00
40	Gavvy Cravath	195.00	100.00	50.00
41	Sam Crawford	715.00	375.00	190.00
42	Jean Dale	195.00	100.00	50.00
43	Jake Daubert	195.00	100.00	50.00
44	Charles Deal	195.00	100.00	50.00
45	Al Demaree	195.00	100.00	50.00
46	Josh Devore	195.00	100.00	50.00
47	William Doak	195.00	100.00	50.00
48	Bill Donovan	195.00	100.00	50.00
49	Charles Dooin	195.00	100.00	50.00
50	Mike Doolan	195.00	100.00	50.00
51	Larry Doyle	195.00	100.00	50.00
52	Jean Dubuc	195.00	100.00	50.00
53	Oscar Dugey	195.00	100.00	50.00
54	Johnny Evers	715.00	375.00	190.00
55	Urban Faber	715.00	375.00	190.00
56	"Hap" Felsch	2,000	860.00	430.00
57	Bill Fischer	195.00	100.00	50.00
58	Ray Fisher	195.00	100.00	50.00
59	Max Flack	195.00	100.00	50.00
60	Art Fletcher	195.00	100.00	50.00
61	Eddie Foster	195.00	100.00	50.00
62	Jacques Fournier	195.00	100.00	50.00
63	Del Gainer (Gainor)	195.00	100.00	50.00
64	"Chic" Gandil	715.00	375.00	190.00
65	Larry Gardner	195.00	100.00	50.00
66	Joe Gedeon	195.00	100.00	50.00
67	Gus Getz	195.00	100.00	50.00
68	Geo. Gibson	195.00	100.00	50.00
69	Wilbur Good	195.00	100.00	50.00
70	Hank Gowdy	195.00	100.00	50.00
71	John Graney	195.00	100.00	50.00
72	Clark Griffith	715.00	375.00	190.00
73	Tom Griffith	195.00	100.00	50.00
74	Heinie Groh	195.00	100.00	50.00
75	Earl Hamilton	195.00	100.00	50.00
76	Bob Harmon	195.00	100.00	50.00
77	Roy Hartzell	195.00	100.00	50.00
78	Claude Hendrix	195.00	100.00	50.00
79	Olaf Henriksen	195.00	100.00	50.00
80	John Henry	195.00	100.00	50.00
81	"Buck" Herzog	195.00	100.00	50.00
82	Hugh High	195.00	100.00	50.00
83	Dick Hoblitzell	195.00	100.00	50.00
84	Harry Hooper	715.00	375.00	190.00
85	Ivan Howard	195.00	100.00	50.00
86	Miller Huggins	715.00	375.00	190.00
87	Joe Jackson	20,000	7,150	3,575
88	William James	195.00	100.00	50.00
89	Harold Janvrin	195.00	100.00	50.00
90	Hugh Jennings	715.00	375.00	190.00
91	Walter Johnson	1,760	835.00	470.00
92	Fielder Jones	195.00	100.00	50.00
93	Joe Judge	195.00	100.00	50.00
94	Bennie Kauff	195.00	100.00	50.00
95	Wm. Killefer Jr.	195.00	100.00	50.00
96	Ed. Konetchy	195.00	100.00	50.00
97	Napoleon Lajoie	715.00	375.00	190.00
98	Jack Lapp	195.00	100.00	50.00
99	John Lavan	195.00	100.00	50.00
100	Jimmy Lavender	195.00	100.00	50.00
101	"Nemo" Leibold	195.00	100.00	50.00
102	H.B. Leonard	195.00	100.00	50.00
103	Duffy Lewis	175.00	100.00	50.00
104	Hans Lobert	195.00	100.00	50.00
105	Tom Long	195.00	100.00	50.00
106	Fred Luderus	195.00	100.00	50.00
107	Connie Mack	715.00	375.00	190.00
108	Lee Magee	195.00	100.00	50.00
109	Sherwood Magee	195.00	100.00	50.00
110	Al. Mamaux	195.00	100.00	50.00
111	Leslie Mann	195.00	100.00	50.00
112	"Rabbit" Maranville	715.00	375.00	190.00
113	Rube Marquard	715.00	375.00	190.00
114	J. Erskine Mayer	195.00	100.00	50.00
115	George McBride	195.00	100.00	50.00
116	John J. McGraw	715.00	375.00	190.00
117	Jack McInnis	195.00	100.00	50.00

118	Fred Merkle	195.00	100.00	50.00
119	Chief Meyers	195.00	100.00	50.00
120	Clyde Milan	195.00	100.00	50.00
121	John Miller	195.00	100.00	50.00
122	Otto Miller	195.00	100.00	50.00
123	Willie Mitchell	195.00	100.00	50.00
124	Fred Mollwitz	195.00	100.00	50.00
125	Pat Moran	195.00	100.00	50.00
126	Ray Morgan	195.00	100.00	50.00
127	Geo. Moriarty	195.00	100.00	50.00
128	Guy Morton	195.00	100.00	50.00
129	Mike Mowrey	195.00	100.00	50.00
130	Ed. Murphy	195.00	100.00	50.00
131	"Hy" Myers	195.00	100.00	50.00
132	J.A. Niehoff	195.00	100.00	50.00
133	Rube Oldring	195.00	100.00	50.00
134	Oliver O'Mara	195.00	100.00	50.00
135	Steve O'Neill	195.00	100.00	50.00
136	"Dode" Paskert	195.00	100.00	50.00
137	Roger Peckinpaugh	195.00	100.00	50.00
138	Walter Pipp	195.00	100.00	50.00
139	Derril Pratt (Derrill)	195.00	100.00	50.00
140	Pat Ragan	195.00	100.00	50.00
141	Bill Rariden	195.00	100.00	50.00
142	Eppa Rixey	715.00	375.00	190.00
143	Davey Robertson	195.00	100.00	50.00
144	Wilbert Robinson	715.00	375.00	190.00
145	Bob Roth	195.00	100.00	50.00
146	Ed. Roush	715.00	375.00	190.00
147	Clarence Rowland	195.00	100.00	50.00
148	"Nap" Rucker	195.00	100.00	50.00
149	Dick Rudolph	195.00	100.00	50.00
150	Reb Russell	195.00	100.00	50.00
151	Babe Ruth	27,500	14,300	7,150
152	Vic Saier	195.00	100.00	50.00
153	"Slim" Sallee	195.00	100.00	50.00
154	Ray Schalk	715.00	375.00	190.00
155	Walter Schang	195.00	100.00	50.00
156	Frank Schulte	195.00	100.00	50.00
157	Everett Scott	195.00	100.00	50.00
158	Jim Scott	195.00	100.00	50.00
159	Tom Seaton	195.00	100.00	50.00
160	Howard Shanks	195.00	100.00	50.00
161	Bob Shawkey	195.00	100.00	50.00
162	Ernie Shore	195.00	100.00	50.00
163	Burt Shotton	195.00	100.00	50.00
164	Geo. Sisler	715.00	375.00	190.00
165	J. Carlisle Smith	195.00	100.00	50.00
166	Fred Snodgrass	195.00	100.00	50.00
167	Geo. Stallings	195.00	100.00	50.00
168	Oscar Stanage	195.00	100.00	50.00
169	Charles Stengel	715.00	375.00	190.00
170	Milton Stock	195.00	100.00	50.00
171	Amos Strunk	195.00	100.00	50.00
172	Billy Sullivan	195.00	100.00	50.00
173	"Jeff" Tesreau	195.00	100.00	50.00
174	Joe Tinker	715.00	375.00	190.00
175	Fred Toney	195.00	100.00	50.00
176	Terry Turner	195.00	100.00	50.00
177	George Tyler	195.00	100.00	50.00
178	Jim Vaughn	195.00	100.00	50.00
179	Bob Veach	195.00	100.00	50.00
180	James Viox	195.00	100.00	50.00
181	Oscar Vitt	195.00	100.00	50.00
182	Hans Wagner	5,000	1,375	690.00
183	Clarence Walker	195.00	100.00	50.00
184	Ed. Walsh	715.00	375.00	190.00
185	W. Wambsganss (Photo actually Fritz Coumbe.)	195.00	100.00	50.00
186	Buck Weaver	1,320	690.00	340.00
187	Carl Weilman	195.00	100.00	50.00
188	Zach Wheat	715.00	375.00	190.00
189	Geo. Whitted	195.00	100.00	50.00
190	Fred Williams	195.00	100.00	50.00
191	Art Wilson	195.00	100.00	50.00
192	J. Owen Wilson	195.00	100.00	50.00
193	Ivy Wingo	195.00	100.00	50.00
194	"Mel" Wolfgang	195.00	100.00	50.00
195	Joe Wood	195.00	100.00	50.00
196	Steve Yerkes	195.00	100.00	50.00
197	"Pep" Young	195.00	100.00	50.00
198	Rollie Zeider	195.00	100.00	50.00
199	Heiny Zimmerman	195.00	100.00	50.00
200	Ed. Zwilling	195.00	100.00	50.00

1917 Weil Baking Co. (D328)

THIS is one of a series of 200 action pictures of Major League Baseball Players, comprising Baseball's Hall of Fame.
H. Weil Baking Co.
4914 PRYTANIA STREET
NEW ORLEANS :: LA.

This set comprises one of several regional advertisers' use of the 200-card issue for promotional purposes. These cards are most often seen with the advertising of the Collins-McCarthy Candy Co. of San Francisco. Cards measure 2" x 3-1/4" and are printed in black-and-white. This set was listed as D328 in the American Card Catalog.

		NM	EX	VG
Complete Set (200):		140,000	70,000	42,500
Common Player:		330.00	165.00	100.00
1	Sam Agnew	330.00	165.00	100.00
2	Grover Alexander	1,320	660.00	395.00
3	W.S. Alexander (W.E.)	330.00	165.00	100.00
4	Leon Ames	330.00	165.00	100.00
5	Fred Anderson	330.00	165.00	100.00
6	Ed Appleton	330.00	165.00	100.00
7	Jimmy Archer	330.00	165.00	100.00
8	Jimmy Austin	330.00	165.00	100.00
9	Jim Bagby	330.00	165.00	100.00
10	H.D. Baird	330.00	165.00	100.00
11	J. Franklin Baker	770.00	385.00	230.00
12	Dave Bancroft	770.00	385.00	230.00
13	Jack Barry	330.00	165.00	100.00
14	Joe Benz	330.00	165.00	100.00
15	Al Betzel	330.00	165.00	100.00
16	Ping Bodie	330.00	165.00	100.00
17	Joe Boehling	330.00	165.00	100.00
18	Eddie Burns	330.00	165.00	100.00
19	George Burns	330.00	165.00	100.00
20	Geo. J. Burns	330.00	165.00	100.00
21	Joe Bush	330.00	165.00	100.00
22	Owen Bush	330.00	165.00	100.00
23	Bobby Byrne	330.00	165.00	100.00
24	Forrest Cady	330.00	165.00	100.00
25	Max Carey	770.00	385.00	230.00
26	Ray Chapman	385.00	195.00	115.00
27	Larry Cheney	330.00	165.00	100.00
28	Eddie Cicotte	770.00	385.00	230.00
29	Tom Clarke	330.00	165.00	100.00
30	Ty Cobb	9,900	4,950	3,000
31	Eddie Collins	770.00	385.00	230.00
32	"Shauno" Collins (Shano)	330.00	165.00	100.00
33	Fred Coumbe	330.00	165.00	100.00
34	Harry Coveleskie (Coveleski)	330.00	165.00	100.00
35	Gavvy Cravath	330.00	165.00	100.00
36	Sam Crawford	770.00	385.00	230.00
37	Geo. Cutshaw	330.00	165.00	100.00
38	Jake Daubert	330.00	165.00	100.00
39	Geo. Dauss	330.00	165.00	100.00
40	Charles Deal	330.00	165.00	100.00
41	"Wheezer" Dell	330.00	165.00	100.00
42	William Doak	330.00	165.00	100.00
43	Bill Donovan	330.00	165.00	100.00
44	Larry Doyle	330.00	165.00	100.00
45	Johnny Evers	770.00	385.00	230.00
46	Urban Faber	770.00	385.00	230.00
47	"Hap" Felsch	1,650	825.00	495.00
48	Bill Fischer	330.00	165.00	100.00
49	Ray Fisher	330.00	165.00	100.00
50	Art Fletcher	330.00	165.00	100.00
51	Eddie Foster	330.00	165.00	100.00
52	Jacques Fournier	330.00	165.00	100.00
53	Del Gainer (Gainor)	330.00	165.00	100.00
54	Bert Gallia	330.00	165.00	100.00
55	"Chic" Gandil (Chick)	990.00	495.00	300.00
56	Larry Gardner	330.00	165.00	100.00
57	Joe Gedeon	330.00	165.00	100.00
58	Gus Getz	330.00	165.00	100.00
59	Frank Gilhooley	330.00	165.00	100.00
60	Wm. Gleason	330.00	165.00	100.00
61	M.A. Gonzales (Gonzalez)	330.00	165.00	100.00
62	Hank Gowdy	330.00	165.00	100.00
63	John Graney	330.00	165.00	100.00
64	Tom Griffith	330.00	165.00	100.00
65	Heinie Groh	330.00	165.00	100.00
66	Bob Groom	330.00	165.00	100.00
67	Louis Guisto	330.00	165.00	100.00
68	Earl Hamilton	330.00	165.00	100.00
69	Harry Harper	330.00	165.00	100.00
70	Grover Hartley	330.00	165.00	100.00
71	Harry Heilmann	770.00	385.00	230.00
72	Claude Hendrix	330.00	165.00	100.00
73	Olaf Henriksen	330.00	165.00	100.00
74	John Henry	330.00	165.00	100.00
75	"Buck" Herzog	330.00	165.00	100.00
76	Hugh High	330.00	165.00	100.00
77	Dick Hoblitzell	330.00	165.00	100.00
78	Walter Holke	330.00	165.00	100.00
79	Harry Hooper	770.00	385.00	230.00
80	Rogers Hornsby	1,320	660.00	395.00
81	Ivan Howard	330.00	165.00	100.00
82	Joe Jackson	27,500	13,750	8,250
83	Harold Janvrin	330.00	165.00	100.00
84	William James	330.00	165.00	100.00
85	C. Jamieson	330.00	165.00	100.00
86	Hugh Jennings	770.00	385.00	230.00
87	Walter Johnson	1,650	825.00	495.00
88	James Johnston	330.00	165.00	100.00
89	Fielder Jones	330.00	165.00	100.00
90	Joe Judge	330.00	165.00	100.00
91	Hans Lobert	330.00	165.00	100.00
92	Benny Kauff	330.00	165.00	100.00
93	Wm. Killefer Jr.	330.00	165.00	100.00
94	Ed. Konetchy	330.00	165.00	100.00
95	John Lavan	330.00	165.00	100.00
96	Jimmy Lavender	330.00	165.00	100.00
97	"Nemo" Leibold	330.00	165.00	100.00
98	H.B. Leonard	330.00	165.00	100.00
99	Duffy Lewis	330.00	165.00	100.00
100	Tom Long	330.00	165.00	100.00
101	Wm. Louden	330.00	165.00	100.00
102	Fred Luderus	330.00	165.00	100.00
103	Lee Magee	330.00	165.00	100.00
104	Sherwood Magee	330.00	165.00	100.00
105	Al Mamaux	330.00	165.00	100.00
106	Leslie Mann	330.00	165.00	100.00
107	"Rabbit" Maranville	770.00	385.00	230.00
108	Rube Marquard	770.00	385.00	230.00
109	Armando Marsans	330.00	165.00	100.00
110	J. Erskine Mayer	330.00	165.00	100.00
111	George McBride	330.00	165.00	100.00
112	Lew McCarty	330.00	165.00	100.00
113	John J. McGraw	770.00	385.00	230.00
114	Jack McInnis	330.00	165.00	100.00
115	Lee Meadows	330.00	165.00	100.00
116	Fred Merkle	330.00	165.00	100.00
117	"Chief" Meyers	330.00	165.00	100.00
118	Clyde Milan	330.00	165.00	100.00
119	Otto Miller	330.00	165.00	100.00
120	Clarence Mitchell	330.00	165.00	100.00
121	Ray Morgan	330.00	165.00	100.00
122	Guy Morton	330.00	165.00	100.00
123	"Mike" Mowrey	330.00	165.00	100.00
124	Elmer Myers	330.00	165.00	100.00
125	"Hy" Myers	330.00	165.00	100.00
126	A.E. Neale	385.00	195.00	115.00
127	Arthur Nehf	330.00	165.00	100.00
128	J.A. Niehoff	330.00	165.00	100.00
129	Steve O'Neill	330.00	165.00	100.00
130	"Dode" Paskert	330.00	165.00	100.00
131	Roger Peckinpaugh	330.00	165.00	100.00
132	"Pol" Perritt	330.00	165.00	100.00
133	"Jeff" Pfeffer	330.00	165.00	100.00
134	Walter Pipp	330.00	165.00	100.00
135	Derril Pratt (Derrill)	330.00	165.00	100.00
136	Bill Rariden	330.00	165.00	100.00
137	E.C. Rice	770.00	385.00	230.00
138	Wm. A. Ritter (Wm. H.)	330.00	165.00	100.00
139	Eppa Rixey	770.00	385.00	230.00
140	Davey Robertson	330.00	165.00	100.00
141	"Bob" Roth	330.00	165.00	100.00
142	Ed. Roush	770.00	385.00	230.00
143	Clarence Rowland	330.00	165.00	100.00
144	Dick Rudolph	330.00	165.00	100.00
145	William Rumler	330.00	165.00	100.00
146	Reb Russell	330.00	165.00	100.00
147	"Babe" Ruth	22,000	11,000	6,600
148	Vic Saier	330.00	165.00	100.00
149	"Slim" Sallee	330.00	165.00	100.00
150	Ray Schalk	770.00	385.00	230.00
151	Walter Schang	330.00	165.00	100.00
152	Frank Schulte	330.00	165.00	100.00
153	Ferd Schupp	330.00	165.00	100.00
154	Everett Scott	330.00	165.00	100.00
155	Hank Severeid	330.00	165.00	100.00
156	Howard Shanks	330.00	165.00	100.00
157	Bob Shawkey	330.00	165.00	100.00
158	Jas. Sheckard	330.00	165.00	100.00
159	Ernie Shore	330.00	165.00	100.00
160	C.H. Shorten	330.00	165.00	100.00
161	Burt Shotton	330.00	165.00	100.00
162	Geo. Sisler	770.00	385.00	230.00
163	Elmer Smith	330.00	165.00	100.00
164	J. Carlisle Smith	330.00	165.00	100.00
165	Fred Snodgrass	330.00	165.00	100.00
166	Tris Speaker	1,320	660.00	395.00
167	Oscar Stanage	330.00	165.00	100.00
168	Charles Stengel	770.00	385.00	230.00
169	Milton Stock	330.00	165.00	100.00
170	Amos Strunk	330.00	165.00	100.00
171	"Zeb" Terry	330.00	165.00	100.00
172	"Jeff" Tesreau	330.00	165.00	100.00
173	Chester Thomas	330.00	165.00	100.00
174	Fred Toney	330.00	165.00	100.00
175	Terry Turner	330.00	165.00	100.00
176	George Tyler	330.00	165.00	100.00
177	Jim Vaughn	330.00	165.00	100.00
178	Bob Veach	330.00	165.00	100.00
179	Oscar Vitt	330.00	165.00	100.00
180	Hans Wagner	7,700	3,850	2,300
181	Clarence Walker	330.00	165.00	100.00
182	Jim Walsh	330.00	165.00	100.00
183	Al Walters	330.00	165.00	100.00
184	W. Wambsganss	330.00	165.00	100.00
185	Buck Weaver	2,200	1,100	660.00
186	Carl Weilman	330.00	165.00	100.00
187	Zack Wheat	770.00	385.00	230.00
188	Geo. Whitted	330.00	165.00	100.00
189	Joe Wilhoit	330.00	165.00	100.00
190	Claude Williams	1,650	825.00	495.00
191	Fred Williams	330.00	165.00	100.00
192	Art Wilson	330.00	165.00	100.00
193	Lawton Witt	330.00	165.00	100.00
194	Joe Wood	495.00	250.00	150.00
195	William Wortman	330.00	165.00	100.00
196	Steve Yerkes	330.00	165.00	100.00
197	Earl Yingling	330.00	165.00	100.00
198	"Pep" (Ralph) Young	330.00	165.00	100.00
199	Rollie Zeider	330.00	165.00	100.00
200	Henry Zimmerman	330.00	165.00	100.00

1886 Welton Cigars N.Y. Giants (H812)

(See "1886 New York Base Ball Club" for checklist and values.)

1977 Wendy's Discs

Virtually identical in format to the several locally sponsored disc sets of the previous year, these 3-3/8" diameter

player discs were given away at participating stores in the fast-food hamburger chain. Discs once again feature black-and-white player portrait photos in the center of a baseball design. The left and right panels are in one of several bright colors. Licensed by the Players Association through Mike Schechter Associates, the player photos carry no uniform logos. Backs are printed in green. The unnumbered discs are checklisted here alphabetically.

		NM	EX	VG
Complete Set (70):		325.00	165.00	100.00
Common Player:		3.00	1.50	.90
(1)	Sal Bando	3.00	1.50	.90
(2)	Buddy Bell	3.00	1.50	.90
(3)	Johnny Bench	20.00	10.00	6.00
(4)	Larry Bowa	3.00	1.50	.90
(5)	Steve Braun	3.00	1.50	.90
(6)	George Brett	50.00	25.00	15.00
(7)	Lou Brock	12.50	6.25	3.75
(8)	Jeff Burroughs	3.00	1.50	.90
(9)	Bert Campaneris	3.00	1.50	.90
(10)	John Candelaria	3.00	1.50	.90
(11)	Jose Cardenal	3.00	1.50	.90
(12)	Rod Carew	12.50	6.25	3.75
(13)	Steve Carlton	12.50	6.25	3.75
(14)	Dave Cash	3.00	1.50	.90
(15)	Cesar Cedeno	3.00	1.50	.90
(16)	Ron Cey	3.00	1.50	.90
(17)	Dave Concepcion	3.00	1.50	.90
(18)	Dennis Eckersley	12.50	6.25	3.75
(19)	Mark Fidrych	6.00	3.00	1.75
(20)	Rollie Fingers	12.50	6.25	3.75
(21)	Carlton Fisk	12.50	6.25	3.75
(22)	George Foster	3.00	1.50	.90
(23)	Wayne Garland	3.00	1.50	.90
(24)	Ralph Garr	3.00	1.50	.90
(25)	Steve Garvey	4.50	2.25	1.25
(26)	Cesar Geronimo	3.00	1.50	.90
(27)	Bobby Grich	3.00	1.50	.90
(28)	Ken Griffey Sr.	3.00	1.50	.90
(29)	Don Gullett	3.00	1.50	.90
(30)	Mike Hargrove	3.00	1.50	.90
(31)	Al Hrabosky	3.00	1.50	.90
(32)	Jim Hunter	12.50	6.25	3.75
(33)	Reggie Jackson	45.00	22.50	13.50
(34)	Randy Jones	3.00	1.50	.90
(35)	Dave Kingman	3.00	1.50	.90
(36)	Jerry Koosman	3.00	1.50	.90
(37)	Dave LaRoche	3.00	1.50	.90
(38)	Greg Luzinski	3.00	1.50	.90
(39)	Fred Lynn	3.00	1.50	.90
(40)	Bill Madlock	3.00	1.50	.90
(41)	Rick Manning	3.00	1.50	.90
(42)	Jon Matlock	3.00	1.50	.90
(43)	John Mayberry	3.00	1.50	.90
(44)	Hal McRae	3.00	1.50	.90
(45)	Andy Messersmith	3.00	1.50	.90
(46)	Rick Monday	3.00	1.50	.90
(47)	John Montefusco	3.00	1.50	.90
(48)	Joe Morgan	12.50	6.25	3.75
(49)	Thurman Munson	12.50	6.25	3.75
(50)	Bobby Murcer	3.00	1.50	.90
(51)	Bill North	3.00	1.50	.90
(52)	Jim Palmer	12.50	6.25	3.75
(53)	Tony Perez	12.50	6.25	3.75
(54)	Jerry Reuss	3.00	1.50	.90
(55)	Brooks Robinson	15.00	7.50	4.50
(56)	Pete Rose	55.00	27.50	16.50
(57)	Joe Rudi	3.00	1.50	.90
(58)	Nolan Ryan	65.00	32.50	20.00
(59)	Manny Sanguillen	3.00	1.50	.90
(60)	Mike Schmidt	50.00	25.00	15.00
(61)	Tom Seaver	20.00	10.00	6.00
(62)	Bill Singer	3.00	1.50	.90
(63)	Willie Stargell	12.50	6.25	3.75
(64)	Rusty Staub	4.00	2.00	1.25
(65)	Luis Tiant	3.00	1.50	.90
(66)	Bob Watson	3.00	1.50	.90
(67)	Butch Wynegar	3.00	1.50	.90
(68)	Carl Yastrzemski	20.00	10.00	6.00
(69)	Robin Yount	12.50	6.25	3.75
(70)	Richie Zisk	3.00	1.50	.90

1963 Western Oil Minnesota Twins

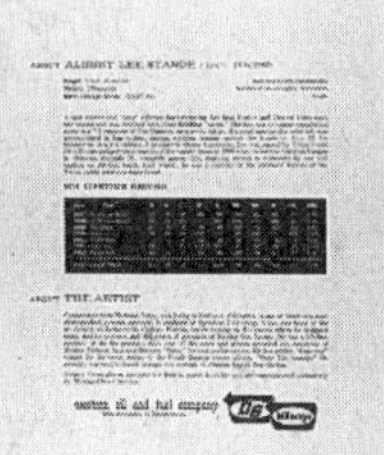

Issued by Mileage and DS gas stations, these 8-1/2" x 11" heavy paper portraits are the work of sports/entertainment artist Nicholas Volpe, who had done a similar series earlier for the Los Angeles Dodgers, and would do several more in the future for other baseball and NFL teams. The 1963 Twins issue features pastel portrait and action renderings against a black background on front. The player's name appears as a facsimile autograph in white on the painting and is printed in black in the white bottom border. Backs have biographical data and a career summary of the player at top. At center is a black box with complete major and minor league stats. At lower center is a biography of the artist, and, on most pictures, his portrait. The DS and Mileage logos of the Western Oil and Fuel Co. appear at bottom.

		NM	EX	VG
Complete Set (24):		150.00	75.00	45.00
Common Player:		10.00	5.00	3.00
(1)	Bernie Allen	10.00	5.00	3.00
(2)	Bob Allison	15.00	7.50	4.50
(3)	George Banks	10.00	5.00	3.00
(4)	Earl Battey	12.50	6.25	3.75
(5)	Bill Dailey	10.00	5.00	3.00
(6)	John Goryl	10.00	5.00	3.00
(7)	Lenny Green	10.00	5.00	3.00
(8)	Jimmie Hall	10.00	5.00	3.00
(9)	Jim Kaat	15.00	7.50	4.50
(10)	Harmon Killebrew	30.00	15.00	9.00
(11)	Sam Mele	10.00	5.00	3.00
(12)	Don Mincher	10.00	5.00	3.00
(13)	Ray Moore	10.00	5.00	3.00
(14)	Camilo Pascual	12.50	6.25	3.75
(15)	Jim Perry	10.00	5.00	3.00
(16)	Bill Pleis	10.00	5.00	3.00
(17)	Vic Power	12.00	6.00	3.50
(18)	Garry Roggenburk	10.00	5.00	3.00
(19)	Jim Roland	10.00	5.00	3.00
(20)	Rich Rollins	10.00	5.00	3.00
(21)	Lee Stange	10.00	5.00	3.00
(22)	Dick Stigman	10.00	5.00	3.00
(23)	Zoilo Versalles	12.50	6.25	3.75
(24)	Jerry Zimmerman	10.00	5.00	3.00

1964 Western Oil Minnesota Twins

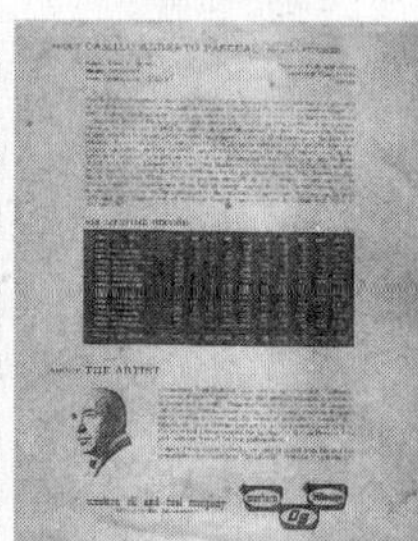

Identical in format to the previous year's issue, the 1964 set of Twins pictures features the use of a second portrait of the player in civilian dress rather than an action picture. The 1964 issue also has background of pastel colors, rather than all-black, and, on back, an oval/arrow logo for Western brand gas, along with the Mileage and DS logos.

		NM	EX	VG
Complete Set (15):		120.00	60.00	35.00
Common Player:		10.00	5.00	3.00
(1)	Bernie Allen	10.00	5.00	3.00
(2)	Bob Allison	12.50	6.25	3.75
(3)	Earl Battey	12.50	6.25	3.75
(4)	Bill Dailey	10.00	5.00	3.00
(5)	Jimmie Hall	10.00	5.00	3.00
(6)	Jim Kaat	15.00	7.50	4.50
(7)	Harmon Killebrew	30.00	15.00	9.00
(8)	Don Mincher	10.00	5.00	3.00
(9)	Tony Oliva	25.00	12.50	7.50
(10)	Camilo Pascual	12.50	6.25	3.75
(11)	Bill Pleis	10.00	5.00	3.00
(12)	Jim Roland	10.00	5.00	3.00
(13)	Rich Rollins	10.00	5.00	3.00
(14)	Dick Stigman	10.00	5.00	3.00
(15)	Zoilo Versalles	12.50	6.25	3.75

1974 Weston Expos

This 10-card set features members of the Montreal Expos. Each full-color card measures 3-1/2" x 5-1/2" and includes a facsimile autograph in black ink with the player's name printed along the bottom. The backs are distinct because they are divided in half. The top of the card lists player data and 1973 statistics in English, while the bottom carries the same information in French. The cards are numbered according to the player's uniform number.

		NM	EX	VG
Complete Set (10):		10.00	5.00	3.00
Common Player:		1.50	.75	.45
3	Bob Bailey	1.50	.75	.45
8	Boots Day	1.50	.75	.45
12	John Boccabella	1.50	.75	.45
16	Mike Jorgensen	1.50	.75	.45
18	Steve Renko	1.50	.75	.45
19	Tim Foli	1.50	.75	.45
21	Ernie McAnally	1.50	.75	.45
26	Bill Stoneman	1.50	.75	.45
29	Ken Singleton	1.50	.75	.45
33	Ron Hunt	1.50	.75	.45

1888 WG1 Base Ball Playing Cards

This little-known set of playing cards featuring drawings of real baseball players in action poses was issued in 1888 and includes members of the eight National League teams of the day. Each club is represented by nine players - one at each position - making the set complete at 72 cards. The cards measure 2-1/2" x 3-1/2" and have a blue-on-blue lathework pattern on back. The cards were sold as a boxed set. They were designed to resemble a deck of regular playing cards, and the various positions were all assigned the same denomination (for example, all of the pitchers were kings, catchers were aces, etc.). There are no cards numbered either two, three, four or five; and rather than the typical hearts, clubs, diamonds and spades, each team represents a different "suit." The American Card Catalog designation is WG1.

		NM	EX	VG
Complete Set (72):		90,000	35,000	17,500
Common Player:		900.00	360.00	180.00
Box:		5,000	2,500	1,500
(1)	Ed Andrews	900.00	360.00	180.00
(2)	Cap Anson	6,250	2,500	1,250
(3)	Charles Bassett	900.00	360.00	180.00
(4)	Charles Bastian	900.00	360.00	180.00
(5)	Charles Bennett	900.00	360.00	180.00
(6)	Henry Boyle	900.00	360.00	180.00
(7)	Dan Brouthers	3,000	1,200	600.00
(8)	Tom Brown	900.00	360.00	180.00
(9)	Tom Burns	900.00	360.00	180.00
(10)	Fred Carroll	900.00	360.00	180.00
(11)	Dan Casey	900.00	360.00	180.00
(12)	John Clarkson	3,000	1,200	600.00
(13)	Jack Clements	900.00	360.00	180.00
(14)	John Coleman	900.00	360.00	180.00
(15)	Roger Connor	3,000	1,200	600.00
(16)	Abner Dalrymple	900.00	360.00	180.00
(17)	Jerry Denny	900.00	360.00	180.00
(18)	Jim Donelly	900.00	360.00	180.00
(19)	Fred Dunlap	900.00	360.00	180.00
(20)	Dude Esterbrook	900.00	360.00	180.00
(21)	Buck Ewing	3,000	1,200	600.00
(22)	Sid Farrar	900.00	360.00	180.00
(23)	Silver Flint	900.00	360.00	180.00
(24)	Jim Fogarty	900.00	360.00	180.00
(25)	Elmer Foster	900.00	360.00	180.00
(26)	Pud Galvin	3,000	1,200	600.00
(27)	Charlie Getzein (Getzien)	900.00	360.00	180.00
(28)	Jack Glasscock	900.00	360.00	180.00
(29)	George Gore	900.00	360.00	180.00
(30)	Ned Hanlon	3,000	1,200	600.00
(31)	Paul Hines	900.00	360.00	180.00
(32)	Joe Hornung	900.00	360.00	180.00
(33)	Dummy Hoy	1,350	550.00	275.00
(34)	Arthur Irwin (Philadelphia)	900.00	360.00	180.00
(35)	John Irwin (Washington)	900.00	360.00	180.00
(36)	Dick Johnston	900.00	360.00	180.00
(37)	Tim Keefe	3,000	1,200	600.00
(38)	King Kelly	4,250	1,700	850.00
(39)	Willie Kuehne	900.00	360.00	180.00
(40)	Connie Mack	3,250	1,300	650.00
(41)	Al Maul	900.00	360.00	180.00
(42)	Al Meyers (Myers) (Washington)	900.00	360.00	180.00
(43)	George Meyers (Myers) (Indianapolis)	900.00	360.00	180.00
(44)	John Morrill	900.00	360.00	180.00
(45)	Joseph Mulvey	900.00	360.00	180.00
(46)	Billy Nash	900.00	360.00	180.00
(47)	Billy O'Brien	900.00	360.00	180.00
(48)	Orator Jim O'Rourke	3,000	1,200	600.00
(49)	Bob Pettit	900.00	360.00	180.00
(50)	Fred Pfeffer	900.00	360.00	180.00
(51)	Danny Richardson (New York)	900.00	360.00	180.00
(52)	Hardy Richardson (Detroit)	900.00	360.00	180.00
(53)	Jack Rowe	900.00	360.00	180.00
(54)	Jimmy Ryan	900.00	360.00	180.00
(55)	Emmett Seery	900.00	360.00	180.00
(56)	George Shoch	900.00	360.00	180.00
(57)	Otto Shomberg (Schomberg)	900.00	360.00	180.00
(58)	Pap Smith	900.00	360.00	180.00
(59)	Marty Sullivan	900.00	360.00	180.00
(60)	Billy Sunday	3,000	1,200	600.00
(61)	Ezra Sutton	900.00	360.00	180.00
(62)	Sam Thompson	3,000	1,200	600.00
(63)	Mike Tiernan	900.00	360.00	180.00
(64)	Larry Twitchell	900.00	360.00	180.00
(65)	Rip Van Haltren	900.00	360.00	180.00
(66)	John Ward	3,000	1,200	600.00
(67)	Deacon White	900.00	360.00	180.00
(68)	Jim Whitney	900.00	360.00	180.00

		NM	EX	VG
(69)	Ned Williamson	900.00	360.00	180.00
(70)	Walt Wilmot	900.00	360.00	180.00
(71)	Medoc Wise	900.00	360.00	180.00
(72)	George Wood	900.00	360.00	180.00

1932 Wheaties Babe Ruth Flip Book

This novelty item measures about 1-3/4" x 2-1/2" and is stapled at the bottom. When properly thumbed, the individual black-and-white pages inside present a simulated moving picture, "Babe Ruth Shows You How to Hit a Home Run". The covers feature orange and blue artwork.

	NM	EX	VG
Babe Ruth	750.00	375.00	225.00

1933-1934 Wheaties

Sponsored by Wheaties via mail-in offers heard on baseball games on half a dozen radio stations, these black-and-white cards are blank-backed and feature posed action photo with facsimile autographs bordered in white. In a 3-1/4" x 5-3/8" format, they are similar in design to the later 1936 National Chicle "Fine Pens" (R313) and the Gold Medal Foods World Series (R313A) issue of 1934, though each of the photos found in this set are unique. To date, this likely incomplete checklist comprises on players from the Browns, Cardinals, Cubs, White Sox, Indians and the Des Moines Demons of the Western League.

		NM	EX	VG
Common Player:				
(1)	Earl Averill	275.00	135.00	80.00
(2)	Geo. E. Blaeholder	45.00	22.50	13.50
(3)	Irving "Jack" Burns	45.00	22.50	13.50
(4)	Bruce Campbell	45.00	22.50	13.50
(5)	"Tex" Carleton	45.00	22.50	13.50
(6)	George Earnshaw	45.00	22.50	13.50
(7)	Red Faber	80.00	40.00	24.00
(8)	Fabian Gaffke	45.00	22.50	13.50
(9)	Odell Hale	180.00	90.00	55.00
(10)	Mel Harder	45.00	22.50	13.50
(11)	Roy Hudson	45.00	22.50	13.50
(12)	Chuck Klein	80.00	40.00	24.00
(13)	Jack Knott	45.00	22.50	13.50
(14)	Al Marchand	45.00	22.50	13.50
(15)	Ossie Orwoll	45.00	22.50	13.50
(16)	Al Simmons	80.00	40.00	24.00
(17)	Hal Trosky	45.00	22.50	13.50
(18)	Joe Vosmik	45.00	22.50	13.50
(19)	Bill Walker	45.00	22.50	13.50

1935 Wheaties - Series 1

This set of major leaguers (plus fictional sports hero Jack Armstrong) was issued on the back of Wheaties cereal boxes in 1935 and because of its design, is known as "Fancy Frame with Script Signature." The unnumbered cards measure 6" x 6-1/4" with frame, and 5" x 5-1/2" without the frame. The player photo is tinted blue, while the background is blue and orange. A facsimile autograph appears at the bottom of the photo. Illinois high school track star Herman "Jack" Waddlington posed for the photos of fictional Jack Armstrong "All-American Boy."

		NM	EX	VG
Complete Set (27):		3,000	1,500	900.00
Common Player:		50.00	25.00	15.50
(1)	Jack Armstrong/Btg	50.00	25.00	15.00
(2)	Jack Armstrong/Throwing	50.00	25.00	15.00
(3)	Wally Berger	50.00	25.00	15.00
(4)	Tommy Bridges	50.00	25.00	15.00
(5)	Mickey Cochrane (Black hat.)	90.00	45.00	27.00
(6)	Michey Cochrane (White hat.)	425.00	210.00	125.00
(7)	James "Rip" Collins	50.00	25.00	15.00
(8)	Dizzy Dean	325.00	160.00	97.00
(9)	Dizzy Dean, Paul Dean	250.00	125.00	75.00
(10)	Paul Dean	55.00	27.50	16.50
(11)	William Delancey	50.00	25.00	15.00
(12)	"Jimmie" Foxx	190.00	95.00	60.00
(13)	Frank Frisch	75.00	37.50	22.00
(14)	Lou Gehrig	475.00	235.00	140.00
(15)	Goose Goslin	75.00	37.50	22.00
(16)	Lefty Grove	125.00	65.00	35.00
(17)	Carl Hubbell	85.00	40.00	25.00
(18)	Travis C. Jackson	75.00	37.50	22.00
(19)	"Chuck" Klein	75.00	37.50	22.00
(20)	Gus Mancuso	50.00	25.00	15.00
(21)	Pepper Martin/Btg	55.00	27.00	16.50
(22)	Pepper Martin/Portrait	55.00	27.00	16.50
(23)	Joe Medwick	75.00	37.50	22.00
(24)	Melvin Ott	90.00	45.00	27.00
(25)	Harold Schumacher	50.00	25.00	15.00
(26)	Al Simmons	75.00	37.50	22.00
(27)	"Jo Jo" White	50.00	25.00	15.00

1936 Wheaties - Series 3

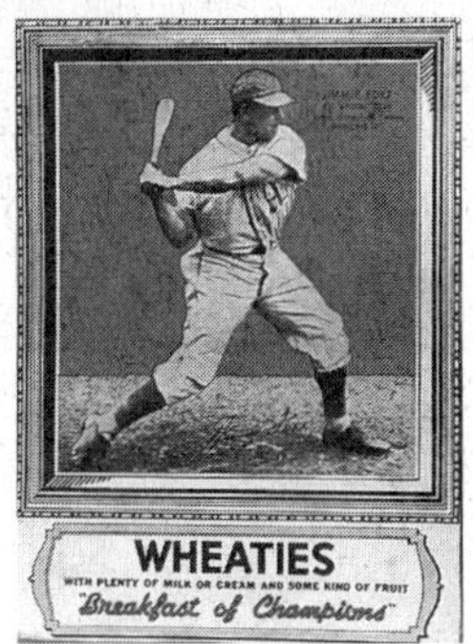

Consisting of 12 unnumbered cards, this set is similar in size (6" x 6-1/4" with frame) and design to the Wheaties of the previous year, but is known as "Fancy Frame with Printed Name and Data" because the cards also include a few printed words describing the player.

		NM	EX	VG
Complete Set (12):		1,600	800.00	475.00
Common Player:		45.00	22.00	13.50
(1)	Earl Averill	60.00	30.00	18.00
(2)	Mickey Cochrane	60.00	30.00	18.00
(3)	Jimmy Foxx	200.00	100.00	60.00
(4)	Lou Gehrig	750.00	375.00	225.00
(5)	Hank Greenberg	175.00	90.00	50.00
(6)	"Gabby" Hartnett	60.00	30.00	18.00
(7)	Carl Hubbell	65.00	32.50	20.00
(8)	"Pepper" Martin	50.00	25.00	15.00
(9)	Van L. Mungo	45.00	22.50	13.50
(10)	"Buck" Newsom	45.00	22.50	13.50
(11)	"Arky" Vaughan	60.00	30.00	18.00
(12)	Jimmy Wilson	45.00	22.50	13.50

1936 Wheaties - Series 4

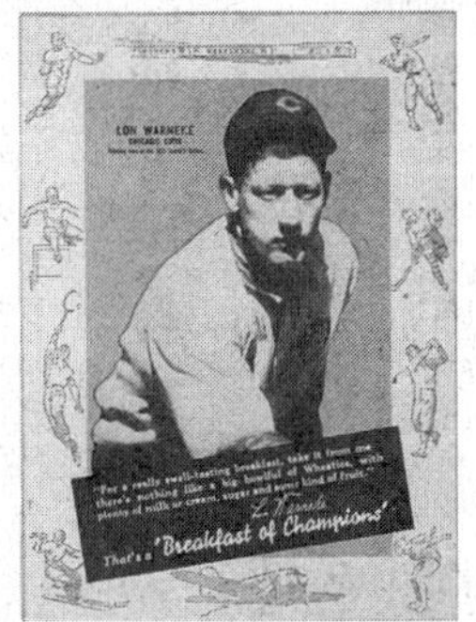

This larger size (8-1/2" x 6") card also made up the back of a Wheaties box, and because of its distinctive border which featured drawings of small athletic figures, it is referred to as "Thin Orange Border/Figures in Border." Twelve major leaguers are pictured in the unnumbered set. The photos are enclosed in a 4" x 6-1/2" box. Below the photo is an endorsement for Wheaties, the "Breakfast of Champions," and a facsimile autograph.

		NM	EX	VG
Complete Set (12):		1,200	600.00	350.00
Common Player:		45.00	22.00	13.50
(1)	Curt Davis	45.00	22.50	13.50
(2)	Lou Gehrig	500.00	250.00	150.00
(3)	Charley Gehringer	75.00	37.50	22.00
(4)	Lefty Grove	165.00	85.00	50.00
(5)	Rollie Hemsley	45.00	22.50	13.50
(6)	Billy Herman	75.00	37.50	22.00
(7)	Joe Medwick	75.00	37.50	22.00
(8)	Mel Ott	80.00	40.00	25.00
(9)	Schoolboy Rowe	45.00	22.50	13.50
(10)	Arky Vaughan	75.00	37.50	22.00
(11)	Joe Vosmik	45.00	22.50	13.50
(12)	Lon Warneke	45.00	22.50	13.50

1936 Wheaties - Series 5

Often referred to as "How to Play Winning Baseball," this 12-card set features a large player photo surrounded by blue and white drawings that illustrate various playing tips. Different major leaguers offer advice on different aspects of the game. The cards again made up the back panel of a Wheaties box and measure 8-1/2" x 6-1/2". The cards are numbered from 1 through 12, and it is now believed that each can be found with or without a small number "28" followed by a letter from "A" through "L."

		NM	EX	VG
Complete Set (12)		1,000	500.00	300.00
Common Player:		45.00	22.50	13.50
1	Lefty Gomez	85.00	45.00	25.00
2	Billy Herman	75.00	37.50	22.00
3	Luke Appling	75.00	37.50	22.00
4	Jimmie Foxx	90.00	45.00	27.00
5	Joe Medwick	75.00	37.50	22.00
6	Charles Gehringer	75.00	37.50	22.00
7a	Mel Ott (Tips in vertical sequence.)	95.00	45.00	25.00
7b	Mel Ott (Tips in two horizontal rows.)	95.00	45.00	25.00
8	Odell Hale	45.00	22.50	13.50
9	Bill Dickey	85.00	45.00	25.00
10	"Lefty" Grove	85.00	45.00	25.00
11	Carl Hubbell	80.00	40.00	25.00
12	Earl Averill	75.00	37.50	22.00

1937 Wheaties - Series 6

Similar to the Series 5 set, this numbered, 12-card series is known as "How to Star in Baseball" and again includes a large player photo with small instructional drawings to illustrate playing tips. The cards measure 8-1/4" x 6" and include a facsimile autograph.

		NM	EX	VG
Complete Set (12):		1,000	500.00	300.00
Common Player:		35.00	17.50	10.00
1	Bill Dickey	75.00	37.50	22.00
2	Red Ruffing	60.00	30.00	18.00
3	Zeke Bonura	35.00	17.50	10.00
4	Charlie Gehringer	60.00	30.00	18.00
5	"Arky" Vaughn (Vaughan)	60.00	30.00	18.00
6	Carl Hubbell	60.00	30.00	18.00
7	John Lewis	35.00	17.50	10.00
8	Heinie Manush	60.00	30.00	18.00
9	"Lefty" Grove	75.00	37.50	22.00
10	Billy Herman	60.00	30.00	18.00
11	Joe DiMaggio	400.00	200.00	120.00
12	Joe Medwick	60.00	30.00	18.00

1937 Wheaties - Series 7

This set of 6" x 8-1/4" panels contains several different card designs. One style (picturing Lombardi, Travis and Mungo) has a white background with an orange border and a large orange circle behind the player. Another design (showing Bonura, DiMaggio and Bridges) has the player outlined against a bright orange background with a Wheaties endorsement along the bottom. A third format (picturing Moore, Radcliff and Martin) has a distinctive red, white and blue border. And a fourth design (featuring Trosky, Demaree and Vaughan) has a tilted picture against an orange background framed in blue and white. The

set also includes four Pacific Coast League Players (#29M-29P). The cards are numbered with a small "29" followed by a letter from "A" through "P."

		NM	EX	VG
Complete Set (16):		1,200	600.00	350.00
Common Player:		45.00	22.50	13.50
29A	"Zeke" Bonura	45.00	22.50	13.50
29B	Cecil Travis	45.00	22.50	13.50
29C	Frank Demaree	45.00	22.50	13.50
29D	Joe Moore	45.00	22.50	13.50
29E	Ernie Lombardi	60.00	30.00	18.00
29F	John L. "Pepper" Martin	50.00	25.00	15.00
29G	Harold Trosky	45.00	22.50	13.50
29H	Raymond Radcliff	45.00	22.50	13.50
29I	Joe DiMaggio	300.00	150.00	90.00
29J	Tom Bridges	45.00	22.50	13.50
29K	Van L. Mungo	45.00	22.50	13.50
29L	"Arky" Vaughn (Vaughan)	60.00	30.00	18.00
29M	Arnold Statz	100.00	50.00	30.00
29N	Wes Schulmerich	100.00	50.00	30.00
29O	Fred Mueller	100.00	50.00	30.00
29P	Gene Lillard	100.00	50.00	30.00

1937 Wheaties - Series 8

Another series printed on the back of Wheaties boxes in 1937, the eight cards in this set are unnumbered and measure 8-1/2" x 6". There are several different designs, but in all of them the player photo is surrounded by speckles of color, causing this series to be known as the "Speckled Orange, White and Blue" series. A facsimile autograph is included, along with brief printed 1936 season statistics.

		NM	EX	VG
Complete Set (8):		1,300	650.00	400.00
Common Player:		120.00	60.00	36.00
(1)	Luke Appling	100.00	50.00	30.00
(2)	Earl Averill	100.00	50.00	30.00
(3)	Joe DiMaggio	450.00	225.00	135.00
(4)	Robert Feller	225.00	110.00	65.00
(5)	Chas. Gehringer	100.00	50.00	30.00
(6)	Lefty Grove	125.00	65.00	35.00
(7)	Carl Hubbell	125.00	65.00	35.00
(8)	Joe Medwick	100.00	50.00	30.00

1937 Wheaties - Series 9

This unnumbered set includes one player from each of the 16 major league teams and is generally referred to as the "Color Series." The cards measure 8-1/2" x 6" and were the back panels of Wheaties boxes. The player photos are shown inside or against large stars, circles, "V" shapes, rectangles and other geometric designs. A facsimile autograph and team designation are printed near the photo, while a Wheaties endorsement and a line of player stats appear along the bottom.

		NM	EX	VG
Complete Set (16):		1,600	800.00	480.00
Common Player:		50.00	25.00	15.00
(1)	Zeke Bonura	50.00	25.00	15.00
(2)	Tom Bridges	50.00	25.00	15.00
(3)	Harland Clift (Harlond)	50.00	25.00	15.00
(4)	Kiki Cuyler	75.00	37.50	22.50
(5)	Joe DiMaggio	600.00	300.00	180.00
(6)	Robert Feller	175.00	85.00	50.00
(7)	Lefty Grove	100.00	50.00	30.00
(8)	Billy Herman	75.00	37.50	22.50
(9)	Carl Hubbell	90.00	45.00	27.50
(10)	Buck Jordan	50.00	25.00	15.00
(11)	"Pepper" Martin	60.00	30.00	18.00
(12)	John Moore	50.00	25.00	15.00
(13)	Wally Moses	50.00	25.00	15.00
(14)	Van L. Mungo	50.00	25.00	15.00
(15)	Cecil Travis	50.00	25.00	15.00
(16)	Arky Vaughan	75.00	37.50	22.50

1937 Wheaties - Series 14

Much reduced in size (2-5/8" x 3-7/8"), these unnumbered cards made up the back panels of single-serving size Wheaties boxes. The player photo (which is sometimes identical to the photos used in the larger series) is set against an orange or white background. The player's name appears in large capital letters with his position and team in smaller capitals. A facsimile autograph and Wheaties endorsement are also included. Some cards are also found with the number "29" followed by a letter.

		NM	EX	VG
Complete Set (16):		5,000	2,500	1,500
Common Player:		200.00	100.00	60.00
(1)	"Zeke" Bonura	200.00	100.00	60.00
(2)	Tom Bridges	200.00	100.00	60.00
(3)	Dolph Camilli	200.00	100.00	60.00
(4)	Frank Demaree	200.00	100.00	60.00
(5)	Joe DiMaggio	1,300	650.00	390.00
(6)	Billy Herman	300.00	150.00	90.00
(7)	Carl Hubbell	350.00	175.00	105.00
(8)	Ernie Lombardi	300.00	150.00	90.00
(9)	"Pepper" Martin	250.00	125.00	75.00
(10)	Joe Moore	200.00	100.00	60.00
(11)	Van Mungo	200.00	100.00	60.00
(12)	Mel Ott	350.00	175.00	105.00
(13)	Raymond Radcliff	200.00	100.00	60.00
(14)	Cecil Travis	200.00	100.00	60.00
(15)	Harold Trosky	200.00	100.00	60.00
(16a)	"Arky" Vaughan (29L on card)	350.00	175.00	105.00
(16b)	"Arky" Vaughan (No 29L on card.)	350.00	175.00	105.00

1938 Wheaties - Series 10

FIRST BIG LEAGUE HIT, A HOMER!
... and Camilli gets biggest baseball thrill!
Breakfast of Champions

One player from each major league team is included in this 16-card set, referred to as the "Biggest Thrills in Baseball" series. Measuring 8-1/2" x 6", each numbered card was the back panel of a Wheaties box and pictures a player along with a printed description of his biggest thrill in baseball and facsimile autograph. All 16 cards in this series have also been found on paper stock.

		NM	EX	VG
Complete Set (16):		1,700	850.00	500.00
Common Player:		45.00	22.50	13.50
1	Bob Feller	160.00	80.00	45.00
2	Cecil Travis	45.00	22.50	13.50
3	Joe Medwick	65.00	32.50	20.00
4	Gerald Walker	45.00	22.50	13.50
5	Carl Hubbell	65.00	32.50	20.00
6	Bob Johnson	45.00	22.50	13.50
7	Beau Bell	45.00	22.50	13.50
8	Ernie Lombardi	65.00	32.50	20.00
9	Lefty Grove	80.00	40.00	24.00
10	Lou Fette	45.00	22.50	13.50
11	Joe DiMaggio	600.00	300.00	180.00
12	Pinky Whitney	45.00	22.50	13.50
13	Dizzy Dean	175.00	85.00	55.00
14	Charley Gehringer	65.00	32.50	20.00
15	Paul Waner	65.00	32.50	20.00
16	Dolf Camilli	45.00	22.50	13.50

1938 Wheaties - Series 11

Cards in this unnumbered, eight-card series measure 8-1/2" x 6" and show the players in street clothes either eating or getting ready to enjoy a bowl of Wheaties. Sometimes a waitress or other person also appears in the photo. The set is sometimes called the "Dress Clothes" or "Civies" series.

		NM	EX	VG
Complete Set (8):		750.00	375.00	225.00
Common Player:		60.00	30.00	18.00
(1)	Lou Fette	60.00	30.00	18.00
(2)	Jimmie Foxx	145.00	75.00	45.00
(3)	Charlie Gehringer	115.00	55.00	35.00
(4)	Lefty Grove	115.00	55.00	35.00
(5)	Hank Greenberg, Roxie Lawson	115.00	55.00	35.00
(6)	Lee Grissom, Ernie Lombardi	85.00	40.00	25.00
(7)	Joe Medwick	85.00	40.00	25.00
(8)	Lon Warneke	60.00	30.00	18.00

1938 Wheaties - Series 15

Another set of small (2-5/8" x 3-7/8") cards, the photos in this unnumbered series made up the back panels of single-serving size Wheaties boxes. The panels have orange, blue and white backgrounds. Some of the photos are the same as those used in the larger Wheaties panels.

		NM	EX	VG
Complete Set (11):		4,500	2,250	1,350
Common Player:		160.00	80.00	45.00
(1)	"Zeke" Bonura	160.00	80.00	45.00
(2)	Joe DiMaggio	1,300	650.00	390.00
(3)	Charles Gehringer/Btg	400.00	200.00	120.00
(4)	Chas. Gehringer/Leaping	400.00	200.00	120.00
(5)	Hank Greenberg	500.00	250.00	150.00
(6)	Lefty Grove	400.00	200.00	120.00
(7)	Carl Hubbell	325.00	160.00	97.00
(8)	John (Buddy) Lewis	160.00	80.00	45.00
(9)	Heinie Manush	300.00	150.00	90.00
(10)	Joe Medwick	300.00	150.00	90.00
(11)	Arky Vaughan	300.00	150.00	90.00

1939 Wheaties - Series 12

The nine cards in this numbered series, known as the "Personal Pointers" series, measure 8-1/4" x 6" and feature an instructional format similar to earlier Wheaties issues. The cards feature a player photo along with printed tips on various aspects of hitting and pitching.

		NM	EX	VG
Complete Set (9):		1,500	750.00	450.00
Common Player:		100.00	50.00	30.00
1	Ernie Lombardi	160.00	80.00	45.00
2	Johnny Allen	100.00	50.00	30.00
3	Lefty Gomez	185.00	90.00	55.00
4	Bill Lee	100.00	50.00	30.00
5	Jimmie Foxx	250.00	125.00	75.00
6	Joe Medwick	160.00	80.00	45.00
7	Hank Greenberg	250.00	125.00	75.00
8	Mel Ott	185.00	90.00	55.00
9	Arky Vaughn (Vaughan)	160.00	80.00	45.00

1939 Wheaties - Series 13

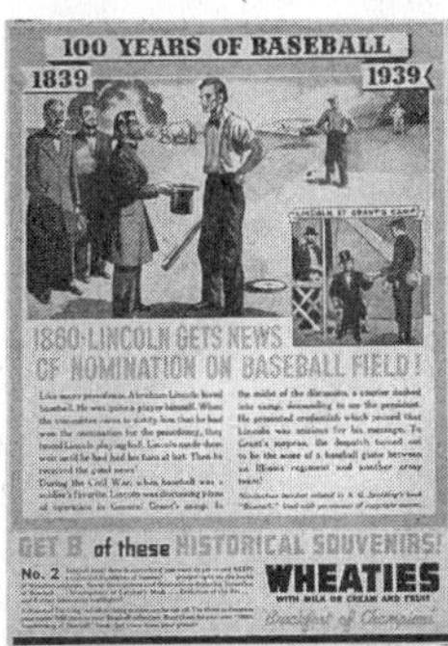

Issued in baseball's centennial year of 1939, this set of eight 6" x 6-3/4" cards commemorates "100 Years of Baseball." Each of the numbered panels illustrates a significant event in baseball history.

		NM	EX	VG
Complete Set (8):		650.00	325.00	200.00
Common Panel:		75.00	37.50	22.50
1	Design of First Diamond - 1838 (Abner Doubleday)	75.00	37.50	22.50
2	Gets News of Nomination on Field - 1860 (Abraham Lincoln)	125.00	62.50	37.50
3	Crowd Boos First Baseball Glove/1869	75.00	37.50	22.50
4	Curve Ball Just an Illusion/ 1877	75.00	37.50	22.50
5	Fencer's Mask is Pattern/1877	75.00	37.50	22.50
6	Baseball Gets "All Dressed Up"/1895	75.00	37.50	22.50
7	Modern Bludgeon Enters Game/1895	75.00	37.50	22.50
8	"Casey at the Bat"	100.00	50.00	30.00

1940 Wheaties Champs of the USA

This set consists of 13 numbered panels (plus seven variations). Each pictures three athletes, including one, two or three baseball players; the others include football stars, golfers, skaters, racers, etc. The entire panel measures approximately 8-1/4" x 6", while the actual card measures approximately 6" square. Each athlete is pictured in what looks like a postage stamp with a serrated edge. A brief biography appears alongside the "stamp." Some variations are known to exist among the first nine panels. The cards are numbered in the upper right corner.

		NM	EX	VG
Complete Set (20):		1,400	700.00	425.00
Common Panel:		50.00	25.00	15.00
1A	Bob Feller, Lynn Patrick, Charles "Red" Ruffing	135.00	67.00	40.00
1B	Leo Durocher, Lynn Patrick, Charles "Red" Ruffing	90.00	45.00	27.00
2A	Joe DiMaggio, Don Budge, Hank Greenberg	300.00	150.00	90.00
2B	Joe DiMaggio, Mel Ott, Ellsworth Vines	200.00	100.00	60.00
3	Bernie Bierman, Bill Dickey, Jimmie Foxx	125.00	62.00	37.00
4	Morris Arnovich, Capt R.K. Baker, Earl "Dutch" Clark	50.00	25.00	15.00
5	Madison (Matty) Bell, Ab Jenkins, Joe Medwick	50.00	25.00	15.00
6A	Ralph Guldahl, John Mize, Davey O'Brien	50.00	25.00	15.00
6B	Bob Feller, John Mize, Rudy York	90.00	45.00	27.00
6C	Ralph Guldahl, Gabby Hartnett, Davey O'Brien	50.00	25.00	15.00
7A	Joe Cronin, Cecil Isbell, Byron Nelson	50.00	25.00	15.00
7B	Joe Cronin, Hank Greenberg, Byron Nelson	75.00	37.00	22.00
7C	Paul Derringer, Cecil Isbell, Byron Nelson	50.00	25.00	15.00
8A	Ernie Lombardi, Jack Manders, George I. Myers	50.00	25.00	15.00
8B	Paul Derringer, Ernie Lombardi, George I. Myers	50.00	25.00	15.00
9	Bob Bartlett, Captain R.C. Hanson, Terrell Jacobs	50.00	25.00	15.00
10	Lowell "Red" Dawson, Billy Herman, Adele Inge	50.00	25.00	15.00
11	Dolph Camilli, Antoinette Concello, Wallace Wade	50.00	25.00	15.00
12	Luke Appling, Stanley Hack, Hugh McManus	50.00	25.00	15.00
13	Felix Adler, Hal Trosky, Mabel Vinson	50.00	25.00	15.00

1941 Wheaties Champs of the USA

This eight-card series is actually a continuation of the previous year's Wheaties set, and the format is identical. The set begins with number 14, starting where the 1940 set ended.

		NM	EX	VG
Complete Set (8):		800.00	400.00	240.00
Common Panel:		50.00	25.00	15.00
14	Felix Adler, Jimmie Foxx, Capt. R.G. Hanson	90.00	45.00	27.00
15	Bernie Bierman, Bob Feller, Jessie McLeod	90.00	45.00	27.00
16	Lowell "Red" Dawson, Hank Greenberg, J.W. Stoker	80.00	40.00	24.00
17	Antoniette Concello, Joe DiMaggio, Byron Nelson	300.00	150.00	90.00
18	Capt. R.L. Baker, Frank "Buck" McCormick, Harold "Pee Wee" Reese	90.00	45.00	27.00
19	William W. Robbins, Gene Sarazen, Gerald "Gee" Walker	50.00	25.00	15.00
20	Harry Danning, Barney McCosky, Bucky Walters	50.00	25.00	15.00
21	Joe "Flash" Gordon, Stan Hack, George I. Myers	50.00	25.00	15.00

1951 Wheaties

Printed as the backs of single-serving size boxes of Wheaties, the six-card 1951 set includes three baseball players and one football player, basketball player and golfer. Well-trimmed cards measure 2-1/2" x 3-1/4". The cards feature blue line drawings of the athletes with a facsimile autograph and descriptive title below. There is a wide white border. A small hoard of complete sets of unused boxes made its way into the hobby in the early 1990s. Complete boxes should be priced at 1.5X the values shown here.

		NM	EX	VG
Complete Set (6):		650.00	325.00	195.00
Common Player:		85.00	42.00	25.00
(1)	Bob Feller (Baseball)	100.00	50.00	30.00
(2)	John Lujack (Football)	55.00	27.50	16.50
(3)	George Mikan (Basketball)	110.00	55.00	35.00
(4)	Stan Musial (Baseball)	150.00	75.00	45.00
(5)	Sam Snead (Golfer)	65.00	32.50	20.00
(6)	Ted Williams (Baseball)	200.00	100.00	60.00

1951 Wheaties Premium Photos

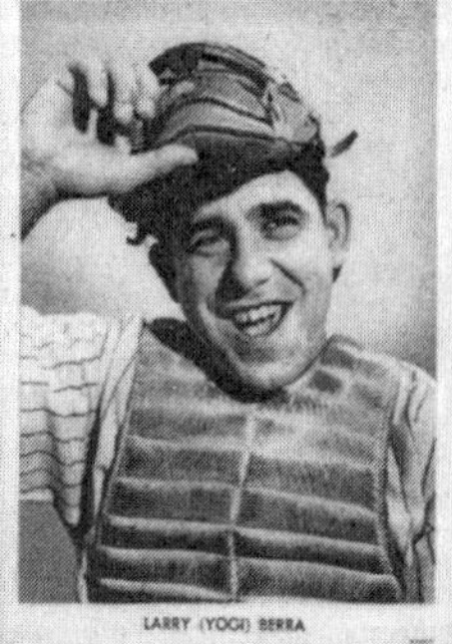
LARRY (YOGI) BERRA

Whether or not these 5" x 7" black-and-white, blank-back photos were ever issued at all, or only on a test basis is unknown. Despite being unmarked, they are reliably attributed to General Mills, possibly intended for use as a Wheaties premium. The photos found on several of the pictures are the same pictures used on the box-back Wheaties cards of 1952. The pictures appear in most cases to be re-uses of team-issued images from photo packs and the like. Player names are in the bottom border in capital letters. Each picture has a small alpha-numeric identifier in the lower-right corner. The scope of the issue is unknown as several letters from the sequence are missing. The letter shown in this checklist is preceded in each case by "A8491."

		NM	EX	VG
Complete Baseball Set (8):		2,600	1,300	775.00
Common Player:		66.00	33.00	20.00
A	Stan Musial	325.00	160.00	95.00
C	Richie Ashburn	120.00	60.00	36.00
D	Bob Feller	120.00	60.00	36.00
E	Al Rosen	65.00	32.50	20.00
F	Larry (Yogi) Berra	175.00	85.00	50.00
G	Mickey Mantle	1,600	800.00	480.00
H	Betty Schalow (Ice skater.)	15.00	7.50	4.50
J	Bob Lemon	65.00	32.50	20.00
K	Roy Campanella	150.00	75.00	45.00

1952 Wheaties

BOB FELLER
PITCHER, CLEVELAND INDIANS

These 2" x 2-3/4" cards appeared on the back of the popular cereal boxes. Actually, sports figures had been appearing on the backs of the boxes for many years, but in 1952, of the 30 athletes depicted, 10 were baseball players. That means there are 20 baseball cards, as each player appears in both a portrait and an action drawing. The cards have a blue line drawing on an orange background with a white border. The player's name, team, and position appear at the bottom. The cards have rounded corners, but are often found poorly cut from the boxes. This set was extensively counterfeited circa 2002, which had a chilling effect on values of cards not professionally graded by a major certification company.

		NM	EX	VG
Complete (Baseball) Set (20):		650.00	325.00	195.00
Common Player:		20.00	10.00	6.00
(1)	Larry "Yogi" Berra/Portrait	50.00	25.00	15.00
(2)	Larry "Yogi" Berra/Action	50.00	25.00	15.00
(3)	Roy Campanella/Portrait	50.00	25.00	15.00
(4)	Roy Campanella/Action	50.00	25.00	15.00
(5)	Bob Feller/Portrait	30.00	15.00	9.00
(6)	Bob Feller/Action	30.00	15.00	9.00
(7)	George Kell/Portrait	25.00	12.50	7.50
(8)	George Kell/Action	25.00	12.50	7.50
(9)	Ralph Kiner/Portrait	25.00	12.50	7.50
(10)	Ralph Kiner/Action	25.00	12.50	7.50
(11)	Bob Lemon/Portrait	25.00	12.50	7.50
(12)	Bob Lemon/Action	25.00	12.50	7.50
(13)	Stan Musial/Portrait	60.00	30.00	18.00
(14)	Stan Musial/Action	60.00	30.00	18.00
(15)	Phil Rizzuto/Portrait	30.00	15.00	9.00
(16)	Phil Rizzuto/Action	30.00	15.00	9.00
(17)	Elwin "Preacher" Roe/Portrait	20.00	10.00	6.00
(18)	Elwin "Preacher" Roe/Action	20.00	10.00	6.00
(19)	Ted Williams/Portrait	100.00	50.00	30.00
(20)	Ted Williams/Action	100.00	50.00	30.00

1952 Wheaties Tin Trays

This unique cereal box premium took the shape of a 4-7/8" x 5-1/8" tin tray which was glued to the back of Wheaties boxes. A cream-colored border surrounded the 3" x 4" color photo debossed at center. A black facsimile autograph appears across the photo. At top a small hole was punched for hanging the plaque. Backs were blank, and are often found with glue and paper residue on the gold-tone metal. Most of the plates have acquired numerous scratches and dings over the years, making true Near Mint examples very scarce. The unnumbered trays are checklisted alphabetically. A George Kell tray was long believed to exist but has never been verified.

		NM	EX	VG
Complete Set (4):		1,200	600.00	350.00
Common Player:		50.00	25.00	15.00
(1)	Ralph Kiner	50.00	25.00	15.00
(2)	Stan Musial	125.00	65.00	35.00
(3)	Phil Rizzuto	60.00	30.00	18.00
(4)	Jackie Robinson	1,100	550.00	330.00

1964 Wheaties Stamps

This General Mills' promotion included 50 player stamps and a 48-page orange album called "Wheaties Major League All-Star Baseball Player Stamp Album." The 2-1/2" x 2-3/4" stamps have a color player photo at center with a facsimile autograph and surrounded by a white border. Backs are blank. The unnumbered set is checklisted here in alphabetical order.

		NM	EX	VG
Complete Set (50):		325.00	160.00	95.00
Complete Set, In Album:		125.00	65.00	35.00
Common Player:		4.00	2.00	1.25
Album:		40.00	20.00	12.00
(1)	Hank Aaron	30.00	15.00	9.00
(2)	Bob Allison	4.00	2.00	1.25
(3)	Luis Aparicio	7.50	3.75	2.25
(4)	Ed Bailey	4.00	2.00	1.25
(5)	Steve Barber	4.00	2.00	1.25
(6)	Earl Battey	4.00	2.00	1.25
(7)	Jim Bouton	5.00	2.50	1.50
(8)	Ken Boyer	5.00	2.50	1.50
(9)	Jim Bunning	7.50	3.75	2.25
(10)	Orlando Cepeda	10.00	5.00	3.00
(11)	Roberto Clemente	45.00	22.50	13.50
(12)	Ray Culp	4.00	2.00	1.25
(13)	Tommy Davis	4.00	2.00	1.25
(14)	John Edwards	4.00	2.00	1.25
(15)	Whitey Ford	20.00	10.00	6.00
(16)	Nellie Fox	10.00	5.00	3.00
(17)	Bob Friend	4.00	2.00	1.25
(18)	Jim Gilliam	5.00	2.50	1.50
(19)	Jim Grant	4.00	2.00	1.25
(20)	Dick Groat	4.00	2.00	1.25
(21)	Elston Howard	5.00	2.50	1.50
(22)	Larry Jackson	4.00	2.00	1.25
(23)	Julian Javier	4.00	2.00	1.25
(24)	Al Kaline	12.50	6.25	3.75
(25)	Harmon Killebrew	12.50	6.25	3.75
(26)	Don Leppert	4.00	2.00	1.25
(27)	Frank Malzone	4.00	2.00	1.25
(28)	Juan Marichal	7.50	3.75	2.25
(29)	Willie Mays	30.00	15.00	9.00
(30)	Ken McBride	4.00	2.00	1.25
(31)	Willie McCovey	10.00	5.00	3.00
(32)	Jim O'Toole	4.00	2.00	1.25
(33)	Albie Pearson	4.00	2.00	1.25
(34)	Joe Pepitone	5.00	2.50	1.50
(35)	Ron Perranoski	4.00	2.00	1.25
(36)	Juan Pizzaro	4.00	2.00	1.25
(37)	Dick Radatz	4.00	2.00	1.25
(38)	Bobby Richardson	6.00	3.00	1.75
(39)	Brooks Robinson	12.50	6.25	3.75
(40)	Ron Santo	6.00	3.00	1.75
(41)	Norm Siebern	4.00	2.00	1.25
(42)	Duke Snider	20.00	10.00	6.00
(43)	Warren Spahn	12.50	6.25	3.75
(44)	Joe Torre	6.00	3.00	1.75
(45)	Tom Tresh	5.00	2.50	1.50
(46)	Zoilo Versailles (Versalles)	4.00	2.00	1.25
(47)	Leon Wagner	4.00	2.00	1.25
(48)	Bill White	4.00	2.00	1.25
(49)	Hal Woodeshick	4.00	2.00	1.25
(50)	Carl Yastrzemski	20.00	10.00	6.00

1937 WHIO-Sy Burick Cincinnati Reds Postcards

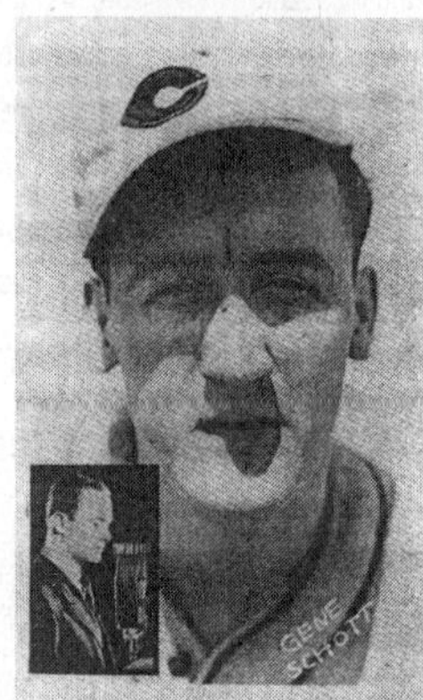

(See 1937-39 Orcajo Cincinnati Reds postcards for checklist, values.)

1889 C.S. White & Co. Boston N.L.

(See 1889 Number 7 Cigars for checklist and value information.)

1977 Wiffle Insert Discs

Similar in concept and format to the many contemporary MSA baseball player disc sets, the pieces inserted within Wiffle brand baseball, softball and bat boxes differ in that they are smaller, at 2-3/8" diameter, and feature a larger checklist. The discs feature black-and-white player portrait photos in the center of a baseball design. The left and right panels are in one of several bright colors. Licensed by the players' association through Mike Schechter Associates, the player photos carry no uniform logos. Backs are printed in black and orange. The unnumbered discs are checklisted here alphabetically.

		NM	EX	VG
Complete Set (80):		325.00	160.00	100.00
Common Player:		2.50	1.25	.70
(1)	Sal Bando	2.50	1.25	.70
(2)	Buddy Bell	2.50	1.25	.70
(3)	Johnny Bench	7.50	3.75	2.25
(4)	Vida Blue	2.50	1.25	.70
(5)	Bert Blyleven	3.00	1.50	.90
(6)	Bobby Bonds	2.50	1.25	.70
(7)	George Brett	12.00	6.00	3.50
(8)	Lou Brock	6.00	3.00	1.75
(9)	Bill Buckner	2.50	1.25	.70
(10)	Ray Burris	2.50	1.25	.70
(11)	Jeff Burroughs	2.50	1.25	.70
(12)	Bert Campaneris	2.50	1.25	.70
(13)	Rod Carew	6.00	3.00	1.75
(14)	Steve Carlton	6.00	3.00	1.75
(15)	Dave Cash	2.50	1.25	.70
(16)	Cesar Cedeno	2.50	1.25	.70
(17)	Ron Coy	2.50	1.25	.70
(18)	Chris Chambliss	2.50	1.25	.70
(19)	Dave Concepcion	2.50	1.25	.70
(20)	Dennis Eckersley	6.00	3.00	1.75
(21)	Mark Fidrych	3.50	1.75	1.00
(22)	Rollie Fingers	6.00	3.00	1.75
(23)	Carlton Fisk	6.00	3.00	1.75
(24)	George Foster	2.50	1.25	.70
(25)	Wayne Garland	2.50	1.25	.70
(26)	Ralph Garr	2.50	1.25	.70
(27)	Steve Garvey	5.00	2.50	1.50
(28)	Don Gullett	2.50	1.25	.70
(29)	Larry Hisle	2.50	1.25	.70
(30)	Al Hrabosky	2.50	1.25	.70
(31)	Catfish Hunter	6.00	3.00	1.75
(32)	Reggie Jackson	12.00	6.00	3.50
(33)	Randy Jones	2.50	1.25	.70
(34)	Dave Kingman	2.50	1.25	.70
(35)	Jerry Koosman	2.50	1.25	.70
(36)	Ed Kranepool	2.50	1.25	.70
(37)	Ron LeFlore	2.50	1.25	.70
(38)	Sixto Lezcano	2.50	1.25	.70
(39)	Davey Lopes	2.50	1.25	.70
(40)	Greg Luzinski	2.50	1.25	.70
(41)	Fred Lynn	2.50	1.25	.70
(42)	Garry Maddox	2.50	1.25	.70
(43)	Jon Matlock	2.50	1.25	.70
(44)	Gary Matthews	2.50	1.25	.70
(45)	Lee May	2.50	1.25	.70
(46)	John Mayberry	2.50	1.25	.70
(47)	Bake McBride	2.50	1.25	.70
(48)	Tug McGraw	2.50	1.25	.70
(49)	Hal McRae	2.50	1.25	.70
(50)	Andy Messersmith	2.50	1.25	.70
(51)	Randy Moffitt	2.50	1.25	.70
(52)	John Montefusco	2.50	1.25	.70
(53)	Joe Morgan	6.00	3.00	1.75
(54)	Thurman Munson	6.00	3.00	1.75
(55)	Graig Nettles	2.50	1.25	.70
(56)	Al Oliver	2.50	1.25	.70
(57)	Jorge Orta	2.50	1.25	.70
(58)	Jim Palmer	6.00	3.00	1.75
(59)	Dave Parker	2.50	1.25	.70
(60)	Tony Perez	6.00	3.00	1.75
(61)	Gaylord Perry	6.00	3.00	1.75
(62)	Jim Rice	3.00	1.50	.90
(63)	Steve Rogers	2.50	1.25	.70
(64)	Pete Rose	15.00	7.50	4.50
(65)	Joe Rudi	2.50	1.25	.70
(66)	Nolan Ryan	30.00	15.00	9.00
(67)	Manny Sanguillen	2.50	1.25	.70
(68)	Mike Schmidt	12.00	6.00	3.50
(69)	Tom Seaver	7.50	3.75	2.25
(70)	Ted Simmons	2.50	1.25	.70
(71)	Reggie Smith	2.50	1.25	.70
(72)	Willie Stargell	6.00	3.00	1.75
(73)	Rusty Staub	2.50	1.25	.70
(74)	Frank Tanana	2.50	1.25	.70
(75)	Gene Tenace	2.50	1.25	.70
(76)	Luis Tiant	2.50	1.25	.70
(77)	Manny Trillo	2.50	1.25	.70
(78)	Bob Watson	2.50	1.25	.70
(79)	Carl Yastrzemski	7.50	3.75	2.25
(80)	Richie Zisk	2.50	1.25	.70

1978 Wiffle Box-Side Discs

Similar in concept and format to the many contemporary MSA baseball player disc sets, the pieces printed on the sides of Wiffle-brand baseball boxes differ in that they are smaller, at 2-3/8" diameter, and feature a larger checklist. The discs feature black-and-white player portrait photos in the center of a baseball design. The left and right panels are in one of several bright colors. Licensed by the players' association through Mike Schechter Associates, the player photos carry no uniform logos. Backs are printed in black and orange. The unnumbered discs are checklisted here alphabetically.

		NM	EX	VG
Complete Set (88):		325.00	160.00	100.00
Common Player:		2.50	1.25	.70
(1)	Sal Bando	2.50	1.25	.70
(2)	Buddy Bell	2.50	1.25	.70
(3)	Johnny Bench	7.50	3.75	2.25
(4)	Vida Blue	2.50	1.25	.70
(5)	Bert Blyleven	3.00	1.50	.90
(6)	Bobby Bonds	2.50	1.25	.70
(7)	George Brett	12.00	6.00	3.50
(8)	Lou Brock	6.00	3.00	1.75
(9)	Bill Buckner	2.50	1.25	.70
(10)	Ray Burris	2.50	1.25	.70
(11)	Jeff Burroughs	2.50	1.25	.70
(12)	Bert Campaneris	2.50	1.25	.70
(13)	John Candelaria	2.50	1.25	.70
(14)	Jose Cardenal	2.50	1.25	.70
(15)	Rod Carew	6.00	3.00	1.75
(16)	Steve Carlton	6.00	3.00	1.75
(17)	Dave Cash	2.50	1.25	.70
(18)	Cesar Cedeno	2.50	1.25	.70
(19)	Ron Cey	2.50	1.25	.70
(20)	Chris Chambliss	2.50	1.25	.70
(21)	Dave Concepcion	2.50	1.25	.70
(22)	Dennis Eckersley	6.00	3.00	1.75
(23)	Mark Fidrych	3.50	1.75	1.00
(24)	Rollie Fingers	6.00	3.00	1.75
(25)	Carlton Fisk	6.00	3.00	1.75
(26)	George Foster	2.50	1.25	.70
(27)	Wayne Garland	2.50	1.25	.70
(28)	Ralph Garr	2.50	1.25	.70
(29)	Steve Garvey	5.00	2.50	1.50
(30)	Don Gullett	2.50	1.25	.70
(31)	Larry Hisle	2.50	1.25	.70
(32)	Al Hrabosky	2.50	1.25	.70
(33)	Catfish Hunter	6.00	3.00	1.75
(34)	Reggie Jackson	12.00	6.00	3.50
(35)	Randy Jones	2.50	1.25	.70
(36)	Von Joshua	2.50	1.25	.70
(37)	Dave Kingman	2.50	1.25	.70
(38)	Jerry Koosman	2.50	1.25	.70
(39)	Ed Kranepool	2.50	1.25	.70
(40)	Ron LeFlore	2.50	1.25	.70
(41)	Sixto Lezcano	2.50	1.25	.70
(42)	Davey Lopes	2.50	1.25	.70
(43)	Greg Luzinski	2.50	1.25	.70
(44)	Fred Lynn	2.50	1.25	.70
(45)	Garry Maddox	2.50	1.25	.70
(46)	Jon Matlock	2.50	1.25	.70
(47)	Gary Matthews	2.50	1.25	.70
(48)	Lee May	2.50	1.25	.70
(49)	John Mayberry	2.50	1.25	.70
(50)	Bake McBride	2.50	1.25	.70
(51)	Tug McGraw	2.50	1.25	.70
(52)	Hal McRae	2.50	1.25	.70
(53)	Andy Messersmith	2.50	1.25	.70
(54)	Randy Moffitt	2.50	1.25	.70
(55)	John Montefusco	2.50	1.25	.70
(56)	Joe Morgan	6.00	3.00	1.75
(57)	Thurman Munson	6.00	3.00	1.75
(58)	Graig Nettles	2.50	1.25	.70
(59)	Bill North	2.50	1.25	.70
(60)	Al Oliver	2.50	1.25	.70
(61)	Jorge Orta	2.50	1.25	.70
(62)	Jim Palmer	6.00	3.00	1.75
(63)	Dave Parker	2.50	1.25	.70
(64)	Tony Perez	6.00	3.00	1.75
(65)	Gaylord Perry	6.00	3.00	1.75
(66)	Jim Rice	3.00	1.50	.90
(67)	Ellie Rodriguez	2.50	1.25	.70
(68)	Steve Rogers	2.50	1.25	.70
(69)	Pete Rose	15.00	7.50	4.50
(70)	Joe Rudi	2.50	1.25	.70
(71)	Nolan Ryan	30.00	15.00	9.00
(72)	Manny Sanguillen	2.50	1.25	.70
(73)	Mike Schmidt	12.00	6.00	3.50
(74)	Tom Seaver	7.50	3.75	2.25
(75)	Ted Simmons	2.50	1.25	.70
(76)	Reggie Smith	2.50	1.25	.70
(77)	Jim Spencer	2.50	1.25	.70
(78)	Willie Stargell	6.00	3.00	1.75
(79)	Rusty Staub	2.50	1.25	.70
(80)	Rennie Stennett	2.50	1.25	.70
(81)	Frank Tanana	2.50	1.25	.70
(82)	Gene Tenace	2.50	1.25	.70
(83)	Luis Tiant	2.50	1.25	.70
(84)	Manny Trillo	2.50	1.25	.70
(85)	Bob Watson	2.50	1.25	.70
(86)	Butch Wynegar	2.50	1.25	.70
(87)	Carl Yastrzemski	7.50	3.75	2.25
(88)	Richie Zisk	2.50	1.25	.70

1922 Willard's Chocolates Premium

Details on distribution of this 7-1/8" x 11-1/4" premium are unclear, likely involving some sort of wrapper or coupon redemption. The blank-back piece has a central photo of Babe Ruth in action. A facsimile autograph appears in a panel at bottom.

	NM	EX	VG
Babe Ruth	4,000	2,000	1,200

1923 Willard's Chocolate (V100)

Issued circa 1923, this set was produced by the Willard Chocolate Co. of Canada and features sepia-toned photographs on cards measuring about 2" x 3-1/4". The cards are blank-backed and feature the player's name in script on the front, along with a tiny credit line: "Photo by International." The set is complete at 180 cards and nearly one-fourth of the photos used in the set are identical to the better known E120 American Caramel set. The Willard set is identified as V100 in the American Card Catalog.

		NM	EX	VG
Complete Set (180):		30,000	15,000	9,000
Common Player:		100.00	50.00	30.00
(1)	Chas. B. Adams	100.00	50.00	30.00
(2)	Grover C. Alexander	400.00	200.00	125.00
(3)	J.P. Austin	100.00	50.00	30.00
(4)	J.C. Bagby	100.00	50.00	30.00
(5)	J. Franklin Baker	300.00	150.00	90.00
(6)	David J. Bancroft	300.00	150.00	90.00
(7)	Turner Barber	100.00	50.00	30.00
(8)	Jesse L. Barnes	100.00	50.00	30.00
(9)	J.C. Bassler	100.00	50.00	30.00
(10)	L.A. Blue	100.00	50.00	30.00
(11)	Norman D. Boeckel	100.00	50.00	30.00
(12)	F.L. Brazil (Brazill)	100.00	50.00	30.00
(13)	G.H. Burns	100.00	50.00	30.00
(14)	Geo. J. Burns	100.00	50.00	30.00
(15)	Leon Cadore	100.00	50.00	30.00
(16)	Max G. Carey	300.00	150.00	90.00
(17)	Harold G. Carlson	100.00	50.00	30.00
(18)	Lloyd R Christenberry (Christenbury)	100.00	50.00	30.00
(19)	Vernon J. Clemons	100.00	50.00	30.00
(20)	T.R. Cobb	2,400	1,200	750.00
(21)	Bert Cole	100.00	50.00	30.00
(22)	John F. Collins	100.00	50.00	30.00
(23)	S. Coveleskie (Coveleski)	300.00	150.00	90.00
(24)	Walton E. Cruise	100.00	50.00	30.00
(25)	G.W. Cutshaw	100.00	50.00	30.00
(26)	Jacob E. Daubert	100.00	50.00	30.00
(27)	Geo. Dauss	100.00	50.00	30.00
(28)	F.T. Davis	100.00	50.00	30.00
(29)	Chas. A. Deal	100.00	50.00	30.00
(30)	William L. Doak	100.00	50.00	30.00
(31)	William E. Donovan	100.00	50.00	30.00
(32)	Hugh Duffy	300.00	150.00	90.00
(33)	J.A. Dugan	100.00	50.00	30.00
(34)	Louis B. Duncan	100.00	50.00	30.00
(35)	James Dykes	100.00	50.00	30.00
(36)	H.J. Ehmke	100.00	50.00	30.00
(37)	F.R. Ellerbe	100.00	50.00	30.00
(38)	E.G. Erickson	100.00	50.00	30.00
(39)	John J. Evers	300.00	150.00	90.00
(40)	U.C. Faber	300.00	150.00	90.00
(41)	B.A. Falk	100.00	50.00	30.00
(42)	Max Flack	100.00	50.00	30.00
(43)	Lee Fohl	100.00	50.00	30.00
(44)	Jacques F. Fournier	100.00	50.00	30.00
(45)	Frank F. Frisch	300.00	150.00	90.00
(46)	C.E. Galloway	100.00	50.00	30.00
(47)	W.C. Gardner	100.00	50.00	30.00
(48)	E.P. Gharrity	100.00	50.00	30.00
(49)	Geo. Gibson	100.00	50.00	30.00
(50)	Wm. Gleason	100.00	50.00	30.00
(51)	William Gleason	100.00	50.00	30.00
(52)	Henry M. Gowdy	100.00	50.00	30.00
(53)	I.M. Griffin	100.00	50.00	30.00
(54)	Tom Griffith	100.00	50.00	30.00
(55)	Burleigh A. Grimes	300.00	150.00	90.00
(56)	Charles J. Grimm	100.00	50.00	30.00
(57)	Jesse J. Haines	300.00	150.00	90.00
(58)	S.R. Harris	300.00	150.00	90.00
(59)	W.B. Harris	100.00	50.00	30.00
(60)	R.K. Hasty	100.00	50.00	30.00
(61)	H.E. Heilman (Heilmann)	300.00	150.00	90.00
(62)	Walter J. Henline	100.00	50.00	30.00
(63)	Walter L. Holke	100.00	50.00	30.00
(64)	Charles J. Hollocher	100.00	50.00	30.00
(65)	H.B. Hooper	300.00	150.00	90.00
(66)	Rogers Hornsby	400.00	200.00	125.00
(67)	W.C. Hoyt	300.00	150.00	90.00
(68)	Miller Huggins	300.00	150.00	90.00
(69)	W.C. Jacobsen (Jacobson)	100.00	50.00	30.00
(70)	C.D. Jamieson	100.00	50.00	30.00
(71)	Ernest Johnson	100.00	50.00	30.00
(72)	W.P. Johnson	750.00	375.00	225.00
(73)	James H. Johnston	100.00	50.00	30.00
(74)	R.W. Jones	100.00	50.00	30.00
(75)	Samuel Pond Jones	100.00	50.00	30.00
(76)	J.I. Judge	100.00	50.00	30.00
(77)	James W. Keenan	100.00	50.00	30.00
(78)	Geo. L. Kelly	300.00	150.00	90.00
(79)	Peter J. Kilduff	100.00	50.00	30.00
(80)	William Killefer	100.00	50.00	30.00
(81)	Lee King	100.00	50.00	30.00
(82)	Ray Kolp	100.00	50.00	30.00
(83)	John Lavan	100.00	50.00	30.00
(84)	H.L. Leibold	100.00	50.00	30.00
(85)	Connie Mack	300.00	150.00	90.00
(86)	J.W. Mails	100.00	50.00	30.00
(87)	Walter J. Maranville	300.00	150.00	90.00
(88)	Richard W. Marquard	300.00	150.00	90.00
(89)	C.W. Mays	100.00	50.00	30.00
(90)	Geo. F. McBride	100.00	50.00	30.00
(91)	H.M. McClellan	100.00	50.00	30.00
(92)	John J. McGraw	300.00	150.00	90.00
(93)	Austin B. McHenry	100.00	50.00	30.00
(94)	J. McInnis	100.00	50.00	30.00
(95)	Douglas McWeeney (McWeeny)	100.00	50.00	30.00
(96)	M. Menosky	100.00	50.00	30.00
(97)	Emil F. Meusel	100.00	50.00	30.00
(98)	R. Meusel	100.00	50.00	30.00
(99)	Henry W. Meyers	100.00	50.00	30.00
(100)	J.C. Milan	100.00	50.00	30.00
(101)	John K. Miljus	100.00	50.00	30.00
(102)	Edmund J. Miller	100.00	50.00	30.00
(103)	Elmer Miller	100.00	50.00	30.00
(104)	Otto L. Miller	100.00	50.00	30.00
(105)	Fred Mitchell	100.00	50.00	30.00
(106)	Geo. Mogridge	100.00	50.00	30.00
(107)	Patrick J. Moran	100.00	50.00	30.00
(108)	John D. Morrison	100.00	50.00	30.00
(109)	J.A. Mostil	100.00	50.00	30.00
(110)	Clarence F. Mueller	100.00	50.00	30.00
(111)	A. Earle Neale	100.00	50.00	30.00
(112)	Joseph Oeschger	100.00	50.00	30.00
(113)	Robert J. O'Farrell	100.00	50.00	30.00
(114)	J.C. Oldham	100.00	50.00	30.00
(115)	I.M. Olson	100.00	50.00	30.00
(116)	Geo. M. O'Neil	100.00	50.00	30.00
(117)	S.F. O'Neill	100.00	50.00	30.00
(118)	Frank J. Parkinson	100.00	50.00	30.00
(119)	Geo. H. Paskert	100.00	50.00	30.00
(120)	R.T. Peckinpaugh	100.00	50.00	30.00
(121)	H.J. Pennock	300.00	150.00	90.00
(122)	Ralph Perkins	100.00	50.00	30.00
(123)	Edw. J. Pfeffer	100.00	50.00	30.00
(124)	W.C. Pipp	100.00	50.00	30.00
(125)	Charles Elmer Ponder	100.00	50.00	30.00
(126)	Raymond R. Powell	100.00	50.00	30.00
(127)	D.B. Pratt	100.00	50.00	30.00
(128)	Joseph Rapp	100.00	50.00	30.00
(129)	John H. Rawlings	100.00	50.00	30.00
(130)	E.S. Rice (Should be E.C.)	300.00	150.00	90.00
(131)	Branch Rickey	350.00	175.00	110.00
(132)	James J. Ring	100.00	50.00	30.00
(133)	Eppa J. Rixey	300.00	150.00	90.00
(134)	Davis A. Robertson	100.00	50.00	30.00
(135)	Edwin Rommel	100.00	50.00	30.00
(136)	Edd J. Roush	300.00	150.00	90.00
(137)	Harold Ruel (Herold)	100.00	50.00	30.00
(138)	Allen Russell	100.00	50.00	30.00
(139)	G.H. Ruth	4,500	2,250	1,400
(140)	Wilfred D. Ryan	100.00	50.00	30.00
(141)	Henry F. Sallee	100.00	50.00	30.00
(142)	W.H. Schang	100.00	50.00	30.00
(143)	Raymond H. Schmandt	100.00	50.00	30.00
(144)	Everett Scott	100.00	50.00	30.00
(145)	Henry Severeid	100.00	50.00	30.00
(146)	Jos. W. Sewell	300.00	150.00	90.00
(147)	Howard S. Shanks	100.00	50.00	30.00
(148)	E.H. Sheely	100.00	50.00	30.00
(149)	Ralph Shinners	100.00	50.00	30.00
(150)	U.J. Shocker	100.00	50.00	30.00
(151)	G.H. Sisler	300.00	150.00	90.00
(152)	Earl L. Smith	100.00	50.00	30.00
(153)	Earl S. Smith	100.00	50.00	30.00
(154)	Geo. A. Smith	100.00	50.00	30.00
(155)	J.W. Smith	100.00	50.00	30.00
(156)	Tris E. Speaker	400.00	200.00	125.00
(157)	Arnold Staatz (Statz)	100.00	50.00	30.00
(158)	J.R. Stephenson	100.00	50.00	30.00
(159)	Milton J. Stock	100.00	50.00	30.00
(160)	John L. Sullivan	100.00	50.00	30.00
(161)	H.F. Tormahlen	100.00	50.00	30.00
(162)	Jas. A. Tierney	100.00	50.00	30.00
(163)	J.T. Tobin	100.00	50.00	30.00
(164)	Jas. L. Vaughn	100.00	50.00	30.00
(165)	R.H. Veach	100.00	50.00	30.00
(166)	C.W. Walker	100.00	50.00	30.00
(167)	A.L. Ward	100.00	50.00	30.00
(168)	Zack D. Wheat	300.00	150.00	90.00
(169)	George B. Whitted	100.00	50.00	30.00
(170)	Irvin K. Wilhelm	100.00	50.00	30.00
(171)	Roy H. Wilkinson	100.00	50.00	30.00
(172)	Fred C. Williams	100.00	50.00	30.00
(173)	K.R. Williams	100.00	50.00	30.00
(174)	Sam'l W. Wilson	100.00	50.00	30.00
(175)	Ivy B. Wingo	100.00	50.00	30.00
(176)	L.W. Witt	100.00	50.00	30.00
(177)	Joseph Wood	200.00	100.00	60.00
(178)	E. Yaryan	100.00	50.00	30.00
(179)	R.S. Young	100.00	50.00	30.00
(180)	Ross Young (Youngs)	300.00	150.00	90.00

1924 Willard's Chocolate Sports Champions (V122)

Three baseball players are featured among this 56-card Canadian set. The black-and-white cards are printed on thin paper measuring 1-3/8" x 3-3/8". Backs are blank. The set features male and female athletes from many different sports, with a distinct Canadian flavor. The candy company was headquartered in Toronto.

		NM	EX	VG
2	Eddie Collins	600.00	300.00	180.00
5	Babe Ruth	3,250	1,625	975.00
39	Ty Cobb	2,250	1,125	675.00

1911 Williams Baking Philadelphia A's (D359)

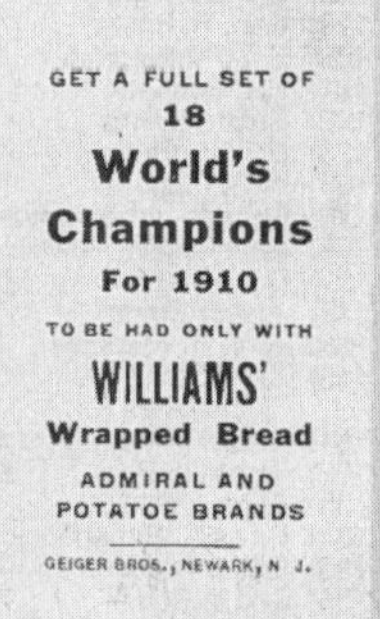

This Philadelphia Athletics team set is among the scarcest early 20th Century baking company issues. It commemorates the A's 1910 Championship season, and, except for pitcher Jack Coombs, the checklist includes nearly all key members of the club, including manager Connie Mack. The cards are the standard size for the era, 1-1/2" x 2-5/8". Fronts feature a player portrait set against a colored background. The player's name and the word "Athletics" appear at the bottom, while "World's Champions 1910" is printed along the top. Backs of the cards advertise the set as the "Athletics Series." Collectors should be aware that the same checklist was used for a similar Athletics set issued by Rochester Baking and Cullivan's Fireside tobacco (T208) and also that blank-backed versions are also known to exist, cataloged as E104 in the American Card Catalog.

		NM	EX	VG
Complete Set (18):		85,000	35,000	17,000
Common Player:		4,000	2,000	1,000
(1)	Home Run Baker	7,000	3,500	1,750
(2)	Jack Barry	4,000	2,000	1,000
(3)	Chief Bender	7,000	3,500	1,750
(4)	Eddie Collins	7,000	3,500	1,750
(5)	Harry Davis	6,000	3,000	1,500
(6)	Jimmy Dygert	4,000	2,000	1,000
(7)	Topsy Hartsel	4,000	2,000	1,000
(8)	Harry Krause	4,000	2,000	1,000
(9)	Jack Lapp	4,000	2,000	1,000
(10)	Paddy Livingston	4,000	2,000	1,000
(11)	Bris Lord	4,000	2,000	1,000
(12)	Connie Mack	14,000	7,900	4,575
(13)	Cy Morgan	4,000	2,000	1,000
(14)	Danny Murphy	6,000	3,000	1,500
(15)	Rube Oldring	4,000	2,000	1,000
(16)	Eddie Plank	14,000	7,900	4,575
(17)	Amos Strunk	4,000	2,000	1,000
(18a)	Ira Thomas (1910 at top)	4,000	2,000	1,000
(18b)	Ira Thomas (1910 at right)	4,000	2,000	1,000

1910 Williams Caramels (E103)

N. LAJOIE, 2d B., Cleveland
The Williams Caramel Co. Oxford, Pa.

This 30-card set issued by the Williams Caramel Co. of Oxford, Pa., in 1910 can be differentiated from other similar sets because it was printed on a thin paper stock rather than cardboard. Measuring approximately 1-3/4" x 2-5/8", each card features a player portrait set against a red background. The bottom of the card lists the player's last name, position and team; beneath that is the line, "The Williams Caramel Co. Oxford Pa." Nearly all of the photos in the set, which is designated E103 by the ACC, are identical to those in the M116 Sporting Life set.

		NM	EX	VG
Complete Set (30):		156,000	60,000	30,000
Common Player:		1,175	475.00	225.00
(1)	Chas. Bender	5,400	2,150	1,100
(2)	Roger Bresnahan	5,400	2,150	1,100
(3)	Mordecai Brown	5,400	2,150	1,100
(4)	Frank Chance	5,400	2,150	1,100
(5)	Hal Chase	3,600	1,450	700.00
(6)	Ty Cobb	45,000	18,000	9,000
(7)	Edward Collins	5,400	2,150	1,100
(8)	Sam Crawford	5,400	2,150	1,100
(9)	Harry Davis	1,175	475.00	225.00
(10)	Arthur Devlin	1,175	475.00	225.00
(11)	William Donovan	1,175	475.00	225.00
(12)	Chas. Dooin	1,175	475.00	225.00
(13)	L. Doyle	1,175	475.00	225.00
(14)	John Ewing	1,175	475.00	225.00
(15)	George Gibson	1,175	475.00	225.00
(16)	Hugh Jennings	5,400	2,150	1,100
(17)	David Jones	1,175	475.00	225.00
(18)	Tim Jordan	1,175	475.00	225.00
(19)	N. Lajoie	5,400	2,150	1,100
(20)	Thomas Leach	1,175	475.00	225.00
(21)	Harry Lord	1,175	475.00	225.00
(22)	Chris. Mathewson	18,000	7,200	3,600
(23)	John McLean	1,175	475.00	225.00
(24)	Geo. W. McQuillan	1,175	475.00	225.00
(25)	Pastorius	1,175	475.00	225.00
(26)	N. Rucker	1,175	475.00	225.00
(27)	Fred Tenny (Tenney)	1,175	475.00	225.00
(28)	Ira Thomas	1,175	475.00	225.00
(29)	Hans Wagner	36,000	14,400	7,200
(30)	Robert Wood	1,175	475.00	225.00

1889 E.R. Williams Card Game

This set of 52 playing cards came packed in its own box that advertised the set as the "Egerton R. Williams Popular Indoor Base Ball Game." Designed to look like a conventional deck of playing cards, the set included various players from the National League and the American Association. Although the set contains 52 cards (like a typical deck of playing cards) only 19 actually feature color drawings of players. Each of these cards pictures two different players (one at the top and a second at the bottom, separated by sepia-colored crossed bats in the middle), resulting in 38 different players. The remaining 33 cards in the deck are strictly game cards showing a specific baseball play (such as "Batter Out on Fly" or "Two Base Hit," etc.). The cards have green-tinted backs and measure 2-7/16" x 3-1/2". Each one carries an 1889 copyright line by E.R. Williams.

		NM	EX	VG
Complete Boxed Set:		24,000	12,000	7,250
Common Player Card:		600.00	300.00	175.00
Common Game Action Card:		110.00	55.00	30.00
(1)	Cap Anson, Buck Ewing	2,400	1,200	720.00
(2)	Dan Brouthers, Arlie Latham	900.00	450.00	275.00
(3)	Charles Buffinton, Bob Carruthers	600.00	300.00	175.00
(4)	Hick Carpenter, Cliff Carroll	600.00	300.00	175.00
(5)	Charles Comiskey, Roger Connor	1,200	600.00	360.00
(6)	Pop Corkhill, Jim Fogarty	600.00	300.00	175.00
(7)	John Clarkson, Tim Keefe	1,200	600.00	360.00
(8)	Jerry Denny, Mike Tiernan	600.00	300.00	175.00
(9)	Dave Foutz, King Kelly	2,200	1,100	660.00
(10)	Pud Galvin, Dave Orr	900.00	450.00	275.00
(11)	Jack Glasscock, Tommy Tucker	600.00	300.00	175.00
(12)	Mike Griffin, Ed McKean	600.00	300.00	175.00
(13)	Dummy Hoy, Long John Reilley (Reilly)	900.00	450.00	275.00
(14)	Arthur Irwin, Ned Williamson	600.00	300.00	175.00
(15)	Silver King, John Tener	900.00	450.00	275.00
(16)	Al Myers, Cub Stricker	600.00	300.00	175.00
(17)	Fred Pfeffer, Chicken Wolf	600.00	300.00	175.00
(18)	Tom Ramsey, Gus Weyhing	600.00	300.00	175.00
(19)	John Ward, Curt Welch	1,000	500.00	300.00

1961 J.B. Williams Co. Roger Maris Lithograph

The maker of Lectric Shave and Aqua Velva offered fans a lithograph of Roger Maris hitting his 59th home run at Baltimore, Sept. 20, 1961. The 16" x 11" black-and-white print on parchment paper was available by mail for 25 cents and a box top from either of the shaving products. The artwork is by Robert Riger.

	NM	EX	VG
Roger Maris	200.00	100.00	60.00

1908 R.C. Williams Cy Young Postcard

A mature Cy Young, about age 42, is pictured on this postcard bearing the imprint of R.C. Williams. No other contemporary cards with this imprint have been reported.

	NM	EX	VG
Cy Young	800.00	400.00	240.00

1954 Wilson Franks

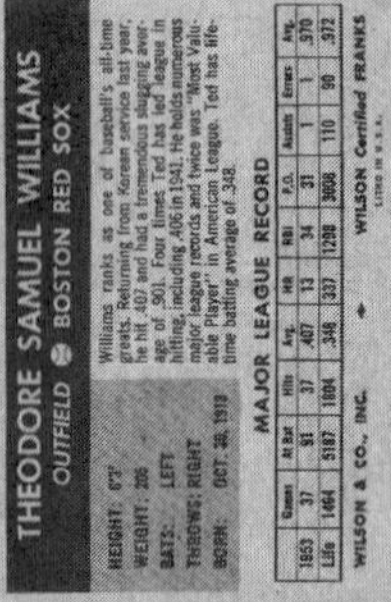

The 2-5/8" x 3-3/4" cards are among the most popular and scarcest baseball card sets issued with hot dogs during the 1950s. The cards feature color-added photos on the front along with a facsimile autograph and a package of frankfurters. Backs feature personal information, a career summary and 1953 and career statistics. Cards were packaged in direct contact with the meat, resulting in many exhibiting grease stains. Survival rates of the various players differ widely, probably based on the geography of initial distribution. A small hoard of roughly half the players was discovered in unissued condition in the late 1990s, temporarily influencing the market.

		NM	EX	VG
Complete Set (20):		30,000	12,000	6,000
Common Player:		650.00	260.00	130.00
Advertising Poster:		7,500	3,500	2,000
(1)	Roy Campanella	1,800	725.00	350.00
(2)	Del Ennis	650.00	260.00	130.00
(3)	Carl Erskine	675.00	275.00	135.00
(4)	Ferris Fain	650.00	260.00	130.00
(5)	Bob Feller	1,250	500.00	250.00
(6)	Nelson Fox	1,250	500.00	250.00
(7)	Johnny Groth	750.00	300.00	150.00
(8)	Stan Hack	1,100	440.00	220.00
(9)	Gil Hodges	2,750	1,100	550.00
(10)	Ray Jablonski	1,250	500.00	250.00
(11)	Harvey Kuenn	1,350	550.00	275.00
(12)	Roy McMillan	650.00	260.00	130.00
(13)	Andy Pafko	650.00	260.00	130.00
(14)	Paul Richards	900.00	360.00	180.00
(15)	Hank Sauer	900.00	360.00	180.00
(16)	Red Schoendienst	1,000	400.00	200.00
(17)	Enos Slaughter	800.00	320.00	160.00
(18)	Vern Stephens	650.00	260.00	130.00
(19)	Sammy White	650.00	260.00	130.00
(20)	Ted Williams	13,500	6,500	3,500

1961 Wilson Meats L.A.Dodgers/Angels

It is likely these 5-1/2" x 8-1/2" photos were prepared for promotional appearances by players on behalf of the meat company. The player name appears at the bottom of the photo and the sponsor's message appears at bottom, "Courtesy of WILSON & CO., Inc., Fine Meat Products." Backs are blank. The pictures are often found with player autographs, another indicator of their use at personal appearances.

		NM	EX	VG
(1)	Ron Fairly	50.00	25.00	15.00
(2)	Gil Hodges	75.00	37.00	22.00
(3)	Frank Howard	50.00	25.00	15.00
(4)	Ted Kluszewski	60.00	30.00	18.00

1950s-70s Wilson Advisory Staff Photos

Advisory staff photos were a promotional item which debuted in the early 1950s, flourished in the 1960s and died in the early 1970s. Generally 8" x 10" (sometimes a little larger), these black-and-white (a few later were color) glossy photos picture players who had contracted with a major baseball equipment company to endorse and use their product. Usually the product - most often a glove - was prominently displayed in the photo. The pictures were often displayed in the windows of sporting goods stores or the walls of sports departments and were sometimes made available to customers. Because the companies tended to stick with players over the years, some photos were reissued, sometimes with and sometimes without a change of team, pose or style. The photos are checklisted here in alphabetical order. A pose description is given where known. It is unlikely this list is complete. Gaps have been left in the assigned numbering to accommodate future additions. In general, Wilson advisory staff photos feature the player name and a line of type indicating the player's status as an advisory staffer in the bottom border.

		NM	EX	VG
Common Player:		14.00	7.00	4.00
(1)	Bob Allison (Twins, full-length.)	20.00	10.00	6.00
(2)	Felipe Alou (Braves, neck-to-cap.)	25.00	12.50	7.50
(3)	Felipe Alou (Braves, upper body.)	25.00	12.50	7.50
(4)	Max Alvis (Indians, hands on knees.)	20.00	10.00	6.00
(5)	Max Alvis (Indians, upper body.)	20.00	10.00	6.00
(6)	Luis Aparicio/Fldg (White Sox, horizontal)	50.00	25.00	15.00
(7)	Luis Aparicio/Fldg (White Sox, full-length.)	40.00	20.00	12.00
(8)	Luis Aparicio (Orioles, full-length.)	50.00	25.00	15.00
(9)	Gerry Arrigo (Reds, full-length pitching.)	20.00	10.00	6.00
(10)	Ernie Banks/Btg	75.00	37.00	22.00
(11)	Ernie Banks/Fldg (Horizontal)	60.00	30.00	18.00
(12)	Glenn Beckert/Fldg (Cubs, ball in hand.)	25.00	12.50	7.50
(13)	Glenn Beckert/Fldg (Cubs, no ball.)	25.00	12.50	7.50
(14)	Paul Blair (Orioles, full-length.)	25.00	12.50	7.50
(15)	Don Blasingame (Cardinals, belt-up.)	20.00	10.00	6.00
(16)	Bob Bolin (Giants, pitching follow-through.)	20.00	10.00	6.00
(17)	Dave Boswell (Twins, full-length.)	20.00	10.00	6.00
(18)	Dave Boswell (Twins, waist-up, stretch position.)	20.00	10.00	6.00
(19)	Jackie Brandt (Orioles, full-length.)	20.00	10.00	6.00
(20)	Smoky Burgess (Pirates, sitting on step w/ three bats.)	20.00	10.00	6.00
(21)	Rico Carty/Btg (Milwaukee Braves)	20.00	10.00	6.00
(22)	Rico Carty (Milwaukee Braves, dugout step.)	20.00	10.00	6.00
(23)	Rico Carty/Btg (Atlanta Braves)	20.00	10.00	6.00
(24)	Paul Casanova (Senators, catching crouch.)	20.00	10.00	6.00
(25)	Norm Cash/Btg (Tigers, waist-up.)	25.00	12.50	7.50
(26)	Orlando Cepeda/Btg (Braves)	30.00	15.00	9.00
(27)	Orlando Cepeda (Cardinals, dugout step.)	25.00	12.50	7.50
(28)	Orlando Cepeda/Fldg (Cardinals)	25.00	12.50	7.50
(29)	Jim Davenport/Fldg (Giants)	20.00	10.00	6.00
(30)	Vic Davalillo (Indians, upper body.)	20.00	10.00	6.00
(31)	Willie Davis (Dodgers, full-length.)	20.00	10.00	6.00
(32)	Chuck Dobson (A's, full-length.)	20.00	10.00	6.00
(35)	"Moe" Drabowsky (Cubs, thighs-up.)	20.00	10.00	6.00
(36)	Don Drysdale (L.A. Dodgers, follow-through.)	25.00	12.50	7.50
(37)	Dick Ellsworth (Cubs, pitching follow-through.)	20.00	10.00	6.00
(38)	Dick Ellsworth (Phillies, full-length.)	20.00	10.00	6.00
(39)	Del Ennis/Kneeling (Cardinals)	20.00	10.00	6.00
(40)	Bob Feller (Seated, glove on knee.)	120.00	60.00	36.00
(41)	Nellie Fox (White Sox, chest-up.)	35.00	17.50	10.50
(42)	Nellie Fox (White Sox, fielding grounder.)	50.00	25.00	15.00
(43)	Nelson Fox/Seated (White Sox)	50.00	25.00	15.00
(44)	Nelson Fox/Btg (Colt .45s)	50.00	25.00	15.00
(45)	Bill Freehan (Catching crouch.)	20.00	10.00	6.00
(46)	Bill Freehan (Two pictures.)	20.00	10.00	6.00
(47)	Phil Gagliano/Fldg (Cardinals, photo actually Ed Spiezio.)	25.00	12.50	7.50
(48)	Jim Gentile/Btg (Orioles, chest-up.)	20.00	10.00	6.00
(49)	Vernon "Lefty" Gomez (w/ glasses.)	25.00	12.50	7.50
(50)	Lefty Gomez (No glasses.)	25.00	12.50	7.50
(51)	Jim Hall/Fldg (Angels)	25.00	12.50	7.50
(52a)	Don Hoak (Pirates, full-length, waist up.)	20.00	10.00	6.00
(52b)	Don Hoak (Pirates, waist up.)	20.00	10.00	6.00
(53)	Gil Hodges (L.A. Dodgers, belt-up batting.)	50.00	25.00	15.00
(54)	Willie Horton (Tigers, full-length.)	20.00	10.00	6.00
(55)	Bruce Howard (White Sox, pitching follow-through.)	20.00	10.00	6.00
(56)	Jim Hunter (K.C. A's, beginning wind-up.)	25.00	12.50	7.50
(57)	Jim Hunter (Oakland A's, full-length, photo actually Chuck Dobson.)	25.00	12.50	7.50
(58)	Mack Jones (Reds, full-length.)	20.00	10.00	6.00
(59)	Duane Josephson (White Sox, catching crouch.)	20.00	10.00	6.00
(61)	Jim Kaat (Twins, upper body.)	25.00	12.50	7.50
(62)	Al Kaline/Btg (Full-length)	75.00	37.00	22.00
(63)	Al Kaline/Btg (Upper body)	75.00	37.00	22.00
(64)	Al Kaline (Upper body, hands on knees.)	75.00	37.00	22.00
(65)	Al Kaline (Upper body.)	75.00	37.00	22.00
(66)	Al Kaline (Upper body, looking right.)	75.00	37.00	22.00
(67)	Harmon Killebrew/Btg (Twins, upper body)	50.00	25.00	15.00
(68)	Harmon Killebrew/Btg (Twins, looking front.)	50.00	25.00	15.00
(69)	Harmon Killebrew/Kneeling (Twins)	50.00	25.00	15.00
(70)	Cal Koonce (Cubs, pitching follow-through.)	20.00	10.00	6.00
(71)	Harvey Kuenn/Btg (Tigers)	25.00	12.50	7.50
(72)	Harvey Kuenn (Tigers, upper body.)	25.00	12.50	7.50
(73)	Hal Lanier/Throwing (Giants)	20.00	10.00	6.00
(74)	Juan Marichal (Giants, upper body.)	25.00	12.50	7.50
(75)	Willie McCovey/Btg (Giants)	25.00	12.50	7.50
(76)	Sam McDowell (Indians, seated, no cap.)	25.00	12.50	7.50
(77)	Dennis McLain (Tigers, hands at chest.)	25.00	12.50	7.50
(78)	Roy McMillan/Btg (Braves)	20.00	10.00	6.00
(79)	Roy McMillan (Reds, belt-up.)	20.00	10.00	6.00
(81)	Denis Menke/Fldg (Braves)	20.00	10.00	6.00
(82)	Denis Menke (Braves, upper body.)	20.00	10.00	6.00
(83)	Don Mincher (Angels, full-length.)	20.00	10.00	6.00
(84)	Joe Morgan/Btg (Astros)	40.00	20.00	12.00
(85)	Joe Morgan/Fldg (Astros)	40.00	20.00	12.00
(86)	Jim Nash/Pitching (A's)	20.00	10.00	6.00
(87)	Rich Nye/Pitching (Cubs)	20.00	10.00	6.00
(88)	John Odom/Pitching (Kansas City A's)	20.00	10.00	6.00
(89)	John Odom (Oakland A's, belt-up pose.)	20.00	10.00	6.00
(90)	John Orsino/Kneeling (Orioles)	20.00	10.00	6.00
(91)	Jim O'Toole (Reds, upper body, warm-up jacket.)	20.00	10.00	6.00
(92)	Jim O'Toole (White Sox, upper body.)	20.00	10.00	6.00
(93)	Ray Oyler/Fldg (Tigers)	20.00	10.00	6.00
(94)	Milt Pappas/Pitching (Orioles, full-length.)	20.00	10.00	6.00
(95)	Milt Pappas/Pitching (Orioles, knees-up.)	20.00	10.00	6.00
(96)	Don Pavletich (Reds, full-length.)	20.00	10.00	6.00
(97)	Don Pavletich/Squatting (Reds)	20.00	10.00	6.00
(98)	Albie Pearson (Angels, glove under left arm.)	20.00	10.00	6.00
(99)	Ron Perranoski (Dodgers, upper body.)	20.00	10.00	6.00
(100)	Ron Perranoski (Twins, belt-up from side.)	25.00	12.50	7.50
(101)	Ron Perranoski/Pitching (Twins)	20.00	10.00	6.00
(102)	Gaylord Perry/Pitching (Giants)	25.00	12.50	7.50
(103)	Billy Pierce (White Sox, knees-up.)	25.00	12.50	7.50
(104)	Bob Purkey (Reds, waist-up.)	20.00	10.00	6.00
(105)	Doug Rader/Fldg (Astros)	20.00	10.00	6.00
(106)	Dick Rodatz (Radatz) (Red Sox, upper body.)	20.00	10.00	6.00
(107)	Dick Radatz (Red Sox, upper body.)	20.00	10.00	6.00
(108)	Pete Runnels (Red Sox, kneeling on deck.)	25.00	12.50	7.50
(109)	Ron Santo/Fldg (Cubs)	25.00	12.50	7.50
(110)	George Scott (Red Sox, upper body.)	20.00	10.00	6.00
(111)	Larry Sherry (Dodgers, full-length.)	20.00	10.00	6.00
(112)	Chris Short (Phillies, upper body.)	20.00	10.00	6.00
(113)	Hal Smith/Btg (Pirates)	25.00	12.50	7.50
(114)	Mickey Stanley (Tigers, full-length.)	20.00	10.00	6.00
(115)	Tony Taylor (Phillies, bat on shoulder.)	20.00	10.00	6.00
(116)	Frank Thomas (Pirates, waist-up.)	20.00	10.00	6.00
(117)	Frank Thomas/Btg (Cubs)	20.00	10.00	6.00
(119)	Jeff Torborg (Dodgers, holding mask.)	20.00	10.00	6.00
(121)	Al Weis (White Sox, ready to throw.)	20.00	10.00	6.00
(122)	Al Weis/Fldg (Mets)	20.00	10.00	6.00
(123)	Ted Williams/Btg	125.00	62.00	37.00
(125)	Bobby Wine (Phillies, ready to throw.)	20.00	10.00	6.00
(126)	Rick Wise (Phillies, upper body.)	20.00	10.00	6.00
(128)	Woody Woodward (Reds, belt-to-cap.)	25.00	12.50	7.50

(130)	Early Wynn (White Sox, full-length.)	25.00	12.50	7.50
(131)	Jim Wynn/Btg (Colt .45s, upper body.)	20.00	10.00	6.00
(132)	Jim Wynn/Btg (Astros, full-length.)	20.00	10.00	6.00
(133)	Don Zimmer (Cubs, waist-up batting.)	20.00	10.00	6.00

1961 Wilson Advisory Staff Cards

Similar in format to the contemporary 8" x 10" photos, these 2-3/4" x 4" cards have black-and-white player poses on front, prominently displaying a Wilson glove. In the white bottom border is: "Member-Advisory Staff, Wilson Sporting Goods Co." A blue facsimile autograph is printed across the picture. Backs are blank. The checklist, presented here alphabetically, may not be complete.

		NM	EX	VG
Common Player:		10.00	5.00	3.00
(1)	Dick Ellsworth	10.00	5.00	3.00
(2)	Don Hoak	12.00	6.00	3.50
(3)	Harvey Kuenn	12.00	6.00	3.50
(4)	Roy McMillan	10.00	5.00	3.00
(5)	Jim Piersall	12.00	6.00	3.50
(6)	Ron Santo	16.00	8.00	4.75

1977 Wilson Sporting Goods Mini-Posters

Though unmarked as such, these 6" x 9" cards are a promotion from Wilson. The blank-back cards have a color action photo with white borders and a facsimile autograph.

		NM	EX	VG
Complete Set (10):		200.00	100.00	60.00
Common Player:		10.00	5.00	3.00
(1)	Johnny Bench	35.00	17.50	10.50
(2)	George Brett	50.00	25.00	15.00
(3)	Rod Carew	30.00	15.00	9.00
(4)	Dave Concepcion	10.00	5.00	3.00
(5)	Steve Garvey	15.00	7.50	4.50
(6)	Reggie Jackson	40.00	20.00	12.00
(7)	Greg Luzinski	10.00	5.00	3.00
(8)	Pete Rose	75.00	37.00	22.00
(9)	Mike Schmidt	40.00	20.00	12.00
(10)	Tom Seaver	40.00	17.50	10.50

1955-1958 Don Wingfield Washington Nationals Postcards

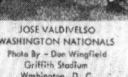

This series of 3-1/2" x 5-1/2" black-and-white glossy postcards provided Nationals' players with a vehicle for accommodating fan requests. Player portraits or action poses are bordered in white with three (or in the case of Valdivielso, five) lines of type at bottom identifying the player, team and copyright holder. Most have "Photo Post Card" at top on back and "Devolite Peerless" in the stamp box. The unnumbered cards are checklisted here in alphabetical order.

		NM	EX	VG
Complete Set (12):		1,800	900.00	550.00
Common Player:		150.00	75.00	45.00
(1)	Jim Busby	150.00	75.00	45.00
(2)	Chuck Dressen	150.00	75.00	45.00
(3)	Ed Fitz Gerald	150.00	75.00	45.00
(4)	Jim Lemon	175.00	85.00	55.00
(5)	Bob Porterfield	150.00	75.00	45.00
(6)	Pete Runnels	150.00	75.00	45.00
(7)	Roy Sievers	175.00	85.00	55.00
(8)	Chuck Stobbs	150.00	75.00	45.00
(9)	Dean Stone	150.00	75.00	45.00
(10)	Jose Valdivelso (Valdivielso)	175.00	85.00	55.00
(11)	Mickey Vernon	175.00	85.00	55.00
(12)	Ed Yost	150.00	75.00	45.00

1957-1959 Don Wingfield Photocards

These black-and-white glossy photocards are usually blank-back, evidently for use as in-person handouts, rather than by mail. In 3-1/2" x 5-1/2" size, the player photos are bordered in white with an especially wide white bottom border for affixing an autograph. Other than the autograph which may appear, the player is not identified on the card. Wingfield's name may appear in white letters in the lower-right corner of the photo, may be on a credit line on back or may not appear at all.

		NM	EX	VG
Common Player:		50.00	25.00	15.00
(1)	Ted Abernathy	50.00	25.00	15.00
(2)	Bobby Allison	50.00	25.00	15.00
(3)	Tex Clevenger	50.00	25.00	15.00
(4)	Russ Kemmerer	50.00	25.00	15.00
(5)	Harmon Killebrew	100.00	50.00	30.00
(6)	Bob Usher	50.00	25.00	15.00
(7)	Hal Woodeshick	50.00	25.00	15.00

1960s Don Wingfield Postcards - B/W

A second type of player photo postcards was produced by Alexandria, Va., photographer Don Wingfield beginning around 1960. Also black-and-white, the 3-1/2" x 5-1/2" cards have (usually) borderless poses on front with no extraneous graphics. Backs have standard postcard indicia plus (on most cards) the player name and team and a copyright line with Wingfield's name and address. At top on back is "Post Card," with "Place Stamp Here" in the postage box. Washington Senators players dominate the checklist which also includes stars of other teams. The autograph on the pictured card was added by the player after printing and is not part of the design. The currently known checklist is presented here alphabetically.

		NM	EX	VG
Common Player:		50.00	25.00	15.00
(1)	Bob Allison	55.00	27.50	16.50
(2)	Ernie Banks	100.00	50.00	30.00
(3)	Earl Battey/Btg (Chest to cap.)	50.00	25.00	15.00
(4)	Earl Battey (Kneeling w/bat.)	50.00	25.00	15.00
(5)	Norm Cash	60.00	30.00	18.00
(6)	Jim Coates	50.00	25.00	15.00
(7)	Rocky Colavito	60.00	30.00	18.00
(8)	Chuck Cottier	50.00	25.00	15.00
(9)	Bennie Daniels	50.00	25.00	15.00
(10)	Dan Dobbek	50.00	25.00	15.00
(11)	Nellie Fox	60.00	30.00	18.00
(12)	Jim Gentile	50.00	25.00	15.00
(13)	Gene Green	50.00	25.00	15.00
(14)	Steve Hamilton	50.00	25.00	15.00
(15)	Ken Hamlin	50.00	25.00	15.00
(16a)	Rudy Hernandez (Postcard back.)	50.00	25.00	15.00
(16b)	Rudy Hernandez (Restuarant ad on back.)	60.00	30.00	18.00
(17)	Ed Hobaugh	50.00	25.00	15.00
(18)	Elston Howard	60.00	30.00	18.00
(19)	Bob Johnson	50.00	25.00	15.00
(20)	Russ Kemmerer	50.00	25.00	15.00
(21)	Harmon Killebrew	100.00	50.00	30.00
(22)	Dale Long	50.00	25.00	15.00
(23)	Mickey Mantle	325.00	160.00	100.00
(24)	Roger Maris	200.00	100.00	60.00
(25)	Willie Mays	250.00	125.00	75.00
(26)	Stan Musial	200.00	100.00	60.00
(27)	Claude Osteen	50.00	25.00	15.00
(28)	Ken Retzer	50.00	25.00	15.00
(29)	Brooks Robinson	100.00	50.00	30.00
(30)	Don Rudolph	50.00	25.00	15.00
(31)	Bill Skowron	60.00	30.00	18.00
(32)	Dave Stenhouse	50.00	25.00	15.00
(33)	Jose Valdivielso	50.00	25.00	15.00
(34)	Gene Woodling	50.00	25.00	15.00
(35)	Bud Zipfel	50.00	25.00	15.00

1960s Don Wingfield Postcards - Color

Similar in format to the contemporary series of black-and-white player photo postcards, only a single player is known to have been issued in color by Alexandria, Va., photographer Don Wingfield. The card is 3-1/2" x 5-1/2" with standard postcard indicia on back.

	NM	EX	VG
C14711 Harmon Killebrew	110.00	55.00	33.00

1951-53 Wisconsin's Athletic Hall of Fame Postcards

This set of black-and-white postcards reproduces the plaques of athletes in the state's Hall of Fame, as displayed in Milwaukee's Arena during the 1950s. Backs have typical postcard markings.

		NM	EX	VG
Complete Set (12):		150.00	75.00	45.00
Common Player:		10.00	5.00	3.00
(1)	Addie Joss	20.00	10.00	6.00
(2)	Alvin Kraenzlein (Track)	10.00	5.00	3.00
(3)	"Strangler" Lewis (Wrestling)	12.50	6.25	3.75
(4)	George McBride	10.00	5.00	3.00
(5)	Ralph Metcalfe (Track)	10.00	5.00	3.00
(6)	Ernie Nevers	20.00	10.00	6.00
(7)	"Kid" Nichols	20.00	10.00	6.00
(8)	"Pa" O'Dea (Football)	10.00	5.00	3.00
(9)	Dave Schreiner (Football)	10.00	5.00	3.00

		NM	EX	VG
(10)	Al Simmons	20.00	10.00	6.00
(11)	Billy Sullivan	12.50	6.25	3.75
(12)	Bob Zuppke (Basketball)	10.00	5.00	3.00

1922 Witmor Candy Co.

Two types of Witmor issues are known, both of which utilize the format of the 1921-22 W575-1 blank-back strip cards. Printed in black-and-white and measuring about 2" x 3-1/4" the two types of Witmor issues are differentiated by the ads on back for the San Francisco candy company. One type has the advertising in a horizontal format, the other has the advertising in a vertical design. Values of Witmor Candy cards carry a premium over the more common blank-back versions. The extent to which the Witmors and W575-1 share a checklist, particularly the latter's variations, is unknown.

PREMIUMS:
Common Players: 3-4X
Hall of Famers: 3-4X
(See 1921-22 W575-1 for checklist and value information.)

1907 Wolverine News Co. Detroit Tigers

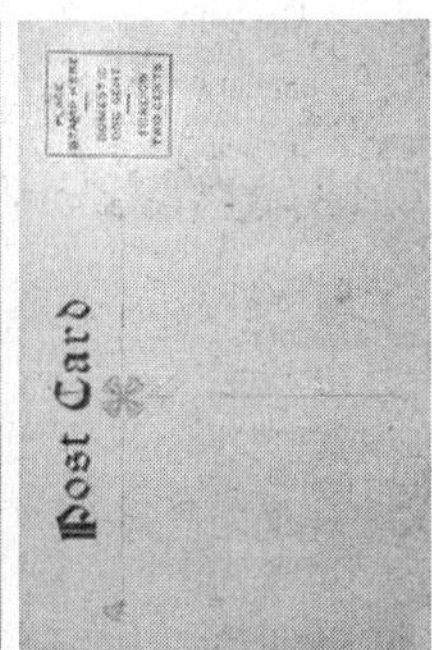

This series of postcards depicts members of the A.L. champ Tigers. The 3-5/16" x 5-5/16" black-and-white cards have poses or posed action photos on front, with a narrow white border at bottom carrying player identification. Backs are standard postcard format with a credit line to Wolverine News Co.

		NM	EX	VG
Complete Set (20):		9,000	4,500	2,700
Common Player:		100.00	50.00	30.00
(1)	Ty Cobb/Btg	3,000	1,500	900.00
(2)	Ty Cobb/Portrait	3,500	1,750	1,000
(3)	Bill Coughlin	100.00	50.00	30.00
(4)	Sam Crawford/Bunting	250.00	125.00	75.00
(5)	Sam Crawford (Chest-to-cap portrait.)	250.00	125.00	75.00
(6)	"Wild Bill" Donovan/Pitching	100.00	50.00	30.00
(7)	"Wild Bill" Donovan ("at the Water Wagon")	150.00	75.00	45.00
(8)	Jerry Downs	100.00	50.00	30.00
(9)	Hughie Jennings (Manager)	250.00	125.00	75.00
(10)	Hughie Jennings (On the Coaching line.)	300.00	150.00	90.00
(11)	Davy Jones	100.00	50.00	30.00
(12)	Ed Killian	100.00	50.00	30.00
(13)	George Mullin	100.00	50.00	30.00
(14)	Charlie O'Leary	100.00	50.00	30.00
(15)	Fred Payne	100.00	50.00	30.00
(16)	Claude Rossman	100.00	50.00	30.00
(17)	Herman Schaefer	100.00	50.00	30.00
(18)	Herman Schaefer, Charley O'Leary	100.00	50.00	30.00
(19)	Charlie Schmidt	100.00	50.00	30.00
(20)	Eddie Siever	100.00	50.00	30.00

1886 J. Wood Studio N.Y. Giants Cabinets

Members of the 1886 N.Y. Giants were immportalized in this series of 4-1/4" x 6-7/8" studio cabinets. The sepia portraits are bordered in gold. The photos were likely available singly from the studio or as a complete set, with an advertising frontpiece and a 6-9/16" x 4-3/16" composite photo. It is interesting to note that on one version of the composite card, baseball caps were artificially added to the portraits. The photos became the basis for the same players' cards in several late 1880s card series.

		NM	EX	VG
Common Player:		10,000	5,000	3,000
(1)	Roger Connor	25,000	7,500	4,500
(2)	Larry Corcoran	10,000	5,000	3,000
(3)	Pat Deasley	10,000	5,000	3,000
(4)	Mike Dorgan	10,000	5,000	3,000
(5)	Dude Esterbrook	10,000	5,000	3,000
(6)	Buck Ewing	35,000	7,500	4,500
(7)	Joe Gerhardt	10,000	5,000	3,000
(8)	Pete Gillespie	10,000	5,000	3,000
(9)	Tim Keefe	25,000	7,500	4,500
(10)	Jim Mutrie	10,000	5,000	3,000
(11)	Jim O'Rourke	30,000	7,500	4,500
(12)	Danny Richardson	10,000	5,000	3,000
(13)	John Ward	30,000	7,500	4,500
(14)	Mickey Welch	25,000	7,500	4,500
(15)	N.Y. Giants Team Composite (No caps.)	25,000	10,000	6,000
(16)	N.Y. Giants Team Composite (With caps.)	25,000	10,000	6,000

1886 J. Wood Studio N.Y. Metropolitans Cabinets

Nattily attired in dress shirts and sporty dotted ties, members of the 1886 N.Y. Metropolitans of the American Association were immortalized in this series of 4-1/2" x 6-1/2" studio cabinets. The vignetted sepia portraits are framed in gold. The photos became the basis for the same players' cards in the "dotted tie" subset of the 1887 Old Judge cigarette card issue, indicating that more of the cabinet-size photos may yet be added to this checklist.

	NM	EX	VG
Common Player:	12,500	6,250	3,750
Jos. Crotty	12,500	6,250	3,750
E.L. Cushman	12,500	6,250	3,750
E.E. Foster	12,500	6,250	3,750
Al. Mays	12,500	6,250	3,750
Jas. Roseman	12,500	6,250	3,750

1921 Wool's American-Maid Bread

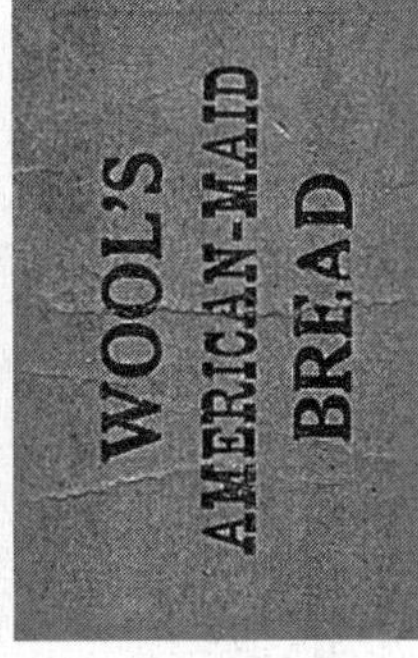

This seldom-seen variation of the W551 strip-card set appears to have been locally overprinted at an unknown location for use as a bread purchase premium. It is presumed the same checklist for W551 can be found with the Wool's back advertising. If ideally cut from the strip, the cards would measure 1-3/8" x 2-1/4". They feature color drawings and are unnumbered.

		NM	EX	VG
Complete Set (10):		6,000	3,000	1,800
Common Player:		160.00	80.00	48.00
(1)	Frank Baker	400.00	200.00	120.00
(2)	Dave Bancroft	400.00	200.00	120.00
(3)	Jess Barnes	250.00	125.00	75.00
(4)	Ty Cobb	2,000	1,000	600.00
(5)	Walter Johnson	750.00	375.00	225.00
(6)	Wally Pipp	300.00	150.00	90.00
(7)	Babe Ruth	2,500	1,250	750.00
(8)	George Sisler	400.00	200.00	120.00
(9)	Tris Speaker	600.00	300.00	180.00
(10)	Casey Stengel	450.00	225.00	135.00

1933 Worch Cigar

This set of unnumbered postcard-size (3-7/16" x 5-7/16") cards, utilizing photos from the Minneapolis Star and St. Paul Dispatch newspapers, was used as a promotion by Worch Cigar Co. of St. Paul, Minn. Although there is no advertising for Worch Cigars on the cards themselves, the cards were mailed in envelopes bearing the Worch name. The cards feature portrait or posed action photos. Player identification, which may be full name or last name, with or without team, may be found in several different styles, either printed on the background, or in a white or black box. Sometimes a photo credit is also present. Many pictures have the top of the background whited out.

		NM	EX	VG
Common Player:		90.00	40.00	25.00
(1)	Sparky Adams	90.00	40.00	25.00
(2)	Dale Alexander	90.00	40.00	25.00
(3)	Ivy Paul Andrews	90.00	40.00	25.00
(4a)	Earl Averill (Cleveland)	400.00	180.00	100.00
(4b)	Earl Averill (No team designation.)	400.00	180.00	100.00
(5)	Richard Bartell	90.00	40.00	25.00
(6)	Herman Bell	90.00	40.00	25.00
(7)	Walter Berger	90.00	40.00	25.00
(8)	Huck Betts	90.00	40.00	25.00
(9)	Max Bishop	90.00	40.00	25.00
(10)	Jim Bottomley	400.00	180.00	100.00
(11a)	Tom Bridges (Name and team in box.)	90.00	40.00	25.00
(11b)	Tom Bridges (No box.)	90.00	40.00	25.00
(12)	Clint Brown	90.00	40.00	25.00
(13a)	Donie Bush	90.00	40.00	25.00
(13b)	Donie Bush	90.00	40.00	25.00
(14a)	Max Carey (Brooklyn)	400.00	180.00	100.00
(14b)	Max Carey (No team designation.)	400.00	180.00	100.00
(15)	Tex Carlton	90.00	40.00	25.00
(16)	Ben Chapman	90.00	40.00	25.00
(17)	Chalmer Cissell	90.00	40.00	25.00
(18)	Mickey Cochrane	400.00	180.00	100.00
(19)	Ripper Collins	90.00	40.00	25.00
(20)	Earle Combs	400.00	180.00	100.00
(21)	Adam Comorosky	90.00	40.00	25.00
(22)	Estel Crabtree	90.00	40.00	25.00
(23)	Rodger Cramer (Roger)	90.00	40.00	25.00
(24)	Pat Crawford	90.00	40.00	25.00
(25)	Hugh Critz	90.00	40.00	25.00
(26a)	Joe Cronin (Name and team in box.)	400.00	180.00	100.00
(26b)	Joe Cronin (No box.)	400.00	180.00	100.00
(27)	Frank Crosetti	150.00	67.00	37.00
(28)	Alvin Crowder	90.00	40.00	25.00
(29a)	Tony Cuccinello (Photo background.)	90.00	40.00	25.00
(29b)	Tony Cuccinello (Blank background.)	90.00	40.00	25.00
(30)	KiKi Cuyler	400.00	180.00	100.00
(31)	Geo. Davis	90.00	40.00	25.00
(32)	Dizzy Dean	750.00	335.00	185.00
(33)	Wm. Dickey	450.00	200.00	110.00
(34)	Leo Durocher	400.00	180.00	100.00
(35)	James Dykes	90.00	40.00	25.00
(36)	George Earnshaw	90.00	40.00	25.00
(37)	Woody English	90.00	40.00	25.00
(38a)	Richard Ferrell (Name and team in box.)	400.00	180.00	100.00
(38b)	Richard Ferrell (No box.)	400.00	180.00	100.00
(39a)	Wesley Ferrell (Name and team in box.)	90.00	40.00	25.00
(39b)	Wesley Ferrell (No box.)	90.00	40.00	25.00
(40)	Fred Fitzsimmons	90.00	40.00	25.00
(41)	Lew Fonseca	90.00	40.00	25.00
(42)	Bob Fothergill	90.00	40.00	25.00
(43)	James Foxx	750.00	335.00	185.00
(44)	Fred Frankhouse	90.00	40.00	25.00
(45)	Frank Frisch	400.00	180.00	100.00
(46a)	Leon Gaslin (Name incorrect.)	400.00	180.00	100.00
(46b)	Leon Goslin (Name correct.)	400.00	180.00	100.00
(47)	Lou Gehrig	1,500	675.00	375.00
(48)	Charles Gehringer	400.00	180.00	100.00
(49)	George Gibson	90.00	40.00	25.00
(50)	Vernon Gomez	400.00	180.00	100.00
(51)	George Grantham	90.00	40.00	25.00
(52)	Grimes The Lord Of Burleigh (Burleigh Grimes)	400.00	180.00	100.00
(53)	Charlie Grimm	90.00	40.00	25.00
(54)	Robt. Grove	600.00	270.00	150.00
(55)	Frank Grube	90.00	40.00	25.00
(56)	Chic Hafey (Chick)	400.00	180.00	100.00
(57)	Jess Haines	400.00	180.00	100.00
(58)	Bill Hallahan	90.00	40.00	25.00
(59)	Mel Harder	90.00	40.00	25.00
(60)	Dave Harris	90.00	40.00	25.00

#	Player	NM	EX	VG
(61a)	Gabby Hartnett (Small projection.)	400.00	180.00	100.00
(61b)	Gabby Hartnett (Large projection.)	400.00	180.00	100.00
(62)	George Hass (Haas)	90.00	40.00	25.00
(63)	Ray Hayworth	90.00	40.00	25.00
(64)	Harvey Hendrick	90.00	40.00	25.00
(65)	Dutch Henry	90.00	40.00	25.00
(66)	"Babe" Herman	150.00	67.00	37.00
(67)	Bill Herman	400.00	180.00	100.00
(68)	Frank Higgins	90.00	40.00	25.00
(69)	Oral Hildebrand	90.00	40.00	25.00
(70)	"Shanty" Hogan	90.00	40.00	25.00
(71)	Roger Hornsby (Rogers)	600.00	270.00	150.00
(72)	Carl Hubbell	450.00	200.00	110.00
(73)	Travis Jackson	400.00	180.00	100.00
(74)	Hank Johnson	90.00	40.00	25.00
(75)	Syl Johnson	90.00	40.00	25.00
(76)	Smead Jolley	90.00	40.00	25.00
(77)	Wm. Kamm	90.00	40.00	25.00
(78)	Wes Kingdon	90.00	40.00	25.00
(79a)	Charles Klein (Philadelphia, N.L.)	400.00	180.00	100.00
(79b)	Charles Klein (Chicago, N.L.)	400.00	180.00	100.00
(80)	Jos. Kuhel	90.00	40.00	25.00
(81a)	Tony Lazzeri (Name and team in box.)	400.00	180.00	100.00
(81b)	Tony Lazzeri (No box.)	400.00	180.00	100.00
(82)	Sam Leslie	90.00	40.00	25.00
(83)	Ernie Lombardi	400.00	180.00	100.00
(84)	Al Lopez	400.00	180.00	100.00
(85)	Red Lucas	90.00	40.00	25.00
(86)	Adolfo Luque	90.00	40.00	22.00
(87)	Ted Lyons	400.00	180.00	100.00
(88)	Connie Mack	400.00	180.00	100.00
(89)	Gus Mancuso	90.00	40.00	25.00
(90)	Henry Manush	400.00	180.00	100.00
(91)	Fred Marberry	90.00	40.00	25.00
(92)	Pepper Martin	200.00	90.00	50.00
(93)	Wm. McKechnie	400.00	180.00	100.00
(94)	Joe Medwick	400.00	180.00	100.00
(95)	Jim Mooney	90.00	40.00	25.00
(96)	Joe Moore	90.00	40.00	25.00
(97)	Joe Mowry	90.00	40.00	25.00
(98)	Van Mungo	90.00	40.00	25.00
(99)	Buddy Myer	90.00	40.00	25.00
(100)	"Lefty" O'Doul	200.00	90.00	50.00
(101)	Bob O'Farrell	90.00	40.00	25.00
(102)	Ernie Orsatti	90.00	40.00	25.00
(103)	Melvin Ott	450.00	200.00	110.00
(104)	Roy Parmelee	90.00	40.00	25.00
(105)	Homer Peel	90.00	40.00	25.00
(106)	George Pipgras	90.00	40.00	25.00
(107)	Harry Rice	90.00	40.00	25.00
(108)	Paul Richards	90.00	40.00	25.00
(109)	Eppa Rixey	400.00	180.00	100.00
(110)	Charles Ruffing	400.00	180.00	100.00
(111)	Jack Russell	90.00	40.00	25.00
(112)	Babe Ruth	2,000	900.00	500.00
(113)	"Blondy" Ryan	90.00	40.00	25.00
(114)	Wilfred Ryan	90.00	40.00	25.00
(115)	Fred Schulte	90.00	40.00	25.00
(116)	Hal Schumacher	90.00	40.00	25.00
(117a)	Luke Sewel (Sewell) (Name and team in box.)	90.00	40.00	25.00
(117b)	Luke Sewel (Sewell) (No box.)	90.00	40.00	25.00
(118)	Al Simmons	400.00	180.00	100.00
(119)	Ray Spencer	90.00	40.00	25.00
(120)	Casey Stengel	400.00	180.00	100.00
(121)	Riggs Stephenson	90.00	40.00	25.00
(122)	Walter Stewart	90.00	40.00	25.00
(123)	John Stone	90.00	40.00	25.00
(124)	Gabby Street	90.00	40.00	25.00
(125)	Gus Suhr	90.00	40.00	25.00
(126)	Evar Swanson	90.00	40.00	25.00
(127)	Dan Taylor	90.00	40.00	25.00
(128)	Bill Terry	400.00	180.00	100.00
(129)	Al Todd	90.00	40.00	25.00
(130)	Pie Traynor	400.00	180.00	100.00
(131)	William Urbanski	90.00	40.00	25.00
(132)	Dazzy Vance	400.00	180.00	100.00
(133)	Lloyd (Floyd) Vaughan	400.00	180.00	100.00
(134)	Johnny Vergez	90.00	40.00	25.00
(135)	George Walberg	90.00	40.00	25.00
(136)	Bill Walker	90.00	40.00	25.00
(137)	Gerald Walker	90.00	40.00	25.00
(138a)	Lloyd Waner (Photo background.)	400.00	180.00	100.00
(138b)	Lloyd Waner (Blank background.)	400.00	180.00	100.00
(139a)	Paul Waner (Photo background.)	400.00	180.00	100.00
(139b)	Paul Waner (Blank background, small projection.)	400.00	180.00	100.00
(139c)	Lloyd Waner (Blank background, large projection.)	400.00	180.00	100.00
(140)	Lon Warneke	90.00	40.00	25.00
(141)	George Watkins	90.00	40.00	25.00
(142)	Monte Weaver	90.00	40.00	25.00
(143)	Sam West	90.00	40.00	25.00
(144)	Earl Whitehill	90.00	40.00	25.00
(145)	Hack Wilson	400.00	180.00	100.00
(146)	Jimmy Wilson	90.00	40.00	25.00

1933 World Wide Gum (Canadian Goudey, V353)

Also known as "Canadian Goudeys," this 94-card set drew heavily on its U.S. contemporary. Card fronts are identical to the '33 Goudeys and the backs are nearly so. The first 52 cards in the set carry the same card numbers as their American counterparts, while cards #53-94 have different numbers than the U.S. version. Card backs can be found printed entirely in English, or in English and French; the former being somewhat scarcer. Cards measure approximately 2-3/8" x 2-7/8".

		NM	EX	VG
Complete Set (94):		20,000	10,000	6,000
Common Player:		60.00	30.00	18.00
1	Benny Bengough	550.00	60.00	20.00
2	Arthur (Dazzy) Vance	250.00	110.00	60.00
3	Hugh Critz	60.00	30.00	18.00
4	Henry (Heinie) Schuble	60.00	30.00	18.00
5	Floyd (Babe) Herman	110.00	50.00	25.00
6	Jimmy Dykes	60.00	30.00	18.00
7	Ted Lyons	250.00	110.00	60.00
8	Roy Johnson	60.00	30.00	18.00
9	Dave Harris	60.00	30.00	18.00
10	Glenn Myatt	60.00	30.00	18.00
11	Billy Rogell	60.00	30.00	18.00
12	George Pipgras	60.00	30.00	18.00
13	Lafayette Thompson	60.00	30.00	18.00
14	Henry Johnson	60.00	30.00	18.00
15	Victor Sorrell	60.00	30.00	18.00
16	George Blaeholder	60.00	30.00	18.00
17	Watson Clark	60.00	30.00	18.00
18	Herold (Muddy) Ruel	60.00	30.00	18.00
19	Bill Dickey	275.00	125.00	70.00
20	Bill Terry	250.00	110.00	60.00
21	Phil Collins	60.00	30.00	18.00
22	Harold (Pie) Traynor	250.00	110.00	60.00
23	Hazen (Ki-Ki) Cuyler	250.00	110.00	60.00
24	Horace Ford	60.00	30.00	18.00
25	Paul Waner	250.00	110.00	60.00
26	Chalmer Cissell	60.00	30.00	18.00
27	George Connally	60.00	30.00	18.00
28	Dick Bartell	60.00	30.00	18.00
29	Jimmy Foxx	350.00	155.00	85.00
30	Frank Hogan	60.00	30.00	18.00
31	Tony Lazzeri	250.00	110.00	60.00
32	John (Bud) Clancy	60.00	30.00	18.00
33	Ralph Kress	60.00	30.00	18.00
34	Bob O'Farrell	60.00	30.00	18.00
35	Al Simmons	250.00	110.00	60.00
36	Tommy Thevenow	60.00	30.00	18.00
37	Jimmy Wilson	60.00	30.00	18.00
38	Fred Brickell	60.00	30.00	18.00
39	Mark Koenig	60.00	30.00	18.00
40	Taylor Douthit	60.00	30.00	18.00
41	Gus Mancuso	60.00	30.00	18.00
42	Eddie Collins	250.00	110.00	60.00
43	Lew Fonseca	60.00	30.00	18.00
44	Jim Bottomley	250.00	110.00	60.00
45	Larry Benton	60.00	30.00	18.00
46	Ethan Allen	60.00	30.00	18.00
47	Henry "Heinie" Manush	250.00	110.00	60.00
48	Marty McManus	60.00	30.00	18.00
49	Frank Frisch	250.00	110.00	60.00
50	Ed Brandt	60.00	30.00	18.00
51	Charlie Grimm	60.00	30.00	18.00
52	Andy Cohen	60.00	30.00	18.00
53	Jack Quinn	60.00	30.00	18.00
54	Urban (Red) Faber	250.00	110.00	60.00
55	Lou Gehrig	2,100	950.00	525.00
56	John Welch	60.00	30.00	18.00
57	Bill Walker	60.00	30.00	18.00
58	Frank (Lefty) O'Doul	90.00	40.00	22.50
59	Edmund (Bing) Miller	60.00	30.00	18.00
60	Waite Hoyt	250.00	110.00	60.00
61	Max Bishop	60.00	30.00	18.00
62	"Pepper" Martin	90.00	40.00	22.50
63	Joe Cronin	250.00	110.00	60.00
64	Burleigh Grimes	250.00	110.00	60.00
65	Milton Gaston	60.00	30.00	18.00
66	George Grantham	60.00	30.00	18.00
67	Guy Bush	60.00	30.00	18.00
68	Willie Kamm	60.00	30.00	18.00
69	Gordon (Mickey) Cochrane	250.00	110.00	60.00
70	Adam Comorosky	60.00	30.00	18.00
71	Alvin Crowder	60.00	30.00	18.00
72	Willis Hudlin	60.00	30.00	18.00
73	Eddie Farrell	60.00	30.00	18.00
74	Leo Durocher	250.00	110.00	60.00
75	Walter Stewart	60.00	30.00	18.00
76	George Walberg	60.00	30.00	18.00
77	Glenn Wright	60.00	30.00	18.00
78	Charles (Buddy) Myer	60.00	30.00	18.00
79	James (Zack) Taylor	60.00	30.00	18.00
80	George Herman (Babe) Ruth	4,000	1,800	1,000
81	D'Arcy (Jake) Flowers	60.00	30.00	18.00
82	Ray Kolp	60.00	30.00	18.00
83	Oswald Bluege	60.00	30.00	18.00
84	Morris (Moe) Berg	600.00	275.00	150.00
85	Jimmy Foxx	400.00	180.00	100.00
86	Sam Byrd	60.00	30.00	11.00
87	Danny Mcfayden (McFayden)	60.00	30.00	18.00
88	Joe Judge	60.00	30.00	18.00
89	Joe Sewell	250.00	110.00	60.00
90	Lloyd Waner	250.00	110.00	60.00
91	Luke Sewell	60.00	30.00	18.00
92	Leo Mangum	60.00	30.00	18.00
93	George Herman (Babe) Ruth	3,600	1,625	900.00
94	Al Spohrer	60.00	30.00	18.00

1934 World Wide Gum (Canadian Goudey, V354)

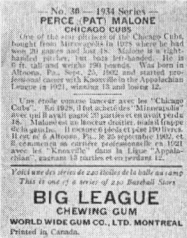

Again a near-clone of the American issue, the '34 "Canadian Goudeys" feature the same number (96) and size (2-3/8" x 2-7/8") of cards. Player selection is considerably different, however. Cards #1-48 feature the same front design as the '33 World Wide/Goudey sets. Cards #49-96 have the "Lou Gehrig says..." graphic on the front. Unlike the 1933 cards, backs are only found with bi-lingual text.

		NM	EX	VG
Complete Set (96):		19,000	8,500	4,500
Common Player:		75.00	35.00	20.00
1	Rogers Hornsby	900.00	400.00	250.00
2	Eddie Morgan	75.00	35.00	20.00
3	Valentine J. (Val) Picinich	75.00	35.00	20.00
4	Rabbit Maranville	250.00	120.00	75.00
5	Flint Rhem	75.00	35.00	20.00
6	Jim Elliott	75.00	35.00	20.00
7	Fred (Red) Lucas	75.00	35.00	20.00
8	Fred Marberry	75.00	35.00	20.00
9	Clifton Heathcote	75.00	35.00	20.00
10	Bernie Friberg	75.00	35.00	20.00
11	Elwood (Woody) English	75.00	35.00	20.00
12	Carl Reynolds	75.00	35.00	20.00
13	Ray Benge	75.00	35.00	20.00
14	Ben Cantwell	75.00	35.00	20.00
15	Irvin (Bump) Hadley	75.00	35.00	20.00
16	Herb Pennock	250.00	120.00	75.00
17	Fred Lindstrom	250.00	120.00	75.00
18	Edgar (Sam) Rice	250.00	120.00	75.00
19	Fred Frankhouse	75.00	35.00	20.00
20	Fred Fitzsimmons	75.00	35.00	20.00
21	Earl Coombs (Earle Combs)	250.00	120.00	75.00
22	George Uhle	75.00	35.00	20.00
23	Richard Coffman	75.00	35.00	20.00
24	Travis C. Jackson	250.00	120.00	75.00
25	Robert J. Burke	75.00	35.00	20.00
26	Randy Moore	75.00	35.00	20.00
27	John Henry (Heinie) Sand	75.00	35.00	20.00
28	George Herman (Babe) Ruth	4,200	2,000	1,600
29	Tris Speaker	300.00	145.00	90.00
30	Perce (Pat) Malone	75.00	35.00	20.00
31	Sam Jones	75.00	35.00	20.00
32	Eppa Rixey	250.00	120.00	75.00
33	Floyd (Pete) Scott	75.00	35.00	20.00
34	Pete Jablonowski	75.00	35.00	20.00
35	Clyde Manion	75.00	35.00	20.00
36	Dibrell Williams	75.00	35.00	20.00
37	Glenn Spencer	75.00	35.00	20.00
38	Ray Kremer	75.00	35.00	20.00
39	Phil Todt	75.00	35.00	20.00
40	Russell Rollings	75.00	35.00	20.00
41	Earl Clark	75.00	35.00	20.00
42	Jess Petty	75.00	35.00	20.00
43	Frank O'Rourke	75.00	35.00	20.00
44	Jesse Haines	250.00	120.00	75.00
45	Horace Lisenbee	75.00	35.00	20.00
46	Owen Carroll	75.00	35.00	20.00
47	Tom Zachary	75.00	35.00	20.00
48	Charlie Ruffing	250.00	120.00	75.00
49	Ray Benge	75.00	35.00	20.00
50	Elwood (Woody) English	75.00	35.00	20.00
51	Ben Chapman	75.00	35.00	20.00
52	Joe Kuhel	75.00	35.00	20.00
53	Bill Terry	250.00	120.00	75.00
54	Robert (Lefty) Grove	300.00	145.00	90.00
55	Jerome (Dizzy) Dean	450.00	220.00	140.00
56	Charles (Chuck) Klein	250.00	120.00	75.00
57	Charley Gehringer	250.00	120.00	75.00
58	Jimmy Foxx	400.00	195.00	125.00
59	Gordon (Mickey) Cochrane	250.00	120.00	75.00
60	Willie Kamm	75.00	35.00	20.00
61	Charlie Grimm	75.00	35.00	20.00
62	Ed Brandt	75.00	35.00	20.00
63	Tony Piet	75.00	35.00	20.00
64	Frank Frisch	250.00	120.00	75.00
65	Alvin Crowder	75.00	35.00	20.00
66	Frank Hogan	75.00	35.00	20.00
67	Paul Waner	250.00	120.00	75.00
68	Henry (Heinie) Manush	250.00	120.00	75.00
69	Leo Durocher	250.00	120.00	75.00
70	Floyd Vaughan	250.00	120.00	75.00
71	Carl Hubbell	275.00	135.00	85.00
72	Hugh Critz	75.00	35.00	20.00
73	John (Blondy) Ryan	75.00	35.00	20.00
74	Roger Cramer	75.00	35.00	20.00
75	Baxter Jordan	75.00	35.00	20.00
76	Ed Coleman	75.00	35.00	20.00
77	Julius Solters	75.00	35.00	20.00
78	Charles (Chick) Hafey	250.00	120.00	75.00
79	Larry French	75.00	35.00	20.00
80	Frank (Don) Hurst	75.00	35.00	20.00
81	Gerald Walker	75.00	35.00	20.00
82	Ernie Lombardi	250.00	120.00	75.00
83	Walter (Huck) Betts	75.00	35.00	20.00
84	Luke Appling	250.00	120.00	75.00
85	John Frederick	75.00	35.00	20.00

86	Fred Walker	75.00	35.00	20.00
87	Tom Bridges	75.00	35.00	20.00
88	Dick Porter	75.00	35.00	20.00
89	John Stone	75.00	35.00	20.00
90	James (Tex) Carleton	75.00	35.00	20.00
91	Joe Stripp	75.00	35.00	20.00
92	Lou Gehrig	2,500	1,225	775.00
93	George Earnshaw	75.00	35.00	20.00
94	Oscar Melillo	75.00	35.00	20.00
95	Oral Hildebrand	75.00	35.00	20.00
96	John Allen	75.00	35.00	20.00

1936 World Wide Gum (Canadian Goudey, V355)

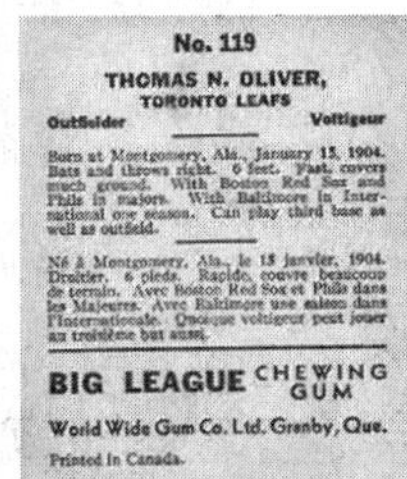
No. 119

THOMAS N. OLIVER,
TORONTO LEAFS

Outfielder Voltigeur

Born at Montgomery, Ala., January 15, 1904. Bats and throws right. 6 feet. Fast, covers much ground. With Boston Red Sox and Phils in majors. With Baltimore in International one season. Can play third base as well as outfield.

Né à Montgomery, Ala., le 15 janvier, 1904. Droitier. 6 pieds. Rapide, couvre beaucoup de terrain. Avec Boston Red Sox et Phils dans les Majeures. Avec Baltimore une saison dans l'Internationale. Quoique voltigeur peut jouer au troisième but aussi.

BIG LEAGUE CHEWING GUM

World Wide Gum Co. Ltd. Granby, Que.

Printed in Canada.

This black and white Canadian set was issued by World Wide Gum in 1936. The cards measure approximately 2-1/2" x 2-7/8", and the set includes both portrait and action photos. The card number and player's name (appearing in all capital letters) are printed inside a white box below the photo.

		NM	EX	VG
Complete Set (135):		40,000	20,000	12,000
Common Player:		125.00	55.00	30.00
1	Jimmy Dykes	300.00	75.00	30.00
2	Paul Waner	250.00	125.00	75.00
3	Cy Blanton	125.00	55.00	30.00
4	Sam Leslie	125.00	55.00	30.00
5	Johnny Louis Vergez	125.00	55.00	30.00
6	Arky Vaughan	250.00	125.00	75.00
7	Bill Terry	250.00	125.00	75.00
8	Joe Moore	125.00	55.00	30.00
9	Gus Mancuso	125.00	55.00	30.00
10	Fred Marberry	125.00	55.00	30.00
11	George Selkirk	125.00	55.00	30.00
12	Spud Davis	125.00	55.00	30.00
13	Chuck Klein	250.00	125.00	75.00
14	Fred Fitzsimmons	125.00	55.00	30.00
15	Bill Delancey	125.00	55.00	30.00
16	Billy Herman	250.00	125.00	75.00
17	George Davis	125.00	55.00	30.00
18	Rip Collins	125.00	55.00	30.00
19	Dizzy Dean	400.00	200.00	120.00
20	Roy Parmelee	125.00	55.00	30.00
21	Vic Sorrell	125.00	55.00	30.00
22	Harry Danning	125.00	55.00	30.00
23	Hal Schumacher	125.00	55.00	30.00
24	Cy Perkins	125.00	55.00	30.00
25	Speedy Durocher	250.00	125.00	75.00
26	Glenn Myatt	125.00	55.00	30.00
27	Bob Seeds	125.00	55.00	30.00
28	Jimmy Ripple	125.00	55.00	30.00
29	Al Schacht	125.00	55.00	30.00
30	Pete Fox	125.00	55.00	30.00
31	Del Baker	125.00	55.00	30.00
32	Flea Clifton	125.00	55.00	30.00
33	Tommy Bridges	125.00	55.00	30.00
34	Bill Dickey	250.00	115.00	65.00
35	Wally Berger	125.00	55.00	30.00
36	Slick Castleman	125.00	55.00	30.00
37	Dick Bartell	125.00	55.00	30.00
38	Red Rolfe	125.00	55.00	30.00
39	Waite Hoyt	250.00	125.00	75.00
40	Wes Ferrell	125.00	55.00	30.00
41	Hank Greenberg	400.00	190.00	105.00
42	Charlie Gehringer	250.00	125.00	75.00
43	Goose Goslin	250.00	125.00	75.00
44	Schoolboy Rowe	125.00	55.00	30.00
45	Mickey Cochrane	250.00	125.00	75.00
46	Joe Cronin	250.00	125.00	75.00
47	Jimmie Foxx	475.00	225.00	125.00
48	Jerry Walker	125.00	55.00	30.00
49	Charlie Gelbert	125.00	55.00	30.00
50	Roy Hayworth (Ray)	125.00	55.00	30.00
51	Joe DiMaggio	15,000	7,000	4,000
52	Billy Rogell	125.00	55.00	30.00
53	Joe McCarthy	250.00	125.00	75.00
54	Phil Cavaretta (Cavarretta)	125.00	55.00	30.00
55	Kiki Cuyler	250.00	125.00	75.00
56	Lefty Gomez	250.00	125.00	75.00
57	Gabby Hartnett	250.00	125.00	75.00
58	Johnny Marcum	125.00	55.00	30.00
59	Burgess Whitehead	125.00	55.00	30.00
60	Whitey Whitehill	125.00	55.00	30.00
61	Buckey Walters	125.00	55.00	30.00
62	Luke Sewell	125.00	55.00	30.00
63	Joey Kuhel	125.00	55.00	30.00
64	Lou Finney	125.00	55.00	30.00
65	Fred Lindstrom	250.00	125.00	75.00
66	Paul Derringer	125.00	55.00	30.00
67	Steve O'Neil (O'Neill)	125.00	55.00	30.00
68	Mule Haas	125.00	55.00	30.00
69	Freck Owen	125.00	55.00	30.00
70	Wild Bill Hallahan	125.00	55.00	30.00
71	Bill Urbanski	125.00	55.00	30.00
72	Dan Taylor	125.00	55.00	30.00
73	Heinie Manush	250.00	125.00	75.00
74	Jo-Jo White	125.00	55.00	30.00
75	Mickey Medwick (Ducky)	250.00	125.00	75.00
76	Joe Vosmik	125.00	55.00	30.00
77	Al Simmons	250.00	125.00	75.00
78	Shag Shaughnessy	125.00	55.00	30.00
79	Harry Smythe	125.00	55.00	30.00
80	Benny Tate	125.00	55.00	30.00
81	Billy Rhiel	125.00	55.00	30.00
82	Lauri Myllykangas	125.00	55.00	30.00
83	Ben Sankey	125.00	55.00	30.00
84	Crip Polli	125.00	55.00	30.00
85	Jim Bottomley	250.00	125.00	75.00
86	William Clark	125.00	55.00	30.00
87	Ossie Bluege	125.00	55.00	30.00
88	Lefty Grove	250.00	115.00	65.00
89	Charlie Grimm	125.00	55.00	30.00
90	Ben Chapman	125.00	55.00	30.00
91	Frank Crosetti	125.00	60.00	30.00
92	John Pomorski	125.00	55.00	30.00
93	Jesse Haines	250.00	125.00	75.00
94	Chick Hafey	250.00	125.00	75.00
95	Tony Piet	125.00	55.00	30.00
96	Lou Gehrig	4,000	2,000	1,400
97	Bill Jurges	125.00	55.00	30.00
98	Smead Jolley	125.00	55.00	30.00
99	Jimmy Wilson	125.00	55.00	30.00
100	Lonnie Warneke	125.00	55.00	30.00
101	Lefty Tamulis	125.00	55.00	30.00
102	Charlie Ruffing	250.00	125.00	75.00
103	Earl Grace	125.00	55.00	30.00
104	Rox Lawson	125.00	55.00	30.00
105	Stan Hack	125.00	55.00	30.00
106	August Galan	125.00	55.00	30.00
107	Frank Frisch	250.00	125.00	75.00
108	Bill McKechnie	250.00	125.00	75.00
109	Bill Lee	125.00	55.00	30.00
110	Connie Mack	250.00	125.00	75.00
111	Frank Reiber	125.00	55.00	30.00
112	Zeke Bonura	125.00	55.00	30.00
113	Luke Appling	250.00	125.00	75.00
114	Monte Pearson	125.00	55.00	30.00
115	Bob O'Farrell	125.00	55.00	30.00
116	Marvin Duke	125.00	55.00	30.00
117	Paul Florence	125.00	55.00	30.00
118	John Berley	125.00	55.00	30.00
119	Tom Oliver	125.00	55.00	30.00
120	Norman Kies	125.00	55.00	30.00
121	Hal King	125.00	55.00	30.00
122	Tom Abernathy	125.00	55.00	30.00
123	Phil Hensick	125.00	55.00	30.00
124	Roy Schalk (Ray)	250.00	125.00	75.00
125	Paul Dunlap	125.00	55.00	30.00
126	Benny Bates	125.00	55.00	30.00
127	George Puccinelli	125.00	55.00	30.00
128	Stevie Stevenson	125.00	55.00	30.00
129	Rabbit Maranville	250.00	125.00	75.00
130	Bucky Harris	250.00	125.00	75.00
131	Al Lopez	250.00	125.00	75.00
132	Buddy Myer	125.00	55.00	30.00
133	Cliff Bolton	125.00	55.00	30.00
134	Estel Crabtree	125.00	55.00	30.00
135	Phil Weintraub	3,000	1,500	900.00

1939 World Wide Gum (Canadian Goudey, V351)

These premium pictures are analogous to the R303-A issue in the U.S. The 4" x 5-3/4" pictures were given away with the purchase of World Wide gum. The pictures are printed in sepia on cream-colored paper. Fronts have a bordered photo with facsimile autograph. Backs have a "How to . . ." baseball playing tip illustrated with drawings. Backs of the Canadian version differ from the U.S. pieces in the absence of a border line around the playing tip, and the use of a "Lithographed in Canada" notice at lower-right. The unnumbered pictures are checklisted here in alphabetical order.

		NM	EX	VG
Complete Set (25):		5,500	2,750	1,650
Common Player:		100.00	50.00	30.00
(1)	Morris Arnovich	100.00	50.00	30.00
(2)	Sam Bell	130.00	65.00	40.00
(3)	Zeke Bonura	100.00	50.00	30.00
(4)	Earl Caldwell	100.00	50.00	30.00
(5)	Flea Clifton	100.00	50.00	30.00
(6)	Frank Crosetti	140.00	70.00	40.00
(7)	Harry Danning	100.00	50.00	30.00
(8)	Dizzy Dean	250.00	125.00	75.00
(9)	Emile De Jonghe	130.00	65.00	40.00
(10)	Paul Derringer	100.00	50.00	30.00
(11)	Joe DiMaggio	1,500	750.00	450.00
(12)	Vince DiMaggio	100.00	50.00	30.00
(13)	Charlie Gehringer	225.00	110.00	67.00
(14)	Gene Hasson	130.00	65.00	40.00
(15)	Tommy Henrich	150.00	75.00	45.00
(16)	Fred Hutchinson	100.00	50.00	30.00
(17)	Phil Marchildon	100.00	50.00	30.00
(18)	Mike Meola	100.00	50.00	30.00
(19)	Arnold Moser	130.00	65.00	40.00
(20)	Frank Pytlak	100.00	50.00	30.00
(21)	Frank Reiber	100.00	50.00	30.00
(22)	Lee Rogers	100.00	50.00	30.00
(23)	Cecil Travis	100.00	50.00	30.00
(24)	Hal Trosky	100.00	50.00	30.00
(25)	Ted Williams	1,500	750.00	450.00

1975 WTMJ Milwaukee Brewers Broadcasters

To promote its schedule of radio and television broadcasts of Brewers baseball, WTMJ issued this set of broadcaster and schedule cards to potential sponsors. The standard 2-1/2" x 3-1/2" cards are printed in team colors of blue and gold. The on-air talent cards have portraits and facsimile autographs on front, with career summaries on back. The schedule cards have game-action photos on front along with the slogan, "Brewers 75: It's Gonna' Be A Whole New Ballgame!" The cards were distributed in a wax pack with gum.

		NM	EX	VG
Complete Set (7):		25.00	12.50	7.50
Common Card:		2.50	1.25	.70
1	Jim Irwin	4.00	2.00	1.25
2	Gary Bender	4.00	2.00	1.25
3	Bob Uecker	12.50	6.25	3.75
4	Merle Harmon	4.00	2.00	1.25
(5)	TV Schedule	2.50	1.25	.70
(6)	Radio Schedule, Part 1	2.50	1.25	.70
(7)	Radio Schedule, Part 2	2.50	1.25	.70

1910 W-UNC Strip Cards

Considerably earlier than most known strip cards, these pieces were cut from a notebook cover. The known players point to a 1910 issue date. Crudely printed on flimsy stock, the cards feature familiar colorized portraits of players on brightly colored backgrounds. The format is about 1-3/8" x 2-3/8" and some cards have evidence of a 1-16th" yellow strip around the outside of the black border. Player name and city are printed in the white border at bottom. Backs are blank. The unnumbered cards are listed here in alphabetical order, though the checklist may or may not be complete.

		NM	EX	VG
Common Player:		300.00	120.00	60.00
(1)	Babe Adams	300.00	120.00	60.00
(2)	Chief Bender	600.00	240.00	120.00
(3)	Roger Bresnahan	600.00	240.00	120.00
(4)	Donie Bush	300.00	120.00	60.00
(5)	Bobby Byrne	300.00	120.00	60.00
(6)	Bill Carrigan	300.00	120.00	60.00
(7)	Frank Chance	600.00	240.00	120.00
(8)	Hal Chase	450.00	180.00	90.00
(9)	Ty Cobb	2,750	1,100	550.00
(10)	Willis Cole	300.00	120.00	60.00
(11)	Eddie Collins	600.00	240.00	120.00
(12)	Jack Coombs	300.00	120.00	60.00
(13)	Sam Crawford	600.00	240.00	120.00
(14)	Johnny Evers	600.00	240.00	120.00
(15)	Solly Hoffman	300.00	120.00	60.00
(16)	Hughie Jennings	600.00	240.00	120.00
(17)	Walter Johnston (Johnson)	1,500	600.00	300.00
(18)	Johnny Kling	300.00	120.00	60.00
(19)	Ed Konetchy	300.00	120.00	60.00
(20)	Harry Lord	300.00	120.00	60.00
(21)	Sherry Magee	300.00	120.00	60.00
(22)	Christy Mathewson	1,600	650.00	325.00
(23)	Mike Mitchell	300.00	120.00	60.00
(24)	Tris Speaker	750.00	300.00	150.00
(25)	Oscar Stanage	300.00	120.00	60.00
(26)	Honus Wagner	2,000	800.00	400.00

1912 W-UNC Strip Cards

The attributed issue date is speculative, based on the limited known roster. In much the same size and format as W555, these small (photo image area is 1-3/8" x 1-1/2") blank-back cards appear to have been cut off a box or other packaging and may actually be candy cards. Black-and-white photos are framed in dark green with the player's last name in white capital letters below.

		NM	EX	VG
Common Player:		2,000	800.00	400.00
(1)	Bill Carrigan	2,000	800.00	400.00
(2)	Tommy Leach	2,000	800.00	400.00
(3)	Oscar Stanage	2,000	800.00	400.00
(4)	Honus Wagner	7,500	3,000	1,500
(5)	Cy Young	6,500	2,600	1,300

1915 W-UNC Strip Cards

Utilizing many photos familiar to collectors from contemporary card sets, including pictures that were several years old at the time of issue, this appears to be a strip-card issue whose scarcity has caused it to elude cataloging efforts heretofore. Cards are printed in black-and-white, blank-backed and are nominally 1-3/4" x 2-3/4". Player or photo identification appears in the bottom border, or at right on horizontally formatted cards.

		NM	EX	VG
Common Player:		500.00	250.00	150.00
(1)	Ty Cobb	6,500	2,600	1,300
(2)	Larry Doyle	500.00	200.00	100.00
(3)	Johnny Evers	1,500	600.00	300.00
(4)	Joe Jackson	16,000	6,400	3,200
(5)	Walter Johnson	2,500	1,000	500.00
(6)	Sherwood Magee	500.00	200.00	100.00
(7)	Fred Maisel	500.00	200.00	100.00
(8)	Walter (Rabbit) Maranville	1,500	600.00	300.00
(9)	Rube Marquard	1,500	600.00	300.00
(10)	Christy Mathewson	2,750	1,100	550.00
(11)	Phila. Athletics, Champ.	750.00	300.00	150.00
(12)	Ready for the Wallop (Honus Wagner, Bresnahan)	1,500	600.00	300.00
(13)	Nap Rucker	500.00	200.00	100.00
(14)	Hans Wagner	3,500	1,400	700.00
(15)	Joe Wood	600.00	240.00	120.00

1916-20 W-UNC "Big Head" Strip Cards

Given the known player content (perhaps not complete as listed here) and the fact that no team designations are printed on the cards, it is impossible to more accurately date this blank-back strip card issue. The 1-3/8" x 2-1/2" cards have color artwork of the players in full-body poses. The pictures are unusual in that the players' heads are out of proportion to the rest of the body. Whether the portraits were meant to be accurate portrayals is conjecture. Player names given here are as printed on the cards.

		NM	EX	VG
Complete Set (20):		16,000	6,400	3,200
Common Player:		500.00	350.00	150.00
(1)	Jim Bagby	500.00	350.00	150.00
(2)	Home Run Baker	800.00	475.00	300.00
(3)	Dave Bancroft	800.00	475.00	300.00
(4)	Ping Bodie	500.00	350.00	150.00
(5)	Geo. Burns	500.00	350.00	150.00
(6)	Leon Cadore	500.00	350.00	150.00
(7)	Ty Cobb	4,000	2,500	1,250
(8)	Larry Doyle	500.00	350.00	150.00
(9)	Hinie Groh	500.00	350.00	150.00
(10)	R. Hornsby	2,000	1,000	750.00
(11)	Johnston (Walter Johnson)	1,500	850.00	500.00
(12)	Joe Judge	500.00	350.00	150.00
(13)	Eddy Konetchy	500.00	350.00	150.00
(14)	Carl Mays	500.00	350.00	150.00
(15)	Zeb Milan	500.00	350.00	150.00
(16)	Sam Rice	800.00	475.00	300.00
(17)	Babe Ruth	14,000	8,000	3,000
(18)	Ray Schalk	800.00	475.00	300.00
(19)	Wally Schang	500.00	350.00	150.00
(20)	Geo. Sisler	1,500	850.00	500.00

1921 W-UNC Self-Developing Strip Cards

The technology of a self-developing photographic baseball card was popularized in the early 1930s by Ray-O-Print and again in the late late 1940s and early 1950s by Topps, but appears to have been pioneered circa 1921 by an unknown company which produced this series. Individual cards measure between 1-1/16" and 1-3/16" in width and 1-13/16" in depth. In black-and-white, they feature action poses on a dark background with the player name and team in white. A white border surrounds the picture. Backs are blank. The unnumbered cards are checklisted here alphabetically, though the list is probably incomplete.

		NM	EX	VG
Common Player:		100.00	40.00	20.00
(1)	Grover Alexander	450.00	180.00	90.00
(2)	Ty Cobb	2,000	800.00	400.00
(3)	Eddie Collins	300.00	120.00	60.00
(4)	Jake Daubert	100.00	40.00	20.00
(5)	Red Faber	250.00	100.00	50.00
(6)	Max Flack	100.00	40.00	20.00
(7)	"Roger (Rogers) Hornsby"	350.00	140.00	70.00
(8)	Doc Johnston	100.00	40.00	20.00
(9)	Walter Johnston (Johnson)	900.00	360.00	180.00
(10)	Bill Killifer (Killefer)	100.00	40.00	20.00
(11)	Steve O'Neill	100.00	40.00	20.00
(12)	Derrill Pratt	100.00	40.00	20.00
(13)	"Babe" Ruth	3,500	1,400	700.00
(14)	Wallie Schang	100.00	40.00	20.00

1929 W-UNC Playing Strip Cards (1)

Recent discoveries indicate that this issue was produced by Universal Toy & Novelty circa 1929. Likely printed on a sheet similar to other playing card/strip card sets of the era, the individual cards are about 1-1/2" x 2-1/2". The front has a crude black-and-white drawing of the player inside a suit-shaped design on a red background. Back is blank.

		NM	EX	VG
6C	Shanty Hogan	150.00	75.00	45.00
7S	Doug McWeeny	150.00	75.00	45.00

1920s W-UNC Playing Strip Cards (2)

Because only three players have thus far been checklisted from this set, it is not possible to more precisely date this issue. Likely printed on a sheet similar to other playing card/strip card sets of the era, the individual cards are about 1-1/2" x 2-1/2", printed in either red (hearts, diamonds) or black (clubs, spades), with a player photo at center. Backs are blank.

Values Undetermined

6C	Bob Meusel
9S	Tris Speaker
AD	Babe Ruth

1926 W-UNC Strip Cards

Ruth is the only baseball player known in this set of athletic, cinematic and historical subjects. The approximately 1-1/2" x 2-1/2" black-and-white, blue-and-white, or maroon-and-white blank-backed card identifies the player, position and team typographically within the photo and has the card number and name in the bottom border. The card has been seen with numbers 1, 52 and 71, as well as unnumbered.

		NM	EX	VG
1	Babe Ruth (Black-and-white.)	800.00	400.00	240.00
52	Babe Ruth (Blue duotone.)	800.00	400.00	240.00
71	Babe Ruth (Blue duotone.)	800.00	400.00	240.00
71	Babe Ruth (Maroon duotone.)	800.00	400.00	240.00
---	Babe Ruth (Unnumbered, maroon.)	1,100	550.00	330.00

1931 W-UNC Strip Cards

(14) ROBERT GROVE

This issue is virtually identical in format to the various 1928-1931 issues cataloged as W502, York Caramel, Yuengling Ice Cream, etc. The black-and-white, cards measure about 1-3/8" (give or take a 1/16") x 2-1/2". Player photos are bordered in white with the name printed in capital letters at bottom. At bottom-left is a card number in parentheses. This issue's checklist is identical to the 1931 W502. the only difference being these cards have blank backs.

		NM	EX	VG
Complete Set (60):		12,500	5,000	2,500
Common Player:		75.00	30.00	15.00
1	Muddy Ruel	75.00	30.00	15.00
2	John Grabowski	75.00	30.00	15.00
3	Mickey Cochrane	150.00	60.00	30.00
4	Bill Cissell	75.00	30.00	15.00
5	Carl Reynolds	75.00	30.00	15.00
6	Luke Sewell	75.00	30.00	15.00
7	Ted Lyons	150.00	60.00	30.00
8	Harvey Walker	75.00	30.00	15.00
9	Gerald Walker	75.00	30.00	15.00
10	Sam Byrd	75.00	30.00	15.00
11	Joe Vosmik	75.00	30.00	15.00
12	Dan MacFayden	75.00	30.00	15.00
13	William Dickey	150.00	60.00	30.00
14	Robert Grove	300.00	120.00	60.00
15	Al Simmons	150.00	60.00	30.00
16	Jimmy Foxx	300.00	120.00	60.00
17	Nick Altrock	75.00	30.00	15.00
18	Charlie Grimm	75.00	30.00	15.00
19	Bill Terry	150.00	60.00	30.00
20	Clifton Heathcote	75.00	30.00	15.00
21	Burleigh Grimes	150.00	60.00	30.00
22	Red Faber	150.00	60.00	30.00
23	Gabby Hartnett	150.00	60.00	30.00
24	Earl (Earle) Combs	150.00	60.00	30.00
25	Hack Wilson	150.00	60.00	30.00
26	Stanley Harris	150.00	60.00	30.00
27	John J. McGraw	150.00	60.00	30.00
28	Paul Waner	150.00	60.00	30.00
29	Babe Ruth	4,000	1,600	800.00
30	Herb Pennock	150.00	60.00	30.00
31	Joe Sewell	150.00	60.00	30.00
32	Lou Gehrig	2,000	800.00	400.00
33	Tony Lazzeri	150.00	60.00	30.00
34	Waite Hoyt	150.00	60.00	30.00
35	Glenn Wright	75.00	30.00	15.00
36	Leon (Goose) Goslin	150.00	60.00	30.00
37	Frank Frisch	150.00	60.00	30.00
38	George Uhle	75.00	30.00	15.00
39	Bob O'Farrell	75.00	30.00	15.00
40	Rogers Hornsby	200.00	80.00	40.00
41	"Pie" Traynor	150.00	60.00	30.00
42	Clarence Mitchell	75.00	30.00	15.00

#	Player	NM	EX	VG
43	Sherwood Smith	75.00	30.00	15.00
44	Miguel A. Gonzalez	75.00	30.00	15.00
45	Joe Judge	75.00	30.00	15.00
46	Eppa Rixey	150.00	60.00	30.00
47	Adolfo Luque	75.00	30.00	15.00
48	E.C. (Sam) Rice	150.00	60.00	30.00
49	Earl Sheely	75.00	30.00	15.00
50	Sam Jones	75.00	30.00	15.00
51	Bib A. Falk	75.00	30.00	15.00
52	Willie Kamm	75.00	30.00	15.00
53	Roger Peckinpaugh	75.00	30.00	15.00
54	Lester Bell	75.00	30.00	15.00
55	L. Waner	150.00	60.00	30.00
56	Eugene Hargrave	75.00	30.00	15.00
57	Harry Heilmann	150.00	60.00	30.00
58	Earl Smith	75.00	30.00	15.00
59	Dave Bancroft	150.00	60.00	30.00
60	George Kelly	150.00	60.00	30.00

1922 W501

This "strip card" set, known as W501 in the American Card Catalog, is closely connected to the more popular E121 American Caramel set of 1921 and 1922. Because they were handcut from strips, measurements are relative, with well-cut cards typically about 1-7/8" to 2" by about 3-3/8". The W501 cards are numbered in the upper-right corner and have the notation "G-4-22" in the upper-left corner, apparrently indicating the cards were issued in April of 1922.

#	Player	NM	EX	VG
	Complete Set (122):	30,000	12,000	6,000
	Common Player:	100.00	40.00	20.00
1	Ed Rounnel (Rommel)	100.00	40.00	20.00
2	Urban Shocker	100.00	40.00	20.00
3	Dixie Davis	100.00	40.00	20.00
4	George Sisler	350.00	140.00	70.00
5	Bob Veach	100.00	40.00	20.00
6	Harry Heilman (Heilmann)	350.00	140.00	70.00
7a	Ira Falgstead (Name incorrect.)	100.00	40.00	20.00
7b	Ira Flagstead (Name correct.)	100.00	40.00	20.00
8	Ty Cobb	3,750	1,500	750.00
9	Oscar Vitt	100.00	40.00	20.00
10	Muddy Ruel	100.00	40.00	20.00
11	Derrill Pratt	100.00	40.00	20.00
12	Ed Gharrity	100.00	40.00	20.00
13	Joe Judge	100.00	40.00	20.00
14	Sam Rice	350.00	140.00	70.00
15	Clyde Milan	100.00	40.00	20.00
16	Joe Sewell	350.00	140.00	70.00
17	Walter Johnson	900.00	360.00	180.00
18	Jack McInnis	100.00	40.00	20.00
19	Tris Speaker	450.00	180.00	90.00
20	Jim Bagby	100.00	40.00	20.00
21	Stanley Coveleskie (Coveleski)	350.00	140.00	70.00
22	Bill Wambsganss	100.00	40.00	20.00
23	Walter Mails	100.00	40.00	20.00
24	Larry Gardner	100.00	40.00	20.00
25	Aaron Ward	100.00	40.00	20.00
26	Miller Huggins	350.00	140.00	70.00
27	Wally Schang	100.00	40.00	20.00
28	Tom Rogers	100.00	40.00	20.00
29	Carl Mays	125.00	50.00	25.00
30	Everett Scott	100.00	40.00	20.00
31	Robert Shawkey	100.00	40.00	20.00
32	Waite Hoyt	350.00	140.00	70.00
33	Mike McNally	100.00	40.00	20.00
34	Joe Bush	100.00	40.00	20.00
35	Bob Meusel	100.00	40.00	20.00
36	Elmer Miller	100.00	40.00	20.00
37	Dick Kerr	100.00	40.00	20.00
38	Eddie Collins	350.00	140.00	70.00
39	Kid Gleason	100.00	40.00	20.00
40	Johnny Mostil	100.00	40.00	20.00
41	Bib Falk (Bibb)	100.00	40.00	20.00
42	Clarence Hodge	100.00	40.00	20.00
43	Ray Schalk	350.00	140.00	70.00
44	Amos Strunk	100.00	40.00	20.00
45	Eddie Mulligan	100.00	40.00	20.00
46	Earl Sheely	100.00	40.00	20.00
47	Harry Hooper	350.00	140.00	70.00
48	Urban Faber	350.00	140.00	70.00
49	Babe Ruth	6,000	2,400	1,200
50	Ivy B. Wingo	100.00	40.00	20.00
51	Earle Neale	125.00	50.00	25.00
52	Jake Daubert	100.00	40.00	20.00
53	Ed Roush	350.00	140.00	70.00
54	Eppa J. Rixey	350.00	140.00	70.00
55	Elwood Martin	100.00	40.00	20.00
56	Bill Killifer (Killefer)	100.00	40.00	20.00
57	Charles Hollocher	100.00	40.00	20.00
58	Zeb Terry	100.00	40.00	20.00
59	G.C. Alexander (Arms above head.)	600.00	240.00	120.00
60	Turner Barber	100.00	40.00	20.00
61	John Rawlings	100.00	40.00	20.00
62	Frank Frisch	350.00	140.00	70.00
63	Pat Shea	100.00	40.00	20.00
64	Dave Bancroft	350.00	140.00	70.00
65	Cecil Causey	100.00	40.00	20.00
66	Frank Snyder	100.00	40.00	20.00
67	Heinie Groh	100.00	40.00	20.00
68	Ross Young (Youngs)	350.00	140.00	70.00
69	Fred Toney	100.00	40.00	20.00
70	Arthur Nehf	100.00	40.00	20.00
71	Earl Smith	100.00	40.00	20.00
72	George Kelly	350.00	140.00	70.00
73	John J. McGraw	350.00	140.00	70.00
74	Phil Douglas	100.00	40.00	20.00
75	Bill Ryan	100.00	40.00	20.00
76	Jess Haines	350.00	140.00	70.00
77	Milt Stock	100.00	40.00	20.00
78	William Doak	100.00	40.00	20.00
79	George Toporcer	100.00	40.00	20.00
80	Wilbur Cooper	100.00	40.00	20.00
81	George Whitted	100.00	40.00	20.00
82	Chas. Grimm	100.00	40.00	20.00
83	Rabbit Maranville	350.00	140.00	70.00
84	Babe Adams	100.00	40.00	20.00
85	Carson Bigbee	100.00	40.00	20.00
86	Max Carey	350.00	140.00	70.00
87	Whitey Glazner	100.00	40.00	20.00
88	George Gibson	100.00	40.00	20.00
89	Bill Southworth	100.00	40.00	20.00
90	Hank Gowdy	100.00	40.00	20.00
91	Walter Holke	100.00	40.00	20.00
92	Joe Oeschger	100.00	40.00	20.00
93	Pete Kilduff	100.00	40.00	20.00
94	Hy Myers	100.00	40.00	20.00
95	Otto Miller	100.00	40.00	20.00
96	Wilbert Robinson	350.00	140.00	70.00
97	Zach Wheat	350.00	140.00	70.00
98	Walter Ruether	100.00	40.00	20.00
99	Curtis Walker	100.00	40.00	20.00
100	Fred Williams	100.00	40.00	20.00
101	Dave Danforth	100.00	40.00	20.00
102	Ed Rounnel (Rommel)	100.00	40.00	20.00
103	Carl Mays	125.00	50.00	25.00
104	Frank Frisch	350.00	140.00	70.00
105	Lou DeVormer	100.00	40.00	20.00
106	Tom Griffith	100.00	40.00	20.00
107	Harry Harper	100.00	40.00	20.00
108a	John Lavan	100.00	40.00	20.00
108b	John J. McGraw	350.00	140.00	70.00
109	Elmer Smith	100.00	40.00	20.00
110	George Dauss	100.00	40.00	20.00
111	Alexander Gaston	100.00	40.00	20.00
112	John Graney	100.00	40.00	20.00
113	Emil Muesel	100.00	40.00	20.00
114	Rogers Hornsby	450.00	180.00	90.00
115	Leslie Nunamaker	100.00	40.00	20.00
116	Steve O'Neill	100.00	40.00	20.00
117	Max Flack	100.00	40.00	20.00
118	Bill Southworth	100.00	40.00	20.00
119	Arthur Nehf	100.00	40.00	20.00
120	Chick Fewster	100.00	40.00	20.00

1928 W502

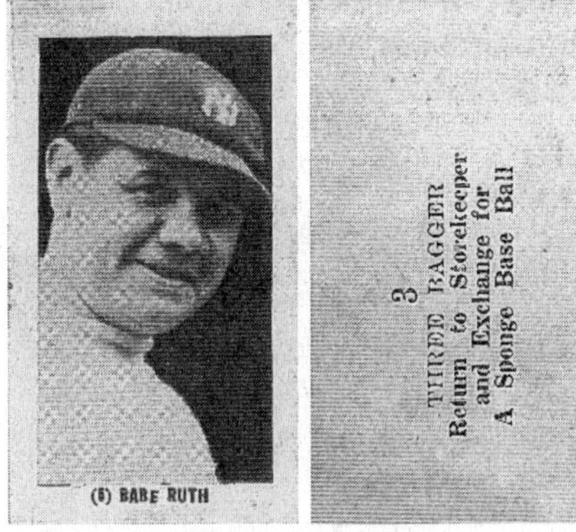

Issued in 1928, the manner of distribution for this set is unknown. Because some of the cards' backs indicate they were redeemable for prizes, they were most likely issued inside of a package of candy or similar product, or perhaps in an opaque envelope. The black-and-white cards measure about 1-3/8" x 2-1/2" and display the player's name at the bottom in capital letters preceded by a number in parentheses. The backs of the cards read either "One Bagger," "Three Bagger" or "Home Run." The listings here show two cards known to exist for numbers 38 and 40, which do not correspond to those numbers in 1931 W502. This raises the possibility there may have been a similar set issued in 1929 and/or 1930. The set carries the American Card Catalog designation W502.

#	Player	NM	EX	VG
	Complete Set (62):	13,500	5,400	2,700
	Common Player:	75.00	30.00	15.00
1	Burleigh Grimes	150.00	60.00	30.00
2	Walter Reuther (Ruether)	75.00	30.00	15.00
3	Joe Dugan	75.00	30.00	15.00
4	Red Faber	150.00	60.00	30.00
5	Gabby Hartnett	150.00	60.00	30.00
6	Babe Ruth	4,500	1,800	900.00
7	Bob Meusel	75.00	30.00	15.00
8	Herb Pennock	150.00	60.00	30.00
9	George Burns (Photo is George J., not George H. Burns.)	75.00	30.00	15.00
10	Joe Sewell	150.00	60.00	30.00
11	George Uhle	75.00	30.00	15.00
12	Bob O'Farrell	75.00	30.00	15.00
13	Rogers Hornsby	200.00	80.00	40.00
14	"Pie" Traynor	150.00	60.00	30.00
15	Clarence Mitchell	75.00	30.00	15.00
16	Eppa Jepha Rixey	150.00	60.00	30.00
17	Carl Mays	90.00	35.00	17.50
18	Adolfo Luque	75.00	30.00	15.00
19	Dave Bancroft	150.00	60.00	30.00
20	George Kelly	150.00	60.00	30.00
21	Earl Combs (Earle)	150.00	60.00	30.00
22	Harry Heilmann	150.00	60.00	30.00
23	Ray W. Schalk	150.00	60.00	30.00
24	Johnny Mostil	75.00	30.00	15.00
25	Hack Wilson (Photo actually Art Wilson.)	150.00	60.00	30.00
26	Lou Gehrig	1,750	700.00	350.00
27	Ty Cobb	1,750	700.00	350.00
28	Tris Speaker	200.00	80.00	40.00
29	Tony Lazzeri	150.00	60.00	30.00
30	Waite Hoyt	150.00	60.00	30.00
31	Sherwood Smith	75.00	30.00	15.00
32	Max Carey	150.00	60.00	30.00
33	Eugene Hargrave	75.00	30.00	15.00
34	Miguel L. Gonzales (Miguel A. Gonzalez)	75.00	30.00	15.00
35	Joe Judge	75.00	30.00	15.00
36	E.C. (Sam) Rice	150.00	60.00	30.00
37	Earl Sheely	75.00	30.00	15.00
38a	Sam Jones	75.00	30.00	15.00
38b	Emory E. Rigney	75.00	30.00	15.00
39	Bib A. Falk (Bibb)	75.00	30.00	15.00
40a	Nick Altrock	75.00	30.00	15.00
40b	Willie Kamm	75.00	30.00	15.00
41	Stanley Harris	150.00	60.00	30.00
42	John J. McGraw	150.00	60.00	30.00
43	Artie Nehf	75.00	30.00	15.00
44	Grover Alexander	250.00	100.00	50.00
45	Paul Waner	150.00	60.00	30.00
46	William H. Terry	150.00	60.00	30.00
47	Glenn Wright	75.00	30.00	15.00
48	Earl Smith	75.00	30.00	15.00
49	Leon (Goose) Goslin	150.00	60.00	30.00
50	Frank Frisch	150.00	60.00	30.00
51	Joe Harris	75.00	30.00	15.00
52	Fred (Cy) Williams	75.00	30.00	15.00
53	Eddie Roush	150.00	60.00	30.00
54	George Sisler	150.00	60.00	30.00
55	Ed Rommel	75.00	30.00	15.00
56	Rogers Peckinpaugh (Roger)	75.00	30.00	15.00
57	Stanley Coveleskie (Coveleski)	150.00	60.00	30.00
58	Lester Bell	75.00	30.00	15.00
59	Dave Bancroft	150.00	60.00	30.00
60	John P. McInnis	75.00	30.00	15.00

1931 W502

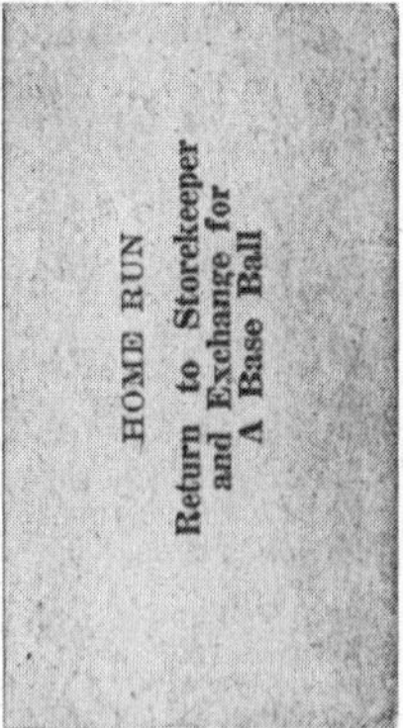

Issued in 1931, the manner of distribution for this set is unknown. Because some of the cards' backs indicate they were redeemable for prizes, they were most likely issued inside of a package of candy or similar product, or perhaps in an opaque envelope. The black-and-white cards measure about 1-3/8" x 2-1/2" and display the player's name at the bottom in capital letters preceded by a number in parentheses. The backs of the cards read either "One Bagger," "Three Bagger" or "Home Run." The set carries the American Card Catalog designation W502.

#	Player	NM	EX	VG
	Complete Set (60):	12,500	5,500	2,750
	Common Player:	90.00	35.00	17.50
1	Muddy Ruel	90.00	35.00	17.50
2	John Grabowski	90.00	35.00	17.50
3	Mickey Cochrane	150.00	60.00	30.00
4	Bill Cissell	90.00	35.00	17.50
5	Carl Reynolds	90.00	35.00	17.50
6	Luke Sewell	90.00	35.00	17.50
7	Ted Lyons	150.00	60.00	30.00
8	Harvey Walker	90.00	35.00	17.50
9	Gerald Walker	90.00	35.00	17.50
10	Sam Byrd	90.00	35.00	17.50
11	Joe Vosmik	90.00	35.00	17.50

12	Dan MacFayden	90.00	35.00	17.50
13	William Dickey	150.00	60.00	30.00
14	Robert Grove	250.00	100.00	50.00
15	Al Simmons	150.00	60.00	30.00
16	Jimmy Foxx	300.00	120.00	60.00
17	Nick Altrock	90.00	35.00	17.50
18	Charlie Grimm	90.00	35.00	17.50
19	Bill Terry	150.00	60.00	30.00
20	Clifton Heathcote	90.00	35.00	17.50
21	Burleigh Grimes	150.00	60.00	30.00
22	Red Faber	150.00	60.00	30.00
23	Gabby Hartnett	150.00	60.00	30.00
24	Earl (Earle) Combs	150.00	60.00	30.00
25	Hack Wilson	150.00	60.00	30.00
26	Stanley Harris	150.00	60.00	30.00
27	John J. McGraw	150.00	60.00	30.00
28	Paul Waner	150.00	60.00	30.00
29	Babe Ruth	4,500	1,800	900.00
30	Herb Pennock	150.00	60.00	30.00
31	Joe Sewell	150.00	60.00	30.00
32	Lou Gehrig	2,000	800.00	400.00
33	Tony Lazzeri	150.00	60.00	30.00
34	Waite Hoyt	150.00	60.00	30.00
35	Glenn Wright	90.00	35.00	17.50
36	Leon (Goose) Goslin	150.00	60.00	30.00
37	Frank Frisch	150.00	60.00	30.00
38	George Uhle	90.00	35.00	17.50
39	Bob O'Farrell	90.00	35.00	17.50
40	Rogers Hornsby	200.00	80.00	40.00
41	"Pie" Traynor	150.00	60.00	30.00
42	Clarence Mitchell	90.00	35.00	17.50
43	Sherwood Smith	90.00	35.00	17.50
44	Miguel A. Gonzalez	90.00	35.00	17.50
45	Joe Judge	90.00	35.00	17.50
46	Eppa Rixey	150.00	60.00	30.00
47	Adolfo Luque	90.00	35.00	17.50
48	E.C. (Sam) Rice	150.00	60.00	30.00
49	Earl Sheely	90.00	35.00	17.50
50	Sam Jones	90.00	35.00	17.50
51	Bib A. Falk	90.00	35.00	17.50
52	Willie Kamm	90.00	35.00	17.50
53	Roger Peckinpaugh	90.00	35.00	17.50
54	Lester Bell	90.00	35.00	17.50
55	L. Waner	150.00	60.00	30.00
56	Eugene Hargrave	90.00	35.00	17.50
57	Harry Heilmann	150.00	60.00	30.00
58	Earl Smith	90.00	35.00	17.50
59	Dave Bancroft	150.00	60.00	30.00
60	George Kelly	150.00	60.00	30.00

1922 W503

Issued circa 1923, this 64-card set of blank-backed cards, measuring 1-3/4" x 2-3/4", feature black and white player photos surrounded by a white border. The player's name and team appear on the card, along with a card number in either the left or right bottom corner. There is no indication of the set's producer, although it is believed the cards were issued with candy or gum. The set carries a W503 American Card Catalog designation.

		NM	EX	VG
Complete Set (64):		40,000	16,000	8,000
Common Player:		350.00	140.00	70.00
1	Joe Bush	350.00	140.00	70.00
2	Wally Schang	350.00	140.00	70.00
3	Dave Robertson	350.00	140.00	70.00
4	Wally Pipp	375.00	150.00	75.00
5	Bill Ryan	350.00	140.00	70.00
6	George Kelly	900.00	360.00	180.00
7	Frank Snyder	350.00	140.00	70.00
8	Jimmy O'Connell	350.00	140.00	70.00
9	Bill Cunningham	350.00	140.00	70.00
10	Norman McMillan	350.00	140.00	70.00
11	Waite Hoyt	900.00	360.00	180.00
12	Art Nehf	350.00	140.00	70.00
13	George Sisler	900.00	360.00	180.00
14	Al DeVormer	350.00	140.00	70.00
15	Casey Stengel	900.00	360.00	180.00
16	Ken Williams	350.00	140.00	70.00
17	Joe Dugan	350.00	140.00	70.00
18	"Irish" Meusel	350.00	140.00	70.00
19	Bob Meusel	350.00	140.00	70.00
20	Carl Mays	375.00	150.00	75.00
21	Frank Frisch	900.00	360.00	180.00
22	Jess Barnes	350.00	140.00	70.00
23	Walter Johnson	1,500	600.00	300.00
24	Claude Jonnard	350.00	140.00	70.00
25	Dave Bancroft	900.00	360.00	180.00
26	Johnny Rawlings	350.00	140.00	70.00
27	"Pep" Young	350.00	140.00	70.00
28	Earl Smith	350.00	140.00	70.00
29	Willie Kamm	350.00	140.00	70.00
30	Art Fletcher	350.00	140.00	70.00
31	"Kid" Gleason	350.00	140.00	70.00
32	"Babe" Ruth	12,000	4,800	2,400
33	Guy Morton	350.00	140.00	70.00
34	Heinie Groh	350.00	140.00	70.00
35	Leon Cadore	350.00	140.00	70.00
36	Joe Tobin	350.00	140.00	70.00
37	"Rube" Marquard	900.00	360.00	180.00
38	Grover Alexander	1,200	480.00	240.00
39	George Burns	350.00	140.00	70.00
40	Joe Oeschger	350.00	140.00	70.00
41	"Chick" Shorten	350.00	140.00	70.00
42	Roger Hornsby (Rogers)	1,100	440.00	220.00
43	Adolfo Luque	350.00	140.00	70.00
44	Zack Wheat	900.00	360.00	180.00
45	Herb Pruett (Hub)	350.00	140.00	70.00
46	Rabbit Maranville	900.00	360.00	180.00
47	Jimmy Ring	350.00	140.00	70.00
48	Sherrod Smith	350.00	140.00	70.00
49	Lea Meadows (Lee)	350.00	140.00	70.00
50	Aaron Ward	350.00	140.00	70.00
51	Herb Pennock	900.00	360.00	180.00
52	Carlson Bigbee (Carson)	350.00	140.00	70.00
53	Max Carey	900.00	360.00	180.00
54	Charles Robertson	350.00	140.00	70.00
55	Urban Shocker	350.00	140.00	70.00
56	Dutch Ruether	350.00	140.00	70.00
57	Jake Daubert	350.00	140.00	70.00
58	Louis Guisto	350.00	140.00	70.00
59	Ivy Wingo	350.00	140.00	70.00
60	Bill Pertica	350.00	140.00	70.00
61	Luke Sewell	350.00	140.00	70.00
62	Hank Gowdy	350.00	140.00	70.00
63	Jack Scott	350.00	140.00	70.00
64	Stan Coveleskie (Coveleski)	900.00	360.00	180.00

1926 W511

Ruth is the only baseball player known in this set of athletic, cinematic and historical subjects. The approximately 1-1/2" x 2-1/2" black-and-white, blue-and-white, or maroon-and-white blank-backed card identifies the player, position and team typographically within the photo and has the card number and name in the bottom border. The card has been seen with numbers 1, 52 and 71, as well as unnumbered.

		NM	EX	VG
1	Babe Ruth (Black-and-white.)	800.00	400.00	240.00
52	Babe Ruth (Blue duotone.)	800.00	400.00	240.00
71	Babe Ruth (Blue duotone.)	800.00	400.00	240.00
71	Babe Ruth (Maroon duotone.)	800.00	400.00	240.00
---	Babe Ruth (Unnumbered, maroon.)	1,100	550.00	330.00

1926-27 W512

One of the many "strip card" sets of the period, the W512 set was initially issued in 1926 and includes 10 baseball players among its 50 cards. Also featured are boxers, golfers, tennis players, aviators, movie stars and other celebrities. The 1-3/8" x 2-1/4" cards feature crude color drawings of the subjects with their names below. A card number appears in the lower-left corner. Baseball players lead off the set and are numbered from 1 to 10. Like most strip cards, they have blank backs. At least four of the baseball player cards have been found in a second type, on which the team name is presented in a typewriter style font on the second line; these changes reflect player status as of 1927. Reprints of Ruth, Cobb, Johnson and Speaker are known.

		NM	EX	VG
Common Player:		55.00	22.50	10.00
1	Dave Bancroft	75.00	30.00	15.00
2a	Grover Alexander (Cubs)	190.00	75.00	35.00
2b	Grover Alexander (Cardinals)	95.00	40.00	20.00
3a	"Ty" Cobb	325.00	130.00	65.00
3b	"Ty" Cobb (Ex-Mgr. Detroit A.L.)	350.00	140.00	70.00
4a	Tris Speaker	95.00	40.00	20.00
4b	Tris Speaker (Ex-Mgr. Cleveland A.L.)	95.00	40.00	20.00
5	Glen Wright (Glenn)	55.00	22.50	10.00
6	"Babe" Ruth	360.00	145.00	70.00
7a	Everett Scott (Yankees)	75.00	30.00	15.00
7b	Everett Scott (White Sox)	55.00	22.50	10.00
8a	Frank Frisch (Giants)	75.00	30.00	15.00
8b	Frank Frisch (Cardinals)	75.00	30.00	15.00
9a	Rogers Hornsby (Cardinals)	95.00	40.00	20.00
9b	Rogers Hornsby (Giants)	95.00	40.00	20.00
10	Dazzy Vance	75.00	30.00	15.00

1928 W513

69
Rube Benton
Giants Pitcher
New York National

This "strip card" set, issued in 1928 was actually a continuation of the W512 set issued two years earlier and is numbered starting with number 61 where the W512 set ended. The blank-backed cards measure 1-3/8" x 2-1/4" and display color drawings of the athletes, which include 14 boxers and the 26 baseball players listed here. The cards are numbered in the lower-left corner.

		NM	EX	VG
Complete (Baseball) Set (26):		1,600	650.00	325.00
Common Player:		50.00	20.00	10.00
61	Eddie Roush	75.00	30.00	15.00
62	Waite Hoyt	75.00	30.00	15.00
63	"Gink" Hendrick	50.00	20.00	10.00
64	"Jumbo" Elliott	50.00	20.00	10.00
65	John Miljus	50.00	20.00	10.00
66	Jumping Joe Dugan	50.00	20.00	10.00
67	Smiling Bill Terry	75.00	30.00	15.00
68	Herb Pennock	75.00	30.00	15.00
69	Rube Benton	50.00	20.00	10.00
70	Paul Waner	75.00	30.00	15.00
71	Adolfo Luque	50.00	20.00	10.00
72	Burleigh Grimes	75.00	30.00	15.00
73	Lloyd Waner	75.00	30.00	15.00
74	Hack Wilson	75.00	30.00	15.00
75	Hal Carlson	50.00	20.00	10.00
76	L. Grantham	50.00	20.00	10.00
77	Wilcey Moore (Wilcy)	50.00	20.00	10.00
78	Jess Haines	75.00	30.00	15.00
79	Tony Lazzeri	75.00	30.00	15.00
80	Al DeVormer	50.00	20.00	10.00
81	Joe Harris	50.00	20.00	10.00
82	Pie Traynor	75.00	30.00	15.00
83	Mark Koenig	50.00	20.00	10.00
84	Babe Herman	60.00	24.00	12.00
85	George Harper	50.00	20.00	10.00
86	Earl Coombs (Earle Combs)	75.00	30.00	15.00

1919-21 W514

Consisting of 120 cards, the W514 set is the largest of the various "strip card" issues of its era. Issued between 1919-1921, it is also one of the earliest and most widely-collected. The 1-3/8" x 2-1/2" cards feature color drawings of the players and display the card number in the lower-left corner. The player's name, position and team appear in the bottom border of the blank-backed cards. The set holds special interest for baseball historians because it includes seven of the eight Chicago "Black Sox" who were banned from baseball for their alleged role in throwing the 1919 World Series. The most famous of them, "Shoeless" Joe Jackson, makes his only strip card appearance in this set.

		NM	EX	VG
Complete Set (124):		30,000	12,000	6,000
Common Player:		75.00	30.00	15.00
1	Ira Flagstead	75.00	30.00	15.00
2	Babe Ruth	1,900	750.00	375.00
	(HOME RUN KING)			
3	Happy Felsch	1,200	475.00	250.00
4	Doc Lavan	75.00	30.00	15.00
5	Phil Douglas	75.00	30.00	15.00
6	Earle Neale	75.00	30.00	15.00
7	Leslie Nunamaker	75.00	30.00	15.00
8	Sam Jones	75.00	30.00	15.00
9	Claude Hendrix	75.00	30.00	15.00
10	Frank Schulte	75.00	30.00	15.00
11	Cactus Cravath	75.00	30.00	15.00
12	Pat Moran	75.00	30.00	15.00
13	Dick Rudolph	75.00	30.00	15.00
14	Arthur Fletcher	75.00	30.00	15.00
15	Joe Jackson	5,000	2,000	1,000
16	Bill Southworth	75.00	30.00	15.00
17	Ad Luque	75.00	30.00	15.00
18	Charlie Deal	75.00	30.00	15.00
19	Al Mamaux	75.00	30.00	15.00
20	Stuffy McInness (McInnis)	75.00	30.00	15.00
21a	Rabbit Maranville (Braves)	200.00	80.00	40.00
21b	Rabbit Maranville (Pirates)	200.00	80.00	40.00
22	Max Carey	200.00	80.00	40.00
23	Dick Kerr	75.00	30.00	15.00
24	George Burns	75.00	30.00	15.00
25	Eddie Collins	200.00	80.00	40.00
26	Steve O'Neil (O'Neill)	75.00	30.00	15.00
27	Bill Fisher	75.00	30.00	15.00
28	Rube Bressler	75.00	30.00	15.00
29	Bob Shawkey	75.00	30.00	15.00
30	Donie Bush	75.00	30.00	15.00
31	Chick Gandil	700.00	280.00	140.00
32	Ollie Zeider	75.00	30.00	15.00
33	Vean Gregg	75.00	30.00	15.00
34	Miller Huggins	200.00	80.00	40.00
35	Lefty Williams	800.00	325.00	160.00
36	Tub Spencer	75.00	30.00	15.00
37	Lew McCarty	75.00	30.00	15.00
38	Hod Eller	75.00	30.00	15.00
39	Joe Gedeon	75.00	30.00	15.00
40a	Dave Bancroft (Quakers)	200.00	80.00	40.00
40b	Dave Bancroft (Giants)	200.00	80.00	40.00
41	Clark Griffith	200.00	80.00	40.00
42	Wilbur Cooper	75.00	30.00	15.00
43	Ty Cobb	1,750	700.00	350.00
44	Roger Peckinpaugh	75.00	30.00	15.00
45	Nic Carter (Nick)	75.00	30.00	15.00
46	Heinie Groh	75.00	30.00	15.00
47a	Bob Roth (Indians)	75.00	30.00	15.00
47b	Bob Roth (Yankees)	75.00	30.00	15.00
48	Frank Davis	75.00	30.00	15.00
49	Leslie Mann	75.00	30.00	15.00
50	Fielder Jones	75.00	30.00	15.00
51	Bill Doak	75.00	30.00	15.00
52	John J. McGraw	200.00	80.00	40.00
53	Charles Hollocher	75.00	30.00	15.00
54	Babe Adams	75.00	30.00	15.00
55	Dode Paskert	75.00	30.00	15.00
56	Roger Hornsby (Rogers)	250.00	100.00	50.00
57	Max Rath	75.00	30.00	15.00
58	Jeff Pfeffer	75.00	30.00	15.00
59	Nick Cullop	75.00	30.00	15.00
60	Ray Schalk	200.00	80.00	40.00
61	Bill Jacobson	75.00	30.00	15.00
62	Nap Lajoie	225.00	90.00	45.00
63	George Gibson	75.00	30.00	15.00
64	Harry Hooper	200.00	80.00	40.00
65	Grover Alexander	300.00	120.00	60.00
66	Ping Bodie	75.00	30.00	15.00
67	Hank Gowdy	75.00	30.00	15.00
68	Jake Daubert	75.00	30.00	15.00
69	Red Faber	200.00	80.00	40.00
70	Ivan Olson	75.00	30.00	15.00
71	Pickles Dilhoefer	75.00	30.00	15.00
72	Christy Mathewson	900.00	350.00	175.00
73	Ira Wingo (Ivy)	75.00	30.00	15.00
74	Fred Merkle	75.00	30.00	15.00
75	Frank Baker	200.00	80.00	40.00
76	Bert Gallia	75.00	30.00	15.00
77	Milton Watson	75.00	30.00	15.00
78	Bert Shotten (Shotton)	75.00	30.00	15.00
79	Sam Rice	200.00	80.00	40.00
80	Dan Greiner	75.00	30.00	15.00
81	Larry Doyle	75.00	30.00	15.00
82	Eddie Cicotte	750.00	300.00	150.00
83	Hugo Bezdek	75.00	30.00	15.00
84	Wally Pipp	90.00	35.00	17.50
85	Eddie Rousch (Roush)	200.00	80.00	40.00
86	Slim Sallee	75.00	30.00	15.00
87	Bill Killifer (Killefer)	75.00	30.00	15.00
88	Bob Veach	75.00	30.00	15.00
89	Jim Burke	75.00	30.00	15.00
90	Everett Scott	75.00	30.00	15.00
91	Buck Weaver	1,100	450.00	225.00
92	George Whitted	75.00	30.00	15.00
93	Ed Konetchy	75.00	30.00	15.00
94	Walter Johnson	600.00	240.00	120.00
95	Sam Crawford	200.00	80.00	40.00
96	Fred Mitchell	75.00	30.00	15.00
97	Ira Thomas	75.00	30.00	15.00
98	Jimmy Ring	75.00	30.00	15.00
99	Wally Shange (Schang)	75.00	30.00	15.00
100	Benny Kauff	75.00	30.00	15.00
101	George Sisler	200.00	80.00	40.00
102	Tris Speaker	250.00	100.00	50.00
103	Carl Mays	90.00	35.00	17.50
104	Buck Herzog	75.00	30.00	15.00
105	Swede Risberg	2,750	1,100	550.00
106a	Hugh Jennings (Tigers)	200.00	80.00	40.00
106b	Hughie Jennings (Giants)	200.00	80.00	40.00
107	Pep Young	75.00	30.00	15.00
108	Walter Reuther (Ruether)	75.00	30.00	15.00
109	Joe Gharrity (Ed)	75.00	30.00	15.00
110	Zach Wheat	200.00	80.00	40.00
111	Jim Vaughn	75.00	30.00	15.00
112	Kid Gleason	75.00	30.00	15.00
113	Casey Stengel	200.00	80.00	40.00
114	Hal Chase	150.00	60.00	30.00
115	Oscar Stange (Stanage)	75.00	30.00	15.00
116	Larry Shean	75.00	30.00	15.00
117	Steve Pendergast	75.00	30.00	15.00
118	Larry Kopf	75.00	30.00	15.00
119	Charles Whiteman	75.00	30.00	15.00
120	Jess Barnes	75.00	30.00	15.00

1923 W515-1

11. GEORGE SISLER
First Base
St. Louis Browns, A. L.

Cards in the 60-card "strip set" measure about 1-3/8" x 2-1/4" and feature color drawings. Backs are blank. The card number along with the player's name, position and team appear in the bottom border. Most cards also display a "U&U" copyright line, indicating that the photos on which the drawings were based were provided by Underwood & Underwood, a major news photo service of the day. The set has a heavy emphasis on New York players with 39 of the 60 cards depicting members of the Yankees, Dodgers or Giants. Babe Ruth appears on two cards and two other cards picture two players each.

		NM	EX	VG
Complete Set (60):		8,000	3,200	1,600
Common Player:		50.00	20.00	10.00
1	Bill Cunningham	50.00	20.00	10.00
2	Al Mamaux	50.00	20.00	10.00
3	"Babe" Ruth	1,600	650.00	325.00
4	Dave Bancroft	100.00	40.00	20.00
5	Ed Rommel	50.00	20.00	10.00
6	"Babe" Adams	50.00	20.00	10.00
7	Clarence Walker	50.00	20.00	10.00
8	Waite Hoyt	100.00	40.00	20.00
9	Bob Shawkey	50.00	20.00	10.00
10	"Ty" Cobb	750.00	300.00	150.00
11	George Sisler	100.00	40.00	20.00
12	Jack Bentley	50.00	20.00	10.00
13	Jim O'Connell	50.00	20.00	10.00
14	Frank Frisch	100.00	40.00	20.00
15	Frank Baker	100.00	40.00	20.00
16	Burleigh Grimes	100.00	40.00	20.00
17	Wally Schang	50.00	20.00	10.00
18	Harry Heilman (Heilmann)	100.00	40.00	20.00
19	Aaron Ward	50.00	20.00	10.00
20	Carl Mays	60.00	24.00	12.00
21	The Meusel Bros.	60.00	24.00	12.00
	(Bob Meusel, Irish Meusel)			
22	Arthur Nehf	50.00	20.00	10.00
23	Lee Meadows	50.00	20.00	10.00
24	"Casey" Stengel	100.00	40.00	20.00
25	Jack Scott	50.00	20.00	10.00
26	Kenneth Williams	50.00	20.00	10.00
27	Joe Bush	50.00	20.00	10.00
28	Tris Speaker	150.00	60.00	30.00
29	Ross Young (Youngs)	100.00	40.00	20.00
30	Joe Dugan	50.00	20.00	10.00
31	The Barnes Bros. (Jesse	60.00	24.00	12.00
	Barnes, Virgil Barnes)			
32	George Kelly	100.00	40.00	20.00
33	Hugh McQuillen (McQuillan)	50.00	20.00	10.00
34	Hugh Jennings	100.00	40.00	20.00
35	Tom Griffith	50.00	20.00	10.00
36	Miller Huggins	100.00	40.00	20.00
37	"Whitey" Witt	50.00	20.00	10.00
38	Walter Johnson	400.00	160.00	80.00
39	"Wally" Pipp	50.00	20.00	10.00
40	"Dutch" Reuther (Ruether)	50.00	20.00	10.00
41	Jim Johnston	50.00	20.00	10.00
42	Willie Kamm	50.00	20.00	10.00
43	Sam Jones	50.00	20.00	10.00
44	Frank Snyder	50.00	20.00	10.00
45	John McGraw	100.00	40.00	20.00
46	Everett Scott	50.00	20.00	10.00
47	"Babe" Ruth	1,600	650.00	325.00
48	Urban Shocker	50.00	20.00	10.00
49	Grover Alexander	150.00	60.00	30.00
50	"Rabbit" Maranville	100.00	40.00	20.00
51	Ray Schalk	100.00	40.00	20.00
52	"Heinie" Groh	50.00	20.00	10.00
53	Wilbert Robinson	100.00	40.00	20.00
54	George Burns	50.00	20.00	10.00
55	Rogers Hornsby	150.00	60.00	30.00
56	Zack Wheat	100.00	40.00	20.00
57	Eddie Roush	100.00	40.00	20.00
58	Eddie Collins	100.00	40.00	20.00
59	Charlie Hollocher	50.00	20.00	10.00
60	Red Faber	100.00	40.00	20.00

1923 W515-2

A near duplicate of the W515-1 set in every respect except size, the W515-2 strip cards are larger in format, at about 1-1/2" x 2-1/2". Placement of the U&U copyright also differs between some players' cards in each set. Cards may be found with letters in the top border from the title, "THE LITTLE WONDER PICTURE SERIES."

		NM	EX	VG
Complete Set (60):		8,000	3,200	1,600
Common Player:		50.00	25.00	15.00
1	Bill Cunningham	50.00	25.00	15.00
2	Al Mamaux	50.00	25.00	15.00
3	"Babe" Ruth	1,600	800.00	480.00
4	Dave Bancroft	100.00	50.00	30.00
5	Ed Rommel	50.00	25.00	15.00
6	"Babe" Adams	50.00	25.00	15.00
7	Clarence Walker	50.00	25.00	15.00
8	Waite Hoyt	100.00	50.00	30.00
9	Bob Shawkey	50.00	25.00	15.00
10	"Ty" Cobb	750.00	375.00	225.00
11	George Sisler	100.00	50.00	30.00
12	Jack Bentley	50.00	25.00	15.00
13	Jim O'Connell	50.00	25.00	15.00
14	Frank Frisch	100.00	50.00	30.00
15	Frank Baker	100.00	50.00	30.00
16	Burleigh Grimes	100.00	50.00	30.00
17	Wally Schang	50.00	25.00	15.00
18	Harry Heilman (Heilmann)	100.00	50.00	30.00
19	Aaron Ward	50.00	25.00	15.00
20	Carl Mays	60.00	30.00	18.00
21	The Meusel Bros.	60.00	30.00	18.00
	(Bob Meusel, Irish Meusel)			
22	Arthur Nehf	50.00	25.00	15.00
23	Lee Meadows	50.00	25.00	15.00
24	"Casey" Stengel	100.00	50.00	30.00
25	Jack Scott	50.00	25.00	15.00
26	Kenneth Williams	50.00	25.00	15.00
27	Joe Bush	50.00	25.00	15.00
28	Tris Speaker	150.00	75.00	45.00
29	Ross Young (Youngs)	100.00	50.00	30.00
30	Joe Dugan	50.00	25.00	15.00
31	The Barnes Bros. (Jesse	60.00	30.00	18.00
	Barnes, Virgil Barnes)			
32	George Kelly	100.00	50.00	30.00
33	Hugh McQuillen	50.00	25.00	15.00
	(McQuillan)			
34	Hugh Jennings	100.00	50.00	30.00
35	Tom Griffith	50.00	25.00	15.00
36	Miller Huggins	100.00	50.00	30.00
37	"Whitey" Witt	50.00	25.00	15.00
38	Walter Johnson	400.00	200.00	120.00
39	"Wally" Pipp	50.00	25.00	15.00
40	"Dutch" Reuther (Ruether)	50.00	25.00	15.00
41	Jim Johnston	50.00	25.00	15.00
42	Willie Kamm	50.00	25.00	15.00
43	Sam Jones	50.00	25.00	15.00
44	Frank Snyder	50.00	25.00	15.00
45	John McGraw	100.00	50.00	30.00
46	Everett Scott	50.00	25.00	15.00
47	"Babe" Ruth	1,600	800.00	480.00
48	Urban Shocker	50.00	25.00	15.00
49	Grover Alexander	150.00	75.00	45.00
50	"Rabbit" Maranville	100.00	50.00	30.00
51	Ray Schalk	100.00	50.00	30.00
52	"Heinie" Groh	50.00	25.00	15.00
53	Wilbert Robinson	100.00	50.00	30.00
54	George Burns	50.00	25.00	15.00
55	Rogers Hornsby	150.00	75.00	45.00
56	Zack Wheat	100.00	50.00	30.00
57	Eddie Roush	100.00	50.00	30.00
58	Eddie Collins	100.00	50.00	30.00
59	Charlie Hollocher	50.00	25.00	15.00
60	Red Faber	100.00	50.00	30.00

1920 W516-1

This "strip card" set consists of 30 cards featuring colored drawings - either portraits or full-length action poses. The blank-backed cards measure 1-1/2" x 2-1/2". The player's name, position and team appear beneath the picture in hand-printed style. To the right of the name is the card number. The set can be identified by an "IFS" copyright symbol. representing International Feature Service.

		NM	EX	VG
Complete Set (30):		5,250	2,000	1,000
Common Player:		50.00	25.00	10.00
1	Babe Ruth	2,000	800.00	400.00
2	Heinie Groh	50.00	25.00	10.00
3	Ping Bodie	50.00	25.00	10.00
4	Ray Shalk (Schalk)	100.00	40.00	20.00
5	Tris Speaker	150.00	60.00	30.00
6	Ty Cobb	750.00	300.00	150.00
7	Roger Hornsby (Rogers)	150.00	60.00	30.00
8	Walter Johnson	300.00	120.00	60.00
9	Grover Alexander	150.00	60.00	30.00
10	George Burns	50.00	25.00	10.00
11	Jimmy Ring	50.00	25.00	10.00
12	Jess Barnes	50.00	25.00	10.00
13	Larry Doyle	50.00	25.00	10.00
14	Arty Fletcher	50.00	25.00	10.00
15	Dick Rudolph	50.00	25.00	10.00
16	Benny Kauf (Kauff)	50.00	25.00	10.00
17	Art Nehf	50.00	25.00	10.00
18	Babe Adams	50.00	25.00	10.00
19	Will Cooper	50.00	25.00	10.00
20	R. Peckinpaugh	50.00	25.00	10.00
21	Eddie Cicotte	100.00	40.00	20.00
22	Hank Gowdy	50.00	25.00	10.00
23	Eddie Collins	100.00	40.00	20.00
24	Christy Mathewson	400.00	160.00	80.00
25	Clyde Milan	50.00	25.00	10.00
26	M. Kelley (should be G. Kelly)	100.00	40.00	20.00
27	Ed Hooper (Harry)	100.00	40.00	20.00
28	Pep. Young	50.00	25.00	10.00
29	Eddie Rousch (Roush)	100.00	40.00	20.00
30	Geo. Bancroft (Dave)	100.00	40.00	20.00

1920 W516-1-2

This set is a re-issue of the W516-1-1 set, with several changes: The pictures are reverse images of W516-1-1, and are printed only in black, red and yellow. Well cut, the blank-back cards measure a nominal 1-1/2" x 2-3/8". The cards display a backwards "IFC" copyright symbol.

		NM	EX	VG
Complete Set (30):		5,250	2,000	1,000
Common Player:		50.00	25.00	10.00
1	Babe Ruth	2,000	1,000	600.00
2	Heinie Groh	50.00	25.00	10.00
3	Ping Bodie	50.00	25.00	10.00
4	Ray Shalk (Schalk)	100.00	40.00	20.00
5	Tris Speaker	150.00	60.00	30.00
6	Ty Cobb	750.00	300.00	150.00
7	Roger Hornsby (Rogers)	150.00	75.00	45.00
8	Walter Johnson	300.00	150.00	90.00
9	Grover Alexander	150.00	60.00	30.00
10	George Burns	50.00	25.00	10.00
11	Jimmy Ring	50.00	25.00	10.00
12	Jess Barnes	50.00	25.00	10.00
13	Larry Doyle	50.00	25.00	10.00
14	Arty Fletcher	50.00	25.00	10.00
15	Dick Rudolph	50.00	25.00	10.00
16	Benny Kauf (Kauff)	50.00	25.00	10.00
17	Art Nehf	50.00	25.00	10.00
18	Babe Adams	50.00	25.00	10.00
19	Will Cooper	50.00	25.00	10.00
20	R. Peckinpaugh	50.00	25.00	10.00
21	Eddie Cicotte	100.00	50.00	30.00
22	Hank Gowdy	50.00	25.00	10.00
23	Eddie Collins	100.00	40.00	20.00
24	Christy Mathewson	400.00	200.00	120.00
25	Clyde Milan	50.00	25.00	10.00
26	M. Kelley (Should be G. Kelly.)	100.00	40.00	20.00
27	Ed Hooper (Harry)	100.00	40.00	20.00
28	Pep. Young	50.00	25.00	10.00
29	Eddie Rousch (Roush)	100.00	40.00	20.00
30	Geo. Bancroft (Dave)	100.00	40.00	20.00

1921 W516-2-1

This set is essentially a re-issue of the W516-1 set, with several changes: The pictures are reverse images of W516-1, and are printed only in red and blue. Cards have been renumbered and have player identification in typeset serifed style. The blank-backed cards measure about 1-1/2" x 2-3/8". The cards display a backwards "IFC" copyright symbol.

		NM	EX	VG
Complete Set (30):		4,500	1,800	900.00
Common Player:		50.00	25.00	10.00
1	George Burns	50.00	25.00	10.00
2	Grover Alexander	150.00	60.00	30.00
3	Walter Johnson	250.00	100.00	50.00
4	Roger Hornsby (Rogers)	125.00	50.00	25.00
5	Ty Cobb	750.00	300.00	150.00
6	Tris Speaker	125.00	50.00	25.00
7	Ray Shalk (Schalk)	75.00	30.00	15.00
8	Ping Bodie	50.00	25.00	10.00
9	Heinie Groh	50.00	25.00	10.00
10	Babe Ruth	1,500	600.00	300.00
11	R. Peckinpaugh	50.00	25.00	10.00
12	Will. Cooper	50.00	25.00	10.00
13	Babe Adams	50.00	25.00	10.00
14	Art Nehf	50.00	25.00	10.00
15	Benny Kauf (Kauff)	50.00	25.00	10.00
16	Dick Rudolph	50.00	25.00	10.00
17	Arty. Fletcher	50.00	25.00	10.00
18	Larry Doyle	50.00	25.00	10.00
19	Jess Barnes	50.00	25.00	10.00
20	Jimmy Ring	50.00	25.00	10.00
21	George Bancroft (Dave)	75.00	30.00	15.00
22	Eddie Rousch (Roush)	75.00	30.00	15.00
23	Pep Young	50.00	25.00	10.00
24	Ed Hooper (Harry)	75.00	30.00	15.00
25	M. Kelley (Should be G. Kelly.)	75.00	30.00	15.00
26	Clyde Milan	50.00	25.00	10.00
27	Christy Mathewson	350.00	140.00	70.00
28	Eddie Collins	75.00	30.00	15.00
29	Hank Gowdy	50.00	25.00	10.00
30	Eddie Cicotte	125.00	50.00	25.00

1921 W516-2-2

This set is yet another variation in the W516 "family." In numbering it parallels W516-2-1, though the typography is in the same sans-serif font as W516-1. Like W516-2-1, the player pictures have been reversed. Well cut, the blank-backed cards measure a nominal 1-1/2" x 2-1/4". The cards display a backwards "IFC" copyright symbol in the picture portion.

		NM	EX	VG
Complete Set (30):		5,000	2,500	1,500
Common Player:		50.00	25.00	10.00
1	George Burns	50.00	25.00	10.00
2	Grover Alexander	150.00	75.00	45.00
3	Walter Johnson	300.00	150.00	90.00
4	Roger Hornsby (Rogers)	125.00	62.00	37.00
5	Ty Cobb	750.00	375.00	225.00
6	Tris Speaker	125.00	62.00	37.00
7	Ray Shalk (Schalk)	75.00	37.50	22.50
8	Ping Bodie	50.00	25.00	10.00
9	Heinie Groh	50.00	25.00	10.00
10	Babe Ruth	2,000	1,000	600.00
11	R. Peckinpaugh	50.00	25.00	10.00
12	Will. Cooper	50.00	25.00	10.00
13	Babe Adams	50.00	25.00	10.00
14	Art Nehf	50.00	25.00	10.00
15	Benny Kauf (Kauff)	50.00	25.00	10.00
16	Dick Rudolph	50.00	25.00	10.00
17	Arty. Fletcher	50.00	25.00	10.00
18	Larry Doyle	50.00	25.00	10.00
19	Jess Barnes	50.00	25.00	10.00
20	Jimmy Ring	50.00	25.00	10.00
21	George Bancroft (Dave)	75.00	37.50	22.50
22	Eddie Rousch (Roush)	75.00	37.50	22.50
23	Pep Young	50.00	25.00	10.00
24	Ed Hooper (Harry)	75.00	37.50	22.50
25	M. Kelley (Should be G. Kelly.)	75.00	37.50	22.50
26	Clyde Milan	50.00	25.00	10.00
27	Christy Mathewson	400.00	200.00	120.00
28	Eddie Collins	75.00	37.50	22.50
29	Hank Gowdy	50.00	25.00	10.00
30	Eddie Cicotte	100.00	50.00	30.00

1921 W516-2-3

This issue shares a checklist with W516-2-1, and is likewise printed only in red and blue, with typography in a serifed typeface. Unlike W516-2-1, however, the images on these cards are not reversed, as can easily be ascertained by looking at the copyright symbol and letters.

		NM	EX	VG
Complete Set (30):		5,000	2,500	1,500
Common Player:				
1	George Burns	50.00	25.00	10.00
2	Grover Alexander	150.00	75.00	45.00
3	Walter Johnson	300.00	150.00	90.00
4	Roger Hornsby (Rogers)	125.00	62.00	37.00
5	Ty Cobb	750.00	375.00	225.00
6	Tris Speaker	125.00	62.00	37.00
7	Ray Shalk (Schalk)	75.00	30.00	15.00
8	Ping Bodie	50.00	25.00	10.00
9	Heinie Groh	50.00	25.00	10.00
10	Babe Ruth	2,000	1,000	600.00
11	R. Peckinpaugh	50.00	25.00	10.00
12	Will. Cooper	50.00	25.00	10.00
13	Babe Adams	50.00	25.00	10.00
14	Art Nehf	50.00	25.00	10.00
15	Benny Kauf (Kauff)	50.00	25.00	10.00
16	Dick Rudolph	50.00	25.00	10.00
17	Arty. Fletcher	50.00	25.00	10.00
18	Larry Doyle	50.00	25.00	10.00
19	Jess Barnes	50.00	25.00	10.00
20	Jimmy Ring	50.00	25.00	10.00
21	George Bancroft (Dave)	75.00	30.00	15.00
22	Eddie Rousch (Roush)	75.00	30.00	15.00
23	Pep Young	50.00	25.00	10.00
24	Ed Hooper (Harry)	75.00	30.00	15.00
25	M. Kelley (Should be G. Kelly.)	75.00	30.00	15.00
26	Clyde Milan	50.00	25.00	10.00
27	Christy Mathewson	400.00	200.00	120.00
28	Eddie Collins	75.00	30.00	15.00
29	Hank Gowdy	50.00	25.00	10.00
30	Eddie Cicotte	100.00	50.00	30.00

1931 W517

The 54-player W517 set is an issue of 3" x 4" cards generally found in a sepia color, though other colors are known. The cards feature a player photo as well as his name and team. The card number appears in a small circle on the front, while the backs are blank. The set is heavy in stars of the period including two Babe Ruths (#4 and 20). The cards were sold in vertical strips of three cards; some cards are found with baseball plays in a line at top. Complete set prices do not include variations. The set was reprinted in three-card-strip format in 1997, with "W-517" printed in the lower-left corner of the reprints.

		NM	EX	VG
Complete Set (59):		11,000	4,400	2,200
Common Player:		75.00	35.00	20.00
1	Earl Combs (Earle)	160.00	70.00	40.00
2	Pie Traynor	160.00	70.00	40.00
3	Eddie Rausch (Roush)	160.00	70.00	40.00
4	Babe Ruth/Throwing	1,500	675.00	375.00
5a	Chalmer Cissell (Chicago)	75.00	35.00	20.00
5b	Chalmer Cissell (Cleveland)	75.00	35.00	20.00
6	Bill Sherdel	75.00	35.00	20.00
7	Bill Shore	75.00	35.00	20.00
8	Geo. Earnshaw	75.00	35.00	20.00
9	Bucky Harris	160.00	70.00	40.00
10	Charlie Klein	160.00	70.00	40.00
11a	Geo. Kelly (Reds)	75.00	35.00	20.00
11b	Geo. Kelly (Brooklyn)	75.00	35.00	20.00
12	Travis Jackson	160.00	70.00	40.00
13	Willie Kamm	75.00	35.00	20.00
14	Harry Heilman (Heilmann)	160.00	70.00	40.00
15	Grover Alexander	250.00	110.00	60.00
16	Frank Frisch	160.00	70.00	40.00
17	Jack Quinn	75.00	35.00	20.00
18	Cy Williams	75.00	35.00	20.00
19	Kiki Cuyler	160.00	70.00	40.00
20	Babe Ruth (Portrait)	1,750	785.00	435.00
21	Jimmie Foxx	350.00	155.00	85.00
22	Jimmy Dykes	75.00	35.00	20.00
23	Bill Terry	160.00	70.00	40.00
24	Freddy Lindstrom	160.00	72.00	40.00
25	Hughey Critz	75.00	35.00	20.00
26	Pete Donahue	75.00	35.00	20.00
27	Tony Lazzeri	160.00	70.00	40.00
28	Heine Manush (Heinie)	160.00	70.00	40.00
29a	Chick Hafey (Cardinals)	160.00	70.00	40.00
29b	Chick Hafey (Cincinnati)	160.00	70.00	40.00
30	Melvin Ott	200.00	90.00	50.00
31	Bing Miller	75.00	35.00	20.00
32	Geo. Haas	75.00	35.00	20.00
33a	Lefty O'Doul (Phillies)	95.00	45.00	25.00
33b	Lefty O'Doul (Brooklyn)	95.00	45.00	25.00
(34)	Paul Waner (No card number.)	160.00	70.00	40.00
34	Paul Waner (W/card number.)	160.00	70.00	40.00
35	Lou Gehrig	900.00	400.00	225.00
36	Dazzy Vance	160.00	70.00	40.00
37	Mickey Cochrane	160.00	70.00	40.00
38	Rogers Hornsby	225.00	100.00	55.00
39	Lefty Grove	200.00	90.00	50.00
40	Al Simmons	160.00	70.00	40.00
41	Rube Walberg	75.00	35.00	20.00
42	Hack Wilson	160.00	70.00	40.00
43	Art Shires	75.00	35.00	20.00
44	Sammy Hale	75.00	35.00	20.00
45	Ted Lyons	160.00	70.00	40.00
46	Joe Sewell	160.00	70.00	40.00
47	Goose Goslin	160.00	70.00	40.00
48	Lou Fonseca (Lew)	75.00	35.00	20.00
49	Bob Muesel (Meusel)	75.00	35.00	20.00
50	Lu Blue	75.00	35.00	20.00
51	Earl Averill	160.00	70.00	40.00
52	Eddy Collins (Eddie)	160.00	70.00	40.00
53	Joe Judge	75.00	35.00	20.00
54	Mickey Cochrane	160.00	70.00	40.00

1931 W517 Mini

Little is known about these smaller-format (1-3/4" x 2-3/4") versions of the W517 strip cards. They are identical in design to the more common 3" x 4" cards, although some, if not all, do not have the card number-in-circle found on regular W517s. It is presumed, though not confirmed, that all 54 of the regular versions can be found in the mini size, as well as several color variations.

PREMIUM: 2-3X
(See W517 for checklist and base card values.)

1920 W519 - Numbered 1

Cards in this 20-card "strip set" measure 1-1/2" x 2-1/2" and feature player drawings set against a brightly colored background. A card number appears in the lower-left corner followed by the player's name, printed in capital letters. The player drawings are all posed portraits, except for Joe Murphy and Ernie Kreuger, who are shown catching. Like all strip cards, the cards were sold in strips and have blank backs. The date of issue may be approximate.

		NM	EX	VG
Complete Set (20):		5,500	2,200	1,100
Common Player:		100.00	40.00	20.00
1	Guy Morton	100.00	40.00	20.00
2	Rube Marquard	300.00	120.00	60.00
3	Gabby Cravath (Gavvy)	100.00	40.00	20.00
4	Ernie Krueger	100.00	40.00	20.00
5	Babe Ruth	2,400	960.00	480.00
6	George Sisler	300.00	120.00	60.00
7	Rube Benton	100.00	40.00	20.00
8	Jimmie Johnston	100.00	40.00	20.00
9	Wilbur Robinson (Wilbert)	300.00	120.00	60.00
10	Johnny Griffith	100.00	40.00	20.00
11	Frank Baker	300.00	120.00	60.00
12	Bob Veach	100.00	40.00	20.00
13	Jesse Barnes	100.00	40.00	20.00
14	Leon Cadore	100.00	40.00	20.00
15	Ray Schalk	300.00	120.00	60.00
16	Kid Gleasen (Gleason)	100.00	40.00	20.00
17	Joe Murphy	100.00	40.00	20.00
18	Frank Frisch	300.00	120.00	60.00
19	Eddie Collins	300.00	120.00	60.00
20	Wallie (Wally) Schang	100.00	40.00	20.00

1920 W519 - Numbered 2

A second type of numbered version of W519 exists on which the style of the card numbers differs as does, apparently, the numbering of the players. On Type 1 cards, the card number to the left of the player name is printed in the same heavy sans-serif style as the name. Type 2 cards have the number in a lighter typewriter-style font. While 10 Type 2 cards are currently confirmed to exist, it is expected the other 10 players from W519 were also issued.

		NM	EX	VG
12	Joe Murphy	100.00	40.00	20.00
12	Bobby Veach	100.00	40.00	20.00
13	Jesse Barnes	100.00	40.00	20.00
13	Frank Frisch	300.00	120.00	60.00
14	Eddie Collins	300.00	120.00	60.00
16	Guy Morton	100.00	40.00	20.00
17	Rube Marquard	300.00	120.00	60.00
19	Ernie Kreuger	100.00	40.00	20.00
20a	Babe Ruth	2,400	960.00	480.00
20b	Wallie Schange (Wally Schang)	100.00	40.00	20.00

1920 W519 - Unnumbered

Cards in this 10-card set are identical in design and size (1-1/2" x 2-1/2") to the W519 Numbered set, except the player drawings are all set against a blue background and the cards are not numbered. With the lone exception of Eddie Ciotte, all of the subjects in the unnumbered set also appear in the numbered set.

		NM	EX	VG
Complete Set (10):		3,600	1,450	725.00
Common Player:		90.00	40.00	20.00
(1)	Eddie Cicotte	350.00	140.00	70.00
(2)	Eddie Collins	275.00	110.00	55.00
(3)	Gabby Cravath (Gavvy)	90.00	40.00	20.00
(4)	Frank Frisch	275.00	110.00	55.00
(5)	Kid Gleasen (Gleason)	90.00	40.00	20.00
(6)	Ernie Kreuger	90.00	40.00	20.00
(7)	Rube Marquard	275.00	110.00	55.00
(8)	Guy Morton	90.00	40.00	20.00
(9)	Joe Murphy	90.00	40.00	20.00
(10)	Babe Ruth	2,000	800.00	400.00

1920 W520

Another "strip card" set issued circa 1920, cards in this set measure 1-3/8" x 2-1/4" and are numbered in the lower-right corner. The first nine cards in the set display portrait poses, while the rest are full-length action poses. Some of the poses in this set are the same as those in the W516 issue with the pictures reversed. The player's last name appears in the border beneath the picture. The cards are blank-backed.

		NM	EX	VG
Complete Set (20):		4,000	1,600	800.00
Common Player:		50.00	20.00	10.00
1	Dave Bancroft	150.00	60.00	30.00
2	Christy Mathewson	400.00	160.00	80.00
3	Larry Doyle	50.00	20.00	10.00
4	Jess Barnes	50.00	20.00	10.00
5	Art Fletcher	50.00	20.00	10.00
6	Wilbur Cooper	50.00	20.00	10.00
7	Mike Gonzales (Gonzalez)	50.00	20.00	10.00
8	Zach Wheat	150.00	60.00	30.00
9	Tris Speaker	200.00	80.00	40.00
10	Benny Kauff	50.00	20.00	10.00
11	Zach Wheat	150.00	60.00	30.00
12	Phil Douglas	50.00	20.00	10.00
13	Babe Ruth	2,000	800.00	400.00
14	Stan Koveleski (Coveleski)	150.00	60.00	30.00
15	Goldie Rapp	50.00	20.00	10.00
16	Pol Perritt	50.00	20.00	10.00
17	Otto Miller	50.00	20.00	10.00
18	George Kelly	150.00	60.00	30.00
19	Mike Gonzales (Gonzalez)	50.00	20.00	10.00
20	Les Nunamaker	50.00	20.00	10.00

1921 W521

This issue is closely related to the W519 Numbered set. In fact, it uses the same color drawings as that set with the pictures reversed, resulting in a mirror-image of the W519 cards. The player poses and the numbering system are identical, as are the various background colors. The W521 cards are blank-backed and were sold in strips.

		NM	EX	VG
Complete Set (20):		3,000	1,200	600.00
Common Player:		50.00	20.00	10.00
1	Guy Morton	50.00	20.00	10.00
2	Rube Marquard	150.00	60.00	30.00
3	Gabby Cravath (Gavvy)	50.00	20.00	10.00
4	Ernie Krueger	50.00	20.00	10.00
5	Babe Ruth	1,500	600.00	300.00
6	George Sisler	150.00	60.00	30.00
7	Rube Benton	50.00	20.00	10.00
8	Jimmie Johnston	50.00	20.00	10.00
9	Wilbur Robinson (Wilbert)	150.00	60.00	30.00
10	Johnny Griffith	50.00	20.00	10.00
11	Frank Baker	150.00	60.00	30.00
12	Bob Veach	50.00	20.00	10.00
13	Jesse Barnes	50.00	20.00	10.00
14	Leon Cadore	50.00	20.00	10.00
15	Ray Schalk	150.00	60.00	30.00
16	Kid Gleasen (Gleason)	50.00	20.00	10.00
17	Joe Murphy	50.00	20.00	10.00
18	Frank Frisch	150.00	60.00	30.00
19	Eddie Collins	150.00	60.00	30.00
20	Wallie (Wally) Schang	50.00	20.00	10.00

1920 W522

The 20 cards in this "strip card" set, issued circa 1920, are numbered from 31-50 and use the same players and drawings as the W520 set, issued about the same time. The cards measure 1-3/8" x 2-1/4" and are numbered in the lower left corner followed by the player's name. The cards have blank backs.

		NM	EX	VG
Complete Set (20):		5,000	2,000	1,000
Common Player:		75.00	30.00	15.00
31	Benny Kauf (Kauff)	75.00	30.00	15.00
32	Tris Speaker	300.00	120.00	60.00
33	Zach Wheat	225.00	90.00	45.00
34	Mike Gonzales (Gonzalez)	75.00	30.00	15.00
35	Wilbur Cooper	75.00	30.00	15.00
36	Art Fletcher	75.00	30.00	15.00
37	Jess Barnes	75.00	30.00	15.00
38	Larry Doyle	75.00	30.00	15.00
39	Christy Mathewson	900.00	360.00	180.00
40	Dave Bancroft	225.00	90.00	45.00
41	Les Nunamaker	75.00	30.00	15.00
42	Mike Gonzales (Gonzalez)	75.00	30.00	15.00
43	George Kelly	225.00	90.00	45.00
44	Otto Miller	75.00	30.00	15.00
45	Pol Perritt	75.00	30.00	15.00
46	Goldie Rapp	75.00	30.00	15.00
47	Stan Koveleski (Coveleski)	225.00	90.00	45.00
48	Babe Ruth	2,250	900.00	450.00
49	Phil Douglas	75.00	30.00	15.00
50	Zach Wheat	225.00	90.00	45.00

1921 W551

Another "strip set" issued circa 1920, these ten cards measure 1-3/8" x 2-1/4" and feature color drawings. The cards are unnumbered and blank-backed.

		NM	EX	VG
Complete Set (10):		2,000	800.00	400.00
Complete Set, Uncut Strip:		2,500	1,000	500.00
Common Player:		50.00	20.00	10.00
(1)	Frank Baker	125.00	50.00	25.00
(2)	Dave Bancroft	125.00	50.00	25.00
(3)	Jess Barnes	50.00	20.00	10.00
(4)	Ty Cobb	400.00	160.00	80.00
(5)	Walter Johnson	175.00	70.00	35.00
(6)	Wally Pipp	50.00	20.00	10.00
(7)	Babe Ruth	1,100	450.00	225.00
(8)	George Sisler	125.00	50.00	25.00
(9)	Tris Speaker	150.00	60.00	30.00
(10)	Casey Stengel	125.00	50.00	25.00

1929 W553

One of the more obscure strip card sets, and one of the last of the genre, this issue also is one of the most attractive. Player photos - the same pictures used in the contemporary Kashin Publications (R316) boxed set and anonymous W554 strip cards - are printed in either black on white or as duotones (blue, green and magenta seen thus far), with an ornate frame. Cards measure 1-3/4" x 2-3/4". There is a facsimile autograph on front and the player's team and league are also spelled out. Backs are blank. This checklist is probably incomplete. Gaps have been left in the assigned numbering for future additions.

		NM	EX	VG
Common Player:		100.00	50.00	30.00
(1)	Lu Blue	100.00	50.00	30.00
(2)	Mickey Cochrane	200.00	100.00	60.00
(4)	Jimmie Foxx	300.00	150.00	90.00
(5)	Frank Frisch	200.00	100.00	60.00
(6)	Lou Gehrig	750.00	375.00	225.00
(7)	Goose Goslin	200.00	100.00	60.00
(8)	Burleigh Grimes	200.00	100.00	60.00
(9)	Lefty Grove	250.00	125.00	75.00
(11)	Rogers Hornsby	250.00	125.00	75.00
(13)	Rabbit Maranville	200.00	100.00	60.00
(14)	Bing Miller	100.00	50.00	30.00
(15)	Lefty O'Doul	150.00	75.00	45.00
(16)	Babe Ruth	1,200	600.00	360.00
(17)	Al Simmons	200.00	100.00	60.00
(18)	Pie Traynor	200.00	100.00	60.00

1930 W554

This unidentified set of black-and-white cards features most of the era's stars in action poses. A facsimile autograph appears on the front of each of the blank-back 5" x 7" pictures. Cards can be found either with and/or without player name and, sometimes, team spelled out in all-capital letters in the

bottom white border, with the position in upper- and lower-case between. The unnumbered pictures are checklisted here in alphabetical order. A version of the issue has been seen with advertising for "Big Prize" on the back, printed in red. Another known back stamp is a round black ad for "A. Bonemery / ICE CREAM / CONFECTIONERY."

		NM	EX	VG
Complete Set (18):		3,500	1,400	700.00
Common Player:		60.00	25.00	12.50
(1)	Gordon S. (Mickey) Cochrane	100.00	40.00	20.00
(2)	Lewis A. Fonseca	60.00	25.00	12.50
(3)	Jimmy Foxx	200.00	80.00	40.00
(4)	Lou Gehrig	950.00	380.00	190.00
(5)	Burleigh Grimes	100.00	40.00	20.00
(6)	Robert M. Grove	125.00	50.00	25.00
(7)	Waite Hoyt	100.00	40.00	20.00
(8)	Joe Judge	60.00	25.00	12.50
(9)	Charles (Chuck) Klein	100.00	40.00	20.00
(10)	Douglas McWeeny	60.00	25.00	12.50
(11)	Frank O'Doul	75.00	25.00	15.00
(12)	Melvin Ott	125.00	50.00	25.00
(13)	Herbert Pennock	100.00	40.00	20.00
(14)	Eddie Rommel	60.00	25.00	12.50
(15)	Babe Ruth	1,200	480.00	240.00
(16)	Al Simmons	100.00	40.00	20.00
(17)	Lloyd Waner	100.00	40.00	20.00
(18)	Hack Wilson	125.00	50.00	25.00

1909-1910 W555

Designated as W555 in the American Card Catalog, the nearly square cards measure only 1-1/8" x 1-3-16" and feature a sepia-colored player photo. Sixty-six different cards have been discovered to date, but others may exist. A recent discovery indicates these cards were produced by Jay S. Meyer confectioners of Philly. The sets appear to be related to a series of contemporary candy cards (E93, E94, E97, and E98) because, with only two exceptions, the players and poses are the same. Recent discoveries also indicate the cards were issued four per box of Base Ball Snap Shots candy.

		NM	EX	VG
Complete Set (67):		25,000	10,000	5,000
Common Player:		125.00	50.00	25.00
(1)	Red Ames	125.00	50.00	25.00
(2)	Jimmy Austin	125.00	50.00	25.00
(3)	Johnny Bates	125.00	50.00	25.00
(4)	Chief Bender	375.00	150.00	75.00
(5)	Bob Bescher	125.00	50.00	25.00
(6)	Joe Birmingham	125.00	50.00	25.00
(7)	Bill Bradley	125.00	50.00	25.00
(8)	Kitty Bransfield	125.00	50.00	25.00
(9)	Mordecai Brown	375.00	150.00	75.00
(10)	Bobby Byrne	125.00	50.00	25.00
(11)	Frank Chance	375.00	150.00	75.00
(12)	Hal Chase	375.00	150.00	75.00
(13)	Ed Cicotte	375.00	150.00	75.00
(14)	Fred Clarke	375.00	150.00	75.00
(15)	Ty Cobb	4,500	1,800	900.00
(16)	Eddie Collins (Dark uniform.)	375.00	150.00	75.00
(17)	Eddie Collins (Light uniform.)	375.00	150.00	75.00
(18)	Harry Coveleskie (Coveleski)	125.00	50.00	25.00
(19)	Sam Crawford	375.00	150.00	75.00
(20)	Harry Davis	125.00	50.00	25.00
(21)	Jim Delehanty (Delahanty)	125.00	50.00	25.00
(22)	Art Devlin	125.00	50.00	25.00
(23)	Josh Devore	125.00	50.00	25.00
(24)	Wild Bill Donovan	125.00	50.00	25.00
(25)	Red Dooin	125.00	50.00	25.00
(26)	Mickey Doolan	125.00	50.00	25.00
(27)	Bull Durham	125.00	50.00	25.00
(28)	Jimmy Dygert	125.00	50.00	25.00

#	Player	NM	EX	VG
(29)	Johnny Evers	375.00	150.00	75.00
(30)	Russ Ford	125.00	50.00	25.00
(31)	George Gibson	125.00	50.00	25.00
(32)	Clark Griffith	375.00	150.00	75.00
(33)	Topsy Hartsell (Hartsel)	125.00	50.00	25.00
(34)	Bill Heinchman (Hinchman)	125.00	50.00	25.00
(35)	Ira Hemphill	125.00	50.00	25.00
(36)	Hughie Jennings	375.00	150.00	75.00
(37)	Davy Jones	125.00	50.00	25.00
(38)	Addie Joss	500.00	200.00	100.00
(39)	Wee Willie Keeler	375.00	150.00	75.00
(40)	Red Kleinow	125.00	50.00	25.00
(41)	Nap Lajoie	375.00	150.00	75.00
(42)	Joe Lake	125.00	50.00	25.00
(43)	Tommy Leach	125.00	50.00	25.00
(44)	Harry Lord	125.00	50.00	25.00
(45)	Sherry Magee	125.00	50.00	25.00
(46)	Christy Mathewson	2,000	800.00	400.00
(47)	Amby McConnell	125.00	50.00	25.00
(48)	John McGraw	375.00	150.00	75.00
(49)	Chief Meyers	125.00	50.00	25.00
(50)	Earl Moore	125.00	50.00	25.00
(51)	Mike Mowery	125.00	50.00	25.00
(52)	George Mullin	125.00	50.00	25.00
(53)	Red Murray	125.00	50.00	25.00
(54)	Nichols	125.00	50.00	25.00
(55)	Jim Pastorious (Pastorius)	125.00	50.00	25.00
(56)	Deacon Phillippi (Phillippe)	125.00	50.00	25.00
(57)	Eddie Plank	375.00	150.00	75.00
(58)	Fred Snodgrass	125.00	50.00	25.00
(59)	Harry Steinfeldt	125.00	50.00	25.00
(60)	Joe Tinker	375.00	150.00	75.00
(61)	Hippo Vaughn	125.00	50.00	25.00
(62)	Honus Wagner	2,500	1,000	500.00
(63)	Rube Waddell	375.00	150.00	75.00
(64)	Hooks Wiltse	125.00	50.00	25.00
(65)	Cy Young/Standing (Full name on front.)	1,500	600.00	300.00
(66)	Cy Young/Standing (Last name on front.)	1,500	600.00	300.00
(67)	Cy Young/Portrait	1,650	660.00	330.00

1927 W560

Although assigned a "W" number by the American Card Catalog, this is not a "strip card" issue in the same sense as most other "W" sets, although W560 cards are frequently found in uncut sheets of 16 cards. Cards measure a nominal 1-3/4" x 2-3/4" and are designed like a deck of playing cards, with the pictures on the various suits. The set includes aviators and other athletes in addition to baseball players. Cards can be found with designs printed in red or black, or less commonly with both and red and black on each card. Some players will also be found with different suit/value combinations.

		NM	EX	VG
	Complete Set, Sheets (64):	3,250	1,625	975.00
	Complete (Baseball) Set (49):	2,400	1,200	725.00
	Common Player:	25.00	12.50	7.50
(1)	Vic Aldridge	25.00	12.50	7.50
(2)	Lester Bell	25.00	12.50	7.50
(3)	Larry Benton	25.00	12.50	7.50
(4)	Max Bishop	25.00	12.50	7.50
(5)	Del Bissonette	25.00	12.50	7.50
(6)	Jim Bottomley	45.00	22.50	13.50
(7)	Guy Bush	25.00	12.50	7.50
(8)	W. Clark	25.00	12.50	7.50
(9)	Andy Cohen	25.00	12.50	7.50
(10)	Mickey Cochrane	45.00	22.50	13.50
(11)	Hugh Critz	25.00	12.50	7.50
(12)	Kiki Cuyler	45.00	22.50	13.50
(13)	Taylor Douthit	25.00	12.50	7.50
(14)	Fred Fitzsimmons	25.00	12.50	7.50
(15)	Jim Foxx	110.00	55.00	35.00
(16)	Lou Gehrig	325.00	160.00	100.00
(17)	Goose Goslin	45.00	22.50	13.50
(18)	Sam Gray	25.00	12.50	7.50
(19)	Lefty Grove	60.00	30.00	18.00
(20)	Jesse Haines	45.00	22.50	13.50
(21)	Babe Herman	30.00	15.00	9.00
(22)	Roger Hornsby (Rogers)	60.00	30.00	18.00
(23)	Waite Hoyt	45.00	22.50	13.50
(24)	Henry Johnson	25.00	12.50	7.50
(25)	Walter Johnson	150.00	75.00	45.00
(26)	Willie Kamm	25.00	12.50	7.50
(27)	Remy Kremer	25.00	12.50	7.50
(28)	Fred Lindstrom	45.00	22.50	13.50
(29)	Fred Maguire	25.00	12.50	7.50
(30)	Fred Marberry	25.00	12.50	7.50
(31)	Johnny Mostil	25.00	12.50	7.50
(32)	Buddy Myer	25.00	12.50	7.50
(33)	Herb Pennock	45.00	22.50	13.50
(34)	George Pipgras	25.00	12.50	7.50
(35)	Flint Rhem	25.00	12.50	7.50
(36)	Babe Ruth	400.00	200.00	120.00
(37)	Luke Sewell	25.00	12.50	7.50
(38)	Willie Sherdel	25.00	12.50	7.50
(39)	Al Simmons	45.00	22.50	13.50
(40)	Thomas Thevenow	25.00	12.50	7.50
(41)	Fresco Thompson	25.00	12.50	7.50
(42)	George Uhle	25.00	12.50	7.50
(43)	Dazzy Vance	45.00	22.50	13.50
(44)	Rube Walberg	25.00	12.50	7.50
(45)	Lloyd Waner	45.00	22.50	13.50
(46)	Paul Waner	45.00	22.50	13.50
(47)	Fred "Cy" Williams	25.00	12.50	7.50
(48)	Jim Wilson	25.00	12.50	7.50
(49)	Glen Wright (Glenn)	25.00	12.50	7.50

1928 W565

Similar in concept to W560, the 50 cards comprising this set were printed on two 7" x 10-1/2" sheets of cheap cardboard, one in black-and-white and one in red-and-white, each with navy blue backs. Most of the cards in the issue are of movie stars, with a few boxers, ballplayers and other notables included. While most of the cards depict the person in the center of a playing card format, it is interesting to note that a full deck of cards cannot be made up by cutting the sheets. Individual cards are 1-1/4" x 2-1/8". Only the baseball players are listed here.

		NM	EX	VG
	Complete Set, Sheets (50):	450.00	225.00	135.00
	Common Player:	75.00	37.50	22.50
(1)	Lou Gehrig	300.00	150.00	90.00
(2)	Harry Heilmann	75.00	37.50	22.50
(3)	Tony Lazzeri	75.00	37.50	22.50
(4)	Al Simmons	75.00	37.50	22.50

1947 W571

(See 1947 Bond Bread.)

1923 W572

These cards, designated as W572 by the American Card Catalog, measure 1-5/16" x 2-1/2" and are blank-backed. Fronts feature black-and-white or sepia player photos. The set is closely related to the popular E120 American Caramel set issued in 1922 and, with the exception of Ty Cobb, it uses the same photos. The cards were originally issued as strips of 10, with baseball players and boxers often mixed. They are found on either a white, slick stock or a dark, coarser cardboard. The player's name on the front of the cards appears in script. All cards have on front a copyright symbol and one of several alphabetical combinations indicating the source of the photo. The baseball players from the set are checklisted here in alphabetical order.

		NM	EX	VG
	Complete (Baseball) Set (121):	12,500	6,250	3,750
	Common Player:	50.00	25.00	15.00
(1)	Eddie Ainsmith	50.00	25.00	15.00
(2)	Vic Aldridge	50.00	25.00	15.00
(3)	Grover Alexander	250.00	125.00	75.00
(4)	Dave Bancroft	150.00	75.00	45.00
(5)	Walt Barbare	50.00	25.00	15.00
(6)	Jess Barnes	50.00	25.00	15.00
(7)	John Bassler	50.00	25.00	15.00
(8)	Lu Blue	50.00	25.00	15.00
(9)	Norman Boeckel	50.00	25.00	15.00
(10)	George Burns	50.00	25.00	15.00
(11)	Joe Bush	50.00	25.00	15.00
(12)	Leon Cadore	50.00	25.00	15.00
(13)	Virgil Cheevers (Cheeves)	50.00	25.00	15.00
(14)	Ty Cobb	1,350	675.00	400.00
(15)	Eddie Collins	150.00	75.00	45.00
(16)	John Collins	50.00	25.00	15.00
(17)	Wilbur Cooper	50.00	25.00	15.00
(18)	Stanley Coveleski	150.00	75.00	45.00
(19)	Walton Cruise	50.00	25.00	15.00
(20)	Dave Danforth	50.00	25.00	15.00
(21)	Jake Daubert	50.00	25.00	15.00
(22)	Hank DeBerry	50.00	25.00	15.00
(23)	Lou DeVormer	50.00	25.00	15.00
(24)	Bill Doak	50.00	25.00	15.00
(25)	Pete Donohue	50.00	25.00	15.00
(26)	Pat Duncan	50.00	25.00	15.00
(27)	Jimmy Dykes	50.00	25.00	15.00
(28)	Urban Faber	150.00	75.00	45.00
(29)	Bib Falk (Bibb)	50.00	25.00	15.00
(30)	Frank Frisch	150.00	75.00	45.00
(31)	C. Galloway	50.00	25.00	15.00
(32)	Ed Gharrity	50.00	25.00	15.00
(33)	Chas. Glazner	50.00	25.00	15.00
(34)	Hank Gowdy	50.00	25.00	15.00
(35)	Tom Griffith	50.00	25.00	15.00
(36)	Burleigh Grimes	150.00	75.00	45.00
(37)	Ray Grimes	50.00	25.00	15.00
(38)	Heinie Groh	50.00	25.00	15.00
(39)	Joe Harris	50.00	25.00	15.00
(40)	Stanley Harris	150.00	75.00	45.00
(41)	Joe Hauser	50.00	25.00	15.00
(42)	Harry Heilmann	150.00	75.00	45.00
(43)	Walter Henline	50.00	25.00	15.00
(44)	Chas. Hollocher	50.00	25.00	15.00
(45)	Harry Hooper	150.00	75.00	45.00
(46)	Rogers Hornsby	150.00	75.00	45.00
(47)	Waite Hoyt	150.00	75.00	45.00
(48)	Wilbur Hubbell	50.00	25.00	15.00
(49)	Wm. Jacobson	50.00	25.00	15.00
(50)	Chas. Jamieson	50.00	25.00	15.00
(51)	S. Johnson	50.00	25.00	15.00
(52)	Walter Johnson	500.00	250.00	150.00
(53)	Jimmy Johnston	50.00	25.00	15.00
(54)	Joe Judge	50.00	25.00	15.00
(55)	Geo. Kelly	150.00	75.00	45.00
(56)	Lee King	50.00	25.00	15.00
(57)	Larry Kopff (Kopf)	50.00	25.00	15.00
(58)	Geo. Leverette	50.00	25.00	15.00
(59)	Al Mamaux	50.00	25.00	15.00
(60)	"Rabbit" Maranville	150.00	75.00	45.00
(61)	"Rube" Marquard	150.00	75.00	45.00
(62)	Martin McManus	50.00	25.00	15.00
(63)	Lee Meadows	50.00	25.00	15.00
(64)	Mike Menosky	50.00	25.00	15.00
(65)	Bob Meusel	50.00	25.00	15.00
(66)	Emil Meusel	50.00	25.00	15.00
(67)	Geo. Mogridge	50.00	25.00	15.00
(68)	John Morrison	50.00	25.00	15.00
(69)	Johnny Mostil	50.00	25.00	15.00
(70)	Roliene Naylor	50.00	25.00	15.00
(71)	Art Nehf	50.00	25.00	15.00
(72)	Joe Oeschger	50.00	25.00	15.00
(73)	Bob O'Farrell	50.00	25.00	15.00
(74)	Steve O'Neill	50.00	25.00	15.00
(75)	Frank Parkinson	50.00	25.00	15.00
(76)	Ralph Perkins	50.00	25.00	15.00
(77)	H. Pillette	50.00	25.00	15.00
(78)	Ralph Pinelli	50.00	25.00	15.00
(79)	Wallie Pipp (Wally)	60.00	30.00	18.00
(80)	Ray Powell	50.00	25.00	15.00
(81)	Jack Quinn	50.00	25.00	15.00
(82)	Goldie Rapp	50.00	25.00	15.00
(83)	Walter Reuther (Ruether)	50.00	25.00	15.00
(84)	Sam Rice	150.00	75.00	45.00
(85)	Emory Rigney	50.00	25.00	15.00
(86)	Eppa Rixey	150.00	75.00	45.00
(87)	Ed Rommel	50.00	25.00	15.00
(88)	Eddie Roush	150.00	75.00	45.00
(89)	Babe Ruth	3,500	1,750	1,000
(90)	Ray Schalk	150.00	75.00	45.00
(91)	Wallie Schang (Wally)	50.00	25.00	15.00
(92)	Walter Schmidt	50.00	25.00	15.00
(93)	Joe Schultz	50.00	25.00	15.00
(94)	Hank Severeid	50.00	25.00	15.00
(95)	Joe Sewell	150.00	75.00	45.00
(96)	Bob Shawkey	50.00	25.00	15.00
(97)	Earl Sheely	50.00	25.00	15.00
(98)	Will Sherdel	50.00	25.00	15.00
(99)	Urban Shocker	50.00	25.00	15.00
(100)	George Sisler	150.00	75.00	45.00
(101)	Earl Smith	50.00	25.00	15.00
(102)	Elmer Smith	50.00	25.00	15.00
(103)	Jack Smith	50.00	25.00	15.00
(104)	Bill Southworth	50.00	25.00	15.00
(105)	Tris Speaker	150.00	75.00	45.00
(106)	Arnold Statz	50.00	25.00	15.00
(107)	Milton Stock	50.00	25.00	15.00
(108)	Jim Tierney	50.00	25.00	15.00
(109)	Harold Traynor	150.00	75.00	45.00
(110)	Geo. Uhle	50.00	25.00	15.00
(111)	Bob Veach	50.00	25.00	15.00
(112)	Clarence Walker	50.00	25.00	15.00
(113)	Curtis Walker	50.00	25.00	15.00
(114)	Bill Wambsganss	50.00	25.00	15.00
(115)	Aaron Ward	50.00	25.00	15.00
(116)	Zach Wheat	150.00	75.00	45.00
(117)	Fred Williams	50.00	25.00	15.00

(118)	Ken Williams	50.00	25.00	15.00
(119)	Ivy Wingo	50.00	25.00	15.00
(120)	Joe Wood	75.00	37.50	22.50
(121)	J.T. Zachary	50.00	25.00	15.00

1922 W573

DAVE (BEAUTY) BANCROFT
SHORT STOP, NEW YORK NATIONALS

These cards, identified as W573 in the American Card Catalog, are blank-backed, black-and-white versions of the popular E120 American Caramel set. These "strip cards," were sold in strips of 10 for a penny. The cards measure about 2-1/16" x 3-3/8", but allowances in width must be made because the cards were hand-cut from a horizontal strip. Some cards have been found with the advertising of various firms on back.

		NM	EX	VG
Complete Set (240):		22,500	11,250	6,750
Common Player:		75.00	37.50	22.50
(1)	Charles (Babe) Adams	75.00	37.50	22.50
(2)	Eddie Ainsmith	75.00	37.50	22.50
(3)	Vic Aldridge	75.00	37.50	22.50
(4)	Grover C. Alexander	300.00	150.00	90.00
(5)	Jim Bagby	75.00	37.50	22.50
(6)	Frank (Home Run) Baker	200.00	100.00	60.00
(7)	Dave (Beauty) Bancroft	200.00	100.00	60.00
(8)	Walt Barbare	75.00	37.50	22.50
(9)	Turnor Barbor	75.00	37.50	22.50
(10)	Jess Barnes	75.00	37.50	22.50
(11)	Clyde Barnhart	75.00	37.50	22.50
(12)	John Bassler	75.00	37.50	22.50
(13)	Will Bayne	75.00	37.50	22.50
(14)	Walter (Huck) Betts	75.00	37.50	22.50
(15)	Carson Bigbee	75.00	37.50	22.50
(16)	Lu Blue	75.00	37.50	22.50
(17)	Norman Boeckel	75.00	37.50	22.50
(18)	Sammy Bohne	75.00	37.50	22.50
(19)	George Burns	75.00	37.50	22.50
(20)	George Burns	75.00	37.50	22.50
(21)	"Bullet Joe" Bush	75.00	37.50	22.50
(22)	Leon Cadore	75.00	37.50	22.50
(23)	Marty Callaghan	75.00	37.50	22.50
(24)	Frank Calloway (Callaway)	75.00	37.50	22.50
(25)	Max Carey	200.00	100.00	60.00
(26)	Jimmy Caveney	75.00	37.50	22.50
(27)	Virgil Cheeves	75.00	37.50	22.50
(28)	Vern Clemons	75.00	37.50	22.50
(29)	Ty Cob (Cobb)	1,350	675.00	400.00
(30)	Bert Cole	75.00	37.50	22.50
(31)	Eddie Collins	200.00	100.00	60.00
(32)	John (Shano) Collins	75.00	37.50	22.50
(33)	T.P. (Pat) Collins	75.00	37.50	22.50
(34)	Wilbur Cooper	75.00	37.50	22.50
(35)	Harry Courtney	75.00	37.50	22.50
(36)	Stanley Coveleskie (Coveleski)	200.00	100.00	60.00
(37)	Elmer Cox	75.00	37.50	22.50
(38)	Sam Crane	75.00	37.50	22.50
(39)	Walton Cruise	75.00	37.50	22.50
(40)	Bill Cunningham	75.00	37.50	22.50
(41)	George Cutshaw	75.00	37.50	22.50
(42)	Dave Danforth	75.00	37.50	22.50
(43)	Jake Daubert	75.00	37.50	22.50
(44)	George Dauss	75.00	37.50	22.50
(45)	Frank (Dixie) Davis	75.00	37.50	22.50
(46)	Hank DeBerry	75.00	37.50	22.50
(47)	Albert Devormer (Lou DeVormer)	75.00	37.50	22.50
(48)	Bill Doak	75.00	37.50	22.50
(49)	Pete Donohue	75.00	37.50	22.50
(50)	"Shufflin" Phil Douglas	75.00	37.50	22.50
(51)	Joe Dugan	75.00	37.50	22.50
(52)	Louis (Pat) Duncan	75.00	37.50	22.50
(53)	Jimmy Dykes	75.00	37.50	22.50
(54)	Howard Ehmke	75.00	37.50	22.50
(55)	Frank Ellerbe	75.00	37.50	22.50
(56)	Urban (Red) Faber	200.00	100.00	60.00
(57)	Bib Falk (Bibb)	75.00	37.50	22.50
(58)	Dana Fillingim	75.00	37.50	22.50
(59)	Max Flack	75.00	37.50	22.50
(60)	Ira Flagstead	75.00	37.50	22.50
(61)	Art Fletcher	75.00	37.50	22.50
(62)	Horace Ford	75.00	37.50	22.50
(63)	Jack Fournier	75.00	37.50	22.50
(64)	Frank Frisch	200.00	100.00	60.00
(65)	Ollie Fuhrman	75.00	37.50	22.50
(66)	Clarance Galloway	75.00	37.50	22.50
(67)	Larry Gardner	75.00	37.50	22.50
(68)	Walter Gerber	75.00	37.50	22.50
(69)	Ed Gharrity	75.00	37.50	22.50
(70)	John Gillespie	75.00	37.50	22.50
(71)	Chas. (Whitey) Glazner	75.00	37.50	22.50
(72)	Johnny Gooch	75.00	37.50	22.50
(73)	Leon Goslin	200.00	100.00	60.00
(74)	Hank Gowdy	75.00	37.50	22.50
(75)	John Graney	75.00	37.50	22.50
(76)	Tom Griffith	75.00	37.50	22.50
(77)	Burleigh Grimes	200.00	100.00	60.00
(78)	Oscar Ray Grimes	75.00	37.50	22.50
(79)	Charlie Grimm	75.00	37.50	22.50
(80)	Heinie Groh	75.00	37.50	22.50
(81)	Jesse Haines	200.00	100.00	60.00
(82)	Earl Hamilton	75.00	37.50	22.50
(83)	Gene (Bubbles) Hargrave	75.00	37.50	22.50
(84)	Bryan Harris (Harriss)	75.00	37.50	22.50
(85)	Joe Harris	75.00	37.50	22.50
(86)	Stanley Harris	200.00	100.00	60.00
(87)	Chas. (Dowdy) Hartnett	200.00	100.00	60.00
(88)	Bob Hasty	75.00	37.50	22.50
(89)	Joe Hauser	100.00	50.00	30.00
(90)	Clif Heathcote	75.00	37.50	22.50
(91)	Harry Heilmann	200.00	100.00	60.00
(92)	Walter (Butch) Henline	75.00	37.50	22.50
(93)	Clarence (Shovel) Hodge	75.00	37.50	22.50
(94)	Walter Holke	75.00	37.50	22.50
(95)	Charles Hollocher	75.00	37.50	22.50
(96)	Harry Hooper	200.00	100.00	60.00
(97)	Rogers Hornsby	250.00	125.00	75.00
(98)	Waite Hoyt	200.00	100.00	60.00
(99)	Wilbur Hubbell (Wilbert)	75.00	37.50	22.50
(100)	Bernard (Bud) Hungling	75.00	37.50	22.50
(101)	Will Jacobson	75.00	37.50	22.50
(102)	Charlie Jamieson	75.00	37.50	22.50
(103)	Ernie Johnson	75.00	37.50	22.50
(104)	Sylvester Johnson	75.00	37.50	22.50
(105)	Walter Johnson	750.00	375.00	225.00
(106)	Jimmy Johnston	75.00	37.50	22.50
(107)	W.R. (Doc) Johnston	75.00	37.50	22.50
(108)	"Deacon" Sam Jones	75.00	37.50	22.50
(109)	Bob Jones	75.00	37.50	22.50
(110)	Percy Jones	75.00	37.50	22.50
(111)	Joe Judge	75.00	37.50	22.50
(112)	Ben Karr	75.00	37.50	22.50
(113)	Johnny Kelleher	75.00	37.50	22.50
(114)	George Kelly	200.00	100.00	60.00
(115)	Lee King	75.00	37.50	22.50
(116)	Wm (Larry) Kopff (Kopf)	75.00	37.50	22.50
(117)	Marty Krug	75.00	37.50	22.50
(118)	Johnny Lavan	75.00	37.50	22.50
(119)	Nemo Leibold	75.00	37.50	22.50
(120)	Roy Leslie	75.00	37.50	22.50
(121)	George Leverette (Leverett)	75.00	37.50	22.50
(122)	Adolfo Luque	75.00	37.00	22.00
(123)	Walter Mails	75.00	37.50	22.50
(124)	Al Mamaux	75.00	37.50	22.50
(125)	"Rabbit" Maranville	200.00	100.00	60.00
(126)	Cliff Markle	75.00	37.50	22.50
(127)	Richard (Rube) Marquard	200.00	100.00	60.00
(128)	Carl Mays	75.00	37.50	22.50
(129)	Hervey McClellan (Harvey)	75.00	37.50	22.50
(130)	Austin McHenry	75.00	37.50	22.50
(131)	"Stuffy" McInnis	75.00	37.50	22.50
(132)	Martin McManus	75.00	37.50	22.50
(133)	Mike McNally	75.00	37.50	22.50
(134)	Hugh McQuillan	75.00	37.50	22.50
(135)	Lee Meadows	75.00	37.50	22.50
(136)	Mike Menosky	75.00	37.50	22.50
(137)	Bob (Dutch) Meusel	75.00	37.50	22.50
(138)	Emil (Irish) Meusel	75.00	37.50	22.50
(139)	Clyde Milan	75.00	37.50	22.50
(140)	Edmund (Bing) Miller	75.00	37.50	22.50
(141)	Elmer Miller	75.00	37.50	22.50
(142)	Lawrence (Hack) Miller	75.00	37.50	22.50
(143)	Clarence Mitchell	75.00	37.50	22.50
(144)	George Mogridge	75.00	37.50	22.50
(145)	Roy Moore	75.00	37.50	22.50
(146)	John L. Mokan	75.00	37.50	22.50
(147)	John Morrison	75.00	37.50	22.50
(148)	Johnny Mostil	75.00	37.50	22.50
(149)	Elmer Myers	75.00	37.50	22.50
(150)	Hy Myers	75.00	37.50	22.50
(151)	Roliene Naylor (Roleine)	75.00	37.50	22.50
(152)	Earl "Greasy" Neale	75.00	37.50	22.50
(153)	Art Nehf	75.00	37.50	22.50
(154)	Les Nunamaker	75.00	37.50	22.50
(155)	Joe Oeschger	75.00	37.50	22.50
(156)	Bob O'Farrell	75.00	37.50	22.50
(157)	Ivan Olson	75.00	37.50	22.50
(158)	George O'Neil	75.00	37.50	22.50
(159)	Steve O'Neill	75.00	37.50	22.50
(160)	Frank Parkinson	75.00	37.50	22.50
(161)	Roger Peckinpaugh	75.00	37.50	22.50
(162)	Herb Pennock	200.00	100.00	60.00
(163)	Ralph (Cy) Perkins	75.00	37.50	22.50
(164)	Will Pertica	75.00	37.50	22.50
(165)	Jack Peters	75.00	37.50	22.50
(166)	Tom Phillips	75.00	37.50	22.50
(167)	Val Picinich	75.00	37.50	22.50
(168)	Herman Pillette	75.00	37.50	22.50
(169)	Ralph Pinelli	75.00	37.50	22.50
(170)	Wallie Pipp	75.00	37.50	22.50
(171)	Clark Pittenger (Clarke)	75.00	37.50	22.50
(172)	Raymond Powell	75.00	37.50	22.50
(173)	Derrill Pratt	75.00	37.50	22.50
(174)	Jack Quinn	75.00	37.50	22.50
(175)	Joe (Goldie) Rapp	75.00	37.50	22.50
(176)	John Rawlings	75.00	37.50	22.50
(177)	Walter (Dutch) Reuther (Ruether)	75.00	37.50	22.50
(178)	Sam Rice	200.00	100.00	60.00
(179)	Emory Rigney	75.00	37.50	22.50
(180)	Jimmy Ring	75.00	37.50	22.50
(181)	Eppa Rixey	200.00	100.00	60.00
(182)	Charles Robertson	75.00	37.50	22.50
(183)	Ed Rommel	75.00	37.50	22.50
(184)	Eddie Roush	200.00	100.00	60.00
(185)	Harold (Muddy) Ruel (Herold)	75.00	37.50	22.50
(186)	Babe Ruth	2,750	1,375	825.00
(187)	Ray Schalk	200.00	100.00	60.00
(188)	Wallie Schang	75.00	37.50	22.50
(189)	Ray Schmandt	75.00	37.50	22.50
(190)	Walter Schmidt	75.00	37.50	22.50
(191)	Joe Schultz	75.00	37.50	22.50
(192)	Everett Scott	75.00	37.50	22.50
(193)	Henry Severeid	75.00	37.50	22.50
(194)	Joe Sewell	200.00	100.00	60.00
(195)	Howard Shanks	75.00	37.50	22.50
(196)	Bob Shawkey	75.00	37.50	22.50
(197)	Earl Sheely	75.00	37.50	22.50
(198)	Will Sherdel	75.00	37.50	22.50
(199)	Ralph Shinners	75.00	37.50	22.50
(200)	Urban Shocker	75.00	37.50	22.50
(201)	Charles (Chick) Shorten	75.00	37.50	22.50
(202)	George Sisler	200.00	100.00	60.00
(203)	Earl Smith	75.00	37.50	22.50
(204)	Earl Smith	75.00	37.50	22.50
(205)	Elmer Smith	75.00	37.50	22.50
(206)	Jack Smith	75.00	37.50	22.50
(207)	Sherrod Smith	75.00	37.50	22.50
(208)	Colonel Snover	75.00	37.50	22.50
(209)	Frank Snyder	75.00	37.50	22.50
(210)	Al Sothoron	75.00	37.50	22.50
(211)	Bill Southworth	75.00	37.50	22.50
(212)	Tris Speaker	250.00	125.00	75.00
(213)	Arnold Statz	75.00	37.50	22.50
(214)	Milton Stock	75.00	37.50	22.50
(215)	Amos Strunk	75.00	37.50	22.50
(216)	Jim Tierney	75.00	37.50	22.50
(217)	John Tobin	75.00	37.50	22.50
(218)	Fred Toney	75.00	37.50	22.50
(219)	George Toporcer	75.00	37.50	22.50
(220)	Harold (Pie) Traynor	200.00	100.00	60.00
(221)	George Uhle	75.00	37.50	22.50
(222)	Elam Vangilder	75.00	37.50	22.50
(223)	Bob Veach	75.00	37.50	22.50
(224)	Clarence (Tillie) Walker	75.00	37.50	22.50
(225)	Curtis Walker	75.00	37.50	22.50
(226)	Al Walters	75.00	37.50	22.50
(227)	Bill Wambsganss	75.00	37.50	22.50
(228)	Aaron Ward	75.00	37.50	22.50
(229)	John Watson	75.00	37.50	22.50
(230)	Frank Welch	75.00	37.50	22.50
(231)	Zach Wheat	200.00	100.00	60.00
(232)	Fred (Cy) Williams	75.00	37.50	22.50
(233)	Kenneth Williams	75.00	37.50	22.50
(234)	Ivy Wingo	75.00	37.50	22.50
(235)	Joe Wood	75.00	37.50	22.50
(236)	Lawrence Woodall	75.00	37.50	22.50
(237)	Russell Wrightstone	75.00	37.50	22.50
(238)	Everett Yaryan	75.00	37.50	22.50
(239)	Ross Young (Youngs)	200.00	100.00	60.00
(240)	J.T. Zachary	75.00	37.50	22.50

1933 W574

Cards in this set measure an unusual 2-1/4" x 2-7/8". They are unnumbered and are listed here in alphabetical order. The black-and-white photos have a facsimile autograph and team name at bottom.

		NM	EX	VG
Complete Set (29):		3,000	1,500	900.00
Common Player:		60.00	30.00	18.00
(1)	Dale Alexander	60.00	30.00	18.00
(2)	Ivy Paul Andrews	60.00	30.00	18.00
(3)	Luke Appling	250.00	100.00	50.00
(4)	Earl Averill	250.00	100.00	50.00
(5)	George Blaeholder	60.00	30.00	18.00
(6)	Irving Burns	60.00	30.00	18.00
(7)	Pat Caraway	60.00	30.00	18.00
(8)	Chalmer Cissell	60.00	30.00	18.00
(9)	Harry Davis	60.00	30.00	18.00
(10)	Jimmy Dykes	60.00	30.00	18.00
(11)	George Earnshaw	60.00	30.00	18.00
(12)	Urban Faber	250.00	100.00	50.00
(13)	Lewis Fonseca	60.00	30.00	18.00
(14)	Jimmy Foxx	450.00	180.00	90.00
(15)	Victor Frasier	60.00	30.00	18.00
(16)	Robert Grove	350.00	140.00	70.00
(17)	Frank Grube	60.00	30.00	18.00
(18)	Irving Hadley	60.00	30.00	18.00
(19)	Willie Kamm	60.00	30.00	18.00
(20)	Bill Killefer	60.00	30.00	18.00
(21)	Ralph Kress	60.00	30.00	18.00
(22)	Fred Marberry	60.00	30.00	18.00
(23)	Roger Peckinpaugh	60.00	30.00	18.00
(24)	Frank Reiber	60.00	30.00	18.00
(25)	Carl Reynolds	60.00	30.00	18.00
(26)	Al Simmons	250.00	100.00	50.00
(27)	Joe Vosmik	60.00	30.00	18.00
(28)	Gerald Walker	60.00	30.00	18.00
(29)	Whitlow Wyatt	60.00	30.00	18.00

1921-1922 W575-1

The known variations indicate this set was issued over a period of time, likely encompassing more than one calendar year or baseball season. Designated as W575 in the American Card Catalog, these "strip cards" are essentially blank-backed versions of the contemporary American Caramel E121 set, though the checklists do not exactly correspond. Ideally cut cards in W575-1 measure 2" x 3-1/4" and are printed in black-and-white. It is almost impossible to distinguish W575-1 cards from the blank-backed Koester's Bread Yankees and Giants cards issued to commemorate the 1921 "Subway" World Series. This checklist may not be complete. Gaps have been left among the assigned numbers to accommodate future additions.

		NM	EX	VG
Common Player:		40.00	20.00	12.00
(1)	Chas. "Babe" Adams	40.00	20.00	12.00
(2)	G.C. Alexander	350.00	175.00	100.00
(3)	Grover Alexander	350.00	175.00	100.00
(4)	Jim Bagby	40.00	20.00	12.00
(5)	J. Franklin Baker	175.00	85.00	50.00
(6)	Frank Baker	175.00	85.00	50.00
(7)	Dave Bancroft/Btg	175.00	85.00	50.00
(8)	Dave Bancroft/Fldg	175.00	85.00	50.00
(9)	Turner Barber	40.00	20.00	12.00
(10)	Jesse Barnes	40.00	20.00	12.00
(11)	Howard Berry	40.00	20.00	12.00
(12)	L. Bigbee (Should be C.)	40.00	20.00	12.00
(13)	Ping Bodie	40.00	20.00	12.00
(14)	"Ed" Brown	40.00	20.00	12.00
(15)	George Burns	40.00	20.00	12.00
(16)	Geo. J. Burns	40.00	20.00	12.00
(17)	"Bullet Joe" Bush	40.00	20.00	12.00
(18)	Owen Bush	40.00	20.00	12.00
(19)	Max Carey/Btg	175.00	85.00	50.00
(20)	Max Carey (Hands on hips.)	175.00	85.00	50.00
(21)	Ty Cobb	2,000	1,000	600.00
(22)	Eddie Collins	175.00	85.00	50.00
(23)	"Rip" Collins	40.00	20.00	12.00
(24)	Stanley Coveleskie (Coveleski)	175.00	85.00	50.00
(25)	Bill Cunningham	40.00	20.00	12.00
(26a)	Jake Daubert (1B.)	40.00	20.00	12.00
(26b)	Jake Daubert (1st B.)	40.00	20.00	12.00
(28)	George Dauss	40.00	20.00	12.00
(29)	Dixie Davis	40.00	20.00	12.00
(30)	Charles Deal (Dark uniform.)	40.00	20.00	12.00
(31)	Charles Deal (Light uniform.)	40.00	20.00	12.00
(32)	Lou DeVormer (Photo actually Emil "Irish" Meusel)	40.00	20.00	12.00
(33)	William Doak	40.00	20.00	12.00
(34)	Bill Donovan/Pitching	40.00	20.00	12.00
(35)	Bill Donovan/Portrait	40.00	20.00	12.00
(36)	Phil Douglas	40.00	20.00	12.00
(37a)	Johnny Evers (Mgr.)	175.00	85.00	50.00
(37b)	Johnny Evers (Manager)	175.00	85.00	50.00
(39)	Urban Faber (Dark uniform.)	175.00	85.00	50.00
(40)	Urban Faber (White uniform.)	175.00	85.00	50.00
(42)	Bib Falk (Bibb)	40.00	20.00	12.00
(43)	Alex Ferguson	40.00	20.00	12.00
(44)	Wm. Fewster	40.00	20.00	12.00
(45)	Ira Flagstead	40.00	20.00	12.00
(46)	Art Fletcher	40.00	20.00	12.00
(47)	Eddie Foster	40.00	20.00	12.00
(48)	Frank Frisch	175.00	85.00	50.00
(49)	W.L. Gardner	40.00	20.00	12.00
(50)	Alexander Gaston	40.00	20.00	12.00
(51)	E.P. Gharrity	40.00	20.00	12.00
(52)	Chas. "Whitey" Glazner	40.00	20.00	12.00
(53)	"Kid" Gleason	40.00	20.00	12.00
(54)	"Mike" Gonzalez	40.00	20.00	12.00
(55)	Hank Gowdy	40.00	20.00	12.00
(56a)	John Graney (Util. o.f.)	40.00	20.00	12.00
(56b)	John Graney (O.F.)	40.00	20.00	12.00
(57)	Tom Griffith	40.00	20.00	12.00
(58)	Chas. Grimm	40.00	20.00	12.00
(59a)	Heinie Groh (Cincinnati)	40.00	20.00	12.00
(59b)	Heinie Groh (New York)	40.00	20.00	12.00
(62)	Jess Haines	175.00	85.00	50.00
(63)	Harry Harper	40.00	20.00	12.00
(64)	"Chicken" Hawks	40.00	20.00	12.00
(65)	Harry Heilman (Heilmann) (Holding bat.)	175.00	85.00	50.00
(66)	Harry Heilman/Running (Heilmann)	175.00	85.00	50.00
(67)	John Henry	40.00	20.00	12.00
(68)	Clarence Hodge	40.00	20.00	12.00
(69)	Fred Hoffman	40.00	20.00	12.00
(70a)	Walter Holke/Portrait (1st B)	40.00	20.00	12.00
(70b)	Walter Holke/Portrait (1B)	40.00	20.00	12.00
(71)	Walter Holke/Throwing	40.00	20.00	12.00
(72a)	Charles Hollacher (Name incorrect.)	40.00	20.00	12.00
(72b)	Charles Hollocher (Name correct.)	40.00	20.00	12.00
(73)	Harry Hooper	175.00	85.00	50.00
(74a)	Rogers Hornsby (2nd B.)	250.00	125.00	75.00
(74b)	Rogers Hornsby (O.F.)	250.00	125.00	75.00
(75)	Waite Hoyt	175.00	85.00	50.00
(76)	Miller Huggins	175.00	85.00	50.00
(78)	Wm. C. Jacobson	40.00	20.00	12.00
(79)	Hugh Jennings	175.00	85.00	50.00
(80)	Walter Johnson (Arms at chest.)	500.00	250.00	150.00
(81)	Walter Johnson/Throwing	500.00	250.00	150.00
(82)	James Johnston	40.00	20.00	12.00
(84)	Joe Judge/Btg	40.00	20.00	12.00
(85)	Joe Judge/Fldg	40.00	20.00	12.00
(86a)	George Kelly (1st B.)	175.00	85.00	50.00
(86b)	George Kelly (1B.)	175.00	85.00	50.00
(88)	Dick Kerr	40.00	20.00	12.00
(89)	P.J. Kilduff	40.00	20.00	12.00
(90a)	Bill Killefer	40.00	20.00	12.00
(90b)	Bill Killifer (Killefer)	40.00	20.00	12.00
(92)	John Lavan	40.00	20.00	12.00
(93)	"Nemo" Leibold	40.00	20.00	12.00
(94)	Duffy Lewis	40.00	20.00	12.00
(95)	Walter Mails	40.00	20.00	12.00
(96)	Al. Mamaux	40.00	20.00	12.00
(97)	"Rabbit" Maranville	175.00	85.00	50.00
(98)	Elwood Martin	40.00	20.00	12.00
(99a)	Carl Mays (Name correct.)	40.00	20.00	12.00
(99b)	Carl May (Mays)	40.00	20.00	12.00
(100)	John McGraw (Mgr.)	175.00	85.00	50.00
(101)	John McGraw (Manager)	175.00	85.00	50.00
(102)	Jack McInnis	40.00	20.00	12.00
(103a)	M.J. McNally (3B.)	40.00	20.00	12.00
(103b)	M.J. McNally (3rd B.)	40.00	20.00	12.00
(104)	Lee Meadows	40.00	20.00	12.00
(105)	Emil Meusel	40.00	20.00	12.00
(106)	R. Meusel	40.00	20.00	12.00
(107)	Clyde Milan	40.00	20.00	12.00
(108)	Elmer Miller	40.00	20.00	12.00
(109)	Otto Miller	40.00	20.00	12.00
(110)	John Mitchell (S.S.)	40.00	20.00	12.00
(111)	John Mitchell (3rd B.)	40.00	20.00	12.00
(112)	Guy Morton	40.00	20.00	12.00
(113)	Johnny Mostil	40.00	20.00	12.00
(114)	Eddie Mulligan	40.00	20.00	12.00
(115)	Eddie Murphy	40.00	20.00	12.00
(116a)	"Hy" Myers (C.F./O.F.)	40.00	20.00	12.00
(116b)	Hy Myers (O.F.)	40.00	20.00	12.00
(117a)	A.E. Neale	75.00	37.50	22.50
(117b)	Earl Neale	75.00	37.00	22.00
(119)	Arthur Nehf	40.00	20.00	12.00
(120)	Joe Oeschger	40.00	20.00	12.00
(122)	Chas. O'Leary	40.00	20.00	12.00
(123)	Steve O'Neill	40.00	20.00	12.00
(124a)	Roger Peckinbaugh (Name incorrect.)	40.00	20.00	12.00
(124b)	Roger Peckinpaugh (Name correct.)	40.00	20.00	12.00
(125a)	Jeff Pfeffer (Brooklyn)	40.00	20.00	12.00
(125b)	Jeff Pfeffer (St. Louis)	40.00	20.00	12.00
(127)	William Piercy	40.00	20.00	12.00
(128)	Walter Pipp	40.00	20.00	12.00
(129)	D.B. Pratt	40.00	20.00	12.00
(130)	Jack Quinn	40.00	20.00	12.00
(131a)	John Rawlings (2nd B.)	40.00	20.00	12.00
(131b)	John Rawlings (2B.)	40.00	20.00	12.00
(133a)	E.S. Rice (Name incorrect.)	175.00	85.00	50.00
(133b)	E.C. Rice (Name correct.)	175.00	85.00	50.00
(134a)	Eppa Rixey	175.00	85.00	50.00
(134b)	Eppa Rixey, Jr.	175.00	85.00	50.00
(136)	Wilbert Robinson	175.00	85.00	50.00
(137)	Tom Rogers	40.00	20.00	12.00
(139)	Ed Rounnel (Rommel)	40.00	20.00	12.00
(140)	Robert Roth	40.00	20.00	12.00
(142a)	Ed Roush (O.F.)	175.00	85.00	50.00
(142b)	Ed Roush (C.F.)	175.00	85.00	50.00
(144)	"Muddy" Ruel	40.00	20.00	12.00
(145)	Walter Ruether	40.00	20.00	12.00
(146a)	"Babe" Ruth (R.F.)	3,500	1,750	1,000
(146b)	Babe Ruth (L.F.)	3,500	1,750	1,000
(147)	"Babe" Ruth (W/man, bird.)	3,500	1,750	1,000
(148a)	Bill Ryan	40.00	20.00	12.00
(148b)	"Bill" Ryan	40.00	20.00	12.00
(149a)	"Slim" Sallee (Ball in hand.)	40.00	20.00	12.00
(149b)	"Slim" Sallee (No ball in hand.)	40.00	20.00	12.00
(151)	Ray Schalk/Bunting	175.00	85.00	50.00
(152)	Ray Schalk/Catching	175.00	85.00	50.00
(153a)	Walter Schang	40.00	20.00	12.00
(153b)	Wally Schang	40.00	20.00	12.00
(154a)	Fred Schupp (Name incorrect.)	40.00	20.00	12.00
(154b)	Ferd Schupp (Name correct.)	40.00	20.00	12.00
(155a)	Everett Scott (Boston)	40.00	20.00	12.00
(155b)	Everett Scott (New York)	40.00	20.00	12.00
(157)	Hank Severeid	40.00	20.00	12.00
(159)	Robert Shawkey	40.00	20.00	12.00
(160a)	"Pat" Shea	40.00	20.00	12.00
(160b)	Pat Shea	40.00	20.00	12.00
(161)	Earl Sheely	40.00	20.00	12.00
(163)	Urban Shocker	40.00	20.00	12.00
(165)	George Sisler/Btg	175.00	85.00	50.00
(166)	George Sisler/Throwing	175.00	85.00	50.00
(168)	Earl Smith	40.00	20.00	12.00
(169)	Elmer Smith	40.00	20.00	12.00
(170)	J. Carlisle Smith	40.00	20.00	12.00
(171)	Frank Snyder	40.00	20.00	12.00
(172)	Bill Southworth	40.00	20.00	12.00
(173a)	Tris Speaker (Large projection.)	250.00	125.00	75.00
(173b)	Tris Speaker (Small projection.)	250.00	125.00	75.00
(175a)	Charles Stengel/Btg	175.00	85.00	50.00
(175b)	Charles Stengel/Portrait	175.00	85.00	50.00
(177)	Milton Stock	40.00	20.00	12.00
(178a)	Amos Strunk (C.F.)	40.00	20.00	12.00
(178b)	Amos Strunk (O.F.)	40.00	20.00	12.00
(180a)	Zeb Terry (Dark uniform, 2nd B.)	40.00	20.00	12.00
(180b)	Zeb Terry (Dark uniform, 2B.)	40.00	20.00	12.00
(181)	Zeb Terry (White uniform.)	40.00	20.00	12.00
(182)	Chester Thomas	40.00	20.00	12.00
(183)	Fred Toney (Both feet on ground.)	40.00	20.00	12.00
(184)	Fred Toney (One foot in air.)	40.00	20.00	12.00
(185)	George Toporcer	40.00	20.00	12.00
(186)	George Tyler	40.00	20.00	12.00
(187)	Jim Vaughn (Plain uniform.)	40.00	20.00	12.00
(188)	Jim Vaughn (Striped uniform.)	40.00	20.00	12.00
(189)	Bob Veach (Arm raised.)	40.00	20.00	12.00
(190)	Bob Veach (Arms folded.)	40.00	20.00	12.00
(191a)	Oscar Vitt (3rd B.)	40.00	20.00	12.00
(191b)	Oscar Vitt (3B.)	40.00	20.00	12.00
(192)	Curtis Walker	40.00	20.00	12.00
(193)	W. Wambsganss	40.00	20.00	12.00
(194)	Carl Weilman	40.00	20.00	12.00
(195)	Zach Wheat	175.00	85.00	50.00
(196)	George Whitted	40.00	20.00	12.00
(197)	Fred Williams	40.00	20.00	12.00
(198)	Ivy B. Wingo	40.00	20.00	12.00
(199)	Lawton Witt	40.00	20.00	12.00
(200)	Joe Wood	100.00	50.00	30.00
(202)	Pep Young	40.00	20.00	12.00
(203)	Ross Young (Youngs)	175.00	85.00	50.00

1922 W575-2

The blank-back, black-and-white cards in this set measure a nominal 2-1/8" x 3-3/8". Because of the design of the cards the set is sometimes called the "autograph on shoulder" series. Some cards have the player's position and team added to the name inscription. The cards were produced by Kromo Gravue Photo Co., Detroit, Mich.

		NM	EX	VG
Complete Set (40):		10,000	5,000	3,000
Common Player:		75.00	37.50	22.50
(1)	Dave Bancroft	200.00	100.00	60.00
(2)	Johnnie Bassler	75.00	37.50	22.50
(3)	Joe Bush	75.00	37.50	22.50
(4)	Ty Cobb	2,000	1,000	600.00
(5)	Eddie Collins	200.00	100.00	60.00
(6)	Stan Coveleskie (Coveleski)	200.00	100.00	60.00
(7)	Jake Daubert	75.00	37.50	22.50
(8)	Joe Dugan	75.00	37.50	22.50
(9)	Red Faber	200.00	100.00	60.00
(10)	Frank Frisch	200.00	100.00	60.00
(11)	Walter H. Gerber	75.00	37.50	22.50
(12)	Harry Heilmann	200.00	100.00	60.00
(13)	Harry Hooper	200.00	100.00	60.00
(14)	Rogers Hornsby	300.00	150.00	90.00
(15)	Waite Hoyt	200.00	100.00	60.00
(16)	Joe Judge	75.00	37.50	22.50
(17)	Geo. Kelly	200.00	100.00	60.00
(18)	Rabbit Maranville	200.00	100.00	60.00
(19)	Rube Marquard	200.00	100.00	60.00
(20)	Guy Morton	75.00	37.50	22.50
(21)	Art Nehf	75.00	37.50	22.50
(22)	Derrill B. Pratt	75.00	37.50	22.50
(23)	Jimmy Ring	75.00	37.50	22.50
(24)	Eppa Rixey	200.00	100.00	60.00
(25)	Gene Robertson	75.00	37.50	22.50
(26)	Ed Rommell (Rommel)	75.00	37.50	22.50
(27)	Babe Ruth	3,500	1,750	1,050
(28)	Wally Schang	75.00	37.50	22.50
(29)	Everett Scott	75.00	37.50	22.50
(30)	Henry Severeid	75.00	37.50	22.50
(31)	Joe Sewell	200.00	100.00	60.00
(32)	Geo. Sisler	200.00	100.00	60.00
(33)	Tris Speaker	300.00	150.00	90.00
(34)	(Riggs) Stephenson	75.00	37.50	22.50
(35)	Zeb Terry	75.00	37.50	22.50
(36)	Bobbie Veach	75.00	37.50	22.50
(37)	Clarence Walker	75.00	37.50	22.50
(38)	Johnnie Walker	75.00	37.50	22.50
(39)	Zach Wheat	200.00	100.00	60.00
(40)	Kenneth Williams	75.00	37.50	22.50

1925-31 W590

Originally unlisted in the American Card Catalog, this strip-card set was given the number W590 in later editions. It is part of a larger set cataloged as W580 which includes movie stars, boxers and other athletes. These cards measure approximately 1-3/8" x 2-1/2". Fronts have black-and-white

player photos with a white border. In the bottom border is the player name, position, city and league or team nickname. Some cards can be found with a "Former" designation before the position. Several variations are known in team designations, indicating the set was probably reissued at least once between 1927-31. Backs are blank. Only the baseball players are listed here, in alphabetical order.

		NM	EX	VG
Common Player:		75.00	37.00	22.00
(1a)	Grover C. Alexander (Chicago N.L.)	300.00	150.00	90.00
(1b)	Grover C. Alexander (House of David)	600.00	300.00	180.00
(2a)	Dave Bancroft (Boston N.L.)	150.00	75.00	45.00
(2b)	Dave Bancroft (New York N.L.)	150.00	75.00	45.00
(3a)	Jess Barnes ("Pitcher" Boston N.L.)	75.00	37.50	22.50
(3b)	Jess Barnes ("Former Pitcher" Boston N.L.)	75.00	37.50	22.50
(4)	Ray Blades (St. Louis Cardinals)	75.00	37.50	22.50
(5)	Pictbred Bluege (Ossie)(Third Baseman)	75.00	37.50	22.50
(6a)	George Burns (New York N.L.)	75.00	37.50	22.50
(6b)	George Burns (Philadolphia N.L.)	75.00	37.50	22.50
(7a)	George Burns (Cleveland A.L. - 1st Baseman)	75.00	37.50	22.50
(7b)	George Burns (Cleveland A.L. - Former 1st Baseman)	75.00	37.50	22.50
(8)	Max Carey (Pittsburg N.L.)	150.00	75.00	45.00
(9a)	Caveney (Jimmy) (Short Stop)	75.00	37.50	22.50
(9b)	Caveney (Jimmy) (Former Short Stop)	75.00	37.50	22.50
(10)	"Ty" Cobb	1,300	650.00	390.00
(11a)	Eddie Collins (Chicago White Sox)	175.00	85.00	50.00
(11b)	Eddie Collins (Philadelphia A.L.)	175.00	85.00	50.00
(12)	George Dauss (Former Pitcher - Detroit)	75.00	37.50	22.50
(13)	"Red" Faber	150.00	75.00	45.00
(14a)	Frankie Frisch (New York N.L.)	175.00	85.00	50.00
(14b)	Frank Frisch (St. Louis N.L.)	175.00	85.00	50.00
(15)	Lou Gehrig (1st Baseman)	1,125	560.00	335.00
(17a)	Hank Gowdy (Catcher)	75.00	37.50	22.50
(17b)	Hank Gowdy (Former Catcher)	75.00	37.50	22.50
(18)	Sam Gray	75.00	37.50	22.50
(19)	Charley Grimm (Chicago N.L.)	75.00	37.50	22.50
(20)	"Buckey" Harris (Manager, Washington A.L.)	150.00	75.00	45.00
(21a)	Rogers Hornsby (St. Louis N.L.)	200.00	100.00	60.00
(21b)	Rogers Hornsby (Boston N.L.)	200.00	100.00	60.00
(22)	Travis Jackson (Short Stop, New York N.L.)	150.00	75.00	45.00
(23)	Walter Johnson (Pitcher)	600.00	300.00	180.00
(24a)	George Kelly (New York N.L.)	150.00	75.00	45.00
(24b)	George Kelly (Chicago N.L.)	150.00	75.00	45.00
(25)	Fred Lindstrom	150.00	75.00	45.00
(26a)	Rabbit Maranville (Chicago N.L.)	150.00	75.00	45.00
(26b)	Rabbit Maranville (Boston N.L.)	150.00	75.00	45.00
(27)	Bob Meusel/Fielder (New York A.L.)	75.00	37.50	22.50
(28)	Jack Quinn	75.00	37.50	22.50
(29)	Eppa Rixey (Cincinnati N.L.)	150.00	75.00	45.00
(31)	Eddie Rommel	75.00	37.50	22.50
(32)	"Babe" Ruth (King of the Bat)	2,250	1,125	675.00
(33)	Heinie Sand	75.00	37.50	22.50
(34)	Geo. Sissler (Sisler)	150.00	75.00	45.00
(35)	Earl Smith	75.00	37.50	22.50
(36a)	Tris Speaker (Cleveland A.L.)	200.00	100.00	60.00
(36b)	Tris Speaker (Manager, Newark)	200.00	100.00	60.00
(37)	Roy Spencer	75.00	37.50	22.50
(38)	Milton Stock	75.00	37.50	22.50
(39a)	Phil Todt (Boston A.L.)	75.00	37.50	22.50
(39b)	Phil Todt (Philadelphia A.L.)	75.00	37.50	22.50
(40)	Dazzy Vance	150.00	75.00	45.00
(41)	Zach Wheat (Brooklyn N.L.)	150.00	75.00	45.00
(42a)	Kenneth Williams (St. Louis A.L.)	75.00	37.50	22.50
(42b)	Kenneth Williams (Boston A.L.)	75.00	37.50	22.50
(43a)	Ross Young (Youngs) (Right Fielder)	150.00	75.00	45.00
(43b)	Ross Young (Youngs) (Former Right Fielder)	150.00	75.00	45.00

1921 W9316

As crude as many of the strip cards of the era were, this issue is the worst. In the same blank-back format and size (about 1-1/2" x 2-1/2") as many contemporary strip cards, the set features 10 of the players from W519/W521. The artwork on these cards is very crudely done, almost child-like. The most striking feature about the pictures is the ruby red lips on the players. Unlisted in the American Card Catalog, this set was given the designation W9316 in John Stirling's Sports Card Catalog.

		NM	EX	VG
Complete Set (10):		2,000	800.00	400,00
Common Player:		175.00	70.00	35.00
1	Bob Veach	175.00	70.00	35.00
2	Frank Baker	275.00	110.00	55.00
3	Wilbur (Wilbert) Robinson	275.00	110.00	55.00
4	Johnny Griffith	175.00	70.00	35.00
5	Jimmie Johnston	175.00	70.00	35.00
6	Wallie Schange (Wally Schang)	175.00	70.00	35.00
7	Leon Cadore	175.00	70.00	35.00
8	George Sisler	275.00	110.00	55.00
9	Ray Schalk	275.00	110.00	55.00
10	Jesse Barnes	175.00	70.00	35.00

1972 The Yawkey Red Sox

Morris Berg
BRTR Catcher
6'1",185 B:3-2-02
("Moe")
(Died 5-29-72)
Moe managed to build a 15 year career out of being a back-up catcher. The last 5 seasons of that career were in a BoSox uniform, 1935-1939. During that time he was in total of 148 games, with 107 hits, in 406 AB's, for .262.

HELP FIGHT CANCER IN CHILDREN
GIVE TO THE JIMMY FUND

Boston Red Sox players of the 1930s are featured in this collectors' issue. The issue date given is only a guess. The 2-1/2" x 3-1/2" cards have black-and-whie player photos with brown borders and black graphics. Backs are also in black-and-white with personal data, a career summary and a promotion for the Red Sox long-time charity, The Jimmy Fund. The unnumbered cards are listed here alphabetically.

		NM	EX	VG
Complete Set (45):		45.00	22.50	13.50
Common Player:		3.00	1.50	.90
(1)	Mel Almada	4.50	2.25	1.25
(2)	Morris "Moe" Berg	9.00	4.50	2.75
(3)	Max Bishop	3.00	1.50	.90
(4)	Doc Bowers	3.00	1.50	.90
(5)	Joe Cascarella	3.00	1.50	.90
(6)	Ben Chapman	3.00	1.50	.90
(7)	Bill Cissell	3.00	1.50	.90
(8)	Dusty Cooke	3.00	1.50	.90
(9)	Doc Cramer	3.00	1.50	.90
(10)	Joe Cronin	4.50	2.25	1.25
(11)	George Dickey	3.00	1.50	.90
(12)	Emerson Dickman	3.00	1.50	.90
(13)	Bobby Doerr	4.50	2.25	1.25
(14)	Rick Ferrell	4.50	2.25	1.25
(15)	Wes Ferrell	3.00	1.50	.90
(16)	Jimmie Foxx	7.50	3.75	2.25
(17)	Joe Gonzales	3.00	1.50	.90
(18)	Lefty Grove	6.00	3.00	1.75
(19)	Bucky Harris	4.50	2.25	1.25
(20)	Jim Henry	3.00	1.50	.90
(21)	Pinky Higgins	3.00	1.50	.90
(22)	Lefty Hockette	3.00	1.50	.90
(23)	Roy Johnson	3.00	1.50	.90
(24)	John Kroner	3.00	1.50	.90
(25)	Heinie Manush	4.50	2.25	1.25
(26)	Archie McKain	3.00	1.50	.90
(27)	Eric McNair	3.00	1.50	.90
(28)	Oscar Melillo	3.00	1.50	.90
(29)	Bing Miller	3.00	1.50	.90
(30)	Joe Mulligan	3.00	1.50	.90
(31)	Bobo Newsom	3.00	1.50	.90
(32)	Ted Olson	3.00	1.50	.90
(33)	Fritz Ostermueller	3.00	1.50	.90
(34)	George Pipgras	3.00	1.50	.90
(35)	Dusty Rhodes	3.00	1.50	.90
(36)	Walt Ripley	3.00	1.50	.90
(37)	Buck Rogers	3.00	1.50	.90
(38)	Jack Russell	3.00	1.50	.90
(39)	Tommy Thomas	3.00	1.50	.90
(40)	Hy Vandenberg	3.00	1.50	.90
(41)	Rube Walberg	3.00	1.50	.90
(42)	Johnny Welch	3.00	1.50	.90
(43)	Bill Werber	3.00	1.50	.90
(44)	Dib Williams	3.00	1.50	.90
(45)	Black Jack Wilson	3.00	1.50	.90

1959 Yoo-Hoo

Issued as a promotion for Yoo-Hoo chocolate flavored soft drink (it's a New York thing), this issue features five New York Yankees players. The black-and-white blank-backed cards measure 2-7/16" x 5-1/8", including a tab at the bottom which could be redeemed for various prizes. The top of the card features a posed spring training photo and includes a facsimile autograph and "Me for Yoo-Hoo" slogan. Prices shown here are for complete cards; cards without tabs would be valued at one-half of these figures. A Mickey Mantle advertising piece in larger size is often collected as an adjunct to the set, but no card of Mantle was issued. The Berra card is considerably scarcer than the others.

		NM	EX	VG
Complete Set, W/Tabs (5):		4,500	2,250	1,350
Complete Set, No Tabs (5):		1,350	675.00	415.00
Common Player, W/Tab:		800.00	400.00	240.00
Common Player, No Tab:				
	WITH TAB			
(1)	Yogi Berra	1,200	600.00	360.00
(2)	Whitey Ford	1,200	600.00	360.00
(3)	Tony Kubek	800.00	400.00	240.00
(4)	Gil McDougald	800.00	400.00	240.00
(5)	Bill Skowron	800.00	400.00	240.00
	NO TAB			
(1)	Yogi Berra	300.00	150.00	90.00
(2)	Whitey Ford	300.00	150.00	90.00
(3)	Tony Kubek	250.00	125.00	75.00
(4)	Gil McDougald	250.00	125.00	75.00
(5)	Bill Skowron	250.00	125.00	75.00

1959 Yoo-Hoo Mickey Mantle

In a different format than the other contemporary Yoo-Hoo Yankees cards, the manner of original distribution of this card is unclear. The 2-5/8" x 3-5/8" black-and-white card has a portrait photo and endorsement for the product on front. Back is blank.

	NM	EX	VG
Mickey Mantle	1,600	800.00	480.00

1959 Yoo-Hoo Bottle Caps

These lids for the chocolate soft drink feature black-and-white player portraits with the player name across the chest and "ME FOR" above with "YOO-HOO" below. Caps come in two styles, the older pry-off style and a later screw-top.

		NM	EX	VG
Complete Set (6):		2,000	1,000	450.00
Common Player:		200.00	100.00	60.00
Screw-Tops: +25 Percent				
(1)	Yogi Berra	400.00	200.00	90.00
(2)	Whitey Ford	400.00	200.00	90.00
(3)	Tony Kubek	225.00	110.00	50.00
(4)	Mickey Mantle	800.00	400.00	175.00
(5)	Gil McDougald	200.00	100.00	45.00
(6)	Moose Skowron	225.00	110.00	50.00

1964 Yoo-Hoo Counter Sign

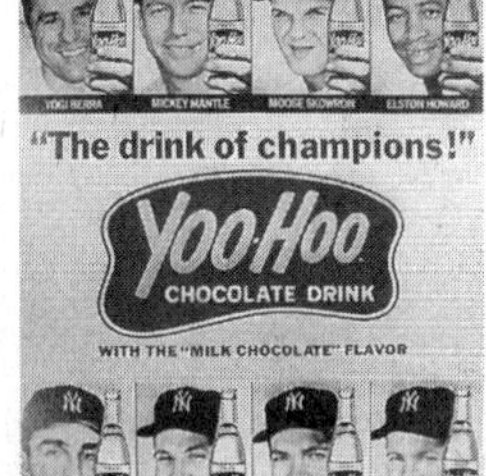

Seven N.Y. Yankees and Bill Skowron in a Senators' cap are pictured on this 11" x 14" easel-back counter display for the chocolate soft drink. Printed in brown, yellow and white, the sign has a hand holding a bottle in front of each player's portrait.

	NM	EX	VG
Yogi Berra, Whitey Ford, Elston Howard, Mickey Mantle, Joe Pepitone, Bobby Richardson, Moose Skowron, Tom Tresh	2,000	1,000	600.00

1927 York Caramels Type 1 (E210)

Issued in 1927 by the York Caramel Co. of York, Pa., these black-and-white cards are among the last of the caramel issues. Measuring 1-3/8" x 2-1/2", they are similar in appearance to earlier candy and tobacco cards. Fronts have the player's name in capital letters beneath the photo preceded by a number in parentheses. The back also lists the player's name in capital letters, along with a brief phrase describing him and the line, "This is one of a series of sixty of the most prominent stars in baseball." The bottom of the cards reads "York Caramel Co. York, Pa." The set includes several variations and is designated in the ACC as E210. It is closely related to the W502 set of the same year. Cards can be found on white or gray card stock. Type 1 cards can be differentiated from Type 2s by the orientation of the back printing. On Type 1 cards, the player name on back is at right when a normally-viewed front is turned over.

		NM	EX	VG
Complete Set (60):		40,000	16,000	8,000
Common Player:		250.00	100.00	50.00
1	Burleigh Grimes	500.00	200.00	100.00
2	Walter Reuther (Ruether)	500.00	200.00	100.00
3	Joe Duggan (Dugan)	250.00	100.00	50.00
4	Red Faber	500.00	200.00	100.00
5	Gabby Hartnett	500.00	200.00	100.00
6	Babe Ruth	15,000	4,800	2,400
7	Bob Meusel	250.00	100.00	50.00
8a	Herb Pennock (Team name on jersey.)	500.00	200.00	100.00
8b	Herb Pennock (No team name.)	500.00	200.00	100.00
9	George Burns	250.00	100.00	50.00
10	Joe Sewell	500.00	200.00	100.00
11	George Uhle	250.00	100.00	50.00
12a	Bob O'Farrel (O'Farrell) (Team name on jersey.)	250.00	100.00	50.00
12b	Bob O'Farrel (O'Farrell) (No team name.)	250.00	100.00	50.00
13	Rogers Hornsby	600.00	240.00	120.00
14	Pie Traynor	500.00	200.00	100.00
15	Clarence Mitchell	250.00	100.00	50.00
16	Eppa Jepha Rixey (Jeptha)	500.00	200.00	100.00
17	Carl Mays	250.00	100.00	50.00
18	Adolph Luque (Adolfo)	250.00	100.00	50.00
19	Dave Bancroft	500.00	200.00	100.00
20	George Kelly	500.00	200.00	100.00
21	Ira Flagstead	250.00	100.00	50.00
22	Harry Heilmann	500.00	200.00	100.00
23	Raymond W. Shalk (Schalk)	500.00	200.00	100.00
24	Johnny Mostil	250.00	100.00	50.00
25	Hack Wilson (Photo actually Art Wilson.)	500.00	200.00	100.00
26	Tom Zachary	250.00	100.00	50.00
27	Ty Cobb	6,500	2,600	1,300
28	Tris Speaker	600.00	240.00	120.00
29	Ralph Perkins	250.00	100.00	50.00
30	Jess Haines	500.00	200.00	100.00
31	Sherwood Smith (Photo actually Jack Coombs.)	250.00	100.00	50.00
32	Max Carey	500.00	200.00	100.00
33	Eugene Hargraves (Hargrave)	250.00	100.00	50.00
34	Miguel L. Gonzales (Miguel A. Gonzalez)	250.00	100.00	50.00
35a	Clifton Heathcot (Heathcote) (Team name on jersey.)	250.00	100.00	50.00
35b	Clifton Heathcot (Heathcote) (No team name.)	250.00	100.00	50.00
35c	Clifton Heathcote (Correct spelling.) (Team Name on jersey.)	250.00	100.00	50.00
36	E.C. (Sam) Rice	500.00	200.00	100.00
37	Earl Sheely	250.00	100.00	50.00
38a	Emory E. Rigney (Team name on jersey.)	250.00	100.00	50.00
38b	Emory E. Rigney (No team name.)	250.00	100.00	50.00
39	Bib A. Falk (Bibb)	250.00	100.00	50.00
40	Nick Altrock	250.00	100.00	50.00
41	Stanley Harris	500.00	200.00	100.00
42	John J. McGraw	500.00	200.00	100.00
43	Wilbert Robinson	500.00	200.00	100.00
44	Grover Alexander	750.00	300.00	150.00
45	Walter Johnson	1,000	400.00	200.00
46	William H. Terry (Photo actually Zeb Terry.)	500.00	200.00	100.00
47	Edward Collins	500.00	200.00	100.00
48	Marty McManus	250.00	100.00	50.00
49	Leon (Goose) Goslin	500.00	200.00	100.00
50	Frank Frisch	500.00	200.00	100.00
51	Jimmie Dykes	250.00	100.00	50.00
52	Fred (Cy) Williams	250.00	100.00	50.00
53	Eddie Roush	500.00	200.00	100.00
54	George Sisler	500.00	200.00	100.00
55	Ed Rommel	250.00	100.00	50.00
56a	Rogers Peckinpaugh (Roger) (Card number upside-down.)	250.00	100.00	50.00
56b	Rogers Peckinpaugh (Roger) (Card number corrected.)	250.00	100.00	50.00
57	Stanley Coveleskie (Coveleski)	500.00	200.00	100.00
58	Clarence Gallaway (Galloway)	250.00	100.00	50.00
59	Bob Shawkey	250.00	100.00	50.00
60	John P. McInnis	250.00	100.00	50.00

1927 York Caramels Type 2 (E210)

Type 2 York Caramels are in the same size and format as the Type 1 cards. They can be differentiated from Type 1 cards by the orientation of the back printing. On Type 2 cards, the player name appears at left when a normally-held card is turned over. Type 2 cards are all printed on white stock. Some players and photos were changed, and the descriptive lines about the players were changed on most cards.

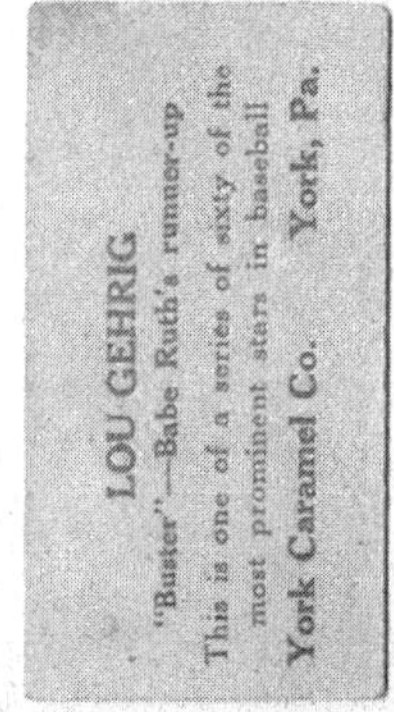

		NM	EX	VG
Complete Set (60):		45,000	18,000	9,000
Common Player:		250.00	100.00	50.00
1	Burleigh Grimes	500.00	200.00	100.00
2	Walter Reuther (Ruether)	250.00	100.00	50.00
3	Joe Dugan	250.00	100.00	50.00
4	Red Faber	500.00	200.00	100.00
5	Gabby Hartnett	500.00	200.00	100.00
6	Babe Ruth	12,000	4,800	2,400
7	Bob Meusel	250.00	100.00	50.00
8	Herb Pennock (Profile)	500.00	200.00	100.00
9	George Burns	250.00	100.00	50.00
10	Joe Sewell	500.00	200.00	100.00
11	George Uhle	250.00	100.00	50.00
12	Bob O'Farrell	250.00	100.00	50.00
13	Rogers Hornsby	600.00	240.00	120.00
14	Pie Traynor	500.00	200.00	100.00
15	Clarence Mitchell	250.00	100.00	50.00
16	Eppa Rixey	500.00	200.00	100.00
17	Carl Mays	250.00	100.00	50.00
18	Adolfo Luque	250.00	100.00	50.00
19	Dave Bancroft	500.00	200.00	100.00
20	George Kelly	500.00	200.00	100.00
21	Earle Combs	500.00	200.00	100.00
22	Harry Heilmann	500.00	200.00	100.00
23	Ray W. Schalk	500.00	200.00	100.00
24	Johnny Mostil	250.00	100.00	50.00
25	Hack Wilson	500.00	200.00	100.00
26	Lou Gehrig	10,000	2,600	1,300
27	Ty Cobb	6,500	2,600	1,300
28	Tris Speaker	600.00	240.00	120.00
29	Tony Lazzeri	500.00	200.00	100.00
30	Waite Hoyt	500.00	200.00	100.00
31	Sherwood Smith (Photo actually Jack Coombs.)	250.00	100.00	50.00
32	Max Carey	500.00	200.00	100.00
33	Eugene Hargrave (Hargraves)	250.00	100.00	50.00
34	Miguel L. Gonzales (Miguel A. Gonzalez)	250.00	100.00	50.00
35	Joe Judge	250.00	100.00	50.00
36	E.C. (Sam) Rice	500.00	200.00	100.00
37	Earl Sheely	250.00	100.00	50.00
38	Sam Jones	250.00	100.00	50.00
39	Bib (Bibb) A. Falk	250.00	100.00	50.00
40	Willie Kamm	250.00	100.00	50.00
41	Stanley Harris	500.00	200.00	100.00
42	John J. McGraw	500.00	200.00	100.00
43	Artie Nehf	250.00	100.00	50.00
44	Grover Alexander	750.00	300.00	150.00
45	Paul Waner	500.00	200.00	100.00
46	William H. Terry (Photo actually Zeb Terry.)	500.00	200.00	100.00
47	Glenn Wright	250.00	100.00	50.00
48	Earl Smith	250.00	100.00	50.00
49	Leon (Goose) Goslin	500.00	200.00	100.00
50	Frank Frisch	500.00	200.00	100.00
51	Joe Harris	250.00	100.00	50.00
52	Fred (Cy) Williams	250.00	100.00	50.00
53	Eddie Roush	500.00	200.00	100.00
54	George Sisler	500.00	200.00	100.00
55	Ed Rommel	250.00	100.00	50.00
56	Rogers Peckinpaugh (Roger)	250.00	100.00	50.00
57	Stanley Coveleskie (Coveleski)	500.00	200.00	100.00
58	Lester Bell	250.00	100.00	50.00
59	L. Waner	500.00	200.00	100.00
60	John P. McInnis	250.00	100.00	50.00

1917 Youth's Companion Stamps

The date attributed is speculative. This set of poster-stamps was issued to promote a Boston-based weekly magazine. Although he is not named, the left-handed pitcher depicted in very Red Sox-like uniform on one of the color litho stamps evidently looks enough like Babe Ruth that collectors have been willing to pay hundreds of dollars for examples of this scarce issue. The 1-7/8" x 2-1/2" stamp is, of course, blank-backed and is part of a set which featured other sporting activities, hobbys and topics suitable for young readers.

	NM	EX	VG
(Babe Ruth?)	600.00	300.00	180.00

1928 Yuengling's Ice Cream (F50)

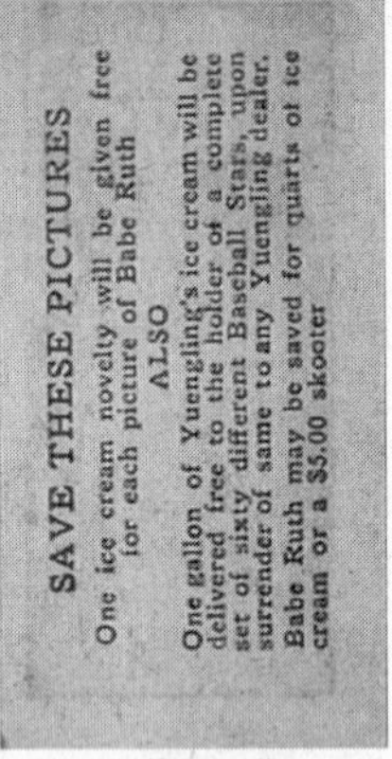
SAVE THESE PICTURES

One ice cream novelty will be given free for each picture of Babe Ruth

ALSO

One gallon of Yuengling's ice cream will be delivered free to the holder of a complete set of sixty different Baseball Stars, upon surrender of same to any Yuengling dealer. Babe Ruth may be saved for quarts of ice cream or a $5.00 skooter

Issued in 1928, the Yuengling's Ice Cream issue consists of 60 black-and-white cards measuring 1-3/8" x 2-1/2". The photos are similar to those used in the E210 and W502 sets. Other ice cream companies such as Harrington's and Tharp's produced nearly identical cards. Two types of cards are seen, though whether either or both can be found for all players is unknown. Besides typographical placement differences on front, the back of one type mentions a "$5.00 skooter" as a redemption, while the other type has no mention of the toy. Collectors could redeem an entire set of Yuengling's cards for a gallon of ice cream.

		NM	EX	VG
Complete Set (60):		45,000	18,000	9,000
Common Player:		250.00	100.00	50.00
1	Burleigh Grimes	500.00	200.00	100.00
2	Walter Reuther (Ruether)	250.00	100.00	50.00
3	Joe Dugan	250.00	100.00	50.00
4	Red Faber	500.00	200.00	100.00
5	Gabby Hartnett	500.00	200.00	100.00
6	Babe Ruth	12,000	4,800	2,400
7	Bob Meusel	250.00	100.00	50.00
8	Herb Pennock	500.00	200.00	100.00
9	George Burns	250.00	100.00	50.00
10	Joe Sewell	500.00	200.00	100.00
11	George Uhle	250.00	100.00	50.00
12	Bob O'Farrell	250.00	100.00	50.00
13	Rogers Hornsby	600.00	240.00	120.00
14	"Pie" Traynor	500.00	200.00	100.00
15	Clarence Mitchell	250.00	100.00	50.00
16	Eppa Jepha Rixey	500.00	200.00	100.00
17	Carl Mays	250.00	100.00	50.00
18	Adolfo Luque	250.00	100.00	50.00
19	Dave Bancroft	500.00	200.00	100.00
20	George Kelly	500.00	200.00	100.00
21	Earl (Earle) Combs	500.00	200.00	100.00
22	Harry Heilmann	500.00	200.00	100.00
23	Ray W. Schalk	500.00	200.00	100.00
24	Johnny Mostil	250.00	100.00	50.00
25	Hack Wilson	500.00	200.00	100.00
26	Lou Gehrig	6,500	2,600	1,300
27	Ty Cobb	6,500	2,600	1,300
28	Tris Speaker	600.00	240.00	120.00
29	Tony Lazzeri	500.00	200.00	100.00
30	Waite Hoyt	500.00	200.00	100.00
31	Sherwood Smith	250.00	100.00	50.00
32	Max Carey	500.00	200.00	100.00
33	Eugene Hargrave	250.00	100.00	50.00
34	Miguel L. Gonzales (Miguel A. Gonzalez)	250.00	100.00	50.00
35	Joe Judge	250.00	100.00	50.00
36	E.C. (Sam) Rice	500.00	200.00	100.00
37	Earl Sheely	250.00	100.00	50.00
38	Sam Jones	250.00	100.00	50.00
39	Bib (Bibb) A. Falk	250.00	100.00	50.00
40	Willie Kamm	250.00	100.00	50.00
41	Stanley Harris	500.00	200.00	100.00
42	John J. McGraw	500.00	200.00	100.00
43	Artie Nehf	250.00	100.00	50.00
44	Grover Alexander	750.00	300.00	150.00
45	Paul Waner	500.00	200.00	100.00
46	William H. Terry	500.00	200.00	100.00
47	Glenn Wright	250.00	100.00	50.00
48	Earl Smith	250.00	100.00	50.00
49	Leon (Goose) Goslin	500.00	200.00	100.00
50	Frank Frisch	500.00	200.00	100.00
51	Joe Harris	250.00	100.00	50.00
52	Fred (Cy) Williams	250.00	100.00	50.00
53	Eddie Roush	500.00	200.00	100.00
54	George Sisler	500.00	200.00	100.00
55	Ed. Rommel	250.00	100.00	50.00
56	Rogers Peckinpaugh (Roger)	250.00	100.00	50.00
57	Stanley Coveleskie (Coveleski)	500.00	200.00	100.00
58	Lester Bell	250.00	100.00	50.00
59	L. Waner	500.00	200.00	100.00
60	John P. McInnis	250.00	100.00	50.00

1888 Yum Yum Tobacco (N403)

An extremely rare series of tobacco cards, this set was issued in 1888 by August Beck & Co., Chicago. The cards vary slightly in size but average 1-3/8" x 2-3/4". They were distributed in packages of the company's Yum Yum smoking and chewing tobacco and are found in two distinct types: photographic portraits and full-length action drawings copied from photos used in the Old Judge sets of the same period. In both types, the player's name and position appear in capital letters below the photo, while the very bottom of the card states: "Smoke and Chew "Yum Yum" Tobacco. A. Beck & Co. Chicago, Ill." Players from all eight National League clubs, plus Brooklyn of the American Association, are included in the set. The checklist here has gaps left to accommodate future additions.

		NM	EX	VG
Common Player:		9,000	4,500	2,725
(3)	Cap Anson/Portrait	45,000	22,500	13,500
(4)	Cap Anson/Btg	23,750	11,250	6,750
(7)	Lady Baldwin (Left arm extended.)	9,750	4,875	2,925
(11)	Dan Brouthers/Btg	18,000	9,000	5,400
(13)	Willard "California" Brown	9,750	4,875	2,925
(15)	Charles Buffington (Buffinton)	9,750	4,875	2,925
(17)	Tom Burns/Portrait	16,500	8,250	4,950
(18)	Tom Burns (With bat.)	9,750	4,875	2,925
(21)	John Clarkson/Portrait	30,000	15,000	9,000
(22)	John Clarkson/Throwing (Arm back.)	18,000	9,000	5,400
(25)	John Coleman/Portrait	16,500	8,250	4,950
(27)	Roger Connor/Btg	18,000	9,000	5,400
(28)	Roger Connor/Portrait	30,000	15,000	9,000
(30)	Larry Corcoran/Portrait	16,500	8,250	4,950
(34)	Tom Daily/Portrait (Daly) (Photo actually Billy Sunday.)	17,250	8,625	5,175
(36)	Tom Deasley/Portrait	16,500	8,250	4,950
(39)	Mike Dorgan/Portrait	16,500	8,250	4,950
(40)	Dude Esterbrook/Portrait	16,500	8,250	4,950
(41)	Buck Ewing/Portrait	30,000	15,000	9,000
(42)	Buck Ewing (With bat.)	18,000	9,000	5,400
(45)	Silver Flint/Portrait	16,500	8,250	4,950
(47)	Jim Fogarty/Throwing	9,750	4,875	2,925
(49)	Pud Galvin (Ball in hands at chest.)	18,000	9,000	5,400
(51)	Joe Gerhardt	16,500	8,250	4,950
(53)	Charlie Getzein (Getzien) (Holding ball.))	9,750	4,875	2,925
(55)	Pete Gillespie/Portrait	16,500	8,250	4,950
(57)	Jack Glasscock	9,750	4,875	2,925
(59)	George Gore (Leaning on bat.)	9,750	4,875	2,925
(61)	Ed Greer/Portrait	16,500	8,250	4,950
(65)	Tim Keefe/Pitching	18,000	9,000	5,400
(66)	Tim Keefe/Portrait	30,000	15,000	9,000
(67)	King Kelly/Btg	18,000	9,000	5,400
(68)	King Kelly (Photo, standing by urn.)	45,000	22,500	13,500
(70)	Gus Krock/Portrait	16,500	8,250	4,950
(72)	Connie Mack	18,000	9,000	5,400
(74)	Kid Madden (Ball in raised right hand.)	9,750	4,875	2,925
(76)	Doggie Miller (Leaning on bat.)	9,750	4,875	2,925
(78)	John Morrill (Leaning on bat.)	9,750	4,875	2,925
(80)	James Mutrie/Portrait	16,500	8,250	4,950
(82)	Billy Nash (Holding bat.)	9,750	4,875	2,925
(84)	Jim O'Rourke/Portrait	30,000	15,000	9,000
(85)	Jim O'Rourke (With bat.)	18,000	9,000	5,400
(87)	Fred Pfeffer (Bat on shoulder.)	9,750	4,875	2,925
(90)	Danny Richardson/Portrait	16,500	8,250	4,950
(92)	Chief Roseman/Portrait	16,500	8,250	4,950
(94)	Jimmy Ryan/Portrait	16,500	8,250	4,950
(95)	Jimmy Ryan/Throwing	9,750	4,875	2,925
(97)	Bill Sowders (Ball in hands at chest.)	9,750	4,875	2,925
(100)	Marty Sullivan/Portrait	16,500	8,250	4,950
(102)	Billy Sunday/Fldg	18,000	9,000	5,400
(103)	Billy Sunday/Portrait (Photo actually Mark Baldwin.)	18,000	9,000	5,400
(105)	Ezra Sutton/Btg	9,750	4,875	2,925
(110)	Mike Tiernan/Portrait	16,500	8,250	4,950
(111)	Mike Tiernan (With bat.)	9,750	4,875	2,925
(115)	Rip Van Haltren (Photo not Van Haltren.)	16,500	8,250	4,950
(119)	John Ward/Portrait	30,000	15,000	9,000
(123)	Mickey Welch (Ball in hands at chest.)	18,000	9,000	5,400
(124)	Mickey Welch/Portrait	30,000	15,000	9,000
(125)	Mickey Welch (Right arm extended.)	18,000	9,000	5,400
(129)	Jim Whitney/Throwing	9,750	4,875	2,925
(133)	George Wood/Throwing (Arm behind head.)	9,750	4,875	2,925

Z

1977 Zip'z discs

Virtually identical in format to the several locally sponsored disc sets of the previous year, these 3-3/8" diameter player discs were given away at the sponsor's sundae bars around the cvountry. Some are found with a black rubber-stamp on back of the specific Zip's location. Discs once again feature black-and-white player portrait photos in the center of a baseball design. The left and right panels are in one of several bright colors. Licensed by the players' association through Mike Schechter Associates, the player photos carry no uniform logos. Backs are printed in reddish-orange. The unnumbered discs are checklisted here alphabetically.

		NM	EX	VG
Complete Set (70):		120.00	60.00	35.00
Common Player:		2.00	1.00	.60
(1)	Sal Bando	2.00	1.00	.60
(2)	Buddy Bell	2.00	1.00	.60
(3)	Johnny Bench	7.50	3.75	2.25
(4)	Larry Bowa	2.00	1.00	.60
(5)	Steve Braun	2.00	1.00	.60
(6)	George Brett	20.00	10.00	6.00
(7)	Lou Brock	6.00	3.00	1.75
(8)	Jeff Burroughs	2.00	1.00	.60
(9)	Bert Campaneris	2.00	1.00	.60
(10)	John Candelaria	2.00	1.00	.60
(11)	Jose Cardenal	2.00	1.00	.60
(12)	Rod Carew	6.00	3.00	1.75
(13)	Steve Carlton	6.00	3.00	1.75
(14)	Dave Cash	2.00	1.00	.60
(15)	Cesar Cedeno	2.00	1.00	.60
(16)	Ron Cey	2.00	1.00	.60
(17)	Dave Concepcion	2.00	1.00	.60
(18)	Dennis Eckersley	6.00	3.00	1.75
(19)	Mark Fidrych	3.00	1.50	.90
(20)	Rollie Fingers	6.00	3.00	1.75
(21)	Carlton Fisk	6.00	3.00	1.75
(22)	George Foster	2.00	1.00	.60
(23)	Wayne Garland	2.00	1.00	.60
(24)	Ralph Garr	2.00	1.00	.60
(25)	Steve Garvey	5.00	2.50	1.50
(26)	Cesar Geronimo	2.00	1.00	.60
(27)	Bobby Grich	2.00	1.00	.60
(28)	Ken Griffey Sr.	2.00	1.00	.60
(29)	Don Gullett	2.00	1.00	.60
(30)	Mike Hargrove	2.00	1.00	.60
(31)	Al Hrabosky	2.00	1.00	.60
(32)	Jim Hunter	6.00	3.00	1.75
(33)	Reggie Jackson	15.00	7.50	4.50
(34)	Randy Jones	2.00	1.00	.60
(35)	Dave Kingman	2.00	1.00	.60
(36)	Jerry Koosman	2.00	1.00	.60
(37)	Dave LaRoche	2.00	1.00	.60
(38)	Greg Luzinski	2.00	1.00	.60
(39)	Fred Lynn	2.00	1.00	.60
(40)	Bill Madlock	2.00	1.00	.60
(41)	Rick Manning	2.00	1.00	.60
(42)	Jon Matlock	2.00	1.00	.60
(43)	John Mayberry	2.00	1.00	.60
(44)	Hal McRae	2.00	1.00	.60
(45)	Andy Messersmith	2.00	1.00	.60
(46)	Rick Monday	2.00	1.00	.60
(47)	John Montefusco	2.00	1.00	.60
(48)	Joe Morgan	6.00	3.00	1.75
(49)	Thurman Munson	5.00	2.50	1.50
(50)	Bobby Murcer	2.00	1.00	.60
(51)	Bill North	2.00	1.00	.60
(52)	Jim Palmer	6.00	3.00	1.75
(53)	Tony Perez	6.00	3.00	1.75
(54)	Jerry Reuss	2.00	1.00	.60
(55)	Brooks Robinson	7.50	3.75	2.25
(56)	Pete Rose	25.00	12.50	7.50
(57)	Joe Rudi	2.00	1.00	.60
(58)	Nolan Ryan	35.00	17.50	10.00
(59)	Manny Sanguillen	2.00	1.00	.60
(60)	Mike Schmidt	15.00	7.50	4.50
(61)	Tom Seaver	7.50	3.75	2.25
(62)	Bill Singer	2.00	1.00	.60
(63)	Willie Stargell	6.00	3.00	1.75
(64)	Rusty Staub	2.00	1.00	.60
(65)	Luis Tiant	2.00	1.00	.60
(66)	Bob Watson	2.00	1.00	.60
(67)	Butch Wynegar	2.00	1.00	.60
(68)	Carl Yastrzemski	10.00	5.00	3.00
(69)	Robin Yount	6.00	3.00	1.75
(70)	Richie Zisk	2.00	1.00	.60

1950s Bill Zuber's Restaurant

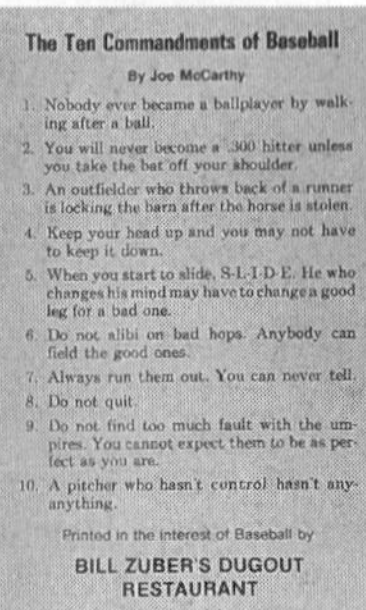
The Ten Commandments of Baseball

By Joe McCarthy

1. Nobody ever became a ballplayer by walking after a ball.
2. You will never become a .300 hitter unless you take the bat off your shoulder.
3. An outfielder who throws back of a runner is locking the barn after the horse is stolen.
4. Keep your head up and you may not have to keep it down.
5. When you start to slide, S-L-I-D-E. He who changes his mind may have to change a good leg for a bad one.
6. Do not alibi on bad hops. Anybody can field the good ones.
7. Always run them out. You can never tell.
8. Do not quit.
9. Do not find too much fault with the umpires. You cannot expect them to be as perfect as you are.
10. A pitcher who hasn't control hasn't any-anything.

Printed in the interest of Baseball by

BILL ZUBER'S DUGOUT RESTAURANT

Homestead, Iowa

These 3-1/2" x 5-1/2" black-and-white cards were produced as a promotional item for an Iowa restaurant owned by the former big league pitcher (1936-47). The semi-gloss front has a portrait and facsimile autograph. One type has an advertising message at left and the inscription, "Good Hitting." On back are printed Joe McCarthy's "Ten Commandments of Baseball." A second type has the inscription, "Sincerest Wishes," with a postcard-style back featuring an advertising message in the top-left corner.

		NM	EX	VG
(1)	Bill Zuber (Ten Commandments back.)	8.00	4.00	2.50
(2)	Bill Zuber (Postcard back.)	8.00	4.00	2.50

MODERN MAJOR LEAGUE (1981-2008)

The vast majority of cards and collectibles listed in this section were issued between 1981 and May 2008 and feature only major league players.

Because modern cards are generally not collected in lower grades, cards in this section carry only a Near Mint-to-Mint (NM/M) value quote. In general, post-1980 cards that grade Near Mint will retail at about 75 percent of the NM/M price, while Excellent condition cards bring about 40 percent. Cards in lesser condition are generally not considered collectible.

Values shown are for "raw" cards, that is, cards not authenticated, graded and encapsulated by an independent certification firm. Many cards that have been graded Mint, Gem Mint or Pristine by recognized major grading companies (SCD, SGC, BGS, GAI or PSA) will sell at a premium over the values quoted here. Because the standards and reputations of these companies vary widely, prices listed here cannot be correlated to values for "slabbed" cards

1991 Acme Reproductions Ryan-Seaver

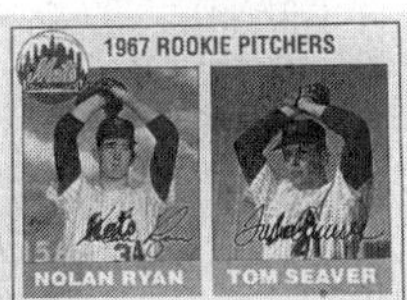

This collectors' issue was produced in an edition of 10,000 in an over-size (4-1/4" x 3") format and style approximating a 1967 Topps card. The future Hall of Famers are pictured in their early days with the Mets. Facsimile autographs appear at the bottom of each photo. A total of 420 of the cards was authentically autographed by both players. Backs have a cartoon and biographical data on each player, plus a career summary up to 1967. Original issue price was $29, or $109 for the autographed card. Each came in a lucite holder with numbered certificate of authenticity. A 17-1/2" x 12-1/2" lithograph was produced in an edition of 3,000, with the first 1,000 autographed by each player. The litho sold for $219 autographed and $109 unsigned.

	NM/M
Nolan Ryan, Tom Seaver	10.00
Nolan Ryan, Tom Seaver/Auto.	200.00

1988 Action Packed

Action Packed released this test set in an effort to receive a license from Major League Baseball. The cards are styled like the Action Packed football issues on the card fronts. The flip sides are styled like Score baseball cards. The Ozzie Smith card is considered scarcer than the other five cards in the test set, while a hoard of Mattingly cards revealed in 1998 drove down the price of his card. Action Packed did not receive a license to produce baseball cards.

		NM/M
Complete Set (6):		45.00
Common Player:		6.00
(1)	Wade Boggs	12.50
(2)	Andre Dawson	7.50
(3)	Dwight Gooden	6.00
(4)	Carney Lansford	6.00
(5)	Don Mattingly	6.00
(6)	Ozzie Smith	30.00

1992 Action Packed Promos

This set was produced to preview Action Packed's All-Star Gallery card issue. The promo cards are identical in format to the regularly issued cards and use the same player photos. The only differences in the promos are found on the back, where the card number is missing from the lower-left corner and where a white "1992 Prototype" is overprinted on the gray background beneath the black career highlights. The promos were widely distributed at trade shows and to Action Packed's dealer network. The unnumbered promo cards are checklisted here alphabetically.

		NM/M
Complete Set (5):		6.00
Common Player:		1.00
(1)	Yogi Berra	1.50
(2)	Bob Gibson	1.00
(3)	Willie Mays	3.00
(4)	Warren Spahn	1.00
(5)	Willie Stargell	1.00

1992 Action Packed All-Star Gallery Series 1

Action Packed, makers of a high quality, embossed style football card for several years,

entered the baseball card field in 1992 with its 84-card All-Star Gallery Series 1. The cards feature former baseball greats, with 72 of the 84 cards in color and the remaining in sepia tone. Each foil pack of seven cards reportedly contained at least one Hall of Famer, and the company also made special 24K gold leaf stamped cards of all of the HOFers that were randomly inserted in the packs.

		NM/M
Complete Set (84):		15.00
Common Player:		.10
Wax Pack (7):		.75
Wax Box (24):		12.50
1	Yogi Berra	.50
2	Lou Brock	.25
3	Bob Gibson	.25
4	Ferguson Jenkins	.25
5	Ralph Kiner	.25
6	Al Kaline	.40
7	Lou Boudreau	.25
8	Bobby Doerr	.25
9	Billy Herman	.25
10	Monte Irvin	.25
11	George Kell	.25
12	Robin Roberts	.25
13	Johnny Mize	.25
14	Willie Mays	1.00
15	Enos Slaughter	.25
16	Warren Spahn	.25
17	Willie Stargell	.25
18	Billy Williams	.25
19	Vernon Law	.10
20	Virgil Trucks	.10
21	Mel Parnell	.10
22	Wally Moon	.10
23	Gene Woodling	.10
24	Richie Ashburn	.25
25	Mark Fidrych	.25
26	Elroy Face	.10
27	Larry Doby	.25
28	Dick Groat	.10
29	Cesar Cedeno	.10
30	Bob Horner	.10
31	Bobby Richardson	.25
32	Bobby Murcer	.10
33	Gil McDougald	.10
34	Roy White	.10
35	Bill Skowron	.25
36	Mickey Lolich	.10
37	Minnie Minoso	.10
38	Billy Pierce	.10
39	Ron Santo	.25
40	Sal Bando	.10
41	Ralph Branca	.10
42	Bert Campaneris	.10
43	Joe Garagiola	.25
44	Vida Blue	.10
45	Frank Crosetti	.10
46	Luis Tiant	.10
47	Maury Wills	.10
48	Sam McDowell	.10
49	Jimmy Piersall	.10
50	Jim Lonborg	.10
51	Don Newcombe	.15
52	Bobby Thomson	.10
53	Wilbur Wood	.10
54	Carl Erskine	.10
55	Chris Chambliss	.10
56	Dave Kingman	.10
57	Ken Holtzman	.10
58	Bud Harrelson	.10
59	Clem Labine	.10
60	Tony Oliva	.10
61	George Foster	.10
62	Bobby Bonds	.10
63	Harvey Haddix	.10
64	Steve Garvey	.15
65	Rocky Colavito	.15
66	Orlando Cepeda	.25
67	Ed Lopat	.10
68	Al Oliver	.10
69	Bill Mazeroski	.25
70	Al Rosen	.10
71	Bob Grich	.10
72	Curt Flood	.10
73	Willie Horton	.10
74	Rico Carty	.10
75	Davey Johnson	.10
76	Don Kessinger	.10
77	Frank Thomas	.10
78	Bobby Shantz	.10
79	Herb Score	.10
80	Boog Powell	.15
81	Rusty Staub	.15
82	Bill Madlock	.10
83	Manny Mota	.10
84	Bill White	.10

1993 Action Packed All-Star Gallery Series 2

The Second Series of Action Packed All-Star Gallery was released in 1993, with cards numbered from 85 to 168. In a similar fashion to the First Series, Series Two features 52 cards in color, 31 in sepia tone and one as a colorized black and white. The series also includes two tongue-in-cheek cards - "Who's on First?" duo Bud Abbot and Lou Costello, and a card highlighting the TV and radio career of Bob Uecker.

		NM/M
Complete Set (84):		10.00
Common Player:		.10
Wax Pack (7):		1.00
Wax Box (24):		17.50
85	Cy Young	.15
86	Honus Wagner	.25
87	Christy Mathewson	.15
88	Ty Cobb	1.00
89	Eddie Collins	.10
90	Walter Johnson	.15
91	Tris Speaker	.15
92	Grover Alexander	.10
93	Edd Roush	.10
94	Babe Ruth	2.00
95	Rogers Hornsby	.15
96	Pie Traynor	.10
97	Lou Gehrig	1.00
98	Mickey Cochrane	.10
99	Lefty Grove	.10
100	Jimmie Foxx	.15
101	Tony Lazzeri	.10
102	Mel Ott	.10
103	Carl Hubbell	.10
104	Al Lopez	.10
105	Lefty Gomez	.10
106	Dizzy Dean	.15
107	Hank Greenberg	.10
108	Joe Medwick	.10
109	Arky Vaughan	.10
110	Bob Feller	.15
111	Hal Newhouser	.10
112	Early Wynn	.10
113	Bob Lemon	.10
114	Red Schoendienst	.10
115	Satchel Paige	.25
116	Whitey Ford	.15
117	Eddie Mathews	.15
118	Harmon Killebrew	.15
119	Roberto Clemente	1.50
120	Brooks Robinson	.15
121	Don Drysdale	.15
122	Luis Aparicio	.15
123	Willie McCovey	.15
124	Juan Marichal	.10
125	Gaylord Perry	.10
126	Catfish Hunter	.10
127	Jim Palmer	.15
128	Rod Carew	.15
129	Tom Seaver	.15
130	Rollie Fingers	.10
131	Joe Jackson	2.00
132	Pepper Martin	.10
133	Joe Gordon	.10
134	Marty Marion	.10
135	Allie Reynolds	.10
136	Johnny Sain	.10
137	Gil Hodges	.15
138	Ted Kluszewski	.15
139	Nellie Fox	.15
140	Billy Martin	.10
141	Smoky Burgess	.10
142	Lew Burdette	.10
143	Joe Black	.10
144	Don Larsen	.10
145	Ken Boyer	.10
146	Johnny Callison	.10
147	Norm Cash	.10
148	Keith Hernandez	.10
149	Jim Kaat	.10
150	Bill Freehan	.10
151	Joe Torre	.10
152	Bob Uecker	.15
153	Dave McNally	.10
154	Denny McLain	.10
155	Dick Allen	.10
156	Jimmy Wynn	.10
157	Tommy John	.10
158	Paul Blair	.10
159	Reggie Smith	.10
160	Jerry Koosman	.10
161	Thurman Munson	.15
162	Graig Nettles	.10
163	Ron Cey	.10
164	Cecil Cooper	.10
165	Dave Parker	.10
166	Jim Rice	.10
167	Kent Tekulve	.10
168	Who's on First? (Bud Abbott, Lou Costello)	.75

1992 Action Packed Diamond Stars

The first 18 cards from Series 1 Action Packed ASG were produced in a gold-enhanced boxed-set version which included a diamond chip in 14-Karat gold setting. Each card was serially numbered from within an edition of 500.

		NM/M
Complete Set (18):		80.00
Common Player:		4.00
1G	Yogi Berra	7.50
2G	Lou Brock	4.00
3G	Bob Gibson	4.00
4G	Ferguson Jenkins	4.00
5G	Ralph Kiner	4.00
6G	Al Kaline	5.00
7G	Lou Boudreau	4.00
8G	Bobby Doerr	4.00
9G	Billy Herman	4.00
10G	Monte Irvin	4.00
11G	George Kell	4.00
12G	Robin Roberts	4.00
13G	Johnny Mize	4.00
14G	Willie Mays	12.50
15G	Enos Slaughter	4.00
16G	Warren Spahn	4.00
17G	Willie Stargell	4.00
18G	Billy Williams	4.00

1992-93 Action Packed Gold

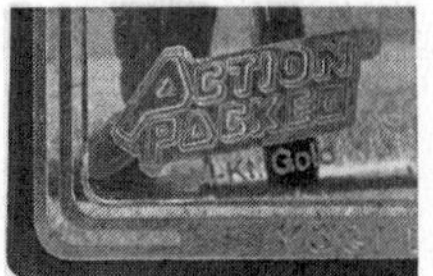

Essentially identical to the regular-issue Action Packed All-Star Gallery cards, these premium inserts are specially numbered with a "G" prefix and highlighted with 24-Karat gold detailing.

		NM/M
Complete Set (65):		175.00
Common Player:		2.50
Series 1		
1	Yogi Berra	4.00
2	Lou Brock	2.50
3	Bob Gibson	2.50
4	Ferguson Jenkins	2.50
5	Ralph Kiner	2.50
6	Al Kaline	3.50
7	Lou Boudreau	2.50
8	Bobby Doerr	2.50
9	Billy Herman	2.50
10	Monte Irvin	2.50
11	George Kell	2.50
12	Robin Roberts	2.50
13	Johnny Mize	2.50
14	Willie Mays	7.50
15	Enos Slaughter	2.50
16	Warren Spahn	2.50
17	Willie Stargell	2.50
18	Billy Williams	2.50
Series 2		
19	Cy Young	3.50
20	Honus Wagner	5.00
21	Christy Mathewson	3.50
22	Ty Cobb	6.00
23	Eddie Collins	2.50
24	Walter Johnson	3.50
25	Tris Speaker	3.50

26	Grover Alexander	3.25
27	Edd Roush	2.50
28	Babe Ruth	12.50
29	Rogers Hornsby	3.50
30	Pie Traynor	2.50
31	Lou Gehrig	10.00
32	Mickey Cochrane	3.25
33	Lefty Grove	3.25
34	Jimmie Foxx	3.50
35	Tony Lazzeri	2.50
36	Mel Ott	2.50
37	Carl Hubbell	2.50
38	Al Lopez	2.50
39	Lefty Gomez	2.50
40	Dizzy Dean	3.50
41	Hank Greenberg	3.50
42	Joe Medwick	2.50
43	Arky Vaughan	2.50
44	Bob Feller	3.50
45	Hal Newhouser	2.50
46	Early Wynn	2.50
47	Bob Lemon	2.50
48	Red Schoendienst	2.50
49	Satchel Paige	6.00
50	Whitey Ford	3.25
51	Eddie Mathews	3.25
52	Harmon Killebrew	3.25
53	Roberto Clemente	15.00
54	Brooks Robinson	3.25
55	Don Drysdale	3.25
56	Luis Aparicio	2.50
57	Willie McCovey	3.25
58	Juan Marichal	2.50
59	Gaylord Perry	2.50
60	Catfish Hunter	2.50
61	Jim Palmer	3.25
62	Rod Carew	3.25
63	Tom Seaver	3.25
64	Rollie Fingers	2.50
65	Who's on First? (Bud Abbott, Lou Costello)	3.50

1992 Action Packed 24-Kt. Gold

At least the first 18 cards in 1992 AP All-Star Gallery Series 1 were also issued in a full-coverage gold-foil version (as opposed to the gold-highlighted parallels). The cards are embossed front and back in gold-foil and numbered identically to the regular-issue cards. Each has a "24-Kt. Gold" imprint on front and is ink-jet serially numbered on back within an edition of 1,000.

		NM/M
Complete Set (18):		35.00
Common Player:		2.00
1	Yogi Berra	3.50
2	Lou Brock	2.50
3	Bob Gibson	2.50
4	Ferguson Jenkins	2.50
5	Ralph Kiner	2.50
6	Al Kaline	2.50
7	Lou Boudreau	2.00
8	Bobby Doerr	2.00
9	Billy Herman	2.00
10	Monte Irvin	2.00
11	George Kell	2.00
12	Robin Roberts	2.50
13	Johnny Mize	2.50
14	Willie Mays	7.50
15	Enos Slaughter	2.50
16	Warren Spahn	2.50
17	Willie Stargell	2.50
18	Billy Williams	2.50

1993 Action Packed Amoco/Coke

A special version of 18 of its All-Star Gallery cards was created by Action Packed for use as a premium by Amoco gas stations and Coca-Cola. Card fronts feature the same embossed color or sepia player photos with a heavily lacquered finish and gold-foil and black borders. Gray backs have biographical and career data, a few stats and sponsors' logos. Complete sets were available via a mail-in offer from Coke products. Most of these cards share card numbers and photos with AP's Series I ASG cards.

AL KALINE

		NM/M
Complete Set (18):		4.00
Common Player:		.50
1	Yogi Berra	1.00
2	Lou Brock	.50
3	Bob Gibson	.50
4	Red Schoendienst	.50
5	Ralph Kiner	.50
6	Al Kaline	.75
7	Lou Boudreau	.50
8	Bobby Doerr	.50
9	Gaylord Perry	.50
10	Monte Irvin	.50
11	George Kell	.50
12	Robin Roberts	.60
13	Johnny Mize	.60
14	Willie Mays	2.00
15	Enos Slaughter	.50
16	Warren Spahn	.60
17	Willie Stargell	.60
18	Billy Williams	.50

1993 Action Packed 24-Kt. Gold

EARLY WYNN

The first 46 cards of AP's All-Star Gallery Series II, along with the special Abbott & Costello card were produced in a limited gold edition as random pack inserts. Labeled "24-Kt. Gold" on front, the cards have the same format and design as the regular-issue, except the embossed front photo and incuse stats on back are on solid-gold foil. Each gold card carries a black ink-jetted serial number on back from within an edition of either 500 or 1,000.

		NM/M
Complete Set (47):		80.00
Common Player:		2.00
85	Cy Young	3.00
86	Honus Wagner	4.00
87	Christy Mathewson	4.00
88	Ty Cobb	6.00
89	Eddie Collins	2.00
90	Walter Johnson	4.00
91	Tris Speaker	2.00
92	Grover Alexander	2.00
93	Edd Roush	2.00
94	Babe Ruth	16.00
95	Rogers Hornsby	2.00
96	Pie Traynor	2.00
97	Lou Gehrig	10.00
98	Mickey Cochrane	2.00
99	Lefty Grove	2.00
100	Jimmie Foxx	3.00
101	Tony Lazzeri	2.00
102	Mel Ott	2.00
103	Carl Hubbell	2.00
104	Al Lopez	2.00
105	Lefty Gomez	2.00
106	Dizzy Dean	3.00
107	Hank Greenberg	3.00
108	Joe Medwick	2.00
109	Arky Vaughan	2.00
110	Bob Feller	3.00
111	Hal Newhouser	2.00
112	Early Wynn	2.00
113	Bob Lemon	2.00
114	Red Schoendienst	2.00
115	Satchel Paige	4.00
116	Whitey Ford	4.00
117	Eddie Mathews	2.00
118	Harmon Killebrew	2.00
119	Roberto Clemente	12.00
120	Brooks Robinson	2.00
121	Don Drysdale	2.00
122	Luis Aparicio	2.00
123	Willie McCovey	2.00
124	Juan Marichal	2.00
125	Gaylord Perry	2.00
126	Catfish Hunter	2.00
127	Jim Palmer	2.00
128	Rod Carew	2.00
129	Tom Seaver	2.00
130	Rollie Fingers	2.00
168	Who's on First? (Lou Costello, Bud Abbott)	3.00

1993 Action Packed Tom Seaver Prototypes

TOM SEAVER

Tom Seaver's career was highlighted in this five-card promo set. Each card has an embossed front color photo surrounded by three gold pinstripes and a red border. Seaver's name is in red in a gold bar at bottom. Backs are printed in black and gold with a white undertype reading "1993 Prototype." Backs have biographical and career data, lifetime stats and a few sentences of career highlights. Cards have a "TS" prefix to the card number.

		NM/M
Complete Set (5):		8.00
Common Card:		2.00
1	The Franchise	2.00
2	Amazin' Mets	3.25
3	A Tearful Goodbye	2.00
4	Tom Terrific	2.00
5	Dazzling the Windy City	2.00

1983 Affiliated Food Rangers

This set, featuring the Texas Rangers, was issued as a promotion by the Affiliated Food Stores chain of Arlington, Texas. Complete sets were given to youngsters 13 and under at the September 3 Rangers game. Cards measure 2-3/8" x 3-1/2" and feature a full-color photo on the front. Also on the front, located inside a blue box, is the player's name, uniform number, and "1983 Rangers." Backs have a small player photo plus biographical and statistical information, along with the Affiliated logo and a brief promotional message. A total of 10,000 sets was reportedly printed. Cards are numbered by the players' uniform numbers in the checklist that follows.

		NM/M
Complete Set (28):		6.00
Common Player:		.25
1	Bill Stein	.25
2	Mike Richardt	.25
3	Wayne Tolleson	.25
5	Billy Sample	.25
6	Bobby Jones	.25
7	Bucky Dent	.35
8	Bobby Johnson	.25
9	Pete O'Brien	.25
10	Jim Sundberg	.25
11	Doug Rader	.25
12	Dave Hostetler	.25
14	Larry Biittner	.25
15	Larry Parrish	.25
17	Mickey Rivers	.30
21	Odell Jones	.25
24	Dave Schmidt	.25
25	Buddy Bell	.35
26	George Wright	.25
28	Frank Tanana	.25
29	John Butcher	.25
32	Jon Matlack	.25
40	Rick Honeycutt	.25
41	Dave Tobik	.25
44	Danny Darwin	.25
46	Jim Anderson	.25
48	Mike Smithson	.25
49	Charlie Hough	.30
---	Coaching Staff (Rich Donnelly, Glenn Ezell, Merv Rettenmund, Dick Such, Wayne Terwilliger)	.25

1990 Agfa Film

Rollie Fingers

This "old-timers" set was distributed in three-card packs with the purchase of Agfa film. Produced by Michael Schecter Associates, whose logo appears on the back, the cards were not licensed by Major League Baseball, so team logos had to be eliminated from the photos. Cards have a white background with the film company's logos in the upper corners. Backs are in black-and-white and have full major league regular season and post-season stats.

		NM/M
Complete Set (22):		7.50
Common Player:		.50
1	Willie Mays	2.00
2	Carl Yastrzemski	1.00
3	Harmon Killebrew	1.00
4	Joe Torre	.50
5	Al Kaline	1.00
6	Hank Aaron	2.00
7	Rod Carew	.75
8	Roberto Clemente	2.50
9	Luis Aparicio	.75
10	Roger Maris	1.00
11	Joe Morgan	.75
12	Maury Wills	.50
13	Brooks Robinson	1.00
14	Tom Seaver	.75
15	Steve Carlton	.75
16	Whitey Ford	.75
17	Jim Palmer	.75
18	Rollie Fingers	.75
19	Bruce Sutter	.75
20	Willie McCovey	.75
21	Mike Schmidt	1.50
22	Yogi Berra	1.00

1990 All American Baseball Team

KENT HRBEK
Minnesota Twins

Produced by Mike Schecter Associates, this 24-card set includes many of the top players in the game. Team logos are airbrushed from the color photo on front, which is surrounded by a red, white and blue border and the MLB Players Association logo. The backs are printed in blue on white stock, with a facsimile autograph appearing above the statistics.

		NM/M
Complete Set (24):		20.00
Common Player:		.50
1	George Brett	1.50
2	Mark McGwire	3.00
3	Wade Boggs	1.25
4	Cal Ripken, Jr.	4.00
5	Rickey Henderson	1.00
6	Dwight Gooden	.50
7	Bo Jackson	.75
8	Roger Clemens	1.50
9	Orel Hershiser	.50
10	Ozzie Smith	1.25
11	Don Mattingly	2.00
12	Kirby Puckett	1.25
13	Robin Yount	1.00
14	Tony Gwynn	1.25
15	Jose Canseco	.60
16	Nolan Ryan	4.00
17	Ken Griffey Jr.	2.50
18	Will Clark	.50
19	Ryne Sandberg	1.25
20	Kent Hrbek	.50
21	Carlton Fisk	1.00
22	Paul Molitor	1.00
23	Dave Winfield	1.00
24	Andre Dawson	.60

1987 Allstate Insurance

This six-card set was the second promotional series of baseball cards created by Allstate Insurance graphic artist Ray Lending for internal use by the company. Modeled after the famous "Diamond Stars" from the 1930s, this set features full-color player portraits of legendary sluggers. "Life Grand Slam" (the promotion theme) is printed beneath the player portrait and the player's name appears in an upper corner. Black and white backs provide personal information, player profiles and career highlights; 15,000 sets of the cards were distributed, although only a few filtered into the collecting hobby. Cards measure 2-3/4" x 3-5/8" in size. Full-color 22" x 28" reproductions of the cards in this set were produced in poster format.

		NM/M
Complete Set (6):		75.00
Common Player:		10.00
(1)	Hank Aaron	12.00
(2)	Joe DiMaggio	15.00
(3)	Jimmie Foxx	10.00
(4)	Lou Gehrig	15.00
(5)	Babe Ruth	20.00
(6)	Ted Williams	15.00

1994 AMC Theaters S.F. Giants

This series of large-format (about 4-1/4" x 11"), blank-back photocards was sponsored by a Bay Area movie house chain. Cards have black-and-white action photos at center with player identification below. At top is a team logo, at bottom is a sponsor's logo. The unnumbered cards are checklisted here in alphabetical order.

		NM/M
Complete Set (33)		30.00
Common Player:		1.00
(1)	Dusty Baker	1.25
(2)	Rod Beck (Ready to pitch.)	1.00
(3)	Rod Beck (Piching follow through.)	1.00
(4)	Mike Benjamin	1.00
(5)	Todd Benzinger	1.00
(6)	Barry Bonds ('93 jersey)	9.00
(7)	Barry Bonds ('94 jersey)	9.00
(8)	Dave Burba	1.00
(9)	John Burkett	1.00
(10)	Mark Carreon	1.00
(11)	Royce Clayton	1.00
(12)	Steve Frey	1.00
(13)	Bryan Hickerson	1.00
(14)	Mike Jackson	1.00
(15)	Darren Lewis	1.00
(16)	Kirt Manwaring	1.00
(17)	Dave Martinez ('93 jersey)	1.00
(18)	Dave Martinez ('94 jersey)	1.00
(19)	Willie McGee	1.00
(20)	Rich Monteleone	1.00
(21)	John Patterson	1.00
(22)	Mark Portugal (Negative reversed, pitching lefty.)	1.00
(23)	Mark Portugal (Correct, pitching righty.)	1.00
(24)	Jeff Reed	1.00
(25)	Kevin Rogers/Standing	1.00
(26)	Kevin Rogers/Pitching	1.00
(27)	Steve Scarsone	1.00
(28)	Bill Swift	1.00
(29)	Robby Thompson ('93 jersey)	1.00
(30)	Robby Thompson ('94 jersey)	1.00
(31)	Salomon Torres	1.00
(32)	Matt Williams/Btg	1.50
(33)	Matt William/Fldg	1.50

1994 American Archives Origins of Baseball

This collectors' issue presents the history of baseball in America from 1744-1899. Sold in box-set form only, the cards are in standard 2-1/2" x 3-1/2" format. Fronts feature sepia-toned photos and line-art on a black background. Backs have a lengthy narrative, also printed in sepia on black. Both sides are UV coated. Individual cards feature early players, team photos, game action scenes or other historical vignettes. The set was produced by American Archives.

	NM/M
Complete Set (101):	6.00
Common Card:	.10
1 Abner Doubleday	.10
2 Doubleday Field	.10
3 Rounders 1744	.10
4 Early Baseball 700 A.D.	.10
5 The Knickerbockers	.10
6 Alex Cartwright	.10
7 Baseball in the 1850s	.10
8 Social Clubs	.10
9 Brooklyn Eckfords	.10
10 New England Baseball	.10
11 Henry Chadwick	.10
12 Brooklyn Excelsiors	.10
13 Abraham Lincoln	.10
14 Andrew Johnson	.10
15 First Enclosed Park	.10
16 Brooklyn Atlantics	.10
17 James Creighton	.10
18 Baseball in the 1860s	.10
19 1869 Red Stockings	.10
20 Cincinnati Celebration	.10
21 Harry Wright	.10
22 Boston Ball Club 1872	.10
23 Arthur Cummings	.10
24 William Hulbert	.10
25 George Wright	.10
26 Albert Spalding	.10
27 Albert Bushong	.10
28 Bid McPhee	.10
29 James O'Rourke	.10
30 Pud Galvin	.10
31 Edwin Bligh	.10
32 William Purcell	.10
33 Roger Connor	.10
34 Cincinnati Ball Club 1882	.10
35 Peter Browning	.10
36 William Gleason	.10
37 Paul Hines	.10
38 Baseball in the 1880s	.10
39 Robert Carruthers	.10
40 New York Metropolitans	.10
41 St. George's Field	.10
42 Charles Radbourne	.10
43 George Andrews	.10
44 William Hoy	.10
45 Chicago Ball Club 1886	.10
46 Cap Anson	.10
47 John Clarkson	.10
48 Mike Kelly	.10
49 Buffalo Bisons 1887	.10
50 Moses Walker	.10
51 Detroit Ball Club 1887	.10
52 Little League	.10
53 Louisville Ball Club 1888	.10
54 John Farrell	.10
55 Walter Latham	.10
56 Fred Dunlap	.10
57 Tim Keefe	.10
58 Cincinnati Ball Club 1888	.10
59 1889 World Tour	.10
60 Dan Brouthers	.10
61 John M. Ward	.10
62 Albert Spalding	.10
63 The Baseball Cap	.10
64 Tom Esterbrook	.10
65 Mark Baldwin	.10
66 Tony Mullane	.10
67 John Glasscock	.10
68 Amos Rusie	.10
69 Jake Beckley	.10
70 Jimmy Collins	.10
71 Charles Comiskey	.10
72 Tom Connolly	.10
73 Mickey Welch	.10
74 Ed Delahanty	.10
75 Hugh Duffy	.10
76 Buck Ewing	.10
77 Clark Griffith	.10
78 Kid Nichols	.10
79 Billy Hamilton	.10
80 Ban Johnson	.10
81 Willie Keeler	.10
82 Bobby Wallace	.10
83 Napoleon Lajoie	.10
84 Connie Mack	.10
85 Fred Clarke	.10
86 Tommy McCarthy	.10
87 John McGraw	.10
88 Jesse Burkett	.10
89 Frank Chance	.10
90 Mordecai Brown	.10
91 New York Nationals	.10
92 Jack Chesbro	.10
93 Sam Thompson	.10
94 Boston v. New York 1891	.10
95 Rube Waddell	.10
96 Joel Kelley	.10
97 Addie Joss	.10
98 The Boston Beaneaters	.10
99 Baltimore Baseball Club	.10
100 The Game in 1899	.10
---- Bibliography	.10

1989 Ames 20/20 Club

This 33-card set was produced by Topps for the Ames toy store chain. As its name implies, the special boxed set highlights players who have recorded 20 home runs and 20 stolen bases in the same season. The glossy cards feature action or posed photos on the front with the player's name at the top and "Ames 20/20 Club" along the bottom. The Topps logo appears in the upper-right corner. Backs have lifetime stats, biographical data and career highlights.

	NM/M
Complete Set (33):	4.00
Common Player:	.10
1 Jesse Barfield	.10
2 Kevin Bass	.10
3 Don Baylor	.10
4 George Bell	.10
5 Barry Bonds	2.00
6 Phil Bradley	.10
7 Ellis Burks	.10
8 Jose Canseco	.25
9 Joe Carter	.10
10 Kal Daniels	.10
11 Eric Davis	.10
12 Mike Davis	.10
13 Andre Dawson	.25
14 Kirk Gibson	.10
15 Pedro Guerrero	.10
16 Rickey Henderson	.45
17 Bo Jackson	.25
18 Howard Johnson	.10
19 Jeffrey Leonard	.10
20 Kevin McReynolds	.10
21 Dale Murphy	.25
22 Dwayne Murphy	.10
23 Dave Parker	.10
24 Kirby Puckett	.60
25 Juan Samuel	.10
26 Ryne Sandberg	.60
27 Mike Schmidt	.75
28 Darryl Strawberry	.10
29 Alan Trammell	.10
30 Andy Van Slyke	.10
31 Devon White	.10
32 Dave Winfield	.45
33 Robin Yount	.45

1990 Ames All-Stars

This 33-card boxed set was the second annual issue produced by Topps for the Ames toy store chain. The cards measure 2-1/2" x 3-1/2" and have a high-gloss finish on front. The set's checklist comprises the active career leaders in runs produced per game. Backs have a green striped background and present player personal data and seasonal major league stats. Issue price for the set was $2.

	NM/M
Complete Set (33):	4.00
Common Player:	.10
1 Dave Winfield	.50
2 George Brett	.75
3 Jim Rice	.25
4 Dwight Evans	.10
5 Robin Yount	.50
6 Dave Parker	.10
7 Eddie Murray	.50
8 Keith Hernandez	.10
9 Andre Dawson	.25
10 Fred Lynn	.10
11 Dale Murphy	.35
12 Jack Clark	.10
13 Rickey Henderson	.50
14 Paul Molitor	.50
15 Cal Ripken	1.50
16 Wade Boggs	.60
17 Tim Raines	.10
18 Don Mattingly	.75
19 Kent Hrbek	.10
20 Kirk Gibson	.10
21 Julio Franco	.10
22 George Bell	.10
23 Darryl Strawberry	.10
24 Kirby Puckett	.60
25 Juan Samuel	.10
26 Alvin Davis	.10
27 Joe Carter	.10
28 Eric Davis	.10
29 Jose Canseco	.40
30 Wally Joyner	.10
31 Will Clark	.10
32 Ruben Sierra	.10
33 Danny Tartabull	.10

1999 Anaheim Angels Police

Sponsored by the Santa Ana district of the California Highway Patrol, five of the cards in this set feature players photographed with police officers. The 2-1/2" x 3-1/2" cards have borderless photos on two sides, with dark blue and gold stripes bearing player identification. The team and CHP logos are in opposite corners. Backs have a smaller version of the front photo along with player data, career information and a safety message.

	NM/M
Complete Set (10):	12.50
Common Player:	.50
1 Chuck Finley	.50
2 Shigetosi Hasegawa	.50
3 Gary DiSarcina	.50
4 Darin Erstad	2.00
5 Mo Vaughn	.50
6 Tim Salmon (W/officers.)	1.00
7 Troy Percival (W/officers.)	.50
8 Jim Edmonds (W/officers.)	3.00
9 Troy Glaus (W/officers.)	5.00
10 Santa Ana CHPs	.25

2000 Anaheim Angels Police

The California Highway Patrol sponsored this promotional set given away at an Angels game. Standard-size cards have color game-action photos which are borderless on top and right. At left and bottom are dark blue and gold stripes. A CHP badge logo appears in the lower-right. Backs have a monochrome version of the front photo, player personal data and career information and a CHP Designated Driver logo at bottom. The back photos on Jim Edmonds' and Troy Percival's cards were switched.

	NM/M
Complete Set (10):	12.50
Common Player:	1.00
1 Chuck Finley	1.00
2 Shigetosi Hasegawa	1.00
3 Gary Disarcina	1.00
4 Darin Erstad	2.00
5 Mo Vaughn	1.00
6 Tim Salmon	2.00
7 Troy Percival	1.00
8 Jim Edmonds	2.00
9 Troy Glaus	4.00
10 CHP San Ana Area Police Officers	1.00

2000 APBA Super Stars Baseball

In the premiere edition of its board game for children, APBA included six player-image game pieces and 30 player cards, one from each team. The irregularly shaped game pieces are 1-11/16" at their widest point and 2-5/16" tall. The same player action picture appears on each side on a brightly colored background. The player cards are round-cornered, 2-1/2" x 3-1/2", with a game-action photo and green borders. The game's APBA Andy logo appears at lower-left. Backs have a few personal data and dice-throw results chart used to play the game. Player cards are unnumbered and listed here in alphabetical order. Retail price at time of issue was $19.95.

	NM/M
Complete Game:	10.00
Common Game Piece:	.50
Common Player Card:	.25
(1) Barry Bonds	.75
(2) Nomar Garciaparra	.45
(3) Ken Griffey Jr.	.50
(4) Mark McGwire	.60
(5) Mike Piazza	.50
(6) Alex Rodriguez	.60
(1) Roberto Alomar	.30
(2) Jeff Bagwell	.40
(3) Barry Bonds	.75
(4) Jeromy Burnitz	.25
(5) Carlos Delgado	.35
(6) Jermaine Dye	.25
(7) Cliff Floyd	.25
(8) Jason Giambi	.35
(9) Juan Gonzalez	.30
(10) Shawn Green	.30
(11) Ken Griffey Jr.	.50
(12) Vladimir Guerrero	.40
(13) Tony Gwynn	.45
(14) Todd Helton	.30
(15) Derek Jeter	.75
(16) Randy Johnson	.40
(17) Chipper Jones	.45
(18) Jason Kendall	.25
(19) Matt Lawton	.25
(20) Pedro Martinez	.40
(21) Mark McGwire	.60
(22) Mike Piazza	.50
(23) Cal Ripken Jr.	.75
(24) Alex Rodriguez	.60
(25) Ivan Rodriguez	.30
(26) Scott Rolen	.30
(27) Sammy Sosa	.45
(28) Frank Thomas	.35
(29) Greg Vaughn	.25
(30) Mo Vaughn	.25

1996 Arby's Cleveland Indians

These cards honor, according to the logo on front, "1995 Tribe Milestones." Fronts are bordered in black with the action photo vignetted in black. The player's milestone is printed in white on a red strip at bottom. Backs have a large baseball, bat and glove in the background with a color portrait at top. A diamond shaped area at center has stats. Cello-wrapped cards were available one per week with a purchase.

	NM/M
Complete Set (8):	10.00
Common Player:	1.00
1 Eddie Murray (3,000th Hit)	3.00
2 Orel Hershiser (L.C.S. MVP in Both Leagues)	1.00
3 Manny Ramirez (Silver Slugger)	3.00
4 Jose Mesa (Saves Record)	1.00
5 Kenny Lofton (Gold Glove/Most Steals)	1.00
6 Omar Vizquel (3rd Straight Gold Glove)	1.00
7 Albert Belle (50/50 Season)	1.00
8 Carlos Baerga (.310+ Ave. Four Straight Years)	1.00

2004 Archway Seattle Mariners

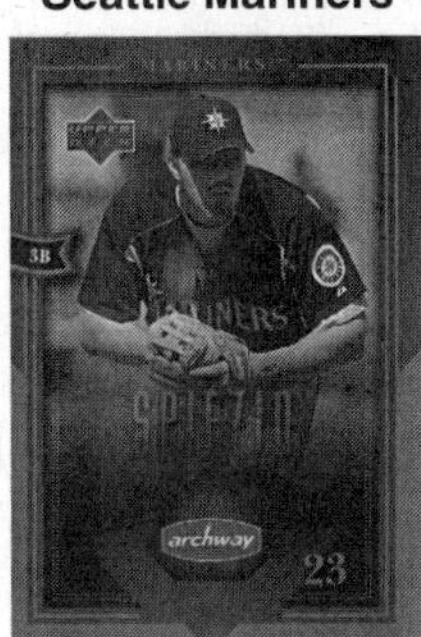

This stadium give-away set was sponsored by Archway Cookies and produced by Upper Deck. Fronts have green and tan borders and game-action photos. Backs repeat the color scheme and include Major League stats and licensor logos.

	NM/M
Complete Set (16):	8.00
Common Player:	.25
1 Ichiro	6.00
2 Raul Ibanez	.25
3 Randy Winn	.25
4 John Olerud	.25
5 Bret Boone	.50
6 Rich Aurilia	.25
7 Scott Spiezio	.25
8 Dan Wilson	.25
9 Edgar Martinez	.50
10 Freddy Garcia	.25
11 Jamie Moyer	.25
12 Joel Pineiro	.50
13 Gil Meche	.25
14 Ryan Franklin	.25
15 Shigetoshi Hasegawa	.25
16 Eddie Guardado	.25

2005 Arizona Republic Diamondbacks Deck

This stadium giveaway was sponsored by a local newspaper. Cards are 2-3/16" x 3-3/8" with rounded corners. Backs have a sponsor's logo. Each player appears four times in the deck, with an identical portrait photo on the same value card in each suit. Two Jokers complete the boxed set.

	NM/M
Complete Set (54):	10.00
Common Player:	.25
2 Koyie Hill	.25
3 Chad Tracy	.50
4 Craig Counsell	.25
5 Troy Glaus	.35
6 Royce Clayton	.25
7 Luis Gonzalez	.35
8 Jose Cruz, Jr.	.25
9 Shawn Green	.45
10 Brandon Webb	.35
J Russ Ortiz	.25
Q Mascot	.25
K Bob Melvin	.25
A Javier Vasquez	.35
JOKER Mascot	.25
JOKER Mascot	.25

2003 Arizona Diamondbacks Can Kickers Club

The attributed date is speculative, since there is no copyright date on the cards. The method of the cards' distrubtion is also unknown. These are high-tech chromium cards issued to support the team's anti-chewing tobacco program aimed at children. Fronts have color or colorized player photos with the player name at bottom. Backs are identical and feature a Peanuts cartoon, an anti-chew message and the club logo.

	NM/M
Complete Set (3):	10.00
Common Player:	2.00
(1) Steve Finley	2.00
(2) Joe Garagiola	3.00
(3) Mark McGwire	6.00

1996 Arizona Lottery

To promote its Diamond Bucks scratch-off lottery game, the Arizona Lottery issued this three-card set of Hall of Fame players' cards. Fronts have black-and-white photos which have had uniform logos airbrushed away. Borders are black. Backs are also in black-and-white, with player data and career highlights, along with the sponsors logos. Sets were given with the purchase of $5 in lottery tickets.

		NM/M
Complete Set (3):		7.50
Common Player:		2.00
(1)	Ernie Banks	4.00
(2)	Gaylord Perry	2.00
(3)	Brooks Robinson	3.00

2001 Armour Stars

The manner of distribution for this seven-card cello wrapped set is unknown. Produced by Playoff, the cards have game-action photos on front with red and black borders. A gold-foil Armour Stars logo is at bottom. Backs have a portrait photo, biographical data, 2000 and career stats and a trivia question about which condiments the player prefers on his hot dogs. All photos have had team logos removed.

		NM/M
Complete Set (7):		6.00
Common Player:		.50
1	Roberto Alomar	.50
2	Barry Bonds	2.00
3	Kevin Brown	.50
4	Roger Clemens	1.00
5	Greg Maddux	.75
6	Alex Rodriguez	1.50
7	Frank Thomas	.65

1997 AT&T Ambassadors of Baseball

Taking over for the tour previously sponsored by MCI, AT&T brought a visiting team of former major league ballplayers to overseas military bases in 1997, where they played base teams in exhibition games. Card fronts feature photos (with uniform logos airbrushed away) from the players' major league days, with AT&T and Ambassadors Tour logos. Backs have typical player data.

		NM/M
Complete Set (4):		30.00
Common Player:		6.00
(1)	Jesse Barfield	6.00
(2)	Darrell Evans	12.00
(3)	Al Hrabosky	6.00
(4)	Jerry Koosman	12.00

1981 Atlanta Braves Police

The first Atlanta Braves police set was a cooperative effort of the team, Hostess, Coca-Cola and the Atlanta Police Department. Card fronts feature full-color photos of 27 different Braves and manager Bobby Cox. Police and team logos are on the card backs. Card backs offer capsule biographies of the players, along with a tip for youngsters. The 2-5/8" x 4-1/8" cards are numbered by uniform number. Terry Harper (#19) appears to be somewhat scarcer than the other cards in the set. Reportedly, 33,000 sets were printed.

		NM/M
Complete Set (27):		10.00
Common Player:		.25
1	Jerry Royster	.25
3	Dale Murphy	3.00
4	Biff Pocoroba	.25
5	Bob Horner	.75
6	Bob Cox	.35
9	Luis Gomez	.25
10	Chris Chambliss	.25
15	Bill Nahorodny	.25
16	Rafael Ramirez	.25
17	Glenn Hubbard	.25
18	Claudell Washington	.25
19	Terry Harper/SP	.75
20	Bruce Benedict	.25
24	John Montefusco	.25
25	Rufino Linares	.25
26	Gene Garber	.25
30	Brian Asselstine	.25
34	Larry Bradford	.25
35	Phil Niekro	1.50
37	Rick Camp	.25
39	Al Hrabosky	.25
40	Tommy Boggs	.25
42	Rick Mahler	.25
45	Ed Miller	.25
46	Gaylord Perry	1.50
49	Preston Hanna	.25
---	Hank Aaron	5.00

1982 Atlanta Braves Police

After their successful debut in 1981, the Atlanta Braves, the Atlanta Police Department, Coca-Cola and Hostess issued another card set in '82. This 30- card set is extremely close in format to the 1981 set and again measures 2-5/8" x 4-1/8". The full-color player photos are outstanding, and each card front also bears a statement marking the 1982 Braves' record-breaking 13-game win streak at the season's beginning. Card backs offer short biographies and "Tips from the Braves." Sponsors logos are also included. Reportedly, only 8,000 of these sets were printed.

		NM/M
Complete Set (30):		10.00
Common Player:		.25
1	Jerry Royster	.25
3	Dale Murphy	4.00
4	Biff Pocoroba	.25
5	Bob Horner	.50
6	Randy Johnson	.25
8	Bob Watson	.25
9	Joe Torre	1.00
10	Chris Chambliss	.25
15	Claudell Washington	.25
16	Rafael Ramirez	.25
17	Glenn Hubbard	.25
20	Bruce Benedict	.25
22	Brett Butler	.50
23	Tommie Aaron	.25
25	Rufino Linares	.50
26	Gene Garber	.25
27	Larry McWilliams	.25
28	Larry Whisenton	.25
32	Steve Bedrosian	.25
35	Phil Niekro	1.50
37	Rick Camp	.25
38	Joe Cowley	.25
39	Al Hrabosky	.25
42	Rick Mahler	.25
43	Bob Walk	.25
45	Bob Gibson	3.00
49	Preston Hanna	.25
52	Joe Pignatano	.25
53	Dal Maxvill	.25
54	Rube Walker	.25

1983 Atlanta Braves Police

An almost exact replica of their 1982 set, the 1983 Atlanta Braves police set includes 30 cards numbered by uniform. Sponsors Hostess, Coca-Cola and the Atlanta Police Department returned for the third year. The cards are again 2-5/8" x 4-1/8", with full-color photos and police and team logos on the card fronts. A statement noting the team's 1982 National League Western Division title in the upper right corner is the key difference on the card fronts. As in 1982, 8,000 sets were reportedly printed.

		NM/M
Complete Set (30):		6.00
Common Player:		.15
1	Jerry Royster	.15
3	Dale Murphy	3.00
4	Biff Pocoroba	.15
5	Bob Horner	.25
6	Randy G. Johnson	.15
8	Bob Watson	.15
9	Joe Torre	.50
10	Chris Chambliss	.15
11	Ken Smith	.15
15	Claudell Washington	.15
16	Rafael Ramirez	.15
17	Glenn Hubbard	.15
19	Terry Harper	.15
20	Bruce Benedict	.15
22	Brett Butler	.15
24	Larry Owen	.15
26	Gene Garber	.15
27	Pascual Perez	.15
29	Craig McMurtry	.15
32	Steve Bedrosian	.15
33	Pete Falcone	.15
35	Phil Niekro	1.00
36	Sonny Jackson	.15
37	Rick Camp	.15
45	Bob Gibson	2.00
49	Rick Behenna	.15
51	Terry Forster	.15
52	Joe Pignatano	.15
53	Dal Maxvill	.15
54	Rube Walker	.15

1984 Atlanta Braves Police

A fourth annual effort by the Braves, the Atlanta Police Department, Coca-Cola and Hostess, this 30-card set continued to be printed in a 2-5/8" x 4-1/8" format, with full-color photos plus team and police logos on the card fronts. For the first time, the cards also have a large logo and date in the upper right corner. Hostess and Coke logos again are on the card backs, with brief player information and a safety tip. Two cards in the set (Pascual Perez and Rafael Ramirez) were issued in Spanish. Cards were distributed two per week by Atlanta police officers. As in 1982 and 1983, a reported 8,000 sets were printed.

		NM/M
Complete Set (30):		8.00
Common Player:		.25
1	Jerry Royster	.25
3	Dale Murphy	3.00
5	Bob Horner	.40
6	Randy Johnson	.25
8	Bob Watson	.25
9	Joe Torre	.75
10	Chris Chambliss	.25
11	Mike Jorgensen	.25
15	Claudell Washington	.25
16	Rafael Ramirez	.25
17	Glenn Hubbard	.25
19	Terry Harper	.25
20	Bruce Benedict	.25
25	Alex Trevino	.25
26	Gene Garber	.25
27	Pascual Perez	.25
28	Gerald Perry	.25
29	Craig McMurtry	.25
31	Donnie Moore	.25
32	Steve Bedrosian	.25
33	Pete Falcone	.25
37	Rick Camp	.25
39	Len Barker	.25
42	Rick Mahler	.25
45	Bob Gibson	2.50
51	Terry Forster	.25
52	Joe Pignatano	.25
53	Dal Maxvill	.25
54	Rube Walker	.25
55	Luke Appling	2.00

1985 Atlanta Braves Police

There are again 30 full-color cards in this fifth annual set. Hostess, Coca-Cola and the Atlanta Police Department joined the team as sponsors again for the 2-5/8" x 4-1/8" set. Card backs are similar to previous years, with the only difference on the fronts being a swap in position for the year and team logo. The cards are checklisted by uniform number.

		NM/M
Complete Set (30):		4.00
Common Player:		.25
2	Albert Hall	.25
3	Dale Murphy	3.00
5	Rick Cerone	.25
7	Bobby Wine	.25
10	Chris Chambliss	.25
11	Bob Horner	.45
12	Paul Runge	.25
15	Claudell Washington	.25
16	Rafael Ramirez	.25
17	Glenn Hubbard	.25
18	Paul Zuvella	.25
19	Terry Harper	.25
20	Bruce Benedict	.25
22	Eddie Haas	.25
24	Ken Oberkfell	.25
26	Gene Garber	.25
27	Pascual Perez	.25
28	Gerald Perry	.25
29	Craig McMurtry	.25
32	Steve Bedrosian	.25
33	Johnny Sain	.30
34	Zane Smith	.25
36	Brad Komminsk	.25
37	Rick Camp	.25
39	Len Barker	.25
40	Bruce Sutter	1.50
42	Rick Mahler	.25
51	Terry Forster	.25
52	Leo Mazzone	.25
53	Bobby Dews	.25

1986 Atlanta Braves Police

The Police Athletic League of Atlanta issued a 30-card full-color set featuring Braves players and personnel. Cards measure 2-5/8" x 4-1/8". Fronts include player photos with name, uniform number and position below the photo. Backs offer the 100th Anniversary Coca-Cola logo, player information, statistics and a safety related tip. This was the sixth consecutive year that the Braves issued a safety set available from police officers in Atlanta.

		NM/M
Complete Set (30):		4.00
Common Player:		.25
2	Russ Nixon	.25
3	Dale Murphy	3.00
4	Bob Skinner	.25
5	Billy Sample	.25
7	Chuck Tanner	.25
8	Willie Stargell	1.50
9	Ozzie Virgil	.25
10	Chris Chambliss	.25
11	Bob Horner	.25
14	Andres Thomas	.25
15	Claudell Washington	.25
16	Rafael Ramirez	.25
17	Glenn Hubbard	.25
18	Omar Moreno	.25
19	Terry Harper	.25
20	Bruce Benedict	.25
23	Ted Simmons	.25
24	Ken Oberkfell	.25
26	Gene Garber	.25
29	Craig McMurtry	.25
30	Paul Assenmacher	.25
33	Johnny Sain	.25
34	Zane Smith	.25
38	Joe Johnson	.25
40	Bruce Sutter	2.00
42	Rick Mahler	.25
46	David Palmer	.25
48	Duane Ward	.25
49	Jeff Dedmon	.25
52	Al Monchak	.25

1987 Atlanta Braves Fire Safety

These fire safety cards were given out at several different Atlanta games, with about 25,000 sets in all being distributed. The 4" x 6" cards feature Braves players in an oval frame, bordered in red, white and blue. Only the player's last name is shown on front. Backs contain the player's name, position and personal data plus a Smokey Bear cartoon fire safety message.

		NM/M
Complete Set (27):		4.00
Common Player:		.25
1	Zane Smith	.25
2	Charlie Puleo	.25
3	Randy O'Neal	.25
4	David Palmer	.25
5	Rick Mahler	.25
6	Ed Olwine	.25
7	Jeff Dedmon	.25
8	Paul Assenmacher	.25
9	Gene Garber	.25
10	Jim Acker	.25
11	Bruce Benedict	.25
12	Ozzie Virgil	.25
13	Ted Simmons	.25
14	Dale Murphy	3.00
15	Graig Nettles	.35
16	Ken Oberkfell	.25
17	Gerald Perry	.25
18	Rafael Ramirez	.25
19	Ken Griffey	.25
20	Andres Thomas	.25
21	Glenn Hubbard	.25
22	Damaso Garcia	.25
23	Gary Roenicke	.25
24	Dion James	.25
25	Albert Hall	.25
26	Chuck Tanner	.25
---	Smokey Bear Logo Card/Checklist	.10

1986 Ault Foods Blue Jays stickers

The Ault Foods Blue Jays set is comprised of 24 full-color stickers. Designed to be placed in a special album, the stickers measure 2" x 3" in size. The attractive album measures 9" x 12" and is printed on glossy stock. While the stickers carry no information except for the player's last name and uniform number, the 20-page album contains extensive personal and statistical information about each of the 24 players.

		NM/M
Complete Set (24):		12.50
Common Player:		.50
Album:		4.00
1	Tony Fernandez	1.00
5	Rance Mulliniks	.50
7	Damaso Garcia	.50
11	George Bell	1.50
12	Ernie Whitt	.50
13	Buck Martinez	.50
15	Lloyd Moseby	.50
16	Garth Iorg	.50
17	Kelly Gruber	.50
18	Jim Clancy	.50
22	Jimmy Key	1.00
23	Cecil Fielder	5.00
25	Steve Davis	.50
26	Willie Upshaw	.50
29	Jesse Barfield	.50
31	Jim Acker	.50
33	Doyle Alexander	.50
36	Bill Caudill	.50
37	Dave Stieb	1.00
39	Don Gordon	.50
44	Cliff Johnson	.50
46	Gary Lavelle	.50
50	Tom Henke	.50
53	Dennis Lamp	.50

1982 Authentic Sports Autographs Mickey Mantle Story

This 72-card set chronicles the life of Mickey Mantle in contemporary photos, many from Mantle's own collection and many picturing him with such stars of the era as Maris, DiMaggio, Ted Williams, Mays, etc. A total of 20,000 sets was produced; 5,000 of them feature a genuine Mantle autograph on card #1 and 15,000 sets have no autograph. Backs of cards from the autographed sets are printed in blue while the unautographed sets have backs printed in red. Issue price was $25 for the autographed set, $13 for the unsigned version.

		NM/M
Comp. Set, #1 Autographed (72):		200.00
Comp. Set, Unautographed (72):		45.00
Common Card:		1.00
1	Header card	1.00
2	Mickey & Merlyn 12/23/51	1.00
3	Spring Training 1951	1.50
4	Spring Training 1951	1.50
5	Mickey's Mom, Mickey & Merlyn	1.00
6	4/15/51 1st Homer in NY	1.00
7	1951 - DiMaggio, Mantle, Williams	1.50
8	1951- Mickey signs for 1952	1.00
9	Martin & Mickey Jr. 4/12/52	1.00
10	Brothers Roy and Ray	1.00
11	Spring Training 1952	1.00
12	1952- Bauer, Hopp, Mantle	1.50
13	1952 Season	1.00
14	Mantle & Martin 1952 Series	1.50
15	Billy & Mickey 1953	1.50
16	Knee Injury 1953	1.00
17	1953 - Before knee surgery	1.00
18	New business 1953	1.00
19	1953 World Series Power	1.00
20	1953 The long Home Run	1.50
21	1955 Hall of Fame Game	1.50
22	1955	1.00
23	1955 - Skowron, Rizzuto, Mantle	1.50
24	1954 - Jackie Robinson at 1st	1.00
25	1956 - Mickey with Ted Williams	1.50
26	1955 - Skowron, Berra, Mantle	1.50
27	1956 - Mickey safe at first	1.00
28	1956 World Series	1.00
29	1957 - Yogi, Whitey, Mickey	1.00
30	1957 - Roy Sievers with Mickey	1.00
31	1957 World Series	1.00
32	1957 Hitchcock Award	1.50
33	1957 - Mickey with Cardinal Spellman	1.00
34	1957 - Singing with Teresa Brewer	1.00
35	1957 - Brooks Robinson & Mickey	1.50
36	1958 World Series	1.00
37	1958 All Star Game with Banks	1.50
38	With Stengel 1959	1.50
39	1960 - With Roger Maris	1.50
40	1960 World Series	1.00
41	1961 All Star Game with Maris & Mays	1.00
42	Blanchard	1.50
43	1961 - with Maris & Mrs. Babe Ruth	1.50
44	1961 - Mickey Congratulates Maris	1.00
45	1961 - Maris & Mantle	1.00
46	400th Career HR 9/11/62	1.00
47	1962 World Series	1.50
48	1963 season	1.50
49	1963 World Series	1.50
50	1964 World Series	1.50
51	1964 - Pepitone, Ford, Mantle	1.00
52	1964 season	1.50
53	1965 Mickey's Day	1.50
54	1965 season	1.50
55	1966 - with Joe DiMaggio	1.50
56	Mantle family	1.00
57	1967 season	1.50
58	1968 - hits HR No. 529	1.00
59	1968 - Retirement	1.00
60	1968 - His farewell	1.50
61	Mickey's trophy room	1.00
62	1970 - Welcome back Coach	1.00
63	1973 - TV commercial	1.00
64	1974 visit	1.00
65	1974 visit	1.00
66	1974 Hall of Fame inductees	1.00
67	1979 Old Timers Game	1.00
68	1981 Old Timers Game	1.00
69	Family Day	1.00
70	The Mantle Swing	1.00
71	The Mantle Swing	1.00
72	The Mantle Swing	1.00

1983 Authentic Sports Autographs

These collectors' issue sets of a dozen cards each present the careers of 11 Hall of Famers in pictures and words. Each 2-1/2" x 3-1/2" card has a black-and-white or color photo on front with a card title and red or green border graphics. Backs present a narrative of the player's career and some include a small portrait photo. Each set was made available in both an unautographed version and a version in which the No. 1 card was authentically autographed.

		NM/M
(1)	Hank Aaron Story	15.00
(1a)	Hank Aaron Story, Autographed	50.00
(2)	Yogi Berra Story	6.00
(2a)	Yogi Berra Story, Autographed	20.00
(3)	Joe DiMaggio Story	15.00
(3a)	Joe DiMaggio Story, Autographed	150.00
(4)	Bob Feller Story	7.50
(4a)	Bob Feller Story, Autographed	15.00
(5)	Juan Marichal Story	7.50
(5a)	Juan Marichal Story, Autographed	20.00
(6)	Willie Mays Story	10.00
(6a)	Willie Mays Story, Autographed	50.00
(7)	Johnny Mize Story	6.00
(7a)	Johnny Mize Story, Autogrphed	15.00
(8)	Brooks Robinson Story	6.00
(8a)	Brooks Robinson Story, Autographed	15.00
(9)	Frank Robinson Story	6.00
(9a)	Frank Robinson Story, Autographed	20.00
(10)	Duke Snider Story	6.00
(10a)	Duke Snider Story, Autographed	20.00
(11)	Warren Spahn Story	6.00
(11a)	Warren Spahn Story, Autographed	20.00

2005 Azteca Seattle Mariners Hispanic Heroes

This set of M's Latino players was a stadium giveaway to 20,000 fans at the 3rd annual Latin American Beisbol Night, September 13 at Safeco Field.

		NM/M
Complete Set (9):		10.00
Common Player:		.50
1	Adrian Beltre	1.00
2	Yuniesky Betancourt	1.00
3	Eddie Guardado	.50
4	Felix Hernandez	5.00
5	Raul Ibanez	.50
6	Jose Lopez	1.00
7	Julio Mateo	.50
8	Joel Pineiro	.50
9	Yorvit Torrealba	.50

B

1998 Ball Park Detroit Tigers

Fans in attendance at the August 9 game at Tiger Stadium received this team set sponsored by Ball Park franks, the stadium hot dog concessionairre. Cards are standard 2-1/2" x 3-1/2" format printed on light cardboard. Fronts have color posed or action photos with white borders. Player identification is in a strip at left. Backs have a light blue background, overprinted in dark blue with the player's personal data, stats and a 1997 season highlight, along with the sponsor's logo and a picture of a moving baseball.

		NM/M
Complete Set (26):		9.00
Common Player:		.50
01	Gabe Alvarez	.50
02	Matt Anderson	.50
03	Paul Bako	.50
04	Trey Beamon	.50
05	Buddy Bell	.50
06	Geronimo Berroa	.50
07	Doug Bochtler	.50
08	Doug Brocail	.50
09	Raul Casanova	.50
10	Frank Castillo	.50
11	Frank Catalanotto	.50
12	Tony Clark	.50
13	Dean Crow	.50
14	Deivi Cruz	.50
15	Damion Easley	.50
16	Bryce Florie	.50
17	Luis Gonzalez	2.50
18	Seth Greisinger	.50
19	Bobby Higginson	.75
20	Brian Hunter	.50
21	Todd Jones	.50
22	Brian Moehler	.50
23	Brian Powell	.50
24	Joe Randa	.50
25	Sean Runyan	.50
26	Justin Thompson	.50

1994 Baltimore Orioles Program Cards

Virtually the entire O's organization, major and minor leaguers, was included in this season-long promotion. One of 12 nine-card sheets was inserted into the team's programs, which sold for $3. A reported 17,000 sets were produced. The sheets are unperforated and measure 7-1/2" x 10-1/2". Fronts have color game-action or posed photos within an orange border. A team logo is at top-right. At bottom is a black strip with the player's number (if a major leaguer), name and position in white. Backs are printed in black and orange on white with biographical details and complete major and minor league stats. The unnumbered cards are checklisted here alphabetically.

		NM/M
Complete Set, Sheets (12):		25.00
Complete Set, Singles (108):		25.00
Common Player:		.25
(1)	Manny Alexander	.25
(2)	Brady Anderson	.25
(3)	Matt Anderson	.25
(4)	Harold Baines	.25
(5)	Myles Barnden	.25
(6)	Kimera Bartee	.25
(7)	Juan Bautista	.25
(8)	Armando Benitez	.25
(9)	Joe Borowski	.25
(10)	Brian Brewer	.25
(11)	Brandon Bridgers	.25
(12)	Cory Brown	.25
(13)	Damon Buford	.25
(14)	Philip Byrne	.25
(15)	Rocco Cafaro	.25
(16)	Paul Carey	.25
(17)	Carlos Chavez	.25
(18)	Eric Chavez	.25
(19)	Steve Chitren	.25
(20)	Mike Cook	.25
(21)	Shawn Curran	.25
(22)	Kevin Curtis	.25
(23)	Joey Dawley	.25
(24)	Jim Dedrick	.25
(25)	Cesar Devarez	.25
(26)	Mike Devereaux	.25
(27)	Brian DuBois	.25
(28)	Keith Eaddy	.25
(29)	Mark Eichhorn	.25
(30)	Scott Emerson	.25
(31)	Vaughn Eshelman	.25
(32)	Craig Faulkner	.25
(33)	Sid Fernandez	.25
(34)	Rick Forney	.25
(35)	Jim Foster	.25
(36)	Jesse Garcia	.25
(37)	Mike Garguilo	.25
(38)	Rich Gedman	.25
(39)	Leo Gomez	.25
(40)	Rene Gonzalez	.25
(41)	Curtis Goodwin	.25
(42)	Kris Gresham	.25
(43)	Shane Hale	.25
(44)	Jeffrey Hammonds	.25
(45)	Jimmy Haynes	.25
(46)	Chris Hoiles	.25
(47)	Tim Hullett	.25
(48)	Matt Jarvis	.25
(49)	Scott Klingenbeck	.25
(50)	Rick Krivda	.25
(51)	David Lamb	.25
(52)	Chris Lemp	.25
(53)	T.R. Lewis	.25
(54)	Brian Link	.25
(55)	John Lombardi	.25
(56)	Rob Lukachyk	.25
(57)	Calvin Maduro	.25
(58)	Barry Manuel	.25
(59)	Lincoln Martin	.25
(60)	Scott McClain	.25
(61)	Ben McDonald	.25
(62)	Kevin McGehee	.25
(63)	Mark McLemore	.25
(64)	Miguel Mejia	.25
(65)	Feliciano Mercedes	.25
(66)	Jose Millares	.25
(67)	Brent Miller	.25
(68)	Alan Mills	.25
(69)	Jamie Moyer	.25
(70)	Mike Mussina	1.50
(71)	Sherman Obando	.25
(72)	Alex Ochoa	.25
(73)	John O'Donoghue	.25
(74)	Mike Oquist	.25
(75)	Bo Ortiz	.25
(76)	Billy Owens	.25
(77)	Rafael Palmeiro	2.00
(78)	Dave Paveloff	.25
(79)	Brad Pennington	.25
(80)	Bill Percibel	.25
(81)	Jim Poole	.25
(82)	Jay Powell	.25
(83)	Arthur Rhodes	.25
(84)	Matt Riemer	.25
(85)	Cal Ripken Jr.	5.00
(86)	Kevin Ryan	.25
(87)	Chris Sabo	.25
(88)	Brian Sackinsky	.25
(89)	Francisco Saneaux	.25
(90)	Jason Satre	.25
(91)	David Segui	.25
(92)	Jose Serra	.25
(93)	Larry Shenk	.25
(94)	Lee Smith	.25
(95)	Lonnie Smith	.25
(96)	Mark Smith	.25
(97)	Garrett Stephenson	.25
(98)	Jeff Tackett	.25
(99)	Brad Tyler	.25
(100)	Pedro Ulises	.25
(101)	Jack Voight	.25
(102)	Jim Walker	.25
(103)	B.J. Waszgis	.25
(104)	Jim Wawruck	.25
(105)	Mel Wearing	.25
(106)	Mark Williamson	.25
(107)	Brian Wood	.25
(108)	Gregg Zaun	.25

1984 Baseball Cards Magazine Repli-Cards

With its August 1984 issue, Baseball Cards Magazine pioneered the use of "repli-cards" to enhance feature articles and increase sales. The cards were printed on cardboard stock and stapled into the magazines. Most of the cards were done in the style of earlier popular card issues, though some featured original designs and others were reproductions of actual cards. Some of baseball's best artists' and photographers' work appears on the cards. The inclusion of repli-cards ceased after 1993 when abuses by other "publishers" caused baseball's licensors to threaten legal action. Values quoted are for single cards cut from the panel; complete panels or magazines command a premium. Cards are grouped by magazine issue and numbered with a month-designation.

		NM/M
Complete Set (3):		10.00
Aug.	Ted Williams (1953 Topps style)	4.50
Aug.	Dale Murphy (1953 Topps style)	3.50
Oct.	Mickey Mantle (1949 Bowman style)	6.00

1985 Baseball Cards Magazine Repli-Cards

In three of its 1985 issues, Baseball Cards Magazine offered "repli-cards" to enhance feature articles and increase sales. The cards were printed on cardboard stock and stapled into the magazines. Original designs and reproductions of earlier cards were used. Values quoted are for single cards cut from the panel; complete panels or magazines command a premium. Cards are grouped by magazine issue and numbered with a month-designation.

		NM/M
Complete Set (6):		12.00
Common Player:		2.00
April	Chuck Connors (Original design.)	2.00
April	Chuck Connors (1952 Topps style)	2.00
June	Pete Rose (Reproduction 1965 Topps.)	3.00
June	Fritz Ackley, Steve Carlton (Reproduction 1965 Topps.)	2.00
Oct.	Mickey Mantle (Reproduction 1955 Bowman #202.)	4.00
Oct.	Ernie Banks (Reproduction 1955 Bowman #242.)	2.00

1986 Baseball Cards Magazine Repli-Cards

In three of its 1986 issues, Baseball Cards Magazine offered "repli-cards" to enhance feature articles and increase sales. The cards were printed on cardboard stock and stapled into the magazines. Reproductions of existing cards and modern player cards done in the style of vintage issues were used. Values quoted are for single cards cut from the panel; complete panels or magazines command a premium. Cards are grouped by magazine issue and numbered with a month-designation.

		NM/M
	Complete Set (12):	12.00
	Common Player:	.50
April	Vince Coleman (Kondritz Trading Cards sample.)	.50
April	Vince Coleman (Kondritz Trading Cards sample.)	.50
June	Stan Musial (Reproduction 1953 Bowman.)	2.00
June	Roy Campanella (Reproduction 1953 Bowman.)	1.00
June	Yogi Berra (Reproduction 1953 Bowman.)	1.50
Dec.	Don Mattingly (1951 Topps Red Back style)	3.00
Dec.	Wally Joyner (1951 Topps Red Back style)	.50
Dec.	Wade Boggs (1951 Topps All-Stars style)	1.50
Dec.	Dwight Gooden (1951 Topps All-Stars style)	.50
Dec.	George Brett (Reproduction 1981 Donruss proof.)	3.00
Dec.	Reggie Jackson (Reproduction 1981 Donruss proof.)	2.50
Dec.	Lou Piniella (Reproduction 1982 Fleer proof.)	.75

1987 Baseball Cards Magazine Repli-Cards

In four of its 1987 issues, Baseball Cards Magazine offered "repli-cards" to enhance feature articles and increase sales. The cards were printed on cardboard stock and stapled into the magazines. Original designs and modern player cards done in the style of vintage issues were used. Values quoted are for single cards cut from the panel; complete panels or magazines command a premium. Cards are grouped by magazine issue and numbered with a month-designation.

		NM/M
	Complete Set (10):	14.00
	Common Player:	.40
April	Don Mattingly (1983 Donruss style)	5.00
April	Don Mattingly (1983 Topps style)	5.00
Sept.	Ozzie Canseco (Original "Future Stars" design.)	.40
Sept.	Patrick Lennon (Original "Future Stars" design.)	.40
Oct.	Eric Davis (1951 Bowman style)	.75
Oct.	Bo Jackson (1951 Bowman style)	.75
Oct.	Stan Musial (1951 Bowman style)	1.50
Dec.	Dale Murphy (1981 Fleer style)	1.50
Dec.	Tim Raines (1981 Fleer style)	.50
Dec.	Double Trouble (Eric Davis, Mark McGwire (1981 Fleer style)	2.50

1988 Baseball Cards Magazine Repli-Cards

In six of its 1988 issues, Baseball Cards Magazine offered "repli-cards" to enhance feature articles and increase sales. The cards were printed on cardboard stock and stapled into the magazines. Original designs, reproductions and modern player cards done in the style of vintage issues were used. Values quoted are for single cards cut from the panel; complete panels or magazines command a premium. Cards are grouped by magazine issue and numbered with a month-designation.

		NM/M
	Complete Set (16):	27.50
	Common Player:	.40
Feb.	Babe Ruth (1936 Diamond Stars style)	1.50
Feb.	Wade Boggs (1936 Diamond Stars style)	1.50
Feb.	Mark McGwire (1936 Diamond Stars style; available only via mail-in offer)	4.00
April	Ted Williams (1952 Topps style)	1.50
April	Ted Williams (Reproduction 1954 Bowman #66.)	2.50
June	Joey Meyer (Original design.)	.40
June	Sam Horn (Original design.)	.40
Aug.	Roger "Rocket" Clemens (1941 Play Ball style)	2.50
Aug.	Kirk Gibson (1941 Play Ball style)	.40
Aug.	Jack Clark (1941 Play Ball style)	.40
Oct.	Mickey Mantle (1956 Bowman proof style)	7.50
Oct.	Jackie Robinson (1952 Bowman style)	1.50
Oct.	Dave Winfield (1974 Topps "Washington" style)	1.25
Dec.	Mickey Mantle (Reproduction 1952 Bowman.)	2.50
Dec.	Mickey Mantle (Reproduction 1951 Bowman.)	4.50
Dec.	Mickey Mantle (Reproduction 1952 Topps.)	6.00

1989 Baseball Cards Magazine Repli-Cards

Beginning with its January 1989 issue, Baseball Cards Magazine began issuing its repli-cards in panels of six cards per month, creating an annual set of 72 insert cards. Contemporary players were presented in the designs of classic Topps sets of the 1950s-1970s. In 1989 the magazine's cards were in the style of 1959 Topps. Besides the individual player's

cards, specialty cards included "Rookie Stars of 1989" and multi-player feature cards.

		NM/M
	Complete Set (72):	20.00
	Common Player:	.15
1	Keith Hernandez	.15
2	Will Clark	.15
3	Andres Galarraga	.15
4	Mark McGwire	1.50
5	Don Mattingly	1.00
6	Ricky Jordan (Rookie Stars)	.15
7	Juan Samuel	.15
8	Julio Franco	.15
9	Harold Reynolds	.15
10	Gregg Jefferies (Rookie Stars)	.15
11	Ryne Sandberg	.75
12	Lou Whitaker	.15
13	Ozzie Smith	.75
14	Gary Sheffield (Rookie Stars)	.25
15	Alan Trammell	.15
16	Cal Ripken Jr.	2.00
17	Barry Larkin	.15
18	Tony Fernandez	.15
19	Mike Schmidt	1.00
20	Wade Boggs	.75
21	Gary Gaetti	.15
22	Chris Sabo (Rookie Stars)	.15
23	Paul Molitor	.60
24	Carney Lansford	.15
25	Dave Winfield	.60
26	Darryl Strawberry	.15
27	Tony Gwynn	.75
28	Darryl Hamilton	.15
29	Jose Canseco	.45
30	Andre Dawson	.25
31	Kirby Puckett	.75
32	Cameron Drew (Rookie Stars)	.15
33	Robin Yount	.60
34	Ellis Burks	.15
35	Eric Davis	.15
36	Joe Carter	.15
37	George Bell	.15
38	Kevin McReynolds	.15
39	Tim Raines	.15
40	Luis Medina (Rookie Stars)	.15
41	Mike Greenwell	.15
42	Kal Daniels	.15
43	Dwight Gooden	.15
44	Roger Clemens	1.00
45	Nolan Ryan	2.00
46	Erik Hanson	.15
47	Orel Hershiser	.15
48	Bret Saberhagen	.15
49	Jimmy Key	.15
50	Frank Viola	.15
51	Bruce Hurst	.15
52	Norm Charlton (Rookie Stars)	.15
53	Ted Higuera	.15
54	Mark Langston	.15
55	Damon Berryhill	.15
56	Carlton Fisk	.60
57	Terry Steinbach	.15
58	Sandy Alomar (Rookie Stars)	.15
59	Benito Santiago	.15
60	Bob Boone	.15
61	Jerome Walton (Rookie Stars)	.15
62	Jaime Navarro (Rookie Stars)	.15
63	Ken Griffey Jr. (Rookie Stars)	1.50
64	Jim Abbott (Rookie Stars)	.15
65	Junior Felix (Rookie Stars)	.15
66	Tom Gordon	.15
67	Power Plus (Kirby Puckett, Don Mattingly)	.65
68	Fence Busters (Julio Franco, Eric Davis, Ruben Sierra)	.15
69	N.L. Hitting Kings (Will Clark, Tony Gwynn)	.25
70	Keystone Combo (Ozzie Smith, Ryne Sandberg)	.50
71	Dinger Duo (Howard Johnson, Kevin Mitchell)	.15
72	Texas Heat (Nolan Ryan, Mike Scott)	.75

1990 Baseball Cards Magazine Repli-Cards

Beginning with its January 1989 issue, Baseball Cards Magazine began issuing its repli-cards in panels of six cards per month, creating an annual set of 72 insert cards. Contemporary players were presented in the designs of classic Topps sets of the 1950s-1970s. In 1990 the magazine's cards were in the style of 1969 Topps. Besides the individual player's cards, there were a number of multi-player "Rookie Stars" cards.

		NM/M
	Complete Set (72):	25.00
	Common Player:	.15
1	Craig Biggio	.15
2	Kevin Mitchell	.15
3	Orel Hershiser	.15
4	Will Clark	.15
5	Eric Davis	.15
6	Tony Gwynn	.75
7	Mike Scott	.15
8	Barry Larkin	.15
9	John Smoltz	.15
10	Glenn Davis	.15
11	Roberto Alomar	.25
12	Rick Reuschel	.15
13	N.L. West Rookie Stars (Eric Anthony, Ed Whited)	.15
14	N.L. West Rookie Stars (Andy Benes, Steve Avery)	.15
15	N.L. West Rookie Stars (John Wetteland, Joe Oliver)	.15
16	Giants Rookie Stars (Randy McCament, Greg Litton)	.15
17	Dodgers Rookie Stars (Jose Offerman, Jose Vizcaino)	.15
18	Reds Rookie Stars (Scott Scudder, Rosario Rodriguez)	.15
19	Darryl Strawberry	.15
20	Von Hayes	.15
21	Dwight Smith	.15
22	Howard Johnson	.15
23	Pedro Guerrero	.15
24	Tim Raines	.15
25	Ozzie Smith	.75
26	Barry Bonds	2.00
27	Jerome Walton	.15
28	Ryne Sandberg	.75
29	Bobby Bonilla	.15
30	Mark Grace	.15
31	Cards Rookie Stars (Todd Zeile, Alex Cole)	.15
32	N.L. East Rookie Stars (Pat Combs, Dean Wilkins)	.15
33	N.L. East Rookie Stars (Steve Carter, Jeff Huson)	.15
34	Cubs Rookie Stars (Greg Smith, Derrick May)	.15
35	Expos Rookie Stars (Marquis Grissom, Larry Walker)	.45
36	Mets Rookie Stars (Wally Whitehurst, Blaine Beatty)	.15
37	Ken Griffey Jr.	1.50
38	Kirby Puckett	.75
39	Julio Franco	.15
40	Ruben Sierra	.15
41	Bo Jackson	.25
42	Jose Canseco	.35
43	Dennis Eckersley	.50
44	Bret Saberhagen	.15
45	Wally Joyner	.15
46	Carlton Fisk	.60
47	Nolan Ryan	2.00
48	Rickey Henderson	.60
49	White Sox Rookie Stars (Robin Ventura, Sammy Sosa)	7.50
50	A.L. West Rookie Stars (John Orton, Scott Radinsky)	.15
51	A.L. West Rookie Stars (Bobby Rose, Bob Hamelin)	.15
52	Rangers Rookie Stars (Monty Fariss, Juan Gonzalez)	.50
53	Mariners Rookie Stars (Tino Martinez, Roger Salkeld)	.15
54	Twins Rookie Stars (Terry Jorgensen, Paul Sorrento)	.15
55	Don Mattingly	1.00
56	Roger Clemens	1.00
57	Cal Ripken	2.00
58	Robin Yount	.60
59	Wade Boggs	.75
60	Fred McGriff	.15
61	Cecil Fielder	.15
62	Ellis Burks	.15
63	Sandy Alomar	.15
64	Alan Trammell	.15
65	Steve Sax	.15
66	Paul Molitor	.60
67	Brewers Rookie Stars (Bert Hefferman, Matias Carillo)	.15
68	A.L. East Rookie Stars (Ben McDonald, John Olerud)	.25
69	A.L. East Rookie Stars (Mark Whiten, Phil Clark)	.15
70	Yankees Rookie Stars (Jim Leyritz, Kevin Maas)	.15
71	Indians Rookie Stars (Mark Lewis, Carlos Baerga)	.15
72	Orioles Rookie Stars (David Segui, Chris Hoiles)	.15

1991 Baseball Cards Magazine Repli-Cards

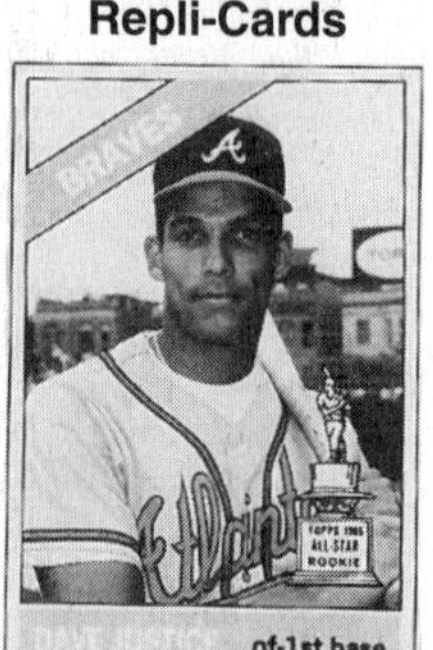

For the third year in 1991, Baseball Cards Magazine issued its repli-cards in panels of six cards per month, creating an annual set of 72 insert cards. Contemporary players were presented in the classic Topps design of 1966. Besides the individual players' cards, there are a number of multi-player feature cards and "Rookie Stars of 1991" multi-player cards, plus a 1952 Topps style card of Don Mattingly.

		NM/M
	Complete Set (72):	18.00
	Common Player:	.15
1	Eric Davis	.15
2	Cubs Rookie Stars (Lance Dickson, Hector Villanueva)	.15
3	Bobby Bonilla	.15
4	Len Dykstra	.15
5	John Franco	.15
6	Matt Williams	.15
7	Barry Bonds	2.00
8	Cards Rookie Stars (Geronimo Pena, Ray Lankford, Bernard Gilkey)	.15
9	Andre Dawson	.25
10	Dave Justice	.15
11	Triple Expos-ure (Larry Walker, Marquis Grissom, Delino DeShields)	.20
12	Howard Johnson	.15
13	Darryl Strawberry	.15
14	Astros Rookie Stars (Karl Rhodes, Andujar Cedeno, Mike Simms)	.15
15	Will Clark	.15
16	Barry Larkin	.15
17	Ramon Martinez	.15
18	Ron Gant	.15
19	Gregg Jefferies	.15
20	Giants Rookie Stars (Steve Decker, Steve Hosey, Mark Leonard)	.15
21	Todd Zeile	.15
22	Benito Santiago	.15
23	Eddie Murray	.60
24	Randy Myers	.15
25	Greg Maddux	.75
26	Phillies Rookie Stars (Mickey Morandini, Wes Chamberlain)	.15
27	Tim Wallach	.15
28	Dale Murphy	.25
29	Doug Drabek	.15
30	Kevin Mitchell	.15
31	Frank Viola	.15
32	Padres Rookie Stars (Rafael Valdez, Paul Faries)	.15
33	Hal Morris	.15
34	Pedro Guerrero	.15
35	Dwight Gooden	.15
36	Shawon Dunston	.15
37	Ken Griffey Jr.	1.00
38	Royals Rookie Stars (Sean Berry, Brian McRae)	.15
39	Roger Clemens	.85
40	Ellis Burks	.15
41	Robin Yount	.60
42	Frank Thomas	.60
43	Ruben Sierra	.15
44	Red Sox Rookie Stars (Mo Vaughn, Phil Plantier, Tim Naehring)	.15
45	Tim Raines	.15
46	Dave Parker	.15
47	Jose Canseco	.35
48	Glenn Davis	.15
49	Dave Winfield	.60
50	Chuck Knoblauch, Scott Leius, Willie Banks (Twins Rookie Stars)	.15
51	Joe Carter	.15
52	Cal Ripken	2.00
53	Carlton Fisk	.60
54	Julio Franco	.15
55	Don Mattingly	.85
56	Blue Jays Rookie Stars (Eddie Zosky, William Suero, Derek Bell)	.15
57	Sandy Alomar	.15
58	Juan Gonzalez	.30
59	Don Mattingly (1952 Topps style)	1.50
60	Mike Greenwell	.15
61	Chuck Finley	.15
62	Rangers Rookie Stars (Dean Palmer, Ivan Rodriguez, Gerald Alexander)	1.00
63	Scott Erickson	.15
64	Paul Molitor	.60
65	Triple Terrors (Cecil Fielder, Jose Canseco, Mark McGwire)	.60
66	Dennis Eckersley	.50
67	Brian Harper	.15
68	A.L. Rookie Stars (Bernie Williams, Wilson Alvarez) (No designation on front banner.)	.25
69	Robin Ventura	.15
70	Kirby Puckett	.75
71	Rafael Palmeiro	.50
72	Roberto Alomar	.25

1992 Baseball Cards Magazine Repli-Cards

The annual repli-card series inserted in Baseball Cards Magazine began in January with six-card panels each month. In May, panels were increased to eight cards and a UV coating was added to the front. Contemporary players were presented in the designs of classic Topps sets of the 1950s-1970s. In 1992 the magazine's cards were in the style of 1970 Topps. Besides the individual player's cards, specialty cards included "1992 Rookie Stars" multi-player and Team USA cards.

#	Player	NM/M
	Complete Set (88):	20.00
	Common Player:	.15
1	Eddie Murray	.50
2	Braves Rookie Stars (Ryan Klesko, Mark Wohlers)	.15
3	Barry Bonds	1.50
4	Will Clark	.15
5	Jose Canseco	.35
6	Ron Gant	.15
7	Ruben Sierra	.15
8	Reds Rookie Stars (Reggie Sanders, Mo Sanford)	.15
9	Terry Pendleton	.15
10	Hal Morris	.15
11	Kirby Puckett	.60
12	Paul Molitor	.50
13	Jack McDowell	.15
14	Dodgers Rookie Stars (Eric Karros, Tom Goodwin)	.15
15	Ramon Martinez	.15
16	Steve Avery	.15
17	Roger Clemens	.75
18	Jim Abbott	.15
19	Phil Plantier	.15
20	Giants Rookie Stars (Royce Clayton, Ted Wood)	.15
21	Frank Thomas	.50
22	Juan Gonzalez	.25
23	Felix Jose	.15
24	Chuck Knoblauch	.15
25	Tony Gwynn	.60
26	Julio Franco	.15
27	Greg Blosser, Frankie Rodriguez	.15
28	Wade Boggs	.60
29	Robin Ventura	.15
30	Shane Mack	.15
31	Roberto Alomar	.25
32	Don Mattingly	.75
33	Astros Rookie Stars (Ryan Bowen, Jeff Juden)	.15
34	Cal Ripken Jr.	1.50
35	Ozzie Smith	.60
36	Ken Griffey Jr.	1.00
37	Ivan Rodriguez	.40
38	Matt Williams	.15
39	Craig Biggio	.15
40	John Kruk	.15
41	George Brett	.75
42	Carlton Fisk	.50
43	Indians Rookie Stars (Kenny Lofton, Jim Thome)	.50
44	Andre Dawson	.25
45	Nolan Ryan	1.50
46	Robin Yount	.50
47	Ryne Sandberg	.60
48	Rickey Henderson	.50
49	Bobby Thigpen	.15
50	Dennis Eckersley	.40
51	Cards Rookie Stars (Brian Jordan, Dmitri Young)	.15
52	Jeff Reardon	.15
53	Bryan Harvey	.15
54	Tom Henke	.15
55	Lee Smith	.15
56	John Franco	.15
57	Cecil Fielder	.15
58	Darryl Strawberry	.15
59	Twins Rookie Stars (David McCarty, Scott Stahoviak)	.15
60	Mark McGwire	1.00
61	George Bell	.15
62	Fred McGriff	.15
63	Danny Tartabull	.15
64	Joe Carter	.15
65	Deion Sanders	.15
66	Roberto Alomar	.25
67	A.L. Rookie Stars (Eduardo Perez, Joe Vitiello, Bret Boone)	.15
68	Bip Roberts	.15
69	Ray Lankford	.15
70	Brady Anderson	.15
71	Tim Raines	.15
72	Marquis Grissom	.15
73	Dave Fleming	.15
74	Andy Benes	.15
75	Yankees Rookie Stars (Bob Wickman, Mark Hutton)	.15
76	Bill Swift	.15
77	Mike Mussina	.25
78	Donovan Osborne	.15
79	Juan Guzman	.15
80	Kevin Brown	.15
81	Charles Johnson (USA)	.15
82	Jeffrey Hammonds (USA)	.15
83	Rick Helling (USA)	.15
84	Chris Wimmer (USA)	.15
85	Darren Dreifort (USA)	.15
86	Calvin Murray (USA)	.15
87	Phil Nevin (USA)	.15
88	B.J. Wallace (USA)	.15

1993 Baseball Cards/Sports Cards Magazine Repli-Cards

The annual repli-card series began in Baseball Cards Magazine in 1989 continued in 1993 with eight-card panels of UV-coated repli-cards stapled into each monthly issue. (Only seven cards were included in July; there are two #32 and no #40.) Contemporary players were presented in the design of the classic 1968 Topps set. Backs are printed in black, white and yellow and include an investment advisory about the player's cards. Besides the individual player's repli-cards, there is a group of "1993 Rookie Stars" multi-player cards. Effective with its May issue, the magazine's title was changed to Sports Cards, the copyright line on back reflecting that change.

#	Player	NM/M
	Complete Set (95):	25.00
	Common Player:	.15
1	Andy Van Slyke	.15
2	Ruben Sierra	.15
3	Carlos Baerga	.15
4	Gary Sheffield	.30
5	Chuck Knoblauch	.15
6	Danny Tartabull	.15
7	Angels Rookie Stars (Chad Curtis, Tim Salmon)	.45
8	Darren Daulton	.15
9	Deion Sanders	.20
10	Pat Listach	.15
11	Albert Belle	.15
12	Frank Thomas	.60
13	Dave Hollins	.15
14	Braves Rookie Stars (Javy Lopez, Mike Kelly)	.15
15	Travis Fryman	.15
16	Edgar Martinez	.15
17	Barry Bonds	1.50
18	Dennis Eckersley	.50
19	Brady Anderson	.15
20	Fred McGriff	.15
21	Paul Molitor	.60
22	Juan Gonzalez	.30
23	Dodgers Rookie Stars (Bill Ashley, Mike Piazza)	1.50
24	Larry Walker	.15
25	Dave Winfield	.60
26	Robin Yount	.60
27	George Brett	.85
28	Jack Morris	.15
29	Eddie Murray	.60
30	Nolan Ryan	1.50
31	Carlton Fisk	.60
32a	Dale Murphy	.30
32b	Jeff Bagwell	.60
33	Eric Karros	.15
34	Roberto Alomar	.25
35	Robin Ventura	.15
36	Delino DeShields	.15
37	Ken Griffey Jr.	1.00
38	Eric Anthony	.15
39	Marquis Grissom	.15
41	Cecil Fielder	.15
42	Mark McGwire	1.25
43	Ryne Sandberg	.75
44	Kirby Puckett	.75
45	Cal Ripken Jr.	1.50
46	David McCarty	.15
47	Joe Carter	.15
48	Dean Palmer	.15
49	Jack McDowell	.15
50	Roger Clemens	.85
51	Cal Eldred	.15
52	Tom Glavine	.25
53	Steve Avery	.15
54	Mike Mussina	.35
55	Brien Taylor	.15
56	Mark Grace	.15
57	Ray Lankford	.15
58	Shane Mack	.15
59	Terry Pendleton	.15
60	Tony Gwynn	.75
61	Rafael Palmeiro	.50
62	Will Clark	.15
63	Wil Cordero	.15
64	Cliff Floyd	.15
65	Aaron Sele	.15
66	Chipper Jones	.75
67	Frank Rodriguez	.15
68	Ryan Klesko	.15
69	Manny Ramirez	.60
70	Carlos Delgado	.30
71	Paul Shuey	.15
72	Barry Bonds	1.50
73	Andre Dawson	.30
74	Paul Molitor	.60
75	Greg Maddux	.75
76	Wade Boggs	.75
77	Bryan Harvey	.15
78	Andres Galarraga	.15
79	Gregg Jefferies	.15
80	Mike Piazza	1.00
81	J.T. Snow	.15
82	Ivan Rodriguez	.50
83	Derrick May	.15
84	Tim Salmon	.15
85	Greg Vaughn	.15
86	Kenny Lofton	.15
87	John Olerud	.15
88	Sammy Sosa	.75
89	Lee Smith	.15
90	Matt Williams	.15
91	Don Mattingly	.85
92	Willie Greene	.15
93	Jim Abbott	.15
94	Mo Vaughn	.15
95	Randy Johnson	.60

1990-92 Baseball Cards Presents Repli-Cards

Taking advantage of the boom in sports card collecting, Baseball Cards Magazine began a series of special newsstand magazine titles. Beginning with "Baseball Card Boom," dated February 1990, the series, officially known as "Baseball Cards Presents . . ." included baseball (and other sports) repli-cards in most of its issues through August 1992. Cards are listed here by issue in which they were inserted.

#	Player	NM/M
	Complete Set (61):	27.50
	Common Player:	.25
1	Don Mattingly	1.25
2	Dwight Gooden	.25
3	Jose Canseco	.35
4	Bo Jackson	.35
5	Ken Griffey Jr.	1.50
1	John Olerud	.25
2	Eric Anthony	.25
3	Greg Vaughn	.25
4	Todd Zeile	.25
5	Ben McDonald	.25
6	Deion Sanders (Mail-in offer only.)	.75
1	Mark Davis	.25
2	Bret Saberhagen	.25
3	Kirby Puckett	.65
4	Rickey Henderson	.50
5	Kevin Mitchell	.25
1	Cecil Fielder	.25
2	Rickey Henderson	.50
3	Barry Bonds	2.00
4	Ryne Sandberg	.65
5	Roger Clemens	1.00
1	Nolan Ryan	2.00
2	Eric Davis	.25
3	Ryne Sandberg	.65
4	Rickey Henderson	.50
5	Kevin Maas	.25
6	Dave Justice	.25
7	Jose Canseco	.35
8	Bo Jackson	.35
9	Roger Clemens	1.00
10	Ken Griffey Jr.	1.50
1	Babe Ruth (1936 Diamond Stars style)	1.00
1	Ted Williams (1952 Topps style)	.75
2	Rickey Henderson (1933 Goudey style)	.50
5	Roger Clemens (1941 Play Ball style)	1.00
325	Stan Musial (1951 Bowman style)	.65
11	Frank Thomas	.50
12	Dwight Gooden	.25
13	David Robinson/Basketball	.25
14	Will Clark	.25
15	Darryl Strawberry	.25
16	Kevin Mitchell	.25
17	Tony Gwynn	.65
18	Cal Ripken Jr.	2.00
19	Michael Jordan	1.50
20	Don Mattingly	1.25
1	Frank Thomas	.50
2	Scott Erickson	.25
3	Terry Pendleton	.25
4	Cal Ripken	2.00
5	Barry Bonds	2.00
1	Frank Thomas	.50
2	Jeff Bagwell	.50
3	Cecil Fielder	.25
4	Ken Griffey Jr.	1.50
5	Juan Gonzalez	.35
1	Ryne Sandberg	.65
2	Phil Plantier	.25
3	Barry Larkin	.25
4	Cecil Fielder	.25
5	Dave Justice	.25

1992 The Baseball Enquirer

This set of "Mystery Interview" cards parodies baseball players and baseball cards. The 2-1/2" x 3-1/2" cards have caricatures of well-known players on front, surrounded by a gray border and a blank white name box. A blue "Fun Stuff" trademark is at bottom-right. Backs are printed in blue and black on white with a card number, another blank name box, issuer's trademarks and a mock interview with the player. Actual player names are not seen anywhere on the cards. Issued in 10-card poly-packs at 49 cents, complete sets - 184,000 of them - were also issued at $5.

#	Player	NM/M
	Complete Set (64):	7.50
	Common Player:	.50
	Pack (10):	.25
	Box (36):	7.50
1	Bo Jackson	.65
2	Jose Canseco	.60
3	Mark Langston	.50
4	Billy Ripken	.60
5	David Justice	.50
6	Rob Deer	.50
7	Jack McDowell	.50
8	Cecil Fielder	.50
9	John Smoltz	.50
10	Will Clark	.50
11	Ken Caminiti	.50
12	Kent Hrbek	.50
13	Gregg Jefferies	.50
14	Bob Uecker	.75
15	Mike Greenwell	.50
16	No player	.05
17	Ken Griffey Jr.	2.00
18	Robin Yount	.75
19	Joe DiMaggio	2.00
20	Mackey Sasser	.50
21	Dave Stewart	.50
22	Barry Bonds	3.00
23	Don Zimmer	.50
24	Jack Morris	.50
25	George Brett	1.50
26	Tommy Lasorda	.50
27	Whitey Ford	.50
28	Bill Buckner	.50
29	Ozzie Smith	1.00
30	Stump Merrill	.50
31	Randy Johnson	.75
32	George Bell	.50
33	Johnny Bench	1.00
34	Rickey Henderson	.75
35	Jack Clark	.50
36	Jim Palmer	.50
37	Lenny Dykstra	.50
38	George Steinbrenner	.50
39	Dave Stieb	.50
40	Nolan Ryan	3.00
41	Chris Sabo	.50
42	Unidentified Player	.50
43	Kirby Puckett	1.00
44	Lou Piniella	.50
45	Wade Boggs	1.00
46	Andre Dawson	.60
47	Roger Clemens	1.25
48	Pete Rose	2.00
49	David Cone	.50
50	Warren Cromartie	.50
51	Unidentified Umpire	.50
52	Phil Rizzuto	.50
53	Dan Gladden	.50
54	Mark Lemke	.50
55	Buck Rodgers	.50
56	Darryl Strawberry	.50
57	Rob Dibble	.50
58	Deion Sanders	.50
59	Tony Gwynn	1.00
60	Dale Murphy	.60
61	Albert Belle	.50
62	Don Mattingly	1.50
63	Andres Galarraga	.50
64	Babe Ruth	2.00

1980-88 Baseball Immortals

One of the most popular of the "collectors' issues," this set is produced with the permission of Major League Baseball by Renata Galasso Inc. and TCMA. The set features players in the Baseball Hall of Fame and was first issued in 1980. For several years thereafter the set was updated to include new inductees. The cards measure 2-1/2" x 3-1/2" and have colorful borders. The card fronts include the player's name, position and year of induction. The backs feature a short biography and a trivia question. The photos used are color; most players who were active before 1950 have colored black-and-white photos. The designation "first printing" appears on all cards issued in 1981 and after.

#	Player	NM/M
	Complete 1980 Set (173):	15.00
	Complete Set (199):	30.00
	Common Player:	.10
1	Babe Ruth	2.00
2	Ty Cobb	1.00
3	Walter Johnson	.20
4	Christy Mathewson	.20
5	Honus Wagner	.20
6	Morgan Bulkeley	.10
7	Ban Johnson	.10
8	Larry Lajoie	.10
9	Connie Mack	.10
10	John McGraw	.10
11	Tris Speaker	.10
12	George Wright	.10
13	Cy Young	.10
14	Grover Alexander	.10
15	Alexander Cartwright	.10
16	Henry Chadwick	.10
17	Cap Anson	.10
18	Eddie Collins	.10
19	Charles Comiskey	.10
20	Candy Cummings	.10
21	Buck Ewing	.10
22	Lou Gehrig	1.50
23	Willie Keeler	.10
24	Hoss Radbourne	.10
25	George Sisler	.10
26	Albert Spalding	.10
27	Rogers Hornsby	.10
28	Judge Landis	.10
29	Roger Bresnahan	.10
30	Dan Brouthers	.10
31	Fred Clarke	.10
32	James Collins	.10
33	Ed Delahanty	.10
34	Hugh Duffy	.10
35	Hughie Jennings	.10
36	Mike "King" Kelly	.10
37	James O'Rourke	.10
38	Wilbert Robinson	.10
39	Jesse Burkett	.10
40	Frank Chance	.10
41	Jack Chesbro	.10
42	John Evers	.10
43	Clark Griffith	.10
44	Thomas McCarthy	.10
45	Joe McGinnity	.10
46	Eddie Plank	.10
47	Joe Tinker	.10
48	Rube Waddell	.10
49	Ed Walsh	.10
50	Mickey Cochrane	.10
51	Frankie Frisch	.10
52	Lefty Grove	.10
53	Carl Hubbell	.10
54	Herb Pennock	.10
55	Pie Traynor	.10
56	Three Finger Brown	.10
57	Charlie Gehringer	.10
58	Kid Nichols	.10
59	Jimmie Foxx	.10
60	Mel Ott	.10
61	Harry Heilmann	.10
62	Paul Waner	.10
63	Ed Barrow	.10
64	Chief Bender	.10
65	Tom Connolly	.10
66	Dizzy Dean	.10
67	Bill Klem	.10
68	Al Simmons	.10
69	Bobby Wallace	.10
70	Harry Wright	.10
71	Bill Dickey	.10
72	Rabbit Maranville	.10
73	Bill Terry	.10
74	Home Run Baker	.10
75	Joe DiMaggio	2.00
76	Gabby Hartnett	.10
77	Ted Lyons	.10
78	Ray Schalk	.10
79	Dazzy Vance	.10
80	Joe Cronin	.10
81	Hank Greenberg	.10
82	Sam Crawford	.10
83	Joe McCarthy	.10
84	Zack Wheat	.10
85	Max Carey	.10
86	Billy Hamilton	.10
87	Bob Feller	.10
88	Bill McKechnie	.10
89	Jackie Robinson	1.00
90	Edd Roush	.10
91	John Clarkson	.10
92	Elmer Flick	.10
93	Sam Rice	.10
94	Eppa Rixey	.10
95	Luke Appling	.10
96	Red Faber	.10
97	Burleigh Grimes	.10
98	Miller Huggins	.10
99	Tim Keefe	.10
100	Heinie Manush	.10
101	John Ward	.10
102	Pud Galvin	.10
103	Casey Stengel	.10
104	Ted Williams	1.00
105	Branch Rickey	.10
106	Red Ruffing	.10
107	Lloyd Waner	.10
108	Kiki Cuyler	.10
109	Goose Goslin	.10
110	Joe (Ducky) Medwick	.10
111	Roy Campanella	.20
112	Stan Coveleski	.10
113	Waite Hoyt	.10
114	Stan Musial	.50
115	Lou Boudreau	.10
116	Earle Combs	.10
117	Ford Frick	.10
118	Jesse Haines	.10
119	Dave Bancroft	.10
120	Jake Beckley	.10
121	Chick Hafey	.10
122	Harry Hooper	.10
123	Joe Kelley	.10
124	Rube Marquard	.10
125	Satchel Paige	.50
126	George Weiss	.10

#	Player	NM/M
127	Yogi Berra	.20
128	Josh Gibson	.10
129	Lefty Gomez	.10
130	Will Harridge	.10
131	Sandy Koufax	1.00
132	Buck Leonard	.10
133	Early Wynn	.10
134	Ross Youngs	.10
135	Roberto Clemente	2.00
136	Billy Evans	.10
137	Monte Irvin	.10
138	George Kelly	.10
139	Warren Spahn	.10
140	Mickey Welch	.10
141	Cool Papa Bell	.10
142	Jim Bottomley	.10
143	Jocko Conlan	.10
144	Whitey Ford	.10
145	Mickey Mantle	5.00
146	Sam Thompson	.10
147	Earl Averill	.10
148	Bucky Harris	.10
149	Billy Herman	.10
150	Judy Johnson	.10
151	Ralph Kiner	.10
152	Oscar Charleston	.10
153	Roger Connor	.10
154	Cal Hubbard	.10
155	Bob Lemon	.10
156	Fred Lindstrom	.10
157	Robin Roberts	.10
158	Ernie Banks	.25
159	Martin Dihigo	.10
160	Pop Lloyd	.10
161	Al Lopez	.10
162	Amos Rusie	.10
163	Joe Sewell	.10
164	Addie Joss	.10
165	Larry MacPhail	.10
166	Eddie Mathews	.10
167	Warren Giles	.10
168	Willie Mays	1.00
169	Hack Wilson	.10
170	Duke Snider	.20
171	Al Kaline	.10
172	Chuck Klein	.10
173	Tom Yawkey	.10
174	Bob Gibson	.10
175	Rube Foster	.10
176	Johnny Mize	.10
177	Hank Aaron	1.00
178	Frank Robinson	.10
179	Happy Chandler	.10
180	Travis Jackson	.10
181	Brooks Robinson	.10
182	Juan Marichal	.10
183	George Kell	.10
184	Walter Alston	.10
185	Harmon Killebrew	.10
186	Luis Aparicio	.10
187	Don Drysdale	.10
188	Pee Wee Reese	.10
189	Rick Ferrell	.10
190	Willie McCovey	.10
191	Ernie Lombardi	.10
192	Bobby Doerr	.10
193	Arky Vaughan	.10
194	Enos Slaughter	.10
195	Lou Brock	.10
196	Hoyt Wilhelm	.10
197	Billy Williams	.10
198	"Catfish" Hunter	.10
199	Ray Dandridge	.10

1990 Baseball Wit

This 108-card set was released in two printings. The first printing featured unnumbered cards and several errors. The second printing featured corrections and numbered cards. The set was available at several retail chains and feature trivia questions on the card backs. The set was dedicated to Little League baseball.

#	Player	NM/M
	Complete Set (108):	12.50
	Common Player:	.10
1	Orel Hershiser	.10
2	Tony Gwynn	.60
3	Mickey Mantle	2.50
4	Willie Stargell	.10
5	Don Baylor	.10
6	Hank Aaron	1.00
7	Don Larsen	.10
8	Lee Mazzilli	.10
9	Boog Powell	.10
10	Little League World Series	.10
11	Jose Canseco	.30
12	Mike Scott	.10
13	Bob Feller	.10
14	Ron Santo	.10
15	Mel Stottlemyre	.10
16	Shea Stadium	.10
17	Brooks Robinson	.25
18	Willie Mays	1.00
19	Ernie Banks	.30
20	Keith Hernandez	.10
21	Bret Saberhagen	.10
22	Hall of Fame	.10
23	Luis Aparicio	.10
24	Yogi Berra	.30
25	Manny Mota	.10
26	Steve Garvey	.10
27	Bill Shea	.10
28	Fred Lynn	.10
29	Todd Worrell	.10
30	Roy Campanella	.30
31	Bob Gibson	.10
32	Gary Carter	.10
33	Jim Palmer	.25
34	Carl Yastrzemski	.25
35	Dwight Gooden	.10
36	Stan Musial	.50
37	Rickey Henderson	.25
38	Dale Murphy	.25
39	Mike Schmidt	.75
40	Gaylord Perry	.10
41	Ozzie Smith	.60
42	Reggie Jackson	.75
43	Steve Carlton	.25
44	Jim Perry	.10
45	Vince Coleman	.10
46	Tom Seaver	.25
47	Marty Marion	.10
48	Frank Robinson	.25
49	Joe DiMaggio	1.50
50	Ted Williams	1.00
51	Rollie Fingers	.10
52	Jackie Robinson	1.00
53	Victor Raschi	.10
54	Johnny Bench	.25
55	Nolan Ryan	1.50
56	Ty Cobb	1.00
57	Harry Steinfeldt	.10
58	James O'Rourke	.10
59	John McGraw	.10
60	Candy Cummings	.10
61	Jimmie Foxx	.10
62	Walter Johnson	.25
63	1903 World Series	.10
64	Satchel Paige	.40
65	Bobby Wallace	.10
66	Cap Anson	.10
67	Hugh Duffy	.10
68	Buck Ewing	.10
69	Bobo Holloman	.10
70	Ed Delehanty (Delahanty)	.10
71	Dizzy Dean	.25
72	Tris Speaker	.10
73	Lou Gehrig	1.50
74	Wee Willie Keeler	.10
75	Cal Hubbard	.10
76	Eddie Collins	.10
77	Chris Von Der Ahe	.10
78	Sam Crawford	.10
79	Cy Young	.25
80	Johnny Vander Meer	.10
81	Joey Jay	.10
82	Zack Wheat	.10
83	Jim Bottomley	.10
84	Honus Wagner	.30
85	Casey Stengel	.10
86	Babe Ruth	1.50
87	John Lindemuth	.10
88	Max Carey	.10
89	Mordecai Brown	.10
90	1869 Red Stockings	.10
91	Rube Marquard	.10
92	Horse Radbourne	.10
93	Hack Wilson	.10
94	Lefty Grove	.10
95	Carl Hubbell	.10
96	A.J. Cartwright	.10
97	Rogers Hornsby	.10
98	Ernest Thayer	.10
99	Connie Mack	.10
100	1939 Centennial Celebration	.10
101	Branch Rickey	.10
102	Dan Brouthers	.10
103	First Baseball Uniform	.10
104	Christy Mathewson	.25
105	Joe Nuxhall	.10
106	1939 Centennial Celebration	.10
107	President Taft	.10
108	Abner Doubleday	.10

1987 Baseball's All-Time Greats

Though the producer is not identified anywhere on the cards, this collectors' issue was created primarily for insertion in beginner's baseball card kits. One series of 50 cards was produced about 1987, a second series some years later. All cards have bright green or orange borders with a "window" at center in which players are pictured in either color or black-and-white photos, or artwork. The player's major league career span is in a tan oval towards bottom. Horizontal backs have a red strip at top with personal data and also include a career summary. The unnumbered cards are checklisted here in alphabetical order. Variations in photos and the presence or absence of team logos have been observed on some cards. Gaps have been left in the checklist to accommodate additions; "g" for green or "o" for orange borders is shown in parentheses where verified.

#	Player	NM/M
	Common Player:	.10
(1)	Henry Aaron	1.00
(2)	Joe Adcock	.10
(3)	Richie Allen	.10
(4)	Grover C. Alexander	.10
(5)	Luis Aparicio	.10
(6)	Luke Appling	.10
(7)	Ernie Banks	.25
(8)	Hank Bauer	.10
(9)	Johnny Bench	.15
(10)	"Yogi" Berra	.15
(11)	Lou Boudreau	.10
(12)	Lou Brock	.10
(13)	"Three Finger" Brown	.10
(14)	Jim Bunning	.10
(15)	Roy Campanella	.25
(16)	Rod Carew	.10
(17)	Orlando Cepeda	.10
(18)	Roberto Clemente	1.00
(19a)	Ty Cobb/g	1.00
(19b)	Ty Cobb/o	1.00
(20)	Mickey Cochrane	.10
(21)	Rocky Colavito	.10
(22)	Eddie Collins	.10
(23)	Sam Crawford	.10
(24)	Joe Cronin	.10
(25)	Alvin Dark	.10
(26)	Dizzy Dean	.10
(27)	Bill Dickey	.10
(28)	Joe DiMaggio	1.00
(29)	Larry Doby	.10
(30)	Don Drysdale	.10
(31)	Leo Durocher	.10
(32)	Carl Erskine	.10
(33)	Bob Feller	.10
(34)	Curt Flood	.10
(35a)	Whitey Ford/g (Chest, cap logos.)	.10
(36)	Jimmie Foxx	.10
(37a)	Frankie Frisch/g (Jersey logo.)	.10
(38)	Carl Furillo	.10
(39a)	Lou Gehrig/g	1.25
(39b)	Lou Gehrig/o	1.25
(40)	Charlie Gehringer	.10
(41)	Bob Gibson/g	.25
(42)	Hank Greenberg	.10
(43)	"Lefty" Grove	.10
(44)	"Gabby" Hartnett	.10
(45)	Gil Hodges	.10
(46)	Rogers Hornsby	.10
(47)	Carl Hubbell	.10
(48)	Jim Hunter	.10
(49)	Monte Irvin	.10
(50)	Ferguson Jenkins	.10
(51)	Walter Johnson	.10
(52)	Jim Kaat	.10
(54)	George Kell	.10
(55)	Ralph Kiner	.10
(56)	Ted Kluszewski	.10
(57)	Don Larsen	.10
(58)	Bob Lemon	.10
(59)	Ernie Lombardi	.10
(61)	Eddie Lopat	.10
(62a)	Mickey Mantle/o (Chest-up portrait.)	2.00
(63)	Juan Marichal	.10
(64)	Roger Maris	.50
(65)	Billy Martin	.10
(66)	Eddie Mathews	.10
(67)	Christy Mathewson	.25
(68)	Willie Mays	1.00
(69)	Bill Mazeroski	.10
(70)	Joe Morgan	.10
(71)	Thurman Munson	.10
(72)	Stan Musial	.50
(73)	Tony Oliva	.10
(74)	Mel Ott	.10
(75)	Jim Palmer	.10
(76)	Gaylord Perry	.10
(77)	Boog Powell	.10
(78)	Pee Wee Reese	.10
(79)	Robin Roberts	.10
(80a)	Brooks Robinson (g)(Baltimore jersey.)	.25
(81)	Frank Robinson/g	.25
(82a)	Jackie Robinson/g	1.00
(82b)	Jackie Robinson/o	1.00
(83a)	Babe Ruth/g	1.50
(83b)	Babe Ruth/o	1.50
(84)	Tom Seaver	.10
(85)	Bobby Shantz	.10
(86)	Al Simmons	.10
(87)	George Sisler	.10
(88)	Enos Slaughter	.10
(89)	Duke Snider	.10
(91)	Warren Spahn/g	.25
(92)	Tris Speaker	.10
(93)	Willie Stargell	.10
(94)	Bill Terry	.10
(95)	Bobby Thomson	.10
(96)	Pie Traynor	.10
(97)	Honus Wagner	.25
(98)	Ed Walsh	.10
(99)	Paul Waner	.10
(100)	Hoyt Wilhelm	.10
(101)	Billy Williams	.10
(102)	Ted Williams	1.00
(103)	Maury Wills	.10
(104)	Early Wynn	.10
(105)	Carl Yastrzemski	.25
(106)	Cy Young/o	.25
(107)	Ross Youngs	.10

1988 Bazooka

This 22-card set from Topps marks the first Bazooka issue since 1971. Full-color player photos are bordered in white, with the player name printed on a red, white and blue bubble gum box in the lower right corner. Flip sides are also red, white and blue, printed vertically. A large, but faint, Bazooka logo backs the Topps baseball logo team name, card number, player's name and position, followed by batting records, personal information and brief career highlights. Cards were sold inside specially marked 59¢ and 79¢ Bazooka gum and candy boxes, one card per box.

#	Player	NM/M
	Complete Set (22):	3.00
	Common Player:	.10
1	George Bell	.10
2	Wade Boggs	.50
3	Jose Canseco	.25
4	Roger Clemens	.60
5	Vince Coleman	.10
6	Eric Davis	.10
7	Tony Fernandez	.10
8	Dwight Gooden	.10
9	Tony Gwynn	.50
10	Wally Joyner	.10
11	Don Mattingly	.60
12	Willie McGee	.10
13	Mark McGwire	.75
14	Kirby Puckett	.50
15	Tim Raines	.10
16	Dave Righetti	.10
17	Cal Ripken, Jr.	1.00
18	Juan Samuel	.10
19	Ryne Sandberg	.50
20	Benny Santiago	.10
21	Darryl Strawberry	.10
22	Todd Worrell	.10

1989 Bazooka

Topps produced this 22-card set in 1989 to be included

(one card per box) in specially-marked boxes of its Bazooka brand bubblegum. The player photos have the words "Shining Star" along the top, while the player's name appears along the bottom of the card, along with the Topps Bazooka logo in the lower right corner. The cards are numbered alphabetically.

#	Player	NM/M
	Complete Set (22):	3.00
	Common Player:	.10
1	Tim Belcher	.10
2	Damon Berryhill	.10
3	Wade Boggs	.75
4	Jay Buhner	.10
5	Jose Canseco	.25
6	Vince Coleman	.10
7	Cecil Espy	.10
8	Dave Gallagher	.10
9	Ron Gant	.10
10	Kirk Gibson	.10
11	Paul Gibson	.10
12	Mark Grace	.10
13	Tony Gwynn	.75
14	Rickey Henderson	.50
15	Orel Hershiser	.10
16	Gregg Jefferies	.10
17	Ricky Jordan	.10
18	Chris Sabo	.10
19	Gary Sheffield	.40
20	Darryl Strawberry	.10
21	Frank Viola	.10
22	Walt Weiss	.10

1990 Bazooka

For the second consecutive year, Bazooka entitled its set "Shining Stars." Full-color action and posed player shots are featured on the card fronts. The flip sides feature player statistics in a style much like the cards from the previous two Bazooka issues. Unlike the past two releases, the cards are not numbered alphabetically. The cards measure 2-1/2" x 3-1/2" in size and 22 cards complete the set.

#	Player	NM/M
	Complete Set (22):	3.00
	Common Player:	.10
1	Kevin Mitchell	.10
2	Robin Yount	.40
3	Mark Davis	.10
4	Bret Saberhagen	.10
5	Fred McGriff	.10
6	Tony Gwynn	.50
7	Kirby Puckett	.50
8	Vince Coleman	.10
9	Rickey Henderson	.40
10	Ben McDonald	.10
11	Gregg Olson	.10
12	Todd Zeile	.10
13	Carlos Martinez	.10
14	Gregg Jefferies	.10
15	Craig Worthington	.10
16	Gary Sheffield	.25
17	Greg Briley	.10
18	Ken Griffey Jr.	1.50
19	Jerome Walton	.10
20	Bob Geren	.10
21	Tom Gordon	.10
22	Jim Abbott	.10

1991 Bazooka

For the third consecutive year Bazooka entitled its set "Shining Stars." The cards are styled like the 1990 issue, but include the Topps "40th Anniversary" logo. The 1991 issue is considered much scarcer than the previous releases. The cards measure 2-1/2" x 3-1/2" in size and 22 cards complete the set.

#	Player	NM/M
	Complete Set (22):	5.00
	Common Player:	.10
1	Barry Bonds	3.50
2	Rickey Henderson	.50
3	Bob Welch	.10
4	Doug Drabek	.10
5	Alex Fernandez	.10
6	Jose Offerman	.10
7	Frank Thomas	.50
8	Cecil Fielder	.10
9	Ryne Sandberg	.75
10	George Brett	1.00
11	Willie McGee	.10
12	Vince Coleman	.10
13	Hal Morris	.10
14	Delino DeShields	.10
15	Robin Ventura	.10
16	Jeff Huson	.10
17	Felix Jose	.10
18	Dave Justice	.10
19	Larry Walker	.10
20	Sandy Alomar, Jr.	.10
21	Kevin Appier	.10
22	Scott Radinsky	.10

1992 Bazooka

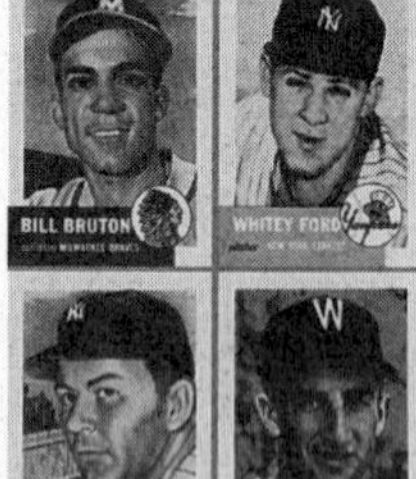

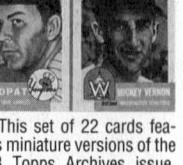

This set of 22 cards features miniature versions of the 1953 Topps Archives issue. The mini-cards are set against a blue background on front and back. Besides reproductions of issued 1953 Topps cards, these "Quadracards" include miniature versions of many of the special cards created for the Archives set. Cards feature the Bazooka logo on back, and were distributed in boxes of that bubble gum.

		NM/M
	Complete Tin-Box Set (22):	16.00
	Complete Set (22):	8.00
	Common Player:	.25
1	Joe Adcock, Bob Lemon, Willie Mays, Vic Wertz	1.50
2	Carl Furillo, Don Newcombe, Phil Rizzuto, Hank Sauer	.25
3	Ferris Fain, John Logan, Ed Mathews, Bobby Shantz	.25

4	Yogi Berra, Del Crandall, Howie Pollett, Gene Woodling	.25
5	Richie Ashburn, Leo Durocher, Allie Reynolds, Early Wynn	.25
6	Hank Aaron, Ray Boone, Luke Easter, Dick Williams	1.50
7	Ralph Branca, Bob Feller, Rogers Hornsby, Bobby Thomson	.25
8	Jim Gilliam, Billy Martin, Orestes Minoso, Hal Newhouser	.25
9	Smoky Burgess, John Mize, Preacher Roe, Warren Spahn	.25
10	Monte Irvin, Bobo Newsom, Duke Snider, Wes Westrum	.25
11	Carl Erskine, Jackie Jensen, George Kell, Al Schoendienst	.25
12	Bill Bruton, Whitey Ford, Ed Lopat, Mickey Vernon	.25
13	Joe Black, Lew Burdette, Johnny Pesky, Enos Slaughter	.25
14	Gus Bell, Mike Garcia, Mel Parnell, Jackie Robinson	1.25
15	Alvin Dark, Dick Groat, Pee Wee Reese, John Sain	.25
16	Gil Hodges, Sal Maglie, Wilmer Mizell, Billy Pierce	.45
17	Nellie Fox, Ralph Kiner, Ted Kluszewski, Eddie Stanky	.25
18	Ewell Blackwell, Vern Law, Satchell Paige, Jim Wilson	.45
19	Lou Boudreau, Roy Face, Harvey Haddix, Bill Rigney	.25
20	Roy Campanella, Walt Dropo, Harvey Kuenn, Al Rosen	.45
21	Joe Garagiola, Robin Roberts, Casey Stengel, Hoyt Wilhelm	.25
22	John Antonelli, Bob Friend, Dixie Walker, Ted Williams	1.00

1993 Bazooka Team USA

The members of Team USA are featured on this boxed set. The 2-1/2" x 3-1/2" cards feature the same basic design as 1993 Topps baseball, except for a Bazooka gum logo in one of the upper corners. Both front and back feature posed player photos. Backs have a design simulating the U.S. flag and include amateur stats, biographical details and career highlights. The cards are virtually identical to the same players' cards in the 1993 Topps Traded set, with the addition of the Bazooka logo on front and the differences in card numbers. A special tin-boxed edition with 50 pieces of gum was produced in an edition reported as 750.

		NM/M
Complete Set (22):		100.00
Complete Tin Set (22):		150.00
Common Player:		.50
1	Terry Harvey	.50
2	Dante Powell	.50
3	Andy Barkett	.50
4	Steve Reich	.50
5	Charlie Nelson	.50
6	Todd Walker	1.00
7	Dustin Hermanson	1.00
8	Pat Clougherty	.50
9	Danny Graves	.50
10	Paul Wilson	.75
11	Todd Helton	90.00
12	Russ Johnson	.50
13	Darren Grass	.50
14	A.J. Hinch	.50
15	Mark Merila	.50
16	John Powell	.50
17	Bob Scafa	.50
18	Matt Beaumont	.50
19	Todd Dunn	.50
20	Mike Martin	.50
21	Carlton Loewer	.50
22	Bret Wagner	.50

1995 Bazooka

Topps returned to the beginner's level baseball card niche in 1995 by resurrecting its Bazooka brand name. The set was unabashedly aimed at the younger collector, offering five cards and a Bazooka Joe cartoon-wrapped chunk of bubblegum for 50 cents. Cards feature on their backs a "roulette" wheel design based on the player's 1994 stats, to be used to play a game of spinner baseball. A game instruction card and cardboard spinner was included in each pack. Limiting the set to 132 cards allowed for a concentration of established stars and hot youngsters. A 22-card Red Hot insert set is found at the rate of one card per six packs, on average. Factory sets offering the 132 base cards, five Red Hot inserts and 10 pieces of bubblegum were produced.

		NM/M
Complete Set (132):		3.00
Factory Set (132+5):		5.00
Common Player:		.05
Pack (5):		.30
Wax Box (36):		7.00
1	Greg Maddux	.50
2	Cal Ripken Jr	1.00
3	Lee Smith	.05
4	Sammy Sosa	.50
5	Jason Bere	.05
6	Dave Justice	.05
7	Kevin Mitchell	.05
8	Ozzie Guillen	.05
9	Roger Clemens	.60
10	Mike Mussina	.30
11	Sandy Alomar	.05
12	Cecil Fielder	.05
13	Dennis Martinez	.05
14	Randy Myers	.05
15	Jay Buhner	.05
16	Ivan Rodriguez	.35
17	Mo Vaughn	.05
18	Ryan Klesko	.05
19	Chuck Finley	.05
20	Barry Bonds	1.00
21	Dennis Eckersley	.35
22	Kenny Lofton	.05
23	Rafael Palmeiro	.35
24	Mike Stanley	.05
25	Gregg Jefferies	.05
26	Robin Ventura	.05
27	Mark McGwire	.75
28	Ozzie Smith	.50
29	Troy Neel	.05
30	Tony Gwynn	.50
31	Ken Griffey Jr.	.65
32	Will Clark	.05
33	Craig Biggio	.05
34	Shawon Dunston	.05
35	Wilson Alvarez	.05
36	Bobby Bonilla	.05
37	Marquis Grissom	.05
38	Ben McDonald	.05
39	Delino DeShields	.05
40	Barry Larkin	.05
41	John Olerud	.05
42	Jose Canseco	.30
43	Greg Vaughn	.05
44	Gary Sheffield	.20
45	Paul O'Neill	.05
46	Bob Hamelin	.05
47	Don Mattingly	.60
48	John Franco	.05
49	Bret Boone	.05
50	Rick Aguilera	.05
51	Tim Wallach	.05
52	Roberto Kelly	.05
53	Danny Tartabull	.05
54	Randy Johnson	.40
55	Greg McMichael	.05
56	Bip Roberts	.05
57	David Cone	.05
58	Raul Mondesi	.05
59	Travis Fryman	.05
60	Jeff Conine	.05
61	Jeff Bagwell	.40
62	Rickey Henderson	.40
63	Fred McGriff	.05
64	Matt Williams	.05
65	Rick Wilkins	.05
66	Eric Karros	.05
67	Mel Rojas	.05
68	Juan Gonzalez	.20
69	Chuck Carr	.05
70	Moises Alou	.05
71	Mark Grace	.05
72	Alex Fernandez	.05
73	Rod Beck	.05
74	Ray Lankford	.05
75	Dean Palmer	.05
76	Joe Carter	.05
77	Mike Piazza	.65
78	Eddie Murray	.40
79	Dave Nilsson	.05
80	Brett Butler	.05
81	Roberto Alomar	.10
82	Jeff Kent	.05
83	Andres Galarraga	.05
84	Brady Anderson	.05
85	Jimmy Key	.05
86	Bret Saberhagen	.05
87	Chili Davis	.05
88	Jose Rijo	.05
89	Wade Boggs	.50
90	Len Dykstra	.05
91	Steve Howe	.05
92	Hal Morris	.05
93	Larry Walker	.05
94	Jeff Montgomery	.05
95	Wil Cordero	.05
96	Jay Bell	.05
97	Tom Glavine	.15
98	Chris Hoiles	.05
99	Steve Avery	.05
100	Ruben Sierra	.05
101	Mickey Tettleton	.05
102	Paul Molitor	.40
103	Carlos Baerga	.05
104	Walt Weiss	.05
105	Darren Daulton	.05
106	Jack McDowell	.05
107	Doug Drabek	.05
108	Mark Langston	.05
109	Manny Ramirez	.40
110	Kevin Appier	.05
111	Andy Benes	.05
112	Chuck Knoblauch	.05
113	Kirby Puckett	.50
114	Dante Bichette	.05
115	Deion Sanders	.10
116	Albert Belle	.05
117	Todd Zeile	.05
118	Devon White	.05
119	Tim Salmon	.05
120	Frank Thomas	.40
121	John Wetteland	.05
122	James Mouton	.05
123	Javy Lopez	.05
124	Carlos Delgado	.25
125	Cliff Floyd	.05
126	Alex Gonzalez	.05
127	Billy Ashley	.05
128	Rondell White	.05
129	Rico Brogna	.05
130	Melvin Nieves	.05
131	Jose Oliva	.05
132	J.R. Phillips	.05

1995 Bazooka Red Hot Inserts

Twenty-two of the game's biggest stars were chosen for inclusion in 1995 Bazooka's only insert set - Red Hots. The chase cards are found at an average rate of one per six packs. Red Hots are identical to the players' cards in the regular set except that the background has been rendered in shades of red, and the player name printed in gold foil. Card numbers have an "RH" prefix.

		NM/M
Complete Set (22):		7.00
Common Player:		.15
1	Greg Maddux	1.00
2	Cal Ripken Jr.	2.00
3	Barry Bonds	2.00
4	Kenny Lofton	.15
5	Mike Stanley	.15
6	Tony Gwynn	1.00
7	Ken Griffey Jr.	1.50
8	Barry Larkin	.15
9	Jose Canseco	.35
10	Paul O'Neill	.15
11	Randy Johnson	.75
12	David Cone	.15
13	Jeff Bagwell	.75
14	Matt Williams	.15
15	Mike Piazza	1.50
16	Roberto Alomar	.25
17	Jimmy Key	.15
18	Wade Boggs	1.00
19	Paul Molitor	.75
20	Carlos Baerga	.15
21	Albert Belle	.15
22	Frank Thomas	.75

1996 Bazooka

Topps' 1996 Bazooka set offers collectors interactive fun with its cards geared for a flipping game. Each front has an action photo of the player. The back contains one of five different Bazooka Joe characters, along with the Bazooka Ball game, the player's biographical data, and 1995 and career stats. Cards were available five per pack for 50 cents. The complete set was also offered in a factory set, packaged in an attractive gift box. As an exclusive bonus, one 1959 Bazooka Mickey Mantle reprint card is found in every factory set, along with 10 pieces of bubble gum.

		NM/M
Unopened Fact. Set (133):		9.00
Complete Set (132):		6.00
Common Player:		.05
Pack (5):		.40
Wax Box (36):		9.00
1	Ken Griffey Jr.	.75
2	J.T. Snow	.05
3	Rondell White	.05
4	Reggie Sanders	.05
5	Jeff Montgomery	.05
6	Mike Stanley	.05
7	Bernie Williams	.05
8	Mike Piazza	.75
9	Brian Hunter	.05
10	Len Dykstra	.05
11	Ray Lankford	.05
12	Kenny Lofton	.05
13	Robin Ventura	.05
14	Devon White	.05
15	Cal Ripken Jr.	1.50
16	Heathcliff Slocumb	.05
17	Ryan Klesko	.05
18	Terry Steinbach	.05
19	Travis Fryman	.05
20	Sammy Sosa	.50
21	Jim Thome	.35
22	Kenny Rogers	.05
23	Don Mattingly	.60
24	Kirby Puckett	.50
25	Matt Williams	.05
26	Larry Walker	.05
27	Tim Wakefield	.05
28	Greg Vaughn	.05
29	Denny Neagle	.05
30	Ken Caminiti	.05
31	Garret Anderson	.05
32	Brady Anderson	.05
33	Carlos Baerga	.05
34	Wade Boggs	.50
35	Roberto Alomar	.15
36	Eric Karros	.05
37	Jay Buhner	.05
38	Dante Bichette	.05
39	Darren Daulton	.05
40	Jeff Bagwell	.40
41	Jay Bell	.05
42	Dennis Eckersley	.35
43	Will Clark	.05
44	Tom Glavine	.20
45	Rick Aguilera	.05
46	Kevin Seitzer	.05
47	Bret Boone	.05
48	Mark Grace	.05
49	Ray Durham	.05
50	Rico Brogna	.05
51	Kevin Appier	.05
52	Moises Alou	.05
53	Jeff Conine	.05
54	Marty Cordova	.05
55	Jose Mesa	.05
56	Rod Beck	.05
57	Marquis Grissom	.05
58	David Cone	.05
59	Albert Belle	.05
60	Lee Smith	.05
61	Frank Thomas	.40
62	Roger Clemens	.60
63	Bobby Bonilla	.05
64	Paul Molitor	.40
65	Chuck Knoblauch	.05
66	Steve Finley	.05
67	Craig Biggio	.05
68	Ramon Martinez	.05
69	Jason Isringhausen	.05
70	Mark Wohlers	.05
71	Vinny Castilla	.05
72	Ron Gant	.05
73	Juan Gonzalez	.20
74	Mark McGwire	1.00
75	Jeff King	.05
76	Pedro Martinez	.40
77	Chad Curtis	.05
78	John Olerud	.05
79	Greg Maddux	.50
80	Derek Jeter	1.50
81	Mike Mussina	.25
82	Gregg Jefferies	.05
83	Jim Edmonds	.05
84	Carlos Perez	.05
85	Mo Vaughn	.05
86	Todd Hundley	.05
87	Roberto Hernandez	.05
88	Derek Bell	.05
89	Andres Galarraga	.05
90	Brian McRae	.05
91	Joe Carter	.05
92	Orlando Merced	.05
93	Cecil Fielder	.05
94	Dean Palmer	.05
95	Randy Johnson	.40
96	Chipper Jones	.50
97	Barry Larkin	.05
98	Hideo Nomo	.25
99	Gary Gaetti	.05
100	Edgar Martinez	.05
101	John Wetteland	.05
102	Rafael Palmeiro	.35
103	Chuck Finley	.05
104	Ivan Rodriguez	.35
105	Shawn Green	.10
106	Manny Ramirez	.40
107	Lance Johnson	.05
108	Jose Canseco	.20
109	Fred McGriff	.05
110	David Segui	.05
111	Tim Salmon	.05
112	Hal Morris	.05
113	Tino Martinez	.05
114	Bret Saberhagen	.05
115	Brian Jordan	.05
116	David Justice	.05
117	Jack McDowell	.05
118	Barry Bonds	1.50
119	Mark Langston	.05
120	John Valentin	.05
121	Raul Mondesi	.05
122	Quilvio Veras	.05
123	Randy Myers	.05
124	Tony Gwynn	.50
125	Johnny Damon	.20
126	Doug Drabek	.05
127	Bill Pulsipher	.05
128	Paul O'Neill	.05
129	Rickey Henderson	.40
130	Deion Sanders	.10
131	Orel Hershiser	.05
132	Gary Sheffield	.20

1996 Bazooka Mickey Mantle 1959 Reprint

Continuing its tribute to the late Mickey Mantle across all of its product lines, Topps produced a special reprint of

the 1959 Bazooka Mantle card exclusively for inclusion in factory sets of its 1996 Bazooka cards. While the original '59 Mantle was printed in nearly 3" x 5" size on the bottom of gum boxes, the reprint is in the current 2-1/2" x 3-1/2" size.

	NM/M
Mickey Mantle	7.50

1992 Ben's Bakery Super Hitters Discs

Ben's Bakery, a small, eastern Canadian bakery, inserted promotional discs in its hot dog and hamburger buns in 1992. As in the case of 1991, which was the company's first year in the promotion, the 1992 set contained 20 different players, including many of the top stars in the country. Twenty of the game's top hitters, with a special emphasis on Blue Jays players, are featured in this regional issue by a small Eastern Canada bakery. The 2-3/4" diameter discs were packaged in the company's hot dog and hamburger buns. Fronts feature a color photo on which team logos have been airbrushed away. The bakery logo is flanked by a red "Super Hitters" in the white border at top. The player's name appears in white in an orange banner beneath the photo, with his team and position in blue at bottom. Backs are printed in black and include a few biographical details and 1991 stats, along with a card number and appropriate logos and copyright notices.

		NM/M
Complete Set (20):		15.00
Common Player:		.75
1	Cecil Fielder	.75
2	Joe Carter	.75
3	Roberto Alomar	1.00
4	Devon White	.75
5	Kelly Gruber	.75
6	Cal Ripken, Jr.	3.50
7	Kirby Puckett	2.00
8	Paul Molitor	1.50
9	Julio Franco	.75
10	Ken Griffey Jr.	3.00
11	Frank Thomas	1.50
12	Jose Canseco	1.25
13	Danny Tartabull	.75
14	Terry Pendleton	.75
15	Tony Gwynn	2.00
16	Howard Johnson	.75
17	Will Clark	.75
18	Barry Bonds	3.50
19	Ryne Sandberg	2.00
20	Bobby Bonilla	.75

1993 Ben's Bakery Super Pitchers Discs

An emphasis on Toronto's pitchers is noted in the checklist for this regional bakery issue. The 2-3/4" diameter discs were packed with hot dog and hamburger buns and follow a 1991 issue by the company featuring super hitters. A color player portrait at center has had the uniform logos airbrushed away. "Super Pitchers" in red flanks the bakery logo in the white border above the photo. The player's name appears in white in an orange banner beneath the photo, with his team and position in blue at bottom. Backs are printed in black and include minimal biographical data, a card number, 1992 stats and copyright information.

		NM/M
Complete Set (20):		10.00
Common Player:		.45
1	Dennis Eckersley	1.50
2	Chris Bosio	.45
3	Jack Morris	.45
4	Greg Maddux	2.50
5	Dennis Martinez	.45
6	Tom Glavine	.75
7	Doug Drabek	.45
8	John Smoltz	.45
9	Randy Myers	.45
10	Jack McDowell	.45
11	John Wetteland	.45
12	Roger Clemens	3.00
13	Mike Mussina	.75
14	Juan Guzman	.45
15	Jose Rijo	.45
16	Tom Henke	.45
17	Gregg Olson	.45
18	Jim Abbott	.45
19	Jimmy Key	.45
20	Rheal Cormier	.45

1987 David Berg Hot Dogs Cubs

Changing sponsors from Gatorade to David Berg Pure Beef Hot Dogs, the Chicago Cubs handed out a 26-card set of baseball cards to fans attending the July 29th game at Wrigley Field. The cards are printed in full-color on white stock and measure 2-7/8" x 4-1/4" in size. The set is numbered by the players' uniform numbers. The card backs contain player personal and statistical information, plus a full-color picture of a David Berg hot dog in a bun with all the garnishings. The set marked the sixth consecutive year the Cubs held a baseball card giveaway promotion.

		NM/M
Complete Set (26):		10.00
Common Player:		.40
1	Dave Martinez	.40
4	Gene Michael	.40
6	Keith Moreland	.40
7	Jody Davis	.40
8	Andre Dawson	1.00
10	Leon Durham	.40
11	Jim Sundberg	.40
12	Shawon Dunston	.40
19	Manny Trillo	.40
20	Bob Dernier	.40
21	Scott Sanderson	.40
22	Jerry Mumphrey	.40
23	Ryne Sandberg	5.00
24	Brian Dayett	.40
29	Chico Walker	.40
31	Greg Maddux	5.00
33	Frank DiPino	.40
34	Steve Trout	.40
36	Gary Matthews	.40
37	Ed Lynch	.40
39	Ron Davis	.40
40	Rick Sutcliffe	.40
46	Lee Smith	.40
47	Dickie Noles	.40
49	Jamie Moyer	.40
---	The Coaching Staff (Johnny Oates, Jim Snyder, Herm Starrette, John Vukovich, Billy Williams)	.40

1988 David Berg Hot Dogs Cubs

This oversized (2-7/8" x 4-1/2") set of 26 cards was distributed to fans at Wrigley Field on August 24th. The set includes cards for the manager and coaching staff, as well as players. Full-color action photos are framed in red and blue on a white background. The backs feature small black and white player close-ups, colorful team logos, statistics and sponsor logos (David Berg Hot Dogs and Venture Store Restaurants). The numbers in the following checklist refer to players' uniforms.

		NM/M
Complete Set (27):		17.50
Common Player:		.40
2	Vance Law	.40
4	Don Zimmer	.40
7	Jody Davis	.40
8	Andre Dawson	1.00
9	Damon Berryhill	.40
12	Shawon Dunston	.40
17	Mark Grace	1.00
18	Angel Salazar	.40
19	Manny Trillo	.40
21	Scott Sanderson	.40
22	Jerry Mumphrey	.40
23	Ryne Sandberg	4.00
24	Gary Varsho	.40
25	Rafael Palmeiro	2.50
28	Mitch Webster	.40
30	Darrin Jackson	.40
31	Greg Maddux	4.00
32	Calvin Schiraldi	.40
33	Frank DiPino	.40
37	Pat Perry	.40
40	Rick Sutcliffe	.40
41	Jeff Pico	.40
45	Al Nipper	.40
49	Jamie Moyer	.40
50	Les Lancaster	.40
54	Rich Gossage	.40
---	The Coaching Staff (Joe Altobelli, Chuck Cottier, Larry Cox, Jose Martinez, Dick Pole)	.40

1994 Big Apple 1969 Mets Discs

Big Apple Collector, Inc. released the "1969 World Champion Miracle Mets Com-

memorative Cap Sheet," which has likenesses of each of the 31 members of the squad captured in oil paintings by sports artist Ron Lewis. The player's likeness is centered in a 1-5/8" diameter round commemorative cap which is die cut but remains in place on the sheet. Each cap is gold foil accented, and each 11" x 14" sheet is produced in full color on 48-point card stock. The sheet has a suggested retail price of $39.95.

		NM/M
Complete Set (31):		12.00
Common Player:		.25
(1)	Gil Hodges	1.50
(2)	Rube Walker	.25
(3)	Yogi Berra	1.50
(4)	Joe Pignatano	.25
(5)	Ed Yost	.25
(6)	Tommie Agee	.25
(7)	Ken Boswell	.25
(8)	Don Cardwell	.25
(9)	Ed Charles	.25
(10)	Donn Clendenon	.25
(11)	Jack DiLauro	.25
(12)	Duffy Dyer	.25
(13)	Wayne Garrett	.25
(14)	Rod Gaspar	.25
(15)	Gary Gentry	.25
(16)	Jerry Grote	.25
(17)	Bud Harrelson	.30
(18)	Cleon Jones	.25
(19)	Cal Koonce	.25
(20)	Jerry Koosman	.30
(21)	Ed Kranepool	.25
(22)	J.C. Martin	.25
(23)	Jim McAndrew	.25
(24)	Tug McGraw	.40
(25)	Bob Pfeil	.25
(26)	Nolan Ryan	4.00
(27)	Tom Seaver	2.00
(28)	Art Shamsky	.25
(29)	Ron Swoboda	.25
(30)	Ron Taylor	.25
(31)	Al Weis	.25

2001 The Big Book of Jewish Baseball

To promote its book on Jewish ballplayers, S.P.I. Books of Ft. Lee, N.J., issued a nine-card sheet. The sheet measures 8-1/2" x 12". At top on a purple background are nine cards which, if cut out on the yellow dotted lines, would each measure 2-11/16" x 3-3/8". Card #1 pictures the book's cover with its picture of Sandy Koufax. The other cards have color photos or colorized photos of some of the players featured in the book. Black-and-white backs have minimal player data and stats. At the bottom of the sheet is a coupon for ordering the book.

		NM/M
Sheet:		6.00
Complete Set (9):		6.00
Common Player:		.50
(1)	Book Cover (Sandy Koufax)	2.00
2	Lipman Pike	1.00
3	Moe Berg	2.00
4	Jesse Levis	.50
5	Harry Shuman	.50
6	Hank Greenberg	1.00
7	Harry Danning	.50
8	Cy Malis	.50
9	Hy Cohen	.50

1980s Big League Cards

Former major league pitcher and author Jim Bouton was a principal in the most successful of many "vanity" card manufacturers which sprang up in the 1980s and 1990s. For a price, anybody could send a picture to the New Jersey company and have it placed on a run of baseball cards. Persons could, and did, also send photos of ballplayers to create fantasy cards and at least several ballplayers who never appeared on cards contemporary with their careers had cards made up for themselves retroactively. Fronts have black, blue and red graphics. Backs are printed in blue on white with personal data, stats and other information provided by person ordering the cards. Unlike most other contemporary vanity cards, the Big League Cards are printed on thick quality similar to vintage baseball cards. There is no way to document the individual issue of these cards.

1986 Big League Chew

The 1986 Big League Chew set consists of 12 cards featuring the players who have hit 500 or more career home runs. The cards, which measure 2-1/2" x 3-1/2", were inserted in specially marked packages of Big League Chew, the shredded bubble gum developed by former major leaguer Jim Bouton. The set is entitled "Home Run Legends" and was available through a write-in offer on the package. Recent-day players in the set are shown in color photos, while the older sluggers are pictured in black and white.

		NM/M
Complete Set (12):		10.00
Common Player:		1.00
1	Hank Aaron	2.00
2	Babe Ruth	3.00
3	Willie Mays	2.00
4	Frank Robinson	1.00
5	Harmon Killebrew	1.00
6	Mickey Mantle	4.00
7	Jimmie Foxx	1.00
8	Ted Williams	2.00
9	Ernie Banks	1.00
10	Eddie Mathews	1.00
11	Mel Ott	1.00
12	500-HR Group Card	.50

1997 Big League Chew Alumni

Autographed cards of three Hall of Famers were available through a mail-in offer by Big League Chew shredded bubble gum. Cards could be obtained by sending in proofs of purchase from pouches with the players' photos on them. Each card comes with a certificate of authenticity from Major League Baseball Players Alumni, which licensed the issue. Because the cards are not licensed by Major League Baseball, uniform logos have been removed from the color photos. Cards have a green, orange and white color scheme on front and back and are standard 2-1/2" x 3-1/2". Backs include career highlights and lifetime stats.

		NM/M
Complete Set (3):		20.00
Common Player:		7.50
(1)	Juan Marichal	7.50
(2)	Brooks Robinson	7.50
(3)	Billy Williams	7.50

1982 Big League Collectibles Diamond Classics, Series 1

Attempting to recapture the flavor of vintage baseball cards, this collectors set presents former stars in a 2-1/2" x 3-3/4" format on thick white cardboard stock. Fronts have a painted player portrait in color with no other graphic elements. Backs are in black and blue and include in-depth biographical sketches and career stats. The edition was limited to 10,000 sets.

		NM/M
Complete Set (56):		30.00
Common Player:		.60
1	Joe DiMaggio	5.00
2	Enos Slaughter	.60
3	Smokey Joe Wood (Smoky)	.60
4	Roy Campanella	1.25
5	Charlie Gehringer	.60
6	Carl Hubbell	.60
7	Rogers Hornsby	.60
8	Arky Vaughan	.60
9	Al Simmons	.60
10	Wally Berger	.60
11	Sam Rice	.60
12	Dizzy Dean	.60
13	Babe Ruth	5.00
14	Frankie Frisch	.60
15	George Kell	.60
16	Pee Wee Reese	.60
17	Earl Averill	.60
18	Willie Mays	2.50
19	Frank Baker	.60
20	Hack Wilson	.60
21	Ted Williams	3.00
22	Chuck Klein	.60
23	Bill Dickey	.60
24	Johnny Mize	.60
25	Luke Appling	.60
26	Duke Snider	.60
27	Wahoo Sam Crawford	.60
28	Waite Hoyt	.60
29	Eddie Collins	.60
30	Warren Spahn	.60
31	Satchel Paige	1.25
32	Ernie Lombardi	.60
33	Dom DiMaggio	.60
34	Joe Garagiola	.60
35	Lou Gehrig	2.50
36	Burleigh Grimes	.60
37	Walter Johnson	.60
38	Bill Terry	.60
39	Ty Cobb	2.50
40	Pie Traynor	.60
41	Ted Lyons	.60
42	Richie Ashburn	.60
43	Lefty Grove	.60
44	Edd Roush	.60
45	Phil Rizzuto	.60
46	Stan Musial	2.00
47	Bob Feller	.60
48	Jackie Robinson	2.50
49	Hank Greenberg	1.25
50	Mel Ott	.60
51	Joe Cronin	.60
52	Lefty O'Doul	.60
53	Indian Bob Johnson	.60
54	Kiki Cuyler	.60
55	Mickey Mantle	7.50
---	Checklist	.10

1983 Big League Collectibles Diamond Classics, Series 2

A second series of cards featuring past greats was issued by Big League Collectibles in 1983. Again at 55 cards, the set featured painted portraits of the players on front, devoid of any other graphics. Backs are in red and black and include a lengthy career summary along with innovative stats and a few biographical bits. The 2-1/2" x 3-3/4" cards are printed on a heavy white cardboard stock. The series was produced in an edition of 10,000 sets.

		NM/M
Complete Set (56):		20.00
Common Player:		.60
56	Ernie Banks	1.50
57	Stan Coveleski	.60
58	Vince DiMaggio	.60
59	Sunny Jim Bottomley	.60
60	Sandy Koufax	4.00
61	Doc Cramer	.60
62	Ted Kluszewski	.60
63	Zeke Bonura	.60
64	Spud Davis	.60
65	Jackie Jensen	.60
66	Honus Wagner	.75
67	Brooks Robinson	1.25
68	Dazzy Vance	.60
69	George Uhle	.60
70	Juan Marichal	.60
71	Bobo Newsom	.60

72 Billy Herman .60
73 Al Rosen .60
74 Roberto Clemente 4.00
75 George Case .60
76 Bill Nicholson .60
77 Tommy Bridges .60
78 Rabbit Maranville .60
79 Bob Lemon .60
80 Heinie Groh .60
81 Tris Speaker .60
82 Hank Aaron 4.00
83 Whitey Ford 1.25
84a Guy Bush (Ernie Banks back.) .60
84b Guy Bush (Correct back.) .60
85 Jimmie Foxx .60
86 Marty Marion .60
87a Hal Newhouser (Charlie Grimm back.) .60
87b Hal Newhouser (Correct back.) .60
88 George Kelley (Kelly) .60
89 Harmon Killebrew .60
90 Willie McCovey .60
91 Mel Harder .60
92 Vada Pinson .60
93 Luis Aparicio .60
94 Grover Alexander .60
95 Joe Kuhel .60
96 Casey Stengel .60
97 Joe Sewell .60
98 Red Lucas .60
99 Luke Sewell .60
100 Charlie Grimm .60
101 Cecil Travis .60
102 Travis Jackson .60
103 Lou Boudreau .60
104 Nap Rucker .60
105 Chief Bender .60
106 Riggs Stephenson .60
107 Red Ruffing .60
108 Robin Roberts .60
109 Harland Clift (Harlond) .60
110 Ralph Kiner .60
--- Checklist .10

1983 Big League Collectibles Original All-Stars

Players in the first modern All-Star Game, staged in conjunction with the Chicago World's Fair in 1933, are featured in this collectors issue. The 2-1/2" x 3-3/4" cards feature pastel paintings of the players on front. A circled baseball at lower-left has player and set identification. Backs are printed in blue and black and include All-Star Game and overall 1933 season performance.

		NM/M
Complete Set (38):		20.00
Common Player:		.50
2	Connie Mack	.50
3	Alvin Crowder	.50
4	Lefty Gomez	.50
5	Jimmy Dykes	.50
6	Earl Averill	.50
7	Charlie Gehringer	.50
8	Lefty Grove	.50
9	Lou Gehrig	2.00
10	Al Simmons	.50
11	Ben Chapman	.50
12	Jimmie Foxx	.75
13	Oral Hildebrand	.50
14	Joe Cronin	.50
15	Bill Dickey	.50
16	Sam West	.50
17	Rick Ferrell	.50
18	Tony Lazzeri	.50
19	Wes Ferrell	.50
20	Babe Ruth	2.50
22	John McGraw	.50
23	Pepper Martin	.50
24	Woody English	.50
25	Paul Waner	.50
26	Lefty O'Doul	.50
27	Chuck Klein	.50
28	Tony Cuccinello	.50
29	Frankie Frisch	.50
30	Gabby Hartnett	.50
31	Carl Hubbell	.50
32	Chick Hafey	.50
33	Dick Bartell	.50
34	Bill Hallahan	.50
35	Hal Schumacher	.50
36	Lon Warneke	.50
37	Wally Berger	.50
38	Bill Terry	.50
39	Jimmy Wilson	.50
40	Pie Traynor	.50

1985 Big League Collectibles National Pastime 1930-1939

Major league baseball in the 1930s is chronicled in this boxed collectors set. In 2-1/8" x 3-1/8" format (the same size as the 1951-52 Bowmans), the cards feature painted player portraits on front with identification in the white border at bottom. Backs are in black and red on thick white cardboard stock and feature in-depth career summaries and unique stats. The edition was limited to 5,000 sets, with a serially numbered header card.

		NM/M
Complete Set (90):		45.00
Common Player:		.60
1	Header card	.10
2	William H. Walters	.60
3	Montgomery M. Pearson	.60
4	Stanley C. Hack	.60
5	Joseph E. Cronin	.60
6	Leo E. Durocher	.60
7	Max F. Bishop	.60
8	Frank O'Donnell Hurst	.60
9	W. Barney McCosky	.60
10	Remy P. Kremer	.60
11	Julius J. Solters	.60
12	Daniel K. MacFayden	.60
13	Gordon S. Cochrane	.60
14	Ethan N. Allen	.60
15	Luzerne A. Blue	.60
16	John R. Mize	.60
17	Joseph P. DiMaggio	3.50
18	George F. Grantham	.60
19	William E. Kamm	.60
20	Charles A. Root	.60
21	Morris Berg	2.00
22	Floyd C. Herman	.60
23	Henry E. Manush	.60
24	Adolf L. Camilli	.60
25	Rudolph P. York	.60
26	Truett B. Sewell	.60
27	Richard B. Ferrell	.60
28	Arthur C. Whitney	.60
29	Edmund J. Miller	.60
30	August R. Mancuso	.60
31	John B. Conlan	.60
32	Joseph M. Medwick	.60
33	John T. Allen	.60
34	John S. Vander Meer	.60
35	H. Earl Averill	.60
36	Taylor L. Douthit	.60
37	Charles S. Myer	.60
38	Van Lingle Mungo	.60
39	Smead P. Jolley	.60
40	C. Flint Rhem	.60
41	Leon A. Goslin	.60
42	Adam A. Comorosky	.60
43	Jack I. Burns	.60
44	Edward A. Brandt	.60
45	Robert L. Johnson	.60
46	Melvin T. Ott	.60
47	Monty F.P. Stratton	.60
48	Paul D. Dean	.60
49	H. Louis Gehrig	3.50
50	Frank A. McCormick	.60
51	J. Geoffrey Heath	.60
52	Charles L. Hartnett	.60
53	Oswald L. Bluege	.60
54	George H. Ruth	6.00
55	Robert P. Doerr	.60
56	Virgil L. Davis	.60
57	D. Dale Alexander	.60
58	James A. Tobin	.60
59	Joseph F. Vosmik	.60
60	Alfonso R. Lopez	.60
61	James E. Foxx	.60
62	Frederick L. Fitzsimmons	.60
63	Robert R. Fothergill	.60
64	Morton C. Cooper	.60
65	George A. Selkirk	.60
66	Burton E. Shotton	.60
67	Robert W.A. Feller	.60
68	Lawrence H. French	.60
69	Joseph I. Judge	.60
70	Clyde L. Sukeforth	.60
71	James R. Tabor	.60
72	Silas K. Johnson	.60
73	W. Earl Webb	.60
74	Charles F. Lucas	.60
75	Ralph Kress	.60
76	Charles D. Stengel	.60
77	George W. Haas	.60
78	Joe G. Moore	.60
79	Carl N. Reynolds	.60
80	James O. Carleton	.60
81	John J. Murphy	.60
82	Paul Derringer	.60
83	Harold A. Trosky, Sr.	.60
84	Fred C. Lindstrom	.60
85	Jack E. Russell	.60
86	Stanley G. Bordagaray	.60
87	Roy C. Johnson	.60
88	Sylvester W. Johnson	.60
89	Michael F. Higgins	.60
90	J. Floyd Vaughan	.60

1989 Bimbo Cookies Super Stars Discs

A dozen Hispanic players are featured in this set of 2-3/4" diameter discs distributed in Puerto Rico in boxes of cookies. Color portrait photos at center have cap logos removed because the discs are licensed only by the players' union, not MLB; typical for issues from Michael Schechter Associates. The Bimbo bear logo is at top-center, with the player name in a yellow strip at bottom; team and position are in blue in the white border beneath that. Yellow stars, blue baseballs and red words "SUPER STARS" flank the player photo. Backs are printed in blue and have a few biographical details, 1988 and career stats, card number and appropriate logos.

		NM/M
Complete Set (12):		15.00
Common Player:		1.50
1	Carmelo Martinez	1.50
2	Candy Maldonado	1.50
3	Benito Santiago	1.50
4	Rey Quinones	1.50
5	Jose Oquendo	1.50
6	Ruben Sierra	1.50
7	Jose Lind	1.50
8	Juan Beniquez	1.50
9	Willie Hernandez	1.50
10	Juan Nieves	1.50
11	Jose Guzman	1.50
12	Roberto Alomar (Photo actually Sandy Alomar Jr.)	3.50

1991-1992 Bleachers Promos

To introduce its 1992 lineup of single-player 23-Karat gold trimmed card sets, Bleachers produced a series of promo cards. Fronts have color portraits of the players. Backs have another picture of the player and information about ordering and coming releases. The Nolan Ryan card, showing him winding up in a tuxedo, is known in several variations with different card show names stamped on

front in gold, representing venues at which sample cards were given away.

		NM/M
Complete Set (3):		3.00
(1)	Ken Griffey Jr.	1.00
(2)	David Justice	.50
(3)	Nolan Ryan	2.00

1991 Bleachers Frank Thomas

This limited edition three-card set features 23-Karat gold cards. The photos feature Frank Thomas at different stages of his baseball career before the big leagues. Production was limited to 10,000 sets and 1,500 uncut strips. All are numbered and feature a gold facsimile autograph on the back.

		NM/M
Complete Set (3):		4.00
Common Card:		2.00
1	Frank Thomas (Auburn Tigers)	2.00
2	Frank Thomas (Sarasota White Sox)	2.00
3	Frank Thomas (Birmingham Barons)	2.00

1992 Bleachers Ken Griffey, Jr.

Young superstar Ken Griffey, Jr. is honored in this three-card set featuring him at different stages of his baseball career. The 23-Karat gold cards feature full-color photos and a facsimile autograph on the back. Production was limited to 10,000 cut sets and 1,500 uncut strips.

		NM/M
Complete Set (3):		10.00
Common Card:		3.00
1	Ken Griffey Jr. (Moeller High School)	4.00
2	Ken Griffey Jr. (Bellingham Mariners)	4.00
3	Ken Griffey Jr. (San Bernadino Spirit)	4.00

1992 Bleachers David Justice

Atlanta Brave slugger David Justice is the subject of this three card 23-Karat gold set. The cards depict Justice at different stages of his baseball career. Like the other Bleachers issues, production was limited to 10,000 cut card sets and 1,500 uncut strips.

		NM/M
Complete Set (3):		6.00
Common Card:		2.50
1	David Justice (Durham Bulls)	2.50
2	David Justice (Greenville Braves)	2.50
3	David Justice (Richmond Braves)	2.50

1992 Bleachers Nolan Ryan

Three stops along Ryan's minor league trail are recalled in this collectors issue. The 2-1/2" x 3-1/2" cards have photos of Ryan at center with different colored borders and trim on each card. "23KT," his name and team are gold-foil stamped on front. Backs have career information and highlights, along with a serial number from within an edition of 10,000. Cards with silver prismatic foil on front rather than gold were random inserts in sets. Three-card uncut strips were made available in an edition of 1,500.

		NM/M
Complete Set (3):		6.00
Common Card:		2.00
Silver-foil:		2X
1	Nolan Ryan (Marion Mets)	2.00
2	Nolan Ryan (Greenville Mets)	2.00
3	Nolan Ryan (Jacksonville Suns)	2.00

1993 Bleachers Promos

To introduce its 1993 issues, Bleachers distributed large quantities of promo cards within the hobby to dealers and to the public at several large card shows. Most of the '93 promos can be found with several different show logos overprinted in gold foil on the front. All cards carry a 1993 copyright date on back, except the plain

Ryan/tuxedo card, which has a 1992 date on back, but 1993 card-show indicia on front.

		NM/M
Common Card:		1.00
(1)	Barry Bonds (Arizona State)	2.00
(2)	Ken Griffey Jr. (Moeller High School uniform.)	2.00
(3)	Nolan Ryan (Triple-exposure pitching.)	2.00
(4)	Nolan Ryan (Tuxedo, '92 copyright.)	2.00
(5)	Nolan Ryan (Tuxedo, gold background.)	2.00
(6)	Nolan Ryan (Tuxedo, silver speckled background.)	2.00
(7)	Nolan Ryan (Tuxedo, wavy silver background.)	2.00
(8)	Nolan Ryan (Western clothing.)	2.00
(9)	Nolan Ryan (W/glove and ball in Bleachers cap.)	2.00
(10)	Nolan Ryan (With Yellow Lab puppy.)	2.00
(11)	Ryne Sandberg (Three-sport high school photos.)	1.00

1993 Bleachers Barry Bonds

The pre-major league career of Barry Bonds is featured on this trio of collectors cards. Fronts have color photos of Bonds within a gold border. His name, team and the notation "23KT" are printed in gold foil. Backs have career data and highlights, along with a serial number. It was reported that 10,000 sets and 1,500 three-card strips were issued. Cards found with silver prismatic borders on front are random inserts in sets.

		NM/M
Complete Set (3):		9.00
Common Card:		4.00
Silver:		2X
1	Barry Bonds (Arizona State University)	4.00
2	Barry Bonds (Price Williams Pirates)	4.00
3	Barry Bonds (Hawaii Islanders)	4.00

1993 Bleachers Nolan Ryan

Nolan Ryan's career is recapped in this set of collectors issues. Fronts have prismatic foil borders around color or colorized photos. Information on front is stamped in gold foil. Backs have a photo of a young Ryan along with career data and stats, and a serial number

from within an announced edition of 10,000 sets and 1,500 three-card uncut strips.

		NM/M
Complete Set (6):		15.00
Common Card:		3.00
1	Nolan Ryan (Little League)	3.00
2	Nolan Ryan (High school.)	3.00
3	Nolan Ryan (Minor league highlights.)	3.00
4	Nolan Ryan (Minor league stats.)	3.00
5	Nolan Ryan (Strikeout record.)	3.00
6	Nolan Ryan (Career highlights.)	3.00

1993 Bleachers Nolan Ryan 23KT

"The Express" is pictured with each of his four major league teams in this collectors issue. Each 2-1/2" x 3-1/2" card has a color photo of Ryan at center with variously colored borders and gold-foil graphic highlights. Backs have his stats with that team, a facsimile autograph and a serial number from within an edition of 10,000 sets. Uncut strips were also issued, numbered to 1,500.

		NM/M
Complete Set (4):		15.00
Uncut Strip:		20.00
Common Card:		4.00
1	Nolan Ryan/Mets	4.00
2	Nolan Ryan/Angels	4.00
3	Nolan Ryan/Astros	4.00
4	Nolan Ryan/Rangers	4.00

1993 Bleachers Ryne Sandberg

Ryno's pre-major league career is featured on this trio of collectors cards. Fronts have color photos of Sandberg within a gold border. His name, team and the notation "23KT" are printed in gold foil. Backs have career data and highlights, along with a serial number. It was reported that 10,000 sets and 1,500 three-card, gold highlighted strips were issued. Cards found with silver prismatic borders on front are random inserts in sets.

		NM/M
Complete Set (3):		9.00
Common Card:		3.00
Gold Strip:		12.00
Silver:		3X
1	Ryne Sandberg (North Central H.S.)	3.00
2	Ryne Sandberg (Helena Phillies)	3.00
3	Ryne Sandberg (Reading Phillies)	3.00

1992 Blockbuster Video Pin/Cards

Given away at special promotional games, these combination collectibles feature a 2-3/4" x 4" card, beneath which is a perforated tab of 2-3/4" x 1-9/16". The card has a borderless photo with the player name and his uniform number. The tab has a sponsor's logo. Attached to the tab is an enameled pin, about 1-1/4" square, which has a representation of the player's jersey. The black-and-white back has a portrait photo, player biographical details and career highlights. On back of the tab is a list of the Blockbuster locations participating in the promotion.

		NM/M
Common Player:		3.00
3	Jay Bell	3.00
6	Orlando Merced	3.00
15	Doug Drabek	3.00
24	Barry Bonds	15.00

1988 Blue Cross/ Blue Shield Bob Uecker Reprint

Issued as a fund-raiser and sold for $3 to benefit Bob Uecker's Ride for the Arts bicycling event in 1988, this 2-1/2" x 3-1/2" card features on its front a reprint of Uecker's card from the 1963 Topps set. Back has history and details of the fund-raiser and the logos of Blue Cross and Blue Shield.

		NM/M
(1)	Bob Uecker	6.00

1987 Bluegrass State Games

Athletes with ties to Kentucky and public figures from the state are featured on this set issued in conjunction with the 1987 Bluegrass State Games. Fronts have color photos on a blue background with white borders. Beneath the photo are the logos of Champions Against Drugs and sponsors Coke and Valvoline. Backs have an anti-drug

message from the pictured celebrity. Cards were handed out over the period May 25-October 19 by law enforcement officers. Only the baseball-related cards are listed here.

		NM/M
Complete Set (24):		50.00
Common Player:		.50
5	Doug Flynn	1.00
13	Pee Wee Reese	5.00
22	A.B. (Happy) Chandler	1.00

1987 Boardwalk and Baseball All Time Record Holders

This boxed set was a repackaging of the cards produced by Topps for Woolworth stores in 1985. Fronts have "framed" black-and-white or color photos with player identification in a "plaque" at bottom. Blue-on-orange backs have brief biographical data, a listing of the player's record and career highlights, and lifetime stats.

(See 1985 Woolworth for checklist and values.)

1987 Boardwalk and Baseball Top Run Makers

Created by Topps for distribution at the Boardwalk and Baseball theme park near Orlando, Fla., the cards are standard size with a thin, pink border around a color action photo. The backs are printed in black and light red, with the Topps and B/B logos at the bottom. There are 33-cards in the "Top Run Makers" boxed set, all hitters. A checklist appears on the back panel of the box. A much scarcer version of each card can be found with no slash between the "B"s on front.

		NM/M
Complete Set (33):		4.00
Common Player:		.10
No Slash:		3X
1	Mike Schmidt	1.00
2	Eddie Murray	.45
3	Dale Murphy	.25
4	Dave Winfield	.45
5	Jim Rice	.25
6	Cecil Cooper	.10
7	Dwight Evans	.10
8	Rickey Henderson	.45
9	Robin Yount	.45
10	Andre Dawson	.25
11	Gary Carter	.45
12	Keith Hernandez	.10
13	George Brett	1.00
14	Bill Buckner	.10
15	Tony Armas	.10
16	Harold Baines	.10
17	Don Baylor	.10
18	Steve Garvey	.10
19	Lance Parrish	.10
20	Dave Parker	.10
21	Buddy Bell	.10
22	Cal Ripken, Jr.	1.50
23	Bob Horner	.10
24	Tim Raines	.10
25	Jack Clark	.10
26	Leon Durham	.10
27	Pedro Guerrero	.10
28	Kent Hrbek	.10
29	Kirk Gibson	.10
30	Ryne Sandberg	.60
31	Wade Boggs	.60
32	Don Mattingly	.75
33	Darryl Strawberry	.10

1987 Bohemian Hearth Bread Padres

Bohemian Hearth Bread of San Diego issued this Padres team set. Produced in conjunction with Mike Schechter Associates, the cards are 2-1/2" x 3-1/2". Fronts have a color portrait photo encompassed by a yellow border. The Bohemian Hearth logo is located in the upper-left corner. Card backs are printed in light brown on a cream stock and carry player personal and statistical information, along with a facsimile autograph.

		NM/M
Complete Set (22):		20.00
Common Player:		.50
1	Garry Templeton	.50
4	Jose Cora	.50
5	Randy Ready	.50
6	Steve Garvey	3.00
7	Kevin Mitchell	.50
8	John Kruk	.65
9	Benito Santiago	.75
10	Larry Bowa	.50
11	Tim Flannery	.50
14	Carmelo Martinez	.50
16	Marvell Wynne	.50
19	Tony Gwynn	15.00
21	James Steels	.50
22	Stan Jefferson	.50
30	Eric Show	.50
31	Ed Whitson	.50
34	Storm Davis	.50
37	Craig Lefferts	.50
40	Andy Hawkins	.50
41	Lance McCullers	.50
43	Dave Dravecky	.50
54	Rich Gossage	.50

1984 Borden's Reds Stickers

This regional set of eight Reds stickers was issued by Borden Dairy in the Cincinnati area in 1984. Originally issued in two perforated sheets of

four stickers each, the individual stickers measure 2-1/2" x 3-7/8", while a full sheet measures 5-1/2" x 8". The colorful stickers feature a player photo surrounded by a bright red border with the Reds logo and the Borden logo in the corners. The backs display coupons for Borden dairy products. The set is numbered according to the players' uniform numbers.

		NM/M
Complete Panel Set (2):		8.00
Complete Singles Set (8):		8.00
Common Player:		.50
PANEL (1)		5.00
2	Gary Redus	.50
20	Eddie Milner	.50
24	Tony Perez	3.00
46	Jeff Russell	.50
PANEL (2)		3.00
16	Ron Oester	.50
36	Mario Soto	.50
39	Dave Parker	.60
44	Eric Davis	1.00

1983 Boston Herald Sox Stamps

Current and former Red Sox stars are featured in this set of stamps issued by one of Boston's daily newspapers. Coupons in the paper could be redeemed for packets of stamps which could be mounted on a large (34" x 22") colorful wallchart. Persons completing the set could enter a contest for various prizes. Stamps #1-26 and 39-42 are in color and feature portrait photos of the '83 team. They measure 1" x 1-3/4". Stamps #27-38 and 43-50 are 1" x 1-1/8" and may have either color or black-and-white photos of current and former players. Values shown are for unused stamps.

		NM/M
Complete Set (50):		30.00
Common Player:		.50
Wallchart:		15.00
1	Jerry Remy	.50
2	Glenn Hoffman	.50
3	Luis Aponte	.50
4	Jim Rice	1.00
5	Mark Clear	.50
6	Reid Nichols	.50
7	Wade Boggs	5.00
8	Dennis Eckersley	2.00
9	Jeff Newman	.50
10	Bob Ojeda	.50
11	Ed Jurak	.50
12	Rick Miller	.50
13	Carl Yastrzemski	7.50
14	Mike Brown	.50
15	Bob Stanley	.50
16	John Tudor	.50
17	Gary Allenson	.50
18	Rich Gedman	.50
19	Tony Armas	.75
20	Doug Bird	.50
21	Bruce Hurst	.50
22	Dave Stapleton	.50
23	Dwight Evans	1.00
24	Julio Valdez	.50
25	John Henry Johnson	.50
26	Ralph Houk	.50
27	George Scott	.75
28	Bobby Doerr	.60
29	Frank Malzone	.50
30	Rico Petrocelli	.75
31	Carl Yastrzemski	5.00
32	Ted Williams	7.50
33	Dwight Evans	.75
34	Carlton Fisk	4.00
35	Dick Radatz	.50
36	Luis Tiant	.75
37	Mel Parnell	.50
38	Jim Rice	.75
39	Dennis Boyd	.60
40	Marty Barrett	.50
41	Brian Denman	.50
42	Steve Crawford	.50
43	Cy Young	.75
44	Jimmy Collins	.50
45	Tris Speaker	.75
46	Harry Hooper	.50
47	Lefty Grove	.60
48	Joe Cronin	.50
49	Jimmie Foxx	.75
50	Ted Williams	7.50

1982 Boston Red Sox Favorites

No issuer is identified on this collectors set, though some attribute it to the Boston Globe newspaper. The 2-1/2" x 3-1/2" cards are black-and-white with rather wide white borders on front. There is no player identification on front. Backs are roughly in the style of 1955 Bowmans and have player identification, personal data, stats, career highlights and a trivia question.

		NM/M
Complete Set (128):		35.00
Common Player:		.25
1	Harry Agganis	2.00
2	Ken Aspromonte	.25
3	Bobby Avila	.25
4	Frank Baumann	.25
5	Lou Berberet	.25
6	Milt Bolling	.25
7	Lou Boudreau	.50
8	Ted Bowsfield	.25
9	Tom Brewer	.25
10	Don Buddin	.25
11	Jerry Casale	.25
12	Billy Consolo	.25
13	Pete Daley	.25
14	Ike Delock	.25
15	Dom DiMaggio	1.00
16	Bobby Doerr	.50
17	Walt Dropo	.50
18	Arnold Earley	.25
19	Hoot Evers	.25
20	Mike Fornieles	.25
21	Gary Geiger	.25
22	Don Gile	.25
23	Joe Ginsberg	.25
24	Billy Goodman	.25
25	Pumpsie Green	.35
26	Grady Hatten	.25
27	Mike Higgins	.25
28	Jackie Jensen	.50
29	George Kell	.50
30	Marty Keough	.25
31	Leo Kiely	.25
32	Ellis Kinder	.25
33	Billy Klaus	.25
34	Don Lenhardt	.25
35	Ted Lepcio	.25
36	Frank Malzone	.35
37	Gene Mauch	.25
38	Maury McDermott	.25
39	Bill Monbouquette	.25
40	Chet Nichols	.25
41	Willard Nixon	.25
42	Jim Pagliaroni	.25
43	Mel Parnell	.25
44	Johnny Pesky	.25
45	Jimmy Piersall	.50
46	Bob Porterfield	.25

47	Pete Runnels	.25
48	Dave Sisler	.25
49	Riverboat Smith	.25
50	Gene Stephens	.25
51	Vern Stephens	.25
52	Chuck Stobbs	.25
53	Dean Stone	.25
54	Frank Sullivan	.25
55	Haywood Sullivan	.25
56	Birdie Tebbetts	.25
57	Mickey Vernon	.35
58	Vic Wertz	.25
59	Sammy White	.25
60	Ted Williams	6.00
61	Ted Wills	.25
62	Earl Wilson	.25
63	Al Zarilla	.25
64	Norm Zauchin	.25
65	Ted Williams, Carl Yastrzemski	4.00
66	Jim Lonborg, George Scott, Dick Williams, Carl Yastrzemski	2.00
67	Billy Conigliaro, Tony Conigliaro	.75
68	Jerry Adair	.25
69	Mike Andrews	.25
70	Gary Bell	.25
71	Dennis Bennett	.25
72	Ed Bressoud	.25
73	Ken Brett	.25
74	Lu Clinton	.25
75	Tony Conigliaro	1.00
76	Billy Conigliaro	.25
77	Gene Conley	.25
78	Ray Culp	.25
79	Dick Ellsworth	.25
80	Joe Foy	.25
81	Russ Gibson	.25
82	Jim Gosger	.25
83	Lennie Green	.25
84	Ken Harrelson	.25
85	Tony Horton	.35
86	Elston Howard	.35
87	Dalton Jones	.25
88	Eddie Kasko	.25
89	Joe Lahoud	.25
90	Jack Lamabe	.25
91	Jim Lonborg	.50
92	Sparky Lyle	.50
93	Felix Mantilla	.25
94	Roman Mejias	.25
95	Don McMahon	.25
96	Dave Morehead	.25
97	Gerry Moses	.25
98	Mike Nagy	.25
99	Russ Nixon	.25
100	Gene Oliver	.25
101	Dan Osinski	.25
102	Rico Petrocelli	.50
103	Juan Pizzaro	.25
104	Dick Radatz	.35
105	Vicente Romo	.25
106	Mike Ryan	.25
107	Jose Santiago	.25
108	Chuck Schilling	.35
109	Dick Schofield	.25
110	Don Schwall	.25
111	George Scott	.35
112	Norm Siebern	.25
113	Sonny Seibert	.25
114	Reggie Smith	.35
115	Bill Spanswick	.25
116	Tracy Stallard	.25
117	Lee Stange	.25
118	Jerry Stephenson	.25
119	Dick Stuart	.25
120	Tom Sturdivant	.25
121	Jose Tartabull	.25
122	George Thomas	.25
123	Lee Thomas	.25
124	Bob Tillman	.25
125	Gary Waslewski	.25
126	Dick Williams	.25
127	John Wyatt	.25
128	Carl Yastrzemski	4.00

1993 Boston Red Sox Police

This police set was issued by the police department and local sponsors around the Red Sox spring training base in Florida. Card fronts have studio poses of the players. The Winter Haven P.D. and Police Athletic League logos are at top, while the Red Sox logo, player ID and uniform number are beneath the portrait. Backs have a little personal data, some stats, a safety message and the names of sponsoring businesses.

		NM/M
Complete Set (28):		10.00
Common Player:		.50
1	Checklist	.10
2	Scott Bankhead	.50
3	Danny Darwin	.50
4	Andre Dawson	.75
5	Scott Fletcher	.50
6	Billy Hatcher	.50
7	Jack Clark	.50
8	Roger Clemens	5.00
9	Scott Cooper	.50
10	John Dopson	.50
11	Paul Quantrill	.50
12	Mike Greenwell	.50
13	Greg A. Harris	.50
14	Joe Hesketh	.50
15	Peter Hoy	.50
16	Daryl Irvine	.50
17	John Marzano	.50
18	Jeff McNeeley	.50
19	Tim Naehring	.50
20	Matt Young	.50
21	Jeff Plympton	.50
22	Bob Melvin	.50
23	Tony Pena	.50
24	Luis Rivera	.50
25	Scott Taylor	.50
26	John Valentin	.50
27	Mo Vaughn	.50
28	Frank Viola	.50

2001 Boston Red Sox 100 Seasons

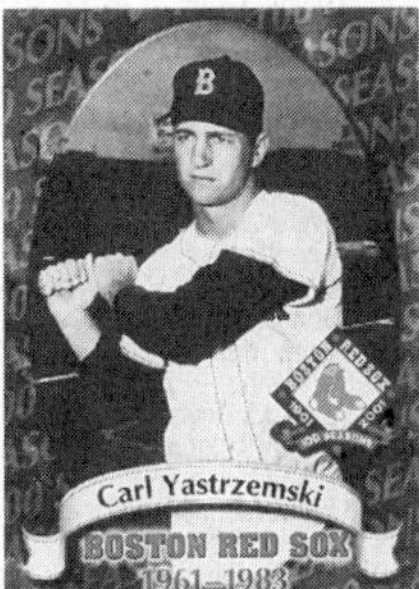

This limited edition card set was issued by the team as part of its 100 seasons anniversary. One card was designated as a give-away at each of 16 home games during spring training. The first 4,000 fans at each game received that day's card. An additional 1,000 sets was reserved for team use. The 2-1/2" x 3-1/2" cards have sepia photos on front, along with a 100 seasons logo and the years the player was with the Red Sox. Backs have a Grapefruit League logo, a few career highlights and the logos of the sponsors, Aramark and gulf-coasting.com.

		NM/M
Complete Set (16):		25.00
Common Player:		1.00
1	Jimmy Collins	1.00
2	Cy Young	2.00
3	Tris Speaker	1.50
4	Babe Ruth	7.50
5	Lefty Grove	1.00
6	Joe Cronin	1.00
7	Jimmie Foxx	1.50
8	Bobby Doerr	1.00
9	Ted Williams	6.00
10	Dom DiMaggio	1.00
11	Johnny Pesky	1.00
12	Carl Yastrzemski	4.00
13	Carlton Fisk	3.00
14	Jim Rice	1.50
15	Nomar Garciaparra	4.50
16	Pedro Martinez	2.50

1987 Bowery Bank Joe DiMaggio

These cards were issued to promote the New York City bank's relationship with spokesman Joe DiMaggio. The 2-1/2" x 3-1/2" cards have a posed color photo on front. The back has

biographical data, career highlights and stats printed in black and red.

	NM/M
Joe DiMaggio	17.50

1989 Bowman

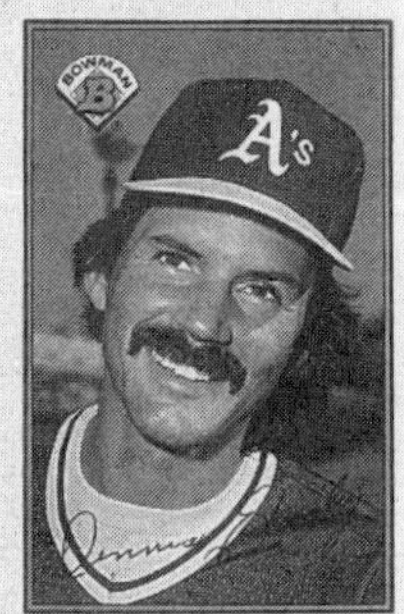

Topps, which purchased Bowman in 1955, revived the brand name in 1989, issuing a 484-card set. The 2-1/2" x 3-3/4" cards are slightly taller than current standard. Fronts contain a full-color player photo, with facsimile autograph and the Bowman logo in an upper corner. Backs include a breakdown of the player's stats against each team in his league. A series of "Hot Rookie Stars" highlights the set. The cards were distributed in both wax packs and rack packs. Each pack included a special reproduction of a classic Bowman card with a sweepstakes on the back.

		NM/M
Unopened Fact. Set (484):		20.00
Complete Set (484):		15.00
Common Player:		.05
Wax Pack (12+1):		.75
Wax Box (36):		15.00
Rack Pack (40):		1.00
Rack Box (24):		20.00
1	Oswald Peraza	.05
2	Brian Holton	.05
3	Jose Bautista	.05
4	Pete Harnisch **RC**	.10
5	Dave Schmidt	.05
6	Gregg Olson	.05
7	Jeff Ballard	.05
8	Bob Melvin	.05
9	Cal Ripken, Jr.	.75
10	Randy Milligan	.05
11	Juan Bell **RC**	.05
12	Billy Ripken	.05
13	Jim Traber	.05
14	Pete Stanicek	.05
15	Steve Finley **RC**	.25
16	Larry Sheets	.05
17	Phil Bradley	.05
18	Brady Anderson	.05
19	Lee Smith	.05
20	Tom Fischer	.05
21	Mike Boddicker	.05
22	Rob Murphy	.05
23	Wes Gardner	.05
24	John Dopson	.05
25	Bob Stanley	.05
26	Roger Clemens	.60
27	Rich Gedman	.05
28	Marty Barrett	.05
29	Luis Rivera	.05
30	Jody Reed	.05
31	Nick Esasky	.05
32	Wade Boggs	.50
33	Jim Rice	.20
34	Mike Greenwell	.05
35	Dwight Evans	.05
36	Ellis Burks	.05
37	Chuck Finley	.05
38	Kirk McCaskill	.05
39	Jim Abbott	.05
40	Bryan Harvey **RC**	.05
41	Bert Blyleven	.05
42	Mike Witt	.05
43	Bob McClure	.05
44	Bill Schroeder	.05
45	Lance Parrish	.05
46	Dick Schofield	.05
47	Wally Joyner	.05
48	Jack Howell	.05
49	Johnny Ray	.05
50	Chili Davis	.05
51	Tony Armas	.05
52	Claudell Washington	.05
53	Brian Downing	.05
54	Devon White	.05
55	Bobby Thigpen	.05
56	Bill Long	.05
57	Jerry Reuss	.05
58	Shawn Hillegas	.05
59	Melido Perez	.05
60	Jeff Bittiger	.05
61	Jack McDowell	.05
62	Carlton Fisk	.40
63	Steve Lyons	.05
64	Ozzie Guillen	.05
65	Robin Ventura	.05
66	Fred Manrique	.05
67	Dan Pasqua	.05
68	Ivan Calderon	.05
69	Ron Kittle	.05
70	Daryl Boston	.05
71	Dave Gallagher	.05
72	Harold Baines	.05
73	Charles Nagy **RC**	.15
74	John Farrell	.05
75	Kevin Wickander	.05
76	Greg Swindell	.05
77	Mike Walker	.05
78	Doug Jones	.05
79	Rich Yett	.05
80	Tom Candiotti	.05
81	Jesse Orosco	.05
82	Bud Black	.05
83	Andy Allanson	.05
84	Pete O'Brien	.05
85	Jerry Browne	.05
86	Brook Jacoby	.05
87	Mark Lewis **RC**	.05
88	Luis Aguayo	.05
89	Cory Snyder	.05
90	Oddibe McDowell	.05
91	Joe Carter	.05
92	Frank Tanana	.05
93	Jack Morris	.05
94	Doyle Alexander	.05
95	Steve Searcy	.05
96	Randy Bockus	.05
97	Jeff Robinson	.05
98	Mike Henneman	.05
99	Paul Gibson	.05
100	Frank Williams	.05
101	Matt Nokes	.05
102	Rico Brogna	.05
103	Lou Whitaker	.05
104	Al Pedrique	.05
105	Alan Trammell	.05
106	Chris Brown	.05
107	Pat Sheridan	.05
108	Gary Pettis	.05
109	Keith Moreland	.05
110	Mel Stottlemyre, Jr.	.05
111	Bret Saberhagen	.05
112	Floyd Bannister	.05
113	Jeff Montgomery	.05
114	Steve Farr	.05
115	Tom Gordon	.05
116	Charlie Leibrandt	.05
117	Mark Gubicza	.05
118	Mike MacFarlane	.05
119	Bob Boone	.05
120	Kurt Stillwell	.05
121	George Brett	.60
122	Frank White	.05
123	Kevin Seitzer	.05
124	Willie Wilson	.05
125	Pat Tabler	.05
126	Bo Jackson	.10
127	Hugh Walker	.05
128	Danny Tartabull	.05
129	Teddy Higuera	.05
130	Don August	.05
131	Juan Nieves	.05
132	Mike Birkbeck	.05
133	Dan Plesac	.05
134	Chris Bosio	.05
135	Bill Wegman	.05
136	Chuck Crim	.05
137	B.J. Surhoff	.05
138	Joey Meyer	.05
139	Dale Sveum	.05
140	Paul Molitor	.40
141	Jim Gantner	.05
142	Gary Sheffield **RC**	.75
143	Greg Brock	.05
144	Robin Yount	.40
145	Glenn Braggs	.05
146	Rob Deer	.05
147	Fred Toliver	.05
148	Jeff Reardon	.05
149	Allan Anderson	.05
150	Frank Viola	.05
151	Shane Rawley	.05
152	Juan Berenguer	.05
153	Johnny Ard	.05
154	Tim Laudner	.05
155	Brian Harper	.05
156	Al Newman	.05
157	Kent Hrbek	.05
158	Gary Gaetti	.05
159	Wally Backman	.05
160	Gene Larkin	.05
161	Greg Gagne	.05
162	Kirby Puckett	.50
163	Danny Gladden	.05
164	Randy Bush	.05
165	Dave LaPoint	.05
166	Andy Hawkins	.05
167	Dave Righetti	.05
168	Lance McCullers	.05
169	Jimmy Jones	.05
170	Al Leiter	.05
171	John Candelaria	.05
172	Don Slaught	.05
173	Jamie Quirk	.05
174	Rafael Santana	.05
175	Mike Pagliarulo	.05
176	Don Mattingly	.60
177	Ken Phelps	.05
178	Steve Sax	.05
179	Dave Winfield	.40
180	Stan Jefferson	.05
181	Rickey Henderson	.40
182	Bob Brower	.05
183	Roberto Kelly	.05
184	Curt Young	.05
185	Gene Nelson	.05
186	Bob Welch	.05
187	Rick Honeycutt	.05
188	Dave Stewart	.05
189	Mike Moore	.05
190	Dennis Eckersley	.35
191	Eric Plunk	.05
192	Storm Davis	.05
193	Terry Steinbach	.05
194	Ron Hassey	.05
195	Stan Royer	.05
196	Walt Weiss	.05
197	Mark McGwire	.65
198	Carney Lansford	.05
199	Glenn Hubbard	.05
200	Dave Henderson	.05
201	Jose Canseco	.30
202	Dave Parker	.05
203	Scott Bankhead	.05
204	Tom Niedenfuer	.05
205	Mark Langston	.05
206	Erik Hanson **RC**	.05
207	Mike Jackson	.05
208	Dave Valle	.05
209	Scott Bradley	.05
210	Harold Reynolds	.05
211	Tino Martinez	.05
212	Rich Renteria	.05
213	Rey Quinones	.05
214	Jim Presley	.05
215	Alvin Davis	.05
216	Edgar Martinez	.05
217	Darnell Coles	.05
218	Jeffrey Leonard	.05
219	Jay Buhner	.05
220	Ken Griffey Jr. **RC**	6.00
221	Drew Hall	.05
222	Bobby Witt	.05
223	Jamie Moyer	.05
224	Charlie Hough	.05
225	Nolan Ryan	.75
226	Jeff Russell	.05
227	Jim Sundberg	.05
228	Julio Franco	.05
229	Buddy Bell	.05
230	Scott Fletcher	.05
231	Jeff Kunkel	.05
232	Steve Buechele	.05
233	Monty Fariss	.05
234	Rick Leach	.05
235	Ruben Sierra	.05
236	Cecil Espy	.05
237	Rafael Palmeiro	.35
238	Pete Incaviglia	.05
239	Dave Steib	.05
240	Jeff Musselman	.05
241	Mike Flanagan	.05
242	Todd Stottlemyre	.05
243	Jimmy Key	.05
244	Tony Castillo	.05
245	Alex Sanchez	.05
246	Tom Henke	.05
247	John Cerutti	.05
248	Ernie Whitt	.05
249	Bob Brenly	.05
250	Rance Mulliniks	.05
251	Kelly Gruber	.05
252	Ed Sprague	.05
253	Fred McGriff	.05
254	Tony Fernandez	.05
255	Tom Lawless	.05
256	George Bell	.05
257	Jesse Barfield	.05
258	Sandy Alomar, Sr.	.05
259	Ken Griffey (With Ken Griffey Jr.)	.30
260	Cal Ripken, Sr.	.05
261	Mel Stottlemyre, Sr.	.05
262	Zane Smith	.05
263	Charlie Puleo	.05
264	Derek Lilliquist	.05
265	Paul Assenmacher	.05
266	John Smoltz	.05
267	Tom Glavine	.25
268	Steve Avery **RC**	.05
269	Pete Smith **RC**	.05
270	Jody Davis	.05
271	Bruce Benedict	.05
272	Andres Thomas	.05
273	Gerald Perry	.05
274	Ron Gant	.05
275	Darrell Evans	.05
276	Dale Murphy	.25
277	Dion James	.05
278	Lonnie Smith	.05
279	Geronimo Berroa	.05
280	Steve Wilson	.05
281	Rick Suctcliffe	.05
282	Kevin Coffman	.05
283	Mitch Williams	.05
284	Greg Maddux	.50
285	Paul Kilgus	.05
286	Mike Harkey	.05
287	Lloyd McClendon	.05
288	Damon Berryhill	.05
289	Ty Griffin	.05
290	Ryne Sandberg	.50
291	Mark Grace	.05
292	Curt Wilkerson	.05
293	Vance Law	.05
294	Shawon Dunston	.05
295	Jerome Walton	.05
296	Mitch Webster	.05
297	Dwight Smith	.05
298	Andre Dawson	.25
299	Jeff Sellers	.05
300	Jose Rijo	.05
301	John Franco	.05
302	Rick Mahler	.05
303	Ron Robinson	.05
304	Danny Jackson	.05
305	Rob Dibble	.05
306	Tom Browning	.05
307	Bo Diaz	.05
308	Manny Trillo	.05
309	Chris Sabo **RC**	.05
310	Ron Oester	.05
311	Barry Larkin	.05
312	Todd Benzinger	.05
313	Paul O'Neill	.05
314	Kal Daniels	.05
315	Joel Youngblood	.05
316	Eric Davis	.05
317	Dave Smith	.05
318	Mark Portugal	.05
319	Brian Meyer	.05
320	Jim Deshaies	.05
321	Juan Agosto	.05
322	Mike Scott	.05
323	Rick Rhoden	.05
324	Jim Clancy	.05
325	Larry Andersen	.05
326	Alex Trevino	.05
327	Alan Ashby	.05
328	Craig Reynolds	.05
329	Bill Doran	.05
330	Rafael Ramirez	.05
331	Glenn Davis	.05
332	Willie Ansley **RC**	.05
333	Gerald Young	.05
334	Cameron Drew	.05
335	Jay Howell	.05
336	Tim Belcher	.05
337	Fernando Valenzuela	.05
338	Ricky Horton	.05
339	Tim Leary	.05
340	Bill Bene	.05
341	Orel Hershiser	.05
342	Mike Scioscia	.05
343	Rick Dempsey	.05
344	Willie Randolph	.05
345	Alfredo Griffin	.05
346	Eddie Murray	.40
347	Mickey Hatcher	.05
348	Mike Sharperson	.05
349	John Shelby	.05
350	Mike Marshall	.05
351	Kirk Gibson	.05
352	Mike Davis	.05
353	Bryn Smith	.05
354	Pascual Perez	.05
355	Kevin Gross	.05
356	Andy McGaffigan	.05
357	Brian Holman	.05
358	Dave Wainhouse	.05
359	Denny Martinez	.05
360	Tim Burke	.05
361	Nelson Santovenia	.05
362	Tim Wallach	.05
363	Spike Owen	.05
364	Rex Hudler	.05
365	Andres Galarraga	.05
366	Otis Nixon	.05
367	Hubie Brooks	.05
368	Mike Aldrete	.05
369	Rock Raines	.05
370	Dave Martinez	.05
371	Bob Ojeda	.05
372	Ron Darling	.05
373	Wally Whitehurst	.05
374	Randy Myers	.05
375	David Cone	.05
376	Dwight Gooden	.05
377	Sid Fernandez	.05
378	Dave Proctor	.05
379	Gary Carter	.40
380	Keith Miller	.05
381	Gregg Jefferies	.05
382	Tim Teufel	.05
383	Kevin Elster	.05
384	Dave Magadan	.05
385	Keith Hernandez	.05
386	Mookie Wilson	.05
387	Darryl Strawberry	.05
388	Kevin McReynolds	.05
389	Mark Carreon	.05
390	Jeff Parrett	.05
391	Mike Maddux	.05

No.	Player	Value
392	Don Carman	.05
393	Bruce Ruffin	.05
394	Ken Howell	.05
395	Steve Bedrosian	.05
396	Floyd Youmans	.05
397	Larry McWilliams	.05
398	Pat Combs	.05
399	Steve Lake	.05
400	Dickie Thon	.05
401	Ricky Jordan	.05
402	Mike Schmidt	.60
403	Tom Herr	.05
404	Chris James	.05
405	Juan Samuel	.05
406	Von Hayes	.05
407	Ron Jones	.05
408	Curt Ford	.05
409	Bob Walk	.05
410	Jeff Robinson	.05
411	Jim Gott	.05
412	Scott Medvin	.05
413	John Smiley	.05
414	Bob Kipper	.05
415	Brian Fisher	.05
416	Doug Drabek	.05
417	Mike Lavalliere	.05
418	Ken Oberkfell	.05
419	Sid Bream	.05
420	Austin Manahan	.05
421	Jose Lind	.05
422	Bobby Bonilla	.05
423	Glenn Wilson	.05
424	Andy Van Slyke	.05
425	Gary Redus	.05
426	Barry Bonds	.75
427	Don Heinkel	.05
428	Ken Dayley	.05
429	Todd Worrell	.05
430	Brad DuVall	.05
431	Jose DeLeon	.05
432	Joe Magrane	.05
433	John Ericks	.05
434	Frank DiPino	.05
435	Tony Pena	.05
436	Ozzie Smith	.50
437	Terry Pendleton	.05
438	Jose Oquendo	.05
439	Tim Jones	.05
440	Pedro Guerrero	.05
441	Milt Thompson	.05
442	Willie McGee	.05
443	Vince Coleman	.05
444	Tom Brunansky	.05
445	Walt Terrell	.05
446	Eric Show	.05
447	Mark Davis	.05
448	Andy Benes **RC**	.10
449	Eddie Whitson	.05
450	Dennis Rasmussen	.05
451	Bruce Hurst	.05
452	Pat Clements	.05
453	Benito Santiago	.05
454	Sandy Alomar, Jr.	.05
455	Garry Templeton	.05
456	Jack Clark	.05
457	Tim Flannery	.05
458	Roberto Alomar	.25
459	Camelo Martinez	.05
460	John Kruk	.05
461	Tony Gwynn	.50
462	Jerald Clark	.05
463	Don Robinson	.05
464	Craig Lefferts	.05
465	Kelly Downs	.05
466	Rick Rueschel	.05
467	Scott Garrelts	.05
468	Wil Tejada	.05
469	Kirt Manwaring	.05
470	Terry Kennedy	.05
471	Jose Uribe	.05
472	Royce Clayton **RC**	.10
473	Robby Thompson	.05
474	Kevin Mitchell	.05
475	Ernie Riles	.05
476	Will Clark	.05
477	Donnell Nixon	.05
478	Candy Maldonado	.05
479	Tracy Jones	.05
480	Brett Butler	.05
481	Checklist 1-121	.05
482	Checklist 122-242	.05
483	Checklist 243-363	.05
484	Checklist 364-484	.05

Tiffany

A special collectors' version of the revitalized Bowman cards was produced in 1989, differing from the regular-issue cards in the application of a high-gloss finish to the front and the use of a white cardboard stock. The "Tiffany" version (as the glossies are known to collectors), was sold only in complete boxed sets, with an estimated production of 6,000 sets.

	NM/M
Unopened Set (495):	165.00
Complete Set (495):	100.00
Common Player:	.25

Inserts

Bowman inserted sweepstakes cards in its 1989 packs. Each sweepstakes card reproduces a classic Bowman card on the front, with a prominent "REPRINT" notice. With one card in each pack, they are by no means scarce. A "Tiffany" version of the reprints was produced for inclusion in the factory set of 1989 Bowman cards. The glossy-front inserts are valued at 10X the standard version.

		NM/M
Complete Set (11):		3.50
Common Player:		.10
(1)	Richie Ashburn	.10
(2)	Yogi Berra	.10
(3)	Whitey Ford	.10
(4)	Gil Hodges	.10
(5)	Mickey Mantle/1951	2.00
(6)	Mickey Mantle/1953	1.50
(7)	Willie Mays	.50
(8)	Satchel Paige	.25
(9)	Jackie Robinson	1.00
(10)	Duke Snider	.10
(11)	Ted Williams	1.00

1990 Bowman

Bowman followed its 1989 rebirth with a 528-card set in 1990. The 1990 cards follow the classic Bowman style featuring a full-color photo bordered in white. The Bowman logo appears in the upper-left corner. The player's team nickname and name appear on the bottom border of the card photo. Unlike the 1989 set, the 1990 cards are standard 2-1/2" x 3-1/2". Backs are horizontal and display the player's statistics against the teams in his league.

	NM/M
Unopened Factory Set (528):	20.00
Complete Set (528):	15.00
Common Player:	.05
Wax Pack (15):	.75
Wax Box (36):	15.00
Jumbo Pack (31):	1.00
Jumbo Box (24):	15.00
Rack Pack (39):	1.50
Rack Box (24):	20.00

No.	Player	Value
1	Tommy Greene **RC**	.05
2	Tom Glavine	.30
3	Andy Nezelek	.05
4	Mike Stanton	.05
5	Rick Lueken	.05
6	Kent Mercker	.05
7	Derek Lilliquist	.05
8	Charlie Liebrandt	.05
9	Steve Avery	.05
10	John Smoltz	.05
11	Mark Lemke	.05
12	Lonnie Smith	.05
13	Oddibe McDowell	.05
14	Tyler Houston **RC**	.05
15	Jeff Blauser	.05
16	Ernie Whitt	.05
17	Alexis Infante	.05
18	Jim Presley	.05
19	Dale Murphy	.25
20	Nick Esasky	.05
21	Rick Sutcliffe	.05
22	Mike Bielecki	.05
23	Steve Wilson	.05
24	Kevin Blankenship	.05
25	Mitch Williams	.05
26	Dean Wilkins	.05
27	Greg Maddux	.50
28	Mike Harkey	.05
29	Mark Grace	.05
30	Ryne Sandberg	.50
31	Greg Smith	.05
32	Dwight Smith	.05
33	Damon Berryhill	.05
34	Earl Cunningham	.05
35	Jerome Walton	.05
36	Lloyd McClendon	.05
37	Ty Griffin	.05
38	Shawon Dunston	.05
39	Andre Dawson	.25
40	Luis Salazar	.05
41	Tim Layana	.05
42	Rob Dibble	.05
43	Tom Browning	.05
44	Danny Jackson	.05
45	Jose Rijo	.05
46	Scott Scudder	.05
47	Randy Myers	.05
48	Brian Lane	.05
49	Paul O'Neill	.05
50	Barry Larkin	.05
51	Reggie Jefferson	.05
52	Jeff Branson	.05
53	Chris Sabo	.05
54	Joe Oliver	.05
55	Todd Benzinger	.05
56	Rolando Roomes	.05
57	Hal Morris	.05
58	Eric Davis	.05
59	Scott Bryant	.05
60	Ken Griffey	.05
61	Darryl Kile **RC**	.05
62	Dave Smith	.05
63	Mark Portugal	.05
64	Jeff Juden **RC**	.05
65	Bill Gullickson	.05
66	Danny Darwin	.05
67	Larry Andersen	.05
68	Jose Cano	.05
69	Dan Schatzeder	.05
70	Jim Deshaies	.05
71	Mike Scott	.05
72	Gerald Young	.05
73	Ken Caminiti	.05
74	Ken Oberkfell	.05
75	Dave Rhode	.05
76	Bill Doran	.05
77	Andujar Cedeno	.05
78	Craig Biggio	.05
79	Karl Rhodes	.05
80	Glenn Davis	.05
81	Eric Anthony **RC**	.05
82	John Wetteland	.05
83	Jay Howell	.05
84	Orel Hershiser	.05
85	Tim Belcher	.05
86	Kiki Jones	.05
87	Mike Hartley	.05
88	Ramon Martinez	.05
89	Mike Scioscia	.05
90	Willie Randolph	.05
91	Juan Samuel	.05
92	Jose Offerman **RC**	.05
93	Dave Hansen	.05
94	Jeff Hamilton	.05
95	Alfredo Griffin	.05
96	Tom Goodwin	.05
97	Kirk Gibson	.05
98	Jose Vizcaino	.05
99	Kal Daniels	.05
100	Hubie Brooks	.05
101	Eddie Murray	.40
102	Dennis Boyd	.05
103	Tim Burke	.05
104	Bill Sampen	.05
105	Brett Gideon	.05
106	Mark Gardner	.05
107	Howard Farmer	.05
108	Mel Rojas	.05
109	Kevin Gross	.05
110	Dave Schmidt	.05
111	Denny Martinez	.05
112	Jerry Goff	.05
113	Andres Galarraga	.05
114	Tim Welch	.05
115	Marquis Grissom **RC**	.25
116	Spike Owen	.05
117	Larry Walker **RC**	1.00
118	Rock Raines	.05
119	Delino DeShields **RC**	.10
120	Tom Foley	.05
121	Dave Martinez	.05
122	Frank Viola	.05
123	Julio Valera	.05
124	Alejandro Pena	.05
125	David Cone	.05
126	Dwight Gooden	.05
127	Kevin Brown	.05
128	John Franco	.05
129	Terry Bross	.05
130	Blaine Beatty	.05
131	Sid Fernandez	.05
132	Mike Marshall	.05
133	Howard Johnson	.05
134	Jaime Roseboro	.05
135	Alan Zinter	.05
136	Keith Miller	.05
137	Kevin Elster	.05
138	Kevin McReynolds	.05
139	Barry Lyons	.05
140	Gregg Jefferies	.05
141	Darryl Strawberry	.05
142	Todd Hundley **RC**	.10
143	Scott Service	.05
144	Chuck Malone	.05
145	Steve Ontiveros	.05
146	Roger McDowell	.05
147	Ken Howell	.05
148	Pat Combs	.05
149	Jeff Parrett	.05
150	Chuck McElroy	.05
151	Jason Grimsley	.05
152	Len Dykstra	.05
153	Mickey Morandini	.05
154	John Kruk	.05
155	Dickie Thon	.05
156	Ricky Jordan	.05
157	Jeff Jackson	.05
158	Darren Daulton	.05
159	Tom Herr	.05
160	Von Hayes	.05
161	Dave Hollins **RC**	.05
162	Carmelo Martinez	.05
163	Bob Walk	.05
164	Doug Drabek	.05
165	Walt Terrell	.05
166	Bill Landrum	.05
167	Scott Ruskin	.05
168	Bob Patterson	.05
169	Bobby Bonilla	.05
170	Jose Lind	.05
171	Andy Van Slyke	.05
172	Mike LaValliere	.05
173	Willie Greene **RC**	.05
174	Jay Bell	.05
175	Sid Bream	.05
176	Tom Prince	.05
177	Wally Backman	.05
178	Moises Alou **RC**	.25
179	Steve Carter	.05
180	Gary Redus	.05
181	Barry Bonds	1.00
182	Don Slaught	.05
183	Joe Magrane	.05
184	Bryn Smith	.05
185	Todd Worrell	.05
186	Jose Deleon	.05
187	Frank DiPino	.05
188	John Tudor	.05
189	Howard Hilton	.05
190	John Ericks	.05
191	Ken Dayley	.05
192	Ray Lankford **RC**	.10
193	Todd Zeile	.05
194	Willie McGee	.05
195	Ozzie Smith	.50
196	Milt Thompson	.05
197	Terry Pendleton	.05
198	Vince Coleman	.05
199	Paul Coleman	.05
200	Jose Oquendo	.05
201	Pedro Guerrero	.05
202	Tom Brunansky	.05
203	Roger Smithberg	.05
204	Eddie Whitson	.05
205	Dennis Rasmussen	.05
206	Craig Lefferts	.05
207	Andy Benes	.05
208	Bruce Hurst	.05
209	Eric Show	.05
210	Rafael Valdez	.05
211	Joey Cora	.05
212	Thomas Howard	.05
213	Rob Nelson	.05
214	Jack Clark	.05
215	Garry Templeton	.05
216	Fred Lynn	.05
217	Tony Gwynn	.50
218	Benny Santiago	.05
219	Mike Pagliarulo	.05
220	Joe Carter	.05
221	Roberto Alomar	.25
222	Bip Roberts	.05
223	Rick Reuschel	.05
224	Russ Swan	.05
225	Eric Gunderson	.05
226	Steve Bedrosian	.05
227	Mike Remlinger	.05
228	Scott Garrelts	.05
229	Ernie Camacho	.05
230	Andres Santana	.05
231	Will Clark	.05
232	Kevin Mitchell	.05
233	Robby Thompson	.05
234	Bill Bathe	.05
235	Tony Perezchica	.05
236	Gary Carter	.40
237	Brett Butler	.05
238	Matt Williams	.05
239	Ernie Riles	.05
240	Kevin Bass	.05
241	Terry Kennedy	.05
242	Steve Hosey **RC**	.05
243	Ben McDonald **RC**	.15
244	Jeff Ballard	.05
245	Joe Price	.05
246	Curt Schilling	.30
247	Pete Harnisch	.05
248	Mark Williamson	.05
249	Gregg Olson	.05
250	Chris Myers	.05
251a	David Segui (No bio. data on back.)	3.50
251b	David Segui (Bio. data on back.)	.05
252	Joe Orsulak	.05
253	Craig Worthington	.05
254	Mickey Tettleton	.05
255	Cal Ripken, Jr.	1.00
256	Billy Ripken	.05
257	Randy Milligan	.05
258	Brady Anderson	.05
259	Chris Hoiles **RC**	.05
260	Mike Devereaux	.05
261	Phil Bradley	.05
262	Leo Gomez **RC**	.05
263	Lee Smith	.05
264	Mike Rochford	.05
265	Jeff Reardon	.05
266	Wes Gardner	.05
267	Mike Boddicker	.05
268	Roger Clemens	.60
269	Rob Murphy	.05
270	Mickey Pina	.05
271	Tony Pena	.05
272	Jody Reed	.05
273	Kevin Romine	.05
274	Mike Greenwell	.05
275	Mo Vaughn **RC**	.60
276	Danny Heep	.05
277	Scott Cooper	.05
278	Greg Blosser **RC**	.05
279	Dwight Evans	.05
280	Ellis Burks	.05
281	Wade Boggs	.50
282	Marty Barrett	.05
283	Kirk McCaskill	.05
284	Mark Langston	.05
285	Bert Blyleven	.05
286	Mike Fetters	.05
287	Kyle Abbott	.05
288	Jim Abbott	.05
289	Chuck Finley	.05
290	Gary DiSarcina	.05
291	Dick Schofield	.05
292	Devon White	.05
293	Bobby Rose	.05
294	Brian Downing	.05
295	Lance Parrish	.05
296	Jack Howell	.05
297	Claudell Washington	.05
298	John Orton	.05
299	Wally Joyner	.05
300	Lee Stevens	.05
301	Chili Davis	.05
302	Johnny Ray	.05
303	Greg Hibbard	.05
304	Eric King	.05
305	Jack McDowell	.05
306	Bobby Thigpen	.05
307	Adam Peterson	.05
308	Scott Radinsky **RC**	.05
309	Wayne Edwards	.05
310	Melido Perez	.05
311	Robin Ventura	.05
312	Sammy Sosa **RC**	2.00
313	Dan Pasqua	.05
314	Carlton Fisk	.40
315	Ozzie Guillen	.05
316	Ivan Calderon	.05
317	Daryl Boston	.05
318	Craig Grebeck	.05
319	Scott Fletcher	.05
320	Frank Thomas **RC**	3.00
321	Steve Lyons	.05
322	Carlos Martinez	.05
323	Joe Skalski	.05
324	Tom Candiotti	.05
325	Greg Swindell	.05
326	Steve Olin	.05
327	Kevin Wickander	.05
328	Doug Jones	.05
329	Jeff Shaw	.05
330	Kevin Bearse	.05
331	Dion James	.05
332	Jerry Browne	.05
333	Albert Belle	.05
334	Felix Fermin	.05
335	Candy Maldonado	.05
336	Cory Snyder	.05
337	Sandy Alomar	.05
338	Mark Lewis	.05
339	Carlos Baerga **RC**	.10
340	Chris James	.05
341	Brook Jacoby	.05
342	Keith Hernandez	.05
343	Frank Tanana	.05
344	Scott Aldred	.05
345	Mike Henneman	.05
346	Steve Wapnick	.05
347	Greg Gohr	.05
348	Eric Stone	.05
349	Brian DuBois	.05
350	Kevin Ritz	.05
351	Rico Brogna	.05
352	Mike Heath	.05
353	Alan Trammell	.05
354	Chet Lemon	.05
355	Dave Bergman	.05
356	Lou Whitaker	.05
357	Cecil Fielder	.05
358	Milt Cuyler	.05
359	Tony Phillips	.05
360	Travis Fryman **RC**	.10
361	Ed Romero	.05
362	Lloyd Moseby	.05
363	Mark Gubicza	.05
364	Bret Saberhagen	.05
365	Tom Gordon	.05
366	Steve Farr	.05
367	Kevin Appier	.05
368	Storm Davis	.05
369	Mark Davis	.05
370	Jeff Montgomery	.05
371	Frank White	.05
372	Brent Mayne	.05
373	Bob Boone	.05
374	Jim Eisenreich	.05
375	Danny Tartabull	.05
376	Kurt Stillwell	.05
377	Bill Pecota	.05
378	Bo Jackson	.10
379	Bob Hamelin **RC**	.05
380	Kevin Seitzer	.05
381	Rey Palacios	.05
382	George Brett	.60
383	Gerald Perry	.05
384	Teddy Higuera	.05
385	Tom Filer	.05
386	Dan Plesac	.05
387	Cal Eldred **RC**	.05
388	Jaime Navarro	.05
389	Chris Bosio	.05
390	Randy Veres	.05
391	Gary Sheffield	.25
392	George Canale	.05
393	B.J. Surhoff	.05
394	Tim McIntosh	.05
395	Greg Brock	.05
396	Greg Vaughn	.05
397	Darryl Hamilton	.05
398	Dave Parker	.05
399	Paul Molitor	.40
400	Jim Gantner	.05
401	Rob Deer	.05
402	Billy Spiers	.05
403	Glenn Braggs	.05
404	Robin Yount	.40
405	Rick Aguilera	.05
406	Johnny Ard	.05
407	Kevin Tapani **RC**	.10
408	Park Pittman	.05
409	Allan Anderson	.05
410	Juan Berenguer	.05
411	Willie Banks	.05
412	Rich Yett	.05
413	Dave West	.05
414	Greg Gagne	.05
415	Chuck Knoblauch **RC**	.50
416	Randy Bush	.05
417	Gary Gaetti	.05
418	Kent Hrbek	.05
419	Al Newman	.05
420	Danny Gladden	.05
421	Paul Sorrento	.05
422	Derek Parks	.05
423	Scott Leius	.05
424	Kirby Puckett	.50
425	Willie Smith	.05
426	Dave Righetti	.05
427	Jeff Robinson	.05
428	Alan Mills	.05
429	Tim Leary	.05
430	Pascual Perez	.05
431	Alvaro Espinoza	.05
432	Dave Winfield	.40
433	Jesse Barfield	.05
434	Randy Velarde	.05
435	Rick Cerone	.05
436	Steve Balboni	.05
437	Mel Hall	.05
438	Bob Geren	.05
439	Bernie Williams **RC**	1.00
440	Kevin Maas **RC**	.05
441	Mike Blowers	.05
442	Steve Sax	.05
443	Don Mattingly	.60
444	Roberto Kelly	.05
445	Mike Moore	.05
446	Reggie Harris	.05
447	Scott Sanderson	.05
448	Dave Otto	.05
449	Dave Stewart	.05
450	Rick Honeycutt	.05
451	Dennis Eckersley	.35
452	Carney Lansford	.05
453	Scott Hemond	.05
454	Mark McGwire	.75
455	Felix Jose	.05
456	Terry Steinbach	.05
457	Rickey Henderson	.40
458	Dave Henderson	.05
459	Mike Gallego	.05
460	Jose Canseco	.30
461	Walt Weiss	.05
462	Ken Phelps	.05
463	Darren Lewis **RC**	.05
464	Ron Hassey	.05
465	Roger Salkeld **RC**	.05
466	Scott Bankhead	.05
467	Keith Comstock	.05
468	Randy Johnson	.40
469	Erik Hanson	.05
470	Mike Schooler	.05
471	Gary Eave	.05
472	Jeffrey Leonard	.05
473	Dave Valle	.05
474	Omar Vizquel	.05
475	Pete O'Brien	.05
476	Henry Cotto	.05
477	Jay Buhner	.05
478	Harold Reynolds	.05
479	Alvin Davis	.05
480	Darnell Coles	.05
481	Ken Griffey Jr.	.65
482	Greg Briley	.05

483	Scott Bradley	.05
484	Tino Martinez	.05
485	Jeff Russell	.05
486	Nolan Ryan	1.00
487	Robb Nen	.05
488	Kevin Brown	.05
489	Brian Bohanon	.05
490	Ruben Sierra	.05
491	Pete Incaviglia	.05
492	Juan Gonzalez **RC**	1.00
493	Steve Buechele	.05
494	Scott Coolbaugh	.05
495	Geno Petralli	.05
496	Rafael Palmeiro	.35
497	Julio Franco	.05
498	Gary Pettis	.05
499	Donald Harris	.05
500	Monty Fariss	.05
501	Harold Baines	.05
502	Cecil Espy	.05
503	Jack Daugherty	.05
504	Willie Blair	.05
505	Dave Steib	.05
506	Tom Henke	.05
507	John Cerutti	.05
508	Paul Kilgus	.05
509	Jimmy Key	.05
510	John Olerud **RC**	.75
511	Ed Sprague	.05
512	Manny Lee	.05
513	Fred McGriff	.05
514	Glenallen Hill	.05
515	George Bell	.05
516	Mookie Wilson	.05
517	Luis Sojo	.05
518	Nelson Liriano	.05
519	Kelly Gruber	.05
520	Greg Myers	.05
521	Pat Borders	.05
522	Junior Felix	.05
523	Eddie Zosky	.05
524	Tony Fernandez	.05
525	Checklist	.05
526	Checklist	.05
527	Checklist	.05
528	Checklist	.05

Tiffany

Reported production of fewer than 10,000 sets has created a significant premium for these glossy "Tiffany" versions of Bowman's 1990 baseball card set. The use of white cardboard stock and high-gloss front finish distinguishes these cards from regular-issue Bowmans.

	NM/M
Unopened Set (539):	200.00
Complete Set (539):	60.00
Common Player:	.25

Inserts

Bowman inserted sweepstakes cards in its 1990 packs, much like in 1989. This 11-card set features current players displayed in drawings by Craig Pursley.

		NM/M
Complete Set (11):		1.00
Common Player:		.05
(1)	Will Clark	.05
(2)	Mark Davis	.05
(3)	Dwight Gooden	.05
(4)	Bo Jackson	.10
(5)	Don Mattingly	.40
(6)	Kevin Mitchell	.05
(7)	Gregg Olson	.05
(8)	Nolan Ryan	.50
(9)	Bret Saberhagen	.05
(10)	Jerome Walton	.05
(11)	Robin Yount	.25

Lithographs

The paintings which were the basis for the sweepstakes insert cards in 1990 Bowman were also used in the creation of a set of 11" x 14" lithographs. The lithographs were

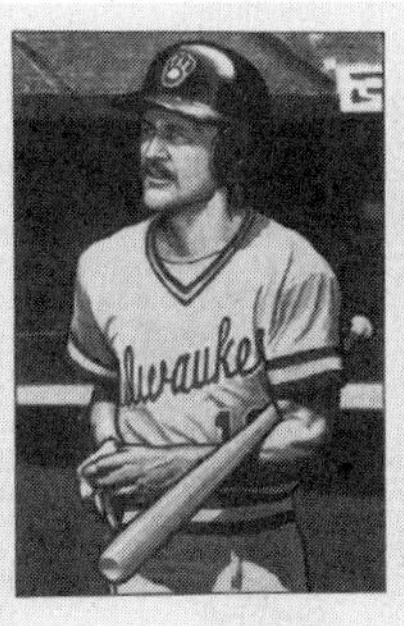

offered as a prize in the sweepstakes or could be purchased from hobby dealers for a retail price in the $400-450 range.

		NM/M
Complete Set (11):		250.00
Common Player:		10.00
(1)	Will Clark	10.00
(2)	Mark Davis	10.00
(3)	Dwight Gooden	10.00
(4)	Bo Jackson	20.00
(5)	Don Mattingly	50.00
(6)	Kevin Mitchell	10.00
(7)	Gregg Olson	10.00
(8)	Nolan Ryan	100.00
(9)	Bret Saberhagen	10.00
(10)	Jerome Walton	10.00
(11)	Robin Yount	25.00

1991 Bowman

The 1991 Bowman set features 704 cards compared to 528 cards in the 1990 issue. The cards imitate the 1953 Bowman style. Special Rod Carew cards and gold foil-stamped cards are included. The set is numbered by teams. Like the 1989 and 1990 issues, the card backs feature a breakdown of performance against each other's team in the league.

		NM/M
Unopened Factory Set (704):		30.00
Complete Set (704):		20.00
Common Player:		.05
Wax Pack (14):		.75
Wax Box (36):		17.50
Cello Pack (29):		1.50
Cello Box (24):		25.00
1	Rod Carew-I	.10
2	Rod Carew-II	.10
3	Rod Carew-III	.10
4	Rod Carew-IV	.10
5	Rod Carew-V	.10
6	Willie Fraser	.05
7	John Olerud	.05
8	William Suero	.05
9	Roberto Alomar	.20
10	Todd Stottlemyre	.05
11	Joe Carter	.05
12	Steve Karsay **RC**	.10
13	Mark Whiten	.05
14	Pat Borders	.05
15	Mike Timlin	.05
16	Tom Henke	.05
17	Eddie Zosky	.05
18	Kelly Gruber	.05
19	Jimmy Key	.05
20	Jerry Schunk	.05
21	Manny Lee	.05
22	Dave Steib	.05
23	Pat Hentgen	.05
24	Glenallen Hill	.05
25	Rene Gonzales	.05
26	Ed Sprague	.05
27	Ken Dayley	.05
28	Pat Tabler	.05
29	Denis Boucher **RC**	.05
30	Devon White	.05
31	Dante Bichette	.05
32	Paul Molitor	.40
33	Greg Vaughn	.05
34	Dan Plesac	.05
35	Chris George	.05
36	Tim McIntosh	.05
37	Franklin Stubbs	.05
38	Bo Dodson	.05
39	Ron Robinson	.05
40	Ed Nunez	.05
41	Greg Brock	.05
42	Jaime Navarro	.05
43	Chris Bosio	.05
44	B.J. Surhoff	.05
45	Chris Johnson	.05
46	Willie Randolph	.05
47	Narciso Elvira	.05
48	Jim Gantner	.05
49	Kevin Brown	.05
50	Julio Machado	.05
51	Chuck Crim	.05
52	Gary Sheffield	.30
53	Angel Miranda	.05
54	Teddy Higuera	.05
55	Robin Yount	.40
56	Cal Eldred	.05
57	Sandy Alomar	.05
58	Greg Swindell	.05
59	Brook Jacoby	.05
60	Efrain Valdez	.05
61	Ever Magallanes	.05
62	Tom Candiotti	.05
63	Eric King	.05
64	Alex Cole	.05
65	Charles Nagy	.05
66	Mitch Webster	.05
67	Chris James	.05
68	Jim Thome **RC**	3.00
69	Carlos Baerga	.05
70	Mark Lewis	.05
71	Jerry Browne	.05
72	Jesse Orosco	.05
73	Mike Huff	.05
74	Jose Escobar	.05
75	Jeff Manto	.05
76	Turner Ward **RC**	.05
77	Doug Jones	.05
78	Bruce Egloff **RC**	.05
79	Tim Costo	.05
80	Beau Allred	.05
81	Albert Belle	.05
82	John Farrell	.05
83	Glenn Davis	.05
84	Joe Orsulak	.05
85	Mark Williamson	.05
86	Ben McDonald	.05
87	Billy Ripken	.05
88	Leo Gomez	.05
89	Bob Melvin	.05
90	Jeff Robinson	.05
91	Jose Mesa	.05
92	Gregg Olson	.05
93	Mike Devereaux	.05
94	Luis Mercedes	.05
95	Arthur Rhodes **RC**	.10
96	Juan Bell	.05
97	Mike Mussina **RC**	3.00
98	Jeff Ballard	.05
99	Chris Hoiles	.05
100	Brady Anderson	.05
101	Bob Milacki	.05
102	David Segui	.05
103	Dwight Evans	.05
104	Cal Ripken, Jr.	1.00
105	Mike Linskey	.05
106	Jeff Tackett **RC**	.05
107	Jeff Reardon	.05
108	Dana Kiecker	.05
109	Ellis Burks	.05
110	Dave Owen	.05
111	Danny Darwin	.05
112	Mo Vaughn	.05
113	Jeff McNeely	.05
114	Tom Bolton	.05
115	Greg Blosser	.05
116	Mike Greenwell	.05
117	Phil Plantier **RC**	.05
118	Roger Clemens	.60
119	John Marzano	.05
120	Jody Reed	.05
121	Scott Taylor	.05
122	Jack Clark	.05
123	Derek Livernois	.05
124	Tony Pena	.05
125	Tom Brunansky	.05
126	Carlos Quintana	.05
127	Tim Naehring	.05
128	Matt Young	.05
129	Wade Boggs	.50
130	Kevin Morton	.05
131	Pete Incaviglia	.05
132	Rob Deer	.05
133	Bill Gullickson	.05
134	Rico Brogna	.05
135	Lloyd Moseby	.05
136	Cecil Fielder	.05
137	Tony Phillips	.05
138	Mark Leiter	.05
139	John Cerutti	.05
140	Mickey Tettleton	.05
141	Milt Cuyler	.05
142	Greg Gohr	.05
143	Tony Bernazard	.05
144	Dan Gakeler	.05
145	Travis Fryman	.05
146	Dan Petry	.05
147	Scott Aldred	.05
148	John DeSilva	.05
149	Rusty Meacham	.05
150	Lou Whitaker	.05
151	Dave Haas	.05
152	Luis de los Santos	.05
153	Ivan Cruz	.05
154	Alan Trammell	.05
155	Pat Kelly	.05
156	Carl Everett **RC**	.25
157	Greg Cadaret	.05
158	Kevin Maas	.05
159	Jeff Johnson	.05
160	Willie Smith	.05
161	Gerald Williams	.05
162	Mike Humphreys	.05
163	Alvaro Espinoza	.05
164	Matt Nokes	.05
165	Wade Taylor	.05
166	Roberto Kelly	.05
167	John Habyan	.05
168	Steve Farr	.05
169	Jesse Barfield	.05
170	Steve Sax	.05
171	Jim Leyritz	.05
172	Robert Eenhoorn	.05
173	Bernie Williams	.05
174	Scott Lusader	.05
175	Torey Lovullo	.05
176	Chuck Cary	.05
177	Scott Sanderson	.05
178	Don Mattingly	.60
179	Mel Hall	.05
180	Juan Gonzalez	.30
181	Hensley Meulens	.05
182	Jose Offerman	.05
183	Jeff Bagwell **RC**	2.50
184	Jeff Conine **RC**	.25
185	Henry Rodriguez **RC**	.05
186	Jimmie Reese	.05
187	Kyle Abbott	.05
188	Lance Parrish	.05
189	Rafael Montalvo	.05
190	Floyd Bannister	.05
191	Dick Schofield	.05
192	Scott Lewis	.05
193	Jeff Robinson	.05
194	Kent Anderson	.05
195	Wally Joyner	.05
196	Chuck Finley	.05
197	Luis Sojo	.05
198	Jeff Richardson	.05
199	Dave Parker	.05
200	Jim Abbott	.05
201	Junior Felix	.05
202	Mark Langston	.05
203	Tim Salmon **RC**	1.00
204	Cliff Young	.05
205	Scott Bailes	.05
206	Bobby Rose	.05
207	Gary Gaetti	.05
208	Ruben Amaro	.05
209	Luis Polonia	.05
210	Dave Winfield	.40
211	Bryan Harvey	.05
212	Mike Moore	.05
213	Rickey Henderson	.40
214	Steve Chitren	.05
215	Bob Welch	.05
216	Terry Steinbach	.05
217	Ernie Riles	.05
218	Todd Van Poppel **RC**	.10
219	Mike Gallego	.05
220	Curt Young	.05
221	Todd Burns	.05
222	Vance Law	.05
223	Eric Show	.05
224	Don Peters **RC**	.05
225	Dave Stewart	.05
226	Dave Henderson	.05
227	Jose Canseco	.30
228	Walt Weiss	.05
229	Dann Howitt	.05
230	Willie Wilson	.05
231	Harold Baines	.05
232	Scott Hemond	.05
233	Joe Slusarski	.05
234	Mark McGwire	.75
235	Kirk Dressendorfer **RC**	.05
236	Craig Paquette **RC**	.05
237	Dennis Eckersley	.35
238	Dana Allison	.05
239	Scott Bradley	.05
240	Brian Holman	.05
241	Mike Schooler	.05
242	Rich Delucia	.05
243	Edgar Martinez	.05
244	Henry Cotto	.05
245	Omar Vizquel	.05
246a	Ken Griffey Jr.	.65
246b	Ken Griffey Sr. (Should be #255.)	.10
247	Jay Buhner	.05
248	Bill Krueger	.05
249	Dave Fleming **RC**	.05
250	Patrick Lennon **RC**	.05
251	Dave Valle	.05
252	Harold Reynolds	.05
253	Randy Johnson	.40
254	Scott Bankhead	.05
256	Greg Briley	.05
257	Tino Martinez	.05
258	Alvin Davis	.05
259	Pete O'Brien	.05
260	Erik Hanson	.05
261	Bret Boone **RC**	.50
262	Roger Salkeld	.05
263	Dave Burba	.05
264	Kerry Woodson **RC**	.05
265	Julio Franco	.05
266	Dan Peltier	.05
267	Jeff Russell	.05
268	Steve Buechele	.05
269	Donald Harris	.05
270	Robb Nen	.05
271	Rich Gossage	.05
272	Ivan Rodriguez **RC**	3.00
273	Jeff Huson	.05
274	Kevin Brown	.05
275	Dan Smith **RC**	.05
276	Gary Pettis	.05
277	Jack Daugherty	.05
278	Mike Jeffcoat	.05
279	Brad Arnsberg	.05
280	Nolan Ryan	1.00
281	Eric McCray	.05
282	Scott Chiamparino	.05
283	Ruben Sierra	.05
284	Geno Petralli	.05
285	Monty Fariss	.05
286	Rafael Palmeiro	.35
287	Bobby Witt	.05
288	Dean Palmer	.05
289	Tony Scruggs	.05
290	Kenny Rogers	.05
291	Bret Saberhagen	.05
292	Brian McRae **RC**	.05
293	Storm Davis	.05
294	Danny Tartabull	.05
295	David Howard	.05
296	Mike Boddicker	.05
297	Joel Johnston	.05
298	Tim Spehr	.05
299	Hector Wagner	.05
300	George Brett	.60
301	Mike Macfarlane	.05
302	Kirk Gibson	.05
303	Harvey Pulliam	.05
304	Jim Eisenreich	.05
305	Kevin Seitzer	.05
306	Mark Davis	.05
307	Kurt Stillwell	.05
308	Jeff Montgomery	.05
309	Kevin Appier	.05
310	Bob Hamelin	.05
311	Tom Gordon	.05
312	Kerwin Moore **RC**	.05
313	Hugh Walker	.05
314	Terry Shumpert	.05
315	Warren Cromartie	.05
316	Gary Thurman	.05
317	Steve Bedrosian	.05
318	Danny Gladden	.05
319	Jack Morris	.05
320	Kirby Puckett	.50
321	Kent Hrbek	.05
322	Kevin Tapani	.05
323	Denny Neagle	.05
324	Rich Garces	.05
325	Larry Casian	.05
326	Shane Mack	.05
327	Allan Anderson	.05
328	Junior Ortiz	.05
329	Paul Abbott **RC**	.05
330	Chuck Knoblauch	.05
331	Chili Davis	.05
332	Todd Ritchie **RC**	.05
333	Brian Harper	.05
334	Rick Aguilera	.05
335	Scott Erickson	.05
336	Pedro Munoz	.05
337	Scott Leuis	.05
338	Greg Gagne	.05
339	Mike Pagliarulo	.05
340	Terry Leach	.05
341	Willie Banks	.05
342	Bobby Thigpen	.05
343	Roberto Hernandez **RC**	.10
344	Melido Perez	.05
345	Carlton Fisk	.40
346	Norberto Martin **RC**	.05
347	Johnny Ruffin **RC**	.05
348	Jeff Carter **RC**	.05
349	Lance Johnson	.05
350	Sammy Sosa	.50
351	Alex Fernandez	.05
352	Jack McDowell	.05
353	Bob Wickman	.05
354	Wilson Alvarez	.05
355	Charlie Hough	.05
356	Ozzie Guillen	.05
357	Cory Snyder	.05
358	Robin Ventura	.05
359	Scott Fletcher	.05
360	Cesar Bernhardt	.05
361	Dan Pasqua	.05
362	Tim Raines	.05
363	Brian Drahman	.05
364	Wayne Edwards	.05
365	Scott Radinsky	.05
366	Frank Thomas	.40
367	Cecil Fielder	.05
368	Julio Franco	.05
369	Kelly Gruber	.05
370	Alan Trammell	.05
371	Rickey Henderson	.30
372	Jose Canseco	.15
373	Ellis Burks	.05
374	Lance Parrish	.05
375	Dave Parker	.05
376	Eddie Murray	.30
377	Ryne Sandberg	.35
378	Matt Williams	.05
379	Barry Larkin	.05
380	Barry Bonds	.75
381	Bobby Bonilla	.05
382	Darryl Strawberry	.05
383	Benny Santiago	.05
384	Don Robinson	.05
385	Paul Coleman	.05
386	Milt Thompson	.05
387	Lee Smith	.05
388	Ray Lankford	.05
389	Tom Pagnozzi	.05
390	Ken Hill	.05
391	Jamie Moyer	.05
392	Greg Carmona **RC**	.05
393	John Ericks	.05
394	Bob Tewksbury	.05
395	Jose Oquendo	.05
396	Rheal Cormier	.05
397	Mike Milchin **RC**	.05
398	Ozzie Smith	.50
399	Aaron Holbert **RC**	.05
400	Jose DeLeon	.05
401	Felix Jose	.05
402	Juan Agosto	.05
403	Pedro Guerrero	.05
404	Todd Zeile	.05
405	Gerald Perry	.05
407	Bryn Smith	.05
408	Bernard Gilkey	.05
409	Rex Hudler	.05
410a	Ralph Branca, Bobby Thomson	.10
410b	Donovan Osborne	.05
411	Lance Dickson	.05
412	Danny Jackson	.05
413	Jerome Walton	.05
414	Sean Cheetham	.05
415	Joe Girardi	.05
416	Ryne Sandberg	.50
417	Mike Harkey	.05
418	George Bell	.05
419	Rick Wilkins **RC**	.05
420	Earl Cunningham	.05
421	Heathcliff Slocumb	.05
422	Mike Bielecki	.05
423	Jessie Hollins **RC**	.05
424	Shawon Dunston	.05
425	Dave Smith	.05
426	Greg Maddux	.50
427	Jose Vizcaino	.05
428	Luis Salazar	.05
429	Andre Dawson	.25
430	Rick Sutcliffe	.05
431	Paul Assenmacher	.05
432	Erik Pappas	.05
433	Mark Grace	.05
434	Denny Martinez	.05
435	Marquis Grissom	.05
436	Wil Cordero **RC**	.05
437	Tim Wallach	.05
438	Brian Barnes **RC**	.05
439	Barry Jones	.05
440	Ivan Calderon	.05
441	Stan Spencer **RC**	.05
442	Larry Walker	.05
443	Chris Haney **RC**	.05
444	Hector Rivera	.05
445	Delino DeShields	.05
446	Andres Galarraga	.05
447	Gilberto Reyes	.05
448	Willie Greene	.05
449	Greg Colbrunn	.05
450	Rondell White **RC**	.25
451	Steve Frey	.05
452	Shane Andrews **RC**	.10
453	Mike Fitzgerald	.05
454	Spike Owen	.05
455	Dave Martinez	.05
456	Dennis Boyd	.05
457	Eric Bullock	.05
458	Reid Cornelius **RC**	.05
459	Chris Nabholz	.05
460	David Cone	.05
461	Hubie Brooks	.05
462	Sid Fernandez	.05
463	Doug Simons **RC**	.05
464	Howard Johnson	.05
465	Chris Donnels	.05
466	Anthony Young	.05
467	Todd Hundley	.05
468	Rick Cerone	.05
469	Kevin Elster	.05
470	Wally Whitehurst	.05
471	Vince Coleman	.05
472	Dwight Gooden	.05
473	Charlie O'Brien	.05
474	Jeromy Burnitz **RC**	.50
475	John Franco	.05
476	Daryl Boston	.05
477	Frank Viola	.05
478	D.J. Dozier	.05
479	Kevin McReynolds	.05
480	Tom Herr	.05
481	Gregg Jefferies	.05
482	Pete Schourek	.05
483	Ron Darling	.05
484	Dave Magadan	.05
485	Andy Ashby **RC**	.05
486	Dale Murphy	.20
487	Von Hayes	.05
488	Kim Batiste **RC**	.05
489	Tony Longmire **RC**	.05
490	Wally Backman	.05
491	Jeff Jackson	.05
492	Mickey Morandini	.05
493	Darrel Akerfelds	.05
494	Ricky Jordan	.05
495	Randy Ready	.05
496	Darrin Fletcher	.05
497	Chuck Malone	.05
498	Pat Combs	.05
499	Dickie Thon	.05
500	Roger McDowell	.05
501	Len Dykstra	.05
502	Joe Boever	.05

503 John Kruk .05
504 Terry Mulholland .05
505 Wes Chamberlain .05
506 Mike Lieberthal **RC** .75
507 Darren Daulton .05
508 Charlie Hayes .05
509 John Smiley .05
510 Gary Varsho .05
511 Curt Wilkerson .05
512 Orlando Merced **RC** .05
513 Barry Bonds 1.00
514 Mike Lavalliere .05
515 Doug Drabek .05
516 Gary Redus .05
517 William Pennyfeather **RC** .05
518 Randy Tomlin .05
519 Mike Zimmerman **RC** .05
520 Jeff King .05
521 Kurt Miller **RC** .05
522 Jay Bell .05
523 Bill Landrum .05
524 Zane Smith .05
525 Bobby Bonilla .05
526 Bob Walk .05
527 Austin Manahan .05
528 Joe Ausanio **RC** .05
529 Andy Van Slyke .05
530 Jose Lind .05
531 Carlos Garcia **RC** .05
532 Don Slaught .05
533 Colin Powell .25
534 Frank Bolick **RC** .05
535 Gary Scott **RC** .05
536 Nikco Riesgo .05
537 Reggie Sanders **RC** .25
538 Tim Howard **RC** .05
539 Ryan Bowen **RC** .05
540 Eric Anthony .05
541 Jim Deshaies .05
542 Tom Nevers .05
543 Ken Caminiti .05
544 Karl Rhodes .05
545 Xavier Hernandez .05
546 Mike Scott .05
547 Jeff Juden .05
548 Darryl Kile .05
549 Willie Ansley .05
550 Luis Gonzalez **RC** 1.00
551 Mike Simms **RC** .05
552 Mark Portugal .05
553 Jimmy Jones .05
554 Jim Clancy .05
555 Pete Harnisch .05
556 Craig Biggio .05
557 Eric Yelding .05
558 Dave Rohde .05
559 Casey Candaele .05
560 Curt Schilling .25
561 Steve Finley .05
562 Javier Ortiz .05
563 Andujar Cedeno .05
564 Rafael Ramirez .05
565 Kenny Lofton **RC** .50
566 Steve Avery .05
567 Lonnie Smith .05
568 Kent Mercker .05
569 Chipper Jones **RC** 3.00
570 Terry Pendleton .05
571 Otis Nixon .05
572 Juan Berenguer .05
573 Charlie Leibrandt .05
574 Dave Justice .05
575 Keith Mitchell .05
576 Tom Glavine .25
577 Greg Olson .05
578 Rafael Belliard .05
579 Ben Rivera .05
580 John Smoltz .05
581 Tyler Houston .05
582 Mark Wohlers **RC** .05
583 Ron Gant .05
584 Ramon Caraballo .05
585 Sid Bream .05
586 Jeff Treadway .05
587 Javier Lopez **RC** .75
588 Deion Sanders .10
589 Mike Heath .05
590 Ryan Klesko **RC** .20
591 Bob Ojeda .05
592 Alfredo Griffin .05
593 Raul Mondesi **RC** .25
594 Greg Smith .05
595 Orel Hershiser .05
596 Juan Samuel .05
597 Brett Butler .05
598 Gary Carter .40
599 Stan Javier .05
600 Kal Daniels .05
601 Jamie McAndrew **RC** .05
602 Mike Sharperson .05
603 Jay Howell .05
604 Eric Karros **RC** .25
605 Tim Belcher .05
606 Dan Opperman .05
607 Lenny Harris .05
608 Tom Goodwin .05
609 Darryl Strawberry .05
610 Ramon Martinez .05
611 Kevin Gross .05
612 Zakary Shinall .05
613 Mike Scioscia .05
614 Eddie Murray .40
615 Ronnie Walden .05
616 Will Clark .05
617 Adam Hyzdu .05
618 Matt Williams .05
619 Don Robinson .05
620 Jeff Brantley .05
621 Greg Litton .05
622 Steve Decker .05
623 Robby Thompson .05
624 Mark Leonard **RC** .05
625 Kevin Bass .05
626 Scott Garrelts .05
627 Jose Uribe .05
628 Eric Gunderson .05
629 Steve Hosey .05
630 Trevor Wilson .05
631 Terry Kennedy .05
632 Dave Righetti .05
633 Kelly Downs .05
634 Johnny Ard .05
635 Eric Christopherson **RC** .05
636 Kevin Mitchell .05
637 John Burkett .05
638 Kevin Rogers **RC** .05
639 Bud Black .05
640 Willie McGee .05
641 Royce Clayton .05
642 Tony Fernandez .05
643 Ricky Bones .05
644 Thomas Howard .05
645 Dave Staton .05
646 Jim Presley .05
647 Tony Gwynn .50
648 Marty Barrett .05
649 Scott Coolbaugh .05
650 Craig Lefferts .05
651 Eddie Whitson .05
652 Oscar Azocar .05
653 Wes Gardner .05
654 Bip Roberts .05
655 Robbie Beckett **RC** .05
656 Benny Santiago .05
657 Greg W. Harris .05
658 Jerald Clark .05
659 Fred McGriff .05
660 Larry Andersen .05
661 Bruce Hurst .05
662 Steve Martin .05
663 Rafael Valdez .05
664 Paul Faries **RC** .05
665 Andy Benes .05
666 Randy Myers .05
667 Rob Dibble .05
668 Glenn Sutko .05
669 Glenn Braggs .05
670 Billy Hatcher .05
671 Joe Oliver .05
672 Freddie Benavides .05
673 Barry Larkin .05
674 Chris Sabo .05
675 Mariano Duncan .05
676 Chris Jones **RC** .05
677 Gino Minutelli **RC** .05
678 Reggie Jefferson .05
679 Jack Armstrong .05
680 Chris Hammond .05
681 Jose Rijo .05
682 Bill Doran .05
683 Terry Lee .05
684 Tom Browning .05
685 Paul O'Neill .05
686 Eric Davis .05
687 Dan Wilson **RC** .05
688 Ted Power .05
689 Tim Layana .05
690 Norm Charlton .05
691 Hal Morris .05
692 Rickey Henderson .35
693 Sam Militello **RC** .05
694 Matt Mieske **RC** .05
695 Paul Russo **RC** .05
696 Domingo Mota **RC** .05
697 Todd Guggiana **RC** .05
698 Marc Newfield .05
699 Checklist .05
700 Checklist .05
701 Checklist .05
702 Checklist .05
703 Checklist .05
704 Checklist .05

1992 Bowman

Topps introduced several changes with the release of its 1992 Bowman set. The 705-card set features 45 special insert cards stamped with gold foil. The cards are printed with a premium UV coated glossy card stock. Several players without major league experience are featured in the set. Included in this group are 1991 MVP's of the minor leagues and first round draft choices. Eighteen of the gold-foil enchanced cards have been identified as short-prints (designated SP in the listings), printed in quantities one-half the other foils.

	NM/M
Complete Set (705):	120.00
Common Player:	.10
Pack (15):	6.00
Wax Box (36):	160.00
Jumbo Pack (25):	8.00
Jumbo Box (36):	220.00

1 Ivan Rodriguez 1.25
2 Kirk McCaskill .10
3 Scott Livingstone .10
4 Salomon Torres **RC** .10
5 Carlos Hernandez .10
6 Dave Hollins .10
7 Scott Fletcher .10
8 Jorge Fabregas .10
9 Andujar Cedeno .10
10 Howard Johnson .10
11 Trevor Hoffman **RC** 2.00
12 Roberto Kelly .10
13 Gregg Jefferies .10
14 Marquis Grissom .10
15 Mike Ignasiak .10
16 Jack Morris .10
17 William Pennyfeather .10
18 Todd Stottlemyre .10
19 Chito Martinez .10
20 Roberto Alomar .30
21 Sam Militello .10
22 Hector Fajardo .10
23 Paul Quantrill **RC** .10
24 Chuck Knoblauch .10
25 Reggie Jefferson .10
26 Jeremy McGarity .10
27 Jerome Walton .10
28 Chipper Jones 8.00
29 Brian Barber **RC** .10
30 Ron Darling .10
31 Roberto Petagine **RC** .10
32 Chuck Finley .10
33 Edgar Martinez .10
34 Napolean Robinson .10
35 Andy Van Slyke .10
36 Bobby Thigpen .10
37 Travis Fryman .10
38 Eric Christopherson .10
39 Terry Mulholland .10
40 Darryl Strawberry .10
41 Manny Alexander **RC** .10
42 Tracey Sanders **RC** .10
43 Pete Incaviglia .10
44 Kim Batiste .10
45 Frank Rodriguez .10
46 Greg Swindell .10
47 Delino DeShields .10
48 John Ericks .10
49 Franklin Stubbs .10
50 Tony Gwynn 2.00
51 Clifton Garrett **RC** .10
52 Mike Gardella .10
53 Scott Erickson .10
54 Gary Caballo .10
55 Jose Oliva **RC** .10
56 Brook Fordyce .10
57 Mark Whiten .10
58 Joe Slusarski .10
59 J.R. Phillips **RC** .10
60 Barry Bonds 4.00
61 Bob Milacki .10
62 Keith Mitchell .10
63 Angel Miranda .10
64 Raul Mondesi .10
65 Brian Koelling .10
66 Brian McRae .10
67 John Patterson .10
68 John Wetteland .10
69 Wilson Alvarez .10
70 Wade Boggs 2.00
71 Darryl Ratliff .10
72 Jeff Jackson .10
73 Jeremy Hernandez .10
74 Darryl Hamilton .10
75 Rafael Belliard .10
76 Ricky Trilcek .10
77 Felipe Crespo **RC** .10
78 Carney Lansford .10
79 Ryan Long .10
80 Kirby Puckett 2.00
81 Earl Cunningham .10
82 Pedro Martinez 1.50
83 Scott Hatteberg .10
84 Juan Gonzalez .75
85 Robert Nutting .10
86 Calvin Reese **RC** .50
87 Dave Silvestri .10
88 Scott Ruffcorn **RC** .10
89 Rick Aguilera .10
90 Cecil Fielder .10
91 Kirk Dressendorfer .10
92 Jerry DiPoto .10
93 Mike Felder .10
94 Craig Paquette .10
95 Elvin Paulino .10
96 Donovan Osborne .10
97 Hubie Brooks .10
98 Derek Lowe **RC** 4.00
99 David Zancanaro .10
100 Ken Griffey Jr. 2.75
101 Todd Hundley .10
102 Mike Trombley .10
103 Ricky Gutierrez **RC** .10
104 Braulio Castillo .10
105 Craig Lefferts .10
106 Rick Sutcliffe .10
107 Dean Palmer .10
108 Henry Rodriguez .10
109 Mark Clark **RC** .10
110 Kenny Lofton .10
111 Mark Carreon .10
112 J.T. Bruett **RC** .10
113 Gerald Williams .10
114 Frank Thomas 1.50
115 Kevin Reimer .10
116 Sammy Sosa 2.00
117 Mickey Tettleton .10
118 Reggie Sanders .10
119 Trevor Wilson .10
120 Cliff Brantley .10
121 Spike Owen .10
122 Jeff Montgomery .10
123 Alex Sutherland .10
124 Brien Taylor **RC** .10
125 Brian Williams .10
126 Kevin Seitzer .10
127 Carlos Delgado **RC** 15.00
128 Gary Scott .10
129 Scott Cooper .10
130 Domingo Jean **RC** .10
131 Pat Mahomes **RC** .10
132 Mike Boddicker .10
133 Roberto Hernandez .10
134 Dave Valle .10
135 Kurt Stillwell .10
136 Brad Pennington **RC** .10
137 Jermaine Swifton .10
138 Ryan Hawblitzel .10
139 Tito Navarro .10
140 Sandy Alomar .10
141 Todd Benzinger .10
142 Danny Jackson .10
143 Melvin Nieves **RC** .25
144 Jim Campanis .10
145 Luis Gonzalez .10
146 Dave Doorneweerd .10
147 Charlie Hayes .10
148 Greg Maddux 2.00
149 Brian Harper .10
150 Brent Miller .10
151 Shawn Estes **RC** .75
152 Mike Williams .10
153 Charlie Hough .10
154 Randy Myers .10
155 Kevin Young **RC** .10
156 Rick Wilkins .10
157 Terry Schumpert .10
158 Steve Karsay .10
159 Gary DiSarcina .10
160 Deion Sanders .10
161 Tom Browning .10
162 Dickie Thon .10
163 Luis Mercedes .10
164 Ricardo Ingram .10
165 Tavo Alavarez **RC** .10
166 Rickey Henderson 1.50
167 Jaime Navarro .10
168 Billy Ashley **RC** .10
169 Phil Dauphin .10
170 Ivan Cruz .10
171 Harold Baines .10
172 Bryan Harvey .10
173 Alex Cole .10
174 Curtis Shaw .10
175 Matt Williams .10
176 Felix Jose .10
177 Sam Horn .10
178 Randy Johnson 1.50
179 Ivan Calderon .10
180 Steve Avery .10
181 William Suero .10
182 Bill Swift .10
183 Howard Battle **RC** .10
184 Ruben Amaro .10
185 Jim Abbott .10
186 Mike Fitzgerald .10
187 Bruce Hurst .10
188 Jeff Juden .10
189 Jeromy Burnitz .10
190 Dave Burba .10
191 Kevin Brown .10
192 Patrick Lennon .10
193 Jeffrey McNeely .10
194 Wil Cordero .10
195 Chili Davis .10
196 Milt Cuyler .10
197 Von Hayes .10
198 Todd Revening **RC** .10
199 Joel Johnson .10
200 Jeff Bagwell 1.50
201 Alex Fernandez .10
202 Todd Jones .10
203 Charles Nagy .10
204 Tim Raines .10
205 Kevin Maas .10
206 Julio Franco .10
207 Randy Velarde .10
208 Lance Johnson .10
209 Scott Leius .10
210 Derek Lee .10
211 Joe Sondrini .10
212 Royce Clayton .10
213 Chris George .10
214 Gary Sheffield .60
215 Mark Gubicza .10
216 Mike Moore .10
217 Rick Huisman .10
218 Jeff Russell .10
219 D.J. Dozier .10
220 Dave Martinez .10
221 Al Newman .10
222 Nolan Ryan 4.00
223 Teddy Higuera .10
224 Damon Buford **RC** .10
225 Ruben Sierra .10
226 Tom Nevers .10
227 Tommy Greene .10
228 Nigel Wilson **RC** .10
229 John DeSilva .10
230 Bobby Witt .10
231 Greg Cadaret .10
232 John VanderWal .10
233 Jack Clark .10
234 Bill Doran .10
235 Bobby Bonilla .10
236 Steve Olin .10
237 Derek Bell .10
238 David Cone .10
239 Victor Cole .10
240 Rod Bolton .10
241 Tom Pagnozzi .10
242 Rob Dibble .10
243 Michael Carter .10
244 Don Peters .10
245 Mike LaValliere .10
246 Joe Perona .10
247 Mitch Williams .10
248 Jay Buhner .10
249 Andy Benes .10
250 Alex Ochoa **RC** .10
251 Greg Blosser .10
252 Jack Armstrong .10
253 Juan Samuel .10
254 Terry Pendleton .10
255 Ramon Martinez .10
256 Rico Brogna .10
257 John Smiley .10
258 Carl Everett .10
259 Tim Salmon .10
260 Will Clark .10
261 Ugueth Urbina **RC** .40
262 Jason Wood .10
263 Dave Magadan .10
264 Dante Bichette .10
265 Jose DeLeon .10
266 Mike Neill **RC** .10
267 Paul O'Neill .10
268 Anthony Young .10
269 Greg Harris .10
270 Todd Van Poppel .10
271 Pete Castellano .10
272 Tony Phillips .10
273 Mike Gallego .10
274 Steve Cooke **RC** .10
275 Robin Ventura .10
276 Kevin Mitchell .10
277 Doug Linton .10
278 Robert Eenhorn .10
279 Gabe White **RC** .10
280 Dave Stewart .10
281 Mo Sanford .10
282 Greg Perschke .10
283 Kevin Flora .10
284 Jeff Williams .10
285 Keith Miller .10
286 Andy Ashby .10
287 Doug Dascenzo .10
288 Eric Karros .10
289 Glenn Murray **RC** .10
290 Troy Percival **RC** .75
291 Orlando Merced .10
292 Peter Hoy .10
293 Tony Fernandez .10
294 Juan Guzman .10
295 Jesse Barfield .10
296 Sid Fernandez .10
297 Scott Cepicky .10
298 Garret Anderson **RC** 6.00
299 Cal Eldred .10
300 Ryne Sandberg 2.00
301 Jim Gantner .10
302 Mariano Rivera **RC** 25.00
303 Ron Lockett .10
304 Jose Offerman .10
305 Denny Martinez .10
306 Luis Ortiz **RC** .10
307 David Howard .10
308 Russ Springer .10
309 Chris Howard .10
310 Kyle Abbott .10
311 Aaron Sele **RC** 1.00
312 Dave Justice .10
313 Pete O'Brien .10
314 Greg Hansell .10
315 Dave Winfield 1.50
316 Lance Dickson .10
317 Eric King .10
318 Vaughn Eshelman .10
319 Tim Belcher .10
320 Andres Galarraga .10
321 Scott Bullett .10
322 Doug Strange .10
323 Jerald Clark .10
324 Dave Righetti .10
325 Greg Hibbard .10
326 Eric Dillman .10
327 Shane Reynolds **RC** .25
328 Chris Hammond .10
329 Albert Belle .10
330 Rich Becker **RC** .10
331 Eddie Williams .10
332 Donald Harris .10
333 Dave Smith .10
334 Steve Fireovid .10
335 Steve Buechele .10
336 Mike Schooler .10
337 Kevin McReynolds .10
338 Hensley Meulens .10
339 Benji Gil **RC** .10
340 Don Mattingly 2.50
341 Alvin Davis .10
342 Alan Mills .10
343 Kelly Downs .10
344 Leo Gomez .10
345 Tarrik Brock **RC** .10
346 Ryan Turner .10
347 John Smoltz .10
348 Bill Sampen .10
349 Paul Byrd .10
350 Mike Bordick .10
351 Jose Lind .10
352 David Wells .10
353 Barry Larkin .10
354 Bruce Ruffin .10
355 Luis Rivera .10
356 Sid Bream .10
357 Julian Vasquez .10
358 Jason Bere **RC** .10
359 Ben McDonald .10
360 Scott Stahoviak .10
361 Kirt Manwaring .10
362 Jeff Johnson .10
363 Rob Deer .10
364 Tony Pena .10
365 Melido Perez .10
366 Clay Parker .10
367 Dale Sveum .10
368 Mike Scioscia .10
369 Roger Salkeld .10
370 Mike Stanley .10
371 Jack McDowell .10
372 Tim Wallach .10
373 Billy Ripken .10
374 Mike Christopher .10
375 Paul Molitor 1.50
376 Dave Stieb .10
377 Pedro Guerrero .10
378 Russ Swan .10
379 Bob Ojeda .10
380 Donn Pall .10
381 Eddie Zosky .10
382 Darnell Coles .10
383 Tom Smith .10
384 Mark McGwire 3.00
385 Gary Carter 1.50
386 Rich Amaral .10
387 Alan Embree .10
388 Jonathan Hurst .10
389 Bobby Jones **RC** .10
390 Rico Rossy .10
391 Dan Smith .10
392 Terry Steinbach .10
393 Jon Farrell .10
394 Dave Anderson .10
395 Benito Santiago .10
396 Mark Wohlers .10
397 Mo Vaughn .10
398 Randy Kramer .10
399 John Jaha **RC** .10
400 Cal Ripken, Jr. 4.00
401 Ryan Bowen .10
402 Tim McIntosh .10
403 Bernard Gilkey .10
404 Junior Felix .10
405 Cris Colon .10
406 Marc Newfield .10
407 Bernie Williams .10
408 Jay Howell .10
409 Zane Smith .10
410 Jeff Shaw .10
411 Kerry Woodson .10
412 Wes Chamberlain .10
413 Dave Mlicki .10
414 Benny Distefano .10
415 Kevin Rogers .10
416 Tim Naehring .10
417 Clemente Nunez .10
418 Luis Sojo .10
419 Kevin Ritz .10
420 Omar Oliveras .10
421 Manuel Lee .10
422 Julio Valera .10
423 Omar Vizquel .10
424 Darren Burton .10
425 Mel Hall .10
426 Dennis Powell .10
427 Lee Stevens .10
428 Glenn Davis .10
429 Willie Greene .10
430 Kevin Wickander .10
431 Dennis Eckersley 1.25
432 Joe Orsulak .10
433 Eddie Murray 1.50
434 Matt Stairs **RC** .10
435 Wally Joyner .10
436 Rondell White .10
437 Rob Mauer .10
438 Joe Redfield .10
439 Mark Lewis .10
440 Darren Daulton .10
441 Mike Henneman .10
442 John Cangelosi .10
443 Vince Moore **RC** .10
444 John Wehner .10
445 Kent Hrbek .10
446 Mark McLemore .10
447 Bill Wegman .10
448 Robby Thompson .10
449 Mark Anthony .10
450 Archi Cianfrocco .10
451 Johnny Ruffin .10
452 Javier Lopez .10
453 Greg Gohr .10

454 Tim Scott .10
455 Stan Belinda .10
456 Darrin Jackson .10
457 Chris Gardner .10
458 Esteban Beltre .10
459 Phil Plantier .10
460 Jim Thome 1.25
461 Mike Piazza **RC** 25.00
462 Matt Sinatro .10
463 Scott Servais .10
464 Brian Jordan **RC** .75
465 Doug Drabek .10
466 Carl Willis .10
467 Bret Barbarie .10
468 Hal Morris .10
469 Steve Sax .10
470 Jerry Willard .10
471 Dan Wilson .10
472 Chris Hoiles .10
473 Rheal Cormier .10
474 John Morris .10
475 Jeff Reardon .10
476 Mark Leiter .10
477 Tom Gordon .10
478 Kent Bottenfield **RC** .10
479 Gene Larkin .10
480 Dwight Gooden .10
481 B.J. Surhoff .10
482 Andy Stankiewicz .10
483 Tino Martinez .10
484 Craig Biggio .10
485 Denny Neagle .10
486 Rusty Meacham .10
487 Kal Daniels .10
488 Dave Henderson .10
489 Tim Costo .10
490 Doug Davis .10
491 Frank Viola .10
492 Cory Snyder .10
493 Chris Martin .10
494 Dion James .10
495 Randy Tomlin .10
496 Greg Vaughn .10
497 Dennis Cook .10
498 Rosario Rodriguez .10
499 Dave Staton .10
500 George Brett 2.50
501 Brian Barnes .10
502 Butch Henry .10
503 Harold Reynolds .10
504 David Nied **RC** .10
505 Lee Smith .10
506 Steve Chitren .10
507 Ken Hill .10
508 Robbie Beckett .10
509 Troy Afenir .10
510 Kelly Gruber .10
511 Bret Boone .10
512 Jeff Branson .10
513 Mike Jackson .10
514 Pete Harnisch .10
515 Chad Kreuter .10
516 Joe Vitko .10
517 Orel Hershiser .10
518 John Doherty **RC** .10
519 Jay Bell .10
520 Mark Langston .10
521 Dann Howitt .10
522 Bobby Reed .10
523 Roberto Munoz .10
524 Todd Ritchie .10
525 Bip Roberts .10
526 Pat Listach **RC** .10
527 Scott Brosius **RC** .10
528 John Roper **RC** .10
529 Phil Hiatt **RC** .10
530 Denny Walling .10
531 Carlos Baerga .10
532 Manny Ramirez **RC** 20.00
533 Pat Clements .10
534 Ron Gant .10
535 Pat Kelly .10
536 Billy Spiers .10
537 Darren Reed .10
538 Ken Caminiti .10
539 Butch Huskey **RC** .10
540 Matt Nokes .10
541 John Kruk .10
542 John Jaha/SP (Foil) .35
543 Justin Thompson **RC** .10
544 Steve Hosey .10
545 Joe Kmak .10
546 John Franco .10
547 Devon White .10
548 Elston Hanse/SP (Foil) .35
549 Ryan Klesko .10
550 Danny Tartabull .10
551 Frank Thomas/SP (Foil) 1.50
552 Kevin Tapani .10
553a Willie Banks .10
553b Pat Clements .10
554 B.J. Wallace/SP (Foil) **RC** .35
555 Orlando Miller **RC** .10
556 Mark Smith **RC** .10
557 Tim Wallach (Foil) .10
558 Bill Gullickson .10
559 Derek Bell (Foil) .10
560 Joe Randa (Foil) .10
561 Frank Seminara .10
562 Mark Gardner .10
563 Rick Greene (Foil) .10
564 Gary Gaetti .10
565 Ozzie Guillen .10
566 Charles Nagy (Foil) .10
567 Mike Milchin .10
568 Ben Shelton (Foil) .10
569 Chris Roberts (Foil) .10
570 Ellis Burks .10
571 Scott Scudder .10
572 Jim Abbott (Foil) .10
573 Joe Carter .10
574 Steve Finley .10
575 Jim Olander (Foil) .10
576 Carlos Garcia .10
577 Greg Olson .10
578 Greg Swindell (Foil) .10
579 Matt Williams (Foil) .10
580 Mark Grace .10
581 Howard House (Foil) .10
582 Luis Polonia .10
583 Erik Hanson .10
584 Salomon Torres (Foil) .10
585 Carlton Fisk 1.50
586 Bret Saberhagen .10
587 Chad McDonnell **RC** (Foil) .10
588 Jimmy Key .10
589 Mike MacFarlane .10
590 Barry Bonds (Foil) 3.50
591 Jamie McAndrew .10
592 Shane Mack .10
593 Kerwin Moore .10
594 Joe Oliver .10
595 Chris Sabo .10
596 Alex Gonzalez **RC** .50
597 Brett Butler .10
598 Mark Hutton .10
599 Andy Benes (Foil) .10
600 Jose Canseco .60
601 Darryl Kile .10
602 Matt Stairs/SP (Foil) .35
603 Rob Butler (Foil) .10
604 Willie McGee .10
605 Jack McDowell .10
606 Tom Candiotti .10
607 Ed Martel .10
608 Matt Mieske (Foil) .10
609 Darrin Fletcher .10
610 Rafael Palmeiro 1.25
611 Bill Swift (Foil) .10
612 Mike Mussina .65
613 Vince Coleman .10
614 Scott Cepicky (Foil) .10
615 Mike Greenwell .10
616 Kevin McGehee .10
617 Jeffrey Hammonds (Foil) .10
618 Scott Taylor .10
619 Dave Otto .10
620 Mark McGwire (Foil) 3.00
621 Kevin Tatar .10
622 Steve Farr .10
623 Ryan Klesko (Foil) .10
625 Andre Dawson .40
626 Tino Martinez/SP (Foil) .35
627 Chad Curtis **RC** .50
628 Mickey Morandini .10
629 Gregg Olson/SP (Foil) .35
630 Lou Whitaker .10
631 Arthur Rhodes .10
632 Brandon Wilson .10
633 Lance Jennings **RC** .10
634 Allen Watson **RC** .10
635 Len Dykstra .10
636 Joe Girardi .10
637 Kiki Hernandez/SP (Foil) .35
638 Mike Hampton **RC** 1.00
639 Al Osuna .10
640 Kevin Appier .10
641 Rick Helling/SP (Foil) .35
642 Jody Reed .10
643 Ray Lankford .10
644 John Olerud .10
645 Paul Molitor/SP (Foil) 1.50
646 Pat Borders .10
647 Mike Morgan .10
648 Larry Walker .10
649 Pete Castellano/SP (Foil) .35
650 Fred McGriff .10
651 Walt Weiss .10
652 Calvin Murray/SP **RC** Foil) .35
653 Dave Nilsson .10
654 Greg Pirkl .10
655 Robin Ventura/SP (Foil) .35
656 Mark Portugal .10
657 Roger McDowell .10
658 Rick Hirtensteiner/SP (Foil) .35
659 Glenallen Hill .10
660 Greg Gagne .10
661 Charles Johnson/SP (Foil) .35
662 Brian Hunter .10
663 Mark Lemke .10
664 Tim Belcher/SP (Foil) .35
665 Rich DeLucia .10
666 Bob Walk .10
667 Joe Carter/SP (Foil) .35
668 Jose Guzman .10
669 Otis Nixon .10
670 Phil Nevin (Foil) .10
671 Eric Davis .10
672 Damion Easley **RC** .25
673 Will Clark (Foil) .10
674 Mark Kiefer .10
675 Ozzie Smith 2.00
676 Manny Ramirez (Foil) 6.00
677 Gregg Olson .10
678 Cliff Floyd **RC** 1.00
679 Duane Singleton .10
680 Jose Rijo .10
681 Willie Randolph .10
682 Michael Tucker **RC** (Foil) .25
683 Darren Lewis .10
684 Dale Murphy .35
685 Mike Pagliarulo .10
686 Paul Miller .10
687 Mike Robertson .10
688 Mike Devereaux .10
689 Pedro Astacio .10
690 Alan Trammell .10
691 Roger Clemens 2.50
692 Bud Black .10
693 Turk Wendell .10
694 Barry Larkin/SP (Foil) .35
695 Todd Zeile .10
696 Pat Hentgen .10
697 Eddie Taubensee **RC** .10
698 Guillermo Vasquez .10
699 Tom Glavine .30
700 Robin Yount 1.50
701 Checklist .10
702 Checklist .10
703 Checklist .10
704 Checklist .10
705 Checklist .10

1993 Bowman

Bowman's 708-card 1993 set once again features a premium UV-coated glossy stock. There are also 48 special insert cards, with gold foil stamping, randomly inserted one per pack or two per jumbo pack. The foil cards, numbered 339-374 and 693-704, feature top prospects and rookie-of-the-year candidates, as do several regular cards in the set. Cards are standard size.

NM/M
Complete Set (708): 35.00
Common Player: .10
Pack (15): 1.50
Wax Box (24): 35.00
Jumbo Pack (22): 2.50
Jumbo Box (20): 40.00
1 Glenn Davis .10
2 Hector Roa **RC** .10
3 Ken Ryan **RC** .10
4 Derek Wallace **RC** .10
5 Jorge Fabregas .10
6 Joe Oliver .10
7 Brandon Wilson .10
8 Mark Thompson **RC** .10
9 Tracy Sanders .10
10 Rich Renteria .10
11 Lou Whitaker .10
12 Brian Hunter **RC** .10
13 Joe Vitiello .10
14 Eric Karros .10
15 Joe Kmak .10
16 Tavo Alvarez .10
17 Steve Dunn **RC** .10
18 Tony Fernandez .10
19 Melido Perez .10
20 Mike Lieberthal .10
21 Terry Steinbach .10
22 Stan Belinda .10
23 Jay Buhner .10
24 Allen Watson .10
25 Daryl Henderson **RC** .10
26 Ray McDavid **RC** .10
27 Shawn Green .30
28 Bud Black .10
29 Sherman Obando **RC** .10
30 Mike Hostetler **RC** .10
31 Nate Hinchey **RC** .10
32 Randy Myers .10
33 Brian Grebeck **RC** .10
34 John Roper .10
35 Larry Thomas .10
36 Alex Cole .10
37 Tom Kramer **RC** .10
38 Matt Whisenant **RC** .10
39 Chris Gomez **RC** .10
40 Luis Gonzalez .10
41 Kevin Appier .10
42 Omar Daal **RC** .10
43 Duane Singleton .10
44 Bill Risley .10
45 Pat Meares **RC** .10
46 Butch Huskey .10
47 Bobby Munoz .10
48 Juan Bell .10
49 Scott Lydy **RC** .10
50 Dennis Moeller .10
51 Marc Newfield .10
52 Tripp Cromer **RC** .10
53 Kurt Miller .10
54 Jim Pena .10
55 Juan Guzman .10
56 Matt Williams .10
57 Harold Reynolds .10
58 Donnie Elliott **RC** .10
59 Jon Shave **RC** .10
60 Kevin Roberson **RC** .10
61 Hilly Hathaway **RC** .10
62 Jose Rijo .10
63 Kerry Taylor **RC** .10
64 Ryan Hawblitzel .10
65 Glenallen Hill .10
66 Ramon D. Martinez **RC** .10
67 Travis Fryman .10
68 Tom Nevers .10
69 Phil Hiatt .10
70 Tim Wallach .10
71 B.J. Surhoff .10
72 Rondell White .10
73 Denny Hocking **RC** .10
74 Mike Oquist **RC** .10
75 Paul O'Neill .10
76 Willie Banks .10
77 Bob Welch .10
78 Jose Sandoval **RC** .10
79 Bill Haselman .10
80 Rheal Cormier .10
81 Dean Palmer .10
82 Pat Gomez **RC** .10
83 Steve Karsay .10
84 Carl Hanselman **RC** .10
85 T.R. Lewis **RC** .10
86 Chipper Jones 2.00
87 Scott Hatteberg .10
88 Greg Hibbard .10
89 Lance Painter **RC** .10
90 Chad Mottola **RC** .10
91 Jason Bere .10
92 Dante Bichette .10
93 Sandy Alomar .10
94 Carl Everett .10
95 Danny Bautista **RC** .10
96 Steve Finley .10
97 David Cone .10
98 Todd Hollandsworth .10
99 Matt Mieske .10
100 Larry Walker .10
101 Shane Mack .10
102 Aaron Ledesma **RC** .10
103 Andy Pettitte **RC** 4.00
104 Kevin Stocker .10
105 Mike Mobler .10
106 Tony Menedez .10
107 Derek Lowe .10
108 Basil Shabazz .10
109 Dan Smith .10
110 Scott Sanders **RC** .10
111 Todd Stottlemyre .10
112 Benji Sikonton **RC** .10
113 Rick Sutcliffe .10
114 Lee Heath **RC** .10
115 Jeff Russell .10
116 Dave Stevens **RC** .10
117 Mark Holzemer **RC** .10
118 Tim Belcher .10
119 Bobby Thigpen .10
120 Roger Bailey **RC** .10
121 Tony Mitchell **RC** .10
122 Junior Felix .10
123 Rich Robertson **RC** .10
124 Andy Cook **RC** .10
125 Brian Bevil **RC** .10
126 Darryl Strawberry .10
127 Cal Eldred .10
128 Cliff Floyd .10
129 Alan Newman .10
130 Howard Johnson .10
131 Jim Abbott .10
132 Chad McConnell .10
133 Miguel Jimenez **RC** .10
134 Brett Backlund **RC** .10
135 John Cummings **RC** .10
136 Brian Barber .10
137 Rafael Palmeiro 1.25
138 Tim Worrell **RC** .10
139 Jose Pett **RC** .10
140 Barry Bonds 4.00
141 Damon Buford .10
142 Jeff Blauser .10
143 Frankie Rodriguez .10
144 Mike Morgan .10
145 Gary DeSarcina .10
146 Calvin Reese .10
147 Johnny Ruffin .10
148 David Nied .10
149 Charles Nagy .10
150 Mike Myers **RC** .10
151 Kenny Carlyle **RC** .10
152 Eric Anthony .10
153 Jose Lind .10
154 Pedro Martinez 1.50
155 Mark Kiefer .10
156 Tim Laker **RC** .10
157 Pat Mahomes .10
158 Bobby Bonilla .10
159 Domingo Jean .10
160 Darren Daulton .10
161 Mark McGwire 3.50
162 Jason Kendall **RC** 1.00
163 Desi Relaford .10
164 Ozzie Canseco .10
165 Rick Helling .10
166 Steve Pegues **RC** .10
167 Paul Molitor 1.50
168 Larry Carter **RC** .10
169 Arthur Rhodes .10
170 Damon Hollins **RC** .10
171 Frank Viola .10
172 Steve Trachsel **RC** .25
173 J.T. Snow **RC** .50
174 Keith Gordon **RC** .10
175 Carlton Fisk 1.50
176 Jason Bates **RC** .10
177 Mike Crosby **RC** .10
178 Benny Santiago .10
179 Mike Moore .10
180 Jeff Juden .10
181 Darren Burton .10
182 Todd Williams **RC** .10
183 John Jaha .10
184 Mike Lansing **RC** .50
185 Pedro Grifol **RC** .10
186 Vince Coleman .10
187 Pat Kelly .10
188 Clemente Alvarez **RC** .10
189 Ron Darling .10
190 Orlando Merced .10
191 Chris Bosio .10
192 Steve Dixon **RC** .10
193 Doug Dascenzo .10
194 Ray Holbert **RC** .10
195 Howard Battle .10
196 Willie McGee .10
197 John O'Donoghue **RC** .10
198 Steve Avery .10
199 Greg Blosser .10
200 Ryne Sandberg 2.00
201 Joe Grahe .10
202 Dan Wilson .10
203 Domingo Martinez **RC** .10
204 Andres Galarraga .10
205 Jamie Taylor **RC** .10
206 Darrell Whitmore **RC** .10
207 Ben Blomdahl **RC** .10
208 Doug Drabek .10
209 Keith Miller .10
210 Billy Ashley .10
211 Mike Farrell **RC** .10
212 John Wetteland .10
213 Randy Tomlin .10
214 Sid Fernandez .10
215 Quilvio Veras **RC** .10
216 Dave Hollins .10
217 Mike Neill .10
218 Andy Van Slyke .10
219 Bret Boone .10
220 Tom Pagnozzi .10
221 Mike Welch **RC** .10
222 Frank Seminara .10
223 Ron Villone .10
224 D.J. Thielen **RC** .10
225 Cal Ripken, Jr. 4.00
226 Pedro Borbon **RC** .10
227 Carlos Quintana .10
228 Tommy Shields **RC** .10
229 Tim Salmon .10
230 John Smiley .10
231 Ellis Burks .10
232 Pedro Castellano .10
233 Paul Byrd .10
234 Bryan Harvey .10
235 Scott Livingstone .10
236 James Mouton **RC** .10
237 Joe Randa .10
238 Pedro Astacio .10
239 Darryl Hamilton .10
240 Joey Eischen **RC** .10
241 Edgar Herrera **RC** .10
242 Dwight Gooden .10
243 Sam Militello .10
244 Ron Blazier **RC** .10
245 Ruben Sierra .10
246 Al Martin .10
247 Mike Felder .10
248 Bob Tewksbury .10
249 Craig Lefferts .10
250 Luis Lopez .10
251 Devon White .10
252 Will Clark .10
253 Mark Smith .10
254 Terry Pendleton .10
255 Aaron Sele .10
256 Jose Viera **RC** .10
257 Damion Easley .10
258 Rod Lofton **RC** .10
259 Chris Snopek **RC** .10
260 Quinton McCracken **RC** .10
261 Mike Matthews **RC** .10
262 Hector Carrasco **RC** .10
263 Rick Greene .10
264 Chris Bolt **RC** .10
265 George Brett 2.50
266 Rick Gorecki **RC** .10
267 Francisco Gamez **RC** .10
268 Marquis Grissom .10
269 Kevin Tapani .10
270 Ryan Thompson .10
271 Gerald Williams .10
272 Paul Fletcher **RC** .10
273 Lance Blankenship .10
274 Marty Heff **RC** .10
275 Shawn Estes .10
276 Rene Arocha **RC** .10
277 Scott Evre **RC** .10
278 Phil Plantier .10
279 Paul Spoljaric **RC** .10
280 Chris Gahbs .10
281 Harold Baines .10
282 Jose Oliva **RC** .10
283 Matt Whiteside .10
284 Brant Brown **RC** .10
285 Russ Springer .10
286 Chris Sabo .10
287 Ozzie Guillen .10
288 Marcus Moore **RC** .10
289 Chad Ogea .10
290 Walt Weiss .10
291 Brian Edmondson .10
292 Jimmy Gonzalez .10
293 Danny Miceli **RC** .10
294 Jose Offerman .10
295 Greg Vaughn .10
296 Frank Bolick .10
297 Mike Maksudian **RC** .10
298 John Franco .10
299 Danny Tartabull .10
300 Len Dykstra .10
301 Bobby Witt .10
302 Trey Beamon **RC** .10
303 Tino Martinez .10
304 Aaron Holbert .10
305 Juan Gonzalez .75
306 Billy Hall **RC** .10
307 Duane Ward .10
308 Rod Beck .10
309 Jose Mercedes **RC** .10
310 Otis Nixon .10
311 Gettys Glaze **RC** .10
312 Candy Maldonado .10
313 Chad Curtis .10
314 Tim Costo .10
315 Mike Robertson .10
316 Nigel Wilson .10
317 Greg McMichael **RC** .10
318 Scott Pose **RC** .10
319 Ivan Cruz .10
320 Greg Swindell .10
321 Kevin McReynolds .10
322 Tom Candiotti .10
323 Bob Wishnevski **RC** .10
324 Ken Hill .10
325 Kirby Puckett 2.00
326 Tim Bogar **RC** .10
327 Mariano Rivera .30
328 Mitch Williams .10
329 Craig Paquette .10
330 Jay Bell .10
331 Jose Martinez **RC** .10
332 Rob Deer .10
333 Brook Fordyce .10
334 Matt Nokes .10
335 Derek Lee .10
336 Paul Ellis **RC** .10
337 Desi Wilson **RC** .10
338 Roberto Alomar .30
339 Jim Tatum (Foil) .10
340 J.T. Snow (Foil) .10
341 Tim Salmon (Foil) .10
342 Russ Davis **RC** (Foil) .25
343 Javier Lopez (Foil) .10
344 Troy O'Leary **RC** (Foil) .10
345 Marty Cordova **RC** (Foil) .60
346 Bubba Smith **RC** (Foil) .10
347 Chipper Jones (Foil) 1.50
348 Jessie Hollins (Foil) .10
349 Willie Greene (Foil) .10
350 Mark Thompson (Foil) .10
351 Nigel Wilson (Foil) .10
352 Todd Jones (Foil) .10
353 Raul Mondesi (Foil) .10
354 Cliff Floyd (Foil) .10
355 Bobby Jones (Foil) .10
356 Kevin Stocker (Foil) .10
357 Midre Cummings (Foil) .10
358 Allen Watson (Foil) .10
359 Ray McDavid (Foil) .10
360 Steve Hosey (Foil) .10
361 Brad Pennington (Foil) .10
362 Frankie Rodriguez (Foil) .10
363 Troy Percival (Foil) .10
364 Jason Bere (Foil) .10
365 Manny Ramirez (Foil) .75
366 Justin Thompson (Foil) .10
367 Joe Vitello (Foil) .10
368 Tyrone Hill (Foil) .10
369 David McCarty (Foil) .10
370 Brien Taylor (Foil) .10
371 Todd Van Poppel (Foil) .10
372 Marc Newfield (Foil) .10
373 Terrell Lowery **RC** (Foil) .10
374 Alex Gonzalez (Foil) .10
375 Ken Griffey Jr. 3.00
376 Donovan Osborne .10
377 Ritchie Moody **RC** .10
378 Shane Andrews .10
379 Carlos Delgado .65
380 Bill Swift .10
381 Leo Gomez .10
382 Ron Gant .10
383 Scott Fletcher .10
384 Matt Walbeck **RC** .10
385 Chuck Finley .10
386 Kevin Mitchell .10
387 Wilson Alvarez .10
388 John Burke **RC** .10
389 Alan Embree .10
390 Trevor Hoffman .10
391 Alan Trammell .10
392 Todd Jones .10
393 Felix Jose .10
394 Orel Hershiser .10
395 Pat Listach .10
396 Gabe White .10
397 Dan Serafini **RC** .10
398 Todd Hundley .10
399 Wade Boggs 2.00

No.	Player	Price
400	Tyler Green	.10
401	Mike Bordick	.10
402	Scott Bullett	.10
403	Lagrande Russell **RC**	.10
404	Ray Lankford	.10
405	Nolan Ryan	4.00
406	Robbie Beckett	.10
407	Brent Bowers **RC**	.10
408	Adell Davenport **RC**	.10
409	Brady Anderson	.10
410	Tom Glavine	.35
411	Doug Hecker **RC**	.10
412	Jose Guzman	.10
413	Luis Polonia	.10
414	Brian Williams	.10
415	Bo Jackson	.15
416	Eric Young	.10
417	Kenny Lofton	.10
418	Orestes Destrade	.10
419	Tony Phillips	.10
420	Jeff Bagwell	1.50
421	Hark Gardner	.10
422	Brett Butler	.10
423	Graeme Lloyd **RC**	.10
424	Delino DeShields	.10
425	Scott Erickson	.10
426	Jeff Kent	.10
427	Jimmy Key	.10
428	Mickey Morandini	.10
429	Marcos Arkas **RC**	.10
430	Don Slaught	.10
431	Randy Johnson	1.50
432	Omar Olivares	.10
433	Charlie Leibrandt	.10
434	Kurt Stillwell	.10
435	Scott Brow **RC**	.10
436	Robby Thompson	.10
437	Ben McDonald	.10
438	Deion Sanders	.10
439	Tony Pena	.10
440	Mark Grace	.10
441	Eduardo Perez	.10
442	Tim Pugh **RC**	.10
443	Scott Ruffcorn	.10
444	Jay Gainer **RC**	.10
445	Albert Belle	.10
446	Bret Barberie	.10
447	Justin Mashore	.10
448	Pete Harnisch	.10
449	Greg Gagne	.10
450	Eric Davis	.10
451	Dave Mlicki	.10
452	Moises Alou	.10
453	Rick Aguilera	.10
454	Eddie Murray	1.50
455	Bob Wickman	.10
456	Wes Chamberlain	.10
457	Bront Gates	.10
458	Paul Weber	.10
459	Mike Hampton	.10
460	Ozzie Smith	2.00
461	Tom Henke	.10
462	Ricky Gutuerrez	.10
463	Jack Morris	.10
464	Joel Chimelis **RC**	.10
465	Gregg Olson	.10
466	Javier Lopez	.10
467	Scott Cooper	.10
468	Willie Wilson	.10
469	Mark Langston	.10
470	Barry Larkin	.10
471	Rod Bolton	.10
472	Freddie Benavides	.10
473	Ken Ramos **RC**	.10
474	Chuck Carr	.10
475	Cecil Fielder	.10
476	Eddie Taubensee	.10
477	Chris Eddy **RC**	.10
478	Greg Hansell	.10
479	Kevin Reimer	.10
480	Denny Martinez	.10
481	Chuck Knoblauch	.10
482	Mike Draper	.10
483	Spike Owen	.10
484	Terry Mulholland	.10
485	Dennis Eckersley	1.25
486	Blas Minor	.10
487	Dave Fleming	.10
488	Dan Cholonsky	.10
489	Ivan Rodriguez	1.25
490	Gary Sheffield	.45
491	Ed Sprague	.10
492	Steve Hosey	.10
493	Jimmy Haynes **RC**	.10
494	John Smoltz	.10
495	Andre Dawson	.35
496	Rey Sanchez	.10
497	Ty Van Burkleo **RC**	.10
498	Bobby Ayala **RC**	.10
499	Tim Raines	.10
500	Charlie Hayes	.10
501	Paul Sorrento	.10
502	Richie Lewis **RC**	.10
503	Jason Pfaff **RC**	.10
504	Ken Caminiti	.10
505	Mike Macfarlane	.10
506	Jody Reed	.10
507	Bobby Hughes **RC**	.10
508	Wil Cordero	.10
509	George Tsanis **RC**	.10
510	Bret Saberhagen	.10
511	Derek Jeter **RC**	20.00
512	Gene Schall	.10
513	Curtis Shaw	.10
514	Steve Cooke	.10
515	Edgar Martinez	.10
516	Mike Milchin	.10
517	Billy Ripken	.10
518	Andy Benes	.10
519	Juan de la Rosa **RC**	.10
520	John Burkett	.10
521	Alex Ochoa	.10
522	Tony Tarasco **RC**	.10
523	Luis Ortiz	.10
524	Rick Williams	.10
525	Chris Turner **RC**	.10
526	Rob Dibble	.10
527	Jack McDowell	.10
528	Daryl Boston	.10
529	Bill Wertz **RC**	.10
530	Charlie Hough	.10
531	Sean Bergman	.10
532	Doug Jones	.10
533	Jeff Montgomery	.10
534	Roger Cedeno **RC**	.25
535	Robin Yount	1.50
536	Mo Vaughn	.10
537	Brian Harper	.10
538	Juan Castillo	.10
539	Steve Farr	.10
540	John Kruk	.10
541	Troy Neel	.10
542	Danny Clyburn **RC**	.10
543	Jim Converse **RC**	.10
544	Gregg Jefferies	.10
545	Jose Canseco	.40
546	Julio Bruno **RC**	.10
547	Rob Butler	.10
548	Royce Clayton	.10
549	Chris Hoiles	.10
550	Greg Maddux	2.00
551	Joe Ciccarella **RC**	.10
552	Ozzie Timmons	.10
553	Chili Davis	.10
554	Brian Koelling	.10
555	Frank Thomas	1.50
556	Vinny Castilla	.10
557	Reggie Jefferson	.10
558	Rob Natal	.10
559	Mike Henneman	.10
560	Craig Biggio	.10
561	Billy Brewer **RC**	.10
562	Dan Melendez	.10
563	Kenny Felder **RC**	.10
564	Miguel Batista **RC**	.10
565	Dave Winfield	1.50
566	Al Shirley	.10
567	Robert Eenhoorn	.10
568	Mike Williams	.10
569	Tanyon Sturtze **RC**	.10
570	Tim Wakefield	.10
571	Greg Pirkl	.10
572	Sean Lowe **RC**	.25
573	Terry Burows **RC**	.10
574	Kevin Higgins **RC**	.10
575	Joe Carter	.10
576	Kevin Rogers	.10
577	Manny Alexander	.10
578	Dave Justice	.10
579	Brian Conroy **RC**	.10
580	Jessie Hollins **RC**	.10
581	Ron Watson **RC**	.10
582	Bip Roberts	.10
583	Tom Urbani **RC**	.10
584	Jason Hutchins **RC**	.10
585	Carlos Baerga	.10
586	Jeff Mutis	.10
587	Justin Thompson	.10
588	Orlando Miller	.10
589	Brian McRae	.10
590	Ramon Martinez	.10
591	Dave Nilsson	.10
592	Jose Vidro **RC**	1.50
593	Rich Becker	.10
594	Preston Wilson **RC**	1.50
595	Don Mattingly	2.50
596	Tony Longmire	.10
597	Kevin Seitzer	.10
598	Midre Cummings **RC**	.10
599	Omar Vizquel	.10
600	Lee Smith	.10
601	David Hulse **RC**	.10
602	Darrell Sherman **RC**	.10
603	Alex Gonzalez	.10
604	Geronimo Pena	.10
605	Mike Devereaux	.10
606	Sterling Hitchcock **RC**	.25
607	Mike Greenwell	.10
608	Steve Buechele	.10
609	Troy Percival	.10
610	Bobby Kelly	.10
611	James Baldwin **RC**	.10
612	Jerald Clark	.10
613	Albie Lopez **RC**	.10
614	Dave Magadan	.10
615	Mickey Tettleton	.10
616	Sean Runyan **RC**	.10
617	Bob Hamelin	.10
618	Raul Mondesi	.10
619	Tyrone Hill	.10
620	Darrin Fletcher	.10
621	Mike Trombley	.10
622	Jeromy Burnitz	.10
623	Bernie Williams	.10
624	Mike Farmer **RC**	.10
625	Rickey Henderson	1.50
626	Carlos Garcia	.10
627	Jeff Darwin **RC**	.10
628	Todd Zeile	.10
629	Benji Gil	.10
630	Tony Gwynn	2.00
631	Aaron Small **RC**	.10
632	Joe Rosselli **RC**	.10
633	Mike Mussina	1.00
634	Ryan Klesko	.10
635	Roger Clemens	2.50
636	Sammy Sosa	2.00
637	Orlando Palmeiro **RC**	.10
638	Willie Greene	.10
639	George Bell	.10
640	Garvin Alston **RC**	.10
641	Pete Janicki **RC**	.10
642	Chris Sheff **RC**	.10
643	Felipe Lira **RC**	.10
644	Roberto Petagine	.10
645	Wally Joyner	.10
646	Mike Piazza	3.00
647	Jaime Navarro	.10
648	Jeff Hartsock **RC**	.10
649	David McCarty	.10
650	Bobby Jones	.10
651	Mark Hutton	.10
652	Kyle Abbott	.10
653	Steve Cox **RC**	.10
654	Jeff King	.10
655	Norm Charlton	.10
656	Mike Gulan **RC**	.10
657	Julio Franco	.10
658	Cameron Cairncross **RC**	.10
659	John Olerud	.10
660	Salomon Torres	.10
661	Brad Pennington	.10
662	Melvin Nieves	.10
663	Ivan Calderon	.10
664	Turk Wendell	.10
665	Chris Pritchett	.10
666	Reggie Sanders	.10
667	Robin Ventura	.10
668	Joe Girardi	.10
669	Manny Ramirez	1.50
670	Jeff Conine	.10
671	Greg Gohr	.10
672	Andujar Cedeno	.10
673	Les Norman **RC**	.10
674	Mike James **RC**	.10
675	Marshall Boze **RC**	.10
676	B.J. Wallace	.10
677	Kent Hrbek	.10
678	Jack Voight	.10
679	Brien Taylor	.10
680	Curt Schilling	.35
681	Todd Van Poppel	.10
682	Kevin Young	.10
683	Tommy Adams	.10
684	Bernard Gilkey	.10
685	Kevin Brown	.10
686	Fred McGriff	.10
687	Pat Borders	.10
688	Kirt Manwaring	.10
689	Sid Bream	.10
690	John Valentin	.10
691	Steve Olsen **RC**	.10
692	Roberto Mejia **RC**	.10
693	Carlos Delgado (Foil)	.50
694	Steve Gibralter **RC** (Foil)	.10
695	Gary Mota (Foil)	.10
696	Jose Malave **RC** (Foil)	.10
697	Larry Sutton **RC** (Foil)	.10
698	Dan Frye **RC** (Foil)	.10
699	Tim Clark **RC** (Foil)	.10
700	Brian Rupp **RC** (Foil)	.10
701	Felipe Alou, Moises Alou (Foil)	.10
702	Bobby Bonds, Barry Bonds (Foil)	1.00
703	Ken Griffey Sr., Ken Griffey Jr. (Foil)	1.00
704	Hal McRae, Brian McRae (Foil)	.10
705	Checklist 1	.10
706	Checklist 2	.10
707	Checklist 3	.10
708	Checklist 4	.10

1994 Bowman Previews

Bowman Preview cards were randomly inserted into Stadium Club 1994 Baseball Series II at a rate of one every 24 packs. This 10-card set featured several proven major league stars, as well as minor league players. Card number 10, James Mouton, is designed as a special MVP foil card.

		NM/M
Complete Set (10):		7.00
Common Player:		.50
1	Frank Thomas	1.50
2	Mike Piazza	3.00
3	Albert Belle	.50
4	Javier Lopez	.50
5	Cliff Floyd	.50
6	Alex Gonzalez	.50
7	Ricky Bottalico	.50
8	Tony Clark	.50
9	Mac Suzuki	.50
10	James Mouton (Foil)	.50

1994 Bowman

Bowman baseball for 1994 was a 682-card set issued all in one series, including a 52-card foil subset. There were 11 regular cards plus one foil card in each pack, with a suggested retail price of $2. The cards have a full-bleed design, with gold-foil stamping on every card. As in the past, the set includes numerous rookies and prospects, along with the game's biggest stars. The 52-card foil subset features 28 Top Prospects, with the player's team logo in the background; 17 Minor League MVPs, with a stadium in the background; and seven Diamonds in the Rough, with, you guessed it, a diamond as a backdrop.

		NM/M
Complete Set (682):		40.00
Common Player:		.10
Pack (12):		1.50
Wax Box (24):		30.00
1	Joe Carter	.10
2	Marcus Moore	.10
3	Doug Creek **RC**	.10
4	Pedro Martinez	1.50
5	Ken Griffey Jr.	3.00
6	Greg Swindell	.10
7	J.J. Johnson	.10
8	Homer Bush **RC**	.10
9	Arquimedez Pozo **RC**	.10
10	Bryan Harvey	.10
11	J.T. Snow	.10
12	Alan Benes **RC**	.10
13	Chad Kreuter	.10
14	Eric Karros	.10
15	Frank Thomas	1.50
16	Bret Saberhagen	.10
17	Terrell Lowery	.10
18	Rod Bolton	.10
19	Harold Baines	.10
20	Matt Walbeck	.10
21	Tom Glavine	.30
22	Todd Jones	.10
23	Alberto Castillo	.10
24	Ruben Sierra	.10
25	Don Mattingly	2.50
26	Mike Morgan	.10
27	Jim Musselwhite **RC**	.10
28	Matt Brunson **RC**	.10
29	Adam Meinershagen **RC**	.10
30	Joe Girardi	.10
31	Shane Halter	.10
32	Jose Paniagua **RC**	.10
33	Paul Perkins	.10
34	John Hudek **RC**	.10
35	Frank Viola	.10
36	David Lamb **RC**	.10
37	Marshall Boze	.10
38	Jorge Posada **RC**	6.00
39	Brian Anderson **RC**	.25
40	Mark Whiten	.10
41	Sean Bergman	.10
42	Jose Parra **RC**	.10
43	Mike Robertson	.10
44	Pete Walker **RC**	.10
45	Juan Gonzalez	.75
46	Cleveland Ladell **RC**	.10
47	Mark Smith	.10
48	Kevin Jarvis **RC**	.10
49	Amaury Telemaco **RC**	.10
50	Andy Van Slyke	.10
51	Rikkert Faneyte **RC**	.10
52	Curtis Shaw	.10
53	Matt Drews **RC**	.10
54	Wilson Alvarez	.10
55	Manny Ramirez	1.50
56	Bobby Munoz	.10
57	Ed Sprague	.10
58	Jamey Wright **RC**	.10
59	Jeff Montgomery	.10
60	Kirk Rueter	.10
61	Edgar Martinez	.10
62	Luis Gonzalez	.10
63	Tim Vanegmond **RC**	.10
64	Bip Roberts	.10
65	John Jaha	.10
66	Chuck Carr	.10
67	Chuck Finley	.10
68	Aaron Holbert	.10
69	Cecil Fielder	.10
70	Tom Engle **RC**	.10
71	Ron Karkovice	.10
72	Joe Orsulak	.10
73	Duff Brumley **RC**	.10
74	Craig Clayton **RC**	.10
75	Cal Ripken, Jr.	4.00
76	Brad Fullmer **RC**	.50
77	Tony Tarasco	.10
78	Terry Farrar **RC**	.10
79	Matt Williams	.10
80	Rickey Henderson	1.50
81	Terry Mulholland	.10
82	Sammy Sosa	2.00
83	Paul Sorrento	.10
84	Pete Incaviglia	.10
85	Darren Hall **RC**	.10
86	Scott Klingenbeck	.10
87	Dario Perez **RC**	.10
88	Ugueth Urbina	.10
89	Dave Vanhof **RC**	.10
90	Domingo Jean	.10
91	Otis Nixon	.10
92	Andres Berumen	.10
93	Jose Valentin	.10
94	Edgar Renteria **RC**	5.00
95	Chris Turner	.10
96	Ray Lankford	.10
97	Danny Bautista	.10
98	Chan Ho Park **RC**	1.00
99	Glenn DiSarcina **RC**	.10
100	Butch Huskey	.10
101	Ivan Rodriguez	1.00
102	Johnny Ruffin	.10
103	Alex Ochoa	.10
104	Torii Hunter **RC**	6.00
105	Ryan Klesko	.10
106	Jay Bell	.10
107	Kurt Peltzer **RC**	.10
108	Miguel Jimenez	.10
109	Russ Davis	.10
110	Derek Wallace	.10
111	Keith Lockhart **RC**	.10
112	Mike Lieberthal	.10
113	Dave Stewart	.10
114	Tom Schmidt	.10
115	Brian McRae	.10
116	Moises Alou	.10
117	Dave Fleming	.10
118	Jeff Bagwell	1.50
119	Luis Ortiz	.10
120	Tony Gwynn	2.00
121	Jaime Navarro	.10
122	Benny Santiago	.10
123	Darrel Whitmore	.10
124	John Mabry **RC**	.15
125	Mickey Tettleton	.10
126	Tom Candiotti	.10
127	Tim Raines	.10
128	Bobby Bonilla	.10
129	John Dettmer	.10
130	Hector Carrasco	.10
131	Chris Hoiles	.10
132	Rick Aguilera	.10
133	Dave Justice	.10
134	Esteban Loaiza **RC**	1.50
135	Barry Bonds	4.00
136	Bob Welch	.10
137	Mike Stanley	.10
138	Roberto Hernandez	.10
139	Sandy Alomar	.10
140	Darren Daulton	.10
141	Angel Martinez **RC**	.10
142	Howard Johnson	.10
143	Bob Hamelin	.10
144	J.J. Thobe **RC**	.10
145	Roger Salkeld	.10
146	Orlando Miller	.10
147	Dmitri Young	.10
148	Tim Hyers **RC**	.10
149	Mark Loretta **RC**	3.00
150	Chris Hammond	.10
151	Joel Moore **RC**	.10
152	Todd Zeile	.10
153	Wil Cordero	.10
154	Chris Smith	.10
155	James Baldwin	.10
156	Edgardo Alfonzo **RC**	1.00
157	Kym Ashworth **RC**	.10
158	Paul Bako **RC**	.10
159	Rick Krivda **RC**	.10
160	Pat Mahomes	.10
161	Damon Hollins	.10
162	Felix Martinez **RC**	.10
163	Jason Myers **RC**	.10
164	Izzy Molina **RC**	.10
165	Brien Taylor	.10
166	Kevin Orie **RC**	.10
167	Casey Whitten **RC**	.10
168	Tony Longmire	.10
169	John Olerud	.10
170	Mark Thompson	.10
171	Jorge Fabregas	.10
172	John Wetteland	.10
173	Dan Wilson	.10
174	Doug Drabek	.10
175	Jeffrey McNeely	.10
176	Melvin Nieves	.10
177	Doug Glanville **RC**	.10
178	Javier De La Hoya **RC**	.10
179	Chad Curtis	.10
180	Brian Barber	.10
181	Mike Henneman	.10
182	Jose Offerman	.10
183	Robert Ellis **RC**	.10
184	John Franco	.10
185	Benji Gil	.10
186	Hal Morris	.10
187	Chris Sabo	.10
188	Blaise Ilsley **RC**	.10
189	Steve Avery	.10
190	Rick White **RC**	.10
191	Rod Beck	.10
(192)	Mark McGwire (No card number.)	3.00
193	Jim Abbott	.10
194	Randy Myers	.10
195	Kenny Lofton	.10
196	Mariano Duncan	.10
197	Lee Daniels **RC**	.10
198	Armando Reynoso	.10
199	Joe Randa	.10
200	Cliff Floyd	.10
201	Tim Harkrider **RC**	.10
202	Kevin Gallaher **RC**	.10
203	Scott Cooper	.10
204	Phil Stidham **RC**	.10
205	Jeff D'Amico **RC**	.25
206	Matt Whisenant	.10
207	De Shawn Warren	.10
208	Rene Arocha	.10
209	Tony Clark **RC**	.50
210	Jason Jacome **RC**	.10
211	Scott Christman **RC**	.10
212	Bill Pulsipher	.10
213	Dean Palmer	.10
214	Chad Mottola	.10
215	Manny Alexander	.10
216	Rich Becker	.10
217	Andre King **RC**	.10
218	Carlos Garcia	.10
219	Ron Pezzoni **RC**	.10
220	Steve Karsay	.10
221	Jose Musset **RC**	.10
222	Karl Rhodes	.10
223	Frank Cimorelli **RC**	.10
224	Kevin Jordan **RC**	.10
225	Duane Ward	.10
226	John Burke	.10
227	Mike MacFarlane	.10
228	Mike Lansing	.10
229	Chuck Knoblauch	.10
230	Ken Caminiti	.10
231	Gar Finnvold **RC**	.10
232	Derrek Lee **RC**	12.00
233	Brady Anderson	.10
234	Vic Darensbourg **RC**	.10
235	Mark Langston	.10
236	T.J. Mathews **RC**	.10
237	Lou Whitaker	.10
238	Roger Cedeno	.10
239	Alex Fernandez	.10
240	Ryan Thompson	.10
241	Kerry Lacy **RC**	.10
242	Reggie Sanders	.10
243	Brad Pennington	.10
244	Bryan Eversgerd **RC**	.10
245	Greg Maddux	2.00
246	Jason Kendall	.10
247	J.R. Phillips	.10
248	Bobby Witt	.10
249	Paul O'Neill	.10
250	Ryne Sandberg	2.00
251	Charles Nagy	.10
252	Kevin Stocker	.10
253	Shawn Green	.30
254	Charlie Hayes	.10
255	Donnie Elliott	.10
256	Rob Fitzpatrick **RC**	.10
257	Tim Davis	.10
258	James Mouton	.10
259	Mike Greenwell	.10
260	Ray McDavid	.10
261	Mike Kelly	.10
262	Andy Larkin **RC**	.10
(263)	Marquis Riley (No card number.)	.10
264	Bob Tewksbury	.10
265	Brian Edmondson	.10
266	Eduardo Lantigua **RC**	.10
267	Brandon Wilson	.10
268	Mike Welch	.10
269	Tom Henke	.10
270	Calvin Reese	.10
271	Gregg Zaun **RC**	.10
272	Todd Ritchie	.10
273	Javier Lopez	.10
274	Kevin Young	.10
275	Kirt Manwaring	.10
276	Bill Taylor **RC**	.10
277	Robert Eenhoorn	.10
278	Jessie Hollins	.10
279	Julian Tavarez **RC**	.10
280	Gene Schall	.10
281	Paul Molitor	1.50
282	Neifi Perez **RC**	.10
283	Greg Gagne	.10
284	Marquis Grissom	.10
285	Randy Johnson	1.50
286	Pete Harnisch	.10
287	Joel Bennett **RC**	.10
288	Derek Bell	.10

289 Darryl Hamilton .10
290 Gary Sheffield .40
291 Eduardo Perez .10
292 Basil Shabazz .10
293 Eric Davis .10
294 Pedro Astacio .10
295 Robin Ventura .10
296 Jeff Kent .10
297 Rick Helling .10
298 Joe Oliver .10
299 Lee Smith .10
300 Dave Winfield 1.50
301 Deion Sanders .10
302 Ravelo Manzanillo **RC** .10
303 Mark Portugal .10
304 Brent Gates .10
305 Wade Boggs 2.00
306 Rick Wilkins .10
307 Carlos Baerga .10
308 Curt Schilling .35
309 Shannon Stewart .10
310 Darren Holmes .10
311 Robert Toth **RC** .10
312 Gabe White .10
313 Mac Suzuki **RC** .10
314 Alvin Morman **RC** .10
315 Mo Vaughn .10
316 Bryce Florie **RC** .10
317 Gabby Martinez **RC** .10
318 Carl Everett .10
319 Kerwin Moore .10
320 Tom Pagnozzi .10
321 Chris Gomez .10
322 Todd Williams .10
323 Pat Hentgen .10
324 Kirk Presley **RC** .10
325 Kevin Brown .10
326 Jason Isringhausen **RC** 1.50
327 Rick Forney **RC** .10
328 Carlos Pulido **RC** .10
329 Terrell Wade **RC** .10
330 Al Martin .10
331 Dan Carlson **RC** .10
332 Mark Acre **RC** .10
333 Sterling Hitchcock .10
334 Jon Ratliff **RC** .10
335 Alex Ramirez **RC** .10
336 Phil Geisler **RC** .10
337 Eddie Zambrano **RC** (Foil) .10
338 Jim Thome (Foil) .60
339 James Mouton (Foil) .10
340 Cliff Floyd (Foil) .10
341 Carlos Delgado (Foil) .40
342 Roberto Petagine (Foil) .10
343 Tim Clark (Foil) .10
344 Bubba Smith (Foil) .10
345 Randy Curtis **RC** (Foil) .10
346 Joe Biasucci **RC** (Foil) .10
347 D.J. Boston **RC** (Foil) .10
348 Ruben Rivera **RC** (Foil) .75
349 Bryan Link **RC** (Foil) .10
350 Mike Bell **RC** (Foil) .25
351 Marty Watson **RC** (Foil) .10
352 Jason Myers (Foil) .10
353 Chipper Jones (Foil) 1.25
354 Brooks Kieschnick (Foil) .10
355 Calvin Reese (Foil) .10
356 John Burke (Foil) .10
357 Kurt Miller (Foil) .10
358 Orlando Miller (Foil) .10
359 Todd Hollandsworth (Foil) .10
360 Rondell White (Foil) .10
361 Bill Pulsipher (Foil) .10
362 Tyler Green (Foil) .10
363 Midre Cummings (Foil) .10
364 Brian Barber (Foil) .10
365 Melvin Nieves (Foil) .10
366 Salomon Torres (Foil) .10
367 Alex Ochoa (Foil) .10
368 Frank Rodriguez (Foil) .10
369 Brian Anderson (Foil) .10
370 James Baldwin (Foil) .10
371 Manny Ramirez (Foil) .75
372 Justin Thompson (Foil) .10
373 Johnny Damon (Foil) .50
374 Jeff D'Amico (Foil) .10
375 Rich Becker (Foil) .10
376 Derek Jeter (Foil) 3.00
377 Steve Karsay (Foil) .10
378 Mac Suzuki (Foil) .10
379 Benji Gil (Foil) .10
380 Alex Gonzalez (Foil) .10
381 Jason Bere (Foil) .10
382 Brett Butler (Foil) .10
383 Jeff Conine (Foil) .10
384 Darren Daulton (Foil) .10
385 Jeff Kent (Foil) .10
386 Don Mattingly (Foil) 1.50
387 Mike Piazza (Foil) 2.00
388 Ryne Sandberg (Foil) 1.25
389 Rich Amaral .10
390 Craig Biggio .10
391 Jeff Suppan **RC** .35
392 Andy Benes .10
393 Cal Eldred .10
394 Jeff Conine .10
395 Tim Salmon .10
396 Ray Suplee **RC** .10
397 Tony Phillips .10
398 Ramon Martinez .10
399 Julio Franco .10
400 Dwight Gooden .10
401 Kevin Lomon **RC** .10
402 Jose Rijo .10
403 Mike Devereaux .10
404 Mike Zolecki **RC** .10
405 Fred McGriff .10
406 Danny Clyburn .10
407 Robby Thompson .10
408 Terry Steinbach .10
409 Luis Polonia .10
410 Mark Grace .10
411 Albert Belle .10
412 John Kruk .10
413 Scott Spiezio **RC** .25
414 Ellis Burks .10
415 Joe Vitiello .10
416 Tim Costo .10
417 Marc Newfield .10
418 Oscar Henriquez **RC** .10
419 Matt Perisho **RC** .10
420 Julio Bruno .10
421 Kenny Felder .10
422 Tyler Green .10
423 Jim Edmonds .10
424 Ozzie Smith 2.00
425 Rick Greene .10
426 Todd Hollandsworth .10
427 Eddie Pearson **RC** .10
428 Quilvio Veras .10
429 Kenny Rogers .10
430 Willie Greene .10
431 Vaughn Eshelman .10
432 Pat Meares .10
433 Jermaine Dye **RC** 8.00
434 Steve Cooke .10
435 Bill Swift .10
436 Fausto Cruz **RC** .10
437 Mark Hutton .10
438 Brooks Kieschnick **RC** .10
439 Yorkis Perez .10
440 Len Dykstra .10
441 Pat Borders .10
442 Doug Walls **RC** .10
443 Wally Joyner .10
444 Ken Hill .10
445 Eric Anthony .10
446 Mitch Williams .10
447 Cory Bailey **RC** .10
448 Dave Staton .10
449 Greg Vaughn .10
450 Dave Magadan .10
451 Chili Davis .10
452 Gerald Santos **RC** .10
453 Joe Perona .10
454 Delino DeShields .10
455 Jack McDowell .10
456 Todd Hundley .10
457 Ritchie Moody .10
458 Bret Boone .10
459 Ben McDonald .10
460 Kirby Puckett 2.00
461 Gregg Olson .10
462 Rich Aude **RC** .10
463 John Burkett .10
464 Troy Neel .10
465 Jimmy Key .10
466 Ozzie Timmons .10
467 Eddie Murray 1.50
468 Mark Tranberg **RC** .10
469 Alex Gonzalez .10
470 David Nied .10
471 Barry Larkin .10
472 Brian Looney **RC** .10
473 Shawn Estes .10
474 A.J. Sager **RC** .10
475 Roger Clemens 2.50
476 Vince Moore .10
477 Scott Karl **RC** .10
478 Kurt Miller .10
479 Garret Anderson .10
480 Allen Watson .10
481 Jose Lima **RC** .10
482 Rick Gorecki .10
483 Jimmy Hurst **RC** .10
484 Preston Wilson .10
485 Will Clark .10
486 Mike Ferry **RC** .10
487 Curtis Goodwin **RC** .10
488 Mike Myers .10
489 Chipper Jones 2.00
490 Jeff King .10
491 Bill Van Landingham **RC** .10
492 Carlos Reyes **RC** .10
493 Andy Pettitte .30
494 Brant Brown .10
495 Daron Kirkreit .10
496 Ricky Bottalico **RC** .25
497 Devon White .10
498 Jason Johnson **RC** .10
499 Vince Coleman .10
500 Larry Walker .10
501 Bobby Ayala .10
502 Steve Finley .10
503 Scott Fletcher .10
504 Brad Ausmus .10
505 Scott Talanoa **RC** .10
506 Orestes Destrade .10
507 Gary DiSarcina .10
508 Willie Smith **RC** .10
509 Alan Trammell .10
510 Mike Piazza 3.00
511 Ozzie Guillen .10
512 Jeromy Burnitz .10
513 Darren Oliver .10
514 Kevin Mitchell .10
515 Rafael Palmeiro 1.00
516 David McCarty .10
517 Jeff Blauser .10
518 Trey Beamon .10
519 Royce Clayton .10
520 Dennis Eckersley 1.00
521 Bernie Williams .10
522 Steve Buechele .10
523 Denny Martinez .10
524 Dave Hollins .10
525 Joey Hamilton .10
526 Andres Galarraga .10
527 Jeff Granger .10
528 Joey Eischen .10
529 Desi Relaford .10
530 Roberto Petagine .10
531 Andre Dawson .30
532 Ray Holbert .10
533 Duane Singleton .10
534 Kurt Abbott **RC** .20
535 Bo Jackson .20
536 Gregg Jefferies .10
537 David Mysel .10
538 Raul Mondesi .10
539 Chris Snopek .10
540 Brook Fordyce .10
541 Ron Frazier **RC** .10
542 Brian Koelling .10
543 Jimmy Haynes .10
544 Marty Cordova .10
545 Jason Green **RC** .10
546 Orlando Merced .10
547 Lou Pote **RC** .10
548 Todd Van Poppel .10
549 Pat Kelly .10
550 Turk Wendell .10
551 Herb Perry **RC** .10
552 Ryan Karp **RC** .10
553 Juan Guzman .10
554 Bryan Rekar **RC** .10
555 Kevin Appier .10
556 Chris Schwab **RC** .10
557 Jay Buhner .10
558 Andujar Cedeno .10
559 Ryan McGuire **RC** .10
560 Ricky Gutierrez .10
561 Keith Kimsey **RC** .10
562 Tim Clark .10
563 Damion Easley .10
564 Clint Davis **RC** .10
565 Mike Moore .10
566 Orel Hershiser .10
567 Jason Bere .10
568 Kevin McReynolds .10
569 Leland Macon **RC** .10
570 John Courtright **RC** .10
571 Sid Fernandez .10
572 Chad Roper .10
573 Terry Pendleton .10
574 Danny Miceli .10
575 Joe Rosselli .10
576 Mike Bordick .10
577 Danny Tartabull .10
578 Jose Guzman .10
579 Omar Vizquel .10
580 Tommy Greene .10
581 Paul Spoljaric .10
582 Walt Weiss .10
583 Oscar Jimenez **RC** .10
584 Rod Henderson .10
585 Derek Lowe .10
586 Richard Hidalgo **RC** 1.00
587 Shayne Bennett **RC** .10
588 Tim Belk **RC** .10
589 Matt Mieske .10
590 Nigel Wilson .10
591 Jeff Knox **RC** .10
592 Bernard Gilkey .10
593 David Cone .10
594 Paul LoDuca **RC** 5.00
595 Scott Ruffcorn .10
596 Chris Roberts .10
597 Oscar Munoz **RC** .10
598 Scott Sullivan **RC** .10
599 Matt Jarvis **RC** .10
600 Jose Canseco .35
601 Tony Graffanino **RC** .10
602 Don Slaught .10
603 Brett King **RC** .10
604 Jose Herrera **RC** .10
605 Melido Perez .10
606 Mike Hubbard **RC** .10
607 Chad Ogea .10
608 Wayne Gomes **RC** .10
609 Roberto Alomar .25
610 Angel Echevarria **RC** .10
611 Jose Lind .10
612 Darrin Fletcher .10
613 Chris Bosio .10
614 Darryl Kile .10
615 Frank Rodriguez .10
616 Phil Plantier .10
617 Pat Listach .10
618 Charlie Hough .10
619 Ryan Hancock **RC** .10
620 Darrel Deak **RC** .10
621 Travis Fryman .10
622 Brett Butler .10
623 Lance Johnson .10
624 Pete Smith .10
625 James Hurst .10
626 Roberto Kelly .10
627 Mike Mussina .50
628 Kevin Tapani .10
629 John Smoltz .10
630 Midre Cummings .10
631 Salomon Torres .10
632 Willie Adams .10
633 Derek Jeter 4.00
634 Steve Trachsel .10
635 Albie Lopez .10
636 Jason Moler .10
637 Carlos Delgado .50
638 Roberto Mejia .10
639 Darren Burton .10
640 B.J. Wallace .10
641 Brad Clontz **RC** .10
642 Billy Wagner **RC** 1.00
643 Aaron Sele .10
644 Cameron Cairncross .10
645 Brian Harper .10
(646) Marc Valdes (No card number.) .10
647 Mark Ratekin .10
648 Terry Bradshaw **RC** .10
649 Justin Thompson .10
650 Mike Busch **RC** .10
651 Joe Hall **RC** .10
652 Bobby Jones .10
653 Kelly Stinnett **RC** .10
654 Rod Steph **RC** .10
655 Jay Powell **RC** .10
(656) Keith Garagozzo **RC** (No card number.) .10
657 Todd Dunn .10
658 Charles Peterson **RC** .10
659 Darren Lewis .10
660 John Wasdin **RC** .10
661 Tate Seefried **RC** .10
662 Hector Trinidad **RC** .10
663 John Carter **RC** .10
664 Larry Mitchell .10
665 David Catlett **RC** .10
666 Dante Bichette .10
667 Felix Jose .10
668 Rondell White .10
669 Tino Martinez .10
670 Brian Hunter .10
671 Jose Malave .10
672 Archi Cianfrocco .10
673 Mike Matheny **RC** .15
674 Bret Barberie .10
675 Andrew Lorraine **RC** .10
676 Brian Jordan .10
677 Tim Belcher .10
678 Antonio Osuna **RC** .10
679 Checklist I .10
680 Checklist II .10
681 Checklist III .10
682 Checklist IV .10

Superstar Sampler

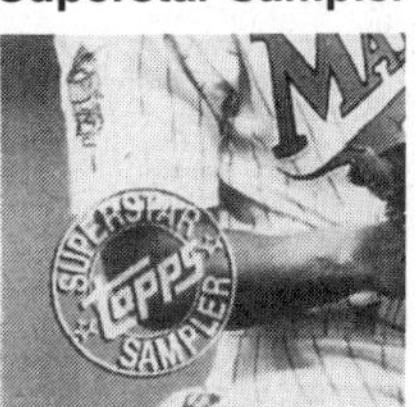

As an insert in 1994 Topps retail factory sets, three-card cello packs of "Superstar Sampler" cards were included. The packs contained special versions of the same player's 1994 Bowman, Finest and Stadium Club cards. Forty-five of the game's top stars are represented in the issue. The Bowman cards in this issue are identical to the cards in the regular set except for the appearance of a round "Topps Superstar Sampler" logo on back.

NM/M
Complete Set (45): 275.00
Common Player: 2.00
1 Joe Carter 2.00
5 Ken Griffey Jr. 20.00
15 Frank Thomas 10.00
21 Tom Glavine 3.00
25 Don Mattingly 17.50
45 Juan Gonzalez 6.00
50 Andy Van Slyke 2.00
55 Manny Ramirez 10.00
69 Cecil Fielder 2.00
75 Cal Ripken Jr. 35.00
79 Matt Williams 2.00
118 Jeff Bagwell 10.00
120 Tony Gwynn 15.00
128 Bobby Bonilla 2.00
133 Dave Justice 2.00
135 Barry Bonds 35.00
140 Darren Daulton 2.00
169 John Olerud 2.00
200 Cliff Floyd 2.00
245 Greg Maddux 15.00
250 Ryne Sandberg 15.00
281 Paul Molitor 10.00
284 Marquis Grissom 2.00
285 Randy Johnson 10.00
290 Gary Sheffield 4.00
307 Carlos Baerga 2.00
315 Mo Vaughn 2.00
395 Tim Salmon 2.00
405 Fred McGriff 2.00
410 Mark Grace 2.00
411 Albert Belle 2.00
440 Len Dykstra 2.00
455 Jack McDowell 2.00
460 Kirby Puckett 15.00
471 Barry Larkin 2.00
475 Roger Clemens 17.50
485 Will Clark 2.00
500 Larry Walker 2.00
510 Mike Piazza 20.00
515 Rafael Palmeiro 9.00
526 Andres Galarraga 2.00
536 Gregg Jefferies 2.00
538 Raul Mondesi 2.00
600 Jose Canseco 6.00
609 Roberto Alomar 4.00

1994 Bowman's Best

The debut Bowman's Best consists of 90 red cards (largely veterans), 90 blue cards (rookies and young players) and 20 Mirror Images combining veteran and young stars by position. Utilizing Topps Finest technology, cards are full-color front and back with high-gloss surfaces. Cards were sold in eight-card foil packs with one Mirror Image card in each pack. A 200-card parallel version officially called "Special Effects," uses Topps refractor technology. Red and Blue sets each contain cards numbered 1-90, while the Mirror Image cards are numbered 91-110.

NM/M
Complete Set (200): 30.00
Red Set (90): 10.00
Blue Set (90): 20.00
Common Player: .15
Pack (8): 1.50
Wax Box (24): 30.00
1 Paul Molitor 1.50
2 Eddie Murray 1.50
3 Ozzie Smith 2.00
4 Rickey Henderson 1.50
5 Lee Smith .15
6 Dave Winfield 1.50
7 Roberto Alomar .30
8 Matt Williams .15
9 Mark Grace .15
10 Lance Johnson .15
11 Darren Daulton .15
12 Tom Glavine .35
13 Gary Sheffield .40
14 Rod Beck .15
15 Fred McGriff .15
16 Joe Carter .15
17 Dante Bichette .15
18 Danny Tartabull .15
19 Juan Gonzalez .75
20 Steve Avery .15
21 John Wetteland .15
22 Ben McDonald .15
23 Jack McDowell .15
24 Jose Canseco .65
25 Tim Salmon .15
26 Wilson Alvarez .15
27 Gregg Jefferies .15
28 John Burkett .15
29 Greg Vaughn .15
30 Robin Ventura .15
31 Paul O'Neill .15
32 Cecil Fielder .15
33 Kevin Mitchell .15
34 Jeff Conine .15
35 Carlos Baerga .15
36 Greg Maddux 2.00
37 Roger Clemens 2.25
38 Deion Sanders .15
39 Delino DeShields .15
40 Ken Griffey Jr. 2.50
41 Albert Belle 1.50
42 Wade Boggs 2.00
43 Andres Galarraga .15
44 Aaron Sele .15
45 Don Mattingly 2.25
46 David Cone .15
47 Lenny Dykstra .15
48 Brett Butler .15
49 Bill Swift .15
50 Bobby Bonilla .15
51 Rafael Palmeiro 1.25
52 Moises Alou .15
53 Jeff Bagwell 1.50
54 Mike Mussina .50
55 Frank Thomas 1.50
56 Jose Rijo .15
57 Ruben Sierra .15
58 Randy Myers .15
59 Barry Bonds 4.00
60 Jimmy Key .15
61 Travis Fryman .15
62 John Olerud .15
63 David Justice .15
64 Ray Lankford .15
65 Bob Tewksbury .15
66 Chuck Carr .15
67 Jay Buhner .15
68 Kenny Lofton .15
69 Marquis Grissom .15
70 Sammy Sosa 2.00
71 Cal Ripken Jr. 4.00
72 Ellis Burks .15
73 Jeff Montgomery .15
74 Julio Franco .15
75 Kirby Puckett 2.00
76 Larry Walker .15
77 Andy Van Slyke .15
78 Tony Gwynn 2.00
79 Will Clark .15
80 Mo Vaughn .15
81 Mike Piazza 2.50
82 James Mouton .15
83 Carlos Delgado .60
84 Ryan Klesko .15
85 Javy Lopez .15
86 Raul Mondesi .15
87 Cliff Floyd .15
88 Manny Ramirez 1.50
89 Hector Carrasco .15
90 Jeff Granger .15
1 Chipper Jones 2.00
2 Derek Jeter 4.00
3 Bill Pulsipher .15
4 James Baldwin .15
5 Brooks Kieschnick **RC** .50
6 Justin Thompson .15
7 Midre Cummings .15
8 Joey Hamilton .15
9 Calvin Reese .15
10 Brian Barber .15
11 John Burke .15
12 De Shawn Warren .15
13 Edgardo Alfonzo **RC** .75
14 Eddie Pearson **RC** .15
15 Jimmy Haynes .15
16 Danny Bautista .15
17 Roger Cedeno .15
18 Jon Lieber .15
19 Billy Wagner **RC** .75
20 Tate Seefried **RC** .15
21 Chad Mottola .15
22 Jose Malave .15
23 Terrell Wade **RC** .15
24 Shane Andrews .15
25 Chan Ho Park **RC** .75
26 Kirk Presley **RC** .15
27 Robbie Beckett .15
28 Orlando Miller .15
29 Jorge Posada **RC** 8.00
30 Frank Rodriguez .15
31 Brian Hunter .15
32 Billy Ashley .15
33 Rondell White .15
34 John Roper .15
35 Marc Valdes .15
36 Scott Ruffcorn .15
37 Rod Henderson .15
38 Curt Goodwin .15
39 Russ Davis .15
40 Rick Gorecki .15
41 Johnny Damon .60
42 Roberto Petagine .15
43 Chris Snopek .15
44 Mark Acre .15
45 Todd Hollandsworth .15
46 Shawn Green .35
47 John Carter .15
48 Jim Pittsley .15
49 John Wasdin **RC** .15
50 D.J. Boston .15
51 Tim Clark .15
52 Alex Ochoa .15
53 Chad Roper .15
54 Mike Kelly .15
55 Brad Fullmer **RC** .50
56 Carl Everett .15
57 Tim Belk **RC** .15
58 Jimmy Hurst **RC** .15
59 Mac Suzuki **RC** .15
60 Michael Moore .15
61 Alan Benes **RC** .15
62 Tony Clark **RC** 1.00
63 Edgar Renteria **RC** 8.00
64 Trey Beamon .15
65 LaTroy Hawkins **RC** .15
66 Wayne Gomes **RC** .15
67 Ray McDavid .15
68 John Dettmer .15
69 Willie Greene .15
70 Dave Stevens .15
71 Kevin Orie **RC** .15
72 Chad Ogea .15
73 Ben Van Ryn .15
74 Kym Ashworth .15
75 Dmitri Young .15
76 Herb Perry .15
77 Joey Eischen .15
78 Arquimedez Pozo **RC** .15
79 Ugueth Urbina .15
80 Keith Williams .15

81 John Frascatore **RC** .15
82 Garey Ingram .15
83 Aaron Small .15
84 Olmedo Saenz **RC** .15
85 Jesus Tavarez .15
86 Jose Silva **RC** .15
87 Gerald Witasick Jr. **RC** .15
88 Jay Maldonado .15
89 Keith Heberling .15
90 Rusty Greer **RC** .50
91 Frank Thomas, Kevin Young .60
92 Fred McGriff, Brooks Kieschnick **RC** .15
93 Matt Williams, Shane Andrews .15
94 Cal Ripken Jr., Kevin Orie **RC** 1.50
95 Barry Larkin, Derek Jeter 1.50
96 Ken Griffey Jr., Johnny Damon 1.50
97 Barry Bonds, Rondell White 1.50
98 Albert Belle, Jimmy Hurst **RC** .15
99 Raul Mondesi, Ruben Rivera **RC** .15
100 Roger Clemens, Scott Ruffcorn 1.00
101 Greg Maddux, John Wasdin **RC** .75
102 Tim Salmon, Chad Mottola .15
103 Carlos Baerga, Arquimedez Pozo **RC** .15
104 Mike Piazza, Bobby Hughes 1.00
105 Carlos Delgado, Melvin Nieves .50
106 Javy Lopez, Jorge Posada **RC** 2.00
107 Manny Ramirez, Jose Malave .65
108 Travis Fryman, Chipper Jones .75
109 Steve Avery, Bill Pulsipher .15
110 John Olerud, Shawn Green .50

Refractors

This 200-card parallel set, officially titled "Special Effects," uses Topps' refractor technology. The refractors were packed at the rate of three per wax box of Bowman's Best, but are very difficult to differentiate from the regular high-tech cards.

Superstars: 8-10X
Stars: 4-8X

1995 Bowman

Large numbers of rookie cards and a lengthy run of etched-foil cards distinguishes the 1995 Bowman set. The set's basic cards share a design with a large color photo flanked at left by a severely horizontally compressed mirror image in green, and at bottom by a similar version in brown. Most of the bottom image is covered by the player's last name printed in silver (cards #1-220, rookies) or gold (cards #275-439, veterans) foil. A color team logo is in the lower-left corner of all cards, and the Bowman logo is in red foil at top. In between are the foil-etched subsets of "Minor League MVPs," "1st Impressions," and "Prime Prospects." Each of these cards, seeded one per regular pack and two per jumbo, has the player photo set against a background of textured color foil, with a prismatic silver border. Each of the foil cards can also be found in a gold-toned version, in a ratio of six silver to one gold. Backs of the rookies' cards have a portrait photo at right and a scouting report at left. Veterans' cards have either a scouting report for younger players, or a chart of stats versus each team played in 1994. Backs of all the foil cards have a scouting report.

	NM/M
Complete Set (439):	150.00
Common Player:	.10
Pack (10):	6.00
Wax Box (24):	125.00
Rack Pack (15):	5.00
Rack Box (24):	125.00

1 Billy Wagner .10
2 Chris Widger .10
3 Brent Bowers .10
4 Bob Abreu **RC** 10.00
5 Lou Collier **RC** .10
6 Juan Acevedo **RC** .25
7 Jason Kelley **RC** .10
8 Brian Sackinsky .10
9 Scott Christman .10
10 Damon Hollins .10
11 Willis Otanez **RC** .10
12 Jason Ryan **RC** .10
13 Jason Giambi .75
14 Andy Taulbee **RC** .10
15 Mark Thompson .10
16 Hugo Pivaral **RC** .10
17 Brien Taylor .10
18 Antonio Osuna .10
19 Edgardo Alfonzo .10
20 Carl Everett .10
21 Matt Drews .10
22 Bartolo Colon **RC** 4.00
23 Andruw Jones **RC** 30.00
24 Robert Person **RC** .40
25 Derrek Lee .75
26 John Ambrose **RC** .10
27 Eric Knowles **RC** .10
28 Chris Roberts .10
29 Don Wengert .10
30 Marcus Jensen **RC** .10
31 Brian Barber .10
32 Kevin Brown .10
33 Benji Gil .10
34 Mike Hubbard .10
35 Bart Evans **RC** .10
36 Enrique Wilson **RC** .50
37 Brian Buchanan **RC** .10
38 Ken Ray **RC** .10
39 Micah Franklin **RC** .10
40 Ricky Otero **RC** .10
41 Jason Kendall .10
42 Jimmy Hurst .10
43 Jerry Wolak **RC** .10
44 Jayson Peterson **RC** .10
45 Allen Battle **RC** .10
46 Scott Stahoviak .10
47 Steve Schrenk **RC** .10
48 Travis Miller **RC** .25
49 Eddie Rios **RC** .10
50 Mike Hampton .10
51 Chad Frontera **RC** .10
52 Tom Evans **RC** .10
53 C.J. Nitkowski .10
54 Clay Caruthers **RC** .10
55 Shannon Stewart .10
56 Jorge Posada .50
57 Aaron Holbert .10
58 Harry Berrios **RC** .10
59 Steve Rodriguez .10
60 Shane Andrews .10
61 Will Cunnane **RC** .10
62 Richard Hidalgo .10
63 Bill Selby **RC** .10
64 Jay Cranford **RC** .10
65 Jeff Suppan .10
66 Curtis Goodwin .10
67 John Thomson **RC** .10
68 Justin Thompson .10
69 Troy Percival .10
70 Matt Wagner **RC** .10
71 Terry Bradshaw .10
72 Greg Hansell .10
73 John Burke .10
74 Jeff D'Amico .10
75 Ernie Young .10
76 Jason Bates .10
77 Chris Stynes .10
78 Cade Gaspar **RC** .10
79 Melvin Nieves .10
80 Rick Gorecki .10
81 Felix Rodriguez **RC** .50
82 Ryan Hancock .10
83 Chris Carpenter **RC** 6.00
84 Ray McDavid .10
85 Chris Wimmer .10
86 Doug Glanville .10
87 DeShawn Warren .10
88 Damian Moss **RC** .50
89 Rafael Orellano **RC** .10
90 Vladimir Guerrero **RC** 50.00
91 Raul Casanova **RC** .40
92 Karim Garcia **RC** .75
93 Bryce Florie .10
94 Kevin Orie .10
95 Ryan Nye **RC** .10
96 Matt Sachse **RC** .10
97 Ivan Arteaga **RC** .10
98 Glenn Murray .10
99 Stacy Hollins **RC** .10
100 Jim Pittsley .10
101 Craig Mattson **RC** .10
102 Neifi Perez .10
103 Keith Williams .10
104 Roger Cedeno .10
105 Tony Terry **RC** .10
106 Jose Malave .10
107 Joe Rosselli .10
108 Kevin Jordan .10
109 Sid Roberson **RC** .10
110 Alan Embree .10
111 Terrell Wade .10
112 Bob Wolcott .10
113 Carlos Perez **RC** .10
114 Mike Bovee **RC** .10
115 Tommy Davis **RC** .10
116 Jeremey Kendall **RC** .10
117 Rich Aude .10
118 Rick Huisman .10
119 Tim Belk .10
120 Edgar Renteria .25
121 Calvin Maduro **RC** .10
122 Jerry Martin **RC** .10
123 Ramon Fermin **RC** .10
124 Kimera Bartee **RC** .10
125 Mark Farris .10
126 Frank Rodriguez .10
127 Bobby Higginson **RC** .50
128 Bret Wagner .10
129 Edwin Diaz **RC** .10
130 Jimmy Haynes .10
131 Chris Weinke **RC** .75
132 Damian Jackson **RC** .10
133 Felix Martinez .10
134 Edwin Hurtado **RC** .25
135 Matt Raleigh **RC** .10
136 Paul Wilson .10
137 Ron Villone .10
138 Eric Stuckenschneider **RC** .10
139 Tate Seefried .10
140 Rey Ordonez **RC** .75
141 Eddie Pearson .10
142 Kevin Gallaher .10
143 Torii Hunter .25
144 Daron Kirkreit .10
145 Craig Wilson .10
146 Ugueth Urbina .10
147 Chris Snopek .10
148 Kym Ashworth .10
149 Wayne Gomes .10
150 Mark Loretta .10
151 Ramon Morel **RC** .10
152 Trot Nixon .20
153 Desi Relaford .10
154 Scott Sullivan .10
155 Marc Barcelo .10
156 Willie Adams .10
157 Derrick Gibson **RC** .10
158 Brian Meadows **RC** .10
159 Julian Tavarez .10
160 Bryan Rekar .10
161 Steve Gibralter .10
162 Esteban Loaiza .10
163 John Wasdin .10
164 Kirk Presley .10
165 Mariano Rivera .50
166 Andy Larkin .10
167 Sean Whiteside **RC** .10
168 Matt Apana **RC** .10
169 Shawn Senior **RC** .10
170 Scott Gentile .10
171 Quilvio Veras .10
172 Elieser Marrero **RC** 1.00
173 Mendy Lopez **RC** .10
174 Homer Bush .10
175 Brian Stephenson **RC** .10
176 Jon Nunnally .10
177 Jose Herrera .10
178 Corey Avrard **RC** .10
179 David Bell .10
180 Jason Isringhausen .10
181 Jamey Wright .10
182 Lonell Roberts **RC** .10
183 Marty Cordova .10
185 Amaury Telemaco .10
185 John Mabry .10
186 Andrew Vessel **RC** .10
187 Jim Cole **RC** .10
188 Marquis Riley .10
189 Todd Dunn .10
190 John Carter .10
191 Donnie Sadler **RC** .25
192 Mike Bell .10
193 Chris Cumberland **RC** .10
194 Jason Schmidt .25
195 Matt Brunson .10
196 James Baldwin .10
197 Bill Simas **RC** .10
198 Gus Gandarillas .10
199 Mac Suzuki .10
200 Rick Holifield **RC** .10
201 Fernando Lunar **RC** .10
202 Kevin Jarvis .10
203 Everett Stull **RC** .10
204 Steve Wojciechowski .10
205 Shawn Estes .10
206 Jermaine Dye .10
207 Marc Kroon .10
208 Peter Munro **RC** .10
209 Pat Watkins .10
210 Matt Smith .10
211 Joe Vitiello .10
212 Gerald Witasick Jr. .10
213 Freddy Garcia **RC** .10
214 Glenn Dishman **RC** .10
215 Jay Canizaro **RC** .10
216 Angel Martinez .10
217 Yamil Benitez **RC** .10
218 Fausto Macey **RC** .10
219 Eric Owens .10
220 Checklist .10
221 Dwayne Hosey **RC** (Minor League MVPs) .10
222 Brad Woodall **RC** (Minor League MVPs) .25
223 Billy Ashley (Minor League MVPs) .10
224 Mark Grudzielanek **RC** (Minor League MVPs) 2.00
225 Mark Johnson **RC** (Minor League MVPs) .10
226 Tim Unroe **RC** (Minor League MVPs) .10
227 Todd Greene (Minor League MVPs) .10
228 Larry Sutton (Minor League MVPs) .10
229 Derek Jeter (Minor League MVPs) 3.00
230 Sal Fasano **RC** (Minor League MVPs) .10
231 Ruben Rivera (Minor League MVPs) .10
232 Chris Truby **RC** (Minor League MVPs) .10
233 John Donati (Minor League MVPs) .10
234 Decomba Conner **RC** (Minor League MVPs) .10
235 Sergio Nunez **RC** (Minor League MVPs) .10
236 Ray Brown **RC** (Minor League MVPs) .10
237 Juan Melo **RC** (Minor League MVPs) .10
238 Hideo Nomo **RC** (First Impressions) 4.00
239 Jaime Bluma **RC** (First Impressions) .10
240 Jay Payton **RC** (First Impressions) 1.50
241 Paul Konerko (First Impressions) .75
242 Scott Elarton **RC** (First Impressions) .50
243 Jeff Abbott **RC** (First Impressions) .25
244 Jim Brower **RC** (First Impressions) .10
245 Geoff Blum **RC** (First Impressions) .40
246 Aaron Boone **RC** (First Impressions) 1.00
247 J.R. Phillips (Top Prospects) .10
248 Alex Ochoa (Top Prospects) .10
249 Nomar Garciaparra (Top Prospects) 5.00
250 Garret Anderson (Top Prospects) .25
251 Ray Durham (Top Prospects) .10
252 Paul Shuey (Top Prospects) .10
253 Tony Clark (Top Prospects) .10
254 Johnny Damon (Top Prospects) 1.00
255 Duane Singleton (Top Prospects) .10
256 LaTroy Hawkins (Top Prospects) .10
257 Andy Pettitte (Top Prospects) .40
258 Ben Grieve (Top Prospects) .10
259 Marc Newfield (Top Prospects) .10
260 Terrell Lowery (Top Prospects) .10
261 Shawn Green (Top Prospects) .40
262 Chipper Jones (Top Prospects) 1.50
263 Brooks Kieschnick (Top Prospects) .10
264 Calvin Reese (Top Prospects) .10
265 Doug Million (Top Prospects) .10
266 Marc Valdes (Top Prospects) .10
267 Brian Hunter (Top Prospects) .10
268 Todd Hollandsworth (Top Prospects) .10
269 Rod Henderson (Top Prospects) .10
270 Bill Pulsipher (Top Prospects) .10
271 Scott Rolen **RC** (Top Prospects) 15.00
272 Trey Beamon (Top Prospects) .10
273 Alan Benes (Top Prospects) .10
274 Dustin Hermanson (Top Prospects) .10
275 Ricky Bottalico .10
276 Albert Belle .10
277 Deion Sanders .25
278 Matt Williams .10
279 Jeff Bagwell .75
280 Kirby Puckett 1.50
281 Dave Hollins .10
282 Don Mattingly 1.50
283 Joey Hamilton .10
284 Bobby Bonilla .10
285 Moises Alou .25
286 Tom Glavine .25
287 Brett Butler .10
288 Chris Hoiles .10
289 Kenny Rogers .10
290 Larry Walker .25
291 Tim Raines .10
292 Kevin Appier .10
293 Roger Clemens 2.00
294a Chuck Carr .10
294b Cliff Floyd (Should be #394.) .10
295 Randy Myers .10
296 Dave Nilsson .10
297 Joe Carter .10
298 Chuck Finley .10
299 Ray Lankford .10
300 Roberto Kelly .10
301 Jon Lieber .10
302 Travis Fryman .10
303 Mark McGwire 1.50
304 Tony Gwynn 1.00
305 Kenny Lofton .10
306 Mark Whiten .10
307 Doug Drabek .10
308 Terry Steinbach .10
309 Ryan Klesko .10
310 Mike Piazza 1.50
311 Ben McDonald .10
312 Reggie Sanders .10
313 Alex Fernandez .10
314 Aaron Sele .10
315 Gregg Jefferies .10
316 Rickey Henderson .75
317 Brian Anderson .10
318 Jose Valentin .10
319 Rod Beck .10
320 Marquis Grissom .10
321 Ken Griffey Jr. 2.00
322 Bret Saberhagen .10
323 Juan Gonzalez .50
324 Paul Molitor .75
325 Gary Sheffield .40
326 Darren Daulton .10
327 Bill Swift .10
328 Brian McRae .10
329 Robin Ventura .10
330 Lee Smith .10
331 Fred McGriff .20
332 Delino DeShields .10
333 Edgar Martinez .10
334 Mike Mussina .50
335 Orlando Merced .10
336 Carlos Baerga .10
337 Wil Cordero .10
338 Tom Pagnozzi .10
339 Pat Hentgen .10
340 Chad Curtis .10
341 Darren Lewis .10
342 Jeff Kent .20
343 Bip Roberts .10
344 Ivan Rodriguez .50
345 Jeff Montgomery .10
346 Hal Morris .10
347 Danny Tartabull .10
348 Raul Mondesi .10
349 Ken Hill .10
350 Pedro Martinez 1.00
351 Frank Thomas .75
352 Manny Ramirez 1.00
353 Tim Salmon .10
354 William Van Landingham .10
355 Andres Galarraga .10
356 Paul O'Neill .25
357 Brady Anderson .10
358 Ramon Martinez .10
359 John Olerud .10
360 Ruben Sierra .10
361 Cal Eldred .10
362 Jay Buhner .10
363 Jay Bell .10
364 Wally Joyner .10
365 Chuck Knoblauch .10
366 Len Dykstra .10
367 John Wetteland .10
368 Roberto Alomar .25
369 Craig Biggio .25
370 Ozzie Smith 1.50
371 Terry Pendleton .10
372 Sammy Sosa 1.00
373 Carlos Garcia .10
374 Jose Rijo .10
375 Chris Gomez .10
376 Barry Bonds 2.00
377 Steve Avery .10
378 Rick Wilkins .10
379 Pete Harnisch .10
380 Dean Palmer .10
381 Bob Hamelin .10
382 Jason Bere .10
383 Jimmy Key .10
384 Dante Bichette .10
385 Rafael Palmeiro .50
386 David Justice .10
387 Chili Davis .10
388 Mike Greenwell .10
389 Todd Zeile .10
390 Jeff Conine .10
391 Rick Aguilera .10
392 Eddie Murray .50
393 Mike Stanley .10
395 Randy Johnson 1.00
396 David Nied .10
397 Devon White .10
398 Royce Clayton .10
399 Andy Benes .10
400 John Hudek .10
401 Bobby Jones .10
402 Eric Karros .10
403 Will Clark .25
404 Mark Langston .10
405 Kevin Brown .10
406 Greg Maddux 1.50
407 David Cone .10
408 Wade Boggs .75
409 Steve Trachsel .10
410 Greg Vaughn .10
411 Mo Vaughn .10
412 Wilson Alvarez .10
413 Cal Ripken Jr. 3.00
414 Rico Brogna .10
415 Barry Larkin .40
416 Cecil Fielder .10
417 Jose Canseco .50
418 Jack McDowell .10
419 Mike Lieberthal .10
420 Andrew Lorraine .10
421 Rich Becker .10
422 Tony Phillips .10
423 Scott Ruffcorn .10
424 Jeff Granger .10
425 Greg Pirkl .10
426 Dennis Eckersley .50
427 Jose Lima .10
428 Russ Davis .10
429 Armando Benitez .10
430 Alex Gonzalez .10
431 Carlos Delgado .75
432 Chan Ho Park .10
433 Mickey Tettleton .10
434 Dave Winfield .75
435 John Burkett .10
436 Orlando Miller .10
437 Rondell White .10
438 Jose Oliva .10
439 Checklist .10

Gold

The only chase cards in the '95 Bowman set are gold versions of the foil-etched "Minor League MVPs," "1st Impressions" and "Prime Prospects." The gold cards are found in every 6th (regular) or 12th (jumbo) pack, on average, in place of the silver versions.

	NM/M
Complete Set (54):	100.00
Common Player:	.50
Stars/RC's:	2.5X

1995 Bowman's Best

Actually made up of three subsets, all cards feature a player photo set against a silver foil background. The 90 veterans' cards have a broad red-foil stripe in the background beneath the team logo; the 90 rookies' cards have a similar stripe in tones of blue. All of those cards are printed in Topps' Finest technology. The 15 Mirror Image cards are in horizontal format, printed more conventionally on metallic foil, and have a rookie and veteran sharing the card. Backs of each card continue the color theme, have '94 and career stats and a highlight or two. Standard packaging was seven-card foil packs with inserts consisting of higher-tech parallel sets of the regular issue.

	NM/M
Complete Set (195):	200.00
Common Player:	.25
Pack (7):	12.00
Wax Box (24):	275.00
Complete Set Red (90):	45.00

1 Randy Johnson 1.50
2 Joe Carter .25
3 Chili Davis .25
4 Moises Alou .25
5 Gary Sheffield .40
6 Kevin Appier .25
7 Denny Neagle .25
8 Ruben Sierra .25
9 Darren Daulton .25
10 Cal Ripken Jr. 4.00
11 Bobby Bonilla .25
12 Manny Ramirez 1.50
13 Barry Bonds 4.00
14 Eric Karros .25
15 Greg Maddux 2.00
16 Jeff Bagwell 1.50
17 Paul Molitor 1.50
18 Ray Lankford .25
19 Mark Grace .25
20 Kenny Lofton .25
21 Tony Gwynn 2.00
22 Will Clark .25
23 Roger Clemens 2.25
24 Dante Bichette .25
25 Barry Larkin .25
26 Wade Boggs 2.00
27 Kirby Puckett 2.00
28 Cecil Fielder .25
29 Jose Canseco .50
30 Juan Gonzalez .75
31 David Cone .25
32 Craig Biggio .25
33 Tim Salmon .25
34 David Justice .25
35 Sammy Sosa 2.00
36 Mike Piazza 2.50
37 Carlos Baerga .25
38 Jeff Conine .25
39 Rafael Palmeiro 1.25
40 Bret Saberhagen .25
41 Len Dykstra .25
42 Mo Vaughn .25
43 Wally Joyner .25
44 Chuck Knoblauch .25
45 Robin Ventura .25
46 Don Mattingly 2.25
47 Dave Hollins .25
48 Andy Benes .25
49 Ken Griffey Jr. 2.50
50 Albert Belle .25
51 Matt Williams .25
52 Rondell White .25
53 Raul Mondesi .25
54 Brian Jordan .25
55 Greg Vaughn .25
56 Fred McGriff .25
57 Roberto Alomar .40
58 Dennis Eckersley 1.25
59 Lee Smith .25
60 Eddie Murray 1.50
61 Kenny Rogers .25
62 Ron Gant .25
63 Larry Walker .25
64 Chad Curtis .25
65 Frank Thomas 1.50
66 Paul O'Neill .25
67 Kevin Seitzer .25
68 Marquis Grissom .25
69 Mark McGwire 3.00
70 Travis Fryman .25
71 Andres Galarraga .25
72 Carlos Perez **RC** .25
73 Tyler Green .25
74 Marty Cordova .25
75 Shawn Green .40
76 Vaughn Eshelman .25
77 John Mabry .25
78 Jason Bates .25
79 Jon Nunnally .25
80 Ray Durham .25
81 Edgardo Alfonzo .25
82 Esteban Loaiza .25
83 Hideo Nomo **RC** 10.00
84 Orlando Miller .25
85 Alex Gonzalez .25
86 Mark Grudzielanek **RC** .65
87 Julian Tavarez .25
88 Benji Gil .25
89 Quilvio Veras .25
90 Ricky Bottalico .25

Complete Set Blue (90): 150.00

1 Derek Jeter 3.00
2 Vladimir Guerrero **RC** 80.00
3 Bob Abreu **RC** 25.00
4 Chan Ho Park .25
5 Paul Wilson .25
6 Chad Ogea .25
7 Andruw Jones **RC** 50.00
8 Brian Barber .25
9 Andy Larkin .25
10 Richie Sexson **RC** 10.00
11 Everett Stull **RC** .25
12 Brooks Kieschnick .25
13 Matt Murray .25
14 John Wasdin .25
15 Shannon Stewart .25
16 Luis Ortiz .25
17 Marc Kroon .25
18 Todd Greene .25
19 Juan Acevedo .25
20 Tony Clark .25
21 Jermaine Dye .25
22 Derrek Lee 1.00
23 Pat Watkins .25
24 Calvin Reese .25
25 Ben Grieve .25
26 Julio Santana **RC** .25
27 Felix Rodriguez **RC** .50
28 Paul Konerko .25
29 Nomar Garciaparra 2.00
30 Pat Ahearne .25
31 Jason Schmidt .25
32 Billy Wagner .25
33 Rey Ordonez **RC** 1.00
34 Curtis Goodwin .25
35 Sergio Nunez **RC** .25
36 Tim Belk .25
37 Scott Elarton **RC** 1.00
38 Jason Isringhausen .25
39 Trot Nixon .35
40 Sid Roberson .25
41 Ron Villone .25
42 Ruben Rivera .25
43 Rick Huisman .25
44 Todd Hollandsworth .25
45 Johnny Damon 1.00
46 Garret Anderson .25
47 Jeff D'Amico .25
48 Dustin Hermanson .25
49 Juan Encarnacion **RC** 4.00
50 Andy Pettitte .50
51 Chris Stynes .25
52 Troy Percival .25
53 LaTroy Hawkins .25
54 Roger Cedeno .25
55 Alan Benes .25
56 Karim Garcia **RC** 1.50
57 Andrew Lorraine .25
58 Gary Rath **RC** .25
59 Bret Wagner .25
60 Jeff Suppan .25
61 Bill Pulsipher .25
62 Jay Payton **RC** 3.00
63 Alex Ochoa .25
64 Ugueth Urbina .25
65 Armando Benitez .25
66 George Arias .25
67 Raul Casanova **RC** .50
68 Matt Drews .25
69 Jimmy Haynes .25
70 Jimmy Hurst .25
71 C.J. Nitkowski .25
72 Tommy Davis **RC** .25
73 Bartolo Colon **RC** 5.00
74 Chris Carpenter **RC** 10.00
75 Trey Beamon .25
76 Bryan Rekar .25
77 James Baldwin .25
78 Marc Valdes .25
79 Tom Fordham **RC** .25
80 Marc Newfield .25
81 Angel Martinez .25
82 Brian Hunter .25
83 Jose Herrera .25
84 Glenn Dishman **RC** .25
85 Jacob Cruz **RC** .25
86 Paul Shuey .25
87 Scott Rolen **RC** 25.00
88 Doug Million .25
89 Desi Relaford .25
90 Michael Tucker .25

Mirror Image: .50

1 Ben Davis **RC**, Ivan Rodriguez 1.00
2 Mark Redman **RC**, Manny Ramirez 1.50
3 Reggie Taylor **RC**, Deion Sanders .50
4 Ryan Jaroncyk, Shawn Green .50
5 Juan LeBron, Juan Gonzalez 1.00
6 Toby McKnight, Craig Biggio .50
7 Michael Barrett **RC**, Travis Fryman 1.00
8 Corey Jenkins, Mo Vaughn .50
9 Ruben Rivera, Frank Thomas 1.50
10 Curtis Goodwin, Kenny Lofton .50
11 Brian Hunter, Tony Gwynn 1.75
12 Todd Greene, Ken Griffey Jr. 2.50
13 Karim Garcia, Matt Williams .75
14 Billy Wagner, Randy Johnson 1.50
15 Pat Watkins, Jeff Bagwell 1.50

Refractors

The large volume of silver foil in the background of the red and blue subsets in '95 Best make the Refractor technology much easier to see than in past issues. The chase cards, found one per six packs on average, also have a small "REFRACTOR" printed near the lower-left corner on back. The 15-card Mirror Image subset was not paralleled in Refractor technology, but in a process Topps calls "diffraction-foil" which creates a strong vertical-stripe rainbow effect in the background. Cards #72 (Carlos Perez) and 84 (Orlando Miller) can be found both with and without the "REFRACTOR" notice on back; neither version commands a premium.

	NM/M
Common Player:	1.00
Stars:	3-6X
Rookies:	2-3X

Refractors - Jumbo

These super-size versions of Bowman's Best Refractors were produced exclusively for inclusion as a one-per-box insert in retail boxes of the product distributed by ANCO to large retail chains. The 4-1/4" x 5-3/4" cards are identical in all ways except size to the regular refractors. The jumbo inserts were not produced in equal quantities, with the most popular players being printed in greater numbers.

	NM/M
Complete Set (10):	35.00
Common Player:	2.00

10 Cal Ripken Jr. 10.00
15 Greg Maddux 4.00
21 Tony Gwynn 4.00
35 Sammy Sosa 5.00
36 Mike Piazza 6.00
42 Mo Vaughn 2.00
49 Ken Griffey Jr. 6.00
50 Albert Belle 2.00
65 Frank Thomas 3.50
83 Hideo Nomo 3.00

1996 Bowman

In a "Guaranteed Value Program," Topps stated it would pay $100 for this set in 1999, if collectors mail in a request form (one per three packs), a $5 fee and the complete set in numerical order (only one per person). Every set redeemed was destroyed. The 385-card set has 110 veteran stars and 275 prospects. Backs of the prospects' cards provide a detailed scouting report. A "1st Bowman Card" gold-foil stamped logo was included on the card front for 156 players making their first appearance in a Bowman set. Insert sets include Bowman's Best Previews (along with Refractor and Atomic Refractor versions), a 1952 Mickey Mantle Bowman reprint (1 in 48 packs) and Minor League Player of the Year candidates. A 385-card parallel version of the entire base set was also produced on 18-point foilboard; seeded one per pack.

	NM/M
Complete Set (385):	50.00
Common Player:	.10
Foils:	1.5X
Pack (11):	2.00
Wax Box (24):	40.00

1 Cal Ripken Jr. 2.00
2 Ray Durham .10
3 Ivan Rodriguez .50
4 Fred McGriff .20
5 Hideo Nomo .50
6 Troy Percival .10
7 Moises Alou .20
8 Mike Stanley .10
9 Jay Buhner .10
10 Shawn Green .25
11 Ryan Klesko .10
12 Andres Galarraga .10
13 Dean Palmer .10
14 Jeff Conine .10
15 Brian Hunter .10
16 J.T. Snow .10
17 Larry Walker .25
18 Barry Larkin .40
19 Alex Gonzalez .10
20 Edgar Martinez .10
21 Mo Vaughn .10
22 Mark McGwire 1.50
23 Jose Canseco .50
24 Jack McDowell .10
25 Dante Bichette .10
26 Wade Boggs .50
27 Mike Piazza 1.00
28 Ray Lankford .10
29 Craig Biggio .25
30 Rafael Palmeiro .50
31 Ron Gant .10
32 Javy Lopez .10
33 Brian Jordan .10
34 Paul O'Neill .20
35 Mark Grace .25
36 Matt Williams .20
37 Pedro Martinez .75
38 Rickey Henderson .50
39 Bobby Bonilla .10
40 Todd Hollandsworth .10
41 Jim Thome .75
42 Gary Sheffield .40
43 Tim Salmon .10
44 Gregg Jefferies .10
45 Roberto Alomar .25
45p Roberto Alomar (Unmarked promo card, fielding photo on front.) 3.00
46 Carlos Baerga .10
47 Mark Grudzielanek .10
48 Randy Johnson .75
49 Tino Martinez .10
50 Robin Ventura .10
51 Ryne Sandberg 1.50
52 Jay Bell .10
53 Jason Schmidt .10
54 Frank Thomas .75
55 Kenny Lofton .10
56 Ariel Prieto .10
57 David Cone .10
58 Reggie Sanders .10
59 Michael Tucker .10
60 Vinny Castilla .10
61 Lenny Dykstra .10
62 Todd Hundley .10
63 Brian McRae .10
64 Dennis Eckersley .40
65 Rondell White .10
66 Eric Karros .10
67 Greg Maddux 1.50
68 Kevin Appier .10
69 Eddie Murray .50
70 John Olerud .10
71 Tony Gwynn .75
72 David Justice .10
73 Ken Caminiti .10
74 Terry Steinbach .10
75 Alan Benes .10
76 Chipper Jones 1.00
77 Jeff Bagwell .50
77p Jeff Bagwell (Unmarked promo card, name in gold.) 6.00
78 Barry Bonds 2.00
79 Ken Griffey Jr. 1.50
80 Roger Cedeno .10
81 Joe Carter .10
82 Henry Rodriguez .10
83 Jason Isringhausen .10
84 Chuck Knoblauch .10
85 Manny Ramirez .75
86 Tom Glavine .30
87 Jeffrey Hammonds .10
88 Paul Molitor .75
89 Roger Clemens 2.00
90 Greg Vaughn .10
91 Marty Cordova .10
92 Albert Belle .10
93 Mike Mussina .40
94 Garret Anderson .10
95 Juan Gonzalez .40
96 John Valentin .10
97 Jason Giambi .50
98 Kirby Puckett 1.50
99 Jim Edmonds .25
100 Cecil Fielder .10
101 Mike Aldrete .10
102 Marquis Grissom .10
103 Derek Bell .10
104 Raul Mondesi .10
105 Sammy Sosa 1.00
106 Travis Fryman .10
107 Rico Brogna .10
108 Will Clark .25
109 Bernie Williams .40
110 Brady Anderson .10
111 Torii Hunter .10
112 Derek Jeter 2.00
113 Mike Kusiewicz **RC** .10
114 Scott Rolen 1.00
115 Ramon Castro .10
116 Jose Guillen **RC** 2.50
117 Wade Walker **RC** .10
118 Shawn Senior .10
119 Onan Masaoka **RC** .10
120 Marlon Anderson **RC** .75
121 Katsuhiro Maeda **RC** .25
122 Garrett Stephenson **RC** .25
123 Butch Huskey .10
124 D'Angelo Jimenez **RC** .50
125 Tony Mounce **RC** .20
126 Jay Canizaro .10
127 Juan Melo .10
128 Steve Gibralter .10
129 Freddy Garcia .10
130 Julio Santana .10
131 Richard Hidalgo .10
132 Jermaine Dye .10
133 Willie Adams .10
134 Everett Stull .10
135 Ramon Morel .10
136 Chan Ho Park .10
137 Jamey Wright .10
138 Luis Garcia **RC** .10
139 Dan Serafini .10
140 Ryan Dempster **RC** .50
141 Tate Seefried .10
142 Jimmy Hurst .10
143 Travis Miller .10
144 Curtis Goodwin .10
145 Rocky Coppinger **RC** .10
146 Enrique Wilson .10
147 Jaime Bluma .10
148 Andrew Vessel .10
149 Damian Moss .10
150 Shawn Gallagher **RC** .10
151 Pat Watkins .10
152 Jose Paniagua .10
153 Danny Graves .10
154 Bryon Gainey **RC** .10
155 Steve Soderstrom .10
156 Cliff Brumbaugh **RC** .10
157 Eugene Kingsale **RC** .10
158 Lou Collier .10
159 Todd Walker .10
160 Kris Detmers **RC** .10
161 Josh Booty **RC** .25
162 Greg Whiteman **RC** .10
163 Damian Jackson .10
164 Tony Clark .10
165 Jeff D'Amico .10
166 Johnny Damon .50
167 Rafael Orellano .10
168 Ruben Rivera .10
169 Alex Ochoa .10
170 Jay Powell .10
171 Tom Evans .10
172 Ron Villone .10
173 Shawn Estes .10
174 John Wasdin .10
175 Bill Simas .10
176 Kevin Brown .10
177 Shannon Stewart .10
178 Todd Greene .10
179 Bob Wolcott .10
180 Chris Snopek .10
181 Nomar Garciaparra 1.00
182 Cameron Smith **RC** .10
183 Matt Drews .10
184 Jimmy Haynes .10
185 Chris Carpenter .25
186 Desi Relaford .10
187 Ben Grieve .10
188 Mike Bell .10
189 Luis Castillo **RC** .75
190 Ugueth Urbina .10
191 Paul Wilson .10
191p Paul Wilson (Unmarked promo card, name in gold.) 1.00
192 Andruw Jones .75
193 Wayne Gomes .10
194 Craig Counsell **RC** .75
195 Jim Cole .10
196 Brooks Kieshnick .10
197 Trey Beamon .10
198 Marino Santana **RC** .10
199 Bob Abreu .25
200 Calvin Reese .10
201 Dante Powell .10
202 George Arias .10
202p George Arias (Unmarked promo card, name in gold.) 1.00
203 Jorge Velandia **RC** .10
204 George Lombard **RC** .10
205 Byron Browne **RC** .10
206 John Frascatore .10
207 Terry Adams .10
208 Wilson Delgado **RC** .10
209 Billy McMillon .10
210 Jeff Abbott .10
211 Trot Nixon .10
212 Amaury Telemaco .10
213 Scott Sullivan .10
214 Justin Thompson .10
215 Decomba Conner .10
216 Ryan McGuire .10
217 Matt Luke **RC** .10
218 Doug Million .10
219 Jason Dickson **RC** .25
220 Ramon Hernandez **RC** .50
221 Mark Bellhorn **RC** .25
222 Eric Ludwick **RC** .10
223 Luke Wilcox **RC** .10
224 Marty Malloy **RC** .10
225 Gary Coffee **RC** .10
226 Wendell Magee **RC** .10
227 Brett Tomko **RC** .25
228 Derek Lowe .10
229 Jose Rosado **RC** .10
230 Steve Bourgeois **RC** .10
231 Neil Weber **RC** .10
232 Jeff Ware .10
233 Edwin Diaz .10
234 Greg Norton .10
235 Aaron Boone .10
236 Jeff Suppan .10
237 Bret Wagner .10
238 Elieser Marrero .10
239 Will Cunnane .10
240 Brian Barkley **RC** .10
241 Jay Payton .10
242 Marcus Jensen .10
243 Ryan Nye .10
244 Chad Mottola .10
245 Scott McClain **RC** .10
246 Jesse Ibarra **RC** .10
247 Mike Darr **RC** .10
248 Bobby Estalella **RC** .50
249 Michael Barrett .10
250 Jamie Lopiccolo **RC** .10
251 Shane Spencer **RC** .40
252 Ben Petrick **RC** .50
253 Jason Bell **RC** .10
254 Arnold Gooch **RC** .10
255 T.J. Mathews .10
256 Jason Ryan .10
257 Pat Cline **RC** .10
258 Rafael Carmona **RC** .10
259 Carl Pavano **RC** 1.00
260 Ben Davis .10
261 Matt Lawton **RC** 1.00
262 Kevin Sefcik **RC** .10
263 Chris Fussell **RC** .10
264 Mike Cameron **RC** 1.50
265 Marty Janzen **RC** .10
266 Livan Hernandez **RC** 1.00
267 Raul Ibanez **RC** 1.50
268 Juan Encarnacion .10

269 David Yocum **RC** .10
270 Jonathan Johnson **RC** .10
271 Reggie Taylor .10
272 Danny Buxbaum **RC** .10
273 Jacob Cruz .10
274 Bobby Morris **RC** .10
275 Andy Fox **RC** .10
276 Greg Keagle .10
277 Charles Peterson .10
278 Derrek Lee .50
279 Bryant Nelson **RC** .10
280 Antone Williamson .10
281 Scott Elarton .10
282 Shad Williams **RC** .10
283 Rich Hunter **RC** .10
284 Chris Sheff .10
285 Derrick Gibson .10
286 Felix Rodriguez .10
287 Brian Banks **RC** .10
288 Jason McDonald .10
289 Glendon Rusch **RC** .50
290 Gary Rath .10
291 Peter Munro .10
292 Tom Fordham .10
293 Jason Kendall .10
294 Russ Johnson .10
295 Joe Long **RC** .10
296 Robert Smith **RC** .10
297 Jarrod Washburn **RC** .75
298 Dave Coggin **RC** .10
299 Jeff Yoder **RC** .10
300 Jed Hansen **RC** .10
301 Matt Morris **RC** 1.00
302 Josh Bishop **RC** .10
303 Dustin Hermanson .10
304 Mike Gulan .10
305 Felipe Crespo .10
306 Quinton McCracken .10
307 Jim Bonnici **RC** .10
308 Sal Fasano .10
309 Gabe Alvarez **RC** .10
310 Heath Murray **RC** .10
311 Jose Valentin **RC** .10
312 Bartolo Colon .10
313 Olmedo Saenz .10
314 Norm Hutchins **RC** .10
315 Chris Holt **RC** .10
316 David Doster **RC** .10
317 Robert Person .10
318 Donne Wall **RC** .10
319 Adam Riggs **RC** .10
320 Homer Bush .10
321 Brad Rigby **RC** .10
322 Lou Merloni **RC** .25
323 Neifi Perez .10
324 Chris Cumberland .10
325 Alvie Shepherd **RC** .10
326 Jarrod Patterson **RC** .10
327 Ray Ricken **RC** .10
328 Danny Klassen **RC** .10
329 David Miller **RC** .10
330 Chad Alexander **RC** .10
331 Matt Beaumont .10
332 Damon Hollins .10
333 Todd Dunn .10
334 Mike Sweeney **RC** 1.50
335 Richie Sexson .40
336 Billy Wagner .10
337 Ron Wright **RC** .10
338 Paul Konerko .25
339 Tommy Phelps **RC** .10
340 Karim Garcia .10
341 Mike Grace **RC** .10
342 Russell Branyan **RC** .40
343 Randy Winn **RC** .50
344 A.J. Pierzynski **RC** 1.50
345 Mike Busby **RC** .10
346 Matt Beech **RC** .10
347 Jose Cepeda **RC** .10
348 Brian Stephenson .10
349 Rey Ordonez .10
350 Rich Aurilia **RC** 1.00
351 Edgard Velazquez **RC** .25
352 Raul Casanova .10
353 Carlos Guillen **RC** 1.00
354 Bruce Aven **RC** .10
355 Ryan Jones **RC** .10
356 Derek Aucoin **RC** .10
357 Brian Rose **RC** .10
358 Richard Almanzar **RC** .10
359 Fletcher Bates **RC** .10
360 Russ Ortiz **RC** .75
361 Wilton Guerrero **RC** .10
362 Geoff Jenkins **RC** 1.00
363 Pete Janicki .10
364 Yamil Benitez .10
365 Aaron Holbert .10
366 Tim Belk .10
367 Terrell Wade .10
368 Terrence Long .10
369 Brad Fullmer .10
370 Matt Wagner .10
371 Craig Wilson .10
372 Mark Loretta .10
373 Eric Owens .10
374 Vladimir Guerrero 1.00
375 Tommy Davis .10
376 Donnie Sadler .10
377 Edgar Renteria .25
378 Todd Helton .50
379 Ralph Milliard **RC** .10
380 Darin Blood **RC** .10
381 Shayne Bennett .10
382 Mark Redman .10
383 Felix Martinez .10
384 Sean Watkins **RC** .10
385 Oscar Henriquez .10

Minor League Player of the Year

Fifteen prospects who were candidates for Minor League Player of the Year are featured in this 1996 Bowman baseball insert set. Cards were seeded one per every 12 packs.

		NM/M
Complete Set (15):		12.50
Common Player:		.50
1	Andruw Jones	4.00
2	Derrick Gibson	.50
3	Bob Abreu	.75
4	Todd Walker	.50
5	Jamey Wright	.50
6	Wes Helms	.50
7	Karim Garcia	.75
8	Bartolo Colon	2.00
9	Alex Ochoa	.50
10	Mike Sweeney	2.00
11	Ruben Rivera	.50
12	Gabe Alvarez	.50
13	Billy Wagner	.50
14	Vladimir Guerrero	4.00
15	Edgard Velazquez	.50

1952 Mickey Mantle Reprints

Reprints of Mickey Mantle's 1952 Bowman baseball card were created for insertion in Bowman and Bowman's Best products for 1996. The 2-1/2" x 3-1/2" card can be found in regular (gold seal on front), Finest, Finest Refractor and Atomic Refractor versions.

		NM/M
Complete Set (4):		20.00
Common Card:		2.50
20	Mickey Mantle/Reprint	2.50
20	Mickey Mantle/Finest	5.00
20	Mickey Mantle/ Refractor	7.50
20	Mickey Mantle/ Atomic Refractor	10.00

1996 Bowman's Best Preview

These cards use Topps' Finest technology. The cards were seeded one per every 12 packs of 1996 Bowman baseball. Fifteen veterans and 15 prospects are featured in the set. Refractor versions are found one per 24 packs, with Atomic Refractors a 1:48 pick.

		NM/M
Complete Set (30):		18.50
Common Player:		.25
Refractors:		1.5X
Atomic Refractors:		2X
1	Chipper Jones	1.50
2	Alan Benes	.25
3	Brooks Kieshnick	.25
4	Barry Bonds	3.00
5	Rey Ordonez	.25
6	Tim Salmon	.25
7	Mike Piazza	2.00
8	Billy Wagner	.25
9	Andruw Jones	1.00
10	Tony Gwynn	1.50
11	Paul Wilson	.25
12	Calvin Reese	.25
13	Frank Thomas	1.00
14	Greg Maddux	1.50
15	Derek Jeter	3.00
16	Jeff Bagwell	1.00
17	Barry Larkin	.25
18	Todd Greene	.25
19	Ruben Rivera	.25
20	Richard Hidalgo	.25
21	Larry Walker	.25
22	Carlos Baerga	.25
23	Derrick Gibson	.25
24	Richie Sexson	.25
25	Mo Vaughn	.25
26	Hideo Nomo	.50
27	Nomar Garciaparra	1.50
28	Cal Ripken Jr.	3.00
29	Karim Garcia	.25
30	Ken Griffey Jr.	2.00

1996 Bowman's Best

Bowman's Best returns in its traditional format of 180 cards: 90 established stars and 90 up-and-coming prospects and rookies. Three types of insert sets are found in Bowman's Best: Mirror Image, Bowman's Best Cuts and the 1952 Bowman Mickey Mantle reprints. There are also parallel sets of Refractors and Atomic Refractors randomly seeded in packs. Refractors are found on average of one per 12 packs; Atomic Refractors are seeded one per 48 packs. Mirror Image Refractors are found one per 96 packs, while Mirror Image Atomic Refractors are seeded one per 192 packs. Refractor versions of the Mantle reprint are seeded one per every 96 packs; Atomic Refractor Mantle reprints are seeded in every 192nd pack.

		NM/M
Complete Set (180):		30.00
Common Player:		.25
Refractors:		2X
Atomics:		15X
1952 Mickey Mantle:		2.50
1952 Mantle Finest:		5.00
1952 Mantle Refractor:		7.50
1952 Mantle Atomic:		10.00
Pack (6):		2.50
Wax Box (24):		40.00
1	Hideo Nomo	.75
2	Edgar Martinez	.25
3	Cal Ripken Jr.	4.00
4	Wade Boggs	1.00
5	Cecil Fielder	.25
6	Albert Belle	.25
7	Chipper Jones	1.50
8	Ryne Sandberg	2.00
9	Tim Salmon	.25
10	Barry Bonds	3.00
11	Ken Caminiti	.25
12	Ron Gant	.25
13	Frank Thomas	1.00
14	Dante Bichette	.25
15	Jason Kendall	.25
16	Mo Vaughn	.25
17	Rey Ordonez	.25
18	Henry Rodriguez	.25
19	Ryan Klesko	.25
20	Jeff Bagwell	1.00
21	Randy Johnson	1.50
22	Jim Edmonds	.50
23	Kenny Lofton	.25
24	Andy Pettitte	.50
25	Brady Anderson	.25
26	Mike Piazza	2.50
27	Greg Vaughn	.25
28	Joe Carter	.25
29	Jason Giambi	1.00
30	Ivan Rodriguez	1.00
31	Jeff Conine	.25
32	Rafael Palmeiro	.75
33	Roger Clemens	3.00
34	Chuck Knoblauch	.25
35	Reggie Sanders	.25
36	Andres Galarraga	.25
37	Paul O'Neill	.50
38	Tony Gwynn	2.00
39	Paul Wilson	.25
40	Garret Anderson	.25
41	David Justice	.25
42	Eddie Murray	1.00
43	Mike Grace **RC**	.25
44	Marty Cordova	.25
45	Kevin Appier	.25
46	Raul Mondesi	.25
47	Jim Thome	1.00
48	Sammy Sosa	2.00
49	Craig Biggio	.50
50	Marquis Grissom	.25
51	Alan Benes	.25
52	Manny Ramirez	1.50
53	Gary Sheffield	.75
54	Mike Mussina	.50
55	Robin Ventura	.25
56	Johnny Damon	1.00
57	Jose Canseco	.75
58	Juan Gonzalez	.75
59	Tino Martinez	.25
60	Brian Hunter	.25
61	Fred McGriff	.25
62	Jay Buhner	.25
63	Carlos Delgado	.75
64	Moises Alou	.50
65	Roberto Alomar	.50
66	Barry Larkin	.50
67	Vinny Castilla	.25
68	Ray Durham	.25
69	Travis Fryman	.25
70	Jason Isringhausen	.25
71	Ken Griffey Jr.	2.50
72	John Smoltz	.50
73	Matt Williams	.25
74	Chan Ho Park	.25
75	Mark McGwire	2.50
76	Jeffrey Hammonds	.25
77	Will Clark	.50
78	Kirby Puckett	2.00
79	Derek Jeter	4.00
80	Derek Bell	.25
81	Eric Karros	.25
82	Lenny Dykstra	.25
83	Larry Walker	.50
84	Mark Grudzielanek	.25
85	Greg Maddux	2.50
86	Carlos Baerga	.25
87	Paul Molitor	1.00
88	John Valentin	.25
89	Mark Grace	.50
90	Ray Lankford	.25
91	Andruw Jones	1.50
92	Nomar Garciaparra	2.00
93	Alex Ochoa	.25
94	Derrick Gibson	.25
95	Jeff D'Amico	.25
96	Ruben Rivera	.25
97	Vladimir Guerrero	1.50
98	Calvin Reese	.25
99	Richard Hidalgo	.25
100	Bartolo Colon	.25
101	Karim Garcia	.25
102	Ben Davis	.25
103	Jay Powell	.25
104	Chris Snopek	.25
105	Glendon Rusch **RC**	1.00
106	Enrique Wilson	.25
107	Antonio Alfonseca **RC**	.75
108	Wilton Guerrero **RC**	.50
109	Jose Guillen **RC**	3.00
110	Miguel Mejia **RC**	.25
111	Jay Payton	.25
112	Scott Elarton	.25
113	Brooks Kieschnick	.25
114	Dustin Hermanson	.25
115	Roger Cedeno	.25
116	Matt Wagner	.25
117	Lee Daniels	.25
118	Ben Grieve	.25
119	Ugueth Urbina	.25
120	Danny Graves	.25
121	Dan Donato **RC**	.25
122	Matt Ruebel **RC**	.25
123	Mark Sievert **RC**	.25
124	Chris Stynes	.25
125	Jeff Abbott	.25
126	Rocky Coppinger **RC**	.25
127	Jermaine Dye	.25
128	Todd Greene	.15
129	Chris Carpenter	1.00
130	Edgar Renteria	.50
131	Matt Drews	.25
132	Edgard Velazquez **RC**	.50
133	Casey Whitten	.25
134	Ryan Jones **RC**	.25
135	Todd Walker	.20
136	Geoff Jenkins **RC**	2.00
137	Matt Morris **RC**	2.00
138	Richie Sexson	.75
139	Todd Dunwoody **RC**	.50
140	Gabe Alvarez **RC**	.50
141	J.J. Johnson	.25
142	Shannon Stewart	.25
143	Brad Fullmer	.25
144	Julio Santana	.25
145	Scott Rolen	1.00
146	Amaury Telemaco	.25
147	Trey Beamon	.25
148	Billy Wagner	.20
149	Todd Hollandsworth	.25
150	Doug Million	.25
151	Jose Valentin **RC**	.25
152	Wes Helms **RC**	.50
153	Jeff Suppan	.25
154	Luis Castillo **RC**	1.50
155	Bob Abreu	.50
156	Paul Konerko	.50
157	Jamey Wright	.25
158	Eddie Pearson	.25
159	Jimmy Haynes	.25
160	Derrek Lee	.75
161	Damian Moss	.15
162	Carlos Guillen **RC**	2.00
163	Chris Fussell **RC**	.25
164	Mike Sweeney **RC**	3.00
165	Donnie Sadler	.15
166	Desi Relaford	.25
167	Steve Gibralter	.25
168	Neifi Perez	.25
169	Antone Williamson	.25
170	Marty Janzen **RC**	.25
171	Todd Helton	1.00
172	Raul Ibanez **RC**	2.00
173	Bill Selby	.25
174	Shane Monahan **RC**	.35
175	Robin Jennings **RC**	.25
176	Bobby Chouinard **RC**	.25
177	Einar Diaz	.25
178	Jason Thompson	.15
179	Rafael Medina **RC**	.25
100	Kevin Orie	.25

Cuts

Bowman's Best Cuts gave collectors the first die-cut chromium cards in a 15-card set of top stars. The cards were seeded one per 24 packs. Refractor versions are inserted on average of one per 48 packs; Atomic Refractor versions are found one per 96 packs.

		NM/M
Complete Set (15):		15.00
Common Player:		.25
Refractors:		1.5X
Atomic Refractors:		2X
1	Ken Griffey Jr.	2.50
2	Jason Isringhausen	.25
3	Derek Jeter	4.00
4	Andruw Jones	1.00
5	Chipper Jones	2.00
6	Ryan Klesko	.25
7	Raul Mondesi	.25
8	Hideo Nomo	.50
9	Mike Piazza	2.50
10	Manny Ramirez	1.00
11	Cal Ripken Jr.	4.00
12	Ruben Rivera	.25
13	Tim Salmon	.25
14	Frank Thomas	1.00
15	Jim Thome	.75

Mirror Image

Mirror Image inserts feature four top players at 10 different positions, pairing an American League veteran and a prospect on one side and a National League veteran and

prospect on the other. These cards are seeded one per every 48 packs. Mirror Image Refractors (one in every 96 packs) and Mirror Image Atomic Refractors (one in every 192 packs) were also produced.

		NM/M
Complete Set (10):		24.00
Common Card:		1.50
Refractors:		1.5X
Atomics:		2X
1	Jeff Bagwell, Todd Helton, Frank Thomas, Richie Sexson	3.00
2	Craig Biggio, Luis Castillo, Roberto Alomar, Desi Relaford	1.50
3	Chipper Jones, Scott Rolen, Wade Boggs, George Arias	3.50
4	Barry Larkin, Neifi Perez, Cal Ripken Jr., Mark Bellhorn	6.00
5	Larry Walker, Karim Garcia, Albert Belle, Ruben Rivera	1.50
6	Barry Bonds, Andruw Jones, Kenny Lofton, Donnie Sadler	6.00
7	Tony Gwynn, Vladimir Guerrero, Ken Griffey Jr., Ben Grieve	4.50
8	Mike Piazza, Ben Davis, Ivan Rodriguez, Jose Valentin	4.50
9	Greg Maddux, Jamey Wright, Mike Mussina, Bartolo Colon	3.50
10	Tom Glavine, Billy Wagner, Randy Johnson, Jarrod Washburn	1.50

1997 Bowman Pre-Production

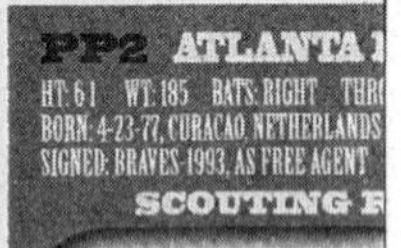

The format for 1997 Bowman's base set was previewed in this sample issue distributed to card dealers and the hobby press. The samples are virtually identical to the issued versions of the same players' cards, except they carry a "PP" prefix to the number on back.

		NM/M
Complete Set (4):		9.00
Common Player:		1.50
PP1	Jose Cruz, Jr.	1.50
PP2	Andruw Jones	2.00
PP3	Derek Jeter	4.50
PP4	Sammy Sosa	3.00

1997 Bowman

The 1997 Bowman set consists of 440 base cards, an increase of 55 cards from the '96 set. Fronts have a player photo within a red or blue frame with black borders. Backs feature another color photo, along with 1996 statistics broken down by opponent. Players making their first appearance in a Bowman set have a "1st Bowman Card" designation on the card. Prospects' cards have red foil on front; vet-

erans have blue. Inserts include International parallels, Certified Autographs, Scout's Honor Roll and Bowman's Best Previews. Cards were sold in 10-card packs with a suggested retail price of $2.50. Topps offered collectors a $125 guarantee on the value of the set through the year 2000.

NM/M

Complete Set (440): 50.00
Complete Series 1 (221): 25.00
Complete Series 2 (219): 25.00
Common Player: .10
Series 1 Pack (10): 2.00
Series 1 Wax Box (24): 35.00
Series 2 Pack (10): 2.00
Series 2 Wax Box (24): 35.00
1 Derek Jeter 2.00
2 Edgar Renteria .10
3 Chipper Jones 1.00
4 Hideo Nomo .40
5 Tim Salmon .10
6 Jason Giambi .50
7 Robin Ventura .10
8 Tony Clark .10
9 Barry Larkin .25
10 Paul Molitor .75
11 Bernard Gilkey .10
12 Jack McDowell .10
13 Andy Benes .10
14 Ryan Klesko .10
15 Mark McGwire 1.50
16 Ken Griffey Jr. 1.50
17 Robb Nen .10
18 Cal Ripken Jr. 2.00
19 John Valentin .10
20 Ricky Bottalico .10
21 Mike Lansing .10
22 Ryne Sandberg 1.00
23 Carlos Delgado .50
24 Craig Biggio .25
25 Eric Karros .10
26 Kevin Appier .10
27 Mariano Rivera .50
28 Vinny Castilla .10
29 Juan Gonzalez .40
30 Al Martin .10
31 Jeff Cirillo .10
32 Eddie Murray .75
33 Ray Lankford .10
34 Manny Ramirez .75
35 Roberto Alomar .25
36 Will Clark .25
37 Chuck Knoblauch .10
38 Harold Baines .10
39 Trevor Hoffman .10
40 Edgar Martinez .10
41 Geronimo Berroa .10
42 Rey Ordonez .10
43 Mike Stanley .10
44 Mike Mussina .40
45 Kevin Brown .10
46 Dennis Eckersley .50
47 Henry Rodriguez .10
48 Tino Martinez .10
49 Eric Young .10
50 Bret Boone .10
51 Raul Mondesi .10
52 Sammy Sosa 1.00
53 John Smoltz .25
54 Billy Wagner .10
55 Jeff D'Amico .10
56 Ken Caminiti .10
57 Jason Kendall .10
58 Wade Boggs .75
59 Andres Galarraga .10
60 Jeff Brantley .10
61 Mel Rojas .10
62 Brian Hunter .10
63 Bobby Bonilla .10
64 Roger Clemens 1.50
65 Jeff Kent .20
66 Matt Williams .10
67 Albert Belle .10
68 Jeff King .10
69 John Wetteland .10
70 Deion Sanders .25
71 Bubba Trammell **RC** .25
72 Felix Heredia **RC** .25
73 Billy Koch **RC** .25
74 Sidney Ponson **RC** .25
75 Ricky Ledee **RC** .25
76 Brett Tomko .10
77 Braden Looper **RC** .25
78 Damian Jackson .10
79 Jason Dickson .10
80 Chad Green **RC** .10
81 R.A. Dickey **RC** .10
82 Jeff Liefer .10
83 Matt Wagner .10
84 Richard Hidalgo .10
85 Adam Riggs .10
86 Robert Smith .10
87 Chad Hermansen **RC** .10
88 Felix Martinez .10
89 J.J. Johnson .10
90 Todd Dunwoody .10
91 Katsuhiro Maeda .10
92 Darin Erstad .25
93 Elieser Marrero .10
94 Bartolo Colon .10
95 Chris Fussell .10
96 Ugueth Urbina .10
97 Josh Paul **RC** .10
98 Jaime Bluma .10
99 Seth Greisinger **RC** .10
100 Jose Cruz **RC** .25
101 Todd Dunn .10
102 Joe Young **RC** .10
103 Jonathan Johnson .10
104 Justin Towle **RC** .10
105 Brian Rose .10
106 Jose Guillen .10
107 Andruw Jones .75
108 Mark Kotsay **RC** 1.00
109 Wilton Guerrero .10
110 Jacob Cruz .10
111 Mike Sweeney .10
112 Julio Mosquera .10
113 Matt Morris .10
114 Wendell Magee .10
115 John Thomson .10
116 Javier Valentin **RC** .10
117 Tom Fordham .10
118 Ruben Rivera .10
119 Mike Drumright **RC** .10
120 Chris Holt .10
121 Sean Maloney **RC** .10
122 Michael Barrett .10
123 Tony Saunders **RC** .10
124 Kevin Brown .10
125 Richard Almanzar .10
126 Mark Redman .10
127 Anthony Sanders **RC** .10
128 Jeff Abbott .10
129 Eugene Kingsale .10
130 Paul Konerko .40
131 Randall Simon **RC** .25
132 Andy Larkin .10
133 Rafael Medina .10
134 Mendy Lopez .10
135 Freddy Garcia .10
136 Karim Garcia .15
137 Larry Rodriguez **RC** .10
138 Carlos Guillen .10
139 Aaron Boone .15
140 Donnie Sadler .10
141 Brooks Kieschnick .10
142 Scott Spiezio .10
143 Everett Stull .10
144 Enrique Wilson .10
145 Milton Bradley **RC** 1.50
146 Kevin Orie .10
147 Derek Wallace .10
148 Russ Johnson .10
149 Joe Lagarde **RC** .10
150 Luis Castillo .10
151 Jay Payton .10
152 Joe Long .10
153 Livan Hernandez .10
154 Vladimir Nunez **RC** .15
156a George Arias .10
156b Calvin Reese (Should be #155.) .10
157 Homer Bush .10
159a Eric Milton **RC** .50
159b Chris Carpenter (Should be #158.) .50
160 Richie Sexson .40
161 Carl Pavano .10
162 Chris Gissell **RC** .10
163 Mac Suzuki .10
164 Pat Cline .10
165 Ron Wright .10
166 Dante Powell .10
167 Mark Bellhorn .10
168 George Lombard .10
169 Pee Wee Lopez **RC** .10
170 Paul Wilder **RC** .10
171 Brad Fullmer .10
172 Willie Martinez **RC** .10
173 Dario Veras **RC** .10
174 Dave Coggin .10
175 Kris Benson **RC** 1.00
176 Torii Hunter .25
177 D.T. Cromer **RC** .10
178 Nelson Figueroa **RC** .10
179 Hiram Bocachica **RC** .15
180 Shane Monahan .10
181 Jimmy Anderson **RC** .10
182 Juan Melo .10
183 Pablo Ortega **RC** .10
184 Calvin Pickering **RC** .50
185 Reggie Taylor .10
186 Jeff Farnsworth **RC** .10
187 Terrence Long .10
188 Geoff Jenkins .10
189 Steve Rain **RC** .10
190 Nerio Rodriguez **RC** .10
191 Derrick Gibson .10
192 Darin Blood .10
193 Ben Davis .10
194 Adrian Beltre **RC** 2.00
195 Damian Sapp **RC** .10
196 Kerry Wood **RC** 3.00
197 Nate Rolison **RC** .10
198 Fernando Tatis **RC** .25
199 Brad Penny **RC** 2.00
200 Jake Westbrook **RC** .15
201 Edwin Diaz .10
202 Joe Fontenot **RC** .10
203 Matt Halloran **RC** .10
204 Blake Stein **RC** .10
205 Onan Masaoka .10
206 Ben Petrick .10
207 Matt Clement **RC** 1.00
208 Todd Greene .10
209 Ray Ricken .10
210 Eric Chavez **RC** 3.00
211 Edgard Velazquez .10
212 Bruce Chen **RC** .10
213 Danny Patterson **RC** .10
214 Jeff Yoder .10
215 Luis Ordaz **RC** .10
216 Chris Widger .10
217 Jason Brester .10
218 Carlton Loewer .10
219 Chris Reitsma **RC** .10
220 Neifi Perez .10
221 Hideki Irabu **RC** .25
222 Ellis Burks .10
223 Pedro Martinez .75
224 Kenny Lofton .10
225 Randy Johnson .75
226 Terry Steinbach .10
227 Bernie Williams .25
228 Dean Palmer .10
229 Alan Benes .10
230 Marquis Grissom .10
231 Gary Sheffield .40
232 Curt Schilling .40
233 Reggie Sanders .10
234 Bobby Higginson .10
235 Moises Alou .20
236 Tom Glavine .25
237 Mark Grace .25
238 Ramon Martinez .10
239 Rafael Palmeiro .50
240 John Olerud .10
241 Dante Bichette .10
242 Greg Vaughn .10
243 Jeff Bagwell .50
244 Barry Bonds 2.00
245 Pat Hentgen .10
246 Jim Thome .50
247 Jermaine Allensworth .10
248 Andy Pettitte .25
249 Jay Bell .10
250 John Jaha .10
251 Jim Edmonds .25
252 Ron Gant .10
253 David Cone .10
254 Jose Canseco .40
255 Jay Buhner .10
256 Greg Maddux 1.50
257 Brian McRae .10
258 Lance Johnson .10
259 Travis Fryman .10
260 Paul O'Neill .20
261 Ivan Rodriguez .50
262 Gregg Jefferies .10
263 Fred McGriff .20
264 Derek Bell .10
265 Jeff Conine .10
266 Mike Piazza 1.50
267 Mark Grudzielanek .10
268 Brady Anderson .10
269 Marty Cordova .10
270 Ray Durham .10
271 Joe Carter .10
272 Brian Jordan .10
273 David Justice .10
274 Tony Gwynn 1.00
275 Larry Walker .20
276 Cecil Fielder .10
277 Mo Vaughn .10
278 Alex Fernandez .10
279 Michael Tucker .10
280 Jose Valentin .10
281 Sandy Alomar .10
282 Todd Hollandsworth .10
283 Rico Brogna .10
284 Rusty Greer .10
285 Roberto Hernandez .10
286 Hal Morris .10
287 Johnny Damon .75
288 Todd Hundley .10
289 Rondell White .10
290 Frank Thomas .75
291 Don Denbow **RC** .10
292 Derrek Lee .50
293 Todd Walker .10
294 Scott Rolen .50
295 Wes Helms .10
296 Bob Abreu .25
297 John Patterson **RC** 1.50
298 Alex Gonzalez **RC** .25
299 Grant Roberts **RC** .25
300 Jeff Suppan .10
301 Luke Wilcox .10
302 Marlon Anderson .10
303 Ray Brown .10
304 Mike Caruso **RC** .25
305 Sam Marsonek **RC** .10
306 Brady Raggio **RC** .10
307 Kevin McGlinchy **RC** .25
308 Roy Halladay **RC** 3.00
309 Jeremi Gonzalez **RC** .25
310 Aramis Ramirez **RC** 4.00
311 Dermal Brown **RC** .10
312 Justin Thompson .10
313 Jay Tessmer **RC** .10
314 Mike Johnson .10
315 Danny Clyburn .10
316 Bruce Aven .10
317 Keith Foulke **RC** 1.50
318 Jimmy Osting **RC** .10
319 Valerio De Los Santos **RC** .25
320 Shannon Stewart .10
321 Willie Adams .10
322 Larry Barnes .10
323 Mark Johnson .10
324 Chris Stowers **RC** .10
325 Brandon Reed .10
326 Randy Winn .10
327 Steven Chavez .10
328 Nomar Garciaparra 1.00
329 Jacque Jones **RC** 1.00
330 Chris Clemons .10
331 Todd Helton .50
332 Ryan Brannan **RC** .10
333 Alex Sanchez **RC** .25
334 Arnold Gooch .10
335 Russell Branyan .10
336 Daryle Ward .10
337 John LeRoy **RC** .10
338 Steve Cox .10
339 Kevin Witt .10
340 Norm Hutchins .10
341 Gabby Martinez .10
342 Kris Detmers .10
343 Mike Villano **RC** .10
344 Preston Wilson .10
345 Jim Manias **RC** .10
346 Deivi Cruz **RC** .25
347 Donzell McDonald **RC** .10
348 Rod Myers **RC** .10
349 Shawn Chacon **RC** .25
350 Elvin Hernandez **RC** .10
351 Orlando Cabrera **RC** 1.00
352 Brian Banks .10
353 Robbie Bell .10
354 Brad Rigby .10
355 Scott Elarton .10
356 Kevin Sweeney **RC** .10
357 Steve Soderstrom .10
358 Ryan Nye .10
359 Marlon Allen **RC** .10
360 Donny Leon **RC** .10
361 Garrett Neubart **RC** .10
362 Abraham Nunez **RC** .25
363 Adam Eaton **RC** .50
364 Octavio Dotel **RC** .40
365 Dean Crow **RC** .10
366 Jason Baker **RC** .10
367 Sean Casey .10
368 Joe Lawrence **RC** .10
369 Adam Johnson **RC** .10
370 Scott Schoeneweis **RC** .25
371 Gerald Witasick Jr. .10
372 Ronnie Belliard **RC** .25
373 Russ Ortiz .10
374 Robert Stratton **RC** .10
375 Bobby Estalella .10
376 Corey Lee **RC** .10
377 Carlos Beltran .50
378 Mike Cameron .10
379 Scott Randall **RC** .10
380 Corey Erickson **RC** .10
381 Jay Canizaro .10
382 Kerry Robinson **RC** .10
383 Todd Noel **RC** .10
384 A.J. Zapp **RC** .10
385 Jarrod Washburn .10
386 Ben Grieve .10
387 Javier Vazquez **RC** 1.50
388 Tony Graffanino .10
389 Travis Lee **RC** .50
390 DaRond Stovall .10
391 Dennis Reyes **RC** .25
392 Danny Buxbaum .10
393 Marc Lewis **RC** .10
394 Kelvim Escobar **RC** .25
395 Danny Klassen .10
396 Ken Cloude **RC** .25
397 Gabe Alvarez .10
398 Jaret Wright **RC** .50
399 Raul Casanova .10
400 Clayton Brunner **RC** .10
401 Jason Marquis **RC** .50
402 Marc Kroon .10
403 Jamey Wright .10
404 Matt Snyder **RC** .10
405 Josh Garrett **RC** .10
406 Juan Encarnacion .10
407 Heath Murray .10
408 Brett Herbison **RC** .10
409 Brent Butler **RC** .25
410 Danny Peoples **RC** .25
411 Miguel Tejada **RC** 10.00
412 Damian Moss .10
413 Jim Pittsley .10
414 Dmitri Young .10
415 Glendon Rusch .10
416 Vladimir Guerrero .75
417 Cole Liniak **RC** .10
418 Ramon Hernandez .10
419 Cliff Politte **RC** .25
420 Mel Rosario **RC** .10
421 Jorge Carrion **RC** .10
422 John Barnes **RC** .10
423 Chris Stowe **RC** .10
424 Vernon Wells **RC** 4.00
425 Brett Caradonna **RC** .10
426 Scott Hodges **RC** .10
427 Jon Garland **RC** 1.50
428 Nathan Haynes **RC** .25
429 Geoff Goetz **RC** .25
430 Adam Kennedy **RC** .50
431 T.J. Tucker **RC** .10
432 Aaron Akin **RC** .10
433 Jayson Werth **RC** .50
434 Glenn Davis **RC** .10
435 Mark Mangum **RC** .10
436 Troy Cameron **RC** .10
437 J.J. Davis **RC** .10
438 Lance Berkman **RC** 4.00
439 Jason Standridge **RC** .25
440 Jason Dellaero **RC** .10
441 Hideki Irabu **RC** .25

Certified Autographs

Ninety players signed autographs for inclusion in Series 1 and 2 packs. Each autograph card features a gold-foil Certified Autograph stamp on front and can be found in one of three versions: Blue, 1:96 packs; black, 1:503 packs and gold, 1:1,509 packs. Derek Jeter's card can also be found in a green-ink autographed version, inserted one per 1,928 packs. Card numbers have a "CA" prefix.

NM/M

Common Blue: 2.00
Black: 1.5X
Gold: 4X
Derek Jeter Green: 1.5X
1 Jeff Abbott 2.00
2 Bob Abreu 40.00
3 Willie Adams 2.00
4 Brian Banks 2.00
5 Kris Benson 15.00
6 Darin Blood 2.00
7 Jaime Bluma 2.00
8 Kevin Brown 5.00
9 Ray Brown 2.00
10 Homer Bush 4.00
11 Mike Cameron 8.00
12 Jay Canizaro 3.00
13 Luis Castillo 5.00
14 Dave Coggin 2.00
15 Bartolo Colon 15.00
16 Rocky Coppinger 3.00
17 Jacob Cruz 5.00
18 Jose Cruz 8.00
19 Jeff D'Amico 5.00
20 Ben Davis 5.00
21 Mike Drumbright 5.00
22 Scott Elarton 5.00
23 Darin Erstad 10.00
24 Bobby Estalella 5.00
25 Joe Fontenot 4.00
26 Tom Fordham 2.00
27 Brad Fullmer 5.00
28 Chris Fussell 2.00
29 Karim Garcia 5.00
30 Kris Detmers 2.00
31 Todd Greene 4.00
32 Ben Grieve 5.00
33 Vladimir Guerrero 75.00
34 Jose Guillen 15.00
35 Roy Halladay 65.00
36 Wes Helms 5.00
37 Chad Hermansen 3.00
38 Richard Hidalgo 8.00
39 Todd Hollandsworth 3.00
40 Damian Jackson 3.00
41 Derek Jeter 120.00
42 Andruw Jones 40.00
43 Brooks Kieschnick 3.00
44 Eugene Kingsale 5.00
45 Paul Konerko 15.00
46 Marc Kroon 2.00
47 Derrek Lee 40.00
48 Travis Lee 5.00
49 Terrence Long 4.00
50 Curt Lyons 3.00
51 Elieser Marrero 3.00
52 Rafael Medina 2.00
53 Juan Melo 3.00
54 Shane Monahan 2.00
55 Julio Mosquera 2.00
56 Heath Murray 2.00
57 Ryan Nye 2.00
58 Kevin Orie 4.00
59 Russ Ortiz 5.00
60 Carl Pavano 30.00
61 Jay Payton 5.00
62 Neifi Perez 3.00
63 Sidney Ponson 10.00
64 Calvin Reese 8.00
65 Ray Ricken 3.00
66 Brad Rigby 3.00
67 Adam Riggs 3.00
68 Ruben Rivera 4.00
69 J.J. Johnson 2.00
70 Scott Rolen 40.00
71 Tony Saunders 3.00
72 Donnie Sadler 5.00
73 Richie Sexson 15.00
74 Scott Spiezio 6.00
75 Everett Stull 2.00
76 Mike Sweeney 15.00
77 Fernando Tatis 4.00
78 Miguel Tejada 80.00
79 Justin Thompson 5.00
80 Justin Towle 6.00
81 Billy Wagner 20.00
82 Todd Walker 5.00
83 Luke Wilcox 2.00
84 Paul Wilder 4.00
85 Enrique Wilson 5.00
86 Kerry Wood 60.00
87 Jamey Wright 5.00
88 Ron Wright 5.00
89 Dmitri Young 10.00
90 Nelson Figueroa 2.00

International

Inserted at the rate of one per pack, the International parallel set replaces the regular photo background on front and back with the flag of the player's native land. Card #441 from the regular-issue version does not exist as an International parallel.

NM/M

Complete Set (440): 75.00
Complete Series 1 (221): 40.00
Complete Series 2 (219): 40.00
Common Player: .25
Stars and Rookies: 1.5X
(See 1997 Bowman for checklist base card values.)

International Best

This Series 2 insert set features a flag design in the background of each card front depicting the player's country of origin. On back is another color photo, player personal data, a record of his best season and colored flags representing 14 nations which have sent players to the major leagues. One International Best card was inserted in every second series pack. Card numbers carry a "BBI" prefix. Refractor versions are a 1:48 parallel with Atomic Refractors found 1:96.

NM/M

Complete Set (20): 20.00
Common Player: .60
Refractors: 1.5X
Atomic Refractors: 2X
1 Frank Thomas 1.50
2 Ken Griffey Jr. 2.50
3 Juan Gonzalez 1.50
4 Bernie Williams .60
5 Hideo Nomo 1.50
6 Sammy Sosa 3.50
7 Larry Walker .60
8 Vinny Castilla .60
9 Mariano Rivera .75
10 Rafael Palmeiro 1.00
11 Nomar Garciaparra 3.50
12 Todd Walker .60
13 Andruw Jones 1.50
14 Vladimir Guerrero 1.50
15 Ruben Rivera .60
16 Bob Abreu .75
17 Karim Garcia .75
18 Katsuhiro Maeda .60
19 Jose Cruz Jr. 1.00
20 Damian Moss .60

Rookie of the Year Candidates

This 15-card insert was inserted in one per 12 packs of Bowman Series 2. Fronts feature a color shot of the player over a textured foil background, with the player's name across the bottom and the words "Rookie of the Year Favorites" across the top with the word "Rookie" in large script letters. Card numbers have a "ROY" prefix.

		NM/M
Complete Set (15):		9.00
Common Player:		.50
1	Jeff Abbott	.50
2	Karim Garcia	.50
3	Todd Helton	2.50
4	Richard Hidalgo	.50
5	Geoff Jenkins	.50
6	Russ Johnson	.50
7	Paul Konerko	.75
8	Mark Kotsay	.50
9	Ricky Ledee	.50
10	Travis Lee	.75
11	Derrek Lee	1.50
12	Elieser Marrero	.50
13	Juan Melo	.50
14	Brian Rose	.50
15	Fernando Tatis	.50

Scout's Honor Roll

This insert features 15 prospects deemed to have the most potential by Topps' scouts. Each card features a double-etched foil design and is inserted 1:12 packs.

		NM/M
Complete Set (15):		12.50
Common Player:		.50
1	Dmitri Young	.50
2	Bob Abreu	.75
3	Vladimir Guerrero	2.00
4	Paul Konerko	.75
5	Kevin Orie	.50
6	Todd Walker	.50
7	Ben Grieve	.50
8	Darin Erstad	1.00
9	Derrek Lee	1.00
10	Jose Cruz	.50
11	Scott Rolen	1.00
12	Travis Lee	.75
13	Andruw Jones	2.00
14	Wilton Guerrero	.50
15	Nomar Garciaparra	2.50

1997 Bowman's Best Preview

This 20-card set, featuring 10 veterans and 10 prospects, is a preview of the format used in the Bowman's Best product. Three different versions of the Preview cards

were available: Regular (1:12 packs), Refractors (1:48) and Atomic Refractors (1:96).

		NM/M
Complete Set (20):		30.00
Common Player:		.75
Refractors:		1.5X
Atomic Refractors:		2X
1	Frank Thomas	1.50
2	Ken Griffey Jr.	3.00
3	Barry Bonds	5.00
4	Derek Jeter	5.00
5	Chipper Jones	2.00
6	Mark McGwire	4.00
7	Cal Ripken Jr.	5.00
8	Kenny Lofton	.75
9	Gary Sheffield	.75
10	Jeff Bagwell	1.50
11	Wilton Guerrero	.75
12	Scott Rolen	1.00
13	Todd Walker	.75
14	Ruben Rivera	.75
15	Andruw Jones	1.50
16	Nomar Garciaparra	2.00
17	Vladimir Guerrero	1.50
18	Miguel Tejada	1.00
19	Bartolo Colon	.75
20	Katsuhiro Maeda	.75

1997 Bowman Chrome

Bowman Chrome was released in one 300-card series following the conclusion of the 1997 season. Four-card foil packs carried an SRP of $3. Each card reprints one of the regular Bowman set, utilizing chromium technology on front. Inserts include: International parallels, Rookie of the Year Favorites and Scout's Honor Roll.

		NM/M
Complete Set (300):		150.00
Common Player:		.25
Pack (3):		5.00
Wax Box (24):		100.00
1	Derek Jeter	4.00
2	Chipper Jones	2.00
3	Hideo Nomo	.75
4	Tim Salmon	.25
5	Robin Ventura	.25
6	Tony Clark	.25
7	Barry Larkin	.50
8	Paul Molitor	1.00
9	Andy Benes	.25
10	Ryan Klesko	.25
11	Mark McGwire	3.00
12	Ken Griffey Jr.	2.50
13	Robb Nen	.25
14	Cal Ripken Jr.	4.00
15	John Valentin	.25
16	Ricky Bottalico	.25
17	Mike Lansing	.25
18	Ryne Sandberg	2.00
19	Carlos Delgado	1.00
20	Craig Biggio	.50
21	Eric Karros	.25
22	Kevin Appier	.25
23	Mariano Rivera	.75
24	Vinny Castilla	.25
25	Juan Gonzalez	.50
26	Al Martin	.25
27	Jeff Cirillo	.25
28	Ray Lankford	.25
29	Manny Ramirez	1.50
30	Roberto Alomar	.40
31	Will Clark	.50
32	Chuck Knoblauch	.25
33	Harold Baines	.25
34	Edgar Martinez	.25
35	Mike Mussina	.50
36	Kevin Brown	.25
37	Dennis Eckersley	.75
38	Tino Martinez	.25
39	Raul Mondesi	.25
40	Sammy Sosa	1.50
41	John Smoltz	.75
42	Billy Wagner	.25
43	Ken Caminiti	.25
44	Wade Boggs	1.50
45	Andres Galarraga	.25
46	Roger Clemens	3.00
47	Matt Williams	.25
48	Albert Belle	.25
49	Jeff King	.25
50	John Wetteland	.25
51	Deion Sanders	.50
52	Ellis Burks	.25
53	Pedro Martinez	1.50
54	Kenny Lofton	.25
55	Randy Johnson	1.50
56	Bernie Williams	.50
57	Marquis Grissom	.25
58	Gary Sheffield	.50
59	Curt Schilling	1.00
60	Reggie Sanders	.25
61	Bobby Higginson	.25
62	Moises Alou	.50
63	Tom Glavine	.50
64	Mark Grace	.50
65	Rafael Palmeiro	1.00
66	John Olerud	.25
67	Dante Bichette	.25
68	Jeff Bagwell	1.00
69	Barry Bonds	3.00
70	Pat Hentgen	.25
71	Jim Thome	1.00
72	Andy Pettitte	.50
73	Jay Bell	.25
74	Jim Edmonds	.50
75	Ron Gant	.25
76	David Cone	.25
77	Jose Canseco	.75
78	Jay Buhner	.25
79	Greg Maddux	2.50
80	Lance Johnson	.25
81	Travis Fryman	.25
82	Paul O'Neill	.50
83	Ivan Rodriguez	1.00
84	Fred McGriff	.25
85	Mike Piazza	2.50
86	Brady Anderson	.25
87	Marty Cordova	.25
88	Joe Carter	.25
89	Brian Jordan	.25
90	David Justice	.25
91	Tony Gwynn	2.00
92	Larry Walker	.40
93	Mo Vaughn	.25
94	Sandy Alomar	.25
95	Rusty Greer	.25
96	Roberto Hernandez	.25
97	Hal Morris	.25
98	Todd Hundley	.25
99	Rondell White	.25
100	Frank Thomas	1.50
101	Bubba Trammell **RC**	.75
102	Sidney Ponson **RC**	1.50
103	Ricky Ledee **RC**	.50
104	Brett Tomko	.25
105	Braden Looper **RC**	.50
106	Jason Dickson	.25
107	Chad Green **RC**	.25
108	R.A. Dickey **RC**	.25
109	Jeff Liefer	.25
110	Richard Hidalgo	.25
111	Chad Hermansen **RC**	.50
112	Felix Martinez	.25
113	J.J. Johnson	.25
114	Todd Dunwoody	.25
115	Katsuhiro Maeda	.25
116	Darin Erstad	.50
117	Elieser Marrero	.25
118	Bartolo Colon	.25
119	Ugueth Urbina	.25
120	Jaime Bluma	.25
121	Seth Greisinger **RC**	.50
122	Jose Cruz Jr. **RC**	1.50
123	Todd Dunn	.25
124	Justin Towle **RC**	.25
125	Brian Rose	.25
126	Jose Guillen	.25
127	Andruw Jones	1.50
128	Mark Kotsay **RC**	2.50
129	Wilton Guerrero	.25
130	Jacob Cruz	.25
131	Mike Sweeney	.25
132	Matt Morris	.25
133	John Thomson	.25
134	Javier Valentin **RC**	.25
135	Mike Drumright **RC**	.25
136	Michael Barrett	.25
137	Tony Saunders **RC**	.25
138	Kevin Brown	.25
139	Anthony Sanders **RC**	.25
140	Jeff Abbott	.25
141	Eugene Kingsale	.25
142	Paul Konerko	.50
143	Randall Simon **RC**	.50
144	Freddy Garcia	.25
145	Karim Garcia	.25
146	Carlos Guillen	.25
147	Aaron Boone	.25
148	Donnie Sadler	.25
149	Brooks Kieschnick	.25
150	Scott Spiezio	.25
151	Kevin Orie	.25
152	Russ Johnson	.25
153	Livan Hernandez	.25
154	Vladimir Nunez **RC**	.75
155	Calvin Reese	.25
156	Chris Carpenter	.25
157	Eric Milton **RC**	1.50
158	Richie Sexson	.50
159	Carl Pavano	.25
160	Pat Cline	.25
161	Ron Wright	.25
162	Dante Powell	.25
163	Mark Bellhorn	.25
164	George Lombard	.25
165	Paul Wilder **RC**	.25
166	Brad Fullmer	.25
167	Kris Benson **RC**	2.00
168	Torii Hunter	.50
169	D.T. Cromer	.25
170	Nelson Figueroa **RC**	.50
171	Hiram Bocachica **RC**	.50
172	Shane Monahan	.25
173	Juan Melo	.25
174	Calvin Pickering **RC**	1.50
175	Reggie Taylor	.25
176	Geoff Jenkins	.25
177	Steve Rain **RC**	.25
178	Nerio Rodriguez	.25
179	Derrick Gibson	.25
180	Darin Blood	.25
181	Ben Davis	.25
182	Adrian Beltre **RC**	8.00
183	Kerry Wood **RC**	8.00
184	Nate Rolison	.25
185	Fernando Tatis **RC**	.50
186	Jake Westbrook **RC**	2.00
187	Edwin Diaz	.25
188	Joe Fontenot **RC**	.50
189	Matt Halloran **RC**	.25
190	Matt Clement **RC**	3.00
191	Todd Greene	.25
192	Eric Chavez **RC**	10.00
193	Edgard Velazquez	.25
194	Bruce Chen **RC**	.25
195	Jason Brester	.25
196	Chris Reitsma **RC**	.50
197	Neifi Perez	.25
198	Hideki Irabu **RC**	.50
199	Don Denbow **RC**	.25
200	Derrek Lee	.75
201	Todd Walker	.25
202	Scott Rolen	1.00
203	Wes Helms	.25
204	Bob Abreu	.50
205	John Patterson **RC**	2.00
206	Alex Gonzalez **RC**	1.00
207	Grant Roberts **RC**	.50
208	Jeff Suppan	.25
209	Luke Wilcox	.25
210	Marlon Anderson	.25
211	Mike Caruso **RC**	.75
212	Roy Halladay **RC**	8.00
213	Jeremi Gonzalez **RC**	.50
214	Aramis Ramirez **RC**	10.00
215	Dermal Brown **RC**	.25
216	Justin Thompson	.25
217	Danny Clyburn	.25
218	Bruce Aven	.25
219	Keith Foulke **RC**	2.00
220	Shannon Stewart	.25
221	Larry Barnes	.25
222	Mark Johnson **RC**	.25
223	Randy Winn	.25
224	Nomar Garciaparra	2.00
225	Jacque Jones **RC**	4.00
226	Chris Clemons	.25
227	Todd Helton	1.00
228	Ryan Brannan **RC**	.25
229	Alex Sanchez **RC**	.50
230	Russell Branyan	.25
231	Daryle Ward	.25
232	Kevin Witt	.25
233	Gabby Martinez	.25
234	Preston Wilson	.25
235	Donzell McDonald **RC**	.25
236	Orlando Cabrera **RC**	5.00
237	Brian Banks	.25
238	Robbie Bell	.25
239	Brad Rigby	.25
240	Scott Elarton	.25
241	Donny Leon **RC**	.25
242	Abraham Nunez **RC**	1.00
243	Adam Eaton **RC**	2.00
244	Octavio Dotel **RC**	1.00
245	Sean Casey	.35
246	Joe Lawrence **RC**	.50
247	Adam Johnson **RC**	.25
248	Ronnie Belliard **RC**	1.00
249	Bobby Estalella	.25
250	Corey Lee **RC**	.25
251	Mike Cameron	.25
252	Kerry Robinson **RC**	.25
253	A.J. Zapp **RC**	.25
254	Jarrod Washburn	.25
255	Ben Grieve	.25
256	Javier Vazquez **RC**	3.00
257	Travis Lee **RC**	1.00
258	Dennis Reyes **RC**	.50
259	Danny Buxbaum	.25
260	Kelvim Escobar **RC**	1.00
261	Danny Klassen	.25
262	Ken Cloude **RC**	.50
263	Gabe Alvarez	.25
264	Clayton Brunner **RC**	.25
265	Jason Marquis **RC**	1.50
266	Jamey Wright	.25
267	Matt Snyder **RC**	.25
268	Josh Garrett **RC**	.25
269	Juan Encarnacion	.25
270	Heath Murray	.25
271	Brent Butler **RC**	1.00
272	Danny Peoples **RC**	.50
273	Miguel Tejada **RC**	20.00
274	Jim Pittsley	.25
275	Dmitri Young	.25
276	Vladimir Guerrero	1.50
277	Cole Liniak **RC**	.50
278	Ramon Hernandez	.25
279	Cliff Politte **RC**	.50
280	Mel Rosario **RC**	.25
281	Jorge Carrion **RC**	.25
282	John Barnes **RC**	.25
283	Chris Stowe **RC**	.25
284	Vernon Wells **RC**	15.00
285	Brett Caradonna **RC**	.25
286	Scott Hodges **RC**	.25
287	Jon Garland **RC**	4.00
288	Nathan Haynes **RC**	.50
289	Geoff Goetz **RC**	.50
290	Adam Kennedy **RC**	1.00
291	T.J. Tucker **RC**	.25
292	Aaron Akin **RC**	.25
293	Jayson Werth **RC**	2.50
294	Glenn Davis **RC**	.25
295	Mark Mangum **RC**	.25
296	Troy Cameron **RC**	.25
297	J.J. Davis **RC**	.25
298	Lance Berkman **RC**	15.00
299	Jason Standridge **RC**	.75
300	Jason Dellaero **RC**	.25

Refractors

All 300 cards in Bowman Chrome were reprinted in Refractor versions and inserted one per 12 packs. The cards are very similar to the base cards, but feature a refractive foil finish on front.

	NM/M
Common Player:	1.00
Stars:	4X

(See 1997 Bowman Chrome for checklist and base card values.)

International

Internationals paralleled all 300 cards in the base set with a flag from the player's native country in the background. These inserts were seeded one per four packs.

	NM/M
Common Player:	1.00
Stars:	3X

Inserted 1:4

(See 1997 Bowman Chrome for checklist and base card values.)

International Refractors

Each International parallel card was also reprinted in a Refractor version. International Refractors were seeded one per 24 packs.

	NM/M
Common Player:	2.00
Stars:	6X

ROY Candidates

This 15-card insert set features color action photos of 1998 Rookie of the Year candidates printed on chromium finish cards. Card backs are numbered with a "ROY" prefix and were inserted one per 24 packs of Bowman Chrome. Refractor versions are seeded one per 72 packs.

		NM/M
Complete Set (15):		9.00
Common Player:		.50
Refractors:		1.5X
1	Jeff Abbott	.50
2	Karim Garcia	.75
3	Todd Helton	2.50
4	Richard Hidalgo	.50
5	Geoff Jenkins	.50
6	Russ Johnson	.50
7	Paul Konerko	1.00
8	Mark Kotsay	.50
9	Ricky Ledee	.50
10	Travis Lee	.75
11	Derrek Lee	1.50
12	Elieser Marrero	.50
13	Juan Melo	.50
14	Brian Rose	.50
15	Fernando Tatis	.50

Scout's Honor Roll

This 15-card set features top prospects and rookies as selected by the Topps' scouts. These chromium cards are numbered with a "SHR" prefix and are inserted one per 12 packs, while Refractor versions are seeded one per 36 packs.

		NM/M
Complete Set (15):		12.00
Common Player:		.50
Refractors:		1.5X
1	Dmitri Young	.50
2	Bob Abreu	.75
3	Vladimir Guerrero	2.00
4	Paul Konerko	.75
5	Kevin Orie	.50
6	Todd Walker	.50
7	Ben Grieve	.50
8	Darin Erstad	1.00
9	Derrek Lee	1.00
10	Jose Cruz, Jr.	.50
11	Scott Rolen	1.00
12	Travis Lee	.50
13	Andruw Jones	2.00
14	Wilton Guerrero	.50
15	Nomar Garciaparra	2.50

1997 Bowman's Best

The 200-card base set is divided into a 100-card subset featuring current stars on a gold-chromium stock, and 100 cards of top prospects in silver chromium. Packs contain six cards and were issued with a suggested retail price of $5. Autographed cards of 10 different players were randomly inserted into packs, with each player signing regular, Refractor and Atomic Refractor versions of their cards. Bowman's Best Laser Cuts and Mirror

Image are the two other inserts, each with Refractor and Atomic Refractor editions.

NM/M
Complete Set (200): 25.00
Common Player: .25
Star Refractors: 4X
Star Atomics: 6X
Pack (6): 2.00
Wax Box (24): 40.00
1 Ken Griffey Jr. 1.50
2 Cecil Fielder .25
3 Albert Belle .25
4 Todd Hundley .25
5 Mike Piazza 1.00
6 Matt Williams .25
7 Mo Vaughn .25
8 Ryne Sandberg 1.50
9 Chipper Jones 1.00
10 Edgar Martinez .25
11 Kenny Lofton .25
12 Ron Gant .25
13 Moises Alou .25
14 Pat Hentgen .25
15 Steve Finley .25
16 Mark Grace .25
17 Jay Buhner .25
18 Jeff Conine .25
19 Jim Edmonds .25
20 Todd Hollandsworth .25
21 Andy Petitte .50
22 Jim Thome .75
23 Eric Young .25
24 Ray Lankford .25
25 Marquis Grissom .25
26 Tony Clark .25
27 Jermaine Allensworth .25
28 Ellis Burks .25
29 Tony Gwynn 1.50
30 Barry Larkin .25
31 John Olerud .25
32 Mariano Rivera .40
33 Paul Molitor 1.00
34 Ken Caminiti .25
35 Gary Sheffield .45
36 Al Martin .25
37 John Valentin .25
38 Frank Thomas .75
39 John Jaha .25
40 Greg Maddux 1.50
41 Alex Fernandez .25
42 Dean Palmer .25
43 Bernie Williams .25
44 Deion Sanders .25
45 Mark McGwire 2.00
46 Brian Jordan .25
47 Bernard Gilkey .25
48 Will Clark .25
49 Kevin Appier .25
50 Tom Glavine .40
51 Chuck Knoblauch .25
52 Rondell White .25
53 Greg Vaughn .25
54 Mike Mussina .50
55 Brian McRae .25
56 Chili Davis .25
57 Wade Boggs 1.50
58 Jeff Bagwell .75
59 Roberto Alomar .35
60 Dennis Eckersley .50
61 Ryan Klesko .25
62 Manny Ramirez 1.00
63 John Wetteland .25
64 Cal Ripken Jr. 2.00
65 Edgar Renteria .25
66 Tino Martinez .25
67 Larry Walker .25
68 Gregg Jefferies .25
69 Lance Johnson .25
70 Carlos Delgado .50
71 Craig Biggio .25
72 Jose Canseco .50
73 Barry Bonds 2.00
74 Juan Gonzalez .50
75 Eric Karros .25
76 Reggie Sanders .25
77 Robin Ventura .25
78 Hideo Nomo .50
79 David Justice .25
80 Vinny Castilla .25
81 Travis Fryman .25
82 Derek Jeter 2.00
83 Sammy Sosa 1.50
84 Ivan Rodriguez .75
85 Rafael Palmeiro .75
86 Roger Clemens 2.00
87 Jason Giambi .50
88 Andres Galarraga .25
89 Jermaine Dye .25
90 Joe Carter .25
91 Brady Anderson .25
92 Derek Bell .25
93 Randy Johnson 1.00
94 Fred McGriff .25
95 John Smoltz .25
96 Harold Baines .25
97 Raul Mondesi .25
98 Tim Salmon .25
99 Carlos Baerga .25
100 Dante Bichette .25
101 Vladimir Guerrero 1.00
102 Richard Hidalgo .25
103 Paul Konerko .25
104 Alex Gonzalez **RC** .50
105 Jason Dickson .25
106 Jose Rosado .25
107 Todd Walker .25
108 Seth Greisinger **RC** .40
109 Todd Helton .75
110 Ben Davis .25
111 Bartolo Colon .25
112 Elieser Marrero .25
113 Jeff D'Amico .25
114 Miguel Tejada **RC** 8.00
115 Darin Erstad .50
116 Kris Benson **RC** 1.00
117 Adrian Beltre **RC** 2.00
118 Neifi Perez .25
119 Calvin Reese .25
120 Carl Pavano .25
121 Juan Melo .25
122 Kevin McGlinchy **RC** .50
123 Pat Cline .25
124 Felix Heredia **RC** .40
125 Aaron Boone .25
126 Glendon Rusch .25
127 Mike Cameron .25
128 Justin Thompson .25
129 Chad Hermansen **RC** .25
130 Sidney Ponson **RC** 1.00
131 Willie Martinez **RC** .25
132 Paul Wilder **RC** .25
133 Geoff Jenkins .25
134 Roy Halladay **RC** 2.00
135 Carlos Guillen .25
136 Tony Batista .25
137 Todd Greene .25
138 Luis Castillo .25
139 Jimmy Anderson **RC** .25
140 Edgard Velazquez .25
141 Chris Snopek .25
142 Ruben Rivera .25
143 Javier Valentin **RC** .25
144 Brian Rose .25
145 Fernando Tatis **RC** .50
146 Dean Crow **RC** .25
147 Karim Garcia .25
148 Dante Powell .25
149 Hideki Irabu **RC** .40
150 Matt Morris .25
151 Wes Helms .25
152 Russ Johnson .25
153 Jarrod Washburn .25
154 Kerry Wood **RC** 4.00
155 Joe Fontenot **RC** .25
156 Eugene Kingsale .25
157 Terrence Long .25
158 Calvin Maduro .25
159 Jeff Suppan .25
160 DaRond Stovall .25
161 Mark Redman .25
162 Ken Cloude **RC** .25
163 Bobby Estalella .25
164 Abraham Nunez **RC** .75
165 Derrick Gibson .25
166 Mike Drumright **RC** .25
167 Katsuhiro Maeda .25
168 Jeff Liefer .25
169 Ben Grieve .25
170 Bob Abreu .25
171 Shannon Stewart .25
172 Braden Looper **RC** .40
173 Brant Brown .25
174 Marlon Anderson .25
175 Brad Fullmer .25
176 Carlos Beltran .25
177 Nomar Garciaparra 1.50
178 Derrek Lee .75
179 Valerio De Los Santos **RC** .25
180 Dmitri Young .25
181 Jamey Wright .25
182 Hiram Bocachica **RC** .25
183 Wilton Guerrero .25
184 Chris Carpenter .25
185 Scott Spiezio .25
186 Andruw Jones 1.00
187 Travis Lee **RC** .75
188 Jose Cruz Jr. **RC** 1.00
189 Jose Guillen .25
190 Jeff Abbott .25
191 Ricky Ledee **RC** .40
192 Mike Sweeney .25
193 Donnie Sadler .25
194 Scott Rolen .75
195 Kevin Orie .25
196 Jason Conti **RC** .25
197 Mark Kotsay **RC** .75
198 Eric Milton **RC** 1.00
199 Russell Branyan .25
200 Alex Sanchez **RC** .50

Autographs

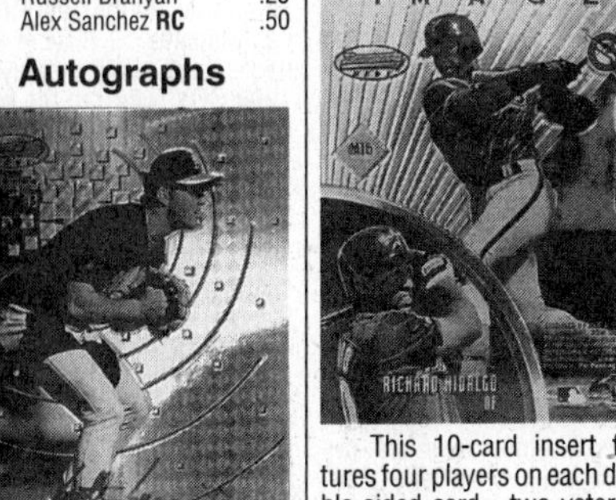

Ten different players each signed 10 regular versions of their respective Bowman's Best cards (1:170 packs), 10 of their Bowman's Best Refractors (1:2,036 packs) and 10 of their Bowman's Best Atomic Refractors (1:6,107 packs). Each autograph card features a special Certified Autograph stamp on the front.

NM/M
Complete Set (10): 150.00
Common Player: 5.00
Refractors: 1.5X
Atomics: 2X
29 Tony Gwynn 30.00
33 Paul Molitor 20.00
82 Derek Jeter 100.00
91 Brady Anderson 7.50
98 Tim Salmon 10.00
107 Todd Walker 5.00
183 Wilton Guerrero 5.00
185 Scott Spiezio 5.00
188 Jose Cruz Jr. 6.00
194 Scott Rolen 20.00

Cuts

Each of these 20-card inserts features a laser-cut pattern in the chromium stock. Backs have another color photo and list several of the player's career "Bests." Three different versions of each card are available: Regular (1:24 packs), Refractor (1:48) and Atomic Refractor (1:96). Cards are numbered with a "BC" prefix.

NM/M
Complete Set (20): 20.00
Common Player: .35
Refractors: 1.5X
Atomic Refractors: 2X
1 Derek Jeter 4.00
2 Chipper Jones 1.50
3 Frank Thomas 1.00
4 Cal Ripken Jr. 4.00
5 Mark McGwire 3.00
6 Ken Griffey Jr. 2.00
7 Jeff Bagwell 1.00
8 Mike Piazza 2.00
9 Ken Caminiti .35
10 Albert Belle .35
11 Jose Cruz Jr. .35
12 Wilton Guerrero .35
13 Darin Erstad .50
14 Andruw Jones 1.00
15 Scott Rolen .75
16 Jose Guillen .35
17 Bob Abreu .35
18 Vladimir Guerrero 1.00
19 Todd Walker .35
20 Nomar Garciaparra 1.50

Mirror Image

This 10-card insert features four players on each double-sided card - two veterans and two rookies - utilizing Finest technology. Regular Mirror Image cards are found 1:48 packs, while Refractor versions are seeded 1:96 packs and Atomic Refractors are found 1:192 packs. Cards are numbered with an "MI" prefix.

NM/M
Complete Set (10): 35.00
Common Card: 2.00
Refractors: 1.5X
Atomic Refractors: 2X
1 Nomar Garciaparra, Derek Jeter, Hiram Bocachica, Barry Larkin 7.50
2 Travis Lee, Frank Thomas, Derrek Lee, Jeff Bagwell 3.50
3 Kerry Wood, Greg Maddux, Kris Benson, John Smoltz 3.50
4 Kevin Brown, Ivan Rodriguez, Elieser Marrero, Mike Piazza 5.00
5 Jose Cruz Jr., Ken Griffey Jr., Andruw Jones, Barry Bonds 7.50
6 Jose Guillen, Juan Gonzalez, Richard Hidalgo, Gary Sheffield 2.00
7 Paul Konerko, Mark McGwire, Todd Helton, Rafael Palmeiro 6.00
8 Wilton Guerrero, Craig Biggio, Donnie Sadler, Chuck Knoblauch 2.00
9 Russell Branyan, Matt Williams, Adrian Beltre, Chipper Jones 3.50
10 Bob Abreu, Kenny Lofton, Vladimir Guerrero, Albert Belle 3.00

Jumbos

This large-format (4" x 5-5/8") version of 1997 Bowman's Best features 16 of the season's top stars and hottest rookies. Utilizing chromium, Refractor and Atomic Refractor technologies, the cards are identical in every way except size to the regular-issue Bowman's Best. The jumbos were sold only through Topps Stadium Club. Each of the sets consists of 12 chromium cards, plus three randomly packaged Refractors and one Atomic Refractor. About 900 sets were produced according to Topps sales literature, which breaks down to 700 regular cards, 170 Refractors and 60 Atomic Refractors of each player.

NM/M
Complete Set (16): 90.00
Common Player: 4.50
Refractor: 1.5X
Atomic Refractor: 2X
1 Ken Griffey Jr. 7.50
5 Mike Piazza 7.50
9 Chipper Jones 6.00
11 Kenny Lofton 4.50
29 Tony Gwynn 6.00
33 Paul Molitor 5.00
38 Frank Thomas 5.00
45 Mark McGwire 9.00
64 Cal Ripken Jr. 12.00
73 Barry Bonds 12.00
74 Juan Gonzalez 4.50
82 Derek Jeter 12.00
101 Vladimir Guerrero 5.00
177 Nomar Garciaparra 6.00
186 Andruw Jones 5.00
188 Jose Cruz, Jr. 4.50

1998 Bowman

Bowman was a 441-card set released in a pair of 220-card series in 1998 (Orlando Hernandez, #221, was a late Series 1 addition.) Within each series are 150 prospects printed in a silver and blue design and 70 veterans printed in silver and red. Cards feature a Bowman seal, and in cases of a player's first Bowman card, a "Bowman Rookie Card" stamp is applied. The player's facsimile signature from his first contract runs down the side. The entire set was paralleled twice in Bowman International (one per pack) and Golden Anniversary (serially numbered to 50). Inserts in Series 1 include Autographs, Scout's Choice, and Japanese Rookies. Inserts in Series 2 include Autographs, 1999 Rookie of the Year Favorites, Minor League MVPs and Japanese Rookies.

NM/M
Complete Set (441): 40.00
Series 1 (221): 20.00
Series 2 (220): 20.00
Common Player: .10
Internationals: 1.5X
Inserted 1:1
Series 1 Pack (10): 2.00
Series 1 Wax Box (24): 30.00
Series 2 Pack (10): 1.50
Series 2 Wax Box (24): 25.00
1 Nomar Garciaparra 1.50
2 Scott Rolen .75
3 Andy Pettitte .30
4 Ivan Rodriguez .65
5 Mark McGwire 2.50
6 Jason Dickson .10
7 Jose Cruz Jr. .10
8 Jeff Kent .10
9 Mike Mussina .30
10 Jason Kendall .10
11 Brett Tomko .10
12 Jeff King .10
13 Brad Radke .10
14 Robin Ventura .10
15 Jeff Bagwell 1.00
16 Greg Maddux 1.50
17 John Jaha .10
18 Mike Piazza 2.00
19 Edgar Martinez .10
20 David Justice .10
21 Todd Hundley .10
22 Tony Gwynn 1.50
23 Larry Walker .10
24 Bernie Williams .10
25 Edgar Renteria .10
26 Rafael Palmeiro .75
27 Tim Salmon .10
28 Matt Morris .10
29 Shawn Estes .10
30 Vladimir Guerrero 1.00
31 Fernando Tatis .10
32 Justin Thompson .10
33 Ken Griffey Jr. 2.00
34 Edgardo Alfonzo .10
35 Mo Vaughn .10
36 Marty Cordova .10
37 Craig Biggio .10
38 Roger Clemens 1.75
39 Mark Grace .10
40 Ken Caminiti .10
41 Tony Womack .10
42 Albert Belle .10
43 Tino Martinez .10
44 Sandy Alomar .10
45 Jeff Cirillo .10
46 Jason Giambi .50
47 Darin Erstad .25
48 Livan Hernandez .10
49 Mark Grudzielanek .10
50 Sammy Sosa 1.50
51 Curt Schilling .30
52 Brian Hunter .10
53 Neifi Perez .10
54 Todd Walker .10
55 Jose Guillen .10
56 Jim Thome .10
57 Tom Glavine .30
58 Todd Greene .10
59 Rondell White .10
60 Roberto Alomar .25
61 Tony Clark .10
62 Vinny Castilla .10
63 Barry Larkin .10
64 Hideki Irabu .10
65 Johnny Damon .35
66 Juan Gonzalez .50
67 John Olerud .10
68 Gary Sheffield .25
69 Raul Mondesi .10
70 Chipper Jones 1.50
71 David Ortiz .50
72 Warren Morris **RC** .50
73 Alex Gonzalez .10
74 Nick Bierbrodt .10
75 Roy Halladay .10
76 Danny Buxbaum .10
77 Adam Kennedy .10
78 Jared Sandberg **RC** .75
79 Michael Barrett .10
80 Gil Meche .10
81 Jayson Werth .10
82 Abraham Nunez .10
83 Ben Petrick .10
84 Brett Caradonna .10
85 Mike Lowell **RC** 3.00
86 Clay Bruner **RC** .10
87 John Curtice **RC** .10
88 Bobby Estalella .10
89 Juan Melo .10
90 Arnold Gooch .10
91 Kevin Millwood **RC** 1.00
92 Richie Sexson .10
93 Orlando Cabrera .10
94 Pat Cline .10
95 Anthony Sanders .10
96 Russ Johnson .10
97 Ben Grieve .10
98 Kevin McGlinchy .10
99 Paul Wilder .10
100 Russ Ortiz .10
101 Ryan Jackson **RC** .10
102 Heath Murray .10
103 Brian Rose .10
104 Ryan Radmanovich **RC** .10
105 Ricky Ledee .10
106 Jeff Wallace **RC** .10
107 Ryan Minor **RC** .10
108 Dennis Reyes .10
109 James Manias **RC** .10
110 Chris Carpenter .10
111 Daryle Ward .10
112 Vernon Wells .10
113 Chad Green .10
114 Mike Stoner **RC** .10
115 Brad Fullmer .10
116 Adam Eaton .10
117 Jeff Liefer .10
118 Corey Koskie **RC** 1.00
119 Todd Helton .75
120 Jaime Jones **RC** .10
121 Mel Rosario .10
122 Geoff Goetz .10
123 Adrian Beltre .40
124 Jason Dellaero .10
125 Gabe Kapler **RC** .50
126 Scott Schoeneweis .10
127 Ryan Brannan .10
128 Aaron Akin .10
129 Ryan Anderson **RC** .25
130 Brad Penny .10
131 Bruce Chen .10
132 Eli Marrero .10
133 Eric Chavez .30
134 Troy Glaus **RC** 3.00
135 Troy Cameron .10
136 Brian Sikorski **RC** .10
137 Mike Kinkade **RC** .25
138 Braden Looper .10
139 Mark Mangum .10
140 Danny Peoples .10
141 J.J. Davis .10
142 Ben Davis .10
143 Jacque Jones .10
144 Derrick Gibson .10
145 Bronson Arroyo .10
146 Cristian Guzman **RC** .50
147 Jeff Abbott .10
148 Mike Cuddyer **RC** 1.00
149 Jason Romano .10
150 Shane Monahan .10
151 Ntema Ndungidi **RC** .10
152 Alex Sanchez .10
153 Jack Cust **RC** 1.50
154 Brent Butler .10
155 Ramon Hernandez .10
156 Norm Hutchins .10
157 Jason Marquis .10
158 Jacob Cruz .10
159 Rob Burger **RC** .10
160 Eric Milton .10
161 Preston Wilson .10
162 Jason Fitzgerald **RC** .10
163 Dan Serafini .10
164 Peter Munro .10
165 Trot Nixon .10
166 Homer Bush .10
167 Dermal Brown .10
168 Chad Hermansen .10
169 Julio Moreno **RC** .10
170 John Roskos **RC** .10
171 Grant Roberts .10

172 Ken Cloude .10
173 Jason Brester .10
174 Jason Conti .10
175 Jon Garland .10
176 Robbie Bell .10
177 Nathan Haynes .10
178 Ramon Ortiz **RC** .50
179 Shannon Stewart .10
180 Pablo Ortega .10
181 Jimmy Rollins **RC** 4.00
182 Sean Casey .30
183 Ted Lilly **RC** .25
184 Chris Enochs **RC** .10
185 Magglio Ordonez **RC** 3.00
186 Mike Drumright .10
187 Aaron Boone .10
188 Matt Clement .10
189 Todd Dunwoody .10
190 Larry Rodriguez .10
191 Todd Noel .10
192 Geoff Jenkins .10
193 George Lombard .10
194 Lance Berkman .10
195 Marcus McCain **RC** .10
196 Ryan McGuire .10
197 Jhensy Sandoval **RC** .10
198 Corey Lee .10
199 Mario Valdez .10
200 Robert Fick **RC** .20
201 Donnie Sadler .10
202 Marc Kroon .10
203 David Miller .10
204 Jarrod Washburn .10
205 Miguel Tejada .30
206 Raul Ibanez .10
207 John Patterson .10
208 Calvin Pickering .10
209 Felix Martinez .10
210 Mark Redman .10
211 Scott Elarton .10
212 Jose Amado **RC** .10
213 Kerry Wood .40
214 Dante Powell .10
215 Aramis Ramirez .10
216 A.J. Hinch .10
217 Dustin Carr **RC** .10
218 Mark Kotsay .10
219 Jason Standridge .10
220 Luis Ordaz .10
221 Orlando Hernandez **RC** .50
222 Cal Ripken Jr. 3.00
223 Paul Molitor 1.00
224 Derek Jeter 3.00
225 Barry Bonds 3.00
226 Jim Edmonds .10
227 John Smoltz .10
228 Eric Karros .10
229 Ray Lankford .10
230 Rey Ordonez .10
231 Kenny Lofton .10
232 Alex Rodriguez 2.50
233 Dante Bichette .10
234 Pedro Martinez 1.00
235 Carlos Delgado .45
236 Rod Beck .10
237 Matt Williams .10
238 Charles Johnson .10
239 Rico Brogna .10
240 Frank Thomas 1.00
241 Paul O'Neill .10
242 Jaret Wright .10
243 Brant Brown .10
244 Ryan Klesko .10
245 Chuck Finley .10
246 Derek Bell .10
247 Delino DeShields .10
248 Chan Ho Park .10
249 Wade Boggs 1.50
250 Jay Buhner .10
251 Butch Huskey .10
252 Steve Finley .10
253 Will Clark .10
254 John Valentin .10
255 Bobby Higginson .10
256 Darryl Strawberry .10
257 Randy Johnson 1.00
258 Al Martin .10
259 Travis Fryman .10
260 Fred McGriff .10
261 Jose Valentin .10
262 Andruw Jones 1.00
263 Kenny Rogers .10
264 Moises Alou .10
265 Denny Neagle .10
266 Ugueth Urbina .10
267 Derrek Lee .45
268 Ellis Burks .10
269 Mariano Rivera .30
270 Dean Palmer .10
271 Eddie Taubensee .10
272 Brady Anderson .10
273 Brian Giles .10
274 Quinton McCracken .10
275 Henry Rodriguez .10
276 Andres Galarraga .10
277 Jose Canseco .45
278 David Segui .10
279 Bret Saberhagen .10
280 Kevin Brown .10
281 Chuck Knoblauch .10
282 Jeromy Burnitz .10
283 Jay Bell .10
284 Manny Ramirez 1.00
285 Rick Helling .10
286 Francisco Cordova .10
287 Bob Abreu .20
288 J.T. Snow Jr. .10
289 Hideo Nomo .50
290 Brian Jordan .10
291 Javy Lopez .10
292 Travis Lee .10
293 Russell Branyan .10
294 Paul Konerko .10
295 Masato Yoshii **RC** .50
296 Kris Benson .10
297 Juan Encarnacion .10
298 Eric Milton .10
299 Mike Caruso .10
300 Ricardo Aramboles **RC** .10
301 Bobby Smith .10
302 Billy Koch .10
303 Richard Hidalgo .10
304 Justin Baughman **RC** .10
305 Chris Gissell .10
306 Donnie Bridges **RC** .10
307 Nelson Lara **RC** .10
308 Randy Wolf **RC** 1.00
309 Jason LaRue **RC** .25
310 Jason Gooding **RC** .10
311 Edgar Clemente **RC** .10
312 Andrew Vessel .10
313 Chris Reitsma .10
314 Jesus Sanchez **RC** .10
315 Buddy Carlyle **RC** .10
316 Randy Winn .10
317 Luis Rivera .10
318 Marcus Thames **RC** 1.50
319 A.J. Pierzynski .10
320 Scott Randall .10
321 Damian Sapp .10
322 Eddie Yarnell **RC** .10
323 Luke Allen **RC** .10
324 J.D. Smart .10
325 Willie Martinez .10
326 Alex Ramirez .10
327 Eric DuBose **RC** .10
328 Kevin Witt .10
329 Dan McKinley **RC** .10
330 Cliff Politte .10
331 Vladimir Nunez .10
332 John Halama **RC** .25
333 Nerio Rodriguez .10
334 Desi Relaford .10
335 Robinson Checo .10
336 John Nicholson **RC** .10
337 Tom LaRosa **RC** .10
338 Kevin Nicholson **RC** .10
339 Javier Vazquez .10
340 A.J. Zapp .10
341 Tom Evans .10
342 Kerry Robinson .10
343 Gabe Gonzalez **RC** .10
344 Ralph Milliard .10
345 Enrique Wilson .10
346 Elvin Hernandez .10
347 Mike Lincoln **RC** .10
348 Cesar King **RC** .10
349 Cristian Guzman **RC** 1.00
350 Donzell McDonald .10
351 Jim Parque **RC** .25
352 Mike Saipe **RC** .10
353 Carlos Febles **RC** .40
354 Dernell Stenson **RC** .25
355 Mark Osborne **RC** .10
356 Odalis Perez **RC** .40
357 Jason Dewey **RC** .10
358 Joe Fontenot .10
359 Jason Grilli **RC** .40
360 Kevin Haverbusch **RC** .25
361 Jay Yennaco **RC** .10
362 Brian Buchanan .10
363 John Barnes .10
364 Chris Fussell .10
365 Kevin Gibbs **RC** .10
366 Joe Lawrence .10
367 DaRond Stovall .10
368 Brian Fuentes **RC** .10
369 Jimmy Anderson .10
370 Laril Gonzalez **RC** .10
371 Scott Williamson **RC** .40
372 Milton Bradley .10
373 Jason Halper **RC** .10
374 Brent Billingsley **RC** .10
375 Joe DePastino **RC** .10
376 Jake Westbrook .10
377 Octavio Dotel .10
378 Jason Williams **RC** .10
379 Julio Ramirez **RC** .10
380 Seth Greisinger .10
381 Mike Judd **RC** .10
382 Ben Ford **RC** .10
383 Tom Bennett .10
384 Adam Butler **RC** .10
385 Wade Miller **RC** .75
386 Kyle Peterson **RC** .10
387 Tommy Peterman **RC** .10
388 Onan Masaoka .10
389 Jason Rakers **RC** .10
390 Rafael Medina .10
391 Luis Lopez .10
392 Jeff Yoder .10
393 Vance Wilson **RC** .25
394 Fernando Seguignol **RC** .25
395 Ron Wright .10
396 Ruben Mateo **RC** .40
397 Steve Lomasney **RC** .25
398 Damian Jackson .10
399 Mike Jerzembeck **RC** .10
400 Luis Rivas **RC** .25
401 Kevin Burford **RC** .10
402 Glenn Davis .10
403 Robert Luce **RC** .10
404 Cole Liniak .10
405 Matthew LeCroy **RC** .20
406 Jeremy Giambi **RC** .40
407 Shawn Chacon .10
408 Dewayne Wise **RC** .10
409 Steve Woodard **RC** .25
410 Francisco Cordero **RC** .25
411 Damon Minor **RC** .20
412 Lou Collier .10
413 Justin Towle .10
414 Juan LeBron .10
415 Michael Coleman .10
416 Felix Rodriguez .10
417 Paul Ah Yat **RC** .10
418 Kevin Barker **RC** .25
419 Brian Meadows .10
420 Darnell McDonald **RC** .20
421 Matt Kinney **RC** .25
422 Mike Vavrek **RC** .10
423 Courtney Duncan **RC** .10
424 Kevin Millar **RC** .50
425 Ruben Rivera .10
426 Steve Shoemaker **RC** .10
427 Dan Reichert **RC** .10
428 Carlos Lee **RC** 2.00
429 Rod Barajas .10
430 Pablo Ozuna **RC** .20
431 Todd Belitz **RC** .10
432 Sidney Ponson .10
433 Steve Carver **RC** .10
434 Esteban Yan .10
435 Cedrick Bowers **RC** .10
436 Marlon Anderson .10
437 Carl Pavano .10
438 Jae Weong Seo **RC** .50
439 Jose Taveras **RC** .10
440 Matt Anderson **RC** .25
441 Darron Ingram **RC** .10

Golden Anniversary

This 441-card parallel set celebrates Bowman's 50th anniversary with a gold, rather than black, facsimile autograph on each card. Golden Anniversary cards were inserted in both Series 1 (1:237) and Series 2 (1:194) packs and are sequentially numbered to 50.

NM/M
Common Player: 4.00
Veteran Stars: 15-30X
Young Stars: 5-10X
Rookie Cards: 5-10X
(See 1998 Bowman for checklist and base card values.)

International

All 441 cards in Bowman Series 1 and 2 are paralleled in an International version, with the player's native country highlighted. Background map designs and vital information were translated into the player's native language on these one per pack parallel cards.

NM/M
Common Player: .25
Stars: 1.5X
Inserted 1:1
(See 1998 Bowman for checklist and base card values.)

Autographs

Rookies and prospects are featured on the certified autograph cards found as '98 Bowman inserts. Each player signed cards in blue, silver and gold ink. The front of each autographed card bears a certification seal. Relative values in the current market come nowhere near reflecting those scarcities.

NM/M
Common Player: 3.00
Inserted 1:149
Silvers (1:992): 1.5-2.5X
Golds (1:2,976): 2-4X
1 Adrian Beltre 15.00
2 Brad Fullmer 5.00
3 Ricky Ledee 5.00
4 David Ortiz 35.00
5 Fernando Tatis 3.00
6 Kerry Wood 20.00
7 Mel Rosario 3.00
8 Cole Liniak 5.00
9 A.J. Hinch 5.00
10 Jhensy Sandoval 3.00
11 Jose Cruz Jr. 5.00
12 Richard Hidalgo 6.00
13 Geoff Jenkins 8.00
14 Carl Pavano 10.00
15 Richie Sexson 12.00
16 Tony Womack 5.00
17 Scott Rolen 20.00
18 Ryan Minor 5.00
19 Elieser Marrero 5.00
20 Jason Marquis 5.00
21 Mike Lowell 20.00
22 Todd Helton 20.00
23 Chad Green 3.00
24 Scott Elarton 3.00
25 Russell Branyan 6.00
26 Mike Drumright 3.00
27 Ben Grieve 5.00
28 Jacque Jones 8.00
29 Jared Sandberg 5.00
30 Grant Roberts 5.00
31 Mike Stoner 3.00
32 Brian Rose 3.00
33 Randy Winn 5.00
34 Justin Towle 3.00
35 Anthony Sanders 3.00
36 Rafael Medina 3.00
37 Corey Lee 3.00
38 Mike Kinkade 5.00
39 Norm Hutchins 3.00
40 Jason Brester 3.00
41 Ben Davis 5.00
42 Nomar Garciaparra 75.00
43 Jeff Liefer 3.00
44 Eric Milton 6.00
45 Preston Wilson 8.00
46 Miguel Tejada 30.00
47 Luis Ordaz 3.00
48 Travis Lee 5.00
49 Kris Benson 6.00
50 Jacob Cruz 5.00
51 Dermal Brown 3.00
52 Marc Kroon 3.00
53 Chad Hermansen 5.00
54 Roy Halladay 15.00
55 Eric Chavez 10.00
56 Jason Conti 3.00
57 Juan Encarnacion 5.00
58 Paul Wilder 3.00
59 Aramis Ramirez 15.00
60 Cliff Politte 3.00
61 Todd Dunwoody 3.00
62 Paul Konerko 10.00
63 Shane Monahan 3.00
64 Alex Sanchez 3.00
65 Jeff Abbott 3.00
66 John Patterson 3.00
67 Peter Munro 3.00
68 Jarrod Washburn 5.00
69 Derrek Lee 20.00
70 Ramon Hernandez 5.00

Japanese Rookies

Bowman offered collectors a chance to receive original 1991 BBM-brand Japanese rookie cards of three players. Series 1 had rookie cards of Hideo Nomo and Shigetoshi Hasegawa inserted in one per 2,685 packs, while Series 2 offered Hideki Irabu seeded one per 4,411 packs. Card numbers have a "BBM" prefix.

NM/M
Complete Set (3): 15.00
Common Player: 5.00
11 Hideo Nomo 10.00
17 Shigetosi Hasegawa 5.00
Hideki Irabu 5.00

Minor League MVP

This 11-card insert set features players who are former Minor League MVPs who had graduated to the majors. Minor League MVPs are seeded one per 12 packs of Series 2 and are numbered with a "MVP" prefix.

NM/M
Complete Set (11): 9.00
Common Player: .50
1 Jeff Bagwell 1.00
2 Andres Galarraga .50
3 Juan Gonzalez .60
4 Tony Gwynn 1.50
5 Vladimir Guerrero 1.00
6 Derek Jeter 3.00
7 Andruw Jones 1.00
8 Tino Martinez .50
9 Manny Ramirez 1.00
10 Gary Sheffield .60
11 Jim Thome .65

Rookie of the Year Favorites

Rookie of the Year Favorites displays 10 players who had a legitimate shot at the 1999 ROY award in the opinion of the Bowman scouts. The insert was seeded one per 12 packs of Series 2 and numbered with an "ROY" prefix.

NM/M
Complete Set (10): 6.00
Common Player: .50
1 Adrian Beltre .75
2 Troy Glaus 3.00
3 Chad Hermansen .50
4 Matt Clement .50
5 Eric Chavez .75
6 Kris Benson .50
7 Richie Sexson .50
8 Randy Wolf .50
9 Ryan Minor .50
10 Alex Gonzalez .50

Scout's Choice

This Series 1 insert has players with potential for Major League stardom. Fronts have action photos with gold-foil highlights. Backs have a portrait photo and an assessment of the player's skills in the traditional five areas of raw talent. Cards are numbered with an "SC" prefix.

NM/M
Complete Set (21): 8.00
Common Player: .25
Inserted 1:12
1 Paul Konerko .50
2 Richard Hidalgo .25
3 Mark Kotsay .25
4 Ben Grieve .25
5 Chad Hermansen .25
6 Matt Clement .25
7 Brad Fullmer .25
8 Eli Marrero .25
9 Kerry Wood 1.50
10 Adrian Beltre 1.50
11 Ricky Ledee .25
12 Travis Lee .25
13 Abraham Nunez .25
14 Ryan Anderson .25
15 Dermal Brown .25
16 Juan Encarnacion .25
17 Aramis Ramirez .25
18 Todd Helton 2.50
19 Kris Benson .25
20 Russell Branyan .25
21 Mike Stoner .25

1998 Bowman Chrome

All 441 cards in Bowman 1 and 2 were reprinted with a chromium finish for Bowman Chrome. Chrome contains International and Golden Anniversary parallels, like Bowman. Internationals are seeded one per four packs, with Refractor versions every 24 packs. Golden Anniversary parallels are exclusive to hobby packs and inserted one per 164 packs and sequentially numbered to 50 sets. Refractor versions are seeded one per 1,279 packs and numbered to just five sets. In addition, 50 Bowman Chrome Reprints were inserted with 25 in each series.

NM/M
Complete Set (441): 100.00
Complete Series 1 (221): 60.00
Complete Series 2 (220): 50.00
Common Player: .20
Series 1 Pack (4): 2.50
Series 2 Pack (4): 2.00
Series 1 Box (24): 45.00
Series 2 Box (24): 35.00
1 Nomar Garciaparra 1.00
2 Scott Rolen .75
3 Andy Pettitte .40

4 Ivan Rodriguez .75
5 Mark McGwire 2.50
6 Jason Dickson .20
7 Jose Cruz Jr. .20
8 Jeff Kent .20
9 Mike Mussina .50
10 Jason Kendall .20
11 Brett Tomko .20
12 Jeff King .20
13 Brad Radke .20
14 Robin Ventura .20
15 Jeff Bagwell 1.00
16 Greg Maddux 1.50
17 John Jaha .20
18 Mike Piazza 2.00
19 Edgar Martinez .20
20 David Justice .20
21 Todd Hundley .20
22 Tony Gwynn 1.50
23 Larry Walker .20
24 Bernie Williams .20
25 Edgar Renteria .20
26 Rafael Palmeiro .75
27 Tim Salmon .20
28 Matt Morris .20
29 Shawn Estes .20
30 Vladimir Guerrero 1.00
31 Fernando Tatis .20
32 Justin Thompson .20
33 Ken Griffey Jr. 2.00
34 Edgardo Alfonzo .20
35 Mo Vaughn .20
36 Marty Cordova .20
37 Craig Biggio .20
38 Roger Clemens 2.00
39 Mark Grace .20
40 Ken Caminiti .20
41 Tony Womack .20
42 Albert Belle .20
43 Tino Martinez .20
44 Sandy Alomar .20
45 Jeff Cirillo .20
46 Jason Giambi .50
47 Darin Erstad .45
48 Livan Hernandez .20
49 Mark Grudzielanek .20
50 Sammy Sosa 1.50
51 Curt Schilling .50
52 Brian Hunter .20
53 Neifi Perez .20
54 Todd Walker .20
55 Jose Guillen .20
56 Jim Thome .20
57 Tom Glavine .40
58 Todd Greene .20
59 Rondell White .20
60 Roberto Alomar .35
61 Tony Clark .20
62 Vinny Castilla .20
63 Barry Larkin .20
64 Hideki Irabu .20
65 Johnny Damon .60
66 Juan Gonzalez .50
67 John Olerud .20
68 Gary Sheffield .45
69 Raul Mondesi .20
70 Chipper Jones 1.50
71 David Ortiz .75
72 Warren Morris **RC** .50
73 Alex Gonzalez .20
74 Nick Bierbrodt .20
75 Roy Halladay .20
76 Danny Buxbaum .20
77 Adam Kennedy .20
78 Jared Sandberg **RC** .50
79 Michael Barrett .20
80 Gil Meche .20
81 Jayson Werth .20
82 Abraham Nunez .20
83 Ben Petrick .20
84 Brett Caradonna .20
85 Mike Lowell **RC** 5.00
86 Clay Bruner **RC** .20
87 John Curtice **RC** .20
88 Bobby Estalella .20
89 Juan Melo .20
90 Arnold Gooch .20
91 Kevin Millwood **RC** 4.00
92 Richie Sexson .20
93 Orlando Cabrera .20
94 Pat Cline .20
95 Anthony Sanders .20
96 Russ Johnson .20
97 Ben Grieve .20
98 Kevin McGlinchy .20
99 Paul Wilder .20
100 Russ Ortiz .20
101 Ryan Jackson **RC** .50
102 Heath Murray .20
103 Brian Rose .20
104 Ryan Radmanovich **RC** .20
105 Ricky Ledee .20
106 Jeff Wallace **RC** .20
107 Ryan Minor **RC** .45
108 Dennis Reyes .20
109 James Manias **RC** .20
110 Chris Carpenter .20
111 Daryle Ward .20
112 Vernon Wells .20
113 Chad Green .20
114 Mike Stoner **RC** .20
115 Brad Fullmer .20
116 Adam Eaton .20
117 Jeff Liefer .20
118 Corey Koskie **RC** 1.50
119 Todd Helton .75
120 Jaime Jones **RC** .20
121 Mel Rosario .20
122 Geoff Goetz .20
123 Adrian Beltre .40
124 Jason Dellaero .20
125 Gabe Kapler **RC** 1.00
126 Scott Schoeneweis .20
127 Ryan Brannan .20
128 Aaron Akin .20
129 Ryan Anderson **RC** .50
130 Brad Penny .20
131 Bruce Chen .20
132 Eli Marrero .20
133 Eric Chavez .35
134 Troy Glaus **RC** 10.00
135 Troy Cameron .20
136 Brian Sikorski **RC** .20
137 Mike Kinkade **RC** .50
138 Braden Looper .20
139 Mark Mangum .20
140 Danny Peoples .20
141 J.J. Davis .20
142 Ben Davis .20
143 Jacque Jones .20
144 Derrick Gibson .20
145 Bronson Arroyo .20
146 Luis De Los Santos **RC** .20
147 Jeff Abbott .20
148 Mike Cuddyer **RC** 1.50
149 Jason Romano .20
150 Shane Monahan .20
151 Ntema Ndungidi **RC** .20
152 Alex Sanchez .20
153 Jack Cust **RC** 5.00
154 Brent Butler .20
155 Ramon Hernandez .20
156 Norm Hutchins .20
157 Jason Marquis .20
158 Jacob Cruz .20
159 Rob Burger **RC** .20
160 Eric Milton .20
161 Preston Wilson .20
162 Jason Fitzgerald **RC** .20
163 Dan Serafini .20
164 Peter Munro .20
165 Trot Nixon .40
166 Homer Bush .20
167 Dermal Brown .20
168 Chad Hermansen .20
169 Julio Moreno **RC** .20
170 John Roskos **RC** .20
171 Grant Roberts .20
172 Ken Cloude .20
173 Jason Brester .20
174 Jason Conti .20
175 Jon Garland .20
176 Robbie Bell .20
177 Nathan Haynes .20
178 Ramon Ortiz **RC** .50
179 Shannon Stewart .20
180 Pablo Ortega .20
181 Jimmy Rollins **RC** 10.00
182 Sean Casey .45
183 Ted Lilly **RC** .20
184 Chris Enochs **RC** .20
185 Magglio Ordonez **RC** 3.00
186 Mike Drumright .20
187 Aaron Boone .20
188 Matt Clement .20
189 Todd Dunwoody .20
190 Larry Rodriguez .20
191 Todd Noel .20
192 Geoff Jenkins .20
193 George Lombard .20
194 Lance Berkman .20
195 Marcus McCain **RC** .20
196 Ryan McGuire .20
197 Jhensy Sandoval **RC** .20
198 Corey Lee .20
199 Mario Valdez .20
200 Robert Fick **RC** .20
201 Donnie Sadler .20
202 Marc Kroon .20
203 David Miller .20
204 Jarrod Washburn .20
205 Miguel Tejada .40
206 Raul Ibanez .20
207 John Patterson .20
208 Calvin Pickering .20
209 Felix Martinez .20
210 Mark Redman .20
211 Scott Elarton .20
212 Jose Amado **RC** .20
213 Kerry Wood .50
214 Dante Powell .20
215 Aramis Ramirez .20
216 A.J. Hinch .20
217 Dustin Carr **RC** .20
218 Mark Kotsay .20
219 Jason Standridge .20
220 Luis Ordaz .20
221 Orlando Hernandez **RC** 3.00
222 Cal Ripken Jr. 3.00
223 Paul Molitor 1.00
224 Derek Jeter 3.00
225 Barry Bonds 3.00
226 Jim Edmonds .20
227 John Smoltz .20
228 Eric Karros .20
229 Ray Lankford .20
230 Rey Ordonez .20
231 Kenny Lofton .20
232 Alex Rodriguez 2.50
233 Dante Bichette .20
234 Pedro Martinez 1.00
235 Carlos Delgado .50
236 Rod Beck .20
237 Matt Williams .20
238 Charles Johnson .20
239 Rico Brogna .20
240 Frank Thomas 1.00
241 Paul O'Neill .20
242 Jaret Wright .20
243 Brant Brown .20
244 Ryan Klesko .20
245 Chuck Finley .20
246 Derek Bell .20
247 Delino DeShields .20
248 Chan Ho Park .20
249 Wade Boggs 1.50
250 Jay Buhner .20
251 Butch Huskey .20
252 Steve Finley .20
253 Will Clark .20
254 John Valentin .20
255 Bobby Higginson .20
256 Darryl Strawberry .20
257 Randy Johnson 1.00
258 Al Martin .20
259 Travis Fryman .20
260 Fred McGriff .20
261 Jose Valentin .20
262 Andruw Jones 1.00
263 Kenny Rogers .20
264 Moises Alou .20
265 Denny Neagle .20
266 Ugueth Urbina .20
267 Derrek Lee .50
268 Ellis Burks .20
269 Mariano Rivera .40
270 Dean Palmer .20
271 Eddie Taubensee .20
272 Brady Anderson .20
273 Brian Giles .20
274 Quinton McCracken .20
275 Henry Rodriguez .20
276 Andres Galarraga .20
277 Jose Canseco .40
278 David Segui .20
279 Bret Saberhagen .20
280 Kevin Brown .20
281 Chuck Knoblauch .20
282 Jeromy Burnitz .20
283 Jay Bell .20
284 Manny Ramirez 1.00
285 Rick Helling .20
286 Francisco Cordova .20
287 Bob Abreu .30
288 J.T. Snow Jr. .20
289 Hideo Nomo .50
290 Brian Jordan .20
291 Javy Lopez .20
292 Aaron Akin **RC** .20
293 Russell Branyan .20
294 Paul Konerko .20
295 Masato Yoshii **RC** 1.00
296 Kris Benson .20
297 Juan Encarnacion .20
298 Eric Milton .20
299 Mike Caruso .20
300 Ricardo Aramboles **RC** .20
301 Bobby Smith .20
302 Billy Koch .20
303 Richard Hidalgo .20
304 Justin Baughman **RC** .20
305 Chris Gissell .20
306 Donnie Bridges **RC** .20
307 Nelson Lara **RC** .20
308 Randy Wolf **RC** 1.00
309 Jason LaRue **RC** .50
310 Jason Gooding **RC** .20
311 Edgar Clemente **RC** .20
312 Andrew Vessel .20
313 Chris Reitsma .20
314 Jesus Sanchez **RC** .20
315 Buddy Carlyle **RC** .20
316 Randy Winn .20
317 Luis Rivera .20
318 Marcus Thames **RC** 5.00
319 A.J. Pierzynski .20
320 Scott Randall .20
321 Damian Sapp .20
322 Eddie Yarnell **RC** .20
323 Luke Allen **RC** .20
324 J.D. Smart .20
325 Willie Martinez .20
326 Alex Ramirez .20
327 Eric DuBose **RC** .20
328 Kevin Witt .20
329 Dan McKinley **RC** .20
330 Cliff Politte .20
331 Vladimir Nunez .20
332 John Halama **RC** .50
333 Nerio Rodriguez .20
334 Desi Relaford .20
335 Robinson Checo .20
336 John Nicholson **RC** .20
337 Tom LaRosa **RC** .20
338 Kevin Nicholson **RC** .20
339 Javier Vazquez .20
340 A.J. Zapp .20
341 Tom Evans .20
342 Kerry Robinson .20
343 Gabe Gonzalez **RC** .20
344 Ralph Milliard .20
345 Enrique Wilson .20
346 Elvin Hernandez .20
347 Mike Lincoln **RC** .35
348 Cesar King **RC** .20
349 Cristian Guzman **RC** .50
350 Donzell McDonald .20
351 Jim Parque **RC** .20
352 Mike Saipe **RC** .20
353 Carlos Febles **RC** .50
354 Dernell Stenson **RC** .20
355 Mark Osborne **RC** .20
356 Odalis Perez **RC** 2.00
357 Jason Dewey **RC** .20
358 Joe Fontenot .20
359 Jason Grilli **RC** .40
360 Kevin Haverbusch **RC** .20
361 Jay Yennaco **RC** .20
362 Brian Buchanan .20
363 John Barnes .20
364 Chris Fussell .20
365 Kevin Gibbs **RC** .20
366 Joe Lawrence .20
367 DaRond Stovall .20
368 Brian Fuentes **RC** .20
369 Jimmy Anderson .20
370 Laril Gonzalez **RC** .20
371 Scott Williamson **RC** 1.00
372 Milton Bradley .20
373 Jason Halper **RC** .20
374 Brent Billingsley **RC** .20
375 Joe DePastino **RC** .20
376 Jake Westbrook .20
377 Octavio Dotel .20
378 Jason Williams **RC** .20
379 Julio Ramirez **RC** .20
380 Seth Greisinger .20
381 Mike Judd **RC** .20
382 Ben Ford **RC** .20
383 Tom Bennett **RC** .20
384 Adam Butler **RC** .20
385 Wade Miller **RC** 1.50
386 Kyle Peterson **RC** .20
387 Tommy Peterman **RC** .20
388 Onan Masaoka .20
389 Jason Rakers **RC** .20
390 Rafael Medina .20
391 Luis Lopez .20
392 Jeff Yoder .20
393 Vance Wilson **RC** .20
394 Fernando Seguignol **RC** .35
395 Ron Wright .20
396 Ruben Mateo **RC** 1.00
397 Steve Lomasney **RC** .50
398 Damian Jackson .20
399 Mike Jerzembeck **RC** .20
400 Luis Rivas **RC** .50
401 Kevin Burford **RC** .20
402 Glenn Davis .20
403 Robert Luce **RC** .20
404 Cole Liniak .20
405 Matthew LeCroy **RC** .50
406 Jeremy Giambi **RC** .50
407 Shawn Chacon .20
408 Dewayne Wise **RC** .20
409 Steve Woodard **RC** .50
410 Francisco Cordero **RC** .20
411 Damon Minor **RC** .20
412 Lou Collier .20
413 Justin Towle .20
414 Juan LeBron .20
415 Michael Coleman .20
416 Felix Rodriguez .20
417 Paul Ah Yat **RC** .20
418 Kevin Barker **RC** .20
419 Brian Meadows .20
420 Darnell McDonald **RC** .40
421 Matt Kinney **RC** .40
422 Mike Vavrek **RC** .20
423 Courtney Duncan **RC** .20
424 Kevin Millar **RC** 1.50
425 Ruben Rivera .20
426 Steve Shoemaker **RC** .20
427 Dan Reichert **RC** .20
428 Carlos Lee **RC** 6.00
429 Rod Barajas **RC** .20
430 Pablo Ozuna **RC** .50
431 Todd Belitz **RC** .20
432 Sidney Ponson .20
433 Steve Carver **RC** .20
434 Esteban Yan **RC** .20
435 Cedrick Bowers **RC** .20
436 Marlon Anderson .20
437 Carl Pavano .20
438 Jae Weong Seo **RC** 1.00
439 Jose Taveras **RC** .20
440 Matt Anderson **RC** .50
441 Darron Ingram **RC** .20

Refractors

Refractor versions for all 441 cards in Bowman Chrome Series 1 and 2 were created. The cards contained the word "Refractor" on the back in black letters directly under the card number.

	NM/M
Common Player:	2.00
Stars:	3X
Inserted 1:12	
Int'l Refractors:	6X
Inserted 1:24	

(See 1998 BowmanChrome for checklist and base card values.)

Golden Anniversary

Golden Anniversary parallels were printed for all 441 cards in Bowman Chrome. They are exclusive to hobby packs, seeded one per 164 packs and sequentially numbered to 50 sets. Refractor

versions were also available, numbered to just five sets and inserted one per 1,279 packs.

	NM/M
Common Player:	5.00
Stars:	20X
Common Refractor:	20.00

(See 1998 BowmanChrome for checklist and base card values.)

International

All 441 cards throughout Bowman Chrome Series 1 and 2 were paralleled in International versions. Cards fronts have the regular background replaced by a map denoting the player's birthplace. Backs are written in the player's native language.

	NM/M
Common Player:	.50
Stars and Rookies:	1.5X
Inserted 1:4	

(See 1998 BowmanChrome for checklist and base card values.)

Reprints

Bowman Chrome Reprints showcase 50 of the most popular rookie cards to appear in the brand since 1948. The 25 odd-numbered cards are found in Series 1; the evens in Series 2. The Reprints are numbered with a "BC" prefix.

	NM/M
Complete Set (50):	20.00
Common Player:	.25
Inserted 1:12	
Refractors:	1.5X
Inserted 1:36	

1 Yogi Berra .75
2 Jackie Robinson 2.00
3 Don Newcombe .50
4 Satchel Paige .50
5 Willie Mays 2.00
6 Gil McDougald .25
7 Don Larsen .50
8 Elston Howard .25
9 Robin Ventura .25
10 Brady Anderson .25
11 Gary Sheffield .50
12 Tino Martinez .25
13 Ken Griffey Jr. 1.50
14 John Smoltz .50
15 Sandy Alomar Jr. .25
16 Larry Walker .25
17 Todd Hundley .25
18 Mo Vaughn .25
19 Sammy Sosa 1.00
20 Frank Thomas .50
21 Chuck Knoblauch .25
22 Bernie Williams .25
23 Juan Gonzalez .25
24 Mike Mussina .50
25 Jeff Bagwell .50
26 Tim Salmon .25
27 Ivan Rodriguez .50
28 Kenny Lofton .25
29 Chipper Jones 1.00
30 Javier Lopez .25
31 Ryan Klesko .25
32 Raul Mondesi .25
33 Jim Thome .50
34 Carlos Delgado .25
35 Mike Piazza 1.00
36 Manny Ramirez .50
37 Andy Pettitte .50
38 Derek Jeter 2.00
39 Brad Fullmer .25
40 Richard Hidalgo .25
41 Tony Clark .25
42 Andruw Jones .50
43 Vladimir Guerrero .75
44 Nomar Garciaparra .75
45 Paul Konerko .50
46 Ben Grieve .25
47 Hideo Nomo .25
48 Scott Rolen .50
49 Jose Guillen .25
50 Livan Hernandez .25

1998 Bowman's Best

Bowman's Best was issued in a single 200-card series comprised of 100 prospects and 100 veterans. Prospects are shown on a silver background, while the veterans are showcased on gold. The set was paralleled twice: A Refractor version is seeded one per 20 packs and sequentially numbered to 400, while an Atomic Refractor version is a 1:82 find and numbered to 100 sets. Inserts include regular, Refractor and Atomic Refractor versions of: Autographs, Mirror Image and Performers.

	NM/M
Complete Set (200):	30.00
Common Player:	.25
Refractors:	8X
Production 400 Sets	
Atomic Refractors:	12X
Production 100 Sets	
Pack (6):	2.50
Wax Box (24):	35.00

1 Mark McGwire 2.00
2 Hideo Nomo .50
3 Barry Bonds 3.00
4 Dante Bichette .25
5 Chipper Jones 1.50
6 Frank Thomas 1.00
7 Kevin Brown .25
8 Juan Gonzalez .50
9 Jay Buhner .25
10 Chuck Knoblauch .25
11 Cal Ripken Jr. 3.00
12 Matt Williams .25
13 Jim Edmonds .25
14 Manny Ramirez 1.00
15 Tony Clark .25
16 Mo Vaughn .25
17 Bernie Williams .25
18 Scott Rolen .75
19 Gary Sheffield .40
20 Albert Belle .25
21 Mike Piazza 2.00
22 John Olerud .25
23 Tony Gwynn 1.50
24 Jay Bell .25
25 Jose Cruz Jr. .25
26 Justin Thompson .25
27 Ken Griffey Jr. 2.00
28 Sandy Alomar .25
29 Mark Grudzielanek .25
30 Mark Grace .25
31 Ron Gant .25
32 Javy Lopez .25
33 Jeff Bagwell 1.00
34 Fred McGriff .25
35 Rafael Palmeiro .75
36 Vinny Castilla .25
37 Andy Benes .25
38 Pedro Martinez 1.00
39 Andy Pettitte .40
40 Marty Cordova .25
41 Rusty Greer .25
42 Kevin Orie .25
43 Chan Ho Park .25
44 Ryan Klesko .25
45 Alex Rodriguez 2.50

46 Travis Fryman .25
47 Jeff King .25
48 Roger Clemens 2.00
49 Darin Erstad .50
50 Brady Anderson .25
51 Jason Kendall .25
52 John Valentin .25
53 Ellis Burks .25
54 Brian Hunter .25
55 Paul O'Neill .25
56 Ken Caminiti .25
57 David Justice .25
58 Eric Karros .25
59 Pat Hentgen .25
60 Greg Maddux 1.50
61 Craig Biggio .25
62 Edgar Martinez .25
63 Mike Mussina .50
64 Larry Walker .25
65 Tino Martinez .25
66 Jim Thome .60
67 Tom Glavine .40
68 Raul Mondesi .25
69 Marquis Grissom .25
70 Randy Johnson 1.00
71 Steve Finley .25
72 Jose Guillen .25
73 Nomar Garciaparra 1.50
74 Wade Boggs 1.50
75 Bobby Higginson .25
76 Robin Ventura .25
77 Derek Jeter 3.00
78 Andruw Jones 1.00
79 Ray Lankford .25
80 Vladimir Guerrero 1.00
81 Kenny Lofton .50
82 Ivan Rodriguez .75
83 Neifi Perez .25
84 John Smoltz .25
85 Tim Salmon .25
86 Carlos Delgado .50
87 Sammy Sosa 1.50
88 Jaret Wright .25
89 Roberto Alomar .40
90 Paul Molitor 1.00
91 Dean Palmer .25
92 Barry Larkin .25
93 Jason Giambi .50
94 Curt Schilling .40
95 Eric Young .25
96 Denny Neagle .25
97 Moises Alou .25
98 Livan Hernandez .25
99 Todd Hundley .25
100 Andres Galarraga .25
101 Travis Lee .25
102 Lance Berkman .25
103 Orlando Cabrera .25
104 Mike Lowell **RC** 2.00
105 Ben Grieve .25
106 Jae Weong Seo **RC** .50
107 Richie Sexson .25
108 Eli Marrero .25
109 Aramis Ramirez .25
110 Paul Konerko .25
111 Carl Pavano .25
112 Brad Fullmer .25
113 Matt Clement .25
114 Donzell McDonald .25
115 Todd Helton .75
116 Mike Caruso .25
117 Donnie Sadler .25
118 Bruce Chen .25
119 Jarrod Washburn .25
120 Adrian Beltre .40
121 Ryan Jackson **RC** .50
122 Kevin Millar **RC** 1.50
123 Corey Koskie **RC** 1.00
124 Dermal Brown .25
125 Kerry Wood .50
126 Juan Melo .25
127 Ramon Hernandez .25
128 Roy Halladay .25
129 Ron Wright .25
130 Darnell McDonald **RC** .50
131 Odalis Perez **RC** .75
132 Alex Cora **RC** .25
133 Justin Towle .25
134 Juan Encarnacion .25
135 Brian Rose .25
136 Russell Branyan .25
137 Cesar King **RC** .25
138 Ruben Rivera .25
139 Ricky Ledee .25
140 Vernon Wells .25
141 Luis Rivas **RC** .50
142 Brent Butler .25
143 Karim Garcia .25
144 George Lombard .25
145 Masato Yoshii **RC** .50
146 Braden Looper .25
147 Alex Sanchez .25
148 Kris Benson .25
149 Mark Kotsay .25
150 Richard Hidalgo .25
151 Scott Elarton .25
152 Ryan Minor **RC** .25
153 Troy Glaus **RC** 5.00
154 Carlos Lee **RC** 2.00
155 Michael Coleman .25
156 Jason Grilli **RC** .50
157 Julio Ramirez **RC** .50
158 Randy Wolf **RC** .75
159 Ryan Brannan .25
160 Edgar Clemente **RC** .50
161 Miguel Tejada .40
162 Chad Hermansen .25
163 Ryan Anderson **RC** .50
164 Ben Petrick .25
165 Alex Gonzalez .25
166 Ben Davis .25
167 John Patterson .25
168 Cliff Politte .25
169 Randall Simon .25
170 Javier Vazquez .25
171 Kevin Witt .25
172 Geoff Jenkins .25
173 David Ortiz .60
174 Derrick Gibson .25
175 Abraham Nunez .25
176 A.J. Hinch .25
177 Ruben Mateo **RC** .75
178 Magglio Ordonez **RC** 2.50
179 Todd Dunwoody .25
180 Daryle Ward .25
181 Mike Kinkade **RC** .50
182 Willie Martinez .25
183 Orlando Hernandez **RC** 1.50
184 Eric Milton .25
185 Eric Chavez .50
186 Damian Jackson .25
187 Jim Parque **RC** .50
188 Dan Reichert **RC** .25
189 Mike Drumright .25
190 Todd Walker .25
191 Shane Monahan .25
192 Derrek Lee .65
193 Jeremy Giambi **RC** .50
194 Dan McKinley **RC** .25
195 Tony Armas **RC** .75
196 Matt Anderson **RC** .50
197 Jim Chamblee **RC** .25
198 Francisco Cordero **RC** .25
199 Calvin Pickering .25
200 Reggie Taylor .25

Refractors

Refractor versions for all 200 cards in Bowman's Best were available. Fronts featured a reflective finish, while backs were numbered to 400 and inserted one per 20 packs.

	NM/M
Common Player:	4.00
Stars:	8X
Production 400 Sets	

(See 1998 Bowman Best for checklist and base card values.)

Atomic Refractors

Atomic Refractor versions were available for all 200 cards in Bowman's Best. The cards were printed in a prismatic foil on the front, sequentially numbered to 100 sets on the back and inserted one per 82 packs.

	NM/M
Common Player:	6.00
Stars:	12X
Production 100 Sets	

(See 1998 Bowman Best for checklist and base card values.)

Autographs

This 10-card set offers autographs from five prospects and five veteran stars. Each card has on front the Topps "Certified Autograph Issue" logo for authentication.

	NM/M
Complete Set (10):	65.00
Common Player:	5.00
Inserted 1:180	
Refractors:	1.5X
Inserted 1:2,158	
Atomics:	2X
Inserted 1:6,437	

5 Chipper Jones 30.00
10 Chuck Knoblauch 5.00
15 Tony Clark 5.00
20 Albert Belle 8.00
25 Jose Cruz Jr. 5.00
105 Ben Grieve 5.00
110 Paul Konerko 15.00
115 Todd Helton 15.00
120 Adrian Beltre 15.00
125 Kerry Wood 20.00

Mirror Image Fusion

This 20-card die-cut insert features a veteran star on one side and a young player at the same position on the other. Regular versions are seeded one per 12 packs, while Refractors are found 1:809 packs and numbered within an edition of 100, and Atomic Refractors are

a 1:3,237 find numbered to 25. All have a "MI" prefix to the card number.

	NM/M
Complete Set (20):	35.00
Common Player (1:12):	.50
Refractor (1:809):	6X
Atomic Refractor (1:3,237):	12X

1 Frank Thomas, David Ortiz 2.00
2 Chuck Knoblauch, Enrique Wilson .50
3 Nomar Garciaparra, Miguel Tejada 2.50
4 Alex Rodriguez, Mike Caruso 3.50
5 Cal Ripken Jr., Ryan Minor 4.50
6 Ken Griffey Jr., Ben Grieve 3.00
7 Juan Gonzalez, Juan Encarnacion .75
8 Jose Cruz Jr., Ruben Mateo .50
9 Randy Johnson, Ryan Anderson 1.50
10 Ivan Rodriguez, A.J. Hinch 1.25
11 Jeff Bagwell, Paul Konerko 1.50
12 Mark McGwire, Travis Lee 3.50
13 Craig Biggio, Chad Hermanson .50
14 Mark Grudzielanek, Alex Gonzalez .50
15 Chipper Jones, Adrian Beltre 2.50
16 Larry Walker, Mark Kotsay .50
17 Tony Gwynn, Preston Wilson 2.50
18 Barry Bonds, Richard Hidalgo 4.50
19 Greg Maddux, Kerry Wood 2.50
20 Mike Piazza, Ben Petrick 3.00

Performers

Performers are 10 players who had the best minor league seasons in 1997. Regular versions were inserted one per six packs, while Refractors are seeded 1:809 and serially numbered to 200, and Atomic Refractors are 1:3,237 and numbered to 50 sets. All versions have card numbers with a "BP" prefix.

	NM/M
Complete Set (10):	4.00
Common Player:	.35
Refractor (1:309):	3X
Atomic Refractor (1:3,237):	5X

1 Ben Grieve .35
2 Travis Lee .35
3 Ryan Minor .35
4 Todd Helton 2.00
5 Brad Fullmer .35
6 Paul Konerko .50
7 Adrian Beltre .75
8 Richie Sexson .35
9 Aramis Ramirez .35
10 Russell Branyan .35

1999 Bowman Pre-Production

Bowman's 1999 issue was introduced with this group of sample cards. Format is nearly identical to the issued cards, except for the use of a "PP" prefix to the card number on back.

	NM/M
Complete Set (6):	4.00
Common Player:	.60

1 Andres Galarraga .60
2 Raul Mondesi .60
3 Vinny Castilla .60
4 Corey Koskie 2.00
5 Octavio Dotel .60
6 Dernell Stenson .60

1999 Bowman

The set was issued in two 220-card series, each comprised of 70 veterans and 150 rookies and prospects. Rookie/prospect cards have blue metallic foil highlights; veteran cards are highlighted with red foil. On each card is the player's facsimile autograph, reproduced from their initial Topps contract.

	NM/M
Complete Set (440):	60.00
Complete Series 1 (220):	30.00
Complete Series 2 (220):	35.00
Common Player:	.10
Series 1 Pack (10):	2.00
Series 1 Box (24):	35.00
Series 2 Pack (10):	3.00
Series 2 Box (24):	50.00

1 Ben Grieve .10
2 Kerry Wood .40
3 Ruben Rivera .10
4 Sandy Alomar .10
5 Cal Ripken Jr. 2.00
6 Mark McGwire 1.75
7 Vladimir Guerrero .75
8 Moises Alou .10
9 Jim Edmonds .10
10 Greg Maddux 1.00
11 Gary Sheffield .40
12 John Valentin .10
13 Chuck Knoblauch .10
14 Tony Clark .10
15 Rusty Greer .10
16 Al Leiter .10
17 Travis Lee .10
18 Jose Cruz Jr. .10
19 Pedro Martinez .75
20 Paul O'Neill .10
21 Todd Walker .10
22 Vinny Castilla .10
23 Barry Larkin .10
24 Curt Schilling .40
25 Jason Kendall .10
26 Scott Erickson .10
27 Andres Galarraga .10
28 Jeff Shaw .10
29 John Olerud .10
30 Orlando Hernandez .10
31 Larry Walker .10
32 Andruw Jones .75
33 Jeff Cirillo .10
34 Barry Bonds 2.00
35 Manny Ramirez .75
36 Mark Kotsay .10
37 Ivan Rodriguez .60
38 Jeff King .10
39 Brian Hunter .10
40 Ray Durham .10
41 Bernie Williams .10
42 Darin Erstad .30
43 Chipper Jones 1.00
44 Pat Hentgen .10
45 Eric Young .10
46 Jaret Wright .10
47 Juan Guzman .10
48 Jorge Posada .10
49 Bobby Higginson .10
50 Jose Guillen .10
51 Trevor Hoffman .10
52 Ken Griffey Jr. 1.50
53 David Justice .10
54 Matt Williams .10
55 Eric Karros .10
56 Derek Bell .10
57 Ray Lankford .10
58 Mariano Rivera .25
59 Brett Tomko .10
60 Mike Mussina .40
61 Kenny Lofton .10
62 Chuck Finley .10
63 Alex Gonzalez .10
64 Mark Grace .10
65 Raul Mondesi .10
66 David Cone .10
67 Brad Fullmer .10
68 Andy Benes .10
69 John Smoltz .10
70 Shane Reynolds .10
71 Bruce Chen .10
72 Adam Kennedy .10
73 Jack Cust .10
74 Matt Clement .10
75 Derrick Gibson .10
76 Darnell McDonald .10
77 Adam Everett **RC** .50
78 Ricardo Aramboles .10
79 Mark Quinn **RC** .25
80 Jason Rakers .10
81 Seth Etherton **RC** .35
82 Jeff Urban **RC** .25
83 Manny Aybar .10
84 Mike Nannini **RC** .25
85 Onan Masaoka .10
86 Rod Barajas .10
87 Mike Frank .10
88 Scott Randall .10
89 Justin Bowles **RC** .25
90 Chris Haas .10
91 Arturo McDowell **RC** .25
92 Matt Belisle **RC** .35
93 Scott Elarton .10
94 Vernon Wells .10
95 Pat Cline .10
96 Ryan Anderson .10
97 Kevin Barker .10
98 Ruben Mateo .10
99 Robert Fick .10
100 Corey Koskie .10
101 Ricky Ledee .10
102 Rick Elder **RC** .25
103 Jack Cressend **RC** .25
104 Joe Lawrence .10
105 Mike Lincoln .10
106 Kit Pellow **RC** .35
107 Matt Burch **RC** .25
108 Brent Butler .10
109 Jason Dewey .10
110 Cesar King .10
111 Julio Ramirez .10
112 Jake Westbrook .10
113 Eric Valent **RC** .35
114 Roosevelt Brown **RC** .35
115 Choo Freeman **RC** .50
116 Juan Melo .10
117 Jason Grilli .10
118 Jared Sandberg .10
119 Glenn Davis .10
120 David Riske **RC** .25
121 Jacque Jones .10
122 Corey Lee .10
123 Michael Barrett .10
124 Lariel Gonzalez .10
125 Mitch Meluskey .10
126 Freddy Garcia .10
127 Tony Torcato **RC** .25
128 Jeff Liefer .10
129 Ntema Ndungidi .10
130 Andy Brown **RC** .35
131 Ryan Mills **RC** .25
132 Andy Abad **RC** .25
133 Carlos Febles .10
134 Jason Tyner **RC** .25
135 Mark Osborne .10
136 Phil Norton **RC** .25
137 Nathan Haynes .10
138 Roy Halladay .10
139 Juan Encarnacion .10
140 Brad Penny .10
141 Grant Roberts .10
142 Aramis Ramirez .10
143 Cristian Guzman .10
144 Mamon Tucker **RC** .25
145 Ryan Bradley .10
146 Brian Simmons .10
147 Dan Reichert .10
148 Russ Branyon .10
149 Victor Valencia **RC** .25
150 Scott Schoeneweis .10
151 Sean Spencer **RC** .25
152 Odalis Perez .10
153 Joe Fontenot .10
154 Milton Bradley .10
155 Josh McKinley **RC** .25
156 Terrence Long .10
157 Danny Klassen .10
158 Paul Hoover **RC** .25
159 Ron Belliard .10
160 Armando Rios .10
161 Ramon Hernandez .10
162 Jason Conti .10
163 Chad Hermansen .10
164 Jason Standridge .10
165 Jason Dellaero .10
166 John Curtice .10
167 Clayton Andrews **RC** .25
168 Jeremy Giambi .10
169 Alex Ramirez .10
170 Gabe Molina **RC** .25
171 Mario Encarnacion **RC** .25
172 Mike Zywica **RC** .25
173 Chip Ambres **RC** .25
174 Trot Nixon .10
175 Pat Burrell **RC** 2.00
176 Jeff Yoder .10
177 Chris Jones **RC** .25
178 Kevin Witt .10
179 Keith Luuloa **RC** .25
180 Billy Koch .10
181 Damaso Marte **RC** .25
182 Ryan Glynn **RC** .25
183 Calvin Pickering .10
184 Michael Cuddyer .10
185 Nick Johnson **RC** .75
186 Doug Mientkiewicz **RC** 1.00
187 Nate Cornejo **RC** .35
188 Octavio Dotel .10
189 Wes Helms .10
190 Nelson Lara .10
191 Chuck Abbott **RC** .25
192 Tony Armas Jr. .10
193 Gil Meche .10
194 Ben Petrick .10
195 Chris George **RC** .25
196 Scott Hunter **RC** .25
197 Ryan Brannan .10
198 Amaury Garcia **RC** .25
199 Chris Gissell .10
200 Austin Kearns **RC** 1.50
201 Alex Gonzalez .10
202 Wade Miller .10
203 Scott Williamson .10
204 Chris Enochs .10
205 Fernando Seguignol .10
206 Marlon Anderson .10
207 Todd Sears **RC** .25
208 Nate Bump **RC** .25
209 J.M. Gold **RC** .25
210 Matt LeCroy .10
211 Alex Hernandez .10
212 Luis Rivera .10
213 Troy Cameron .10
214 Alex Escobar **RC** .50
215 Jason LaRue .10
216 Kyle Peterson .10
217 Brent Butler .10
218 Dernell Stenson .10
219 Adrian Beltre .40
220 Daryle Ward .10
---- Series 1 Checklist Folder .10
221 Jim Thome .60
222 Cliff Floyd .10
223 Rickey Henderson .75
224 Garret Anderson .10
225 Ken Caminiti .10
226 Bret Boone .10
227 Jeromy Burnitz .10
228 Steve Finley .10
229 Miguel Tejada .40
230 Greg Vaughn .10
231 Jose Offerman .10
232 Andy Ashby .10
233 Albert Belle .10
234 Fernando Tatis .10
235 Todd Helton .65
236 Sean Casey .25
237 Brian Giles .10
238 Andy Pettitte .25
239 Fred McGriff .10
240 Roberto Alomar .30
241 Edgar Martinez .10
242 Lee Stevens .10
243 Shawn Green .25
244 Ryan Klesko .10
245 Sammy Sosa 1.00
246 Todd Hundley .10
247 Shannon Stewart .10
248 Randy Johnson .75
249 Rondell White .10
250 Mike Piazza 1.50
251 Craig Biggio .10
252 David Wells .10
253 Brian Jordan .10
254 Edgar Renteria .10
255 Bartolo Colon .10
256 Frank Thomas .75
257 Will Clark .10
258 Dean Palmer .10
259 Dmitri Young .10
260 Scott Rolen .60
261 Jeff Kent .10
262 Dante Bichette .10
263 Nomar Garciaparra 1.00
264 Tony Gwynn 1.00

265	Alex Rodriguez	1.75
266	Jose Canseco	.45
267	Jason Giambi	.40
268	Jeff Bagwell	.75
269	Carlos Delgado	.40
270	Tom Glavine	.40
271	Eric Davis	.10
272	Edgardo Alfonzo	.10
273	Tim Salmon	.10
274	Johnny Damon	.35
275	Rafael Palmeiro	.65
276	Denny Neagle	.10
277	Neifi Perez	.10
278	Roger Clemens	1.25
279	Brant Brown	.10
280	Kevin Brown	.10
281	Jay Bell	.10
282	Jay Buhner	.10
283	Matt Lawton	.10
284	Robin Ventura	.10
285	Juan Gonzalez	.35
286	Mo Vaughn	.10
287	Kevin Millwood	.10
288	Tino Martinez	.10
289	Justin Thompson	.10
290	Derek Jeter	2.00
291	Ben Davis	.10
292	Mike Lowell	.10
293	Joe Crede **RC**	.75
294	Micah Bowie **RC**	.25
295	Lance Berkman	.10
296	Jason Marquis	.10
297	Chad Green	.10
298	Dee Brown	.10
299	Jerry Hairston Jr.	.10
300	Gabe Kapler	.10
301	Brent Stentz **RC**	.25
302	Scott Mullen **RC**	.25
303	Brandon Reed	.10
304	Shea Hillenbrand **RC**	.50
305	J.D. Closser **RC**	.25
306	Gary Matthews Jr.	.10
307	Toby Hall **RC**	.25
308	Jason Phillips **RC**	.25
309	Jose Macias **RC**	.25
310	Jung Bong **RC**	.25
311	Ramon Soler **RC**	.25
312	Kelly Dransfeldt **RC**	.25
313	Carlos Hernandez **RC**	.25
314	Kevin Haverbusch	.10
315	Aaron Myette **RC**	.25
316	Chad Harville **RC**	.35
317	Kyle Farnsworth **RC**	.50
318	Travis Dawkins **RC**	.50
319	Willie Martinez	.10
320	Carlos Lee	.10
321	Carlos Pena **RC**	1.00
322	Peter Bergeron **RC**	.25
323	A.J. Burnett **RC**	.50
324	Bucky Jacobsen **RC**	.25
325	Mo Bruce **RC**	.25
326	Reggie Taylor	.10
327	Jackie Rexrode	.10
328	Alvin Morrow **RC**	.25
329	Carlos Beltran	.40
330	Eric Chavez	.25
331	John Patterson	.10
332	Jayson Werth	.10
333	Richie Sexson	.10
334	Randy Wolf	.10
335	Eli Marrero	.10
336	Paul LoDuca	.10
337	J.D. Smart	.10
338	Ryan Minor	.10
339	Kris Benson	.10
340	George Lombard	.10
341	Troy Glaus	.75
342	Eddie Yarnell	.10
343	Kip Wells **RC**	.50
344	C.C. Sabathia **RC**	1.00
345	Sean Burroughs **RC**	.50
346	Felipe Lopez **RC**	1.50
347	Ryan Rupe **RC**	.25
348	Orber Moreno **RC**	.25
349	Rafael Roque **RC**	.25
350	Alfonso Soriano **RC**	5.00
351	Pablo Ozuna	.10
352	Corey Patterson **RC**	1.00
353	Braden Looper	.10
354	Robbie Bell	.10
355	Mark Mulder **RC**	2.00
356	Angel Pena	.10
357	Kevin McGlinchy	.10
358	Michael Restovich **RC**	.35
359	Eric DuBose	.10
360	Geoff Jenkins	.10
361	Mark Harriger **RC**	.25
362	Junior Herndon **RC**	.25
363	Tim Raines Jr. **RC**	.25
364	Rafael Furcal **RC**	.75
365	Marcus Giles **RC**	1.00
366	Ted Lilly	.10
367	Jorge Toca **RC**	.25
368	David Kelton **RC**	.35
369	Adam Dunn **RC**	5.00
370	Guillermo Mota **RC**	.35
371	Brett Laxton **RC**	.25
372	Travis Harper **RC**	.25
373	Tom Davey **RC**	.25
374	Darren Blakely **RC**	.25
375	Tim Hudson **RC**	3.00
376	Jason Romano	.10
377	Dan Reichert	.10
378	Julio Lugo **RC**	.75
379	Jose Garcia **RC**	.25
380	Erubiel Durazo **RC**	.25
381	Jose Jimenez	.10
382	Chris Fussell	.10
383	Steve Lomasney	.10
384	Juan Pena **RC**	.25
385	Allen Levrault **RC**	.25
386	Juan Rivera **RC**	.25
387	Steve Colyer **RC**	.25
388	Joe Nathan **RC**	.25
389	Ron Walker **RC**	.10
390	Nick Bierbrodt	.10
391	Luke Prokopec **RC**	.25
392	Dave Roberts **RC**	.40
393	Mike Darr	.10
394	Abraham Nunez **RC**	.35
395	Giuseppe Chiaramonte **RC**	.25
396	Jermaine Van Buren **RC**	.25
397	Mike Kusiewicz	.10
398	Matt Wise **RC**	.25
399	Joe McEwing **RC**	.40
400	Matt Holliday **RC**	5.00
401	Willi Mo Pena **RC**	1.50
402	Ruben Quevedo **RC**	.25
403	Rob Ryan **RC**	.25
404	Freddy Garcia **RC**	1.00
405	Kevin Eberwein **RC**	.25
406	Jesus Colome **RC**	.25
407	Chris Singleton **RC**	.25
408	Bubba Crosby **RC**	.50
409	Jesus Cordero **RC**	.25
410	Donny Leon	.10
411	Goefrey Tomlinson **RC**	.25
412	Jeff Winchester **RC**	.25
413	Adam Piatt **RC**	.50
414	Robert Stratton	.10
415	T.J. Tucker	.10
416	Ryan Langerhans **RC**	.25
417	Anthony Shumaker **RC**	.25
418	Matt Miller **RC**	.25
419	Doug Clark **RC**	.25
420	Kory DeHaan **RC**	.25
421	David Eckstein **RC**	.75
422	Brian Cooper **RC**	.25
423	Brady Clark **RC**	.25
424	Chris Magruder **RC**	.25
425	Bobby Seay **RC**	.25
426	Aubrey Huff **RC**	1.00
427	Mike Jerzembeck	.10
428	Matt Blank **RC**	.25
429	Benny Agbayani **RC**	.25
430	Kevin Beirne **RC**	.25
431	Josh Hamilton **RC**	4.00
432	Josh Girdley **RC**	.25
433	Kyle Snyder **RC**	.25
434	Mike Paradis **RC**	.25
435	Jason Jennings **RC**	.25
436	David Walling **RC**	.25
437	Omar Ortiz **RC**	.25
438	Jay Gehrke **RC**	.25
439	Casey Burns **RC**	.25
440	Carl Crawford **RC**	2.50

Gold

Gold, rather than black, ink for the facsimile autograph, Bowman logo and player name on front, and a serial number on back from within an edition of 99, designate these parallels. Stated odds of finding the Gold cards were one per 111 packs of Series 1, and 1:59 in Series 2.

	NM/M
Common Player:	3.00
Gold Stars:	10X

(See 1999 Bowman for checklist and base card values.)

International

International parallels are a one-per-pack insert. Fronts are printed in metallic silver on which the photo's background has been replaced with a scenic picture supposed to be indicative of the player's native land. That location is spelled out at the lower-left corner of the photo. Backs of the Internationals are printed in the player's native language.

	NM/M
Common Player:	.25
Int'l Stars:	1.5X

(See 1999 Bowman for checklist and base card values.)

Autographs

Autographs were randomly seeded in Series 1 and 2 packs, with each card bearing a Topps Certified Autograph seal on the front and numbered with a "BA" prefix on back. Levels of scarcity are color coded by the metallic-foil highlights on front: Golds are the most difficult to find at 1:1,941 Series 1 packs and 1:1,024 Series 2. Silvers are seeded 1:485 in Series 1, 1:256 Series 2. Blues are found at an average rate of 1:162 in first series and 1:85 in second series.

		NM/M
Common Player:		3.00
Blues inserted 1:162 or 1:85		
Silvers inserted 1:485 or 1:256		
Golds inserted 1:1,954 or 1:1,024		
1	Ruben Mateo/B	5.00
2	Troy Glaus/G	40.00
3	Ben Davis/G	8.00
4	Jayson Werth/B	5.00
5	Jerry Hairston Jr./S	6.00
6	Darnell McDonald/B	4.00
7	Calvin Pickering/S	8.00
8	Ryan Minor/S	4.00
9	Alex Escobar/B	6.00
10	Grant Roberts/B	5.00
11	Carlos Guillen/B	10.00
12	Ryan Anderson/S	6.00
13	Gil Meche/S	5.00
14	Russell Branyan/S	5.00
15	Alex Ramirez/S	5.00
16	Jason Rakers/S	5.00
17	Eddie Yarnall/B	5.00
18	Freddy Garcia/B	20.00
19	Jason Conti/B	3.00
20	Corey Koskie/B	5.00
21	Roosevelt Brown/B	5.00
22	Willie Martinez/B	3.00
23	Mike Jerzembeck/B	3.00
24	Lariel Gonzalez/B	3.00
25	Fernando Seguignol/B	3.00
26	Robert Fick/S	5.00
27	J.D. Smart/B	3.00
28	Ryan Mills/B	3.00
29	Chad Hermansen/G	6.00
30	Jason Grilli/B	5.00
31	Michael Cuddyer/B	5.00
32	Jacque Jones/S	10.00
33	Reggie Taylor/B	3.00
34	Richie Sexson/G	15.00
35	Michael Barrett/B	8.00
36	Paul LoDuca/B	8.00
37	Adrian Beltre/G	30.00
38	Peter Bergeron/B	4.00
39	Joe Fontenot/B	3.00
40	Randy Wolf/B	6.00
41	Nick Johnson/B	12.00
42	Ryan Bradley/B	4.00
43	Mike Lowell/S	10.00
44	Ricky Ledee/B	5.00
45	Mike Lincoln/S	4.00
46	Jeremy Giambi/B	5.00
47	Dermal Brown/S	3.00
48	Derrick Gibson/B	3.00
49	Scott Randall/B	3.00
50	Ben Petrick/S	5.00
51	Jason LaRue/B	3.00
52	Cole Liniak/B	3.00
53	John Curtice/B	3.00
54	Jackie Rexrode/B	3.00
55	John Patterson/B	4.00
56	Brad Penny/S	6.00
57	Jared Sandberg/B	6.00
58	Kerry Wood/G	20.00
59	Eli Marrero/B	5.00
60	Jason Marquis/B	8.00
61	George Lombard/S	5.00
62	Bruce Chen/S	3.00
63	Kevin Witt/S	4.00
64	Vernon Wells/B	15.00
65	Billy Koch/B	3.00
66	Roy Halladay/B	20.00
67	Nathan Haynes/B	3.00
68	Ben Grieve/G	8.00
69	Eric Chavez/G	10.00
70	Lance Berkman/S	15.00

Early Risers

This insert set features 11 current baseball superstars who have already won a Rookie of the Year award and who continue to excel. Cards have an "ER" prefix to the number on back.

		NM/M
Complete Set (11):		8.00
Common Player:		.25
Inserted 1:12		
1	Mike Piazza	1.00
2	Cal Ripken Jr.	2.00
3	Jeff Bagwell	.50
4	Ben Grieve	.25
5	Kerry Wood	.40
6	Mark McGwire	1.50
7	Nomar Garciaparra	.75
8	Derek Jeter	2.00
9	Scott Rolen	.50
10	Jose Canseco	.45
11	Raul Mondesi	.25

Late Bloomers

This 10-card set features late-round picks from previous drafts who have emerged as bona fide stars. These inserts are numbered with an "LB" prefix.

		NM/M
Complete Set (10):		4.00
Common Player:		.25
Inserted 1:12		
LB1	Mike Piazza	2.00
LB2	Jim Thome	.75
LB3	Larry Walker	.25
LB4	Vinny Castilla	.25
LB5	Andy Pettitte	.50
LB6	Jim Edmonds	.25
LB7	Kenny Lofton	.25
LB8	John Smoltz	.25
LB9	Mark Grace	.25
LB10	Trevor Hoffman	.25

Scout's Choice

Scout's Choice inserts were randomly inserted in Series 1 packs and feature a borderless, double-etched design. The 21-card set focuses on prospects who have potential to win a future Rookie of the Year award.

		NM/M
Complete Set (21):		12.00
Common Player:		.40
Inserted 1:12		
SC1	Ruben Mateo	.40
SC2	Ryan Anderson	.40
SC3	Pat Burrell	3.00
SC4	Troy Glaus	4.00
SC5	Eric Chavez	1.00
SC6	Adrian Beltre	1.00
SC7	Bruce Chen	.40
SC8	Carlos Beltran	1.00
SC9	Alex Gonzalez	.40
SC10	Carlos Lee	.50
SC11	George Lombard	.40
SC12	Matt Clement	.40
SC13	Calvin Pickering	.40
SC14	Marlon Anderson	.40
SC15	Chad Hermansen	.40
SC16	Russell Branyan	.40
SC17	Jeremy Giambi	.40
SC18	Ricky Ledee	.40
SC19	John Patterson	.40
SC20	Roy Halladay	.75
SC21	Michael Barrett	.40

2000 Rookie of the Year

Randomly inserted in Series 2 packs, these cards have a borderless, double-etched foil design. The 10-card set focuses on players that have potential to win the 2000 Rookie of the Year award.

		NM/M
Complete Set (10):		7.00
Common Player:		.50
Inserted 1:12		
1	Ryan Anderson	.50
2	Pat Burrell	2.50
3	A.J. Burnett	.50
4	Ruben Mateo	.50
5	Alex Escobar	.50
6	Pablo Ozuna	.50
7	Mark Mulder	1.00
8	Corey Patterson	1.00
9	George Lombard	.50
10	Nick Johnson	1.00

1999 Bowman Chrome

Bowman Chrome was released in two 220-card series as an upscale chromium parallel version of Bowman Baseball. Like Bowman, each series has 150 prospect cards with blue foil, while 70 veteran cards have red foil. Packs contain four cards with an original SRP of $3.

		NM/M
Complete Set (440):		175.00
Complete Series 1 (220):		65.00
Complete Series 2 (220):		125.00
Common Player:		.25
Series 1 Pack (4):		3.00
Series 1 Wax Box (24):		50.00
Series 2 Pack (4):		5.00
Series 2 Wax Box (24):		100.00
1	Ben Grieve	.25
2	Kerry Wood	.45
3	Ruben Rivera	.25
4	Sandy Alomar	.25
5	Cal Ripken Jr.	3.00
6	Mark McGwire	2.50
7	Vladimir Guerrero	1.00
8	Moises Alou	.25
9	Jim Edmonds	.25
10	Greg Maddux	1.50
11	Gary Sheffield	.50
12	John Valentin	.25
13	Chuck Knoblauch	.25
14	Tony Clark	.25
15	Rusty Greer	.25
16	Al Leiter	.25
17	Travis Lee	.25
18	Jose Cruz Jr.	.25
19	Pedro Martinez	1.00
20	Paul O'Neill	.25
21	Todd Walker	.25
22	Vinny Castilla	.25
23	Barry Larkin	.25
24	Curt Schilling	.40
25	Jason Kendall	.25
26	Scott Erickson	.25
27	Andres Galarraga	.25
28	Jeff Shaw	.25
29	John Olerud	.25
30	Orlando Hernandez	.40
31	Larry Walker	.25
32	Andruw Jones	1.00
33	Jeff Cirillo	.25
34	Barry Bonds	3.00
35	Manny Ramirez	1.00
36	Mark Kotsay	.25
37	Ivan Rodriguez	.75
38	Jeff King	.25
39	Brian Hunter	.25
40	Ray Durham	.25
41	Bernie Williams	.25
42	Darin Erstad	.50
43	Chipper Jones	1.50
44	Pat Hentgen	.25
45	Eric Young	.25
46	Jaret Wright	.25
47	Juan Guzman	.25
48	Jorge Posada	.25
49	Bobby Higginson	.25
50	Jose Guillen	.25
51	Trevor Hoffman	.25
52	Ken Griffey Jr.	2.00
53	David Justice	.25
54	Matt Williams	.25
55	Eric Karros	.25
56	Derek Bell	.25
57	Ray Lankford	.25
58	Mariano Rivera	.40
59	Brett Tomko	.25
60	Mike Mussina	.50
61	Kenny Lofton	.25
62	Chuck Finley	.25
63	Alex Gonzalez	.25
64	Mark Grace	.25
65	Raul Mondesi	.25
66	David Cone	.25
67	Brad Fullmer	.25
68	Andy Benes	.25
69	John Smoltz	.25
70	Shane Reynolds	.25
71	Bruce Chen	.25
72	Adam Kennedy	.25
73	Jack Cust	.25
74	Matt Clement	.25
75	Derrick Gibson	.25
76	Darnell McDonald	.25
77	Adam Everett **RC**	.75
78	Ricardo Aramboles	.25
79	Mark Quinn **RC**	.50
80	Jason Rakers	.25
81	Seth Etherton **RC**	.50
82	Jeff Urban **RC**	.35
83	Manny Aybar	.25
84	Mike Nannini **RC**	.35
85	Onan Masaoka	.25
86	Rod Barajas	.25
87	Mike Frank	.25
88	Scott Randall	.25
89	Justin Bowles **RC**	.35
90	Chris Haas	.25
91	Arturo McDowell **RC**	.35
92	Matt Belisle **RC**	.50
93	Scott Elarton	.25
94	Vernon Wells	.25
95	Pat Cline	.25
96	Ryan Anderson	.25

97 Kevin Barker .25
98 Ruben Mateo .25
99 Robert Fick .25
100 Corey Koskie .25
101 Ricky Ledee .25
102 Rick Elder **RC** .35
103 Jack Cressend **RC** .35
104 Joe Lawrence .25
105 Mike Lincoln .25
106 Kit Pellow **RC** .50
107 Matt Burch **RC** .35
108 Brent Butler .25
109 Jason Dewey .25
110 Cesar King .25
111 Julio Ramirez .25
112 Jake Westbrook .25
113 Eric Valent **RC** 1.00
114 Roosevelt Brown **RC** .50
115 Choo Freeman **RC** 1.50
116 Juan Melo .25
117 Jason Grilli .25
118 Jared Sandberg .25
119 Glenn Davis .25
120 David Riske **RC** .35
121 Jacque Jones .25
122 Corey Lee .25
123 Michael Barrett .25
124 Lariel Gonzalez .25
125 Mitch Meluskey .25
126 Freddy Garcia **RC** .25
127 Tony Torcato **RC** .35
128 Jeff Liefer .25
129 Ntema Ndungidi .25
130 Andy Brown **RC** .50
131 Ryan Mills **RC** .35
132 Andy Abad **RC** .50
133 Carlos Febles .25
134 Jason Tyner **RC** .50
135 Mark Osborne .25
136 Phil Norton **RC** .35
137 Nathan Haynes .25
138 Roy Halladay .25
139 Juan Encarnacion .25
140 Brad Penny .25
141 Grant Roberts .25
142 Aramis Ramirez .25
143 Cristian Guzman .25
144 Mamon Tucker **RC** .35
145 Ryan Bradley .25
146 Brian Simmons .25
147 Dan Reichert .25
148 Russ Branyon .25
149 Victor Valencia **RC** .35
150 Scott Schoeneweis .25
151 Sean Spencer **RC** .35
152 Odalis Perez .25
153 Joe Fontenot .25
154 Milton Bradley .25
155 Josh McKinley **RC** .35
156 Terrence Long .25
157 Danny Klassen .25
158 Paul Hoover **RC** .35
159 Ron Belliard .25
160 Armando Rios .25
161 Ramon Hernandez .25
162 Jason Conti .25
163 Chad Hermansen .25
164 Jason Standridge .25
165 Jason Dellaero .25
166 John Curtice .25
167 Clayton Andrews **RC** .35
168 Jeremy Giambi .25
169 Alex Ramirez .25
170 Gabe Molina **RC** .35
171 Mario Encarnacion **RC** .35
172 Mike Zywica **RC** .35
173 Chip Ambres **RC** .35
174 Trot Nixon .25
175 Pat Burrell **RC** 10.00
176 Jeff Yoder .25
177 Chris Jones **RC** .35
178 Kevin Witt .25
179 Keith Luuloa **RC** .35
180 Billy Koch .25
181 Damaso Marte **RC** .35
182 Ryan Glynn **RC** .35
183 Calvin Pickering .25
184 Michael Cuddyer .25
185 Nick Johnson **RC** 4.00
186 Doug Mientkiewicz **RC** 2.00
187 Nate Cornejo **RC** 1.00
188 Octavio Dotel .25
189 Wes Helms .25
190 Nelson Lara .25
191 Chuck Abbott **RC** .35
192 Tony Armas Jr. .25
193 Gil Meche .25
194 Ben Petrick .25
195 Chris George **RC** .35
196 Scott Hunter **RC** .35
197 Ryan Brannan .25
198 Amaury Garcia **RC** .35
199 Chris Gissell .25
200 Austin Kearns **RC** 5.00
201 Alex Gonzalez .25
202 Wade Miller .25
203 Scott Williamson .25
204 Chris Enochs .25
205 Fernando Seguignol .25
206 Marlon Anderson .25
207 Todd Sears **RC** .35
208 Nate Bump **RC** .35
209 J.M. Gold **RC** .50
210 Matt LeCroy **RC** .35
211 Alex Hernandez .25
212 Luis Rivera .25
213 Troy Cameron .25
214 Alex Escobar **RC** 1.00
215 Jason LaRue .25
216 Kyle Peterson .25
217 Brent Butler .25
218 Dernell Stenson .25
219 Adrian Beltre .40
220 Daryle Ward .25
221 Jim Thome .65
222 Cliff Floyd .25
223 Rickey Henderson 1.00
224 Garret Anderson .25
225 Ken Caminiti .25
226 Bret Boone .25
227 Jeromy Burnitz .25
228 Steve Finley .25
229 Miguel Tejada .40
230 Greg Vaughn .25
231 Jose Offerman .25
232 Andy Ashby .25
233 Albert Belle .25
234 Fernando Tatis .25
235 Todd Helton .75
236 Sean Casey .40
237 Brian Giles .25
238 Andy Pettitte .40
239 Fred McGriff .25
240 Roberto Alomar .40
241 Edgar Martinez .25
242 Lee Stevens .25
243 Shawn Green .40
244 Ryan Klesko .25
245 Sammy Sosa 1.50
246 Todd Hundley .25
247 Shannon Stewart .25
248 Randy Johnson 1.00
249 Rondell White .25
250 Mike Piazza 2.00
251 Craig Biggio .25
252 David Wells .25
253 Brian Jordan .25
254 Edgar Renteria .25
255 Bartolo Colon .25
256 Frank Thomas 1.00
257 Will Clark .25
258 Dean Palmer .25
259 Dmitri Young .25
260 Scott Rolen .65
261 Jeff Kent .25
262 Dante Bichette .25
263 Nomar Garciaparra 1.50
264 Tony Gwynn 1.50
265 Alex Rodriguez 2.00
266 Jose Canseco .50
267 Jason Giambi .50
268 Jeff Bagwell 1.00
269 Carlos Delgado .65
270 Tom Glavine .50
271 Eric Davis .25
272 Edgardo Alfonzo .25
273 Tim Salmon .25
274 Johnny Damon .50
275 Rafael Palmeiro .75
276 Denny Neagle .25
277 Neifi Perez .25
278 Roger Clemens 1.75
279 Brant Brown .25
280 Kevin Brown .25
281 Jay Bell .25
282 Jay Buhner .25
283 Matt Lawton .25
284 Robin Ventura .25
285 Juan Gonzalez .50
286 Mo Vaughn .25
287 Kevin Millwood .25
288 Tino Martinez .25
289 Justin Thompson .25
290 Derek Jeter 3.00
291 Ben Davis .25
292 Mike Lowell .25
293 Joe Crede **RC** 3.00
294 Micah Bowie **RC** .50
295 Lance Berkman .25
296 Jason Marquis .25
297 Chad Green .25
298 Dee Brown .25
299 Jerry Hairston Jr. .25
300 Gabe Kapler .25
301 Brent Stentz **RC** .35
302 Scott Mullen **RC** .35
303 Brandon Reed .25
304 Shea Hillenbrand **RC** 2.50
305 J.D. Closser **RC** 1.00
306 Gary Matthews Jr. .25
307 Toby Hall **RC** 1.00
308 Jason Phillips **RC** .50
309 Jose Macias **RC** .50
310 Jung Bong **RC** .35
311 Ramon Soler **RC** .35
312 Kelly Dransfeldt **RC** .75
313 Carlos Hernandez **RC** .50
314 Kevin Haverbusch .75
315 Aaron Myette **RC** .75
316 Chad Harville **RC** .75
317 Kyle Farnsworth **RC** 1.00
318 Travis Dawkins **RC** .75
319 Willie Martinez .25
320 Carlos Lee .35
321 Carlos Pena **RC** 4.00
322 Peter Bergeron **RC** .50
323 A.J. Burnett **RC** 4.00
324 Bucky Jacobsen **RC** 1.00
325 Mo Bruce **RC** .35
326 Reggie Taylor .25
327 Jackie Rexrode .25
328 Alvin Morrow **RC** .35
329 Carlos Beltran .50
330 Eric Chavez .50
331 John Patterson .25
332 Jayson Werth .25
333 Richie Sexson .25
334 Randy Wolf .25
335 Eli Marrero .25
336 Paul LoDuca .25
337 J.D. Smart .25
338 Ryan Minor .25
339 Kris Benson .25
340 George Lombard .25
341 Troy Glaus .75
342 Eddie Yarnell .25
343 Kip Wells **RC** 1.00
344 C.C. Sabathia **RC** 4.00
345 Sean Burroughs **RC** 1.00
346 Felipe Lopez **RC** 5.00
347 Ryan Rupe **RC** .75
348 Orber Moreno **RC** .50
349 Rafael Roque **RC** .35
350 Alfonso Soriano **RC** 25.00
351 Pablo Ozuna .25
352 Corey Patterson **RC** 3.00
353 Braden Looper .25
354 Robbie Bell .25
355 Mark Mulder **RC** 4.00
356 Angel Pena .25
357 Kevin McGlinchy .25
358 Michael Restovich **RC** 1.00
359 Eric DuBose .25
360 Geoff Jenkins .25
361 Mark Harriger **RC** .35
362 Junior Herndon **RC** .35
363 Tim Raines Jr. **RC** .35
364 Rafael Furcal **RC** 3.00
365 Marcus Giles **RC** 2.00
366 Ted Lilly .25
367 Jorge Toca **RC** .35
368 David Kelton **RC** 1.50
369 Adam Dunn **RC** 25.00
370 Guillermo Mota **RC** .35
371 Brett Laxton **RC** .35
372 Travis Harper **RC** .35
373 Tom Davey **RC** .35
374 Darren Blakely **RC** .35
375 Tim Hudson **RC** 10.00
376 Jason Romano .25
377 Dan Reichert .25
378 Julio Lugo **RC** .35
379 Jose Garcia **RC** .35
380 Erubiel Durazo **RC** 1.50
381 Jose Jimenez .25
382 Chris Fussell .25
383 Steve Lomasney .25
384 Juan Pena **RC** .75
385 Allen Levrault **RC** .35
386 Juan Rivera **RC** .35
387 Steve Colyer **RC** .35
388 Joe Nathan **RC** 1.50
389 Ron Walker **RC** .35
390 Nick Bierbrodt .25
391 Luke Prokopec **RC** .35
392 Dave Roberts **RC** .50
393 Mike Darr .25
394 Abraham Nunez **RC** 1.00
395 Giuseppe Chiaramonte **RC** .35
396 Jermaine Van Buren **RC** .35
397 Mike Kusiewicz .25
398 Matt Wise **RC** .35
399 Joe McEwing **RC** .50
400 Matt Holliday **RC** 20.00
401 Willi Mo Pena **RC** 4.00
402 Ruben Quevedo **RC** .35
403 Rob Ryan **RC** .35
404 Freddy Garcia **RC** 3.00
405 Kevin Eberwein **RC** .35
406 Jesus Colome **RC** .35
407 Chris Singleton **RC** .35
408 Bubba Crosby **RC** 1.50
409 Jesus Cordero **RC** .35
410 Donny Leon .35
411 Goefrey Tomlinson **RC** .35
412 Jeff Winchester **RC** .35
413 Adam Piatt **RC** .50
414 Robert Stratton .25
415 T.J. Tucker .25
416 Ryan Langerhans **RC** 1.50
417 Chris Wakeland **RC** .35
418 Matt Miller **RC** .35
419 Doug Clark **RC** .35
420 Kory DeHaan **RC** .35
421 David Eckstein **RC** 2.00
422 Brian Cooper **RC** .35
423 Brady Clark **RC** 1.50
424 Chris Magruder **RC** .35
425 Bobby Seay **RC** .50
426 Aubrey Huff **RC** 5.00
427 Mike Jerzembeck .25
428 Matt Blank **RC** .35
429 Benny Agbayani **RC** .35
430 Kevin Beirne **RC** .35
431 Josh Hamilton **RC** 15.00
432 Josh Girdley **RC** .35
433 Kyle Snyder **RC** .35
434 Mike Paradis **RC** .35
435 Jason Jennings **RC** .75
436 David Walling **RC** .35
437 Omar Ortiz **RC** .35
438 Jay Gehrke **RC** .35
439 Casey Burns **RC** .35
440 Carl Crawford **RC** 12.00

Refractors

Refractor versions of all Bowman Chrome base cards and inserts were also created. Base card Refractors are found at the average rate of one per 12 packs. Scout's Choice Refractors are a 1:48 find; International Refractors (serially numbered within an edition of 100 each) are 1:76 and Diamond Aces Refractors are 1:84.

	NM/M
Common Player:	1.00
Refractor Stars:	5X

(See 1999 Bowman Chrome for checklist and base card values.)

Gold

A gold, rather than black, facsimile signature differentiates this parallel from the base-card issue. At an average insertion rate of 1:12, the Series 1 Golds are twice as easy as the Series 2 (1:24). Conversely, a Refractor version which is limited to 25 serially numbered sets, is an easier pull in Series 2 (1:200) than in Series 1 (1:305).

	NM/M
Common Player, Series 1:	1.50
Common Player, Series 2:	2.00
Stars:	3X
Gold Refractors:	30X

(See 1999 Bowman Chrome for checklist and base card values.)

International

Replacing the regular-card background with a scene from the player's native land gives this parallel issue an international flavor. For the geographically challenged, the place of birth is spelled out in the lower-left corner of the photo. In addition, the card backs are printed in the player's native language. Series 1 Internationals are found on the average of one per four packs, while the scarcer Series 2 Internationals are a 1:12 pick. Conversely, the Refractor version, individually numbered within an edition of 100 each is scarcer in Series 1 (1:76) than in Series 2 (1:50).

	NM/M
Common Player, Series 1:	.25
Common Player, Series 2:	.50
Stars:	1.5X
Common Refractor:	5.00
Refractors:	12X

(See 1999 Bowman Chrome for checklist and base card values.)

Diamond Aces

This 18-card set features nine emerging stars along with nine proven veterans. The cards have a prismatic look with "Diamond Aces" across the top. They are inserted in Series 1 packs. A parallel Refractor version is also randomly inserted.

		NM/M
Complete Set (18):		24.00
Common Player:		.50
Inserted 1:21		
Refractors:		1.5X
Inserted 1:84		
DA1	Troy Glaus	1.50
DA2	Eric Chavez	.75
DA3	Fernando Seguignol	.50
DA4	Ryan Anderson	.50
DA5	Ruben Mateo	.50
DA6	Carlos Beltran	1.00
DA7	Adrian Beltre	.75
DA8	Bruce Chen	.50
DA9	Pat Burrell	2.00
DA10	Mike Piazza	3.00
DA11	Ken Griffey Jr.	3.00
DA12	Chipper Jones	2.00
DA13	Derek Jeter	4.00
DA14	Mark McGwire	3.50
DA15	Nomar Garciaparra	2.00
DA16	Sammy Sosa	2.00
DA17	Juan Gonzalez	.75
DA18	Alex Rodriguez	3.50

Early Impact

The checklist of this Series 2 insert mixes a dozen youngsters - labeled "Early Impact" on front - who are already making a mark in the majors with eight veteran stars, whose cards are labeled "Lasting Impact." A Refractor version is a parallel.

		NM/M
Complete Set (20):		35.00
Common Player:		.75
Inserted 1:15		
Refractor:		1.5X
Inserted 1:75		
1	Alfonso Soriano	2.00
2	Pat Burrell	2.00
3	Ruben Mateo	.75
4	A.J. Burnett	.75
5	Corey Patterson	1.00
6	Daryle Ward	.75
7	Eric Chavez	1.00
8	Troy Glaus	2.00
9	Sean Casey	1.00
10	Joe McEwing	.75
11	Gabe Kapler	.75
12	Michael Barrett	.75
13	Sammy Sosa	2.50
14	Alex Rodriguez	4.00
15	Mark McGwire	4.00
16	Derek Jeter	5.00
17	Nomar Garciaparra	2.50
18	Mike Piazza	3.00
19	Chipper Jones	2.50
20	Ken Griffey Jr.	3.00

Scout's Choice

This is a chromium parallel of the inserts found in Series 1 Bowman. The 21-card set showcases prospects that have potential to win a future Rookie of the Year award. Refractor parallels are also randomly inserted.

		NM/M
Complete Set (21):		20.00
Common Player:		.75
Inserted 1:12		
Refractors:		1.5X
Inserted 1:48		
SC1	Ruben Mateo	.75
SC2	Ryan Anderson	.75
SC3	Pat Burrell	3.00
SC4	Troy Glaus	4.00
SC5	Eric Chavez	2.00
SC6	Adrian Beltre	1.50
SC7	Bruce Chen	.75
SC8	Carlos Beltran	2.50
SC9	Alex Gonzalez	.75
SC10	Carlos Lee	1.00
SC11	George Lombard	.75
SC12	Matt Clement	.75
SC13	Calvin Pickering	.75
SC14	Marlon Anderson	.75
SC15	Chad Hermansen	.75
SC16	Russell Branyan	.75
SC17	Jeremy Giambi	.75
SC18	Ricky Ledee	.75
SC19	John Patterson	.75
SC20	Roy Halladay	1.00
SC21	Michael Barrett	.75

2000 Rookie of the Year

This is a chromium parallel of the inserts found in Series 2 Bowman. The 10-card set is inserted in Series 2 Chrome packs and showcases prospects that have potential to win the 2000 Rookie of the Year award. Refractor parallels are also randomly inserted.

		NM/M
Complete Set (10):		12.00
Common Player:		1.00
Inserted 1:20		
Refractors:		1.5-3X
Inserted 1:100		
1	Ryan Anderson	1.00
2	Pat Burrell	4.00
3	A.J. Burnett	1.00
4	Ruben Mateo	1.00
5	Alex Escobar	1.00
6	Pablo Ozuna	1.00
7	Mark Mulder	1.50
8	Corey Patterson	2.00
9	George Lombard	1.00
10	Nick Johnson	2.00

1999 Bowman's Best Pre-Production

These cards were issued to draw interest to the '99 Bowman's Best issue. The promos are virtually identical to the issued version of each player's card except for the card number which is preceeded by a "PP" prefix.

		NM/M
Complete Set (3):		3.00
Common Player:		2.00
PP1	Javy Lopez	1.00
PP2	Marlon Anderson	1.00
PP3	J.M. Gold	1.00

1999 Bowman's Best

Bowman's Best consists of 200 cards printed on thick 27-point stock. Within the base set are 85 veteran stars printed on gold foil, 15 Best Performers on bronze foil, 50 Prospects on silver foil and 50 rookies on blue foil. The rookies are seeded one per pack. There are also two parallel versions: Refractors and Atomic Refractors. Refractors are inserted 1:15 packs and are sequentially numbered to 400, while Atomic Refractors are found 1:62 packs and are sequentially numbered to 100.

		NM/M
Complete Set (200):		30.00
Common Player:		.25
Pack (6):		2.00
Wax Box (24):		40.00
1	Chipper Jones	1.50
2	Brian Jordan	.25
3	David Justice	.25
4	Jason Kendall	.25
5	Mo Vaughn	.25
6	Jim Edmonds	.25
7	Wade Boggs	1.50
8	Jeromy Burnitz	.25
9	Todd Hundley	.25
10	Rondell White	.25
11	Cliff Floyd	.25
12	Sean Casey	.40
13	Bernie Williams	.25
14	Dante Bichette	.25
15	Greg Vaughn	.25
16	Andres Galarraga	.25
17	Ray Durham	.25
18	Jim Thome	.60
19	Gary Sheffield	.45
20	Frank Thomas	1.00
21	Orlando Hernandez	.35
22	Ivan Rodriguez	.75
23	Jose Cruz Jr.	.25
24	Jason Giambi	.50
25	Craig Biggio	.25
26	Kerry Wood	.45
27	Manny Ramirez	1.00
28	Curt Schilling	.45
29	Mike Mussina	.45
30	Tim Salmon	.25
31	Mike Piazza	2.00
32	Roberto Alomar	.40
33	Larry Walker	.25
34	Barry Larkin	.25
35	Nomar Garciaparra	1.50
36	Paul O'Neill	.25
37	Todd Walker	.25
38	Eric Karros	.25
39	Brad Fullmer	.25
40	John Olerud	.25
41	Todd Helton	.75
42	Raul Mondesi	.25
43	Jose Canseco	.50
44	Matt Williams	.25
45	Ray Lankford	.25
46	Carlos Delgado	.50
47	Darin Erstad	.50
48	Vladimir Guerrero	1.00
49	Robin Ventura	.25
50	Alex Rodriguez	2.50
51	Vinny Castilla	.25
52	Tony Clark	.25
53	Pedro Martinez	1.00
54	Rafael Palmeiro	.65
55	Scott Rolen	.65
56	Tino Martinez	.25
57	Tony Gwynn	1.50
58	Barry Bonds	3.00
59	Kenny Lofton	.25
60	Javy Lopez	.25
61	Mark Grace	.25
62	Travis Lee	.25
63	Kevin Brown	.25
64	Al Leiter	.25
65	Albert Belle	.25
66	Sammy Sosa	1.50
67	Greg Maddux	1.50
68	Mark Kotsay	.25
69	Dmitri Young	.25
70	Mark McGwire	2.50
71	Juan Gonzalez	.50
72	Andruw Jones	1.00
73	Derek Jeter	3.00
74	Randy Johnson	1.00
75	Cal Ripken Jr.	3.00
76	Shawn Green	.35
77	Moises Alou	.25
78	Tom Glavine	.45
79	Sandy Alomar	.25
80	Ken Griffey Jr.	2.00
81	Ryan Klesko	.25
82	Jeff Bagwell	1.00
83	Ben Grieve	.25
84	John Smoltz	.25
85	Roger Clemens	1.75
86	Ken Griffey Jr.	1.00
87	Roger Clemens	.85
88	Derek Jeter	1.50
89	Nomar Garciaparra	.75
90	Mark McGwire	1.25
91	Sammy Sosa	.75
92	Alex Rodriguez	1.25
93	Greg Maddux	.75
94	Vladimir Guerrero	1.00
95	Chipper Jones	.75
96	Kerry Wood	.30
97	Ben Grieve	.25
98	Tony Gwynn	.75
99	Juan Gonzalez	.30
100	Mike Piazza	1.00
101	Eric Chavez	.40
102	Billy Koch	.25
103	Dernell Stenson	.25
104	Marlon Anderson	.25
105	Ron Belliard	.25
106	Bruce Chen	.25
107	Carlos Beltran	.40
108	Chad Hermansen	.25
109	Ryan Anderson	.25
110	Michael Barrett	.25
111	Matt Clement	.25
112	Ben Davis	.25
113	Calvin Pickering	.25
114	Brad Penny	.25
115	Paul Konerko	.35
116	Alex Gonzalez	.25
117	George Lombard	.25
118	John Patterson	.25
119	Rob Bell	.25
120	Ruben Mateo	.25
121	Troy Glaus	.75
122	Ryan Bradley	.25
123	Carlos Lee	.35
124	Gabe Kapler	.25
125	Ramon Hernandez	.25
126	Carlos Febles	.25
127	Mitch Meluskey	.25
128	Michael Cuddyer	.25
129	Pablo Ozuna	.25
130	Jayson Werth	.25
131	Ricky Ledee	.25
132	Jeremy Giambi	.25
133	Danny Klassen	.25
134	Mark DeRosa	.25
135	Randy Wolf	.25
136	Roy Halladay	.35
137	Derrick Gibson	.25
138	Ben Petrick	.25
139	Warren Morris	.25
140	Lance Berkman	.25
141	Russell Branyan	.25
142	Adrian Beltre	.40
143	Juan Encarnacion	.25
144	Fernando Seguignol	.25
145	Corey Koskie	.25
146	Preston Wilson	.25
147	Homer Bush	.25
148	Daryle Ward	.25
149	Joe McEwing **RC**	.50
150	Peter Bergeron **RC**	.50
151	Pat Burrell **RC**	3.00
152	Choo Freeman **RC**	.50
153	Matt Belisle **RC**	.50
154	Carlos Pena **RC**	1.00
155	A.J. Burnett **RC**	.75
156	Doug Mientkiewicz **RC**	.75
157	Sean Burroughs **RC**	.50
158	Mike Zywica **RC**	.35
159	Corey Patterson **RC**	1.50
160	Austin Kearns **RC**	2.00
161	Chip Ambres **RC**	.35
162	Kelly Dransfeldt **RC**	.35
163	Mike Nannini **RC**	.35
164	Mark Mulder **RC**	2.00
165	Jason Tyner **RC**	.35
166	Bobby Seay **RC**	.50
167	Alex Escobar **RC**	.75
168	Nick Johnson **RC**	1.00
169	Alfonso Soriano **RC**	4.00
170	Clayton Andrews **RC**	.35
171	C.C. Sabathia **RC**	1.00
172	Matt Holliday **RC**	5.00
173	Brad Lidge **RC**	1.00
174	Kit Pellow **RC**	.50
175	J.M. Gold **RC**	.50
176	Roosevelt Brown **RC**	.50
177	Eric Valent **RC**	.50
178	Adam Everett **RC**	.75
179	Jorge Toca **RC**	.35
180	Matt Roney **RC**	.35
181	Andy Brown **RC**	.35
182	Phil Norton **RC**	.35
183	Mickey Lopez **RC**	.35
184	Chris George **RC**	.35
185	Arturo McDowell **RC**	.35
186	Jose Fernandez **RC**	.35
187	Seth Etherton **RC**	.50
188	Josh McKinley **RC**	.50
189	Nate Cornejo **RC**	.50
190	Giuseppe Chiaramonte **RC**	.35
191	Mamon Tucker **RC**	.35
192	Ryan Mills **RC**	.50
193	Chad Moeller **RC**	.50
194	Tony Torcato **RC**	.35
195	Jeff Winchester **RC**	.35
196	Rick Elder **RC**	.35
197	Matt Burch **RC**	.35
198	Jeff Urban **RC**	.35
199	Chris Jones **RC**	.35
200	Masao Kida **RC**	.50

Refractors

Inserted at an average rate of about one per 15 packs, Best Refractor's are so marked on the back in the card-number box at upper-right. Also found on back is a serial numbered stamped in gold-foil from within an edition of 400.

	NM/M
Complete Set (200):	250.00
Common Player:	1.00
Stars:	6X
Production 400 Sets	

(See 1999 Bowman Best for checklist and base card values.)

Atomic Refractors

The vibrant refractive background on front announces these parallels which are found on average of about once per 62 packs. Backs identify the variation in the card-number box at upper-right and with a serial number from within an edition of 100 per card.

	NM/M
Common Player:	3.00
Stars:	12X
Production 100 Sets	

(See 1999 Bowman Best for checklist and base card values.)

Franchise Best

Ten league leaders are featured in this insert set on three different technologies: Mach I, Mach II and Mach III. Mach I features die-cut Serillusion stock and is numbered to 3,000. Mach II features die-cut refractive styrene stock, numbered to 1,000; and, Mach III

features die-cut polycarbonate stock and is limited to 500 numbered sets. All cards numbers have an "FB" prefix.

		NM/M
Complete Set (10):		15.00
Common Player:		.75
Production 3,000 Sets		
Mach II (1,000):		1.5X
Mach III (500):		2.5X
1	Mark McGwire	2.50
2	Ken Griffey Jr.	1.50
3	Sammy Sosa	1.25
4	Nomar Garciaparra	1.25
5	Alex Rodriguez	2.50
6	Derek Jeter	3.50
7	Mike Piazza	1.50
8	Frank Thomas	1.00
9	Chipper Jones	1.25
10	Juan Gonzalez	.75

Franchise Favorites

This six-card set features retired legends and current stars in three versions. Version A features a current star, Version B features a retired player and Version C pairs the current star with the retired player. Cards have an "FR" prefix to the number on back.

		NM/M
Complete Set (6):		12.00
Common Player:		.50
Inserted 1:75		
1A	Derek Jeter	5.00
1B	Don Mattingly	2.00
1C	Derek Jeter, Don Mattingly	5.00
2A	Scott Rolen	.50
2B	Mike Schmidt	1.50
2C	Scott Rolen, Mike Schmidt	1.00

Franchise Favorites Autographs

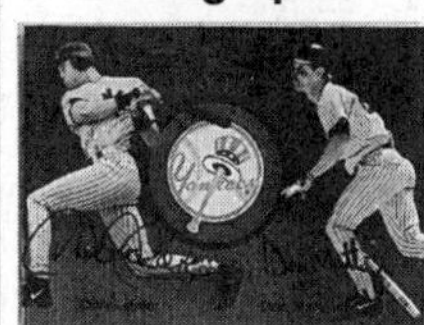

This is a parallel autographed version of the regular Franchise Favorites inserts.

		NM/M
Common Player:		15.00
Version A & B 1:1,548		
Version C 1:6,191		
1A	Derek Jeter	100.00
1B	Don Mattingly	60.00
1C	Derek Jeter, Don Mattingly	300.00
2A	Scott Rolen	20.00
2B	Mike Schmidt	50.00
2C	Scott Rolen, Mike Schmidt	100.00

Future Foundations

Ten up-and-coming players are featured in this set that has the same technologies as the Franchise Best inserts and broken down the same way.

The insert rates are 1:41 packs for Mach I, 1:124 for Mach II and 1:248 for Mach III.

		NM/M
Complete Set (10):		16.00
Common Player:		.75
Production 3,000 Sets		
Mach II (1,000):		1.5X
Mach III (500):		2.5X
1	Ruben Mateo	.75
2	Troy Glaus	4.00
3	Eric Chavez	1.50
4	Pat Burrell	4.00
5	Adrian Beltre	1.50
6	Ryan Anderson	.75
7	Alfonso Soriano	3.00
8	Brad Penny	.75
9	Derrick Gibson	.75
10	Bruce Chen	.75

Mirror Image

These inserts feature a veteran player on one side and a prospect on the other side for a total of 10 double-sided cards featuring 20 players. There are also parallel Refractor and Atomic Refractor versions.

		NM/M
Complete Set (10):		20.00
Common Player:		1.50
Inserted 1:24		
Refractors (1:96):		1.5X
Atomic Refractors (1:192):		2X
1	Alex Rodriguez, Alex Gonzalez	2.50
2	Ken Griffey Jr., Ruben Mateo	2.00
3	Derek Jeter, Alfonso Soriano	4.00
4	Sammy Sosa, Corey Patterson	1.50
5	Greg Maddux, Bruce Chen	1.50
6	Chipper Jones, Eric Chavez	1.50
7	Vladimir Guerrero, Carlos Beltran	1.50
8	Frank Thomas, Nick Johnson	1.50
9	Nomar Garciaparra, Pablo Ozuna	1.50
10	Mark McGwire, Pat Burrell	3.00

Rookie Locker Room Autographs

This five-card set features autographs of baseball's current hot prospects. Each card is branded with a "Topps Certified Autograph Issue" stamp.

		NM/M
Common Player:		4.00
Inserted 1:248		
1	Pat Burrell	10.00
2	Michael Barrett	4.00
3	Troy Glaus	10.00
4	Gabe Kapler	4.00
5	Eric Chavez	7.50

Rookie Locker Room Game-Worn Jerseys

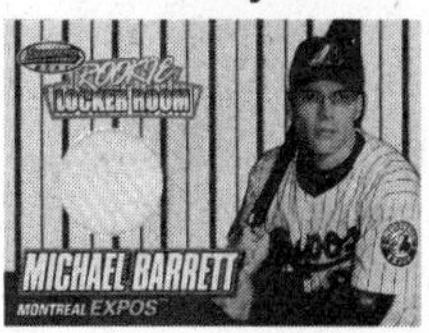

This four-card set spotlights hot prospects and has a swatch of game-used jersey from the featured player embedded into the card.

		NM/M
Common Player:		3.00
Inserted 1:270		
1	Richie Sexson	5.00
2	Michael Barrett	3.00
3	Troy Glaus	8.00
4	Eric Chavez	5.00

Rookie Locker Room Game-Used Lumber

This six-card set features actual pieces of each player's game-used bat embedded into the cards.

		NM/M
Complete Set (6):		35.00
Common Player:		4.00
Inserted 1:258		
1	Pat Burrell	10.00
2	Michael Barrett	4.00
3	Troy Glaus	10.00
4	Gabe Kapler	4.00
5	Eric Chavez	7.50
6	Richie Sexson	5.00

Rookie of the Year

This set salutes 1998 AL and NL Rookie of Year award winners Kerry Wood and Ben Grieve. They are inserted 1:95 packs and are numbered with a ROY prefix. Ben Grieve also autographed some of the inserts which feature a "Topps Certified Autograph Issue" stamp. Autographs are seeded 1:1,241 packs.

		NM/M
Complete Set (2):		4.00
1	Ben Grieve	2.00
2	Kerry Wood	2.00
A1	Ben Grieve/Auto.	6.00

2000 Bowman

Released in one 440-card series. The card fronts are foil stamped to differentiate Veterans (gold foil) from Rookies and Prospects (silver). All card fronts feature facsimile signatures from the players' original Topps contracts. All bona fide rookie cards also exhibit the "Bowman Rookie Card" stamped under the 2000 Bowman logo.

	NM/M
Complete Set (440):	65.00

Common Player: .15
Common Rookie: .25
Pack (10): 2.50
Box (24): 40.00
1 Vladimir Guerrero .75
2 Chipper Jones .75
3 Todd Walker .15
4 Barry Larkin .25
5 Bernie Williams .40
6 Todd Helton .75
7 Jermaine Dye .15
8 Brian Giles .15
9 Freddy Garcia .15
10 Greg Vaughn .15
11 Alex Gonzalez .15
12 Luis Gonzalez .25
13 Ron Belliard .15
14 Ben Grieve .15
15 Carlos Delgado .50
16 Brian Jordan .15
17 Fernando Tatis .15
18 Ryan Rupe .15
19 Miguel Tejada .50
20 Mark Grace .30
21 Kenny Lofton .15
22 Eric Karros .15
23 Cliff Floyd .15
24 John Halama .15
25 Cristian Guzman .15
26 Scott Williamson .15
27 Mike Lieberthal .15
28 Tim Hudson .40
29 Warren Morris .15
30 Pedro Martinez 1.00
31 John Smoltz .15
32 Ray Durham .15
33 Chad Allen .15
34 Tony Clark .15
35 Tino Martinez .15
36 J.T. Snow Jr. .15
37 Kevin Brown .25
38 Bartolo Colon .15
39 Rey Ordonez .15
40 Jeff Bagwell .50
41 Ivan Rodriguez .50
42 Eric Chavez .25
43 Eric Milton .15
44 Jose Canseco .50
45 Shawn Green .25
46 Rich Aurilia .15
47 Roberto Alomar .40
48 Brian Daubach .15
49 Magglio Ordonez .25
50 Derek Jeter 2.00
51 Kris Benson .15
52 Albert Belle .15
53 Rondell White .15
54 Justin Thompson .15
55 Nomar Garciaparra .75
56 Chuck Finley .15
57 Omar Vizquel .15
58 Luis Castillo .15
59 Richard Hidalgo .15
60 Barry Bonds 2.00
61 Craig Biggio .15
62 Doug Glanville .15
63 Gabe Kapler .15
64 Johnny Damon .15
65 Pokey Reese .15
66 Andy Pettitte .25
67 B.J. Surhoff .15
68 Richie Sexson .40
69 Javy Lopez .15
70 Raul Mondesi .15
71 Darin Erstad .25
72 Kevin Millwood .15
73 Ricky Ledee .15
74 John Olerud .15
75 Sean Casey .25
76 Carlos Febles .15
77 Paul O'Neill .15
78 Bob Abreu .15
79 Neifi Perez .15
80 Tony Gwynn .75
81 Russ Ortiz .15
82 Matt Williams .15
83 Chris Carpenter .15
84 Roger Cedeno .15
85 Tim Salmon .30
86 Billy Koch .15
87 Jeromy Burnitz .15
88 Edgardo Alfonzo .15
89 Jay Bell .15
90 Manny Ramirez .75
91 Frank Thomas .75
92 Mike Mussina .50
93 J.D. Drew .25
94 Adrian Beltre .25
95 Alex Rodriguez 2.00
96 Larry Walker .15
97 Juan Encarnacion .15
98 Mike Sweeney .15
99 Rusty Greer .15
100 Randy Johnson .75
101 Jose Vidro .15
102 Preston Wilson .15
103 Greg Maddux 1.50
104 Jason Giambi .50
105 Cal Ripken Jr. 2.00
106 Carlos Beltran .50
107 Vinny Castilla .15
108 Mariano Rivera .25
109 Mo Vaughn .15
110 Rafael Palmeiro .50
111 Shannon Stewart .15
112 Mike Hampton .15
113 Joe Nathan .15
114 Ben Davis .15
115 Andruw Jones .50
116 Robin Ventura .15
117 Damion Easley .15
118 Jeff Cirillo .15
119 Kerry Wood .25
120 Scott Rolen .75
121 Sammy Sosa .75
122 Ken Griffey Jr. 1.50
123 Shane Reynolds .15
124 Troy Glaus .40
125 Tom Glavine .35
126 Michael Barrett .15
127 Al Leiter .15
128 Jason Kendall .15
129 Roger Clemens 2.00
130 Juan Gonzalez .40
131 Corey Koskie .15
132 Curt Schilling .50
133 Mike Piazza 1.00
134 Gary Sheffield .40
135 Jim Thome .40
136 Orlando Hernandez .25
137 Ray Lankford .15
138 Geoff Jenkins .15
139 Jose Lima .15
140 Mark McGwire 1.50
141 Adam Piatt .15
142 Pat Manning **RC** .25
143 Marcos Castillo **RC** .25
144 Lesli Brea **RC** .25
145 Humberto Cota **RC** .25
146 Ben Petrick .15
147 Kip Wells .15
148 Willi Mo Pena .25
149 Chris Wakeland .15
150 Brad Baker **RC** .25
151 Robbie Morrison **RC** .25
152 Reggie Taylor .15
153 Brian Cole **RC** .25
154 Peter Bergeron .15
155 Roosevelt Brown .15
156 Matt Cepicky **RC** .25
157 Ramon Castro .25
158 Brad Baisley **RC** .25
159 Jeff Goldbach **RC** .25
160 Mitch Meluskey .15
161 Chad Harville .15
162 Brian Cooper .15
163 Marcus Giles .15
164 Jim Morris .50
165 Geoff Goetz .15
166 Bobby Bradley **RC** .25
167 Rob Bell .15
168 Joe Crede .15
169 Michael Restovich .15
170 Quincy Foster **RC** .25
171 Enrique Cruz **RC** .25
172 Mark Quinn .15
173 Nick Johnson .15
174 Jeff Liefer .15
175 Kevin Mench **RC** .75
176 Steve Lomasney .15
177 Jayson Werth .15
178 Tim Drew .15
179 Chip Ambres .15
180 Ryan Anderson .15
181 Matt Blank .15
182 Giuseppe Chiaramonte .15
183 Corey Myers **RC** .25
184 Jeff Yoder .15
185 Craig Dingman **RC** .25
186 Jon Hamilton **RC** .25
187 Toby Hall .15
188 Russell Branyan .15
189 Brian Falkenborg **RC** .25
190 Aaron Harang **RC** .75
191 Juan Pena .15
192 Travis Thompson **RC** .25
193 Alfonso Soriano .50
194 Alejandro Diaz **RC** .25
195 Carlos Pena .15
196 Kevin Nicholson .15
197 Mo Bruce .15
198 C.C. Sabathia .15
199 Carl Crawford .15
200 Rafael Furcal .15
201 Andrew Beinbrink **RC** .25
202 Jimmy Osting .15
203 Aaron McNeal **RC** .25
204 Brett Laxton .15
205 Chris George .15
206 Felipe Lopez .15
207 Ben Sheets **RC** 2.00
208 Mike Meyers **RC** .40
209 Jason Conti .15
210 Milton Bradley .15
211 Chris Mears **RC** .25
212 Carlos Hernandez **RC** .50
213 Jason Romano .15
214 Goefrey Tomlinson .15
215 Jimmy Rollins .40
216 Pablo Ozuna .15
217 Steve Cox .15
218 Terrence Long .15
219 Jeff DaVanon **RC** .40
220 Rick Ankiel .25
221 Jason Standridge .15
222 Tony Armas .15
223 Jason Tyner .15
224 Ramon Ortiz .15
225 Daryle Ward .15
226 Enger Veras **RC** .25
227 Chris Jones **RC** .25
228 Eric Cammack **RC** .25
229 Ruben Mateo .15
230 Ken Harvey **RC** .50
231 Jake Westbrook .15
232 Rob Purvis **RC** .25
233 Choo Freeman .15
234 Aramis Ramirez .15
235 A.J. Burnett .15
236 Kevin Barker .15
237 Chance Caple **RC** .25
238 Jarrod Washburn .15
239 Lance Berkman .15
240 Michael Wenner **RC** .25
241 Alex Sanchez .15
242 Jake Esteves **RC** .25
243 Grant Roberts .15
244 Mark Ellis **RC** .50
245 Donny Leon .15
246 David Eckstein .15
247 Dicky Gonzalez **RC** .25
248 John Patterson .15
249 Chad Green .15
250 Scot Shields **RC** .25
251 Troy Cameron .15
252 Jose Molina .15
253 Rob Pugmire **RC** .25
254 Rick Elder .15
255 Sean Burroughs .25
256 Josh Kalinowski **RC** .25
257 Matt LeCroy .15
258 Alex Graman **RC** .50
259 Tomokazu Ohka **RC** .50
260 Brady Clark .15
261 Rico Washington **RC** .25
262 Gary Matthews Jr. .15
263 Matt Wise .15
264 Keith Reed **RC** .50
265 Santiago Ramirez **RC** .25
266 Ben Broussard **RC** .50
267 Ryan Langerhans .15
268 Juan Rivera .15
269 Shawn Gallagher .15
270 Jorge Toca .15
271 Brad Lidge .15
272 Leo Estrella **RC** .25
273 Ruben Quevedo .15
274 Jack Cust .15
275 T.J. Tucker .15
276 Mike Colangelo .15
277 Brian Schneider .15
278 Calvin Murray .15
279 Josh Girdley .15
280 Mike Paradis .15
281 Chad Hermansen .15
282 Ty Howington **RC** .50
283 Aaron Myette .15
284 D'Angelo Jimenez .15
285 Dernell Stenson .15
286 Jerry Hairston Jr. .15
287 Gary Majewski **RC** .25
288 Derrin Ebert **RC** .25
289 Steve Fish **RC** .25
290 Carlos Hernandez .15
291 Allen Levrault .15
292 Sean McNally **RC** .25
293 Randey Dorame **RC** .25
294 Wes Anderson **RC** .50
295 B.J. Ryan .15
296 Alan Webb **RC** .25
297 Brandon Inge **RC** .75
298 David Walling .15
299 Sun-Woo Kim **RC** .40
300 Pat Burrell .25
301 Rick Guttormson **RC** .25
302 Gil Meche .15
303 Carlos Zambrano **RC** 3.00
304 Eric Byrnes **RC** (Photo actually Bo Porter.) 1.00
305 Robb Quinlan **RC** .25
306 Jackie Rexrode .15
307 Nate Bump .15
308 Sean DePaula **RC** .25
309 Matt Riley .15
310 Ryan Minor .15
311 J.J. Davis .15
312 Randy Wolf .15
313 Jason Jennings .15
314 Scott Seabol **RC** .25
315 Doug Davis .15
316 Todd Moser **RC** .25
317 Rob Ryan .15
318 Bubba Crosby .15
319 Lyle Overbay **RC** 1.00
320 Mario Encarnacion .15
321 Francisco Rodriguez **RC** 2.00
322 Michael Cuddyer .15
323 Eddie Yarnall .15
324 Cesar Saba **RC** .25
325 Travis Dawkins .15
326 Alex Escobar .15
327 Julio Zuleta **RC** .40
328 Josh Hamilton .25
329 Nick Neugebauer **RC** .25
330 Matt Belisle .15
331 Kurt Ainsworth **RC** .50
332 Tim Raines Jr. .15
333 Eric Munson .15
334 Donzell McDonald .15
335 Larry Bigbie **RC** .25
336 Matt Watson .15
337 Aubrey Huff .15
338 Julio Ramirez .15
339 Jason Grabowski **RC** .25
340 Jon Garland .15
341 Austin Kearns .25
342 Josh Pressley .15
343 Miguel Olivo **RC** .25
344 Julio Lugo .15
345 Roberto Vaz .15
346 Ramon Soler .15
347 Brandon Phillips **RC** 2.00
348 Vince Faison **RC** .25
349 Mike Venafro .15
350 Rick Asadoorian **RC** .25
351 B.J. Garbe **RC** .25
352 Dan Reichert .15
353 Jason Stumm **RC** .25
354 Ruben Salazar **RC** .25
355 Francisco Cordero .15
356 Juan Guzman **RC** .25
357 Mike Bacsik **RC** .25
358 Jared Sandberg .15
359 Rod Barajas .15
360 Junior Brignac **RC** .25
361 J.M. Gold .15
362 Octavio Dotel .15
363 David Kelton .15
364 Scott Morgan **RC** .25
365 Wascar Serrano **RC** .25
366 Wilton Veras .15
367 Eugene Kingsale .15
368 Ted Lilly .15
369 George Lombard .15
370 Chris Haas .15
371 Wilton Pena **RC** .50
372 Vernon Wells .15
373 Jason Royer **RC** .25
374 Jeff Heaverlo **RC** .25
375 Calvin Pickering .15
376 Mike Lamb **RC** .40
377 Kyle Snyder .15
378 Javier Cardona **RC** .25
379 Aaron Rowand **RC** 1.00
380 Dee Brown .15
381 Brett Myers **RC** 1.00
382 Abraham Nunez .20
383 Eric Valent .15
384 Jody Gerut **RC** .25
385 Adam Dunn .50
386 Jay Gehrke .15
387 Omar Ortiz .15
388 Darnell McDonald .15
389 Chad Alexander .15
390 J.D. Closser .15
391 Ben Christensen **RC** .25
392 Adam Kennedy .15
393 Nick Green **RC** .25
394 Ramon Hernandez .15
395 Roy Oswalt **RC** 4.00
396 Andy Tracy **RC** .50
397 Eric Gagne .15
398 Michael Tejera **RC** .25
399 Adam Everett .15
400 Corey Patterson .25
401 Gary Knotts **RC** .25
402 Ryan Christianson **RC** .50
403 Eric Ireland **RC** .25
404 Andrew Good **RC** .25
405 Brad Penny .15
406 Jason LaRue .15
407 Kit Pellow .15
408 Kevin Beirne .15
409 Kelly Dransfeldt .15
410 Jason Grilli .15
411 Scott Downs **RC** .25
412 Jesus Colome .15
413 John Sneed **RC** .25
414 Tony McKnight **RC** .25
415 Luis Rivera .15
416 Adam Eaton .15
417 Mike MacDougal **RC** .50
418 Mike Nannini .15
419 Barry Zito **RC** 2.00
420 Dewayne Wise .15
421 Jason Dellaero .15
422 Chad Moeller .15
423 Jason Marquis .15
424 Tim Redding **RC** .50
425 Mark Mulder .15
426 Josh Paul .15
427 Chris Enochs .15
428 Wilfredo Rodriguez **RC** .50
429 Kevin Witt .15
430 Scott Sobkowiak **RC** .25
431 McKay Christensen .15
432 Jung Bong .15
433 Keith Evans **RC** .25
434 Garry Maddox Jr. .15
435 Ramon Santiago **RC** .50
436 Alex Cora .15
437 Carlos Lee .15
438 Jason Repko **RC** .25
439 Matt Burch .15
440 Shawn Sonnier **RC** .25

Gold

Golds are a 440-card parallel to the base set and are highlighted by gold-stamped facsimile autographs on the card front. Golds are limited to 99 serial numbered sets.

Stars: 10-20X
Rookies: 4-8X
Production 99 Sets
(See 2000 Bowman for checklist and base card values.)

Retro/Future

These inserts are a parallel to the 440-card base set. The foiled card fronts have a horizontal format and a design reminiscent of the 1955 Bowman "television set" design. They were seeded one per pack.

NM/M
Common Player: .25
Stars: 2-3X
Rookies: .75-2X
Inserted 1:1
(See 2000 Bowman for checklist and base card values.)

Autographs

This set consists of 40 players with card rarity differentiated by either a Blue, Silver or Gold foil Topps "Certified Autograph Issue" stamp. Card backs are numbered using the player initials and have a Topps serial numbered foil hologram to ensure the authenticity of the autograph.

NM/M
Common Autograph: 5.00
Blue Inserted 1:144
Silver 1:312
Gold 1:1,604
CA Chip Ambres/B 5.00
RA Rick Ankiel/G 15.00
CB Carlos Beltran/G 40.00
LB Lance Berkman/S 20.00
DB Dee Brown/S 8.00
SB Sean Burroughs/S 8.00
JDC J.D. Closser/B 5.00
SC Steve Cox/B 5.00
MC Michael Cuddyer/S 10.00
JC Jack Cust/S 15.00
SD Scott Downs/S 10.00
JDD J.D. Drew/G 25.00
AD Adam Dunn/B 25.00
CF Choo Freeman/B 5.00
RF Rafael Furcal/S 15.00
AH Aubrey Huff/B 8.00
JJ Jason Jennings/B 8.00
NJ Nick Johnson/S 10.00
AK Austin Kearns/B 15.00
DK David Kelton/B 5.00
RM Ruben Mateo/G 15.00
MM Mike Meyers/B 5.00
CP Corey Patterson/S 20.00
BWP Brad Penny/B 5.00
BP Ben Petrick/G 10.00
AP Adam Piatt/S 8.00
MQ Mark Quinn/S 8.00
MR Mike Restovich/B 5.00
MR Matt Riley/S 8.00
JR Jason Romano/B 5.00
BS Ben Sheets/B 30.00
AS Alfonso Soriano/S 40.00
EV Eric Valent/B 5.00
JV Jose Vidro/S 10.00
VW Vernon Wells/G 20.00
SW Scott Williamson/G 10.00
KJW Kevin Witt/S 10.00
KLW Kerry Wood/S 25.00
EY Eddie Yarnall/S 10.00
JZ Julio Zuleta/B 5.00

2000 Bowman Bowman's Best Previews

This 10-card insert set is identical in design to 2000 Bowman's Best. The card fronts have a Refractor like sheen and the card backs are numbered with a "BBP" prefix.

NM/M
Complete Set (10): 15.00
Common Player: .50
Inserted 1:18
1 Derek Jeter 4.00
2 Ken Griffey Jr. 3.00
3 Nomar Garciaparra 2.00
4 Mike Piazza 2.00
5 Alex Rodriguez 4.00
6 Sammy Sosa 2.00
7 Mark McGwire 3.00
8 Pat Burrell 1.00
9 Josh Hamilton .50
10 Adam Piatt .50

Early Indications

This 10-card set has a blue foiled card front with red foil stamping. Card backs are numbered with an "E" prefix.

NM/M
Complete Set (10): 18.00
Common Player: 1.00
Inserted 1:24
1 Nomar Garciaparra 1.50
2 Cal Ripken Jr. 4.00
3 Derek Jeter 4.00
4 Mark McGwire 3.00
5 Alex Rodriguez 3.00
6 Chipper Jones 1.50
7 Todd Helton 1.00
8 Vladimir Guerrero 1.50
9 Mike Piazza 1.50
10 Jose Canseco 1.00

Major Power

This 10-card set spotlights the top home run hitters. Card fronts have a red border on a full foiled card front. These are numbered with an "MP" prefix on the card back.

		NM/M
Complete Set (10):		20.00
Common Player:		1.00
Inserted 1:24		
1	Mark McGwire	4.00
2	Chipper Jones	2.50
3	Alex Rodriguez	4.00
4	Sammy Sosa	3.00
5	Rafael Palmeiro	1.00
6	Ken Griffey Jr.	3.00
7	Nomar Garciaparra	3.00
8	Barry Bonds	5.00
9	Derek Jeter	5.00
10	Jeff Bagwell	1.50

Tool Time

This 20-card set focuses on the top minor league Prospects in five different categories: batting, power, speed, arm strength and defense. These are seeded 1:8 packs. Backs are numbered with a "TT" prefix.

		NM/M
Complete Set (20):		8.00
Common Player:		.40
Inserted 1:8		
1	Pat Burrell	1.00
2	Aaron Rowand	.40
3	Chris Wakeland	.40
4	Ruben Mateo	.40
5	Pat Burrell	1.00
6	Adam Piatt	.50
7	Nick Johnson	1.00
8	Jack Cust	.40
9	Rafael Furcal	.40
10	Julio Ramirez	.40
11	Travis Dawkins	.40
12	Corey Patterson	1.00
13	Ruben Mateo	.40
14	Jason Dellaero	.40
15	Sean Burroughs	.40
16	Ryan Langerhans	.40
17	D'Angelo Jimenez	.40
18	Corey Patterson	1.00
19	Troy Cameron	.40
20	Michael Cuddyer	.50

2000 Bowman Chrome

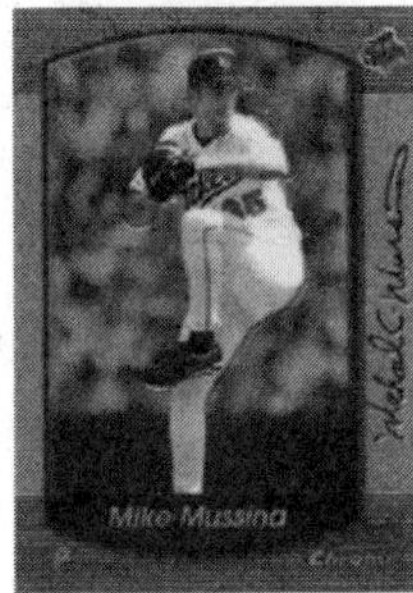

Released as a single series 440-card set, Bowman Chrome is identical in design to 2000 Bowman besides the Chromium finish on all cards. Foil highlights differentiate rookies and prospects (blue) from veterans (red). Three parallels to the base set are randomly seeded: Refractors, Retro/Future and Retro/Future Refractors.

		NM/M
Complete Set (440):		120.00
Common Player:		.25
Common Rookie:		.50
Pack (4):		2.50
Box (24):		50.00
1	Vladimir Guerrero	1.00
2	Chipper Jones	1.00
3	Todd Walker	.25
4	Barry Larkin	.25
5	Bernie Williams	.50
6	Todd Helton	.75
7	Jermaine Dye	.25
8	Brian Giles	.25
9	Freddy Garcia	.25
10	Greg Vaughn	.25
11	Alex Gonzalez	.25
12	Luis Gonzalez	.25
13	Ron Belliard	.25
14	Ben Grieve	.25
15	Carlos Delgado	.75
16	Brian Jordan	.25
17	Fernando Tatis	.25
18	Ryan Rupe	.25
19	Miguel Tejada	.40
20	Mark Grace	.35
21	Kenny Lofton	.25
22	Eric Karros	.25
23	Cliff Floyd	.25
24	John Halama	.25
25	Cristian Guzman	.25
26	Scott Williamson	.25
27	Mike Lieberthal	.25
28	Tim Hudson	.40
29	Warren Morris	.25
30	Pedro Martinez	1.00
31	John Smoltz	.25
32	Ray Durham	.25
33	Chad Allen	.25
34	Tony Clark	.25
35	Tino Martinez	.25
36	J.T. Snow Jr.	.25
37	Kevin Brown	.40
38	Bartolo Colon	.25
39	Rey Ordonez	.25
40	Jeff Bagwell	.50
41	Ivan Rodriguez	.75
42	Eric Chavez	.50
43	Eric Milton	.25
44	Jose Canseco	.50
45	Shawn Green	.50
46	Rich Aurilia	.25
47	Roberto Alomar	.50
48	Brian Daubach	.25
49	Magglio Ordonez	.50
50	Derek Jeter	2.00
51	Kris Benson	.25
52	Albert Belle	.25
53	Rondell White	.25
54	Justin Thompson	.25
55	Nomar Garciaparra	1.00
56	Chuck Finley	.25
57	Omar Vizquel	.25
58	Luis Castillo	.25
59	Richard Hidalgo	.25
60	Barry Bonds	2.00
61	Craig Biggio	.25
62	Doug Glanville	.25
63	Gabe Kapler	.25
64	Johnny Damon	.40
65	Pokey Reese	.25
66	Andy Pettitte	.50
67	B.J. Surhoff	.25
68	Richie Sexson	.50
69	Javy Lopez	.25
70	Raul Mondesi	.25
71	Darin Erstad	.40
72	Kevin Millwood	.40
73	Ricky Ledee	.25
74	John Olerud	.25
75	Sean Casey	.25
76	Carlos Febles	.25
77	Paul O'Neill	.25
78	Bob Abreu	.25
79	Neifi Perez	.25
80	Tony Gwynn	1.00
81	Russ Ortiz	.25
82	Matt Williams	.25
83	Chris Carpenter	.25
84	Roger Cedeno	.25
85	Tim Salmon	.35
86	Billy Koch	.25
87	Jeromy Burnitz	.25
88	Edgardo Alfonzo	.25
89	Jay Bell	.15
90	Manny Ramirez	.75
91	Frank Thomas	.75
92	Mike Mussina	.50
93	J.D. Drew	.40
94	Adrian Beltre	.40
95	Alex Rodriguez	2.00
96	Larry Walker	.25
97	Juan Encarnacion	.25
98	Mike Sweeney	.25
99	Rusty Greer	.25
100	Randy Johnson	.75
101	Jose Vidro	.25
102	Preston Wilson	.25
103	Greg Maddux	1.50
104	Jason Giambi	.75
105	Cal Ripken Jr.	3.00
106	Carlos Beltran	.25
107	Vinny Castilla	.25
108	Mariano Rivera	.35
109	Mo Vaughn	.25
110	Rafael Palmeiro	.50
111	Shannon Stewart	.25
112	Mike Hampton	.25
113	Joe Nathan	.25
114	Ben Davis	.25
115	Andruw Jones	.75
116	Robin Ventura	.25
117	Damion Easley	.25
118	Jeff Cirillo	.25
119	Kerry Wood	.40
120	Scott Rolen	.75
121	Sammy Sosa	1.00
122	Ken Griffey Jr.	2.00
123	Shane Reynolds	.25
124	Troy Glaus	.50
125	Tom Glavine	.40
126	Michael Barrett	.25
127	Al Leiter	.25
128	Jason Kendall	.25
129	Roger Clemens	2.00
130	Juan Gonzalez	.50
131	Corey Koskie	.25
132	Curt Schilling	.75
133	Mike Piazza	1.00
134	Gary Sheffield	.50
135	Jim Thome	.50
136	Orlando Hernandez	.40
137	Ray Lankford	.25
138	Geoff Jenkins	.25
139	Jose Lima	.25
140	Mark McGwire	1.50
141	Adam Piatt	.25
142	Pat Manning **RC**	.50
143	Marcos Castillo **RC**	.50
144	Lesli Brea **RC**	.50
145	Humberto Cota **RC**	.50
146	Ben Petrick	.25
147	Kip Wells	.25
148	Willi Mo Pena	.40
149	Chris Wakeland	.25
150	Brad Baker **RC**	.50
151	Robbie Morrison **RC**	.50
152	Reggie Taylor	.25
153	Matt Ginter **RC**	.50
154	Peter Bergeron	.25
155	Roosevelt Brown	.25
156	Matt Cepicky **RC**	.50
157	Ramon Castro	.25
158	Brad Baisley **RC**	.50
159	Jason Hart **RC**	1.00
160	Mitch Meluskey	.25
161	Chad Harville	.25
162	Brian Cooper	.25
163	Marcus Giles	.25
164	Jim Morris	.50
165	Geoff Goetz	.25
166	Bobby Bradley **RC**	.50
167	Rob Bell	.25
168	Joe Crede	.25
169	Michael Restovich	.25
170	Quincy Foster **RC**	.50
171	Enrique Cruz **RC**	.50
172	Mark Quinn	.25
173	Nick Johnson	.40
174	Jeff Liefer	.25
175	Kevin Mench **RC**	3.00
176	Steve Lomasney	.25
177	Jayson Werth	.25
178	Tim Drew	.25
179	Chip Ambres	.25
180	Ryan Anderson	.25
181	Matt Blank	.25
182	Giuseppe Chiaramonte	.25
183	Corey Myers **RC**	.50
184	Jeff Yoder	.25
185	Craig Dingman **RC**	.50
186	Jon Hamilton **RC**	.50
187	Toby Hall	.25
188	Russell Branyan	.25
189	Brian Falkenborg **RC**	.50
190	Aaron Harang **RC**	3.00
191	Juan Pena	.25
192	Chin-Hui Tsao **RC**	3.00
193	Alfonso Soriano	.75
194	Alejandro Diaz **RC**	.50
195	Carlos Pena	.25
196	Kevin Nicholson	.25
197	Mo Bruce	.25
198	C.C. Sabathia	.25
199	Carl Crawford	.25
200	Rafael Furcal	.25
201	Andrew Beinbrink **RC**	.50
202	Jimmy Osting	.25
203	Aaron McNeal **RC**	.50
204	Brett Laxton	.25
205	Chris George	.25
206	Felipe Lopez	.25
207	Ben Sheets **RC**	6.00
208	Mike Meyers **RC**	.50
209	Jason Conti	.25
210	Milton Bradley	.25
211	Chris Mears **RC**	.50
212	Carlos Hernandez **RC**	.50
213	Jason Romano	.25
214	Goefrey Tomlinson	.25
215	Jimmy Rollins	.75
216	Pablo Ozuna	.25
217	Steve Cox	.25
218	Terrence Long	.25
219	Jeff DaVanon **RC**	.50
220	Rick Ankiel	.50
221	Jason Standridge	.25
222	Tony Armas	.25
223	Jason Tyner	.25
224	Ramon Ortiz	.25
225	Daryle Ward	.25
226	Enger Veras **RC**	.50
227	Chris Jones **RC**	.50
228	Eric Cammack **RC**	.50
229	Ruben Mateo	.25
230	Ken Harvey **RC**	1.00
231	Jake Westbrook	.25
232	Rob Purvis **RC**	.50
233	Choo Freeman	.25
234	Aramis Ramirez	.25
235	A.J. Burnett	.25
236	Kevin Barker	.25
237	Chance Caple **RC**	.50
238	Jarrod Washburn	.25
239	Lance Berkman	.25
240	Michael Wenner **RC**	.50
241	Alex Sanchez	.25
242	Jake Esteves **RC**	.50
243	Grant Roberts	.25
244	Mark Ellis **RC**	.50
245	Donny Leon	.25
246	David Eckstein	.25
247	Dicky Gonzalez **RC**	.50
248	John Patterson	.25
249	Chad Green	.25
250	Scot Shields **RC**	.50
251	Troy Cameron	.25
252	Jose Molina	.25
253	Rob Pugmire **RC**	.50
254	Rick Elder	.25
255	Sean Burroughs	.50
256	Josh Kalinowski **RC**	.50
257	Matt LeCroy	.25
258	Alex Graman **RC**	.50
259	Juan Silvestre **RC**	.50
260	Brady Clark	.25
261	Rico Washington **RC**	.50
262	Gary Matthews Jr.	.25
263	Matt Wise	.25
264	Keith Reed **RC**	.50
265	Santiago Ramirez **RC**	.50
266	Ben Broussard **RC**	.50
267	Ryan Langerhans	.25
268	Juan Rivera	.25
269	Shawn Gallagher	.25
270	Jorge Toca	.25
271	Brad Lidge	.25
272	Leo Estrella **RC**	.50
273	Ruben Quevedo	.25
274	Jack Cust	.25
275	T.J. Tucker	.25
276	Mike Colangelo	.25
277	Brian Schneider	.25
278	Calvin Murray	.25
279	Josh Girdley	.25
280	Mike Paradis	.25
281	Chad Hermansen	.25
282	Ty Howington **RC**	.50
283	Aaron Myette	.25
284	D'Angelo Jimenez	.25
285	Dernell Stenson	.25
286	Jerry Hairston Jr.	.25
287	Gary Majewski **RC**	.50
288	Derrin Ebert **RC**	.50
289	Steve Fish **RC**	.50
290	Carlos Hernandez	.25
291	Allen Levrault	.25
292	Sean McNally **RC**	.50
293	Randey Dorame **RC**	.50
294	Wes Anderson **RC**	.50
295	B.J. Ryan	.25
296	Alan Webb **RC**	.50
297	Brandon Inge **RC**	2.00
298	David Walling	.25
299	Sun-Woo Kim **RC**	1.00
300	Pat Burrell	.50
301	Rick Guttormson **RC**	.50
302	Gil Meche	.25
303	Carlos Zambrano **RC**	10.00
304	Eric Byrnes **RC** (Photo actually Bo Porter.)	5.00
305	Robb Quinlan **RC**	.50
306	Jackie Rexrode	.25
307	Nate Bump	.25
308	Sean DePaula **RC**	.50
309	Matt Riley	.25
310	Ryan Minor	.25
311	J.J. Davis	.25
312	Randy Wolf	.25
313	Jason Jennings	.25
314	Scott Seabol **RC**	.50
315	Doug Davis	.25
316	Todd Moser **RC**	.50
317	Rob Ryan	.25
318	Bubba Crosby	.25
319	Lyle Overbay **RC**	2.50
320	Mario Encarnacion	.25
321	Francisco Rodriguez **RC**	6.00
322	Michael Cuddyer	.25
323	Eddie Yarnall	.25
324	Cesar Saba **RC**	.50
325	Travis Dawkins	.25
326	Alex Escobar	.25
327	Julio Zuleta **RC**	.50
328	Josh Hamilton	.50
329	Carlos Urquiola **RC**	.50
330	Matt Belisle	.25
331	Kurt Ainsworth **RC**	1.00
332	Tim Raines Jr.	.25
333	Eric Munson	.25
334	Donzell McDonald	.25
335	Larry Bigbie **RC**	.50
336	Matt Watson	.50
337	Aubrey Huff	.25
338	Julio Ramirez	.25
339	Jason Grabowski **RC**	.50
340	Jon Garland	.25
341	Austin Kearns	.50
342	Josh Pressley	.25
343	Miguel Olivo **RC**	.50
344	Julio Lugo	.25
345	Roberto Vaz	.25
346	Ramon Soler	.25
347	Brandon Phillips **RC**	5.00
348	Vince Faison **RC**	.50
349	Mike Venafro	.25
350	Rick Asadoorian **RC**	.50
351	B.J. Garbe **RC**	.50
352	Dan Reichert	.25
353	Jason Stumm **RC**	.50
354	Ruben Salazar **RC**	.50
355	Francisco Cordero	.25
356	Juan Guzman **RC**	.50
357	Mike Bacsik **RC**	.50
358	Jared Sandberg	.25
359	Rod Barajas	.25
360	Junior Brignac **RC**	.50
361	J.M. Gold	.25
362	Octavio Dotel	.25
363	David Kelton	.25
364	Scott Morgan **RC**	.50
365	Wascar Serrano **RC**	.50
366	Wilton Veras	.25
367	Eugene Kingsale	.25
368	Ted Lilly	.25
369	George Lombard	.25
370	Chris Haas	.25
371	Wilton Pena **RC**	.50
372	Vernon Wells	.50
373	Keith Ginter **RC**	.50
374	Jeff Heaverlo **RC**	.50
375	Calvin Pickering	.25
376	Mike Lamb **RC**	.50
377	Kyle Snyder	.25
378	Javier Cardona **RC**	.50
379	Aaron Rowand **RC**	3.00
380	Dee Brown	.25
381	Brett Myers **RC**	4.00
382	Abraham Nunez	.25
383	Eric Valent	.25
384	Jody Gerut **RC**	.50
385	Adam Dunn	.50
386	Jay Gehrke	.25
387	Omar Ortiz	.25
388	Darnell McDonald	.25
389	Chad Alexander	.25
390	J.D. Closser	.25
391	Ben Christensen **RC**	.50
392	Adam Kennedy	.25
393	Nick Green **RC**	.50
394	Ramon Hernandez	.25
395	Roy Oswalt **RC**	20.00
396	Andy Tracy **RC**	1.00
397	Eric Gagne	.25
398	Michael Tejera **RC**	.50
399	Adam Everett	.25
400	Corey Patterson	.50
401	Gary Knotts **RC**	.50
402	Ryan Christianson **RC**	.50
403	Eric Ireland **RC**	.50
404	Andrew Good **RC**	.50
405	Brad Penny	.25
406	Jason LaRue	.25
407	Kit Pellow	.25
408	Kevin Beirne	.25
409	Kelly Dransfeldt	.25
410	Jason Grilli	.25
411	Scott Downs **RC**	.50
412	Jesus Colome	.25
413	John Sneed **RC**	.50
414	Tony McKnight **RC**	.50
415	Luis Rivera	.25
416	Adam Eaton	.25
417	Mike MacDougal **RC**	1.00
418	Mike Nannini	.25
419	Barry Zito **RC**	6.00
420	Dewayne Wise	.25
421	Jason Dellaero	.25
422	Chad Moeller	.25
423	Jason Marquis	.25
424	Tim Redding **RC**	.50
425	Mark Mulder	.25
426	Josh Paul	.25
427	Chris Enochs	.25
428	Wilfredo Rodriguez **RC**	.50
429	Kevin Witt	.25
430	Scott Sobkowiak **RC**	.50
431	McKay Christensen	.25
432	Jung Bong	.25
433	Keith Evans **RC**	.50
434	Garry Maddox Jr.	.25
435	Ramon Santiago **RC**	.50
436	Alex Cora	.25
437	Carlos Lee	.25
438	Jason Repko **RC**	.50
439	Matt Burch	.25
440	Shawn Sonnier **RC**	1.00

Refractors

A parallel to the 440-card base set, these inserts have a mirror like sheen to them on the card front and are listed Refractor underneath the card number on the back. These were seeded 1:12 packs.

Stars:	4-8X
Rookies:	2-4X
Inserted 1:12	

(See 2000 Bowman Chrome for checklist and base card values.)

Retro/Future

This 440-card parallel to the base set is modeled after the 1955 Bowman "television set" design and are seeded 1:6 packs, with Refractors seeded 1:60 packs.

Stars:	1.5-3X
Rookies:	.75X
Inserted 1:6	
Refractors:	6-8X
Rookies:	1-30X
Inserted 1:60	

(See 2000 Bowman Chrome for checklist and base card values.)

Bidding for the Call

Top minor league prospects are highlighted on a design with gold foil background on an all chromium finish. Card backs are numbered with a "BC" prefix. A Refractor parallel version was also produced.

		NM/M
Complete Set (15):		10.00
Common Player:		.50
Inserted 1:16		
Refractors:		2-4X
Inserted 1:160		
1	Adam Piatt	.50
2	Pat Burrell	1.00
3	Mark Mulder	1.00
4	Nick Johnson	1.00
5	Alfonso Soriano	2.00
6	Chin-Feng Chen	2.50
7	Scott Sobkowiak	.50
8	Corey Patterson	1.00
9	Jack Cust	.50
10	Sean Burroughs	.50
11	Josh Hamilton	1.00
12	Corey Myers	.50
13	Eric Munson	.50
14	Wes Anderson	.50
15	Lyle Overbay	1.00

Meteoric Rise

This 10-card set spotlights players who all made their first All-Star team within their first two years. Card fronts have a futuristic background, with the player in an intergalactic setting. Card backs are numbered with a "MR" prefix. A Refractor parallel version also exists.

		NM/M
Complete Set (10):		20.00
Common Player:		1.00
Inserted 1:24		

Refractors: 2-4X
Inserted 1:240
1 Nomar Garciaparra 3.00
2 Mark McGwire 4.00
3 Ken Griffey Jr. 3.00
4 Chipper Jones 2.50
5 Manny Ramirez 2.00
6 Mike Piazza 3.00
7 Cal Ripken Jr. 5.00
8 Ivan Rodriguez 1.00
9 Greg Maddux 3.00
10 Randy Johnson 2.00

Oversize

NM/M
Complete Set (8): 8.00
Common Player: .75
Inserted 1:Box
1 Pat Burrell 2.00
2 Josh Hamilton 1.00
3 Rafael Furcal 1.00
4 Corey Patterson 1.50
5 A.J. Burnett .75
6 Eric Munson .75
7 Nick Johnson 1.00
8 Alfonso Soriano 2.00

Rookie Class 2000

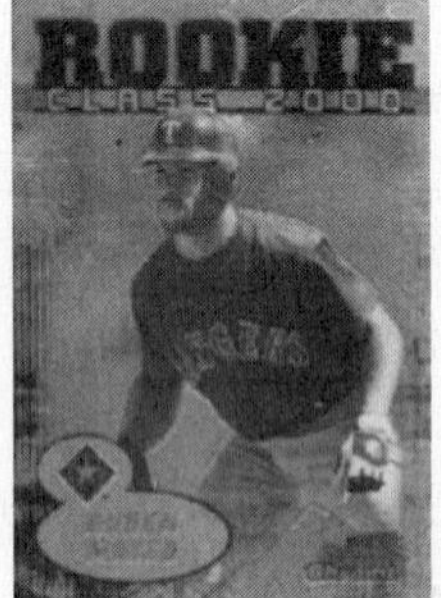

This set highlighted 10 prospects who were thought to contend for the 2000 Rookie of the Year awards. Backs are numbered with a "RC" prefix. A Refractor parallel version was also issued.

NM/M
Complete Set (10): 8.00
Common Player: .75
Inserted 1:24
Refractors: 2-4X
Inserted 1:240
1 Pat Burrell 2.00
2 Rick Ankiel .75
3 Ruben Mateo .75
4 Vernon Wells 1.50
5 Mark Mulder 1.50
6 A.J. Burnett .75
7 Chad Hermansen .75
8 Corey Patterson 1.50
9 Rafael Furcal 1.00
10 Mike Lamb .75

Teen Idols

This 15-card set highlights top teenagers who are predicted to emerge as major league standouts.

NM/M
Complete Set (15): 15.00
Common Player: .75
Inserted 1:16
Refractors: 2-4X
Inserted 1:160
1 Alex Rodriguez 5.00
2 Andruw Jones 1.50
3 Juan Gonzalez 1.00
4 Ivan Rodriguez 1.50
5 Ken Griffey Jr. 3.00
6 Bobby Bradley .75
7 Brett Myers .75
8 C.C. Sabathia .75
9 Ty Howington .75
10 Brandon Phillips 1.00
11 Rick Asadoorian .75
12 Wily Pena 1.00
13 Sean Burroughs .75
14 Josh Hamilton 1.00
15 Rafael Furcal 1.00

2000 Bowman Draft Picks and Prospects

NM/M
Complete Set (110): 40.00
Common Player: .15
1 Pat Burrell .25
2 Rafael Furcal .15
3 Grant Roberts .15
4 Barry Zito .50
5 Julio Zuleta .15
6 Mark Mulder .25
7 Rob Bell .15
8 Adam Piatt .15
9 Mike Lamb .15
10 Pablo Ozuna .15
11 Jason Tyner .15
12 Jason Marquis .15
13 Eric Munson .15
14 Seth Etherton .15
15 Milton Bradley .15
16 Nick Green .15
17 Chin-Feng Chen **RC** 1.00
18 Matt Boone **RC** .25
19 Kevin Gregg **RC** .25
20 Eddy Garabito **RC** .25
21 Aaron Capista **RC** .25
22 Esteban German **RC** .25
23 Derek Thompson **RC** .25
24 Phil Merrell **RC** .25
25 Brian O'Connor **RC** .25
26 Yamid Haad .15
27 Hector Mercado **RC** .25
28 Jason Woolf **RC** .25
29 Eddie Furniss **RC** .25
30 Cha Sueng Baek **RC** .25
31 Colby Lewis **RC** .25
32 Pasqual Coco **RC** .25
33 Jorge Cantu **RC** .50
34 Erasmo Ramirez **RC** .25
35 Bobby Kielty **RC** .50
36 Joaquin Benoit **RC** .25
37 Brian Esposito **RC** .25
38 Michael Wenner .15
39 Juan Rincon **RC** .25
40 Yorvit Torrealba **RC** .25
41 Chad Durham **RC** .25
42 Jim Mann **RC** .25
43 Shane Loux **RC** .25
44 Luis Rivas .15
45 Ken Chenard **RC** .25
46 Mike Lockwood **RC** .25
47 Yovanny Lara **RC** .25
48 Bubba Carpenter **RC** .25
49 Jeremy Griffiths **RC** .25
50 John Stephens **RC** .25
51 Pedro Feliz **RC** .75
52 Kenny Kelly **RC** .25
53 Neil Jenkins **RC** .25
54 Mike Glendenning **RC** .25
55 Bo Porter .15
56 Eric Byrnes .15
57 Tony Alvarez **RC** .25
58 Kazuhiro Sasaki **RC** .50
59 Chad Durbin **RC** .25
60 Mike Bynum **RC** .25
61 Travis Wilson **RC** .25
62 Jose Leon **RC** .25
63 Bill Ortega **RC** .25
64 Geraldo Guzman **RC** .25
65 Craig Anderson **RC** .25
66 Carlos Silva **RC** .50
67 Brad Thomas **RC** .25
68 Chin-Hui Tsao **RC** .75
69 Mark Buehrle **RC** 2.00
70 Juan Salas **RC** .25
71 Denny Abreu **RC** .25
72 Keith McDonald **RC** .25
73 Chris Richard **RC** .25
74 Tomas de la Rosa **RC** .25
75 Vicente Padilla .50
76 Justin Brunette **RC** .25
77 Scott Linebrink **RC** .25
78 Jeff Sparks **RC** .25
79 Tike Redman **RC** .25
80 John Lackey **RC** 1.50
81 Joe Strong **RC** .25
82 Brian Tollberg **RC** .25
83 Steve Sisco **RC** .25
84 Chris Clapinski .15
85 Augie Ojeda **RC** .25
86 Adrian Gonzalez **RC** (Draft Picks) 2.50
87 Mike Stodolka **RC** (Draft Picks) .25
88 Adam Johnson **RC** (Draft Picks) .25
89 Matt Wheatland **RC** (Draft Picks) .25
90 Corey Smith **RC** (Draft Picks) .25
91 Rocco Baldelli **RC** (Draft Picks) 3.00
92 Keith Bucktrot **RC** (Draft Picks) .25
93 Adam Wainwright **RC** (Draft Picks) 1.50
94 Blaine Boyer **RC** (Draft Picks) .25
95 Aaron Herr **RC** (Draft Picks) .25
96 Scott Thorman **RC** (Draft Picks) 1.50
97 Brian Digby **RC** (Draft Picks) .25
98 Josh Shortslef **RC** (Draft Picks) .25
99 Sean Smith **RC** (Draft Picks) .25
100 Alex Cruz **RC** (Draft Picks) .25
101 Marc Love **RC** (Draft Picks) .25
102 Kevin Lee **RC** (Draft Picks) .25
103 Victor Ramos **RC** (Draft Picks) .25
104 Jason Kanoi **RC** (Draft Picks) .25
105 Luis Escobar **RC** (Draft Picks) .25
106 Tripper Johnson **RC** (Draft Picks) .25
107 Phil Dumatrait **RC** (Draft Picks) .25
108 Bryan Edwards **RC** (Draft Picks) .25
109 Grady Sizemore **RC** (Draft Picks) 20.00
110 Thomas Mitchell **RC** (Draft Picks) .25

Autograph

NM/M
Common Autograph: 5.00
Inserted 1:Set
1 Pat Burrell 20.00
2 Rafael Furcal 15.00
3 Grant Roberts 5.00
4 Barry Zito 40.00
5 Julio Zuleta 5.00
6 Mark Mulder 15.00
7 Bob Bell 5.00
8 Adam Piatt 5.00
9 Mike Lamb 15.00
10 Pablo Ozuna 5.00
11 Jason Tyner 5.00
12 Jason Marquis 10.00
13 Eric Munson 6.00
14 Seth Etherton 5.00
15 Milton Bradley 15.00
17 Michael Wenner 5.00
18 Mike Glendenning 5.00
19 Tony Alvarez 5.00
20 Adrian Gonzalez 80.00
21 Corey Smith 10.00
22 Matt Wheatland 5.00
23 Adam Johnson 8.00
24 Mike Stodolka 5.00
25 Rocco Baldelli 40.00
26 Juan Rincon 5.00
27 Chad Durbin 5.00
28 Yorvit Torrealba 5.00
29 Nick Green 10.00
30 Derek Thompson 5.00
31 John Lackey 40.00
33 Kevin Gregg 5.00
35 Denny Abreu 5.00
36 Brian Tollberg 5.00
37 Yamid Haad 5.00
38 Grady Sizemore 300.00
39 Carlos Silva 10.00
40 Jorge Cantu 20.00
41 Bobby Kielty 8.00
42 Scott Thorman 30.00
43 Juan Salas 10.00
44 Phil Dumatrait 5.00
46 Mike Lockwood 5.00
47 Yovanny Lara 5.00
48 Tripper Johnson 10.00
49 Colby Lewis 5.00
50 Neil Jenkins 5.00
51 Keith Bucktrot 5.00
52 Eric Byrnes 30.00
53 Aaron Herr 5.00
54 Erasmo Ramirez 5.00
55 Chris Richard 5.00
57 Mike Bynum 5.00
58 Brian Esposito 5.00
59 Chris Clapinski 5.00
60 Augie Ojeda 5.00

2000 Bowman Chrome Draft Picks and Prospects

NM/M
Complete Set (110): 50.00
Common Player: .25
1 Pat Burrell .50
2 Rafael Furcal .50
3 Grant Roberts .25
4 Barry Zito 2.00
5 Julio Zuleta .50
6 Mark Mulder .25
7 Rob Bell .25
8 Adam Piatt .50
9 Mike Lamb .25
10 Pablo Ozuna .25
11 Jason Tyner .25
12 Jason Marquis .25
13 Eric Munson .25
14 Seth Etherton .25
15 Milton Bradley .25
16 Nick Green .25
17 Chin-Feng Chen **RC** 2.00
18 Matt Boone **RC** .50
19 Kevin Gregg **RC** .50
20 Eddy Garabito **RC** .50
21 Aaron Capista **RC** .50
22 Esteban German **RC** .50
23 Derek Thompson **RC** .50
24 Phil Merrell **RC** .50
25 Brian O'Connor **RC** .50
26 Yamid Haad .25
27 Hector Mercado **RC** .50
28 Jason Woolf **RC** .50
29 Eddie Furniss **RC** .50
30 Cha Sueng Baek **RC** .50
31 Colby Lewis **RC** .50
32 Pasqual Coco **RC** .50
33 Jorge Cantu **RC** 2.00
34 Erasmo Ramirez **RC** .50
35 Bobby Kielty **RC** 1.00
36 Joaquin Benoit **RC** .50
37 Brian Esposito **RC** .50
38 Michael Wenner .25
39 Juan Rincon **RC** .50
40 Yorvit Torrealba **RC** .50
41 Chad Durham **RC** .50
42 Jim Mann **RC** .50
43 Shane Loux **RC** .50
44 Luis Rivas .25
45 Ken Chenard **RC** .50
46 Mike Lockwood **RC** .50
47 Giovanni Lara **RC** .50
48 Bubba Carpenter **RC** .50
49 Ryan Dittfurth **RC** .50
50 John Stephens **RC** .50
51 Pedro Feliz **RC** 2.00
52 Kenny Kelly **RC** .50
53 Neil Jenkins **RC** .50
54 Mike Glendenning **RC** .50
55 Bo Porter .25
56 Eric Byrnes .25
57 Tony Alvarez **RC** .50
58 Kazuhiro Sasaki **RC** 1.00
59 Chad Durbin **RC** .50
60 Mike Bynum **RC** .50
61 Travis Wilson **RC** .50
62 Jose Leon **RC** .50
63 Ryan Vogelsong **RC** .50
64 Geraldo Guzman **RC** .50
65 Craig Anderson **RC** .50
66 Carlos Silva **RC** 1.00
67 Brad Thomas **RC** .50
68 Chin-Hui Tsao 1.50
69 Mark Buehrle **RC** 6.00
70 Juan Salas **RC** .50
71 Denny Abreu **RC** .50
72 Keith McDonald **RC** .50
73 Chris Richard **RC** .50
74 Tomas de la Rosa **RC** .50
75 Vicente Padilla 1.00
76 Justin Brunette **RC** .50
77 Scott Linebrink **RC** .50
78 Jeff Sparks **RC** .50
79 Tike Redman **RC** .50
80 John Lackey **RC** 3.00
81 Joe Strong **RC** .50
82 Brian Tollberg **RC** .50
83 Steve Sisco **RC** .50
84 Chris Clapinski .25
85 Augie Ojeda **RC** .50
86 Adrian Gonzalez **RC** (Draft Picks) 6.00
87 Mike Stodolka **RC** (Draft Picks) .50
88 Adam Johnson **RC** (Draft Picks) .50
89 Matt Wheatland **RC** (Draft Picks) .50
90 Corey Smith **RC** (Draft Picks) .50
91 Rocco Baldelli **RC** (Draft Picks) 4.00
92 Keith Bucktrot **RC** (Draft Picks) .50
93 Adam Wainwright **RC** (Draft Picks) 4.00
94 Blaine Boyer **RC** (Draft Picks) .50
95 Aaron Herr **RC** (Draft Picks) .50
96 Scott Thorman **RC** (Draft Picks) 2.00
97 Brian Digby **RC** (Draft Picks) .50
98 Josh Shortslef **RC** (Draft Picks) .50
99 Sean Smith **RC** (Draft Picks) .50
100 Alex Cruz **RC** (Draft Picks) .50
101 Marc Love **RC** (Draft Picks) .50
102 Kevin Lee **RC** (Draft Picks) .50
103 Timoniel Perez **RC** (Draft Picks) .50
104 Alex Cabrera **RC** (Draft Picks) 1.00
105 Shane Heams **RC** (Draft Picks) .50
106 Tripper Johnson **RC** (Draft Picks) .50
107 Brent Abernathy **RC** (Draft Picks) .50
108 John Cotton **RC** (Draft Picks) .50
109 Brad Wilkerson **RC** (Draft Picks) 3.00
110 Jon Rauch **RC** (Draft Picks) .50

2000 Bowman's Best Pre-Production

Three-card cello packs of promotional cards introduced the Bowman's Best issue for 2000. The cards are virtually identical to the regularly issued version except for the numbering on the back which includes a "PP" prefix.

NM/M
Complete Set (3): 6.00
Common Player: 2.00
PP1 Larry Walker 2.00
PP2 Adam Dunn 2.00
PP3 Brett Myers 2.00

2000 Bowman's Best

The base set consists of 200-cards on a mirror like sheen, reminiscent of Refractors. Veteran cards have gold highlights while rookies and prospects have blue highlights. There are three subsets: Best Performers (86-100), Prospects (101-150) and Rookies (151-200). Rookies are serially numbered

to 2,999 on the card back and are randomly inserted on the average of 1:7 packs.

NM/M
Complete Set (200): 275.00
Common Player: .20
Common Rookie (151-200): 5.00
Production 2,999 Sets
Pack (4): 4.00
Box (24): 75.00
1 Nomar Garciaparra 2.00
2 Chipper Jones 1.50
3 Damion Easley .20
4 Bernie Williams .40
5 Barry Bonds 3.00
6 Jermaine Dye .20
7 John Olerud .20
8 Mike Hampton .20
9 Cal Ripken Jr. 3.00
10 Jeff Bagwell 1.00
11 Troy Glaus 1.00
12 J.D. Drew .40
13 Jeromy Burnitz .20
14 Carlos Delgado .75
15 Shawn Green .40
16 Kevin Millwood .40
17 Rondell White .20
18 Scott Rolen .75
19 Jeff Cirillo .20
20 Barry Larkin .20
21 Brian Giles .20
22 Roger Clemens 1.75
23 Manny Ramirez 1.00
24 Alex Gonzalez .20
25 Mark Grace .35
26 Fernando Tatis .20
27 Randy Johnson 1.00
28 Roger Cedeno .20
29 Brian Jordan .20
30 Kevin Brown .40
31 Greg Vaughn .20
32 Roberto Alomar .50
33 Larry Walker .20
34 Rafael Palmeiro .75
35 Curt Schilling .50
36 Orlando Hernandez .20
37 Todd Walker .20
38 Juan Gonzalez 1.00
39 Sean Casey .35
40 Tony Gwynn 1.50
41 Albert Belle .20
42 Gary Sheffield .40
43 Michael Barrett .20
44 Preston Wilson .20
45 Jim Thome .40
46 Shannon Stewart .20
47 Mo Vaughn .20
48 Ben Grieve .20
49 Adrian Beltre .35
50 Sammy Sosa 2.00
51 Bob Abreu .20
52 Edgardo Alfonzo .20
53 Carlos Febles .20
54 Frank Thomas 1.00
55 Alex Rodriguez 2.50
56 Cliff Floyd .20
57 Jose Canseco .40
58 Erubiel Durazo .20
59 Tim Hudson .50
60 Craig Biggio .20
61 Eric Karros .20
62 Mike Mussina .50
63 Robin Ventura .20
64 Carlos Beltran .50
65 Pedro Martinez 1.00
66 Gabe Kapler .20
67 Jason Kendall .20
68 Derek Jeter 3.00
69 Magglio Ordonez .50
70 Mike Piazza 2.00
71 Mike Lieberthal .20
72 Andres Galarraga .20
73 Raul Mondesi .20
74 Eric Chavez .40
75 Greg Maddux 1.50
76 Matt Williams .30
77 Kris Benson .20
78 Ivan Rodriguez .50
79 Pokey Reese .20
80 Vladimir Guerrero 1.00
81 Mark McGwire 2.50
82 Vinny Castilla .20
83 Todd Helton 1.00
84 Andruw Jones .75
85 Ken Griffey Jr. 2.00

86 Mark McGwire (Best Performers) 1.25
87 Derek Jeter (Best Performers) 1.50
88 Chipper Jones (Best Performers) .75
89 Nomar Garciaparra (Best Performers) 1.00
90 Sammy Sosa (Best Performers) .75
91 Cal Ripken Jr. (Best Performers) 1.50
92 Juan Gonzalez (Best Performers) .50
93 Alex Rodriguez (Best Performers) 1.25
94 Barry Bonds (Best Performers) 1.50
95 Sean Casey (Best Performers) .25
96 Vladimir Guerrero (Best Performers) .50
97 Mike Piazza (Best Performers) 1.00
98 Shawn Green (Best Performers) .25
99 Jeff Bagwell (Best Performers) .50
100 Ken Griffey Jr. (Best Performers) 1.00
101 Rick Ankiel (Prospects) .35
102 John Patterson (Prospects) .20
103 David Walling (Prospects) .20
104 Michael Restovich (Prospects) .20
105 A.J. Burnett (Prospects) .20
106 Matt Riley (Prospects) .20
107 Chad Hermansen (Prospects) .20
108 Choo Freeman (Prospects) .20
109 Mark Quinn (Prospects) .20
110 Corey Patterson (Prospects) .40
111 Ramon Ortiz (Prospects) .20
112 Vernon Wells (Prospects) .40
113 Milton Bradley (Prospects) .20
114 Travis Dawkins (Prospects) .20
115 Sean Burroughs (Prospects) .35
116 Willi Mo Pena (Prospects) .40
117 Dee Brown (Prospects) .20
118 C.C. Sabathia (Prospects) .20
119 Larry Bigbie **RC** (Prospects) .20
120 Octavio Dotel (Prospects) .20
121 Kip Wells (Prospects) .20
122 Ben Petrick (Prospects) .20
123 Mark Mulder (Prospects) .40
124 Jason Standridge (Prospects) .20
125 Adam Piatt (Prospects) .20
126 Steve Lomasney (Prospects) .20
127 Jayson Werth (Prospects) .20
128 Alex Escobar (Prospects) .20
129 Ryan Anderson (Prospects) .20
130 Adam Dunn (Prospects) .50
131 Omar Ortiz (Prospects) .20
132 Brad Penny (Prospects) .20
133 Daryle Ward (Prospects) .20
134 Eric Munson (Prospects) .20
135 Nick Johnson (Prospects) .50
136 Jason Jennings (Prospects) .20
137 Tim Raines Jr. (Prospects) .20
138 Ruben Mateo (Prospects) .20
139 Jack Cust (Prospects) .20
140 Rafael Furcal (Prospects) .20
141 Eric Gagne (Prospects) .35
142 Tony Armas (Prospects) .20
143 Mike Paradis (Prospects) .20
144 Chris George (Prospects) .20
145 Alfonso Soriano (Prospects) .75
146 Josh Hamilton (Prospects) .50
147 Michael Cuddyer (Prospects) .35
148 Jay Gehrke (Prospects) .20
149 Josh Girdley (Prospects) .20
150 Pat Burrell (Prospects) .75
151 Brett Myers **RC** 10.00
152 Scott Seabol **RC** 5.00
153 Keith Reed **RC** 5.00
154 Francisco Rodriguez **RC** 20.00
155 Barry Zito **RC** 20.00
156 Pat Manning **RC** 5.00
157 Ben Christensen **RC** 5.00
158 Corey Myers **RC** 5.00
159 Wascar Serrano **RC** 5.00
160 Wes Anderson **RC** 5.00
161 Andy Tracy **RC** 5.00
162 Cesar Saba **RC** 5.00
163 Mike Lamb **RC** 5.00
164 Bobby Bradley **RC** 5.00
165 Vince Faison **RC** 5.00
166 Ty Howington **RC** 8.00
167 Ken Harvey **RC** 8.00
168 Josh Kalinowski **RC** 5.00
169 Ruben Salazar **RC** 5.00
170 Aaron Rowand **RC** 10.00
171 Ramon Santiago **RC** 5.00
172 Scott Sobkowiak **RC** 5.00
173 Lyle Overbay **RC** 10.00
174 Rico Washington **RC** 5.00
175 Rick Asadoorian **RC** 5.00
176 Matt Ginter **RC** 5.00
177 Jason Stumm **RC** 5.00
178 B.J. Garbe **RC** 5.00
179 Mike MacDougal **RC** 5.00
180 Ryan Christianson **RC** 5.00
181 Kurt Ainsworth **RC** 5.00
182 Brad Baisley **RC** 5.00
183 Ben Broussard **RC** 5.00
184 Aaron McNeal **RC** 5.00
185 John Sneed **RC** 5.00
186 Junior Brignac **RC** 5.00
187 Chance Caple **RC** 5.00
188 Scott Downs **RC** 5.00
189 Matt Cepicky **RC** 5.00
190 Chin-Feng Chen **RC** 20.00
191 Johan Santana **RC** 100.00
192 Brad Baker **RC** 5.00
193 Jason Repko **RC** 5.00
194 Craig Dingman **RC** 5.00
195 Chris Wakeland 5.00
196 Rogelio Arias **RC** 5.00
197 Luis Matos **RC** 8.00
198 Robert Ramsay **RC** 5.00
199 Willie Bloomquist **RC** 20.00
200 Tony Pena Jr. **RC** 5.00

Bets

This 10-card set highlighted prospects who had the best chance of making the big league. The upper left corner and bottom right corner are die-cut. A small action photo is superimposed over a larger background shot of the featured player. Backs are numbered with a "BBB" prefix.

NM/M
Complete Set (10): 10.00
Common Player: .75
Inserted 1:15
1 Pat Burrell 2.00
2 Alfonso Soriano 2.00
3 Corey Patterson 1.50
4 Eric Munson .75
5 Sean Burroughs 1.00
6 Rafael Furcal .75
7 Rick Ankiel 1.00
8 Nick Johnson 1.50
9 Ruben Mateo .75
10 Josh Hamilton 1.00

Franchise Favorites

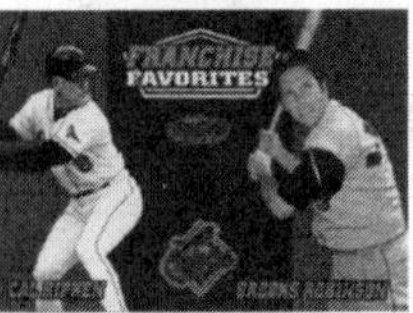

Two current players and two retired stars are featured in this six-card set. Card backs are numbered with a "FR" prefix.

NM/M
Complete Set (6): 15.00
Common Player: 1.00
Inserted 1:17
1A Sean Casey 1.00
1B Johnny Bench 3.00
1C Sean Casey, Johnny Bench 3.00
2A Cal Ripken Jr. 5.00
2B Brooks Robinson 2.00
2C Cal Ripken Jr., Brooks Robinson 5.00

Franchise Favorites Autograph

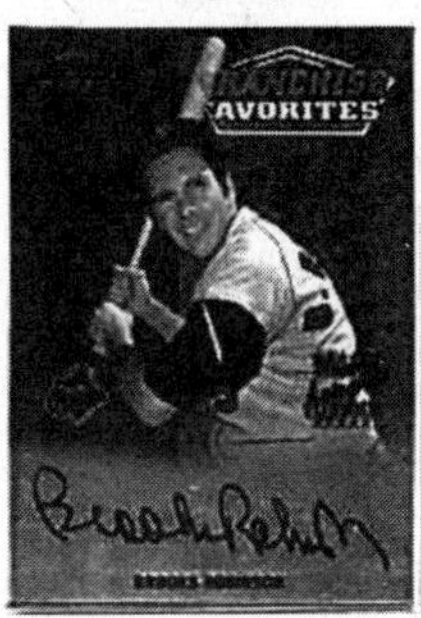

These autographs are seeded 1:1,291 packs, while the two dual autographed versions are inserted 1:5,153 packs.

NM/M
Common Player: 20.00
Version A & B 1:1,291
Version C 1:5,153
1A Sean Casey 20.00
1B Johnny Bench 50.00
1C Sean Casey, Johnny Bench 100.00
2A Cal Ripken Jr. 125.00
2B Brooks Robinson 50.00
2C Cal Ripken Jr., Brooks Robinson 250.00

Franchise 2000

Each of the 25-cards in this set have rounded corners on a holographic silver design. Backs are numbered with a "F" prefix.

NM/M
Complete Set (25): 60.00
Common Player: 1.00
Inserted 1:18
1 Cal Ripken Jr. 8.00
2 Nomar Garciaparra 6.00
3 Frank Thomas 2.00
4 Manny Ramirez 2.00
5 Juan Gonzalez 1.50
6 Carlos Beltran 2.00
7 Derek Jeter 8.00
8 Alex Rodriguez 6.00
9 Ben Grieve 1.00
10 Jose Canseco 1.50
11 Ivan Rodriguez 1.50
12 Mo Vaughn 1.00
13 Randy Johnson 3.00
14 Chipper Jones 4.00
15 Sammy Sosa 5.00
16 Ken Griffey Jr. 5.00
17 Larry Walker 1.00
18 Preston Wilson 1.00
19 Jeff Bagwell 2.00
20 Shawn Green 1.00
21 Vladimir Guerrero 2.00
22 Mike Piazza 5.00
23 Scott Rolen 2.00
24 Tony Gwynn 3.50
25 Barry Bonds 8.00

Locker Room Collection Autographs

Part of the Locker Room Collection, these autographs feature 19 players. Backs are numbered with a "LRCA" prefix.

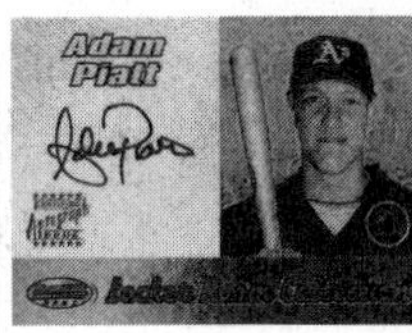

NM/M
Common Player: 8.00
Inserted 1:57
1 Carlos Beltran 25.00
2 Rick Ankiel 8.00
3 Vernon Wells 12.00
4 Ruben Mateo 8.00
5 Ben Petrick 8.00
6 Adam Piatt 8.00
7 Eric Munson 8.00
8 Alfonso Soriano 40.00
9 Kerry Wood 25.00
10 Jack Cust 8.00
11 Rafael Furcal 15.00
12 Josh Hamilton 10.00
13 Brad Penny 8.00
14 Dee Brown 8.00
15 Milton Bradley 12.00
16 Ryan Anderson 8.00
17 John Patterson 8.00
18 Nick Johnson 10.00
19 Peter Bergeron 8.00

Locker Room Collection Jerseys

These inserts have a piece of game-worn jersey embedded into them and are numbered with a "LRCJ" prefix.

NM/M
Common Player: 4.00
Inserted 1:206
1 Carlos Beltran 12.00
2 Rick Ankiel 5.00
3 Adam Kennedy 4.00
4 Ben Petrick 4.00
5 Adam Piatt 4.00

Locker Room Collection Lumber

These inserts have a piece of game-used bat embedded into them. They are numbered with a "LRCL" prefix on the back.

NM/M
Common Player: 5.00
Inserted 1:376
1 Carlos Beltran 15.00
2 Rick Ankiel 5.00
3 Vernon Wells 10.00
4 Adam Kennedy 5.00
5 Ben Petrick 5.00
6 Adam Piatt 5.00
7 Eric Munson 5.00
8 Rafael Furcal 8.00
9 J.D. Drew 8.00
10 Pat Burrell 10.00

Rookie Signed Baseballs

Redemption inserts, redeemable for Rookie Signed Baseballs, were randomly inserted. Signed baseball displays the Bowman "Rookie Autograph" logo and the Topps "Genuine Issue" sticker.

NM/M
Complete Set (5): 75.00
Common Player: 15.00
Inserted 1:688
1 Josh Hamilton 30.00
2 Rick Ankiel 15.00
3 Alfonso Soriano 50.00
4 Nick Johnson 30.00
5 Corey Patterson 20.00

Selections

This 15-card set is printed on a luminescent, die-cut design. The set features former Rookies of the Year and former No. 1 overall Draft Picks. These are seeded 1:30 packs. Backs are numbered with a "BBS" prefix.

NM/M
Complete Set (15): 50.00
Common Player: 1.00
Inserted 1:30
1 Alex Rodriguez 7.50
2 Ken Griffey Jr. 6.00
3 Pat Burrell 2.00
4 Mark McGwire 7.50
5 Derek Jeter 10.00
6 Nomar Garciaparra 6.00
7 Mike Piazza 6.00
8 Josh Hamilton 1.00
9 Cal Ripken Jr. 10.00
10 Jeff Bagwell 2.50
11 Chipper Jones 4.50
12 Jose Canseco 1.50
13 Carlos Beltran 2.00
14 Kerry Wood 2.00
15 Ben Grieve 1.00

Year By Year

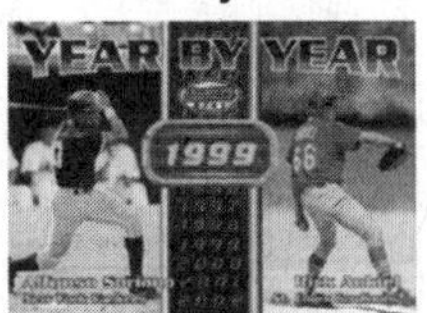

This 10-card set highlights 10 duos who began their careers in the same year. They have a horizontal format on a mirror foiled card front. Backs are numbered with a "YY" prefix.

NM/M
Complete Set (10): 25.00
Common Card: 1.50
Inserted 1:23
1 Sammy Sosa, Ken Griffey Jr. 4.00
2 Nomar Garciaparra, Vladimir Guerrero 4.00
3 Alex Rodriguez, Jeff Cirillo 5.00
4 Mike Piazza, Pedro Martinez 4.00
5 Derek Jeter, Edgardo Alfonzo 6.00
6 Alfonso Soriano, Rick Ankiel 2.00
7 Mark McGwire, Barry Bonds 6.00
8 Juan Gonzalez, Larry Walker 1.50
9 Ivan Rodriguez, Jeff Bagwell 1.50
10 Shawn Green, Manny Ramirez 1.50

2001 Bowman

NM/M
Complete Set (440): 140.00
Common Player: .15
Common Rookie: .25
Golds: 1-2X
Inserted 1:1
Pack (10): 8.00
Box (24): 160.00
1 Jason Giambi .40
2 Rafael Furcal .15
3 Rick Ankiel .15
4 Freddy Garcia .15
5 Magglio Ordonez .25
6 Bernie Williams .40
7 Kenny Lofton .15
8 Al Leiter .15
9 Albert Belle .15
10 Craig Biggio .15
11 Mark Mulder .15
12 Carlos Delgado .40
13 Darin Erstad .25
14 Richie Sexson .15
15 Randy Johnson .75
16 Greg Maddux 1.50
17 Cliff Floyd .15
18 Mark Buehrle .15
19 Chris Singleton .15
20 Orlando Hernandez .20
21 Javier Vazquez .15
22 Jeff Kent .15
23 Jim Thome .50
24 John Olerud .15
25 Jason Kendall .15
26 Scott Rolen .50
27 Tony Gwynn .75
28 Edgardo Alfonzo .15
29 Pokey Reese .15
30 Todd Helton .50
31 Mark Quinn .15
32 Dan Tosca **RC** .25
33 Dean Palmer .15
34 Jacque Jones .15
35 Ray Durham .15
36 Rafael Palmeiro .50
37 Carl Everett .15
38 Ryan Dempster .15
39 Randy Wolf .15
40 Vladimir Guerrero .75
41 Livan Hernandez .15
42 Mo Vaughn .15
43 Shannon Stewart .15
44 Preston Wilson .15
45 Jose Vidro .15
46 Fred McGriff .15
47 Kevin Brown .25
48 Peter Bergeron .15
49 Miguel Tejada .50
50 Chipper Jones .75
51 Edgar Martinez .15
52 Tony Batista .15
53 Jorge Posada .40
54 Ricky Ledee .15
55 Sammy Sosa 1.00
56 Steve Cox .15
57 Tony Armas Jr. .15
58 Gary Sheffield .40
59 Bartolo Colon .15
60 Pat Burrell .40
61 Jay Payton .15
62 Sean Casey .25
63 Larry Walker .15
64 Mike Mussina .40
65 Nomar Garciaparra 1.00
66 Darren Dreifort .15
67 Richard Hidalgo .15
68 Troy Glaus .40
69 Ben Grieve .15
70 Jim Edmonds .40
71 Raul Mondesi .15
72 Andruw Jones .50
73 Luis Castillo .15
74 Mike Sweeney .15
75 Derek Jeter 2.00
76 Ruben Mateo .15
77 Carlos Lee .15
78 Cristian Guzman .15
79 Mike Hampton .25
80 J.D. Drew .25
81 Matt Lawton .15
82 Moises Alou .15
83 Terrence Long .15
84 Geoff Jenkins .15
85 Manny Ramirez .75
86 Johnny Damon .15
87 Barry Larkin .15
88 Pedro Martinez .75
89 Juan Gonzalez .40
90 Roger Clemens 2.00
91 Carlos Beltran .50
92 Brad Radke .15
93 Orlando Cabrera .15
94 Roberto Alomar .50
95 Barry Bonds 2.00
96 Tim Hudson .25
97 Tom Glavine .25
98 Jeromy Burnitz .15
99 Adrian Beltre .15
100 Mike Piazza 1.00
101 Kerry Wood .40
102 Steve Finley .15
103 Alex Cora .15
104 Bob Abreu .15
105 Neifi Perez .15
106 Mark Redman .15
107 Paul Konerko .15
108 Jermaine Dye .15
109 Brian Giles .15
110 Ivan Rodriguez .50
111 Vinny Castilla .15
112 Adam Kennedy .15
113 Eric Chavez .25
114 Billy Koch .15
115 Shawn Green .25
116 Matt Williams .15
117 Greg Vaughn .15
118 Gabe Kapler .15
119 Jeff Cirillo .15
120 Frank Thomas .50
121 David Justice .15
122 Cal Ripken Jr. 3.00
123 Rich Aurilia .15
124 Curt Schilling .40

125 Barry Zito .25
126 Brian Jordan .15
127 Chan Ho Park .15
128 J.T. Snow Jr. .15
129 Kazuhiro Sasaki .15
130 Alex Rodriguez 2.00
131 Mariano Rivera .25
132 Eric Milton .15
133 Andy Pettitte .25
134 Scott Elarton .15
135 Ken Griffey Jr. 1.50
136 Bengie Molina .15
137 Jeff Bagwell .50
138 Kevin Millwood .15
139 Tino Martinez .15
140 Mark McGwire 1.50
141 Larry Barnes .15
142 John Buck **RC** .25
143 Freddie Bynum **RC** .25
144 Abraham Nunez .15
145 Felix Diaz **RC** .25
146 Horatio Estrada **RC** .25
147 Ben Diggins .15
148 Tsuyoshi Shinjo **RC** .50
149 Rocco Baldelli .25
150 Rod Barajas .15
151 Luis Terrero .15
152 Milton Bradley .15
153 Kurt Ainsworth .15
154 Russell Branyan .15
155 Ryan Anderson .15
156 Mitch Jones **RC** .25
157 Chip Ambres .15
158 Steve Bennett **RC** .25
159 Ivanon Coffie .15
160 Sean Burroughs .15
161 Keith Bucktrot .15
162 Tony Alvarez .15
163 Joaquin Benoit .15
164 Rick Asadoorian .15
165 Ben Broussard .15
166 Ryan Madson **RC** 1.50
167 Dee Brown .15
168 Sergio Contreras **RC** .25
169 John Barnes .15
170 Ben Washburn **RC** .50
171 Erick Almonte **RC** .25
172 Shawn Fagan **RC** .25
173 Gary Johnson **RC** .25
174 Brady Clark .15
175 Grant Roberts .15
176 Tony Torcato .15
177 Ramon Castro .15
178 Esteban German .15
179 Joe Hamer **RC** .25
180 Nick Neugebauer .25
181 Dernell Stenson .15
182 Yhency Brazoban **RC** .40
183 Aaron Myette .15
184 Juan Sosa .15
185 Brandon Inge .15
186 Domingo Guante **RC** .25
187 Adrian Brown .15
188 Deivi Mendez **RC** .25
189 Luis Matos .15
190 Pedro Liriano **RC** .50
191 Donnie Bridges .15
192 Alex Cintron .15
193 Jace Brewer .15
194 Ron Davenport **RC** .50
195 Jason Belcher **RC** .25
196 Adrian Hernandez **RC** .25
197 Bobby Kielty .15
198 Reggie Griggs **RC** .25
199 Reggie Abercrombie **RC** 1.00
200 Troy Farnsworth **RC** .50
201 Matt Belisle .15
202 Miguel Villilo **RC** .50
203 Adam Everett .15
204 John Lackey .15
205 Pasqual Coco .15
206 Adam Wainwright .25
207 Matt White **RC** .25
208 Chin-Feng Chen .25
209 Jeff Andra **RC** .25
210 Willie Bloomquist .15
211 Wes Anderson .15
212 Enrique Cruz .15
213 Jerry Hairston Jr. .15
214 Mike Bynum .15
215 Brian Hitchcox **RC** .25
216 Ryan Christianson .15
217 J.J. Davis .15
218 Jovanny Cedeno .15
219 Elvin Nina .15
220 Alex Graman .15
221 Arturo McDowell .15
222 Deivi Santos **RC** .25
223 Jody Gerut .25
224 Sun-Woo Kim .15
225 Jimmy Rollins .25
226 Pappy Ndungidi .15
227 Ruben Salazar .15
228 Josh Girdley .15
229 Carl Crawford .15
230 Luis Montanez **RC** .50
231 Ramon Carvajal **RC** .25
232 Matt Riley .15
233 Ben Davis .15
234 Jason Grabowski .15
235 Chris George .15
236 Hank Blalock **RC** 5.00
237 Roy Oswalt .25
238 Eric Reynolds **RC** .25
239 Brian Cole .15
240 Denny Bautista **RC** .75
241 Hector Garcia **RC** .25
242 Joe Thurston **RC** .25
243 Brad Cresse .25
244 Corey Patterson .25
245 Brett Evert **RC** .25
246 Elpidio Guzman **RC** .25
247 Vernon Wells .25
248 Roberto Miniel **RC** .25
249 Brian Bass **RC** .50
250 Mark Burnett **RC** .25
251 Juan Silvestre .15
252 Pablo Ozuna .15
253 Jayson Werth .15
254 Russ Jacobsen **RC** .25
255 Chad Hermansen .15
256 Travis Hafner **RC** 8.00
257 Bradley Baker .15
258 Gookie Dawkins .15
259 Michael Cuddyer .15
260 Mark Buehrle .15
261 Ricardo Aramboles .15
262 Esix Snead **RC** .25
263 Wilson Betemit **RC** .50
264 Albert Pujols **RC** 85.00
265 Joe Lawrence .15
266 Ramon Ortiz .15
267 Ben Sheets .50
268 Luke Lockwood **RC** .25
269 Toby Hall .15
270 Jack Cust .15
271 Pedro Feliz .15
272 Noel Devarez **RC** .25
273 Josh Beckett .15
274 Alex Escobar .15
275 Doug Gredvig **RC** .25
276 Marcus Giles .15
277 Jon Rauch .15
278 Brian Schmitt **RC** .25
279 Seung Song **RC** .50
280 Kevin Mench .15
281 Adam Eaton .15
282 Shawn Sonnier .15
283 Andy Van Hekken **RC** .25
284 Aaron Rowand .15
285 Tony Blanco **RC** .25
286 Ryan Kohlmeier .15
287 C.C. Sabathia .15
288 Bubba Crosby .15
289 Josh Hamilton .25
290 Dee Haynes **RC** .25
291 Jason Marquis .15
292 Julio Zuleta .15
293 Carlos Hernandez .15
294 Matt LeCroy .15
295 Andy Beal **RC** .25
296 Carlos Pena .15
297 Reggie Taylor .15
298 Bob Keppel **RC** .25
299 Miguel Cabrera (Photo actually Manuel Esquivia.) .75
300 Ryan Franklin .15
301 Brandon Phillips .15
302 Victor Hall **RC** .25
303 Tony Pena Jr. .15
304 Jim Journell **RC** .25
305 Cristian Guerrero .25
306 Miguel Olivo .15
307 Jin Ho Cho .15
308 Choo Freeman .15
309 Danny Borrell **RC** .25
310 Doug Mientkiewicz .15
311 Aaron Herr .15
312 Keith Ginter .15
313 Felipe Lopez .15
314 Jeff Goldbach **RC** .25
315 Travis Harper .15
316 Paul LoDuca .15
317 Joe Torres .15
318 Eric Byrnes .15
319 George Lombard .15
320 David Krynzel .15
321 Ben Christensen .15
322 Aubrey Huff .15
323 Lyle Overbay .15
324 Sean McGowan .15
325 Jeff Heaverlo .15
326 Timo Perez .15
327 Octavio Martinez **RC** .25
328 Vince Faison .15
329 David Parrish **RC** .25
330 Bobby Bradley .15
331 Jason Miller **RC** .25
332 Corey Spencer **RC** .25
333 Craig House .15
334 Maxim St. Pierre **RC** .25
335 Adam Johnson .15
336 Joe Crede .15
337 Greg Nash **RC** .25
338 Chad Durbin .15
339 Pat Magness **RC** .25
340 Matt Wheatland .15
341 Julio Lugo .15
342 Grady Sizemore .50
343 Adrian Gonzalez .25
344 Tim Raines Jr. .15
345 Rainier Olmedo **RC** .25
346 Phil Dumatrait .15
347 Brandon Mims **RC** .25
348 Jason Jennings .15
349 Phil Wilson **RC** .25
350 Jason Hart .15
351 Cesar Izturis .15
352 Matt Butler **RC** .25
353 David Kelton .15
354 Luke Prokopec .15
355 Corey Smith .15
356 Joel Pineiro **RC** .75
357 Ken Chenard .15
358 Keith Reed .15
359 David Walling .15
360 Alexis Gomez **RC** .50
361 Justin Morneau **RC** 10.00
362 Josh Fogg **RC** .50
363 J.R. House .15
364 Andy Tracy .15
365 Kenny Kelly .15
366 Aaron McNeal .15
367 Nick Johnson .15
368 Brian Esposito .15
369 Charles Frazier **RC** .25
370 Scott Heard .15
371 Patrick Strange .15
372 Mike Meyers .15
373 Ryan Ludwick **RC** .50
374 Brad Wilkerson .15
375 Allen Levrault .15
376 Seth McClung **RC** .40
377 Joe Nathan .15
378 Rafael Soriano **RC** .75
379 Chris Richard .15
380 Xavier Nady .15
381 Tike Redman .15
382 Adam Dunn .15
383 Jared Abruzzo **RC** .25
384 Jason Richardson **RC** .25
385 Matt Holliday .50
386 Darwin Cubillian **RC** .25
387 Mike Nannini .15
388 Blake Williams **RC** .25
389 Valentino Pascucci **RC** .25
390 Jon Garland .15
391 Josh Pressley .15
392 Jose Ortiz .15
393 Ryan Hannaman **RC** .25
394 Steve Smyth **RC** .25
395 John Patterson .15
396 Chad Petty **RC** .25
397 Jake Peavy **RC** 10.00
398 Onix Mercado **RC** .25
399 Jason Romano .15
400 Luis Torres **RC** .25
401 Casey Fossum **RC** .25
402 Eduardo Figueroa **RC** .25
403 Bryan Barnowski **RC** .25
404 Tim Redding .15
405 Jason Standridge .15
406 Marvin Seale **RC** .25
407 Todd Moser .15
408 Alex Gordon .15
409 Steve Smitherman **RC** .75
410 Ben Petrick .15
411 Eric Munson .15
412 Luis Rivas .15
413 Matt Ginter .15
414 Alfonso Soriano .50
415 Rafael Boitel **RC** .25
416 Dany Morban **RC** .25
417 Justin Woodrowc **RC** .25
418 Wilfredo Rodriguez .15
419 Derrick Van Dusen **RC** .25
420 Josh Spoerl **RC** .25
421 Juan Pierre .15
422 J.C. Romero .15
423 Ed Rogers **RC** .25
424 Tomokazu Ohka .15
425 Ben Hendrickson **RC** .25
426 Carlos Zambrano .15
427 Brett Myers .15
428 Scott Seabol .15
429 Thomas Mitchell .15
430 Jose Reyes **RC** 35.00
431 Kip Wells .15
432 Willi Mo Pena .15
433 Adam Pettyjohn **RC** .25
434 Austin Kearns .15
435 Rico Washington .15
436 Doug Nickle **RC** .25
437 Steve Lomasney .15
438 Jason Jones **RC** .25
439 Bobby Seay .15
440 Justin Wayne **RC** .50

Autographs

NM/M
Common Autograph: 5.00
Inserted 1:74
BB Brian Barnowski 5.00
WB Wilson Betemit 15.00
JB Jason Botts 15.00
SB Sean Burroughs 5.00
FB Freddie Bynum 5.00
ND Noel Devarez 5.00
JD Jose Diaz 5.00
BD Ben Diggins 5.00
AE Alex Escobar 8.00
RF Rafael Furcal 10.00
AG Adrian Gonzalez 15.00
AKG Alex Gordon 5.00
AJG Alex Graman 5.00
CG Cristian Guerrero 5.00
TH Travis Hafner 100.00
JH Josh Hamilton 30.00
JWH Jason Hart 5.00
JRH J.R. House 5.00
RJ Russ Jacobson 5.00
AJ Adam Johnson 5.00
TJ Tripper Johnson 5.00
DWK David Kelton 5.00
DK David Krynzel 5.00
PR Pedro Liriano 5.00
SM Sean McGowan 5.00
KM Kevin Mench 8.00
LM Luis Montanez 8.00
JM Justin Morneau 140.00
LO Lyle Overbay 12.00
ADP Adam Piatt 8.00
JP Josh Pressley 6.00
AP Albert Pujols 650.00
BS Ben Sheets 20.00
SDS Steve Smyth 5.00
SS Shawn Sonnier 5.00
SU Sixto Urena 5.00
MV Miguel Villilo 5.00
BW Brad Wilkerson 10.00
BZ Barry Zito 25.00

Autoproofs

Common Player:
Inserted 1:18,259H
Inserted 1:8,306HTA
Redemption Expired 4/30/03
Values Undetermined

Futures Game-Worn Jersey

NM/M
Common Player: 5.00
Inserted 1:82
KA Kurt Ainsworth 6.00
CA Craig Anderson 5.00
RA Ryan Anderson 5.00
BB Bobby Bradley 5.00
MB Mike Bynum 5.00
RC Ramon Castro 5.00
CC Chin-Feng Chen 25.00
JC Jack Cust 5.00
TD Travis Dawkins 5.00
RD Randey Dorame 5.00
AE Alex Escobar 5.00
CG Chris George 5.00
MG Marcus Giles 6.00
JH Josh Hamilton 8.00
CH Carlos Hernandez 5.00
SK Sun-Woo Kim 5.00
FL Felipe Lopez 5.00
EM Eric Munson 5.00
AM Aaron Myette 5.00
NN Ntema Ndungidi 5.00
TO Tomokazu Ohka 6.00
RO Ramon Ortiz 5.00
DCP Corey Patterson 8.00
CP Carlos Pena 5.00
BP Ben Petrick 5.00
GR Grant Roberts 5.00
JR Jason Romano 5.00
BS Ben Sheets 6.00
CT Chin-Hui Tsao 15.00
VW Vernon Wells 8.00
BW Brad Wilkerson 5.00
TW Travis Wilson 5.00
BZ Barry Zito 15.00
JZ Julio Zuleta 5.00

Futures Game Three-Piece Game-Used

NM/M
Common Player: 20.00
RC Ramon Castro 20.00
CC Chin-Feng Chen 80.00
JC Jack Cust 20.00
TD Travis Dawkins 20.00
AE Alex Escobar 20.00
MG Marcus Giles 20.00
JH Josh Hamilton 20.00
FL Felipe Lopez 20.00
EM Eric Munson 25.00
NN Ntema Ndungidi 20.00
DCP Corey Patterson 25.00
CP Carlos Pena 20.00
BP Ben Petrick 20.00
JR Jason Romano 20.00
VW Vernon Wells 30.00
BW Brad Wilkerson 20.00
TW Travis Wilson 20.00
JZ Julio Zuleta 20.00

Autographed Three-Piece Game-Used

No pricing due to scarcity.

Rookie of the Year Dual Jersey

NM/M
Inserted 1:2,202
ROYR Kazuhiro Sasaki, Rafael Furcal 30.00

Rookie Reprints

NM/M
Complete Set (25): 50.00
Common Player: 1.50
Inserted 1:12
1 Yogi Berra 5.00
2 Ralph Kiner 2.50
3 Stan Musial 6.00
4 Warren Spahn 4.00
5 Roy Campanella 4.00
6 Bob Lemon 1.50
7 Robin Roberts 2.00
8 Duke Snider 4.00
9 Early Wynn 1.50
10 Richie Ashburn 1.50
11 Gil Hodges 2.00
12 Hank Bauer 2.00
13 Don Newcombe 1.50
14 Al Rosen 1.50
15 Willie Mays 8.00
16 Joe Garagiola 2.00
17 Whitey Ford 4.00
18 Lew Burdette 1.50
19 Gil McDougald 1.50
20 Minnie Minoso 1.50
21 Eddie Mathews 4.00
22 Harvey Kuenn 2.00
23 Don Larsen 3.00
24 Elston Howard 2.00
25 Don Zimmer 1.50

Autographed Rookie Reprints

NM/M
Common Autograph: 20.00
Inserted 1:2,467
1 Yogi Berra 70.00
2 Willie Mays 200.00
3 Stan Musial 100.00
4 Duke Snider 35.00
5 Warren Spahn 50.00
6 Ralph Kiner 25.00
8 Don Larsen 30.00
9 Don Zimmer 20.00
10 Minnie Minoso 20.00

Game-Used Bat Rookie Reprints

NM/M
Common Player: 10.00
Inserted 1:1,954
1 Willie Mays 60.00
2 Duke Snider 25.00
3 Minnie Minoso 10.00
4 Hank Bauer 10.00
5 Al Rosen 10.00

Autographed Game-Used Bat Rookie Reprints

Inserted 1:18,259
No pricing due to scarcity.

2001 Bowman Chrome

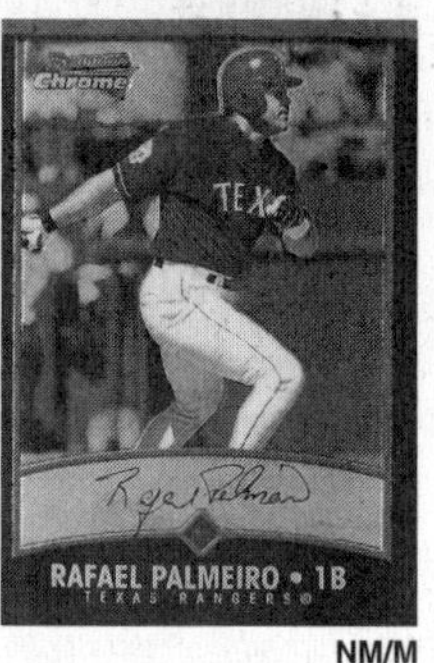

NM/M
Complete Set (351):
Common (1-110, 201-310): .20
Common Ref. (111-200, 311-330): 4.00
Inserted 1:4
Common Ref. Auto. (331-350): 25.00
Production 500
Pack (4): 15.00
Box (24): 350.00
1 Jason Giambi .60
2 Rafael Furcal .40
3 Bernie Williams .50
4 Kenny Lofton .20
5 Al Leiter .20
6 Albert Belle .20
7 Craig Biggio .40
8 Mark Mulder .40
9 Carlos Delgado .75
10 Darin Erstad .75
11 Richie Sexson .40
12 Randy Johnson 1.00
13 Greg Maddux 1.50
14 Orlando Hernandez .20
15 Javier Vazquez .20
16 Jeff Kent .40
17 Jim Thome .50
18 John Olerud .20
19 Jason Kendall .20
20 Scott Rolen .75
21 Tony Gwynn 1.00
22 Edgardo Alfonzo .20
23 Pokey Reese .20
24 Todd Helton .75
25 Mark Quinn .20
26 Dean Palmer .20
27 Ray Durham .20
28 Rafael Palmeiro .75
29 Carl Everett .20
30 Vladimir Guerrero 1.00
31 Livan Hernandez .20
32 Preston Wilson .20
33 Jose Vidro .20
34 Fred McGriff .20
35 Kevin Brown .20
36 Miguel Tejada .50
37 Chipper Jones 1.00
38 Edgar Martinez .20
39 Tony Batista .20
40 Jorge Posada .50
41 Sammy Sosa 1.00
42 Gary Sheffield .50
43 Bartolo Colon .20
44 Pat Burrell .50
45 Jay Payton .20
46 Mike Mussina .60
47 Nomar Garciaparra 1.00
48 Darren Dreifort .20
49 Richard Hidalgo .20
50 Troy Glaus .50
51 Ben Grieve .20
52 Jim Edmonds .40
53 Raul Mondesi .20
54 Andruw Jones .75
55 Mike Sweeney .20
56 Derek Jeter 3.00
57 Ruben Mateo .20
58 Cristian Guzman .20
59 Mike Hampton .20
60 J.D. Drew .40
61 Matt Lawton .20
62 Moises Alou .40
63 Terrence Long .20
64 Geoff Jenkins .20
65 Manny Ramirez 1.00
66 Johnny Damon 1.00
67 Pedro Martinez 1.00
68 Juan Gonzalez .50
69 Roger Clemens 2.00
70 Carlos Beltran .75
71 Roberto Alomar .50
72 Barry Bonds 3.00
73 Tim Hudson .50
74 Tom Glavine .50
75 Jeromy Burnitz .20
76 Adrian Beltre .40

77 Mike Piazza 1.00
78 Kerry Wood .40
79 Steve Finley .20
80 Bobby Abreu .40
81 Neifi Perez .20
82 Mark Redman .20
83 Paul Konerko .40
84 Jermaine Dye .20
85 Brian Giles .20
86 Ivan Rodriguez .75
87 Adam Kennedy .20
88 Eric Chavez .40
89 Billy Koch .20
90 Shawn Green .40
91 Matt Williams .20
92 Greg Vaughn .20
93 Jeff Cirillo .20
94 Frank Thomas .75
95 David Justice .20
96 Cal Ripken Jr. 3.00
97 Curt Schilling .75
98 Barry Zito .40
99 Brian Jordan .20
100 Chan Ho Park .20
101 J.T. Snow Jr. .20
102 Kazuhiro Sasaki .20
103 Alex Rodriguez 2.50
104 Mariano Rivera .50
105 Eric Milton .20
106 Andy Pettitte .50
107 Ken Griffey Jr. 2.00
108 Bengie Molina .20
109 Jeff Bagwell .75
110 Mark McGwire 2.00
111 Dan Tosca **RC** 4.00
112 Sergio Contreras **RC** 4.00
113 Mitch Jones **RC** 4.00
114 Ramon Carvajal **RC** 4.00
115 Ryan Madson **RC** 12.00
116 Hank Blalock **RC** 30.00
117 Ben Washburn **RC** 4.00
118 Erick Almonte **RC** 4.00
119 Shawn Fagan **RC** 4.00
120 Gary Johnson **RC** 4.00
121 Brett Evert **RC** 4.00
122 Joe Hamer **RC** 4.00
123 Yhency Brazoban **RC** 6.00
124 Domingo Guante **RC** 4.00
125 Deivi Mendez **RC** 4.00
126 Adrian Hernandez **RC** 4.00
127 Reggie Abercrombie **RC** 8.00
128 Steve Bennett **RC** 4.00
129 Matt White **RC** 4.00
130 Brian Hitchcox **RC** 4.00
131 Deivis Santos **RC** 4.00
132 Luis Montanez **RC** 4.00
133 Eric Reynolds **RC** 4.00
134 Denny Bautista **RC** 8.00
135 Hector Garcia **RC** 4.00
136 Joe Thurston **RC** 8.00
137 Tsuyoshi Shinjo **RC** 8.00
138 Elpidio Guzman **RC** 4.00
139 Brian Bass **RC** 4.00
140 Mark Burnett **RC** 4.00
141 Russ Jacobsen **RC** 4.00
142 Travis Hafner **RC** 50.00
143 Wilson Betemit **RC** 12.00
144 Luke Lockwood **RC** 4.00
145 Noel Devarez **RC** 4.00
146 Doug Gredvig **RC** 4.00
147 Seung Jun Song **RC** 6.00
148 Andy Van Hekken **RC** 4.00
149 Ryan Kohlmeier 4.00
150 Dee Haynes **RC** 6.00
151 Jim Journell **RC** 6.00
152 Chad Petty **RC** 4.00
153 Danny Borrell **RC** 4.00
154 David Kryznel 4.00
155 Octavio Martinez **RC** 4.00
156 David Parrish **RC** 4.00
157 Jason Miller **RC** 4.00
158 Corey Spencer **RC** 4.00
159 Maxim St. Pierre **RC** 4.00
160 Pat Magness **RC** 4.00
161 Rainier Olmedo **RC** 4.00
162 Brandon Mims **RC** 4.00
163 Phil Wilson **RC** 4.00
164 Jose Reyes **RC** 150.00
165 Matt Butler **RC** 4.00
166 Joel Pineiro 4.00
167 Ken Chenard 4.00
168 Alexis Gomez **RC** 6.00
169 Justin Morneau **RC** 75.00
170 Josh Fogg **RC** 5.00
171 Charles Frazier **RC** 4.00
172 Ryan Ludwick **RC** 15.00
173 Seth McClung **RC** 6.00
174 Justin Wayne **RC** 6.00
175 Rafael Soriano **RC** 6.00
176 Jared Abruzzo **RC** 4.00
177 Jason Richardson **RC** 4.00
178 Darwin Cubillan **RC** 4.00
179 Blake Williams **RC** 4.00
180 Valentino Pascucci **RC** 4.00
181 Ryan Hannaman **RC** 4.00
182 Steve Smyth **RC** 4.00
183 Jake Peavy **RC** 65.00
184 Onix Mercado **RC** 4.00
185 Luis Torres **RC** 4.00
186 Casey Fossum **RC** 6.00
187 Eduardo Figueroa **RC** 4.00
188 Bryan Barnowski **RC** 4.00
189 Jason Standridge 4.00
190 Marvin Seale **RC** 4.00
191 Steve Smitherman **RC** 8.00
192 Rafael Boitel **RC** 4.00
193 Dany Morban **RC** 4.00
194 Justin Woodrowc **RC** 4.00
195 Ed Rogers **RC** 4.00
196 Ben Hendrickson **RC** 4.00
197 Thomas Mitchell 4.00
198 Adam Pettyjohn **RC** 4.00
199 Doug Nickle **RC** 4.00
200 Jason Jones **RC** 4.00
201 Larry Barnes .20
202 Ben Diggins .20
203 Dee Brown .20
204 Rocco Baldelli 1.00
205 Luis Terrero .20
206 Milton Bradley .20
207 Kurt Ainsworth .20
208 Sean Burroughs .20
209 Rick Asadoorian .20
210 Ramon Castro .20
211 Nick Neugebauer .20
212 Aaron Myette .20
213 Luis Matos .20
214 Donnie Bridges .20
215 Alex Cintron .20
216 Bobby Kielty .20
217 Matt Belisle .20
218 Adam Everett .20
219 John Lackey .20
220 Adam Wainwright .50
221 Jerry Hairston Jr. .20
222 Mike Bynum .20
223 Ryan Christianson .20
224 J.J. Davis .20
225 Alex Graman .20
226 Abraham Nunez .20
227 Sun-Woo Kim .20
228 Jimmy Rollins .50
229 Ruben Salazar .20
230 Josh Girdley .20
231 Carl Crawford .20
232 Ben Davis .20
233 Jason Grabowski .20
234 Chris George .20
235 Roy Oswalt .75
236 Brian Cole .20
237 Corey Patterson .40
238 Vernon Wells .20
239 Bradley Baker .20
240 Gookie Dawkins .20
241 Michael Cuddyer .20
242 Ricardo Aramboles .20
243 Ben Sheets .50
244 Toby Hall .20
245 Jack Cust .20
246 Pedro Feliz .20
247 Josh Beckett .50
248 Alex Escobar .20
249 Marcus Giles .20
250 Jon Rauch .20
251 Kevin Mench .20
252 Shawn Sonnier .20
253 Aaron Rowand .20
254 C.C. Sabathia .20
255 Bubba Crosby .20
256 Josh Hamilton .25
257 Carlos Hernandez .20
258 Carlos Pena .20
259 Miguel Cabrera (Photo actually Manuel Esquivia.) 2.50
260 Brandon Phillips .20
261 Tony Pena Jr. .20
262 Cristian Guerrero .20
263 Jin Ho Cho .20
264 Aaron Herr .20
265 Keith Ginter .20
266 Felipe Lopez .20
267 Travis Harper .20
268 Joe Torres .20
269 Eric Byrnes .20
270 Ben Christensen .20
271 Aubrey Huff .20
272 Lyle Overbay .20
273 Vince Faison .20
274 Bobby Bradley .20
275 Joe Crede .20
276 Matt Wheatland .20
277 Grady Sizemore 1.50
278 Adrian Gonzalez .50
279 Timothy Raines Jr. .20
280 Phil Dumatrait .20
281 Jason Hart .20
282 David Kelton .20
283 David Walling .20
284 J.R. House .50
285 Kenny Kelly .20
286 Aaron McNeal .20
287 Nick Johnson .20
288 Scott Heard .20
289 Brad Wilkerson .20
290 Allen Levrault .20
291 Chris Richard .20
292 Jared Sandberg .20
293 Tike Redman .20
294 Adam Dunn .75
295 Josh Pressley .20
296 Jose Ortiz .20
297 Jason Romano .20
298 Tim Redding .20
299 Alex Gordon .20
300 Ben Petrick .20
301 Eric Munson .20
302 Luis Rivas .20
303 Matt Ginter .20
304 Alfonso Soriano .75
305 Wilfredo Rodriguez .20
306 Brett Myers .20
307 Scott Seabol .20
308 Tony Alvarez .20
309 Donzell McDonald .20
310 Austin Kearns .20
311 Will Ohman **RC** 4.00
312 Ryan Soules **RC** 4.00
313 Cody Ross **RC** 4.00
314 Bill Whitecotton **RC** 4.00
315 Mike Burns **RC** 4.00
316 Manuel Acosta **RC** 4.00
317 Lance Niekro **RC** 10.00
318 Travis Thompson **RC** 4.00
319 Zach Sorensen **RC** 4.00
320 Austin Evans **RC** 4.00
321 Brad Stiles **RC** 4.00
322 Joe Kennedy **RC** 4.00
323 Luke Martin **RC** 4.00
324 Juan Diaz **RC** 4.00
325 Pat Hallmark **RC** 4.00
326 Christian Parker **RC** 4.00
327 Ronny Corona **RC** 4.00
328 Jermaine Clark **RC** 4.00
329 Scott Dunn **RC** 4.00
330 Scott Chiasson **RC** 4.00
331 Greg Nash/Auto. **RC** 25.00
332 Brad Cresse/Auto. 25.00
333 John Buck/Auto. **RC** 50.00
334 Freddie Bynum/ Auto. **RC** 25.00
335 Felix Diaz/Auto. **RC** 25.00
336 Jason Belcher/ Auto. **RC** 25.00
337 Troy Farnsworth **RC** 25.00
338 Roberto Miniel **RC** 25.00
339 Esix Snead **RC** 25.00
340 Albert Pujols **RC** 2,500
341 Jeff Andra **RC** 25.00
342 Victor Hall **RC** 25.00
343 Pedro Liriano **RC** 25.00
344 Andy Beal **RC** 25.00
345 Bob Keppel **RC** 40.00
346 Brian Schmitt **RC** 25.00
347 Ron Davenport **RC** 150.00
348 Tony Blanco **RC** 50.00
349 Reggie Griggs **RC** 25.00
350 Derrick Van Dusen **RC** 25.00
351a Ichiro Suzuki Eng. **RC** 100.00
351b Ichiro Suzuki Japanese **RC** 100.00

Gold Refractors

Stars: 8-15X
Rookies: 1.5-3X
Production 99 Sets

X-Fractors

Stars: 4-8X
Rookies: .75-1.5X
Inserted 1:23

Futures Game Memorabilia

NM/M
Common Player: 6.00
Inserted 1:460
KA Kurt Ainsworth 8.00
CA Craig Anderson 6.00
RA Ryan Anderson 6.00
BB Bobby Bradley 6.00
MB Mike Bynum 6.00
RC Ramon Castro 6.00
CC Chin-Feng Chen 30.00
JC Jack Cust 6.00
RD Randey Dorame 6.00
AE Alex Escobar 6.00
CG Chris George 6.00
MG Marcus Giles 6.00
JH Josh Hamilton 8.00
CH Carlos Hernandez 6.00
SK Sun-Woo Kim 6.00
FL Felipe Lopez 8.00
EM Eric Munson 6.00
AM Aaron Myette 6.00
NN Ntema Ndungidi 6.00
TO Tomokazu Ohka 6.00
DCP Corey Patterson 10.00
CP Carlos Pena 6.00
BP Ben Petrick 6.00
JR Jason Romano 6.00
BS Ben Sheets 8.00
CT Chin-Hui Tsao 40.00
BW Brad Wilkerson 6.00
TW Travis Wilson 6.00
BZ Barry Zito 15.00
JZ Julio Zuleta 6.00

Rookie Reprints

NM/M
Complete Set (25): 50.00
Common Player: 2.00
Inserted 1:12
Refractors: 2-3X
Production 299 Sets
1 Yogi Berra 5.00
2 Ralph Kiner 3.00
3 Stan Musial 6.00
4 Warren Spahn 4.00
5 Roy Campanella 4.00
6 Bob Lemon 2.00
7 Robin Roberts 2.00
8 Duke Snider 4.00
9 Early Wynn 2.00
10 Richie Ashburn 3.00
11 Gil Hodges 3.00
12 Hank Bauer 2.00
13 Don Newcombe 2.00
14 Al Rosen 2.00
15 Willie Mays 8.00
16 Joe Garagiola 3.00
17 Whitey Ford 4.00
18 Lew Burdette 2.00
19 Gil McDougald 2.00
20 Minnie Minoso 2.00
21 Eddie Mathews 4.00
22 Harvey Kuenn 2.00
23 Don Larsen 3.00
24 Elston Howard 2.00
25 Don Zimmer 2.00

Rookie Reprint Relics

NM/M
Common Player: 8.00
Inserted 1:244
1 David Justice 8.00
2 Richie Sexson 12.00
3 Sean Casey 8.00
4 Mike Piazza 50.00
5 Carlos Delgado 8.00
6 Chipper Jones 25.00

2001 Bowman Draft Picks & Prospects

NM/M
Complete Set (110): 35.00
Complete Factory Set (112): 40.00
Common Player: .10
1 Alfredo Amezaga **RC** .25
2 Andrew Good .10
3 Kelly Johnson **RC** 3.00
4 Larry Bigbie .10

5 Matt Thompson **RC** .40
6 Wilton Chavez **RC** .40
7 Joe Borchard **RC** .50
8 David Espinosa .10
9 Zach Day **RC** .50
10 Brad Hawpe **RC** 3.00
11 Nate Cornejo .10
12 Jim Kavourias **RC** .25
13 Brad Lidge .10
14 Angel Berroa **RC** .75
15 Lamont Matthews **RC** .25
16 Jose Garcia .10
17 Grant Balfour **RC** .25
18 Ron Chiavacci **RC** .25
19 Jae Seo .10
20 Juan Rivera .10
21 D'Angelo Jimenez .10
22 Aaron Harang .10
23 Marlon Byrd **RC** .50
24 Sean Burnett .10
25 Josh Pearce **RC** .25
26 Brandon Duckworth **RC** .25
27 Jack Taschner **RC** .25
28 Bo Robinson **RC** .25
29 Brent Abernathy .10
30 David Elder **RC** .25
31 Scott Cassidy **RC** .25
32 Dennis Tankersley **RC** .40
33 Denny Stark .10
34 Dave Williams **RC** .25
35 Boof Bonser **RC** 1.00
36 Kris Foster **RC** .25
37 Neal Musser **RC** .25
38 Shawn Chacon .10
39 Mike Rivera **RC** .25
40 Will Smith **RC** .25
41 Morgan Ensberg **RC** 1.50
42 Ken Harvey .10
43 Ricardo Rodriguez **RC** .25
44 Jose Mieses **RC** .25
45 Luis Maza **RC** .25
46 Julio Perez **RC** .25
47 Billy Traber **RC** .25
48 David Martinez **RC** .25
49 Covelli Crisp **RC** 2.00
50 Mario Ramos **RC** .25
51 Matt Thornton **RC** .25
52 Xavier Nady .10
53 Ryan Vogelsong .10
54 Jim Magrane **RC** .25
55 Domingo Valdez **RC** .25
56 Brent Butler .10
57 Brian Tallet **RC** .25
58 Brian Reith **RC** .25
59 Mario Valenzuela **RC** .25
60 Bobby Hill **RC** .50
61 Rich Rundles **RC** .25
62 Rick Elder .10
63 J.D. Closser .10
64 Scot Shields .10
65 Miguel Olivo .10
66 Stubby Clapp **RC** .25
67 Jerome Williams **RC** .40
68 Jason Lane **RC** .75
69 Chase Utley **RC** 20.00
70 Erik Bedard **RC** 5.00
71 Alex Herrera **RC** .20
72 Juan Cruz **RC** .40
73 Billy Martin **RC** .20
74 Ronnie Merrill **RC** .20
75 Jason Kinchen **RC** .20
76 Wilken Ruan **RC** .20
77 Cody Ransom **RC** .20
78 Bud Smith **RC** .25
79 Wily Mo Pena .10
80 Jeff Nettles **RC** .20
81 Jamal Strong **RC** .25
82 Bill Ortega .10
83 Junior Zamora .10
84 Ichiro Suzuki **RC** 10.00
85 Fernando Rodney **RC** .20
86 Chris Smith **RC** .40
87 John Van Benschoten **RC** .50
88 Bobby Crosby **RC** 3.00
89 Kenny Baugh **RC** .25
90 Jake Gautreau **RC** .40
91 Gabe Gross **RC** .75
92 Kris Honel **RC** .40
93 Daniel Denham **RC** .25
94 Aaron Heilman **RC** 1.00
95 Irvin Guzman **RC** 5.00
96 Mike Jones **RC** .50
97 John-Ford Griffin **RC** .25
98 Macay McBride **RC** .50
99 John Rheineckar **RC** .50
100 Bronson Sardinha **RC** .25
101 Jason Weintraub **RC** .25
102 J.D. Martin **RC** .25
103 Jayson Nix **RC** .40
104 Noah Lowry **RC** 3.00
105 Richard Lewis **RC** .25
106 Brad Hennessey **RC** .40
107 Jeff Mathis **RC** .75
108 Jon Skaggs **RC** .40
109 Justin Pope **RC** .25
110 Josh Burrus **RC** .25

Autographs

Thirteen players on the original checklist from Bowman were never issued.

NM/M
Common Autograph: 5.00
Inserted 1:Set
JA Jared Abruzzo 5.00
AA Alfredo Amezaga 10.00
GA Garrett Atkins 50.00
BB Bobby Bradley 5.00
ANC Antoine Cameron 5.00
ROC Ramon Carvajal 5.00
RC Ryan Church 15.00
AC Alex Cintron 5.00
RD Ryan Dittfurth 5.00
AE Adam Everett 5.00
AF Alex Fernandez 5.00
AG Alexis Gomez 10.00
CG Cristian Guerrero 5.00
BH Beau Hale 5.00
SH Scott Heard 5.00
AH Aaron Herr 5.00
CI Cesar Izturis 5.00
GJ Gary Johnson 5.00
NJ Nick Johnson 10.00
AK Austin Kearns 15.00
JK Joe Kennedy 5.00
JL John Lackey 12.00
FL Felipe Lopez 8.00
RI Ryan Ludwick 10.00
RMM Ryan Madson 15.00
TO Tomo Ohka 8.00
RO Roy Oswalt 35.00
CP Christian Parra 5.00
BP Brandon Phillips 15.00
JP Joel Pineiro 15.00
NR Nick Regilio 5.00
ER Ed Rogers 5.00
SS Scott Seabol 5.00
BS Bud Smith 5.00
BJS Brian Specht 5.00
JT Joe Torres 5.00
JMW Justin Wayne 8.00

Draft Pick Relics

NM/M
Common Player: 4.00
One per factory set.
CI Cesar Izturis 4.00
GJ Gary Johnson 4.00
NR Nick Regilio 4.00
RC Ryan Church 4.00
BJS Brian Specht 4.00
JRH J.R. House 4.00

Futures Game Relics

NM/M
Common Player: 4.00
One per factory set.
AA Alfredo Amezaga 4.00
AD Adam Dunn 10.00
AG Adrian Gonzalez 8.00

AH Alex Herrera 4.00
BM Brett Myers 8.00
CD Cody Ransom 4.00
CG Chris George 4.00
CH Carlos Hernandez 5.00
CU Chase Utley 25.00
EB Eric Bedard 15.00
GB Grant Balfour 4.00
HB Hank Blalock 18.00
JB Joe Borchard 10.00
JC Juan Cruz 5.00
JP Josh Pearce 4.00
JR Juan Rivera 4.00
LG Luis Garcia 4.00
MC Miguel Cabrera 10.00
MR Mike Rivera 4.00
RR Ricardo Rodriguez 4.00
SC Scott Chiasson 4.00
SS Seung Jun Song 6.00
TB Toby Hall 4.00
WB Wilson Betemit 4.00
WP Wily Mo Pena 5.00
JAP Juan Pena 4.00

2001 Bowman Heritage Promos

To introduce its Heritage issue, Topps produced this five-card promo set for distribution at the National Sports Collectors Convention in Cleveland, June 28 through July 1. The three Indians cards were available from the PSA booth, the Pujols card from the Beckett booth and the McGwire card from the SCD booth. Only 500 of each card were produced. Styled after the 1948 Bowman cards with black-and-white photos on front and gray cardboard backs, the promos are in the standard 2-1/2" x 3-1/2" size and were given away in a cello pack with a cello-wrapped piece of bubblegum.

NM/M
Complete Set (5): 60.00
Common Player: 6.00
1 Roberto Alomar 6.00
2 Albert Pujols 50.00
3 C.C. Sabathia 6.00
4 Mark McGwire 12.50
5 Juan Gonzalez 6.00

2001 Bowman Heritage

NM/M
Complete Set (440): 200.00
Common Player: .15
Common (331-440): 1.00
Inserted 1:2
Pack (10): 5.00
Box (24): 100.00
1 Chipper Jones 1.25
2 Pete Harnisch .15
3 Brian Giles .15
4 J.T. Snow .15
5 Bartolo Colon .15
6 Jorge Posada .25
7 Shawn Green .25
8 Derek Jeter 2.50
9 Benito Santiago .15
10 Ramon Hernandez .15
11 Bernie Williams .40
12 Greg Maddux 1.50
13 Barry Bonds 2.50
14 Roger Clemens 2.00
15 Miguel Tejada .50
16 Pedro Feliz .15
17 Jim Edmonds .40
18 Tom Glavine .40
19 David Justice .25
20 Rich Aurilia .15
21 Jason Giambi .75
22 Orlando Hernandez .15
23 Shawn Estes .15
24 Nelson Figueroa .15
25 Terrence Long .15
26 Mike Mussina .50
27 Eric Davis .15
28 Jimmy Rollins .50
29 Andy Pettitte .50
30 Shawon Dunston .15
31 Tim Hudson .40
32 Jeff Kent .25
33 Scott Brosius .15
34 Livan Hernandez .15
35 Alfonso Soriano 1.00
36 Mark McGwire 1.50
37 Russ Ortiz .15
38 Fernando Vina .15
39 Ken Griffey Jr. 1.50
40 Edgar Renteria .15
41 Kevin Brown .15
42 Robb Nen .15
43 Paul LoDuca .15
44 Bobby Abreu .25
45 Adam Dunn .50
46 Osvaldo Fernandez .15
47 Marvin Benard .15
48 Mark Gardner .15
49 Alex Rodriguez 2.00
50 Preston Wilson .15
51 Roberto Alomar .40
52 Ben Davis .15
53 Derek Bell .15
54 Ken Caminiti .15
55 Barry Zito .40
56 Scott Rolen .75
57 Geoff Jenkins .15
58 Mike Cameron .15
59 Ben Grieve .15
60 Chuck Knoblauch .15
61 Matt Lawton .15
62 Chan Ho Park .15
63 Lance Berkman .40
64 Carlos Beltran .50
65 Dean Palmer .15
66 Alex Gonzalez .15
67 Larry Walker .25
68 Magglio Ordonez .25
69 Ellis Burks .15
70 Mark Mulder .25
71 Randy Johnson .75
72 John Smoltz .40
73 Jerry Hairston Jr. .15
74 Pedro Martinez .75
75 Fred McGriff .15
76 Sean Casey .25
77 C.C. Sabathia .15
78 Todd Helton .75
79 Brad Penny .15
80 Mike Sweeney .15
81 Billy Wagner .15
82 Mark Buehrle .25
83 Cristian Guzman .15
84 Jose Vidro .15
85 Pat Burrell .40
86 Jermaine Dye .15
87 Brandon Inge .15
88 David Wells .15
89 Mike Piazza 1.00
90 Jose Cabrera .15
91 Cliff Floyd .15
92 Matt Morris .15
93 Raul Mondesi .15
94 Joe Kennedy **RC** .50
95 Jack Wilson **RC** 1.00
96 Andruw Jones .75
97 Mariano Rivera .50
98 Mike Hampton .15
99 Roger Cedeno .15
100 Jose Cruz .15
101 Mike Lowell .15
102 Pedro Astacio .15
103 Joe Mays .15
104 John Franco .15
105 Tim Redding .15
106 Sandy Alomar .15
107 Bret Boone .15
108 Josh Towers **RC** .50
109 Matt Stairs .15
110 Chris Truby .15
111 Jeff Suppan .15
112 J.C. Romero .15
113 Felipe Lopez .15
114 Ben Sheets .40
115 Frank Thomas .75
116 A.J. Burnett .15
117 Tony Clark .15
118 Mac Suzuki .15
119 Brad Radke .15
120 Jeff Shaw .15
121 Nick Neugebauer .15
122 Kenny Lofton .15
123 Jacque Jones .15
124 Brent Mayne .15
125 Carlos Hernandez .15
126 Shane Spencer .15
127 John Lackey .15
128 Sterling Hitchcock .15
129 Darren Dreifort .15
130 Rusty Greer .15
131 Michael Cuddyer .15
132 Tyler Houston .15
133 Chin-Feng Chen .15
134 Ken Harvey .15
135 Marquis Grissom .15
136 Russell Branyan .15
137 Eric Karros .15
138 Josh Beckett .25
139 Todd Zeile .15
140 Corey Koskie .15
141 Steve Sparks .15
142 Bobby Seay .15
143 Tim Raines .15
144 Julio Zuleta .15
145 Jose Lima .15
146 Dante Bichette .15
147 Randy Keisler .15
148 Brent Butler .15
149 Antonio Alfonseca .15
150 Bryan Rekar .15
151 Jeffrey Hammonds .15
152 Larry Bigbie .15
153 Blake Stein .15
154 Robin Ventura .15
155 Rondell White .15
156 Juan Silvestre .15
157 Marcus Thames .15
158 Sidney Ponson .15
159 Juan Pena .15
160 Charles Johnson .15
161 Adam Everett .15
162 Eric Munson .15
163 Jason Isringhausen .15
164 Brad Fullmer .15
165 Miguel Olivo .15
166 Fernando Tatis .15
167 Freddy Garcia .15
168 Tom Goodwin .15
169 Armando Benitez .15
170 Paul Konerko .40
171 Jeff Cirillo .15
172 Shane Reynolds .15
173 Kevin Tapani .15
174 Joe Crede .25
175 Omar Infante **RC** .50
176 Jake Peavy **RC** 5.00
177 Corey Patterson .25
178 Alfredo Amezaga **RC** .25
179 Jeromy Burnitz .15
180 David Segui .15
181 Marcus Giles .15
182 Paul O'Neill .25
183 John Olerud .15
184 Andy Benes .15
185 Brad Cresse **RC** .25
186 Ricky Ledee .15
187 Allen Levrault .15
188 Royce Clayton .15
189 Kelly Johnson **RC** 4.00
190 Quilvio Veras .15
191 Mike Williams .15
192 Jason Lane **RC** 1.00
193 Rick Helling .15
194 Tim Wakefield .15
195 James Baldwin .15
196 Cody Ransom **RC** .25
197 Bobby Kielty .15
198 Bobby Jones .15
199 Steve Cox .15
200 Jamal Strong **RC** .25
201 Steve Lomasney .15
202 Bill Ortega .15
203 Mike Matheny .15
204 Jeff Randazzo **RC** .25
205 Aubrey Huff .15
206 Chuck Finley .15
207 Denny Bautista **RC** 1.50
208 Terry Mulholland .15
209 Rey Ordonez .15
210 Jason Belcher **RC** .25
211 Orlando Cabrera .15
212 Juan Encarnacion .15
213 Dustin Hermanson .15
214 Luis Rivas .15
215 Mark Quinn .15
216 Randy Velarde .15
217 Billy Koch .15
218 Ryan Rupe .15
219 Keith Ginter .15
220 Woody Williams .15
221 Blake Williams **RC** .25
222 Aaron Myette .15
223 Joe Borchard **RC** .75
224 Nate Cornejo .15
225 Julian Tavarez .15
226 Kevin Millwood .15
227 Travis Hafner **RC** 5.00
228 Charles Nagy .15
229 Mike Lieberthal .15
230 Jeff Nelson .15
231 Ryan Dempster .15
232 Andres Galarraga .15
233 Chad Durbin .15
234 Timoniel Perez .15
235 Troy O'Leary .15
236 Kevin Young .15
237 Gabe Kapler .15
238 Juan Cruz **RC** .50
239 Masato Yoshii .15
240 Aramis Ramirez .40
241 Matt Cooper **RC** .25
242 Randy Flores **RC** .25
243 Rafael Furcal .25
244 David Eckstein .15
245 Matt Clement .15
246 Craig Biggio .40
247 Rick Reed .15
248 Jose Macias .15
249 Alex Escobar .15
250 Roberto Hernandez .15
251 Andy Ashby .15
252 Tony Armas .15
253 Jamie Moyer .15
254 Jason Tyner .15
255 Ryan Ludwick **RC** .50
256 Jeff Conine .15
257 Francisco Cordova .15
258 Ted Lilly .15
259 Joe Randa .15
260 Jeff D'Amico .15
261 Albie Lopez .15
262 Kevin Appier .15
263 Richard Hidalgo .15
264 Omar Daal .15
265 Ricky Gutierrez .15
266 John Rocker .15
267 Ray Lankford .15
268 Beau Hale **RC** .25
269 Tony Blanco **RC** .25
270 Derrek Lee .75
271 Jamey Wright .15
272 Alex Gordon .15
273 Jeff Weaver .15
274 Jaret Wright .15
275 Jose Hernandez .15
276 Bruce Chen .15
277 Todd Hollandsworth .15
278 Wade Miller .15
279 Luke Prokopec .15
280 Rafael Soriano **RC** .75
281 Damion Easley .15
282 Darren Oliver .15
283 Brandon Duckworth **RC** .50
284 Aaron Herr .15
285 Ray Durham .15
286 Adrian Hernandez **RC** .40
287 Ugueth Urbina .15
288 Scott Seabol .15
289 Lance Niekro **RC** 1.00
290 Trot Nixon .15
291 Adam Kennedy .15
292 Brian Schmitt **RC** .25
293 Grant Roberts .15
294 Benny Agbayani .15
295 Travis Lee .15
296 Erick Almonte **RC** .40
297 Jim Thome .50
298 Eric Young .15
299 Daniel Denham **RC** .25
300 Boof Bonser **RC** 2.00
301 Denny Neagle .15
302 Kenny Rogers .15
303 J.D. Closser .15
304 Chase Utley **RC** 15.00
305 Rey Sanchez .15
306 Sean McGowan .15
307 Justin Pope **RC** .25
308 Torii Hunter .40
309 B.J. Surhoff .15
310 Aaron Heilman **RC** .50
311 Gabe Gross **RC** .75
312 Lee Stevens .15
313 Todd Hundley .15
314 Macay McBride **RC** .50
315 Edgar Martinez .15
316 Omar Vizquel .15
317 Reggie Sanders .15
318 John-Ford Griffin **RC** .50
319 Tim Salmon (Photo actually Troy Glaus.) .50
320 Pokey Reese .15
321 Jay Payton .15
322 Doug Glanville .15
323 Greg Vaughn .15
324 Ruben Sierra .15
325 Kip Wells .15
326 Carl Everett .15
327 Garret Anderson .15
328 Jay Bell .15
329 Barry Larkin .15
330 Jeff Mathis **RC** .75
331 Adrian Gonzalez 2.00
332 Juan Rivera 1.00
333 Tony Alvarez 1.00
334 Xavier Nady 1.00
335 Josh Hamilton 1.00
336 Will Smith **RC** 1.50
337 Israel Alcantara 1.00
338 Chris George 1.00
339 Sean Burroughs 1.00
340 Jack Cust 1.00
341 Eric Byrnes 1.00
342 Carlos Pena 1.00
343 J.R. House 1.00
344 Carlos Silva 1.00
345 Mike Rivera **RC** 1.00
346 Adam Johnson 1.00
347 Scott Heard 1.00
348 Alex Cintron 1.00
349 Miguel Cabrera 3.00
350 Nick Johnson 1.00
351 Albert Pujols **RC** 60.00
352 Ichiro Suzuki **RC** 30.00
353 Carlos Delgado 1.50
354 Troy Glaus 2.00
355 Sammy Sosa 3.00
356 Ivan Rodriguez 2.00
357 Vladimir Guerrero 2.00
358 Manny Ramirez 2.00
359 Luis Gonzalez 1.00
360 Roy Oswalt 1.50
361 Moises Alou 1.00
362 Juan Gonzalez 1.50
363 Tony Gwynn 2.00
364 Hideo Nomo 2.00
365 Tsuyoshi Shinjo **RC** 1.00
366 Kazuhiro Sasaki 1.00
367 Cal Ripken Jr. 8.00
368 Rafael Palmeiro 2.00
369 J.D. Drew 1.50
370 Doug Mientkiewicz 1.00
371 Jeff Bagwell 2.00
372 Darin Erstad 2.00
373 Tom Gordon 1.00
374 Ben Petrick 1.00
375 Eric Milton 1.00
376 Nomar Garciaparra 3.00
377 Julio Lugo 1.00
378 Tino Martinez 1.50
379 Javier Vazquez 1.00
380 Jeremy Giambi 1.00
381 Marty Cordova 1.00
382 Adrian Beltre 1.50
383 John Burkett 1.00
384 Aaron Boone 1.00
385 Eric Chavez 1.00
386 Curt Schilling 1.50
387 Cory Lidle 1.00
388 Jason Schmidt 1.00
389 Johnny Damon 3.00
390 Steve Finley 1.00
391 Edgardo Alfonzo 1.00
392 Jose Valentin 1.00
393 Jose Canseco 1.50
394 Ryan Klesko 1.00
395 David Cone 1.00
396 Jason Kendall 1.00
397 Placido Polanco 1.00
398 Glendon Rusch 1.00
399 Aaron Sele 1.00
400 D'Angelo Jimenez 1.00
401 Mark Grace 1.50
402 Al Leiter 1.00
403 Brian Jordan 1.00
404 Phil Nevin 1.00
405 Brent Abernathy 1.00
406 Kerry Wood 1.00
407 Alex Gonzalez 1.00
408 Robert Fick 1.00
409 Dmitri Young 1.00
410 Wes Helms 1.00
411 Trevor Hoffman 1.00
412 Rickey Henderson 2.00
413 Bobby Higginson 1.00
414 Gary Sheffield 1.50
415 Darryl Kile 1.00
416 Richie Sexson 1.50
417 Frank Menechino 1.00
418 Javy Lopez 1.00
419 Carlos Lee 1.00
420 Jon Lieber 1.00
421 Hank Blalock **RC** 6.00
422 Marlon Byrd **RC** 1.50
423 Jason Kinchen **RC** 1.00
424 Morgan Ensberg **RC** 5.00
425 Greg "Toe" Nash **RC** 1.00
426 Dennis Tankersley **RC** 1.00
427 Joel Pineiro 1.00
428 Chris Smith **RC** 1.00
429 Jake Gautreau **RC** 1.00
430 John Van Benschoten **RC** 1.50
431 Travis Thompson 1.00
432 Orlando Hudson **RC** 3.00
433 Jerome Williams **RC** 2.00
434 Kevin Reese 1.00
435 Ed Rogers **RC** 1.00
436 Grant Balfour **RC** 1.00
437 Adam Pettyjohn **RC** 1.00
438 Hee Seop Choi **RC** 2.00
439 Justin Morneau **RC** 15.00
440 Mitch Jones **RC** 1.00

Autographs

NM/M
Common Player: 90.00
BB Barry Bonds 180.00
RC Roger Clemens 120.00
AR Alex Rodriguez 90.00

Team Topps Legends Autographs

NM/M
Common Autograph: 30.00
Inserted 1:332
TT13F Warren Spahn/1965 40.00
TT21R Bob Feller/1952 30.00

1948 Bowman Reprints

NM/M
Complete Set (13): 10.00
Common Player: .75
Inserted 1:2
1 Ralph Kiner .75
2 Johnny Mize .75
3 Bobby Thomson .75
4 Yogi Berra 1.50
5 Phil Rizzuto 1.00
6 Bob Feller 1.00
7 Enos Slaughter .75
8 Stan Musial 2.00
9 Hank Sauer .75
10 Ferris Fain .75
11 Red Schoendienst .75
12 Allie Reynolds .75
13 Johnny Sain .75

1948 Bowman Reprint Autographs

NM/M
1 Warren Spahn 40.00
2 Bob Feller 40.00

1948 Reprint Relics

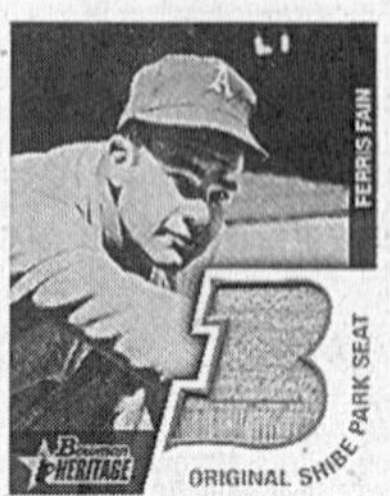

NM/M
Common Player: 8.00
Inserted 1:44
YB1 Yogi Berra 20.00
YB2 Yogi Berra 35.00
FF Ferris Fain 8.00
BF Bob Feller 12.00
RK Ralph Kiner 15.00
JM Johnny Mize 15.00
SM1 Stan Musial 30.00
PR Phil Rizzuto 15.00
HS Hank Sauer 8.00
RS Red Schoendienst 10.00
ES Enos Slaughter 10.00
BT Bobby Thomson 8.00

Chrome

Stars: 4-8X
SP's: 2-4X
Inserted 1:12

(See 2001 Bowman Heritage for checklist and base card values.)

2001 Bowman's Best Pre-Production

The flashy new look for Bowman's Best in 2001 was debuted in this three-card sample set. Identical in format to the issued cards, they have textured foil printing on front and a matte back.

		NM/M
Complete Set (3):		6.00
Common Player:		2.00
PP1	Todd Helton	3.00
PP2	Tim Hudson	2.00
PP3	Vernon Wells	2.00

2001 Bowman's Best

		NM/M
Complete Set (200):		
Common Player:		.20
Common SP (151-200):		5.00
Production 2,999		
Pack (5):		10.00
Box (24):		200.00
1	Vladimir Guerrero	1.00
2	Miguel Tejada	.50
3	Geoff Jenkins	.20
4	Jeff Bagwell	.75
5	Todd Helton	.75
6	Ken Griffey Jr.	2.00
7	Nomar Garciaparra	1.00
8	Chipper Jones	1.00
9	Darin Erstad	.40
10	Frank Thomas	1.00
11	Jim Thome	.50
12	Preston Wison	.20
13	Kevin Brown	.20
14	Derek Jeter	3.00
15	Scott Rolen	1.00
16	Ryan Klesko	.20
17	Jeff Kent	.40
18	Raul Mondesi	.20
19	Greg Vaughn	.20
20	Bernie Williams	.40
21	Mike Piazza	1.00
22	Richard Hidalgo	.20
23	Dean Palmer	.20
24	Roberto Alomar	.40
25	Sammy Sosa	1.00
26	Randy Johnson	1.00
27	Manny Ramirez	1.00
28	Roger Clemens	2.00
29	Terrence Long	.20
30	Jason Kendall	.20
31	Richie Sexson	.40
32	David Wells	.20
33	Andruw Jones	1.00
34	Pokey Reese	.20
35	Juan Gonzalez	.50
36	Carlos Beltran	.75
37	Shawn Green	.40
38	Mariano Rivera	.50
39	John Olerud	.20
40	Jim Edmonds	.40
41	Andres Galarraga	.20
42	Carlos Delgado	.75
43	Kris Benson	.20
44	Andy Pettitte	.40
45	Jeff Cirillo	.20
46	Maggilo Ordonez	.40
47	Tom Glavine	.40
48	Garret Anderson	.20
49	Cal Ripken Jr.	3.00
50	Pedro Martinez	1.00
51	Barry Bonds	3.00
52	Alex Rodriguez	2.50
53	Ben Grieve	.20
54	Edgar Martinez	.20
55	Jason Giambi	.75
56	Jeromy Burnitz	.20
57	Mike Mussina	.75
58	Moises Alou	.40
59	Sean Casey	.40
60	Greg Maddux	1.50
61	Tim Hudson	.50
62	Mark McGwire	2.00
63	Rafael Palmeiro	.75
64	Tony Batista	.20
65	Kazuhiro Sasaki	.20
66	Jorge Posada	.50
67	Johnny Damon	1.00
68	Brian Giles	.20
69	Jose Vidro	.20
70	Jermaine Dye	.20
71	Craig Biggio	.40
72	Larry Walker	.40
73	Eric Chavez	.40
74	David Segui	.20
75	Tim Salmon	.40
76	Javy Lopez	.20
77	Paul Konerko	.40
78	Barry Larkin	.40
79	Mike Hampton	.20
80	Bobby Higginson	.20
81	Mark Mulder	.40
82	Pat Burrell	.50
83	Kerry Wood	.50
84	J.T. Snow	.20
85	Ivan Rodriguez	.75
86	Edgardo Alfonzo	.20
87	Orlando Hernandez	.20
88	Gary Sheffield	.50
89	Mike Sweeney	.20
90	Carlos Lee	.20
91	Rafael Furcal	.40
92	Troy Glaus	.50
93	Bartolo Colon	.20
94	Cliff Floyd	.20
95	Barry Zito	.50
96	J.D. Drew	.40
97	Eric Karros	.20
98	Jose Valentin	.20
99	Ellis Burks	.20
100	David Justice	.20
101	Larry Barnes	.20
102	Rod Barajas	.20
103	Tony Pena	.20
104	Jerry Hairston Jr.	.20
105	Keith Ginter	.20
106	Corey Patterson	.40
107	Aaron Rowand	.20
108	Miguel Olivo	.20
109	Gookie Dawkins	.20
110	C.C. Sabathia	.20
111	Ben Petrick	.20
112	Eric Munson	.20
113	Ramon Castro	.20
114	Alex Escobar	.20
115	Josh Hamilton	.40
116	Jason Marquis	.20
117	Ben Davis	.20
118	Alex Cintron	.20
119	Julio Zuleta	.20
120	Ben Broussard	.20
121	Adam Everett	.20
122	Ramon Carvajal **RC**	.75
123	Felipe Lopez	.20
124	Alfonso Soriano	1.00
125	Jayson Werth	.20
126	Donzell McDonald	.20
127	Jason Hart	.25
128	Joe Crede	.50
129	Sean Burroughs	.20
130	Jack Cust	.20
131	Corey Smith	.20
132	Adrian Gonzalez	.40
133	J.R. House	.20
134	Steve Lomasney	.20
135	Tim Raines Jr.	.20
136	Tony Alvarez	.20
137	Doug Mientkiewicz	.20
138	Rocco Baldelli	.75
139	Jason Romano	.20
140	Vernon Wells	.40
141	Mike Bynum	.20
142	Xavier Nady	.20
143	Brad Wilkerson	.20
144	Ben Diggins	.20
145	Aubrey Huff	.20
146	Eric Byrnes	.20
147	Alex Gordon	.20
148	Roy Oswalt	.50
149	Brian Esposito	.20
150	Scott Seabol	.20
151	Erick Almonte **RC**	5.00
152	Gary Johnson **RC**	5.00
153	Pedro Liriano **RC**	5.00
154	Matt White **RC**	5.00
155	Luis Montanez **RC**	5.00
156	Brad Cresse	5.00
157	Wilson Betemit **RC**	6.00
158	Octavio Martinez **RC**	5.00
159	Adam Pettyjohn **RC**	5.00
160	Corey Spencer **RC**	5.00
161	Mark Burnett **RC**	5.00
162	Ichiro Suzuki **RC**	60.00
163	Alexis Gomez **RC**	5.00
164	Greg "Toe" Nash **RC**	5.00
165	Roberto Miniel **RC**	5.00
166	Justin Morneau **RC**	50.00
167	Ben Washburn **RC**	5.00
168	Bob Keppel **RC**	5.00
169	Deivi Mendez **RC**	5.00
170	Tsuyoshi Shinjo **RC**	5.00
171	Jared Abruzzo **RC**	5.00
172	Derrick Van Dusen **RC**	5.00
173	Hee Seop Choi **RC**	8.00
174	Albert Pujols **RC**	200.00
175	Travis Hafner **RC**	25.00
176	Ron Davenport **RC**	6.00
177	Luis Torres **RC**	5.00
178	Jake Peavy **RC**	30.00
179	Elvis Corporan **RC**	5.00
180	David Krynzel	5.00
181	Tony Blanco **RC**	5.00
182	Elpidio Guzman **RC**	5.00
183	Matt Butler **RC**	5.00
184	Joe Thurston **RC**	5.00
185	Andy Beal **RC**	5.00
186	Kevin Nulton **RC**	5.00
187	Sneideer Santos **RC**	5.00
188	Joe Dillon **RC**	5.00
189	Jeremy Blevins **RC**	5.00
190	Chris Amador **RC**	5.00
191	Mark Hendrickson **RC**	5.00
192	Willy Aybar **RC**	10.00
193	Antoine Cameron **RC**	5.00
194	Jonathan Johnson **RC**	5.00
195	Ryan Ketchner **RC**	5.00
196	Bjorn Ivy **RC**	5.00
197	Josh Kroeger **RC**	5.00
198	Ty Wigginton **RC**	5.00
199	Stubby Clapp **RC**	5.00
200	Jerrod Riggan **RC**	5.00

Autographs

		NM/M
Common Player:		8.00
Inserted 1:95		
SB	Sean Burroughs	8.00
BC	Brad Cresse	8.00
AG	Adrian Gonzalez	15.00
JH	Josh Hamilton	30.00
JRH	J.R. House	8.00
TL	Terrence Long	8.00
JR	Jon Rauch	8.00

Exclusive Rookie Autographs

		NM/M
Common Player:		6.00
Inserted 1:50		
WA	Willy Aybar	25.00
SC	Stubby Clapp	6.00
BI	Bjorn Ivy	6.00
JJ	Jonathan Johnson	6.00
TW	Ty Wigginton	6.00
JR	Jerrod Riggan	6.00
SS	Sneideer Santos	6.00
JB	Jeremy Blevins	6.00
MH	Mark Hendrickson	6.00

Franchise Favorites

		NM/M
Complete Set (8):		30.00
Common Player:		1.50
Inserted 1:16		
DM	Don Mattingly	6.00
AR	Alex Rodriguez	6.00
DE	Darin Erstad	1.50
DW	Dave Winfield	1.50
NR	Nolan Ryan	8.00
RJ	Reggie Jackson	2.00
MW	Don Mattingly, Dave Winfield	4.00
RR	Nolan Ryan, Alex Rodriguez	8.00
EJ	Darin Erstad, Reggie Jackson	2.00

Franchise Favorites Autographs

		NM/M
Common Player:		20.00
Inserted 1:556		
Combo 1:4,436		
DE	Darin Erstad	20.00
RJ	Reggie Jackson	40.00
EJ	Darin Erstad, Reggie Jackson	65.00
DM	Don Mattingly	60.00
MW	Don Mattingly, Dave Winfield	150.00
AR	Alex Rodriguez	80.00
NR	Nolan Ryan	80.00
RR	Nolan Ryan, Alex Rodriguez	300.00
DW	Dave Winfield	25.00

Franchise Favorites Relics

		NM/M
Common Player:		6.00
Jersey 1:139		
Pants 1:307		
Combo Relic 1:1,114		
JB	Jeff Bagwell	10.00
CB	Craig Biggio	6.00
BB	Craig Biggio, Jeff Bagwell	25.00
DE	Darin Erstad	6.00
RJ	Reggie Jackson	10.00
EJ	Reggie Jackson, Darin Erstad	25.00
DM	Don Mattingly	30.00
MW	Don Mattingly, Dave Winfield	65.00
AR	Alex Rodriguez	20.00
NR	Nolan Ryan	40.00
RR	Nolan Ryan, Alex Rodriguez	60.00
DW	Dave Winfield	8.00

Franchise Futures

		NM/M
Complete Set (12):		15.00
Common Player:		1.00
Inserted 1:24		
FF1	Josh Hamilton	1.00
FF2	Wes Helms	1.00
FF3	Alfonso Soriano	4.00
FF4	Nick Johnson	1.50
FF5	Jose Ortiz	1.00
FF6	Ben Sheets	1.50
FF7	Sean Burroughs	1.50
FF8	Ben Petrick	1.00
FF9	Corey Patterson	1.50
FF10	J.R. House	1.00
FF11	Alex Escobar	1.00
FF12	Travis Hafner	1.50

Game-Used Bats

		NM/M
Common Player:		5.00
Inserted 1:267		
PB	Pat Burrell	10.00
SB	Sean Burroughs	5.00
AG	Adrian Gonzalez	10.00
EM	Eric Munson	5.00
CP	Corey Patterson	8.00

Game-Worn Jerseys

		NM/M
Common Player:		5.00
Inserted 1:133		
EC	Eric Chavez	8.00
MM	Mark Mulder	8.00
JP	Jay Payton	5.00
PR	Pokey Reese	5.00
PW	Preston Wilson	5.00

Impact Players

		NM/M
Complete Set (20):		15.00
Common Player:		.50
Inserted 1:7		
IP1	Mark McGwire	3.00
IP2	Sammy Sosa	2.00
IP3	Manny Ramirez	1.00
IP4	Troy Glaus	1.00
IP5	Ken Griffey Jr.	2.00
IP6	Gary Sheffield	.75
IP7	Vladimir Guerrero	1.00
IP8	Carlos Delgado	.75
IP9	Jason Giambi	.75
IP10	Frank Thomas	1.50
IP11	Vernon Wells	.60
IP12	Carlos Pena	.50
IP13	Joe Crede	.50
IP14	Keith Ginter	.50
IP15	Aubrey Huff	.50
IP16	Brad Cresse	.50
IP17	Austin Kearns	.75
IP18	Nick Johnson	.50
IP19	Josh Hamilton	.50
IP20	Corey Patterson	.60

Rookie Fever

		NM/M
Complete Set (10):		10.00
Common Player:		.50
Inserted 1:10		
RF1	Chipper Jones	2.00
RF2	Preston Wilson	.50
RF3	Todd Helton	1.00
RF4	Jay Payton	.50
RF5	Ivan Rodriguez	.75
RF6	Manny Ramirez	1.00
RF7	Derek Jeter	4.00
RF8	Orlando Hernandez	.50
RF9	Marcus Quinn	.50
RF10	Terrence Long	.50

Team Topps

		NM/M
Common Player:		10.00
Overall odds 1:71.		
13R	Warren Spahn/1952	40.00
37R	Tug McGraw/1965	10.00
48R	Bobby Richardson/1957	15.00
25R	Luis Tiant/1965 + Exchange	10.00
31R	Clete Boyer/1957	15.00
23R	Gil McDougald/1952	15.00
27R	Andy Pafko/1952	15.00
28R	Herb Score/1956	15.00
18R	Bob Gibson/1959	40.00
29R	Moose Skowron/1954	15.00
37F	Tug McGraw/1985	10.00
28F	Herb Score/1962	15.00

2002 Bowman

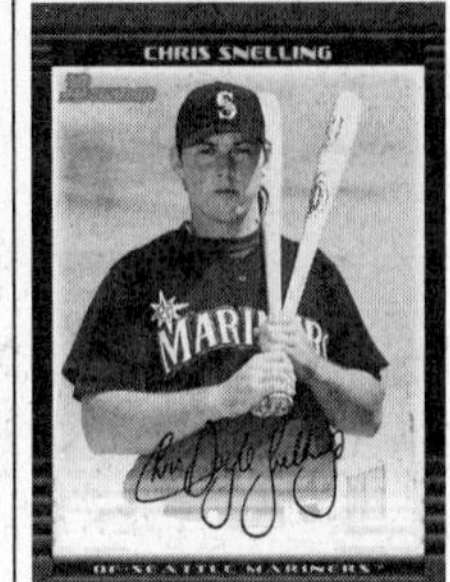

		NM/M
Complete Set (440):		70.00
Common Player:		.15
Common Rookie:		.40
Pack (10):		4.50
Box (24):		90.00
1	Adam Dunn	.50
2	Derek Jeter	2.00
3	Alex Rodriguez	1.50
4	Miguel Tejada	.50
5	Nomar Garciaparra	1.00
6	Toby Hall	.15
7	Brandon Duckworth	.15
8	Paul LoDuca	.15
9	Brian Giles	.15
10	C.C. Sabathia	.15
11	Curt Schilling	.75
12	Tsuyoshi Shinjo	.15
13	Ramon Hernandez	.15
14	Jose Cruz Jr.	.15

15 Albert Pujols 2.00
16 Joe Mays .15
17 Javy Lopez .15
18 J.T. Snow .15
19 David Segui .15
20 Jorge Posada .40
21 Doug Mientkiewicz .15
22 Jerry Hairston Jr. .15
23 Bernie Williams .40
24 Mike Sweeney .15
25 Jason Giambi .50
26 Ryan Dempster .15
27 Ryan Klesko .15
28 Mark Quinn .15
29 Jeff Kent .25
30 Eric Chavez .30
31 Adrian Beltre .25
32 Andruw Jones .50
33 Alfonso Soriano 1.00
34 Aramis Ramirez .40
35 Greg Maddux 1.00
36 Andy Pettitte .50
37 Bartolo Colon .15
38 Ben Sheets .40
39 Bobby Higginson .15
40 Ivan Rodriguez .50
41 Brad Penny .15
42 Carlos Lee .25
43 Damion Easley .15
44 Preston Wilson .15
45 Jeff Bagwell .50
46 Eric Milton .15
47 Rafael Palmeiro .50
48 Gary Sheffield .40
49 J.D. Drew .25
50 Jim Thome .50
51 Ichiro Suzuki 1.50
52 Bud Smith .15
53 Chan Ho Park .15
54 D'Angelo Jimenez .15
55 Ken Griffey Jr. 1.50
56 Wade Miller .15
57 Vladimir Guerrero .50
58 Troy Glaus .40
59 Shawn Green .40
60 Kerry Wood .40
61 Jack Wilson .15
62 Kevin Brown .25
63 Marcus Giles .15
64 Pat Burrell .40
65 Larry Walker .25
66 Sammy Sosa .75
67 Raul Mondesi .15
68 Tim Hudson .25
69 Lance Berkman .40
70 Mike Mussina .40
71 Barry Zito .40
72 Jimmy Rollins .40
73 Barry Bonds 2.00
74 Craig Biggio .40
75 Todd Helton .50
76 Roger Clemens 1.50
77 Frank Catalanotto .15
78 Josh Towers .15
79 Roy Oswalt .40
80 Chipper Jones 1.00
81 Cristian Guzman .15
82 Darin Erstad .40
83 Freddy Garcia .15
84 Jason Tyner .15
85 Carlos Delgado .40
86 Jon Lieber .15
87 Juan Pierre .15
88 Matt Morris .15
89 Phil Nevin .15
90 Jim Edmonds .40
91 Magglio Ordonez .25
92 Mike Hampton .15
93 Rafael Furcal .25
94 Richie Sexson .40
95 Luis Gonzalez .25
96 Scott Rolen .50
97 Tim Redding .15
98 Moises Alou .25
99 Jose Vidro .15
100 Mike Piazza 1.00
101 Pedro Martinez .75
102 Geoff Jenkins .15
103 Johnny Damon .75
104 Mike Cameron .15
105 Randy Johnson .75
106 David Eckstein .15
107 Javier Vazquez .15
108 Mark Mulder .25
109 Robert Fick .15
110 Roberto Alomar .40
111 Wilson Betemit .15
112 Chris Tritle **RC** .50
113 Ed Rogers .15
114 Juan Pena .15
115 Josh Beckett .50
116 Juan Cruz .15
117 Noochie Varner **RC** .50
118 Taylor Buchholz **RC** .50
119 Mike Rivera .15
120 Hank Blalock .40
121 Hansel Izquierdo **RC** .50
122 Orlando Hudson .15
123 Bill Hall .15
124 Jose Reyes .50
125 Juan Rivera .15
126 Eric Valent .15
127 Scotty Layfield **RC** .40
128 Austin Kearns .50
129 Nic Jackson **RC** .50
130 Chris Baker **RC** .50
131 Chad Qualls **RC** .40
132 Marcus Thames .15
133 Nathan Haynes .15
134 Brett Evert .15
135 Joe Borchard .15
136 Ryan Christianson .15
137 Josh Hamilton .15
138 Corey Patterson .15
139 Travis Wilson .15
140 Alex Escobar .15
141 Alexis Gomez .15
142 Nick Johnson .15
143 Kenny Kelly .15
144 Marlon Byrd .15
145 Kory DeHaan .15
146 Matt Belisle .15
147 Carlos Hernandez .15
148 Sean Burroughs .15
149 Angel Berroa .15
150 Aubrey Huff .15
151 Travis Hafner .40
152 Brandon Berger .15
153 David Krynzel .15
154 Ruben Salazar .15
155 J.R. House .15
156 Juan Silvestre .15
157 Dewon Brazelton .15
158 Jayson Werth .15
159 Larry Barnes .15
160 Elvis Pena .15
161 Ruben Gotay **RC** .40
162 Tommy Marx **RC** .50
163 John Suomi **RC** .40
164 Javier Colina .15
165 Greg Sain **RC** .40
166 Robert Cosby **RC** .40
167 Angel Pagan **RC** 2.00
168 Ralph Santana **RC** .40
169 Joe Orloski **RC** .40
170 Shayne Wright **RC** .40
171 Jay Caligiuri **RC** .25
172 Greg Montalbano **RC** .50
173 Rich Harden **RC** 3.00
174 Rich Thompson **RC** .40
175 Fred Bastardo **RC** .50
176 Alejandro Giron **RC** .40
177 Jesus Medrano **RC** .40
178 Kevin Deaton **RC** .40
179 Mike Rosamond **RC** .50
180 Jon Guzman **RC** .40
181 Gerard Oakes **RC** .40
182 Francisco Liriano **RC** 8.00
183 Matt Allegra **RC** .50
184 Mike Snyder **RC** .40
185 James Shanks **RC** .40
186 Anderson Hernandez **RC** .40
187 Dan Trumble **RC** .40
188 Luis DePaula **RC** .40
189 Randall Shelley **RC** .40
190 Richard Lane **RC** .40
191 Antwon Rollins **RC** .50
192 Ryan Bukvich **RC** .40
193 Derrick Lewis .15
194 Eric Miller **RC** .40
195 Justin Schuda **RC** .40
196 Brian West **RC** .40
197 Adam Roller **RC** .40
198 Neal Frendling **RC** .40
199 Jeremy Hill **RC** .40
200 James Barrett **RC** .50
201 Brett Kay **RC** .50
202 Ryan Mottl **RC** .50
203 Brad Nelson **RC** .50
204 Juan Gonzalez .15
205 Curtis Legendre **RC** .40
206 Ronald Acuna **RC** .40
207 Chris Flinn **RC** .40
208 Nick Alvarez **RC** .40
209 Jason Ellison **RC** .40
210 Blake McGinley **RC** .40
211 Dan Phillips **RC** .50
212 Demetrius Heath **RC** .40
213 Eric Bruntlett **RC** .40
214 Joe Jiannetti **RC** .40
215 Mike Hill **RC** .40
216 Ricardo Cordova **RC** .40
217 Mark Hamilton **RC** .50
218 David Mattox **RC** .40
219 Jose Morban **RC** .50
220 Scott Wiggins **RC** .50
221 Steve Green .15
222 Brian Rogers .15
223 Chin-Hui Tsao .40
224 Kenny Baugh .15
225 Nate Teut .15
226 Josh Wilson **RC** .40
227 Christian Parker .15
228 Tim Raines Jr. .15
229 Anastacio Martinez **RC** .40
230 Richard Lewis .15
231 Tim Kalita **RC** .40
232 Edwin Almonte **RC** .40
233 Hee Seop Choi .25
234 Ty Howington .15
235 Victor Alvarez **RC** .40
236 Morgan Ensberg .15
237 Jeff Austin **RC** .40
238 Luis Terrero .15
239 Adam Wainwright .15
240 Clint Weibl **RC** .40
241 Eric Cyr **RC** .40
242 Marlyn Tisdale **RC** .40
243 John VanBenschoten .15
244 Ryan Raburn **RC** .40
245 Miguel Cabrera .75
246 Jung Bong .15
247 Raul Chavez **RC** .50
248 Erik Bedard .15
249 Chris Snelling **RC** .50
250 Joe Rogers **RC** .40
251 Nate Field **RC** .40
252 Matt Herges .15
253 Matt Childers **RC** .50
254 Erick Almonte .15
255 Nick Neugebauer .15
256 Ron Calloway **RC** .40
257 Seung Jun Song .15
258 Brandon Phillips .15
259 Cole Barthel .25
260 Jason Lane .15
261 Jae Weong Seo .15
262 Randy Flores .15
263 Scott Chiasson .15
264 Chase Utley 1.00
265 Tony Alvarez .15
266 Ben Howard **RC** .40
267 Nelson Castro **RC** .40
268 Mark Lukasiewicz .15
269 Eric Glaser **RC** .40
270 Rob Henkel **RC** .40
271 Jose Valverde **RC** .40
272 Ricardo Rodriguez .15
273 Chris Smith .15
274 Mark Prior .75
275 Miguel Olivo .15
276 Ben Broussard .15
277 Zach Sorensen .15
278 Brian Mallette **RC** .40
279 Brad Wilkerson .15
280 Carl Crawford .15
281 Chone Figgins **RC** .40
282 Jimmy Alvarez **RC** .40
283 Gavin Floyd 1.50
284 Josh Bonifay **RC** .50
285 Garrett Guzman **RC** .50
286 Blake Williams .15
287 Matt Holliday .50
288 Ryan Madson .15
289 Luis Torres .15
290 Jeff Verplancke **RC** .40
291 Nate Espy **RC** .40
292 Jeff Lincoln **RC** .40
293 Ryan Snare **RC** .40
294 Jose Ortiz .15
295 Eric Munson .15
296 Denny Bautista .15
297 Willy Aybar .15
298 Kelly Johnson .15
299 Justin Morneau .50
300 Derrick Van Dusen .15
301 Chad Petty .15
302 Mike Restovich .15
303 Shawn Fagan .15
304 Yurendell DeCaster **RC** .40
305 Justin Wayne .15
306 Mike Peeples **RC** .40
307 Joel Guzman **RC** .75
308 Ryan Vogelsong .15
309 Jorge Padilla **RC** .50
310 Grady Sizemore .75
311 Joe Jester **RC** .40
312 Jim Journell .15
313 Bobby Seay .15
314 Ryan Church **RC** 1.00
315 Grant Balfour .15
316 Mitch Jones .15
317 Travis Foley .50
318 Bobby Crosby .15
319 Adrian Gonzalez .15
320 Ronnie Merrill .15
321 Joel Pineiro .15
322 John-Ford Griffin .15
323 Brian Forystek **RC** .40
324 Sean Douglass .15
325 Manny Delcarmen **RC** .40
326 Donnie Bridges .15
327 Jim Kavourias .15
328 Gabe Gross .15
329 Greg "Toe" Nash .15
330 Bill Ortega .15
331 Joey Hammond **RC** .40
332 Ramon Moreta **RC** .40
333 Ron Davenport .15
334 Brett Myers .15
335 Carlos Pena .15
336 Ezequiel Astacio **RC** .40
337 Edwin Yan **RC** .50
338 Josh Girdley .15
339 Shaun Boyd .15
340 Juan Rincon .15
341 Chris Duffy **RC** .50
342 Jason Kinchen .15
343 Brad Thomas .15
344 David Kelton .15
345 Rafael Soriano .15
346 Colin Young **RC** .50
347 Eric Byrnes .15
348 Chris Narveson **RC** .50
349 John Rheinecker **RC** .40
350 Mike Wilson **RC** .40
351 Justin Sherrod **RC** .50
352 Deivi Mendez .15
353 Wily Mo Pena .15
354 Brett Roneberg **RC** .50
355 Trey Lunsford **RC** .40
356 Jimmy Gobble **RC** .50
357 Brent Butler .15
358 Aaron Heilman .15
359 Wilkin Ruan .15
360 Brian Wolfe **RC** .40
361 Cody Ransom .15
362 Koyie Hill .40
363 Scott Cassidy .15
364 Tony Fontana **RC** .50
365 Mark Teixeira .50
366 Doug Sessions **RC** .40
367 Victor Hall .15
368 Josh Cisneros **RC** .40
369 Kevin Mench .15
370 Tike Redman .15
371 Jeff Heaverlo .15
372 Carlos Brackley **RC** .40
373 Brad Hawpe .50
374 Jesus Colome .15
375 David Espinosa .15
376 Jesse Foppert .75
377 Ross Peeples **RC** .40
378 Alexander Requena **RC** .40
379 Joe Mauer **RC** 10.00
380 Carlos Silva .15
381 David Wright 40.00
382 Craig Kuzmic **RC** .50
383 Peter Zamora **RC** .40
384 Matt Parker **RC** .40
385 Ricardo Rodriguez .15
386 Gary Cates Jr. **RC** .40
387 Justin Reid **RC** .50
388 Jake Mauer **RC** .50
389 John-Ford Griffin .15
390 Josh Barfield 2.00
391 Luis Maza .15
392 Henry Pichardo **RC** .40
393 Michael Floyd **RC** .40
394 Clint Nageotte **RC** .75
395 Jim Warden .15
396 Mauricio Lara **RC** .50
397 Alejandro Cadena **RC** .40
398 Jonny Gomes **RC** 3.00
399 Jason Bulger **RC** .50
400 Bobby Jenks **RC** 1.00
401 David Gil **RC** .40
402 Joel Crump **RC** .40
403 Kazuhisa Ishii **RC** .75
404 So Taguchi **RC** .75
405 Ryan Doumit **RC** 1.00
406 Macay McBride .15
407 Brandon Claussen .15
408 Chin-Feng Chen .15
409 Josh Phelps .25
410 Freddie Money **RC** .40
411 Clifford Bartosh **RC** .40
412 Josh Pearce .15
413 Lyle Overbay .15
414 Ryan Anderson .15
415 Terrance Hill **RC** .40
416 John Rodriguez **RC** .40
417 Richard Stahl **RC** .40
418 Brian Specht .15
419 Chris Latham **RC** .50
420 Carlos Cabrera **RC** .40
421 Jose Bautista **RC** .50
422 Kevin Frederick **RC** .40
423 Jerome Williams .50
424 Napoleon Calzado **RC** .50
425 Benito Baez .15
426 Xavier Nady .15
427 Jason Botts **RC** .40
428 Steve Bechler **RC** .50
429 Reed Johnson **RC** .50
430 Mark Outlaw **RC** .40
431 Billy Sylvester .15
432 Luke Lockwood .15
433 Jake Peavy .25
434 Alfredo Amezega .15
435 Aaron Cook **RC** .50
436 Josh Shaffer **RC** .40
437 Dan Wright .15
438 Ryan Gripp **RC** .50
439 Alex Herrera .15
440 Jason Bay **RC** 4.00

Gold

Stars: 1-2.5X
Rookies: 1-2X
Inserted 1:1

Uncirculated

NM/M
Common Player: 4.00
Production 1,000 Sets
112 Chris Tritle 6.00
113 Ed Rogers 4.00
114 Juan Pena 4.00
115 Josh Beckett 8.00
116 Juan Cruz 4.00
117 Noochie Varner 6.00
118 Taylor Buchholz 4.00
119 Mike Rivera 4.00
120 Hank Blalock 8.00
121 Hansel Izquierdo 4.00
122 Orlando Hudson 4.00
123 Bill Hall 4.00
124 Jose Reyes 8.00
125 Juan Rivera 4.00
126 Eric Valent 4.00
127 Scotty Layfield 4.00
128 Austin Kearns 8.00
129 Nic Jackson 4.00
130 Chris Baker 4.00
131 Chad Qualls 4.00

Autographs

NM/M
Common Autograph: 5.00
Inserted 1:37
AA Alfredo Amezaga 5.00
GA Garrett Atkins 20.00
JB Josh Beckett 35.00
WB Wilson Betemit 5.00
LB Larry Bigbie 5.00
HB Hank Blalock 20.00
TB Tony Blanco 5.00
JAB Jason Botts 5.00
MB Marlon Byrd 10.00
BDC Brian Cardwell 5.00
BC Ben Christensen 5.00
BAC Brandon Claussen 8.00
JD Jeff Davanon 5.00
MD Manny Delcarmen 8.00
RF Randy Flores 5.00
RF Ryan Franklin 5.00
KG Keith Ginter 5.00
TH Toby Hall 5.00
AH Aubrey Huff 10.00
GJ Gary Johnson 5.00
NJ Nick Johnson 10.00
CK Charles Kegley 5.00
JL Jason Lane 10.00
NN Nick Neugebauer 5.00
RO Roy Oswalt 15.00
JP Juan Pena 5.00
MP Mark Prior 20.00
CR Cody Ransom 5.00
JS Juan Silvestre 5.00
TS Termel Sledge 8.00
BS Bud Smith 5.00
CS Chris Smith 5.00
WS Will Smith 5.00
BJS Brian Specht 5.00
CT Chris Tritle 8.00
CU Chase Utley 75.00
DV Domingo Valdez 5.00
NV Noochie Varner 5.00
RV Ryan Vogelsong 5.00
JLW Jerome Williams 8.00
DW Dan Wright 5.00

Autographed Futures Game Game-Used Base

NM/M
Randomly Inserted
TB Toby Hall 15.00

Autographed Futures Game Game-Worn Jersey

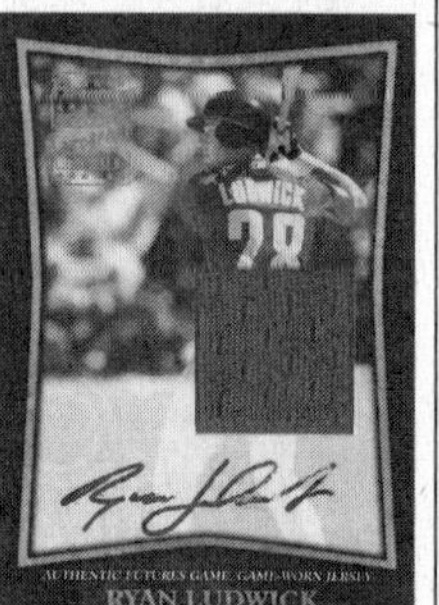

NM/M
Common Player: 15.00
Inserted 1:193
WB Wilson Betemit 15.00
CH Carlos Hernandez 15.00
JRH J.R. House 15.00
NJ Nick Johnson 20.00
RL Ryan Ludwick 15.00
CP Carlos Pena 15.00
DT Dennis Tankersley 15.00
JW Jerome Williams 20.00

Game-Used Relics

NM/M
Common Player: 4.00
Inserted 1:165
JA1 Jared Abruzzo 4.00
JA2 Jared Abruzzo 4.00
GA Garrett Atkins 8.00
AB Angel Berroa 6.00
AC Antoine Cameron 4.00
RC Ryan Church 6.00
ALC Alex Cintron 4.00
NC Nate Cornejo 4.00
RD Ryan Dittfurth 4.00
AE Adam Everett 4.00
AF1 Alex Fernandez 4.00
AF2 Alex Fernandez 4.00
AG Alexis Gomez 4.00
CG Cristian Guerrero 4.00
CI Cesar Izturis 4.00
DJ D'Angelo Jimenez 4.00
FJ Forrest Johnson 4.00
AK Austin Kearns 6.00
JL Jason Lane 4.00
RM Ryan Madson 4.00
NN Nick Neugebauer 4.00
CP Corey Patterson 6.00
RS Ruben Salazar 4.00
RST Richard Stahl 4.00
JS Jamal Strong 4.00
CY Colin Young 4.00

2002 Bowman Chrome

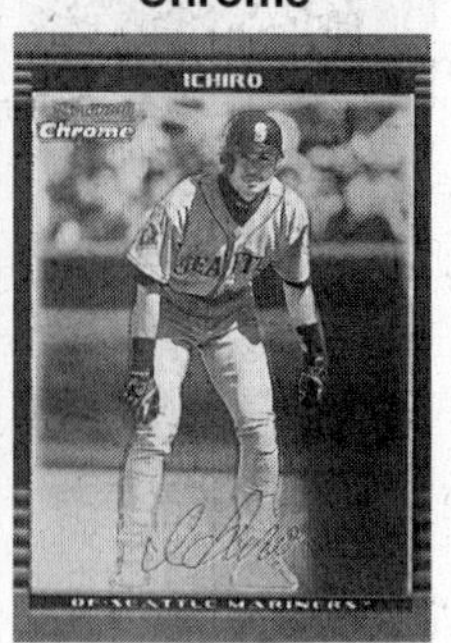

NM/M
Complete Set (405):
Common Player: .25
Common SP: 3.00
Inserted 1:3
Common Auto. (384-402,405) 10.00
Inserted 1:18
Pack (4): 12.00
Box (18): 200.00
1 Adam Dunn .50
2 Derek Jeter 3.00
3 Alex Rodriguez 2.50
4 Miguel Tejada .50
5 Nomar Garciaparra 1.00
6 Toby Hall .25
7 Brandon Duckworth .25
8 Paul LoDuca .25
9 Brian Giles .25
10 C.C. Sabathia .25
11 Curt Schilling .75
12 Tsuyoshi Shinjo .25
13 Ramon Hernandez .25
14 Jose Cruz Jr. .25
15 Albert Pujols 3.00
16 Joe Mays .25
17 Javy Lopez .25
18 J.T. Snow .25
19 David Segui .25
20 Jorge Posada .50
21 Doug Mientkiewicz .25
22 Jerry Hairston Jr. .25
23 Bernie Williams .50
24 Mike Sweeney .25
25 Jason Giambi .75
26 Ryan Dempster .25
27 Ryan Klesko .25
28 Mark Quinn .25
29 Jeff Kent .25
30 Eric Chavez .40
31 Adrian Beltre .40
32 Andruw Jones 1.00
33 Alfonso Soriano 1.00
34 Aramis Ramirez .50
35 Greg Maddux 1.50
36 Andy Pettitte .50
37 Bartolo Colon .25
38 Ben Sheets .40
39 Bobby Higginson .25
40 Ivan Rodriguez .60
41 Brad Penny .25
42 Carlos Lee .40
43 Damion Easley .25
44 Preston Wilson .25
45 Jeff Bagwell 1.00
46 Eric Milton .25
47 Rafael Palmeiro .75
48 Gary Sheffield .50
49 J.D. Drew .40
50 Jim Thome .75
51 Ichiro Suzuki 2.00
52 Bud Smith .25
53 Chan Ho Park .25
54 D'Angelo Jimenez .25
55 Ken Griffey Jr. 2.00
56 Wade Miller .25
57 Vladimir Guerrero 1.00
58 Troy Glaus .50
59 Shawn Green .40
60 Kerry Wood .50
61 Jack Wilson .25
62 Kevin Brown .25
63 Marcus Giles .25
64 Pat Burrell .50
65 Larry Walker .40
66 Sammy Sosa 1.00
67 Raul Mondesi .25
68 Tim Hudson .40
69 Lance Berkman .50
70 Mike Mussina .50
71 Barry Zito .50
72 Jimmy Rollins .75

73 Barry Bonds 3.00
74 Craig Biggio .40
75 Todd Helton .75
76 Roger Clemens 2.00
77 Frank Catalanotto .25
78 Josh Towers .25
79 Roy Oswalt .40
80 Chipper Jones 1.00
81 Cristian Guzman .25
82 Darin Erstad .60
83 Freddy Garcia .25
84 Jason Tyner .25
85 Carlos Delgado .50
86 Jon Lieber .25
87 Juan Pierre .25
88 Matt Morris .25
89 Phil Nevin .25
90 Jim Edmonds .40
91 Magglio Ordonez .40
92 Mike Hampton .25
93 Rafael Furcal .40
94 Richie Sexson .40
95 Luis Gonzalez .40
96 Scott Rolen .75
97 Tim Redding .25
98 Moises Alou .40
99 Jose Vidro .25
100 Mike Piazza 1.50
101 Pedro Martinez 1.00
102 Geoff Jenkins .25
103 Johnny Damon 1.00
104 Mike Cameron .25
105 Randy Johnson 1.00
106 David Eckstein .25
107 Javier Vazquez .25
108 Mark Mulder .40
109 Robert Fick .25
110 Roberto Alomar .40
111 Wilson Betemit .25
112 Chris Tritle/SP **RC** 4.00
113 Ed Rogers .25
114 Juan Pena .25
115 Josh Beckett .50
116 Juan Cruz .25
117 Noochie Varner/SP **RC** 5.00
118 Blake Williams .25
119 Mike Rivera .25
120 Hank Blalock .50
121 Hansel Izquierdo/ SP **RC** 4.00
122 Orlando Hudson .25
123 Bill Hall .25
124 Jose Reyes 1.00
125 Juan Rivera .25
126 Eric Valent .25
127 Scotty Layfield/SP **RC** 3.00
128 Austin Kearns .50
129 Nic Jackson/SP **RC** 5.00
130 Scott Chiasson .25
131 Chad Qualls/SP **RC** 4.00
132 Marcus Thames .25
133 Nathan Haynes .25
134 Joe Borchard .25
135 Josh Hamilton .25
136 Corey Patterson .25
137 Travis Wilson .25
138 Alex Escobar .25
139 Alexis Gomez .25
140 Nick Johnson .25
141 Marlon Byrd .25
142 Kory DeHaan .25
143 Carlos Hernandez .25
144 Sean Burroughs .25
145 Angel Berroa .25
146 Aubrey Huff .25
147 Travis Hafner .75
148 Brandon Berger .25
149 J.R. House .25
150 Dewon Brazelton .25
151 Jayson Werth .25
152 Larry Barnes .25
153 Ruben Gotay/SP **RC** 6.00
154 Tommy Marx/SP **RC** 3.00
155 John Suomi/SP **RC** 4.00
156 Javier Colina/SP 3.00
157 Greg Sain/SP **RC** 3.00
158 Robert Cosby/SP **RC** 4.00
159 Angel Pagan/SP **RC** 8.00
160 Ralph Santana **RC** 1.50
161 Joe Orloski **RC** 1.50
162 Shayne Wright/SP **RC** 3.00
163 Jay Caligiuri/SP **RC** 4.00
164 Greg Montalbano/ SP **RC** 5.00
165 Rich Harden/SP **RC** 25.00
166 Rich Thompson/ SP **RC** 3.00
167 Fred Bastardo/SP **RC** 3.00
168 Alejandro Giron/SP **RC** 3.00
169 Jesus Medrano/SP **RC** 3.00
170 Kevin Deaton/SP **RC** 4.00
171 Mike Rosamond **RC** 1.50
172 Jon Guzman/SP **RC** 3.00
173 Gerard Oakes/SP **RC** 4.00
174 Francisco Liriano/ SP **RC** 40.00
175 Matt Allegra/SP **RC** 4.00
176 Mike Snyder/SP **RC** 4.00
177 James Shanks/SP **RC** 3.00
178 Anderson Hernandez/ SP **RC** 4.00
179 Dan Trumble/SP **RC** 3.00
180 Luis DePaula/SP **RC** 4.00
181 Randall Shelley/SP **RC** 4.00
182 Richard Lane/SP **RC** 3.00
183 Antwon Rollins/SP **RC** 4.00
184 Ryan Bukvich/SP **RC** 4.00
185 Derrick Lewis/SP 3.00
186 Eric Miller/SP **RC** 3.00
187 Justin Schuda/SP **RC** 3.00
188 Brian West/SP **RC** 4.00
189 Brad Wilkerson .25
190 Neal Frendling/SP **RC** 3.00
191 Jeremy Hill/SP **RC** 3.00
192 James Barrett/SP **RC** 4.00
193 Brett Kay/SP **RC** 3.00
194 Ryan Mottl/SP **RC** 4.00
195 Brad Nelson/SP **RC** 5.00
196 Juan Gonzalez/SP 3.00
197 Curtis Legendre/ SP **RC** 3.00
198 Ronald Acuna/SP **RC** 3.00
199 Chris Flinn/SP **RC** 3.00
200 Nick Alvarez/SP **RC** 3.00
201 Jason Ellison/SP **RC** 4.00
202 Blake McGinley/SP **RC** 3.00
203 Dan Phillips/SP **RC** 3.00
204 Demetrius Heath/ SP **RC** 3.00
205 Eric Bruntlett/SP **RC** 3.00
206 Joe Jiannetti/SP **RC** 3.00
207 Mike Hill/SP **RC** 3.00
208 Ricardo Cordova/ SP **RC** 3.00
209 Mark Hamilton/SP **RC** 3.00
210 David Mattox/SP **RC** 3.00
211 Jose Morban/SP **RC** 5.00
212 Scott Wiggins/SP **RC** 3.00
213 Steve Green .25
214 Brian Rogers/SP 3.00
215 Kenny Baugh .25
216 Anastacio Martinez/ SP **RC** 3.00
217 Richard Lewis .25
218 Tim Kalita/SP **RC** 3.00
219 Edwin Almonte/SP **RC** 3.00
220 Hee Seop Choi .25
221 Ty Howington .25
222 Victor Alvarez/SP **RC** 3.00
223 Morgan Ensberg .25
224 Jeff Austin/SP **RC** 3.00
225 Clint Weibl/SP **RC** 4.00
226 Eric Cyr **RC** 1.00
227 Marlyn Tisdale/SP **RC** 3.00
228 John VanBenschoten .25
229 Ruben Salazar .25
230 Raul Chavez/SP **RC** 4.00
231 Brett Evert .25
232 Joe Rogers/SP **RC** 4.00
233 Adam Wainwright .50
234 Matt Herges .50
235 Matt Childers/SP **RC** 4.00
236 Nick Neugebauer .25
237 Carl Crawford 1.00
238 Seung Jun Song .25
239 Randy Flores .25
240 Jason Lane .25
241 Chase Utley 4.00
242 Ben Howard/SP **RC** 3.00
243 Eric Glaser/SP **RC** 3.00
244 Josh Wilson **RC** 1.00
245 Jose Valverde/SP **RC** 4.00
246 Chris Smith .25
247 Mark Prior 1.00
248 Brian Mallette/SP **RC** 3.00
249 Chone Figgins/SP **RC** 8.00
250 Jimmy Alvarez/SP **RC** 3.00
251 Luis Terrero .25
252 Josh Bonifay/SP **RC** 4.00
253 Garrett Guzman/SP **RC** 3.00
254 Jeff Verplancke/SP **RC** 3.00
255 Nate Espy/SP **RC** 4.00
256 Jeff Lincoln/SP **RC** 3.00
257 Ryan Snare/SP **RC** 4.00
258 Jose Ortiz .25
259 Denny Bautista .25
260 Willy Aybar .25
261 Kelly Johnson 1.00
262 Shawn Fagan .25
263 Yurendell DeCaster/ SP **RC** 3.00
264 Mike Peeples/SP **RC** 3.00
265 Joel Guzman **RC** 3.00
266 Ryan Vogelsong .25
267 Jorge Padilla/SP **RC** 3.00
268 Joe Jester/SP **RC** 3.00
269 Ryan Church/SP **RC** 10.00
270 Mitch Jones .25
271 Travis Foley/SP 3.00
272 Bobby Crosby 2.00
273 Adrian Gonzalez .75
274 Ronnie Merrill .25
275 Joel Pineiro .25
276 John-Ford Griffin .25
277 Brian Forystek/SP **RC** 3.00
278 Sean Douglass .25
279 Manny Delcarmen/ SP **RC** 5.00
280 Jim Kavourias/SP 3.00
281 Gabe Gross .25
282 Bill Ortega .25
283 Joey Hammond/SP **RC** 3.00
284 Brett Myers .50
285 Carlos Pena .50
286 Ezequiel Astacio/ SP **RC** 3.00
287 Edwin Yan/SP **RC** 3.00
288 Chris Duffy/SP **RC** 6.00
289 Jason Kinchen .25
290 Rafael Soriano .25
291 Colin Young **RC** .50
292 Eric Byrnes .25
293 Chris Narveson/SP **RC** 5.00
294 John Rheinecker **RC** .50
295 Mike Wilson/SP **RC** 4.00
296 Justin Sherrod/SP **RC** 5.00
297 Deivi Mendez .25
298 Wily Mo Pena .25
299 Brett Roneberg/SP **RC** 4.00
300 Trey Lunsford/SP **RC** 3.00
301 Christian Parker .25
302 Brent Butler .25
303 Aaron Heilman .25
304 Wilkin Ruan .25
305 Kenny Kelly .25
306 Cody Ransom .25
307 Koyie Hill/SP 3.00
308 Tony Fontana/SP **RC** 3.00
309 Mark Teixeira 2.00
310 Doug Sessions/SP **RC** 3.00
311 Josh Cisneros/SP **RC** 3.00
312 Carlos Brackley/SP **RC** 3.00
313 Tim Raines Jr. .25
314 Ross Peeples/SP **RC** 5.00
315 Alexander Requena/ SP **RC** 5.00
316 Chin-Hui Tsao .25
317 Tony Alvarez .25
318 Craig Kuzmic/SP **RC** 3.00
319 Peter Zamora/SP **RC** 3.00
320 Matt Parker/SP **RC** 3.00
321 Keith Ginter .25
322 Gary Cates Jr./SP **RC** 3.00
323 Matt Belisle .25
324 Ben Broussard .25
324 Jake Mauer/auto **RC** 10.00
325 Dennis Tankersley .25
326 Juan Silvestre .25
327 Henry Pichardo/SP **RC** 3.00
328 Michael Floyd/SP **RC** 3.00
329 Clint Nageotte/SP **RC** 6.00
330 Raymond Cabrera/ SP **RC** 3.00
331 Mauricio Lara/SP **RC** 4.00
332 Alejandro Cadena/ SP **RC** 3.00
333 Jonny Gomes/SP **RC** 15.00
334 Jason Bulger/SP **RC** 4.00
335 Nate Teut .25
336 David Gil/SP **RC** 3.00
337 Joel Crump/SP **RC** 3.00
338 Brandon Phillips .25
339 Macay McBride .50
340 Brandon Claussen 1.00
341 Josh Phelps .25
342 Freddie Money/SP **RC** 4.00
343 Clifford Bartosh/SP **RC** 3.00
344 Terrance Hill/SP **RC** 3.00
345 John Rodriguez/ SP **RC** 4.00
346 Chris Latham/SP **RC** 3.00
347 Carlos Cabrera/SP **RC** 3.00
348 Jose Bautista/SP **RC** 5.00
349 Kevin Frederick/SP **RC** 3.00
350 Jerome Williams .75
351 Napoleon Calzado/ SP **RC** 3.00
352 Benito Baez/SP 3.00
353 Xavier Nady .25
354 Jason Botts/SP **RC** 8.00
355 Steve Bechler/SP **RC** 4.00
356 Reed Johnson/SP **RC** 8.00
357 Mark Outlaw/SP **RC** 3.00
358 Jake Peavy 1.00
359 Josh Shaffer/SP **RC** 3.00
360 Dan Wright/SP 3.00
361 Ryan Gripp/SP **RC** 3.00
362 Nelson Castro/SP **RC** 3.00
363 Jason Bay/SP **RC** 30.00
364 Franklin German/ SP **RC** 3.00
365 Corwin Malone/SP 3.00
366 Kelly Ramos/SP **RC** 3.00
367 John Ennis/SP **RC** 3.00
368 George Perez/SP 3.00
369 Rene Reyes/SP **RC** 3.00
370 Rolando Viera/SP **RC** 3.00
371 Earl Snyder/SP **RC** 4.00
372 Kyle Kane/SP **RC** 3.00
373 Mario Ramos/SP 3.00
374 Tyler Yates/SP **RC** 3.00
375 Jason Young/SP **RC** 5.00
376 Chris Bootcheck/ SP **RC** 5.00
377 Jesus Cota/SP **RC** 5.00
378 Corky Miller/SP 3.00
379 Matt Erickson/SP **RC** 3.00
380 Justin Huber/SP **RC** 5.00
381 Felix Escalona/SP **RC** 3.00
382 Kevin Cash/SP **RC** 3.00
383 J.J. Putz/SP **RC** 3.00
384 Chris Snelling **RC** 20.00
385 David Wright 450.00
386 Brian Wolfe **RC** 10.00
387 Justin Reid **RC** 10.00
389 Ryan Raburn **RC** 10.00
390 Josh Barfield 30.00
391 Joe Mauer **RC** 150.00
392 Bobby Jenks **RC** 25.00
393 Rob Henkel **RC** 10.00
394 Jimmy Gobble **RC** 10.00
395 Jesse Foppert 15.00
396 Gavin Floyd 25.00
397 Nate Field **RC** 10.00
398 Ryan Doumit **RC** 25.00
399 Ron Calloway **RC** 10.00
400 Taylor Buchholz **RC** 15.00
401 Adam Roller **RC** 10.00
402 Cole Barthel 10.00
403 Kazuhisa Ishii/SP **RC** 6.00
404 So Taguchi/SP **RC** 4.00
405 Chris Baker **RC** 10.00

Refractors

Star Refractors (1-220): 2-3X
SP Refractors: .5-1.5X
Production 500
X-Fractors (1-220): 3-5X
SP X-Fractors: .75-2X
Production 250:
Gold Refractors (1-220): 8-15X
SP Gold Refractors: 2-4X
Production 50
Refractor Autos. (384-402,405) .75-1.5X
Production 500
X-Fractor Autos.: .75-2X
Production 250
Gold Autographs: 2-4X
Production 50

Uncirculated

Cards: 1-30X
Production 350
Autos. 10 cards of each player.
No Pricing

Ishii & Taguchi Autographs

NM/M
Refractors: .75-1.5X
Production 100
X-Fractors: 2-4X
Production 50
Golds: Production 10
403 Kazuhisa Ishii 50.00
404 So Taguchi 25.00

Rookie Reprints

NM/M
Complete Set (20): 25.00
Common Player: 1.00
Inserted 1:6
Refractors: 1.5-2X
Inserted 1:18
JB Jeff Bagwell 1.50
BC Bartolo Colon 1.00
CD Carlos Delgado 1.00
JG Juan Gonzalez 1.50
LG Luis Gonzalez 1.00
KG Ken Griffey Jr. 3.00
VG Vladimir Guerrero 2.00
DJ Derek Jeter 5.00
AJ Andruw Jones 1.50
CJ Chipper Jones 2.50
JK Jason Kendall 1.00
MP Mike Piazza 3.00
JP Jorge Posada 1.00
IR Ivan Rodriguez 1.00
SR Scott Rolen 1.00
GS Gary Sheffield 1.00
MS Mike Sweeney 1.00
FT Frank Thomas 1.50
LW Larry Walker 1.00
BW Bernie Williams 1.00

2002 Bowman Draft Picks & Prospects

NM/M
Complete Set (165): 35.00
Common Player: .15
Common RC: .25
Pack: (4 + 2 Chrome: 10.00
Box (24): 200.00
BDP1 Clint Everts **RC** .75
BDP2 Fred Lewis **RC** 1.00
BDP3 Jonathan Broxton **RC** .75
BDP4 Jason Anderson **RC** .25
BDP5 Mike Eusebio **RC** .25
BDP6 Zack Greinke **RC** 2.00
BDP7 Joe Blanton **RC** 2.00
BDP8 Sergio Santos **RC** .50
BDP9 Jason Cooper **RC** .50
BDP10 Delwyn Young **RC** 1.00
BDP11 Jeremy Hermida **RC** 3.00
BDP12 Dan Ortmeyer **RC** .40
BDP13 Kevin Jepsen **RC** .50
BDP14 Russ Adams **RC** 1.00
BDP15 Mike Nixon **RC** .40
BDP16 Nick Swisher **RC** 4.00
BDP17 Cole Hamels **RC** 10.00
BDP18 Brian Dopirak **RC** 1.00
BDP19 James Loney **RC** 4.00
BDP20 Denard Span **RC** .50
BDP21 Billy Petrick **RC** .25
BDP22 Jared Doyle **RC** .25
BDP23 Jeff Francoeur **RC** 15.00
BDP24 Nick Bourgeois **RC** .25
BDP25 Matt Cain **RC** 8.00
BDP26 John McCurdy **RC** .40
BDP27 Mark Kiger **RC** .15
BDP28 Bill Murphy **RC** .40
BDP29 Matt Craig **RC** .25
BDP30 Mike Megrew **RC** .50
BDP31 Ben Crockett **RC** .25
BDP32 Luke Hagerty **RC** .50
BDP33 Matt Whitney **RC** 1.00
BDP34 Dan Meyer **RC** .50
BDP35 Jeremy Brown **RC** .50
BDP36 Doug Johnson **RC** .25
BDP37 Steve Obenchain **RC** .25
BDP38 Matt Clanton **RC** .40
BDP39 Mark Teahen **RC** 1.50
BDP40 Thomas Carrow **RC** .25
BDP41 Micah Schilling **RC** .50
BDP42 Blair Johnson **RC** .25
BDP43 Jason Pridie **RC** .75
BDP44 Joey Votto **RC** 4.00
BDP45 Taber Lee **RC** .25
BDP46 Adam Peterson **RC** .25
BDP47 Adam Donachie **RC** .40
BDP48 Josh Murray **RC** .40
BDP49 Brent Clevlen **RC** 1.50
BDP50 Chad Pleiness **RC** .40
BDP51 Zach Hammes **RC** .50
BDP52 Chris Snyder **RC** .50
BDP53 Chris Smith .25
BDP54 Justin Maureau **RC** .25
BDP55 David Bush **RC** 1.00
BDP56 Tim Gilhooly **RC** .25
BDP57 Blair Barbier **RC** .25
BDP58 Zach Segovia **RC** .50
BDP59 Jeremy Reed **RC** 2.00
BDP60 Matt Pender **RC** .25
BDP61 Eric Thomas **RC** .25
BDP62 Justin Jones **RC** 1.00
BDP63 Brian Slocum **RC** .40
BDP64 Larry Broadway **RC** 1.00
BDP65 Bo Flowers **RC** .25
BDP66 Scott White **RC** .75
BDP67 Steve Stanley **RC** .25
BDP68 Alex Merricks **RC** .25
BDP69 Josh Womack **RC** .40
BDP70 Dave Jensen **RC** .25
BDP71 Curtis Granderson **RC** 4.00
BDP72 Pat Osborn **RC** .40
BDP73 Nic Carter **RC** .25
BDP74 Mitch Talbot **RC** .25
BDP75 Don Murphy **RC** .25
BDP76 Val Majewski **RC** .50
BDP77 Javy Rodriguez **RC** .25
BDP78 Fernando Pacheco **RC** .40
BDP79 Steve Russell **RC** .25
BDP80 Jon Slack **RC** .25
BDP81 John Baker **RC** .25
BDP82 Aaron Coonrod **RC** .25
BDP83 Josh Johnson **RC** 2.00
BDP84 Jake Blalock **RC** .75
BDP85 Alex Hart **RC** .50
BDP86 Wes Bankston **RC** 1.50
BDP87 Josh Rupe **RC** .40
BDP88 Dan Cevette **RC** .75
BDP89 Kiel Fisher **RC** .50
BDP90 Alan Rick **RC** .25
BDP91 Charlie Morton **RC** .50
BDP92 Chad Spann **RC** .50
BDP93 Kyle Boyer **RC** .25
BDP94 Bob Malek **RC** .25
BDP95 Ryan Rodriguez **RC** .25
BDP96 Jordan Renz **RC** .25
BDP97 Randy Frye **RC** .25
BDP98 Rich Hill **RC** 3.00
BDP99 B.J. Upton **RC** 5.00
BDP100 Dan Christensen **RC** .50
BDP101 Casey Kotchman 1.00
BDP102 Eric Good **RC** .25
BDP103 Mike Fontenot **RC** .75
BDP104 John Webb **RC** .25
BDP105 Jason Dubois **RC** .75
BDP106 Ryan Kibler **RC** .25
BDP107 Jhonny Peralta **RC** 2.50
BDP108 Kirk Saarloos .75
BDP109 Rhett Parrott **RC** .25
BDP110 Jason Grove **RC** .25
BDP111 Colt Griffin .50
BDP112 Dallas McPherson 1.00
BDP113 Oliver Perez **RC** 1.50
BDP114 Marshall McDougall **RC** .25
BDP115 Mike Wood **RC** .40
BDP116 Scott Hairston 1.00
BDP117 Jason Simontacchi **RC** .50
BDP118 Taggert Bozied **RC** 1.00
BDP119 Shelley Duncan **RC** 2.00
BDP120 Dontrelle Willis **RC** 6.00
BDP121 Sean Burnett .15
BDP122 Aaron Cook **RC** .25
BPD123 Brett Evert .15
BDP124 Jimmy Journell .15
BDP125 Brett Myers .15
BDP126 Brad Baker .15
BDP127 Billy Traber .50
BDP128 Adam Wainwright .15
BDP129 Jason Young **RC** .40
BDP130 John Buck .15
BDP131 Kevin Cash **RC** .25
BDP132 Jason Stokes **RC** .50
BDP133 Drew Henson .25
BDP134 Chad Tracy **RC** 1.50
BDP135 Orlando Hudson .15
BDP136 Brandon Phillips .15
BDP137 Joe Borchard .15
BDP138 Marlon Byrd .15
BDP139 Carl Crawford .25
BDP140 Michael Restovich .15
BDP141 Corey Hart **RC** 1.50
BDP142 Edwin Almonte .15
BDP143 Francis Beltran **RC** .25
BDP144 Jorge De La Rosa **RC** .50
BDP145 Gerardo Garcia **RC** .25
BDP146 Franklyn German **RC** .25
BDP147 Francisco Liriano 4.00
BDP148 Francisco Rodriguez .50
BDP149 Ricardo Rodriguez .15
BDP150 Seung Jun Song .15
BDP151 John Stephens .15
BDP152 Justin Huber **RC** 1.00
BDP153 Victor Martinez .50
BDP154 Hee Seop Choi .15
BDP155 Justin Morneau .50
BDP156 Miguel Cabrera .75
BDP157 Victor Diaz **RC** 1.00
BDP158 Jose Reyes .50
BDP159 Omar Infante **RC** .25
BDP160 Angel Berroa .15
BDP161 Tony Alvarez .15
BDP162 Shin-Soo Choo **RC** 1.00
BDP163 Wily Mo Pena .15
BDP164 Andres Torres .15
BDP165 Jose Lopez **RC** 2.00

Gold

Rookies: .75-1.5X
Inserted 1:1

Fabric of Future

NM/M
Common Player: 4.00
Inserted 1:55
EA Edwin Almonte 4.00
TA Tony Alvarez 4.00
FB Francis Beltran 4.00
AB Angel Berroa 5.00
SB Sean Burnett 4.00
KC Kevin Cash 4.00
HC Hee Seop Choi 5.00
SC Shin-Soo Choo 10.00
CC Carl Crawford 6.00
JR Jorge de la Rosa 4.00
VD Victor Diaz 6.00
GG Gerardo Garcia 4.00
FG Franklyn German 4.00
CH Corey Hart 10.00
DH Drew Henson 6.00
JH Justin Huber 6.00
JK Josh Karp 4.00
FL Francisco Liriano 15.00
JL Jose Lopez 8.00
BM Brett Meyers 6.00
WP Wily Mo Pena 6.00
MR Michael Restovich 4.00
JS John Stephens 4.00
JS Jason Stokes 5.00
AT Andres Torres 4.00
BT Billy Traber 4.00
CT Chad Tracy 8.00
AW Adam Wainwright 10.00

Freshman Fiber

NM/M
Common Player: 4.00
Bat inserted 1:605
Jersey 1:45
BA Brent Abernathy 4.00

DB Dewon Brazelton 4.00
MB Marlon Byrd/Bat 4.00
TH Toby Hall 4.00
JH Josh Hamilton 8.00
AH Aubrey Huff 6.00
AK Austin Kearns/Bat 4.00
JK Joe Kennedy 4.00
JS Jared Sandberg 4.00
JWS Jason Standridge 4.00
MT Mark Teixeira/Bat 10.00
JV John Van Benschoten 4.00

Signs of the Future

NM/M
Common Autograph: 5.00
EB Erik Bedard 40.00
LB Larry Bigbie 5.00
TB Taylor Buchholz 5.00
DD Daniel Denham 5.00
ME Morgan Ensberg 10.00
MF Mike Fontenot 8.00
KH Kris Honel 5.00
BI Brandon Inge 10.00
NJ Nic Jackson 5.00
MJ Mitch Jones 5.00
BK Bob Keppel 5.00
TL Todd Linden 8.00
JM Jake Mauer 8.00
JEM Justin Morneau 25.00
LN Lance Niekro 8.00
CP Christian Parra 5.00
BP Brandon Phillips 15.00
JR Juan Rivera 5.00
BS Bud Smith 5.00
AT Chad Tracy 15.00
JW Jerome Williams 8.00

2002 Bowman Chrome Draft Picks & Prospects

NM/M
Complete Set (175): 275.00
Common Player: .25
Common RC: .75
1-165 Two Per Pack
Common Auto.(166-175): 10.00
Auto.'s Inserted 1:45
BDP1 Clint Everts **RC** 2.00
BDP2 Fred Lewis **RC** 4.00
BDP3 Jonathan Broxton **RC** 2.00
BDP4 Jason Anderson **RC** .75
BDP5 Mike Eusebio **RC** .75
BDP6 Zack Greinke **RC** 5.00
BDP7 Joe Blanton **RC** 5.00
BDP8 Sergio Santos **RC** 1.50
BDP9 Jason Cooper **RC** 1.50
BDP10 Delwyn Young **RC** 3.00
BDP11 Jeremy Hermida **RC** 15.00
BDP12 Dan Ortmeyer **RC** 1.50
BDP13 Kevin Jepsen **RC** 2.00
BDP14 Russ Adams **RC** 2.00
BDP15 Mike Nixon **RC** .75
BDP16 Nick Swisher **RC** 15.00
BDP17 Cole Hamels **RC** 35.00
BDP18 Brian Dopirak **RC** 3.00
BDP19 James Loney **RC** 15.00
BDP20 Denard Span **RC** 2.00
BDP21 Billy Petrick **RC** .75
BDP22 Jared Doyle **RC** .75
BDP23 Jeff Francoeur **RC** 50.00
BDP24 Nick Bourgeois **RC** .75
BDP25 Matt Cain **RC** 30.00
BDP26 John McCurdy **RC** .75
BDP27 Mark Kiger **RC** .75
BDP28 Bill Murphy **RC** 1.00
BDP29 Matt Craig **RC** 1.00
BDP30 Mike Megrew **RC** 1.00
BDP31 Ben Crockett **RC** .75
BDP32 Luke Hagerty **RC** 1.50
BDP33 Matt Whitney **RC** 1.00
BDP34 Dan Meyer **RC** 1.50
BDP35 Jeremy Brown **RC** 1.00
BDP36 Doug Johnson **RC** .75
BDP37 Steve Obenchain **RC** .75
BDP38 Matt Clanton **RC** 1.00
BDP39 Mark Teahen **RC** 4.00
BDP40 Thomas Carrow **RC** .75
BDP41 Micah Schilling **RC** 1.00
BDP42 Blair Johnson **RC** 1.00
BDP43 Jason Pridie **RC** 1.00
BDP44 Joey Votto **RC** 15.00
BDP45 Taber Lee **RC** .75
BDP46 Adam Peterson **RC** .75
BDP47 Adam Donachie **RC** 1.00
BDP48 Josh Murray **RC** 1.00
BDP49 Brent Clevlen **RC** 4.00
BDP50 Chad Pleiness **RC** 1.00
BDP51 Zach Hammes **RC** 1.50
BDP52 Chris Snyder **RC** 1.50
BDP53 Chris Smith .50
BDP54 Justin Maureau **RC** .75
BDP55 David Bush **RC** 3.00
BDP56 Tim Gilhooly **RC** .75
BDP57 Blair Barbier **RC** .75
BDP58 Zach Segovia **RC** 1.00
BDP59 Jeremy Reed **RC** 4.00
BDP60 Matt Pender **RC** .75
BDP61 Eric Thomas **RC** .75
BDP62 Justin Jones **RC** 1.50
BDP63 Brian Slocum **RC** 1.00
BDP64 Larry Broadway **RC** 1.50
BDP65 Bo Flowers **RC** .75
BDP66 Scott White **RC** 1.00
BDP67 Steve Stanley **RC** .75
BDP68 Alex Merricks **RC** .75
BDP69 Josh Womack **RC** .75
BDP70 Dave Jensen **RC** .75
BDP71 Curtis Granderson **RC** 15.00
BDP72 Pat Osborn **RC** 1.50
BDP73 Nic Carter **RC** .75
BDP74 Mitch Talbot **RC** .75
BDP75 Don Murphy **RC** .75
BDP76 Val Majewski **RC** 1.50
BDP77 Javy Rodriguez **RC** .75
BDP78 Fernando Pacheco **RC** 1.00
BDP79 Steve Russell **RC** .75
BDP80 Jon Slack **RC** .75
BDP81 John Baker **RC** .75
BDP82 Aaron Coonrod **RC** .75
BDP83 Josh Johnson **RC** 6.00
BDP84 Jake Blalock **RC** 1.50
BDP85 Alex Hart **RC** 1.50
BDP86 Wes Bankston **RC** 5.00
BDP87 Josh Rupe **RC** 1.00
BDP88 Dan Cevette **RC** 1.00
BDP89 Kiel Fisher **RC** 1.00
BDP90 Alan Rick **RC** .75
BDP91 Charlie Morton **RC** 1.00
BDP92 Chad Spann **RC** 1.00
BDP93 Kyle Boyer **RC** 1.00
BDP94 Bob Malek **RC** .75
BDP95 Ryan Rodriguez **RC** .75
BDP96 Jordan Renz **RC** .75
BDP97 Randy Frye **RC** .75
BDP98 Rich Hill **RC** 10.00
BDP99 B.J. Upton **RC** 15.00
BDP100 Dan Christensen **RC** 1.00
BDP101 Casey Kotchman 4.00
BDP102 Eric Good **RC** .75
BDP103 Mike Fontenot **RC** 2.00
BDP104 John Webb **RC** .75
BDP105 Jason Dubois **RC** 1.50
BDP106 Ryan Kibler **RC** .75
BDP107 Jhonny Peralta **RC** 8.00
BDP108 Kirk Saarloos 1.50
BDP109 Rhett Parrott **RC** .75
BDP110 Jason Grove **RC** .75
BDP111 Colt Griffin 1.00
BDP112 Dallas McPherson 2.50
BDP113 Oliver Perez **RC** 4.00
BDP114 Marshall McDougall **RC** .75
BDP115 Mike Wood **RC** 1.00
BDP116 Scott Hairston 1.50
BDP117 Jason Simontacchi **RC** 1.00
BDP118 Taggert Bozied **RC** 1.50
BDP119 Shelley Duncan **RC** 4.00
BDP120 Dontrelle Willis **RC** 15.00
BDP121 Sean Burnett .25
BDP122 Aaron Cook **RC** .75
BPD123 Brett Evert .25
BDP124 Jimmy Journell .25
BDP125 Brett Myers .25
BDP126 Brad Baker .25
BDP127 Billy Traber 1.50
BDP128 Adam Wainwright .50
BDP129 Jason Young 1.00
BDP130 John Buck .25
BDP131 Kevin Cash .25
BDP132 Jason Stokes **RC** 1.50
BDP133 Drew Henson .50
BDP134 Chad Tracy **RC** 4.00
BDP135 Orlando Hudson .50
BDP136 Brandon Phillips .25
BDP137 Joe Borchard .25
BDP138 Marlon Byrd .25
BDP139 Carl Crawford .25
BDP140 Michael Restovich .25
BDP141 Corey Hart **RC** 6.00
BDP142 Edwin Almonte .25
BDP143 Francis Beltran **RC** 1.00
BDP144 Jorge De La Rosa **RC** .75
BDP145 Gerardo Garcia **RC** .75
BDP146 Franklyn German **RC** .75
BDP147 Francisco Liriano 10.00
BDP148 Francisco Rodriguez .50
BDP149 Ricardo Rodriguez .25
BDP150 Seung Jun Song .25
BDP151 John Stephens .25
BDP152 Justin Huber 2.00
BDP153 Victor Martinez .50
BDP154 Hee Seop Choi .25
BDP155 Justin Morneau .25
BDP156 Miguel Cabrera 2.00
BDP157 Victor Diaz **RC** .75
BDP158 Jose Reyes .75
BDP159 Omar Infante **RC** .75
BDP160 Angel Berroa .25
BDP161 Tony Alvarez .25
BDP162 Shin-Soo Choo **RC** 4.00
BDP163 Wily Mo Pena .25
BDP164 Andres Torres .25
BDP165 Jose Lopez **RC** 4.00
BDP166 Scott Moore/Auto. **RC** 15.00
BDP167 Chris Gruler/Auto. **RC** 15.00
BDP168 Joe Saunders/Auto. **RC** 20.00
BDP169 Jeff Francis/Auto. **RC** 30.00
BDP170 Royce Ring/Auto. **RC** 10.00
BDP171 Greg Miller/Auto. 20.00
BDP172 Brandon Weeden/Auto. **RC** 10.00
BDP173 Drew Meyer/Auto. **RC** 10.00
BDP174 Khalil Greene/Auto. **RC** 50.00
BDP175 Mark Schramek/Auto. **RC** 10.00

Refractor

Cards 1-165: 2-4X
Rookies 1-175: 2-3X
1-165 Production 300 Sets
166-175 Inserted 1:154

Gold Refractor

Cards 1-165: 8-15X
Rookies 1-165: 5-10X
1-165 Production 50 Sets
166-175: No Pricing

X-Fractor

Cards 1-165: 2-5X
Rookies 1-165: 3-4X
Rookies 166-175: .75-1.5X
1-165 Production 150 Sets
166-175 Inserted 1:309

2002 Bowman Heritage

NM/M
Complete Set (439): 190.00
Common Player: .25
Common SP: 1.00
Inserted 1:2
Black Box Variations: 2-3X
Inserted 1:2
Pack (10): 3.00
Box (24): 60.00
1 Brent Abernathy .25
2 Jermaine Dye .25
3 James Shanks **RC** .40
4 Chris Flinn **RC** .40
5 Mike Peeples/SP **RC** 1.50
6 Gary Sheffield .50
7 Livan Hernandez/SP 1.00
8 Jeff Austin **RC** .40
9 Jeremy Giambi .25
10 Adam Roller **RC** .50
11 Sandy Alomar Jr./SP 1.00
12 Matt Williams/SP 1.00
13 Hee Seop Choi .25
14 Jose Offerman .25
15 Robin Ventura .25
16 Craig Biggio .50
17 David Wells .40
18 Rob Henkel **RC** .40
19 Edgar Martinez .25
20 Matt Morris/SP 2.00
21 Jose Valentin .25
22 Barry Bonds 2.50
23 Justin Schuda **RC** .50
24 Josh Phelps .25
25 John Rodriguez **RC** .50
26 Angel Pagan **RC** 1.50
27 Aramis Ramirez .50
28 Jack Wilson .25
29 Roger Clemens 2.00
30 Kazuhisa Ishii **RC** .50
31 Carlos Beltran .75
32 Drew Henson/SP 1.50
33 Kevin Young/SP 1.00
34 Juan Cruz .25
35 Curtis Legendre **RC** .40
36 Jose Morban **RC** .50
37 Ricardo Cordova/SP **RC** 1.50
38 Adam Everett .25
39 Mark Prior .75
40 Jose Bautista **RC** .75
41 Travis Foley .25
42 Kerry Wood .50
43 B.J. Surhoff .25
44 Moises Alou .40
45 Joey Hammond **RC** .50
46 Eric Bruntlett **RC** .50
47 Carlos Guillen .25
48 Joe Crede .40
49 Dan Phillips **RC** .50
50 Jason LaRue .25
51 Javy Lopez .25
52 Larry Bigbie/SP 1.00
53 Chris Baker **RC** .75
54 Marty Cordova .25
55 C.C. Sabathia .25
56 Mike Piazza 1.00
57 Brian Giles .25
58 Mike Bordick/SP 1.00
59 Tyler Houston/SP 1.00
60 Gabe Kapler .25
61 Ben Broussard .25
62 Steve Finley/SP 1.50
63 Koyie Hill .25
64 Jeff D'Amico .25
65 Edwin Almonte **RC** .50
66 Pedro J. Martinez 1.00
67 Travis Fryman/SP 1.50
68 Brady Clark .25
69 Reed Johnson/SP **RC** 2.00
70 Mark Grace/SP 4.00
71 Tony Batista/SP 1.00
72 Roy Oswalt .50
73 Pat Burrell .50
74 Dennis Tankersley .25
75 Ramon Ortiz .25
76 Neal Frendling/SP **RC** 1.50
77 Omar Vizquel/SP 2.00
78 Hideo Nomo .50
79 Orlando Hernandez/SP 1.50
80 Andy Pettitte .50
81 Cole Barthel .25
82 Bret Boone .25
83 Alfonso Soriano 1.00
84 Brandon Duckworth .25
85 Ben Grieve .25
86 Mike Rosamond/SP **RC** 1.50
87 Luke Prokopec .25
88 Chone Figgins **RC** 1.50
89 Rick Ankiel/SP 1.50
90 David Eckstein .25
91 Corey Koskie .25
92 David Justice .25
93 Jimmy Alvarez **RC** .40
94 Jason Schmidt .40
95 Reggie Sanders .25
96 Victor Alvarez **RC** .40
97 Brett Roneberg **RC** .40
98 D'Angelo Jimenez .25
99 Hank Blalock .50
100 Juan Rivera .25
101 Mark Buehrle/SP 1.50
102 Juan Uribe .25
103 Royce Clayton/SP 1.00
104 Brett Kay **RC** .50
105 John Olerud .25
106 Richie Sexson .40
107 Chipper Jones 1.00
108 Adam Dunn .75
109 Tim Salmon/SP 1.50
110 Eric Karros .25
111 Jose Vidro .25
112 Jerry Hairston Jr. .25
113 Anastacio Martinez **RC** .50
114 Robert Fick/SP 1.50
115 Randy Johnson 1.00
116 Trot Nixon/SP 2.00
117 Nick Bierbrodt/SP 1.00
118 Jim Edmonds .40
119 Rafael Palmeiro .75
120 Jose Macias .25
121 Josh Beckett .50
122 Sean Douglass .25
123 Jeff Kent .25
124 Tim Redding .25
125 Xavier Nady .25
126 Carl Everett .25
127 Joe Randa .25
128 Luke Hudson/SP 1.00
129 Eric Miller **RC** .40
130 Melvin Mora .25
131 Adrian Gonzalez .25
132 Larry Walker/SP 1.50
133 Nic Jackson/SP **RC** 2.00
134 Mike Lowell/SP 1.00
135 Jim Thome .75
136 Eric Milton .25
137 Rich Thompson/SP **RC** 1.50
138 Placido Polanco/SP 1.00
139 Juan Pierre .25
140 David Segui .25
141 Chuck Finley .25
142 Felipe Lopez .25
143 Toby Hall .25
144 Fred Bastardo **RC** .50
145 Troy Glaus .75
146 Todd Helton .75
147 Ruben Gotay/SP **RC** 1.50
148 Darin Erstad .40
149 Ryan Gripp/SP **RC** 1.50
150 Orlando Cabrera .25
151 Jason Young **RC** .50
152 Sterling Hitchcock/SP 1.00
153 Miguel Tejada .75
154 Al Leiter .25
155 Taylor Buchholz **RC** .40
156 Juan Gonzalez .50
157 Damion Easley .25
158 Jimmy Gobble **RC** 1.00
159 Dennis Ulacia/SP 1.00
160 Shane Reynolds/SP 1.00
161 Javier Colina .25
162 Frank Thomas 1.00
163 Chuck Knoblauch .25
164 Sean Burroughs .25
165 Greg Maddux 1.50
166 Jason Ellison **RC** .50
167 Tony Womack .25
168 Randall Shelley/SP **RC** 1.50
169 Jason Marquis .25
170 Brian Jordan .25
171 Darryl Kile .25
172 Barry Zito .50
173 Matt Allegra/SP **RC** 1.50
174 Ralph Santana/SP **RC** 1.50
175 Carlos Lee .40
176 Richard Hidalgo/SP 1.00
177 Kevin Deaton **RC** .50
178 Juan Encarnacion .25
179 Mark Quinn .25
180 Rafael Furcal .40
181 Garret Anderson .50
182 David Wright 15.00
183 Jose Reyes .50
184 Mario Ramos/SP 1.00
185 J.D. Drew .50
186 Juan Gonzalez .50
187 Nick Neugebauer .25
188 Alejandro Giron **RC** .50
189 John Burkett .25
190 Ben Sheets .50
191 Vinny Castilla/SP 1.00
192 Cory Lidle .25
193 Fernando Vina .25
194 Russell Branyan/SP 1.00
195 Ben Davis .25
196 Angel Berroa .25
197 Alex Gonzalez .25
198 Jared Sandberg .25
199 Travis Lee/SP 1.00
200 Luis DePaula/SP **RC** 1.50
201 Ramon Hernandez/SP 1.00
202 Brandon Inge .25
203 Aubrey Huff .25
204 Mike Rivera .25
205 Brad Nelson **RC** .50
206 Colt Griffin/SP 2.00
207 Joel Pineiro .25
208 Adam Pettyjohn .25
209 Mark Redman .25
210 Roberto Alomar/SP 3.00
211 Denny Neagle .25
212 Adam Kennedy .25
213 Jason Arnold/SP 2.00
214 Jamie Moyer .25
215 Aaron Boone .25
216 Doug Glanville .25
217 Nick Johnson/SP 1.00
218 Mike Cameron/SP 1.50
219 Tim Wakefield/SP 1.50
220 Todd Stottlemyre/SP 1.00
221 Mo Vaughn .25
222 Vladimir Guerrero 1.00
223 Bill Ortega .25
224 Kevin Brown .25
225 Peter Bergeron/SP 1.00
226 Shannon Stewart/SP 1.50
227 Eric Chavez .50
228 Clint Weibl **RC** .40
229 Todd Hollandsworth/SP 1.00
230 Jeff Bagwell .75
231 Chad Qualls **RC** .40
232 Ben Howard **RC** 1.00
233 Rondell White/SP 1.50
234 Fred McGriff .20
235 Steve Cox/SP 1.00
236 Chris Tritle **RC** 1.50
237 Eric Valent .25
238 Joe Mauer **RC** 5.00
239 Shawn Green .40
240 Jimmy Rollins .75
241 Edgar Renteria .25
242 Edwin Yan **RC** .40
243 Noochie Varner **RC** .40
244 Kris Benson/SP 1.50
245 Mike Hampton .25
246 So Taguchi **RC** 1.00
247 Sammy Sosa 1.00
248 Terrence Long .25
249 Jason Bay **RC** 4.00
250 Kevin Millar/SP 1.00
251 Albert Pujols 2.50
252 Chris Latham **RC** .40
253 Eric Byrnes .25
254 Napoleon Calzado/SP **RC** 1.50
255 Bobby Higginson .25
256 Ben Molina .25
257 Torii Hunter/SP 3.00
258 Jason Giambi .75
259 Bartolo Colon .25
260 Benito Baez .25
261 Ichiro Suzuki 2.00
262 Mike Sweeney .25
263 Brian West **RC** .40
264 Brad Penny .25
265 Kevin Millwood/SP 2.00
266 Orlando Hudson .25
267 Doug Mientkiewicz .25
268 Luis Gonzalez/SP 1.50
269 Jay Caligiuri **RC** .40
270 Nate Cornejo/SP 1.00
271 Lee Stevens .25
272 Eric Hinske .25
273 Antwon Rollins **RC** .50
274 Bobby Jenks **RC** 1.00
275 Joe Mays .25
276 Josh Shaffer **RC** .40
277 Jonny Gomes **RC** 3.00
278 Bernie Williams .50
279 Ed Rogers .25
280 Carlos Delgado .50
281 Raul Mondesi/SP 1.50
282 Jose Ortiz .25
283 Cesar Izturis .25
284 Ryan Dempster/SP 1.00
285 Brian Daubach .25
286 Hansel Izquierdo **RC** .40
287 Mike Lieberthal/SP 1.00
288 Marcus Thames .25
289 Nomar Garciaparra 1.00
290 Brad Fullmer .25
291 Tino Martinez .25
292 James Barrett **RC** .40
293 Jacque Jones .25
294 Nick Alvarez/SP **RC** 1.50
295 Jason Grove/SP **RC** 1.50
296 Mike Wilson/SP **RC** 1.50
297 J.T. Snow .25
298 Cliff Floyd .25
299 Todd Hundley/SP 1.00
300 Tony Clark/SP 1.00
301 Demetrius Heath **RC** .40
302 Morgan Ensberg .25
303 Cristian Guzman .25
304 Frank Catalanotto .25
305 Jeff Weaver .25
306 Tim Hudson .50
307 Scott Wiggins/SP **RC** 1.50
308 Shea Hillenbrand/SP 2.00
309 Todd Walker/SP 1.00
310 Tsuyoshi Shinjo .25
311 Adrian Beltre .40
312 Craig Kuzmic **RC** .40
313 Paul Konerko .40
314 Scott Hairston 1.50
315 Chan Ho Park .25
316 Jorge Posada .40
317 Chris Snelling **RC** .75
318 Keith Foulke .25
319 John Smoltz .50
320 Ryan Church/SP **RC** 3.00
321 Mike Mussina .75
322 Tony Armas Jr/SP 1.00
323 Craig Counsell .25
324 Marcus Giles .25
325 Greg Vaughn .25
326 Curt Schilling .75
327 Jeromy Burnitz .25
328 Eric Byrnes .25
329 Johnny Damon .75
330 Michael Floyd/SP **RC** 1.50
331 Edgardo Alfonzo .25
332 Jeremy Hill **RC** .40
333 Josh Bonifay **RC** .40
334 Byung-Hyun Kim .25
335 Keith Ginter .25
336 Richard Acuna/SP **RC** 1.50
337 Mike Hill/SP **RC** 1.50
338 Sean Casey .25
339 Matt Anderson/SP 1.00
340 Dan Wright .25
341 Ben Petrick .25
342 Mike Sirotka/SP 1.00
343 Alex Rodriguez 2.50
344 Einar Diaz .25
345 Derek Jeter 2.50
346 Jeff Conine .25
347 Ray Durham/SP 1.00
348 Wilson Betemit/SP 1.00
349 Jeffrey Hammonds .25
350 Dan Trumble **RC** .40
351 Phil Nevin/SP 1.50
352 A.J. Burnett .25
353 Bill Mueller .25
354 Charles Nagy .25
355 Rusty Greer/SP 1.00
356 Jason Botts **RC** .25
357 Magglio Ordonez .50
358 Kevin Appier .25
359 Brad Radke .25
360 Chris George .25
361 Chris Piersoll **RC** .25
362 Ivan Rodriguez .75
363 Jim Kavourias .25
364 Rick Helling/SP 1.00
365 Dean Palmer .25
366 Rich Aurilia/SP 1.00
367 Ryan Vogelsong .25
368 Matt Lawton .25
369 Wade Miller .25
370 Dustin Hermanson .25

371 Craig Wilson .25
372 Todd Zeile/SP 1.00
373 Jon Guzman **RC** .40
374 Ellis Burks .25
375 Robert Cosby/SP **RC** 1.50
376 Jason Kendall .25
377 Scott Rolen/SP 4.00
378 Andruw Jones 1.00
379 Greg Sain **RC** .40
380 Paul LoDuca .25
381 Scotty Layfield **RC** .40
382 Drew Henson .50
383 Garrett Guzman **RC** .40
384 Jack Cust .25
385 Shayne Wright **RC** .40
386 Derrek Lee .75
387 Jesus Medrano **RC** .40
388 Javier Vazquez .25
389 Preston Wilson/SP 1.50
390 Gavin Floyd 1.50
391 Sidney Ponson/SP 1.00
392 Jose Hernandez .25
393 Scott Erickson/SP 1.00
394 Jose Valverde **RC** .40
395 Mark Hamilton/SP **RC** 1.50
396 Brad Cresse .25
397 Danny Bautista .25
398 Ray Lankford/SP 1.00
399 Miguel Batista/SP 1.00
400 Brent Butler .25
401 Manny Delcarmen/SP **RC** 1.50
402 Kyle Farnsworth/SP 1.00
403 Freddy Garcia .25
404 Joe Jiannetti **RC** .40
405 Josh Barfield 2.00
406 Corey Patterson .25
407 Josh Towers .25
408 Carlos Pena .25
409 Jeff Cirillo .25
410 Jon Lieber .25
411 Woody Williams/SP 1.00
412 Richard Lane/SP **RC** 1.50
413 Alex Gonzalez .25
414 Wilkin Ruan .25
415 Geoff Jenkins .25
416 Carlos Hernandez .25
417 Matt Clement/SP 1.50
418 Jose Cruz Jr. .25
419 Jake Mauer **RC** .50
420 Matt Childers **RC** .50
421 Tom Glavine/SP 2.50
422 Ken Griffey Jr. 2.00
423 Anderson Hernandez **RC** .40
424 John Suomi **RC** .40
425 Doug Sessions **RC** .40
426 Jaret Wright .25
427 Rolando Viera/SP **RC** 1.50
428 Aaron Sele .25
429 Dmitri Young .25
430 Ryan Klesko .25
431 Kevin Tapani/SP 1.00
432 Joe Kennedy .25
433 Austin Kearns .40
434 Roger Cedeno .25
435 Lance Berkman .50
436 Frank Menechino .25
437 Brett Myers .25
438 Bobby Abreu .50
439 Shawn Estes .25

Relics

NM/M
Common Player: 4.00
Inserted 1:47
EA Edgardo Alfonzo 4.00
JB Josh Beckett 8.00
BB Barry Bonds 20.00
EC Eric Chavez 6.00
CD Carlos Delgado 6.00
JE Jim Edmonds 8.00
DE Darin Erstad 4.00
NG Nomar Garciaparra 15.00
TG Tony Gwynn 10.00
TH Todd Helton 8.00
CJ Chipper Jones 10.00
PK Paul Konerko 8.00
GM Greg Maddux 15.00
EM Edgar Martinez 8.00
MP Mike Piazza 10.00
AP Albert Pujols 20.00
MR Mariano Rivera 8.00
IR Ivan Rodriguez 8.00
SR Scott Rolen 10.00
TS Tim Salmon 5.00
KS Kazuhiro Sasaki 4.00
JS John Smoltz 8.00
FT Frank Thomas 8.00
JT Jim Thome 8.00

LW Larry Walker 4.00
PW Preston Wilson 4.00

Autographs

NM/M
Common Player: 8.00
Inserted 1:45
LB Lance Berkman 20.00
HB Hank Blalock 15.00
KG Keith Ginter 8.00
TH Toby Hall 8.00
DH Drew Henson 15.00
KI Kazuhisa Ishii 25.00
CI Cesar Izturis 10.00
PL Paul LoDuca 15.00
JM Joe Mauer 75.00
RO Roy Oswalt 15.00
MP Mark Prior 20.00
AP Albert Pujols 250.00
JR Juan Rivera 8.00

1954 Bowman Reprints

NM/M
Complete Set (20): 40.00
Common Player: 2.00
Inserted 1:12
RA Richie Ashburn 2.00
YB Yogi Berra 4.00
DC Del Crandell 2.00
BF Bob Feller 2.50
WF Whitey Ford 4.00
NF Nellie Fox 2.00
CL Clem Labine 2.00
DL Don Larsen 3.00
JL Johnny Logan 2.00
WM Willie Mays 6.00
GM Gil McDougald 2.00
DM Don Mueller 2.00
JP Jimmy Piersall 2.00
AR Allie Reynolds 2.00
PR Phil Rizzuto 3.00
ES Enos Slaughter 2.00
DS Duke Snider 4.00
WW Wes Westrum 2.00
HW Hoyt Wilhelm 2.00
DW Davey Williams 2.00

1954 Bowman Reprint Autographs

NM/M
Common Player: 10.00
Inserted 1:118
YB Yogi Berra 50.00
DC Del Crandell 15.00
CL Clem Labine 15.00
JL Johnny Logan 15.00
DM Don Mueller 10.00
DW Davey Williams 10.00

Team Topps Legends Autographs

NM/M
Common Player: 8.00
Gil McDougald 8.00
Joe Pepitone 8.00
Bobby Richardson 8.00
Robin Roberts 12.00
Warren Spahn 30.00
Luis Tiant 8.00
Carl Yastrzemski 40.00

Chrome Refractor

Stars: 3-6X
SP's: 1-2X
Inserted 1:16
Gold Refractors: 4-8X
SP's: 2-3X
Inserted 1:32

2002 Bowman's Best

NM/M
Complete Set (181):
Common Player: .40
Common (91-181): 4.00
Inserted 1:Pack
Blue (1-90): 1-2X
Production 300
Red (1-90): 1-2X
Production 200
Gold (1-90): 3-6X
Production 50
Blue (91-181): .75-1X
Production 500
Red (91-181): 1-1.5X
Production 150
Gold (91-181): 1-2X
Production 50
Pack (5): 20.00
Box (10): 180.00
1 Josh Beckett .75
2 Derek Jeter 4.00
3 Alex Rodriguez 3.00
4 Miguel Tejada 1.00
5 Nomar Garciaparra 1.50
6 Aramis Ramirez .75
7 Jeremy Giambi .40
8 Bernie Williams .50
9 Juan Pierre .40
10 Chipper Jones 1.50
11 Jimmy Rollins .75
12 Alfonso Soriano 1.00
13 Daryle Ward .40
14 Paul Konerko .75
15 Tim Hudson .75
16 Doug Mientkiewicz .40
17 Todd Helton 1.00
18 Moises Alou .75
19 Juan Gonzalez .75
20 Jorge Posada .75
21 Jeff Kent .50
22 Roger Clemens 3.00
23 Phil Nevin .40
24 Brian Giles .40
25 Carlos Delgado 1.00
26 Jason Giambi .75
27 Vladimir Guerrero 1.50
28 Cliff Floyd .40
29 Shea Hillenbrand .40
30 Ken Griffey Jr. 2.50
31 Mike Piazza 1.50
32 Carlos Pena .40
33 Larry Walker .50
34 Magglio Ordonez .50
35 Mike Mussina .75
36 Andruw Jones 1.00
37 Mark Teixeira .75
38 Curt Schilling 1.00
39 Eric Chavez .60
40 Bartolo Colon .40
41 Eric Hinske .40
42 Sean Burroughs .40
43 Randy Johnson 1.00
44 Adam Dunn .75
45 Pedro Martinez 1.50
46 Garret Anderson .40
47 Jim Thome 1.00
48 Gary Sheffield 1.00
49 Tsuyoshi Shinjo .40
50 Albert Pujols 4.00
51 Ichiro Suzuki 3.00
52 C.C. Sabathia .40
53 Bobby Abreu .75
54 Ivan Rodriguez .75
55 J.D. Drew .50
56 Jacque Jones .40
57 Jason Kendall .40
58 Javier Vazquez .40
59 Jeff Bagwell .75
60 Greg Maddux 2.50
61 Jim Edmonds .50
62 Austin Kearns .50
63 Jose Vidro .40
64 Kevin Brown .40
65 Preston Wilson .40
66 Sammy Sosa 1.50
67 Lance Berkman .75
68 Mark Mulder .60
69 Marty Cordova .40
70 Frank Thomas 1.00
71 Mike Cameron .40
72 Mike Sweeney .40
73 Barry Bonds 4.00
74 Troy Glaus .75
75 Barry Zito .75
76 Pat Burrell .50
77 Paul LoDuca .40
78 Rafael Palmeiro .75
79 Mark Prior 1.00
80 Darin Erstad .50
81 Richie Sexson .75
82 Roberto Alomar .75
83 Roy Oswalt .75
84 Ryan Klesko .40
85 Luis Gonzalez .50
86 Scott Rolen 1.00
87 Shannon Stewart .40
88 Shawn Green .60
89 Toby Hall .40
90 Bret Boone .40
91 Casey Kotchman/Bat 10.00
92 Jose Valverde/Auto. **RC** 8.00
93 Cole Barthel/Bat 4.00
94 Brad Nelson/Auto. **RC** 8.00
95 Mauricio Lara/Auto. **RC** 8.00
96 Ryan Gripp/Bat **RC** 4.00
97 Brian West/Auto. **RC** 8.00
98 Chris Piersoll/Auto. **RC** 8.00
99 Ryan Church/Auto. **RC** 15.00
100 Javier Colina/Auto. 8.00
101 Juan Gonzalez/Auto. 8.00
102 Benito Baez/Auto. 8.00
103 Mike Hill/Bat **RC** 4.00
104 Jason Grove/Auto. **RC** 8.00
105 Koyie Hill/Auto. 8.00
106 Mark Outlaw/Auto. **RC** 8.00
107 Jason Bay/Bat **RC** 15.00
108 Jorge Padilla/Auto. **RC** 8.00
109 Peter Zamora/Auto. **RC** 8.00
110 Joe Mauer/Auto. **RC** 80.00
111 Franklyn German/Auto. **RC** 8.00
112 Chris Flinn/Auto. **RC** 8.00
113 David Wright/Bat 80.00
114 Anastacio Martinez/Auto. **RC** 8.00
115 Nic Jackson/Bat **RC** 8.00
116 Rene Reyes/Auto. **RC** 8.00
117 Colin Young/Auto. **RC** 8.00
118 Joe Orloski/Auto. **RC** 8.00
119 Mike Wilson/Auto. **RC** 8.00
120 Rich Thompson/Auto. **RC** 8.00
121 Jake Mauer/Auto. **RC** 8.00
122 Mario Ramos/Auto. 8.00
123 Doug Sessions/Auto. **RC** 8.00
124 Doug DeVore/Bat **RC** 4.00
125 Travis Foley/Auto. 10.00
126 Chris Baker/Auto. **RC** 8.00
127 Michael Floyd/Auto. **RC** 8.00
128 Josh Barfield/Bat 15.00
129 Jose Bautista/Bat **RC** 6.00
130 Gavin Floyd/Auto. 15.00
131 Jason Botts/Bat **RC** 4.00
132 Clint Nageotte/Auto. **RC** 10.00
133 Jesus Cota/Auto. **RC** 10.00
134 Ron Calloway/Bat **RC** 4.00
135 Kevin Cash/Bat **RC** 4.00
136 Jonny Gomes/Auto. **RC** 15.00
137 Dennis Ulacia/Auto. 8.00
138 Ryan Snare/Auto. **RC** 8.00
139 Kevin Deaton/Auto. **RC** 8.00
140 Bobby Jenks/Auto. **RC** 15.00
141 Casey Kotchman/Auto. 25.00
142 Adam Walker/Auto. **RC** 8.00
143 Mike Gonzalez/Auto. **RC** 8.00
144 Ruben Gotay/Bat **RC** 6.00
145 Jason Grove/Bat **RC** 4.00
146 Freddy Sanchez/Auto. **RC** 20.00
147 Jason Arnold/Auto. 10.00
148 Scott Hairston/Auto. 10.00
149 Jason St. Clair/Auto. **RC** 8.00
150 Chris Tritle/Bat **RC** 4.00
151 Edwin Yan/Bat **RC** 4.00
152 Freddy Sanchez/Bat **RC** 10.00
153 Greg Sain/Bat **RC** 4.00
154 Yurendell DeCaster/Bat **RC** 6.00
155 Noochie Varner/Bat **RC** 6.00
156 Nelson Castro/Auto. **RC** 8.00
157 Randall Shelley/Bat **RC** 6.00
158 Reed Johnson/Bat **RC** 10.00
159 Ryan Raburn/Auto. **RC** 8.00
160 Jose Morban/Bat **RC** 5.00
161 Justin Schuda/Auto. **RC** 8.00
162 Henry Pichardo/Auto. **RC** 8.00
163 Josh Bard/Auto. **RC** 10.00
164 Josh Bonifay/Auto. **RC** 8.00
165 Brandon League/Auto. 8.00
166 Julio DePaula/Auto. **RC** 10.00
167 Todd Linden/Auto. **RC** 10.00
168 Francisco Liriano/Auto. **RC** 100.00
169 Chris Snelling/Auto. **RC** 15.00
170 Blake McGinley/Auto. **RC** 8.00
171 Cody McKay/Auto. **RC** 8.00
172 Jason Stanford/Auto. **RC** 8.00
173 Lenny Dinardo/Auto. **RC** 8.00
174 Greg Montalbano/Auto. **RC** 8.00
175 Earl Snyder/Auto. **RC** 8.00
176 Justin Huber/Auto. **RC** 10.00
177 Chris Narveson/Auto. **RC** 8.00
178 Jon Switzer/Auto. 8.00
179 Ronald Acuna/Auto. **RC** 8.00
180 Chris Duffy/Bat **RC** 8.00
181 Kazuhisa Ishii/Bat **RC** 8.00

2003 Bowman

NM/M
Complete Set (330): 75.00
Common Player: .15
Common Rookie: .40
Pack (10): 3.00
Box (24): 60.00
1 Garret Anderson .15
2 Derek Jeter 2.00
3 Gary Sheffield .40
4 Matt Morris .25
5 Derek Lowe .15
6 Andy Van Hekken .15
7 Sammy Sosa 1.00
8 Ken Griffey Jr. 1.50
9 Omar Vizquel .15
10 Jorge Posada .40
11 Lance Berkman .40
12 Mike Sweeney .15
13 Adrian Beltre .25
14 Richie Sexson .25
15 A.J. Pierzynski .15
16 Bartolo Colon .15
17 Mike Mussina .40
18 Paul Byrd .15
19 Bobby Abreu .40
20 Miguel Tejada .50
21 Aramis Ramirez .40
22 Edgardo Alfonzo .15
23 Edgar Martinez .15
24 Albert Pujols 2.00
25 Carl Crawford .25
26 Eric Hinske .15
27 Tim Salmon .25
28 Luis Gonzalez .25
29 Jay Gibbons .15
30 John Smoltz .40
31 Tim Wakefield .15
32 Mark Prior .75
33 Magglio Ordonez .25
34 Adam Dunn .50
35 Larry Walker .25
36 Luis Castillo .15
37 Wade Miller .15
38 Carlos Beltran .50
39 Odalis Perez .15
40 Alex Sanchez .15
41 Torii Hunter .25
42 Cliff Floyd .15
43 Andy Pettitte .25
44 Francisco Rodriguez .15
45 Eric Chavez .40
46 Kevin Millwood .25
47 Dennis Tankersley .15
48 Hideo Nomo .25
49 Freddy Garcia .15
50 Randy Johnson .75
51 Aubrey Huff .15
52 Carlos Delgado .40
53 Troy Glaus .50
54 Junior Spivey .15
55 Mike Hampton .15
56 Sidney Ponson .15
57 Aaron Boone .15
58 Kerry Wood .40
59 Willie Harris .15
60 Nomar Garciaparra 1.00
61 Todd Helton .50
62 Mike Lowell .15
63 Roy Oswalt .40
64 Raul Ibanez .15
65 Brian Jordan .15
66 Geoff Jenkins .15
67 Jermaine Dye .15
68 Tom Glavine .25
69 Bernie Williams .40
70 Vladimir Guerrero .75
71 Mark Mulder .25
72 Jimmy Rollins .40
73 Oliver Perez .15
74 Rich Aurilia .15
75 Joel Pineiro .15
76 J.D. Drew .25
77 Ivan Rodriguez .50
78 Josh Phelps .15
79 Darin Erstad .40
80 Curt Schilling .75
81 Paul LoDuca .15
82 Marty Cordova .15
83 Manny Ramirez .75
84 Bobby Hill .15
85 Paul Konerko .40
86 Austin Kearns .25
87 Jason Jennings .15
88 Brad Penny .15
89 Jeff Bagwell .75
90 Shawn Green .40
91 Jason Schmidt .40
92 Doug Mientkiewicz .15
93 Jose Vidro .15
94 Bret Boone .15
95 Jason Giambi .50
96 Barry Zito .40
97 Roy Halliday .40
98 Pat Burrell .40
99 Sean Burroughs .15
100 Barry Bonds 2.00
101 Kazuhiro Sasaki .15
102 Fernando Vina .15
103 Chan Ho Park .15
104 Andruw Jones .75
105 Adam Kennedy .15
106 Shea Hillenbrand .15
107 Greg Maddux 1.50
108 Jim Edmonds .40
109 Pedro J. Martinez 1.00
110 Moises Alou .25
111 Jeff Weaver .15
112 C.C. Sabathia .15
113 Robert Fick .15
114 A.J. Burnett .15
115 Jeff Kent .25
116 Kevin Brown .25
117 Rafael Furcal .25
118 Cristian Guzman .15
119 Brad Wilkerson .15
120 Mike Piazza 1.00
121 Alfonso Soriano .75
122 Mark Ellis .15
123 Vicente Padilla .15
124 Eric Gagne .15
125 Ryan Klesko .15
126 Ichiro Suzuki 1.50
127 Tony Batista .15
128 Roberto Alomar .40
129 Alex Rodriguez 2.00
130 Jim Thome .75
131 Jarrod Washburn .15
132 Orlando Hudson .15
133 Chipper Jones 1.00
134 Rodrigo Lopez .15
135 Johnny Damon .75
136 Matt Clement .15
137 Frank Thomas .75
138 Ellis Burks .15
139 Carlos Pena .15
140 Josh Beckett .25
141 Joe Randa .15
142 Brian Giles .25
143 Kazuhisa Ishii .15
144 Corey Koskie .15
145 Orlando Cabrera .15
146 Mark Buehrle .25
147 Roger Clemens 2.00
148 Tim Hudson .40
149 Randy Wolf .15
150 Josh Fogg .15
151 Phil Nevin .15
152 John Olerud .15
153 Scott Rolen .75
154 Joe Kennedy .15
155 Rafael Palmeiro .75
156 Chad Hutchinson .40
157 Quincy Carter .15
158 Hee Seop Choi .15
159 Joe Borchard .15
160 Brandon Phillips .15
161 Wily Mo Pena .15
162 Victor Martinez .25
163 Jason Stokes .15
164 Ken Harvey .15
165 Juan Rivera .15
166 Jose Contreras **RC** 1.00
167 Dan Haren 1.00
168 Michel Hernandez **RC** .50
169 Eider Torres **RC** .40
170 Chris De La Cruz **RC** .50
171 Ramon A. Martinez **RC** .50
172 Mike Adams **RC** .40
173 Justin Arneson **RC** .50
174 Jamie Athas **RC** .40
175 Dwaine Bacon **RC** .40
176 Clint Barmes **RC** .50
177 B.J. Barns **RC** .40
178 Tyler Johnson **RC** .40

179 Bobby Basham **RC** .50
180 T.J. Bohn **RC** .50
181 J.D. Durbin **RC** .50
182 Brandon Bowe **RC** .40
183 Craig Brazell **RC** .50
184 Dusty Brown **RC** .50
185 Brian Bruney **RC** .50
186 Greg Bruso **RC** .40
187 Jaime Bubela **RC** .50
188 Bryan Bullington **RC** .50
189 Brian Burgamy **RC** .40
190 Eny Cabreja **RC** .50
191 Daniel Cabrera **RC** 1.00
192 Ryan Cameron **RC** .40
193 Lance Caracciolli **RC** .50
194 David Cash **RC** .40
195 Bernie Castro **RC** .40
196 Ismael Castro **RC** .40
197 Daryl Clark **RC** .50
198 Jeff Clark **RC** .50
199 Chris Colton **RC** .40
200 Dexter Cooper **RC** .40
201 Callix Crabbe **RC** .40
202 Chien-Ming Wang **RC** 5.00
203 Eric Crozier **RC** .50
204 Nook Logan **RC** .40
205 David DeJesus **RC** .75
206 Matt DeMarco **RC** .40
207 Chris Duncan **RC** 3.00
208 Eric Eckenstahler .40
209 Willie Eyre **RC** .40
210 Evel Bastida-Martinez **RC** .40
211 Chris Fallon **RC** .75
212 Mike Flannery **RC** .40
213 Mike O'Keefe **RC** .40
214 Ben Francisco **RC** .50
215 Kason Gabbard **RC** 1.00
216 Mike Gallo **RC** .40
217 Jairo Garcia **RC** .40
218 Angel Garcia **RC** .40
219 Michael Garciaparra .50
220 Joey Gomes .40
221 Dusty Gomon **RC** .40
222 Bryan Grace **RC** .40
223 Tyson Graham **RC** .40
224 Henry Guerrero **RC** .40
225 Franklin Gutierrez **RC** .50
226 Carlos Guzman **RC** .50
227 Matthew Hagen **RC** .40
228 Josh Hall **RC** .50
229 Rob Hammock **RC** .50
230 Brendan Harris **RC** .75
231 Gary Harris **RC** .40
232 Clay Hensley **RC** .75
233 Michael Hinckley **RC** .40
234 Luis Hodge **RC** .40
235 Donnie Hood **RC** .50
236 Travis Ishikawa **RC** .50
237 Edwin Jackson **RC** .75
238 Ardley Jansen **RC** .50
239 Ferenc Jongejan **RC** .40
240 Matt Kata **RC** .50
241 Kazuhiro Takeoka **RC** .40
242 Beau Kemp **RC** .40
243 Il Kim **RC** .40
244 Brennan King **RC** .40
245 Cris Kroski **RC** .40
246 Jason Kubel **RC** 2.00
247 Pete LaForest **RC** .40
248 Wilfredo Ledezma **RC** .40
249 Jeremy Bonderman 3.00
250 Gonzalo Lopez **RC** .40
251 Brian Luderer **RC** .50
252 Ruddy Lugo **RC** .40
253 Wayne Lydon **RC** .40
254 Mark Malaska **RC** .40
255 Andy Marte **RC** 1.00
256 Tyler Martin **RC** .40
257 Branden Florence **RC** .40
258 Aneudis Mateo **RC** .40
259 Derell McCall **RC** .40
260 Brian McCann 5.00
261 Mike McNutt **RC** .40
262 Jacabo Meque **RC** .40
263 Derek Michaelis **RC** .50
264 Aaron Miles **RC** 1.00
265 Jose Morales .40
266 Dustin Moseley **RC** .40
267 Adrian Myers **RC** .40
268 Dan Neil **RC** .40
269 Jon Nelson **RC** .50
270 Mike Neu **RC** .40
271 Leigh Neuage **RC** .40
272 Weston O'Brien **RC** .40
273 Trent Oeltjen **RC** .50
274 Tim Olson **RC** .50
275 David Pahucki **RC** .40
276 Nathan Panther **RC** .50
277 Arnie Munoz **RC** .40
278 David Pember **RC** .40
279 Jason Perry **RC** .50
280 Matthew Peterson **RC** .40
281 Ryan Shealy **RC** 1.50
282 Jorge Piedra **RC** .40
283 Simon Pond **RC** .40
284 Aaron Rakers **RC** .40
285 Hanley Ramirez **RC** 5.00
286 Manuel Ramirez **RC** .40
287 Kevin Randel **RC** .50
288 Darrell Rasner .40
289 Prentice Redman **RC** .40
290 Eric Reed **RC** .50
291 Wilton Reynolds **RC** .40
292 Eric Riggs **RC** .40
293 Carlos Rijo **RC** .40
294 Rajai Davis **RC** .40
295 Aron Weston **RC** .40
296 Arturo Rivas **RC** .50
297 Kyle Roat **RC** .40
298 Bubba Nelson **RC** .50
299 Levi Robinson **RC** .40
300 Ray Sadler **RC** .40
301 Gary Schneidmiller **RC** .50
302 Jon Schuerholz **RC** .75
303 Corey Shafer **RC** .50
304 Brian Shackelford **RC** .40
305 Bill Simon **RC** .40
306 Haj Turay **RC** .40
307 Sean Smith .40
308 Ryan Spataro **RC** .40
309 Jemel Spearman **RC** .50
310 Keith Stamler **RC** .40
311 Luke Steidlmayer **RC** .40
312 Adam Stern .50
313 Jay Sitzman **RC** .40
314 Thomari Story-Harden **RC** .50
315 Terry Tiffee **RC** .40
316 Nick Trzesniak **RC** .50
317 Denny Tussen **RC** .40
318 Scott Tyler .40
319 Shane Victorino **RC** .40
320 Doug Waechter **RC** .50
321 Brandon Watson **RC** .50
322 Todd Wellemeyer **RC** .50
323 Eli Whiteside **RC** .50
324 Josh Willingham **RC** 1.00
325 Travis Wong **RC** .50
326 Brian Wright **RC** .40
327 Kevin Youkilis **RC** 3.00
328 Andy Sisco .50
329 Dustin Yount **RC** .50
330 Andrew Dominique **RC** .40

Gold

Stars (1-165): 1-2X
Rookies (166-330): 1-2X
Inserted 1:1

Uncirculated

Stars (1-165): 3-5X
Rookies (166-330): 2-4X
Production 250 Sets

Future Fiber Relics

NM/M
Common Player: 4.00
RB Rocco Baldelli 10.00
WB Wilson Betemit 6.00
HB Hank Blalock 10.00
JB Jason Botts 5.00
SB Sean Burroughs 8.00
KC Kevin Cash 4.00
KD Kory DeHaan 5.00
CD Chris Duffy 4.00
PF Pedro Feliz 5.00
AG Adrian Gonzalez 5.00
JG Jason Grove 5.00
JH Josh Hamilton 8.00
NH Nathan Haynes 4.00
DH Drew Henson 8.00
AH Aubrey Huff 5.00
RJ Reed Johnson 6.00
AK Austin Kearns 5.00
CK Casey Kotchman 8.00
RK Ryan Langerhans 5.00
JDM Jake Mauer 6.00
JM Joe Mauer 15.00
XN Xavier Nady 6.00
MR Michael Restovich 6.00
WR Wilkin Ruan 6.00
FS Freddy Sanchez 8.00
RS Randall Shelley 4.00
BS Bud Smith 4.00
ES Esix Snead 6.00
ST So Taguchi 8.00
JW Justin Wayne 5.00
TW Travis Wilson 6.00
DW David Wright 15.00
EY Edwin Yan 4.00

Futures Game Gear Relics

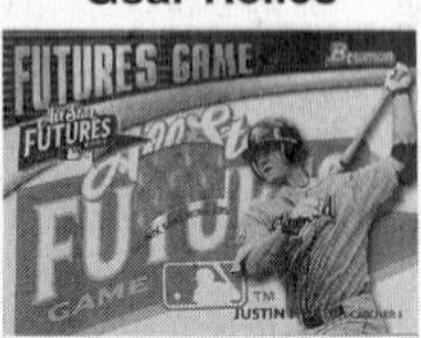

NM/M
Common Player: 4.00
Inserted 1:26
EA Edwin Almonte 4.00
TA Tony Alvarez 4.00
BB Brad Baker 4.00
FB Francis Beltran 4.00
JEB Joe Borchard 4.00
JB John Buck 4.00
SB Sean Burnett 6.00
MB Marlon Byrd 4.00
MC Miguel Cabrera 10.00
KC Kevin Cash 4.00
HC Hee Seop Choi 5.00
SC Shin-Soo Choo 6.00
AC Aaron Cook 5.00
CC Carl Crawford 5.00
JDR Jorge De La Rosa 4.00
VD Victor Diaz 4.00
RD Ryan Dittfurth 4.00
BE Brett Evert 4.00
GG Gerardo Garcia 4.00
BH Bill Hall 4.00
CH Corey Hart 4.00
DH Drew Henson 8.00
JH Justin Huber 6.00
OH Orlando Hudson 4.00
OI Omar Infante 4.00
JJ Jimmy Journell 4.00
JK Josh Karp 4.00
FL Francisco Liriano 4.00
JL Jose Lopez 4.00
VM Victor Martinez 8.00
JM Justin Morneau 10.00
BM Brett Myers 6.00
LO Lyle Overbay 6.00
WP Wily Mo Pena 6.00
BP Brandon Phillips 6.00
MR Mike Restovich 8.00
JR Jose Reyes 10.00
FR Francisco Rodriguez 5.00
RR Ricardo Rodriguez 4.00
SS Seung Jun Song 6.00
JMS John Stephens 4.00
JS Jason Stokes 8.00
BT Billy Traber 5.00
CT Chad Tracey 4.00
AW Adam Wainwright 10.00
JY Jason Young 4.00

Futures Game MVP Autograph

NM/M
Complete Set (1):
JR Jose Reyes 40.00

ROY Dual Relic

NM/M
Inserted 1:765
JH Eric Hinske, Jason Jennings 10.00

Signs of the Future

NM/M
Common Autograph: 5.00
Red Autographs: 1-2.5X
Production 50 Sets
JA Jason Arnold 8.00
JB John Buck 10.00
BB Bryan Bullington 10.00
QC Quincy Carter 10.00
NC Nelson Castro 8.00
RC Ryan Church 10.00
JC Jesus Cota 5.00
JOG Jonny Gomes 20.00
DG Doug Gredvig 5.00
KG Khalil Greene 25.00
ZG Zack Greinke 15.00
JG Jason Grove 5.00
JGU Jeremy Guthrie 10.00
CH Cole Hamels 80.00
JRH Joel Hanrahan 8.00
CJH Corey Hart 30.00
KH Koyie Hill 8.00
CMH Chad Hutchinson 10.00
BJ Bobby Jenks 15.00
BK Ben Kozlowski 5.00
BL Brandon League 5.00
DL Donald Levinski 5.00
FL Fred Lewis 25.00
TL Todd Linden 5.00
JL James Loney 35.00
VM Val Majewski 8.00
DHM Dustin McGowan 20.00
CP Chris Piersoll 8.00
HR Hanley Ramirez 40.00
PR Prentice Redman 8.00
JR Jose Reyes 40.00
JSC Jason St. Clair 6.00
FS Freddy Sanchez 15.00
ZS Zach Segovia 8.00
DS Doug Sessions 5.00
BS Brian Slocum 6.00
RS Ryan Snare 8.00
MT Mitch Talbot 5.00
AT Andres Torres 5.00
AV Andy Van Hekken 5.00
OV Oscar Villarreal 8.00

Dual Signs of the Future Autograph

NM/M
Inserted 1:9,220
CH Quincy Carter, Chad Hutchinson 85.00

2003 Bowman Chrome

NM/M
Complete Set (351): 400.00
Common Player: .25
Common Rookie: 1.00
Common RC Auto. (331-350): 10.00
Pack (4): 7.00
Box (18): 100.00
1 Garret Anderson .25
2 Derek Jeter 3.00
3 Gary Sheffield .50
4 Matt Morris .35
5 Derek Lowe .25
6 Andy Van Hekken .25
7 Sammy Sosa 1.00
8 Ken Griffey Jr. 2.00
9 Omar Vizquel .40
10 Jorge Posada .50
11 Lance Berkman .50
12 Mike Sweeney .25
13 Adrian Beltre .50
14 Richie Sexson .50
15 A.J. Pierzynski .25
16 Bartolo Colon .25
17 Mike Mussina .75
18 Paul Byrd .25
19 Bobby Abreu .50
20 Miguel Tejada .75
21 Aramis Ramirez .50
22 Edgardo Alfonzo .25
23 Edgar Martinez .40
24 Albert Pujols 3.00
25 Carl Crawford .40
26 Eric Hinske .25
27 Tim Salmon .40
28 Luis Gonzalez .40
29 Jay Gibbons .25
30 John Smoltz .50
31 Tim Wakefield .25
32 Mark Prior 1.00
33 Magglio Ordonez .40
34 Adam Dunn .75
35 Larry Walker .40
36 Luis Castillo .25
37 Wade Miller .25
38 Carlos Beltran .75
39 Odalis Perez .25
40 Alex Sanchez .25
41 Torii Hunter .50
42 Cliff Floyd .25
43 Andy Pettitte .50
44 Francisco Rodriguez .25
45 Eric Chavez .50
46 Kevin Millwood .40
47 Dennis Tankersley .25
48 Hideo Nomo .50
49 Freddy Garcia .25
50 Randy Johnson 1.00
51 Aubrey Huff .25
52 Carlos Delgado .50
53 Troy Glaus .50
54 Junior Spivey .25
55 Mike Hampton .25
56 Sidney Ponson .25
57 Aaron Boone .25
58 Kerry Wood .50
59 Willie Harris .25
60 Nomar Garciaparra 1.00
61 Todd Helton .75
62 Mike Lowell .25
63 Roy Oswalt .50
64 Raul Ibanez .25
65 Brian Jordan .25
66 Geoff Jenkins .25
67 Jermaine Dye .25
68 Tom Glavine .50
69 Bernie Williams .50
70 Vladimir Guerrero 1.00
71 Mark Mulder .40
72 Jimmy Rollins .50
73 Oliver Perez .25
74 Rich Aurilia .25
75 Joel Pineiro .25
76 J.D. Drew .40
77 Ivan Rodriguez .75
78 Josh Phelps .25
79 Darin Erstad .40
80 Curt Schilling 1.00
81 Paul LoDuca .25
82 Marty Cordova .25
83 Manny Ramirez 1.00
84 Bobby Hill .25
85 Paul Konerko .50
86 Austin Kearns .40
87 Jason Jennings .25
88 Brad Penny .25
89 Jeff Bagwell .75
90 Shawn Green .40
91 Jason Schmidt .40
92 Doug Mientkiewicz .25
93 Jose Vidro .25
94 Bret Boone .25
95 Jason Giambi .75
96 Barry Zito .50
97 Roy Halliday .50
98 Pat Burrell .50
99 Sean Burroughs .25
100 Barry Bonds 3.00
101 Kazuhiro Sasaki .25
102 Fernando Vina .25
103 Chan Ho Park .25
104 Andruw Jones 1.00
105 Adam Kennedy .25
106 Shea Hillenbrand .25
107 Greg Maddux 2.00
108 Jim Edmonds .40
109 Pedro J. Martinez 1.00
110 Moises Alou .40
111 Jeff Weaver .25
112 C.C. Sabathia .25
113 Robert Fick .25
114 A.J. Burnett .25
115 Jeff Kent .40
116 Kevin Brown .25
117 Rafael Furcal .40
118 Cristian Guzman .25
119 Brad Wilkerson .25
120 Mike Piazza 1.00
121 Alfonso Soriano 1.00
122 Mark Ellis .25
123 Vicente Padilla .25
124 Eric Gagne .50
125 Ryan Klesko .25
126 Ichiro Suzuki 2.00
127 Tony Batista .25
128 Roberto Alomar .50
129 Alex Rodriguez 2.50
130 Jim Thome .75
131 Jarrod Washburn .25
132 Orlando Hudson .25
133 Chipper Jones 1.00
134 Rodrigo Lopez .25
135 Johnny Damon 1.00
136 Matt Clement .25
137 Frank Thomas 1.00
138 Ellis Burks .25
139 Carlos Pena .25
140 Josh Beckett .50
141 Joe Randa .25
142 Brian Giles .25
143 Kazuhisa Ishii .25
144 Corey Koskie .25
145 Orlando Cabrera .25
146 Mark Buehrle .40
147 Roger Clemens 2.00
148 Tim Hudson .50
149 Randy Wolf .25
150 Josh Fogg .25
151 Phil Nevin .25
152 John Olerud .25
153 Scott Rolen 1.00
154 Joe Kennedy .25
155 Rafael Palmeiro .75
156 Chad Hutchinson .50
157 Quincy Carter .50
158 Hee Seop Choi .40
159 Joe Borchard .25
160 Brandon Phillips .25
161 Wily Mo Pena .25
162 Victor Martinez .50
163 Jason Stokes .25
164 Ken Harvey .25
165 Juan Rivera .25
166 Joe Valentine **RC** 1.50
167 Dan Haren 4.00
168 Michel Hernandez **RC** 1.00
169 Eider Torres **RC** 1.00
170 Chris De La Cruz **RC** 1.00
171 Ramon A. Martinez **RC** 1.50
172 Mike Adams **RC** 1.00
173 Justin Arneson **RC** 1.00
174 Jamie Athas **RC** 1.00
175 Dwaine Bacon **RC** 1.00
176 Clint Barmes **RC** 1.50
177 B.J. Barns **RC** 1.00
178 Tyler Johnson **RC** 1.00
179 Brandon Webb **RC** 8.00
180 T.J. Bohn **RC** 1.00
181 Ozzie Chavez **RC** 1.50
182 Brandon Bowe **RC** 1.00
183 Craig Brazell **RC** 1.00
184 Dusty Brown **RC** 1.50
185 Brian Bruney **RC** 1.00
186 Greg Bruso **RC** 1.00
187 Jaime Bubela **RC** 1.00
188 Matt Diaz **RC** 2.00
189 Brian Burgamy **RC** 1.00
190 Eny Cabreja **RC** 2.00
191 Daniel Cabrera **RC** 3.00
192 Ryan Cameron **RC** 1.00
193 Lance Caracciolli **RC** 1.50
194 David Cash **RC** 1.00
195 Bernie Castro **RC** 1.00
196 Ismael Castro **RC** 1.00
197 Cory Doyne **RC** 2.00
198 Jeff Clark **RC** 1.00
199 Chris Colton **RC** 1.00
200 Dexter Cooper **RC** 1.00
201 Callix Crabbe **RC** 1.00
202 Chien-Ming Wang **RC** 15.00
203 Eric Crozier **RC** 1.50
204 Nook Logan **RC** 1.50
205 David DeJesus **RC** 4.00
206 Matt DeMarco **RC** 1.00
207 Chris Duncan **RC** 12.00
208 Eric Eckenstahler 1.00
209 Willie Eyre **RC** 1.00
210 Evel Bastida-Martinez **RC** 1.00
211 Chris Fallon **RC** 1.50
212 Mike Flannery **RC** 1.00
213 Mike O'Keefe **RC** 1.00
214 Lew Ford **RC** 1.50
215 Kason Gabbard **RC** 3.00
216 Mike Gallo **RC** 1.00
217 Jairo Garcia **RC** 1.00
218 Angel Garcia **RC** 1.00
219 Michael Garciaparra 1.00
220 Jeremy Griffiths 1.50
221 Dusty Gomon **RC** 1.50
222 Bryan Grace **RC** 1.00
223 Tyson Graham **RC** 1.00
224 Henry Guerrero **RC** 1.00
225 Franklin Gutierrez **RC** 4.00
226 Carlos Guzman **RC** 2.00
227 Matthew Hagen **RC** 2.00
228 Josh Hall **RC** 1.50
229 Rob Hammock **RC** 1.50
230 Brendan Harris **RC** 2.00
231 Gary Harris **RC** 1.00
232 Clay Hensley **RC** 1.50
233 Michael Hinckley **RC** 2.00
234 Luis Hodge **RC** 1.00
235 Donnie Hood **RC** 2.00
236 Matt Hensley **RC** 2.00
237 Edwin Jackson **RC** 1.50
238 Ardley Jansen **RC** 2.00
239 Ferenc Jongejan **RC** 1.00
240 Matt Kata **RC** 1.50
241 Kazuhiro Takeoka **RC** 1.00
242 Charlie Manning **RC** 1.00
243 Il Kim **RC** 1.00
244 Brennan King **RC** 1.00
245 Cris Kroski **RC** 1.00
246 David Martinez 1.50
247 Pete LaForest **RC** 1.00
248 Wilfredo Ledezma **RC** 1.00
249 Jeremy Bonderman 12.00
250 Gonzalo Lopez **RC** 1.00
251 Brian Luderer **RC** 1.50
252 Ruddy Lugo **RC** 1.50
253 Wayne Lydon **RC** 1.00
254 Mark Malaska **RC** 1.00
255 Andy Marte **RC** 8.00
256 Tyler Martin **RC** 1.00
257 Branden Florence **RC** 1.00
258 Aneudis Mateo **RC** 1.00
259 Derell McCall **RC** 1.00
260 Elizardo Ramirez **RC** 2.00
261 Mike McNutt **RC** 1.00
262 Jacabo Meque **RC** 1.00
263 Derek Michaelis **RC** 1.50
264 Aaron Miles **RC** 2.00
265 Jose Morales 1.00
266 Dustin Moseley **RC** 1.00
267 Adrian Myers **RC** 1.00
268 Dan Neil **RC** 1.00
269 Jon Nelson **RC** 2.00
270 Mike Neu **RC** 1.00
271 Leigh Neuage **RC** 1.00
272 Weston O'Brien **RC** 1.00
273 Trent Oeltjen **RC** 2.00
274 Tim Olson **RC** 2.00
275 David Pahucki **RC** 1.00
276 Nathan Panther **RC** 1.50
277 Arnie Munoz **RC** 1.00
278 David Pember **RC** 1.00
279 Jason Perry **RC** 2.00
280 Matthew Peterson **RC** 1.00
281 Greg Aquino **RC** 1.50
282 Jorge Piedra **RC** 1.00
283 Simon Pond **RC** 1.50
284 Aaron Rakers **RC** 1.00
285 Felix Sanchez **RC** 1.50
286 Manuel Ramirez **RC** 1.00
287 Kevin Randel **RC** 1.00
288 Kelly Shoppach **RC** 3.00
289 Prentice Redman **RC** 2.00
290 Eric Reed **RC** 2.00
291 Wilton Reynolds **RC** 1.00
292 Eric Riggs **RC** 1.00
293 Carlos Rijo **RC** 1.00
294 Tyler Adamczyk **RC** 2.00
295 Jon-Mark Sprowl **RC** 2.00
296 Arturo Rivas **RC** 2.00
297 Kyle Roat **RC** 1.00
298 Bubba Nelson **RC** 2.00
299 Levi Robinson **RC** 1.00
300 Ray Sadler **RC** 1.00
301 Ryan Reed **RC** 2.00
302 Jon Schuerholz **RC** 1.00
303 Nobuaki Yoshida **RC** 1.50
304 Brian Shackelford **RC** 1.00
305 Bill Simon **RC** 1.00
306 Haj Turay **RC** 1.00
307 Sean Smith 1.00
308 Ryan Spataro **RC** 1.00
309 Jemel Spearman **RC** 1.50
310 Keith Stamler **RC** 1.00
311 Luke Steidlmayer **RC** 1.00
312 Adam Stern 1.00
313 Jay Sitzman **RC** 1.00
314 Mike Wodnicki **RC** 1.50
315 Terry Tiffee **RC** 1.00
316 Nick Trzesniak **RC** 1.00
317 Denny Tussen **RC** 1.00
318 Scott Tyler 1.00
319 Shane Victorino **RC** 3.00
320 Doug Waechter **RC** 1.50
321 Brandon Watson **RC** 1.50
322 Todd Wellemeyer **RC** 1.50

323 Eli Whiteside RC 1.50
324 Josh Willingham RC 4.00
325 Travis Wong RC 1.50
326 Brian Wright RC 1.00
327 Felix Pie RC 10.00
328 Andy Sisco 1.00
329 Dustin Yount RC 1.00
330 Andrew Dominique RC 1.50
331 Brian McCann 80.00
332 Jose Contreras RC 75.00
333 Corey Shafer RC 10.00
334 Hanley Ramirez RC 180.00
335 Ryan Shealy RC 25.00
336 Kevin Youkilis RC 50.00
337 Jason Kubel RC 25.00
338 Aron Weston RC 10.00
339 J.D. Durbin RC 10.00
340 Gary Schneidmiller RC 10.00
341 Travis Ishikawa RC 15.00
342 Ben Francisco RC 10.00
343 Bobby Basham RC 10.00
344 Joey Gomes 10.00
345 Beau Kemp RC 10.00
346 Thomari Story-Harden RC 10.00
347 Daryl Clark RC 10.00
348 Bryan Bullington RC 25.00
349 Rajai Davis RC 10.00
350 Darrell Rasner 10.00
351 Willie Mays 3.00

Refractors

Stars (1-165, 351): 2-4X
Rookies (166-350): .5-1.5X
X-Fractors (1-165, 351): 3-6X
X-Fractors (166-350): 1-2X
Uncirc.Gold Refractors (1-165): 5-10X
Gold Refractors (166-350): 2-3X
Production 170 Sets
Gold Refractors (331-350): 1-30X

Willie Mays Autograph

NM/M
Production 150
351AU Willie Mays 225.00

2003 Bowman Draft Picks & Prospects

NM/M
Complete Set (165): 35.00
Common Player: .15
Common Rookie: .25
Pack (5 + 2 Chrome): 10.00
Box (24): 220.00
BDP1 Dontrelle Willis .40
BDP2 Freddy Sanchez .15
BDP3 Miguel Cabrera .50
BDP4 Ryan Ludwick .15
BDP5 Ty Wigginton .15
BDP6 Mark Teixeira .50
BDP7 Trey Hodges .15
BDP8 Laynce Nix .15
BDP9 Antonio Perez .15
BDP10 Jody Gerut .15
BDP11 Jae Weong Seo .15
BDP12 Erick Almonte .15
BDP13 Lyle Overbay .15
BDP14 Billy Traber .15
BDP15 Andres Torres .15
BDP16 Jose Valverde .15
BDP17 Aaron Heilman .15
BDP18 Brandon Larson .15
BDP19 Jung Bong .15
BDP20 Jesse Foppert .15
BDP21 Angel Berroa .15
BDP22 Jeff DaVanon .15
BDP23 Kurt Ainsworth .15
BDP24 Brandon Claussen .15
BDP25 Xavier Nady .15
BDP26 Travis Hafner .40
BDP27 Jerome Williams .15
BDP28 Jose Reyes .40
BDP29 Sergio Mitre RC .25
BDP30 Bo Hart RC .50
BDP31 Adam Miller RC 4.00
BDP32 Brian Finch RC .25
BDP33 Taylor Mattingly RC .75
BDP34 Daric Barton RC 3.00
BDP35 Chris Ray RC .25
BDP36 Jarrod Saltalamacchia RC 4.00
BDP37 Dennis Dove RC .25
BDP38 James Houser RC .50
BDP39 Clinton King RC .50
BDP40 Lou Palmisano RC .50
BDP41 Dan Moore RC .25
BDP42 Craig Stansberry RC .50
BDP43 Jo Jo Reyes RC .75
BDP44 Jake Stevens RC .50
BDP45 Tom Gorzelanny RC 1.00
BDP46 Brian Marshall RC .50
BDP47 Scott Beerer RC .25
BDP48 Javi Herrera RC .50
BDP49 Steve Lerud RC .75
BDP50 Josh Banks RC .75
BDP51 Jonathan Papelbon RC 10.00
BDP52 Juan Valdes RC .50
BDP53 Beau Vaghan .50
BDP54 Matt Chico RC .25
BDP55 Todd Jennings RC .50
BDP56 Tony Gwynn Jr. RC 1.00
BDP57 Matt Harrison RC .25
BDP58 Aaron Mardsen .25
BDP59 Casey Abrams RC .25
BDP60 Cory Stuart RC .25
BDP61 Mike Wagner RC .25
BDP62 Jordan Pratt RC .50
BDP63 Andre Randolph RC .25
BDP64 Blake Balkcom RC .25
BDP65 Josh Muecke RC .25
BDP66 Jamie D'Antona RC 1.00
BDP67 Cole Seifrig RC .50
BDP68 Josh Anderson RC .25
BDP69 Matt Lorenzo RC .25
BDP70 Nate Spears RC .50
BDP71 Chris Goodman RC .50
BDP72 Brian McFall RC .50
BDP73 Billy Hogan RC .50
BDP74 Jamie Romak RC .50
BDP75 Jeff Cook RC .50
BDP76 Brooks McNiven RC .25
BDP77 Xavier Paul RC 1.00
BDP78 Bob Zimmerman RC .25
BDP79 Mickey Hall RC .50
BDP80 Shaun Marcum RC .25
BDP81 Matt Nachreiner RC .25
BDP82 Chris Kinsey RC .25
BDP83 Jonathan Fulton RC .50
BDP84 Edgardo Baez RC .50
BDP85 Robert Valido RC .75
BDP86 Kenny Lewis RC .50
BDP87 Trent Peterson RC .25
BDP88 Johnny Woodard RC .25
BDP89 Wes Littleton RC .50
BDP90 Sean Rodriguez RC 1.00
BDP91 Kyle Pearson RC .25
BDP92 Josh Rainwater RC .75
BDP93 Travis Schlichting RC .50
BDP94 Tim Battle RC .75
BDP95 Aaron Hill RC .75
BDP96 Bob McCrory RC .25
BDP97 Rick Guarno RC .25
BDP98 Brandon Yarbrough RC .25
BDP99 Peter Stonard RC .50
BDP100 Darin Downs RC .50
BDP101 Matt Bruback RC .25
BDP102 Danny Garcia RC .25
BDP103 Cory Stewart RC .25
BDP104 Ferdin Tejeda RC .50
BDP105 Kade Johnson RC .25
BDP106 Andrew Brown RC .25
BDP107 Aquilino Lopez RC .25
BDP108 Stephen Randolph RC .25
BDP109 Dave Matranga RC .25
BDP110 Dustin McGowan RC 1.00
BDP111 Juan Camacho RC .50
BDP112 Cliff Lee .15
BDP113 Jeff Duncan RC .50
BDP114 C.J. Wilson .25
BDP115 Brandon Roberson RC .25
BDP116 David Corrente RC .25
BDP117 Kevin Beavers RC .25
BDP118 Anthony Webster RC .25
BDP119 Oscar Villarreal RC .25
BDP120 Hong-Chih Kuo RC 2.00
BDP121 Josh Barfield .15
BDP122 Denny Bautista .15
BDP123 Chris Burke .75
BDP124 Robinson Cano RC 10.00
BDP125 Jose Castillo .15
BDP126 Neal Cotts .15
BDP127 Jorge De La Rosa .15
BDP128 J.D. Durbin .15
BDP129 Edwin Encarnacion .50
BDP130 Gavin Floyd .15
BDP131 Alexis Gomez .15
BDP132 Edgar Gonzalez RC .25
BDP133 Khalil Greene .25
BDP134 Zack Greinke .15
BDP135 Franklin Gutierrez .40
BDP136 Rich Harden .15
BDP137 J.J. Hardy 3.00
BDP138 Ryan Howard 20.00
BDP139 Justin Huber .15
BDP140 David Kelton .15
BDP141 David Krynzel .15
BDP142 Pete LaForest .15
BDP143 Adam LaRoche .15
BDP144 Preston Larrison .15
BDP145 John Maine RC 4.00
BDP146 Andy Marte 1.00
BDP147 Jeff Mathis .15
BDP148 Joe Mauer .50
BDP149 Clint Nageotte .15
BDP150 Chris Narveson .15
BDP151 Ramon Nivar RC .25
BDP152 Felix Pie RC 4.00
BDP153 Guillermo Quiroz RC .50
BDP154 Rene Reyes .15
BDP155 Royce Ring .15
BDP156 Alexis Rios .75
BDP157 Grady Sizemore .75
BDP158 Stephen Smitherman .15
BDP159 Seung Jun Song .15
BDP160 Scott Thorman .15
BDP161 Chad Tracy .15
BDP162 Chin-Hui Tsao .15
BDP163 John Van Benschoten RC .25
BDP164 Kevin Youkilis 1.00
BDP165 Chien-Ming Wang 3.00

Gold

Cards (1-165): 1-2X
Inserted 1:1

Fabric of Future

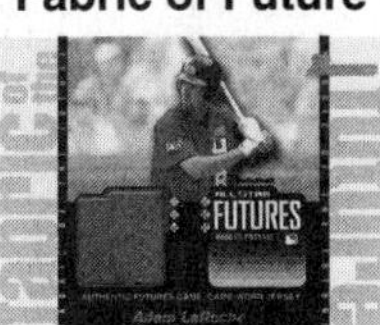

NM/M
Common Player: 4.00
JB Josh Barfield 6.00
RC Robinson Cano 25.00
JD J.D. Durbin 4.00
GF Gavin Floyd 4.00
EG Edgar Gonzalez 4.00
KG Khalil Greene 8.00
ZG Zack Greinke 4.00
FG Franklin Gutierrez 4.00
RH Rich Harden 6.00
RJH Ryan Howard 50.00
JH Justin Huber 5.00
AL Adam LaRoche 8.00
AM Andy Marte 8.00
JSM Jeff Mathis 6.00
JM Joe Mauer 10.00
CN Chris Narveson 4.00
FP Felix Pie 15.00
RR Rene Reyes 4.00
RRR Royce Ring 4.00
GS Grady Sizemore 10.00

Prospect Premiums

NM/M
Common Player: 4.00
RB Rocco Baldelli 6.00
HB Hank Blalock 6.00
CC Carl Crawford 5.00
TH Travis Hafner 8.00
BH Brendan Harris 4.00
NH Nathan Haynes 4.00
JM Justin Morneau 6.00
CS Chris Snelling 4.00
JT Joe Thurston 4.00
CU Chase Utley 10.00

Signs of the Future

NM/M
Common Player: 5.00
JA Jason Arnold 5.00
ZG Zack Greinke 15.00
CS Cory Stewart 5.00
DT Dennis Tankersley 5.00
AT Andres Torres 8.00

2003 Bowman Chrome Draft Picks & Prospects

NM/M
Complete Set (176): 500.00
Common Player: .25
Common Rookie: 1.00
Common Rk Autograph (166-176): 10.00
BDP1 Dontrelle Willis .75
BDP2 Freddy Sanchez .25
BDP3 Miguel Cabrera .75
BDP4 Ryan Ludwick .25
BDP5 Ty Wigginton .25
BDP6 Mark Teixeira .75
BDP7 Trey Hodges .25
BDP8 Laynce Nix .25
BDP9 Antonio Perez .25
BDP10 Jody Gerut .25
BDP11 Jae Weong Seo .25
BDP12 Erick Almonte .25
BDP13 Lyle Overbay .25
BDP14 Billy Traber .25
BDP15 Andres Torres .25
BDP16 Jose Valverde .25
BDP17 Aaron Heilman .25
BDP18 Brandon Larson .25
BDP19 Jung Bong .25
BDP20 Jesse Foppert .25
BDP21 Angel Berroa .25
BDP22 Jeff DaVanon .25
BDP23 Kurt Ainsworth .25
BDP24 Brandon Claussen .25
BDP25 Xavier Nady .25
BDP26 Travis Hafner .75
BDP27 Jerome Williams .25
BDP28 Jose Reyes .50
BDP29 Sergio Mitre RC 1.00
BDP30 Bo Hart RC 1.00
BDP31 Adam Miller RC 12.00
BDP32 Brian Finch RC 1.00
BDP33 Taylor Mattingly RC 2.00
BDP34 Daric Barton RC 6.00
BDP35 Chris Ray RC 2.00
BDP36 Jarrod Saltalamacchia RC 15.00
BDP37 Dennis Dove RC 1.00
BDP38 James Houser RC 1.50
BDP39 Clinton King RC 2.00
BDP40 Lou Palmisano RC 2.00
BDP41 Dan Moore RC 1.00
BDP42 Craig Stansberry RC 1.50
BDP43 Jo Jo Reyes RC 2.00
BDP44 Jake Stevens RC 1.00
BDP45 Tom Gorzelanny RC 3.00
BDP46 Brian Marshall RC 1.50
BDP47 Scott Beerer RC 1.00
BDP48 Javi Herrera RC 1.50
BDP49 Steve Lerud RC 2.00
BDP50 Josh Banks RC 2.00
BDP51 Jonathan Papelbon RC 30.00
BDP52 Juan Valdes RC 1.50
BDP53 Beau Vaghan 1.50
BDP54 Matt Chico RC 2.00
BDP55 Todd Jennings RC 1.50
BDP56 Tony Gwynn Jr. RC 5.00
BDP57 Matt Harrison RC 2.00
BDP58 Aaron Mardsen 1.00
BDP59 Casey Abrams RC 1.00
BDP60 Cory Stuart RC 1.00
BDP61 Mike Wagner RC 1.00
BDP62 Jordan Pratt RC 1.50
BDP63 Andre Randolph RC 1.00
BDP64 Blake Balkcom RC 1.00
BDP65 Josh Muecke RC 1.00
BDP66 Jamie D'Antona RC 3.00
BDP67 Cole Seifrig RC 2.00
BDP68 Josh Anderson RC 1.00
BDP69 Matt Lorenzo RC 1.00
BDP70 Nate Spears RC 1.00
BDP71 Chris Goodman RC 1.50
BDP72 Brian McFall RC 1.50
BDP73 Billy Hogan RC 1.50
BDP74 Jamie Romak RC 1.50
BDP75 Jeff Cook RC 1.50
BDP76 Brooks McNiven RC 1.00
BDP77 Xavier Paul RC 1.50
BDP78 Bob Zimmerman RC 1.00
BDP79 Mickey Hall RC 1.00
BDP80 Shaun Marcum RC 1.00
BDP81 Matt Nachreiner RC 1.00
BDP82 Chris Kinsey RC 1.00
BDP83 Jonathan Fulton RC 1.50
BDP84 Edgardo Baez RC 1.50
BDP85 Robert Valido RC 2.00
BDP86 Kenny Lewis RC 1.50
BDP87 Trent Peterson RC 1.00
BDP88 Johnny Woodard RC 1.00
BDP89 Wes Littleton RC 1.50
BDP90 Sean Rodriguez RC 4.00
BDP91 Kyle Pearson RC 1.00
BDP92 Josh Rainwater RC 2.00
BDP93 Travis Schlichting RC 1.50
BDP94 Tim Battle RC 2.00
BDP95 Aaron Hill RC 3.00
BDP96 Bob McCrory RC 1.00
BDP97 Rick Guarno RC 1.00
BDP98 Brandon Yarbrough RC 1.00
BDP99 Peter Stonard RC 1.50
BDP100 Darin Downs RC 1.50
BDP101 Matt Bruback RC 1.00
BDP102 Danny Garcia RC 1.00
BDP103 Cory Stewart RC 1.00
BDP104 Ferdin Tejeda RC 1.50
BDP105 Kade Johnson RC 1.00
BDP106 Andrew Brown RC 2.00
BDP107 Aquilino Lopez RC 1.00
BDP108 Stephen Randolph RC 1.00
BDP109 Dave Matranga RC 1.00
BDP110 Dustin McGowan RC 3.00
BDP111 Juan Camacho RC 1.50
BDP112 Cliff Lee .15
BDP113 Jeff Duncan RC 1.00
BDP114 C.J. Wilson .50
BDP115 Brandon Roberson RC 1.00
BDP116 David Corrente RC 1.00
BDP117 Kevin Beavers RC 1.00
BDP118 Anthony Webster RC 1.50
BDP119 Oscar Villarreal RC 1.00
BDP120 Hong-Chih Kuo RC 6.00
BDP121 Josh Barfield .15
BDP122 Denny Bautista .15
BDP123 Chris Burke 2.50
BDP124 Robinson Cano RC 20.00
BDP125 Jose Castillo .15
BDP126 Neal Cotts .15
BDP127 Jorge De La Rosa .15
BDP128 J.D. Durbin .15
BDP129 Edwin Encarnacion 2.00
BDP130 Gavin Floyd .15
BDP131 Alexis Gomez .15
BDP132 Edgar Gonzalez RC 1.00
BDP133 Khalil Greene .50
BDP134 Zack Greinke .15
BDP135 Franklin Gutierrez 1.50
BDP136 Rich Harden .15
BDP137 J.J. Hardy 8.00
BDP138 Ryan Howard 50.00
BDP139 Justin Huber .15
BDP140 David Kelton .15
BDP141 David Krynzel .15
BDP142 Pete LaForest .15
BDP143 Adam LaRoche .15
BDP144 Preston Larrison 1.00
BDP145 John Maine RC 15.00
BDP146 Andy Marte 4.00
BDP147 Jeff Mathis .15
BDP148 Joe Mauer 1.00
BDP149 Clint Nageotte .15
BDP150 Chris Narveson .15
BDP151 Ramon Nivar RC 1.00
BDP152 Felix Pie 6.00
BDP153 Guillermo Quiroz RC 1.00
BDP154 Rene Reyes .15
BDP155 Royce Ring .15
BDP156 Alexis Rios 2.50
BDP157 Grady Sizemore 1.00
BDP158 Stephen Smitherman .15
BDP159 Seung Jun Song .15
BDP160 Scott Thorman .15
BDP161 Chad Tracy .15
BDP162 Chin-Hui Tsao .15
BDP163 John Van Benschoten RC 1.00
BDP164 Kevin Youkilis 5.00
BDP165 Chien-Ming Wang 6.00
BDP166 Chris Lubanski/Auto. RC 40.00
BDP167 Ryan Harvey/Auto. RC 20.00
BDP168 Matt Murton/Auto. RC 20.00
BDP169 Jay Sborz/Auto. RC 10.00
BDP170 Brandon Wood/Auto. RC 60.00
BDP171 Nicholas Markakis/Auto. RC 75.00
BDP172 Rickie Weeks/Auto. RC 40.00
BDP173 Eric Duncan/Auto. RC 20.00
BDP174 Chad Billingsley/Auto. RC 50.00
BDP175 Ryan Wagner/Auto. RC 10.00
BDP176 Delmon Young/Auto. RC 125.00

Refractor

Rookies (29-165): 2-4X

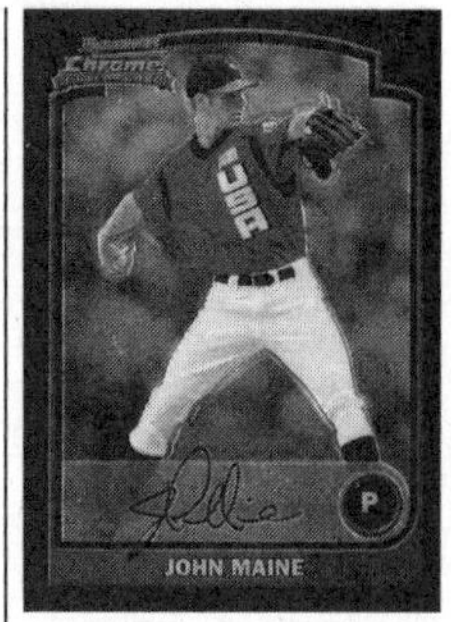

Inserted 1:11
Autos (166-176): .75-1.5X
Inserted 1:196

Gold Refractor

Rookies (29-165): 3-5X
Production 50 Sets
Autos (166-176): No Pricing
Inserted 1:1,479

X-Fractor

Rookies (29-165): 2-4X
Production 130 Sets
Autos (166-176): .75-2X
Inserted 1:393

2003 Bowman Heritage

NM/M
Complete Set (280): 60.00
Common Player: .25
Cards 171-180 have three versions.
Pack (8): 3.00
Box (24): 65.00
1 Jorge Posada .50
2 Todd Helton .75
3 Marcus Giles .25
4 Eric Chavez .40
5 Edgar Martinez .25
6 Luis Gonzalez .40
7 Corey Patterson .25
8 Preston Wilson .25
9 Ryan Klesko .25
10 Randy Johnson 1.00
11 Eric Byrnes .25
12 Carlos Lee .40
13 Steve Finley .25
14 A.J. Pierzynski .25
15 Troy Glaus .50
16 Darin Erstad .40
17 Moises Alou .40
18 Torii Hunter .50
19 Marlon Byrd .25
20 Mark Prior .75
21 Shannon Stewart .25
22 Craig Biggio .40
23 Johnny Damon .75
24 Robert Fick .25
25 Jason Giambi .75
26 Fernando Vina .25
27 Aubrey Huff .25
28 Benito Santiago .25
29 Jay Gibbons .25
30 Ken Griffey Jr. 2.00
31 Rocco Baldelli .50
32 Pat Burrell .50
33 A.J. Burnett .25
34 Omar Vizquel .25
35 Greg Maddux 1.50
36 Jae Weong Seo .25
37 C.C. Sabathia .25
38 Geoff Jenkins .25
39 Ty Wigginton .25
40 Jeff Kent .40
41 Orlando Hudson .25
42 Edgardo Alfonzo .25

43	Greg Myers	.25
44	Melvin Mora	.25
45	Sammy Sosa	1.00
46	Russ Ortiz	.25
47	Josh Beckett	.50
48	David Wells	.25
49	Woody Williams	.25
50	Alex Rodriguez	2.00
51	Randy Wolf	.25
52	Carlos Beltran	.75
53	Austin Kearns	.40
54	Trot Nixon	.25
55	Ivan Rodriguez	.75
56	Shea Hillenbrand	.25
57	Roberto Alomar	.40
58	John Olerud	.25
59	Michael Young	.25
60	Garret Anderson	.25
61	Mike Lieberthal	.25
62	Adam Dunn	.50
63	Raul Ibanez	.25
64	Kenny Lofton	.25
65	Ichiro Suzuki	1.50
66	Jarrod Washburn	.25
67	Shawn Chacon	.25
68	Alex Gonzalez	.25
69	Roy Halladay	.40
70	Vladimir Guerrero	1.00
71	Hee Seop Choi	.25
72	Brandon Phillips	.25
73	Ray Durham	.25
74	Mark Teixeira	.75
75	Hank Blalock	.40
76	Jerry Hairston Jr.	.25
77	Erubiel Durazo	.25
78	Frank Catalanotto	.25
79	Jacque Jones	.25
80	Bobby Abreu	.50
81	Mike Hampton	.25
82	Zach Day	.25
83	Jimmy Rollins	.50
84	Joel Pineiro	.25
85	Brett Myers	.25
86	Frank Thomas	.75
87	Aramis Ramirez	.40
88	Paul LoDuca	.25
89	Bobby Higginson	.25
90	Brian Giles	.25
91	Jose Cruz Jr.	.25
92	Derek Lowe	.25
93	Mark Buehrle	.25
94	Wade Miller	.25
95	Derek Jeter	2.00
96	Bret Boone	.25
97	Tony Batista	.25
98	Sean Casey	.25
99	Eric Hinske	.25
100	Albert Pujols	2.00
101	Runelvys Hernandez	.25
102	Vernon Wells	.40
103	Kerry Wood	.40
104	Lance Berkman	.50
105	Alfonso Soriano	1.00
106	Ken Harvey	.25
107	Bartolo Colon	.25
108	Andy Pettitte	.40
109	Rafael Furcal	.40
110	Dontrelle Willis	.40
111	Carl Crawford	.40
112	Scott Rolen	.75
113	Chipper Jones	1.00
114	Magglio Ordonez	.50
115	Bernie Williams	.50
116	Roy Oswalt	.50
117	Kevin Brown	.35
118	Cristian Guzman	.25
119	Kazuhisa Ishii	.25
120	Larry Walker	.40
121	Miguel Tejada	.50
122	Manny Ramirez	1.00
123	Mike Mussina	.50
124	Mike Lowell	.25
125	Barry Bonds	2.00
126	Aaron Boone	.25
127	Carlos Delgado	.60
128	Jose Vidro	.25
129	Brad Radke	.25
130	Rafael Palmeiro	.75
131	Mark Mulder	.40
132	Jason Schmidt	.40
133	Gary Sheffield	.50
134	Richie Sexson	.40
135	Barry Zito	.50
136	Tom Glavine	.40
137	Jim Edmonds	.40
138	Andruw Jones	.75
139	Pedro J. Martinez	1.00
140	Curt Schilling	.75
141	Joe Kennedy	.25
142	Nomar Garciaparra	1.00
143	Vicente Padilla	.25
144	Kevin Millwood	.40
145	Shawn Green	.40
146	Jeff Bagwell	.75
147	Hideo Nomo	.50
148	Fred McGriff	.25
149	Matt Morris	.25
150	Roger Clemens	2.00
151	Damian Moss	.25
152	Orlando Cabrera	.25
153	Tim Hudson	.40
154	Mike Sweeney	.25
155	Jim Thome	.75
156	Rich Aurilia	.25
157	Mike Piazza	1.00
158	Edgar Renteria	.25
159	Javy Lopez	.25
160	Jamie Moyer	.25
161	Miguel Cabrera	.75
162	Adam Loewen **RC**	1.00
163	Jose Reyes	.50
164	Zack Greinke	.25
165	Cole Hamels	.25
166	Jeremy Guthrie	.25
167	Victor Martinez	.40
168	Rich Harden	.25
169	Joe Mauer	.50
170	Khalil Greene	.25
171	Willie Mays	2.00
172	Phil Rizzuto	.50
173	Al Kaline	1.00
174	Warren Spahn	1.00
175	Jimmy Piersall	.50
176	Luis Aparicio	.50
177	Whitey Ford	1.00
178	Harmon Killebrew	1.00
179	Duke Snider	1.00
180	Bobby Richardson	.50
181	David Martinez	.25
182	Felix Pie **RC**	3.00
183	Kevin Correia **RC**	.50
184	Brandon Webb **RC**	2.50
185	Matt Diaz **RC**	.50
186	Lew Ford **RC**	.50
187	Jeremy Griffiths	.25
188	Matt Hensley **RC**	.75
189	Danny Garcia **RC**	.50
190	Elizardo Ramirez **RC**	.50
191	Greg Aquino **RC**	.50
192	Felix Sanchez **RC**	.50
193	Kelly Shoppach **RC**	.75
194	Bubba Nelson **RC**	.50
195	Mike O'Keefe **RC**	.50
196	Hanley Ramirez **RC**	5.00
197	Todd Wellemeyer **RC**	.50
198	Dustin Moseley **RC**	.75
199	Eric Crozier **RC**	.50
200	Ryan Shealy **RC**	1.50
201	Jeremy Bonderman	2.00
202	Bo Hart **RC**	.50
203	Dusty Brown **RC**	.50
204	Rob Hammock **RC**	.50
205	Jorge Piedra **RC**	.50
206	Jason Kubel **RC**	1.00
207	Stephen Randolph **RC**	.50
208	Andy Sisco	.50
209	Matt Kata **RC**	.50
210	Robinson Cano **RC**	10.00
211	Ben Francisco **RC**	.50
212	Arnie Munoz **RC**	.50
213	Ozzie Chavez **RC**	.50
214	Beau Kemp **RC**	.50
215	Travis Wong **RC**	.50
216	Brian McCann	5.00
217	Aquilino Lopez **RC**	.50
218	Bobby Basham **RC**	.50
219	Tim Olson **RC**	.50
220	Nathan Panther **RC**	.50
221	Wilfredo Ledezma **RC**	.50
222	Josh Willingham **RC**	1.00
223	David Cash **RC**	.50
224	Oscar Villarreal **RC**	.50
225	Jeff Duncan **RC**	.75
226	Dan Haren	2.00
227	Michel Hernandez **RC**	.50
228	Matt Murton **RC**	1.50
229	Clay Hensley **RC**	.75
230	Tyler Johnson **RC**	.50
231	Tyler Martin **RC**	.50
232	J.D. Durbin **RC**	.75
233	Shane Victorino **RC**	.50
234	Rajai Davis **RC**	.50
235	Chien-Ming Wang **RC**	6.00
236	Travis Ishikawa **RC**	.50
237	Eric Eckenstahler	.25
238	Dustin McGowan **RC**	1.00
239	Prentice Redman **RC**	.50
240	Haj Turay **RC**	.50
241	Matt DeMarco **RC**	.50
242	Lou Palmisano **RC**	.50
243	Eric Reed **RC**	.50
244	Willie Eyre **RC**	.50
245	Ferdin Tejeda **RC**	.75
246	Michael Garciaparra	.25
247	Michael Hinckley **RC**	.50
248	Branden Florence **RC**	.50
249	Trent Oeltjen **RC**	.50
250	Mike Neu **RC**	.75
251	Chris Lubanski **RC**	1.50
252	Brandon Wood **RC**	5.00
253	Delmon Young **RC**	5.00
253	Delmon Young/ Auto. **RC**	75.00
254	Matt Harrison **RC**	.50
255	Chad Billingsley **RC**	2.50
256	Josh Anderson **RC**	.50
257	Brian McFall	.75
258	Ryan Wagner **RC**	.50
259	Billy Hogan **RC**	.50
260	Nate Spears **RC**	.75
261	Ryan Harvey **RC**	2.00
262	Wes Littleton **RC**	.50
263	Xavier Paul **RC**	.75
264	Sean Rodriguez **RC**	1.50
265	Brian Finch **RC**	.50
266	Josh Rainwater **RC**	.50
267	Brian Snyder **RC**	.75
268	Eric Duncan **RC**	1.50
269	Rickie Weeks **RC**	3.00
270	Tim Battle **RC**	.50
271	Scott Beerer **RC**	.50
272	Aaron Hill **RC**	.75
273	Casey Abrams **RC**	.50
274	Jonathan Fulton **RC**	.50
275	Todd Jennings **RC**	.50
276	Jordan Pratt **RC**	.50
277	Tom Gorzelanny **RC**	1.00
278	Matt Lorenzo **RC**	.75
279	Jarrod Saltalamacchia **RC**	3.00
280	Mike Wagner **RC**	.50

Diamond Cuts

		NM/M
Common Player:		4.00
Red:		1-2X
Production 56 Sets		
JA	Jeremy Affeldt	4.00
MA	Moises Alou	5.00
TA	Tony Armas Jr.	4.00
JB	Jeff Bagwell	6.00
CB	Craig Biggio	6.00
HB	Hank Blalock	6.00
BB	Bret Boone	4.00
EC	Eric Chavez	4.00
JE	Jim Edmonds	6.00
JG	Jason Giambi	8.00
TG	Troy Glaus	6.00
MG	Mark Grace	6.00
VG	Vladimir Guerrero	8.00
CG	Cristian Guzman	4.00
TH	Todd Helton	6.00
RH	Rickey Henderson	12.00
JJ	Jason Jennings	4.00
AJ	Andruw Jones	6.00
CJ1	Chipper Jones/Jsy	8.00
CJ2	Chipper Jones/Bat	8.00
AK	Austin Kearns	6.00
PL	Paul LoDuca	4.00
JL	Javy Lopez	4.00
PM	Pedro J. Martinez	8.00
KM	Kevin Millwood	4.00
MM	Mark Mulder	4.00
BM	Brett Myers	4.00
HN	Hideo Nomo	8.00
RP1	Rafael Palmeiro/Jsy	8.00
RP2	Rafael Palmeiro/Bat	8.00
JLP	Josh Phelps	4.00
AP	Albert Pujols	15.00
JR	Jose Reyes	6.00
AR1	Alex Rodriguez/Jsy	10.00
AR2	Alex Rodriguez/Bat	10.00
SR1	Scott Rolen/Jsy	8.00
SR2	Scott Rolen/Bat	10.00
KI	Kazuhiro Sasaki	4.00
GS	Gary Sheffield	6.00
AS	Alfonso Soriano	8.00
SS1	Sammy Sosa/Jsy	10.00
SS2	Sammy Sosa/Bat	10.00
MS	Mike Sweeney	4.00
MT	Miguel Tejada	6.00
JV	Javier Vazquez	4.00
JW	Jarrod Washburn	4.00
VW	Vernon Wells	4.00
BW	Bernie Williams	6.00
KW	Kerry Wood	5.00
BZ	Barry Zito	6.00

Keith Olbermann Autograph

		NM/M
Inserted 1:1,421		
KO	Keith Olbermann	50.00

Signs of Greatness

		NM/M
Common Player:		6.00
Inserted 1:30		
Red Ink:		No Pricing
Production One Set		
CB	Chad Billingsley	25.00
RC	Robinson Cano	125.00
JD	Jeff Duncan	8.00
BF	Brian Finch	8.00
TG	Tom Gorzelanny	15.00
RH	Rich Harden	15.00
MM	Matt Murton	15.00
FP	Felix Pie	25.00
BS	Brian Snyder	8.00
RW	Rickie Weeks	20.00

DW	Dontrelle Willis	25.00
KY	Kevin Youkilis	20.00

2003 Bowman's Best

		NM/M
Complete Set:		
Common Player:		.50
Pack (5):		50.00
Box (10):		450.00
Veterans		
GJA	Garret Anderson	.50
LB	Lance Berkman	.75
BLB	Barry Bonds	4.00
PB	Pat Burrell	.50
WRC	Roger Clemens	3.00
NG	Nomar Garciaparra	1.50
JGG	Jason Giambi	1.00
BSG	Brian Giles	.50
SG	Shawn Green	.50
KG	Ken Griffey Jr.	2.50
VG	Vladimir Guerrero	1.50
TH	Todd Helton	1.00
TKH	Torii Hunter	.75
DJ	Derek Jeter	4.00
RJ	Randy Johnson	1.50
CJ	Chipper Jones	1.50
AK	Austin Kearns	.50
JFK	Jeff Kent	.50
GM	Greg Maddux	2.50
PM	Pedro J. Martinez	1.50
MOR	Magglio Ordonez	.50
MJP	Mike Piazza	1.50
MP	Mark Prior	1.00
AP	Albert Pujols	4.00
MR	Manny Ramirez	1.50
AR	Alex Rodriguez	3.00
CMS	Curt Schilling	1.50
AS	Alfonso Soriano	1.50
SS	Sammy Sosa	2.50
IS	Ichiro Suzuki	2.50
MS	Mike Sweeney	.50
MT	Miguel Tejada	1.00
JT	Jim Thome	1.00
LW	Larry Walker	.50
BZ	Barry Zito	.75
First-Year Players		
JB	Jeremy Bonderman	4.00
TJB	T.J. Bohn	1.00
MB	Matt Bruback **RC**	1.00
BC	Bernie Castro **RC**	1.00
JC	Jose Contreras **RC**	2.00
MD	Matt Diaz **RC**	2.00
BJH	Bo Hart **RC**	1.00
RM	Ramon Martinez	1.00
MO	Mike O'Keefe **RC**	1.00
JMS	Jon-Mark Sprowl **RC**	1.00
TT	Terry Tiffee	1.00
HT	Haj Turay **RC**	2.00
SV	Shane Victorino **RC**	3.00
CW	Chien-Ming Wang **RC**	15.00
DY	Dustin Yount **RC**	1.00
First-Year Player Autographs		
Common Auto.:		8.00
Inserted 1:1		
TA	Tyler Adamczyk **RC**	8.00
GA	Greg Aquino **RC**	8.00
BWB	Bobby Basham **RC**	10.00
GB	Gregor Blanco **RC**	10.00
AB	Andrew Brown **RC**	8.00
BB	Bryan Bullington **RC**	20.00
RC	Ryan Cameron **RC**	8.00
DC	David Cash **RC**	8.00
OC	Ozzie Chavez **RC**	8.00
RD	Rajai Davis **RC**	10.00
CDC	Chris De La Cruz **RC**	10.00
MD	Matt Diaz **RC**	10.00
CAD	Carlos Duran **RC**	10.00
JDD	J.D. Durbin **RC**	10.00
WE	Willie Eyre **RC**	8.00
BF	Branden Florence **RC**	8.00
LF	Lew Ford **RC**	10.00
BLF	Ben Francisco **RC**	10.00
JG	Joey Gomes	10.00
JRG	Jeremy Griffiths	10.00
MNH	Matt Hagen **RC**	10.00
RWH	Robby Hammock **RC**	10.00
DH	Dan Haren	30.00
BH	Brendan Harris **RC**	15.00
MDH	Matt Hensley **RC**	8.00
MH	Michel Hernandez **RC**	10.00
MHI	Michael Hinckley **RC**	10.00
RH	Ryan Howard	350.00
TI	Travis Ishikawa **RC**	10.00
KJ	Kade Johnson **RC**	8.00
TJ	Tyler Johnson **RC**	8.00
MK	Matt Kata **RC**	10.00
BK	Beau Kemp **RC**	8.00
JK	Jason Kubel **RC**	15.00
PL	Pete LaForest **RC**	10.00
WL	Wilfredo Ledezma **RC**	10.00
NL	Nook Logan **RC**	10.00
MDM	Mark Malaska **RC**	8.00
CM	Charlie Manning **RC**	8.00
DM	David Martinez	10.00
AM	Aneudis Mateo **RC**	8.00
BM	Brian McCann	60.00
DMM	Dustin McGowan **RC**	30.00
JM	Jose Morales	10.00
DAM	Dustin Moseley **RC**	10.00
TO	Tim Olson **RC**	10.00
FP	Felix Pie **RC**	60.00
ER	Elizardo Ramirez **RC**	10.00
HR	Hanley Ramirez **RC**	100.00
DR	Darrell Rasner	8.00
PR	Prentice Redman **RC**	8.00
FS	Felix Sanchez **RC**	10.00
GS	Gary Schneidmiller **RC**	8.00
CSS	Corey Shafer **RC**	10.00
RS	Ryan Shealy **RC**	15.00
KS	Kelly Shoppach **RC**	15.00
CS	Cory Stewart **RC**	10.00
TSH	Thomari Story-Harden **RC**	8.00
FT	Ferdin Tejeda **RC**	10.00
ET	Eider Torres **RC**	10.00
ST	Scott Tyler	10.00
JV	Joe Valentine **RC**	8.00
DW	Doug Waechter **RC**	10.00
AW	Aron Weston **RC**	8.00
JW	Josh Willingham **RC**	20.00
CJW	C.J. Wilson	0.00
KY	Kevin Youkilis **RC**	40.00
CW	Chien-Ming Wang **RC**	250.00

Blue

Blue Autographs:	1-1.5X
Inserted 1:32	
Blue Base Card:	3-5X
Blue Rookies:	1-2X
Production 100	

Red

Red Autographs:	2-4X
Inserted 1:63	
Red Base Card:	4-8X
Red Rookies:	2-3X
Production 50	

Double Play

		NM/M
Common Card:		20.00
Inserted 1:55		
EB	Elizardo Ramirez, Bryan Bullington	25.00
GK	Joey Gomes, Jason Kubel	50.00
SR	Felix Sanchez, Darrell Rasner	20.00
YS	Kevin Youkilis, Kelly Shoppach	40.00
HV	Dan Haren, Joe Valentine	25.00
GM	Jeremy Griffiths, David Martinez	20.00
HM	Michael Hinckley, Brian McCann	20.00
RS	Prentice Redman, Gary Schneidmiller	20.00
LL	Nook Logan, Wilfredo Ledezma	25.00
SB	Corey Shafer, Gregor Blanco	25.00

Triple Play

		NM/M
Inserted 1:219		
DRS	Rajai Davis, Hanley Ramirez, Ryan Shealy	85.00
BCS	Andrew Brown, David Cash, Cory Stewart	30.00

First-Year Player Relics

		NM/M
Common Player:		5.00
RLD	Rajai Davis	5.00
JLF	Lew Ford	8.00
JGG	Joey Gomes	5.00
RJH	Ryan Howard	60.00
JJK	Jason Kubel	8.00
HRB	Hanley Ramirez	20.00
RNS	Ryan Shealy	8.00
KBS	Kelly Shoppach	8.00
KEY	Kevin Youkilis	10.00

2004 Bowman

		NM/M
Complete Set (330):		70.00
Common Player:		.15
Common Rookie:		.50
Pack (10):		3.00
Box (24):		60.00
1	Garret Anderson	.15
2	Larry Walker	.25
3	Derek Jeter	2.00
4	Curt Schilling	.75
5	Carlos Zambrano	.40
6	Shawn Green	.25
7	Manny Ramirez	.75
8	Randy Johnson	.75
9	Jeremy Bonderman	.25
10	Alfonso Soriano	.75
11	Scott Rolen	.75
12	Kerry Wood	.25
13	Eric Gagne	.25
14	Ryan Klesko	.15
15	Kevin Millar	.15
16	Ty Wigginton	.15
17	David Ortiz	.75
18	Luis Castillo	.15
19	Bernie Williams	.40
20	Edgar Renteria	.25
21	Matt Kata	.15
22	Bartolo Colon	.25
23	Derrek Lee	.50
24	Gary Sheffield	.40
25	Nomar Garciaparra	.75
26	Kevin Millwood	.25
27	Corey Patterson	.25
28	Carlos Beltran	.50
29	Mike Lieberthal	.15
30	Troy Glaus	.40
31	Preston Wilson	.15
32	Jorge Posada	.50
33	Bo Hart	.15
34	Mark Prior	.40
35	Hideo Nomo	.25
36	Jason Kendall	.15
37	Shea Hillenbrand	.15
38	Dmitri Young	.15
39	Aaron Boone	.15
40	Jim Edmonds	.40
41	Ryan Ludwick	.15
42	Brandon Webb	.25
43	Todd Helton	.50
44	Jacque Jones	.15
45	Xavier Nady	.15
46	Tim Salmon	.25
47	Kelvim Escobar	.15
48	Tony Batista	.15
49	Nick Johnson	.15
50	Jim Thome	.50
51	Casey Blake	.15
52	Trot Nixon	.25
53	Luis Gonzalez	.25
54	Dontrelle Willis	.25
55	Mike Mussina	.40
56	Carl Crawford	.25
57	Mark Buehrle	.25
58	Scott Podsednik	.25
59	Brian Giles	.15
60	Rafael Furcal	.25
61	Miguel Cabrera	.75
62	Rich Harden	.15
63	Mark Teixeira	.50
64	Frank Thomas	.75
65	Johan Santana	.50
66	Jason Schmidt	.25
67	Aramis Ramirez	.40
68	Jose Reyes	.75
69	Magglio Ordonez	.25
70	Mike Sweeney	.15
71	Eric Chavez	.25
72	Rocco Baldelli	.25
73	Sammy Sosa	.50
74	Javy Lopez	.15
75	Roy Oswalt	.25
76	Raul Ibanez	.15
77	Ivan Rodriguez	.50
78	Jerome Williams	.15
79	Carlos Lee	.25
80	Geoff Jenkins	.15
81	Sean Burroughs	.15
82	Marcus Giles	.15
83	Mike Lowell	.15

84 Barry Zito .40
85 Aubrey Huff .15
86 Esteban Loaiza .15
87 Torii Hunter .25
88 Phil Nevin .15
89 Andruw Jones .50
90 Josh Beckett .40
91 Mark Mulder .25
92 Hank Blalock .25
93 Jason Phillips .15
94 Russ Ortiz .15
95 Juan Pierre .15
96 Tom Glavine .25
97 Gil Meche .15
98 Ramon Ortiz .15
99 Richie Sexson .40
100 Albert Pujols 2.00
101 Javier Vazquez .15
102 Johnny Damon .75
103 Alex Rodriguez 1.50
104 Omar Vizquel .25
105 Chipper Jones .75
106 Lance Berkman .40
107 Tim Hudson .40
108 Carlos Delgado .40
109 Austin Kearns .25
110 Orlando Cabrera .25
111 Edgar Martinez .25
112 Melvin Mora .15
113 Jeff Bagwell .50
114 Marlon Byrd .15
115 Vernon Wells .25
116 C.C. Sabathia .25
117 Cliff Floyd .15
118 Ichiro Suzuki 1.00
119 Miguel Olivo .15
120 Mike Piazza .75
121 Adam Dunn .40
122 Paul Lo Duca .15
123 Brett Myers .25
124 Michael Young .25
125 Larry Bigbie .15
126 Greg Maddux 1.00
127 Vladimir Guerrero .75
128 Miguel Tejada .40
129 Andy Pettitte .40
130 Jose Cruz .15
131 Ken Griffey Jr. 1.50
132 Shannon Stewart .15
133 Joel Pineiro .15
134 Luis Matos .15
135 Jeff Kent .25
136 Randy Wolf .15
137 Chris Woodward .15
138 Jody Gerut .15
139 Jose Vidro .15
140 Bret Boone .15
141 Bill Mueller .15
142 Angel Berroa .15
143 Bobby Abreu .25
144 Roy Halladay .25
145 Delmon Young .50
146 Jonny Gomes .15
147 Rickie Weeks .40
148 Edwin Jackson .15
149 Neal Cotts .15
150 Jason Bay .40
151 Khalil Greene .25
152 Joe Mauer .40
153 Bobby Jenks .15
154 Chin-Feng Chen .15
154 Chin-Feng Chen/Jsy 10.00
155 Chien-Ming Wang .75
155 Chien-Ming Wang/ Jsy 25.00
156 Mickey Hall .15
156 Mickey Hall/Jersey 5.00
157 James Houser .15
157 James Houser/Jsy 5.00
158 Jay Sborz .15
158 Jay Sborz/Jersey 5.00
159 Jonathan Fulton .15
159 Jonathan Fulton/Jsy 5.00
160 Steve Lerud .15
160 Steve Lerud/Jersey 5.00
161 Grady Sizemore .50
161 Grady Sizemore/ Auto. 40.00
162 Felix Pie .50
162 Felix Pie/Auto. 15.00
163 Dustin McGowan .15
163 Dustin McGowan/ Auto. 10.00
164 Chris Lubanski .15
164 Chris Lubanski/Auto. 10.00
164 Chris Lubanski/Jsy 5.00
165 Tom Gorzelanny .15
165 Tom Gorzelanny/ Auto. 15.00
166 Rudy Guillen **RC** 1.00
166 Rudy Guillen/auto **RC** 10.00
167 Bobby Brownlie **RC** 1.00
167 Bobby Brownlie/ Auto. **RC** 10.00
168 Conor Jackson 1.50
168 Conor Jackson/Auto. 30.00
169 Matt Moses 1.00
169 Matt Moses/Auto. 20.00
170 Ervin Santana **RC** 1.50
170 Ervin Santana/ Auto. **RC** 15.00
171 Merkin Valdez **RC** .50
171 Merkin Valdez/ Auto. **RC** 10.00
172 Erick Aybar **RC** 1.00
172 Erick Aybar/Auto. **RC** 15.00
173 Brad Sullivan .50
173 Brad Sullivan/Auto. 10.00
174 David Aardsma .50
174 David Aardsma/Auto. 10.00
175 Brad Snyder .75
175 Brad Snyder/Auto. 10.00
176 Alberto Callaspo **RC** .75
177 Brandon Medders **RC** .50
178 Zach Miner **RC** 1.00
179 Charlie Zink **RC** .40
180 Adam Greenberg .75
181 Kevin Howard **RC** .50
182 Wanell Severino **RC** .50
183 Kevin Kouzmanoff 2.00
184 Joel Zumaya **RC** 4.00
185 Skip Schumaker **RC** .50
186 Nic Ungs **RC** .50
187 Todd Self **RC** .50
188 Brian Steffek **RC** .50
189 Brock Peterson **RC** .50
190 Greg Thissen **RC** .50
191 Frank Brooks **RC** .50
192 Estee Harris **RC** .50
192 Estee Harris/Jersey **RC** 5.00
193 Chris Mabeus **RC** .50
194 Daniel Giese **RC** .50
195 Jared Wells **RC** .50
196 Carlos Sosa **RC** .50
197 Bobby Madritsch .50
198 Calvin Hayes **RC** .50
199 Omar Quintanilla .50
200 Chris O'Riordan **RC** .50
201 Tim Hutting **RC** .50
202 Carlos Quentin 3.00
203 Brayan Pena **RC** .50
204 Jeff Salazar **RC** 1.00
205 David Murphy 1.00
206 Alberto Garcia **RC** .50
207 Ramon Ramirez **RC** .50
208 Luis Bolivar **RC** .50
209 Rodney Choy Foo **RC** .50
210 Kyle Sleeth .50
211 Anthony Acevedo **RC** .50
212 Chad Santos **RC** .50
213 Jason Frasor **RC** .75
214 Jesse Roman **RC** .50
215 James Tomlin **RC** .50
216 Josh Labandeira **RC** .75
217 Joaquin Arias **RC** .50
218 Don Sutton **RC** (Photo actually Nick Swisher.) 1.50
219 Danny Gonzalez **RC** .50
220 Javier Guzman **RC** .50
221 Anthony Lerew **RC** .50
221 Anthony Lerew/Jsy **RC** 5.00
222 Jon Knott **RC** .50
223 Jesse English **RC** .50
224 Felix Hernandez **RC** 5.00
225 Travis Hanson .50
226 Jesse Floyd **RC** .50
227 Nick Gorneault **RC** .50
228 Craig Ansman **RC** .50
229 Wardell Starling **RC** .50
230 Carl Loadenthal **RC** .50
231 David Crouthers .50
232 Harvey Garcia **RC** .50
233 Casey Kopitzke **RC** .50
234 Ricky Nolasco 1.00
235 Miguel Perez **RC** .50
236 Ryan Mulhern **RC** .50
237 Chris Aguila **RC** .50
238 Brooks Conrad **RC** .50
239 Damaso Espino **RC** .50
240 Jereme Milons **RC** .50
241 Luke Hughes **RC** .50
242 Kory Casto .50
243 Jose Valdez **RC** .50
244 J.T. Stotts .50
245 Lee Gwaltney **RC** .50
246 Yoann Torrealba **RC** .50
247 Omar Falcon **RC** .50
248 Jon Coutlangus **RC** .50
249 George Sherrill **RC** .50
250 John Santor **RC** .50
251 Tony Richie **RC** .50
252 Kevin Richardson **RC** .50
253 Tim Bittner **RC** .50
254 Dustin Nippert **RC** 1.00
255 Jose Capellan **RC** .50
256 Donald Levinski .50
257 Jerome Gamble **RC** .50
258 Jeff Keppinger **RC** 1.00
259 Jason Szuminski **RC** .50
260 Akinori Otsuka **RC** .75
261 Ryan Budde .50
262 Shingo Takatsu **RC** .75
263 Jeffrey Allison .40
264 Hector Gimenez **RC** .50
265 Tim Frend **RC** .50
266 Tom Farmer **RC** .50
267 Shawn Hill **RC** .50
268 Lastings Milledge 5.00
269 Scott Proctor **RC** .75
270 Jorge Mejia **RC** .50
271 Terry Jones **RC** .50
272 Zachary Duke **RC** 1.50
273 Tim Stauffer .75
274 Luke Anderson **RC** .50
275 Hunter Brown **RC** .50
276 Matt Lemanczyk **RC** .50
277 Fernando Cortez **RC** .50
278 Vince Perkins **RC** .50
279 Tommy Murphy **RC** .50
280 Mike Gosling .50
281 Paul Bacot .50
282 Matt Capps **RC** .75
283 Juan Gutierrez **RC** .50
284 Teodoro Encarnacion **RC** .50
285 Juan Cedeno **RC** .50
286 Matt Creighton **RC** .50
287 Ryan Hankins **RC** .50
288 Leo Nunez **RC** .50
289 Dave Wallace **RC** .50
290 Rob Tejeda **RC** .75
291 Lincoln Holdzkom **RC** .50
292 Jason Hirsh 1.50
293 Tydus Meadows **RC** .50
294 Khalid Ballouli **RC** .50
295 Benji DeQuin **RC** .50
296 Tyler Davidson 1.00
297 Brent Colamarino **RC** .50
298 Marcus McBeth **RC** .50
299 Brad Eldred **RC** .75
300 David Pauley **RC** .50
301 Yadier Molina **RC** 1.00
302 Chris Shelton **RC** 1.00
303 Travis Blackley **RC** .50
304 Jon DeVries .50
305 Sheldon Fulse **RC** .50
306 Vito Chiaravalloti **RC** .50
307 Warner Madrigal **RC** .75
308 Reid Gorecki **RC** .50
309 Sung Jung **RC** .50
310 Peter Shier **RC** .50
311 Michael Mooney **RC** .50
312 Kenny Perez **RC** .50
313 Mike Mallory **RC** .50
314 Ben Himes **RC** .50
315 Ivan Ochoa **RC** .50
316 Donald Kelly **RC** .50
317 Logan Kensing **RC** .50
318 Kevin Davidson **RC** .50
319 Brian Pilkington .50
320 Alex Romero **RC** .50
321 Chad Chop **RC** .50
322 Dioner Navarro **RC** .75
323 Casey Myers **RC** .50
324 Mike Rouse .50
325 Sergio Silva **RC** .50
326 J.J. Furmaniak **RC** .75
327 Brad Vericker **RC** .50
328 Blake Hawksworth **RC** 1.00
329 Brock Jacobsen **RC** .50
330 Alec Zumwalt **RC** .50

Gold

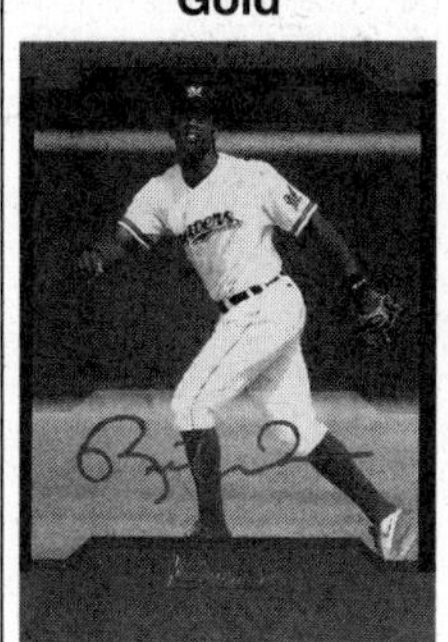

Stars: 1-2X
Rookies: 1-2X
Inserted 1:1

Uncirculated

Stars: 4-8X
Rookies: 3-5X
Production 245 Sets

1st Edition

NM/M
Stars: 3-5X
Rookies: 1-2X
HTA Exclusive
Pack (10): 4.00
Box (20): 75.00

Base of the Future Autographed Relic

NM/M
HTA Exclusive
GS Grady Sizemore 40.00

Futures Game Gear

NM/M
Common Player: 4.00
DB Denny Bautista 6.00
CB Chris Burke 6.00
JC Jose Castillo 4.00
NC Neal Cotts 5.00
JD Jorge De La Rosa 4.00
EE Edwin Encarnacion 8.00
SH Shawn Hill 4.00
EJ Edwin Jackson 4.00
DK David Kelton 4.00
DBK David Krynzel 4.00
PL Pete LaForest 4.00
JM John Maine 10.00
CN Clint Nageotte 6.00
RN Ramon Nivar 4.00
GQ Guillermo Quiroz 4.00
AR Alexis Rios 8.00
ES Ervin Santana 8.00
SS Stephen Smitherman 4.00
SJS Seung Jun Song 4.00
CT Chad Tracy 8.00
ST Scott Thorman 8.00
MV Merkin Valdez 4.00
JV John VanBenschoten 6.00
CW Chien-Ming Wang 40.00
KY Kevin Youkilis 10.00

Rookie of the Year Dual Relic

NM/M
Inserted 1:829
BW Angel Berroa, Dontrelle Willis 15.00

Signs of Future

NM/M
Common Autograph: 8.00
Red Ink: No Pricing
Production 25 Sets
JB Justin Backsmeyer 10.00
IC Ismael Castro 8.00
BC Brent Clevelen 15.00
ED Eric Duncan 15.00
BF Brian Finch 8.00
RH Ryan Harvey 15.00
AH Aaron Hill 15.00
JH James Houser 8.00
TJ Tyler Johnson 8.00
TL Todd Linden 8.00
NM Nicholas Markakis 25.00
BM Brandon Medders 8.00
MM Matt Murton 15.00
CS Corey Shafer 8.00
GS Grady Sizemore 40.00
BS Brian Snyder 8.00
DS Denard Span 8.00
JV Joey Votto 30.00
BW Brandon Wood 20.00

2004 Bowman Chrome

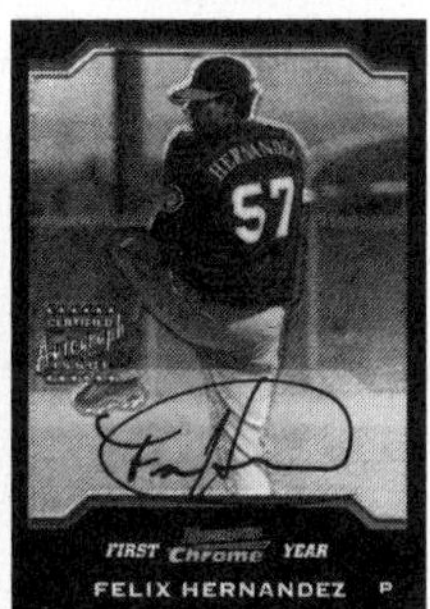

NM/M
Complete Set (350):
Common Player: .25
Common Rookie: 1.00
Common Rookie Auto. (331-350): 10.00
Inserted 1:18
Pack (4): 7.00
Box (18): 120.00
1 Garret Anderson .50
2 Larry Walker .50
3 Derek Jeter 2.50
4 Curt Schilling .75
5 Carlos Zambrano .50
6 Shawn Green .50
7 Manny Ramirez 1.00
8 Randy Johnson 1.00
9 Jeremy Bonderman .50
10 Alfonso Soriano 1.00
11 Scott Rolen 1.00
12 Kerry Wood .50
13 Eric Gagne .50
14 Ryan Klesko .25
15 Kevin Millar .25
16 Ty Wigginton .25
17 David Ortiz 1.50
18 Luis Castillo .25
19 Bernie Williams .50
20 Edgar Renteria .50
21 Matt Kata .25
22 Bartolo Colon .50
23 Derrek Lee .75
24 Gary Sheffield .75
25 Nomar Garciaparra 1.00
26 Kevin Millwood .25
27 Corey Patterson .50
28 Carlos Beltran .75
29 Mike Lieberthal .25
30 Troy Glaus .50
31 Preston Wilson .25
32 Jorge Posada .50
33 Bo Hart .25
34 Mark Prior .75
35 Hideo Nomo .50
36 Jason Kendall .25
37 Roger Clemens 2.50
38 Dmitri Young .25
39 Jason Giambi .75
40 Jim Edmonds .75
41 Ryan Ludwick .25
42 Brandon Webb .50
43 Todd Helton .75
44 Jacque Jones .25
45 Jamie Moyer .25
46 Tim Salmon .50
47 Kelvim Escobar .25
48 Tony Batista .25
49 Nick Johnson .25
50 Jim Thome 1.00
51 Casey Blake .25
52 Trot Nixon .50
53 Luis Gonzalez .50
54 Dontrelle Willis .50
55 Mike Mussina .50
56 Carl Crawford .50
57 Mark Buehrle .50
58 Scott Podsednik .50
59 Brian Giles .50
60 Rafael Furcal .50
61 Miguel Cabrera 1.00
62 Rich Harden .50
63 Mark Teixeira .75
64 Frank Thomas .75
65 Johan Santana .75
66 Jason Schmidt .50
67 Aramis Ramirez .50
68 Jose Reyes .75
69 Magglio Ordonez .50
70 Mike Sweeney .25
71 Eric Chavez .50
72 Rocco Baldelli .50
73 Sammy Sosa .75
74 Javy Lopez .25
75 Roy Oswalt .50
76 Raul Ibanez .25
77 Ivan Rodriguez .75
78 Jerome Williams .25
79 Carlos Lee .50
80 Geoff Jenkins .25
81 Sean Burroughs .25
82 Marcus Giles .25
83 Mike Lowell .50
84 Barry Zito .50
85 Aubrey Huff .25
86 Esteban Loaiza .25
87 Torii Hunter .50
88 Phil Nevin .25
89 Andruw Jones .75
90 Josh Beckett .75
91 Mark Mulder .50
92 Hank Blalock .50
93 Jason Phillips .25
94 Russ Ortiz .25
95 Juan Pierre .25
96 Tom Glavine .50
97 Gil Meche .25
98 Ramon Ortiz .25
99 Richie Sexson .75
100 Albert Pujols 2.50
101 Javier Vazquez .50
102 Johnny Damon 1.00
103 Alex Rodriguez 2.50
104 Omar Vizquel .50
105 Chipper Jones 1.00
106 Lance Berkman .50
107 Tim Hudson .50
108 Carlos Delgado .50
109 Austin Kearns .40
110 Orlando Cabrera .25
111 Edgar Martinez .50
112 Melvin Mora .25
113 Jeff Bagwell .75
114 Marlon Byrd .25
115 Vernon Wells .50
116 C.C. Sabathia .50
117 Cliff Floyd .25
118 Ichiro Suzuki 2.00
119 Miguel Olivo .25
120 Mike Piazza 1.00
121 Adam Dunn .75
122 Paul Lo Duca .25
123 Brett Myers .25
124 Michael Young .50
125 Sidney Ponson .25
126 Greg Maddux 2.00
127 Vladimir Guerrero 1.00
128 Miguel Tejada .50
129 Andy Pettitte .50
130 Rafael Palmeiro .75
131 Ken Griffey Jr. 2.00
132 Shannon Stewart .25
133 Joel Pineiro .25
134 Luis Matos .25
135 Jeff Kent .50
136 Randy Wolf .25
137 Chris Woodward .25
138 Jody Gerut .25
139 Jose Vidro .25
140 Bret Boone .25
141 Bill Mueller .25
142 Angel Berroa .25
143 Bobby Abreu .50
144 Roy Halladay .50
145 Delmon Young .50
146 Jonny Gomes .25
147 Rickie Weeks .50
148 Edwin Jackson .25
149 Neal Cotts .25
150 Jason Bay .50
151 Khalil Greene .50
152 Joe Mauer .50
153 Bobby Jenks .25
154 Chin-Feng Chen .25
155 Chien-Ming Wang .75
156 Mickey Hall .25
157 James Houser .25
158 Jay Sborz .25
159 Jonathan Fulton .25
160 Steve Lerud .25
161 Grady Sizemore .75
162 Felix Pie .50
163 Dustin McGowan .25
164 Chris Lubanski .25
165 Tom Gorzelanny .50
166 Rudy Guillen **RC** 3.00
167 Aarom Baldiris **RC** 2.00
168 Conor Jackson 8.00
169 Matt Moses 2.00
170 Ervin Santana **RC** 2.00
171 Merkin Valdez **RC** 2.00
172 Erick Aybar **RC** 3.00
173 Brad Sullivan 1.00
174 Joey Gathright **RC** 2.00
175 Brad Snyder 2.00
176 Alberto Callaspo **RC** 3.00
177 Brandon Medders **RC** 1.00
178 Zach Miner **RC** 3.00
179 Charlie Zink **RC** 1.50
180 Adam Greenberg 2.50
181 Kevin Howard **RC** 1.00
182 Wanell Severino **RC** 1.00
183 Chin-Lung Hu **RC** 3.00
184 Joel Zumaya **RC** 10.00
185 Skip Schumaker **RC** 1.00
186 Nic Ungs **RC** 1.00
187 Todd Self **RC** 2.00
188 Brian Steffek **RC** 1.00
189 Brock Peterson **RC** 2.00
190 Greg Thissen **RC** 1.00
191 Frank Brooks **RC** 1.00
192 Scott Olsen **RC** 3.00
193 Chris Mabeus **RC** 1.00
194 Daniel Giese **RC** 2.00
195 Jared Wells **RC** 1.00
196 Carlos Sosa **RC** 2.00
197 Bobby Madritsch 1.00
198 Calvin Hayes **RC** 1.50
199 Omar Quintanilla 2.00
200 Chris O'Riordan **RC** 1.00
201 Tim Hutting **RC** 1.00
202 Carlos Quentin 10.00
203 Brayan Pena **RC** 1.00
204 Jeff Salazar **RC** 2.00
205 David Murphy 3.00
206 Alberto Garcia **RC** 2.00
207 Ramon Ramirez **RC** 2.00
208 Luis Bolivar **RC** 1.00
209 Rodney Choy Foo **RC** 1.00
210 Fausto Carmona **RC** 5.00
211 Anthony Acevedo **RC** 2.00
212 Chad Santos **RC** 1.00
213 Jason Frasor **RC** 1.50
214 Jesse Roman **RC** 1.00
215 James Tomlin **RC** 1.00
216 Josh Labandeira **RC** 1.00
217 Ryan Meaux **RC** 1.00
218 Don Sutton **RC** 3.00
219 Danny Gonzalez **RC** 1.00
220 Javier Guzman **RC** 2.00
221 Anthony Lerew **RC** 2.00
222 Jon Connolly **RC** 3.00
223 Jesse English **RC** 1.00
224 Hector Made **RC** 2.50
225 Travis Hanson 1.50
226 Jesse Floyd **RC** 1.00
227 Nick Gorneault **RC** 1.00
228 Craig Ansman **RC** 1.00
229 Paul McAnulty **RC** 2.50
230 Carl Loadenthal **RC** 1.50
231 David Crouthers 1.00
232 Harvey Garcia **RC** 1.00
233 Casey Kopitzke **RC** 1.00
234 Ricky Nolasco 3.00
235 Miguel Perez **RC** 1.00
236 Ryan Mulhern **RC** 1.00
237 Chris Aguila **RC** 1.00
238 Brooks Conrad **RC** 1.00
239 Damaso Espino **RC** 1.00
240 Jereme Milons **RC** 1.50
241 Luke Hughes **RC** 1.00
242 Kory Casto 1.50
243 Jose Valdez **RC** 1.00
244 J.T. Stotts 1.50
245 Lee Gwaltney **RC** 1.50
246 Yoann Torrealba **RC** 1.00
247 Omar Falcon **RC** 1.00
248 Jon Coutlangus **RC** 1.00
249 George Sherrill **RC** 2.00
250 John Santor **RC** 1.00
251 Tony Richie **RC** 1.00
252 Kevin Richardson **RC** 1.00
253 Tim Bittner **RC** 1.00

254 Chris Saenz **RC** 1.50
255 Jose Capellan **RC** 2.00
256 Donald Levinski 1.00
257 Jerome Gamble **RC** 1.00
258 Jeff Keppinger **RC** 4.00
259 Jason Szuminski **RC** 1.00
260 Akinori Otsuka **RC** 1.50
261 Ryan Budde 1.00
262 Marland Williams **RC** 2.00
263 Jeffrey Allison 1.00
264 Hector Gimenez **RC** 1.00
265 Tim Frend **RC** 1.00
266 Tom Farmer **RC** 1.00
267 Shawn Hill **RC** 1.00
268 Mike Huggins **RC** 2.00
269 Scott Proctor **RC** 1.50
270 Jorge Mejia **RC** 1.00
271 Terry Jones **RC** 1.50
272 Zachary Duke **RC** 4.00
273 Jesse Crain 3.00
274 Luke Anderson **RC** 1.00
275 Hunter Brown **RC** 1.50
276 Matt Lemanczyk **RC** 1.00
277 Fernando Cortez **RC** 1.00
278 Vince Perkins **RC** 1.00
279 Tommy Murphy **RC** 1.00
280 Mike Gosling 1.00
281 Paul Bacot 1.50
282 Matt Capps **RC** 2.00
283 Juan Gutierrez **RC** 1.00
284 Teodoro Encarnacion **RC** 2.00
285 Chad Bentz **RC** 1.50
286 Kazuo Matsui **RC** 1.50
287 Ryan Hankins **RC** 1.00
288 Leo Nunez **RC** 1.00
289 Dave Wallace **RC** 1.00
290 Rob Tejeda **RC** 2.50
291 Paul Maholm **RC** 3.00
292 Casey Daigle **RC** 1.00
293 Tydus Meadows **RC** 1.00
294 Khalid Ballouli **RC** 1.00
295 Benji DeQuin **RC** 2.00
296 Tyler Davidson 2.00
297 Brent Colamarino **RC** 3.00
298 Marcus McBeth **RC** 1.00
299 Brad Eldred **RC** 2.50
300 David Pauley **RC** 3.00
301 Yadier Molina **RC** 4.00
302 Chris Shelton **RC** 2.00
303 Nyjer Morgan **RC** 1.00
304 Jon DeVries 1.00
305 Sheldon Fulse **RC** 1.00
306 Vito Chiaravalloti **RC** 1.50
307 Warner Madrigal **RC** 3.00
308 Reid Gorecki **RC** 1.00
309 Sung Jung **RC** 1.00
310 Peter Shier **RC** 1.00
311 Michael Mooney **RC** 1.00
312 Kenny Perez **RC** 1.00
313 Mike Mallory **RC** 1.00
314 Ben Himes **RC** 1.00
315 Ivan Ochoa **RC** 1.00
316 Donald Kelly **RC** 1.00
317 Tom Mastny **RC** 1.00
318 Kevin Davidson **RC** 1.50
319 Brian Pilkington 1.00
320 Alex Romero **RC** 1.00
321 Chad Chop **RC** 1.00
322 Kody Kirkland **RC** 2.50
323 Casey Myers **RC** 1.00
324 Mike Rouse 1.00
325 Sergio Silva **RC** 1.00
326 J.J. Furmaniak **RC** 3.00
327 Brad Vericker **RC** 1.00
328 Blake Hawksworth **RC** 2.00
329 Brock Jacobsen **RC** 1.00
330 Alec Zumwalt **RC** 1.00
331 Wardell Starling **RC** 10.00
332 Estee Harris **RC** 10.00
333 Kyle Sleeth 15.00
334 Dioner Navarro **RC** 15.00
335 Logan Kensing **RC** 10.00
336 Travis Blackley **RC** 10.00
337 Lincoln Holdzkom **RC** 10.00
338 Jason Hirsh 20.00
339 Juan Cedeno **RC** 10.00
340 Matt Creighton **RC** 10.00
341 Tim Stauffer 10.00
342 Shingo Takatsu **RC** 10.00
343 Lastings Milledge 60.00
344 Dustin Nippert **RC** 10.00
345 Felix Hernandez **RC** 100.00
346 Joaquin Arias **RC** 10.00
347 Kevin Kouzmanoff 30.00
348 Bobby Brownlie **RC** 10.00
349 David Aardsma 10.00
350 Jon Knott **RC** 10.00

Refractor

Stars (1-165): 2-4X
Rookies (166-330): 1-2X
Inserted 1:4
Autograph (331-350): 1-2X
Inserted 1:100

Gold Refractor

Stars (1-165): 4-8X
Rookies (166-330): 3-5X
Production 50
Autograph (331-350): No Pricing
Inserted 1:1,003

X-Fractor

Stars (1-165): 3-5X
Rookies (166-330): 2-4X

Production 173
Autograph (331-350): No Pricing
Inserted 1:200

Stars Of The Future

NM/M

Inserted 1:600
YSS Delmon Young, Kyle Sleeth, Tim Stauffer 70.00
LHC Chris Lubanski, Ryan Harvey, Chad Cordero 50.00
MHD Nicholas Markakis, Aaron Hill, Eric Duncan 50.00

2004 Bowman Draft Picks & Prospects

NM/M

Complete Set (1-165): 30.00
Common Player: .15
Common Rookie: .25
Pack (5 Bowman + 2 Chrome): 7.00
Box (24): 140.00
BDP1 Lyle Overbay .25
BDP2 David Newhan .15
BDP3 J.R. House .15
BDP4 Chad Tracy .15
BDP5 Humberto Quintero .15
BDP6 David Bush .15
BDP7 Scott Hairston .15
BDP8 Mike Wood .15
BDP9 Alexis Rios .25
BDP10 Sean Burnett .15
BDP11 Wilson Valdez .15
BDP12 Lew Ford .15
BDP13 Freddy Thon **RC** .25
BDP14 Zack Greinke .15
BDP15 Bucky Jacobsen .15
BDP16 Kevin Youkilis .25
BDP17 Grady Sizemore .25
BDP18 Denny Bautista .15
BDP19 David DeJesus .15
BDP20 Casey Kotchman .15
BDP21 David Kelton .15
BDP22 Charles Thomas **RC** .25
BDP23 Kazuhito Tadano **RC** .50
BDP24 Justin Leone **RC** .25
BDP25 Eduardo Villacis .25
BDP26 Brian Dallimore **RC** .25
BDP27 Nick Green .25
BDP28 Sam McConnell .25
BDP29 Brad Halsey **RC** .25
BDP30 Roman Colon **RC** .25
BDP31 Josh Fields **RC** 2.00
BDP32 Cody Bunkelman .50
BDP33 Jay Rainville **RC** 1.00
BDP34 Richie Robnett **RC** 1.00
BDP35 Jon Poterson **RC** .75
BDP36 Huston Street **RC** 1.00
BDP37 Erick San Pedro **RC** .25
BDP38 Cory Dunlap 1.00
BDP39 Kurt Suzuki **RC** .75
BDP40 Anthony Swarzak .50
BDP41 Ian Desmond 1.00
BDP42 Chris Covington .40
BDP43 Christian Garcia .40
BDP44 Gaby Hernandez **RC** 1.00
BDP45 Steven Register .25
BDP46 Eduardo Morlan .25
BDP47 Collin Balester .25
48 Nathan Phillips .25
49 Dan Schwartzbauer .25
50 Rafael Gonzalez .25
51 K.C. Herren **RC** .50
52 William Susdorf .25
53 Rob Johnson .25
54 Louis Marson .50
55 Joe Koshansky **RC** 1.50
56 Jamar Walton 1.00
57 Mark Lowe .75
58 Matt Macri **RC** .75
59 Donny Lucy .25
60 Mike Ferris .50
61 Mike Nickeas .50
62 Eric Hurley **RC** .75
63 Scott Elbert **RC** 1.00
64 Blake DeWitt **RC** 1.50
65 Danny Putnam **RC** .50
66 J.P. Howell **RC** .75
67 John Wiggins .25
68 Justin Orenduff **RC** .50
69 Ray Liotta **RC** .75
70 Billy Buckner **RC** .25
71 Eric Campbell **RC** 1.50
72 Olin Wick .25
73 Sean Gamble .40
74 Seth Smith 1.00
75 Wade Davis **RC** 1.00
76 Joe Jacobitz .25
77 J.A. Happ .50
78 Eric Ridener .25
79 Matt Tuiasosopo **RC** 1.00
80 Bradley Bergesen .25
81 Javy Guerra .40
82 Buck Shaw .50
83 Paul Janish .50
84 Sean Kazmar .25
85 Josh Johnson **RC** .50
86 Angel Salome .75
87 Jordan Parraz **RC** .50
88 Kelvin Vazquez .25
89 Grant Hansen .25
90 Matt Fox **RC** .50
91 Trevor Plouffe **RC** 1.50
92 Wes Whisler .50
93 Curtis Thigpen .50
94 Donnie Smith **RC** .25
95 Luis Rivera .40
96 Jesse Hoover .25
97 Jason Vargas **RC** 1.00
98 Clary Carlsen .25
99 Mark Robinson .25
100 J.C. Holt **RC** .40
101 Chad Blackwell .25
102 Daryl Jones **RC** .75
103 Jonathan Tierce .25
104 Patrick Bryant .25
105 Eddie Prasch .40
106 Mitch Einertson **RC** .75
107 Kyle Waldrop **RC** .75
108 Jeff Marquez **RC** .50
109 Zach Jackson **RC** .50
110 Josh Wahpepah .25
111 Adam Lind **RC** 2.00
112 Kyle Bloom .25
113 Ben Harrison .25
114 Taylor Tankersley **RC** .75
115 Steven Jackson .25
116 David Purcey **RC** .50
117 Jacob McGee 1.50
118 Lucas Harrell **RC** .25
119 Brandon Allen .75
120 Van Pope .50
121 Jeff Francis .15
122 Joe Blanton .15
123 Wilfredo Ledezma .15
124 Bryan Bullington .15
125 Jairo Garcia .15
126 Matt Cain .40
127 Arnie Munoz .15
128 Clint Everts .15
129 Jesus Cota .15
130 Gavin Floyd .15
131 Edwin Encarnacion .15
132 Koyie Hill .15
133 Ruben Gotay .15
134 Jeff Mathis .15
135 Andy Marte .25
136 Dallas McPherson .15
137 Justin Morneau .40
138 Rickie Weeks .25
139 Joel Guzman .15
140 Shin-Soo Choo .15
141 Yusmeiro Petit **RC** 2.00
142 Jorge Cortes .25
143 Val Majewski .15
144 Felix Pie .15
145 Aaron Hill .15
146 Jose Capellan .25
147 Dioner Navarro **RC** .25
148 Fausto Carmona **RC** .50
149 Robinzon Diaz .25
150 Felix Hernandez 2.00
151 Andres Blanco .25
152 Jason Kubel .15
153 Willy Taveras **RC** 1.00
154 Merkin Valdez .40
155 Robinson Cano .50
156 Bill Murphy .25
157 Chris Burke .15
158 Kyle Sleeth .25
159 B.J. Upton .25
160 Tim Stauffer .25
161 David Wright 1.00
162 Conor Jackson .25
163 Brad Thompson **RC** .25
164 Delmon Young .40
165 Jeremy Reed .15

Gold

Rookies: .75-1.5X
Inserted 1:1

Red

No Pricing
Production One Set

AFLAC All-Americans

Complete Set (40):
Common Player:

Printing Plates

No Pricing
Production one for each color.

Prospect Premiums

NM/M

Common Player: 4.00
AB Angel Berroa 4.00
KC Kevin Cash 4.00
RH Ryan Harvey 6.00
CJ Conor Jackson 10.00
EJ Edwin Jackson 4.00
LM Lastings Milledge 15.00
DN Dioner Navarro 4.00
CQ Carlos Quentin 8.00
JR Jeremy Reed 6.00
NS Nick Swisher 8.00
BU B.J. Upton 8.00
DY Delmon Young 8.00

Signs of the Future

NM/M

Common Player: 8.00
CC Chad Cordero 10.00
JH James Houser 8.00
AL Adam Loewen 15.00
PM Paul Maholm 8.00
TP Tyler Pelland 8.00
TT Terry Tiffee 8.00

2004 Bowman Chrome Draft Picks & Prospects

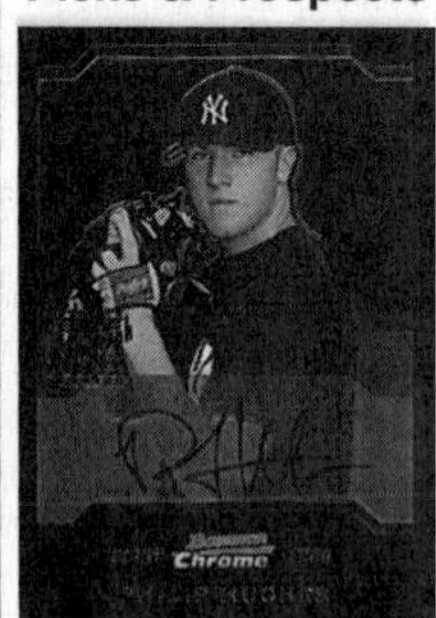

NM/M

Complete Set (175):
Common Player: .25
Common Rookie: 1.00
Common RC Auto. (166-175): 15.00
Inserted 1:60
BDP1 Lyle Overbay .50
BDP2 David Newhan .25
BDP3 J.R. House .25
BDP4 Chad Tracy .25
BDP5 Humberto Quintero .25
BDP6 David Bush .25
BDP7 Scott Hairston .25
BDP8 Mike Wood .25
BDP9 Alexis Rios .50
BDP10 Sean Burnett .25
BDP11 Wilson Valdez .25
BDP12 Lew Ford .25
BDP13 Freddie Thon **RC** 1.00
BDP14 Zack Greinke .25
BDP15 Bucky Jacobsen .25
BDP16 Kevin Youkilis .50
BDP17 Grady Sizemore .75
BDP18 Denny Bautista .25
BDP19 David DeJesus .25
BDP20 Casey Kotchman .25
BDP21 David Kelton .25
BDP22 Charles Thomas **RC** 1.00
BDP23 Kazuhito Tadano **RC** 1.50
BDP24 Justin Leone **RC** 1.00
BDP25 Eduardo Villacis **RC** 1.00
BDP26 Brian Dallimore **RC** 1.00
BDP27 Nick Green **RC** 1.00
BDP28 Sam McConnell **RC** 1.00
BDP29 Brad Halsey **RC** 1.00
BDP30 Roman Colon **RC** 1.00
BDP31 Josh Fields **RC** 6.00
BDP32 Cody Bunkelman **RC** 1.00
BDP33 Jay Rainville **RC** 4.00
BDP34 Richie Robnett **RC** 3.00
BDP35 Jon Poterson **RC** 2.50
BDP36 Huston Street **RC** 5.00
BDP37 Erick San Pedro **RC** 1.00
BDP38 Cory Dunlap **RC** 3.00
BDP39 Kurt Suzuki **RC** 3.00
BDP40 Anthony Swarzak **RC** 2.00
BDP41 Ian Desmond **RC** 3.00
BDP42 Chris Covington **RC** 1.50
BDP43 Christian Garcia **RC** 1.50
BDP44 Gaby Hernandez **RC** 5.00
BDP45 Steven Register **RC** 1.00
BDP46 Eduardo Morlan **RC** 2.50
BDP47 Collin Balester **RC** 2.00
BDP48 Nathan Phillips **RC** 1.00
BDP49 Dan Schwartzbauer **RC** 1.00
BDP50 Rafael Gonzalez **RC** 1.00
BDP51 K.C. Herren **RC** 2.00
BDP52 William Susdorf **RC** 1.00
BDP53 Rob Johnson **RC** 1.00
BDP54 Louis Marson **RC** 2.00
BDP55 Joe Koshansky **RC** 5.00
BDP56 Jamar Walton **RC** 3.00
BDP57 Mark Lowe **RC** 2.50
BDP58 Matt Macri **RC** 3.00
BDP59 Donny Lucy **RC** 1.00
BDP60 Mike Ferris **RC** 2.00
BDP61 Mike Nickeas **RC** 1.50
BDP62 Eric Hurley **RC** 3.00
BDP63 Scott Elbert **RC** 4.00
BDP64 Blake DeWitt **RC** 5.00
BDP65 Danny Putnam **RC** 2.00
BDP66 J.P. Howell **RC** 3.00
BDP67 John Wiggins **RC** 1.00
BDP68 Justin Orenduff **RC** 2.00
BDP69 Ray Liotta **RC** 2.00
BDP70 Billy Buckner **RC** 1.00
BDP71 Eric Campbell **RC** 4.00
BDP72 Olin Wick **RC** 2.00
BDP73 Sean Gamble **RC** 1.50
BDP74 Seth Smith **RC** 3.00
BDP75 Wade Davis **RC** 4.00
BDP76 Joe Jacobitz **RC** 1.00
BDP77 J.A. Happ **RC** 2.00
BDP78 Eric Ridener **RC** 1.00
BDP79 Matt Tuiasosopo **RC** 3.00
BDP80 Bradley Bergesen **RC** 1.00
BDP81 Javy Guerra **RC** 1.50
BDP82 Buck Shaw **RC** 2.00
BDP83 Paul Janish **RC** 2.00
BDP84 Sean Kazmar **RC** 1.00
BDP85 Josh Johnson **RC** 1.50
BDP86 Angel Salome **RC** 2.00
BDP87 Jordan Parraz **RC** 1.00
BDP88 Kelvin Vazquez **RC** 1.00
BDP89 Grant Hansen **RC** 1.00
BDP90 Matt Fox **RC** 2.00
BDP91 Trevor Plouffe **RC** 4.00
BDP92 Wes Whisler **RC** 1.00
BDP93 Curtis Thigpen **RC** 2.00
BDP94 Donnie Smith **RC** 1.00
BDP95 Luis Rivera **RC** 1.50
BDP96 Jesse Hoover **RC** 1.00
BDP97 Jason Vargas **RC** 4.00
BDP98 Clary Carlsen **RC** 1.00
BDP99 Mark Robinson **RC** 1.00
BDP100 J.C. Holt **RC** 1.50
BDP101 Chad Blackwell **RC** 1.00
BDP102 Daryl Jones **RC** 2.00
BDP103 Jonathan Tierce **RC** 1.00
BDP104 Patrick Bryant **RC** 1.00
BDP105 Eddie Prasch **RC** 1.50
BDP106 Mitch Einertson **RC** 2.00
BDP107 Kyle Waldrop **RC** 4.00
BDP108 Jeff Marquez **RC** 2.00
BDP109 Zach Jackson **RC** 2.00
BDP110 Josh Wahpepah **RC** 1.00
BDP111 Adam Lind **RC** 5.00
BDP112 Kyle Bloom **RC** 1.00
BDP113 Ben Harrison **RC** 1.00
BDP114 Taylor Tankersley **RC** 2.00
BDP115 Steven Jackson **RC** 1.00
BDP116 David Purcey **RC** 1.50
BDP117 Jacob McGee **RC** 4.00
BDP118 Lucas Harrell **RC** 1.00
BDP119 Brandon Allen **RC** 2.50
BDP120 Van Pope **RC** 1.50
BDP121 Jeff Francis .25
BDP122 Joe Blanton .25
BDP123 Wilfredo Ledezma .25
BDP124 Bryan Bullington .25
BDP125 Jairo Garcia .25
BDP126 Matt Cain .75
BDP127 Arnie Munoz .25
BDP128 Clint Everts .25
BDP129 Jesus Cota .25
BDP130 Gavin Floyd .25
BDP131 Edwin Encarnacion .25
BDP132 Koyie Hill .25
BDP133 Ruben Gotay .25
BDP134 Jeff Mathis .25
BDP135 Andy Marte .50
BDP136 Dallas McPherson .25
BDP137 Justin Morneau .50
BDP138 Rickie Weeks .40
BDP139 Joel Guzman .25
BDP140 Shin-Soo Choo .25
BDP141 Yusmeiro Petit **RC** 6.00
BDP142 Jorge Cortes **RC** 1.00
BDP143 Val Majewski .25
BDP144 Felix Pie .50
BDP145 Aaron Hill .25
BDP146 Jose Capellan .25
BDP147 Dioner Navarro **RC** 1.00
BDP148 Fausto Carmona 1.00
BDP149 Robinzon Diaz **RC** 1.00
BDP150 Felix Hernandez 5.00
BDP151 Andres Blanco **RC** 1.00
BDP152 Jason Kubel .25
BDP153 Willy Taveras **RC** 2.50
BDP154 Merkin Valdez 1.00
BDP155 Robinson Cano 1.00
BDP156 Bill Murphy **RC** .50
BDP157 Chris Burke .25
BDP158 Kyle Sleeth .75
BDP159 B.J. Upton .75
BDP160 Tim Stauffer 1.00
BDP161 David Wright 2.50
BDP162 Conor Jackson 3.00
BDP163 Brad Thompson **RC** 2.00
BDP164 Delmon Young .50
BDP165 Jeremy Reed .25
BDP166 Matt Bush **RC** 20.00
BDP167 Mark Rogers **RC** 15.00
BDP168 Thomas Diamond **RC** 15.00
BDP169 Greg Golson **RC** 20.00
BDP170 Homer Bailey **RC** 60.00
BDP171 Chris Lambert **RC** 10.00
BDP172 Neil Walker **RC** 30.00
BDP173 Bill Bray **RC** 10.00
BDP174 Phillip Hughes **RC** 140.00
BDP175 Gio Gonzalez **RC** 40.00

Refractor

Rookies: 2-4X
Inserted 1:11
Rookie Autos. (166-175): .75-1.5X
Inserted 1:204

Gold Refractor

Rookies: 10-20X
Production 50
Rookie Autos. (166-175): 3-5X
Inserted 1:2,045

X-Fractor

Rookies: 3-6X
Production 125
Rookie Autos. (166-175): 1-2X
Inserted 1:407

2004 Bowman Heritage

NM/M

Complete Set (347):
Common Player: .15
Common SP: 4.00
Common SP Rookie: 4.00
SP's inserted 1:3
Pack (8): 5.00
Box (24): 100.00
1 Tom Glavine .40
2 Mike Piazza/SP 8.00
3 Sidney Ponson .15
4 Jerry Hairston Jr. .15
5 Jermaine Dye .25
6 Bobby Crosby .15
7 Carlos Zambrano .25
8 Moises Alou .25
9 Alex Rodriguez/SP 10.00
10 Derek Jeter 2.00
11 Rafael Furcal .25
12 J.D. Drew .25
13 Joe Mauer/SP 6.00

14 Brad Radke .15
15 Johnny Damon .75
16 Derek Lowe .15
17 Pat Burrell .25
18 Mike Lieberthal .15
19 Cliff Lee .15
20 Ronnie Belliard .15
21 Eric Gagne/SP 4.00
22 Brad Penny .15
23 Al Kaline .50
24 Mike Maroth .15
25 Magglio Ordonez/SP 4.00
26 Mark Buehrle .25
27 Jack Wilson .15
28 Oliver Perez .15
29 Al "Red" Schoendienst .15
30 Yadier Molina **RC** 1.50
31 Ryan Freel .15
32 Adam Dunn .50
33 Paul Konerko .40
34 Esteban Loaiza .15
35 Ivan Rodriguez .50
36 Carlos Guillen .15
37 Adrian Beltre .25
38 C.C. Sabathia .25
39 Hideo Nomo .40
40 Victor Martinez/SP 4.00
41 Bobby Abreu .25
42 Randy Wolf .15
43 Johnny Estrada .15
44 Russ Ortiz .15
45 Kenny Rogers .15
46 Hank Blalock/SP 4.00
47 David Ortiz 1.00
48 Pedro Martinez/SP 6.00
49 Austin Kearns .25
50 Ken Griffey Jr./SP 6.00
51 Mark Prior .50
52 Kerry Wood .40
53 Eric Chavez .25
54 Tim Hudson .25
55 Rafael Palmeiro/SP 5.00
56 Javy Lopez .15
57 Jason Bay .40
58 Craig Wilson .15
59 Ed "Whitey" Ford .50
60 Jason Giambi .50
61 Scott Rolen/SP 6.00
62 Matt Morris .15
63 Javier Vazquez .15
64 Jim Thome .50
65 Don Zimmer .25
66 Shawn Green .25
67 Don Larsen .50
68 Gary Sheffield .40
69 Jorge Posada .50
70 Bernie Williams .40
71 Chipper Jones .75
72 Andruw Jones .50
73 John Thomson .15
74 Jim Edmonds .40
75 Albert Pujols 2.00
76 Chris Carpenter .50
77 Aubrey Huff/SP 4.00
78 Carl Crawford .40
79 Victor Zambrano .15
80 Alfonso Soriano/SP 5.00
81 Lance Berkman .40
82 Mike Sweeney .15
83 Ken Harvey .15
84 Angel Berroa .15
85 A.J. Burnett .15
86 Mike Lowell .15
87 Miguel Cabrera/SP 5.00
88 Preston Wilson .15
89 Todd Helton/SP 4.00
90 Larry Walker .25
91 Vladimir Guerrero .75
92 Garret Anderson .15
93 Bartolo Colon .15
94 Scott Hairston .15
95 Richie Sexson/SP 4.00
96 Sean Casey .25
97 Johnny Podres .40
98 Andy Pettitte .40
99 Roy Oswalt .25
100 Roger Clemens/SP 8.00
101 Scott Podsednik .25
102 Ben Sheets .25
103 Lyle Overbay .25
104 Nick Johnson/SP 4.00
105 Zach Day .15
106 Jose Reyes .75
107 Khalil Greene .25
108 Sean Burroughs .15
109 David Wells/SP 4.00
110 Jason Schmidt .25
111 Neifi Perez .15
112 Edgar Renteria .25
113 Rich Aurilia .15
114 Edgar Martinez .15
115 Joel Pineiro .15
116 Mark Teixeira .40
117 Michael Young .25
118 Ricardo Rodriguez .15
119 Carlos Delgado .50
120 Roy Halladay .25
121 Jose Guillen .15
122 Troy Glaus .40
123 Shea Hillenbrand .15
124 Luis Gonzalez .25
125 Horacio Ramirez .15
126 Melvin Mora .15
127 Miguel Tejada/SP 4.00
128 Manny Ramirez .75
129 Tim Wakefield .15
130 Curt Schilling/SP 5.00
131 Aramis Ramirez .40
132 Sammy Sosa/SP 6.00
133 Matt Clement .15
134 Juan Uribe .15
135 Dontrelle Willis .25
136 Paul LoDuca .15
137 Juan Pierre .15
138 Kevin Brown .15
139 Brian Giles,
Marcus Giles .15
140 Brian Giles .15
141 Nomar Garciaparra/SP 6.00
142 Cesar Izturis .15
143 Don Newcombe .15
144 Craig Biggio .25
145 Carlos Beltran .50
146 Torii Hunter .25
147 Livan Hernandez .15
148 Cliff Floyd .15
149 Barry Zito .40
150 Mark Mulder .25
151 Rocco Baldelli .25
152 Bret Boone .15
153 Jamie Moyer .15
154 Ichiro Suzuki 1.50
155 Brett Myers .25
156 Carl Pavano .15
157 Josh Beckett .25
158 Randy Johnson .75
159 Trot Nixon .15
160 Dmitri Young .15
161 Jacque Jones .15
162 Lew Ford .15
163 Jose Vidro .15
164 Mark Kotsay .15
165 A.J. Pierzynski .15
166 Dewon Brazelton .15
167 Jeromy Burnitz .15
168 Johan Santana .50
169 Greg Maddux 1.00
170 Carl Erskine .15
171 Robin Roberts .15
172 Freddy Garcia .15
173 Carlos Lee .25
174 Jeff Bagwell .40
175 Jeff Kent .25
176 Kazuhisa Ishii .15
177 Orlando Cabrera .25
178 Shannon Stewart .15
179 Mike Cameron .15
180 Mike Mussina .40
181 Frank Thomas .75
182 Jaret Wright .15
183 Alex Gonzalez/SP 4.00
184 Matt Lawton .15
185 Derrek Lee .50
186 Omar Vizquel .25
187 Jeremy Bonderman .25
188 Jake Westbrook .15
189 Zack Greinke/SP 4.00
190 Chad Tracy .15
191 Rondell White .15
192 Alex Gonzalez .15
193 Geoff Jenkins .15
194 Ralph Kiner .40
195 Al Leiter .15
196 Kevin Millwood .25
197 Jason Kendall .15
198 Kris Benson .15
199 Ryan Klesko .15
200 Mark Loretta .15
201 Richard Hidalgo .15
202 Reed Johnson .15
203 Luis Castillo .15
204 Jon Zeringue/SP **RC** 6.00
205 Matt Bush **RC** 2.00
206 Kurt Suzuki/SP **RC** 5.00
207 Mark Rogers **RC** 2.00
208 Jason Vargas/SP **RC** 5.00
209 Homer Bailey **RC** 5.00
210 Ray Liotta/SP **RC** 5.00
211 Eric Campbell **RC** 2.00
212 Thomas Diamond **RC** 2.00
213 Gaby Hernandez/
SP **RC** 8.00
214 Neil Walker **RC** 2.00
215 Bill Bray **RC** 1.00
216 Wade Davis/SP **RC** 5.00
217 David Purcey **RC** 2.00
218 Scott Elbert **RC** 2.00
219 Josh Fields **RC** 3.00
220 Josh Johnson/SP 4.00
221 Chris Lambert **RC** 2.00
222 Trevor Plouffe **RC** 3.00
223 Bruce Froemming .15
224 Matt Macri/SP **RC** 5.00
225 Greg Golson **RC** 2.00
226 Phillip Hughes **RC** 10.00
227 Kyle Waldrop **RC** 2.00
228 Matt Tuiasosopo/
SP **RC** 5.00
229 Richie Robnett **RC** 2.00
230 Taylor Tankersley **RC** 1.50
231 Blake DeWitt **RC** 2.50
232 Charlie Reliford .15
233 Eric Hurley **RC** 1.00
234 Jordan Parraz/SP **RC** 4.00
235 J.P. Howell **RC** 2.00
236 Dana DeMuth .15
237 Zach Jackson **RC** 1.00
238 Justin Orenduff **RC** 1.00
239 Brad Thompson **RC** 1.00
240 J.C. Holt/SP **RC** 5.00
241 Matt Fox **RC** 1.00
242 Danny Putnam **RC** 1.00
243 Daryl Jones/SP **RC** 5.00
244 Jon Poterson **RC** 1.00
245 Gio Gonzalez **RC** 2.00
246 Lucas Harrell/SP **RC** 4.00
247 Jerry Crawford .15
248 Jay Rainville **RC** 2.00
249 Donnie Smith/SP **RC** 5.00
250 Huston Street **RC** 2.00
251 Jeff Marquez **RC** 1.00
252 Reid Brignac **RC** 3.00
253 Yusmeiro Petit **RC** 2.00
254 K.C. Herren **RC** 1.00
255 Dale Scott .15
256 Erick San Pedro **RC** 1.00
257 Ed Montague .15
258 Billy Buckner **RC** 1.00
259 Mitch Einertson/
SP **RC** 4.00
260 Aarom Baldiris **RC** 1.00
261 Conor Jackson 2.00
262 Rick Reed .15
263 Ervin Santana **RC** 2.00
264 Gerry Davis .15
265 Merkin Valdez **RC** 1.00
266 Joey Gathright **RC** 1.00
267 Alberto Callaspo **RC** .75
268 Carlos Quentin/SP 6.00
269 Gary Darling .15
270 Jeff Salazar/SP **RC** 4.00
271 Akinori Otsuka/SP **RC** 4.00
272 Joe Brinkman .15
273 Omar Quintanilla .50
274 Brian Runge .15
275 Tom Mastny **RC** .50
276 John Hirschbeck .15
277 Warner Madrigal **RC** .50
278 Joe West .15
279 Paul Maholm **RC** 1.00
280 Larry Young .15
281 Mike Reilly .15
282 Kazuo Matsui/SP **RC** 4.00
283 Randy Marsh .15
284 Frank Francisco **RC** .50
285 Zachary Duke **RC** 2.00
286 Tim McClelland .15
287 Jesse Crain .75
288 Hector Gimenez **RC** .50
289 Marland Williams **RC** .50
290 Brian Gorman .25
291 Jose Capellan/SP **RC** 4.00
292 Tim Welke .15
293 Javier Guzman **RC** .50
294 Paul McAnulty **RC** .50
295 Hector Made **RC** .50
296 Jon Connolly **RC** .50
297 Don Sutton **RC** 1.00
298 Fausto Carmona **RC** 1.00
299 Ramon Ramirez **RC** .50
300 Brad Snyder 1.00
301 Chin-Lung Hu **RC** 1.00
302 Rudy Guillen **RC** .50
303 Matt Moses 1.00
304 Brad Halsey/SP **RC** 4.00
305 Erick Aybar **RC** 1.50
306 Brad Sullivan 1.00
307 Nick Gorneault **RC** 1.00
308 Craig Ansman **RC** 1.00
309 Ricky Nolasco 1.00
310 Luke Hughes **RC** 1.00
311 Danny Gonzalez **RC** 1.00
312 Josh Labandeira **RC** .50
313 Donald Levinski .50
314 Vince Perkins **RC** .50
315 Tommy Murphy **RC** .50
316 Chad Bentz **RC** .50
317 Chris Shelton **RC** 2.00
318 Nyjer Morgan/SP **RC** 4.00
319 Kody Kirkland **RC** 6.00
320 Blake Hawksworth **RC** .50
321 Alex Romero **RC** .50
322 Mike Gosling .50
323 Ryan Budde .50
324 Kevin Howard **RC** .50
325 Wanell Macia **RC** .50
326 Travis Blackley **RC** 1.00
327 Kazuhito Tadano/
SP **RC** 4.00
328 Shingo Takatsu **RC** 1.00
329 Joaquin Arias **RC** 1.00
330 Juan Cedeno **RC** .75
331 Bobby Brownlie **RC** 1.00
332 Lastings Milledge 5.00
333 Estee Harris **RC** .75
334 Tim Stauffer/SP 5.00
335 Jon Knott .50
336 David Aardsma .50
337 Wardell Starling **RC** .50
338 Dioner Navarro **RC** 1.00
339 Logan Kensing **RC** .50
340 Jason Hirsh 1.50
341 Matt Creighton **RC** .50
342 Felix Hernandez/
SP **RC** 10.00
343 Kyle Sleeth .50
344 Dustin Nippert **RC** .50
345 Anthony Lerew **RC** .50
346 Chris Saenz **RC** .50
347 Steve Palermo .15
348 Barry Bonds 20.00

Black & White

Stars: 2X
SP Stars: .5-1X
Rookies: 1-2X
SP Rookies: .5-.75X
Inserted 1:1

Mohagany

Stars: 15-25X
SP Stars: 3-4X
Rookies: 4-8X
SP Rookies: 3-5X
Production 25 Sets

Printing Plates

No Pricing
Production One Set

Commissioner's Cut

Production One

Signs of Authority

NM/M
Common Autograph: 15.00
Inserted 1:49
Red Ink: 1.5-2X
Production 55 Sets
JB Joe Brinkman 15.00
JC Jerry Crawford 15.00
GDA Gary Darling 15.00
GD Gerry Davis 15.00
DD Dana DeMuth 15.00
BF Bruce Froemming 20.00
BG Brian Gorman 15.00
JH John Hirschbeck 15.00
RM Randy Marsh 15.00
TM Tim McClelland 15.00
EM Ed Montague 15.00
SP Steve Palermo 15.00
ER Rick Reed 15.00
MR Mike Reilly 15.00
CM Charlie Reliford 15.00
BR Brian Runge 15.00
DS Dale Scott 20.00
TW Tim Welke 15.00
JW Joe West 20.00
LY Larry Young 15.00

Signs of Glory

NM/M
Common Autograph: 25.00
Inserted 1:246
Red Ink: 2X
Production 55 Sets
GK George Kell 25.00
BK Bob Kuzava 25.00
PR Elwin "Preacher Roe 30.00
BS Bobby Shantz 25.00
MS Bill "Moose" Skowron 30.00

Signs of Greatness

NM/M
Common Autograph: 10.00
Inserted 1:57
Red Ink: 2-4X
Production 55 Sets
MB Matt Bush 15.00
TD Thomas Diamond 15.00
GG Greg Golson 15.00
PH Phillip Hughes 100.00
CL Chris Lambert 10.00
JM Jeff Marquez 10.00
TP Trevor Plouffe 15.00
JR Jay Rainville 15.00
MR Mark Rogers 15.00
NW Neil Walker 20.00

Threads of Greatness

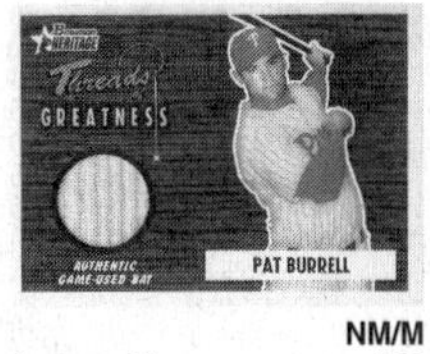

NM/M
Common Player: 4.00
Inserted 1:12
Gold: 2-3X
Production 55 Sets
MA Moises Alou 5.00
JB Jeff Bagwell 8.00
JB2 Jeff Bagwell 8.00
RB Rocco Baldelli 4.00
TB Tony Batista 4.00
JB Josh Beckett 4.00
JB2 Josh Beckett 4.00
AB Adrian Beltre 6.00
AGB Armando Benitez 4.00
LB Lance Berkman 6.00
LB2 Lance Berkman 6.00
AMB Angel Berroa 4.00
HB Hank Blalock 6.00
HB2 Hank Blalock 6.00
WB3 Wade Boggs 8.00
BB Bret Boone 4.00
BB2 Bret Boone 4.00
PB Pat Burrell 4.00
MC Miguel Cabrera 8.00
EC Eric Chavez 4.00
EC2 Eric Chavez 4.00
RC Roger Clemens 10.00
BC Bobby Cox 4.00
JD Johnny Damon 15.00
CE Carl Everett 4.00
NG Nomar Garciaparra 8.00
JG Jason Giambi 6.00
JG2 Jason Giambi 6.00
JAG Juan Gonzalez 6.00
RH Roy Halladay 6.00
TH Todd Helton 6.00
AJ Andruw Jones 6.00
DJ David Justice 4.00
PL Paul LoDuca 4.00
JL Javy Lopez 4.00
ML Mike Lowell 4.00
JM Joe Mauer 10.00
MCD Mike McDougal 4.00
KM Kevin Millwood 4.00
MM Mark Mulder 4.00
MM2 Mark Mulder 4.00
HN Hideo Nomo 8.00
JO John Olerud 4.00
JO2 John Olerud 4.00
AEP Andy Pettitte 4.00
MP Mike Piazza 10.00
MP2 Mike Piazza 10.00
AP Albert Pujols 15.00
AP2 Albert Pujols 15.00
MR Manny Ramirez 8.00
MR2 Manny Ramirez 8.00
JR Jose Reyes 10.00
AR Alex Rodriguez 15.00
CS C.C. Sabathia 6.00
JDS Jason Schmidt 6.00
GS Gary Sheffield 6.00
RS Ruben Sierra 4.00
JS John Smoltz 6.00
JS2 John Smoltz 6.00
AS Alfonso Soriano 8.00
SS Sammy Sosa 8.00
SS2 Sammy Sosa 8.00
SS3 Sammy Sosa 8.00
MS Mike Sweeney 4.00
MCT Mark Teixeira 6.00
MT Miguel Tejada 6.00
MT2 Miguel Tejada 6.00
MT3 Miguel Tejada 6.00
FT Frank Thomas 8.00
JT Jim Thome 8.00
JT2 Jim Thome 8.00
OV Omar Vizquel 4.00
JW Jarrod Washburn 4.00
VW Vernon Wells 6.00
BW Bernie Williams 6.00
DW Dontrelle Willis 6.00
KW Kerry Wood 4.00
KW2 Kerry Wood 4.00
MY Michael Young 4.00
BZ Barry Zito 4.00

2004 Bowman Sterling

NM/M
Common Rookie: 5.00
Pack (5): 60.00
Box (6): 325.00
ABA Aarom Baldiris **RC** 5.00
BBR Bill Bray **RC** 5.00
RBR Reid Brignac **RC** 15.00
BBU Billy Buckner **RC** 5.00
JC Jose Capellan **RC** 5.00
FC Fausto Carmona **RC** 10.00
JCR Jesse Crain **RC** 6.00
TD Thomas Diamond **RC** 10.00
ZD Zachary Duke **RC** 5.00
ME Mitch Einertson **RC** 5.00
BE Brad Eldred **RC** 5.00
MF Mike Ferris **RC** 5.00
JFI Josh Fields **RC** 10.00
MFO Matt Fox **RC** 5.00
JG Joey Gathright **RC** 5.00
GG Greg Golson **RC** 8.00
GIG Gio Gonzalez **RC** 10.00
FG Freddy Guzman **RC** 5.00
GH Gaby Hernandez **RC** 8.00
FH Felix Hernandez **RC** 20.00
KCH K.C. Herren **RC** 5.00
JH Jesse Hoover **RC** 5.00
JPH J.P. Howell **RC** 5.00
PH Phillip Hughes **RC** 30.00
EH Eric Hurley **RC** 5.00
CJ Conor Jackson 15.00
ZJ Zach Jackson **RC** 5.00
CLA Chris Lambert **RC** 5.00
CH Chin-Lung Hu **RC** 8.00
MMC Matt Macri **RC** 5.00
HM Hector Made **RC** 5.00
PGM Paul Maholm **RC** 6.00
NM Nyjer Morgan **RC** 5.00
CN Chris Nelson **RC** 8.00
JO Justin Orenduff **RC** 5.00
YP Yusmeiro Petit **RC** 15.00
DPU David Purcey **RC** 5.00
OQ Omar Quintanilla **RC** 5.00
MRO Mark Rogers **RC** 8.00
ESP Erick San Pedro **RC** 5.00
NS Nate Schierholtz **RC** 8.00
SSM Seth Smith **RC** 8.00
KS Kurt Suzuki **RC** 8.00
KT Kazuhito Tadano **RC** 5.00
CT Curtis Thigpen **RC** 5.00
BT Brad Thompson **RC** 5.00
NW Neil Walker **RC** 10.00
AWH Anthony Whittington **RC** 5.00
MW Marland Williams **RC** 5.00
JZ Jon Zeringue **RC** 5.00

Rookie Relic Autographs

HB Homer Bailey **RC** 40.00
BB Brian Bixler **RC** 10.00
MB Matt Bush **RC** 15.00
BD Blake DeWitt **RC** 20.00
CG Christian Garcia **RC** 10.00
SK Scott Kazmir 35.00
JM Jeff Marquez **RC** 10.00
SO Scott Olsen **RC** 15.00
TP Trevor Plouffe **RC** 20.00
DP Danny Putnam **RC** 10.00
HS Huston Street **RC** 20.00
TT Taylor Tankersley **RC** 10.00
MT Matt Tuiasosopo **RC** 15.00
KWA Kyle Waldrop **RC** 15.00

Prospect Relic Autographs

RC Robinson Cano 50.00
CC Chad Cordero 10.00
DD David DeJesus 15.00
RH Ryan Harvey 15.00
CL Chris Lubanski 15.00
FP Felix Pie 20.00
BU B.J. Upton 25.00
AW Adam Wainwright 20.00
DW David Wright 50.00
DY Delmon Young 20.00

Rookie Autographs:

CA Chris Aguila **RC** 8.00
AC Alberto Callaspo **RC** 15.00
HG Hector Gimenez **RC** 10.00
BH Blake Hawksworth **RC** 10.00
LH Lincoln Holdzkom **RC** 10.00
RM Ryan Meaux **RC** 8.00
MM Matt Moses **RC** 10.00
VP Vince Perkins **RC** 8.00
CQ Carlos Quentin 25.00
JR Jay Rainville **RC** 10.00
AR Alex Romero **RC** 8.00
MR Mike Rouse 8.00
JS Jeremy Sowers **RC** 15.00
AZ Alec Zumwalt **RC** 8.00

Relics: 5.00

MA Moises Alou 5.00
JB Jeff Bagwell 8.00
RB Rocco Baldelli 5.00
CIB Carlos Beltran 10.00
LB Lance Berkman 5.00
AB Angel Berroa 5.00
CB Craig Biggio 5.00
HJB Hank Blalock 5.00
MC Miguel Cabrera 8.00
LC Luis Castillo 5.00
HC Hee Seop Choi 5.00
BC2 Bobby Crosby 5.00
JD Johnny Damon 10.00
AD Adam Dunn 8.00
JE Johnny Estrada 5.00
EG Eric Gagne 5.00
TG Troy Glaus 5.00
TMG Tom Glavine 8.00
VG Vladimir Guerrero 10.00
TLH Todd Helton 8.00
RJH Richard Hidalgo 5.00
NJ Nick Johnson 5.00
AJ Andruw Jones 8.00
AK Austin Kearns 5.00
JK Jason Kendall 5.00
PL Paul LoDuca 5.00
TM Tino Martinez 5.00
MAM Mark Mulder 5.00
LN Laynce Nix 5.00
RO Russ Ortiz 5.00
RP Rafael Palmeiro 6.00
MJP Mike Piazza 10.00
JP Juan Pierre 5.00
MP Mark Prior 8.00
AP Albert Pujols 20.00
ANR Aramis Ramirez 8.00
MAR Manny Ramirez 8.00
PR Pokey Reese 5.00
AER Alex Rodriguez 15.00
IR Ivan Rodriguez 8.00
GS Gary Sheffield 8.00
SS Sammy Sosa 10.00
MCT Mark Teixeira 6.00
MT1 Miguel Tejada/Bat 8.00
MT2 Miguel Tejada/Jsy 8.00
FT Frank Thomas 10.00
BW Bernie Williams 8.00
DWW Dontrelle Willis 5.00
KW Kerry Wood 5.00
MY Michael Young 5.00

Refractors

Regular Rookies: 1.5-2X
Rookie Relic Autos.: 1-2X
Rookie Autos.: 1-2X
Prospect Relic Autos.: 1-2X
Relics: 1-2X
Production 199 Sets

Black Refractors

No Pricing
Production 25 Sets

Red Refractor

No Pricing
Production One Set

Uncirculated

No Pricing
Production 16 Sets

Autographed Originals

Complete Set (51):
Common Player:

2004 Bowman's Best

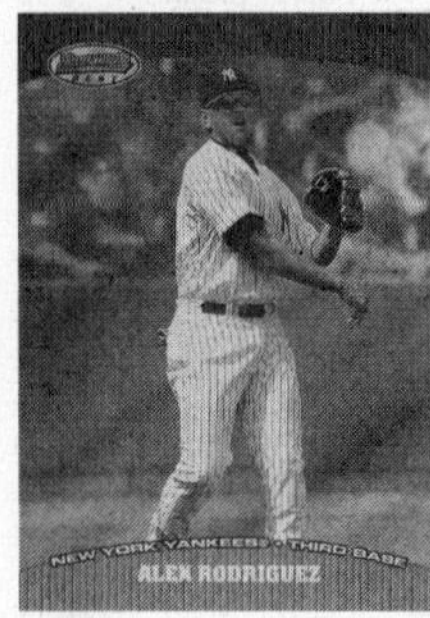

NM/M
Complete Set:
Common Player: .25
Pack (5): 15.00
Box (10): 125.00

Veterans
GA Garret Anderson .25
CB Carlos Beltran .75
HB Hank Blalock .50
MTC Miguel Cabrera 1.00
EC Eric Chavez .50
RC Roger Clemens 2.50
CD Carlos Delgado .50
NAG Nomar Garciaparra 1.00
JGG Jason Giambi .75
BG Brian Giles .25
VG Vladimir Guerrero 1.00
TLH Todd Helton .75
RJ Randy Johnson 1.00
LWJ Chipper Jones 1.00
JLO Javy Lopez .25
MO Magglio Ordonez .25
LO Lyle Overbay .25
MJP Mike Piazza 1.50
JP Jorge Posada .50
MWP Mark Prior .75
AP Albert Pujols 3.00
MAR Manny Ramirez 1.00
AER Alex Rodriguez 2.50
IR Ivan Rodriguez .75
SR Scott Rolen 1.00
CMS Curt Schilling 1.00
JDS Jason Schmidt .50
RS Richie Sexson .50
AS Alfonso Soriano 1.00
SS Sammy Sosa 1.00
IS Ichiro Suzuki 2.00
MT Miguel Tejada .50
JT Jim Thome .75
JAV Jose Vidro .25
MY Michael Young .25

First-Year Players
Common Rookie 1.00
JJC Jon Connolly **RC** 2.00
JRG Joey Gathright **RC** 2.00
DG Danny Gonzalez **RC** 1.00
NG Nick Gorneault **RC** 1.00
MG Mike Gosling 1.00
CH Chin-Lung Hu **RC** 2.00
TJ Terry Jones 1.00
AL Anthony Lerew **RC** 1.00
HM Hector Made **RC** 2.00
WM Warner Madrigal **RC** 2.00
PMM Paul McAnulty **RC** 2.00
AO Akinori Otsuka **RC** 1.00
TS Todd Self **RC** 1.00
KS Kyle Sleeth 1.00
DS Don Sutton **RC** 1.00

First-Year Player Autographs
Common Autograph: 8.00
DA David Aardsma 10.00
CMA Craig Ansman **RC** 10.00
JA Joaquin Arias **RC** 10.00
EA Erick Aybar **RC** 15.00
BB Bobby Brownlie **RC** 10.00
RB Ryan Budde 10.00
KC Kory Casto 10.00
JC Juan Cedeno **RC** 10.00
VC Vito Chiaravalloti **RC** 10.00
MDC Matt Creighton **RC** 8.00
DC David Crouthers 10.00
TD Tyler Davidson 10.00
ZD Zachary Duke **RC** 15.00
JE Jesse English **RC** 10.00
AG Adam Greenberg 10.00
RG Rudy Guillen **RC** 10.00
TOH Travis Hanson 10.00
EH Estee Harris **RC** 10.00
FH Felix Hernandez **RC** 75.00
SH Shawn Hill 10.00
JH Jason Hirsh 15.00
LTH Luke Hughes **RC** 8.00
CJ Conor Jackson 25.00
LK Logan Kensing **RC** 10.00
JK Jon Knott **RC** 10.00
KK Kevin Kouzmanoff 20.00
JL Josh Labandeira **RC** 8.00
DL Donald Levinski 10.00
PM Paul Maholm **RC** 15.00
TRM Tom Mastny **RC** 10.00
BEM Brandon Medders **RC** 8.00
LM Lastings Milledge 50.00
YM Yadier Molina **RC** 20.00
DM David Murphy 20.00
DN Dioner Navarro **RC** 15.00
DDN Dustin Nippert **RC** 10.00
RN Ricky Nolasco 15.00
BP Brayan Pena **RC** 8.00
QQ Omar Quintanilla 10.00
RR Ramon Ramirez **RC** 10.00
JS Jeff Salazar **RC** 10.00
ES Ervin Santana **RC** 15.00
BMS Brad Snyder 15.00
WS Wardell Starling **RC** 10.00
TJS Tim Stauffer 10.00
BS Brad Sullivan 10.00
JSZ Jason Szuminski **RC** 10.00
RT Rob Tejeda **RC** 10.00
NU Nic Ungs **RC** 10.00
MV Merkin Valdez **RC** 10.00
CZ Charlie Zink **RC** 10.00

First-Year Player Relics
TB Travis Blackley **RC** 5.00
KRK Kody Kirkland **RC** 6.00
KM Kazuo Matsui **RC** 6.00
KT Kazuhito Tadano **RC** 6.00
ST Shingo Takatsu **RC** 8.00

Green

Green Stars: 4-8X
Green Non-Auto. RC's: 1.5-3X
Production 100
Green RC Autos.: 1-2X

Red

Red Stars: No Pricing
Production 20
Red Non-Auto. RC's: No Pricing
Red RC Autos.: No Pricing

Double Play Autographs

NM/M
Common Duo: 20.00
Inserted 1:33
MH Lastings Milledge, Estee Harris 40.00
QS Omar Quintanilla, Brad Snyder 20.00
SC Tim Stauffer, Vito Chiaravalloti 20.00
HJ Travis Hanson, Conor Jackson 25.00
MN Brandon Medders, Dustin Nippert 20.00
UK Nic Ungs, Kevin Kouzmanoff 25.00
CC Matt Creighton, David Crouthers 20.00
EN Jesse English, Ricky Nolasco 20.00
SV Ervin Santana, Merkin Valdez 30.00
SK Jeff Salazar, Jon Knott 20.00

Triple Play Autographs

NM/M
Common Trio: 30.00
Inserted 1:109
CBA Juan Cedeno, Bobby Brownlie, Joaquin Arias 30.00
ALS David Aardsma, Donald Levinski, Brad Sullivan 25.00
SSV Tim Stauffer, Ervin Santana, Merkin Valdez 50.00

2005 Bowman

NM/M
Complete Set (330): 60.00
Common Player: .15
Common Rookie: .50
Pack (10): 3.00
Box (24): 60.00
1 Gavin Floyd .15
2 Eric Chavez .25
3 Miguel Tejada .50
4 Dmitri Young .15
5 Hank Blalock .25
6 Kerry Wood .25
7 Andy Pettitte .40
8 Pat Burrell .25
9 Johnny Estrada .15
10 Frank Thomas .50
11 Juan Pierre .25
12 Tom Glavine .40
13 Lyle Overbay .25
14 Jim Edmonds .40
15 Steve Finley .15
16 Jermaine Dye .25
17 Omar Vizquel .15
18 Nick Johnson .15
19 Brian Giles .25
20 Justin Morneau .50
21 Preston Wilson .15
22 Wily Mo Pena .15
23 Rafael Palmeiro .50
24 Scott Kazmir .25
25 Derek Jeter 2.00
26 Barry Zito .25
27 Mike Lowell .15
28 Jason Bay .25
29 Ken Harvey .15
30 Nomar Garciaparra .75
31 Roy Halladay .25
32 Todd Helton .50
33 Mark Kotsay .15
34 Jake Peavy .40
35 David Wright 1.00
36 Dontrelle Willis .40
37 Marcus Giles .15
38 Chone Figgins .15
39 Sidney Ponson .15
40 Randy Johnson .75
41 John Smoltz .25
42 Kevin Millar .15
43 Mark Teixeira .50
44 Alex Rios .25
45 Mike Piazza 1.00
46 Victor Martinez .25
47 Jeff Bagwell .50
48 Shawn Green .25
49 Ivan Rodriguez .50
50 Alex Rodriguez 1.50
51 Kazuo Matsui .25
52 Mark Mulder .40
53 Michael Young .25
54 Javy Lopez .15
55 Johnny Damon .75
56 Jeff Francis .15
57 Rich Harden .15
58 Bobby Abreu .40
59 Mark Loretta .15
60 Gary Sheffield .40
61 Jamie Moyer .15
62 Garret Anderson .25
63 Vernon Wells .25
64 Orlando Cabrera .25
65 Magglio Ordonez .15
66 Ronnie Belliard .15
67 Carlos Lee .25
68 Carl Pavano .25
69 Jon Lieber .15
70 Aubrey Huff .15
71 Rocco Baldelli .25
72 Jason Schmidt .25
73 Bernie Williams .40
74 Hideki Matsui 1.50
75 Ken Griffey Jr. 1.50
76 Josh Beckett .25
77 Mark Buehrle .25
78 David Ortiz .75
79 Luis Gonzalez .25
80 Scott Rolen .75
81 Joe Mauer .50
82 Jose Reyes .75
83 Adam Dunn .50
84 Greg Maddux 1.00
85 Bartolo Colon .25
86 Bret Boone .15
87 Mike Mussina .50
88 Ben Sheets .40
89 Lance Berkman .40
90 Miguel Cabrera .75
91 C.C. Sabathia .25
92 Mike Maroth .15
93 Andruw Jones .50
94 Jack Wilson .15
95 Ichiro Suzuki 1.50
96 Geoff Jenkins .15
97 Zack Greinke .15
98 Jorge Posada .40
99 Travis Hafner .40
100 Barry Bonds 2.00
101 Aaron Rowand .15
102 Aramis Ramirez .40
103 Curt Schilling .75
104 Melvin Mora .15
105 Albert Pujols 2.00
106 Austin Kearns .25
107 Shannon Stewart .15
108 Carl Crawford .40
109 Carlos Zambrano .40
110 Roger Clemens 2.00
111 Javier Vazquez .15
112 Randy Wolf .15
113 Chipper Jones .75
114 Larry Walker .25
115 Alfonso Soriano .75
116 Brad Wilkerson .15
117 Bobby Crosby .15
118 Jim Thome .75
119 Oliver Perez .25
120 Vladimir Guerrero .75
121 Roy Oswalt .40
122 Torii Hunter .25
123 Rafael Furcal .25
124 Luis Castillo .15
125 Carlos Beltran .50
126 Mike Sweeney .15
127 Johan Santana .50
128 Tim Hudson .40
129 Troy Glaus .40
130 Manny Ramirez .75
131 Jeff Kent .25
132 Jose Vidro .15
133 Edgar Renteria .25
134 Russ Ortiz .15
135 Sammy Sosa .75
136 Carlos Delgado .40
137 Richie Sexson .25
138 Pedro Martinez .75
139 Adrian Beltre .25
140 Mark Prior .40
141 Omar Quintanilla .15
142 Carlos Quentin .25
143 Dan Johnson .15
144 Jake Stevens .15
145 Nate Schierholtz .15
146 Neil Walker .15
147 Bill Bray .15
148 Taylor Tankersley .15
149 Trevor Plouffe .15
150 Felix Hernandez .50
151 Phillip Hughes .50
152 James Houser .15
153 David Murphy .15
154 Ervin Santana .15
155 Anthony Whittington .15
156 Chris Lambert .15
157 Jeremy Sowers .15
158 Gio Gonzalez .15
159 Blake DeWitt .15
160 Thomas Diamond .15
161 Greg Golson .15
162 David Aardsma .15
163 Paul Maholm .15
164 Mark Rogers .15
165 Homer Bailey .50
166 Chip Cannon **RC** 1.00
167 Tony Giarratano **RC** .75
168 Darren Fenster **RC** .50
169 Elvys Quezada **RC** .75
170 Glen Perkins **RC** 1.00
171 Ian Kinsler **RC** 3.00
172 Michael Bourn 1.00
173 Jeremy West **RC** .75
174 Justin Verlander **RC** 3.00
175 Kevin West **RC** .50
176 Luis Hernandez **RC** 1.00
177 Matt Campbell **RC** .75
178 Nate McLouth **RC** 1.00
179 Ryan Goleski **RC** .50
180 Matt Lindstrom **RC** .50
181 Matt DeSalvo **RC** 1.00
182 Kole Strayhorn .50
183 Jose Vaquedano **RC** .50
184 James Jurries **RC** .50
185 Ian Bladergroen **RC** .75
186 Eric Nielsen **RC** .75
187 Chris Vines **RC** 1.00
188 Chris Denorfia **RC** .50
189 Kevin Melillo **RC** .50
190 Melky Cabrera **RC** 2.00
191 Ryan Sweeney 1.50
192 Sean Marshall **RC** 1.00
193 Andy LaRoche **RC** 3.00
194 Tyler Pelland **RC** 1.50
195 Mike Morse **RC** .75
196 Wes Swackhamer **RC** .50
197 Wade Robinson **RC** .50
198 Dan Santin **RC** .50
199 Steven Doetsch **RC** .50
200 Shane Costa .75
201 Scott Mathieson **RC** .75
202 Ben Jones **RC** .75
203 Michael Rogers **RC** .50
204 Matt Rogelstad **RC** .50
205 Luis Ramirez **RC** 1.00
206 Landon Powell **RC** .75
207 Erik Cordier **RC** 1.00
208 Chris Seddon **RC** .75
209 Chris Roberson **RC** .75
210 Tom Oldham **RC** .50
211 Dana Eveland **RC** 1.00
212 Cody Haerther **RC** .75
213 Danny Core **RC** .50
214 Craig Tatum **RC** .75
215 Elliot Johnson **RC** .75
216 Ender Chavez **RC** .75
217 Errol Simonitsch **RC** .75
218 Matt Van Der Bosch **RC** .75
219 Eulogio de la Cruz **RC** .50
220 C.J. Smith **RC** .50
221 Adam Boeve **RC** .75
222 Adam Harben **RC** .75
223 Baltazar Lopez **RC** .75
224 Russ Martin **RC** 2.50
225 Brian Bannister **RC** 1.00
226 Brian Miller **RC** .50
227 Casey McGehee **RC** .50
228 Humberto Sanchez **RC** 1.50
229 Javon Moran **RC** .50
230 Brandon McCarthy **RC** 1.50
231 Danny Zell **RC** .50
232 Jake Postlewait **RC** .50
233 Juan Tejeda **RC** .50
234 Keith Ramsey **RC** .50
235 Lorenzo Scott **RC** .75
236 Wladimir Balentien **RC** 1.50
237 Martin Prado **RC** .50
238 Matt Albers **RC** 1.00
239 Brian Schweiger **RC** .50
240 Brian Stavisky **RC** .50
241 Pat Misch **RC** .50
242 Pat Osborn **RC** .50
243 Ryan Feierabend **RC** 1.00
244 Shaun Marcum .50
245 Kevin Collins **RC** .50
246 Stuart Pomeranz **RC** .50
247 Tetsu Yofu **RC** .75
248 Hernan Iribarren **RC** 1.00
249 Miko Spiegel **RC** .50
250 Tony Arnerich **RC** .50
251 Manny Parra **RC** .75
252 Drew Anderson **RC** .75
253 T.J. Beam **RC** 1.00
254 Pedro Lopez **RC** .75
255 Andy Sides **RC** .75
256 Bear Bay **RC** .50
257 Bill McCarthy **RC** 1.00
258 Daniel Haigwood **RC** 1.50
259 Brian Sprout **RC** .75
260 Bryan Triplett .75
261 Steve Bondurant .50
262 Darwinson Salazar **RC** .75
263 David Shepard **RC** .50
264 Johan Silva **RC** .75
265 J.B. Thurmond **RC** .50
266 Brandon Moorhead **RC** .50
267 Kyle Nichols **RC** .50
268 Jonathan Sanchez **RC** 1.00
269 Mike Esposito **RC** .50
270 Erik Schindewolf **RC** .75
271 Peeter Ramos **RC** .75
272 Juan Senreiso **RC** .50
273 Matthew Kemp **RC** 3.00
274 Vinny Rottino **RC** .50
275 Micah Furtado **RC** .50
276 George Kottaras **RC** 1.00
277 Billy Butler **RC** 5.00
278 Buck Coats **RC** .50
279 Ken Durost **RC** .50
280 Nic Touchstone **RC** .50
281 Jerry Owens **RC** 1.00
282 Stefan Bailie .50
283 Jesse Gutierrez **RC** .75
284 Chuck Tiffany **RC** 1.00
285 Brendan Ryan **RC** .50
286 Hayden Penn **RC** 2.00
287 Shawn Bowman **RC** .50
288 Alexander Smit **RC** .50
289 Micah Schnurstein **RC** .75
290 Jared Gothreaux **RC** .50
291 Jair Jurrjens **RC** 1.50
292 Bobby Livingston **RC** .75
293 Ryan Speier **RC** .50
294 Zachary Parker **RC** .50
295 Christian Colonel **RC** .75
296 Scott Mitchinson **RC** .50
297 Neil Wilson **RC** .50
298 Chuck James **RC** 2.00
299 Heath Totten **RC** .50
300 Sean Tracey **RC** .75
301 Ismael Ramirez **RC** .50
302 Matt Brown **RC** .50
303 Franklin Morales **RC** 1.00
304 Brandon Sing **RC** 1.00
305 D.J. Houlton **RC** .50
306 Jayce Tingler **RC** .50
307 Mitchell Arnold **RC** .50
308 Jim Burt **RC** .75
309 Jason Motte **RC** .50
310 David Gassner **RC** .75
311 Andy Santana **RC** .50
312 Kelvin Pichardo **RC** .50
313 Carlos Carrasco **RC** 1.50
314 Willy Mota **RC** .50
315 Frank Mata **RC** .50
316 Carlos Gonzalez **RC** 2.50
317 Jeff Niemann **RC** 1.00
318 Chris Young **RC** 3.00
319 Billy Sadler .50
320 Ricky Barrett .50
321 Benjamin Harrison .50
322 Steve Nelson **RC** .50
323 Daryl Thompson **RC** .75
324 Philip Humber **RC** 1.50
325 Jeremy Harts **RC** .50
326 Nick Masset **RC** .50
327 Mike Rodriguez **RC** .50
328 Mike Garber **RC** .50
329 Kennard Bibbs **RC** .50
330 Ryan Garko **RC** 1.50

Gold

Stars: 1-2X
Rookies: 1-2X
Inserted 1:1

White

Stars: 3-6X
Rookies: 3-6X
Production 240 Sets

1st Edition

NM/M
Stars: 3-5X
Rookies: 1-2X
HTA Exclusive
Pack (10): 3.50
Box (20): 60.00

A-Rod Throwbacks

NM/M
Complete Set (4): 6.00
Common A-Rod: 2.00
94-AR - 97 Alex Rodriguez 2.00

A-Rod Throwbacks Autographs

NM/M
Production 1-225
96A-AR Alex Rodriguez/99 150.00
97A-AR Alex Rodriguez/225 150.00

A-Rod Throwbacks Relic

NM/M
Quantity produced listed
96R-AR Alex Rodriguez/99 20.00
97R-AR Alex Rodriguez/800 15.00

Autographed Base Card Variations

NM/M
Inserted 1:1,599
141 Omar Quintanilla 8.00
142 Carlos Quentin 20.00
143 Dan Johnson 10.00
144 Jake Stevens 10.00
145 Nate Schierholtz 10.00
146 Neil Walker 15.00
147 Bill Bray 8.00
148 Taylor Tankersley 10.00
149 Trevor Plouffe 12.00
150 Felix Hernandez 30.00
151 Phillip Hughes 50.00
152 James Houser 10.00

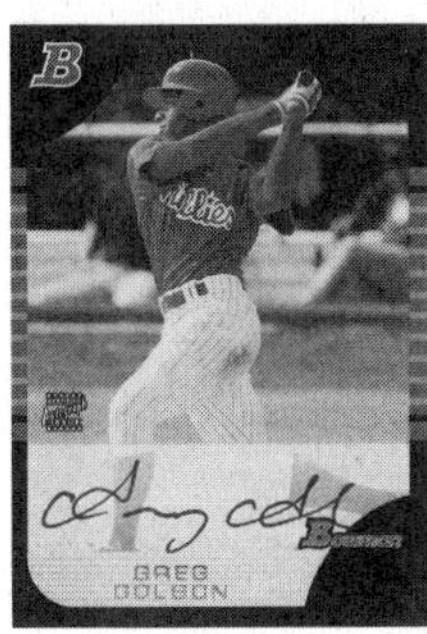

153 David Murphy 15.00
154 Ervin Santana 15.00
155 Anthony Whittington 8.00
156 Chris Lambert 12.00
157 Jeremy Sowers 15.00
158 Gio Gonzalez 15.00
159 Blake DeWitt 15.00
160 Thomas Diamond 15.00
161 Greg Golson 12.00
162 David Aardsma 10.00
163 Paul Maholm 12.00
164 Mark Rogers 15.00
165 Homer Bailey 25.00

Dual Rookie of the Year Relic

NM/M

Inserted 1:668
ROY-BC Jason Bay, Bobby Crosby 15.00

Futures Game Gear

NM/M

JB Joe Blanton 5.00
BB Bryan Bullington 5.00
MC Matt Cain 5.00
SC Shin-Soo Choo 6.00
JCO Jorge Cortes 5.00
JC Jesus Cota 5.00
EE Edwin Encarnacion 5.00
CE Clint Everts 5.00
GF Gavin Floyd 5.00
JF Jeff Francis 5.00
JG Jairo Garcia 5.00
RG Ruben Gotay 5.00
JGU Joel Guzman 5.00
AH Aaron Hill 5.00
KH Koyie Hill 5.00
WL Wilfredo Ledezma 5.00
VM Val Majewski 5.00
AMA Andy Marte 8.00
JM Jeff Mathis 5.00
DM Dallas McPherson 8.00
JMO Justin Morneau 8.00
AM Arnie Munoz 5.00
YP Yusmeiro Petit 8.00
FP Felix Pie 8.00
RW Rickie Weeks 8.00

Printing Plates

No Pricing
Production One Set

Relic Base Card Variations

NM/M

Inserted 1:50
2 Eric Chavez 5.00
5 Hank Blalock 8.00
23 Rafael Palmeiro 8.00
43 Mark Teixeira 8.00
49 Ivan Rodriguez 8.00
50 Alex Rodriguez 15.00
60 Gary Sheffield 8.00
65 Magglio Ordonez 5.00
78 David Ortiz 10.00
83 Adam Dunn 8.00
90 Miguel Cabrera 8.00
93 Andruw Jones 5.00
100 Barry Bonds 25.00
104 Melvin Mora 5.00
105 Albert Pujols 20.00
115 Alfonso Soriano 8.00
120 Vladimir Guerrero 8.00
125 Carlos Beltran 10.00
130 Manny Ramirez 8.00
135 Sammy Sosa 12.00

Signs of the Future

NM/M

BB Brian Bixler 10.00
MC Melky Cabrera 25.00
RC Robinson Cano 45.00
CC Chad Cordero 10.00
BC Bobby Crosby 15.00
BD Blake DeWitt 20.00
CG Christian Garcia 10.00
TG Tom Gorzelanny 10.00
PH Phillip Hughes 40.00
TH Tim Hutting 10.00
SK Scott Kazmir 15.00
AL Adam Loewen 10.00
PM Paul Maholm 10.00
DM Dallas McPherson 10.00
SO Scott Olson 10.00
TP Trevor Plouffe 15.00
DP Dan Putnam 10.00
JR Jay Rainville 15.00
RR Richie Robnett 8.00
ES Ervin Santana 15.00
JS Jay Sborz 10.00
BMS Brad Snyder 10.00
HS Huston Street 25.00
BS Brad Sullivan 10.00
TT Taylor Tankersley 12.00
RW Ryan Wagner 10.00
KW Kyle Waldrop 10.00
AW Anthony Whittington 10.00
DW David Wright 70.00

Two of a Kind Autograph

No Pricing
Production 13

2005 Bowman Chrome

NM/M

Complete Set (352):
Common Player: .25
Common Rookie: 1.00
Common RC Auto. (331-352): 10.00
Pack (4): 8.00
Box (18): 125.00
1 Gavin Floyd .25
2 Eric Chavez .50
3 Miguel Tejada .75
4 Dmitri Young .25
5 Hank Blalock .50
6 Kerry Wood .50
7 Andy Pettitte .50
8 Pat Burrell .50
9 Johnny Estrada .25
10 Frank Thomas .75
11 Juan Pierre .25
12 Tom Glavine .50
13 Lyle Overbay .25
14 Jim Edmonds .50
15 Steve Finley .25
16 Jermaine Dye .25
17 Omar Vizquel .25
18 Nick Johnson .25
19 Brian Giles .25
20 Justin Morneau .50
21 Preston Wilson .25
22 Wily Mo Pena .25
23 Rafael Palmeiro .75
24 Scott Kazmir .50
25 Derek Jeter 3.00
26 Barry Zito .50
27 Mike Lowell .25
28 Jason Bay .50
29 Ken Harvey .25
30 Nomar Garciaparra 1.00
31 Roy Halladay .50
32 Todd Helton .75
33 Mark Kotsay .25
34 Jake Peavy .50
35 David Wright 1.00
36 Dontrelle Willis .50
37 Marcus Giles .25
38 Chone Figgins .25
39 Sidney Ponson .25
40 Randy Johnson 1.00
41 John Smoltz .50
42 Kevin Millar .25
43 Mark Teixeira .75
44 Alex Rios .25
45 Mike Piazza 1.00
46 Victor Martinez .50
47 Jeff Bagwell .75
48 Shawn Green .50
49 Ivan Rodriguez .75
50 Alex Rodriguez 2.50
51 Kazuo Matsui .25
52 Mark Mulder .50
53 Michael Young .50
54 Javy Lopez .25
55 Johnny Damon 1.00
56 Jeff Francis .25
57 Rich Harden .50
58 Bobby Abreu .50
59 Mark Loretta .25
60 Gary Sheffield .50
61 Jamie Moyer .25
62 Garret Anderson .50
63 Vernon Wells .50
64 Orlando Cabrera .25
65 Magglio Ordonez .25
66 Ronnie Belliard .25
67 Carlos Lee .50
68 Carl Pavano .25
69 Jon Lieber .25
70 Aubrey Huff .25
71 Rocco Baldelli .25
72 Jason Schmidt .50
73 Bernie Williams .50
74 Hideki Matsui 2.00
75 Ken Griffey Jr. 2.00
76 Josh Beckett .50
77 Mark Buehrle .40
78 David Ortiz 1.00
79 Luis Gonzalez .25
80 Scott Rolen 1.00
81 Joe Mauer .75
82 Jose Reyes .75
83 Adam Dunn .75
84 Greg Maddux 2.00
85 Bartolo Colon .40
86 Bret Boone .25
87 Mike Mussina .50
88 Ben Sheets .50
89 Lance Berkman .50
90 Miguel Cabrera 1.00
91 C.C. Sabathia .25
92 Mike Maroth .25
93 Andruw Jones .50
94 Jack Wilson .25
95 Ichiro Suzuki 2.00
96 Geoff Jenkins .25
97 Zack Greinke .25
98 Jorge Posada .50
99 Travis Hafner .50
100 Barry Bonds 3.00
101 Aaron Rowand .25
102 Aramis Ramirez .50
103 Curt Schilling 1.00
104 Melvin Mora .25
105 Albert Pujols 3.00
106 Austin Kearns .40
107 Shannon Stewart .25
108 Carl Crawford .50
109 Carlos Zambrano .50
110 Roger Clemens 3.00
111 Javier Vazquez .25
112 Randy Wolf .25
113 Chipper Jones 1.00
114 Larry Walker .50
115 Alfonso Soriano 1.00
116 Brad Wilkerson .25
117 Bobby Crosby .25
118 Jim Thome .75
119 Oliver Perez .25
120 Vladimir Guerrero 1.00
121 Roy Oswalt .50
122 Torii Hunter .40
123 Rafael Furcal .25
124 Luis Castillo .25
125 Carlos Beltran .75
126 Mike Sweeney .25
127 Johan Santana .75
128 Tim Hudson .50
129 Troy Glaus .50
130 Manny Ramirez 1.00
131 Jeff Kent .40
132 Jose Vidro .25
133 Edgar Renteria .40
134 Russ Ortiz .25
135 Sammy Sosa 1.00
136 Carlos Delgado .50
137 Richie Sexson .50
138 Pedro Martinez 1.00
139 Adrian Beltre .50
140 Mark Prior .75
141 Omar Quintanilla .25
142 Carlos Quentin .25
143 Dan Johnson .25
144 Jake Stevens .25
145 Nate Schierholtz .25
146 Neil Walker .25
147 Bill Bray .25
148 Taylor Tankersley .25
149 Trevor Plouffe .25
150 Felix Hernandez 1.00
151 Phillip Hughes .50
152 James Houser .25
153 David Murphy .25
154 Ervin Santana .25
155 Anthony Whittington .25
156 Chris Lambert .25
157 Jeremy Sowers .25
158 Gio Gonzalez .25
159 Blake DeWitt .25
160 Thomas Diamond .25
161 Greg Golson .25
162 David Aardsma .25
163 Paul Maholm .25
164 Mark Rogers .25
165 Homer Bailey .50
166 Elvin Puello **RC** 1.00
167 Tony Giarratano **RC** 1.50
168 Darren Fenster **RC** 1.00
169 Elvys Quezada **RC** 1.00
170 Glen Perkins **RC** 2.50
171 Ian Kinsler **RC** 10.00
172 Adam Bostick **RC** 1.00
173 Jeremy West **RC** 2.00
174 Brett Harper **RC** 2.00
175 Kevin West **RC** 1.00
176 Luis Hernandez **RC** 1.00
177 Matt Campbell **RC** 1.00
178 Nate McLouth **RC** 2.50
179 Ryan Goleski **RC** 2.00
180 Matt Lindstrom **RC** 1.00
181 Matt DeSalvo **RC** 3.00
182 Kole Strayhorn **RC** 1.00
183 Jose Vaquedano **RC** 1.00
184 James Jurries **RC** 2.00
185 Ian Bladergroen **RC** 2.50
186 Kila Kaaihue **RC** 4.00
187 Luke Scott **RC** 4.00
188 Chris Denorfia **RC** 3.00
189 Jai Miller **RC** 1.50
190 Melky Cabrera **RC** 6.00
191 Ryan Sweeney 4.00
192 Sean Marshall **RC** 2.00
193 Eric Abreu **RC** 2.00
194 Tyler Pelland **RC** 1.50
195 Cole Armstrong **RC** 1.50
196 John Hudgins **RC** 1.00
197 Wade Robinson **RC** 1.00
198 Dan Santin **RC** 1.50
199 Steven Doetsch **RC** 1.50
200 Shane Costa **RC** 1.00
201 Scott Mathieson **RC** 2.00
202 Ben Jones **RC** 2.00
203 Michael Rogers **RC** 1.00
204 Matt Rogelstad **RC** 1.50
205 Luis Ramirez **RC** 1.00
206 Landon Powell **RC** 2.00
207 Erik Cordier **RC** 1.50
208 Chris Seddon **RC** 1.00
209 Chris Roberson **RC** 1.50
210 Tom Oldham **RC** 1.00
211 Dana Eveland **RC** 2.50
212 Cody Haerther **RC** 1.00
213 Danny Core **RC** 1.00
214 Craig Tatum **RC** 1.00
215 Elliot Johnson **RC** 2.50
216 Ender Chavez **RC** 1.00
217 Errol Simonitsch **RC** 1.50
218 Matt Van Der Bosch **RC** 1.00
219 Eulogio de la Cruz **RC** 1.00
220 Drew Toussaint **RC** 1.50
221 Adam Boeve **RC** 2.00
222 Adam Harben **RC** 1.50
223 Baltazar Lopez **RC** 2.00
224 Russell Martin **RC** 8.00
225 Brian Bannister **RC** 2.00
226 Chris Walker **RC** 1.00
227 Casey McGehee **RC** 1.50
228 Humberto Sanchez **RC** 6.00
229 Javon Moran **RC** 1.00
230 Brandon McCarthy **RC** 2.00
231 Danny Zell **RC** 1.00
232 Kevin Barry **RC** 1.00
233 Juan Tejeda **RC** 1.50
234 Keith Ramsey **RC** 1.00
235 Lorenzo Scott **RC** 1.00
236 Jonathan Barratt **RC** 1.00
237 Martin Prado **RC** 2.00
238 Matt Albers **RC** 3.00
239 Brian Schweiger **RC** 1.00
240 Raul Tablado **RC** 1.00
241 Pat Misch **RC** 1.00
242 Pat Osborn **RC** 1.00
243 Ryan Feierabend **RC** 1.00
244 Shaun Marcum 1.00
245 Kevin Collins **RC** 1.00
246 Stuart Pomeranz **RC** 1.00
247 Tetsu Yofu **RC** 1.00
248 Hernan Iribarren **RC** 3.00
249 Michael Spidale **RC** 1.00
250 Tony Americh **RC** 1.00
251 Manny Parra **RC** 1.00
252 Drew Anderson **RC** 1.00
253 T.J. Beam **RC** 3.00
254 Claudio Arias **RC** 2.00
255 Andy Sides **RC** 1.00
256 Bear Bay **RC** 2.00
257 Bill McCarthy **RC** 1.00
258 Daniel Haigwood **RC** 2.00
259 Brian Sprout **RC** 1.00
260 Bryan Triplett **RC** 1.00
261 Steve Bondurant **RC** 1.00
262 Darwinson Salazar **RC** 1.00
263 David Shepard **RC** 1.00
264 Johan Silva **RC** 1.50
265 J.B. Thurmond **RC** 1.00
266 Brandon Moorhead **RC** 1.00
267 Kyle Nichols **RC** 2.00
268 Jonathan Sanchez **RC** 3.00
269 Mike Esposito **RC** 1.00
270 Erik Schindewolf **RC** 2.00
271 Peeter Ramos **RC** 1.00
272 Juan Senreiso **RC** 1.00
273 Travis Chick **RC** 2.00
274 Vinny Rottino **RC** 1.00
275 Micah Furtado **RC** 1.00
276 George Kottaras **RC** 2.00
277 Abel Gomez **RC** 1.50
278 Buck Coats **RC** 1.00
279 Ken Durost **RC** 1.00
280 Nick Touchstone **RC** 1.00
281 Jerry Owens **RC** 2.00
282 Stefan Bailie **RC** 1.00
283 Jesse Gutierrez **RC** 1.00
284 Chuck Tiffany **RC** 3.00
285 Brendan Ryan **RC** 1.00
286 Julio Pimentel **RC** 1.50
287 Shawn Bowman **RC** 1.50
288 Alexander Smit **RC** 1.50
289 Micah Schnurstein **RC** 1.50
290 Jared Gothreaux **RC** 1.00
291 Jair Jurrjens **RC** 4.00
292 Bobby Livingston **RC** 1.00
293 Ryan Speier **RC** 1.00
294 Zachary Parker **RC** 1.00
295 Christian Colonel **RC** 1.00
296 Scott Mitchinson **RC** 1.00
297 Neil Wilson **RC** 1.00
298 Chuck James **RC** 5.00
299 Heath Totten **RC** 1.00
300 Sean Tracey **RC** 1.00
301 Tadahito Iguchi **RC** 2.50
302 Matt Brown **RC** 1.00
303 Franklin Morales **RC** 3.00
304 Brandon Sing **RC** 3.00
305 D.J. Houlton **RC** 1.50
306 Jayce Tingler **RC** 1.00
307 Mitchell Arnold **RC** 1.00
308 Jim Burt **RC** 1.00
309 Jason Motte **RC** 1.00
310 David Gassner **RC** 1.00
311 Andy Santana **RC** 1.00
312 Kelvin Pichardo **RC** 1.00
313 Carlos Carrasco **RC** 5.00
314 Willy Mota **RC** 2.00
315 Frank Mata **RC** 1.00
316 Carlos Gonzalez **RC** 10.00
317 Jesse Floyd **RC** 1.00
318 Chris Young **RC** 6.00
319 Billy Sadler 1.00
320 Ricky Barrett **RC** 1.00
321 Benjamin Harrison **RC** 1.00
322 Steve Nelson **RC** 1.00
323 Daryl Thompson **RC** 1.00
324 Davis Romero **RC** 1.00
325 Jeremy Harts **RC** 1.00
326 Nick Masset **RC** 1.00
327 Thomas Pauly **RC** 1.00
328 Mike Garber **RC** 1.00
329 Kennard Bibbs **RC** 1.00
330 Colter Bean **RC** 1.00
331 Justin Verlander **RC** 80.00
332 Chip Cannon **RC** 25.00
333 Kevin Melillo **RC** 20.00
334 Jake Postlewait **RC** 10.00
335 Wes Swackhamer **RC** 15.00
336 Mike Rodriguez **RC** 15.00
337 Philip Humber **RC** 30.00
338 Jeff Niemann **RC** 30.00
339 Brian Miller **RC** 10.00
340 Chris Vines **RC** 10.00
341 Andy LaRoche **RC** 40.00
342 Michael Bourn 30.00
343 Eric Nielsen **RC** 15.00
344 Wladimir Balentien **RC** 40.00
345 Ismael Ramirez **RC** 15.00
346 Pedro Lopez **RC** 10.00
347 Shawn Bowman **RC** 15.00
348 Hayden Penn **RC** 20.00
349 Matthew Kemp **RC** 70.00
350 Brian Stavisky **RC** 10.00
351 C.J. Smith **RC** 10.00
352 Mike Morse **RC** 15.00
353 Billy Butler **RC** 100.00

Refractor

Stars (1-165): 2-4X
Rookies (166-330): 1-2X
Inserted 1:4
Autograph (331-353): 1-2X
Production 500

Blue Refractor

Stars (1-165): 3-5X
Rookies (166-330): 3-5X
Autograph (331-353): 1-2.5X
Production 150 Sets

Gold Refractor

Stars (1-165): 8-15X
Rookies (166-330): 15-25X
Autograph (331-353): 3-6X
Production 50 Sets

Red Refractor

No Pricing
Production Five Sets

Superfractor

No Pricing
Production One Set

X-Fractor

Stars (1-165): 3-5X
Rookies (166-330): 2-5X
Autograph (331-353): 1-2.5X
Production 225 Sets

Printing Plates

No Pricing
Production one set per color.

A-Rod Throwback

NM/M

Complete Set (4): 6.00
Common A-Rod 2.00
Inserted 1:9
Refractor: 2-3X
Production 499 Sets
X-Fractor: 3-5X
Production 99 Sets
Superfractor: No Pricing
Production One Set
94AR Alex Rodriguez 2.00
95AR Alex Rodriguez 2.00
96AR Alex Rodriguez 2.00
97AR Alex Rodriguez 2.00

A-Rod Throwback Autograph

NM/M

Quantity produced listed
96AR Alex Rodriguez/50 160.00
97AR Alex Rodriguez/99 150.00

One Of A Kind Autograph

No Pricing
Production 13

2005 Bowman Draft Picks & Prospects

NM/M

Complete Set (165): 30.00
Commmon Player: .15
Common Rookie .25
Pack (5 + 2 Chrome): 7.00
Box (24): 140.00
BDP1 Rickie Weeks .15
BDP2 Kyle Davies .15
BDP3 Garrett Atkins .15
BDP4 Chien-Ming Wang .50
BDP5 Dallas McPherson .15
BDP6 Dan Johnson .15
BDP7 Andy Sisco .15
BDP8 Ryan Doumit .15
BDP9 J.P. Howell .15
BDP10 Tim Stauffer .15
BDP11 Willy Taveras .15
BDP12 Aaron Hill .15
BDP13 Victor Diaz .15
BDP14 Wilson Betemit .15
BDP15 Ervin Santana .15
BDP16 Mike Morse .15
BDP17 Yadier Molina .15
BDP18 Kelly Johnson .15
BDP19 Clint Barmes .15
BDP20 Robinson Cano .40
BDP21 Brad Thompson .15
BDP22 Jorge Cantu .15
BDP23 Brad Halsey .15
BDP24 Lance Niekro .15
BDP25 D.J. Houlton .15
BDP26 Ryan Church .15
BDP27 Hayden Penn .15
BDP28 Chris Young .50
BDP29 Chad Orvella .15
BDP30 Mark Teahen .15
BDP31 Mark McCormick **RC** .25
BDP32 Jay Bruce **RC** 6.00
BDP33 Beau Jones **RC** .75
BDP34 Tyler Greene **RC** .40
BDP35 Zach Ward **RC** .75
BDP36 Josh Bell **RC** 1.00
BDP37 Josh Wall **RC** .50

BDP38 Nick Webber **RC** .25
BDP39 Travis Buck **RC** 1.00
BDP40 Kyle Winters **RC** .25
BDP41 Mitch Boggs **RC** .25
BDP42 Tommy Mendoza **RC** .50
BDP43 Brad Corley **RC** .40
BDP44 Drew Butera **RC** .25
BDP45 Ryan Mount **RC** .40
BDP46 Tyler Herron **RC** .50
BDP47 Nick Weglarz **RC** 1.00
BDP48 Brandon Erbe **RC** 1.00
BDP49 Cody Allen **RC** .25
BDP50 Eric Fowler **RC** .25
BDP51 James Boone **RC** .50
BDP52 Josh Flores **RC** .75
BDP53 Brandon Monk **RC** .50
BDP54 Kieron Pope **RC** .75
BDP55 Kyle Cofield **RC** .40
BDP56 Brent Lillibridge **RC** .75
BDP57 Daryl Jones **RC** .40
BDP58 Eli Iorg **RC** .50
BDP59 Brett Hayes **RC** .25
BDP60 Mike Durant **RC** .75
BDP61 Michael Bowden **RC** 1.50
BDP62 Paul Kelly **RC** .50
BDP63 Andrew McCutchen **RC** 1.50
BDP64 Travis Wood **RC** .75
BDP65 Cesar Ramos **RC** .25
BDP66 Chaz Roe **RC** .40
BDP67 Matt Torra **RC** .50
BDP68 Kevin Slowey **RC** 2.00
BDP69 Trayvon Robinson **RC** .40
BDP70 Reid Engel **RC** .40
BDP71 Kris Harvey **RC** .50
BDP72 Craig Italiano **RC** .50
BDP73 Matt Maloney **RC** 1.00
BDP74 Sean West **RC** 1.00
BDP75 Henry Sanchez **RC** .50
BDP76 Scott Blue **RC** .25
BDP77 Jordan Schafer **RC** 1.00
BDP78 Chris Robinson **RC** .25
BDP79 Chris Hobdy **RC** .25
BDP80 Brandon Durden **RC** .25
BDP81 Clay Buchholz **RC** 5.00
BDP82 Josh Geer **RC** .25
BDP83 Sam LeCure **RC** .25
BDP84 Justin Thomas **RC** .25
BDP85 Brett Gardner **RC** .50
BDP86 Tommy Manzella **RC** .25
BDP87 Matt Green **RC** .25
BDP88 Yunel Escobar **RC** .75
BDP89 Mike Costanzo **RC** .75
BDP90 Nick Hundley **RC** .25
BDP91 Zach Simons **RC** .25
BDP92 Jacob Marceaux **RC** .25
BDP93 Jed Lowrie **RC** .75
BDP94 Brandon Snyder **RC** 1.00
BDP95 Matt Goyen **RC** .25
BDP96 Jon Egan **RC** .40
BDP97 Drew Thompson **RC** .40
BDP98 Bryan Anderson **RC** 1.00
BDP99 Clayton Richard **RC** .25
BDP100 Jimmy Shull **RC** .25
BDP101 Mark Pawelek **RC** 1.00
BDP102 P.J. Phillips **RC** .40
BDP103 John Drennen **RC** .75
BDP104 Nolan Reimold **RC** 1.50
BDP105 Troy Tulowitzki **RC** 4.00
BDP106 Kevin Whelan **RC** .25
BDP107 Wade Townsend **RC** .50
BDP108 Micah Owings **RC** 1.50
BDP109 Ryan Tucker **RC** .40
BDP110 Jeff Clement **RC** 1.50
BDP111 Josh Sullivan **RC** .25
BDP112 Jeff Lyman **RC** .25
BDP113 Brian Bogusevic **RC** .40
BDP114 Trevor Bell **RC** .50
BDP115 Brent Cox **RC** .75
BDP116 Michael Billek **RC** .25
BDP117 Garrett Olson **RC** 1.00
BDP118 Steven Johnson **RC** .25
BDP119 Chase Headley **RC** .75
BDP120 Daniel Carte **RC** .50
BDP121 Francisco Liriano .75
BDP122 Fausto Carmona .15
BDP123 Zach Jackson .15
BDP124 Adam Loewen .15
BDP125 Chris Lambert .15
BDP126 Scott Mathieson **RC** .25
BDP127 Paul Maholm .15
BDP128 Fernando Nieve .15
BDP129 Justin Verlander .75
BDP130 Yusmeiro Petit .40
BDP131 Joel Zumaya .25
BDP132 Merkin Valdez .15
BDP133 Ryan Garko **RC** .75
BDP134 Edinson Volquez **RC** 1.00
BDP135 Russell Martin .50
BDP136 Conor Jackson .15
BDP137 Miguel Montero **RC** .50
BDP138 Josh Barfield .15
BDP139 Delmon Young .25
BDP140 Andy LaRoche .75
BDP141 William Bergolla .15
BDP142 B.J. Upton .15
BDP143 Hernan Iribarren **RC** .25
BDP144 Brandon Wood .40
BDP145 Jose Bautista .15
BDP146 Edwin Encarnacion .15
BDP147 Javier Herrera **RC** 1.00
BDP148 Jeremy Hermida .25
BDP149 Frank Diaz **RC** .25
BDP150 Chris Young .50
BDP151 Shin-Soo Choo .15
BDP152 Kevin Thompson .15
BDP153 Hanley Ramirez .50
BDP154 Lastings Milledge .25
BDP155 Luis Montanez .15
BDP156 Justin Huber .15
BDP157 Zachary Duke .15
BDP158 Jeff Francoeur .25
BDP159 Melky Cabrera 1.00
BDP160 Bobby Jenks .15
BDP161 Ian Snell .15
BDP162 Fernando Cabrera .15
BDP163 Troy Patton .50
BDP164 Anthony Lerew .15
BDP165 Nelson Cruz **RC** .75

White

Rookies: 3-5X
Production 225 Sets

Red

No Pricing
Production One Set

Base Relic Variation

NM/M
Common Player: 4.00
BDP121 Francisco Liriano 8.00
BDP122 Fausto Carmona 4.00
BDP123 Zach Jackson 4.00
BDP124 Adam Loewen 4.00
BDP125 Chris Lambert 4.00
BDP126 Scott Mathieson 4.00
BDP127 Paul Maholm 4.00
BDP128 Fernando Nieve 4.00
BDP129 Justin Verlander 8.00
BDP130 Yusmeiro Petit 6.00
BDP131 Joel Zumaya 10.00
BDP132 Merkin Valdez 4.00
BDP133 Ryan Garko 6.00
BDP134 Edinson Volquez 15.00
BDP135 Russell Martin 6.00
BDP136 Conor Jackson 6.00
BDP137 Miguel Montero 6.00
BDP138 Josh Barfield 4.00
BDP139 Delmon Young 6.00
BDP140 Andy LaRoche 6.00
BDP141 William Bergolla 4.00
BDP142 B.J. Upton 4.00
BDP143 Hernan Iribarren 4.00
BDP144 Brandon Wood 10.00
BDP145 Jose Bautista 4.00
BDP146 Edwin Encarnacion 4.00
BDP147 Javier Herrera 6.00
BDP148 Jeremy Hermida 6.00
BDP149 Frank Diaz 4.00
BDP150 Chris Young 6.00

Signs of the Future

NM/M
Common Player: 8.00
HB Homer Bailey 25.00
BB Bill Bray 8.00
JF Jeff Frazier 8.00
GG Greg Golson 8.00
AG Angel Guzman 10.00
JH Justin Hoyman 8.00
JJ Justin Jones 8.00
DL Donald Lucey 8.00
TL Tyler Lumsden 8.00
DM David Murphy 10.00
JP Jonathan Poterson 8.00
DP David Purcey 8.00
RR Richie Robnett 8.00
JS Jeremy Sowers 10.00

2005 Bowman Chrome Draft Picks & Prospects

NM/M
Complete Set (180):
Common Player: .25
Common Rookie: 1.00
Common Rk Auto. (166-180): 15.00
BDP1 Rickie Weeks .40
BDP2 Kyle Davies .25
BDP3 Garrett Atkins .25
BDP4 Chien-Ming Wang .75
BDP5 Dallas McPherson .25
BDP6 Dan Johnson .25
BDP7 Andy Sisco .25
BDP8 Ryan Doumit .25
BDP9 J.P. Howell .25
BDP10 Tim Stauffer .25
BDP11 Willy Taveras .25
BDP12 Aaron Hill .25
BDP13 Victor Diaz .25
BDP14 Wilson Betemit .25
BDP15 Ervin Santana .25
BDP16 Mike Morse .25
BDP17 Yadier Molina .25
BDP18 Kelly Johnson .25
BDP19 Clint Barmes .25
BDP20 Robinson Cano .75
BDP21 Brad Thompson .25
BDP22 Jorge Cantu .25
BDP23 Brad Halsey .25
BDP24 Lance Niekro .25
BDP25 D.J. Houlton .25
BDP26 Ryan Church .25
BDP27 Hayden Penn .25
BDP28 Chris Young 1.00
BDP29 Chad Orvella .50
BDP30 Mark Teahen .25
BDP31 Mark McCormick **RC** 1.00
BDP32 Jay Bruce **RC** 15.00
BDP33 Beau Jones **RC** 2.50
BDP34 Tyler Greene **RC** 1.50
BDP35 Zach Ward **RC** 2.50
BDP36 Josh Bell **RC** 4.00
BDP37 Josh Wall **RC** 2.00
BDP38 Nick Webber **RC** 1.00
BDP39 Travis Buck **RC** 3.00
BDP40 Kyle Winters **RC** 1.00
BDP41 Mitch Boggs **RC** 1.00
BDP42 Tommy Mendoza **RC** 2.00
BDP43 Brad Corley **RC** 1.50
BDP44 Drew Butera **RC** 1.00
BDP45 Ryan Mount **RC** 1.50
BDP46 Tyler Herron **RC** 1.50
BDP47 Nick Weglarz **RC** 3.00
BDP48 Brandon Erbe **RC** 4.00
BDP49 Cody Allen **RC** 1.00
BDP50 Eric Fowler **RC** 1.00
BDP51 James Boone **RC** 1.50
BDP52 Josh Flores **RC** 1.00
BDP53 Brandon Monk **RC** 2.00
BDP54 Kieron Pope **RC** 2.50
BDP55 Kyle Cofield **RC** 1.50
BDP56 Brent Lillibridge **RC** 2.50
BDP57 Daryl Jones **RC** 1.50
BDP58 Eli Iorg **RC** 2.00
BDP59 Brett Hayes **RC** 1.00
BDP60 Mike Durant **RC** 3.00
BDP61 Michael Bowden **RC** 5.00
BDP62 Paul Kelly **RC** 2.00
BDP63 Andrew McCutchen **RC** 8.00
BDP64 Travis Wood **RC** 3.00
BDP65 Cesar Ramos **RC** 1.00
BDP66 Chaz Roe **RC** 1.50
BDP67 Matt Torra **RC** 2.00
BDP68 Kevin Slowey **RC** 6.00
BDP69 Trayvon Robinson **RC** 1.50
BDP70 Reid Engel **RC** 1.50
BDP71 Kris Harvey **RC** 2.00
BDP72 Craig Italiano **RC** 2.50
BDP73 Matt Maloney **RC** 3.00
BDP74 Sean West **RC** 4.00
BDP75 Henry Sanchez **RC** 2.50
BDP76 Scott Blue **RC** 1.00
BDP77 Jordan Schafer **RC** 4.00
BDP78 Chris Robinson **RC** 1.00
BDP79 Chris Hobdy **RC** 1.00
BDP80 Brandon Durden **RC** 1.00
BDP81 Clay Buchholz **RC** 20.00
BDP82 Josh Geer **RC** 1.00
BDP83 Sam LeCure **RC** 1.00
BDP84 Justin Thomas **RC** 1.00
BDP85 Brett Gardner **RC** 1.50
BDP86 Tommy Manzella **RC** 1.00
BDP87 Matt Green **RC** 1.00
BDP88 Yunel Escobar **RC** 3.00
BDP89 Mike Costanzo **RC** 3.00
BDP90 Nick Hundley **RC** 1.00
BDP91 Zach Simons **RC** 1.00
BDP92 Jacob Marceaux **RC** 1.00
BDP93 Jed Lowrie **RC** 3.00
BDP94 Brandon Snyder **RC** 4.00
BDP95 Matt Goyen **RC** 1.00
BDP96 Jon Egan **RC** 1.50
BDP97 Drew Thompson **RC** 1.50
BDP98 Bryan Anderson **RC** 4.00
BDP99 Clayton Richard **RC** 1.00
BDP100 Jimmy Shull **RC** 1.00
BDP101 Mark Pawelek **RC** 5.00
BDP102 P.J. Phillips **RC** 1.50
BDP103 John Drennen **RC** 3.00
BDP104 Nolan Reimold **RC** 4.00
BDP105 Troy Tulowitzki **RC** 15.00
BDP106 Kevin Whelan **RC** 1.00
BDP107 Wade Townsend **RC** 2.00
BDP108 Micah Owings **RC** 4.00
BDP109 Ryan Tucker **RC** 1.50
BDP110 Jeff Clement **RC** 4.00
BDP111 Josh Sullivan **RC** 1.00
BDP112 Jeff Lyman **RC** 1.00
BDP113 Brian Bogusevic **RC** 1.50
BDP114 Trevor Bell **RC** 2.00
BDP115 Brent Cox **RC** 1.50
BDP116 Michael Billek **RC** 1.00
BDP117 Garrett Olson **RC** 4.00
BDP118 Steven Johnson **RC** 1.00
BDP119 Chase Headley **RC** 4.00
BDP120 Daniel Carte **RC** 2.00
BDP121 Francisco Liriano 1.50
BDP122 Fausto Carmona .25
BDP123 Zach Jackson .25
BDP124 Adam Loewen .25
BDP125 Chris Lambert .25
BDP126 Scott Mathieson **RC** 1.00
BDP127 Paul Maholm .25
BDP128 Fernando Nieve .25
BDP129 Justin Verlander 3.00
BDP130 Yusmeiro Petit .25
BDP131 Joel Zumaya 1.00
BDP132 Merkin Valdez .25
BDP133 Ryan Garko **RC** 4.00
BDP134 Edinson Volquez **RC** 10.00
BDP135 Russell Martin 3.00
BDP136 Conor Jackson .25
BDP137 Miguel Montero **RC** 3.00
BDP138 Josh Barfield .25
BDP139 Delmon Young .50
BDP140 Andy LaRoche 2.00
BDP141 William Bergolla .25
BDP142 B.J. Upton .25
BDP143 Hernan Iribarren 1.00
BDP144 Brandon Wood 1.00
BDP145 Jose Bautista .25
BDP146 Edwin Encarnacion .25
BDP147 Javier Herrera **RC** 4.00
BDP148 Jeremy Hermida .25
BDP149 Frank Diaz **RC** 1.00
BDP150 Chris Young 2.00
BDP151 Shin-Soo Choo .25
BDP152 Kevin Thompson .25
BDP153 Hanley Ramirez 1.00
BDP154 Lastings Milledge .50
BDP155 Luis Montanez .25
BDP156 Justin Huber .25
BDP157 Zachary Duke .25
BDP158 Jeff Francoeur .50
BDP159 Melky Cabrera 3.00
BDP160 Bobby Jenks .25
BDP161 Ian Snell .25
BDP162 Fernando Cabrera .25
BDP163 Troy Patton 2.00
BDP164 Anthony Lerew .25
BDP165 Nelson Cruz **RC** 3.00
BDP166 Stephen Drew **RC** 75.00
BDP167 Jered Weaver **RC** 60.00
BDP168 Ryan Braun **RC** 200.00
BDP169 John Mayberry Jr. **RC** 25.00
BDP170 Aaron Thompson **RC** 20.00
BDP171 Cesar Carrillo **RC** 25.00
BDP172 Jacoby Ellsbury **RC** 150.00
BDP173 Matt Garza **RC** 40.00
BDP174 Cliff Pennington **RC** 10.00
BDP175 Colby Rasmus **RC** 120.00
BDP176 Chris Volstad **RC** 30.00
BDP177 Ricky Romero **RC** 15.00
BDP178 Ryan Zimmerman **RC** 100.00
BDP179 C.J. Henry **RC** 30.00
BDP180 Eddy Martinez **RC** 25.00

Refractor

Rookies: 2-4X
Inserted 1:11
Rk Autos (166-180): 1-1.5X
Production 500

Blue Refractor

Rookies: 4-6X
Rk Autos (166-180): 1.5-3X
Production 150 Sets

Gold Refractor

Rookies: 8-15X
Rk Autos (166-180): 4-6X
Production 50 Sets

Red Refractor

No Pricing
Production One Set

SuperFractor

No Pricing
Production One Set

X-Fractor

Rookies: 4-6X
Rk Autos (166-180): 1-2X
Production 250 Sets

2005 Bowman Heritage

NM/M
Complete Set (349):
Common Player (1-300): .15
Common SP (301-349): 3.00
Inserted 1:3
Draft Pick Variations (325-349) 1-1.5X
One DPV pack per hobby box.
Pack (8): 4.00
Box (24): 85.00
1 Steven White **RC** .75
2 Jorge Posada .25
3 Brett Myers .15
4 Pat Burrell .25
5 Grady Sizemore .50
6 Jeff Weaver .15
7 Jeff Kent .25
8 Mark Kotsay .15
9 Nick Swisher .25
10 Scott Rolen .50
11 Matt Morris .25
12 Luis Castillo .15
13 Pedro Feliz .15
14 Omar Vizquel .15
15 Edgar Renteria .25
16 David Wells .15
17 Chad Cordero .15
18 Brad Wilkerson .15
19 Kelly Johnson .15
20 Johnny Estrada .15
21 Brian Roberts .25
22 Jeromy Burnitz .15
23 Magglio Ordonez .15
24 Adam Dunn .50
25 Randy Johnson .75
26 Derek Jeter 2.00
27 Jon Lieber .15
28 Jim Thome .50
29 Ronnie Belliard .15
30 Jake Westbrook .15
31 Bengie Molina .15
32 J.D. Drew .25
33 Rich Harden .25
34 David Eckstein .15
35 Scott Podsednik .25
36 Mark Buehrle .25
37 Barry Bonds 2.00
38 Brian Schneider .15
39 Tim Wakefield .15
40 Craig Wilson .15
41 Jose Vidro .15
42 Jacque Jones .15
43 Felix Hernandez .50
44 Nomar Garciaparra .75
45 Neifi Perez .15
46 Brandon Inge .15
47 Felipe Lopez .15
48 Ken Griffey Jr. 1.50
49 Robinson Cano .40
50 Jason Giambi .50
51 Mike Lieberthal .15
52 Bobby Abreu .25
53 C.C. Sabathia .15
54 Aaron Boone .15
55 Milton Bradley .15
56 Derek Lowe .15
57 Barry Zito .25
58 Jim Edmonds .40
59 Jon Garland .15
60 Tadahito Iguchi **RC** 1.50
61 Jason Schmidt .25
62 David Ortiz .75
63 Matt Lawton .15
64 Zachary Duke .25
65 Gary Sheffield .40
66 Chipper Jones .75
67 Sammy Sosa .75
68 Rafael Palmeiro .50
69 Carlos Zambrano .25
70 Aramis Ramirez .25
71 Chris Shelton .15
72 Wily Mo Pena .15
73 Mike Mussina .25
74 Chien-Ming Wang .50
75 Randy Wolf .15
76 Jimmy Rollins .25
77 Chase Utley .25
78 Kevin Millwood .15
79 Victor Martinez .25
80 Morgan Ensberg .25
81 Bartolo Colon .25
82 Bobby Crosby .15
83 Dan Johnson .15
84 Danny Haren .15
85 Yadier Molina .15
86 Mark Mulder .25
87 Russell Branyan .15
88 Lyle Overbay .15
89 Edgardo Alfonzo .15
90 Mike Matheny .15
91 J.T. Snow .15
92 Curt Schilling .75
93 Oliver Perez .15
94 Mark Redman .15
95 Esteban Loaiza .15
96 Livan Hernandez .15
97 Ryan Church .15
98 Kyle Davies .15
99 Mike Hampton .15
100 Jeff Francoeur .25
101 Javy Lopez .15
102 Mark Prior .75
103 Kerry Wood .25
104 Carlos Guillen .15
105 Dmitri Young .15
106 David Wright 1.00
107 Cliff Floyd .15
108 Carlos Beltran .50
109 Melky Cabrera **RC** 2.00
110 Carl Pavano .15
111 Jamie Moyer .15
112 Joel Pineiro .15
113 Adrian Beltre .25
114 Jhonny Peralta .15
115 Travis Hafner .40
116 Cesar Izturis .15
117 Brad Penny .15
118 Garret Anderson .25
119 Scott Kazmir .15
120 Aubrey Huff .15
121 Larry Walker .25
122 Albert Pujols 2.00
123 Paul Konerko .25
124 Frank Thomas .50
125 Phil Nevin .15
126 Brian Giles .15
127 Ramon Hernandez .15
128 Johnny Damon .75
129 Trot Nixon .15
130 Rocco Baldelli .15
131 Carl Crawford .25
132 Alfonso Soriano .50
133 Mark Teixeira .50
134 Gustavo Chacin .15
135 Vernon Wells .25
136 Erik Bedard .15
137 Daniel Cabrera .15
138 Michael Barrett .15
139 Greg Maddux 1.00
140 Javier Vazquez .15
141 Chad Tracy .15
142 Michael Young .15
143 Kenny Rogers .15
144 Mike Piazza .75
145 Jose Reyes .40
146 Geoff Jenkins .15
147 Carlos Lee .25
148 Brady Clark .15
149 Torii Hunter .25
150 Johan Santana .75
151 Steve Finley .15
152 Darin Erstad .25
153 Jake Peavy .25
154 Xavier Nady .15
155 Ryan Klesko .15
156 Ichiro Suzuki 1.50
157 Richie Sexson .40
158 Raul Ibanez .15
159 Freddy Garcia .15
160 Brad Hawpe .15
161 Jeff Francis .15
162 Todd Helton .40
163 Clint Barmes .15
164 Rodrigo Lopez .15
165 Melvin Mora .15
166 Brandon Webb .15
167 Shawn Green .25
168 Moises Alou .25
169 Matt Clement .25
170 John Smoltz .40
171 Rafael Furcal .25
172 Jeff Bagwell .25
173 Roger Clemens 2.00
174 Dontrelle Willis .40
175 Paul LoDuca .15
176 Zack Greinke .15
177 David DeJesus .15
178 Mike Sweeney .15
179 Ben Sheets .25
180 Doug Davis .15
181 Mike Cameron .15
182 Lance Berkman .40
183 Craig Biggio .25
184 Shannon Stewart .15
185 Joe Mauer .50
186 Justin Morneau .25
187 Mike Maroth .15
188 Ivan Rodriguez .50
189 Luis Gonzalez .15
190 Troy Glaus .25
191 Adam Eaton .15
192 Khalil Greene .25
193 Mike Lowell .15
194 Miguel Cabrera .75
195 Roy Halladay .25
196 Ted Lilly .15
197 Alex Rios .15
198 Josh Beckett .25
199 A.J. Burnett .15
200 Juan Pierre .15
201 Marcus Giles .15
202 Craig Tatum **RC** .50
203 Hayden Penn **RC** .50
204 C.J. Smith **RC** .25
205 Matt Albers **RC** 1.00
206 Jared Gothreaux **RC** .25
207 Mike Rodriguez **RC** .25
208 Hernan Iribarren **RC** .25
209 Manny Parra **RC** .25
210 Kevin Collins **RC** .25
211 Buck Coats **RC** .50
212 Jeremy West **RC** .50
213 Ian Bladergroen **RC** .25
214 Chuck Tiffany **RC** 1.50
215 Andy LaRoche **RC** 2.00
216 Frank Diaz **RC** .25
217 Jai Miller **RC** .25
218 Tony Giarratano **RC** .50
219 Danny Zell **RC** .25
220 Justin Verlander **RC** 5.00
221 Ryan Sweeney 1.00
222 Brandon McCarthy **RC** 1.00
223 Jerry Owens **RC** .25
224 Glen Perkins **RC** .50
225 Kevin West **RC** .25
226 Billy Butler **RC** 4.00
227 Shane Costa **RC** .50
228 Erik Schindewolf **RC** .50

229 Miguel Montero **RC** .75
230 Stephen Drew **RC** 4.00
231 Matt DeSalvo **RC** 1.00
232 Ben Jones **RC** .75
233 Bill McCarthy **RC** .25
234 Chuck James **RC** 2.00
235 Brandon Sing **RC** .75
236 Andy Santana **RC** .75
237 Brendan Ryan **RC** .50
238 Wes Swackhamer **RC** .50
239 Jeff Niemann **RC** 1.00
240 Ian Kinsler **RC** 3.00
241 Micah Furtado **RC** .50
242 Ryan Mount **RC** 1.00
243 P.J. Phillips **RC** .50
244 Trevor Bell **RC** 1.00
245 Jered Weaver **RC** 4.00
246 Eddy Martinez-Esteve **RC** .75
247 Brian Bannister **RC** 1.00
248 Philip Humber **RC** 1.00
249 Michael Rogers **RC** .50
250 Landon Powell **RC** .50
251 Kennard Bibbs **RC** .50
252 Nelson Cruz **RC** 1.00
253 Paul Kelly **RC** .75
254 Kevin Slowey **RC** 2.00
255 Brandon Snyder **RC** 1.00
256 Nolan Reimold **RC** 1.50
257 Brian Stavisky **RC** .25
258 Javier Herrera **RC** 1.50
259 Russell Martin **RC** 3.00
260 Matthew Kemp **RC** 3.00
261 Wade Townsend **RC** .75
262 Nick Touchstone **RC** .50
263 Ryan Feierabend **RC** .50
264 Bobby Livingston **RC** .50
265 Wladimir Balentien **RC** .75
266 Keiichi Yabu **RC** 1.00
267 Craig Italiano **RC** .50
268 Ryan Goleski **RC** .50
269 Ryan Garko **RC** 1.50
270 Michael Bourn .50
271 Scott Mathieson **RC** .75
272 Scott Mitchinson **RC** .75
273 Tyler Greene **RC** 1.00
274 Mark McCormick **RC** .50
275 Daryl Jones **RC** .50
276 Travis Chick **RC** .50
277 Luis Hernandez **RC** .25
278 Steven Doetsch **RC** .25
279 Chris Vines **RC** .50
280 Mike Costanzo **RC** 1.00
281 Matt Maloney **RC** 1.00
282 Matt Goyen **RC** .25
283 Jacob Marceaux **RC** .25
284 David Gassner **RC** .25
285 Ricky Barrett **RC** .50
286 Jon Egan **RC** .50
287 Scott Blue **RC** .50
288 Steve Bondurant **RC** .50
289 Kevin Melillo **RC** .50
290 Brad Corley **RC** .50
291 Brent Lillibridge **RC** 1.00
292 Mike Morse **RC** .25
293 Justin Thomas **RC** .50
294 Nick Webber **RC** .25
295 Mitch Boggs **RC** .25
296 Jeff Lyman **RC** .50
297 Jordan Schafer **RC** 1.50
298 Ismael Ramirez **RC** .25
299 Chris Young **RC** 2.50
300 Brian Miller **RC** .50
301 Jason Bay 4.00
302 Tim Hudson 3.00
303 Miguel Tejada 4.00
304 Jeremy Bonderman 3.00
305 Alex Rodriguez 8.00
306 Rickie Weeks 3.00
307 Manny Ramirez 6.00
308 Nick Johnson 3.00
309 Andruw Jones 4.00
310 Hideki Matsui 6.00
311 Jeremy Reed 5.00
312 Dallas McPherson 3.00
313 Vladimir Guerrero 5.00
314 Eric Chavez 3.00
315 Chris Carpenter 4.00
316 Aaron Hill 3.00
317 Derrek Lee 5.00
318 Mark Loretta 3.00
319 Garrett Atkins 3.00
320 Hank Blalock 3.00
321 Chris Young 5.00
322 Roy Oswalt 3.00
323 Carlos Delgado 4.00
324 Pedro Martinez 5.00
325 Jeff Clement **RC** 4.00
326 Jimmy Shull **RC** 4.00
327 Daniel Carte **RC** 4.00
328 Travis Buck **RC** 4.00
329 Chris Volstad **RC** 3.00
330 Andrew McCutchen **RC** 8.00
331 Cliff Pennington **RC** 4.00
332 John Mayberry Jr. **RC** 4.00
333 C.J. Henry **RC** 4.00
334 Ricky Romero **RC** 5.00
335 Aaron Thompson **RC** 5.00
336 Cesar Carrillo **RC** 4.00
337 Jacoby Ellsbury **RC** 12.00
338 Matt Garza **RC** 8.00
339 Colby Rasmus **RC** 8.00
340 Ryan Zimmerman **RC** 12.00
341 Ryan Braun **RC** 20.00
342 Brent Lillibridge **RC** 3.00
343 Jay Bruce **RC** 12.00
344 Matt Green **RC** 4.00
345 Brent Cox **RC** 6.00
346 Jed Lowrie **RC** 4.00
347 Beau Jones **RC** 3.00
348 Eli Iorg **RC** 4.00
349 Chaz Roe **RC** 4.00

Mahogany

Stars (1-300): 1-2X
SP's (301-349): .5-1X
Inserted 1:1

Mini

Stars (1-300): 1-2X
SP's (301-349): .5-1X
Inserted 1:1

Red

No Pricing
Production One Set

Draft Pick Variation

NM/M

Variations (325-349): 1-1.5X Base
One DPV pack per hobby box.
325 Jeff Clement 10.00
326 Jimmy Shull 6.00
327 Daniel Carte 6.00
328 Travis Buck 5.00
329 Chris Volstad 5.00
330 Andrew McCutchen 12.00
331 Cliff Pennington 6.00
332 John Mayberry Jr. 6.00
333 C.J. Henry 8.00
334 Ricky Romero 6.00
335 Aaron Thompson 6.00
336 Cesar Carrillo 6.00
337 Jacoby Ellsbury 20.00
338 Matt Garza 10.00
339 Colby Rasmus 15.00
340 Ryan Zimmerman 15.00
341 Ryan Braun 30.00
342 Brent Lillibridge 6.00
343 Jay Bruce 15.00
344 Matt Green 6.00
345 Brent Cox 6.00
346 Jed Lowrie 6.00
347 Beau Jones 5.00
348 Eli Iorg 6.00
349 Chaz Roe 6.00

Future Greatness

NM/M

Common Player: 4.00
TB Tony Blanco 4.00
JB Joe Blanton 4.00
BB Bryan Bullington 4.00
MC Matt Cain 8.00
FC Fausto Carmona 4.00
SC Shin-Soo Choo 4.00
JC Jorge Cortes 4.00
JCO Jesus Cota 4.00
EE Edwin Encarnacion 4.00
CE Clint Everts 4.00
GF Gavin Floyd 4.00
JF Jeff Francis 4.00
JGA Jairo Garcia 4.00
RG Ruben Gotay 6.00
JG Joel Guzman 4.00
AH Aaron Hill 4.00
KH Koyie Hill 4.00
JK Jason Kubel 4.00
WL Wilfredo Ledezma 4.00
VM Val Majewski 4.00
AMA Andy Marte 8.00
JMA Jeff Mathis 8.00
DM Dallas McPherson 4.00
JM Justin Morneau 8.00
AM Arnie Munoz 4.00
JP Juan Perez 4.00
YP Yusmeiro Petit 4.00
FP Felix Pie 6.00
BT Brad Thompson 15.00
RW Rickie Weeks 6.00
DY Delmon Young 8.00

Pieces of Greatness

NM/M

Common Player: 4.00
JB Josh Beckett 4.00
CB Carlos Beltran 6.00
BB Barry Bonds 20.00
MC Miguel Cabrera 8.00
EC Eric Chavez 4.00
RC Roger Clemens 10.00
BC Bobby Crosby 4.00
JD Johnny Damon 8.00
CD Carlos Delgado 6.00
AD Adam Dunn 8.00
JG Josh Gibson 15.00
TG Troy Glaus 4.00
RH Rich Harden 4.00
TH Todd Helton 6.00
JK Jeff Kent 4.00
PK Paul Konerko 6.00
PM Pedro Martinez 8.00
MMO Melvin Mora 4.00
MM Mark Mulder 4.00
BM Brett Myers 4.00
AP Albert Pujols 20.00
MR Manny Ramirez 8.00
BR Brian Roberts 4.00
AR Alex Rodriguez 15.00
JS John Smoltz 8.00
IS Ichiro Suzuki 15.00
MT Miguel Tejada 6.00
JT Jim Thome 6.00
DW Dontrelle Willis 6.00
DWR David Wright 15.00
BZ Barry Zito 4.00

Printing Plates

No Pricing
Production one set per color.

Signs of Greatness

NM/M

Common Player: 6.00
RB Ryan Braun 100.00
JB Jay Bruce 50.00
PB Patrick Bryant 10.00
MB Matt Bush 15.00
TC Travis Chick 6.00
TD Thomas Diamond 10.00
SE Scott Elbert 15.00
MG Matt Green 8.00
AG Angel Guzman 8.00
JH J.P. Howell 8.00
PH Philip Humber 20.00
ZJ Zach Jackson 8.00
JJ Jason Jaramillo 10.00
DJ Dan Johnson 8.00
BL Brent Lillibridge 10.00
DL Donald Lucey 8.00
EM Eddy Martinez-Esteve 8.00
JM John Mayberry Jr. 20.00
AM Andrew McCutchen 35.00
JP Jonathan Papelbon 40.00
DP David Purcey 8.00
RR Ricky Romero 10.00
HS Huston Street 20.00
CT Curtis Thigpen 10.00
WW Wes Whisler 10.00
JZ Jon Zeringue 8.00
RZ Ryan Zimmerman 40.00

51 Topps Heritage Blue Back

NM/M

Common Player: 1.00
1 Adam Dunn 3.00
2 Zachary Duke 1.50
3 Alex Rodriguez 8.00
4 Vladimir Guerrero 3.00
5 Andruw Jones 2.00
6 Travis Chick 2.00
7 Alfonso Soriano 2.00
8 Scott Rolen 3.00
9 Brian Bannister 2.00
10 Randy Johnson 3.00
11 Barry Bonds 8.00
12 Pat Burrell 1.50
13 Barry Zito 1.50
14 Nomar Garciaparra 3.00
15 C.C. Sabathia 1.00
16 Miguel Tejada 2.00
17 Hideki Matsui 6.00
18 John Smoltz 2.00
19 Ken Griffey Jr. 5.00
20 Chris Carpenter 1.50
21 Ian Kinsler 2.00
22 Chuck Tiffany 1.50
23 Gary Sheffield 2.00
24 Mark Mulder 1.50
25 Ichiro Suzuki 5.00
26 Kerry Wood 1.50
27 Jose Reyes 1.00
28 Derrek Lee 2.00
29 Justin Verlander 2.00
30 Johnny Damon 3.00
31 Chris Volstad 1.00
32 Jeremy Bonderman 1.00
33 David Ortiz 3.00
34 Morgan Ensberg 1.00
35 Mark Buehrle 1.00
36 Chuck James 2.00
37 Miguel Cabrera 3.00
38 Magglio Ordonez 1.00
39 Michael Young 1.00
40 Carlos Beltran 2.00
41 Nick Johnson 1.00
42 Billy Butler 2.00
43 Brian Giles 1.00
44 Paul Konerko 1.50
45 Roy Oswalt 1.50
46 Bobby Abreu 1.50
47 Sammy Sosa 3.00
48 Aramis Ramirez 1.50
49 Torii Hunter 1.00
50 Aubrey Huff 1.00
51 Vernon Wells 1.00
52 Joe Mauer 1.50

51 Topps Heritage Red Back

NM/M

Common Player: 1.00
1 Andy LaRoche 3.00
2 Mike Piazza 4.00
3 Pedro Martinez 3.00
4 Wladimir Balentien 1.00
5 Tim Hudson 1.50
6 Richie Sexson 1.50
7 Carlos Delgado 1.00
8 Derek Jeter 8.00
9 Ryan Zimmerman 6.00
10 Mark Teixeira 2.00
11 David Wright 3.00
12 Jake Peavy 1.50
13 Jose Vidro 1.00
14 Jim Thome 2.00
15 Carlos Zambrano 1.50
16 Hank Blalock 1.50
17 Johan Santana 2.00
18 Cliff Pennington 1.00
19 Rafael Palmeiro 1.50
20 Curt Schilling 2.00
21 Brandon McCarthy 2.00
22 Stephen Drew 8.00
23 Jeff Niemann 2.00
24 Eric Chavez 1.00
25 Hernan Iribarren 1.00
26 Jered Weaver 2.00
27 Edgar Renteria 1.00
28 Travis Hafner 1.00
29 Frank Thomas 1.50
30 Brian Roberts 1.00
31 Anthony Reyes 1.00
32 Scott Kazmir 1.00
33 Carlos Lee 1.00
34 Jimmy Rollins 1.00
35 Garret Anderson 1.00
36 Jason Schmidt 1.00
37 Jon Garland 1.00
38 Dontrelle Willis 1.50
39 C.J. Henry 3.00
40 Greg Maddux 4.00
41 Todd Helton 2.00
42 Ivan Rodriguez 2.00
43 Chipper Jones 3.00
44 Rich Harden 1.50
45 Mark Prior 3.00
46 Roy Halladay 1.50
47 Albert Pujols 8.00
48 Roger Clemens 8.00
49 Andrew McCutchen 4.00
50 Scott Podsednik 1.50
51 Manny Ramirez 3.00
52 Carl Crawford 1.00
53 Jim Edmonds 1.50
54 Wily Mo Pena 1.00

2005 Bowman Sterling

NM/M

Pack (5): 45.00
Box (6): 250.00

First Year Autographs

MA Matt Albers **RC** 20.00
RB Ryan Braun **RC** 125.00
TC Travis Chick **RC** 10.00
MG Matt Green **RC** 10.00
CH C.J. Henry **RC** 15.00
GK George Kottaras **RC** 20.00
EM Eddy Martinez-Esteve **RC** 15.00
JM John Mayberry Jr. **RC** 20.00
GO Garrett Olson **RC** 20.00
CP Cliff Pennington **RC** 10.00
HS Humberto Sanchez **RC** 25.00
BS Brandon Sing **RC** 15.00
AT Aaron Thompson **RC** 15.00
CV Chris Volstad **RC** 20.00
SW Steven White **RC** 10.00

Autographed First Year Relics

TB Trevor Bell **RC** 15.00
MB Michael Bowden **RC** 30.00
JB Jay Bruce **RC** 80.00
MC Mike Conroy **RC** 15.00
BC J. Brent Cox **RC** 15.00
JE Jacoby Ellsbury **RC** 100.00
JG Josh Geer **RC** 15.00
PH Philip Humber **RC** 25.00
EI Eli Iorg **RC** 15.00
BJ Beau Jones **RC** 15.00
BL Bobby Livingston **RC** 15.00
JL Jed Lowrie **RC** 25.00
SM Steve Marek **RC** 15.00
RM Russell Martin **RC** 40.00
BM Brandon McCarthy **RC** 15.00
AM Andrew McCutchen **RC** 40.00
TM Tyler Minges **RC** 15.00
JCN John Nelson **RC** 15.00
JN Jeff Niemann **RC** 20.00
JO Justin Olson **RC** 10.00
CPP Carmen Pignatiello **RC** 15.00
CR Colby Rasmus **RC** 80.00
CRO Chaz Roe **RC** 15.00
CS C.J. Smith **RC** 10.00
RT Raul Tablado **RC** 15.00
JV Justin Verlander **RC** 60.00

Autographed Prospect Base Relics

BB Billy Buckner 15.00
SE Scott Elbert 15.00
BE Brad Eldred 15.00
JF Josh Fields 20.00
AL Adam Lind 15.00
CN Chris Nelson 15.00
DP Dustin Pedroia 60.00
CT Curtis Thigpen 10.00

First Year Base Cards

BA Brian Anderson 4.00
BRB Brian Bogusevic **RC** 4.00
CBU Clay Buchholz **RC** 30.00
TBU Travis Buck **RC** 6.00
BBU Billy Butler **RC** 20.00
CC Cesar Carrillo **RC** 6.00
DC Daniel Carte **RC** 4.00
JC Jeff Clement **RC** 15.00
MCO Mike Constanzo **RC** 6.00
BCR Brad Corley **RC** 4.00
JDR John Drennen **RC** 8.00
SD Stephen Drew **RC** 10.00
JEG Jon Egan **RC** 6.00
YE Yunel Escobar **RC** 6.00
MGA Matt Garza **RC** 10.00
TG Tyler Greene **RC** 6.00
BH Brett Hayes **RC** 4.00
CHE Chase Headley **RC** 6.00
THE Tyler Herron **RC** 5.00
NH Nick Hundley **RC** 4.00
TI Tadahito Iguchi **RC** 6.00
HI Hernan Iribarren **RC** 4.00
CI Craig Italiano **RC** 6.00
CJ Chuck James **RC** 8.00
PK Paul Kelly **RC** 8.00
ACL Andy LaRoche **RC** 10.00
JLY Jeff Lyman **RC** 6.00
MAM Matt Maloney **RC** 8.00
JMA Jacob Marceaux **RC** 4.00
MMC Mark McCormick **RC** 4.00
RMO Ryan Mount **RC** 6.00
PP P.J. Phillips **RC** 4.00
CRA Cesar Ramos **RC** 4.00
NR Nolan Reimold **RC** 8.00
RR Ricky Romero **RC** 6.00
HAS Henry Sanchez **RC** 6.00
ZS Zach Simons **RC** 4.00
KS Kevin Slowey **RC** 15.00
BSN Brandon Snyder **RC** 8.00
DT Drew Thompson **RC** 4.00
CLT Chuck Tiffany **RC** 6.00
MTO Matt Torra **RC** 6.00
WT Wade Townsend **RC** 4.00
TT Troy Tulowitzki **RC** 20.00
JW Josh Wall **RC** 6.00
JWE Jered Weaver **RC** 15.00
NW Nick Webber **RC** 4.00
KW Kevin Whelan **RC** 4.00
TW Travis Wood **RC** 4.00
RZ Ryan Zimmerman **RC** 25.00

Refractors

Rookies: 1.5-2X
Rookie Auto.: 1-2X
Rookie Relic Auto.: 1-2X
Production 199 Sets

Black Refractors

No Pricing
Production 25 Sets

Red Refractor

No Pricing
Production One Set

MLB Logo Patch

No Pricing
Production One Set

Original Autographs

NM/M

Production 1-160
AJ4 Andruw Jones 02 B/122 25.00
AJ6 Andruw Jones 03 B/112 25.00
AJ8 Andruw Jones 04 B/71 25.00
DL1 Derrek Lee 95 B/27 25.00
DL2 Derrek Lee 96 B/29 25.00
DL5 Derrek Lee 98 B/22 25.00
DL6 Derrek Lee 04 B/92 20.00
DL7 Derrek Lee 04 BC/26 25.00
DW1 David Wright 04 BD/98 85.00
DW3 David Wright 05 B/139 85.00
GA1 Garret Anderson 04 BC/36 20.00
GA2 Garret Anderson 05 B/48 20.00
JR1 Jeremy Reed 04 BD/82 15.00
JR2 Jeremy Reed 04 BCD/48 20.00
MC2 Miguel Cabrera 02 BD/26 50.00
MC4 Miguel Cabrera 03 BD/27 50.00
MC5 Miguel Cabrera 03 BCD/25 50.00
MC6 Miguel Cabrera 04 B/127 25.00
MC7 Miguel Cabrera 04 BC/25 50.00
MC8 Miguel Cabrera 05 B/154 25.00
MC9 Miguel Cabrera 05 BC/25 50.00
MK3 Mark Kotsay 98 B/56 15.00
MK5 Mark Kotsay 99 B/75 15.00
MK7 Mark Kotsay 05 B/160 10.00
MK8 Mark Kotsay 05 BC/46 15.00
MY1 Michael Young 04 B/148 15.00
MY2 Michael Young 04 BC/64 15.00
MY3 Michael Young 05 B/92 15.00

Relics

NM/M

Common Player: 4.00
Refractor: 1-1.5X
Production 199 Sets
Black Refractor: 2-4X
Production 25 Sets
JBE Josh Beckett 4.00
RBE Ronnie Belliard 4.00
CB Carlos Beltran 6.00
HB Hank Blalock 4.00
BLB Barry Bonds 20.00
MCA Miguel Cabrera 8.00
EC Eric Chavez 4.00
JD Johnny Damon 8.00
CD Carlos Delgado 4.00
JPE Jim Edmonds 6.00
RF Rafael Furcal 4.00
JGI Josh Gibson 15.00
MGI Marcus Giles 4.00
KG Khalil Greene 6.00
VG Vladimir Guerrero 8.00
TLH Todd Helton 6.00
THU Tim Hudson 4.00
TH Torii Hunter 4.00
LWJ Chipper Jones 8.00
DL Derrek Lee 6.00
PL Paul LoDuca 4.00
GM Greg Maddux 10.00
PM Pedro Martinez 8.00
TM Tino Martinez 4.00
VM Victor Martinez 4.00
HM Hideki Matsui 15.00
KM Kevin Millar 4.00
BMU Bill Mueller 4.00
MM Mark Mulder 4.00
TN Trot Nixon 4.00
DO David Ortiz 10.00
MP Mike Piazza 8.00
JP Jorge Posada 6.00
MPR Mark Prior 6.00
AP Albert Pujols 20.00
ARA Aramis Ramirez 4.00
MR Manny Ramirez 8.00
AR Alex Rodriguez 20.00
IR Ivan Rodriguez 6.00
SR Scott Rolen 8.00
CSU Curt Schilling 6.00
GS Gary Sheffield 6.00
JS John Smoltz 6.00
AS Alfonso Soriano 6.00
SS Sammy Sosa 8.00
MTE Mark Teixeira 8.00
MT Miguel Tejada 6.00
DW Dontrelle Willis 6.00
MY Michael Young 4.00
BZ Barry Zito 4.00

2005 Bowman's Best

NM/M

Common Player: .25
Common Rookie: 1.00
Common Rookie Auto. (101-143): 10.00
Production 974
Pack (5): 14.00
Box (10): 120.00
1 Jose Vidro .25
2 Adam Dunn .50
3 Manny Ramirez .75
4 Miguel Tejada .50
5 Ken Griffey Jr. 1.00
6 Pedro Martinez 1.00
7 Alex Rodriguez 1.50
8 Ichiro Suzuki 1.50
9 Alfonso Soriano .75

10 Brian Giles .25
11 Roger Clemens 2.00
12 Todd Helton .50
13 Ivan Rodriguez .50
14 David Ortiz .75
15 Sammy Sosa 1.00
16 Chipper Jones .75
17 Mark Buehrle .50
18 Miguel Cabrera .75
19 Johan Santana .75
20 Randy Johnson .75
21 Jim Thome .50
22 Vladimir Guerrero .75
23 Dontrelle Willis .50
24 Nomar Garciaparra .75
25 Barry Bonds 2.00
26 Curt Schilling .75
27 Carlos Beltran .50
28 Albert Pujols 2.00
29 Mark Prior .75
30 Derek Jeter 2.00
31 Ryan Garko **RC** 4.00
32 Eulogio de la Cruz **RC** 1.00
33 Luke Scott **RC** 3.00
34 Shane Costa **RC** 1.00
35 Casey McGehee **RC** 1.00
36 Jered Weaver **RC** 8.00
37 Kevin Melillo **RC** 2.00
38 D.J. Houlton **RC** 2.00
39 Brandon Moorhead **RC** 1.00
40 Jerry Owens **RC** 1.00
41 Elliot Johnson **RC** 1.50
42 Kevin West **RC** 2.00
43 Hernan Iribarren **RC** 1.00
44 Miguel Montero **RC** 6.00
45 Craig Tatum **RC** 1.00
46 Ryan Sweeney 2.00
47 Micah Furtado **RC** 1.00
48 Cody Haerther **RC** 1.00
49 Erik Abreu **RC** 1.00
50 Chuck Tiffany **RC** 2.00
51 Tadahito Iguchi **RC** 4.00
52 Frank Diaz **RC** 3.00
53 Errol Simonitsch **RC** 1.00
54 Wade Robinson **RC** 2.00
55 Adam Boeve **RC** 1.00
56 Steve Bondurant **RC** 1.00
57 Jason Motte **RC** 1.00
58 Juan Senreiso **RC** 1.00
59 Vinny Rottino **RC** 1.00
60 Jai Miller **RC** 1.00
61 Thomas Pauly **RC** 1.00
62 Tony Giarratano **RC** 1.00
63 Alexander Smit **RC** 1.00
64 Keiichi Yabu **RC** 1.00
65 Brian Bannister **RC** 2.50
66 Kennard Bibbs **RC** 1.00
67 Anthony Reyes **RC** 4.00
68 Tom Oldham **RC** 1.00
69 Benjamin Harrison **RC** 1.00
70 Daryl Thompson **RC** 1.00
71 Kevin Collins **RC** 1.00
72 Wes Swackhamer **RC** 1.50
73 Landon Powell **RC** 1.50
74 Matt Brown **RC** 1.00
75 Russell Martin **RC** 6.00
76 Nick Touchstone **RC** 1.00
77 Steven White **RC** 1.00
78 Ian Bladergroen **RC** 1.00
79 Sean Marshall **RC** 2.00
80 Nick Masset **RC** 1.00
81 Ryan Goleski **RC** 1.50
82 Matt Campbell **RC** 1.00
83 Manny Parra **RC** 1.00
84 Melky Cabrera **RC** 5.00
85 Ryan Feierabend **RC** 1.50
86 Nate McLouth **RC** 1.50
87 Glen Perkins **RC** 2.50
88 Kila Kaaihue **RC** 1.50
89 Dana Eveland **RC** 1.50
90 Tyler Pelland **RC** 1.00
91 Matt Van Der Bosch **RC** 1.00
92 Andy Santana **RC** 1.00
93 Eric Nielsen **RC** 1.00
94 Brendan Ryan **RC** 1.00
95 Ian Kinsler **RC** 4.00
96 Matthew Kemp **RC** 8.00
97 Stephen Drew **RC** 10.00
98 Peeter Ramos **RC** 2.00
99 Chris Seddon **RC** 2.00
100 Chuck James **RC** 6.00
101 Travis Chick **RC** 10.00
102 Justin Verlander **RC** 60.00
103 Billy Butler **RC** 50.00
104 Chris Young **RC** 80.00
105 Jake Postlewait **RC** 10.00
106 C.J. Smith **RC** 10.00
107 Mike Rodriguez **RC** 12.00
108 Philip Humber **RC** 25.00
109 Jeff Niemann **RC** 20.00
110 Brian Miller **RC** 10.00
111 Chris Vines **RC** 12.00
112 Andy LaRoche **RC** 30.00
113 Mike Bourn 15.00
114 Wladimir Balentien **RC** 30.00
115 Ismael Ramirez **RC** 10.00
116 Hayden Penn **RC** 15.00
117 Pedro Lopez **RC** 10.00
118 Shawn Bowman **RC** 15.00
119 Chad Orvella **RC** 10.00
120 Sean Tracey **RC** 10.00
121 Bobby Livingston **RC** 10.00
122 Michael Rogers **RC** 10.00
123 Willy Mota **RC** 15.00
124 Brandon McCarthy **RC** 15.00
125 Mike Morse **RC** 10.00
126 Matt Lindstrom **RC** 10.00
127 Brian Stavisky **RC** 10.00
128 Rich Gardner **RC** 10.00
129 Scott Mitchinson **RC** 10.00
130 Billy McCarthy **RC** 10.00
131 Brandon Sing **RC** 15.00
132 Matt Albers **RC** 12.00
133 George Kottaras **RC** 15.00
134 Luis Hernandez **RC** 10.00
135 Humberto Sanchez **RC** 20.00
136 Buck Coats **RC** 12.00
137 Jonathan Barratt **RC** 10.00
138 Raul Tablado **RC** 12.00
139 Jake Mullinax **RC** 15.00
140 Edgar Varela **RC** 12.00
141 Ryan Garko **RC** 25.00
142 Nate McLouth **RC** 15.00
143 Shane Costa **RC** 10.00

Green Refractor

Stars: 2-3X
Rookies: 1-2X
Production 899
Rookie Autos. 1-1.5X
Production 399

Blue Refractor

Stars: 2-4X
Rookies: 1-2X
Production 499
Rookie Autos. 1-1.5X
Production 299

Red Refractor

Stars: 3-5X
Rookies: 2-3X
Rookie Autos. 1.5-2X
Production 199 Sets

Silver Refractor

Stars: 4-6X
Rookies: 2-3X
Rookie Autos. 1.5-3X
Production 99 Sets

Gold Refractor

No Pricing
Production 25 Sets

Printing Plates

No Pricing
Production one set for each color.

Printing Plates Autograph

No Pricing
Production one set for each color.

A-Rod Throwback Autograph

NM/M
Production 100
AR Alex Rodriguez 150.00
Production 100
AR Alex Rodriguez 150.00

Bowman's Best Shortstops

Production 25

Mirror Image Spokesmen

Production 10

Mirror Image Throwback

NM/M
Production 50
RR Cal Ripken Jr., Alex Rodriguez 450.00

2006 Bowman

NM/M
Complete Set (231):
Common Player (1-200): .15
Common RC (201-220): .25
Common Auto. (219-231): 10.00
Pack (10): 4.00
Box (24): 85.00
1 Nick Swisher .15
2 Ted Lilly .15
3 John Smoltz .25
4 Lyle Overbay .15
5 Alfonso Soriano .50
6 Javier Vazquez .15
7 Ronnie Belliard .15
8 Jose Reyes .50
9 Brian Roberts .25
10 Curt Schilling .75
11 Adam Dunn .50
12 Zack Greinke .15
13 Carlos Guillen .15
14 Jon Garland .15
15 Robinson Cano .25
16 Chris Burke .15
17 Barry Zito .25
18 Russ Adams .15
19 Chris Capuano .15
20 Scott Rolen .50
21 Kerry Wood .25
22 Scott Kazmir .25
23 Brandon Webb .25
24 Jeff Kent .25
25 Albert Pujols 2.00
26 C.C. Sabathia .15
27 Adrian Beltre .15
28 Brad Wilkerson .15
29 Randy Wolf .15
30 Jason Bay .25
31 Austin Kearns .25
32 Clint Barmes .15
33 Mike Sweeney .15
34 Justin Verlander **(RC)** .25
35 Justin Morneau .15
36 Scott Podsednik .25
37 Jason Giambi .50
38 Steve Finley .15
39 Morgan Ensberg .25
40 Eric Chavez .25
41 Roy Halladay .25
42 Horacio Ramirez .15
43 Ben Sheets .25
44 Chris Carpenter .40
45 Andruw Jones .50
46 Carlos Zambrano .25
47 Jonny Gomes .25
48 Shawn Green .15
49 Moises Alou .25
50 Ichiro Suzuki 1.50
51 Juan Pierre .15
52 Grady Sizemore .40
53 Kazuo Matsui .15
54 Jose Vidro .15
55 Jake Peavy .25
56 Dallas McPherson .15
57 Ryan Howard 1.00
58 Zachary Duke .15
59 Michael Young .15
60 Todd Helton .50
61 David DeJesus .15
62 Ivan Rodriguez .50
63 Johan Santana .50
64 Danny Haren .15
65 Derek Jeter 2.00
66 Greg Maddux 1.00
67 Jorge Cantu .15
68 Conor Jackson **(RC)** .15
69 Victor Martinez .25
70 David Wright 1.00
71 Ryan Church .15
72 Khalil Greene .15
73 Jimmy Rollins .25
74 Hank Blalock .25
75 Pedro Martinez .75
76 Jonathan Papelbon **(RC)** 3.00
77 Felipe Lopez .15
78 Jeff Francis .15
79 Andrew Sisco .15
80 Hideki Matsui 1.50
81 Ken Griffey Jr. 1.50
82 Nomar Garciaparra .75
83 Kevin Millwood .25
84 Paul Konerko .25
85 A.J. Burnett .15
86 Mike Piazza .75
87 Brian Giles .25
88 Johnny Damon .75
89 Jim Thome .50
90 Roger Clemens 2.00
91 Aaron Rowand .15
92 Rafael Furcal .25
93 Gary Sheffield .50
94 Mike Cameron .15
95 Carlos Delgado .50
96 Jorge Posada .40
97 Denny Bautista .15
98 Mike Maroth .15
99 Brad Radke .15
100 Alex Rodriguez 2.00
101 Freddy Garcia .15
102 Oliver Perez .15
103 Jon Lieber .15
104 Melvin Mora .25
105 Travis Hafner .40
106 Matt Cain **(RC)** .25
107 Derek Lowe .15
108 Luis Castillo .15
109 Livan Hernandez .15
110 Tadahito Iguchi .15
111 Shawn Chacon .15
112 Frank Thomas .40
113 Josh Beckett .25
114 Aubrey Huff .15
115 Derrek Lee .50
116 Chien-Ming Wang .25
117 Joe Crede .15
118 Torii Hunter .25
119 J.D. Drew .25
120 Troy Glaus .40
121 Sean Casey .15
122 Edgar Renteria .25
123 Craig Wilson .15
124 Adam Eaton .15
125 Jeff Francoeur .15
126 Bruce Chen .15
127 Cliff Floyd .15
128 Jeremy Reed .15
129 Jake Westbrook .15
130 Wily Mo Pena .15
131 Toby Hall .15
132 David Ortiz .75
133 David Eckstein .15
134 Brady Clark .15
135 Marcus Giles .15
136 Aaron Hill .15
137 Mark Kotsay .15
138 Carlos Lee .40
139 Roy Oswalt .40
140 Chone Figgins .15
141 Mike Mussina .50
142 Orlando Hernandez .15
143 Magglio Ordonez .15
144 Jim Edmonds .40
145 Bobby Abreu .40
146 Nick Johnson .15
147 Carlos Beltran .50
148 Jhonny Peralta .15
149 Pedro Feliz .15
150 Miguel Tejada .50
151 Luis Gonzalez .15
152 Carl Crawford .25
153 Yadier Molina .15
154 Rich Harden .25
155 Tim Wakefield .15
156 Rickie Weeks .25
157 Johnny Estrada .15
158 Gustavo Chacin .15
159 Dan Johnson .15
160 Willy Taveras .15
161 Garret Anderson .25
162 Randy Johnson .75
163 Jermaine Dye .15
164 Joe Mauer .50
165 Ervin Santana .15
166 Jeremy Bonderman .15
167 Garrett Atkins .15
168 Manny Ramirez .75
169 Brad Eldred .15
170 Chase Utley .25
171 Mark Loretta .15
172 John Patterson .15
173 Tom Glavine .40
174 Dontrelle Willis .25
175 Mark Teixeira .50
176 Felix Hernandez .40
177 Cliff Lee .15
178 Jason Schmidt .25
179 Chad Tracy .15
180 Rocco Baldelli .15
181 Aramis Ramirez .25
182 Andy Pettitte .25
183 Mark Mulder .25
184 Geoff Jenkins .15
185 Chipper Jones .75
186 Vernon Wells .25
187 Bobby Crosby .15
188 Lance Berkman .40
189 Vladimir Guerrero .75
190 Jose Capellan **(RC)** .15
191 Brad Penny .15
192 Jose Guillen .15
193 Brett Myers .15
194 Miguel Cabrera .75
195 Bartolo Colon .15
196 Craig Biggio .25
197 Tim Hudson .25
198 Mark Prior .50
199 Mark Buehrle .25
200 Barry Bonds 2.00
201 Anderson Hernandez **(RC)** .25
202 Charlton Jimerson **(RC)** .25
203 Jeremy Accardo **RC** .50
204 Hanley Ramirez **(RC)** .50
205 Matt Capps **(RC)** .25
206 John-Ford Griffin **(RC)** .25
207 Chuck James **(RC)** .25
208 Jaime Bubela **(RC)** .25
209 Mark Woodyard **(RC)** .25
210 Jason Botts **(RC)** .25
211 Chris Demaria **RC** .75
212 Miguel Perez **(RC)** .25
213 Tom Gorzelanny **(RC)** .25
214 Adam Wainwright **(RC)** .25
215 Ryan Garko **(RC)** .25
216 Jason Bergmann **RC** 1.00
217 J.J. Furmaniak **(RC)** .25
218 Francisco Liriano **(RC)** .50
219 Kenji Johjima **RC** 2.50
219 Kenji Johjima/Auto. **RC** 75.00
220 Craig Hansen **RC** 1.50
220 Craig Hansen/Auto. **RC** 15.00
221 Ryan Zimmerman/Auto. **(RC)** 40.00
222 Joey Devine/Auto. **RC** 10.00
223 Scott Olsen/Auto. **(RC)** 10.00
224 Darrell Rasner/Auto. **(RC)** 10.00
225 Craig Breslow/Auto. **RC** 10.00
226 Reggie Abercrombie/Auto. **(RC)** 10.00
227 Dan Uggla/Auto. **(RC)** 20.00
228 Willie Eyre/Auto. **(RC)** 10.00
229 Joel Zumaya/Auto. **(RC)** 20.00
230 Ricky Nolasco/Auto. **(RC)** 10.00
231 Ian Kinsler/Auto. **(RC)** 20.00

White

Stars: 3-6X
Rookies (201-220): 3-6X
RC Auto. (219-231): 1-2X
Production 120 Sets

Blue

Stars: 2-4X
Rookies (201-220): 2-4X
RC Auto. (219-231): 1-1.5X
Production 500 Sets

Gold

Stars: 1-2X
Rookies (201-220): 1-2X
Inserted 1:1

Red

No Pricing
Production One Set

Base of the Future

NM/M
JH Justin Huber 20.00

Prospects

NM/M
Common Player: .25
B1 Alex Gordon 10.00
B2 Jonathan George .25
B3 Scott Walter .25
B4 Brian Holliday .25
B5 Ben Copeland .50
B6 Bobby Wilson .50
B7 Mayker Sandoval .50
B8 Alejandro de Aza .25
B9 David Munoz .25
B10 Josh LeBlanc .50
B11 Philippe Valiquette .50
B12 Edwin Bellorin .50
B13 Jason Quarles .50
B14 Mark Trumbo .75
B15 Steve Kelly .25
B16 Jamie Hoffman .25
B17 Joseph Bauserman .50
B18 Nick Adenhart 2.50
B19 Mike Butia .25
B20 Jon Weber .25
B21 Luis Valdez .50
B22 Rafael Rodriguez .75
B23 Wyatt Toregas .75
B24 John Vanden Berg .25
B25 Mike Connolly .25
B26 Mike O'Connor 1.00
B27 Garrett Mock .25
B28 Bill Layman .25
B29 Luis Pena .25
B30 Billy Killian .50
B31 Ross Ohlendorf .25
B32 Mark Kaiser .25
B33 Ryan Costello .25
B34 Dale Thayer .25
B35 Steve Garrabrants .25
B36 Samuel Deduno .25
B37 Juan Portes 1.00
B38 Javier Martinez .25
B39 Clint Sammons .25
B40 Andrew Kown .75
B41 Matt Tolbert .25
B42 Michael Ekstrom .25
B43 Shawn Norris .25
B44 Diory Hernandez .25
B45 Chris Maples .25
B46 Aaron Hathaway .50
B47 Steven Baker .25
B48 Greg Creek .50
B49 Collin Mahoney .25
B50 Corey Ragsdale .25
B51 Ariel Nunez .25
B52 Max Ramirez 1.50
B53 Eric Rodland .50
B54 Dante Brinkley .50
B55 Casey Craig .50
B56 Ryan Spilborghs 1.00
B57 Fredy Deza .25
B58 Jeff Frazier .25
B59 Vince Cordova .25
B60 Oswaldo Navarro .75
B61 Jarod Rine .25
B62 Jordan Tata .75
B63 Ben Julianel .50
B64 Yung-Chi Chen 1.50
B65 Carlos Torres .50
B66 Juan Francia .50
B67 Brett Smith .50
B68 Francisco Leandro .50
B69 Chris Turner 1.00
B70 Matt Joyce .50
B71 Jason Jones .25
B72 Jose Diaz .25
B73 Kevin Ool .25
B74 Nate Bumstead .25
B75 Omir Santos .25
B76 Shawn Riggans .25
B77 Ofilio Castro .25
B78 Mike Rozier .75
B79 Wilkin Ramirez .75
B80 Yobal Duenas .25
B81 Adam Bourassa .50
B82 Tony Granadillo .25
B83 Brad McCann 1.50
B84 Dustin Majewski .50
B85 Kelvin Jimenez .25
B86 Mark Reed 1.50
B87 Asdrubal Cabrera 1.00
B88 James Barthmaier .25
B89 Brandon Boggs .25
B90 Raul Valdez .25
B91 Jose Campusano .50
B92 Henry Owens .25
B93 Tug Hulett .50
B94 Nate Gold .25
B95 Lee Mitchell .25
B96 John Hardy .25
B97 Aaron Wideman .25
B98 Brandon Roberts .50
B99 Lou Santangelo .25
B100 Kyle Kendrick .75
B101 Michael Collins .75
B102 Camilo Vazquez .25
B103 Mark McLemore .25
B104 Alexander Peralta .25
B105 Josh Whitesell .50
B106 Carlos Guevara .25
B107 Michael Aubrey .50
B108 Brandon Chaves .25
B109 Leonard Davis .25
B110 Kendry Morales 1.50
B111 Koby Clemens 25.00
B112 Lance Broadway 15.00
B113 Cameron Maybin 100.00
B114 Mike Aviles 10.00
B115 Kyle Blanks 40.00
B116 Chris Dickerson 15.00
B117 Sean Gallagher 20.00
B118 Jamar Hill 15.00
B119 Garrett Mock 15.00
B120 Kendry Morales 15.00
B121 Russel Rohlicek 15.00
B122 Clete Thomas 15.00
B123 Josh Kinney 15.00
B124 Justin Huber 10.00

Prospects White

White: 4-6X
White Autos.: 1.5-2X
Production 120 Sets

Prospects Blue

Blue: 2-3X
Blue Autos.: 1.5X
Production 500 Sets

Prospects Gold

Gold: 1-1.5X
Inserted 1:1

2006 Bowman Chrome Prospects

		NM/M
Common Prospect:		.50
BC1	Alex Gordon	25.00
BC2	Jonathan George	.50
BC3	Scott Walter	.50
BC4	Brian Holliday	.50
BC5	Ben Copeland	1.00
BC6	Bobby Wilson	1.50
BC7	Mayker Sandoval	1.50
BC8	Alejandro de Aza	2.00
BC9	David Munoz	.75
BC10	Josh LeBlanc	1.00
BC11	Philippe Valiquette	1.00
BC12	Edwin Bellorin	1.00
BC13	Jason Quarles	1.00
BC14	Mark Trumbo	2.00
BC15	Steve Kelly	.75
BC16	Jamie Hoffman	.75
BC17	Joseph Bauserman	1.00
BC18	Nick Adenhart	8.00
BC19	Mike Butia	.75
BC20	Jon Weber	.75
BC21	Luis Valdez	1.00
BC22	Rafael Rodriguez	1.50
BC23	Wyatt Toregas	1.50
BC24	John Vanden Berg	.75
BC25	Mike Connolly	.75
BC26	Mike O'Connor	3.00
BC27	Garrett Mock	.75
BC28	Bill Layman	.75
BC29	Luis Pena	.75
BC30	Billy Killian	1.00
BC31	Ross Ohlendorf	.50
BC32	Mark Kaiser	.75
BC33	Ryan Costello	.75
BC34	Dale Thayer	.75
BC35	Steve Garrabrants	.75
BC36	Samuel Deduno	.75
BC37	Juan Portes	3.00
BC38	Javier Martinez	.75
BC39	Clint Sammons	1.00
BC40	Andrew Kown	1.50
BC41	Matt Tolbert	.75
BC42	Michael Ekstrom	.75
BC43	Shawn Norris	.75
BC44	Diory Hernandez	.75
BC45	Chris Maples	.75
BC46	Aaron Hathaway	1.00
BC47	Steven Baker	.75
BC48	Greg Creek	1.00
BC49	Collin Mahoney	.75
BC50	Corey Ragsdale	1.50
BC51	Ariel Nunez	.50
BC52	Max Ramirez	4.00
BC53	Eric Rodland	1.00
BC54	Dante Brinkley	1.00
BC55	Casey Craig	1.00
BC56	Ryan Spilborghs	2.50
BC57	Fredy Deza	.75
BC58	Jeff Frazier	.50
BC59	Vince Cordova	.50
BC60	Oswaldo Navarro	1.50
BC61	Jarod Rine	.75
BC62	Jordan Tata	1.50
BC63	Ben Julianel	1.00
BC64	Yung-Chi Chen	5.00
BC65	Carlos Torres	1.50
BC66	Juan Francia	1.50
BC67	Brett Smith	1.00
BC68	Francisco Leandro	1.00
BC69	Chris Turner	3.00
BC70	Matt Joyce	2.00
BC71	Jason Jones	1.00
BC72	Jose Diaz	.50
BC73	Kevin Ool	.75
BC74	Nate Bumstead	1.00
BC75	Omir Santos	1.00
BC76	Shawn Riggans	1.00
BC77	Ofilio Castro	.50
BC78	Mike Rozier	1.50
BC79	Wilkin Ramirez	2.00
BC80	Yobal Duenas	1.00
BC81	Adam Bourassa	1.00
BC82	Tony Granadillo	1.00
BC83	Brad McCann	4.00
BC84	Dustin Majewski	1.00
BC85	Kelvin Jimenez	.50
BC86	Mark Reed	4.00
BC87	Asdrubal Cabrera	3.00
BC88	James Barthmaier	1.00
BC89	Brandon Boggs	.75
BC90	Raul Valdez	.50
BC91	Jose Campusano	1.50
BC92	Henry Owens	1.00
BC93	Tug Hulett	1.00
BC94	Nate Gold	1.00
BC95	Lee Mitchell	1.00
BC96	John Hardy	.75
BC97	Aaron Wideman	.75
BC98	Brandon Roberts	1.50
BC99	Lou Santangelo	.50
BC100	Kyle Kendrick	2.50
BC101	Michael Collins	2.00
BC102	Camilo Vazquez	.75
BC103	Mark McLemore	.50
BC104	Alexander Peralta	.75
BC105	Josh Whitesell	1.00
BC106	Carlos Guevara	.50
BC107	Michael Aubrey	1.50
BC108	Brandon Chaves	1.00
BC109	Leonard Davis	1.00
BC110	Kendry Morales	2.00

Refractor

Refractor (1-110): 2-4X
Production 500 Sets

X-Fractor

X-Fractor (1-110): 3-6X
Production 250 Sets

Red Refractor

No Pricing
Production Five Sets

Gold Refractor

Gold Refractor (1-110): 8-15X
Production 50 Sets

Blue Refractor

Blue Refractor (1-110): 4-6X
Production 150 Sets

Orange Refractor

No Pricing
Production 25 Sets

Signs of the Future

		NM/M
Common Auto.:		10.00
BB	Brian Bogusevic	10.00
MB	Michael Bowden	20.00
RB	Ryan Braun	60.00
TB	Travis Buck	15.00
JC	Jeff Clement	15.00
BC	Ben Copeland	15.00
MC	Mike Costanzo	10.00
TC	Trevor Crowe	15.00
JD	John Drennen	10.00
JE	Jacoby Ellsbury	30.00
YE	Yunel Escobar	15.00
JM	John Mayberry Jr.	15.00
GO	Garrett Olson	10.00
CR	Cesar Ramos	10.00
RR	Ricky Romero	10.00
HS	Henry Sanchez	10.00
DS	Denard Span	10.00
AT	Aaron Thompson	15.00
RT	Ryan Tucker	10.00
TT	Troy Tulowitzki	30.00
SW	Sean West	10.00

2006 Bowman Chrome

		NM/M
Complete Set (224):		
Common Player:		.25
Common Rookie (201-220):		.50
Pack (4):		8.00
Box (18):		125.00
1	Nick Swisher	.25
2	Ted Lilly	.25
3	John Smoltz	.50
4	Lyle Overbay	.25
5	Alfonso Soriano	.75
6	Javier Vazquez	.25
7	Ronnie Belliard	.25
8	Jose Reyes	.75
9	Brian Roberts	.25
10	Curt Schilling	.75
11	Adam Dunn	.75
12	Zack Greinke	.25
13	Carlos Guillen	.25
14	Jon Garland	.25
15	Robinson Cano	.50
16	Chris Burke	.25
17	Barry Zito	.50
18	Russ Adams	.25
19	Chris Capuano	.25
20	Scott Rolen	.75
21	Kerry Wood	.25
22	Scott Kazmir	.50
23	Brandon Webb	.50
24	Jeff Kent	.40
25	Albert Pujols	2.50
26	C.C. Sabathia	.25
27	Adrian Beltre	.25
28	Brad Wilkerson	.25
29	Randy Wolf	.25
30	Jason Bay	.50
31	Austin Kearns	.25
32	Clint Barmes	.25
33	Mike Sweeney	.25
34	Kevin Youkilis	.50
35	Justin Morneau	.50
36	Scott Podsednik	.40
37	Jason Giambi	.75
38	Steve Finley	.25
39	Morgan Ensberg	.25
40	Eric Chavez	.40
41	Roy Halladay	.50
42	Horacio Ramirez	.25
43	Ben Sheets	.40
44	Chris Carpenter	.50
45	Andruw Jones	.75
46	Carlos Zambrano	.40
47	Jonny Gomes	.40
48	Shawn Green	.40
49	Moises Alou	.40
50	Ichiro Suzuki	1.50
51	Juan Pierre	.25
52	Grady Sizemore	.75
53	Kazuo Matsui	.25
54	Jose Vidro	.25
55	Jake Peavy	.50
56	Dallas McPherson	.25
57	Ryan Howard	2.00
58	Zachary Duke	.25
59	Michael Young	.50
60	Todd Helton	.75
61	David DeJesus	.25
62	Ivan Rodriguez	.75
63	Johan Santana	.75
64	Danny Haren	.25
65	Derek Jeter	2.50
66	Greg Maddux	1.50
67	Jorge Cantu	.25
68	J.J. Hardy	.25
69	Victor Martinez	.50
70	David Wright	1.50
71	Ryan Church	.25
72	Khalil Greene	.25
73	Jimmy Rollins	.40
74	Hank Blalock	.40
75	Pedro Martinez	1.00
76	Chris Shelton	.25
77	Felipe Lopez	.25
78	Jeff Francis	.25
79	Andrew Sisco	.25
80	Hideki Matsui	1.50
81	Ken Griffey Jr.	1.50
82	Nomar Garciaparra	.75
83	Kevin Millwood	.25
84	Paul Konerko	.50
85	A.J. Burnett	.25
86	Mike Piazza	1.00
87	Brian Giles	.40
88	Johnny Damon	1.00
89	Jim Thome	.75
90	Roger Clemens	2.50
91	Aaron Rowand	.25
92	Rafael Furcal	.40
93	Gary Sheffield	.50
94	Mike Cameron	.25
95	Carlos Delgado	.50
96	Jorge Posada	.50
97	Denny Bautista	.25
98	Mike Maroth	.25
99	Brad Radke	.25
100	Alex Rodriguez	2.50
101	Freddy Garcia	.25
102	Oliver Perez	.25
103	Jon Lieber	.25
104	Melvin Mora	.25
105	Travis Hafner	.50
106	Alex Rios	.25
107	Derek Lowe	.25
108	Luis Castillo	.25
109	Livan Hernandez	.25
110	Tadahito Iguchi	.25
111	Shawn Chacon	.25
112	Frank Thomas	.75
113	Josh Beckett	.50
114	Aubrey Huff	.25
115	Derrek Lee	.75
116	Chien-Ming Wang	.50
117	Joe Crede	.50
118	Torii Hunter	.50
119	J.D. Drew	.40
120	Troy Glaus	.40
121	Sean Casey	.40
122	Edgar Renteria	.40
123	Craig Wilson	.25
124	Adam Eaton	.25
125	Jeff Francoeur	.40
126	Bruce Chen	.25
127	Cliff Floyd	.25
128	Jeremy Reed	.25
129	Jake Westbrook	.25
130	Wily Mo Pena	.25
131	Toby Hall	.25
132	David Ortiz	1.00
133	David Eckstein	.25
134	Brady Clark	.25
135	Marcus Giles	.25
136	Aaron Hill	.25
137	Mark Kotsay	.25
138	Carlos Lee	.50
139	Roy Oswalt	.50
140	Chone Figgins	.25
141	Mike Mussina	.75
142	Orlando Hernandez	.25
143	Magglio Ordonez	.40
144	Jim Edmonds	.50
145	Bobby Abreu	.50
146	Nick Johnson	.25
147	Carlos Beltran	.75
148	Jhonny Peralta	.25
149	Pedro Feliz	.25
150	Miguel Tejada	.75
151	Luis Gonzalez	.40
152	Carl Crawford	.50
153	Yadier Molina	.25
154	Rich Harden	.40
155	Tim Wakefield	.25
156	Rickie Weeks	.50
157	Johnny Estrada	.25
158	Gustavo Chacin	.25
159	Dan Johnson	.25
160	Willy Taveras	.25
161	Garret Anderson	.40
162	Randy Johnson	1.00
163	Jermaine Dye	.25
164	Joe Mauer	.75
165	Ervin Santana	.25
166	Jeremy Bonderman	.50
167	Garrett Atkins	.25
168	Manny Ramirez	1.00
169	Brad Eldred	.25
170	Chase Utley	.75
171	Mark Loretta	.25
172	John Patterson	.25
173	Tom Glavine	.50
174	Dontrelle Willis	.50
175	Mark Teixeira	.50
176	Felix Hernandez	.50
177	Cliff Lee	.25
178	Jason Schmidt	.40
179	Chad Tracy	.25
180	Rocco Baldelli	.25
181	Aramis Ramirez	.40
182	Andy Pettitte	.50
183	Mark Mulder	.40
184	Geoff Jenkins	.25
185	Chipper Jones	.75
186	Vernon Wells	.50
187	Bobby Crosby	.25
188	Lance Berkman	.50
189	Vladimir Guerrero	.75
190	Coco Crisp	.25
191	Brad Penny	.25
192	Jose Guillen	.25
193	Brett Myers	.25
194	Miguel Cabrera	.75
195	Bartolo Colon	.25
196	Craig Biggio	.40
197	Tim Hudson	.50
198	Mark Prior	.50
199	Mark Buehrle	.40
200	Barry Bonds	2.50
201	Anderson Hernandez **(RC)**	.50
202	Jose Capellan **(RC)**	.50
203	Jeremy Accardo **RC**	1.00
204	Hanley Ramirez **(RC)**	1.00
205	Matt Capps **(RC)**	.50
206	Jonathan Papelbon **(RC)**	4.00
207	Chuck James **(RC)**	.50
208	Matt Cain **(RC)**	1.00
209	Cole Hamels **(RC)**	1.00
210	Jason Botts **(RC)**	.50
211	Lastings Milledge **(RC)**	.50
212	Conor Jackson **(RC)**	.50
213	Yusmeiro Petit **(RC)**	.50
214	Alay Soler **RC**	2.00
215	Willy Aybar **(RC)**	.50
216	Adam Loewen **(RC)**	.50
217	Justin Verlander **(RC)**	1.00
218	Francisco Liriano **(RC)**	4.00
219	Kenji Johjima **RC**	4.00
219	Kenji Johjima/Auto. **RC**	75.00
220	Craig Hansen **RC**	2.00
221	Prince Fielder/Auto. **(RC)**	100.00
222	Josh Barfield/Auto. **(RC)**	15.00
223	Fausto Carmona/Auto. **(RC)**	30.00
224	James Loney/Auto. **(RC)**	40.00

Refractor

Refractor (1-200): 2-4X
Refractor (201-220): 2-3X
Inserted 1:4
Autograph (219, 221-224): 1-1.5X
Production 500

X-Fractor

X-Refractor (1-200): 3-5X
X-Refractor (201-220): 3-5X
Production 250
X-Fractor Auto. (219, 221-224): 1-2X
Production 225

Blue Refractor

Blue Refractor (1-200): 3-6X
Blue Refractor (201-220): 4-6X
Production 150
Blue Ref. Auto. (219, 221-224): 1-2.5X
Production 150

Gold Refractor

Gold Refractor (1-200): 8-15X
Gold Refractor (201-220): 8-15X
Production 50
Gold Ref Auto. (219, 221-224): 3-5X
Production 50

Orange Refractor

Orange Refractor (1-200): 15-25X
Orange Refractor (201-220): 15-25X
Production 25
Orange Ref Auto (221-224): No Pricing
Production 25

Red Refractor

No Pricing
Production Five Sets

Super Fractor

No Pricing
Production One Set

Printing Plates

No Pricing
Production One Set

Bowman Chrome Prospects

		NM/M
Common Prospect:		.50
BC111	Koby Clemens	2.00
BC112	Lance Broadway	1.50
BC113	Cameron Maybin	15.00
BC114	Mike Aviles	.50
BC115	Kyle Blanks	2.00
BC116	Chris Dickerson	1.00
BC117	Sean Gallagher	3.00
BC118	Jamar Hill	.50
BC119	Garrett Mock	.75
BC120	Russel Rohlicek	.50
BC121	Clete Thomas	1.00
BC122	Elvis Andrus	5.00
BC123	Brandon Moss	.75
BC124	Mark Holliman	3.00
BC125	Jose Tabata	15.00
BC126	Corey Wimberly	2.00
BC127	Bobby Wilson	1.00
BC128	Edward Mujica	1.50
BC129	Hunter Pence	6.00
BC130	Adam Heether	.50
BC131	Andy Wilson	.50
BC132	Radhames Liz	3.00
BC133	Garrett Patterson	.50
BC134	Carlos Gomez	15.00
BC135	Jared Lansford	1.00
BC136	Jose Arredondo	2.00
BC137	Renee Cortez	1.00
BC138	Francisco Rosario	.50
BC139	Brian Stokes	.50
BC140	Will Thompson	.50
BC141	Ernesto Frieri	1.00
BC142	Jose Mijares	1.00
BC143	Jeremy Slayden	2.00
BC144	Brandon Fahey	1.00
BC145	Jason Windsor	1.50
BC146	Shawn Nottingham	1.00
BC147	Dallas Trahern	1.00
BC148	Jon Niese	3.00
BC149	A.J. Shappi	.50
BC150	Jordan Pals	.50
BC151	Tim Moss	.50
BC152	Stephen Marek	1.00
BC153	Mat Gamel	3.00
BC154	Sean Henn	.50
BC155	Matt Guillory	.50
BC156	Brandon Jones	4.00
BC157	Gary Galvez	1.00
BC158	Shane Lindsay	1.50
BC159	Jesus Reina	.50
BC160	Lorenzo Cain	4.00
BC161	Chris Britton	1.00
BC162	Yovani Gallardo	4.00
BC163	Matt Walker	1.00
BC164	Shaun Cumberland	1.00
BC165	Ryan Patterson	2.00
BC166	Michael Hollimon	1.00
BC167	Eude Brito	.50
BC168	John Bowker	.50
BC169	James Avery	.50
BC170	John Bannister	.50
BC171	Juan Ciriaco	.50
BC172	Manuel Corpas	1.00
BC173	Leo Rosales	.50
BC174	Tim Kennelly	.50
BC175	Adam Russell	.50
BC176	Jeremy Hellickson	4.00
BC177	Ryan Klosterman	.50
BC178	Evan Meek	1.00
BC179	Steve Murphy	2.00
BC180	Scott Feldman	.50
BC181	Pablo Sandoval	1.50
BC182	Dexter Fowler	2.00
BC183	Jairo Cuevas	1.50
BC184	Andrew Pinckney	1.00
BC185	Marino Salas	.50
BC186	Justin Christian	.50
BC187	Ching-Lung Lo	3.00
BC188	Randy Roth	2.00
BC189	Andrew Sonnanstine	3.00
BC190	Josh Outman	3.00
BC191	Yuber A. Rodriguez	1.00
BC192	Hainley Statia	2.00
BC193	Kevin Estrada	1.50
BC194	Jeff Karstens	1.50
BC195	Corey Coles	.50
BC196	Gustavo Espinoza	1.00
BC197	Brian Horwitz	.50
BC198	Landon Jacobsen	.50
BC199	Ben Krosschell	1.00
BC200	Jason Jaramillo	1.00
BC201	Josh Wilson	.50
BC202	Jason Ray	.50
BC203	Brent Dlugach	1.00
BC204	Cesar Jimenez	1.00
BC205	Eric Haberer	.50
BC206	Felipe Paulino	.50
BC207	Alcides Escobar	2.00
BC208	Jose Ascanio	1.00
BC209	Yoel Hernandez	1.00
BC210	Geoff Vandel	1.00
BC211	Travis Denker	1.50
BC212	Ramon Alvarado	1.00
BC213	Welinson Baez	1.50
BC214	Chris Kolkhorst	.50
BC215	Emiliano Fruto	1.00
BC216	Luis Cota	1.00
BC217	Mark Worrell	.50
BC218	Cla Meredith	1.50
BC219	Emmanuel Garcia	1.50
BC220	B.J. Szymanski	1.00
BC221	Alex Gordon/Auto.	125.00
BC222	Mark Pawelek/Auto.	25.00
BC223	Justin Upton/Auto.	160.00
BC224	Sean West/Auto.	15.00
BC225	Tyler Greene/Auto.	15.00
BC226	Josh Kinney/Auto.	15.00
BC227	Pedro Lopez/Auto.	10.00
BC228	Troy Patton/Auto.	25.00
BC229	Chris Iannetta/Auto.	20.00
BC230	Jared Wells/Auto.	10.00
BC231	Brandon Wood/Auto.	20.00
BC232	Josh Geer/Auto.	15.00
BC233	Cesar Carrillo/Auto.	10.00
BC234	Franklin Gutierrez/Auto.	15.00
BC235	Matt Garza/Auto.	25.00
BC236	Eli Iorg/Auto.	15.00
BC237	Trevor Bell/Auto.	10.00
BC238	Jeff Lyman/Auto.	15.00
BC239	Jon Lester/Auto.	40.00
BC240	Kendry Morales/Auto.	15.00
BC241	J. Brent Cox/Auto.	15.00
BC242	Jose Bautista/Auto.	15.00
BC243	Josh Sullivan/Auto.	15.00
BC244	Brandon Snyder/Auto.	15.00
BC245	Elvin Puello/Auto.	10.00
BC246	Henry Sanchez/Auto.	15.00
BC247	Jacob Marceaux/Auto.	15.00

Prospects Refractors

Refractor (111-220): 2-4X
Refractor Auto. (221-247): 1-1.5X
Production 500 Sets

Prospects X-Fractors

X-Refractor (111-220): 3-5X
Production 250
X-Refractor Auto. (221-247): 1-2X
Production 225

Prospects Blue Refractors

Blue Refractor (111-220): 4-6X

Blue Refractor Auto. (221-247): 1-2.5X
Production 150 Sets

Prospects Gold Refractors

Gold Refractor (111-220): 8-15X
Gold Refractor Auto. (221-247): 3-5X
Production 50 Sets

Prospects Orange Refractors

Orange Refractor (111-220): 15-25X
Orange Refractor Auto. (221-247): 4-6X
Production 25 Sets

Prospects Red Refractors

No Pricing
Production Five Sets

Prospects Super Fractors

No Pricing
Production One Set

2006 Bowman Chrome Draft

NM/M
Complete Set (55): 25.00
Common Player: .50
1 Matthew Kemp **(RC)** 1.50
2 Taylor Tankersley **(RC)** .50
3 Michael Napoli **RC** 1.50
4 Brian Bannister **(RC)** .50
5 Melky Cabrera **(RC)** .50
6 Bill Bray **(RC)** .50
7 Brian Anderson **(RC)** .50
8 Jered Weaver **(RC)** 2.00
9 Chris Duncan **(RC)** .50
10 Boof Bonser **(RC)** 1.00
11 Mike Rouse **(RC)** .50
12 David Pauley **(RC)** .50
13 Russell Martin **(RC)** 1.00
14 Jeremy Sowers **(RC)** .50
15 Kevin Reese **(RC)** .50
16 John Rheinecker **(RC)** .50
17 Tommy Murphy **(RC)** .50
18 Sean Marshall **(RC)** .50
19 Jason Kubel **(RC)** .50
20 Chad Billingsley **(RC)** 1.50
21 Kendry Morales **(RC)** 1.00
22 Jon Lester **(RC)** 2.00
23 Brandon Fahey **RC** .50
24 Josh Johnson **(RC)** .50
25 Kevin Frandsen **(RC)** .50
26 Casey Janssen **RC** .50
27 Scott Thorman **(RC)** 1.00
28 Scott Mathieson **(RC)** .50
29 Jeremy Hermida **(RC)** .50
30 Dustin Nippert **(RC)** .50
31 Kevin Thompson **(RC)** .50
32 Bobby Livingston **(RC)** .50
33 Travis Ishikawa **(RC)** .50
34 Jeff Mathis **(RC)** .50
35 Charlie Haeger **RC** 1.00
36 Josh Willingham **(RC)** .50
37 Taylor Buchholz **(RC)** .50
38 Joel Guzman **(RC)** .50
39 Zach Jackson **(RC)** .50
40 Howie Kendrick **(RC)** 1.00
41 T.J. Beam **(RC)** 1.00
42 Ty Taubenheim **RC** 1.00
43 Erick Aybar **(RC)** .50
44 Anibal Sanchez **(RC)** 1.00
45 Mike Pelfrey **RC** 6.00
46 Shawn Hill **(RC)** .50
47 Chris Roberson **(RC)** .50
48 Carlos Villanueva **RC** .50
49 Andre Ethier **(RC)** 1.50
50 Anthony Reyes **(RC)** 1.00
51 Franklin Gutierrez **(RC)** .50
52 Angel Guzman **(RC)** .50
53 Michael O'Connor **RC** .50
54 James Shields **RC** 2.50
55 Nate McLouth **(RC)** .50

SuperFractor

No Pricing
Production One Set

Red Refractor

No Pricing
Production Five Sets

Orange Refractor

Orange Refractor (1-55): 15-25X
Production 25 Sets

Gold Refractor

Gold Refractor (1-55): 8-15X
Production 50 Sets

Blue Refractor

Blue Refractor (1-55): 4-8X
Production 199 Sets

X-Fractor

X-Fractor (1-55): 3-6X
Production 299 Sets

Refractor

Refractor (1-55): 2-4X

Draft Picks

NM/M
Complete Set (90):
Common Draft Pick (1-65): 1.00
Common Auto. (66-90): 20.00
1 Tyler Colvin 3.00
2 Chris Marrero 4.00
3 Hank Conger 4.00
4 Chris Parmelee 5.00
5 Jason Place 5.00
6 Billy Rowell 6.00
7 Travis Snider 8.00
8 Colton Willems 3.00
9 Chase Fontaine 2.00
10 Jon Jay 2.00
11 Wade Leblanc 3.00
12 Justin Masterson 5.00
13 Gary Daley 1.50
14 Justin Edwards 1.00
15 Charlie Yarbrough 1.50
16 Cyle Hankerd 4.00
17 Zach McAllister 1.50
18 Tyler Robertson 1.00
19 Joe Smith 1.00
20 Nate Culp 1.00
21 John Holdzkom 1.00
22 Patrick Bresnehan 1.00
23 Chad Lee 1.00
24 Ryan Morris 1.00
25 D'Arby Myers 2.50
26 Garrett Olson 2.00
27 Jon Still 1.50
28 Brandon Rice 1.00
29 Chris Davis 4.00
30 Zack Daeges 1.50
31 Bobby Henson 1.50
32 George Kontos 2.00
33 Jermaine Mitchell 2.50
34 Adam Coe 2.00
35 Dustin Richardson 1.50
36 Allen Craig 1.00
37 Austin McClune 1.50
38 Doug Fister 1.00
39 Corey Madden 1.00
40 Justin Jacobs 1.50
41 Jim Negrych 1.00
42 Tyler Norrick 1.50
43 Adam Davis 1.00
44 Brett Logan 1.00
45 Brian Omogrosso 1.50
46 Kyle Drabek 4.00
47 Jamie Ortiz 2.00
48 Alex Presley 2.00
49 Terrance Warren 1.50
50 David Christensen 2.00
51 Helder Velazquez 2.00
52 Matt McBride 1.50
53 Quintin Berry 2.00
54 Michael Eisenberg 1.00
55 Dan Garcia 1.00
56 Scott Cousins 1.00
57 Sean Land 1.00
58 Kristopher Medlen 1.00
59 Tyler Reves 1.00
60 John Shelby 1.50
61 Jordan Newton 1.50
62 Ricky Orta 1.00
63 Jason Donald 1.00
64 David Huff 1.50
65 Brett Sinkbeil 2.00
66 Evan Longoria/Auto. 140.00
67 Cody Johnson/Auto. 40.00
68 Kris Johnson/Auto. 25.00
69 Kasey Kiker/Auto. 20.00
70 Ronny Bourquin/Auto. 20.00
71 Adrian Cardenas/Auto. 40.00
72 Matt Antonelli/Auto. 50.00
73 Brooks Brown/Auto. 20.00
74 Steven Evarts/Auto. 25.00
75 Joshua Butler/Auto. 20.00
76 Chad Huffman/Auto. 20.00
77 Steven Wright/Auto. 15.00
78 Cory Rasmus/Auto. 20.00
79 Brad Furnish/Auto. 15.00
80 Andrew Carpenter/Auto. 20.00
81 Dustin Evans/Auto. 15.00
82 Tommy Hickman/Auto. 25.00
83 Matt Long/Auto. 15.00
84 Clayton Kershaw/Auto. 125.00
85 Kyle McCulloch/Auto. 20.00
86 Pedro Beato/Auto. 30.00
87 Kyler Burke/Auto. 25.00
88 Stephen Englund/Auto. 20.00
89 Michael Felix/Auto. 15.00
90 Sean Watson/Auto. 20.00

Draft Picks X-Fractor

X-Fractor (1-65): 3-6X
Production 299 Sets
X-Fractor Auto. (66-90): 1-2X
Production 225 Sets

Draft Picks Refractor

Refractor (1-65): 2-4X
Refractor Auto. (66-90): 1-1.5X
Production 500 for #'s 66-90

Draft Picks SuperFractor

No Pricing
Production One Set

Draft Picks Red Refractor

No Pricing
Production Five Sets

Draft Picks Orange Refractor

Orange Refractor (1-65): 15-25X
Production 25 Sets
Orange Auto. (66-90): No Pricing
Production 25 Sets

Draft Picks Gold Refractor

Gold Refractor (1-65): 8-15X
Production 50 Sets
Gold Auto. (66-90): 3-5X
Production 50 Sets

Draft Picks Blue Refractor

Blue Refractor (1-65): 4-8X
Production 199 Sets
Blue Auto. (66-90): 1-2.5X
Production 150 Sets

Future's Game Prospects

NM/M
Complete Set (45): 20.00
Common Player: .50
1 Nick Adenhart 1.00
2 Joel Guzman .50
3 Ryan Braun .50
4 Carlos Carrasco .50
5 Neil Walker .50
6 Pablo Sandoval .50
7 Gio Gonzalez .50
8 Joey Votto .50
9 Luis Cruz .50
10 Nolan Reimold .50
11 Juan Salas .50
12 Josh Fields 1.00
13 Yovani Gallardo 1.00
14 Radhames Liz .50
15 Eric Patterson .50
16 Cameron Maybin 2.50
17 Edgar Martinez .50
18 Hunter Pence 1.50
19 Phillip Hughes 2.00
20 Trent Oeltjen .50
21 Nick Pereira .50
22 Wladimir Balentien .50
23 Stephen Drew 1.50
24 Davis Romero .50
25 Joe Koshansky .50
26 Chin-Lung Hu 2.00
27 Jason Hirsh .50
28 Jose Tabata 2.00
29 Eric Hurley .50
30 Yung-Chi Chen 2.50
31 Howie Kendrick 1.00
32 Humberto Sanchez 1.00
33 Alex Gordon 4.00
34 Yunel Escobar .50
35 Travis Buck .75
36 Billy Butler 1.00
37 Homer Bailey 1.00
38 George Kottaras .50
39 Kurt Suzuki .50
40 Joaquin Arias .50
41 Matt Lindstrom .50
42 Sean Smith .50
43 Carlos Gonzalez .50
44 Jaime Garcia 1.00
45 Jose Garcia 1.00

Future's Game Red Refractor

No Pricing
Production Five Sets

Future's Game Orange Refractor

Orange (1-45): 15-30X
Production 25 Sets

Future's Game Gold Refractor

Gold (1-45): 8-15X
Production 50 Sets

Future's Game Blue Refractor

Blue (1-45): 4-8X
Production 199 Sets

Future's Game X-Fractor

X-Fractor (1-45): 3-6X
Production 299 Sets

Future's Game Refractor

Refractor (1-45): 2-4X

Head of the Class Dual Autograph

NM/M
Production 174
Refractor: 1-1.5X
Production 50
Gold Refractor: No Pricing
Production 25
RU Alex Rodriguez, Justin Upton 150.00

2006 Bowman Draft

NM/M
Complete Set (55): 10.00
Common Player: .25
Pack (5 + 2 Chrome): 3.50
Box (24): 75.00
1 Matthew Kemp **(RC)** .50
2 Taylor Tankersley **(RC)** .25
3 Michael Napoli **RC** .50
4 Brian Bannister **(RC)** .25
5 Melky Cabrera **(RC)** .25
6 Bill Bray **(RC)** .25
7 Brian Anderson **(RC)** .25
8 Jered Weaver **(RC)** .75
9 Chris Duncan **(RC)** .25
10 Boof Bonser **(RC)** .50
11 Mike Rouse **(RC)** .25
12 David Pauley **(RC)** .25
13 Russell Martin **(RC)** .25
14 Jeremy Sowers **(RC)** .25
15 Kevin Reese **(RC)** .25
16 John Rheinecker **(RC)** .25
17 Tommy Murphy **(RC)** .25
18 Sean Marshall **(RC)** .25
19 Jason Kubel **(RC)** .25
20 Chad Billingsley **(RC)** .75
21 Kendry Morales **(RC)** .50
22 Jon Lester **(RC)** .75
23 Brandon Fahey **RC** .25
24 Josh Johnson **(RC)** .25
25 Kevin Frandsen **(RC)** .25
26 Casey Janssen **RC** .25
27 Scott Thorman **(RC)** .25
28 Scott Mathieson **(RC)** .25
29 Jeremy Hermida **(RC)** .25
30 Dustin Nippert **(RC)** .25
31 Kevin Thompson **(RC)** .25
32 Bobby Livingston **(RC)** .25
33 Travis Ishikawa **(RC)** .25
34 Jeff Mathis **(RC)** .25
35 Charlie Haeger **RC** .50
36 Josh Willingham **(RC)** .25
37 Taylor Buchholz **(RC)** .25
38 Joel Guzman **(RC)** .25
39 Zach Jackson **(RC)** .25
40 Howie Kendrick **(RC)** .50
41 T.J. Beam **(RC)** .50
42 Ty Taubenheim **RC** .50
43 Erick Aybar **(RC)** .25
44 Anibal Sanchez **(RC)** .25
45 Mike Pelfrey **RC** 2.00
46 Shawn Hill **(RC)** .25
47 Chris Roberson **(RC)** .25
48 Carlos Villanueva **RC** .25
49 Andre Ethier **(RC)** .50
50 Anthony Reyes **(RC)** .25
51 Franklin Gutierrez **(RC)** .25
52 Angel Guzman **(RC)** .25
53 Michael O'Connor **RC** .25
54 James Shields **RC** .50
55 Nate McLouth **(RC)** .25

Printing Plates

No Pricing
Production one set per color.

Red

No Pricing
Production One Set

White

White (1-55): 2-5X
Production 225 Sets

Gold

Gold (1-55): 1-2X
Inserted 1:1

Draft Picks

NM/M
Complete Set (65): 20.00
Common Draft Pick (1-65): .50
1 Tyler Colvin 1.00
2 Chris Marrero 1.00
3 Hank Conger 1.00
4 Chris Parmelee 1.00
5 Jason Place 1.00
6 Billy Rowell 1.00
7 Travis Snider 2.00
8 Colton Willems .75
9 Chase Fontaine .50
10 Jon Jay .50
11 Wade Leblanc 1.00
12 Justin Masterson 1.50
13 Gary Daley .50
14 Justin Edwards .50
15 Charlie Yarbrough .50
16 Cyle Hankerd 1.00
17 Zach McAllister .50
18 Tyler Robertson .50
19 Joe Smith .50
20 Nate Culp .50
21 John Holdzkom .50
22 Patrick Bresnehan .50
23 Chad Lee .50
24 Ryan Morris .50
25 D'Arby Myers .75
26 Garrett Olson .75
27 Jon Still .50
28 Brandon Rice .50
29 Chris Davis 1.00
30 Zack Daeges .50
31 Bobby Henson .50
32 George Kontos .50
33 Jermaine Mitchell .75
34 Adam Coe .50
35 Dustin Richardson .50
36 Allen Craig .50
37 Austin McClune .50
38 Doug Fister .50
39 Corey Madden .50
40 Justin Jacobs .50
41 Jim Negrych .50
42 Tyler Norrick .50
43 Adam Davis .50
44 Brett Logan .50
45 Brian Omogrosso .50
46 Kyle Drabek 1.00
47 Jamie Ortiz .50
48 Alex Presley .50
49 Terrance Warren .50
50 David Christensen .50
51 Helder Velazquez .50
52 Matt McBride .50
53 Quintin Berry .50
54 Michael Eisenberg .50
55 Dan Garcia .50
56 Scott Cousins .50
57 Sean Land .50
58 Kristopher Medlen .50
59 Tyler Reves .50
60 John Shelby .50
61 Jordan Newton .50
62 Ricky Orta .50
63 Jason Donald .50
64 David Huff .50
65 Brett Sinkbeil .50

Future's Game Prospects

NM/M
Complete Set (45): 10.00
Common Player: .25
1 Nick Adenhart .50
2 Joel Guzman .25
3 Ryan Braun .50
4 Carlos Carrasco .25
5 Neil Walker .25
6 Pablo Sandoval .25
7 Gio Gonzalez .25
8 Joey Votto .25
9 Luis Cruz .25
10 Nolan Reimold .25
11 Juan Salas .25
12 Josh Fields .50
13 Yovani Gallardo .50
14 Radhames Liz .25
15 Eric Patterson .25
16 Cameron Maybin 1.00
17 Edgar Martinez .25
18 Hunter Pence .75
19 Phillip Hughes .75
20 Trent Oeltjen .25
21 Nick Pereira .25
22 Wladimir Balentien .25
23 Stephen Drew .50
24 Davis Romero .25
25 Joe Koshansky .25
26 Chin-Lung Hu .50
27 Jason Hirsh .25
28 Jose Tabata .75
29 Eric Hurley .25
30 Yung-Chi Chen .75
31 Howie Kendrick .50
32 Humberto Sanchez .50
33 Alex Gordon 1.50
34 Yunel Escobar .25
35 Travis Buck .25
36 Billy Butler .50
37 Homer Bailey .50
38 George Kottaras .25
39 Kurt Suzuki .25
40 Joaquin Arias .25
41 Matt Lindstrom .25
42 Sean Smith .25
43 Carlos Gonzalez .25
44 Jaime Garcia .25
45 Jose Garcia .50

Future's Game Prospects Relics

NM/M
Common Player: 4.00
1 Nick Adenhart 8.00
2 Joel Guzman 4.00
3 Ryan Braun 8.00
4 Carlos Carrasco 4.00
5 Neil Walker 4.00
6 Pablo Sandoval 4.00
7 Gio Gonzalez 4.00
8 Joey Votto 6.00
9 Luis Cruz 4.00
10 Nolan Reimold 4.00
11 Juan Salas 4.00
12 Josh Fields 6.00
13 Yovani Gallardo 6.00
14 Radhames Liz 4.00
15 Eric Patterson 6.00
16 Cameron Maybin 10.00
17 Edgar Martinez 4.00
18 Hunter Pence 8.00
19 Phillip Hughes 20.00
20 Trent Oeltjen 4.00
21 Nick Pereira 4.00
22 Wladimir Balentien 4.00
23 Stephen Drew 8.00
24 Davis Romero 4.00
25 Joe Koshansky 4.00
26 Chin-Lung Hu 25.00
27 Jason Hirsh 4.00
28 Jose Tabata 15.00
29 Eric Hurley 4.00
30 Yung-Chi Chen 35.00
31 Howie Kendrick 8.00
32 Humberto Sanchez 6.00
33 Alex Gordon 20.00
34 Yunel Escobar 4.00
35 Travis Buck 4.00
36 Billy Butler 8.00
37 Homer Bailey 10.00
38 George Kottaras 4.00
39 Kurt Suzuki 4.00
40 Joaquin Arias 4.00
41 Matt Lindstrom 4.00
42 Sean Smith 4.00
43 Carlos Gonzalez 4.00
44 Jaime Garcia 4.00
45 Jose Garcia 4.00

Signs of the Future

NM/M
Common Autograph: 6.00
BS Brandon Snyder 8.00
KC Koby Clemens 15.00
AG Alex Gordon 80.00
CI Chris Iannetta 15.00
MO Micah Owings 15.00
JC Jeff Clement 15.00
CR Clayton Richard 8.00
TB Travis Buck 15.00
BJ Beau Jones 15.00
DJ Daryl Jones 8.00
CDR Chaz Roe 8.00
JM Jacob Marceaux 8.00
CTI Craig Italiano 6.00
JB Jay Bruce 25.00
WT Wade Townsend 8.00
MM Mark McCormick 8.00
HS Henry Sanchez 6.00
MC Mike Costanzo 8.00
CRA Cesar Ramos 8.00

2006 Bowman Heritage

NM/M
Complete Set (300): .15
Common Player (1-200): .15
Common SP (even #'s 202-300): 3.00
Inserted 1:3
Pack (8): 3.00
Box (24): 60.00
1 David Wright 1.00
2 Andruw Jones .50
3 Ryan Howard 1.50

4 Jason Bay .25
5 Paul Konerko .25
6 Jake Peavy .25
7 Todd Jones .15
8 Troy Glaus .25
9 Rocco Baldelli .15
10 Rafael Furcal .25
11 Freddy Sanchez .15
12 Jermaine Dye .15
13 A.J. Burnett .15
14 Michael Cuddyer .15
15 Barry Zito .25
16 Chipper Jones .75
17 Paul LoDuca .15
18 Mark Mulder .15
19 Raul Ibanez .15
20 Carlos Delgado .40
21 Marcus Giles .15
22 Danny Haren .15
23 Justin Morneau .40
24 Livan Hernandez .15
25 Ken Griffey Jr. 1.50
26 Aaron Hill .15
27 Tadahito Iguchi .15
28 Nate Robertson .15
29 Kevin Millwood .15
30 Jim Thome .50
31 Aubrey Huff .15
32 Dontrelle Willis .25
33 Khalil Greene .25
34 Doug Davis .15
35 Ivan Rodriguez .50
36 Rickie Weeks .25
37 Jhonny Peralta .15
38 Yadier Molina .15
39 Eric Chavez .25
40 Alfonso Soriano .75
41 Pat Burrell .25
42 B.J. Ryan .15
43 Carl Crawford .25
44 Preston Wilson .15
45 Jorge Posada .40
46 Carlos Zambrano .25
47 Mark Teahen .15
48 Nick Johnson .15
49 Mark Kotsay .15
50 Derek Jeter 2.00
51 Moises Alou .25
52 Ryan Freel .15
53 Shannon Stewart .15
54 Casey Blake .15
55 Edgar Renteria .25
56 Frank Thomas .50
57 Ty Wigginton .15
58 Jeff Kent .25
59 Chien-Ming Wang .50
60 Josh Beckett .25
61 Chase Utley .40
62 Gary Matthews .15
63 Torii Hunter .25
64 Bobby Jenks .15
65 Wilson Betemit .15
66 Jeremy Bonderman .25
67 Scott Rolen .75
68 Brad Penny .15
69 Jacque Jones .15
70 Jose Reyes .50
71 Brian Roberts .15
72 John Smoltz .25
73 Johnny Estrada .15
74 Ronnie Belliard .15
75 Vladimir Guerrero .75
76 A.J. Pierzynski .15
77 Garrett Atkins .15
78 Adam LaRoche .15
79 Mark Loretta .15
80 Todd Helton .50
81 Jose Vidro .15
82 Carlos Guillen .15
83 Michael Barrett .15
84 Lyle Overbay .15
85 Travis Hafner .25
86 Shea Hillenbrand .15
87 Julio Lugo .15
88 Tim Hudson .25
89 Scott Podsednik .15
90 Roy Halladay .25
91 Bartolo Colon .15
92 Ryan Langerhans .15
93 Tom Glavine .40
94 Ken Rogers .15
95 Robinson Cano .50
96 Mark Prior .50
97 Jason Schmidt .25
98 Bengie Molina .15
99 Jon Lieber .15
100 Alex Rodriguez 2.00
101 Scott Kazmir .25
102 Jeff Francoeur .25
103 Chris Carpenter .40
104 Juan Uribe .15
105 Mariano Rivera .40
106 Rich Harden .15
107 Jack Wilson .15
108 Austin Kearns .15
109 Marcus Thames .15
110 Miguel Tejada .25
111 Chone Figgins .15
112 Bronson Arroyo .15
113 Chad Cordero .15
114 Bill Hall .15
115 Curt Schilling .50
116 David Eckstein .15
117 Ramon Hernandez .15
118 Eric Byrnes .15
119 Clint Barmes .15
120 Bobby Abreu .25
121 Joe Crede .25
122 Derek Lowe .15
123 Jason Marquis .15
124 Erik Bedard .15
125 Derrek Lee .50
126 Brian McCann .25
127 Magglio Ordonez .25
128 Ben Sheets .25
129 Brandon Inge .15
130 Miguel Cabrera .75
131 Jim Edmonds .25
132 John Lackey .15
133 Kevin Mench .15
134 Adrian Beltre .25
135 Curtis Granderson .15
136 Shawn Green .25
137 Jose Contreras .15
138 Joe Nathan .15
139 Bobby Crosby .15
140 Johnny Damon .50
141 Brad Hawpe .15
142 Brandon Phillips .15
143 Victor Martinez .15
144 Jimmy Rollins .50
145 Corey Patterson .15
146 Grady Sizemore .40
147 Placido Polanco .15
148 Mike Lowell .15
149 Francisco Rodriguez .15
150 Ichiro Suzuki 1.50
151 Kris Benson .15
152 Scott Hatteberg .15
153 Akinori Otsuka .15
154 Cesar Izturis .15
155 Roger Clemens 2.00
156 Kerry Wood .25
157 Tom Gordon .15
158 Sean Casey .15
159 Jose Lopez .15
160 Orlando Hernandez .15
161 Aramis Ramirez .25
162 J.D. Drew .25
163 David DeJesus .15
164 Craig Biggio .25
165 Brad Myers .15
166 C.C. Sabathia .15
167 Zachary Duke .15
168 Luis Castillo .15
169 Hideki Matsui 1.00
170 Brian Giles .15
171 Coco Crisp .15
172 Richie Sexson .25
173 Nomar Garciaparra .75
174 Roy Oswalt .25
175 David Ortiz .75
176 Matt Morris .15
177 Felipe Lopez .15
178 Garret Anderson .15
179 Kevin Youkilis .25
180 Alex Rios .15
181 John Garland .15
182 Luis Gonzalez .15
183 Cliff Floyd .15
184 Juan Encarnacion .15
185 Nick Swisher .25
186 Mike Cameron .15
187 Jose Castillo .15
188 Ray Durham .15
189 Jorge Cantu .15
190 Andy Pettitte .25
191 Chad Tracy .15
192 Adrian Gonzalez .15
193 Jose Valentin .15
194 Mark Buehrle .25
195 Huston Street .15
196 Chris Capuano .15
197 Aaron Rowand .15
198 Billy Wagner .15
199 Orlando Cabrera .15
200 Albert Pujols 2.00
201 Dan Uggla **(RC)** .50
202 Alay Soler **RC** 3.00
203 Matthew Kemp **(RC)** 1.00
204 Michael Napoli **RC** 3.00
205 Joel Zumaya **(RC)** 3.00
206 Mike Pelfrey **RC** 4.00
207 Ian Kinsler **(RC)** .50
208 Josh Willingham **(RC)** 3.00
209 Erick Aybar **(RC)** .50
210 Willie Eyre **(RC)** 3.00
211 Kendry Morales **(RC)** .50
212 Scott Thorman **(RC)** 3.00
213 Hanley Ramirez **(RC)** 1.00
214 Boof Bonser **(RC)** 4.00
215 Anthony Reyes **(RC)** .50
216 Justin Huber **(RC)** 3.00
217 Yusmeiro Petit **(RC)** .50
218 Jason Bartlett **(RC)** 3.00
219 Shin-Soo Choo **(RC)** 1.00
220 Francisco Liriano **(RC)** 5.00
221 Craig Hansen **RC** 2.00
222 Ricky Nolasco **(RC)** 3.00
223 Adam Loewen **(RC)** .50
224 Scott Olsen **(RC)** 3.00
225 Cole Hamels **(RC)** 1.50
226 Martin Prado **(RC)** 3.00
227 James Loney **(RC)** 1.00
228 Kevin Thompson **(RC)** 3.00
229 Adam Jones **(RC)** 1.00
230 Josh Johnson **(RC)** 3.00
231 Anderson Hernandez **(RC)** .40
232 Tony Gwynn Jr. **(RC)** 3.00
233 Casey Janssen **RC** .50
234 Taylor Tankersley **(RC)** 3.00
235 Mike Thompson **RC** .50
236 Jeremy Sowers **(RC)** 3.00
237 Anibal Sanchez **(RC)** .50
238 Adam Wainwright **(RC)** 4.00
239 Rich Hill **(RC)** .50
240 Russell Martin **(RC)** 4.00
241 Joe Inglett **RC** .50
242 Tony Pena **(RC)** 3.00
243 Joshua Sharpless **RC** .50
244 Darrell Rasner **(RC)** 3.00
245 Joe Saunders **(RC)** .50
246 Jon Lester **(RC)** 6.00
247 Jeremy Hermida **(RC)** .50
248 Chad Billingsley **(RC)** 4.00
249 Bobby Livingston **(RC)** .50
250 Justin Verlander **(RC)** 5.00
251 Mickey Mantle 10.00
252 Hank Blalock 3.00
253 Manny Ramirez 1.00
254 Mike Mussina 5.00
255 Greg Maddux 2.00
256 Jason Giambi 4.00
257 Mark Teixeira .75
258 Carlos Beltran 4.00
259 Matt Holliday 1.00
260 Pedro Martinez 5.00
261 Joe Mauer 1.00
262 Melvin Mora 3.00
263 Mike Piazza 1.50
264 B.J. Upton 4.00
265 Vernon Wells .75
266 Gary Sheffield 4.00
267 Randy Johnson 1.00
268 Ryan Zimmerman 4.00
269 Lance Berkman .75
270 Johan Santana 5.00
271 Carlos Lee .50
272 Brandon Webb 3.00
273 Adam Dunn .75
274 Michael Young 3.00
275 Barry Bonds 2.00
276 Jonathan Papelbon **(RC)** 6.00
277 Howie Kendrick **(RC)** 1.00
278 Melky Cabrera **(RC)** 3.00
279 Jered Weaver **(RC)** 2.00
280 Josh Barfield **(RC)** 3.00
281 Chuck James **(RC)** 1.00
282 Lastings Milledge **(RC)** 5.00
283 Nicholas Markakis **(RC)** 1.00
284 Jose Capellan **(RC)** 3.00
285 Prince Fielder **(RC)** 3.00
286 Jason Botts **(RC)** 3.00
287 Eliezer Alfonzo **RC** .50
288 Sean Marshall **(RC)** 3.00
289 Ryan Garko **(RC)** .75
290 Stephen Drew **(RC)** 5.00
291 Joel Guzman **(RC)** .50
292 Hong-Chih Kuo **(RC)** 3.00
293 Zach Miner **(RC)** .50
294 Angel Guzman **(RC)** 3.00
295 Andre Ethier **(RC)** 1.00
296 Fausto Carmona **(RC)** 3.00
297 Ronny Paulino **(RC)** .75
298 Matt Cain **(RC)** 5.00
299 Carlos Quentin **(RC)** .75
300 Kenji Johjima **RC** 5.00

Mini

Mini (1-300): 1-2X
Inserted 1:1

Foil

Foil (1-300): 1-2X
Foil (301-350): .5-1X
Inserted 1:1

Black

No Pricing
Production One Set

Printing Plates

No Pricing
Production One Set

Signs of Greatness

NM/M
Common Autograph: 10.00
White: No Pricing
Production Five Sets
Black: No Pricing
Production One Set
BB Brian Bogusevic 10.00
LB Lance Broadway 15.00
KC Koby Clemens 20.00
JCL Jeff Clement 15.00
JC Jesus Cota 10.00
TC Trevor Crowe 15.00
JD John Drennen 15.00
SG Sean Gallagher 15.00
AG Alex Gordon 60.00
JH Justin Huber 15.00
CI Craig Italiano 15.00
SL Sam LeCure 10.00
MM Matt Maloney 15.00
CM Cameron Maybin 50.00
JS Jarrod Saltalamacchia 25.00
BS Brandon Snyder 10.00
ST Steve Tolleson 15.00
WT Wade Townsend 15.00
RT Ryan Tucker 15.00
JU Justin Upton 80.00
KW Kevin Whelan 10.00
BW Brandon Wood 25.00

Pieces of Greatness

NM/M
Common Player: 5.00
Inserted 1:12
White: 1.5-3X
Production 49 Sets
Black: No Pricing
Production One Set
LB Lance Berkman 5.00
CB Craig Biggio 8.00
HB Hank Blalock 5.00
BB Barry Bonds 25.00
MB Milton Bradley 5.00
RC Robinson Cano 20.00
AD Adam Dunn 5.00
JD Jermaine Dye 5.00
DE David Eckstein 15.00
EE Edwin Encarnacion 5.00
ME Morgan Ensberg 5.00
CF Cliff Floyd 5.00
JF Jeff Francoeur 10.00
RF Rafael Furcal 5.00
VG Vladimir Guerrero 10.00
THE Todd Helton 8.00
RH Ryan Howard 25.00
TH Torii Hunter 5.00
AJ Andruw Jones 8.00
AJ2 Andruw Jones 8.00
CJ Chipper Jones 8.00
CJ2 Chipper Jones 8.00
NJ Nick Johnson 5.00
JK Jeff Kent 5.00
AL Adam LaRoche 5.00
DL Derrek Lee 8.00
JL Javy Lopez 5.00
ML Mike Lowell 5.00
GM Greg Maddux 10.00
VM Victor Martinez 5.00
XN Xavier Nady 5.00
MO Magglio Ordonez 5.00
DO David Ortiz 15.00
AJP A.J. Pierzynski 5.00
SP Scott Podsednik 10.00
AP Albert Pujols 25.00
AP2 Albert Pujols 25.00
ARA Aramis Ramirez 5.00
MR Manny Ramirez 8.00
BR Brian Roberts 5.00
AR Alex Rodriguez 20.00
CS Curt Schilling 8.00
GS Gary Sheffield 8.00
NS Nick Swisher 8.00
JT Jim Thome 8.00
CU Chase Utley 8.00
BW Brad Wilkerson 5.00
DW Dontrelle Willis 5.00
MY Michael Young 5.00
BZ Barry Zito 5.00

Prospects

NM/M
Common Prospect: .50
Inserted 2:Pack
Black: No Pricing
Production One Set
BHP1 Justin Upton 5.00
BHP2 Koby Clemens 6.00
BHP3 Lance Broadway 1.00
BHP4 Cameron Maybin 8.00
BHP5 Garrett Mock 1.00
BHP6 Alex Gordon 6.00
BHP7 Ben Copeland 1.00
BHP8 Nick Adenhart 2.00
BHP9 Yung-Chi Chen 3.00
BHP10 Tim Moss .50
BHP11 Francisco Leandro .50
BHP12 Brad McCann 1.00
BHP13 Dallas Trahern 1.00
BHP14 Dustin Majewski 2.00
BHP15 James Barthmaier 1.00
BHP16 Nate Gold 1.00
BHP17 John Hardy .50
BHP18 Mark McLemore .50
BHP19 Michael Aubrey 1.00
BHP20 Mark Holliman 2.00
BHP21 Bobby Wilson .50
BHP22 Radhames Liz 1.00
BHP23 Jose Tabata 8.00
BHP24 Jared Lansford .50
BHP25 Brent Dlugach 1.00
BHP26 Steve Garrabrants .50
BHP27 Eric Haberer 1.00
BHP28 Chris Dickerson .50
BHP29 Welinson Baez 1.00
BHP30 Chris Kolkhorst .50
BHP31 Brandon Moss 2.00
BHP32 Corey Wimberly .50
BHP33 Ryan Patterson 2.00
BHP34 Michael Hollimon 1.00
BHP35 John Bannister .50
BHP36 Pablo Sandoval .50
BHP37 Dexter Fowler .50
BHP38 Elvis Andrus 2.00
BHP39 Jason Windsor 1.00
BHP40 B.J. Szymanski 1.00
BHP41 Yovani Gallardo 4.00
BHP42 John Bowker .50
BHP43 Justin Christian 2.00
BHP44 Andrew Sonnanstine 2.00
BHP45 Jeremy Slayden .50
BHP46 Brandon Jones .50
BHP47 Travis Denker 2.00
BHP48 Emmanuel Garcia 3.00
BHP49 Landon Jacobsen 6.00
BHP50 Kevin Estrada 1.00
BHP51 Ross Ohlendorf .50
BHP52 Wyatt Toregas .50
BHP53 Andrew Kown 1.00
BHP54 Steve Kelly .50
BHP55 Mike Butia .50
BHP56 Mike Connolly .50
BHP57 Brian Horwitz .50
BHP58 Dale Thayer .50
BHP59 Diory Hernandez 1.00
BHP60 Samuel Deduno .50
BHP61 Jamie Hoffman 1.00
BHP62 Matt Tolbert 3.00
BHP63 Michael Ekstrom .50
BHP64 Chris Maples 1.00
BHP65 Adam Coe 1.00
BHP66 Max Ramirez .50
BHP67 Evan MacLane .50
BHP68 Jose Campusano .50
BHP69 Lou Santangelo 1.00
BHP70 Shawn Riggans 1.00
BHP71 Kyle Kendrick .75
BHP72 Oswaldo Navarro .50
BHP73 Eric Rodland 1.00
BHP74 Omir Santos 2.00
BHP75 Kyle McCulloch .50
BHP76 Evan Longoria 5.00
BHP77 Adrian Cardenas 1.00
BHP78 Steven Wright .50
BHP79 Andrew Carpenter 2.00
BHP80 Dustin Evans 1.50
BHP81 Chad Tracy .50
BHP82 Matthew Sulentic 4.00
BHP83 Adam Ottavino 2.00
BHP84 Matt Long .50
BHP85 Clayton Kershaw 4.00
BHP86 Matt Antonelli 2.00
BHP87 Chris Parmelee 2.00
BHP88 Billy Rowell 3.00
BHP89 Chase Fontaine 1.00
BHP90 Chris Murrero 2.00
BHP91 Jamie Ortiz 2.00
BHP92 Sean Watson 1.00
BHP93 Brooks Brown 1.00
BHP94 Brad Furnish 3.00
BHP95 Chad Huffman 2.00
BHP96 Pedro Beato 3.00
BHP97 Kyler Burke 1.00
BHP98 Stephen Englund 1.00
BHP99 Tyler Norrick .50
BHP100 Brent Sinkbeil .50

Draft Pick Variations

NM/M
One five card pack per box.
BHP76 Evan Longoria 6.00
BHP77 Adrian Cardenas 1.00
BHP78 Steven Wright 1.00
BHP79 Andrew Carpenter 2.00
BHP80 Dustin Evans 2.00
BHP81 Chad Tracy 1.00
BHP82 Matthew Sulentic 4.00
BHP83 Adam Ottavino 2.00
BHP84 Matt Long 1.00
BHP85 Clayton Kershaw 5.00
BHP86 Matt Antonelli 3.00
BHP87 Chris Parmelee 2.00
BHP88 Billy Rowell 3.00
BHP89 Chase Fontaine 1.00
BHP90 Chris Murrero 2.00
BHP91 Jamie Ortiz 2.00
BHP92 Sean Watson 1.00
BHP93 Brooks Brown 1.00
BHP94 Brad Furnish 3.00
BHP95 Chad Huffman 2.00
BHP96 Pedro Beato 3.00
BHP97 Kyler Burke 1.00
BHP98 Stephen Englund 1.00
BHP99 Tyler Norrick 1.00
BHP100 Brent Sinkbeil 1.00

2006 Bowman Originals

NM/M
Complete Set (55): 50.00
Common Player (1-35): 1.00
Common Player (36-55): 2.00
Pack (7): 60.00
Box (6): 350.00
1 David Wright 3.00
2 Derek Jeter 5.00
3 Eric Chavez 1.00
4 Ken Griffey Jr. 4.00
5 Albert Pujols 5.00
6 Ryan Howard 5.00
7 Joe Mauer 1.50
8 Andruw Jones 1.50
9 Nomar Garciaparra 2.00
10 Michael Young 1.00
11 Miguel Tejada 1.50
12 Alfonso Soriano 2.00
13 Alex Rodriguez 5.00
14 Paul Konerko 1.50
15 Carl Crawford 1.00
16 Nick Johnson 1.00
17 Jim Thome 1.50
18 Ivan Rodriguez 1.50
19 Chipper Jones 2.00
20 Pedro Martinez 2.00
21 Carlos Delgado 1.50
22 Roger Clemens 5.00
23 Mark Teixeira 1.50
24 Manny Ramirez 2.00
25 Barry Bonds 5.00
26 Vernon Wells 1.00
27 Vladimir Guerrero 2.00
28 Miguel Cabrera 2.00
29 Victor Martinez 1.00
30 Derrek Lee 1.50
31 Carlos Lee 1.00
32 Ichiro Suzuki 3.00
33 Johan Santana 1.50
34 David Ortiz 2.00
35 Jason Bay 1.50
36 Kendry Morales **(RC)** 3.00
37 Nicholas Markakis **(RC)** 5.00
38 Conor Jackson **(RC)** 2.00
39 Justin Verlander **(RC)** 5.00
40 Ryan Zimmerman **(RC)** 5.00
41 Jeremy Hermida **(RC)** 2.00
42 Dan Uggla **(RC)** 3.00
43 Matthew Kemp **(RC)** 3.00
44 Lastings Milledge **(RC)** 5.00
45 Kenji Johjima **RC** 5.00
46 Ian Kinsler **(RC)** 3.00
47 Hanley Ramirez **(RC)** 3.00
48 Melky Cabrera **(RC)** 3.00
49 Willy Aybar **(RC)** 2.00
50 Jonathan Papelbon **(RC)** 6.00
51 Prince Fielder **(RC)** 5.00
52 Cole Hamels **(RC)** 5.00
53 Josh Barfield **(RC)** 2.00
54 Alay Soler **RC** 3.00
55 Russell Martin **(RC)** 3.00

Blue

Blue (1-55): 2-3X
Production 249 Sets

Black

Black (1-55): 3-5X
Production 99 Sets

Red

No Pricing
Production One Set

Printing Plates

No Pricing
Production one set per color.

Buyback Autographs

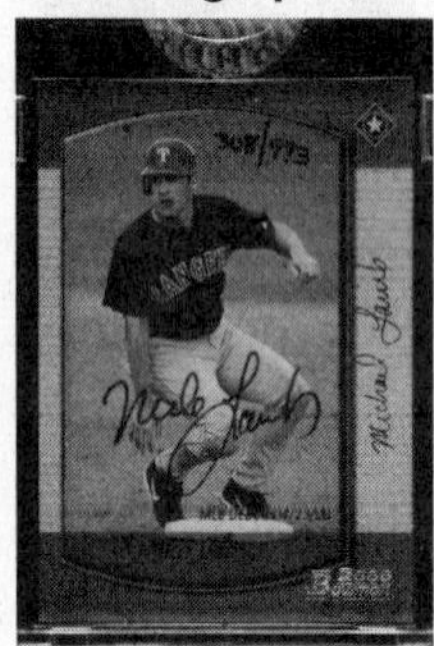

	NM/M
Adam Loewen/68	15.00
Adam Loewen/719	10.00
Adam Loewen/198	15.00
Adrian Gonzalez/976	20.00
Albert Pujols/44	250.00
Albert Pujols/50	250.00
Alex Gordon/49	250.00
Alex Gordon/32	280.00
Andrew McCutchen/391	40.00
Andrew McCutchen/33	60.00
Andrew McCutchen/561	35.00
Andruw Jones/34	50.00
Andruw Jones/22	60.00
Andruw Jones/24	60.00
Andruw Jones/28	60.00
Andruw Jones/48	50.00
Andy LaRoche/109	40.00
Andy LaRoche/60	40.00
Andy LaRoche/66	40.00
Andy LaRoche/734	25.00
Alex Rodriguez/21	150.00
Alex Rodriguez/22	150.00
B.J. Upton/58	30.00
B.J. Upton/136	25.00
B.J. Upton/667	20.00
B.J. Upton/120	25.00
Beau Jones/576	15.00
Beau Jones/63	30.00
Beau Jones/329	20.00
Beau Jones/33	30.00
Billy Buckner/99	25.00
Billy Buckner/432	20.00
Billy Buckner/182	20.00
Billy Buckner/33	30.00
Billy Wagner/56	30.00
Billy Wagner/47	30.00
Billy Wagner/64	25.00
Billy Wagner/90	20.00
Billy Wagner/99	20.00
Billy Wagner/37	30.00
Billy Wagner/38	30.00
Brandon Phillips/46	15.00
Brandon Phillips/26	20.00
Brandon Phillips/67	10.00
Brandon Phillips/28	20.00
Brandon Phillips/32	15.00
Brandon Phillips/140	10.00
Brandon Phillips/35	15.00
Brandon Phillips/335	10.00
Brandon Phillips/257	10.00
Brandon Snyder/461	15.00
Brandon Wood/70	30.00
Brandon Wood/100	30.00
Brandon Wood/627	20.00
Brandon Wood/239	30.00
Brent Cox/240	15.00
Brent Cox/66	20.00
Brent Cox/688	15.00
Carl Crawford/37	25.00
Carl Crawford/40	25.00
Carl Crawford/20	30.00
Carl Crawford/30	25.00
Carl Crawford/71	20.00
Carl Crawford/71	20.00
Carl Crawford/334	15.00
Carl Crawford/279	15.00
Carlos Silva/996	10.00
Cesar Ramos/25	25.00
Cesar Ramos/76	25.00
Cesar Ramos/161	15.00
Cesar Ramos/732	10.00
Chase Utley/23	75.00
Chase Utley/150	40.00
Chase Utley/303	40.00
Chase Utley/23	75.00
Chaz Roe/73	15.00
Chaz Roe/774	10.00
Chaz Roe/132	10.00
Chien-Ming Wang/25	500.00
Chien-Ming Wang/25	600.00
Chien-Ming Wang/25	500.00
Chien-Ming Wang/25	600.00
Chipper Jones/20	80.00
Chipper Jones/20	80.00
Chipper Jones/20	80.00
Chipper Jones/20	80.00
Chipper Jones/20	80.00
Chris Young/70	20.00
Chris Young/772	20.00
Chris Young/146	20.00
Chris Young/211	20.00
Chris Young/44	75.00
Chris Young/88	40.00
Chris Young/81	40.00
Chris Young/558	25.00
Clint Barmes/61	20.00
Clint Barmes/113	15.00
Clint Barmes/375	10.00
Clint Barmes/430	10.00
Conor Jackson/70	30.00
Conor Jackson/78	50.00
Conor Jackson/457	20.00
Conor Jackson/360	20.00
Craig Italiano/160	15.00
Craig Italiano/650	10.00
Craig Italiano/163	15.00
Dan Johnson/276	15.00
Dan Johnson/575	15.00
Dan Johnson/101	15.00
Dan Johnson/29	20.00
David Wright/543	60.00
David Wright/264	150.00
David Wright/45	80.00
David Wright/64	80.00
Derrek Lee/61	20.00
Dontrelle Willis/147	20.00
Dontrelle Willis/55	25.00
Dontrelle Willis/525	20.00
Dontrelle Willis/79	25.00
Dontrelle Willis/78	25.00
Dontrelle Willis/24	25.00
Dontrelle Willis/36	25.00
Eli Iorg/167	15.00
Eli Iorg/151	15.00
Eli Iorg/672	15.00
Eric Chavez/34	20.00
Eric Chavez/301	15.00
Eric Chavez/25	20.00
Eric Chavez/70	20.00
Eric Chavez/62	20.00
Ervin Santana/369	15.00
Ervin Santana/544	15.00
Ervin Santana/51	20.00
Ervin Santana/109	20.00
Ervin Santana/76	20.00
Ervin Santana/67	20.00
Ervin Santana/62	50.00
Fausto Carmona/131	10.00
Fausto Carmona/56	15.00
Fausto Carmona/263	10.00
Francisco Cordero/64	10.00
Francisco Cordero/87	10.00
Francisco Cordero/49	10.00
Francisco Cordero/138	10.00
Francisco Cordero/140	10.00
Francisco Liriano/142	35.00
Francisco Liriano/63	40.00
Francisco Liriano/47	35.00
Francisco Liriano/222	30.00
Francisco Liriano/350	25.00
Francisco Liriano/212	65.00
Garrett Atkins/121	15.00
Garrett Atkins/27	20.00
Garrett Atkins/209	15.00
Garrett Atkins/581	15.00
Garrett Atkins/38	15.00
Hanley Ramirez/435	20.00
Hanley Ramirez/98	25.00
Hanley Ramirez/466	20.00
Jason Bay/24	30.00
Jason Bay/298	25.00
Jason Bay/50	25.00
Jason Bay/58	25.00
Jason Bay/70	25.00
Jason Botts/29	15.00
Jason Botts/31	15.00
Jason Botts/269	10.00
Jason Botts/46	15.00
Jason Botts/59	15.00
Jason Botts/577	10.00
Jason Kubel/232	15.00
Jason Kubel/127	15.00
Jason Kubel/25	25.00
Jason Kubel/77	20.00
Jason Marquis/944	8.00
Jason Marquis/26	20.00
Jay Bruce/66	80.00
Jay Bruce/434	50.00
Jed Lowrie/123	15.00
Jed Lowrie/141	15.00
Jed Lowrie/716	15.00
Jeff Mathis/127	15.00
Jeff Mathis/185	15.00
Jeff Mathis/97	15.00
Jerome Williams/292	8.00
Jerome Williams/48	10.00
Jerome Williams/45	10.00
Jerome Williams/97	8.00
Joel Guzman/274	15.00
Joel Guzman/54	20.00
Joel Guzman/53	20.00
Joel Zumaya/233	50.00
Joel Zumaya/57	50.00
Joel Zumaya/96	80.00
Joel Zumaya/582	40.00
Joel Zumaya/163	50.00
John Drennen/78	30.00
John Drennen/387	15.00
John Van Benschoten/51	15.00
John Van Benschoten/24	20.00
John Van Benschoten/130	15.00
John Van Benschoten/272	10.00
Jonny Gomes/341	15.00
Jonny Gomes/27	50.00
Jonny Gomes/175	15.00
Jonny Gomes/363	10.00
Josh Barfield/158	20.00
Josh Barfield/557	15.00
Josh Barfield/178	30.00
Josh Geer/343	10.00
Josh Geer/138	10.00
Justin Huber/32	15.00
Justin Huber/99	15.00
Justin Huber/572	10.00
Justin Huber/212	10.00
Justin Huber/26	20.00
Justin Huber/37	15.00
Justin Upton/1000	100.00
Kevin Gregg/988	10.00
Lastings Milledge/166	35.00
Lastings Milledge/166	35.00
Lastings Milledge/632	25.00
Mark Mulder/20	25.00
Mark Mulder/20	25.00
Mark Mulder/20	25.00
Mark Mulder/20	25.00
Mark Mulder/20	25.00
Matt Cain/36	30.00
Matt Cain/389	20.00
Matt Maloney/350	25.00
Matt Maloney/50	60.00
Matt Maloney/20	75.00
Matt Maloney/60	60.00
Matt Torra/456	15.00
Matt Torra/37	30.00
Melky Cabrera/606	30.00
Melky Cabrera/191	35.00
Melky Cabrera/60	50.00
Melky Cabrera/24	70.00
Melky Cabrera/95	40.00
Melky Cabrera/12	12.00
Merkin Valdez/41	15.00
Merkin Valdez/325	8.00
Merkin Valdez/70	15.00
Merkin Valdez/66	15.00
Micah Owings/138	30.00
Micah Owings/648	20.00
Michael Bowden/27	40.00
Michael Bowden/24	40.00
Michael Bowden/449	20.00
Miguel Cabrera/70	30.00
Miguel Cabrera/70	30.00
Miguel Cabrera/69	30.00
Miguel Cabrera/98	30.00
Miguel Cabrera/63	30.00
Miguel Cabrera/130	40.00
Mike Costanzo/466	15.00
Mike Lamb/993	10.00
Morgan Ensberg/74	15.00
Morgan Ensberg/334	10.00
Morgan Ensberg/64	15.00
Nick Swisher/342	20.00
Nick Swisher/73	25.00
Nick Swisher/31	30.00
Nolan Reimold/41	60.00
Nolan Reimold/419	20.00
Nolan Reimold/30	60.00
Rich Harden/87	20.00
Rich Harden/82	20.00
Rich Harden/70	20.00
Rich Harden/68	20.00
Rich Harden/68	30.00
Ricky Nolasco/52	15.00
Ricky Nolasco/256	10.00
Ricky Nolasco/148	15.00
Robinson Cano/90	50.00
Robinson Cano/72	50.00
Robinson Cano/101	50.00
Robinson Cano/222	40.00
Roy Oswalt/96	25.00
Roy Oswalt/42	30.00
Roy Oswalt/61	30.00
Roy Oswalt/63	40.00
Roy Oswalt/25	50.00
Roy Oswalt/199	25.00
Russell Martin/33	40.00
Russell Martin/96	30.00
Russell Martin/577	25.00
Russell Martin/252	25.00
Ryan Howard/50	350.00
Scott Elbert/79	50.00
Scott Elbert/330	35.00
Scott Elbert/60	50.00
Scott Kazmir/99	25.00
Scott Kazmir/36	30.00
Scott Kazmir/153	20.00
Scott Kazmir/26	30.00
Scott Kazmir/661	20.00
Scott Mathieson/472	8.00
Scott Mathieson/108	20.00
Scott Mathieson/72	25.00
Scott Thorman/980	10.00
Sean West/394	20.00
Sean West/70	30.00
Shaun Marcum/133	15.00
Shaun Marcum/26	20.00
Shaun Marcum/138	20.00
Shaun Marcum/153	20.00
Shaun Marcum/33	25.00
Travis Buck/60	40.00
Travis Buck/44	60.00
Travis Buck/747	20.00
Travis Hafner/114	20.00
Travis Hafner/96	20.00
Travis Hafner/386	20.00
Travis Hafner/45	25.00
Travis Hafner/280	20.00
Trevor Bell/146	15.00
Trevor Bell/28	15.00
Trevor Bell/689	15.00
Troy Patton/211	15.00
Troy Patton/50	30.00
Troy Patton/736	15.00
Vernon Wells/52	25.00
Vernon Wells/100	25.00
Vernon Wells/25	40.00
Vernon Wells/96	25.00
Vernon Wells/68	25.00
Vernon Wells/56	25.00
Vernon Wells/40	40.00
Vernon Wells/29	40.00
Vernon Wells/426	20.00
Vladimir Guerrero/21	80.00
Vladimir Guerrero/45	60.00
Vladimir Guerrero/20	80.00
Wade Townsend/423	15.00
Wade Townsend/53	20.00
Wily Mo Pena/79	20.00
Wily Mo Pena/70	20.00
Wily Mo Pena/69	20.00
Wily Mo Pena/134	20.00
Wily Mo Pena/62	20.00
Xavier Nady/105	20.00
Xavier Nady/72	20.00
Xavier Nady/192	15.00
Xavier Nady/213	15.00
Xavier Nady/294	15.00
Xavier Nady/41	20.00
Yunel Escobar/69	30.00
Yunel Escobar/395	20.00
Yusmeiro Petit/68	20.00
Yusmeiro Petit/102	20.00
Yusmeiro Petit/160	15.00
Yusmeiro Petit/630	15.00

2006 Bowman Sterling

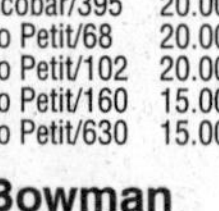

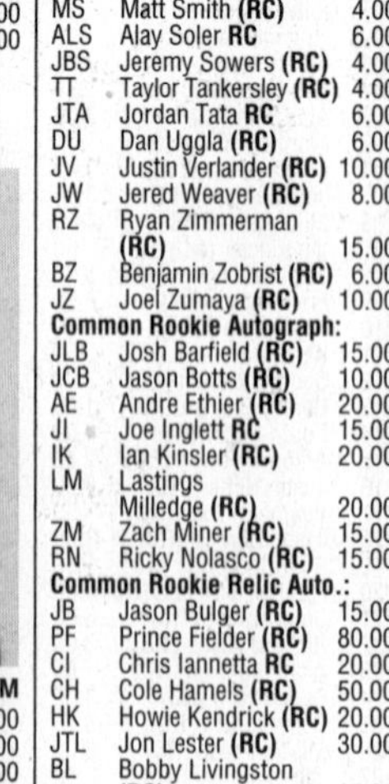

		NM/M
Common Relic:		5.00
Pack (5):		50.00
Box (6):		260.00
CB	Carlos Beltran	8.00
CB2	Carlos Beltran	8.00
LB	Lance Berkman	5.00
HB	Hank Blalock	5.00
BLB	Barry Bonds	20.00
MC	Miguel Cabrera	10.00
MC2	Miguel Cabrera	10.00
RC	Robinson Cano	15.00
CC	Chris Carpenter	8.00
EC	Eric Chavez	5.00
JDD	Johnny Damon	8.00
AD	Adam Dunn	5.00
ME	Morgan Ensberg	5.00
VG	Vladimir Guerrero	10.00
JRH	Rich Harden	5.00
TH	Todd Helton	8.00
RH	Ryan Howard	25.00
AJ	Andruw Jones	8.00
LWJ	Chipper Jones	8.00
PK	Paul Konerko	8.00
MCM	Mickey Mantle	120.00
PM	Pedro Martinez	8.00
HM	Hideki Matsui	20.00
MM	Mark Mulder	5.00
DO	David Ortiz	10.00
MJP	Mike Piazza	10.00
AP	Albert Pujols	25.00
AP2	Albert Pujols	25.00
AR	Aramis Ramirez	8.00
MR	Manny Ramirez	10.00
MR2	Manny Ramirez	10.00
BR	Brian Roberts	5.00
AER	Alex Rodriguez	20.00
IR	Ivan Rodriguez	8.00
SR	Scott Rolen	8.00
JAS	Johan Santana	8.00
CS	Curt Schilling	8.00
GS	Grady Sizemore	8.00
APS	Alfonso Soriano	10.00
IS	Ichiro Suzuki	25.00
MCT	Mark Teixeira	8.00
MT	Miguel Tejada	8.00
JHT	Jim Thome	8.00
DWW	Dontrelle Willis	5.00
DW	David Wright	20.00
Common Rookie:		4.00
BA	Brian Anderson **(RC)**	4.00
WA	Willy Aybar **(RC)**	4.00
BB	Brian Bannister **(RC)**	4.00
CRB	Chad Billingsley **(RC)**	10.00
BON	Boof Bonser **(RC)**	6.00
MCC	Melky Cabrera **(RC)**	6.00
JD	Joey Devine **RC**	4.00
SD	Stephen Drew **(RC)**	10.00
KF	Kevin Frandsen **(RC)**	4.00
RK	Ryan Garko **(RC)**	6.00
DG	David Gassner **(RC)**	4.00
EG	Enrique Gonzalez **(RC)**	4.00
FG	Franklin Gutierrez **(RC)**	4.00
TGJ	Tony Gwynn Jr. **(RC)**	6.00
CRH	Craig Hansen **RC**	8.00
CJ	Conor Jackson **(RC)**	4.00
CHJ	Chuck James **(RC)**	6.00
CJJ	Casey Janssen **RC**	4.00
KJ	Kenji Johjima **RC**	10.00
JJ	Josh Johnson **(RC)**	6.00
JK	Jeff Karstens **RC**	6.00
MK	Matthew Kemp **(RC)**	6.00
HK	Howie Kendrick **(RC)**	6.00
FL	Francisco Liriano **(RC)**	10.00
JL	James Loney **(RC)**	6.00
NM	Nicholas Markakis **(RC)**	8.00
RM	Russell Martin **(RC)**	6.00
SM	Scott Mathieson **(RC)**	6.00
JM	Jeff Mathis **(RC)**	6.00
KM	Kendry Morales **(RC)**	4.00
SO	Scott Olsen **(RC)**	4.00
JP	Jonathan Papelbon **(RC)**	10.00
DP	David Pauley **(RC)**	6.00
MPP	Mike Pelfrey **RC**	15.00
HP	Hayden Penn **(RC)**	4.00
CQ	Carlos Quentin **(RC)**	4.00
HR	Hanley Ramirez **(RC)**	6.00
AS	Anibal Sanchez **(RC)**	4.00
JS	James Shields **RC**	8.00
MS	Matt Smith **(RC)**	4.00
ALS	Alay Soler **RC**	6.00
JBS	Jeremy Sowers **(RC)**	4.00
TT	Taylor Tankersley **(RC)**	4.00
JTA	Jordan Tata **RC**	6.00
DU	Dan Uggla **(RC)**	6.00
JV	Justin Verlander **(RC)**	10.00
JW	Jered Weaver **(RC)**	8.00
RZ	Ryan Zimmerman **(RC)**	15.00
BZ	Benjamin Zobrist **(RC)**	6.00
JZ	Joel Zumaya **(RC)**	10.00
Common Rookie Autograph:		
JLB	Josh Barfield **(RC)**	15.00
JCB	Jason Botts **(RC)**	10.00
AE	Andre Ethier **(RC)**	20.00
JI	Joe Inglett **RC**	15.00
IK	Ian Kinsler **(RC)**	20.00
LM	Lastings Milledge **(RC)**	20.00
ZM	Zach Miner **(RC)**	15.00
RN	Ricky Nolasco **(RC)**	15.00
Common Rookie Relic Auto.:		
JB	Jason Bulger **(RC)**	15.00
PF	Prince Fielder **(RC)**	80.00
CI	Chris Iannetta **RC**	20.00
CH	Cole Hamels **(RC)**	50.00
HK	Howie Kendrick **(RC)**	20.00
JTL	Jon Lester **(RC)**	30.00
BL	Bobby Livingston **(RC)**	15.00
MN	Erik Naposki **RC**	20.00
RP	Ronny Paulino **(RC)**	15.00
YP	Yusmeiro Petit **(RC)**	20.00
MP	Martin Prado **(RC)**	20.00
ALR	Anthony Reyes **(RC)**	20.00
JT	Jack Taschner **(RC)**	15.00
ST	Scott Thorman **(RC)**	15.00

Prospects

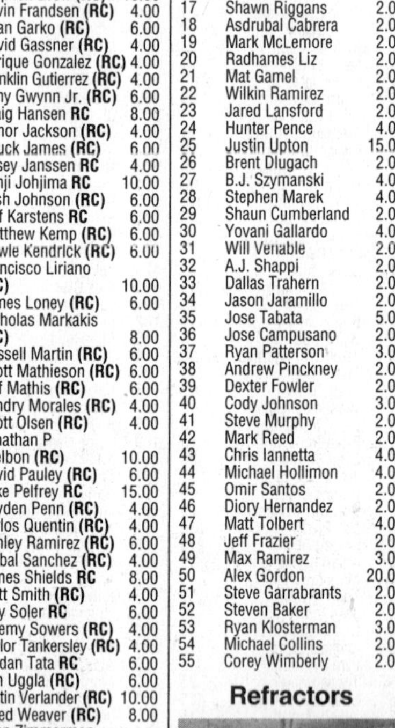

		NM/M
Common Player:		2.00
Blue:		1.5-2X
Production 249 Sets		
Black:		2-4X
Production 99 Sets		
Red:		No Pricing
Production One Set		
1	Cameron Maybin	15.00
2	Koby Clemens	5.00
3	Lance Broadway	2.00
4	Chris Dickerson	2.00
5	Garrett Mock	2.00
6	Ben Copeland	2.00
7	Nick Adenhart	2.00
8	Brad McCann	3.00
9	Dustin Majewski	2.00
10	Jimmy Barthmaier	2.00
11	Michael Aubrey	2.00
12	Evan Longoria	20.00
13	Clayton Kershaw	12.00
14	Juan Francia	2.00
15	Elvis Andrus	6.00
16	Mark Trumbo	2.00
17	Shawn Riggans	2.00
18	Asdrubal Cabrera	2.00
19	Mark McLemore	2.00
20	Radhames Liz	2.00
21	Mat Gamel	2.00
22	Wilkin Ramirez	2.00
23	Jared Lansford	2.00
24	Hunter Pence	4.00
25	Justin Upton	15.00
26	Brent Dlugach	2.00
27	B.J. Szymanski	4.00
28	Stephen Marek	4.00
29	Shaun Cumberland	2.00
30	Yovani Gallardo	4.00
31	Will Venable	2.00
32	A.J. Shappi	2.00
33	Dallas Trahern	2.00
34	Jason Jaramillo	2.00
35	Jose Tabata	5.00
36	Jose Campusano	2.00
37	Ryan Patterson	3.00
38	Andrew Pinckney	2.00
39	Dexter Fowler	2.00
40	Cody Johnson	3.00
41	Steve Murphy	2.00
42	Mark Reed	2.00
43	Chris Iannetta	4.00
44	Michael Hollimon	4.00
45	Omir Santos	2.00
46	Diory Hernandez	2.00
47	Matt Tolbert	4.00
48	Jeff Frazier	2.00
49	Max Ramirez	3.00
50	Alex Gordon	20.00
51	Steve Garrabrants	2.00
52	Steven Baker	2.00
53	Ryan Klosterman	3.00
54	Michael Collins	2.00
55	Corey Wimberly	2.00

Refractors

Rookies: 1.5-2X
Rookie Auto.: 1-2X
Rookie Relic Auto.: 1-2X
Relics: 1-2X
Prospects: 1.5-2X
Prospect Auto.: 1-2X
Production 199 Sets

Black Refractors

No Pricing
Production 25 Sets

Printing Plates

No Pricing
Production One Set

Red Refractors

No Pricing
Production One Set

Gold Refractors

No Pricing
Production 10 Sets

Prospect Autographs

		NM/M
BA	Brandon Allen	8.00
MAA	Matt Antonelli	25.00
MA	Mike Aviles	10.00
PB	Pedro Beato	20.00
RB	Ronny Bourquin	15.00
BB	Brooks Brown	15.00
TB	Travis Buck	15.00
KB	Kyler Burke	15.00
JBU	Joshua Butler	15.00
AC	Adrian Cardenas	25.00
KC	Koby Clemens	20.00
JC	Jeff Clement	15.00
TC	Tyler Colvin	35.00
HC	Hank Conger	25.00
TC	Trevor Crowe	20.00
CD	Chris Dickerson	10.00
KD	Kyle Drabek	25.00
DE	Dustin Evans	15.00
SE	Steven Evarts	15.00
MF	Michael Felix	15.00
BF	Brad Furnish	15.00
AG	Alex Gordon	80.00
DH	Daniel Haigwood	15.00
BH	Brett Hayes	15.00
CH	Chase Headley	20.00
LH	Luke Hochevar	40.00
DHU	David Huff	15.00
CHH	Chad Huffman	15.00
JJ	Jeremy Jeffress	20.00
CJ	Cody Johnson	20.00
KJ	Kris Johnson	15.00
CK	Clayton Kershaw	60.00
KK	Kasey Kiker	15.00
EL	Evan Longoria	75.00
PL	Pedro Lopez	8.00
CM	Cameron Maybin	70.00
MM	Mark McCormick	15.00
KM	Kyle McCulloch	15.00
GM	Garrett Mock	15.00
BM	Brandon Moss	20.00
JN	Jason Neighborgall	10.00
AO	Adam Ottavino	15.00
MO	Micah Owings	20.00
CP	Chris Parmelee	35.00
TP	Troy Patton	25.00
EP	Elvin Puello	10.00
CR	Cory Rasmus	15.00
JR	Joshua Rodriguez	15.00
BR	Billy Rowell	60.00
JS	Jarrod Saltalamacchia	20.00
BSI	Brett Sinkbeil	20.00
BS	Brandon Snyder	15.00
WT	Wade Townsend	15.00
CT	Chad Tracy	15.00
JU	Justin Upton	90.00
SWA	Sean Watson	15.00
JW	Johnny Whittleman	20.00
CW	Colten Willems	15.00
BW	Brandon Wood	25.00
SW	Steven Wright	15.00

Prospect

		NM/M
NA	Nick Adenhart	5.00
EA	Elvis Andrus	15.00
MRA	Michael Aubrey	5.00
JRB	Jimmy Barthmaier	5.00
AJC	Asdrubal Cabrera	6.00
JAC	Jose Campusano	5.00
YC	Yung-Chi Chen	20.00
ADC	Adam Coe	8.00
MC	Michael Collins	8.00
BC	Ben Copeland	5.00
SC	Shaun Cumberland	5.00
CD	Chris Dickerson	5.00
BD	Brent Dlugach	5.00
DF	Dexter Fowler	6.00
JF	Juan Francia	5.00
JKF	Jeff Frazier	5.00
YG	Yovani Gallardo	8.00
MG	Mat Gamel	5.00
SGG	Steve Garrabrants	8.00
DIH	Diory Hernandez	5.00
MH	Michael Hollimon	5.00
JJ	Jason Jaramillo	5.00
BJ	Brandon Jones	5.00
RK	Ryan Klosterman	8.00
JTL	Jared Lansford	5.00
RL	Radhames Liz	8.00
EM	Evan MacLane	5.00
DM	Dustin Majewski	6.00
SM	Stephen Marek	5.00
BWM	Brad McCann	5.00
MSM	Mark McLemore	5.00
GLM	Garrett Mock	5.00
SMM	Steve Murphy	5.00
ON	Oswaldo Navarro	5.00
RP	Ryan Patterson	6.00
HP	Hunter Pence	5.00
AP	Andrew Pinckney	8.00
MRR	Max Ramirez	6.00
WR	Wilkin Ramirez	5.00
MR	Mark Reed	5.00
SR	Shawn Riggans	5.00
OS	Omir Santos	5.00
AS	A.J. Shappi	5.00
BJS	B.J. Szymanski	5.00
JT	Jose Tabata	25.00
CMT	Matt Tolbert	8.00
DT	Dallas Trahern	5.00
MT	Mark Trumbo	6.00
WV	Will Venable	5.00
CW	Corey Wimberly	5.00

2007 Bowman

		NM/M
Complete Set (237):		
Common Player:		.15
Common RC (201-220):		.25
Common RC Auto.:		10.00
Pack (10):		3.50
Box (24):		75.00
1	Hanley Ramirez	.50
2	Justin Verlander	.50
3	Ryan Zimmerman	.40
4	Jered Weaver	.50
5	Stephen Drew	.50
6	Jonathan Papelbon	.50
7	Melky Cabrera	.25
8	Francisco Liriano	.25
9	Prince Fielder	.75
10	Dan Uggla	.15
11	Jeremy Sowers	.15
12	Carlos Quentin	.15
13	Chuck James	.15
14	Andre Ethier	.15
15	Cole Hamels	.50
16	Kenji Johjima	.25
17	Chad Bilingsley	.15
18	Ian Kinsler	.25
19	Jason Hirsh	.15
20	Nicholas Markakis	.25
21	Jeremy Hermida	.15
22	Ryan Shealy	.15
23	Scott Olsen	.15
24	Russell Martin	.25
25	Conor Jackson	.15
26	Erik Bedard	.25
27	Brian McCann	.15
28	Michael Barrett	.25
29	Brandon Phillips	.15
30	Garrett Atkins	.25
31	Freddy Garcia	.15
32	Mark Loretta	.15
33	Craig Biggio	.25
34	Jeremy Bonderman	.25
35	Johan Santana	.75
36	Jorge Posada	.40
37	Brian Bannister	.15
38	Carlos Delgado	.50
39	Gary Mathews Jr.	.15
40	Mike Cameron	.15
41	Adrian Beltre	.25
42	Freddy Sanchez	.15
43	Austin Kearns	.15
44	Mark Buehrle	.15
45	Miguel Cabrera	.75
46	Josh Beckett	.25
47	Chone Figgins	.15
48	Edgar Renteria	.25
49	Derek Lowe	.15
50	Ryan Howard	1.50
51	Shawn Green	.15
52	Jason Giambi	.50
53	Ervin Santana	.15
54	Jack Wilson	.15
55	Roy Oswalt	.50
56	Danny Haren	.25
57	Jose Vidro	.15
58	Kevin Millwood	.15
59	Jim Edmonds	.25
60	Carl Crawford	.50
61	Randy Wolf	.15
62	Paul LoDuca	.15
63	Johnny Estrada	.15
64	Brian Roberts	.25
65	Manny Ramirez	.75
66	Jose Contreras	.15
67	Josh Barfield	.15
68	Juan Pierre	.15
69	David DeJesus	.15
70	Gary Sheffield	.40
71	Jon Lieber	.15
72	Randy Johnson	.75
73	Rickie Weeks	.25
74	Brian Giles	.15
75	Ichiro Suzuki	1.00
76	Nick Swisher	.25
77	Justin Morneau	.50
78	Scott Kazmir	.25
79	Lyle Overbay	.15
80	Alfonso Soriano	.75
81	Brandon Webb	.25
82	Joe Crede	.15
83	Corey Patterson	.15
84	Kenny Rogers	.15
85	Ken Griffey Jr.	1.50
86	Cliff Lee	.15
87	Mike Lowell	.15
88	Marcus Giles	.15
89	Orlando Cabrera	.15
90	Derek Jeter	2.00
91	Josh Johnson	.15
92	Carlos Guillen	.15
93	Bill Hall	.25
94	Michael Cuddyer	.15
95	Miguel Tejada	.50
96	Todd Helton	.50
97	C.C. Sabathia	.25
98	Tadahito Iguchi	.15
99	Jose Reyes	.75
100	David Wright	1.00
101	Barry Zito	.25
102	Jake Peavy	.25
103	Richie Sexson	.40
104	A.J. Burnett	.15
105	Eric Chavez	.25
106	Jorge Cantu	.15
107	Grady Sizemore	.50
108	Bronson Arroyo	.15
109	Mike Mussina	.40
110	Magglio Ordonez	.25
111	Anibal Sanchez	.15
112	Jeff Francoeur	.25
113	Kevin Youkilis	.25
114	Aubrey Huff	.15
115	Carlos Zambrano	.25
116	Mark Teahen	.15
117	Carlos Silva	.15
118	Pedro Martinez	.50
119	Hideki Matsui	.75
120	Mike Piazza	.75
121	Jason Schmidt	.25
122	Greg Maddux	1.50
123	Joe Blanton	.15
124	Chris Carpenter	.75
125	David Ortiz	.75
126	Alex Rios	.15
127	Nick Johnson	.15
128	Carlos Lee	.25
129	Pat Burrell	.25
130	Ben Sheets	.25
131	Kazuo Matsui	.15
132	Adam Dunn	.50
133	Jermaine Dye	.25
134	Curt Schilling	.75
135	Chad Tracy	.15
136	Vladimir Guerrero	.75
137	Melvin Mora	.15
138	John Smoltz	.25
139	Craig Monroe	.15
140	Dontrelle Willis	.25
141	Jeff Francis	.15
142	Chipper Jones	.75
143	Frank Thomas	.50
144	Brett Myers	.15
145	Xavier Nady	.15
146	Robinson Cano	.40
147	Jeff Kent	.15
148	Scott Rolen	.50
149	Roy Halladay	.25
150	Joe Mauer	.25
151	Bobby Abreu	.25
152	Matt Cain	.25
153	Hank Blalock	.15
154	Chris Capuano	.15
155	Jake Westbrook	.15
156	Javier Vazquez	.15
157	Garret Anderson	.15
158	Aramis Ramirez	.40
159	Mark Kotsay	.15
160	Matthew Kemp	.15
161	Adrian Gonzalez	.25
162	Felix Hernandez	.25
163	David Eckstein	.15
164	Curtis Granderson	.15
165	Paul Konerko	.25
166	Orlando Hudson	.15
167	Tim Hudson	.25
168	J.D. Drew	.25
169	Chien-Ming Wang	.50
170	Jimmy Rollins	.50
171	Matt Morris	.15
172	Raul Ibanez	.15
173	Mark Teixeira	.40
174	Ted Lilly	.15
175	Albert Pujols	2.00
176	Carlos Beltran	.50
177	Lance Berkman	.40
178	Ivan Rodriguez	.50
179	Torii Hunter	.25
180	Johnny Damon	.50
181	Chase Utley	.75
182	Jason Bay	.40
183	Jeff Weaver	.15
184	Troy Glaus	.25
185	Rocco Baldelli	.15
186	Rafael Furcal	.25
187	Jim Thome	.50
188	Travis Hafner	.40
189	Matt Holliday	.50
190	Andruw Jones	.50
191	Ramon Hernandez	.15
192	Victor Martinez	.25
193	Aaron Hill	.15
194	Michael Young	.25
195	Vernon Wells	.25
196	Mark Mulder	.15
197	Derrek Lee	.50
198	Tom Glavine	.40
199	Chris Young	.25
200	Alex Rodriguez	2.00
201	Delmon Young **(RC)**	.50
202	Alexi Casilla **RC**	.25
203	Shawn Riggans **(RC)**	.25
204	Jeff Baker **(RC)**	.25
205	Hector Gimenez **(RC)**	.25
206	Ubaldo Jimenez **(RC)**	.25
207	Adam Lind **(RC)**	.25
208	Joaquin Arias **(RC)**	.25
209	David Murphy **(RC)**	.25
210	Daisuke Matsuzaka **RC**	10.00
211	Jerry Owens **(RC)**	.25
212	Ryan Sweeney **(RC)**	.25
213	Kei Igawa **RC**	1.00
214	Fred Lewis **(RC)**	.25
215	Philip Humber **(RC)**	.25
216	Kevin Hooper **(RC)**	.25
217	Jeff Fiorentino **(RC)**	.25
218	Michael Bourn **(RC)**	.25
219	Hideki Okajima **RC**	3.00
219	Hideki Okajima/ Aut.o **RC**	50.00
220	Josh Fields **(RC)**	.25
221	Andrew Miller/ Auto. **RC**	40.00
222	Troy Tulowitzki/ Auto. **(RC)**	20.00
223	Ryan Braun/Auto. **RC**	15.00
224	Oswaldo Navarro/ Auto. **RC**	10.00
225	Philip Humber/ Auto. **(RC)**	15.00
226	Mitch Maier/ Auto. **(RC)**	15.00
227	Jerry Owens/ Auto. **(RC)**	15.00
228	Mike Rabelo/Auto. **RC**	20.00
229	Delwyn Young/ Auto. **(RC)**	10.00
230	Miguel Montero/ Auto. **(RC)**	15.00
231	Akinori Iwamura/ Auto. **RC**	30.00
232	Matt Lindstrom/ Auto. **(RC)**	10.00
233	Josh Hamilton/ Auto. **(RC)**	20.00
235	Elijah Dukes/Auto. **RC**	20.00
236	Sean Henn/ Auto. **(RC)**	15.00
237	Barry Bonds	2.00

Chrome Prospects

		NM/M
Complete Set (110):		50.00
Common Player:		.50
Inserted 2:Hobby Pack		
1	Cooper Brannon	1.00
2	Jason Taylor	2.50
3	Shawn O'Malley	1.00
4	Robert Alcombrack	1.00
5	Dellin Betances	4.00
6	Jeremy Papelbon	2.00
7	Adam Carr	1.00
8	Matthew Clarkson	.50
9	Darin McDonald	1.00
10	Brandon Rice	1.00
11	Matthew Sweeney	2.50
12	Scott Deal	.50
13	Brennan Boesch	1.00
14	Scott Taylor	1.00
15	Michael Brantley	2.00
16	Yahmed Yema	1.00
17	Brandon Morrow	5.00
18	Cole Garner	1.00
19	Erik Lis	1.50
20	Lucas French	1.00
21	Aaron Cunningham	3.00
22	Ryan Schreppel	.50
23	Kevin Russo	1.00
24	Yohan Pino	1.00
25	Michael Sullivan	.50
26	Trey Shields	.50
27	Danny Matienzo	.50
28	Chuck Lofgren	2.00
29	Gerrit Simpson	.50
30	David Haehnel	.50
31	Marvin Lowrance	1.00
32	Kevin Ardoin	.50
33	Edwin Maysonet	.50
34	Derek Griffith	.50
35	Sam Fuld	1.00
36	Chase Wright	1.50
37	Brandon Roberts	.50
38	Kyle Aselton	.50
39	Steven Sollmann	1.00
40	Michael Devaney	1.00
41	Charlie Fermaint	.50
42	Jesse Litsch	1.50
43	Bryan Hansen	1.00
44	Ramon Garcia	.50
45	John Otness	1.50
46	Trey Hearne	.50
47	Habelito Hernandez	.50
48	Edgar Garcia	1.50
49	Seth Fortenberry	1.00
50	Reid Brignac	2.00
51	Derek Rodriguez	.50
52	Ervin Alcantara	1.00
53	Tom Hottovy	1.00
54	Jesus Flores	1.00
55	Matt Palmer	.50
56	Brian Henderson	.50
57	John Gragg	.50
58	Jay Garthwaite	1.00
59	Esmerling Vasquez	.50
60	Gilberto Mejia	.50
61	Aaron Jensen	.50
62	Cedric Brooks	.50
63	Brandon Mann	.50
64	Myron Leslie	1.00
65	Ray Aguilar	.50
66	Jesus Guzman	1.00
67	Sean Thompson	.50
68	Jarrett Hoffpauir	1.00
69	Matt Goodson	.50
70	Neal Musser	.50
71	Tony Abreu	4.00
72	Tony Peguero	.50
73	Michael Bertram	1.00
74	Randy Wells	1.00
75	Bradley Davis	.50
76	Jay Sawatski	1.00
77	Vic Buttler	.50
78	Jose Oyervidez	.50
79	Doug Deeds	1.00
80	Daniel Dement	1.00
81	Spike Lundberg	.50
82	Ricardo Nanita	.50
83	Brad Knox	1.00
84	Will Venable	1.00
85	Greg Smith	1.50
86	Pedro Powell	1.00
87	Gabriel Medina	1.00
88	Duke Sardinha	.50
89	Mike Madsen	1.50
90	Rayner Bautista	.50
91	T.J. Nall	.50
92	Neil Sellers	1.00
93	Andrew Dobies	1.00
94	Leo Daigle	.50
95	Brian Duensing	1.50
96	Vincent Blue	1.00
97	Fernando Rodriguez	1.00
98	Derin McMains	.50
99	Adam Bass	1.00
100	Justin Ruggiano	1.50
101	Jared Burton	1.00
102	Mike Parisi	1.00
103	Aaron Peel	1.00
104	Evan Englebrook	1.00
105	Sendy Vasquez	.50
106	Desmond Jennings	3.00
107	Clay Harris	1.00
108	Cody Strait	1.00
109	Ryan Mullins	1.00
110	Ryan Webb	1.00

2007 Bowman Prospects

		NM/M
Complete Set (135):		
Common Player (1-110):		.25
Common Auto. (111-135):		10.00
1	Cooper Brannon	.25
2	Jason Taylor	.75
3	Shawn O'Malley	.25
4	Robert Alcombrack	.25
5	Dellin Betances	1.00
6	Jeremy Papelbon	.50
7	Adam Carr	.25
8	Matthew Clarkson	.25
9	Darin McDonald	.25
10	Brandon Rice	.25
11	Matthew Sweeney	.50
12	Scott Deal	.25
13	Brennan Boesch	.25
14	Scott Taylor	.25
15	Michael Brantley	.50
16	Yahmed Yema	.25
17	Brandon Morrow	1.50
18	Cole Garner	.25
19	Erik Lis	.50
20	Lucas French	.25
21	Aaron Cunningham	1.00
22	Ryan Schreppel	.25
23	Kevin Russo	.25
24	Yohan Pino	.25
25	Michael Sullivan	.25
26	Trey Shields	.25
27	Danny Matienzo	.25
28	Chuck Lofgren	.50
29	Gerrit Simpson	.25
30	David Haehnel	.25
31	Marvin Lowrance	.25
32	Kevin Ardoin	.25
33	Edwin Maysonet	.25
34	Derek Griffith	.25
35	Sam Fuld	.25
36	Chase Wright	.50
37	Brandon Roberts	.25
38	Kyle Aselton	.25
39	Steven Sollmann	.25
40	Michael Devaney	.25
41	Charlie Fermaint	.25
42	Jesse Litsch	.50
43	Bryan Hansen	.25
44	Ramon Garcia	.25
45	John Otness	.50
46	Trey Hearne	.25
47	Habelito Hernandez	.25
48	Edgar Garcia	.50
49	Seth Fortenberry	.25
50	Reid Brignac	.50
51	Derek Rodriguez	.25
52	Ervin Alcantara	.25
53	Tom Hottovy	.25
54	Jesus Flores	.25
55	Matt Palmer	.25
56	Brian Henderson	.25
57	John Gragg	.25
58	Jay Garthwaite	.25
59	Esmerling Vasquez	.25
60	Gilberto Mejia	.25
61	Aaron Jensen	.25
62	Cedric Brooks	.25
63	Brandon Mann	.25
64	Myron Leslie	.25
65	Ray Aguilar	.25
66	Jesus Guzman	.25
67	Sean Thompson	.25
68	Jarrett Hoffpauir	.25
69	Matt Goodson	.25
70	Neal Musser	.25
71	Tony Abreu	1.50
72	Tony Peguero	.25
73	Michael Bertram	.25
74	Randy Wells	.25
75	Bradley Davis	.25
76	Jay Sawatski	.25
77	Vic Buttler	.25
78	Jose Oyervidez	.25
79	Doug Deeds	.25
80	Daniel Dement	.25
81	Spike Lundberg	.25
82	Ricardo Nanita	.25
83	Brad Knox	.25
84	Will Venable	.25
85	Greg Smith	.50
86	Pedro Powell	.25
87	Gabriel Medina	.25
88	Duke Sardinha	.25
89	Mike Madsen	.50
90	Rayner Bautista	.25
91	T.J. Nall	.25
92	Neil Sellers	.25
93	Andrew Dobies	.25
94	Leo Daigle	.25
95	Brian Duensing	.50
96	Vincent Blue	.25
97	Fernando Rodriguez	.25
98	Derin McMains	.25
99	Adam Bass	.25
100	Justin Ruggiano	.50
101	Jared Burton	.25
102	Mike Parisi	.25
103	Aaron Peel	.25
104	Evan Englebrook	.25
105	Sendy Vasquez	.25
106	Desmond Jennings	.75
107	Clay Harris	.25
108	Cody Strait	.25
109	Ryan Mullins	.25
110	Ryan Webb	.25
111	Kyle Drabek	20.00
112	Evan Longoria	30.00
113	Tyler Colvin	20.00
114	Matt Long	10.00
115	Jeremy Jeffress	15.00
116	Kasey Kiker	15.00
117	Hank Conger	15.00
118	Cody Johnson	15.00
119	David Huff	15.00
120	Tommy Hickman	10.00
121	Chris Parmelee	20.00
122	Dustin Evans	10.00
123	Brett Sinkbeil	10.00
124	Andrew Carpenter	15.00
125	Colton Willems	10.00
126	Matt Antonelli	15.00
127	Marcus Sanders	15.00
128	Joshua Rodriguez	15.00
129	Keith Weiser	20.00
130	Chad Tracy	15.00
131	Matthew Sulentic	20.00
132	Adam Ottavino	15.00
133	Jarrod Saltalamacchia	25.00
134	Kyle Blanks	15.00
135	Brad Eldred	10.00

Chrome Prospects Refractor

Refractor (1-110): 2-4X
Production 500 Sets

Chrome Prospects Blue Refractor

Blue Refractor (1-110): 4-6X
Production 150 Sets

Chrome Prospects Gold Refractor

Gold Refractor (1-110): 10-20X
Production 50 Sets

Chrome Prospects Orange Refractor

Orange Refractor (1-110): No Pricing
Production 25 Sets

Chrome Prospects Red Refractor

Red Refractor (1-110): No Pricing
Production Five Sets

Chrome Prospects SuperFractor

Superfractor (1-110): No Pricing
Production One Set

Chrome Prospects X-Fractor

X-Fractor (1-110): 3-6X
Production 275 Sets

Printing Plates

No Pricing
Production one set per color.

Orange

Orange: 3-6X
Orange RC Auto.: 1-1.5X
Production 250 Sets

Blue

Blue: 2-4X
Blue RC Auto.: 1X
Production 500 Sets

Gold

Gold (1-220): 1-2X
Inserted 1:1

Red

No Pricing
Production One Set

Prospects Orange

Orange (1-110): 3-6X
Orange RC Auto. (111-135): 1-1.5X
Production 250 Sets

Prospects Blue

Blue (1-110): 2-4X
Blue RC Auto. (111-135): 1X
Production 500 Sets

Prospects Red

No Pricing
Production One Set

Prospects Gold

Gold (1-110): 1-2X
Inserted 1:1

Alex Rodriguez Road to 500

NM/M
Common Rodriguez: 2.00
Inserted 2:Box
Autograph: No Pricing
Production One Set

2007 Bowman Signs of the Future

NM/M
KD Kyle Drabek 20.00
DB Dellin Betances 60.00
JBC J. Brent Cox 15.00
JD John Drennen 10.00
DS Denard Span 15.00
KC Koby Clemens 25.00
EH Estee Harris 20.00
MN Mike Neu 15.00
RO Ross Ohlendorf 15.00
CG Chris Getz 10.00
AR Adam Russell 15.00
JC Jesus Cota 10.00
JB John Baker 10.00
BM Brandon Moss 10.00
CS Chad Santos 10.00
KS Kurt Suzuki 10.00
JJ Jair Jurrjens 20.00
MA Mike Aviles 10.00
TT Taylor Teagarden 15.00
SK Shane Komine 15.00
ME Mike Edwards 10.00
MM Matthew Merricks 10.00
JDA Jamie D'Antona 10.00
JBB John Bowker 10.00
CR Chris Robinson 10.00
JW Jared Wells 10.00
BF Ben Fritz 10.00
BB Brian Bixler 10.00
CM Christopher McConnell 10.00
JCB Jordan Brown 15.00
FP Felix Pie 20.00
ER Eric Reed 10.00
AM Andrew McCutchen 20.00
MR Michael Rogers 10.00
RB Reid Brignac 20.00
RG Rich Gardner 10.00
SG Sean Gallagher 10.00
CJS Chris Seddon 10.00

2007 Bowman Chrome

NM/M
Common Player: .25
Common RC: .50
Pack (4): 5.00
Box (18): 85.00
1 Hanley Ramirez .75
2 Justin Verlander .50
3 Ryan Zimmerman .50
4 Jered Weaver .50
5 Stephen Drew .40
6 Jonathan Papelbon .50
7 Melky Cabrera .50
8 Francisco Liriano .25
9 Prince Fielder 1.00
10 Dan Uggla .25
11 Jeremy Sowers .25
12 Carlos Quentin .25
13 Chuck James .25
14 Andre Ethier .25
15 Cole Hamels .50
16 Kenji Johjima .25
17 Chad Billingsley .50
18 Ian Kinsler .50
19 Jason Hirsh .25
20 Nicholas Markakis .50
21 Jeremy Hermida .25
22 Ryan Shealy .25
23 Scott Olsen .25
24 Russell Martin .50
25 Conor Jackson .25
26 Erik Bedard .50
27 Brian McCann .50
28 Michael Barrett .25
29 Brandon Phillips .25
30 Garrett Atkins .50
31 Freddy Garcia .25
32 Mark Loretta .25
33 Craig Biggio .50
34 Jeremy Bonderman .50
35 Johan Santana .75
36 Jorge Posada .75
37 Victor Martinez .50
38 Carlos Delgado .75
39 Gary Matthews .50
40 Mike Cameron .25
41 Adrian Beltre .25
42 Freddy Sanchez .25
43 Austin Kearns .25
44 Mark Buehrle .25
45 Miguel Cabrera 1.00
46 Josh Beckett .75
47 Chone Figgins .50
48 Edgar Renteria .50
49 Derek Lowe .25
50 Ryan Howard 2.00
51 Shawn Green .25
52 Jason Giambi .50
53 Ervin Santana .25
54 Aaron Hill .25
55 Roy Oswalt .50
56 Danny Haren .25
57 Jose Vidro .25
58 Kevin Millwood .25
59 Jim Edmonds .50
60 Carl Crawford .50
61 Randy Wolf .25
62 Paul LoDuca .25
63 Johnny Estrada .25
64 Brian Roberts .50
65 Manny Ramirez 1.00
66 Jose Contreras .25
67 Josh Barfield .25
68 Juan Pierre .25
69 David DeJesus .25
70 Gary Sheffield .75
71 Michael Young .50
72 Randy Johnson .75
73 Rickie Weeks .25
74 Brian Giles .25
75 Ichiro Suzuki 1.50
76 Nick Swisher .50
77 Justin Morneau .75
78 Scott Kazmir .50
79 Lyle Overbay .25
80 Alfonso Soriano 1.00
81 Brandon Webb .50
82 Joe Crede .25
83 Corey Patterson .25
84 Kenny Rogers .25
85 Ken Griffey Jr. 2.00
86 Cliff Lee .25
87 Mike Lowell .50
88 Marcus Giles .25
89 Orlando Cabrera .50
90 Derek Jeter 2.50
91 Ramon Hernandez .25
92 Carlos Guillen .25
93 Bill Hall .25
94 Michael Cuddyer .25
95 Miguel Tejada .75
96 Todd Helton .75
97 C.C. Sabathia .50
98 Tadahito Iguchi .25
99 Jose Reyes 1.00
100 David Wright 1.00
101 Barry Zito .50
102 Jake Peavy .50
103 Richie Sexson .50
104 A.J. Burnett .25
105 Eric Chavez .25
106 Vernon Wells .50
107 Grady Sizemore .75
108 Bronson Arroyo .25
109 Mike Mussina .50
110 Magglio Ordonez .50
111 Anibal Sanchez .25
112 Jeff Francoeur .50
113 Kevin Youkilis .50
114 Aubrey Huff .25
115 Carlos Zambrano .50
116 Mark Teahen .25
117 Mark Mulder .50
118 Pedro Martinez 1.00
119 Hideki Matsui 1.50
120 Mike Piazza 1.00
121 Jason Schmidt .25
122 Greg Maddux 2.00
123 Joe Blanton .25
124 Chris Carpenter .75
125 David Ortiz 1.00
126 Alex Rios .25
127 Nick Johnson .25
128 Carlos Lee .50
129 Pat Burrell .50
130 Ben Sheets .50
131 Derrek Lee .50
132 Adam Dunn .50
133 Jermaine Dye .25
134 Curt Schilling .75
135 Chad Tracy .25
136 Vladimir Guerrero 1.00
137 Melvin Mora .25
138 John Smoltz .50
139 Craig Monroe .25
140 Dontrelle Willis .25
141 Jeff Francis .25
142 Chipper Jones 1.00
143 Frank Thomas 1.00
144 Brett Myers .25
145 Tom Glavine .75
146 Robinson Cano .75
147 Jeff Kent .50
148 Scott Rolen .75
149 Roy Halladay .50
150 Joe Mauer .50
151 Bobby Abreu .50
152 Matt Cain .50
153 Hank Blalock .50
154 Chris Young .50
155 Jake Westbrook .25
156 Javier Vazquez .25
157 Garret Anderson .25
158 Aramis Ramirez .50
159 Mark Kotsay .25
160 Matthew Kemp .50
161 Adrian Gonzalez .50
162 Felix Hernandez .50
163 David Eckstein .25
164 Curtis Granderson .50
165 Paul Konerko .50
166 Alex Rodriguez 2.50
167 Tim Hudson .50
168 J.D. Drew .25
169 Chien-Ming Wang 1.00
170 Jimmy Rollins .75
171 Matt Morris .25
172 Raul Ibanez .25
173 Mark Teixeira .75
174 Ted Lilly .25
175 Albert Pujols 2.50
176 Carlos Beltran 1.00
177 Lance Berkman .50
178 Ivan Rodriguez .75
179 Torii Hunter .50
180 Johnny Damon .75
181 Chase Utley 1.00
182 Jason Bay .50
183 Jeff Weaver .25
184 Troy Glaus .50
185 Rocco Baldelli .25
186 Rafael Furcal .50
187 Jim Thome .75
188 Travis Hafner .50
189 Matt Holliday .50
190 Andruw Jones .50
191 Andrew Miller **RC** 5.00
192 Ryan Braun **RC** .50
193 Oswaldo Navarro **RC** .50
194 Mike Rabelo **RC** .50
195 Delwyn Young **(RC)** .50
196 Miguel Montero **(RC)** .60
197 Matt Lindstrom **(RC)** .50
198 Josh Hamilton **(RC)** 2.00
199 Elijah Dukes **RC** 1.00
200 Sean Henn **(RC)** .50
201 Delmon Young **(RC)** 1.00
202 Alexi Casilla **RC** .50
203 Hunter Pence **(RC)** 10.00
204 Jeff Baker **(RC)** .50
205 Hector Gimenez **(RC)** .50
206 Ubaldo Jimenez **(RC)** .50
207 Adam Lind **(RC)** 1.00
208 Joaquin Arias **(RC)** 1.00
209 David Murphy **(RC)** .50
210 Daisuke Matsuzaka **RC** 8.00
211 Jerry Owens **(RC)** .50
212 Ryan Sweeney **(RC)** .50
213 Kei Igawa **RC** 1.00
214 Mitch Maier **RC** .50
215 Philip Humber **(RC)** 1.00
216 Troy Tulowitzki **(RC)** 2.00
217 Tim Lincecum **RC** 10.00
218 Michael Bourn **(RC)** .50
219 Hideki Okajima **RC** 2.00
220 Josh Fields **(RC)** 1.00

Chrome Prospects

NM/M
Common Player: .50
Common Auto. (221-256): 10.00
BC1 Cooper Brannon 1.00
BC2 Jason Taylor 1.00
BC3 Shawn O'Malley .50
BC4 Robert Alcombrack .50
BC5 Dellin Betances 4.00
BC6 Jeremy Papelbon 1.00
BC7 Adam Carr .50
BC8 Matthew Clarkson .50
BC9 Darin McDonald .50
BC10 Brandon Rice .50
BC11 Matthew Sweeney 3.00
BC12 Scott Deal .50
BC13 Brennan Boesch .50
BC14 Scott Taylor .50
BC15 Michael Brantley 1.00
BC16 Yahmed Yema .50
BC17 Brandon Morrow 1.00
BC18 Cole Garner .50
BC19 Erik Lis 1.00
BC20 Lucas French .50
BC21 Aaron Cunningham 2.00
BC22 Ryan Schreppel .50
BC23 Kevin Russo .50
BC24 Yohan Pino 1.00
BC25 Michael Sullivan 1.00
BC26 Trey Shields 1.00
BC27 Danny Matienzo .50
BC28 Chuck Lofgren .50
BC29 Gerrit Simpson .50
BC30 David Haehnel .50
BC31 Marvin Lowrance .50
BC32 Kevin Ardoin .50
BC33 Edwin Maysonet .50
BC34 Derek Griffith .50
BC35 Sam Fuld 1.00
BC36 Chase Wright 2.00
BC37 Brandon Roberts .50
BC38 Kyle Aselton .50
BC39 Steven Sollmann .50
BC40 Michael Devaney .50
BC41 Charlie Fermaint .50
BC42 Jesse Litsch 1.00
BC43 Bryan Hansen .50
BC44 Ramon Garcia 1.00
BC45 John Otness .50
BC46 Trey Hearne .50
BC47 Habelito Hernandez .50
BC48 Edgar Garcia .50
BC49 Seth Fortenberry .50
BC50 Reid Brignac 1.00
BC51 Derek Rodriguez .50
BC52 Ervin Alcantara .50
BC53 Tom Hottovy .50
BC54 Jesus Flores 1.00
BC55 Matt Palmer .50
BC56 Brian Henderson .50
BC57 John Gragg .50
BC58 Jay Garthwaite .50
BC59 Esmerling Vasquez .50
BC60 Gilberto Mejia 1.00
BC61 Aaron Jensen .50
BC62 Cedric Brooks 1.00
BC63 Brandon Mann .50
BC64 Myron Leslie 1.00
BC65 Ray Aguilar .50
BC66 Jesus Guzman 2.00
BC67 Sean Thompson .50
BC68 Jarrett Hoffpauir 1.00
BC69 Matt Goodson .50
BC70 Neal Musser .50
BC71 Tony Abreu 1.50
BC72 Tony Peguero 1.00
BC73 Michael Bertram .50
BC74 Randy Wells .50
BC75 Bradley Davis .50
BC76 Jay Sawatski .50
BC77 Vic Buttler 1.00
BC78 Jose Oyervidez 1.00
BC79 Doug Deeds 1.00
BC80 Daniel Dement .50
BC81 Spike Lundberg .50
BC82 Ricardo Nanita 1.00
BC83 Brad Knox 1.00
BC84 Will Venable 1.00
BC85 Greg Smith .50
BC86 Pedro Powell .50
BC87 Gabriel Medina .50
BC88 Duke Sardinha .50
BC89 Mike Madsen .50
BC90 Rayner Bautista .50
BC91 T.J. Nall .50
BC92 Neil Sellers .50
BC93 Andrew Dobies .50
BC94 Leo Daigle .50
BC95 Brian Duensing 2.00
BC96 Vincent Blue .50
BC97 Fernando Rodriguez .50
BC98 Derin McMains .50
BC99 Adam Bass .50
BC100 Justin Ruggiano 1.00
BC101 Jared Burton 1.00
BC102 Mike Parisi .50
BC103 Aaron Peel 1.00
BC104 Evan Englebrook .50
BC105 Sendy Vasquez .50
BC106 Desmond Jennings 1.50
BC107 Clay Harris 1.00
BC108 Cody Strait .50
BC109 Ryan Mullins .50
BC110 Ryan Webb .50
BC111 Mike Carp 1.00
BC112 Greg Porter .50
BC113 Joe Ness .50
BC114 Matt Camp .50
BC115 Carlos Fisher .50
BC116 Bryan Bass .50
BC117 Jeff Baisley 1.00
BC118 Burke Badenhop 1.00
BC119 Grant Psomas .50
BC120 Eric Young Jr. 1.00
BC121 Henry Rodriguez 1.00
BC122 Carlos Fernandez 1.00
BC123 Chris Errecart 1.00
BC124 Brandon Hynick 1.50
BC125 Jose Constanza .50
BC126 Steve Delabar .50
BC127 Raul Barron .50
BC128 Nick DeBarr .50
BC129 Reegie Corona 1.00
BC130 Thomas Fairchild .50
BC131 Bryan Byrne .50
BC132 Kurt Mertins .50
BC133 Erik Averill .50
BC134 Matt Young .50
BC135 Ryan Rogowski .50
BC136 Andrew Bailey 2.00
BC137 Jonathan Van Every .50
BC138 Scott Shoemaker .50
BC139 Steve Singleton .50
BC140 Mitch Atkins .50
BC141 Robert Rohrbaugh 1.00
BC142 Ole Sheldon .50
BC143 Adam Ricks .50
BC144 Daniel Mayora 1.50
BC145 Johnny Cueto 15.00
BC146 Jim Fasano .50
BC147 Jared Goedert 1.50
BC148 Jonathan Ash .50
BC149 Derek Miller .50
BC150 Juan Miranda 1.50
BC151 J.R. Mathes .50
BC152 Craig Cooper .50
BC153 Drew Locke .50
BC154 Michael MacDonald .50
BC155 Ryan Norwood .50
BC156 Tony Butler 1.50
BC157 Pat Dobson .50
BC158 Cody Ehlers .50
BC159 Dan Fournier .50
BC160 Joe Gaetti .50
BC161 Mark Wagner 1.50
BC162 Tommy Hanson 2.00
BC163 Sharlon Schoop .50
BC164 Woods Fines .50
BC165 Chad Boyd .50
BC166 Kala Kaaihu 2.00
BC167 Chris Salamida 1.00
BC168 Brendan Katin 1.00
BC169 Terrance Blunt .50
BC170 Tobi Stoner 1.00
BC171 Phil Coke .50
BC172 O.D. Gonzalez .50
BC173 Christopher Cody .50
BC174 Cedric Hunter 2.00
BC175 Whit Robbins .50
BC176 Chris Begg .50
BC177 Nathan Southard .50
BC178 Dan Brauer .50
BC179 Jared Keel .50
BC180 Chance Douglass 1.00
BC181 Daniel Murphy 1.00
BC182 Anthony Hatch .50
BC183 Justin Byler 1.00
BC184 Scott Lewis .50
BC185 Andrew Fie 1.00
BC186 Chorye Spoone 1.00
BC187 Cole Bruce .50
BC188 Adam Cowart 1.00
BC189 Chris Nowak .50
BC190 Gorkys Hernandez 5.00
BC191 Devin Ivany .50
BC192 Jordan Smith .50
BC193 Philip Britton .50
BC194 Cole Gillespie 1.00
BC195 Brett Anderson 2.00
BC196 Joe Mather 1.00
BC197 Eddie Degerman .50
BC198 Ronald Prettyman .50
BC199 Patrick Reilly .50
BC200 Tyler Clippard 1.00
BC201 Nick Van Stratten .50
BC202 Todd Redmond .50
BC203 Michael Martinez .50
BC204 Alberto Bastardo .50
BC205 Vasili Spanos .50
BC206 Shane Benson .50
BC207 Brent Johnson .50
BC208 Brett Campbell .50
BC209 Dustin Martin .50
BC210 Chris Carter 4.00
BC211 Alfred Joseph .50
BC212 Carlos Leon .50
BC213 Gabriel Sanchez 1.00
BC214 Carlos Corporan .50
BC215 Emerson Frostad .50
BC216 Karl Gelinas .50
BC217 Ryan Finan .50
BC218 Noe Rodriguez .50
BC219 Archie Gilbert .50
BC220 Jeff Locke 3.00
BC221 Fernando Martinez 100.00
BC222 Jeremy Papelbon 20.00
BC223 Ryan Adams 10.00
BC224 Chris Perez 10.00
BC225 J.R. Towles 30.00
BC226 Tommy Mendoza 15.00
BC227 Jeff Samardzija 40.00
BC228 Sergio Perez 20.00
BC229 Justin Reed 20.00
BC230 Luke Hochevar 30.00
BC231 Ivan DeJesus 20.00
BC232 Kevin Mulvey 30.00
BC233 Chris Coghlan 20.00
BC234 Trevor Cahill 40.00
BC235 Peter Bourjos 20.00
BC236 Joba Chamberlain 180.00
BC237 Josh Rodriguez 15.00
BC238 Tim Lincecum 100.00
BC239 Josh Papelbon 20.00
BC240 Greg Reynolds 25.00
BC241 Wes Hodges 25.00
BC242 Chad Reineke 20.00
BC243 Emmanuel Burriss 20.00
BC244 Henry Sosa 25.00
BC245 Cesar Nicolas 15.00
BC246 Young Il Jung 20.00
BC247 Eric Patterson 15.00
BC248 Hunter Pence 40.00
BC249 Dellin Betances 60.00
BC250 Will Venable 20.00
BC251 Zach McAllister 25.00
BC252 Mark Hamilton 20.00
BC253 Paul Estrada 15.00
BC254 Brad Lincoln 20.00
BC255 Cedric Hunter 50.00
BC256 Chad Rodgers 20.00

Printing Plates

Production One Set

Refractors

Refractor (1-190): 2-4X
Refractor RC (191-220): 1.5-2X
Inserted 4:Box

X-Fractor

X-Fractor (1-190): 3-5X
X-Fractor RC (191-220): 2-4X
Production 250 Sets

Blue Refractor

Blue Refractor (1-190): 4-6X
Blue Refractor RC (191-220): 3-5X
Production 150 Sets

2007 Bowman Chrome Gold Refractor

Gold Refractor (1-190): 10-15X
Gold Refractor RC (191-220): 8-15X
Production 50 Sets

Orange Refractor

Orange Refractor (1-190): 10-20X
Orange Refractor RC (191-220): 10-20X
Production 25 Sets

Red Refractor

Production Five Sets

Super-Fractor

Production One Set

Chrome Prospects Refractor

Refractor (1-200): 3-5X
Refractor Auto. (201-256): 1-1.5X
Production 500 Sets

Chrome Prospects X-Fractor

X-Fractor (1-200): 4-8X
Production 250 Sets
X-Fractor Auto. (201-256): 1-2X
Production 225 Sets

Chrome Prospects Blue Refractor

Blue Refractor (1-200): 5-10X
Blue Refractor Auto. (201-256): 1.5-2.5X
Production 150 Sets

Chrome Prospects Gold Refractor

Gold Refractor (1-200): 15-25X
Gold Refractor Auto. (201-256): 3-5X
Production 50 Sets

Chrome Prospects Orange Refractor

Orange Refractor (1-200): No Pricing
Orange Refract Auto. (201-256): No Pricing
Production 25 Sets

Chrome Prospects Red Refractor

No Pricing
Production Five Sets

2007 Bowman Heritage

NM/M
Complete Set (251):
Common Player (1-200): .25
Common RC (201-251): .50
Common SP: 3.00
Inserted 1:3
SP's don't have Auto. on front.
Pack (8):
Box (24):
1 Jeff Francoeur .50
2 Jered Weaver .40
3 Derrek Lee .50
4 Todd Helton .50
5 Shawn Hill .25
6 Ivan Rodriguez .50
7 Mickey Mantle 5.00
8 Ramon Hernandez .25
9 Randy Johnson .75
10 Jermaine Dye .25
11 Brian Roberts .40
12 Hank Blalock .40
13 Chien-Ming Wang .75
14 Mike Lowell .50
15 Brandon Webb .50
16 Kelly Johnson .25
17 Nick Johnson .25
18 Zach Duke .25
19 Aaron Hill .25
20 Miguel Tejada .50
21 Mark Buehrle .40
22 Michael Young .40
23 Carlos Delgado .50
24 Anibal Sanchez .25
25 Vladimir Guerrero .75
26 Russell Martin .40
27 Lance Berkman .40
28 Bobby Crosby .25
29 Javier Vazquez .25
30 Manny Ramirez .75
31 Rich Hill .25
32 Mike Sweeney .25
33 Jeff Kent .40

34 Noah Lowry .25
35 Alfonso Soriano .75
36 Paul LoDuca .25
37 J.D. Drew .25
38 C.C. Sabathia .50
39 Craig Biggio .40
40 Adam Dunn .50
41 Josh Beckett .50
42 Carlos Guillen .25
43 Jeff Francis .25
44 Orlando Hudson .25
45 Grady Sizemore .75
46 Jason Jennings .25
47 Mark Teixeira .50
48 Freddy Garcia .25
49 Adrian Gonzalez .40
50 Albert Pujols 2.00
51 Tom Glavine .50
52 J.J. Hardy .40
53 Bobby Abreu .40
54 Bartolo Colon .25
55 Garrett Atkins .40
56 Moises Alou .40
57 Cliff Lee .25
58 Mike Cuddyer .25
59 Brandon Phillips .40
60 Jeremy Bonderman .40
61 Rickie Weeks .40
62 Chris Carpenter .50
63 Frank Thomas .75
64 Victor Martinez .50
65 Dontrelle Willis .40
66 Jim Thome .50
67 Aaron Rowand .40
68 Andy Pettitte .50
69 Brian McCann .40
70 Roger Clemens 2.00
71 Gary Matthews .25
72 Bronson Arroyo .25
73 Jeremy Hermida .25
74 Eric Chavez .40
75 David Ortiz .75
76 Stephen Drew .50
77 Ronnie Belliard .25
78 James Shields .25
79 Richie Sexson .40
80 Johan Santana .75
81 Orlando Cabrera .25
82 Aramis Ramirez .50
83 Greg Maddux 1.00
84 Reggie Sanders .25
85 Carlos Zambrano .50
86 Bengie Molina .25
87 David DeJesus .25
88 Adam Wainwright .40
89 Conor Jackson .25
90 David Wright 1.00
91 Ryan Garko .25
92 Bill Hall .25
93 Marcus Giles .25
94 Kenny Rogers .25
95 Joe Mauer .40
96 Hanley Ramirez .75
97 Brian Giles .25
98 Danny Haren .25
99 Robinson Cano .50
100 Ryan Howard 1.00
101 Andruw Jones .40
102 Aaron Harang .25
103 Hideki Matsui 1.50
104 Nick Swisher .40
105 Pedro Martinez .75
106 Felipe Lopez .25
107 Erik Bedard .25
108 Rafael Furcal .40
109 Curt Schilling .50
110 Jose Reyes .75
111 Adam LaRoche .40
112 Mike Mussina .50
113 Melvin Mora .25
114 Zack Greinke .25
115 Justin Morneau .75
116 Ervin Santana .25
117 Ken Griffey Jr. 1.50
118 David Eckstein .25
119 Jamie Moyer .25
120 Jorge Posada .50
121 Justin Verlander .50
122 Sammy Sosa .75
123 Jason Schmidt .25
124 Josh Willingham .25
125 Roy Oswalt .50
126 Travis Hafner .40
127 John Maine .40
128 Willy Taveras .25
129 Magglio Ordonez .50
130 Barry Zito .40
131 Prince Fielder 1.00
132 Michael Barrett .25
133 Livan Hernandez .25
134 Troy Glaus .40
135 Rocco Baldelli .40
136 Jason Giambi .50
137 Austin Kearns .25
138 Dan Uggla .25
139 Pat Burrell .40
140 Carlos Beltran .50
141 Carlos Quentin .25
142 Johnny Estrada .25
143 Torii Hunter .40
144 Carlos Lee .50
145 Mike Piazza .75
146 Mark Teahen .25
147 Juan Pierre .40
148 Paul Konerko .50
149 Freddy Sanchez .25
150 Derek Jeter 2.00
151 Orlando Hernandez .25
152 Raul Ibanez .25
153 John Smoltz .50
154 Scott Rolen .50
155 Jimmy Rollins .50
156 A.J. Burnett .25
157 Jason Varitek .50
158 Ben Sheets .40
159 Matt Cain .40
160 Carl Crawford .40
161 Jeff Suppan .25
162 Tadahito Iguchi .25
163 Kevin Millwood .25
164 Chris Duncan .25
165 Rich Harden .25
166 Joe Crede .25
167 Chipper Jones .75
168 Gary Sheffield .50
169 Cole Hamels .50
170 Jason Bay .40
171 Jhonny Peralta .40
172 Aubrey Huff .25
173 Xavier Nady .25
174 Kazuo Matsui .25
175 Vernon Wells .40
176 Johnny Damon .50
177 Jim Edmonds .40
178 Jose Vidro .25
179 Garret Anderson .25
180 Alex Rios .40
181 Ichiro Suzuki 1.50
181 Ichiro Suzuki/SP 6.00
182 Jake Peavy .50
182 Jake Peavy/SP 4.00
183 Ian Kinsler .50
183 Ian Kinsler/SP 3.00
184 Tom Gorzelanny .25
184 Tom Gorzelanny/SP 3.00
185 Miguel Cabrera .75
185 Miguel Cabrera/SP 5.00
186 Scott Kazmir .40
186 Scott Kazmir/SP 3.00
187 Matt Holliday .50
187 Matt Holliday/SP 5.00
188 Roy Halladay .50
188 Roy Halladay/SP 4.00
189 Ryan Zimmerman .50
189 Ryan Zimmerman/SP 4.00
190 Alex Rodriguez 2.00
190 Alex Rodriguez/SP 8.00
191 Kenji Johjima .25
191 Kenji Johjima/SP 3.00
192 Gil Meche .25
192 Gil Meche/SP 3.00
193 Chase Utley .75
193 Chase Utley/SP 5.00
194 Jeremy Sowers .25
194 Jeremy Sowers/SP 3.00
195 John Lackey .25
195 John Lackey/SP 3.00
196 Nick Markakis .50
196 Nick Markakis/SP 4.00
197 Tim Hudson .40
197 Tim Hudson/SP 3.00
198 B.J. Upton .50
198 B.J. Upton/SP 4.00
199 Felix Hernandez .50
199 Felix Hernandez/SP 4.00
200 Barry Bonds 2.00
200 Barry Bonds/SP 8.00
201 Jarrod Saltalamacchia **(RC)** .50
202 Tim Lincecum **RC** 5.00
203 Kory Casto **(RC)** .50
204 Sean Henn **(RC)** .50
205 Hector Gimenez **(RC)** .50
206 Homer Bailey **(RC)** 1.00
207 Yunel Escobar **(RC)** .50
208 Matt Lindstrom **(RC)** .50
209 Tyler Clippard **(RC)** .50
210 Joe Smith **RC** .50
211 Tony Abreu **RC** .50
212 Billy Butler **(RC)** 1.00
213 Gustavo Molina **RC** .50
214 Brian Stokes **(RC)** .50
215 Kevin Slowey **(RC)** .50
216 Curtis Thigpen **(RC)** .50
217 Carlos Gomez **RC** 2.00
218 Rick Vanden Hurk **RC** .50
219 Michael Bourn **(RC)** .50
220 Jeff Baker **(RC)** .50
221 Andy LaRoche **(RC)** 1.00
222 Andrew Sonnanstine **RC** .50
223 Chase Wright **RC** .50
224 Mark Reynolds **RC** 2.00
225 Matt Chico **(RC)** .50
226 Hunter Pence **(RC)** 2.00
226 Hunter Pence/SP 6.00
227 John Danks **(RC)** .50
227 John Danks/SP 3.00
228 Elijah Dukes **RC** .50
228 Elijah Dukes/SP 3.00
229 Kei Igawa **RC** 1.00
229 Kei Igawa/SP 4.00
230 Felix Pie **(RC)** .75
230 Felix Pie/SP 3.00
231 Jesus Flores **RC** .50
231 Jesus Flores/SP 3.00
232 Dallas Braden **RC** .50
232 Dallas Braden/SP 3.00
233 Akinori Iwamura **RC** 1.00
233 Akinori Iwamura/SP 4.00
234 Ryan Braun **(RC)** 2.50
234 Ryan Braun/SP 8.00
235 Alex Gordon **RC** 2.00
235 Alex Gordon/SP 6.00
236 Micah Owings **(RC)** .50
236 Micah Owings/SP 3.00
237 Kevin Kouzmanoff **(RC)** .75
237 Kevin Kouzmanoff/SP 3.00
238 Glen Perkins **(RC)** .50
238 Glen Perkins/SP 3.00
239 Danny Putnam **(RC)** .50
239 Danny Putnam/SP 3.00
240 Phil Hughes **(RC)** 2.00
240 Phil Hughes/SP 6.00
241 Ryan Sweeney **(RC)** .50
241 Ryan Sweeney/SP 3.00
242 Josh Hamilton **(RC)** 1.00
242 Josh Hamilton/SP 4.00
243 Hideki Okajima **RC** 1.00
243 Hideki Okajima/SP 4.00
244 Adam Lind **(RC)** .50
244 Adam Lind/SP 3.00
245 Travis Buck **(RC)** .50
245 Travis Buck/SP 3.00
246 Miguel Montero **(RC)** .50
246 Miguel Montero/SP 3.00
247 Brandon Morrow **RC** 1.00
247 Brandon Morrow/SP 4.00
248 Troy Tulowitzki **(RC)** 2.00
248 Troy Tulowitzki/SP 6.00
249 Delmon Young **(RC)** 1.00
249 Delmon Young/SP 4.00
250 Daisuke Matsuzaka **RC** 5.00
250 Daisuke Matsuzaka/SP 15.00
251 Joba Chamberlain **RC** 10.00

Signs of Greatness

NM/M
Common Autograph: 8.00
Black: 1.5-2X
Production 52 Sets
Red: No Pricing
Production One Set
DW David Wright 75.00
CJ Chipper Jones 50.00
CC Carl Crawford 15.00
CH Cole Hamels 30.00
JH J.P. Howell 8.00
BJ Blake Johnson 15.00
JP Jorge Posada 35.00
NR Nolan Reimold 15.00
CA Carlos Arroyo 15.00
JB John Buck 15.00
JC Jorge Cantu 8.00
GM Garrett Mock 10.00
AO Adam Ottavino 20.00
RD Rajai Davis 8.00
MM Matt Maloney 10.00
WJB Joe Benson 15.00
JCB Jordan Brown 20.00
TG Tony Giarratano 8.00
GG Glenn Gibson 15.00
EJ Elliot Johnson 10.00
JM Jeff Manship 20.00
SS Scott Sizemore 15.00
MT Mike Thompson 8.00
SE Stephen Englund 10.00
AF Andrew Fie 15.00
SJ Seth Johnston 10.00
SK Sean Kazmar 10.00
JL Jeff Locke 20.00
SP Steve Pearce 30.00
CS Chorye Spoone 15.00
WCS Cody Strait 10.00
JT J.R. Towles 15.00
JW Johnny Whittleman 10.00

Prospects

NM/M
Common Prospect: .50
Inserted 2:Pack
Black: 10-15X
Production 52 Sets
Red: No Pricing
Production One Set
1 Thomas Fairchild .50
2 Peter Bourjos .50
3 Brett Campbell .50
4 Cesar Nicolas .50
5 Kala Kaaihu 1.00
6 Zach McAllister 1.00
7 Chad Reineke .50
8 Anthony Hatch .50
9 Cedric Hunter 1.00
10 Chris Carter 1.50
11 Tommy Hanson 2.00
12 Dellin Betances 2.00
13 John Otness .50
14 Derin McMains .50
15 Greg Reynolds .50
16 Jonathan Van Every .50
17 Eddie Degerman .50
18 Cody Strait .50
19 Noe Rodriguez .50
20 Young-Il Jung .50
21 Reegie Corona 1.00
22 Carlos Corporan .50
23 Chance Douglass .50
24 Leo Daigle .50
25 Jeff Samardzija 2.00
26 Mark Wagner .50
27 Chuck Lofgren 1.00
28 Bryan Byrne 1.00
29 Daniel Mayora 1.00
30 Gorkys Hernandez 2.00
31 Joshua Rodriguez .50
32 Brad Knox .50
33 Scott Lewis .50
34 Joe Gaetti .50
35 Mike Saunders .50
36 Brendan Katin .50
37 Brennan Boesch .50
38 Jay Garthwaite .50
39 Michael Devaney .50
40 J.R. Towles 1.50
41 Joe Ness 1.00
42 Michael Martinez 1.00
43 Justin Byler 1.00
44 Chris Coghlan 1.00
45 Eric Young Jr. 1.00
46 J.R. Mathes 1.00
47 Ivan DeJesus Jr. .50
48 Woods Fines .50
49 Andrew Fie .50
50 Luke Hochevar 2.00
51 Will Venable .50
52 Todd Redmond .50
53 Matthew Sweeney .50
54 Trevor Cahill 2.00
55 Mike Carp .50
56 Henry Sosa .50
57 Emerson Frostad .50
58 Jeremy Jeffress 1.00
59 Whit Robbins .50
60 Joba Chamberlain 10.00
61 Raul Barron .50
62 Aaron Cunningham 1.00
63 Greg Smith 1.00
64 Jeff Baisley .50
65 Vic Buttler .50
66 Steve Singleton .50
67 Josh Papelbon 1.00
68 Ryan Finan .50
69 Deolis Guerra 1.50
70 Vasili Spanos 1.00
71 Patrick Reilly .50
72 Tom Hottovy 1.00
73 Daniel Murphy .50
74 Matt Young 1.00
75 Brian Bocock 1.00
76 Chris Salamida .50
77 Nathan Southard .50
78 Brandon Hynick 1.50
79 Chris Nowak .50
80 Reid Brignac 1.00
81 Cole Garner .50
82 Nick Van Stratten 1.00
83 Jeremy Papelbon 1.00
84 Jarrett Hoffpauir .50
85 Kevin Mulvey 1.00
86 Matt Miller .50
87 Devin Ivany 1.00
88 Marcus Sanders .50
89 Michael MacDonald .50
90 Gabriel Sanchez .50
91 Ryan Norwood .50
92 Jim Fasano .50
93 Ryan Adams .50
94 Evan Englebrook .50
95 Juan Miranda 2.00
96 Greg Porter .50
97 Shane Benson .50
98 Sam Fuld 1.00
99 Cooper Brannon .50
100 Fernando Martinez 4.00

Mickey Mantle Shortprints

NM/M
Complete Set (5): 40.00
Common Mantle: 10.00
Black: 4-8X
Production 52 Sets
Red: No Pricing
Production One Set
1-5 Mickey Mantle 10.00

Rainbow

Rainbow: 1-2X
Rainbow SP's: .5-1X
Inserted 1:1

Red

Production One Set

Black

Black: 10-15X
Black SP's: 3-5X
Production 52 Sets

Printing Plates

Production one set per color.

A-Rod Road to 500

NM/M
Common A-Rod (351-375): 2.00
Inserted 2:Box
Autograph: No Pricing
Production One Set

Box Topper

NM/M
Common Player: 3.00
Inserted 1:Box
1 Alex Rodriguez 10.00
2 Barry Bonds 10.00
3 Ryan Howard 6.00
4 David Wright 6.00
5 Ichiro Suzuki 6.00
6 Hideki Matsui 6.00
7 Mickey Mantle 15.00
8 Manny Ramirez 3.00
9 David Ortiz 4.00
10 Vladimir Guerrero 3.00
11 Jose Reyes 5.00
12 Albert Pujols 10.00
13 Alfonso Soriano 3.00
14 Matt Holliday 3.00
15 Miguel Cabrera 3.00
16 Phil Hughes 8.00
17 Daisuke Matsuzaka 10.00
18 Delmon Young 3.00
19 Troy Tulowitzki 5.00
20 Felix Pie 3.00
21 Alex Gordon 8.00
22 Hunter Pence 5.00
23 Akinori Iwamura 3.00
24 Josh Hamilton 3.00
25 Kei Igawa 3.00

Pieces of Greatness

NM/M
Common Player: 4.00
Black: 2-3X
Production 52 Sets
Red: No Pricing
RB Rocco Baldelli 4.00
LB Lance Berkman 6.00
CB Craig Biggio 6.00
JB Jeremy Bonderman 4.00
BB Barry Bonds 20.00
MC Miguel Cabrera 8.00
RC Robinson Cano 8.00
RC2 Robinson Cano 8.00
EC Eric Chavez 4.00
BC Bobby Crosby 4.00
JD Johnny Damon 8.00
JDD J.D. Drew 4.00
AD Adam Dunn 6.00
JE Juan Encarnacion 4.00
DE Darin Erstad 4.00
AE Andre Ethier 4.00
JF Jeff Francoeur 10.00
JFR Jeff Francis 4.00
RF Rafael Furcal 4.00
BG Brian Giles 4.00
AG Alex Gonzalez 4.00
LG Luis Gonzalez 4.00
SG Shawn Green 4.00
VG Vladimir Guerrero 8.00
CH Cole Hamels 10.00
RH Rich Harden 4.00
TH Todd Helton 8.00
TH2 Todd Helton 8.00
THU Tim Hudson 6.00
TI Tadahito Iguchi 4.00
AJ Andruw Jones 6.00
JK Jeff Kent 4.00
PK Paul Konerko 6.00
PK2 Paul Konerko 6.00
CK Corey Koskie 4.00
AL Adam LaRoche 4.00
BL Brad Lidge 4.00
ML Mike Lowell 6.00
GM Greg Maddux 10.00
HM Hideki Matsui 15.00
JM Joe Mauer 6.00
YM Yadier Molina 4.00
MM Mark Mulder 4.00
TN Trot Nixon 4.00
MO Magglio Ordonez 4.00
DO David Ortiz 8.00
DO2 David Ortiz 8.00
CP Corey Patterson 4.00
MP Mike Piazza 8.00
AR Aramis Ramirez 8.00
MR Manny Ramirez 8.00
MR2 Manny Ramirez 8.00
JR Jose Reyes 10.00
ARO Alex Rodriguez 15.00
IR Ivan Rodriguez 6.00
CS Curt Schilling 8.00
GS Gary Sheffield 6.00
GSI Grady Sizemore 10.00
NS Nick Swisher 4.00
MT Mark Teixeira 8.00
MTE Miguel Tejada 6.00
FT Frank Thomas 8.00
CU Chase Utley 8.00
TW Tim Wakefield 4.00
DW Dontrelle Willis 4.00
DWR David Wright 10.00
4.00
BZ Barry Zito 4.00
CBE Carlos Beltran 8.00
CT Chad Tracy 4.00

2007 Bowman Draft

NM/M
Complete Set (54): 15.00
Common RC: .25
Pack (7): 3.00
Box (24): 65.00
1 Travis Buck **(RC)** .25
2 Matt Chico **(RC)** .25
3 Justin Upton **RC** 1.00
4 Chase Wright **RC** .50
5 Kevin Kouzmanoff **(RC)** .25
6 John Danks **RC** .25
7 Alejandro De Aza **RC** .25
8 Jamie Vermilyea **RC** .25
9 Jesus Flores **RC** .25
10 Glen Perkins **(RC)** .25
11 Tim Lincecum **RC** 1.00
12 Cameron Maybin **RC** 1.00
13 Brandon Morrow **RC** .25
14 Mike Rabelo **RC** .25
15 Alex Gordon **RC** 1.00
16 Zack Segovia **(RC)** .25
17 Jon Knott **(RC)** .25
18 Joba Chamberlain **RC** 2.50
19 Danny Putnam **(RC)** .25
20 Matt DeSalvo **(RC)** .25
21 Fred Lewis **(RC)** .25
22 Sean Gallagher **(RC)** .25
23 Brandon Wood **(RC)** .25
24 Dennis Dove **(RC)** .25
25 Hunter Pence **(RC)** 1.00
26 Jarrod Saltalamacchia **(RC)** .25
27 Ben Francisco **(RC)** .25
28 Doug Slaten **RC** .25
29 Tony Abreu **RC** .25
30 Billy Butler **(RC)** .50
31 Jesse Litsch **RC** .25
32 Nate Schierholtz **(RC)** .25
33 Jared Burton **RC** .25
34 Matt Brown **RC** .25
35 Dallas Braden **RC** .25
36 Carlos Gomez **RC** .50
37 Brian Stokes **(RC)** .25
38 Kory Casto **(RC)** .25
39 Mark McLemore **(RC)** .25
40 Andy LaRoche **(RC)** .50
41 Tyler Clippard **(RC)** .25
42 Curtis Thigpen **(RC)** .25
43 Yunel Escobar **(RC)** .25
44 Andrew Sonnanstine **RC** .25
45 Felix Pie **(RC)** .25
46 Homer Bailey **(RC)** .50
47 Kyle Kendrick **RC** .25
48 Angel Sanchez **RC** .25
49 Phil Hughes **(RC)** 1.00
50 Ryan Braun **(RC)** 1.00
51 Kevin Slowey **(RC)** .25
52 Brendan Ryan **(RC)** .25
53 Yovani Gallardo **(RC)** .50
54 Mark Reynolds **RC** .25
237 Barry Bonds 1.00

Blue

Blue: 2-4X
Production 399 Sets

Gold

Gold: 1-2X
Inserted 1:1

Red

Production One Set

Printing Plates

No Pricing
Production one set per color.

Draft Picks Blue

Blue: 2-4X
Production 399 Sets

Draft Picks Gold

Gold: 1-2X
Inserted 1:1

Draft Picks Red

No Pricing
Production One Set

Draft Picks Printing Plates

Production one set per color.

Future's Game Prospects Blue

Blue: 2-4X
Production 399 Sets

Future's Game Prospects Gold

Gold: 1-2X
Inserted 1:1

Future's Game Prospects Red

No Pricing
Production One Set

Future's Game Prospect Printing Plate

Production one set per color.

Head of the Class Dual Autograph

NM/M
Production 174 Sets
Refractor: 1-1.5X
Production 50 Sets
Gold Refractor: No Pricing
Production 25 Sets
SuperFractor: No Pricing
Production One Set

GH Jonathan Gilmore, Jason Heyward 100.00
HP Luke Hochevar, David Price 100.00

Refractor

Refractor: 2-3X
Inserted 1:11

Blue Refractor

Blue Refractor: 3-5X
Production 199 Sets

Gold Refractor

Gold Refractor: 8-15X
Production 50 Sets

Orange Refractor

Orange Refractor: No Pricing
Production 25 Sets

Red Refractor

No Pricing
Production Five Sets

Draft SuperFractor

No Pricing
Production One Set

Draft X-Fractor

X-Fractor: 3-4X
Production 299 Sets

Draft Picks Blue Refractor

Blue Refract.(1-65): 6-12X
Production 199
Blue Refr. Auto. (111-140): 2-3X
Production 150 Sets

Draft Picks Gold Refractor

Gold Refract.(1-65): 20-30X
Gold Refr. Auto. (111-140): 4-8X
Production 50 Sets

Draft Picks Orange Refractor

No Pricing
Production 25 Sets

Draft Picks Printing Plate

No Pricing
Production one set per color.

Draft Picks Red Refractor

No Pricing
Production Five Sets

Draft Picks Refractor

Refractor (1-65): 2-4X
Inserted 1:11
Refractor Auto. (111-140): 1-1.5X
Production 500 for autos.

Draft Picks X-Fractor

X-Fractor (1-65): 4-8X
Production 299
X-Fractor Auto. (111-140): 1-2X
Production 225

Draft Picks SuperFractor

No Pricing
Production One Set

Draft Future's Game Blue Refractor

Blue Refractor: 3-5X
Production 199 Sets

Draft Future's Game Gold Refractor

Gold Refractor: 8-15X
Production 50 Sets

Draft Future's Game Orange Refractor

No Pricing
Production 25 Sets

Draft Future's Game Red Refractor

No Pricing
Production Five Sets

Draft Future's Game Refractor

Refractor: 2-3X
Inserted 1:11

Draft Future's Game Superfractor

No Pricing
Production One Set

Draft Future's Game X-Fractor

X-Fractor: 3-4X
Production 299 Sets

2007 Bowman Chrome Draft

NM/M
Complete Set (54): 25.00
Common RC: .50
1 Travis Buck **(RC)** .50
2 Matt Chico **(RC)** .50
3 Justin Upton **RC** 2.50
4 Chase Wright **RC** 1.00
5 Kevin Kouzmanoff **(RC)** .50
6 John Danks **RC** .50
7 Alejandro De Aza **RC** .50
8 Jamie Vermilyea **RC** .50
9 Jesus Flores **RC** .50
10 Glen Perkins **(RC)** .50
11 Tim Lincecum **RC** 2.50
12 Cameron Maybin **RC** 2.00
13 Brandon Morrow **RC** .50
14 Mike Rabelo **RC** .50
15 Alex Gordon **RC** 2.00
16 Zack Segovia **(RC)** .50
17 Jon Knott **(RC)** .50
18 Joba Chamberlain **RC** 6.00
19 Danny Putnam **(RC)** .50
20 Matt DeSalvo **(RC)** .50
21 Fred Lewis **(RC)** .50
22 Sean Gallagher **(RC)** .50
23 Brandon Wood **(RC)** .50
24 Dennis Dove **(RC)** .50
25 Hunter Pence **(RC)** 2.00
26 Jarrod Saltalamacchia **(RC)** .50
27 Ben Francisco **(RC)** .50
28 Doug Slaten **RC** .50
29 Tony Abreu **RC** .50
30 Billy Butler **(RC)** 1.00
31 Jesse Litsch **RC** .50
32 Nate Schierholtz **(RC)** .50
33 Jared Burton **RC** .50
34 Matt Brown **RC** .50
35 Dallas Braden **RC** .50
36 Carlos Gomez **RC** 1.00
37 Brian Stokes **(RC)** .50
38 Kory Casto **(RC)** .50
39 Mark McLemore **(RC)** .50
40 Andy LaRoche **(RC)** 1.00
41 Tyler Clippard **(RC)** .50
42 Curtis Thigpen **(RC)** .50
43 Yunel Escobar **(RC)** .50
44 Andrew Sonnanstine **RC** .50
45 Felix Pie **(RC)** .50
46 Homer Bailey **(RC)** 1.00
47 Kyle Kendrick **RC** .50
48 Angel Sanchez **RC** .50
49 Phil Hughes **(RC)** 2.00
50 Ryan Braun **(RC)** 2.00
51 Kevin Slowey **(RC)** .50
52 Brendan Ryan **(RC)** .50
53 Yovani Gallardo **(RC)** 1.00
54 Mark Reynolds **RC** .50
237 Barry Bonds 2.00

Future's Game Prospects

NM/M
Complete Set (66-110): 8.00
Common Prospect: .25
66 Pedro Beato .25
67 Collin Balester .25
68 Carlos Carrasco .25
69 Clay Buchholz .50
70 Emiliano Fruto .25
71 Joba Chamberlain 2.00
72 Deolis Guerra .25
73 Kevin Mulvey .25
74 Franklin Morales .25
75 Luke Hochevar .50
76 Henry Sosa .25
77 Clayton Kershaw .50
78 Rich Thompson .25
79 Chuck Lofgren .25
80 Rick Vanden Hurk .25
81 Mike Madsen .25
82 Robinzon Diaz .25
83 Jeff Niemann .25
84 Max Ramirez .25
85 Geovany Soto .25
86 Elvis Andrus .25
87 Bryan Anderson .25
88 German Duran .25
89 J.R. Towles .50
90 Alcides Escobar .25
91 Brian Bocock .25
92 Chin-Lung Hu .25
93 Adrian Cardenas .25
94 Freddy Sandoval .25
95 Chris Coghlan .25
96 Craig Stansberry .25
97 Brent Lillibridge .25
98 Joey Votto .25
99 Evan Longoria 1.00
100 Wladimir Balentien .25
101 Johnny Whittleman .25
102 Gorkys Hernandez .25
103 Jay Bruce .50
104 Matt Tolbert .25
105 Jacoby Ellsbury 1.00
106 Mike Saunders .25
107 Cameron Maybin 1.00
108 Carlos Gonzalez .25
109 Colby Rasmus .50
110 Justin Upton 1.00

Future's Game Prospects

NM/M
Complete Set (66-110): 15.00
Common Prospect: .50
66 Pedro Beato .50
67 Collin Balester .50
68 Carlos Carrasco .50
69 Clay Buchholz 1.00
70 Emiliano Fruto .50
71 Joba Chamberlain 5.00
72 Deolis Guerra .50
73 Kevin Mulvey .50
74 Franklin Morales .50
75 Luke Hochevar 1.00
76 Henry Sosa .50
77 Clayton Kershaw 1.00
78 Rich Thompson .50
79 Chuck Lofgren .50
80 Rick Vanden Hurk .50
81 Mike Madsen .50
82 Robinzon Diaz .50
83 Jeff Niemann .50
84 Max Ramirez .50
85 Geovany Soto .50
86 Elvis Andrus 1.00
87 Bryan Anderson .50
88 German Duran .50
89 J.R. Towles .50
90 Alcides Escobar .50
91 Brian Bocock .50
92 Chin-Lung Hu .50
93 Adrian Cardenas .50
94 Freddy Sandoval .50
95 Chris Coghlan .50
96 Craig Stansberry .50
97 Brent Lillibridge .50
98 Joey Votto .50
99 Evan Longoria 2.00
100 Wladimir Balentien .50
101 Johnny Whittleman .50
102 Gorkys Hernandez .50
103 Jay Bruce 1.00
104 Matt Tolbert .50
105 Jacoby Ellsbury 2.50
106 Mike Saunders .50
107 Cameron Maybin 2.00
108 Carlos Gonzalez .50
109 Colby Rasmus 1.00
110 Justin Upton 2.00

Draft Future's Game Prospects Patch

NM/M
Common Player: 15.00
Production 99 Sets
66 Pedro Beato 25.00
67 Collin Balester 15.00
68 Carlos Carrasco 15.00
69 Clay Buchholz 35.00
70 Emiliano Fruto 15.00
71 Joba Chamberlain 75.00
72 Deolis Guerra 30.00
73 Kevin Mulvey 15.00
74 Franklin Morales 15.00
75 Luke Hochevar 30.00
76 Henry Sosa 20.00
77 Clayton Kershaw 20.00
78 Rich Thompson 15.00
79 Chuck Lofgren 20.00
80 Rick Vanden Hurk 20.00
81 Mike Madsen 15.00
82 Robinzon Diaz 15.00
83 Jeff Niemann 15.00
84 Max Ramirez 15.00
85 Geovany Soto 25.00
86 Elvis Andrus 25.00
87 Bryan Anderson 20.00
88 German Duran 25.00
89 J.R. Towles 25.00
90 Alcides Escobar 15.00
91 Brian Bocock 15.00
92 Chin-Lung Hu 60.00
93 Adrian Cardenas 20.00
94 Freddy Sandoval 15.00
95 Chris Coghlan 15.00
96 Craig Stansberry 15.00
97 Brent Lillibridge 15.00
98 Joey Votto 20.00
99 Evan Longoria 25.00
100 Wladimir Balentien 20.00
101 Johnny Whittleman 20.00
102 Gorkys Hernandez 20.00
103 Jay Bruce 30.00
104 Matt Tolbert 20.00
105 Jacoby Ellsbury 65.00
106 Mike Saunders 15.00
107 Cameron Maybin 25.00
108 Carlos Gonzalez 20.00
109 Colby Rasmus 30.00
110 Justin Upton 40.00

Future's Game Prospects Jersey

NM/M
Complete Player: 5.00
68 Carlos Carrasco 5.00
69 Clay Buchholz 15.00
71 Joba Chamberlain 30.00
73 Kevin Mulvey 5.00
74 Franklin Morales 5.00
75 Luke Hochevar 8.00
78 Rich Thompson 5.00
83 Jeff Niemann 8.00
84 Max Ramirez 5.00
89 J.R. Towles 8.00
95 Chris Coghlan 5.00
96 Craig Stansberry 5.00
97 Brent Lillibridge 5.00
98 Joey Votto 10.00
102 Gorkys Hernandez 8.00
105 Jacoby Ellsbury 25.00
106 Mike Saunders 5.00
107 Cameron Maybin 10.00
108 Carlos Gonzalez 8.00
110 Justin Upton 15.00

Draft Future's Game Prospects Base

NM/M
Common Player: 8.00
Production 135 Sets .50
86 Elvis Andrus 8.00
87 Bryan Anderson 8.00
88 German Duran 8.00
89 J.R. Towles 10.00
91 Brian Bocock 8.00
92 Chin-Lung Hu 25.00
93 Adrian Cardenas 10.00
94 Freddy Sandoval 8.00
95 Chris Coghlan 8.00
97 Brent Lillibridge 8.00
98 Joey Votto 10.00
99 Evan Longoria 20.00
101 Johnny Whittleman 8.00
102 Gorkys Hernandez 8.00
103 Jay Bruce 20.00
105 Jacoby Ellsbury 25.00
106 Mike Saunders 10.00
108 Carlos Gonzalez 8.00
109 Colby Rasmus 20.00
110 Justin Upton 20.00

Signs of the Future

NM/M
Common Auto.: 10.00
HC Hank Conger 20.00
AL Anthony Lerew 10.00
BA Brandon Allen 10.00
CM Casey McGehee 10.00
PH Philip Humber 10.00
CMM Carlos Marmol 20.00
RD Ryan Delaughter 10.00
AM Adam Miller 15.00
CD Chris Dickerson 10.00
CMC Chris McConnell 15.00
JK John Koronka 15.00
JR John Rheinecker 10.00
JV Jonathan Van Every 15.00
TC Trevor Crowe 15.00
FM Fernando Martinez 40.00
JGA Jaime Garcia 15.00

Draft Picks

NM/M
Complete Set (65): 15.00
Common Draft Pick: .25
1 Cody Crowell .25
2 Karl Bolt .25
3 Corey Brown .25
4 Tyler Mach .25
5 Trevor Pippin .25
6 Ed Easley .25
7 Cory Luebke .25
8 Darin Mastroianni .25
9 Ryan Zink .25
10 Brandon Hamilton .50
11 Kyle Lotzkar .50
12 Freddie Freeman .50
13 Nicholas Barnese .50
14 Travis d'Arnaud .50
15 Eric Eiland .50
16 John Ely .25
17 Oliver Marmol .25
18 Eric Sogard .25
19 Lars Davis .25
20 Sam Runion .50
21 Austin Gallagher .50
22 Matt West .50
23 Derek Norris .25
24 Taylor Holiday .25
25 Dustin Biell .25
26 Julio Borbon .50
27 Brant Rustich .50
28 Andrew Lambo 1.00
29 Corey Kluber .25
30 Justin Jackson .50
31 Scott Carroll .25
32 Danny Rams .25
33 Thomas Eager .25
34 Matt Dominguez 1.00
35 Steven Souza .50
36 Craig Heyer .25
37 Michael Taylor .50
38 Drew Bowman .25
39 Frank Gailey .25
40 Jeremy Hefner .25
41 Reynaldo Navarro .25
42 Daniel Descalso .25
43 Leroy Hunt .25
44 Jason Kiley .25
45 Ryan Pope .50
46 Josh Horton .25
47 Jason Monti .25
48 Richard Lucas .25
49 Jonathan Lucroy .50
50 Sean Doolittle .50
51 Mike McDade .25
52 Charlie Culberson .50
53 Michael Moustakas 1.50
54 Jason Heyward 1.50
55 David Price 1.50
56 Brad Mills .25
57 John Tolisano .50
58 Jarrod Parker .75
59 Wendell Fairley 1.00
60 Gary Gattis .50
61 Madison Bumgarner 1.00
62 Danny Payne .25
63 Jake Smolinski .50
64 Matt LaPorta 2.00
65 Jackson Williams .25

Draft Picks

NM/M
Common Draft Pick (1-65): .50
Common DP Auto. (111-140): 15.00
1 Cody Crowell .75
2 Karl Bolt .50
3 Corey Brown .50
4 Tyler Mach .50
5 Trevor Pippin .50
6 Ed Easley .50
7 Cory Luebke .50
8 Darin Mastroianni .50
9 Ryan Zink .75
10 Brandon Hamilton 1.00
11 Kyle Lotzkar 1.00
12 Freddie Freeman 1.50
13 Nicholas Barnese 1.50
14 Travis d'Arnaud .75
15 Eric Eiland 1.00
16 John Ely .50
17 Oliver Marmol .50
18 Eric Sogard .50
19 Lars Davis .50
20 Sam Runion 1.50
21 Austin Gallagher 1.00
22 Matt West 1.50
23 Derek Norris .75
24 Taylor Holiday .50
25 Dustin Biell .50
26 Julio Borbon 1.00
27 Brant Rustich .50
28 Andrew Lambo 3.00
29 Corey Kluber .50
30 Justin Jackson 1.50
31 Scott Carroll .50
32 Danny Rams .75
33 Thomas Eager .50
34 Matt Dominguez 3.00
35 Steven Souza 1.00
36 Craig Heyer .50
37 Michael Taylor 1.50
38 Drew Bowman .50
39 Frank Gailey .50
40 Jeremy Hefner .50
41 Reynaldo Navarro .75
42 Daniel Descalso 1.00
43 Leroy Hunt .50
44 Jason Kiley .50
45 Ryan Pope 1.50
46 Josh Horton .75
47 Jason Monti .50
48 Richard Lucas .50
49 Jonathan Lucroy 1.50
50 Sean Doolittle 1.00
51 Mike McDade .50
52 Charlie Culberson 1.50
53 Michael Moustakas 5.00
54 Jason Heyward 5.00
55 David Price 5.00
56 Brad Mills .50
57 John Tolisano 1.00
58 Jarrod Parker 2.00
59 Wendell Fairley 3.00
60 Gary Gattis 1.00
61 Madison Bumgarner 3.00
62 Danny Payne .50
63 Jake Smolinski 1.50
64 Matt LaPorta 6.00
65 Jackson Williams .50
111 Daniel Moskos 20.00
112 Ross Detwiler 25.00
113 Tim Alderson 30.00
114 Beau Mills 35.00
115 Devin Mesoraco 25.00
116 Kyle Lotzkar 20.00
117 Blake Beavan 30.00
118 Peter Kozma 20.00
119 Chris Withrow 25.00
120 Cory Luebke 20.00
121 Nick Schmidt 20.00
122 Michael Main 25.00
123 Aaron Poreda 20.00
124 James Simmons 15.00
125 Ben Revere 25.00
126 Joe Savery 20.00
127 Jonathan Gilmore 25.00
128 Todd Frazier 25.00
129 Matt Mangini 20.00
130 Casey Weathers 20.00
131 Nick Noonan 35.00
132 Kellen Kulbacki 30.00
133 Michael Burgess 50.00
134 Nick Hagadone 30.00
135 Clayton Mortensen 20.00
136 Justin Jackson 25.00
137 Ed Easley 15.00
138 Corey Brown 25.00
139 Danny Payne 20.00
140 Travis d'Arnaud 15.00

A-Rod Road to 500

NM/M
Common A-Rod (426-450): 2.00
Inserted 2:Box
Autographs: No Pricing
Production One Set

2007 Bowman's Best

NM/M
Common Player (1-33): .75
Common Auto. (23-51): 15.00
Common RC (52-81): 4.00
Production 799
Common RC Auto. (71-99): 10.00
Pack (5): 20.00
Box (15): 240.00
1 Jose Reyes 2.00
2 Derek Jeter 4.00
3 Vladimir Guerrero 1.50
4 Ichiro Suzuki 3.00
5 Jason Bay .75
6 Joe Mauer .75
7 Alfonso Soriano 1.50
8 David Ortiz 1.50
9 Andruw Jones .75
10 Roger Clemens 3.00
11 Grady Sizemore 1.50
12 Magglio Ordonez .75
13 Carl Crawford .75
14 Chase Utley 1.50
15 Mark Teixeira 1.00
16 Ryan Zimmerman 1.00
17 Ken Griffey Jr. 3.00
18 Derrek Lee 1.00
19 Barry Bonds 4.00
20 Chipper Jones 1.50
21 Vernon Wells .75
22 Manny Ramirez 1.50
23 Alex Rodriguez 4.00
23 Alex Rodriguez/Auto. 150.00
24 Ryan Howard 2.50
24 Ryan Howard/Auto. 65.00
25 Tom Glavine 1.00
25 Tom Glavine/Auto. 60.00
26 Gary Sheffield 1.00
26 Gary Sheffield/Auto. 25.00
27 Miguel Cabrera 1.50
27 Miguel Cabrera/Auto. 25.00
28 Robinson Cano 1.00
28 Robinson Cano/Auto. 30.00
29 David Wright 2.00
29 David Wright/Auto. 40.00
30 Jim Thome 1.00
30 Jim Thome/Auto. 35.00
31 Albert Pujols 4.00
31 Albert Pujols/Auto. 160.00
32 Jorge Posada .75
33 Brian McCann .75
33 Brian McCann/Auto. 35.00
34 Josh Barfield/Auto. 10.00
35 Melky Cabrera/Auto. 25.00
36 Bill Hall/Auto. 15.00
37 Cole Hamels/Auto. 30.00
38 Adam LaRoche/Auto. 15.00
39 Matt Holliday/Auto. 25.00
40 Jeremy Hermida/Auto. 10.00
41 Jonathan Papelbon/Auto. 25.00
42 Hanley Ramirez/Auto. 20.00
43 Justin Verlander/Auto. 25.00
44 Andre Ethier/Auto. 15.00
46 Erik Bedard/Auto. 20.00
47 Freddy Sanchez/Auto. 15.00
48 Adrian Gonzalez/Auto. 15.00
49 Russell Martin/Auto. 20.00
50 B.J. Upton/Auto. 15.00
51 Prince Fielder/Auto. 40.00
52 Tony Abreu **RC** 4.00
53 Ben Francisco **(RC)** 4.00
54 Billy Butler **(RC)** 8.00
55 Phil Hughes **(RC)** 15.00
56 Josh Fields **(RC)** 4.00
57 Carlos Gomez **RC** 6.00
58 Akinori Iwamura **RC** 6.00
59 Matt Brown **RC** 4.00
60 Jesus Flores **RC** 6.00
61 Mike Fontenot **(RC)** 4.00
62 Ryan Feierabend **(RC)** 4.00
63 Miguel Montero **(RC)** 4.00
64 Daisuke Matsuzaka **RC** 25.00
64 Daisuke Matsuzaka/Jsy **RC** 40.00
65 Kei Igawa **RC** 6.00

66 Shawn Riggans **(RC)** 6.00
67 Masumi Kuwata **RC** 15.00
68 Kevin Slowey **(RC)** 4.00
69 Josh Hamilton **(RC)** 6.00
70 Curtis Thigpen **(RC)** 6.00
71 Justin Upton **RC** 12.00
71 Justin Upton/Auto. **RC** 60.00
72 Delmon Young **(RC)** 6.00
72 Delmon Young/Auto. **(RC)** 20.00
73 Brandon Wood **(RC)** 6.00
73 Brandon Wood/Auto. **(RC)** 15.00
74 Felix Pie **(RC)** 6.00
74 Felix Pie/Auto. **(RC)** 15.00
75 Alex Gordon **RC** 10.00
75 Alex Gordon/Auto. **RC** 40.00
76 Mark Reynolds **RC** 6.00
76 Mark Reynolds/Auto. **RC** 30.00
77 Tyler Clippard **(RC)** 6.00
77 Tyler Clippard/Auto. 20.00
78 Adam Lind **(RC)** 4.00
78 Adam Lind/Auto. **(RC)** 15.00
79 Hunter Pence **(RC)** 10.00
79 Hunter Pence/Auto. **(RC)** 40.00
81 Jarrod Saltalamacchia **(RC)** 6.00
81 Jarrod Saltalamacchia/Auto. **(RC)** 15.00
82 Kevin Kouzmanoff/Auto. **(RC)** 15.00
83 Glen Perkins/Auto. **(RC)** 10.00
84 Michael Bourn/Auto. **(RC)** 10.00
85 Andrew Miller/Auto. **RC** 25.00
86 Fred Lewis/Auto. **(RC)** 15.00
88 Joba Chamberlain/Auto. **RC** 120.00
89 Hideki Okajima/Auto. **RC** 35.00
90 Troy Tulowitzki/Auto. **(RC)** 40.00
91 Ryan Sweeney/Auto. **(RC)** 10.00
92 Matt Lindstrom/Auto. **(RC)** 10.00
93 Tim Lincecum/Auto. **RC** 50.00
94 Homer Bailey/Auto. **(RC)** 20.00
95 Matt DeSalvo/Auto. **(RC)** 15.00
96 Alejandro De Aza/Auto. **RC** 10.00
97 Ryan Braun/Auto. **(RC)** 50.00
99 Andy LaRoche **(RC)** 15.00

Prospects

NM/M
Common Player (1-40): 4.00
Production 499
Common Auto. (37-60): 10.00
1 Greg Smith 15.00
2 J.R. Towles 6.00
3 Jeff Locke 15.00
4 Henry Sosa 6.00
5 Ivan DeJesus Jr. 8.00
6 Brad Lincoln 6.00
7 Josh Papelbon 8.00
8 Mark Hamilton 6.00
9 Sam Fuld 10.00
10 Thomas Fairchild 4.00
11 Chris Carter 6.00
12 Chuck Lofgren 4.00
13 Joe Gaetti 4.00
14 Zach McAllister 4.00
15 Cole Gillespie 10.00
16 Jeremy Papelbon 6.00
17 Mike Carp 4.00
18 Cody Strait 4.00
19 Gorkys Hernandez 8.00
20 Andrew Fie 4.00
21 Erik Lis 4.00
22 Chance Douglass 4.00
23 Vasili Spanos 4.00
24 Desmond Jennings 4.00
25 Vic Buttler 4.00
26 Cedric Hunter 4.00
27 Emerson Frostad 4.00
28 Michael Devaney 6.00
29 Eric Young Jr. 4.00
30 Evan Englebrook 4.00
31 Aaron Cunningham 6.00
32 Dellin Betances 10.00
33 Mike Saunders 4.00
34 Deolis Guerra 10.00
35 Brian Bocock 8.00
36 Rich Thompson 6.00
37 Greg Reynolds 4.00
37 Greg Reynolds/Auto. 10.00
38 Jeff Samardzija 8.00
38 Jeff Samardzija/Auto. 25.00
39 Evan Longoria 8.00
39 Evan Longoria/Auto. 30.00
40 Luke Hochevar 8.00
40 Luke Hochevar/Auto. 25.00
41 James Avery/Auto. 8.00
42 Joe Mather/Auto. 15.00
43 Hank Conger/Auto. 15.00
44 Adam Miller/Auto. 15.00
45 Clayton Kershaw/Auto. 25.00
46 Adam Ottavino/Auto. 15.00
47 Jason Place/Auto. 20.00
48 Billy Rowell/Auto. 20.00
49 Brett Sinkbeil/Auto. 10.00
50 Colton Willems/Auto. 15.00
51 Cameron Maybin/Auto. 25.00
52 Jeremy Jeffress/Auto. 15.00
53 Fernando Martinez/Auto. 40.00
54 Chris Marrero/Auto. 50.00
55 Kyle McCulloch/Auto. 15.00
56 Chris Parmelee/Auto. 15.00
57 Emmanuel Burris/Auto. 15.00
58 Chris Coghlan/Auto. 15.00
59 Chris Perez/Auto. 15.00
60 David Huff/Auto. 10.00

Green

Green (1-33): 2-4X
Green RC (52-99): 1-2X
Production 249

Blue

NM/M
Blue (1-33): 3-5X
Blue Auto. (23-51): 1-1.5X
Blue RC (52-81): 1-2X
Blue RC Auto. (71-99): 1-1.5X
Matsuzaka Blue Jersey 40.00
Production 99 Sets

Gold

NM/M
Gold (1-33): 4-6X
Gold Auto. (23-51): 1-2X
Gold RC (52-81): 2-4X
Gold RC Auto. (71-99): 1-2X
Matsuzaka Gold Jersey 60.00
Production 50 Sets

Red

No Pricing
Production One Set

Printing Plates

Production one set per color.

Prospects Blue

Blue (1-40): 1-2X
Blue Auto. (37-60): 1-1.5X
Production 99 Sets

Prospects Green

Green (1-40): 1-1.5X
Production 249 Sets

Prospects Gold

Gold (1-40): 2-3X
Gold Auto. (37-60): 1.5-3X
Production 50 Sets

Prospects Red

Production One Set

Barry Bonds 756

NM/M
Inserted 1:20
BB756 Barry Bonds 8.00

AROD 500

NM/M
Inserted 1:20
AR500 Alex Rodriguez 8.00

A-Rod Road to 500

NM/M
Common A-Rod (401-425): 15.00
Autographs: No Pricing
Production One Set

2007 Bowman Sterling

NM/M
Common RC: 3.00
Common RC Auto.: 10.00
Pack (5): 50.00
Box (6): 250.00
AAL Adam Lind **(RC)** 3.00
AG Alex Gordon **RC** 8.00
AI Akinori Iwamura **RC** 4.00
AL Andy LaRoche **(RC)** 4.00
AM Andrew Miller **RC** 8.00
AS Andrew Sonnanstine **RC** 5.00
BB Billy Butler **(RC)** 5.00
BF Ben Francisco **(RC)** 3.00
BS Brian Stokes **(RC)** 6.00
BW Brandon Wood **(RC)** 4.00
CG Carlos Gomez **RC** 5.00
CH Chase Headley/Auto. **(RC)** 10.00
CM Cameron Maybin/Auto. **RC** 25.00
CT Curtis Thigpen **(RC)** 3.00
DM Daisuke Matsuzaka **RC** 10.00
DMM David Murphy **(RC)** 3.00
DP Danny Putnam **(RC)** 3.00
DY Delmon Young **(RC)** 4.00
FL Fred Lewis **(RC)** 3.00
FP Felix Pie/Auto. **(RC)** 15.00
GO Garrett Olson **(RC)** 3.00
GP Glen Perkins/Auto. **(RC)** 10.00
HB Homer Bailey/Auto. **(RC)** 15.00
HG Hector Gimenez **(RC)** 3.00
HO Hideki Okajima **RC** 5.00
HP Hunter Pence **(RC)** 8.00
JB Jeff Baker **(RC)** 3.00
JC1 Joba Chamberlain **RC** 15.00
JC2 Joba Chamberlain/Auto. **RC** 100.00
JD John Danks/Auto. **RC** 10.00
JDF Josh Fields **(RC)** 3.00
JE Jacoby Ellsbury **(RC)** 10.00
JF Jesus Flores **RC** 4.00
JH Josh Hamilton/Auto. **(RC)** 15.00
JL Jesse Litsch/Auto. **RC** 10.00
JQF Jake Fox **RC** 4.00
JR Jo Jo Reyes **(RC)** 4.00
JS Jarrod Saltalamacchia/Auto. **(RC)** 15.00
JU Justin Upton **RC** 8.00
KI Kei Igawa **RC** 3.00
KK Kevin Kouzmanoff **(RC)** 3.00
KKS Kurt Suzuki/Auto. **(RC)** 10.00
KRK Kyle Kendrick/Auto. **RC** 15.00
KS Kevin Slowey/Auto. **(RC)** 15.00
MB Michael Bourn **(RC)** 3.00
MC Matt Chico/Auto. **(RC)** 10.00
MF Mike Fontenot **(RC)** 4.00
MK Masumi Kuwata **RC** 8.00
MM Miguel Montero **(RC)** 3.00
MO Micah Owings **(RC)** 3.00
MP Manny Parra **(RC)** 4.00
MR Mark Reynolds **RC** 5.00
MSM Mark McLemore **(RC)** 3.00
NG Nick Gorneault/Auto. **(RC)** 10.00
NS Nate Schierholtz/Auto. **(RC)** 10.00
PH Phil Hughes **(RC)** 6.00
PH Phil Hughes/Auto. **(RC)** 35.00
RB Ryan Braun/Auto. **(RC)** 40.00
RS Ryan Sweeney **(RC)** 3.00
RV Rick Vanden Hurk **RC** 4.00
SD Shelley Duncan **(RC)** 4.00
SG Sean Gallagher **(RC)** 3.00
TA Tony Abreu **RC** 3.00
TB Travis Buck **(RC)** 3.00
TC Tyler Clippard **(RC)** 3.00
TL Tim Lincecum/Auto. **RC** 50.00
TM Travis Metcalf **RC** 4.00
UJ Ubaldo Jimenez **(RC)** 3.00
YE Yunel Escobar **(RC)** 3.00
YG Yovani Gallardo/Auto. **(RC)** 20.00
Common Memorabilia: 4.00
AER Alex Rodriguez 20.00
AJ Andruw Jones 6.00
AP Albert Pujols 15.00
AR Alex Rios 8.00
AS Alfonso Soriano 8.00
BLB Barry Bonds 15.00
BP Brad Penny 4.00
BR Brian Roberts 6.00
BU B.J. Upton 6.00
BW Brandon Webb 6.00
CAB Craig Biggio 6.00
CAG Carlos Guillen 6.00
CH Cole Hamels 8.00
CL Carlos Lee 6.00
CMS Curt Schilling 6.00
DDY Dmitri Young 4.00
DO David Ortiz 8.00
DW David Wright 10.00
DWW Dontrelle Willis 4.00
EC Eric Chavez 4.00
IS Ichiro Suzuki 20.00
JAV Jason Varitek 10.00
JBR Jose Reyes 10.00
JE Jim Edmonds 4.00
JS Johan Santana 8.00
JV Justin Verlander 10.00
LB Lance Berkman 6.00
MAR Manny Ramirez 8.00
MC Melky Cabrera 8.00
MCT Mark Teixeira 8.00
MH Matt Holliday 8.00
MJO Magglio Ordonez 6.00
MM Mickey Mantle 80.00
MT Miguel Tejada 6.00
MY Michael Young 6.00
OC Orlando Cabrera 4.00
PF Prince Fielder 10.00
RB Rocco Baldelli 4.00
RC Roger Clemens 15.00
RJC Robinson Cano 10.00
RJH Ryan Howard 15.00
RZ Ryan Zimmerman 8.00
SK Scott Kazmir 6.00
TH Tim Hudson 6.00
TLH Todd Helton 6.00
TW Tim Wakefield 6.00
VG Vladimir Guerrero 8.00

Refractors

RC's: 1-2X
RC Auto.: 1-2X
Relics: 1-2X

Black Refractors

No Pricing
Production 25 Sets

Red Refractors

Production One Set

Printing Plates

Production one set per color.

Dual Autographs

NM/M
Common Dual Auto.: 20.00
Refractors: 1-1.5X
Production 199 Sets
Black Refractor: No Pricing
Production 25 Sets
Red Refractors: No Pricing
Production One Set
BV Jay Bruce, Joey Votto 50.00
CH Shin-Soo Choo, Chin-Lung Hu 30.00
GM Deolis Guerra, Fernando Martinez 50.00
HC Phil Hughes, Joba Chamberlain 180.00
HP Luke Hochevar, David Price 50.00
LC Evan Longoria, Carl Crawford 30.00
MM John Maine, Lastings Milledge 20.00
PB Hunter Pence, Ryan Braun 60.00
PP Jeremy Papelbon, Josh Papelbon 25.00
PS Felix Pie, Jeff Samardzija 30.00

Prospects

NM/M
Common Prospect: 3.00
Common Prospect Auto.: 8.00
AC Adrian Cardenas/Jsy Auto. 10.00
AF Andrew Fie 3.00
ALC Aaron Cunningham 3.00
AP Aaron Poreda Auto 15.00
BB Brian Bocock/Jsy Auto. 15.00
BB Blake Beavan/Auto. 15.00
BEL Brad Lincoln 3.00
BH Brandon Hamilton 3.00
BHB Burke Badenhop 3.00
BL Bryan LaHair/Auto. 8.00
BM Brandon MaGee/Auto. 8.00
BMI Beau Mills/Auto. 20.00
BR Ben Revere/Auto. 15.00
BWH Brandon Hynick 5.00
CB Collin Balester/Jsy Auto. 10.00
CC Chris Carter 8.00
CD Chance Douglass 3.00
CG Cole Gillespie/Auto. 15.00
CH Chin-Lung Hu/Jsy Auto. 50.00
CH Cedric Hunter 3.00
CK Clayton Kershaw/Jsy Auto. 30.00
CL Chuck Lofgren/Jsy Auto. 15.00
CM Clayton Mortensen/Auto. 10.00
CN Chris Nowak 3.00
CR Colby Rasmus/Jsy Auto. 35.00
CS Cody Strait 3.00
CW Chris Withrow/Auto. 20.00
CWW Casey Weathers/Auto. 10.00
DB Daniel Bard/Auto. 20.00
DBE Dellin Betances 8.00
DG Deolis Guerra/Jsy Auto. 30.00
DI Devin Ivany 3.00
DJ Desmond Jennings 5.00
DL Drew Locke 3.00
DM Daniel Moskos/Auto. 15.00
DME Devin Mesoraco/Auto. 15.00
DMM Derek Miller 5.00
DPP David Price/Auto. 50.00
DS James Simmons/Auto. 10.00
EE Ed Easley 3.00
EL Evan Longoria/Jsy Auto. 30.00
EL Erik Lis/Auto. 10.00
EM Emerson Frostad 3.00
EY Eric Young Jr. 3.00
FF Freddie Freeman 5.00
GD German Duran/Jsy Auto. 15.00
GH Gorkys Hernandez 6.00
GP Greg Porter 3.00
GR Greg Reynolds 3.00
GS Greg Smith 3.00
HS Henry Sosa/Jsy Auto. 20.00
ID Ivan DeJesus 4.00
IS Ian Stewart/Jsy Auto. 25.00
JA J.P. Arencibia/Auto. 15.00
JAA James Avery/Auto. 8.00
JB Jay Bruce/Jsy Auto. 35.00
JB Joe Benson/Auto. 15.00
JBO Julio Borbon/Auto. 15.00
JG Jonathan Gilmore/Auto. 15.00
JGA Joe Gaetti 3.00
JGO Jared Goedert 3.00
JH Jason Heyward/Auto. 50.00
JJ Justin Jackson 3.00
JL Jeff Locke 8.00
JM Joe Mather 5.00
JO Josh Outman/Auto. 10.00
JP Jason Place 3.00
JPA Jeremy Papelbon 5.00
JPP Josh Papelbon 5.00
JS Joe Savery/Auto. 15.00
JS Jeff Samardzija 5.00
JSM Jake Smolinski 5.00
JT J.R. Towles 6.00
JV Joey Votto/Jsy Auto. 20.00
JV Josh Vitters/Auto. 40.00
JVE Jonathan Van Every 3.00
JW Johnny Whittleman/Jsy Auto. 10.00
KA Kevin Ahrens/Auto. 20.00
KK Kellen Kulbacki/Auto. 15.00
KK Kala Kaaihu 4.00
MB Michael Burgess/Auto. 30.00
MBB Madison Bumgarner/Auto. 25.00
MC Mike Carp 3.00
MCA Mitch Canham/Auto. 10.00
MD Mike Daniel/Auto. 10.00
MDE Michael Devaney 3.00
MDO Matt Dominguez/Auto. 25.00
MH Mark Hamilton 3.00
MIM Michael Main/Auto. 15.00
MLP Matt LaPorta/Auto. 50.00
MM Mike Madsen/Jsy Auto. 10.00
MM Matt McBride/Auto. 10.00
MMG Matt Mangini/Auto/ 15.00
MP Mike Parisi/Auto. 10.00
MS Mike Saunders 4.00
MY Matt Young 3.00
NH Nick Hagadone/Auto. 20.00
NN Nick Noonan/Auto. 20.00
NS Nick Schmidt/Auto. 10.00
OS Ole Sheldon 3.00
PB Pedro Beato/Jsy Auto. 10.00
PK Peter Kozma/Auto. 15.00
RD Ross Detwiler/Auto. 20.00
RM Ryan Mount/Auto. 8.00
RT Rich Thompson 3.00
SF Sam Fuld 6.00
SP Steve Pearce/Jsy Auto. 30.00
TA Tim Alderson/Auto. 20.00
TF Todd Frazier/Auto. 20.00
TF Thomas Fairchild 3.00
TM Tommy Manzella/Auto. 8.00
TS Travis Snider/Auto. 30.00
TW Ty Weeden/Auto. 15.00
VB Vic Buttler 3.00
VS Vasili Spanos 3.00
WF Wendell Fairley/Auto. 25.00
WT Wade Townsend/Auto. 8.00
ZM Zach McAllister 3.00

Prospects Refractors

Prospects: 1-2X
Autos: 1-2X
Production 199 Sets

Prospects Black Refractors

No Pricing
Production 25 Sets

Prospects Red Refractors

Production One Set

A-Rod Road to 500

NM/M
Common A-Rod (450-475): 10.00
Autographs: No Pricing
Production One Set

1992-2004 Boy Scouts of America Atlanta Braves

In 1992 the Atlanta-area Boy Scouts of America began a "Collector's Edition" series of commemorative baseball cards featuring Braves players. The 2-1/2" x 3-1/2" cards have a variety of designs with color photos, usually game-action. Red, white and blue backs have player information and stats and logos of the team, sponsor(s), and/or BSA.

NM/M
Complete Set (13): 50.00
Common Player: 2.00
(1) Jeff Treadway/1992 3.00
(2) Dale Murphy/1993 15.00
(3) Deion Sanders/1994 8.00
(4) Gregory McMichael/1995 3.00
(5) Ryan Klesko/1996 5.00
(6) Jeff Blauser/1997 3.00
(7) Greg Maddux/1998 12.00
(8) John Rocker/1999 5.00
(9) John Smoltz/2000 3.00
(10) Tom Glavine/2001 3.00
(11) Kevin Millwood/2002 2.00
(12) Marcus Giles/2003 2.00
(13) Russ Ortiz/2004 2.00

1998 Bryan Braves Team Photo Set

After a one-year absence and a change of stadium hot dog vendors, the Braves again distributed a team photo foldout in 1998. The 10-5/8" x 31-3/8" three-panel perforated sheet has a large team photo and individual 2-1/8" x 3-1/8" cards of 35 players and staff. The player cards have a portrait photo on a background of brown baseballs and faded red "A"s. The player name is in gold at the bottom; his position vertically in a blue strip at left. A red Bryan logo is at top-left. Backs are in red, white and blue with biographical and career notes and stats. The unnumbered cards are checklisted here alpabetically.

NM/M
Complete Foldout Set: 8.00
Common Player: .10
(1) Danny Bautista .10
(2) Jim Beauchamp .10
(3) Rafael Belliard .10
(4) Adam Butler .10
(5) Norm Charlton .10
(6) Greg Colbrunn .10
(7) Pat Corrales .10
(8) Bobby Cox .10
(9) Bobby Dews .10
(10) Frank Fultz .10
(11) Andres Galarraga .10
(12) Tom Glavine 1.00
(13) Tony Graffanino .10
(14) Ozzie Guillen .10
(15) Andruw Jones 1.50
(16) Chipper Jones 3.00
(17) Clarence Jones .10
(18) Ryan Klesko .10
(19) Kerry Ligtenberg .10
(20) Keith Lockhart .10
(21) Javy Lopez .10

(22) Greg Maddux 2.00
(23) Dennis Martinez .10
(24) Leo Mazzone .10
(25) Kevin Millwood .50
(26) Denny Neagle .10
(27) Eddie Perez .10
(28) John Rocker .10
(29) Rudy Seanez .10
(30) John Smoltz 1.00
(31) Russ Springer .10
(32) Michael Tucker .10
(33) Walt Weiss .10
(34) Gerald Williams .10
(35) Ned Yost .10
(36) Team Photo .50

1999 Bryan Braves

These Tuesday-night homestand give-away cards were sponsored by the team's hot dog vendor and given away three players at a time to children only. Completion of a set is thus a challenge. The cards of Hernandez, Mulholland and Myers were late-season additions and differ from the rest of the set in that the player names in gold vertically at left are in upper- and lower-case type, while most cards have the name in all-caps. The 2-1/2" x 3-1/2" cards have player portraits bordered in blue at left and bottom. The position is in gold at bottom; the uniform number in gold at top. A red Bryan logo is at lower-left. Black, white and blue backs have minimal player vitae and full professional stats. The unnumbered cards are checklisted here in alphabetical order.

NM/M
Complete Set (30): 32.50
Common Player: 1.00
(1) Don Baylor 1.00
(2) Bret Boone 1.00
(3) Pat Corrales 1.00
(4) Bobby Cox 1.00
(5) Bobby Dews 1.00
(6) Tom Glavine 1.50
(7) Ozzie Guillen 1.00
(8) Jose Hernandez 1.00
(9) Glenn Hubbard 1.00
(10) Brian Hunter 1.00
(11) Andruw Jones 2.50
(12) Chipper Jones 4.00
(13) Brian Jordan 1.00
(14) Ryan Klesko 1.00
(15) Keith Lockhart 1.00
(16) Javy Lopez 1.00
(17) Greg Maddux 3.00
(18) Leo Mazzone 1.00
(19) Kevin Millwood 1.00
(20) Terry Mulholland 1.00
(21) Greg Myers 1.00
(22) Otis Nixon 1.00
(23) Eddie Perez 1.00
(24) Odalis Perez 1.00
(25) Mike Remlinger 1.00
(26) John Rocker 1.00
(27) Rudy Seanez 1.00
(28) John Smoltz 1.50
(29) Walt Weiss 1.00
(30) Ned Yost 1.00

Team Photo Set

Children visiting Turner Field for a late-season game received this foldout sponsored by the team's hot dog vendor. The 10-5/8" x 31-3/8" three-panel perforated sheet has a large team photo and individual 2-1/8" x 3-1/8" cards of 35 players and staff. The player cards have a portrait photo on a baseball back-

ground. The player name and position are at left. A large red Bryan logo is at top-right. Backs are in red, white and black with biographical and career notes and stats. The unnumbered cards are checklisted here alpabetically.

NM/M
Complete Foldout Set: 8.00
Common Player: .10
(1) Don Baylor .10
(2) Bret Boone .25
(3) Bruce Chen .10
(4) Pat Corrales .10
(5) Bobby Cox .10
(6) Bobby Dews .10
(7) Frank Fultz .10
(8) Tom Glavine 1.00
(9) Ozzie Guillen .10
(10) Jose Hernandez .10
(11) Glenn Hubbard .10
(12) Brian Hunter .10
(13) Andruw Jones 1.50
(14) Chipper Jones 3.00
(15) Brian Jordan .10
(16) Ryan Klesko .10
(17) Keith Lockhart .10
(18) Javy Lopez .10
(19) Greg Maddux 2.00
(20) Leo Mazzone .10
(21) Kevin McGlinchy .10
(22) Kevin Millwood .50
(23) Terry Mulholland .10
(24) Greg Myers .10
(25) Otis Nixon .10
(26) Eddie Perez .10
(27) Mike Remlinger .10
(28) John Rocker .10
(29) Rudy Seanez .10
(30) Randall Simon .10
(31) John Smoltz 1.00
(32) Russ Springer .10
(33) Walt Weiss .10
(34) Gerald Williams .10
(35) Ned Yost .10
(36) Team Photo .50

2000 Bryan Braves

For the first time since the Braves hot dog concessionaires began issuing annual stadium give-away card sets in 1989, the number of Tuesday home games in 2000 dictated that some players be issued in more than one variation to allow for three cards to be given away each date. The 2-1/2" x 3-1/2" cards have game-action photos vignetted with blue borders. The player's full name and position are in red at left, and his last name in white at right. His uniform number is at top. A red Bryan logo is at bottom. Black, white and blue backs have a few bits of personal data and complete minor and major league stats. The unnumbered cards are checklisted here alphabetically.

NM/M
Complete Set (39): 45.00
Common Player: 1.00
(1) Andy Ashby 1.00
(2) Bobby Bonilla 1.00
(3) John Burkett 1.00
(4) Pat Corrales 1.00
(5) Bobby Cox 1.00
(6) Bobby Dews 1.00
(7) Rafael Furcal 1.50
(8) Andres Galarraga/Bat 1.00
(9) Andres Galarraga/Fldg 1.00
(10) Tom Glavine 2.00
(11) Glenn Hubbard 1.00
(12) Andruw Jones (Batting stance.) 2.50
(13) Andruw Jones (Follow-through.) 2.50
(14) Chipper Jones (Back turned.) 4.00
(15) Chipper Jones/Fldg 4.00
(16) Brian Jordan/Btg 1.00
(17) Brian Jordan/Portrait 1.00
(18) Wally Joyner 1.00
(19) Kerry Ligtenberg 1.00
(20) Keith Lockhart 1.00
(21) Javy Lopez/Btg 1.00
(22) Javy Lopez/Catching 1.00
(23) Greg Maddux 3.00
(24) Leo Mazzone 1.00
(25) Kevin McGlinchy 1.00
(26) Kevin Millwood 1.00
(27) Terry Mulholland 1.00
(28) Eddie Perez 1.00
(29) Odalis Perez 1.00
(30) Mike Remlinger 1.00
(31) Merv Rettenmund 1.00
(32) John Rocker 1.00
(33) Reggie Sanders 1.00
(34) Rudy Seanez 1.00
(35) John Smoltz 2.00
(36) B.J. Surhoff 1.00
(37) Quilvio Veras 1.00
(38) Walt Weiss 1.00
(39) Ned Yost 1.00

Team Photo Set

Children visiting Turner Field for a late-season game received this foldout sponsored by the team's hot dog vendor. The 10-5/8" x 31-3/8" three-panel perforated sheet has a large team photo and individual 2-1/8" x 3-1/8" cards of 35 players and staff. The staff cards have a portrait photo on a blue background. The player cards have game-action photos. All cards are bordered in brown with a nameplate design at bottom with identification and a Bryan logo. Backs are in red, white and black with biographical and career notes and stats. The unnumbered cards are checklisted here alpabetically.

NM/M
Complete Foldout Set: 8.00
Common Player: .10
(1) Andy Ashby .10
(2) Bobby Bonilla .10
(3) John Burkett .10
(4) Bobby Cox .10
(5) Pat Corrales .10
(6) Bobby Dews .10
(7) Frank Fultz .10
(8) Rafael Furcal .75
(9) Andres Galarraga .10
(10) Tom Glavine 1.00
(11) Glenn Hubbard .10
(12) Andruw Jones 1.00
(13) Chipper Jones 3.00
(14) Brian Jordan .10
(15) Wally Joyner .10
(16) Kerry Ligtenberg .10
(17) Keith Lockhart .10
(18) Javy Lopez .10
(19) Greg Maddux 1.50
(20) Leo Mazzone .10
(21) Kevin McGlinchy .10
(22) Kevin Millwood .10
(23) Terry Mulholland .10
(24) Eddie Perez .10
(25) Odalis Perez .10
(26) Mike Remlinger .10
(27) Merv Rettenmund .10
(28) John Rocker .10
(29) Reggie Sanders .10
(30) Rudy Seanez .10
(31) John Smoltz 1.00
(32) B.J. Surhoff .10
(33) Quilvio Veras .10
(34) Walt Weiss .10
(35) Ned Yost .10

2001 Bryan Braves

Three cards were given out at each Tuesday home game to children 12 and under from this set sponsored by Turner Field's hot dog vendor. The 2-1/2" x 3-1/2" cards have game-action photos with a team logo at top, a sponsor's logo at bottom, a trio of ghost-image baseballs at left and the player name and position at right. Black, white and blue backs have minimal player personal data and complete pro stats. The unnumbered cards are checklisted here in alphabetical order. Due to the manner of their distribution, assembly of a complete set is difficult.

NM/M
Complete Set (29): 30.00
Common Player: 1.00
(1) Rico Brogna 1.00
(2) John Burkett 1.00
(3) Jose Cabrera 1.00
(4) Ken Caminiti 1.00
(5) Bobby Cox 1.00
(6) Mark DeRosa 1.00
(7) Bobby Dews 1.00
(8) Rafael Furcal 1.50
(9) Marcus Giles 1.00
(10) Tom Glavine 2.00
(11) Wes Helms 1.00
(12) Andruw Jones 2.50
(13) Chipper Jones 4.00
(14) Brian Jordan 1.00
(15) Kerry Ligtenberg 1.00
(16) Keith Lockhart 1.00
(17) George Lombard 1.00
(18) Javy Lopez 1.00
(19) Greg Maddux 3.00
(20) Jason Marquis 1.00
(21) Dave Martinez 1.00
(22) Leo Mazzone 1.00
(23) Kevin Millwood 1.50
(24) Odalis Perez 1.00
(25) Mike Remlinger 1.00
(26) John Rocker 1.00
(27) John Smoltz 2.00
(28) B.J. Surhoff 1.00
(29) Quilvio Veras 1.00

Team Photo Set

Children visiting Turner Field for a late-season game received this foldout sponsored by the team's hot dog vendor. The 10-5/8" x 31-3/8" three-panel perforated sheet has a large team photo and individual 2-1/8" x 3-1/8" cards of 35 players and staff. The staff cards have a portrait photo; the player cards have game-action photos. All photos are in the "sweet spot" on a baseball background with name and position in red at left and a large Bryan logo at lower-right. Backs are in red, white and black with biographical and career notes and stats on a ghost image of the front photo. The unnumbered cards are checklisted here alpabetically.

NM/M
Complete Foldout Set: 8.00
Common Player: .10
(1) Paul Bako .10
(2) John Burkett .10
(3) Jose Cabrera .10
(4) Ken Caminiti .10
(5) Pat Corrales .10
(6) Bobby Cox .10
(7) Mark DeRosa .10
(8) Bobby Dews .10
(9) Frank Fultz .10
(10) Marcus Giles .10
(11) Bernard Gilkey .10
(12) Tom Glavine .75
(13) Wes Helms .10
(14) Glenn Hubbard .10
(15) Andruw Jones 1.00
(16) Chipper Jones 3.00
(17) Brian Jordan .10
(18) Steve Karsay .10
(19) Kerry Ligtenberg .10
(20) Keith Lockhart .10
(21) George Lombard .10
(22) Javy Lopez .10
(23) Greg Maddux 2.00
(24) Jason Marquis .10
(25) Dave Martinez .10
(26) Leo Mazzone .10
(27) Kevin Millwood .35
(28) Odalis Perez .10
(29) Steve Reed .10
(30) Mike Remlinger .10
(31) Merv Rettenmund .10
(32) Rey Sanchez .10
(33) John Smoltz .75
(34) B.J. Surhoff .10
(35) Ned Yost .10
(36) Team Photo .50

2002 Bryan Braves Team Photo Set

Children visiting Turner Field for a September game received this foldout sponsored by the team's hot dog vendor. The 10-5/8" x 31-3/8" three-panel perforated sheet has a large team photo and individual 2-1/8" x 3-1/8" cards of 35 players and staff. The staff cards have a portrait photo; the player cards have game-action photos. All photos are framed in blue and bordered in white. Name and position are at bottom, a red "A" at top and a large Bryan logo at lower-left. Backs are in blue, white and black with biographical and career notes and stats on a ghost image of the front photo. The unnumbered cards are checklisted here alpabetically.

NM/M
Complete Foldout Set: 8.00
Common Player: .10
(1) Henry Blanco .10
(2) Darren Bragg .10
(3) Vinny Castilla .10
(4) Pat Corrales .10
(5) Bobby Cox .10
(6) Mark DeRosa .10
(7) Bobby Dews .10
(8) Julio Franco .10
(9) Matt Franco .10
(10) Frank Fultz .10
(11) Rafael Furcal .10
(12) Jesse Garcia .10
(13) Marcus Giles .10
(14) Tom Glavine 1.00
(15) Chris Hammond .10
(16) Wes Helms .10
(17) Darren Holmes .10
(18) Glenn Hubbard .10
(19) Andruw Jones 1.00
(20) Chipper Jones 3.00
(21) Kerry Ligtenberg .10
(22) Keith Lockhart .10
(23) Albie Lopez .10
(24) Javy Lopez .10
(25) Greg Maddux 2.00
(26) Jason Marquis .10
(27) Leo Mazzone .10
(28) Kevin Millwood .35
(29) Damian Moss .25
(30) Terry Pendleton .10
(31) Mike Remlinger .10
(32) Gary Sheffield .35
(33) John Smoltz 1.00
(34) Tim Spooneybarger .10
(35) Ned Yost .10
(36) Team Photo .50

1982 Builders Emporium Los Angeles Dodgers

Shoppers at this chain of building supply stores in Southern California were able to receive one of this seven-card set with each visit. Cards are printed in black-and-white in 11" x 8-1/2" format with blank backs. Fronts of the player cards have both portrait and action photos, the manager's card has only a portrait. Team and sponsors' logos are at bottom-right. The unnumbered cards are checklisted here in alphabetical order.

NM/M
Complete Set (7): 35.00
Common Player: 6.00
(1) Dusty Baker 6.00
(2) Ron Cey 6.00
(3) Steve Garvey 9.00
(4) Pedro Guerrero 6.00
(5) Tommy Lasorda 6.00
(6) Jerry Reuss 6.00
(7) Steve Sax 6.00

1982 Burger King Braves

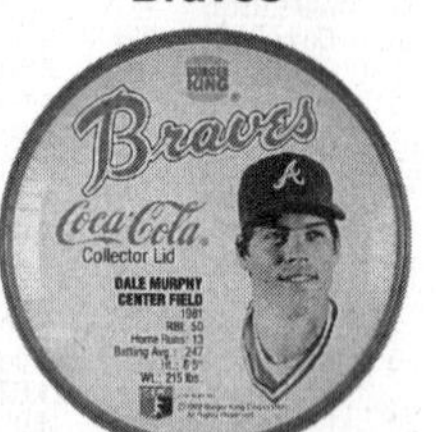

A set consisting of 27 "Collector Lids" featuring the Atlanta Braves was issued by Burger King restaurants in 1982. The plastic lids, 3-5/8" in diameter, were placed on a special Coca-Cola cup which listed the scores of the Braves' season-opening 13-game win streak. A black-and-white photo plus the player's name, position, height, weight, and 1981 statistics are found on the lid front. The unnumbered, blank-backed lids also contain logos for Burger King, Coca-Cola, and the Major League Baseball Players Association.

	NM/M
Complete Set (27):	20.00
Common Player:	1.00
(1) Steve Bedrosian	1.00
(2) Bruce Benedict	1.00
(3) Tommy Boggs	1.00
(4) Brett Butler	1.50
(5) Rick Camp	1.00
(6) Chris Chambliss	1.00
(7) Ken Dayley	1.00
(8) Gene Garber	1.00
(9) Preston Hanna	1.00
(10) Terry Harper	1.00
(11) Bob Horner	1.50
(12) Al Hrabosky	1.00
(13) Glenn Hubbard	1.00
(14) Randy Johnson	1.00
(15) Rufino Linares	1.00
(16) Rick Mahler	1.00
(17) Larry McWilliams	1.00
(18) Dale Murphy	12.50
(19) Phil Niekro	3.00
(20) Biff Pocoroba	1.00
(21) Rafael Ramirez	1.00
(22) Jerry Royster	1.00
(23) Ken Smith	1.00
(24) Bob Walk	1.00
(25) Claudell Washington	1.00
(26) Bob Watson	1.00
(27) Larry Whisenton	1.00

1982 Burger King Indians

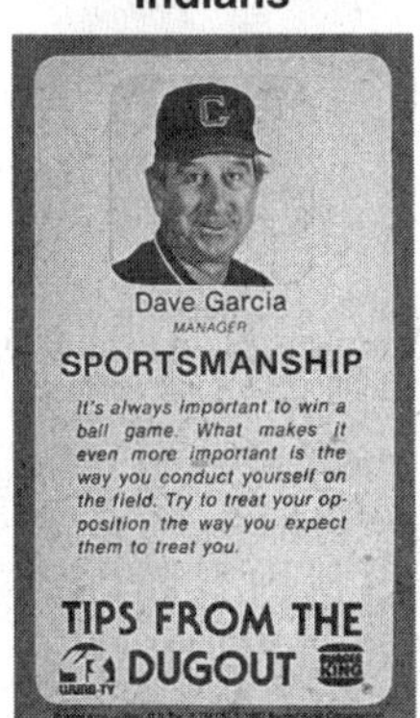

Dave Garcia
MANAGER
SPORTSMANSHIP
It's always important to win a ball game. What makes it even more important is the way you conduct yourself on the field. Try to treat your opposition the way you expect them to treat you.
TIPS FROM THE DUGOUT

This set was sponsored by WUAB-TV and Burger Kings in the Cleveland vicinity. The cards' green borders encompass a large yellow area which contains a black-and-white photo plus a baseball tip. Manager Dave Garcia and his coaches provide the baseball hints. The cards, which measure 3" x 5", are unnumbered and blank-backed.

	NM/M
Complete Set (12):	7.00
Common Player:	.75
(1) Dave Garcia (Be In The Game)	.75
(2) Dave Garcia (Sportsmanship)	.75
(3) Johnny Goryl (Rounding The Bases)	.75
(4) Johnny Goryl (3rd Base Running)	.75
(5) Tom McCraw (Follow Thru)	.75
(6) Tom McCraw (Selecting A Bat)	.75
(7) Tom McCraw (Watch The Ball)	.75
(8) Mel Queen (Master One Pitch)	.75
(9) Mel Queen (Warm Up)	.75
(10) Dennis Sommers (Get Down On A Ground Ball)	.75
(11) Dennis Sommers (Protect Your Fingers)	.75
(12) Dennis Sommers (Tagging First Base)	.75

1986 Burger King

Burger King restaurants in the Pennsylvania and New Jersey areas issued a set entitled "All-Pro Series." Cards were issued with the purchase of a Whopper sandwich and came in folded panels of two cards each, along with a coupon

card. Fronts feature a color photo and identification plus the Burger King logo. Due to a lack of MLB licensing, team insignias on the players' uniforms were airbrushed away. Backs are in black-and-white and contain brief biographical and statistical information.

	NM/M
Complete Panel Set (10):	3.00
Complete Singles Set (20):	3.00
Common Panel:	.25
Common Single Player:	.05
PANEL (1)	.40
1 Tony Pena	.05
2 Dave Winfield	.20
PANEL (2)	1.00
3 Fernando Valenzuela	.05
4 Pete Rose	.45
PANEL (3)	1.00
5 Mike Schmidt	.40
6 Steve Carlton	.20
PANEL (4)	.25
7 Glenn Wilson	.05
8 Jim Rice	.15
PANEL (5)	.50
9 Wade Boggs	.25
10 Juan Samuel	.05
PANEL (6)	.50
11 Dale Murphy	.10
12 Reggie Jackson	.35
PANEL (7)	.40
13 Kirk Gibson	.05
14 Eddie Murray	.20
PANEL (8)	1.00
15 Cal Ripken Jr.	.50
16 Willie McGee	.05
PANEL (9)	.40
17 Dwight Gooden	.05
18 Steve Garvey	.10
PANEL (10)	1.00
19 Don Mattingly	.40
20 George Brett	.40

1987 Burger King

#5 OF 20
ALL-PRO
2ND EDITION SERIES
STEVE GARVEY
SAN DIEGO PADRES
FIRST BASE

The 1987 "All-Pro 2nd Edition Series" set was part of a giveaway promotion at participating Burger King restaurants. The set is comprised of 20 players on ten different panels. Cards measure 2-1/2" x 3-1/2" each with a three-card panel (includes a coupon card) measuring 7-5/8" x 3-1/2". Fronts feature a full-color photo and Burger King logo surrounded by a blue stars-and-stripes border. Backs are black-and-white with a brief biography and 1986/Career statistics. The set was produced by Mike Schecter Associates and, as with many MSA issues, all team insignias were airbrushed away.

	NM/M
Complete Panel Set (10):	3.00
Complete Singles Set (20):	3.00
Common Panel:	.30
Common Single Player:	.05
PANEL (1)	.75
1 Wade Boggs	.40
2 Gary Carter	.30
PANEL (2)	.75
3 Will Clark	.05
4 Roger Clemens	.50
PANEL (3)	.40
5 Steve Garvey	.20
6 Ron Darling	.05
PANEL (4)	.30
7 Pedro Guerrero	.05
8 Von Hayes	.05
PANEL (5)	.40
9 Rickey Henderson	.30
10 Keith Hernandez	.05
PANEL (6)	.30
11 Wally Joyner	.05
12 Mike Krukow	.05
PANEL (7)	1.00
13 Don Mattingly	.50
14 Ozzie Smith	.40
PANEL (8)	.30
15 Tony Pena	.05
16 Jim Rice	.20
PANEL (9)	1.00
17 Ryne Sandberg	.40
18 Mike Schmidt	.50
PANEL (10)	.30
19 Darryl Strawberry	.05
20 Fernando Valenzuela	.05

1994 Burger King Cal Ripken Jr.

Although the cards themselves do not indicate it, this issue was co-sponsored by Burger King and Coke, and distributed in BK restaurants in the Baltimore-Washington area. Cards were available in three-card packs for 25 cents with the purchase of a Coke product. Each pack contains two regular cards and a gold card. Each of the nine cards could be found in a regular and gold version. Cards feature color photos with a semi-circular black border at top or left. "Score '94" appears in orange in one of the upper corners, along with an Orioles logo. Cal Ripken, Jr.'s name appears at the bottom. On the gold premium version, there is a gold-foil circle around the Orioles logo and Ripken's name appears in gold, rather than white. Backs have a smaller color photo, again meeting at a semi-circular edge with the black border at left and bottom. In the black are another Score logo, a card number, an Orioles logo, a headline and a few career details and/or stats. Cards are UV coated on each side. Several hundred of the cards were personally autographed by Ripken and distributed in a drawing.

	NM/M
Complete Set (9):	5.00
Complete Set, Gold (9):	9.00
Common Card:	.75
Common Card, Gold:	1.25
Autographed Card:	185.00
1 Double Honors	.75
1a Double Honors/Gold	1.25
2 Perennial All-Star	.75
2a Perennial All-Star/Gold	1.25
3 Peerless Power	.75
3a Peerless Power/Gold	1.25
4 Fitness Fan	.75
4a Fitness Fan/Gold	1.25
5 Prime Concerns	.75
5a Prime Concerns/Gold	1.25
6 Home Run Club	.75
6a Home Run Club/Gold	1.25
7 The Iron Man	.75
7a The Iron Man/Gold	1.25
8 Heavy Hitter	.75
8a Heavy Hitter/Gold	1.25
9 Gold Glover	.75
9a Gold Glover/Gold	1.25

1997 Burger King Cal Ripken Jr.

Three years after its 1994 tribute, Burger King in 1997 created an eight-card set honoring the future Hall of Famer. Participating BK outlets in Maryland, the District of Columbia, Delaware, Pennsylvania, Virginia and West Virginia offered the cards for 99¢ with a meal purchase or $1.15 without. Each card was produced in two forms: with and without a gold holographic foil facsimile autograph and "1 of 10,000" notation. The 2-1/2" x 3-1/2" cards have action photos of Ripken on front with muted backgrounds. His name, uniform number and team logo also appear. Backs, numbered "X/8" have another color photo with ghosted background and a paragraph of a career highlight. Autographed cards were part of a prize structure explained on information cards accompanying the Ripken card in each pack.

	NM/M
Complete Set (8):	5.00
Complete Gold Set (8):	10.00
Common Card:	1.00
Common Gold Card:	2.00
Autographed Card:	185.00
1-8 Cal Ripken Jr.	1.00
-- Autograph Information Card	.25

1999 Burger King N.Y. Yankees

Members of the World Champion 1998 N.Y. Yankees are featured on this three-sheet set of cards sold by metropolitan New York Burger King restaurants in April-May, 1999. The 12-1/2" x 10-1/2" perforated sheets each include nine standard-size cards. Fronts feature action photos with the Yankees and Fleer logos. Backs have the same photo along with season and career stats and highlights, printed on a ghosted background of a Yankees pinstriped jersey. The Fleer and team logos appear on back, as do those of the players union and the restaurant chain. On the sheet along with the player cards are a checklist, team schedule, mention of the BK Cancer Foundation of New York and a kids' club offer.

	NM/M
Complete Sheet Set (3):	7.50
Complete Singles Set (27):	7.50
Common Player:	.25
SHEET 1	6.00
1 Derek Jeter	4.00
2 Paul O'Neill	.25
3 Scott Brosius	.25
4 Mariano Rivera	.50
5 Chuck Knoblauch	.25
6 Graeme Lloyd	.25
7 Joe Girardi	.25
8 Orlando Hernandez	.25
9 Tim Raines	.25
SHEET 2	3.50
10 Bernie Williams	.45
11 Tino Martinez	.25
12 Andy Pettitte	.40
13 Hideki Irabu	.25
14 Ramiro Mendoza	.25
15 Jeff Nelson	.25
16 Homer Bush	.25
17 Darren Holmes	.25
18 Yankees Championship History	.25
SHEET 3	3.50
19 David Cone	.25
20 David Wells	.25
21 Chili Davis	.25
22 Darryl Strawberry	.25
23 Ricky Ledee	.25
24 Jorge Posada	.25
25 Luis Sojo	.25
26 Chad Curtis	.25
27 Mike Stanton	.25

C

1989 Cadaco All-Star Baseball Discs

This set of player discs was sold with and intended for use in a board game. Fronts of the 3-1/2" diameter position players' discs have a yellow border sectioned with numbers from 1 to 14, indicating that player's likelihood of performing a specific baseball result based on career stats. At center is a color player photo from which the uniform details have been airbrushed. Logos of the game's producer and the Major League Players Association flank the portrait. The player's name, team and position are below the photo. Backs have up to five years of recent stats and lifetime totals, along with a few biographical data. Several of the discs have player names misspelled. Each disc can be found either with or without the team name and league on back. Four error discs from the initial print run (with team, league on back) were corrected. The unnumbered discs are checklisted alphabetically.

	NM/M
Complete Set (63):	20.00
Common Player:	.25
(1) Harold Baines	.25
(2) Wade Boggs	2.00
(3) Bobby Bonilla	.25
(4) George Brett	2.50
(5) Jose Canseco	1.00
(6) Gary Carter	1.50
(7) Joe Carter	.25
(8) Will Clark	.25
(9a) Rodger Clemens (First name misspelled.)	3.00
(9b) Roger Clemens (Corrected)	3.00
(10) Vince Coleman	.25
(11) David Cone	.25
(12) Alvin Davis	.25
(13) Eric Davis	.25
(14) Glenn Davis	.25
(15) Andre Dawson	.65
(16) Shawon Dunston	.25
(17) Dennis Eckersley	.60
(18) Carlton Fisk	1.50
(19) Scott Fletcher	.25
(20a) John Frannko (Last name misspelled.)	.35
(20b) John Franco (Corrected)	.25
(21) Julio Franko (Franco)	.25
(22) Gary Gaetti	.25
(23) Andres Galarraga	.25
(24) Kirk Gibson	.25
(25) Mike Greenwell	.25
(26) Mark Gubicza	.25
(27) Pedro Guerrero	.25
(28) Tony Gwynn	2.00
(29) Rickey Henderson	1.50
(30) Orel Hershiser	.25
(31) Kent Hrbek	.25
(32) Danny Jackson	.25
(33a) Barry Larkin (Wrong photo.)	.65
(33b) Barry Larkin (Corrected)	.25
(34) Greg Maddux	2.00
(35) Don Mattingly	2.50
(36a) Mark McGuire (Last name misspelled.)	4.50
(36b) Mark McGwire (Corrected)	4.50
(37) Fred McGriff	.25
(38) Paul Molitor	1.50
(39) Tony Pena	.25
(40) Gerald Perry	.25
(41) Dan Plesac	.25
(42) Kirby Puckett	2.00
(43) Johnny Ray	.25
(44) Jeff Reardon	.25
(45) Cal Ripken, Jr.	4.50
(46) Babe Ruth	3.50
(47) Nolan Ryan	4.50
(48) Juan Samuel	.25
(49) Ryne Sandberg	2.00
(50) Benito Santiago	.25
(51) Steve Sax	.25
(52) Mike Schmidt	2.25
(53) Kevin Seitzer	.25
(54) Ozzie Smith	2.00
(55) Terry Steinbach	.25
(56) Dave Stewart	.25
(57) Darryl Strawberry	.25
(58) Andres Thomas	.25
(59) Alan Trammell (Trammell)	.25
(60) Andy Van Slyke	.25
(61) Frank Viola	.25
(62) Dave Winfield	1.50
(63) Todd Worrell	.25

1990 Cadaco All-Star Baseball Discs

This set of player discs was sold with and intended for use in a board game. Fronts of the 3-1/2" diameter position players' discs have a border sectioned with numbers from 1 to 14, indicating that player's likelihood of performing a specific baseball result based on career stats. At center is a color player photo from which the uniform details have been airbrushed. Logos of the game's producer and the Major League Players Association flank the portrait. The player's name, team and position are below the photo. Backs have up to five years of recent stats and lifetime totals, along with brief biographical data. A handful of the game's past greats were included among the contemporary players which make up the bulk of the disc set. The unnumbered discs are checklisted alphabetically.

	NM/M
Complete Set (63):	20.00
Common Player:	.25
(1) Harold Baines	.25
(2) Damon Berryhill	.25
(3) Craig Biggio	.25
(4) Wade Boggs	2.00

(5)	Bobby Bonilla	.25
(6)	Jose Canseco	1.00
(7)	Will Clark	.25
(8)	Roger Clemens	2.50
(9)	Roberto Clemente	4.00
(10)	Ty Cobb	2.50
(11)	Vince Coleman	.25
(12)	Eric Davis	.25
(13)	Glenn Davis	.25
(14)	Andre Dawson	.65
(15)	Shawon Dunston	.25
(16)	Tony Fernandez	.25
(17)	Carlton Fisk	1.50
(18)	Julio Franco	.25
(19)	Gary Gaetti	.25
(20)	Lou Gehrig	4.00
(21)	Kirk Gibson	.25
(22)	Mark Grace	.25
(23)	Ken Griffey Jr.	3.00
(24)	Pedro Guerrero	.25
(25)	Tony Gwynn	2.00
(26)	Rickey Henderson	1.50
(27)	Orel Hershiser	.25
(28)	Bo Jackson	.60
(29)	Howard Johnson	.25
(30)	Carney Lansford	.25
(31)	Barry Larkin	.25
(32)	Greg Maddux	2.00
(33)	Don Mattingly	2.50
(34)	Fred McGriff	.25
(35)	Mark McGwire	3.50
(36)	Kevin Mitchell	.25
(37)	Tony Pena	.25
(38)	Kirby Puckett	2.00
(39)	Willie Randolph	.25
(40)	Cal Ripken Jr.	4.50
(41)	Babe Ruth	4.00
(42)	Nolan Ryan	4.50
(43)	Bret Saberhagen	.25
(44)	Chris Sabo	.25
(45)	Ryne Sandberg	2.00
(46)	Benito Santiago	.25
(47)	Steve Sax	.25
(48)	Mike Scott	.25
(49)	Kevin Seitzer	.25
(50)	Ruben Sierra	.25
(51)	Ozzie Smith	2.00
(52)	Terry Steinbach	.25
(53)	Dave Stewart	.25
(54)	Mickey Tettleton	.25
(55)	Robby Thompson	.25
(56)	Alan Trammell	.25
(57)	Jose Uribe	.25
(58)	Andy Van Slyke	.25
(59)	Honus Wagner	1.50
(60)	Jerome Walton	.25
(61)	Lou Whitaker	.25
(62)	Matt Williams	.25
(63)	Robin Yount	1.50

1991 Cadaco All-Star Baseball Discs

This set of player discs was sold with and intended for use in a board game. Fronts of the 3-1/2" diameter discs have a yellow border sectioned with numbers from 1 to 14, indicating that player's likelihood of performing a specific baseball result based on career stats. At center is a color player photo from which the uniform details have been airbrushed. Logos of the game's producer and the Major League Players Association flank the portrait. The player's name, team and position are below the photo. Backs have up to five years of recent stats and lifetime totals, along with a few biographical data. The unnumbered discs are checklisted alphabetically.

		NM/M
Complete Set (62):		20.00
Common Player:		.25
(1)	Roberto Alomar	.35
(2)	Harold Baines	.25
(3)	Craig Biggio	.25
(4)	Wade Boggs	2.00
(5)	Barry Bonds	4.50
(6)	Bobby Bonilla	.25
(7)	Jose Canseco	.75
(8)	Will Clark	.25
(9)	Roger Clemens	2.50
(10)	Roberto Clemente	4.00
(11)	Ty Cobb	2.50
(12)	Vince Coleman	.25
(13)	Eric Davis	.25
(14)	Glenn Davis	.25
(15)	Andre Dawson	.65
(16)	Delino DeShields	.25
(17)	Shawon Dunston	.25
(18)	Tony Fernandez	.25
(19)	Cecil Fielder	.25
(20)	Carlton Fisk	1.50
(21)	Julio Franco	.25
(22)	Gary Gaetti	.25
(23)	Lou Gehrig	3.00
(24)	Kirk Gibson	.25
(25)	Mark Grace	.25
(26)	Ken Griffey Jr.	3.00
(27)	Kelly Gruber	.25
(28)	Tony Gwynn	2.00
(29)	Rickey Henderson	1.50
(30)	Orel Hershiser	.25
(31)	David Justice	.25
(32)	Bo Jackson	.50
(33)	Howard Johnson	.25
(34)	Barry Larkin	.25
(35)	Ramon Martinez	.25
(36)	Don Mattingly	2.50
(37)	Fred McGriff	.25
(38)	Mark McGwire	3.50
(39)	Kevin Mitchell	.25
(40)	Lance Parrish	.25
(41)	Tony Pena	.25
(42)	Kirby Puckett	2.00
(43)	Cal Ripken Jr.	4.50
(44)	Babe Ruth	4.00
(45)	Nolan Ryan	4.50
(46)	Bret Saberhagen	.25
(47)	Chris Sabo	.25
(48)	Ryne Sandberg	2.00
(49)	Benito Santiago	.25
(50)	Steve Sax	.25
(51)	Gary Sheffield	.75
(52)	Ruben Sierra	.25
(53)	Ozzie Smith	2.00
(54)	Terry Steinbach	.25
(55)	Dave Stewart	.25
(56)	Mickey Tettleton	.25
(57)	Alan Trammell	.25
(58)	Jose Uribe	.25
(59)	Honus Wagner	1.50
(60)	Lou Whitaker	.25
(61)	Matt Williams	.25
(62)	Robin Yount	1.50

1993 Cadaco All-Star Baseball Discs

This set of player discs was sold with and intended for use in a board game. Fronts of the 3-1/2" diameter discs have a yellow border sectioned with numbers from 1 to 14, indicating that player's likelihood of performing a specific baseball result based on career stats. At center is a color player photo from which the uniform details have been airbrushed. Logos of the game's producer and the Major League Players Association flank the portrait. The player's name, team and position are below the photo. Backs have up to five years of recent stats and lifetime totals, along with a few biographical data. The unnumbered discs are checklisted alphabetically.

		NM/M
Complete Set (62):		20.00
Common Player:		.25
(1)	Kevin Appier	.25
(2)	Carlos Baerga	.25
(3)	Harold Baines	.25
(4)	Derek Bell	.25
(5)	George Bell	.25
(6)	Jay Bell	.25
(7)	Mike Boddicker	.25
(8)	Wade Boggs	2.00
(9)	Hubie Brooks	.25
(10)	Jose Canseco	.75
(11)	Roger Clemens	2.50
(12)	Roberto Clemente	4.00
(13)	Ty Cobb	2.50
(14)	Alex Cole	.25
(15)	Jeff Conine	.25
(16)	Andre Dawson	.65
(17)	Shawon Dunston	.25
(18)	Lenny Dykstra	.25
(19)	Carlton Fisk	1.50
(20)	Darrin Fletcher	.25
(21)	Gary Gaetti	.25
(22)	Greg Gagne	.25
(23)	Mike Gallego	.25
(24)	Lou Gehrig	4.00
(25)	Kirk Gibson	.25
(26)	Tom Glavine	.50
(27)	Mark Grace	.25
(28)	Ken Griffey Jr.	3.00
(29)	Tony Gwynn	2.00
(30)	Charlie Hayes	.25
(31)	Rickey Henderson	1.50
(32)	Orel Hershiser	.25
(33)	Bo Jackson	.50
(34)	Howard Johnson	.25
(35)	Randy Johnson	1.50
(36)	Ricky Jordan	.25
(37)	David Justice	.25
(38)	Ray Lankford	.25
(39)	Ramon Martinez	.25
(40)	Don Mattingly	2.50
(41)	Mark McGwire	3.50
(42)	Brian McRae	.25
(43)	Joe Oliver	.25
(44)	Tony Pena	.25
(45)	Kirby Puckett	2.00
(46)	Cal Ripken Jr.	4.50
(47)	Babe Ruth	4.00
(48)	Nolan Ryan	4.50
(49)	Bret Saberhagen	.25
(50)	Chris Sabo	.25
(51)	Ryne Sandberg	2.00
(52)	Benito Santiago	.25
(53)	Steve Sax	.25
(54)	Gary Sheffield	.75
(55)	Ozzie Smith	2.00
(56)	Dave Stewart	.25
(57)	Darryl Strawberry	.25
(58)	Frank Thomas	1.50
(59)	Robin Ventura	.25
(60)	Hector Villanueva	.25
(61)	Honus Wagner	1.50
(62)	Lou Whitaker	.25

1985 Cain's Potato Chips Tigers

This set commemorating the 1984 World Champion Tigers was issued in bags of Cain's Potato Chips in the Michigan area in 1985. The yellow-bordered, unnumbered cards measure 2-3/4" in diameter and feature full-color oval photos inside a diamond. The word "Cain's" appears in the upper left corner, while the player's name appears in the lower left with his position directly below the photo. The words "1984 World Champions" are printed in the upper right corner. Backs include 1984 statistics.

		NM/M
Complete Set (20):		10.00
Common Player:		.50
(1)	Doug Bair	.50
(2)	Juan Berenguer	.50
(3)	Dave Bergman	.50
(4)	Tom Brookens	.50
(5)	Marty Castillo	.50
(6)	Darrell Evans	1.00
(7)	Barbaro Garbey	.50
(8)	Kirk Gibson	1.00
(9)	John Grubb	.50
(10)	Willie Hernandez	.50
(11)	Larry Herndon	.50
(12)	Chet Lemon	.50
(13)	Aurelio Lopez	.50
(14)	Jack Morris	1.00
(15)	Lance Parrish	1.00
(16)	Dan Petry	.50
(17)	Bill Scherrer	.50
(18)	Alan Trammell	2.50
(19)	Lou Whitaker	1.50
(20)	Milt Wilcox	.50

1986 Cain's Potato Chips Tigers

For the second year in a row, player discs of the Detroit Tigers were found in boxes of Cain's Potato Chips sold in the

Detroit area. Twenty discs make up the set which is branded as a "1986 Annual Collectors' Edition." Discs, measuring 2-3/4" in diameter, have fronts which contain a color photo plus the player's name, team and position. The Cain's logo and the Major League Baseball Players Association's logo also appear. The backs, which display black print on white stock, contain player information plus the card number.

		NM/M
Complete Set (20):		7.50
Common Player:		.50
1	Tom Brookens	.50
2	Willie Hernandez	.50
3	Dave Bergman	.50
4	Lou Whitaker	1.25
5	Dave LaPoint	.50
6	Lance Parrish	.75
7	Randy O'Neal	.50
8	Nelson Simmons	.50
9	Larry Herndon	.50
10	Doug Flynn	.50
11	Jack Morris	.75
12	Dan Petry	.50
13	Walt Terrell	.50
14	Chet Lemon	.50
15	Frank Tanana	.50
16	Kirk Gibson	.75
17	Darrell Evans	.75
18	Dave Collins	.50
19	John Grubb	.50
20	Alan Trammell	2.00

1987 Cain's Potato Chips Tigers

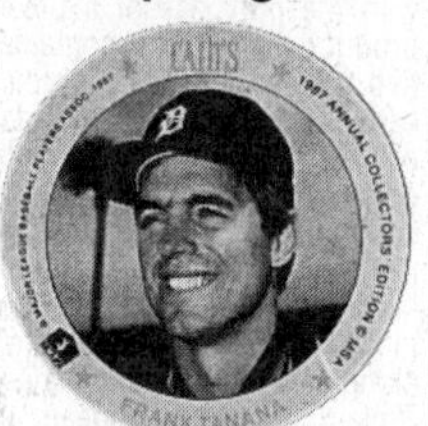

Player discs of the Detroit Tigers were inserted in boxes of Cain's Potato Chips for the third consecutive year. The 1987 edition is made up of cards each measuring 2-3/4" in diameter. The discs, which were packaged in a cellophane wrapper, feature a full-color photo surrounded by an orange border. Backs are printed in red on white stock. The set was produced by Mike Schechter and Associates.

		NM/M
Complete Set (20):		12.50
Common Player:		.60
1	Tom Brookens	.60
2	Darnell Coles	.60
3	Mike Heath	.60
4	Dave Bergman	.60
5	Dwight Lowry	.60
6	Darrell Evans	1.00
7	Alan Trammell	2.50
8	Lou Whitaker	1.75
9	Kirk Gibson	1.00
10	Chet Lemon	.60
11	Larry Herndon	.60
12	John Grubb	.60
13	Willie Hernandez	.60
14	Jack Morris	1.00
15	Dan Petry	.60
16	Walt Terrell	.60
17	Mark Thurmond	.60
18	Pat Sheridan	.60
19	Eric King	.60
20	Frank Tanana	.60

1984 California Angels Fire Safety

This 32-card set was distributed at a June home game to fans 14 and under. Cards measure 2-1/2" x 3-1/2". Fronts have full-color action photos along a portrait of Smokey the Bear and U.S. and California Forest Service logos commemorating Smokey's 40th birthday. Black-and-white backs have minimal player data and stats and a tip for preventing forest fires.

		NM/M
Complete Set (32):		4.00
Common Player:		.25
(1)	Don Aase	.25
(2)	Juan Beniquez	.25
(3)	Bob Boone	.45
(4)	Rick Burleson	.25
(5)	Rod Carew	1.50
(6)	John Curtis	.25
(7)	Doug DeCinces	.25
(8)	Brian Downing	.25
(9)	Ken Forsch	.25
(10)	Bobby Grich	.25
(11)	Reggie Jackson	2.00
(12)	Ron Jackson	.25
(13)	Tommy John	.50
(14)	Curt Kaufman	.25
(15)	Bruce Kison	.25
(16)	Frank LaCorte	.25
(17)	Fred Lynn	.45
(18)	John McNamara	.25
(19)	Jerry Narron	.25
(20)	Gary Pettis	.25
(21)	Robert Picciolo	.25
(22)	Ron Romanick	.25
(23)	Luis Sanchez	.25
(24)	Dick Schofield	.25
(25)	Daryl Sconiers	.25
(26)	Jim Slaton	.25
(27)	Ellis Valentine	.25
(28)	Robert Wilfong	.25
(29)	Mike Witt	.25
(30)	Geoff Zahn	.25
---	Forestry Dept. Logo Card	.10
---	Smokey Logo Card	.10

1985 California Angels Fire Safety

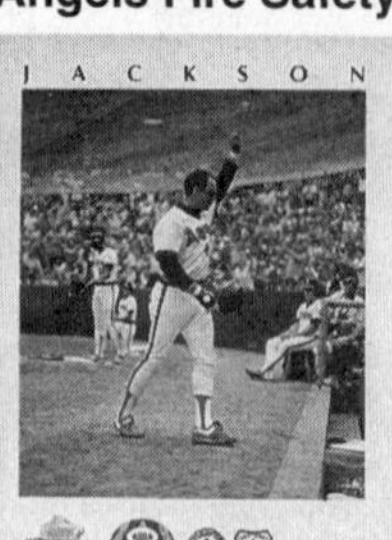

This full-color set of large-format cards was given to fans attending the July 14 game at Anaheim Stadium. Fronts feature player photos with their last name at the top above the picture. In the bottom border are a portrait of Smokey the Bear, and logos of the Angels, California Forestry Service and U.S. Forestry Service. Cards measure 4-1/4" x 6". On back, printed in black-and-white, are personal data, a few stats and a wildfire safety tip.

		NM/M
Complete Set (24):		5.00
Common Player:		.25
1	Mike Witt	.25
2	Reggie Jackson	1.50
3	Bob Boone	.45
4	Mike Brown	.25
5	Rod Carew	1.00
6	Doug DeCinces	.25
7	Brian Downing	.25
8	Ken Forsch	.25
9	Gary Pettis	.25
10	Jerry Narron	.25
11	Ron Romanick	.25
12	Bobby Grich	.25
13	Dick Schofield	.25
14	Juan Beniquez	.25
15	Geoff Zahn	.25
16	Luis Sanchez	.25
17	Jim Slaton	.25
18	Doug Corbett	.25
19	Ruppert Jones	.25
20	Rob Wilfong	.25
21	Donnie Moore	.25
22	Pat Clements	.25
23	Tommy John	.50
24	Gene Mauch	.25

1986 California Angels Fire Safety

The Angels, in conjuction with the U.S. and California Forestry Services, issued this set promoting Wildfire Prevention. Cards measure 4-1/4" x 6" and offer a full-color front with the player's picture in an oval frame. Backs have player stats with a drawing and fire safety tip. The sets were given out August 9 at the game in Anaheim Stadium.

		NM/M
Complete Set (24):		5.00
Common Player:		.25
1	Mike Witt	.25
2	Reggie Jackson	1.50
3	Bob Boone	.40
4	Don Sutton	1.00
5	Kirk McCaskill	.25
6	Doug DeCinces	.25
7	Brian Downing	.25
8	Doug Corbett	.25
9	Gary Pettis	.25
10	Jerry Narron	.25
11	Ron Romanick	.25
12	Bobby Grich	.25
13	Dick Schofield	.25
14	George Hendrick	.25
15	Rick Burleson	.25
16	John Candelaria	.25
17	Jim Slaton	.25
18	Darrell Miller	.25
19	Ruppert Jones	.25
20	Rob Wilfong	.25
21	Donnie Moore	.25
22	Wally Joyner	1.00
23	Terry Forster	.25
24	Gene Mauch	.25

1987 California Angels Fire Safety

The U.S. Forestry Service distributed this set to 25,000 fans in attendance at Anaheim Stadium on August 1. The full-color cards measure 4" x 6". Fronts carry a design of baseballs and bats framing the player photo. Only the player's last name is given. At bottom is a Smokey Bear portrait and team logo. Backs contain the player's name, position and personal data along with a Smokey Bear cartoon fire prevention tip and sponsors' logos.

		NM/M
Complete Set (24):		5.00
Common Player:		.25
1	John Candelaria	.25
2	Don Sutton	1.00
3	Mike Witt	.25
4	Gary Lucas	.25
5	Kirk McCaskill	.25
6	Chuck Finley	.25
7	Willie Fraser	.25
8	Donnie Moore	.25
9	Urbano Lugo	.25
10	Butch Wynegar	.25
11	Darrell Miller	.25
12	Wally Joyner	.75
13	Mark McLemore	.25
14	Mark Ryal	.25
15	Dick Schofield	.25
16	Jack Howell	.25
17	Doug DeCinces	.25
18	Gus Polidor	.25
19	Brian Downing	.25
20	Gary Pettis	.25
21	Ruppert Jones	.25
22	George Hendrick	.25
23	Devon White	.25
---	Smokey Bear Logo Card/Checklist	.10

1988 California Angels Fire Safety

These borderless full-color cards (2-1/2" x 3-1/2") are highlighted by a thin white outline on front. The player name, team logo and a Smokey Bear picture logo appear in the photo's lower-right corner. Backs are black-and-white and include personal information and a large cartoon fire prevention tip. Part of the U.S. Forest Service fire prevention campaign, the cards were distributed in three separate in-stadium giveaways during August and September games.

		NM/M
Complete Set (25):		4.50
Common Player:		.25
1	Cookie Rojas	.25
2	Johnny Ray	.25
3	Jack Howell	.25
4	Mike Witt	.25
5	Tony Armas	.25
6	Gus Polidor	.25
7	DeWayne Buice	.25
8	Dan Petry	.25
9	Bob Boone	.50
10	Chili Davis	.25
11	Greg Minton	.25
12	Kirk McCaskill	.25
13	Devon White	.25
14	Willie Fraser	.25
15	Chuck Finley	.25
16	Dick Schofield	.25
17	Wally Joyner	.50
18	Brian Downing	.25
19	Stewart Cliburn	.25
20	Donnie Moore	.25
21	Bryan Harvey	.25
22	Mark McLemore	.25
23	Butch Wynegar	.25
24	George Hendrick	.25
---	Team Logo/Checklist	.10

1989 California Angels All-Stars Fire Safety

The U.S. Forest Service, in conjunction with the California Angels, issued this all-time team set. The 2-1/2" x 3-1/2" cards have a silver border with the player photo outlined in red. Beneath the photo a banner across homeplate reads "Angels All-Stars," along with the player's name and position, which are flanked by Smokey Bear on the left and the Angels 1989 All-Star Game logo on the right. Card backs highlight the player's career with the Angels and include an illustrated fire prevention tip.

		NM/M
Complete Set (20):		6.00
Common Player:		.25
1	Bill Rigney	.25
2	Dean Chance	.40
3	Jim Fregosi	.25
4	Bobby Knoop	.25
5	Don Mincher	.25
6	Clyde Wright	.25
7	Nolan Ryan	4.00
8	Frank Robinson	1.00
9	Frank Tanana	.25
10	Rod Carew	1.00
11	Bobby Grich	.25
12	Brian Downing	.25
13	Don Baylor	.25
14	Fred Lynn	.35
15	Reggie Jackson	1.50
16	Doug DeCinces	.25
17	Bob Boone	.35
18	Wally Joyner	.50
19	Mike Witt	.25
20	Johnny Ray	.25

1990 California Angels Fire Safety

This set was released by the U.S. Forestry Service in conjunction with the California Angels. The sets were distributed at the May 27 home game. The 2-1/2" x 3-1/2" cards feature full-color action photos surrounded by metallic silver borders. Team and Smokey Bear logos appear on front. Backs contain player data and a cartoon Smokey Bear message urging the prevention of forest fires.

		NM/M
Complete Set (20):		5.00
Common Player:		.25
1	Jim Abbott	.50
2	Bert Blyleven	.50
3	Chili Davis	.25
4	Brian Downing	.25
5	Chuck Finley	.25
6	Willie Fraser	.25
7	Bryan Harvey	.25
8	Jack Howell	.25
9	Wally Joyner	.50
10	Mark Langston	.25
11	Kirk McCaskill	.25
12	Mark McLemore	.25
13	Lance Parrish	.25
14	Johnny Ray	.25
15	Dick Schofield	.25
16	Mike Witt	.25
17	Claudell Washington	.25
18	Devon White	.25
19	Scott Bailes	.25
20	Bob McClure	.25

1991 California Angels Fire Safety

This set was sponsored by the California Department of Forestry. Front of the 2-1/2" x 3-1/2" cards features gray borders surrounding full-color action photos. The flip sides feature a fire safety cartoon and biographical information, along with sponsor logos, printed in blue and red on white.

		NM/M
Complete Set (20):		6.00
Common Player:		.25
1	Luis Polonia	.25
2	Junior Felix	.25
3	Dave Winfield	2.00
4	Dave Parker	.25
5	Lance Parrish	.25
6	Wally Joyner	.35
7	Jim Abbott	.45
8	Mark Langston	.25
9	Dick Schofield	.25
10	Kirk McCaskill	.25
11	Jack Howell	.25
12	Donnie Hill	.25
13	Gary Gaetti	.25
14	Chuck Finley	.25
15	Luis Sojo	.25
16	Mark Eichhorn	.25
17	Bryan Harvey	.25
18	Jeff Robinson	.25
19	Scott Lewis	.25
20	John Orton	.25

1992 California Angels Police

This safety set was sponsored by Carl's Jr. fast food restaurants and distributed by the Orange County Sheriff's Dept. Single cards were distributed to children over the course of the season and complete sets were handed out at the Angels' September 19 game. Fronts have color player action photos on a star-studded red, white and blue border. Backs have a small black-and-white portrait photo, stats, career highlights, an anti-drug message and sponsors' logos.

		NM/M
Complete Set (18):		8.00
Common Player:		.50
1	Jim Abbott	.60
2	Gene Autry	1.00
3	Bert Blyleven	.75
4	Hubie Brooks	.50
5	Chad Curtis	.50
6	Alvin Davis	.50
7	Gary DiSarcina	.50
8	Junior Felix	.50
9	Chuck Finley	.50
10	Gary Gaetti	.50
11	Rene Gonzalez	.50
12	Von Hayes	.50
13	Carl Karcher	.50
14	Mark Langston	.50
15	Luis Polonia	.50
16	Bobby Rose	.50
17	Lee Stevens	.50
18	Happy Star (Mascot)	.50

1993 California Angels Police

Sponsored by the Carl's Jr. hamburger restaurant chain and distributed through the California Chiefs & Sheriffs Assn., it was reported that 20,000-25,000 sets were produced. The 2-1/2" x 3-1/2" cards have a player action photo on front. Backs are printed in blue and black and include a portrait photo, career highlights, stats and an anti-drug message.

		NM/M
Complete Set (21):		16.00
Common Player:		.50
1	Gene Autry	1.00
2	Carl Karcher	.50
3	Buck Rodgers	.50
4	Rod Carew	3.50
5	Kelly Gruber	.50
6	Chili Davis	.50
7	Chad Curtis	.50
8	Mark Langston	.50
9	Scott Sanderson	.50
10	J.T. Snow	2.00
11	Rene Gonzalez	.50
12	Jimmie Reese	.50
13	Damion Easley	.50
14	Julio Valera	.50
15	Luis Polonia	.50
16	John Orton	.50
17	Gary DiSarcina	.50
18	Greg Myers	.50
19	Chuck Finley	.50
20	Tim Salmon	2.50
21	Happy Star (Mascot)	.50

1995 California Angels Police

The California Highway Patrol sponsored this safety set to coincide with the Angels 35th anniversary. Cards have action photos bordered in gray and dark blue. The team's anniversary logo and CHP logo appear in opposite corners. Black-and-white backs have a few bit of player data and a safety tip.

		NM/M
Complete Set (16):		20.00
Common Player:		1.00
1	Tim Salmon	2.00
2	Chuck Finley	1.00
3	Mark Langston	1.00
4	Gary Disarcina	1.00
5	Damion Easley	1.00
6	Spike Owen	1.00
7	Troy Percival	1.00
8	Chili Davis	1.00
9	Jim Edmonds	2.00
10	Rex Hudler	1.00
11	Greg Myers	1.00
12	Brian Anderson	1.00
13	J.T. Snow	1.50
14	Tony Phillips	1.00
15	Lee Smith	1.50
16	Marcel Lachemann, Don Watkins (Chief, CHP)	1.00

2004 California Angels Card Deck

This stadium giveaway was sponsored by Coast Plaza Doctors Hospital and Redio Disney. Cards are 2-1/4" x 3-7/16" with rounded corners. Red backs have team and sponsors' logos. Each player appears four times in the deck, with an identical portrait photo on the same value card in each suit. Two Rally Monkey jokers complete the boxed set.

		NM/M
Complete Set (54):		10.00
Common Player:		.25
2	Adam Kennedy	.25
3	Garret Anderson	.25
4	Bartolo Colon	.25
5	David Eckstein	.25
6	Jose Guillen	.35
7	Darin Erstad	.25
8	Kelvim Escobar	.25
9	Tim Salmon	.25
10	Bengie Molina	.25
J	Troy Percival	.25
Q	Troy Glaus	.40
K	Vladimir Guerrero	.50
A	Mike Scioscia	.25
Joker	Rally Monkey	.25

1992-93 Canadian Card News Repli-Cards

Krause Publications short-lived attempt to service the Canadian card collecting market with a newsstand magazine included the use of replicard panels of five in each of the magazine's five issues. The cards feature a mix of hockey players, CFL stars and Blue Jays and Expos. Only the baseball players are listed here.

		NM/M
Complete (Baseball) Set (12):		6.50
Common Player:		.50
2	Kelly Gruber	.50
3	Roberto Alomar	.75
5	Larry Walker, Marquis Grissom, Delino DeShields	.50
8	Dave Winfield	2.00
14	Ken Hill	.50
16	Jimmy Key	.50
17	Pat Borders	.50
21	Joe Carter	.50
22	Larry Walker	.75
23	Delino DeShields	.50
24	Derek Bell	.50
25	Wil Cordero	.50

1996 Canadian Club Classic Stars of the Game

A promotion for Canadian Club's Classic 12 whisky offered a series of autographed Hall of Famer cards. One card was included in a special folder attached to bottles. An offer sheet inside gave details for ordering other cards for $5 each plus proof of purchase. Also in the bottle-hanger was a certificate of authenticity for the enclosed signed card. In standard 2-1/2" x 3-1/2" format, cards feature vintage color player photos on which uniform logos have been deleted. Cards have a black border, are highlighted in gold foil and have an authentic autograph on front. Backs have career stats and summary. Cards #1-4 were labeled as Series I, cards #5-6 are Series II.

		NM/M
Complete Set (6):		60.00
Common Player:		6.00
1	Brooks Robinson	12.00
2	Billy Williams	6.00
3	Willie Stargell	13.50
4	Ernie Banks	17.50
5	Frank Robinson	15.00
6	Rollie Fingers	6.00

2000 CaP Cure Home Run Challenge

As part of its fund-raising "Home Run Challenge" promotion June 15-20, 2000, the Association for the Cure of Cancer of the Prostate issued a nine-card perforated sheet of 2-1/2" x 3-1/2" cards. Fronts have an action photo with black borders. At top-left is the CaP Cure logo, at lower-right is the MLBPA logo. Backs have messages promoting the cause, along with contact information for the organization.

		NM/M
Complete Sheet:		20.00
Complete Set (9):		20.00
Common Player:		2.00
(1)	Jason Giambi	2.00
(2)	Ken Griffey Jr.	3.00
(3)	Tony Gwynn	2.50
(4)	Derek Jeter	5.00
(5)	Mark McGwire	4.00
(6)	Alex Rodriguez	4.00
(7)	Sammy Sosa	2.50
(8)	Robin Ventura	1.00
(9)	Header Card	.25

2001 CaP Cure Home Run Challenge

As part of its fund-raising "Home Run Challenge" promotion, the Association for the Cure of Cancer of the Prostate issued a nine-card perforated sheet of 2-1/2" x 3-1/2" cards. Each card has two fronts, with each side having an action photo which is borderless at top, bottom and right. The CaP Cure logo is at lower-right, the player name and uniform number in a colored strip at right and the MLB Players Choice logo at top-left. The association phone number is at left. The center card on the sheet offers a contest to win autographed baseballs, utilizing the individual serial number on the back.

		NM/M
Complete Sheet:		15.00
Common Card:		1.50
(1)	Jeff Bagwell, Carlos Delgado	1.50
(2)	Jay Bell, Alex Rodriguez	3.00
(3)	Nomar Garciaparra, Sammy Sosa	2.00
(4)	Jason Giambi, Mark McGwire	2.50
(5)	Ken Griffey Jr., Robin Ventura	2.25
(6)	Tony Gwynn, Ivan Rodriguez	2.00
(7)	Derek Jeter, Mike Sweeney	3.00
(8)	Chipper Jones, Jim Thome	2.00
(9)	Contest Card	.25

2002 CaP Cure Home Run Challenge

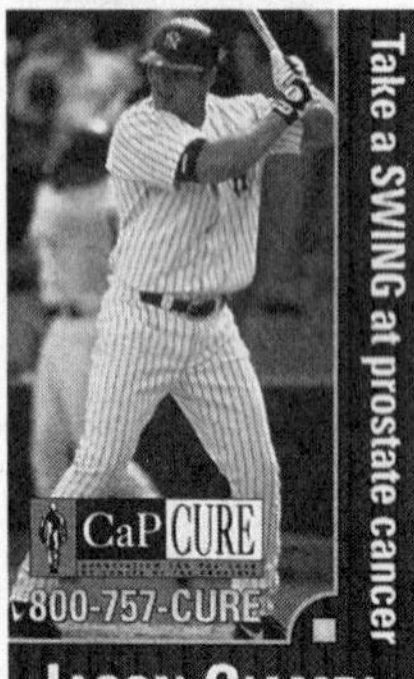

In its third season, the Association for the Cure of Cancer of the Prostate reduced the number of cards to four and the size of the cards to 1-5/8" x 2-3/4". Cards have action photos on front, which are repeated in ghost-image form on back. A Q-and-A about prostate cancer is presented on back.

		NM/M
Complete Set (4):		8.00
Common Player:		1.50
(1)	Derek Jeter	3.50
(2)	Jason Giambi	1.50
(3)	Ken Griffey Jr.	2.50
(4)	Sammy Sosa	2.00

1994 Capital Cards 1969 Mets Postcards

Nolan Ryan

Capital Cards, produced a 32-card postcard set of members of the 1969 World Champion New York Mets from Ron Lewis paintings, limited to 25,000 sets. Capital Cards also produced 5,000 uncut sheets that are individually numbered and carried a suggested retail price of $99.95. The boxed postcard set retailed for $39.95. The cards could also be purchased with autographs.

		NM/M
Complete Set (32):		15.00
Common Player:		.35
Uncut Sheet:		15.00
1	Logo Card	.35
2	Gil Hodges	2.00
3	Rube Walker	.35
4	Yogi Berra	2.00
5	Joe Pignatano	.35
6	Ed Yost	.35
7	Tommie Agee	.35
8	Ken Boswell	.35
9	Don Cardwell	.35
10	Ed Charles	.35
11	Donn Clendenon	.35
12	Jack DiLauro	.35
13	Duffy Dyer	.35
14	Wayne Garrett	.35
15	Rod Gaspar	.35
16	Gary Gentry	.35
17	Jerry Grote	.35
18	Bud Harrelson	.50
19	Cleon Jones	.50
20	Cal Koonce	.35
21	Jerry Koosman	.50
22	Ed Kranepool	.35
23	J.C. Martin	.35
24	Jim McAndrew	.35
25	Tug McGraw	.50
26	Bob Pfeil	.35
27	Nolan Ryan	6.00
28	Tom Seaver	3.00
29	Art Shamsky	.35
30	Ron Swoboda	.35
31	Ron Taylor	.35
32	Al Weis	.35

1989 Cap 'n Crunch

This 22-card set was produced by Topps for Cap 'n Crunch cereal boxes. Two cards and a stick of gum were included in each cereal box while the offer was active. The fronts of these 2-1/2" x 3-1/2" cards feature red, white and blue borders. The card backs are horizontal and feature lifetime statistics. The set was not offered in any complete set deal.

		NM/M
Complete Set (22):		5.00
Common Player:		.10
1	Jose Canseco	.40
2	Kirk Gibson	.10
3	Orel Hershiser	.10
4	Frank Viola	.10
5	Tony Gwynn	.65
6	Cal Ripken	1.50
7	Darryl Strawberry	.10
8	Don Mattingly	.75
9	George Brett	.75
10	Andre Dawson	.25
11	Dale Murphy	.25
12	Alan Trammell	.10
13	Eric Davis	.10
14	Jack Clark	.10
15	Eddie Murray	.50
16	Mike Schmidt	.75
17	Dwight Gooden	.10
18	Roger Clemens	.75
19	Will Clark	.10
20	Kirby Puckett	.65
21	Robin Yount	.50
22	Mark McGwire	1.00

1995 Cardtoons

Just about everything related to baseball comes in for the jab in this set of parody cards. Players, teams, attitudes, owners, mascots, Hall of Famers, announcers and the business of baseball are all panned. Besides a base set of 95 cards, there are several insert issues and send-away prizes. Cards are standard 2-1/2" x 3-1/2" with easily identifiable caricatures on front and sophomoric humor on the back. The cards make a point of stating they are parodies and not licensed either by the players or Major League Baseball. While they carry a 1993 copyright date, the cards were not issued until 1995.

		NM/M
Complete Set (95):		10.00
Common Card:		.25
1	Hey Abbott	.25
2	Robin Adventura	.25
3	Roberto Alamode	.30
4	Don Battingly	1.25
5	Cow Belle	.25
6	Jay Bellhop	.25
7	Fowl Boggs	1.00
8	Treasury Bonds	2.50
9	True Brett	1.25
10	Wild Pitch Mitch	.25
11	Balou's Brothers (Felipe Balou, Moises Balou)	.25
12	Charlie Bustle	2.00
13	Brett Butter	.25
14	Rambo Canseco	.40
15	Roberto Cementie	2.50
16	Roger Clemency	1.25
17	Will Clock	.25
18	David Clone	.25
19	Tom Clowning	.25
20	Mr. Club	1.00
21	Joe Crater	.25
22	Doolin' Daulton	.25
23	Chili Dog Davis	.25
24	Doug Drawback	.25
25	Dennis Excellency	.65
26	Silly Fanatic	.25
27	Wand Gonzalez	.40
28	Amazing Grace	.25
29	Tom Grapevine	.25
30	Marquis Gruesome	.25
31	Homerin' Hank	2.00
32	Kevin Happier	.25
33	Pete Harness	.25
34	Charlie Haze	.25
35	Egotisticky Henderson	.75
36	Sayanora Infielder	.25
37	Snoozin' Ted & Tarzan Jane	.25
38	Cloud Johnson	.75
39	Sandy K-Fax	2.00
40	The Say What Kid	2.00
41	Tommy Lasagna	.25
42	Greg Maddogs	1.00
43	Stamp the Man	1.00
44	Mark McBash	2.00
45	Fred McGruff	.25
46	Mount Mick	3.00
47	Pat Moustache	.25
48	Ozzie Myth	1.00
49	Bob Nukesbury	.25
50	Reggie October	1.00
51	Doctor OK	.25
52	Rafael Palmist	.65
53	Lose Piniella	.25
54	Vince Poleman	.25
55	Charlie Puff	.25
56	Rob Quibble	.25
57	Darryl Razzberry	.25
58	Cal Ripkenwinkle	2.50
59	Budge Rodriguez	.65
60	Ryne Sandbox	1.00
61	Steve Saxophone	.25
62	Harry Scary	.25
63	Scary Sheffield	.45
64	Ruben Siesta	.25
65	Dennis Smartinez	.25
66	Lee Smite	.25
67	Ken Spiffey Jr.	1.50
68	Nails Spikestra	.25
69	The Splendid Spinner	2.00
70	Toad Stottlemyre	.25
71	Raging Tartabull	.25
72	Robbery Thompson	.25
73	Alan Trampoline	.25
74	Monster Truk	.25
75	Shawon Tungsten	.25
76	Tony Twynn	1.00
77	Andy Van Tyke	.25
78	Derrick Ventriloquist	.25
79	Frank Violin	.25
80	Rap Winfielder	.75
81	Robinhood Yount	.75
82	Swift Justice	.25
83	Brat Saberhagen	.25
84	Mike Pizazz	1.50
85	Andres Colorado	.25
86	Money Bagswell	.75
87	Video Nomo	.40
88	Out of the Park	.25
89	Tim Wallet	.25
90	Checklist	.10
91	Greenback Jack	.25
92	Mighty Matt Power Hitter	.25
93	Frankenthomas	.75
94	Neon Peon Slanders	.35
95	Just Air Jordan	2.50
---	Replacement Card No. 1 (Redeemable for "Cardtoons Annual Awards" set with payment of $26.95.)	.10
---	Replacement Card No. 2 (Redeemable for Cardtoons binder and plastic sheets with payment of $18.95.)	.13
---	Replacement card No. 3 (Redeemable for Cardtoons phone card set of four with payment of $39.95.)	.13

Awards Replacement Set

This set was available via a mail-in offer for $26.95.

		NM/M
Complete Set (8):		6.25
Common Card:		1.00
R1	No Ball Peace Prize	1.00
R2	Forrest Grump	1.00
R3	Most Virtous Player	1.00
R4	Golden Glove Award	1.00
R5	Comdown Player of the Year	1.00
R6	Corkville Slugger	1.00
R7	Can't Get No Relief	1.00
R8	1994 World Series Champ	1.00

Big Bang Bucks

This insert set lampoons baseball's top 20 salaried players. Fronts resemble U.S. currency overprinted with gold foil in denominations of five, six and seven million. A player caricature portrait is in color at center of the 3-1/2" x 2-1/2" card. Backs give the player's salary history and rationale for his being overpaid. A statement on back says the cards are intended to be a parody and that they are not licensed by MLB or the players union. The cards are numbered with the "BB" prefix.

		NM/M
Complete Set (20):		20.00
Common Card:		1.00
1	Treasury Bonds	4.00
2	Sayanora Infielder	1.00
3	Cal Ripkenwinkle	4.00
4	Bobby Bonus	1.00
5	Joe Crater	1.00
6	Kirby Plunkit	2.00
7	David Clone	1.00
8	Ken Spiffey Jr.	3.00
9	Ruben Siesta	1.00
10	Greg Maddogs	2.00
11	Mark McBash	3.50
12	Rafael Palmist	1.50
13	Roberto Alamode	1.00
14	Greenback Jack	1.00
15	Raging Tartabull	1.00
16	Jimmy Kiwi	1.00
17	Roger Clemency	2.25
18	Rambo Canseco	1.25
19	Tom Grapevine	1.00
20	John Smileyface	1.00

Field of Greed Puzzle Set

These nine-cards are inserts which form a "Field of Greed" picture when the individual cards are aligned. Fronts have 1/9th of the cartoon puzzle, backs have a history of baseball's recent labor problems. Cards have an "FOG" prefix to their number.

		NM/M
Complete Set (9):		1.50
Common Card:		.25
1	1972 Strike	.25
2	1973 Lockout	.25
3	1976 Lockout	.25
4	1980 Strike	.25
5	1981 Strike	.25
6	1985 Strike	.25
7	1990 Lockout	.25
8	1994 Strike	.25
9	Future Problems	.25

Grand Slam Foils

This insert set utilizes foil printing technology to give a high-tech look to the caricatures of major leaguers. Fronts have cartoon parodies of the players, backs attempt to be humorous. A note on back says the cards are not licensed by either the players or Major League Baseball. Cards are numbered with a "F" prefix.

		NM/M
Complete Set (10):		12.00
Common Player:		1.00
1	Bo Action	1.50
2	Andre Awesome	1.25
3	Bobby Bonus	1.00
4	Steve Bravery	1.00
5	Carlton Fist	2.00
6	E.T. McGee	1.00
7	Kirby Plunkit	4.00
8	Jose Rheostat	1.00
9	Sir Noble Ryan	6.00
10	Day-Glo Sabo	1.00

Politics in Baseball

This insert set takes a poke at the perceived problems of baseball during the 1994-95 strike. Fronts have cartoons, backs have pointed commentary. Cards are numbered with the "S" prefix.

		NM/M
Complete Set (11):		3.00
Common Card:		.15
1	Pledge of Allegiance	.15
2	The Wave	.15
3	Slick Willie	1.50
4	Umpires Convention	.15
5	The Slide	.15
6	SH-H-H-H-H-H-H	.15
7	Throwing Out the First Contract	.15
8	Babe Rush	1.00
9	Hot Prospect	.15
10	Let's Play Ball	.15
11	Role Model	.15

1992 Carl's Jr. Padres

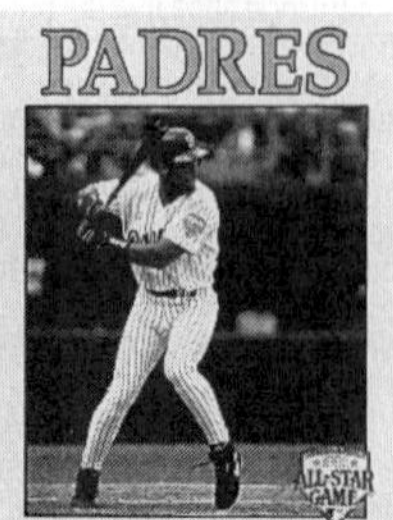

For the fifth consecutive year the San Diego Padres issued a card set in conjunction with the Jr. Padres program. Carl's Jr., a fast food chain, began sponsoring the set in 1991. The set contains 25 cards and was available in either nine-card perforated sheets or precut. At 2-9/16" x 3-9/16" the cards are slightly larger than current standard. Player photos feature an All-Star Game logo in the lower-right corner. On the white border, the player's name and position are printed in dark blue beneath the photo. The team name is in light brown above the photo. On back, the player's stats, career highlights and biographical data are printed in dark blue. The unnumbered cards are checklisted here in alphabetical order.

		NM/M
Complete Set (25):		6.00
Common Player:		.25
(1)	Larry Anderson	.25
(2)	Oscar Azocar	.25
(3)	Andy Benes	.25
(4)	Dann Bilardello	.25
(5)	Jerald Clark	.25
(6)	Tony Fernandez	.25
(7)	Tony Gwynn	4.00
(8)	Greg Harris	.25
(9)	Bruce Hurst	.25
(10)	Darrin Jackson	.25
(11)	Craig Lefferts	.25
(12)	Mike Maddux	.25
(13)	Fred McGriff	.25
(14)	Jose Melendez	.25
(15)	Randy Myers	.25
(16)	Greg Riddoch	.25
(17)	Rich Rodriguez	.25
(18)	Benito Santiago	.25
(19)	Gary Sheffield	.50
(20)	Craig Shipley	.25
(21)	Kurt Stillwell	.25
(22)	Tim Teufel	.25
(23)	Kevin Ward	.25
(24)	Ed Whitson	.25
(25)	All-Star Logo	.25

2003 Carl's Jr. San Diego Padres

Marking the team's 35th anniversary, the fast-food chain sponsored a card giveaway at Qualcomm on September 6. A baker's dozen past and current Padres stars are featured in the set, in several designs in 2-1/2" x 3-1/2" format on thin cardboard. Fronts have game-action color photos. On a two-toned blue background on back stats for the player's tenure with the Pads, printed in white, along with team and sponsor logos are presented. The unnumbered cards are listed here in alphabetical order.

		NM/M
Complete Set (13):		8.00
Common Player:		.25
(1)	Roberto Alomar	.40
(2)	Bruce Bochy	.25
(3)	Kevin Brown	.25
(4)	Ken Caminiti	.25
(5)	Steve Finley	.25
(6)	Steve Garvey	.50
(7)	Tony Gwynn	3.00
(8)	Trevor Hoffman	.25
(9)	Randy Jones	.25
(10)	Gaylord Perry	.50
(11)	Benito Santiago	.25
(12)	Ozzie Smith	3.00
(13)	Dave Winfield	2.00

1992 Carlson Travel 1982 Brewers

The team's American League Championship season of 1982 was commemorated a decade later with this card set given away at a Brewers promotional date. The cards were sponsored by Carlson Travel and United Airlines, whose logos appear on the front of the cards, along with Channel 6 television, whose logo is on the back. Fronts feature game-action photos of

the '82 Brewers, borderless at top and sides. Beneath the photo is a thin gold stripe, then a blue stripe with the player's name and position in white. A red, white and blue 1982 World Series logo appears in the lower-left corner. Backs are printed in blue, and include 1982 stats and a summary of the player's season. Player cards are numbered by uniform number in the upper-left.

		NM/M
Complete Set (31):		12.00
Common Player:		.25
4	Paul Molitor	5.00
5	Ned Yost	.25
7	Don Money	.25
10	Bob McClure	.25
11	Ed Romero	.25
13	Roy Howell	.25
15	Cecil Cooper	.25
16	Marshall Edwards	.25
17	Jim Gantner	.25
19	Robin Yount	5.00
20	Gorman Thomas	.25
21	Don Sutton	1.00
22	Charlie Moore	.25
23	Ted Simmons	.25
24	Ben Oglivie	.25
27	Pete Ladd	.25
29	Mark Brouhard	.25
30	Moose Haas	.25
32	Harvey Kuenn	.25
33	Doc Medich	.25
34	Rollie Fingers	1.00
41	Jim Slaton	.25
46	Jerry Augustine	.25
47	Dwight Bernard	.25
48	Mike Caldwell	.25
50	Pete Vuckovich	.25
---	Coaches (Pat Dobson, Larry Haney, Ron Hansen, Cal McLish, Harry Warner)	.25
---	Team Card	.25
---	Bernie Brewer (Mascot)	.25
---	Post-season Rally	.25
---	$50 Travel Coupon	.25

1985 CBS Radio Game of the Week

To promote its Game of the Week radio broadcasts, CBS issued a six-card set picturing network announcers, including Hall of Famer Johnny Bench. The cards, standard 2-1/2" x 3-1/2" format, were sent to CBS affiliate stations only. Fronts of the full-color cards picture the announcers in CBS Radio Sports baseball-style uniforms.

		NM/M
Complete Set (6):		55.00
Common Player:		3.00
(1)	Johnny Bench	35.00
(2)	Brent Musburger	15.00
(3)	Lindsey Nelson	7.50
(4)	John Rooney	3.00
(5)	Dick Stockton	4.50
(6)	Bill White	7.50

1986 CBS Radio Game of the Week

For the second consecutive year, CBS Radio Sports issued a five-card set featuring announcers used by the network for the Game of the Week and post-season broadcasts. The cards, packaged in a custom-designed wax wrapper, were sent to CBS radio affiliates as a promotion. The color cards measure 2-1/2" x 3-1/2".

		NM/M
Complete Set (5):		35.00
Common Player:		3.00
(1)	Sparky Anderson	15.00
(2)	Jack Buck	10.00
(3)	Howard David	3.00
(4)	Ernie Harwell	10.00
(5)	Ted Robinson	3.00

1987 Champion Phillies

This four card set is interesting in that the players are not identified on the card fronts or backs. The full-color cards, which measure 2-3/4" x 4-5/16", were produced by the Champion Spark Plug Co. as part of a contest held at participating Big A, Car Quest and Pep Boys auto parts stores. Entrants were advised to return the scratch-off coupon portion of the card for a chance to win a Blackbird Racer. Each card contains a scratch-off portion which may have contained an instant prize. Each card can be found with either a Big A, Car Quest or Pep Boys logo in the lower left corner on the card front. The contest was also sponsored in part by the Philadelphia Phillies and radio station WIP.

		NM/M
Complete Set (4):		15.00
Common Player:		1.00
(1)	Von Hayes (Glove on knee.)	1.00
(2)	Steve Jeltz (#30 on uniform)	1.00
(3)	Juan Samuel (Laying on base.)	1.00
(4)	Mike Schmidt (Making throw.)	12.00

1981 Champions of American Sport

From June 1981, through June 1982, Phillip Morris and Miller Beer sponsored a travel-

ing exhibition of sporting art and artifacts from The National Portrait Gallery and the Smithsonian Institution. In conjunction with the exhibitions in Washington, D.C., Chicago, Los Angeles and New York, an 18-card souvenir set was issued featuring many of the top athletes featured in the exhibits. The set was released in the form of an 8" x 11" eight-page booklet. Inside were two sheets of nine cards each. The perforated cards could be separated into individual cards of 2-1/2" x 3-3/4" dimensions. Fronts featured colored photos or artwork, backs had quotes about the athlete and stats. The unnumbered cards are checklisted here alphabetically.

		NM/M
Complete Set, Booklet:		60.00
Complete Set, Singles (18):		40.00
Common Player:		2.00
(1)	Muhammad Ali	6.00
(2)	Arthur Ashe	2.00
(3)	Peggy Fleming	2.00
(4)	A.J. Foyt	2.00
(5)	Eric Heiden	2.00
(6)	Bobby Hull	4.00
(7)	Sandy Koufax	6.00
(8)	Joe Louis	3.00
(9)	Bob Mathias	2.00
(10)	Willie Mays	6.00
(11)	Joe Namath	5.00
(12)	Jack Nicklaus	5.00
(13)	Knute Rockne	2.00
(14)	Bill Russell	5.00
(15)	Jim Ryun	2.00
(16)	Willie Shoemaker	2.00
(17)	Casey Stengel	2.00
(18)	Johnny Unitas	2.00

1988 Chef Boyardee

This uncut sheet features 12 each American and National League players. Color player portraits are printed beneath a red, white and blue "1988 1st Annual Collector's Edition" header. The player name, team and position appear beneath his photo. Card backs are printed in blue on red and include biographical information, stats and career highlights. The set was produced by American Home Food Products for distribution via a mail-in offer involving proofs of purchase from the company's Chef Boyardee products. Photos, licensed only by the players union, have had uniform logos airbrushed off.

		NM/M
Complete Set, Sheet:		6.00
Complete Set, Singles (24):		6.00
Common Player:		.10
1	Mark McGwire	1.00
2	Eric Davis	.10
3	Jack Morris	.10
4	George Bell	.10
5	Ozzie Smith	.60
6	Tony Gwynn	.60
7	Cal Ripken, Jr.	1.50
8	Todd Worrell	.10
9	Larry Parrish	.10
10	Gary Carter	.50
11	Ryne Sandberg	.60
12	Keith Hernandez	.10
13	Kirby Puckett	.60
14	Mike Schmidt	.75
15	Frank Viola	.10
16	Don Mattingly	.75
17	Dale Murphy	.25
18a	Andre Dawson (1987 team is Expos)	.25
18b	Andre Dawson (1987 team is Cubs)	.25
19	Mike Scott	.10
20	Rickey Henderson	.50
21	Jim Rice	.25
22	Wade Boggs	.60
23	Roger Clemens	.75
24	Fernando Valenzuela	.10

1996 Chevrolet/ Geo Pirates Team Sheet

Western Pennsylvania Chevy/Geo dealers sponsored this issue of a team card set given away at the May 12 game vs. the Giants. The individual 2-1/4" x 3-1/4" cards are perforated for removal from the sheet. Individual cards have a color player photo at center with team name and '96 logo at top in a red stripe and the player name and Chev logo at bottom in an orange stripe. Backs are in black-and-white. The cards are checklisted here in alphabetical order.

		NM/M
Complete Set, Uncut Sheet:		9.00
Complete Set, Singles (30):		7.00
Common Player:		.25
(1)	Jay Bell	.25
(2)	Cam Bonifay	.25
(3)	Jacob Brumfield	.25
(4)	Jason Christiansen	.25
(5)	Dave Clark	.25
(6)	Steve Cooke	.25
(7)	Francisco Cordova	.25
(8)	Danny Darwin	.25
(9)	John Ericks	.25
(10)	Carlos Garcia	.25
(11)	Lee Hancock	.25
(12)	Charlie Hayes	.25
(13)	Mark Johnson	.25
(14)	Jason Kendall	.75
(15)	Jim Leyland	.25
(16)	Jeff King	.25
(17)	Mike Kingery	.25
(18)	Nelson Liriano	.25
(19)	Jon Lieber	.25
(20)	Al Martin	.25
(21)	Orlando Merced	.25
(22)	Dan Miceli	.25
(23)	Denny Neagle	.25
(24)	Keith Osik	.25
(25)	Steve Parris	.25
(26)	Dan Plesac	.25
(27)	Zane Smith	.25
(28)	Paul Wagner	.25
(29)	John Wehner	.25
(30)	Pirate Parrot (Mascot)	.25

1992 Chevron Giants Hall of Fame Pins

This series of card/pin combinations was distributed by Chevron gas stations hon-

oring San Francisco Giants enshrined in baseball's Hall of Fame. Fronts of the 2-1/2" x 5" cards have a color player photo in an oval frame with an orange border. The player name and team logo are in a large white strip at bottom. Black-and-white backs have a small player portrait photo, some personal data, career highlights and pictures of the pins in the set. An enameled pin, about 1-1/8" x 1-1/4", with a representation of the player in action, is attached at the bottom of the card.

		NM/M
Complete Set (3):		15.00
Common Player:		4.00
24	Willie Mays	7.50
36	Gaylord Perry	4.00
44	Willie McCovey	4.00

2004 Chevron Clean Outta' Here

This premium set was regionally marketed with customers receiving a one-card pack with each $8 fuel purchase. Fronts have game-action photos and a Chevron "Clean Outta' Here" logo. Red, white and blue backs have stats, player data and career highlights. Printed on thin cardboard, the cards were produced by Upper Deck.

		NM/M
Complete Set (12):		3.00
Common Player:		.25
1	Andruw Jones	.50
2	Hank Blalock	.35
3	Jeff Bagwell	.50
4	Vladimir Guerrero	.50
5	Shawn Green	.35
6	Mike Lowell	.25
7	Aubrey Huff	.25
8	Richie Sexson	.25
9	Brian Giles	.25
10	Bret Boone	.25
11	A.J. Pierzynski	.25
12	Eric Chavez	.25

1985 Chicago Cubs Playing Cards

A regular 52-card deck plus two jokers comprise this set produced by long-time Cubs broadcaster Jack Brick-

house, whose photo and trademark phrase "Hey Hey!" are featured on the back of each card. Card fronts have a black-and-white photo with player(s) names and a date beneath. Traditional suit and value marking of a playing card deck are included in the corners of the 2-1/2" x 3-1/2" round-cornered cards. The cards are arranged in roughly chronological order.

		NM/M
Complete Set (54):		10.00
Common Player:		.25
AH	Jack Brickhouse	.25
2H	1876 Champions (Team composite photo.)	.25
3H	Cap Anson	.25
4H	Joe Tinker, Johnny Evers, Frank Chance, Harry Steinfeldt	2.00
5H	Ed Reulbach	.25
6H	Mordecai Brown	.25
7H	Jim Vaughn	.25
8H	Joe McCarthy	.25
9H	Jimmy Cooney	.25
10H	Rogers Hornsby	.50
JH	Hack Wilson	.25
QH	"Homers Row" (Hack Wilson, Babe Ruth, Lou Gehrig)	.50
KH	Babe Ruth ("Called the Shot")	4.00
AC	Lon Warneke	.25
2C	Augie Galan	.25
3C	1935 Pennant Winning Cubs (Team photo.)	.25
4C	Dizzy Dean	.50
5C	Gabby Hartnett	.25
6C	Billy Herman	.25
7C	Charlie Root	.25
8C	Charlie Grimm	.25
9C	Andy Pafko	.25
10C	Stan Hack	.25
JC	Phil Cavarretta	.25
QC	National League Champs 1945 (Team photo.)	.25
KC	Bill Nicholson	.25
KD	Hank Sauer	.25
QD	Ernie Banks	4.00
JD	Sam Jones	.25
10D	Dale Long	.25
9D	Lou Boudreau	.30
8D	Don Cardwell	.25
7D	Ken Hubbs	.50
6D	Billy Williams	.30
5D	1969 Cubs - The Team That Almost Made It (Composite photo.)	.25
4D	Ken Holtzman	.25
3D	Ron Santo	.30
2D	Fergie Jenkins	.40
AD	Burt Hooten (Hooton)	.25
KS	Milt Pappas	.25
QS	Rick Reuschel	.25
JS	Bill Madlock	.25
10S	Dallas Green	.25
9S	Jody Davis	.25
8S	Rick Sutcliffe	.25
7S	Jim Frey	.25
6S	Ryne Sandberg	4.00
5S	Eastern Division Champs 1984 (Team photo.)	.25
4S	Bob Dernier	.25
3S	Gary Matthews	.25
2S	Keith Moreland	.25
AS	Leon Durham	.25
Joker	Ron Cey	.25
Joker	Hey Hey! and Holy Cow! (Jack Brickhouse, Harry Caray)	.25

1988 Chicago Cubs Fire Safety

This set of four oversize (approximately 3-7/8" x 5-1/2") cards was produced on a single perforated sheet for distribution to fans as part of a U.S. Forest Service fire prevention campaign. Card fronts feature color player photos framed with vertical blue and pink borders and the player's name in light blue at bottom. Team and Smokey logos flank the name while the team name is printed in red above the photo. Backs have a bit of player biography and a large cartoon fire safety message.

		NM/M
Complete Set (4):		7.00
Common Card:		1.00
1	Vance Law (With Smokey.)	2.00
2	Vance Law/Fldg	2.00
3	Vance Law/Btg	2.00
4	Smokey Bear	1.00

1992 Chicago White Sox 1917 Team Issue Reprints

Card dealer Greg Manning, who purchased the unique original set of 1917 White Sox team-issue cards in 1991 issued a collectors' reprint set a year later. The reprints are in 2" x 3" format, slightly larger than the originals. The cards of the banned "Black Sox" have had a black frame added around the picture and have career information and 1919 stats on back. The other cards have blank backs. A second, colorized, card of Joe Jackson was added to the reprint set. The unnumbered cards are checklisted here in alphabetical order.

		NM/M
Complete Set (26):		9.00
Common Player:		.25
(1)	Joe Benz	.25
(2)	Eddie Cicotte	1.00
(3)	Eddie Collins	.25
(4)	Shano Collins	.25
(5)	Charles Comiskey	.25
(6)	Dave Danforth	.25
(7)	Red Faber	.25
(8)	Happy Felsch	.50
(9)	Chick Gandil	1.00
(10)	Kid Gleason	.25
(11)	Joe Jackson (Black-and-white.)	3.00
(12)	Joe Jackson (Colorized)	3.00
(12)	Joe Jenkins	.25
(13)	Ted Jourdan	.25
(14)	Nemo Leibold	.25
(15)	Byrd Lynn	.25
(16)	Fred McMullin	.50
(17)	Eddie Murphy	.25
(18)	Swede Risberg	.50
(19)	Pants Rowland	.25
(20)	Reb Russell	.25
(21)	Ray Schalk	.25
(22)	James Scott	.25
(23)	Buck Weaver	1.00
(24)	Lefty Williams	.50
(25)	Mellie Wolfgang	.25

2005 Chicago White Sox Carlton Fisk

This oversize (8-1/2" x 11") card was a Comiskey Park stadium giveaway on August 7 when the Hall of Famer's uniform number was retired by the White Sox. Sponsored by Nike, the back of the card has personal data and career stats.

	NM/M
Carlton Fisk	7.50

1994 Churchs Chicken Hometown Stars

Produced by Pinnacle Brands for distribution in the fried chicken restaurant chain, the cards were distributed in packs of four with the purchase of a nine-piece family meal or were sold separately for 69 cents. Each foil pack contained three regular cards and one card with gold foil instead of regular printing on the player's name and "Hometown Stars." Every fourth pack contains one of 10 "Show Stoppers" Dufex-process chase cards. In standard 2-1/2" x 3-1/2", the cards featured full-bleed front action photos with the Churchs logo at lower-left and the player's name at lower-right. "Hometown Stars" is printed vertically at top-left. Backs have a portrait photo at left, a career summary and 1993 and career stats. Because the cards were licensed by the Major League Baseball Players Association, but not Major League Baseball, both the front and the back photos on each card have had the uniform logos airbrushed away.

		NM/M
Complete Set (28):		7.00
Complete Set (Gold) (28):		15.00
Common Player:		.10
Common Player (Gold):		.25
1	Brian McRae	.10
1a	Brian McRae/Gold	.25
2	Dwight Gooden	.10
2a	Dwight Gooden/Gold	.25
3	Ruben Sierra	.10
3a	Ruben Sierra/Gold	.25
4	Greg Maddux	1.00
4a	Greg Maddux/Gold	1.50
5	Kirby Puckett	1.00
5a	Kirby Puckett/Gold	1.50
6	Jeff Bagwell	.75
6a	Jeff Bagwell/Gold	1.00
7	Cal Ripken, Jr.	1.50
7a	Cal Ripken, Jr./Gold	2.50
8	Lenny Dykstra	.10
8a	Lenny Dykstra/Gold	.25
9	Tim Salmon	.10
9a	Tim Salmon/Gold	.25
10	Matt Williams	.10
10a	Matt Williams/Gold	.25
11	Roberto Alomar	.30
11a	Roberto Alomar/Gold	.45
12	Barry Larkin	.10
12a	Barry Larkin/Gold	.25
13	Roger Clemens	1.00
13a	Roger Clemens/Gold	1.75
14	Mike Piazza	1.25
14a	Mike Piazzav	2.00
15	Travis Fryman	.10
15a	Travis Fryman/Gold	.25
16	Ryne Sandberg	1.00
16a	Ryne Sandberg/Gold	1.50
17	Robin Ventura	.10
17a	Robin Ventura/Gold	.25
18	Gary Sheffield	.35
18a	Gary Sheffield/Gold	.50
19	Carlos Baerga	.10
19a	Carlos Baerga/Gold	.25
20	Jay Bell	.10
20a	Jay Bell/Gold	.25
21	Edgar Martinez	.10
21a	Edgar Martinez/Gold	.25
22	Phil Plantier	.10
22a	Phil Plantier/Gold	.25
23	Danny Tartabull	.10
23a	Danny Tartabull/Gold	.25
24	Marquis Grissom	.10
24a	Marquis Grissom/Gold	.25
25	Robin Yount	.75
25a	Robin Yount/Gold	1.00
26	Ozzie Smith	1.00
26a	Ozzie Smith/Gold	1.50
27	Ivan Rodriguez	.60
27a	Ivan Rodriguez/Gold	.75
28	Dante Bichette	.10
28a	Dante Bichette/Gold	.25

Show Stoppers

Ten of baseball's top home-run hitters are featured in this insert set. Found approximately once every four packs in the four-card packs distributed by the fried chicken chain, the cards were produced by Pinnacle Brands using its foil-printing Dufex process. A player action photo is depicted inside a home-plate shaped frame at right. "Show Stoppers" is printed vertically at left in red and yellow tones. The background merges from green at left to purple at right, with the player's name in black in a yellow-to-red rainbow effect box beneath the photo. The Churchs logo is at bottom-left. On back is a portrait photo in a light blue box. There is a description of the player's home run prowess along with gold boxes showing his 1993 homers, slugging percentage and at bat/home run ratio. The border mirrors the front's green-to-purple effect. Because the cards are not licensed by Major League Baseball, the uniform logos have been removed from both the front and back photos.

		NM/M
Complete Set (10):		7.50
Common Player:		.50
1	Juan Gonzalez	.75
2	Barry Bonds	2.50
3	Ken Griffey Jr.	2.00
4	David Justice	.50
5	Frank Thomas	1.50
6	Fred McGriff	.50
7	Albert Belle	.50
8	Joe Carter	.50
9	Cecil Fielder	.50
10	Mickey Tettleton	.50

1998 CHW San Francisco Giants

At four special Senior Citizens Days at 3Com Park Giants home games, cards of four Hall of Famers were given away. The promotion was sponsored by Catholic Healthcare West, whose logo and name appear at top-left on the cards' fronts. Fronts combine vintage action photos with recent portrait shots and include a facsimile autograph. Backs provide a tip for healthy living and the phone numbers of various health care providers.

		NM/M
Complete Set (4):		20.00
Common Player:		4.00
(1)	Orlando Cepeda	4.00
(2)	Juan Marichal	4.00
(3)	Willie Mays	12.00
(4)	Willie McCovey	4.00

1982 Cincinnati Reds Yearbook Cards

In 1982 the Reds began a series of yearbook inserts consisting of two nine-card sheets. The 16-3/4" x 10-7/8" sheet contains 18 perforated 2-5/8" x 3-3/4" cards. Fronts have color photos wth red graphics and a white border. Backs are in black-and-white and include complete major and minor league stats. The cards are checklisted here by uniform number.

		NM/M
Complete Set, Sheet:		7.50
Complete Set, Singles (18):		6.00
Common Player:		.25
3	John McNamara	.25
5	Johnny Bench	3.00
13	Dave Concepcion	.25
16	Ron Oester	.25
21	Paul Householder	.25
22	Dan Driessen	.25
28	Cesar Cedeno	.25
29	Alex Trevino	.25
30	Clint Hurdle	.25
35	Frank Pastore	.25
36	Mario Soto	.25
38	Bruce Berenyi	.25
41	Tom Seaver	2.00
47	Tom Hume	.25
49	Joe Price	.25
51	Mike LaCoss	.25
---	Best in Baseball	.25
---	Riverfront Stadium	.25

1983 Cincinnati Reds Yearbook Cards

This 16-3/4" x 10-7/8" cardboard sheet was stapled into the Reds 1983 yearbook. The sheet contains 18 2-5/8" x 3-3/4" cards perforated for removal. Fronts have color game-action photos with red graphics. Backs are in black-and-white and include complete career stats. Cards are checklisted here by uniform number.

		NM/M
Complete Set, Sheet:		6.00
Complete Set, Singles (18):		5.00
Common Player:		.25
2	Gary Redus	.25
5	Johnny Bench	3.00
7	Russ Nixon	.25
13	Dave Concepcion	.25
16	Ron Oester	.25
20	Eddie Milner	.25
21	Paul Householder	.25
22	Dan Driessen	.25
25	Charlie Puleo	.25
28	Cesar Cedeno	.25
29	Alex Trevino	.25
32	Rich Gale	.25
35	Frank Pastore	.25
36	Mario Soto	.25
38	Bruce Berenyi	.25
47	Tom Hume	.25
49	Joe Price	.25
---	Riverfront Stadium	.25

1984 Cincinnati Reds Yearbook Cards

Once again in 1984 the Reds inserted a 16-3/4" x 11" cardboard panel into their yearbook. The sheet contains 18 cards, 2-5/8" x 3-3/4", perforated for removal. Fronts have color phots with a large red frame and white borders. Backs are in black-and-white with complete major and minor league stats. Cards are checklisted here by uniform number.

		NM/M
Complete Set, Sheet:		5.00
Complete Set, Singles (18):		3.00
Common Player:		.25
2	Gary Redus	.25
9	Vern Rapp	.25
11	Dann Bilardello	.25
12	Nick Esasky	.25
13	Dave Concepcion	.25
16	Ron Oester	.25
20	Eddie Milner	.25
22	Dan Driessen	.25
24	Tony Perez	1.00
26	Duane Walker	.25
34	Bill Scherrer	.25
35	Frank Pastore	.25
36	Mario Soto	.25
38	Bruce Berenyi	.25

39	Dave Parker	.35
47	Tom Hume	.25
49	Joe Price	.25
---	Bob Howsam (President)	.25

1985 Cincinnati Reds Yearbook Cards

Once again in 1985 the Reds inserted a 16-3/4" x 11" cardboard panel into their yearbook. The sheet contains 18 cards, 2-5/8" x 3-3/4", perforated for removal. Fronts have color phots with red and white graphics. Backs are in black-and-white with complete major and minor league stats. Cards are checklisted here alphabetically.

		NM/M
Complete Sheet:		6.00
Complete Set (18):		5.00
Common Player:		.25
(1)	Cesar Cedeno	.25
(2)	Dave Concepcion	.25
(3)	Eric Davis	.75
(4)	Nick Esasky	.25
(5)	Tom Foley	.25
(6)	John Franco	.25
(7)	Brad Gulden	.25
(8)	Wayne Krenchicki	.25
(9)	Eddie Milner	.25
(10)	Ron Oester	.25
(11)	Dave Parker	.25
(12)	Ted Power	.25
(13)	Joe Price	.25
(14)	Pete Rose	3.00
(15)	Jeff Russell	.25
(16)	Mario Soto	.25
(17)	Jay Tibbs	.25
(18)	Duane Walker	.25

2003 Cincinnati Reds Scratch-Offs

The first 10,000 fans entering the newly opened Great American Ball Park for a trio of promotional dates received a special scratch-off card. The card has a game-action borderless photo on front. At top left is the sponsor's (Klosterman or Kroger) logo, with a silver box beneath. Scratching off the box revealed whether the fan won one of 500 player-autographed balls which were given away that day. The team's 2003 logo is at bottom-right. The back has the same logos, along with a career summary and an ink-jetted serial number.

		NM/M
Complete Set (3):		4.00
Common Player:		1.00
(1)	Johnny Bench	2.00
(2)	Aaron Boone	1.00
(3)	Adam Dunn	1.50

1996 Circa

This hobby-exclusive product was limited to 2,000 sequentially numbered cases. The regular-issue set has 196 player cards, including 18 top prospects and four prospects. Circa also has a 200-card parallel set called Rave which is limited to 150 sets. Each Rave card is sequentially numbered from 1-150. Two other insert sets were also produced - Access and Boss.

		NM/M
Complete Set (200):		15.00
Common Player:		.10
Raves:		30X
Pack (8):		1.50
Wax Box (24):		25.00
1	Roberto Alomar	.25
2	Brady Anderson	.10
3	Rocky Coppinger **RC**	.10
4	Eddie Murray	.75
5	Mike Mussina	.35
6	Randy Myers	.10
7	Rafael Palmeiro	.65
8	Cal Ripken Jr.	2.00
9	Jose Canseco	.50
10	Roger Clemens	1.00
11	Mike Greenwell	.10
12	Tim Naehring	.10
13	John Valentin	.10
14	Mo Vaughn	.10
15	Tim Wakefield	.10
16	Jim Abbott	.10
17	Garret Anderson	.10
18	Jim Edmonds	.10
19	Darin Erstad **RC**	2.00
20	Chuck Finley	.10
21	Troy Percival	.10
22	Tim Salmon	.10
23	J.T. Snow	.10
24	Wilson Alvarez	.10
25	Harold Baines	.10
26	Ray Durham	.10
27	Alex Fernandez	.10
28	Tony Phillips	.10
29	Frank Thomas	.75
30	Robin Ventura	.10
31	Sandy Alomar Jr.	.10
32	Albert Belle	.10
33	Kenny Lofton	.10
34	Dennis Martinez	.10
35	Jose Mesa	.10
36	Charles Nagy	.10
37	Manny Ramirez	.75
37p	Manny Ramirez/OPS	2.00
38	Jim Thome	.60
39	Travis Fryman	.10
40	Bob Higginson	.10
41	Melvin Nieves	.10
42	Alan Trammell	.10
43	Kevin Appier	.10
44	Johnny Damon	.30
45	Keith Lockhart	.10
46	Jeff Montgomery	.10
47	Joe Randa	.10
48	Bip Roberts	.10
49	Ricky Bones	.10
50	Jeff Cirillo	.10
51	Marc Newfield	.10
52	Dave Nilsson	.10
53	Kevin Seitzer	.10
54	Ron Coomer	.10
55	Marty Cordova	.10
56	Roberto Kelly	.10
57	Chuck Knoblauch	.10
58	Paul Molitor	.75
59	Kirby Puckett	1.00
60	Scott Stahoviak	.10
61	Wade Boggs	1.00
62	David Cone	.10
63	Cecil Fielder	.10
64	Dwight Gooden	.10
65	Derek Jeter	2.00
66	Tino Martinez	.10
67	Paul O'Neill	.10
68	Andy Pettitte	.35
69	Ruben Rivera	.10
70	Bernie Williams	.10
71	Geronimo Berroa	.10
72	Jason Giambi	.45
73	Mark McGwire	1.50
74	Terry Steinbach	.10
75	Todd Van Poppel	.10
76	Jay Buhner	.10
77	Norm Charlton	.10
78	Ken Griffey Jr.	1.25
79	Randy Johnson	.75
80	Edgar Martinez	.10
81	Alex Rodriguez	1.50
82	Paul Sorrento	.10
83	Dan Wilson	.10
84	Will Clark	.10
85	Kevin Elster	.10
86	Juan Gonzalez	.40
87	Rusty Greer	.10
88	Ken Hill	.10
89	Mark McLemore	.10
90	Dean Palmer	.10
91	Roger Pavlik	.10
92	Ivan Rodriguez	.65
93	Joe Carter	.10
94	Carlos Delgado	.35
95	Juan Guzman	.10
96	John Olerud	.10
97	Ed Sprague	.10
98	Jermaine Dye	.10
99	Tom Glavine	.30
100	Marquis Grissom	.10
101	Andruw Jones	.75
102	Chipper Jones	1.00
103	David Justice	.10
104	Ryan Klesko	.10
105	Greg Maddux	1.00
106	Fred McGriff	.10
107	John Smoltz	.10
108	Brant Brown	.10
109	Mark Grace	.10
110	Brian McRae	.10
111	Ryne Sandberg	1.00
112	Sammy Sosa	1.00
113	Steve Trachsel	.10
114	Bret Boone	.10
115	Eric Davis	.10
116	Steve Gibralter	.10
117	Barry Larkin	.10
118	Reggie Sanders	.10
119	John Smiley	.10
120	Dante Bichette	.10
121	Ellis Burks	.10
122	Vinny Castilla	.10
123	Andres Galarraga	.10
124	Larry Walker	.10
125	Eric Young	.10
126	Kevin Brown	.10
127	Greg Colbrunn	.10
128	Jeff Conine	.10
129	Charles Johnson	.10
130	Al Leiter	.10
131	Gary Sheffield	.50
132	Devon White	.10
133	Jeff Bagwell	.75
134	Derek Bell	.10
135	Craig Biggio	.10
136	Doug Drabek	.10
137	Brian Hunter	.10
138	Darryl Kile	.10
139	Shane Reynolds	.10
140	Brett Butler	.10
141	Eric Karros	.10
142	Ramon Martinez	.10
143	Raul Mondesi	.10
144	Hideo Nomo	.40
145	Chan Ho Park	.10
146	Mike Piazza	1.25
147	Moises Alou	.10
148	Yamil Benitez	.10
149	Mark Grudzielanek	.10
150	Pedro Martinez	.75
151	Henry Rodriguez	.10
152	David Segui	.10
153	Rondell White	.10
154	Carlos Baerga	.10
155	John Franco	.10
156	Bernard Gilkey	.10
157	Todd Hundley	.10
158	Jason Isringhausen	.10
159	Lance Johnson	.10
160	Alex Ochoa	.10
161	Rey Ordonez	.10
162	Paul Wilson	.10
163	Ron Blazier	.10
164	Ricky Bottalico	.10
165	Jim Eisenreich	.10
166	Pete Incaviglia	.10
167	Mickey Morandini	.10
168	Ricky Otero	.10
169	Curt Schilling	.25
170	Jay Bell	.10
171	Charlie Hayes	.10
172	Jason Kendall	.10
173	Jeff King	.10
174	Al Martin	.10
175	Alan Benes	.10
176	Royce Clayton	.10
177	Brian Jordan	.10
178	Ray Lankford	.10
179	John Mabry	.10
180	Willie McGee	.10
181	Ozzie Smith	1.00
182	Todd Stottlemyre	.10
183	Andy Ashby	.10
184	Ken Caminiti	.10
185	Steve Finley	.10
186	Tony Gwynn	1.00
187	Rickey Henderson	.75
188	Wally Joyner	.10
189	Fernando Valenzuela	.10
190	Greg Vaughn	.10
191	Rod Beck	.10
192	Barry Bonds	2.00
193	Shawon Dunston	.10
194	Chris Singleton	.10
195	Robby Thompson	.10
196	Matt Williams	.10
197	Checklist (Barry Bonds)	.75
198	Checklist (Ken Griffey Jr.)	.65
199	Checklist (Cal Ripken Jr.)	.75
200	Checklist (Frank Thomas)	.40

Rave

Rainbow metallic foil highlights on front and a serial number on back from within an edition of 150 of each card differentiate this parallel issue from the Circa base cards. Announced insertion rate for Raves was one per 60 packs.

	NM/M
Common Player:	2.00
Stars:	30X

Access

This 1996 Fleer Circa insert set highlights 30 players on a three-panel foldout design that includes multiple photographs, personal information and statistics. The cards were seeded about one every 12 packs.

		NM/M
Complete Set (30):		50.00
Common Player:		.60
1	Cal Ripken Jr.	6.00
2	Mo Vaughn	.60
3	Tim Salmon	.75
4	Frank Thomas	2.00
5	Albert Belle	.75
6	Kenny Lofton	.60
7	Manny Ramirez	2.00
8	Paul Molitor	2.00
9	Kirby Puckett	3.00
10	Paul O'Neill	.60
11	Mark McGwire	5.00
12	Ken Griffey Jr.	4.00
13	Randy Johnson	2.00
14	Greg Maddux	3.00
15	John Smoltz	.60
16	Sammy Sosa	4.00
17	Barry Larkin	.60
18	Gary Sheffield	1.00
19	Jeff Bagwell	2.00
20	Hideo Nomo	2.00
21	Mike Piazza	4.00
22	Moises Alou	.60
23	Henry Rodriguez	.60
24	Rey Ordonez	.60
25	Jay Bell	.60
26	Ozzie Smith	3.00
27	Tony Gwynn	3.00
28	Rickey Henderson	2.00
29	Barry Bonds	6.00
30	Matt Williams	.60
30p	Matt Williams/OPS	1.00

Boss

This insert set showcases the game's top stars on an embossed design. Cards were seeded one per six packs.

		NM/M
Complete Set (50):		50.00
Common Player:		.45
1	Roberto Alomar	1.00
2	Cal Ripken Jr.	5.00
2p	Cal Ripken Jr./OPS	3.00
3	Jose Canseco	1.50
4	Mo Vaughn	.45
5	Tim Salmon	.60
6	Frank Thomas	2.00
7	Robin Ventura	.45
8	Albert Belle	.60
9	Kenny Lofton	.45
10	Manny Ramirez	2.00
11	Dave Nilsson	.45
12	Chuck Knoblauch	.45
13	Paul Molitor	2.00
14	Kirby Puckett	3.00
15	Wade Boggs	3.00
16	Dwight Gooden	.45
17	Paul O'Neill	.45
18	Mark McGwire	4.00
19	Jay Buhner	.45
20	Ken Griffey Jr.	3.50
21	Randy Johnson	2.00
22	Will Clark	.60
23	Juan Gonzalez	2.00
24	Joe Carter	.45
25	Tom Glavine	.45
26	Ryan Klesko	.45
27	Greg Maddux	3.00
28	John Smoltz	.45
29	Ryne Sandberg	3.00
30	Sammy Sosa	3.50
31	Barry Larkin	.45
32	Reggie Sanders	.45
33	Dante Bichette	.45
34	Andres Galarraga	.45
35	Charles Johnson	.45
36	Gary Sheffield	1.50
37	Jeff Bagwell	2.00
38	Hideo Nomo	2.00
39	Mike Piazza	3.50
40	Moises Alou	.45
41	Henry Rodriguez	.45
42	Rey Ordonez	.45
43	Ricky Otero	.45
44	Jay Bell	.45
45	Royce Clayton	.45
46	Ozzie Smith	3.00
47	Tony Gwynn	3.00
48	Rickey Henderson	2.00
49	Barry Bonds	5.00
50	Matt Williams	.45

1997 Circa

Circa baseball returned for the second year in 1997, with a 400-card set, including 393 player cards and seven checklists. Cards feature action photos on a dynamic graphic arts background, and arrived in eight-card packs. The set was paralelled in a Rave insert and was accompanied by five inserts: Boss, Fast Track, Icons, Limited Access and Rave Reviews.

		NM/M
Complete Set (400):		15.00
Common Player:		.10
Pack (8):		1.00
Retail Wax Box (18):		15.00
Hobby Wax Box (36):		30.00
1	Kenny Lofton	.10
2	Ray Durham	.10
3	Mariano Rivera	.20
4	Jon Lieber	.10
5	Tim Salmon	.10
6	Mark Grudzielanek	.10
7	Neifi Perez	.10
8	Cal Ripken Jr.	3.00
9	John Olerud	.10
10	Edgar Renteria	.10
11	Jose Rosado	.10
12	Mickey Morandini	.10
13	Orlando Miller	.10
14	Ben McDonald	.10
15	Hideo Nomo	.40
16	Fred McGriff	.10
17	Sean Berry	.10
18	Roger Pavlik	.10
19	Aaron Sele	.10
20	Joey Hamilton	.10
21	Roger Clemens	1.25
22	Jose Herrera	.10
23	Ryne Sandberg	1.00
24	Ken Griffey Jr.	1.50
25	Barry Bonds	3.00
26	Dan Naulty	.10
27	Wade Boggs	1.00
28	Ray Lankford	.10
29	Rico Brogna	.10
30	Wally Joyner	.10
31	F.P. Santangelo	.10
32	Vinny Castilla	.10
33	Eddie Murray	.75
34	Kevin Elster	.10
35	Mike Macfarlane	.10
36	Jeff Kent	.10
37	Orlando Merced	.10
38	Jason Isringhausen	.10
39	Chad Ogea	.10
40	Greg Gagne	.10
41	Curt Lyons	.10
42	Mo Vaughn	.10
43	Rusty Greer	.10
44	Shane Reynolds	.10
45	Frank Thomas	.75
46	Chris Hoiles	.10
47	Scott Sanders	.10
48	Mark Lemke	.10
49	Fernando Vina	.10
50	Mark McGwire	2.00
51	Bernie Williams	.10
52	Bobby Higginson	.10
53	Kevin Tapani	.10
54	Rich Becker	.10
55	Felix Heredia **RC**	.30
56	Delino DeShields	.10
57	Rick Wilkins	.10
58	Edgardo Alfonzo	.10
59	Brett Butler	.10
60	Ed Sprague	.10
61	Joe Randa	.10
62	Ugueth Urbina	.10
63	Todd Greene	.10
64	Devon White	.10
65	Bruce Ruffin	.10
66	Mark Gardner	.10
67	Omar Vizquel	.10
68	Luis Gonzalez	.10
69	Tom Glavine	.25
70	Cal Eldred	.10
71	William Van Landingham	.10
72	Jay Buhner	.10
73	James Baldwin	.10
74	Robin Jennings	.10
75	Terry Steinbach	.10
76	Billy Taylor	.10
77	Armando Benitez	.10
78	Joe Girardi	.10
79	Jay Bell	.10
80	Damon Buford	.10
81	Deion Sanders	.15
82	Bill Haselman	.10
83	John Flaherty	.10
84	Todd Stottlemyre	.10
85	J.T. Snow	.10
86	Felipe Lira	.10
87	Steve Avery	.10
88	Trey Beamon	.10
89	Alex Gonzalez	.10
90	Mark Clark	.10
91	Shane Andrews	.10
92	Randy Myers	.10
93	Gary Gaetti	.10
94	Jeff Blauser	.10
95	Tony Batista	.10
96	Todd Worrell	.10
97	Jim Edmonds	.10
98	Eric Young	.10
99	Roberto Kelly	.10
100	Alex Rodriguez	2.00
100p	Alex Rodriguez/OPS	2.00
101	Julio Franco	.10
102	Jeff Bagwell	.75
103	Bobby Witt	.10
104	Tino Martinez	.10
105	Shannon Stewart	.10
106	Brian Banks	.10
107	Eddie Taubensee	.10
108	Terry Mulholland	.10
109	Lyle Mouton	.10
110	Jeff Conine	.10
111	Johnny Damon	.30
112	Quilvio Veras	.10
113	Wilton Guerrero	.10
114	Dmitri Young	.10
115	Garret Anderson	.10
116	Bill Pulsipher	.10
117	Jacob Brumfield	.10
118	Mike Lansing	.10
119	Jose Canseco	.50
120	Mike Bordick	.10
121	Kevin Stocker	.10
122	Frank Rodriguez	.10
123	Mike Cameron	.10
124	Tony Womack **RC**	.25
125	Bret Boone	.10
126	Moises Alou	.10
127	Tim Naehring	.10
128	Brant Brown	.10
129	Todd Zeile	.10
130	Dave Nilsson	.10

131	Donne Wall	.10
132	Jose Mesa	.10
133	Mark McLemore	.10
134	Mike Stanton	.10
135	Dan Wilson	.10
136	Jose Offerman	.10
137	David Justice	.10
138	Kirt Manwaring	.10
139	Raul Casanova	.10
140	Ron Coomer	.10
141	Dave Hollins	.10
142	Shawn Estes	.10
143	Darren Daulton	.10
144	Turk Wendell	.10
145	Darrin Fletcher	.10
146	Marquis Grissom	.10
147	Andy Benes	.10
148	Nomar Garciaparra	1.00
149	Andy Pettitte	.30
150	Tony Gwynn	1.00
151	Robb Nen	.10
152	Kevin Seitzer	.10
153	Ariel Prieto	.10
154	Scott Karl	.10
155	Carlos Baerga	.10
156	Wilson Alvarez	.10
157	Thomas Howard	.10
158	Kevin Appier	.10
159	Russ Davis	.10
160	Justin Thompson	.10
161	Pete Schourek	.10
162	John Burkett	.10
163	Roberto Alomar	.25
164	Darren Holmes	.10
165	Travis Miller	.10
166	Mark Langston	.10
167	Juan Guzman	.10
168	Pedro Astacio	.10
169	Mark Johnson	.10
170	Mark Leiter	.10
171	Heathcliff Slocumb	.10
172	Dante Bichette	.10
173	Brian Giles **RC**	1.00
174	Paul Wilson	.10
175	Eric Davis	.10
176	Charles Johnson	.10
177	Willie Greene	.10
178	Geronimo Berroa	.10
179	Mariano Duncan	.10
180	Robert Person	.10
181	David Segui	.10
182	Ozzie Guillen	.10
183	Osvaldo Fernandez	.10
184	Dean Palmer	.10
185	Bob Wickman	.10
186	Eric Karros	.10
187	Travis Fryman	.10
188	Andy Ashby	.10
189	Scott Stahoviak	.10
190	Norm Charlton	.10
191	Craig Paquette	.10
192	John Smoltz	.10
193	Orel Hershiser	.10
194	Glenallen Hill	.10
195	George Arias	.10
196	Brian Jordan	.10
197	Greg Vaughn	.10
198	Rafael Palmeiro	.60
199	Darryl Kile	.10
200	Derek Jeter	3.00
201	Jose Vizcaino	.10
202	Rick Aguilera	.10
203	Jason Schmidt	.10
204	Trot Nixon	.10
205	Tom Pagnozzi	.10
206	Mark Wohlers	.10
207	Lance Johnson	.10
208	Carlos Delgado	.40
209	Cliff Floyd	.10
210	Kent Mercker	.10
211	Matt Mieske	.10
212	Ismael Valdes	.10
213	Shawon Dunston	.10
214	Melvin Nieves	.10
215	Tony Phillips	.10
216	Scott Spiezio	.10
217	Michael Tucker	.10
218	Matt Williams	.10
219	Ricky Otero	.10
220	Kevin Ritz	.10
221	Darryl Strawberry	.10
222	Troy Percival	.10
223	Eugene Kingsale	.10
224	Julian Tavarez	.10
225	Jermaine Dye	.10
226	Jason Kendall	.10
227	Sterling Hitchcock	.10
228	Jeff Cirillo	.10
229	Roberto Hernandez	.10
230	Ricky Bottalico	.10
231	Bobby Bonilla	.10
232	Edgar Martinez	.10
233	John Valentin	.10
234	Ellis Burks	.10
235	Benito Santiago	.10
236	Terrell Wade	.10
237	Armando Reynoso	.10
238	Danny Graves	.10
239	Ken Hill	.10
240	Dennis Eckersley	.65
241	Darin Erstad	.25
242	Lee Smith	.10
243	Cecil Fielder	.10
244	Tony Clark	.10
245	Scott Erickson	.10
246	Bob Abreu	.10
247	Ruben Sierra	.10
248	Chili Davis	.10
249	Darryl Hamilton	.10
250	Albert Belle	.10
251	Todd Hollandsworth	.10
252	Terry Adams	.10
253	Rey Ordonez	.10
254	Steve Finley	.10
255	Jose Valentin	.10
256	Royce Clayton	.10
257	Sandy Alomar	.10
258	Mike Lieberthal	.10
259	Ivan Rodriguez	.65
260	Rod Beck	.10
261	Ron Karkovice	.10
262	Mark Gubicza	.10
263	Chris Holt	.10
264	Jaime Bluma	.10
265	Francisco Cordova	.10
266	Javy Lopez	.10
267	Reggie Jefferson	.10
268	Kevin Brown	.10
269	Scott Brosius	.10
270	Dwight Gooden	.10
271	Marty Cordova	.10
272	Jeff Brantley	.10
273	Joe Carter	.10
274	Todd Jones	.10
275	Sammy Sosa	1.00
276	Randy Johnson	.75
277	B.J. Surhoff	.10
278	Chan Ho Park	.10
279	Jamey Wright	.10
280	Manny Ramirez	.75
281	John Franco	.10
282	Tim Worrell	.10
283	Scott Rolen	.60
284	Reggie Sanders	.10
285	Mike Fetters	.10
286	Tim Wakefield	.10
287	Trevor Hoffman	.10
288	Donovan Osborne	.10
289	Phil Nevin	.10
290	Jermaine Allensworth	.10
291	Rocky Coppinger	.10
292	Tim Raines	.10
293	Henry Rodriguez	.10
294	Paul Sorrento	.10
295	Tom Goodwin	.10
296	Raul Mondesi	.10
297	Allen Watson	.10
298	Derek Bell	.10
299	Gary Sheffield	.45
300	Paul Molitor	.75
301	Shawn Green	.15
302	Darren Oliver	.10
303	Jack McDowell	.10
304	Denny Neagle	.10
305	Doug Drabek	.10
306	Mel Rojas	.10
307	Andres Galarraga	.10
308	Alex Ochoa	.10
309	Gary DiSarcina	.10
310	Ron Gant	.10
311	Gregg Jefferies	.10
312	Ruben Rivera	.10
313	Vladimir Guerrero	.75
314	Willie Adams	.10
315	Bip Roberts	.10
326	Mark Grace	.10
317	Bernard Gilkey	.10
318	Marc Newfield	.10
319	Al Leiter	.10
320	Otis Nixon	.10
321	Tom Candiotti	.10
322	Mike Stanley	.10
323	Jeff Fassero	.10
324	Billy Wagner	.10
325	Todd Walker	.10
326	Chad Curtis	.10
327	Quinton McCracken	.10
328	Will Clark	.10
329	Andruw Jones	.75
330	Robin Ventura	.10
331	Curtis Pride	.10
332	Barry Larkin	.10
333	Jimmy Key	.10
334	David Wells	.10
335	Mike Holtz	.10
336	Paul Wagner	.10
337	Greg Maddux	1.00
338	Curt Schilling	.35
339	Steve Trachsel	.10
340	John Wetteland	.10
341	Rickey Henderson	.75
342	Ernie Young	.10
343	Harold Baines	.10
344	Bobby Jones	.10
345	Jeff D'Amico	.10
346	John Mabry	.10
347	Pedro Martinez	.75
348	Mark Lewis	.10
349	Dan Miceli	.10
350	Chuck Knoblauch	.10
351	John Smiley	.10
352	Brady Anderson	.10
353	Jim Leyritz	.10
354	Al Martin	.10
355	Pat Hentgen	.10
356	Mike Piazza	1.50
357	Charles Nagy	.10
358	Luis Castillo	.10
359	Paul O'Neill	.10
360	Steve Reed	.10
361	Tom Gordon	.10
362	Craig Biggio	.10
363	Jeff Montgomery	.10
364	Jamie Moyer	.10
365	Ryan Klesko	.10
366	Todd Hundley	.10
367	Bobby Estalella	.10
368	Jason Giambi	.50
369	Brian Hunter	.10
370	Ramon Martinez	.10
371	Carlos Garcia	.10
372	Hal Morris	.10
373	Juan Gonzalez	.40
374	Brian McRae	.10
375	Mike Mussina	.40
376	John Ericks	.10
377	Larry Walker	.10
378	Chris Gomez	.10
379	John Jaha	.10
380	Rondell White	.10
381	Chipper Jones	1.00
382	David Cone	.10
383	Alan Benes	.10
384	Troy O'Leary	.10
385	Ken Caminiti	.10
386	Jeff King	.10
387	Mike Hampton	.10
388	Jaime Navarro	.10
389	Brad Radke	.10
390	Joey Cora	.10
391	Jim Thome	.60
392	Alex Fernandez	.10
393	Chuck Finley	.10
394	Andruw Jones Checklist	.35
395	Ken Griffey Jr. Checklist	.60
396	Frank Thomas Checklist	.35
397	Alex Rodriguez Checklist	.75
398	Cal Ripken Jr. Checklist	1.00
399	Mike Piazza Checklist	.60
400	Greg Maddux Checklist	.45

Rave

In its second year, Circa Rave parallel inserts were limited to inclusion only in hobby packs at the stated rate of one card per "30 to 40" packs. Raves are distinguished from regular-edition Circa cards by the use of purple metallic foil for the brand name and player identification on front. Rave backs carry a silver-foil serial number detailing its position within a production of 150 for each card.

		NM/M
Common Player:		3.00
Stars/Rookies:		10-15X

Boss

Boss was Circa's most common insert series. Twenty embossed cards were seeded one per six packs, displaying some of baseball's best players. A Super Boss parallel insert features metallic-foil background and graphics on front, and is inserted at a rate of one per 36 packs.

		NM/M
Complete Set (20):		10.00
Common Player:		.15
Super Boss:		2X
1	Jeff Bagwell	.60
2	Albert Belle	.15
3	Barry Bonds	2.00
4	Ken Caminiti	.15
5	Juan Gonzalez	.30
6	Ken Griffey Jr.	1.00
7	Tony Gwynn	.75
8	Derek Jeter	2.00
9	Andruw Jones	.60
10	Chipper Jones	.75
11	Greg Maddux	.75
12	Mark McGwire	1.50
13	Mike Piazza	1.00
14	Manny Ramirez	.60
15	Cal Ripken Jr.	2.00
16	Alex Rodriguez	1.50
17	John Smoltz	.15
18	Frank Thomas	.60
19	Mo Vaughn	.15
20	Bernie Williams	.15

Emerald Autograph Redemption Cards

These box-topper cards were a hobby exclusive redeemable until May 31, 1998, for autographed special cards of six young stars. Fronts have a green-foil enhanced player action photo. Backs provide details of the redemption program.

		NM/M
Complete Set (6):		6.50
Common Player:		.50
(1)	Darin Erstad	1.25
(2)	Todd Hollandsworth	.50
(3)	Alex Ochoa	.50
(4)	Alex Rodriguez	6.00
(5)	Scott Rolen	1.50
(6)	Todd Walker	.50

Emerald Autographs

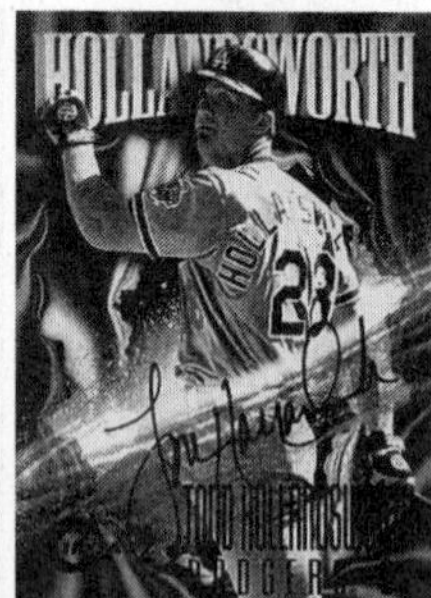

Special green-foil enhanced cards of six top young stars were available via a mail-in redemption. The cards feature authentic player signatures on front and an embossed authentication seal. Backs are identical to the regular card of each featured player.

		NM/M
Complete Set (6):		100.00
Common Player:		6.00
100	Alex Rodriguez	75.00
241	Darin Erstad	9.00
251	Todd Hollandsworth	6.00
283	Scott Rolen	12.00
308	Alex Ochoa	6.00
325	Todd Walker	6.00

Fast Track

Fast Track highlights 10 top rookies and young stars on a flocked background simulating grass. Cards were inserted every 24 packs.

		NM/M
Complete Set (10):		12.00
Common Player:		.50
1	Vladimir Guerrero	1.50
2	Todd Hollandsworth	.50
3	Derek Jeter	4.00
4	Andruw Jones	1.50
5	Chipper Jones	2.50
6	Andy Pettitte	1.00
7	Mariano Rivera	.75
8	Alex Rodriguez	3.00
9	Scott Rolen	1.25
10	Todd Walker	.50

Icons

Twelve of baseball's top sluggers were displayed on 100-percent holofoil cards in Icons. Icons were found at a rate of one per 36 packs.

		NM/M
Complete Set (12):		25.00
Common Player:		.50
1	Juan Gonzalez	.75
2	Ken Griffey Jr.	3.00
3	Tony Gwynn	2.00
4	Derek Jeter	5.00
5	Chipper Jones	2.00
6	Greg Maddux	2.00
7	Mark McGwire	4.00
8	Mike Piazza	3.00
9	Cal Ripken Jr.	5.00
10	Alex Rodriguez	4.00
11	Frank Thomas	1.50
12	Matt Williams	.50

Limited Access

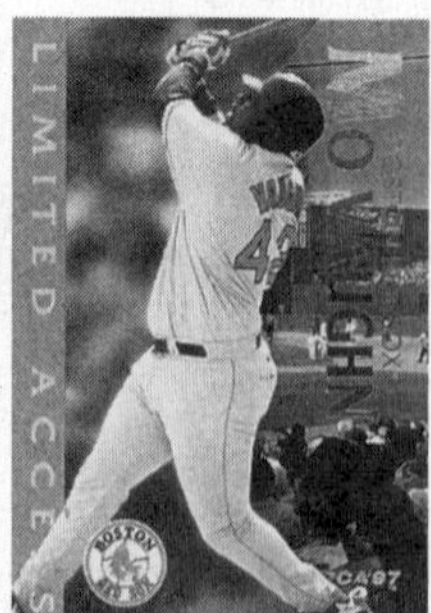

Limited Access was a retail-only insert found every 18 packs. Cards feature an in-depth, statistical analysis including the player's favorite pitcher to hit and each pitcher's least favorite hitter to face. Limited Access is formatted as a die-cut, bi-fold design resembling a book.

		NM/M
Complete Set (15):		30.00
Common Player:		1.25
1	Jeff Bagwell	2.00
2	Albert Belle	1.25
3	Barry Bonds	5.00
4	Juan Gonzalez	1.50
5	Ken Griffey Jr.	3.25
6	Tony Gwynn	2.50
7	Derek Jeter	5.00
8	Chipper Jones	2.50
9	Greg Maddux	2.50
10	Mark McGwire	4.00
11	Mike Piazza	3.50
12	Cal Ripken Jr.	5.00
13	Alex Rodriguez	4.00
14	Frank Thomas	2.00
15	Mo Vaughn	1.25

Rave Reviews

Hitters that continually put up great numbers were selected for Rave Reviews. The insert was found every 288 packs and was printed on 100-percent holofoil.

		NM/M
Complete Set (12):		75.00
Common Player:		3.00
1	Albert Belle	3.00
2	Barry Bonds	12.00
3	Juan Gonzalez	3.00
4	Ken Griffey Jr.	7.50
5	Tony Gwynn	6.00
6	Greg Maddux	6.00
7	Mark McGwire	9.00
8	Eddie Murray	4.00
9	Mike Piazza	7.50
10	Cal Ripken Jr.	12.00
11	Alex Rodriguez	9.00
12	Frank Thomas	4.50

1998 Circa Thunder

Circa Thunder was issued as one series of 300 cards, sold in packs of eight for $1.59. The set marked SkyBox's brand transition from Circa to Thunder so the cards are labeled with both names. Inserts include: Rave and Super Rave parallels, Boss, Fast Track, Quick Strike, Limited Access, Rave Review and Thunder Boomers.

		NM/M
Complete Set (300):		10.00
Common Player:		.10
Pack (8):		1.00
Wax Box (36):		20.00
1	Ben Grieve	.10
2	Derek Jeter	2.50
3	Alex Rodriguez	2.00
4	Paul Molitor	.75
5	Nomar Garciaparra	1.00
6	Fred McGriff	.10
7	Kenny Lofton	.10
8a	Cal Ripken Jr.	2.50
8b	Marquis Grissom (Should be #280.)	.10
8s	Cal Ripken Jr. ("PROMOTIONAL SAMPLE" on back.)	2.50
9	Matt Williams	.10
10	Chipper Jones	1.00
11	Barry Larkin	.10
12	Steve Finley	.10
13	Billy Wagner	.10
14	Rico Brogna	.10
15	Tim Salmon	.10

No.	Player	Value
16	Hideo Nomo	.40
17	Tony Clark	.10
18	Jason Kendall	.10
19	Juan Gonzalez	.40
20	Jeromy Burnitz	.10
21	Roger Clemens	1.25
22	Mark Grace	.10
23	Robin Ventura	.10
24	Manny Ramirez	.75
25	Mark McGwire	2.00
26	Gary Sheffield	.50
27	Vladimir Guerrero	.75
28	Butch Huskey	.10
29	Cecil Fielder	.10
30	Roderick Myers	.10
31	Greg Maddux	1.00
32	Bill Mueller	.10
33	Larry Walker	.10
34	Henry Rodriguez	.10
35	Mike Mussina	.35
36	Ricky Ledee	.10
37	Bobby Bonilla	.10
38	Curt Schilling	.35
39	Luis Gonzalez	.10
40	Troy Percival	.10
41	Eric Milton	.10
42	Mo Vaughn	.10
43	Raul Mondesi	.10
44	Kenny Rogers	.10
45	Frank Thomas	.75
46	Jose Canseco	.50
47	Tom Glavine	.35
48	Rich Butler **RC**	.10
49	Jay Buhner	.10
50	Jose Cruz Jr.	.10
51	Bernie Williams	.10
52	Doug Glanville	.10
53	Travis Fryman	.10
54	Rey Ordonez	.10
55	Jeff Conine	.10
56	Trevor Hoffman	.10
57	Kirk Rueter	.10
58	Ron Gant	.10
59	Carl Everett	.10
60	Joe Carter	.10
61	Livan Hernandez	.10
62	John Jaha	.10
63	Ivan Rodriguez	.65
64	Willie Blair	.10
65	Todd Helton	.65
66	Kevin Young	.10
67	Mike Caruso	.10
68	Steve Trachsel	.10
69	Marty Cordova	.10
70	Alex Fernandez	.10
71	Eric Karros	.10
72	Reggie Sanders	.10
73	Russ Davis	.10
74	Roberto Hernandez	.10
75	Barry Bonds	2.50
76	Alex Gonzalez	.10
77	Roberto Alomar	.25
78	Troy O'Leary	.10
79	Bernard Gilkey	.10
80	Ismael Valdes	.10
81	Travis Lee	.10
82	Brant Brown	.10
83	Gary DiSarcina	.10
84	Joe Randa	.10
85	Jaret Wright	.10
86	Quilvio Veras	.10
87	Rickey Henderson	.75
88	Randall Simon	.10
89	Mariano Rivera	.25
90	Ugueth Urbina	.10
91	Fernando Vina	.10
92	Alan Benes	.10
93	Dante Bichette	.10
94	Karim Garcia	.10
95	A.J. Hinch	.10
96	Shane Reynolds	.10
97	Kevin Stocker	.10
98	John Wetteland	.10
99	Terry Steinbach	.10
100	Ken Griffey Jr.	1.50
101	Mike Cameron	.10
102	Damion Easley	.10
103	Randy Myers	.10
104	Jason Schmidt	.10
105	Jeff King	.10
106	Gregg Jefferies	.10
107	Sean Casey	.15
108	Mark Kotsay	.10
109	Brad Fullmer	.10
110	Wilson Alvarez	.10
111	Sandy Alomar Jr.	.10
112	Walt Weiss	.10
113	Doug Jones	.10
114	Andy Benes	.10
115	Paul O'Neill	.10
116	Dennis Eckersley	.65
117	Todd Greene	.10
118	Bobby Jones	.10
119	Darrin Fletcher	.10
120	Eric Young	.10
121	Jeffrey Hammonds	.10
122	Mickey Morandini	.10
123	Chuck Knoblauch	.10
124	Moises Alou	.10
125	Miguel Tejada	.15
126	Brian Anderson	.10
127	Edgar Renteria	.10
128	Mike Lansing	.10
129	Quinton McCracken	.10
130	Ray Lankford	.10
131	Andy Ashby	.10
132	Kelvin Escobar	.10
133	Mike Lowell **RC**	.40
134	Randy Johnson	.75
135	Andres Galarraga	.10
136	Armando Benitez	.10
137	Rusty Greer	.10
138	Jose Guillen	.10
139	Paul Konerko	.15
140	Edgardo Alfonzo	.10
141	Jim Leyritz	.10
142	Mark Clark	.10
143	Brian Johnson	.10
144	Scott Rolen	.60
145	David Cone	.10
146	Jeff Shaw	.10
147	Shannon Stewart	.10
148	Brian Hunter	.10
149	Garret Anderson	.10
150	Jeff Bagwell	.75
151	James Baldwin	.10
152	Devon White	.10
153	Jim Thome	.60
154	Wally Joyner	.10
155	Mark Wohlers	.10
156	Jeff Cirillo	.10
157	Jason Giambi	.60
158	Royce Clayton	.10
159	Dennis Reyes	.10
160	Raul Casanova	.10
161	Pedro Astacio	.10
162	Todd Dunwoody	.10
163	Sammy Sosa	1.00
164	Todd Hundley	.10
165	Wade Boggs	1.00
166	Robb Nen	.10
167	Dan Wilson	.10
168	Hideki Irabu	.10
169	B.J. Surhoff	.10
170	Carlos Delgado	.40
171	Fernando Tatis	.10
172	Bob Abreu	.15
173	David Ortiz	.50
174	Tony Womack	.10
175	Magglio Ordonez **RC**	1.00
176	Aaron Boone	.10
177	Brian Giles	.10
178	Kevin Appier	.10
179	Chuck Finley	.10
180	Brian Rose	.10
181	Ryan Klesko	.10
182	Mike Stanley	.10
183	Dave Nilsson	.10
184	Carlos Perez	.10
185	Jeff Blauser	.10
186	Richard Hidalgo	.10
187	Charles Johnson	.10
188	Vinny Castilla	.10
189	Joey Hamilton	.10
190	Bubba Trammell	.10
191	Eli Marrero	.10
192	Scott Erickson	.10
193	Pat Hentgen	.10
194	Jorge Fabregas	.10
195	Tino Martinez	.10
196	Bobby Higginson	.10
197	Dave Hollins	.10
198	Rolando Arrojo **RC**	.25
199	Joey Cora	.10
200	Mike Piazza	1.50
201	Reggie Jefferson	.10
202	John Smoltz	.10
203	Bobby Smith	.10
204	Tom Goodwin	.10
205	Omar Vizquel	.10
206	John Olerud	.10
207	Matt Stairs	.10
208	Bobby Estalella	.10
209	Miguel Cairo	.10
210	Shawn Green	.20
211	Jon Nunnally	.10
212	Al Leiter	.10
213	Matt Lawton	.10
214	Brady Anderson	.10
215	Jeff Kent	.10
216	Ray Durham	.10
217	Al Martin	.10
218	Jeff D'Amico	.10
219	Kevin Tapani	.10
220	Jim Edmonds	.10
221	Jose Vizcaino	.10
222	Jay Bell	.10
223	Ken Caminiti	.10
224	Craig Biggio	.10
225	Bartolo Colon	.10
226	Neifi Perez	.10
227	Delino DeShields	.10
228	Javier Lopez	.10
229	David Wells	.10
230	Brad Rigby	.10
231	John Franco	.10
232	Michael Coleman	.10
233	Edgar Martinez	.10
234	Francisco Cordova	.10
235	Johnny Damon	.30
236	Deivi Cruz	.10
237	J.T. Snow	.10
238	Enrique Wilson	.10
239	Rondell White	.10
240	Aaron Sele	.10
241	Tony Saunders	.10
242	Ricky Bottalico	.10
243	Cliff Floyd	.10
244	Chili Davis	.10
245	Brian McRae	.10
246	Brad Radke	.10
247	Chan Ho Park	.10
248	Lance Johnson	.10
249	Rafael Palmeiro	.65
250	Tony Gwynn	1.00
251	Denny Neagle	.10
252	Dean Palmer	.10
253	Jose Valentin	.10
254	Matt Morris	.10
255	Ellis Burks	.10
256	Jeff Suppan	.10
257	Jimmy Key	.10
258	Justin Thompson	.10
259	Brett Tomko	.10
260	Mark Grudzielanek	.10
261	Mike Hampton	.10
262	Jeff Fassero	.10
263	Charles Nagy	.10
264	Pedro Martinez	.75
265	Todd Zeile	.10
266	Will Clark	.10
267	Abraham Nunez	.10
268	Dave Martinez	.10
269	Jason Dickson	.10
270	Eric Davis	.10
271	Kevin Orie	.10
272	Derrek Lee	.50
273	Andruw Jones	.75
274	Juan Encarnacion	.10
275	Carlos Baerga	.10
276	Andy Pettitte	.35
277	Brent Brede	.10
278	Paul Sorrento	.10
279	Mike Lieberthal	.10
280	(Not issued, see #8)	.10
281	Darin Erstad	.25
282	Willie Greene	.10
283	Derek Bell	.10
284	Scott Spiezio	.10
285	David Segui	.10
286	Albert Belle	.10
287	Ramon Martinez	.10
288	Jeremi Gonzalez	.10
289	Shawn Estes	.10
290	Ron Coomer	.10
291	John Valentin	.10
292	Kevin Brown	.10
293	Michael Tucker	.10
294	Brian Jordan	.10
295	Darryl Kile	.10
296	David Justice	.10
297	Jose Cruz Jr. Checklist	.10
298	Alex Rodriguez Checklist	1.00
299	Ken Griffey Jr. Checklist	.75
300	Frank Thomas Checklist	.65

Rave

Rave parallels each card in Circa Thunder except for the four checklist cards. A special silver sparkling foil is used on the player's name and the Thunder logo on front. This 296-card set was inserted approximately one per 36 packs and sequentially numbered to 150 sets on the back.

	NM/M
Common Player:	2.00
Stars:	15X

Super Rave

Only 25 Super Rave parallel sets were printed and they were inserted approximately one per 216 packs. The set contains 296 player cards (no checklist cards). Fronts are identified by sparkling gold foil on the player's name and the Thunder logo, with sequential numbering on the back to 25.

	NM/M
Common Player:	6.00
Stars:	40X

Boss

This insert set has cards embossed with the player's last name in large letters across the top.

		NM/M
Complete Set (20):		10.00
Common Player:		.25
Inserted 1:6		
1B	Jeff Bagwell	.75
2B	Barry Bonds	2.00
3B	Roger Clemens	1.00
4B	Jose Cruz Jr.	.25
5B	Nomar Garciaparra	1.00
6B	Juan Gonzalez	.40
7B	Ken Griffey Jr.	1.25
8B	Tony Gwynn	1.00
9B	Derek Jeter	2.00
10B	Chipper Jones	1.00
11B	Travis Lee	.25
12B	Greg Maddux	1.00
13B	Pedro Martinez	.75
14B	Mark McGwire	1.50
15B	Mike Piazza	1.25
16B	Cal Ripken Jr.	2.00
17B	Alex Rodriguez	1.50
18B	Scott Rolen	.65
19B	Frank Thomas	.75
20B	Larry Walker	.25

Fast Track

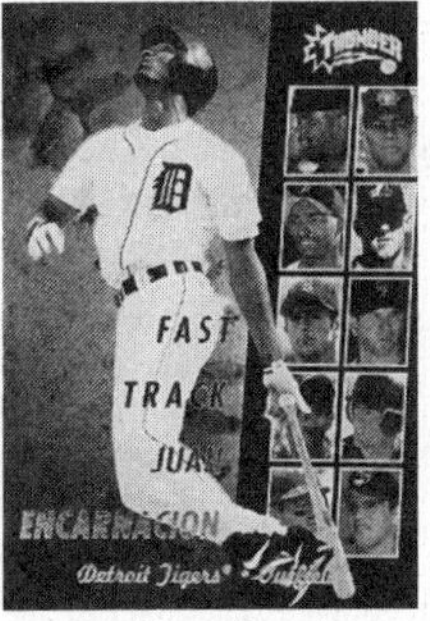

This 10-card insert showcases some of the top young stars in baseball. Fronts picture the player over a closeup of a gold foil baseball on the left. The right side has smaller head shots of all 10 players with the featured player's head in gold foil.

		NM/M
Complete Set (10):		8.00
Common Player:		.25
Inserted 1:24		
1FT	Jose Cruz Jr.	.25
2FT	Juan Encarnacion	.25
3FT	Brad Fullmer	.25
4FT	Nomar Garciaparra	4.00
5FT	Todd Helton	2.50
6FT	Livan Hernandez	.25
7FT	Travis Lee	.25
8FT	Neifi Perez	.25
9FT	Scott Rolen	1.50
10FT	Jaret Wright	.25

Limited Access

These retail-exclusive insert cards are bi-fold and die-cut with foil stamping on front. The theme of the insert was to provide an in-depth statistical scouting analysis of each player.

		NM/M
Complete Set (15):		17.50
Common Player:		.50
Inserted 1:18		
1LA	Jeff Bagwell	1.25
2LA	Roger Clemens	1.75
3LA	Jose Cruz Jr.	.50
4LA	Nomar Garciaparra	1.50
5LA	Juan Gonzalez	1.00
6LA	Ken Griffey Jr.	2.00
7LA	Tony Gwynn	1.50
8LA	Derek Jeter	3.00
9LA	Greg Maddux	1.50
10LA	Pedro Martinez	1.25
11LA	Mark McGwire	2.50
12LA	Mike Piazza	2.00
13LA	Alex Rodriguez	2.50
14LA	Frank Thomas	1.25
15LA	Larry Walker	.50

Quick Strike

This insert pictures players over a colorful die-cut foil-board front.

		NM/M
Complete Set (12):		20.00
Common Player:		.50
Inserted 1:36		
1QS	Jeff Bagwell	2.00
2QS	Roger Clemens	2.75
3QS	Jose Cruz Jr.	.50
4QS	Nomar Garciaparra	2.50
5QS	Ken Griffey Jr.	3.00
6QS	Greg Maddux	2.50
7QS	Pedro Martinez	2.00
8QS	Mark McGwire	4.00
9QS	Mike Piazza	3.00
10QS	Alex Rodriguez	4.00
11QS	Frank Thomas	2.00
12QS	Larry Walker	.50

Rave Reviews

Rave Reviews cards are die-cut in a horizontal design with bronze foil etching and the image of a ballfield in the background.

		NM/M
Complete Set (15):		100.00
Common Player:		2.00
Inserted 1:288		
1RR	Jeff Bagwell	5.00
2RR	Barry Bonds	15.00
3RR	Roger Clemens	7.50
4RR	Jose Cruz Jr.	2.00
5RR	Nomar Garciaparra	6.00
6RR	Juan Gonzalez	3.50
7RR	Ken Griffey Jr.	10.00
8RR	Tony Gwynn	6.00
9RR	Derek Jeter	15.00
10RR	Greg Maddux	6.00
11RR	Mark McGwire	12.50
12RR	Mike Piazza	10.00
13RR	Alex Rodriguez	12.50
14RR	Frank Thomas	5.00
15RR	Larry Walker	2.00

Thunder Boomers

Thunder Boomers feature top power hitters imposed over a see-through cloud-like plastic center with the imagery of a wooden fence with a large hole blasted through the middle of it.

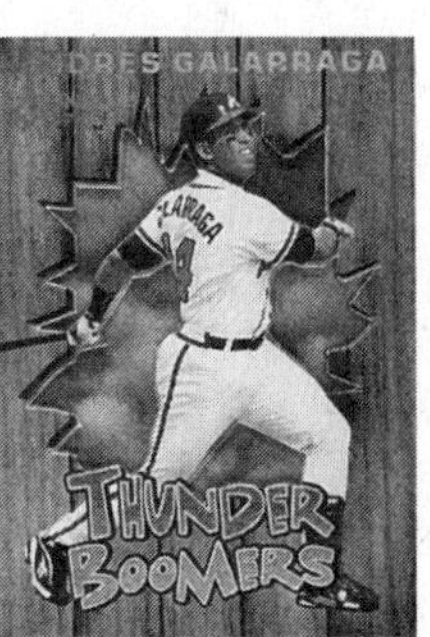

		NM/M
Complete Set (12):		50.00
Common Player:		1.50
Inserted 1:96		
1TB	Jeff Bagwell	6.00
2TB	Barry Bonds	10.00
3TB	Jay Buhner	1.50
4TB	Andres Galarraga	1.50
5TB	Juan Gonzalez	3.00
6TB	Ken Griffey Jr.	7.50
7TB	Tino Martinez	1.50
8TB	Mark McGwire	9.00
9TB	Mike Piazza	7.50
10TB	Frank Thomas	6.00
11TB	Jim Thome	4.50
12TB	Larry Walker	1.50

1985 Circle K

Produced by Topps for Circle K stores, this set is titled "Baseball All Time Home Run Kings." The 2-1/2" x 3-1/2" cards are numbered on the back according to the player's position on the all-time career home run list. Joe DiMaggio, who ranked 31st, was not included in the set. Glossy card fronts generally feature a color photo, although black-and-whites were utilized for a few of the homer kings who played before 1960. Backs have blue and red print on white stock and contain the player's career batting statistics. The set was issued in a specially designed box.

		NM/M
Complete Set (33):		5.00
Common Player:		.10
1	Hank Aaron	1.25
2	Babe Ruth	2.00
3	Willie Mays	1.25
4	Frank Robinson	.15
5	Harmon Killebrew	.15
6	Mickey Mantle	2.50
7	Jimmie Foxx	.15
8	Willie McCovey	.15
9	Ted Williams	1.25
10	Ernie Banks	.30
11	Eddie Mathews	.15
12	Mel Ott	.15
13	Reggie Jackson	.60
14	Lou Gehrig	1.25
15	Stan Musial	.75
16	Willie Stargell	.15
17	Carl Yastrzemski	.25
18	Billy Williams	.15
19	Mike Schmidt	.60
20	Duke Snider	.30
21	Al Kaline	.25
22	Johnny Bench	.25
23	Frank Howard	.15
24	Orlando Cepeda	.15
25	Norm Cash	.15
26	Dave Kingman	.15
27	Rocky Colavito	.15
28	Tony Perez	.15
29	Gil Hodges	.30
30	Ralph Kiner	.15
32	Johnny Mize	.15
33	Yogi Berra	.30
34	Lee May	.15

1993 City Pride Roberto Clemente

To assist in the building of the statue of Roberto Clemente which was unveiled at Three Rivers Stadium during All-Star festivities in 1994, Pittsburgh's City Pride bakery contributed a portion of sales proceeds from a special run of bread loaves featuring Roberto Clemente cards. The cards came in a special plastic pouch within the bread wrapper to protect them from stains. The wrapper itself included a portrait of Clemente and details of the statue project. The 2-1/2" x 3-1/2" cards featured sepia-toned or color photos of Clemente inside black and gold borders. A color team logo appears in the lower-right corner with his name in an orange stripe at the bottom of the photo. Backs are in black-and-white and contain a narrative of Clemente's career, with one card containing his lifetime stats. The unnumbered cards are checklisted here in chronological order.

		NM/M
Complete Set (6):		6.00
Common Card:		1.50
(1)	Roberto Clemente/Btg (1934-1958, sepia photo)	1.50
(2)	Roberto Clemente/Btg (1960-1966, color photo)	1.50
(3)	Roberto Clemente (1971-1972, running to first base)	1.50
(4)	Roberto Clemente/Portrait (1972-1973)	1.50
(5)	Roberto Clemente (Fielding records, kneeling with one bat.)	1.50
(6)	Roberto Clemente (Batting record, kneeling with five bats.)	1.50

1993 Clark Candy Reggie Jackson

The reintroduction of the "Reggie" candy bar by the Clark company was accompanied by a three-card set highlighting his career produced by Upper Deck. One card was found in each candy bar. Cards have a color photo of Jackson on front, on which uniform logos have been removed. Backs have an equipment montage and a paragraph about the slugger. Clark and UD logos appear on front, with an UD hologram on back. A limited number (200) of autographed cards were randomly inserted.

		NM/M
Complete Set (3):		3.00
Common Player:		1.00
Autographed Card:		75.00
C1	Reggie Jackson (Hall of Fame, 1993)	1.00
C2	Reggie Jackson (Mr. October, 1977)	1.00
C3	Reggie Jackson (A.L. MVP, 1973)	1.00

1987 Classic Major League Baseball Game

The "Classic Major League Baseball Board Game" set consists of 100 full-color cards used to play the game in which participants answer trivia questions found on the card backs. Cards measure 2-1/2" x 3-1/2" and are printed on semi-gloss stock. Backs carry the player's career stats besides the trivia questions. The game was produced by Game Time, Ltd. of Marietta, Ga., and sold for $19.95 in most retail outlets. In 1991-92 the set was selling for $200 or more, with the Bo Jackson card advertised as high as $80.

		NM/M
Complete Boxed Set:		25.00
Complete Set (100):		20.00
Common Player:		.05
1	Pete Rose	2.00
2	Len Dykstra	.05
3	Darryl Strawberry	.05
4	Keith Hernandez	.05
5	Gary Carter	.65
6	Wally Joyner	.05
7	Andres Thomas	.05
8	Pat Dodson	.05
9	Kirk Gibson	.05
10	Don Mattingly	1.00
11	Dave Winfield	.65
12	Rickey Henderson	.65
13	Dan Pasqua	.05
14	Don Baylor	.05
15	Bo Jackson	2.50
16	Pete Incaviglia	.05
17	Kevin Bass	.05
18	Barry Larkin	.05
19	Dave Magadan	.05
20	Steve Sax	.05
21	Eric Davis	.05
22	Mike Pagliarulo	.05
23	Fred Lynn	.05
24	Reggie Jackson	1.00
25	Larry Parrish	.05
26	Tony Gwynn	.75
27	Steve Garvey	.20
28	Glenn Davis	.05
29	Tim Raines	.05
30	Vince Coleman	.05
31	Willie McGee	.05
32	Ozzie Smith	.75
33	Dave Parker	.05
34	Tony Pena	.05
35	Ryne Sandberg	.75
36	Brett Butler	.05
37	Dale Murphy	.25
38	Bob Horner	.05
39	Pedro Guerrero	.05
40	Brook Jacoby	.05
41	Carlton Fisk	.65
42	Harold Baines	.05
43	Rob Deer	.05
44	Robin Yount	.65
45	Paul Molitor	.65
46	Jose Canseco	.50
47	George Brett	1.00
48	Jim Presley	.05
49	Rich Gedman	.05
50	Lance Parrish	.05
51	Eddie Murray	.65
52	Cal Ripken, Jr.	3.00
53	Kent Hrbek	.05
54	Gary Gaetti	.05
55	Kirby Puckett	.75
56	George Bell	.05
57	Tony Fernandez	.05
58	Jesse Barfield	.05
59	Jim Rice	.25
60	Wade Boggs	.75
61	Marty Barrett	.05
62	Mike Schmidt	1.00
63	Von Hayes	.05
64	Jeff Leonard	.05
65	Chris Brown	.05
66	Dave Smith	.05
67	Mike Krukow	.05
68	Ron Guidry	.05
69	Rob Woodward (Photo actually Pat Dodson.)	.05
70	Rob Murphy	.05
71	Andres Galarraga	.05
72	Dwight Gooden	.05
73	Bob Ojeda	.05
74	Sid Fernandez	.05
75	Jesse Orosco	.05
76	Roger McDowell	.05
77	John Tutor (Tudor)	.05
78	Tom Browning	.05
79	Rick Aguilera	.05
80	Lance McCullers	.05
81	Mike Scott	.05
82	Nolan Ryan	3.00
83	Bruce Hurst	.05
84	Roger Clemens	1.00
85	Oil Can Boyd	.05
86	Dave Righetti	.05
87	Dennis Rasmussen	.05
88	Bret Saberhagan (Saberhagen)	.05
89	Mark Langston	.05
90	Jack Morris	.05
91	Fernando Valenzuela	.05
92	Orel Hershiser	.05
93	Rick Honeycutt	.05
94	Jeff Reardon	.05
95	John Habyan	.05
96	Goose Gossage	.05
97	Todd Worrell	.05
98	Floyd Youmans	.05
99	Don Aase	.05
100	John Franco	.05

Travel Update (Yellow)

Game Time, Ltd. of Marietta, Ga., issued as an update to its Classic Baseball Board Game a 50-card set entitled "Travel Edition." Cards measure 2-1/2" x 3-1/2" in the same format as the first release, though with yellow, rather than green, borders. Numbered from 101 to 150, the "Travel Edition," besides updating player trades and showcasing rookies, offers several highlights from the 1987 season. All new trivia questions are found on the card backs. It was reported that about 50,000 of the set's 150,000 press run was mistakenly printed with green, rather than yellow backs; the green-back errors sell for a premium.

		NM/M
Complete Set (50):		15.00
Common Player:		.05
Green-backs:		1.5X
101	Mike Schmidt	.75
102	Eric Davis	.05
103	Pete Rose	1.50
104	Don Mattingly	.75
105	Wade Boggs	.60
106	Dale Murphy	.20
107	Glenn Davis	.05
108	Wally Joyner	.05
109	Bo Jackson	.15
110	Cory Snyder	.05
111	Jim Lindeman	.05
112	Kirby Puckett	.60
113	Barry Bonds	10.00
114	Roger Clemens	.75
115	Oddibe McDowell	.05
116	Bret Saberhagen	.05
117	Joe Magrane	.05
118	Scott Fletcher	.05
119	Mark McLemore	.05
120	Who Me? (Joe Niekro)	.25
121	Mark McGwire	2.00
122	Darryl Strawberry	.05
123	Mike Scott	.05
124	Andre Dawson	.20
125	Jose Canseco	.50
126	Kevin McReynolds	.05
127	Joe Carter	.05
128	Casey Candaele	.05
129	Matt Nokes	.05
130	Kal Daniels	.05
131	Pete Incaviglia	.05
132	Benito Santiago	.05
133	Barry Larkin	.05
134	Gary Pettis	.05
135	B.J. Surhoff	.05
136	Juan Nieves	.05
137	Jim Deshaies	.05
138	Pete O'Brien	.05
139	Kevin Seitzer	.05
140	Devon White	.05
141	Rob Deer	.05
142	Kurt Stillwell	.05
143	Edwin Correa	.05
144	Dion James	.05
145	Danny Tartabull	.05
146	Jerry Browne	.05
147	Ted Higuera	.05
148	Jack Clark	.05
149	Ruben Sierra	.05
150	Mark McGwire, Eric Davis	.60

Travel Update 1 (Red)

This set was produced for use with the travel edition of Game Time's Classic Baseball Board Game. Special cards in the set include a McGwire/Mattingly, an instruction card with McGwire/Canseco and three different cards featuring Phil Niekro (in different uniforms). Update I card fronts have red borders, a yellow Classic logo in the upper-left corner and a black and beige name banner beneath the photo. Backs are printed in red and pink on white and include the player name, personal info, major league records, a baseball question and space for the player autograph. Classic card series sold via hobby dealers and retail toy stores nationwide. Game Time Ltd., the set's producer, was purchased by Scoreboard of Cherry Hill, N.J. in 1988.

		NM/M
Complete Set (50):		4.00
Common Player:		.05
151	Don Mattingly, Mark McGwire	.45
152	Don Mattingly	.65
153	Mark McGwire	1.00
154	Eric Davis	.05
155	Wade Boggs	.50
156	Dale Murphy	.15
157	Andre Dawson	.15
158	Roger Clemens	.65
159	Kevin Seitzer	.05
160	Benito Santiago	.05
161	Kal Daniels	.05
162	John Kruk	.05
163	Bill Ripken	.05
164	Kirby Puckett	.50
165	Jose Canseco	.30
166	Matt Nokes	.05
167	Mike Schmidt	.60
168	Tim Raines	.05
169	Ryne Sandberg	.50
170	Dave Winfield	.40
171	Dwight Gooden	.05
172	Bret Saberhagen	.05
173	Willie McGee	.05
174	Jack Morris	.05
175	Jeff Leonard	.05
176	Cal Ripken, Jr.	1.50
177	Pete Incaviglia	.05
178	Devon White	.05
179	Nolan Ryan	1.50
180	Ruben Sierra	.05
181	Todd Worrell	.05
182	Glenn Davis	.05
183	Frank Viola	.05
184	Cory Snyder	.05
185	Tracy Jones	.05
186	Terry Steinbach	.05
187	Julio Franco	.05
188	Larry Sheets	.05
189	John Marzano	.05
190	Kevin Elster	.05
191	Vincente Palacios	.05
192	Kent Hrbek	.05
193	Eric Bell	.05
194	Kelly Downs	.05
195	Jose Lind	.05
196	Dave Stewart	.05
197	Jose Canseco, Mark McGwire	.45
198	Phil Niekro	.10
199	Phil Niekro	.10
200	Phil Niekro	.10

Travel Update 2 (Blue)

This set was produced for use with the travel edition of Game Time's Classic Baseball Board Game. Fronts have blue borders, a yellow Classic logo in the upper-left corner and a black and beige name banner beneath the photo. Backs are printed in blue on white and include the player name, personal info, major league records, a baseball question and space for the player autograph. Classic card series are sold via hobby dealers and retail toy stores nationwide. Game Time Ltd., the set's producer, was purchased by Scoreboard of Cherry Hill, N.J. in 1988.

		NM/M
Complete Set (50):		4.00
Common Player:		.05
201	Dale Murphy, Eric Davis	.10
202	B.J. Surhoff	.05
203	John Kruk	.05
204	Sam Horn	.05
205	Jack Clark	.05
206	Wally Joyner	.05
207	Matt Nokes	.05
208	Bo Jackson	.10
209	Darryl Strawberry	.05
210	Ozzie Smith	.60
211	Don Mattingly	.75
212	Mark McGwire	1.50
213	Eric Davis	.05
214	Wade Boggs	.60
215	Dale Murphy	.25
216	Andre Dawson	.25
217	Roger Clemens	.75
218	Kevin Seitzer	.05
219	Benito Santiago	.05
220	Tony Gwynn	.60
221	Mike Scott	.05
222	Steve Bedrosian	.05
223	Vince Coleman	.05
224	Rick Sutcliffe	.05
225	Will Clark	.05
226	Pete Rose	1.00
227	Mike Greenwell	.05
228	Ken Caminiti	.05
229	Ellis Burks	.05
230	Dave Magadan	.05
231	Alan Trammell	.05
232	Paul Molitor	.50
233	Gary Gaetti	.05
234	Rickey Henderson	.50
235	Danny Tartabull	.05
236	Bobby Bonilla	.05
237	Mike Dunne	.05
238	Al Leiter	.05
239	John Farrell	.05
240	Joe Magrane	.05
241	Mike Henneman	.05
242	George Bell	.05
243	Gregg Jefferies	.10
244	Jay Buhner	.05
245	Todd Benzinger	.05
246	Matt Williams	.05
(247)	Don Mattingly, Mark McGwire (No card number on back.)	.50
248	George Brett	.75
249	Jimmy Key	.05
250	Mark Langston	.05

1989 Classic

This 100-card set was released by The Score Board to accompany trivia board games. Fronts have a wide border which graduates from pink at the top to blue at the bottom. Card backs are printed in blue. The flip side includes personal information, and major league record in a boxed area. Another boxed area below the record presents five trivia questions. The lower border on back provides an autograph space. The Classic card series was sold by retail stores and hobby dealers nationwide.

		NM/M
Complete Set (100):		6.00
Common Player:		.05
1	Orel Hershiser	.05
2	Wade Boggs	.50
3	Jose Canseco	.30
4	Mark McGwire	1.00
5	Don Mattingly	.60
6	Gregg Jefferies	.05
7	Dwight Gooden	.05
8	Darryl Strawberry	.05
9	Eric Davis	.05
10	Joey Meyer	.05
11	Joe Carter	.05
12	Paul Molitor	.40
13	Mark Grace	.05
14	Kurt Stillwell	.05
15	Kirby Puckett	.50
16	Keith Miller	.05
17	Glenn Davis	.05
18	Will Clark	.05
19	Cory Snyder	.05
20	Jose Lind	.05
21	Andres Thomas	.05
22	Dave Smith	.05
23	Mike Scott	.05
24	Kevin McReynolds	.05
25	B.J. Surhoff	.05
26	Mackey Sasser	.05
27	Chad Kreuter	.05
28	Hal Morris	.05
29	Wally Joyner	.05
30	Tony Gwynn	.50
31	Kevin Mitchell	.05
32	Dave Winfield	.40
33	Billy Bean	.05
34	Steve Bedrosian	.05
35	Ron Gant	.05
36	Len Dykstra	.05
37	Andre Dawson	.25
38	Brett Butler	.05
39	Rob Deer	.05
40	Tommy John	.05
41	Gary Gaetti	.05
42	Tim Raines	.05
43	George Bell	.05
44	Dwight Evans	.05
45	Denny Martinez	.05
46	Andres Galarraga	.05
47	George Brett	.60
48	Mike Schmidt	.60
49	Dave Steib	.05
50	Rickey Henderson	.40
51	Craig Biggio	.05
52	Mark Lemke	.05
53	Chris Sabo	.05
54	Jeff Treadway	.05
55	Kent Hrbek	.05
56	Cal Ripken, Jr.	1.50
57	Tim Belcher	.05

58 Ozzie Smith .50
59 Keith Hernandez .05
60 Pedro Guerrero .05
61 Greg Swindell .05
62 Bret Saberhagen .05
63 John Tudor .05
64 Gary Carter .40
65 Kevin Seitzer .05
66 Jesse Barfield .05
67 Luis Medina .05
68 Walt Weiss .05
69 Terry Steinbach .05
70 Barry Larkin .05
71 Pete Rose .75
72 Luis Salazar .05
73 Benito Santiago .05
74 Kal Daniels .05
75 Kevin Elster .05
76 Rob Dibble .05
77 Bobby Witt .05
78 Steve Searcy .05
79 Sandy Alomar (Photo is Roberto Alomar.) .05
80 Chili Davis .05
81 Alvin Davis .05
82 Charlie Leibrandt .05
83 Robin Yount .40
84 Mark Carreon .05
85 Pascual Perez .05
86 Dennis Rasmussen .05
87 Ernie Riles .05
88 Melido Perez .05
89 Doug Jones .05
90 Dennis Eckersley .35
91 Bob Welch .05
92 Bob Milacki .05
93 Jeff Robinson .05
94 Mike Henneman .05
95 Randy Johnson 1.00
96 Ron Jones .05
97 Jack Armstrong .05
98 Willie McGee .05
99 Ryne Sandberg .50
100 David Cone, Danny Jackson .05

Travel Update 1 (Orange)

Roberto Alomar

Sold only as a 50-card complete set under the official name of "Travel Update I," these cards are identical in format to the 1989 Classic 100-card set with the exception that the borders are orange at the top, graduating to maroon at the bottom. Backs are maroon.

NM/M
Complete Set (50): 5.00
Common Player: .05
101 Gary Sheffield .25
102 Wade Boggs .50
103 Jose Canseco .30
104 Mark McGwire 1.00
105 Orel Hershiser .05
106 Don Mattingly .60
107 Dwight Gooden .05
108 Darryl Strawberry .05
109 Eric Davis .05
110 Bam Bam Meulens .05
111 Andy Van Slyke .05
112 Al Leiter .05
113 Matt Nokes .05
114 Mike Krukow .05
115 Tony Fernandez .05
116 Fred McGriff .05
117 Barry Bonds 1.50
118 Gerald Perry .05
119 Roger Clemens .60
120 Kirk Gibson .05
121 Greg Maddux .50
122 Bo Jackson .10
123 Danny Jackson .05
124 Dale Murphy .20
125 David Cone .05
126 Tom Browning .05
127 Roberto Alomar .25
128 Alan Trammell .05
129 Ricky Jordan .05
130 Ramon Martinez .05
131 Ken Griffey Jr. 3.00
132 Gregg Olson .05
133 Carlos Quintana .05
134 Dave West .05
135 Cameron Drew .05
136 Ted Higuera .05
137 Sil Campusano .05
138 Mark Gubicza .05
139 Mike Boddicker .05
140 Paul Gibson .05
141 Jose Rijo .05
142 John Costello .05
143 Cecil Espy .05
144 Frank Viola .05
145 Erik Hanson .05
146 Juan Samuel .05
147 Harold Reynolds .05
148 Joe Magrane .05
149 Mike Greenwell .05
150 Darryl Strawberry, Will Clark .05

Travel Update 2 (Purple)

Jerome Walton

Numbered from 151-200, this set features rookies and traded players with their new teams. The cards are purple and gray and were sold as part of a board game with baseball trivia questions.

NM/M
Complete Set (50): 5.00
Common Player: .05
151 Jim Abbott .05
152 Ellis Burks .05
153 Mike Schmidt .75
154 Gregg Jefferies .05
155 Mark Grace .05
156 Jerome Walton .05
157 Bo Jackson .10
158 Jack Clark .05
159 Tom Glavine .20
160 Eddie Murray .45
161 John Dopson .05
162 Ruben Sierra .05
163 Rafael Palmeiro .40
164 Nolan Ryan 1.50
165 Barry Larkin .05
166 Tommy Herr .05
167 Roberto Kelly .05
168 Glenn Davis .05
169 Glenn Braggs .05
170 Juan Bell .05
171 Todd Burns .05
172 Derek Lilliquist .05
173 Orel Hershiser .05
174 John Smoltz .05
175 Ozzie Guillen, Ellis Burks .05
176 Kirby Puckett .60
177 Robin Ventura .05
178 Allan Anderson .05
179 Steve Sax .05
180 Will Clark .05
181 Mike Devereaux .05
182 Tom Gordon .05
183 Rob Murphy .05
184 Pete O'Brien .05
185 Cris Carpenter .05
186 Tom Brunansky .05
187 Bob Boone .05
188 Lou Whitaker .05
189 Dwight Gooden .05
190 Mark McGwire 1.00
191 John Smiley .05
192 Tommy Gregg .05
193 Ken Griffey Jr. 3.00
194 Bruce Hurst .05
195 Greg Swindell .05
196 Nelson Liriano .05
197 Randy Myers .05
198 Kevin Mitchell .05
199 Dante Bichette .05
200 Deion Sanders .10

1990 Classic

Classic baseball returned in 1990 with a 150-card set. Cards have a blue border on front, with splashes of pink. The cards were again sold as part of a baseball trivia game.

NM/M
Complete Set (150): 4.00
Common Player: .05
1 Nolan Ryan 1.00
2 Bo Jackson .10

Ozzie Smith

3 Gregg Olson .05
4 Tom Gordon .05
5 Robin Ventura .05
6 Will Clark .05
7 Ruben Sierra .05
8 Mark Grace .05
9 Luis de los Santos .05
10 Bernie Williams .05
11 Eric Davis .05
12 Carney Lansford .05
13 John Smoltz .05
14 Gary Sheffield .20
15 Kent Merker .05
16 Don Mattingly .60
17 Tony Gwynn .50
18 Ozzie Smith .50
19 Fred McGriff .05
20 Ken Griffey Jr. .65
21a Deion Sanders ("Prime Time") .30
21b Deion Sanders (Deion "Prime Time" Sanders) .15
22 Jose Canseco .25
23 Mitch Williams .05
24 Cal Ripken, Jr. 1.00
25 Bob Geren .05
26 Wade Boggs .50
27 Ryne Sandberg .50
28 Kirby Puckett .50
29 Mike Scott .05
30 Dwight Smith .05
31 Craig Worthington .05
32 Ricky Jordan .05
33 Darryl Strawberry .05
34 Jerome Walton .05
35 John Olerud .05
36 Tom Glavine .15
37 Rickey Henderson .30
38 Rolando Roomes .05
39 Mickey Tettleton .05
40 Jim Abbott .05
41 Dave Righetti .05
42 Mike LaValliere .05
43 Rob Dibble .05
44 Pete Harnisch .05
45 Jose Offerman .05
46 Walt Weiss .05
47 Mike Greenwell .05
48 Barry Larkin .05
49 Dave Gallagher .05
50 Junior Felix .05
51 Roger Clemens .60
52 Lonnie Smith .05
53 Jerry Browne .05
54 Greg Briley .05
55 Delino DeShields .05
56 Carmelo Martinez .05
57 Craig Biggio .05
58 Dwight Gooden .05
59a Bo, Ruben, Mark (Bo Jackson, Ruben Sierra, Mark McGwire) .25
59b A.L. Fence Busters (Bo Jackson, Ruben Sierra, Mark McGwire) .15
60 Greg Vaughn .05
61 Roberto Alomar .20
62 Steve Bedrosian .05
63 Devon White .05
64 Kevin Mitchell .05
65 Marquis Grissom .05
66 Brian Holman .05
67 Julio Franco .05
68 Dave West .05
69 Harold Baines .05
70 Eric Anthony .05
71 Glenn Davis .05
72 Mark Langston .05
73 Matt Williams .05
74 Rafael Palmeiro .25
75 Pete Rose, Jr. .25
76 Ramon Martinez .05
77 Dwight Evans .05
78 Mackey Sasser .05
79 Mike Schooler .05
80 Dennis Cook .05
81 Orel Hershiser .05
82 Barry Bonds 1.00
83 Geronimo Berroa .05
84 George Bell .05
85 Andre Dawson .25
86 John Franco .05
87a Clark/Gwynn (Will Clark, Tony Gwynn) .25
87b N.L. Hit Kings (Will Clark, Tony Gwynn) .15
88 Glenallen Hill .05
89 Jeff Ballard .05
90 Todd Zeile .05
91 Frank Viola .05
92 Ozzie Guillen .05
93 Jeff Leonard .05
94 Dave Smith .05
95 Dave Parker .05
96 Jose Gonzalez .05
97 Dave Steib .05
98 Charlie Hayes .05
99 Jesse Barfield .05
100 Joey Belle .15
101 Jeff Reardon .05
102 Bruce Hurst .05
103 Luis Medina .05
104 Mike Moore .05
105 Vince Coleman .05
106 Alan Trammell .05
107 Randy Myers .05
108 Frank Tanana .05
109 Craig Lefferts .05
110 John Wetteland .05
111 Chris Gwynn .05
112 Mark Carreon .05
113 Von Hayes .05
114 Doug Jones .05
115 Andres Galarraga .05
116 Carlton Fisk .30
117 Paul O'Neill .05
118 Tim Raines .05
119 Tom Brunansky .05
120 Andy Benes .05
121 Mark Portugal .05
122 Willie Randolph .05
123 Jeff Blauser .05
124 Don August .05
125 Chuck Cary .05
126 John Smiley .05
127 Terry Mullholland .05
128 Harold Reynolds .05
129 Hubie Brooks .05
130 Ben McDonald .05
131 Kevin Ritz .05
132 Luis Quinones .05
133a Bam Bam Muelens (Last name incorrect.) .25
133b Bam Bam Meulens (Last name correct.) .05
134 Bill Spiers .05
135 Andy Hawkins .05
136 Alvin Davis .05
137 Lee Smith .05
138 Joe Carter .05
139 Bret Saberhagen .05
140 Sammy Sosa 1.00
141 Matt Nokes .05
142 Bert Blyleven .05
143 Bobby Bonilla .05
144 Howard Johnson .05
145 Joe Magrane .05
146 Pedro Guerrero .05
147 Robin Yount .30
148 Dan Gladden .05
149 Steve Sax .05
150a Clark/Mitchell (Will Clark, Kevin Mitchell) .25
150b Bay Bombers (Will Clark, Kevin Mitchell) .25

Series 2

Juan Gonzalez

As in previous years, Classic released a 50-card second series set for use with its trivia board game. Unlike earlier update sets, the 1990 Series II set is numbered 1-50 with a "T" designation accompanying the card number. Cards measure 2-1/2" x 3-1/2" and share the format of the original 1990 Classic cards; Series II cards have pink borders with blue highlights. The cards were issued only in complete set form.

NM/M
Complete Set (50): 3.00
Common Player: .05
1 Gregg Jefferies .05
2 Steve Adkins .05
3 Sandy Alomar, Jr. .05
4 Steve Avery .05
5 Mike Blowers .05
6 George Brett .75
7 Tom Browning .05
8 Ellis Burks .05
9 Joe Carter .05
10 Jerald Clark .05
11 "Hot Corners" (Matt Williams, Will Clark) .10
12 Pat Combs .05
13 Scott Cooper .05
14 Mark Davis .05
15 Storm Davis .05
16 Larry Walker .05
17 Brian DuBois .05
18 Len Dykstra .05
19 John Franco .05
20 Kirk Gibson .05
21 Juan Gonzalez .20
22 Tommy Greene .05
23 Kent Hrbek .05
24 Mike Huff .05
25 Bo Jackson .10
26 Nolan Knows Bo (Bo Jackson, Nolan Ryan) 1.50
27 Roberto Kelly .05
28 Mark Langston .05
29 Ray Lankford .05
30 Kevin Maas .05
31 Julio Machado .05
32 Greg Maddux .60
33 Mark McGwire 1.00
34 Paul Molitor .40
35 Hal Morris .05
36 Dale Murphy .20
37 Eddie Murray .40
38 Jaime Navarro .05
39 Dean Palmer .05
40 Derek Parks .05
41 Bobby Rose .05
42 Wally Joyner .05
43 Chris Sabo .05
44 Benito Santiago .05
45 Mike Stanton .05
46 Terry Steinbach .05
47 Dave Stewart .05
48 Greg Swindell .05
49 Jose Vizcaino .05
--- "Royal Flush" (Bret Saberhagen, Mark Davis) .05

Series 3

Scott Coolbaugh

Classic's third series of 1990 features the same format as the previous two releases. Series 3 borders are yellow with blue accents. The cards have trivia questions on back and are numbered 1T-100T. No card 51T or 57T exists. Two cards in the set are unnumbered. Like other Classic issues, the cards are designed for use with the trivia board game and were sold only as complete sets.

NM/M
Complete Set (100): 4.00
Common Player: .05
1 Ken Griffey Jr. .75
2 John Tudor .05
3 John Kruk .05
4 Mark Gardner .05
5 Scott Radinsky .05
6 John Burkett .05
7 Will Clark .05
8 Gary Carter .40
9 Ted Higuera .05
10 Dave Parker .05
11 Dante Bichette .05
12 Don Mattingly .60
13 Greg Harris .05
14 David Hollins .05
15 Matt Nokes .05
16 Kevin Tapani .05
17 Shane Mack .05
18 Randy Myers .05
19 Greg Olson .05
20 Shawn Abner .05
21 Jim Presley .05
22 Randy Johnson .40
23 Edgar Martinez .05
24 Scott Coolbaugh .05
25 Jeff Treadway .05
26 Joe Klink .05
27 Rickey Henderson .40
28 Sam Horn .05
29 Kurt Stillwell .05
30 Andy Van Slyke .05
31 Willie Banks .05
32 Jose Canseco .35
33 Felix Jose .05
34 Candy Maldonado .05
35 Carlos Baerga .05
36 Keith Hernandez .05
37 Frank Viola .05
38 Pete O'Brien .05
39 Pat Borders .05
40 Mike Heath .05
41 Kevin Brown .05
42 Chris Bosio .05
43 Shawn Boskie .05
44 Carlos Quintana .05
45 Juan Samuel .05
46 Tim Layana .05
47 Mike Harkey .05
48 Gerald Perry .05
49 Mike Witt .05
50 Joe Orsulak .05
52 Willie Blair .05
53 Gene Larkin .05
54 Jody Reed .05
55 Jeff Reardon .05
56 Kevin McReynolds .05
58 Eric Yelding .05
59 Fred Lynn .05
60 Jim Leyritz .05
61 John Orton .05
62 Mike Lieberthal .05
63 Mike Hartley .05
64 Kal Daniels .05
65 Terry Shumpert .05
66 Sil Campusano .05
67 Tony Pena .05
68 Barry Bonds 1.00
69 Oddibe McDowell .05
70 Kelly Gruber .05
71 Willie Randolph .05
72 Rick Parker .05
73 Bobby Bonilla .05
74 Jack Armstrong .05
75 Hubie Brooks .05
76 Sandy Alomar, Jr. .05
77 Ruben Sierra .05
78 Erik Hanson .05
79 Tony Phillips .05
80 Rondell White .05
81 Bobby Thigpen .05
82 Ron Walden .05
83 Don Peters .05
84 #6 (Nolan Ryan) 1.00
85 Lance Dickson .05
86 Ryne Sandberg .60
87 Eric Christopherson .05
88 Shane Andrews .05
89 Marc Newfield .05
90 Adam Hyzdu .05
91 "Texas Heat" (Nolan Ryan, Reid Ryan) 1.00
92 Chipper Jones .75
93 Frank Thomas .75
94 Cecil Fielder .05
95 Delino DeShields .05
96 John Olerud .05
97 Dave Justice .05
98 Joe Oliver .05
99 Alex Fernandez .05
100 Todd Hundley .05
--- Mike Marshall (Game instructions on back.) .05
--- 4 in 1 (Frank Viola, Nolan/Reid Ryan, Chipper Jones, Don Mattingly) .50

1991 Classic

Kirby Puckett

Top rookies and draft picks highlight this set from Classic. The cards come with a trivia board game and accessories. Fronts have fading blue borders with a touch of red. A blank-back "4-in-1" micro-player card is included with each game set.

NM/M
Complete Set (99): 4.00
Common Player: .05
1 John Olerud .05
2 Tino Martinez .05
3 Ken Griffey Jr. .65

4	Jeromy Burnitz	.05
5	Ron Gant	.05
6	Mike Benjamin	.05
7	Steve Decker	.05
8	Matt Williams	.05
9	Rafael Novoa	.05
10	Kevin Mitchell	.05
11	Dave Justice	.05
12	Leo Gomez	.05
13	Chris Hoiles	.05
14	Ben McDonald	.05
15	David Segui	.05
16	Anthony Telford	.05
17	Mike Mussina	.30
18	Roger Clemens	.60
19	Wade Boggs	.50
20	Tim Naehring	.05
21	Joe Carter	.05
22	Phil Plantier	.05
23	Rob Dibble	.05
24	Mo Vaughn	.05
25	Lee Stevens	.05
26	Chris Sabo	.05
27	Mark Grace	.05
28	Derrick May	.05
29	Ryne Sandberg	.50
30	Matt Stark	.05
31	Bobby Thigpen	.05
32	Frank Thomas	.40
33	Don Mattingly	.60
34	Eric Davis	.05
35	Reggie Jefferson	.05
36	Alex Cole	.05
37	Mark Lewis	.05
38	Tim Costo	.05
39	Sandy Alomar, Jr.	.05
40	Travis Fryman	.05
41	Cecil Fielder	.05
42	Milt Cuyler	.05
43	Andujar Cedeno	.05
44	Danny Darwin	.05
45	Randy Henis	.05
46	George Brett	.60
47	Jeff Conine	.05
48	Bo Jackson	.10
49	Brian McRae	.05
50	Brent Mayne	.05
51	Eddie Murray	.40
52	Ramon Martinez	.05
53	Jim Neidlinger	.05
54	Jim Poole	.05
55	Tim McIntosh	.05
56	Randy Veres	.05
57	Kirby Puckett	.50
58	Todd Ritchie	.05
59	Rich Garces	.05
60	Moises Alou	.05
61	Delino DeShields	.05
62	Oscar Azocar	.05
63	Kevin Maas	.05
64	Alan Mills	.05
65	John Franco	.05
66	Chris Jelic	.05
67	Dave Magadan	.05
68	Darryl Strawberry	.05
69	Hensley Meulens	.05
70	Juan Gonzalez	.20
71	Reggie Harris	.05
72	Rickey Henderson	.40
73	Mark McGwire	.75
74	Willie McGee	.05
75	Todd Van Poppel	.05
76	Bob Welch	.05
77	"Future Aces" (Todd Van Poppel, Don Peters, David Zancanaro, Kirk Dressendorfer)	.05
78	Lenny Dykstra	.05
79	Mickey Morandini	.05
80	Wes Chamberlain	.05
81	Barry Bonds	1.00
82	Doug Drabek	.05
83	Randy Tomlin	.05
84	Scott Chiamparino	.05
85	Rafael Palmeiro	.35
86	Nolan Ryan	1.00
87	Bobby Witt	.05
88	Fred McGriff	.05
89	Dave Steib	.05
90	Ed Sprague	.05
91	Vince Coleman	.05
92	Rod Brewer	.05
93	Bernard Gilkey	.05
94	Roberto Alomar	.20
95	Chuck Finley	.05
96	Dale Murphy	.20
97	Jose Rijo	.05
98	Hal Morris	.05
99	"Friendly Foes" (Dwight Gooden, Darryl Strawberry)	.05
---	John Olerud, Dwight Gooden, Jose Canseco, Darryl Strawberry	.10

Series 2

Classic released a 100-card second series in 1991. Cards feature the same format as the first series, with the exception of border color; Series II features maroon borders. The cards are designed for trivia game use. Series II includes

several players with new teams and top rookies. Special Four-In-One, 300 Game Winner and Strikout Kings cards are included with each set.

		NM/M
Complete Set (100):		4.50
Common Player:		.05
1	Ken Griffey Jr.	.75
2	Wilfredo Cordero	.05
3	Cal Ripken, Jr.	1.00
4	D.J. Dozier	.05
5	Darrin Fletcher	.05
6	Glenn Davis	.05
7	Alex Fernandez	.05
8	Cory Snyder	.05
9	Tim Raines	.05
10	Greg Swindell	.05
11	Mark Lewis	.05
12	Rico Brogna	.05
13	Gary Sheffield	.30
14	Paul Molitor	.50
15	Kent Hrbek	.05
16	Scott Erickson	.05
17	Steve Sax	.05
18	Dennis Eckersley	.40
19	Jose Canseco	.30
20	Kirk Dressendorfer	.05
21	Ken Griffey Sr.	.05
22	Erik Hanson	.05
23	Dan Peltier	.05
24	John Olerud	.05
25	Eddie Zosky	.05
26	Steve Avery	.05
27	John Smoltz	.05
28	Frank Thomas	.50
29	Jerome Walton	.05
30	George Bell	.05
31	Jose Rijo	.05
32	Randy Myers	.05
33	Barry Larkin	.05
34	Eric Anthony	.05
35	Dave Hansen	.05
36	Eric Karros	.05
37	Jose Offerman	.05
38	Marquis Grissom	.05
39	Dwight Gooden	.05
40	Gregg Jefferies	.05
41	Pat Combs	.05
42	Todd Zeile	.05
43	Benito Santiago	.05
44	Dave Staton	.05
45	Tony Fernandez	.05
46	Fred McGriff	.05
47	Jeff Brantley	.05
48	Junior Felix	.05
49	Jack Morris	.05
50	Chris George	.05
51	Henry Rodriguez	.05
52	Paul Marak	.05
53	Ryan Klesko	.05
54	Darren Lewis	.05
55	Lance Dickson	.05
56	Anthony Young	.05
57	Willie Banks	.05
58	Mike Bordick	.05
59	Roger Salkeld	.05
60	Steve Karsay	.05
61	Bernie Williams	.05
62	Mickey Tettleton	.05
63	Dave Justice	.05
64	Steve Decker	.05
65	Roger Clemens	.65
66	Phil Plantier	.05
67	Ryne Sandberg	.60
68	Sandy Alomar,Jr.	.05
69	Cecil Fielder	.05
70	George Brett	.65
71	Delino DeShields	.05
72	Dave Magadan	.05
73	Darryl Strawberry	.05
74	Juan Gonzalez	.25
75	Rickey Henderson	.50
76	Willie McGee	.05
77	Todd Van Poppel	.05
78	Barry Bonds	1.00
79	Doug Drabek	.05
80	Nolan Ryan (300 games)	1.00
81	Roberto Alomar	.20
82	Ivan Rodriguez	.50
83	Dan Opperman	.05
84	Jeff Bagwell	.50
85	Braulio Castillo	.05
86	Doug Simons	.05
87	Wade Taylor	.05
88	Gary Scott	.05
89	Dave Stewart	.05
90	Mike Simms	.05
91	Luis Gonzalez	.05
92	Bobby Bonilla	.05
93	Tony Gwynn	.60
94	Will Clark	.05
95	Rich Rowland	.05
96	Alan Trammell	.05
97	"Strikeout Kings" (Nolan Ryan, Roger Clemens)	.50
98	Joe Carter	.05
99	Jack Clark	.05
100	Four-In-One	.20

Series 3

Green borders highlight Classic's third series of cards for 1991. The set includes a gameboard and player cards featuring trivia questions on the back. Statistics and biographical information are also found on back.

		NM/M
Complete Set (100):		4.50
Common Player:		.05
1	Jim Abbott	.05
2	Craig Biggio	.05
3	Wade Boggs	.45
4	Bobby Bonilla	.05
5	Ivan Calderon	.05
6	Jose Canseco	.25
7	Andy Benes	.05
8	Wes Chamberlain	.05
9	Will Clark	.05
10	Royce Clayton	.05
11	Gerald Alexander	.05
12	Chili Davis	.05
13	Eric Davis	.05
14	Andre Dawson	.25
15	Rob Dibble	.05
16	Chris Donnels	.05
17	Scott Erickson	.05
18	Monty Fariss	.05
19	Ruben Amaro Jr.	.05
20	Chuck Finley	.05
21	Carlton Fisk	.35
22	Carlos Baerga	.05
23	Ron Gant	.05
24	Dave Justice, Ron Gant	.05
25	Mike Gardiner	.05
26	Tom Glavine	.15
27	Joe Grahe	.05
28	Derek Bell	.05
29	Mike Greenwell	.05
30	Ken Griffey Jr.	.75
31	Leo Gomez	.05
32	Tom Goodwin	.05
33	Tony Gwynn	.45
34	Mel Hall	.05
35	Brian Harper	.05
36	Dave Henderson	.05
37	Albert Belle	.05
38	Orel Hershiser	.05
39	Brian Hunter	.05
40	Howard Johnson	.05
41	Felix Jose	.05
42	Wally Joyner	.05
43	Jeff Juden	.05
44	Pat Kelly	.05
45	Jimmy Key	.05
46	Chuck Knoblauch	.05
47	John Kruk	.05
48	Ray Lankford	.05
49	Ced Landrum	.05
50	Scott Livingstone	.05
51	Kevin Maas	.05
52	Greg Maddux	.45
53	Dennis Martinez	.05
54	Edgar Martinez	.05
55	Pedro Martinez	.50
56	Don Mattingly	.50
57	Orlando Merced	.05
58	Keith Mitchell	.05
59	Kevin Mitchell	.05
60	Paul Molitor	.35
61	Jack Morris	.05
62	Hal Morris	.05
63	Kevin Morton	.05
64	Pedro Munoz	.05
65	Eddie Murray	.35
66	Jack McDowell	.05
67	Jeff McNeely	.05
68	Brian McRae	.05
69	Kevin McReynolds	.05
70	Gregg Olson	.05
71	Rafael Palmeiro	.30
72	Dean Palmer	.05
73	Tony Phillips	.05
74	Kirby Puckett	.45
75	Carlos Quintana	.05
76	Pat Rice	.05
77	Cal Ripken, Jr.	1.00
78	Ivan Rodriguez	.30
79	Nolan Ryan	1.00
80	Bret Saberhagen	.05
81	Tim Salmon	.05
82	Juan Samuel	.05
83	Ruben Sierra	.05
84	Heathcliff Slocumb	.05
85	Joe Slusarski	.05
86	John Smiley	.05
87	Dave Smith	.05
88	Ed Sprague	.05
89	Todd Stottlemyre	.05
90	Mike Timlin	.05
91	Greg Vaughn	.05
92	Frank Viola	.05
93	John Wehner	.05
94	Devon White	.05
95	Matt Williams	.05
96	Rick Wilkins	.05
97	Bernie Williams	.05
98	Starter & Stopper (Goose Gossage, Nolan Ryan)	.20
99	Gerald Williams	.05
----	4-in-1 (Bobby Bonilla, Will Clark, Cal Ripken Jr., Scott Erickson)	.25

Collector's Edition

The Classic Collector's edition made its debut in 1991. This package includes a board game, trivia baseball player cards, a baseball tips booklet and a certificate of authenticity, all packaged in a collector's edition box. Each box is individually and sequentially numbered on the outside, with a reported 100,000 available.

		NM/M
Complete Set (200):		7.50
Common Player:		.05
1	Frank Viola	.05
2	Tim Wallach	.05
3	Lou Whitaker	.05
4	Brett Butler	.05
5	Jim Abbott	.05
6	Jack Armstrong	.05
7	Craig Biggio	.05
8	Brian Barnes	.05
9	Dennis "Oil Can" Boyd	.05
10	Tom Browning	.05
11	Tom Brunansky	.05
12	Ellis Burks	.05
13	Harold Baines	.05
14	Kal Daniels	.05
15	Mark Davis	.05
16	Storm Davis	.05
17	Tom Glavine	.25
18	Mike Greenwell	.05
19	Kelly Gruber	.05
20	Mark Gubicza	.05
21	Pedro Guerrero	.05
22	Mike Harkey	.05
23	Orel Hershiser	.05
24	Ted Higuera	.05
25	Von Hayes	.05
26	Andre Dawson	.25
27	Shawon Dunston	.05
28	Roberto Kelly	.05
29	Joe Magrane	.05
30	Dennis Martinez	.05
31	Kevin McReynolds	.05
32	Matt Nokes	.05
33	Dan Plesac	.05
34	Dave Parker	.05
35	Randy Johnson	.40
36	Bret Saberhagen	.05
37	Mackey Sasser	.05
38	Mike Scott	.05
39	Ozzie Smith	.50
40	Kevin Seitzer	.05
41	Ruben Sierra	.05
42	Kevin Tapani	.05
43	Danny Tartabull	.05
44	Robby Thompson	.05
45	Andy Van Slyke	.05
46	Greg Vaughn	.05
47	Harold Reynolds	.05
48	Will Clark	.05
49	Gary Gaetti	.05
50	Joe Grahe	.05
51	Carlton Fisk	.40
52	Robin Ventura	.05
53	Ozzie Guillen	.05
54	Tom Candiotti	.05
55	Doug Jones	.05
56	Eric King	.05
57	Kirk Gibson	.05
58	Tim Costo	.05
59	Robin Yount	.40
60	Sammy Sosa	.50
61	Jesse Barfield	.05
62	Marc Newfield	.05
63	Jimmy Key	.05
64	Felix Jose	.05
65	Mark Whiten	.05
66	Tommy Greene	.05
67	Kent Mercker	.05
68	Greg Maddux	.50
69	Danny Jackson	.05
70	Reggie Sanders	.05
71	Eric Yelding	.05
72	Karl Rhodes	.05
73	Fernando Valenzuela	.05
74	Chris Nabholz	.05
75	Andres Galarraga	.05
76	Howard Johnson	.05
77	Hubie Brooks	.05
78	Terry Mulholland	.05
79	Paul Molitor	.40
80	Roger McDowell	.05
81	Darren Daulton	.05
82	Zane Smith	.05
83	Ray Lankford	.05
84	Bruce Hurst	.05
85	Andy Benes	.05
86	John Burkett	.05
87	Dave Righetti	.05
88	Steve Karsay	.05
89	D.J. Dozier	.05
90	Jeff Bagwell	.40
91	Joe Carter	.05
92	Wes Chamberlain	.05
93	Vince Coleman	.05
94	Pat Combs	.05
95	Jerome Walton	.05
96	Jeff Conine	.05
97	Alan Trammell	.05
98	Don Mattingly	.66
99	Ramon Martinez	.05
100	Dave Magadan	.05
101	Greg Swindell	.05
102	Dave Stewart	.05
103	Gary Sheffield	.30
104	George Bell	.05
105	Mark Grace	.05
106	Steve Sax	.05
107	Ryne Sandberg	.50
108	Chris Sabo	.05
109	Jose Rijo	.05
110	Cal Ripken, Jr.	1.00
111	Kirby Puckett	.50
112	Eddie Murray	.40
113	Roberto Alomar	.20
114	Randy Myers	.05
115	Rafael Palmeiro	.35
116	John Olerud	.05
117	Gregg Jefferies	.05
118	Kent Hrbek	.05
119	Marquis Grissom	.05
120	Ken Griffey Jr.	.60
121	Dwight Gooden	.05
122	Juan Gonzalez	.20
123	Ron Gant	.05
124	Travis Fryman	.05
125	John Franco	.05
126	Dennis Eckersley	.35
127	Cecil Fielder	.05
128	Phil Plantier	.05
129	Kevin Mitchell	.05
130	Kevin Maas	.05
131	Mark McGwire	.75
132	Ben McDonald	.05
133	Lenny Dykstra	.05
134	Delino DeShields	.05
135	Jose Canseco	.30
136	Eric Davis	.05
137	George Brett	.55
138	Steve Avery	.05
139	Eric Anthony	.05
140	Bobby Thigpen	.05
141	Ken Griffey Sr.	.05
142	Barry Larkin	.05
143	Jeff Brantley	.05
144	Bobby Bonilla	.05
145	Jose Offerman	.05
146	Mike Mussina	.30
147	Erik Hanson	.05
148	Dale Murphy	.15
149	Roger Clemens	.55
150	Tino Martinez	.05
151	Todd Van Poppel	.05
152	Mo Vaughn	.05
153	Derrick May	.05
154	Jack Clark	.05
155	Dave Hansen	.05
156	Tony Gwynn	.50
157	Brian McRae	.05
158	Matt Williams	.05
159	Kirk Dressendorfer	.05
160	Scott Erickson	.05
161	Tony Fernandez	.05
162	Willie McGee	.05
163	Fred McGriff	.05
164	Leo Gomez	.05
165	Bernard Gilkey	.05
166	Bobby Witt	.05
167	Doug Drabek	.05
168	Rob Dibble	.05
169	Glenn Davis	.05
170	Danny Darwin	.05
171	Eric Karros	.05
172	Eddie Zosky	.05
173	Todd Zeile	.05
174	Tim Raines	.05
175	Benito Santiago	.05
176	Dan Peltier	.05
177	Darryl Strawberry	.05
178	Hal Morris	.05
179	Hensley Meulens	.05
180	John Smoltz	.05
181	Frank Thomas	.40
182	Dave Staton	.05
183	Scott Chiamparino	.05
184	Alex Fernandez	.05
185	Mark Lewis	.05
186	Bo Jackson	.10
187	Mickey Morandini (Photo actually Darren Daulton.)	.05
188	Cory Snyder	.05
189	Rickey Henderson	.40
190	Junior Felix	.05
191	Milt Cuyler	.05
192	Wade Boggs	.50
193	"Justice Prevails" (David Justice)	.05
194	Sandy Alomar, Jr.	.05
195	Barry Bonds	1.00
196	Nolan Ryan	1.00
197	Rico Brogna	.05
198	Steve Decker	.05
199	Bob Welch	.05
200	Andujar Cedeno	.05

1991 Classic/ American Collectables Nolan Ryan

This set of Nolan Ryan highlights was produced by Classic for American Collectables and sold as a limited-edition issue. The cards feature color photos of Ryan bordered in a garish green and yellow design. Backs have personal data and stats printed in black on green, along with a color MLB logo.

		NM/M
Complete Set (10):		7.50
Common Card:		1.00
1	Nolan Ryan (Mets '66-'71)	1.00
2	Nolan Ryan (Angels '72-'79)	1.00
3	Nolan Ryan (Astros '80-'88)	1.00
4	Nolan Ryan (Rangers '89-'90)	1.00
5	Nolan Ryan (5000 K's)	1.00
6	Nolan Ryan (6th No-No)	1.00
7	Nolan Ryan (Angels '72-'79)	1.00
8	Nolan Ryan (Astros '80-'88)	1.00
9	Nolan Ryan (Rangers '89-'90)	1.00
10	Nolan Ryan (300 Wins)	1.00

1992 Classic Series 1

Classic introduced an innovative design with the release of its 1992 set. Fronts feature full-color photos bordered in white, while backs feature statistics, biographical information and trivia ques-

tions accented by a fading stadium shot. The cards were released with a gameboard and are numbered on back with a "T" prefix.

NM/M
Complete Set (100): 4.50
Common Player: .05
1 Jim Abbott .05
2 Kyle Abbott .05
3 Scott Aldred .05
4 Roberto Alomar .20
5 Wilson Alvarez .05
6 Andy Ashby .05
7 Steve Avery .05
8 Jeff Bagwell .40
9 Bret Barberie .05
10 Kim Batiste .05
11 Derek Bell .05
12 Jay Bell .05
13 Albert Belle .05
14 Andy Benes .05
15 Sean Berry .05
16 Barry Bonds 1.00
17 Ryan Bowen .05
18 Trifecta (Alejandro Pena, Mark Wohlers, Kent Mercker) .05
19 Scott Brosius .05
20 Jay Buhner .05
21 David Burba .05
22 Jose Canseco .35
23 Andujar Cedeno .05
24 Will Clark .05
25 Royce Clayton .05
26 Roger Clemens .50
27 David Cone .05
28 Scott Cooper .05
29 Chris Cron .05
30 Len Dykstra .05
31 Cal Eldred .05
32 Hector Fajardo .05
33 Cecil Fielder .05
34 Dave Fleming .05
35 Steve Foster .05
36 Julio Franco .05
37 Carlos Garcia .05
38 Tom Glavine .15
39 Tom Goodwin .05
40 Ken Griffey Jr. .65
41 Chris Haney .05
42 Bryan Harvey .05
43 Rickey Henderson .40
44 Carlos Hernandez .05
45 Roberto Hernandez .05
46 Brook Jacoby .05
47 Howard Johnson .05
48 Pat Kelly .05
49 Darryl Kile .05
50 Chuck Knoblauch .05
51 Ray Lankford .05
52 Mark Leiter .05
53 Darren Lewis .05
54 Scott Livingstone .05
55 Shane Mack .05
56 Chito Martinez .05
57 Dennis Martinez .05
58 Don Mattingly .50
59 Paul McClellan .05
60 Chuck McElroy .05
61 Fred McGriff .05
62 Orlando Merced .05
63 Luis Mercedes .05
64 Kevin Mitchell .05
65 Hal Morris .05
66 Jack Morris .05
67 Mike Mussina .30
68 Denny Neagle .05
69 Tom Pagnozzi .05
70 Terry Pendleton .05
71 Phil Plantier .05
72 Kirby Puckett .45
73 Carlos Quintana .05
74 Willie Randolph .05
75 Arthur Rhodes .05
76 Cal Ripken 1.00
77 Ivan Rodriguez .35
78 Nolan Ryan 1.00
79 Ryne Sandberg .45
80 Deion Sanders .10
81 Reggie Sanders .05
82 Mo Sanford .05
83 Terry Shumpert .05
84 Tim Spehr .05
85 Lee Stevens .05
86 Darryl Strawberry .05
87 Kevin Tapani .05
88 Danny Tartabull .05
89 Frank Thomas .40
90 Jim Thome .30
91 Todd Van Poppel .05
92 Andy Van Slyke .05
93 John Wehner .05
94 John Wetteland .05
95 Devon White .05
96 Brian Williams .05
97 Mark Wohlers .05
98 Robin Yount .40
99 Eddie Zosky .05
--- 4-in-1 (Barry Bonds, Roger Clemens, Steve Avery, Nolan Ryan) .50

Series 2

The 100-cards in Classic's 1992 Series II came packaged with a gameboard and spinner. In a completely different format from Classic's other '92 issues, Series II features player photos bordered at left and right with red or blue color bars which fade toward top and bottom. Backs have biographical data, previous-year and career statistics and five trivia questions, along with a color representation of the team's uniform. Cards, except the 4-In-1, are numbered with a "T" prefix.

NM/M
Complete Set (100): 4.50
Common Player: .05
1 Jim Abbott .05
2 Jeff Bagwell .40
3 Jose Canseco .30
4 Julio Valera .05
5 Scott Brosius .05
6 Mark Langston .05
7 Andy Stankiewicz .05
8 Gary DiSarcina .05
9 Pete Harnisch .05
10 Mark McGwire .75
11 Ricky Bones .05
12 Steve Avery .05
13 Deion Sanders .10
14 Mike Mussina .25
15 Dave Justice .05
16 Pat Hentgen .05
17 Tom Glavine .20
18 Juan Guzman .05
19 Ron Gant .05
20 Kelly Gruber .05
21 Eric Karros .05
22 Derrick May .05
23 Dave Hansen .05
24 Andre Dawson .25
25 Eric Davis .05
26 Ozzie Smith .45
27 Sammy Sosa .45
28 Lee Smith .05
29 Ryne Sandberg .45
30 Robin Yount .40
31 Matt Williams .05
32 John Vander Wal .05
33 Bill Swift .05
34 Delino DeShields .05
35 Royce Clayton .05
36 Moises Alou .05
37 Will Clark .05
38 Darryl Strawberry .05
39 Larry Walker .05
40 Ramon Martinez .05
41 Howard Johnson .05
42 Tino Martinez .05
43 Dwight Gooden .05
44 Ken Griffey Jr. .60
45 David Cone .05
46 Kenny Lofton .05
47 Bobby Bonilla .05
48 Carlos Baerga .05
49 Don Mattingly .50
50 Sandy Alomar, Jr. .05
51 Lenny Dykstra .05
52 Tony Gwynn .45
53 Felix Jose .05
54 Rick Sutcliffe .05
55 Wes Chamberlain .05
56 Cal Ripken, Jr. 1.00
57 Kyle Abbott .05
58 Leo Gomez .05
59 Gary Sheffield .20
60 Anthony Young .05
61 Roger Clemens .50
62 Rafael Palmeiro .35
63 Wade Boggs .45
64 Andy Van Slyke .05
65 Ruben Sierra .05
66 Denny Neagle .05
67 Nolan Ryan 1.00
68 Doug Drabek .05
69 Ivan Rodriguez .35
70 Barry Bonds 1.00
71 Chuck Knoblauch .05
72 Reggie Sanders .05
73 Cecil Fielder .05
74 Barry Larkin .05
75 Scott Aldred .05
76 Rob Dibble .05
77 Brian McRae .05
78 Tim Belcher .05
79 George Brett .50
80 Frank Viola .05
81 Roberto Kelly .05
82 Jack McDowell .05
83 Mel Hall .05
84 Esteban Beltre .05
85 Robin Ventura .05
86 George Bell .05
87 Frank Thomas .40
88 John Smiley .05
89 Bobby Thigpen .05
90 Kirby Puckett .45
91 Kevin Mitchell .05
92 Peter Hoy .05
93 Russ Springer .05
94 Donovan Osborne .05
95 Dave Silvestri .05
96 Chad Curtis .05
97 Pat Mahomes .05
98 Danny Tartabull .05
99 John Doherty .05
--- 4-in-1 (Ryne Sandberg, Mike Mussina, Reggie Sanders, Jose Canseco) .25

Collector's Edition

The second annual 200-card "Collector's Edition" set was packaged with a gameboard, spinner, generic player pieces, a mechanical scoreboard and a book of tips from star players. The UV-coated card fronts feature color player photos against a deep purple border. Backs have a few biographical details, previous season and career stats, plus five trivia questions in case anyone actually wanted to play the game.

NM/M
Complete Set (200): 9.00
Common Player: .05
1 Chuck Finley .05
2 Craig Biggio .05
3 Luis Gonzalez .05
4 Pete Harnisch .05
5 Jeff Juden .05
6 Harold Baines .05
7 Kirk Dressendorfer .05
8 Dennis Eckersley .35
9 Dave Henderson .05
10 Dave Stewart .05
11 Joe Carter .05
12 Juan Guzman .05
13 Dave Stieb .05
14 Todd Stottlemyre .05
15 Ron Gant .05
16 Brian Hunter .05
17 Dave Justice .05
18 John Smoltz .05
19 Mike Stanton .05
20 Chris George .05
21 Paul Molitor .40
22 Omar Olivares .05
23 Lee Smith .05
24 Ozzie Smith .50
25 Todd Zeile .05
26 George Bell .05
27 Andre Dawson .25
28 Shawon Dunston .05
29 Mark Grace .05
30 Greg Maddux .50
31 Dave Smith .05
32 Brett Butler .05
33 Orel Hershiser .05
34 Eric Karros .05
35 Ramon Martinez .05
36 Jose Offerman .05
37 Juan Samuel .05
38 Delino DeShields .05
39 Marquis Grissom .05
40 Tim Wallach .05
41 Eric Gunderson .05
42 Willie McGee .05
43 Dave Righetti .05
44 Robby Thompson .05
45 Matt Williams .05
46 Sandy Alomar, Jr. .05
47 Reggie Jefferson .05
48 Mark Lewis .05
49 Robin Ventura .05
50 Tino Martinez .05
51 Roberto Kelly .05
52 Vince Coleman .05
53 Dwight Gooden .05
54 Todd Hundley .05
55 Kevin Maas .05
56 Wade Taylor .05
57 Bryan Harvey .05
58 Leo Gomez .05
59 Ben McDonald .05
60 Ricky Bones .05
61 Tony Gwynn .50
62 Benito Santiago .05
63 Wes Chamberlain .05
64 Tommy Greene .05
65 Dale Murphy .15
66 Steve Buechele .05
67 Doug Drabek .05
68 Joe Grahe .05
69 Rafael Palmeiro .35
70 Wade Boggs .50
71 Ellis Burks .05
72 Mike Greenwell .05
73 Mo Vaughn .05
74 Derek Bell .05
75 Rob Dibble .05
76 Barry Larkin .05
77 Jose Rijo .05
78 Doug Henry .05
79 Chris Sabo .05
80 Pedro Guerrero .05
81 George Brett .60
82 Tom Gordon .05
83 Mark Gubicza .05
84 Mark Whiten .05
85 Brian McRae .05
86 Danny Jackson .05
87 Milt Cuyler .05
88 Travis Fryman .05
89 Mickey Tettleton .05
90 Alan Trammell .05
91 Lou Whitaker .05
92 Chili Davis .05
93 Scott Erickson .05
94 Kent Hrbek .05
95 Alex Fernandez .05
96 Carlton Fisk .40
97 Ramon Garcia .05
98 Ozzie Guillen .05
99 Tim Raines .05
100 Bobby Thigpen .05
101 Kirby Puckett .50
102 Bernie Williams .05
103 Dave Hansen .05
104 Kevin Tapani .05
105 Don Mattingly .60
106 Frank Thomas .40
107 Monty Fariss .05
108 Bo Jackson .10
109 Jim Abbott .05
110 Jose Canseco .25
111 Phil Plantier .05
112 Brian Williams .05
113 Mark Langston .05
114 Wilson Alvarez .05
115 Roberto Hernandez .05
116 Darryl Kile .05
117 Ryan Bowen .05
118 Rickey Henderson .40
119 Mark McGwire 1.00
120 Devon White .05
121 Roberto Alomar .20
122 Kelly Gruber .05
123 Eddie Zosky .05
124 Tom Glavine .25
125 Kal Daniels .05
126 Cal Eldred .05
127 Deion Sanders .10
128 Robin Yount .40
129 Cecil Fielder .05
130 Ray Lankford .05
131 Ryne Sandberg .50
132 Darryl Strawberry .05
133 Chris Haney .05
134 Dennis Martinez .05
135 Bryan Hickerson .05
136 Will Clark .05
137 Hal Morris .05
138 Charles Nagy .05
139 Jim Thome .35
140 Albert Belle .05
141 Reggie Sanders .05
142 Scott Cooper .05
143 David Cone .05
144 Anthony Young .05
145 Howard Johnson .05
146 Arthur Rhodes .05
147 Scott Aldred .05
148 Mike Mussina .25
149 Fred McGriff .05
150 Andy Benes .05
151 Ruben Sierra .05
152 Len Dykstra .05
153 Andy Van Slyke .05
154 Orlando Merced .05
155 Barry Bonds 1.50
156 John Smiley .05
157 Julio Franco .05
158 Juan Gonzalez .20
159 Ivan Rodriguez .35
160 Willie Banks .05
161 Eric Davis .05
162 Eddie Murray .40
163 Dave Fleming .05
164 Wally Joyner .05
165 Kevin Mitchell .05
166 Ed Taubensee .05
167 Danny Tartabull .05
168 Ken Hill .05
169 Willie Randolph .05
170 Kevin McReynolds .05
171 Gregg Jefferies .05
172 Patrick Lennon .05
173 Luis Mercedes .05
174 Glenn Davis .05
175 Bret Saberhagen .05
176 Bobby Bonilla .05
177 Kenny Lofton .05
178 Jose Lind .05
179 Royce Clayton .05
180 Scott Scudder .05
181 Chuck Knoblauch .05
182 Terry Pendleton .05
183 Nolan Ryan 1.50
184 Rob Maurer .05
185 Brian Bohanon .05
186 Ken Griffey Jr. .75
187 Jeff Bagwell .40
188 Steve Avery .05
189 Roger Clemens .60
190 Cal Ripken, Jr. 1.50
191 Kim Batiste .05
192 Bip Roberts .05
193 Greg Swindell .05
194 Dave Winfield .40
195 Steve Sax .05
196 Frank Viola .05
197 Mo Sanford .05
198 Kyle Abbott .05
199 Jack Morris .05
200 Andy Ashby .05

1993 Classic

A 100-card travel edition of Classic's baseball trivia cards was produced for 1993. Cards feature game-action player photos with dark blue borders. Backs have previous season and career stats along with five trivia questions. Card numbers have a "T" prefix.

NM/M
Complete Set (100): 4.00
Common Player: .05
1 Jim Abbott .05
2 Roberto Alomar .20
3 Moises Alou .05
4 Brady Anderson .05
5 Eric Anthony .05
6 Alex Arias .05
7 Pedro Astacio .05
8 Steve Avery .05
9 Carlos Baerga .05
10 Jeff Bagwell .40
11 George Bell .05
12 Albert Belle .05
13 Craig Biggio .05
14 Barry Bonds 1.00
15 Bobby Bonilla .05
16 Mike Bordick .05
17 George Brett .55
18 Jose Canseco .30
19 Joe Carter .05
20 Royce Clayton .05
21 Roger Clemens .55
22 Greg Colbrunn .05
23 David Cone .05
24 Darren Daulton .05
25 Delino DeShields .05
26 Rob Dibble .05
27 Dennis Eckersley .35
28 Cal Eldred .05
29 Scott Erickson .05
30 Junior Felix .05
31 Tony Fernandez .05
32 Cecil Fielder .05
33 Steve Finley .05
34 Dave Fleming .05
35 Travis Fryman .05
36 Tom Glavine .25
37 Juan Gonzalez .20
38 Ken Griffey Jr. .60
39 Marquis Grissom .05
40 Juan Guzman .05
41 Tony Gwynn .50
42 Rickey Henderson .40
43 Felix Jose .05
44 Wally Joyner .05
45 David Justice .05
46 Eric Karros .05
47 Roberto Kelly .05
48 Ryan Klesko .05
49 Chuck Knoblauch .05
50 John Kruk .05
51 Ray Lankford .05
52 Barry Larkin .05
53 Pat Listach .05
54 Kenny Lofton .05
55 Shane Mack .05
56 Greg Maddux .50
57 Dave Magadan .05
58 Edgar Martinez .05
59 Don Mattingly .55
60 Ben McDonald .05
61 Jack McDowell .05
62 Fred McGriff .05
63 Mark McGwire .75
64 Kevin McReynolds .05
65 Sam Militello .05
66 Paul Molitor .40
67 Jeff Montgomery .05
68 Jack Morris .05
69 Eddie Murray .40
70 Mike Mussina .30
71 Otis Nixon .05
72 Donovan Osborne .05
73 Terry Pendleton .05
74 Mike Piazza .60
75 Kirby Puckett .50
76 Cal Ripken, Jr. 1.00
77 Bip Roberts .05
78 Ivan Rodriguez .35
79 Nolan Ryan 1.00
80 Ryne Sandberg .50
81 Deion Sanders .10
82 Reggie Sanders .05
83 Frank Seminara .05
84 Gary Sheffield .30
85 Ruben Sierra .05
86 John Smiley .05
87 Lee Smith .05
88 Ozzie Smith .50
89 John Smoltz .05
90 Danny Tartabull .05
91 Bob Tewksbury .05
92 Frank Thomas .40
93 Andy Van Slyke .05
94 Mo Vaughn .05
95 Robin Ventura .05
96 Tim Wakefield .05
97 Larry Walker .05
98 Dave Winfield .40
99 Robin Yount .40
--- 4-in-1 (Mark McGwire, Sam Militello, Ryan Klesko, Greg Maddux) .50

1996 Classic/ Metallic Impressions Nolan Ryan

Nolan Ryan's career is traced in this set of 2-5/8" x 3-5/8" embossed metal cards produced for Classic by Metallic Impressions. The center of each card's front is a raised color photo which continues in muted tones of yellow and orange to the edges. The Classic and The Metal Edge logos are embossed, as well. Horizontal backs are identical in design with a color portrait of Ryan at left and a paragraph describing a highlight or milestone at right. Classic and Cooperstown Collection logos are in opposite corners. Each of 14,950 sets was sold with a numbered certificate of authenticity in an embossed lithographed metal box.

		NM/M
Complete Boxed Set (10):		7.50
Single Card:		1.00
1	Nolan Ryan (Career ends with Rangers)	1.00
2	Nolan Ryan (1970s, California Angels)	1.00
3	Nolan Ryan (Major League debut.)	1.00
4	Nolan Ryan (Over-40 no-hitters.)	1.00
5	Nolan Ryan (Rangers no-hitters.)	1.00
6	Nolan Ryan (Mets trade Ryan).	1.00
7	Nolan Ryan (Joins Astros.)	1.00
8	Nolan Ryan (Career records.)	1.00
9	Nolan Ryan (Lean years in Houston.)	1.00
10	Nolan Ryan ("Ryan Express" returns to A.L.)	1.00

1989 Cleveland Indians Team Issue

(28) Cory Snyder, OF

The Cleveland Indians released this oversized (2-3/4" x 4-1/2") set in 1989. Cards feature a full-color player photo on front with the "Tribe" logo in the upper left corner. Card backs include major and minor league statistics and a facsimile autograph.

		NM/M
Complete Set (28):		6.00
Common Player:		.25
(1)	Doc Edwards	.25
(2)	Joel Skinner	.25
(3)	Andy Allanson	.25
(4)	Tom Candiotti	.25
(5)	Doug Jones	.25
(6)	Keith Atherton	.25
(7)	Rich Yett	.25
(8)	John Farrell	.25
(9)	Rod Nichols	.25
(10)	Joe Skalski	.25
(11)	Pete O'Brien	.25
(12)	Jerry Browne	.25
(13)	Brook Jacoby	.25
(14)	Felix Fermin	.25
(15)	Bud Black	.25
(16)	Brad Havens	.25
(17)	Greg Swindell	.25
(18)	Scott Bailes	.25
(19)	Jesse Orosco	.25
(20)	Oddibe McDowell	.25
(21)	Joe Carter	.50
(22)	Cory Snyder	.25
(23)	Louie Medina	.25
(24)	Dave Clark	.25
(25)	Brad Komminsk	.25
(26)	Luis Aguayo	.25
(27)	Pat Keedy	.25
(28)	Tribe Coaches	.25

1990 Cleveland Indians Team Issue

The Cleveland Indians released this oversized (2-7/8" x 4-1/4") set in 1990. Cards feature a full-color portrait photo on front with the "Tribe" logo in the top-left corner. Player

(17) Keith Hernandez, 1B

name, uniform number and position are in the bottom border. Backs are blank.

		NM/M
Complete Set (46):		12.00
Common Player:		.25
(1)	Beau Allred	.25
(2)	Sandy Alomar Jr.	.50
(3)	Carlos Baerga	.25
(4)	Kevin Bearse	.25
(5)	Joey (Albert) Belle	2.00
(6)	Bud Black	.25
(7)	Tom Brookens	.25
(8)	Jerry Browne	.25
(9)	Tom Candiotti	.25
(10)	Colin Charland	.25
(11)	Rich Dauer	.25
(12)	John Farrell	.25
(13)	Felix Fermin	.25
(14)	Cecilio Guante	.25
(15)	Mike Hargrove	.35
(16)	Keith Hernandez	.40
(17)	Luis Isaac	.25
(18)	Brook Jacoby	.25
(19)	Chris James	.25
(20)	Dion James	.25
(21)	Doug Jones	.25
(22)	Carl Kelipuleole	.25
(23)	Tom Lampkin	.25
(24)	Tom Magrann	.25
(25)	Candy Maldonado	.25
(26)	Jeff Manto	.25
(27)	John McNamara	.25
(28)	Jose Morales	.25
(29)	Rod Nichols	.25
(30)	Al Nipper	.25
(31)	Steve Olin	.25
(32)	Jesse Orosco	.25
(33)	Doug Robertson	.25
(34)	Rudy Seanez	.25
(35)	Jeff Shaw	.25
(36)	Doug Sisk	.25
(37)	Joe Skalski	.25
(38)	Joel Skinner	.25
(39)	Cory Snyder	.25
(40)	Greg Swindell	.25
(41)	Sergio Valdez	.25
(42)	Mike Walker	.25
(43)	Mitch Webster	.25
(44)	Kevin Wickander	.25
(45)	Mark Wiley	.25
(46)	Billy Williams	.25

1993 Cleveland Indians Team Issue

Only the mascot's card carries the logo of the television station which sponsored this team set. In 2-1/2" x 3-1/2" format printed on thin cardboard, the fronts feature color game-action photos with borders of red, white and blue. The player's uniform number appears in the lower-left corner. Backs are in black-and-white with major league career stats and a log commemorating the team's 61 years at Municipal Stadium. The set is checklisted here alphabetically.

		NM/M
Complete Set (34):		12.00
Common Player:		.25
(1)	Sandy Alomar Jr.	.50
(2)	Carlos Baerga	.25
(3)	Albert Belle	1.00
(4)	Mike Bielecki	.25
(5)	Mike Christopher	.25
(6)	Mark Clark	.25
(7)	Dennis Cook	.25
(8)	Alvaro Espinoza	.25
(9)	Felix Fermin	.25
(10)	Mike Hargrove	.25
(11)	Glenallen Hill	.25
(12)	Thomas Howard	.25
(13)	Reggie Jefferson	.25
(14)	Wayne Kirby	.25
(15)	Tom Kramer	.25
(16)	Mark Lewis	.25
(17)	Derek Lilliquist	.25
(18)	Kenny Lofton	.35
(19)	Carlos Martinez	.25
(20)	Jose Mesa	.25
(21)	Jeff Mutis	.25
(22)	Charles Nagy	.25
(23)	Bob Ojeda	.25
(24)	Junior Ortiz	.25
(25)	Eric Plunk	.25
(26)	Ted Power	.25
(27)	Scott Scudder	.25
(28)	Joel Skinner	.25
(29)	Paul Sorrento	.25
(30)	Jim Thome	2.00
(31)	Jeff Treadway	.25
(32)	Kevin Wickander	.25
(33)	Indians Coaches (Rick Adair, Ken Bolke, Dom Chiti, Ron Clark, Jose Morales, Dave Nelson, Jeff Newman)	.25
(34)	Slider (Mascot)	.25

2005 Cloverdale Meats Seattle Mariners

Cloverdale Mets sponsored a kids' trading card stadium giveaway on June 16, distributing 27-card packs to fans 14 and under. Each pack contained 20 different cards and seven duplicates to trade in an effort to complete the set. Fronts of the 2-1/2" x 3-1/2" cards have game-action photos. Full-color backs have a portrait photo, player data and trivia, and team and sponsor's logos.

		NM/M
Complete Set (27):		10.00
Common Player:		.35
1	Mike Hargrove	.35
2	Adrian Beltre	.75
3	Willie Bloomquist	.35
4	Bret Boone	.35
5	Ryan Franklin	.35
6	Eddie Guardado	.35
7	Shigetoshi Hasegawa	.35
8	Raul Ibanez	.35
9	Bobby Madritsch	.35
10	Julio Mateo	.35
11	Gil Meche	.35
12	Jamie Moyer	.35
13	Jeff Nelson	.35
14	Miguel Olivo	.35
15	Joel Pineiro	.35
16	J.J. Putz	.35
17	Jeremy Reed	.75
18	Pokey Reese	.35
19	Aaron Sele	.35
20	Richie Sexson	.35
21	Scott Spiezio	.35
22	Ichiro Suzuki	3.00
23	Matt Thornton	.35
24	Wilson Valdez	.35
25	Ron Villone	.35
26	Dan Wilson	.35
27	Randy Winn	.35

1992 Clovis Police Department Mark's Moments

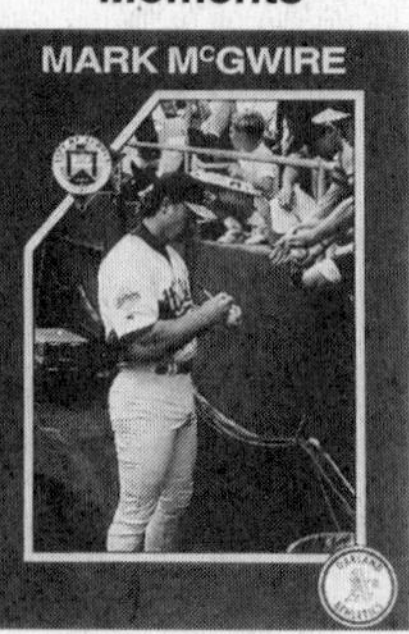

Highlights of Mark McGwire's career to that point are shown and/or described in this set of police cards from the Clovis, Calif., P.D. Cards have color photos framed in gold with green borders. The city seal is at upper-left, the Oakland description of a "Moment," a safety tip, the description of the "Moment" on front, a safety tip, the logo of the Clovis P.D., another team logo and sponsors' credits.

	NM/M
Complete Set (24):	35.00
Common Card:	1.50

1981 Coca-Cola

In 1981 Topps produced for Coca-Cola 12-card sets for 11 American and National League teams. The sets include 11 player cards and one unnumbered header card. The 2-1/2" x 3-1/2" cards are identical in format to the 1981 Topps regular issue with an added Coca-Cola logo. Backs differ from the '81 Topps regular set in that they are numbered 1-11 and carry the Coca-Cola trademark and copyright line. The header cards contain an offer for 132-card uncut sheets of 1981 Topps baseball cards. Some New York Yankees' cards were prepared, but never issued; to date, only three of the players are known.

		NM/M
Complete Set (No Yankees) (132):		20.00
Common Player:		.10
Boston Red Sox Team Set		3.00
1	Tom Burgmeier	.10
2	Dennis Eckersley	.35
3	Dwight Evans	.20
4	Bob Stanley	.10
5	Glenn Hoffman	.10
6	Carney Lansford	.10
7	Frank Tanana	.10
8	Tony Perez	.75
9	Jim Rice	.50
10	Dave Stapleton	.10
11	Carl Yastrzemski	2.00
----	Red Sox Header Card	.05
Chicago Cubs Team Set		1.25
1	Tim Blackwell	.10
2	Bill Buckner	.35
3	Ivan DeJesus	.10
4	Leon Durham	.10
5	Steve Henderson	.10
6	Mike Krukow	.10
7	Ken Reitz	.10
8	Rick Reuschel	.10
9	Scot Thompson	.10
10	Dick Tidrow	.10
11	Mike Tyson	.10
----	Cubs Header Card	.05
Chicago White Sox Team Set		1.00
1	Britt Burns	.10
2	Todd Cruz	.10
3	Rich Dotson	.10
4	Jim Essian	.10
5	Ed Farmer	.10
6	Lamar Johnson	.10
7	Ron LeFlore	.10
8	Chet Lemon	.10
9	Bob Molinaro	.10
10	Jim Morrison	.10
11	Wayne Nordhagen	.10
----	White Sox Header Card	.05
Cincinnati Reds Team Set		3.50
1	Johnny Bench	2.75
2	Dave Collins	.10
3	Dave Concepcion	.20
4	Dan Driessen	.10
5	George Foster	.20
6	Ken Griffey	.20
7	Tom Hume	.10
8	Ray Knight	.20
9	Ron Oester	.10
10	Tom Seaver	1.75
11	Mario Soto	.10
----	Reds Header Card	.05
Detroit Tigers Team Set		2.25
1	Champ Summers	.10
2	Al Cowens	.10
3	Rich Hebner	.10
4	Steve Kemp	.10
5	Aurelio Lopez	.10
6	Jack Morris	.20
7	Lance Parrish	.35
8	Johnny Wockenfuss	.10
9	Alan Trammell	.75
10	Lou Whitaker	.35
11	Kirk Gibson	.35
----	Tigers Header Card	.05
Houston Astros Team Set		5.00
1a	Alan Ashby	.10
1b	Nolan Ryan	25.00
2	Cesar Cedeno	.10
3	Jose Cruz	.10
4	Art Howe	.10
5	Rafael Landestoy	.10
6	Joe Niekro	.20
7	Terry Puhl	.10
8	J.R. Richard	.20
9	Nolan Ryan	4.00
10	Joe Sambito	.10
11	Don Sutton	.75
----	Astros Header Card	.05
Kansas City Royals Team Set		3.00
1	Willie Aikens	.10
2	George Brett	2.00
3	Larry Gura	.10
4	Dennis Leonard	.10
5	Hal McRae	.20
6	Amos Otis	.10
7	Dan Quisenberry	.10
8	U.L. Washington	.10
9	John Wathan	.10
10	Frank White	.10
11	Willie Wilson	.20
----	Royals Header Card	.05
New York Mets Team Set		1.25
1	Neil Allen	.10
2	Doug Flynn	.10
3	Dave Kingman	.35
4	Randy Jones	.10
5	Pat Zachry	.10
6	Lee Mazzilli	.10
7	Rusty Staub	.20
8	Craig Swan	.10
9	Frank Taveras	.10
10	Alex Trevino	.10
11	Joel Youngblood	.10
----	Mets Header Card	.05
New York Yankees Team Set		75.00
1	Rich Gossage	15.00
2	Reggie Jackson	60.00
3	Rick Cerone	12.50
----	Yankees Header Card	4.00
Philadelphia Phillies Team Set		6.00
1	Bob Boone	.35
2	Larry Bowa	.20
3	Steve Carlton	1.25
4	Greg Luzinski	.10
5	Garry Maddox	.10
6	Bake McBride	.10
7	Tug McGraw	.20
8	Pete Rose	2.75
9	Mike Schmidt	2.75
10	Lonnie Smith	.10
11	Manny Trillo	.10
----	Phillies Header Card	.05
Pittsburgh Pirates Team Set		3.00
1	Jim Bibby	.10
2	John Candelaria	.10
3	Mike Easler	.10
4	Tim Foli	.10
5	Phil Garner	.10
6	Bill Madlock	.20
7	Omar Moreno	.10
8	Ed Ott	.10
9	Dave Parker	.30
10	Willie Stargell	2.00
11	Kent Tekulve	.10
----	Pirates Header Card	.05
St. Louis Cardinals Team Set		1.25
1	Bob Forsch	.10
2	George Hendrick	.10
3	Keith Hernandez	.20
4	Tom Herr	.10
5	Sixto Lezcano	.10
6	Ken Oberkfell	.10
7	Darrell Porter	.10
8	Tony Scott	.10
9	Lary Sorensen	.10
10	Bruce Sutter	.50
11	Garry Templeton	.10
----	Cardinals Header Card	.05

Brigham's Red Sox Ad Signs

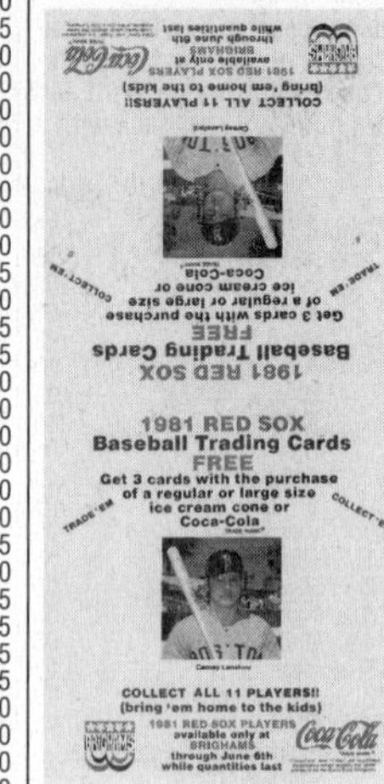

These 6" x 17-1/2" blank-back cardboard ad pieces were designed to be folded into a countertop tent card, identical on each side. The color player photos on the ad pieces are different than those found on the issued cards.

		NM/M
Complete Set (11):		35.00
Common Player:		2.00
(1)	Tom Burgmeier	2.00
(2)	Dennis Eckersley	4.00
(3)	Dwight Evans	3.00
(4)	Bob Stanley	2.00
(5)	Glenn Hoffman	2.00
(6)	Carney Lansford	2.00
(7)	Frank Tanana	2.00
(8)	Tony Perez	6.00
(9)	Jim Rice	8.00
(10)	Dave Stapleton	2.00
(11)	Carl Yastrzemski	15.00

1982 Coca-Cola Brigham's Red Sox

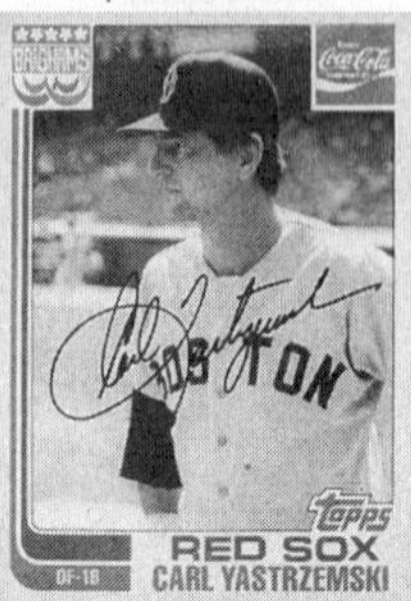

Coca-Cola, in conjunction with Brigham's Ice Cream stores, issued a 23-card set in the Boston area featuring Red Sox players. The Topps-produced cards, 2-1/2" x 3-1/2", are identical in format to the regular 1982 Topps set but contain the Coca-Cola and Brigham's logos in the corners. The cards were distributed in three-card cello packs, including an unnumbered header card.

		NM/M
Complete Set (23):		5.00
Common Player:		.25
1	Gary Allenson	.25

2 Tom Burgmeier .25
3 Mark Clear .25
4 Steve Crawford .25
5 Dennis Eckersley 1.50
6 Dwight Evans .35
7 Rich Gedman .25
8 Garry Hancock .25
9 Glen Hoffman (Glenn) .25
10 Carney Lansford .25
11 Rick Miller .25
12 Reid Nichols .25
13 Bob Ojeda .25
14 Tony Perez 1.50
15 Chuck Rainey .25
16 Jerry Remy .25
17 Jim Rice 1.00
18 Bob Stanley .25
19 Dave Stapleton .25
20 Mike Torrez .25
21 John Tudor .25
22 Carl Yastrzemski 3.00
--- Header Card .10

Reds

Produced by Topps for Coca-Cola, the set consists of 23 cards featuring the Cincinnati Reds and was distributed in the Cincinnati area. The cards, which are 2-1/2" x 3-1/2" in size, are identical in design to the regular 1982 Topps set but have a Coca-Cola logo on the front and red backs. An unnumbered header card is included in the set.

NM/M
Complete Set (23): 3.00
Common Player: .25
1 Johnny Bench 2.00
2 Bruce Berenyi .25
3 Larry Biittner .25
4 Cesar Cedeno .35
5 Dave Concepcion .35
6 Dan Driessen .25
7 Greg Harris .25
8 Paul Householder .25
9 Tom Hume .25
10 Clint Hurdle .25
11 Jim Kern .25
12 Wayne Krenchicki .25
13 Rafael Landestoy .25
14 Charlie Leibrandt .25
15 Mike O'Berry .25
16 Ron Oester .25
17 Frank Pastore .25
18 Joe Price .25
19 Tom Seaver 1.00
20 Mario Soto .25
21 Alex Trevino .25
22 Mike Vail .25
---- Header Card .05

1985 Coca-Cola Dodgers Photocards

©1985 L.A. Dodgers All Rights Reserved
Mariano Duncan

The first of two annual player photocard sets sponsored by Coke, these 3-1/2" x 5-1/2" cards feature color player action photos on front, surrounded by a white border. Below the photo is a 1985 copyright notice; the player's name is at bottom. Backs have a Coca-Cola logo in the lower-right corner, and may be found both with and without a printed message. The unnumbered cards are checklisted here in alphabetical order.

NM/M
Complete Set (34): 15.00
Common Player: .50
(1) Joe Amalfitano .50
(2) Dave Anderson .50
(3) Bob Bailor .50
(4) Monty Basgall .50
(5) Tom Brennan .50
(6) Greg Brock .50
(7) Bobby Castillo .50
(8) Mark Cresse .50
(9) Carlos Diaz .50
(10) Mariano Duncan .60
(11) Pedro Guerrero .50
(12) Orel Hershiser 2.00
(13) Rick Honeycutt .50
(14) Steve Howe .60
(15) Ken Howell .50
(16) Jay Johnstone .50
(17) Ken Landreaux .50
(18) Tommy Lasorda .75
(19) Candy Maldonado .50
(20) Mike Marshall .50
(21) Manny Mota .50
(22) Tom Niedenfuer .50
(23) Al Oliver .60
(24) Alejandro Pena .50
(25) Ron Perranoski .50
(26) Jerry Reuss .50
(27) R.J. Reynolds .50
(28) Bill Russell .50
(29) Steve Sax .50
(30) Mike Scioscia .50
(31) Fernando Valenzuela .75
(32) Bob Welch .50
(33) Terry Whitfield .50
(34) Steve Yeager .50

Pirates

A companion set to the cards issued in the 1985 Pirates yearbook, this set was given away to the first 10,000 youngsters attending May 18 and July 13 home games. The card of Kent Tekulve was withdrawn after his trade to the Phillies, making it quite scarce. The 2-1/2" x 3-1/2" cards have a color photo at center, surrounded by black and gold borders. A white panel at bottom has the player's name, position and uniform number. Backs are in black-and-white and feature complete major and minor league stats, plus the Cameron/Coca-Cola sponsors' logos.

NM/M
Complete Set (29) (No Tekulve.): 12.00
Complete Set (30) (W/ Tekulve.): 20.00
Common Player: .50
2 Jim Morrison .50
3 Johnny Ray .50
5 Bill Madlock 1.00
6 Tony Pena .60
7 Chuck Tanner .50
10 Tim Foli .50
11 Joe Orsulak .50
12 Bill Almon .50
13 Steve Kemp .50
15 George Hendrick .50
16 Lee Mazzilli .50
17 Jerry Dybzinski .50
19 Rod Scurry .50
22 Lee Tunnell .50
25 Jose DeLeon .50
27 Kent Tekulve 7.50
28 Sixto Lezcano .50
29 Rick Rhoden .50
30 Jason Thompson .50
34 Mike Bielecki .50
35 Al Holland .50
36 Marvell Wynne .50
37 Rafael Belliard .50
43 Don Robinson .50
45 John Candelaria .50
47 Cecilio Guante .50
49 Larry McWilliams .50
51 Doug Frobel .50
-- Pirates Coaches .50

White Sox

Featuring past and present White Sox players, the cards in this set were given out on Tuesday night home games. The 2-5/8" x 4-1/8" cards contain a color photo of a current Sox member. A red box at the bottom of the card carries the team logo, player name, uniform number and position, plus a small oval portrait of a past Sox player. Backs contain the Coca-Cola logo and lifetime stats for the current and past player. The set is listed here by the player's uniform number with the last three cards being unnumbered. Complete sets were available through a fan club offer found in White Sox programs.

NM/M
Complete Set (30): 7.50
Common Player: .25
0 Oscar Gamble, Zeke Bonura .25
1 Scott Fletcher, Luke Appling .60
3 Harold Baines, Bill Melton .75
5 Luis Salazar, Chico Carrasquel .25
7 Marc Hill, Sherman Lollar .25
8 Daryl Boston, Jim Landis .25
10 Tony LaRussa, Al Lopez .75
12 Julio Cruz, Nellie Fox 1.50
13 Ozzie Guillen, Luis Aparicio 2.00
17 Jerry Hairston Sr., Smoky Burgess .50
20 Joe DeSa, Carlos May .25
22 Joel Skinner, J.C. Martin .25
23 Rudy Law, Bill Skowron .50
24 Floyd Bannister, Red Faber .25
29 Greg Walker, Dick Allen 1.00
30 Gene Nelson, Early Wynn .50
32 Tim Hulett, Pete Ward .25
34 Richard Dotson, Ed Walsh .25
37 Dan Spillner, Thornton Lee .25
40 Britt Burns, Gary Peters .25
41 Tom Seaver, Ted Lyons 2.00
42 Ron Kittle, Minnie Minoso 1.00
43 Bob James, Hoyt Wilhelm .25
44 Tom Paciorek, Eddie Collins .25
46 Tim Lollar, Billy Pierce .25
50 Juan Agosto, Wilbur Wood .25
72 Carlton Fisk, Ray Schalk 1.50
--- Comiskey Park .50
--- Ribbie and Roobarb (Mascots) .25
--- Nancy Faust (Organist) .25

1986 Coca-Cola Dodgers Photocards

©1986 L.A. Dodgers All Rights Reserved
Dave Anderson

For a second year Coke sponsored this set of 3-1/2" x 5-1/2" color cards. Fronts feature an action photo with white borders. Beneath the photo is a 1986 copyright line; the player's name is at bottom. Backs have a red Coca-Cola logo in the lower-right corner, and can be found either otherwise blank or with a message to fans from the pictured player, along with a facsimile autograph. The unnumbered cards are checklisted here alphabetically.

NM/M
Complete Set (34): 15.00
Common Player: .50
(1) Joe Amalfitano .50
(2) Dave Anderson .50
(3) Monty Basgall .50
(4) Greg Brock .50
(5) Enos Cabell .50
(6) Cesar Cedeno .50
(7) Mark Cresse .50
(8) Carlos Diaz .50
(9) Mariano Duncan .50
(10) Pedro Guerrero .50
(11) Orel Hershiser 1.00
(12) Ben Hines .50
(13) Rick Honeycutt .50
(14) Ken Howell .50
(15) Ken Landreaux .50
(16) Tom Lasorda .75
(17) Bill Madlock .50
(18) Mike Marshall .50
(19) Len Matuszek .50
(20) Manny Mota .50
(21) Tom Niedenfuer .50
(22) Alejandro Pena .50
(23) Ron Perranoski .50
(24) Dennis Powell .50
(25) Jerry Reuss .50
(26) Bill Russell .50
(27) Steve Sax .50
(28) Mike Scioscia .50
(29) Franklin Stubbs .50
(30) Alex Trevino .50
(31) Fernando Valenzuela .75
(32) Ed Vande Berg .50
(33) Bob Welch .50
(34) Terry Whitfield .50

White Sox

For the second year in a row, Coca-Cola, in conjunction with the Chicago White Sox, issued a 30-card set. As in 1985, cards were given out at the park on Tuesday night games. Full sets were available through a fan club offer found in the White Sox program. The 2-5/8" x 4-1/8" cards feature 25 players plus other team personnel. Fronts have a color photo (a game-action shot in most instances) and a white bar at the bottom. A black and white bat with "SOX" shown on the barrel is located within the white bar, along with the player's name, position and uniform number. The white and gray backs with black print include the Coca-Cola trademark. Lifetime statistics are shown on all player cards, but there is no personal information such as height, weight or age. The non-player cards are blank-backed save for the name and logo at the top. The cards in the checklist that follows are numbered by the players' uniform numbers, with the last five cards of the set being unnumbered.

NM/M
Complete Set (30): 12.00
Common Player: .25
1 Wayne Tolleson .25
3 Harold Baines .75
7 Marc Hill .25
8 Daryl Boston .25
12 Julio Cruz .25
13 Ozzie Guillen .50
17 Jerry Hairston Sr. .25
19 Floyd Bannister .25
20 Reid Nichols .25
22 Joel Skinner .25
24 Dave Schmidt .25
26 Bobby Bonilla 1.00
29 Greg Walker .25
30 Gene Nelson .25
32 Tim Hulett .25
33 Neil Allen .25
34 Richard Dotson .25
40 Joe Cowley .25
41 Tom Seaver 3.00
42 Ron Kittle .35
43 Bob James .25
44 John Cangelosi .25
50 Juan Agosto .25
52 Joel Davis .25
72 Carlton Fisk 3.00
--- Ribbie & Roobarb (Mascots) .25
--- Nancy Faust (Organist) .25
--- Ken "Hawk" Harrelson .35
--- Tony LaRussa .60
--- Minnie Minoso 1.50

1987 Coca-Cola Tigers

Coca-Cola and S. Abraham & Sons, Inc. issued a set of 18 baseball cards featuring members of the Detroit Tigers. The set is comprised of six four-part folding panels. Each panel includes three player cards (each 2-1/2" x 3-1/2") and one team logo card. A bright yellow border surrounds the full-color photo. The backs are designed on a vertical format and contain personal data and career statistics. The set was produced by Mike Schechter and Associates.

NM/M
Complete Panel Set (6): 4.00
Complete Singles Set (18): 2.00
Common Panel: .50
Common Player: .05
Panel .85
1 Kirk Gibson .30
2 Larry Herndon .05
3 Walt Terrell .05
Panel 1.50
4 Alan Trammell .50
5 Frank Tanana .05
6 Pat Sheridan .05
Panel .85
7 Jack Morris .30
8 Mike Heath .05
9 Dave Bergman .05
Panel .50
10 Chet Lemon .05
11 Dwight Lowry .05
12 Dan Petry .05
Panel .85
13 Darrell Evans .25
14 Darnell Coles .05
15 Willie Hernandez .05
Panel 1.00
16 Lou Whitaker .25
17 Tom Brookens .05
18 John Grubb .05

White Sox

The Chicago White Sox Fan Club, in conjunction with Coca-Cola, offered members a set of 30 trading cards. For the $10 membership fee, fans received the set plus additional fan club gifts and privileges. The cards, 2-5/8" x 4", feature full-color photos inside a blue and red border. Backs include the player's name, position, uniform number and statistics, plus the Coca-Cola logo. Cards are checklisted here by uniform number.

NM/M
Complete Set (30): 7.50
Common Player: .25
1 Jerry Royster .25
3 Harold Baines .50
5 Ron Karkovice .25
8 Daryl Boston .25
10 Fred Manrique .25
12 Steve Lyons .25
13 Ozzie Guillen .50
14 Russ Morman .25
15 Donnie Hill .25
16 Jim Fregosi .25
17 Jerry Hairston Sr. .25
19 Floyd Bannister .25
21 Gary Redus .25
22 Ivan Calderon .25
25 Ron Hassey .25
26 Jose DeLeon .25
29 Greg Walker .25
32 Tim Hulett .25
33 Neil Allen .25
34 Rich Dotson .25
36 Ray Searage .25
37 Bobby Thigpen .25
40 Jim Winn .25
43 Bob James .25
50 Joel McKeon .25
52 Joel Davis .25
72 Carlton Fisk 3.00
--- Ribbie & Roobarb (Mascots) .25
--- Nancy Faust (Organist) .25
--- Minnie Minoso .75

1988 Coca-Cola Padres

A 20-card set sponsored by Coca-Cola was designed as part of the San Diego Padres Junior Fan Club promotion for 1988. This set was distributed as a nine-card starter sheet, with 11 additional single cards handed out during various home games. The standard-size cards feature full-color player photos framed by a black and orange border. The player's name is printed above the photo; uniform number and position appear at lower-right. A large Padres logo curves upward from the lower-left corner. Backs are brown on white and include the Padres logo at upper-left opposite the player's name and personal information. Career highlights and 1987 stats appear in the center of the card back above the Coca-Cola and Junior Padres Fan Club logos.

		NM/M
Complete Set (21):		20.00
Common Player:		.50
Panel		
1	Garry Templeton	.60
5	Randy Ready	.50
10	Larry Bowa	.60
11	Tim Flannery	.50
35	Chris Brown	.50
45	Jimmy Jones	.50
48	Mark Davis	.50
55	Mark Grant	.50
----	20th Anniversary Logo Card	.10
Singles		
7	Keith Moreland	1.00
8	John Kruk	2.00
9	Benito Santiago	2.00
14	Carmelo Martinez	1.00
15	Jack McKeon	1.00
19	Tony Gwynn	6.00
22	Stan Jefferson	1.00
27	Mark Parent	1.00
30	Eric Show	1.00
31	Ed Whitson	1.00
41	Lance McCullers	1.00
51	Greg Booker	1.00

White Sox

Part of a fan club membership package, this unnumbered 30-card set features full-color photos of 27 players, the team mascot, team organist and Comiskey Park. Cards have a bright red border, with team logo in the photo's lower-left corner. The player name fills the bottom border. Backs are printed in black on gray and white and include player name, personal info and career summary. The set was included in the $10 membership package, with a portion of the cost going to the ChiSox Kids Charity.

		NM/M
Complete Set (30):		5.00
Common Player:		.25
(1)	Harold Baines	.50
(2)	Daryl Boston	.25
(3)	Ivan Calderon	.25
(4)	John Davis	.25
(5)	Jim Fregosi	.25
(6)	Carlton Fisk	2.50
(7)	Ozzie Guillen	.50
(8)	Donnie Hill	.25
(9)	Rick Horton	.25
(10)	Lance Johnson	.25
(11)	Dave LaPoint	.25
(12)	Bill Long	.25
(13)	Steve Lyons	.25
(14)	Jack McDowell	.30
(15)	Fred Manrique	.25
(16)	Minnie Minoso	.75
(17)	Dan Pasqua	.25
(18)	John Pawlowski	.25
(19)	Melido Perez	.25
(20)	Billy Pierce	.25
(21)	Gary Redus	.25
(22)	Jerry Reuss	.25
(23)	Mark Salas	.25
(24)	Jose Segura	.25
(25)	Bobby Thigpen	.25
(26)	Greg Walker	.25
(27)	Kenny Williams	.25
(28)	Nancy Faust (Organist)	.25
(29)	Ribbie & Roobarb (Mascots)	.25
(30)	Comiskey Park	.40

1989 Coca-Cola Padres

This 20-card set is part of the Junior Padres Fan Club membership package. Members receive a nine-card starter set printed on one large perforated sheet. Additional cards are distributed to kids at specially designated games (free admission for kids). Fronts feature an orange-and-brown double border, with a bright orange Padres logo printed at lower-left. Uniform number and position are printed diagonally across the upper-left corner, with the player's name in large block letters along the bottom border.

		NM/M
Complete Set (21):		26.00
Common Player:		.50
Panel		
1	Garry Templeton	.60
5	Randy Ready	.50
12	Roberto Alomar	4.50
14	Carmelo Martinez	.50
15	Jack McKeon	.50
30	Eric Show	.50
31	Ed Whitson	.50
43	Dennis Rasmussen	.50
----	Logo Card	.10
Singles		
6	Luis Salazar	1.00
9	Benito Santiago	1.00
10	Leon Roberts	1.00
11	Tim Flannery	1.00
18	Chris James	1.00
19	Tony Gwynn	8.00
25	Jack Clark	1.00
27	Mark Parent	1.00
35	Walt Terrell	1.00
47	Bruce Hurst	1.00
48	Mark Davis	1.00
55	Mark Grant	1.00

White Sox

For the fifth straight year, Coca-Cola sponsored a set of cards featuring the Chicago White Sox. The 30-card set was distributed to fans attending a special promotional game at Comiskey Park and was also available by mail to members of the ChiSox fan club. Card fronts feature blue borders with red and white graphics and a pair of crossed bats. Horizontal backs include player biographies, personal data and the Coca-Cola logo. Cards measure 2-5/8" x 3-1/2".

		NM/M
Complete Set (30):		5.00
Common Player:		.20
1	New Comiskey Park, 1991	.40
2	Comiskey Park	.40
3	Jeff Torborg	.20
4	Coaching staff (Dave LaRoche, Terry Bevington, Walt Hriniak, Sammy Ellis, Glenn Rosenbaum, Ron Clark)	.20
5	Harold Baines	.45
6	Daryl Boston	.20
7	Ivan Calderon	.20
8	Carlton Fisk	2.50
9	Dave Gallagher	.20
10	Ozzie Guillen	.50
11	Shawn Hillegas	.20
12	Barry Jones	.20
13	Ron Karkovice	.20
14	Eric King	.20
15	Ron Kittle	.20
16	Bill Long	.20
17	Steve Lyons	.20
18	Donn Pall	.20
19	Dan Pasqua	.20
20	Ken Patterson	.20
21	Melido Perez	.20
22	Jerry Reuss	.20
23	Billy Jo Robidoux	.20
24	Steve Rosenberg	.20
25	Jeff Schaefer	.20
26	Bobby Thigpen	.20
27	Greg Walker	.20
28	Eddie Williams	.20
29	Nancy Faust (Organist)	.20
30	Minnie Minoso	.75

1990 Coca-Cola Padres

This set was designed for members of the Junior Padres Club sponsored by Coca-Cola. Each member received an eight-card panel and then received two different single cards at every Junior Padres Club game attended. Card fronts feature full-color photos with the Padres logo in the upper-right corner of the card. Backs feature statistics, career highlights and a red Coca-Cola logo. The cards are numbered by the player's uniform number.

		NM/M
Complete Set (21):		16.00
Common Player:		.35
Panel		
10	Bip Roberts	.35
15	Jack McKeon	.35
30	Eric Show	.35
31	Ed Whitson	.35
40	Andy Benes	.75
43	Dennis Rasmussen	.35
55	Mark Grant	.35
----	Logo Card	.35
Singles		
1	Garry Templeton	.50
8	Fred Lynn	.75
9	Benito Santiago	1.00
11	Craig Lefferts	.50
12	Roberto Alomar	4.00
13	Mike Pagliarulo	.50
17	Joe Carter	1.00
19	Tony Gwynn	6.00
25	Jack Clark	.50
27	Mark Parent	.50
38	Calvin Schiraldi	.50
46	Greg Harris	.50
47	Bruce Hurst	.50

Garry Templeton

Coca-Cola, Vons stores and the Padres joined forces to release this special pin/baseball card collectible in honor of Garry Templeton becoming the club's all-time leader in games played. The card front features a full-color photo of Templeton and displays "Most Games Played" and "The Captain" in orange at the top of the photo. "Templeton" appears vertically in white along the left border. The Coca-Cola and Padre logos also appear on the card front. The bottom of the card features a perforated edge where the pin is attached as an extension of the card. The card back is printed in black and white and displays biographical information, career highlights and career statistics.

		NM/M
Card/Pin Combination:		1.50
(1)	Most Games Played Card (Garry Templeton)	.50
(2)	Most Games Played Pin (Garry Templeton)	1.00

Tigers

Once again utilizing the larger 2-7/8" x 4-1/4" format, this set was jointly sponsored by Coke and Kroger grocery stores and distributed at the July 14 game. Cards feature color action photos on front, surrounded by green borders. Backs have a black-and-white portrait photo, the appropriate logos and complete minor and major league stats. The player's uniform number appears in the upper-left corner.

		NM/M
Complete Set (28):		6.00
Common Player:		.15
(1)	Sparky Anderson	.50
(2)	Dave Bergman	.15
(3)	Brian DuBois	.15
(4)	Cecil Fielder	.25
(5)	Paul Gibson	.15
(6)	Jerry D. Gleaton	.15
(7)	Mike Heath	.15
(8)	Mike Henneman	.15
(9)	Tracy Jones	.15
(10)	Chet Lemon	.15
(11)	Urbano Lugo	.15
(12)	Jack Morris	.20
(13)	Lloyd Moseby	.15
(14)	Matt Nokes	.15
(15)	Edwin Nunez	.15
(16)	Dan Petry	.15
(17)	Tony Phillips	.25
(18)	Kevin Ritz	.15
(19)	Jeff Robinson	.15
(20)	Ed Romero	.15
(21)	Mark Salas	.15
(22)	Larry Sheets	.15
(23)	Frank Tanana	.15
(24)	Alan Trammell	.75
(25)	Gary Ward	.15
(26)	Lou Whitaker	.40
(27)	Ken Williams	.15
(28)	Coaches (Billy Consolo, Alex Grammas, Billy Muffett, Vada Pinson, Dick Tracewski)	.15

White Sox

An attractive "Comiskey Park 1910-1990" logo is featured on the front of each card in this set. Fronts also feature full-color photos with a thin white inner border. The cards are numbered according to uniform number, with the exception of four special cards including Top Prospect Frank Thomas. Horizontal card backs feature black print on white and gray stock; 1989 statistics and career highlights are provided. The 1990 set marks the sixth straight year that Coca-Cola sponsored a White Sox set.

		NM/M
Complete Set (30):		80.00
Common Player:		.25
1	Lance Johnson	.25
7	Scott Fletcher	.25
10	Jeff Torborg	.25
12	Steve Lyons	.25
13	Ozzie Guillen	.50
14	Craig Grebeck	.25
17	Dave Gallagher	.25
20	Ron Karkovice	.25
22	Ivan Calderon	.25
23	Robin Ventura	1.00
24	Carlos Martinez	.25
25	Sammy Sosa	65.00
27	Greg Hibbard	.25
29	Jack McDowell	.25
30	Donn Pall	.25
31	Scott Radinsky	.25
33	Melido Perez	.25
34	Ken Patterson	.25
36	Eric King	.25
37	Bobby Thigpen	.25
42	Ron Kittle	.25
44	Dan Pasqua	.25
45	Wayne Edwards	.25
50	Barry Jones	.25
52	Jerry Kutzler	.25
72	Carlton Fisk	5.00
---	Top Prospect (Frank Thomas)	15.00
---	White Sox Manager, Coaches (Jeff Torborg)	.25
---	Captains (Ozzie Guillen, Carlton Fisk)	1.00
---	Rookies (Wayne Edwards, Craig Greback, Jerry Kutzler, Scott Radinsky, Robin Ventura)	.35

1991 Coca-Cola Don Mattingly

Though sponsored by Coca-Cola, the manner of distribution of this issue is unclear. The "Mattingly's 23" logo on each side of the card suggests a connection to his Evansville, Ind., restaurant. Fronts of the 2-1/2" x 3-1/2" cards have photos in black-and-white or color, or artwork.

The border is white with blue pinstripes. The year of the picture is at top of the photo and there is a Coke logo at bottom. Backs are printed in red and blue and contain career highlights and stats, along with a card number and logos.

		NM/M
Complete Set (15):		10.00
Common Card:		1.00
1	Don Mattingly/1978	1.00
2	Don Mattingly/1979	1.00
3	Don Mattingly/1980	1.00
4	Don Mattingly/1981	1.00
5	Don Mattingly/1982	1.00
6	Don Mattingly/1983	1.00
7	Don Mattingly ('83-'84)	1.00
8	Don Mattingly/1984	1.00
9	Don Mattingly/1985	1.00
10	Don Mattingly/1986	1.00
11	Don Mattingly/1987	1.00
12	Don Mattingly/1990	1.00
13	Don Mattingly/1991 (Photo)	1.00
14	Don Mattingly/1991 (Artwork)	1.00
15	Don Mattingly/1991 (Coca-Cola logo.)	1.00

Tigers

This set was sponsored by Coca-Cola and Kroger, whose logos appear on the red, white and blue backs. The oversize (2-7/8" x 4-1/4") cards feature game-action or portrait color photos on front along with the player's name vertically printed on the right border and the Tigers logo in the lower-left corner. Backs are printed horizontally and feature complete minor and major league statistics. The set is numbered according to uniform number, which appears in an orange triangle on front.

		NM/M
Complete Set (28):		7.00
Common Player:		.35
1	Lou Whitaker	.75
3	Alan Trammell	1.00
4	Tony Phillips	.35
10	Andy Allanson	.35
11	Sparky Anderson	.75
14	Dave Bergman	.35
15	Lloyd Moseby	.35
19	Jerry Don Gleaton	.35
20	Mickey Tettleton	.35
22	Milt Cuyler	.35
23	Mark Leiter	.35
24	Travis Fryman	.35
25	John Shelby	.35
26	Frank Tanana	.35
27	Mark Salas	.35
29	Pete Incaviglia	.35
31	Kevin Ritz	.35
35	Walt Terrell	.35
36	Bill Gullickson	.35

39 Mike Henneman .35
42 Mike Dalton .35
44 Rob Deer .35
45 Cecil Fielder .50
46 Dan Petry .35
48 Paul Gibson .35
49 Steve Searcy .35
55 John Cerutti .35
Tigers Coaches (Billy Consolo, Jim Davenport, Alex Grammas, Billy Muffett, Vada Pinson, Dick Tracewski) .35

1992 Coca-Cola Nolan Ryan Career Series

This 26-card set was produced by Donruss in conjunction with Coca-Cola to honor Nolan Ryan's 26 major league seasons. One Nolan Ryan card was packaged with three regular 1992 Donruss cards in special 12-packs of Coke. Complete sets, in a black, red and gold box, were available through a mail-in offer. The 2-1/2" x 3-1/2" cards have a full-color photo on front, framed by a gold border. Ryan's name is printed in gold toward the bottom, above a blue bar which presents a team and year. The Coke logo is at upper right. On back there are details of Ryan's performance in the indicated year, the card number, and team and Coke logos. An 18" x 12" color poster picturing the cards and a photo of a Ryan-autographed ball was issued as a point-of-purchase display.

NM/M
Complete Set (26): 7.50
Common Card: .50
Display Poster: 15.00
1 1966 Breaking In .50
2 1968 Record-Setting Rookie .50
3 1969 World Champions .50
4 1970 Growing Pains .50
5 1971 Traded .50
6 1972 Fitted for a Halo .50
7 1973 First Two No-Nos and a Record .50
8 1974 No-Hitter No. 3/Another K Record .50
9 1975 Tying Koufax .50
10 1976 Back on Track .50
11 1977 Carrying the Load .50
12 1978 A Year of Injuries .50
13 1979 California Farewell .50
14 1980 Coming Home .50
15 1981 A Gusher in Houston .50
16 1982 Mounting 'Em Up .50
17 1983 Passing the Big Train .50
18 1984 Misleading Signs of Age .50
19 1985 Another Milestone/ A New Contract .50
20 1986 The Elbow Flares Up Again .50
21 1987 Another ERA/Strikeout Crown at 40 .50
22 1988 Leaving Home Again .50
23 1989 5,000 Strikeouts .50
24 1990 Win No. 300, No-Hitter No. 6 .50
25 1991 No-Hitter No. 7 .50
26 1992 Man of Records .50

Tigers

This set of large-format (2-7/8" x 4-1/4") cards features central photos of the Bengals in action. Dark blue

stripes at top and bottom have the team name in white, while the player name, uniform number and position are printed in black on an orange stripe directly beneath the photo. A color team logo in the upper-right completes the front design. Backs have complete major and minor league stats, a few personal data and color logos of Coke and the Kroger grocery chain.

NM/M
Complete Set (28): 5.00
Common Player: .15
1 Lou Whitaker .35
3 Alan Trammell .75
4 Tony Phillips .15
7 Scott Livingstone .15
9 Skeeter Barnes .15
11 Sparky Anderson .50
14 Dave Bergman .15
15 Mark Carreon .15
18 Gary Pettis .15
19 Chad Kreuter .15
20 Mickey Tettleton .15
22 Milt Cuyler .15
23 Mark Leiter .15
24 Travis Fryman .25
26 Frank Tanana .15
27 Kurt Knudsen .15
28 Rob Deer .15
31 Kevin Ritz .15
32 Dan Gladden .15
35 Walt Terrell .15
36 Bill Gullickson .15
39 Mike Henneman .15
43 Mike Munoz .15
44 John Doherty .15
45 Cecil Fielder .25
46 John Kiely .15
48 Les Lancaster .15
--- Tigers Coaches (Billy Consolo, Gene Roof, Larry Herndon, Dick Tracewksi, Billy Muffett, Dan Whitmer) .15

1992 Coca-Cola/ Hardees Major League Line-Up Discs

This set of 3" diameter "Major League Line-Up" cardboard discs was a regional give-away sponsored by Coca-Cola and distributed by Hardee's restaurants. The glossy discs have player photos at center with position and uniform numbers at the sides. Backs are in black-and-white with a few stats and career highlights and various logos. A checklist disc was also distributed.

NM/M
Complete Set (24): 12.00
Common Player: .50
1 Roger Clemens 2.50
2 Sandy Alomar Jr. .50
3 Rafael Palmeiro 1.25
4 Roberto Alomar .75
5 Kelly Gruber .50
6 Ozzie Guillen .50
7 Devon White .50
8 David Henderson .50
9 Robin Yount 1.50
10 Chili Davis .50
11 Chuck Knoblauch .50
12 Paul Molitor 1.50
13 Tom Glavine .75
14 Benito Santiago .50
15 Hal Morris .50
16 Delino DeShields .50
17 Matt Williams .50
18 Ozzie Smith 2.00
19 Andy Van Slyke .50
20 Andre Dawson .75
21 Ron Gant .50
22 Jeff Bagwell 1.50
23 Terry Pendleton .50
24 Brett Butler .50

1993 Coca-Cola Commanders of the Hill

Coca-Cola and Topps teamed up to print a 30-card Commanders of the Hill set in 1993. The cards were available in five-card packages with soft-drink purchases on military bases at base exchange food court concessions. The set was divided into three areas: Cy Young Winners, Strikeout Leaders and Team ERA Leaders, with the National League player's names in yellow on a red background and the American League in red on yellow.

NM/M
Complete Set (30): 5.00
Common Player: .10
1 Dennis Eckersley .50
2 Mike Mussina .40
3 Roger Clemens 1.00
4 Jim Abbott .10
5 Jack McDowell .10
6 Charles Nagy .10
7 Bill Gullickson .10
8 Kevin Appier .10
9 Bill Wegman .10
10 John Smiley .10
11 Melido Perez .10
12 Dave Stewart .10
13 Dave Fleming .10
14 Kevin Brown .10
15 Juan Guzman .10
16 Randy Johnson .60
17 Greg Maddux .75
18 Tom Glavine .35
19 Greg Maddux .75
20 Jose Rijo .10
21 Pete Harnisch .10
22 Tom Candiotti .10
23 Denny Martinez .10
24 Sid Fernandez .10
25 Curt Schilling .35
26 Doug Drabek .10
27 Bob Tewksbury .10
28 Andy Benes .10
29 Bill Swift .10
30 John Smoltz .10

1995 Coca-Cola Minnesota Twins POGs

Over the course of three games in July 1995, the Twins issued a three-sheet series of POGs, 15,000 at each game. The souvenir measures about 10-1/4" x 9-1/2" and features a large color game photo, around and above which are POGs, about 1-1/8" diameter, of players, coaches and sponsors. The POGs are die-cut for removal from the sheets. Each sheet has 11 players or coaches, and each has the same four sponsors' POGs. Fronts have player portrait photos while backs have a repeating Coca-Cola logo. The POGs are unnumbered and listed here alphabetically by sheet. The players are not identified on the POGs themselves.

NM/M
Complete Set, Sheets (3): 12.00
Complete Set, Singles (33): 9.00
Common Player: .25
Series 1, July 1 4.00
(1) Rick Aguilera .25
(2) Rich Becker .25
(3) Marty Cordova .25
(4) Terry Crowley .25
(5) Eddie Guardado .25
(6) Jeff Reboulet .25
(7) Rich Robertson .25
(8) Scott Stahoviak .25
(9) Dick Such .25
(10) Kevin Tapani .25
(11) Matt Walbeck .25
Series 2, July 17 3.00
(12) Alex Cole .25
(13) Scott Erickson .25
(14) Ron Gardenhire .25
(15) Chip Hale .25
(16) Chuck Knoblauch .25
(17) Scott Leius .25
(18) Pat Mahomes .25
(19) Pedro Munoz .25
(20) Erik Schullstrom .25
(21) Dave Stevens .25
(22) Scott Ullger .25
Series 3, July 28 5.00
(23) Jerald Clark .25
(24) Mark Guthrie .25
(25) Tom Kelly .25
(26) Kevin Maas .25
(27) Pat Meares .25
(28) Matt Merullo .25
(29) Kirby Puckett 3.50
(30) Brad Radke .25
(31) Rick Stelmaszek .25
(32) Mike Trombley .25
(33) Jerry White .25
--- Coca-Cola .05
--- Fox 29 TV .05
--- Minnesota Twins Logo .10
--- Nestle .05

Pittsburgh Pirates POGs

To celebrate the 25th anniversary of Three Rivers Stadium, Coca-Cola and the Pirates issued a set of POGs marking the 25 greatest baseball moments at the stadium. The POGs were issued nine apiece on heavy 6" x 8" cardboard panels. Individual POGs measure about 1-3/4" diameter and are perforated at the edge so they can be removed from the panel. Most fronts have a border of team-color orange and black, with central photos in black-and-white or color. Backs of #1-8 have a green Fruitopia ad; backs of #10-18 have an ad for Sprite in green, while #9, 19-25 have a red Coca-Cola ad on back.

NM/M
Complete Set Panels (3): 15.00
Complete Set Singles (27): 9.00
Common POG: .25
1 1994 All-Star Game (All-Star logo) .25
2 Roberto Clemente (3,000th Hit) 2.00
3 Roberto Clemente (Uniform #21 retired.) 2.00
4 Pirates Win 1979 N.L. Pennant (We Are Family logo) .25
5 John Candelaria (No-Hitss Dodgers) .25
6 Willie Stargell (Uniform #8 retired.) .50
7 Mike Schmidt (500th Home Run) .75
8 Kent Tekulve (First Game, 7/16/70) .25
-- Coke/Fruitopia Logos .05
9 First World Series Night Game .25
10 Nellie Briles (1971 World Series 2-Hitter) .25
11 Pirates Win 1971 N.L. Pennant .25
12 Pirates Clinch N.L. East, 1979 .25
13 Pirates Clinch N.L. East, 1992 (Jim Leyland) .25
14 Bob Gibson (No-Hits Pirates 8/14/71) .40
15 1979 World Series Game 5 (Jim Rooker) .25
16 Pirates Clinch N.L. East, 1971 .25
17 Beat Braves in NLCS Game 5, 1992 .25
18 John Milner (Grand Slam Beats Phillis 8/5/79) .25
19 Barry Bonds (11th Inning HR Beats St. Louis 8/12/91) .75
20 Jeff King (5 Runs in 9th to Beat Dodgers, 5/28/90) .25
21 Danny Murtaugh (Murtaugh, Joe L. Brown Retire) .25
22 "Gunner" Returns to Broadcast Booth .25
23 Sweep Phillies in 9/29/78 Doubleheader .25
24 Jim Leyland (Makes Pittsburgh Debut) .25
25 1974 All-Star Game (Program) .25
--- Coke Logos .05

1995 Coca-Cola/ Publix Florida Marlins

Coca-Cola and the Publix grocery store chain sponsored this team set issue. Fronts of the standard-size (2-1/2" x 3-1/2") cards have color player action photos on a large background of the team logo. Backs have a color portrait photo and stats. Cards are checklisted here by uniform number.

NM/M
Complete Set (27): 7.50
Common Player: .50
3 Quilvio Veras .50
4 Greg Colbrunn .50
6 Tommy Gregg .50
7 Kurt Abbott .50
8 Andre Dawson 2.50
9 Terry Pendleton .50
10 Gary Sheffield 2.50
11 Chris Hammond .50
14 Jerry Browne .50
15 Marcel Lacheman .50
17 Darrell Whitmore .50
21 Chuck Carr .50
23 Charles Johnson .50
26 Alex Arias .50
28 Mark Gardner .50
29 Mario Diaz .50
31 Robb Nen .50
33 John Burkett .50
34 Bryan Harvey .50
35 David Weathers .50
42 Jeremy Hernandez .50
48 Pat Rapp .50
51 Terry Mathews .50
52 Randy Veres .50
58 Yorkis Perez .50
--- Coaches .50
--- Billy the Marlin (Mascot) .50

1996 Coca-Cola/ Kroger Nolan Ryan Card/Pin

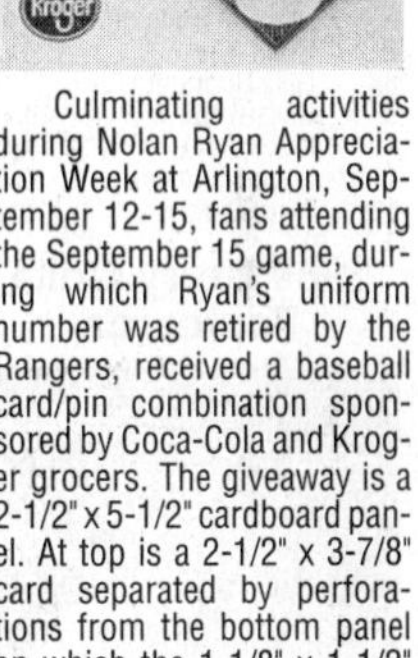

Culminating activities during Nolan Ryan Appreciation Week at Arlington, September 12-15, fans attending the September 15 game, during which Ryan's uniform number was retired by the Rangers, received a baseball card/pin combination sponsored by Coca-Cola and Kroger grocers. The giveaway is a 2-1/2" x 5-1/2" cardboard panel. At top is a 2-1/2" x 3-7/8" card separated by perforations from the bottom panel on which the 1-1/8" x 1-1/2" enameled jersey pin is affixed. The front has a spring-training game-action color photo of Ryan. The back is in black-and-white with a career summary, sponsor' logos and a picture of the pin.

NM/M
Card/Pin Combination: 7.00

1998 Coca-Cola Chipper Jones

This 2-1/2" x 3-1/2" card was an Atlanta-area exclusive. The front shows the Braves' star enjoying a Coke. On back is a coupon for a free 20-oz. Coca-Cola.

NM/M
Chipper Jones 10.00

2002 Coca-Cola S.F. Giants

A dozen of the most popular Giants are pictured in game-action photos on the fronts of these regionally issued cards. Two-card cello packs were inserted in each specially marked 24-can case of Coke, making acquisition of the set an expensive proposition. The glossy fronts have red borders with Coca-Cola and team logos in the lower corners. Backs have a portrait photo, a few bits of personal data and stats, and a host of appropriate logos.

		NM/M
Complete Set (12):		20.00
Common Player:		1.00
1	Jeff Kent	1.00
2	Rich Aurilia	1.00
3	J.T. Snow	1.00
4	Marvin Benard	1.00
5	Pedro Feliz	1.00
6	Shawon Dunston	1.00
7	Robb Nen	1.00
8	Felix Rodriguez	1.00
9	Russ Ortiz	1.00
10	Kirk Reuter	1.00
11	Livan Hernandez	1.00
12	Barry Bonds	12.00

1989 Barry Colla Postcards

In 1989 California baseball photographer Barry Colla began a series of player postcard sets. Each set contains eight postcards of the player and was sold in a white paper envelope with the team logo. The postcards are identical in format, measuring 3-1/2" x 5-1/2". Fronts feature borderless color photos on high-gloss stock. Backs are printed in black-and-white and feature a team logo at center. The player's name, uniform number, team and position are printed in the upper-left. A card number appears at top-center.

		NM/M
1-8	Will Clark	3.00
1-8	Jose Canseco	4.00
1-8	Andre Dawson	4.00
1-8	Mike Greenwell	3.00
1-8	Don Mattingly	5.00
1-8	Mark McGwire	6.00
1-8	Kevin Mitchell	3.00
1-8	Ozzie Smith	4.50

1990 Barry Colla Promos

Each of the 12-card single-player sets produced by photographer Barry Colla in 1990 was preceded by a promo card. The promos feature the same borderless color photography as the issued cards. Backs have information on date and size of the limited-

edition issues and ordering information printed in black and white. Checklist of the unnumbered cards is presented here in alphabetical order.

		NM/M
Complete Set (4):		6.00
Common Player:		1.00
(1)	Jose Canseco	2.00
(2)	Will Clark	1.00
(3)	Kevin Maas	1.00
(4)	Don Mattingly	3.00

1990 Barry Colla

In 1990 baseball photographer Barry Colla began production of a series of single-player card sets. In standard 2-1/2" x 3-1/2" size, the cards featured high-gloss borderless photos on front, with no extraneous graphics. Backs feature stats, career notes, personal data and team logos. The 12-card sets were sold in small decorative cardboard boxes. Production figures are noted in parentheses.

		NM/M
1-12	Jose Canseco/20,000	3.00
1-12	Will Clark/15,000	2.00
1-12	Kevin Maas/7,500	2.00
1-12	Don Mattingly/15,000	7.50

Postcards

Barry Colla continued his series of single-player postcard sets 1990. The basic format continued unchanged. The 3-1/2" x 5-1/2" card feature borderless color game-action and posed photos on high-gloss stock. Black-and-white backs feature a team logo at center, a card number at top and, in the upper-left, the player's name, uniform number, team and position. Sets were sold in white paper envelopes with color team logos on the front.

		NM/M
1-8	Mark Grace	3.00

1991 Barry Colla Promos

Each of the eight 12-card single-player sets produced by California photographer Barry Colla in 1991 was preceded by the issue of a promo card. Identical in format, the promos feature high quality borderless photos on glossy stock. Backs are printed in black-and-white and include information on the size and release date of the limited-edition set, along with ordering information and appropriate logos. The checklist of the unnumbered promo cards is presented here alphabetically.

		NM/M
Complete Set (10):		12.00
Common Player:		1.00
(1a)	Roberto Alomar	1.25
(1b)	Roberto Alomar (French)	1.50
(2)	Barry Bonds	4.00
(3a)	Joe Carter	1.00
(3b)	Joe Carter (French)	1.00
(4)	Dwight Gooden	1.00
(5)	Ken Griffey Jr.	3.00
(6)	Dave Justice	1.00
(7)	Ryne Sandberg	2.50
(8)	Darryl Strawberry	1.00

1991 Barry Colla

In 1991 baseball photographer Barry Colla continued production of a series of single-player card sets. In standard 2-1/2" x 3-1/2" size, the cards featured high-gloss borderless photos on front, with no extraneous graphics. Backs feature stats, career notes, personal data and team logos. The 12-card sets were sold in small decorative cardboard boxes. Production figures are noted in parentheses.

		NM/M
1-12	Roberto Alomar/ 7,500	2.00
1-12	Barry Bonds/7,500	12.00
1-12	Joe Carter/7,500	1.50
1-12	Dwight Gooden/ 15,000	1.50
1-12	Ken Griffey Jr./ 15,000	6.00
1-12	David Justice/15,000	1.50
1-12	Ryne Sandberg/ 15,000	4.00
1-12	Darryl Strawberry/ 15,000	1.50

Postcards

Only one single-player postcard set was produced by Barry Colla in 1991: Ryne Sandberg. The eight-card set, like the 1989-90 issues, features full-color game-action and posed photos presented on a borderless, high-gloss 3-1/2" x 5-1/2" format. Back design was changed for the 1991 issue. The team logo now appears in the upper-left corner with the player's name at top and his uniform number, team and position beneath. Sets were sold in a white paper envelope featuring a color Cubs logo.

		NM/M
1-8	Ryne Sandberg	5.00

1992 Barry Colla Promos

Each of the seven card sets produced by California photographer Barry Colla in 1992 was preceded by a promo card. In standard 2-1/2" x 3-1/2" size, the promos follow the format of the regular-issue cards with a borderless color photo on high-gloss stock. All of the card backs are printed in black-and-white and feature ordering information about the sets, expected release date and issue size and appropriate logos. Some promo cards feature checklists of all existing Colla Collection card sets. The unnumbered promo cards are checklisted here alphabetically.

		NM/M
Complete Set (7):		7.50
Common Player:		1.00
(1)	All-Star Set (Juan Guzman)	1.00
(2)	Steve Avery	1.00
(3)	Jeff Bagwell	1.50
(4)	Tony Gwynn	1.50
(5)	Mark McGwire	2.00
(6)	Frank Thomas	1.50
(7)	Nolan Ryan	2.50

1992 Barry Colla

In 1992 photographer Barry Colla continued production of a series of single-player card sets. In standard 2-1/2" x 3-1/2" size, the cards featured high-gloss borderless photos on front, with no extraneous graphics. Backs feature stats, career notes, personal data, team logos and/or a cartoon. Card #1 in each set was serially numbered on the back. The 12-card sets were sold in small decorative cardboard boxes. Production figures are noted in parentheses. One in every 125 Mark McGwire sets contained an autographed card numbered from an edition of 200, but since the cards are not otherwise marked, caution should be exercised in paying a significant premium for such a set.

		NM/M
1-12	Steve Avery/7,500	2.00
1-12	Jeff Bagwell/25,000	4.00
1-12	Tony Gwynn/7,500	6.00
1-12	Mark McGwire/ 15,000	6.00
1-12	Mark McGwire (Autographed edition.)	300.00
1-12	Nolan Ryan/25,000	6.00
1-12	Frank Thomas/25,000	4.00

All-Stars

The 1992 Colla All-Star set consists of 24 players from the All-Star game in San Diego that year, packaged in a collector's box. Limited to 25,000 sets, the first card in each set is numbered and collectors had the opportunity to win numbered and autographed Roberto Alomar cards. Two hundred autographed Frank Thomas cards were also created for use as a premium, but he did not play in the 1992 All-Star Game due to injury.

		NM/M
Complete Set (24):		7.00
Common Player:		.25
1	Mark McGwire	1.50
2	Will Clark	.25
3	Roberto Alomar	.35
3a	Roberto Alomar/ Auto.	10.00
4	Ryne Sandberg	1.00
5	Cal Ripken, Jr.	2.00
6	Ozzie Smith	1.00
7	Wade Boggs	1.00
8	Terry Pendleton	.25
9	Kirby Puckett	1.00
10	Chuck Knoblauch	.25
11	Ken Griffey Jr.	1.25
12	Joe Carter	.25
13	Sandy Alomar, Jr.	.25
14	Benito Santiago	.25
15	Mike Mussina	.35
16	Fred McGriff	.25
17	Dennis Eckersley	.75
18	Tony Gwynn	1.00
19	Roger Clemens	1.00
20	Gary Sheffield	.35
21	Jose Canseco	.35
22	Barry Bonds	2.00
23	Ivan Rodriguez	.75
24	Tony Fernandez	.25
---	Frank Thomas/Auto.	25.00

Postcards

Only one single-player postcard set was produced by Barry Colla in 1992: Ivan Rodriguez. The four-card set, like

KEN GRIFFEY, JR.

the 1989-91 issues, features full-color game-action and posed photos presented on a borderless, high gloss 3 1/2" x 5-1/2" format. Besides the I-Rod set, Colla also produced at least one one-card "set," apparently on special order. These cards are in the same format as his other issues and are individually serially numbered on back from within an edition of 4,000.

		NM/M
1-4	Ivan Rodriguez	4.00
6492	Ken Griffey Jr.	6.00

1993 Barry Colla All-Stars

For the second year in 1993 California photographer Barry Colla produced a 24-card All-Star set commemorating the game played in Baltimore on July 13. The specially boxed collector's edition includes an unnumbered All-Star logo/ checklist card. Cards feature black borders on the UV-coated front, featuring game-action or posed photos. Team logos are centered beneath the photo, with the player's name and position in white at bottom. Backs are also bordered in black and include another player color photo, league and All-Star logos and information and stats on prior All-Star Game appearances.

		NM/M
Complete Set (25):		4.00
Common Player:		.15
1	Roberto Alomar	.30
2	Barry Bonds	.75
3	Ken Griffey Jr.	.50
4	John Kruk	.15
5	Kirby Puckett	.45
6	Darren Daulton	.15
7	Wade Boggs	.45
8	Matt Williams	.15
9	Cal Ripken, Jr.	.75
10	Ryne Sandberg	.45
11	Ivan Rodriguez	.30
12	Andy Van Slyke	.15
13	John Olerud	.15
14	Tom Glavine	.25
15	Juan Gonzalez	.30
16	David Justice	.15
17	Mike Mussina	.25
18	Tony Gwynn	.45
19	Joe Carter	.15
20	Barry Larkin	.15
21	Brian Harper	.15
22	Ozzie Smith	.45
23	Mark McGwire	.60
24	Mike Piazza	.50
	Checklist	.05

Postcards

Following a one-year lay-off, Barry Colla continued his single-player, eight-card postcard series in 1993 with a pair of sets. Like the earlier issues, the cards are 3-1/2" x 5-1/2" and feature high-gloss fronts with borderless game-action and posed photos. Black-and-white backs have a more traditional postcard format than earlier issues. The sets were sold in white paper envelopes with color team logos on front. A version of each set was made with an embossed gold-foil team logo on front; they are valued about 5X the regular issue.

		NM/M
1-8	Mike Piazza	3.50
1-8	Cal Ripken Jr.	6.00

1994 Collector's Choice Promos

Upper Deck used a pair of promo cards to preview its new 1994 Collector's Choice brand. Ken Griffey Jr. was featured on the promos, though the photos differ from those which appear on his regular-issue card, as does the card number. "For Promotional Use Only" is printed diagonally in black on both the front and back of the regular-size card. The 5" x 7-3/8" promo card uses the same front photo as the smaller promo and has advertising on the back describing the Collector's Choice issue.

		NM/M
50	Ken Griffey Jr.	5.00
---	Ken Griffey Jr. (Jumbo)	5.00

1994 Collector's Choice

This base-brand set, released in two series, was more widely available than the regular 1994 Upper Deck issue. Cards feature UD production staples such as UV coating and hologram and have large photos with a narrow pinstripe border. Backs have stats and a color photo. Series 1 has 320 cards and subsets titled Rookie Class, Draft Picks and Top Performers. Series 2 subsets are Up Close and Personal, Future Foundation and Rookie Class. Each of the set's player cards can also be found with either a gold- (1 in 36 packs) or silver-foil replica-autograph card; one silver-signature card appears in every pack. Factory sets include five randomly selected gold-signature cards.

	NM/M
Unopened Fact. Set (675):	25.00
Complete Set (670):	20.00
Common Player:	.05
Silver Signature:	2.5X
Gold Signature:	15X
Series 1 Pack (12):	.35
Series 1 Box (36):	8.00
Series 2 Pack (12):	.75
Series 2 Box (36):	17.50

No.	Player	Price
1	Rich Becker **RC**	.05
2	Greg Blosser	.05
3	Midre Cummings	.05
4	Carlos Delgado	.30
5	Steve Dreyer **RC**	.05
6	Carl Everett **RC**	.50
7	Cliff Floyd	.05
8	Alex Gonzalez	.05
9	Shawn Green	.10
10	Butch Huskey	.05
11	Mark Hutton	.05
12	Miguel Jimenez	.05
13	Steve Karsay	.05
14	Marc Newfield	.05
15	Luis Ortiz	.05
16	Manny Ramirez	.60
17	Johnny Ruffin	.05
18	Scott Stahoviak **RC**	.05
19	Salomon Torres	.05
20	Gabe White **RC**	.10
21	Brian Anderson **RC**	.05
22	Wayne Gomes **RC**	.05
23	Jeff Granger	.05
24	Steve Soderstrom **RC**	.05
25	Trot Nixon **RC**	.50
26	Kirk Presley **RC**	.05
27	Matt Brunson **RC**	.05
28	Brooks Kieschnick **RC**	.05
29	Billy Wagner **RC**	.50
30	Matt Drews **RC**	.05
31	Kurt Abbott **RC**	.05
32	Luis Alicea	.05
33	Roberto Alomar	.20
34	Sandy Alomar Jr.	.05
35	Moises Alou	.05
36	Wilson Alvarez	.05
37	Rich Amaral	.05
38	Eric Anthony	.05
39	Luis Aquino	.05
40	Jack Armstrong	.05
41	Rene Arocha	.05
42	Rich Aude **RC**	.05
43	Brad Ausmus	.05
44	Steve Avery	.05
45	Bob Ayrault	.05
46	Willie Banks	.05
47	Bret Barberie	.05
48	Kim Batiste	.05
49	Rod Beck	.05
50	Jason Bere	.05
51	Sean Berry	.05
52	Dante Bichette	.05
53	Jeff Blauser	.05
54	Mike Blowers	.05
55	Tim Bogar	.05
56	Tom Bolton	.05
57	Ricky Bones	.05
58	Bobby Bonilla	.05
59	Bret Boone	.05
60	Pat Borders	.05
61	Mike Bordick	.05
62	Daryl Boston	.05
63	Ryan Bowen	.05
64	Jeff Branson	.05
65	George Brett	.85
66	Steve Buechele	.05
67	Dave Burba	.05
68	John Burkett	.05
69	Jeromy Burnitz	.05
70	Brett Butler	.05
71	Rob Butler	.05
72	Ken Caminiti	.05
73	Cris Carpenter	.05
74	Vinny Castilla	.05
75	Andujar Cedeno	.05
76	Wes Chamberlain	.05
77	Archi Cianfrocco	.05
78	Dave Clark	.05
79	Jerald Clark	.05
80	Royce Clayton	.05
81	David Cone	.05
82	Jeff Conine	.05
83	Steve Cooke	.05
84	Scott Cooper	.05
85	Joey Cora	.05
86	Tim Costa	.05
87	Chad Curtis	.05
88	Ron Darling	.05
89	Danny Darwin	.05
90	Rob Deer	.05
91	Jim Deshaies	.05
92	Delino DeShields	.05
93	Rob Dibble	.05
94	Gary DiSarcina	.05
95	Doug Drabek	.05
96	Scott Erickson	.05
97	Rikkert Faneyte **RC**	.05
98	Jeff Fassero	.05
99	Alex Fernandez	.05
100	Cecil Fielder	.05
101	Dave Fleming	.05
102	Darrin Fletcher	.05
103	Scott Fletcher	.05
104	Mike Gallego	.05
105	Carlos Garcia	.05
106	Jeff Gardner	.05
107	Brent Gates	.05
108	Benji Gil	.05
109	Bernard Gilkey	.05
110	Chris Gomez	.05
111	Luis Gonzalez	.05
112	Tom Gordon	.05
113	Jim Gott	.05
114	Mark Grace	.05
115	Tommy Greene	.05
116	Willie Greene	.05
117	Ken Griffey Jr.	1.00
118	Bill Gullickson	.05
119	Ricky Gutierrez	.05
120	Juan Guzman	.05
121	Chris Gwynn	.05
122	Tony Gwynn	.75
123	Jeffrey Hammonds	.05
124	Erik Hanson	.05
125	Gene Harris	.05
126	Greg Harris	.05
127	Bryan Harvey	.05
128	Billy Hatcher	.05
129	Hilly Hathaway	.05
130	Charlie Hayes	.05
131	Rickey Henderson	.60
132	Mike Henneman	.05
133	Pat Hentgen	.05
134	Roberto Hernandez	.05
135	Orel Hershiser	.05
136	Phil Hiatt	.05
137	Glenallen Hill	.05
138	Ken Hill	.05
139	Eric Hillman	.05
140	Chris Hoiles	.05
141	Dave Hollins	.05
142	David Hulse	.05
143	Todd Hundley	.05
144	Pete Incaviglia	.05
145	Danny Jackson	.05
146	John Jaha	.05
147	Domingo Jean	.05
148	Gregg Jefferies	.05
149	Reggie Jefferson	.05
150	Lance Johnson	.05
151	Bobby Jones	.05
152	Chipper Jones	.75
153	Todd Jones	.05
154	Brian Jordan	.05
155	Wally Joyner	.05
156	Dave Justice	.05
157	Ron Karkovice	.05
158	Eric Karros	.05
159	Jeff Kent	.05
160	Jimmy Key	.05
161	Mark Kiefer	.05
162	Darryl Kile	.05
163	Jeff King	.05
164	Wayne Kirby	.05
165	Ryan Klesko	.05
166	Chuck Knoblauch	.05
167	Chad Kreuter	.05
168	John Kruk	.05
169	Mark Langston	.05
170	Mike Lansing	.05
171	Barry Larkin	.05
172	Manuel Lee	.05
173	Phil Leftwich **RC**	.05
174	Darren Lewis	.05
175	Derek Lilliquist	.05
176	Jose Lind	.05
177	Albie Lopez	.05
178	Javier Lopez	.05
179	Torey Lovullo	.05
180	Scott Lydy	.05
181	Mike Macfarlane	.05
182	Shane Mack	.05
183	Greg Maddux	.75
184	Dave Magadan	.05
185	Joe Magrane	.05
186	Kirt Manwaring	.05
187	Al Martin	.05
188	Pedro A. Martinez **RC**	.05
189	Pedro Martinez	.60
190	Ramon Martinez	.05
191	Tino Martinez	.05
192	Don Mattingly	.85
193	Derrick May	.05
194	David McCarty	.05
195	Ben McDonald	.05
196	Roger McDowell	.05
197	Fred McGriff	.05
198	Mark McLemore	.05
199	Greg McMichael	.05
200	Jeff McNeely	.05
201	Brian McRae	.05
202	Pat Meares	.05
203	Roberto Mejia	.05
204	Orlando Merced	.05
205	Jose Mesa	.05
206	Blas Minor	.05
207	Angel Miranda	.05
208	Paul Molitor	.60
209	Raul Mondesi	.05
210	Jeff Montgomery	.05
211	Mickey Morandini	.05
212	Mike Morgan	.05
213	Jamie Moyer	.05
214	Bobby Munoz	.05
215	Troy Neel	.05
216	Dave Nilsson	.05
217	John O'Donoghue	.05
218	Paul O'Neill	.05
219	Jose Offerman	.05
220	Joe Oliver	.05
221	Greg Olson	.05
222	Donovan Osborne	.05
223	Jayhawk Owens	.05
224	Mike Pagliarulo	.05
225	Craig Paquette	.05
226	Roger Pavlik	.05
227	Brad Pennington	.05
228	Eduardo Perez	.05
229	Mike Perez	.05
230	Tony Phillips	.05
231	Hipolito Pichardo	.05
232	Phil Plantier	.05
233	Curtis Pride **RC**	.05
234	Tim Pugh	.05
235	Scott Radinsky	.05
236	Pat Rapp	.05
237	Kevin Reimer	.05
238	Armando Reynoso	.05
239	Jose Rijo	.05
240	Cal Ripken, Jr.	2.00
241	Kevin Roberson	.05
242	Kenny Rogers	.05
243	Kevin Rogers	.05
244	Mel Rojas	.05
245	John Roper	.05
246	Kirk Rueter	.05
247	Scott Ruffcorn	.05
248	Ken Ryan	.05
249	Nolan Ryan	2.00
250	Bret Saberhagen	.05
251	Tim Salmon	.05
252	Reggie Sanders	.05
253	Curt Schilling	.20
254	David Segui	.05
255	Aaron Sele	.05
256	Scott Servais	.05
257	Gary Sheffield	.30
258	Ruben Sierra	.05
259	Don Slaught	.05
260	Lee Smith	.05
261	Cory Snyder	.05
262	Paul Sorrento	.05
263	Sammy Sosa	.75
264	Bill Spiers	.05
265	Mike Stanley	.05
266	Dave Staton	.05
267	Terry Steinbach	.05
268	Kevin Stocker	.05
269	Todd Stottlemyre	.05
270	Doug Strange	.05
271	Bill Swift	.05
272	Kevin Tapani	.05
273	Tony Tarasco	.05
274	Julian Tavarez **RC**	.05
275	Mickey Tettleton	.05
276	Ryan Thompson	.05
277	Chris Turner	.05
278	John Valentin	.05
279	Todd Van Poppel	.05
280	Andy Van Slyke	.05
281	Mo Vaughn	.05
282	Robin Ventura	.05
283	Frank Viola	.05
284	Jose Vizcaino	.05
285	Omar Vizquel	.05
286	Larry Walker	.05
287	Duane Ware	.05
288	Allen Watson	.05
289	Bill Wegman	.05
290	Turk Wendell	.05
291	Lou Whitaker	.05
292	Devon White	.05
293	Rondell White	.05
294	Mark Whiten	.05
295	Darrell Whitmore	.05
296	Bob Wickman	.05
297	Rick Wilkins	.05
298	Bernie Williams	.05
299	Matt Williams	.05
300	Woody Williams	.05
301	Nigel Wilson	.05
302	Dave Winfield	.60
303	Anthony Young	.05
304	Eric Young	.05
305	Todd Zeile	.05
306	Jack McDowell, John Burkett, Tom Glavine/TP	.05
307	Randy Johnson/TP	.25
308	Randy Myers/TP	.05
309	Jack McDowell/TP	.05
310	Mike Piazza/TP	.40
311	Barry Bonds/TP	.60
312	Andres Galarraga/TP	.05
313	Juan Gonzalez, Barry Bonds/TP	.45
314	Albert Belle/TP	.05
315	Kenny Lofton/TP	.05
316	Checklist 1-64 (Barry Bonds)	.50
317	Checklist 65-128 (Ken Griffey Jr.)	.35
318	Checklist 129-192 (Mike Piazza)	.35
319	Checklist 193-256 (Kirby Puckett)	.25
320	Checklist 257-320 (Nolan Ryan)	.50
321	Checklist 321-370 (Roberto Alomar)	.10
322	Checklist 371-420 (Roger Clemens)	.30
323	Checklist 421-470 (Juan Gonzalez)	.10
324	Checklist 471-520 (Ken Griffey Jr.)	.35
325	Checklist 521-570 (David Justice)	.05
326	Checklist 571-620 (John Kruk)	.05
327	Checklist 621-670 (Frank Thomas)	.20
328	Angels Checklist (Tim Salmon)	.05
329	Astros Checklist (Jeff Bagwell)	.20
330	Athletics Checklist (Mark McGwire)	.45
331	Blue Jays Checklist (Roberto Alomar)	.10
332	Braves Checklist (David Justice)	.05
333	Brewers Checklist (Pat Listach)	.05
334	Cardinals Checklist (Ozzie Smith)	.25
335	Cubs Checklist (Ryne Sandberg)	.25
336	Dodgers Checklist (Mike Piazza)	.35
337	Expos Checklist (Cliff Floyd)	.05
338	Giants Checklist (Barry Bonds)	.50
339	Indians Checklist (Albert Belle)	.05
340	Mariners Checklist (Ken Griffey Jr.)	.35
341	Marlins Checklist (Gary Sheffield)	.10
342	Mets Checklist (Dwight Gooden)	.05
343	Orioles Checklist (Cal Ripken, Jr.)	.50
344	Padres Checklist (Tony Gwynn)	.25
345	Phillies Checklist (Lenny Dykstra)	.05
346	Pirates Checklists (Andy Van Slyke)	.05
347	Rangers Checklist (Juan Gonzalez)	.10
348	Red Sox Checklist (Roger Clemens)	.30
349	Reds Checklist (Barry Larkin)	.05
350	Rockies Checklist (Andres Galarraga)	.05
351	Royals Checklist (Kevin Appier)	.05
352	Tigers Checklist (Cecil Fielder)	.05
353	Twins Checklist (Kirby Puckett)	.25
354	White Sox Checklist (Frank Thomas)	.20
355	Yankees Checklist (Don Mattingly)	.30
356	Bo Jackson	.10
357	Randy Johnson	.60
358	Darren Daulton	.05
359	Charlie Hough	.05
360	Andres Galarraga	.05
361	Mike Felder	.05
362	Chris Hammond	.05
363	Shawon Dunston	.05
364	Junior Felix	.05
365	Ray Lankford	.05
366	Darryl Strawberry	.05
367	Dave Magadan	.05
368	Gregg Olson	.05
369	Len Dykstra	.05
370	Darrin Jackson	.05
371	Dave Stewart	.05
372	Terry Pendleton	.05
373	Arthur Rhodes	.05
374	Benito Santiago	.05
375	Travis Fryman	.05
376	Scott Brosius	.05
377	Stan Belinda	.05
378	Derek Parks	.05
379	Kevin Seitzer	.05
380	Wade Boggs	.75
381	Wally Whitehurst	.05
382	Scott Leius	.05
383	Danny Tartabull	.05
384	Harold Reynolds	.05
385	Tim Raines	.05
386	Darryl Hamilton	.05
387	Felix Fermin	.05
388	Jim Eisenreich	.05
389	Kurt Abbott	.05
390	Kevin Appier	.05
391	Chris Bosio	.05
392	Randy Tomlin	.05
393	Bob Hamelin	.05
394	Kevin Gross	.05
395	Wil Cordero	.05
396	Joe Girardi	.05
397	Orestes Destrade	.05
398	Chris Haney	.05
399	Xavier Hernandez	.05
400	Mike Piazza	1.00
401	Alex Arias	.05
402	Tom Candiotti	.05
403	Kirk Gibson	.05
404	Chuck Carr	.05
405	Brady Anderson	.05
406	Greg Gagne	.05
407	Bruce Ruffin	.05
408	Scott Hemond	.05
409	Keith Miller	.05
410	John Wetteland	.05
411	Eric Anthony	.05
412	Andre Dawson	.25
413	Doug Henry	.05
414	John Franco	.05
415	Julio Franco	.05
416	Dave Hansen	.05
417	Mike Harkey	.05
418	Jack Armstrong	.05
419	Joe Orsulak	.05
420	John Smoltz	.05
421	Scott Livingstone	.05
422	Darren Holmes	.05
423	Ed Sprague	.05
424	Jay Buhner	.05
425	Kirby Puckett	.75
426	Phil Clark	.05
427	Anthony Young	.05
428	Reggie Jefferson	.05
429	Mariano Duncan	.05
430	Tom Glavine	.20
431	Dave Henderson	.05
432	Melido Perez	.05
433	Paul Wagner	.05
434	Tim Worrell	.05
435	Ozzie Guillen	.05
436	Mike Butcher	.05
437	Jim Deshaies	.05
438	Kevin Young	.05
439	Tom Browning	.05
440	Mike Greenwell	.05
441	Mike Stanton	.05
442	John Doherty	.05
443	John Dopson	.05
444	Carlos Baerga	.05
445	Jack McDowell	.05
446	Kent Mercker	.05
447	Ricky Jordan	.05
448	Jerry Browne	.05
449	Fernando Vina	.05
450	Jim Abbott	.05
451	Teddy Higuera	.05
452	Tim Naehring	.05
453	Jim Leyritz	.05
454	Frank Castillo	.05
455	Joe Carter	.05
456	Craig Biggio	.05
457	Geronimo Pena	.05
458	Alejandro Pena	.05
459	Mike Moore	.05
460	Randy Myers	.05
461	Greg Myers	.05
462	Greg Hibbard	.05
463	Jose Guzman	.05
464	Tom Pagnozzi	.05
465	Marquis Grissom	.05
466	Tim Wallach	.05
467	Joe Grahe	.05
468	Bob Tewksbury	.05
469	B.J. Surhoff	.05
470	Kevin Mitchell	.05
471	Bobby Witt	.05
472	Milt Thompson	.05
473	John Smiley	.05
474	Alan Trammell	.05
475	Mike Mussina	.30
476	Rick Aguilera	.05
477	Jose Valentin	.05
478	Harold Baines	.05
479	Bip Roberts	.05
480	Edgar Martinez	.05
481	Rheal Cormier	.05
482	Hal Morris	.05
483	Pat Kelly	.05
484	Roberto Kelly	.05
485	Chris Sabo	.05
486	Kent Hrbek	.05
487	Scott Kamieniecki	.05
488	Walt Weiss	.05
489	Karl Rhodes	.05
490	Derek Bell	.05
491	Chili Davis	.05
492	Brian Harper	.05
493	Felix Jose	.05
494	Trevor Hoffman	.05
495	Dennis Eckersley	.50
496	Pedro Astacio	.05
497	Jay Bell	.05
498	Randy Velarde	.05
499	David Wells	.05
500	Frank Thomas	.60
501	Mark Lemke	.05
502	Mike Devereaux	.05
503	Chuck McElroy	.05
504	Luis Polonia	.05

505 Damion Easley .05
506 Greg A. Harris .05
507 Chris James .05
508 Terry Mulholland .05
509 Pete Smith .05
510 Rickey Henderson .60
511 Sid Fernandez .05
512 Al Leiter .05
513 Doug Jones .05
514 Steve Farr .05
515 Chuck Finley .05
516 Bobby Thigpen .05
517 Jim Edmonds .05
518 Graeme Lloyd .05
519 Dwight Gooden .05
520 Pat Listach .05
521 Kevin Bass .05
522 Willie Banks .05
523 Steve Finley .05
524 Delino DeShields .05
525 Mark McGwire 1.50
526 Greg Swindell .05
527 Chris Nabholz .05
528 Scott Sanders .05
529 David Segui .05
530 Howard Johnson .05
531 Jaime Navarro .05
532 Jose Vizcaino .05
533 Mark Lewis .05
534 Pete Harnisch .05
535 Robby Thompson .05
536 Marcus Moore .05
537 Kevin Brown .05
538 Mark Clark .05
539 Sterling Hitchcock .05
540 Will Clark .05
541 Denis Boucher .05
542 Jack Morris .05
543 Pedro Munoz .05
544 Bret Boone .05
545 Ozzie Smith .75
546 Dennis Martinez .05
547 Dan Wilson .05
548 Rick Sutcliffe .05
549 Kevin McReynolds .05
550 Roger Clemens .85
551 Todd Benzinger .05
552 Bill Haselman .05
553 Bobby Munoz .05
554 Ellis Burks .05
555 Ryne Sandberg .75
556 Lee Smith .05
557 Danny Bautista .05
558 Rey Sanchez .05
559 Norm Charlton .05
560 Jose Canseco .35
561 Tim Belcher .05
562 Denny Neagle .05
563 Eric Davis .05
564 Jody Reed .05
565 Kenny Lofton .05
566 Gary Gaetti .05
567 Todd Worrell .05
568 Mark Portugal .05
569 Dick Schofield .05
570 Andy Benes .05
571 Zane Smith .05
572 Bobby Ayala .05
573 Chip Hale .05
574 Bob Welch .05
575 Deion Sanders .10
576 Dave Nied .05
577 Pat Mahomes .05
578 Charles Nagy .05
579 Otis Nixon .05
580 Dean Palmer .05
581 Roberto Petagine .05
582 Dwight Smith .05
583 Jeff Russell .05
584 Mark Dewey .05
585 Greg Vaughn .05
586 Brian Hunter .05
587 Willie McGee .05
588 Pedro J. Martinez .60
589 Roger Salkeld .05
590 Jeff Bagwell .60
591 Spike Owen .05
592 Jeff Reardon .05
593 Erik Pappas .05
594 Brian Williams .05
595 Eddie Murray .60
596 Henry Rodriguez .05
597 Erik Hanson .05
598 Stan Javier .05
599 Mitch Williams .05
600 John Olerud .05
601 Vince Coleman .05
602 Damon Berryhill .05
603 Tom Brunansky .05
604 Robb Nen .05
605 Rafael Palmeiro .50
606 Cal Eldred .05
607 Jeff Brantley .05
608 Alan Mills .05
609 Jeff Nelson .05
610 Barry Bonds 2.00
611 Carlos Pulido **RC** .05
612 Tim Hyers **RC** .05
613 Steve Howe .05
614 Brian Turang **RC** .05
615 Leo Gomez .05
616 Jesse Orosco .05
617 Dan Pasqua .05
618 Marvin Freeman .05
619 Tony Fernandez .05
620 Albert Belle .05
621 Eddie Taubensee .05
622 Mike Jackson .05
623 Jose Bautista .05
624 Jim Thome .40
625 Ivan Rodriguez .50
626 Ben Rivera .05
627 Dave Valle .05
628 Tom Henke .05
629 Omar Vizquel .05
630 Juan Gonzalez .30
631 Roberto Alomar (Up Close) .10
632 Barry Bonds (Up Close) .60
633 Juan Gonzalez (Up Close) .15
634 Ken Griffey Jr. (Up Close) .50
635 Michael Jordan (Up Close) 1.50
636 Dave Justice (Up Close) .05
637 Mike Piazza (Up Close) .50
638 Kirby Puckett (Up Close) .25
639 Tim Salmon (Up Close) .05
640 Frank Thomas (Up Close) .35
641 Alan Benes/FF **RC** .05
642 Johnny Damon/FF .35
643 Brad Fullmer/FF **RC** .25
644 Derek Jeter/FF 2.00
645 Derrek Lee/FF **RC** .75
646 Alex Ochoa/FF .05
647 Alex Rodriguez/FF **RC** 6.00
648 Jose Silva/FF **RC** .05
649 Terrell Wade/FF **RC** .05
650 Preston Wilson/FF .05
651 Shane Andrews (Rookie Class) .05
652 James Baldwin (Rookie Class) .05
653 Ricky Bottalico **RC** (Rookie Class) .10
654 Tavo Alvarez (Rookie Class) .05
655 Donnie Elliott (Rookie Class) .05
656 Joey Eischen (Rookie Class) .05
657 Jason Giambi (Rookie Class) .50
658 Todd Hollandsworth (Rookie Class) .05
659 Brian Hunter (Rookie Class) .05
660 Charles Johnson (Rookie Class) .05
661 Michael Jordan **RC** (Rookie Class) 3.00
662 Jeff Juden (Rookie Class) .05
663 Mike Kelly (Rookie Class) .05
664 James Mouton (Rookie Class) .05
665 Ray Holbert (Rookie Class) .05
666 Pokey Reese (Rookie Class) .05
667 Ruben Santana **RC** (Rookie Class) .05
668 Paul Spoljaric (Rookie Class) .05
669 Luis Lopez (Rookie Class) .05
670 Matt Walbeck (Rookie Class) .05

Silver Signature

Each of the cards in the debut edition of Upper Deck's Collector's Choice brand was also issued in a parallel edition bearing a facsimile silver-foil signature on front. The silver-signature cards were inserted at a one-per-pack rate in the set's foil packs, and proportionately in other types of packaging.

	NM/M
Common Player:	.15
Stars:	2.5X

647 Alex Rodriguez (White Letters. Some A-Rod Silver Signature parallels were mistakenly printed on base cards with his name and other details on front and back printed in white, rather than gray.) 100.00

Gold Signature

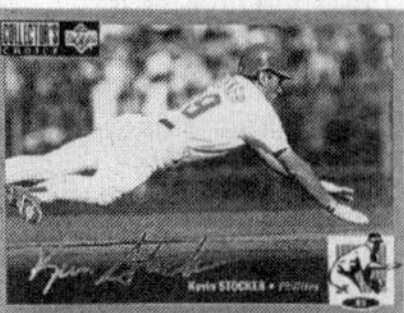

A super-scarce parallel set of the premiere-issue Collector's Choice in 1994 was the gold-signature version found on average of only once per 36 foil packs. In addition to a gold-foil facsimile signature on the card front, this edition features gold-colored borders on the regular player cards.

	NM/M
Common Player:	2.00
Stars:	15X

Home Run All-Stars

Among the most attractive of the 1994 chase cards, the perceived high production (over a million sets according to stated odds of winning) of this set keeps it affordable. Sets were available by a mail-in offer to persons who found a winner card in Series 1 foil packs (about one per box). Cards feature a combination of brick-bordered hologram and color player photo on front, along with a gold-foil facsimile autograph. On back the brick border is repeated, as is the photo on the hologram, though this time in full color. There is a stadium photo in the background, over which is printed a description of the player's home run prowess. A numbering error resulted in two cards numbered HA4 and no card with the HA5 number.

		NM/M
Complete Set (8):		4.00
Common Player:		.25
1HA	Juan Gonzalez	.50
2HA	Ken Griffey Jr.	1.50
3HA	Barry Bonds	2.50
4HAa	Bobby Bonilla	.25
4HAb	Cecil Fielder	.25
6HA	Albert Belle	.25
7HA	David Justice	.25
8HA	Mike Piazza	1.50

Team vs. Team Scratchoff

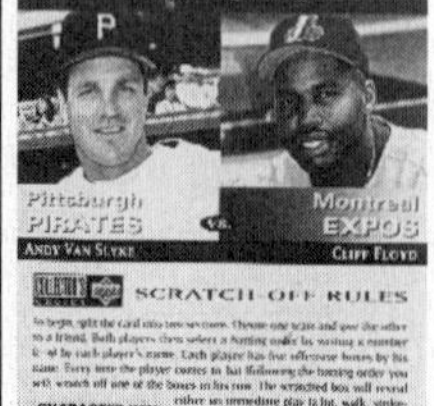

Team vs. Team scratch-offs are a 15-card set, with one game card being inserted into every pack of Collector's Choice 1994 baseball. Each card allowed two persons to play a nine-inning baseball game. Game cards also double as a prize card in the "You Crash The Deck" contest.

		NM/M
Complete Set (15):		4.50
Common Card:		.25
1	Blue Jays-White Sox (Roberto Alomar, Frank Thomas)	.30
2	Phillies-Braves (Lenny Dykstra, David Justice)	.25
3	Mariners-Rangers (Ken Griffey Jr., Juan Gonzalez)	.50
4	Dodgers-Giants (Mike Piazza, Barry Bonds)	.75
5	Red Sox-Yankees (Roger Clemens, Don Mattingly)	.45
6	Reds-Astros (Barry Larkin, Jeff Bagwell)	.25
7	Orioles-Tigers (Cal Ripken Jr., Cecil Fielder)	.75
8	Cubs-Cardinals (Ryne Sandberg, Ozzie Smith)	.35
9	Athletics-Angels (Mark McGwire, Tim Salmon)	.60
10	Pirates-Expos (Andy Van Slyke, Cliff Floyd)	.25
11	Brewers-Indians (Pat Listach, Albert Belle)	.25
12	Rockies-Padres (Andres Galarraga, Tony Gwynn)	.35
13	Twins-Royals (Kirby Puckett, Brian McRae)	.35
14	Mets-Marlins (Dwight Gooden, Gary Sheffield)	.25
15	N.L. All-Stars-A.L. All-Stars (Barry Bonds, Ken Griffey Jr.)	.75

1995 Collector's Choice

Issued in a single series, Upper Deck's base-brand baseball series features a number of subsets within the main body of the issue, as well as several insert sets. Basic cards feature large photos on front and back, with the back having full major league stats. The set opens with a 27-card Rookie Class subset featuring front photos on which the background has been rendered in hot pink tones. Backs have a lime-green box with a scouting report on the player and a box featuring 1994 minor and major league stats. The next 18 cards are Future Foundation cards which have the prospects pictured with a posterized background on front, with backs similar to the Rookie Class cards. Career finale cards of five retired superstars follow, then a run of Best of the '90s cards honoring record-setting achievements, followed by cards depicting major award winners of the previous season. Each of the last three named subsets features borderless color photos on front, with backs similar to the regular cards. Immediately preceding the regular cards, which are arranged in team-set order, is a five-card What's the Call? subset featuring cartoon representations of the players. A set of five checklist cards marking career highlights ends the set.

	NM/M
Unopened Fact. Set (545):	17.50
Complete Set (530):	12.50
Common Player:	.05
Silver Stars:	2X
Gold Stars:	6X
Pack (12):	1.00
Wax Box (36):	20.00

1 Charles Johnson (Rookie Class) .05
2 Scott Ruffcorn (Rookie Class) .05
3 Ray Durham (Rookie Class) .05
4 Armando Benitez (Rookie Class) .05
5 Alex Rodriguez (Rookie Class) 1.25
6 Julian Tavarez (Rookie Class) .05
7 Chad Ogea (Rookie Class) .05
8 Quilvio Veras (Rookie Class) .05
9 Phil Nevin (Rookie Class) .05
10 Michael Tucker (Rookie Class) .05
11 Mark Thompson (Rookie Class) .05
12 Rod Henderson (Rookie Class) .05
13 Andrew Lorraine (Rookie Class) .05
14 Joe Randa (Rookie Class) .05
15 Derek Jeter (Rookie Class) 1.50
16 Tony Clark (Rookie Class) .05
17 Juan Castillo (Rookie Class) .05
18 Mark Acre (Rookie Class) .05
19 Orlando Miller (Rookie Class) .05
20 Paul Wilson (Rookie Class) .05
21 John Mabry (Rookie Class) .05
22 Garey Ingram (Rookie Class) .05
23 Garret Anderson (Rookie Class) .05
24 Dave Stevens (Rookie Class) .05
25 Dustin Hermanson (Rookie Class) .05
26 Paul Shuey (Rookie Class) .05
27 J.R. Phillips (Rookie Class) .05
28 Ruben Rivera/FF .05
29 Nomar Garciaparra/FF .75
30 John Wasdin/FF .05
31 Jim Pittsley/FF .05
32 Scott Elarton/FF **RC** .15
33 Raul Casanova/FF **RC** .05
34 Todd Greene/FF .05
35 Bill Pulsipher/FF .05
36 Trey Beamon/FF .05
37 Curtis Goodwin/FF .05
38 Doug Million/FF .05
39 Karim Garcia/FF **RC** 1.00
40 Ben Grieve/FF .05
41 Mark Farris/FF .05
42 Juan Acevedo/FF **RC** .05
43 C.J. Nitkowski/FF .05
44 Travis Miller/FF **RC** .10
45 Reid Ryan/FF .10
46 Nolan Ryan 1.50
47 Robin Yount .50
48 Ryne Sandberg .75
49 George Brett .85
50 Mike Schmidt .85
51 Cecil Fielder (Best of the 90's) .05
52 Nolan Ryan (Best of the 90's) .75
53 Rickey Henderson (Best of the 90's) .20
54 George Brett, Robin Yount, Dave Winfield (Best of the 90's) .25
55 Sid Bream (Best of the 90's) .05
56 Carlos Baerga (Best of the 90's) .05
57 Lee Smith (Best of the 90's) .05
58 Mark Whiten (Best of the 90's) .05
59 Joe Carter (Best of the 90's) .05
60 Barry Bonds (Best of the 90's) .75
61 Tony Gwynn (Best of the 90's) .40
62 Ken Griffey Jr. (Best of the 90's) .50
63 Greg Maddux (Best of the 90's) .40
64 Frank Thomas (Best of the 90's) .35
65 Dennis Martinez, Kenny Rogers (Best of the 90's) .05
66 David Cone (Cy Young) .05
67 Greg Maddux (Cy Young) .75
68 Jimmy Key (Most Victories) .05
69 Fred McGriff (All-Star MVP) .05
70 Ken Griffey Jr. (HR Champ) 1.00
71 Matt Williams (HR Champ) .05
72 Paul O'Neill (Batting Title) .05
73 Tony Gwynn (Batting Title) .40
74 Randy Johnson (Ks Leader) .60
75 Frank Thomas (MVP) .60
76 Jeff Bagwell (MVP) .60
77 Kirby Puckett (RBI leader) .75
78 Bob Hamelin (ROY) .05
79 Raul Mondesi (ROY) .05
80 Mike Piazza/AS 1.00
81 Kenny Lofton (SB Leader) .05
82 Barry Bonds (Gold Glove) 1.50
83 Albert Belle/AS .05
84 Juan Gonzalez (HR Champ) .30
85 Cal Ripken Jr. (2,000 Straight Games) 1.50
86 Barry Bonds (What's the Call?) .75
87 Mike Piazza (What's the Call?) .60
88 Ken Griffey Jr. (What's the Call?) .50
89 Frank Thomas (What's the Call?) .35
90 Juan Gonzalez (What's the Call?) .10
91 Jorge Fabregas .05
92 J.T. Snow .05
93 Spike Owen .05
94 Eduardo Perez .05
95 Bo Jackson .10
96 Damion Easley .05
97 Gary DiSarcina .05
98 Jim Edmonds .05
99 Chad Curtis .05
100 Tim Salmon .05
101 Chili Davis .05
102 Chuck Finley .05
103 Mark Langston .05
104 Brian Anderson .05
105 Lee Smith .05
106 Phil Leftwich .05
107 Chris Donnels .05
108 John Hudek .05
109 Craig Biggio .05
110 Luis Gonzalez .05
111 Brian L. Hunter .05
112 James Mouton .05
113 Scott Servais .05
114 Tony Eusebio .05
115 Derek Bell .05
116 Doug Drabek .05
117 Shane Reynolds .05
118 Darryl Kile .05
119 Greg Swindell .05
120 Phil Plantier .05
121 Todd Jones .05
122 Steve Ontiveros .05
123 Bobby Witt .05
124 Brent Gates .05
125 Rickey Henderson .60
126 Scott Brosius .05
127 Mike Bordick .05
128 Fausto Cruz .05
129 Stan Javier .05
130 Mark McGwire 1.25
131 Geronimo Berroa .05
132 Terry Steinbach .05
133 Steve Karsay .05
134 Dennis Eckersley .50
135 Ruben Sierra .05
136 Ron Darling .05
137 Todd Van Poppel .05
138 Alex Gonzalez .05
139 John Olerud .05
140 Roberto Alomar .20
141 Darren Hall .05
142 Ed Sprague .05
143 Devon White .05
144 Shawn Green .20
145 Paul Molitor .60
146 Pat Borders .05
147 Carlos Delgado .35
148 Juan Guzman .05
149 Pat Hentgen .05
150 Joe Carter .05
151 Dave Stewart .05
152 Todd Stottlemyre .05
153 Dick Schofield .05
154 Chipper Jones .75
155 Ryan Klesko .05
156 Dave Justice .05

157 Mike Kelly .05
158 Roberto Kelly .05
159 Tony Tarasco .05
160 Javier Lopez .05
161 Steve Avery .05
162 Greg McMichael .05
163 Kent Mercker .05
164 Mark Lemke .05
165 Tom Glavine .20
166 Jose Oliva .05
167 John Smoltz .05
168 Jeff Blauser .05
169 Troy O'Leary .05
170 Greg Vaughn .05
171 Jody Reed .05
172 Kevin Seitzer .05
173 Jeff Cirillo .05
174 B.J. Surhoff .05
175 Cal Eldred .05
176 Jose Valentin .05
177 Turner Ward .05
178 Darryl Hamilton .05
179 Pat Listach .05
180 Matt Mieske .05
181 Brian Harper .05
182 Dave Nilsson .05
183 Mike Fetters .05
184 John Jaha .05
185 Ricky Bones .05
186 Geronimo Pena .05
187 Bob Tewksbury .05
188 Todd Zeile .05
189 Danny Jackson .05
190 Ray Lankford .05
191 Bernard Gilkey .05
192 Brian Jordan .05
193 Tom Pagnozzi .05
194 Rick Sutcliffe .05
195 Mark Whiten .05
196 Tom Henke .05
197 Rene Arocha .05
198 Allen Watson .05
199 Mike Perez .05
200 Ozzie Smith .75
201 Anthony Young .05
202 Rey Sanchez .05
203 Steve Buechele .05
204 Shawon Dunston .05
205 Mark Grace .05
206 Glenallen Hill .05
207 Eddie Zambrano .05
208 Rick Wilkins .05
209 Derrick May .05
210 Sammy Sosa .75
211 Kevin Roberson .05
212 Steve Trachsel .05
213 Willie Banks .05
214 Kevin Foster .05
215 Randy Myers .05
216 Mike Morgan .05
217 Rafael Bournigal .05
218 Delino DeShields .05
219 Tim Wallach .05
220 Eric Karros .05
221 Jose Offerman .05
222 Tom Candiotti .05
223 Ismael Valdes .05
224 Henry Rodriguez .05
225 Billy Ashley .05
226 Darren Dreifort .05
227 Ramon Martinez .05
228 Pedro Astacio .05
229 Orel Hershiser .05
230 Brett Butler .05
231 Todd Hollandsworth .05
232 Chan Ho Park .05
233 Mike Lansing .05
234 Sean Berry .05
235 Rondell White .05
236 Ken Hill .05
237 Marquis Grissom .05
238 Larry Walker .05
239 John Wetteland .05
240 Cliff Floyd .05
241 Joey Eischen .05
242 Lou Frazier .05
243 Darrin Fletcher .05
244 Pedro J. Martinez .60
245 Wil Cordero .05
246 Jeff Fassero .05
247 Butch Henry .05
248 Mel Rojas .05
249 Kirk Rueter .05
250 Moises Alou .05
251 Rod Beck .05
252 John Patterson .05
253 Robby Thompson .05
254 Royce Clayton .05
255 William Van Landingham .05
256 Darren Lewis .05
257 Kirt Manwaring .05
258 Mark Portugal .05
259 Bill Swift .05
260 Rikkert Faneyte .05
261 Mike Jackson .05
262 Todd Benzinger .05
263 Bud Black .05
264 Salomon Torres .05
265 Eddie Murray .60
266 Mark Clark .05
267 Paul Sorrento .05
268 Jim Thome .45
269 Omar Vizquel .05
270 Carlos Baerga .05
271 Jeff Russell .05
272 Herbert Perry .05
273 Sandy Alomar Jr. .05
274 Dennis Martinez .05
275 Manny Ramirez .60
276 Wayne Kirby .05
277 Charles Nagy .05
278 Albie Lopez .05
279 Jeromy Burnitz .05
280 Dave Winfield .60
281 Tim Davis .05
282 Marc Newfield .05
283 Tino Martinez .05
284 Mike Blowers .05
285 Goose Gossage .05
286 Luis Sojo .05
287 Edgar Martinez .05
288 Rich Amaral .05
289 Felix Fermin .05
290 Jay Buhner .05
291 Dan Wilson .05
292 Bobby Ayala .05
293 Dave Fleming .05
294 Greg Pirkl .05
295 Reggie Jefferson .05
296 Greg Hibbard .05
297 Yorkis Perez .05
298 Kurt Miller .05
299 Chuck Carr .05
300 Gary Sheffield .30
301 Jerry Browne .05
302 Dave Magadan .05
303 Kurt Abbott .05
304 Pat Rapp .05
305 Jeff Conine .05
306 Benito Santiago .05
307 Dave Weathers .05
308 Robb Nen .05
309 Chris Hammond .05
310 Bryan Harvey .05
311 Charlie Hough .05
312 Greg Colbrunn .05
313 David Segui .05
314 Rico Brogna .05
315 Jeff Kent .05
316 Jose Vizcaino .05
317 Jim Lindeman .05
318 Carl Everett .05
319 Ryan Thompson .05
320 Bobby Bonilla .05
321 Joe Orsulak .05
322 Pete Harnisch .05
323 Doug Linton .05
324 Todd Hundley .05
325 Bret Saberhagen .05
326 Kelly Stinnett .05
327 Jason Jacome .05
328 Bobby Jones .05
329 John Franco .05
330 Rafael Palmeiro .50
331 Chris Hoiles .05
332 Leo Gomez .05
333 Chris Sabo .05
334 Brady Anderson .05
335 Jeffrey Hammonds .05
336 Dwight Smith .05
337 Jack Voigt .05
338 Harold Baines .05
339 Ben McDonald .05
340 Mike Mussina .30
341 Bret Barberie .05
342 Jamie Moyer .05
343 Mike Oquist .05
344 Sid Fernandez .05
345 Eddie Williams .05
346 Joey Hamilton .05
347 Brian Williams .05
348 Luis Lopez .05
349 Steve Finley .05
350 Andy Benes .05
351 Andujar Cedeno .05
352 Bip Roberts .05
353 Ray McDavid .05
354 Ken Caminiti .05
355 Trevor Hoffman .05
356 Mel Nieves .05
357 Brad Ausmus .05
358 Andy Ashby .05
359 Scott Sanders .05
360 Gregg Jefferies .05
361 Mariano Duncan .05
362 Dave Hollins .05
363 Kevin Stocker .05
364 Fernando Valenzuela .05
365 Lenny Dykstra .05
366 Jim Eisenreich .05
367 Ricky Bottalico .05
368 Doug Jones .05
369 Ricky Jordan .05
370 Darren Daulton .05
371 Mike Lieberthal .05
372 Bobby Munoz .05
373 John Kruk .05
374 Curt Schilling .20
375 Orlando Merced .05
376 Carlos Garcia .05
377 Lance Parrish .05
378 Steve Cooke .05
379 Jeff King .05
380 Jay Bell .05
381 Al Martin .05
382 Paul Wagner .05
383 Rick White .05
384 Midre Cummings .05
385 Jon Lieber .05
386 Dave Clark .05
387 Don Slaught .05
388 Denny Neagle .05
389 Zane Smith .05
390 Andy Van Slyke .05
391 Ivan Rodriguez .50
392 David Hulse .05
393 John Burkett .05
394 Kevin Brown .05
395 Dean Palmer .05
396 Otis Nixon .05
397 Rick Helling .05
398 Kenny Rogers .05
399 Darren Oliver .05
400 Will Clark .05
401 Jeff Frye .05
402 Kevin Gross .05
403 John Dettmer .05
404 Manny Lee .05
405 Rusty Greer .05
406 Aaron Sele .05
407 Carlos Rodriguez .05
408 Scott Cooper .05
409 John Valentin .05
410 Roger Clemens .85
411 Mike Greenwell .05
412 Tim Vanegmond .05
413 Tom Brunansky .05
414 Steve Farr .05
415 Jose Canseco .35
416 Joe Hesketh .05
417 Ken Ryan .05
418 Tim Naehring .05
419 Frank Viola .05
420 Andre Dawson .25
421 Mo Vaughn .05
422 Jeff Brantley .05
423 Pete Schourek .05
424 Hal Morris .05
425 Deion Sanders .10
426 Brian L. Hunter .05
427 Bret Boone .05
428 Willie Greene .05
429 Ron Gant .05
430 Barry Larkin .05
431 Reggie Sanders .05
432 Eddie Taubensee .05
433 Jack Morris .05
434 Jose Rijo .05
435 Johnny Ruffin .05
436 John Smiley .05
437 John Roper .05
438 David Nied .05
439 Roberto Mejia .05
440 Andres Galarraga .05
441 Mike Kingery .05
442 Curt Leskanic .05
443 Walt Weiss .05
444 Marvin Freeman .05
445 Charlie Hayes .05
446 Eric Young .05
447 Ellis Burks .05
448 Joe Girardi .05
449 Lance Painter .05
450 Dante Bichette .05
451 Bruce Ruffin .05
452 Jeff Granger .05
453 Wally Joyner .05
454 Jose Lind .05
455 Jeff Montgomery .05
456 Gary Gaetti .05
457 Greg Gagne .05
458 Vince Coleman .05
459 Mike Macfarlane .05
460 Brian McRae .05
461 Tom Gordon .05
462 Kevin Appier .05
463 Billy Brewer .05
464 Mark Gubicza .05
465 Travis Fryman .05
466 Danny Bautista .05
467 Sean Bergman .05
468 Mike Henneman .05
469 Mike Moore .05
470 Cecil Fielder .05
471 Alan Trammell .05
472 Kirk Gibson .05
473 Tony Phillips .05
474 Mickey Tettleton .05
475 Lou Whitaker .05
476 Chris Gomez .05
477 John Doherty .05
478 Greg Gohr .05
479 Bill Gullickson .05
480 Rick Aguilera .05
481 Matt Walbeck .05
482 Kevin Tapani .05
483 Scott Erickson .05
484 Steve Dunn .05
485 David McCarty .05
486 Scott Leius .05
487 Pat Meares .05
488 Jeff Reboulet .05
489 Pedro Munoz .05
490 Chuck Knoblauch .05
491 Rich Becker .05
492 Alex Cole .05
493 Pat Mahomes .05
494 Ozzie Guillen .05
495 Tim Raines .05
496 Kirk McCaskill .05
497 Olmedo Saenz .05
498 Scott Sanderson .05
499 Lance Johnson .05
500 Michael Jordan 1.50
501 Warren Newson .05
502 Ron Karkovice .05
503 Wilson Alvarez .05
504 Jason Bere .05
505 Robin Ventura .05
506 Alex Fernandez .05
507 Roberto Hernandez .05
508 Norberto Martin .05
509 Bob Wickman .05
510 Don Mattingly .85
511 Melido Perez .05
512 Pat Kelly .05
513 Randy Velarde .05
514 Tony Fernandez .05
515 Jack McDowell .05
516 Luis Polonia .05
517 Bernie Williams .05
518 Danny Tartabull .05
519 Mike Stanley .05
520 Wade Boggs .75
521 Jim Leyritz .05
522 Steve Howe .05
523 Scott Kamieniecki .05
524 Russ Davis .05
525 Jim Abbott .05
526 Checklist 1-106 (Eddie Murray) .20
527 Checklist 107-212 (Alex Rodriguez) .40
528 Checklist 213-318 (Jeff Bagwell) .20
529 Checklist 319-424 (Joe Carter) .05
530 Checklist 425-530 (Fred McGriff) .05
--- National Packtime Offer Card .05

Silver Signature

A silver-foil facsimile autograph added to the card front is the only difference between these chase cards and regular-issue Collector's Choice cards. The silver-signature inserts are found one per pack in regular foil packs, and two per pack in retail jumbo packs.

	NM/M
Common Player:	.10
Stars:	2X

Gold Signature

The top-of-the-line chase card in 1995 Collector's Choice is the Gold Signature parallel set. Each of the 530 cards in the set was created in a special gold version that was found on average only one per box of foil packs. Other than the addition of a gold-foil facsimile autograph on front, the cards are identical to regular-issue Collector's Choice.

	NM/M
Common Player:	.50
Stars:	6X

Trade Cards

A series of five mail-in redemption cards was included as inserts into UD Collector's Choice, at the rate of approximately one per 11 packs. The cards could be sent in with $2 to receive 11 Collector's Choice Update cards, as specified on the front of the card.

The trade offer expired on Feb. 1, 1996. Cards are numbered with the "TC" prefix.

		NM/M
Complete Set (5):		1.00
Common Player:		.25
1	Larry Walker (#531-541)	.25
2	David Cone (#542-552)	.25
3	Marquis Grissom (#553-563)	.25
4	Terry Pendleton (#564-574)	.25
5	Fernando Valenzuela (#575-585)	.25

Redemption Cards

These update cards were available only via a mail-in offer involving trade cards found in foil packs. Each trade card was redeemable for a specific 11-card set of players shown in their new uniforms as a result of rookie call-ups, trades and free agent signings. The cards are in the same format as the regular 1995 Collector's Choice issue. The update redemption cards are numbered by team nickname from Angels through Yankees, the numbers running contiguously from the body of the CC set.

		NM/M
Complete Set (55):		2.50
Common Player:		.10
531	Tony Phillips	.10
532	Dave Magadan	.10
533	Mike Gallego	.10
534	Dave Stewart	.10
535	Todd Stottlemyre	.10
536	David Cone	.10
537	Marquis Grissom	.10
538	Derrick May	.10
539	Joe Oliver	.10
540	Scott Cooper	.10
541	Ken Hill	.10
542	Howard Johnson	.10
543	Brian McRae	.10
544	Jaime Navarro	.10
545	Ozzie Timmons	.10
546	Roberto Kelly	.10
547	Hideo Nomo	1.50
548	Shane Andrews	.10
549	Mark Grudzielanek	.10
550	Carlos Perez	.10
551	Henry Rodriguez	.10
552	Tony Tarasco	.10
553	Glenallen Hill	.10
554	Terry Mulholland	.10
555	Orel Hershiser	.10
556	Darren Bragg	.10
557	John Burkett	.10
558	Bobby Witt	.10
559	Terry Pendleton	.10
560	Andre Dawson	.50
561	Brett Butler	.10
562	Kevin Brown	.10
563	Doug Jones	.10
564	Andy Van Slyke	.10
565	Jody Reed	.10
566	Fernando Valenzuela	.10
567	Charlie Hayes	.10
568	Benji Gil	.10
569	Mark McLemore	.10
570	Mickey Tettleton	.10
571	Bob Tewksbury	.10
572	Rheal Cormier	.10
573	Vaughn Eshelman	.10
574	Mike Macfarlane	.10
575	Mark Whiten	.10
576	Benito Santiago	.10
577	Jason Bates	.10
578	Bill Swift	.10
579	Larry Walker	.10
580	Chad Curtis	.10
581	Bobby Higginson	.10
582	Marty Cordova	.10
583	Mike Devereaux	.10
584	John Kruk	.10
585	John Wetteland	.10

Crash the Game

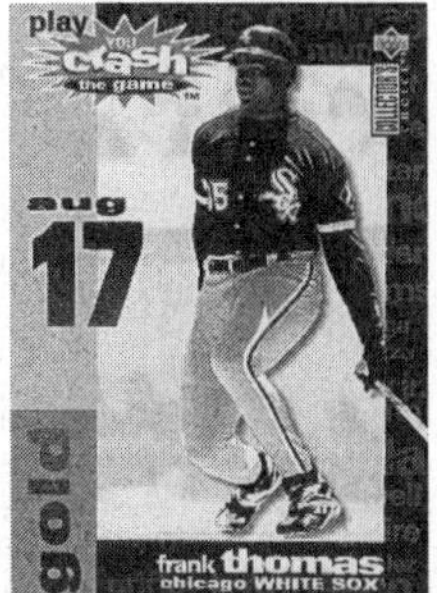

These insert cards gave collectors a reason to follow box scores around the major leagues between June 18-October 1. Each of 20 noted home run hitters can be found with three different dates foil-stamped on the card front. If the player hit a home run on that day, the card could be redeemed for a set of 20 special prize cards. Stated odds of finding a You Crash the Game card were one in five packs. Most of the inserts are silver-foil enhanced, with about one in eight being found with gold foil. Winning cards are much scarcer than the others since they had to be mailed in for redemption.

		NM/M
Complete Set, Silver (20):		5.00
Common Player, Silver:		.15
Complete Set, Gold (20):		12.00
Common Player, Gold:		.35
CG1	Jeff Bagwell (July 30)	.25
CG1	Jeff Bagwell (Aug. 13)	.25
CG1	Jeff Bagwell (Sept. 28)	.25
CG2	Albert Belle (June 18)	.15
CG2	Albert Belle (Aug. 26)	.15
CG2	Albert Belle (Sept. 20)	.15
CG3	Barry Bonds (June 28)	1.00
CG3	Barry Bonds (July 9)	1.00
CG3	Barry Bonds (Sept. 6)	1.00
CG4	Jose Canseco (June 30)(Winner)	1.00
CG4	Jose Canseco (July 30)(Winner)	1.00
CG4	Jose Canseco (Sept. 3)	.35
CG5	Joe Carter (July 14)	.15
CG5	Joe Carter (Aug. 9)	.15
CG5	Joe Carter (Sept. 23)	.15
CG6	Cecil Fielder (July 4)	.15
CG6	Cecil Fielder (Aug. 2)	.15
CG6	Cecil Fielder (Oct. 1)	.15
CG7	Juan Gonzalez (June 29)	.30
CG7	Juan Gonzalez (Aug. 13)	.30
CG7	Juan Gonzalez (Sept. 3)(Winner)	1.00
CG8	Ken Griffey Jr. (July 2)	.60
CG8	Ken Griffey Jr. (Aug. 24)(Winner)	2.50
CG8	Ken Griffey Jr. (Sept. 15)	.60
CG9	Bob Hamelin (July 23)	.15
CG9	Bob Hamelin (Aug. 1)	.15
CG9	Bob Hamelin (Sept. 29)	.15
CG10	David Justice (June 24)	.15
CG10	David Justice (July 25)	.15
CG10	David Justice (Sept. 17)	.15
CG11	Ryan Klesko (July 13)	.15
CG11	Ryan Klesko (Aug. 20)	.15
CG11	Ryan Klesko (Sept. 10)	.15
CG12	Fred McGriff (Aug. 25)	.15
CG12	Fred McGriff (Sept. 8)	.15
CG12	Fred McGriff (Sept. 24)	.15
CG13	Mark McGwire (July 23)	.75
CG13	Mark McGwire (Aug. 3)(Winner)	3.00

CG13 Mark McGwire (Sept. 27) .75
CG14 Raul Mondesi (July 27)(Winner) .75
CG14 Raul Mondesi (Aug. 13) .15
CG14 Raul Mondesi (Sept. 15)(Winner) .75
CG15 Mike Piazza (July 23)(Winner) 2.00
CG15 Mike Piazza (Aug. 27)(Winner) 2.00
CG15 Mike Piazza (Sept. 19) .60
CG16 Manny Ramirez (June 21) .35
CG16 Manny Ramirez (Aug. 13) .35
CG16 Manny Ramirez (Sept. 26) .35
CG17 Alex Rodriguez (Sept. 10) .75
CG17 Alex Rodriguez (Sept. 18) .75
CG17 Alex Rodriguez (Sept. 24) .75
CG18 Gary Sheffield (July 5) .30
CG18 Gary Sheffield (Aug. 13) .30
CG18 Gary Sheffield (Sept. 4)(Winner) 1.00
CG19 Frank Thomas (July 26) .50
CG19 Frank Thomas (Aug. 17) .50
CG19 Frank Thomas (Sept. 23) .50
CG20 Matt Williams (July 29) .15
CG20 Matt Williams (Aug. 12) .15
CG20 Matt Williams (Sept. 19) .15
CG1 Jeff Bagwell (July 30) .75
CG1 Jeff Bagwell (Aug. 13) .75
CG1 Jeff Bagwell (Sept. 28) .75
CG2 Albert Belle (June 18) .35
CG2 Albert Belle (Aug. 26) .35
CG2 Albert Belle (Sept. 20) .35
CG3 Barry Bonds (June 28) 2.50
CG3 Barry Bonds (July 9) 2.50
CG3 Barry Bonds (Sept. 6) 2.50
CG4 Jose Canseco (June 30)(Winner) 2.00
CG4 Jose Canseco (July 30)(Winner) 2.00
CG4 Jose Canseco (Sept. 3) .75
CG5 Joe Carter (July 14) .35
CG5 Joe Carter (Aug. 9) .35
CG5 Joe Carter (Sept. 23) .35
CG6 Cecil Fielder (July 4) .35
CG6 Cecil Fielder (Aug. 2) .35
CG6 Cecil Fielder (Oct. 1) .35
CG7 Juan Gonzalez (June 29) .45
CG7 Juan Gonzalez (Aug. 13) .45
CG7 Juan Gonzalez (Sept. 3)(Winner) 1.50
CG8 Ken Griffey Jr. (July 2) 1.50
CG8 Ken Griffey Jr. (Aug. 24)(Winner) 3.00
CG8 Ken Griffey Jr. (Sept. 15) 1.50
CG9 Bob Hamelin (July 23) .35
CG9 Bob Hamelin (Aug. 1) .35
CG9 Bob Hamelin (Sept. 29) .35
CG10 David Justice (June 24) .35
CG10 David Justice (July 25) .35
CG10 David Justice (Sept. 17) .35
CG11 Ryan Klesko (July 13) .35
CG11 Ryan Klesko (Aug. 20) .35
CG11 Ryan Klesko (Sept. 10) .35
CG12 Fred McGriff (Aug. 25) .35
CG12 Fred McGriff (Sept. 8) .35
CG12 Fred McGriff (Sept. 24) .35
CG13 Mark McGwire (July 23) 2.00
CG13 Mark McGwire (Aug. 3)(Winner) 4.00
CG13 Mark McGwire (Sept. 27) 2.00
CG14 Raul Mondesi (July 27)(Winner) 1.25
CG14 Raul Mondesi (Aug. 13) .45
CG14 Raul Mondesi (Sept. 15)(Winner) 1.25
CG15 Mike Piazza (July 23)(Winner) 3.00
CG15 Mike Piazza (Aug. 27)(Winner) 3.00
CG15 Mike Piazza (Sept. 19) 1.00
CG16 Manny Ramirez (June 21) .75
CG16 Manny Ramirez (Aug. 13) .75
CG16 Manny Ramirez (Sept. 26) .75
CG17 Alex Rodriguez (Sept. 10) 1.00
CG17 Alex Rodriguez (Sept. 18) 1.00
CG17 Alex Rodriguez (Sept. 24) 1.00
CG18 Gary Sheffield (July 5) .75
CG18 Gary Sheffield (Aug. 13) .75
CG18 Gary Sheffield (Sept. 4)(Winner) 2.00
CG19 Frank Thomas (July 26) .65
CG19 Frank Thomas (Aug. 17) .65
CG19 Frank Thomas (Sept. 23) .65
CG20 Matt Williams (July 29) .45
CG20 Matt Williams (Aug. 12) .45
CG20 Matt Williams (Sept. 19) .45

Crash Winners

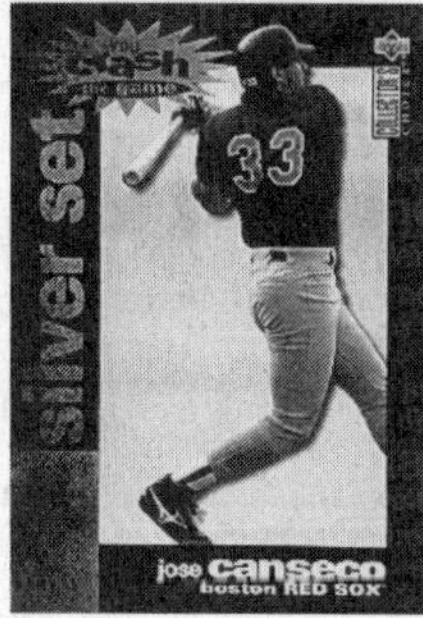

These 20-card sets were awarded to collectors who redeemed "You Crash the Game" winners cards. A silver-foil enhanced set was sent to winners with silver redemption cards, a gold version was sent to gold winners. A $3 redemption fee was required. Fronts are similar to the game cards, except for the foil printing down the left side in the place of the game date. Instead of redemption rules on the back of award cards there are career highlights at left and a panel at right with the names of the players in the set.

NM/M

Complete Set, Silver (20): 6.00
Complete Set, Gold (20): 25.00
Common Player, Silver: .25
Common Player, Gold: 1.00
CR1 Jeff Bagwell .60
CR2 Albert Belle .25
CR3 Barry Bonds 2.50
CR4 Jose Canseco .50
CR5 Joe Carter .25
CR6 Cecil Fielder .25
CR7 Juan Gonzalez .50
CR8 Ken Griffey Jr. 1.50
CR9 Bob Hamelin .25
CR10 Dave Justice .25
CR11 Ryan Klesko .25
CR12 Fred McGriff .25
CR13 Mark McGwire 2.00
CR14 Raul Mondesi .25
CR15 Mike Piazza 1.50
CR16 Manny Ramirez .60
CR17 Alex Rodriguez 2.00
CR18 Gary Sheffield .50
CR19 Frank Thomas .60
CR20 Matt Williams .25
CR1 Jeff Bagwell 2.00
CR2 Albert Belle 1.00
CR3 Barry Bonds 4.00
CR4 Jose Canseco 1.50
CR5 Joe Carter 1.00
CR6 Cecil Fielder 1.00
CR7 Juan Gonzalez 1.50
CR8 Ken Griffey Jr. 3.00
CR9 Bob Hamelin 1.00
CR10 Dave Justice 1.00
CR11 Ryan Klesko 1.00
CR12 Fred McGriff 1.00
CR13 Mark McGwire 3.00
CR14 Raul Mondesi 1.00
CR15 Mike Piazza 3.00
CR16 Manny Ramirez 2.00
CR17 Alex Rodriguez 3.50
CR18 Gary Sheffield 1.50
CR19 Frank Thomas 2.00
CR20 Matt Williams 1.00

Michael Jordan Jumbo

A limited edition of 10,000 of these 3" x 5" cards was produced for direct sales to consumers. The card is in the format of the 1995 Collector's Choice Rookie Class subset and includes a silver foil facsimile of Jordan's autograph on front. Back includes a serial number in the lower-right corner.

NM/M

661 Michael Jordan 15.00

Ichiro Suzuki

This card was part of a set produced by Upper Deck's Collector's Choice brand in conjunction with a series of NBA games held in Japan. The cards were made for various members of the media, sports dignitaries, etc., to be used as personal business cards. Cards are in standard 2-1/2" x 3-1/2" format.

NM/M

59 Ichiro Suzuki 1,000

1995 Collector's Choice/SE

The first Upper Deck baseball card issue for 1995 was this 265-card set which uses blue borders and a blue foil "Special Edition" trapezoidal logo to impart a premium look. The set opens with a Rookie Class subset of 25 cards on which the background has been rendered in orange hues. A series of six Record Pace cards, horizontal with blue and yellow backgrounds, immediately precedes the regular cards. Base cards in the set are arranged in team-alpha order. Front and back have large color photos, while backs offer complete major league stats. Interspersed within the teams are special cards with borderless front designs honoring players who won significant awards in the 1994 season. Another subset, Stat Leaders, pictures various players in a silver dollar-sized circle at the center of the card and lists the 1994 leaders in that category on the back. A dozen-card Fantasy Team subset near the end of the set lists on back the top-rated players at each position, picturing one of them on front, with a giant blue baseball. The set closes with five checklists honoring career highlights from the '94 season.

NM/M

Complete Set (265): 17.50
Common Player: .05
Silver Stars: 1.5X
Gold Stars: 8X
Pack (12): 1.25
Wax Box (36): 25.00
1 Alex Rodriguez 1.50
2 Derek Jeter 2.00
3 Dustin Hermanson .05
4 Bill Pulsipher .05
5 Terrell Wade .05
6 Darren Dreifort .05
7 LaTroy Hawkins .05
8 Alex Ochoa .05
9 Paul Wilson .05
10 Ernie Young .05
11 Alan Benes .05
12 Garret Anderson .05
13 Armando Benitez .05
14 Robert Perez .05
15 Herbert Perry .05
16 Jose Silva .05
17 Orlando Miller .05
18 Russ Davis .05
19 Jason Isringhausen .05
20 Ray McDavid .05
21 Duane Singleton .05
22 Paul Shuey .05
23 Steve Dunn .05
24 Mike Lieberthal .05
25 Chan Ho Park .05
26 Ken Griffey Jr. (Record Pace) .65
27 Tony Gwynn (Record Pace) .40
28 Chuck Knoblauch (Record Pace) .05
29 Frank Thomas (Record Pace) .35
30 Matt Williams (Record Pace) .05
31 Chili Davis .05
32 Chad Curtis .05
33 Brian Anderson .05
34 Chuck Finley .05
35 Tim Salmon .05
36 Bo Jackson .10
37 Doug Drabek .05
38 Craig Biggio .05
39 Ken Caminiti .05
40 Jeff Bagwell .65
41 Darryl Kile .05
42 John Hudek .05
43 Brian L. Hunter .05
44 Dennis Eckersley .60
45 Mark McGwire 1.50
46 Brent Gates .05
47 Steve Karsay .05
48 Rickey Henderson .65
49 Terry Steinbach .05
50 Ruben Sierra .05
51 Roberto Alomar .25
52 Carlos Delgado .25
53 Alex Gonzalez .05
54 Joe Carter .05
55 Paul Molitor .65
56 Juan Guzman .05
57 John Olerud .05
58 Shawn Green .25
59 Tom Glavine .25
60 Greg Maddux .75
61 Roberto Kelly .05
62 Ryan Klesko .05
63 Javier Lopez .05
64 Jose Oliva .05
65 Fred McGriff .05
66 Steve Avery .05
67 Dave Justice .05
68 Ricky Bones .05
69 Cal Eldred .05
70 Greg Vaughn .05
71 Dave Nilsson .05
72 Jose Valentin .05
73 Matt Mieske .05
74 Todd Zeile .05
75 Ozzie Smith .75
76 Bernard Gilkey .05
77 Ray Lankford .05
78 Bob Tewksbury .05
79 Mark Whiten .05
80 Gregg Jefferies .05
81 Randy Myers .05
82 Shawon Dunston .05
83 Mark Grace .05
84 Derrick May .05
85 Sammy Sosa .75
86 Steve Trachsel .05
87 Brett Butler .05
88 Delino DeShields .05
89 Orel Hershiser .05
90 Mike Piazza 1.00
91 Todd Hollandsworth .05
92 Eric Karros .05
93 Ramon Martinez .05
94 Tim Wallach .05
95 Raul Mondesi .05
96 Larry Walker .05
97 Wil Cordero .05
98 Marquis Grissom .05
99 Ken Hill .05
100 Cliff Floyd .05
101 Pedro J. Martinez .65
102 John Wetteland .05
103 Rondell White .05
104 Moises Alou .05
105 Barry Bonds 2.00
106 Darren Lewis .05
107 Mark Portugal .05
108 Matt Williams .05
109 William Van Landingham .05
110 Bill Swift .05
111 Robby Thompson .05
112 Rod Beck .05
113 Darryl Strawberry .05
114 Jim Thome .50
115 Dave Winfield .65
116 Eddie Murray .65
117 Manny Ramirez .75
118 Carlos Baerga .05
119 Kenny Lofton .05
120 Albert Belle .05
121 Mark Clark .05
122 Dennis Martinez .05
123 Randy Johnson .65
124 Jay Buhner .05
125 Ken Griffey Jr. 1.00
125a Ken Griffey Jr./OPS 1.50
126 Rich Gossage .05
127 Tino Martinez .05
128 Reggie Jefferson .05
129 Edgar Martinez .05
130 Gary Sheffield .30
131 Pat Rapp .05
132 Bret Barberie .05
133 Chuck Carr .05
134 Jeff Conine .05
135 Charles Johnson .05
136 Benito Santiago .05
137 Matt Williams (Stat Leaders) .05
138 Jeff Bagwell (Stat Leaders) .35
139 Kenny Lofton (Stat Leaders) .05
140 Tony Gwynn (Stat Leaders) .40
141 Jimmy Key (Stat Leaders) .05
142 Greg Maddux (Stat Leaders) .40
143 Randy Johnson (Stat Leaders) .25
144 Lee Smith (Stat Leaders) .05
145 Bobby Bonilla .05
146 Jason Jacome .05
147 Jeff Kent .05
148 Ryan Thompson .05
149 Bobby Jones .05
150 Bret Saberhagen .05
151 John Franco .05
152 Lee Smith .05
153 Rafael Palmeiro .60
154 Brady Anderson .05
155 Cal Ripken Jr. 2.00
156 Jeffrey Hammonds .05
157 Mike Mussina .35
158 Chris Hoiles .05
159 Ben McDonald .05
160 Tony Gwynn .75
161 Joey Hamilton .05
162 Andy Benes .05
163 Trevor Hoffman .05
164 Phil Plantier .05
165 Derek Bell .05
166 Bip Roberts .05
167 Eddie Williams .05
168 Fernando Valenzuela .05
169 Mariano Duncan .05
170 Lenny Dykstra .05
171 Darren Daulton .05
172 Danny Jackson .05
173 Bobby Munoz .05
174 Doug Jones .05
175 Jay Bell .05
176 Zane Smith .05
177 Jon Lieber .05
178 Carlos Garcia .05
179 Orlando Merced .05
180 Andy Van Slyke .05
181 Rick Helling .05
182 Rusty Greer .05
183 Kenny Rogers .05
184 Will Clark .05
185 Jose Canseco .40
186 Juan Gonzalez .35
187 Dean Palmer .05
188 Ivan Rodriguez .60
189 John Valentin .05
190 Roger Clemens .85
191 Aaron Sele .05
192 Scott Cooper .05
193 Mike Greenwell .05
194 Mo Vaughn .05
195 Andre Dawson .25
196 Ron Gant .05
197 Jose Rijo .05
198 Bret Boone .05
199 Deion Sanders .10
200 Barry Larkin .05
201 Hal Morris .05
202 Reggie Sanders .05
203 Kevin Mitchell .05
204 Marvin Freeman .05
205 Andres Galarraga .05
206 Walt Weiss .05
207 Charlie Hayes .05
208 David Nied .05
209 Dante Bichette .05
210 David Cone .05
211 Jeff Montgomery .05
212 Felix Jose .05
213 Mike Macfarlane .05
214 Wally Joyner .05
215 Bob Hamelin .05
216 Brian McRae .05
217 Kirk Gibson .05
218 Lou Whitaker .05
219 Chris Gomez .05
220 Cecil Fielder .05
221 Mickey Tettleton .05
222 Travis Fryman .05
223 Tony Phillips .05
224 Rick Aguilera .05
225 Scott Erickson .05
226 Chuck Knoblauch .05
227 Kent Hrbek .05
228 Shane Mack .05
229 Kevin Tapani .05
230 Kirby Puckett .75
231 Julio Franco .05
232 Jack McDowell .05
233 Jason Bere .05
234 Alex Fernandez .05
235 Frank Thomas .65
236 Ozzie Guillen .05
237 Robin Ventura .05
238 Michael Jordan 2.00
239 Wilson Alvarez .05
240 Don Mattingly .85
241 Jim Abbott .05
242 Jim Leyritz .05
243 Paul O'Neill .05
244 Melido Perez .05
245 Wade Boggs .75
246 Mike Stanley .05
247 Danny Tartabull .05
248 Jimmy Key .05
249 Greg Maddux (Fantasy Team) .40
250 Randy Johnson (Fantasy Team) .20
251 Bret Saberhagen (Fantasy Team) .05
252 John Wetteland (Fantasy Team) .05
253 Mike Piazza (Fantasy Team) .50
254 Jeff Bagwell (Fantasy Team) .35
255 Craig Biggio (Fantasy Team) .05
256 Matt Williams (Fantasy Team) .05
257 Wil Cordero (Fantasy Team) .05
258 Kenny Lofton (Fantasy Team) .05
259 Barry Bonds (Fantasy Team) .75
260 Dante Bichette (Fantasy Team) .05
261 Checklist 1-53 (Ken Griffey Jr.) .35
262 Checklist 54-106 (Goose Gossage) .05
263 Checklist 107-159 (Cal Ripken Jr.) .45
264 Checklist 160-212 (Kenny Rogers) .05
265 Checklist 213-265 (John Valentin) .05

Silver

The cards in this parallel edition feature the addition of a silver-foil facsimile autograph on the card front. Also, the blue SE logo and card borders have been replaced with silver on the chase cards, which are found on average of one per pack.

NM/M

Common Player: .15
Stars: 1.5X

Gold

Each of the cards in the SE issue can be found in a premium chase card version which replaces the blue border and SE logo with gold, and adds a

gold-foil facsimile autograph to the front of the card. The gold-version SE inserts are found on average of one per 36 packs.

	NM/M
Common Player:	1.00
Stars:	8X

1996 Collector's Choice Promo

To introduce its base-brand set, Upper Deck issued a promotional sample card of Ken Griffey, Jr. Numbered 100 (he's #310 in the issued set), the back is overprinted "For Promotional Use Only."

		NM/M
100	Ken Griffey Jr.	4.00

1996 Collector's Choice

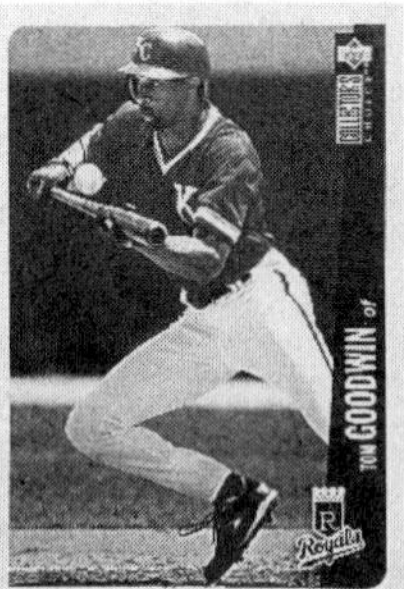

The third year for Collector's Choice includes 730 cards in two series with packs formatted in retail and hobby versions. The 280 regular player cards are joined by subsets of Rookie Class, International Flavor, Traditional Threads, Fantasy Team, Stat Leaders, Season Highlights, First Class, Arizona Fall League, Awards and Checklists. Packs feature a number of different insert sets including silver and gold signature parallel sets, interactive "You Make the Play" cards, four cards from the cross-brand Cal Ripken Collection and three postseason trade cards redeemable for 10-card sets recalling the League Championships and World Series. An additional 30 cards (#761-790) featuring traded players in their new uniforms was issued only in factory sets.

		NM/M
Unopened Fact. Set (790):		17.50
Complete Set: (760):		12.50
Traded Set (366T-395T):		3.00
Common Player:		.05
Series 1 Pack (12):		.75
Series 1 Wax Box (36):		22.50
Series 2 Pack (14):		1.00
Series 2 Wax Box (40):		25.00
1	Cal Ripken Jr.	2.00
2	Edgar Martinez, Tony Gwynn (1995 Stat Leaders)	.05
3	Albert Belle, Dante Bichette (1995 Stat Leaders)	.05
4	Albert Belle, Mo Vaughn, Dante Bichette (1995 Stat Leaders)	.05
5	Kenny Lofton, Quilvio Veras (1995 Stat Leaders)	.05
6	Mike Mussina, Greg Maddux (1995 Stat Leaders)	.40
7	Randy Johnson, Hideo Nomo (1995 Stat Leaders)	.25
8	Randy Johnson, Greg Maddux (1995 Stat Leaders)	.40
9	Jose Mesa, Randy Myers (1995 Stat Leaders)	.05
10	Johnny Damon (Rookie Class)	.35
11	Rick Krivda (Rookie Class)	.05
12	Roger Cedeno (Rookie Class)	.05
13	Angel Martinez (Rookie Class)	.05
14	Ariel Prieto (Rookie Class)	.05
15	John Wasdin (Rookie Class)	.05
16	Edwin Hurtado (Rookie Class)	.05
17	Lyle Mouton (Rookie Class)	.05
18	Chris Snopek (Rookie Class)	.05
19	Mariano Rivera (Rookie Class)	.15
20	Ruben Rivera (Rookie Class)	.05
21	Juan Castro **RC** (Rookie Class)	.05
22	Jimmy Haynes (Rookie Class)	.05
23	Bob Wolcott (Rookie Class)	.05
24	Brian Barber (Rookie Class)	.05
25	Frank Rodriguez (Rookie Class)	.05
26	Jesus Tavarez (Rookie Class)	.05
27	Glenn Dishman (Rookie Class)	.05
28	Jose Herrera (Rookie Class)	.05
29	Chan Ho Park (Rookie Class)	.05
30	Jason Isringhausen (Rookie Class)	.05
31	Doug Johns (Rookie Class)	.05
32	Gene Schall (Rookie Class)	.05
33	Kevin Jordan (Rookie Class)	.05
34	Matt Lawton **RC** (Rookie Class)	.10
35	Karim Garcia (Rookie Class)	.05
36	George Williams (Rookie Class)	.05
37	Orlando Palmeiro (Rookie Class)	.05
38	Jamie Brewington (Rookie Class)	.05
39	Robert Person (Rookie Class)	.05
40	Greg Maddux	.75
41	Marquis Grissom	.05
42	Chipper Jones	.75
43	David Justice	.05
44	Mark Lemke	.05
45	Fred McGriff	.05
46	Javy Lopez	.05
47	Mark Wohlers	.05
48	Jason Schmidt	.05
49	John Smoltz	.05
50	Curtis Goodwin	.05
51	Gregg Zaun	.05
52	Armando Benitez	.05
53	Manny Alexander	.05
54	Chris Hoiles	.05
55	Harold Baines	.05
56	Ben McDonald	.05
57	Scott Erickson	.05
58	Jeff Manto	.05
59	Luis Alicea	.05
60	Roger Clemens	.85
61	Rheal Cormier	.05
62	Vaughn Eshelman	.05
63	Zane Smith	.05
64	Mike Macfarlane	.05
65	Erik Hanson	.05
66	Tim Naehring	.05
67	Lee Tinsley	.05
68	Troy O'Leary	.05
69	Garret Anderson	.05
70	Chili Davis	.05
71	Jim Edmonds	.05
72	Troy Percival	.05
73	Mark Langston	.05
74	Spike Owen	.05
75	Tim Salmon	.05
76	Brian Anderson	.05
77	Lee Smith	.05
78	Jim Abbott	.05
79	Jim Bullinger	.05
80	Mark Grace	.05
81	Todd Zeile	.05
82	Kevin Foster	.05
83	Howard Johnson	.05
84	Brian McRae	.05
85	Randy Myers	.05
86	Jaime Navarro	.05
87	Luis Gonzalez	.05
88	Ozzie Timmons	.05
89	Wilson Alvarez	.05
90	Frank Thomas	.60
91	James Baldwin	.05
92	Ray Durham	.05
93	Alex Fernandez	.05
94	Ozzie Guillen	.05
95	Tim Raines	.05
96	Roberto Hernandez	.05
97	Lance Johnson	.05
98	John Kruk	.05
99	Mark Portugal	.05
100	Don Mattingly (Traditional Threads)	.65
101	Jose Canseco (Traditional Threads)	.15
102	Raul Mondesi (Traditional Threads)	.05
103	Cecil Fielder (Traditional Threads)	.05
104	Ozzie Smith (Traditional Threads)	.40
105	Frank Thomas (Traditional Threads)	.45
106	Sammy Sosa (Traditional Threads)	.50
107	Fred McGriff (Traditional Threads)	.05
108	Barry Bonds (Traditional Threads)	1.00
109	Thomas Howard	.05
110	Ron Gant	.05
111	Eddie Taubensee	.05
112	Hal Morris	.05
113	Jose Rijo	.05
114	Pete Schourek	.05
115	Reggie Sanders	.05
116	Benito Santiago	.05
117	Jeff Brantley	.05
118	Julian Tavarez	.05
119	Carlos Baerga	.05
120	Jim Thome	.40
121	Jose Mesa	.05
122	Dennis Martinez	.05
123	Dave Winfield	.60
124	Eddie Murray	.60
125	Manny Ramirez	.60
126	Paul Sorrento	.05
127	Kenny Lofton	.05
128	Eric Young	.05
129	Jason Bates	.05
130	Bret Saberhagen	.05
131	Andres Galarraga	.05
132	Joe Girardi	.05
133	John Vander Wal	.05
134	David Nied	.05
135	Dante Bichette	.05
136	Vinny Castilla	.05
137	Kevin Ritz	.05
138	Felipe Lira	.05
139	Joe Boever	.05
140	Cecil Fielder	.05
141	John Flaherty	.05
142	Kirk Gibson	.05
143	Brian Maxcy	.05
144	Lou Whitaker	.05
145	Alan Trammell	.05
146	Bobby Higginson	.05
147	Chad Curtis	.05
148	Quilvio Veras	.05
149	Jerry Browne	.05
150	Andre Dawson	.25
151	Robb Nen	.05
152	Greg Colbrunn	.05
153	Chris Hammond	.05
154	Kurt Abbott	.05
155	Charles Johnson	.05
156	Terry Pendleton	.05
157	Dave Weathers	.05
158	Mike Hampton	.05
159	Craig Biggio	.05
160	Jeff Bagwell	.60
161	Brian L. Hunter	.05
162	Mike Henneman	.05
163	Dave Magadan	.05
164	Shane Reynolds	.05
165	Derek Bell	.05
166	Orlando Miller	.05
167	James Mouton	.05
168	Melvin Bunch	.05
169	Tom Gordon	.05
170	Kevin Appier	.05
171	Tom Goodwin	.05
172	Greg Gagne	.05
173	Gary Gaetti	.05
174	Jeff Montgomery	.05
175	Jon Nunnally	.05
176	Michael Tucker	.05
177	Joe Vitiello	.05
178	Billy Ashley	.05
179	Tom Candiotti	.05
180	Hideo Nomo	.30
181	Chad Fonville	.05
182	Todd Hollandsworth	.05
183	Eric Karros	.05
184	Roberto Kelly	.05
185	Mike Piazza	1.00
186	Ramon Martinez	.05
187	Tim Wallach	.05
188	Jeff Cirillo	.05
189	Sid Roberson	.05
190	Kevin Seitzer	.05
191	Mike Fetters	.05
192	Steve Sparks	.05
193	Matt Mieske	.05
194	Joe Oliver	.05
195	B.J. Surhoff	.05
196	Alberto Reyes	.05
197	Fernando Vina	.05
198	LaTroy Hawkins	.05
199	Marty Cordova	.05
200	Kirby Puckett	.75
201	Brad Radke	.05
202	Pedro Munoz	.05
203	Scott Klingenbeck	.05
204	Pat Meares	.05
205	Chuck Knoblauch	.05
206	Scott Stahoviak	.05
207	Dave Stevens	.05
208	Shane Andrews	.05
209	Moises Alou	.05
210	David Segui	.05
211	Cliff Floyd	.05
212	Carlos Perez	.05
213	Mark Grudzielanek	.05
214	Butch Henry	.05
215	Rondell White	.05
216	Mel Rojas	.05
217	Ugueth Urbina	.05
218	Edgardo Alfonzo	.05
219	Carl Everett	.05
220	John Franco	.05
221	Todd Hundley	.05
222	Bobby Jones	.05
223	Bill Pulsipher	.05
224	Rico Brogna	.05
225	Jeff Kent	.05
226	Chris Jones	.05
227	Butch Huskey	.05
228	Robert Eenhoorn	.05
229	Sterling Hitchcock	.05
230	Wade Boggs	.75
231	Derek Jeter	2.00
232	Tony Fernandez	.05
233	Jack McDowell	.05
234	Andy Pettitte	.35
235	David Cone	.05
236	Mike Stanley	.05
237	Don Mattingly	.85
238	Geronimo Berroa	.05
239	Scott Brosius	.05
240	Rickey Henderson	.60
241	Terry Steinbach	.05
242	Mike Gallego	.05
243	Jason Giambi	.40
244	Steve Ontiveros	.05
245	Dennis Eckersley	.50
246	Dave Stewart	.05
247	Don Wengert	.05
248	Paul Quantrill	.05
249	Ricky Bottalico	.05
250	Kevin Stocker	.05
251	Lenny Dykstra	.05
252	Tony Longmire	.05
253	Tyler Green	.05
254	Mike Mimbs	.05
255	Charlie Hayes	.05
256	Mickey Morandini	.05
257	Heathcliff Slocumb	.05
258	Jeff King	.05
259	Midre Cummings	.05
260	Mark Johnson	.05
261	Freddy Garcia	.05
262	Jon Lieber	.05
263	Esteban Loaiza	.05
264	Danny Miceli	.05
265	Orlando Merced	.05
266	Denny Neagle	.05
267	Steve Parris	.05
268	Fantasy Team '95 (Greg Maddux)	.35
269	Fantasy Team '95 (Randy Johnson)	.20
270	Fantasy Team '95 (Hideo Nomo)	.15
271	Fantasy Team '95 (Jose Mesa)	.05
272	Fantasy Team '95 (Mike Piazza)	.60
273	Fantasy Team '95 (Mo Vaughn)	.05
274	Fantasy Team '95 (Craig Biggio)	.05
275	Fantasy Team '95 (Edgar Martinez)	.05
276	Fantasy Team '95 (Barry Larkin)	.05
277	Fantasy Team '95 (Sammy Sosa)	.50
278	Fantasy Team '95 (Dante Bichette)	.05
279	Fantasy Team '95 (Albert Belle)	.05
280	Ozzie Smith	.75
281	Mark Sweeney	.05
282	Terry Bradshaw	.05
283	Allen Battle	.05
284	Danny Jackson	.05
285	Tom Henke	.05
286	Scott Cooper	.05
287	Tripp Cromer	.05
288	Bernard Gilkey	.05
289	Brian Jordan	.05
290	Tony Gwynn	.75
291	Brad Ausmus	.05
292	Bryce Florie	.05
293	Andres Berumen	.05
294	Ken Caminiti	.05
295	Bip Roberts	.05
296	Trevor Hoffman	.05
297	Roberto Petagine	.05
298	Jody Reed	.05
299	Fernando Valenzuela	.05
300	Barry Bonds	2.00
301	Mark Leiter	.05
302	Mark Carreon	.05
303	Royce Clayton	.05
304	Kirt Manwaring	.05
305	Glenallen Hill	.05
306	Deion Sanders	.10
307	Joe Rosselli	.05
308	Robby Thompson	.05
309	William Van Landingham	.05
310	Ken Griffey Jr.	1.00
311	Bobby Ayala	.05
312	Joey Cora	.05
313	Mike Blowers	.05
314	Darren Bragg	.05
315	Randy Johnson	.60
316	Alex Rodriguez	1.50
317	Andy Benes	.05
318	Tino Martinez	.05
319	Dan Wilson	.05
320	Will Clark	.05
321	Jeff Frye	.05
322	Benji Gil	.05
323	Rick Helling	.05
324	Mark McLemore	.05
325	Dave Nilsson (International Flavor)	.05
326	Larry Walker (International Flavor)	.05
327	Jose Canseco (International Flavor)	.15
328	Raul Mondesi (International Flavor)	.05
329	Manny Ramirez (International Flavor)	.30
330	Robert Eenhoorn (International Flavor)	.05
331	Chili Davis (International Flavor)	.05
332	Hideo Nomo (International Flavor)	.15
333	Benji Gil (International Flavor)	.05
334	Fernando Valenzuela (International Flavor)	.05
335	Dennis Martinez (International Flavor)	.05
336	Roberto Kelly (International Flavor)	.05
337	Carlos Baerga (International Flavor)	.05
338	Juan Gonzalez (International Flavor)	.15
339	Roberto Alomar (International Flavor)	.10
340	Chan Ho Park (International Flavor)	.05
341	Andres Galarraga (International Flavor)	.05
342	Midre Cummings (International Flavor)	.05
343	Otis Nixon	.05
344	Jeff Russell	.05
345	Ivan Rodriguez	.50
346	Mickey Tettleton	.05
347	Bob Tewksbury	.05
348	Domingo Cedeno	.05
349	Lance Parrish	.05
350	Joe Carter	.05
351	Devon White	.05
352	Carlos Delgado	.35
353	Alex Gonzalez	.05
354	Darren Hall	.05
355	Paul Molitor	.60
356	Al Leiter	.05
357	Randy Knorr	.05
358	Checklist 1-46 (12-player Astros-Padres trade)	.05
359	Checklist 47-92 (Hideo Nomo)	.15
360	Checklist 93-138 (Ramon Martinez)	.05
361	Checklist 139-184 (Robin Ventura)	.05
362	Checklist 185-230 (Cal Ripken Jr.)	.30
363	Checklist 231-275 (Ken Caminiti)	.05
364	Checklist 276-320 (Eddie Murray)	.20
365	Checklist 321-365 (Randy Johnson)	.15
366	A.L. Divisional Series (Tony Pena)	.10
367	A.L. Divisional Series (Jim Thome)	.25
368	A.L. Divisional Series (Don Mattingly)	.60
369	A.L. Divisional Series (Jim Leyritz)	.10
370	A.L. Divisional Series (Ken Griffey Jr.)	.60
371	A.L. Divisional Series (Edgar Martinez)	.10
372	N.L. Divisional Series (Pete Schourek)	.10
373	N.L. Divisional Series (Mark Lewis)	.10
374	N.L. Divisonal Series (Chipper Jones)	.50
375	N.L. Divisonal Series (Fred McGriff)	.10
376	N.L. Championship Series (Javy Lopez)	.10
377	N.L. Championship Series (Fred McGriff)	.10
378	N.L. Championship Series (Charlie O'Brien)	.10
379	N.L. Championship Series (Mike Devereaux)	.10
380	N.L. Championship Series (Mark Wohlers)	.10
381	A.L. Championship Series (Bob Wolcott)	.10
382	A.L. Championship Series (Manny Ramirez)	.25
383	A.L. Championship Series (Jay Buhner)	.10
384	A.L. Championship Series (Orel Hershiser)	.10
385	A.L. Championship Series (Kenny Lofton)	.10
386	World Series (Greg Maddux)	.50
387	World Series (Javy Lopez)	.10
388	World Series (Kenny Lofton)	.10
389	World Series (Eddie Murray)	.10
390	World Series (Luis Polonia)	.10
391	World Series (Pedro Borbon)	.10
392	World Series (Jim Thome)	.25
393	World Series (Orel Hershiser)	.10
394	World Series (David Justice)	.10
395	World Series (Tom Glavine)	.10
396	Braves Team Checklist (Greg Maddux)	.25
397	Mets Team Checklist (Brett Butler)	.05
398	Phillies Team Checklist (Darren Daulton)	.05
399	Marlins Team Checklist (Gary Sheffield)	.05
400	Expos Team Checklist (Moises Alou)	.05
401	Reds Team Checklist (Barry Larkin)	.05
402	Astros Team Checklist (Jeff Bagwell)	.20
403	Cubs Team Checklist (Sammy Sosa)	.35
404	Cardinals Team Checklist (Ozzie Smith)	.25
405	Pirates Team Checklist (Jeff King)	.05
406	Dodgers Team Checklist (Mike Piazza)	.50
407	Rockies Team Checklist (Dante Bichette)	.05
408	Padres Team Checklist (Tony Gwynn)	.25
409	Giants Team Checklist (Barry Bonds)	.45
410	Indians Team Checklist (Kenny Lofton)	.05
411	Royals Team Checklist (Jon Nunnally)	.05
412	White Sox Team Checklist (Frank Thomas)	.20
413	Brewers Team Checklist (Greg Vaughn)	.05
414	Twins Team Checklist (Paul Molitor)	.20
415	Mariners Team Checklist (Ken Griffey Jr.)	.35
416	Angels Team Checklist (Jim Edmonds)	.05
417	Rangers Team Checklist (Juan Gonzalez)	.15
418	Athletics Team Checklist (Mark McGwire)	.75
419	Red Sox Team Checklist (Roger Clemens)	.30
420	Yankees Team Checklist (Wade Boggs)	.35
421	Orioles Team Checklist (Cal Ripken Jr.)	.40
422	Tigers Team Checklist (Cecil Fielder)	.05
423	Blue Jays Team Checklist (Joe Carter)	.05
424	Osvaldo Fernandez **RC** (Rookie Class)	.15

425 Billy Wagner (Rookie Class) .05
426 George Arias (Rookie Class) .05
427 Mendy Lopez (Rookie Class) .05
428 Jeff Suppan (Rookie Class) .05
429 Rey Ordonez (Rookie Class) .05
430 Brooks Kieschnick (Rookie Class) .05
431 Raul Ibanez **RC** (Rookie Class) .05
432 Livan Hernandez **RC** (Rookie Class) .20
433 Shannon Stewart (Rookie Class) .05
434 Steve Cox (Rookie Class) .05
435 Trey Beamon (Rookie Class) .05
436 Sergio Nunez (Rookie Class) .05
437 Jermaine Dye (Rookie Class) .05
438 Mike Sweeney **RC** (Rookie Class) .45
439 Richard Hidalgo (Rookie Class) .05
440 Todd Greene (Rookie Class) .05
441 Robert Smith **RC** (Rookie Class) .05
442 Rafael Orellano (Rookie Class) .05
443 Wilton Guerrero **RC** (Rookie Class) .05
444 David Doster **RC** (Rookie Class) .05
445 Jason Kendall (Rookie Class) .05
446 Edgar Renteria (Rookie Class) .05
447 Scott Spiezio (Rookie Class) .05
448 Jay Canizaro (Rookie Class) .05
449 Enrique Wilson (Rookie Class) .05
450 Bob Abreu (Rookie Class) .10
451 Dwight Smith .05
452 Jeff Blauser .05
453 Steve Avery .05
454 Brad Clontz .05
455 Tom Glavine .20
456 Mike Mordecai .05
457 Rafael Belliard .05
458 Greg McMichael .05
459 Pedro Borbon .05
460 Ryan Klesko .05
461 Terrell Wade .05
462 Brady Anderson .05
463 Roberto Alomar .20
464 Bobby Bonilla .05
465 Mike Mussina .40
466 Cesar Devarez **RC** .05
467 Jeffrey Hammonds .05
468 Mike Devereaux .05
469 B.J. Surhoff .05
470 Rafael Palmeiro .50
471 John Valentin .05
472 Mike Greenwell .05
473 Dwayne Hosey .05
474 Tim Wakefield .05
475 Jose Canseco .35
476 Aaron Sele .05
477 Stan Belinda .05
478 Mike Stanley .05
479 Jamie Moyer .05
480 Mo Vaughn .05
481 Randy Velarde .05
482 Gary DiSarcina .05
483 Jorge Fabregas .05
484 Rex Hudler .05
485 Chuck Finley .05
486 Tim Wallach .05
487 Eduardo Perez .05
488 Scott Sanderson .05
489 J.T. Snow .05
490 Sammy Sosa .75
491 Terry Adams .05
492 Matt Franco .05
493 Scott Servais .05
494 Frank Castillo .05
495 Ryne Sandberg .75
496 Rey Sanchez .05
497 Steve Trachsel .05
498 Jose Hernandez .05
499 Dave Martinez .05
500 Babe Ruth (First Class) 1.00
501 Ty Cobb (First Class) .50
502 Walter Johnson (First Class) .10
503 Christy Mathewson (First Class) .10
504 Honus Wagner (First Class) .25
505 Robin Ventura .05
506 Jason Bere .05
507 Mike Cameron **RC** .25
508 Ron Karkovice .05
509 Matt Karchner .05
510 Harold Baines .05
511 Kirk McCaskill .05
512 Larry Thomas .05
513 Danny Tartabull .05
514 Steve Gibralter .05
515 Bret Boone .05
516 Jeff Branson .05
517 Kevin Jarvis .05
518 Xavier Hernandez .05
519 Eric Owens .05
520 Barry Larkin .05
521 Dave Burba .05
522 John Smiley .05
523 Paul Assenmacher .05
524 Chad Ogea .05
525 Orel Hershiser .05
526 Alan Embree .05
527 Tony Pena .05
528 Omar Vizquel .05
529 Mark Clark .05
530 Albert Belle .05
531 Charles Nagy .05
532 Herbert Perry .05
533 Darren Holmes .05
534 Ellis Burks .05
535 Bill Swift .05
536 Armando Reynoso .05
537 Curtis Leskanic .05
538 Quinton McCracken .05
539 Steve Reed .05
540 Larry Walker .05
541 Walt Weiss .05
542 Bryan Rekar .05
543 Tony Clark .05
544 Steve Rodriguez .05
545 C.J. Nitkowski .05
546 Todd Steverson .05
547 Jose Lima .05
548 Phil Nevin .05
549 Chris Gomez .05
550 Travis Fryman .05
551 Mark Lewis .05
552 Alex Arias .05
553 Marc Valdes .05
554 Kevin Brown .05
555 Jeff Conine .05
556 John Burkett .05
557 Devon White .05
558 Pat Rapp .05
559 Jay Powell .05
560 Gary Sheffield .30
561 Jim Dougherty .05
562 Todd Jones .05
563 Tony Eusebio .05
564 Darryl Kile .05
565 Doug Drabek .05
566 Mike Simms .05
567 Derrick May .05
568 Donne Wall **RC** .05
569 Greg Swindell .05
570 Jim Pittsley .05
571 Bob Hamelin .05
572 Mark Gubicza .05
573 Chris Haney .05
574 Keith Lockhart .05
575 Mike Macfarlane .05
576 Les Norman .05
577 Joe Randa .05
578 Chris Stynes .05
579 Greg Gagne .05
580 Raul Mondesi .05
581 Delino DeShields .05
582 Pedro Astacio .05
583 Antonio Osuna .05
584 Brett Butler .05
585 Todd Worrell .05
586 Mike Blowers .05
587 Felix Rodriguez .05
588 Ismael Valdes .05
589 Ricky Bones .05
590 Greg Vaughn .05
591 Mark Loretta .05
592 Cal Eldred .05
593 Chuck Carr .05
594 Dave Nilsson .05
595 John Jaha .05
596 Scott Karl .05
597 Pat Listach .05
598 Jose Valentin **RC** .05
599 Mike Trombley .05
600 Paul Molitor .60
601 Dave Hollins .05
602 Ron Coomer .05
603 Matt Walbeck .05
604 Roberto Kelly .05
605 Rick Aguilera .05
606 Pat Mahomes .05
607 Jeff Reboulet .05
608 Rich Becker .05
609 Tim Scott .05
610 Pedro J. Martinez .60
611 Kirk Rueter .05
612 Tavo Alvarez .05
613 Yamil Benitez .05
614 Darrin Fletcher .05
615 Mike Lansing .05
616 Henry Rodriguez .05
617 Tony Tarasco .05
618 Alex Ochoa .05
619 Tim Bogar .05
620 Bernard Gilkey .05
621 Dave Mlicki .05
622 Brent Mayne .05
623 Ryan Thompson .05
624 Pete Harnisch .05
625 Lance Johnson .05
626 Jose Vizcaino .05
627 Doug Henry .05
628 Scott Kamieniecki .05
629 Jim Leyritz .05
630 Ruben Sierra .05
631 Pat Kelly .05
632 Joe Girardi .05
633 John Wetteland .05
634 Melido Perez .05
635 Paul O'Neill .05
636 Jorge Posada .05
637 Bernie Williams .05
638 Mark Acre .05
639 Mike Bordick .05
640 Mark McGwire 1.50
641 Fausto Cruz .05
642 Ernie Young .05
643 Todd Van Poppel .05
644 Craig Paquette .05
645 Brent Gates .05
646 Pedro Munoz .05
647 Andrew Lorraine .05
648 Sid Fernandez .05
649 Jim Eisenreich .05
650 Johnny Damon (Arizona Fall League) .30
651 Dustin Hermanson (Arizona Fall League) .05
652 Joe Randa (Arizona Fall League) .05
653 Michael Tucker (Arizona Fall League) .05
654 Alan Benes (Arizona Fall League) .05
655 Chad Fonville (Arizona Fall League) .05
656 David Bell (Arizona Fall League) .05
657 Jon Nunnally (Arizona Fall League) .05
658 Chan Ho Park (Arizona Fall League) .05
659 LaTroy Hawkins (Arizona Fall League) .05
660 Jamie Brewington (Arizona Fall League) .05
661 Quinton McCracken (Arizona Fall League) .05
662 Tim Unroe (Arizona Fall League) .05
663 Jeff Ware (Arizona Fall League) .05
664 Todd Greene (Arizona Fall League) .05
665 Andrew Lorraine (Arizona Fall League) .05
666 Ernie Young (Arizona Fall League) .05
667 Toby Borland .05
668 Lenny Webster .05
669 Benito Santiago .05
670 Gregg Jefferies .05
671 Darren Daulton .05
672 Curt Schilling .25
673 Mark Whiten .05
674 Todd Zeile .05
675 Jay Bell .05
676 Paul Wagner .05
677 Dave Clark .05
678 Nelson Liriano .05
679 Ramon Morel .05
680 Charlie Hayes .05
681 Angelo Encaracion .05
682 Al Martin .05
683 Jacob Brumfield .05
684 Mike Kingery .05
685 Carlos Garcia .05
686 Tom Pagnozzi .05
687 David Bell .05
688 Todd Stottlemyre .05
689 Jose Oliva .05
690 Ray Lankford .05
691 Mike Morgan .05
692 John Frascatore .05
693 John Mabry .05
694 Mark Petkovsek .05
695 Alan Benes .05
696 Steve Finley .05
697 Marc Newfield .05
698 Andy Ashby .05
699 Marc Kroon .05
700 Wally Joyner .05
701 Joey Hamilton .05
702 Dustin Hermanson .05
703 Scott Sanders .05
704 Marty Cordova (Award Win.-ROY) .05
705 Hideo Nomo (Award Win.-ROY) .15
706 Mo Vaughn (Award Win.-MVP) .05
707 Barry Larkin (Award Win.-MVP) .05
708 Randy Johnson (Award Win.-CY) .20
709 Greg Maddux (Award Win.-CY) .35
710 Mark McGwire (Award-Comeback) .75
711 Ron Gant (Award-Comeback) .05
712 Andujar Cedeno .05
713 Brian Johnson .05
714 J.R. Phillips .05
715 Rod Beck .05
716 Sergio Valdez .05
717 Marvin Benard **RC** .25
718 Steve Scarsone .05
719 Rich Aurilia **RC** .10
720 Matt Williams .05
721 John Patterson .05
722 Shawn Estes .05
723 Russ Davis .05
724 Rich Amaral .05
725 Edgar Martinez .05
726 Norm Charlton .05
727 Paul Sorrento .05
728 Luis Sojo .05
729 Arquimedez Pozo .05
730 Jay Buhner .05
731 Chris Bosio .05
732 Chris Widger .05
733 Kevin Gross .05
734 Darren Oliver .05
735 Dean Palmer .05
736 Matt Whiteside .05
737 Luis Ortiz .05
738 Roger Pavlik .05
739 Damon Buford .05
740 Juan Gonzalez .30
741 Rusty Greer .05
742 Lou Frazier .05
743 Pat Hentgen .05
744 Tomas Perez .05
745 Juan Guzman .05
746 Otis Nixon .05
747 Robert Perez .05
748 Ed Sprague .05
749 Tony Castillo .05
750 John Olerud .05
751 Shawn Green .10
752 Jeff Ware .05
753 Checklist 396-441/Blake St. Bombers (Dante Bichette, Larry Walker, Andres Galarraga, Vinny Castilla) .05
754 Checklist 442-487 (Greg Maddux) .25
755 Checklist 488-533 (Marty Cordova) .05
756 Checklist 534-579 (Ozzie Smith) .35
757 Checklist 580-625 (John Vander Wal) .05
758 Checklist 626-670 (Andres Galarraga) .05
759 Checklist 671-715 (Frank Thomas) .20
760 Checklist 716-760 (Tony Gwynn) .25
761 Randy Myers .10
762 Kent Mercker .10
763 David Wells .10
764 Tom Gordon .10
765 Wil Cordero .10
766 Dave Magadan .10
767 Doug Jones .10
768 Kevin Tapani .10
769 Curtis Goodwin .10
770 Julio Franco .10
771 Jack McDowell .10
772 Al Leiter .10
773 Sean Berry .10
774 Bip Roberts .10
775 Jose Offerman .10
776 Ben McDonald .10
777 Dan Serafini .10
778 Ryan McGuire .10
779 Tim Raines .10
780 Tino Martinez .10
781 Kenny Rogers .10
782 Bob Tewksbury .10
783 Rickey Henderson .60
784 Ron Gant .10
785 Gary Gaetti .10
786 Andy Benes .10
787 Royce Clayton .10
788 Darryl Hamilton .10
789 Ken Hill .10
790 Erik Hanson .10

Silver Signature

A silver border instead of white, and a facsimile autograph in silver ink on the card front differentiate these parallel insert cards from the regular-issue Collector's Choice. The inserts are seeded at the rate of one per pack.

	NM/M
Common Player:	.10
Stars:	1.5X

Gold Signature

This insert set parallels each card in the regular Collector's Choice set. Found on

average of one per 35 packs, the cards are nearly identical to the regular version except for the presence of a facsimile autograph in gold ink on the front and gold, instead of white, borders.

	NM/M
Common Player:	1.00
Stars:	10X

A Cut Above

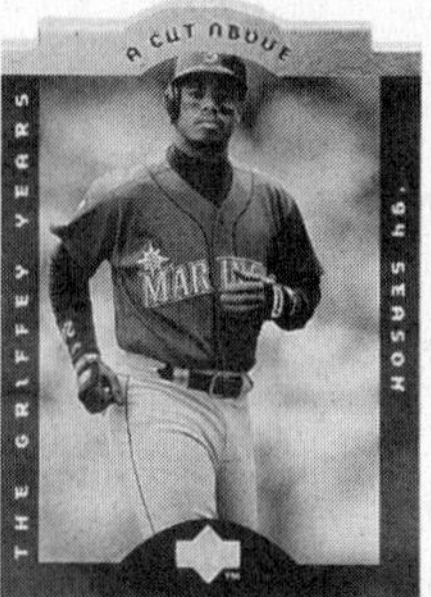

This 10-card set highlights the career of Ken Griffey Jr. The front has a color photo with "The Griffey Years" printed in the left border and a title in the right border. Die-cut gold-foil tops have "A CUT ABOVE" in black. Backs have a portrait photo on a marbled border and a narrative. This set was inserted one per six-card Wal-Mart exclusive pack.

		NM/M
Complete Set (10):		8.00
Common Card:		1.00
CA1	Ken Griffey Jr. (Teenage Rookie)	1.00
CA2	Ken Griffey Jr. (Great Defense)	1.00
CA3	Ken Griffey Jr. (Fun-Loving)	1.00
CA4	Ken Griffey Jr. (All-Star Games)	1.00
CA5	Ken Griffey Jr. ('93 Season)	1.00
CA6	Ken Griffey Jr. ('94 HR Records)	1.00
CA7	Ken Griffey Jr. ('94 Season)	1.00
CA8	Ken Griffey Jr. ('95 Season)	1.00
CA9	Ken Griffey Jr. ('95 Postseason)	1.00
CA10	Ken Griffey Jr. ('96: A Look Ahead)	1.00

Crash the Game

For a second season, UD continued its interactive chase card series, "You Crash the Game." At a ratio of about one per five packs for a silver version and one per 49 packs for a gold version, cards of the game's top sluggers can be found bearing one of three date ranges representing a three- or four-game series in which that player was scheduled to play during the 1996 season. If the player hit a home run during the series shown on the card, the card could be redeemed (for $1.75) by mail for a "Super Premium" wood-and-plastic card of the player. Both silver and gold Crash cards feature silver and red prismatic foil behind the player action photo. Silver versions have the Crash logo, series dates and player ID in silver foil on front; those details are in gold foil on the gold cards. Backs have contest rules printed on a gray (silver) or yellow (gold) background. Card numbers are preceded by a "CG" prefix. Cards were redeemable only until Nov. 25, 1996. Winning cards are indicated with an asterisk; they would be in shorter supply than those which could not be redeemed.

		NM/M
Complete Set (90):		75.00
Common Silver Player:		.50
Golds:		2X
1a	Chipper Jones (July 11-14*)	2.50
1b	Chipper Jones (Aug. 27-29*)	2.50
1c	Chipper Jones (Sept. 19-23)	1.50
2a	Fred McGriff (July 1-3)	.50
2b	Fred McGriff (Aug. 30-Sept. 1)	.50
2c	Fred McGriff (Sept. 10-12*)	1.00
3a	Rafael Palmeiro (July 4-7*)	1.75
3b	Rafael Palmeiro (Aug. 29-Sept. 1)	.75
3c	Rafael Palmeiro (Sept. 26-29)	.75
4a	Cal Ripken Jr. (June 27-30)	2.50
4b	Cal Ripken Jr. (July 25-28*)	5.00
4c	Cal Ripken Jr. (Sept. 2-4)	2.50
5a	Jose Canseco (June 27-30)	.65
5b	Jose Canseco (July 11-14*)	1.50
5c	Jose Canseco (Aug. 23-25)	.65
6a	Mo Vaughn (June 21-23*)	1.00
6b	Mo Vaughn (July 18-21*)	1.00
6c	Mo Vaughn (Sept. 20-22)	.50
7a	Jim Edmonds (July 18-21*)	1.00
7b	Jim Edmonds (Aug. 16-18*)	1.00
7c	Jim Edmonds (Sept. 20-22)	.50
8a	Tim Salmon (June 20-23)	.50
8b	Tim Salmon (July 30-Aug. 1)	.50
8c	Tim Salmon (Sept. 9-12)	.50
9a	Sammy Sosa (July 4-7*)	2.50
9b	Sammy Sosa (Aug. 1-4*)	2.50
9c	Sammy Sosa (Sept. 2-4)	1.50
10a	Frank Thomas (June 27-30)	1.00
10b	Frank Thomas (July 4-7)	1.00
10c	Frank Thomas (Sept. 2-4*)	2.00
11a	Albert Belle (June 25-26)	.50
11b	Albert Belle (Aug. 2-5*)	1.00
11c	Albert Belle (Sept. 6-8)	.50
12a	Manny Ramirez (July 18-21*)	2.00
12b	Manny Ramirez (Aug. 26-28)	1.00
12c	Manny Ramirez (Sept. 9-12*)	2.00
13a	Jim Thome (June 27-30)	.75
13b	Jim Thome (July 4-7*)	1.25
13c	Jim Thome (Sept. 23-25)	.75
14a	Dante Bichette (July 11-14*)	1.00
14b	Dante Bichette (Aug. 9-11)	.50
14c	Dante Bichette (Sept. 9-12)	.50
15a	Vinny Castilla (July 1-3)	.50

15b	Vinny Castilla (Aug. 23-25*)	1.00
15c	Vinny Castilla (Sept. 13-15*)	1.00
16a	Larry Walker (June 24-26)	.50
16b	Larry Walker (July 18-21)	.50
16c	Larry Walker (Sept. 27-29)	.50
17a	Cecil Fielder (June 27-30)	.50
17b	Cecil Fielder (July 30-Aug. 1*)	1.00
17c	Cecil Fielder (Sept. 17-19*)	1.00
18a	Gary Sheffield (July 4-7)	.65
18b	Gary Sheffield (Aug. 2-4)	.65
18c	Gary Sheffield (Sept. 5-8*)	1.50
19a	Jeff Bagwell (July 4-7*)	2.00
19b	Jeff Bagwell (Aug. 16-18)	1.00
19c	Jeff Bagwell (Sept. 13-15)	1.00
20a	Eric Karros (July 4-7*)	1.00
20b	Eric Karros (Aug. 13-15*)	1.00
20c	Eric Karros (Sept. 16-18)	.50
21a	Mike Piazza (June 27-30*)	3.00
21b	Mike Piazza (July 26-28)	1.75
21c	Mike Piazza (Sept. 12-15*)	3.00
22a	Ken Caminiti (July 11-14*)	1.00
22b	Ken Caminiti (Aug. 16-18*)	1.00
22c	Ken Caminiti (Sept. 19-22*)	1.00
23a	Barry Bonds (June 27-30*)	5.00
23b	Barry Bonds (July 22-24)	2.50
23c	Barry Bonds (Sept. 24-26)	2.50
24a	Matt Williams (July 11-14*)	1.00
24b	Matt Williams (Aug. 19-21)	.50
24c	Matt Williams (Sept. 27-29)	.50
25a	Jay Buhner (June 20-23)	.50
25b	Jay Buhner (July 25-28)	.50
25c	Jay Buhner (Aug. 29-Sept. 1*)	1.00
26a	Ken Griffey Jr. (July 18-21*)	3.00
26b	Ken Griffey Jr. (Aug. 16-18*)	3.00
26c	Ken Griffey Jr. (Sept. 20-22*)	3.00
27a	Ron Gant (June 24-27*)	1.00
27b	Ron Gant (July 11-14*)	1.00
27c	Ron Gant (Sept. 27-29*)	1.00
28a	Juan Gonzalez (June 28-30*)	1.25
28b	Juan Gonzalez (July 15-17*)	1.25
28c	Juan Gonzalez (Aug. 6-8)	.60
29a	Mickey Tettleton (July 4-7*)	1.00
29b	Mickey Tettleton (Aug. 6-8)	.50
29c	Mickey Tettleton (Sept. 6-8*)	1.00
30a	Joe Carter (June 25-27)	.50
30b	Joe Carter (Aug. 5-8)	.50
30c	Joe Carter (Sept. 23-25)	.50

Crash Winners

Collectors who held "You Crash The Game" insert cards with date ranges on which the pictured player hit a home run could redeem them (for $1.75 per card) for a premium card of that player. The redemption cards have a layer of clear plastic bonded to a wood-laminate front. Within a starburst cutout at center is the player photo with a red background. Cards have a Crash/Game logo in the lower-right corner, in either silver or gold, depending on which winning card was submitted for exchange. Backs have 1995 and career stats along with licensing and copyright data. There were no winning cards of Tim Salmon, Larry Walker or Joe Carter.

		NM/M
Complete Set (27):		35.00
Common Player:		1.00
Golds:		2X
CR1	Chipper Jones	2.50
CR2	Fred McGriff	1.00
CR3	Rafael Palmeiro	1.75
CR4	Cal Ripken Jr.	4.00
CR5	Jose Canseco	1.50
CR6	Mo Vaughn	1.00
CR7	Jim Edmonds	1.00
CR9	Sammy Sosa	2.50
CR10	Frank Thomas	2.00
CR11	Albert Belle	1.00
CR12	Manny Ramirez	2.00
CR13	Jim Thome	1.50
CR14	Dante Bichette	1.00
CR15	Vinny Castilla	1.00
CR17	Cecil Fielder	1.00
CR18	Gary Sheffield	1.50
CR19	Jeff Bagwell	2.00
CR20	Eric Karros	1.00
CR21	Mike Piazza	3.00
CR22	Ken Caminiti	1.00
CR23	Barry Bonds	4.00
CR24	Matt Williams	1.00
CR25	Jay Buhner	1.00
CR26	Ken Griffey Jr.	3.00
CR27	Ron Gant	1.00
CR28	Juan Gonzalez	1.50
CR29	Mickey Tettleton	1.00

Nomo Scrapbook

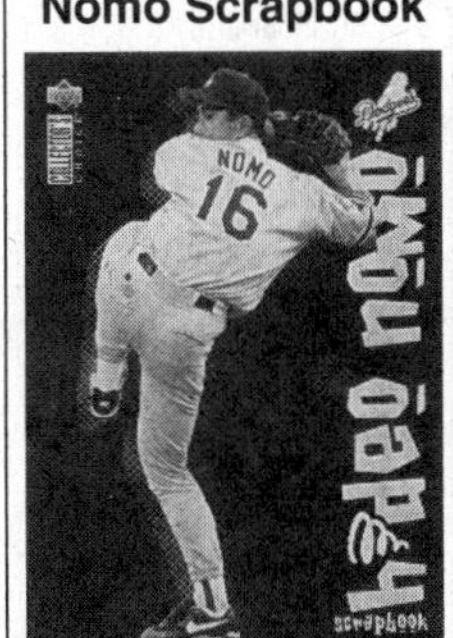

The five-card, regular-sized set was randomly inserted in 1996 Collector's Choice baseball. Fronts depict the Dodgers pitcher in action with his name in atypical lower-case type up the right border. Backs feature in-depth text below Nomo's name. A version featuring Japanese text was issued in Japan.

		NM/M
Complete Set (5):		10.00
Common Card:		2.00
Japanese:		3X
1-5	Hideo Nomo	2.00

Ripken Collection

The 23-card, regular-sized Cal Ripken Collection was randomly inserted in various Upper Deck baseball releases in 1996. Cards #1-4 were found in Series 1 Collector's Choice; cards 5-8 were found in Upper Deck Series 1; cards 9-12 in Collector's Choice Series 2; cards 13-17 in Upper Deck Series 2; cards 18-22 in SP baseball and the header card in Collector's Choice.

	NM/M
Complete Set (1-4, 9-12)	15.00
Common Card:	2.50
Header Card:	2.00

Cal Ripken Jr. Jumbo

This 5" x 3-1/2" card is a virtual parallel to the #1 card in the multi-brand Ripken set which was issued to mark his career to the point of his 2,131st consecutive game. This version, however, was sold only through a television shopping program. The front has a silver facsimile autograph. On back is a "Limited Edition" seal and a serial number within an edition of 21,310.

		NM/M
1	Cal Ripken Jr.	5.00

You Make the Play

This insert series of interactive game cards was packaged with Series 1 Collector's Choice. Each player's card can be found with one of two play outcomes printed thereon, which are then used to play a baseball card game utilizing a playing field and scorecard found on box bottoms. Regular versions of the cards are seeded one per pack, while gold-signature versions are found one per 36 packs.

		NM/M
Complete Set (45):		60.00
Common Player:		.50
Gold:		4X
1a	Kevin Appier (Strike out.)	.50
1b	Kevin Appier (Pick off)	.50
2a	Carlos Baerga (Home run.)	.50
2b	Carlos Baerga (Ground out.)	.50
3a	Jeff Bagwell (Walk)	1.00
3b	Jeff Bagwell (Strike out.)	1.00
4a	Jay Bell (Sacrifice)	.50
4b	Jay Bell (Walk)	.50
5a	Albert Belle (Fly out.)	.50
5b	Albert Belle (Home run.)	.50
6a	Craig Biggio (Single)	.50
6b	Craig Biggio (Strike out.)	.50
7a	Wade Boggs (Single)	1.50
7b	Wade Boggs (Ground out.)	1.50
8a	Barry Bonds (Strike out.)	3.00
8b	Barry Bonds (Reach on error.)	3.00
9a	Bobby Bonilla (Walk)	.50
9b	Bobby Bonilla (Strike out.)	.50
10a	Jose Canseco (Strike out.)	.75
10b	Jose Canseco (Double)	.75
11a	Joe Carter (Double)	.50
11b	Joe Carter (Fly out.)	.50
12a	Darren Daulton (Ground out.)	.50
12b	Darren Daulton (Catcher's interference.)	.50
13a	Cecil Fielder (Stolen base.)	.50
13b	Cecil Fielder (Home run.)	.50
14a	Ron Gant (Home run.)	.50
14b	Ron Gant (Fly out.)	.50
15a	Juan Gonzalez (Double)	.65
15b	Juan Gonzalez (Fly out)	.65
16a	Ken Griffey Jr. (Home run.)	2.00
16b	Ken Griffey Jr. (Hit by pitch.)	2.00
17a	Tony Gwynn (Single)	1.50
17b	Tony Gwynn (Ground out.)	1.50
18a	Randy Johnson (Strike out.)	1.00
18b	Randy Johnson (K - reach on wild pitch.)	1.00
19a	Chipper Jones (Walk)	1.50
19b	Chipper Jones (Strike out.)	1.50
20a	Barry Larkin (Ground out.)	.50
20b	Barry Larkin (Stolen base.)	.50
21a	Kenny Lofton (Triple)	.50
21b	Kenny Lofton (Stolen base.)	.50
22a	Greg Maddux (Single)	1.50
22b	Greg Maddux (Strike out.)	1.50
23a	Don Mattingly (Fly out.)	1.75
23b	Don Mattingly (Double)	1.75
24a	Fred McGriff (Double)	.50
24b	Fred McGriff (Home run.)	.50
25a	Mark McGwire (Strike out.)	2.50
25b	Mark McGwire (Home run.)	2.50
26a	Paul Molitor (Ground out.)	1.00
26b	Paul Molitor (Single)	1.00
27a	Raul Mondesi (Single)	.50
27b	Raul Mondesi (Fly out.)	.50
28a	Eddie Murray (Sacrifice fly.)	1.00
28b	Eddie Murray (Ground out.)	1.00
29a	Hideo Nomo (Strike out.)	.65
29b	Hideo Nomo (Balk)	.65
30a	Jon Nunnally (Single)	.50
30b	Jon Nunnally (Error)	.50
31a	Mike Piazza (Strike out.)	2.00
31b	Mike Piazza (Single)	2.00
32a	Kirby Puckett (Walk)	1.50
32b	Kirby Puckett (Ground out.)	1.50
33a	Cal Ripken Jr. (Home run.)	3.00
33b	Cal Ripken Jr. (Double)	3.00
34a	Alex Rodriguez (Strike out.)	2.50
34b	Alex Rodriguez (Triple)	2.50
35a	Tim Salmon (Sacrifice fly.)	.50
35b	Tim Salmon (Strike out.)	.50
36a	Gary Sheffield (Fly out.)	.65
36b	Gary Sheffield (Single)	.65
37a	Lee Smith (Strike out.)	.50
37b	Lee Smith (Pick off of lead runner.)	.50
38a	Ozzie Smith (Ground out.)	1.50
38b	Ozzie Smith (Single)	1.50
39a	Sammy Sosa (Stolen base.)	1.50
39b	Sammy Sosa (Single)	1.50
40a	Frank Thomas (Walk)	1.00
40b	Frank Thomas (Home run.)	1.00
41a	Greg Vaughn (Sacrifice fly.)	.50
41b	Greg Vaughn (Strike out.)	.50
42a	Mo Vaughn (Hit by Pitch.)	.50
42b	Mo Vaughn (Stolen base.)	.50
43a	Larry Walker (Strike out.)	.50
43b	Larry Walker (Walk)	.50
44a	Rondell White (Triple)	.50
44b	Rondell White (Fly out.)	.50
45a	Matt Williams (Home run.)	.50
45b	Matt Williams (Single)	.50

1997 Collector's Choice

The 506-card, standard-size set contains five subsets: Rookie Class (1-27), Leaders (56-63), Postseason (218-224), Ken Griffey Jr. Checklists (244-249) and Griffey Hot List (325-334). Insert sets are: All-Star Connection, Big Shots, Stick'Ums, Premier Power, Clearly Dominant, The Big Show. Toast of the Town and New Frontier. Basic card fronts feature a color action shot with the player's name appearing on the bottom edge. The team logo is located in the lower-left corner and each card features a white border. Backs contain another action shot on the upper half with biography, and career/season stats. The cards were issued in 12-card packs retailing for 99 cents. A factory set was issued that includes 10 Premier Power jumbo cards.

		NM/M
Factory Set (516):		16.00
Complete Set (506):		12.00
Common Player:		.05
Pack (12):		1.00
Wax Box (36):		20.00
1	Andruw Jones (Rookie Class)	1.00
2	Rocky Coppinger (Rookie Class)	.05
3	Jeff D'Amico (Rookie Class)	.05
4	Dmitri Young (Rookie Class)	.05
5	Darin Erstad (Rookie Class)	.75
6	Jermaine Allensworth (Rookie Class)	.05
7	Damian Jackson (Rookie Class)	.05
8	Bill Mueller (Rookie Class)	.05
9	Jacob Cruz (Rookie Class)	.05
10	Vladimir Guerrero (Rookie Class)	1.00
11	Marty Janzen (Rookie Class)	.05
12	Kevin L. Brown (Rookie Class)	.05
13	Willie Adams (Rookie Class)	.05
14	Wendell Magee (Rookie Class)	.05
15	Scott Rolen (Rookie Class)	.65
16	Matt Beech (Rookie Class)	.05
17	Neifi Perez (Rookie Class)	.05
18	Jamey Wright (Rookie Class)	.05
19	Jose Paniagua (Rookie Class)	.05
20	Todd Walker (Rookie Class)	.05
21	Justin Thompson (Rookie Class)	.05
22	Robin Jennings (Rookie Class)	.05
23	Dario Veras **RC** (Rookie Class)	.05
24	Brian Lesher (Rookie Class)	.05
25	Nomar Garciaparra (Rookie Class)	1.25
26	Luis Castillo (Rookie Class)	.05
27	Brian Giles **RC** (Rookie Class)	.75
28	Jermaine Dye	.05
29	Terrell Wade	.05
30	Fred McGriff	.05
31	Marquis Grissom	.05
32	Ryan Klesko	.05
33	Javier Lopez	.05
34	Mark Wohlers	.05
35	Tom Glavine	.25
36	Denny Neagle	.05
37	Scott Erickson	.05
38	Chris Hoiles	.05
39	Roberto Alomar	.25
40	Eddie Murray	.75
41	Cal Ripken Jr.	2.00
42	Randy Myers	.05
43	B.J. Surhoff	.05
44	Rick Krivda	.05
45	Jose Canseco	.50
46	Heathcliff Slocumb	.05
47	Jeff Suppan	.05
48	Tom Gordon	.05
49	Aaron Sele	.05
50	Mo Vaughn	.05
51	Darren Bragg	.05
52	Wil Cordero	.05
53	Scott Bullett	.05
54	Terry Adams	.05
55	Jackie Robinson	.35
56	Tony Gwynn, Alex Rodriguez (Batting Leaders)	.35
57	Andres Galarraga, Mark McGwire (Homer Leaders)	.50
58	Andres Galarraga, Albert Belle (RBI Leaders)	.05
59	Eric Young, Kenny Lofton (SB Leaders)	.05
60	John Smoltz, Andy Pettitte (Victory Leaders)	.05
61	John Smoltz, Roger Clemens (Strikout Leaders)	.20
62	Kevin Brown, Juan Guzman (ERA Leaders)	.05
63	John Wetteland, Todd Worrell, Jeff Brantley (Save Leaders)	.05
64	Scott Servais	.05
65	Sammy Sosa	1.00
66	Ryne Sandberg	1.00
67	Frank Castillo	.05
68	Rey Sanchez	.05
69	Steve Trachsel	.05
70	Robin Ventura	.05
71	Wilson Alvarez	.05
72	Tony Phillips	.05
73	Lyle Mouton	.05
74	Mike Cameron	.05
75	Harold Baines	.05
76	Albert Belle	.05
77	Chris Snopek	.05
78	Reggie Sanders	.05
79	Jeff Brantley	.05
80	Barry Larkin	.05
81	Kevin Jarvis	.05
82	John Smiley	.05
83	Pete Schourek	.05
84	Thomas Howard	.05
85	Lee Smith	.05
86	Omar Vizquel	.05
87	Julio Franco	.05
88	Orel Hershiser	.05
89	Charles Nagy	.05
90	Matt Williams	.05
91	Dennis Martinez	.05
92	Jose Mesa	.05
93	Sandy Alomar Jr.	.05
94	Jim Thome	.50
95	Vinny Castilla	.05
96	Armando Reynoso	.05
97	Kevin Ritz	.05
98	Larry Walker	.05
99	Eric Young	.05
100	Dante Bichette	.05
101	Quinton McCracken	.05
102	John Vander Wal	.05
103	Phil Nevin	.05
104	Tony Clark	.05
105	Alan Trammell	.05
106	Felipe Lira	.05
107	Curtis Pride	.05
108	Bobby Higginson	.05
109	Mark Lewis	.05
110	Travis Fryman	.05
111	Al Leiter	.05
112	Devon White	.05
113	Jeff Conine	.05
114	Charles Johnson	.05
115	Andre Dawson	.25
116	Edgar Renteria	.05
117	Robb Nen	.05
118	Kevin Brown	.05
119	Derek Bell	.05
120	Bob Abreu	.10
121	Mike Hampton	.05
122	Todd Jones	.05
123	Billy Wagner	.05
124	Shane Reynolds	.05
125	Jeff Bagwell	.75
126	Brian L. Hunter	.05
127	Jeff Montgomery	.05
128	Rod Myers **RC**	.05
129	Tim Belcher	.05
130	Kevin Appier	.05
131	Mike Sweeney	.05
132	Craig Paquette	.05

133 Joe Randa .05
134 Michael Tucker .05
135 Raul Mondesi .05
136 Tim Wallach .05
137 Brett Butler .05
138 Karim Garcia .10
139 Todd Hollandsworth .05
140 Eric Karros .05
141 Hideo Nomo .40
142 Ismael Valdes .05
143 Cal Eldred .05
144 Scott Karl .05
145 Matt Mieske .05
146 Mike Fetters .05
147 Mark Loretta .05
148 Fernando Vina .05
149 Jeff Cirillo .05
150 Dave Nilsson .05
151 Kirby Puckett 1.00
152 Rich Becker .05
153 Chuck Knoblauch .05
154 Marty Cordova .05
155 Paul Molitor .75
156 Rick Aguilera .05
157 Pat Meares .05
158 Frank Rodriguez .05
159 David Segui .05
160 Henry Rodriguez .05
161 Shane Andrews .05
162 Pedro J. Martinez .75
163 Mark Grudzielanek .05
164 Mike Lansing .05
165 Rondell White .05
166 Ugueth Urbina .05
167 Rey Ordonez .05
168 Robert Person .05
169 Carlos Baerga .05
170 Bernard Gilkey .05
171 John Franco .05
172 Pete Harnisch .05
173 Butch Huskey .05
174 Paul Wilson .05
175 Bernie Williams .05
176 Dwight Gooden .05
177 Wade Boggs 1.00
178 Ruben Rivera .05
179 Jim Leyritz .05
180 Derek Jeter 2.00
181 Tino Martinez .05
182 Tim Raines .05
183 Scott Brosius .05
184 Jason Giambi .60
185 Geronimo Berroa .05
186 Ariel Prieto .05
187 Scott Spiezio .05
188 John Wasdin .05
189 Ernie Young .05
190 Mark McGwire 1.50
191 Jim Eisenreich .05
192 Ricky Bottalico .05
193 Darren Daulton .05
194 David Doster .05
195 Gregg Jefferies .05
196 Lenny Dykstra .05
197 Curt Schilling .20
198 Todd Stottlemyre .05
199 Willie McGee .05
200 Ozzie Smith 1.00
201 Dennis Eckersley .65
202 Ray Lankford .05
203 John Mabry .05
204 Alan Benes .05
205 Ron Gant .05
206 Archi Cianfrocco .05
207 Fernando Valenzuela .05
208 Greg Vaughn .05
209 Steve Finley .05
210 Tony Gwynn 1.00
211 Rickey Henderson .75
212 Trevor Hoffman .05
213 Jason Thompson .05
214 Osvaldo Fernandez .05
215 Glenallen Hill .05
216 William Van Landingham .05
217 Marvin Benard .05
218 Juan Gonzalez (Postseason) .10
219 Roberto Alomar (Postseason) .05
220 Brian Jordan (Postseason) .05
221 John Smoltz (Postseason) .05
222 Javy Lopez (Postseason) .05
223 Bernie Williams (Postseason) .05
224 Jim Leyritz, John Wetteland (Postseason) .05
225 Barry Bonds 2.00
226 Rich Aurilia .05
227 Jay Canizaro .05
228 Dan Wilson .05
229 Bob Wolcott .05
230 Ken Griffey Jr. 1.25
231 Sterling Hitchcock .05
232 Edgar Martinez .05
233 Joey Cora .05
234 Norm Charlton .05
235 Alex Rodriguez 1.50
236 Bobby Witt .05
237 Darren Oliver .05
238 Kevin Elster .05
239 Rusty Greer .05
240 Juan Gonzalez .40
241 Will Clark .05
242 Dean Palmer .05
243 Ivan Rodriguez .65
244 Checklist (Ken Griffey Jr.) .25
245 Checklist (Ken Griffey Jr.) .25
246 Checklist (Ken Griffey Jr.) .25
247 Checklist (Ken Griffey Jr.) .25
248 Checklist (Ken Griffey Jr.) .25
249 Checklist (Ken Griffey Jr.) .25
250 Eddie Murray .75
251 Troy Percival .05
252 Garret Anderson .05
253 Allen Watson .05
254 Jason Dickson .05
255 Jim Edmonds .05
256 Chuck Finley .05
257 Randy Velarde .05
258 Shigetosi Hasegawa .05
259 Todd Greene .05
260 Tim Salmon .05
261 Mark Langston .05
262 Dave Hollins .05
263 Gary DiSarcina .05
264 Kenny Lofton .05
265 John Smoltz .05
266 Greg Maddux 1.00
267 Jeff Blauser .05
268 Alan Embree .05
269 Mark Lemke .05
270 Chipper Jones 1.00
271 Mike Mussina .65
272 Rafael Palmeiro .65
273 Jimmy Key .05
274 Mike Bordick .05
275 Brady Anderson .05
276 Eric Davis .05
277 Jeffrey Hammonds .05
278 Reggie Jefferson .05
279 Tim Naehring .05
280 John Valentin .05
281 Troy O'Leary .05
282 Shane Mack .05
283 Mike Stanley .05
284 Tim Wakefield .05
285 Brian McRae .05
286 Brooks Kieschnick .05
287 Shawon Dunston .05
288 Kevin Foster .05
289 Mel Rojas .05
290 Mark Grace .05
291 Brant Brown .05
292 Amaury Telemaco .05
293 Dave Martinez .05
294 Jaime Navarro .05
295 Ray Durham .05
296 Ozzie Guillen .05
297 Roberto Hernandez .05
298 Ron Karkovice .05
299 James Baldwin .05
300 Frank Thomas .75
301 Eddie Taubensee .05
302 Bret Boone .05
303 Willie Greene .05
304 Dave Burba .05
305 Deion Sanders .10
306 Reggie Sanders .05
307 Hal Morris .05
308 Pokey Reese .05
309 Tony Fernandez .05
310 Manny Ramirez .75
311 Chad Ogea .05
312 Jack McDowell .05
313 Kevin Mitchell .05
314 Chad Curtis .05
315 Steve Kline .05
316 Kevin Seitzer .05
317 Kirt Manwaring .05
318 Bill Swift .05
319 Ellis Burks .05
320 Andres Galarraga .05
321 Bruce Ruffin .05
322 Mark Thompson .05
323 Walt Weiss .05
324 Todd Jones .05
325 Andruw Jones (Griffey Hot List) .50
326 Chipper Jones (Griffey Hot List) .65
327 Mo Vaughn (Griffey Hot List) .05
328 Frank Thomas (Griffey Hot List) .50
329 Albert Belle (Griffey Hot List) .10
330 Mark McGwire (Griffey Hot List) 1.00
331 Derek Jeter (Griffey Hot List) 1.50
332 Alex Rodriguez (Griffey Hot List) 1.00
333 Jay Buhner (Griffey Hot List) .05
334 Ken Griffey Jr. (Griffey Hot List) .75
335 Brian L. Hunter .05
336 Brian Johnson .05
337 Omar Olivares .05
338 Deivi Cruz **RC** .05
339 Damion Easley .05
340 Melvin Nieves .05
341 Moises Alou .05
342 Jim Eisenreich .05
343 Mark Hutton .05
344 Alex Fernandez .05
345 Gary Sheffield .35
346 Pat Rapp .05
347 Brad Ausmus .05
348 Sean Berry .05
349 Darryl Kile .05
350 Craig Biggio .05
351 Chris Holt .05
352 Luis Gonzalez .05
353 Pat Listach .05
354 Jose Rosado .05
355 Mike Macfarlane .05
356 Tom Goodwin .05
357 Chris Haney .05
358 Chili Davis .05
359 Jose Offerman .05
360 Johnny Damon .30
361 Bip Roberts .05
362 Ramon Martinez .05
363 Pedro Astacio .05
364 Todd Zeile .05
365 Mike Piazza 1.25
366 Greg Gagne .05
367 Chan Ho Park .05
368 Wilton Guerrero .05
369 Todd Worrell .05
370 John Jaha .05
371 Steve Sparks .05
372 Mike Matheny .05
373 Marc Newfield .05
374 Jeromy Burnitz .05
375 Jose Valentin .05
376 Ben McDonald .05
377 Roberto Kelly .05
378 Bob Tewksbury .05
379 Ron Coomer .05
380 Brad Radke .05
381 Matt Lawton .05
382 Dan Naulty .05
383 Scott Stahoviak .05
384 Matt Wagner .05
385 Jim Bullinger .05
386 Carlos Perez .05
387 Darrin Fletcher .05
388 Chris Widger .05
389 F.P. Santangelo .05
390 Lee Smith .05
391 Bobby Jones .05
392 John Olerud .05
393 Mark Clark .05
394 Jason Isringhausen .05
395 Todd Hundley .05
396 Lance Johnson .05
397 Edgardo Alfonzo .05
398 Alex Ochoa .05
399 Darryl Strawberry .05
400 David Cone .05
401 Paul O'Neill .05
402 Joe Girardi .05
403 Charlie Hayes .05
404 Andy Pettitte .25
405 Mariano Rivera .25
406 Mariano Duncan .05
407 Kenny Rogers .05
408 Cecil Fielder .05
409 George Williams .05
410 Jose Canseco .35
411 Tony Batista .05
412 Steve Karsay .05
413 Dave Telgheder .05
414 Billy Taylor .05
415 Mickey Morandini .05
416 Calvin Maduro .05
417 Mark Leiter .05
418 Kevin Stocker .05
419 Mike Lieberthal .05
420 Rico Brogna .05
421 Mark Portugal .05
422 Rex Hudler .05
423 Mark Johnson .05
424 Esteban Loiaza .05
425 Lou Collier .05
426 Kevin Elster .05
427 Francisco Cordova .05
428 Marc Wilkins .05
429 Joe Randa .05
430 Jason Kendall .05
431 Jon Lieber .05
432 Steve Cooke .05
433 Emil Brown **RC** .05
434 Tony Womack **RC** .25
435 Al Martin .05
436 Jason Schmidt .05
437 Andy Benes .05
438 Delino DeShields .05
439 Royce Clayton .05
440 Brian Jordan .05
441 Donovan Osborne .05
442 Gary Gaetti .05
443 Tom Pagnozzi .05
444 Joey Hamilton .05
445 Wally Joyner .05
446 John Flaherty .05
447 Chris Gomez .05
448 Sterling Hitchcock .05
449 Andy Ashby .05
450 Ken Caminiti .05
451 Tim Worrell .05
452 Jose Vizcaino .05
453 Rod Beck .05
454 Wilson Delgado .05
455 Darryl Hamilton .05
456 Mark Lewis .05
457 Mark Gardner .05
458 Rick Wilkins .05
459 Scott Sanders .05
460 Kevin Orie .05
461 Glendon Rusch .05
462 Juan Melo .05
463 Richie Sexson .05
464 Bartolo Colon .05
465 Jose Guillen .05
466 Heath Murray .05
467 Aaron Boone .05
468 Bubba Trammell **RC** .05
469 Jeff Abbott .05
470 Derrick Gibson .05
471 Matt Morris .05
472 Ryan Jones .05
473 Pat Cline .05
474 Adam Riggs .05
475 Jay Payton .05
476 Derrek Lee .50
477 Elieser Marrero .05
478 Lee Tinsley .05
479 Jamie Moyer .05
480 Jay Buhner .05
481 Bob Wells .05
482 Jeff Fassero .05
483 Paul Sorrento .05
484 Russ Davis .05
485 Randy Johnson .75
486 Roger Pavlik .05
487 Damon Buford .05
488 Julio Santana .05
489 Mark McLemore .05
490 Mickey Tettleton .05
491 Ken Hill .05
492 Benji Gil .05
493 Ed Sprague .05
494 Mike Timlin .05
495 Pat Hentgen .05
496 Orlando Merced .05
497 Carlos Garcia .05
498 Carlos Delgado .35
499 Juan Guzman .05
500 Roger Clemens 1.00
501 Erik Hanson .05
502 Otis Nixon .05
503 Shawn Green .10
504 Charlie O'Brien .05
505 Joe Carter .05
506 Alex Gonzalez .05

All-Star Connection

This 45-card insert from Series 2 highlights All-Star caliber players. Cards feature a large starburst pattern on a metallic-foil background behind the player's photo. They were inserted one per pack.

		NM/M
Complete Set (45):		10.00
Common Player:		.10
1	Mark McGwire	1.00
2	Chuck Knoblauch	.10
3	Jim Thome	.35
4	Alex Rodriguez	1.00
5	Ken Griffey Jr.	.75
6	Brady Anderson	.10
7	Albert Belle	.10
8	Ivan Rodriguez	.40
9	Pat Hentgen	.10
10	Frank Thomas	.50
11	Roberto Alomar	.25
12	Robin Ventura	.10
13	Cal Ripken Jr.	1.50
14	Juan Gonzalez	.25
15	Manny Ramirez	.50
16	Bernie Williams	.10
17	Terry Steinbach	.10
18	Andy Pettitte	.25
19	Jeff Bagwell	.50
20	Craig Biggio	.10
21	Ken Caminiti	.10
22	Barry Larkin	.10
23	Tony Gwynn	.60
24	Barry Bonds	1.50
25	Kenny Lofton	.10
26	Mike Piazza	.75
27	John Smoltz	.10
28	Andres Galarraga	.10
29	Ryne Sandberg	.60
30	Chipper Jones	.60
31	Mark Grudzielanek	.10
32	Sammy Sosa	.60
33	Steve Finley	.10
34	Gary Sheffield	.25
35	Todd Hundley	.10
36	Greg Maddux	.60
37	Mo Vaughn	.10
38	Eric Young	.10
39	Vinny Castilla	.10
40	Derek Jeter	1.50
41	Lance Johnson	.10
42	Ellis Burks	.10
43	Dante Bichette	.10
44	Javy Lopez	.10
45	Hideo Nomo	.25

Big Shots

This 20-card insert depicts the game's top stars in unique photos. Cards were inserted 1:12 packs. Gold Signature Editions, featuring a gold foil-stamped facsimile autograph, were inserted 1:144 packs. Fronts are highlighted in silver foil. Backs repeat a portion of the front photo, have a picture of the photographer and his comments about the picture.

		NM/M
Complete Set (19):		15.00
Common Player:		.25
Gold Signature Edition:		2X
1	Ken Griffey Jr.	2.00
2	Nomar Garciaparra	1.50
3	Brian Jordan	.25
4	Scott Rolen	.75
5	Alex Rodriguez	2.50
6	Larry Walker	.25
7	Mariano Rivera	.35
8	Cal Ripken Jr.	3.00
9	Deion Sanders	.25
10	Frank Thomas	1.00
11	Dean Palmer	.25
12	Ken Caminiti	.25
13	Derek Jeter	3.00
14	Barry Bonds	3.00
15	Chipper Jones	1.50
16	Mo Vaughn	.25
17	Jay Buhner	.25
18	Mike Piazza	2.00
19	Tony Gwynn	1.50

Big Show

The 45-card, regular-sized set was inserted one per pack of Series 1. Backs feature player comments written by ESPN SportsCenter hosts Keith Olbermann and Dan Patrick, whose portraits appear both front and back. On front, printed on metallic foil, is an action shot of the player, with his name printed along the left border of the horizontal cards. The cards are numbered "X/45." A parallel set to this chase-card series carries a gold-foil "World Headquarters Edition" seal at lower-right and was a 1:35 insert.

		NM/M
Complete Set (45):		7.00
Common Player:		.10
World Headquarters:		8X
1	Greg Maddux	.50
2	Chipper Jones	.50
3	Andruw Jones	.40
4	John Smoltz	.10
5	Cal Ripken Jr.	1.00
6	Roberto Alomar	.25
7	Rafael Palmeiro	.35
8	Eddie Murray	.40
9	Jose Canseco	.30
10	Roger Clemens	.55
11	Mo Vaughn	.10
12	Jim Edmonds	.10
13	Tim Salmon	.10
14	Sammy Sosa	.50
15	Albert Belle	.10
16	Frank Thomas	.40
17	Barry Larkin	.10
18	Kenny Lofton	.10
19	Manny Ramirez	.40
20	Matt Williams	.10
21	Dante Bichette	.10
22	Gary Sheffield	.30
23	Craig Biggio	.10
24	Jeff Bagwell	.40
25	Todd Hollandsworth	.10
26	Raul Mondesi	.10
27	Hideo Nomo	.25
28	Mike Piazza	.60
29	Paul Molitor	.40
30	Kirby Puckett	.50
31	Rondell White	.10
32	Rey Ordonez	.10
33	Paul Wilson	.10
34	Derek Jeter	1.00
35	Andy Pettitte	.25
36	Mark McGwire	.75
37	Jason Kendall	.10
38	Ozzie Smith	.50
39	Tony Gwynn	.50
40	Barry Bonds	1.00
41	Alex Rodriguez	.75
42	Jay Buhner	.10
43	Ken Griffey Jr.	.60
44	Randy Johnson	.40
45	Juan Gonzalez	.25

Big Show World Headquarters

The 45-card chase set in Series 2 is also found in a special parallel version which carries a "World Headquarters Edition" gold-foil seal on front at the lower-right.

	NM/M
Complete Set (45):	50.00
Common Player:	1.50
Stars:	8X

Clearly Dominant

The five-card, regular-sized set features Seattle outfielder Ken Griffey Jr. on each card and was inserted every 144 packs of 1997 Collector's Choice baseball.

		NM/M
Complete Set (5):		16.00
Common Card:		4.00
CD1-5	Ken Griffey Jr.	4.00

Clearly Dominant Jumbos

Each of the five Ken Griffey Jr. cards from the Collector's Choice insert set was also produced in a special retail-only 5" x 3-1/2" jumbo version. The supersize Clearly Dominant cards were packaged in a special collectors' kit which also included a Griffey stand-up figure and eight packs of CC cards, retailing for about $15. The cards could also be purchased as a complete set for $10. Cards are numbered with a "CD" prefix.

		NM/M
Complete Set (5):		10.00
Common Card:		2.00
1-5	Ken Griffey Jr.	2.00

Hot List Jumbos

These 5" x 7" versions of the "Ken Griffey Jr.'s Hot List" subset from Series 2 are an exclusive box-topper in certain retail packaging of Collector's Choice. Other than size, the jumbos are identical to the regular Hot List cards, including foil background printing on front.

		NM/M
Complete Set (10):		15.00
Common Player:		.50
325	Andruw Jones	1.50
326	Chipper Jones	2.00
327	Mo Vaughn	.50
328	Frank Thomas	1.50
329	Albert Belle	.50
330	Mark McGwire	3.00
331	Derek Jeter	4.00
332	Alex Rodriguez	3.00
333	Jay Buhner	.50
334	Ken Griffey Jr.	2.50

New Frontier

This is a 40-card Series 2 insert highlighting anticipated interleague matchups. Cards were designed with each player's action photo superimposed on a metallic-foil background depicting half of a ballfield. Pairs could then be displayed side-by-side. Cards were inserted 1:69 packs. They are numbered and carry a "NF" prefix.

		NM/M
Complete Set (40):		75.00
Common Player:		1.00
1	Alex Rodriguez	5.00
2	Tony Gwynn	3.00
3	Jose Canseco	1.25
4	Hideo Nomo	1.25
5	Mark McGwire	5.00
6	Barry Bonds	6.00
7	Juan Gonzalez	1.25
8	Ken Caminiti	1.00
9	Tim Salmon	1.00
10	Mike Piazza	4.00
11	Ken Griffey Jr.	4.00
12	Andres Galarraga	1.00
13	Jay Buhner	1.00
14	Dante Bichette	1.00
15	Frank Thomas	2.00
16	Ryne Sandberg	3.00
17	Roger Clemens	3.50
18	Andruw Jones	2.00
19	Jim Thome	1.50
20	Sammy Sosa	3.00
21	David Justice	1.00
22	Deion Sanders	1.00
23	Todd Walker	1.00
24	Kevin Orie	1.00
25	Albert Belle	1.00
26	Jeff Bagwell	2.00
27	Manny Ramirez	2.00
28	Brian Jordan	1.00
29	Derek Jeter	6.00
30	Chipper Jones	3.00
31	Mo Vaughn	1.00
32	Gary Sheffield	1.50
33	Carlos Delgado	1.50
34	Vladimir Guerrero	2.00
35	Cal Ripken Jr.	6.00
36	Greg Maddux	3.00
37	Cecil Fielder	1.00
38	Todd Hundley	1.00
39	Mike Mussina	1.25
40	Scott Rolen	1.50

Premier Power

The 20-card, regular-sized set was included one per 15 packs of Series 1. Fronts feature an action photo with the "Premier Power" logo in silver foil in the lower half and "spotlights" aiming out toward the sides. The bottom portion of the card is transparent red. Backs are bordered in red with the same card front shot appearing in black-and-white above a brief description and "Power Facts." The cards are numbered with a "PP" prefix. A parallel gold-foil version was available every 69 packs.

		NM/M
Complete Set (20):		20.00
Common Player:		.40
Gold:		2X
1	Mark McGwire	3.00
2	Brady Anderson	.40
3	Ken Griffey Jr.	2.50
4	Albert Belle	.40
5	Juan Gonzalez	.60
6	Andres Galarraga	.40
7	Jay Buhner	.40
8	Mo Vaughn	.40
9	Barry Bonds	3.50
10	Gary Sheffield	.75
11	Todd Hundley	.40
12	Frank Thomas	1.50
13	Sammy Sosa	2.00
14	Ken Caminiti	.40
15	Vinny Castilla	.40
16	Ellis Burks	.40
17	Rafael Palmeiro	1.00
18	Alex Rodriguez	3.00
19	Mike Piazza	2.50
20	Eddie Murray	1.50

Premier Power Jumbo

Each factory set of 1997 Collector's Choice included 10 super-size (3" x 5") versions of the Premier Power inserts. Besides the size, the jumbos differ from the insert version in the addition of a metallic facsimile autograph on front.

		NM/M
Complete Set (20):		15.00
Common Player:		.50
1	Mark McGwire	2.50
2	Brady Anderson	.50
3	Ken Griffey Jr.	2.00
4	Albert Belle	.50
5	Juan Gonzalez	.75
6	Andres Galarraga	.50
7	Jay Buhner	.50
8	Mo Vaughn	.50
9	Barry Bonds	3.00
10	Gary Sheffield	.65
11	Todd Hundley	.50
12	Frank Thomas	1.00
13	Sammy Sosa	1.50
14	Ken Caminiti	.50
15	Vinny Castilla	.50
16	Ellis Burks	.50
17	Rafael Palmeiro	.75
18	Alex Rodriguez	2.50
19	Mike Piazza	2.00
20	Eddie Murray	1.00

Stick'Ums

The 30-piece 2-1/2" x 3-1/2" sticker set was inserted one per three packs of Series 1 Collector's Choice. Fronts feature a bright background color and include five different peel-off stickers: An action shot of the player, a pennant in team colors featuring the player's name, a team logo, an Upper Deck Collector's Choice logo and a "Super Action Stick'Ums" decal. Backs feature the player checklist in black ink over a gray background. An unnumbered version of the stickers (without Smith and Puckett) was sold in a special retail-only package.

		NM/M
Complete Set (30):		5.00
Common Player:		.05
1	Ozzie Smith	.50
2	Andruw Jones	.40
3	Alex Rodriguez	.75
4	Paul Molitor	.40
5	Jeff Bagwell	.40
6	Manny Ramirez	.40
7	Kenny Lofton	.05
8	Albert Belle	.05
9	Jay Buhner	.05
10	Chipper Jones	.50
11	Barry Larkin	.05
12	Dante Bichette	.05
13	Mike Piazza	.60
14	Andres Galarraga	.05
15	Barry Bonds	1.00
16	Brady Anderson	.05
17	Gary Sheffield	.20
18	Jim Thome	.35
19	Tony Gwynn	.50
20	Cal Ripken Jr.	1.00
21	Sammy Sosa	.50
22	Juan Gonzalez	.20
23	Greg Maddux	.50
24	Ken Griffey Jr.	.60
25	Mark McGwire	.75
26	Kirby Puckett	.50
27	Mo Vaughn	.05
28	Vladimir Guerrero	.40
29	Ken Caminiti	.05
30	Frank Thomas	.40

Toast of the Town

This 30-card Series 2 insert features top stars on foil-enhanced cards. Odds of finding one are 1:35 packs. Cards are numbered with a "T" prefix.

		NM/M
Complete Set (30):		40.00
Common Player:		.30
1	Andruw Jones	2.00
2	Chipper Jones	2.50
3	Greg Maddux	2.50
4	John Smoltz	.30
5	Kenny Lofton	.30
6	Brady Anderson	.30
7	Cal Ripken Jr.	6.00
8	Mo Vaughn	.30
9	Sammy Sosa	2.50
10	Albert Belle	.30
11	Frank Thomas	2.00
12	Barry Larkin	.30
13	Manny Ramirez	2.00
14	Jeff Bagwell	2.00
15	Mike Piazza	4.00
16	Paul Molitor	2.00
17	Vladimir Guerrero	2.00
18	Todd Hundley	.30
19	Derek Jeter	6.00
20	Andy Pettitte	.45
21	Bernie Williams	.30
22	Mark McGwire	5.00
23	Scott Rolen	1.00
24	Ken Caminiti	.30
25	Tony Gwynn	2.50
26	Barry Bonds	6.00
27	Ken Griffey Jr.	4.00
28	Alex Rodriguez	5.00
29	Juan Gonzalez	.75
30	Roger Clemens	3.00

Update

This update set was offered via a mail-in redemption offer. Traded players in their new uniforms and 1997 rookies are the focus of the set. Fronts are color photos which are borderless at top and sides. Beneath each photo the player's name and team logo appear in a red (A.L.) or blue (N.L.) baseball design. Backs have another photo, major and minor league career stats and a trivia question. Cards are numbered with a "U" prefix.

		NM/M
Complete Set (30):		2.00
Common Player:		.10
1	Jim Leyritz	.10
2	Matt Perisho	.10
3	Michael Tucker	.10
4	Mike Johnson	.10
5	Jaime Navarro	.10
6	Doug Drabek	.10
7	Terry Mulholland	.10
8	Brett Tomko	.10
9	Marquis Grissom	.10
10	David Justice	.10
11	Brian Moehler	.10
12	Bobby Bonilla	.10
13	Todd Dunwoody	.10
14	Tony Saunders	.10
15	Jay Bell	.10
16	Jeff King	.10
17	Terry Steinbach	.10
18	Steve Bieser	.10
19	Takashi Kashiwada **RC**	.10
20	Hideki Irabu	.10
21	Damon Mashore	.10
22	Quilvio Veras	.10
23	Will Cunnane	.10
24	Jeff Kent	.50
25	J.T. Snow	.10
26	Dante Powell	.10
17	Jose Cruz Jr.	.10
28	John Burkett	.10
29	John Wetteland	.10
30	Benito Santiago	.10

You Crash the Game

A 30-player interactive set found in Series 2 packs features the game's top home run hitters. Cards were inserted 1:5 packs. Fronts feature a red-foil Crash logo and a range of game dates. Those holding cards of players who homered in that span could (for $2 per card handling fee) redeem them for high-tech versions. Instant winner cards (seeded 1:721) were redeemable for complete 30-card upgrade sets. Winning cards are marked with an asterisk; theoretically they would be scarcer than losing cards because many were redeemed. The contest cards expired on Sept. 8, 1997. Cards are numbered with a "CG" prefix.

	NM/M
Complete Set (90):	65.00
Common Player:	.25
July 28-30	.25
August 8-11	.25
Sept. 19-21	.25
August 15-17	1.00
August 29-31	1.00
Sept. 12-14	1.00
August 22-24*	1.50
Sept. 1-3	.75
Sept. 19-22	.75
July 31-Aug. 3*	.50
Sept. 4-7	.25
Sept. 19-22	.25
July 29-30	.60
Aug. 29-31	.60
Sept. 26-28	.60
August 8-10*	4.00
Sept. 1-3*	4.00
Sept. 11-14	2.00
August 14-17	.25
August 29-31*	.50
Sept. 23-25*	.50
August 1-3*	2.00
August 29-31	1.00
Sept. 19-21*	2.00
August 7-10	.25
Sept. 11-14	.25
Sept. 19-21*	.50
August 29-31	.75
Sept. 1-3	.75
Sept. 23-25*	1.50
August 12-14*	1.50
August 29-31	.75
Sept. 11-14*	1.50
July 28-30	.50
August 15-18*	1.00
Sept. 19-22	.50
August 4-5	.25
Sept. 1-3*	.50
Sept. 23-25	.25
July 24-27*	.50
August 28-29	.25
Sept. 26-28*	.50
August 12-13	.25
Sept. 4-7*	.50
Sept. 19-21	.25
August 8-10*	.50
August 30-31	.25
Sept. 12-14	.25
August 1-3*	.75
Sept. 1-3*	.75
Sept. 12-14*	.75
Sept. 9-10	.75
Sept. 19-22*	1.50
Sept. 23-25*	1.50
August 1-3	.25
August 15-17	.25
Sept. 25-28*	.50
August 11-12	1.25
Sept. 5-8*	2.50
Sept. 19-21*	2.50
August 22-24	.75
August 29-31	.75
Sept. 19-22	.75
August 29-31	.25
Sept. 4-7	.25
Sept. 26-28*	.50
August 22-24	.35
Sept. 12-14	.35
Sept. 26-28	.35
July 31-Aug. 3	1.50
August 30-31	1.50
Sept. 19-22*	3.00
August 8-10	.25
Sept. 4-7	.25
Sept. 17-18*	.50
August 5-7	2.00
Sept. 4-7*	4.00
Sept. 23-24*	4.00
August 7-10	.25
August 28-29	.25
Sept. 1-3	.25
August 22-24*	2.50
August 28-29	1.25
Sept. 19-22*	2.50
July 29-31	1.50
August 30-31	1.50
Sept. 12-15	1.50
August 11-13*	.75
August 30-31	.40
Sept. 19-21*	.75

You Crash the Game Winners

These are the prize cards from CC's interactive "You Crash the Game" cards in Se-

ries 2. Persons who redeemed a Crash card with the correct date(s) on which the pictured player homered received (for a $2 handling fee) this high-end version of the Crash card. The redemption cards have the same basic design as the contest cards, but use different player photos with fronts printed on metallic-foil stock, and a team logo in place of the Crash foil logo. Where the contest cards have game rules on back, the redemption cards have another photo of the player and career highlights. Complete redemption sets were available upon redeeming an instant winner card, found on average of one per 721 packs. Because some cards were only available in complete redemption sets (marked with an "SP" here), and others might have been available for more than one date range, some cards will be scarcer than others.

		NM/M
Complete Set (30):		55.00
Common Player:		.50
CG1	Ryan Klesko/SP	1.25
CG2	Chipper Jones/SP	12.00
CG3	Andruw Jones	.75
CG4	Brady Anderson	.50
CG5	Rafael Palmeiro/SP	2.50
CG6	Cal Ripken Jr.	10.00
CG7	Mo Vaughn	.50
CG8	Sammy Sosa	3.00
CG9	Albert Belle	.50
CG10	Frank Thomas	1.00
CG11	Manny Ramirez	.75
CG12	Jim Thome	.65
CG13	Matt Williams	.50
CG14	Dante Bichette	.50
CG15	Vinny Castilla	.50
CG16	Andres Galarraga	.50
CG17	Gary Sheffield	.65
CG18	Jeff Bagwell	.75
CG19	Eric Karros	.50
CG20	Mike Piazza	2.50
CG21	Vladimir Guerrero/SP	3.00
CG22	Cecil Fielder/SP	1.25
CG23	Jose Canseco/SP	2.00
CG24	Mark McGwire	7.50
CG25	Ken Caminiti	.50
CG26	Barry Bonds	10.00
CG27	Jay Buhner/SP	1.25
CG28	Ken Griffey Jr.	2.50
CG29	Alex Rodriguez/SP	9.00
CG30	Juan Gonzalez	.60

Instant Winner

Found on average of one per 721 packs, these Instant Winner cards could be redeemed (with a $2 handling fee) for a complete set of You Crash the Game exchange cards - the only way eight of the Crash winner cards could be obtained. These special cards have a red foil "instant winner!" logo on front and a congratulatory message on back, along with instructions for redemption prior to the Dec. 8, 1997, deadline.

	NM/M
Complete Set (30):	300.00
Common Player:	2.00

Team Sets

A special version of Collector's Choice cards for several popular major league teams was produced in two retail packages by Upper Deck. In one version, blister packs containing 13 player cards and a metallic-foil team logo/checklist card was sold for a suggested retail price of $1.99. The second version, exclusive to Wal-Mart, is a hard plastic blister pack containing two cello-wrapped packages. One holds a random assortment of 15 Series 1 Collector's Choice cards. The other has 13 player cards and a foil logo/checklist card for a specific team. The team-set cards are identical to the regular-issue cards, from either Series 1 or Series 2, except each of the team-set cards has a number on back which differs from the regular edition. Packaged with the Wal-Mart version is a 3-1/2" x 5" "Home Team Heroes" card, listed seperately.

NM/M

Common Player: .10
Atlanta Braves Team Set: 3.00
AB Team Logo/Checklist .10
AB1 Andruw Jones .60
AB2 Kenny Lofton .10
AB3 Fred McGriff .10
AB4 Michael Tucker .10
AB5 Ryan Klesko .10
AB6 Javy Lopez .10
AB7 Mark Wohlers .10
AB8 Tom Glavine .25
AB9 Denny Neagle .10
AB10 Chipper Jones .75
AB11 Jeff Blauser .10
AB12 Greg Maddux .75
AB13 John Smoltz .10
Baltimore Orioles Team Set: 2.00
BO Team Logo/Checklist .10
BO1 Rocky Coppinger .10
BO2 Scott Erickson .10
BO3 Chris Hoiles .10
BO4 Roberto Alomar .30
BO5 Cal Ripken Jr. 1.50
BO6 Randy Myers .10
BO7 B.J. Surhoff .10
BO8 Mike Mussina .40
BO9 Rafael Palmeiro .50
BO10 Jimmy Key .10
BO11 Mike Bordick .10
BO12 Brady Anderson .10
BO13 Eric Davis .10
Chicago White Sox Team Set: 2.50
CW Team Logo/Checklist .10
CW1 Robin Ventura .10
CW2 Wilson Alvarez .10
CW3 Tony Phillips .10
CW4 Lyle Mouton .10
CW5 James Baldwin .10
CW6 Harold Baines .10
CW7 Albert Belle .10
CW8 Chris Snopek .10
CW9 Ray Durham .10
CW10 Frank Thomas .60
CW11 Ozzie Guillen .10
CW12 Roberto Hernandez .10
CW13 Jaime Navarro .10
Cleveland Indians Team Set: 1.50
CI Team Logo/Checklist .10
CI1 Brian Giles .10
CI2 Omar Vizquel .10
CI3 Julio Franco .10
CI4 Orel Hershiser .10
CI5 Charles Nagy .10
CI6 Matt Williams .10
CI7 Jose Mesa .10
CI8 Sandy Alomar .10
CI9 Jim Thome .50
CI10 David Justice .10
CI11 Marquis Grissom .10
CI12 Chad Ogea .10
CI13 Manny Ramirez .60
Colorado Rockies Team Set: 1.25
CR Team Logo/Checklist .10
CR1 Dante Bichette .10
CR2 Vinny Castilla .10
CR3 Kevin Ritz .10
CR4 Larry Walker .10
CR5 Eric Young .10
CR6 Quinton McCracken .10
CR7 John Vander Wal .10
CR8 Jamey Wright .10
CR9 Mark Thompson .10
CR10 Andres Galarraga .10
CR11 Ellis Burks .10
CR12 Kirt Manwaring .10
CR13 Walt Weiss .10
Florida Marlins Team Set: 2.00
FM Team Logo/Checklist .10
FM1 Luis Castillo .10
FM2 Al Leiter .10
FM3 Devon White .10
FM4 Jeff Conine .10
FM5 Charles Johnson .10
FM6 Edgar Renteria .10
FM7 Robb Nen .10
FM8 Kevin Brown .10
FM9 Gary Sheffield .45
FM10 Alex Fernandez .10
FM11 Pat Rapp .10
FM12 Moises Alou .10
FM13 Bobby Bonilla .10
L.A. Dodgers Team Set: 3.00
LA Team Logo/Checklist .10
LA1 Raul Mondesi .10
LA2 Brett Butler .10
LA3 Todd Hollandsworth .10
LA4 Eric Karros .10
LA5 Hideo Nomo .30
LA6 Ismael Valdes .10
LA7 Wilton Guerrero .10
LA8 Ramon Martinez .10
LA9 Greg Gagne .10
LA10 Mike Piazza 1.00
LA11 Chan Ho Park .10
LA12 Todd Worrell .10
LA13 Todd Zeile .10
New York Yankees Team Set: 3.00
NY Team Logo/Checklist .10
NY1 Bernie Williams .10
NY2 Dwight Gooden .10
NY3 Wade Boggs .75
NY4 Ruben Rivera .10
NY5 Derek Jeter 1.50
NY6 Tino Martinez .10
NY7 Tim Raines .10
NY8 Joe Girardi .10
NY9 Charlie Hayes .10
NY10 Andy Pettitte .30
NY11 Cecil Fielder .10
NY12 Paul O'Neill .10
NY13 David Cone .10
Seattle Mariners Team Set: 3.00
SM Team Logo/Checklist .10
SM1 Dan Wilson .10
SM2 Ken Griffey Jr. 1.00
SM3 Edgar Martinez .10
SM4 Joey Cora .10
SM5 Norm Charlton .10
SM6 Alex Rodriguez 1.25
SM7 Randy Johnson .60
SM8 Paul Sorrento .10
SM9 Jamie Moyer .10
SM10 Jay Buhner .10
SM11 Russ Davis .10
SM12 Jeff Fassero .10
SM13 Bob Wells .10
Texas Rangers Team Set: 3.00
TR Team Logo/Checklist .10
TR1 Bobby Witt .10
TR2 Darren Oliver .10
TR3 Rusty Greer .10
TR4 Juan Gonzalez .30
TR5 Will Clark .10
TR6 Dean Palmer .10
TR7 Ivan Rodriguez .50
TR8 John Wetteland .10
TR9 Mark McLemore .10
TR10 John Burkett .10
TR11 Benji Gil .10
TR12 Ken Hill .10
TR13 Mickey Tettleton .10

1998 Collector's Choice

The 530-card Collectors Choice set was issued in two 265-card series. Series 1 features 197 regular cards, five checklists and four subsets: Cover Story features 18 of the leagues' top stars, Rookie Class has 27 young players, the nine-card Top of the Charts subset honors 1997's statistical leaders and Masked Marauders is a nine-card subset. Inserts in Series 1 are Super Action Stick-Ums, Evolution Revolution and StarQuest. Series 2 has 233 regular cards, five checklist cards, an 18-card Rookie Class subset and the nine-card Golden Jubilee subset. Inserts in Series 2 include Mini Bobbing Head Cards, You Crash the Game and StarQuest. Factory sets include a random assortment of 10 StarQuest cards.

NM/M

Unopened Fact. Set (540): 15.00
Complete Set (530): 10.00
Common Player: .05
Pack (14): 1.00
Wax Box (36): 15.00
1 Nomar Garciaparra (Cover Glory) .50
2 Roger Clemens (Cover Glory) .50
3 Larry Walker (Cover Glory) .05
4 Mike Piazza (Cover Glory) .60
5 Mark McGwire (Cover Glory) .75
6 Tony Gwynn (Cover Glory) .45
7 Jose Cruz Jr. (Cover Glory) .05
8 Frank Thomas (Cover Glory) .40
9 Tino Martinez (Cover Glory) .05
10 Ken Griffey Jr. (Cover Glory) .60
11 Barry Bonds (Cover Glory) .85
12 Scott Rolen (Cover Glory) .30
13 Randy Johnson (Cover Glory) .15
14 Ryne Sandberg (Cover Glory) .35
15 Eddie Murray (Cover Glory) .15
16 Kevin Brown (Cover Glory) .05
17 Greg Maddux (Cover Glory) .35
18 Sandy Alomar Jr. (Cover Glory) .05
19 Checklist (Ken Griffey Jr., Adam Riggs) .40
20 Checklist (Nomar Garciaparra, Charlie O'Brien) .10
21 Checklist (Ben Grieve, Ken Griffey Jr., Larry Walker, Mark McGwire) .50
22 Checklist (Mark McGwire, Cal Ripken Jr.) .50
23 Checklist (Tino Martinez) .05
24 Jason Dickson .05
25 Darin Erstad .25
26 Todd Greene .05
27 Chuck Finley .05
28 Garret Anderson .05
29 Dave Hollins .05
30 Rickey Henderson .60
31 John Smoltz .05
32 Michael Tucker .05
33 Jeff Blauser .05
34 Javier Lopez .05
35 Andruw Jones .60
36 Denny Neagle .05
37 Randall Simon .05
38 Mark Wohlers .05
39 Harold Baines .05
40 Cal Ripken Jr. 1.50
41 Mike Bordick .05
42 Jimmy Key .05
43 Armando Benitez .05
44 Scott Erickson .05
45 Eric Davis .05
46 Bret Saberhagen .05
47 Darren Bragg .05
48 Steve Avery .05
49 Jeff Frye .05
50 Aaron Sele .05
51 Scott Hatteberg .05
52 Tom Gordon .05
53 Kevin Orie .05
54 Kevin Foster .05
55 Ryne Sandberg .75
56 Doug Glanville .05
57 Tyler Houston .05
58 Steve Trachsel .05
59 Mark Grace .05
60 Frank Thomas .60
61 Scott Eyre **RC** .05
62 Jeff Abbott .05
63 Chris Clemons .05
64 Jorge Fabregas .05
65 Robin Ventura .05
66 Matt Karchner .05
67 Jon Nunnally .05
68 Aaron Boone .05
69 Pokey Reese .05
70 Deion Sanders .10
71 Jeff Shaw .05
72 Eduardo Perez .05
73 Brett Tomko .05
74 Bartolo Colon .05
75 Manny Ramirez .60
76 Jose Mesa .05
77 Brian Giles .05
78 Richie Sexson .05
79 Orel Hershiser .05
80 Matt Williams .05
81 Walt Weiss .05
82 Jerry DiPoto .05
83 Quinton McCracken .05
84 Neifi Perez .05
85 Vinny Castilla .05
86 Ellis Burks .05
87 John Thomson .05
88 Willie Blair .05
89 Bob Hamelin .05
90 Tony Clark .05
91 Todd Jones .05
92 Deivi Cruz .05
93 Frank Catalanotto **RC** .15
94 Justin Thompson .05
95 Gary Sheffield .25
96 Kevin Brown .05
97 Charles Johnson .05
98 Bobby Bonilla .05
99 Livan Hernandez .05
100 Paul Konerko (Rookie Class) .10
101 Craig Counsell (Rookie Class) .05
102 Magglio Ordonez **RC** (Rookie Class) 1.00
103 Garrett Stephenson (Rookie Class) .05
104 Ken Cloude (Rookie Class) .05
105 Miguel Tejada (Rookie Class) .25
106 Juan Encarnacion (Rookie Class) .05
107 Dennis Reyes (Rookie Class) .05
108 Orlando Cabrera (Rookie Class) .05
109 Kelvim Escobar (Rookie Class) .05
110 Ben Grieve (Rookie Class) .05
111 Brian Rose (Rookie Class) .05
112 Fernando Tatis (Rookie Class) .05
113 Tom Evans (Rookie Class) .05
114 Tom Fordham (Rookie Class) .05
115 Mark Kotsay (Rookie Class) .05
116 Mario Valdez (Rookie Class) .05
117 Jeremi Gonzalez (Rookie Class) .05
118 Todd Dunwoody (Rookie Class) .05
119 Javier Valentin (Rookie Class) .05
120 Todd Helton (Rookie Class) .50
121 Jason Varitek (Rookie Class) .10
122 Chris Carpenter (Rookie Class) .05
123 Kevin Millwood **RC** (Rookie Class) .75
124 Brad Fullmer (Rookie Class) .05
125 Jaret Wright (Rookie Class) .05
126 Brad Rigby (Rookie Class) .05
127 Edgar Renteria .05
128 Robb Nen .05
129 Tony Pena .05
130 Craig Biggio .05
131 Brad Ausmus .05
132 Shane Reynolds .05
133 Mike Hampton .05
134 Billy Wagner .05
135 Richard Hidalgo .05
136 Jose Rosado .05
137 Yamil Benitez .05
138 Felix Martinez .05
139 Jeff King .05
140 Jose Offerman .05
141 Joe Vitiello .05
142 Tim Belcher .05
143 Brett Butler .05
144 Greg Gagne .05
145 Mike Piazza 1.00
146 Ramon Martinez .05
147 Raul Mondesi .05
148 Adam Riggs .05
149 Eddie Murray .50
150 Jeff Cirillo .05
151 Scott Karl .05
152 Mike Fetters .05
153 Dave Nilsson .05
154 Antone Williamson .05
155 Jeff D'Amico .05
156 Jose Valentin .05
157 Brad Radke .05
158 Torii Hunter .05
159 Chuck Knoblauch .05
160 Paul Molitor .60
161 Travis Miller .05
162 Rich Robertson .05
163 Ron Coomer .05
164 Mark Grudzielanek .05
165 Lee Smith .05
166 Vladimir Guerrero .60
167 Dustin Hermanson .05
168 Ugueth Urbina .05
169 F.P. Santangelo .05
170 Rondell White .05
171 Bobby Jones .05
172 Edgardo Alfonzo .05
173 John Franco .05
174 Carlos Baerga .05
175 Butch Huskey .05
176 Rey Ordonez .05
177 Matt Franco .05
178 Dwight Gooden .05
179 Chad Curtis .05
180 Tino Martinez .05
181 Charlie O'Brien (Masked Marauders) .05
182 Sandy Alomar Jr. (Masked Marauders) .05
183 Raul Casanova (Masked Marauders) .05
184 Jim Leyritz (Masked Marauders) .05
185 Mike Piazza (Masked Marauders) .60
186 Ivan Rodriguez (Masked Marauders) .25
187 Charles Johnson (Masked Marauders) .05
188 Brad Ausmus (Masked Marauders) .05
189 Brian Johnson (Masked Marauders) .05
190 Wade Boggs .75
191 David Wells .05
192 Tim Raines .05
193 Ramiro Mendoza .05
194 Willie Adams .05
195 Matt Stairs .05
196 Jason McDonald .05
197 Dave Magadan .05
198 Mark Bellhorn .05
199 Ariel Prieto .05
200 Jose Canseco .35
201 Bobby Estalella .05
202 Tony Barron **RC** .05
203 Midre Cummings .05
204 Ricky Bottalico .05
205 Mike Grace .05
206 Rico Brogna .05
207 Mickey Morandini .05
208 Lou Collier .05
209 Kevin Polcovich **RC** .05
210 Kevin Young .05
211 Jose Guillen .05
212 Esteban Loaiza .05
213 Marc Wilkins .05
214 Jason Schmidt .05
215 Gary Gaetti .05
216 Fernando Valenzuela .05
217 Willie McGee .05
218 Alan Benes .05
219 Eli Marrero .05
220 Mark McGwire 1.25
221 Matt Morris .05
222 Trevor Hoffman .05
223 Will Cunnane .05
224 Joey Hamilton .05
225 Ken Caminiti .05
226 Derrek Lee .35
227 Mark Sweeney .05
228 Carlos Hernandez .05
229 Brian Johnson .05
230 Jeff Kent .05
231 Kirk Rueter .05
232 Bill Mueller .05
233 Dante Powell .05
234 J.T. Snow .05
235 Shawn Estes .05
236 Dennis Martinez .05
237 Jamie Moyer .05
238 Dan Wilson .05
239 Joey Cora .05
240 Ken Griffey Jr. 1.00
241 Paul Sorrento .05
242 Jay Buhner .05
243 Hanley Frias **RC** .05
244 John Burkett .05
245 Juan Gonzalez .30
246 Rick Helling .05
247 Darren Oliver .05
248 Mickey Tettleton .05
249 Ivan Rodriguez .45
250 Joe Carter .05
251 Pat Hentgen .05
252 Marty Janzen .05
253 Frank Thomas, Tony Gwynn (Top of the Charts) .25
254 Mark McGwire, Ken Griffey Jr., Larry Walker (Top of the Charts) .50
255 Ken Griffey Jr., Andres Galarraga (Top of the Charts) .40
256 Brian Hunter, Tony Womack (Top of the Charts) .05
257 Roger Clemens, Denny Neagle (Top of the Charts) .10
258 Roger Clemens, Curt Schilling (Top of the Charts) .30
259 Roger Clemens, Pedro J. Martinez (Top of the Charts) .25
260 Randy Myers, Jeff Shaw (Top of the Charts) .05
261 Nomar Garciaparra, Scott Rolen (Top of the Charts) .25
262 Charlie O'Brien .05
263 Shannon Stewart .05
264 Robert Person .05
265 Carlos Delgado .25
266 Checklist (Matt Williams, Travis Lee) .05
267 Checklist (Nomar Garciaparra, Cal Ripken Jr.) .50
268 Checklist (Mark McGwire, Mike Piazza) .50
269 Checklist (Tony Gwynn, Ken Griffey Jr.) .40
270 Checklist (Fred McGriff, Jose Cruz Jr.) .05
271 Andruw Jones (Golden Jubilee) .25
272 Alex Rodriguez (Golden Jubilee) .65
273 Juan Gonzalez (Golden Jubilee) .15
274 Nomar Garciaparra (Golden Jubilee) .50
275 Ken Griffey Jr. (Golden Jubilee) .60
276 Tino Martinez (Golden Jubilee) .05
277 Roger Clemens (Golden Jubilee) .40
278 Barry Bonds (Golden Jubilee) .85
279 Mike Piazza (Golden Jubilee) .60
280 Tim Salmon (Golden Jubilee) .05
281 Gary DiSarcina .05
282 Cecil Fielder .05
283 Ken Hill .05
284 Troy Percival .05
285 Jim Edmonds .05
286 Allen Watson .05
287 Brian Anderson .05
288 Jay Bell .05
289 Jorge Fabregas .05
290 Devon White .05
291 Yamil Benitez .05
292 Jeff Suppan .05
293 Tony Batista .05
294 Brent Brede .05
295 Andy Benes .05
296 Felix Rodriguez .05
297 Karim Garcia .05
298 Omar Daal .05
299 Andy Stankiewicz .05
300 Matt Williams .05
301 Willie Blair .05
302 Ryan Klesko .05
303 Tom Glavine .25
304 Walt Weiss .05
305 Greg Maddux .75
306 Chipper Jones .75
307 Keith Lockhart .05
308 Andres Galarraga .05
309 Chris Hoiles .05
310 Roberto Alomar .25
311 Joe Carter .05
312 Doug Drabek .05
313 Jeffrey Hammonds .05
314 Rafael Palmeiro .40
315 Mike Mussina .40
316 Brady Anderson .05
317 B.J. Surhoff .05
318 Dennis Eckersley .45
319 Jim Leyritz .05
320 Mo Vaughn .05
321 Nomar Garciaparra .75
322 Reggie Jefferson .05
323 Tim Naehring .05
324 Troy O'Leary .05
325 Pedro J. Martinez .50
326 John Valentin .05
327 Mark Clark .05
328 Rod Beck .05
329 Mickey Morandini .05
330 Sammy Sosa .75
331 Jeff Blauser .05
332 Lance Johnson .05
333 Scott Servais .05
334 Kevin Tapani .05
335 Henry Rodriguez .05
336 Jaime Navarro .05
337 Benji Gil .05
338 James Baldwin .05
339 Mike Cameron .05

340 Ray Durham .05
341 Chris Snopek .05
342 Eddie Taubensee .05
343 Bret Boone .05
344 Willie Greene .05
345 Barry Larkin .05
346 Chris Stynes .05
347 Pete Harnisch .05
348 Dave Burba .05
349 Sandy Alomar Jr. .05
350 Kenny Lofton .05
351 Geronimo Berroa .05
352 Omar Vizquel .05
353 Travis Fryman .05
354 Dwight Gooden .05
355 Jim Thome .40
356 David Justice .05
357 Charles Nagy .05
358 Chad Ogea .05
359 Pedro Astacio .05
360 Larry Walker .05
361 Mike Lansing .05
362 Kirt Manwaring .05
363 Dante Bichette .05
364 Jamey Wright .05
365 Darryl Kile .05
366 Luis Gonzalez .05
367 Joe Randa .05
368 Raul Casanova .05
369 Damion Easley .05
370 Brian L. Hunter .05
371 Bobby Higginson .05
372 Brian Moehler .05
373 Scott Sanders .05
374 Jim Eisenreich .05
375 Derrek Lee .35
376 Jay Powell .05
377 Cliff Floyd .05
378 Alex Fernandez .05
379 Felix Heredia .05
380 Jeff Bagwell .60
381 Bill Spiers .05
382 Chris Holt .05
383 Carl Everett .05
384 Derek Bell .05
385 Moises Alou .05
386 Ramon Garcia .05
387 Mike Sweeney .05
388 Glendon Rusch .05
389 Kevin Appier .05
390 Dean Palmer .05
391 Jeff Conine .05
392 Johnny Damon .25
393 Jose Vizcaino .05
394 Todd Hollandsworth .05
395 Eric Karros .05
396 Todd Zeile .05
397 Chan Ho Park .05
398 Ismael Valdes .05
399 Eric Young .05
400 Hideo Nomo .25
401 Mark Loretta .05
402 Doug Jones .05
403 Jeromy Burnitz .05
404 John Jaha .05
405 Marquis Grissom .05
406 Mike Matheny .05
407 Todd Walker .05
408 Marty Cordova .05
409 Matt Lawton .05
410 Terry Steinbach .05
411 Pat Meares .05
412 Rick Aguilera .05
413 Otis Nixon .05
414 Derrick May .05
415 Carl Pavano (Rookie Class) .05
416 A.J. Hinch (Rookie Class) .05
417 David Dellucci **RC** (Rookie Class) .10
418 Bruce Chen (Rookie Class) .05
419 Darron Ingram **RC** (Rookie Class) .05
420 Sean Casey (Rookie Class) .20
421 Mark L. Johnson (Rookie Class) .05
422 Gabe Alvarez (Rookie Class) .05
423 Alex Gonzalez (Rookie Class) .05
424 Daryle Ward (Rookie Class) .05
425 Russell Branyan (Rookie Class) .05
426 Mike Caruso (Rookie Class) .05
427 Mike Kinkade **RC** (Rookie Class) .20
428 Ramon Hernandez (Rookie Class) .05
429 Matt Clement (Rookie Class) .05
430 Travis Lee (Rookie Class) .05
431 Shane Monahan (Rookie Class) .05
432 Rich Butler **RC** (Rookie Class) .05
433 Chris Widger .05
434 Jose Vidro .05
435 Carlos Perez .05
436 Ryan McGuire .05
437 Brian McRae .05
438 Al Leiter .05
439 Rich Becker .05
440 Todd Hundley .05
441 Dave Mlicki .05
442 Bernard Gilkey .05
443 John Olerud .05
444 Paul O'Neill .05
445 Andy Pettitte .30
446 David Cone .05
447 Chili Davis .05
448 Bernie Williams .05
449 Joe Girardi .05
450 Derek Jeter 1.50
451 Mariano Rivera .20
452 George Williams .05
453 Kenny Rogers .05
454 Tom Candiotti .05
455 Rickey Henderson .60
456 Jason Giambi .40
457 Scott Spiezio .05
458 Doug Glanville .05
459 Desi Relaford .05
460 Curt Schilling .20
461 Bob Abreu .10
462 Gregg Jefferies .05
463 Scott Rolen .40
464 Mike Lieberthal .05
465 Tony Womack .05
466 Jermaine Allensworth .05
467 Francisco Cordova .05
468 Jon Lieber .05
469 Al Martin .05
470 Jason Kendall .05
471 Todd Stottlemyre .05
472 Royce Clayton .05
473 Brian Jordan .05
474 John Mabry .05
475 Ray Lankford .05
476 Delino DeShields .05
477 Ron Gant .05
478 Mark Langston .05
479 Steve Finley .05
480 Tony Gwynn .75
481 Andy Ashby .05
482 Wally Joyner .05
483 Greg Vaughn .05
484 Sterling Hitchcock .05
485 J. Kevin Brown .05
486 Orel Hershiser .05
487 Charlie Hayes .05
488 Darryl Hamilton .05
489 Mark Gardner .05
490 Barry Bonds 1.50
491 Robb Nen .05
492 Kirk Rueter .05
493 Randy Johnson .50
494 Jeff Fassero .05
495 Alex Rodriguez 1.25
496 David Segui .05
497 Rich Amaral .05
498 Russ Davis .05
499 Bubba Trammell .05
500 Wade Boggs .75
501 Roberto Hernandez .05
502 Dave Martinez .05
503 Dennis Springer .05
504 Paul Sorrento .05
505 Wilson Alvarez .05
506 Mike Kelly .05
507 Albie Lopez .05
508 Tony Saunders .05
509 John Flaherty .05
510 Fred McGriff .05
511 Quinton McCracken .05
512 Terrell Wade .05
513 Kevin Stocker .05
514 Kevin Elster .05
515 Will Clark .05
516 Bobby Witt .05
517 Tom Goodwin .05
518 Aaron Sele .05
519 Lee Stevens .05
520 Rusty Greer .05
521 John Wetteland .05
522 Darrin Fletcher .05
523 Jose Canseco .35
524 Randy Myers .05
525 Jose Cruz Jr. .05
526 Shawn Green .15
527 Tony Fernandez .05
528 Alex Gonzalez .05
529 Ed Sprague .05
530 Roger Clemens .85

Cover Glory 5x7

NM/M
Complete Set (10): 10.00
Common Player: 1.00
1 Nomar Garciaparra 1.50
2 Roger Clemens 2.00
3 Larry Walker 1.00
4 Mike Piazza 2.50
5 Mark McGwire 3.00
6 Tony Gwynn 1.50
7 Jose Cruz Jr. 1.00
8 Frank Thomas 1.25
9 Tino Martinez 1.00
10 Ken Griffey Jr. 2.50

Evolution Revolution

This 28-card insert features one player from each Major League team. The fronts picture the team jersey and open to reveal the player's top 1997 accomplishment. Evolution Revolution was inserted in Series 1 packs. Cards are numbered with an "ER" prefix.

NM/M
Complete Set (28): 36.00
Common Player: .40
Inserted 1:13
1 Tim Salmon .40
2 Greg Maddux 2.50
3 Cal Ripken Jr. 6.00
4 Mo Vaughn .40
5 Sammy Sosa 2.50
6 Frank Thomas 1.50
7 Barry Larkin .40
8 Jim Thome .65
9 Larry Walker .40
10 Travis Fryman .40
11 Gary Sheffield .65
12 Jeff Bagwell 1.50
13 Johnny Damon .65
14 Mike Piazza 4.00
15 Jeff Cirillo .40
16 Paul Molitor 1.50
17 Vladimir Guerrero 1.50
18 Todd Hundley .40
19 Tino Martinez .40
20 Jose Canseco .65
21 Scott Rolen .75
22 Al Martin .40
23 Mark McGwire 5.00
24 Tony Gwynn 2.50
25 Barry Bonds 6.00
26 Ken Griffey Jr. 4.00
27 Juan Gonzalez .75
28 Roger Clemens 3.00

Golden Jubilee Jumbos

The Golden Jubilee subset cards from Series 2 C.C. were reproduced in 4X (5" x 7") size as one-per-box inserts in special versions of retail packaging.

NM/M
Complete Set (9): 17.50
Common Player: 1.00
271 Andruw Jones 1.50
272 Alex Rodriguez 4.00
273 Juan Gonzalez 1.00
274 Nomar Garciaparra 2.00
275 Ken Griffey Jr. 3.00
276 Tino Martinez 1.00
277 Roger Clemens 2.00
278 Barry Bonds 5.00
279 Mike Piazza 3.00

Jumbos (3.5x5)

These double-size versions of various Series 1 cards were available one per special blister pack of Collector's Choice sold in retail chains.

NM/M
Complete Set (15): 17.50
Common Player: 1.00
35 Andruw Jones 1.50
40 Cal Ripken Jr. 3.00
55 Ryne Sandberg 1.75
60 Frank Thomas 1.50
95 Gary Sheffield 1.25
97 Charles Johnson 1.00
145 Mike Piazza 2.00
160 Paul Molitor 1.50
180 Tino Martinez 1.00
220 Mark McGwire 2.50
225 Ken Caminiti 1.00
240 Ken Griffey Jr. 2.00
242 Jay Buhner 1.00
245 Juan Gonzalez 1.25
249 Ivan Rodriguez 1.25

Jumbos (5x7)

These super-size (5" x 7") cards were one-per-box inserts in Series 2 retail packaging. Besides being four times the size of a normal card, the 5x7s are identical to the regular versions.

NM/M
Complete Set (10): 15.00
Common Player: 1.00
306 Chipper Jones 2.00
321 Nomar Garciaparra 2.00
360 Larry Walker 1.00
450 Derek Jeter 4.00
463 Scott Rolen 1.25
480 Tony Gwynn 2.00
490 Barry Bonds 4.00
495 Alex Rodriguez 3.00
525 Jose Cruz Jr. 1.00
530 Roger Clemens 2.50

Mini Bobbing Heads

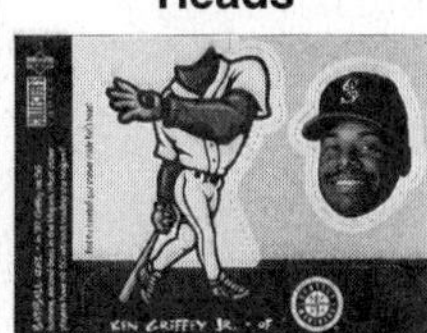

The cards in this 30-card insert series can be punched out and assembled into a stand-up figure with a removable bobbing head. They are a Series 2 insert.

NM/M
Complete Set (30): 20.00
Common Player: .25
Inserted 1:3
1 Tim Salmon .25
2 Travis Lee .25
3 Matt Williams .25
4 Chipper Jones 1.00
5 Greg Maddux 1.00
6 Cal Ripken Jr. 2.50
7 Nomar Garciaparra 1.00
8 Mo Vaughn .25
9 Sammy Sosa 1.00
10 Frank Thomas .75
11 Kenny Lofton .25
12 Jaret Wright .25
13 Larry Walker .25
14 Tony Clark .25
15 Edgar Renteria .25
16 Jeff Bagwell .75
17 Mike Piazza 1.50
18 Vladimir Guerrero .75
19 Derek Jeter 2.50
20 Ben Grieve .25
21 Scott Rolen .50
22 Mark McGwire 2.00
23 Tony Gwynn 1.00
24 Barry Bonds 2.50
25 Ken Griffey Jr. 1.50
26 Alex Rodriguez 2.00
27 Fred McGriff .25
28 Juan Gonzalez .40
29 Roger Clemens 1.25
30 Jose Cruz Jr. .25

Rookie Class: Prime Choice

This 18-card set is a parallel of the Rookie Class subset. Each card is foil-stamped with the words "Prime Choice Reserve." This hobby-only set is sequentially numbered to 500 and was inserted in Series 2 packs.

NM/M
Complete Set (18): 30.00
Common Player: 2.00
415 Carl Pavano 2.00
416 A.J. Hinch 2.00
417 David Dellucci 2.00
418 Bruce Chen 2.00
419 Darron Ingram 2.00
420 Sean Casey 5.00
421 Mark L. Johnson 2.00
422 Gabe Alvarez 2.00
423 Alex Gonzalez 2.00
424 Daryle Ward 2.00
425 Russell Branyan 2.00
426 Mike Caruso 2.00
427 Mike Kinkade 2.00
428 Ramon Hernandez 2.00
429 Matt Clement 2.00
430 Travis Lee 2.50
431 Shane Monahan 2.00
432 Rich Butler 2.00

StarQuest - Series 1

The StarQuest insert in Series 1 consists of 90 cards within four tiers. The tiers are designated by the number of stars found on front, the more the better: Special Delivery (#1-45, one star), Students of the Game (two stars, #46-65), Super Powers (three stars, #66-80) and Super Star Domain (four stars, #81-90). All cards are numbered with a "SQ" prefix.

NM/M
Complete Set (90): 185.00
Common Special Delivery (1-45): .25
Inserted 1:1
Common Student of the Game (46-65): .75
Inserted 1:21
Common Super Power (66-80): 2.00
Inserted 1:71
Common Superstar Domain (81-90): 3.00
Inserted 1:145
1 Nomar Garciaparra 1.50
2 Scott Rolen .75
3 Jason Dickson .25
4 Jaret Wright .25
5 Kevin Orie .25
6 Jose Guillen .25
7 Matt Morris .25
8 Mike Cameron .25
9 Kevin Polcovich .25
10 Jose Cruz Jr. .25
11 Miguel Tejada .40
12 Fernando Tatis .25
13 Todd Helton .65
14 Ken Cloude .25
15 Ben Grieve .25
16 Dante Powell .25
17 Bubba Trammell .25
18 Juan Encarnacion .25
19 Derrek Lee .50
20 Paul Konerko .35
21 Richard Hidalgo .25
22 Denny Neagle .25
23 David Justice .25
24 Pedro J. Martinez 1.00
25 Greg Maddux 1.50
26 Edgar Martinez .25
27 Cal Ripken Jr. 2.50
28 Tim Salmon .25
29 Shawn Estes .25
30 Ken Griffey Jr. 2.00
31 Brad Radke .25
32 Andy Pettitte .40
33 Curt Schilling .50
34 Raul Mondesi .25
35 Alex Rodriguez 2.25
36 Jeff Kent .25
37 Jeff Bagwell 1.00
38 Juan Gonzalez .50
39 Barry Bonds 2.50
40 Mark McGwire 2.00
41 Frank Thomas 1.00
42 Ray Lankford .25
43 Tony Gwynn 1.50
44 Mike Piazza 1.75
45 Tino Martinez .25
46 Nomar Garciaparra 3.00
47 Paul Molitor 1.50
48 Chuck Knoblauch .75
49 Rusty Greer .75
50 Cal Ripken Jr. 6.00
51 Roberto Alomar 1.00
52 Scott Rolen 1.00
53 Derek Jeter 6.00
54 Mark Grace .75
55 Randy Johnson 1.50
56 Craig Biggio .75
57 Kenny Lofton .75
58 Eddie Murray 1.50
59 Ryne Sandberg 2.00
60 Rickey Henderson 1.50
61 Darin Erstad 1.00
62 Jim Edmonds .75
63 Ken Caminiti .75
64 Ivan Rodriguez 1.25
65 Tony Gwynn 2.00
66 Tony Clark 2.00
67 Andres Galarraga 2.00
68 Rafael Palmeiro 3.00
69 Manny Ramirez 6.00
70 Albert Belle 2.00
71 Jay Buhner 2.00
72 Mo Vaughn 2.00
73 Barry Bonds 15.00
74 Chipper Jones 7.50
75 Jeff Bagwell 6.00
76 Jim Thome 3.00
77 Sammy Sosa 7.50
78 Todd Hundley 2.00
79 Matt Williams 2.00
80 Vinny Castilla 2.00
81 Jose Cruz Jr. 3.00
82 Frank Thomas 7.50
83 Juan Gonzalez 4.00
84 Mike Piazza 15.00
85 Alex Rodriguez 20.00
86 Larry Walker 3.00
87 Tino Martinez 3.00
88 Greg Maddux 12.50
89 Mark McGwire 20.00
90 Ken Griffey Jr. 15.00

StarQuest - Series 2

The 30-card StarQuest insert was included in Series 2 packs. The insert has four parallel tiers - Single, Double, Triple and Home Run - designat-

ed by the number of baseball diamond icons on the card front. Single cards were inserted 1:1, Doubles 1:21, Triples 1:71 and Home Runs are sequentially numbered to 100. The second series SQ cards feature a front design with the letters "QSUTEASRT" in color blocks vertically at left.

		NM/M
Complete Set (30):		17.50
Common Player:		.25
Singles 1:1		
Doubles 1:21		2X
Triples 1:71		6X
Home Runs:		15X
1	Ken Griffey Jr.	1.25
2	Jose Cruz Jr.	.25
3	Cal Ripken Jr.	2.00
4	Roger Clemens	1.00
5	Frank Thomas	.75
6	Derek Jeter	2.00
7	Alex Rodriguez	1.50
8	Andruw Jones	.75
9	Vladimir Guerrero	.75
10	Mark McGwire	1.50
11	Kenny Lofton	.25
12	Pedro J. Martinez	.75
13	Greg Maddux	1.00
14	Larry Walker	.25
15	Barry Bonds	2.00
16	Chipper Jones	1.00
17	Jeff Bagwell	.75
18	Juan Gonzalez	.50
19	Tony Gwynn	1.00
20	Mike Piazza	1.25
21	Tino Martinez	.25
22	Mo Vaughn	.20
23	Ben Grieve	.25
24	Scott Rolen	.60
25	Nomar Garciaparra	1.00
26	Paul Konerko	.35
27	Jaret Wright	.25
28	Gary Sheffield	.50
29	Travis Lee	.25
30	Todd Helton	.65

StarQuest Super Powers Jumbos

This enlarged (3-1/2" x 5") version of the StarQuest Super Powers cards from Series 1 were a retail-only variation found one per blister pack of specially marked Collector's Choice product.

		NM/M
Complete Set (10):		17.50
Common Player:		1.00
SQ67	Andres Galarraga	1.00
SQ68	Rafael Palmeiro	2.00
SQ69	Manny Ramirez	2.50
SQ70	Albert Belle	1.00
SQ71	Jay Buhner	1.00
SQ72	Mo Vaughn	1.00
SQ73	Barry Bonds	5.00
SQ74	Chipper Jones	3.00
SQ75	Jeff Bagwell	2.50
SQ76	Jim Thome	1.50

Stickums

This 30-card insert was seeded 1:3 Series 1 packs. The stickers can be peeled off the card and reused.

		NM/M
Complete Set (30):		7.00
Common Player:		.10
Inserted 1:3		
1	Andruw Jones	.35
2	Chipper Jones	.45
3	Cal Ripken Jr.	1.00
4	Nomar Garciaparra	.45
5	Mo Vaughn	.10
6	Ryne Sandberg	.45
7	Sammy Sosa	.45
8	Frank Thomas	.35
9	Albert Belle	.10
10	Jim Thome	.30
11	Manny Ramirez	.35
12	Larry Walker	.10
13	Gary Sheffield	.20
14	Jeff Bagwell	.35
15	Mike Piazza	.60
16	Paul Molitor	.35
17	Pedro J. Martinez	.35
18	Todd Hundley	.10
19	Derek Jeter	1.00
20	Tino Martinez	.10
21	Curt Schilling	.25
22	Mark McGwire	.75
23	Tony Gwynn	.45
24	Barry Bonds	1.00
25	Ken Griffey Jr.	.60
26	Alex Rodriguez	.75
27	Juan Gonzalez	.20
28	Ivan Rodriguez	.30
29	Roger Clemens	.50
30	Jose Cruz Jr.	.10

You Crash the Game

These 90 game cards were inserted one per five Series 2 packs. Each card features a player and a list of dates. If the pictured player hit a home run on one of those days, collectors with the card could mail it in for a graphically enhanced prize version. Instant Winner cards of each player were also inserted at the rate of 1:721 and could be exchanged for the complete 30-card prize set. Deadline for exchange of all winning cards was Dec. 1, 1998. Winning cards are designated here with an asterisk and can be expected to be somewhat scarcer than non-winning dates.

		NM/M
Complete Set (90):		75.00
Common Player:		.50
Instant Winner:		8X
Inserted 1:5		
CG1	Ken Griffey Jr. (June 26-28*)	3.00
CG1	Ken Griffey Jr. (July 7)	1.25
CG1	Ken Griffey Jr. (Sept. 21-24*)	3.00
CG2	Travis Lee (July 27-30)	.50
CG2	Travis Lee (Aug. 27-30)	.50
CG2	Travis Lee (Sept. 17-20)	.50
CG3	Larry Walker (July 17-19)	.50
CG3	Larry Walker (Aug. 27-30*)	1.00
CG3	Larry Walker (Sept. 25-27*)	1.00
CG4	Tony Clark (July 9-12*)	1.00
CG4	Tony Clark (June 30-July 2)	.50
CG4	Tony Clark (Sept. 4-6)	.50
CG5	Cal Ripken Jr. (June 22-25*)	4.00
CG5	Cal Ripken Jr. (July 7)	2.00
CG5	Cal Ripken Jr. (Sept. 4-6)	2.00
CG6	Tim Salmon (June 22-25)	.50
CG6	Tim Salmon (Aug. 28-30)	.50
CG6	Tim Salmon (Sept. 14-15)	.50
CG7	Vinny Castilla (June 30-July 2*)	1.00
CG7	Vinny Castilla (Aug. 27-30*)	1.00
CG7	Vinny Castilla (Sept. 7-10*)	1.00
CG8	Fred McGriff (June 22-25)	.50
CG8	Fred McGriff (July 3-5)	.50
CG8	Fred McGriff (Sept. 18-20*)	1.00
CG9	Matt Williams (July 17-29)	.50
CG9	Matt Williams (Sept. 14-16*)	1.00
CG9	Matt Williams (Sept. 18-20)	.50
CG10	Mark McGwire (July 7)	1.50
CG10	Mark McGwire (July 24-26*)	3.50
CG10	Mark McGwire (Aug. 18-19*)	3.50
CG11	Albert Belle (July 3-5)	.50
CG11	Albert Belle (Aug. 21-23*)	1.00
CG11	Albert Belle (Sept. 11-13)	.50
CG12	Jay Buhner (July 9-12*)	1.00
CG12	Jay Buhner (Aug. 6-9)	.50
CG12	Jay Buhner (Sept. 25-27)	.50
CG13	Vladimir Guerrero (June 22-25)	.75
CG13	Vladimir Guerrero (Aug. 10-12*)	1.50
CG13	Vladimir Guerrero (Sept. 14-16*)	1.50
CG14	Andruw Jones (July 16-19*)	1.50
CG14	Andruw Jones (Aug. 27-30*)	1.50
CG14	Andruw Jones (Sept. 17-20)	.75
CG15	Nomar Garciaparra (July 9-12)	1.00
CG15	Nomar Garciaparra (Aug. 13-16*)	2.50
CG15	Nomar Garciaparra (Sept. 24-27)	1.00
CG16	Ken Caminiti (June 26-28*)	1.00
CG16	Ken Caminiti (July 13-15*)	1.00
CG16	Ken Caminiti (Sept. 10-13)	.50
CG17	Sammy Sosa (July 9-12*)	2.50
CG17	Sammy Sosa (Aug. 27-30*)	2.50
CG17	Sammy Sosa (Sept. 18-20)	1.00
CG18	Ben Grieve (June 30-July 2*)	1.00
CG18	Ben Grieve (Aug. 14-16)	.50
CG18	Ben Grieve (Sept. 24-27)	.50
CG19	Mo Vaughn (July 7)	.50
CG19	Mo Vaughn (Sept. 7-9)	.50
CG19	Mo Vaughn (Sept. 24-27*)	1.00
CG20	Frank Thomas (July 7)	.75
CG20	Frank Thomas (July 17-19*)	1.50
CG20	Frank Thomas (Sept. 4-6)	.75
CG21	Manny Ramirez (July 9-12)	.75
CG21	Manny Ramirez (Aug. 13-16*)	1.50
CG21	Manny Ramirez (Sept. 18-20*)	1.50
CG22	Jeff Bagwell (July 7)	.75
CG22	Jeff Bagwell (Aug. 28-30*)	1.50
CG22	Jeff Bagwell (Sept. 4-6*)	1.50
CG23	Jose Cruz Jr. (July 9-12)	.50
CG23	Jose Cruz Jr. (Aug. 13-16)	.50
CG23	Jose Cruz Jr. (Sept. 18-20)	.50
CG24	Alex Rodriguez (July 7*)	3.50
CG24	Alex Rodriguez (Aug. 6-9*)	3.50
CG24	Alex Rodriguez (Sept. 21-23*)	3.50
CG25	Mike Piazza (June 22-25*)	3.00
CG25	Mike Piazza (July 7)	1.25
CG25	Mike Piazza (Sept. 10-13*)	3.00
CG26	Tino Martinez (June 26-28*)	1.00
CG26	Tino Martinez (July 9-12)	.50
CG26	Tino Martinez (Aug. 13-16)	.50
CG27	Chipper Jones (July 3-5)	1.00
CG27	Chipper Jones (Aug. 27-30)	1.00
CG27	Chipper Jones (Sept. 17-20)	1.00
CG28	Juan Gonzalez (July 7)	.60
CG28	Juan Gonzalez (Aug. 6-9*)	1.25
CG28	Juan Gonzalez (Sept. 11-13*)	1.25
CG29	Jim Thome (June 22-23)	.60
CG29	Jim Thome (July 23-26*)	1.25
CG29	Jim Thome (Sept. 24-27)	.60
CG30	Barry Bonds (July 7*)	4.00
CG30	Barry Bonds (Sept. 4-6)	2.00
CG30	Barry Bonds (Sept. 18-20*)	4.00

You Crash the Game Winners

Collectors who redeemed winning "Crash" cards prior to the Dec. 1, 1998 deadline received an upgraded version of that player's card. Similar in format, the winners' cards have an action photo on front (different than the game card), with a metallic foil background. Instead of dates in the three circles at bottom are the letters "W I N." Backs have a career summary and stats, instead of the redemption instructions found on the game cards. The cards are numbered with a "CG" prefix. Cards of players who didn't homer during their designated dates were available only by redeeming a scarce (1:721 packs) Instant Win card. They are indicated here by "SP."

		NM/M
Complete Set (30):		9.00
Common Player:		.25
CG1	Ken Griffey Jr.	1.00
CG2	Travis Lee/SP	.75
CG3	Larry Walker	.25
CG4	Tony Clark	.25
CG5	Cal Ripken Jr.	1.50
CG6	Tim Salmon/SP	.60
CG7	Vinny Castilla	.25
CG8	Fred McGriff	.25
CG9	Matt Williams	.25
CG10	Mark McGwire	1.25
CG11	Albert Belle	.25
CG12	Jay Buhner	.25
CG13	Vladimir Guerrero	.50
CG14	Andruw Jones	.50
CG15	Nomar Garciaparra	.75
CG16	Ken Caminiti	.25
CG17	Sammy Sosa	.75
CG18	Ben Grieve	.25
CG19	Mo Vaughn	.25
CG20	Frank Thomas	.50
CG21	Manny Ramirez	.50
CG22	Jeff Bagwell	.50
CG23	Jose Cruz Jr./SP	.60
CG24	Alex Rodriguez	1.25
CG25	Mike Piazza	1.00
CG26	Tino Martinez	.25
CG27	Chipper Jones/SP	1.50
CG28	Juan Gonzalez	.35
CG29	Jim Thome	.35
CG30	Barry Bonds	1.50

You Crash/Game Instant Winner

Found on average of one per 721 packs, these Instant Winner cards could be redeemed (with a $2 handling fee) for a complete set of You Crash the Game exchange cards - the only way Crash winner cards of Travis Lee, Jose Cruz Jr. and Chipper Jones could be obtained. These special cards have an instant winner logo on front in place of game dates, and a congratulatory message on back along with instructions for redemption prior to the Dec. 1, 1998 deadline.

	NM/M
Complete Set (30):	250.00
Common Player:	4.00

1995 Collector's Edge Ball Park Franks Baseball Legends

"Baseball Legends" Yogi Berra and Brooks Robinson are featured in this hot dog promotional set. Sunday newspapers on March 5 featured a coupon used to obtain the pair of autographed cards for eight proofs-of-purchase, or $2.50 with four UPCs or $5 with two UPCs. Cards have color photos, with uniform logos removed, and marbled borders. An authentic autograph is across the front of the card. Backs have a portrait photo and career summary. Each card was accompanied by a card-like certificate of authenticity.

		NM/M
Complete Set (2):		20.00
(1)	Yogi Berra	16.00
(2)	Frank Robinson	8.00

1993 Colorado Fever Rockies

In its inaugural issue, a fan magazine titled "Colorado Fever" issued a sheet of nine baseball cards in both its "Regional" and "Metro" editions. Stapled into the center of the magazine is an 8-3/8" x 11" cardboard insert. One panel has nine Rockies cards which are not perforated and would measure about 2-5/8" x 3-5/8" if cut from the sheet. Cards from the Metro edition feature players in uniform; most of the cards from the Regional edition show the players in street clothes. It is not known whether future editions of the announced twice-annual magazine were ever published or if they contained baseball card inserts.

		NM/M
Complete Set (18):		8.00
Common Player:		.50
1M	David Nied	.50
2M	Charlie Hayes	.50
3M	Andy Ashby	.50
4M	Joe Girardi	.50
5M	Don Baylor	.60
6M	Andres Galarraga	.50
7M	Jim Tatum	.50
8M	Eric Young	.50
9M	Dante Bichette	.50
1R	Alex Cole	.50
2R	Don Baylor	.60
3R	Dante Bichette	.50
4R	Jeff Parrett	.50
5R	David Nied	.50
6R	Butch Henry	.50
7R	Andres Galarraga	.50
8R	Daryl Boston	.50
9R	Joe Girardi	.50

1994 Colorado Rockies Police

The Rockies' premiere police set is an oversized (2-5/8" x 4") effort with posed and action player photos on a yellow and purple background on front. Team logo and name are above the photo, while ID and uniform number are beneath the photo. Backs are printed in purple with a few bits of personal data and stats, a safety message and sponsors' logos. The cards are checklisted here in alphabetical order.

		NM/M
Complete Set (27):		6.00
Common Player:		.50
(1)	Don Baylor	.75
(2)	Dante Bichette	.75
(3)	Willie Blair	.50
(4)	Kent Bottenfield	.50
(5)	Ellis Burks	.50
(6)	Vinny Castilla	.50
(7)	Marvin Freeman	.50
(8)	Andres Galarraga	.75
(9)	Andres Galarraga (Batting champion.)	.75
(10)	Joe Girardi	.50
(11)	Mike Harkey	.50
(12)	Greg Harris	.50
(13)	Charlie Hayes	.50
(14)	Darren Holmes	.50
(15)	Howard Johnson	.50
(16)	Nelson Liriano	.50
(17)	Roberto Mejia	.50
(18)	Mike Munoz	.50
(19)	David Nied	.50
(20)	Steve Reed	.50
(21)	Armando Reynoso	.50
(22)	Bruce Ruffin	.50
(23)	Danny Sheaffer	.50
(24)	Darrell Sherman	.50
(25)	Walt Weiss	.50
(26)	Eric Young	.50
(27)	Rockies Coaches (Larry Bearnarth, Dwight Evans, Gene Glynn, Ron Hassey, Bill Plummer, Don Zimmer)	.50

1995 Colorado Rockies Police

With only a dozen players included, this is one of the smallest safety sets of the genre. The 2-5/8" x 4" cards have color player action photos on front, bordered in black with the team logo in the lower-right corner. The player's last name and year appear in orange in the upper-right. Backs are in black-and-white and include a safety message or cartoon, and a few biographical data and stats. Cards are checklisted by uniform number.

		NM/M
Complete Set (12):		5.00
Common Player:		.50
6	Jason Bates	.50
7	Joe Girardi	.50
9	Vinny Castilla	.50
10	Dante Bichette	.50
12	Mike Kingery	.50
14	Andres Galarraga	.75
20	Bill Swift	.50
21	Eric Young	.50
22	Walt Weiss	.50
25	Don Baylor	.75
26	Ellis Burks	.50
33	Larry Walker	1.50

1996 Colorado Rockies Police

The Rockies third annual safety set is the team's largest, at 27 cards. The set's format is 2-5/8" x 4" and is sponsored by Kansas City Life Insurance. Fronts have game-action photos, with the team logo, player last name and uniform number at bottom. Backs are printed in purple and feature a safety-message cartoon. The set was initially distributed to fans attending an April game. The set is checklisted here by uniform number. A Spanish-language version of the set was also issued.

		NM/M
Complete Set (27):		5.00
Common Player:		.25
Spanish:		2X
1	Trenidad Hubbard	.25
3	Quinton McCracken	.25
6	Jason Bates	.25
9	Vinny Castilla	.25
10	Dante Bichette	.25
14	Andres Galarraga	.50
16	Curtis Leskanic	.25
18	Bruce Ruffin	.25
20	Bill Swift	.25
21	Eric Young	.25
22	Walt Weiss	.25
23	Bryan Rekar	.25
25	Don Baylor	.35
26	Ellis Burks	.25
28	Lance Painter	.25
30	Kevin Ritz	.25
31	Bret Saberhagen	.35
32	Mark Thompson	.25
33	Larry Walker	1.00
34	Jayhawk Owens	.25
35	John Vander Wal	.25
38	Roger Bailey	.25
39	Steve Reed	.25
40	Darren Holmes	.25
42	Armando Reynoso	.25
43	Mike Munoz	.25
44	Marvin Freeman	.25

1997 Colorado Rockies Police

In conjunction with the Colorado Association of Chiefs of Police, the Rockies handed out this safety set at a designated home game early in the season. It is the team's fourth annual safety set. The 2-1/2" x 3-1/2" cards feature game-action photos on front surrounded by a white border. The team logo is at upper-left;

player identification is in purple and gray stripes diagonally at bottom. Backs are in black-and-white and have some player personal data, a career-best stat lines and a safety message. Cards are numbered by uniform number in a baseball at upper-right.

		NM/M
Complete Set (12):		5.00
Common Player:		.60
3	Quinton McCracken	.60
8	Kirt Manwaring	.60
9	Vinny Castilla	.60
10	Dante Bichette	.60
14	Andres Galarraga	.75
20	Bill Swift	.60
21	Eric Young	.60
22	Walt Weiss	.60
25	Don Baylor	.75
26	Ellis Burks	.60
33	Larry Walker	1.50
00	Dinger (Mascot)	.60

1998 Colorado Rockies Police

Children attending a May 31 promotional game at Coors Field received this set of Rockies cards. Game-action color photos are featured on front, borderless at top, bottom and left. At right is a vertical gray stripe with the player's name and position; team logo and name are at bottom. On back is a player portrait photo, identification, biographical details, an inspirational message and logos of the sponsoring organizations.

		NM/M
Complete Set (12):		6.00
Common Player:		.35
3	Mike Lansing	.50
5	Neifi Perez	.50
8	Kirt Manwaring	.50
9	Vinny Castilla	.50
10	Dante Bichette	.50
17	Todd Helton	4.00
25	Don Baylor	.60
26	Ellis Burks	.50
33	Larry Walker	1.00
34	Pedro Astacio	.50
57	Darryl Kile	.50
00	Dinger (Mascot)	.50

1999 Colorado Rockies Police

Children attending a promotional game at Coors Field received this set of Rockies cards. Borderless game-action color photos are featured on front. At right is a vertical strip with the team name; the player name and position are at bottom. On back is a player portrait photo, identification,

biographical details, a safety message and logos of the sponsoring organizations.

		NM/M
Complete Set (12):		6.00
Common Player:		1.00
(1)	Dante Bichette	1.00
(2)	Vinny Castilla	1.00
(3)	Dinger (Mascot)	1.00
(4)	Jerry DiPoto	1.00
(5)	Darryl Hamilton	1.00
(6)	Todd Helton	2.50
(7)	Darryl Kile	1.00
(8)	Mike Lansing	1.00
(9)	Jim Leyland	1.00
(10)	Kirt Manwaring	1.00
(11)	Neifi Perez	1.00
(12)	Larry Walker	1.50

2000 Colorado Rockies Police

Children attending a May 28 promotional game at Coors Field received this set of Rockies cards. Borderless game-action color photos are featured on front. On back is a player portrait photo, identification, biographical details, an inspirational message and a credit line for the Colorado Association of Chiefs of Police.

		NM/M
Complete Set (12):		6.00
Common Player:		.75
3	Mike Lansing	.75
4	Jeffrey Hammonds	.75
5	Neifi Perez	.75
7	Jeff Cirillo	.75
8	Brent Mayne	.75
17	Todd Helton	3.00
24	Tom Goodwin	.75
25	Buddy Bell	.75
30	Rolando Arrojo	.75
33	Larry Walker	1.50
00	Dinger (Mascot)	.75
---	Coors Field	.75

2002 Colorado Rockies Police

The Rockies hot dog vendor sponsored this stadium give-away safety set featuring the manager and 11 popular players. The 2-1/2" x 3-1/2" cards have game-action photos vignetted on front with white borders. A 10-year team anniversary logo is lower-left. Horizontal backs have a portrait photo in the top-right corner and a ghosted image of the front photo at left, which is overprinted with player data, 2001 stats, career highlights and a safety or inspirational message in English or Spanish. The sponsor and team logos are at right.

		NM/M
Complete Set (12):		6.00
Common Player:		.50
2	Jose Ortiz	.50
4	Juan Uribe	.50
9	Juan Pierre	1.50
10	Mike Hampton	.50
12	Todd Zeile	.50
13	Clint Hurdle	.50
15	Denny Neagle	.50
17	Todd Helton	2.50
27	Todd Hollandsworth	.50
29	Gary Bennett	.50
33	Larry Walker	1.00
00	Dinger (Mascot)	.50

2005 Comcast Oakland A's

Sponsored by Comcast, 15,000 of these team sets were given away at the September 24 game. Fronts have a gold border. Green-and-gold backs have player personal data.

		NM/M
Complete Set (32):		10.00
Common Player:		.25
(1)	Team Photo/Checklist	.25
2	Ken Macha	.25
3	Eric Chavez	.75
4	Barry Zito	.75
5	Mark Kotsay	.25
6	Rich Harden	.75
7	Jason Kendall	.25
8	Bobby Crosby	1.00
9	Jay Payton	.25
10	Scott Hatteberg	.25
11	Huston Street	1.00
12	Mark Ellis	.25
13	Dan Haren	.75
14	Nick Swisher	.25
15	Joe Blanton	.75
16	Marco Scutaro	.25
17	Kirk Saarloos	.25
18	Dan Johnson	.75
19	Kiko Calero	.25
20	Bobby Kielty	.25
21	Justin Duchscherer	.25
22	Adam Melhuse	.25
23	Ricardo Rincon	.25
24	Joe Kennedy	.25
25	Keiichi Yabu	.25
26	Erubiel Durazo	.25
27	Juan Cruz	.25
28	Keith Ginter	.25
29	Octavio Dotel	.25
30	Charles Thomas	.25
31	Jay Witasick	.25
32	Coaching Staff (Brad Fischer, Bob Geren, Dave Hudgens, Rene Lachemann, Curt Young, Ron Washington)	.25

1995 Comic Images National Pastime Promo

This unnumbered card was issued to promote Comic Images' set of baseball history cards.

The 2-1/2" x 3-1/2" card has a familiar color photo of company spokesman Phil Rizzuto on front, done up in chromium technology and with the Yankees team logos removed from the uniform. The back advertises the forthcoming card set.

	NM/M
Phil Rizzuto	3.00

1995 Comic Images The National Pastime

This set is principally made up of 19th Century baseball images done up in 20th Century chromium card technology to detail the history of baseball from the 1860s through the 1950s. As might be expected, there was little positive reaction from collectors. Photos of old baseball collectibles, including a few vintage baseball cards are scattered throughout the set as are a few actual player photos. Hall of Famer Phil Rizzuto was tapped to promote the issue, but his name was misspelled on the cards' box. A number of special inserts including Rizzuto autographed cards were part of the issue.

		NM/M
Complete Set (90):		8.00
Common Card:		.10
Autographed Rizzuto Card:		35.00
MagnaChrome Rizzuto Career Card (6):		2.00
MagnaChrome Diamond Cover (3):		1.00
Medallion Card:		2.00
Six-card Case-Topper Sheet:		6.00
1	Sportsman's Park	.10
2	Harper's Weekly, August, 1913	.10
3	Shibe Park	.10
4	Polo Grounds Print	.10
5	Forbes Field	.10
6	Hall of Fame (Phil Rizzuto)	.25
7	League Park	.10
8	Highlander Park	.10
9	South Side Park	.10
10	Catchers' Mitt	.10
11	Baseball Trophy	.10
12	Baseball Plate	.10
13	Bisque Figure	.10
14	Beanbag	.10
15	Tobacco Carved Figure	.10
16	Sunday Magazine	.10
17	Street & Smith Sport	.10
18	Collier's	.10
19	Bluebook	.10
20	Chadwick's	.10
21	Harper's Weekly	.10
22	American Magazine	.10
23	Crazy Baseball Stories	.10
24	New York Giants, 1892	.10
25	Cincinnati American Association, 1882	.10
26	Chicago White Stockings, 1885	.10
27	Baltimore Blues, 1890	.10
28	Chicago & All-Americans, 1889	.10
29	Philadelphia Baseball Team, 1910	.10
30	1887 Goodwin & Co. Champions	.25
31	John McGraw	.15
32	Home Run (1885 trade card)	.10
33	Lorillard Chicago BBC	.10
34	Boston BBC	.10
35	Out at First (Trade card.)	.10
36	"Coffee Cards"	.10
37	Uncut Sheet - Detail	.10
38	Tobin Lithographers	.10
39	Uncut Sheet - Die Cut	.10
40	Patsy Dougherty (T207)	.10
41	A Regular Corker (1885 trade card)	.10
42	Barker's Advertising Book	.10
43	Toledo BBC Tobacco Poster	.10
44	Shredded Wheat Advertisement	.10
45	BVD Advertisement	.10
46	Police Gazette Poster	.10
47	Japanese Poster	.10
48	Safe Hit Vegetable Crate Label	.10
49	Slide, Kelly, Slide Poster	.10
50	Peck & Snyder Hat Advertisement	.10
51	Reach Gloves Catalog	.10
52	New York Giants Scorecard	.10
53	Game Card	.10
54	Wright & Ditson Guide	.10
55	1933 All-Star Game Program	.10
56	Stadium Scene	.10
57	Currier & Ives Print	.10
58	Scorecard Artwork	.10
59	Folk Art	.10
60	Batter (Wrong front, belongs to #73.)	.10
61	Cartoon	.10
62	Teddy Roosevelt Cartoon	.10
63	Uncle Sam Cartoon	.10
64	Casey at the Bat	.15
65	Seymour Church Print	.10
66	Valentine Card	.10
67	Pinup Book	.10
68	Uncle Sam WWI Sheet Music	.10
69	Baseball Sheet Music	.10
70	Saturday Globe	.10
71	Ft. Wayne Woman Player	.15
72	Spalding Baseball Guide	.10
73	Rally Day Postcard (Wrong front, belongs to #60.)	.10
74	Spalding Advertisement Die Cut	.10
75	Our Baseball Club Cover	.10
76	Jake Beckley	.15
77	Cap Anson (Allen & Ginter album page)	.25
78	St. Louis Player	.10
79	Sam Thompson (Scrap's Die Cut)	.15
80	Bobby Wallace (Turkey Red cabinet)	.15
81	Fogarty & McGuire (Jim Fogarty, Deacon McGuire (1887 Kalamazoo Bats detail)	.15
82	Yank Robinson (1887 die-cut game card)	.15
83	Charles Comiskey (1887 Scrap's tobacco die-cut)	.15
84	Picked Off! (Action photo.)	.10
85	Error (Action photo.)	.10
86	Third Base (Action photo.)	.10
87	Safe at Home (Action photo.)	.10
88	Baseball Action (Action photo.)	.10
89	Great Fielding (Action photo.)	.10
90	Checklist	.10

1991 Conlon Collection Prototypes

The cards which previewed the debut set of Conlon Collection cards in the 1990s can generally be identified by the lack of Major League Baseball logo and Curtis Management copyright information on back. Except for the colorized Babe Ruth card, they

are not otherwise marked as prototypes. While most of the 1991 Conlon prototypes were distributed in relatively small quantities, reportedly 2,940, the colorized Ty Cobbs was an edition of 60,000 and the colorized Babe Ruth card was produced for the 12th National Sports Collectors Convention in Anaheim, Calif., to the tune of 225,000 cards.

NM/M
Complete Set (6): 9.00
Common Player: 2.00
13 Ty Cobb (Colorized edition of 60,000.) 4.50
34 Dizzy Dean 2.00
111 Lou Gehrig 3.50
145 Babe Ruth 4.50
145 Babe Ruth (Colorized, edition of 225,000.) 3.00
250 Ty Cobb 3.00

1991 Conlon Collection

This 330-card set features the photography of Charles Martin Conlon, who was active from before 1910 through the early 1940s. Black-and-white photos are set against black borders on the UV-coated card fronts. Megacards worked with The Sporting News (owners of the Conlon photos) to release the set. Several subsets are featured such as Hall of Famers, 1927 New York Yankees, MVPs and more. The backs feature statistics and career highlights and can be found either with or without the MLB logo.

NM/M
Complete Factory Set (330): 13.50
Factory Set w/Autographed Feller: 16.00
Complete Set (330): 9.00
Common Player: .10
Wax Pack (18): .50
Wax Box (36): 15.00
1 Rogers Hornsby .25
2 James E. Foxx .25
3 Jay H. Dean .25
4 Walter J.V. Maranville .10
5 Paul G. Waner .10
6 Lloyd J. Waner .10
7 Melvin T. Ott .15
8 John P. Wagner .30
9 Walter P. Johnson .25
10 Carl O. Hubbell .15
11 Frank F. Frisch .15
12 Hazen S. Cuyler .10
13 Charles H. Ruffing .15
14 Henry B. Greenberg .15
15 John J. Evers .10
16 Hugh A. Jennings .10
17 David J. Bancroft .10
18 Joseph M. Medwick .10
19 Theodore A. Lyons .10
20 Charles A. Bender .10
21 Edward T. Collins .10
22 James L. Bottomley .10
23 Robert M. Grove .15
24 Max Carey .10
25 Burleigh A. Grimes .10
26 Ross M. Youngs .10
27 Ernest N. Lombardi .10
28 Joseph V. McCarthy .10
29 Lewis R. Wilson .10
30 Charles H. Klein .10
31 Howard E. Averill Sr. .10
32 Grover C. Alexander .15
33 Charles J. Hafey .10
34 William B. McKechnie .10
35 Robert W.A. Feller .15
36 Harold J. Traynor .10
37 Charles D. Stengel .15
38 Joseph F. Vaughan .10
39 Eppa Rixey .10
40 Joseph W. Sewell .10
41 Urban C. Faber .10
42 Travis C. Jackson .10
43 Jesse J. Haines .10
44 Tristram E. Speaker .25
45 Cornelius Mack .10
46 Cornelius Mack .10
47 Cornelius Mack .10
48 Raymond W. Schalk .10
49 Aloysius H. Simmons .10
50 Joseph E. Cronin .10
51 Gordon S. Cochrane .10
52 Harry E. Heilmann .10
53 John R. Mize .15
54 Edgar C. Rice .10
55 Edd J. Roush .10
56 Enos B. Slaughter .10
57 Christopher Mathewson .25
58 Fred C. Lindstrom .10
59 Charles L. Hartnett .10
60 George L. Kelly .10
61 Stanley R. Harris .10
62 Leon A. Goslin .10
63 Henry E. Manush .10
64 William H. Terry .10
65 John J. McGraw .10
66 George H. Sisler .10
67 Vernon L. Gomez .10
68 Joseph I. Judge .10
69 Thomas J. Thevenow .10
70 Charles M. Gelbert .10
71 Minter C. Hayes .10
72 Robert R. Fothergill .10
73 Adam A. Comorosky .10
74 Earl S. Smith .10
75 Samuel D. Gray .10
76 Peter W. Appleton .10
77 Eugene Moore Jr. .10
78 Arndt L. Jorgens .10
79 William H. Knickerbocker .10
80 Carl N. Reynolds .10
81 Oscar D. Melillo .10
82 John H. Burnett .10
83 Alvin J. Powell .10
84 John J. Murphy .10
85 Leroy E. Parmelee .10
86 James A. Ripple .10
87 Gerald H. Walker .10
88 George L. Earnshaw .10
89 William H. Southworth .10
90 Wallace Moses .10
91 George E. Walberg .10
92 James J. Dykes .10
93 Charles H. Root .10
94 John W. Cooney .10
95 Charles J. Grimm .10
96 Robert L. Johnson .10
97 John W. Scott .10
98 Raymond A. Radcliff .10
99 Frederick R. Ostermueller .10
100 Julian V. Wera .10
101 Miller J. Huggins .10
102 Raymond A. Morehart .10
103 Bernard O. Bengough .10
104 Walter H. Ruether .10
105 Earle B. Combs .10
106 Myles L. Thomas .10
107 Benjamin E. Paschal .10
108 Cedric M. Durst .10
109 William W. Moore .10
110 George H. Ruth 1.00
111 Louis H. Gehrig .50
112 Joseph A. Dugan .10
113 Anthony M. Lazzeri .10
114 Urban J. Shocker .10
115 Waite C. Hoyt .10
116 Charles T. O'Leary .10
117 Arthur Fletcher .10
118 Tharon L. Collins .10
119 Joseph O. Giard .10
120 Herbert J. Pennock .10
121 Michael Gazella .10
122 Robert W. Meusel .10
123 George W. Pipgras .10
124 John P. Grabowski .10
125 Mark A. Koenig .10
126 Stanley C. Hack .10
127 Earl O. Whitehill .10
128 William C. Lee .10
129 Frank O. Mancuso .10
130 Francis R. Blades .10
131 John I. Burns .10
132 Clinton H. Brown .10
133 William J. Dietrich .10
134 Darrell E. Blanton .10
135 Harry B. Hooper .10
136 Charles H. Shorten .10
137 Clarence W. Walker .10
138 George Foster .10
139 John J. Barry .10
140 Samuel P. Jones .10
141 Ernest G. Shore .10
142 Hubert B. Leonard .10
143 Herbert J. Pennock .10
144 Harold C. Janvrin .10
145 George H. Ruth 1.00
146 George E. Lewis .10
147 William L. Gardner .10
148 Richard C. Hoblitzel .10
149 Lewis E. Scott .10
150 Carl W. Mays .10
151 John A. Niehoff .10
152 Burton E. Shotton .10
153 Leon K. Ames .10
154 Fred Williams .10
155 William W. Hinchman .10
156 James R. Shawkey .10
157 Walter C. Pipp .10
158 George J. Burns .10
159 Robert H. Veach .10
160 Harold H. Chase .10
161 Thomas L. Hughes .10
162 Derrill B. Pratt .10
163 Henry K. Groh .10
164 Zachariah D. Wheat .10
165 Francis J. O'Doul .10
166 William E. Kamm .10
167 Paul G. Waner .10
168 Fred C. Snodgrass .10
169 Floyd C. Herman .10
170 Albert H. Bridwell .10
171 John T. Meyers .10
172 John B. Lobert .10
173 Raymond B. Bressler .10
174 Samuel P. Jones .10
175 Robert A. O'Farrell .10
176 George Toporcer .10
177 George E. McNeely .10
178 John H. Knott .10
179 Clarence F. Mueller .10
180 Thomas J.D. Bridges .10
181 Lloyd A. Brown .10
182 Lawrence J. Benton .10
183 Max F. Bishop .10
184 Morris Berg .20
185 Ralph F. Perkins .10
186 Stephen F. O'Neill .10
187 Glenn C. Myatt .10
188 Joseph A. Kuhel .10
189 Martin J. McManus .10
190 Charles F. Lucas .10
191 John P. McInnis .10
192 Edmund J. Miller .10
193 James L. Sewell .10
194 William H. Sherdel .10
195 Harold J. Rhyne .10
196 Guy T. Bush .10
197 Ervin Fox .10
198 Wesley C. Ferrell .10
199 Roy C. Johnson .10
200 William Wambsganss .10
201 George H. Burns .10
202 Clarence E. Mitchell .10
203 Cornelius Ball .10
204 John H. Neun .10
205 Homer W. Summa .10
206 Ernest K. Padgett .10
207 Walter H. Holke .10
208 Forrest G. Wright .10
209 Henry M. Gowdy .10
210 James W. Taylor .10
211 Benjamin C. Cantwell .10
212 Joseph F. Demaree .10
213 Samuel P. Derringer .10
214 William A. Hallahan .10
215 Daniel K. MacFayden .10
216 Harry F. Rice .10
217 Robert Eldridge Smith .10
218 Jackson R. Stephenson .10
219 Perce L. Malone .10
220 Henry B. Tate .10
221 Joseph F. Vosmik .10
222 George A. Watkins .10
223 James Wilson .10
224 George E. Uhle .10
225 Melvin T. Ott .15
226 Nicholas Altrock .10
227 Charles H. Ruffing .10
228 Joseph V.L. Krakauskas .10
229 Walter A. Berger .10
230 Norman L. Newsom .10
231 Lonnie Warneke .10
232 Frank E. Snyder .10
233 Myril O. Hoag .10
234 Baldomero M. Almada .10
235 Ivy B. Wingo .10
236 James P. Austin .10
237 Henry J. Bonura .10
238 Russell G. Wrightstone .10
239 Alfred C. Todd .10
240 Harold B. Warstler .10
241 Samuel F. West .10
242 Arthur C. Reinhart .10
243 Walter C. Stewart .10
244 John B. Gooch .10
245 Eugene F. Hargrave .10
246 George W. Harper .10
247 George W. Connally .10
248 Edgar G. Braxton .10
249 Walter H. Schang .10
250 Tyrus R. Cobb .50
251 Rogers Hornsby .15
252 Richard W. Marquard .10
253 Carl O. Hubbell .15
254 Joe Wood .10
255 Robert M. Grove .15
256 Lynwood T. Rowe .10
257 Alvin F. Crowder .10
258 Walter P. Johnson .15
259 Charles J. Hafey .10
260 Frederick L. Fitzsimmons .10
261 William E. Webb .10
262 Earle B. Combs .10
263 Edward J. Konetchy .10
264 Taylor L. Douthit .10
265 Lloyd J. Waner .10
266 Gordon S. Cochrane .10
267 John O. Wilson .10
268 Harold J. Traynor .10
269 Virgil L. Davis .10
270 Henry E. Manush .10
271 Michael F. Higgins .10
272 Adrian Joss .10
273 Edward Augustine Walsh .10
274 Johnny L.R. Martin .10
275 Joseph W. Sewell .10
276 Hubert B. Leonard .10
277 Clifford C. Cravath .10
278 Oral C. Hildebrand .10
279 Remy P. Kremer .10
280 Frank A. Pytlak .10
281 Samuel D. Byrd .10
282 Curtis B. Davis .10
283 Lewis A. Fonseca .10
284 Herold D. Ruel .10
285 Julius J. Solters .10
286 Fred W. Schulte .10
287 John P. Quinn .10
288 Arthur C. Whitney .10
289 Jonathon T. Stone .10
290 Hugh M. Critz .10
291 Ira J. Flagstead .10
292 George F. Grantham .10
293 Samuel D. Hale .10
294 James F. Hogan .10
295 Oswald L. Bluege .10
296 Debs Garms .10
297 Augistaf B. Friberg .10
298 Edward A. Brandt .10
299 Ralston B. Hemsley .10
300 Charles H. Klein .10
301 Morton C. Cooper .10
302 James L. Bottomley .10
303 James E. Foxx .15
304 Frank Schulte .10
305 Frank F. Frisch .15
306 Frank A. McCormick .10
307 Jacob E. Daubert .10
308 Roger T. Peckinpaugh .10
309 George H. Burns .10
310 Louis H. Gehrig .50
311 Aloysius H. Simmons .10
312 Edward T. Collins .10
313 Charles L. Hartnett .10
314 Joseph E. Cronin .10
315 Paul G. Waner .10
316 Robert A. O'Farrell .10
317 Lawrence J. Doyle .10
318 Lynford H. Lary .10
319 Frank S. May .10
320 Roy H. Spencer .10
321 Samuel R. Coffman .10
322 Peter J. Donohue .10
323 George W. Haas .10
324 Edward S. Farrell .10
325 Charles F. Rhem .10
326 Frederick Marberry .10
327 Charles Martin Conlon .10
328 Checklist 1-110 .10
329 Checklist 111-220 .10
330 Checklist 221-330 .10

1992 Conlon Collection Prototypes

Along with the 1991 Babe Ruth prototype card, these five cards were distributed at the Anaheim National Sports Collectors Convention in 1991. The announced distribution was 20,000 of each card except the Joe Jackson, which had a press run of 67,000. Except for card 331, all the prototypes have different numbers than the same card in the regular-issue Conlon set. Each of the 1992 cards has a gray "PROTOTYPE" overprinted diagonally on the back.

NM/M
Complete Set (6): 9.00
Common Player: .50
14 Joe Jackson (Colorized, edition of 60,000.) 3.00
331 Christy Mathewson 1.50
400 Joe Jackson 2.50
450 Hughie Jennings .50
500 Ty Cobb 2.00
520 Goose Goslin .50

1992 Conlon Collection

In their second season, the 330 cards of the Conlon Collection were numbered consecutively where the 1991 premiere issue ended. Cards 331-660 also maintained the high-gloss black-and-white format of the previous year. Many subsets within the issue carry special designations on the card fronts. Subsets included no-hitters, Triple Crown winners, "Great Stories," nicknames and more.

NM/M
Factory Set (330): 25.00
Complete Set (330): 15.00
Common Player: .10
Wax Pack: .50
Wax Box (36): 15.00
331 Christopher Mathewson .15
332 George L. Wiltse .10
333 George N. Rucker .10
334 Leon K. Ames .10
335 Charles A. Bender .10
336 Joe Wood .10
337 Edward Augustine Walsh .10
338 George J. Mullin .10
339 Earl A. Hamilton .10
340 Charles M Tesreau .10
341 James Scott .10
342 Richard W. Marquard .10
343 Claude R. Hendrix .15
344 James S. Lavender .10
345 Leslie A. Bush .10
346 Hubert B. Leonard .10
347 Fred A. Toney .10
348 James L. Vaughn .10
349 Ernest G. Koob .10
350 Robert Groom .10
351 Ernest G. Shore .10
352 Horace O. Eller .10
353 Walter P. Johnson .15
354 Charles C. Robertson .10
355 Jesse L. Barnes .10
356 Samuel P. Jones .10
357 Howard J. Ehmke .10
358 Jesse J. Haines .10
359 Theodore A. Lyons .10
360 Carl O. Hubbell .15
361 Wesley C. Ferrell .10
362 Robert J. Burke .10
363 Paul D. Dean .10
364 Norman L. Newsom .10
365 Lloyd V. Kennedy .10
366 William J. Dietrich .10
367 John S. Vander Meer .10
368 John S. Vander Meer .10
369 Montgomery M. Pearson .10
370 Robert W.A. Feller .15
371 Lonnie Warneke .10
372 James A. Tobin .10
373 Earl A. Moore .10
374 William H. Dineen .10
375 Malcolm W. Eason .10
376 George A. Mogridge .10
377 Clarence A. Vance .10
378 James O. Carleton .10
379 Clyde M. Shoun .10
380 Franklin W. Hayes .10
381 Benjamin R. Frey .10
382 Henry W. Johnson .10
383 Ralph Kress .10
384 John T. Allen .10
385 Harold A. Trosky Sr. .10
386 Eugene E. Robertson .10
387 Lemuel F. Young .10
388 George A. Selkirk .10
389 Edwin L. Wells .10
390 James D. Weaver .10
391 George H. McQuinn .10
392 John B. Lobert .10
393 Ernest E. Swanson .10
394 Ernest A. Nevers .10
395 James J. Levey .10
396 Hugo F. Bezdek .10
397 Walter E. French .10
398 Charles F. Berry .10
399 Franklin T. Grube .10
400 Charles W. Dressen .10
401 Alfred E. Neale .10
402 Henry A. Vick .10
403 James F. Thorpe .50
404 Walter J. Gilbert .10
405 John L. Urban .10
406 Everett V. Purdy .10
407 Albert O. Wright .10
408 William M. Urbanski .10
409 Charles W. Fischer .10
410 John R. Warner .10
411 Chalmer W. Cissell .10
412 Mervin D.J. Shea .10
413 Adolfo Luque .10
414 John L. Bassler .10
415 Arvel O. Hale .10
416 Lawrence R. French .10
417 William C. Walker .10
418 Allen L. Cooke .10
419 Philip J. Todt .10
420 Ivy P. Andrews .10
421 William J. Herman .10
422 Tristram E. Speaker .15
423 Aloysius H. Simmons .10
424 Lewis R. Wilson .10
425 Tyrus R. Cobb .40
426 George H. Ruth .50
427 Ernest N. Lombardi .10
428 Jay H. Dean .15
429 Lloyd J. Waner .10
430 Henry B. Greenberg .15
431 Robert M. Grove .15
432 Gordon S. Cochrane .10
433 Burleigh A. Grimes .10
434 Harold J. Traynor .10
435 John R. Mize .15
436 Edgar C. Rice .10
437 Leon A. Goslin .10
438 Charles H. Klein .10
439 Cornelius Mack .10
440 James L. Bottomley .10
441 Jackson R. Stephenson .10
442 Kenneth Williams .10
443 Charles B. Adams .10
444 Joseph J. Jackson .50
445 Harold Newhouser .10
446 Wesley C. Ferrell .10
447 Francis J. O'Doul .10
448 Walter H. Schang .10
449 Sherwood R. Magee .10
450 Michael J. Donlin .10
451 Roger M. Cramer .10
452 Richard W. Bartell .10
453 Earle T. Mack .10
454 Walter G. Brown .10
455 John A. Heving .10
456 Percy L. Jones .10
457 Theodore Blankenship .10
458 Absalom H. Wingo .10
459 Roger P. Bresnahan .10
460 William J. Klem .10
461 Charles L. Gehringer .10
462 Stanley A. Coveleski .10
463 Edward S. Plank .10
464 Clark C.F. Griffith .10
465 Herbert J. Pennock .10
466 Earle B. Combs .10
467 Robert P. Doerr .10
468 Waite C. Hoyt .10
469 Thomas H. Connolly .10
470 Harry B. Hooper .10
471 Richard B. Ferrell .10
472 William G. Evans .10
473 William J. Herman .10
474 William M. Dickey .15
475 Lucius B. Appling .15
476 Ralph A. Pinelli .10
477 Donald E. McNair .10
478 John F. Blake .10
479 Valentine J. Picinich .10
480 Fred A. Heimach .10
481 John G. Graney .10
482 Ewell A. Russell .10
483 Urban C. Faber .10
484 Benjamin M. Kauff .10
485 Clarence L. Rowland .10
486 Robert H. Veach .10
487 James C. Bagby .10
488 William D. Perritt .10
489 Charles L. Herzog .10
490 Arthur Fletcher .10
491 Walter H. Holke .10
492 Arthur N. Nehf .10
493 Lafayette F. Thompson .10
494 James D. Welsh .10
495 Oscar J. Vitt .10
496 Owen T. Carroll .10
497 James K. O'Dea .10
498 Fredrick M. Frankhouse .10
499 Jewel W. Ens .10
500 Morris Arnovich .10
501 Walter Gerber .10
502 George W. Davis .10

503 Charles S. Myer .10
504 Samuel A. Leslie .10
505 William C. Bolton .10
506 Fred Walker .10
507 John W. Smith .10
508 Irving D. Hadley .10
509 Clyde E. Crouse .10
510 Joseph C. Glenn .10
511 Clyde E. Kimsey .10
512 Louis K. Finney .10
513 Alfred V. Lawson .10
514 Charles P. Fullis .10
515 Earl H. Sheely .10
516 George Gibson .10
517 John J. Broaca .10
518 Bibb A. Falk .10
519 Frank O. Hurst .10
520 Grover A. Hartley .10
521 Donald H. Heffner .10
522 Harvey L. Hendrick .10
523 Allen S. Sothoron .10
524 Anthony F. Piet .10
525 Tyrus R. Cobb .40
526 James E. Foxx .15
527 Rogers Hornsby .15
528 Napoleon LaJoie .15
529 Louis H. Gehrig .40
530 Henry Zimmerman .10
531 Charles H. Klein .10
532 Hugh Duffy .10
533 Robert M. Grove .15
534 Grover C. Alexander .15
535 Amos W. Rusie .10
536 Vernon L. Gomez .10
537 William H. Walters .10
538 Urban J. Hodapp .10
539 Bruce D. Campbell .10
540 Horace M. Lisenbee .10
541 John F. Fournier .10
542 James R. Tabor .10
543 John H. Burnett .10
544 Roy A. Hartzell .10
545 Walter P. Gautreau .10
546 Emil O. Yde .10
547 Robert L. Johnson .10
548 Joseph J. Hauser .10
549 Edward M. Reulbach .10
550 Baldomero M. Almada .10
551 Gordon S. Cochrane .10
552 Carl O. Hubbell .15
553 Charles L. Gehringer .10
554 Aloysius H. Simmons .10
555 Mordecai P.C. Brown .10
556 Hugh A. Jennings .10
557 Norman A. Elberfeld .10
558 Charles D. Stengel .10
559 Alexander Schacht .10
560 James E. Foxx .15
561 George L. Kelly .10
562 Lloyd J. Waner .10
563 Paul G. Waner .10
564 Walter P. Johnson .15
565 John Franklin Baker .10
566 Roy J. Hughes .10
567 Lewis S. Riggs .10
568 John H. Whitehead .10
569 Elam R. Vangilder .10
570 William A. Zitzmann .10
571 Walter J. Schmidt .10
572 John A. Tavener .10
573 Joseph E. Genewich .10
574 John A. Marcum .10
575 Fred Hofmann .10
576 Robert A. Rolfe .10
577 Victor G. Sorrell .10
578 Floyd J. Scott .10
579 Alphonse Thomas .10
580 Alfred J. Smith .10
581 Walter J. Henline .10
582 Edward T. Collins .10
583 Earle B. Combs .10
584 John J. McGraw .10
585 Lewis R. Wilson .10
586 Charles L. Hartnett .10
587 Hazen S. Cuyler .10
588 William H. Terry .10
589 Joseph V. McCarthy .10
590 Henry B. Greenberg .15
591 Tristram E. Speaker .15
592 William B. McKechnie .10
593 Stanley R. Harris .10
594 Herbert J. Pennock .10
595 George H. Sisler .10
596 Fred C. Lindstrom .10
597 Howard E. Averill Sr. .10
598 David J. Bancroft .10
599 Cornelius Mack .10
600 Joseph E. Cronin .10
601 Kenneth L. Ash .10
602 Alfred R. Spohrer .10
603 Lee R. Mahaffey .10
604 James F. O'Rourke .10
605 Ulysses S.G. Stoner .10
606 Frank H. Gabler .10
607 Thomas F. Padden .10
608 Charles A. Shires .10
609 Sherrod M. Smith .10
610 Philip Weintraub .10
611 Russell Van Atta .10
612 Joyner C. White .10
613 Clifford G. Melton .10
614 James J. Ring .10
615 John H. Sand .10
616 David D. Alexander .10
617 Kent Greenfield .10
618 Edwin H. Dyer .10
619 William H. Sherdel .10
620 Hubert M. Lanier .10
621 Robert A. O'Farrell .10
622 Rogers Hornsby .15
623 William A. Beckman .10
624 Morton C. Cooper .10
625 William P. Delancey .10
626 Martin W. Marion .10
627 William H. Southworth .10
628 John R. Mize .15
629 Joseph M. Medwick .10
630 Grover C. Alexander .15
631 Paul D. Dean .10
632 Herman S. Bell .10
633 William W. Cooper .10
634 Frank F. Frisch .10
635 Jay H. Dean .15
636 Donald J. Gutteridge .10
637 Johnny L.R. Martin .10
638 Edward J. Konetchy .10
639 William A. Hallahan .10
640 Lonnie Warneke .10
641 Terry B. Moore .10
642 Enos B. Slaughter .10
643 Clarence F. Mueller .10
644 George Toporcer .10
645 James L. Bottomely .10
646 Francis R. Blades .10
647 Jesse J. Haines .10
648 Andrew A. High .10
649 Miller J. Huggins .10
650 Ernesto R. Orsatti .10
651 Lester R. Bell .10
652 Charles E. Street .10
653 Walter H. Roettger .10
654 Sylvester W. Johnson .10
655 Miguel A. Gonzalez .10
656 James A. Collins .10
657 Charles J. Hafey .10
658 Checklist 331-440 .10
659 Checklist 441-550 .10
660 Checklist 551-660 .10

1992-94 Conlon Collection Gold

Four of the heroes of the inaugural All-Star Game of 1933 were featured in a pop-up ad in the program for the 1992 Game in San Diego. One card was inserted into each of the programs printed for distribution at the game and by mail order. Each card was reported printed in an edition of 34,000. Cards are similar in format to the regular Conlon Collection issues except for the gold-foil border around the player photo on front and the use of a "G" suffix to the card number. A banner at top front reads, "Game of the Century." On back is a summary of the player's 1933 All-Star performance and his stats. Gold editions of other Conlon cards were also issued in several different venues in 1993-94. Six cards (#665-880) were included in 1992 Conlon factory sets in editions of up to 90,000. The Johnson-Ryan gold card was available only in packaging sold in Eckerd stores, while the 1994 Cobb gold card was only available at Toys R Us. Cards are numbered with a "G" suffix.

NM/M

Complete Set (12): 50.00
Common Player: 2.00
661 Bill Terry 2.00
662 Lefty Gomez 2.00
663 Babe Ruth 12.00
664 Frankie Frisch 2.00
665 Carl Hubbell 2.00
667 Charlie Gehringer (Edition of 20,000.) 4.00
730 Luke Appling (Edition of 20,000.) 4.00
770 Tommy Henrich 2.00
820 John McGraw 2.00
880 Gabby Hartnett 2.00
934 Walter Johnson, Nolan Ryan (Edition of 100,000.) 12.00
1000 Ty Cobb (Edition of 100,000.) 6.00

1992 Conlon Collection 13th National

These samples of the 1993 Conlon Collection series were distributed at the National Sports Collectors Convention in Atlanta in 1992. Other than the Joe Jackson card, they carry the same numbers as the regularly issued versions. Designs are also identical except for the overprint on back in outline letters, "13TH NATIONAL."

NM/M

Complete Set (4): 4.00
Common Player: .50
14 Joe Jackson 1.00
663 George H. Ruth 2.00
775 John T. Meyers .50
800 James L. Vaughn .50

1993 Conlon Collection Prototypes

The cards in this issue were produced to preview the basic set and various subsets of the 1993 Conlon Collection issue. Cards are similar to the regular-issue set with the exception that the word "PROTOTYPE" is printed in gray diagonally on back. Production of most of the black-and-white cards was 60,000, though Gomez and Frisch were limited to 10,000 apiece. Three of the cards can be found with "All Star FanFest" notations on back, having been distributed as samples there.

NM/M

Complete Set (8): 3.00
Common Player: 1.00
661 Bill Terry 1.00
661 Bill Terry (All Star FanFest) 2.00
662 Lefty Gomez 1.00
663 Babe Ruth 6.00
664 Frankie Frisch 1.00
710 Red Faber 1.00
710 Red Faber (All Star FanFest) 2.00
775 Chief Meyers 1.00
800 Hippo Vaughn 1.00
888 Babe Ruth (Colorized, edition of 52,000.) 5.00
905 Lena Blackburne 1.00
905 Lena Blackbourne (All Star FanFest) 2.00
934 Walter Johnson, Nolan Ryan (Colorized edition of 52,000.) 4.00

1993 Conlon Collection

The third annual Conlon Collection issue of 330 cards is numbered 661-990, a continuation of the series produced in 1991-92. The format of black-and-white photos produced 50-90 years ago by Charles Martin Conlon and surrounded by a wide black border and UV coating was

continued. As with earlier issues, card backs contain brief biographical data, a few stats and well-written career highlights. The 1993 set also featured many subsets arranged by topic, such as spitballers, native Americans, players who overcame handicaps, etc. One subset compared Nolan Ryan with star pitchers in baseball history and included a fantasy photo of Ryan shaking hands in the dugout with Walter Johnson (card #934).

NM/M

Complete Set in Commemorative Tin: 20.00
Complete Set (330): 15.00
Common Player: .10
Wax Pack: .50
Wax Box (36): 15.00
661 William H. Terry .10
662 Vernon L. Gomez .10
663 George H. Ruth .50
664 Frank F. Frisch .10
665 Carl O. Hubbell .10
666 Aloysius H. Simmons .15
667 Charles L. Gehringer .15
668 Howard E. Averill Sr. .15
669 Robert M. Grove .15
670 Harold J. Traynor .15
671 Charles H. Klein .15
672 Paul G. Waner .10
673 Louis H. Gehrig .40
674 Richard B. Ferrell .10
675 Charles L. Hartnett .10
676 Joseph E. Cronin .10
677 Charles J. Hafey .10
678 James J. Dykes .10
679 Samuel F. West .10
680 Johnny L.R. Martin .10
681 Francis J. O'Doul .10
682 Alvin F. Crowder .10
683 James Wilson .10
684 Richard W. Bartell .10
685 William A. Hallahan .10
686 Walter A. Berger .10
687 Lonnie Warneke .10
688 William B. Chapman .10
689 Elwood G. English .10
690 James H. Reese .10
691 Roscoe A. Holm .10
692 Charles D. Jamieson .10
693 Jonathan T.W. Zachary .10
694 John C. Ryan .10
695 Earl J. Adams .10
696 William E. Hunnefield .10
697 Henry L. Meadows .10
698 Thomas F. Carey .10
699 John W. Rawlings .10
700 Kenneth E. Holloway .10
701 Lance C. Richbourg .10
702 Raymond L. Fisher .10
703 Edward Augustine Walsh .10
704 Richard Rudolph .10
705 Raymond B. Caldwell .10
706 Burleigh A. Grimes .10
707 Stanley A. Coveleski .10
708 George A. Hildebrand .10
709 John P. Quinn .10
710 Urban C. Faber .10
711 Urban J. Shocker .10
712 Hubert B. Leonard .10
713 Louis L. Koupal .10
714 James C. Wasdell .10
715 John H. Lindell .10
716 Don W. Padgett .10
717 Nelson T. Potter .10
718 Lynwood T. Rowe .10
719 David C. Danforth .10
720 Claude W. Passeau .10
721 Harry L. Kelley .10
722 John T. Allen .10
723 Thomas J.D. Bridges .10
724 William C. Lee .10
725 Fredrick M. Frankhouse .10
726 John J. McCarthy .10
727 Glen D. Russell .10
728 Emory E. Rigney .10
729 Howard S. Shanks .10
730 Lucius B. Appling .10
731 William J. Byron .10
732 Earle B. Combs .10
733 Henry B. Greenberg .15
734 Walter W. Beck .10
735 Hollis J. Thurston .10
736 Lewis R. Wilson .10
737 William A. McGowan .10
738 Henry J. Bonura .10
739 Thomas C. Baker .10
740 William C. Jacobson .10
741 Hazen S. Cuyler .10
742 George F. Blaeholder .10
743 Wilson D. Miles .10
744 Lee E. Handley .10
745 John F. Collins .10
746 Wilfred P. Ryan .10
747 Aaron L. Ward .10
748 Montgomery M. Pearson .10
749 Jacob W. Early .10
750 William F. Atwood .10
751 Mark A. Koenig .10
752 John A. Hassett .10
753 David J. Jones .10
754 John P. Wagner .25
755 William M. Dickey .15
756 Albert M. Butcher .10
757 Waite C. Hoyt .10
758 Walter P. Johnson .15
759 Howard J. Ehmke .10
760 Norman L. Newsom .10
761 Anthony M. Lazzeri .10
762 Anthony M. Lazzeri .10
763 Spurgeon F. Chandler .10
764 Walter K. Higbe .10
765 Paul R. Richards .10
766 Rogers Hornsby .15
767 Joseph F. Vosmik .10
768 Jesse J. Haines .10
769 William H. Walters .10
770 Thomas D. Henrich .10
771 James F. Thorpe .40
772 Euel W. Moore .10
773 Rudolph P. York .10
774 Charles A. Bender .10
775 John T. Meyers .10
776 Robert L. Johnson .10
777 Roy C. Johnson .10
778 Richard T. Porter .10
779 Ethan N. Allen .10
780 Harry F. Sallee .10
781 Roy C. Bell .10
782 Arnold J. Statz .10
783 Frank J. Henry .10
784 Charles L. Woodall .10
785 Philip E. Collins .10
786 Joseph W. Sewell .10
787 William J. Herman .10
788 Rueben H. Oldring .10
789 William H. Walker .10
790 Joseph C. Schultz .10
791 Fred E. Maguire .10
792 Claude W. Willoughby .10
793 James A. Ferguson .10
794 John D. Morrison .10
795 Tristram E. Speaker .15
796 Tyrus R. Cobb .40
797 Max Carey .10
798 George H. Sisler .10
799 Charles J. Hollocher .10
800 James L. Vaughn .10
801 Samuel P. Jones .10
802 Harry B. Hooper .10
803 Clifford C. Cravath .10
804 Walter P. Johnson .15
805 Jacob E. Daubert .10
806 Jesse C. Milan .10
807 Hugh A. McQuillan .10
808 George F. Brickell .10
809 Joseph V. Stripp .10
810 Urban J. Hodapp .10
811 John L. Vergez .10
812 Linus R. Frey .10
813 William W. Regan .10
814 Norman R. Young .10
815 Charles C. Robertson .10
816 Walter F. Judnich .10
817 Joseph B. Tinker .15
818 John Evers .15
819 Frank L. Chance .15
820 John J. McGraw .10
821 Charles J. Grimm .10
822 Ted Lyons .10
823 Joe McCarthy .10
824 Connie Mack .10
825 George Gibson .10
826 Steve O'Neill .10
827 Tristram E. Speaker .15
828 William F. Carrigan .10
829 Charles D. Stengel .15
830 Miller J. Huggins .10
831 William B. McKechnie .10
832 Charles W. Dressen .10
833 Charles E. Street .10
834 Melvin T. Ott .15
835 Frank F. Frisch .10
836 George H. Sisler .10
837 Napoleon LaJoie .15
838 Tyrus R. Cobb .40
839 William H. Southworth .10
840 Clark C.F. Griffith .10
841 William H. Terry .10
842 Rogers Hornsby .15
843 Joseph E. Cronin .10
844 Alfonso R. Lopez .10
845 Stanley R. Harris .10
846 Wilbert Robinson .10
847 Hugh A. Jennings .10
848 James J. Dykes .10
849 Roy J. Cullenbine .10
850 Graham E. Moore .10
851 John H. Rothrock .10
852 William H. Lamar .10
853 Monte Weaver .10
854 Ival R. Goodman .10
855 Henry L. Severeid .10
856 Fred G. Haney .10
857 Joseph B. Shaute .10
858 Smead P. Jolley .10
859 Edwin D. Williams .10
860 Bernard O. Bengough .10
861 Richard B. Ferrell .10
862 Robert A. O'Farrell .10
863 Virgil L. Davis .10
864 Franklin W. Hayes .10
865 Herold D. Ruel .10
866 Gordon S. Cochrane .10
867 John Kling .10
868 Ivy B. Wingo .10
869 William M. Dickey .15
870 Frank E. Snyder .10
871 Roger P. Bresnahan .10
872 Walter H. Schang .10
873 Alfonso R. Lopez .10
874 James Wilson .10
875 Valentine J. Picinich .10
876 Stephen F. O'Neill .10
877 Ernest N. Lombardi .10
878 John L. Bassler .10
879 Raymond W. Schalk .10
880 Charles L. Hartnett .10
881 Bruce D. Campbell .10
882 Charles H. Ruffing .10
883 Mordecai P.C. Brown .10
884 Peter J. Archer .10
885 David E. Keefe .10
886 Nathan H. Andrews .10
887 Edgar C. Rice .10
888 George H. Ruth .50
889 Charles J. Hafey .10
890 Oscar D. Melillo .10
891 Joe Wood .10
892 John J. Evers .10
893 George Toporcer .10
894 Myril O. Hoag .10
895 Robert G. Weiland .10
896 Joseph A. Marty .10
897 Sherwood R. Magee .10
898 Daniel T. Taylor .10
899 William E. Kamm .10
900 Samuel J.T. Sheckard .10
901 Sylvester W. Johnson .10
902 Stephen R. Sundra .10
903 Roger M. Cramer .10
904 Hubert S. Pruett .10
905 Russell A. Blackburne .10
906 Eppa Rixey .10
907 Leon A. Goslin .10
908 George L. Kelly .10
909 James L. Bottomley .10
910 Christopher Mathewson .15
911 Anthony M. Lazzeri .10
912 John A. Mostil .10
913 Robert P. Doerr .10
914 Walter J.V. Maranville .10
915 Harry E. Heilmann .10
916 Rodrick J. Wallace .10
917 James E. Foxx .15
918 John R. Mize .10
919 John N. Bentley .10
920 Alexander Schacht .10
921 Parke E. Coleman .10
922 George H. Paskert .10
923 Horace H. Ford .10
924 Randolph E. Moore .10
925 Milburn J. Shoffner .10
926 Richard W. Siebert .10
927 Anthony C. Kaufmann .10
928 Jay H. Dean, Nolan Ryan .25
929 Clarence A. Vance, Nolan Ryan .25
930 Robert M. Grove, Nolan Ryan .25
931 George E. Waddell, Nolan Ryan .25
932 Grover C. Alexander, Nolan Ryan .25
933 Robert W.A. Feller, Nolan Ryan .25
934 Walter P. Johnson, Nolan Ryan .50
935 Theodore A. Lyons, Nolan Ryan .25
936 James C. Bagby .10
937 Joseph Sugden .10
938 Robert E. Grace .10
939 John G. Heath .10
940 Kenneth Williams .10
941 Marvin J. Owen .10
942 Cyril R. Weatherly .10
943 Edward C. Morgan .10
944 John C. Rizzo .10
945 Archie R. McKain .10
946 Robert M. Garbark .10
947 John B. Osborn .10
948 John S. Podgajny .10
949 Joseph P. Evans .10
950 George A. Rensa .10
951 John H. Humphries .10
952 Merritt P. Cain .10
953 Roy E. Hansen .10
954 John A. Niggeling .10
955 Harold J. Wiltse .10
956 Alejandro A.A.E. Carrasquel .10
957 George A. Grant .10

958 Philip W. Weinert .10
959 Ervin B. Brame .10
960 Raymond J. Harrell .10
961 Edward K. Linke .10
962 Samuel B. Gibson .10
963 John C. Watwood .10
964 James T. Prothro .10
965 Julio G. Bonetti .10
966 Howard R. Mills .10
967 Clarence E. Galloway .10
968 Harold J. Kelleher .10
969 Elon C. Hogsett .10
970 Edward B. Heusser .10
971 Edward J. Baecht .10
972 Otto H. Saltzgaver .10
973 Leroy G. Herrmann .10
974 Beveric B. Bean .10
975 Harry Seibold .10
976 Howard V. Keen .10
977 William J. Barrett .10
978 Patrick H. McNulty .10
979 George E. Turbeville .10
980 Edward D. Phillips .10
981 Garland M. Buckeye .10
982 Victor P. Frasier .10
983 John G. Rhodes .10
984 Emile D. Barnes .10
985 James C. Edwards .10
986 Herschel E. Bennett .10
987 Carmen P. Hill .10
988 Checklist 661-770 .10
989 Checklist 771-880 .10
990 Checklist 881-990 .10

1993-95 Conlon Collection Color

The cards in this set were previously released in black-and-white in regular 1991-94 Conlon sets. Cards 1-12 were issued as bonus cards in Megacards accessory items; 250,000 of each were produced. Cards 13-20 were randomly inserted in 1993 Conlon counter and blister packs; 100,000 of those were produced. Cards 21-22, in an edition of 75,000, were only available through a send-away offer. Card 23 was available exclusively as an insert in the 7th Edition SCD Baseball Card Price Guide, in an edition of 60,000. Cards 24-39 were issued in 1994. Numbers 24-28 were random inserts printed to the number of 84,000 apiece. Cards 29-30 were a send-away premium; #31-33 were hobby foil inserts. All were issued in quantities of 12,000. Cards 34-37 - 48,000 of each - were a Toys R Us exclusive insert. Cards 38-39 were special-offer premiums. A special printing of 24,000 of #28 were issued with a "Conlon Collection Day" overprint on back and were distributed at the Sept. 11, 1994, St. Louis Cardinals game.

NM/M
Complete Set (47): 100.00
Common Player: 2.00
1 Sunny Jim Bottomley 2.00
2 Lefty Grove 2.00
3 Lou Gehrig 10.00
4 Babe Ruth 10.00
5 Casey Stengel 3.00
6 Rube Marquard 2.00
7 Walter Johnson 3.00
8 Lou Gehrig 5.00
9 Christy Mathewson 3.00
10 Ty Cobb 5.00
11 Mel Ott 2.00
12 Carl Hubbell 2.00
13 Al Simmons 2.00
14 Connie Mack 2.00
15 Grover C. Alexander 2.00
16 Jimmie Foxx 3.00
17 Lloyd Waner 2.00
18 Tris Speaker 4.00
19 Dizzy Dean 5.00
20 Rogers Hornsby 3.00
21 Shoeless Joe Jackson 7.50
22 Jim Thorpe 7.50
23 Bob Feller 8.00
24 Hal Newhouser 2.00
25 Hughie Jennings 2.00
26 Red Faber 2.00
27 Enos Slaughter 2.00
28 Johnny Mize 2.00
28CCD Johnny Mize 4.00
29 Pie Traynor 2.00
30 Walter Johnson, Nolan Ryan 4.00
31 Lou Gehrig 2.00
32 Benny Bengough 2.00
33 Babe Ruth 2.00
34 Charlie Gehringer 2.00
35 Babe Ruth 2.00
36 Bill Dickey 2.00
37 Mordecai Brown 2.00
38 Ray Schalk 4.00
39 Home Run Baker 5.00
40 Frank Frisch 2.00
41 Hack Wilson 2.00
42 Ty Cobb 6.00
43 Honus Wagner 4.00
44 John McGraw 2.00
45 Reds vs. Giants 2.00
46 Indians vs. Yanks 2.00
47 Babe Ruth 12.00

1993 Conlon Collection Master Series

"The Best There Was" was the subtitle on this portfolio of oversized (10" x 8") cards produced from the photos of Charles Martin Conlon. On the high-gloss card fronts, a wide black border surrounds the black-and-white photo, with a gold-foil pinstripe border between the two. The player's name appears in gold at the bottom. Backs are printed in black-and-white and feature a large player portrait, complete major league stats and a career summary. A serial numbered certificate placing the set within an edition of 25,000 was included with the set; a deluxe portfolio album to house the collection was available for $10.

NM/M
Complete Set (9): 15.00
Common Card: 1.50
1 Title card .50
2 Babe Ruth 6.00
3 Lou Gehrig, Walter Johnson 4.00
4 Honus Wagner 3.00
5 Mickey Cochrane 1.50
6 Tris Speaker 1.50
7 Ty Cobb 4.00
8 Rogers Hornsby 1.50
9 Pie Traynor 1.50

1993 Conlon Collection Color Masters

Some of the premier photography of Charles Martin Conlon was computer color-enhanced and placed on these oversized (10" x 8") cards in a special edition of 25,000. High-gloss fronts feature the colorized photos separated by a thin white pinstripe from the dark blue background. Backs are printed in black and blue on white and feature a career summary or other historical data, along with a description of the front photo. A serially numbered certificate of authenticity accompanied the set and could be redeemed, along with $10, for a deluxe portfolio to house the collection.

NM/M
Complete Set (9): 15.00
Common Player: 1.50
1 Title Card .50
2 Napoleon Lajoie 1.50
3 Walter Johnson, Nolan Ryan (Fantasy photo.) 6.00
4 Action at Hilltop Park .50
5 Babe Ruth 6.00
6 Frank Baker 1.50
7 John McGraw 1.50
8 John McGraw, Wilbert Robinson, Christy Mathewson 1.50
9 Hughie Jennings 1.50

1994 Conlon Collection Prototypes

A large gray "PROTOTYPE" overprint on back identifies these cards as sample of the fourth annual edition of Conlon Collection cards by Megacards. Cards carry the same number as issued versions. It was reported that 26,000 prototypes were issued of Martin, Traynor, Hubbell, Klem and Koenig; while 52,000 each were issued of Jackson and the Deans.

NM/M
Complete Set (8): 8.00
Common Player 1.00
991 Pepper Martin 1.00
1030 Joe Jackson 3.00
1050 Pie Traynor 1.00
1105 Carl Hubbell 1.00
1140 Lefty Grove 1.00
1170 Dizzy Dean, Paul Dean 1.50
1190 Bill Klem 1.00
1230 Mark Koenig 1.00

1994 Conlon Collection

DAFFY & DIZZY DEAN

The production of "old-timers" cards based on the baseball photography of Charles M. Conlon from the 1910s through the 1930s continued into a fourth year in 1994 with another 330-card series, numbered 991-1320. Once again the format of previous years was continued. Subsets included the 1919 Chicago White Sox, major league brothers and action photos.

NM/M
Complete Set in Commemorative Tin: 40.00
Complete Set (330): 30.00
Common Player: .10
Wax Box (36): 40.00
991 Johnny L.R. Martin .10
992 Joseph W. Sewell .10
993 Edd J. Roush .10
994 Richard B. Ferrell .10
995 John J. Broaca .10
996 James L. Sewell .10
997 Burleigh A. Grimes .10
998 Lewis R. Wilson .10
999 Robert M. Grove .15
1000 Tyrus R. Cobb .40
1001 John J. McGraw .10
1002 Edward S. Plank .10
1003 Samuel P. Jones .10
1004 James L. Bottomley .10
1005 Henry B. Greenberg .15
1006 Lloyd J. Waner .10
1007 William W. Moore .10
1008 Lucius B. Appling .10
1009 Harold Newhouser .10
1010 Alfonso R. Lopez .10
1011 Tyrus R. Cobb .40
1012 Charles A. Nichols .10
1013 Edward Augustine Walsh .10
1014 Hugh Duffy .10
1015 Richard W. Marquard .10
1016 Adrian Joss .10
1017 Rodrick J. Wallace .10
1018 William H. Keeler .10
1019 Jacob E. Daubert .10
1020 Harry F. Sallee .10
1021 Adolfo Luque .10
1022 Ivy B. Wingo .10
1023 Edd J. Roush .10
1024 William A. Rariden .10
1025 Sherwood R. Magee .10
1026 Louis B. Duncan .10
1027 Horace O. Eller .10
1028 Alfred E. Neale .10
1029 George D. Weaver .10
1030 Joseph J. Jackson .50
1031 Arnold Gandil .10
1032 Charles A. Risberg .10
1033 Raymond W. Schalk .10
1034 Edward V. Cicotte .10
1035 William H. James .10
1036 Harry L. Leibold .10
1037 Richard H. Kerr .10
1038 William J. Gleason .10
1039 Frederick W. McMullin (Middle initial actually "D.") .10
1040 Edward T. Collins .10
1041 Sox Pitchers (Lefty Williams, Bill James, Ed Cicotte, Dicky Kerr) .10
1042 Sox Outfielders (Nemo Leibold, Happy Felsch, Shano Collins) .10
1043 Kenneth F. Keltner .10
1044 Charles F. Berry .10
1045 Walter J. Lutzke .10
1046 John C. Schulte .10
1047 John V. Welch .10
1048 Jack E. Russell .10
1049 John J. Murray .10
1050 Harold J. Traynor .10
1051 Michael J. Donlin .10
1052 Charles L. Hartnett .10
1053 Anthony M. Lazzeri .10
1054 Lawrence H. Miller .10
1055 Clarence A. Vance .10
1056 Williams F. Carrigan .10
1057 John J. Murphy .10
1058 Clifton E Heathcote .10
1059 Joseph A. Dugan .10
1060 Walter J.V. Maranville .10
1061 Thomas D. Henrich .10
1062 Leroy E. Parmelee .10
1063 Vernon L. Gomez .10
1064 Ernest N. Lombardi .10
1065 David J. Bancroft .10
1066 William B. McKechnie .10
1067 John A. Hassett .10
1068 Spurgeon F. Chandler .10
1069 Roy J. Hughes .10
1070 George A. Dauss .10
1071 Joseph J. Hauser .10
1072 Virgil L. Davis .10
1073 Albert M. Butcher .10
1074 Louis P. Chiozza .10
1075 Center Field Bleachers .10
1076 Charles L. Gehringer .10
1077 Henry E. Manush .10
1078 Charles H. Ruffing .10
1079 Melvin L. Harder .10
1080 George H. Ruth .50
1081 William B. Chapman .10
1082 Louis H. Gehrig .40
1083 James E. Foxx .15
1084 Aloysius H. Simmons .10
1085 Joseph E. Cronin .10
1086 William M. Dickey .15
1087 Gordon S. Cochrane .10
1088 Vernon L. Gomez .10
1089 Howard E. Averill Sr. .10
1090 Samuel F. West .10
1091 Frank F. Frisch .10
1092 William J. Herman .10
1093 Harold J. Traynor .10
1094 Joseph M. Medwick .10
1095 Charles H. Klein .10
1096 Hazen S. Cuyler .10
1097 Melvin T. Ott .15
1098 Walter T. Berger .10
1099 Paul G. Waner .10
1100 William H. Terry .10
1101 Travis C. Jackson .10
1102 Joseph F. Vaughan .10
1103 Charles L. Hartnett .10
1104 Alfonso R. Lopez .10
1105 Carl O. Hubbell .15
1106 Lonnie Warneke .10
1107 Van L. Mungo .10
1108 Johnny J.R. Martin .10
1109 Jay H. Dean .15
1110 Fredrick M. Frankhouse .10
1111 Giullaedeau Spink Heydler .10
1112 JG Taylor Spink/ Mrs. Spink .10
1113 Hirchman, Keller .10
1114 Victor E. Aldridge .10
1115 Michael F. Higgins .10
1116 Harold G. Carlson .10
1117 Frederick L. Fitzsimmons .10
1118 William H. Walters .10
1119 Nicholas Altrock .10
1120 Charles W. Dressen .10
1121 Mark A. Koenig .10
1122 Charles L. Gehringer .10
1123 Lloyd V. Kennedy .10
1124 Harlond B. Clift .10
1125 Ernest G. Phelps .10
1126 John R. Mize .15
1127 Harold H. Schumacher .10
1128 Ethan N. Allen .10
1129 William A. Wambsganss .10
1130 Frederick Leach .10
1131 John W. Clancy .10
1132 John F. Stewart .10
1133 Wilbur L. Brubaker .10
1134 Leslie Mann .10
1135 Howard J. Ehmke .10
1136 Aloysius H. Simmons .10
1137 George L. Earnshaw .10
1138 George W. Haas .10
1139 Edmund J. Miller .10
1140 Robert M. Grove .15
1141 John P. Boley .10
1142 Edward T. Collins Sr. .10
1143 Walter E. French .10
1144 Donald E. McNair .10
1145 William D. Shores .10
1146 Gordon S. Cochrane .10
1147 Homer W. Summa .10
1148 John P. Quinn .10
1149 Max F. Bishop .10
1150 James J. Dykes .10
1151 George E. Walberg .10
1152 James E. Foxx .15
1153 George H. Burns .10
1154 Roger M. Cramer .10
1155 Samuel D. Hale .10
1156 Edwin A. Rommel .10
1157 Ralph F. Perkins .10
1158 James J. Cronin .10
1159 Cornelius Mack .10
1160 Raymond C. Kolp .10
1161 Clyde J. Manion .10
1162 Franklin T. Grube .10
1163 Stephen A. Swetonic .10
1164 Joseph B. Tinker .15
1165 John J. Evers .15
1166 Frank L. Chance .15
1167 Emerson Dickman .10
1168 John T. Tobin .10
1169 Wesley C. Ferrell .10
1170 Jay H. Dean .15
1171 Tony & Al Cuccinello (Tony Cuccinello, Al Cuccinello) .10
1172 Harry Coveleski, Stan Coveleski .10
1173 Bob Johnson, Roy Johnson .10
1174 Andy & Hugh High .10
1175 Joe Sewell, Luke Sewell .10
1176 Joe Heving, John Heving .10
1177 Ab & Ivy Wingo .10
1178 Wade Killefer, Bill Killefer .10
1179 Bubbles Hargrave, Pinky Hargrave .10
1180 Paul Waner, Lloyd Waner .10
1181 John S. Vander Meer .10
1182 Joe G. Moore .10
1183 Robert J. Burke .10
1184 John F. Moore .10
1185 John J. Egan .10
1186 Thomas H. Connolly .10
1187 Frank H. O'Loughlin .10
1188 John E. Reardon .10
1189 Charles B. Moran .10
1190 William J. Klem .10
1191 Albert D. Stark .10
1192 Albert L. Orth .10
1193 William E. Bransfield .10
1194 Roy Van Graflan .10
1195 Eugene F. Hart .10
1196 John B. Conlan .10
1197 Ralph A. Pinelli .10
1198 John F. Sheridan .10
1199 Richard F. Nallin .10
1200 William H. Dineen .10
1201 Henry F. O'Day .10
1202 Charles Rigler .10
1203 Robert D. Emslie .10
1204 Charles H. Pfirman .10
1205 Harry C. Geisel .10
1206 Ernest C. Quigley .10
1207 Emmett T. Ormsby .10
1208 George A. Hildebrand .10
1209 George J. Moriarty .10
1210 William G. Evans .10
1211 Clarence B. Owens .10
1212 William A. McGowan .10
1213 Walter K. Higbe .10
1214 Taylor L. Douthit .10
1215 Delmar D. Baker .10
1216 Albert W. Demaree .10
1217 Cornelius Mack .10
1218 Napoleon Lajoie .15
1219 John P. Wagner .25
1220 Christopher Mathewson .15
1221 Samuel E. Crawford .10
1222 Tristram E. Speaker .15
1223 Grover C. Alexander .15
1224 Joseph E. Bowman .10
1225 John D. Rigney .10
1226 William E. Webb .10
1227 Lloyd A. Moore .10
1228 Bruce D. Campbell .10
1229 Luzerne A. Blue .10
1230 Mark A. Koenig .10
1231 Walter H. Schang .10
1232 Max Carey .10
1233 Frank F. Frisch .10
1234 Owen J. Bush .10
1235 Goerge S. Davis .10
1236 William G. Rogell .10
1237 James A. Collins .10
1238 Mauricel L. Burrus .10
1239 Ernest E. Swanson .10
1240 Elwood G. English .10
1241 Joseph Harris .10
1242 Harry H. McCurdy .10
1243 Richard W. Bartell .10
1244 Rupert L. Thompson .10
1245 Charles B. Adams .10
1246 Arthur N. Nehf .10
1247 John G. Graney .10
1248 Theodore A. Lyons .10
1249 Louis H. Gehrig .40
1250 Michael F. Welch .10
1251 Urban C. Faber .10
1252 Joseph J. McGinnity .10
1253 Rogers Hornsby .15
1254 Melvin T. Ott .15
1255 Walter P. Johnson .15
1256 Edgar C. Rice .10
1257 James A. Tobin .10
1258 Roger T. Peckinpaugh .10
1259 George T. Stovall .10
1260 Fredrick C. Merkle .10
1261 Harry W. Collins .10
1262 Henry C. Lind .10
1263 George N. Rucker .10
1264 Hollis J. Thurston .10
1265 Alexander Metzler .10
1266 Charles Martin Conlon .10
1267 McCarty Gets Magee (Lew McCarty, Lee Magee) .10
1268 Sliding Home .10
1269 Kauff Safe at 3rd (Benny Kauff) .10
1270 Groh Out at 3rd (Heine Groh) .10
1271 Mollwitz Out at the Plate (Fred Mollwitz) .10
1272 Burns Safe at Home .10
1273 Lee Magee Out Stealing 3rd (Lee Magee) .10
1274 Killefer Out at Plate (Bill Killefer) .10
1275 John M. Warhop .10
1276 Emil J. Leonard .10
1277 Alvin F. Crowder .10
1278 Chester P. Laabs .10
1279 Leslie A. Bush .10
1280 Raymond B. Bressler .10
1281 Robret M. Brown .10
1282 Bernard Deviveiros .10
1283 Leslie W. Tietje .10
1284 Charles Devens .10
1285 Elliott A. Bigelow .10
1286 John O. Dickshot .10
1287 Charles L. Chatham .10
1288 Walter E. Beall .10
1289 Richard D. Attreau .10
1290 Anthony V. Brief .10
1291 James J. Gleason .10
1292 Walter D. Shaner .10
1293 Clifford R. Crawford .10
1294 Manuel Salvo .10
1295 Calvin L. Dorsett .10
1296 Russell D. Peters .10
1297 John D. Couch .10
1298 Frank W. Ulrich .10
1299 James M. Bivin .10
1300 Paul E. Strand .10
1301 John Y. Lanning .10
1302 William R. Brenzel .10
1303 Don Songer .10
1304 Emil H. Levsen .10
1305 Otto A. Bluege .10
1306 Fabian S. Gaffke .10
1307 Maurice J. Archdeacon .10
1308 James B. Chaplin .10
1309 Lawrence J. Rosenthal .10
1310 William M. Bagwell .10
1311 Ralph F. Dawson .10
1312 John P.J. Sturm .10
1313 Haskell C. Billings .10
1314 Vernon S. Wilshere .10
1315 Robert A. Asbjornson .10
1316 Henry J. Steinbacher .10
1317 Stanwood F. Baumgartner .10
1318 Checklist 991-1100 .10
1319 Checklist 1101-1210 .10
1320 Checklist 1211-1320 .10

1994 Conlon Collection Burgundy

A parallel version of the 1994 Conlon series with burgundy, rather than black, borders was issued as a one-per-pack insert.

	NM/M
Complete Set (330):	30.00
Common Player:	.50

1995 Conlon Collection Prototypes

Megacards issued this 10-card series of prototypes to introduce its basic series for 1995. Cards are similar to the issued versions except that they lack the gold-foil enhancements on front and have different card numbers on some of the card backs. Cards have "PROMOTIONAL" printed diagonally on the back. Prototypes are listed here alphabetically.

		NM/M
Complete Set (10):		12.00
Common Player:		2.00
(1)	Lou Boudreau	2.00
(2)	Ray Chapman	2.00
(3)	Charles Comiskey	2.00
(4)	Bill Dickey	2.00
(5)	Bob Feller	2.00
(6)	Lou Gehrig	3.00
(7)	Charles L. Hartnett	2.00
(8)	Walter J.V. Maranville	2.00
(9)	Babe Ruth	4.00
(10)	Tris Speaker	2.00

1995 Conlon Collection

Gold-foil enhanced printing was a first for the Conlon Collection in 1995. For the first time, each regular card in the issue featured gold frames around the black-and-white photos, and a gold Conlon Collection seal at lower-right. Background for the 1995 cards is in dark green, with typography in white. Backs are black-and-white and feature an in-depth historical vignette. In its fifth year, numbers for Conlon Collection cards continued from previous years, beginning at #1321. The first series, cards 1321-1430, were issued in February, a second series, #1431-1540, was announced for August release but was never issued. A special Babe Ruth 100th birthday anniversary card was included with the issue, bearing a combined Topps/Conlon Collection logo and paralleling card #3 in the 1995 Topps issue. Conlon cards for 1995 were issued in plastic clam-shell packaging of 22, 55 or 110 cards. Once again, many of the cards in the set were grouped into themes such as "Baseball Goes to War," "Nicknames" and "Beating the Odds."

		NM/M
Complete Set, Commemorative Tin:		100.00
Complete Set (111):		80.00
Common Player:		1.00
1321	Grover Alexander	1.00
1322	Christy Mathewson	1.50
1323	Eddie Grant	1.00
1324	Gabby Street	1.00
1325	Hank Gowdy	1.00
1326	Jack Bentley	1.00
1327	Eppa Rixey	1.00
1328	Bob Shawkey	1.00
1329	Rabbit Maranville	1.00
1330	Casey Stengel	1.00
1331	Herb Pennock	1.00
1332	Eddie Collins	1.00
1333	Buddy Hassett	1.00
1334	Andy Cohen	1.00
1335	Hank Greenberg	1.50
1336	Andy High	1.00
1337	Bob Feller	1.00
1338	George Earnshaw	1.00
1339	Jack Knott	1.00
1340	Larry French	1.00
1341	Skippy Roberge	1.00
1342	Boze Berger	1.00
1343	Bill Posedel	1.00
1344	Kirby Higbe	1.00
1345	Bob Neighbors	1.00
1346	Hugh Mulcahy	1.00
1347	Harry Walker	1.00
1348	Buddy Lewis	1.00
1349	Cecil Travis	1.00
1350	Moe Berg	2.00
1351	Nixey Callahan	1.00
1352	Heinie Peitz	1.00
1353	Doc White	1.00
1354	Smokey Joe Wood	1.00
1355	Larry Gardner	1.00
1356	Steve O'Neill	1.00
1357	Tris Speaker	1.00
1358	Bill Wambsganss	1.00
1359	Geo. H. Burns	1.00
1360	Charlie Jamieson	1.00
1361	Les Nunamaker	1.00
1362	Stan Coveleski	1.00
1363	Joe Sewell	1.00
1364	Jim Bagby	1.00
1365	Duster Mails	1.00
1366	Jack Graney	1.00
1367	Elmer Smith	1.00
1368	Tommy Leach	1.00
1369	Russ Ford	1.00
1370	Harry Wolter	1.00
1371	Dazzy Vance	1.00
1372	Germany Schaefer	1.00
1373	Elbie Fletcher	1.00
1374	Clark Griffith	1.00
1375	Al Simmons	1.00
1376	Billy Jurges	1.00
1377	Earl Averill	1.00
1378	Bill Klem	1.00
1379	Armando Marsans	1.00
1380	Mike Gonzalez	1.00
1381	Jacques Fournier	1.00
1382	Ol' Stubblebeard (Burleigh Grimes)	1.00
1383	Freshest Man on Earth (Arlie Latham)	1.00
1384	Cracker (Ray Schalk)	1.00
1385	Goose (Goose Goslin)	1.00
1386	Unser Choe (Joe Hauser)	1.00
1387	The People's Cherce (Dixie Walker)	1.00
1388	The Crab (Jesse Burkett)	1.00
1389	Mountain Music (Cliff Melton)	1.00
1390	Gee (Gee Walker)	1.00
1391	Tony Cuccinello	1.00
1392	Vern Kennedy	1.00
1393	Tuck Stainback	1.00
1394	Ed Barrow	1.00
1395	Ford Frick	1.00
1396	Ban Johnson	1.00
1397	Charles Comiskey	1.00
1398	Jacob Ruppert	1.00
1399	Branch Rickey	1.00
1400	Jack Kieran	1.00
1401	Mike Ryba	1.00
1402	Stan Spence	1.00
1403	Red Barrett	1.00
1404	Gabby Hartnett	1.00
1405	Babe Ruth	3.00
1406	Fred Merkle	1.00
1407	Claude Passeau	1.00
1408	Smokey Joe Wood	1.00
1409	Cliff Heathcote	1.00
1410	Walt Cruise	1.00
1411	Cookie Lavagetto	1.00
1412	Tony Lazzari	1.00
1413	Atley Donald	1.00
1414	Ken Raffensberger	1.00
1415	Dizzy Trout	1.00
1416	Augie Galan	1.00
1417	Monty Stratton	1.00
1418	Claude Passeau	1.00
1419	Oscar Grimes Jr.	1.00
1420	Rollie Hemsley	1.00
1421	Lou Gehrig	2.00
1422	Tom Sunkel	1.00
1423	Tris Speaker	1.00
1424	Chick Fewster	1.00
1425	Lou Boudreau	1.00
1426	Hank Leiber	1.00
1427	Eddie Mayo	1.00
1428	Charley Gelbert	1.00
1429	Jackie Hayes	1.00
1430	Checklist 1321-1430	1.00
3C	Babe Ruth (100th Birthday)	4.00

In the Zone

An eight-card set comparing Ken Griffey Jr. with superstars of the past was randomly inserted into 1995 Conlon Collection packs. Fronts feature a colorized background photo of the player with whom Griffey is being compared. A smaller color photo of Griffey is in the foreground. An "In the Zone" logo is at lower-left. Backs share a background photo of Griffey and have a black-and-white portrait of the comparison player in the upper-left. Narrative describes how the two players compare. A card number is at upper-right in the Zone logo. Megacard and Cooperstown Collection logos are at bottom. The first six cards of the series coould be found in Conlon Collection packs, cards 7 and 8 were available only through a mail-in offer for $2 plus five proofs-of-purchase. The print run was announced as no more than 50,000 sets.

		NM/M
Complete Set (8):		12.00
Common Card:		2.00
1	Ken Griffey Jr., Babe Ruth	3.50
2	Ken Griffey Jr., Lou Gehrig	3.00
3	Ken Griffey Jr., Ty Cobb	3.00
4	Ken Griffey Jr., Jimmie Foxx	2.00
5	Ken Griffey Jr., Mel Ott	2.00
6	Ken Griffey Jr., Joe Jackson	3.00
7	Ken Griffey Jr., Tris Speaker	2.00
8	Ken Griffey Jr., Jim Bottomley	2.00

1979-83 Coral-Lee Postcards

A number of baseball subjects were among a series of sports postcards published by Coral-Lee of California. Two formats are seen, standard postcard size of 3-1/2" x 5-1/2", and a larger 4" x 6" style seen on cards numbered 14 or higher. The standard-size cards have borderless color portrait photos on front, with no identification. Postcard style backs have the player's id, along with publisher, printer and copyright information in black-and-white. Most are dated. The larger cards have action photos on front, with backs similar to the smaller type. This list may not be complete as far as baseball-related cards within the series.

		NM/M
Common Player:		.25
1	Pete Rose	3.00
2	Davey Lopes	.25
3	Dave Winfield	1.50
4	Billy Martin	1.00
5	George Steinbrenner, Billy Martin, Reggie Jackson, Thurman Munson	1.50
6	Reggie Jackson	1.50
7	Bruce Kison	.25
8	Bobby Grich	.25
9	Rod Carew	.50
10	Tommy John	.25
11	Dick Howser	.25
12	George Brett	1.00
14-C	Cal Ripken Jr.	2.00
15-C	Carl Yastrzemski	1.00
16-C	Joe Morgan	.50
18-C	Graig Nettles	.25
69	Willie Mays, Ronald Reagan, Edward Stack	1.00
81	Fernando Valenzuela, Jose Lopez Portillo	1.00

1988-93 Costacos Brothers Ad Cards

During the hey-day of sports hero personality posters in the late 1980s and early 1990s, one of the industry's major players, Costacos Brothers, issued a series of 4" x 6" cards to advertise their poster offerings. Card fronts duplicate the issued poster, while backs contain an ad for the poster company. Players in many sports were included in the series but only the baseball players are listed here.

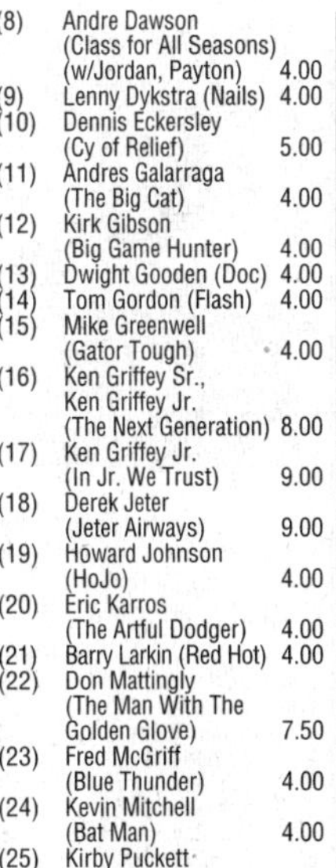

		NM/M
Complete Set (31):		125.00
Common Player:		4.00
(1)	Barry Bonds (License to Thrill)	10.00
(2)	Bobby Bonilla (Bobby Bo)	4.00
(3)	Will Clark (Thriller)	4.00
(4)	Will Clark (Willpower)	4.00
(5)	Roger Clemens (The Rocket)	8.00
(6)	Darren Daulton (D-Day)	4.00
(7)	Glenn Davis (The Big Bopper)	4.00
(8)	Andre Dawson (Class for All Seasons) (w/Jordan, Payton)	4.00
(9)	Lenny Dykstra (Nails)	4.00
(10)	Dennis Eckersley (Cy of Relief)	5.00
(11)	Andres Galarraga (The Big Cat)	4.00
(12)	Kirk Gibson (Big Game Hunter)	4.00
(13)	Dwight Gooden (Doc)	4.00
(14)	Tom Gordon (Flash)	4.00
(15)	Mike Greenwell (Gator Tough)	4.00
(16)	Ken Griffey Sr., Ken Griffey Jr. (The Next Generation)	8.00
(17)	Ken Griffey Jr. (In Jr. We Trust)	9.00
(18)	Derek Jeter (Jeter Airways)	9.00
(19)	Howard Johnson (HoJo)	4.00
(20)	Eric Karros (The Artful Dodger)	4.00
(21)	Barry Larkin (Red Hot)	4.00
(22)	Don Mattingly (The Man With The Golden Glove)	7.50
(23)	Fred McGriff (Blue Thunder)	4.00
(24)	Kevin Mitchell (Bat Man)	4.00
(25)	Kirby Puckett (The Wrecking Ball)	7.50
(26)	Tim Raines (Steal Wheels)	4.00
(27)	Harold Reynolds (Turning Point)	4.00
(28)	Benito Santiago (Thou Shalt Not Steal!)	4.00
(29)	Steve Sax (Sax Appeal)	4.00
(30)	Darryl Strawberry (Straw-Some)	4.00
(31)	Greg Swindell, Pete Harnisch, Doug Drabek (Shooting Stars)	4.00

1991 Country Hearth Mariners

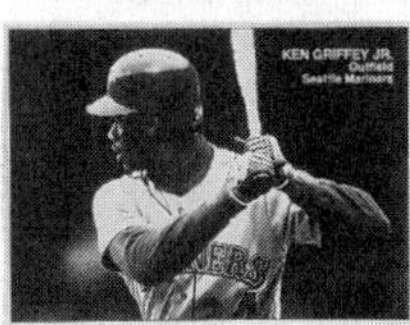

This 29-card set was inserted in loaves of bread and also given away at a Mariner home game. The card fronts feature full-color glossy photos, while the flip sides feature statistics.

		NM/M
Complete Set (29):		15.00
Common Player:		.50
1	Jim Lefebvre	.50
2	Jeff Schaefer	.50
3	Harold Reynolds	.75
4	Greg Briley	.50
5	Scott Bradley	.50
6	Dave Valle	.50
7	Edgar Martinez	1.00
8	Pete O'Brien	.50
9	Omar Vizquel	1.00
10	Tino Martinez	1.00
11	Scott Bankhead	.50
12	Bill Swift	.50
13	Jay Buhner	1.00
14	Alvin Davis	.50
15	Ken Griffey, Jr.	10.00
16	Tracy Jones	.50
17	Brent Knackert	.50
18	Henry Cotto	.50
19	Ken Griffey Sr.	.50
20	Keith Comstock	.50
21	Brian Holman	.50
22	Russ Swan	.50
23	Mike Jackson	.50
24	Erik Hanson	.50
25	Mike Schooler	.50
26	Randy Johnson	3.00
27	Rich DeLucia	.50
28	The Griffeys (Ken Griffey Jr., Ken Griffey Sr.)	2.00
29	Mascot	.50

1993 Country Time Brooks Robinson

Sponsored by Country Time drink mix, this set honors the career of the Orioles' Hall of Fame third baseman. The 2-1/2" x 3-5/8" cards feature color and colorized action photos with pale yellow frames, black diamond and textured green backgrounds and red and black borders. "Country Time Legends" and MLB logos appear in one of the bottom corners. Backs are printed in black, green and yellow and have a few sentences about some phase of Robinson's career. The cards are not numbered.

		NM/M
Complete Set (8):		7.00
Common Card:		1.00
(1)	Title Card	.25
(2)	Brooks Robinson/Btg (Back view.)	1.00
(3)	Brooks Robinson/Btg (Front view.)	1.00
(4)	Brooks Robinson/Btg (Horizontal.)	1.00
(5)	Brooks Robinson/Fldg (Horizontal white jersey.)	1.00
(6)	Brooks Robinson/Fldg (Horizontal orange jersey.)	1.00
(7)	Brooks Robinson/Fldg (Vertical.)	1.00
(8)	Brooks Robinson (Saluting crowd.)	1.00

1982 Cracker Jack

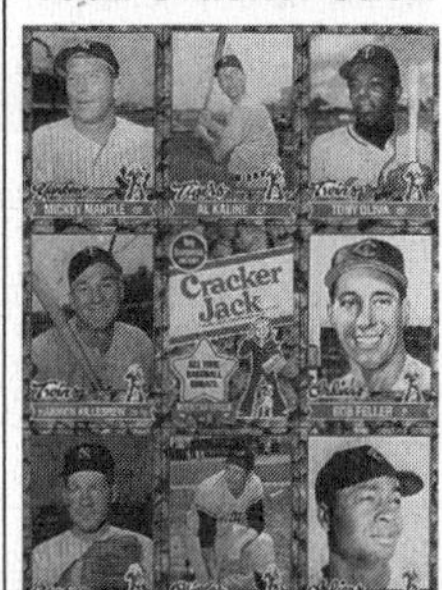

The Topps-produced 1982 Cracker Jack set was issued to promote the first "Old Timers Baseball Classic," held in Washington, D.C. The set was issued in two sheets of eight player cards, plus an advertising card located in the center. Individual cards are 2-1/2" x 3-1/2," with the complete sheets measuring 7-1/2" x 10-1/2". Cards #1-8 feature American League players with #9-16 being former National League stars. Fronts feature a full-color photo inside a Cracker Jack border. Backs contain the sponsor's logo plus a short player biography and his lifetime pitching or batting record. Complete sheets were available through a write-in offer.

		NM/M
Complete Panel Set (2):		12.00
Complete Singles Set (17):		10.00
Common Single Player:		.50
A.L. Panel		6.00
1	Larry Doby	.50
2	Bob Feller	.50
3	Whitey Ford	.50
4	Al Kaline	.50
5	Harmon Killebrew	.50
6	Mickey Mantle	5.00
7	Tony Oliva	.50
8	Brooks Robinson	.50
---	Advertising Card	.05
N.L. Panel		4.00
9	Hank Aaron	2.00

10	Ernie Banks	.50
11	Ralph Kiner	.50
12	Eddie Mathews	.50
13	Willie Mays	2.00
14	Robin Roberts	.50
15	Duke Snider	.50
16	Warren Spahn	.50
---	Advertising Card	.05

1991 Cracker Jack Topps 1st Series

In their first issue in almost 10 years, Cracker Jack inserted miniature cards (1-1/4" x 1-3/4") as the toy surprise in packages of the famous snack. The company produced two 36-card series, portraying many of the top stars in the game. Card fronts are identical to the corresponding regular-issue Topps cards, but the backs are significantly different because of the small amount of space available for statistics. The Cracker Jack sailor logo appears on the bright red backs, along with copyright information listing Borden, Cracker Jack's parent company. These are sometimes found on 2-1/2" x 3-1/2" cards bearing four different of the mini-cards; these were cut from sheets illegally removed from the printer.

		NM/M
Complete Set (36):		10.00
Common Player:		.25
1	Nolan Ryan	3.00
2	Paul Molitor	.60
3	Tim Raines	.25
4	Frank Viola	.25
5	Sandy Alomar Jr.	.25
6	Ryne Sandberg	.75
7	Don Mattingly	1.00
8	Pedro Guerrero	.25
9	Jose Rijo	.25
10	Jose Canseco	.40
11	Dave Parker	.25
12	Doug Drabek	.25
13	Cal Ripken	3.00
14	Dave Justice	.25
15	George Brett	1.00
16	Eric Davis	.25
17	Mark Langston	.25
18	Rickey Henderson	.60
19	Barry Bonds	3.00
20	Kevin Maas	.25
21	Len Dykstra	.25
22	Roger Clemens	1.00
23	Robin Yount	.60
24	Mark Grace	.25
25	Bo Jackson	.40
26	Tony Gwynn	.75
27	Mark McGwire	2.00
28	Dwight Gooden	.25
29	Wade Boggs	.75
30	Kevin Mitchell	.25
31	Cecil Fielder	.25
32	Bobby Thigpen	.25
33	Benito Santiago	.25
34	Kirby Puckett	.75
35	Will Clark	.25
36	Ken Griffey Jr.	1.50

Topps 2nd Series

A second series of 36 micro cards was found in Cracker Jack boxes later in the 1991 season. Again numbered from 1-18, the 1-1/4" x 1-3/4" cards carry a "2nd Series" designation on the back above the card number. Like the first series, these cards replicate the front of the 1991 Topps issue and have modified back design which includes the "Sailor Jack" logo of the candy com-

pany. Four-card panels, believed to have been cut from sheets illegally removed from the printer, are known.

		NM/M
Complete Set (36):		5.00
Common Player:		.35
1	Eddie Murray	.75
2	Carlton Fisk	.75
3	Eric Anthony	.40
4	Kelly Gruber	.40
5	Von Hayes	.40
6	Ben McDonald	.40
7	Andre Dawson	.60
8	Ellis Burks	.40
9	Matt Williams	.40
10	Dave Stewart	.40
11	Barry Larkin	.40
12	Chuck Finley	.40
13	Shane Andrews	.40
14	Bret Saberhagen	.40
15	Bobby Bonilla	.40
16	Roberto Kelly	.40
17	Orel Hershiser	.40
18	Ruben Sierra	.40
19	Ron Gant	.40
20	Frank Thomas	1.00
21	Tim Wallach	.40
22	Gregg Olson	.40
23	Shawon Dunston	.40
24	Kent Hrbek	.40
25	Ramon Martinez	.40
26	Alan Trammell	.40
27	Ozzie Smith	2.00
28	Bob Welch	.40
29	Chris Sabo	.40
30	Steve Sax	.40
31	Bip Roberts	.40
32	Dave Steib	.40
33	Howard Johnson	.40
34	Mike Greenwell	.40
35	Delino DeShields	.40
36	Alex Fernandez	.40

1992 Cracker Jack Donruss Series 1

In 1992, Cracker Jack turned to Donruss to produce the cards for the surprise in their packages. The first series of micro cards (1-1/4" x 1-3/4") was numbered 1-36 and features many top players. Card fronts are identical to the regular-issue '92 Donruss, but the backs have a different format and much less information because of the tiny space available. The backs have a blue border, with some spot red printing and the Cracker Jack sailor logo in the lower-left corner.

		NM/M
Complete Set (36):		20.00
Common Player:		.50
Album:		10.00
1	Dennis Eckersley	1.00
2	Jeff Bagwell	1.25
3	Jim Abbott	.50
4	Steve Avery	.50
5	Kelly Gruber	.50
6	Ozzie Smith	1.50
7	Lance Dickson	.50
8	Robin Yount	1.25
9	Brett Butler	.50
10	Sandy Alomar Jr.	.50
11	Travis Fryman	.50
12	Ken Griffey Jr.	2.00
13	Cal Ripken, Jr.	4.00
14	Will Clark	.50
15	Nolan Ryan	4.00
16	Tony Gwynn	1.50
17	Roger Clemens	1.75
18	Wes Chamberlain	.50
19	Barry Larkin	.50
20	Brian McRae	.50
21	Marquis Grissom	.50
22	Cecil Fielder	.50
23	Dwight Gooden	.50
24	Chuck Knoblauch	.50
25	Jose Çanseco	.65
26	Terry Pendleton	.50
27	Ivan Rodriguez	1.00
28	Ryne Sandberg	1.50
29	Kent Hrbek	.50
30	Ramon Martinez	.50
31	Todd Zeile	.50
32	Hal Morris	.50
33	Robin Ventura	.50
34	Doug Drabek	.50
35	Frank Thomas	1.25
36	Don Mattingly	1.75

Donruss Series 2

The Second Series of the 1992 Crack Jack Donruss set is almost identical to the first series, with the only change being different players and red border on the back instead of blue. The micro cards are numbered 1-36, just as in the first series.

		NM/M
Complete Set (36):		15.00
Common Player:		.50
1	Craig Biggio	.50
2	Tom Glavine	.65
3	David Justice	.50
4	Lee Smith	.50
5	Mark Grace	.50
6	George Bell	.50
7	Darryl Strawberry	.50
8	Eric Davis	.50
9	Ivan Calderon	.50
10	Royce Clayton	.50
11	Matt Williams	.50
12	Fred McGriff	.50
13	Len Dykstra	.50
14	Barry Bonds	3.00
15	Reggie Sanders	.50
16	Chris Sabo	.50
17	Howard Johnson	.50
18	Bobby Bonilla	.50
19	Rickey Henderson	.75
20	Mark Langston	.50
21	Joe Carter	.50
22	Paul Molitor	.75
23	Glenallen Hill	.50
24	Edgar Martinez	.50
25	Gregg Olson	.50
26	Ruben Sierra	.50
27	Julio Franco	.50
28	Phil Plantier	.50
29	Wade Boggs	1.00
30	George Brett	1.25
31	Alan Trammell	.50
32	Kirby Puckett	1.00
33	Scott Erickson	.50
34	Matt Nokes	.50
35	Danny Tartabull	.50
36	Jack McDowell	.50

1993 Cracker Jack Anniversary

In 1993, as part of the company's 100th anniversary celebration, Cracker Jack issued a 24-card set of mini replicas of its famous 1915 cards. The cards, 1-1/4" x 1-3/4", were included in specially-marked packages of the famous snack. The set features Hall of Famers such as Cobb, Mathewson, Walter Johnson and others, plus the Joe Jackson card. A red plastic album, with color pictures of the replicas inside, was also available.

		NM/M
Complete Set (24):		10.00
Common Player:		.50
Album:		5.00
1	Ty Cobb	1.50
2	Joe Jackson	3.00
3	Honus Wagner	1.00
4	Christy Mathewson	.75
5	Walter Johnson	.75
6	Tris Speaker	.50
7	Grover Alexander	.50
8	Nap Lajoie	.50
9	Rube Marquard	.50
10	Connie Mack	.50
11	Johnny Evers	.50
12	Branch Rickey	.50
13	Fred Clarke	.50
14	Harry Hooper	.50
15	Zack Wheat	.50
16	Joe Tinker	.50
17	Eddie Collins	.50
18	Mordecai Brown	.50
19	Eddie Plank	.50
20	Rabbit Maranville	.50
21	John McGraw	.50
22	Miller Huggins	.50
23	Ed Walsh	.50
24	Leslie Bush	.50

1997 Cracker Jack All Stars

After an hiatus of three years, Cracker Jack resumed the use of baseball cards as premiums in 1997 with a 20-card All Stars set. Like the other CJ issues of the 1990s, this set features miniature (1-5/16" x 1-3/4") cards. Cards feature player action photos on front along with a Cracker Jack All Stars logo. Photos have uniform logos removed as the set is licensed only by the Players Association and not Major League Baseball. Backs are printed in red and blue with Cracker Jack and MLBPA logos, a few stats and personal data. Cards were also distributed as prizes in various promotional contests conducted by American Sports Classics, which inserted a logo card within the regular Cracker Jack prize wrapping.

		NM/M
Complete Set (20):		15.00
Common Player:		.50
1	Jeff Bagwell	1.00
2	Chuck Knoblauch	.50
3	Cal Ripken Jr.	3.00
4	Chipper Jones	1.50
5	Derek Jeter	3.00
6	Barry Larkin	.50
7	Bernie Williams	.50
8	Barry Bonds	3.00
9	Kenny Lofton	.50
10	Gary Sheffield	.65
11	Sammy Sosa	1.50
12	Paul Molitor	1.00
13	Andres Galarraga	.50
14	Ivan Rodriguez	.75
15	Mike Piazza	2.00
16	Andy Pettitte	.65
17	Tom Glavine	.65
18	Albert Belle	.50
19	Mark McGwire	2.50
20	Mo Vaughn	.50
Album:		2.00

1999 Cracker Jack Mac Stickers

In conjunction with its season-long promotion with Rawlings in which various Big

Mac equipment items were given away, individual boxes of the snack could be found bearing one of 10 different McGwire stickers. The 1-1/2" x 2-1/8" stickers each include some type of interactive play element. Values shown are for opened, but complete, prize booklets. The color photos of McGwire on the stickers have had uniform logos removed.

	NM/M
Complete Set (10):	5.00
Common Sticker:	.50

1999 Cracker Jack Mark McGwire Home Run Record

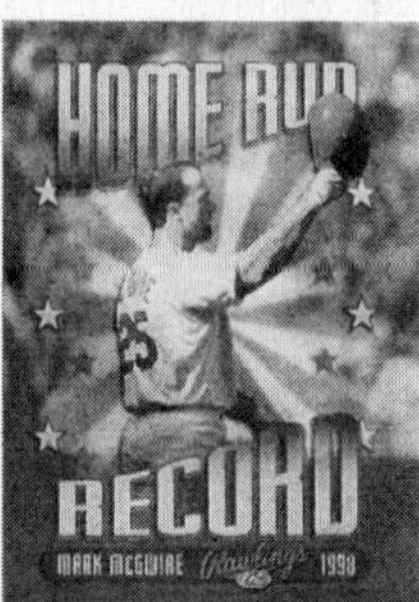

One of several premiums which were part of a Rawlings promotion in boxes of Cracker Jack and related mail-in offers, this card marks McGwire's 70-HR season of 1998. The front is optical-variable, offering an image of McGwire in his home run-followthrough and, with a change in viewing angle, tipping his helmet to the crowd. Back has the date and distance of each of his 1998 homers, along with Rawling and Cracker Jack logos. The card is in standard 2-1/2" x 3-1/2" format.

	NM/M
Mark McGwire	10.00

1999 Cracker Jack Mark McGwire Spinners

"Home Run Around" is the name given to these spinner discs found as prizes in Cracker Jack boxes. The 1-5/8" plastic discs have a "magic motion" picture of McGwire on front with a large "70." Around the front rim are segments with other numbers. Instructions on back are to spin the disc and stop it to see if the player can hit more homers than McGwire. A raised spot at center allow the disc to be spun. While the Rawlings logo appears on front and back, Cardinals uniform logos have been deleted from the photos.

	NM/M
Complete Set (5):	10.00
Common Disc:	2.00

2002 Cracker Jack All-Stars

After skipping four years, Cracker Jack resumed the use of baseball cards as premiums in 2002 with a 30-card All-Stars set produced by Topps. Like the CJ issues of the 1990s, this set features miniature (1-5/8" x 2-1/8") cards with player action photos on front along with a Cracker Jack All-Stars logo. The checklist shows one player from each team. Backs are printed in color with Cracker Jack, Topps and MLB/MLBPA logos, a few stats and personal data. Complete sets in a customer holder were available by mail for $9.99.

		NM/M
Complete Set (30):		12.00
Common Player:		.25
1	Roger Clemens	.75
2	Pedro Martinez	.50
3	Carlos Delgado	.35
4	Jeff Conine	.25
5	Greg Vaughn	.25
6	Jim Thome	.40
7	Brad Radke	.25
8	Frank Thomas	.50
9	Steve Sparks	.25
10	Carlos Beltran	.35
11	Ichiro	2.00
12	Mark Mulder	.25
13	Troy Glaus	.45
14	Alex Rodriguez	1.50
15	Chipper Jones	.65
16	Bobby Abreu	.25
17	Mike Piazza	1.00
18	Cliff Floyd	.25
19	Vladimir Guerrero	.50
20	Jeff Bagwell	.50
21	Albert Pujols	1.50
22	Sammy Sosa	.65
23	Richie Sexson	.25
24	Sean Casey	.25
25	Brian Giles	.25
26	Randy Johnson	.50
27	Barry Bonds	2.00
28	Kevin Brown	.25
29	Phil Nevin	.25
30	Todd Helton	.40

2003 Cracker Jack All-Stars

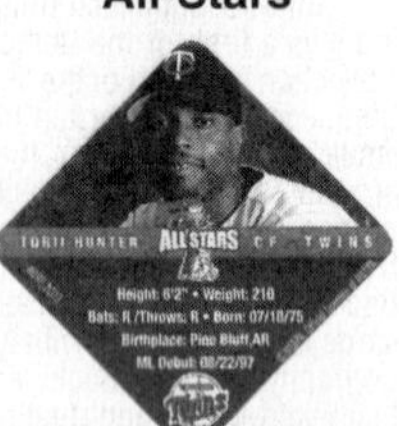

The baseball cards inserted in boxes of Cracker Jack for 2003 were an entirely new format, printed on round-cornered 1-5/8" x 1-5/8" plastic squares. The printing is formatted to give the cards a diamond shape. Fronts have a player portrait in the upper half with personal data below.

Team and sponsor logos also appear. Backs have team and sponsor logos, along with those of the licensors. The unnumbered cards are checklisted here alphabetically. Besides product insertion, the complete set was available by mail, along with a color 10-1/2" x 21" poster in which the cards could be displayed, for about $12.

		NM/M
Complete Set (32):		12.00
Common Player:		.50
Poster:		5.00
(1)	Roberto Alomar	.60
(2)	Jeff Bagwell	.75
(3)	Tony Batista	.50
(4)	Carlos Beltran	.60
(5)	Bret Boone	.50
(6)	Ellis Burks	.50
(7)	A.J. Burnett	.50
(8)	Pat Burrell	.50
(9)	Sean Casey	.50
(10)	Carlos Delgado	.65
(11)	Damion Easley	.50
(12)	Jason Giambi	.65
(13)	Brian Giles	.50
(14)	Troy Glaus	.65
(15)	Shawn Green	.60
(16)	Ben Grieve	.50
(17)	Vladimir Guerrero	.75
(18)	Todd Helton	.65
(19)	Torii Hunter	.50
(20)	Randy Johnson	.75
(21)	Chipper Jones	1.00
(22)	Ryan Klesko	.50
(23)	Paul Konerko	.60
(24)	Pedro Martinez	.75
(25)	Mark Mulder	.50
(26)	Robb Nen	.50
(27)	Rafael Palmeiro	.65
(28)	Albert Pujols	2.00
(29)	Ben Sheets	.50
(30)	Sammy Sosa	1.00
(31)	All-Star Game Logo	.15
(32)	Cracker Jack Logo	.15

2004 Cracker Jack Baseball History

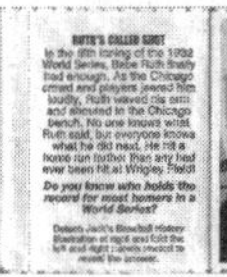

Illustrations of great moments in baseball history are reproduced in this set of Cracker Jack prize inserts. When opened, each 2" x 2-1/2" prize wrapper has the illustration on one side and narrative on the other. If detached and folded, the illustration reveals the answer to a trivia question.

		NM/M
Complete Set (10):		10.00
Common Player:		.50
(1)	Aaron Hits #715 (Hank Aaron)	1.00
(2)	Back to Back (Johnny Vander Meer)	.50
(3)	Jackie Robinson	1.00
(4)	Joe DiMaggio - The Streak	1.00
(5)	Larsen's Perfect Game (Don Larsen)	.50
(6)	Pete Gray	.50
(7)	Roberto Clemente	2.00
(8)	Ruth's Called Shot (Babe Ruth)	2.00
(9)	Shot Heard Round the World (Bobby Thomson)	.50
(10)	The Catch (Willie Mays)	1.00

2005 Cracker Jack Ballpark Legends

A set of 10 small booklets featuring past stars was produced for inclusion in 99-cent packages of Cracker Jack. The prize was in the form of a small (about 1-1/2" x 2-1/8" booklet about the individual player, with a baseball card in the center. The booklet has a career summary and checklist. The card has a heavily retouched photo with uniform details removed, "BALLPARK LEGENDS" at top and the player name between stars at bottom. Backs have biographical data, career highlights and lifetime stats.

Complete Set, Booklets (10):
Common Player Booklet:
Unattached Cards: 50 Percent

1980-83 Cramer Baseball Legends

Consecutively numbered, this set was issued over a period of four years by Cramer Sports Promotions, the forerunner of today's Pacific card company. Sold in wax packs and measuring the standard 2-1/2" x 3-1/2", the cards have a sepia-toned photo on front with a black frame. In the background is a weathered wooden slat design with the player's name on a hanging board beneath. The borders are dull yellow. Backs are printed in brown and include a few personal data, career stats and a career summary. Cards 1-30 were issued in 1980; #31-60 in 1981; #61-90 in 1982 and #90-124 in 1983. Cards #121-124 were issued on the 1983 wax box.

		NM/M
Complete Set (124):		45.00
Complete Set (120):		
Common Player:		.25
1980		
1	Babe Ruth	3.00
2	Heinie Manush	.25
3	Rabbit Maranville	.25
4	Earl Averill	.25
5	Joe DiMaggio	2.00
6	Mickey Mantle	3.00
7	Hank Aaron	1.50
8	Stan Musial	1.25
9	Bill Terry	.25
10	Sandy Koufax	1.50
11	Ernie Lombardi	.25
12	Dizzy Dean	.25
13	Lou Gehrig	2.00
14	Walter Alston	.25
15a	Jackie Robinson/Portrait	4.00
15b	Jackie Robinson/Btg	1.00
16	Jimmie Foxx	.25
17	Billy Southworth	.25
18	Honus Wagner	.50
19	Duke Snider	.25
20	Rogers Hornsby	.25
21	Paul Waner	.25
22	Luke Appling	.25
23	Billy Herman	.25
24	Lloyd Waner	.25
25	Fred Hutchinson	.25
26	Eddie Collins	.25
27	Lefty Grove	.25
28	Chuck Connors	.25
29	Lefty O'Doul	.25
30	Hank Greenberg	.25
1981		
31	Ty Cobb	2.50
32	Enos Slaughter	.25
33	Ernie Banks	.45
34	Christy Mathewson	.35
35	Mel Ott	.25
36	Pie Traynor	.25
37	Clark Griffith	.25
38	Mickey Cochrane	.25
39	Joe Cronin	.25
40	Leo Durocher	.25
41	Frank Baker	.25
42	Joe Tinker	.25
43	John McGraw	.25
44	Bill Dickey	.25
45	Walter Johnson	.35
46	Frankie Frisch	.25
47	Casey Stengel	.25
48	Willie Mays	2.00
49	Johnny Mize	.25
50	Roberto Clemente	4.00
51	Burleigh Grimes	.25
52	Pee Wee Reese	.25
53	Bob Feller	.25
54	Brooks Robinson	.25
55	Sam Crawford	.25
56	Robin Roberts	.25
57	Warren Spahn	.25
58	Joe McCarthy	.25
59	Jocko Conlan	.25
60	Satchel Paige	.75
1982		
61	Ted Williams	3.00
62	George Kelly	.25
63	Gil Hodges	.25
64	Jim Bottomley	.25
65	Al Kaline	.25
66	Harvey Kuenn	.25
67	Yogi Berra	.25
68	Nellie Fox	.25
69	Harmon Killebrew	.25
70	Edd Roush	.25
71	Mordecai Brown	.25
72	Gabby Hartnett	.25
73	Early Wynn	.25
74	Nap Lajoie	.25
75	Charlie Grimm	.25
76	Joe Garagiola	.25
77	Ted Lyons	.25
78	Mickey Vernon	.25
79	Lou Boudreau	.25
80	Al Dark	.25
81	Ralph Kiner	.25
82	Phil Rizzuto	.25
83	Stan Hack	.25
84	Frank Chance	.25
85	Ray Schalk	.25
86	Bill McKechnie	.25
87	Travis Jackson	.25
88	Pete Reiser	.25
89	Carl Hubbell	.25
90	Roy Campanella	.25
1983		
91	Cy Young	.25
92	Kiki Cuyler	.25
93	Chief Bender	.25
94	Richie Ashburn	.25
95	Riggs Stephenson	.25
96	Minnie Minoso	.25
97	Hack Wilson	.25
98	Al Lopez	.25
99	Willie Keeler	.25
100	Fred Lindstrom	.25
101	Roger Maris	.25
102	Roger Bresnahan	.25
103	Monty Stratton	.25
104	Goose Goslin	.25
105	Earle Combs	.25
106	Pepper Martin	.25
107	Joe Jackson	3.00
108	George Sisler	.25
109	Red Ruffing	.25
110	Johnny Vander Meer	.25
111	Herb Pennock	.25
112	Chuck Klein	.25
113	Paul Derringer	.25
114	Addie Joss	.25
115	Bobby Thomson	.25
116	Chick Hafey	.25
117	Lefty Gomez	.25
118	George Kell	.25
119	Al Simmons	.25
120	Bob Lemon	.25
121	Hoyt Wilhelm	1.00
122	Arky Vaughan	1.00
123	Frank Robinson	1.50
124	Grover Alexander	1.50

1991 Crown/Coke Orioles

Claiming to include every player for the modern (1954-1991) Baltimore Orioles, this 501-card set was issued in four series. The first three series contain 120 cards each in a format of a dozen perforated cards on each of 10 sheets. Those series were given away at May 17, June 28 and August 11 home games. The fourth series, 12 sheets of 12 cards each, including three blank cards, was available only at participating Crown gas stations, which also sold the first three series following the giveaway days at the ballpark. Cards measure 2-1/2" x 3-3/16" and are perforated on two, three or four sides, depending on their position on the sheet. All players are featured in sepia-toned head shots, virtually all in Orioles' uniform. Around the photos are borders of, successively, green, orange, black and white. The player's name and position appear in a black banner above the photo. In the lower-left corner is a 1954-1991 Memorial Stadium "Season to Remember" logo. That logo is repeated at bottom-center of the black-and-white backs, flanked by the logos of Coca-Cola and Crown. A card number appears in the lower-right. Most cards were numbered alphabetically. Backs include stats for the player's major league career and time with the Orioles.

		NM/M
Complete Set (501):		30.00
Common Player:		.15
1	Don Aase	.15
2	Cal Abrams	.15
3	Jerry Adair	.15
4	Bobby Adams	.15
5	Mike Adamson	.15
6	Jay Aldrich	.15
7	Bob Alexander	.15
8	Doyle Alexander	.15
9	Brady Anderson	.40
10	John Anderson	.15
11	Mike Anderson	.15
12	Luis Aparicio	1.25
13	Tony Arnold	.15
14	Bobby Avila	.15
15	Benny Ayala	.15
16	Bob Bailor	.15
17	Frank Baker	.15
18	Jeff Ballard	.15
19	George Bamberger	.15
20	Steve Barber	.15
21	Ray "Buddy" Barker	.15
22	Ed Barnowski	.15
23	Jose Bautista	.15
24	Don Baylor	.40
25	Charlie Beamon	.15
26	Fred Beene	.15
27	Mark Belanger	.25
28	Eric Bell	.15
29	Juan Bell	.15
30	Juan Beniquez	.15
31	Neil Berry	.15
32	Frank Bertaina	.15
33	Fred Besana	.15
34	Vern Bickford	.15
35	Babe Birrer	.15
36	Paul Blair	.15
37	Curt Blefary	.15
38	Mike Blyzka	.15
39	Mike Boddicker	.15
40	Juan Bonilla	.15
41	Bob Bonner	.15
42	Dan Boone	.15
43	Rich Bordi	.15
44	Dave Boswell	.15
45	Sam Bowens	.15
46	Bob Boyd	.15
47	Gene Brabender	.15
48	Phil Bradley	.15
49	Jackie Brandt	.15
50	Marv Breeding	.15
51	Jim Brideweser	.15
52	Nellie Briles	.15
53	Dick Brown	.15
54	Hal Brown	.15
55	Larry Brown	.15
56	Mark Brown	.15
57	Marty Brown	.15
58	George Brunet	.15
59	Don Buford	.25
60	Al Bumbry	.15
61	Wally Bunker	.15
62	Leo Burke	.15
63	Rick Burleson	.15
64	Pete Burnside	.15
65	Jim Busby	.15
66	John Buzhardt	.15
67	Harry Byrd	.15
68	Enos Cabell	.15
69	Chico Carrasquel	.15
70	Camilo Carreon	.15
71	Foster Castleman	.15
72	Wayne Causey	.15
73	Art Ceccarelli	.15
74	Bob Chakales	.15
75	Tony Chevez	.15
76	Tom Chism	.15
77	Gino Cimoli	.15
78	Gil Coan	.15
79	Rich Coggins	.15
80	Joe Coleman	.15
81	Rip Coleman	.15
82	Fritz Connally	.15
83	Sandy Consuegra	.15
84	Doug Corbett	.15
85	Mark Corey	.15
86	Clint Courtney	.15
87	Billy Cox	.15
88	Dave Criscione	.15
89	Terry Crowley	.15
90	Todd Cruz	.15
91	Mike Cuellar	.30
92	Angie Dagres	.15
93	Clay Dalrymple	.15
94	Rich Dauer	.15
95	Jerry DaVanon	.15
96	Butch Davis	.15
97	Storm Davis	.15
98	Tommy Davis	.15
99	Doug DeCinces	.25
100	Luis DeLeon	.15
101	Ike Delock	.15
102	Rick Dempsey	.25
103	Mike Devereaux	.15
104	Chuck Diering	.15
105	Gordon Dillard	.15
106	Bill Dillman	.15
107	Mike Dimmel	.15
108	Ken Dixon	.15
109	Pat Dobson	.15
110	Tom Dodd	.15
111	Harry Dorish	.15
112	Moe Drabowsky	.15
113	Dick Drago	.15
114	Walt Dropo	.15
115	Tom Dukes	.15
116	Dave Duncan	.15
117	Ryne Duren	.15
118	Joe Durham	.15
119	Jim Dwyer	.15
120	Jim Dyck	.15
121	Mike Epstein	.15
122	Chuck Essegian	.15
123	Chuck Estrada	.15
124	Andy Etchebarren	.15
125	Hoot Evers	.15
126	Ed Farmer	.15
127	Chico Fernandez	.15
128	Don Ferrarese	.15
129	Jim Finigan	.15
130	Steve Finley	.15
131	Mike Fiore	.15
132	Eddie Fisher	.15
133	Jack Fisher	.15
134	Tom Fisher	.15
135	Mike Flanagan	.15
136	John Flinn	.15
137	Bobby Floyd	.15
138	Hank Foiles	.15
139	Dan Ford	.15
140	Dave Ford	.15
141	Mike Fornieles	.15
142	Howie Fox	.15
143	Tito Francona	.15
144	Joe Frazier	.15
145	Roger Freed	.15
146	Jim Fridley	.15
147	Jim Fuller	.15
148	Joe Gaines	.15
149	Vinicio "Chico" Garcia	.15
150	Kiko Garcia	.15
151	Billy Gardner	.15
152	Wayne Garland	.15
153	Tommy Gastall	.15
154	Jim Gentile	.25
155	Ken Gerhart	.15
156	Paul Gilliford	.15
157	Joe Ginsberg	.15
158	Leo Gomez	.15
159	Rene Gonzales	.15
160	Billy Goodman	.15
161	Dan Graham	.15
162	Ted Gray	.15
163	Gene Green	.15
164	Lenny Green	.15
165	Bobby Grich	.30
166	Mike Griffin	.15
167	Ross Grimsley	.15
168	Wayne Gross	.15
169	Glenn Gulliver	.15
170	Jackie Gutierrez	.15
171	John Habyan	.15
172	Harvey Haddix	.15
173	Bob Hale	.15
174	Dick Hall	.15
175	Bert Hamric	.15
176	Larry Haney	.15
177	Ron Hansen	.15
178	Jim Hardin	.15
179	Larry Harlow	.15
180	Pete Harnisch	.15
181	Tommy Harper	.15
182	Bob Harrison	.15
183	Roric Harrison	.15
184	Jack Harshman	.15
185	Mike Hart	.15
186	Paul Hartzell	.15
187	Grady Hatton	.15
188	Brad Havens	.15
189	Drungo Hazewood	.15
190	Jehosie Heard	.15
191	Mel Held	.15
192	Woodie Held	.15
193	Ellie Hendricks	.25
194	Leo Hernandez	.15
195	Whitey Herzog	.15
196	Kevin Hickey	.15
197	Billy Hoeft	.15
198	Chris Hoiles	.15
199	Fred Holdsworth	.15
200	Brian Holton	.15
201	Ken Holtzman	.15
202	Don Hood	.15
203	Sam Horn	.15
204	Art Houtteman	.15
205	Bruce Howard	.15
206	Rex Hudler	.15
207	Phil Huffman	.15
208	Keith Hughes	.15
209	Mark Huismann	.15
210	Tim Hulett	.15
211	Billy Hunter	.15
212	Dave Huppert	.15
213	Jim Hutto	.15
214	Dick Hyde	.15
215	Grant Jackson	.15
216	Lou Jackson	.15
217	Reggie Jackson	5.00
218	Ron Jackson	.15
219	Jesse Jefferson	.15
220	Stan Jefferson	.15
221	Bob Johnson	.15
222	Connie Johnson	.15
223	Darrell Johnson	.15
224	Dave Johnson	.15
225	Davey Johnson	.25
226	David Johnson	.15
227	Don Johnson	.15
228	Ernie Johnson	.15
229	Gordon Jones	.15
230	Ricky Jones	.15
231	O'Dell Jones	.15
232	Sam Jones	.15
233	George Kell	.75
234	Frank Kellert	.15
235	Pat Kelly	.15
236	Bob Kennedy	.15
237	Terry Kennedy	.15
238	Joe Kerrigan	.15
239	Mike Kinnunen	.15
240	Willie Kirkland	.15
241	Ron Kittle	.15
242	Billy Klaus	.15
243	Ray Knight	.25
244	Darold Knowles	.15
245	Dick Kokos	.15
246	Brad Komminsk	.15
247	Dave Koslo	.15
248	Wayne Krenchicki	.15
249	Lou Kretlow	.15
250	Dick Kryhoski	.15
251	Bob Kuzava	.15
252	Lee Lacy	.15
253	Hobie Landrith	.15
254	Tito Landrum	.15
255	Don Larsen	.25
256	Charlie Lau	.25
257	Jim Lehew	.15
258	Ken Lehman	.15
259	Don Lenhardt	.15
260	Dave Leonhard	.15
261	Don Leppert	.15
262	Dick Littlefield	.15
263	Charlie Locke	.15
264	Whitey Lockman	.15
265	Billy Loes	.15
266	Ed Lopat	.15
267	Carlos Lopez	.15
268	Marcelino Lopez	.15
269	John Lowenstein	.15
270	Steve Luebber	.15
271	Dick Luebke	.15
272	Fred Lynn	.45
273	Bobby Mabe	.15
274	Elliott Maddox	.15
275	Hank Majeski	.15
276	Roger Marquis	.15
277	Freddie Marsh	.15
278	Jim Marshall	.15
279	Morrie Martin	.15
280	Dennis Martinez	.25
281	Tippy Martinez	.25
282	Tom Matchick	.15
283	Charlie Maxwell	.15
284	Dave May	.15
285	Lee May	.15
286	Rudy May	.15
287	Mike McCormick	.15
288	Ben McDonald	.15
289	Jim McDonald	.15
290	Scott McGregor	.25
291	Mickey McGuire	.15
292	Jeff McKnight	.15
293	Dave McNally	.25
294	Sam Mele	.15
295	Francisco Melendez	.15
296	Bob Melvin	.15
297	Jose Mesa	.15
298	Eddie Miksis	.15
299	Bob Milacki	.15
300	Bill Miller	.15
301	Dyar Miller	.15
302	John Miller	.15
303	Randy Miller	.15
304	Stu Miller	.15

305	Randy Milligan	.15
306	Paul Mirabella	.15
307	Willy Miranda	.15
308	John Mitchell	.15
309	Paul Mitchell	.15
310	Ron Moeller	.15
311	Bob Molinaro	.15
312	Ray Moore	.15
313	Andres Mora	.15
314	Jose Morales	.15
315	Keith Moreland	.15
316	Mike Morgan	.15
317	Dan Morogiello	.15
318	John Morris	.15
319	Les Moss	.15
320	Curt Motton	.15
321	Eddie Murray	1.50
322	Ray Murray	.15
323	Tony Muser	.15
324	Buster Narum	.15
325	Bob Nelson	.15
326	Roger Nelson	.15
327	Carl Nichols	.15
328	Dave Nicholson	.15
329	Tom Niedenfuer	.15
330	Bob Nieman	.15
331	Donell Nixon	.15
332	Joe Nolan	.15
333	Dickie Noles	.15
334	Tim Nordbrook	.15
335	Jim Northrup	.15
336	Jack O'Connor	.15
337	Billy O'Dell	.15
338	John O'Donoghue	.15
339	Tom O'Malley	.15
340	Johnny Oates	.15
341	Chuck Oertel	.15
342	Bob Oliver	.15
343	Gregg Olson	.15
344	John Orsino	.15
345	Joe Orsulak	.15
346	John Pacella	.15
347	Dave Pagan	.15
348	Erv Palica	.15
349	Jim Palmer	1.50
350	John Papa	.15
351	Milt Pappas	.15
352	Al Pardo	.15
353	Kelly Paris	.15
354	Mike Parrott	.15
355	Tom Patton	.15
356	Albie Pearson	.15
357	Orlando Pena	.15
358	Oswaldo Peraza	.15
359	Buddy Peterson	.15
360	Dave Philley	.15
361	Tom Phoebus	.15
362	Al Pilarcik	.15
363	Duane Pillette	.15
364	Lou Piniella	.25
365	Dave Pope	.15
366	Arnie Portocarrero	.15
367	Boog Powell	1.00
368	Johnny Powers	.15
369	Carl Powis	.15
370	Joe Price	.15
371	Jim Pyburn	.15
372	Art Quirk	.15
373	Jamie Quirk	.15
374	Allan Ramirez	.15
375	Floyd Rayford	.15
376	Mike Reinbach	.15
377	Merv Rettenmund	.15
378	Bob Reynolds	.15
379	Del Rice	.15
380	Pete Richert	.15
381	Jeff Rineer	.15
382	Bill Ripken	.15
383	Cal Ripken	9.00
384	Robin Roberts	1.25
385	Brooks Robinson	4.00
386	Earl Robinson	.15
387	Eddie Robinson	.15
388	Frank Robinson	3.00
389	Sergio Robles	.15
390	Aurelio Rodriguez	.15
391	Vic Rodriguez	.15
392	Gary Roenicke	.15
393	Saul Rogovin	.15
394	Wade Rowdon	.15
395	Ken Rowe	.15
396	Willie Royster	.15
397	Vic Roznovsky	.15
398	Ken Rudolph	.15
399	Lenn Sakata	.15
400	Chico Salmon	.15
401	Orlando Sanchez	.15
402	Bob Saverine	.15
403	Art Schallock	.15
404	Bill Scherrer	.15
405	Curt Schilling	.75
406	Dave Schmidt	.15
407	Johnny Schmitz	.15
408	Jeff Schneider	.15
409	Rick Schu	.15
410	Mickey Scott	.15
411	Kal Segrist	.15
412	David Segui	.15
413	Al Severinsen	.15
414	Larry Sheets	.15
415	John Shelby	.15
416	Barry Shetrone	.15
417	Tom Shopay	.15
418	Bill Short	.15
419	Norm Siebern	.15
420	Nelson Simmons	.15
421	Ken Singleton	.25
422	Doug Sisk	.15
423	Dave Skaggs	.15
424	Lou Sleater	.15
425	Al Smith	.15
426	Billy Smith	.15
427	Hal Smith	.15
428	"Texas" Mike Smith	.15
429	Nate Smith	.15
430	Nate Snell	.15
431	Russ Snyder	.15
432	Don Stanhouse	.15
433	Pete Stanicek	.15
434	Herm Starrette	.15
435	John Stefero	.15
436	Gene Stephens	.15
437	Vern Stephens	.15
438	Earl Stephenson	.15
439	Sammy Stewart	.15
440	Royle Stillman	.15
441	Wes Stock	.15
442	Tim Stoddard	.15
443	Dean Stone	.15
444	Jeff Stone	.15
445	Steve Stone	.25
446	Marlin Stuart	.15
447	Gordie Sundin	.15
448	Bill Swaggerty	.15
449	Willie Tasby	.15
450	Joe Taylor	.15
451	Dorn Taylor	.15
452	Anthony Telford	.15
453	Johnny Temple	.15
454	Mickey Tettleton	.15
455	Valmy Thomas	.15
456	Bobby Thomson	.25
457	Marv Thorneberry	.15
458	Mark Thurmond	.15
459	Jay Tibbs	.15
460	Mike Torrez	.15
461	Jim Traber	.15
462	Gus Triandos	.15
463	Paul "Dizzy" Trout	.15
464	Bob Turley	.15
465	Tom Underwood	.15
466	Fred Valentine	.15
467	Dave Van Gorder	.15
468	Dave Vineyard	.15
469	Ozzie Virgil	.15
470	Eddie Waitkus	.15
471	Greg Walker	.15
472	Jerry Walker	.15
473	Pete Ward	.15
474	Carl Warwick	.15
475	Ron Washington	.15
476	Eddie Watt	.15
477	Don Welchel	.15
478	George Werley	.15
479	Vic Wertz	.15
480	Wally Westlake	.15
481	Mickey Weston	.15
482	Alan Wiggins	.15
483	Bill Wight	.15
484	Hoyt Wilhelm	.50
485	Dallas Williams	.15
486	Dick Williams	.15
487	Earl Williams	.15
488	Mark Williamson	.15
489	Jim Wilson	.15
490	Gene Woodling	.15
491	Craig Worthington	.15
492	Bobby Young	.15
493	Mike Young	.15
494	Frank Zupo	.15
495	George Zuverink	.15
496	Glenn Davis	.15
497	Dwight Evans	.25
498	Dave Gallagher	.15
499	Paul Kilgus	.15
500	Jeff Robinson	.15
501	Ernie Whitt	.15

1992 Crown Orioles Action Standups

Crown Petroleum released a set of standup cards in 1992 of 12 Oriole greats, most retired, that was sold at service stations in three series. The 4-1/4" x 9" cards have color photos on a white background on front; backs have black-and-white stats, logos, and career highlights. Cal Ripken, Jr. and Tippy Martinez were the only active players portrayed in the set. Suggested retail price at issue was $4 per series; about $2 with a gasoline purchase. A collector's album could also be purchased.

		NM/M
Complete Set (12):		20.00
Common Player:		1.00
SET 1		10.00
(1)	Frank Robinson	3.00
(2)	Brooks Robinson	4.00
(3)	Jim Palmer	3.00
(4)	Rick Dempsey	1.00
SET 2		12.00
(5)	Cal Ripken Jr.	10.00
(6)	Tippy Martinez	1.00
(7)	Bobby Grich	1.00
(8)	Earl Weaver	1.00
SET 3		4.00
(9)	Boog Powell	1.50
(10)	Paul Blair	1.00
(11)	Terry Crowley	1.00
(12)	Ken Singleton	1.00

1998 CyberAction

During the 1998 National Sports Collectors Convention in Chicago, CyberAction gave away samples of its product. The cards are printed on flimsy cardboard in standard 2-1/2" x 3-1/2" format. Fronts have a blue-bordered action photo at center. In the background is a large team logo. The firm's website address is at top; its logo at bottom. Backs have details on winning a World Series trip.

		NM/M
Complete Set (6):		11.00
Common Player:		1.50
1	Ken Griffey Jr.	2.25
2	Mark McGwire	2.50
3	Barry Bonds	3.00
4	Derek Jeter	3.00
5	Greg Maddux	2.00
6	Larry Walker	1.50

1992 Dairy Queen Team USA

In 1992, in conjunction with the Dairy Queen Team USA Sundae-in-a-Helmet promotion, customers received a four-card pack of Team USA cards, part of a 33-card set manufactured by Topps for the company. Included in the set are Team USA players from the 1984 and 1988 Olympics, many of whom have gone on to major league stardom. The set also has 15 Team USA Prospects, a 1988 Gold Medal team celebration card and a card of 1992 coach Ron Fraser. Fronts feature each player in their Team USA uniform and the backs include statistics from amateur, Team USA and professional competition.

		NM/M
Complete Set (33):		13.50
Common Player:		.25
1	Mark McGwire/1984	4.00
2	Will Clark/1984	1.00
3	John Marzano/1984	.25
4	Barry Larkin/1984	1.00
5	Bobby Witt/1984	.25
6	Scott Bankhead/1984	.25
7	B.J. Surhoff/1984	.25
8	Shane Mack/1984	.25
9	Jim Abbott/1988	.35
10	Ben McDonald/1988	.25
11	Robin Ventura/1988	.50
12	Charles Nagy/1988	.25
13	Andy Benes/1988	.25
14	Joe Slusarski /1988	.25
15	Ed Sprague/1988	.25
16	Bret Barberie/1988	.25
17	Gold Medal - 1988/1988	.25
18	Jeff Granger/1992	.25
19	John Dettmer/1992	.25
20	Todd Greene/1992	.25
21	Jeffrey Hammonds/1992	.25
22	Dan Melendez /1992	.25
23	Kennie Steenstra/1992	.25
24	Todd Johnson/1992	.25
25	Chris Roberts/1992	.25
26	Steve Rodriguez/1992	.25
27	Charles Johnson/1992	.25
28	Chris Wimmer/1992	.25
29	Tony Phillips/1992	.25
30	Craig Wilson/1992	.25
31	Jason Giambi/1992	6.00
32	Paul Shuey/1992	.25
33	Ron Fraser (1992 coach)	.25

1993 Dairy Queen Magic Mariner Moments Pin/Cards

		NM/M
Complete Set (4):		10.00
Common Player:		2.00
1	Randy Johnson ('92 AL K King)	3.25
2	Edgar Martinez ('92 AL Batting Champ)	2.00
3	Chris Bosio (No-Hitter)	2.00
4	Ken Griffey Jr. ('92 All-Star MVP)	4.00

1994 Dairy Queen Ken Griffey, Jr.

Distributed by Dairy Queen stores in the Pacific Northwest, this set was issued in two different versions, with green borders and with gold borders. All cards feature a "Ken Griffey Jr. Golden Moments" logo in the upper-left corner. His name and the DQ logo appear at the bottom. Backs have another photo of Griffey along with a description of the career highlight depicted on front, sponsors' logos and a card number. Values shown here are for green-bordered cards; gold-bordered cards sell for about twice those figures.

		NM/M
Complete Set (10):		7.50
Common Player:		.75
Gold:		2X
1	Ken Griffey Jr. ("The Spider Man Catch")	.75
2	Ken Griffey Jr. ("Back to Back Homeruns")	.75
3	Ken Griffey Jr. (Hit .327 in 1991)	.75
4	Ken Griffey Jr. (1992 All-Star MVP)	.75
5	Ken Griffey Jr. ("Dialing Long Distance")	.75
6	Ken Griffey Jr. ("8 Straight Homeruns")	.75
7	Ken Griffey Jr. (4-Time Golden Glove Winner)	.75
8	Ken Griffey Jr. (45 Homeruns in 1993)	.75
9	Ken Griffey Jr. (Major League Career Hitting Record)	.75
10	Ken Griffey Jr. ("Looking to 1994")	.75

1996-2003 Danbury Mint 22kt Gold Cooperstown Collection

A series of embossed 22kt. gold-foil cards was offered by the private mint beginning in 1996. Each month two cards were sent to subscribers. The standard-size cards have a player picture on front with team logo and player identification at bottom. Backs have career stats. Each card was sealed in acrylic. An album for the set has identification labels with name in both printed and facsimile autograph form. Only persons who completed Set 1 were allowed to purchase subsequent sets. While each card is numbered, they are checklisted here alphabetically within series. Because the Babe Ruth card was used as a free promotional give-away, it is more common than the others.

		NM/M
Complete Set (200):		750.00
Common Player (1-50):		5.00
Common Player (51-100):		6.00
Common Player (101-150):		7.50
Common Player (151-200):		7.50
(1)	Richie Allen	4.00
(2)	Paul Blair	3.00
(3)	Vida Blue	3.00
(4)	Bert Blyleven	3.00
(5)	Roy Campanella	6.00
(6)	Bert Campaneris	3.00
(7)	Gary Carter	4.00
(8)	Cesar Cedeno	3.00
(9)	Orlando Cepeda	4.00
(10)	Ty Cobb	7.50
(11)	Mickey Cochrane	3.00
(12)	Eddie Collins	3.00
(13)	Dizzy Dean	5.00
(14)	Bob Feller	4.00
(15)	George Foster	3.00
(16)	Steve Garvey	3.00
(17)	Lou Gehrig	7.50
(18)	Lefty Gomez	3.00
(19)	Gil Hodges	4.00
(20)	Carl Hubbell	3.00
(21)	Walter Johnson	5.00
(22)	Jim Kaat	3.00
(23)	Don Kessinger	3.00
(24)	Harmon Killebrew	4.00
(25)	Jerry Koosman	3.00
(26)	Mickey Lolich	3.00
(27)	Sparky Lyle	3.00
(28)	Fred Lynn	3.00
(29)	Bill Mazeroski	4.00
(30)	Minnie Minoso	3.00
(31)	Johnny Mize	3.00
(32)	Thurman Munson	5.00
(33)	Graig Nettles	3.00
(34)	Phil Niekro	3.00
(35)	Tony Oliva	3.00
(36)	Al Oliver	3.00
(37)	Satchel Paige	7.50
(38)	Jim Palmer	3.00
(39)	Herb Pennock	3.00
(40)	Tony Perez	3.00
(41)	Boog Powell	3.00
(42)	Brooks Robinson	4.00
(43)	Babe Ruth	2.50
(44)	Duke Snider	3.00
(45)	Tris Speaker	3.00
(46)	Willie Stargell	3.00
(47)	Luis Tiant	3.00
(48)	Honus Wagner	5.00
(49)	Maury Wills	3.00
(50)	Cy Young	5.00
(51)	Grover Alexander	6.00
(52)	Sandy Alomar Jr.	6.00
(53)	Jeff Bagwell	9.00
(54)	Dusty Baker	6.00
(55)	Albert Belle	6.00
(56)	Wade Boggs	10.00
(57)	Barry Bonds	17.50
(58)	Joe Carter	6.00
(59)	Will Clark	6.00
(60)	Roger Clemens	12.00
(61)	Dwight Evans	6.00
(62)	Jim Fregosi	6.00
(63)	Andres Galarraga	6.00
(64)	Bob Gibson	6.00
(65)	Ken Griffey Jr.	13.50
(66)	Tony Gwynn	10.00
(67)	Rogers Hornsby	6.00
(68)	Catfish Hunter	6.00
(69)	Joe Jackson	17.50
(70)	Ferguson Jenkins	6.00
(71)	Derek Jeter	17.50
(72)	Randy Johnson	9.00
(73)	Jimmy Key	6.00
(74)	Ralph Kiner	6.00
(75)	Don Larsen	6.00
(76)	Greg Maddux	10.00
(77)	Juan Marichal	6.00
(78)	Eddie Mathews	7.50
(79)	Christy Mathewson	9.00
(80)	Fred McGriff	6.00
(81)	Mark McGwire	15.00
(82)	Dave McNally	6.00
(83)	Bobby Murcer	6.00
(84)	Dale Murphy	7.50
(85)	Gaylord Perry	6.00
(86)	Rico Petrocelli	6.00
(87)	Andy Pettitte	7.50
(88)	Mike Piazza	13.50
(89)	Cal Ripken Jr.	17.50
(90)	Alex Rodriguez	15.00
(91)	Joe Rudi	6.00
(92)	Ron Santo	6.00
(93)	Gary Sheffield	6.00
(94)	John Smoltz	6.00
(95)	Sammy Sosa	10.00
(96)	Warren Spahn	6.00
(97)	Billy Williams	6.00
(98)	Bobby Thomson	6.00
(99)	Mo Vaughn	6.00
(100)	Hoyt Wilhelm	6.00
(101)	Brady Anderson	7.50
(102)	Luis Aparicio	7.50
(103)	Kevin Appier	7.50
(104)	Richie Ashburn	9.00
(105)	Lou Boudreau	7.50
(106)	Lou Brock	7.50
(107)	Kevin Brown	7.50

(108)	Jim Bunning	7.50
(109)	Jose Canseco	9.00
(110)	David Cone	7.50
(111)	Rollie Fingers	7.50
(112)	Chuck Finley	7.50
(113)	Curt Flood	7.50
(114)	Jimmie Foxx	10.00
(115)	Nomar Garciaparra	12.00
(116)	Tom Glavine	7.50
(117)	Juan Gonzalez	7.50
(118)	Luis Gonzalez	7.50
(119)	Mark Grace	7.50
(120)	Shawn Green	7.50
(121)	Burleigh Grimes	7.50
(122)	Lefty Grove	7.50
(123)	Al Hrabosky	7.50
(124)	Chipper Jones	12.00
(125)	Al Kaline	9.00
(126)	Tony Lazzeri	7.50
(127)	Bill Lee	7.50
(128)	Jose Lima	7.50
(129)	Bill Madlock	7.50
(130)	Roger Maris	9.00
(131)	Pedro Martinez	10.00
(132)	Tino Martinez	7.50
(133)	Tug McGraw	7.50
(134)	Kevin Millwood	7.50
(135)	Joe Morgan	7.50
(136)	Charles Nagy	7.50
(137)	Mel Ott	7.50
(138)	Rafael Palmeiro	7.50
(139)	Manny Ramirez	9.00
(140)	Jim Rice	7.50
(141)	Ivan Rodriguez	7.50
(142)	Edd Roush	7.50
(143)	Manny Sanguillen	7.50
(144)	Curt Schilling	7.50
(145)	Ron Swoboda	7.50
(146)	Greg Vaughn	7.50
(147)	Larry Walker	7.50
(148)	Zack Wheat	7.50
(149)	Bernie Williams	7.50
(150)	Jim Wynn	7.50
(151)	Bobby Abreu	7.50
(152)	Roberto Alomar	7.50
(153)	Moises Alou	7.50
(154)	Carlos Beltran	7.50
(155)	Armando Benitez	7.50
(156)	Lance Berkman	7.50
(157)	Bret Boone	7.50
(158)	Ellis Burks	7.50
(159)	Sean Casey	7.50
(160)	Carlos Delgado	10.00
(161)	J.D. Drew	10.00
(162)	Jim Edmonds	7.50
(163)	Cliff Floyd	7.50
(164)	Freddy Garcia	7.50
(165)	Jason Giambi	10.00
(166)	Brian Giles	7.50
(167)	Troy Glaus	10.00
(168)	Vladimir Guerrero	12.50
(169)	Mike Hampton	7.50
(170)	Todd Helton	10.00
(171)	Trevor Hoffman	7.50
(172)	Tim Hudson	10.00
(173)	Andruw Jones	12.50
(174)	Jeff Kent	7.50
(175)	Ryan Klesko	7.50
(176)	Al Leiter	7.50
(177)	Edgar Martinez	7.50
(178)	Raul Mondesi	7.50
(179)	Matt Morris	7.50
(180)	Jamie Moyer	7.50
(181)	Mark Mulder	7.50
(182)	Mike Mussina	9.00
(183)	Robb Nen	7.50
(184)	Phil Nevin	7.50
(185)	John Olerud	7.50
(186)	Magglio Ordonez	7.50
(187)	Roy Oswalt	7.50
(188)	Chan Ho Park	7.50
(189)	Troy Percival	7.50
(190)	Albert Pujols	15.00
(191)	Brad Radke	7.50
(192)	Mariano Rivera	7.50
(193)	Kazuhiro Sasaki	7.50
(194)	Jeff Shaw	7.50
(195)	Alfonso Soriano	9.00
(196)	Frank Thomas	12.50
(197)	Jim Thome	7.50
(198)	Billy Wagner	7.50
(199)	Kerry Wood	9.00
(200)	Barry Zito	9.00

1991 Jimmy Dean

Baseball cards were inserted into packages of Jimmy Dean sausages in 1991. The complete set consists of 25 star players' cards. Red and yellow borders surround color player photos on the card fronts. No team logos appear on the cards. The card backs feature statistics, biographical information and a facsimile autograph. The set is entitled the "Signature Edition." An uncut sheet was also available via special offer.

		NM/M
Complete Set (25):		5.00
Common Player:		.15
Uncut Sheet:		6.00
1	Will Clark	.15
2	Ken Griffey Jr.	.75
3	Dale Murphy	.25
4	Barry Bonds	1.00
5	Darryl Strawberry	.15
6	Ryne Sandberg	.50
7	Gary Sheffield	.25
8	Sandy Alomar, Jr.	.15
9	Frank Thomas	.45
10	Barry Larkin	.15
11	Kirby Puckett	.50
12	George Brett	.60
13	Kevin Mitchell	.15
14	Dave Justice	.15
15	Cal Ripken, Jr.	1.00
16	Craig Biggio	.15
17	Rickey Henderson	.45
18	Roger Clemens	.60
19	Jose Canseco	.25
20	Ozzie Smith	.50
21	Cecil Fielder	.15
22	Dave Winfield	.45
23	Kevin Maas	.15
24	Nolan Ryan	1.00
25	Dwight Gooden	.15

1992 Jimmy Dean

For the second year in a row, baseball cards were inserted into packages of Jimmy Dean sausage in 1992. Featuring 18 star players, the set portrays the player's name on a vertical panel at the left of the card, along with his team name and position. The Jimmy Dean logo appears in the lower-right corner. Major League team logos have been eliminated from the photos.

		NM/M
Complete Set (18):		5.00
Common Player:		.15
1	Jim Abbott	.15
2	Barry Bonds	1.50
3	Jeff Bagwell	.45
4	Frank Thomas	.45
5	Steve Avery	.15
6	Chris Sabo	.15
7	Will Clark	.15
8	Don Mattingly	.60
9	Darryl Strawberry	.15
10	Roger Clemens	.60
11	Ken Griffey Jr.	1.00
12	Chuck Knoblauch	.15
13	Tony Gwynn	.50
14	Juan Gonzalez	.30
15	Cecil Fielder	.15
16	Bobby Bonilla	.15
17	Wes Chamberlain	.15
18	Ryne Sandberg	.50

Living Legends

Approximately 100,000 of these six-card sets were made available via a mail-in offer for $1 and proofs of purchase from the company's breakfast meats. Color photos on front have had uniform logos removed and are over-

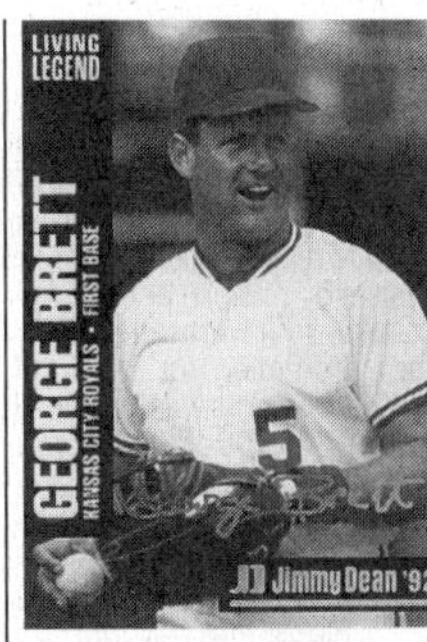

printed with a gold-foil facsimile autograph. Other gold foil highlights the player, team and sponsor names on front. Backs are printed in black and yellow and include a few biographical details, career highlights and summary statistics.

		NM/M
Complete Set (6):		8.00
Common Player:		1.00
1	George Brett	2.00
2	Carlton Fisk	1.00
3	Ozzie Smith	1.50
4	Robin Yount	1.00
5	Cal Ripken, Jr.	3.00
6	Nolan Ryan	3.00

Rookie Stars

Nine of 1992's hottest rookies were featured in this set issued as inserts into various Jimmy Dean meat products. Cards feature full-bleed photos on which uniform logos have been airbrushed away. A 1992 Rookie Star logo appears at upper-left, atop a black vertical strip containing the player's name, team and position. A white strip at bottom has the Jimmy Dean logo. On back, personal data and minor and major league stats are featured in a center panel, surrounded by a light blue border.

		NM/M
Complete Set (9):		3.00
Common Player:		.50
1	Andy Stankiewicz	.50
2	Pat Listach	.50
3	Brian Jordan	.50
4	Eric Karros	.50
5	Reggie Sanders	.50
6	Dave Fleming	.50
7	Donovan Osborne	.50
8	Kenny Lofton	.50
9	Moises Alou	.50

1993 Jimmy Dean

Issued in the company's meat products and via a mail-in offer, this set once again features player photos on which the uniform logos have been airbrushed away, due to lack of a license from Major League Baseball. A pair of horizontal color bars in one of the lower corners contains a Jimmy Dean logo and the player's name. Backs have a line drawing portrait of the player, along with stats, personal data and logos.

		NM/M
Complete Set (28):		6.00
Common Player:		.15
1	Frank Thomas	.50
2	Barry Larkin	.15
3	Cal Ripken, Jr.	1.25
4	Andy Van Slyke	.15
5	Darren Daulton	.15
6	Don Mattingly	.65
7	Roger Clemens	.65
8	Juan Gonzalez	.35
9	Mark Langston	.15
10	Barry Bonds	1.25
11	Ken Griffey Jr.	.75
12	Cecil Fielder	.15
13	Kirby Puckett	.60
14	Tom Glavine	.25
15	George Brett	.65
16	Nolan Ryan	1.25
17	Eddie Murray	.50
18	Gary Sheffield	.35
19	Doug Drabek	.15
20	Ray Lankford	.15
21	Benito Santiago	.15
22	Mark McGwire	1.00
23	Kenny Lofton	.15
24	Eric Karros	.15
25	Ryne Sandberg	.60
26	Charlie Hayes	.15
27	Mike Mussina	.25
28	Pat Listach	.15

Rookie Cards

Jimmy Dean Foods issued a Rookie Stars baseball card set in 1993. The nine-card set features promising rookies, with players highlighted against a marblized background with color photos on both sides of the cards. The cards were distributed randomly in three-card sets in specially-marked packages of Jimmy Dean products.

		NM/M
Complete Set (9):		3.00
Common Player:		.10
(1)	Rich Amaral	.10
(2)	Vinny Castilla	.15
(3)	Jeff Conine	.25
(4)	Brent Gates	.10
(5)	Wayne Kirby	.10
(6)	Mike Lansing	.25
(7)	David Nied	.10
(8)	Mike Piazza	2.00
(9)	Tim Salmon	.75

1995 Jimmy Dean All Time Greats

Six Hall of Famers are featured in this promotion for the country singer's breakfast meats. Besides inclusion of regular cards in food packages, a send-away deal offered autographed cards of three of the players for proofs of purchase and $7 apiece. Cards feature action photos on which team uniform logos have been removed; while the cards are licensed by the Major League

Baseball Players Alumni, they are not sanctioned by MLB. A large "1995 All Time Greats Collectors Set" logo appears in the upper-right corner on front, while the Jimmy Dean logo and player name are in the lower-left. Full color backs offer a career summary and lifetime stats, along with a ghost image of the front photo.

		NM/M
Complete Set (6):		5.00
Common Player:		.50
1	Rod Carew	1.00
2	Jim "Catfish" Hunter	.50
2a	Jim "Catfish" Hunter/ Auto.	15.00
3	Al Kaline	1.50
3a	Al Kaline/Auto.	8.00
4	Mike Schmidt	1.50
5	Billy Williams	.50
5a	Billy Williams/Auto.	8.00
6	Carl Yastrzemski	1.50

1997 Jimmy Dean Great Moments

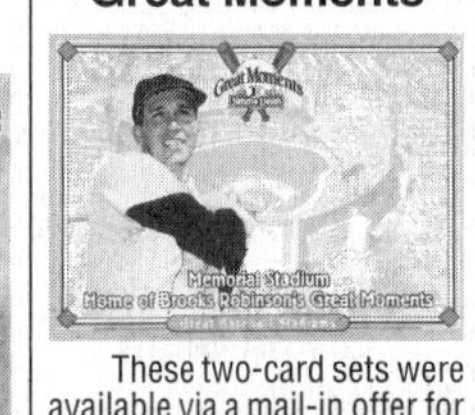

These two-card sets were available via a mail-in offer for $12.95 apiece plus proofs of purchase. Each set consists of an autographed "Great Moments in Baseball" card with an action photo and a "Great Baseball Stadiums" card featuring a player photo set against the stadium background. All pictures are sepia toned with uniform logos removed. Cards have player or stadium information on the backs and came with a certificate of authenticity.

		NM/M
Complete Set (4):		35.00
(1)	Yogi Berra/Auto.	20.00
(2)	Yogi Berra (Yankee Stadium)	5.00
(3)	Brooks Robinson/ Auto.	10.00
(4)	Brooks Robinson (Memorial Stadium)	3.00

1984 Decathlon Negro League Baseball Stars

According to contemporary advertising, this set was produced in conjunction with the Negro Baseball Hall of History in Kentucky, to a total of 2,000 sets and 300 uncut sheets. The cards and checklist are identical to the 1986 issue by Larry Fritsch Cards, which purchased rights to the set, except for the copyright line at bottom on back.

	NM/M
Complete Set (119):	35.00
Common Player:	.30
Stars:	3X

1985 Decathlon Ultimate Baseball Card Set

Originally intended to be a six-series, 90-card issue, this collectors' set was cut short after the first series. The large-format (4" x 5-5/8") cards feature on front color artwork by former Topps artist Gerry Dvorak. The portraits are surrounded by a white border. Black-and-white backs have a career capsule. Announced as an edition of 10,000 sets, original issue price was about $11.

		NM/M
Complete Set (15):		20.00
Common Player:		1.00
1	Ty Cobb	3.00
2	Honus Wagner	3.00
3	Babe Ruth	5.00
4	Lou Gehrig	4.00
5	Frank Baker	1.00
6	Casey Stengel	1.00
7	Moses Walker	1.00
8	Cy Young	1.00
9	Joe DiMaggio	4.00
10	John McGraw	1.00
11	Josh Gibson	1.00
12	Johnny Mize	1.00
13	Walter Johnson	1.00
14	Walter Alston	1.00
15	Enos Slaughter	1.00

1993 Dempster's Blue Jays

One of several Canadian baseball card issues marking the 1992 World Series victory of the Toronto Blue Jays, the Dempster's stores set is a 25-card issue in standard 2-1/2" x 3-1/2", UV-coatd on both sides. Fronts have a large dark blue border with white horizontal white pinstripes. An action photo is at center, with the player's name and position below. The Jays World Championship logo and Players Association logo are at top; the sponsor's logo at lower-right.

A baseball at bottom center has the card number. Backs feature a large portrait photo at top, against a dark blue background. Color bars carry the player's '92 and career stats. A facsimile autograph appears beneath the team logo at right.

		NM/M
Complete Set (25):		6.50
Common Player:		.25
1	Juan Guzman	.25
2	Roberto Alomar	.75
3	Danny Cox	.25
4	Paul Molitor	4.00
5	Todd Stottlemyre	.25
6	Joe Carter	.50
7	Jack Morris	.35
8	Ed Sprague	.25
9	Turner Ward	.25
10	John Olerud	.75
11	Duane Ward	.25
12	Alfredo Griffin	.25
13	Cito Gaston	.25
14	Dave Stewart	.25
15	Mark Eichhorn	.25
16	Darnell Coles	.25
17	Randy Knorr	.25
18	Al Leiter	.25
19	Pat Hentgen	.25
20	Devon White	.25
21	Pat Borders	.25
22	Darrin Jackson	.25
23	Dick Schofield	.25
24	Luis Sojo	.25
25	Mike Timlin	.25

1991 Denny's Grand Slam

This 26-card set was produced by Upper Deck and features one player from each Major League team. One hologram card was distributed with the purchase of a Grand Slam meal. The cards are numbered on the front and are 3-D. The card backs describe grand slams hit by the featured player.

		NM/M
Complete Set (26):		12.50
Common Player:		.50
1	Ellis Burks	.50
2	Cecil Fielder	.50
3	Will Clark	.50
4	Eric Davis	.50
5	Dave Parker	.50
6	Kelly Gruber	.50
7	Kent Hrbek	.50
8	Don Mattingly	1.50
9	Brook Jacoby	.50
10	Mark McGwire	2.00
11	Howard Johnson	.50
12	Tim Wallach	.50
13	Ricky Jordan	.50
14	Andre Dawson	.75
15	Eddie Murray	1.00
16	Danny Tartabull	.50
17	Bobby Bonilla	.50
18	Benito Santiago	.50
19	Alvin Davis	.50
20	Cal Ripken	2.50
21	Ruben Sierra	.50
22	Pedro Guerrero	.50
23	Wally Joyner	.50
24	Craig Biggio	.50
25	Dave Justice	.50
26	Tim Raines	.50

1992 Denny's Grand Slam

The second year of the Denny's Gland Slam promotion featured one power hitter from each major league team, portrayed on a hologram in front of a scene from his team's city. As in the first year, the cards were produced by

Upper Deck and given away, one at a time, with a Denny's purchase during the middle of the summer. An album with plastic pages holding four cards each was also available.

		NM/M
Complete Set (26):		7.50
Common Player:		.25
Album:		3.00
1	Marquis Grissom	.25
2	Ken Caminiti	.25
3	Fred McGriff	.25
4	Felix Jose	.25
5	Jack Clark	.25
6	Albert Belle	.25
7	Sid Bream	.25
8	Robin Ventura	.25
9	Cal Ripken, Jr.	2.00
10	Ryne Sandberg	1.00
11	Paul O'Neill	.25
12	Luis Polonia	.25
13	Cecil Fielder	.25
14	Kal Daniels	.25
15	Brian McRae	.25
16	Howard Johnson	.25
17	Greg Vaughn	.25
18	Dale Murphy	.60
19	Kent Hrbek	.25
20	Barry Bonds	2.00
21	Matt Nokes	.25
22	Jose Canseco	.50
23	Jay Buhner	.25
24	Will Clark	.25
25	Ruben Sierra	.25
26	Joe Carter	.25

1993 Denny's Grand Slam

The 1993 Denny's Grand Slam set expanded to 28 cards with the addition of the Florida and Colorado expansion teams. The featured color photos of one grand slam slugger for each team superimposed over a hologram background. The reverse of each card gives anecdotes about the player's grand slams along with his career total. The cards were distributed at participating Denny's restaurants during mid-summer.

		NM/M
Complete Set (28):		7.50
Common Player:		.25
1	Chili Davis	.25
2	Eric Anthony	.25
3	Rickey Henderson	.60
4	Joe Carter	.25
5	Terry Pendleton	.25
6	Robin Yount	.60
7	Ray Lankford	.25
8	Ryne Sandberg	.75
9	Darryl Strawberry	.25
10	Marquis Grissom	.25
11	Will Clark	.25
12	Albert Belle	.25
13	Edgar Martinez	.25
14	Benito Santiago	.25
15	Eddie Murray	.60
16	Cal Ripken, Jr.	2.00
17	Gary Sheffield	.45
18	Dave Hollins	.25
19	Andy Van Slyke	.25
20	Juan Gonzalez	.45
21	John Valentin	.25
22	Joe Oliver	.25
23	Dante Bichette	.25
24	Wally Joyner	.25
25	Cecil Fielder	.25
26	Kirby Puckett	.75
27	Robin Ventura	.25
28	Danny Tartabull	.25

1994 Denny's Grand Slam

For its fourth annual hologram card promotion, Denny's chose a horizontal format with portrait and action photos of one player from each major league team. Designated the "Anniversary Edition," the set features the 125th year logo at bottom center, with the player's name at left; Upper Deck and Denny's logos are at top. On back the same two photos are conventionally printed along with a brief player biography, appropriate logos and copyright notices. The cards are numbered alphabetically. Cards were available with certain menu items from July 1 through Aug. 31. Each restaurant received one special boxed set for use as a contest prize. These sets include a special Reggie Jackson "Route to Cooperstown" hologram card; the edition was limited to about 1,500.

		NM/M
Complete Set (28 / No Jackson):		7.50
Common Player:		.25
1	Jim Abbott	.25
2	Roberto Alomar	.35
3	Kevin Appier	.25
4	Jeff Bagwell	.60
5	Albert Belle	.25
6	Barry Bonds	2.00
7	Bobby Bonilla	.25
8	Lenny Dykstra	.25
9	Cal Eldred	.25
10	Cecil Fielder	.25
11	Andres Galarraga	.25
12	Juan Gonzalez	.40
13	Ken Griffey Jr.	1.00
14	Tony Gwynn	.75
15	Rickey Henderson	.60
16	Kent Hrbek	.25
17	David Justice	.25
18	Mike Piazza	1.50
19	Jose Rijo	.25
20	Cal Ripken, Jr.	2.00
21	Tim Salmon	.25
22	Ryne Sandberg	.75
23	Gary Sheffield	.35
24	Ozzie Smith	.75
25	Frank Thomas	.60
26	Andy Van Slyke	.25
27	Mo Vaughn	.25
28	Larry Walker	.25
---	Reggie Jackson	60.00

1995 Denny's Classic Hits

For the fifth consecutive year, this August 1-September 30 promotion offered a hologram baseball card with the purchase of selected items from the restaurant's "Classic Hits" menu. The cards were produced for Denny's by Upper Deck and combine photographic and holographic images of the player on the horizontal-format front. Backs have another color photo, career highlights, and past-season/lifetime stats. Each Major League team is represented in the set by one player card. According to advertisements for the promotion, a total of 8,000,000 cards was produced - about 286,000 of each player.

		NM/M
Complete Set (28):		6.00
Common Player:		.15
1	Roberto Alomar	.30
2	Moises Alou	.15
3	Jeff Bagwell	.35
4	Albert Belle	.15
5	Jason Bere	.15
6	Roger Clemens	.60
7	Darren Daulton	.15
8	Cecil Fielder	.15
9	Andres Galarraga	.15
10	Juan Gonzalez	.35
11	Ken Griffey Jr.	.75
12	Tony Gwynn	.50
13	Barry Larkin	.15
14	Greg Maddux	.50
15	Don Mattingly	.50
16	Mark McGwire	1.00
17	Orlando Merced	.15
18	Jeff Montgomery	.15
19	Rafael Palmeiro	.35
20	Mike Piazza	1.00
21	Kirby Puckett	.50
22	Bret Saberhagen	.15
23	Tim Salmon	.15
24	Gary Sheffield	.30
25	Ozzie Smith	.50
26	Sammy Sosa	.50
27	Greg Vaughn	.15
28	Matt Williams	.15

1996 Denny's Instant Replay Holograms

Pinnacle, in its first year as supplier for Denny's annual baseball card promotion, attempted breakthrough technology that didn't quite hit the mark. The hologram portion of the card front was supposed to show as much as four seconds of on-field action, but unless viewed at exactly the right distance and angle, and under exacting light requirements, the action is little more than a silver-foil streak. Card fronts also included a color player photo. Another color photo appears on the back, along with a description of the action on front for those who couldn't master the "Full Motion" hologram. Cards were sold in single-card foil packs for 49 cents (limit two) with a qualifying purchase. Besides the hologram card, each pack includes a card explaining "How To View a Full Motion Hologram." Besides the regular cards, two "Grand Slam" chase sets were issued along with instant winner cards for complete card sets or trips to the World Series. Stated odds on the chase cards would indicate about 750,000 of each regular card were produced. One player from each team is represented in the checklist.

		NM/M
Complete Set (28):		5.00
Common Player:		.15
1	Greg Maddux	.50
2	Cal Ripken Jr.	1.00
3	Frank Thomas	.45
4	Albert Belle	.15
5	Mo Vaughn	.15
6	Jeff Bagwell	.45
7	Jay Buhner	.15
8	Barry Bonds	1.00
9	Ryne Sandberg	.50
10	Hideo Nomo	.35
11	Kirby Puckett	.50
12	Gary Sheffield	.30
13	Barry Larkin	.15
14	Wade Boggs	.50
15	Tony Gwynn	.50
16	Tim Salmon	.15
17	Jason Isringhausen	.15
18	Cecil Fielder	.15
19	Dante Bichette	.15
20	Ozzie Smith	.50
21	Ivan Rodriguez	.35
22	Kevin Appier	.15
23	Joe Carter	.15
24	Moises Alou	.15
25	Mark McGwire	.75
26	Kevin Seitzer	.15
27	Darren Daulton	.15
28	Jay Bell	.15

1996 Denny's Grand Slam

Exploding fireworks in the background are an allegory for the firepower brought to the plate by the sluggers featured in this chase set from Denny's annual baseball card promotion. A Grand Slam card is randomly substituted for the standard hologram card about once every 56 packs.

		NM/M
Complete Set (10):		13.50
Common Player:		1.00
1	Cal Ripken Jr.	2.50
2	Frank Thomas	1.50
3	Mike Piazza	2.25
4	Tony Gwynn	2.00
5	Sammy Sosa	2.00
6	Barry Bonds	2.50
7	Jeff Bagwell	1.50
8	Albert Belle	1.00
9	Mo Vaughn	1.00
10	Kirby Puckett	2.00

Artist's Proofs

A specially marked Artist's Proof version of the Grand Slam chase cards are substituted for the standard hologram card in about every 360 packs, according to stated odds.

		NM/M
Complete Set (10):		50.00
Common Player:		2.00
1	Cal Ripken Jr.	10.00
2	Frank Thomas	5.00
3	Mike Piazza	7.50
4	Tony Gwynn	6.00
5	Sammy Sosa	6.00
6	Barry Bonds	10.00
7	Jeff Bagwell	5.00
8	Albert Belle	2.00
9	Mo Vaughn	2.00
10	Kirby Puckett	6.00

1997 Denny's 3-D Holograms

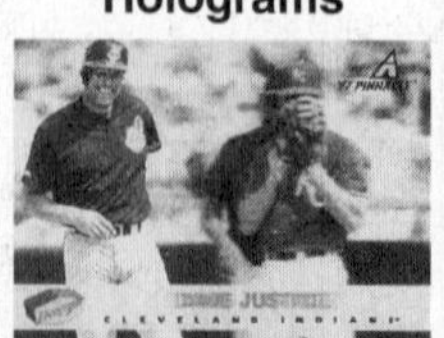

Denny's seventh annual baseball card issue was produced by Pinnacle and showcases two popular card technologies. Fronts of the 3-1/2" x 2-1/2" horizontal cards feature a deep 3D look. Backs have a player portrait hologram at the right. A partial baseball at left is the background for player data and stats along with sponsor and licensor logos. Cards were distributed one per pack for 59 cents from June 26-September 3, with 10 cents from the sale of each card being donated to children's charities. The set features one player from each major league team, plus a Jackie Robinson tribute card.

		NM/M
Complete Set (29):		8.00
Common Player:		.20
1	Tim Salmon	.20
2	Rafael Palmeiro	.45
3	Mo Vaughn	.20
4	Frank Thomas	.50
5	David Justice	.20
6	Travis Fryman	.20
7	Johnny Damon	.35
8	John Jaha	.20
9	Chuck Knoblauch	.20
10	Mark McGwire	1.00
11	Alex Rodriguez	1.00
12	Juan Gonzalez	.35
13	Roger Clemens	.65
14	Derek Jeter	1.50
15	Andruw Jones	.50
16	Sammy Sosa	.60
17	Barry Larkin	.20
18	Dante Bichette	.20
19	Jeff Bagwell	.50
20	Mike Piazza	.75
21	Gary Sheffield	.35
22	Vladimir Guerrero	.50
23	Todd Hundley	.20
24	Jason Kendall	.20
25	Ray Lankford	.20
26	Ken Caminiti	.20
27	Barry Bonds	1.50
28	Scott Rolen	.40
29	Jackie Robinson (50th Anniversary Commemorative)	1.50

Larry Doby

In the same format as the restaurant chain's regular set of 1997, this card honors the first black player to appear in the American League. The card was available only at the All-Star FanFest and All-Star Game in Cleveland in early July. Fronts have a black-and-white 3-D image; backs have a color hologram at right and a 50th anniversary logo at upper-left. Personal data, career highlights and stats are included, as well as appropriate logos.

		NM/M
1	Larry Doby	6.00

1981 Detroit News Tigers Centennial

The 100th anniversary of professional baseball in Detroit was marked by "The Detroit News" with the issue of this set honoring "The Boys of Summer." The 2-1/2" x 3-1/2" cards have black-and-white photos on front, over a mock sports page. Cards can be found either with or without a red border on front, though the relative scarcity of each version is not known. Black-and-white backs have player data, career summary and stats, or a description of the front photo/highlight.

	NM/M
Complete Set (135):	30.00

Common Player: .25
1 Detroit Boys of Summer 100th Anniversary .25
2 Charles W. Bennett .25
3 Mickey Cochrane .25
4 Harry Heilmann .25
5 Walter O. Briggs .25
6 Mark Fidrych .75
7 1887 Tigers .25
8 Tiger Stadium .25
9 Rudy York .25
10 George Kell .25
11 Steve O'Neill .25
12 John Hiller .25
13 1934 Tigers .25
14 Charlie Gehringer .45
15 Denny McLain .60
16 Billy Rogell .25
17 Ty Cobb 5.00
18 Sparky Anderson .60
19 Davy Jones .25
20 Kirk Gibson .45
21 Pat Mullin .25
22 1972 Tigers .25
23 What a Night .25
24 "Doc" Cramer .25
25 Mickey Stanley .25
26 Johnny Lipon .25
27 Jo Jo White .25
28 Recreation Park .25
29 Wild Bill Donovan .25
30 Ray Oyler .25
31 Earl Whitehill .25
32 Billy Hoeft .25
33 Johnny Groth .25
34 Hughie Jennings .25
35 Mayo Smith .25
36 Bennett Park .25
37 Tigers Win .25
38 Donie Bush .25
39 Harry Coveleski .25
40 Paul Richards .25
41 Jonathan Stone .25
42 Bill Swift .25
43 Roy Cullenbine .25
44 Hoot Evers .25
45 Tigers Win Series .25
46 Art Houtteman .25
47 Aurelio Rodriguez .25
48 Fred Hutchinson .25
49 Don Mossi .25
50 Gehrig's Streak Ends in Detroit (Lou Gehrig) 2.50
51 Earl Wilson .25
52 Jim Northrup .25
53 1907 Tigers .25
54 Greenberg's Two Homers Ties Ruth (Hank Greenberg) .45
55 Mickey Lolich .45
56 Tommy Bridges .25
57 Al Benton .25
58 Del Baker .25
59 Lou Whitaker .45
60 Navin Field .25
61 1945 Tigers .25
62 Ernie Harwell .25
63 League Champs .25
64 Bobo Newsom .25
65 Don Wert .25
66 Ed Summers .25
67 Billy Martin .45
68 Alan Trammell 1.50
69 Dale Alexander .25
70 Ed Brinkman .25
71 Right Man in Right Place Wins (Ted Williams) 2.00
72 Bill Freehan .25
73 Norm Cash .60
74 George Dauss .25
75 Aurelio Lopez .25
76 Charlie Maxwell .25
77 Ed Barrow .25
78 Willie Horton .25
79 Denny Sets Record (Denny McLain) .45
80 Dan Brouthers .25
81 John E. Fetzer .25
82 Heinie Manush .25
83 1935 Tigers .25
84 Ray Boone .25
85 Bob Fothergill .25
86 Steve Kemp .25
87 Ed Killian .25
88 Giebell is Ineligible (Floyd Giebell) .25
89 Pinky Higgins .25
90 Lance Parrish .25
91 Eldon Auker .25
92 Birdie Tebbetts .25
93 Schoolboy Rowe .25
94 McLain Wins 30th (Denny McLain) .45
95 1909 Tigers .25
96 Harvey Kuenn .40
97 Jim Bunning .60
98 1940 Tigers .25
99 Rocky Colavito 2.50
100 Kaline Enters Hall of Fame (Al Kaline) 1.00
101 Billy Bruton .25
102 Germany Schaefer .25
103 Frank Bolling .25
104 Briggs Stadium .25
105 Bucky Harris .25
106 Gates Brown .25
107 Martin Made the Difference (Billy Martin) .25
108 1908 Tigers .25
109 "Gee" Walker .25
110 Pete Fox .25
111 Virgil Trucks .25
112 1968 Tigers 1.50
113 Dizzy Trout .25
114 Barney McCosky .25
115 Lu Blue .25
116 Hal Newhouser .25
117 Tigers are Home for Series .25
118 Bobby Veach .25
119 George Mullins (Mullin) .25
120 Reggie's Super Homer (Reggie Jackson) .60
121 Sam Crawford .25
122 Hank Aguirre .25
123 Vic Wertz .25
124 Goose Goslin .25
125 Frank Lary .25
126 Joe Coleman .25
127 Ed Katalinas .25
128 Jack Morris .25
129 3 Time AL Leaders .25
130 James A. Campbell .25
131 Ted Gray .25
132 Al Kaline 5.00
133 Hank Greenberg 2.50
134 Dick McAuliffe .25
135 Ozzie Virgil .25

1988 Detroit Tigers Police

This unnumbered issue, sponsored by the Michigan State Police features 13 players and manager Sparky Anderson in full-color standard-size (2-1/2" x 3-1/2") cards. Player photos are framed by a blue border, with the Detroit logo upper left and a large name block that lists the player's name, position batting/throwing preference, height, weight and birthday beneath the photo. The backs carry an anti-drug or anti-crime message.

NM/M
Complete Set (14): 7.00
Common Player: .50
(1) Doyle Alexander .50
(2) Sparky Anderson 1.00
(3) Dave Bergman .50
(4) Tom Brookens .50
(5) Darrell Evans .60
(6) Larry Herndon .50
(7) Chet Lemon .50
(8) Jack Morris .60
(9) Matt Nokes .50
(10) Jeff Robinson .50
(11) Frank Tanana .50
(12) Walt Terrell .50
(13) Alan Trammell 1.00
(14) Lou Whitaker .75

1989 Detroit Tigers Police

(21) GUILLERMO HERNANDEZ—P
B-L, T-L, HT: 6'2", WT: 185, BORN: 11-14-54

This unnumbered issue, distributed and sponsored by the Michigan State Police Department features 14 full-color 2-1/2" x 3-1/2" cards. Player photos are framed by a blue and orange border, with the team logo in the upper left and biographical information below the photo. The card backs featue anti-drug or anti-crime messages.

NM/M
Complete Set (14): 4.00
Common Player: .25
(1) Doyle Alexander .25
(2) Sparky Anderson .75
(3) Dave Bergman .25
(4) Mike Henneman .25
(5) Guillermo Hernandez .25
(6) Chet Lemon .25
(7) Fred Lynn .25
(8) Jack Morris .35
(9) Matt Nokes .25
(10) Jeff Robinson .25
(11) Pat Sheridan .25
(12) Frank Tanana .25
(13) Alan Trammell .75
(14) Lou Whitaker .50

1991 Detroit Tigers Police

One of the scarcer safety issues is this Tigers team issue. Cards have a color player action photo on front with orange and blue team-color graphics. Backs have a safety message and the logos of sponsors HSP and Team Michigan, along with the Michigan State Police. The unnumbered cards are checklisted here alphabetically.

NM/M
Complete Set (14): 7.00
Common Player: .50
(1) Sparky Anderson .75
(2) Dave Bergman .50
(3) Cecil Fielder .75
(4) Travis Fryman .50
(5) Paul Gibson .50
(6) Jerry Don Gleaton .50
(7) Lloyd Moseby .50
(8) Dan Petry .50
(9) Tony Phillips .50
(10) Mark Salas .50
(11) John Shelby .50
(12) Frank Tanana .50
(13) Alan Trammell .75
(14) Lou Whitaker .75

1993 DiamondMarks Prototypes

In the same format as the regular-issue DiamondMark cards, these promos were produced to preview the concept for dealers and collectors. The promo cards feature different photos than those used on the issued version. The unnumbered cards are listed here alphabetically. On the back of the promos, the phrase "1993 PROTOTYPE" appears vertically at left.

NM/M
Complete Set (8): 40.00
Common Player: 3.00
(1) Roberto Alomar 4.00
(2) Will Clark 3.00
(3) Dennis Eckersley 5.00
(4) Juan Gonzalez 4.00
(5) Ken Griffey Jr. 10.00
(6) Kirby Puckett 7.50
(7) Ryne Sandberg 6.00
(8) Frank Thomas 6.00

1993 DiamondMarks

While they look like baseball cards and were sold in foil packs like baseball cards, DiamondMarks were licensed as book marks. Issued by Barry Colla Productions, the 2-1/2" x 5" cards feature Barry Colla's trademark high-quality player photos on front and back. The UV-coated fronts feature black borders with the player's name in white above the photo and a color team logo beneath. Backs, also bordered in black, feature two color player photos in an open book design. There is a portrait photo on the left and a head-and-shoulders reproduction of the front photo at right. A bookmark with team logo is incorporated in the design. The 120-card set is unnumbered and is arranged in the checklist below alphabetically within league and team.

NM/M
Complete Set (120): 12.00
Common Player: .15
Wax Box (48): 20.00

Atlanta Braves
(1) Steve Avery .15
(2) Ron Gant .15
(3) Tom Glavine .35
(4) David Justice .15
(5) Terry Pendleton .15
(6) Deion Sanders .25
(7) John Smoltz .15

Chicago Cubs
(8) Mark Grace .15
(9) Randy Myers .15
(10) Ryne Sandberg .75
(11) Jose Vizcaino .15

Cincinnati Reds
(12) Bobby Kelly .15
(13) Barry Larkin .15
(14) Kevin Mitchell .15
(15) Jose Rijo .15
(16) Reggie Sanders .15

Colorado Rockies
(17) Dante Bichette .15
(18) Daryl Boston .15
(19) Andres Galarraga .15
(20) Charlie Hayes .15

Florida Marlins
(21) Orestes Destrade .15
(22) Benito Santiago .15
(23) Gary Sheffield .35
(24) Walt Weiss .15

Houston Astros
(25) Jeff Bagwell .60
(26) Craig Biggio .15
(27) Ken Caminiti .15
(28) Luis Gonzalez .15

Los Angeles Dodgers
(29) Brett Butler .15
(30) Eric Davis .15
(31) Orel Hershiser .15
(32) Eric Karros .15
(33) Ramon Martinez .15
(34) Mike Piazza 1.50
(35) Darryl Strawberry .15

Montreal Expos
(36) Moises Alou .15
(37) Delino DeShields .15
(38) Marquis Grissom .15
(39) Dennis Martinez .15
(40) Larry Walker .15

New York Mets
(41) Bobby Bonilla .15
(42) Dwight Gooden .15
(43) Howard Johnson .15
(44) Eddie Murray .60

Philadelphia Phillies
(45) Darren Daulton .15
(46) Lenny Dykstra .15
(47) Dave Hollins .15
(48) John Kruk .15

Pittsburgh Pirates
(49) Jay Bell .15
(50) Al Martin .15
(51) Orlando Merced .15
(52) Andy Van Slyke .15

St. Louis Cardinals
(53) Gregg Jefferies .15
(54) Tom Pagnozzi .15
(55) Ozzie Smith .75
(56) Todd Zeile .15

San Diego Padres
(57) Derek Bell .15
(58) Tony Gwynn .75
(59) Fred McGriff .15

San Francisco Giants
(60) Barry Bonds 2.00
(61) John Burkett .15
(62) Will Clark .15
(63) Matt Williams .15

Baltimore Orioles
(64) Brady Anderson .15
(65) Mike Mussina .30
(66) Cal Ripken, Jr. 2.00

Boston Red Sox
(67) Roger Clemens 1.00
(68) Andre Dawson .30
(69) Mike Greenwell .15
(70) Mo Vaughn .15

Detroit Tigers
(71) Cecil Fielder .15
(72) Tony Phillips .15
(73) Mickey Tettleton .15
(74) Alan Trammell .15

Cleveland Indians
(75) Sandy Alomar Jr. .15
(76) Carlos Baerga .15
(77) Albert Belle .15
(78) Kenny Lofton .15

Chicago White Sox
(79) Bo Jackson .25
(80) Frank Thomas .60
(81) Robin Ventura .15

California Angels
(82) Chad Curtis .15
(83) Gary DiSarcina .15
(84) Tim Salmon .15
(85) J.T. Snow .15

Kansas City Royals
(86) George Brett 1.00
(87) Wally Joyner .15
(88) Mike MacFarlane .15
(89) Brian McRae .15

Milwaukee Brewers
(90) Darryl Hamilton .15
(91) Pat Listach .15
(92) B.J. Surhoff .15
(93) Robin Yount .60

Minnesota Twins
(94) Kent Hrbek .15
(95) Chuck Knoblauch .15
(96) Kirby Puckett .75
(97) Dave Winfield .60

New York Yankees
(98) Wade Boggs .75
(99) Don Mattingly 1.00
(100) Danny Tartabull .15

Oakland Athletics
(101) Dennis Eckersley .50
(102) Rickey Henderson .60
(103) Mark McGwire 1.50
(104) Ruben Sierra .15
(105) Terry Steinbach .15

Seattle Mariners
(106) Ken Griffey Jr. 1.50
(107) Edgar Martinez .15
(108) Pete O'Brien .15
(109) David Valle .15

Texas Rangers
(110) Jose Canseco .35
(111) Juan Gonzalez .35
(112) Ivan Rodriguez .50
(113) Nolan Ryan 2.00

Toronto Blue Jays
(114) Roberto Alomar .30
(115) Pat Borders .15
(116) Joe Carter .15
(117) Juan Guzman .15
(118) Paul Molitor .60
(119) John Olerud .15
(120) Dave Stewart .15

Inserts

Randomly inserted into packs of DiamondMarks cards at the rate of one per 48-pack carton was a series of eight cards featuring the baseball artwork of Terry Smith. The inserts are the same 2-1/2" x 5" size as the regular issue and carry on with the basic black bordered design, though the inserts are UV-

coated both front and back. Beneath the fantasy-design player art on the front is the player's name. On back the open book design is seen again, with a short player profile on the left and a Barry Colla photo portrait on the right, along with the appropriate team logo.

NM/M
Complete Set (8): 50.00
Common Player: 5.00
(1) Roberto Alomar 6.00
(2) Barry Bonds 15.00
(3) Ken Griffey Jr. 10.00
(4) David Justice 5.00
(5) John Olerud 5.00
(6) Nolan Ryan 15.00
(7) Frank Thomas 7.50
(8) Robin Yount 7.50

1981 Diamond Stars Extension Set

About 1980 an uncut sheet of artwork apparently intended for use in the original Diamond Stars series (1934-36) was discovered. The art was used to create a collectors' issue "extension" set by Den's Collectors Den of Maryland. The new cards were printed in the same 2-3/8" x 2-7/8" format as the 1930s issue with the player name on front. Backs are printed in blue with a career summary, biographical details and a 1981 copyright line. The set was sold in a heavy paper wrapper patterned after the original.

NM/M
Complete Set (12): 5.00
Uncut Sheet: 25.00
Common Player: .25
109 Benny Frey .25
110 Pete Fox .25
111 Phil Cavarretta .35
112 Leon Goslin .50
113 Mel Harder .35
114 Roger Cramer .35
115 Gene Moore .25
116 Rip Collins .35
117 Linus Frey .25
118 Vernon Gomez 1.00
119 Jim Bottomley, Rogers Hornsby 1.50
120 Lon Warneke .25

1993 Diamond Stars Extension Set

In the style of the 1934-36 Diamond Stars bubblegum cards from National Chicle

Co., this collectors' issue features colorful painting of players from the mid-1930s. Cards measure about 2-3/8" x 2-7/8" with white borders on front with no player identification or other graphics. The artwork is by D'August Roth Martin. Backs have player id, personal data and a career summary purporting to have been written by Travis Lake in Aug., 1936, the man who wrote the backs for the original cards. A copyright line at bottom identifies the "Extended Edition" as a 1993 issue of "The Chicle Fantasy Co." According to the set's producer, 4,166 were printed with 1,936 cut into hand-numbered sets which were originally sold at $19.95. Promo versions of each card in the set have a red rubber-stamped ad on back.

		NM/M
Complete Set, Uncut Sheet:		15.00
Complete Set (36):		10.00
Common Player:		.25
121	Moe Berg	2.00
122	Harlond Clift	.25
123	Joe Cronin	.50
124	Dizzy Dean	1.00
125	Paul Dean	.50
126	Joe DiMaggio	3.00
127	Leo Durocher	.50
128	Bob Feller	1.00
129	Carl Fisher	.25
130	Lou Gehrig	2.00
131	Bump Hadley	.25
132	Jesse Haines	.25
133	Bad News Hale	.25
134	Gabby Hartnett	.25
135	Babe Herman	.25
136	Billy Herman	.25
137	Waite Hoyt	.25
138	Bob Johnson	.25
139	Chuck Klein	.50
140	Mike Kreevich	.25
141	Fred Lindstrom	.25
142	Connie Mack	.50
143	Joe McCarthy	.25
144	Bill McKechnie	.25
145	Johnny Mize	.60
146	Johnny Moore	.25
147	Hugh Mulcahy	.25
148	Buck Newsom	.25
149	Al Smith	.25
150	Casey Stengel	1.00
151	Arky Vaughan	.25
152	Gee Walker	.25
153	Kenesaw M. Landis	.25
	Cool Papa Bell	.25
	Josh Gibson	.50
	Satchel Paige	1.00
	Title Card	.10

1992 Diet Pepsi Collector Series

This Canadian issue includes 30 top stars, with a slight emphasis on the two Canadian teams. Because the set is licensed only by the players' association, and not Major League Baseball, all photos had team logos eliminated. Fronts feature action photo with Diet Pepsi logos in a strip below. Backs have a portrait photo, recent stats and a facsimile autograph. Card number 5 of Tom Glavine can be found showing him pitching right-handed (error) or left-handed (right). Cards are UV coated on both sides. A poster picturing all 30 cards was also issued. Cards were issued in three-card packs.

		NM/M
Complete Set (30):		7.00
Poster:		7.50
Common Player:		.15
1	Roger Clemens	.60
2	Dwight Gooden	.15
3	Tom Henke	.15
4	Dennis Martinez	.15
5a	Tom Glavine (Pitching right-handed.)	.25
5b	Tom Glavine (Pitching left-handed.)	.75
6	Jack Morris	.15
7	Dennis Eckersley	.35
8	Jeff Reardon	.15
9	Bryan Harvey	.15
10	Sandy Alomar Jr.	.15
11	Carlton Fisk	.40
12	Gary Carter	.40
13	Cecil Fielder	.15
14	Will Clark	.15
15	Roberto Alomar	.30
16	Ryne Sandberg	.50
17	Cal Ripken Jr.	1.50
18	Barry Larkin	.15
19	Ozzie Smith	.50
20	Kelly Gruber	.15
21	Wade Boggs	.50
22	Tim Wallach	.15
23	Howard Johnson	.15
24	Jose Canseco	.30
25	Joe Carter	.15
26	Ken Griffey Jr.	.65
27	Kirby Puckett	.50
28	Rickey Henderson	.40
29	Barry Bonds	1.50
30	Dave Winfield	.40

2002 Disabled American Veterans

In conjunction with its "DAV at the Ballpark" program, the vets' service organization and many Major League teams had special promotions during the 2002 season. Baseball cards featuring one or more members of the home team were distributed to fans. Cards share a format of standard 2-1/2" x 3-1/2" size with glossy coating on both sides. Fronts have action pictures against a ghosted image of the home ballpark. A small portrait photo also appears, along with team and DAV logos and a card number. Backs have information about the DAV and contact data. This checklist is not complete.

		NM/M
Common Player:		1.00
2	Ben Sheets	1.00
5	Trevor Hoffman	1.00
12	Steve Cox	1.00
13	Jay Gibbons	1.00
14	Rusty Greer	1.00
15	Danny Graves	1.00
16	Todd Helton	1.50
17	Eddie Guardado	1.00
20	Kazuhiro Sasaki	1.00
21	Ichiro Suzuki	2.50
22	Mike Cameron, Mark McLemore	1.00
23	Mike Scioscia	1.00

2003 Disabled American Veterans

In conjunction with its "DAV at the Ballpark" program, the vets' service organization and several Major League teams had special promotions during the 2003 season. Baseball cards featuring one or more members of the home team were distributed to fans. Cards share a format of standard 2-1/2" x 3-1/2" size with glossy coating on both sides. Fronts have action pictures against a ghosted image of the home ballpark. A team and DAV logo also appear, along with uniform and "Limited Edition" card numbers. Backs have information about the DAV and contact data. This checklist is not complete.

		NM/M
Common Player:		
3	Richie Sexson	1.00
9	Rocco Baldelli	1.50
12	Edgar Martinez	1.00
16	Preston Wilson	1.00
26	Adam Dunn	1.00

2004 Disabled American Veterans

In conjunction with its "DAV at the Ballpark" program, the vets' service organization and several Major League teams had special promotions during the 2004 season. Baseball cards featuring one or more members of the home team were distributed to fans. Cards share a format of standard 2-1/2" x 3-1/2" size with glossy coating on both sides. Fronts have a large portrait photo and smaller action photo. A team logo and uniform number are at top, at bottom is "Limited Edition" and a card number. Backs have information about the DAV and contact data.

		NM/M
Complete Set (42):		30.00
Common Player:		1.00
1	Robby Hammock	1.00
2	Austin Kearns	2.00
3	Larry Bigbie	1.00
4	Wes Helms	1.00
5	Scott Podsednik	2.00
6	Ben Sheets	1.00
7	Brian Giles	1.00
8	Joel Pineiro	1.50
9	Dan Wilson	1.00
10	Ron Gardenhire	1.00
11	Eddie Guardado	1.00
12	Raul Ibanez	1.00
13	Hank Blalock	4.00
14	Mark Teixeira	2.00
15	Michael Young	1.00
16	Danys Baez	1.00
17	Jose Cruz Jr.	1.00
18	Robert Fick	1.00
19	Toby Hall	1.00
20	Tino Martinez	1.00
21	Mike Maroth	1.00
22	Lou Piniella	1.00
23	Damian Rolls	1.00
24	Doug Waechter	1.00
25	Victor Zambrano	1.00
26	Don Zimmer	1.00
27	J.D. Drew	3.00
28	Horacio Ramirez	1.00
29	Jeff Kent	1.00
30	John Thomson	1.00
31	John Estrada	1.00
32	Rafael Furcal	1.00
33	John Smoltz	1.00
34	Chipper Jones	5.00
35	Marcus Giles	1.00
36	Andruw Jones	4.00
37	Josh Beckett	2.00
38	Miguel Cabrera	1.50
39	Hee Seop Choi	1.00
40	Brad Penny	1.00
41	Juan Pierre	1.50
42	Dontrelle Willis	1.00

2005 Disabled American Veterans

These cards were issued by vets' service organization and several Major League teams in special promotions during the 2005 season. Baseball cards featuring one or more members of the home team were distributed to fans. Cards share a format of standard 2-1/2" x 3-1/2" size with glossy coating on both sides. Fronts have an action photo on a ball-and-glove background with team logo. At bottom is "Limited Edition" and a card number. Backs have information about the DAV and contact data.

Common Player:

1988 Domino's Pizza Tigers

Domino's Pizza produced a 28-card set commemorating the 20th anniversary of the 1968 World Champion Detroit Tigers. The cards were given away at an Old Timers Game at Tiger Stadium in 1988. The cards, which measure 2-1/2" x 3-1/2", feature black and white photos semi-surrounded by a two-stripe band. The stripes on the card's left side are the same color (red and light blue) as the Domino's Pizza logo in the upper corner. The stripes on the card's right side match the colors of the Tigers logo (red and dark blue). The backs of all the cards (except for Ernie Harwell) contain a brief summary of the Tigers' 1968 season. Located at the bottom on the card backs are the players' major league records through 1968 plus their 1968 World Series statistics.

		NM/M
Complete Set (29):		8.00
Common Player:		.25
(1)	Gates Brown	.25
(2)	Norm Cash	1.00
(3)	Wayne Comer	.25
(4)	Pat Dobson	.25
(5)	Bill Freehan	.60
(6)	John Hiller	.25
(7)	Ernie Harwell (Announcer)	.30
(8)	Willie Horton	.40
(9a)	Al Kaline/Btg	3.00
(9b)	Al Kaline (In outfield.)	3.00
(10)	Fred Lasher	.25
(11)	Mickey Lolich	.75
(12)	Tom Matchick	.25
(13)	Ed Mathews	1.25
(14)	Dick McAuliff (McAuliffe)	.25
(15)	Denny McLain	.75
(16)	Don McMahon	.25
(17)	Jim Northrup	.25
(18)	Ray Oyler	.25
(19)	Daryl Patterson	.25
(20)	Jim Price	.25
(21)	Joe Sparma	.25
(22)	Mickey Stanley	.25
(23)	Dick Tracewski	.25
(24)	Jon Warden	.25
(25)	Don Wert	.25
(26)	Earl Wilson	.25
(27)	Header Card	.05
(28)	Coupon Card	.05

1980 Donruss Prototypes

When it became apparent that Topps' monopoly on baseball card production was going to be ended by the courts, Memphis-based Donruss began work to produce a bubblegum card set for 1981. As part of its research, Donruss created a three-card prototype panel in three different sizes to test collector preference. Two of the prototypes have player pictures, the third does not. Backs are blank.

	NM/M
Small Panel (About 6" x 2-3/4".):	75.00
Regular Panel(About 7-1/2" x 3-1/2".):	75.00
Large Panel (About 10-1/2" x 4-3/4".):	75.00
George Brett (2" x 2-3/4")	35.00
George Brett (2-1/2" x 3-1/2")	35.00
George Brett (3-1/2" x 4-3/4")	30.00
Reggie Jackson (2" x 2-3/4")	35.00
Reggie Jackson (2-1/2" x 3-1/2")	35.00
Reggie Jackson (3-1/2" x 4-3/4")	30.00
No Player Pictured (2" x 2-3/4")	7.50
No Player Pictured (2-1/2" x 3-1/2")	5.00
No Player Pictured (3-1/2" x 4-3/4")	5.00

1981 Donruss Promo Sheet

Rookie sensation Joe Charbonneau was the featured attraction when this sample sheet was issued to introduce Donruss' debut baseball card issue. The 10" x 7" sheet is comprised of eight of the cards which appeared in the set.

	NM/M
Complete Sheet:	35.00

1981 Donruss

The Donruss Co. of Memphis, Tenn., produced its premiere baseball card issue in 1981 with a set that consisted of 600 numbered cards and five unnumbered checklists. The cards, which measure 2-1/2" x 3-1/2", are printed on thin stock. The card fronts contain the Donruss logo plus the year of issue. The card backs are designed on a vertical format and have black print on red and white. The set, entitled "First Edition Collector Series," contains nearly 40 variations, those being first-printing errors that were corrected in a subsequent print run. The cards were sold in wax packs with bubblegum. The complete set price does not include the higher priced variations.

		NM/M
Complete Set (605):		25.00
Uncut Sheet Set (5):		65.00
Common Player:		.10
Wax Pack (18):		2.00
Wax Box (36):		60.00
1	Ozzie Smith	2.00
2	Rollie Fingers	1.00
3	Rick Wise	.10
4	Gene Richards	.10
5	Alan Trammell	.10
6	Tom Brookens	.10
7a	Duffy Dyer (1980 Avg. .185)	.25
7b	Duffy Dyer (1980 Avg. 185)	.10
8	Mark Fidrych	.15
9	Dave Rozema	.10
10	Ricky Peters	.10
11	Mike Schmidt	3.00
12	Willie Stargell	1.25
13	Tim Foli	.10
14	Manny Sanguillen	.10
15	Grant Jackson	.10
16	Eddie Solomon	.10
17	Omar Moreno	.10
18	Joe Morgan	1.25
19	Rafael Landestoy	.10
20	Bruce Bochy	.10
21	Joe Sambito	.10
22	Manny Trillo	.10
23a	Dave Smith **RC** (Incomplete box around stats.)	.10
23b	Dave Smith **RC** (Complete box around stats.)	.15
24	Terry Puhl	.10
25	Bump Wills	.10
26a	John Ellis (Danny Walton photo - with bat.)	.30
26b	John Ellis (John Ellis photo - with glove.)	.10
27	Jim Kern	.10
28	Richie Zisk	.10

29 John Mayberry .10
30 Bob Davis .10
31 Jackson Todd .10
32 Al Woods .10
33 Steve Carlton 1.50
34 Lee Mazzilli .10
35 John Stearns .10
36 Roy Jackson .10
37 Mike Scott .10
38 Lamar Johnson .10
39 Kevin Bell .10
40 Ed Farmer .10
41 Ross Baumgarten .10
42 Leo Sutherland .10
43 Dan Meyer .10
44 Ron Reed .10
45 Mario Mendoza .10
46 Rick Honeycutt .10
47 Glenn Abbott .10
48 Leon Roberts .10
49 Rod Carew 1.50
50 Bert Campaneris .10
51a Tom Donahue (Incorrect spelling.) .25
51b Tom Donohue (Donohue on front.) .10
52 Dave Frost .10
53 Ed Halicki .10
54 Dan Ford .10
55 Garry Maddox .10
56a Steve Garvey (Surpassed 25 HR..) 1.25
56b Steve Garvey (Surpassed 21 HR..) .60
57 Bill Russell .10
58 Don Sutton 1.00
59 Reggie Smith .10
60 Rick Monday .10
61 Ray Knight .10
62 Johnny Bench 1.50
63 Mario Soto .10
64 Doug Bair .10
65 George Foster .10
66 Jeff Burroughs .10
67 Keith Hernandez .10
68 Tom Herr .10
69 Bob Forsch .10
70 John Fulgham .10
71a Bobby Bonds (Lifetime HR 986.) .35
71b Bobby Bonds (Lifetime HR 326.) .15
72a Rennie Stennett ("...breaking broke leg..." on back) .25
72b Rennie Stennett ("...breaking leg..." on back) .10
73 Joe Strain .10
74 Ed Whitson .10
75 Tom Griffin .10
76 Bill North .10
77 Gene Garber .10
78 Mike Hargrove .10
79 Dave Rosello .10
80 Ron Hassey .10
81 Sid Monge .10
82a Joe Charboneau **RC** ("For some reason, Phillies..." on back.) 2.00
82b Joe Charboneau **RC** ("Phillies..." on back.) .25
83 Cecil Cooper .10
84 Sal Bando .10
85 Moose Haas .10
86 Mike Caldwell .10
87a Larry Hisle ("...Twins with 28 RBI." on back.) .25
87b Larry Hisle ("...Twins with 28 HR" on back.) .10
88 Luis Gomez .10
89 Larry Parrish .10
90 Gary Carter 1.25
91 Bill Gullickson **RC** .15
92 Fred Norman .10
93 Tommy Hutton .10
94 Carl Yastrzemski 1.50
95 Glenn Hoffman .10
96 Dennis Eckersley 1.25
97a Tom Burgmeier (Throws: Right) .25
97b Tom Burgmeier (Throws: Left) .10
98 Win Remmerswaal .10
99 Bob Horner .10
100 George Brett 3.00
101 Dave Chalk .10
102 Dennis Leonard .10
103 Renie Martin .10
104 Amos Otis .10
105 Graig Nettles .15
106 Eric Soderholm .10
107 Tommy John .10
108 Tom Underwood .10
109 Lou Piniella .15
110 Mickey Klutts .10
111 Bobby Murcer .10
112 Eddie Murray 1.50
113 Rick Dempsey .10
114 Scott McGregor .10
115 Ken Singleton .10
116 Gary Roenicke .10
117 Dave Revering .10
118 Mike Norris .10
119 Rickey Henderson 2.00
120 Mike Heath .10
121 Dave Cash .10
122 Randy Jones .10
123 Eric Rasmussen .10
124 Jerry Mumphrey .10
125 Richie Hebner .10
126 Mark Wagner .10
127 Jack Morris .10
128 Dan Petry .10
129 Bruce Robbins .10
130 Champ Summers .10
131a Pete Rose ("See card 251" on back.) 2.00
131b Pete Rose ("See card 371" on back.) 2.00
132 Willie Stargell 1.25
133 Ed Ott .10
134 Jim Bibby .10
135 Bert Blyleven .10
136 Dave Parker .10
137 Bill Robinson .10
138 Enos Cabell .10
139 Dave Bergman .10
140 J.R. Richard .10
141 Ken Forsch .10
142 Larry Bowa .10
143 Frank LaCorte (Photo actually Randy Niemann.) .10
144 Dennis Walling .10
145 Buddy Bell .10
146 Fergie Jenkins 1.00
147 Danny Darwin .10
148 John Grubb .10
149 Alfredo Griffin .10
150 Jerry Garvin .10
151 Paul Mirabella **RC** .10
152 Rick Bosetti .10
153 Dick Ruthven .10
154 Frank Taveras .10
155 Craig Swan .10
156 Jeff Reardon **RC** 1.00
157 Steve Henderson .10
158 Jim Morrison .10
159 Glenn Borgmann .10
160 Lamarr Hoyt (LaMarr) **RC** .10
161 Rich Wortham .10
162 Thad Bosley .10
163 Julio Cruz .10
164a Del Unser (No 3B in stat heads.) .25
164b Del Unser (3B in stat heads) .10
165 Jim Anderson .10
166 Jim Beattie .10
167 Shane Rawley .10
168 Joe Simpson .10
169 Rod Carew 1.50
170 Fred Patek .10
171 Frank Tanana .10
172 Alfredo Martinez .10
173 Chris Knapp .10
174 Joe Rudi .10
175 Greg Luzinski .10
176 Steve Garvey .60
177 Joe Ferguson .10
178 Bob Welch .10
179 Dusty Baker .10
180 Rudy Law .10
181 Dave Concepcion .10
182 Johnny Bench 1.50
183 Mike LaCoss .10
184 Ken Griffey .10
185 Dave Collins .10
186 Brian Asselstine .10
187 Garry Templeton .10
188 Mike Phillips .10
189 Pete Vukovich .10
190 John Urrea .10
191 Tony Scott .10
192 Darrell Evans .10
193 Milt May .10
194 Bob Knepper .10
195 Randy Moffitt .10
196 Larry Herndon .10
197 Rick Camp .10
198 Andre Thornton .10
199 Tom Veryzer .10
200 Gary Alexander .10
201 Rick Waits .10
202 Rick Manning .10
203 Paul Molitor 1.25
204 Jim Gantner .10
205 Paul Mitchell .10
206 Reggie Cleveland .10
207 Sixto Lezcano .10
208 Bruce Benedict .10
209 Rodney Scott .10
210 John Tamargo .10
211 Bill Lee .10
212 Andre Dawson .75
213 Rowland Office .10
214 Carl Yastrzemski 1.50
215 Jerry Remy .10
216 Mike Torrez .10
217 Skip Lockwood .10
218 Fred Lynn .10
219 Chris Chambliss .10
220 Willie Aikens .10
221 John Wathan .10
222 Dan Quisenberry .10
223 Willie Wilson .10
224 Clint Hurdle .10
225 Bob Watson .10
226 Jim Spencer .10
227 Ron Guidry .15
228 Reggie Jackson 2.00
229 Oscar Gamble .10
230 Jeff Cox .10
231 Luis Tiant .10
232 Rich Dauer .10
233 Dan Graham .10
234 Mike Flanagan .10
235 John Lowenstein .10
236 Benny Ayala .10
237 Wayne Gross .10
238 Rick Langford .10
239 Tony Armas .10
240a Bob Lacy (Incorrect spelling.) .25
240b Bob Lacey (Correct spelling.) .10
241 Gene Tenace .10
242 Bob Shirley .10
243 Gary Lucas .10
244 Jerry Turner .10
245 John Wockenfuss .10
246 Stan Papi .10
247 Milt Wilcox .10
248 Dan Schatzeder .10
249 Steve Kemp .10
250 Jim Lentine .10
251 Pete Rose 2.00
252 Bill Madlock .10
253 Dale Berra .10
254 Kent Tekulve .10
255 Enrique Romo .10
256 Mike Easler .10
257 Chuck Tanner .10
258 Art Howe .10
259 Alan Ashby .10
260 Nolan Ryan 5.00
261a Vern Ruhle (Ken Forsch photo - head shot.) .25
261b Vern Ruhle (Vern Ruhle photo - waist to head shot.) .10
262 Bob Boone .10
263 Cesar Cedeno .10
264 Jeff Leonard .10
265 Pat Putnam .10
266 Jon Matlack .10
267 Dave Rajsich .10
268 Billy Sample .10
269 Damaso Garcia **RC** .10
270 Tom Buskey .10
271 Joey McLaughlin .10
272 Barry Bonnell .10
273 Tug McGraw .10
274 Mike Jorgensen .10
275 Pat Zachry .10
276 Neil Allen .10
277 Joel Youngblood .10
278 Greg Pryor .10
279 Britt Burns **RC** .10
280 Rich Dotson **RC** .25
281 Chet Lemon .10
282 Rusty Kuntz .10
283 Ted Cox .10
284 Sparky Lyle .10
285 Larry Cox .10
286 Floyd Bannister .10
287 Byron McLaughlin .10
288 Rodney Craig .10
289 Bobby Grich .10
290 Dickie Thon .10
291 Mark Clear .10
292 Dave Lemanczyk .10
293 Jason Thompson .10
294 Rick Miller .10
295 Lonnie Smith .10
296 Ron Cey .10
297 Steve Yeager .10
298 Bobby Castillo .10
299 Manny Mota .10
300 Jay Johnstone .10
301 Dan Driessen .10
302 Joe Nolan .10
303 Paul Householder .10
304 Harry Spilman .10
305 Cesar Geronimo .10
306a Gary Mathews (Mathews on front.) .35
306b Gary Matthews (Matthews on front.) .10
307 Ken Reitz .10
308 Ted Simmons .10
309 John Littlefield .10
310 George Frazier .10
311 Dane Iorg .10
312 Mike Ivie .10
313 Dennis Littlejohn .10
314 Gary LaVelle (Lavelle) .10
315 Jack Clark .10
316 Jim Wohlford .10
317 Rick Matula .10
318 Toby Harrah .10
319a Dwane Kuiper (Dwane on front.) .25
319b Duane Kuiper (Duane on front.) .10
320 Len Barker .10
321 Victor Cruz .10
322 Dell Alston .10
323 Robin Yount 1.25
324 Charlie Moore .10
325 Lary Sorensen .10
326a Gorman Thomas ("...30-HR mark 4th..." on back) .25
326b Gorman Thomas ("...30-HR mark 3rd..." on back) .10
327 Bob Rodgers .10
328 Phil Niekro 1.00
329 Chris Speier .10
330a Steve Rodgers (Rodgers on front.) .25
330b Steve Rogers (Rogers on front.) .10
331 Woodie Fryman .10
332 Warren Cromartie .10
333 Jerry White .10
334 Tony Perez 1.25
335 Carlton Fisk 1.25
336 Dick Drago .10
337 Steve Renko .10
338 Jim Rice .75
339 Jerry Royster .10
340 Frank White .10
341 Jamie Quirk .10
342a Paul Spittorff (Spittorff on front.) .25
342b Paul Splittorff (Splittorff on front.) .10
343 Marty Pattin .10
344 Pete LaCock .10
345 Willie Randolph .10
346 Rick Cerone .10
347 Rich Gossage .10
348 Reggie Jackson 2.00
349 Ruppert Jones .10
350 Dave McKay .10
351 Yogi Berra .50
352 Doug Decinces (DeCinces) .10
353 Jim Palmer 1.25
354 Tippy Martinez .10
355 Al Bumbry .10
356 Earl Weaver .50
357a Bob Picciolo (Bob on front.) .25
357b Rob Picciolo (Rob on front.) .10
358 Matt Keough .10
359 Dwayne Murphy .10
360 Brian Kingman .10
361 Bill Fahey .10
362 Steve Mura .10
363 Dennis Kinney .10
364 Dave Winfield 1.25
365 Lou Whitaker .10
366 Lance Parrish .10
367 Tim Corcoran .10
368 Pat Underwood .10
369 Al Cowens .10
370 Sparky Anderson .50
371 Pete Rose 3.00
372 Phil Garner .10
373 Steve Nicosia .10
374 John Candelaria .10
375 Don Robinson .10
376 Lee Lacy .10
377 John Milner .10
378 Craig Reynolds .10
379a Luis Pujois (Pujois on front.) .25
379b Luis Pujols (Pujols on front.) .10
380 Joe Niekro .10
381 Joaquin Andujar .10
382 Keith Moreland **RC** .15
383 Jose Cruz .10
384 Bill Virdon .10
385 Jim Sundberg .10
386 Doc Medich .10
387 Al Oliver .10
388 Jim Norris .10
389 Bob Bailor .10
390 Ernie Whitt .10
391 Otto Velez .10
392 Roy Howell .10
393 Bob Walk **RC** .10
394 Doug Flynn .10
395 Pete Falcone .10
396 Tom Hausman .10
397 Elliott Maddox .10
398 Mike Squires .10
399 Marvis Foley .10
400 Steve Trout .10
401 Wayne Nordhagen .10
402 Tony Larussa (LaRussa) .10
403 Bruce Bochte .10
404 Bake McBride .10
405 Jerry Narron .10
406 Rob Dressler .10
407 Dave Heaverlo .10
408 Tom Paciorek .10
409 Carney Lansford .10
410 Brian Downing .10
411 Don Aase .10
412 Jim Barr .10
413 Don Baylor .10
414 Jim Fregosi .10
415 Dallas Green .10
416 Dave Lopes .10
417 Jerry Reuss .10
418 Rick Sutcliffe .10
419 Derrel Thomas .10
420 Tommy LaSorda (Lasorda) .50
421 Charlie Leibrandt **RC** .25
422 Tom Seaver 1.50
423 Ron Oester .10
424 Junior Kennedy .10
425 Tom Seaver 1.50
426 Bobby Cox .10
427 Leon Durham **RC** .20
428 Terry Kennedy .10
429 Silvio Martinez .10
430 George Hendrick .10
431 Red Schoendienst .50
432 John LeMaster .10
433 Vida Blue .10
434 John Montefusco .10
435 Terry Whitfield .10
436 Dave Bristol .10
437 Dale Murphy .75
438 Jerry Dybzinski .10
439 Jorge Orta .10
440 Wayne Garland .10
441 Miguel Dilone .10
442 Dave Garcia .10
443 Don Money .10
444a Buck Martinez (Photo reversed.) .35
444b Buck Martinez (Photo correct.) .10
445 Jerry Augustine .10
446 Ben Oglivie .10
447 Jim Slaton .10
448 Doyle Alexander .10
449 Tony Bernazard .10
450 Scott Sanderson .10
451 Dave Palmer .10
452 Stan Bahnsen .10
453 Dick Williams .10
454 Rick Burleson .10
455 Gary Allenson .10
456 Bob Stanley .10
457a John Tudor **RC** (Lifetime W/L 9.7.) .40
457b John Tudor **RC** (Lifetime W/L 9-7.) .20
458 Dwight Evans .10
459 Glenn Hubbard .10
460 U L Washington .10
461 Larry Gura .10
462 Rich Gale .10
463 Hal McRae .10
464 Jim Frey .10
465 Bucky Dent .10
466 Dennis Werth .10
467 Ron Davis .10
468 Reggie Jackson 2.50
469 Bobby Brown .10
470 Mike Davis **RC** .10
471 Gaylord Perry 1.25
472 Mark Belanger .10
473 Jim Palmer 1.25
474 Sammy Stewart .10
475 Tim Stoddard .10
476 Steve Stone .10
477 Jeff Newman .10
478 Steve McCatty .10
479 Billy Martin .10
480 Mitchell Page .10
481 Steve Carlton (CY) .40
482 Bill Buckner .10
483a Ivan DeJesus (Lifetime hits 702.) .25
483b Ivan DeJesus (Lifetime hits 642.) .10
484 Cliff Johnson .10
485 Lenny Randle .10
486 Larry Milbourne .10
487 Roy Smalley .10
488 John Castino .10
489 Ron Jackson .10
490a Dave Roberts (1980 highlights begins "Showed pop...") .25
490b Dave Roberts (1980 highlights begins "Declared himself...") .10
491 George Brett (MVP) 1.50
492 Mike Cubbage .10
493 Rob Wilfong .10
494 Danny Goodwin .10
495 Jose Morales .10
496 Mickey Rivers .10
497 Mike Edwards .10
498 Mike Sadek .10
499 Lenn Sakata .10
500 Gene Michael .10
501 Dave Roberts .10
502 Steve Dillard .10
503 Jim Essian .10
504 Rance Mulliniks .10
505 Darrell Porter .10
506 Joe Torre .50
507 Terry Crowley .10
508 Bill Travers .10
509 Nelson Norman .10
510 Bob McClure .10
511 Steve Howe **RC** .15
512 Dave Rader .10
513 Mick Kelleher .10
514 Kiko Garcia .10
515 Larry Biittner .10
516a Willie Norwood (1980 highlights begins "Spent most...") .25
516b Willie Norwood (1980 highlights begins "Traded to...") .10
517 Bo Diaz .10
518 Juan Beniquez .10
519 Scot Thompson .10
520 Jim Tracy .10
521 Carlos Lezcano .10
522 Joe Amalfitano .10
523 Preston Hanna .10
524a Ray Burris (1980 highlights begins "Went on...") .25
524b Ray Burris (1980 highlights begins "Drafted by...") .10
525 Broderick Perkins .10
526 Mickey Hatcher .10
527 John Goryl .10
528 Dick Davis .10
529 Butch Wynegar .10
530 Sal Butera .10
531 Jerry Koosman .10
532a Jeff (Geoff) Zahn (1980 highlights begins "Was 2nd in...") .25
532b Jeff (Geoff) Zahn (1980 highlights begins "Signed a 3 year ...") .10
533 Dennis Martinez .10
534 Gary Thomasson .10
535 Steve Macko .10
536 Jim Kaat .15
537 Best Hitters (George Brett, Rod Carew) 1.50
538 Tim Raines **RC** 3.00
539 Keith Smith .10
540 Ken Macha .10
541 Burt Hooton .10
542 Butch Hobson .10
543 Bill Stein .10
544 Dave Stapleton .10
545 Bob Pate .10
546 Doug Corbett .10
547 Darrell Jackson .10
548 Pete Redfern .10
549 Roger Erickson .10
550 Al Hrabosky .10
551 Dick Tidrow .10
552 Dave Ford .10
553 Dave Kingman .10
554a Mike Vail (1980 highlights begins "After...") .25
554b Mike Vail (1980 highlights begins "Traded...") .10
555a Jerry Martin (1980 highlights begins "Overcame...") .25
555b Jerry Martin (1980 highlights begins "Traded...") .10
556a Jesus Figueroa (1980 highlights begins "Had...") .25
556b Jesus Figueroa (1980 highlights begins "Traded...") .10
557 Don Stanhouse .10
558 Barry Foote .10
559 Tim Blackwell .10
560 Bruce Sutter 1.25
561 Rick Reuschel .10
562 Lynn McGlothen .10
563a Bob Owchinko (1980 highlights begins "Traded...") .25
563b Bob Owchinko (1980 highlights begins "Involved...") .10
564 John Verhoeven .10
565 Ken Landreaux .10
566a Glen Adams (Glen on front.) .25
566b Glenn Adams (Glenn on front.) .10
567 Hosken Powell .10
568 Dick Noles .10
569 Danny Ainge **RC** 2.00
570 Bobby Mattick .10
571 Joe LeFebvre (Lefebvre) .10
572 Bobby Clark .10
573 Dennis Lamp .10
574 Randy Lerch .10
575 Mookie Wilson **RC** .30
576 Ron LeFlore .10
577 Jim Dwyer .10
578 Bill Castro .10
579 Greg Minton .10
580 Mark Littell .10
581 Andy Hassler .10
582 Dave Stieb .10
583 Ken Oberkfell .10
584 Larry Bradford .10
585 Fred Stanley .10
586 Bill Caudill .10
587 Doug Capilla .10
588 George Riley .10
589 Willie Hernandez .10
590 Mike Schmidt (MVP) 1.50
591 Steve Stone (Cy Young 1980) .10
592 Rick Sofield .10
593 Bombo Rivera .10
594 Gary Ward .10
595a Dave Edwards (1980 highlights begins "Sidelined...") .25
595b Dave Edwards (1980 highlights begins "Traded...") .10
596 Mike Proly .10
597 Tommy Boggs .10
598 Greg Gross .10
599 Elias Sosa .10
600 Pat Kelly .10
---- Checklist 1-120 (51 Tom Donohue) .25
---- Checklist 1-120 (51 Tom Donahue) .10
---- Checklist 121-240 .10
---- Checklist 241-360 (306 Gary Mathews) .25
---- Checklist 241-360 (306 Gary Matthews) .10
---- Checklist 361-480 (379 Luis Pujois) .25
---- Checklist 361-480 (379 Luis Pujols) .10
---- Checklist 481-600 (566 Glen Adams) .25
---- Checklist 481-600 (566 Glenn Adams) .10

1982 Donruss

Using card stock thicker than the previous year, Donruss issued a 660-card set which includes 653 numbered cards and seven unnumbered checklists. The cards were sold with puzzle pieces rather than gum as a result of a lawsuit by Topps. The puzzle pieces (three pieces on one card per pack) feature Babe Ruth. The first 26 cards of the set, entitled Diamond Kings, showcase the artwork of Dick Perez. Card fronts display the Donruss logo and the year of issue. Backs have black and blue ink on white stock and include the player's career highlights. The complete set price does not include the higher priced variations.

	NM/M
Unopened Fact. Set (660):	50.00
Complete Set (660):	45.00
Complete Set, Uncut Sheets (5):	175.00
Common Player:	.10
Babe Ruth Puzzle:	1.00
Wax Pack (15):	2.50
Wax Box (36):	80.00

No.	Player	Price
1	Pete Rose/DK	4.00
2	Gary Carter/DK	1.25
3	Steve Garvey/DK	.45
4	Vida Blue/DK	.10
5a	Alan Trammel/DK (Last name incorrect.)	1.00
5b	Alan Trammell/DK (Corrected)	.30
6	Len Barker/DK	.10
7	Dwight Evans/DK	.15
8	Rod Carew/DK	1.25
9	George Hendrick/DK	.10
10	Phil Niekro/DK	1.00
11	Richie Zisk/DK	.10
12	Dave Parker/DK	.10
13	Nolan Ryan/DK	5.00
14	Ivan DeJesus/DK	.10
15	George Brett/DK	2.00
16	Tom Seaver/DK	1.25
17	Dave Kingman/DK	.15
18	Dave Winfield/DK	1.25
19	Mike Norris/DK	.10
20	Carlton Fisk/DK	1.25
21	Ozzie Smith/DK	1.50
22	Roy Smalley/DK	.10
23	Buddy Bell/DK	.10
24	Ken Singleton/DK	.10
25	John Mayberry/DK	.10
26	Gorman Thomas/DK	.10
27	Earl Weaver	.50
28	Rollie Fingers	1.00
29	Sparky Anderson	.50
30	Dennis Eckersley	1.25
31	Dave Winfield	1.25
32	Burt Hooton	.10
33	Rick Waits	.10
34	George Brett	2.00
35	Steve McCatty	.10
36	Steve Rogers	.10
37	Bill Stein	.10
38	Steve Renko	.10
39	Mike Squires	.10
40	George Hendrick	.10
41	Bob Knepper	.10
42	Steve Carlton	1.25
43	Larry Biittner	.10
44	Chris Welsh	.10
45	Steve Nicosia	.10
46	Jack Clark	.10
47	Chris Chambliss	.10
48	Ivan DeJesus	.10
49	Lee Mazzilli	.10
50	Julio Cruz	.10
51	Pete Redfern	.10
52	Dave Stieb	.10
53	Doug Corbett	.10
54	George Bell **RC**	.50
55	Joe Simpson	.10
56	Rusty Staub	.10
57	Hector Cruz	.10
58	Claudell Washington **RC**	.10
59	Enrique Romo	.10
60	Gary Lavelle	.10
61	Tim Flannery	.10
62	Joe Nolan	.10
63	Larry Bowa	.10
64	Sixto Lezcano	.10
65	Joe Sambito	.10
66	Bruce Kison	.10
67	Wayne Nordhagen	.10
68	Woodie Fryman	.10
69	Billy Sample	.10
70	Amos Otis	.10
71	Matt Keough	.10
72	Toby Harrah	.10
73	Dave Righetti **RC**	.30
74	Carl Yastrzemski	1.50
75	Bob Welch	.10
76a	Alan Trammel (Last name misspelled.)	1.00
76b	Alan Trammell (Corrected)	.10
77	Rick Dempsey	.10
78	Paul Molitor	1.25
79	Dennis Martinez	.10
80	Jim Slaton	.10
81	Champ Summers	.10
82	Carney Lansford	.10
83	Barry Foote	.10
84	Steve Garvey	.45
85	Rick Manning	.10
86	John Wathan	.10
87	Brian Kingman	.10
88	Andre Dawson	.50
89	Jim Kern	.10
90	Bobby Grich	.10
91	Bob Forsch	.10
92	Art Howe	.10
93	Marty Bystrom	.10
94	Ozzie Smith	1.50
95	Dave Parker	.10
96	Doyle Alexander	.10
97	Al Hrabosky	.10
98	Frank Taveras	.10
99	Tim Blackwell	.10
100	Floyd Bannister	.10
101	Alfredo Griffin	.10
102	Dave Engle	.10
103	Mario Soto	.10
104	Ross Baumgarten	.10
105	Ken Singleton	.10
106	Ted Simmons	.10
107	Jack Morris	.10
108	Bob Watson	.10
109	Dwight Evans	.10
110	Tom Lasorda	.50
111	Bert Blyleven	.10
112	Dan Quisenberry	.10
113	Rickey Henderson	1.25
114	Gary Carter	1.25
115	Brian Downing	.10
116	Al Oliver	.10
117	LaMarr Hoyt	.10
118	Cesar Cedeno	.10
119	Keith Moreland	.10
120	Bob Shirley	.10
121	Terry Kennedy	.10
122	Frank Pastore	.10
123	Gene Garber	.10
124	Tony Pena **RC**	.10
125	Allen Ripley	.10
126	Randy Martz	.10
127	Richie Zisk	.10
128	Mike Scott	.10
129	Lloyd Moseby **RC**	.10
130	Rob Wilfong	.10
131	Tim Stoddard	.10
132	Gorman Thomas	.10
133	Dan Petry	.10
134	Bob Stanley	.10
135	Lou Piniella	.15
136	Pedro Guerrero **RC**	.10
137	Len Barker	.10
138	Richard Gale	.10
139	Wayne Gross	.10
140	Tim Wallach **RC**	.50
141	Gene Mauch	.10
142	Doc Medich	.10
143	Tony Bernazard	.10
144	Bill Virdon	.10
145	John Littlefield	.10
146	Dave Bergman	.10
147	Dick Davis	.10
148	Tom Seaver	1.50
149	Matt Sinatro	.10
150	Chuck Tanner	.10
151	Leon Durham	.10
152	Gene Tenace	.10
153	Al Bumbry	.10
154	Mark Brouhard	.10
155	Rick Peters	.10
156	Jerry Remy	.10
157	Rick Reuschel	.10
158	Steve Howe	.10
159	Alan Bannister	.10
160	U L Washington	.10
161	Rick Langford	.10
162	Bill Gullickson	.10
163	Mark Wagner	.10
164	Geoff Zahn	.10
165	Ron LeFlore	.10
166	Dane Iorg	.10
167	Joe Niekro	.10
168	Pete Rose	3.00
169	Dave Collins	.10
170	Rick Wise	.10
171	Jim Bibby	.10
172	Larry Herndon	.10
173	Bob Horner	.10
174	Steve Dillard	.10
175	Mookie Wilson	.10
176	Dan Meyer	.10
177	Fernando Arroyo	.10
178	Jackson Todd	.10
179	Darrell Jackson	.10
180	Al Woods	.10
181	Jim Anderson	.10
182	Dave Kingman	.10
183	Steve Henderson	.10
184	Brian Asselstine	.10
185	Rod Scurry	.10
186	Fred Breining	.10
187	Danny Boone	.10
188	Junior Kennedy	.10
189	Sparky Lyle	.10
190	Whitey Herzog	.10
191	Dave Smith	.10
192	Ed Ott	.10
193	Greg Luzinski	.10
194	Bill Lee	.10
195	Don Zimmer	.10
196	Hal McRae	.10
197	Mike Norris	.10
198	Duane Kuiper	.10
199	Rick Cerone	.10
200	Jim Rice	.45
201	Steve Yeager	.10
202	Tom Brookens	.10
203	Jose Morales	.10
204	Roy Howell	.10
205	Tippy Martinez	.10
206	Moose Haas	.10
207	Al Cowens	.10
208	Dave Stapleton	.10
209	Bucky Dent	.10
210	Ron Cey	.10
211	Jorge Orta	.10
212	Jamie Quirk	.10
213	Jeff Jones	.10
214	Tim Raines	.25
215	Jon Matlack	.10
216	Rod Carew	1.50
217	Jim Kaat	.15
218	Joe Pittman	.10
219	Larry Christenson	.10
220	Juan Bonilla	.10
221	Mike Easler	.10
222	Vida Blue	.10
223	Rick Camp	.10
224	Mike Jorgensen	.10
225	Jody Davis **RC**	.15
226	Mike Parrott	.10
227	Jim Clancy	.10
228	Hosken Powell	.10
229	Tom Hume	.10
230	Britt Burns	.10
231	Jim Palmer	1.25
232	Bob Rodgers	.10
233	Milt Wilcox	.10
234	Dave Revering	.10
235	Mike Torrez	.10
236	Robert Castillo	.10
237	Von Hayes **RC**	.25
238	Renie Martin	.10
239	Dwayne Murphy	.10
240	Rodney Scott	.10
241	Fred Patek	.10
242	Mickey Rivers	.10
243	Steve Trout	.10
244	Jose Cruz	.10
245	Manny Trillo	.10
246	Lary Sorensen	.10
247	Dave Edwards	.10
248	Dan Driessen	.10
249	Tommy Boggs	.10
250	Dale Berra	.10
251	Ed Whitson	.10
252	Lee Smith **RC**	4.00
253	Tom Paciorek	.10
254	Pat Zachry	.10
255	Luis Leal	.10
256	John Castino	.10
257	Rich Dauer	.10
258	Cecil Cooper	.10
259	Dave Rozema	.10
260	John Tudor	.10
261	Jerry Mumphrey	.10
262	Jay Johnstone	.10
263	Bo Diaz	.10
264	Dennis Leonard	.10
265	Jim Spencer	.10
266	John Milner	.10
267	Don Aase	.10
268	Jim Sundberg	.10
269	Lamar Johnson	.10
270	Frank LaCorte	.10
271	Barry Evans	.10
272	Enos Cabell	.10
273	Del Unser	.10
274	George Foster	.10
275	Brett Butler **RC**	.50
276	Lee Lacy	.10
277	Ken Reitz	.10
278	Keith Hernandez	.10
279	Doug DeCinces	.10
280	Charlie Moore	.10
281	Lance Parrish	.10
282	Ralph Houk	.10
283	Rich Gossage	.10
284	Jerry Reuss	.10
285	Mike Stanton	.10
286	Frank White	.10
287	Bob Owchinko	.10
288	Scott Sanderson	.10
289	Bump Wills	.10
290	Dave Frost	.10
291	Chet Lemon	.10
292	Tito Landrum	.10
293	Vern Ruhle	.10
294	Mike Schmidt	2.00
295	Sam Mejias	.10
296	Gary Lucas	.10
297	John Candelaria	.10
298	Jerry Martin	.10
299	Dale Murphy	.50
300	Mike Lum	.10
301	Tom Hausman	.10
302	Glenn Abbott	.10
303	Roger Erickson	.10
304	Otto Velez	.10
305	Danny Goodwin	.10
306	John Mayberry	.10
307	Lenny Randle	.10
308	Bob Bailor	.10
309	Jerry Morales	.10
310	Rufino Linares	.10
311	Kent Tekulve	.10
312	Joe Morgan	1.25
313	John Urrea	.10
314	Paul Householder	.10
315	Garry Maddox	.10
316	Mike Ramsey	.10
317	Alan Ashby	.10
318	Bob Clark	.10
319	Tony LaRussa	.15
320	Charlie Lea	.10
321	Danny Darwin	.10
322	Cesar Geronimo	.10
323	Tom Underwood	.10
324	Andre Thornton	.10
325	Rudy May	.10
326	Frank Tanana	.10
327	Davey Lopes	.10
328	Richie Hebner	.10
329	Mike Flanagan	.10
330	Mike Caldwell	.10
331	Scott McGregor	.10
332	Jerry Augustine	.10
333	Stan Papi	.10
334	Rick Miller	.10
335	Graig Nettles	.15
336	Dusty Baker	.10
337	Dave Garcia	.10
338	Larry Gura	.10
339	Cliff Johnson	.10
340	Warren Cromartie	.10
341	Steve Comer	.10
342	Rick Burleson	.10
343	John Martin	.10
344	Craig Reynolds	.10
345	Mike Proly	.10
346	Ruppert Jones	.10
347	Omar Moreno	.10
348	Greg Minton	.10
349	Rick Mahler **RC**	.10
350	Alex Trevino	.10
351	Mike Krukow	.10
352a	Shane Rawley (Jim Anderson photo - shaking hands.)	.50
352b	Shane Rawley (Correct photo - kneeling.)	.15
353	Garth Iorg	.10
354	Pete Mackanin	.10
355	Paul Moskau	.10
356	Richard Dotson	.10
357	Steve Stone	.10
358	Larry Hisle	.10
359	Aurelio Lopez	.10
360	Oscar Gamble	.10
361	Tom Burgmeier	.10
362	Terry Forster	.10
363	Joe Charboneau	.25
364	Ken Brett	.10
365	Tony Armas	.10
366	Chris Speier	.10
367	Fred Lynn	.10
368	Buddy Bell	.10
369	Jim Essian	.10
370	Terry Puhl	.10
371	Greg Gross	.10
372	Bruce Sutter	1.25
373	Joe Lefebvre	.10
374	Ray Knight	.10
375	Bruce Benedict	.10
376	Tim Foli	.10
377	Al Holland	.10
378	Ken Kravec	.10
379	Jeff Burroughs	.10
380	Pete Falcone	.10
381	Ernie Whitt	.10
382	Brad Havens	.10
383	Terry Crowley	.10
384	Don Money	.10
385	Dan Schatzeder	.10
386	Gary Allenson	.10
387	Yogi Berra	.50
388	Ken Landreaux	.10
389	Mike Hargrove	.10
390	Darryl Motley	.10
391	Dave McKay	.10
392	Stan Bahnsen	.10
393	Ken Forsch	.10
394	Mario Mendoza	.10
395	Jim Morrison	.10
396	Mike Ivie	.10
397	Broderick Perkins	.10
398	Darrell Evans	.10
399	Ron Reed	.10
400	Johnny Bench	1.50
401	Steve Bedrosian **RC**	.20
402	Bill Robinson	.10
403	Bill Buckner	.10
404	Ken Oberkfell	.10
405	Cal Ripken, Jr. **RC**	40.00
406	Jim Gantner	.10
407	Kirk Gibson **RC**	.10
408	Tony Perez	1.00
409	Tommy John	.10
410	Dave Stewart **RC**	2.50
411	Dan Spillner	.10
412	Willie Aikens	.10
413	Mike Heath	.10
414	Ray Burris	.10
415	Leon Roberts	.10
416	Mike Witt **RC**	.15
417	Bobby Molinaro	.10
418	Steve Braun	.10
419	Nolan Ryan	4.00
420	Tug McGraw	.10
421	Dave Concepcion	.10
422a	Juan Eichelberger (Gary Lucas photo - white player.)	.50
422b	Juan Eichelberger (Correct photo - black player.)	.10
423	Rick Rhoden	.10
424	Frank Robinson	.50
425	Eddie Miller	.10
426	Bill Caudill	.10
427	Doug Flynn	.10
428	Larry Anderson (Andersen)	.10
429	Al Williams	.10
430	Jerry Garvin	.10
431	Glenn Adams	.10
432	Barry Bonnell	.10
433	Jerry Narron	.10
434	John Stearns	.10
435	Mike Tyson	.10
436	Glenn Hubbard	.10
437	Eddie Solomon	.10
438	Jeff Leonard	.10
439	Randy Bass	.10
440	Mike LaCoss	.10
441	Gary Matthews	.10
442	Mark Littell	.10
443	Don Sutton	1.00
444	John Harris	.10
445	Vada Pinson	.10
446	Elias Sosa	.10
447	Charlie Hough	.10
448	Willie Wilson	.10
449	Fred Stanley	.10
450	Tom Veryzer	.10
451	Ron Davis	.10
452	Mark Clear	.10
453	Bill Russell	.10
454	Lou Whitaker	.10
455	Dan Graham	.10
456	Reggie Cleveland	.10
457	Sammy Stewart	.10
458	Pete Vuckovich	.10
459	John Wockenfuss	.10
460	Glenn Hoffman	.10
461	Willie Randolph	.10
462	Fernando Valenzuela	.10
463	Ron Hassey	.10
464	Paul Splittorff	.10
465	Rob Picciolo	.10
466	Larry Parrish	.10
467	Johnny Grubb	.10
468	Dan Ford	.10
469	Silvio Martinez	.10
470	Kiko Garcia	.10
471	Bob Boone	.10
472	Luis Salazar	.10
473	Randy Niemann	.10
474	Tom Griffin	.10
475	Phil Niekro	1.00
476	Hubie Brooks **RC**	.10
477	Dick Tidrow	.10
478	Jim Beattie	.10
479	Damaso Garcia	.10
480	Mickey Hatcher	.10
481	Joe Price	.10
482	Ed Farmer	.10
483	Eddie Murray	1.25
484	Ben Oglivie	.10
485	Kevin Saucier	.10
486	Bobby Murcer	.10
487	Bill Campbell	.10
488	Reggie Smith	.10
489	Wayne Garland	.10
490	Jim Wright	.10
491	Billy Martin	.10
492	Jim Fanning	.10
493	Don Baylor	.10
494	Rick Honeycutt	.10
495	Carlton Fisk	1.25
496	Denny Walling	.10
497	Bake McBride	.10
498	Darrell Porter	.10
499	Gene Richards	.10
500	Ron Oester	.10
501	Ken Dayley **RC**	.10
502	Jason Thompson	.10
503	Milt May	.10
504	Doug Bird	.10
505	Bruce Bochte	.10
506	Neil Allen	.10
507	Joey McLaughlin	.10
508	Butch Wynegar	.10
509	Gary Roenicke	.10
510	Robin Yount	1.25
511	Dave Tobik	.10
512	Rich Gedman **RC**	.15
513	Gene Nelson **RC**	.10
514	Rick Monday	.10
515	Miguel Dilone	.10
516	Clint Hurdle	.10
517	Jeff Newman	.10
518	Grant Jackson	.10
519	Andy Hassler	.10
520	Pat Putnam	.10
521	Greg Pryor	.10
522	Tony Scott	.10
523	Steve Mura	.10
524	Johnnie LeMaster	.10
525	Dick Ruthven	.10
526	John McNamara	.10
527	Larry McWilliams	.10
528	Johnny Ray **RC**	.15
529	Pat Tabler **RC**	.15
530	Tom Herr	.10
531a	San Diego Chicken (W/trademark symbol.)	.75
531b	San Diego Chicken (No trademark symbol.)	.50
532	Sal Butera	.10
533	Mike Griffin	.10
534	Kelvin Moore	.10
535	Reggie Jackson	2.00
536	Ed Romero	.10
537	Derrel Thomas	.10
538	Mike O'Berry	.10
539	Jack O'Connor	.10
540	Bob Ojeda **RC**	.25
541	Roy Lee Jackson	.10
542	Lynn Jones	.10
543	Gaylord Perry	1.00
544a	Phil Garner (Photo reversed.)	.50
544b	Phil Garner (Photo correct.)	.10
545	Garry Templeton	.10
546	Rafael Ramirez **RC**	.10
547	Jeff Reardon	.10
548	Ron Guidry	.10
549	Tim Laudner **RC**	.15
550	John Henry Johnson	.10
551	Chris Bando	.10
552	Bobby Brown	.10
553	Larry Bradford	.10
554	Scott Fletcher **RC**	.20
555	Jerry Royster	.10
556	Shooty Babbitt	.10
557	Kent Hrbek **RC**	2.00
558	Yankee Winners (Ron Guidry, Tommy John)	.15
559	Mark Bomback	.10
560	Julio Valdez	.10
561	Buck Martinez	.10
562	Mike Marshall **RC**	.15
563	Rennie Stennett	.10
564	Steve Crawford	.10
565	Bob Babcock	.10
566	Johnny Podres	.10
567	Paul Serna	.10
568	Harold Baines **RC**	1.00
569	Dave LaRoche	.10
570	Lee May	.10
571	Gary Ward **RC**	.10
572	John Denny	.10
573	Roy Smalley	.10
574	Bob Brenly **RC**	.20
575	Bronx Bombers (Reggie Jackson, Dave Winfield)	1.50
576	Luis Pujols	.10
577	Butch Hobson	.10
578	Harvey Kuenn	.10
579	Cal Ripken, Sr.	.10
580	Juan Berenguer	.10
581	Benny Ayala	.10
582	Vance Law **RC**	.10
583	Rick Leach **RC**	.15
584	George Frazier	.10
585	Phillies Finest (Pete Rose, Mike Schmidt)	1.00
586	Joe Rudi	.10
587	Juan Beniquez	.10
588	Luis DeLeon **RC**	.10
589	Craig Swan	.10
590	Dave Chalk	.10
591	Billy Gardner	.10
592	Sal Bando	.10
593	Bert Campaneris	.10
594	Steve Kemp	.10
595a	Randy Lerch (Braves)	.25
595b	Randy Lerch (Brewers)	.10
596	Bryan Clark	.10
597	Dave Ford	.10
598	Mike Scioscia **RC**	.10
599	John Lowenstein	.10
600	Rene Lachmann (Lachemann)	.10
601	Mick Kelleher	.10
602	Ron Jackson	.10
603	Jerry Koosman	.10
604	Dave Goltz	.10
605	Ellis Valentine	.10
606	Lonnie Smith	.10
607	Joaquin Andujar	.10
608	Garry Hancock	.10
609	Jerry Turner	.10
610	Bob Bonner	.10
611	Jim Dwyer	.10
612	Terry Bulling	.10
613	Joel Youngblood	.10
614	Larry Milbourne	.10
615	Phil Roof (Photo actually Gene Roof.)	.10
616	Keith Drumright	.10
617	Dave Rosello	.10
618	Rickey Keeton	.10
619	Dennis Lamp	.10
620	Sid Monge	.10
621	Jerry White	.10
622	Luis Aguayo **RC**	.10

623 Jamie Easterly .10
624 Steve Sax **RC** .50
625 Dave Roberts .10
626 Rick Bosetti .10
627 Terry Francona **RC** .15
628 Pride of the Reds (Johnny Bench, Tom Seaver) 1.00
629 Paul Mirabella .10
630 Rance Mulliniks .10
631 Kevin Hickey .10
632 Reid Nichols .10
633 Dave Geisel .10
634 Ken Griffey .10
635 Bob Lemon .15
636 Orlando Sanchez .10
637 Bill Almon .10
638 Danny Ainge 1.00
639 Willie Stargell 1.25
640 Bob Sykes .10
641 Ed Lynch .10
642 John Ellis .10
643 Fergie Jenkins 1.00
644 Lenn Sakata .10
645 Julio Gonzales .10
646 Jesse Orosco **RC** .10
647 Jerry Dybzinski .10
648 Tommy Davis .10
649 Ron Gardenhire .10
650 Felipe Alou .10
651 Harvey Haddix .10
652 Willie Upshaw **RC** .10
653 Bill Madlock .10
---- Checklist 1-26 DK (5 Trammel) .25
---- Checklist 1-26 DK (5 Trammell) .10
---- Checklist 27-130 .10
---- Checklist 131-234 .10
---- Checklist 235-338 .10
---- Checklist 339-442 .10
---- Checklist 443-544 .10
---- Checklist 545-653 .10

1982-89 Donruss Puzzle Promo Sheets

Part of the advertising materials which Donruss issued each year was a series of approximately 8" x 10-7/8" color glossy sheets picturing the Dick Perez art which appear on the Diamond Kings puzzle pieces inserted into card packs.

		NM/M
Complete Set (10):		20.00
Common Player:		2.50
(1)	Babe Ruth/1982	2.50
(2)	Ty Cobb/1983	2.50
(3)	Mickey Mantle/1983	2.50
(4)	Duke Snider/1984	2.50
(5)	Ted Williams/1984	2.50
(6)	Lou Gehrig/1985	2.50
(7)	Hank Aaron/1986	2.50
(8)	Roberto Clemente/1987	2.50
(9)	Stan Musial/1988	2.50
(10)	Warren Spahn/1989	2.50

1983 Donruss Promo Sheet

To debut its 1983 card design for dealers, Donruss prepared this eight-card sheet, including one Diamond Stars card. Card fronts are identical to the issued versions. Backs of most cards differ in the Career Highlights write-up. The sheet measures 10" x 7".

	NM/M
Uncut Sheet:	10.00

1983 Donruss

The 1983 Donruss set consists of 653 numbered cards plus seven unnumbered checklists. The 2-1/2" x 3-1/2" cards were issued with puzzle pieces (three pieces on one card per pack) that feature Ty Cobb. The first 26 cards in the set were once again the Diamond Kings series. The card fronts display the Donruss logo and the year of issue. The card backs have black print on yellow and white and include statistics, career highlights, and the player's contract status. (DK) in the checklist below indicates cards which belong to the Diamond Kings series.

	NM/M
Unopened Fact. Set (660):	50.00
Complete Set (660):	40.00
Common Player:	.10
Ty Cobb Puzzle:	2.50
Wax Pack (15):	2.50
Wax Box (36):	80.00

1 Fernando Valenzuela/DK .15
2 Rollie Fingers/DK .75
3 Reggie Jackson/DK 2.50
4 Jim Palmer/DK 1.00
5 Jack Morris/DK .15
6 George Foster/DK .15
7 Jim Sundberg/DK .10
8 Willie Stargell/DK 1.00
9 Dave Stieb/DK .15
10 Joe Niekro/DK .15
11 Rickey Henderson/DK 1.25
12 Dale Murphy/DK .50
13 Toby Harrah/DK .10
14 Bill Buckner/DK .15
15 Willie Wilson/DK .10
16 Steve Carlton/DK 1.25
17 Ron Guidry/DK .15
18 Steve Rogers/DK .10
19 Kent Hrbek/DK .10
20 Keith Hernandez/DK .10
21 Floyd Bannister/DK .10
22 Johnny Bench/DK 2.00
23 Britt Burns/DK .10
24 Joe Morgan/DK 1.25
25 Carl Yastrzemski/DK 2.00
26 Terry Kennedy/DK .10
27 Gary Roenicke .10
28 Dwight Bernard .10
29 Pat Underwood .10
30 Gary Allenson .10
31 Ron Guidry .10
32 Burt Hooton .10
33 Chris Bando .10
34 Vida Blue .10
35 Rickey Henderson 1.25
36 Ray Burris .10
37 John Butcher .10
38 Don Aase .10
39 Jerry Koosman .10
40 Bruce Sutter 1.00
41 Jose Cruz .10
42 Pete Rose 3.00
43 Cesar Cedeno .10
44 Floyd Chiffer .10
45 Larry McWilliams .10
46 Alan Fowlkes .10
47 Dale Murphy .50
48 Doug Bird .10
49 Hubie Brooks .10
50 Floyd Bannister .10
51 Jack O'Connor .10
52 Steve Senteney .10
53 Gary Gaetti **RC** 1.00
54 Damaso Garcia .10
55 Gene Nelson .10
56 Mookie Wilson .10
57 Allen Ripley .10
58 Bob Horner .10
59 Tony Pena .10
60 Gary Lavelle .10
61 Tim Lollar .10
62 Frank Pastore .10
63 Garry Maddox .10
64 Bob Forsch .10
65 Harry Spilman .10
66 Geoff Zahn .10
67 Salome Barojas .10
68 David Palmer .10
69 Charlie Hough .10
70 Dan Quisenberry .10
71 Tony Armas .10
72 Rick Sutcliffe .10
73 Steve Balboni **RC** .10
74 Jerry Remy .10
75 Mike Scioscia .10
76 John Wockenfuss .10
77 Jim Palmer 1.00
78 Rollie Fingers .75
79 Joe Nolan .10
80 Pete Vuckovich .10
81 Rick Leach .10
82 Rick Miller .10
83 Graig Nettles .15
84 Ron Cey .10
85 Miguel Dilone .10
86 John Wathan .10
87 Kelvin Moore .10
88a Byrn Smith (First name incorrect.) .35
88b Bryn Smith (First name correct.) .10
89 Dave Hostetler .10
90 Rod Carew 1.50
91 Lonnie Smith .10
92 Bob Knepper .10
93 Marty Bystrom .10
94 Chris Welsh .10
95 Jason Thompson .10
96 Tom O'Malley .10
97 Phil Niekro .75
98 Neil Allen .10
99 Bill Buckner .10
100 Ed Vande Berg **RC** .10
101 Jim Clancy .10
102 Robert Castillo .10
103 Bruce Berenyi .10
104 Carlton Fisk 1.25
105 Mike Flanagan .10
106 Cecil Cooper .10
107 Jack Morris .10
108 Mike Morgan **RC** .10
109 Luis Aponte .10
110 Pedro Guerrero .10
111 Len Barker .10
112 Willie Wilson .10
113 Dave Beard .10
114 Mike Gates .10
115 Reggie Jackson 2.50
116 George Wright .10
117 Vance Law .10
118 Nolan Ryan 4.00
119 Mike Krukow .10
120 Ozzie Smith 2.00
121 Broderick Perkins .10
122 Tom Seaver 1.50
123 Chris Chambliss .10
124 Chuck Tanner .10
125 Johnnie LeMaster .10
126 Mel Hall **RC** .15
127 Bruce Bochte .10
128 Charlie Puleo **RC** .10
129 Luis Leal .10
130 John Pacella .10
131 Glenn Gulliver .10
132 Don Money .10
133 Dave Rozema .10
134 Bruce Hurst **RC** .10
135 Rudy May .10
136 Tom LaSorda (Lasorda) .40
137 Dan Spillner (Photo actually Ed Whitson.) .10
138 Jerry Martin .10
139 Mike Norris .10
140 Al Oliver .10
141 Daryl Sconiers .10
142 Lamar Johnson .10
143 Harold Baines .10
144 Alan Ashby .10
145 Garry Templeton .10
146 Al Holland .10
147 Bo Diaz .10
148 Dave Concepcion .10
149 Rick Camp .10
150 Jim Morrison .10
151 Randy Martz .10
152 Keith Hernandez .10
153 John Lowenstein .10
154 Mike Caldwell .10
155 Milt Wilcox .10
156 Rich Gedman .10
157 Rich Gossage .20
158 Jerry Reuss .10
159 Ron Hassey .10
160 Larry Gura .10
161 Dwayne Murphy .10
162 Woodie Fryman .10
163 Steve Comer .10
164 Ken Forsch .10
165 Dennis Lamp .10
166 David Green .10
167 Terry Puhl .10
168 Mike Schmidt 2.50
169 Eddie Milner **RC** .10
170 John Curtis .10
171 Don Robinson .10
172 Richard Gale .10
173 Steve Bedrosian .10
174 Willie Hernandez .10
175 Ron Gardenhire .10
176 Jim Beattie .10
177 Tim Laudner .10
178 Buck Martinez .10
179 Kent Hrbek .10
180 Alfredo Griffin .10
181 Larry Andersen .10
182 Pete Falcone .10
183 Jody Davis .10
184 Glenn Hubbard .10
185 Dale Berra .10
186 Greg Minton .10
187 Gary Lucas .10
188 Dave Van Gorder .10
189 Bob Dernier **RC** .10
190 Willie McGee **RC** 1.50
191 Dickie Thon .10
192 Bob Boone .10
193 Britt Burns .10
194 Jeff Reardon .10
195 Jon Matlack .10
196 Don Slaught **RC** .15
197 Fred Stanley .10
198 Rick Manning .10
199 Dave Righetti .10
200 Dave Stapleton .10
201 Steve Yeager .10
202 Enos Cabell .10
203 Sammy Stewart .10
204 Moose Haas .10
205 Lenn Sakata .10
206 Charlie Moore .10
207 Alan Trammell .10
208 Jim Rice .40
209 Roy Smalley .10
210 Bill Russell .10
211 Andre Thornton .10
212 Willie Aikens .10
213 Dave McKay .10
214 Tim Blackwell .10
215 Buddy Bell .10
216 Doug DeCinces .10
217 Tom Herr .10
218 Frank LaCorte .10
219 Steve Carlton 1.25
220 Terry Kennedy .10
221 Mike Easler .10
222 Jack Clark .10
223 Gene Garber .10
224 Scott Holman .10
225 Mike Proly .10
226 Terry Bulling .10
227 Jerry Garvin .10
228 Ron Davis .10
229 Tom Hume .10
230 Marc Hill .10
231 Dennis Martinez .10
232 Jim Gantner .10
233 Larry Pashnick .10
234 Dave Collins .10
235 Tom Burgmeier .10
236 Ken Landreaux .10
237 John Denny .10
238 Hal McRae .10
239 Matt Keough .10
240 Doug Flynn .10
241 Fred Lynn .10
242 Billy Sample .10
243 Tom Paciorek .10
244 Joe Sambito .10
245 Sid Monge .10
246 Ken Oberkfell .10
247 Joe Pittman (Photo actually Juan Eichelberger.) .10
248 Mario Soto .10
249 Claudell Washington .10
250 Rick Rhoden .10
251 Darrell Evans .10
252 Steve Henderson .10
253 Manny Castillo .10
254 Craig Swan .10
255 Joey McLaughlin .10
256 Pete Redfern .10
257 Ken Singleton .10
258 Robin Yount 1.25
259 Elias Sosa .10
260 Bob Ojeda .10
261 Bobby Murcer .10
262 Candy Maldonado **RC** .10
263 Rick Waits .10
264 Greg Pryor .10
265 Bob Owchinko .10
266 Chris Speier .10
267 Bruce Kison .10
268 Mark Wagner .10
269 Steve Kemp .10
270 Phil Garner .10
271 Gene Richards .10
272 Renie Martin .10
273 Dave Roberts .10
274 Dan Driessen .10
275 Rufino Linares .10
276 Lee Lacy .10
277 Ryne Sandberg **RC** 12.00
278 Darrell Porter .10
279 Cal Ripken, Jr. 4.00
280 Jamie Easterly .10
281 Bill Fahey .10
282 Glenn Hoffman .10
283 Willie Randolph .10
284 Fernando Valenzuela .10
285 Alan Bannister .10
286 Paul Splittorff .10
287 Joe Rudi .10
288 Bill Gullickson .10
289 Danny Darwin .10
290 Andy Hassler .10
291 Ernesto Escarrega .10
292 Steve Mura .10
293 Tony Scott .10
294 Manny Trillo .10
295 Greg Harris **RC** .10
296 Luis DeLeon .10
297 Kent Tekulve .10
298 Atlee Hammaker **RC** .10
299 Bruce Benedict .10
300 Fergie Jenkins .75
301 Dave Kingman .10
302 Bill Caudill .10
303 John Castino .10
304 Ernie Whitt .10
305 Randy S. Johnson .10
306 Garth Iorg .10
307 Gaylord Perry .75
308 Ed Lynch .10
309 Keith Moreland .10
310 Rafael Ramirez .10
311 Bill Madlock .10
312 Milt May .10
313 John Montefusco .10
314 Wayne Krenchicki .10
315 George Vukovich .10
316 Joaquin Andujar .10
317 Craig Reynolds .10
318 Rick Burleson .10
319 Richard Dotson .10
320 Steve Rogers .10
321 Dave Schmidt **RC** .10
322 Bud Black **RC** .15
323 Jeff Burroughs .10
324 Von Hayes .10
325 Butch Wynegar .10
326 Carl Yastrzemski 1.50
327 Ron Roenicke .10
328 Howard Johnson **RC** 1.00
329 Rick Dempsey .10
330a Jim Slaton (One yellow box on back.) .25
330b Jim Slaton (Two yellow boxes on back.) .10
331 Benny Ayala .10
332 Ted Simmons .10
333 Lou Whitaker .10
334 Chuck Rainey .10
335 Lou Piniella .15
336 Steve Sax .10
337 Toby Harrah .10
338 George Brett 2.50
339 Davey Lopes .10
340 Gary Carter 1.25
341 John Grubb .10
342 Tim Foli .10
343 Jim Kaat .15
344 Mike LaCoss .10
345 Larry Christenson .10
346 Juan Bonilla .10
347 Omar Moreno .10
348 Chili Davis .10
349 Tommy Boggs .10
350 Rusty Staub .15
351 Bump Wills .10
352 Rick Sweet .10
353 Jim Gott **RC** .15
354 Terry Felton .10
355 Jim Kern .10
356 Bill Almon .10
357 Tippy Martinez .10
358 Roy Howell .10
359 Dan Petry .10
360 Jerry Mumphrey .10
361 Mark Clear .10
362 Mike Marshall .10
363 Lary Sorensen .10
364 Amos Otis .10
365 Rick Langford .10
366 Brad Mills .10
367 Brian Downing .10
368 Mike Richardt .10
369 Aurelio Rodriguez .10
370 Dave Smith .10
371 Tug McGraw .10
372 Doug Bair .10
373 Ruppert Jones .10
374 Alex Trevino .10
375 Ken Dayley .10
376 Rod Scurry .10
377 Bob Brenly **RC** .10
378 Scot Thompson .10
379 Julio Cruz .10
380 John Stearns .10
381 Dale Murray .10
382 Frank Viola **RC** 1.50
383 Al Bumbry .10
384 Ben Oglivie .10
385 Dave Tobik .10
386 Bob Stanley .10
387 Andre Robertson .10
388 Jorge Orta .10
389 Ed Whitson .10
390 Don Hood .10
391 Tom Underwood .10
392 Tim Wallach .10
393 Steve Renko .10
394 Mickey Rivers .10
395 Greg Luzinski .10
396 Art Howe .10
397 Alan Wiggins .10
398 Jim Barr .10
399 Ivan DeJesus .10
400 Tom Lawless **RC** .10
401 Bob Walk .10
402 Jimmy Smith .10
403 Lee Smith .20
404 George Hendrick .10
405 Eddie Murray 1.25
406 Marshall Edwards .10
407 Lance Parrish .10
408 Carney Lansford .10
409 Dave Winfield 1.25
410 Bob Welch .10
411 Larry Milbourne .10
412 Dennis Leonard .10
413 Dan Meyer .10
414 Charlie Lea .10
415 Rick Honeycutt .10
416 Mike Witt .10
417 Steve Trout .10
418 Glenn Brummer .10
419 Denny Walling .10
420 Gary Matthews .10
421 Charlie Liebrandt (Leibrandt) .10
422 Juan Eichelberger .10
423 Matt Guante (Cecilio) **RC** .10
424 Bill Laskey .10
425 Jerry Royster .10
426 Dickie Noles .10
427 George Foster .10
428 Mike Moore **RC** .25
429 Gary Ward .10
430 Barry Bonnell .10
431 Ron Washington .10
432 Rance Mulliniks .10
433 Mike Stanton .10
434 Jesse Orosco .10
435 Larry Bowa .10
436 Biff Pocoroba .10
437 Johnny Ray .10
438 Joe Morgan 1.25
439 Eric Show **RC** .15
440 Larry Biittner .10
441 Greg Gross .10
442 Gene Tenace .10
443 Danny Heep .10
444 Bobby Clark .10
445 Kevin Hickey .10
446 Scott Sanderson .10
447 Frank Tanana .10
448 Cesar Geronimo .10
449 Jimmy Sexton .10
450 Mike Hargrove .10
451 Doyle Alexander .10
452 Dwight Evans .10
453 Terry Forster .10
454 Tom Brookens .10
455 Rich Dauer .10
456 Rob Picciolo .10
457 Terry Crowley .10
458 Ned Yost .10
459 Kirk Gibson .10
460 Reid Nichols .10
461 Oscar Gamble .10
462 Dusty Baker .10
463 Jack Perconte .10
464 Frank White .10
465 Mickey Klutts .10
466 Warren Cromartie .10
467 Larry Parrish .10
468 Bobby Grich .10
469 Dane Iorg .10
470 Joe Niekro .10
471 Ed Farmer .10
472 Tim Flannery .10
473 Dave Parker .10
474 Jeff Leonard .10
475 Al Hrabosky .10
476 Ron Hodges .10
477 Leon Durham .10
478 Jim Essian .10
479 Roy Lee Jackson .10
480 Brad Havens .10
481 Joe Price .10
482 Tony Bernazard .10
483 Scott McGregor .10
484 Paul Molitor 1.25
485 Mike Ivie .10
486 Ken Griffey .10
487 Dennis Eckersley 1.00
488 Steve Garvey .40
489 Mike Fischlin .10
490 U.L. Washington .10
491 Steve McCatty .10
492 Roy Johnson .10
493 Don Baylor .10
494 Bobby Johnson .10
495 Mike Squires .10
496 Bert Roberge .10
497 Dick Ruthven .10
498 Tito Landrum .10
499 Sixto Lezcano .10
500 Johnny Bench 1.50
501 Larry Whisenton .10
502 Manny Sarmiento .10
503 Fred Breining .10
504 Bill Campbell .10
505 Todd Cruz .10
506 Bob Bailor .10
507 Dave Stieb .10
508 Al Williams .10
509 Dan Ford .10
510 Gorman Thomas .10
511 Chet Lemon .10
512 Mike Torrez .10
513 Shane Rawley .10
514 Mark Belanger .10
515 Rodney Craig .10
516 Onix Concepcion .10
517 Mike Heath .10
518 Andre Dawson .50
519 Luis Sanchez .10
520 Terry Bogener .10
521 Rudy Law .10
522 Ray Knight .10
523 Joe Lefebvre .10
524 Jim Wohlford .10

525	Julio Franco **RC**	2.00
526	Ron Oester	.10
527	Rick Mahler	.10
528	Steve Nicosia	.10
529	Junior Kennedy	.10
530a	Whitey Herzog (One yellow box on back.)	.25
530b	Whitey Herzog (Two yellow boxes on back.)	.15
531a	Don Sutton (Blue frame.)	.75
531b	Don Sutton (Green frame.)	.75
532	Mark Brouhard	.10
533a	Sparky Anderson (One yellow box on back.)	.50
533b	Sparky Anderson (Two yellow boxes on back.)	.50
534	Roger LaFrancois	.10
535	George Frazier	.10
536	Tom Niedenfuer	.10
537	Ed Glynn	.10
538	Lee May	.10
539	Bob Kearney	.10
540	Tim Raines	.10
541	Paul Mirabella	.10
542	Luis Tiant	.10
543	Ron LeFlore	.10
544	Dave LaPoint **RC**	.15
545	Randy Moffitt	.10
546	Luis Aguayo	.10
547	Brad Lesley	.10
548	Luis Salazar	.10
549	John Candelaria	.10
550	Dave Bergman	.10
551	Bob Watson	.10
552	Pat Tabler	.10
553	Brent Gaff	.10
554	Al Cowens	.10
555	Tom Brunansky **RC**	.10
556	Lloyd Moseby	.10
557a	Pascual Perez (Twins)	.25
557b	Pascual Perez (Braves)	.10
558	Willie Upshaw	.10
559	Richie Zisk	.10
560	Pat Zachry	.10
561	Jay Johnstone	.10
562	Carlos Diaz	.10
563	John Tudor	.10
564	Frank Robinson	.50
565	Dave Edwards	.10
566	Paul Householder	.10
567	Ron Reed	.10
568	Mike Ramsey	.10
569	Kiko Garcia	.10
570	Tommy John	.10
571	Tony LaRussa	.10
572	Joel Youngblood	.10
573	Wayne Tolleson **RC**	.10
574	Keith Creel	.10
575	Billy Martin	.10
576	Jerry Dybzinski	.10
577	Rick Cerone	.10
578	Tony Perez	1.00
579	Greg Brock **RC**	.10
580	Glen Wilson (Glenn)	.10
581	Tim Stoddard	.10
582	Bob McClure	.10
583	Jim Dwyer	.10
584	Ed Romero	.10
585	Larry Herndon	.10
586	Wade Boggs **RC**	10.00
587	Jay Howell **RC**	.10
588	Dave Stewart	.10
589	Bert Blyleven	.10
590	Dick Howser	.10
591	Wayne Gross	.10
592	Terry Francona	.10
593	Don Werner	.10
594	Bill Stein	.10
595	Jesse Barfield	.10
596	Bobby Molinaro	.10
597	Mike Vail	.10
598	Tony Gwynn **RC**	12.00
599	Gary Rajsich	.10
600	Jerry Ujdur	.10
601	Cliff Johnson	.10
602	Jerry White	.10
603	Bryan Clark	.10
604	Joe Ferguson	.10
605	Guy Sularz	.10
606a	Ozzie Virgil **RC** (Green frame around photo.)	.25
606b	Ozzie Virgil **RC** (Orange frame around photo.)	.10
607	Terry Harper **RC**	.10
608	Harvey Kuenn	.10
609	Jim Sundberg	.10
610	Willie Stargell	1.25
611	Reggie Smith	.10
612	Rob Wilfong	.10
613	Niekro Brothers (Joe Niekro, Phil Niekro)	.25
614	Lee Elia	.10
615	Mickey Hatcher	.10
616	Jerry Hairston Sr.	.10
617	John Martin	.10
618	Wally Backman **RC**	.10
619	Storm Davis **RC**	.15
620	Alan Knicely	.10
621	John Stuper	.10
622	Matt Sinatro	.10
623	Gene Petralli **RC**	.10
624	Duane Walker	.10
625	Dick Williams	.10
626	Pat Corrales	.10
627	Vern Ruhle	.10
628	Joe Torre	.10
629	Anthony Johnson	.10
630	Steve Howe	.10
631	Gary Woods	.10
632	Lamarr Hoyt (LaMarr)	.10
633	Steve Swisher	.10
634	Terry Leach **RC**	.10
635	Jeff Newman	.10
636	Brett Butler	.10
637	Gary Gray	.10
638	Lee Mazzilli	.10
639a	Ron Jackson (A's)	2.50
639b	Ron Jackson (Angels - green frame around photo.)	.25
639c	Ron Jackson (Angels - red frame around photo.)	.15
640	Juan Beniquez	.10
641	Dave Rucker	.10
642	Luis Pujols	.10
643	Rick Monday	.10
644	Hosken Powell	.10
645	San Diego Chicken	.20
646	Dave Engle	.10
647	Dick Davis	.10
648	MVP's (Vida Blue, Joe Morgan, Frank Robinson)	.15
649	Al Chambers	.10
650	Jesus Vega	.10
651	Jeff Jones	.10
652	Marvis Foley	.10
653	Ty Cobb (puzzle)	.10
----	DK checklist (Dick Perez (No word "Checklist" on back.)	.25
----	DK Checklist (Dick Perez (Word "Checklist" on back.)	.10
----	Checklist 27-130	.10
----	Checklist 131-234	.10
----	Checklist 235-338	.10
----	Checklist 339-442	.10
----	Checklist 443-546	.10
----	Checklist 547-653	.10

1983 Donruss Action All-Stars Promo Sheet

To introduce its series of large-format star cards, Donruss issued this sample sheet with four players on a 10" x 7" format.

	NM/M
Complete Sheet:	15.00

1983 Donruss Action All-Stars

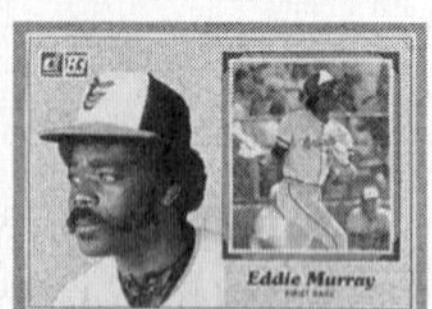

The cards in this 60-card set are designed on a horizontal format and contain a large close-up photo of the player on the left and a smaller action photo on the right. The 5" x 3-1/2" cards have deep red borders and contain the Donruss logo and the year of issue. Backs are printed in black on red and white and contain statistical and biographical information. The cards were sold with puzzle pieces (three pieces on one card per pack) that feature Mickey Mantle.

		NM/M
Complete Set (60):		6.00
Common Player:		.05
Mickey Mantle Puzzle:		6.00
Cello Pack (3):		.35
Cello Box (36):		8.00
1	Eddie Murray	.30
2	Dwight Evans	.05
3a	Reggie Jackson (Red covers part of statistics on back.)	.50
3b	Reggie Jackson (Red does not cover any statistics on back.)	.50
4	Greg Luzinski	.05
5	Larry Herndon	.05
6	Al Oliver	.05
7	Bill Buckner	.05
8	Jason Thompson	.05
9	Andre Dawson	.20
10	Greg Minton	.05
11	Terry Kennedy	.05
12	Phil Niekro	.25
13	Willie Wilson	.05
14	Johnny Bench	.45
15	Ron Guidry	.05
16	Hal McRae	.05
17	Damaso Garcia	.05
18	Gary Ward	.05
19	Cecil Cooper	.05
20	Keith Hernandez	.05
21	Ron Cey	.05
22	Rickey Henderson	.30
23	Nolan Ryan	2.00
24	Steve Carlton	.30
25	John Stearns	.05
26	Jim Sundberg	.05
27	Joaquin Andujar	.05
28	Gaylord Perry	.25
29	Jack Clark	.05
30	Bill Madlock	.05
31	Pete Rose	1.00
32	Mookie Wilson	.05
33	Rollie Fingers	.25
34	Lonnie Smith	.05
35	Tony Pena	.05
36	Dave Winfield	.30
37	Tim Lollar	.05
38	Rod Carew	.30
39	Toby Harrah	.05
40	Buddy Bell	.05
41	Bruce Sutter	.25
42	George Brett	.75
43	Carlton Fisk	.30
44	Carl Yastrzemski	.45
45	Dale Murphy	.20
46	Bob Horner	.05
47	Dave Concepcion	.05
48	Dave Stieb	.05
49	Kent Hrbek	.05
50	Lance Parrish	.05
51	Joe Niekro	.05
52	Cal Ripken, Jr.	2.00
53	Fernando Valenzuela	.05
54	Rickie Zisk	.05
55	Leon Durham	.05
56	Robin Yount	.30
57	Mike Schmidt	.75
58	Gary Carter	.30
59	Fred Lynn	.05
60	Checklist	.05

1983 Donruss Hall of Fame Heroes Promo Sheet

To introduce its series of former star Perez-Steele art cards, Donruss issued this sample sheet which reproduces four of the cards in a 5" x 7" format.

	NM/M
Complete Sheet:	10.00

1983 Donruss Hall of Fame Heroes

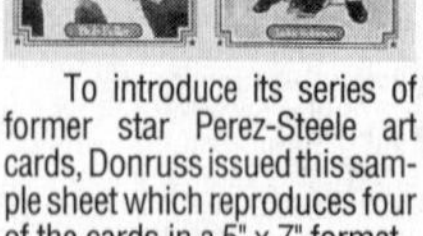

The artwork of Dick Perez is featured in the 44- card Hall of Fame Heroes set issued in 1983. The 2-1/2" x 3-1/2" cards were available in wax packs that contained eight cards plus a Mickey Mantle puzzle piece card (three pieces on one card). Backs display red and blue print on white stock and contain a short biograpical sketch.

		NM/M
Complete Set (44):		5.00
Common Player:		.10
Mickey Mantle Puzzle:		6.00
Wax Pack (8):		.75
Wax Box (36):		15.00
1	Ty Cobb	.75
2	Walter Johnson	.15
3	Christy Mathewson	.15
4	Josh Gibson	.15
5	Honus Wagner	.35
6	Jackie Robinson	.75
7	Mickey Mantle	2.00
8	Luke Appling	.10
9	Ted Williams	.75
10	Johnny Mize	.10
11	Satchel Paige	.35
12	Lou Boudreau	.10
13	Jimmie Foxx	.10
14	Duke Snider	.25
15	Monte Irvin	.10
16	Hank Greenberg	.25
17	Roberto Clemente	1.00
18	Al Kaline	.15
19	Frank Robinson	.15
20	Joe Cronin	.10
21	Burleigh Grimes	.10
22	The Waner Brothers (Lloyd Waner, Paul Waner)	.10
23	Grover Alexander	.10
24	Yogi Berra	.25
25	James Bell	.10
26	Bill Dickey	.10
27	Cy Young	.15
28	Charlie Gehringer	.10
29	Dizzy Dean	.15
30	Bob Lemon	.10
31	Red Ruffing	.10
32	Stan Musial	.60
33	Carl Hubbell	.10
34	Hank Aaron	.75
35	John McGraw	.10
36	Bob Feller	.15
37	Casey Stengel	.10
38	Ralph Kiner	.10
39	Roy Campanella	.25
40	Mel Ott	.10
41	Robin Roberts	.10
42	Early Wynn	.10
43	Mickey Mantle Puzzle Card	.25
---	Checklist	.05

1984 Donruss Promo Sheet

The front designs of nine 1984 Donruss baseball cards were printed on this glossy paper sheet to introduce the company's design for 1994. The 7-1/2" x 10-1/2" sheets are blank-backed. Players are listed here alphabetically.

	NM/M
Complete Sheet:	15.00

1984 Donruss

The 1984 Donruss set consists of 651 numbered cards, seven unnumbered checklists and two "Living Legends" cards (designated A and B). The A and B cards were issued only in wax packs and were not available to hobby dealers purchasing factory sets. The card fronts differ in style from the previous years, however the Donruss logo and year of issue are still included. Backs have black print on green and white and are identical in format to the preceding year. The 2-1/2" x 3-1/2" cards were issued in packs with three pieces of a 63-piece puzzle of Duke Snider. The complete set price in the checklist that follows does not include the higher priced variations. Cards marked with (DK) or (RR) in the checklist refer to the Diamond Kings and Rated Rookies subsets. Each of the Diamond Kings cards and the DK checklist can be found in two varieties. The more common has Frank Steele's name misspelled "Steel" in the credit line at the bottom-right corner on the back. The error was later corrected.

		NM/M
Unopened Fact. Set (658):		150.00
Complete Set (660):		75.00
Common Player:		.15
Duke Snider Puzzle:		2.00
Wax Pack (15):		4.50
Wax Box (36):		150.00
Rack Pack (45):		15.00
A	Living Legends (Rollie Fingers, Gaylord Perry)	1.50
B	Living Legends (Johnny Bench, Carl Yastrzemski)	4.00
1a	Robin Yount/ DK (Steel)	2.50
1b	Robin Yount/ DK (Steele)	3.00
2a	Dave Concepcion/ DK (Steel)	.25
2b	Dave Concepcion/ DK (Steele)	.35
3a	Dwayne Murphy/ DK (Steel)	.25
3b	Dwayne Murphy/DK (Steele)	.35
4a	John Castino/DK (Steel)	.25
4b	John Castino/ DK (Steele)	.35
5a	Leon Durham/ DK (Steel)	.25
5b	Leon Durham/ DK (Steele)	.35
6a	Rusty Staub/DK (Steel)	.30
6b	Rusty Staub/ DK (Steele)	.45
7a	Jack Clark/DK (Steel)	.25
7b	Jack Clark/DK (Steele)	.35
8a	Dave Dravecky/ DK (Steel)	.25
8b	Dave Dravecky/ DK (Steele)	.35
9a	Al Oliver/DK (Steel)	.35
9b	Al Oliver/DK (Steele)	.50
10a	Dave Righetti/ DK (Steel)	.25
10b	Dave Righetti/ DK (Steele)	.35
11a	Hal McRae/DK (Steel)	.25
11b	Hal McRae/DK (Steele)	.35
12a	Ray Knight/DK (Steel)	.25
12b	Ray Knight/DK (Steele)	.35
13a	Bruce Sutter/ DK (Steel)	2.50
13b	Bruce Sutter/ DK (Steele)	3.00
14a	Bob Horner/DK (Steel)	.25
14b	Bob Horner/DK (Steele)	.35
15a	Lance Parrish/ DK (Steel)	.25
15b	Lance Parrish/ DK (Steele)	.35
16a	Matt Young/DK (Steel)	.25
16b	Matt Young/DK (Steele)	.35
17a	Fred Lynn/DK (Steel)	.35
17b	Fred Lynn/DK (Steele)	.50
18a	Ron Kittle/DK (Steel)	.25
18b	Ron Kittle/DK (Steele)	.35
19a	Jim Clancy/DK (Steel)	.25
19b	Jim Clancy/DK (Steele)	.35
20a	Bill Madlock/DK (Steel)	.25
20b	Bill Madlock/ DK (Steele)	.35
21a	Larry Parrish/DK (Steel)	.25
21b	Larry Parrish/ DK (Steele)	.35
22a	Eddie Murray/ DK (Steel)	2.50
22b	Eddie Murray/ DK (Steele)	3.00
23a	Mike Schmidt/ DK (Steel)	3.00
23b	Mike Schmidt/ DK (Steele)	4.00
24a	Pedro Guerrero/ DK (Steel)	.25
24b	Pedro Guerrero/ DK (Steele)	.35
25a	Andre Thornton/ DK (Steel)	.25
25b	Andre Thornton/ DK (Steele)	.35
26a	Wade Boggs/ DK (Steel)	3.00
26b	Wade Boggs/ DK (Steele)	3.00
27	Joel Skinner/RR **RC**	.15
28	Tom Dunbar/RR	.15
29a	Mike Stenhouse/RR (no number on back)	.15
29b	Mike Stenhouse/ RR (29 on back)	1.00
30a	Ron Darling/RR **RC** (no number on back)	1.50
30b	Ron Darling/RR **RC** (30 on back)	2.50
31	Dion James/RR **RC**	.15
32	Tony Fernandez/ RR **RC**	3.00
33	Angel Salazar/RR	.15
34	Kevin McReynolds/ RR **RC**	1.50
35	Dick Schofield/RR **RC**	.20
36	Brad Komminsk/RR **RC**	.15
37	Tim Teufel/RR **RC**	.25
38	Doug Frobel/RR	.15
39	Greg Gagne/RR **RC**	1.00
40	Mike Fuentes/RR	.15
41	Joe Carter/RR **RC**	8.00
42	Mike Brown/RR	.15
43	Mike Jeffcoat/RR	.15
44	Sid Fernandez/RR **RC**	2.00
45	Brian Dayett/RR	.15
46	Chris Smith/RR	.15
47	Eddie Murray	3.00
48	Robin Yount	3.00
49	Lance Parrish	.15
50	Jim Rice	1.00
51	Dave Winfield	3.00
52	Fernando Valenzuela	.15
53	George Brett	5.00
54	Rickey Henderson	3.00
55	Gary Carter	3.00
56	Buddy Bell	.15
57	Reggie Jackson	5.00
58	Harold Baines	.15
59	Ozzie Smith	4.00
60	Nolan Ryan	8.00
61	Pete Rose	7.50
62	Ron Oester	.15
63	Steve Garvey	.75
64	Jason Thompson	.15
65	Jack Clark	.15
66	Dale Murphy	1.50
67	Leon Durham	.15
68	Darryl Strawberry	2.00
69	Richie Zisk	.15
70	Kent Hrbek	.15
71	Dave Stieb	.15
72	Ken Schrom	.15
73	George Bell	.15
74	John Moses	.15
75	Ed Lynch	.15
76	Chuck Rainey	.15
77	Biff Pocoroba	.15
78	Cecilio Guante	.15
79	Jim Barr	.15
80	Kurt Bevacqua	.15
81	Tom Foley	.15
82	Joe Lefebvre	.15
83	Andy Van Slyke **RC**	2.00
84	Bob Lillis	.15
85	Rick Adams	.15
86	Jerry Hairston Sr.	.15
87	Bob James	.15
88	Joe Altobelli	.15
89	Ed Romero	.15
90	John Grubb	.15
91	John Henry Johnson	.15
92	Juan Espino	.15
93	Candy Maldonado	.15
94	Andre Thornton	.15
95	Onix Concepcion	.15
96	Don Hill **RC**	.15
97	Andre Dawson	1.50
98	Frank Tanana	.15
99	Curt Wilkerson **RC**	.15
100	Larry Gura	.15
101	Dwayne Murphy	.15
102	Tom Brennan	.15
103	Dave Righetti	.15
104	Steve Sax	.15
105	Dan Petry	.15
106	Cal Ripken, Jr.	8.00
107	Paul Molitor	3.00
108	Fred Lynn	.15
109	Neil Allen	.15
110	Joe Niekro	.15
111	Steve Carlton	3.00
112	Terry Kennedy	.15
113	Bill Madlock	.15
114	Chili Davis	.15
115	Jim Gantner	.15
116	Tom Seaver	4.00

117 Bill Buckner .15
118 Bill Caudill .15
119 Jim Clancy .15
120 John Castino .15
121 Dave Concepcion .15
122 Greg Luzinski .15
123 Mike Boddicker **RC** .15
124 Pete Ladd .15
125 Juan Berenguer .15
126 John Montefusco .15
127 Ed Jurak .15
128 Tom Niedenfuer .15
129 Bert Blyleven .25
130 Bud Black .15
131 Gorman Heimueller .15
132 Dan Schatzeder .15
133 Ron Jackson .15
134 Tom Henke **RC** 1.00
135 Kevin Hickey .15
136 Mike Scott .15
137 Bo Diaz .15
138 Glenn Brummer .15
139 Sid Monge .15
140 Rich Gale .15
141 Brett Butler .15
142 Brian Harper .15
143 John Rabb .15
144 Gary Woods .15
145 Pat Putnam .15
146 Jim Acker **RC** .15
147 Mickey Hatcher .15
148 Todd Cruz .15
149 Tom Tellmann .15
150 John Wockenfuss .15
151 Wade Boggs 5.00
152 Don Baylor .15
153 Bob Welch .15
154 Alan Bannister .15
155 Willie Aikens .15
156 Jeff Burroughs .15
157 Bryan Little .15
158 Bob Boone .15
159 Dave Hostetler .15
160 Jerry Dybzinski .15
161 Mike Madden .15
162 Luis DeLeon .15
163 Willie Hernandez .15
164 Frank Pastore .15
165 Rick Camp .15
166 Lee Mazzilli .15
167 Scot Thompson .15
168 Bob Forsch .15
169 Mike Flanagan .15
170 Rick Manning .15
171 Chet Lemon .15
172 Jerry Remy .15
173 Ron Guidry .20
174 Pedro Guerrero .15
175 Willie Wilson .15
176 Carney Lansford .15
177 Al Oliver .15
178 Jim Sundberg .15
179 Bobby Grich .15
180 Richard Dotson .15
181 Joaquin Andujar .15
182 Jose Cruz .15
183 Mike Schmidt 5.00
184 Gary Redus **RC** .25
185 Garry Templeton .15
186 Tony Pena .15
187 Greg Minton .15
188 Phil Niekro 1.50
189 Fergie Jenkins 1.50
190 Mookie Wilson .15
191 Jim Beattie .15
192 Gary Ward .15
193 Jesse Barfield .15
194 Pete Filson .15
195 Roy Lee Jackson .15
196 Rick Sweet .15
197 Jesse Orosco .15
198 Steve Lake **RC** .15
199 Ken Dayley .15
200 Manny Sarmiento .15
201 Mark Davis **RC** .15
202 Tim Flannery .15
203 Bill Scherrer .15
204 Al Holland .15
205 David Von Ohlen .15
206 Mike LaCoss .15
207 Juan Beniquez .15
208 Juan Agosto **RC** .15
209 Bobby Ramos .15
210 Al Bumbry .15
211 Mark Brouhard .15
212 Howard Bailey .15
213 Bruce Hurst .15
214 Bob Shirley .15
215 Pat Zachry .15
216 Julio Franco .15
217 Mike Armstrong .15
218 Dave Beard .15
219 Steve Rogers .15
220 John Butcher .15
221 Mike Smithson **RC** .15
222 Frank White .15
223 Mike Heath .15
224 Chris Bando .15
225 Roy Smalley .15
226 Dusty Baker .15
227 Lou Whitaker .15
228 John Lowenstein .15
229 Ben Oglivie .15
230 Doug DeCinces .15
231 Lonnie Smith .15
232 Ray Knight .15
233 Gary Matthews .15
234 Juan Bonilla .15
235 Rod Scurry .15
236 Atlee Hammaker .15
237 Mike Caldwell .15
238 Keith Hernandez .15
239 Larry Bowa .15
240 Tony Bernazard .15
241 Damaso Garcia .15
242 Tom Brunansky .15
243 Dan Driessen .15
244 Ron Kittle **RC** .15
245 Tim Stoddard .15
246 Bob L. Gibson .15
247 Marty Castillo .15
248 Don Mattingly **RC** 25.00
249 Jeff Newman .15
250 Alejandro Pena **RC** .15
251 Toby Harrah .15
252 Cesar Geronimo .15
253 Tom Underwood .15
254 Doug Flynn .15
255 Andy Hassler .15
256 Odell Jones .15
257 Rudy Law .15
258 Harry Spilman .15
259 Marty Bystrom .15
260 Dave Rucker .15
261 Ruppert Jones .15
262 Jeff Jones .15
263 Gerald Perry **RC** .15
264 Gene Tenace .15
265 Brad Wellman .15
266 Dickie Noles .15
267 Jamie Allen .15
268 Jim Gott .15
269 Ron Davis .15
270 Benny Ayala .15
271 Ned Yost .15
272 Dave Rozema .15
273 Dave Stapleton .15
274 Lou Piniella .25
275 Jose Morales .15
276 Brod Perkins .15
277 Butch Davis .15
278 Tony Phillips .15
279 Jeff Reardon .15
280 Ken Forsch .15
281 Pete O'Brien **RC** .15
282 Tom Paciorek .15
283 Frank LaCorte .15
284 Tim Lollar .15
285 Greg Gross .15
286 Alex Trevino .15
287 Gene Garber .15
288 Dave Parker .15
289 Lee Smith .25
290 Dave LaPoint .15
291 John Shelby **RC** .15
292 Charlie Moore .15
293 Alan Trammell .15
294 Tony Armas .15
295 Shane Rawley .15
296 Greg Brock .15
297 Hal McRae .15
298 Mike Davis .15
299 Tim Raines .15
300 Bucky Dent .15
301 Tommy John .25
302 Carlton Fisk 3.00
303 Darrell Porter .15
304 Dickie Thon .15
305 Garry Maddox .15
306 Cesar Cedeno .15
307 Gary Lucas .15
308 Johnny Ray .15
309 Andy McGaffigan .15
310 Claudell Washington .15
311 Ryne Sandberg 5.00
312 George Foster .15
313 Spike Owen **RC** .25
314 Gary Gaetti .15
315 Willie Upshaw .15
316 Al Williams .15
317 Jorge Orta .15
318 Orlando Mercado .15
319 Junior Ortiz **RC** .15
320 Mike Proly .15
321 Randy S. Johnson .15
322 Jim Morrison .15
323 Max Venable .15
324 Tony Gwynn 5.00
325 Duane Walker .15
326 Ozzie Virgil .15
327 Jeff Lahti .15
328 Bill Dawley **RC** .15
329 Rob Wilfong .15
330 Marc Hill .15
331 Ray Burris .15
332 Allan Ramirez .15
333 Chuck Porter .15
334 Wayne Krenchicki .15
335 Gary Allenson .15
336 Bob Meacham **RC** .15
337 Joe Beckwith .15
338 Rick Sutcliffe .15
339 Mark Huismann **RC** .15
340 Tim Conroy **RC** .15
341 Scott Sanderson .15
342 Larry Biittner .15
343 Dave Stewart .15
344 Darryl Motley .15
345 Chris Codiroli **RC** .15
346 Rick Behenna .15
347 Andre Robertson .15
348 Mike Marshall .15
349 Larry Herndon .15
350 Rich Dauer .15
351 Cecil Cooper .15
352 Rod Carew 3.00
353 Willie McGee .15
354 Phil Garner .15
355 Joe Morgan 3.00
356 Luis Salazar .15
357 John Candelaria .15
358 Bill Laskey .15
359 Bob McClure .15
360 Dave Kingman .15
361 Ron Cey .15
362 Matt Young **RC** .15
363 Lloyd Moseby .15
364 Frank Viola .15
365 Eddie Milner .15
366 Floyd Bannister .15
367 Dan Ford .15
368 Moose Haas .15
369 Doug Bair .15
370 Ray Fontenot **RC** .15
371 Luis Aponte .15
372 Jack Fimple .15
373 Neal Heaton **RC** .15
374 Greg Pryor .15
375 Wayne Gross .15
376 Charlie Lea .15
377 Steve Lubratich .15
378 Jon Matlack .15
379 Julio Cruz .15
380 John Mizerock .15
381 Kevin Gross **RC** .15
382 Mike Ramsey .15
383 Doug Gwosdz .15
384 Kelly Paris .15
385 Pete Falcone .15
386 Milt May .15
387 Fred Breining .15
388 Craig Lefferts **RC** .25
389 Steve Henderson .15
390 Randy Moffitt .15
391 Ron Washington .15
392 Gary Roenicke .15
393 Tom Candiotti **RC** .75
394 Larry Pashnick .15
395 Dwight Evans .15
396 Goose Gossage .25
397 Derrel Thomas .15
398 Juan Eichelberger .15
399 Leon Roberts .15
400 Davey Lopes .15
401 Bill Gullickson .15
402 Geoff Zahn .15
403 Billy Sample .15
404 Mike Squires .15
405 Craig Reynolds .15
406 Eric Show .15
407 John Denny .15
408 Dann Bilardello .15
409 Bruce Benedict .15
410 Kent Tekulve .15
411 Mel Hall .15
412 John Stuper .15
413 Rick Dempsey .15
414 Don Sutton 1.50
415 Jack Morris .15
416 John Tudor .15
417 Willie Randolph .15
418 Jerry Reuss .15
419 Don Slaught .15
420 Steve McCatty .15
421 Tim Wallach .15
422 Larry Parrish .15
423 Brian Downing .15
424 Britt Burns .15
425 David Green .15
426 Jerry Mumphrey .15
427 Ivan DeJesus .15
428 Mario Soto .15
429 Gene Richards .15
430 Dale Berra .15
431 Darrell Evans .15
432 Glenn Hubbard .15
433 Jody Davis .15
434 Danny Heep .15
435 Ed Nunez **RC** .15
436 Bobby Castillo .15
437 Ernie Whitt .15
438 Scott Ullger .15
439 Doyle Alexander .15
440 Domingo Ramos .15
441 Craig Swan .15
442 Warren Brusstar .15
443 Len Barker .15
444 Mike Easler .15
445 Renie Martin .15
446 Dennis Rasmussen **RC** .25
447 Ted Power **RC** .15
448 Charlie Hudson **RC** .15
449 Danny Cox **RC** .15
450 Kevin Bass **RC** .15
451 Daryl Sconiers .15
452 Scott Fletcher .15
453 Bryn Smith .15
454 Jim Dwyer .15
455 Rob Picciolo .15
456 Enos Cabell .15
457 Dennis Boyd **RC** .20
458 Butch Wynegar .15
459 Burt Hooton .15
460 Ron Hassey .15
461 Danny Jackson **RC** .15
462 Bob Kearney .15
463 Terry Francona .15
464 Wayne Tolleson .15
465 Mickey Rivers .15
466 John Wathan .15
467 Bill Almon .15
468 George Vukovich .15
469 Steve Kemp .15
470 Ken Landreaux .15
471 Milt Wilcox .15
472 Tippy Martinez .15
473 Ted Simmons .15
474 Tim Foli .15
475 George Hendrick .15
476 Terry Puhl .15
477 Von Hayes .15
478 Bobby Brown .15
479 Lee Lacy .15
480 Joel Youngblood .15
481 Jim Slaton .15
482 Mike Fitzgerald **RC** .15
483 Keith Moreland .15
484 Ron Roenicke .15
485 Luis Leal .15
486 Bryan Oelkers .15
487 Bruce Berenyi .15
488 LaMarr Hoyt .15
489 Joe Nolan .15
490 Marshall Edwards .15
491 Mike Laga **RC** .15
492 Rick Cerone .15
493 Mike Miller (Rick) .15
494 Rick Honeycutt .15
495 Mike Hargrove .15
496 Joe Simpson .15
497 Keith Atherton **RC** .15
498 Chris Welsh .15
499 Bruce Kison .15
500 Bob Johnson .15
501 Jerry Koosman .15
502 Frank DiPino .15
503 Tony Perez 2.00
504 Ken Oberkfell .15
505 Mark Thurmond **RC** .15
506 Joe Price .15
507 Pascual Perez .15
508 Marvell Wynne **RC** .15
509 Mike Krukow .15
510 Dick Ruthven .15
511 Al Cowens .15
512 Cliff Johnson .15
513 Randy Bush **RC** .15
514 Sammy Stewart .15
515 Bill Schroeder **RC** .15
516 Aurelio Lopez .15
517 Mike Brown .15
518 Graig Nettles .25
519 Dave Sax .15
520 Gerry Willard .15
521 Paul Splittorff .15
522 Tom Burgmeier .15
523 Chris Speier .15
524 Bobby Clark .15
525 George Wright .15
526 Dennis Lamp .15
527 Tony Scott .15
528 Ed Whitson .15
529 Ron Reed .15
530 Charlie Puleo .15
531 Jerry Royster .15
532 Don Robinson .15
533 Steve Trout .15
534 Bruce Sutter 2.50
535 Bob Horner .15
536 Pat Tabler .15
537 Chris Chambliss .15
538 Bob Ojeda .15
539 Alan Ashby .15
540 Jay Johnstone .15
541 Bob Dernier .15
542 Brook Jacoby **RC** .15
543 U.L. Washington .15
544 Danny Darwin .15
545 Kiko Garcia .15
546 Vance Law .15
547 Tug McGraw .15
548 Dave Smith .15
549 Len Matuszek .15
550 Tom Hume .15
551 Dave Dravecky .15
552 Rick Rhoden .15
553 Duane Kuiper .15
554 Rusty Staub .20
555 Bill Campbell .15
556 Mike Torrez .15
557 Dave Henderson **RC** .15
558 Len Whitehouse .15
559 Barry Bonnell .15
560 Rick Lysander .15
561 Garth Iorg .15
562 Bryan Clark .15
563 Brian Giles .15
564 Vern Ruhle .15
565 Steve Bedrosian .15
566 Larry McWilliams .15
567 Jeff Leonard .15
568 Alan Wiggins .15
569 Jeff Russell **RC** .15
570 Salome Barojas .15
571 Dane Iorg .15
572 Bob Knepper .15
573 Gary Lavelle .15
574 Gorman Thomas .15
575 Manny Trillo .15
576 Jim Palmer 3.00
577 Dale Murray .15
578 Tom Brookens .15
579 Rich Gedman .15
580 Bill Doran **RC** .25
581 Steve Yeager .15
582 Dan Spillner .15
583 Dan Quisenberry .15
584 Rance Mulliniks .15
585 Storm Davis .15
586 Dave Schmidt .15
587 Bill Russell .15
588 Pat Sheridan **RC** .15
589 Rafael Ramirez .15
590 Bud Anderson .15
591 George Frazier .15
592 Lee Tunnell **RC** .15
593 Kirk Gibson .15
594 Scott McGregor .15
595 Bob Bailor .15
596 Tom Herr .15
597 Luis Sanchez .15
598 Dave Engle .15
599 Craig McMurtry **RC** .15
600 Carlos Diaz .15
601 Tom O'Malley .15
602 Nick Esasky **RC** .15
603 Ron Hodges .15
604 Ed Vande Berg .15
605 Alfredo Griffin .15
606 Glenn Hoffman .15
607 Hubie Brooks .15
608 Richard Barnes (Photo actually Neal Heaton.) .15
609 Greg Walker **RC** .15
610 Ken Singleton .15
611 Mark Clear .15
612 Buck Martinez .15
613 Ken Griffey .20
614 Reid Nichols .15
615 Doug Sisk **RC** .15
616 Bob Brenly .15
617 Joey McLaughlin .15
618 Glenn Wilson .15
619 Bob Stoddard .15
620 Len Sakata (Lenn) .15
621 Mike Young **RC** .15
622 John Stefero .15
623 Carmelo Martinez **RC** .15
624 Dave Bergman .15
625 Runnin' Reds (David Green, Willie McGee, Lonnie Smith, Ozzie Smith) .75
626 Rudy May .15
627 Matt Keough .15
628 Jose DeLeon **RC** .15
629 Jim Essian .15
630 Darnell Coles **RC** .15
631 Mike Warren .15
632 Del Crandall .15
633 Dennis Martinez .15
634 Mike Moore .15
635 Lary Sorensen .15
636 Ricky Nelson .15
637 Omar Moreno .15
638 Charlie Hough .15
639 Dennis Eckersley 2.50
640 Walt Terrell **RC** .15
641 Denny Walling .15
642 Dave Anderson **RC** .15
643 Jose Oquendo **RC** .15
644 Bob Stanley .15
645 Dave Geisel .15
646 Scott Garrelts **RC** .15
647 Gary Pettis **RC** .15
648 Duke Snider Puzzle Card .15
649 Johnnie LeMaster .15
650 Dave Collins .15
651 San Diego Chicken .25
---- Checklist 1-26 DK (Perez-Steel on back.) .15
---- Checklist 1-26 DK (Perez-Steele on back.) .15
---- Checklist 27-130 .15
---- Checklist 131-234 .15
---- Checklist 235-338 .15
---- Checklist 339-442 .15
---- Checklist 443-546 .15
---- Checklist 547-651 .15

Action All-Stars

Full-color photos on the card fronts and backs make the 1984 Donruss Action All-Stars set somewhat unusual. Fronts contain a large action photo plus the Donruss logo and year of issue inside a deep red border. The top half of the backs features a close-up photo with the bottom portion containing biographical and statistical information. The 3-1/2" x 5" cards were sold with Ted Williams puzzle pieces.

NM/M
Complete Set (60): 4.00
Common Player: .05
Ted Williams Puzzle: 2.50
Cello Pack (5): .75
Cello Box (36): 12.50
1 Gary Lavelle .05
2 Willie McGee .05
3 Tony Pena .05
4 Lou Whitaker .05
5 Robin Yount .40
6 Doug DeCinces .05
7 John Castino .05
8 Terry Kennedy .05
9 Rickey Henderson .40
10 Bob Horner .05
11 Harold Baines .05
12 Buddy Bell .05
13 Fernando Valenzuela .05
14 Nolan Ryan 1.00
15 Andre Thornton .05
16 Gary Redus .05
17 Pedro Guerrero .05
18 Andre Dawson .25
19 Dave Stieb .05
20 Cal Ripken, Jr. 1.00
21 Ken Griffey .05
22 Wade Boggs .50
23 Keith Hernandez .05
24 Steve Carlton .40
25 Hal McRae .05
26 John Lowenstein .05
27 Fred Lynn .05
28 Bill Buckner .05
29 Chris Chambliss .05
30 Richie Zisk .05
31 Jack Clark .05
32 George Hendrick .05
33 Bill Madlock .05
34 Lance Parrish .05
35 Paul Molitor .40
36 Reggie Jackson .60
37 Kent Hrbek .05
38 Steve Garvey .15
39 Carney Lansford .05
40 Dale Murphy .15
41 Greg Luzinski .05
42 Larry Parrish .05
43 Ryne Sandberg .50
44 Dickie Thon .05
45 Bert Blyleven .05
46 Ron Oester .05
47 Dusty Baker .05
48 Steve Rogers .05
49 Jim Clancy .05
50 Eddie Murray .40
51 Ron Guidry .05
52 Jim Rice .20
53 Tom Seaver .40
54 Pete Rose .75
55 George Brett .60
56 Dan Quisenberry .05
57 Mike Schmidt .60
58 Ted Simmons .05
59 Dave Righetti .05
60 Checklist .05

Champions

The Champions set includes 10 Hall of Famers, 49 current players and a numbered checklist. Hall of Famers' cards (called Grand Champions) feature the artwork of Dick Perez, while cards of the current players (called Champions) are color photos. All cards measure 3-1/2" x 5". The Grand Champions represent hallmarks of excellence in various statistical categories, while the Champions are the leaders among then-active players in each category. The cards were issued with Duke Snider puzzle pieces.

NM/M
Complete Set (60): 4.00
Common Player: .10
Duke Snider Puzzle: 2.00
Pack (5): .75
Box (36): 12.50
1 Babe Ruth 1.25
2 George Foster .10

3 Dave Kingman .10
4 Jim Rice .25
5 Gorman Thomas .10
6 Ben Oglivie .10
7 Jeff Burroughs .10
8 Hank Aaron .75
9 Reggie Jackson .60
10 Carl Yastrzemski .50
11 Mike Schmidt .60
12 Graig Nettles .10
13 Greg Luzinski .10
14 Ted Williams .75
15 George Brett .60
16 Wade Boggs .50
17 Hal McRae .10
18 Bill Buckner .10
19 Eddie Murray .35
20 Rogers Hornsby .10
21 Rod Carew .35
22 Bill Madlock .10
23 Lonnie Smith .10
24 Cecil Cooper .10
25 Ken Griffey .10
26 Ty Cobb .60
27 Pete Rose .75
28 Rusty Staub .10
29 Tony Perez .15
30 Al Oliver .10
31 Cy Young .25
32 Gaylord Perry .15
33 Ferguson Jenkins .15
34 Phil Niekro .15
35 Jim Palmer .15
36 Tommy John .10
37 Walter Johnson .25
38 Steve Carlton .15
39 Nolan Ryan 1.25
40 Tom Seaver .35
41 Don Sutton .15
42 Bert Blyleven .15
43 Frank Robinson .35
44 Joe Morgan .35
45 Rollie Fingers .15
46 Keith Hernandez .10
47 Robin Yount .35
48 Cal Ripken, Jr. 1.25
49 Dale Murphy .15
50 Mickey Mantle 1.50
51 Johnny Bench .50
52 Carlton Fisk .35
53 Tug McGraw .10
54 Paul Molitor .35
55 Carl Hubbell .10
56 Steve Garvey .15
57 Dave Parker .10
58 Gary Carter .35
59 Fred Lynn .10
60 Checklist .05

1985 Donruss Promo Sheet

To introduce its design for 1985, Donruss distributed this 8-1/2" x 11" paper sample sheet to dealers. The blank-back sheet has examples of nine Donruss cards from the '85 set. Players are listed here in alphabetical order.

NM/M

Complete Sheet: 8.00

1985 Donruss

The black-bordered 1985 Donruss set includes 653 numbered cards and seven unnumbered checklists. Displaying the artwork of Dick Perez for the fourth consecutive year, cards #1-26 feature the Diamond Kings series. Donruss, reacting to the hobby craze over rookie cards, included a Rated Rookies subset (cards #27-46). The cards, in standard 2-1/2" x 3-1/2", were issued with a Lou Gehrig puzzle. Backs repeat the format of previous years with black print on yellow and white. The complete set price does not include the higher priced variations. (DK) and (RR) refer to the Diamond Kings and Rated Rookies subsets.

NM/M

Unopened Fact. Set (660): 75.00
Complete Set (660): 50.00
Common Player: .10
Lou Gehrig Puzzle: 3.00
Wax Pack (15): 4.00
Wax Box (36): 120.00
Rack Pack (45): 7.00

1 Ryne Sandberg/DK 2.50
2 Doug DeCinces/DK .10
3 Rich Dotson/DK .10
4 Bert Blyleven/DK .25
5 Lou Whitaker/DK .10
6 Dan Quisenberry/DK .10
7 Don Mattingly/DK 4.00
8 Carney Lansford/DK .10
9 Frank Tanana/DK .10
10 Willie Upshaw/DK .10
11 Claudell Washington/DK .10
12 Mike Marshall/DK .10
13 Joaquin Andujar/DK .10
14 Cal Ripken, Jr./DK 6.00
15 Jim Rice/DK .75
16 Don Sutton/DK 1.00
17 Frank Viola/DK .10
18 Alvin Davis/DK .10
19 Mario Soto/DK .10
20 Jose Cruz/DK .10
21 Charlie Lea/DK .10
22 Jesse Orosco/DK .10
23 Juan Samuel/DK **RC** .10
24 Tony Pena/DK .10
25 Tony Gwynn/DK 2.50
26 Bob Brenly/DK .10
27 Danny Tartabull/RR **RC** 1.50
28 Mike Bielecki/RR **RC** .10
29 Steve Lyons/RR **RC** .25
30 Jeff Reed/RR **RC** .10
31 Tony Brewer/RR .10
32 John Morris/RR **RC** .10
33 Daryl Boston/RR **RC** .15
34 Alfonso Pulido/RR .10
35 Steve Kiefer/RR **RC** .10
36 Larry Sheets/RR **RC** .10
37 Scott Bradley/RR **RC** .10
38 Calvin Schiraldi/RR **RC** .10
39 Shawon Dunston/RR **RC** 1.50
40 Charlie Mitchell/RR .10
41 Billy Hatcher/RR **RC** .15
42 Russ Stephans/RR .10
43 Alejandro Sanchez/RR .10
44 Steve Jeltz/RR **RC** .10
45 Jim Traber/RR **RC** .10
46 Doug Loman/RR .10
47 Eddie Murray 2.00
48 Robin Yount 2.00
49 Lance Parrish .10
50 Jim Rice .75
51 Dave Winfield 2.00
52 Fernando Valenzuela .10
53 George Brett 3.00
54 Dave Kingman .10
55 Gary Carter 2.00
56 Buddy Bell .10
57 Reggie Jackson 3.00
58 Harold Baines .10
59 Ozzie Smith 2.00
60 Nolan Ryan 6.00
61 Mike Schmidt 3.00
62 Dave Parker .10
63 Tony Gwynn 2.50
64 Tony Pena .10
65 Jack Clark .10
66 Dale Murphy .60
67 Ryne Sandberg 2.50
68 Keith Hernandez .10
69 Alvin Davis .10
70 Kent Hrbek .10
71 Willie Upshaw .10
72 Dave Engle .10
73 Alfredo Griffin .10
74a Jack Perconte (Last line of highlights begins "Batted .346...") .10
74b Jack Perconte (Last line of highlights begins "Led the ...") .15
75 Jesse Orosco .10
76 Jody Davis .10
77 Bob Horner .10
78 Larry McWilliams .10
79 Joel Youngblood .10
80 Alan Wiggins .10
81 Ron Oester .10
82 Ozzie Virgil .10
83 Ricky Horton **RC** .10
84 Bill Doran .10
85 Rod Carew 2.00
86 LaMarr Hoyt .10
87 Tim Wallach .10
88 Mike Flanagan .10
89 Jim Sundberg .10
90 Chet Lemon .10
91 Bob Stanley .10
92 Willie Randolph .10
93 Bill Russell .10
94 Julio Franco .10
95 Dan Quisenberry .10
96 Bill Caudill .10
97 Bill Gullickson .10
98 Danny Darwin .10
99 Curtis Wilkerson .10
100 Bud Black .10
101 Tony Phillips .10
102 Tony Bernazard .10
103 Jay Howell .10
104 Burt Hooton .10
105 Milt Wilcox .10
106 Rich Dauer .10
107 Don Sutton 1.00
108 Mike Witt .10
109 Bruce Sutter 1.50
110 Enos Cabell .10
111 John Denny .10
112 Dave Dravecky .10
113 Marvell Wynne .10
114 Johnnie LeMaster .10
115 Chuck Porter .10
116 John Gibbons .10
117 Keith Moreland .10
118 Darnell Coles .10
119 Dennis Lamp .10
120 Ron Davis .10
121 Nick Esasky .10
122 Vance Law .10
123 Gary Roenicke .10
124 Bill Schroeder .10
125 Dave Rozema .10
126 Bobby Meacham .10
127 Marty Barrett **RC** .10
128 R.J. Reynolds **RC** .15
129 Ernie Camacho .10
130 Jorge Orta .10
131 Lary Sorensen .10
132 Terry Francona .10
133 Fred Lynn .10
134 Bobby Jones .10
135 Jerry Hairston Sr. .10
136 Kevin Bass .10
137 Garry Maddox .10
138 Dave LaPoint .10
139 Kevin McReynolds .10
140 Wayne Krenchicki .10
141 Rafael Ramirez .10
142 Rod Scurry .10
143 Greg Minton .10
144 Tim Stoddard .10
145 Steve Henderson .10
146 George Bell .10
147 Dave Meier .10
148 Sammy Stewart .10
149 Mark Brouhard .10
150 Larry Herndon .10
151 Oil Can Boyd .10
152 Brian Dayett .10
153 Tom Niedenfuer .10
154 Brook Jacoby .10
155 Onix Concepcion .10
156 Tim Conroy .10
157 Joe Hesketh **RC** .15
158 Brian Downing .10
159 Tommy Dunbar .10
160 Marc Hill .10
161 Phil Garner .10
162 Jerry Davis .10
163 Bill Campbell .10
164 John Franco **RC** 1.50
165 Len Barker .10
166 Benny Distefano **RC** .10
167 George Frazier .10
168 Tito Landrum .10
169 Cal Ripken, Jr. 6.00
170 Cecil Cooper .10
171 Alan Trammell .10
172 Wade Boggs 2.50
173 Don Baylor .10
174 Pedro Guerrero .10
175 Frank White .10
176 Rickey Henderson 2.00
177 Charlie Lea .10
178 Pete O'Brien .10
179 Doug DeCinces .10
180 Ron Kittle .10
181 George Hendrick .10
182 Joe Niekro .10
183 Juan Samuel **RC** .10
184 Mario Soto .10
185 Goose Gossage .15
186 Johnny Ray .10
187 Bob Brenly .10
188 Craig McMurtry .10
189 Leon Durham .10
190 Dwight Gooden .25
191 Barry Bonnell .10
192 Tim Teufel .10
193 Dave Stieb .10
194 Mickey Hatcher .10
195 Jesse Barfield .10
196 Al Cowens .10
197 Hubie Brooks .10
198 Steve Trout .10
199 Glenn Hubbard .10
200 Bill Madlock .10
201 Jeff Robinson **RC** .10
202 Eric Show .10
203 Dave Concepcion .10
204 Ivan DeJesus .10
205 Neil Allen .10
206 Jerry Mumphrey .10
207 Mike Brown .10
208 Carlton Fisk 2.00
209 Bryn Smith .10
210 Tippy Martinez .10
211 Dion James .10
212 Willie Hernandez .10
213 Mike Easler .10
214 Ron Guidry .10
215 Rick Honeycutt .10
216 Brett Butler .10
217 Larry Gura .10
218 Ray Burris .10
219 Steve Rogers .10
220 Frank Tanana .10
221 Ned Yost .10
222 Bret Saberhagen .25
223 Mike Davis .10
224 Bert Blyleven .15
225 Steve Kemp .10
226 Jerry Reuss .10
227 Darrell Evans .10
228 Wayne Gross .10
229 Jim Gantner .10
230 Bob Boone .10
231 Lonnie Smith .10
232 Frank DiPino .10
233 Jerry Koosman .10
234 Graig Nettles .15
235 John Tudor .10
236 John Rabb .10
237 Rick Manning .10
238 Mike Fitzgerald .10
239 Gary Matthews .10
240 Jim Presley **RC** .10
241 Dave Collins .10
242 Gary Gaetti .10
243 Dann Bilardello .10
244 Rudy Law .10
245 John Lowenstein .10
246 Tom Tellmann .10
247 Howard Johnson .10
248 Ray Fontenot .10
249 Tony Armas .10
250 Candy Maldonado .10
251 Mike Jeffcoat **RC** .10
252 Dane Iorg .10
253 Bruce Bochte .10
254 Pete Rose 5.00
255 Don Aase .10
256 George Wright .10
257 Britt Burns .10
258 Mike Scott .10
259 Len Matuszek .10
260 Dave Rucker .10
261 Craig Lefferts .10
262 Jay Tibbs **RC** .10
263 Bruce Benedict .10
264 Don Robinson .10
265 Gary Lavelle .10
266 Scott Sanderson .10
267 Matt Young .10
268 Ernie Whitt .10
269 Houston Jimenez .10
270 Ken Dixon **RC** .10
271 Peter Ladd .10
272 Juan Berenguer .10
273 Roger Clemens 25.00
274 Rick Cerone .10
275 Dave Anderson .10
276 George Vukovich .10
277 Greg Pryor .10
278 Mike Warren .10
279 Bob James .10
280 Bobby Grich .10
281 Mike Mason **RC** .10
282 Ron Reed .10
283 Alan Ashby .10
284 Mark Thurmond .10
285 Joe Lefebvre .10
286 Ted Power .10
287 Chris Chambliss .10
288 Lee Tunnell .10
289 Rich Bordi .10
290 Glenn Brummer .10
291 Mike Boddicker .10
292 Rollie Fingers 1.00
293 Lou Whitaker .10
294 Dwight Evans .10
295 Don Mattingly 5.00
296 Mike Marshall .10
297 Willie Wilson .10
298 Mike Heath .10
299 Tim Raines .10
300 Larry Parrish .10
301 Geoff Zahn .10
302 Rich Dotson .10
303 David Green .10
304 Jose Cruz .10
305 Steve Carlton 2.00
306 Gary Redus .10
307 Steve Garvey .40
308 Jose DeLeon .10
309 Randy Lerch .10
310 Claudell Washington .10
311 Lee Smith .25
312 Darryl Strawberry .10
313 Jim Beattie .10
314 John Butcher .10
315 Damaso Garcia .10
316 Mike Smithson .10
317 Luis Leal .10
318 Ken Phelps **RC** .10
319 Wally Backman .10
320 Ron Cey .10
321 Brad Komminsk .10
322 Jason Thompson .10
323 Frank Williams **RC** .10
324 Tim Lollar .10
325 Eric Davis **RC** 1.50
326 Von Hayes .10
327 Andy Van Slyke .10
328 Craig Reynolds .10
329 Dick Schofield .10
330 Scott Fletcher .10
331 Jeff Reardon .10
332 Rick Dempsey .10
333 Ben Oglivie .10
334 Dan Petry .10
335 Jackie Gutierrez .10
336 Dave Righetti .10
337 Alejandro Pena .10
338 Mel Hall .10
339 Pat Sheridan .10
340 Keith Atherton .10
341 David Palmer .10
342 Gary Ward .10
343 Dave Stewart .10
344 Mark Gubicza **RC** .50
345 Carney Lansford .10
346 Jerry Willard .10
347 Ken Griffey .10
348 Franklin Stubbs **RC** .10
349 Aurelio Lopez .10
350 Al Bumbry .10
351 Charlie Moore .10
352 Luis Sanchez .10
353 Darrell Porter .10
354 Bill Dawley .10
355 Charlie Hudson .10
356 Garry Templeton .10
357 Cecilio Guante .10
358 Jeff Leonard .10
359 Paul Molitor 2.00
360 Ron Gardenhire .10
361 Larry Bowa .10
362 Bob Kearney .10
363 Garth Iorg .10
364 Tom Brunansky .10
365 Brad Gulden .10
366 Greg Walker .10
367 Mike Young .10
368 Rick Waits .10
369 Doug Bair .10
370 Bob Shirley .10
371 Bob Ojeda .10
372 Bob Welch .10
373 Neal Heaton .10
374 Danny Jackson (Photo actually Steve Farr.) .10
375 Donnie Hill .10
376 Mike Stenhouse .10
377 Bruce Kison .10
378 Wayne Tolleson .10
379 Floyd Bannister .10
380 Vern Ruhle .10
381 Tim Corcoran .10
382 Kurt Kepshire .10
383 Bobby Brown .10
384 Dave Van Gorder .10
385 Rick Mahler .10
386 Lee Mazzilli .10
387 Bill Laskey .10
388 Thad Bosley .10
389 Al Chambers .10
390 Tony Fernandez .10
391 Ron Washington .10
392 Bill Swaggerty .10
393 Bob L. Gibson .10
394 Marty Castillo .10
395 Steve Crawford .10
396 Clay Christiansen .10
397 Bob Bailor .10
398 Mike Hargrove .10
399 Charlie Leibrandt .10
400 Tom Burgmeier .10
401 Razor Shines .10
402 Rob Wilfong .10
403 Tom Henke .10
404 Al Jones .10
405 Mike LaCoss .10
406 Luis DeLeon .10
407 Greg Gross .10
408 Tom Hume .10
409 Rick Camp .10
410 Milt May .10
411 Henry Cotto **RC** .10
412 Dave Von Ohlen .10
413 Scott McGregor .10
414 Ted Simmons .10
415 Jack Morris .10
416 Bill Buckner .10
417 Butch Wynegar .10
418 Steve Sax .10
419 Steve Balboni .10
420 Dwayne Murphy .10
421 Andre Dawson .65
422 Charlie Hough .10
423 Tommy John .15
424a Tom Seaver (Floyd Bannister photo, left-hander.) 2.00
424b Tom Seaver (Correct photo.) 7.50
425 Tom Herr .10
426 Terry Puhl .10
427 Al Holland .10
428 Eddie Milner .10
429 Terry Kennedy .10
430 John Candelaria .10
431 Manny Trillo .10
432 Ken Oberkfell .10
433 Rick Sutcliffe .10
434 Ron Darling .10
435 Spike Owen .10
436 Frank Viola .10
437 Lloyd Moseby .10
438 Kirby Puckett 8.00
439 Jim Clancy .10
440 Mike Moore .10
441 Doug Sisk .10
442 Dennis Eckersley 1.50
443 Gerald Perry .10
444 Dale Berra .10
445 Dusty Baker .10
446 Ed Whitson .10
447 Cesar Cedeno .10
448 Rick Schu **RC** .10
449 Joaquin Andujar .10
450 Mark Bailey **RC** .10
451 Ron Romanick **RC** .10
452 Julio Cruz .10
453 Miguel Dilone .10
454 Storm Davis .10
455 Jaime Cocanower .10
456 Barbaro Garbey .10
457 Rich Gedman .10
458 Phil Niekro 1.00
459 Mike Scioscia .10
460 Pat Tabler .10
461 Darryl Motley .10
462 Chris Codoroli (Codiroli) .10
463 Doug Flynn .10
464 Billy Sample .10
465 Mickey Rivers .10
466 John Wathan .10
467 Bill Krueger .10
468 Andre Thornton .10
469 Rex Hudler .10
470 Sid Bream **RC** .25
471 Kirk Gibson .10
472 John Shelby .10
473 Moose Haas .10
474 Doug Corbett .10
475 Willie McGee .10
476 Bob Knepper .10
477 Kevin Gross .10
478 Carmelo Martinez .10
479 Kent Tekulve .10
480 Chili Davis .10
481 Bobby Clark .10
482 Mookie Wilson .10
483 Dave Owen .10
484 Ed Nunez .10
485 Rance Mulliniks .10
486 Ken Schrom .10
487 Jeff Russell .10
488 Tom Paciorek .10
489 Dan Ford .10
490 Mike Caldwell .10
491 Scottie Earl .10
492 Jose Rijo .10
493 Bruce Hurst .10
494 Ken Landreaux .10
495 Mike Fischlin .10
496 Don Slaught .10
497 Steve McCatty .10
498 Gary Lucas .10
499 Gary Pettis .10
500 Marvis Foley .10
501 Mike Squires .10
502 Jim Pankovitz **RC** .10
503 Luis Aguayo .10
504 Ralph Citarella .10
505 Bruce Bochy .10
506 Bob Owchinko .10
507 Pascual Perez .10
508 Lee Lacy .10
509 Atlee Hammaker .10
510 Bob Dernier .10
511 Ed Vande Berg .10
512 Cliff Johnson .10
513 Len Whitehouse .10
514 Dennis Martinez .10
515 Ed Romero .10
516 Rusty Kuntz .10
517 Rick Miller .10
518 Dennis Rasmussen .10
519 Steve Yeager .10
520 Chris Bando .10
521 U.L. Washington .10
522 Curt Young **RC** .10
523 Angel Salazar .10
524 Curt Kaufman .10
525 Odell Jones .10
526 Juan Agosto .10
527 Denny Walling .10
528 Andy Hawkins **RC** .10
529 Sixto Lezcano .10
530 Skeeter Barnes .10
531 Randy S. Johnson .10
532 Jim Morrison .10
533 Warren Brusstar .10
534a Jeff Pendleton **RC** (Error) 1.00
534b Terry Pendleton **RC** (Correct) 4.50
535 Vic Rodriguez .10
536 Bob McClure .10
537 Dave Bergman .10
538 Mark Clear .10
539 Mike Pagliarulo **RC** .25
540 Terry Whitfield .10
541 Joe Beckwith .10
542 Jeff Burroughs .10
543 Dan Schatzeder .10
544 Donnie Scott .10

545	Jim Slaton	.10
546	Greg Luzinski	.10
547	Mark Salas **RC**	.10
548	Dave Smith	.10
549	John Wockenfuss	.10
550	Frank Pastore	.10
551	Tim Flannery	.10
552	Rick Rhoden	.10
553	Mark Davis	.10
554	Jeff Dedmon **RC**	.15
555	Gary Woods	.10
556	Danny Heep	.10
557	Mark Langston	.10
558	Darrell Brown	.10
559	Jimmy Key	.10
560	Rick Lysander	.10
561	Doyle Alexander	.10
562	Mike Stanton	.10
563	Sid Fernandez	.10
564	Richie Hebner	.10
565	Alex Trevino	.10
566	Brian Harper	.10
567	Dan Gladden **RC**	.25
568	Luis Salazar	.10
569	Tom Foley	.10
570	Larry Andersen	.10
571	Danny Cox	.10
572	Joe Sambito	.10
573	Juan Beniquez	.10
574	Joel Skinner	.10
575	Randy St. Claire **RC**	.10
576	Floyd Rayford	.10
577	Roy Howell	.10
578	John Grubb	.10
579	Ed Jurak	.10
580	John Montefusco	.10
581	Orel Hershiser **RC**	3.00
582	Tom Waddell **RC**	.10
583	Mark Huismann	.10
584	Joe Morgan	2.00
585	Jim Wohlford	.10
586	Dave Schmidt	.10
587	Jeff Kunkel **RC**	.10
588	Hal McRae	.10
589	Bill Almon	.10
590	Carmen Castillo **RC**	.10
591	Omar Moreno	.10
592	Ken Howell **RC**	.10
593	Tom Brookens	.10
594	Joe Nolan	.10
595	Willie Lozado	.10
596	Tom Nieto **RC**	.10
597	Walt Terrell	.10
598	Al Oliver	.10
599	Shane Rawley	.10
600	Denny Gonzalez **RC**	.10
601	Mark Grant **RC**	.10
602	Mike Armstrong	.10
603	George Foster	.10
604	Davey Lopes	.10
605	Salome Barojas	.10
606	Roy Lee Jackson	.10
607	Pete Filson	.10
608	Duane Walker	.10
609	Glenn Wilson	.10
610	Rafael Santana **RC**	.10
611	Roy Smith	.10
612	Ruppert Jones	.10
613	Joe Cowley **RC**	.10
614	Al Nipper **RC** (Photo actually Mike Brown.)	.15
615	Gene Nelson	.10
616	Joe Carter	.10
617	Ray Knight	.10
618	Chuck Rainey	.10
619	Dan Driessen	.10
620	Daryl Sconiers	.10
621	Bill Stein	.10
622	Roy Smalley	.10
623	Ed Lynch	.10
624	Jeff Stone **RC**	.10
625	Bruce Berenyi	.10
626	Kelvin Chapman	.10
627	Joe Price	.10
628	Steve Bedrosian	.10
629	Vic Mata	.10
630	Mike Krukow	.10
631	Phil Bradley **RC**	.15
632	Jim Gott	.10
633	Randy Bush	.10
634	Tom Browning **RC**	.25
635	Lou Gehrig Puzzle Card	.10
636	Reid Nichols	.10
637	Dan Pasqua **RC**	.25
638	German Rivera	.10
639	Don Schulze **RC**	.10
640a	Mike Jones (Last line of highlights begins "Was 11- 7...")	.10
640b	Mike Jones (Last line of highlights begins "Spent some ...")	.15
641	Pete Rose	4.00
642	Wade Rowdon **RC**	.10
643	Jerry Narron	.10
644	Darrell Miller **RC**	.10
645	Tim Hulett **RC**	.10
646	Andy McGaffigan	.10
647	Kurt Bevacqua	.10
648	John Russell **RC**	.10
649	Ron Robinson **RC**	.10
650	Donnie Moore **RC**	.10
651a	Two for the Title (Don Mattingly, Dave Winfield (Yellow letters.)	3.00
651b	Two for the Title (Don Mattingly, Dave Winfield (White letters.)	4.50
652	Tim Laudner	.10
653	Steve Farr **RC**	.10
----	Checklist 1-26 DK	.10
----	Checklist 27-130	.10
----	Checklist 131-234	.10
----	Checklist 235-338	.10
----	Checklist 339-442	.10
----	Checklist 443-546	.10
----	Checklist 547-653	.10

Box Panels

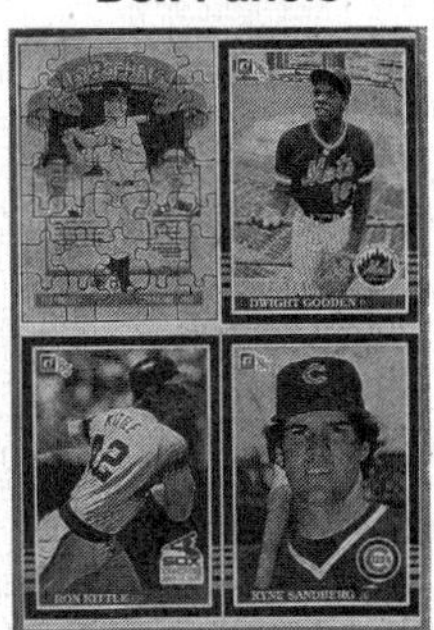

In 1985, Donruss placed on the bottoms of its wax pack boxes a four-card panel which included three player cards and a Lou Gehrig puzzle card. The player cards, numbered PC1 through PC3, have backs identical to the regular 1985 Donruss issue. The card fronts are identical in design to the regular issue, but carry different photos.

		NM/M
Complete Panel:		2.50
Complete Singles Set (4):		2.50
Common Player:		.10
PC1	Dwight Gooden	.25
PC2	Ryne Sandberg	2.50
PC3	Ron Kittle	.10
---	Lou Gehrig (Puzzle card.)	.10

Action All-Stars

In 1985, Donruss issued an Action All-Stars set for the third consecutive year. Card fronts feature an action photo with an inset portrait of the player inside a black border with grey boxes through it. The card backs have black print on blue and white and include statistical and biographical information. The cards were issued with a Lou Gehrig puzzle.

		NM/M
Complete Set (60):		4.00
Common Player:		.05
Lou Gehrig Puzzle:		3.00
Cello Pack (3):		.50
Cello Box (36):		9.00
1	Tim Raines	.05
2	Jim Gantner	.05
3	Mario Soto	.05
4	Spike Owen	.05
5	Lloyd Moseby	.05
6	Damaso Garcia	.05
7	Cal Ripken, Jr.	1.00
8	Dan Quisenberry	.05
9	Eddie Murray	.50
10	Tony Pena	.05
11	Buddy Bell	.05
12	Dave Winfield	.50
13	Ron Kittle	.05
14	Rich Gossage	.05
15	Dwight Evans	.05
16	Al Davis	.05
17	Mike Schmidt	.75
18	Pascual Perez	.05
19	Tony Gwynn	.60
20	Nolan Ryan	1.00
21	Robin Yount	.50
22	Mike Marshall	.05
23	Brett Butler	.05
24	Ryne Sandberg	.60
25	Dale Murphy	.20
26	George Brett	.75
27	Jim Rice	.25
28	Ozzie Smith	.60
29	Larry Parrish	.05
30	Jack Clark	.05
31	Manny Trillo	.05
32	Dave Kingman	.05
33	Geoff Zahn	.05
34	Pedro Guerrero	.05
35	Dave Parker	.05
36	Rollie Fingers	.35
37	Fernando Valenzuela	.05
38	Wade Boggs	.60
39	Reggie Jackson	.75
40	Kent Hrbek	.05
41	Keith Hernandez	.05
42	Lou Whitaker	.05
43	Tom Herr	.05
44	Alan Trammell	.05
45	Butch Wynegar	.05
46	Leon Durham	.05
47	Dwight Gooden	.20
48	Don Mattingly	.75
49	Phil Niekro	.25
50	Johnny Ray	.05
51	Doug DeCinces	.05
52	Willie Upshaw	.05
53	Lance Parrish	.05
54	Jody Davis	.05
55	Steve Carlton	.50
56	Juan Samuel	.05
57	Gary Carter	.50
58	Harold Baines	.05
59	Eric Show	.05
60	Checklist	.04

Diamond Kings Supers

The 1985 Donruss Diamond Kings Supers are enlarged versions of the Diamond Kings cards in the regular 1985 Donruss set. The cards measure 4-15/16" x 6-3/4". The Diamond Kings series features the artwork of Dick Perez. Twenty-eight cards make up the Super set - 26 DK cards, an unnumbered checklist, and an unnumbered Dick Perez card. The back of the Perez card contains a brief history of Dick Perez and the Perez-Steele Galleries. The set could be obtained through a mail-in offer found on wax pack wrappers.

		NM/M
Complete Set (28):		5.00
Common Player:		.10
1	Ryne Sandberg	1.00
2	Doug DeCinces	.10
3	Richard Dotson	.10
4	Bert Blyleven	.10
5	Lou Whitaker	.10
6	Dan Quisenberry	.10
7	Don Mattingly	1.50
8	Carney Lansford	.10
9	Frank Tanana	.10
10	Willie Upshaw	.10
11	Claudell Washington	.10
12	Mike Marshall	.10
13	Joaquin Andujar	.10
14	Cal Ripken, Jr.	2.00
15	Jim Rice	.25
16	Don Sutton	.50
17	Frank Viola	.10
18	Alvin Davis	.10
19	Mario Soto	.10
20	Jose Cruz	.10
21	Charlie Lea	.10
22	Jesse Orosco	.10
23	Juan Samuel	.10
24	Tony Pena	.10
25	Tony Gwynn	1.00
26	Bob Brenly	.10
	Checklist	.03
	Dick Perez (DK artist)	.10

Highlights

Designed in the style of the regular 1985 Donruss set, this issue features the Player of the Month in the major leagues plus highlight cards of special baseball events and milestones of the 1985 season. Fifty-six cards, including an unnumbered checklist, comprise the set which was available only through hobby dealers. The cards measure 2-1/2" x 3-1/2" and have glossy fronts. The last two cards in the set feature Donruss' picks for the A.L. and N.L. Rookies of the Year. The set was issued in a specially designed box.

		NM/M
Complete Set (56):		3.00
Common Player:		.05
1	Sets Opening Day Record (Tom Seaver)	.10
2	Establishes A.L. Save Mark (Rollie Fingers)	.05
3	A.L. Player of the Month - April (Mike Davis)	.05
4	A.L. Pitcher of the Month - April (Charlie Leibrandt)	.05
5	N.L. Player of the Month - April (Dale Murphy)	.10
6	N.L. Pitcher of the Month - April (Fernando Valenzuela)	.05
7	N.L. Shortstop Record (Larry Bowa)	.05
8	Joins Reds 2000 Hit Club (Dave Concepcion)	.05
9	Eldest Grand Slammer (Tony Perez)	.05
10	N.L. Career Run Leader (Pete Rose)	.50
11	A.L. Player of the Month - May (George Brett)	.25
12	A.L. Pitcher of the Month - May (Dave Stieb)	.05
13	N.L. Player of the Month - May (Dave Parker)	.05
14	N.L. Pitcher of the Month - May (Andy Hawkins)	.05
15	Records 11th Straight Win (Andy Hawkins)	.05
16	Two Homers In First Inning (Von Hayes)	.05
17	A.L. Player of the Month - June (Rickey Henderson)	.15
18	A.L. Pitcher of the Month - June (Jay Howell)	.05
19	N.L. Player of the Month - June (Pedro Guerrero)	.05
20	N.L. Pitcher of the Month - June (John Tudor)	.05
21	Marathon Game Iron Men (Gary Carter, Keith Hernandez)	.05
22	Records 4000th K (Nolan Ryan)	.50
23	All-Star Game MVP (LaMarr Hoyt)	.05
24	1st Ranger To Hit For Cycle (Oddibe McDowell)	.05
25	A.L. Player of the Month - July (George Brett)	.25
26	A.L. Pitcher of the Month - July (Bret Saberhagen)	.05
27	N.L. Player of the Month - July (Keith Hernandez)	.05
28	N.L. Pitcher of the Month - July (Fernando Valenzuela)	.05
29	Record Setting Base Stealers (Vince Coleman, Willie McGee)	.05
30	Notches 300th Career Win (Tom Seaver)	.10
31	Strokes 3000th Hit (Rod Carew)	.10
32	Establishes Met Record (Dwight Gooden)	.05
33	Achieves Strikeout Milestone (Dwight Gooden)	.05
34	Explodes For 9 RBI (Eddie Murray)	.10
35	A.L. Career Hbp Leader (Don Baylor)	.05
36	A.L. Player of the Month - August (Don Mattingly)	.50
37	A.L. Pitcher of the Month - August (Dave Righetti)	.05
38	N.L. Player of the Month (Willie McGee)	.05
39	N.L. Pitcher of the Month - August (Shane Rawley)	.05
40	Ty-Breaking Hit (Pete Rose)	.50
41	Hits 3 HRs, Drives In 8 Runs (Andre Dawson)	.05
42	Sets Yankee Theft Mark (Rickey Henderson)	.15
43	20 Wins In Rookie Season (Tom Browning)	.05
44	Yankee Milestone For Hits (Don Mattingly)	.50
45	A.L. Player of the Month - September (Don Mattingly)	.50
46	A.L. Pitcher of the Month - September (Charlie Leibrandt)	.05
47	N.L. Player of the Month - September (Gary Carter)	.05
48	N.L. Pitcher of the Month - September (Dwight Gooden)	.05
49	Major League Record Setter (Wade Boggs)	.25
50	Hurls Shutout For 300th Win (Phil Niekro)	.05
51	Venerable HR King (Darrell Evans)	.05
52	N.L. Switch-hitting Record (Willie McGee)	.05
53	Equals DiMaggio Feat (Dave Winfield)	.10
54	Donruss N.L. Rookie of the Year (Vince Coleman)	.10
55	Donruss A.L. Rookie of the Year (Ozzie Guillen)	.10
----	Checklist	.05

Sluggers of The Hall of Fame

In much the same manner as the 1959-71 Bazooka cards were issued, this eight-player set consists of cards printed on the bottom panel of a box of bubble gum. When cut off the box, cards measure 3-1/2" x 6-1/2", with blank backs. Players are pictured on the cards in paintings done by Dick Perez. Cards were issued on blue Color Bubbles brand boxes and on red Super Bubble boxes, each numbered on a tab at top or bottom; this checklist is arranged by the number on the card front.

		NM/M
Complete Set (8):		6.00
Common Player:		.30
1	Babe Ruth	2.00
2	Ted Williams	1.00
3	Lou Gehrig	1.00
4	Johnny Mize	.30
5	Stan Musial	.60
6	Mickey Mantle	2.50
7	Hank Aaron	.75
8	Frank Robinson	.45

1986 Donruss

In 1986, Donruss issued a 660-card set which included 653 numbered cards and seven unnumbered checklists. The 2-1/2" x 3-1/2" cards have fronts that feature blue borders and backs that have black print on blue and white. For the fifth year in a row, the first 26 cards in the set are Diamond Kings. The Rated Rookies subset (#27-46) appears once again. The cards were distributed with a Hank Aaron puzzle. The complete set price does not include the higher priced variations. In the checklist that follows, (DK) and (RR) refer to the Diamond Kings and Rated Rookies series.

		NM/M
Unopened Factory Set (660):		35.00
Complete Set (660):		30.00
Common Player:		.05
Hank Aaron Puzzle:		3.00
Wax Pack (15):		1.25
Wax Box (36):		35.00
Rack Pack (45):		2.50
1	Kirk Gibson/DK	.15
2	Goose Gossage/DK	.15
3	Willie McGee/DK	.10
4	George Bell/DK	.05
5	Tony Armas/DK	.05
6	Chili Davis/DK	.05
7	Cecil Cooper/DK	.05
8	Mike Boddicker/DK	.05
9	Davey Lopes/DK	.05
10	Bill Doran/DK	.05
11	Bret Saberhagen/DK	.10
12	Brett Butler/DK	.10
13	Harold Baines/DK	.15
14	Mike Davis/DK	.05
15	Tony Perez/DK	1.00
16	Willie Randolph/DK	.05
17	Bob Boone/DK	.10
18	Orel Hershiser/DK	.10
19	Johnny Ray/DK	.05
20	Gary Ward/DK	.05
21	Rick Mahler/DK	.05
22	Phil Bradley/DK	.05
23	Jerry Koosman/DK	.10
24	Tom Brunansky/DK	.05
25	Andre Dawson/DK	.50
26	Dwight Gooden/DK	.10
27	Kal Daniels/RR **RC**	.15
28	Fred McGriff/RR **RC**	4.00
29	Cory Snyder/RR **RC**	.10
30	Jose Guzman/RR **RC**	.05
31	Ty Gainey/RR **RC**	.05
32	Johnny Abrego/RR **RC**	.05
33a	Andres Galarraga/RR **RC** (Accent mark over e of Andres on back.)	2.00
33b	Andres Galarraga/RR **RC** (No accent mark.)	2.00
34	Dave Shipanoff/RR **RC**	.05
35	Mark McLemore/RR **RC**	.50
36	Marty Clary/RR **RC**	.05
37	Paul O'Neill/RR **RC**	2.00
38	Danny Tartabul/RR	.05
39	Jose Canseco/RR **RC**	6.00
40	Juan Nieves/RR **RC**	.05
41	Lance McCullers/RR **RC**	.05
42	Rick Surhoff/RR **RC**	.05
43	Todd Worrell/RR **RC**	.25
44	Bob Kipper/RR **RC**	.05
45	John Habyan/RR **RC**	.05
46	Mike Woodard/RR **RC**	.05
47	Mike Boddicker	.05
48	Robin Yount	1.50
49	Lou Whitaker	.05
50	Dennis Boyd	.05
51	Rickey Henderson	1.50
52	Mike Marshall	.05
53	George Brett	2.50
54	Dave Kingman	.05
55	Hubie Brooks	.05
56	Oddibe McDowell **RC**	.15
57	Doug DeCinces	.05
58	Britt Burns	.05
59	Ozzie Smith	2.00

No.	Player	Value
60	Jose Cruz	.05
61	Mike Schmidt	2.50
62	Pete Rose	3.00
63	Steve Garvey	.40
64	Tony Pena	.05
65	Chili Davis	.05
66	Dale Murphy	.40
67	Ryne Sandberg	2.00
68	Gary Carter	1.50
69	Alvin Davis	.05
70	Kent Hrbek	.05
71	George Bell	.05
72	Kirby Puckett	2.00
73	Lloyd Moseby	.05
74	Bob Kearney	.05
75	Dwight Gooden	.05
76	Gary Matthews	.05
77	Rick Mahler	.05
78	Benny Distefano	.05
79	Jeff Leonard	.05
80	Kevin McReynolds	.05
81	Ron Oester	.05
82	John Russell	.05
83	Tommy Herr	.05
84	Jerry Mumphrey	.05
85	Ron Romanick	.05
86	Daryl Boston	.05
87	Andre Dawson	.50
88	Eddie Murray	1.50
89	Dion James	.05
90	Chet Lemon	.05
91	Bob Stanley	.05
92	Willie Randolph	.05
93	Mike Scioscia	.05
94	Tom Waddell	.05
95	Danny Jackson	.05
96	Mike Davis	.05
97	Mike Fitzgerald	.05
98	Gary Ward	.05
99	Pete O'Brien	.05
100	Bret Saberhagen	.05
101	Alfredo Griffin	.05
102	Brett Butler	.05
103	Ron Guidry	.15
104	Jerry Reuss	.05
105	Jack Morris	.05
106	Rick Dempsey	.05
107	Ray Burris	.05
108	Brian Downing	.05
109	Willie McGee	.05
110	Bill Doran	.05
111	Kent Tekulve	.05
112	Tony Gwynn	2.00
113	Marvell Wynne	.05
114	David Green	.05
115	Jim Gantner	.05
116	George Foster	.05
117	Steve Trout	.05
118	Mark Langston	.05
119	Tony Fernandez	.05
120	John Butcher	.05
121	Ron Robinson	.05
122	Dan Spillner	.05
123	Mike Young	.05
124	Paul Molitor	1.50
125	Kirk Gibson	.05
126	Ken Griffey	.05
127	Tony Armas	.05
128	Mariano Duncan **RC**	.15
129	Pat Tabler (Mr. Clutch)	.05
130	Frank White	.05
131	Carney Lansford	.05
132	Vance Law	.05
133	Dick Schofield	.05
134	Wayne Tolleson	.05
135	Greg Walker	.05
136	Denny Walling	.05
137	Ozzie Virgil	.05
138	Ricky Horton	.05
139	LaMarr Hoyt	.05
140	Wayne Krenchicki	.05
141	Glenn Hubbard	.05
142	Cecilio Guante	.05
143	Mike Krukow	.05
144	Lee Smith	.15
145	Edwin Nunez	.05
146	Dave Stieb	.05
147	Mike Smithson	.05
148	Ken Dixon	.05
149	Danny Darwin	.05
150	Chris Pittaro	.05
151	Bill Buckner	.05
152	Mike Pagliarulo	.05
153	Bill Russell	.05
154	Brook Jacoby	.05
155	Pat Sheridan	.05
156	Mike Gallego **RC**	.05
157	Jim Wohlford	.05
158	Gary Pettis	.05
159	Toby Harrah	.05
160	Richard Dotson	.05
161	Bob Knepper	.05
162	Dave Dravecky	.05
163	Greg Gross	.05
164	Eric Davis	.05
165	Gerald Perry	.05
166	Rick Rhoden	.05
167	Keith Moreland	.05
168	Jack Clark	.05
169	Storm Davis	.05
170	Cecil Cooper	.05
171	Alan Trammell	.05
172	Roger Clemens	2.50
173	Don Mattingly	2.50
174	Pedro Guerrero	.05
175	Willie Wilson	.05
176	Dwayne Murphy	.05
177	Tim Raines	.05
178	Larry Parrish	.05
179	Mike Witt	.05
180	Harold Baines	.05
181	Vince Coleman **RC**	.35
182	Jeff Heathcock **RC**	.05
183	Steve Carlton	1.50
184	Mario Soto	.05
185	Goose Gossage	.10
186	Johnny Ray	.05
187	Dan Gladden	.05
188	Bob Horner	.05
189	Rick Sutcliffe	.05
190	Keith Hernandez	.05
191	Phil Bradley	.05
192	Tom Brunansky	.05
193	Jesse Barfield	.05
194	Frank Viola	.05
195	Willie Upshaw	.05
196	Jim Beattie	.05
197	Darryl Strawberry	.05
198	Ron Cey	.05
199	Steve Bedrosian	.05
200	Steve Kemp	.05
201	Manny Trillo	.05
202	Garry Templeton	.05
203	Dave Parker	.05
204	John Denny	.05
205	Terry Pendleton	.05
206	Terry Puhl	.05
207	Bobby Grich	.05
208	Ozzie Guillen **RC**	2.00
209	Jeff Reardon	.05
210	Cal Ripken, Jr.	3.00
211	Bill Schroeder	.05
212	Dan Petry	.05
213	Jim Rice	.50
214	Dave Righetti	.05
215	Fernando Valenzuela	.05
216	Julio Franco	.05
217	Darryl Motley	.05
218	Dave Collins	.05
219	Tim Wallach	.05
220	George Wright	.05
221	Tommy Dunbar	.05
222	Steve Balboni	.05
223	Jay Howell	.05
224	Joe Carter	.05
225	Ed Whitson	.05
226	Orel Hershiser	.05
227	Willie Hernandez	.05
228	Lee Lacy	.05
229	Rollie Fingers	1.00
230	Bob Boone	.05
231	Joaquin Andujar	.05
232	Craig Reynolds	.05
233	Shane Rawley	.05
234	Eric Show	.05
235	Jose DeLeon	.05
236	Jose Uribe **RC**	.05
237	Moose Haas	.05
238	Wally Backman	.05
239	Dennis Eckersley	1.25
240	Mike Moore	.05
241	Damaso Garcia	.05
242	Tim Teufel	.05
243	Dave Concepcion	.05
244	Floyd Bannister	.05
245	Fred Lynn	.05
246	Charlie Moore	.05
247	Walt Terrell	.05
248	Dave Winfield	1.50
249	Dwight Evans	.05
250	Dennis Powell **RC**	.05
251	Andre Thornton	.05
252	Onix Concepcion	.05
253	Mike Heath	.05
254a	David Palmer (2B on front)	.05
254b	David Palmer (P on front)	.15
255	Donnie Moore	.05
256	Curtis Wilkerson	.05
257	Julio Cruz	.05
258	Nolan Ryan	3.00
259	Jeff Stone	.05
260a	John Tudor (1981 Games is .18)	.05
260b	John Tudor (1981 Games is 18)	.15
261	Mark Thurmond	.05
262	Jay Tibbs	.05
263	Rafael Ramirez	.05
264	Larry McWilliams	.05
265	Mark Davis	.05
266	Bob Dernier	.05
267	Matt Young	.05
268	Jim Clancy	.05
269	Mickey Hatcher	.05
270	Sammy Stewart	.05
271	Bob L. Gibson	.05
272	Nelson Simmons	.05
273	Rich Gedman	.05
274	Butch Wynegar	.05
275	Ken Howell	.05
276	Mel Hall	.05
277	Jim Sundberg	.05
278	Chris Codiroli	.05
279	Herman Winningham **RC**	.05
280	Rod Carew	1.50
281	Don Slaught	.05
282	Scott Fletcher	.05
283	Bill Dawley	.05
284	Andy Hawkins	.05
285	Glenn Wilson	.05
286	Nick Esasky	.05
287	Claudell Washington	.05
288	Lee Mazzilli	.05
289	Jody Davis	.05
290	Darrell Porter	.05
291	Scott McGregor	.05
292	Ted Simmons	.05
293	Aurelio Lopez	.05
294	Marty Barrett	.05
295	Dale Berra	.05
296	Greg Brock	.05
297	Charlie Leibrandt	.05
298	Bill Krueger	.05
299	Bryn Smith	.05
300	Burt Hooton	.05
301	Stu Cliburn **RC**	.05
302	Luis Salazar	.05
303	Ken Dayley	.05
304	Frank DiPino	.05
305	Von Hayes	.05
306a	Gary Redus (1983 2B is .20)	.05
306b	Gary Redus (1983 2B is 20)	.15
307	Craig Lefferts	.05
308	Sam Khalifa	.05
309	Scott Garrelts	.05
310	Rick Cerone	.05
311	Shawon Dunston	.05
312	Howard Johnson	.05
313	Jim Presley	.05
314	Gary Gaetti	.05
315	Luis Leal	.05
316	Mark Salas	.05
317	Bill Caudill	.05
318	Dave Henderson	.05
319	Rafael Santana	.05
320	Leon Durham	.05
321	Bruce Sutter	1.25
322	Jason Thompson	.05
323	Bob Brenly	.05
324	Carmelo Martinez	.05
325	Eddie Milner	.05
326	Juan Samuel	.05
327	Tom Nieto	.05
328	Dave Smith	.05
329	Urbano Lugo **RC**	.05
330	Joel Skinner	.05
331	Bill Gullickson	.05
332	Floyd Rayford	.05
333	Ben Oglivie	.05
334	Lance Parrish	.05
335	Jackie Gutierrez	.05
336	Dennis Rasmussen	.05
337	Terry Whitfield	.05
338	Neal Heaton	.05
339	Jorge Orta	.05
340	Donnie Hill	.05
341	Joe Hesketh	.05
342	Charlie Hough	.05
343	Dave Rozema	.05
344	Greg Pryor	.05
345	Mickey Tettleton	.05
346	George Vukovich	.05
347	Don Baylor	.05
348	Carlos Diaz	.05
349	Barbaro Garbey	.05
350	Larry Sheets	.05
351	Ted Higuera **RC**	.10
352	Juan Beniquez	.05
353	Bob Forsch	.05
354	Mark Bailey	.05
355	Larry Andersen	.05
356	Terry Kennedy	.05
357	Don Robinson	.05
358	Jim Gott	.05
359	Earnest Riles **RC**	.05
360	John Christensen **RC**	.05
361	Ray Fontenot	.05
362	Spike Owen	.05
363	Jim Acker	.05
364a	Ron Davis (Last line in highlights ends with "...in May.")	.05
364b	Ron Davis (Last line in highlights ends with "...relievers (9).")	.15
365	Tom Hume	.05
366	Carlton Fisk	1.50
367	Nate Snell	.05
368	Rick Manning	.05
369	Darrell Evans	.05
370	Ron Hassey	.05
371	Wade Boggs	2.00
372	Rick Honeycutt	.05
373	Chris Bando	.05
374	Bud Black	.05
375	Steve Henderson	.05
376	Charlie Lea	.05
377	Reggie Jackson	2.50
378	Dave Schmidt	.05
379	Bob James	.05
380	Glenn Davis **RC**	.05
381	Tim Corcoran	.05
382	Danny Cox	.05
383	Tim Flannery	.05
384	Tom Browning	.05
385	Rick Camp	.05
386	Jim Morrison	.05
387	Dave LaPoint	.05
388	Davey Lopes	.05
389	Al Cowens	.05
390	Doyle Alexander	.05
391	Tim Laudner	.05
392	Don Aase	.05
393	Jaime Cocanower	.05
394	Randy O'Neal **RC**	.05
395	Mike Easler	.05
396	Scott Bradley	.05
397	Tom Niedenfuer	.05
398	Jerry Willard	.05
399	Lonnie Smith	.05
400	Bruce Bochte	.05
401	Terry Francona	.05
402	Jim Slaton	.05
403	Bill Stein	.05
404	Tim Hulett	.05
405	Alan Ashby	.05
406	Tim Stoddard	.05
407	Garry Maddox	.05
408	Ted Power	.05
409	Len Barker	.05
410	Denny Gonzalez	.05
411	George Frazier	.05
412	Andy Van Slyke	.05
413	Jim Dwyer	.05
414	Paul Householder	.05
415	Alejandro Sanchez	.05
416	Steve Crawford	.05
417	Dan Pasqua	.05
418	Enos Cabell	.05
419	Mike Jones	.05
420	Steve Kiefer	.05
421	Tim Burke **RC**	.05
422	Mike Mason	.05
423	Ruppert Jones	.05
424	Jerry Hairston Sr.	.05
425	Tito Landrum	.05
426	Jeff Calhoun	.05
427	Don Carman **RC**	.05
428	Tony Perez	1.00
429	Jerry Davis	.05
430	Bob Walk	.05
431	Brad Wellman	.05
432	Terry Forster	.05
433	Billy Hatcher	.05
434	Clint Hurdle	.05
435	Ivan Calderon **RC**	.05
436	Pete Filson	.05
437	Tom Henke	.05
438	Dave Engle	.05
439	Tom Filer	.05
440	Gorman Thomas	.05
441	Rick Aguilera **RC**	.25
442	Scott Sanderson	.05
443	Jeff Dedmon	.05
444	Joe Orsulak **RC**	.10
445	Atlee Hammaker	.05
446	Jerry Royster	.05
447	Buddy Bell	.05
448	Dave Rucker	.05
449	Ivan DeJesus	.05
450	Jim Pankovits	.05
451	Jerry Narron	.05
452	Bryan Little	.05
453	Gary Lucas	.05
454	Dennis Martinez	.05
455	Ed Romero	.05
456	Bob Melvin **RC**	.05
457	Glenn Hoffman	.05
458	Bob Shirley	.05
459	Bob Welch	.05
460	Carmen Castillo	.05
461	Dave Leeper	.05
462	Tim Birtsas **RC**	.05
463	Randy St. Claire	.05
464	Chris Welsh	.05
465	Greg Harris	.05
466	Lynn Jones	.05
467	Dusty Baker	.05
468	Roy Smith	.05
469	Andre Robertson	.05
470	Ken Landreaux	.05
471	Dave Bergman	.05
472	Gary Roenicke	.05
473	Pete Vuckovich	.05
474	Kirk McCaskill **RC**	.10
475	Jeff Lahti	.05
476	Mike Scott	.05
477	Darren Daulton **RC**	1.50
478	Graig Nettles	.15
479	Bill Almon	.05
480	Greg Minton	.05
481	Randy Ready **RC**	.05
482	Len Dykstra **RC**	1.50
483	Thad Bosley	.05
484	Harold Reynolds **RC**	1.00
485	Al Oliver	.05
486	Roy Smalley	.05
487	John Franco	.05
488	Juan Agosto	.05
489	Al Pardo	.05
490	Bill Wegman **RC**	.05
491	Frank Tanana	.05
492	Brian Fisher **RC**	.05
493	Mark Clear	.05
494	Len Matuszek	.05
495	Ramon Romero	.05
496	John Wathan	.05
497	Rob Picciolo	.05
498	U.L. Washington	.05
499	John Candelaria	.05
500	Duane Walker	.05
501	Gene Nelson	.05
502	John Mizerock	.05
503	Luis Aguayo	.05
504	Kurt Kepshire	.05
505	Ed Wojna	.05
506	Joe Price	.05
507	Milt Thompson **RC**	.05
508	Junior Ortiz	.05
509	Vida Blue	.05
510	Steve Engel	.05
511	Karl Best	.05
512	Cecil Fielder **RC**	2.00
513	Frank Eufemia	.05
514	Tippy Martinez	.05
515	Billy Robidoux **RC**	.05
516	Bill Scherrer	.05
517	Bruce Hurst	.05
518	Rich Bordi	.05
519	Steve Yeager	.05
520	Tony Bernazard	.05
521	Hal McRae	.05
522	Jose Rijo	.05
523	Mitch Webster **RC**	.05
524	Jack Howell **RC**	.05
525	Alan Bannister	.05
526	Ron Kittle	.05
527	Phil Garner	.05
528	Kurt Bevacqua	.05
529	Kevin Gross	.05
530	Bo Diaz	.05
531	Ken Oberkfell	.05
532	Rick Reuschel	.05
533	Ron Meridith	.05
534	Steve Braun	.05
535	Wayne Gross	.05
536	Ray Searage	.05
537	Tom Brookens	.05
538	Al Nipper	.05
539	Billy Sample	.05
540	Steve Sax	.05
541	Dan Quisenberry	.05
542	Tony Phillips	.05
543	Floyd Youmans **RC**	.05
544	Steve Buechele **RC**	.05
545	Craig Gerber	.05
546	Joe DeSa	.05
547	Brian Harper	.05
548	Kevin Bass	.05
549	Tom Foley	.05
550	Dave Van Gorder	.05
551	Bruce Bochy	.05
552	R.J. Reynolds	.05
553	Chris Brown **RC**	.05
554	Bruce Benedict	.05
555	Warren Brusstar	.05
556	Danny Heep	.05
557	Darnell Coles	.05
558	Greg Gagne	.05
559	Ernie Whitt	.05
560	Ron Washington	.05
561	Jimmy Key	.05
562	Billy Swift **RC**	.05
563	Ron Darling	.05
564	Dick Ruthven	.05
565	Zane Smith **RC**	.05
566	Sid Bream	.05
567a	Joel Youngblood (P on front)	.05
567b	Joel Youngblood (IF on front)	.15
568	Mario Ramirez	.05
569	Tom Runnells	.05
570	Rick Schu	.05
571	Bill Campbell	.05
572	Dickie Thon	.05
573	Al Holland	.05
574	Reid Nichols	.05
575	Bert Roberge	.05
576	Mike Flanagan	.05
577	Tim Leary **RC**	.05
578	Mike Laga	.05
579	Steve Lyons	.05
580	Phil Niekro	1.00
581	Gilberto Reyes	.05
582	Jamie Easterly	.05
583	Mark Gubicza	.05
584	Stan Javier **RC**	.15
585	Bill Laskey	.05
586	Jeff Russell	.05
587	Dickie Noles	.05
588	Steve Farr	.05
589	Steve Ontiveros **RC**	.05
590	Mike Hargrove	.05
591	Marty Bystrom	.05
592	Franklin Stubbs	.05
593	Larry Herndon	.05
594	Bill Swaggerty	.05
595	Carlos Ponce	.05
596	Pat Perry **RC**	.05
597	Ray Knight	.05
598	Steve Lombardozzi **RC**	.05
599	Brad Havens	.05
600	Pat Clements **RC**	.05
601	Joe Niekro	.05
602	Hank Aaron Puzzle Card	.05
603	Dwayne Henry **RC**	.05
604	Mookie Wilson	.05
605	Buddy Biancalana	.05
606	Rance Mulliniks	.05
607	Alan Wiggins	.05
608	Joe Cowley	.05
609a	Tom Seaver (Green stripes around name.)	1.50
609b	Tom Seaver (Yellow stripes around name.)	2.00
610	Neil Allen	.05
611	Don Sutton	1.00
612	Fred Toliver **RC**	.05
613	Jay Baller	.05
614	Marc Sullivan	.05
615	John Grubb	.05
616	Bruce Kison	.05
617	Bill Madlock	.05
618	Chris Chambliss	.05
619	Dave Stewart	.05
620	Tim Lollar	.05
621	Gary Lavelle	.05
622	Charles Hudson	.05
623	Joel Davis **RC**	.05
624	Joe Johnson **RC**	.05
625	Sid Fernandez	.05
626	Dennis Lamp	.05
627	Terry Harper	.05
628	Jack Lazorko	.05
629	Roger McDowell **RC**	.25
630	Mark Funderburk	.05
631	Ed Lynch	.05
632	Rudy Law	.05
633	Roger Mason **RC**	.05
634	Mike Felder **RC**	.05
635	Ken Schrom	.05
636	Bob Ojeda	.05
637	Ed Vande Berg	.05
638	Bobby Meacham	.05
639	Cliff Johnson	.05
640	Garth Iorg	.05
641	Dan Driessen	.05
642	Mike Brown	.05
643	John Shelby	.05
644	Pete Rose (RB)	.50
645	Knuckle Brothers (Joe Niekro, Phil Niekro)	.25
646	Jesse Orosco	.05
647	Billy Beane **RC**	.05
648	Cesar Cedeno	.05
649	Bert Blyleven	.15
650	Max Venable	.05
651	Fleet Feet (Vince Coleman, Willie McGee)	.25
652	Calvin Schiraldi	.05
653	King of Kings (Pete Rose)	3.00
----	Checklist 1-26 DK	.05
----	Checklist 27-130 (45 is Beane)	.05
----	Checklist 27-130 (45 is Habyan)	.05
----	Checklist 131-234	.05
----	Checklist 235-338	.05
----	Checklist 339-442	.05
----	Checklist 443-546	.05
----	Checklist 547-653	.05

Box Panels

For the second year in a row, Donruss placed baseball cards on the bottom of its wax and cello pack boxes. The cards, printed four to a panel, are standard 2-1/2" x 3-1/2". With numbering that begins where Donruss left off in 1985, cards PC4 through PC6 were found on boxes of regular Donruss issue wax packs. Cards PC7 through PC9 were found on boxes of the 1986 All-Star/Pop-up packs. An unnumbered Hank Aaron puzzle card was included on each box.

		NM/M
Complete Panel Set (2):		3.00
Complete Singles Set (8):		3.00
Common Single Player:		.15
Panel		.50
PC4	Kirk Gibson	.15
PC5	Willie Hernandez	.15
PC6	Doug DeCinces	.15
---	Aaron Puzzle Card	.05
Panel		2.00
PC7	Wade Boggs	1.50
PC8	Lee Smith	.20
PC9	Cecil Cooper	.15
---	Aaron Puzzle Card	.05

All-Stars

Issued in conjunction with the 1986 Donruss Pop-Ups set, the All-Stars consist of 60 cards in 3-1/2" x 5" format. Fifty-nine players involved in the 1985 All-Star game plus an unnumbered checklist comprise the set. Card fronts have the same blue border found on the regular 1986 Donruss issue. Retail packs included one Pop-up card, three All-Star cards and one Hank Aaron puzzle-piece card.

		NM/M
	Complete Set (60):	6.00
	Common Player:	.05
	Hank Aaron puzzle:	3.00
	Cello Pack (3):	.50
	Cello Box (36):	6.00
1	Tony Gwynn	.50
2	Tommy Herr	.05
3	Steve Garvey	.20
4	Dale Murphy	.20
5	Darryl Strawberry	.05
6	Graig Nettles	.05
7	Terry Kennedy	.05
8	Ozzie Smith	.50
9	LaMarr Hoyt	.05
10	Rickey Henderson	.35
11	Lou Whitaker	.05
12	George Brett	.75
13	Eddie Murray	.40
14	Cal Ripken, Jr.	1.50
15	Dave Winfield	.40
16	Jim Rice	.25
17	Carlton Fisk	.40
18	Jack Morris	.05
19	Jose Cruz	.05
20	Tim Raines	.05
21	Nolan Ryan	1.50
22	Tony Pena	.05
23	Jack Clark	.05
24	Dave Parker	.05
25	Tim Wallach	.05
26	Ozzie Virgil	.05
27	Fernando Valenzuela	.05
28	Dwight Gooden	.05
29	Glenn Wilson	.05
30	Garry Templeton	.05
31	Goose Gossage	.05
32	Ryne Sandberg	.50
33	Jeff Reardon	.05
34	Pete Rose	1.00
35	Scott Garrelts	.05
36	Willie McGee	.05
37	Ron Darling	.05
38	Dick Williams	.05
39	Paul Molitor	.40
40	Damaso Garcia	.05
41	Phil Bradley	.05
42	Dan Petry	.05
43	Willie Hernandez	.05
44	Tom Brunansky	.05
45	Alan Trammell	.05
46	Donnie Moore	.05
47	Wade Boggs	.50
48	Ernie Whitt	.05
49	Harold Baines	.05
50	Don Mattingly	.75
51	Gary Ward	.05
52	Bert Blyleven	.05
53	Jimmy Key	.05
54	Cecil Cooper	.05
55	Dave Stieb	.05
56	Rich Gedman	.05
57	Jay Howell	.05
58	Sparky Anderson	.05
59	Minneapolis Metrodome	.05
---	Checklist	.03

Diamond Kings Supers

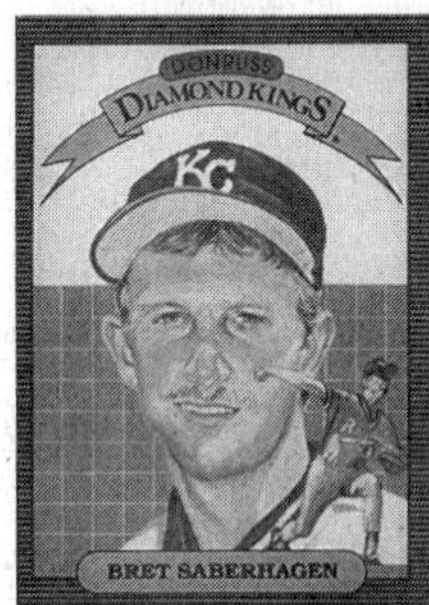

Donruss produced a set of large-format Diamond Kings in 1986 for the second year in a row. The 4-11/16" x 6-3/4" cards are enlarged versions of the 26 Diamond Kings cards found in the regular 1986 Donruss set, plus an unnumbered checklist and an unnumbered Pete Rose "King of Kings" card.

		NM/M
	Complete Set (28):	6.00
	Common Player:	.25
1	Kirk Gibson	.25
2	Goose Gossage	.25
3	Willie McGee	.25
4	George Bell	.25
5	Tony Armas	.25
6	Chili Davis	.25
7	Cecil Cooper	.25
8	Mike Boddicker	.25
9	Davey Lopes	.25
10	Bill Doran	.25
11	Bret Saberhagen	.25
12	Brett Butler	.25
13	Harold Baines	.25
14	Mike Davis	.25
15	Tony Perez	.75
16	Willie Randolph	.25
18	Orel Hershiser	.25
19	Johnny Ray	.25
20	Gary Ward	.25
21	Rick Mahler	.25
22	Phil Bradley	.25
23	Jerry Koosman	.25
24	Tom Brunansky	.25
25	Andre Dawson	.50
26	Dwight Gooden	.25
	Checklist	.05
	King of Kings (Pete Rose)	4.00

Highlights

Donruss, for the second year in a row, issued a 56-card highlights set featuring cards of each league's Player of the Month plus significant events of the 1986 season. The cards, 2-1/2" x 3-1/2," are similar in design to the regular 1986 Donruss set but have a gold border instead of blue. A yellow "Highlights" logo appears in the lower-left corner of each card front. Backs are designed on a vertical format and feature black print on a yellow background. As in 1985, the set includes Donruss' picks for the Rookies of the Year. A new feature was three cards honoring the 1986 Hall of Fame inductees. The set, available only through hobby dealers, was issued in a specially designed box. Each card can also be found with the word "Highlights" in the logo in white, a much scarcer variation that sometimes attracts significant premiums from single-player specialist collectors.

		NM/M
	Complete Set (56):	3.00
	Common Player:	.05
	White "Highlights":	20X
1	Homers In First At-Bat (Will Clark)	.05
2	Oakland Milestone For Strikeouts (Jose Rijo)	.05
3	Royals' All-Time Hit Man (George Brett)	.50
4	Phillies RBI Leader (Mike Schmidt)	.50
5	KKKKKKKKKKKKKKKKKKKK (Roger Clemens)	.50
6	A.L. Pitcher of the Month-April (Roger Clemens)	.50
7	A.L. Player of the Month-April (Kirby Puckett)	.25
8	N.L. Pitcher of the Month-April (Dwight Gooden)	.05
9	N.L. Player of the Month-April (Johnny Ray)	.05
10	Eclipses Mantle HR Record (Reggie Jackson)	.50
11	First Five Hit Game of Career (Wade Boggs)	.25
12	A.L. Pitcher of the Month-May (Don Aase)	.05
13	A.L. Player of the Month-May (Wade Boggs)	.25
14	N.L. Pitcher of the Month-May (Jeff Reardon)	.05
15	N.L. Player of the Month-May (Hubie Brooks)	.05
16	Notches 300th Career Win (Don Sutton)	.05
17	Starts Season 14-0 (Roger Clemens)	.50
18	A.L. Pitcher of the Month-June (Roger Clemens)	.50
19	A.L. Player of the Month-June (Kent Hrbek)	.05
20	N.L. Pitcher of the Month-June (Rick Rhoden)	.05
21	N.L. Player of the Month-June (Kevin Bass)	.05
22	Blasts 4 HRS in 1 Game (Bob Horner)	.05
23	Starting All Star Rookie (Wally Joyner)	.05
24	Starts 3rd Straight All Star Game (Darryl Strawberry)	.05
25	Ties All Star Game Record (Fernando Valenzuela)	.05
26	All Star Game MVP (Roger Clemens)	.50
27	A.L. Pitcher of the Month-July (Jack Morris)	.05
28	A.L. Player of the Month-July (Scott Fletcher)	.05
29	N.L. Pitcher of the Month-July (Todd Worrell)	.05
30	N.L. PLayer of the Month-July (Eric Davis)	.05
31	Records 3000th Strikeout (Bert Blyleven)	.05
32	1986 Hall of Fame Inductee (Bobby Doerr)	.05
33	1986 Hall of Fame Inductee (Ernie Lombardi)	.05
34	1986 Hall of Fame Inductee (Willie McCovey)	.25
35	Notches 4000th K (Steve Carlton)	.25
36	Surpasses DiMaggio Record (Mike Schmidt)	.50
37	Records 3rd "Quadruple Double" (Juan Samuel)	.05
38	A.L. Pitcher of the Month-August (Mike Witt)	.05
39	A.L. Player of the Month-August (Doug DeCinces)	.05
40	N.L. Pitcher of the Month-August (Bill Gullickson)	.05
41	N.L. Player of the Month-August (Dale Murphy)	.15
42	Sets Tribe Offensive Record (Joe Carter)	.05
43	Longest HR In Royals Stadium (Bo Jackson)	.15
44	Majors 1st No-Hitter In 2 Years (Joe Cowley)	.05
45	Sets M.L. Strikeout Record (Jim Deshaies)	.05
46	No Hitter Clinches Division (Mike Scott)	.05
47	A.L. Pitcher of the Month-September (Bruce Hurst)	.05
48	A.L. Player of the Month-September (Don Mattingly)	.50
49	N.L. Pitcher of the Month-September (Mike Krukow)	.05
50	N.L. Player of the Month-September (Steve Sax)	.05
51	A.L. Record For Steals By A Rookie (John Cangelosi)	.05
52	Shatters M.L. Save Mark (Dave Righetti)	.05
53	Yankee Record For Hits & Doubles (Don Mattingly)	.50
54	Donruss N.L. Rookie of the Year (Todd Worrell)	.05
55	Donruss A.L. Rookie of the Year (Jose Canseco)	.50
56	Highlight Checklist	.05

Pop-Ups

Issued in conjunction with the 1986 Donruss All-Stars set, the Pop-Ups (18 unnumbered cards) feature the 1985 All-Star Game starting lineups. The cards, 2-1/2" x 5", are die-cut and fold out to form a three-dimensional stand-up card. The background for the cards is the Minneapolis Metrodome, site of the 1985 All-Star Game. Retail packs in-

cluded one Pop-Up card, three All-Star cards and one Hank Aaron puzzle card.

		NM/M
	Complete Set (18):	4.00
	Common Player:	.05
	Hank Aaron Puzzle:	3.00
	Cello Pack (3):	.50
	Cello Box (36):	6.00
(1)	George Brett	.75
(2)	Carlton Fisk	.40
(3)	Steve Garvey	.20
(4)	Tony Gwynn	.50
(5)	Rickey Henderson	.40
(6)	Tommy Herr	.05
(7)	LaMarr Hoyt	.05
(8)	Terry Kennedy	.05
(9)	Jack Morris	.05
(10)	Dale Murphy	.25
(11)	Eddie Murray	.40
(12)	Graig Nettles	.05
(13)	Jim Rice	.25
(14)	Cal Ripken, Jr.	1.00
(15)	Ozzie Smith	.50
(16)	Darryl Strawberry	.05
(17)	Lou Whitaker	.05
(18)	Dave Winfield	.40

Rookies

Entitled "The Rookies," this 56-card set includes the top 55 rookies of 1986 plus an unnumbered checklist. The cards are similar in format to the 1986 Donruss regular issue, except that the borders are green rather than blue. Several of the rookies who had cards in the regular 1986 Donruss set appear again in "The Rookies" set. The sets, which were only available through hobby dealers, came in a specially designed box.

		NM/M
	Unopened Set (56):	35.00
	Opened Set (56):	30.00
	Common Player:	.05
1	Wally Joyner **RC**	.50
2	Tracy Jones **RC**	.05
3	Allan Anderson **RC**	.05
4	Ed Correa **RC**	.05
5	Reggie Williams	.05
6	Charlie Kerfeld **RC**	.05
7	Andres Galarraga	.15
8	Bob Tewksbury **RC**	.05
9	Al Newman	.05
10	Andres Thomas **RC**	.05
11	Barry Bonds **RC**	25.00
12	Juan Nieves	.05
13	Mark Eichhorn **RC**	.05
14	Dan Plesac **RC**	.05
15	Cory Snyder	.05
16	Kelly Gruber	.05
17	Kevin Mitchell **RC**	.25
18	Steve Lombardozzi	.05
19	Mitch Williams	.05
20	John Cerutti **RC**	.05
21	Todd Worrell	.05
22	Jose Canseco	2.00
23	Pete Incaviglia **RC**	.15
24	Jose Guzman	.05
25	Scott Bailes **RC**	.05
26	Greg Mathews **RC**	.05
27	Eric King **RC**	.05
28	Paul Assenmacher	.05
29	Jeff Sellers	.05
30	Bobby Bonilla **RC**	.25
31	Doug Drabek **RC**	.25
32	Will Clark **RC**	1.00
33	Bip Roberts	.05
34	Jim Deshaies **RC**	.05
35	Mike LaValliere **RC**	.05
36	Scott Bankhead **RC**	.05
37	Dale Sveum **RC**	.05
38	Bo Jackson **RC**	2.00
39	Rob Thompson **RC**	.05
40	Eric Plunk **RC**	.05
41	Bill Bathe	.05
42	John Kruk **RC**	.25
43	Andy Allanson **RC**	.05
44	Mark Portugal	.05
45	Danny Tartabull	.05
46	Bob Kipper	.05
47	Gene Walter	.05
48	Rey Quinonez	.05
49	Bobby Witt **RC**	.05
50	Bill Mooneyham	.05
51	John Cangelosi **RC**	.05
52	Ruben Sierra **RC**	.25
53	Rob Woodward	.05
54	Ed Hearn	.05
55	Joel McKeon	.05
56	Checklist 1-56	.05

1987 Donruss

The 1987 Donruss set consists of 660 numbered cards, each measuring 2-1/2" x 3-1/2." Color photos are surrounded by a bold black border separated by two narrow bands of yellow which enclose a brown area filled with baseballs. The player's name, team and team logo appear on the card fronts along with the words "Donruss '87." The card backs are designed on a horizontal format and contain black print on a yellow and white background. The backs are very similar to those in previous years' sets. Backs of cards issued in wax and rack packs face to the left when turned over, while those issued in factory sets face to the right. Cards were sold with Roberto Clemente puzzle pieces in each pack. Cards checklisted with a (DK) suffix are Diamond Kings; cards with an (RR) suffix are Rated Rookies.

		NM/M
	Unopened Fact. Set (660):	40.00
	Complete Set (660):	30.00
	Common Player:	.05
	Roberto Clemente Puzzle:	2.50
	Wax Pack (15):	1.25
	Wax Box (36):	35.00
	Rack Pack (45):	3.00
	Jumbo Rack (75):	4.00
1	Wally Joyner/DK	.25
2	Roger Clemens/DK	1.00
3	Dale Murphy/DK	.25
4	Darryl Strawberry/DK	.10
5	Ozzie Smith/DK	.75
6	Jose Canseco/DK	.40
7	Charlie Hough/DK	.05
8	Brook Jacoby/DK	.05
9	Fred Lynn/DK	.10
10	Rick Rhoden/DK	.05
11	Chris Brown/DK	.05
12	Von Hayes/DK	.05
13	Jack Morris/DK	.10
14a	Kevin McReynolds/DK (No yellow stripe on back.)	.25
14b	Kevin McReynolds/DK (Yellow stripe on back.)	.25
15	George Brett/DK	1.00
16	Ted Higuera/DK	.05
17	Hubie Brooks/DK	.05
18	Mike Scott/DK	.05
19	Kirby Puckett/DK	.75
20	Dave Winfield/DK	.60
21	Lloyd Moseby/DK	.05
22a	Eric Davis/DK (No yellow stripe on back.)	.25
22b	Eric Davis/DK (Yellow stripe on back.)	.15
23	Jim Presley/DK	.05
24	Keith Moreland/DK	.05
25a	Greg Walker/DK (No yellow stripe on back.)	.25
25b	Greg Walker/DK (Yellow stripe on back.)	.10
26	Steve Sax/DK	.10
27	Checklist 1-27	.05
28	B.J. Surhoff/RR **RC**	.30
29	Randy Myers/RR **RC**	.50
30	Ken Gerhart/RR **RC**	.05
31	Benito Santiago/RR	.15
32	Greg Swindell/RR **RC**	.15
33	Mike Birkbeck/RR **RC**	.05
34	Terry Steinbach/RR **RC**	.25
35	Bo Jackson/RR	1.50
36	Greg Maddux/RR **RC**	8.00
37	Jim Lindeman/RR **RC**	.05
38	Devon White/RR **RC**	.75
39	Eric Bell/RR **RC**	.05
40	Will Fraser/RR **RC**	.05
41	Jerry Browne/RR **RC**	.05
42	Chris James/RR **RC**	.05
43	Rafael Palmeiro/RR **RC**	4.00
44	Pat Dodson/RR **RC**	.05
45	Duane Ward/RR **RC**	.10
46	Mark McGwire/RR	6.00
47	Bruce Fields/RR **RC** (Photo actually Darnell Coles.)	.10
48	Eddie Murray	.60
49	Ted Higuera	.05
50	Kirk Gibson	.05
51	Oil Can Boyd	.05
52	Don Mattingly	1.00
53	Pedro Guerrero	.05
54	George Brett	1.00
55	Jose Rijo	.05
56	Tim Raines	.05
57	Ed Correa **RC**	.05
58	Mike Witt	.05
59	Greg Walker	.05
60	Ozzie Smith	.75
61	Glenn Davis	.05
62	Glenn Wilson	.05
63	Tom Browning	.05
64	Tony Gwynn	.75
65	R.J. Reynolds	.05
66	Will Clark	.25
67	Ozzie Virgil	.05
68	Rick Sutcliffe	.05
69	Gary Carter	.60
70	Mike Moore	.05
71	Bert Blyleven	.10
72	Tony Fernandez	.05
73	Kent Hrbek	.05
74	Lloyd Moseby	.05
75	Alvin Davis	.05
76	Keith Hernandez	.05
77	Ryne Sandberg	.75
78	Dale Murphy	.40
79	Sid Bream	.05
80	Chris Brown	.05
81	Steve Garvey	.25
82	Mario Soto	.05
83	Shane Rawley	.05
84	Willie McGee	.05
85	Jose Cruz	.05
86	Brian Downing	.05
87	Ozzie Guillen	.05
88	Hubie Brooks	.05
89	Cal Ripken, Jr.	2.50
90	Juan Nieves	.05
91	Lance Parrish	.05
92	Jim Rice	.25
93	Ron Guidry	.10
94	Fernando Valenzuela	.05
95	Andy Allanson **RC**	.05
96	Willie Wilson	.05
97	Jose Canseco	.40
98	Jeff Reardon	.05
99	Bobby Witt **RC**	.20
100	Checklist 28-133	.05
101	Jose Guzman	.05
102	Steve Balboni	.05
103	Tony Phillips	.05
104	Brook Jacoby	.05
105	Dave Winfield	.60
106	Orel Hershiser	.05
107	Lou Whitaker	.05
108	Fred Lynn	.05
109	Bill Wegman	.05
110	Donnie Moore	.05
111	Jack Clark	.05
112	Bob Knepper	.05
113	Von Hayes	.05
114	Bip Roberts **RC**	.25
115	Tony Pena	.05
116	Scott Garrelts	.05
117	Paul Molitor	.60

118	Darryl Strawberry	.05
119	Shawon Dunston	.05
120	Jim Presley	.05
121	Jesse Barfield	.05
122	Gary Gaetti	.05
123	Kurt Stillwell **RC**	.10
124	Joel Davis	.05
125	Mike Boddicker	.05
126	Robin Yount	.60
127	Alan Trammell	.05
128	Dave Righetti	.05
129	Dwight Evans	.05
130	Mike Scioscia	.05
131	Julio Franco	.05
132	Bret Saberhagen	.05
133	Mike Davis	.05
134	Joe Hesketh	.05
135	Wally Joyner	.05
136	Don Slaught	.05
137	Daryl Boston	.05
138	Nolan Ryan	2.50
139	Mike Schmidt	1.00
140	Tommy Herr	.05
141	Garry Templeton	.05
142	Kal Daniels	.05
143	Billy Sample	.05
144	Johnny Ray	.05
145	Rob Thompson **RC**	.10
146	Bob Dernier	.05
147	Danny Tartabull	.05
148	Ernie Whitt	.05
149	Kirby Puckett	.75
150	Mike Young	.05
151	Ernest Riles	.05
152	Frank Tanana	.05
153	Rich Gedman	.05
154	Willie Randolph	.05
155a	Bill Madlock (Name in brown band.)	.10
155b	Bill Madlock (Name in red band.)	.25
156a	Joe Carter (Name in brown band.)	.10
156b	Joe Carter (Name in red band.)	.25
157	Danny Jackson	.05
158	Carney Lansford	.05
159	Bryn Smith	.05
160	Gary Pettis	.05
161	Oddibe McDowell	.05
162	John Cangelosi **RC**	.10
163	Mike Scott	.05
164	Eric Show	.05
165	Juan Samuel	.05
166	Nick Esasky	.05
167	Zane Smith	.05
168	Mike Brown	.05
169	Keith Moreland	.05
170	John Tudor	.05
171	Ken Dixon	.05
172	Jim Gantner	.05
173	Jack Morris	.05
174	Bruce Hurst	.05
175	Dennis Rasmussen	.05
176	Mike Marshall	.05
177	Dan Quisenberry	.05
178	Eric Plunk **RC**	.05
179	Tim Wallach	.05
180	Steve Buechele	.05
181	Don Sutton	.50
182	Dave Schmidt	.05
183	Terry Pendleton	.05
184	Jim Deshaies **RC**	.05
185	Steve Bedrosian	.05
186	Pete Rose	2.00
187	Dave Dravecky	.05
188	Rick Reuschel	.05
189	Dan Gladden	.05
190	Rick Mahler	.05
191	Thad Bosley	.05
192	Ron Darling	.05
193	Matt Young	.05
194	Tom Brunansky	.05
195	Dave Stieb	.05
196	Frank Viola	.05
197	Tom Henke	.05
198	Karl Best	.05
199	Dwight Gooden	.05
200	Checklist 134-239	.05
201	Steve Trout	.05
202	Rafael Ramirez	.05
203	Bob Walk	.05
204	Roger Mason	.05
205	Terry Kennedy	.05
206	Ron Oester	.05
207	John Russell	.05
208	Greg Mathews **RC**	.05
209	Charlie Kerfeld	.05
210	Reggie Jackson	1.00
211	Floyd Bannister	.05
212	Vance Law	.05
213	Rich Bordi	.05
214	Dan Plesac **RC**	.10
215	Dave Collins	.05
216	Bob Stanley	.05
217	Joe Niekro	.05
218	Tom Niedenfuer	.05
219	Brett Butler	.05
220	Charlie Leibrandt	.05
221	Steve Ontiveros	.05
222	Tim Burke	.05
223	Curtis Wilkerson	.05
224	Pete Incaviglia **RC**	.10
225	Lonnie Smith	.05
226	Chris Codiroli	.05
227	Scott Bailes **RC**	.05
228	Rickey Henderson	.60
229	Ken Howell	.05
230	Darnell Coles	.05
231	Don Aase	.05
232	Tim Leary	.05
233	Bob Boone	.05
234	Ricky Horton	.05
235	Mark Bailey	.05
236	Kevin Gross	.05
237	Lance McCullers	.05
238	Cecilio Guante	.05
239	Bob Melvin	.05
240	Billy Jo Robidoux	.05
241	Roger McDowell	.05
242	Leon Durham	.05
243	Ed Nunez	.05
244	Jimmy Key	.05
245	Mike Smithson	.05
246	Bo Diaz	.05
247	Carlton Fisk	.60
248	Larry Sheets	.05
249	Juan Castillo **RC**	.05
250	Eric King **RC**	.05
251	Doug Drabek	.05
252	Wade Boggs	.75
253	Mariano Duncan	.05
254	Pat Tabler	.05
255	Frank White	.05
256	Alfredo Griffin	.05
257	Floyd Youmans	.05
258	Rob Wilfong	.05
259	Pete O'Brien	.05
260	Tim Hulett	.05
261	Dickie Thon	.05
262	Darren Daulton	.05
263	Vince Coleman	.05
264	Andy Hawkins	.05
265	Eric Davis	.05
266	Andres Thomas **RC**	.05
267	Mike Diaz **RC**	.05
268	Chili Davis	.05
269	Jody Davis	.05
270	Phil Bradley	.05
271	George Bell	.05
272	Keith Atherton	.05
273	Storm Davis	.05
274	Rob Deer **RC**	.05
275	Walt Terrell	.05
276	Roger Clemens	1.00
277	Mike Easler	.05
278	Steve Sax	.05
279	Andre Thornton	.05
280	Jim Sundberg	.05
281	Bill Bathe	.05
282	Jay Tibbs	.05
283	Dick Schofield	.05
284	Mike Mason	.05
285	Jerry Hairston Sr.	.05
286	Bill Doran	.05
287	Tim Flannery	.05
288	Gary Redus	.05
289	John Franco	.05
290	Paul Assenmacher **RC**	.10
291	Joe Orsulak	.05
292	Lee Smith	.10
293	Mike Laga	.05
294	Rick Dempsey	.05
295	Mike Felder	.05
296	Tom Brookens	.05
297	Al Nipper	.05
298	Mike Pagliarulo	.05
299	Franklin Stubbs	.05
300	Checklist 240-345	.05
301	Steve Farr	.05
302	Bill Mooneyham **RC**	.05
303	Andres Galarraga	.05
304	Scott Fletcher	.05
305	Jack Howell	.05
306	Russ Morman **RC**	.05
307	Todd Worrell	.05
308	Dave Smith	.05
309	Jeff Stone	.05
310	Ron Robinson	.05
311	Bruce Bochy	.05
312	Jim Winn	.05
313	Mark Davis	.05
314	Jeff Dedmon	.05
315	Jamie Moyer **RC**	.10
316	Wally Backman	.05
317	Ken Phelps	.05
318	Steve Lombardozzi	.05
319	Rance Mulliniks	.05
320	Tim Laudner	.05
321	Mark Eichhorn **RC**	.10
322	Lee Guetterman **RC**	.05
323	Sid Fernandez	.05
324	Jerry Mumphrey	.05
325	David Palmer	.05
326	Bill Almon	.05
327	Candy Maldonado	.05
328	John Kruk	.05
329	John Denny	.05
330	Milt Thompson	.05
331	Mike LaValliere **RC**	.10
332	Alan Ashby	.05
333	Doug Corbett	.05
334	Ron Karkovice **RC**	.05
335	Mitch Webster	.05
336	Lee Lacy	.05
337	Glenn Braggs **RC**	.05
338	Dwight Lowry	.05
339	Don Baylor	.05
340	Brian Fisher	.05
341	Reggie Williams **RC**	.05
342	Tom Candiotti	.05
343	Rudy Law	.05
344	Curt Young	.05
345	Mike Fitzgerald	.05
346	Ruben Sierra	.05
347	Mitch Williams **RC**	.25
348	Jorge Orta	.05
349	Mickey Tettleton	.05
350	Ernie Camacho	.05
351	Ron Kittle	.05
352	Ken Landreaux	.05
353	Chet Lemon	.05
354	John Shelby	.05
355	Mark Clear	.05
356	Doug DeCinces	.05
357	Ken Dayley	.05
358	Phil Garner	.05
359	Steve Jeltz	.05
360	Ed Whitson	.05
361	Barry Bonds	10.00
362	Vida Blue	.05
363	Cecil Cooper	.05
364	Bob Ojeda	.05
365	Dennis Eckersley	.50
366	Mike Morgan	.05
367	Willie Upshaw	.05
368	Allan Anderson **RC**	.05
369	Bill Gullickson	.05
370	Bobby Thigpen **RC**	.10
371	Juan Beniquez	.05
372	Charlie Moore	.05
373	Dan Petry	.05
374	Rod Scurry	.05
375	Tom Seaver	.75
376	Ed Vande Berg	.05
377	Tony Bernazard	.05
378	Greg Pryor	.05
379	Dwayne Murphy	.05
380	Andy McGaffigan	.05
381	Kirk McCaskill	.05
382	Greg Harris	.05
383	Rich Dotson	.05
384	Craig Reynolds	.05
385	Greg Gross	.05
386	Tito Landrum	.05
387	Craig Lefferts	.05
388	Dave Parker	.05
389	Bob Horner	.05
390	Pat Clements	.05
391	Jeff Leonard	.05
392	Chris Speier	.05
393	John Moses	.05
394	Garth Iorg	.05
395	Greg Gagne	.05
396	Nate Snell	.05
397	Bryan Clutterbuck **RC**	.05
398	Darrell Evans	.05
399	Steve Crawford	.05
400	Checklist 346-451	.05
401	Phil Lombardi **RC**	.05
402	Rick Honeycutt	.05
403	Ken Schrom	.05
404	Bud Black	.05
405	Donnie Hill	.05
406	Wayne Krenchicki	.05
407	Chuck Finley **RC**	.35
408	Toby Harrah	.05
409	Steve Lyons	.05
410	Kevin Bass	.05
411	Marvell Wynne	.05
412	Ron Roenicke	.05
413	Tracy Jones **RC**	.05
414	Gene Garber	.05
415	Mike Bielecki	.05
416	Frank DiPino	.05
417	Andy Van Slyke	.05
418	Jim Dwyer	.05
419	Ben Oglivie	.05
420	Dave Bergman	.05
421	Joe Sambito	.05
422	Bob Tewksbury **RC**	.30
423	Len Matuszek	.05
424	Mike Kingery **RC**	.05
425	Dave Kingman	.05
426	Al Newman **RC**	.05
427	Gary Ward	.05
428	Ruppert Jones	.05
429	Harold Baines	.05
430	Pat Perry	.05
431	Terry Puhl	.05
432	Don Carman	.05
433	Eddie Milner	.05
434	LaMarr Hoyt	.05
435	Rick Rhoden	.05
436	Jose Uribe	.05
437	Ken Oberkfell	.05
438	Ron Davis	.05
439	Jesse Orosco	.05
440	Scott Bradley	.05
441	Randy Bush	.05
442	John Cerutti **RC**	.05
443	Roy Smalley	.05
444	Kelly Gruber	.05
445	Bob Kearney	.05
446	Ed Hearn **RC**	.05
447	Scott Sanderson	.05
448	Bruce Benedict	.05
449	Junior Ortiz	.05
450	Mike Aldrete **RC**	.05
451	Kevin McReynolds	.05
452	Rob Murphy **RC**	.05
453	Kent Tekulve	.05
454	Curt Ford **RC**	.05
455	Davey Lopes	.05
456	Bobby Grich	.05
457	Jose DeLeon	.05
458	Andre Dawson	.35
459	Mike Flanagan	.05
460	Joey Meyer **RC**	.05
461	Chuck Cary **RC**	.05
462	Bill Buckner	.05
463	Bob Shirley	.05
464	Jeff Hamilton **RC**	.05
465	Phil Niekro	.50
466	Mark Gubicza	.05
467	Jerry Willard	.05
468	Bob Sebra **RC**	.05
469	Larry Parrish	.05
470	Charlie Hough	.05
471	Hal McRae	.05
472	Dave Leiper **RC**	.05
473	Mel Hall	.05
474	Dan Pasqua	.05
475	Bob Welch	.05
476	Johnny Grubb	.05
477	Jim Traber	.05
478	Chris Bosio **RC**	.05
479	Mark McLemore	.05
480	John Morris	.05
481	Billy Hatcher	.05
482	Dan Schatzeder	.05
483	Rich Gossage	.10
484	Jim Morrison	.05
485	Bob Brenly	.05
486	Bill Schroeder	.05
487	Mookie Wilson	.05
488	Dave Martinez **RC**	.10
489	Harold Reynolds	.05
490	Jeff Hearron	.05
491	Mickey Hatcher	.05
492	Barry Larkin **RC**	2.00
493	Bob James	.05
494	John Habyan	.05
495	Jim Adduci **RC**	.05
496	Mike Heath	.05
497	Tim Stoddard	.05
498	Tony Armas	.05
499	Dennis Powell	.05
500	Checklist 452-557	.05
501	Chris Bando	.05
502	David Cone **RC**	2.00
503	Jay Howell	.05
504	Tom Foley	.05
505	Ray Chadwick **RC**	.05
506	Mike Loynd **RC**	.05
507	Neil Allen	.05
508	Danny Darwin	.05
509	Rick Schu	.05
510	Jose Oquendo	.05
511	Gene Walter	.05
512	Terry McGriff **RC**	.05
513	Ken Griffey	.05
514	Benny Distefano	.05
515	Terry Mulholland **RC**	.25
516	Ed Lynch	.05
517	Bill Swift	.05
518	Manny Lee **RC**	.05
519	Andre David	.05
520	Scott McGregor	.05
521	Rick Manning	.05
522	Willie Hernandez	.05
523	Marty Barrett	.05
524	Wayne Tolleson	.05
525	Jose Gonzalez **RC**	.05
526	Cory Snyder	.05
527	Buddy Biancalana	.05
528	Moose Haas	.05
529	Wilfredo Tejada **RC**	.05
530	Stu Cliburn	.05
531	Dale Mohorcic **RC**	.05
532	Ron Hassey	.05
533	Ty Gainey	.05
534	Jerry Royster	.05
535	Mike Maddux **RC**	.05
536	Ted Power	.05
537	Ted Simmons	.05
538	Rafael Belliard **RC**	.05
539	Chico Walker	.05
540	Bob Forsch	.05
541	John Stefero	.05
542	Dale Sveum **RC**	.05
543	Mark Thurmond	.05
544	Jeff Sellers **RC**	.05
545	Joel Skinner	.05
546	Alex Trevino	.05
547	Randy Kutcher **RC**	.05
548	Joaquin Andujar	.05
549	Casey Candaele **RC**	.10
550	Jeff Russell	.05
551	John Candelaria	.05
552	Joe Cowley	.05
553	Danny Cox	.05
554	Denny Walling	.05
555	Bruce Ruffin **RC**	.10
556	Buddy Bell	.05
557	Jimmy Jones **RC**	.05
558	Bobby Bonilla	.05
559	Jeff Robinson	.05
560	Ed Olwine	.05
561	Glenallen Hill **RC**	.25
562	Lee Mazzilli	.05
563	Mike Brown	.05
564	George Frazier	.05
565	Mike Sharperson **RC**	.10
566	Mark Portugal **RC**	.05
567	Rick Leach	.05
568	Mark Langston	.05
569	Rafael Santana	.05
570	Manny Trillo	.05
571	Cliff Speck	.05
572	Bob Kipper	.05
573	Kelly Downs **RC**	.05
574	Randy Asadoor **RC**	.05
575	Dave Magadan **RC**	.25
576	Marvin Freeman **RC**	.05
577	Jeff Lahti	.05
578	Jeff Calhoun	.05
579	Gus Polidor **RC**	.05
580	Gene Nelson	.05
581	Tim Teufel	.05
582	Odell Jones	.05
583	Mark Ryal	.05
584	Randy O'Neal	.05
585	Mike Greenwell **RC**	.50
586	Ray Knight	.05
587	Ralph Bryant **RC**	.05
588	Carmen Castillo	.05
589	Ed Wojna	.05
590	Stan Javier	.05
591	Jeff Musselman **RC**	.05
592	Mike Stanley **RC**	.05
593	Darrell Porter	.05
594	Drew Hall **RC**	.05
595	Rob Nelson **RC**	.05
596	Bryan Oelkers	.05
597	Scott Nielsen **RC**	.05
598	Brian Holton **RC**	.05
599	Kevin Mitchell	.05
600	Checklist 558-660	.05
601	Jackie Gutierrez	.05
602	Barry Jones **RC**	.05
603	Jerry Narron	.05
604	Steve Lake	.05
605	Jim Pankovits	.05
606	Ed Romero	.05
607	Dave LaPoint	.05
608	Don Robinson	.05
609	Mike Krukow	.05
610	Dave Valle **RC**	.05
611	Len Dykstra	.05
612	Roberto Clemente Puzzle Card	.25
613	Mike Trujillo **RC**	.05
614	Damaso Garcia	.05
615	Neal Heaton	.05
616	Juan Berenguer	.05
617	Steve Carlton	.75
618	Gary Lucas	.05
619	Geno Petralli	.05
620	Rick Aguilera	.05
621	Fred McGriff	.05
622	Dave Henderson	.05
623	Dave Clark **RC**	.05
624	Angel Salazar	.05
625	Randy Hunt	.05
626	John Gibbons	.05
627	Kevin Brown **RC**	2.00
628	Bill Dawley	.05
629	Aurelio Lopez	.05
630	Charlie Hudson	.05
631	Ray Soff	.05
632	Ray Hayward **RC**	.05
633	Spike Owen	.05
634	Glenn Hubbard	.05
635	Kevin Elster **RC**	.10
636	Mike LaCoss	.05
637	Dwayne Henry	.05
638	Rey Quinones **RC**	.05
639	Jim Clancy	.05
640	Larry Andersen	.05
641	Calvin Schiraldi	.05
642	Stan Jefferson **RC**	.05
643	Marc Sullivan	.05
644	Mark Grant	.05
645	Cliff Johnson	.05
646	Howard Johnson	.05
647	Dave Sax	.05
648	Dave Stewart	.05
649	Danny Heep	.05
650	Joe Johnson	.05
651	Bob Brower **RC**	.05
652	Rob Woodward	.05
653	John Mizerock	.05
654	Tim Pyznarski **RC**	.05
655	Luis Aquino **RC**	.05
656	Mickey Brantley **RC**	.05
657	Doyle Alexander	.05
658	Sammy Stewart	.05
659	Jim Acker	.05
660	Pete Ladd	.05

Box Panels

Continuing with an idea they initiated in 1985, Donruss once again placed baseball cards on the bottoms of their retail boxes. The cards, which are 2-1/2" x 3-1/2" in size, come four to a panel with each panel containing an unnumbered Roberto Clemente puzzle card. With numbering that begins where Donruss left off in 1986, cards PC 10 through PC 12 were found on boxes of Donruss regular issue wax packs. Cards PC 13 through PC 15 were located on boxes of the 1987 All-Star/Pop-Up packs.

		NM/M
Complete Panel Set (2):		4.00
Complete Singles Set (8):		4.00
Common Single Player:		.15
Panel		1.50
10	Dale Murphy	.40
11	Jeff Reardon	.15
12	Jose Canseco	.60
----	Roberto Clemente Puzzle Card	.15
Panel		3.00
13	Mike Scott	.15
14	Roger Clemens	2.00
15	Mike Krukow	.15
----	Roberto Clemente Puzzle Card	.15

All-Stars

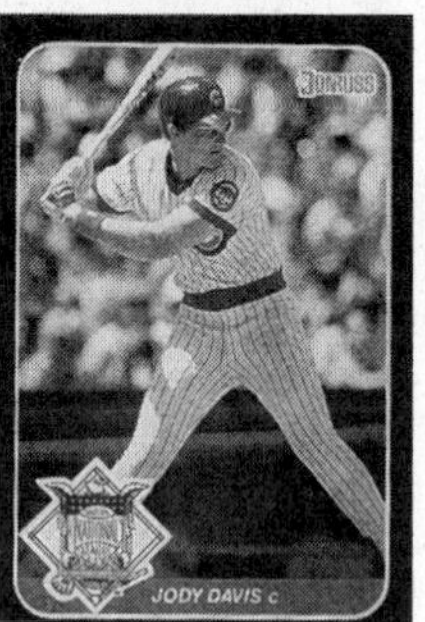

Issued in conjunction with the Donruss Pop-Ups set for the second consecutive year, the 1987 Donruss All-Stars consist of 59 players (plus a checklist) who were selected to the 1986 All-Star Game. Measuring 3-1/2" x 5" in size, the card fronts feature black borders and American or National League logos. Included on back are the player's career highlights and All-Star Game statistics. Retail packs included one Pop-Up card, three All-Star cards and one Roberto Clemente puzzle card.

		NM/M
Complete Set (60):		4.00
Common Player:		.05
Roberto Clemente Puzzle:		2.50
Wax Pack:		.35
Wax Box (48):		5.00
1	Wally Joyner	.05
2	Dave Winfield	.40
3	Lou Whitaker	.05
4	Kirby Puckett	.50
5	Cal Ripken, Jr.	1.00
6	Rickey Henderson	.40
7	Wade Boggs	.50
8	Roger Clemens	.65
9	Lance Parrish	.05
10	Dick Howser	.05
11	Keith Hernandez	.05
12	Darryl Strawberry	.05
13	Ryne Sandberg	.50
14	Dale Murphy	.25
15	Ozzie Smith	.50
16	Tony Gwynn	.50
17	Mike Schmidt	.65
18	Dwight Gooden	.05
19	Gary Carter	.40
20	Whitey Herzog	.05
21	Jose Canseco	.25
22	John Franco	.05
23	Jesse Barfield	.05
24	Rick Rhoden	.05
25	Harold Baines	.05
26	Sid Fernandez	.05
27	George Brett	.65
28	Steve Sax	.05
29	Jim Presley	.05
30	Dave Smith	.05
31	Eddie Murray	.40
32	Mike Scott	.05
33	Don Mattingly	.65
34	Dave Parker	.05
35	Tony Fernandez	.05
36	Tim Raines	.05
37	Brook Jacoby	.05
38	Chili Davis	.05
39	Rich Gedman	.05
40	Kevin Bass	.05
41	Frank White	.05
42	Glenn Davis	.05
43	Willie Hernandez	.05
44	Chris Brown	.05
45	Jim Rice	.25
46	Tony Pena	.05
47	Don Aase	.05
48	Hubie Brooks	.05

49	Charlie Hough	.05
50	Jody Davis	.05
51	Mike Witt	.05
52	Jeff Reardon	.05
53	Ken Schrom	.05
54	Fernando Valenzuela	.05
55	Dave Righetti	.05
56	Shane Rawley	.05
57	Ted Higuera	.05
58	Mike Krukow	.05
59	Lloyd Moseby	.05
60	Checklist	.05

Diamond Kings Supers

For a third season, Donruss produced a set of enlarged Diamond Kings, measuring 4-11/16" x 6-3/4". The 28-cards feature the artwork of Dick Perez, and contain 26 player cards, a checklist and a Roberto Clemente puzzle card. The set was available through a mail-in offer for $9.50 plus three wrappers.

		NM/M
Complete Set (28):		5.00
Common Player:		.15
1	Wally Joyner	.15
2	Roger Clemens	1.50
3	Dale Murphy	.30
4	Darryl Strawberry	.15
5	Ozzie Smith	1.00
6	Jose Canseco	.30
7	Charlie Hough	.15
8	Brook Jacoby	.15
9	Fred Lynn	.15
10	Rick Rhoden	.15
11	Chris Brown	.15
12	Von Hayes	.15
13	Jack Morris	.15
14	Kevin McReynolds	.15
15	George Brett	1.50
16	Ted Higuera	.15
17	Hubie Brooks	.15
18	Mike Scott	.15
19	Kirby Puckett	1.00
20	Dave Winfield	.60
21	Lloyd Moseby	.15
22	Eric Davis	.15
23	Jim Presley	.15
24	Keith Moreland	.15
25	Greg Walker	.15
26	Steve Sax	.15
27	Checklist	.05
---	Roberto Clemente Puzzle Card	.50

Highlights

For a third consecutive year, Donruss produced a 56-card set which highlighted the special events of the 1987 baseball season. The 2-1/2" x 3-1/2" cards have a front design similar to the regular 1987 Donruss set. A blue border and the "Highlights" logo are the significant differences. The backs feature black print on a white background and include the date the event took place plus the particulars. As in the past, the set includes Donruss' picks for the A.L. and N.L. Rookies of the Year. The set was issued in a specially designed box and was available only through hobby dealers.

		NM/M
Complete Set (56):		3.00
Common Player:		.05
1	First No-Hitter For Brewers (Juan Nieves)	.05
2	Hits 500th Homer (Mike Schmidt)	.35
3	N.L. Player of the Month - April (Eric Davis)	.05
4	N.L. Pitcher of the Month - April (Sid Fernandez)	.05
5	A.L. Player of the Month - April (Brian Downing)	.05
6	A.L. Pitcher of the Month - April (Bret Saberhagen)	.05
7	Free Agent Holdout Returns (Tim Raines)	.05
8	N.L. Player of the Month - May (Eric Davis)	.05
9	N.L. Pitcher of the Month - May (Steve Bedrosian)	.05
10	A.L. Player of the Month - May (Larry Parrish)	.05
11	A.L. Pitcher of the Month - May (Jim Clancy)	.05
12	N.L. Player of the Month - June (Tony Gwynn)	.25
13	N.L. Pitcher of the Month - June (Orel Hershiser)	.05
14	A.L. Player of the Month - June (Wade Boggs)	.25
15	A.L. Pitcher of the Month - June (Steve Ontiveros)	.05
16	All Star Game Hero (Tim Raines)	.05
17	Consecutive Game Homer Streak (Don Mattingly)	.35
18	1987 Hall of Fame Inductee (Jim "Catfish" Hunter)	.10
19	1987 Hall of Fame Inductee (Ray Dandridge)	.10
20	1987 Hall of Fame Inductee (Billy Williams)	.10
21	N.L. Player of the Month - July (Bo Diaz)	.05
22	N.L. Pitcher of the Month - July (Floyd Youmans)	.05
23	A.L. Player of the Month - July (Don Mattingly)	.35
24	A.L. Pitcher of the Month - July (Frank Viola)	.05
25	Strikes Out 4 Batters In 1 Inning (Bobby Witt)	.05
26	Ties A.L. 9-Inning Game Hit Mark (Kevin Seitzer)	.05
27	Sets Rookie Home Run Record (Mark McGwire)	.50
28	Sets Cubs' 1st Year Homer Mark (Andre Dawson)	.05
29	Hits In 39 Straight Games (Paul Molitor)	.15
30	Record Weekend (Kirby Puckett)	.25
31	N.L. Player of the Month - August (Andre Dawson)	.05
32	N.L. Pitcher of the Month - August (Doug Drabek)	.05
33	A.L. Player of the Month - August (Dwight Evans)	.05
34	A.L. Pitcher of the Month - August (Mark Langston)	.05
35	100 RBI In 1st 2 Major League Seasons (Wally Joyner)	.05
36	100 SB In 1st 3 Major League Seasons (Vince Coleman)	.05
37	Orioles' All Time Homer King (Eddie Murray)	.15
38	Ends Consecutive Innings Streak (Cal Ripken)	.50
39	Blue Jays Hit Record 10 Homers In 1 Game (Rob Ducey, Fred McGriff, Ernie Whitt)	.05
40	Equal A's RBI Marks (Jose Canseco, Mark McGwire)	.35
41	Sets All-Time Catching Record (Bob Boone)	.05
42	Sets Mets' One-Season HR Mark (Darryl Strawberry)	.05
43	N.L.'s All-Time Switch Hit HR King (Howard Johnson)	.05
44	Five Straight 200-Hit Seasons (Wade Boggs)	.25
45	Eclipses Rookie Game Hitting Streak (Benito Santiago)	.05
46	Eclipses Jackson's A's HR Record (Mark McGwire)	.45
47	13th Rookie To Collect 200 Hits (Kevin Seitzer)	.05
48	Sets Slam Record (Don Mattingly)	.35
49	N.L. Player of the Month - September (Darryl Strawberry)	.05
50	N.L. Pitcher of the Month - September (Pascual Perez)	.05
51	A.L. Player of the Month - September (Alan Trammell)	.05
52	A.L. Pitcher of the Month - September (Doyle Alexander)	.05
53	Strikeout King - Again (Nolan Ryan)	.50
54	Donruss A.L. Rookie of the Year (Mark McGwire)	.50
55	Donruss N.L. Rookie of the Year (Benito Santiago)	.05
56	Highlight Checklist	.05

Opening Day

The Donruss Opening Day set includes all players in major league baseball's starting lineups on the opening day of the 1987 baseball season. Cards in the 272-piece set measure 2-1/2" x 3-1/2" and have a glossy coating. The fronts are identical in design to the regular Donruss set, but new photos were utilized along with maroon borders as opposed to black. The backs carry black printing on white and yellow and offer a brief player biography plus the player's career statistics. The set was packaged in a sturdy 15" by 5" by 2" box with a clear acetate lid.

		NM/M
Unopened Fact. Set (272):		25.00
Complete Set (272):		12.00
Common Player:		.10
1	Doug DeCinces	.10
2	Mike Witt	.10
3	George Hendrick	.10
4	Dick Schofield	.10
5	Devon White	.10
6	Butch Wynegar	.10
7	Wally Joyner	.10
8	Mark McLemore	.10
9	Brian Downing	.10
10	Gary Pettis	.10
11	Bill Doran	.10
12	Phil Garner	.10
13	Jose Cruz	.10
14	Kevin Bass	.10
15	Mike Scott	.10
16	Glenn Davis	.10
17	Alan Ashby	.10
18	Billy Hatcher	.10
19	Craig Reynolds	.10
20	Carney Lansford	.10
21	Mike Davis	.10
22	Reggie Jackson	.75
23	Mickey Tettleton	.10
24	Jose Canseco	.35
25	Rob Nelson	.10
26	Tony Phillips	.10
27	Dwayne Murphy	.10
28	Alfredo Griffin	.10
29	Curt Young	.10
30	Willie Upshaw	.10
31	Mike Sharperson	.10
32	Rance Mulliniks	.10
33	Ernie Whitt	.10
34	Jesse Barfield	.10
35	Tony Fernandez	.10
36	Lloyd Moseby	.10
37	Jimmy Key	.10
38	Fred McGriff	.10
39	George Bell	.10
40	Dale Murphy	.25
41	Rick Mahler	.10
42	Ken Griffey	.10
43	Andres Thomas	.10
44	Dion James	.10
45	Ozzie Virgil	.10
46	Ken Oberkfell	.10
47	Gary Roenicke	.10
48	Glenn Hubbard	.10
49	Bill Schroeder	.10
50	Greg Brock	.10
51	Billy Jo Robidoux	.10
52	Glenn Braggs	.10
53	Jim Gantner	.10
54	Paul Molitor	.50
55	Dale Sveum	.10
56	Ted Higuera	.10
57	Rob Deer	.10
58	Robin Yount	.50
59	Jim Lindeman	.10
60	Vince Coleman	.10
61	Tommy Herr	.10
62	Terry Pendleton	.10
63	John Tudor	.10
64	Tony Pena	.10
65	Ozzie Smith	.60
66	Tito Landrum	.10
67	Jack Clark	.10
68	Bob Dernier	.10
69	Rick Sutcliffe	.10
70	Andre Dawson	.30
71	Keith Moreland	.10
72	Jody Davis	.10
73	Brian Dayett	.10
74	Leon Durham	.10
75	Ryne Sandberg	.60
76	Shawon Dunston	.10
77	Mike Marshall	.10
78	Bill Madlock	.10
79	Orel Hershiser	.10
80	Mike Ramsey	.10
81	Ken Landreaux	.10
82	Mike Scioscia	.10
83	Franklin Stubbs	.10
84	Mariano Duncan	.10
85	Steve Sax	.10
86	Mitch Webster	.10
87	Reid Nichols	.10
88	Tim Wallach	.10
89	Floyd Youmans	.10
90	Andres Galarraga	.10
91	Hubie Brooks	.10
92	Jeff Reed	.10
93	Alonzo Powell	.10
94	Vance Law	.10
95	Bob Brenly	.10
96	Will Clark	.10
97	Chili Davis	.10
98	Mike Krukow	.10
99	Jose Uribe	.10
100	Chris Brown	.10
101	Rob Thompson	.10
102	Candy Maldonado	.10
103	Jeff Leonard	.10
104	Tom Candiotti	.10
105	Chris Bando	.10
106	Cory Snyder	.10
107	Pat Tabler	.10
108	Andre Thornton	.10
109	Joe Carter	.10
110	Tony Bernazard	.10
111	Julio Franco	.10
112	Brook Jacoby	.10
113	Brett Butler	.10
114	Donnell Nixon	.10
115	Alvin Davis	.10
116	Mark Langston	.10
117	Harold Reynolds	.10
118	Ken Phelps	.10
119	Mike Kingery	.10
120	Dave Valle	.10
121	Rey Quinones	.10
122	Phil Bradley	.10
123	Jim Presley	.10
124	Keith Hernandez	.10
125	Kevin McReynolds	.10
126	Rafael Santana	.10
127	Bob Ojeda	.10
128	Darryl Strawberry	.10
129	Mookie Wilson	.10
130	Gary Carter	.50
131	Tim Teufel	.10
132	Howard Johnson	.10
133	Cal Ripken, Jr.	2.00
134	Rick Burleson	.10
135	Fred Lynn	.10
136	Eddie Murray	.50
137	Ray Knight	.10
138	Alan Wiggins	.10
139	John Shelby	.10
140	Mike Boddicker	.10
141	Ken Gerhart	.10
142	Terry Kennedy	.10
143	Steve Garvey	.25
144	Marvell Wynne	.10
145	Kevin Mitchell	.10
146	Tony Gwynn	.60
147	Joey Cora	.10
148	Benito Santiago	.10
149	Eric Show	.10
150	Garry Templeton	.10
151	Carmelo Martinez	.10
152	Von Hayes	.10
153	Lance Parrish	.10
154	Milt Thompson	.10
155	Mike Easler	.10
156	Juan Samuel	.10
157	Steve Jeltz	.10
158	Glenn Wilson	.10
159	Shane Rawley	.10
160	Mike Schmidt	.75
161	Andy Van Slyke	.10
162	Johnny Ray	.10
163a	Barry Bonds (Dark jersey, photo actually Johnny Ray.)	600.00
163b	Barry Bonds (White jersey, correct photo.)	9.00
164	Junior Ortiz	.10
165	Rafael Belliard	.10
166	Bob Patterson	.10
167	Bobby Bonilla	.10
168	Sid Bream	.10
169	Jim Morrison	.10
170	Jerry Browne	.10
171	Scott Fletcher	.10
172	Ruben Sierra	.10
173	Larry Parrish	.10
174	Pete O'Brien	.10
175	Pete Incaviglia	.10
176	Don Slaught	.10
177	Oddibe McDowell	.10
178	Charlie Hough	.10
179	Steve Buechele	.10
180	Bob Stanley	.10
181	Wade Boggs	.60
182	Jim Rice	.30
183	Bill Buckner	.10
184	Dwight Evans	.10
185	Spike Owen	.10
186	Don Baylor	.10
187	Marc Sullivan	.10
188	Marty Barrett	.10
189	Dave Henderson	.10
190	Bo Diaz	.10
191	Barry Larkin	.10
192	Kal Daniels	.10
193	Terry Francona	.10
194	Tom Browning	.10
195	Ron Oester	.10
196	Buddy Bell	.10
197	Eric Davis	.10
198	Dave Parker	.10
199	Steve Balboni	.10
200	Danny Tartabull	.10
201	Ed Hearn	.10
202	Buddy Biancalana	.10
203	Danny Jackson	.10
204	Frank White	.10
205	Bo Jackson	.25
206	George Brett	.75
207	Kevin Seitzer	.10
208	Willie Wilson	.10
209	Orlando Mercado	.10
210	Darrell Evans	.10
211	Larry Herndon	.10
212	Jack Morris	.10
213	Chet Lemon	.10
214	Mike Heath	.10
215	Darnell Coles	.10
216	Alan Trammell	.10
217	Terry Harper	.10
218	Lou Whitaker	.10
219	Gary Gaetti	.10
220	Tom Nieto	.10
221	Kirby Puckett	.60
222	Tom Brunansky	.10
223	Greg Gagne	.10
224	Dan Gladden	.10
225	Mark Davidson	.10
226	Bert Blyleven	.10
227	Steve Lombardozzi	.10
228	Kent Hrbek	.10
229	Gary Redus	.10
230	Ivan Calderon	.10
231	Tim Hulett	.10
232	Carlton Fisk	.50
233	Greg Walker	.10
234	Ron Karkovice	.10
235	Ozzie Guillen	.10
236	Harold Baines	.10
237	Donnie Hill	.10
238	Rich Dotson	.10
239	Mike Pagliarulo	.10
240	Joel Skinner	.10
241	Don Mattingly	.75
242	Gary Ward	.10
243	Dave Winfield	.50
244	Dan Pasqua	.10
245	Wayne Tolleson	.10
246	Willie Randolph	.10
247	Dennis Rasmussen	.10
248	Rickey Henderson	.50
249	Angels Checklist	.05
250	Astros Checklist	.05
251	Athletics Checklist	.05
252	Blue Jays Checklist	.05
253	Braves Checklist	.05
254	Brewers Checklist	.05
255	Cardinals Checklist	.05
256	Dodgers Checklist	.05
257	Expos Checklist	.05
258	Giants Checklist	.05
259	Indians Checklist	.05
260	Mariners Checklist	.05
261	Orioles Checklist	.05
262	Padres Checklist	.05
263	Phillies Checklist	.05
264	Pirates Checklist	.05
265	Rangers Checklist	.05
266	Red Sox Checklist	.05
267	Reds Checklist	.05
268	Royals Checklist	.05
269	Tigers Checklist	.05
270	Twins Checklist	.05
271	White Sox/ Cubs Checklist	.05
272	Yankees/Mets Checklist	.05

Pop-Ups

For the second straight year, Donruss released in conjunction with its All-Stars issue a set of cards designed to fold out to form a three-dimensional stand-up card. Consisting of 20 cards, as opposed to the previous year's 18, the 1987 Donruss Pop-Ups set contains players selected to the 1986 All-Star Game. Background for the 2-1/2" x 5" cards is the Houston Astrodome, site of the 1986 mid-summer classic. Retail packs included one Pop-Up card, three All-Star cards and one Roberto Clemente puzzle card.

		NM/M
Complete Set (20):		3.00
Common Player:		.10
Roberto Clemente Puzzle:		2.50
Wax Pack:		.35
Wax Box (48):		5.00
(1)	Wade Boggs	.50
(2)	Gary Carter	.40
(3)	Roger Clemens	.60
(4)	Dwight Gooden	.10
(5)	Tony Gwynn	.50
(6)	Rickey Henderson	.40
(7)	Keith Hernandez	.10
(8)	Whitey Herzog	.10
(9)	Dick Howser	.10
(10)	Wally Joyner	.10
(11)	Dale Murphy	.25
(12)	Lance Parrish	.10
(13)	Kirby Puckett	.50
(14)	Cal Ripken, Jr.	.75
(15)	Ryne Sandberg	.50
(16)	Mike Schmidt	.60
(17)	Ozzie Smith	.50
(18)	Darryl Strawberry	.10
(19)	Lou Whitaker	.10
(20)	Dave Winfield	.40

Rookies

As they did in 1986, Donruss issued a 56-card set highlighting the major leagues' most promising rookies. The cards are standard 2-1/2" x 3-1/2" and are identical in design to the regular Donruss issue. The card fronts have green borders as opposed to the black found in the regular issue and carry the words "The Rookies" in the lower-left portion of the card. The set came housed in a specially designed box and was available only through hobby dealers.

		NM/M
Unopened Fact. Set (56):		15.00
Complete Set (56):		10.00
Common Player:		.05
1	Mark McGwire	6.00
2	Eric Bell	.05
3	Mark Williamson **RC**	.05
4	Mike Greenwell	.05
5	Ellis Burks	.05
6	DeWayne Buice **RC**	.05
7	Mark Mclemore (McLemore)	.05
8	Devon White	.05
9	Willie Fraser	.05
10	Lester Lancaster **RC**	.05
11	Ken Williams **RC**	.05
12	Matt Nokes	.05
13	Jeff Robinson **RC**	.05
14	Bo Jackson	.25
15	Kevin Seitzer **RC**	.05
16	Billy Ripken **RC**	.05
17	B.J. Surhoff	.05
18	Chuck Crim **RC**	.05
19	Mike Birbeck	.05
20	Chris Bosio	.05
21	Les Straker **RC**	.05
22	Mark Davidson **RC**	.05
23	Gene Larkin **RC**	.05
24	Ken Gerhart	.05
25	Luis Polonia **RC**	.05
26	Terry Steinbach	.05
27	Mickey Brantley	.05
28	Mike Stanley	.05
29	Jerry Browne	.05
30	Todd Benzinger **RC**	.05
31	Fred McGriff	.25
32	Mike Henneman **RC**	.05
33	Casey Candaele	.05
34	Dave Magadan	.05
35	David Cone	.05
36	Mike Jackson **RC**	.05
37	John Mitchell **RC**	.05
38	Mike Dunne **RC**	.05
39	John Smiley	.05
40	Joe Magrane **RC**	.05
41	Jim Lindeman	.05
42	Shane Mack **RC**	.05
43	Stan Jefferson	.05
44	Benito Santiago	.05
45	Matt Williams **RC**	1.50
46	Dave Meads **RC**	.05
47	Rafael Palmeiro	4.00
48	Bill Long **RC**	.05
49	Bob Brower	.05
50	James Steels **RC**	.05
51	Paul Noce **RC**	.05
52	Greg Maddux	5.00
53	Jeff Musselman	.05
54	Brian Holton	.05
55	Chuck Jackson **RC**	.05
56	Checklist 1-56	.03

1988 Donruss Promo Sheet

The full effect of the 1988 Donruss border design of black, blue and red geometric patterns was previewed on this promo sheet. Printed on glossy paper with blank-back, eight regular cards (all pitchers!) and a Diamond King are showcased on the 7-1/2" x 10-1/2" sheet.

	NM/M
Uncut Sheet:	7.50

1988 Donruss

The 1988 Donruss set consists of 660 cards, each measuring 2-1/2" x 3-1/2". Fronts feature a full-color photo surrounded by a colorful border - alternating stripes of black, red, black, blue, black, blue, black, red and black (in that order) - separated by soft-focus edges and airbrushed fades. The player's name and position appear in a red band at the bottom of the card. The Donruss logo is situated in the upper-left corner, while the team logo is located in the lower-right. For the seventh consecutive season, Donruss included a subset of "Diamond Kings" cards (#1-27) in the issue. And for the fifth straight year, Donruss incorporated the popular "Rated Rookies" (card #28-47) with the set. Twenty-six of the cards between #603-660 were short-printed to accommodate the printing of the 26 MVP insert cards.

		NM/M
Unopened Fact. Set (660):		10.00
Complete Set (660):		8.00
Common Player:		.05
Stan Musial Puzzle:		1.00
Wax Pack (15):		.40
Wax Box (36):		10.00
Cello Pack (36):		.75
Cello Box (24):		12.00
Rack Pack (45):		.75
1	Mark McGwire/DK	.75
2	Tim Raines/DK	.05
3	Benito Santiago/DK	.05
4	Alan Trammell/DK	.05
5	Danny Tartabull/DK	.05
6	Ron Darling/DK	.05
7	Paul Molitor/DK	.40
8	Devon White/DK	.05
9	Andre Dawson/DK	.25
10	Julio Franco/DK	.05
11	Scott Fletcher/DK	.05
12	Tony Fernandez/DK	.05
13	Shane Rawley/DK	.05
14	Kal Daniels/DK	.05
15	Jack Clark/DK	.05
16	Dwight Evans/DK	.05
17	Tommy John/DK	.05
18	Andy Van Slyke/DK	.05
19	Gary Gaetti/DK	.05
20	Mark Langston/DK	.05
21	Will Clark/DK	.05
22	Glenn Hubbard/DK	.05
23	Billy Hatcher/DK	.05
24	Bob Welch/DK	.05
25	Ivan Calderon/DK	.05
26	Cal Ripken, Jr./DK	1.00
27	Checklist 1-27	.05
28	Mackey Sasser/RR **RC**	.05
29	Jeff Treadway/RR **RC**	.05
30	Mike Campbell/RR **RC**	.05
31	Lance Johnson/RR **RC**	.15
32	Nelson Liriano/RR **RC**	.05
33	Shawn Abner/RR **RC**	.05
34	Roberto Alomar/RR **RC**	1.00
35	Shawn Hillegas/RR **RC**	.05
36	Joey Meyer/RR	.05
37	Kevin Elster/RR	.05
38	Jose Lind/RR **RC**	.05
39	Kirt Manwaring/RR **RC**	.05
40	Mark Grace/RR **RC**	.50
41	Jody Reed/RR **RC**	.10
42	John Farrell/RR **RC**	.05
43	Al Leiter/RR **RC**	.20
44	Gary Thurman/RR **RC**	.05
45	Vicente Palacios/RR **RC**	.05
46	Eddie Williams/RR **RC**	.05
47	Jack McDowell/RR **RC**	.20
48	Ken Dixon	.05
49	Mike Birkbeck	.05
50	Eric King	.05
51	Roger Clemens	.60
52	Pat Clements	.05
53	Fernando Valenzuela	.05
54	Mark Gubicza	.05
55	Jay Howell	.05
56	Floyd Youmans	.05
57	Ed Correa	.05
58	DeWayne Buice **RC**	.05
59	Jose DeLeon	.05
60	Danny Cox	.05
61	Nolan Ryan	1.00
62	Steve Bedrosian	.05
63	Tom Browning	.05
64	Mark Davis	.05
65	R.J. Reynolds	.05
66	Kevin Mitchell	.05
67	Ken Oberkfell	.05
68	Rick Sutcliffe	.05
69	Dwight Gooden	.05
70	Scott Bankhead	.05
71	Bert Blyleven	.10
72	Jimmy Key	.05
73	Les Straker **RC**	.05
74	Jim Clancy	.05
75	Mike Moore	.05
76	Ron Darling	.05
77	Ed Lynch	.05
78	Dale Murphy	.20
79	Doug Drabek	.05
80	Scott Garrelts	.05
81	Ed Whitson	.05
82	Rob Murphy	.05
83	Shane Rawley	.05
84	Greg Mathews	.05
85	Jim Deshaies	.05
86	Mike Witt	.05
87	Donnie Hill	.05
88	Jeff Reed	.05
89	Mike Boddicker	.05
90	Ted Higuera	.05
91	Walt Terrell	.05
92	Bob Stanley	.05
93	Dave Righetti	.05
94	Orel Hershiser	.05
95	Chris Bando	.05
96	Bret Saberhagen	.05
97	Curt Young	.05
98	Tim Burke	.05
99	Charlie Hough	.05
100a	Checklist 28-137	.05
100b	Checklist 28-133	.05
101	Bobby Witt	.05
102	George Brett	.60
103	Mickey Tettleton	.05
104	Scott Bailes	.05
105	Mike Pagliarulo	.05
106	Mike Scioscia	.05
107	Tom Brookens	.05
108	Ray Knight	.05
109	Dan Plesac	.05
110	Wally Joyner	.05
111	Bob Forsch	.05
112	Mike Scott	.05
113	Kevin Gross	.05
114	Benito Santiago	.05
115	Bob Kipper	.05
116	Mike Krukow	.05
117	Chris Bosio	.05
118	Sid Fernandez	.05
119	Jody Davis	.05
120	Mike Morgan	.05
121	Mark Eichhorn	.05
122	Jeff Reardon	.05
123	John Franco	.05
124	Richard Dotson	.05
125	Eric Bell	.05
126	Juan Nieves	.05
127	Jack Morris	.05
128	Rick Rhoden	.05
129	Rich Gedman	.05
130	Ken Howell	.05
131	Brook Jacoby	.05
132	Danny Jackson	.05
133	Gene Nelson	.05
134	Neal Heaton	.05
135	Willie Fraser	.05
136	Jose Guzman	.05
137	Ozzie Guillen	.05
138	Bob Knepper	.05
139	Mike Jackson **RC**	.05
140	Joe Magrane **RC**	.05
141	Jimmy Jones	.05
142	Ted Power	.05
143	Ozzie Virgil	.05
144	Felix Fermin **RC**	.05
145	Kelly Downs	.05
146	Shawon Dunston	.05
147	Scott Bradley	.05
148	Dave Stieb	.05
149	Frank Viola	.05
150	Terry Kennedy	.05
151	Bill Wegman	.05
152	Matt Nokes **RC**	.10
153	Wade Boggs	.50
154	Wayne Tolleson	.05
155	Mariano Duncan	.05
156	Julio Franco	.05
157	Charlie Leibrandt	.05
158	Terry Steinbach	.05
159	Mike Fitzgerald	.05
160	Jack Lazorko	.05
161	Mitch Williams	.05
162	Greg Walker	.05
163	Alan Ashby	.05
164	Tony Gwynn	.50
165	Bruce Ruffin	.05
166	Ron Robinson	.05
167	Zane Smith	.05
168	Junior Ortiz	.05
169	Jamie Moyer	.05
170	Tony Pena	.05
171	Cal Ripken, Jr.	1.00
172	B.J. Surhoff	.05
173	Lou Whitaker	.05
174	Ellis Burks **RC**	.20
175	Ron Guidry	.10
176	Steve Sax	.05
177	Danny Tartabull	.05
178	Carney Lansford	.05
179	Casey Candaele	.05
180	Scott Fletcher	.05
181	Mark McLemore	.05
182	Ivan Calderon	.05
183	Jack Clark	.05
184	Glenn Davis	.05
185	Luis Aguayo	.05
186	Bo Diaz	.05
187	Stan Jefferson	.05
188	Sid Bream	.05
189	Bob Brenly	.05
190	Dion James	.05
191	Leon Durham	.05
192	Jesse Orosco	.05
193	Alvin Davis	.05
194	Gary Gaetti	.05
195	Fred McGriff	.05
196	Steve Lombardozzi	.05
197	Rance Mulliniks	.05
198	Rey Quinones	.05
199	Gary Carter	.40
200a	Checklist 138-247	.05
200b	Checklist 134-239	.05
201	Keith Moreland	.05
202	Ken Griffey	.05
203	Tommy Gregg **RC**	.05
204	Will Clark	.05
205	John Kruk	.05
206	Buddy Bell	.05
207	Von Hayes	.05
208	Tommy Herr	.05
209	Craig Reynolds	.05
210	Gary Pettis	.05
211	Harold Baines	.05
212	Vance Law	.05
213	Ken Gerhart	.05
214	Jim Gantner	.05
215	Chet Lemon	.05
216	Dwight Evans	.05
217	Don Mattingly	.60
218	Franklin Stubbs	.05
219	Pat Tabler	.05
220	Bo Jackson	.10
221	Tony Phillips	.05
222	Tim Wallach	.05
223	Ruben Sierra	.05
224	Steve Buechele	.05
225	Frank White	.05
226	Alfredo Griffin	.05
227	Greg Swindell	.05
228	Willie Randolph	.05
229	Mike Marshall	.05
230	Alan Trammell	.05
231	Eddie Murray	.40
232	Dale Sveum	.05
233	Dick Schofield	.05
234	Jose Oquendo	.05
235	Bill Doran	.05
236	Milt Thompson	.05
237	Marvell Wynne	.05
238	Bobby Bonilla	.05
239	Chris Speier	.05
240	Glenn Braggs	.05
241	Wally Backman	.05
242	Ryne Sandberg	.50
243	Phil Bradley	.05
244	Kelly Gruber	.05
245	Tom Brunansky	.05
246	Ron Oester	.05
247	Bobby Thigpen	.05
248	Fred Lynn	.05
249	Paul Molitor	.40
250	Darrell Evans	.05
251	Gary Ward	.05
252	Bruce Hurst	.05
253	Bob Welch	.05
254	Joe Carter	.05
255	Willie Wilson	.05
256	Mark McGwire	.75
257	Mitch Webster	.05
258	Brian Downing	.05
259	Mike Stanley	.05
260	Carlton Fisk	.40
261	Billy Hatcher	.05
262	Glenn Wilson	.05
263	Ozzie Smith	.50
264	Randy Ready	.05
265	Kurt Stillwell	.05
266	David Palmer	.05
267	Mike Diaz	.05
268	Rob Thompson	.05
269	Andre Dawson	.25
270	Lee Guetterman	.05
271	Willie Upshaw	.05
272	Randy Bush	.05
273	Larry Sheets	.05
274	Rob Deer	.05
275	Kirk Gibson	.05
276	Marty Barrett	.05
277	Rickey Henderson	.40
278	Pedro Guerrero	.05
279	Brett Butler	.05
280	Kevin Seitzer	.05
281	Mike Davis	.05
282	Andres Galarraga	.05
283	Devon White	.05
284	Pete O'Brien	.05
285	Jerry Hairston Sr.	.05
286	Kevin Bass	.05
287	Carmelo Martinez	.05
288	Juan Samuel	.05
289	Kal Daniels	.05
290	Albert Hall	.05
291	Andy Van Slyke	.05
292	Lee Smith	.10
293	Vince Coleman	.05
294	Tom Niedenfuer	.05
295	Robin Yount	.40
296	Jeff Robinson **RC**	.05
297	Todd Benzinger **RC**	.10
298	Dave Winfield	.40
299	Mickey Hatcher	.05
300a	Checklist 248-357	.05
300b	Checklist 240-345	.05
301	Bud Black	.05
302	Jose Canseco	.25
303	Tom Foley	.05
304	Pete Incaviglia	.05
305	Bob Boone	.05
306	Bill Long **RC**	.05
307	Willie McGee	.05
308	Ken Caminiti **RC**	.20
309	Darren Daulton	.05
310	Tracy Jones	.05
311	Greg Booker	.05
312	Mike LaValliere	.05
313	Chili Davis	.05
314	Glenn Hubbard	.05
315	Paul Noce **RC**	.05
316	Keith Hernandez	.05
317	Mark Langston	.05
318	Keith Atherton	.05
319	Tony Fernandez	.05
320	Kent Hrbek	.05
321	John Cerutti	.05
322	Mike Kingery	.05
323	Dave Magadan	.05
324	Rafael Palmeiro	.35
325	Jeff Dedmon	.05
326	Barry Bonds	1.00
327	Jeffrey Leonard	.05
328	Tim Flannery	.05
329	Dave Concepcion	.05
330	Mike Schmidt	.60
331	Bill Dawley	.05
332	Larry Andersen	.05
333	Jack Howell	.05
334	Ken Williams **RC**	.05
335	Bryn Smith	.05
336	Billy Ripken **RC**	.10
337	Greg Brock	.05
338	Mike Heath	.05
339	Mike Greenwell	.05
340	Claudell Washington	.05
341	Jose Gonzalez	.05
342	Mel Hall	.05
343	Jim Eisenreich	.05
344	Tony Bernazard	.05
345	Tim Raines	.05
346	Bob Brower	.05
347	Larry Parrish	.05
348	Thad Bosley	.05
349	Dennis Eckersley	.35
350	Cory Snyder	.05
351	Rick Cerone	.05
352	John Shelby	.05
353	Larry Herndon	.05
354	John Habyan	.05
355	Chuck Crim **RC**	.05
356	Gus Polidor	.05
357	Ken Dayley	.05
358	Danny Darwin	.05
359	Lance Parrish	.05
360	James Steels **RC**	.05
361	Al Pedrique **RC**	.05
362	Mike Aldrete	.05
363	Juan Castillo	.05
364	Len Dykstra	.05
365	Luis Quinones	.05
366	Jim Presley	.05
367	Lloyd Moseby	.05
368	Kirby Puckett	.50
369	Eric Davis	.05
370	Gary Redus	.05
371	Dave Schmidt	.05
372	Mark Clear	.05
373	Dave Bergman	.05
374	Charles Hudson	.05
375	Calvin Schiraldi	.05
376	Alex Trevino	.05
377	Tom Candiotti	.05
378	Steve Farr	.05
379	Mike Gallego	.05
380	Andy McGaffigan	.05
381	Kirk McCaskill	.05
382	Oddibe McDowell	.05
383	Floyd Bannister	.05
384	Denny Walling	.05
385	Don Carman	.05
386	Todd Worrell	.05
387	Eric Show	.05
388	Dave Parker	.05
389	Rick Mahler	.05
390	Mike Dunne **RC**	.10
391	Candy Maldonado	.05
392	Bob Dernier	.05
393	Dave Valle	.05
394	Ernie Whitt	.05
395	Juan Berenguer	.05
396	Mike Young	.05
397	Mike Felder	.05
398	Willie Hernandez	.05
399	Jim Rice	.25
400a	Checklist 358-467	.05
400b	Checklist 346-451	.05
401	Tommy John	.10
402	Brian Holton	.05
403	Carmen Castillo	.05
404	Jamie Quirk	.05
405	Dwayne Murphy	.05
406	Jeff Parrett **RC**	.05
407	Don Sutton	.35
408	Jerry Browne	.05
409	Jim Winn	.05
410	Dave Smith	.05
411	Shane Mack **RC**	.05
412	Greg Gross	.05
413	Nick Esasky	.05
414	Damaso Garcia	.05
415	Brian Fisher	.05
416	Brian Dayett	.05
417	Curt Ford	.05
418	Mark Williamson **RC**	.05
419	Bill Schroeder	.05
420	Mike Henneman **RC**	.10
421	John Marzano **RC**	.05
422	Ron Kittle	.05
423	Matt Young	.05
424	Steve Balboni	.05
425	Luis Polonia **RC**	.05
426	Randy St. Claire	.05
427	Greg Harris	.05
428	Johnny Ray	.05
429	Ray Searage	.05
430	Ricky Horton	.05
431	Gerald Young **RC**	.05
432	Rick Schu	.05
433	Paul O'Neill	.05
434	Rich Gossage	.10
435	John Cangelosi	.05
436	Mike LaCoss	.05
437	Gerald Perry	.05
438	Dave Martinez	.05
439	Darryl Strawberry	.05
440	John Moses	.05
441	Greg Gagne	.05
442	Jesse Barfield	.05
443	George Frazier	.05
444	Garth Iorg	.05
445	Ed Nunez	.05
446	Rick Aguilera	.05
447	Jerry Mumphrey	.05
448	Rafael Ramirez	.05
449	John Smiley **RC**	.10
450	Atlee Hammaker	.05
451	Lance McCullers	.05
452	Guy Hoffman **RC**	.05
453	Chris James	.05
454	Terry Pendleton	.05
455	Dave Meads **RC**	.05
456	Bill Buckner	.05
457	John Pawlowski **RC**	.05
458	Bob Sebra	.05
459	Jim Dwyer	.05
460	Jay Aldrich **RC**	.05
461	Frank Tanana	.05
462	Oil Can Boyd	.05
463	Dan Pasqua	.05
464	Tim Crews **RC**	.10
465	Andy Allanson	.05
466	Bill Pecota **RC**	.05
467	Steve Ontiveros	.05
468	Hubie Brooks	.05
469	Paul Kilgus **RC**	.05
470	Dale Mohorcic	.05
471	Dan Quisenberry	.05
472	Dave Stewart	.05
473	Dave Clark	.05
474	Joel Skinner	.05
475	Dave Anderson	.05
476	Dan Petry	.05
477	Carl Nichols **RC**	.05
478	Ernest Riles	.05
479	George Hendrick	.05
480	John Morris	.05
481	Manny Hernandez **RC**	.05
482	Jeff Stone	.05
483	Chris Brown	.05
484	Mike Bielecki	.05
485	Dave Dravecky	.05
486	Rick Manning	.05
487	Bill Almon	.05
488	Jim Sundberg	.05
489	Ken Phelps	.05
490	Tom Henke	.05
491	Dan Gladden	.05
492	Barry Larkin	.05
493	Fred Manrique **RC**	.05
494	Mike Griffin	.05
495	Mark Knudson **RC**	.05
496	Bill Madlock	.05
497	Tim Stoddard	.05
498	Sam Horn **RC**	.05
499	Tracy Woodson **RC**	.05
500a	Checklist 468-577	.05
500b	Checklist 452-557	.05
501	Ken Schrom	.05
502	Angel Salazar	.05
503	Eric Plunk	.05
504	Joe Hesketh	.05
505	Greg Minton	.05
506	Geno Petralli	.05
507	Bob James	.05
508	Robbie Wine **RC**	.05
509	Jeff Calhoun	.05
510	Steve Lake	.05
511	Mark Grant	.05
512	Frank Williams	.05
513	Jeff Blauser **RC**	.10
514	Bob Walk	.05
515	Craig Lefferts	.05
516	Manny Trillo	.05
517	Jerry Reed	.05
518	Rick Leach	.05
519	Mark Davidson **RC**	.05
520	Jeff Ballard **RC**	.05
521	Dave Stapleton **RC**	.05
522	Pat Sheridan	.05
523	Al Nipper	.05
524	Steve Trout	.05
525	Jeff Hamilton	.05
526	Tommy Hinzo **RC**	.05
527	Lonnie Smith	.05
528	Greg Cadaret **RC**	.05
529	Rob McClure (Bob)	.05
530	Chuck Finley	.05
531	Jeff Russell	.05
532	Steve Lyons	.05
533	Terry Puhl	.05
534	Eric Nolte **RC**	.05
535	Kent Tekulve	.05
536	Pat Pacillo **RC**	.05
537	Charlie Puleo	.05
538	Tom Prince **RC**	.05
539	Greg Maddux	.50

540	Jim Lindeman	.05
541	Pete Stanicek **RC**	.05
542	Steve Kiefer	.05
543	Jim Morrison	.05
544	Spike Owen	.05
545	Jay Buhner **RC**	.50
546	Mike Devereaux **RC**	.10
547	Jerry Don Gleaton	.05
548	Jose Rijo	.05
549	Dennis Martinez	.05
550	Mike Loynd	.05
551	Darrell Miller	.05
552	Dave LaPoint	.05
553	John Tudor	.05
554	Rocky Childress **RC**	.05
555	Wally Ritchie **RC**	.05
556	Terry McGriff	.05
557	Dave Leiper	.05
558	Jeff Robinson	.05
559	Jose Uribe	.05
560	Ted Simmons	.05
561	Lester Lancaster **RC**	.10
562	Keith Miller **RC**	.05
563	Harold Reynolds	.05
564	Gene Larkin **RC**	.05
565	Cecil Fielder	.05
566	Roy Smalley	.05
567	Duane Ward	.05
568	Bill Wilkinson **RC**	.05
569	Howard Johnson	.05
570	Frank DiPino	.05
571	Pete Smith **RC**	.05
572	Darnell Coles	.05
573	Don Robinson	.05
574	Rob Nelson	.05
575	Dennis Rasmussen	.05
576	Steve Jeltz (Photo actually Juan Samuel.)	.05
577	Tom Pagnozzi **RC**	.05
578	Ty Gainey	.05
579	Gary Lucas	.05
580	Ron Hassey	.05
581	Herm Winningham	.05
582	Rene Gonzales **RC**	.05
583	Brad Komminsk	.05
584	Doyle Alexander	.05
585	Jeff Sellers	.05
586	Bill Gullickson	.05
587	Tim Belcher **RC**	.05
588	Doug Jones **RC**	.05
589	Melido Perez **RC**	.05
590	Rick Honeycutt	.05
591	Pascual Perez	.05
592	Curt Wilkerson	.05
593	Steve Howe	.05
594	John Davis **RC**	.05
595	Storm Davis	.05
596	Sammy Stewart	.05
597	Neil Allen	.05
598	Alejandro Pena	.05
599	Mark Thurmond	.05
600a	Checklist 578-BC26	.05
600b	Checklist 558-660	.05
601	Jose Mesa **RC**	.10
602	Don August **RC**	.05
603	Terry Leach/SP	.10
604	Tom Newell **RC**	.05
605	Randall Byers/SP **RC**	.10
606	Jim Gott	.05
607	Harry Spilman	.05
608	John Candelaria	.05
609	Mike Brumley **RC**	.05
610	Mickey Brantley	.05
611	Jose Nunez/SP **RC**	.10
612	Tom Nieto	.05
613	Rick Reuschel	.05
614	Lee Mazzilli/SP	.10
615	Scott Lusader **RC**	.05
616	Bobby Meacham	.05
617	Kevin McReynolds/SP	.10
618	Gene Garber	.05
619	Barry Lyons/SP **RC**	.10
620	Randy Myers	.05
621	Donnie Moore	.05
622	Domingo Ramos	.05
623	Ed Romero	.05
624	Greg Myers **RC**	.10
625	Ripken Baseball Family (Billy Ripken, Cal Ripken, Jr., Cal Ripken, Sr.)	.40
626	Pat Perry	.05
627	Andres Thomas/SP	.10
628	Matt Williams/SP	.15
629	Dave Hengel **RC**	.05
630	Jeff Musselman/SP	.10
631	Tim Laudner	.05
632	Bob Ojeda/SP	.10
633	Rafael Santana	.05
634	Wes Gardner **RC**	.05
635	Roberto Kelly/SP **RC**	.15
636	Mike Flanagan/SP	.10
637	Jay Bell **RC**	.35
638	Bob Melvin	.05
639	Damon Berryhill **RC**	.05
640	David Wells/SP **RC**	.40
641	Stan Musial Puzzle Card	.05
642	Doug Sisk	.05
643	Keith Hughes **RC**	.05
644	Tom Glavine **RC**	1.00
645	Al Newman	.05
646	Scott Sanderson	.05
647	Scott Terry	.05
648	Tim Teufel/SP	.10
649	Garry Templeton/SP	.10
650	Manny Lee/SP	.10
651	Roger McDowell/SP	.10
652	Mookie Wilson/SP	.10
653	David Cone/SP	.10
654	Ron Gant/SP **RC**	.20
655	Joe Price/SP	.10
656	George Bell /SP	.10
657	Gregg Jefferies/SP **RC**	.25
658	Todd Stottlemyre/SP **RC**	.25
659	Geronimo Berroa/SP **RC**	.20
660	Jerry Royster/SP	.10

MVP

This 26-card set of standard-size player cards replaced the Donruss box-bottom cards in 1988. The bonus cards (numbered BC1 - BC26) were randomly inserted in Donruss wax or rack packs. Cards feature the company's choice of Most Valuable Player for each major league team and are titled "Donruss MVP." The MVP cards were not included in the factory-collated sets. Fronts carry the same basic red-blue-black border design as the 1988 Donruss basic issue. Backs are the same as the regular issue, except for the numbering system.

		NM/M
Complete Set (26):		3.00
Common Player:		.10
1	Cal Ripken, Jr.	1.00
2	Eric Davis	.10
3	Paul Molitor	.40
4	Mike Schmidt	.60
5	Ivan Calderon	.10
6	Tony Gwynn	.50
7	Wade Boggs	.50
8	Andy Van Slyke	.10
9	Joe Carter	.10
10	Andre Dawson	.25
11	Alan Trammell	.10
12	Mike Scott	.10
13	Wally Joyner	.10
14	Dale Murphy	.20
15	Kirby Puckett	.50
16	Pedro Guerrero	.10
17	Kevin Seitzer	.10
18	Tim Raines	.10
19	George Bell	.10
20	Darryl Strawberry	.10
21	Don Mattingly	.60
22	Ozzie Smith	.50
23	Mark McGwire	.75
24	Will Clark	.10
25	Alvin Davis	.10
26	Ruben Sierra	.10

All-Stars

For the third consecutive year, this set of 64 cards was marketed in conjunction with Donruss Pop-Ups. The 1988 issue included a major change - the cards were reduced in size from 3-1/2" x 5" to a standard 2-1/2" x 3-1/2". The set features players from the 1987 All-Star Game starting lineup. Card fronts feature full-color photos, framed in blue, black and white, with a Donruss logo at upper-left. Player name and position appear in a red banner below the photo, along with the appropriate National or American League logo. Backs include player stats and All-Star Game record. In 1988, All-Stars cards were distributed in individual packages containing three All-Stars, one Pop-Up and three Stan Musial puzzle pieces.

		NM/M
Complete Set (64):		5.00
Common Player:		.05
Stan Musial Puzzle:		1.00
Wax Pack:		.50
Wax Box (48):		10.00
1	Don Mattingly	.60
2	Dave Winfield	.40
3	Willie Randolph	.05
4	Rickey Henderson	.40
5	Cal Ripken, Jr.	1.00
6	George Bell	.05
7	Wade Boggs	.50
8	Bret Saberhagen	.05
9	Terry Kennedy	.05
10	John McNamara	.05
11	Jay Howell	.05
12	Harold Baines	.05
13	Harold Reynolds	.05
14	Bruce Hurst	.05
15	Kirby Puckett	.50
16	Matt Nokes	.05
17	Pat Tabler	.05
18	Dan Plesac	.05
19	Mark McGwire	.75
20	Mike Witt	.05
21	Larry Parrish	.05
22	Alan Trammell	.05
23	Dwight Evans	.05
24	Jack Morris	.05
25	Tony Fernandez	.05
26	Mark Langston	.05
27	Kevin Seitzer	.05
28	Tom Henke	.05
29	Dave Righetti	.05
30	Oakland Coliseum	.05
31	Wade Boggs (Top Vote Getter)	.25
32	Checklist 1-32	.05
33	Jack Clark	.05
34	Darryl Strawberry	.05
35	Ryne Sandberg	.50
36	Andre Dawson	.05
37	Ozzie Smith	.50
38	Eric Davis	.05
39	Mike Schmidt	.60
40	Mike Scott	.05
41	Gary Carter	.40
42	Davey Johnson	.05
43	Rick Sutcliffe	.05
44	Willie McGee	.05
45	Hubie Brooks	.05
46	Dale Murphy	.20
47	Bo Diaz	.05
48	Pedro Guerrero	.05
49	Keith Hernandez	.05
50	Ozzie Virgil	.05
51	Tony Gwynn	.50
52	Rick Reuschel	.05
53	John Franco	.05
54	Jeffrey Leonard	.05
55	Juan Samuel	.05
56	Orel Hershiser	.05
57	Tim Raines	.05
58	Sid Fernandez	.05
59	Tim Wallach	.05
60	Lee Smith	.05
61	Steve Bedrosian	.05
62	Tim Raines (MVP)	.05
63	Ozzie Smith (Top Vote Getter)	.25
64	Checklist 33-64	.05

Baseball's Best

The design of this 336-card set is similar to the regular 1988 Donruss issue with the exception of the borders which are orange, instead of blue. Player photos on the glossy front are framed by the Donruss logo upper-left, team logo lower-right and a bright red and white player name that spans the bottom margin. Backs are black and white, framed by a yellow border, and include personal information, year-by-year stats and major league totals. This set was packaged in a bright red cardboard box containing six individually shrink-wrapped packs of 56 cards. Donruss marketed the set via retail chain outlets with a suggested retail price of $21.95.

		NM/M
Complete Set (336):		10.00
Common Player:		.05
1	Don Mattingly	.75
2	Ron Gant	.05
3	Bob Boone	.05
4	Mark Grace	.15
5	Andy Allanson	.05
6	Kal Daniels	.05
7	Floyd Bannister	.05
8	Alan Ashby	.05
9	Marty Barrett	.05
10	Tim Belcher	.05
11	Harold Baines	.05
12	Hubie Brooks	.05
13	Doyle Alexander	.05
14	Gary Carter	.50
15	Glenn Braggs	.05
16	Steve Bedrosian	.05
17	Barry Bonds	1.50
18	Bert Blyleven	.10
19	Tom Brunansky	.05
20	John Candelaria	.05
21	Shawn Abner	.05
22	Jose Canseco	.30
23	Brett Butler	.05
24	Scott Bradley	.05
25	Ivan Calderon	.05
26	Rich Gossage	.05
27	Brian Downing	.05
28	Jim Rice	.25
29	Dion James	.05
30	Terry Kennedy	.05
31	George Bell	.05
32	Scott Fletcher	.05
33	Bobby Bonilla	.05
34	Tim Burke	.05
35	Darrell Evans	.05
36	Mike Davis	.05
37	Shawon Dunston	.05
38	Kevin Bass	.05
39	George Brett	.75
40	David Cone	.05
41	Ron Darling	.05
42	Roberto Alomar	.60
43	Dennis Eckersley	.40
44	Vince Coleman	.05
45	Sid Bream	.05
46	Gary Gaetti	.05
47	Phil Bradley	.05
48	Jim Clancy	.05
49	Jack Clark	.05
50	Mike Krukow	.05
51	Henry Cotto	.05
52	Rich Dotson	.05
53	Jim Gantner	.05
54	John Franco	.05
55	Pete Incaviglia	.05
56	Joe Carter	.05
57	Roger Clemens	.75
58	Gerald Perry	.05
59	Jack Howell	.05
60	Vance Law	.05
61	Jay Bell	.05
62	Eric Davis	.05
63	Gene Garber	.05
64	Glenn Davis	.05
65	Wade Boggs	.60
66	Kirk Gibson	.05
67	Carlton Fisk	.50
68	Casey Candaele	.05
69	Mike Heath	.05
70	Kevin Elster	.05
71	Greg Brock	.05
72	Don Carman	.05
73	Doug Drabek	.05
74	Greg Gagne	.05
75	Danny Cox	.05
76	Rickey Henderson	.50
77	Chris Brown	.05
78	Terry Steinbach	.05
79	Will Clark	.05
80	Mickey Brantley	.05
81	Ozzie Guillen	.05
82	Greg Maddux	.60
83	Kirk McCaskill	.05
84	Dwight Evans	.05
85	Ozzie Virgil	.05
86	Mike Morgan	.05
87	Tony Fernandez	.05
88	Jose Guzman	.05
89	Mike Dunne	.05
90	Andres Galarraga	.05
91	Mike Henneman	.05
92	Alfredo Griffin	.05
93	Rafael Palmeiro	.40
94	Jim Deshaies	.05
95	Mark Gubicza	.05
96	Dwight Gooden	.05
97	Howard Johnson	.05
98	Mark Davis	.05
99	Dave Stewart	.05
100	Joe Magrane	.05
101	Brian Fisher	.05
102	Kent Hrbek	.05
103	Kevin Gross	.05
104	Tom Henke	.05
105	Mike Pagliarulo	.05
106	Kelly Downs	.05
107	Alvin Davis	.05
108	Willie Randolph	.05
109	Rob Deer	.05
110	Bo Diaz	.05
111	Paul Kilgus	.05
112	Tom Candiotti	.05
113	Dale Murphy	.20
114	Rick Mahler	.05
115	Wally Joyner	.05
116	Ryne Sandberg	.60
117	John Farrell	.05
118	Nick Esasky	.05
119	Bo Jackson	.10
120	Bill Doran	.05
121	Ellis Burks	.05
122	Pedro Guerrero	.05
123	Dave LaPoint	.05
124	Neal Heaton	.05
125	Willie Hernandez	.05
126	Roger McDowell	.05
127	Ted Higuera	.05
128	Von Hayes	.05
129	Mike LaValliere	.05
130	Dan Gladden	.05
131	Willie McGee	.05
132	Al Lieter	.05
133	Mark Grant	.05
134	Bob Welch	.05
135	Dave Dravecky	.05
136	Mark Langston	.05
137	Dan Pasqua	.05
138	Rick Sutcliffe	.05
139	Dan Petry	.05
140	Rich Gedman	.05
141	Ken Griffey	.05
142	Eddie Murray	.50
143	Jimmy Key	.05
144	Dale Mohorcic	.05
145	Jose Lind	.05
146	Dennis Martinez	.05
147	Chet Lemon	.05
148	Orel Hershiser	.05
149	Dave Martinez	.05
150	Billy Hatcher	.05
151	Charlie Leibrandt	.05
152	Keith Hernandez	.05
153	Kevin McReynolds	.05
154	Tony Gwynn	.60
155	Stan Javier	.05
156	Tony Pena	.05
157	Andy Van Slyke	.05
158	Gene Larkin	.05
159	Chris James	.05
160	Fred McGriff	.05
161	Rick Rhoden	.05
162	Scott Garrelts	.05
163	Mike Campbell	.05
164	Dave Righetti	.05
165	Paul Molitor	.50
166	Danny Jackson	.05
167	Pete O'Brien	.05
168	Julio Franco	.05
169	Mark McGwire	1.00
170	Zane Smith	.05
171	Johnny Ray	.05
172	Lester Lancaster	.05
173	Mel Hall	.05
174	Tracy Jones	.05
175	Kevin Seitzer	.05
176	Bob Knepper	.05
177	Mike Greenwell	.05
178	Mike Marshall	.05
179	Melido Perez	.05
180	Tim Raines	.05
181	Jack Morris	.05
182	Darryl Strawberry	.05
183	Robin Yount	.50
184	Lance Parrish	.05
185	Darnell Coles	.05
186	Kirby Puckett	.60
187	Terry Pendleton	.05
188	Don Slaught	.05
189	Jimmy Jones	.05
190	Dave Parker	.05
191	Mike Aldrete	.05
192	Mike Moore	.05
193	Greg Walker	.05
194	Calvin Schiraldi	.05
195	Dick Schofield	.05
196	Jody Reed	.05
197	Pete Smith	.05
198	Cal Ripken, Jr.	1.50
199	Lloyd Moseby	.05
200	Ruben Sierra	.05
201	R.J. Reynolds	.05
202	Bryn Smith	.05
203	Gary Pettis	.05
204	Steve Sax	.05
205	Frank DiPino	.05
206	Mike Scott	.05
207	Kurt Stillwell	.05
208	Mookie Wilson	.05
209	Lee Mazzilli	.05
210	Lance McCullers	.05
211	Rick Honeycutt	.05
212	John Tudor	.05
213	Jim Gott	.05
214	Frank Viola	.05
215	Juan Samuel	.05
216	Jesse Barfield	.05
217	Claudell Washington	.05
218	Rick Reuschel	.05
219	Jim Presley	.05
220	Tommy John	.05
221	Dan Plesac	.05
222	Barry Larkin	.05
223	Mike Stanley	.05
224	Cory Snyder	.05
225	Andre Dawson	.25
226	Ken Oberkfell	.05
227	Devon White	.05
228	Jamie Moyer	.05
229	Brook Jacoby	.05
230	Rob Murphy	.05
231	Bret Saberhagen	.05
232	Nolan Ryan	1.50
233	Bruce Hurst	.05
234	Jesse Orosco	.05
235	Bobby Thigpen	.05
236	Pascual Perez	.05
237	Matt Nokes	.05
238	Bob Ojeda	.05
239	Joey Meyer	.05
240	Shane Rawley	.05
241	Jeff Robinson	.05
242	Jeff Reardon	.05
243	Ozzie Smith	.60
244	Dave Winfield	.50
245	John Kruk	.05
246	Carney Lansford	.05
247	Candy Maldonado	.05
248	Ken Phelps	.05
249	Ken Williams	.05
250	Al Nipper	.05
251	Mark McLemore	.05
252	Lee Smith	.05
253	Albert Hall	.05
254	Billy Ripken	.05
255	Kelly Gruber	.05
256	Charlie Hough	.05
257	John Smiley	.05
258	Tim Wallach	.05
259	Frank Tanana	.05
260	Mike Scioscia	.05
261	Damon Berryhill	.05
262	Dave Smith	.05
263	Willie Wilson	.05
264	Len Dykstra	.05
265	Randy Myers	.05
266	Keith Moreland	.05
267	Eric Plunk	.05
268	Todd Worrell	.05
269	Bob Walk	.05
270	Keith Atherton	.05
271	Mike Schmidt	.75
272	Mike Flanagan	.05
273	Rafael Santana	.05
274	Rob Thompson	.05
275	Rey Quinones	.05
276	Cecilio Guante	.05
277	B.J. Surhoff	.05
278	Chris Sabo	.05
279	Mitch Williams	.05
280	Greg Swindell	.05
281	Alan Trammell	.05
282	Storm Davis	.05
283	Chuck Finley	.05
284	Dave Stieb	.05
285	Scott Bailes	.05
286	Larry Sheets	.05
287	Danny Tartabull	.05
288	Checklist	.05
289	Todd Benzinger	.05
290	John Shelby	.05
291	Steve Lyons	.05
292	Mitch Webster	.05
293	Walt Terrell	.05
294	Pete Stanicek	.05
295	Chris Bosio	.05
296	Milt Thompson	.05
297	Fred Lynn	.05
298	Juan Berenguer	.05
299	Ken Dayley	.05
300	Joel Skinner	.05
301	Benito Santiago	.05
302	Ron Hassey	.05
303	Jose Uribe	.05
304	Harold Reynolds	.05
305	Dale Sveum	.05
306	Glenn Wilson	.05
307	Mike Witt	.05
308	Ron Robinson	.05
309	Denny Walling	.05
310	Joe Orsulak	.05
311	David Wells	.05
312	Steve Buechele	.05
313	Jose Oquendo	.05
314	Floyd Youmans	.05
315	Lou Whitaker	.05
316	Fernando Valenzuela	.05
317	Mike Boddicker	.05
318	Gerald Young	.05
319	Frank White	.05
320	Bill Wegman	.05
321	Tom Niedenfuer	.05
322	Ed Whitson	.05
323	Curt Young	.05
324	Greg Mathews	.05
325	Doug Jones	.05
326	Tommy Herr	.05
327	Kent Tekulve	.05
328	Rance Mulliniks	.05
329	Checklist	.05

330 Craig Lefferts .05
331 Franklin Stubbs .05
332 Rick Cerone .05
333 Dave Schmidt .05
334 Larry Parrish .05
335 Tom Browning .05
336 Checklist .05

Diamond Kings Supers

This 28-card set (including the checklist) marks the fourth edition of Donruss' super-size (5" x 7") set. These cards are exact duplicates of the 1988 Diamond Kings that feature player portraits by Dick Perez. A 12-piece Stan Musial puzzle was also included with the purchase of the super-size set which was marketed via a mail-in offer printed on Donruss wrappers.

NM/M
Complete Set (28): 5.00
Common Player: .10
1 Mark McGwire 2.00
2 Tim Raines .10
3 Benito Santiago .10
4 Alan Trammell .10
5 Danny Tartabull .10
6 Ron Darling .10
7 Paul Molitor 1.00
8 Devon White .10
9 Andre Dawson .25
10 Julio Franco .10
11 Scott Fletcher .10
12 Tony Fernandez .10
13 Shane Rawley .10
14 Kal Daniels .10
15 Jack Clark .10
16 Dwight Evans .10
17 Tommy John .15
18 Andy Van Slyke .10
19 Gary Gaetti .10
20 Mark Langston .10
21 Will Clark .10
22 Glenn Hubbard .10
23 Billy Hatcher .10
24 Bob Welch .10
25 Ivan Calderon .10
26 Cal Ripken, Jr. 3.00
27 Checklist .05
641 Stan Musial Puzzle Card .10

Pop-Ups

Donruss' 1988 Pop-Up cards were reduced to the standard 2-1/2" x 3-1/2". The set includes 20 cards that fold out so that the upper portion of the player stands upright, giving a three-dimensional effect. Pop-Ups feature players from the All-Star Game starting lineup. Fronts have the player's name, team and position printed in black on a yellow banner near the bottom. As in previous issues, backs contain only the player's name, league and position and a Leaf copyright. Pop-Ups were distributed in individual packages containing one Pop-Up, five Stan Musial puzzle pieces and three All-Star cards.

NM/M
Complete Set (20): 4.00
Common Player: .05
Stan Musial Puzzle: 1.00
Wax Pack: .50
Wax Box (48): 10.00
(1) George Bell .05
(2) Wade Boggs .50
(3) Gary Carter .40
(4) Jack Clark .05
(5) Eric Davis .05
(6) Andre Dawson .25
(7) Rickey Henderson .40
(8) Davey Johnson .05
(9) Don Mattingly .65
(10) Terry Kennedy .05
(11) John McNamara .05
(12) Willie Randolph .05
(13) Cal Ripken, Jr. 1.00
(14) Bret Saberhagen .05
(15) Ryne Sandberg .50
(16) Mike Schmidt .65
(17) Mike Scott .05
(18) Ozzie Smith .50
(19) Darryl Strawberry .05
(20) Dave Winfield .40

Rookies

For the third consecutive year, Donruss issued a 56-card boxed set highlighting current rookies. The complete set includes a checklist and a 15-piece Stan Musial Diamond Kings puzzle. As in previous years, the set is similar to the company's basic issue, with the exception of the logo and border color. Card fronts feature red, green and black-striped borders, with a red-and-white player name printed in the lower-left corner beneath the photo. "The Rookies" logo is printed in red, white and black in the lower-right corner. Backs are printed in black on bright aqua and include personal data, recent performance stats and major league totals, as well as 1984-88 minor league stats. The cards are the standard 2-1/2" x 3-1/2".

NM/M
Complete Set (56): 4.00
Common Player: .05
1 Mark Grace .25
2 Mike Campbell .05
3 Todd Frowirth **RC** .05
4 Dave Stapleton .05
5 Shawn Abner .05
6 Jose Cecena **RC** .05
7 Dave Gallagher **RC** .05
8 Mark Parent **RC** .05
9 Cecil Espy **RC** .05
10 Pete Smith .05
11 Jay Buhner .25
12 Pat Borders **RC** .05
13 Doug Jennings **RC** .05
14 Brady Anderson **RC** 1.00
15 Pete Stanicek .05
16 Roberto Kelly .05
17 Jeff Treadway .05
18 Walt Weiss **RC** .05
19 Paul Gibson **RC** .05
20 Tim Crews .05
21 Melido Perez .05
22 Steve Peters **RC** .05
23 Craig Worthington **RC** .05
24 John Trautwein **RC** .05
25 DeWayne Vaughn **RC** .05
26 David Wells .15
27 Al Leiter .15
28 Tim Belcher .05
29 Johnny Paredes **RC** .05
30 Chris Sabo **RC** .05
31 Damon Berryhill .05
32 Randy Milligan .05
33 Gary Thurman .05
34 Kevin Elster .05
35 Roberto Alomar 1.50
36 Edgar Martinez **RC** (Photo actually Edwin Nunez.) 1.50
37 Todd Stottlemyre .15
38 Joey Meyer .05
39 Carl Nichols .05
40 Jack McDowell .05
41 Jose Bautista **RC** .05
42 Sil Campusano **RC** .05
43 John Dopson **RC** .05
44 Jody Reed .05
45 Darrin Jackson **RC** .05
46 Mike Capel **RC** .05
47 Ron Gant .05
48 John Davis .05
49 Kevin Coffman **RC** .05
50 Cris Carpenter **RC** .05
51 Mackey Sasser .05
52 Luis Alicea **RC** .05
53 Bryan Harvey **RC** .05
54 Steve Ellsworth **RC** .05
55 Mike Macfarlane **RC** .05
56 Checklist 1-56 .05

Team Books

Three pages of nine cards each and a Stan Musial puzzle highlight these special team collection books. The cards feature the same design as the regular 1988 Donruss cards, but contain a 1988 copyright date instead of 1987 like the regular set. The cards are numbered like the regular issue with the exception of new cards of traded players and rookies produced especially for the team collection books. Books are commonly found complete with the cards and puzzle. The puzzle pieces are perforated for removal, but the card sheets are not.

NM/M
Complete Set, Books (5): 12.00
Common Player: .05
Boston Red Sox Team Book 3.00
NEW Brady Anderson .50
NEW Rick Cerone .05
NEW Steve Ellsworth .05
NEW Dennis Lamp .05
NEW Kevin Romine .05
NEW Lee Smith .25
NEW Mike Smithson .05
NEW John Trautwein .05
41 Jody Reed .05
51 Roger Clemens .75
92 Bob Stanley .05
129 Rich Gedman .05
153 Wade Boggs .65
174 Ellis Burks .05
216 Dwight Evans .05
252 Bruce Hurst .05
276 Marty Barrett .05
297 Todd Benzinger .05
339 Mike Greenwell .05
399 Jim Rice .25
421 John Marzano .05
462 Oil Can Boyd .05
498 Sam Horn .05
544 Spike Owen .05
585 Jeff Sellers .05
623 Ed Romero .05
634 Wes Gardner .05
Chicago Cubs Team Book: 3.00
NEW Mike Bielecki .05
NEW Rich Gossage .25
NEW Drew Hall .05
NEW Darrin Jackson .05
NEW Vance Law .05
NEW Al Nipper .05
NEW Angel Salazar .05
NEW Calvin Schiraldi .05
40 Mark Grace .50
68 Rick Sutcliffe .05
119 Jody Davis .05
146 Shawon Dunston .05
169 Jamie Moyer .05
191 Leon Durham .05
242 Ryne Sandberg .65
269 Andre Dawson .25
315 Paul Noce .05
324 Rafael Palmeiro .40
438 Dave Martinez .05
447 Jerry Mumphrey .05
488 Jim Sundberg .05
516 Manny Trillo .05
539 Greg Maddux .65
561 Les Lancaster .05
570 Frank DiPino .05
639 Damon Berryhill .05
646 Scott Sanderson .05
N.Y. Mets Team Book: 3.00
NEW Jeff Innis .05
NEW Mackey Sasser .05
NEW Gene Walter .05
37 Kevin Elster .05
69 Dwight Gooden .05
76 Ron Darling .05
118 Sid Fernandez .05
199 Gary Carter .50
241 Wally Backman .05
316 Keith Hernandez .05
323 Dave Magadan .05
364 Len Dykstra .05
439 Darryl Strawberry .05
446 Rick Aguilera .05
562 Keith Miller .05
569 Howard Johnson .05
603 Terry Leach .05
614 Lee Mazzilli .05
617 Kevin McReynolds .05
619 Barry Lyons .05
620 Randy Myers .05
632 Bob Ojeda .05
648 Tim Teufel .05
651 Roger McDowell .05
652 Mookie Wilson .05
653 David Cone .05
657 Gregg Jefferies .35
N.Y. Yankees Team Book: 3.00
NEW John Candelaria .05
NEW Jack Clark .05
NEW Jose Cruz .05
NEW Richard Dotson .05
NEW Cecilio Guante .05
NEW Lee Guetterman .05
NEW Rafael Santana .05
NEW Steve Shields .05
NEW Don Slaught .15
43 Al Leiter .05
93 Dave Righetti .05
105 Mike Pagliarulo .05
128 Rick Rhoden .05
175 Ron Guidry .10
217 Don Mattingly .75
228 Willie Randolph .05
251 Gary Ward .05
277 Rickey Henderson .50
278 Dave Winfield .50
340 Claudell Washington .05
374 Charles Hudson .05
401 Tommy John .10
474 Joel Skinner .05
497 Tim Stoddard .05
545 Jay Buhner .10
616 Bobby Meacham .05
635 Roberto Kelly .05
Oakland A's Team Book: 3.00
NEW Don Baylor .25
NEW Ron Hassey .05
NEW Dave Henderson .05
NEW Glenn Hubbard .05
NEW Stan Javier .05
NEW Doug Jennings .05
NEW Ed Jurak .05
NEW Dave Parker .15
NEW Walt Weiss .15
NEW Bob Welch .05
NEW Matt Young .05
97 Curt Young .05
133 Gene Nelson .05
158 Terry Steinbach .05
178 Carney Lansford .05
221 Tony Phillips .05
256 Mark McGwire 1.00
302 Jose Canseco .30
349 Dennis Eckersley .40
379 Mike Gallego .05
425 Luis Polonia .05
467 Steve Ontiveros .05
472 Dave Stewart .05
503 Eric Plunk .05
528 Greg Cadaret .05
590 Rick Honeycutt .05
595 Storm Davis .05

1989 Donruss Promo Sheet

To introduce its card design for 1989, Donruss produced this sheet. Printed on semi-gloss paper, the 7-1/2" x 10-1/2" blank-back sheet has images of seven regular cards, a Diamond King and an MVP.

NM/M
Complete Sheet: 10.00

1989 Donruss

This basic annual issue consists of 660 2-1/2" x 3-1/2" cards, including 26 Diamond Kings (DK) portrait cards and 20 Rated Rookies (RR) cards. Top and bottom borders of the cards are printed in a variety of colors that fade from dark to light. A white-lettered player name is printed across the top margin. The team logo appears upper-right and the Donruss logo lower-left. A black outer stripe varnish gives faintly visible filmstrip texture to the border. Backs are in orange and black, similar to the 1988 design, with personal info, recent stats and major league totals. Team logo sticker cards (22 total) and Warren Spahn puzzle cards (63 total) are included in individual wax packs of cards. Each regular player card can be found with a back variation in the header line above the stats: i.e., "*Denotes" or "*Denotes*." Neither version carries a premium.

NM/M
Unopened Fact. Set (660): 17.50
Complete Set (660): 15.00
Common Player: .05
Warren Spahn Puzzle: .50
Wax Pack (15): .75
Wax Box (36): 15.00
Cello Pack (32): 1.00
Cello Box (24): 15.00
Rack Pack (45): .75
1 Mike Greenwell/DK .05
2 Bobby Bonilla/DK .05
3 Pete Incaviglia/DK .05
4 Chris Sabo/DK .05
5 Robin Yount/DK .40
6 Tony Gwynn/DK .50
7 Carlton Fisk/DK .40
8 Cory Snyder/DK .05
9 David Cone/DK .05
10 Kevin Seitzer/DK .05
11 Rick Reuschel/DK .05
12 Johnny Ray/DK .05
13 Dave Schmidt/DK .05
14 Andres Galarraga/DK .05
15 Kirk Gibson/DK .05
16 Fred McGriff/DK .05
17 Mark Grace/DK .15
18 Jeff Robinson/DK .05
19 Vince Coleman/DK .05
20 Dave Henderson/DK .05
21 Harold Reynolds/DK .05
22 Gerald Perry/DK .05
23 Frank Viola/DK .05
24 Steve Bedrosian/DK .05
25 Glenn Davis/DK .05
26 Don Mattingly/DK .60
27 Checklist 1-27 .05
28 Sandy Alomar, Jr./RR **RC** .35
29 Steve Searcy/RR **RC** .05
30 Cameron Drew/RR **RC** .05
31 Gary Sheffield/RR **RC** 1.00
32 Erik Hanson/RR **RC** .05
33 Ken Griffey Jr./RR **RC** 6.00
34 Greg Harris/RR **RC** .05
35 Gregg Jefferies/RR .05
36 Luis Medina/RR **RC** .05
37 Carlos Quintana/RR **RC** .05
38 Felix Jose/RR **RC** .05
39 Cris Carpenter/RR **RC** .05
40 Ron Jones/RR **RC** .05
41 Dave West/RR **RC** .05
42 Randy Johnson/RR **RC** 3.00
43 Mike Harkey/RR **RC** .05
44 Pete Harnisch/RR **RC** .10
45 Tom Gordon/RR **RC** .25
46 Gregg Olson/RR **RC** .10
47 Alex Sanchez/RR **RC** .05
48 Ruben Sierra .05
49 Rafael Palmeiro .35
50 Ron Gant .05
51 Cal Ripken, Jr. 1.00
52 Wally Joyner .05
53 Gary Carter .40
54 Andy Van Slyke .05
55 Robin Yount .40
56 Pete Incaviglia .05
57 Greg Brock .05
58 Melido Perez .05
59 Craig Lefferts .05
60 Gary Pettis .05
61 Danny Tartabull .05
62 Guillermo Hernandez .05
63 Ozzie Smith .50
64 Gary Gaetti .05
65 Mark Davis .05
66 Lee Smith .05
67 Dennis Eckersley .35
68 Wade Boggs .50
69 Mike Scott .05
70 Fred McGriff .05
71 Tom Browning .05
72 Claudell Washington .05
73 Mel Hall .05
74 Don Mattingly .60
75 Steve Bedrosian .05
76 Juan Samuel .05
77 Mike Scioscia .05
78 Dave Righetti .05
79 Alfredo Griffin .05
80 Eric Davis .05
81 Juan Berenguer .05
82 Todd Worrell .05
83 Joe Carter .05
84 Steve Sax .05
85 Frank White .05
86 John Kruk .05
87 Rance Mulliniks .05
88 Alan Ashby .05
89 Charlie Leibrandt .05
90 Frank Tanana .05
91 Jose Canseco .25
92 Barry Bonds 1.00
93 Harold Reynolds .05
94 Mark McLemore .05
95 Mark McGwire .75
96 Eddie Murray .40
97 Tim Raines .05
98 Rob Thompson .05
99 Kevin McReynolds .05
100 Checklist 28-137 .05
101 Carlton Fisk .40
102 Dave Martinez .05
103 Glenn Braggs .05
104 Dale Murphy .15
105 Ryne Sandberg .50
106 Dennis Martinez .05
107 Pete O'Brien .05
108 Dick Schofield .05
109 Henry Cotto .05
110 Mike Marshall .05
111 Keith Moreland .05
112 Tom Brunansky .05
113 Kelly Gruber .05
114 Brook Jacoby .05
115 Keith Brown **RC** .05
116 Matt Nokes .05
117 Keith Hernandez .05
118 Bob Forsch .05
119 Bert Blyleven .10
120 Willie Wilson .05
121 Tommy Gregg .05
122 Jim Rice .25
123 Bob Knepper .05
124 Danny Jackson .05
125 Eric Plunk .05
126 Brian Fisher .05
127 Mike Pagliarulo .05
128 Tony Gwynn .50
129 Lance McCullers .05
130 Andres Galarraga .05
131 Jose Uribe .05
132 Kirk Gibson .05
133 David Palmer .05
134 R.J. Reynolds .05
135 Greg Walker .05
136 Kirk McCaskill .05
137 Shawon Dunston .05
138 Andy Allanson .05
139 Rob Murphy .05
140 Mike Aldrete .05
141 Terry Kennedy .05
142 Scott Fletcher .05
143 Steve Balboni .05
144 Bret Saberhagen .05
145 Ozzie Virgil .05

146 Dale Sveum .05
147 Darryl Strawberry .05
148 Harold Baines .10
149 George Bell .05
150 Dave Parker .05
151 Bobby Bonilla .05
152 Mookie Wilson .05
153 Ted Power .05
154 Nolan Ryan 1.00
155 Jeff Reardon .05
156 Tim Wallach .05
157 Jamie Moyer .05
158 Rich Gossage .10
159 Dave Winfield .40
160 Von Hayes .05
161 Willie McGee .05
162 Rich Gedman .05
163 Tony Pena .05
164 Mike Morgan .05
165 Charlie Hough .05
166 Mike Stanley .05
167 Andre Dawson .20
168 Joe Boever **RC** .05
169 Pete Stanicek .05
170 Bob Boone .05
171 Ron Darling .05
172 Bob Walk .05
173 Rob Deer .05
174 Steve Buechele .05
175 Ted Higuera .05
176 Ozzie Guillen .05
177 Candy Maldonado .05
178 Doyle Alexander .05
179 Mark Gubicza .05
180 Alan Trammell .05
181 Vince Coleman .05
182 Kirby Puckett .50
183 Chris Brown .05
184 Marty Barrett .05
185 Stan Javier .05
186 Mike Greenwell .05
187 Billy Hatcher .05
188 Jimmy Key .05
189 Nick Esasky .05
190 Don Slaught .05
191 Cory Snyder .05
192 John Candelaria .05
193 Mike Schmidt .60
194 Kevin Gross .05
195 John Tudor .05
196 Neil Allen .05
197 Orel Hershiser .05
198 Kal Daniels .05
199 Kent Hrbek .05
200 Checklist 138-247 .05
201 Joe Magrane .05
202 Scott Bailes .05
203 Tim Belcher .05
204 George Brett .60
205 Benito Santiago .05
206 Tony Fernandez .05
207 Gerald Young .05
208 Bo Jackson .10
209 Chet Lemon .05
210 Storm Davis .05
211 Doug Drabek .05
212 Mickey Brantley (Photo actually Nelson Simmons.) .05
213 Devon White .05
214 Dave Stewart .05
215 Dave Schmidt .05
216 Bryn Smith .05
217 Brett Butler .05
218 Bob Ojeda .05
219 Steve Rosenberg **RC** .05
220 Hubie Brooks .05
221 B.J. Surhoff .05
222 Rick Mahler .05
223 Rick Sutcliffe .05
224 Neal Heaton .05
225 Mitch Williams .05
226 Chuck Finley .05
227 Mark Langston .05
228 Jesse Orosco .05
229 Ed Whitson .05
230 Terry Pendleton .05
231 Lloyd Moseby .05
232 Greg Swindell .05
233 John Franco .05
234 Jack Morris .05
235 Howard Johnson .05
236 Glenn Davis .05
237 Frank Viola .05
238 Kevin Seitzer .05
239 Gerald Perry .05
240 Dwight Evans .05
241 Jim Deshaies .05
242 Bo Diaz .05
243 Carney Lansford .05
244 Mike LaValliere .05
245 Rickey Henderson .40
246 Roberto Alomar .20
247 Jimmy Jones .05
248 Pascual Perez .05
249 Will Clark .05
250 Fernando Valenzuela .05
251 Shane Rawley .05
252 Sid Bream .05
253 Steve Lyons .05
254 Brian Downing .05
255 Mark Grace .05
256 Tom Candiotti .05
257 Barry Larkin .05
258 Mike Krukow .05
259 Billy Ripken .05
260 Cecilio Guante .05
261 Scott Bradley .05
262 Floyd Bannister .05
263 Pete Smith .05
264 Jim Gantner .05
265 Roger McDowell .05
266 Bobby Thigpen .05
267 Jim Clancy .05
268 Terry Steinbach .05
269 Mike Dunne .05
270 Dwight Gooden .05
271 Mike Heath .05
272 Dave Smith .05
273 Keith Atherton .05
274 Tim Burke .05
275 Damon Berryhill .05
276 Vance Law .05
277 Rich Dotson .05
278 Lance Parrish .05
279 Geronimo Berroa .05
280 Roger Clemens .60
281 Greg Mathews .05
282 Tom Niedenfuer .05
283 Paul Kilgus .05
284 Jose Guzman .05
285 Calvin Schiraldi .05
286 Charlie Puleo .05
287 Joe Orsulak .05
288 Jack Howell .05
289 Kevin Elster .05
290 Jose Lind .05
291 Paul Molitor .40
292 Cecil Espy .05
293 Bill Wegman .05
294 Dan Pasqua .05
295 Scott Garrelts .05
296 Walt Terrell .05
297 Ed Hearn .05
298 Lou Whitaker .05
299 Ken Dayley .05
300 Checklist 248-357 .05
301 Tommy Herr .05
302 Mike Brumley .05
303 Ellis Burks .05
304 Curt Young .05
305 Jody Reed .05
306 Bill Doran .05
307 David Wells .05
308 Ron Robinson .05
309 Rafael Santana .05
310 Julio Franco .05
311 Jack Clark .05
312 Chris James .05
313 Milt Thompson .05
314 John Shelby .05
315 Al Leiter .05
316 Mike Davis .05
317 Chris Sabo **RC** .15
318 Greg Gagne .05
319 Jose Oquendo .05
320 John Farrell .05
321 Franklin Stubbs .05
322 Kurt Stillwell .05
323 Shawn Abner .05
324 Mike Flanagan .05
325 Kevin Bass .05
326 Pat Tabler .05
327 Mike Henneman .05
328 Rick Honeycutt .05
329 John Smiley .05
330 Rey Quinones .05
331 Johnny Ray .05
332 Bob Welch .05
333 Larry Sheets .05
334 Jeff Parrett .05
335 Rick Reuschel .05
336 Randy Myers .05
337 Ken Williams .05
338 Andy McGaffigan .05
339 Joey Meyer .05
340 Dion James .05
341 Les Lancaster .05
342 Tom Foley .05
343 Geno Petralli .05
344 Dan Petry .05
345 Alvin Davis .05
346 Mickey Hatcher .05
347 Marvell Wynne .05
348 Danny Cox .05
349 Dave Stieb .05
350 Jay Bell .05
351 Jeff Treadway .05
352 Luis Salazar .05
353 Len Dykstra .05
354 Juan Agosto .05
355 Gene Larkin .05
356 Steve Farr .05
357 Paul Assenmacher .05
358 Todd Benzinger .05
359 Larry Andersen .05
360 Paul O'Neill .05
361 Ron Hassey .05
362 Jim Gott .05
363 Ken Phelps .05
364 Tim Flannery .05
365 Randy Ready .05
366 Nelson Santovenia **RC** .05
367 Kelly Downs .05
368 Danny Heep .05
369 Phil Bradley .05
370 Jeff Robinson .05
371 Ivan Calderon .05
372 Mike Witt .05
373 Greg Maddux .50
374 Carmen Castillo .05
375 Jose Rijo .05
376 Joe Price .05
377 R.C. Gonzalez .05
378 Oddibe McDowell .05
379 Jim Presley .05
380 Brad Wellman .05
381 Tom Glavine .20
382 Dan Plesac .05
383 Wally Backman .05
384 Dave Gallagher **RC** .05
385 Tom Henke .05
386 Luis Polonia .05
387 Junior Ortiz .05
388 David Cone .05
389 Dave Bergman .05
390 Danny Darwin .05
391 Dan Gladden .05
392 John Dopson **RC** .05
393 Frank DiPino .05
394 Al Nipper .05
395 Willie Randolph .05
396 Don Carman .05
397 Scott Terry .05
398 Rick Cerone .05
399 Tom Pagnozzi .05
400 Checklist 358-467 .05
401 Mickey Tettleton .05
402 Curtis Wilkerson .05
403 Jeff Russell .05
404 Pat Perry .05
405 Jose Alvarez **RC** .05
406 Rick Schu .05
407 Sherman Corbett **RC** .05
408 Dave Magadan .05
409 Bob Kipper .05
410 Don August .05
411 Bob Brower .05
412 Chris Bosio .05
413 Jerry Reuss .05
414 Atlee Hammaker .05
415 Jim Walewander **RC** .05
416 Mike Macfarlane **RC** .10
417 Pat Sheridan .05
418 Pedro Guerrero .05
419 Allan Anderson .05
420 Mark Parent **RC** .05
421 Bob Stanley .05
422 Mike Gallego .05
423 Bruce Hurst .05
424 Dave Meads .05
425 Jesse Barfield .05
426 Rob Dibble **RC** .15
427 Joel Skinner .05
428 Ron Kittle .05
429 Rick Rhoden .05
430 Bob Dernier .05
431 Steve Jeltz .05
432 Rick Dempsey .05
433 Roberto Kelly .05
434 Dave Anderson .05
435 Herm Winningham .05
436 Al Newman .05
437 Jose DeLeon .05
438 Doug Jones .05
439 Brian Holton .05
440 Jeff Montgomery **RC** .05
441 Dickie Thon .05
442 Cecil Fielder .05
443 John Fishel **RC** .05
444 Jerry Don Gleaton .05
445 Paul Gibson **RC** .05
446 Walt Weiss .05
447 Glenn Wilson .05
448 Mike Moore .05
449 Chili Davis .05
450 Dave Henderson .05
451 Jose Bautista **RC** .05
452 Rex Hudler .05
453 Bob Brenly .05
454 Mackey Sasser .05
455 Daryl Boston .05
456 Mike Fitzgerald .05
457 Jeffery Leonard .05
458 Bruce Sutter .35
459 Mitch Webster .05
460 Joe Hesketh .05
461 Bobby Witt .05
462 Stew Cliburn .05
463 Scott Bankhead .05
464 Ramon Martinez **RC** .25
465 Dave Leiper .05
466 Luis Alicea **RC** .05
467 John Cerutti .05
468 Ron Washington .05
469 Jeff Reed .05
470 Jeff Robinson .05
471 Sid Fernandez .05
472 Terry Puhl .05
473 Charlie Lea .05
474 Israel Sanchez **RC** .05
475 Bruce Benedict .05
476 Oil Can Boyd .05
477 Craig Reynolds .05
478 Frank Williams .05
479 Greg Cadaret .05
480 Randy Kramer **RC** .05
481 Dave Eiland **RC** .05
482 Eric Show .05
483 Garry Templeton .05
484 Wallace Johnson **RC** .05
485 Kevin Mitchell .05
486 Tim Crews .05
487 Mike Maddux .05
488 Dave LaPoint .05
489 Fred Manrique .05
490 Greg Minton .05
491 Doug Dascenzo **RC** .05
492 Willie Upshaw .05
493 Jack Armstrong **RC** .05
494 Kirt Manwaring .05
495 Jeff Ballard .05
496 Jeff Kunkel .05
497 Mike Campbell .05
498 Gary Thurman .05
499 Zane Smith .05
500 Checklist 468-577 .05
501 Mike Birkbeck .05
502 Terry Leach .05
503 Shawn Hillegas .05
504 Manny Lee .05
505 Doug Jennings **RC** .05
506 Ken Oberkfell .05
507 Tim Teufel .05
508 Tom Brookens .05
509 Rafael Ramirez .05
510 Fred Toliver .05
511 Brian Holman **RC** .05
512 Mike Bielecki .05
513 Jeff Pico **RC** .05
514 Charles Hudson .05
515 Bruce Ruffin .05
516 Larry McWilliams .05
517 Jeff Sellers .05
518 John Costello **RC** .05
519 Brady Anderson .05
520 Craig McMurtry .05
521 Ray Hayward .05
522 Drew Hall .05
523 Mark Lemke **RC** .05
524 Oswald Peraza **RC** .05
525 Bryan Harvey **RC** .05
526 Rick Aguilera .05
527 Tom Prince .05
528 Mark Clear .05
529 Jerry Browne .05
530 Juan Castillo .05
531 Jack McDowell .05
532 Chris Speier .05
533 Darrell Evans .05
534 Luis Aquino .05
535 Eric King .05
536 Ken Hill **RC** .05
537 Randy Bush .05
538 Shane Mack .05
539 Tom Bolton **RC** .05
540 Gene Nelson .05
541 Wes Gardner .05
542 Ken Caminiti .05
543 Duane Ward .05
544 Norm Charlton **RC** .10
545 Hal Morris **RC** .25
546 Rich Yett **RC** .05
547 Hensley Meulens **RC** .10
548 Greg Harris .05
549 Darren Daulton .05
550 Jeff Hamilton .05
551 Luis Aguayo .05
552 Tim Leary .05
553 Ron Oester .05
554 Steve Lombardozzi .05
555 Tim Jones **RC** .05
556 Bud Black .05
557 Alejandro Pena .05
558 Jose DeJesus **RC** .05
559 Dennis Rasmussen .05
560 Pat Borders **RC** .25
561 Craig Biggio .05
562 Luis de los Santos **RC** .05
563 Fred Lynn .05
564 Todd Burns **RC** .05
565 Felix Fermin .05
566 Darnell Coles .05
567 Willie Fraser .05
568 Glenn Hubbard .05
569 Craig Worthington **RC** .05
570 Johnny Paredes **RC** .05
571 Don Robinson .05
572 Barry Lyons .05
573 Bill Long .05
574 Tracy Jones .05
575 Juan Nieves .05
576 Andres Thomas .05
577 Rolando Roomes **RC** .05
578 Luis Rivera **RC** .05
579 Chad Kreuter **RC** .10
580 Tony Armas .05
581 Jay Buhner .05
582 Ricky Horton .05
583 Andy Hawkins .05
584 Sil Campusano **RC** .05
585 Dave Clark .05
586 Van Snider **RC** .05
587 Todd Frohwirth **RC** .05
588 Warren Spahn Puzzle Card .05
589 William Brennan **RC** .05
590 German Gonzalez **RC** .05
591 Ernie Whitt .05
592 Jeff Blauser .05
593 Spike Owen .05
594 Matt Williams .05
595 Lloyd McClendon **RC** .05
596 Steve Ontiveros .05
597 Scott Medvin **RC** .05
598 Hipolito Pena **RC** .05
599 Jerald Clark **RC** .05
600a Checklist 578-BC26 (#635 is Kurt Schilling) .10
600b Checklist 578-BC26 (#635 is Curt Schilling) .05
601 Carmelo Martinez .05
602 Mike LaCoss .05
603 Mike Devereaux .05
604 Alex Madrid **RC** .05
605 Gary Redus .05
606 Lance Johnson .05
607 Terry Clark **RC** .05
608 Manny Trillo .05
609 Scott Jordan **RC** .05
610 Jay Howell .05
611 Francisco Melendez **RC** .05
612 Mike Boddicker .05
613 Kevin Brown .05
614 Dave Valle .05
615 Tim Laudner .05
616 Andy Nezelek **RC** .05
617 Chuck Crim .05
618 Jack Savage **RC** .05
619 Adam Peterson **RC** .05
620 Todd Stottlemyre .05
621 Lance Blankenship **RC** .05
622 Miguel Garcia **RC** .05
623 Keith Miller .05
624 Ricky Jordan **RC** .05
625 Ernest Riles .05
626 John Moses .05
627 Nelson Liriano .05
628 Mike Smithson .05
629 Scott Sanderson .05
630 Dale Mohorcic .05
631 Marvin Freeman .05
632 Mike Young .05
633 Dennis Lamp .05
634 Dante Bichette **RC** .25
635 Curt Schilling **RC** 3.00
636 Scott May **RC** .05
637 Mike Schooler **RC** .05
638 Rick Leach .05
639 Tom Lampkin **RC** .05
640 Brian Meyer **RC** .05
641 Brian Harper .05
642 John Smoltz .05
643 Jose Canseco (40/40) .15
644 Bill Schroeder .05
645 Edgar Martinez **RC** .10
646 Dennis Cook **RC** .05
647 Barry Jones .05
648 Orel Hershiser (59 and Counting) .05
649 Rod Nichols **RC** .05
650 Jody Davis .05
651 Bob Milacki **RC** .05
652 Mike Jackson .05
653 Derek Lilliquist **RC** .05
654 Paul Mirabella .05
655 Mike Diaz .05
656 Jeff Musselman .05
657 Jerry Reed .05
658 Kevin Blankenship **RC** .05
659 Wayne Tolleson .05
660 Eric Hetzel **RC** .05

Grand Slammers

One card from this 12-card set was included in each Donruss cello pack. The complete insert set was included in factory sets. The featured players all hit grand slams in 1988. The 2-1/2" x 3-1/2" cards feature full color action photos. Backs tell the story of the player's grand slam. As many as five border-color variations on the front of each card have been discovered, but the prices are not affected.

		NM/M
Complete Set (12):		2.00
Common Player:		.25
1	Jose Canseco	.35
2	Mike Marshall	.25
3	Walt Weiss	.25
4	Kevin McReynolds	.25
5	Mike Greenwell	.25
6	Dave Winfield	.50
7	Mark McGwire	1.50
8	Keith Hernandez	.25
9	Franklin Stubbs	.25
10	Danny Tartabull	.25
11	Jesse Barfield	.25
12	Ellis Burks	.25

Blue Chip Cards

		NM/M
Complete Set (12):		1,200
Common Player:		60.00
1	Jose Canseco	125.00
2	Mike Marshall	60.00
3	Walt Weiss	60.00
4	Kevin McReynolds	60.00
5	Mike Greenwell	60.00
6	Dave Winfield	150.00
7	Mark McGwire	400.00
8	Keith Hernandez	75.00
9	Franklin Stubbs	60.00
10	Danny Tartabull	60.00
11	Jesse Barfield	60.00
12	Ellis Burks	60.00

MVP

This set, numbered BC1-BC26, was randomly inserted in Donruss wax packs, but not included in factory sets or other card packs. Players highlighted were selected by Donruss, one player per team. MVP cards feature a variation of the design in the basic Donruss issue, with multi-color upper and lower borders and black side borders. The "MVP" designation in large, bright letters serves as a backdrop for the full-color player photo. The cards measure 2-1/2" x 3-1/2".

		NM/M
Complete Set (26):		2.00
Common Player:		.05
1	Kirby Puckett	.40
2	Mike Scott	.05
3	Joe Carter	.05
4	Orel Hershiser	.05
5	Jose Canseco	.25
6	Darryl Strawberry	.05
7	George Brett	.50
8	Andre Dawson	.20
9	Paul Molitor	.30
10	Andy Van Slyke	.05
11	Dave Winfield	.30
12	Kevin Gross	.05
13	Mike Greenwell	.05
14	Ozzie Smith	.40
15	Cal Ripken	1.00
16	Andres Galarraga	.05
17	Alan Trammell	.05
18	Kal Daniels	.05
19	Fred McGriff	.05
20	Tony Gwynn	.40
21	Wally Joyner	.05
22	Will Clark	.05
23	Ozzie Guillen	.05
24	Gerald Perry	.05
25	Alvin Davis	.05
26	Ruben Sierra	.05

All-Stars

For the fourth consecutive year Donruss featured a 64-card set with players from the 1988 All-Star Game. The card fronts include a red-to-gold fade or gold-to-red fade border and blue vertical side borders. The top border features the player's name and position along with the "Donruss 89" logo. Each full-color player photo is highlighted by a thin white line and includes a league logo in the lower right corner. Card backs reveal an orange-gold border and black and white printing. The player's ID and personal information is displayed with a gold star on both sides. The star in the left corner includes the card number. 1988 All-Star game statistics and run totals follow along with a career highlights feature surrounded by the team, All-Star Game MLB, MLBPA, and Leaf Inc. logos. The All-Stars were distributed in wax packages containing five All-Stars, one Pop-Up, and one three-piece Warren Spahn puzzle card.

		NM/M
Complete Set (64):		4.00
Common Player:		.10
Warren Spahn Puzzle:		.50
Wax Pack (5+1):		.30
Wax Box (48):		10.00
1	Mark McGwire	.75
2	Jose Canseco	.25
3	Paul Molitor	.40
4	Rickey Henderson	.40
5	Cal Ripken, Jr.	1.00
6	Dave Winfield	.40
7	Wade Boggs	.50
8	Frank Viola	.10
9	Terry Steinbach	.10
10	Tom Kelly	.10
11	George Brett	.65
12	Doyle Alexander	.10
13	Gary Gaetti	.10
14	Roger Clemens	.65
15	Mike Greenwell	.10
16	Dennis Eckersley	.40
17	Carney Lansford	.10
18	Mark Gubicza	.10
19	Tim Laudner	.10
20	Doug Jones	.10
21	Don Mattingly	.65
22	Dan Plesac	.10
23	Kirby Puckett	.50
24	Jeff Reardon	.10
25	Johnny Ray	.10
26	Jeff Russell	.10
27	Harold Reynolds	.10
28	Dave Stieb	.10
29	Kurt Stillwell	.10
30	Jose Canseco	.25
31	Terry Steinbach	.10
32	A.L. Checklist	.05
33	Will Clark	.10
34	Darryl Strawberry	.10
35	Ryne Sandberg	.50
36	Andre Dawson	.25
37	Ozzie Smith	.50
38	Vince Coleman	.10
39	Bobby Bonilla	.10
40	Dwight Gooden	.10
41	Gary Carter	.40
42	Whitey Herzog	.10
43	Shawon Dunston	.10
44	David Cone	.10
45	Andres Galarraga	.10
46	Mark Davis	.10
47	Barry Larkin	.10
48	Kevin Gross	.10
49	Vance Law	.10
50	Orel Hershiser	.10
51	Willie McGee	.10
52	Danny Jackson	.10
53	Rafael Palmeiro	.35
54	Bob Knepper	.10
55	Lance Parrish	.10
56	Greg Maddux	.50
57	Gerald Perry	.10
58	Bob Walk	.10
59	Chris Sabo	.10
60	Todd Worrell	.10
61	Andy Van Slyke	.10
62	Ozzie Smith	.50
63	Riverfront Stadium	.10
64	N.L. Checklist	.05

Baseball's Best

For the second consecutive year, Donruss issued a "Baseball's Best" set in 1989 to highlight the game's top players. The special 336-card set was packaged in a special box and was sold at various retail chains nationwide following the conclusion of the 1989 baseball season. The cards are styled after the regular 1989 Donruss set with green borders and a glossy finish. The set included a Warren Spahn puzzle.

		NM/M
Unopened Set (336):		30.00
Complete Set (336):		25.00
Common Player:		.05
1	Don Mattingly	.75
2	Tom Glavine	.25
3	Bert Blyleven	.10
4	Andre Dawson	.25
5	Pete O'Brien	.05
6	Eric Davis	.05
7	George Brett	.75
8	Glenn Davis	.05
9	Ellis Burks	.05
10	Kirk Gibson	.05
11	Carlton Fisk	.50
12	Andres Galarraga	.05
13	Alan Trammell	.05
14	Dwight Gooden	.05
15	Paul Molitor	.50
16	Roger McDowell	.05
17	Doug Drabek	.05
18	Kent Hrbek	.05
19	Vince Coleman	.05
20	Steve Sax	.05
21	Roberto Alomar	.20
22	Carney Lansford	.05
23	Will Clark	.05
24	Alvin Davis	.05
25	Bobby Thigpen	.05
26	Ryne Sandberg	.60
27	Devon White	.05
28	Mike Greenwell	.05
29	Dale Murphy	.20
30	Jeff Ballard	.05
31	Kelly Gruber	.05
32	Julio Franco	.05
33	Bobby Bonilla	.05
34	Tim Wallach	.05
35	Lou Whitaker	.05
36	Jay Howell	.05
37	Greg Maddux	.60
38	Bill Doran	.05
39	Danny Tartabull	.05
40	Darryl Strawberry	.05
41	Ron Darling	.05
42	Tony Gwynn	.60
43	Mark McGwire	1.00
44	Ozzie Smith	.60
45	Andy Van Slyke	.05
46	Juan Berenguer	.05
47	Von Hayes	.05
48	Tony Fernandez	.05
49	Eric Plunk	.05
50	Ernest Riles	.05
51	Harold Reynolds	.05
52	Andy Hawkins	.05
53	Robin Yount	.50
54	Danny Jackson	.05
55	Nolan Ryan	1.50
56	Joe Carter	.05
57	Jose Canseco	.35
58	Jody Davis	.05
59	Lance Parrish	.05
60	Mitch Williams	.05
61	Brook Jacoby	.05
62	Tom Browning	.05
63	Kurt Stillwell	.05
64	Rafael Ramirez	.05
65	Roger Clemens	.75
66	Mike Scioscia	.05
67	Dave Gallagher	.05
68	Mark Langston	.05
69	Chet Lemon	.05
70	Kevin McReynolds	.05
71	Rob Deer	.05
72	Tommy Herr	.05
73	Barry Bonds	1.50
74	Frank Viola	.05
75	Pedro Guerrero	.05
76	Dave Righetti	.05
77	Bruce Hurst	.05
78	Rickey Henderson	.50
79	Robby Thompson	.05
80	Randy Johnson	6.00
81	Harold Baines	.05
82	Calvin Schiraldi	.05
83	Kirk McCaskill	.05
84	Lee Smith	.05
85	John Smoltz	1.00
86	Mickey Tettleton	.05
87	Jimmy Key	.05
88	Rafael Palmeiro	.45
89	Sid Bream	.05
90	Dennis Martinez	.05
91	Frank Tanana	.05
92	Eddie Murray	.50
93	Shawon Dunston	.05
94	Mike Scott	.05
95	Bret Saberhagen	.05
96	David Cone	.05
97	Kevin Elster	.05
98	Jack Clark	.05
99	Dave Stewart	.05
100	Jose Oquendo	.05
101	Jose Lind	.05
102	Gary Gaetti	.05
103	Ricky Jordan	.05
104	Fred McGriff	.05
105	Don Slaught	.05
106	Jose Uribe	.05
107	Jeffrey Leonard	.05
108	Lee Guetterman	.05
109	Chris Bosio	.05
110	Barry Larkin	.05
111	Ruben Sierra	.05
112	Greg Swindell	.05
113	Gary Sheffield	1.00
114	Lonnie Smith	.05
115	Chili Davis	.05
116	Damon Berryhill	.05
117	Tom Candiotti	.05
118	Kal Daniels	.05
119	Mark Gubicza	.05
120	Jim Deshaies	.05
121	Dwight Evans	.05
122	Mike Morgan	.05
123	Dan Pasqua	.05
124	Bryn Smith	.05
125	Doyle Alexander	.05
126	Howard Johnson	.05
127	Chuck Crim	.05
128	Darren Daulton	.05
129	Jeff Robinson	.05
130	Kirby Puckett	.60
131	Joe Magrane	.05
132	Jesse Barfield	.05
133	Mark Davis (Photo actually Dave Leiper.)	.05
134	Dennis Eckersley	.45
135	Mike Krukow	.05
136	Jay Buhner	.05
137	Ozzie Guillen	.05
138	Rick Sutcliffe	.05
139	Wally Joyner	.05
140	Wade Boggs	.60
141	Jeff Treadway	.05
142	Cal Ripken	1.50
143	Dave Steib	.05
144	Pete Incaviglia	.05
145	Bob Walk	.05
146	Nelson Santovenia	.05
147	Mike Heath	.05
148	Willie Randolph	.05
149	Paul Kilgus	.05
150	Billy Hatcher	.05
151	Steve Farr	.05
152	Gregg Jefferies	.05
153	Randy Myers	.05
154	Garry Templeton	.05
155	Walt Weiss	.05
156	Terry Pendleton	.05
157	John Smiley	.05
158	Greg Gagne	.05
159	Lenny Dykstra	.05
160	Nelson Liriano	.05
161	Alvaro Espinoza	.05
162	Rick Reuschel	.05
163	Omar Vizquel	.05
164	Clay Parker	.05
165	Dan Plesac	.05
166	John Franco	.05
167	Scott Fletcher	.05
168	Cory Snyder	.05
169	Bo Jackson	.10
170	Tommy Gregg	.05
171	Jim Abbott	.05
172	Jerome Walton	.05
173	Doug Jones	.05
174	Todd Benzinger	.05
175	Frank White	.05
176	Craig Biggio	.50
177	John Dopson	.05
178	Alfredo Griffin	.05
179	Melido Perez	.05
180	Tim Burke	.05
181	Matt Nokes	.05
182	Gary Carter	.50
183	Ted Higuera	.05
184	Ken Howell	.05
185	Rey Quinones	.05
186	Wally Backman	.05
187	Tom Brunansky	.05
188	Steve Balboni	.05
189	Marvell Wynne	.05
190	Dave Henderson	.05
191	Don Robinson	.05
192	Ken Griffey Jr.	9.00
193	Ivan Calderon	.05
194	Mike Bielecki	.05
195	Johnny Ray	.05
196	Rob Murphy	.05
197	Andres Thomas	.05
198	Phil Bradley	.05
199	Junior Felix	.05
200	Jeff Russell	.05
201	Mike LaValliere	.05
202	Kevin Gross	.05
203	Keith Moreland	.05
204	Mike Marshall	.05
205	Dwight Smith	.05
206	Jim Clancy	.05
207	Kevin Seitzer	.05
208	Keith Hernandez	.05
209	Bob Ojeda	.05
210	Ed Whitson	.05
211	Tony Phillips	.05
212	Milt Thompson	.05
213	Randy Kramer	.05
214	Randy Bush	.05
215	Randy Ready	.05
216	Duane Ward	.05
217	Jimmy Jones	.05
218	Scott Garrelts	.05
219	Scott Bankhead	.05
220	Lance McCullers	.05
221	B.J. Surhoff	.05
222	Chris Sabo	.05
223	Steve Buechele	.05
224	Joel Skinner	.05
225	Orel Hershiser	.05
226	Derek Lilliquist	.05
227	Claudell Washington	.05
228	Lloyd McClendon	.05
229	Felix Fermin	.05
230	Paul O'Neill	.05
231	Charlie Leibrandt	.05
232	Dave Smith	.05
233	Bob Stanley	.05
234	Tim Belcher	.05
235	Eric King	.05
236	Spike Owen	.05
237	Mike Henneman	.05
238	Juan Samuel	.05
239	Greg Brock	.05
240	John Kruk	.05
241	Glenn Wilson	.05
242	Jeff Reardon	.05
243	Todd Worrell	.05
244	Dave LaPoint	.05
245	Walt Terrell	.05
246	Mike Moore	.05
247	Kelly Downs	.05
248	Dave Valle	.05
249	Ron Kittle	.05
250	Steve Wilson	.05
251	Dick Schofield	.05
252	Marty Barrett	.05
253	Dion James	.05
254	Bob Milacki	.05
255	Ernie Whitt	.05
256	Kevin Brown	.05
257	R.J. Reynolds	.05
258	Tim Raines	.05
259	Frank Williams	.05
260	Jose Gonzalez	.05
261	Mitch Webster	.05
262	Ken Caminiti	.05
263	Bob Boone	.05
264	Dave Magadan	.05
265	Rick Aguilera	.05
266	Chris James	.05
267	Bob Welch	.05
268	Ken Dayley	.05
269	Junior Ortiz	.05
270	Allan Anderson	.05
271	Steve Jeltz	.05
272	George Bell	.05
273	Roberto Kelly	.05
274	Brett Butler	.05
275	Mike Schooler	.05
276	Ken Phelps	.05
277	Glenn Braggs	.05
278	Jose Rijo	.05
279	Bobby Witt	.05
280	Jerry Browne	.05
281	Kevin Mitchell	.05
282	Craig Worthington	.05
283	Greg Minton	.05
284	Nick Esasky	.05
285	John Farrell	.05
286	Rick Mahler	.05
287	Tom Gordon	.05
288	Gerald Young	.05
289	Jody Reed	.05
290	Jeff Hamilton	.05
291	Gerald Perry	.05
292	Hubie Brooks	.05
293	Bo Diaz	.05
294	Terry Puhl	.05
295	Jim Gantner	.05
296	Jeff Parrett	.05
297	Mike Boddicker	.05
298	Dan Gladden	.05
299	Tony Pena	.05
300	Checklist	.05
301	Tom Henke	.05
302	Pascual Perez	.05
303	Steve Bedrosian	.05
304	Ken Hill	.05
305	Jerry Reuss	.05
306	Jim Eisenreich	.05
307	Jack Howell	.05
308	Rick Cerone	.05
309	Tim Leary	.05
310	Joe Orsulak	.05
311	Jim Dwyer	.05
312	Geno Petralli	.05
313	Rick Honeycutt	.05
314	Tom Foley	.05
315	Kenny Rogers	.05
316	Mike Flanagan	.05
317	Bryan Harvey	.05
318	Billy Ripken	.05
319	Jeff Montgomery	.05
320	Erik Hanson	.05
321	Brian Downing	.05
322	Gregg Olson	.05
323	Terry Steinbach	.05
324	Sammy Sosa	12.00
325	Gene Harris	.05
326	Mike Devereaux	.05
327	Dennis Cook	.05
328	David Wells	.05
329	Checklist	.05
330	Kirt Manwaring	.05
331	Jim Presley	.05
332	Checklist	.05
333	Chuck Finley	.05
334	Rob Dibble	.05
335	Cecil Espy	.05
336	Dave Parker	.05

Diamond King Supers

1989 Donruss Diamond King Supers

Once again for 1989, collectors could acquire a 4-3/4" x 6-3/4" version of the Diamond King subset via a wrapper mail-in offer. Other than size, cards are identical to the DKs in the regular issue.

		NM/M
Complete Set (27):		5.00
Common Player:		.25
1	Mike Greenwell	.25
2	Bobby Bonilla	.25
3	Pete Incaviglia	.25
4	Chris Sabo	.25
5	Robin Yount	1.00
6	Tony Gwynn	1.50
7	Carlton Fisk	1.00
8	Cory Snyder	.25
9	David Cone	.25
10	Kevin Seitzer	.25
11	Rick Reuschel	.25
12	Johnny Ray	.25
13	Dave Schmidt	.25
14	Andres Galarraga	.25
15	Kirk Gibson	.25
16	Fred McGriff	.25
17	Mark Grace	.25
18	Jeff Robinson	.25
19	Vince Coleman	.25
20	Dave Henderson	.25
21	Harold Reynolds	.25
22	Gerald Perry	.25
23	Frank Viola	.25
24	Steve Bedrosian	.25
25	Glenn Davis	.25
26	Don Mattingly	2.00
27	Checklist	.05

Pop-Ups

This set features the starters from the 1988 Major League All-Star game. The cards are designed with a perforated outline so each player can be popped up to stand upright. The flip side features a red, white, and blue "Cincinnati Reds All-Star Game" logo at the top, a league designation, and the player's name and position. The lower portion displays instructions for creating the base of the Pop-Up. The Pop-Ups were marketed in packs with five All-Star cards and Warren Spahn puzzle-piece cards.

		NM/M
Complete Set (20):		2.00
Common Player:		.10
Warren Spahn Puzzle:		.50
Wax Pack (5+1):		.30
Wax Box (48):		10.00
(1)	Mark McGwire	.45
(2)	Jose Canseco	.20
(3)	Paul Molitor	.25
(4)	Rickey Henderson	.25
(5)	Cal Ripken, Jr.	.50
(6)	Dave Winfield	.25
(7)	Wade Boggs	.35
(8)	Frank Viola	.10
(9)	Terry Steinbach	.10
(10)	Tom Kelly	.10
(11)	Will Clark	.10
(12)	Darryl Strawberry	.10
(13)	Ryne Sandberg	.35
(14)	Andre Dawson	.10
(15)	Ozzie Smith	.35
(16)	Vince Coleman	.10
(17)	Bobby Bonilla	.10
(18)	Dwight Gooden	.10
(19)	Gary Carter	.25
(20)	Whitey Herzog	.10

Rookies

For the fourth straight year, Donruss issued a 56-card "Rookies" set in 1989. As in previous years, the set is similar in design to the regular Donruss set, except for a new "The Rookies" logo and a green and black border.

		NM/M
Complete Set (56):		8.00
Common Player:		.05
1	Gary Sheffield	.75
2	Gregg Jefferies	.05
3	Ken Griffey Jr.	5.00
4	Tom Gordon	.05
5	Billy Spiers **RC**	.05
6	Deion Sanders **RC**	.50
7	Donn Pall **RC**	.05
8	Steve Carter **RC**	.05
9	Francisco Oliveras **RC**	.05
10	Steve Wilson **RC**	.05
11	Bob Geren **RC**	.05
12	Tony Castillo **RC**	.05
13	Kenny Rogers	.05
14	Carlos Martinez **RC**	.05
15	Edgar Martinez	.05
16	Jim Abbott **RC**	.05
17	Torey Lovullo **RC**	.05
18	Mark Carreon **RC**	.05
19	Geronimo Berroa	.05
20	Luis Medina	.05
21	Sandy Alomar, Jr.	.05
22	Bob Milacki	.05
23	Joe Girardi **RC**	.10
24	German Gonzalez	.05
25	Craig Worthington	.05
26	Jerome Walton **RC**	.05
27	Gary Wayne **RC**	.05
28	Tim Jones	.05
29	Dante Bichette	.05
30	Alexis Infante **RC**	.05
31	Ken Hill	.05
32	Dwight Smith **RC**	.05
33	Luis de los Santos	.05
34	Eric Yelding **RC**	.05
35	Gregg Olson	.05
36	Phil Stephenson **RC**	.05
37	Ken Patterson **RC**	.05
38	Rick Wrona **RC**	.05
39	Mike Brumley	.05
40	Cris Carpenter	.05
41	Jeff Brantley **RC**	.05
42	Ron Jones	.05
43	Randy Johnson	2.00
44	Kevin Brown	.05
45	Ramon Martinez	.05
46	Greg Harris	.05
47	Steve Finley	.05
48	Randy Kramer	.05
49	Erik Hanson	.05
50	Matt Merullo **RC**	.05
51	Mike Devereaux	.05
52	Clay Parker **RC**	.05
53	Omar Vizquel **RC**	.05
54	Derek Lilliquist	.05
55	Junior Felix **RC**	.05
56	Checklist	.05

Traded

Donruss issued its first "Traded" set in 1989, releasing a 56-card boxed set designed in the same style as the regular 1989 Donruss set. The set included a Stan Musial puzzle card and a checklist.

	NM/M
Complete Set (56):	2.00

Common Player: .05
1 Jeffrey Leonard .05
2 Jack Clark .05
3 Kevin Gross .05
4 Tommy Herr .05
5 Bob Boone .05
6 Rafael Palmeiro .30
7 John Dopson .05
8 Willie Randolph .05
9 Chris Brown .05
10 Wally Backman .05
11 Steve Ontiveros .05
12 Eddie Murray .45
13 Lance McCullers .05
14 Spike Owen .05
15 Rob Murphy .05
16 Pete O'Brien .05
17 Ken Williams .05
18 Nick Esasky .05
19 Nolan Ryan 1.50
20 Brian Holton .05
21 Mike Moore .05
22 Joel Skinner .05
23 Steve Sax .05
24 Rick Mahler .05
25 Mike Aldrete .05
26 Jesse Orosco .05
27 Dave LaPoint .05
28 Walt Terrell .05
29 Eddie Williams .05
30 Mike Devereaux .05
31 Julio Franco .05
32 Jim Clancy .05
33 Felix Fermin .05
34 Curtis Wilkerson .05
35 Bert Blyleven .05
36 Mel Hall .05
37 Eric King .05
38 Mitch Williams .05
39 Jamie Moyer .05
40 Rick Rhoden .05
41 Phil Bradley .05
42 Paul Kilgus .05
43 Milt Thompson .05
44 Jerry Browne .05
45 Bruce Hurst .05
46 Claudell Washington .05
47 Todd Benzinger .05
48 Steve Balboni .05
49 Oddibe McDowell .05
50 Charles Hudson .05
51 Ron Kittle .05
52 Andy Hawkins .05
53 Tom Brookens .05
54 Tom Niedenfuer .05
55 Jeff Parrett .05
56 Checklist .05

1990 Donruss Previews

1990 PREVIEW CARDS
No. 10 of 12
JEROME WALTON
OUTFIELDER
CAREER HIGHLIGHTS

To introduce its 1990 baseball issue, Donruss sent two preview cards from a set of 12 to each member of its dealers' network. Though the photos are different than those used on the issued versions, the front format was the same. Backs are printed in black on white and contain career highlights, but no stats. Issued at the dawn of the "promo card" craze, and succeeding the relatively valueless sample sheets used by most companies in earlier years, little value was attached to these preview cards initially. Today they are among the scarcest of the early-1990s promos.

NM/M
Complete Set (12): 85.00
Common Player: 3.00
1 Todd Zeile 3.00
2 Ben McDonald 3.00
3 Bo Jackson 7.50
4 Will Clark 3.00
5 Dave Stewart 3.00
6 Kevin Mitchell 3.00
7 Nolan Ryan 50.00
8 Howard Johnson 3.00
9 Tony Gwynn 25.00
10 Jerome Walton 3.00
11 Wade Boggs 25.00
12 Kirby Puckett 25.00

1990 Donruss

Donruss marked its 10th anniversary in the baseball card hobby with a 715-card set in 1990, up from previous 660-card sets. The standard-size cards feature bright red borders with the player's name in script at the top. The set includes 26 "Diamond Kings" (DK) in the checklist, 20 "Rated Rookies" (RR) and a Carl Yastrzemski puzzle. Each All-Star card back has two variations. The more common has the stats box headed "All-Star Performance." Slightly scarcer versions say "Recent Major League Performance," and are worth about twice the value of the correct version.

NM/M
Unopened Factory Set (716): 10.00
Complete Set (716): 7.50
Common Player: .05
Carl Yastrzemski Puzzle: 1.00
Wax Pack (16): .50
Wax Box (36): 10.00
Rack Pack (48): 1.00
Blister Rack (78): 1.50
1 Bo Jackson/DK .15
2 Steve Sax/DK .05
3a Ruben Sierra/DK (No vertical black line at top-right on back.) .25
3b Ruben Sierra/DK (Vertical line at top-right on back.) .10
4 Ken Griffey Jr./DK .65
5 Mickey Tettleton/DK .05
6 Dave Stewart /DK .05
7 Jim Deshaies/DK .05
8 John Smoltz/DK .05
9 Mike Bielecki/DK .05
10a Brian Downing/DK (Reversed negative.) .25
10b Brian Downing/DK (Corrected) .05
11 Kevin Mitchell/DK .05
12 Kelly Gruber/DK .05
13 Joe Magrane/DK .05
14 John Franco/DK .05
15 Ozzie Guillen/DK .05
16 Lou Whitaker/DK .05
17 John Smiley/DK .05
18 Howard Johnson/DK .05
19 Willie Randolph/DK .05
20 Chris Bosio/DK .05
21 Tommy Herr/DK .05
22 Dan Gladden/DK .05
23 Ellis Burks/DK .05
24 Pete O'Brien/DK .05
25 Bryn Smith/DK .05
26 Ed Whitson/DK .05
27 Checklist 1-27 .05
28 Robin Ventura/RR .05
29 Todd Zeile/RR **RC** .15
30 Sandy Alomar, Jr./RR .05
31 Kent Mercker/RR **RC** .10
32 Ben McDonald/RR **RC** .25
33a Juan Gonzalez/RR (Reversed negative.) **RC** 2.00
33b Juan Gonzalez/RR **RC** (Corrected) 1.50
34 Eric Anthony/RR **RC** .05
35 Mike Fetters/RR **RC** .05
36 Marquis Grissom/RR **RC** .50
37 Greg Vaughn/RR **RC** .25
38 Brian Dubois/RR **RC** .05
39 Steve Avery/RR **RC** .10
40 Mark Gardner/RR **RC** .05
41 Andy Benes/RR .05
42 Delino DeShields/RR **RC** .15
43 Scott Coolbaugh/RR **RC** .05
44 Pat Combs/RR **RC** .10
45 Alex Sanchez/RR **RC** .05
46 Kelly Mann/RR **RC** .05
47 Julio Machado/RR **RC** .05
48 Pete Incaviglia .05
49 Shawon Dunston .05
50 Jeff Treadway .05
51 Jeff Ballard .05
52 Claudell Washington .05
53 Juan Samuel .05
54 John Smiley .05
55 Rob Deer .05
56 Geno Petralli .05
57 Chris Bosio .05
58 Carlton Fisk .40
59 Kirt Manwaring .05
60 Chet Lemon .05
61 Bo Jackson .10
62 Doyle Alexander .05
63 Pedro Guerrero .05
64 Allan Anderson .05
65 Greg Harris .05
66 Mike Greenwell .05
67 Walt Weiss .05
68 Wade Boggs .50
69 Jim Clancy .05
70 Junior Felix **RC** .05
71 Barry Larkin .05
72 Dave LaPoint .05
73 Joel Skinner .05
74 Jesse Barfield .05
75 Tommy Herr .05
76 Ricky Jordan .05
77 Eddie Murray .40
78 Steve Sax .05
79 Tim Belcher .05
80 Danny Jackson .05
81 Kent Hrbek .05
82 Milt Thompson .05
83 Brook Jacoby .05
84 Mike Marshall .05
85 Kevin Seitzer .05
86 Tony Gwynn .50
87 Dave Steib .05
88 Dave Smith .05
89 Bret Saberhagen .05
90 Alan Trammell .05
91 Tony Phillips .05
92 Doug Drabek .05
93 Jeffrey Leonard .05
94 Wally Joyner .05
95 Carney Lansford .05
96 Cal Ripken, Jr. 1.00
97 Andres Galarraga .05
98 Kevin Mitchell .05
99 Howard Johnson .05
100a Checklist 28-129 .05
100b Checklist 28-125 .05
101 Melido Perez .05
102 Spike Owen .05
103 Paul Molitor .40
104 Geronimo Berroa .05
105 Ryne Sandberg .50
106 Bryn Smith .05
107 Steve Buechele .05
108 Jim Abbott .05
109 Alvin Davis .05
110 Lee Smith .05
111 Roberto Alomar .20
112 Rick Reuschel .05
113a Kelly Gruber (Born 2/22.) .05
113b Kelly Gruber (Born 2/26.) .20
114 Joe Carter .05
115 Jose Rijo .05
116 Greg Minton .05
117 Bob Ojeda .05
118 Glenn Davis .05
119 Jeff Reardon .05
120 Kurt Stillwell .05
121 John Smoltz .05
122 Dwight Evans .05
123 Eric Yelding .05
124 John Franco .05
125 Jose Canseco .20
126 Barry Bonds 1.00
127 Lee Guetterman .05
128 Jack Clark .05
129 Dave Valle .05
130 Hubie Brooks .05
131 Ernest Riles .05
132 Mike Morgan .05
133 Steve Jeltz .05
134 Jeff Robinson .05
135 Ozzie Guillen .05
136 Chili Davis .05
137 Mitch Webster .05
138 Jerry Browne .05
139 Bo Diaz .05
140 Robby Thompson .05
141 Craig Worthington .05
142 Julio Franco .05
143 Brian Holman .05
144 George Brett .60
145 Tom Glavine .20
146 Robin Yount .40
147 Gary Carter .40
148 Ron Kittle .05
149 Tony Fernandez .05
150 Dave Stewart .05
151 Gary Gaetti .05
152 Kevin Elster .05
153 Gerald Perry .05
154 Jesse Orosco .05
155 Wally Backman .05
156 Dennis Martinez .05
157 Rick Sutcliffe .05
158 Greg Maddux .50
159 Andy Hawkins .05
160 John Kruk .05
161 Jose Oquendo .05
162 John Dopson .05
163 Joe Magrane .05
164 Billy Ripken .05
165 Fred Manrique .05
166 Nolan Ryan 1.00
167 Damon Berryhill .05
168 Dale Murphy .20
169 Mickey Tettleton .05
170a Kirk McCaskill (Born 4/19.) .05
170b Kirk McCaskill (Born 4/9.) .10
171 Dwight Gooden .05
172 Jose Lind .05
173 B.J. Surhoff .05
174 Ruben Sierra .05
175 Dan Plesac .05
176 Dan Pasqua .05
177 Kelly Downs .05
178 Matt Nokes .05
179 Luis Aquino .05
180 Frank Tanana .05
181 Tony Pena .05
182 Dan Gladden .05
183 Bruce Hurst .05
184 Roger Clemens .60
185 Mark McGwire .75
186 Rob Murphy .05
187 Jim Deshaies .05
188 Fred McGriff .05
189 Rob Dibble .05
190 Don Mattingly .60
191 Felix Fermin .05
192 Roberto Kelly .05
193 Dennis Cook .05
194 Darren Daulton .05
195 Alfredo Griffin .05
196 Eric Plunk .05
197 Orel Hershiser .05
198 Paul O'Neill .05
199 Randy Bush .05
200a Checklist 130-231 .05
200b Checklist 126-223 .05
201 Ozzie Smith .50
202 Pete O'Brien .05
203 Jay Howell .05
204 Mark Gubicza .05
205 Ed Whitson .05
206 George Bell .05
207 Mike Scott .05
208 Charlie Leibrandt .05
209 Mike Heath .05
210 Dennis Eckersley .35
211 Mike LaValliere .05
212 Darnell Coles .05
213 Lance Parrish .05
214 Mike Moore .05
215 Steve Finley **RC** .20
216 Tim Raines .05
217a Scott Garrelts (Born 10/20.) .05
217b Scott Garrelts (Born 10/30.) .10
218 Kevin McReynolds .05
219 Dave Gallagher .05
220 Tim Wallach .05
221 Chuck Crim .05
222 Lonnie Smith .05
223 Andre Dawson .20
224 Nelson Santovenia .05
225 Rafael Palmeiro .35
226 Devon White .05
227 Harold Reynolds .05
228 Ellis Burks .05
229 Mark Parent .05
230 Will Clark .05
231 Jimmy Key .05
232 John Farrell .05
233 Eric Davis .05
234 Johnny Ray .05
235 Darryl Strawberry .05
236 Bill Doran .05
237 Greg Gagne .05
238 Jim Eisenreich .05
239 Tommy Gregg .05
240 Marty Barrett .05
241 Rafael Ramirez .05
242 Chris Sabo .05
243 Dave Henderson .05
244 Andy Van Slyke .05
245 Alvaro Espinoza .05
246 Garry Templeton .05
247 Gene Harris .05
248 Kevin Gross .05
249 Brett Butler .05
250 Willie Randolph .05
251 Roger McDowell .05
252 Rafael Belliard .05
253 Steve Rosenberg .05
254 Jack Howell .05
255 Marvell Wynne .05
256 Tom Candiotti .05
257 Todd Benzinger .05
258 Don Robinson .05
259 Phil Bradley .05
260 Cecil Espy .05
261 Scott Bankhead .05
262 Frank White .05
263 Andres Thomas .05
264 Glenn Braggs .05
265 David Cone .05
266 Bobby Thigpen .05
267 Nelson Liriano .05
268 Terry Steinbach .05
269 Kirby Puckett .50
270 Gregg Jefferies .05
271 Jeff Blauser .05
272 Cory Snyder .05
273 Roy Smith .05
274 Tom Foley .05
275 Mitch Williams .05
276 Paul Kilgus .05
277 Don Slaught .05
278 Von Hayes .05
279 Vince Coleman .05
280 Mike Boddicker .05
281 Ken Dayley .05
282 Mike Devereaux .05
283 Kenny Rogers **RC** .05
284 Jeff Russell .05
285 Jerome Walton **RC** .10
286 Derek Lilliquist .05
287 Joe Orsulak .05
288 Dick Schofield .05
289 Ron Darling .05
290 Bobby Bonilla .05
291 Jim Gantner .05
292 Bobby Witt .05
293 Greg Brock .05
294 Ivan Calderon .05
295 Steve Bedrosian .05
296 Mike Henneman .05
297 Tom Gordon .05
298 Lou Whitaker .05
299 Terry Pendleton .05
300a Checklist 232-333 .05
300b Checklist 224-321 .05
301 Juan Berenguer .05
302 Mark Davis .05
303 Nick Esasky .05
304 Rickey Henderson .40
305 Rick Cerone .05
306 Craig Biggio .05
307 Duane Ward .05
308 Tom Browning .05
309 Walt Terrell .05
310 Greg Swindell .05
311 Dave Righetti .05
312 Mike Maddux .05
313 Len Dykstra .05
314 Jose Gonzalez .05
315 Steve Balboni .05
316 Mike Scioscia .05
317 Ron Oester .05
318 Gary Wayne **RC** .05
319 Todd Worrell .05
320 Doug Jones .05
321 Jeff Hamilton .05
322 Danny Tartabull .05
323 Chris James .05
324 Mike Flanagan .05
325 Gerald Young .05
326 Bob Boone .05
327 Frank Williams .05
328 Dave Parker .05
329 Sid Bream .05
330 Mike Schooler .05
331 Bert Blyleven .10
332 Bob Welch .05
333 Bob Milacki .05
334 Tim Burke .05
335 Jose Uribe .05
336 Randy Myers .05
337 Eric King .05
338 Mark Langston .05
339 Ted Higuera .05
340 Oddibe McDowell .05
341 Lloyd McClendon .05
342 Pascual Perez .05
343 Kevin Brown .05
344 Chuck Finley .05
345 Erik Hanson .05
346 Rich Gedman .05
347 Bip Roberts .05
348 Matt Williams .05
349 Tom Henke .05
350 Brad Komminsk .05
351 Jeff Reed .05
352 Brian Downing .05
353 Frank Viola .05
354 Terry Puhl .05
355 Brian Harper .05
356 Steve Farr .05
357 Joe Boever .05
358 Danny Heep .05
359 Larry Andersen .05
360 Rolando Roomes .05
361 Mike Gallego .05
362 Bob Kipper .05
363 Clay Parker .05
364 Mike Pagliarulo .05
365 Ken Griffey Jr. .65
366 Rex Hudler .05
367 Pat Sheridan .05
368a Kirk Gibson (May 25 birthdate.) .05
368b Kirk Gibson (May 28 birthdate.) .05
369 Jeff Parrett .05
370 Bob Walk .05
371 Ken Patterson .05
372 Bryan Harvey .05
373 Mike Bielecki .05
374 Tom Magrann **RC** .05
375 Rick Mahler .05
376 Craig Lefferts .05
377 Gregg Olson .05
378 Jamie Moyer .05
379 Randy Johnson .40
380 Jeff Montgomery .05
381 Marty Clary .05
382 Bill Spiers **RC** .05
383 Dave Magadan .05
384 Greg Hibbard **RC** .05
385 Ernie Whitt .05
386 Rick Honeycutt .05
387 Dave West .05
388 Keith Hernandez .05
389 Jose Alvarez .05
390 Albert Belle .05
391 Rick Aguilera .05
392 Mike Fitzgerald .05
393 Dwight Smith **RC** .05
394 Steve Wilson **RC** .05
395 Bob Geren **RC** .05
396 Randy Ready .05
397 Ken Hill .05
398 Jody Reed .05
399 Tom Brunansky .05
400a Checklist 334-435 .05
400b Checklist 322-419 .05
401 Rene Gonzales .05
402 Harold Baines .05
403 Cecilio Guante .05
404 Joe Girardi .05
405a Sergio Valdez **RC** (Black line crosses S in Sergio.) .10
405b Sergio Valdez (Corrected) .05
406 Mark Williamson .05
407 Glenn Hoffman .05
408 Jeff Innis **RC** .05
409 Randy Kramer .05
410 Charlie O'Brien **RC** .05
411 Charlie Hough .05
412 Gus Polidor .05
413 Ron Karkovice .05
414 Trevor Wilson **RC** .05
415 Kevin Ritz **RC** .05
416 Gary Thurman .05
417 Jeff Robinson .05
418 Scott Terry .05
419 Tim Laudner .05
420 Dennis Rasmussen .05
421 Luis Rivera .05
422 Jim Corsi **RC** .05
423 Dennis Lamp .05
424 Ken Caminiti .05
425 David Wells .05
426 Norm Charlton .05
427 Deion Sanders .05
428 Dion James .05
429 Chuck Cary .05
430 Ken Howell .05
431 Steve Lake .05
432 Kal Daniels .05
433 Lance McCullers .05
434 Lenny Harris **RC** .05
435 Scott Scudder **RC** .05
436 Gene Larkin .05
437 Dan Quisenberry .05
438 Steve Olin **RC** .05
439 Mickey Hatcher .05
440 Willie Wilson .05
441 Mark Grant .05
442 Mookie Wilson .05
443 Alex Trevino .05
444 Pat Tabler .05
445 Dave Bergman .05
446 Todd Burns .05
447 R.J. Reynolds .05
448 Jay Buhner .05
449 Lee Stevens **RC** .05
450 Ron Hassey .05
451 Bob Melvin .05
452 Dave Martinez .05
453 Greg Litton **RC** .05
454 Mark Carreon .05
455 Scott Fletcher .05
456 Otis Nixon .05
457 Tony Fossas **RC** .05
458 John Russell .05
459 Paul Assenmacher .05
460 Zane Smith .05
461 Jack Daugherty **RC** .05
462 Rich Monteleone **RC** .05
463 Greg Briley **RC** .05
464 Mike Smithson .05
465 Benito Santiago .05
466 Jeff Brantley **RC** .05
467 Jose Nunez .05
468 Scott Bailes .05
469 Ken Griffey .05
470 Bob McClure .05
471 Mackey Sasser .05
472 Glenn Wilson .05
473 Kevin Tapani **RC** .10
474 Bill Buckner .05
475 Ron Gant .05
476 Kevin Romine **RC** .05
477 Juan Agosto .05
478 Herm Winningham .05
479 Storm Davis .05
480 Jeff King **RC** .05
481 Kevin Mmahat **RC** .05
482 Carmelo Martinez .05
483 Omar Vizquel .05
484 Jim Dwyer .05
485 Bob Knepper .05

486 Dave Anderson .05
487 Ron Jones .05
488 Jay Bell .05
489 Sammy Sosa **RC** 3.00
490 Kent Anderson **RC** .05
491 Domingo Ramos .05
492 Dave Clark .05
493 Tim Birtsas .05
494 Ken Oberkfell .05
495 Larry Sheets .05
496 Jeff Kunkel .05
497 Jim Presley .05
498 Mike Macfarlane .05
499 Pete Smith .05
500a Checklist 436-537 .05
500b Checklist 420-517 .05
501 Gary Sheffield .20
502 Terry Bross **RC** .05
503 Jerry Kutzler **RC** .05
504 Lloyd Moseby .05
505 Curt Young .05
506 Al Newman .05
507 Keith Miller .05
508 Mike Stanton **RC** .20
509 Rich Yett .05
510 Tim Drummond **RC** .05
511 Joe Hesketh .05
512 Rick Wrona **RC** .05
513 Luis Salazar .05
514 Hal Morris .05
515 Terry Mullholland .05
516 John Morris .05
517 Carlos Quintana .05
518 Frank DiPino .05
519 Randy Milligan .05
520 Chad Kreuter .05
521 Mike Jeffcoat .05
522 Mike Harkey .05
523a Andy Nezelek (Born 1985.) .05
523b Andy Nezelek (Born 1965.) .05
524 Dave Schmidt .05
525 Tony Armas .05
526 Barry Lyons .05
527 Rick Reed **RC** .05
528 Jerry Reuss .05
529 Dean Palmer **RC** .10
530 Jeff Peterek **RC** .05
531 Carlos Martinez **RC** .05
532 Atlee Hammaker .05
533 Mike Brumley .05
534 Terry Leach .05
535 Doug Strange **RC** .05
536 Jose DeLeon .05
537 Shane Rawley .05
538 Joey Cora **RC** .05
539 Eric Hetzel .05
540 Gene Nelson .05
541 Wes Gardner .05
542 Mark Portugal .05
543 Al Leiter .05
544 Jack Armstrong .05
545 Greg Cadaret .05
546 Rod Nichols .05
547 Luis Polonia .05
548 Charlie Hayes .05
549 Dickie Thon .05
550 Tim Crews .05
551 Dave Winfield .40
552 Mike Davis .05
553 Ron Robinson .05
554 Carmen Castillo .05
555 John Costello .05
556 Bud Black .05
557 Rick Dempsey .05
558 Jim Acker .05
559 Eric Show .05
560 Pat Borders .05
561 Danny Darwin .05
562 Rick Luecken **RC** .05
563 Edwin Nunez .05
564 Felix Jose .05
565 John Cangelosi .05
566 Billy Swift .05
567 Bill Schroeder .05
568 Stan Javier .05
569 Jim Traber .05
570 Wallace Johnson .05
571 Donell Nixon .05
572 Sid Fernandez .05
573 Lance Johnson .05
574 Andy McGaffigan .05
575 Mark Knudson .05
576 Tommy Greene **RC** .05
577 Mark Grace .05
578 Larry Walker **RC** 1.00
579 Mike Stanley .05
580 Mike Witt .05
581 Scott Bradley .05
582 Greg Harris .05
583a Kevin Hickey (Black stripe over top of "K" vertical stroke.) .05
583b Kevin Hickey (Black stripe under "K.") .05
584 Lee Mazzilli .05
585 Jeff Pico .05
586 Joe Oliver **RC** .05
587 Willie Fraser .05
588 Puzzle card (Carl Yastrzemski) .05
589 Kevin Bass .05
590 John Moses .05
591 Tom Pagnozzi .05
592 Tony Castillo **RC** .05
593 Jerald Clark .05
594 Dan Schatzeder .05
595 Luis Quinones .05
596 Pete Harnisch .05
597 Gary Redus .05
598 Mel Hall .05
599 Rick Schu .05
600a Checklist 538-639 .05
600b Checklist 518-617 .05
601 Mike Kingery .05
602 Terry Kennedy .05
603 Mike Sharperson .05
604 Don Carman .05
605 Jim Gott .05
606 Donn Pall .05
607 Rance Mulliniks .05
608 Curt Wilkerson .05
609 Mike Felder .05
610 Guillermo Hernandez .05
611 Candy Maldonado .05
612 Mark Thurmond .05
613 Rick Leach .05
614 Jerry Reed .05
615 Franklin Stubbs .05
616 Billy Hatcher .05
617 Don August .05
618 Tim Teufel .05
619 Shawn Hillegas .05
620 Manny Lee .05
621 Gary Ward .05
622 Mark Guthrie **RC** .05
623 Jeff Musselman .05
624 Mark Lemke .05
625 Fernando Valenzuela .05
626 Paul Sorrento **RC** .05
627 Glenallen Hill .05
628 Les Lancaster .05
629 Vance Law .05
630 Randy Velarde **RC** .05
631 Todd Frohwirth .05
632 Willie McGee .05
633 Oil Can Boyd .05
634 Cris Carpenter .05
635 Brian Holton .05
636 Tracy Jones .05
637 Terry Steinbach/AS .05
638 Brady Anderson .05
639a Jack Morris (Black line crosses J of Jack.) .10
639b Jack Morris (Corrected) .05
640 Jaime Navarro **RC** .05
641 Darrin Jackson .05
642 Mike Dyer **RC** .05
643 Mike Schmidt .60
644 Henry Cotto .05
645 John Cerutti .05
646 Francisco Cabrera **RC** .05
647 Scott Sanderson .05
648 Brian Meyer .05
649 Ray Searage .05
650 Bo Jackson/AS .25
651 Steve Lyons .05
652 Mike LaCoss .05
653 Ted Power .05
654 Howard Johnson/AS .05
655 Mauro Gozzo **RC** .05
656 Mike Blowers **RC** .05
657 Paul Gibson .05
658 Neal Heaton .05
659a Nolan Ryan 5,000 K's (King of Kings (#665) back.) 1.50
659b Nolan Ryan 5,000 K's (Correct back.) .60
660a Harold Baines/AS (Black line through star on front, Recent Major League Performance on back.) .25
660b Harold Baines/AS (Black line through star on front, All-Star Game Performance on back.) .25
660c Harold Baines/AS (Black line behind star on front, Recent Major League Performance on back.) .25
660d Harold Baines/AS (Black line behind star on front, All-Star Game Performance on back.) .10
661 Gary Pettis .05
662 Clint Zavaras **RC** .05
663 Rick Reuschel/AS .05
664 Alejandro Pena .05
665a Nolan Ryan (King of Kings)(5,000 K's (#659) back.) 1.50
665b Nolan Ryan (King of Kings) (Correct back.) 1.00
665c Nolan Ryan (King of Kings) (No number on back.) 1.00
666 Ricky Horton .05
667 Curt Schilling .05
668 Bill Landrum **RC** .05
669 Todd Stottlemyre .05
670 Tim Leary .05
671 John Wetteland **RC** .25
672 Calvin Schiraldi .05
673 Ruben Sierra/AS .05
674 Pedro Guerrero/AS .05
675 Ken Phelps .05
676 Cal Ripken/AS .50
677 Denny Walling .05
678 Goose Gossage .05
679 Gary Mielke **RC** .05
680 Bill Bathe .05
681 Tom Lawless .05
682 Xavier Hernandez **RC** .05
683 Kirby Puckett/AS .25
684 Mariano Duncan .05
685 Ramon Martinez .05
686 Tim Jones .05
687 Tom Filer .05
688 Steve Lombardozzi .05
689 Bernie Williams **RC** 1.00
690 Chip Hale **RC** .05
691 Beau Allred **RC** .05
692 Ryne Sandberg/AS .25
693 Jeff Huson **RC** .05
694 Curt Ford .05
695 Eric Davis/AS .05
696 Scott Lusader .05
697 Mark McGwire/AS .40
698 Steve Cummings **RC** .05
699 George Canale **RC** .05
700a Checklist 640-715/ BC1-BC26 .05
700b Checklist 640-716/ BC1-BC26 .05
700c Checklist 618-716 .05
701 Julio Franco/AS .05
702 Dave Johnson **RC** .05
703 Dave Stewart/AS .05
704 Dave Justice **RC** .50
705 Tony Gwynn/AS .25
706 Greg Myers .05
707 Will Clark/AS .05
708 Benito Santiago/AS .05
709 Larry McWilliams .05
710 Ozzie Smith/AS .25
711 John Olerud **RC** .50
712 Wade Boggs/AS .25
713 Gary Eave **RC** .05
714 Bob Tewksbury .05
715 Kevin Mitchell/AS .05
716 A. Bartlett Giamatti .25

Grand Slammers

For the second consecutive year Donruss produced a set in honor of players who hit grand slams in the previous season. The cards are styled after the 1990 Donruss regular issue. The cards were inserted into 1990 Donruss factory sets, and one card per cello pack. Each card can be found with blue borders or with blue and green borders, and with or without the split black stripe near the right end on back.

NM/M
Complete Set (12): 2.00
Common Player: .10
1 Matt Williams .10
2 Jeffrey Leonard .10
3 Chris James .10
4 Mark McGwire 1.50
5 Dwight Evans .10
6 Will Clark .10
7 Mike Scioscia .10
8 Todd Benzinger .10
9 Fred McGriff .10
10 Kevin Bass .10
11 Jack Clark .10
12 Bo Jackson .25

MVP

This special 26-card set includes one player from each Major League team. Numbered BC-1 (the "BC" stands for "Bonus Card") through BC-26, the cards from this set were randomly packed in 1990 Donruss wax packs and were not available in factory sets or other types of packaging. The red-bordered cards are similar in design to the regular 1990 Donruss set, except the player photos are set against a special background made up of the "MVP" logo.

NM/M
Complete Set (26): 1.25
Common Player: .10
1 Bo Jackson .20
2 Howard Johnson .10
3 Dave Stewart .10
4 Tony Gwynn .35
5 Orel Hershiser .10
6 Pedro Guerrero .10
7 Tim Raines .10
8 Kirby Puckett .35
9 Alvin Davis .10
10 Ryne Sandberg .35
11 Kevin Mitchell .10
12a John Smoltz (Photo of Tom Glavine.) 1.50
12b John Smoltz (Corrected) .30
13 George Bell .10
14 Julio Franco .10
15 Paul Molitor .25
16 Bobby Bonilla .10
17 Mike Greenwell .10
18 Cal Ripken .50
19 Carlton Fisk .25
20 Chili Davis .10
21 Glenn Davis .10
22 Steve Sax .10
23 Eric Davis .10
24 Greg Swindell .10
25 Von Hayes .10
26 Alan Trammell .10

1990 Donruss Aqueous Test

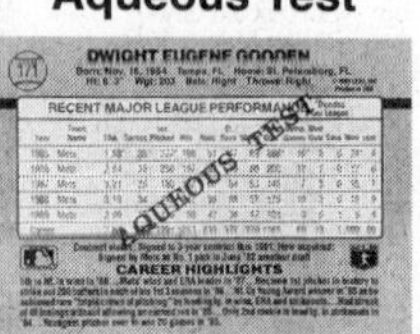

Little is known about this mystery issue which few hobbyists had ever heard of prior to 1999. The cards appear in all major respects to be regular 1990 Donruss cards, but on back have the words "AQUEOUS TEST" printed. The test cards also lack the period after "INC" in the copyright line at upper-right. Approximately 2,000-2,500 cards in total are known, with only part of the '90D checklist represented in the test issue. As few as one specimen each are known for some cards, while a half-dozen or more of others are recorded. Because of limited supply, prices can be volatile depending on the activity of single-player specialist collectors at any given time. It is possible the checklist here is not complete. The cards may have been produced to test a semi-gloss coating known in the printing trade as aqueous.

NM/M
Common Player: 5.00
1 Bo Jackson/DK 17.50
3 Ruben Sierra/DK 5.00
6 Dave Stewart/DK 6.50
8 Mike Bielecki/DK 5.00
9 Mike Bielecki/DK 5.00
16 Lou Whitaker/DK 5.00
18 Howard Johnson/DK 5.00
22 Dan Gladden/DK 5.00
24 Pete O'Brien/DK 5.00
28 Robin Ventura/RR 15.00
29 Todd Zeile/RR 15.00
30 Sandy Alomar Jr./RR 15.00
31 Kent Mercker/RR 5.00
32 Ben McDonald/RR 7.50
33 Juan Gonzalez/RR (Reversed negatives.) 75.00
34 Eric Anthony/RR 5.00
35 Mike Fetters/RR 5.00
48 Pete Incaviglia 5.00
51 Jeff Ballard 5.00
52 Claudell Washington 5.00
55 Rob Deer 5.00
56 Geno Petralli 5.00
57 Chris Bosio 5.00
60 Chet Lemon 5.00
61 Bo Jackson 25.00
63 Pedro Guerrero 5.00
64 Allan Anderson 5.00
65 Greg Harris 5.00
66 Mike Greenwell 5.00
68 Wade Boggs 60.00
70 Junior Felix 5.00
71 Barry Larkin 5.00
72 Dave LaPoint 5.00
74 Jesse Barfield 5.00
77 Eddie Murray 45.00
78 Steve Sax 5.00
79 Tim Belcher 5.00
80 Danny Jackson 5.00
81 Kent Hrbek 5.00
83 Brook Jacoby 5.00
84 Mike Marshall 5.00
85 Kevin Seitzer 5.00
86 Tony Gwynn 60.00
87 Dave Steib 5.00
89 Bret Saberhagen 5.00
90 Alan Trammell 5.00
91 Tony Phillips 5.00
93 Jeff Leonard 5.00
94 Wally Joyner 5.00
95 Carney Lansford 5.00
96 Cal Ripken Jr. 100.00
97 Andres Galarraga 5.00
98 Kevin Mitchell 5.00
100 Checklist 28-129 2.50
102 Spike Owen 5.00
103 Paul Molitor 45.00
105 Ryne Sandberg 60.00
107 Steve Buechele 5.00
108 Jim Abbott 5.00
109 Alvin Davis 5.00
110 Lee Smith 5.00
111 Roberto Alomar 15.00
112 Rick Reuschel 5.00
113 Kelly Gruber 5.00
114 Joe Carter 5.00
115 Jose Rijo 5.00
117 Bobby Ojeda 5.00
118 Glenn Davis 5.00
119 Jeff Reardon 5.00
120 Kurt Stillwell 5.00
122 Dwight Evans 5.00
124 John Franco 5.00
125 Jose Canseco 35.00
126 Barry Bonds 100.00
127 Lee Guetterman 5.00
128 Jack Clark 5.00
129 Dave Valle 5.00
132 Mike Morgan 5.00
133 Steve Jeltz 5.00
134 Jeff Robinson 5.00
139 Bo Diaz 5.00
140 Robby Thompson 5.00
141 Craig Worthington 5.00
144 George Brett 75.00
145 Tom Glavine 15.00
146 Robin Yount 45.00
147 Gary Carter 45.00
148 Ron Kittle 5.00
149 Tony Fernandez 5.00
150 Dave Stewart 5.00
151 Gary Gaetti 5.00
154 Jesse Orosco 5.00
155 Wally Backman 5.00
156 Dennis Martinez 5.00
157 Rick Sutcliffe 6.50
158 Greg Maddux 60.00
160 John Kruk 5.00
162 John Dopson 5.00
164 Billy Ripken 5.00
165 Fred Manrique 5.00
166 Nolan Ryan 100.00
167 Damon Berryhill 5.00
168 Dale Murphy 35.00
169 Mickey Tettleton 5.00
170 Kirk McCaskill 5.00
171 Dwight Gooden 5.00
172 Jose Lind 5.00
173 B.J. Surhoff 5.00
174 Ruben Sierra 5.00
175 Dan Plesac 5.00
176 Dan Pasqua 5.00
177 Kelly Downs 5.00
178 Matt Nokes 5.00
179 Luis Aquino 5.00
180 Frank Tanana 5.00
181 Tony Pena 5.00
182 Dan Gladden 5.00
183 Bruce Hurst 5.00
184 Roger Clemens 75.00
185 Mark McGwire 85.00
186 Rob Murphy 5.00
187 Jim Deshaies 5.00
188 Fred McGriff 5.00
189 Rob Dibble 5.00
190 Don Mattingly 75.00
191 Felix Fermin 5.00
192 Roberto Kelly 5.00
193 Dennis Cook 5.00
194 Darren Daulton 5.00
195 Alfredo Griffin 5.00
196 Eric Plunk 5.00
197 Orel Hershiser 5.00
198 Paul O'Neill 5.00
199 Randy Bush 5.00
201 Ozzie Smith 60.00
202 Pete O'Brien 5.00
203 Jay Howell 5.00
204 Mark Gubicza 5.00
205 Ed Whitson 5.00
206 George Bell 5.00
207 Mike Scott 5.00
208 Charlie Leibrandt 5.00
209 Mike Heath 5.00
210 Dennis Eckersley 45.00
211 Mike LaValliere 5.00
212 Darnell Coles 5.00
213 Lance Parrish 5.00
214 Mike Moore 5.00
215 Steve Finley 5.00
216 Tim Raines 5.00
217 Scott Garrelts 5.00
218 Kevin McReynolds 5.00
219 Dave Gallagher 5.00
220 Tim Wallach 5.00
221 Chuck Crim 5.00
222 Lonnie Smith 5.00
223 Andre Dawson 15.00
224 Nelson Santovenia 5.00
225 Rafael Palmeiro 45.00
226 Devon White 5.00
227 Harold Reynolds 6.50
228 Ellis Burks 5.00
229 Mark Parent 5.00
230 Will Clark 6.50
231 Jimmy Key 5.00
232 John Farrell 5.00
233 Eric Davis 5.00
234 Johnny Ray 5.00
235 Darryl Strawberry 5.00
236 Bill Doran 5.00
237 Greg Gagne 5.00
238 Jim Eisenreich 5.00
239 Tommy Gregg 5.00
240 Marty Barrett 5.00
241 Rafael Ramirez 5.00
242 Chris Sabo 5.00
243 Dave Henderson 5.00
244 Andy Van Slyke 5.00
245 Alvaro Espinoza 5.00
246 Garry Templeton 5.00
247 Gene Harris 5.00
248 Kevin Gross 5.00
249 Brett Butler 5.00
250 Willie Randolph 5.00
251 Roger McDowell 5.00
252 Rafael Belliard 5.00
253 Steve Rosenberg 5.00
254 Jack Howell 5.00
255 Marvell Wynne 5.00
256 Tom Candiotti 5.00
257 Todd Benzinger 5.00
258 Don Robinson 5.00
259 Phil Bradley 5.00
260 Cecil Espy 5.00
261 Scott Bankhead 5.00
262 Frank White 5.00
263 Andre Thomas 5.00
264 Glenn Braggs 5.00
265 David Cone 5.00
266 Bobby Thigpen 5.00
267 Nelson Liriano 5.00
268 Terry Steinbach 5.00
269 Kirby Puckett 60.00
270 Gregg Jeffries 5.00
271 Jeff Blauser 5.00
272 Cory Snyder 5.00
273 Roy Smith 5.00
274 Tom Foley 5.00
275 Mitch Williams 5.00
276 Paul Kilgus 5.00
277 Don Slaught 5.00
278 Von Hayes 5.00
279 Vince Coleman 5.00
280 Mike Boddicker 5.00
281 Ken Dayley 5.00
282 Mike Devereaux 5.00
283 Kenny Rogers 5.00
BC-1 Bo Jackson (MVP) 15.00
BC-2 Howard Johnson (MVP) 5.00
BC-3 Dave Stewart (MVP) 5.00
BC-4 Tony Gwynn (MVP) 45.00
BC-5 Orel Hershiser (MVP) 5.00
BC-6 Pedro Guerrero (MVP) 5.00
BC-7 Tim Raines (MVP) 6.50
BC-8 Kirby Puckett (MVP) 45.00
BC-9 Alvin Davis 5.00

1990 Donruss Blue/White Test Issue

Relatively few examples of this test printing have found their way into the hobby. The cards are "two-headed" with the fronts of two different cards printed back-to back. The cards use the same photos found on the issued versions and differ only in the border colors. Each card can be found with one side bordered in blue and the other bordered in white. The blue side of the card has a glossier finish than the white. The number of different players' cards which can be found in this version is unknown.

Best A.L.

This 144-card set features the top players of the American League. The 2-1/2" x 3-1/2" cards feature the same front design as the regular Donruss set, exception with blue borders instead of red. Backs feature a yellow frame with complete statistics and biographical information provided. This marks the first year that Donruss divided its baseball-best issue into two sets designated by league.

		NM/M
Complete Set (144):		10.00
Common Player:		.05
1	Ken Griffey Jr.	1.00
2	Bob Milacki	.05
3	Mike Boddicker	.05
4	Bert Blyleven	.05
5	Carlton Fisk	.50
6	Greg Swindell	.05
7	Alan Trammell	.05
8	Mark Davis	.05
9	Chris Bosio	.05
10	Gary Gaetti	.05
11	Matt Nokes	.05
12	Dennis Eckersley	.45
13	Kevin Brown	.05
14	Tom Henke	.05
15	Mickey Tettleton	.05
16	Jody Reed	.05
17	Mark Langston	.05
18	Melido Perez	.05
19	John Farrell	.05
20	Tony Phillips	.05
21	Bret Saberhagen	.05
22	Robin Yount	.50
23	Kirby Puckett	.60
24	Steve Sax	.05
25	Dave Stewart	.05
26	Alvin Davis	.05
27	Geno Petralli	.05
28	Mookie Wilson	.05
29	Jeff Ballard	.05
30	Ellis Burks	.05
31	Wally Joyner	.05
32	Bobby Thigpen	.05
33	Keith Hernandez	.05
34	Jack Morris	.05
35	George Brett	.75
36	Dan Plesac	.05
37	Brian Harper	.05
38	Don Mattingly	.75
39	Dave Henderson	.05
40	Scott Bankhead	.05
41	Rafael Palmeiro	.45
42	Jimmy Key	.05
43	Gregg Olson	.05
44	Tony Pena	.05
45	Jack Howell	.05
46	Eric King	.05
47	Cory Snyder	.05
48	Frank Tanana	.05
49	Nolan Ryan	2.00
50	Bob Boone	.05
51	Dave Parker	.05
52	Allan Anderson	.05
53	Tim Leary	.05
54	Mark McGwire	1.50
55	Dave Valle	.05
56	Fred McGriff	.05
57	Cal Ripken	2.00
58	Roger Clemens	.75
59	Lance Parrish	.05
60	Robin Ventura	.05
61	Doug Jones	.05
62	Lloyd Moseby	.05
63	Bo Jackson	.15
64	Paul Molitor	.50
65	Kent Hrbek	.05
66	Mel Hall	.05
67	Bob Welch	.05
68	Erik Hanson	.05
69	Harold Baines	.05
70	Junior Felix	.05
71	Craig Worthington	.05
72	Jeff Reardon	.05
73	Johnny Ray	.05
74	Ozzie Guillen	.05
75	Brook Jacoby	.05
76	Chet Lemon	.05
77	Mark Gubicza	.05
78	B.J. Surhoff	.05
79	Rick Aguilera	.05
80	Pascual Perez	.05
81	Jose Canseco	.30
82	Mike Schooler	.05
83	Jeff Huson	.05
84	Kelly Gruber	.05
85	Randy Milligan	.05
86	Wade Boggs	.60
87	Dave Winfield	.50
88	Scott Fletcher	.05
89	Tom Candiotti	.05
90	Mike Heath	.05
91	Kevin Seitzer	.05
92	Ted Higuera	.05
93	Kevin Tapani	.05
94	Roberto Kelly	.05
95	Walt Weiss	.05
96	Checklist	.05
97	Sandy Alomar	.05
98	Pete O'Brien	.05
99	Jeff Russell	.05
100	John Olerud	.05
101	Pete Harnisch	.05
102	Dwight Evans	.05
103	Chuck Finley	.05
104	Sammy Sosa	6.00
105	Mike Henneman	.05
106	Kurt Stillwell	.05
107	Greg Vaughn	.05
108	Dan Gladden	.05
109	Jesse Barfield	.05
110	Willie Randolph	.05
111	Randy Johnson	.50
112	Julio Franco	.05
113	Tony Fernandez	.05
114	Ben McDonald	.05
115	Mike Greenwell	.05
116	Luis Polonia	.05
117	Carney Lansford	.05
118	Bud Black	.05
119	Lou Whitaker	.05
120	Jim Eisenreich	.05
121	Gary Sheffield	.20
122	Shane Mack	.05
123	Alvaro Espinoza	.05
124	Rickey Henderson	.50
125	Jeffrey Leonard	.05
126	Gary Pettis	.05
127	Dave Steib	.05
128	Danny Tartabull	.05
129	Joe Orsulak	.05
130	Tom Brunansky	.05
131	Dick Schofield	.05
132	Candy Maldonado	.05
133	Cecil Fielder	.05
134	Terry Shumpert	.05
135	Greg Gagne	.05
136	Dave Righetti	.05
137	Terry Steinbach	.05
138	Harold Reynolds	.05
139	George Bell	.05
140	Carlos Quintana	.05
141	Ivan Calderon	.05
142	Greg Brock	.05
143	Ruben Sierra	.05
144	Checklist	.05

Best N.L.

This 144-card set features the top players in the National League for 1990. The 2-1/2" x 3-1/2" cards feature the same design as the regular 1990 Donruss cards, except they have blue, rather than red borders. Traded players are featured with their new teams. This set, along with the A.L. Best set, was available at select retail stores and within the hobby.

		NM/M
Complete Set (144):		7.50
Common Player:		.05
1	Eric Davis	.05
2	Tom Glavine	.20
3	Mike Bielecki	.05
4	Jim Deshaies	.05
5	Mike Scioscia	.05
6	Spike Owen	.05
7	Dwight Gooden	.05
8	Ricky Jordan	.05
9	Doug Drabek	.05
10	Bryn Smith	.05
11	Tony Gwynn	.75
12	John Burkett	.05
13	Nick Esasky	.05
14	Greg Maddux	.75
15	Joe Oliver	.05
16	Mike Scott	.05
17	Tim Belcher	.05
18	Kevin Gross	.05
19	Howard Johnson	.05
20	Darren Daulton	.05
21	John Smiley	.05
22	Ken Dayley	.05
23	Craig Lefferts	.05
24	Will Clark	.05
25	Greg Olson	.05
26	Ryne Sandberg	.75
27	Tom Browning	.05
28	Eric Anthony	.05
29	Juan Samuel	.05
30	Dennis Martinez	.05
31	Kevin Elster	.05
32	Tom Herr	.05
33	Sid Bream	.05
34	Terry Pendleton	.05
35	Roberto Alomar	.20
36	Kevin Bass	.05
37	Jim Presley	.05
38	Les Lancaster	.05
39	Paul O'Neill	.05
40	Dave Smith	.05
41	Kirk Gibson	.05
42	Tim Burke	.05
43	David Cone	.05
44	Ken Howell	.05
45	Barry Bonds	6.00
46	Joe Magrane	.05
47	Andy Benes	.05
48	Gary Carter	.50
49	Pat Combs	.05
50	John Smoltz	.05
51	Mark Grace	.05
52	Barry Larkin	.05
53	Danny Darwin	.05
54	Orel Hershiser	.05
55	Tim Wallach	.05
56	Dave Magadan	.05
57	Roger McDowell	.05
58	Bill Landrum	.05
59	Jose DeLeon	.05
60	Bip Roberts	.05
61	Matt Williams	.05
62	Dale Murphy	.20
63	Dwight Smith	.05
64	Chris Sabo	.05
65	Glenn Davis	.05
66	Jay Howell	.05
67	Andres Galarraga	.05
68	Frank Viola	.05
69	John Kruk	.05
70	Bobby Bonilla	.05
71	Todd Zeile	.05
72	Joe Carter	.05
73	Robby Thompson	.05
74	Jeff Blauser	.05
75	Mitch Williams	.05
76	Rob Dibble	.05
77	Rafael Ramirez	.05
78	Eddie Murray	.50
79	Dave Martinez	.05
80	Darryl Strawberry	.05
81	Dickie Thon	.05
82	Jose Lind	.05
83	Ozzie Smith	.75
84	Bruce Hurst	.05
85	Kevin Mitchell	.05
86	Lonnie Smith	.05
87	Joe Girardi	.05
88	Randy Myers	.05
89	Craig Biggio	.05
90	Fernando Valenzuela	.05
91	Larry Walker	.05
92	John Franco	.05
93	Dennis Cook	.05
94	Bob Walk	.05
95	Pedro Guerrero	.05
96	Checklist	.05
97	Andre Dawson	.25
98	Ed Whitson	.05
99	Steve Bedrosian	.05
100	Oddibe McDowell	.05
101	Todd Benzinger	.05
102	Bill Doran	.05
103	Alfredo Griffin	.05
104	Tim Raines	.05
105	Sid Fernandez	.05
106	Charlie Hayes	.05
107	Mike LaValliere	.05
108	Jose Oquendo	.05
109	Jack Clark	.05
110	Scott Garrelts	.05
111	Ron Gant	.05
112	Shawon Dunston	.05
113	Mariano Duncan	.05
114	Eric Yelding	.05
115	Hubie Brooks	.05
116	Delino DeShields	.05
117	Gregg Jefferies	.05
118	Len Dykstra	.05
119	Andy Van Slyke	.05
120	Lee Smith	.05
121	Benito Santiago	.05
122	Jose Uribe	.05
123	Jeff Treadway	.05
124	Jerome Walton	.05
125	Billy Hatcher	.05
126	Ken Caminiti	.05
127	Kal Daniels	.05
128	Marquis Grissom	.05
129	Kevin McReynolds	.05
130	Wally Backman	.05
131	Willie McGee	.05
132	Terry Kennedy	.05
133	Garry Templeton	.05
134	Lloyd McClendon	.05
135	Daryl Boston	.05
136	Jay Bell	.05
137	Mike Pagliarulo	.05
138	Vince Coleman	.05
139	Brett Butler	.05
140	Von Hayes	.05
141	Ramon Martinez	.05
142	Jack Armstrong	.05
143	Franklin Stubbs	.05
144	Checklist	.05

Diamond Kings Supers

Donruss made this set available through a mail-in offer. Three wrappers, $10 and $2 for postage were necessary to obtain this set. The cards are exactly the same design as the regular Donruss Diamond Kings except they measure approximately 5" x 6-3/4" in size. The artwork of Dick Perez is featured.

		NM/M
Complete Set (26):		5.00
Common Player:		.10
1	Bo Jackson	.25
2	Steve Sax	.10
3	Ruben Sierra	.10
4	Ken Griffey Jr.	4.00
5	Mickey Tettleton	.10
6	Dave Stewart	.10
7	Jim Deshaies	.10
8	John Smoltz	.10
9	Mike Bielecki	.10
10	Brian Downing	.10
11	Kevin Mitchell	.10
12	Kelly Gruber	.10
13	Joe Magrane	.10
14	John Franco	.10
15	Ozzie Guillen	.10
16	Lou Whitaker	.10
17	John Smiley	.10
18	Howard Johnson	.10
19	Willie Randolph	.10
20	Chris Bosio	.10
21	Tommy Herr	.10
22	Dan Gladden	.10
23	Ellis Burks	.10
24	Pete O'Brien	.10
25	Bryn Smith	.10
26	Ed Whitson	.10

Learning Series

Cards from this 55-card set were released as part of an educational package available to schools. The cards are styled like the regular-issue 1990 Donruss cards, but feature a special "learning series" logo on the front. The backs feature career highlights, statistics and card numbers. The cards were not released directly to the hobby.

		NM/M
Complete Set (55):		25.00
Common Player:		.10
1	George Brett/DK	3.00
2	Kevin Mitchell	.10
3	Andy Van Slyke	.10
4	Benito Santiago	.10
5	Gary Carter	1.00
6	Jose Canseco	.50
7	Rickey Henderson	1.00
8	Ken Griffey Jr.	4.00
9	Ozzie Smith	2.00
10	Dwight Gooden	.10
11	Ryne Sandberg/DK	2.00
12	Don Mattingly	2.50
13	Ozzie Guillen	.10
14	Dave Righetti	.10
15	Rick Dempsey	.10
16	Tom Herr	.10
17	Julio Franco	.10
18	Von Hayes	.10
19	Cal Ripken	6.00
20	Alan Trammell	.10
21	Wade Boggs	2.00
22	Glenn Davis	.10
23	Will Clark	.10
24	Nolan Ryan	6.00
25	George Bell	.10
26	Cecil Fielder	.10
27	Gregg Olson	.10
28	Tim Wallach	.10
29	Ron Darling	.10
30	Kelly Gruber	.10
31	Shawn Boskie	.10
32	Mike Greenwell	.10
33	Dave Parker	.10
34	Joe Magrane	.10
35	Dave Stewart	.10
36	Kent Hrbek	.10
37	Robin Yount	1.00
38	Bo Jackson	.15
39	Fernando Valenzuela	.10
40	Sandy Alomar, Jr.	.10
41	Lance Parrish	.10
42	Candy Maldonado	.10
43	Mike LaValliere	.10
44	Jim Abbott	.10
45	Edgar Martinez	.10
46	Kirby Puckett	2.00
47	Delino DeShields	.10
48	Tony Gwynn	2.00
49	Carlton Fisk	1.00
50	Mike Scott	.10
51	Barry Larkin	.10
52	Andre Dawson	.35
53	Tom Glavine	.50
54	Tom Browning	.10
55	Checklist	.05

Rookies

For the fifth straight year, Donruss issued a 56-card "Rookies" set in 1990. As in previous years, the set is similar in design to the regular Donruss set, except for a new "The Rookies" logo and green borders instead of red. The set is packaged in a special box and includes a Carl Yastrzemski puzzle card.

		NM/M
Complete Set (56):		1.00
Common Player:		.05
1	Sandy Alomar	.05
2	John Olerud	.40
3	Pat Combs	.05
4	Brian Dubois	.05
5	Felix Jose	.05
6	Delino DeShields	.05
7	Mike Stanton	.05
8	Mike Munoz **RC**	.05
9	Craig Grebeck **RC**	.05
10	Joe Kraemer **RC**	.05
11	Jeff Huson	.05
12	Bill Sampen **RC**	.05
13	Brian Bohanon **RC**	.05
14	Dave Justice	.40
15	Robin Ventura	.05
16	Greg Vaughn	.05
17	Wayne Edwards **RC**	.05
18	Shawn Boskie	.05
19	Carlos Baerga **RC**	.20
20	Mark Gardner	.05
21	Kevin Appier **RC**	.05
22	Mike Harkey	.05
23	Tim Layana **RC**	.05
24	Glenallen Hill	.05
25	Jerry Kutzler	.05
26	Mike Blowers	.05
27	Scott Ruskin **RC**	.05
28	Dana Kiecker **RC**	.05
29	Willie Blair **RC**	.05
30	Ben McDonald	.05
31	Todd Zeile	.05
32	Scott Coolbaugh	.05
33	Xavier Hernandez	.05
34	Mike Hartley **RC**	.05
35	Kevin Tapani	.05
36	Kevin Wickander **RC**	.05
37	Carlos Hernandez **RC**	.05
38	Brian Traxler **RC**	.05
39	Marty Brown **RC**	.05
40	Scott Radinsky **RC**	.05
41	Julio Machado	.05
42	Steve Avery	.05
43	Mark Lemke	.05
44	Alan Mills **RC**	.05
45	Marquis Grissom	.05
46	Greg Olson **RC**	.05
47	Dave Hollins **RC**	.05
48	Jerald Clark	.05
49	Eric Anthony	.05
50	Tim Drummond	.05
51	John Burkett **RC**	.05
52	Brent Knackert **RC**	.05
53	Jeff Shaw **RC**	.05
54	John Orton **RC**	.05
55	Terry Shumpert **RC**	.05
56	Checklist	.05

1991 Donruss Previews

Once again in late 1990 Donruss distributed individual cards from a 12-card preview issue to its dealer network as an introduction to its 1991 issue. Like the previous year's preview cards, the '91 samples utilized the format which would follow on the regular-issue cards, but the photos were different. This has helped create demand for these cards from superstar collectors. Backs are printed in black-and-white and have little more than a player name, card number and MLB logos.

		NM/M
Complete Set (12):		135.00
Common Player:		2.50
1	Dave Justice	2.50
2	Doug Drabek	2.50
3	Scott Chiamparino	2.50
4	Ken Griffey Jr.	35.00
5	Bob Welch	2.50
6	Tino Martinez	2.50
7	Nolan Ryan	45.00
8	Dwight Gooden	2.50
9	Ryne Sandberg	17.50
10	Barry Bonds	45.00
11	Jose Canseco	7.50
12	Eddie Murray	12.00

1991 Donruss

Donruss used a two-series format in 1991. The first series was released in December 1990, and the second in February 1991. The 1991 design is somewhat reminiscent of the 1986 set, with blue borders on Series I cards; green on Series II. Limited edition cards including an autographed Ryne Sandberg card (5,000) were randomly inserted in wax packs. Other features of the set include 40 Rated Rookies, (RR) in the checklist, Legends and Elite insert series, and another Diamond King (DK) subset. Cards were distributed in packs with Willie Stargell puzzle pieces.

NM/M
Factory Set w/Previews (788): 12.00
Factory Collector's Set (792): 12.00
Complete Set (770): 8.00
Common Player: .05
Willie Stargell Puzzle: .50
Series 1 or 2 Pack (15): .50
Series 1 or 2 Wax Box (36): 12.50

1 Dave Steib/DK .05
2 Craig Biggio/DK .05
3 Cecil Fielder/DK .05
4 Barry Bonds/DK 1.00
5 Barry Larkin/DK .05
6 Dave Parker/DK .05
7 Len Dykstra/DK .05
8 Bobby Thigpen/DK .05
9 Roger Clemens/DK .60
10 Ron Gant/DK .05
11 Delino DeShields/DK .05
12 Roberto Alomar/DK .20
13 Sandy Alomar/DK .05
14 Ryne Sandberg/DK .50
15 Ramon Martinez/DK .05
16 Edgar Martinez/DK .05
17 Dave Magadan/DK .05
18 Matt Williams/DK .05
19 Rafael Palmeiro/DK .40
20 Bob Welch/DK .05
21 Dave Righetti/DK .05
22 Brian Harper/DK .05
23 Gregg Olson/DK .05
24 Kurt Stillwell/DK .05
25 Pedro Guerrero/DK .05
26 Chuck Finley/DK .05
27 Diamond King checklist .05
28 Tino Martinez/RR .05
29 Mark Lewis/RR .05
30 Bernard Gilkey/RR **RC** .10
31 Hensley Meulens/RR .05
32 Derek Bell/RR **RC** .30
33 Jose Offerman/RR .05
34 Terry Bross/RR .05
35 Leo Gomez/RR **RC** .05
36 Derrick May/RR .05
37 Kevin Morton/RR **RC** .05
38 Moises Alou/RR .05
39 Julio Valera/RR **RC** .05
40 Milt Cuyler/RR **RC** .05
41 Phil Plantier/RR **RC** .10
42 Scott Chiamparino/RR **RC** .05
43 Ray Lankford/RR **RC** .20
44 Mickey Morandini/RR **RC** .10
45 Dave Hansen/RR **RC** .05
46 Kevin Belcher/RR **RC** .05
47 Darrin Fletcher/RR **RC** .05
48 Steve Sax/AS .05
49 Ken Griffey Jr./AS .30
50a Jose Canseco/AS (A's in stat line on back.) .10
50b Jose Canseco/AS (AL in stat line on back.) .25
51 Sandy Alomar/AS .05
52 Cal Ripken, Jr./AS .50
53 Rickey Henderson/AS .20
54 Bob Welch/AS .05
55 Wade Boggs/AS .25
56 Mark McGwire/AS .50
57a Jack McDowell (Career Games 30) .05
57b Jack McDowell (Career Games 63) .25
58 Jose Lind .05
59 Alex Fernandez .05
60 Pat Combs .05
61 Mike Walker **RC** .05
62 Juan Samuel .05
63 Mike Blowers .05
64 Mark Guthrie .05
65 Mark Salas .05
66 Tim Jones .05
67 Tim Leary .05
68 Andres Galarraga .05
69 Bob Milacki .05
70 Tim Belcher .05
71 Todd Zeile .05
72 Jerome Walton .05
73 Kevin Seitzer .05
74 Jerald Clark .05
75 John Smoltz .05
76 Mike Henneman .05
77 Ken Griffey Jr. .65
78 Jim Abbott .05
79 Gregg Jefferies .05
80 Kevin Reimer **RC** .05
81 Roger Clemens .60
82 Mike Fitzgerald .05
83 Bruce Hurst .05
84 Eric Davis .05
85 Paul Molitor .40
86 Will Clark .05
87 Mike Bielecki .05
88 Bret Saberhagen .05
89 Nolan Ryan 1.00
90 Bobby Thigpen .05
91 Dickie Thon .05
92 Duane Ward .05
93 Luis Polonia .05
94 Terry Kennedy .05
95 Kent Hrbek .05
96 Danny Jackson .05
97 Sid Fernandez .05
98 Jimmy Key .05
99 Franklin Stubbs .05
100 Checklist 28-103 .05
101 R.J. Reynolds .05
102 Dave Stewart .05
103 Dan Pasqua .05
104 Dan Plesac .05
105 Mark McGwire .75
106 John Farrell .05
107 Don Mattingly .60
108 Carlton Fisk .40
109 Ken Oberkfell .05
110 Darrel Akerfelds .05
111 Gregg Olson .05
112 Mike Scioscia .05
113 Bryn Smith .05
114 Bob Geren .05
115 Tom Candiotti .05
116 Kevin Tapani .05
117 Jeff Treadway .05
118 Alan Trammell .05
119 Pete O'Brien .05
120 Joel Skinner .05
121 Mike LaValliere .05
122 Dwight Evans .05
123 Jody Reed .05
124 Lee Guetterman .05
125 Tim Burke .05
126 Dave Johnson .05
127 Fernando Valenzuela .05
128 Jose DeLeon .05
129 Andre Dawson .20
130 Gerald Perry .05
131 Greg Harris .05
132 Tom Glavine .25
133 Lance McCullers .05
134 Randy Johnson .40
135 Lance Parrish .05
136 Mackey Sasser .05
137 Geno Petralli .05
138 Dennis Lamp .05
139 Dennis Martinez .05
140 Mike Pagliarulo .05
141 Hal Morris .05
142 Dave Parker .05
143 Brett Butler .05
144 Paul Assenmacher .05
145 Mark Gubicza .05
146 Charlie Hough .05
147 Sammy Sosa .50
148 Randy Ready .05
149 Kelly Gruber .05
150 Devon White .05
151 Gary Carter .40
152 Gene Larkin .05
153 Chris Sabo .05
154 David Cone .05
155 Todd Stottlemyre .05
156 Glenn Wilson .05
157 Bob Walk .05
158 Mike Gallego .05
159 Greg Hibbard .05
160 Chris Bosio .05
161 Mike Moore .05
162 Jerry Browne .05
163 Steve Sax .05
164 Melido Perez .05
165 Danny Darwin .05
166 Roger McDowell .05
167 Bill Ripken .05
168 Mike Sharperson .05
169 Lee Smith .05
170 Matt Nokes .05
171 Jesse Orosco .05
172 Rick Aguilera .05
173 Jim Presley .05
174 Lou Whitaker .05
175 Harold Reynolds .05
176 Brook Jacoby .05
177 Wally Backman .05
178 Wade Boggs .50
179 Chuck Cary .05
180 Tom Foley .05
181 Pete Harnisch .05
182 Mike Morgan .05
183 Bob Tewksbury .05
184 Joe Girardi .05
185 Storm Davis .05
186 Ed Whitson .05
187 Steve Avery .05
188 Lloyd Moseby .05
189 Scott Bankhead .05
190 Mark Langston .05
191 Kevin McReynolds .05
192 Julio Franco .05
193 John Dopson .05
194 Oil Can Boyd .05
195 Bip Roberts .05
196 Billy Hatcher .05
197 Edgar Diaz **RC** .05
198 Greg Litton .05
199 Mark Grace .05
200 Checklist 104-179 .05
201 George Brett .60
202 Jeff Russell .05
203 Ivan Calderon .05
204 Ken Howell .05
205 Tom Henke .05
206 Bryan Harvey .05
207 Steve Bedrosian .05
208 Al Newman .05
209 Randy Myers .05
210 Daryl Boston .05
211 Manny Lee .05
212 Dave Smith .05
213 Don Slaught .05
214 Walt Weiss .05
215 Donn Pall .05
216 Jamie Navarro .05
217 Willie Randolph .05
218 Rudy Seanez **RC** .05
219 Jim Leyritz **RC** .15
220 Ron Karkovice .05
221 Ken Caminiti .05
222a Von Hayes (Traded players' first names included in How Acquired on back.) .05
222b Von Hayes (No first names.) .05
223 Cal Ripken, Jr. 1.00
224 Lenny Harris .05
225 Milt Thompson .05
226 Alvaro Espinoza .05
227 Chris James .05
228 Dan Gladden .05
229 Jeff Blauser .05
230 Mike Heath .05
231 Omar Vizquel .05
232 Doug Jones .05
233 Jeff King .05
234 Luis Rivera .05
235 Ellis Burks .05
236 Greg Cadaret .05
237 Dave Martinez .05
238 Mark Williamson .05
239 Stan Javier .05
240 Ozzie Smith .50
241 Shawn Boskie **RC** .05
242 Tom Gordon .05
243 Tony Gwynn .50
244 Tommy Gregg .05
245 Jeff Robinson .05
246 Keith Comstock .05
247 Jack Howell .05
248 Keith Miller .05
249 Bobby Witt .05
250 Rob Murphy .05
251 Spike Owen .05
252 Garry Templeton .05
253 Glenn Braggs .05
254 Ron Robinson .05
255 Kevin Mitchell .05
256 Les Lancaster .05
257 Mel Stottlemyre **RC** .10
258 Kenny Rogers .05
259 Lance Johnson .05
260 John Kruk .05
261 Fred McGriff .05
262 Dick Schofield .05
263 Trevor Wilson .05
264 David West .05
265 Scott Scudder .05
266 Dwight Gooden .05
267 Willie Blair **RC** .05
268 Mark Portugal .05
269 Doug Drabek .05
270 Dennis Eckersley .35
271 Eric King .05
272 Robin Yount .40
273 Carney Lansford .05
274 Carlos Baerga .05
275 Dave Righetti .05
276 Scott Fletcher .05
277 Eric Yelding .05
278 Charlie Hayes .05
279 Jeff Ballard .05
280 Orel Hershiser .05
281 Jose Oquendo .05
282 Mike Witt .05
283 Mitch Webster .05
284 Greg Gagne .05
285 Greg Olson **RC** .05
286 Tony Phillips .05
287 Scott Bradley .05
288 Cory Snyder .05
289 Jay Bell .05
290 Kevin Romine .05
291 Jeff Robinson .05
292 Steve Frey **RC** .05
293 Craig Worthington .05
294 Tim Crews .05
295 Joe Magrane .05
296 Hector Villanueva **RC** .05
297 Terry Shumpert **RC** .05
298 Joe Carter .05
299 Kent Mercker .05
300 Checklist 180-255 .05
301 Chet Lemon .05
302 Mike Schooler .05
303 Dante Bichette .05
304 Kevin Elster .05
305 Jeff Huson .05
306 Greg Harris .05
307 Marquis Grissom .05
308 Calvin Schiraldi .05
309 Mariano Duncan .05
310 Bill Spiers .05
311 Scott Garrelts .05
312 Mitch Williams .05
313 Mike Macfarlane .05
314 Kevin Brown .05
315 Robin Ventura .05
316 Darren Daulton .05
317 Pat Borders .05
318 Mark Eichhorn .05
319 Jeff Brantley .05
320 Shane Mack .05
321 Rob Dibble .05
322 John Franco .05
323 Junior Felix .05
324 Casey Candaele .05
325 Bobby Bonilla .05
326 Dave Henderson .05
327 Wayne Edwards .05
328 Mark Knudson .05
329 Terry Steinbach .05
330 Colby Ward **RC** .05
331 Oscar Azocar **RC** .05
332 Scott Radinsky **RC** .10
333 Eric Anthony .05
334 Steve Lake .05
335 Bob Melvin .05
336 Kal Daniels .05
337 Tom Pagnozzi .05
338 Alan Mills **RC** .05
339 Steve Olin .05
340 Juan Berenguer .05
341 Francisco Cabrera .05
342 Dave Bergman .05
343 Henry Cotto .05
344 Sergio Valdez .05
345 Bob Patterson .05
346 John Marzano .05
347 Dana Kiecker **RC** .05
348 Dion James .05
349 Hubie Brooks .05
350 Bill Landrum .05
351 Bill Sampen **RC** .05
352 Greg Briley .05
353 Paul Gibson .05
354 Dave Eiland .05
355 Steve Finley .05
356 Bob Boone .05
357 Steve Buechele .05
358 Chris Hoiles **RC** .05
359 Larry Walker .05
360 Frank DiPino .05
361 Mark Grant .05
362 Dave Magadan .05
363 Robby Thompson .05
364 Lonnie Smith .05
365 Steve Farr .05
366 Dave Valle .05
367 Tim Naehring **RC** .05
368 Jim Acker .05
369 Jeff Reardon .05
370 Tim Teufel .05
371 Juan Gonzalez .20
372 Luis Salazar .05
373 Rick Honeycutt .05
374 Greg Maddux .50
375 Jose Uribe .05
376 Donnie Hill .05
377 Don Carman .05
378 Craig Grebeck **RC** .05
379 Willie Fraser .05
380 Glenallen Hill .05
381 Joe Oliver .05
382 Randy Bush .05
383 Alex Cole **RC** .05
384 Norm Charlton .05
385 Gene Nelson .05
386a Checklist 256-331 (Blue Borders) .05
386b Checklist 256-331 (Green Borders) .05
387 Rickey Henderson (MVP) .20
388 Lance Parrish (MVP) .05
389 Fred McGriff (MVP) .05
390 Dave Parker (MVP) .05
391 Candy Maldonado (MVP) .05
392 Ken Griffey Jr. (MVP) .50
393 Gregg Olson (MVP) .05
394 Rafael Palmeiro (MVP) .20
395 Roger Clemens (MVP) .30
396 George Brett (MVP) .30
397 Cecil Fielder (MVP) .05
398 Brian Harper (MVP) .05
399 Bobby Thigpen (MVP) .05
400 Roberto Kelly (MVP) .05
401 Danny Darwin (MVP) .05
402 Dave Justice (MVP) .05
403 Lee Smith (MVP) .05
404 Ryne Sandberg (MVP) .25
405 Eddie Murray (MVP) .20
406 Tim Wallach (MVP) .05
407 Kevin Mitchell (MVP) .05
408 Darryl Strawberry (MVP) .05
409 Joe Carter (MVP) .05
410 Len Dykstra (MVP) .05
411 Doug Drabek (MVP) .05
412 Chris Sabo (MVP) .05
413 Paul Marak/RR **RC** .05
414 Tim McIntosh/RR **RC** .05
415 Brian Barnes/RR **RC** .05
416 Eric Gunderson/RR **RC** .05
417 Mike Gardiner/RR **RC** .05
418 Steve Carter/RR .05
419 Gerald Alexander/RR **RC** .05
420 Rich Garces/RR **RC** .05
421 Chuck Knoblauch/RR **RC** .50
422 Scott Aldred/RR **RC** .05
423 Wes Chamberlain/RR **RC** .05
424 Lance Dickson/RR **RC** .05
425 Greg Colbrunn/RR **RC** .10
426 Rich Delucia/RR **RC** .05
427 Jeff Conine/RR **RC** .50
428 Steve Decker/RR **RC** .05
429 Turner Ward/RR **RC** .05
430 Mo Vaughn/RR .05
431 Steve Chitren/RR **RC** .05
432 Mike Benjamin/RR **RC** .05
433 Ryne Sandberg/AS .25
434 Len Dykstra/AS .05
435 Andre Dawson/AS .15
436 Mike Scioscia/AS .05
437 Ozzie Smith/AS .25
438 Kevin Mitchell/AS .05
439 Jack Armstrong/AS .05
440 Chris Sabo/AS .05
441 Will Clark/AS .05
442 Mel Hall .05
443 Mark Gardner .05
444 Mike Devereaux .05
445 Kirk Gibson .05
446 Terry Pendleton .05
447 Mike Harkey .05
448 Jim Eisenreich .05
449 Benito Santiago .05
450 Oddibe McDowell .05
451 Cecil Fielder .05
452 Ken Griffey Sr. .05
453 Bert Blyleven .10
454 Howard Johnson .05
455 Monty Farris **RC** .05
456 Tony Pena .05
457 Tim Raines .05
458 Dennis Rasmussen .05
459 Luis Quinones .05
460 B.J. Surhoff .05
461 Ernest Riles .05
462 Rick Sutcliffe .05
463 Danny Tartabull .05
464 Pete Incaviglia .05
465 Carlos Martinez .05
466 Ricky Jordan .05
467 John Cerutti .05
468 Dave Winfield .40
469 Francisco Oliveras .05
470 Roy Smith .05
471 Barry Larkin .05
472 Ron Darling .05
473 David Wells .05
474 Glenn Davis .05
475 Neal Heaton .05
476 Ron Hassey .05
477 Frank Thomas .40
478 Greg Vaughn .05
479 Todd Burns .05
480 Candy Maldonado .05
481 Dave LaPoint .05
482 Alvin Davis .05
483 Mike Scott .05
484 Dale Murphy .20
485 Ben McDonald .05
486 Jay Howell .05
487 Vince Coleman .05
488 Alfredo Griffin .05
489 Sandy Alomar .05
490 Kirby Puckett .50
491 Andres Thomas .05
492 Jack Morris .05
493 Matt Young .05
494 Greg Myers .05
495 Barry Bonds 1.00
496 Scott Cooper .05
497 Dan Schatzeder .05
498 Jesse Barfield .05
499 Jerry Goff **RC** .05
500 Checklist 332-408 .05
501 Anthony Telford **RC** .05
502 Eddie Murray .40
503 Omar Olivares **RC** .05
504 Ryne Sandberg .50
505 Jeff Montgomery .05
506 Mark Parent .05
507 Ron Gant .05
508 Frank Tanana .05
509 Jay Buhner .05
510 Max Venable .05
511 Wally Whitehurst .05
512 Gary Pettis .05
513 Tom Brunansky .05
514 Tim Wallach .05
515 Craig Lefferts .05
516 Tim Layana **RC** .05
517 Darryl Hamilton .05
518 Rick Reuschel .05
519 Steve Wilson .05
520 Kurt Stillwell .05
521 Rafael Palmeiro .30
522 Ken Patterson .05
523 Len Dykstra .05
524 Tony Fernandez .05
525 Kent Anderson .05
526 Mark Leonard **RC** .05
527 Allan Anderson .05
528 Tom Browning .05
529 Frank Viola .05
530 John Olerud .05
531 Juan Agosto .05
532 Zane Smith .05
533 Scott Sanderson .05
534 Barry Jones .05
535 Mike Felder .05
536 Jose Canseco .20
537 Felix Fermin .05
538 Roberto Kelly .05
539 Brian Holman .05
540 Mark Davidson .05
541 Terry Mulholland .05
542 Randy Milligan .05
543 Jose Gonzalez .05
544 Craig Wilson **RC** .05
545 Mike Hartley .05
546 Greg Swindell .05
547 Gary Gaetti .05
548 Dave Justice .05
549 Steve Searcy .05
550 Erik Hanson .05
551 Dave Stieb .05
552 Andy Van Slyke .05
553 Mike Greenwell .05
554 Kevin Maas .05
555 Delino Deshields .05
556 Curt Schilling .20
557 Ramon Martinez .05
558 Pedro Guerrero .05
559 Dwight Smith .05
560 Mark Davis .05
561 Shawn Abner .05
562 Charlie Leibrandt .05
563 John Shelby .05
564 Bill Swift .05
565 Mike Fetters .05
566 Alejandro Pena .05
567 Ruben Sierra .05
568 Carlos Quintana .05
569 Kevin Gross .05
570 Derek Lilliquist .05
571 Jack Armstrong .05
572 Greg Brock .05
573 Mike Kingery .05
574 Greg Smith **RC** .05
575 Brian McRae **RC** .10
576 Jack Daugherty .05
577 Ozzie Guillen .05
578 Joe Boever .05
579 Luis Sojo .05
580 Chili Davis .05
581 Don Robinson .05
582 Brian Harper .05
583 Paul O'Neill .05
584 Bob Ojeda .05
585 Mookie Wilson .05
586 Rafael Ramirez .05
587 Gary Redus .05
588 Jamie Quirk .05
589 Shawn Hilligas .05
590 Tom Edens **RC** .05
591 Joe Klink **RC** .05
592 Charles Nagy .05
593 Eric Plunk .05
594 Tracy Jones .05
595 Craig Biggio .05
596 Jose DeJesus .05
597 Mickey Tettleton .05
598 Chris Gwynn .05
599 Rex Hudler .05
600 Checklist 409-506 .05
601 Jim Gott .05
602 Jeff Manto **RC** .05
603 Nelson Liriano .05
604 Mark Lemke .05
605 Clay Parker .05
606 Edgar Martinez .05
607 Mark Whiten **RC** .10
608 Ted Power .05
609 Tom Bolton .05
610 Tom Herr .05
611 Andy Hawkins .05
612 Scott Ruskin .05
613 Ron Kittle .05
614 John Wetteland .05
615 Mike Perez **RC** .05
616 Dave Clark .05
617 Brent Mayne **RC** .05
618 Jack Clark .05
619 Marvin Freeman .05
620 Edwin Nunez .05
621 Russ Swan **RC** .05
622 Johnny Ray .05
623 Charlie O'Brien .05
624 Joe Bitker **RC** .05
625 Mike Marshall .05
626 Otis Nixon .05
627 Andy Benes .05
628 Ron Oester .05
629 Ted Higuera .05
630 Kevin Bass .05
631 Damon Berryhill .05
632 Bo Jackson .10
633 Brad Arnsberg .05
634 Jerry Willard .05
635 Tommy Greene .05
636 Bob MacDonald **RC** .05
637 Kirk McCaskill .05
638 John Burkett .05
639 Paul Abbott **RC** .05
640 Todd Benzinger .05
641 Todd Hundley **RC** .05
642 George Bell .05
643 Javier Ortiz **RC** .05
644 Sid Bream .05
645 Bob Welch .05
646 Phil Bradley .05
647 Bill Krueger .05
648 Rickey Henderson .40
649 Kevin Wickander .05
650 Steve Balboni .05
651 Gene Harris .05
652 Jim Deshaies .05
653 Jason Grimsley .05

654	Joe Orsulak	.05
655	Jimmy Poole **RC**	.05
656	Felix Jose	.05
657	Dennis Cook	.05
658	Tom Brookens	.05
659	Junior Ortiz	.05
660	Jeff Parrett	.05
661	Jerry Don Gleaton	.05
662	Brent Knackert	.05
663	Rance Mulliniks	.05
664	John Smiley	.05
665	Larry Andersen	.05
666	Willie McGee	.05
667	Chris Nabholz **RC**	.05
668	Brady Anderson	.05
669	Darren Holmes **RC**	.10
670	Ken Hill	.05
671	Gary Varsho	.05
672	Bill Pecota	.05
673	Fred Lynn	.05
674	Kevin D. Brown **RC**	.05
675	Dan Petry	.05
676	Mike Jackson	.05
677	Wally Joyner	.05
678	Danny Jackson	.05
679	Bill Haselman **RC**	.05
680	Mike Boddicker	.05
681	Mel Rojas **RC**	.05
682	Roberto Alomar	.20
683	Dave Justice (R.O.Y.)	.05
684	Chuck Crim	.05
685a	Matt Williams (Last line of Career Highlights ends, "most DP's in.")	.10
685b	Matt Williams (Last line ends "8/24-27/87.")	.25
686	Shawon Dunston	.05
687	Jeff Schulz **RC**	.05
688	John Barfield **RC**	.05
689	Gerald Young	.05
690	Luis Gonzalez **RC**	.75
691	Frank Wills	.05
692	Chuck Finley	.05
693	Sandy Alomar (R.O.Y.)	.05
694	Tim Drummond	.05
695	Herm Winningham	.05
696	Darryl Strawberry	.05
697	Al Leiter	.05
698	Karl Rhodes **RC**	.05
699	Stan Belinda **RC**	.05
700	Checklist 507-604	.05
701	Lance Blankenship	.05
702	Willie Stargell (Puzzle Card)	.05
703	Jim Gantner	.05
704	Reggie Harris **RC**	.05
705	Rob Ducey	.05
706	Tim Hulett	.05
707	Atlee Hammaker	.05
708	Xavier Hernandez	.05
709	Chuck McElroy **RC**	.05
710	John Mitchell	.05
711	Carlos Hernandez	.05
712	Geronimo Pena **RC**	.05
713	Jim Neidlinger **RC**	.05
714	John Orton	.05
715	Terry Leach	.05
716	Mike Stanton	.05
717	Walt Terrell	.05
718	Luis Aquino	.05
719	Bud Black	.05
720	Bob Kipper	.05
721	Jeff Gray **RC**	.05
722	Jose Rijo	.05
723	Curt Young	.05
724	Jose Vizcaino **RC**	.05
725	Randy Tomlin **RC**	.05
726	Junior Noboa	.05
727	Bob Welch (Award Winner)	.05
728	Gary Ward	.05
729	Rob Deer	.05
730	David Segui **RC**	.05
731	Mark Carreon	.05
732	Vicente Palacios	.05
733	Sam Horn	.05
734	Howard Farmer **RC**	.05
735	Ken Dayley	.05
736	Kelly Mann	.05
737	Joe Grahe **RC**	.05
738	Kelly Downs	.05
739	Jimmy Kremers **RC**	.05
740	Kevin Appier	.05
741	Jeff Reed	.05
742	Jose Rijo (World Series)	.05
743	Dave Rohde **RC**	.05
744	Dr. Dirt/Mr. Clean (Len Dykstra, Dale Murphy)	.10
745	Paul Sorrento	.05
746	Thomas Howard **RC**	.05
747	Matt Stark **RC**	.05
748	Harold Baines	.05
749	Doug Dascenzo	.05
750	Doug Drabek (Award Winner)	.05
751	Gary Sheffield	.20
752	Terry Lee **RC**	.05
753	Jim Vatcher **RC**	.05
754	Lee Stevens	.05
755	Randy Veres **RC**	.05
756	Bill Doran	.05
757	Gary Wayne	.05
758	Pedro Munoz **RC**	.05
759	Chris Hammond **RC**	.05
760	Checklist 605-702	.05
761	Rickey Henderson (MVP)	.20
762	Barry Bonds (MVP)	.50
763	Billy Hatcher (World Series)	.05
764	Julio Machado	.05
765	Jose Mesa	.05
766	Willie Randolph (World Series)	.05
767	Scott Erickson **RC**	.10
768	Travis Fryman	.05
769	Rich Rodriguez **RC**	.05
770	Checklist 703-770; BC1-BC22	.05

Elite

Donruss released a series of special inserts in 1991. Ten thousand of each Elite card was released, while 7,500 Legend cards and 5,000 Signature cards were issued. Cards were inserted in wax packs and feature marble borders. The Legend card features a Dick Perez drawing. Each card is designated with a serial number on the back.

		NM/M
Complete Set (10):		250.00
Common Player:		15.00
1	Barry Bonds	60.00
2	George Brett	40.00
3	Jose Canseco	25.00
4	Andre Dawson	15.00
5	Doug Drabek	7.50
6	Cecil Fielder	7.50
7	Rickey Henderson	25.00
8	Matt Williams	7.50
---	Nolan Ryan (Legend)	65.00
---	Ryne Sandberg (Signature)	100.00

Grand Slammers

This set features players who hit grand slams in 1990. The cards are styled after the 1991 Donruss regular-issue cards. The featured player is showcased with a star in the background. The set was included in factory sets and randomly in jumbo packs.

		NM/M
Complete Set (14):		2.00
Common Player:		.10
1	Joe Carter	.10
2	Bobby Bonilla	.10
3	Kal Daniels	.10
4	Jose Canseco	.30
5	Barry Bonds	1.00
6	Jay Buhner	.10
7	Cecil Fielder	.10
8	Matt Williams	.10
9	Andres Galarraga	.10
10	Luis Polonia	.10
11	Mark McGwire	.75
12	Ron Karkovice	.10
13	Darryl Strawberry	.10
14	Mike Greenwell	.10

Highlights

These inserts feature highlights from the 1990 season. Cards have a "BC" (Bonus Card) prefix to the number and are styled after the 1991 regular-issue Donruss cards. Cards 1-10 feature blue borders due to their release with Series 1 cards. Cards 11-22 feature green borders and were released with Series 2 cards. A highlight logo appears on the front of the card. Each highlight is explained in depth on the card back.

		NM/M
Complete Set (22):		3.00
Common Player:		.10
1	Mark Langston, Mike Witt (No-Hit Mariners)	.10
2	Randy Johnson (No-Hits Tigers)	.25
3	Nolan Ryan (No-Hits A's)	.50
4	Dave Stewart (No-Hits Blue Jays)	.10
5	Cecil Fielder (50 Homer Club)	.10
6	Carlton Fisk (Record Home Run)	.20
7	Ryne Sandberg (Sets Fielding Records)	.25
8	Gary Carter (Breaks Catching Mark)	.20
9	Mark McGwire (Home Run Milestone)	.45
10	Bo Jackson (4 Consecutive HRs)	.15
11	Fernando Valenzuela (No-Hits Cardinals)	.10
12a	Andy Hawkins (PITCHER)	2.50
12b	Andy Hawkins (No-Hits White Sox)	.10
13	Melido Perez (No-Hits Yankees)	.10
14	Terry Mulholland (No-Hits Giants)	.10
15	Nolan Ryan (300th Win)	.50
16	Delino DeShields (4 Hits In Debut)	.10
17	Cal Ripken (Errorless Games)	.50
18	Eddie Murray (Switch Hit Homers)	.20
19	George Brett (3 Decade Champ)	.30
20	Bobby Thigpen (Shatters Save Mark)	.10
21	Dave Stieb (No-Hits Indians)	.10
22	Willie McGee (NL Batting Champ)	.10

Diamond Kings Supers

Donruss made this set available through a mail-in offer. Three wrappers, $12 and postage were necessary to obtain this set. The cards are exactly the same design as the regular Donruss Diamond Kings except they measure approximately 5" x 6-3/4" in size. The artwork of Dick Perez is featured.

		NM/M
Complete Set (26):		8.00
Common Player:		.25
1	Dave Steib	.25
2	Craig Biggio	.25
3	Cecil Fielder	.25
4	Barry Bonds	4.50
5	Barry Larkin	.25
6	Dave Parker	.25
7	Len Dykstra	.25
8	Bobby Thigpen	.25
9	Roger Clemens	2.50
10	Ron Gant	.25
11	Delino DeShields	.25
12	Roberto Alomar	.40
13	Sandy Alomar	.25
14	Ryne Sandberg	1.50
15	Ramon Martinez	.25
16	Edgar Martinez	.25
17	Dave Magadan	.25
18	Matt Williams	.25
19	Rafael Palmeiro	1.00
20	Bob Welch	.25
21	Dave Righetti	.25
22	Brian Harper	.25
23	Gregg Olson	.25
24	Kurt Stillwell	.25
25	Pedro Guerrero	.25
26	Chuck Finley	.25

Rookies

Red borders highlight the 1991 Donruss Rookies cards. This set marks the sixth year that Donruss produced such an issue. As in past years, "The Rookies" logo appears on the card fronts. The set is packaged in a special box and includes a Willie Stargell puzzle card.

		NM/M
Complete Set (56):		4.00
Common Player:		.05
1	Pat Kelly **RC**	.05
2	Rich DeLucia	.05
3	Wes Chamberlain	.05
4	Scott Leius **RC**	.05
5	Darryl Kile **RC**	.05
6	Milt Cuyler	.05
7	Todd Van Poppel	.05
8	Ray Lankford	.05
9	Brian Hunter	.05
10	Tony Perezchica	.05
11	Ced Landrum **RC**	.05
12	Dave Burba **RC**	.05
13	Ramon Garcia	.05
14	Ed Sprague **RC**	.05
15	Warren Newson **RC**	.05
16	Paul Faries **RC**	.05
17	Luis Gonzalez	.15
18	Charles Nagy	.05
19	Chris Hammond	.05
20	Frank Castillo	.05
21	Pedro Munoz	.05
22	Orlando Merced	.05
23	Jose Melendez **RC**	.05
24	Kirk Dressendorfer	.05
25	Heathcliff Slocumb **RC**	.05
26	Doug Simons **RC**	.05
27	Mike Timlin **RC**	.05
28	Jeff Fassero	.05
29	Mark Leiter **RC**	.05
30	Jeff Bagwell **RC**	2.50
31	Brian McRae	.05
32	Mark Whiten	.05
33	Ivan Rodriguez **RC**	1.50
34	Wade Taylor **RC**	.05
35	Darren Lewis	.05
36	Mo Vaughn	.25
37	Mike Remlinger **RC**	.05
38	Rick Wilkins	.05
39	Chuck Knoblauch	.05
40	Kevin Morton	.05
41	Carlos Rodriguez **RC**	.05
42	Mark Lewis	.05
43	Brent Mayne	.05
44	Chris Haney **RC**	.05
45	Denis Boucher **RC**	.05
46	Mike Gardiner	.05
47	Jeff Johnson **RC**	.05
48	Dean Palmer	.05
49	Chuck McElroy	.05
50	Chris Jones **RC**	.05
51	Scott Kamieniecki **RC**	.05
52	Al Osuna **RC**	.05
53	Rusty Meacham **RC**	.05
54	Chito Martinez	.05
55	Reggie Jefferson	.05
56	Checklist	.05

1992 Donruss Previews

Four-card cello packs distributed to members of the Donruss dealers' network previewed the forthcoming 1992 baseball card issue. The preview cards have the same format, front and back photos as their counterparts in the regular set. Only the card number, the security underprinting, "Donruss Preview Card," and the stats, complete only through 1990, differ.

		NM/M
Complete Set (12):		25.00
Common Player:		.50
1	Wade Boggs	2.50
2	Barry Bonds	7.50
3	Will Clark	.50
4	Andre Dawson	.75
5	Dennis Eckersley	1.50
6	Robin Ventura	.50
7	Ken Griffey Jr.	4.00
8	Kelly Gruber	.50
9	Ryan Klesko/RR	.50
10	Cal Ripken, Jr.	7.50
11	Nolan Ryan (Highlight)	7.50
12	Todd Van Poppel	.50

1992 Donruss

For the second consecutive year, Donruss released its card set in two series. The 1992 cards feature improved stock, an anti-counterfeit feature and include both front and back photos. Once again Rated Rookies and All-Stars are included in the set. Special highlight cards also can be found in the 1992 Donruss set. Production was reduced in 1992 compared to 1988-1991. Retail factory sets include four 1992 Leaf preview cards.

		NM/M
Unopened Retail Set (788):		15.00
Unopened Hobby Set (784):		12.50
Unopened "Coca-Cola" Set (784):		25.00
Complete Set (784):		12.00
Common Player:		.05
Rod Carew Puzzle:		.50
Series 1 or 2 Pack (15):		.50
Series 1 or 2 Wax Box (36):		15.00
Blister Rack (92):		1.50
1	Mark Wohlers/RR **RC**	.05
2	Wil Cordero/RR	.05
3	Kyle Abbott/RR	.05
4	Dave Nilsson/RR **RC**	.05
5	Kenny Lofton/RR	.15
6	Luis Mercedes/RR **RC**	.05
7	Roger Salkeld/RR **RC**	.05
8	Eddie Zosky/RR **RC**	.05
9	Todd Van Poppel/RR **RC**	.10
10	Frank Seminara/RR **RC**	.05
11	Andy Ashby/RR **RC**	.10
12	Reggie Jefferson/RR **RC**	.05
13	Ryan Klesko/RR	.05
14	Carlos Garcia/RR **RC**	.10
15	John Ramos/RR **RC**	.05
16	Eric Karros/RR	.05
17	Pat Lennon/RR **RC**	.05
18	Eddie Taubensee/RR **RC**	.05
19	Roberto Hernandez/RR **RC**	.05
20	D.J. Dozier/RR **RC**	.05
21	Dave Henderson/AS	.05
22	Cal Ripken, Jr./AS	.50
23	Wade Boggs/AS	.25
24	Ken Griffey Jr./AS	.35
25	Jack Morris/AS	.05
26	Danny Tartabull/AS	.05
27	Cecil Fielder/AS	.05
28	Roberto Alomar/AS	.10
29	Sandy Alomar/AS	.05
30	Rickey Henderson/AS	.25
31	Ken Hill	.05
32	John Habyan	.05
33	Otis Nixon (Highlight)	.05
34	Tim Wallach	.05
35	Cal Ripken, Jr.	1.00
36	Gary Carter	.35
37	Juan Agosto	.05
38	Doug Dascenzo	.05
39	Kirk Gibson	.05
40	Benito Santiago	.05
41	Otis Nixon	.05
42	Andy Allanson	.05
43	Brian Holman	.05
44	Dick Schofield	.05
45	Dave Magadan	.05
46	Rafael Palmeiro	.35
47	Jody Reed	.05
48	Ivan Calderon	.05
49	Greg Harris	.05
50	Chris Sabo	.05
51	Paul Molitor	.35
52	Robby Thompson	.05
53	Dave Smith	.05
54	Mark Davis	.05
55	Kevin Brown	.05
56	Donn Pall	.05
57	Len Dykstra	.05
58	Roberto Alomar	.15
59	Jeff Robinson	.05
60	Willie McGee	.05
61	Jay Buhner	.05
62	Mike Pagliarulo	.05
63	Paul O'Neill	.05
64	Hubie Brooks	.05
65	Kelly Gruber	.05
66	Ken Caminiti	.05
67	Gary Redus	.05
68	Harold Baines	.05
69	Charlie Hough	.05
70	B.J. Surhoff	.05
71	Walt Weiss	.05
72	Shawn Hillegas	.05
73	Roberto Kelly	.05
74	Jeff Ballard	.05
75	Craig Biggio	.05
76	Pat Combs	.05
77	Jeff Robinson	.05
78	Tim Belcher	.05
79	Cris Carpenter	.05
80	Checklist 1-79	.05
81	Steve Avery	.05
82	Chris James	.05
83	Brian Harper	.05
84	Charlie Leibrandt	.05
85	Mickey Tettleton	.05
86	Pete O'Brien	.05
87	Danny Darwin	.05
88	Bob Walk	.05
89	Jeff Reardon	.05
90	Bobby Rose	.05
91	Danny Jackson	.05
92	John Morris	.05
93	Bud Black	.05
94	Tommy Greene (Highlight)	.05
95	Rick Aguilera	.05
96	Gary Gaetti	.05
97	David Cone	.05
98	John Olerud	.05
99	Joel Skinner	.05
100	Jay Bell	.05
101	Bob Milacki	.05
102	Norm Charlton	.05
103	Chuck Crim	.05
104	Terry Steinbach	.05
105	Juan Samuel	.05
106	Steve Howe	.05
107	Rafael Belliard	.05
108	Joey Cora	.05
109	Tommy Greene	.05
110	Gregg Olson	.05
111	Frank Tanana	.05
112	Lee Smith	.05
113	Greg Harris	.05
114	Dwayne Henry	.05
115	Chili Davis	.05
116	Kent Mercker	.05
117	Brian Barnes	.05
118	Rich DeLucia	.05
119	Andre Dawson	.20
120	Carlos Baerga	.05
121	Mike LaValliere	.05
122	Jeff Gray	.05
123	Bruce Hurst	.05
124	Alvin Davis	.05
125	John Candelaria	.05
126	Matt Nokes	.05
127	George Bell	.05
128	Bret Saberhagen	.05
129	Jeff Russell	.05
130	Jim Abbott	.05
131	Bill Gullickson	.05

132 Todd Zeile .05
133 Dave Winfield .35
134 Wally Whitehurst .05
135 Matt Williams .05
136 Tom Browning .05
137 Marquis Grissom .05
138 Erik Hanson .05
139 Rob Dibble .05
140 Don August .05
141 Tom Henke .05
142 Dan Pasqua .05
143 George Brett .60
144 Jerald Clark .05
145 Robin Ventura .05
146 Dale Murphy .20
147 Dennis Eckersley .30
148 Eric Yelding .05
149 Mario Diaz .05
150 Casey Candaele .05
151 Steve Olin .05
152 Luis Salazar .05
153 Kevin Maas .05
154 Nolan Ryan (Highlight) .50
155 Barry Jones .05
156 Chris Hoiles .05
157 Bobby Ojeda .05
158 Pedro Guerrero .05
159 Paul Assenmacher .05
160 Checklist 80-157 .05
161 Mike Macfarlane .05
162 Craig Lefferts .05
163 Brian Hunter **RC** .05
164 Alan Trammell .05
165 Ken Griffey Jr. .65
166 Lance Parrish .05
167 Brian Downing .05
168 John Barfield .05
169 Jack Clark .05
170 Chris Nabholz .05
171 Tim Teufel .05
172 Chris Hammond .05
173 Robin Yount .35
174 Dave Righetti .05
175 Joe Girardi .05
176 Mike Boddicker .05
177 Dean Palmer .05
178 Greg Hibbard .05
179 Randy Ready .05
180 Devon White .05
181 Mark Eichhorn .05
182 Mike Felder .05
183 Joe Klink .05
184 Steve Bedrosian .05
185 Barry Larkin .05
186 John Franco .05
187 Ed Sprague **RC** .05
188 Mark Portugal .05
189 Jose Lind .05
190 Bob Welch .05
191 Alex Fernandez .05
192 Gary Sheffield .20
193 Rickey Henderson .35
194 Rod Nichols .05
195 Scott Kamieniecki **RC** .05
196 Mike Flanagan .05
197 Steve Finley .05
198 Darren Daulton .05
199 Leo Gomez .05
200 Mike Morgan .05
201 Bob Tewksbury .05
202 Sid Bream .05
203 Sandy Alomar .05
204 Greg Gagne .05
205 Juan Berenguer .05
206 Cecil Fielder .05
207 Randy Johnson .35
208 Tony Pena .05
209 Doug Drabek .05
210 Wade Boggs .45
211 Bryan Harvey .05
212 Jose Vizcaino .05
213 Alonzo Powell **RC** .05
214 Will Clark .05
215 Rickey Henderson (Highlight) .20
216 Jack Morris .05
217 Junior Felix .05
218 Vince Coleman .05
219 Jimmy Key .05
220 Alex Cole .05
221 Bill Landrum .05
222 Randy Milligan .05
223 Jose Rijo .05
224 Greg Vaughn .05
225 Dave Stewart .05
226 Lenny Harris .05
227 Scott Sanderson .05
228 Jeff Blauser .05
229 Ozzie Guillen .05
230 John Kruk .05
231 Bob Melvin .05
232 Milt Cuyler .05
233 Felix Jose .05
234 Ellis Burks .05
235 Pete Harnisch .05
236 Kevin Tapani .05
237 Terry Pendleton .05
238 Mark Gardner .05
239 Harold Reynolds .05
240 Checklist 158-237 .05
241 Mike Harkey .05
242 Felix Fermin .05
243 Barry Bonds 1.00
244 Roger Clemens .60
245 Dennis Rasmussen .05
246 Jose DeLeon .05
247 Orel Hershiser .05
248 Mel Hall .05
249 Rick Wilkins **RC** .05
250 Tom Gordon .05
251 Kevin Reimer .05
252 Luis Polonia .05
253 Mike Henneman .05
254 Tom Pagnozzi .05
255 Chuck Finley .05
256 Mackey Sasser .05
257 John Burkett .05
258 Hal Morris .05
259 Larry Walker .05
260 Billy Swift .05
261 Joe Oliver .05
262 Julio Machado .05
263 Todd Stottlemyre .05
264 Matt Merullo .05
265 Brent Mayne .05
266 Thomas Howard .05
267 Lance Johnson .05
268 Terry Mulholland .05
269 Rick Honeycutt .05
270 Luis Gonzalez .05
271 Jose Guzman .05
272 Jimmy Jones .05
273 Mark Lewis .05
274 Rene Gonzales .05
275 Jeff Johnson **RC** .05
276 Dennis Martinez (Highlight) .05
277 Delino DeShields .05
278 Sam Horn .05
279 Kevin Gross .05
280 Jose Oquendo .05
281 Mark Grace .05
282 Mark Gubicza .05
283 Fred McGriff .05
284 Ron Gant .05
285 Lou Whitaker .05
286 Edgar Martinez .05
287 Ron Tingley .05
288 Kevin McReynolds .05
289 Ivan Rodriguez .30
290 Mike Gardiner .05
291 Chris Haney **RC** .05
292 Darrin Jackson .05
293 Bill Doran .05
294 Ted Higuera .05
295 Jeff Brantley .05
296 Les Lancaster .05
297 Jim Eisenreich .05
298 Ruben Sierra .05
299 Scott Radinsky .05
300 Jose DeJesus .05
301 Mike Timlin **RC** .05
302 Luis Sojo .05
303 Kelly Downs .05
304 Scott Bankhead .05
305 Pedro Munoz .05
306 Scott Scudder .05
307 Kevin Elster .05
308 Duane Ward .05
309 Darryl Kile **RC** .10
310 Orlando Merced .05
311 Dave Henderson .05
312 Tim Raines .05
313 Mark Lee **RC** .05
314 Mike Gallego .05
315 Charles Nagy .45
316 Jesse Barfield .05
317 Todd Frohwirth .05
318 Al Osuna .05
319 Darrin Fletcher .05
320 Checklist 238-316 .05
321 David Segui .05
322 Stan Javier .05
323 Bryn Smith .05
324 Jeff Treadway .05
325 Mark Whiten .05
326 Kent Hrbek .05
327 Dave Justice .05
328 Tony Phillips .05
329 Rob Murphy .05
330 Kevin Morton .05
331 John Smiley .05
332 Luis Rivera .05
333 Wally Joyner .05
334 Heathcliff Slocumb **RC** .05
335 Rick Cerone .05
336 Mike Remlinger **RC** .05
337 Mike Moore .05
338 Lloyd McClendon .05
339 Al Newman .05
340 Kirk McCaskill .05
341 Howard Johnson .05
342 Greg Myers .05
343 Kal Daniels .05
344 Bernie Williams .05
345 Shane Mack .05
346 Gary Thurman .05
347 Dante Bichette .05
348 Mark McGwire .75
349 Travis Fryman .05
350 Ray Lankford .05
351 Mike Jeffcoat .05
352 Jack McDowell .05
353 Mitch Williams .05
354 Mike Devereaux .05
355 Andres Galarraga .05
356 Henry Cotto .05
357 Scott Bailes .05
358 Jeff Bagwell .35
359 Scott Leius .05
360 Zane Smith .05
361 Bill Pecota .05
362 Tony Fernandez .05
363 Glenn Braggs .05
364 Bill Spiers .05
365 Vicente Palacios .05
366 Tim Burke .05
367 Randy Tomlin .05
368 Kenny Rogers .05
369 Brett Butler .05
370 Pat Kelly .05
371 Bip Roberts .05
372 Gregg Jefferies .05
373 Kevin Bass .05
374 Ron Karkovice .05
375 Paul Gibson .05
376 Bernard Gilkey .05
377 Dave Gallagher .05
378 Bill Wegman .05
379 Pat Borders .05
380 Ed Whitson .05
381 Gilberto Reyes .05
382 Russ Swan .05
383 Andy Van Slyke .05
384 Wes Chamberlain .05
385 Steve Chitren .05
386 Greg Olson .05
387 Brian McRae .05
388 Rich Rodriguez .05
389 Steve Decker .05
390 Chuck Knoblauch .05
391 Bobby Witt .05
392 Eddie Murray .35
393 Juan Gonzalez .20
394 Scott Ruskin .05
395 Jay Howell .05
396 Checklist 317-396 .05
397 Royce Clayton/RR .05
398 John Jaha/RR **RC** .05
399 Dan Wilson/RR **RC** .05
400 Archie Corbin/RR **RC** .05
401 Barry Manuel/RR **RC** .05
402 Kim Batiste/RR **RC** .05
403 Pat Mahomes/RR **RC** .05
404 Dave Fleming/RR .05
405 Jeff Juden/RR .05
406 Jim Thome/RR .40
407 Sam Militello/RR **RC** .05
408 Jeff Nelson/RR **RC** .05
409 Anthony Young/RR .05
410 Tino Martinez/RR .05
411 Jeff Mutis/RR **RC** .05
412 Rey Sanchez/RR **RC** .05
413 Chris Gardner/RR **RC** .05
414 John Vander Wal/RR **RC** .10
415 Reggie Sanders/RR .05
416 Brian Williams/RR **RC** .05
417 Mo Sanford/RR **RC** .05
418 David Weathers/RR **RC** .05
419 Hector Fajardo/RR **RC** .05
420 Steve Foster/RR **RC** .05
421 Lance Dickson/RR .05
422 Andre Dawson/AS .15
423 Ozzie Smith/AS .25
424 Chris Sabo/AS .05
425 Tony Gwynn/AS .25
426 Tom Glavine/AS .05
427 Bobby Bonilla/AS .05
428 Will Clark/AS .05
429 Ryne Sandberg/AS .25
430 Benito Santiago/AS .05
431 Ivan Calderon/AS .05
432 Ozzie Smith .45
433 Tim Leary .05
434 Bret Saberhagen (Highlight) .05
435 Mel Rojas .05
436 Ben McDonald .05
437 Tim Crews .05
438 Rex Hudler .05
439 Chico Walker .05
440 Kurt Stillwell .05
441 Tony Gwynn .45
442 John Smoltz .05
443 Lloyd Moseby .05
444 Mike Schooler .05
445 Joe Grahe .05
446 Dwight Gooden .05
447 Oil Can Boyd .05
448 John Marzano .05
449 Bret Barberie .05
450 Mike Maddux .05
451 Jeff Reed .05
452 Dale Sveum .05
453 Jose Uribe .05
454 Bob Scanlan .05
455 Kevin Appier .05
456 Jeff Huson .05
457 Ken Patterson .05
458 Ricky Jordan .05
459 Tom Candiotti .05
460 Lee Stevens .05
461 Rod Beck **RC** .10
462 Dave Valle .05
463 Scott Erickson .05
464 Chris Jones .05
465 Mark Carreon .05
466 Rob Ducey .05
467 Jim Corsi .05
468 Jeff King .05
469 Curt Young .05
470 Bo Jackson .15
471 Chris Bosio .05
472 Jamie Quirk .05
473 Jesse Orosco .05
474 Alvaro Espinoza .05
475 Joe Orsulak .05
476 Checklist 397-477 .05
477 Gerald Young .05
478 Wally Backman .05
479 Juan Bell .05
480 Mike Scioscia .05
481 Omar Olivares .05
482 Francisco Cabrera .05
483 Greg Swindell .05
484 Terry Leach .05
485 Tommy Gregg .05
486 Scott Aldred .05
487 Greg Briley .05
488 Phil Plantier .05
489 Curtis Wilkerson .05
490 Tom Brunansky .05
491 Mike Fetters .05
492 Frank Castillo .05
493 Joe Boever .05
494 Kirt Manwaring .05
495 Wilson Alvarez (Highlight) .05
496 Gene Larkin .05
497 Gary DiSarcina .05
498 Frank Viola .05
499 Manuel Lee .05
500 Albert Belle .05
501 Stan Belinda .05
502 Dwight Evans .05
503 Eric Davis .05
504 Darren Holmes .05
505 Mike Bordick .05
506 Dave Hansen .05
507 Lee Guetterman .05
508 Keith Mitchell **RC** .05
509 Melido Perez .05
510 Dickie Thon .05
511 Mark Williamson .05
512 Mark Salas .05
513 Milt Thompson .05
514 Mo Vaughn .05
515 Jim Deshaies .05
516 Rich Garces .05
517 Lonnie Smith .05
518 Spike Owen .05
519 Tracy Jones .05
520 Greg Maddux .45
521 Carlos Martinez .05
522 Neal Heaton .05
523 Mike Greenwell .05
524 Andy Benes .05
525 Jeff Schaefer .05
526 Mike Sharperson .05
527 Wade Taylor .05
528 Jerome Walton .05
529 Storm Davis .05
530 Jose Hernandez **RC** .05
531 Mark Langston .05
532 Rob Deer .05
533 Geronimo Pena .05
534 Juan Guzman **RC** .10
535 Pete Schourek .05
536 Todd Benzinger .05
537 Billy Hatcher .05
538 Tom Foley .05
539 Dave Cochrane .05
540 Mariano Duncan .05
541 Edwin Nunez .05
542 Rance Mulliniks .05
543 Carlton Fisk .35
544 Luis Aquino .05
545 Ricky Bones .05
546 Craig Grebeck .05
547 Charlie Hayes .05
548 Jose Canseco .25
549 Andujar Cedeno .05
550 Geno Petralli .05
551 Javier Ortiz .05
552 Rudy Seanez .05
553 Rich Gedman .05
554 Eric Plunk .05
555 Nolan Ryan, Rich Gossage (Highlight) .25
556 Checklist 478-555 .05
557 Greg Colbrunn .05
558 Chito Martinez **RC** .05
559 Darryl Strawberry .05
560 Luis Alicea .05
561 Dwight Smith .05
562 Terry Shumpert .05
563 Jim Vatcher .05
564 Deion Sanders .10
565 Walt Terrell .05
566 Dave Burba .05
567 Dave Howard .05
568 Todd Hundley .05
569 Jack Daugherty .05
570 Scott Cooper .05
571 Bill Sampen .05
572 Jose Melendez .05
573 Freddie Benavides .05
574 Jim Gantner .05
575 Trevor Wilson .05
576 Ryne Sandberg .45
577 Kevin Seitzer .05
578 Gerald Alexander .05
579 Mike Huff .05
580 Von Hayes .05
581 Derek Bell .05
582 Mike Stanley .05
583 Kevin Mitchell .05
584 Mike Jackson .05
585 Dan Gladden .05
586 Ted Power .05
587 Jeff Innis .05
588 Bob MacDonald .05
589 Jose Tolentino **RC** .05
590 Bob Patterson .05
591 Scott Brosius **RC** .10
592 Frank Thomas .35
593 Darryl Hamilton .05
594 Kirk Dressendorfer .05
595 Jeff Shaw .05
596 Don Mattingly .60
597 Glenn Davis .05
598 Andy Mota .05
599 Jason Grimsley .05
600 Jimmy Poole .05
601 Jim Gott .05
602 Stan Royer .05
603 Marvin Freeman .05
604 Denis Boucher .05
605 Denny Neagle .05
606 Mark Lemke .05
607 Jerry Don Gleaton .05
608 Brent Knackert .05
609 Carlos Quintana .05
610 Bobby Bonilla .05
611 Joe Hesketh .05
612 Daryl Boston .05
613 Shawon Dunston .05
614 Danny Cox .05
615 Darren Lewis .05
616 Alejandro Pena, Kent Mercker, Mark Wohlers (Highlight) .05
617 Kirby Puckett .45
618 Franklin Stubbs .05
619 Chris Donnels .05
620 David Wells .05
621 Mike Aldrete .05
622 Bob Kipper .05
623 Anthony Telford .05
624 Randy Myers .05
625 Willie Randolph .05
626 Joe Slusarski .05
627 John Wetteland .05
628 Greg Cadaret .05
629 Tom Glavine .20
630 Wilson Alvarez .05
631 Wally Ritchie .05
632 Mike Mussina .25
633 Mark Leiter .05
634 Gerald Perry .05
635 Matt Young .05
636 Checklist 556-635 .05
637 Scott Hemond .05
638 David West .05
639 Jim Clancy .05
640 Doug Piatt **RC** .05
641 Omar Vizquel .05
642 Rick Sutcliffe .05
643 Glenallen Hill .05
644 Gary Varsho .05
645 Tony Fossas .05
646 Jack Howell .05
647 Jim Campanis **RC** .05
648 Chris Gwynn .05
649 Jim Leyritz .05
650 Chuck McElroy .05
651 Sean Berry **RC** .05
652 Donald Harris **RC** .05
653 Don Slaught .05
654 Rusty Meacham **RC** .05
655 Scott Terry .05
656 Ramon Martinez .05
657 Keith Miller .05
658 Ramon Garcia **RC** .05
659 Milt Hill **RC** .05
660 Steve Frey .05
661 Bob McClure .05
662 Ced Landrum **RC** .05
663 Doug Henry **RC** .05
664 Candy Maldonado .05
665 Carl Willis .05
666 Jeff Montgomery .05
667 Craig Shipley **RC** .05
668 Warren Newson **RC** .05
669 Mickey Morandini .05
670 Brook Jacoby .05
671 Ryan Bowen **RC** .05
672 Bill Krueger .05
673 Rob Mallicoat .05
674 Doug Jones .05
675 Scott Livingstone .05
676 Danny Tartabull .05
677 Joe Carter (Highlight) .05
678 Cecil Espy .05
679 Randy Velarde .05
680 Bruce Ruffin .05
681 Ted Wood **RC** .05
682 Dan Plesac .05
683 Eric Bullock .05
684 Junior Ortiz .05
685 Dave Hollins .05
686 Dennis Martinez .05
687 Larry Andersen .05
688 Doug Simons .05
689 Tim Spehr **RC** .05
690 Calvin Jones **RC** .05
691 Mark Guthrie .05
692 Alfredo Griffin .05
693 Joe Carter .05
694 Terry Mathews **RC** .05
695 Pascual Perez .05
696 Gene Nelson .05
697 Gerald Williams .05
698 Chris Cron **RC** .05
699 Steve Buechele .05
700 Paul McClellan **RC** .05
701 Jim Lindeman .05
702 Francisco Oliveras .05
703 Rob Maurer **RC** .05
704 Pat Hentgen **RC** .15
705 Jaime Navarro .05
706 Mike Magnante **RC** .05
707 Nolan Ryan 1.00
708 Bobby Thigpen .05
709 John Cerutti .05
710 Steve Wilson .05
711 Hensley Meulens .05
712 Rheal Cormier **RC** .05
713 Scott Bradley .05
714 Mitch Webster .05
715 Roger Mason .05
716 Checklist 636-716 .05
717 Jeff Fassero **RC** .05
718 Cal Eldred .05
719 Sid Fernandez .05
720 Bob Zupcic **RC** .05
721 Jose Offerman .05
722 Cliff Brantley **RC** .05
723 Ron Darling .05
724 Dave Stieb .05
725 Hector Villanueva .05
726 Mike Hartley .05
727 Arthur Rhodes **RC** .05
728 Randy Bush .05
729 Steve Sax .05
730 Dave Otto .05
731 John Wehner **RC** .05
732 Dave Martinez .05
733 Ruben Amaro **RC** .05
734 Billy Ripken .05
735 Steve Farr .05
736 Shawn Abner .05
737 Gil Heredia **RC** .05
738 Ron Jones .05
739 Tony Castillo .05
740 Sammy Sosa .45
741 Julio Franco .05
742 Tim Naehring .05
743 Steve Wapnick **RC** .05
744 Craig Wilson .05
745 Darrin Chapin **RC** .05
746 Chris George **RC** .05
747 Mike Simms .05
748 Rosario Rodriguez .05
749 Skeeter Barnes .05
750 Roger McDowell .05
751 Dann Howitt .05
752 Paul Sorrento .05
753 Braulio Castillo **RC** .05
754 Yorkis Perez **RC** .05
755 Willie Fraser .05
756 Jeremy Hernandez **RC** .05
757 Curt Schilling .20
758 Steve Lyons .05
759 Dave Anderson .05
760 Willie Banks .05
761 Mark Leonard .05
762 Jack Armstrong .05
763 Scott Servais .05
764 Ray Stephens .05
765 Junior Noboa .05
766 Jim Olander **RC** .05
767 Joe Magrane .05
768 Lance Blankenship .05
769 Mike Humphreys **RC** .05
770 Jarvis Brown **RC** .05
771 Damon Berryhill .05
772 Alejandro Pena .05
773 Jose Mesa .05
774 Gary Cooper **RC** .05
775 Carney Lansford .05
776 Mike Bielecki .05
777 Charlie O'Brien .05
778 Carlos Hernandez .05
779 Howard Farmer .05
780 Mike Stanton .05
781 Reggie Harris .05
782 Xavier Hernandez .05
783 Bryan Hickerson **RC** .05
784 Checklist 717-BC8 .05

Bonus Cards

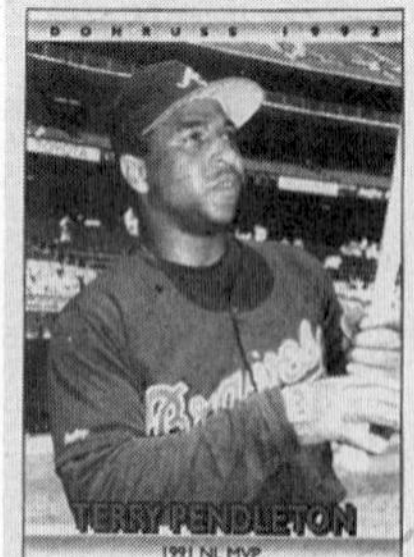

The eight bonus cards were randomly inserted in 1992 foil packs and are numbered with a "BC" prefix. Both leagues' MVPs, Cy Young and Rookie of the Year award winners are featured, as are logo cards for the expansion Colorado Rockies and Florida Marlins. Cards are standard size in a format similar to the regular issue.

		NM/M
Complete Set (8):		5.00
Common Player:		.25
1	Cal Ripken, Jr. (MVP)	2.50
2	Terry Pendleton (MVP)	.25
3	Roger Clemens (Cy Young)	2.00
4	Tom Glavine (Cy Young)	.40

5	Chuck Knoblauch (Rookie of the Year)	.25
6	Jeff Bagwell (Rookie of the Year)	1.50
7	Colorado Rockies	.25
8	Florida Marlins	.25

Diamond Kings

Donruss changed its Diamond Kings style and distribution in 1992. The cards still feature the art of Dick Perez, but quality was improved from past years. The cards were randomly inserted in foil packs. One player from each team is featured. Card numbers have a "DK" prefix.

		NM/M
Complete Set (27):		17.50
Common Player:		.40
1	Paul Molitor	2.00
2	Will Clark	.50
3	Joe Carter	.50
4	Julio Franco	.50
5	Cal Ripken, Jr.	6.00
6	Dave Justice	.50
7	George Bell	.50
8	Frank Thomas	2.00
9	Wade Boggs	4.00
10	Scott Sanderson	.50
11	Jeff Bagwell	2.00
12	John Kruk	.50
13	Felix Jose	.50
14	Harold Baines	.50
15	Dwight Gooden	.50
16	Brian McRae	.50
17	Jay Bell	.50
18	Brett Butler	.50
19	Hal Morris	.50
20	Mark Langston	.50
21	Scott Erickson	.50
22	Randy Johnson	2.00
23	Greg Swindell	.50
24	Dennis Martinez	.50
25	Tony Phillips	.50
26	Fred McGriff	.50
27	Checklist	.10

Diamond Kings Supers

Produced in very limited numbers, possibly as a prototype for use in a sales presentation to a major retail chain, these 4-7/8" x 6-3/4" cards are identical in virtually everything but size to the regular 1992 DK inserts. Both front and back feature a high-gloss finish.

		NM/M
Complete Set (27):		900.00
Common Player:		15.00
1	Paul Molitor	95.00
2	Will Clark	15.00
3	Joe Carter	15.00
4	Julio Franco	15.00
5	Cal Ripken, Jr.	335.00
6	Dave Justice	15.00
7	George Bell	15.00
8	Frank Thomas	100.00
9	Wade Boggs	125.00
10	Scott Sanderson	15.00
11	Jeff Bagwell	95.00
12	John Kruk	15.00
13	Felix Jose	15.00
14	Harold Baines	15.00
15	Dwight Gooden	15.00
16	Brian McRae	15.00
17	Jay Bell	15.00
18	Brett Butler	15.00
19	Hal Morris	15.00
20	Mark Langston	15.00
21	Scott Erickson	15.00
22	Randy Johnson	75.00
23	Greg Swindell	15.00
24	Dennis Martinez	15.00
25	Tony Phillips	15.00
26	Fred McGriff	15.00
27	Checklist (Dick Perez)	5.00

Elite

Donruss continued its Elite series in 1992 by inserting cards in foil packs. Each card was released in the same quantity as the 1991 inserts - 10,000 Elite, 7,500 Legend and 5,000 Signature. The Elite cards, now featuring a prismatic border, are numbered as a continuation of the 1991 issue.

		NM/M
Complete Set (12):		300.00
Common Player:		7.50
9	Wade Boggs	15.00
10	Joe Carter	7.50
11	Will Clark	7.50
12	Dwight Gooden	7.50
13	Ken Griffey Jr.	30.00
14	Tony Gwynn	15.00
15	Howard Johnson	7.50
16	Terry Pendleton	7.50
17	Kirby Puckett	15.00
18	Frank Thomas	15.00
---	Rickey Henderson (Legend)	20.00
---	Cal Ripken, Jr. (Signature)	250.00

Rookies

Donruss increased the size of its Rookies set in 1992 to include 132 cards. In the past the cards were released only in boxed set form, but the 1992 cards were available in packs. Special "Phenoms" cards were randomly inserted into Rookies packs. The Phenoms cards feature black borders, while the Rookies cards are styled after the regular 1992 Donruss issue. The cards are numbered alphabetically.

		NM/M
Complete Set (132):		6.00
Common Player:		.05
Pack (12):		.50
Wax Box (36):		10.00
1	Kyle Abbott	.05
2	Troy Afenir	.05
3	Rich Amaral **RC**	.05
4	Ruben Amaro **RC**	.05
5	Billy Ashley **RC**	.05
6	Pedro Astacio **RC**	.05
7	Jim Austin **RC**	.05
8	Robert Ayrault **RC**	.05
9	Kevin Baez **RC**	.05
10	Estaban Beltre	.05
11	Brian Bohanon **RC**	.05
12	Kent Bottenfield **RC**	.05
13	Jeff Branson **RC**	.05
14	Brad Brink	.05
15	John Briscoe **RC**	.05
16	Doug Brocail **RC**	.05
17	Rico Brogna **RC**	.05
18	J.T. Bruett **RC**	.05
19	Jacob Brumfield	.05
20	Jim Bullinger **RC**	.05
21	Kevin Campbell **RC**	.05
22	Pedro Castellano **RC**	.05
23	Mike Christopher **RC**	.05
24	Archi Cianfrocco **RC**	.05
25	Mark Clark **RC**	.05
26	Craig Colbert **RC**	.05
27	Victor Cole **RC**	.05
28	Steve Cooke **RC**	.05
29	Tim Costo **RC**	.05
30	Chad Curtis **RC**	.05
31	Doug Davis **RC**	.05
32	Gary DiSarcina	.05
33	John Doherty **RC**	.05
34	Mike Draper **RC**	.05
35	Monty Fariss	.05
36	Bien Figueroa **RC**	.05
37	John Flaherty **RC**	.05
38	Tim Fortugno **RC**	.05
39	Eric Fox **RC**	.05
40	Jeff Frye **RC**	.05
41	Ramon Garcia **RC**	.05
42	Brent Gates **RC**	.05
43	Tom Goodwin **RC**	.05
44	Buddy Groom **RC**	.05
45	Jeff Grotewold **RC**	.05
46	Juan Guerrero **RC**	.05
47	Johnny Guzman **RC**	.05
48	Shawn Hare **RC**	.05
49	Ryan Hawblitzel **RC**	.05
50	Bert Heffernan **RC**	.05
51	Butch Henry **RC**	.05
52	Cesar Hernandez **RC**	.05
53	Vince Horsman **RC**	.05
54	Steve Hosey **RC**	.05
55	Pat Howell **RC**	.05
56	Peter Hoy **RC**	.05
57	Jon Hurst **RC**	.05
58	Mark Hutton **RC**	.05
59	Shawn Jeter **RC**	.05
60	Joel Johnston **RC**	.05
61	Jeff Kent **RC**	1.00
62	Kurt Knudsen **RC**	.05
63	Kevin Koslofski **RC**	.05
64	Danny Leon **RC**	.05
65	Jesse Levis **RC**	.05
66	Tom Marsh **RC**	.05
67	Ed Martel **RC**	.05
68	Al Martin **RC**	.05
69	Pedro Martinez **RC**	2.00
70	Derrick May	.05
71	Matt Maysey	.05
72	Russ McGinnis	.05
73	Tim McIntosh	.05
74	Jim McNamara **RC**	.05
75	Jeff McNeely **RC**	.05
76	Rusty Meacham	.05
77	Tony Melendez **RC**	.05
78	Henry Mercedes **RC**	.05
79	Paul Miller **RC**	.05
80	Joe Millette **RC**	.05
81	Blas Minor **RC**	.05
82	Dennis Moeller **RC**	.05
83	Raul Mondesi **RC**	.25
84	Rob Natal **RC**	.05
85	Troy Neel **RC**	.05
86	David Nied **RC**	.05
87	Jerry Nielsen **RC**	.05
88	Donovan Osborne	.05
89	John Patterson **RC**	.05
90	Roger Pavlik **RC**	.05
91	Dan Peltier **RC**	.05
92	Jim Pena **RC**	.05
93	William Pennyfeather **RC**	.05
94	Mike Perez	.05
95	Hipolito Pichardo **RC**	.05
96	Greg Pirkl **RC**	.05
97	Harvey Pulliam **RC**	.05
98	Manny Ramirez **RC**	3.00
99	Pat Rapp **RC**	.05
100	Jeff Reboulet **RC**	.05
101	Darren Reed **RC**	.05
102	Shane Reynolds **RC**	.05
103	Bill Risley **RC**	.05
104	Ben Rivera **RC**	.05
105	Henry Rodriguez **RC**	.05
106	Rico Rossy **RC**	.05
107	Johnny Ruffin **RC**	.05
108	Steve Scarsone **RC**	.05
109	Tim Scott **RC**	.05
110	Steve Shifflett **RC**	.05
111	Dave Silvestri **RC**	.05
112	Matt Stairs **RC**	.05
113	William Suero **RC**	.05
114	Jeff Tackett **RC**	.05
115	Eddie Taubensee **RC**	.05
116	Rick Trlicek **RC**	.05
117	Scooter Tucker **RC**	.05
118	Shane Turner **RC**	.05
119	Julio Valera **RC**	.05
120	Paul Wagner **RC**	.05
121	Tim Wakefield **RC**	.05
122	Mike Walker **RC**	.05
123	Bruce Walton **RC**	.05
124	Lenny Webster	.05
125	Bob Wickman **RC**	.05
126	Mike Williams **RC**	.05
127	Kerry Woodson **RC**	.05
128	Eric Young **RC**	.05
129	Kevin Young **RC**	.05
130	Pete Young **RC**	.05
131	Checklist	.05
132	Checklist	.05

Rookie Phenoms

The first 12 cards in this insert set were available in Donruss Rookies foil packs. Cards 13-20 were found randomly packed in jumbo packs. Predominantly black on both front and back, the borders are highlighted with gold. A gold-foil "Phenoms" appears at top front.

		NM/M
Complete Set (20):		12.50
Common Player:		.25
1	Moises Alou	.25
2	Bret Boone	.50
3	Jeff Conine	.25
4	Dave Fleming	.25
5	Tyler Green	.25
6	Eric Karros	.25
7	Pat Listach	.25
8	Kenny Lofton	.25
9	Mike Piazza	10.00
10	Tim Salmon	.50
11	Andy Stankiewicz	.25
12	Dan Walters	.25
13	Ramon Caraballo	.25
14	Brian Jordan	.25
15	Ryan Klesko	.25
16	Sam Militello	.25
17	Frank Seminara	.25
18	Salomon Torres	.25
19	John Valentin	.25
20	Wil Cordero	.25

Update

Each retail factory set of 1992 Donruss cards contained a cello-wrapped four-card selection from this 22-card Update set. The cards feature the same basic format as the regular '92 Donruss, except they carry a "U" prefix to the card number on back. The cards feature rookies, highlights and traded players from the 1992 season.

		NM/M
Complete Set (22):		15.00
Common Player:		.50
1	Pat Listach/RR	.50
2	Andy Stankiewicz/RR	.50
3	Brian Jordan/RR	.50
4	Dan Walters/RR	.50
5	Chad Curtis/RR	.50
6	Kenny Lofton/RR	1.50
7	Mark McGwire (Highlight)	8.00
8	Eddie Murray (Highlight)	1.00
9	Jeff Reardon (Highlight)	.50
10	Frank Viola	.50
11	Gary Sheffield	.75
12	George Bell	.50
13	Rick Sutcliffe	.50
14	Wally Joyner	.50
15	Kevin Seitzer	.50
16	Bill Krueger	.50
17	Danny Tartabull	.50
18	Dave Winfield	2.00
19	Gary Carter	1.50
20	Bobby Bonilla	.50
21	Cory Snyder	.50
22	Bill Swift	.50

1992 Donruss/ Durivage Montreal Expos

Green borders and posed portrait photos are featured in this custom-published team set which Donruss produced for the Quebec bakery Durivage. Bilingual backs have personal data, recent major league stats and appropriate logos on a gray pinstriped background. Roster changes are reflected in the assignment of the same number to different players in several cases.

		NM/M
Complete Set (26):		50.00
Common Player:		2.00
Album:		5.00
1	Bret Barberie	2.00
2a	Chris Haney	2.00
2b	Brian Barnes	2.00
3a	Bill Sampen	2.00
3b	Phil Bradley	2.00
4	Ivan Calderon	2.00
5	Gary Carter	10.00
6	Delino DeShields	2.00
7	Jeff Fassero	2.00
8	Darrin Fletcher	2.00
9	Mark Gardner	2.00
10	Marquis Grissom	2.00
11	Ken Hill	2.00
12	Dennis Martinez	2.00
13	Chris Nabholz	2.00
14	Spike Owen	2.00
15a	Tom Runnells	2.00
15b	Felipe Alou	3.00
16a	John Vander Wal	2.00
16b	Matt Stairs	2.00
17a	Bill Landrum	2.00
17b	Dave Wainhouse	2.00
18	Larry Walker	10.00
19	Tim Wallach	2.00
20	John Wetteland	2.00
---	Checklist	1.00

1993 Donruss Previews

Twenty-two of the game's biggest stars were selected for inclusion in the preview version of Donruss' 1993 baseball card set. The previews follow the same basic format of the regular-issue 1993 except for the addition of the word "PREVIEW" above the card number in the home plate on back. Front photos are different between the preview and issued versions.

		NM/M
Complete Set (22):		60.00
Common Player:		1.50
1	Tom Glavine	2.00
2	Ryne Sandberg	5.00
3	Barry Larkin	1.50
4	Jeff Bagwell	4.00
5	Eric Karros	1.50
6	Larry Walker	1.50
7	Eddie Murray	4.00
8	Darren Daulton	1.50
9	Andy Van Slyke	1.50
10	Gary Sheffield	2.00
11	Will Clark	1.50
12	Cal Ripken Jr.	9.00
13	Roger Clemens	6.00
14	Frank Thomas	4.00
15	Cecil Fielder	1.50
16	George Brett	6.00
17	Robin Yount	4.00
18	Don Mattingly	6.00
19	Dennis Eckersley	3.50
20	Ken Griffey Jr.	7.50
21	Jose Canseco	2.50
22	Roberto Alomar	2.00

1993 Donruss

Rated Rookies and a randomly inserted Diamond Kings subset once again are featured in the 1993 Donruss set. Series I of the set includes 396 cards. Card fronts feature white borders surrounding a full-color player photo. The flip sides feature an additional photo, biographical information and career statistics. The cards are numbered on the back and the card's series is given with the number. The cards are UV coated. Series II contains a subset of players labeled with an "Expansion Draft" headline over their Marlins or Rockies team logo on front, even though the player photos are in the uniform of their previous team.

		NM/M
Complete Set (792):		10.00
Common Player:		.05
Series 1 or 2 Pack (14):		.50
Series 1 or 2 Box (36):		10.00
1	Craig Lefferts	.05
2	Kent Mercker	.05
3	Phil Plantier	.05
4	Alex Arias **RC**	.05
5	Julio Valera	.05
6	Dan Wilson **RC**	.05
7	Frank Thomas	.50
8	Eric Anthony	.05
9	Derek Lilliquist	.05
10	Rafael Bournigal **RC**	.05
11	Manny Alexander/RR **RC**	.05
12	Bret Barberie	.05
13	Mickey Tettleton	.05
14	Anthony Young	.05
15	Tim Spehr	.05
16	Bob Ayrault **RC**	.05
17	Bill Wegman	.05
18	Jay Bell	.05
19	Rick Aguilera	.05
20	Todd Zeile	.05
21	Steve Farr	.05
22	Andy Benes	.05
23	Lance Blankenship	.05
24	Ted Wood	.05
25	Omar Vizquel	.05
26	Steve Avery	.05
27	Brian Bohanon	.05
28	Rick Wilkins	.05
29	Devon White	.05
30	Bobby Ayala **RC**	.05

31 Leo Gomez .05
32 Mike Simms .05
33 Ellis Burks .05
34 Steve Wilson .05
35 Jim Abbott .05
36 Tim Wallach .05
37 Wilson Alvarez .05
38 Daryl Boston .05
39 Sandy Alomar, Jr. .05
40 Mitch Williams .05
41 Rico Brogna .05
42 Gary Varsho .05
43 Kevin Appier .05
44 Eric Wedge/RR .05
45 Dante Bichette .05
46 Jose Oquendo .05
47 Mike Trombley **RC** .05
48 Dan Walters .05
49 Gerald Williams .05
50 Bud Black .05
51 Bobby Witt .05
52 Mark Davis .05
53 Shawn Barton **RC** .05
54 Paul Assenmacher .05
55 Kevin Reimer .05
56 Billy Ashley/RR **RC** .05
57 Eddie Zosky .05
58 Chris Sabo .05
59 Billy Ripken .05
60 Scooter Tucker **RC** .05
61 Tim Wakefield/RR **RC** .10
62 Mitch Webster .05
63 Jack Clark .05
64 Mark Gardner .05
65 Lee Stevens .05
66 Todd Hundley .05
67 Bobby Thigpen .05
68 Dave Hollins .05
69 Jack Armstrong .05
70 Alex Cole .05
71 Mark Carreon .05
72 Todd Worrell .05
73 Steve Shifflett **RC** .05
74 Jerald Clark .05
75 Paul Molitor .50
76 Larry Carter **RC** .05
77 Rich Rowland **RC** .05
78 Damon Berryhill .05
79 Willie Banks .05
80 Hector Villanueva .05
81 Mike Gallego .05
82 Tim Belcher .05
83 Mike Bordick .05
84 Craig Biggio .05
85 Lance Parrish .05
86 Brett Butler .05
87 Mike Timlin .05
88 Brian Barnes .05
89 Brady Anderson .05
90 D.J. Dozier .05
91 Frank Viola .05
92 Darren Daulton .05
93 Chad Curtis .05
94 Zane Smith .05
95 George Bell .05
96 Rex Hudler .05
97 Mark Whiten .05
98 Tim Teufel .05
99 Kevin Ritz .05
100 Jeff Brantley .05
101 Jeff Conine .05
102 Vinny Castilla .05
103 Greg Vaughn .05
104 Steve Buechele .05
105 Darren Reed .05
106 Bip Roberts .05
107 John Habyan .05
108 Scott Servais .05
109 Walt Weiss .05
110 J.T. Snow/RR **RC** .50
111 Jay Buhner .05
112 Darryl Strawberry .05
113 Roger Pavlik **RC** .05
114 Chris Nabholz .05
115 Pat Borders .05
116 Pat Howell **RC** .05
117 Gregg Olson .05
118 Curt Schilling .25
119 Roger Clemens .65
120 Victor Cole **RC** .05
121 Gary DiSarcina .05
122 Checklist 1-80 .05
123 Steve Sax .05
124 Chuck Carr **RC** .05
125 Mark Lewis .05
126 Tony Gwynn .60
127 Travis Fryman .05
128 Dave Burba .05
129 Wally Joyner .05
130 John Smoltz .05
131 Cal Eldred .05
132 Checklist 81-159 .05
133 Arthur Rhodes .05
134 Jeff Blauser .05
135 Scott Cooper .05
136 Doug Strange .05
137 Luis Sojo .05
138 Jeff Branson **RC** .05
139 Alex Fernandez .05
140 Ken Caminiti .05
141 Charles Nagy .05
142 Tom Candiotti .05
143 Willie Green/RR .05
144 John Vander Wal .05
145 Kurt Knudsen **RC** .05
146 John Franco .05
147 Eddie Pierce **RC** .05
148 Kim Batiste .05
149 Darren Holmes .05
150 Steve Cooke **RC** .05
151 Terry Jorgensen .05
152 Mark Clark **RC** .05
153 Randy Velarde .05
154 Greg Harris .05
155 Kevin Campbell **RC** .05
156 John Burkett .05
157 Kevin Mitchell .05
158 Deion Sanders .05
159 Jose Canseco .25
160 Jeff Hartsock **RC** .05
161 Tom Quinlan **RC** .05
162 Tim Pugh **RC** .05
163 Glenn Davis .05
164 Shane Reynolds **RC** .10
165 Jody Reed .05
166 Mike Sharperson .05
167 Scott Lewis .05
168 Dennis Martinez .05
169 Scott Radinsky .05
170 Dave Gallagher .05
171 Jim Thome .45
172 Terry Mulholland .05
173 Milt Cuyler .05
174 Bob Patterson .05
175 Jeff Montgomery .05
176 Tim Salmon/RR .25
177 Franklin Stubbs .05
178 Donovan Osborne .05
179 Jeff Reboulet **RC** .05
180 Jeremy Hernandez .05
181 Charlie Hayes .05
182 Matt Williams .05
183 Mike Raczka .05
184 Francisco Cabrera .05
185 Rich DeLucia .05
186 Sammy Sosa .60
187 Ivan Rodriguez .45
188 Bret Boone/RR .15
189 Juan Guzman .05
190 Tom Browning .05
191 Randy Milligan .05
192 Steve Finley .05
193 John Patterson/RR .05
194 Kip Gross .05
195 Tony Fossas .05
196 Ivan Calderon .05
197 Junior Felix .05
198 Pete Schourek .05
199 Craig Grebeck .05
200 Juan Bell .05
201 Glenallen Hill .05
202 Danny Jackson .05
203 John Kiely .05
204 Bob Tewksbury .05
205 Kevin Koslofski **RC** .05
206 Craig Shipley .05
207 John Jaha **RC** .05
208 Royce Clayton .05
209 Mike Piazza/RR 2.00
210 Ron Gant .05
211 Scott Erickson .05
212 Doug Dascenzo .05
213 Andy Stankiewicz **RC** .05
214 Geronimo Berroa .05
215 Dennis Eckersley .45
216 Al Osuna .05
217 Tino Martinez .05
218 Henry Rodriguez **RC** .05
219 Ed Sprague .05
220 Ken Hill .05
221 Chito Martinez .05
222 Bret Saberhagen .05
223 Mike Greenwell .05
224 Mickey Morandini .05
225 Chuck Finley .05
226 Denny Neagle .05
227 Kirk McCaskill .05
228 Rheal Cormier .05
229 Paul Sorrento .05
230 Darrin Jackson .05
231 Rob Deer .05
232 Bill Swift .05
233 Kevin McReynolds .05
234 Terry Pendleton .05
235 Dave Nilsson .05
236 Chuck McElroy .05
237 Derek Parks .05
238 Norm Charlton .05
239 Matt Nokes .05
240 Juan Guerrero **RC** .05
241 Jeff Parrett .05
242 Ryan Thompson/RR .05
243 Dave Fleming .05
244 Dave Hansen .05
245 Monty Fariss .05
246 Archi Cianfrocco **RC** .05
247 Pat Hentgen .05
248 Bill Pecota .05
249 Ben McDonald .05
250 Cliff Brantley .05
251 John Valentin **RC** .05
252 Jeff King .05
253 Reggie Williams **RC** .05
254 Checklist 160-238 .05
255 Ozzie Guillen .05
256 Mike Perez .05
257 Thomas Howard .05
258 Kurt Stillwell .05
259 Mike Henneman .05
260 Steve Decker .05
261 Brent Mayne .05
262 Otis Nixon .05
263 Mark Keifer **RC** .05
264 Checklist 239-317 .05
265 Richie Lewis **RC** .05
266 Pat Gomez **RC** .05
267 Scott Taylor **RC** .05
268 Shawon Dunston .05
269 Greg Myers .05
270 Tim Costo .05
271 Greg Hibbard .05
272 Pete Harnisch .05
273 Dave Mlicki **RC** .05
274 Orel Hershiser .05
275 Sean Berry/RR .05
276 Doug Simons .05
277 John Doherty **RC** .05
278 Eddie Murray .50
279 Chris Haney .05
280 Stan Javier .05
281 Jaime Navarro .05
282 Orlando Merced .05
283 Kent Hrbek .05
284 Bernard Gilkey .05
285 Russ Springer .05
286 Mike Maddux .05
287 Eric Fox **RC** .05
288 Mark Leonard .05
289 Tim Leary .05
290 Brian Hunter .05
291 Donald Harris .05
292 Bob Scanlan .05
293 Turner Ward .05
294 Hal Morris .05
295 Jimmy Poole .05
296 Doug Jones .05
297 Tony Pena .05
298 Ramon Martinez .05
299 Tim Fortugno **RC** .05
300 Marquis Grissom .05
301 Lance Johnson .05
302 Jeff Kent **RC** 1.00
303 Reggie Jefferson .05
304 Wes Chamberlain .05
305 Shawn Hare **RC** .05
306 Mike LaValliere .05
307 Gregg Jefferies .05
308 Troy Neel/RR **RC** .05
309 Pat Listach .05
310 Geronimo Pena .05
311 Pedro Munoz .05
312 Guillermo Velasquez **RC** .05
313 Roberto Kelly .05
314 Mike Jackson .05
315 Rickey Henderson .50
316 Mark Lemke .05
317 Erik Hanson .05
318 Derrick May .05
319 Geno Petralli .05
320 Melvin Nieves/RR .05
321 Doug Linton **RC** .05
322 Rob Dibble .05
323 Chris Hoiles .05
324 Jimmy Jones .05
325 Dave Staton/RR .05
326 Pedro Martinez .05
327 Paul Quantrill **RC** .05
328 Greg Colbrunn .05
329 Hilly Hathaway **RC** .05
330 Jeff Innis .05
331 Ron Karkovice .05
332 Keith Shepherd **RC** .05
333 Alan Embree **RC** .05
334 Paul Wagner **RC** .05
335 Dave Haas **RC** .05
336 Ozzie Canseco .05
337 Bill Sampen .05
338 Rich Rodriguez .05
339 Dean Palmer .05
340 Greg Litton .05
341 Jim Tatum/RR .05
342 Todd Haney **RC** .05
343 Larry Casian .05
344 Ryne Sandberg .60
345 Sterling Hitchcock **RC** .10
346 Chris Hammond .05
347 Vince Horsman **RC** .05
348 Butch Henry **RC** .05
349 Dann Howitt .05
350 Roger McDowell .05
351 Jack Morris .05
352 Bill Krueger .05
353 Cris Colon **RC** .05
354 Joe Vitko **RC** .05
355 Willie McGee .05
356 Jay Baller .05
357 Pat Mahomes .05
358 Roger Mason .05
359 Jerry Nielsen **RC** .05
360 Tom Pagnozzi .05
361 Kevin Baez **RC** .05
362 Tim Scott **RC** .05
363 Domingo Martinez **RC** .05
364 Kirt Manwaring .05
365 Rafael Palmeiro .45
366 Ray Lankford .05
367 Tim McIntosh .05
368 Jessie Hollins **RC** .05
369 Scott Leius .05
370 Bill Doran .05
371 Sam Militello **RC** .05
372 Ryan Bowen .05
373 Dave Henderson .05
374 Dan Smith/RR **RC** .05
375 Steve Reed **RC** .05
376 Jose Offerman .05
377 Kevin Brown .05
378 Darrin Fletcher .05
379 Duane Ward .05
380 Wayne Kirby/RR **RC** .05
381 Steve Scarsone **RC** .05
382 Mariano Duncan .05
383 Ken Ryan **RC** .05
384 Lloyd McClendon .05
385 Brian Holman .05
386 Braulio Castillo .05
387 Danny Leon **RC** .05
388 Omar Olivares .05
389 Kevin Wickander .05
390 Fred McGriff .05
391 Phil Clark **RC** .05
392 Darren Lewis .05
393 Phil Hiatt **RC** .10
394 Mike Morgan .05
395 Shane Mack .05
396 Checklist 318-396 .05
397 David Segui .05
398 Rafael Belliard .05
399 Tim Naehring .05
400 Frank Castillo .05
401 Joe Grahe .05
402 Reggie Sanders .05
403 Roberto Hernandez .05
404 Luis Gonzalez .05
405 Carlos Baerga .05
406 Carlos Hernandez .05
407 Pedro Astacio/RR .05
408 Mel Rojas .05
409 Scott Livingstone .05
410 Chico Walker .05
411 Brian McRae .05
412 Ben Rivera .05
413 Ricky Bones .05
414 Andy Van Slyke .05
415 Chuck Knoblauch .05
416 Luis Alicea .05
417 Bob Wickman .05
418 Doug Brocail .05
419 Scott Brosius .05
420 Rod Beck .05
421 Edgar Martinez .05
422 Ryan Klesko .05
423 Nolan Ryan 1.50
424 Rey Sanchez .05
425 Roberto Alomar .20
426 Barry Larkin .05
427 Mike Mussina .30
428 Jeff Bagwell .50
429 Mo Vaughn .05
430 Eric Karros .05
431 John Orton .05
432 Wil Cordero .05
433 Jack McDowell .05
434 Howard Johnson .05
435 Albert Belle .05
436 John Kruk .05
437 Skeeter Barnes .05
438 Don Slaught .05
439 Rusty Meacham .05
440 Tim Laker/RR .05
441 Robin Yount .50
442 Brian Jordan .05
443 Kevin Tapani .05
444 Gary Sheffield .25
445 Rich Monteleone .05
446 Will Clark .05
447 Jerry Browne .05
448 Jeff Treadway .05
449 Mike Schooler .05
450 Mike Harkey .05
451 Julio Franco .05
452 Kevin Young/RR .05
453 Kelly Gruber .05
454 Jose Rijo .05
455 Mike Devereaux .05
456 Andujar Cedeno .05
457 Damion Easley/RR .05
458 Kevin Gross .05
459 Matt Young .05
460 Matt Stairs .05
461 Luis Polonia .05
462 Dwight Gooden .05
463 Warren Newson .05
464 Jose DeLeon .05
465 Jose Mesa .05
466 Danny Cox .05
467 Dan Gladden .05
468 Gerald Perry .05
469 Mike Boddicker .05
470 Jeff Gardner .05
471 Doug Henry .05
472 Mike Benjamin .05
473 Dan Peltier/RR .05
474 Mike Stanton .05
475 John Smiley .05
476 Dwight Smith .05
477 Jim Leyritz .05
478 Dwayne Henry .05
479 Mark McGwire 1.00
480 Pete Incaviglia .05
481 Dave Cochrane .05
482 Eric Davis .05
483 John Olerud .05
484 Ken Bottenfield .05
485 Mark McLemore .05
486 Dave Magadan .05
487 John Marzano .05
488 Ruben Amaro .05
489 Rob Ducey .05
490 Stan Belinda .05
491 Dan Pasqua .05
492 Joe Magrane .05
493 Brook Jacoby .05
494 Gene Harris .05
495 Mark Leiter .05
496 Bryan Hickerson .05
497 Tom Gordon .05
498 Pete Smith .05
499 Chris Bosio .05
500 Shawn Boskie .05
501 Dave West .05
502 Milt Hill .05
503 Pat Kelly .05
504 Joe Boever .05
505 Terry Steinbach .05
506 Butch Huskey/RR .05
507 David Valle .05
508 Mike Scioscia .05
509 Kenny Rogers .05
510 Moises Alou .05
511 David Wells .05
512 Mackey Sasser .05
513 Todd Frohwirth .05
514 Ricky Jordan .05
515 Mike Gardiner .05
516 Gary Redus .05
517 Gary Gaetti .05
518 Checklist 397-476 .05
519 Carlton Fisk .50
520 Ozzie Smith .60
521 Rod Nichols .05
522 Benito Santiago .05
523 Bill Gullickson .05
524 Robby Thompson .05
525 Mike Macfarlane .05
526 Sid Bream .05
527 Darryl Hamilton .05
528 Checklist 477-555 .05
529 Jeff Tackett .05
530 Greg Olson .05
531 Bob Zupcic .05
532 Mark Grace .05
533 Steve Frey .05
534 Dave Martinez .05
535 Robin Ventura .05
536 Casey Candaele .05
537 Kenny Lofton .05
538 Jay Howell .05
539 Fernando Ramsey/RR .05
540 Larry Walker .05
541 Cecil Fielder .05
542 Lee Guetterman .05
543 Keith Miller .05
544 Len Dykstra .05
545 B.J. Surhoff .05
546 Bob Walk .05
547 Brian Harper .05
548 Lee Smith .05
549 Danny Tartabull .05
550 Frank Seminara .05
551 Henry Mercedes .05
552 Dave Righetti .05
553 Ken Griffey Jr. .75
554 Tom Glavine .25
555 Juan Gonzalez .25
556 Jim Bullinger .05
557 Derek Bell .05
558 Cesar Hernandez .05
559 Cal Ripken, Jr. 1.50
560 Eddie Taubensee .05
561 John Flaherty .05
562 Todd Benzinger .05
563 Hubie Brooks .05
564 Delino DeShields .05
565 Tim Raines .05
566 Sid Fernandez .05
567 Steve Olin .05
568 Tommy Greene .05
569 Buddy Groom .05
570 Randy Tomlin .05
571 Hipolito Pichardo .05
572 Rene Arocha/RR .05
573 Mike Fetters .05
574 Felix Jose .05
575 Gene Larkin .05
576 Bruce Hurst .05
577 Bernie Williams .05
578 Trevor Wilson .05
579 Bob Welch .05
580 Dave Justice .05
581 Randy Johnson .50
582 Jose Vizcaino .05
583 Jeff Huson .05
584 Rob Maurer/RR .05
585 Todd Stottlemyre .05
586 Joe Oliver .05
587 Bob Milacki .05
588 Rob Murphy .05
589 Greg Pirkl/RR .05
590 Lenny Harris .05
591 Luis Rivera .05
592 John Wetteland .05
593 Mark Langston .05
594 Bobby Bonilla .05
595 Esteban Beltre .05
596 Mike Hartley .05
597 Felix Fermin .05
598 Carlos Garcia .05
599 Frank Tanana .05
600 Pedro Guerrero .05
601 Terry Shumpert .05
602 Wally Whitehurst .05
603 Kevin Seitzer .05
604 Chris James .05
605 Greg Gohr/RR .05
606 Mark Wohlers .05
607 Kirby Puckett .60
608 Greg Maddux .60
609 Don Mattingly .65
610 Greg Cadaret .05
611 Dave Stewart .05
612 Mark Portugal .05
613 Pete O'Brien .05
614 Bobby Ojeda .05
615 Joe Carter .05
616 Pete Young .05
617 Sam Horn .05
618 Vince Coleman .05
619 Wade Boggs .60
620 Todd Pratt **RC** .05
621 Ron Tingley .05
622 Doug Drabek .05
623 Scott Hemond .05
624 Tim Jones .05
625 Dennis Cook .05
626 Jose Melendez .05
627 Mike Munoz .05
628 Jim Pena .05
629 Gary Thurman .05
630 Charlie Leibrandt .05
631 Scott Fletcher .05
632 Andre Dawson .25
633 Greg Gagne .05
634 Greg Swindell .05
635 Kevin Maas .05
636 Xavier Hernandez .05
637 Ruben Sierra .05
638 Dimitri Young/RR .05
639 Harold Reynolds .05
640 Tom Goodwin .05
641 Todd Burns .05
642 Jeff Fassero .05
643 Dave Winfield .50
644 Willie Randolph .05
645 Luis Mercedes .05
646 Dale Murphy .20
647 Danny Darwin .05
648 Dennis Moeller .05
649 Chuck Crim .05
650 Checklist 556-634 .05
651 Shawn Abner .05
652 Tracy Woodson .05
653 Scott Scudder .05
654 Tom Lampkin .05
655 Alan Trammell .05
656 Cory Snyder .05
657 Chris Gwynn .05
658 Lonnie Smith .05
659 Jim Austin .05
660 Checklist 635-713 .05
661 Tim Hulett .05
662 Marvin Freeman .05
663 Greg Harris .05
664 Heathcliff Slocumb .05
665 Mike Butcher .05
666 Steve Foster .05
667 Donn Pall .05
668 Darryl Kile .05
669 Jesse Levis .05
670 Jim Gott .05
671 Mark Hutton **RC** .05
672 Brian Drahman .05
673 Chad Kreuter .05
674 Tony Fernandez .05
675 Jose Lind .05
676 Kyle Abbott .05
677 Dan Plesac .05
678 Barry Bonds 1.50
679 Chili Davis .05
680 Stan Royer .05
681 Scott Kamieniecki .05
682 Carlos Martinez .05
683 Mike Moore .05
684 Candy Maldanado .05
685 Jeff Nelson .05
686 Lou Whitaker .05
687 Jose Guzman .05
688 Manuel Lee .05
689 Bob MacDonald .05
690 Scott Bankhead .05
691 Alan Mills .05
692 Brian Williams .05
693 Tom Brunansky .05
694 Lenny Webster .05
695 Greg Briley .05
696 Paul O'Neill .05
697 Joey Cora .05
698 Charlie O'Brien .05
699 Junior Ortiz .05
700 Ron Darling .05
701 Tony Phillips .05
702 William Pennyfeather .05
703 Mark Gubicza .05
704 Steve Hosey/RR .05
705 Henry Cotto .05
706 David Hulse **RC** .05
707 Mike Pagliarulo .05
708 Dave Stieb .05
709 Melido Perez .05
710 Jimmy Key .05
711 Jeff Russell .05
712 David Cone .05
713 Russ Swan .05
714 Mark Guthrie .05
715 Checklist 714-792 .05
716 Al Martin/RR .05
717 Randy Knorr .05
718 Mike Stanley .05
719 Rick Sutcliffe .05
720 Terry Leach .05
721 Chipper Jones/RR 1.00
722 Jim Eisenreich .05
723 Tom Henke .05
724 Jeff Frye .05
725 Harold Baines .05
726 Scott Sanderson .05
727 Tom Foley .05
728 Bryan Harvey/ED .05
729 Tom Edens .05
730 Eric Young/ED .05
731 Dave Weathers/ED .05
732 Spike Owen .05
733 Scott Aldred/ED .05
734 Cris Carpenter/ED .05
735 Dion James .05
736 Joe Girardi/ED .05
737 Nigel Wilson/ED .05
738 Scott Chiamparino/ED .05

739	Jeff Reardon	.05
740	Willie Blair/ED	.05
741	Jim Corsi/ED	.05
742	Ken Patterson	.05
743	Andy Ashby/ED	.05
744	Rob Natal/ED	.05
745	Kevin Bass	.05
746	Freddie Benavides/ED	.05
747	Chris Donnels/ED	.05
748	Kerry Woodson **RC**	.05
749	Calvin Jones/ED	.05
750	Gary Scott	.05
751	Joe Orsulak	.05
752	Armando Reynoso/ED	.05
753	Monty Farriss/ED	.05
754	Billy Hatcher	.05
755	Denis Boucher/ED	.05
756	Walt Weiss	.05
757	Mike Fitzgerald	.05
758	Rudy Seanez	.05
759	Bret Barberie/ED	.05
760	Mo Sanford/ED	.05
761	Pedro Castellano/ED **RC**	.05
762	Chuck Carr/ED	.05
763	Steve Howe	.05
764	Andres Galarraga	.05
765	Jeff Conine/ED	.05
766	Ted Power	.05
767	Butch Henry/ED	.05
768	Steve Decker/ED	.05
769	Storm Davis	.05
770	Vinny Castilla/ED	.05
771	Junior Felix/ED	.05
772	Walt Terrell	.05
773	Brad Ausmus/ED	.05
774	Jamie McAndrew/ED	.05
775	Milt Thompson	.05
776	Charlie Hayes/ED	.05
777	Jack Armstrong/ED	.05
778	Dennis Rasmussen	.05
779	Darren Holmes/ED	.05
780	Alex Arias **RC**	.05
781	Randy Bush	.05
782	Javier Lopez/RR	.05
783	Dante Bichette	.05
784	John Johnstone/ED	.05
785	Rene Gonzales	.05
786	Alex Cole/ED	.05
787	Jeromy Burnitz/RR	.05
788	Michael Huff	.05
789	Anthony Telford	.05
790	Jerald Clark/ED	.05
791	Joel Johnston	.05
792	David Nied/RR	.05

Diamond Kings

The traditional Donruss Diamond Kings cards were again used as an insert in Series 2 and Series 2 foil packs in 1993. The first 15 cards were found in Series 1 packs, while cards 16-31 were available in the second series packs.

		NM/M
Complete Set (31):		17.50
Common Player:		.25
1	Ken Griffey Jr.	4.00
2	Ryne Sandberg	3.00
3	Roger Clemens	3.50
4	Kirby Puckett	3.00
5	Bill Swift	.25
6	Larry Walker	.25
7	Juan Gonzalez	.75
8	Wally Joyner	.25
9	Andy Van Slyke	.25
10	Robin Ventura	.25
11	Bip Roberts	.25
12	Roberto Kelly	.25
13	Carlos Baerga	.25
14	Orel Hershiser	.25
15	Cecil Fielder	.25
16	Robin Yount	1.50
17	Darren Daulton	.25
18	Mark McGwire	4.00
19	Tom Glavine	.75
20	Roberto Alomar	.50
21	Gary Sheffield	.75
22	Bob Tewksbury	.25
23	Brady Anderson	.25
24	Craig Biggio	.25
25	Eddie Murray	1.50
26	Luis Polonia	.25
27	Nigel Wilson	.25
28	David Nied	.25
29	Pat Listach	.25
30	Eric Karros	.25
31	Checklist	.05

Elite

Continuing the card numbering from the 1992 Elite set, the Elite '93 inserts utilized a silver-foil prismatic front border with blue back printing. Each card is serial numbered as one of 10,000; this identified production number helping to make the Elites among the more valuable of insert cards.

		NM/M
Complete Set (20):		150.00
Common Player:		10.00
19	Fred McGriff	10.00
20	Ryne Sandberg	20.00
21	Eddie Murray	15.00
22	Paul Molitor	15.00
23	Barry Larkin	10.00
24	Don Mattingly	25.00
25	Dennis Eckersley	15.00
26	Roberto Alomar	12.50
27	Edgar Martinez	10.00
28	Gary Sheffield	12.50
29	Darren Daulton	10.00
30	Larry Walker	10.00
31	Barry Bonds	30.00
32	Andy Van Slyke	10.00
33	Mark McGwire	25.00
34	Cecil Fielder	10.00
35	Dave Winfield	15.00
36	Juan Gonzalez	12.50
---	Robin Yount (Legend)	17.50
---	Will Clark (Signature)	40.00

Elite Supers

A Wal-Mart exclusive, Donruss produced 3-1/2" x 5" versions of its 1993 Elite inserts, added Nolan Ryan and Frank Thomas and a new card of Barry Bonds in his Giants uniform and packaged them one per shrink-wrapped box with Series 1 Donruss leftovers. Each super-size card features a color player photo and silver-foil prismatic borders on front. Backs are printed in blue and include a serial number identifying each of the cards from an edition of 5,000.

		NM/M
Complete Set (20):		150.00
Common Player:		5.00
1	Fred McGriff	5.00
2	Ryne Sandberg	17.50
3	Eddie Murray	10.00
4	Paul Molitor	10.00
5	Barry Larkin	5.00
6	Don Mattingly	20.00
7	Dennis Eckersley	10.00
8	Roberto Alomar	6.50
9	Edgar Martinez	5.00
10	Gary Sheffield	6.50
11	Darren Daulton	5.00
12	Larry Walker	5.00
13	Barry Bonds	25.00
14	Andy Van Slyke	5.00
15	Mark McGwire	25.00
16	Cecil Fielder	5.00
17	Dave Winfield	10.00
18	Juan Gonzalez	7.50
19	Frank Thomas	15.00
20	Nolan Ryan	40.00

Long Ball Leaders

Carrying a prefix of "LL" before the card number, these inserts were released in Series 1 (#1-9) and Series 2 (#10-18) jumbo packs, detailing mammoth home runs of the previous season.

		NM/M
Complete Set (18):		5.00
Common Player:		.10
1	Rob Deer	.10
2	Fred McGriff	.10
3	Albert Belle	.10
4	Mark McGwire	2.00
5	Dave Justice	.10
6	Jose Canseco	.25
7	Kent Hrbek	.10
8	Roberto Alomar	.20
9	Ken Griffey Jr.	1.50
10	Frank Thomas	.50
11	Darryl Strawberry	.10
12	Felix Jose	.10
13	Cecil Fielder	.10
14	Juan Gonzalez	.20
15	Ryne Sandberg	.75
16	Gary Sheffield	.20
17	Jeff Bagwell	.50
18	Larry Walker	.10

MVPs

This set was inserted in jumbo packs of both Series 1 and Series 2. Cards carry a MVP prefix to the card number.

		NM/M
Complete Set (26):		10.00
Common Player:		.10
1	Luis Polonia	.10
2	Frank Thomas	.60
3	George Brett	.75
4	Paul Molitor	.60
5	Don Mattingly	.75
6	Roberto Alomar	.25
7	Terry Pendleton	.10
8	Eric Karros	.10
9	Larry Walker	.10
10	Eddie Murray	.60
11	Darren Daulton	.10
12	Ray Lankford	.10
13	Will Clark	.10
14	Cal Ripken, Jr.	2.00
15	Roger Clemens	.75
16	Carlos Baerga	.10
17	Cecil Fielder	.10
18	Kirby Puckett	.65
19	Mark McGwire	1.50
20	Ken Griffey Jr.	1.25
21	Juan Gonzalez	.30
22	Ryne Sandberg	.65
23	Bip Roberts	.10
24	Jeff Bagwell	.60
25	Barry Bonds	2.00
26	Gary Sheffield	.25

Spirit of the Game

Series 1 and Series 2 foil and jumbo packs could be found with these cards randomly inserted. Several multi-player cards are included in the set. Card numbers bear an SG prefix.

		NM/M
Complete Set (20):		5.00
Common Player:		.25
1	Turning Two (Dave Winfield, Mike Bordick)	.35
2	Play at the Plate (David Justice)	.25
3	In There (Roberto Alomar)	.30
4	Pumped (Dennis Eckersley)	.60
5	Dynamic Duo (Juan Gonzalez, Jose Canseco)	.50
6	Gone (Frank Thomas, George Bell)	.60
7	Safe or Out? (Wade Boggs)	.75
8	The Thrill (Will Clark)	.30
9	Safe at Home (Damon Berryhill, Bip Roberts, Glenn Braggs)	.25
10	Thirty X 31 (Cecil Fielder, Mickey Tettleton, Rob Deer)	.25
11	Bag Bandit (Kenny Lofton)	.25
12	Back to Back (Fred McGriff, Gary Sheffield)	.30
13	Range Rovers (Greg Gagne, Barry Larkin)	.25
14	The Ball Stops Here (Ryne Sandberg)	.75
15	Over the Top (Carlos Baerga, Gary Gaetti)	.25
16	At the Wall (Danny Tartabull)	.25
17	Head First (Brady Anderson)	.25
18	Big Hurt (Frank Thomas)	.65
19	No-Hitter (Kevin Gross)	.25
20	3,000 (Robin Yount)	.65

Elite Dominators

Created as a premium to move left-over boxes of its 1993 product on a home shopping network at $100 apiece, this special edition was produced in standard 2-1/2" x 3-1/2" size in a format similar to the 1991-93 Donruss Elite chase cards. Cards feature green prismatic borders, liberal use of foil stamping, etc. Only 5,000 of each card were produced, and each card is serially numbered on the back. Half of the cards of Nolan Ryan, Juan Gonzalez, Don Mattingly and Paul Molitor were personally autographed by the player.

		NM/M
Complete Set (20):		135.00
Common Player:		3.00
1	Ryne Sandberg	10.00
2	Fred McGriff	3.00
3	Greg Maddux	10.00
4	Ron Gant	3.00
5	Dave Justice	3.00
6	Don Mattingly	12.00
7	Tim Salmon	3.00
8	Mike Piazza	12.00
9	John Olerud	3.00
10	Nolan Ryan	20.00
11	Juan Gonzalez	5.00
12	Ken Griffey Jr.	12.00
13	Frank Thomas	7.50
14	Tom Glavine	4.50
15	George Brett	12.00
16	Barry Bonds	20.00
17	Albert Belle	3.00
18	Paul Molitor	7.50
19	Cal Ripken, Jr.	20.00
20	Roberto Alomar	5.00
Autographed Cards:		
6	Don Mattingly	35.00
10	Nolan Ryan	65.00
11	Juan Gonzalez	20.00
18	Paul Molitor	20.00

Masters of the Game

Donruss issued a series of "Masters of the Game" art cards that were available only at Wal-Mart stores. The oversized cards (3-1/2" x 5") feature the artwork of Dick Perez, creator of the Diamond Kings cards for the same company. The cards came issued one to a pack, along with a foil pack of 1993 Donruss cards for a retail price of about $3.

		NM/M
Complete Set (16):		15.00
Common Player:		1.00
1	Frank Thomas	1.50
2	Nolan Ryan	3.00
3	Gary Sheffield	1.25
4	Fred McGriff	1.00
5	Ryne Sandberg	1.75
6	Cal Ripken, Jr.	3.00
7	Jose Canseco	1.25
8	Ken Griffey Jr.	2.50
9	Will Clark	1.00
10	Roberto Alomar	1.00
11	Juan Gonzalez	1.25
12	David Justice	1.00
13	Kirby Puckett	1.75
14	Barry Bonds	3.00
15	Robin Yount	1.50
16	Deion Sanders	1.00

1992 Blue Jays Commemorative Set

Issued only as a special gold-boxed set, this series commemorates the Toronto Blue Jays 1992 World Championship. Each player on the Jays '92 roster has a card. There are also special cards recalling each game of the Series and a SkyDome card. The World Series highlights cards have a bunting design at top and a gold-foil World Series logo on front. Player cards feature borderless photos; a Blue Jays "Commemorative Set" logo is at lower-left. Backs have a player photo at top and a stat box at bottom with season, career and 1992 LCS and World Series numbers.

		NM/M
Complete Set (54):		5.00
Common Card:		.15
1	Checklist/Logo Card	.15
2	Roberto Alomar	.45
3	Derek Bell	.15
4	Pat Borders	.15
5	Joe Carter	.45
6	Alfredo Griffin	.15
7	Kelly Gruber	.15
8	Manuel Lee	.15
9	Candy Maldonado	.15
10	John Olerud	.45
11	Ed Sprague	.15
12	Pat Tabler	.15
13	Devon White	.15
14	Dave Winfield	1.00
15	David Cone	.25
16	Mark Eichhorn	.15
17	Juan Guzman	.15
18	Tom Henke	.15
19	Jimmy Key	.15
20	Jack Morris	.25
21	Todd Stottlemyre	.15
22	Mike Timlin	.15
23	Duane Ward	.15
24	David Wells	.40
25	Randy Knorr	.15
26	Rance Mulliniks	.15
27	Tom Quinlan	.15
28	Cito Gaston	.15
29	Dave Steib	.15
30	Ken Dayley	.15
31	Turner Ward	.15
32	Eddie Zosky	.15
33	Pat Hentgen	.15
34	Al Leiter	.15
35	Doug Linton	.15
36	Bob MacDonald	.15
37	Rick Trlicek	.15
38	Domingo Martinez	.15
39	Mike Maksudian	.15
40	Rob Ducey	.15
41	Jeff Kent	.60
42	Greg Myers	.15
43	Dave Weathers	.15
44	Skydome	.15
45	Trophy Presentation (Jim Kaat, Cito Gaston, Paul Beeston, Bobby Brown)	.15
World Series Highlights		.10
1WS	Series Opener (Blue Jays vs. Braves)	.10
2WS	Game 1 - Carter Homers in 4th	.25
3WS	Homer	.10
4WS	Game 3 - Maldonado Drives in Game-Winner	.10
5WS	Game 4 - Key's Win Puts Jays Up 3-1	.10
6WS	Game 5 - Olerud Scores Both Jays Runs	.10
7WS	Game 6 - Winfield's Double in 11th Wins	.25
8WS	Pat Border Series MVP	.10
9WS	World Champs Celebration	.10

1994 Donruss Promotional Samples

To introduce both its regular 1994 issue and the "Special Edition" gold cards, Donruss produced this 12-card promo set for distribution to its dealer network. The promos are virtually identical in format to the regular cards except for the large gray diagonal overprint "PROMOTIONAL SAMPLE" on both front and back. Card numbers also differ on the promos.

		NM/M
Complete Set (12):		10.00
Common Player:		.50
1	Barry Bonds	2.00
2	Darren Daulton	.50
3	John Olerud	.50
4	Frank Thomas	1.00
5	Mike Piazza	1.50
6	Tim Salmon	.50
7	Ken Griffey Jr.	1.50
8	Fred McGriff	.50
9	Don Mattingly	1.25
10	Gary Sheffield	.75
Special Edition Gold:		
1G	Barry Bonds (Special Edition Gold)	2.50
4G	Frank Thomas (Special Edition Gold)	1.00

1994 Donruss

Donruss released its 1994 set in two 330-card series. Each series also includes, 50 Special Edition gold cards and several insert sets. Regular cards have full-bleed photos and are UV coated and foil stamped. Special Edition cards are gold-foil stamped on both sides and are included in each pack. Insert sets titled Spirit of the Game and Decade Dominators were produced in regular and super (3-1/2" x 5") formats. Other inserts were MVPs and Long Ball Leaders in regular size and super-size Award Winners. An Elite series of cards, continuing from previous years with #37-48, was also issued as inserts. A 10th Anniversary insert set features 10 popular 1984 Donruss cards in gold-foil enhanced reprint versions.

		NM/M
Complete Set (660):		15.00
Common Player:		.05
Series 1 or 2 Pack (13):		.50
Series 1 or 2 Box (36):		12.50
1	Nolan Ryan (Career Salute 27 Years.)	2.00
2	Mike Piazza	1.00
3	Moises Alou	.05
4	Ken Griffey Jr.	1.00
5	Gary Sheffield	.25
6	Roberto Alomar	.20
7	John Kruk	.05
8	Gregg Olson	.05
9	Gregg Jefferies	.05
10	Tony Gwynn	.65
11	Chad Curtis	.05
12	Craig Biggio	.05
13	John Burkett	.05
14	Carlos Baerga	.05
15	Robin Yount	.60
16	Dennis Eckersley	.50
17	Dwight Gooden	.05
18	Ryne Sandberg	.65
19	Rickey Henderson	.60
20	Jack McDowell	.05
21	Jay Bell	.05
22	Kevin Brown	.05
23	Robin Ventura	.05
24	Paul Molitor	.60
25	Dave Justice	.05
26	Rafael Palmeiro	.50
27	Cecil Fielder	.05
28	Chuck Knoblauch	.05
29	Dave Hollins	.05
30	Jimmy Key	.05
31	Mark Langston	.05
32	Darryl Kile	.05
33	Ruben Sierra	.05
34	Ron Gant	.05
35	Ozzie Smith	.65
36	Wade Boggs	.65
37	Marquis Grissom	.05
38	Will Clark	.05
39	Kenny Lofton	.05
40	Cal Ripken, Jr.	2.00
41	Steve Avery	.05
42	Mo Vaughn	.05
43	Brian McRae	.05
44	Mickey Tettleton	.05
45	Barry Larkin	.05
46	Charlie Hayes	.05
47	Kevin Appier	.05
48	Robby Thompson	.05
49	Juan Gonzalez	.30
50	Paul O'Neill	.05
51	Marcos Armas	.05
52	Mike Butcher	.05
53	Ken Caminiti	.05
54	Pat Borders	.05
55	Pedro Munoz	.05
56	Tim Belcher	.05
57	Paul Assenmacher	.05
58	Damon Berryhill	.05
59	Ricky Bones	.05
60	Rene Arocha	.05
61	Shawn Boskie	.05
62	Pedro Astacio	.05
63	Frank Bolick	.05
64	Bud Black	.05
65	Sandy Alomar, Jr.	.05
66	Rich Amaral	.05
67	Luis Aquino	.05
68	Kevin Baez	.05
69	Mike Devereaux	.05
70	Andy Ashby	.05
71	Larry Andersen	.05
72	Steve Cooke	.05
73	Mario Daiz	.05
74	Rob Deer	.05
75	Bobby Ayala	.05
76	Freddie Benavides	.05
77	Stan Belinda	.05
78	John Doherty	.05
79	Willie Banks	.05
80	Spike Owen	.05
81	Mike Bordick	.05
82	Chili Davis	.05
83	Luis Gonzalez	.05
84	Ed Sprague	.05
85	Jeff Reboulet	.05
86	Jason Bere	.05
87	Mark Hutton	.05
88	Jeff Blauser	.05
89	Cal Eldred	.05
90	Bernard Gilkey	.05
91	Frank Castillo	.05
92	Jim Gott	.05
93	Greg Colbrunn	.05
94	Jeff Brantley	.05
95	Jeremy Hernandez	.05
96	Norm Charlton	.05
97	Alex Arias	.05
98	John Franco	.05
99	Chris Hoiles	.05
100	Brad Ausmus	.05
101	Wes Chamberlain	.05
102	Mark Dewey	.05
103	Benji Gil/RR	.05
104	John Dopson	.05
105	John Smiley	.05
106	David Nied	.05
107	George Brett (Career Salute 21 Years.)	.75
108	Kirk Gibson	.05
109	Larry Casian	.05
110	Checklist (Ryne Sandberg 2,000 Hits)	.25
111	Brent Gates	.05
112	Damion Easley	.05
113	Pete Harnisch	.05
114	Danny Cox	.05
115	Kevin Tapani	.05
116	Roberto Hernandez	.05
117	Domingo Jean	.05
118	Sid Bream	.05
119	Doug Henry	.05
120	Omar Olivares	.05
121	Mike Harkey	.05
122	Carlos Hernandez	.05
123	Jeff Fassero	.05
124	Dave Burba	.05
125	Wayne Kirby	.05
126	John Cummings	.05
127	Bret Barberie	.05
128	Todd Hundley	.05
129	Tim Hulett	.05
130	Phil Clark	.05
131	Danny Jackson	.05
132	Tom Foley	.05
133	Donald Harris	.05
134	Scott Fletcher	.05
135	Johnny Ruffin/RR	.05
136	Jerald Clark	.05
137	Billy Brewer	.05
138	Dan Gladden	.05
139	Eddie Guardado	.05
140	Checklist (Cal Ripken, Jr. 2,000 Hits)	.35
141	Scott Hemond	.05
142	Steve Frey	.05
143	Xavier Hernandez	.05
144	Mark Eichhorn	.05
145	Ellis Burks	.05
146	Jim Leyritz	.05
147	Mark Lemke	.05
148	Pat Listach	.05
149	Donovan Osborne	.05
150	Glenallen Hill	.05
151	Orel Hershiser	.05
152	Darrin Fletcher	.05
153	Royce Clayton	.05
154	Derek Lilliquist	.05
155	Mike Felder	.05
156	Jeff Conine	.05
157	Ryan Thompson	.05
158	Ben McDonald	.05
159	Ricky Gutierrez	.05
160	Terry Mulholland	.05
161	Carlos Garcia	.05
162	Tom Henke	.05
163	Mike Greenwell	.05
164	Thomas Howard	.05
165	Joe Girardi	.05
166	Hubie Brooks	.05
167	Greg Gohr	.05
168	Chip Hale	.05
169	Rick Honeycutt	.05
170	Hilly Hathaway	.05
171	Todd Jones	.05
172	Tony Fernandez	.05
173	Bo Jackson	.10
174	Bobby Munoz	.05
175	Greg McMichael	.05
176	Graeme Lloyd	.05
177	Tom Pagnozzi	.05
178	Derrick May	.05
179	Pedro Martinez	.60
180	Ken Hill	.05
181	Bryan Hickerson	.05
182	Jose Mesa	.05
183	Dave Fleming	.05
184	Henry Cotto	.05
185	Jeff Kent	.05
186	Mark McLemore	.05
187	Trevor Hoffman	.05
188	Todd Pratt	.05
189	Blas Minor	.05
190	Charlie Leibrandt	.05
191	Tony Pena	.05
192	Larry Luebbers **RC**	.05
193	Greg Harris	.05
194	David Cone	.05
195	Bill Gullickson	.05
196	Brian Harper	.05
197	Steve Karsay/RR	.05
198	Greg Myers	.05
199	Mark Portugal	.05
200	Pat Hentgen	.05
201	Mike La Valliere	.05
202	Mike Stanley	.05
203	Kent Mercker	.05
204	Dave Nilsson	.05
205	Erik Pappas	.05
206	Mike Morgan	.05
207	Roger McDowell	.05
208	Mike Lansing	.05
209	Kirt Manwaring	.05
210	Randy Milligan	.05
211	Erik Hanson	.05
212	Orestes Destrade	.05
213	Mike Maddux	.05
214	Alan Mills	.05
215	Tim Mauser	.05
216	Ben Rivera	.05
217	Don Slaught	.05
218	Bob Patterson	.05
219	Carlos Quintana	.05
220	Checklist (Tim Raines 2,000 Hits)	.05
221	Hal Morris	.05
222	Darren Holmes	.05
223	Chris Gwynn	.05
224	Chad Kreuter	.05
225	Mike Hartley	.05
226	Scott Lydy	.05
227	Eduardo Perez	.05
228	Greg Swindell	.05
229	Al Leiter	.05
230	Scott Radinsky	.05
231	Bob Wickman	.05
232	Otis Nixon	.05
233	Kevin Reimer	.05
234	Geronimo Pena	.05
235	Kevin Roberson/RR	.05
236	Jody Reed	.05
237	Kirk Rueter/RR	.05
238	Willie McGee	.05
239	Charles Nagy	.05
240	Tim Leary	.05
241	Carl Everett	.05
242	Charlie O'Brien	.05
243	Mike Pagliarulo	.05
244	Kerry Taylor	.05
245	Kevin Stocker	.05
246	Joel Johnston	.05
247	Geno Petralli	.05
248	Jeff Russell	.05
249	Joe Oliver	.05
250	Robert Mejia	.05
251	Chris Haney	.05
252	Bill Krueger	.05
253	Shane Mack	.05
254	Terry Steinbach	.05
255	Luis Polonia	.05
256	Eddie Taubensee	.05
257	Dave Stewart	.05
258	Tim Raines	.05
259	Bernie Williams	.05
260	John Smoltz	.05
261	Kevin Seitzer	.05
262	Bob Tewksbury	.05
263	Bob Scanlan	.05
264	Henry Rodriguez	.05
265	Tim Scott	.05
266	Scott Sanderson	.05
267	Eric Plunk	.05
268	Edgar Martinez	.05
269	Charlie Hough	.05
270	Joe Orsulak	.05
271	Harold Reynolds	.05
272	Tim Teufel	.05
273	Bobby Thigpen	.05
274	Randy Tomlin	.05
275	Gary Redus	.05
276	Ken Ryan	.05
277	Tim Pugh	.05
278	Jayhawk Owens	.05
279	Phil Hiatt/RR	.05
280	Alan Trammell	.05
281	Dave McCarty/RR	.05
282	Bob Welch	.05
283	J.T. Snow	.05
284	Brian Williams	.05
285	Devon White	.05
286	Steve Sax	.05
287	Tony Tarasco	.05
288	Bill Spiers	.05
289	Allen Watson	.05
290	Checklist (Rickey Henderson 2,000 Hits)	.05
291	Joe Vizcaino	.05
292	Darryl Strawberry	.05
293	John Wetteland	.05
294	Bill Swift	.05
295	Jeff Treadway	.05
296	Tino Martinez	.05
297	Richie Lewis	.05
298	Bret Saberhagen	.05
299	Arthur Rhodes	.05
300	Guillermo Velasquez	.05
301	Milt Thompson	.05
302	Doug Strange	.05
303	Aaron Sele	.05
304	Bip Roberts	.05
305	Bruce Ruffin	.05
306	Jose Lind	.05
307	David Wells	.05
308	Bobby Witt	.05
309	Mark Wohlers	.05
310	B.J. Surhoff	.05
311	Mark Whiten	.05
312	Turk Wendell	.05
313	Raul Mondesi	.05
314	Brian Turang **RC**	.05
315	Chris Hammond	.05
316	Tim Bogar	.05
317	Brad Pennington	.05
318	Tim Worrell	.05
319	Mitch Williams	.05
320	Rondell White/RR	.05
321	Frank Viola	.05
322	Manny Ramirez/RR	.75
323	Gary Wayne	.05
324	Mike Macfarlane	.05
325	Russ Springer	.05
326	Tim Wallach	.05
327	Salomon Torres/RR	.05
328	Omar Vizquel	.05
329	Andy Tomberlin **RC**	.05
330	Chris Sabo	.05
331	Mike Mussina	.30
332	Andy Benes	.05
333	Darren Daulton	.05
334	Orlando Merced	.05
335	Mark McGwire	1.50
336	Dave Winfield	.60
337	Sammy Sosa	.65
338	Eric Karros	.05
339	Greg Vaughn	.05
340	Don Mattingly	.75
341	Frank Thomas	.60
342	Fred McGriff	.05
343	Kirby Puckett	.65
344	Roberto Kelly	.05
345	Wally Joyner	.05
346	Andres Galarraga	.05
347	Bobby Bonilla	.05
348	Benito Santiago	.05
349	Barry Bonds	2.00
350	Delino DeShields	.05
351	Albert Belle	.05
352	Randy Johnson	.60
353	Tim Salmon	.05
354	John Olerud	.05
355	Dean Palmer	.05
356	Roger Clemens	.75
357	Jim Abbott	.05
358	Mark Grace	.05
359	Ozzie Guillen	.05
360	Lou Whitaker	.05
361	Jose Rijo	.05
362	Jeff Montgomery	.05
363	Chuck Finley	.05
364	Tom Glavine	.25
365	Jeff Bagwell	.60
366	Joe Carter	.05
367	Ray Lankford	.05
368	Ramon Martinez	.05
369	Jay Buhner	.05
370	Matt Williams	.05
371	Larry Walker	.05
372	Jose Canseco	.30
373	Len Dykstra	.05
374	Bryan Harvey	.05
375	Andy Van Slyke	.05
376	Ivan Rodriguez	.50
377	Kevin Mitchell	.05
378	Travis Fryman	.05
379	Duane Ward	.05
380	Greg Maddux	.65
381	Scott Servais	.05
382	Greg Olson	.05
383	Rey Sanchez	.05
384	Tom Kramer	.05
385	David Valle	.05
386	Eddie Murray	.60
387	Kevin Higgins	.05
388	Dan Wilson	.05
389	Todd Frohwirth	.05
390	Gerald Williams	.05
391	Hipolito Pichardo	.05
392	Pat Meares	.05
393	Luis Lopez	.05
394	Ricky Jordan	.05
395	Bob Walk	.05
396	Sid Fernandez	.05
397	Todd Worrell	.05
398	Darryl Hamilton	.05
399	Randy Myers	.05
400	Rod Brewer	.05
401	Lance Blankenship	.05
402	Steve Finley	.05
403	Phil Leftwich **RC**	.05
404	Juan Guzman	.05
405	Anthony Young	.05
406	Jeff Gardner	.05
407	Ryan Bowen	.05
408	Fernando Valenzuela	.05
409	David West	.05
410	Kenny Rogers	.05
411	Bob Zupcic	.05
412	Eric Young	.05
413	Bret Boone	.05
414	Danny Tartabull	.05
415	Bob MacDonald	.05
416	Ron Karkovice	.05
417	Scott Cooper	.05
418	Dante Bichette	.05
419	Tripp Cromer	.05
420	Billy Ashley	.05
421	Roger Smithberg	.05
422	Dennis Martinez	.05
423	Mike Blowers	.05
424	Darren Lewis	.05
425	Junior Ortiz	.05
426	Butch Huskey	.05
427	Jimmy Poole	.05
428	Walt Weiss	.05
429	Scott Bankhead	.05
430	Deion Sanders	.05
431	Scott Bullett	.05
432	Jeff Huson	.05
433	Tyler Green	.05
434	Billy Hatcher	.05
435	Bob Hamelin	.05
436	Reggie Sanders	.05
437	Scott Erickson	.05
438	Steve Reed	.05
439	Randy Velarde	.05
440	Checklist (Tony Gwynn 2,000 Hits)	.15
441	Terry Leach	.05
442	Danny Bautista	.05
443	Kent Hrbek	.05
444	Rick Wilkins	.05
445	Tony Phillips	.05
446	Dion James	.05
447	Joey Cora	.05
448	Andre Dawson	.15
449	Pedro Castellano	.05
450	Tom Gordon	.05
451	Rob Dibble	.05
452	Ron Darling	.05
453	Chipper Jones	.65
454	Joe Grahe	.05
455	Domingo Cedeno	.05
456	Tom Edens	.05
457	Mitch Webster	.05
458	Jose Bautista	.05
459	Troy O'Leary	.05
460	Todd Zeile	.05
461	Sean Berry	.05
462	Brad Holman **RC**	.05
463	Dave Martinez	.05
464	Mark Lewis	.05
465	Paul Carey	.05
466	Jack Armstrong	.05
467	David Telgheder	.05
468	Gene Harris	.05
469	Danny Darwin	.05
470	Kim Batiste	.05
471	Tim Wakefield	.05
472	Craig Lefferts	.05
473	Jacob Brumfield	.05
474	Lance Painter	.05
475	Milt Cuyler	.05
476	Melido Perez	.05
477	Derek Parks	.05
478	Gary DiSarcina	.05
479	Steve Bedrosian	.05
480	Eric Anthony	.05
481	Julio Franco	.05
482	Tommy Greene	.05
483	Pat Kelly	.05
484	Nate Minchey/RR	.05
485	William Pennyfeather	.05
486	Harold Baines	.05
487	Howard Johnson	.05
488	Angel Miranda	.05
489	Scott Sanders	.05
490	Shawon Dunston	.05
491	Mel Rojas	.05
492	Jeff Nelson	.05
493	Archi Cianfrocco	.05
494	Al Martin	.05
495	Mike Gallego	.05
496	Mike Henneman	.05
497	Armando Reynoso	.05
498	Mickey Morandini	.05
499	Rick Renteria	.05
500	Rick Sutcliffe	.05
501	Bobby Jones/RR	.05
502	Gary Gaetti	.05
503	Rick Aguilera	.05
504	Todd Stottlemyre	.05
505	Mike Mohler	.05
506	Mike Stanton	.05
507	Jose Guzman	.05
508	Kevin Rogers	.05
509	Chuck Carr	.05
510	Chris Jones	.05
511	Brent Mayne	.05
512	Greg Harris	.05
513	Dave Henderson	.05
514	Eric Hillman	.05
515	Dan Peltier	.05
516	Craig Shipley	.05
517	John Valentin	.05
518	Wilson Alvarez	.05
519	Andujar Cedeno	.05
520	Troy Neel	.05
521	Tom Candiotti	.05
522	Matt Mieske	.05
523	Jim Thome	.50
524	Lou Frazier	.05
525	Mike Jackson	.05
526	Pedro Martinez	.05
527	Roger Pavlik	.05
528	Kent Bottenfield	.05
529	Felix Jose	.05
530	Mark Guthrie	.05
531	Steve Farr	.05
532	Craig Paquette	.05
533	Doug Jones	.05
534	Luis Alicea	.05
535	Cory Snyder	.05
536	Paul Sorrento	.05
537	Nigel Wilson	.05
538	Jeff King	.05
539	Willie Green	.05
540	Kirk McCaskill	.05
541	Al Osuna	.05
542	Greg Hibbard	.05
543	Brett Butler	.05
544	Jose Valentin	.05
545	Wil Cordero	.05
546	Chris Bosio	.05
547	Jamie Moyer	.05
548	Jim Eisenreich	.05
549	Vinny Castilla	.05
550	Checklist (Dave Winfield 3,000 Hits)	.05
551	John Roper	.05
552	Lance Johnson	.05
553	Scott Kamieniecki	.05
554	Mike Moore	.05
555	Steve Buechele	.05
556	Terry Pendleton	.05
557	Todd Van Poppel	.05
558	Rob Butler	.05
559	Zane Smith	.05
560	David Hulse	.05
561	Tim Costo	.05
562	John Habyan	.05
563	Terry Jorgensen	.05
564	Matt Nokes	.05
565	Kevin McReynolds	.05
566	Phil Plantier	.05
567	Chris Turner	.05
568	Carlos Delgado	.40
569	John Jaha	.05
570	Dwight Smith	.05
571	John Vander Wal	.05
572	Trevor Wilson	.05
573	Felix Fermin	.05
574	Marc Newfield/RR	.05
575	Jeromy Burnitz	.05
576	Leo Gomez	.05
577	Curt Schilling	.25
578	Kevin Young	.05
579	Jerry Spradlin **RC**	.05
580	Curt Leskanic	.05
581	Carl Willis	.05
582	Alex Fernandez	.05
583	Mark Holzemer	.05
584	Domingo Martinez	.05
585	Pete Smith	.05
586	Brian Jordan	.05
587	Kevin Gross	.05
588	J.R. Phillips/RR	.05
589	Chris Nabholz	.05
590	Bill Wertz	.05
591	Derek Bell	.05
592	Brady Anderson	.05
593	Matt Turner	.05
594	Pete Incaviglia	.05
595	Greg Gagne	.05
596	John Flaherty	.05
597	Scott Livingstone	.05
598	Rod Bolton	.05
599	Mike Perez	.05
600	Checklist (Roger Clemens 2,000 Strikeouts)	.25
601	Tony Castillo	.05
602	Henry Mercedes	.05
603	Mike Fetters	.05
604	Rod Beck	.05
605	Damon Buford	.05
606	Matt Whiteside	.05
607	Shawn Green	.25
608	Midre Cummings/RR	.05
609	Jeff McNeeley	.05
610	Danny Sheaffer	.05
611	Paul Wagner	.05
612	Torey Lovullo	.05
613	Javier Lopez	.05
614	Mariano Duncan	.05
615	Doug Brocail	.05
616	Dave Hansen	.05

617	Ryan Klesko	.05
618	Eric Davis	.05
619	Scott Ruffcorn/RR	.05
620	Mike Trombley	.05
621	Jaime Navarro	.05
622	Rheal Cormier	.05
623	Jose Offerman	.05
624	David Segui	.05
625	Robb Nen/RR	.05
626	Dave Gallagher	.05
627	Julian Tavarez **RC**	.05
628	Chris Gomez	.05
629	Jeffrey Hammonds/RR	.05
630	Scott Brosius	.05
631	Willie Blair	.05
632	Doug Drabek	.05
633	Bill Wegman	.05
634	Jeff McKnight	.05
635	Rich Rodriguez	.05
636	Steve Trachsel	.05
637	Buddy Groom	.05
638	Sterling Hitchcock	.05
639	Chuck McElroy	.05
640	Rene Gonzales	.05
641	Dan Plesac	.05
642	Jeff Branson	.05
643	Darrell Whitmore	.05
644	Paul Quantrill	.05
645	Rich Rowland	.05
646	Curtis Pride **RC**	.05
647	Erik Plantenberg	.05
648	Albie Lopez	.05
649	Rich Batchelor **RC**	.05
650	Lee Smith	.05
651	Cliff Floyd	.05
652	Pete Schourek	.05
653	Reggie Jefferson	.05
654	Bill Haselman	.05
655	Steve Hosey	.05
656	Mark Clark	.05
657	Mark Davis	.05
658	Dave Magadan	.05
659	Candy Maldonado	.05
660	Checklist (Mark Langston 2,000 Strikeouts)	.05

Special Edition - Gold

In 1994 Donruss added a Special Edition subset of 100 of the game's top players. Fifty cards each were included one or two per pack in all types of Donruss' Series 1 and 2 packaging. The cards use the same photos and format as the regular-issue version, but have special gold-foil stamping on front in the area of the team logo and player name, and on back in a "Special Edition" number box in the upper-left corner.

		NM/M
Complete Set (100):		7.50
Common Player:		.10
1	Nolan Ryan	1.50
2	Mike Piazza	1.00
3	Moises Alou	.10
4	Ken Griffey Jr.	1.00
5	Gary Sheffield	.25
6	Roberto Alomar	.20
7	John Kruk	.10
8	Gregg Olson	.10
9	Gregg Jefferies	.10
10	Tony Gwynn	.65
11	Chad Curtis	.10
12	Craig Biggio	.10
13	John Burkett	.10
14	Carlos Baerga	.10
15	Robin Yount	.60
16	Dennis Eckersley	.50
17	Dwight Gooden	.10
18	Ryne Sandberg	.65
19	Rickey Henderson	.60
20	Jack McDowell	.10
21	Jay Bell	.10
22	Kevin Brown	.10
23	Robin Ventura	.10
24	Paul Molitor	.60
25	David Justice	.10
26	Rafael Palmeiro	.50
27	Cecil Fielder	.10
28	Chuck Knoblauch	.10
29	Dave Hollins	.10
30	Jimmy Key	.10
31	Mark Langston	.10
32	Darryl Kile	.10
33	Ruben Sierra	.10
34	Ron Gant	.10
35	Ozzie Smith	.65
36	Wade Boggs	.65
37	Marquis Grissom	.10
38	Will Clark	.10
39	Kenny Lofton	.10
40	Cal Ripken, Jr.	1.50
41	Steve Avery	.10
42	Mo Vaughn	.10
43	Brian McRae	.10
44	Mickey Tettleton	.10
45	Barry Larkin	.10
46	Charlie Hayes	.10
47	Kevin Appier	.10
48	Robby Thompson	.10
49	Juan Gonzalez	.30
50	Paul O'Neill	.10
51	Mike Mussina	.40
52	Andy Benes	.10
53	Darren Daulton	.10
54	Orlando Merced	.10
55	Mark McGwire	1.25
56	Dave Winfield	.60
57	Sammy Sosa	.65
58	Eric Karros	.10
59	Greg Vaughn	.10
60	Don Mattingly	.75
61	Frank Thomas	.60
62	Fred McGriff	.10
63	Kirby Puckett	.65
64	Roberto Kelly	.10
65	Wally Joyner	.10
66	Andres Galarraga	.10
67	Bobby Bonilla	.10
68	Benito Santiago	.10
69	Barry Bonds	1.50
70	Delino DeShields	.10
71	Albert Belle	.10
72	Randy Johnson	.60
73	Tim Salmon	.10
74	John Olerud	.10
75	Dean Palmer	.10
76	Roger Clemens	.75
77	Jim Abbott	.10
78	Mark Grace	.10
79	Ozzie Guillen	.10
80	Lou Whitaker	.10
81	Jose Rijo	.10
82	Jeff Montgomery	.10
83	Chuck Finley	.10
84	Tom Glavine	.25
85	Jeff Bagwell	.60
86	Joe Carter	.10
87	Ray Lankford	.10
88	Ramon Martinez	.10
89	Jay Buhner	.10
90	Matt Williams	.10
91	Larry Walker	.10
92	Jose Canseco	.25
93	Len Dykstra	.10
94	Bryan Harvey	.10
95	Andy Van Slyke	.10
96	Ivan Rodriguez	.50
97	Kevin Mitchell	.10
98	Travis Fryman	.10
99	Duane Ward	.10
100	Greg Maddux	.65

Anniversary-1984

This set commemorates and features 10 of the most popular cards from Donruss' 1984 set. The cards, inserted in Series I hobby foil packs only, are "holographically enhanced" with foil stamping and UV coating.

		NM/M
Complete Set (10):		20.00
Common Player:		1.00
1	Joe Carter	1.00
2	Robin Yount	1.50
3	George Brett	2.50
4	Rickey Henderson	1.50
5	Nolan Ryan	6.00
6	Cal Ripken, Jr.	6.00
7	Wade Boggs	2.00
8	Don Mattingly	2.50
9	Ryne Sandberg	2.00
10	Tony Gwynn	2.00

Award Winners Supers

Major award winners of the 1993 season are honored in this super-size (3-1/2" x 5") insert set. One card was packaged in each box of U.S. jumbo packs and in each Canadian foil-pack box. On a gold-tone background, the card backs have another player photo, a description of his award winning performance and a white strip with a serial number identifying the card's place in an edition of 10,000.

		NM/M
Complete Set (10):		25.00
Common Player:		1.25
1	Barry Bonds (N.L. MVP)	5.00
2	Greg Maddux (N.L. Cy Young)	2.50
3	Mike Piazza (N.L. ROY)	3.50
4	Barry Bonds (N.L. HR Champ)	5.00
5	Kirby Puckett (All-Star MVP)	2.50
6	Frank Thomas (A.L. MVP)	2.00
7	Jack McDowell (A.L. Cy Young)	1.25
8	Tim Salmon (A.L. ROY)	1.25
9	Juan Gonzalez (A.L. HR Champ)	1.50
10	Paul Molitor (World Series MVP)	2.00

Decade Dominators

Donruss selected 10 top home run hitters (Series I) and 10 RBI leaders of the 1990s for this insert set. Cards were issued in all types of Series I and II packs. Full-bleed UV-coated cards were gold-foil enhanced on the front. Backs featured another full-color player photo and charted information on his 1990s home run or RBI output and ranking.

		NM/M
Complete Set (20):		15.00
Common Player:		.35
Series 1		
1	Cecil Fielder	.35
2	Barry Bonds	2.50
3	Fred McGriff	.35
4	Matt Williams	.35
5	Joe Carter	.35
6	Juan Gonzalez	.40
7	Jose Canseco	.50
8	Ron Gant	.35
9	Ken Griffey Jr.	1.50
10	Mark McGwire	2.00
Series 2		
1	Tony Gwynn	1.00
2	Frank Thomas	.75
3	Paul Molitor	.75
4	Edgar Martinez	.35
5	Kirby Puckett	1.00
6	Ken Griffey, Jr.	1.50
7	Barry Bonds	2.50
8	Willie McGee	.35
9	Len Dykstra	1.50
10	John Kruk	.35

Decade Dominators Supers

Super-size (3-1/2" x 5") versions of the 1994 Donruss Decade Dominators insert cards were produced as a premium, one card being packaged in a paper checklist envelope in each hobby box of Donruss foil packs. The supers are identical in format to the regular-size cards with the exception of a white serial number strip on the back, identifying each card's position in an edition of 10,000.

		NM/M
Complete Set (20):		25.00
Common Player:		1.00
Series 1		
1	Cecil Fielder	1.00
2	Barry Bonds	2.50
3	Fred McGriff	1.00
4	Matt Williams	1.00
5	Joe Carter	1.00
6	Juan Gonzalez	1.00
7	Jose Canseco	1.25
8	Ron Gant	1.00
9	Ken Griffey Jr.	2.00
10	Mark McGwire	2.00
Series 2		
1	Tony Gwynn	2.00
2	Frank Thomas	1.50
3	Paul Molitor	1.50
4	Edgar Martinez	1.00
5	Kirby Puckett	2.00
6	Ken Griffey, Jr.	2.25
7	Barry Bonds	2.50
8	Willie McGee	1.00
9	Lenny Dykstra	2.00
10	John Kruk	1.00

Diamond Kings

The artwork of Dick Perez is again featured on this insert set included in foil packs. Player art is set against garish color backgrounds with a red-and-silver "Diamond Kings" foil logo above, and the player's name in script at bottom. Backs are printed in red on pale yellow and feature a 1993 season summary. Cards have a DK preface to the number. Cards #1-14 and #29, Dave Winfield, were included in Series 1 packs; cards #15-28 were found in Series 2, along with the checklist card (#30), featuring a Dick Perez self-portrait.

		NM/M
Complete Set (30):		12.00
Common Player:		.25
1	Barry Bonds	2.50
2	Mo Vaughn	.25
3	Steve Avery	.25
4	Tim Salmon	.25
5	Rick Wilkins	.25
6	Brian Harper	.25
7	Andres Galarraga	.25
8	Albert Belle	.25
9	John Kruk	.25
10	Ivan Rodriguez	.75
11	Tony Gwynn	1.25
12	Brian McRae	.25
13	Bobby Bonilla	.25
14	Ken Griffey Jr.	2.00
15	Mike Piazza	2.00
16	Don Mattingly	1.50
17	Barry Larkin	.25
18	Ruben Sierra	.25
19	Orlando Merced	.25
20	Greg Vaughn	.25
21	Gregg Jefferies	.25
22	Cecil Fielder	.25
23	Moises Alou	.25
24	John Olerud	.25
25	Gary Sheffield	.25
26	Mike Mussina	.60
27	Jeff Bagwell	1.00
28	Frank Thomas	1.00
29	Dave Winfield (King of Kings)	1.00
30	Dick Perez (Checklist)	.25

Diamond Kings Supers

Each retail box of 1994 Donruss foil packs contains one super-size (4-7/8" x 6-13/16") version of the Diamond Kings inserts. Series 1 boxes offer cards #1-14, while #15-28 are found in Series 2 boxes. A 29th card, honoring Dave Winfield, was also produced. Super DKs are identical in format to the regular-size inserts, with the exception of a white serial number strip on the back which identifies the card within an edition of 10,000.

		NM/M
Complete Set (29):		70.00
Common Player:		2.00
1	Barry Bonds	7.50
2	Mo Vaughn	2.00
3	Steve Avery	2.00
4	Tim Salmon	2.00
5	Rick Wilkins	2.00
6	Brian Harper	2.00
7	Andres Galarraga	2.00
8	Albert Belle	2.00
9	John Kruk	2.00
10	Ivan Rodriguez	3.50
11	Tony Gwynn	5.00
12	Brian McRae	2.00
13	Bobby Bonilla	2.00
14	Ken Griffey Jr.	6.50
15	Mike Piazza	6.50
16	Don Mattingly	6.00
17	Barry Larkin	2.00
18	Ruben Sierra	2.00
19	Orlando Merced	2.00
20	Greg Vaughn	2.00
21	Gregg Jefferies	2.00
22	Cecil Fielder	2.00
23	Moises Alou	2.00
24	John Olerud	2.00
25	Gary Sheffield	3.00
26	Mike Mussina	3.00
27	Jeff Bagwell	4.00
28	Frank Thomas	4.00
29	Dave Winfield (King of Kings)	4.00

Elite

Donruss continued its popular Elite Series with 12 more players in 1994. The cards, numbered #37-48,

were inserted in foil packs only. The cards feature the player in a diamond on the front; the back offers an opinion of why the player is considered an elite and is serially numbered to 10,000.

		NM/M
Complete Set (12):		50.00
Common Player:		4.00
37	Frank Thomas	6.00
38	Tony Gwynn	7.50
39	Tim Salmon	4.00
40	Albert Belle	4.00
41	John Kruk	4.00
42	Juan Gonzalez	5.00
43	John Olerud	4.00
44	Barry Bonds	12.00
45	Ken Griffey Jr.	9.00
46	Mike Piazza	9.00
47	Jack McDowell	4.00
48	Andres Galarraga	4.00

Long Ball Leaders

The "Tale of the Tape" for the 1993 season is chronicled in this Series II hobby-only foil-pack insert. Silver prismatic foil highlights the typography on the front of the card which includes the "Long Ball Leaders" logos (complete with embossed baseball), the player's last name and the distance of his blast. Cards backs have another player photo superimposed on the venue in which the home run was hit. The distance is repeated in silver over the ballpark photo. In a wide silver box at bottom is data about the home run.

		NM/M
Complete Set (10):		6.00
Common Player:		.30
1	Cecil Fielder	.30
2	Dean Palmer	.30
3	Andres Galarraga	.30
4	Bo Jackson	.40
5	Ken Griffey Jr.	1.50
6	Dave Justice	.30
7	Mike Piazza	1.50
8	Frank Thomas	1.00
9	Barry Bonds	3.00
10	Juan Gonzalez	.50

MVPs

These inserts were included in 1994 jumbo packs only. The fronts have a large metallic blue MVP logo, beneath which is a red stripe with the player's name and position in white. Backs have a portrait photo, stats for 1993 and a summary of why the player was selected as team MVP.

	NM/M
Complete Set (28):	20.00

Common Player:		.25
1	Dave Justice	.25
2	Mark Grace	.25
3	Jose Rijo	.25
4	Andres Galarraga	.25
5	Bryan Harvey	.25
6	Jeff Bagwell	1.00
7	Mike Piazza	2.50
8	Moises Alou	.25
9	Bobby Bonilla	.25
10	Len Dykstra	.25
11	Jeff King	.25
12	Gregg Jefferies	.25
13	Tony Gwynn	1.50
14	Barry Bonds	4.00
15	Cal Ripken, Jr.	4.00
16	Mo Vaughn	.25
17	Tim Salmon	.25
18	Frank Thomas	1.00
19	Albert Belle	.25
20	Cecil Fielder	.25
21	Wally Joyner	.25
22	Greg Vaughn	.25
23	Kirby Puckett	1.50
24	Don Mattingly	2.00
25	Ruben Sierra	.25
26	Ken Griffey Jr.	2.50
27	Juan Gonzalez	.50
28	John Olerud	.25

Spirit of the Game

Ten players are featured in this insert set, packaged exclusively in retail boxes. Horizontal in format, fronts feature a color player action photo set against a gold-tone background which has the appearance of a multiple-exposure photo. On back a player portrait photo is set against a backdrop of red, white and blue bunting. There is a short previous-season write-up at right. Cards #1-5 were included with Series I, cards 6-10 were in Series II packs.

		NM/M
Complete Set (10):		10.00
Common Player:		.70
1	John Olerud	.50
2	Barry Bonds	2.50
3	Ken Griffey Jr.	2.00
4	Mike Piazza	2.00
5	Juan Gonzalez	.60
6	Frank Thomas	1.00
7	Tim Salmon	.50
8	Dave Justice	.50
9	Don Mattingly	1.50
10	Len Dykstra	.50

Spirit of the Game Supers

Virtually identical in format to the regular-size "Spirit of the Game" cards, these 3-1/2" x 5" versions have gold-foil, rather than holographic printing on the front, and have a serial number on back identifying it from an edition of 10,000. One super card was inserted in each specially designated retail box.

		NM/M
Complete Set (10):		20.00
Common Player:		1.50
1	John Olerud	1.50
2	Barry Bonds	4.00
3	Ken Griffey Jr.	3.50
4	Mike Piazza	3.50
5	Juan Gonzalez	2.00
6	Frank Thomas	2.50
7	Tim Salmon	1.50
8	Dave Justice	1.50
9	Don Mattingly	3.00
10	Len Dykstra	1.50

1995 Donruss Samples

The cards in this preview release of Donruss' 1995 baseball issue are virtually identical to the issued versions of the same players' cards except for slight picture cropping differences. They are unmakred as to sample status.

		NM/M
Complete Set (7):		10.00
Common Player:		1.00
5	Mike Piazza	2.00
8	Barry Bonds	3.00
20	Jeff Bagwell	1.50
42	Juan Gonzalez	1.00
55	Don Mattingly	2.00
275	Frank Thomas	1.50
331	Greg Maddux	1.50

1995 Donruss

A pair of player photos on the front of each card and silver-foil highlights are featured on the 1995 Donruss set. Besides the main action photo on front, each card has a second photo in a home plate frame at lower-left. A silver-foil ribbon beneath has the player's team and name embossed. Above the small photo is the player's position, with a half-circle of stars over all; both elements in silver foil. Completing the silver-foil highlights is the Donruss logo at upper-left. Full-bleed backs have yet another action photo at center, with a large team logo at left and five years' worth of stats plus career numbers at bottom. Donruss was issued in retail and hobby 12-card packs, magazine distributor packs of 16 and jumbo packs of 20 cards. New to Donruss in 1995 were Super Packs. These were packs that contained complete insert sets and were seeded every 90 packs.

		NM/M
Complete Set (550):		20.00
Common Player:		.05
Press Proofs:		15X
Series 1 or 2 Pack (12):		.75
Series 1 or 2 Wax Box (36):		20.00
1	Dave Justice	.05
2	Rene Arocha	.05
3	Sandy Alomar Jr.	.05
4	Luis Lopez	.05
5	Mike Piazza	1.50
6	Bobby Jones	.05
7	Damion Easley	.05
8	Barry Bonds	2.50
9	Mike Mussina	.40
10	Kevin Seitzer	.05
11	John Smiley	.05
12	W. Van Landingham	.05
13	Ron Darling	.05
14	Walt Weiss	.05
15	Mike Lansing	.05
16	Allen Watson	.05
17	Aaron Sele	.05
18	Randy Johnson	.65
19	Dean Palmer	.05
20	Jeff Bagwell	.65
21	Curt Schilling	.25
22	Darrell Whitmore	.05
23	Steve Trachsel	.05
24	Dan Wilson	.05
25	Steve Finley	.05
26	Bret Boone	.05
27	Charles Johnson	.05
28	Mike Stanton	.05
29	Ismael Valdes	.05
30	Salomon Torres	.05
31	Eric Anthony	.05
32	Spike Owen	.05
33	Joey Cora	.05
34	Robert Eenhoorn	.05
35	Rick White	.05
36	Omar Vizquel	.05
37	Carlos Delgado	.45
38	Eddie Williams	.05
39	Shawon Dunston	.05
40	Darrin Fletcher	.05
41	Leo Gomez	.05
42	Juan Gonzalez	.40
43	Luis Alicea	.05
44	Ken Ryan	.05
45	Lou Whitaker	.05
46	Mike Blowers	.05
47	Willie Blair	.05
48	Todd Van Poppel	.05
49	Roberto Alomar	.25
50	Ozzie Smith	.75
51	Sterling Hitchcock	.05
52	Mo Vaughn	.05
53	Rick Aguilera	.05
54	Kent Mercker	.05
55	Don Mattingly	1.00
56	Bob Scanlan	.05
57	Wilson Alvarez	.05
58	Jose Mesa	.05
59	Scott Kamieniecki	.05
60	Todd Jones	.05
61	John Kruk	.05
62	Mike Stanley	.05
63	Tino Martinez	.05
64	Eddie Zambrano	.05
65	Todd Hundley	.05
66	Jamie Moyer	.05
67	Rich Amaral	.05
68	Jose Valentin	.05
69	Alex Gonzalez	.05
70	Kurt Abbott	.05
71	Delino DeShields	.05
72	Brian Anderson	.05
73	John Vander Wal	.05
74	Turner Ward	.05
75	Tim Raines	.05
76	Mark Acre	.05
77	Jose Offerman	.05
78	Jimmy Key	.05
79	Mark Whiten	.05
80	Mark Gubicza	.05
81	Darren Hall	.05
82	Travis Fryman	.05
83	Cal Ripken, Jr.	2.50
84	Geronimo Berroa	.05
85	Bret Barberie	.05
86	Andy Ashby	.05
87	Steve Avery	.05
88	Rich Becker	.05
89	John Valentin	.05
90	Glenallen Hill	.05
91	Carlos Garcia	.05
92	Dennis Martinez	.05
93	Pat Kelly	.05
94	Orlando Miller	.05
95	Felix Jose	.05
96	Mike Kingery	.05
97	Jeff Kent	.05
98	Pete Incaviglia	.05
99	Chad Curtis	.05
100	Thomas Howard	.05
101	Hector Carrasco	.05
102	Tom Pagnozzi	.05
103	Danny Tartabull	.05
104	Donnie Elliott	.05
105	Danny Jackson	.05
106	Steve Dunn	.05
107	Roger Salkeld	.05
108	Jeff King	.05
109	Cecil Fielder	.05
110	Checklist	.05
111	Denny Neagle	.05
112	Troy Neel	.05
113	Rod Beck	.05
114	Alex Rodriguez	2.00
115	Joey Eischen	.05
116	Tom Candiotti	.05
117	Ray McDavid	.05
118	Vince Coleman	.05
119	Pete Harnisch	.05
120	David Nied	.05
121	Pat Rapp	.05
122	Sammy Sosa	.75
123	Steve Reed	.05
124	Jose Oliva	.05
125	Rick Bottalico	.05
126	Jose DeLeon	.05
127	Pat Hentgen	.05
128	Will Clark	.05
129	Mark Dewey	.05
130	Greg Vaughn	.05
131	Darren Dreifort	.05
132	Ed Sprague	.05
133	Lee Smith	.05
134	Charles Nagy	.05
135	Phil Plantier	.05
136	Jason Jacome	.05
137	Jose Lima	.05
138	J.R. Phillips	.05
139	J.T. Snow	.05
140	Mike Huff	.05
141	Billy Brewer	.05
142	Jeromy Burnitz	.05
143	Ricky Bones	.05
144	Carlos Rodriguez	.05
145	Luis Gonzalez	.05
146	Mark Lemke	.05
147	Al Martin	.05
148	Mike Bordick	.05
149	Robb Nen	.05
150	Wil Cordero	.05
151	Edgar Martinez	.05
152	Gerald Williams	.05
153	Esteban Beltre	.05
154	Mike Moore	.05
155	Mark Langston	.05
156	Mark Clark	.05
157	Bobby Ayala	.05
158	Rick Wilkins	.05
159	Bobby Munoz	.05
160	Checklist	.05
161	Scott Erickson	.05
162	Paul Molitor	.65
163	Jon Lieber	.05
164	Jason Grimsley	.05
165	Norberto Martin	.05
166	Javier Lopez	.05
167	Brian McRae	.05
168	Gary Sheffield	.40
169	Marcus Moore	.05
170	John Hudek	.05
171	Kelly Stinett	.05
172	Chris Gomez	.05
173	Rey Sanchez	.05
174	Juan Guzman	.05
175	Chan Ho Park	.05
176	Terry Shumpert	.05
177	Steve Ontiveros	.05
178	Brad Ausmus	.05
179	Tim Davis	.05
180	Billy Ashley	.05
181	Vinny Castilla	.05
182	Bill Spiers	.05
183	Randy Knorr	.05
184	Brian Hunter	.05
185	Pat Meares	.05
186	Steve Buechele	.05
187	Kirt Manwaring	.05
188	Tim Naehring	.05
189	Matt Mieske	.05
190	Josias Manzanillo	.05
191	Greg McMichael	.05
192	Chuck Carr	.05
193	Midre Cummings	.05
194	Darryl Strawberry	.05
195	Greg Gagne	.05
196	Steve Cooke	.05
197	Woody Williams	.05
198	Ron Karkovice	.05
199	Phil Leftwich	.05
200	Jim Thome	.50
201	Brady Anderson	.05
202	Pedro Martinez	.65
203	Steve Karsay	.05
204	Reggie Sanders	.05
205	Bill Risley	.05
206	Jay Bell	.05
207	Kevin Brown	.05
208	Tim Scott	.05
209	Len Dykstra	.05
210	Willie Greene	.05
211	Jim Eisenreich	.05
212	Cliff Floyd	.05
213	Otis Nixon	.05
214	Eduardo Perez	.05
215	Manuel Lee	.05
216	Armando Benitez **RC**	.10
217	Dave McCarty	.05
218	Scott Livingstone	.05
219	Chad Kreuter	.05
220	Checklist	.05
221	Brian Jordan	.05
222	Matt Whiteside	.05
223	Jim Edmonds	.05
224	Tony Gwynn	.75
225	Jose Lind	.05
226	Marvin Freeman	.05
227	Ken Hill	.05
228	David Hulse	.05
229	Joe Hesketh	.05
230	Roberto Petagine	.05
231	Jeffrey Hammonds	.05
232	John Jaha	.05
233	John Burkett	.05
234	Hal Morris	.05
235	Tony Castillo	.05
236	Ryan Bowen	.05
237	Wayne Kirby	.05
238	Brent Mayne	.05
239	Jim Bullinger	.05
240	Mike Lieberthal	.05
241	Barry Larkin	.05
242	David Segui	.05
243	Jose Bautista	.05
244	Hector Fajardo	.05
245	Orel Hershiser	.05
246	James Mouton	.05
247	Scott Leius	.05
248	Tom Glavine	.25
249	Danny Bautista	.05
250	Jose Mercedes	.05
251	Marquis Grissom	.05
252	Charlie Hayes	.05
253	Ryan Klesko	.05
254	Vicente Palacios	.05
255	Matias Carillo	.05
256	Gary DiSarcina	.05
257	Kirk Gibson	.05
258	Garey Ingram	.05
259	Alex Fernandez	.05
260	John Mabry	.05
261	Chris Howard	.05
262	Miguel Jimenez	.05
263	Heath Slocumb	.05
264	Albert Belle	.05
265	Dave Clark	.05
266	Joe Orsulak	.05
267	Joey Hamilton	.05
268	Mark Portugal	.05
269	Kevin Tapani	.05
270	Sid Fernandez	.05
271	Steve Dreyer	.05
272	Denny Hocking	.05
273	Troy O'Leary	.05
274	Milt Cuyler	.05
275	Frank Thomas	.65
276	Jorge Fabregas	.05
277	Mike Gallego	.05
278	Mickey Morandini	.05
279	Roberto Hernandez	.05
280	Henry Rodriguez	.05
281	Garret Anderson	.05
282	Bob Wickman	.05
283	Gar Finnvold	.05
284	Paul O'Neill	.05
285	Royce Clayton	.05
286	Chuck Knoblauch	.05
287	Johnny Ruffin	.05
288	Dave Nilsson	.05
289	David Cone	.05
290	Chuck McElroy	.05
291	Kevin Stocker	.05
292	Jose Rijo	.05
293	Sean Berry	.05
294	Ozzie Guillen	.05
295	Chris Hoiles	.05
296	Kevin Foster	.05
297	Jeff Frye	.05
298	Lance Johnson	.05
299	Mike Kelly	.05
300	Ellis Burks	.05
301	Roberto Kelly	.05
302	Dante Bichette	.05
303	Alvaro Espinoza	.05
304	Alex Cole	.05
305	Rickey Henderson	.65
306	Dave Weathers	.05
307	Shane Reynolds	.05
308	Bobby Bonilla	.05
309	Junior Felix	.05
310	Jeff Fassero	.05
311	Darren Lewis	.05
312	John Doherty	.05
313	Scott Servais	.05
314	Rick Helling	.05
315	Pedro Martinez	.65
316	Wes Chamberlain	.05
317	Bryan Eversgerd	.05
318	Trevor Hoffman	.05
319	John Patterson	.05
320	Matt Walbeck	.05
321	Jeff Montgomery	.05
322	Mel Rojas	.05
323	Eddie Taubensee	.05
324	Ray Lankford	.05
325	Jose Vizcaino	.05
326	Carlos Baerga	.05
327	Jack Voigt	.05
328	Julio Franco	.05
329	Brent Gates	.05
330	Checklist	.05
331	Greg Maddux	.75
332	Jason Bere	.05
333	Bill Wegman	.05
334	Tuffy Rhodes	.05
335	Kevin Young	.05
336	Andy Benes	.05
337	Pedro Astacio	.05
338	Reggie Jefferson	.05
339	Tim Belcher	.05
340	Ken Griffey Jr.	1.50
341	Mariano Duncan	.05
342	Andres Galarraga	.05
343	Rondell White	.05
344	Cory Bailey	.05
345	Bryan Harvey	.05
346	John Franco	.05
347	Greg Swindell	.05
348	David West	.05
349	Fred McGriff	.05
350	Jose Canseco	.35
351	Orlando Merced	.05
352	Rheal Cormier	.05
353	Carlos Pulido	.05
354	Terry Steinbach	.05
355	Wade Boggs	.75
356	B.J. Surhoff	.05
357	Rafael Palmeiro	.60
358	Anthony Young	.05
359	Tom Brunansky	.05
360	Todd Stottlemyre	.05
361	Chris Turner	.05
362	Joe Boever	.05
363	Jeff Blauser	.05
364	Derek Bell	.05
365	Matt Williams	.05
366	Jeremy Hernandez	.05
367	Joe Girardi	.05
368	Mike Devereaux	.05
369	Jim Abbott	.05
370	Manny Ramirez	.65
371	Kenny Lofton	.05
372	Mark Smith	.05
373	Dave Fleming	.05
374	Dave Stewart	.05
375	Roger Pavlik	.05
376	Hipolito Pichardo	.05
377	Bill Taylor	.05
378	Robin Ventura	.05
379	Bernard Gilkey	.05
380	Kirby Puckett	.75
381	Steve Howe	.05
382	Devon White	.05
383	Roberto Mejia	.05
384	Darrin Jackson	.05
385	Mike Morgan	.05
386	Rusty Meacham	.05
387	Bill Swift	.05
388	Lou Frazier	.05
389	Andy Van Slyke	.05
390	Brett Butler	.05
391	Bobby Witt	.05
392	Jeff Conine	.05
393	Tim Hyers	.05
394	Terry Pendleton	.05
395	Ricky Jordan	.05
396	Eric Plunk	.05
397	Melido Perez	.05
398	Darryl Kile	.05
399	Mark McLemore	.05
400	Greg Harris	.05
401	Jim Leyritz	.05
402	Doug Strange	.05
403	Tim Salmon	.05
404	Terry Mulholland	.05
405	Robby Thompson	.05
406	Ruben Sierra	.05
407	Tony Phillips	.05
408	Moises Alou	.05
409	Felix Fermin	.05
410	Pat Listach	.05
411	Kevin Bass	.05
412	Ben McDonald	.05
413	Scott Cooper	.05
414	Jody Reed	.05
415	Deion Sanders	.05
416	Ricky Gutierrez	.05
417	Gregg Jefferies	.05
418	Jack McDowell	.05
419	Al Leiter	.05
420	Tony Longmire	.05
421	Paul Wagner	.05
422	Geronimo Pena	.05
423	Ivan Rodriguez	.60
424	Kevin Gross	.05
425	Kirk McCaskill	.05
426	Greg Myers	.05
427	Roger Clemens	1.00
428	Chris Hammond	.05
429	Randy Myers	.05
430	Roger Mason	.05
431	Bret Saberhagen	.05
432	Jeff Reboulet	.05
433	John Olerud	.05
434	Bill Gullickson	.05
435	Eddie Murray	.65
436	Pedro Munoz	.05
437	Charlie O'Brien	.05
438	Jeff Nelson	.05
439	Mike Macfarlane	.05
440	Checklist	.05
441	Derrick May	.05
442	John Roper	.05
443	Darryl Hamilton	.05
444	Dan Miceli	.05
445	Tony Eusebio	.05
446	Jerry Browne	.05
447	Wally Joyner	.05
448	Brian Harper	.05
449	Scott Fletcher	.05
450	Bip Roberts	.05
451	Pete Smith	.05
452	Chili Davis	.05
453	Dave Hollins	.05
454	Tony Pena	.05
455	Butch Henry	.05
456	Craig Biggio	.05
457	Zane Smith	.05
458	Ryan Thompson	.05
459	Mike Jackson	.05
460	Mark McGwire	2.00
461	John Smoltz	.05
462	Steve Scarsone	.05
463	Greg Colbrunn	.05
464	Shawn Green	.25
465	David Wells	.05
466	Jose Hernandez	.05
467	Chip Hale	.05
468	Tony Tarasco	.05
469	Kevin Mitchell	.05
470	Billy Hatcher	.05
471	Jay Buhner	.05
472	Ken Caminiti	.05
473	Tom Henke	.05
474	Todd Worrell	.05
475	Mark Eichhorn	.05
476	Bruce Ruffin	.05
477	Chuck Finley	.05
478	Marc Newfield	.05
479	Paul Shuey	.05
480	Bob Tewksbury	.05
481	Ramon Martinez	.05
482	Melvin Nieves	.05
483	Todd Zeile	.05
484	Benito Santiago	.05
485	Stan Javier	.05
486	Kirk Rueter	.05
487	Andre Dawson	.25
488	Eric Karros	.05
489	Dave Magadan	.05
490	Checklist	.05

491	Randy Velarde	.05
492	Larry Walker	.05
493	Cris Carpenter	.05
494	Tom Gordon	.05
495	Dave Burba	.05
496	Darren Bragg	.05
497	Darren Daulton	.05
498	Don Slaught	.05
499	Pat Borders	.05
500	Lenny Harris	.05
501	Joe Ausanio	.05
502	Alan Trammell	.05
503	Mike Fetters	.05
504	Scott Ruffcorn	.05
505	Rich Rowland	.05
506	Juan Samuel	.05
507	Bo Jackson	.10
508	Jeff Branson	.05
509	Bernie Williams	.05
510	Paul Sorrento	.05
511	Dennis Eckersley	.60
512	Pat Mahomes	.05
513	Rusty Greer	.05
514	Luis Polonia	.05
515	Willie Banks	.05
516	John Wetteland	.05
517	Mike LaVaillere	.05
518	Tommy Greene	.05
519	Mark Grace	.05
520	Bob Hamelin	.05
521	Scott Sanderson	.05
522	Joe Carter	.05
523	Jeff Brantley	.05
524	Andrew Lorraine	.05
525	Rico Brogna	.05
526	Shane Mack	.05
527	Mark Wohlers	.05
528	Scott Sanders	.05
529	Chris Bosio	.05
530	Andujar Cedeno	.05
531	Kenny Rogers	.05
532	Doug Drabek	.05
533	Curt Leskanic	.05
534	Craig Shipley	.05
535	Craig Grebeck	.05
536	Cal Eldred	.05
537	Mickey Tettleton	.05
538	Harold Baines	.05
539	Tim Wallach	.05
540	Damon Buford	.05
541	Lenny Webster	.05
542	Kevin Appier	.05
543	Raul Mondesi	.05
544	Eric Young	.05
545	Russ Davis	.05
546	Mike Benjamin	.05
547	Mike Greenwell	.05
548	Scott Brosius	.05
549	Brian Dorsett	.05
550	Checklist	.05

Press Proofs

Designated as Press Proofs, the first 2,000 cards of each player in the '95 Donruss set were enhanced with gold, rather than silver, foil and inserted into packs at an average rate of one per 20 packs.

	NM/M
Complete Set (550):	150.00
Common Player:	1.00
Stars:	15X

All-Stars

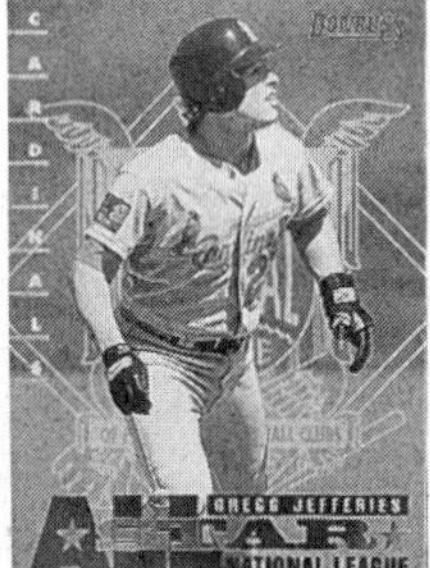

Exclusive to Wal-Mart jumbo packs were Donruss All-Stars. Nine cards featuring American Leaguers were inserted into Series 1, while nine National League All-Stars were inserted into Series 2 jumbos.

		NM/M
Complete Set (18):		26.00
Common Player:		.40
AL1	Jimmy Key	.40
AL2	Ivan Rodriguez	1.25
AL3	Frank Thomas	1.50
AL4	Roberto Alomar	.60
AL5	Wade Boggs	2.00
AL6	Cal Ripken, Jr.	4.50
AL7	Joe Carter	.40
AL8	Ken Griffey Jr.	3.00
AL9	Kirby Puckett	2.00
NL1	Greg Maddux	2.00
NL2	Mike Piazza	3.00
NL3	Gregg Jefferies	.40
NL4	Mariano Duncan	.40
NL5	Matt Williams	.40
NL6	Ozzie Smith	2.00
NL7	Barry Bonds	4.50
NL8	Tony Gwynn	2.00
NL9	Dave Justice	.40

Bomb Squad

Bomb Squad features the top six home run hitters in each league on double-sided cards. These cards were only inserted into Series I retail and magazine distributor packs at a rate of one per 24 retail packs and one per 16 magazine distributor packs.

		NM/M
Complete Set (6):		3.00
Common Player:		.50
1	Ken Griffey Jr., Matt Williams	1.00
2	Frank Thomas, Jeff Bagwell	.75
3	Albert Belle, Barry Bonds	1.50
4	Jose Canseco, Fred McGriff	.60
5	Cecil Fielder, Andres Galarraga	.50
6	Joe Carter, Kevin Mitchell	.50

Diamond Kings

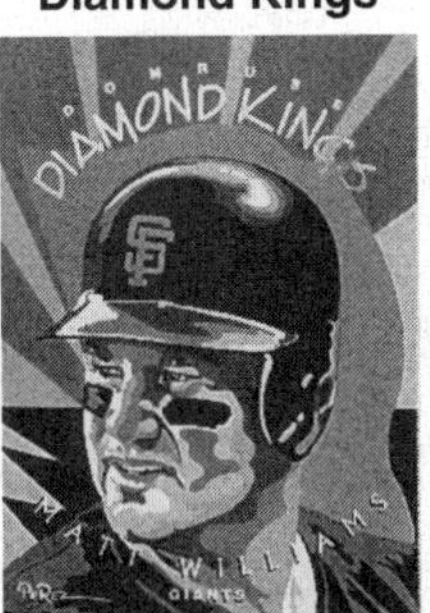

Continuing a tradition begun in 1982, artist Dick Perez painted a series of 28 water colors to produce insert cards of the game's best; 14 in each series. A portrait of the player appears on a party-colored background, with Diamond Kings in gold across the top. DKs were inserted in Series 1 and 2 packs at a rate of one per 10.

		NM/M
Complete Set (29):		35.00
Common Player:		.75
1	Frank Thomas	3.00
2	Jeff Bagwell	3.00
3	Chili Davis	.75
4	Dante Bichette	.75
5	Ruben Sierra	.75
6	Jeff Conine	.75
7	Paul O'Neill	.75
8	Bobby Bonilla	.75
9	Joe Carter	.75
10	Moises Alou	.75
11	Kenny Lofton	.75
12	Matt Williams	.75
13	Kevin Seitzer	.75
14	Sammy Sosa	3.50
15	Scott Cooper	.75
16	Raul Mondesi	.75
17	Will Clark	.75
18	Lenny Dykstra	.75
19	Kirby Puckett	3.50
20	Hal Morris	.75
21	Travis Fryman	.75
22	Greg Maddux	3.50
23	Rafael Palmeiro	2.50
24	Tony Gwynn	3.50
25	David Cone	.75
26	Al Martin	.75
27	Ken Griffey Jr.	5.00
28	Gregg Jefferies	.75
29	Checklist	

Dominators

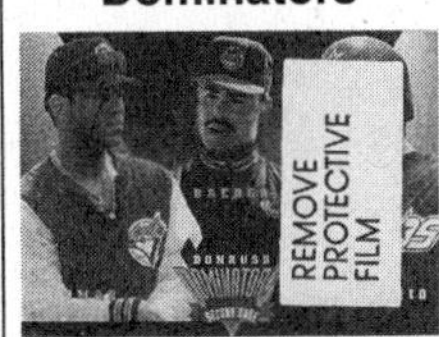

Dominators is a nine-card chase set inserted into hobby packs of Series II Donruss baseball at a rate of one per 24 packs. These acetate cards feature three of the top players at each position on a horizontal format.

		NM/M
Complete Set (9):		7.50
Common Player:		.50
1	David Cone, Mike Mussina, Greg Maddux	1.00
2	Ivan Rodriguez, Mike Piazza, Darren Daulton	2.00
3	Fred McGriff, Frank Thomas, Jeff Bagwell	1.50
4	Roberto Alomar, Carlos Baerga, Craig Biggio	.75
5	Robin Ventura, Travis Fryman, Matt Williams	.50
6	Cal Ripken Jr., Barry Larkin, Wil Cordero	2.50
7	Albert Belle, Barry Bonds, Moises Alou	2.50
8	Ken Griffey Jr., Kenny Lofton, Marquis Grissom	2.00
9	Kirby Puckett, Paul O'Neill, Tony Gwynn	2.00

Elite

Another Donruss insert tradition continues with the fifth annual presentation of the Elite series. Each of the 12 cards (six each Series 1 and 2) is produced in a numbered edition of 10,000 and inserted into all types of packaging at the rate of one per 210 packs.

		NM/M
Complete Set (12):		100.00
Common Player:		6.00
49	Jeff Bagwell	12.00
50	Paul O'Neill	6.00
51	Greg Maddux	15.00
52	Mike Piazza	17.50
53	Matt Williams	6.00
54	Ken Griffey Jr.	17.50
55	Frank Thomas	12.00
56	Barry Bonds	20.00
57	Kirby Puckett	15.00
58	Fred McGriff	6.00
59	Jose Canseco	9.00
60	Albert Belle	6.00

Long Ball Leaders

Exclusive to Series 1 hobby packs, these cards feature the top long-distance home runs of 1994 in an eye-popping holographic foil presentation. Stated odds of picking one from a hobby pack are one in 24.

		NM/M
Complete Set (8):		7.50
Common Player:		.50
1	Frank Thomas	1.50
2	Fred McGriff	.50
3	Ken Griffey Jr.	2.00
4	Matt Williams	.50
5	Mike Piazza	2.00
6	Jose Canseco	.75
7	Barry Bonds	2.50
8	Jeff Bagwell	1.50

Mound Marvels

Mound Marvels is an eight-card insert set containing some of the best pitchers in baseball. Cards were inserted into one per 18 retail and magazine packs of Donruss Series II. Each card features a two-way mirror that allows collectors to see the players' face through the mirror.

		NM/M
Complete Set (8):		7.50
Common Player:		1.00
1	Greg Maddux	4.00
2	David Cone	1.00
3	Mike Mussina	2.00
4	Bret Saberhagen	1.00
5	Jimmy Key	1.00
6	Doug Drabek	1.00
7	Randy Johnson	3.00
8	Jason Bere	1.00

Top of the Order Card Game

In one of the earliest efforts to wed the play factor and collectibility that had made various fantasy card games so successful in 1994-95, Donruss created the interactive Top of the Order baseball card game. Printed on playing card stock with rounded corners and semi-gloss surface, the player cards feature color action photos and all manners of game-action indicators. Backs of each card are printed primarily in green with Donruss logos. Cards were sold in several types of packaging, including 80- and 160-card boxed sets, and 12-card foil "booster" packs. Stars' cards were printed in lesser quantities than those of journeyman players, resulting in values higher than would be the case based on player popularity alone if all cards were printed in equal quantities. The unnumbered cards are checklisted here in alphabetical order within team and league.

		NM/M
Complete Set (360):		125.00
Common Player:		.10
Starter Deck (80):		6.00
Starter Deck (160):		12.00
Wax Pack (12):		1.00
Wax Box (36):		20.00
(1)	Brady Anderson	.10
(2)	Harold Baines	.10
(3)	Bret Barberie	.10
(4)	Armando Benitez	.10
(5)	Bobby Bonilla	.10
(6)	Scott Erickson	.10
(7)	Leo Gomez	.10
(8)	Curtis Goodwin	.10
(9)	Jeffrey Hammonds	.10
(10)	Chris Hoiles	.10
(11)	Doug Jones	.10
(12)	Ben McDonald	.10
(13)	Mike Mussina	1.50
(14)	Rafael Palmeiro	2.50
(15)	Cal Ripken Jr.	10.00
(16)	Rick Aguilera	.10
(17)	Luis Alicea	.10
(18)	Jose Canseco	1.50
(19)	Roger Clemens	5.00
(20)	Mike Greenwell	.10
(21)	Erik Hanson	.10
(22)	Mike Macfarlane	.10
(23)	Tim Naehring	.10
(24)	Troy O'Leary	.10
(25)	Ken Ryan	.10
(26)	Aaron Sele	.10
(27)	Lee Tinsley	.10
(28)	John Valentin	.10
(29)	Mo Vaughn	.10
(30)	Jim Abbott	.10
(31)	Mike Butcher	.10
(32)	Chili Davis	.10
(33)	Gary DiSarcina	.10
(34)	Damion Easley	.10
(35)	Jim Edmonds	.10
(36)	Chuck Finley	.10
(37)	Mark Langston	.10
(38)	Greg Myers	.10
(39)	Spike Owen	.10
(40)	Troy Percival	.10
(41)	Tony Phillips	.10
(42)	Tim Salmon	.10
(43)	Lee Smith	.10
(44)	J.T. Snow	.10
(45)	Jason Bere	.10
(46)	Mike Devereaux	.10
(47)	Ray Durham	.10
(48)	Alex Fernandez	.10
(49)	Ozzie Guillen	.10
(50)	Roberto Hernandez	.10
(51)	Lance Johnson	.10
(52)	Ron Karkovice	.10
(53)	Tim Raines	.10
(54)	Frank Thomas	3.00
(55)	Robin Ventura	.10
(56)	Sandy Alomar Jr.	.10
(57)	Carlos Baerga	.10
(58)	Albert Belle	.10
(59)	Kenny Lofton	.10
(60)	Dennis Martinez	.10
(61)	Jose Mesa	.10
(62)	Eddie Murray	3.00
(63)	Charles Nagy	.10
(64)	Tony Pena	.10
(65)	Eric Plunk	.10
(66)	Manny Ramirez	3.00
(67)	Paul Sorrento	.10
(68)	Jim Thome	2.00
(69)	Omar Vizquel	.10
(70)	Danny Bautista	.10
(71)	Joe Boever	.10
(72)	Chad Curtis	.10
(73)	Cecil Fielder	.10
(74)	John Flaherty	.10
(75)	Travis Fryman	.10
(76)	Kirk Gibson	.10
(77)	Chris Gomez	.10
(78)	Mike Henneman	.10
(79)	Bob Higginson	.10
(80)	Alan Trammell	.10
(81)	Lou Whitaker	.10
(82)	Kevin Appier	.10
(83)	Billy Brewer	.10
(84)	Vince Coleman	.10
(85)	Gary Gaetti	.10
(86)	Greg Gagne	.10
(87)	Tom Goodwin	.10
(88)	Tom Gordon	.10
(89)	Mark Gubicza	.10
(90)	Bob Hamelin	.10
(91)	Phil Hiatt	.10
(92)	Wally Joyner	.10
(93)	Brent Mayne	.10
(94)	Jeff Montgomery	.10
(95)	Ricky Bones	.10
(96)	Mike Fetters	.10
(97)	Darryl Hamilton	.10
(98)	Pat Listach	.10
(99)	Matt Mieske	.10
(100)	Dave Nilsson	.10
(101)	Joe Oliver	.10
(102)	Kevin Seitzer	.10
(103)	B.J. Surhoff	.10
(104)	Jose Valentin	.10
(105)	Greg Vaughn	.10
(106)	Bill Wegman	.10
(107)	Alex Cole	.10
(108)	Marty Cordova	.10
(109)	Chuck Knoblauch	.10
(110)	Scott Leius	.10
(111)	Pat Meares	.10
(112)	Pedro Munoz	.10
(113)	Kirby Puckett	4.00
(114)	Scott Stahoviak	.10
(115)	Mike Trombley	.10
(116)	Matt Walbeck	.10
(117)	Wade Boggs	4.00
(118)	David Cone	.10
(119)	Tony Fernandez	.10
(120)	Don Mattingly	5.00
(121)	Jack McDowell	.10
(122)	Paul O'Neill	.10
(123)	Melido Perez	.10
(124)	Luis Polonia	.10
(125)	Ruben Sierra	.10
(126)	Mike Stanley	.10
(127)	Randy Velarde	.10
(128)	John Wetteland	.10
(129)	Bob Wickman	.10
(130)	Bernie Williams	.10
(131)	Gerald Williams	.10
(132)	Geronimo Berroa	.10
(133)	Mike Bordick	.10
(134)	Scott Brosius	.10
(135)	Dennis Eckersley	.10
(136)	Brent Gates	.10
(137)	Rickey Henderson	3.00
(138)	Stan Javier	.10
(139)	Mark McGwire	8.00
(140)	Steve Ontiveros	.10
(141)	Terry Steinbach	.10
(142)	Todd Stottlemyre	.10
(143)	Danny Tartabull	.10
(144)	Bobby Ayala	.10
(145)	Andy Benes	.10
(146)	Mike Blowers	.10
(147)	Jay Buhner	.10
(148)	Joey Cora	.10
(149)	Alex Diaz	.10
(150)	Ken Griffey Jr.	6.00
(151)	Randy Johnson	3.00
(152)	Edgar Martinez	.10
(153)	Tino Martinez	.10
(154)	Bill Risley	.10
(155)	Alex Rodriguez	8.00
(156)	Dan Wilson	.10
(157)	Will Clark	.10
(158)	Jeff Frye	.10
(159)	Benji Gil	.10
(160)	Juan Gonzalez	1.50
(161)	Rusty Greer	.10
(162)	Mark McLemore	.10
(163)	Otis Nixon	.10
(164)	Dean Palmer	.10
(165)	Ivan Rodriguez	2.50
(166)	Kenny Rogers	.10
(167)	Jeff Russell	.10
(168)	Mickey Tettleton	.10
(169)	Bob Tewksbury	.10
(170)	Bobby Witt	.10
(171)	Roberto Alomar	.30
(172)	Joe Carter	.10
(173)	Alex Gonzalez	.10
(174)	Candy Maldonado	.10
(175)	Paul Molitor	3.00
(176)	John Olerud	.10
(177)	Lance Parrish	.10
(178)	Ed Sprague	.10
(179)	Devon White	.10
(180)	Woody Williams	.10
(181)	Steve Avery	.10
(182)	Jeff Blauser	.10
(183)	Tom Glavine	.50
(184)	Marquis Grissom	.10
(185)	Chipper Jones	4.00
(186)	Dave Justice	.10
(187)	Ryan Klesko	.10
(188)	Mark Lemke	.10
(189)	Javier Lopez	.10
(190)	Greg Maddux	4.00
(191)	Fred McGriff	.10
(192)	Greg McMichael	.10
(193)	John Smoltz	.10
(194)	Mark Wohlers	.10
(195)	Jim Bullinger	.10
(196)	Shawon Dunston	.10
(197)	Kevin Foster	.10
(198)	Luis Gonzalez	.10
(199)	Mark Grace	.10
(200)	Brian McRae	.10
(201)	Randy Myers	.10
(202)	Jaime Navarro	.10
(203)	Rey Sanchez	.10
(204)	Scott Servais	.10
(205)	Sammy Sosa	4.00
(206)	Steve Trachsel	.10
(207)	Todd Zeile	.10
(208)	Bret Boone	.10

(209) Jeff Branson .10
(210) Jeff Brantley .10
(211) Hector Carrasco .10
(212) Ron Gant .10
(213) Lenny Harris .10
(214) Barry Larkin .10
(215) Darren Lewis .10
(216) Hal Morris .10
(217) Mark Portugal .10
(218) Jose Rijo .10
(219) Reggie Sanders .10
(220) Pete Schourek .10
(221) John Smiley .10
(222) Eddie Taubensee .10
(223) Dave Wells .10
(224) Jason Bates .10
(225) Dante Bichette .10
(226) Vinny Castilla .10
(227) Andres Galarraga .10
(228) Joe Girardi .10
(229) Mike Kingery .10
(230) Steve Reed .10
(231) Bruce Ruffin .10
(232) Bret Saberhagen .10
(233) Bill Swift .10
(234) Larry Walker .10
(235) Walt Weiss .10
(236) Eric Young .10
(237) Kurt Abbott .10
(238) John Burkett .10
(239) Chuck Carr .10
(240) Greg Colbrunn .10
(241) Jeff Conine .10
(242) Andre Dawson .35
(243) Chris Hammond .10
(244) Charles Johnson .10
(245) Robb Nen .10
(246) Terry Pendleton .10
(247) Gary Sheffield .50
(248) Quilvio Veras .10
(249) Jeff Bagwell 3.00
(250) Derek Bell .10
(251) Craig Biggio .10
(252) Doug Drabek .10
(253) Tony Eusebio .10
(254) John Hudek .10
(255) Brian Hunter .10
(256) Todd Jones .10
(257) Dave Magadan .10
(258) Orlando Miller .10
(259) James Mouton .10
(260) Shane Reynolds .10
(261) Greg Swindell .10
(262) Billy Ashley .10
(263) Tom Candiotti .10
(264) Delino DeShields .10
(265) Eric Karros .10
(266) Roberto Kelly .10
(267) Ramon Martinez .10
(268) Raul Mondesi .10
(269) Hideo Nomo 1.50
(270) Jose Offerman .10
(271) Mike Piazza 6.00
(272) Kevin Tapani .10
(273) Ismael Valdes .10
(274) Tim Wallach .10
(275) Todd Worrell .10
(276) Moises Alou .10
(277) Sean Berry .10
(278) Wil Cordero .10
(279) Jeff Fassero .10
(280) Darrin Fletcher .10
(281) Mike Lansing .10
(282) Pedro J. Martinez 3.00
(283) Carlos Perez .10
(284) Mel Rojas .10
(285) Tim Scott .10
(286) David Segui .10
(287) Tony Tarasco .10
(288) Rondell White .10
(289) Rico Brogna .10
(290) Brett Butler .10
(291) John Franco .10
(292) Pete Harnisch .10
(293) Todd Hundley .10
(294) Bobby Jones .10
(295) Jeff Kent .10
(296) Joe Orsulak .10
(297) Ryan Thompson .10
(298) Jose Vizcaino .10
(299) Ricky Bottalico .10
(300) Darren Daulton .10
(301) Mariano Duncan .10
(302) Lenny Dykstra .10
(303) Jim Eisenreich .10
(304) Tyler Green .10
(305) Charlie Hayes .10
(306) Dave Hollins .10
(307) Gregg Jefferies .10
(308) Mickey Morandini .10
(309) Curt Schilling .50
(310) Heathcliff Slocumb .10
(311) Kevin Stocker .10
(312) Jay Bell .10
(313) Jacob Brumfield .10
(314) Dave Clark .10
(315) Carlos Garcia .10
(316) Mark Johnson .10
(317) Jeff King .10
(318) Nelson Liriano .10
(319) Al Martin .10
(320) Orlando Merced .10
(321) Dan Miceli .10
(322) Denny Neagle .10
(323) Mark Parent .10
(324) Dan Plesac .10
(325) Scott Cooper .10
(326) Bernard Gilkey .10
(327) Tom Henke .10
(328) Ken Hill .10
(329) Danny Jackson .10
(330) Brian Jordan .10
(331) Ray Lankford .10
(332) John Mabry .10
(333) Jose Oquendo .10
(334) Tom Pagnozzi .10
(335) Ozzie Smith 4.00
(336) Andy Ashby .10
(337) Brad Ausmus .10
(338) Ken Caminiti .10
(339) Andujar Cedeno .10
(340) Steve Finley .10
(341) Tony Gwynn 4.00
(342) Joey Hamilton .10
(343) Trevor Hoffman .10
(344) Jody Reed .10
(345) Bip Roberts .10
(346) Eddie Williams .10
(347) Rod Beck .10
(348) Mike Benjamin .10
(349) Barry Bonds 10.00
(350) Royce Clayton .10
(351) Glenallen Hill .10
(352) Kirt Manwaring .10
(353) Terry Mulholland .10
(354) John Patterson .10
(355) J.R. Phillips .10
(356) Deion Sanders .25
(357) Steve Scarsone .10
(358) Robby Thompson .10
(359) William Van Landingham .10
(360) Matt Williams .10

1996 Donruss Samples

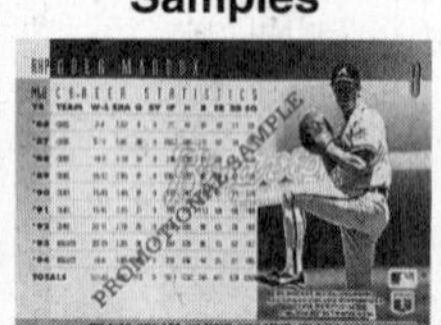

To introduce its 1996 series to dealers and the hobby press, Donruss issued an eight-card sample set. Identical in format to the issued version, the samples are numbered differently from the same players' cards in the regular issue (except #1, Frank Thomas). The samples also differ in that they lack 1995 stats on back, may have slightly different wording in the career highlights, and have printed on front and back a diagonal gray "PROMOTIONAL SAMPLE."

		NM/M
Complete Set (8):		9.00
Common Player:		1.00
1	Frank Thomas	1.00
2	Barry Bonds	2.50
3	Hideo Nomo	1.00
4	Ken Griffey Jr.	1.50
5	Cal Ripken Jr.	2.50
6	Manny Ramirez	1.00
7	Mike Piazza	1.50
8	Greg Maddux	1.25

1996 Donruss

A clean, borderless look marks the 1996 Donruss regular-issue cards. Besides the player name in white inside a fading team-color stripe at top-right, the only graphic enhancement on front is a 7/8" square foil box at bottom-center with the company and team name, team logo, player position and uniform number. The foil box is enhanced with team colors, which are carried over to the horizontal backs. Backs also feature a color action photo, a large gray team logo, stats and career highlights. Basic packaging was 12-card foil packs with a suggested retail price of $1.79. Several types of insert cards were offered, each at a virtually unprecedented rate of scarcity. The set was issued in two series; Series 1 with 330 cards, Series 2 with 220 cards.

		NM/M
Complete Set (550):		20.00
Complete Series 1 (330):		12.00
Complete Series 2 (220):		10.00
Common Player:		.05
Press Proofs:		7X
Series 1 Pack (12):		1.00
Series 1 Wax Box (36):		20.00
Series 2 Pack (12):		1.00
Series 2 Wax Box (18):		12.50

1 Frank Thomas 1.00
2 Jason Bates .05
3 Steve Sparks .05
4 Scott Servais .05
5 Angelo Encarnacion .05
6 Scott Sanders .05
7 Billy Ashley .05
8 Alex Rodriguez 2.00
9 Sean Bergman .05
10 Brad Radke .05
11 Andy Van Slyke .05
12 Joe Girardi .05
13 Mark Grudzielanek .05
14 Rick Aguilera .05
15 Randy Veres .05
16 Tim Bogar .05
17 Dave Veres .05
18 Kevin Stocker .05
19 Marquis Grissom .05
20 Will Clark .05
21 Jay Bell .05
22 Allen Battle .05
23 Frank Rodriguez .05
24 Terry Steinbach .05
25 Gerald Williams .05
26 Sid Roberson .05
27 Gregg Zaun .05
28 Ozzie Timmons .05
29 Vaughn Eshelman .05
30 Ed Sprague .05
31 Gary DiSarcina .05
32 Joe Boever .05
33 Steve Avery .05
34 Brad Ausmus .05
35 Kirt Manwaring .05
36 Gary Sheffield .25
37 Jason Bere .05
38 Jeff Manto .05
39 David Cone .05
40 Manny Ramirez 1.00
41 Sandy Alomar .05
42 Curtis Goodwin/RR .05
43 Tino Martinez .05
44 Woody Williams .05
45 Dean Palmer .05
46 Hipolito Pichardo .05
47 Jason Giambi .60
48 Lance Johnson .05
49 Bernard Gilkey .05
50 Kirby Puckett 1.25
51 Tony Fernandez .05
52 Alex Gonzalez .05
53 Bret Saberhagen .05
54 Lyle Mouton/RR .05
55 Brian McRae .05
56 Mark Gubicza .05
57 Sergio Valdez .05
58 Darrin Fletcher .05
59 Steve Parris .05
60 Johnny Damon/RR .35
61 Rickey Henderson 1.00
62 Darrell Whitmore .05
63 Roberto Petagine .05
64 Trenidad Hubbard .05
65 Heathcliff Slocumb .05
66 Steve Finley .05
67 Mariano Rivera .25
68 Brian Hunter .05
69 Jamie Moyer .05
70 Ellis Burks .05
71 Pat Kelly .05
72 Mickey Tettleton .05
73 Garret Anderson .05
74 Andy Pettitte/RR .75
75 Glenallen Hill .05
76 Brent Gates .05
77 Lou Whitaker .05
78 David Segui .05
79 Dan Wilson .05
80 Pat Listach .05
81 Jeff Bagwell 1.00
82 Ben McDonald .05
83 John Valentin .05
84 John Jaha .05
85 Pete Schourek .05
86 Bryce Florie .05
87 Brian Jordan .05
88 Ron Karkovice .05
89 Al Leiter .05
90 Tony Longmire .05
91 Nelson Liriano .05
92 David Bell .05
93 Kevin Gross .05
94 Tom Candiotti .05
95 Dave Martinez .05
96 Greg Myers .05
97 Rheal Cormier .05
98 Chris Hammond .05
99 Randy Myers .05
100 Bill Pulsipher/RR .05
101 Jason Isringhausen/RR .05
102 Dave Stevens .05
103 Roberto Alomar .20
104 Bob Higginson/RR .05
105 Eddie Murray 1.00
106 Matt Walbeck .05
107 Mark Wohlers .05
108 Jeff Nelson .05
109 Tom Goodwin .05
110 Checklist 1-83 Cal Ripken Jr. (2,131 Consecutive Games) 1.25
111 Rey Sanchez .05
112 Hector Carrasco .05
113 B.J. Surhoff .05
114 Dan Miceli .05
115 Dean Hartgraves .05
116 John Burkett .05
117 Gary Gaetti .05
118 Ricky Bones .05
119 Mike Macfarlane .05
120 Bip Roberts .05
121 Dave Mlicki .05
122 Chili Davis .05
123 Mark Whiten .05
124 Herbert Perry .05
125 Butch Henry .05
126 Derek Bell .05
127 Al Martin .05
128 John Franco .05
129 William Van Landingham .05
130 Mike Bordick .05
131 Mike Mordecai .05
132 Robby Thompson .05
133 Greg Colbrunn .05
134 Domingo Cedeno .05
135 Chad Curtis .05
136 Jose Hernandez .05
137 Scott Klingenbeck .05
138 Ryan Klesko .05
139 John Smiley .05
140 Charlie Hayes .05
141 Jay Buhner .05
142 Doug Drabek .05
143 Roger Pavlik .05
144 Todd Worrell .05
145 Cal Ripken Jr. 2.50
146 Steve Reed .05
147 Chuck Finley .05
148 Mike Blowers .05
149 Orel Hershiser .05
150 Allen Watson .05
151 Ramon Martinez .05
152 Melvin Nieves .05
153 Tripp Cromer .05
154 Yorkis Perez .05
155 Stan Javier .05
156 Mel Rojas .05
157 Aaron Sele .05
158 Eric Karros .05
159 Robb Nen .05
160 Raul Mondesi .05
161 John Wetteland .05
162 Tim Scott .05
163 Kenny Rogers .05
164 Melvin Bunch .05
165 Rod Beck .05
166 Andy Benes .05
167 Lenny Dykstra .05
168 Orlando Merced .05
169 Tomas Perez .05
170 Xavier Hernandez .05
171 Ruben Sierra .05
172 Alan Trammell .05
173 Mike Fetters .05
174 Wilson Alvarez .05
175 Erik Hanson .05
176 Travis Fryman .05
177 Jim Abbott .05
178 Bret Boone .05
179 Sterling Hitchcock .05
180 Pat Mahomes .05
181 Mark Acre .05
182 Charles Nagy .05
183 Rusty Greer .05
184 Mike Stanley .05
185 Jim Bullinger .05
186 Shane Andrews .05
187 Brian Keyser .05
188 Tyler Green .05
189 Mark Grace .05
190 Bob Hamelin .05
191 Luis Ortiz .05
192 Joe Carter .05
193 Eddie Taubensee .05
194 Brian Anderson .05
195 Edgardo Alfonzo .05
196 Pedro Munoz .05
197 David Justice .05
198 Trevor Hoffman .05
199 Bobby Ayala .05
200 Tony Eusebio .05
201 Jeff Russell .05
202 Mike Hampton .05
203 Walt Weiss .05
204 Joey Hamilton .05
205 Roberto Hernandez .05
206 Greg Vaughn .05
207 Felipe Lira .05
208 Harold Baines .05
209 Tim Wallach .05
210 Manny Alexander .05
211 Tim Laker .05
212 Chris Haney .05
213 Brian Maxcy .05
214 Eric Young .05
215 Darryl Strawberry .05
216 Barry Bonds 2.50
217 Tim Naehring .05
218 Scott Brosius .05
219 Reggie Sanders .05
220 Checklist 84-166 Eddie Murray (3,000 Career Hits) .35
221 Luis Alicea .05
222 Albert Belle .05
223 Benji Gil .05
224 Dante Bichette .05
225 Bobby Bonilla .05
226 Todd Stottlemyre .05
227 Jim Edmonds .05
228 Todd Jones .05
229 Shawn Green .25
230 Javy Lopez .05
231 Ariel Prieto .05
232 Tony Phillips .05
233 James Mouton .05
234 Jose Oquendo .05
235 Royce Clayton .05
236 Chuck Carr .05
237 Doug Jones .05
238 Mark Mclemore (McLemore) .05
239 Bill Swift .05
240 Scott Leius .05
241 Russ Davis .05
242 Ray Durham/RR .05
243 Matt Mieske .05
244 Brent Mayne .05
245 Thomas Howard .05
246 Troy O'Leary .05
247 Jacob Brumfield .05
248 Mickey Morandini .05
249 Todd Hundley .05
250 Chris Bosio .05
251 Omar Vizquel .05
252 Mike Lansing .05
253 John Mabry .05
254 Mike Perez .05
255 Delino DeShields .05
256 Wil Cordoro .05
257 Mike James .05
258 Todd Van Poppel .05
259 Joey Cora .05
260 Andre Dawson .25
261 Jerry DiPoto .05
262 Rick Krivda .05
263 Glenn Dishman .05
264 Mike Mimbs .05
265 John Ericks .05
266 Jose Canseco .35
267 Jeff Branson .05
268 Curt Leskanic .05
269 Jon Nunnally .05
270 Scott Stahoviak .05
271 Jeff Montgomery .05
272 Hal Morris .05
273 Esteban Loaiza .05
274 Rico Brogna .05
275 Dave Winfield 1.00
276 J.R. Phillips .05
277 Todd Zeile .05
278 Tom Pagnozzi .05
279 Mark Lemke .05
280 Dave Magadan .05
281 Greg McMichael .05
282 Mike Morgan .05
283 Moises Alou .05
284 Dennis Martinez .05
285 Jeff Kent .05
286 Mark Johnson .05
287 Darren Lewis .05
288 Brad Clontz .05
289 Chad Fonville/RR .05
290 Paul Sorrento .05
291 Lee Smith .05
292 Tom Glavine .25
293 Antonio Osuna .05
294 Kevin Foster .05
295 Sandy Martinez **RC** .05
296 Mark Leiter .05
297 Julian Tavarez .05
298 Mike Kelly .05
299 Joe Oliver .05
300 John Flaherty .05
301 Don Mattingly 1.50
302 Pat Meares .05
303 John Doherty .05
304 Joe Vitiello .05
305 Vinny Castilla .05
306 Jeff Brantley .05
307 Mike Greenwell .05
308 Midre Cummings .05
309 Curt Schilling .25
310 Ken Caminiti .05
311 Scott Erickson .05
312 Carl Everett .05
313 Charles Johnson .05
314 Alex Diaz .05
315 Jose Mesa .05
316 Mark Carreon .05
317 Carlos Perez/RR .05
318 Ismael Valdes .05
319 Frank Castillo .05
320 Tom Henke .05
321 Spike Owen .05
322 Joe Orsulak .05
323 Paul Menhart .05
324 Pedro Borbon .05
325 Checklist 167-249 Paul Molitor (1,000 Career RBI) .35
326 Jeff Cirillo .05
327 Edwin Hurtado .05
328 Orlando Miller .05
329 Steve Ontiveros .05
330 Checklist 250-330 Kirby Puckett (1,000 Career RBI) .75
331 Scott Bullett .05
332 Andres Galarraga .05
333 Cal Eldred .05
334 Sammy Sosa 1.25
335 Don Slaught .05
336 Jody Reed .05
337 Roger Cedeno .05
338 Ken Griffey Jr. 1.75
339 Todd Hollandsworth .05
340 Mike Trombley .05
341 Gregg Jefferies .05
342 Larry Walker .05
343 Pedro Martinez .05
344 Dwayne Hosey .05
345 Terry Pendleton .05
346 Pete Harnisch .05
347 Tony Castillo .05
348 Paul Quantrill .05
349 Fred McGriff .05
350 Ivan Rodriguez .65
351 Butch Huskey .05
352 Ozzie Smith 1.25
353 Marty Cordova .05
354 John Wasdin .05
355 Wade Boggs 1.25
356 Dave Nilsson .05
357 Rafael Palmeiro .65
358 Luis Gonzalez .05
359 Reggie Jefferson .05
360 Carlos Delgado .60
361 Orlando Palmeiro .05
362 Chris Gomez .05
363 John Smoltz .05
364 Marc Newfield .05
365 Matt Williams .05
366 Jesus Tavarez .05
367 Bruce Ruffin .05
368 Sean Berry .05
369 Randy Velarde .05
370 Tony Pena .05
371 Jim Thome .60
372 Jeffrey Hammonds .05
373 Bob Wolcott .05
374 Juan Guzman .05
375 Juan Gonzalez .50
376 Michael Tucker .05
377 Doug Johns .05
378 Mike Cameron **RC** .75
379 Ray Lankford .05
380 Jose Parra .05
381 Jimmy Key .05
382 John Olerud .05
383 Kevin Ritz .05
384 Tim Raines .05
385 Rich Amaral .05
386 Keith Lockhart .05
387 Steve Scarsone .05
388 Cliff Floyd .05
389 Rich Aude .05
390 Hideo Nomo .50
391 Geronimo Berroa .05
392 Pat Rapp .05
393 Dustin Hermanson .05
394 Greg Maddux 1.25
395 Darren Daulton .05
396 Kenny Lofton .05
397 Ruben Rivera .05
398 Billy Wagner .05
399 Kevin Brown .05
400 Mike Kingery .05
401 Bernie Williams .05
402 Otis Nixon .05
403 Damion Easley .05
404 Paul O'Neill .05
405 Deion Sanders .05
406 Dennis Eckersley 1.00
407 Tony Clark .05
408 Rondell White .05
409 Luis Sojo .05
410 David Hulse .05
411 Shane Reynolds .05
412 Chris Hoiles .05
413 Lee Tinsley .05
414 Scott Karl .05
415 Ron Gant .05
416 Brian Johnson .05
417 Jose Oliva .05
418 Jack McDowell .05
419 Paul Molitor 1.00
420 Ricky Bottalico .05
421 Paul Wagner .05
422 Terry Bradshaw .05
423 Bob Tewksbury .05
424 Mike Piazza 1.75
425 Luis Andujar **RC** .05
426 Mark Langston .05
427 Stan Belinda .05
428 Kurt Abbott .05
429 Shawon Dunston .05
430 Bobby Jones .05
431 Jose Vizcaino .05
432 Matt Lawton **RC** .05
433 Pat Hentgen .05
434 Cecil Fielder .05
435 Carlos Baerga .05
436 Rich Becker .05
437 Chipper Jones 1.25

438	Bill Risley	.05
439	Kevin Appier	.05
440	Checklist	.05
441	Jaime Navarro	.05
442	Barry Larkin	.05
443	Jose Valentin **RC**	.05
444	Bryan Rekar	.05
445	Rick Wilkins	.05
446	Quilvio Veras	.05
447	Greg Gagne	.05
448	Mark Kiefer	.05
449	Bobby Witt	.05
450	Andy Ashby	.05
451	Alex Ochoa	.05
452	Jorge Fabregas	.05
453	Gene Schall	.05
454	Ken Hill	.05
455	Tony Tarasco	.05
456	Donnie Wall	.05
457	Carlos Garcia	.05
458	Ryan Thompson	.05
459	Marvin Benard **RC**	.05
460	Jose Herrera	.05
461	Jeff Blauser	.05
462	Chris Hook	.05
463	Jeff Conine	.05
464	Devon White	.05
465	Danny Bautista	.05
466	Steve Trachsel	.05
467	C.J. Nitkowski	.05
468	Mike Devereaux	.05
469	David Wells	.05
470	Jim Eisenreich	.05
471	Edgar Martinez	.05
472	Craig Biggio	.05
473	Jeff Frye	.05
474	Karim Garcia	.05
475	Jimmy Haynes	.05
476	Darren Holmes	.05
477	Tim Salmon	.05
478	Randy Johnson	1.00
479	Eric Plunk	.05
480	Scott Cooper	.05
481	Chan Ho Park	.05
482	Ray McDavid	.05
483	Mark Petkovsek	.05
484	Greg Swindell	.05
485	George Williams	.05
486	Yamil Benitez	.05
487	Tim Wakefield	.05
488	Kevin Tapani	.05
489	Derrick May	.05
490	Checklist (Ken Griffey Jr.)	1.00
491	Derek Jeter	2.50
492	Jeff Fassero	.05
493	Benito Santiago	.05
494	Tom Gordon	.05
495	Jamie Brewington	.05
496	Vince Coleman	.05
497	Kevin Jordan	.05
498	Jeff King	.05
499	Mike Simms	.05
500	Jose Rijo	.05
501	Denny Neagle	.05
502	Jose Lima	.05
503	Kevin Seitzer	.05
504	Alex Fernandez	.05
505	Mo Vaughn	.05
506	Phil Nevin	.05
507	J.T. Snow	.05
508	Andujar Cedeno	.05
509	Ozzie Guillen	.05
510	Mark Clark	.05
511	Mark McGwire	2.00
512	Jeff Reboulet	.05
513	Armando Benitez	.05
514	LaTroy Hawkins	.05
515	Brett Butler	.05
516	Tavo Alvarez	.05
517	Chris Snopek	.05
518	Mike Mussina	.50
519	Darryl Kile	.05
520	Wally Joyner	.05
521	Willie McGee	.05
522	Kent Mercker	.05
523	Mike Jackson	.05
524	Troy Percival	.05
525	Tony Gwynn	1.25
526	Ron Coomer	.05
527	Darryl Hamilton	.05
528	Phil Plantier	.05
529	Norm Charlton	.05
530	Craig Paquette	.05
531	Dave Burba	.05
532	Mike Henneman	.05
533	Terrell Wade	.05
534	Eddie Williams	.05
535	Robin Ventura	.05
536	Chuck Knoblauch	.05
537	Les Norman	.05
538	Brady Anderson	.05
539	Roger Clemens	1.50
540	Mark Portugal	.05
541	Mike Matheny	.05
542	Jeff Parrett	.05
543	Roberto Kelly	.05
544	Damon Buford	.05
545	Chad Ogea	.05
546	Jose Offerman	.05
547	Brian Barber	.05
548	Danny Tartabull	.05
549	Duane Singleton	.05
550	Checklist (Tony Gwynn)	.75

Press Proofs

The first 2,000 of each regular card issued in the 1996 Donruss set are distinguished by the addition of a gold-foil "PRESS PROOF" stamped along the right side. As opposed to regular-issue cards which have silver-and-black card numbers and personal data strip at bottom, the Press Proof cards have those elements printed in black-on-gold. Stated odds of finding a Press Proof are one per 12 packs in Series 1, one per 10 packs in Series 2, on average.

	NM/M
Complete Set (550):	150.00
Common Player:	.50

Diamond Kings

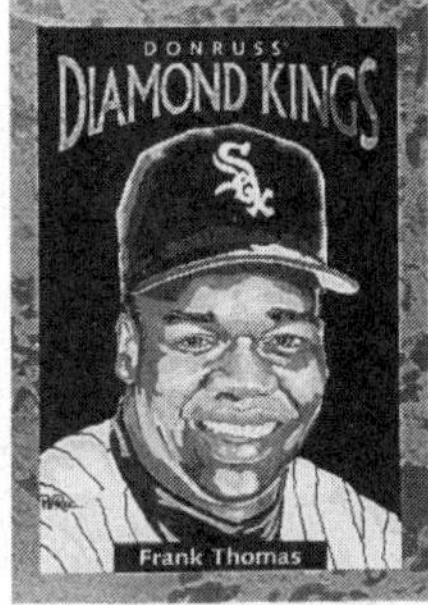

The most "common" of the '96 Donruss inserts are the popular Diamond Kings, featuring the portraits of Dick Perez on a black background within a mottled gold-foil frame. Once again, the DKs feature one player from each team, with 14 issued in each of Series 1 and 2. Like all '96 Donruss inserts, the DKs are numbered on back, within an edition of 10,000. Also on back are color action photos and career highlights. Diamond Kings are inserted at the rate of one per 60 foil packs (Series 1), and one per 30 packs (Series 2), on average.

		NM/M
Complete Set (31):		160.00
Common Player:		2.25
1	Frank Thomas	7.50
2	Mo Vaughn	2.50
3	Manny Ramirez	7.50
4	Mark McGwire	13.50
5	Juan Gonzalez	4.00
6	Roberto Alomar	3.00
7	Tim Salmon	2.50
8	Barry Bonds	15.00
9	Tony Gwynn	10.00
10	Reggie Sanders	2.50
11	Larry Walker	2.50
12	Pedro Martinez	7.50
13	Jeff King	2.50
14	Mark Grace	2.50
15	Greg Maddux	10.00
16	Don Mattingly	12.50
17	Gregg Jefferies	2.50
18	Chad Curtis	2.50
19	Jason Isringhausen	2.50
20	B.J. Surhoff	2.50
21	Jeff Conine	2.50
22	Kirby Puckett	10.00
23	Derek Bell	2.50
24	Wally Joyner	2.50
25	Brian Jordan	2.50
26	Edgar Martinez	2.50
27	Hideo Nomo	4.00
28	Mike Mussina	5.00
29	Eddie Murray	7.50
30	Cal Ripken Jr.	15.00
31	Checklist	.25

Elite

The Elite series continued as a Donruss insert in 1996, and they are the elite of the chase cards, being found on average only once per 140 packs (Series 1) or once per 75 packs (Series 2). The '96 Elite cards have a classic look bespeaking value. Player action photos at top center are framed in mottled silver foil and bordered in bright silver. Backs have another action photo, a few words about the player and a serial number from within an edition of 10,000 cards each. As usual, card numbering continues from the previous year.

		NM/M
Complete Set (12):		55.00
Complete Series 1 (61-66):		25.00
Complete Series 2 (67-72):		30.00
Common Player Series 1:		2.50
Common Player Series 2:		2.00
61	Cal Ripken Jr.	12.00
62	Hideo Nomo	3.00
63	Reggie Sanders	2.00
64	Mo Vaughn	2.00
65	Tim Salmon	2.50
66	Chipper Jones	8.00
67	Manny Ramirez	6.00
68	Greg Maddux	10.00
69	Frank Thomas	6.00
70	Ken Griffey Jr.	10.00
71	Dante Bichette	2.00
72	Tony Gwynn	8.00

Freeze Frame

One of two insert sets exclusive to Series 2 Donruss is the Freeze Frame issue. Printed on heavy, round-cornered cardboard stock, the inserts feature multiple photos of the player on both front and back. Fronts combine matte and glossy finish plus a gold-foil Donruss logo. Backs are conventionally printed, include 1995 season highlights and a serial number from within the edition of 5,000. Stated odds of pulling a Freeze Frame insert are one per 60 packs.

		NM/M
Complete Set (8):		16.00
Common Player:		1.00
1	Frank Thomas	2.00
2	Ken Griffey Jr.	3.00
3	Cal Ripken Jr.	4.00
4	Hideo Nomo	1.50
5	Greg Maddux	2.50
6	Albert Belle	1.00
7	Chipper Jones	2.50
8	Mike Piazza	3.00

Hit List

Printed on metallic foil with gold-foil graphic highlights, players who hit for high average with power or who collected milestone hits are featured in this insert set. Eight inserts were included in each of Series 1 and 2. Backs have a color action photo, a description of the player's batting prowess and a serial number from an edition of 10,000 cards each. Hit List inserts are found at an average rate of once per 106 foil packs in Series 1 and once per 60 packs in Series 2.

		NM/M
Complete Set (16):		30.00
Common Player:		.60
1	Tony Gwynn	3.00
2	Ken Griffey Jr.	5.00
3	Will Clark	.60
4	Mike Piazza	5.00
5	Carlos Baerga	.60
6	Mo Vaughn	.60
7	Mark Grace	.60
8	Kirby Puckett	3.00
9	Frank Thomas	2.00
10	Barry Bonds	6.00
11	Jeff Bagwell	2.00
12	Edgar Martinez	.60
13	Tim Salmon	.60
14	Wade Boggs	3.00
15	Don Mattingly	4.00
16	Eddie Murray	2.00

Long Ball Leaders

Once again the previous season's longest home runs are recalled in this retail-only insert set, found at an average rate of once per 96 packs in Series 1 only. Fronts are bordered and trimmed in bright silver foil and feature the player in his home run stroke against a black background. The date, location and distance of his tape-measure shot are in an arc across the card front. Backs feature another batting action photo, further details of the home run and a serial number within an edition of 5,000.

		NM/M
Complete Set (8):		45.00
Common Player:		1.50
1	Barry Bonds	15.00
2	Ryan Klesko	1.50
3	Mark McGwire	15.00
4	Raul Mondesi	1.50
5	Cecil Fielder	1.50
6	Ken Griffey Jr.	12.00
7	Larry Walker	1.50
8	Frank Thomas	6.00

Power Alley

Among the most visually dazzling of 1996's inserts is this hobby-only chase set featuring baseball's top sluggers. Action batting photos are found within several layers of prismatic foil in geometric patterns on front. Backs are horizontally formatted, feature portrait photos at left and power stats at right and bottom. In the lower-left corner is an individual serial number from within an edition of 5,000 cards each. The first 500 of each player's cards are specially die-cut at left- and right-center. Found only in Series 1 hobby foil packs, Power Alley inserts are a one per 92 pack pick.

		NM/M
Complete Set (10):		30.00
Common Player		2.00
Die-cuts		2X
1	Frank Thomas	4.00
2	Barry Bonds	7.50
3	Reggie Sanders	2.00
4	Albert Belle	2.00
5	Tim Salmon	2.00
6	Dante Bichette	2.00
7	Mo Vaughn	2.00
8	Jim Edmonds	2.00
9	Manny Ramirez	4.00
10	Ken Griffey Jr.	6.00

Pure Power

These cards were random inserts found only in Series 2 retail packs. Fronts are printed on foil backgrounds and at bottom have a die-cut hole giving the impression a baseball has been batted through the card. On back the inserts are individually serial numbered within an edition of 5,000.

		NM/M
Complete Set (8):		25.00
Common Player:		2.25
1	Raul Mondesi	2.25
2	Barry Bonds	10.00
3	Albert Belle	2.25
4	Frank Thomas	4.50
5	Mike Piazza	7.50
6	Dante Bichette	2.25
7	Manny Ramirez	4.50
8	Mo Vaughn	2.25

Round Trippers

An embossed white home plate design bearing the player's 1995 dinger output is featured on this Series 2 insert set. The entire background has been rendered in gold-flecked sepia tones. Typography on front is in bronze foil. Backs repeat the sepia background photo and include a month-by-month bar graph of the player's 1995 and career homers. Within the white home plate frame is the card's unique serial number from within an edition of 5,000. Odds of finding a Round Trippers card are stated at one per 55 packs, in hobby packs only.

		NM/M
Complete Set (10):		35.00
Common Player:		2.50
1	Albert Belle	2.50
2	Barry Bonds	7.50
3	Jeff Bagwell	4.00
4	Tim Salmon	2.50
5	Mo Vaughn	2.50
6	Ken Griffey Jr.	5.00
7	Mike Piazza	5.00
8	Cal Ripken Jr.	7.50
9	Frank Thomas	4.00
9p	Frank Thomas (Promo)	2.50
10	Dante Bichette	2.50

1996 Donruss Showdown

Baseball's top hitters and pitchers are matched on a silver and black foil background in this insert set. Gold-foil graphic highlights complete the horizontal front design. Backs are printed on a black and gold background with color action photos and write-ups about each player. At top is a serial number from within an edition of 10,000 cards each. Showdown inserts are found at an average rate of one per Series 1 foil packs.

		NM/M
Complete Set (8):		22.50
Common Player:		.75
1	Frank Thomas, Hideo Nomo	3.00
2	Barry Bonds, Randy Johnson	6.00
3	Greg Maddux, Ken Griffey Jr.	5.00
4	Roger Clemens, Tony Gwynn	4.50
5	Mike Piazza, Mike Mussina	5.00
6	Cal Ripken Jr., Pedro Martinez	6.00
7	Tim Wakefield, Matt Williams	.75
8	Manny Ramirez, Carlos Perez	2.50

1997 Donruss

Donruss' 1997 Series 1 features 270 base cards with a full-bleed color action photo on the front. Horizontal backs have a photo, career statistics, a brief player profile and biographical tidbits. A Press Proofs parallel was made of the base cards in an edition of 2,000 each. Other Series 1 inserts include the annual Diamond Kings, Elites, Armed and Dangerous cards, Longball Leaders and Rocket Launchers. A 180-card Update set was released later as a follow-up to the regular '97 Donruss series. The Updates are numbered contiguously, #271-450, from the first series. Press Proofs and Gold Press Proof parallel inserts were available; other Update inserts include Dominators, Franchise Futures, Power Alley, Rookie Diamond Kings and a special Cal Ripken Jr. set.

NM/M
Complete Set (450): 20.00
Series 1 Set (270): 10.00
Update Set (180): 10.00
Common Player: .05
Common Press Proof: .50
Press Proof Stars: 5X
Common Press Proof Gold: 2.00
Press Proof Gold Stars: 10X
Wax Pack (10): 1.50
Hobby Wax Box (18): 25.00
Retail Wax Box (36): 40.00
Magazine Pack (13): 1.50
Magazine Box (24): 20.00
Update Pack (10): 1.50
Update Wax Box (24): 30.00
1 Juan Gonzalez .40
2 Jim Edmonds .05
3 Tony Gwynn 1.00
4 Andres Galarraga .05
5 Joe Carter .05
6 Raul Mondesi .05
7 Greg Maddux 1.00
8 Travis Fryman .05
9 Brian Jordan .05
10 Henry Rodriguez .05
11 Manny Ramirez .75
12 Mark McGwire 1.75
13 Marc Newfield .05
14 Craig Biggio .05
15 Sammy Sosa 1.00
16 Brady Anderson .05
17 Wade Boggs 1.00
18 Charles Johnson .05
19 Matt Williams .05
20 Denny Neagle .05
21 Ken Griffey Jr. 1.50
22 Robin Ventura .05
23 Barry Larkin .05
24 Todd Zeile .05
25 Chuck Knoblauch .05
26 Todd Hundley .05
27 Roger Clemens 1.25
28 Michael Tucker .05
29 Rondell White .05
30 Osvaldo Fernandez .05
31 Ivan Rodriguez .65
32 Alex Fernandez .05
33 Jason Isringhausen .05
34 Chipper Jones 1.00
35 Paul O'Neill .05
36 Hideo Nomo .40
37 Roberto Alomar .20
38 Derek Bell .05
39 Paul Molitor .75
40 Andy Benes .05
41 Steve Trachsel .05
42 J.T. Snow .05
43 Jason Kendall .05
44 Alex Rodriguez 1.75
45 Joey Hamilton .05
46 Carlos Delgado .50
47 Jason Giambi .50
48 Larry Walker .05
49 Derek Jeter 2.00
50 Kenny Lofton .05
51 Devon White .05
52 Matt Mieske .05
53 Melvin Nieves .05
54 Jose Canseco .40
55 Tino Martinez .05
56 Rafael Palmeiro .65
57 Edgardo Alfonzo .05
58 Jay Buhner .05
59 Shane Reynolds .05
60 Steve Finley .05
61 Bobby Higginson .05
62 Dean Palmer .05
63 Terry Pendleton .05
64 Marquis Grissom .05
65 Mike Stanley .05
66 Moises Alou .05
67 Ray Lankford .05
68 Marty Cordova .05
69 John Olerud .05
70 David Cone .05
71 Benito Santiago .05
72 Ryne Sandberg 1.00
73 Rickey Henderson .75
74 Roger Cedeno .05
75 Wilson Alvarez .05
76 Tim Salmon .05
77 Orlando Merced .05
78 Vinny Castilla .05
79 Ismael Valdes .05
80 Dante Bichette .05
81 Kevin Brown .05
82 Andy Pettitte .40
83 Scott Stahoviak .05
84 Mickey Tettleton .05
85 Jack McDowell .05
86 Tom Glavine .30
87 Gregg Jefferies .05
88 Chili Davis .05
89 Randy Johnson .75
90 John Mabry .05
91 Billy Wagner .05
92 Jeff Cirillo .05
93 Trevor Hoffman .05
94 Juan Guzman .05
95 Geronimo Berroa .05
96 Bernard Gilkey .05
97 Danny Tartabull .05
98 Johnny Damon .35
99 Charlie Hayes .05
100 Reggie Sanders .05
101 Robby Thompson .05
102 Bobby Bonilla .05
103 Reggie Jefferson .05
104 John Smoltz .05
105 Jim Thome .60
106 Ruben Rivera .05
107 Darren Oliver .05
108 Mo Vaughn .05
109 Roger Pavlik .05
110 Terry Steinbach .05
111 Jermaine Dye .05
112 Mark Grudzielanek .05
113 Rick Aguilera .05
114 Jamey Wright .05
115 Eddie Murray .75
116 Brian Hunter .05
117 Hal Morris .05
118 Tom Pagnozzi .05
119 Mike Mussina .40
120 Mark Grace .05
121 Cal Ripken Jr. 2.00
122 Tom Goodwin .05
123 Paul Sorrento .05
124 Jay Bell .05
125 Todd Hollandsworth .05
126 Edgar Martinez .05
127 George Arias .05
128 Greg Vaughn .05
129 Roberto Hernandez .05
130 Delino DeShields .05
131 Bill Pulsipher .05
132 Joey Cora .05
133 Mariano Rivera .15
134 Mike Piazza 1.50
135 Carlos Baerga .05
136 Jose Mesa .05
137 Will Clark .05
138 Frank Thomas .75
139 John Wetteland .05
140 Shawn Estes .05
141 Garret Anderson .05
142 Andre Dawson .25
143 Eddie Taubensee .05
144 Ryan Klesko .05
145 Rocky Coppinger .05
146 Jeff Bagwell .75
147 Donovan Osborne .05
148 Greg Myers .05
149 Brant Brown .05
150 Kevin Elster .05
151 Bob Wells .05
152 Wally Joyner .05
153 Rico Brogna .05
154 Dwight Gooden .05
155 Jermaine Allensworth .05
156 Ray Durham .05
157 Cecil Fielder .05
158 Ryan Hancock .05
159 Gary Sheffield .30
160 Albert Belle .05
161 Tomas Perez .05
162 David Doster .05
163 John Valentin .05
164 Danny Graves .05
165 Jose Paniagua .05
166 Brian Giles **RC** .50
167 Barry Bonds 2.00
168 Sterling Hitchcock .05
169 Bernie Williams .05
170 Fred McGriff .05
171 George Williams .05
172 Amaury Telemaco .05
173 Ken Caminiti .05
174 Ron Gant .05
175 David Justice .05
176 James Baldwin .05
177 Pat Hentgen .05
178 Ben McDonald .05
179 Tim Naehring .05
180 Jim Eisenreich .05
181 Ken Hill .05
182 Paul Wilson .05
183 Marvin Benard .05
184 Alan Benes .05
185 Ellis Burks .05
186 Scott Servais .05
187 David Segui .05
188 Scott Brosius .05
189 Jose Offerman .05
190 Eric Davis .05
191 Brett Butler .05
192 Curtis Pride .05
193 Yamil Benitez .05
194 Chan Ho Park .05
195 Bret Boone .05
196 Omar Vizquel .05
197 Orlando Miller .05
198 Ramon Martinez .05
199 Harold Baines .05
200 Eric Young .05
201 Fernando Vina .05
202 Alex Gonzalez .05
203 Fernando Valenzuela .05
204 Steve Avery .05
205 Ernie Young .05
206 Kevin Appier .05
207 Randy Myers .05
208 Jeff Suppan .05
209 James Mouton .05
210 Russ Davis .05
211 Al Martin .05
212 Troy Percival .05
213 Al Leiter .05
214 Dennis Eckersley .65
215 Mark Johnson .05
216 Eric Karros .05
217 Royce Clayton .05
218 Tony Phillips .05
219 Tim Wakefield .05
220 Alan Trammell .05
221 Eduardo Perez .05
222 Butch Huskey .05
223 Tim Belcher .05
224 Jamie Moyer .05
225 F.P. Santangelo .05
226 Rusty Greer .05
227 Jeff Brantley .05
228 Mark Langston .05
229 Ray Montgomery .05
230 Rich Becker .05
231 Ozzie Smith 1.00
232 Rey Ordonez .05
233 Ricky Otero .05
234 Mike Cameron .05
235 Mike Sweeney .05
236 Mark Lewis .05
237 Luis Gonzalez .05
238 Marcus Jensen .05
239 Ed Sprague .05
240 Jose Valentin .05
241 Jeff Frye .05
242 Charles Nagy .05
243 Carlos Garcia .05
244 Mike Hampton .05
245 B.J. Surhoff .05
246 Wilton Guerrero .05
247 Frank Rodriguez .05
248 Gary Gaetti .05
249 Lance Johnson .05
250 Darren Bragg .05
251 Darryl Hamilton .05
252 John Jaha .05
253 Craig Paquette .05
254 Jaime Navarro .05
255 Shawon Dunston .05
256 Ron Wright .05
257 Tim Belk .05
258 Jeff Darwin .05
259 Ruben Sierra .05
260 Chuck Finley .05
261 Darryl Strawberry .05
262 Shannon Stewart .05
263 Pedro Martinez .05
264 Neifi Perez .05
265 Jeff Conine .05
266 Orel Hershiser .05
267 Checklist 1-90 (Eddie Murray (500 Career HR)) .05
268 Checklist 91-180 Paul Molitor (3,000 Career Hits) .05
269 Checklist 181-270 Barry Bonds (300 Career HR) .90
270 Checklist - inserts Mark McGwire (300 Career HR) .75
271 Matt Williams .05
272 Todd Zeile .05
273 Roger Clemens 1.25
274 Michael Tucker .05
275 J.T. Snow .05
276 Kenny Lofton .05
277 Jose Canseco .40
278 Marquis Grissom .05
279 Moises Alou .05
280 Benito Santiago .05
281 Willie McGee .05
282 Chili Davis .05
283 Ron Coomer .05
284 Orlando Merced .05
285 Delino DeShields .05
286 John Wetteland .05
287 Darren Daulton .05
288 Lee Stevens .05
289 Albert Belle .05
290 Sterling Hitchcock .05
291 David Justice .05
292 Eric Davis .05
293 Brian Hunter .05
294 Darryl Hamilton .05
295 Steve Avery .05
296 Joe Vitiello .05
297 Jaime Navarro .05
298 Eddie Murray .75
299 Randy Myers .05
300 Francisco Cordova .05
301 Javier Lopez .05
302 Geronimo Berroa .05
303 Jeffrey Hammonds .05
304 Deion Sanders .05
305 Jeff Fassero .05
306 Curt Schilling .25
307 Robb Nen .05
308 Mark McLemore .05
309 Jimmy Key .05
310 Quilvio Veras .05
311 Bip Roberts .05
312 Esteban Loaiza .05
313 Andy Ashby .05
314 Sandy Alomar Jr. .05
315 Shawn Green .20
316 Luis Castillo .05
317 Benji Gil .05
318 Otis Nixon .05
319 Aaron Sele .05
320 Brad Ausmus .05
321 Troy O'Leary .05
322 Terrell Wade .05
323 Jeff King .05
324 Kevin Seitzer .05
325 Mark Wohlers .05
326 Edgar Renteria .05
327 Dan Wilson .05
328 Brian McRae .05
329 Rod Beck .05
330 Julio Franco .05
331 Dave Nilsson .05
332 Glenallen Hill .05
333 Kevin Elster .05
334 Joe Girardi .05
335 David Wells .05
336 Jeff Blauser .05
337 Darryl Kile .05
338 Jeff Kent .05
339 Jim Leyritz .05
340 Todd Stottlemyre .05
341 Tony Clark .05
342 Chris Hoiles .05
343 Mike Lieberthal .05
344 Matt Lawton .05
345 Alex Ochoa .05
346 Chris Snopek .05
347 Rudy Pemberton .05
348 Eric Owens .05
349 Joe Randa .05
350 John Olerud .05
351 Steve Karsay .05
352 Mark Whiten .05
353 Bob Abreu .10
354 Bartolo Colon .05
355 Vladimir Guerrero .75
356 Darin Erstad .30
357 Scott Rolen .60
358 Andruw Jones .75
359 Scott Spiezio .05
360 Karim Garcia .05
361 Hideki Irabu **RC** .25
362 Nomar Garciaparra 1.00
363 Dmitri Young .05
364 Bubba Trammell **RC** .25
365 Kevin Orie .05
366 Jose Rosado .05
367 Jose Guillen .05
368 Brooks Kieschnick .05
369 Pokey Reese .05
370 Glendon Rusch .05
371 Jason Dickson .05
372 Todd Walker .05
373 Justin Thompson .05
374 Todd Greene .05
375 Jeff Suppan .05
376 Trey Beamon .05
377 Damon Mashore .05
378 Wendell Magee .05
379 Shigetosi Hasegawa .05
380 Bill Mueller .05
381 Chris Widger .05
382 Tony Grafannino .05
383 Derrek Lee .50
384 Brian Moehler .05
385 Quinton McCracken .05
386 Matt Morris .05
387 Marvin Benard .05
388 Deivi Cruz **RC** .25
389 Javier Valentin **RC** .05
390 Todd Dunwoody .05
391 Derrick Gibson .05
392 Raul Casanova .05
393 George Arias .05
394 Tony Womack **RC** .25
395 Antone Williamson .05
396 Jose Cruz Jr. **RC** .50
397 Desi Relaford .05
398 Frank Thomas/HL .40
399 Ken Griffey Jr./HL .65
400 Cal Ripken Jr./HL 1.00
401 Chipper Jones/HL .50
402 Mike Piazza/HL .65
403 Gary Sheffield/HL .15
404 Alex Rodriguez/HL .75
405 Wade Boggs/HL .50
406 Juan Gonzalez/HL .20
407 Tony Gwynn/HL .50
408 Edgar Martinez/HL .05
409 Jeff Bagwell/HL .40
410 Larry Walker/HL .05
411 Kenny Lofton/HL .05
412 Manny Ramirez/HL .40
413 Mark McGwire/HL .75
414 Roberto Alomar/HL .10
415 Derek Jeter/HL 1.00
416 Brady Anderson/HL .05
417 Paul Molitor/HL .35
418 Dante Bichette/HL .05
419 Jim Edmonds/HL .05
420 Mo Vaughn/HL .05
421 Barry Bonds/HL .90
422 Rusty Greer/HL .05
423 Greg Maddux (King of the Hill) .50
424 Andy Pettitte (King of the Hill) .15
425 John Smoltz (King of the Hill) .05
426 Randy Johnson (King of the Hill) .40
427 Hideo Nomo (King of the Hill) .20
428 Roger Clemens (King of the Hill) .60
429 Tom Glavine (King of the Hill) .15
430 Pat Hentgen (King of the Hill) .05
431 Kevin Brown (King of the Hill) .05
432 Mike Mussina (King of the Hill) .20
433 Alex Fernandez (King of the Hill) .05
434 Kevin Appier (King of the Hill) .05
435 David Cone (King of the Hill) .05
436 Jeff Fassero (King of the Hill) .05
437 John Wetteland (King of the Hill) .05
438 Barry Bonds, Ivan Rodriguez/IS .90
439 Ken Griffey Jr., Andres Galarraga/IS .65
440 Fred McGriff, Rafael Palmeiro/IS .05
441 Barry Larkin, Jim Thome/IS .05
442 Sammy Sosa, Albert Belle/IS .50
443 Bernie Williams, Todd Hundley/IS .05
444 Chuck Knoblauch, Brian Jordan/IS .05
445 Mo Vaughn, Jeff Conine/IS .05
446 Ken Caminiti, Jason Giambi/IS .25
447 Raul Mondesi, Tim Salmon/IS .05
448 Checklist (Cal Ripken Jr.) .75
449 Checklist (Greg Maddux) .60
450 Checklist (Ken Griffey Jr.) .50

Press Proofs

Each of the 450 cards in the Donruss base set was also produced in a Press Proof parallel edition of 2,000 cards. Virtually identical in design to the regular cards, the Press Proofs are printed on a metallic background with silver-foil highlights. Most Press Proof backs carry the notation "1 of 2000." Stated odds of finding a press proof are one per eight packs. A special "gold" press proof chase set features cards with gold-foil highlights, die-cut at top and bottom and the note "1 of 500" on back. Gold press proofs are found on average of once per 32 packs.

NM/M
Common Player: .50
Stars/Rookies: 5X
Common Gold Player: 2.00
Gold Stars/Rookies: 10X

Armed and Dangerous

These 15 cards are numbered up to 5,000. They were inserted in 1997 Donruss Series 1 retail packs only.

NM/M
Complete Set (15): 35.00
Common Player: 1.00
1 Ken Griffey Jr. 4.00

2 Raul Mondesi 1.00
3 Chipper Jones 3.00
4 Ivan Rodriguez 1.50
5 Randy Johnson 2.00
6 Alex Rodriguez 5.00
7 Larry Walker 1.00
8 Cal Ripken Jr. 6.00
9 Kenny Lofton 1.00
10 Barry Bonds 6.00
11 Derek Jeter 6.00
12 Charles Johnson 1.00
13 Greg Maddux 3.00
14 Roberto Alomar 1.00
15 Barry Larkin 1.00

Diamond Kings

Diamond Kings for 1997 are sequentially numbered from 1 to 10,000. To celebrate 15 years of this popular insert set, Donruss offered collectors a one-of-a-kind piece of artwork if they find one of the 10 cards with the serial number 1,982 (1982 was the first year of the Diamond Kings). Those who find these cards can redeem them for an original artwork provided by artist Dan Gardiner. In addition, Donruss printed the first 500 of each card on canvas stock.

NM/M
Complete Set (10): 30.00
Common Player: 1.00
Canvas (1st 500): 2X
1 Ken Griffey Jr. 6.00
2 Cal Ripken Jr. 10.00
3 Mo Vaughn 1.00
4 Chuck Knoblauch 1.00
5 Jeff Bagwell 2.50
6 Henry Rodriguez 1.00
7 Mike Piazza 6.00
8 Ivan Rodriguez 2.50
9 Frank Thomas 3.00
10 Chipper Jones 5.00

Elite Inserts

There were 2,500 sets of these insert cards made. The cards were randomly included in 1997 Donruss Series I packs. Fronts have a white marbled border and are graphically enhanced with silver foil, including a large script "E." On back is another photo, a career summary and a serial number from within the edition limit of 2,500. A promo card version of each card also exists.

		NM/M
Complete Set (12):		100.00
Common Player:		3.00
Promos: 50 Percent		
1	Frank Thomas	7.50
2	Paul Molitor	7.50
3	Sammy Sosa	10.00
4	Barry Bonds	20.00
5	Chipper Jones	10.00
6	Alex Rodriguez	15.00
7	Ken Griffey Jr.	12.50
8	Jeff Bagwell	7.50
9	Cal Ripken Jr.	20.00
10	Mo Vaughn	3.00
11	Mike Piazza	12.50
12	Juan Gonzalez	4.50

Longball Leaders

These 1997 Donruss Series 1 inserts have an action photo printed on a metallic foil background. Printed on the gold-foil border is a gauge with the player's 1996 home run total indicated. Horizontal backs have a player photo and record of career HRs by season. Each card is serially numbered within an edition of 5,000. The set was seeded in retail packs only.

		NM/M
Complete Set (15):		20.00
Common Player:		.50
1	Frank Thomas	2.00
2	Albert Belle	.50
3	Mo Vaughn	.50
4	Brady Anderson	.50
5	Greg Vaughn	.50
6	Ken Griffey Jr.	3.00
7	Jay Buhner	.50
8	Juan Gonzalez	.75
9	Mike Piazza	3.00
10	Jeff Bagwell	2.00
11	Sammy Sosa	2.50
12	Mark McGwire	4.00
13	Cecil Fielder	.50
14	Ryan Klesko	.50
15	Jose Canseco	.85

Rated Rookies

Although numbered more like an insert set, Rated Rookies are part of the regular-issue set. Cards are numbered 1-30, with no ratio given on packs. The cards are differentiated by a large silver-foil strip on the top right side with the words Rated Rookie.

		NM/M
Complete Set (30):		10.00
Common Player:		.50
1	Jason Thompson	.50
2	LaTroy Hawkins	.50
3	Scott Rolen	1.50
4	Trey Beamon	.50
5	Kimera Bartee	.50
6	Nerio Rodriguez	.50
7	Jeff D'Amico	.50
8	Quinton McCracken	.50
9	John Wasdin	.50
10	Robin Jennings	.50
11	Steve Gibralter	.50
12	Tyler Houston	.50
13	Tony Clark	.50
14	Ugueth Urbina	.50
15	Billy McMillon	.50
16	Raul Casanova	.50
17	Brooks Kieschnick	.50
18	Luis Castillo	.50
19	Edgar Renteria	.50
20	Andruw Jones	2.00
21	Chad Mottola	.50
22	Makoto Suzuki	.50
23	Justin Thompson	.50
24	Darin Erstad	1.00
25	Todd Walker	.50
26	Todd Greene	.50
27	Vladimir Guerrero	2.00
28	Darren Dreifort	.50
29	John Burke	.50
30	Damon Mashore	.50

Jackie Robinson Rookie Reprint

In conjunction with its program of special issues and giveaways honoring the 50th anniversary of Robinson's major league debut, Donruss issued this "Commemorative Rookie Card." Printed in the same size as the 1949 Leaf Robinson, and on heavier, coarser stock than modern cards, the card carries a reprint notice and is serially numbered on back in gold foil from within an edition of 1,948.

		NM/M
79	Jackie Robinson	10.00

Jackie Robinson Sweepstakes Scratch-Off

This pack insert features inside a scratch-off contest in which genuine vintage 1948-49 Leaf Jackie Robinson cards were awarded. The 2-3/8" x 2-7/8" folder has a color photo of the Leaf Robinson rookie card on front. On back is information on ordering numbered lithographs of the Robinson card; an edition of 1,000 selling for $199 apiece, an edition of 500 autographed by his widow selling for $299 apiece.

	NM/M
Jackie Robinson	.50

Rocket Launchers

These 1997 Donruss Series 1 inserts are limited to 5,000 each. They were only included in magazine packs.

		NM/M
Complete Set (15):		25.00
Common Player:		.75
1	Frank Thomas	2.50
2	Albert Belle	.75
3	Chipper Jones	3.00
4	Mike Piazza	4.00
5	Mo Vaughn	.75
6	Juan Gonzalez	1.00
7	Fred McGriff	.75
8	Jeff Bagwell	2.50
9	Matt Williams	.75
10	Gary Sheffield	1.00
11	Barry Bonds	5.00
12	Manny Ramirez	2.00
13	Henry Rodriguez	.75
14	Jason Giambi	1.50
15	Cal Ripken Jr.	5.00

Update Dominators

This 20-card insert highlights players known for being able to "take over a game." Each card features silver-foil highlights on front and stats on back.

		NM/M
Complete Set (20):		22.50
Common Player:		.50
1	Frank Thomas	1.25
2	Ken Griffey Jr.	2.25
3	Greg Maddux	1.50
4	Cal Ripken Jr.	3.00
5	Alex Rodriguez	2.50
6	Albert Belle	.50
7	Mark McGwire	2.50
8	Juan Gonzalez	.65
9	Chipper Jones	1.50
10	Hideo Nomo	.65
11	Roger Clemens	2.00
12	John Smoltz	.50
13	Mike Piazza	2.25
14	Sammy Sosa	1.50
15	Matt Williams	.50
16	Kenny Lofton	.50
17	Barry Larkin	.50
18	Rafael Palmeiro	1.00
19	Ken Caminiti	.50
20	Gary Sheffield	.75

Update Franchise Features

This hobby-exclusive insert consists of 15 cards designed with a movie poster theme. The double-front design highlights a top veteran player on one side with an up-and-coming rookie on the other. The side featuring the veteran has the designation "Now Playing," while the rookie side carries the banner "Coming Attraction." Each card is printed on an all-foil stock and numbered to 3,000.

		NM/M
Complete Set (15):		45.00
Common Player:		2.00
1	Ken Griffey Jr., Andruw Jones	4.00
2	Frank Thomas, Darin Erstad	2.50
3	Alex Rodriguez, Nomar Garciaparra	5.00
4	Chuck Knoblauch, Wilton Guerrero	2.00
5	Juan Gonzalez, Bubba Trammell	2.00
6	Chipper Jones, Todd Walker	3.00
7	Barry Bonds, Vladimir Guerrero	6.00
8	Mark McGwire, Dmitri Young	5.00
9	Mike Piazza, Mike Sweeney	4.00
10	Mo Vaughn, Tony Clark	2.00
11	Gary Sheffield, Jose Guillen	2.00
12	Kenny Lofton, Shannon Stewart	2.00
13	Cal Ripken Jr., Scott Rolen	6.00
14	Derek Jeter, Pokey Reese	6.00
15	Tony Gwynn, Bob Abreu	3.00

Update Power Alley

This 24-card insert is fractured into three different styles: Gold, Blue and Green. Each card is micro-etched and printed on holographic foil board. All cards are sequentially numbered, with the first 250 cards in each level being die-cut. Twelve players' cards feature a green finish and are numbered to 4,000. Eight players are printed on blue cards that are numbered to 2,000. Four players are found on gold cards numbered to 1,000.

		NM/M
Complete Set (24):		100.00
Common Gold:		7.50
Common Blue:		3.00
Common Green:		1.50
Die-Cuts:		3X
1	Frank Thomas/G	7.50
2	Ken Griffey Jr./G	10.00
3	Cal Ripken Jr./G	15.00
4	Jeff Bagwell/B	5.00
5	Mike Piazza/B	7.50
6	Andruw Jones/GR	3.50
7	Alex Rodriguez/G	12.50
8	Albert Belle/GR	1.50
9	Mo Vaughn/GR	1.50
10	Chipper Jones/B	6.00
11	Juan Gonzalez/B	3.00
12	Ken Caminiti/GR	1.50
13	Manny Ramirez/GR	3.50
14	Mark McGwire/GR	6.00
15	Kenny Lofton/B	3.00
16	Barry Bonds/GR	7.50
17	Gary Sheffield/GR	1.50
18	Tony Gwynn/GR	4.50
19	Vladimir Guerrero/B	5.00
20	Ivan Rodriguez/B	3.50
21	Paul Molitor/B	5.00
22	Sammy Sosa/GR	4.50
23	Matt Williams/GR	1.50
24	Derek Jeter/GR	7.50

Update Press Proofs

This 180-card parallel set is printed on an all-foil stock with bright foil accents. Each card is numbered "1 of 2,000." Special die-cut gold versions are numbered as "1 of 500."

	NM/M
Common Player:	.50
Stars:	7X
Common Player, Gold:	2.00
Gold Stars:	15X

Update Cal Ripken

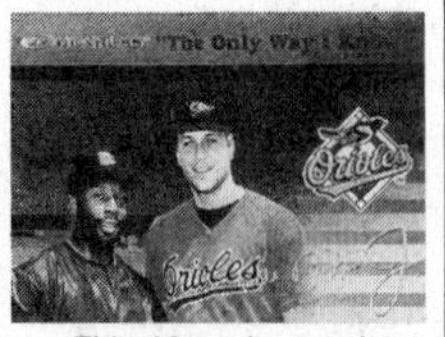

This 10-card set salutes Cal Ripken Jr. and is printed on an all-foil stock with foil highlights. Photos and text are taken from Ripken's autobiography, "The Only Way I Know." The first nine cards of the set were randomly inserted into packs. The 10th card was only available inside the book. Each card found within packs was numbered to 5,000.

		NM/M
Complete Set (10):		75.00
Common Card:		10.00
1-9	Cal Ripken Jr.	10.00
10	Cal Ripken Jr. (Book insert.)	10.00

Update Rookie Diamond Kings

This popular Donruss Update insert set features a new twist - all 10 cards feature promising rookies. Each card is sequentially numbered to 10,000, with the first 500 cards of each player printed on actual canvas.

		NM/M
Complete Set (10):		20.00
Common Player:		1.50
Canvas:		1.5X
1	Andruw Jones	4.00
2	Vladimir Guerrero	10.00
3	Scott Rolen	2.00
4	Todd Walker	1.50
5	Bartolo Colon	2.00
6	Jose Guillen	1.50
7	Nomar Garciaparra	6.00
8	Darin Erstad	2.00
9	Dmitri Young	1.50
10	Wilton Guerrero	1.50

Team Sets

A total of 163 cards were part of the Donruss Team Set issue. Packs consisted solely of players from one of 11 different teams. In addition, a full 163-card parallel set called Pennant Edition was available, featuring red and gold foil and a special "Pennant Edition" logo. Cards were sold in five-card packs for $1.99 each. The Angels and Indians set were sold only at their teams' souvenir outlets. Cards #131 Bernie Williams and #144 Russ Davis were never issued. The Team Set cards utilize team-color foil highlights and the numbers on back differ from the regular-issue version.

		NM/M
Comp. Angels Set (1-15):		1.25
Comp. Braves Set (16-30):		3.00
Comp. Orioles Set (31-45):		2.50
Comp. Red Sox Set (46-60):		1.50
Comp. White Sox Set (61-75):		2.00
Comp. Indians Set (76-90):		1.50
Comp. Rockies Set (91-105):		1.50
Comp. Dodgers Set (106-120):		2.25
Comp. Yankees Set (121-135):		4.50
Comp. Mariners Set (136-150):		4.50
Comp. Cardinals Set (151-165)		2.00
Common Player:		.05
Pennant Edition Stars:		3X
1	Jim Edmonds	.05
2	Tim Salmon	.05
3	Tony Phillips	.05
4	Garret Anderson	.05
5	Troy Percival	.05
6	Mark Langston	.05
7	Chuck Finley	.05
8	Eddie Murray	.75
9	Jim Leyritz	.05
10	Darin Erstad	.30
11	Jason Dickson	.05
12	Allen Watson	.05
13	Shigetosi Hasegawa	.05
14	Dave Hollins	.05
15	Gary DiSarcina	.05
16	Greg Maddux	1.00
17	Denny Neagle	.05
18	Chipper Jones	1.00
19	Tom Glavine	.25
20	John Smoltz	.05
21	Ryan Klesko	.05
22	Fred McGriff	.05
23	Michael Tucker	.05
24	Kenny Lofton	.05
25	Javier Lopez	.05
26	Mark Wohlers	.05
27	Jeff Blauser	.05
28	Andruw Jones	.75
29	Tony Graffanino	.05
30	Terrell Wade	.05
31	Brady Anderson	.05
32	Roberto Alomar	.15
33	Rafael Palmeiro	.65
34	Mike Mussina	.35
35	Cal Ripken Jr.	2.00
36	Rocky Coppinger	.05
37	Randy Myers	.05
38	B.J. Surhoff	.05
39	Eric Davis	.05
40	Armando Benitez	.05
41	Jeffrey Hammonds	.05
42	Jimmy Key	.05
43	Chris Hoiles	.05
44	Mike Bordick	.05
45	Pete Incaviglia	.05
46	Mike Stanley	.05
47	Reggie Jefferson	.05
48	Mo Vaughn	.05
49	John Valentin	.05
50	Tim Naehring	.05
51	Jeff Suppan	.05
52	Tim Wakefield	.05
53	Jeff Frye	.05

54 Darren Bragg .05
55 Steve Avery .05
56 Shane Mack .05
57 Aaron Sele .05
58 Troy O'Leary .05
59 Rudy Pemberton .05
60 Nomar Garciaparra 1.00
61 Robin Ventura .05
62 Wilson Alvarez .05
63 Roberto Hernandez .05
64 Frank Thomas .75
65 Ray Durham .05
66 James Baldwin .05
67 Harold Baines .05
68 Doug Drabek .05
69 Mike Cameron .05
70 Albert Belle .05
71 Jaime Navarro .05
72 Chris Snopek .05
73 Lyle Mouton .05
74 Dave Martinez .05
75 Ozzie Guillen .05
76 Manny Ramirez .75
77 Jack McDowell .05
78 Jim Thome .50
79 Jose Mesa .05
80 Brian Giles .05
81 Omar Vizquel .05
82 Charles Nagy .05
83 Orel Hershiser .05
84 Matt Williams .05
85 Marquis Grissom .05
86 David Justice .05
87 Sandy Alomar .05
88 Kevin Seitzer .05
89 Julio Franco .05
90 Bartolo Colon .05
91 Andres Galarraga .05
92 Larry Walker .05
93 Vinny Castilla .05
94 Dante Bichette .05
95 Jamey Wright .05
96 Ellis Burks .05
97 Eric Young .05
98 Neifi Perez .05
99 Quinton McCracken .05
100 Bruce Ruffin .05
101 Walt Weiss .05
102 Roger Bailey .05
103 Jeff Reed .05
104 Bill Swift .05
105 Kirt Manwaring .05
106 Raul Mondesi .05
107 Hideo Nomo .35
108 Roger Cedeno .05
109 Ismael Valdes .05
110 Todd Hollandsworth .05
111 Mike Piazza 1.50
112 Brett Butler .05
113 Chan Ho Park .05
114 Ramon Martinez .05
115 Eric Karros .05
116 Wilton Guerrero .05
117 Todd Zeile .05
118 Karim Garcia .05
119 Greg Gagne .05
120 Darren Dreifort .05
121 Wade Boggs 1.00
122 Paul O'Neill .05
123 Derek Jeter 2.00
124 Tino Martinez .05
125 David Cone .05
126 Andy Pettitte .25
127 Charlie Hayes .05
128 Mariano Rivera .15
129 Dwight Gooden .05
130 Cecil Fielder .05
132 Darryl Strawberry .05
133 Joe Girardi .05
134 David Wells .05
135 Hideki Irabu .05
136 Ken Griffey Jr. 1.25
137 Alex Rodriguez 1.50
138 Jay Buhner .05
139 Randy Johnson .75
140 Paul Sorrento .05
141 Edgar Martinez .05
142 Joey Cora .05
143 Bob Wells .05
145 Jamie Moyer .05
146 Jeff Fassero .05
147 Dan Wilson .05
148 Jose Cruz, Jr. .05
149 Scott Sanders .05
150 Rich Amaral .05
151 Brian Jordan .05
152 Andy Benes .05
153 Ray Lankford .05
154 John Mabry .05
155 Tom Pagnozzi .05
156 Ron Gant .05
157 Alan Benes .05
158 Dennis Eckersley .65
159 Royce Clayton .05
160 Todd Stottlemyre .05
161 Gary Gaetti .05
162 Willie McGee .05
163 Delino DeShields .05
164 Dmitri Young .05
165 Matt Morris .05

Team Sets MVP

The top players at each position were available in this 18-card insert set. Each card is sequentially numbered to

1,000. Fronts are printed with a textured foil background and holographic foil highlights. Backs have a portrait photo.

NM/M
Complete Set (18). 45.00
Common Player: .50
1 Ivan Rodriguez 1.50
2 Mike Piazza 5.50
3 Frank Thomas 2.50
4 Jeff Bagwell 2.50
5 Chuck Knoblauch .50
6 Eric Young .50
7 Alex Rodriguez 6.00
8 Barry Larkin .50
9 Cal Ripken Jr. 7.50
10 Chipper Jones 4.00
11 Albert Belle .50
12 Barry Bonds 7.50
13 Ken Griffey Jr. 5.50
14 Kenny Lofton .50
15 Juan Gonzalez 1.00
16 Larry Walker .50
17 Roger Clemens 5.00
18 Greg Maddux 4.00

1997 Donruss Elite

Donruss Elite Baseball is a 150-card, single-series set distributed as a hobby-only product. The regular-issue cards feature a silver border around the entire card, with a marblized frame around a color player photo at center. Backs feature a color player photo and minimal statistics and personal data. Elite was accompanied by an Elite Stars parallel set and three inserts: Leather and Lumber, Passing the Torch and Turn of the Century.

NM/M
Complete Set (150): 10.00
Common Player: .10
Common Elite Star: .50
Elite Stars Stars/RC's: 4X
Pack (6): 2.50
Wax Box (18): 35.00
1 Juan Gonzalez .40
2 Alex Rodriguez 2.00
3 Frank Thomas .75
4 Greg Maddux 1.00
5 Ken Griffey Jr. 1.50
6 Cal Ripken Jr. 2.50
7 Mike Piazza 1.50
8 Chipper Jones 1.00
9 Albert Belle .10
10 Andruw Jones .75
11 Vladimir Guerrero .75
12 Mo Vaughn .10
13 Ivan Rodriguez .65
14 Andy Pettitte .40
15 Tony Gwynn 1.00
16 Barry Bonds 2.50
17 Jeff Bagwell .75
18 Manny Ramirez .75
19 Kenny Lofton .10
20 Roberto Alomar .20
21 Mark McGwire 2.00
22 Ryan Klesko .10
23 Tim Salmon .10
24 Derek Jeter 2.50
25 Eddie Murray .75
26 Jermaine Dye .10
27 Ruben Rivera .10
28 Jim Edmonds .10
29 Mike Mussina .40
30 Randy Johnson .75
31 Sammy Sosa 1.00
32 Hideo Nomo .40
33 Chuck Knoblauch .10
34 Paul Molitor .75
35 Rafael Palmeiro .75
36 Brady Anderson .10
37 Will Clark .10
38 Craig Biggio .10
39 Jason Giambi .50
40 Roger Clemens 1.25
41 Jay Buhner .10
42 Edgar Martinez .10
43 Gary Sheffield .35
44 Fred McGriff .10
45 Bobby Bonilla .10
46 Tom Glavine .25
47 Wade Boggs 1.00
48 Jeff Conine .10
49 John Smoltz .10
50 Jim Thome .60
51 Billy Wagner .10
52 Jose Canseco .40
53 Javy Lopez .10
54 Cecil Fielder .10
55 Garret Anderson .10
56 Alex Ochoa .10
57 Scott Rolen .60
58 Darin Erstad .30
59 Rey Ordonez .10
60 Dante Bichette .10
61 Joe Carter .10
62 Moises Alou .10
63 Jason Isringhausen .10
64 Karim Garcia .10
65 Brian Jordan .10
66 Ruben Sierra .10
67 Todd Hollandsworth .10
68 Paul Wilson .10
69 Ernie Young .10
70 Ryne Sandberg 1.00
71 Raul Mondesi .10
72 George Arias .10
73 Ray Durham .10
74 Dean Palmer .10
75 Shawn Green .30
76 Eric Young .10
77 Jason Kendall .10
78 Greg Vaughn .10
79 Terrell Wade .10
80 Bill Pulsipher .10
81 Bobby Higginson .10
82 Mark Grudzielanek .10
83 Ken Caminiti .10
84 Todd Greene .10
85 Carlos Delgado .50
86 Mark Grace .10
87 Rondell White .10
88 Barry Larkin .10
89 J.T. Snow .10
90 Alex Gonzalez .10
91 Raul Casanova .10
92 Marc Newfield .10
93 Jermaine Allensworth .10
94 John Mabry .10
95 Kirby Puckett 1.00
96 Travis Fryman .10
97 Kevin Brown .15
98 Andres Galarraga .10
99 Marty Cordova .10
100 Henry Rodriguez .10
101 Sterling Hitchcock .10
102 Trey Beamon .10
103 Brett Butler .10
104 Rickey Henderson .75
105 Tino Martinez .10
106 Kevin Appier .10
107 Brian Hunter .10
108 Eric Karros .10
109 Andre Dawson .10
110 Darryl Strawberry .10
111 James Baldwin .10
112 Chad Mottola .10
113 Dave Nilsson .10
114 Carlos Baerga .10
115 Chan Ho Park .10
116 John Jaha .10
117 Alan Benes .10
118 Mariano Rivera .20
119 Ellis Burks .10
120 Tony Clark .10
121 Todd Walker .10
122 Dwight Gooden .10
123 Ugueth Urbina .10
124 David Cone .10
125 Ozzie Smith 1.00
126 Kimera Bartee .10
127 Rusty Greer .10
128 Pat Hentgen .10
129 Charles Johnson .10
130 Quinton McCracken .10
131 Troy Percival .10
132 Shane Reynolds .10
133 Charles Nagy .10
134 Tom Goodwin .10
135 Ron Gant .10
136 Dan Wilson .10
137 Matt Williams .10
138 LaTroy Hawkins .10
139 Kevin Seitzer .10
140 Michael Tucker .10
141 Todd Hundley .10
142 Alex Fernandez .10
143 Marquis Grissom .10
144 Steve Finley .10
145 Curtis Pride .10
146 Derek Bell .10
147 Butch Huskey .10
148 Dwight Gooden .10
149 Al Leiter .10
150 Hideo Nomo .40

Stars

Gold, rather than silver, foil differentiates the parallel set of Elite Stars from the regular-issue versions of each of the base cards in the Elite set. The parallels also have a small "Elite Stars" printed at top, flanking the position. Stated odds of finding a Stars insert are about one per five packs.

NM/M
Common Player: 1.00

Leather & Lumber

Leather and Lumber is a 10-card insert set filled with veterans. Genuine leather is featured on one side of the card, while wood card stock is on the other. There were 500 sequentially numbered sets produced.

NM/M
Complete Set (10): 140.00
Common Player: 4.00
1 Ken Griffey Jr. 20.00
2 Alex Rodriguez 25.00
3 Frank Thomas 9.00
4 Chipper Jones 12.50
5 Ivan Rodriguez 7.50
6 Cal Ripken Jr. 35.00
7 Barry Bonds 35.00
8 Chuck Knoblauch 4.00
9 Manny Ramirez 9.00
10 Mark McGwire 25.00

Passing the Torch

Passing the Torch is a 12-card insert limited to 1,500 individually numbered sets. It features eight different stars, each with their own cards and then featured on a double-sided card with another player from the set.

NM/M
Complete Set (12): 110.00
Common Player: 4.50
1 Cal Ripken Jr. 20.00
2 Alex Rodriguez 15.00
3 Cal Ripken Jr., Alex Rodriguez 17.50
4 Kirby Puckett 10.00
5 Andruw Jones 7.50
6 Kirby Puckett, Andruw Jones 7.50
7 Cecil Fielder 4.50
8 Frank Thomas 7.50
9 Cecil Fielder, Frank Thomas 6.00
10 Ozzie Smith 10.00
11 Derek Jeter 20.00
12 Ozzie Smith, Derek Jeter 12.00

Passing the Torch Autographs

The first 150 individually numbered sets of the Passing the Torch insert were autographed. This means that cards 3, 6, 9 and 12 are dual-autographed on their double-sided format.

NM/M
Common Card: 15.00
1 Cal Ripken Jr. 200.00
2 Alex Rodriguez 275.00
3 Cal Ripken Jr., Alex Rodriguez 750.00
4 Kirby Puckett 80.00
5 Andruw Jones 40.00
6 Kirby Puckett, Andruw Jones 140.00
7 Cecil Fielder 45.00
8 Frank Thomas 75.00
9 Cecil Fielder, Frank Thomas 125.00
10 Ozzie Smith 120.00
11 Derek Jeter 160.00
12 Ozzie Smith, Derek Jeter 325.00

Turn of the Century

Turn of the Century includes 20 potential year 2000 superstars on an insert set numbered to 3,500. The first 500 of these sets feature an external die-cut design. Cards feature the player over a framed background image on silver foil board, with black strips down each side. Backs have a color photo, a few words about the player and the serial number. Each card can also be found in an overprinted "SAMPLE" version.

NM/M
Complete Set (20): 55.00
Common Player: 1.00
Die-Cuts: 3X
Samples: 1X
1 Alex Rodriguez 10.00
2 Andruw Jones 6.00
3 Chipper Jones 7.50
4 Todd Walker 1.00
5 Scott Rolen 4.00
6 Trey Beamon 1.00
7 Derek Jeter 12.50
8 Darin Erstad 3.00
9 Tony Clark 1.00
10 Todd Greene 1.00
11 Jason Giambi 3.00
12 Justin Thompson 1.00
13 Ernie Young 1.00
14 Jason Kendall 1.00
15 Alex Ochoa 1.00
16 Brooks Kieschnick 1.00
17 Bobby Higginson 1.00
18 Ruben Rivera 1.00
19 Chan Ho Park 1.00
20 Chad Mottola 1.00

1997 Donruss Limited

Each of the 200 base cards in this set features a double-front design showcasing an action photo on each side. The set is divided into four subsets. Counterparts (100 cards) highlights two different players from the same position; Double Team (40 cards) features some of the majors' top teammate duos; Star Factor (40 cards) consists of two photos of some of the hobby's favorite players; and Unlimited Potential/Talent (20 cards) combines a top veteran with a top prospect. The issue also includes a Limited Exposure parallel set and a multi-tiered insert called Fabric of the Game. Odds of finding any insert card were 1:5 packs. Less than 1,100 base sets were available. Cards were sold in five-card packs for $4.99.

NM/M
Complete Set (200): 450.00
Common Counterpart: .20
Common Double Team: .75
Common Star Factor: 1.50
Common Unlimited Potential: 1.25
Pack (5): 2.00
Wax Box (24): 45.00
1 Ken Griffey Jr., Rondell White (Counterparts) 1.00
2 Greg Maddux, David Cone (Counterparts) .75
3 Gary Sheffield, Moises Alou/DT 1.25
4 Frank Thomas/SF 10.00
5 Cal Ripken Jr., Kevin Orie (Counterparts) 2.00
6 Vladimir Guerrero, Barry Bonds/UPT 20.00
7 Eddie Murray, Reggie Jefferson (Counterparts) .60
8 Manny Ramirez, Marquis Grissom/DT 2.50
9 Mike Piazza/SF 15.00
10 Barry Larkin, Rey Ordonez (Counterparts) .20
11 Jeff Bagwell, Eric Karros (Counterparts) .60
12 Chuck Knoblauch, Ray Durham (Counterparts) .20
13 Alex Rodriguez, Edgar Renteria (Counterparts) 1.50
14 Matt Williams, Vinny Castilla (Counterparts) .20
15 Todd Hollandsworth, Bob Abreu (Counterparts) .20

16 John Smoltz, Pedro Martinez (Counterparts) .60
17 Jose Canseco, Chili Davis (Counterparts) .40
18 Jose Cruz, Jr., Ken Griffey Jr./UPT 15.00
19 Ken Griffey Jr./SF 15.00
20 Paul Molitor, John Olerud (Counterparts) .60
21 Roberto Alomar, Luis Castillo (Counterparts) .35
22 Derek Jeter, Lou Collier (Counterparts) 2.00
23 Chipper Jones, Robin Ventura (Counterparts) .75
24 Gary Sheffield, Ron Gant (Counterparts) .25
25 Ramon Martinez, Bobby Jones (Counterparts) .20
26 Mike Piazza, Raul Mondesi/DT 7.50
27 Darin Erstad, Jeff Bagwell/UPT 7.50
28 Ivan Rodriguez/SF 7.50
29 J.T. Snow, Kevin Young (Counterparts) .20
30 Ryne Sandberg, Julio Franco (Counterparts) .75
31 Travis Fryman, Chris Snopek (Counterparts) .20
32 Wade Boggs, Russ Davis (Counterparts) .75
33 Brooks Kieschnick, Marty Cordova (Counterparts) .20
34 Andy Pettitte, Denny Neagle (Counterparts) .35
35 Paul Molitor, Matt Lawton/DT 2.50
36 Scott Rolen, Cal Ripken Jr./UPT 20.00
37 Cal Ripken Jr./SF 20.00
38 Jim Thome, Dave Nilsson (Counterparts) .50
39 Tony Womack **RC**, Carlos Baerga (Counterparts) .20
40 Nomar Garciaparra, Mark Grudzielanek (Counterparts) .75
41 Todd Greene, Chris Widger (Counterparts) .20
42 Deion Sanders, Bernard Gilkey (Counterparts) .20
43 Hideo Nomo, Charles Nagy (Counterparts) .50
44 Ivan Rodriguez, Rusty Greer/DT 2.00
45 Todd Walker, Chipper Jones/UPT 10.00
46 Greg Maddux/SF 12.00
47 Mo Vaughn, Cecil Fielder (Counterparts) .20
48 Craig Biggio, Scott Spiezio (Counterparts) .20
49 Pokey Reese, Jeff Blauser (Counterparts) .20
50 Ken Caminiti, Joe Randa (Counterparts) .20
51 Albert Belle, Shawn Green (Counterparts) .20
52 Randy Johnson, Jason Dickson (Counterparts) .60
53 Hideo Nomo, Chan Ho Park/DT 2.00
54 Scott Spiezio, Chuck Knoblauch/UPT 1.25
55 Chipper Jones/SF 12.00
56 Tino Martinez, Ryan McGuire (Counterparts) .20
57 Eric Young, Wilton Guerrero (Counterparts) .20
58 Ron Coomer, Dave Hollins (Counterparts) .20
59 Sammy Sosa, Angel Echevarria (Counterparts) .75
60 Dennis Reyes **RC**, Jimmy Key (Counterparts) .20
61 Barry Larkin, Deion Sanders/DT .75
62 Wilton Guerrero, Roberto Alomar/UPT 2.00
63 Albert Belle/SF 1.50
64 Mark McGwire, Andres Galarraga (Counterparts) 1.50
65 Edgar Martinez, Todd Walker (Counterparts) .20
66 Steve Finley, Rich Becker (Counterparts) .20
67 Tom Glavine, Andy Ashby (Counterparts) .30
68 Sammy Sosa, Ryne Sandberg/DT 5.00
69 Nomar Garciaparra, Alex Rodriguez/UPT 15.00
70 Jeff Bagwell/SF 10.00
71 Darin Erstad, Mark Grace (Counterparts) .40
72 Scott Rolen, Edgardo Alfonzo (Counterparts) .50
73 Kenny Lofton, Lance Johnson (Counterparts) .20
74 Joey Hamilton, Brett Tomko (Counterparts) .20
75 Eddie Murray, Tim Salmon/DT 2.50
76 Dmitri Young, Mo Vaughn/UPT 1.25
77 Juan Gonzalez/SF 3.00
78 Frank Thomas, Tony Clark (Counterparts) .60
79 Shannon Stewart, Bip Roberts (Counterparts) .20
80 Shawn Estes, Alex Fernandez (Counterparts) .20
81 John Smoltz, Javier Lopez/DT .75
82 Todd Greene, Mike Piazza/UPT 15.00
83 Derek Jeter/SF 20.00
84 Dmitri Young, Antone Williamson (Counterparts) .20
85 Rickey Henderson, Darryl Hamilton (Counterparts) .60
86 Billy Wagner, Dennis Eckersley (Counterparts) .60
87 Larry Walker, Eric Young/DT .75
88 Mark Kotsay, Juan Gonzalez/UPT 3.00
89 Barry Bonds/SF 20.00
90 Will Clark, Jeff Conine (Counterparts) .20
91 Tony Gwynn, Brett Butler (Counterparts) .75
92 John Wetteland, Rod Beck (Counterparts) .20
93 Bernie Williams, Tino Martinez/DT 1.25
94 Andruw Jones, Kenny Lofton/UPT 7.50
95 Mo Vaughn/SF 1.50
96 Joe Carter, Derrek Lee (Counterparts) .50
97 John Mabry, F.P. Santangelo (Counterparts) .20
98 Esteban Loaiza, Wilson Alvarez (Counterparts) .20
99 Matt Williams, David Justice/DT .75
100 Derrek Lee, Frank Thomas/UPT 7.50
101 Mark McGwire/SF 17.50
102 Fred McGriff, Paul Sorrento (Counterparts) .20
103 Jermaine Allensworth, Bernie Williams (Counterparts) .20
104 Ismael Valdes, Chris Holt (Counterparts) .20
105 Fred McGriff, Ryan Klesko/DT .75
106 Tony Clark, Mark McGwire/UPT 17.50
107 Tony Gwynn/SF 12.00
108 Jeffrey Hammonds, Ellis Burks (Counterparts) .20
109 Shane Reynolds, Andy Benes (Counterparts) .20
110 Roger Clemens, Carlos Delgado/DT 10.00
111 Karim Garcia, Albert Belle/UPT 1.25
112 Paul Molitor/SF 10.00
113 Trey Beamon, Eric Owens (Counterparts) .20
114 Curt Schilling, Darryl Kile (Counterparts) .30
115 Tom Glavine, Michael Tucker/DT .75
116 Pokey Reese, Derek Jeter/UPT 20.00
117 Manny Ramirez/SF 10.00
118 Juan Gonzalez, Brant Brown (Counterparts) .40
119 Juan Guzman, Francisco Cordova (Counterparts) .20
120 Randy Johnson, Edgar Martinez/DT 2.50
121 Hideki Irabu, Greg Maddux/UPT 10.00
122 Alex Rodriguez/SF 17.50
123 Barry Bonds, Quinton McCracken (Counterparts) 2.00
124 Roger Clemens, Alan Benes (Counterparts) .85
125 Wade Boggs, Paul O'Neill/DT 1.75
126 Mike Cameron, Larry Walker/UPT 1.25
127 Gary Sheffield/SF 2.50
128 Andruw Jones, Raul Mondesi (Counterparts) .60
129 Brian Anderson, Terrell Wade (Counterparts) .20
130 Brady Anderson, Rafael Palmeiro/DT 2.00
131 Neifi Perez, Barry Larkin/UPT 1.25
132 Ken Caminiti/SF 1.50
133 Larry Walker, Rusty Greer (Counterparts) .20
134 Mariano Rivera, Mark Wohlers (Counterparts) .30
135 Hideki Irabu, Andy Pettitte/DT 1.50
136 Jose Guillen, Tony Gwynn/UPT 10.00
137 Hideo Nomo/SF 3.00
138 Vladimir Guerrero, Jim Edmonds (Counterparts) .60
139 Justin Thompson, Dwight Gooden (Counterparts) .20
140 Andres Galarraga, Dante Bichette/DT .75
141 Kenny Lofton/SF 1.50
142 Tim Salmon, Manny Ramirez (Counterparts) .60
143 Kevin Brown, Matt Morris (Counterparts) .20
144 Craig Biggio, Bob Abreu/DT .75
145 Roberto Alomar/SF 2.00
146 Jose Guillen, Brian Jordan (Counterparts) .20
147 Bartolo Colon, Kevin Appier (Counterparts) .20
148 Ray Lankford, Brian Jordan/DT .75
149 Chuck Knoblauch/SF 1.50
150 Henry Rodriguez, Ray Lankford (Counterparts) .20
151 Jaret Wright **RC**, Ben McDonald (Counterparts) .20
152 Bobby Bonilla, Kevin Brown/DT .75
153 Barry Larkin/SF 1.50
154 David Justice, Reggie Sanders (Counterparts) .20
155 Mike Mussina, Ken Hill (Counterparts) .40
156 Mark Grace, Brooks Kieschnick/DT .75
157 Jim Thome/SF 2.50
158 Michael Tucker, Curtis Goodwin (Counterparts) .20
159 Jeff Suppan, Jeff Fassero (Counterparts) .20
160 Mike Mussina, Jeffrey Hammonds/DT1.00
161 John Smoltz/SF 1.50
162 Moises Alou, Eric Davis (Counterparts) .20
163 Sandy Alomar Jr., Dan Wilson (Counterparts) .20
164 Rondell White, Henry Rodriguez/DT .75
165 Roger Clemens/SF 12.50
166 Brady Anderson, Al Martin (Counterparts) .20
167 Jason Kendall, Charles Johnson (Counterparts) .20
168 Jason Giambi, Jose Canseco/DT 2.00
169 Larry Walker/SF 1.50
170 Jay Buhner, Geronimo Berroa (Counterparts) .20
171 Ivan Rodriguez, Mike Sweeney (Counterparts) .50
172 Kevin Appier, Jose Rosado/DT .75
173 Bernie Williams/SF 1.50
174 Todd Dunwoody, Brian Giles **RC** (Counterparts) .40
175 Javier Lopez, Scott Hatteberg (Counterparts) .20
176 John Jaha, Jeff Cirillo/DT .75
177 Andy Pettitte/SF 2.00
178 Dante Bichette, Butch Huskey (Counterparts) .20
179 Raul Casanova, Todd Hundley (Counterparts) .20
180 Jim Edmonds, Garret Anderson/DT .75
181 Deion Sanders/SF 1.50
182 Ryan Klesko, Paul O'Neill (Counterparts) .20
183 Joe Carter, Pat Hentgen/DT .75
184 Brady Anderson/SF 1.50
185 Carlos Delgado, Wally Joyner (Counterparts) .50
186 Jermaine Dye, Johnny Damon/DT 1.00
187 Randy Johnson/SF 7.50
188 Todd Hundley, Carlos Baerga/DT .75
189 Tom Glavine/SF 2.50
190 Damon Mashore, Jason McDonald/DT .75
191 Wade Boggs/SF 12.00
192 Al Martin, Jason Kendall/DT .75
193 Matt Williams/SF 1.50
194 Will Clark, Dean Palmer/DT .75
195 Sammy Sosa/SF 12.00
196 Jose Cruz, Jr., Jay Buhner/DT .75
197 Eddie Murray/SF 10.00
198 Darin Erstad, Jason Dickson/DT 1.00
199 Fred McGriff/SF 1.50
200 Bubba Trammell, Bobby Higginson/DT .75

Exposure

A complete 200-card parallel set printed with Holographic Poly-Chromium technology on both sides and featuring a special "Limited Exposure" stamp. Less than 40 sets of the Star Factor Limited Exposures are thought to exist.

	NM/M
Common Counterparts:	.75
Common Double Team:	3.00
Common Star Factor:	6.50
Common Unlimited:	4.50
Stars:	4X

Exposure Non-Glossy

In error, half (100 cards) of the Limited Exposure parallels were produced in regular technology (non-chrome) on regular (non-glossy) cardboard stock. These cards do carry the Limited Exposure identification in the card-number box on back, but do not carry the correct cards' higher values. No checklist of which 100 cards were involved in the error is available.

	NM/M
Common Non-Glossy:	.50
Stars: 25 Percent	

Fabric of the Game

This fractured insert set consists of 69 different cards highlighting three different technologies representing three statistical categories: Canvas (stolen bases), Leather (doubles) and Wood (home runs). Each of the 23 cards in each category are found in varying levels of scarcity: Legendary Material (one card per theme; numbered to 100), Hall of Fame Material (four cards numbered to 250), Superstar Material (five cards numbered to 500), Star Material (six cards numbered to 750), and Major League Material (seven cards numbered to 1,000).

	NM/M
Complete Set: (69):	275.00
Common Player:	1.50
Complete Canvas Set (23):	80.00
Rickey Henderson/100	12.00
Barry Bonds/250	15.00
Kenny Lofton/250	2.50
Roberto Alomar/250	4.50
Ryne Sandberg/250	12.00
Tony Gwynn/500	7.50
Barry Larkin/500	2.00
Brady Anderson/500	2.00
Chuck Knoblauch/500	2.00
Craig Biggio/500	2.00
Sammy Sosa/750	7.50
Gary Sheffield/750	2.00
Eric Young/750	1.50
Larry Walker/750	1.50
Ken Griffey Jr./750	10.00
Deion Sanders/750	1.50
Raul Mondesi/1,000	1.50
Rondell White/1,000	1.50
Derek Jeter/1,000	10.00
Nomar Garciaparra/1,000	6.00
Wilton Guerrero/1,000	1.50
Pokey Reese/1,000	1.50
Darin Erstad/1,000	2.00
Complete Leather Set (23):	90.00
Paul Molitor/100	15.00
Wade Boggs/250	12.00
Cal Ripken Jr./250	20.00
Tony Gwynn/250	12.00
Joe Carter/250	2.50
Rafael Palmeiro/500	5.00
Mark Grace/500	1.50
Bobby Bonilla/500	1.50
Andres Galarraga/500	1.50
Edgar Martinez/500	1.50
Ken Caminiti/750	1.50
Ivan Rodriguez/750	4.50
Frank Thomas/750	6.00
Jeff Bagwell/750	6.00
Albert Belle/750	1.50
Bernie Williams/750	1.50
Chipper Jones/1,000	7.50
Rusty Greer/1,000	1.50
Todd Walker/1,000	1.50
Scott Rolen/1,000	3.00
Bob Abreu/1,000	1.50
Jose Guillen/1,000	1.50
Jose Cruz, Jr./1,000	1.50
Complete Wood Set (23):	110.00
Eddie Murray/100	12.00
Cal Ripken Jr./250	20.00
Barry Bonds/250	20.00
Mark McGwire/250	17.50
Fred McGriff/250	3.50
Ken Griffey Jr./500	7.50
Albert Belle/500	2.00
Frank Thomas/500	6.50
Juan Gonzalez/500	5.00
Matt Williams/500	2.00
Mike Piazza/750	7.50
Jeff Bagwell/750	6.00
Mo Vaughn/750	1.50
Gary Sheffield/750	2.00
Tim Salmon/750	1.50
David Justice/750	1.50
Manny Ramirez/1,000	5.00
Jim Thome/1,000	2.50
Tino Martinez/1,000	1.50
Andruw Jones/1,000	3.50
Vladimir Guerrero/1,000	5.00
Tony Clark/1,000	1.50
Dmitri Young/1,000	1.50

1997 Donruss Preferred

Each of the 200 base cards is printed on all-foil micro-etched stock. Conventional backs have a color player photo and a few stats. The set is fractured into four increasingly scarce levels: 100 Bronze cards, 70 Silver, 20 Gold and 10 Platinum. Instead of traditional packs, cards were sold in five-card collectible tins. Four different inserts were included with the product: Staremaster, X-Ponential Power, Cut To The Chase (a die-cut parallel) and Precious Metals. Odds of finding any insert were 1:4 packs.

		NM/M
Complete Set (200):		225.00
Common Bronze:		.10
Common Silver:		.60
Common Gold:		1.25
Common Platinum:		6.00
Cut to the Chase:		1.5X
Tin Pack (5):		2.50
Tin Box (24):		40.00
1	Frank Thomas/P	7.50
2	Ken Griffey Jr./P	12.50
3	Cecil Fielder/B	.10
4	Chuck Knoblauch/G	1.25
5	Garret Anderson/B	.10
6	Greg Maddux/P	10.00
7	Matt Williams/S	.60
8	Marquis Grissom/S	.60
9	Jason Isringhausen/B	.10
10	Larry Walker/S	.60
11	Charles Nagy/B	.10
12	Dan Wilson/B	.10
13	Albert Belle/G	1.25
14	Javier Lopez/B	.10
15	David Cone/B	.10
16	Bernard Gilkey/B	.10
17	Andres Galarraga/S	.60
18	Bill Pulsipher/B	.10
19	Alex Fernandez/B	.10
20	Andy Pettitte/S	1.25
21	Mark Grudzielanek/B	.10
22	Juan Gonzalez/P	6.00
23	Reggie Sanders/B	.10
24	Kenny Lofton/G	1.25
25	Andy Ashby/B	.10
26	John Wetteland/B	.10
27	Bobby Bonilla/B	.10
28	Hideo Nomo/G	2.50
29	Joe Carter/B	.10
30	Jose Canseco/B	.40
31	Ellis Burks/B	.10
32	Edgar Martinez/S	.60
33	Chan Ho Park/B	.10
34	David Justice/B	.10
35	Carlos Delgado/B	.50
36	Jeff Cirillo/S	.60
37	Charles Johnson/B	.10
38	Manny Ramirez/G	4.50
39	Greg Vaughn/B	.10
40	Henry Rodriguez/B	.10
41	Darryl Strawberry/B	.10
42	Jim Thome/G	2.50
43	Ryan Klesko/S	.60
44	Jermaine Allensworth/B	.10
45	Brian Jordan/G	1.25
46	Tony Gwynn/P	10.00
47	Rafael Palmeiro/G	3.50
48	Dante Bichette/S	.60
49	Ivan Rodriguez/G	3.50
50	Mark McGwire/G	8.00
51	Tim Salmon/S	.60
52	Roger Clemens/B	1.50
53	Matt Lawton/B	.10
54	Wade Boggs/S	3.50
55	Travis Fryman/B	.10
56	Bobby Higginson/S	.60
57	John Jaha/S	.60
58	Rondell White/S	.60
59	Tom Glavine/S	1.25
60	Eddie Murray/S	2.50
61	Vinny Castilla/B	.10
62	Todd Hundley/B	.10
63	Jay Buhner/S	.60
64	Paul O'Neill/B	.10
65	Steve Finley/B	.10
66	Kevin Appier/B	.10
67	Ray Durham/B	.10
68	Dave Nilsson/B	.10
69	Jeff Bagwell/G	4.50
70	Al Martin/S	.60
71	Paul Molitor/G	4.50
72	Kevin Brown/S	.60
73	Ron Gant/B	.10
74	Dwight Gooden/B	.10
75	Quinton McCracken/B	.10
76	Rusty Greer/S	.60
77	Juan Guzman/B	.10
78	Fred McGriff/S	.60
79	Tino Martinez/B	.10
80	Ray Lankford/B	.10
81	Ken Caminiti/G	1.25
82	James Baldwin/B	.10
83	Jermaine Dye/G	1.25
84	Mark Grace/S	.60
85	Pat Hentgen/S	.60
86	Jason Giambi/S	1.50
87	Brian Hunter/B	.10
88	Andy Benes/B	.10

89	Jose Rosado/B	.10
90	Shawn Green/B	.25
91	Jason Kendall/B	.10
92	Alex Rodriguez/P	15.00
93	Chipper Jones/P	10.00
94	Barry Bonds/G	10.00
95	Brady Anderson/G	1.25
96	Ryne Sandberg/S	3.50
97	Lance Johnson/B	.10
98	Cal Ripken Jr./P	17.50
99	Craig Biggio/S	.60
100	Dean Palmer/B	.10
101	Gary Sheffield/G	1.50
102	Johnny Damon/B	.35
103	Mo Vaughn/G	1.25
104	Randy Johnson/S	2.50
105	Raul Mondesi/S	.60
106	Roberto Alomar/G	2.00
107	Mike Piazza/P	12.50
108	Rey Ordonez/B	.10
109	Barry Larkin/G	1.25
110	Tony Clark/S	.60
111	Bernie Williams/S	.60
112	John Smoltz/G	1.25
113	Moises Alou/B	.10
114	Will Clark/B	.10
115	Sammy Sosa/G	6.00
116	Jim Edmonds/S	.60
117	Jeff Conine/B	.10
118	Joey Hamilton/B	.10
119	Todd Hollandsworth/B	.10
120	Troy Percival/B	.10
121	Paul Wilson/B	.10
122	Ken Hill/B	.10
123	Mariano Rivera/S	.75
124	Eric Karros/B	.10
125	Derek Jeter/G	10.00
126	Eric Young/S	.60
127	John Mabry/B	.10
128	Gregg Jefferies/B	.10
129	Ismael Valdes/S	.60
130	Marty Cordova/B	.10
131	Omar Vizquel/B	.10
132	Mike Mussina/S	1.25
133	Darin Erstad/B	.30
134	Edgar Renteria/S	.60
135	Billy Wagner/B	.10
136	Alex Ochoa/B	.10
137	Luis Castillo/B	.10
138	Rocky Coppinger/B	.10
139	Mike Sweeney/B	.10
140	Michael Tucker/B	.10
141	Chris Snopek/B	.10
142	Dmitri Young/S	.60
143	Andruw Jones/P	7.50
144	Mike Cameron/S	.60
145	Brant Brown/B	.10
146	Todd Walker/G	1.25
147	Nomar Garciaparra/G	6.00
148	Glendon Rusch/B	.10
149	Karim Garcia/S	.60
150	Bubba Trammell/S **RC**	.60
151	Todd Greene/B	.10
152	Wilton Guerrero/G	1.25
153	Scott Spiezio/B	.10
154	Brooks Kieschnick/B	.10
155	Vladimir Guerrero/G	4.50
156	Brian Giles/S **RC**	1.50
157	Pokey Reese/B	.10
158	Jason Dickson/G	1.25
159	Kevin Orie/S	.60
160	Scott Rolen/G	3.00
161	Bartolo Colon/S	.60
162	Shannon Stewart/G	1.25
163	Wendell Magee/B	.10
164	Jose Guillen/S	.60
165	Bob Abreu/S	.60
166	Deivi Cruz/B **RC**	.25
167	Alex Rodriguez/B (National Treasures)	3.00
168	Frank Thomas/B (National Treasures)	.75
169	Cal Ripken Jr./B (National Treasures)	4.00
170	Chipper Jones/B (National Treasures)	1.25
171	Mike Piazza/B (National Treasures)	2.50
172	Tony Gwynn/S (National Treasures)	3.50
173	Juan Gonzalez/B (National Treasures)	.40
174	Kenny Lofton/S (National Treasures)	.60
175	Ken Griffey Jr./B (National Treasures)	2.50
176	Mark McGwire/B (National Treasures)	3.00
177	Jeff Bagwell/B (National Treasures)	.75
178	Paul Molitor/S (National Treasures)	2.50
179	Andruw Jones/B (National Treasures)	.75
180	Manny Ramirez/S (National Treasures)	2.50
181	Ken Caminiti/S (National Treasures)	.60
182	Barry Bonds/B (National Treasures)	4.00
183	Mo Vaughn/B (National Treasures)	.10
184	Derek Jeter/B (National Treasures)	4.00
185	Barry Larkin/S (National Treasures)	.60
186	Ivan Rodriguez/B (National Treasures)	.65
187	Albert Belle/S (National Treasures)	.60
188	John Smoltz/S (National Treasures)	.60
189	Chuck Knoblauch/S (National Treasures)	.60
190	Brian Jordan/S (National Treasures)	.60
191	Gary Sheffield/S (National Treasures)	1.00
192	Jim Thome/S (National Treasures)	2.00
193	Brady Anderson/S (National Treasures)	.60
194	Hideo Nomo/S (National Treasures)	1.50
195	Sammy Sosa/S (National Treasures)	3.50
196	Greg Maddux/B (National Treasures)	1.25
197	Checklist (Vladimir Guerrero/B)	.40
198	Checklist (Scott Rolen/B)	.15
199	Checklist (Todd Walker/B)	.10
200	Checklist (Nomar Garciaparra/B)	.60

Cut To The Chase

Each of the cards in the Donruss Preferred series can also be found in this parallel set with die-cut borders, in the same bronze, silver, gold and platinum finishes. Multiplier values of the die-cuts are inverse to that usually found, with platinum cards the lowest, followed by gold, silver and bronze. Besides die-cutting, the chase cards feature a "CUT TO THE CHASE" designation at bottom.

Typical Value: 1.5X

Precious Metals

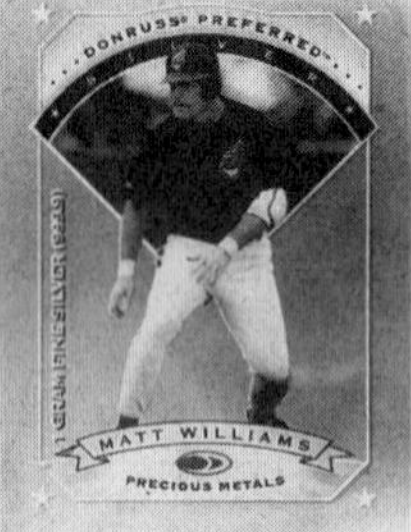

This 25-card partial parallel set features cards printed on actual silver, gold and platinum stock. Only 100 of each card were produced.

		NM/M
	Common Player:	7.50
1	Frank Thomas/P	45.00
2	Ken Griffey Jr./P	75.00
3	Greg Maddux/P	60.00
4	Albert Belle/G	7.50
5	Juan Gonzalez/P	25.00
6	Kenny Lofton/G	7.50
7	Tony Gwynn/P	60.00
8	Ivan Rodriguez/G	30.00
9	Mark McGwire/G	90.00
10	Matt Williams/S	7.50
11	Wade Boggs/S	60.00
12	Eddie Murray/S	45.00
13	Jeff Bagwell/G	45.00
14	Ken Caminiti/G	7.50
15	Alex Rodriguez/P	90.00
16	Chipper Jones/P	60.00
17	Barry Bonds/G	125.00
18	Cal Ripken Jr./P	125.00
19	Mo Vaughn/G	7.50
20	Mike Piazza/P	75.00
21	Derek Jeter/G	125.00
22	Bernie Williams/S	7.50
23	Andruw Jones/P	45.00
24	Vladimir Guerrero/G	45.00
25	Jose Guillen/S	7.50

Staremasters

A 20-card insert printed on foil stock and accented with holographic foil, Staremasters is designed to show upclose "game-face" photography. Each card is sequentially numbered to 1,500. Each of the Staremasters inserts can also be found in a version overprinted with a large diagonal black "SAMPLE" on front and back. These were distributed to dealers and the media. The sample cards have a "PROMO/1500" on back in place of a serial number.

		NM/M
	Complete Set (20):	55.00
	Common Player:	1.00
	Samples: 50 Percent	
1	Alex Rodriguez	6.00
2	Frank Thomas	3.00
3	Chipper Jones	4.00
4	Cal Ripken Jr.	7.50
5	Mike Piazza	4.50
6	Juan Gonzalez	2.25
7	Derek Jeter	7.50
8	Jeff Bagwell	3.00
9	Ken Griffey Jr.	4.50
10	Tony Gwynn	4.00
11	Barry Bonds	7.50
12	Albert Belle	1.00
13	Greg Maddux	4.00
14	Mark McGwire	6.00
15	Ken Caminiti	1.00
16	Hideo Nomo	2.25
17	Gary Sheffield	1.50
18	Andruw Jones	3.00
19	Mo Vaughn	1.00
20	Ivan Rodriguez	2.25

X-Ponential Power

This 20-card die-cut insert contains two top hitters from 10 different teams. Placing the cards of teammates together forms an "X" shape. Cards are printed on thick plastic stock and gold holographic foil stamping and are sequentially numbered to 3,000.

		NM/M
	Complete Set (20):	50.00
	Common Player:	1.00
1A	Manny Ramirez	3.50
1B	Jim Thome	2.00
2A	Paul Molitor	3.50
2B	Chuck Knoblauch	1.00
3A	Ivan Rodriguez	2.50
3B	Juan Gonzalez	2.00
4A	Albert Belle	1.00
4B	Frank Thomas	3.50
5A	Roberto Alomar	1.25
5B	Cal Ripken Jr.	9.00
6A	Tim Salmon	1.00
6B	Jim Edmonds	1.00
7A	Ken Griffey Jr.	6.00
7B	Alex Rodriguez	7.50
8A	Chipper Jones	4.50
8B	Andruw Jones	3.50
9A	Mike Piazza	6.00
9B	Raul Mondesi	1.00
10A	Tony Gwynn	4.50
10B	Ken Caminiti	1.00

Tins

Twenty-five different players are featured on the lithographed steel tins which were the "packs" of Donruss Preferred baseball. The 3" x 4-1/2" x 5/8" tins are hinged along the left side and were produced in two versions. Predominantly blue tins are the standard package. A premium parallel version is gold-colored and serially numbered within an edition of 1,200. Gold tins were packed one per 24-pack box of Preferred. Values shown are for opened tins. Shrink-wrapped unopened tins are valued about 1.5-3X the figures shown.

		NM/M
	Complete Set, Blue (25):	10.00
	Common Tin:	.25
	Gold:	10X
1	Frank Thomas	.40
2	Ken Griffey Jr.	.60
3	Andruw Jones	.40
4	Cal Ripken Jr.	1.00
5	Mike Piazza	.60
6	Chipper Jones	.50
7	Alex Rodriguez	.75
8	Derek Jeter	1.00
9	Juan Gonzalez	.30
10	Albert Belle	.25
11	Tony Gwynn	.50
12	Greg Maddux	.50
13	Jeff Bagwell	.40
14	Roger Clemens	.55
15	Mark McGwire	.75
16	Gary Sheffield	.30
17	Manny Ramirez	.40
18	Hideo Nomo	.30
19	Kenny Lofton	.25
20	Mo Vaughn	.25
21	Ryne Sandberg	.50
22	Barry Bonds	1.00
23	Sammy Sosa	.50
24	John Smoltz	.25
25	Ivan Rodriguez	.35

Tin Boxes

Twenty-five different players are featured on the lithographed steel boxes in which the "packs" of Donruss Preferred baseball were sold. Boxes measure about 5-1/4" x 9-1/4" x 5-3/8". Inside the removable lid is a serial number from within an edition of 1,200 (blue) or 299 (gold). The gold versions were a later, hobby-only release.

		NM/M
	Complete Set, Blue (25):	70.00
	Common Box:	2.00
	Gold:	4X
1	Frank Thomas	3.00
2	Ken Griffey Jr.	5.00
3	Andruw Jones	3.00
4	Cal Ripken Jr.	7.50
5	Mike Piazza	5.00
6	Chipper Jones	4.00
7	Alex Rodriguez	6.00
8	Derek Jeter	7.50
9	Juan Gonzalez	2.50
10	Albert Belle	2.00
11	Tony Gwynn	4.00
12	Greg Maddux	4.00
13	Jeff Bagwell	3.00
14	Roger Clemens	4.50
15	Mark McGwire	6.00
16	Gary Sheffield	2.50
17	Manny Ramirez	3.00
18	Hideo Nomo	2.50
19	Kenny Lofton	2.00
20	Mo Vaughn	2.00
21	Ryne Sandberg	4.00
22	Barry Bonds	7.50
23	Sammy Sosa	4.00
24	John Smoltz	2.00
25	Ivan Rodriguez	2.50

1997 Donruss Signature

Donruss ventured in the autograph-per-pack market with this series featuring 100 base cards (unsigned) and various types and versions of authentically autographed cards. The suggested retail price for each five-card pack was $14.99. Base cards have textured silver-foil borders and highlights on front. Backs have a second photo and lengthy stats. A parallel insert edition of each base card was also issued, labeled "Platinum Press Proof," the parallels have blue metallic foil on front and are designated "1 of 150" on the back.

		NM/M
	Complete Set (100):	15.00
	Common Player:	.10
	Platinum Stars/RC's:	12X
	Pack (5):	7.50
	Wax Box (12):	80.00
1	Mark McGwire	1.25
2	Kenny Lofton	.10
3	Tony Gwynn	.75
4	Tony Clark	.10
5	Tim Salmon	.10
6	Ken Griffey Jr.	1.00
7	Mike Piazza	1.00
8	Greg Maddux	.75
9	Roberto Alomar	.20
10	Andres Galarraga	.10
11	Roger Clemens	.90
12	Bernie Williams	.10
13	Rondell White	.10
14	Kevin Appler	.10
15	Ray Lankford	.10
16	Frank Thomas	.65
17	Will Clark	.10
18	Chipper Jones	.75
19	Jeff Bagwell	.65
20	Manny Ramirez	.65
21	Ryne Sandberg	.75
22	Paul Molitor	.65
23	Gary Sheffield	.10
24	Jim Edmonds	.10
25	Barry Larkin	.10
26	Rafael Palmeiro	.60
27	Alan Benes	.10
28	David Justice	.10
29	Randy Johnson	.65
30	Barry Bonds	1.50
31	Mo Vaughn	.10
32	Michael Tucker	.10
33	Larry Walker	.10
34	Tino Martinez	.10
35	Jose Guillen	.10
36	Carlos Delgado	.40
37	Jason Dickson	.10
38	Tom Glavine	.25
39	Raul Mondesi	.10
40	Jose Cruz Jr. **RC**	.50
41	Johnny Damon	.20
42	Mark Grace	.10
43	Juan Gonzalez	.35
44	Vladimir Guerrero	.65
45	Kevin Brown	.10
46	Justin Thompson	.10
47	Eric Young	.10
48	Ron Coomer	.10
49	Mark Kotsay	.10
50	Scott Rolen	.60
51	Derek Jeter	1.50
52	Jim Thome	.50
53	Fred McGriff	.10
54	Albert Belle	.10
55	Garret Anderson	.10
56	Wilton Guerrero	.10
57	Jose Canseco	.40
58	Cal Ripken Jr.	1.50
59	Sammy Sosa	.75
60	Dmitri Young	.10
61	Alex Rodriguez	1.25
62	Javier Lopez	.10
63	Sandy Alomar Jr.	.10
64	Joe Carter	.10
65	Dante Bichette	.10
66	Al Martin	.10
67	Darin Erstad	.30
68	Pokey Reese	.10
69	Brady Anderson	.10
70	Andruw Jones	.65
71	Ivan Rodriguez	.50
72	Nomar Garciaparra	.75
73	Moises Alou	.10
74	Andy Pettitte	.35
75	Jay Buhner	.10
76	Craig Biggio	.10
77	Wade Boggs	.75
78	Shawn Estes	.10
79	Neifi Perez	.10
80	Rusty Greer	.10
81	Pedro Martinez	.60
82	Mike Mussina	.40
83	Jason Giambi	.40
84	Hideo Nomo	.35
85	Todd Hundley	.10
86	Deion Sanders	.10
87	Mike Cameron	.10
88	Bobby Bonilla	.10
89	Todd Greene	.10
90	Kevin Orie	.10
91	Ken Caminiti	.10
92	Chuck Knoblauch	.10
93	Matt Morris	.10
94	Matt Williams	.10
95	Pat Hentgen	.10
96	John Smoltz	.10
97	Edgar Martinez	.10
98	Jason Kendall	.10
99	Checklist (Ken Griffey Jr.)	.50
100	Checklist (Frank Thomas)	.30

Platinum Press Proofs

This parallel insert set features metallic blue borders and graphics on front and has a "1 of 150" notation on back.

	NM/M
Common Player:	2.00
Stars:	12X

Autographs Promo

The "autograph" on the front of this promo card is a facsimile signature, rather than hand-penned. The sample is identical in format to the common red base level autographs in the set, but Thomas does not appear in that format.

	NM/M
Frank Thomas	6.00

Autographs (Red)

The basic level of authentically autographed cards found one per ($15) pack in Donruss Signature is the unnumbered "red" version. Cards have the background of the front photo printed only in red. For most players, 3,900 cards of the red version were autographed for insertion. Some players, however, signed fewer reds. Exchange cards had to be issued for Raul Mondesi and Edgar Renteria, whose signed cards were not ready when the set was first issued. It has been reported that Mondesi never signed any of the red version autograph cards. Cards are checklisted here in alphabetical order, in concordance with the larger Millenium checklist. The reported number of red cards signed appears in parentheses. This list differs significantly from the original list announced by Donruss in November 1997 due to last minute additions and deletions. Players signed in black and/or blue ink. Some players also added personal touches to some or all of their signatures, such as Bible verse citations, uniform numbers, etc.

		NM/M
Complete Set (116):		700.00
Common Player:		2.00
(1)	Jeff Abbott/3,900	2.00
(2)	Bob Abreu/3,900	8.00
(3)	Edgardo Alfonzo/3,900	3.00
(4)	Roberto Alomar/150	50.00
(5)	Sandy Alomar Jr./1,400	6.00
(6)	Moises Alou/900	10.00
(7)	Garret Anderson/3,900	7.00
(8)	Andy Ashby/3,900	3.00
(10)	Trey Beamon/3,900	2.00
(12)	Alan Benes/3,900	2.00
(13)	Geronimo Berroa/3,900	2.00
(14)	Wade Boggs/150	175.00
(18)	Kevin L. Brown/3,900	2.00
(20)	Brett Butler/1,400	3.50
(21)	Mike Cameron/3,900	7.00
(22)	Giovanni Carrara/2,900	2.00
(23)	Luis Castillo/3,900	4.00
(24)	Tony Clark/3,900	3.00
(25)	Will Clark/1,400	12.00
(27)	Lou Collier/3,900	2.00
(28)	Bartolo Colon/3,900	12.50
(29)	Ron Coomer/3,900	2.00
(30)	Marty Cordova/3,900	3.00
(31)	Jacob Cruz/3,900	2.00
(32)	Jose Cruz Jr./900	8.00
(33)	Russ Davis/3,900	3.00
(34)	Jason Dickson/3,900	2.00
(35)	Todd Dunwoody/3,900	2.00
(36)	Jermaine Dye/3,900	3.00
(37)	Jim Edmonds/3,900	12.00
(38)	Darin Erstad/900	8.00
(39)	Bobby Estalella/3,900	3.00
(40)	Shawn Estes/3,900	3.00
(41)	Jeff Fassero/3,900	2.00
(42)	Andres Galarraga/900	6.00
(43)	Karim Garcia/3,900	3.00
(45)	Derrick Gibson/3,900	2.00
(46)	Brian Giles/3,900	8.00
(47)	Tom Glavine/150	50.00
(49)	Rick Gorecki/900	4.50
(50)	Shawn Green/1,900	15.00
(51)	Todd Greene/3,900	3.00
(52)	Rusty Greer/3,900	3.00
(53)	Ben Grieve/3,900	3.00
(54)	Mark Grudzielanek/3,900	3.00
(55)	Vladimir Guerrero/1,900	20.00
(56)	Wilton Guerrero/2,150	3.00
(57)	Jose Guillen/2,900	8.00
(59)	Jeffrey Hammonds/2,150	3.50
(60)	Todd Helton/1,400	16.00
(61)	Todd Hollandsworth/2,900	3.00
(62)	Trenidad Hubbard/900	4.00
(63)	Todd Hundley/1,400	3.00
(66)	Bobby Jones/3,900	2.00
(68)	Brian Jordan/1,400	4.00
(69)	David Justice/900	10.00
(70)	Eric Karros/650	4.50
(71)	Jason Kendall/3,900	6.00
(72)	Jimmy Key/3,900	5.00
(73)	Brooks Kieschnick/3,900	2.00
(74)	Ryan Klesko/225	10.00
(76)	Paul Konerko/3,900	10.00
(77)	Mark Kotsay/2,400	3.00
(78)	Ray Lankford/3,900	4.00
(79)	Barry Larkin/150	35.00
(80)	Derrek Lee/3,900	10.00
(81)	Esteban Loaiza/3,900	3.00
(82)	Javier Lopez/1,400	10.00
(84)	Edgar Martinez/150	50.00
(85)	Pedro Martinez/900	35.00
(87)	Rafael Medina/3,900	2.00
(88)	Raul Mondesi (Exchange Card)	3.00
(89)	Matt Morris/3,900	10.00
(92)	Paul O'Neill/900	15.00
(93)	Kevin Orie/3,900	2.00
(94)	David Ortiz/3,900	50.00
(95)	Rafael Palmeiro/900	30.00
(96)	Jay Payton/3,900	2.50
(97)	Neifi Perez/3,900	2.00
(99)	Manny Ramirez/900	40.00
(100)	Joe Randa/3,900	2.00
(101)	Calvin Reese/3,900	3.00
(102)	Edgar Renteria (?)	20.00
(102)	Edgar Renteria (Exchange card)	3.00
(103)	Dennis Reyes/3,900	2.00
(106)	Henry Rodriguez/3,900	2.00
(108)	Scott Rolen/1,900	25.00
(109)	Kirk Rueter/2,900	3.00
(110)	Ryne Sandberg/400	60.00
(112)	Dwight Smith/2,900	3.00
(113)	J.T. Snow/900	4.00
(114)	Scott Spiezio/3,900	2.00
(115)	Shannon Stewart/2,900	3.00
(116)	Jeff Suppan/1,900	3.00
(117)	Mike Sweeney/3,900	6.00
(118)	Miguel Tejada/3,900	25.00
(121)	Justin Thompson/2,400	3.00
(122)	Brett Tomko/3,900	3.00
(123)	Bubba Trammell/3,900	2.50
(124)	Michael Tucker/3,900	2.00
(125)	Javier Valentin/3,900	2.00
(126)	Mo Vaughn/150	12.00
(127)	Robin Ventura/1,400	8.00
(128)	Terrell Wade/3,900	2.00
(129)	Billy Wagner/3,900	12.00
(130)	Larry Walker/900	25.00
(131)	Todd Walker/2,400	3.00
(132)	Rondell White/3,900	6.00
(133)	Kevin Wickander/900	4.00
(134)	Chris Widger/3,900	2.00
(136)	Matt Williams/150	25.00
(137)	Antone Williamson/3,900	2.00
(138)	Dan Wilson/3,900	2.00
(139)	Tony Womack/3,900	5.00
(140)	Jaret Wright/3,900	12.00
(141)	Dmitri Young/3,900	8.00
(142)	Eric Young/3,900	2.50
(143)	Kevin Young/3,900	2.50

Century Marks (Blue)

Virtually identical to the more common red and green (Millenium) versions, the Century Marks are identifiable at first glance by the use of blue ink in the background of the front photo and the "Century Marks" designation at top. On back, the cards are numbered from 0001 through 0100 in metallic foil at center. Several players initially had to be represented in the set by exchange cards. The unnumbered cards are checklisted here alphabetically.

		NM/M
Common Player:		20.00
(1)	Jeff Abbott	20.00
(2)	Bob Abreu	30.00
(3)	Edgardo Alfonzo	20.00
(4)	Roberto Alomar	75.00
(5)	Sandy Alomar Jr.	25.00
(6)	Moises Alou	35.00
(7)	Garret Anderson	60.00
(8)	Andy Ashby	20.00
(9)	Jeff Bagwell	80.00
(10)	Trey Beamon	20.00
(11)	Albert Belle	30.00
(12)	Alan Benes	20.00
(13)	Geronimo Berroa	20.00
(14)	Wade Boggs	100.00
(15)	Barry Bonds	300.00
(16)	Bobby Bonilla	20.00
(17)	Kevin Brown	75.00
(18)	Kevin L. Brown	20.00
(19)	Jay Buhner	30.00
(20)	Brett Butler	30.00
(21)	Mike Cameron	25.00
(22)	Giovanni Carrara	20.00
(23)	Luis Castillo	20.00
(24)	Tony Clark	20.00
(25)	Will Clark	100.00
(26)	Roger Clemens	200.00
(27)	Lou Collier	20.00
(28)	Bartolo Colon	30.00
(29)	Ron Coomer	20.00
(30)	Marty Cordova	20.00
(31)	Jacob Cruz	20.00
(32)	Jose Cruz Jr.	30.00
(33)	Russ Davis	20.00
(34)	Jason Dickson	25.00
(35)	Todd Dunwoody	20.00
(36)	Jermaine Dye	20.00
(37)	Jim Edmonds	60.00
(38)	Darin Erstad	40.00
(39)	Bobby Estalella	20.00
(40)	Shawn Estes	20.00
(41)	Jeff Fassero	20.00
(42)	Andres Galarraga	30.00
(43)	Karim Garcia	20.00
(44)	Nomar Garciaparra/SP/62	225.00
(45)	Derrick Gibson	20.00
(46)	Brian Giles	30.00
(47)	Tom Glavine	100.00
(48)	Juan Gonzalez	55.00
(49)	Rick Gorecki	20.00
(50)	Shawn Green	90.00
(51)	Todd Greene	20.00
(52)	Rusty Greer	20.00
(53)	Ben Grieve	20.00
(54)	Mark Grudzielanek	20.00
(55)	Vladimir Guerrero	100.00
(56)	Wilton Guerrero	20.00
(57)	Jose Guillen	30.00
(58)	Tony Gwynn	95.00
(59)	Jeffrey Hammonds	20.00
(60)	Todd Helton	60.00
(61)	Todd Hollandsworth	20.00
(62)	Trenidad Hubbard	20.00
(63)	Todd Hundley	25.00
(64)	Derek Jeter	200.00
(65)	Andruw Jones	50.00
(66)	Bobby Jones	20.00
(67)	Chipper Jones	100.00
(68)	Brian Jordan	35.00
(69)	David Justice	30.00
(70)	Eric Karros	25.00
(71)	Jason Kendall	30.00
(72)	Jimmy Key	50.00
(73)	Brooks Kieschnick	20.00
(74)	Ryan Klesko	25.00
(75)	Chuck Knoblauch	20.00
(76)	Paul Konerko	25.00
(77)	Mark Kotsay	25.00
(78)	Ray Lankford	20.00
(79)	Barry Larkin	60.00
(80)	Derrek Lee	40.00
(81)	Esteban Loaiza	20.00
(82)	Javy Lopez	45.00
(83)	Greg Maddux	175.00
(84)	Edgar Martinez	50.00
(85)	Pedro Martinez	100.00
(86)	Tino Martinez	50.00
(87)	Rafael Medina	20.00
(88)	Raul Mondesi	35.00
(88)	Raul Mondesi (Exchange card.)	5.00
(89)	Matt Morris	40.00
(90)	Eddie Murray	75.00
(91)	Mike Mussina	80.00
(92)	Paul O'Neill	40.00
(93)	Kevin Orie	20.00
(94)	David Ortiz	100.00
(95)	Rafael Palmeiro	80.00
(96)	Jay Payton	20.00
(97)	Neifi Perez	20.00
(98)	Andy Petitte	50.00
(99)	Manny Ramirez	100.00
(100)	Joe Randa	20.00
(101)	Calvin Reese	20.00
(102)	Edgar Renteria	50.00
(102)	Edgar Renteria (Exchange card.)	5.00
(103)	Dennis Reyes	20.00
(104)	Cal Ripken Jr.	225.00
(105)	Alex Rodriguez	180.00
(106)	Henry Rodriguez	20.00
(107)	Ivan Rodriguez	75.00
(108)	Scott Rolen	75.00
(109)	Kirk Rueter	20.00
(110)	Ryne Sandberg	125.00
(111)	Gary Sheffield	50.00
(112)	Dwight Smith	20.00
(113)	J.T. Snow	25.00
(114)	Scott Spiezio	20.00
(115)	Shannon Stewart	25.00
(116)	Jeff Suppan	20.00
(117)	Mike Sweeney	25.00
(118)	Miguel Tejada	120.00
(119)	Frank Thomas	80.00
(120)	Jim Thome	75.00
(120)	Jim Thome (Exchange card.)	5.00
(121)	Justin Thompson	20.00
(122)	Brett Tomko	20.00
(123)	Bubba Trammell	20.00
(124)	Michael Tucker	20.00
(125)	Javier Valentin	20.00
(126)	Mo Vaughn	25.00
(127)	Robin Ventura	30.00
(128)	Terrell Wade	20.00
(129)	Billy Wagner	40.00
(130)	Larry Walker	80.00
(131)	Todd Walker	25.00
(132)	Rondell White	25.00
(133)	Kevin Wickander	20.00
(134)	Chris Widger	20.00
(135)	Bernie Williams	75.00
(136)	Matt Williams	30.00
(137)	Antone Williamson	20.00
(138)	Dan Wilson	20.00
(139)	Tony Womack	25.00
(140)	Jaret Wright	35.00
(141)	Dmitri Young	30.00
(142)	Eric Young	30.00
(143)	Kevin Young	20.00

Millennium Marks (Green)

One thousand cards of most of the players who signed Signature Autographs are found in an edition marked on front as "Millenium Marks." These cards are also distinguished by the use of green ink in the background of the front photo. On back, the cards have a silver-foil serial number between (generally) 0101-1,000. Some cards as noted in the alphabetical checklist here were produced in lower numbers. The MM autographs were a random insert among the one-per-pack autographed cards found in $15 packs of Donruss Signature. Packs carried exchange cards redeemable for autographed cards of Raul Mondesi, Edgar Renteria and Jim Thome. This checklist differs significantly from that released in November 1997 by Donruss due to the last-minute addition, deletion and substitution of players. It is possible that cards exist of players not shown here.

		NM/M
Complete Set (143):		1,450
Common Player:		2.00
(1)	Jeff Abbott	2.00
(2)	Bob Abreu	8.00
(3)	Edgardo Alfonzo	5.00
(4)	Roberto Alomar	20.00
(5)	Sandy Alomar Jr.	8.00
(6)	Moises Alou	15.00
(7)	Garret Anderson	10.00
(8)	Andy Ashby	5.00
(9)	Jeff Bagwell/400	75.00
(10)	Trey Beamon	2.00
(11)	Albert Belle/400	12.50
(12)	Alan Benes	2.00
(13)	Geronimo Berroa	2.00
(14)	Wade Boggs	30.00
(15)	Barry Bonds/400	200.00
(16)	Bobby Bonilla/900	7.50
(17)	Kevin Brown/900	20.00
(18)	Kevin L. Brown	10.00
(19)	Jay Buhner/900	10.00
(20)	Brett Butler	6.00
(21)	Mike Cameron	4.00
(22)	Giovanni Carrara	2.00
(23)	Luis Castillo	5.00
(24)	Tony Clark	5.00
(25)	Will Clark	12.00
(26)	Roger Clemens/400	120.00
(27)	Lou Collier	2.00
(28)	Bartolo Colon	8.00
(29)	Ron Coomer	2.00
(30)	Marty Cordova	2.00
(31)	Jacob Cruz	2.00
(32)	Jose Cruz Jr.	6.00
(33)	Russ Davis	2.00
(34)	Jason Dickson	5.00
(35)	Todd Dunwoody	5.00
(36)	Jermaine Dye	5.00
(37)	Jim Edmonds	30.00
(38)	Darin Erstad	10.00
(39)	Bobby Estalella	3.00
(40)	Shawn Estes	2.00
(41)	Jeff Fassero	4.00
(42)	Andres Galarraga	10.00
(43)	Karim Garcia	3.50
(44)	Nomar Garciaparra/650	75.00
(45)	Derrick Gibson	4.00
(46)	Brian Giles	8.00
(47)	Tom Glavine	25.00
(48)	Juan Gonzalez/900	25.00
(49)	Rick Gorecki	2.00
(50)	Shawn Green	20.00
(51)	Todd Greene	7.50
(52)	Rusty Greer	7.50
(53)	Ben Grieve	5.00
(54)	Mark Grudzielanek	2.00
(55)	Vladimir Guerrero	25.00
(56)	Wilton Guerrero	2.00
(57)	Jose Guillen	6.00
(58)	Tony Gwynn/900	30.00
(59)	Jeffrey Hammonds	2.00
(60)	Todd Helton	30.00
(61)	Todd Hollandsworth	2.00
(62)	Trenidad Hubbard	2.00
(63)	Todd Hundley	6.00
(64)	Derek Jeter/400	100.00
(65)	Andruw Jones/900	15.00
(66)	Bobby Jones	2.00
(67)	Chipper Jones	30.00
(68)	Brian Jordan	7.50
(69)	David Justice	10.00
(70)	Eric Karros	6.00
(71)	Jason Kendall	8.00
(72)	Jimmy Key	2.00
(73)	Brooks Kieschnick	4.00
(74)	Ryan Klesko	5.00
(75)	Chuck Knoblauch/900	5.00
(76)	Paul Konerko	5.00
(77)	Mark Kotsay	6.00
(78)	Ray Lankford	2.00
(79)	Barry Larkin	30.00
(80)	Derrek Lee	20.00
(81)	Esteban Loaiza	2.00
(82)	Javy Lopez	8.00
(83)	Greg Maddux/400	80.00
(84)	Edgar Martinez	25.00
(85)	Pedro Martinez	40.00
(86)	Tino Martinez/900	15.00
(87)	Rafael Medina	2.00
(88)	Raul Mondesi	10.00
(88)	Raul Mondesi (Exchange card.)	2.00
(89)	Matt Morris	15.00
(90)	Eddie Murray/900	27.50
(91)	Mike Mussina/900	20.00
(92)	Paul O'Neill	12.50
(93)	Kevin Orie	2.00
(94)	David Ortiz	40.00
(95)	Rafael Palmeiro	30.00
(96)	Jay Payton	5.00
(97)	Neifi Perez	2.00
(98)	Andy Petitte/900	25.00
(99)	Manny Ramirez	30.00
(100)	Joe Randa	2.00
(101)	Calvin Reese	2.00
(102)	Edgar Renteria	30.00
(102)	Edgar Renteria (Exchange card.)	2.00
(103)	Dennis Reyes	3.00
(104)	Cal Ripken Jr./400	135.00
(105)	Alex Rodriguez/400	100.00
(106)	Henry Rodriguez	3.00
(107)	Ivan Rodriguez/900	20.00
(108)	Scott Rolen	25.00
(109)	Kirk Rueter	2.00
(110)	Ryne Sandberg	40.00
(111)	Gary Sheffield/400	25.00
(112)	Dwight Smith	2.00
(113)	J.T. Snow	7.50
(114)	Scott Spiezio	5.00
(115)	Shannon Stewart	2.00
(116)	Jeff Suppan	2.00
(117)	Mike Sweeney	5.00
(118)	Miguel Tejada	40.00
(119)	Frank Thomas/400	50.00
(120)	Jim Thome/900	30.00
(120)	Jim Thome (Exchange card.)	2.00
(121)	Justin Thompson	2.00
(122)	Brett Tomko	2.00
(123)	Bubba Trammell	4.00
(124)	Michael Tucker	2.00
(125)	Javier Valentin	2.00
(126)	Mo Vaughn	8.00
(127)	Robin Ventura	8.00
(128)	Terrell Wade	2.00
(129)	Billy Wagner	10.00
(130)	Larry Walker	20.00
(131)	Todd Walker	6.00
(132)	Rondell White	6.00
(133)	Kevin Wickander	2.00
(134)	Chris Widger	2.00
(135)	Bernie Williams/400	60.00
(136)	Matt Williams	10.00
(137)	Antone Williamson	2.00
(138)	Dan Wilson	2.00
(139)	Tony Womack	2.00
(140)	Jaret Wright	15.00
(141)	Dmitri Young	5.00
(142)	Eric Young	5.00
(143)	Kevin Young	2.00

Notable Nicknames

Current and former players whose nicknames are instantly recognized are featured in this Signature Series insert. The autographs are generally enhanced by the appearance of those nicknames, though Roger Clemens omitted "The Rocket" from many of his cards. Backs have a serial number from within an edition of 200 of each card.

		NM/M
Common Player:		20.00
(1)	Ernie Banks (Mr. Cub)	150.00
(2)	Tony Clark (The Tiger)	20.00
(3)	Roger Clemens (The Rocket)	300.00
(4)	Reggie Jackson (Mr. October)	125.00
(5)	Randy Johnson (Big Unit)	300.00
(6)	Stan Musial (The Man)	180.00
(7)	Ivan Rodriguez (Pudge)	100.00
(8)	Frank Thomas (The Big Hurt)	125.00
(9)	Mo Vaughn (Hit Dog)	20.00
(10)	Billy Wagner (The Kid)	40.00

Significant Signatures

Retired superstars from the early 1960s through the mid 1990s are featured in this insert series. Cards are horizontal in format with color photos on front and back. Generally autographed on front, each card is serially numbered on back from within an edition of 2,000. The unnumbered cards are listed here in alphabetical order.

	NM/M
Common Player:	15.00
(1) Ernie Banks	25.00
(2) Johnny Bench	30.00
(3) Yogi Berra	30.00
(4) George Brett	40.00
(5) Lou Brock	25.00
(6) Rod Carew	25.00
(7) Steve Carlton	20.00
(8) Larry Doby	35.00
(9) Carlton Fisk	30.00
(10) Bob Gibson	25.00
(11) Reggie Jackson	25.00
(12) Al Kaline	25.00
(13) Harmon Killebrew	30.00
(14) Don Mattingly	40.00
(15) Stan Musial	45.00
(16) Jim Palmer	15.00
(17) Brooks Robinson	30.00
(18) Frank Robinson	15.00
(19) Mike Schmidt	35.00
(20) Tom Seaver	30.00
(21) Duke Snider	20.00
(22) Carl Yastrzemski	40.00

Frank Thomas The Big Heart

In one of several specialty card charitable endeavors, Thomas and Donruss teamed up to issue this set as a fund raiser for "The Big Hurt's" charitable foundation. Each of the cards was available in an edition limited to 2,500 for a $20 donation. Cards are standard 2-1/2" x 3-1/2" with posed photos on front and "THE BIG HEART," a play on his nickname. Backs have information on the foundation, a second photo and a gold-foil serial number.

	NM/M
Complete Set (4):	20.00
Common Card:	5.00
1 Frank Thomas, Rod Carew	5.00
2 Frank Thomas	5.00
3 Frank Thomas	5.00
4 Frank Thomas	5.00

1997 Donruss VXP 1.0

This set was issued to accompany the hobby's first major effort to bring baseball cards into the computer age. The standard-format cards have motion-variable portrait and action photos on front and another photo on back. Cards were sold in packs of 10 with one of six CD ROMs for about $10.

	NM/M
Complete Set (50):	17.50
Common Player:	.25
1 Darin Erstad	.40
2 Jim Thome	.50
3 Alex Rodriguez	1.50
4 Greg Maddux	1.00
5 Scott Rolen	.65
6 Roberto Alomar	.30
7 Tony Clark	.25
8 Randy Johnson	.75
9 Sammy Sosa	1.00
10 Jose Guillen	.25
11 Cal Ripken Jr.	2.00
12 Paul Molitor	.75
13 Jose Cruz Jr.	.20
14 Barry Larkin	.25
15 Ken Caminiti	.25
16 Rafael Palmeiro	.65
17 Chuck Knoblauch	.25
18 Juan Gonzalez	.40
19 Larry Walker	.25
20 Tony Gwynn	1.00
21 Brady Anderson	.25
22 Derek Jeter	2.00
23 Rusty Greer	.25
24 Gary Sheffield	.35
25 Barry Bonds	2.00
26 Mo Vaughn	.20
27 Tino Martinez	.25
28 Ivan Rodriguez	.65
29 Jeff Bagwell	.75
30 Tim Salmon	.25
31 Nomar Garciaparra	1.00
32 Bernie Williams	.25
33 Kenny Lofton	.25
34 Mike Piazza	1.25
35 Jim Edmonds	.25
36 Frank Thomas	.75
37 Andy Pettitte	.35
38 Andruw Jones	.75
39 Raul Mondesi	.25
40 John Smoltz	.25
41 Albert Belle	.25
42 Mark McGwire	1.50
43 Chipper Jones	1.00
44 Hideo Nomo	.40
45 David Justice	.25
46 Manny Ramirez	.75
47 Ken Griffey Jr.	1.25
48 Roger Clemens	1.00
49 Vladimir Guerrero	.75
50 Ryne Sandberg	1.00

CDs

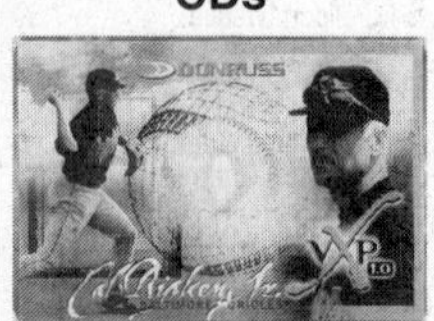

One of the earliest attempts to bring baseball cards into the computer age was Donruss "VXP 1.0 CD ROM" trading cards. Retailed, with 10 special-series player cards for about $10, the 4" x 2-3/4" "card" is a CD with player portrait and action photos on front. The CD was sold in a cardboard folder with the player's picture on front and instructions for use inside. CDs feature player stats, action footage and other interactive elements.

	NM/M
Complete Set (6):	12.00
Common Player:	2.00
(1) Ken Griffey Jr.	2.25
(2) Greg Maddux	2.00
(3) Mike Piazza	2.25
(4) Cal Ripken Jr.	3.00
(5) Alex Rodriguez	2.50
(6) Frank Thomas	2.00

1998 Donruss

This 170-card set includes 155 regular player cards, the 10-card Fan Club subset and five checklists. The cards have color photos and the player's name listed at the bottom. The backs have a horizontal layout with stats and a biography on the left and another photo on the right. The base set is paralleled twice. Silver Press Proofs is a silver foil and die-cut parallel numbered "1 of 1,500." Gold Press Proofs is die-cut, has gold foil and is numbered "1 of 500." The inserts are Crusade, Diamond Kings, Longball Leaders, Production Line and Rated Rookies.

	NM/M
Complete Set (420):	30.00
Complete Series 1 (170):	10.00
Complete Update 2 (250):	15.00
Common Player:	.05
Silver Press Proofs:	3X
Production 1,500 Sets	
Gold Press Proofs:	8X
Production 500 Sets	
Pack (10):	1.00
Wax Box (24):	16.00
1 Paul Molitor	.75
2 Juan Gonzalez	.40
3 Darryl Kile	.05
4 Randy Johnson	.75
5 Tom Glavine	.25
6 Pat Hentgen	.05
7 David Justice	.05
8 Kevin Brown	.05
9 Mike Mussina	.45
10 Ken Caminiti	.05
11 Todd Hundley	.05
12 Frank Thomas	.75
13 Ray Lankford	.05
14 Justin Thompson	.05
15 Jason Dickson	.05
16 Kenny Lofton	.05
17 Ivan Rodriguez	.65
18 Pedro Martinez	.75
19 Brady Anderson	.05
20 Barry Larkin	.05
21 Chipper Jones	1.50
22 Tony Gwynn	1.50
23 Roger Clemens	1.50
24 Sandy Alomar Jr.	.05
25 Tino Martinez	.05
26 Jeff Bagwell	.75
27 Shawn Estes	.05
28 Ken Griffey Jr.	1.75
29 Javier Lopez	.05
30 Denny Neagle	.05
31 Mike Piazza	1.75
32 Andres Galarraga	.05
33 Larry Walker	.05
34 Alex Rodriguez	2.00
35 Greg Maddux	1.50
36 Albert Belle	.05
37 Barry Bonds	2.50
38 Mo Vaughn	.05
39 Kevin Appier	.05
40 Wade Boggs	1.50
41 Garret Anderson	.05
42 Jeffrey Hammonds	.05
43 Marquis Grissom	.05
44 Jim Edmonds	.05
45 Brian Jordan	.05
46 Raul Mondesi	.05
47 John Valentin	.05
48 Brad Radke	.05
49 Ismael Valdes	.05
50 Matt Stairs	.05
51 Matt Williams	.05
52 Reggie Jefferson	.05
53 Alan Benes	.05
54 Charles Johnson	.05
55 Chuck Knoblauch	.05
56 Edgar Martinez	.05
57 Nomar Garciaparra	1.50
58 Craig Biggio	.05
59 Bernie Williams	.05
60 David Cone	.05
61 Cal Ripken Jr.	2.50
62 Mark McGwire	2.00
63 Roberto Alomar	.20
64 Fred McGriff	.05
65 Eric Karros	.05
66 Robin Ventura	.05
67 Darin Erstad	.30
68 Michael Tucker	.05
69 Jim Thome	.60
70 Mark Grace	.05
71 Lou Collier	.05
72 Karim Garcia	.05
73 Alex Fernandez	.05
74 J.T. Snow	.05
75 Reggie Sanders	.05
76 John Smoltz	.05
77 Tim Salmon	.05
78 Paul O'Neill	.05
79 Vinny Castilla	.05
80 Rafael Palmeiro	.65
81 Jaret Wright	.05
82 Jay Buhner	.05
83 Brett Butler	.05
84 Todd Greene	.05
85 Scott Rolen	.65
86 Sammy Sosa	1.50
87 Jason Giambi	.50
88 Carlos Delgado	.50
89 Deion Sanders	.05
90 Wilton Guerrero	.05
91 Andy Pettitte	.30
92 Brian Giles	.05
93 Dmitri Young	.05
94 Ron Coomer	.05
95 Mike Cameron	.05
96 Edgardo Alfonzo	.05
97 Jimmy Key	.05
98 Ryan Klesko	.05
99 Andy Benes	.05
100 Derek Jeter	2.50
101 Jeff Fassero	.05
102 Neifi Perez	.05
103 Hideo Nomo	.40
104 Andruw Jones	.75
105 Todd Helton	.50
106 Livan Hernandez	.05
107 Brett Tomko	.05
108 Shannon Stewart	.05
109 Bartolo Colon	.05
110 Matt Morris	.05
111 Miguel Tejada	.20
112 Pokey Reese	.05
113 Fernando Tatis	.05
114 Todd Dunwoody	.05
115 Jose Cruz Jr.	.05
116 Chan Ho Park	.05
117 Kevin Young	.05
118 Rickey Henderson	.75
119 Hideki Irabu	.05
120 Francisco Cordova	.05
121 Al Martin	.05
122 Tony Clark	.05
123 Curt Schilling	.25
124 Rusty Greer	.05
125 Jose Canseco	.40
126 Edgar Renteria	.05
127 Todd Walker	.05
128 Wally Joyner	.05
129 Bill Mueller	.05
130 Jose Guillen	.05
131 Manny Ramirez	.75
132 Bobby Higginson	.05
133 Kevin Orie	.05
134 Will Clark	.05
135 Dave Nilsson	.05
136 Jason Kendall	.05
137 Ivan Cruz	.05
138 Gary Sheffield	.25
139 Bubba Trammell	.05
140 Vladimir Guerrero	.75
141 Dennis Reyes	.05
142 Bobby Bonilla	.05
143 Ruben Rivera	.05
144 Ben Grieve	.05
145 Moises Alou	.05
146 Tony Womack	.05
147 Eric Young	.05
148 Paul Konerko	.10
149 Dante Bichette	.05
150 Joe Carter	.05
151 Rondell White	.05
152 Chris Holt	.05
153 Shawn Green	.20
154 Mark Grudzielanek	.05
155 Jermaine Dye	.05
156 Ken Griffey Jr. (Fan Club)	.90
157 Frank Thomas (Fan Club)	.50
158 Chipper Jones (Fan Club)	.75
159 Mike Piazza (Fan Club)	.90
160 Cal Ripken Jr. (Fan Club)	1.25
161 Greg Maddux (Fan Club)	.75
162 Juan Gonzalez (Fan Club)	.20
163 Alex Rodriguez (Fan Club)	1.00
164 Mark McGwire (Fan Club)	1.00
165 Derek Jeter (Fan Club)	1.25
166 Checklist (Larry Walker)	.05
167 Checklist (Tony Gwynn)	.60
168 Checklist (Tino Martinez)	.05
169 Checklist (Scott Rolen)	.15
170 Checklist (Nomar Garciaparra)	.60
171 Mike Sweeney	.05
172 Dustin Hermanson	.05
173 Darren Dreifort	.05
174 Ron Gant	.05
175 Todd Hollandsworth	.05
176 John Jaha	.05
177 Kerry Wood	.30
178 Chris Stynes	.05
179 Kevin Elster	.05
180 Derek Bell	.05
181 Darryl Strawberry	.05
182 Damion Easley	.05
183 Jeff Cirillo	.05
184 John Thomson	.05
185 Dan Wilson	.05
186 Jay Bell	.05
187 Bernard Gilkey	.05
188 Marc Valdes	.05
189 Ramon Martinez	.05
190 Charles Nagy	.05
191 Derek Lowe	.05
192 Andy Benes	.05
193 Delino DeShields	.05
194 Ryan Jackson **RC**	.05
195 Kenny Lofton	.05
196 Chuck Knoblauch	.05
197 Andres Galarraga	.05
198 Jose Canseco	.50
199 John Olerud	.05
200 Lance Johnson	.05
201 Darryl Kile	.05
202 Luis Castillo	.05
203 Joe Carter	.05
204 Dennis Eckersley	.65
205 Steve Finley	.05
206 Esteban Loaiza	.05
207 Ryan Christenson **RC**	.05
208 Deivi Cruz	.05
209 Mariano Rivera	.15
210 Mike Judd **RC**	.05
211 Billy Wagner	.05
212 Scott Spiezio	.05
213 Russ Davis	.05
214 Jeff Suppan	.05
215 Doug Glanville	.05
216 Dmitri Young	.05
217 Rey Ordonez	.05
218 Cecil Fielder	.05
219 Masato Yoshii **RC**	.10
220 Raul Casanova	.05
221 Rolando Arrojo **RC**	.20
222 Ellis Burks	.05
223 Butch Huskey	.05
224 Brian Hunter	.05
225 Marquis Grissom	.05
226 Kevin Brown	.05
227 Joe Randa	.05
228 Henry Rodriguez	.05
229 Omar Vizquel	.05
230 Fred McGriff	.05
231 Matt Williams	.05
232 Moises Alou	.05
233 Travis Fryman	.05
234 Wade Boggs	1.50
235 Pedro Martinez	.75
236 Rickey Henderson	.75
237 Bubba Trammell	.05
238 Mike Caruso	.05
239 Wilson Alvarez	.05
240 Geronimo Berroa	.05
241 Eric Milton	.05
242 Scott Erickson	.05
243 Todd Erdos **RC**	.05
244 Bobby Hughes	.05
245 Dave Hollins	.05
246 Dean Palmer	.05
247 Carlos Baerga	.05
248 Jose Silva	.05
249 Jose Cabrera **RC**	.05
250 Tom Evans	.05
251 Marty Cordova	.05
252 Hanley Frias **RC**	.05
253 Javier Valentin	.05
254 Mario Valdez	.05
255 Joey Cora	.05
256 Mike Lansing	.05
257 Jeff Kent	.05
258 David Dellucci **RC**	.10
259 Curtis King **RC**	.05
260 David Segui	.05
261 Royce Clayton	.05
262 Jeff Blauser	.05
263 Manny Aybar **RC**	.05
264 Mike Cather **RC**	.05
265 Todd Zeile	.05
266 Richard Hidalgo	.05
267 Dante Powell	.05
268 Mike DeJean **RC**	.05
269 Ken Cloude	.05
270 Danny Klassen	.05
271 Sean Casey	.15
272 A.J. Hinch	.05
273 Rich Butler **RC**	.05
274 Ben Ford **RC**	.05
275 Billy McMillon	.05
276 Wilson Delgado	.05
277 Orlando Cabrera	.05
278 Geoff Jenkins	.05
279 Enrique Wilson	.05
280 Derrek Lee	.60
281 Marc Pisciotta **RC**	.05
282 Abraham Nunez	.05
283 Aaron Boone	.05
284 Brad Fullmer	.05
285 Rob Stanifer **RC**	.05
286 Preston Wilson	.05
287 Greg Norton	.05
288 Bobby Smith	.05
289 Josh Booty	.05
290 Russell Branyan	.05
291 Jeremi Gonzalez	.05
292 Michael Coleman	.05
293 Cliff Politte	.05
294 Eric Ludwick	.05
295 Rafael Medina	.05
296 Jason Varitek	.05
297 Ron Wright	.05
298 Mark Kotsay	.05
299 David Ortiz	.50
300 Frank Catalanotto **RC**	.20
301 Robinson Checo	.05
302 Kevin Millwood **RC**	.75
303 Jacob Cruz	.05
304 Javier Vazquez	.05
305 Magglio Ordonez **RC**	1.50
306 Kevin Witt	.05
307 Derrick Gibson	.05
308 Shane Monahan	.05
309 Brian Rose	.05
310 Bobby Estalella	.05
311 Felix Heredia	.05
312 Desi Relaford	.05
313 Esteban Yan **RC**	.05
314 Ricky Ledee	.05
315 Steve Woodard **RC**	.05
316 Pat Watkins	.05
317 Damian Moss	.05
318 Bob Abreu	.05
319 Jeff Abbott	.05
320 Miguel Cairo	.05
321 Rigo Beltran **RC**	.05
322 Tony Saunders	.05
323 Randall Simon	.05
324 Hiram Bocachica	.05
325 Richie Sexson	.05
326 Karim Garcia	.05
327 Mike Lowell **RC**	.50
328 Pat Cline	.05
329 Matt Clement	.05
330 Scott Elarton	.05
331 Manuel Barrios **RC**	.05
332 Bruce Chen	.05
333 Juan Encarnacion	.05
334 Travis Lee	.05
335 Wes Helms	.05
336 Chad Fox **RC**	.05
337 Donnie Sadler	.05
338 Carlos Mendoza **RC**	.05
339 Damian Jackson	.05
340 Julio Ramirez **RC**	.05
341 John Halama **RC**	.05
342 Edwin Diaz	.05
343 Felix Martinez	.05
344 Eli Marrero	.05
345 Carl Pavano	.05
346 Vladimir Guerrero/HL	.40
347 Barry Bonds/HL	1.25
348 Darin Erstad/HL	.10
349 Albert Belle/HL	.05
350 Kenny Lofton/HL	.05
351 Mo Vaughn/HL	.05
352 Jose Cruz Jr./HL	.05
353 Tony Clark/HL	.05
354 Roberto Alomar/HL	.10
355 Manny Ramirez/HL	.40
356 Paul Molitor/HL	.40
357 Jim Thome/HL	.05
358 Tino Martinez/HL	.05
359 Tim Salmon/HL	.05
360 David Justice/HL	.05
361 Raul Mondesi/HL	.05
362 Mark Grace/HL	.05
363 Craig Biggio/HL	.05
364 Larry Walker/HL	.05
365 Mark McGwire/HL	1.00
366 Juan Gonzalez/HL	.20
367 Derek Jeter/HL	1.25
368 Chipper Jones/HL	.75
369 Frank Thomas/HL	.50
370 Alex Rodriguez/HL	1.00
371 Mike Piazza/HL	.90
372 Tony Gwynn/HL	.75
373 Jeff Bagwell/HL	.40
374 Nomar Garciaparra/HL	.75
375 Ken Griffey Jr./HL	.90
376 Livan Hernandez (Untouchables)	.05
377 Chan Ho Park (Untouchables)	.05
378 Mike Mussina (Untouchables)	.20
379 Andy Pettitte (Untouchables)	.05
380 Greg Maddux (Untouchables)	.75
381 Hideo Nomo (Untouchables)	.20
382 Roger Clemens (Untouchables)	.80
383 Randy Johnson (Untouchables)	.40
384 Pedro Martinez (Untouchables)	.40
385 Jaret Wright (Untouchables)	.05
386 Ken Griffey Jr. (Spirit of the Game)	.90
387 Todd Helton (Spirit of the Game)	.05
388 Paul Konerko (Spirit of the Game)	.05
389 Cal Ripken Jr. (Spirit of the Game)	1.25
390 Larry Walker (Spirit of the Game)	.05
391 Ken Caminiti (Spirit of the Game)	.05
392 Jose Guillen (Spirit of the Game)	.05
393 Jim Edmonds (Spirit of the Game)	.05
394 Barry Larkin (Spirit of the Game)	.05
395 Bernie Williams (Spirit of the Game)	.05
396 Tony Clark (Spirit of the Game)	.05
397 Jose Cruz Jr. (Spirit of the Game)	.05
398 Ivan Rodriguez (Spirit of the Game)	.30
399 Darin Erstad (Spirit of the Game)	.10
400 Scott Rolen (Spirit of the Game)	.15
401 Mark McGwire (Spirit of the Game)	1.00
402 Andruw Jones (Spirit of the Game)	.40

403 Juan Gonzalez (Spirit of the Game) .20
404 Derek Jeter (Spirit of the Game) 1.25
405 Chipper Jones (Spirit of the Game) .75
406 Greg Maddux (Spirit of the Game) .75
407 Frank Thomas (Spirit of the Game) .50
408 Alex Rodriguez (Spirit of the Game) 1.00
409 Mike Piazza (Spirit of the Game) .90
410 Tony Gwynn (Spirit of the Game) .75
411 Jeff Bagwell (Spirit of the Game) .40
412 Nomar Garciaparra (Spirit of the Game) .75
413 Hideo Nomo (Spirit of the Game) .20
414 Barry Bonds (Spirit of the Game) 1.25
415 Ben Grieve (Spirit of the Game) .05
416 Checklist (Barry Bonds) 1.25
417 Checklist (Mark McGwire) 1.00
418 Checklist (Roger Clemens) .65
419 Checklist (Livan Hernandez) .05
420 Checklist (Ken Griffey Jr.) .75

Silver Press Proofs

Silver Press Proofs paralleled all 420 cards in the Donruss and Donruss Update Baseball. Cards featured silver foil stamping and a die-cut top right corner. Backs had a silver tint and were numbered "1 of 1500" in the bottom left corner.

NM/M
Complete Set (420): 150.00
Common Player: .50
Stars/RC's: 2X
Production 1,500 Sets

Gold Press Proofs

All 420 cards in Donruss and Donruss Update were also issued in Gold Press Proofs. These cards were die-cut on the top right corner and contained gold foil stamping. Backs featured a gold tint and "1 of 500" was printed in black in the bottom-left corner.

NM/M
Common Player: 1.00
Stars/RC's: 6X
Production 500 Sets

Crusade

This 100-card insert was included in 1998 Donruss (40 cards), Leaf (30) and Donruss Update (30). The cards

use refractive technology and the background features heraldic-style lions. The cards are sequentially numbered to 250. Crusade Purple (numbered to 100) and Red (25) parallels were also inserted in the three products.

NM/M
Common Player: 4.00
Production 250 Sets
Purples (100 Sets): 1X
Reds (25 Sets): 4X
5 Jason Dickson 4.00
6 Todd Greene 4.00
7 Roberto Alomar 5.00
8 Cal Ripken Jr. 40.00
12 Mo Vaughn 4.00
13 Nomar Garciaparra 15.00
16 Mike Cameron 4.00
20 Sandy Alomar Jr. 4.00
21 David Justice 4.00
25 Justin Thompson 4.00
27 Kevin Appier 4.00
33 Tino Martinez 4.00
36 Hideki Irabu 4.00
37 Jose Canseco 8.00
39 Ken Griffey Jr. 30.00
42 Edgar Martinez 5.00
45 Will Clark 6.00
47 Rusty Greer 4.00
50 Shawn Green 5.00
51 Jose Cruz Jr. 4.00
52 Kenny Lofton 4.00
53 Chipper Jones 15.00
62 Kevin Orie 4.00
65 Deion Sanders 6.00
67 Larry Walker 6.00
68 Dante Bichette 4.00
71 Todd Helton 10.00
74 Bobby Bonilla 4.00
75 Kevin Brown 4.00
78 Craig Biggio 6.00
82 Wilton Guerrero 4.00
85 Pedro Martinez 15.00
86 Edgardo Alfonzo 4.00
88 Scott Rolen 10.00
89 Francisco Cordova 4.00
90 Jose Guillen 4.00
92 Ray Lankford 4.00
93 Mark McGwire 20.00
94 Matt Morris 4.00
100 Shawn Estes 4.00

Days

Similar in design, but featuring heavier stock, a metallic foil background and gold-foil graphic highlights on front, these cards were part of a ballpark promotion conducted by Donruss during the 1998 baseball season. Fans were given exchange cards at selected ballparks which could be traded at specially designated card shops in those locales for one of these premium star cards. Production was reportedly fewer than 10,000 of each card. Backs are numbered "X of 14," but are otherwise identical to the regular-issue version.

NM/M
Complete Set (14): 16.00
Common Player: .50
1 Frank Thomas 1.00
2 Tony Clark .50
3 Ivan Rodriguez .65
4 David Justice .50
5 Nomar Garciaparra 1.50
6 Mark McGwire 2.50
7 Travis Lee .50
8 Cal Ripken Jr. 3.00
9 Jeff Bagwell 1.00
10 Barry Bonds 3.00
11 Ken Griffey Jr. 2.00
12 Derek Jeter 3.00
13 Raul Mondesi .50
14 Greg Maddux 1.50

Diamond Kings

Diamond Kings is a 20-card insert featuring a painted portrait by Dan Gardiner. Backs have a ghosted image of the portrait with a player biography and the card's number overprinted. A total of 10,000 sets were produced with the first 500 of each card printed on canvas. A Frank Thomas sample card was also created.

NM/M
Complete Set (20): 65.00
Common Player: 2.00
Production 9,500 Sets
Canvas (1st 500 Sets): 2X
1 Cal Ripken Jr. 9.00
2 Greg Maddux 4.50
3 Ivan Rodriguez 2.50
4 Tony Gwynn 4.50
5 Paul Molitor 3.00
6 Kenny Lofton 2.00
7 Andy Pettitte 2.00
8 Darin Erstad 2.00
9 Randy Johnson 3.00
10 Derek Jeter 9.00
11 Hideo Nomo 2.50
12 David Justice 2.00
13 Bernie Williams 2.00
14 Roger Clemens 5.00
15 Barry Larkin 2.00
16 Andruw Jones 3.00
17 Mike Piazza 6.50
18 Frank Thomas 3.00
18s Frank Thomas (Sample) 3.00
19 Alex Rodriguez 7.50
20 Ken Griffey Jr. 6.50

Longball Leaders

Longball Leaders features 24 top home run hitters. The right border features a home run meter with zero at the bottom, 61 at the top and the player's 1997 home run total marked. Each card is sequentially numbered to 5,000.

NM/M
Complete Set (24): 50.00
Common Player: 1.00
Production 5,000 Sets
1 Ken Griffey Jr. 5.00
2 Mark McGwire 6.00
3 Tino Martinez 1.00
4 Barry Bonds 7.50
5 Frank Thomas 3.00
6 Albert Belle 1.00
7 Mike Piazza 5.00
8 Chipper Jones 4.00
9 Vladimir Guerrero 3.00
10 Matt Williams 1.00
11 Sammy Sosa 4.00
12 Tim Salmon 1.00
13 Raul Mondesi 1.00
14 Jeff Bagwell 3.00
15 Mo Vaughn 1.00
16 Manny Ramirez 3.00
17 Jim Thome 2.00
18 Jim Edmonds 1.00
19 Tony Clark 1.00
20 Nomar Garciaparra 4.00
21 Juan Gonzalez 1.50
22 Scott Rolen 2.00
23 Larry Walker 1.00
24 Andres Galarraga 1.00

Production Line-ob

This 20-card insert is printed on holographic foil board. Inserted in magazine packs, this insert features player's with a high on-base percentage in 1997. Each player's card is sequentially numbered to his on-base percentage from that season. The card back has a player photo and a list of the 20 players with their stat.

NM/M
Complete Set (20): 85.00
Common Player: 1.50
1 Frank Thomas/456 6.00
2 Edgar Martinez/456 1.50
3 Roberto Alomar/390 2.00
4 Chuck Knoblauch/390 1.50
5 Mike Piazza/431 10.00
6 Barry Larkin /440 1.50
7 Kenny Lofton/409 1.50
8 Jeff Bagwell/425 6.00
9 Barry Bonds/446 15.00
10 Rusty Greer/405 1.50
11 Gary Sheffield /424 2.00
12 Mark McGwire/393 12.00
13 Chipper Jones/371 8.00
14 Tony Gwynn/409 8.00
15 Craig Biggio/415 1.50
16 Mo Vaughn/420 1.50
17 Bernie Williams/408 1.50
18 Ken Griffey Jr./382 10.00
19 Brady Anderson/393 1.50
20 Derek Jeter/370 15.00

Production Line-pi

This 20-card insert was printed on holographic board. The set features players with a high power index from 1997. Each card is sequentially numbered to that player's power index from that season.

NM/M
Complete Set (20): 85.00
Common Player: 1.50
1 Frank Thomas/1,067 5.00
2 Mark McGwire/1,039 12.00
3 Barry Bonds/1,031 12.50
4 Jeff Bagwell/1,017 5.00
5 Ken Griffey Jr./1,028 10.00
6 Alex Rodriguez/846 12.00
7 Chipper Jones/850 7.00
8 Mike Piazza/1,070 10.00
9 Mo Vaughn/980 1.50
10 Brady Anderson/863 1.50
11 Manny Ramirez/953 5.00
12 Albert Belle/823 1.50
13 Jim Thome/1,001 2.50
14 Bernie Williams/952 1.50
15 Scott Rolen/846 2.00
16 Vladimir Guerrero/833 5.00
17 Larry Walker/1,172 1.50
18 David Justice/1,013 1.50
19 Tino Martinez/948 1.50
20 Tony Gwynn/957 7.00

Production Line-sg

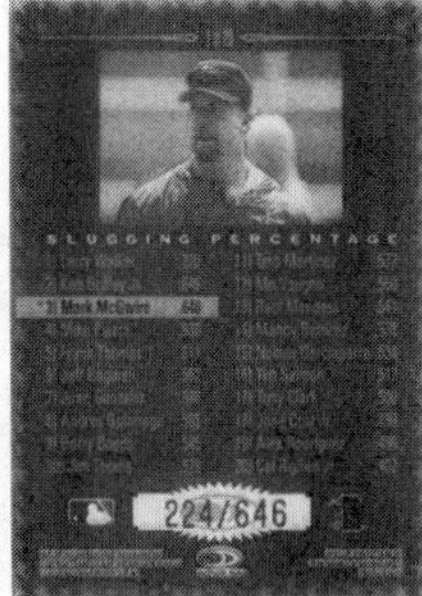

This 20-card insert was printed on holographic board. It featured players with high slugging percentages in 1997. Each card is sequentially numbered to the player's slugging percentage from that season.

NM/M
Complete Set (20): 135.00
Common Player: 3.00
1 Mark McGwire/646 20.00
2 Ken Griffey Jr./646 12.50
3 Andres Galarraga/585 3.00
4 Barry Bonds/585 22.50
5 Juan Gonzalez/589 4.50
6 Mike Piazza/638 12.50
7 Jeff Bagwell/592 7.50
8 Manny Ramirez/538 7.50
9 Jim Thome/579 4.50
10 Mo Vaughn/560 3.00
11 Larry Walker/720 3.00
12 Tino Martinez/577 3.00
13 Frank Thomas/611 7.50
14 Tim Salmon/517 3.00
15 Raul Mondesi/541 3.00
16 Alex Rodriguez/496 15.00
17 Nomar Garciaparra/534 10.00
18 Jose Cruz Jr./499 3.00
19 Tony Clark/500 3.00
20 Cal Ripken Jr./402 25.00

Rated Rookies

This 30-card insert features top young players. The fronts have a color player photo in front of a stars and stripes background, with "Rated Rookies" and the player's name printed on the right. The backs have another photo, basic player information and career highlights. A rare (250 each) Medalist version is micro-etched on gold holographic foil.

NM/M
Complete Set (30): 32.50
Common Player: 1.00
Medalists (250 Sets): 6X
1 Mark Kotsay 1.00
2 Neifi Perez 1.00
3 Paul Konerko 1.50
4 Jose Cruz Jr. 1.00
5 Hideki Irabu 1.00
6 Mike Cameron 1.00
7 Jeff Suppan 1.00
8 Kevin Orie 1.00
9 Pokey Reese 1.00
10 Todd Dunwoody 1.00
11 Miguel Tejada 1.50
12 Jose Guillen 1.00
13 Bartolo Colon 1.50
14 Derrek Lee 2.50
15 Antone Williamson 1.00
16 Wilton Guerrero 1.00
17 Jaret Wright 1.00
18 Todd Helton 4.00
19 Shannon Stewart 1.00
20 Nomar Garciaparra 6.00
21 Brett Tomko 1.00
22 Fernando Tatis 1.00
23 Raul Ibanez 1.00
24 Dennis Reyes 1.00
25 Bobby Estalella 1.00
26 Lou Collier 1.00
27 Bubba Trammell 1.00
28 Ben Grieve 1.00
29 Ivan Cruz 1.00
30 Karim Garcia 1.00

Update Crusade

This 30-card insert is continued from 1998 Donruss and Leaf baseball sets. Each card features a color action photo in front of a Medieval background. The player's name and background are green and each card is serial numbered to 250. Purple (numbered to 100) and Red (25) parallel versions were also created. Crusade is a 130-card cross-brand insert with 40 cards included in 1998 Donruss and 30 each in 1998 Leaf and Leaf Rookies & Stars.

NM/M
Complete Set, Green (30): 325.00
Common Player: 6.00
Production 250 Sets
Purples (100 Sets): 3X
Reds (25 Sets): 10X
1 Tim Salmon 6.00
2 Garret Anderson 6.00
9 Rafael Palmeiro 15.00
10 Brady Anderson 6.00
14 Frank Thomas 15.00
17 Robin Ventura 6.00
22 Matt Williams 6.00
23 Tony Clark 6.00
29 Chuck Knoblauch 6.00
31 Bernie Williams 6.00
32 Derek Jeter 50.00
38 Jason Giambi 10.00
43 Jay Buhner 6.00
44 Juan Gonzalez 7.50
49 Carlos Delgado 9.00
55 Greg Maddux 20.00
57 Tom Glavine 9.00
60 Mark Grace 6.00
61 Sammy Sosa 20.00
63 Barry Larkin 6.00
69 Neifi Perez 6.00
72 Gary Sheffield 7.50
77 Jeff Bagwell 15.00
80 Raul Mondesi 6.00
81 Hideo Nomo 7.50
83 Rondell White 6.00
84 Vladimir Guerrero 15.00
87 Todd Hundley 6.00
96 Brian Jordan 6.00
99 Barry Bonds 50.00

Update Dominators

This 30-card insert features color player photos and holographic foil.

NM/M
Complete Set (30): 25.00
Common Player: .25
Approx: 1:12
1 Roger Clemens 1.50

2 Tony Clark .25
3 Darin Erstad .50
4 Jeff Bagwell 1.00
5 Ken Griffey Jr. 1.75
6 Andruw Jones 1.00
7 Juan Gonzalez .50
8 Ivan Rodriguez .75
9 Randy Johnson 1.00
10 Tino Martinez .25
11 Mark McGwire 2.00
12 Chuck Knoblauch .25
13 Jim Thome .65
14 Alex Rodriguez 2.00
15 Hideo Nomo .50
16 Jose Cruz Jr. .25
17 Chipper Jones 1.50
18 Tony Gwynn 1.50
19 Barry Bonds 2.50
20 Mo Vaughn .25
21 Cal Ripken Jr. 2.50
22 Greg Maddux 1.50
23 Manny Ramirez 1.00
24 Andres Galarraga .25
25 Vladimir Guerrero 1.00
26 Albert Belle .25
27 Nomar Garciaparra 1.50
28 Kenny Lofton .25
29 Mike Piazza 1.75
30 Frank Thomas 1.00

Update Elite

This 20-card insert features color player photos in a diamond-shaped border at the top with the Elite Series logo and player's name at the bottom. The fronts have a cream-colored border.

NM/M
Complete Set (20): 115.00
Common Player: 3.00
Production 2,500 Sets
1 Jeff Bagwell 4.50
2 Andruw Jones 4.50
3 Ken Griffey Jr. 7.50
4 Derek Jeter 15.00
5 Juan Gonzalez 3.50
6 Mark McGwire 10.00
7 Ivan Rodriguez 3.50
8 Paul Molitor 4.50
9 Hideo Nomo 3.50
10 Mo Vaughn 3.00
11 Chipper Jones 6.00
12 Nomar Garciaparra 6.00
13 Mike Piazza 7.50
14 Frank Thomas 4.50
15 Greg Maddux 6.00
16 Cal Ripken Jr. 15.00
17 Alex Rodriguez 10.00
18 Scott Rolen 3.50
19 Barry Bonds 15.00
20 Tony Gwynn 6.00

Update FANtasy Team

This 20-card set features the top vote getters from the Donruss online Fan Club ballot box. The top 10 make up the 1st Team FANtasy Team and are sequentially numbered to 2,000. The other players are included in the 2nd Team FANtasy Team and are numbered to 4,000. The first 250 cards of each player are die-cut. The front of the cards feature a color photo inside a stars and stripes border.

NM/M
Complete Set (20): 35.00
Common Player (1-10) (1,750 Sets): 1.50
Common Player (11-20) (3,750 Sets): 1.00
Die-Cuts (250 Each): 2X
1 Frank Thomas 2.00
2 Ken Griffey Jr. 3.50
3 Cal Ripken Jr. 5.00
4 Jose Cruz Jr. 1.00
5 Travis Lee 1.00
6 Greg Maddux 2.50
7 Alex Rodriguez 4.00
8 Mark McGwire 4.00
9 Chipper Jones 2.50
10 Andruw Jones 2.00
11 Mike Piazza 3.50
12 Tony Gwynn 2.50
13 Larry Walker 1.00
14 Nomar Garciaparra 3.00
15 Jaret Wright 1.00
16 Livan Hernandez 1.00
17 Roger Clemens 2.75
18 Derek Jeter 5.00
19 Scott Rolen 1.25
20 Jeff Bagwell 1.50

Update Rookie Diamond Kings

The Rookie Diamond Kings insert features color portraits by artist Dan Gardiner of young players inside a golden border. Player identification and Rookie Diamond Kings logo are at the bottom. Each card is sequentially numbered to 10,000 with the first 500 printed on canvas.

NM/M
Complete Set (12): 20.00
Common Player: 2.00
Production 9,500 Sets
Canvas (500 Sets): 2X
1 Travis Lee 2.00
2 Fernando Tatis 2.00
3 Livan Hernandez 2.00
4 Todd Helton 5.00
5 Derrek Lee 3.50
6 Jaret Wright 2.00
7 Ben Grieve 2.00
8 Paul Konerko 2.50
9 Jose Cruz Jr. 2.00
10 Mark Kotsay 2.00
11 Todd Greene 2.00
12 Brad Fullmer 2.00

Update Sony MLB 99

This 20-card set promotes the MLB '99 game for Sony PlayStation systems. The card front has a color player photo with a red border on two sides. The Donruss, PlayStation and MLB '99 logos appear on the front as well. The backs have a MLB '99 Tip and instructions on entering the PlayStation MLB '99 Sweepstakes.

NM/M
Complete Set (20): 3.00
Common Player: .05
1 Cal Ripken Jr. .75
2 Nomar Garciaparra .40
3 Barry Bonds .75
4 Mike Mussina .20
5 Pedro Martinez .25
6 Derek Jeter .75
7 Andruw Jones .25
8 Kenny Lofton .05
9 Gary Sheffield .15
10 Raul Mondesi .05
11 Jeff Bagwell .25
12 Tim Salmon .05
13 Tom Glavine .15
14 Ben Grieve .05
15 Matt Williams .05
16 Juan Gonzalez .15
17 Mark McGwire .50
18 Bernie Williams .05
19 Andres Galarraga .05
20 Jose Cruz Jr. .05

Collections

Collections consists of a 750-card base set made up of cards from the Donruss (200 cards), Leaf (200), Donruss Elite (150) and Donruss Preferred (200) sets. The cards were reproduced with a chromium finish and have the scripted word "Collections" vertically at left-front. The Collections logo is repeated on back and each card has a second number within the 750-piece set. The Donruss and Leaf cards were inserted two per pack, Elite was inserted one per pack and Preferred cards had a production run of less than 1,400, averaging one card per two packs. The 200 Collections versions of Donruss cards can be found with a large black "SAMPLE" overprint value on back.

NM/M
Complete Donruss Set (200): 100.00
Complete Leaf Set (200): 125.00
Complete Elite Set (150): 125.00
Complete Preferred Set (200): 300.00
Prized Collections Parallel: 2X
Pack (5): 4.00
Wax Box (20): 75.00
Samples: 6X
1 Paul Molitor 2.00
2 Juan Gonzalez 1.00
3 Darryl Kile .25
4 Randy Johnson 2.00
5 Tom Glavine .50
6 Pat Hentgen .25
7 David Justice .25
8 Kevin Brown .25
9 Mike Mussina .50
10 Ken Caminiti .25
11 Todd Hundley .25
12 Frank Thomas 2.00
13 Ray Lankford .25
14 Justin Thompson .25
15 Jason Dickson .25
16 Kenny Lofton .25
17 Ivan Rodriguez 1.50
18 Pedro Martinez 2.00
19 Brady Anderson .25
20 Barry Larkin .25
21 Chipper Jones 3.00
22 Tony Gwynn 3.00
23 Roger Clemens 3.25
24 Sandy Alomar Jr. .25
25 Tino Martinez .25
26 Jeff Bagwell 2.00
27 Shawn Estes .25
28 Ken Griffey Jr. 3.50
29 Javier Lopez .25
30 Denny Neagle .25
31 Mike Piazza 3.50
32 Andres Galarraga .25
33 Larry Walker .25
34 Alex Rodriguez 4.50
35 Greg Maddux 3.00
36 Albert Belle .25
37 Barry Bonds 6.00
38 Mo Vaughn .25
39 Kevin Appier .25
40 Wade Boggs 3.00
41 Garret Anderson .25
42 Jeffrey Hammonds .25
43 Marquis Grissom .25
44 Jim Edmonds .25
45 Brian Jordan .25
46 Raul Mondesi .25
47 John Valentin .25
48 Brad Radke .25
49 Ismael Valdes .25
50 Matt Stairs .25
51 Matt Williams .25
52 Reggie Jefferson .25
53 Alan Benes .25
54 Charles Johnson .25
55 Chuck Knoblauch .25
56 Edgar Martinez .25
57 Nomar Garciaparra 3.00
58 Craig Biggio .25
59 Bernie Williams .50
60 David Cone .25
61 Cal Ripken Jr. 6.00
62 Mark McGwire 4.50
63 Roberto Alomar .50
64 Fred McGriff .25
65 Eric Karros .25
66 Robin Ventura .25
67 Darin Erstad .50
68 Michael Tucker .25
69 Jim Thome 1.00
70 Mark Grace .25
71 Lou Collier .25
72 Karim Garcia .25
73 Alex Fernandez .25
74 J.T. Snow .25
75 Reggie Sanders .25
76 John Smoltz .25
77 Tim Salmon .25
78 Paul O'Neill .25
79 Vinny Castilla .25
80 Rafael Palmeiro 1.50
81 Jaret Wright .25
82 Jay Buhner .25
83 Brett Butler .25
84 Todd Greene .25
85 Scott Rolen 1.50
86 Sammy Sosa 3.00
87 Jason Giambi 1.00
88 Carlos Delgado .75
89 Deion Sanders .25
90 Wilton Guerrero .25
91 Andy Pettitte .45
92 Brian Giles .25
93 Dmitri Young .25
94 Ron Coomer .25
95 Mike Cameron .25
96 Edgardo Alfonzo .25
97 Jimmy Key .25
98 Ryan Klesko .25
99 Andy Benes .25
100 Derek Jeter 6.00
101 Jeff Fassero .25
102 Neifi Perez .25
103 Hideo Nomo 1.00
104 Andruw Jones 2.00
105 Todd Helton 1.50
106 Livan Hernandez .25
107 Brett Tomko .25
108 Shannon Stewart .25
109 Bartolo Colon .25
110 Matt Morris .25
111 Miguel Tejada .40
112 Pokey Reese .25
113 Fernando Tatis .25
114 Todd Dunwoody .25
115 Jose Cruz Jr. .25
116 Chan Ho Park .25
117 Kevin Young .25
118 Rickey Henderson 2.00
119 Hideki Irabu .25
120 Francisco Cordova .25
121 Al Martin .25
122 Tony Clark .25
123 Curt Schilling .40
124 Rusty Greer .25
125 Jose Canseco .60
126 Edgar Renteria .25
127 Todd Walker .25
128 Wally Joyner .25
129 Bill Mueller .25
130 Jose Guillen .25
131 Manny Ramirez 2.00
132 Bobby Higginson .25
133 Kevin Orie .25
134 Will Clark .25
135 Dave Nilsson .25
136 Jason Kendall .25
137 Ivan Cruz .25
138 Gary Sheffield .40
139 Bubba Trammell .25
140 Vladimir Guerrero 2.00
141 Dennis Reyes .25
142 Bobby Bonilla .25
143 Ruben Rivera .25
144 Ben Grieve .25
145 Moises Alou .25
146 Tony Womack .25
147 Eric Young .25
148 Paul Konerko .35
149 Dante Bichette .25
150 Joe Carter .25
151 Rondell White .25
152 Chris Holt .25
153 Shawn Green .40
154 Mark Grudzielanek .25
155 Jermaine Dye .25
156 Ken Griffey Jr. (Fan Club) 1.75
157 Frank Thomas (Fan Club) 1.00
158 Chipper Jones (Fan Club) 1.50
159 Mike Piazza (Fan Club) 1.75
160 Cal Ripken Jr. (Fan Club) 3.00
161 Greg Maddux (Fan Club) 1.50
162 Juan Gonzalez (Fan Club) .50
163 Alex Rodriguez (Fan Club) 2.25
164 Mark McGwire (Fan Club) 2.25
165 Derek Jeter (Fan Club) 3.00
166 Larry Walker (Checklist) .25
167 Tony Gwynn (Checklist) .75
168 Tino Martinez (Checklist) .25
169 Scott Rolen (Checklist) .40
170 Nomar Garciaparra (Checklist) .75
1 Mark Kotsay .50
2 Neifi Perez .50
3 Paul Konerko 1.00
4 Jose Cruz Jr. .50
5 Hideki Irabu .50
6 Mike Cameron .50
7 Jeff Suppan .50
8 Kevin Orie .50
9 Pokey Reese .50
10 Todd Dunwoody .50
11 Miguel Tejada 1.00
12 Jose Guillen .50
13 Bartolo Colon .50
14 Derrek Lee .75
15 Antone Williamson .50
16 Wilton Guerrero .50
17 Jaret Wright .50
18 Todd Helton 2.00
19 Shannon Stewart .50
20 Nomar Garciaparra 3.00
21 Brett Tomko .50
22 Fernando Tatis .50
23 Raul Ibanez .50
24 Dennis Reyes .50
25 Bobby Estalella .50
26 Lou Collier .50
27 Bubba Trammell .50
28 Ben Grieve .50
29 Ivan Cruz .50
30 Karim Garcia .50
1 Rusty Greer .25
2 Tino Martinez .25
3 Bobby Bonilla .25
4 Jason Giambi .65
5 Matt Morris .25
6 Craig Counsell .25
7 Reggie Jefferson .25
8 Brian Rose .25
9 Ruben Rivera .25
10 Shawn Estes .25
11 Tony Gwynn 3.00
12 Jeff Abbott .25
13 Jose Cruz Jr. .25
14 Francisco Cordova .25
15 Ryan Klesko .25
16 Tim Salmon .25
17 Brett Tomko .25
18 Matt Williams .25
19 Joe Carter .25
20 Harold Baines .25
21 Gary Sheffield .40
22 Charles Johnson .25
23 Aaron Boone .35
24 Eddie Murray 2.00
25 Matt Stairs .25
26 David Cone .25
27 Jon Nunnally .25
28 Chris Stynes .25
29 Enrique Wilson .25
30 Randy Johnson 2.00
31 Garret Anderson .25
32 Manny Ramirez 2.00
33 Jeff Suppan .25
34 Rickey Henderson 2.00
35 Scott Spiezio .25
36 Rondell White .25
37 Todd Greene .25
38 Delino DeShields .25
39 Kevin Brown .25
40 Chili Davis .25
41 Jimmy Key .25
43 Mike Mussina 1.00
44 Joe Randa .25
45 Chan Ho Park .25
46 Brad Radke .25
47 Geronimo Berroa .25
48 Wade Boggs 3.00
49 Kevin Appier .25
50 Moises Alou .25
51 David Justice .25
52 Ivan Rodriguez 1.50
53 J.T. Snow .25
54 Brian Giles .25
55 Will Clark .25
56 Justin Thompson .25
57 Javier Lopez .25
58 Hideki Irabu .25
59 Mark Grudzielanek .25
60 Abraham Nunez .25
61 Todd Hollandsworth .25
62 Jay Bell .25
63 Nomar Garciaparra 3.00
64 Vinny Castilla .25
65 Lou Collier .25
66 Kevin Orie .25
67 John Valentin .25
68 Robin Ventura .25
69 Denny Neagle .25
70 Tony Womack .25
71 Dennis Reyes .25
72 Wally Joyner .25
73 Kevin Brown .35
74 Ray Durham .25
75 Mike Cameron .25
76 Dante Bichette .25
77 Jose Guillen .25
78 Carlos Delgado .60
79 Paul Molitor 2.00
80 Jason Kendall .25
81 Mark Belhorn .25
82 Damian Jackson .25
83 Bill Mueller .25
84 Kevin Young .25
85 Curt Schilling .50
86 Jeffrey Hammonds .25
87 Sandy Alomar Jr. .25
88 Bartolo Colon .25
89 Wilton Guerrero .25
90 Bernie Williams .25
91 Deion Sanders .25
92 Mike Piazza 3.50
93 Butch Huskey .25
94 Edgardo Alfonzo .25
95 Alan Benes .25
96 Craig Biggio .25
97 Mark Grace .25
98 Shawn Green .40
99 Derrek Lee 1.00
100 Ken Griffey Jr. 3.50
101 Tim Raines .25
102 Pokey Reese .25
103 Lee Stevens .25
104 Shannon Stewart .25
105 John Smoltz .25
106 Frank Thomas 2.00
107 Jeff Fassero .25
108 Jay Buhner .25
109 Jose Canseco .45
110 Omar Vizquel .25
111 Travis Fryman .25
112 Dave Nilsson .25
113 John Olerud .25
114 Larry Walker .25
115 Jim Edmonds .25
116 Bobby Higginson .25
117 Todd Hundley .25
118 Paul O'Neill .25
119 Bip Roberts .25
120 Ismael Valdes .25
121 Pedro Martinez 2.00
122 Jeff Cirillo .25
123 Andy Benes .25
124 Bobby Jones .25
125 Brian Hunter .25
126 Darryl Kile .25
127 Pat Hentgen .25
128 Marquis Grissom .25
129 Eric Davis .25
130 Chipper Jones 3.00
131 Edgar Martinez .25
132 Andy Pettitte .50
133 Cal Ripken Jr. 6.00
134 Scott Rolen 1.50
135 Ron Coomer .25
136 Luis Castillo .25
137 Fred McGriff .25
138 Neifi Perez .25
139 Eric Karros .25
140 Alex Fernandez .25
141 Jason Dickson .25
142 Lance Johnson .25
143 Ray Lankford .25
144 Sammy Sosa 3.00
145 Eric Young .25
146 Bubba Trammell .25
147 Todd Walker .25
148 Mo Vaughn/CC .25
149 Jeff Bagwell/CC 2.00
150 Kenny Lofton/CC .25
151 Raul Mondesi/CC .25
152 Mike Piazza/CC 3.50
153 Chipper Jones/CC 3.00
154 Larry Walker/CC .25
155 Greg Maddux/CC 3.00
156 Ken Griffey Jr./CC 3.50
157 Frank Thomas/CC 2.00
158 Darin Erstad/GLS 2.00
159 Roberto Alomar/GLS 1.50
160 Albert Belle/GLS 1.00
161 Jim Thome/GLS 2.00
162 Tony Clark/GLS 1.00
163 Chuck Knoblauch/GLS 1.00
164 Derek Jeter/GLS 12.00
165 Alex Rodriguez/GLS 8.00
166 Tony Gwynn/GLS 6.00
167 Roger Clemens/GLS 7.00
168 Barry Larkin/GLS 1.00

169 Andres Galarraga/GLS 1.00
170 Vladimir Guerrero/GLS 4.50
171 Mark McGwire/GLS 8.00
172 Barry Bonds/GLS 12.00
173 Juan Gonzalez/GLS 2.50
174 Andruw Jones/GLS 4.50
175 Paul Molitor/GLS 4.50
176 Hideo Nomo/GLS 2.50
177 Cal Ripken Jr./GLS 12.50
178 Brad Fullmer/GLR 1.00
179 Jaret Wright/GLR 1.00
180 Bobby Estalella/GLR 1.00
181 Ben Grieve/GLR 1.00
182 Paul Konerko/GLR 1.50
183 David Ortiz/GLR 3.00
184 Todd Helton/GLR 3.00
185 Juan Encarnacion/GLR 1.00
186 Miguel Tejada/GLR 1.50
187 Jacob Cruz/GLR 1.00
188 Mark Kotsay/GLR 1.00
189 Fernando Tatis/GLR 1.00
190 Ricky Ledee/GLR 1.00
191 Richard Hidalgo/GLR 1.00
192 Richie Sexson/GLR 1.00
193 Luis Ordaz/GLR 1.00
194 Eli Marrero/GLR 1.00
195 Livan Hernandez/GLR 1.00
196 Homer Bush/GLR 1.00
197 Raul Ibanez/GLR 1.00
198 Checklist (Nomar Garciaparra) 1.00
199 Checklist (Scott Rolen) .75
200 Checklist (Jose Cruz Jr.) .25
201 Al Martin .25
1 Ken Griffey Jr. 4.00
2 Frank Thomas 2.50
3 Alex Rodriguez 6.00
4 Mike Piazza 4.00
5 Greg Maddux 3.00
6 Cal Ripken Jr. 7.00
7 Chipper Jones 3.00
8 Derek Jeter 7.00
9 Tony Gwynn 3.00
10 Andruw Jones 2.50
11 Juan Gonzalez 1.25
12 Jeff Bagwell 2.50
13 Mark McGwire 6.00
14 Roger Clemens 3.00
15 Albert Belle .50
16 Barry Bonds 7.00
17 Kenny Lofton .50
18 Ivan Rodriguez 2.00
19 Manny Ramirez 2.50
20 Jim Thome 1.50
21 Chuck Knoblauch .50
22 Paul Molitor 2.50
23 Barry Larkin .50
24 Andy Pettitte 1.00
25 John Smoltz .50
26 Randy Johnson 2.50
27 Bernie Williams .50
28 Larry Walker .50
29 Mo Vaughn .50
30 Bobby Higginson .50
31 Edgardo Alfonzo .50
32 Justin Thompson .50
33 Jeff Suppan .50
34 Roberto Alomar 1.00
35 Hideo Nomo 1.25
36 Rusty Greer .50
37 Tim Salmon .50
38 Jim Edmonds .50
39 Gary Sheffield .75
40 Ken Caminiti .50
41 Sammy Sosa 3.00
42 Tony Womack .50
43 Matt Williams .50
44 Andres Galarraga .50
45 Garret Anderson .50
46 Rafael Palmeiro 2.00
47 Mike Mussina 1.00
48 Craig Biggio .50
49 Wade Boggs 3.00
50 Tom Glavine .75
51 Jason Giambi 1.00
52 Will Clark .50
53 David Justice .50
54 Sandy Alomar Jr. .50
55 Edgar Martinez .50
56 Brady Anderson .50
57 Eric Young .50
58 Ray Lankford .50
59 Kevin Brown .60
60 Raul Mondesi .50
61 Bobby Bonilla .50
62 Javier Lopez .50
63 Fred McGriff .50
64 Rondell White .50
65 Todd Hundley .50
66 Mark Grace .50
67 Alan Benes .50
68 Jeff Abbott .50
69 Bob Abreu .50
70 Deion Sanders .50
71 Tino Martinez .50
72 Shannon Stewart .50
73 Homer Bush .50
74 Carlos Delgado 1.50
75 Raul Ibanez .50
76 Hideki Irabu .50
77 Jose Cruz Jr. .50
78 Tony Clark .50
79 Wilton Guerrero .50
80 Vladimir Guerrero 2.50
81 Scott Rolen 2.25
82 Nomar Garciaparra 3.00
83 Darin Erstad 1.00
84 Chan Ho Park .50
85 Mike Cameron .50
86 Todd Walker .50
87 Todd Dunwoody .50
88 Neifi Perez .50
89 Brett Tomko .50
90 Jose Guillen .50
91 Matt Morris .50
92 Bartolo Colon .50
93 Jaret Wright .50
94 Shawn Estes .50
95 Livan Hernandez .50
96 Bobby Estalella .50
97 Ben Grieve .50
98 Paul Konerko .75
99 David Ortiz 1.00
100 Todd Helton 2.00
101 Juan Encarnacion .50
102 Bubba Trammell .50
103 Miguel Tejada 1.00
104 Jacob Cruz .50
105 Todd Greene .50
106 Kevin Orie .50
107 Mark Kotsay .50
108 Fernando Tatis .50
109 Jay Payton .50
110 Pokey Reese .50
111 Derrek Lee 1.50
112 Richard Hidalgo .50
113 Ricky Ledee .50
114 Lou Collier .50
115 Ruben Rivera .50
116 Shawn Green 1.00
117 Moises Alou .50
118 Ken Griffey Jr. (Generations) 2.00
119 Frank Thomas (Generations) 1.25
120 Alex Rodriguez (Generations) 3.00
121 Mike Piazza (Generations) 2.00
122 Greg Maddux (Generations) 1.75
123 Cal Ripken Jr. (Generations) 3.50
124 Chipper Jones (Generations) 1.75
125 Derek Jeter (Generations) 3.50
126 Tony Gwynn (Generations) 1.75
127 Andruw Jones (Generations) 1.25
128 Juan Gonzalez (Generations) .75
129 Jeff Bagwell (Generations) 1.25
130 Mark McGwire (Generations) 3.00
131 Roger Clemens (Generations) 1.75
132 Albert Belle (Generations) .50
133 Barry Bonds (Generations) 3.50
134 Kenny Lofton (Generations) .50
135 Ivan Rodriguez (Generations) 1.00
136 Manny Ramirez (Generations) 1.25
137 Jim Thome (Generations) 1.00
138 Chuck Knoblauch (Generations) .50
139 Paul Molitor (Generations) 1.25
140 Barry Larkin (Generations) .50
141 Mo Vaughn (Generations) .50
142 Hideki Irabu (Generations) .50
143 Jose Cruz Jr. (Generations) .50
144 Tony Clark (Generations) .50
145 Vladimir Guerrero (Generations) 1.25
146 Scott Rolen (Generations) 1.00
147 Nomar Garciaparra (Generations) 2.00
148 Checklist (Nomar Garciaparra) 1.00
149 Checklist (Larry Walker) .50
150 Checklist (Tino Martinez) .50
1 Ken Griffey Jr./EX 12.00
2 Frank Thomas/EX 7.50
3 Cal Ripken Jr./EX 17.50
4 Alex Rodriguez/EX 15.00
5 Greg Maddux/EX 10.00
6 Mike Piazza/EX 12.00
7 Chipper Jones/EX 10.00
8 Tony Gwynn/FB 10.00
9 Derek Jeter/FB 17.50
10 Jeff Bagwell/EX 7.50
11 Juan Gonzalez/EX 4.00
12 Nomar Garciaparra/EX 10.00
13 Andruw Jones/FB 7.50
14 Hideo Nomo/FB 4.00
15 Roger Clemens/FB 13.50
16 Mark McGwire/FB 15.00
17 Scott Rolen/FB 6.00
18 Vladimir Guerrero/FB 7.50
19 Barry Bonds/FB 17.50
20 Darin Erstad/FB 4.00
21 Albert Belle/FB 2.00
22 Kenny Lofton/FB 2.00
23 Mo Vaughn/FB 2.00
24 Tony Clark/FB 2.00
25 Ivan Rodriguez/FB 6.00
26 Larry Walker/CL 2.00
27 Eddie Murray/CL 7.50
28 Andy Pettitte/CL 4.00
29 Roberto Alomar/CL 2.00
30 Randy Johnson/CL 7.50
31 Manny Ramirez/CL 7.50
32 Paul Molitor/FB 7.50
33 Mike Mussina/CL 4.00
34 Jim Thome/FB 2.00
35 Tino Martinez/CL 2.00
36 Gary Sheffield/CL 3.00
37 Chuck Knoblauch/CL 2.00
38 Bernie Williams/CL 2.00
39 Tim Salmon/CL 2.00
40 Sammy Sosa/CL 10.00
41 Wade Boggs/MZ 10.00
42 Will Clark/GS 2.00
43 Andres Galarraga/CL 2.00
44 Raul Mondesi/CL 2.00
45 Rickey Henderson/GS 6.50
46 Jose Canseco/GS 4.00
47 Pedro Martinez/GS 6.50
48 Jay Buhner/GS 2.00
49 Ryan Klesko/GS 2.00
50 Barry Larkin/CL 2.00
51 Charles Johnson/GS 2.00
52 Tom Glavine/GS 3.00
53 Edgar Martinez/CL 2.00
54 Fred McGriff/GS 2.00
55 Moises Alou/MZ 2.00
56 Dante Bichette/GS 2.00
57 Jim Edmonds/CL 2.00
58 Mark Grace/MZ 2.00
59 Chan Ho Park/MZ 2.00
60 Justin Thompson/MZ 2.00
61 John Smoltz/MZ 2.00
62 Craig Biggio/CL 2.00
63 Ken Caminiti/MZ 2.00
64 Deion Sanders/MZ 2.00
65 Carlos Delgado/GS 4.00
66 David Justice/CL 2.00
67 J.T. Snow/GS 2.00
68 Jason Giambi/CL 4.00
69 Garret Anderson/MZ 2.00
70 Rondell White/MZ 2.00
71 Matt Williams/MZ 2.00
72 Brady Anderson/MZ 2.00
73 Eric Karros/GS 2.00
74 Javier Lopez/GS 2.00
75 Pat Hentgen/GS 2.00
76 Todd Hundley/GS 2.00
77 Ray Lankford/GS 2.00
78 Denny Neagle/GS 2.00
79 Henry Rodriguez/GS 2.00
80 Sandy Alomar Jr./MZ 2.00
81 Rafael Palmeiro/MZ 5.00
82 Robin Ventura/GS 2.00
83 John Olerud/GS 2.00
84 Omar Vizquel/GS 2.00
85 Joe Randa/GS 2.00
86 Lance Johnson/GS 2.00
87 Kevin Brown/GS 2.00
88 Curt Schilling/GS 4.00
89 Ismael Valdes/GS 2.00
90 Francisco Cordova/GS 2.00
91 David Cone/GS 2.00
92 Paul O'Neill/GS 2.00
93 Jimmy Key/GS 2.00
94 Brad Radke/GS 2.00
95 Kevin Appier/GS 2.00
96 Al Martin/GS 2.00
97 Rusty Greer/MZ 2.00
98 Reggie Jefferson/GS 2.00
99 Ron Coomer/GS 2.00
100 Vinny Castilla/GS 2.00
101 Bobby Bonilla/MZ 2.00
102 Eric Young/GS 2.00
103 Tony Womack/GS 2.00
104 Jason Kendall/GS 2.00
105 Jeff Suppan/GS 2.00
106 Shawn Estes/MZ 2.00
107 Shawn Green/GS 2.00
108 Edgardo Alfonzo/MZ 2.00
109 Alan Benes/MZ 2.00
110 Bobby Higginson/GS 2.00
111 Mark Grudzielanek/GS 2.00
112 Wilton Guerrero/GS 2.00
113 Todd Greene/MZ 2.00
114 Pokey Reese/GS 2.00
115 Jose Guillen/CL 2.00
116 Neifi Perez/MZ 2.00
117 Luis Castillo/GS 2.00
118 Edgar Renteria/GS 2.00
119 Karim Garcia/GS 2.00
120 Butch Huskey/GS 2.00
121 Michael Tucker/GS 2.00
122 Jason Dickson/GS 2.00
123 Todd Walker/MZ 2.00
124 Brian Jordan/GS 2.00
125 Joe Carter/GS 2.00
126 Matt Morris/MZ 2.00
127 Brett Tomko/MZ 2.00
128 Mike Cameron/CL 2.00
129 Russ Davis/GS 2.00
130 Shannon Stewart/MZ 2.00
131 Kevin Orie/GS 2.00
132 Scott Spiezio/GS 2.00
133 Brian Giles/GS 2.00
134 Raul Casanova/GS 2.00
135 Jose Cruz Jr./CL 2.00
136 Hideki Irabu/GS 2.00
137 Bubba Trammell/GS 2.00
138 Richard Hidalgo/CL 2.00
139 Paul Konerko/CL 2.50
140 Todd Helton/FB 5.00
141 Miguel Tejada/CL 3.00
142 Fernando Tatis/MZ 2.00
143 Ben Grieve/FB 2.00
144 Travis Lee/FB 2.00
145 Mark Kotsay/CL 2.00
146 Eli Marrero/MZ 2.00
147 David Ortiz/CL 4.00
148 Juan Encarnacion/MZ 2.00
149 Jaret Wright/MZ 2.00
150 Livan Hernandez/CL 2.00
151 Ruben Rivera/GS 2.00
152 Brad Fullmer/MZ 2.00
153 Dennis Reyes/GS 2.00
154 Enrique Wilson/MZ 2.00
155 Todd Dunwoody/MZ 2.00
156 Derrick Gibson/MZ 2.00
157 Aaron Boone/MZ 2.00
158 Ron Wright/MZ 2.00
159 Preston Wilson/MZ 2.00
160 Abraham Nunez/GS 2.00
161 Shane Monahan/GS 2.00
162 Carl Pavano/GS 2.00
163 Derrek Lee/GS 4.00
164 Jeff Abbott/GS 2.00
165 Wes Helms/MZ 2.00
166 Brian Rose/GS 2.00
167 Bobby Estalella/GS 2.00
168 Ken Griffey Jr./GS 9.00
169 Frank Thomas/GS 6.00
170 Cal Ripken Jr./GS 15.00
171 Alex Rodriguez/GS 12.00
172 Greg Maddux/GS 7.50
173 Mike Piazza/GS 9.00
174 Chipper Jones/GS 7.50
175 Tony Gwynn/GS 7.50
176 Derek Jeter/GS 15.00
177 Jeff Bagwell/GS 6.00
178 Juan Gonzalez/GS 3.00
179 Nomar Garciaparra/GS 7.50
180 Andruw Jones/GS 6.00
181 Hideo Nomo/GS 3.00
182 Roger Clemens/GS 8.00
183 Mark McGwire/GS 12.00
184 Scott Rolen/GS 3.00
185 Barry Bonds/GS 15.00
186 Darin Erstad/GS 3.00
187 Mo Vaughn/GS 2.00
188 Ivan Rodriguez/GS 5.00
189 Larry Walker/MZ 2.00
190 Andy Pettitte/GS 3.00
191 Randy Johnson/MZ 6.00
192 Paul Molitor/GS 6.00
193 Jim Thome/GS 4.00
194 Tino Martinez/MZ 2.00
195 Gary Sheffield/GS 3.00
196 Albert Belle/GS 2.00
197 Jose Cruz Jr./GS 2.00
198 Todd Helton/GS 5.00
199 Ben Grieve/GS 2.00
200 Paul Konerko/GS 2.50

1998 Donruss Elite

Donruss Elite consists of a 150-card base set with two parallels and five inserts. The base cards feature a foil background with player photo on front. Another photo is on the back with stats and basic player information. The Aspirations parallel is numbered to 750 and the Status parallel is numbered to 100. The base set also includes the 30-card Generations subset and three checklists. The inserts are Back to the Future, Back to the Future Autographs, Craftsmen, Prime Numbers and Prime Numbers Die-Cuts.

NM/M
Complete Set (150): 15.00
Common Player: .10
Aspirations (750 Sets): 2.5X
Status (100 Sets): 15X
Pack (5): 2.50
Wax Box (18): 40.00
1 Ken Griffey Jr. 1.50
2 Frank Thomas .75
3 Alex Rodriguez 2.00
4 Mike Piazza 1.50
5 Greg Maddux 1.00
6 Cal Ripken Jr. 2.50
7 Chipper Jones 1.00
8 Derek Jeter 2.50
9 Tony Gwynn 1.00
10 Andruw Jones .75
11 Juan Gonzalez .40
12 Jeff Bagwell .75
13 Mark McGwire 2.00
14 Roger Clemens 1.25
15 Albert Belle .10
16 Barry Bonds 2.50
17 Kenny Lofton .10
18 Ivan Rodriguez .65
19 Manny Ramirez .75
20 Jim Thome .50
21 Chuck Knoblauch .10
22 Paul Molitor .75
23 Barry Larkin .10
24 Andy Pettitte .40
25 John Smoltz .10
26 Randy Johnson .75
27 Bernie Williams .10
28 Larry Walker .10
29 Mo Vaughn .10
30 Bobby Higginson .10
31 Edgardo Alfonzo .10
32 Justin Thompson .10
33 Jeff Suppan .10
34 Roberto Alomar .30
35 Hideo Nomo .40
36 Rusty Greer .10
37 Tim Salmon .10
38 Jim Edmonds .10
39 Gary Sheffield .25
40 Ken Caminiti .10
41 Sammy Sosa 1.00
42 Tony Womack .10
43 Matt Williams .10
44 Andres Galarraga .10
45 Garret Anderson .10
46 Rafael Palmeiro .65
47 Mike Mussina .40
48 Craig Biggio .10
49 Wade Boggs 1.00
50 Tom Glavine .25
51 Jason Giambi .50
52 Will Clark .10
53 David Justice .10
54 Sandy Alomar Jr. .10
55 Edgar Martinez .10
56 Brady Anderson .10
57 Eric Young .10
58 Ray Lankford .10
59 Kevin Brown .10
60 Raul Mondesi .10
61 Bobby Bonilla .10
62 Javier Lopez .10
63 Fred McGriff .10
64 Rondell White .10
65 Todd Hundley .10
66 Mark Grace .10
67 Alan Benes .10
68 Jeff Abbott .10
69 Bob Abreu .10
70 Deion Sanders .10
71 Tino Martinez .10
72 Shannon Stewart .10
73 Homer Bush .10
74 Carlos Delgado .50
75 Raul Ibanez .10
76 Hideki Irabu .10
77 Jose Cruz Jr. .10
78 Tony Clark .10
79 Wilton Guerrero .10
80 Vladimir Guerrero .75
81 Scott Rolen .60
82 Nomar Garciaparra 1.00
83 Darin Erstad .30
84 Chan Ho Park .10
85 Mike Cameron .10
86 Todd Walker .10
87 Todd Dunwoody .10
88 Neifi Perez .10
89 Brett Tomko .10
90 Jose Guillen .10
91 Matt Morris .10
92 Bartolo Colon .10
93 Jaret Wright .10
94 Shawn Estes .10
95 Livan Hernandez .10
96 Bobby Estalella .10
97 Ben Grieve .10
98 Paul Konerko .15
99 David Ortiz .40
100 Todd Helton .65
101 Juan Encarnacion .10
102 Bubba Trammell .10
103 Miguel Tejada .25
104 Jacob Cruz .10
105 Todd Greene .10
106 Kevin Orie .10
107 Mark Kotsay .10
108 Fernando Tatis .10
109 Jay Payton .10
110 Pokey Reese .10
111 Derrek Lee .10
112 Richard Hidalgo .10
113 Ricky Ledee .10
114 Lou Collier .10
115 Ruben Rivera .10
116 Shawn Green .20
117 Moises Alou .10
118 Ken Griffey Jr. (Generations) .65
119 Frank Thomas (Generations) .40
120 Alex Rodriguez (Generations) .75
121 Mike Piazza (Generations) .65
122 Greg Maddux (Generations) .50
123 Cal Ripken Jr. (Generations) 1.00
124 Chipper Jones (Generations) .50
125 Derek Jeter (Generations) 1.00
126 Tony Gwynn (Generations) .50
127 Andruw Jones (Generations) .40
128 Juan Gonzalez (Generations) .20
129 Jeff Bagwell (Generations) .40
130 Mark McGwire (Generations) .75
131 Roger Clemens (Generations) .65
132 Albert Belle (Generations) .10
133 Barry Bonds (Generations) 1.00
134 Kenny Lofton (Generations) .10
135 Ivan Rodriguez (Generations) .25
136 Manny Ramirez (Generations) .40
137 Jim Thome (Generations) .25
138 Chuck Knoblauch (Generations) .10
139 Paul Molitor (Generations) .40
140 Barry Larkin (Generations) .10
141 Mo Vaughn (Generations) .10
142 Hideki Irabu (Generations) .10
143 Jose Cruz Jr. (Generations) .10
144 Tony Clark (Generations) .10
145 Vladimir Guerrero (Generations) .40
146 Scott Rolen (Generations) .20
147 Nomar Garciaparra (Generations) .50
148 Checklist (Nomar Garciaparra (Hit Streaks)) .40
149 Checklist (Larry Walker (Long HR-Coors)) .10
150 Checklist (Tino Martinez (3 HR in game)) .10

Aspirations

A parallel edition of 750 of each player are found in this die-cut set. Cards have a scalloped treatment cut into the top and sides and red, rather than silver metallic borders. The word "ASPIRATIONS" in printed on front at bottom-right. Backs have the notation "1 of 750."

NM/M
Common Player: .50
Stars/Rookies: 2.5X

Status

Just 100 serially numbered cards of each player are found in this die-cut parallel set. Cards have a scalloped treatment cut into the top and sides and red, rather than silver metallic borders.

NM/M
Common Player: 1.50
Stars/Rookies: 15X

Back to the Future

These double-front cards feature a veteran or retired star on one side and a young player on the other. Each player's name, team and "Back to the Future" are printed in the border. The cards are numbered to 1,500, with the first 100 of each card signed by both players. Exceptions are cards #1 and #6. Ripken and Konerko did not sign the same cards and Frank Thomas did not sign his Back to the Future card. Thomas instead signed 100 copies of his Elite base set card which was specially marked.

NM/M
Complete Set (8): 40.00
Common Player: 2.50
Production 1,400 Sets
1 Cal Ripken Jr., Paul Konerko 9.00
2 Jeff Bagwell, Todd Helton 4.50
3 Eddie Mathews, Chipper Jones 5.00
4 Juan Gonzalez, Ben Grieve 2.50
5 Hank Aaron, Jose Cruz Jr. 7.50
6 Frank Thomas, David Ortiz 4.50
7 Nolan Ryan, Greg Maddux 9.00
8 Alex Rodriguez, Nomar Garciaparra 9.00

Back to the Future Autographs

The first 100 of each card in the Back to the Future insert was autographed by both players. Exceptions are cards #1 and #6. Ripken and Konerko did not sign the same cards and Frank Thomas did not sign his Back to the Future card. Thomas instead signed 100 specially marked copies of his Elite base-set card.

NM/M
Production 100 Sets
1a Paul Konerko 30.00
1b Cal Ripken Jr. 150.00
2 Jeff Bagwell, Todd Helton 120.00
3 Eddie Mathews, Chipper Jones 200.00
4 Juan Gonzalez, Ben Grieve 30.00
5 Hank Aaron, Jose Cruz Jr. 180.00
7 Nolan Ryan, Greg Maddux 850.00
8 Alex Rodriguez, Nomar Garciaparra 450.00
2 Frank Thomas (Specially autographed Elite) 45.00

Craftsmen

This 30-card insert has color player photos on the front and back. The set is sequentially numbered to 3,500. The Master Craftsmen parallel is numbered to 100.

NM/M
Complete Set (30): 40.00
Common Player: .50
Production 3,500 Sets
Master Craftsman (100 Sets): 10X
1 Ken Griffey Jr. 3.00
2 Frank Thomas 1.50
3 Alex Rodriguez 4.00
4 Cal Ripken Jr. 5.00
5 Greg Maddux 2.00
6 Mike Piazza 3.00
7 Chipper Jones 2.00
8 Derek Jeter 5.00
9 Tony Gwynn 2.00
10 Nomar Garciaparra 2.00
11 Scott Rolen 1.25
12 Jose Cruz Jr. .50
13 Tony Clark .50
14 Vladimir Guerrero 1.50
15 Todd Helton 1.25
16 Ben Grieve .50
17 Andruw Jones 1.50
18 Jeff Bagwell 1.50
19 Mark McGwire 4.00
20 Juan Gonzalez .75
21 Roger Clemens 2.50
22 Albert Belle .50
23 Barry Bonds 5.00
24 Kenny Lofton .50
25 Ivan Rodriguez 1.25
26 Paul Molitor 1.50
27 Barry Larkin (Incorrect "CARDINALS" on front.) .50
28 Mo Vaughn .50
29 Larry Walker .50
30 Tino Martinez .50

Prime Numbers

This 36-card insert includes three cards for each of 12 players. Each card has a single number in the background. The three numbers for each player represent a key statistic for the player (ex. Mark McGwire's cards are 3-8-7; his career home run total at the time was 387). Each card in the set is sequentially numbered. The total is dependent upon the player's statistic. Promo versions with no serial number and a large "SAMPLE" on back exist for each card.

NM/M
Common Card: 5.00
Samples: 50 Percent Player's Common
1A Ken Griffey Jr. 2/94 25.00
1B Ken Griffey Jr. 9/204 20.00
1C Ken Griffey Jr. 4/290 17.50
2A Frank Thomas 4/56 25.00
2B Frank Thomas 5/406 7.50
2C Frank Thomas 6/450 7.50
3A Mark McGwire 3/87 30.00
3B Mark McGwire 8/307 20.00
3C Mark McGwire 7/380 20.00
4A Cal Ripken Jr. 5/17 135.00
4B Cal Ripken Jr. 1/507 13.50
4C Cal Ripken Jr. 7/510 13.50
5A Mike Piazza 5/76 30.00
5B Mike Piazza 7/506 12.00
5C Mike Piazza 6/570 12.00
6A Chipper Jones 4/89 25.00
6B Chipper Jones 8/409 9.00
6C Chipper Jones 9/480 9.00
7A Tony Gwynn 3/72 25.00
7B Tony Gwynn 7/302 9.00
7C Tony Gwynn 2/370 9.00
8A Barry Bonds 3/74 45.00
8B Barry Bonds 7/304 12.00
8C Barry Bonds 4/370 12.00
9A Jeff Bagwell 4/25 25.00
9B Jeff Bagwell 2/405 7.50
9C Jeff Bagwell 5/420 7.50
10A Juan Gonzalez 5/89 9.00
10B Juan Gonzalez 8/509 6.00
10C Juan Gonzalez 9/580 6.00
11A Alex Rodriguez 5/34 55.00
11B Alex Rodriguez 3/504 12.00
11C Alex Rodriguez 4/530 12.00
12A Kenny Lofton 3/54 15.00
12B Kenny Lofton 5/304 5.00
12C Kenny Lofton 4/350 5.00

Prime Numbers Die-Cuts

This set is a die-cut parallel of the Prime Numbers insert. Each card is sequentially numbered. The production run for each player is the number featured on his first card times 100, his second card times 10 and his third card is sequentially numbered to the number featured on the card.

NM/M
Common Player: 4.00
1A Ken Griffey Jr. 2/200 20.00
1B Ken Griffey Jr. 9/90 35.00
1C Ken Griffey Jr. 4/4 130.00
2A Frank Thomas 4/400 6.00
2B Frank Thomas 5/50 20.00
2C Frank Thomas 6/6 60.00
3A Mark McGwire 3/300 17.50
3B Mark McGwire 8/80 50.00
3C Mark McGwire 7/7 110.00
4A Cal Ripken Jr. 5/500 12.50
4B Cal Ripken Jr. 1/10 95.00
4C Cal Ripken Jr. 7/7 120.00
5A Mike Piazza 5/500 10.00
5B Mike Piazza 7/70 30.00
5C Mike Piazza 6/6 75.00
6A Chipper Jones 4/400 7.50
6B Chipper Jones 8/80 25.00
6C Chipper Jones 9/9 55.00
7A Tony Gwynn 3/300 9.00
7B Tony Gwynn 7/70 25.00
7C Tony Gwynn 2/2 160.00
8A Barry Bonds 3/300 10.00
8B Barry Bonds 7/70 35.00
8C Barry Bonds 4/4 160.00
9A Jeff Bagwell 4/400 4.00
9B Jeff Bagwell 2/20 25.00
9C Jeff Bagwell 5/5 55.00
10A Juan Gonzalez 5/500 4.00
10B Juan Gonzalez 8/80 15.00
10C Juan Gonzalez 9/9 55.00
11A Alex Rodriguez 5/500 8.00
11B Alex Rodriguez 3/30 60.00
11C Alex Rodriguez 4/4 160.00
12A Kenny Lofton 3/300 4.00
12B Kenny Lofton 5/50 7.50
12C Kenny Lofton 4/4 30.00

1998 Donruss Preferred

The Donruss Preferred 200-card base set is broken down into five subsets: 100 Grand Stand cards (5:1), 40 Mezzanine (1:6), 30 Club Level (1:12), 20 Field Box (1:23) and 10 Executive Suite (1:65). The base set is paralleled in the Preferred Seating set. Each subset has a different die-cut in the parallel. Inserts in this product include Great X-Pectations, Precious Metals and Title Waves.

NM/M
Complete Set (200): 90.00
Common Grand Stand (5:1): .10
Common Mezzanine (1:6): .20
Common Club Level (1:12): .30
Common Field Box: (1:23) .40
Common Executive Suite (1:65): 1.50
Tin Pack (5): 3.00
Tin Box (24): 40.00
1 Ken Griffey Jr./EX 4.00
2 Frank Thomas/EX 2.50
3 Cal Ripken Jr./EX 7.50
4 Alex Rodriguez/EX 5.00
5 Greg Maddux/EX 3.00
6 Mike Piazza/EX 4.00
7 Chipper Jones/EX 3.00
8 Tony Gwynn/FB 2.50
9 Derek Jeter/FB 6.00
10 Jeff Bagwell/EX 2.50
11 Juan Gonzalez/EX 1.50
12 Nomar Garciaparra/EX 3.00
13 Andruw Jones/FB 2.00
14 Hideo Nomo/FB .65
15 Roger Clemens/FB 3.00
16 Mark McGwire/FB 5.00
17 Scott Rolen/FB .75
18 Vladimir Guerrero/FB 2.00
19 Barry Bonds/FB 6.00
20 Darin Erstad/FB .60
21 Albert Belle/FB .40
22 Kenny Lofton/FB .40
23 Mo Vaughn/FB .40
24 Tony Clark/FB .40
25 Ivan Rodriguez/FB 1.50
26 Larry Walker/CL .30
27 Eddie Murray/CL 1.00
28 Andy Pettitte/CL .45
29 Roberto Alomar/CL .40
30 Randy Johnson/CL 1.00
31 Manny Ramirez/CL 1.00
32 Paul Molitor/FB 2.00
33 Mike Mussina/CL .50
34 Jim Thome/FB .75
35 Tino Martinez/CL .30
36 Gary Sheffield/CL .45
37 Chuck Knoblauch/CL .30
38 Bernie Williams/CL .30
39 Tim Salmon/CL .30
40 Sammy Sosa/CL 1.50
41 Wade Boggs/MZ .75
42 Will Clark/GS .10
43 Andres Galarraga/CL .30
44 Raul Mondesi/CL .30
45 Rickey Henderson/GS .50
46 Jose Canseco/GS .35
47 Pedro Martinez/GS .50
48 Jay Buhner/GS .10
49 Ryan Klesko/GS .10
50 Barry Larkin/CL .30
51 Charles Johnson/GS .10
52 Tom Glavine/GS .25
53 Edgar Martinez/CL .30
54 Fred McGriff/GS .10
55 Moises Alou/MZ .20
56 Dante Bichette/GS .10
57 Jim Edmonds/CL .30
58 Mark Grace/MZ .20
59 Chan Ho Park/MZ .20
60 Justin Thompson/MZ .20
61 John Smoltz/MZ .20
62 Craig Biggio/CL .30
63 Ken Caminiti/MZ .20
64 Deion Sanders/MZ .20
65 Carlos Delgado/GS .30
66 David Justice/CL .30
67 J.T. Snow/GS .10
68 Jason Giambi/CL .50
69 Garret Anderson/MZ .20
70 Rondell White/MZ .20
71 Matt Williams/MZ .20
72 Brady Anderson/MZ .20
73 Eric Karros/GS .10
74 Javier Lopez/GS .10
75 Pat Hentgen/GS .10
76 Todd Hundley/GS .10
77 Ray Lankford/GS .10
78 Denny Neagle/GS .10
79 Henry Rodriguez/GS .10
80 Sandy Alomar Jr./MZ .20
81 Rafael Palmeiro/MZ .50
82 Robin Ventura/GS .10
83 John Olerud/GS .10
84 Omar Vizquel/GS .10
85 Joe Randa/GS .10
86 Lance Johnson/GS .10
87 Kevin Brown/GS .10
88 Curt Schilling/GS .25
89 Ismael Valdes/GS .10
90 Francisco Cordova/GS .10
91 David Cone/GS .10
92 Paul O'Neill/GS .10
93 Jimmy Key/GS .10
94 Brad Radke/GS .10
95 Kevin Appier/GS .10
96 Al Martin/GS .10
97 Rusty Greer/MZ .20
98 Reggie Jefferson/GS .10
99 Ron Coomer/GS .10
100 Vinny Castilla/GS .10
101 Bobby Bonilla/MZ .20
102 Eric Young/GS .10
103 Tony Womack/GS .10
104 Jason Kendall/GS .10
105 Jeff Suppan/GS .10
106 Shawn Estes/MZ .20
107 Shawn Green/GS .25
108 Edgardo Alfonzo/MZ .20
109 Alan Benes/MZ .20
110 Bobby Higginson/GS .10
111 Mark Grudzielanek/GS .10
112 Wilton Guerrero/GS .10
113 Todd Greene/MZ .20
114 Pokey Reese/GS .10
115 Jose Guillen/CL .30
116 Neifi Perez/MZ .20
117 Luis Castillo/GS .10
118 Edgar Renteria/GS .10
119 Karim Garcia/GS .10
120 Butch Huskey/GS .10
121 Michael Tucker/GS .10
122 Jason Dickson/GS .10
123 Todd Walker/MZ .20
124 Brian Jordan/GS .10
125 Joe Carter/GS .10
126 Matt Morris/MZ .20
127 Brett Tomko/MZ .20
128 Mike Cameron/CL .30
129 Russ Davis/GS .10
130 Shannon Stewart/MZ .20
131 Kevin Orie/GS .10
132 Scott Spiezio/GS .10
133 Brian Giles/GS .10
134 Raul Casanova/GS .10
135 Jose Cruz Jr./CL .30
136 Hideki Irabu/GS .10
137 Bubba Trammell/GS .10
138 Richard Hidalgo/CL .30
139 Paul Konerko/CL .35
140 Todd Helton/FB 1.00
141 Miguel Tejada/CL .40
142 Fernando Tatis/MZ .20
143 Ben Grieve/FB .40
144 Travis Lee/FB .65
145 Mark Kotsay/CL .30
146 Eli Marrero/MZ .20
147 David Ortiz/CL .50
148 Juan Encarnacion/MZ .20
149 Jaret Wright/MZ .20
150 Livan Hernandez/CL .30
151 Ruben Rivera/GS .10
152 Brad Fullmer/MZ .20
153 Dennis Reyes/GS .10
154 Enrique Wilson/MZ .20
155 Todd Dunwoody/MZ .20
156 Derrick Gibson/MZ .20
157 Aaron Boone/MZ .20
158 Ron Wright/MZ .20
159 Preston Wilson/MZ .20
160 Abraham Nunez/GS .10
161 Shane Monahan/GS .10
162 Carl Pavano/GS .10
163 Derrek Lee/GS .35
164 Jeff Abbott/GS .10
165 Wes Helms/MZ .20
166 Brian Rose/GS .10
167 Bobby Estalella/GS .10
168 Ken Griffey Jr./GS .75
169 Frank Thomas/GS .50
170 Cal Ripken Jr./GS 1.50
171 Alex Rodriguez/GS 1.00
172 Greg Maddux/GS .60
173 Mike Piazza/GS .75
174 Chipper Jones/GS .60
175 Tony Gwynn/GS .60
176 Derek Jeter/GS 1.50
177 Jeff Bagwell/GS .50
178 Juan Gonzalez/GS .30
179 Nomar Garciaparra/GS .60
180 Andruw Jones/GS .50
181 Hideo Nomo/GS .30
182 Roger Clemens/GS .65
183 Mark McGwire/GS 1.00
184 Scott Rolen/GS .35
185 Barry Bonds/GS 1.50
186 Darin Erstad/GS .25
187 Mo Vaughn/GS .10
188 Ivan Rodriguez/GS .40
189 Larry Walker/MZ .20
190 Andy Pettitte/GS .30
191 Randy Johnson/MZ .60
192 Paul Molitor/GS .50
193 Jim Thome/GS .35
194 Tino Martinez/MZ .20
195 Gary Sheffield/GS .30
196 Albert Belle/GS .10
197 Jose Cruz Jr./GS .10
198 Todd Helton/GS .40
199 Ben Grieve/GS .10
200 Paul Konerko/GS .20

Seating

Preferred Seating is a die-cut parallel of the base set. Each section of the base set has a different die-cut.

NM/M
Common Grand Stand: .50
Stars and Rookies: 4X
Common Mezzanine: .50
Stars and Rookies: 2X
Common Club Level: .50

Stars and Rookies: 2X
Common Field Box: 1.00
Stars and Rookies: 1.5X
Common Executive Suite: 2.50
Stars and Rookies: 1X

Great X-pectations

This 26-card insert features a veteran player on one side and a young player on the other. A large "GX" appears in the background on each side. The cards are sequentially numbered to 2,700, with the first 300 of each die-cut around the "GX."

NM/M
Complete Set (26): 35.00
Common Player: .75
Die-Cuts: 3X
Samples: 1X
1 Jeff Bagwell, Travis Lee 1.25
2 Jose Cruz Jr., Ken Griffey Jr. 2.00
3 Larry Walker, Ben Grieve .75
4 Frank Thomas, Todd Helton 1.25
5 Jim Thome, Paul Konerko 1.00
6 Alex Rodriguez, Miguel Tejada 2.50
7 Greg Maddux, Livan Hernandez 1.75
8 Roger Clemens, Jaret Wright 1.75
9 Albert Belle, Juan Encarnacion .75
10 Mo Vaughn, David Ortiz 1.00
11 Manny Ramirez, Mark Kotsay 1.25
12 Tim Salmon, Brad Fullmer .75
13 Cal Ripken Jr., Fernando Tatis 3.50
14 Hideo Nomo, Hideki Irabu 1.50
15 Mike Piazza, Todd Greene 2.00
16 Gary Sheffield, Richard Hidalgo .75
17 Paul Molitor, Darin Erstad 1.25
18 Ivan Rodriguez, Eli Marrero 1.00
19 Ken Caminiti, Todd Walker .75
20 Tony Gwynn, Jose Guillen 1.75
21 Derek Jeter, Nomar Garciaparra 3.50
22 Chipper Jones, Scott Rolen 1.75
23 Juan Gonzalez, Andruw Jones 1.25
24 Barry Bonds, Vladimir Guerrero 3.50
25 Mark McGwire, Tony Clark 2.50
26 Bernie Williams, Mike Cameron .75

Precious Metals

Precious Metals is a 30-card partial parallel of the Preferred base set. Each card was printed on stock using real silver, gold or platinum. Fifty complete sets were produced.

		NM/M
Complete Set (30):		850.00
Common Player:		7.50
1	Ken Griffey Jr.	50.00
2	Frank Thomas	35.00
3	Cal Ripken Jr.	75.00
4	Alex Rodriguez	60.00
5	Greg Maddux	45.00
6	Mike Piazza	50.00
7	Chipper Jones	45.00
8	Tony Gwynn	45.00
9	Derek Jeter	75.00
10	Jeff Bagwell	35.00
11	Juan Gonzalez	15.00
12	Nomar Garciaparra	45.00
13	Andruw Jones	35.00
14	Hideo Nomo	15.00
15	Roger Clemens	45.00
16	Mark McGwire	60.00
17	Scott Rolen	25.00
18	Barry Bonds	75.00
19	Darin Erstad	15.00
20	Kenny Lofton	7.50
21	Mo Vaughn	7.50
22	Ivan Rodriguez	25.00
23	Randy Johnson	35.00
24	Paul Molitor	35.00
25	Jose Cruz Jr.	7.50
26	Paul Konerko	7.50
27	Todd Helton	25.00
28	Ben Grieve	7.50
29	Travis Lee	7.50
30	Mark Kotsay	7.50

Title Waves

This 30-card set features players who won awards or titles between 1993-1997. Printed on plastic stock, each card is sequentially numbered to the year the player won the award. The card fronts feature the Title Waves logo, a color player photo in front of a background of fans and the name of the award the player won.

		NM/M
Complete Set (30):		100.00
Common Player:		1.00
1	Nomar Garciaparra	5.00
2	Scott Rolen	2.50
3	Roger Clemens	5.50
4	Gary Sheffield	1.50
5	Jeff Bagwell	3.50
6	Cal Ripken Jr.	10.00
7	Frank Thomas	3.50
8	Ken Griffey Jr.	6.00
9	Larry Walker	1.00
10	Derek Jeter	10.00
11	Juan Gonzalez	2.00
12	Bernie Williams	1.00
13	Andruw Jones	3.50
14	Andy Pettitte	1.50
15	Ivan Rodriguez	2.50
16	Alex Rodriguez	8.00
17	Mark McGwire	8.00
18	Andres Galarraga	1.00
19	Hideo Nomo	2.00
20	Mo Vaughn	1.00
21	Randy Johnson	3.50
22	Chipper Jones	5.00
23	Greg Maddux	5.00
24	Manny Ramirez	3.50
25	Tony Gwynn	5.00
26	Albert Belle	1.00
27	Kenny Lofton	1.00
28	Mike Piazza	6.00
29	Paul Molitor	3.50
30	Barry Bonds	10.00

Tins

Donruss Preferred was packaged in collectible tins. Each tin contained five cards and featured one of 24 players on the top. Silver (numbered to 999) and gold (199) parallel tins were also produced and included in hobby-only boxes. The values shown are for empty tins.

		NM/M
Complete Set (24):		17.50
Common Player:		.25
Gold Tins (199):		3X
Silver Tins (999):		1.5X
1	Todd Helton	.65
2	Ben Grieve	.25
3	Cal Ripken Jr.	2.50
4	Alex Rodriguez	2.00
5	Greg Maddux	1.00
6	Mike Piazza	1.50
7	Chipper Jones	1.00
8	Travis Lee	.25
9	Derek Jeter	2.50
10	Jeff Bagwell	.75
11	Juan Gonzalez	.50
12	Mark McGwire	2.00
13	Hideo Nomo	.50
14	Roger Clemens	1.25
15	Andruw Jones	.75
16	Paul Molitor	.75
17	Vladimir Guerrero	.75
18	Jose Cruz Jr.	.25
19	Nomar Garciaparra	1.00
20	Scott Rolen	.65
21	Ken Griffey Jr.	1.50
22	Larry Walker	.25
23	Frank Thomas	.75
24	Tony Gwynn	1.00

Double-Wide Tins

Double-wide flip-top tins of Donruss Preferred cards were a reail exclusive with a price tag of about $6. The double-wide retail tins use the same player checklist and photo as the green hobby-version single tins, but have predominantly blue color. Values shown are for opened tins.

		NM/M
Complete Set (12):		12.00
Common Tin:		.65
1	Todd Helton, Ben Grieve	.65
2	Cal Ripken Jr., Alex Rodriguez	2.00
3	Greg Maddux, Mike Piazza	1.25
4	Chipper Jones, Travis Lee	1.00
5	Derek Jeter, Jeff Bagwell	2.00
6	Juan Gonzalez, Mark McGwire	1.50
7	Hideo Nomo, Roger Clemens	1.00
8	Andruw Jones, Paul Molitor	.75
9	Vladimir Guerrero, Jose Cruz Jr.	.75
10	Nomar Garciaparra, Scott Rolen	1.00
11	Ken Griffey Jr., Larry Walker	1.25
12	Tony Gwynn, Frank Thomas	1.00

Tin Boxes

The boxes for 1998 Donruss Preferred consisted of a lithographed steel lidded box which contained 24 tin packs. The basic tin box was green in color and individually serial numbered to 999. A parallel gold box issue was randomly inserted in Preferred cases and had boxes numbered to 199. Values shown are for empty boxes.

		NM/M
Complete Set (24):		85.00
Common Player:		1.00
Gold:		1.5X
1	Todd Helton	2.50
2	Ben Grieve	1.00
3	Cal Ripken Jr.	10.00
4	Alex Rodriguez	7.50
5	Greg Maddux	5.00
6	Mike Piazza	6.00
7	Chipper Jones	5.00
8	Travis Lee	1.00
9	Derek Jeter	10.00
10	Jeff Bagwell	3.00
11	Juan Gonzalez	1.50
12	Mark McGwire	7.50
13	Hideo Nomo	1.50
14	Roger Clemens	5.50
15	Andruw Jones	3.00
16	Paul Molitor	3.00
17	Vladimir Guerrero	3.00
18	Jose Cruz Jr.	1.00
19	Nomar Garciaparra	5.00
20	Scott Rolen	2.00
21	Ken Griffey Jr.	6.00
22	Larry Walker	1.00
23	Frank Thomas	3.00
24	Tony Gwynn	5.00

1998 Donruss Signature Series Preview Autographs

This insert was a surprise addition to Donruss Update. The set features autographs from top rookies and stars. The number of cards produced varies for each player. The card fronts have a color player photo in front of a gold checkered border with the signature in a white area near the bottom. Cards of a number of players (Alou, Casey, Jenkins, Wilson, etc.) were never officially released, having been returned too late by the players; specimens, have, however made their way into the hobby market in unknown numbers.

		NM/M
Common Player:		10.00
(1)	Sandy Alomar Jr./96	30.00
(2)	Moises Alou	50.00
(3)	Andy Benes/135	15.00
(4)	Russell Branyan/188	15.00
(5)	Sean Casey	85.00
(6)	Tony Clark/188	20.00
(7)	Juan Encarnacion/193	15.00
(8)	Brad Fullmer/396	10.00
(9)	Juan Gonzalez/108	115.00
(10)	Ben Grieve/100	35.00
(11)	Todd Helton/101	50.00
(12)	Richard Hidalgo/380	10.00
(13)	A.J. Hinch/400	10.00
(14)	Damian Jackson/15	65.00
(15)	Geoff Jenkins	185.00
(16)	Derek Jeter	1,225
(17)	Chipper Jones/112	125.00
(18)	Chuck Knoblauch/98	50.00
(19)	Travis Lee/101	20.00
(20)	Mike Lowell/450	15.00
(21)	Greg Maddux/92	165.00
(22)	Kevin Millwood/395	30.00
(23)	Magglio Ordonez/420	50.00
(24)	David Ortiz/393	75.00
(25)	Rafael Palmeiro/107	50.00
(26)	Cal Ripken Jr./22	850.00
(27)	Alex Rodriguez/23	1,150
(28)	Curt Schilling/100	100.00
(29)	Randall Simon/380	10.00
(30)	Fernando Tatis/400	10.00
(31)	Miguel Tejada/375	40.00
(32)	Robin Ventura/95	30.00
(33)	Dan Wilson	85.00
(34)	Kerry Wood/373	40.00

1998 Donruss Signature Series

The 140-card base set has a white border encasing the player photo with the logo stamped with silver foil. Card backs have a small photo and complete year-by-year statistics. Signature Proofs are a parallel to the base set utilizing holo-foil treatment and "Signature Proof" written down the left edge of the card front. Each card is numbered "1 of 150" on the card back.

		NM/M
Complete Set (140):		30.00
Common Player:		.10
Signature Proofs:		12X
Pack (5):		12.50
Wax Box (12):		150.00
1	David Justice	.10
2	Derek Jeter	2.50
3	Nomar Garciaparra	1.00
4	Ryan Klesko	.10
5	Jeff Bagwell	.75
6	Dante Bichette	.10
7	Ivan Rodriguez	.65
8	Albert Belle	.10
9	Cal Ripken Jr.	2.50
10	Craig Biggio	.10
11	Barry Larkin	.10
12	Jose Guillen	.10
13	Will Clark	.10
14	J.T. Snow	.10
15	Chuck Knoblauch	.10
16	Todd Walker	.10
17	Scott Rolen	.60
18	Rickey Henderson	.75
19	Juan Gonzalez	.40
20	Justin Thompson	.10
21	Roger Clemens	1.25
22	Ray Lankford	.10
23	Jose Cruz Jr.	.10
24	Ken Griffey Jr.	1.50
25	Andruw Jones	.75
26	Darin Erstad	.30
27	Jim Thome	.50
28	Wade Boggs	1.00
29	Ken Caminiti	.10
30	Todd Hundley	.10
31	Mike Piazza	1.50
32	Sammy Sosa	1.00
33	Larry Walker	.10
34	Matt Williams	.10
35	Frank Thomas	.75
36	Gary Sheffield	.30
37	Alex Rodriguez	2.00
38	Hideo Nomo	.40
39	Kenny Lofton	.10
40	John Smoltz	.10
41	Mo Vaughn	.10
42	Edgar Martinez	.10
43	Paul Molitor	.75
44	Rafael Palmeiro	.65
45	Barry Bonds	2.50
46	Vladimir Guerrero	.75
47	Carlos Delgado	.50
48	Bobby Higginson	.10
49	Greg Maddux	1.00
50	Jim Edmonds	.10
51	Randy Johnson	.75
52	Mark McGwire	2.00
53	Rondell White	.10
54	Raul Mondesi	.10
55	Manny Ramirez	.75
56	Pedro Martinez	.75
57	Tim Salmon	.10
58	Moises Alou	.10
59	Fred McGriff	.10
60	Garret Anderson	.10
61	Sandy Alomar Jr.	.10
62	Chan Ho Park	.10
63	Mark Kotsay	.10
64	Mike Mussina	.50
65	Tom Glavine	.25
66	Tony Clark	.10
67	Mark Grace	.10
68	Tony Gwynn	1.00
69	Tino Martinez	.10
70	Kevin Brown	.10
71	Todd Greene	.10
72	Andy Pettitte	.30
73	Livan Hernandez	.10
74	Curt Schilling	.25
75	Andres Galarraga	.10
76	Rusty Greer	.10
77	Jay Buhner	.10
78	Bobby Bonilla	.10
79	Chipper Jones	1.00
80	Eric Young	.10
81	Jason Giambi	.50
82	Javy Lopez	.10
83	Roberto Alomar	.25
84	Bernie Williams	.10
85	A.J. Hinch	.10
86	Kerry Wood	.40
87	Juan Encarnacion	.10
88	Brad Fullmer	.10
89	Ben Grieve	.10
90	Magglio Ordonez **RC**	2.00
91	Todd Helton	.65
92	Richard Hidalgo	.10
93	Paul Konerko	.15
94	Aramis Ramirez	.10
95	Ricky Ledee	.10
96	Derrek Lee	.50
97	Travis Lee	.15
98	Matt Anderson **RC**	.25
99	Jaret Wright	.10
100	David Ortiz	.35
101	Carl Pavano	.10
102	Orlando Hernandez **RC**	.50
103	Fernando Tatis	.10
104	Miguel Tejada	.30
105	Rolando Arrojo **RC**	.50
106	Kevin Millwood **RC**	1.00
107	Ken Griffey Jr. (Checklist)	.50
108	Frank Thomas (Checklist)	.30
109	Cal Ripken Jr. (Checklist)	.75
110	Greg Maddux (Checklist)	.40
111	John Olerud	.10
112	David Cone	.10
113	Vinny Castilla	.10
114	Jason Kendall	.10
115	Brian Jordan	.10
116	Hideki Irabu	.10
117	Bartolo Colon	.10
118	Greg Vaughn	.10
119	David Segui	.10
120	Bruce Chen	.10
121	Julio Ramirez **RC**	.10
122	Troy Glaus **RC**	4.00
123	Jeremy Giambi **RC**	.50
124	Ryan Minor **RC**	.15
125	Richie Sexson	.10
126	Dermal Brown	.10
127	Adrian Beltre	.15
128	Eric Chavez	.30
129	J.D. Drew **RC**	4.00
130	Gabe Kapler **RC**	.30
131	Masato Yoshii **RC**	.25
132	Mike Lowell **RC**	1.00
133	Jim Parque **RC**	.25
134	Roy Halladay	.10
135	Carlos Lee **RC**	1.00
136	Jin Ho Cho **RC**	.25
137	Michael Barrett	.10
138	Fernando Seguignol **RC**	.40
139	Odalis Perez **RC**	.50
140	Mark McGwire (Checklist)	.65

Proofs

This parallel set differs from the regular issue Signature Series base cards in the presence at left-front of a vertical stack of gold refractive foil strips on which SIGNATURE PROOF is spelled out. Also, backs of the proofs have a gold, rather than white, background.

	NM/M
Complete Set (140):	450.00
Common Player:	1.00
Stars/Rookies:	12X

Autographs Samples

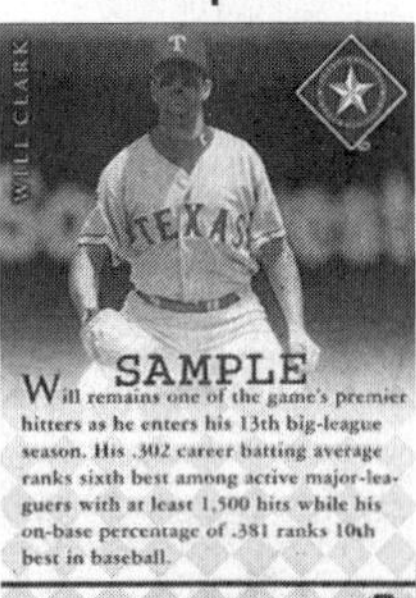

SAMPLE
Will remains one of the game's premier hitters as he enters his 13th big-league season. His .302 career batting average ranks sixth best among active major-leaguers with at least 1,500 hits while his on-base percentage of .381 ranks 10th best in baseball.

An unknown number of cards can be found with facsimile signatures on front and a "SAMPLE" overprint on back.

	NM/M
Adrian Beltre (Century)	12.50
Will Clark (Century)	12.50
Travis Lee (Red)	3.00

Autographs (Red)

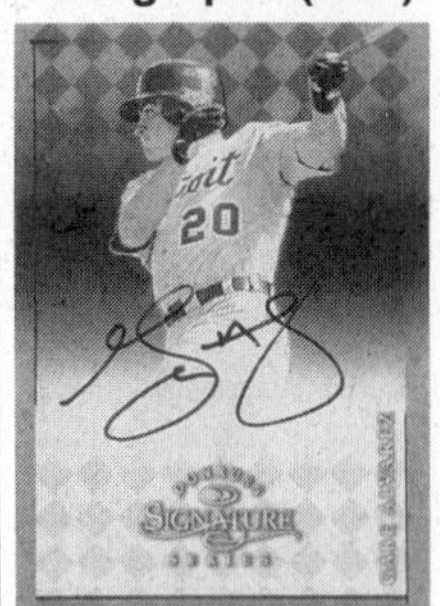

Autographs were inserted one per pack and feature the player photo over a silver and red foil background. The featured player's autograph appears on the bottom portion on front with the Donruss logo stamped in gold foil. Autographs are un-numbered. The first 100 cards signed by each player are blue, sequentially numbered and designated as "Century Marks." The next 1,000 signed are green, sequentially numbered and designated as "Millennium Marks." Greg Maddux signed only 12 regular Donruss Signature Autographs.

		NM/M
Common Player:		2.50
(1)	Roberto Alomar/150	35.00
(2)	Sandy Alomar Jr./700	10.00
(3)	Moises Alou/900	15.00
(4)	Gabe Alvarez/2,900	2.50
(5)	Wilson Alvarez/1,600	4.00
(6)	Jay Bell/1,500	4.00
(7)	Adrian Beltre/1,900	25.00
(8)	Andy Benes/2,600	4.00
(9)	Aaron Boone/3,400	8.00
(10)	Russell Branyan/1,650	4.00
(11)	Orlando Cabrera/3,100	8.00

(12) Mike Cameron/1,150 8.00
(13) Joe Carter/400 10.00
(14) Sean Casey/2,275 8.00
(15) Bruce Chen/150 5.00
(16) Tony Clark/2,275 5.00
(17) Will Clark/1,400 15.00
(18) Matt Clement/1,400 4.00
(19) Pat Cline/400 5.00
(20) Ken Cloude/3,400 2.50
(21) Michael Coleman/2,800 2.50
(22) David Cone/25 50.00
(23) Jeff Conine/1,400 5.00
(24) Jacob Cruz/3,200 2.50
(25) Russ Davis/3,500 2.50
(26) Jason Dickson/1,400 4.00
(27) Todd Dunwoody/3,500 2.50
(28) Juan Encarnacion/3,400 5.00
(29) Darin Erstad/700 10.00
(30) Bobby Estalella/3,400 4.00
(31) Jeff Fassero/3,400 2.50
(32) John Franco/1,800 2.50
(33) Brad Fullmer/3,100 5.00
(34) Jason Giambi/3,100 15.00
(35) Derrick Gibson/1,200 5.00
(36) Todd Greene/1,400 5.00
(37) Ben Grieve/1,400 5.00
(38) Mark Grudzielanek/3,200 4.00
(39) Vladimir Guerrero/2,100 25.00
(40) Wilton Guerrero/1,900 4.00
(41) Jose Guillen/2,400 5.00
(42) Todd Helton/1,300 20.00
(43) Richard Hidalgo/3,400 4.00
(44) A.J. Hinch/2,900 4.00
(45) Butch Huskey/1,900 4.00
(46) Raul Ibanez/3,300 2.50
(47) Damian Jackson/900 2.50
(48) Geoff Jenkins/3,100 6.00
(49) Eric Karros/650 8.00
(50) Ryan Klesko/400 8.00
(51) Mark Kotsay/3,600 5.00
(52) Ricky Ledee/2,200 5.00
(53) Derrek Lee/3,400 15.00
(54) Travis Lee/150 10.00
(54s) Travis Lee (Facsimile autograph, "SAMPLE" on back.) 3.00
(55) Javier Lopez/650 8.00
(56) Mike Lowell/3,500 10.00
(57) Greg Maddux/12 625.00
(58) Eli Marrero/3,400 5.00
(59) Al Martin/1,300 4.00
(60) Rafael Medina/1,400 2.50
(61) Scott Morgan/900 4.50
(62) Abraham Nunez/3,500 2.50
(63) Paul O'Neill/1,000 20.00
(64) Luis Ordaz/2,700 2.50
(65) Magglio Ordonez/3,200 15.00
(66) Kevin Orie/1,350 5.00
(67) David Ortiz/3,400 25.00
(68) Rafael Palmeiro/1,000 25.00
(69) Carl Pavano/2,600 5.00
(70) Neifi Perez/3,300 2.50
(71) Dante Powell/3,050 2.50
(72) Aramis Ramirez/2,800 10.00
(73) Mariano Rivera/900 35.00
(74) Felix Rodriguez/1,400 3.00
(75) Henry Rodriguez/3,400 3.00
(76) Scott Rolen/1,900 30.00
(77) Brian Rose/1,400 3.00
(78) Curt Schilling/900 30.00
(79) Richie Sexson/3,500 8.00
(80) Randall Simon/3,500 3.00
(81) J.T. Snow/400 10.00
(82) Jeff Suppan/1,400 5.00
(83) Fernando Tatis/3,900 3.00
(84) Miguel Tejada/3,800 15.00
(85) Brett Tomko/3,400 2.50
(86) Bubba Trammell/3,900 2.50
(87) Ismael Valdez/1,900 5.00
(88) Robin Ventura/1,400 5.00
(89) Billy Wagner/3,900 10.00
(90) Todd Walker/1,900 5.00
(91) Daryle Ward/400 4.00
(92) Rondell White/3,400 5.00
(93) Antone Williamson/3,350 2.50
(94) Dan Wilson/2,400 4.00
(95) Enrique Wilson/3,400 2.50
(96) Preston Wilson/2,100 5.00
(97) Tony Womack/3,500 2.50
(98) Kerry Wood/3,400 10.00

Century Marks (Blue)

This 121-card set is a serially numbered, blue-foil parallel of the Autographs insert set and limited to 100 cards signed by each featured player (unless otherwise shown in the checklist). Jason Kendall's cards were never signed or returned to Donruss for packaging. A few have made their way into the hobby.

NM/M

Common Player: 10.00

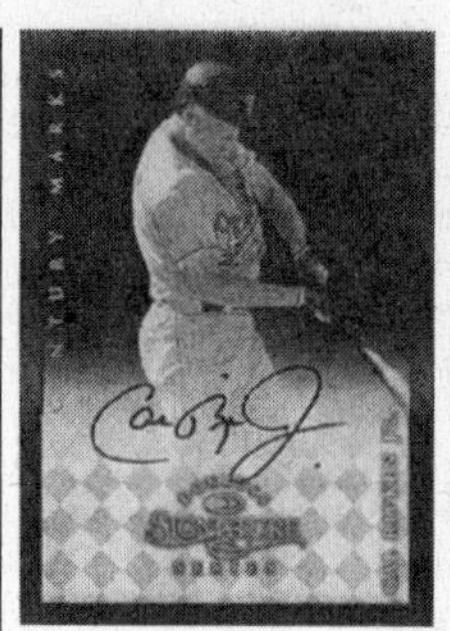

(1) Roberto Alomar 60.00
(2) Sandy Alomar Jr. 15.00
(3) Moises Alou 40.00
(4) Gabe Alvarez 10.00
(5) Wilson Alvarez 10.00
(6) Brady Anderson 15.00
(7) Jay Bell 15.00
(8) Albert Belle 20.00
(9) Adrian Beltre 25.00
(10) Andy Benes 10.00
(11) Wade Boggs 60.00
(12) Barry Bonds 250.00
(13) Aaron Boone 25.00
(14) Russell Branyan 10.00
(15) Jay Buhner 10.00
(16) Ellis Burks 10.00
(17) Orlando Cabrera 25.00
(18) Mike Cameron 10.00
(19) Ken Caminiti 25.00
(20) Joe Carter 20.00
(21) Sean Casey 15.00
(22) Bruce Chen 10.00
(23) Tony Clark 10.00
(24) Will Clark 40.00
(25) Roger Clemens 200.00
(26) Matt Clement 20.00
(27) Pat Cline 10.00
(28) Ken Cloude 10.00
(29) Michael Coleman 10.00
(30) David Cone 25.00
(31) Jeff Conine 10.00
(32) Jacob Cruz 10.00
(33) Jose Cruz Jr. 15.00
(34) Russ Davis 10.00
(35) Jason Dickson 10.00
(36) Todd Dunwoody 10.00
(37) Scott Elarton 10.00
(38) Darin Erstad 25.00
(39) Bobby Estalella 10.00
(40) Jeff Fassero 10.00
(41) John Franco 10.00
(42) Brad Fullmer 10.00
(43) Andres Galarraga 15.00
(44) Nomar Garciaparra 80.00
(45) Jason Giambi 40.00
(46) Derrick Gibson 10.00
(47) Tom Glavine 75.00
(48) Juan Gonzalez 50.00
(49) Todd Greene 10.00
(50) Ben Grieve 10.00
(51) Mark Grudzielanek 10.00
(52) Vladimir Guerrero 75.00
(53) Wilton Guerrero 10.00
(54) Jose Guillen 10.00
(55) Tony Gwynn 80.00
(56) Todd Helton 60.00
(57) Richard Hidalgo 10.00
(58) A.J. Hinch 10.00
(59) Butch Huskey 10.00
(60) Raul Ibanez 10.00
(61) Damian Jackson 10.00
(62) Geoff Jenkins 10.00
(63) Derek Jeter 200.00
(64) Randy Johnson 150.00
(65) Chipper Jones 100.00
(66) Eric Karros/50 15.00
(67) Jason Kendall (Unsigned) 20.00
(68) Ryan Klesko 10.00
(69) Chuck Knoblauch 10.00
(70) Mark Kotsay 10.00
(71) Ricky Ledee 10.00
(72) Derrek Lee 25.00
(73) Travis Lee 15.00
(74) Javier Lopez 25.00
(75) Mike Lowell 30.00
(76) Greg Maddux 150.00
(77) Eli Marrero 10.00
(78) Al Martin 10.00
(79) Rafael Medina 10.00
(80) Paul Molitor 50.00
(81) Scott Morgan 10.00
(82) Mike Mussina 75.00
(83) Abraham Nunez 15.00
(84) Paul O'Neill 40.00
(85) Luis Ordaz 10.00
(86) Magglio Ordonez 30.00
(87) Kevin Orie 10.00
(88) David Ortiz 75.00
(89) Rafael Palmeiro 75.00
(90) Carl Pavano 25.00
(91) Neifi Perez 10.00
(92) Andy Pettitte 50.00
(93) Aramis Ramirez 25.00
(94) Cal Ripken Jr. 200.00
(95) Mariano Rivera 75.00
(96) Alex Rodriguez 200.00
(97) Felix Rodriguez 10.00
(98) Henry Rodriguez 10.00
(99) Scott Rolen 70.00
(100) Brian Rose 10.00
(101) Curt Schilling 50.00
(102) Richie Sexson 20.00
(103) Randall Simon 10.00
(104) J.T. Snow 10.00
(105) Darryl Strawberry 40.00
(106) Jeff Suppan 10.00
(107) Fernando Tatis 10.00
(108) Brett Tomko 10.00
(109) Bubba Trammell 10.00
(110) Ismael Valdez 10.00
(111) Robin Ventura 20.00
(112) Billy Wagner 40.00
(113) Todd Walker 15.00
(114) Daryle Ward 10.00
(115) Rondell White 20.00
(116) Matt Williams/80 35.00
(117) Antone Williamson 10.00
(118) Dan Wilson 15.00
(119) Enrique Wilson 10.00
(120) Preston Wilson 15.00
(121) Tony Womack 10.00
(122) Kerry Wood 40.00

Millennium Marks (Green)

This is a green-foil parallel version of the Autographs insert set and features 1,000 cards signed by the featured player (unless otherwise shown in the checklist). Cards are not numbered.

NM/M

Common Player: 3.00
(1) Roberto Alomar 25.00
(2) Sandy Alomar Jr. 5.00
(3) Moises Alou 10.00
(4) Gabe Alvarez 3.00
(5) Wilson Alvarez 3.00
(6) Brady Anderson/800 8.00
(7) Jay Bell 3.00
(8) Albert Belle/400 10.00
(9) Adrian Beltre 15.00
(10) Andy Benes 3.00
(11) Wade Boggs/900 20.00
(12) Barry Bonds/400 150.00
(13) Aaron Boone 4.00
(14) Russell Branyan 3.00
(15) Jay Buhner/400 10.00
(16) Ellis Burks/900 5.00
(17) Orlando Cabrera 6.00
(18) Mike Cameron 5.00
(19) Ken Caminiti/900 20.00
(20) Joe Carter 8.00
(21) Sean Casey 8.00
(22) Bruce Chen 3.00
(23) Tony Clark 5.00
(24) Will Clark 25.00
(25) Roger Clemens/400 75.00
(26) Matt Clement/900 8.00
(27) Pat Cline 3.00
(28) Ken Cloude 3.00
(29) Michael Coleman 3.00
(30) David Cone 10.00
(31) Jeff Conine 3.00
(32) Jacob Cruz 3.00
(33) Jose Cruz Jr./850 5.00
(34) Russ Davis/950 3.00
(35) Jason Dickson/950 3.00
(36) Todd Dunwoody 3.00
(37) Scott Elarton/900 3.00
(38) Juan Encarnacion 5.00
(39) Darin Erstad 5.00
(40) Bobby Estalella 3.00
(41) Jeff Fassero 3.00
(42) John Franco/950 5.00
(43) Brad Fullmer 3.00
(44) Andres Galarraga/900 10.00
(45) Nomar Garciaparra/400 60.00
(46) Jason Giambi 20.00
(47) Derrick Gibson 3.00
(48) Tom Glavine/700 25.00
(49) Juan Gonzalez 20.00
(50) Todd Greene 3.00
(51) Ben Grieve 4.00
(52) Mark Grudzielanek 3.00
(53) Vladimir Guerrero 30.00
(54) Wilton Guerrero 3.00
(55) Jose Guillen 3.00
(56) Tony Gwynn/900 30.00
(57) Todd Helton 20.00
(58) Richard Hidalgo 3.00
(59) A.J. Hinch 3.00
(60) Butch Huskey 3.00
(61) Raul Ibanez 3.00
(62) Damian Jackson 3.00
(63) Geoff Jenkins 3.00
(64) Derek Jeter/400 100.00
(65) Randy Johnson /800 50.00
(66) Chipper Jones/900 30.00
(67) Eric Karros 5.00
(68) Ryan Klesko 5.00
(69) Chuck Knoblauch/900 10.00
(70) Mark Kotsay 5.00
(71) Ricky Ledee 3.00
(72) Derrek Lee 20.00
(73) Travis Lee 5.00
(74) Javier Lopez/800 10.00
(75) Mike Lowell 10.00
(76) Greg Maddux/400 85.00
(77) Eli Marrero 3.00
(78) Al Martin/950 3.00
(79) Rafael Medina/850 3.00
(80) Paul Molitor/900 20.00
(81) Scott Morgan 3.00
(82) Mike Mussina/900 15.00
(83) Abraham Nunez 3.00
(84) Paul O'Neill/900 20.00
(85) Luis Ordaz 3.00
(86) Magglio Ordonez 15.00
(87) Kevin Orie 3.00
(88) David Ortiz 40.00
(89) Rafael Palmeiro/900 30.00
(90) Carl Pavano 10.00
(91) Neifi Perez 3.00
(92) Andy Pettitte/900 20.00
(93) Dante Powell/950 3.00
(94) Aramis Ramirez 10.00
(95) Cal Ripken Jr./375 100.00
(96) Mariano Rivera 30.00
(97) Alex Rodriguez/350 75.00
(98) Felix Rodriguez 5.00
(99) Henry Rodriguez 3.00
(100) Scott Rolen 20.00
(101) Brian Rose 3.00
(102) Curt Schilling 20.00
(103) Richie Sexson 8.00
(104) Randall Simon 3.00
(105) J.T. Snow 4.00
(106) Darryl Strawberry/900 40.00
(107) Jeff Suppan 3.00
(108) Fernando Tatis 5.00
(109) Miguel Tejada 40.00
(110) Brett Tomko 3.00
(111) Bubba Trammell 3.00
(112) Ismael Valdes 3.00
(113) Robin Ventura 5.00
(114) Billy Wagner/900 10.00
(115) Todd Walker 4.00
(116) Daryle Ward 3.00
(117) Rondell White 5.00
(118) Matt Williams/820 8.00
(119) Antone Williamson 3.00
(120) Dan Wilson 3.00
(121) Enrique Wilson 3.00
(122) Preston Wilson/400 10.00
(123) Tony Womack 3.00
(124) Kerry Wood 20.00

Significant Signatures

This 18-card autographed set features some of baseball's all-time great players. Each card is sequentially numbered to 2,000. The Sandy Koufax autographs weren't received in time prior to release and was redeemable by sending in the Billy Williams autograph, the collector would then receive both the Williams and Koufax back. Exchange cards were also initially released for Nolan Ryan and Ozzie Smith. Early in the 2000s, a large quantity of the Koufax cards found its way into the hobby market.

NM/M

Complete Set (18): 425.00
Common Player: 10.00
Ernie Banks 25.00
Yogi Berra 25.00
George Brett 40.00
Catfish Hunter 35.00
Al Kaline 25.00
Harmon Killebrew 25.00
Ralph Kiner 10.00
Sandy Koufax 100.00
Eddie Mathews 25.00
Don Mattingly 50.00
Willie McCovey 25.00
Stan Musial 40.00
Phil Rizzuto (Edition of 1,000.) 20.00
Nolan Ryan 60.00
Nolan Ryan (Exchange card.) 5.00
Ozzie Smith 20.00
Ozzie Smith (Exchange card.) 5.00
Duke Snider 25.00
Don Sutton 12.00
Billy Williams 12.00

Redemption Baseballs

Redemption cards for authentically autographed baseballs were randomly inserted in Donruss Signature Series packs. Baseballs are laser burned with a Donruss seal to ensure authenticity. Every ball, except Ben Grieve's, is serial numbered within the edition limit shown. Signing Bonus redemption cards, no longer valid, are valued about 10 percent of the corresponding ball.

NM/M

Common Autographed Ball: 15.00
Redemption Card: 10 Percent
(1) Roberto Alomar/60 35.00
(2) Sandy Alomar Jr./60 20.00
(3) Ernie Banks/12 85.00
(4) Ken Caminiti/60 20.00
(5) Tony Clark/60 20.00
(6) Jacob Cruz/12 20.00
(7) Russ Davis/60 15.00
(8) Juan Encarnacion/60 20.00
(9) Bobby Estalella/60 15.00
(10) Jeff Fassero/60 15.00
(11) Mark Grudzielanek/60 15.00
(12) Ben Grieve/30 20.00
(13) Jose Guillen/120 20.00
(14) Tony Gwynn/60 100.00
(15) Al Kaline/12 75.00
(16) Paul Konerko/100 15.00
(17) Travis Lee/100 20.00
(18) Mike Lowell/60 15.00
(19) Eli Marrero/60 15.00
(20) Eddie Mathews/12 80.00
(21) Paul Molitor/60 65.00
(22) Stan Musial/12 125.00
(23) Abraham Nunez/12 20.00
(24) Luis Ordaz/12 20.00
(25) Magglio Ordonez/12 50.00
(26) Scott Rolen/60 45.00
(27) Bubba Trammell/24 25.00
(28) Robin Ventura/60 20.00
(29) Billy Wagner/60 20.00
(30) Rondell White/60 20.00
(31) Antone Williamson/12 15.00
(32) Tony Womack/60 15.00

2001 Donruss

NM/M

Complete Set (220):
Common Player: .15
Common Rated Rookie (151-200): 4.00
Production 2001
Hobby Pack (5): 6.00
Hobby Box (24): 120.00
The Rookies Coupon: 1.00
Inserted 1:72
Baseball's Best Coupon: 1.00
Inserted 1:720
Exchange Deadline 11/01/01
1 Alex Rodriguez 2.00
2 Barry Bonds 2.50
3 Cal Ripken Jr. 2.50
4 Chipper Jones 1.00
5 Derek Jeter 2.50
6 Troy Glaus .50
7 Frank Thomas .75
8 Greg Maddux 1.00
9 Ivan Rodriguez .50
10 Jeff Bagwell .50
11 Jose Canseco .40
12 Todd Helton .50
13 Ken Griffey Jr. 1.50
14 Manny Ramirez .75
15 Mark McGwire 2.00
16 Mike Piazza 1.50
17 Nomar Garciaparra 1.00
18 Pedro Martinez 1.00
19 Randy Johnson .75
20 Rick Ankiel .15
21 Ricky Henderson .75
22 Roger Clemens 2.00
23 Sammy Sosa 1.00
24 Tony Gwynn 1.00
25 Vladimir Guerrero .75
26 Eric Davis .15
27 Roberto Alomar .25
28 Mark Mulder .25
29 Pat Burrell .40
30 Harold Baines .15
31 Carlos Delgado .40
32 J.D. Drew .25
33 Jim Edmonds .40
34 Darin Erstad .25
35 Jason Giambi .50
36 Tom Glavine .30
37 Juan Gonzalez .35
38 Mark Grace .25
39 Shawn Green .25
40 Tim Hudson .25
41 Andruw Jones .75
42 David Justice .15
43 Jeff Kent .25
44 Barry Larkin .25
45 Pokey Reese .15
46 Mike Mussina .40
47 Hideo Nomo .35
48 Rafael Palmeiro .50
49 Adam Piatt .15
50 Scott Rolen .75
51 Gary Sheffield .40
52 Bernie Williams .25
53 Bob Abreu .25
54 Edgardo Alfonzo .15
55 Jermaine Clark RC .15
56 Albert Belle .15
57 Craig Biggio .25
58 Andres Galarraga .15
59 Edgar Martinez .15
60 Fred McGriff .15
61 Magglio Ordonez .15
62 Jim Thome .50
63 Matt Williams .15
64 Kerry Wood .25
65 Moises Alou .25
66 Brady Anderson .15
67 Garret Anderson .15
68 Tony Armas Jr. .15
69 Tony Batista .15
70 Jose Cruz Jr. .15
71 Carlos Beltran .50
72 Adrian Beltre .25
73 Kris Benson .15
74 Lance Berkman .40
75 Kevin Brown .15
76 Jay Buhner .15
77 Jeromy Burnitz .15
78 Ken Caminiti .15
79 Sean Casey .25
80 Luis Castillo .15
81 Eric Chavez .25
82 Jeff Cirillo .15
83 Bartolo Colon .15
84 David Cone .15
85 Freddy Garcia .15
86 Johnny Damon .50
87 Ray Durham .15
88 Jermaine Dye .15
89 Juan Encarnacion .15
90 Terrence Long .15
91 Carl Everett .15
92 Steve Finley .15
93 Cliff Floyd .15
94 Brad Fullmer .15
95 Brian Giles .15
96 Luis Gonzalez .15
97 Rusty Greer .15
98 Jeffrey Hammonds .15
99 Mike Hampton .15
100 Orlando Hernandez .15
101 Richard Hidalgo .15
102 Geoff Jenkins .15
103 Jacque Jones .15
104 Brian Jordan .15
105 Gabe Kapler .15
106 Eric Karros .15
107 Jason Kendall .15
108 Adam Kennedy .15
109 Byung-Hyun Kim .15
110 Ryan Klesko .15
111 Chuck Knoblauch .15
112 Paul Konerko .40
113 Carlos Lee .25
114 Kenny Lofton .15
115 Javy Lopez .15
116 Tino Martinez .15
117 Ruben Mateo .15
118 Kevin Millwood .15
119 Ben Molina .15

120 Raul Mondesi .15
121 Trot Nixon .15
122 John Olerud .15
123 Paul O'Neill .15
124 Chan Ho Park .15
125 Andy Pettitte .25
126 Jorge Posada .25
127 Mark Quinn .15
128 Aramis Ramirez .40
129 Mariano Rivera .25
130 Tim Salmon .15
131 Curt Schilling .75
132 Richie Sexson .40
133 John Smoltz .25
134 J.T. Snow .15
135 Jay Payton .15
136 Shannon Stewart .15
137 B.J. Surhoff .15
138 Mike Sweeney .15
139 Fernando Tatis .15
140 Miguel Tejada .40
141 Jason Varitek .40
142 Greg Vaughn .15
143 Mo Vaughn .15
144 Robin Ventura .15
145 Jose Vidro .15
146 Omar Vizquel .15
147 Larry Walker .15
148 David Wells .15
149 Rondell White .15
150 Preston Wilson .15
151 Brent Abernathy 4.00
152 Cory Aldridge **RC** 4.00
153 Gene Altman **RC** 4.00
154 Josh Beckett 4.00
155 Wilson Betemit **RC** 8.00
156 Albert Pujols/ 500 **RC** 275.00
157 Joe Crede 8.00
158 Jack Cust 4.00
159 Ben Sheets/500 40.00
160 Alex Escobar 4.00
161 Adrian Hernandez **RC** 4.00
162 Pedro Feliz 4.00
163 Nate Frese **RC** 4.00
164 Carlos Garcia **RC** 4.00
165 Marcus Giles 4.00
166 Alexis Gomez **RC** 4.00
167 Jason Hart 4.00
168 Eric Hinske **RC** 8.00
169 Cesar Izturis 4.00
170 Nick Johnson 4.00
171 Mike Young 4.00
172 Brian Lawrence **RC** 6.00
173 Steve Lomasney 4.00
174 Nick Maness **RC** 4.00
175 Jose Mieses **RC** 4.00
176 Greg Miller **RC** 4.00
177 Eric Munson 4.00
178 Xavier Nady 4.00
179 Blaine Neal **RC** 4.00
180 Abraham Nunez 4.00
181 Jose Ortiz 4.00
182 Jeremy Owens **RC** 4.00
183 Pablo Ozuna 4.00
184 Corey Patterson 4.00
185 Carlos Pena 4.00
186 Wily Mo Pena 4.00
187 Timo Perez 4.00
188 Adam Pettyjohn **RC** 4.00
189 Luis Rivas 4.00
190 Jackson Melian **RC** 4.00
191 Wilken Ruan **RC** 4.00
192 Duaner Sanchez **RC** 4.00
193 Alfonso Soriano 5.00
194 Rafael Soriano **RC** 6.00
195 Ichiro Suzuki **RC** 60.00
196 Billy Sylvester **RC** 4.00
197 Juan Uribe **RC** 4.00
198 Eric Valent 4.00
199 Carlos Valderrama **RC** 4.00
200 Matt White **RC** 4.00
201 Alex Rodriguez 2.50
202 Barry Bonds 3.00
203 Cal Ripken Jr. 3.00
204 Chipper Jones 1.00
205 Derek Jeter 2.50
206 Troy Glaus .50
207 Frank Thomas .75
208 Greg Maddux 1.50
209 Ivan Rodriguez .50
210 Jeff Bagwell .50
211 Todd Helton .50
212 Ken Griffey Jr. 1.50
213 Manny Ramirez .75
214 Mark McGwire 1.50
215 Mike Piazza 1.50
216 Pedro Martinez .75
217 Sammy Sosa 1.50
218 Tony Gwynn 1.00
219 Vladimir Guerrero .75
220 Nomar Garciaparra 1.00

Baseball's Best

This up-scale version of 2001 Donruss was available to those who not only beat the 1:720 pack insertion odds, but also paid $105 to redeem the "winning" coupon. The boxed set contains 330 cards comprised of the 220-card '01 Donruss base set, the 105-card The Rookies set and the five Rookies Diamond King

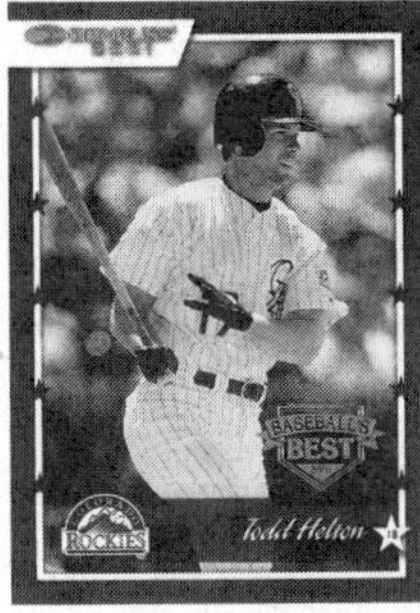

cards. The cards are printed on a thicker, glossy stock and have a "Baseball's Best" logo foil stamped on front in either bronze, silver or gold. Those redeeming coupons had an apparently random chance of receiving one of 999 bronze sets, 499 silver sets or 99 gold sets. Coupons expired in January 2002.

NM/M
Complete Set, Bronze (330): 100.00
999 produced
Stars: 2-3X
Complete Set, Silver (330): 300.00
499 produced
Stars: 2-4X
Complete Set, Gold (330): 550.00
99 produced
Stars: 4-8X

All-Time Diamond Kings

NM/M
Complete Set (10): 150.00
Common Player: 8.00
Production 2,500 Sets
Studio Series: 2-3X
Production 250
#9 Undetermined Redemp.
1a Frank Robinson 8.00
1b Willie Mays (Should have been ATDK-9.) 25.00
2 Harmon Killebrew 8.00
3 Mike Schmidt 20.00
4 Reggie Jackson 8.00
5 Nolan Ryan 35.00
6 George Brett 25.00
7 Tom Seaver 10.00
8 Hank Aaron 25.00
10 Stan Musial 20.00

All-Time Diamond Kings Autograph

NM/M
Production 50 Sets
1 Frank Robinson 100.00
1 Willie Mays 200.00
2 Harmon Killebrew 80.00
3 Mike Schmidt 200.00
4 Reggie Jackson 80.00
5 Nolan Ryan 250.00
6 George Brett 225.00
7 Tom Seaver 85.00
8 Hank Aaron 200.00
10 Stan Musial 120.00

Bat Kings

NM/M
Common Card: 10.00
Production 250 Sets
1 Ivan Rodriguez 10.00
2 Tony Gwynn 25.00
3 Barry Bonds 50.00
4 Todd Helton 10.00
5 Troy Glaus 10.00
6 Mike Schmidt 40.00
7 Reggie Jackson 15.00
8 Harmon Killebrew 15.00
9 Frank Robinson 15.00
10 Hank Aaron 75.00

Bat Kings Autograph

NM/M
Production 50 Sets
1 Ivan Rodriguez 75.00
2 Tony Gwynn 120.00
3 Barry Bonds/ No Auto. 50.00
4 Todd Helton 65.00
5 Troy Glaus 65.00
6 Mike Schmidt 150.00
7 Reggie Jackson 100.00
8 Harmon Killebrew 100.00
9 Frank Robinson 85.00
10 Hank Aaron 200.00

Diamond Kings Hawaii Promo

The first look at the resurrected Donruss brand under Playoff ownership was provided at the 2001 Hawaii trade show where a special promotional Diamond King card was distributed in two versions. The cards feature a Dan Gardiner artwork portrait with gold-foil graphic highlights on front, including a "HAWAII 2001" logo. Cards have a color photo on back. A special autographed version of the card was also created, signed on front and numbered in gold-foil on back from within an edition of 100.

NM/M
HDK-1 Alex Rodriguez 3.00
HDK-1 Alex Rodriguez/ Auto. 150.00

2001 Donruss 2001 Diamond Kings

NM/M
Complete Set (20): 150.00
Common Player: 5.00
Production 2,500 Sets
Studio Canvas Parallel: 1-2X
Production 250
1 Alex Rodriguez 12.50
2 Cal Ripken Jr. 15.00
3 Mark McGwire 12.50
4 Ken Griffey Jr. 10.00
5 Derek Jeter 15.00
6 Nomar Garciaparra 10.00
7 Mike Piazza 10.00
8 Roger Clemens 9.00
9 Greg Maddux 8.00
10 Chipper Jones 8.00
11 Tony Gwynn 8.00
12 Barry Bonds 15.00
13 Sammy Sosa 10.00
14 Vladimir Guerrero 6.00
15 Frank Thomas 6.00
16 Troy Glaus 6.00
17 Todd Helton 6.00
18 Ivan Rodriguez 5.00
19 Pedro Martinez 6.00
20 Carlos Delgado 5.00

Studio Series Autograph

NM/M
Common Autograph: 50.00
Production 50 Sets
1 Alex Rodriguez 180.00
2 Cal Ripken Jr. 250.00
8 Roger Clemens 150.00
9 Greg Maddux 150.00
10 Chipper Jones 85.00
11 Tony Gwynn 80.00
14 Vladimir Guerrero 100.00
16 Troy Glaus 50.00
17 Todd Helton 60.00
18 Ivan Rodriguez 60.00

Reprints

NM/M
Complete Set (20): 160.00
Common Player: 5.00
#'d to yr. produced
1 Rod Carew 5.00
2 Nolan Ryan 25.00
3 Tom Seaver 10.00
4 Carlton Fisk 10.00
5 Reggie Jackson 12.00
6 Steve Carlton 5.00
7 Johnny Bench 10.00
8 Joe Morgan 5.00
9 Mike Schmidt 20.00
10 Wade Boggs 15.00
11 Cal Ripken Jr. 25.00
12 Tony Gwynn 15.00
13 Andre Dawson 5.00
14 Ozzie Smith 15.00
15 George Brett 20.00
16 Dave Winfield 5.00
17 Paul Molitor 10.00
18 Will Clark 5.00
19 Robin Yount 10.00
20 Ken Griffey Jr. 17.50

Reprints Autograph

NM/M
Common Player:
DKR1 Rod Carew/82 40.00
DKR2 Nolan Ryan/82 150.00
DKR3 Tom SeaveR/82 75.00
DKR4 Carlton Fisk/82 65.00
DKR5 Reggie Jackson/83 60.00
DKR6 Steve Carlton/83 40.00
DKR7 Johnny Bench/83 80.00
DKR8 Joe Morgan/83 30.00
DKR9 Mike Schmidt/84 120.00
DKR10 Wade Boggs/84 60.00
DKR11 Cal Ripken Jr./85 180.00
DKR12 Tony Gwynn/86 80.00
DKR13 Andre Dawson/86 35.00
DKR14 Ozzie Smith/87 80.00
DKR15 George Brett/87 120.00
DKR16 Dave Winfield/87 40.00
DKR17 Paul Molitor/88 60.00
DKR18 Will Clark/88 75.00
DKR19 Robin Yount/89 80.00
DKR20 Ken Griffey Jr./ 89/No Auto. 25.00

Elite Series

NM/M
Complete Set (20): 75.00
Common Player: 2.00
Production 2,500 Sets
Dominators: 5-8X
Production 25 Sets
1 Vladimir Guerrero 4.00
2 Cal Ripken Jr. 10.00
3 Greg Maddux 5.00
4 Alex Rodriguez 8.00
5 Barry Bonds 10.00
6 Chipper Jones 5.00
7 Derek Jeter 10.00
8 Ivan Rodriguez 2.50
9 Ken Griffey Jr. 7.00
10 Mark McGwire 8.00
11 Mike Piazza 7.00
12 Nomar Garciaparra 7.00
13 Pedro Martinez 4.00
14 Randy Johnson 4.00
15 Roger Clemens 6.00
16 Sammy Sosa 7.00
17 Tony Gwynn 5.00
18 Darin Erstad 3.00
19 Andruw Jones 4.00
20 Bernie Williams 2.00

Jersey Kings

NM/M
Common Card: 25.00
Production 250 Sets
1 Vladimir Guerrero 15.00
2 Cal Ripken Jr. 50.00
3 Greg Maddux 25.00
4 Chipper Jones 15.00
5 Roger Clemens 25.00
6 George Brett 30.00
7 Tom Seaver 15.00
8 Nolan Ryan 50.00
9 Stan Musial 30.00

Jersey Kings Autographs

NM/M
Production 50 Sets
1 Vladimir Guerrero 90.00
2 Cal Ripken Jr. 225.00
3 Greg Maddux 150.00
4 Chipper Jones 85.00
5 Roger Clemens 175.00
6 George Brett 200.00
7 Tom Seaver 75.00
8 Nolan Ryan 200.00
9 Stan Musial 120.00
10 Ozzie Smith 100.00

Longball Leaders

NM/M
Complete Set (20): 50.00
Common Player: 1.00

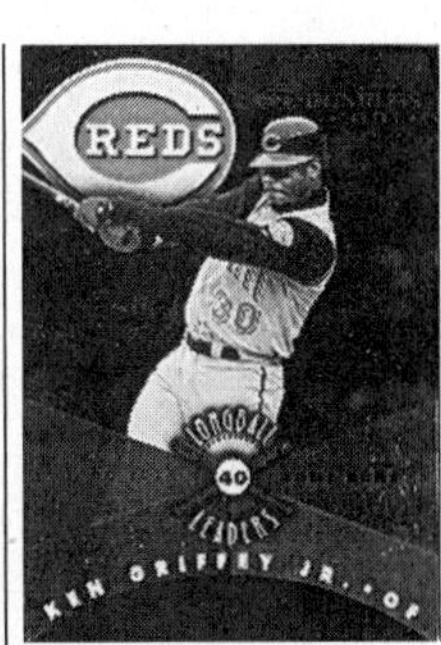

Production 1,000 Sets
Die-Cut Parallel: 3-5X
#'d to '00 HR Total
1 Vladimir Guerrero 4.00
2 Alex Rodriguez 8.00
3 Barry Bonds 10.00
4 Troy Glaus 4.00
5 Frank Thomas 4.00
6 Jeff Bagwell 4.00
7 Todd Helton 4.00
8 Ken Griffey Jr. 6.00
9 Manny Ramirez 4.00
10 Mike Piazza 6.00
11 Sammy Sosa 6.00
12 Carlos Delgado 2.00
13 Jim Edmonds 1.00
14 Jason Giambi 3.00
15 David Justice 1.00
16 Rafael Palmeiro 3.00
17 Gary Sheffield 2.00
18 Jim Thome 1.00
19 Tony Batista 1.00
20 Richard Hidalgo 1.00

Production Line

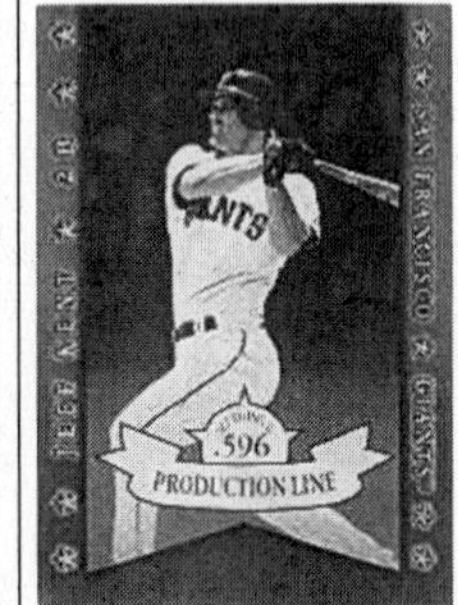

NM/M
Complete Set (60): 150.00
Common Player: .50
Die-Cut OBP (1-20): 1-2X
Die-Cut SLG (21-40): 1-2.5X
Die-Cut PI (41-60): 1.5-3X
Production 100 Sets
1 Jason Giambi/476 3.00
2 Carlos Delgado/470 2.00
3 Todd Helton/463 3.00
4 Manny Ramirez/457 3.00
5 Barry Bonds/440 15.00
6 Gary Sheffield/438 2.00
7 Frank Thomas/436 3.00
8 Nomar Garciaparra/ 434 10.00
9 Brian Giles/432 1.00
10 Edgardo Alfonzo/425 .50
11 Jeff Kent/424 .75
12 Jeff Bagwell/424 3.00
13 Edgar Martinez/423 .75
14 Alex Rodriguez/420 10.00
15 Luis Castillo/418 .50
16 Will Clark/418 2.50
17 Jorge Posada/417 2.00
18 Derek Jeter/416 12.00
19 Bob Abreu/416 1.00
20 Moises Alou/416 .75
21 Todd Helton/698 3.00
22 Manny Ramirez/697 3.00
23 Barry Bonds/688 15.00
24 Carlos Delgado/664 2.00
25 Vladimir Guerrero/664 3.00
26 Jason Giambi/647 3.00
27 Gary Sheffield/643 2.00
28 Richard Hidalgo/636 .50
29 Sammy Sosa/634 8.00
30 Frank Thomas/625 3.00
31 Moises Alou/623 .75
32 Jeff Bagwell/615 3.00
33 Mike Piazza/614 8.00
34 Alex Rodriguez/606 10.00
35 Troy Glaus/604 3.00
36 Nomar Garciaparra/ 599 10.00
37 Jeff Kent/596 .75
38 Brian Giles/594 .75
39 Geoff Jenkins/588 .50
40 Carl Everett/587 .50
41 Todd Helton/1161 3.00
42 Manny Ramirez/1154 3.00
43 Carlos Delgado/1134 2.00
44 Barry Bonds/1128 12.00

45 Jason Giambi/1123 3.00
46 Gary Sheffield/1081 2.00
47 Vladimir Guerrero/ 1074 3.00
48 Frank Thomas/1061 3.00
49 Sammy Sosa/1040 8.00
50 Moises Alou/1039 1.00
51 Jeff Bagwell/1039 3.00
52 Nomar Garciaparra/ 1033 10.00
53 Richard Hidalgo/1027 .50
54 Alex Rodriguez/1026 10.00
55 Brian Giles/1026 1.00
56 Jeff Kent/1020 1.00
57 Mike Piazza/1012 8.00
58 Troy Glaus/1008 3.00
59 Edgar Martinez/1002 1.00
60 Jim Edmonds/994 1.00

Rookie Reprints

NM/M

Complete Set (40): 200.00
Common Player: 3.00
#'d to Original Yr. issued
1 Cal Ripken Jr. 20.00
2 Wade Boggs 10.00
3 Tony Gwynn 10.00
4 Ryne Sandberg 10.00
5 Don Mattingly 12.00
6 Joe Carter 3.00
7 Roger Clemens 15.00
8 Kirby Puckett 10.00
9 Orel Hershiser 3.00
10 Andres Galarraga 3.00
11 Jose Canseco 5.00
12 Fred McGriff 3.00
13 Paul O'Neill 3.00
14 Mark McGwire 15.00
15 Barry Bonds 20.00
16 Kevin Brown 3.00
17 David Cone 3.00
18 Rafael Palmeiro 8.00
19 Barry Larkin 3.00
20 Bo Jackson 5.00
21 Greg Maddux 10.00
22 Roberto Alomar 4.00
23 Mark Grace 3.00
24 David Wells 3.00
25 Tom Glavine 4.00
26 Matt Williams 3.00
27 Ken Griffey Jr. 12.00
28 Randy Johnson 8.00
29 Gary Sheffield 5.00
30 Craig Biggio 3.00
31 Curt Schilling 5.00
32 Larry Walker 3.00
33 Bernie Williams 4.00
34 Sammy Sosa 12.00
35 Juan Gonzalez 8.00
36 David Justice 3.00
37 Ivan Rodriguez 6.00
38 Jeff Bagwell 8.00
39 Jeff Kent 3.00
40 Manny Ramirez 8.00

Rookie Reprints Autographs

NM/M

Common Player:
#'d to last 2 digits of yr. issued
1 Cal Ripken/82 150.00
2 Wade Boggs/83 40.00
3 Tony Gwynn/83 75.00
4 Ryne Sandberg/83 100.00
5 Don Mattingly/84 100.00
6 Joe Carter/84 20.00
7 Roger Clemens/85 200.00
8 Kirby Puckett/85 60.00
9 Orel Hershiser/85 25.00
10 Andres Galarraga/86 30.00
15 Barry Bonds/87 200.00
16 Kevin Brown/87 30.00
17 David Cone/87 30.00
18 Rafael Palmeiro/87 50.00
20 Bo Jackson/87 85.00
21 Greg Maddux/87 150.00
22 Roberto Alomar/88 40.00
24 David Wells/88 25.00
25 Tom Glavine/88 40.00
28 Randy Johnson/89 100.00
29 Gary Sheffield/89 50.00
31 Curt Schilling/89 75.00
35 Juan Gonzalez/90 40.00
36 David Justice/90 25.00
37 Ivan Rodriguez/91 40.00
39 Manny Ramirez/92 100.00

Stat Line Career

NM/M

Cards #1-150 print run 251-400: 3-6X
1-150 p/r 151-250: 4-8X
1-150 p/r 151-200: 4-8X
1-150 p/r 101-150: 5-10X
1-150 p/r 61-100: 10-20X
1-150 p/r 41-60: 20-30X
1-150 p/r 21-40: 25-40X
1-150 p/r 15-20: 30-60X
Common (151-200) p/r 251-400: 1.00
Common (151-200) p/r 151-250: 1.00
Common (151-200) p/r 101-150: 2.00
Common (151-200) p/r 76-100: 2.00
Common (151-200) p/r 31-75: 4.00
Common (151-200) p/r 20-30: 6.00
cards 201-220 p/r 201-400: 1-2X
201-220 p/r 101-200: 2-4X
201-220 p/r 75-100: 3-5X
201-220 p/r 40-74: 4-8X
156 Albert Pujols/154 150.00
190 Jackson Melian/26 50.00
195 Ichiro Suzuki/106 200.00

Stat Line Season

NM/M

Cards #1-150 print run 151-200: 4-8X
1-150 p/r 101-150: 4-8X
1-150 p/r 76-100: 10-20X
1-150 p/r 51-75: 10-20X
1-150 p/r 36-50: 15-25X
1-150 p/r 21-35: 20-40X
Common (151-200) p/r 151-200: 1.00
Common (151-200) p/r 101-150: 1.00
Common (151-200) p/r 101-150: 1.00
Common (151-200) p/r 76-100: 2.00
Common (151-200) p/r 31-75 3.00
Common (151-200) p/r 20-30 6.00
cards 201-220 p/r 151-200: 1-30X
201-220 p/r 101-150: 2-4X
201-220 p/r 75-100: 3-5X
201-220 p/r 40-74: 4-8X
156 Albert Pujols/17 400.00
190 Jackson Melian/73 40.00
195 Ichiro Suzuki/153 150.00

1999 Retro

NM/M

Complete Set (100): 200.00
Common Player: .25
Inserted 1:Hobby Pack
Common (81-100): 3.00
Production 1,999
1 Ken Griffey Jr. 2.00
2 Nomar Garciaparra 2.00
3 Alex Rodriguez 3.00
4 Mark McGwire 2.50
5 Sammy Sosa 2.00
6 Chipper Jones 1.50
7 Mike Piazza 2.00
8 Barry Larkin .50
9 Andruw Jones 1.00
10 Albert Belle .25

11 Jeff Bagwell 1.00
12 Tony Gwynn 1.50
13 Manny Ramirez 1.00
14 Mo Vaughn .25
15 Barry Bonds 4.00
16 Frank Thomas 1.00
17 Vladimir Guerrero 1.00
18 Derek Jeter 3.00
19 Randy Johnson 1.00
20 Greg Maddux 1.50
21 Pedro Martinez 1.00
22 Cal Ripken Jr. 3.00
23 Ivan Rodriguez .75
24 Matt Williams .25
25 Javy Lopez .25
26 Tim Salmon .25
27 Raul Mondesi .25
28 Todd Helton 1.00
29 Magglio Ordonez .75
30 Sean Casey .25
31 Jeromy Burnitz .25
32 Jeff Kent .25
33 Jim Edmonds .25
34 Jim Thome .75
35 Dante Bichette .25
36 Larry Walker .25
37 Will Clark .50
38 Omar Vizquel .25
39 Mike Mussina .50
40 Eric Karros .25
41 Kenny Lofton .25
42 David Justice .25
43 Craig Biggio .50
44 J.D. Drew .25
45 Rickey Henderson 1.00
46 Bernie Williams .50
47 Brian Giles .25
48 Paul O'Neill .50
49 Orlando Hernandez .25
50 Jason Giambi .50
51 Curt Schilling 1.00
52 Scott Rolen 1.00
53 Mark Grace .50
54 Moises Alou .50
55 Jason Kendall .25
56 Ray Lankford .25
57 Kerry Wood .50
58 Gary Sheffield .75
59 Ruben Mateo .50
60 Darin Erstad .50
61 Troy Glaus 1.00
62 Jose Canseco .50
63 Wade Boggs 1.50
64 Tom Glavine .50
65 Gabe Kapler .25
66 Juan Gonzalez 1.00
67 Rafael Palmeiro .75
68 Richie Sexson .50
69 Carl Everett .25
70 David Wells .25
71 Carlos Delgado .75
72 Eric Davis .25
73 Shawn Green .50
74 Andres Galarraga .25
75 Edgar Martinez .25
76 Roberto Alomar .50
77 John Olerud .25
78 Luis Gonzalez .25
79 Kevin Brown .25
80 Roger Clemens 2.00
81 Josh Beckett 5.00
82 Alfonso Soriano 8.00
83 Alex Escobar .50
84 Pat Burrell .50
85 Eric Chavez .50
86 Erubiel Durazo .50
87 Abraham Nunez .50
88 Carlos Pena 2.00
89 Nick Johnson .50
90 Eric Munson .50
91 Corey Patterson .50
92 Wily Mo Pena .50
93 Rafael Furcal 1.00
94 Eric Valent .50
95 Mark Mulder .50
96 Chad Hutchinson 1.00
97 Freddy Garcia .50
98 Tim Hudson 1.00
99 Rick Ankiel 1.00
100 Kip Wells .50

1999 Diamond Kings

NM/M

Complete Set (5): 40.00
Common Player: 8.00
Production 2,500 Sets

1 Scott Rolen 8.00
2 Sammy Sosa 10.00
3 Juan Gonzalez 8.00
4 Ken Griffey Jr. 10.00
5 Derek Jeter 20.00

1999 Retro Stat Line Career

NM/M

Cards #1-80 print run 251-400: 2-3X
(1-80) p/r 151-250: 2-4X
(1-80) p/r 101-150: 3-6X
(1-80) p/r 76-100: 4-8X
(1-80) p/r 51-75: 5-10X
(1-80) p/r 30-50: 8-15X
1 Ken Griffey Jr./350 20.00
2 Nomar Garciaparra/309 20.00
3 Alex Rodriguez/313 20.00
4 Mark McGwire/219 25.00
5 Sammy Sosa/273 12.00
6 Chipper Jones/297 15.00
7 Mike Piazza/333 20.00
8 Barry Larkin/305 5.00
9 Andruw Jones/273 6.00
10 Albert Belle/321 2.50
11 Jeff Bagwell/304 8.00
12 Tony Gwynn/339 12.00
13 Manny Ramirez/154 15.00
14 Mo Vaughn/304 2.50
15 Barry Bonds/290 12.00
16 Frank Thomas/286 10.00
17 Vladimir Guerrero/ 305 10.00
18 Derek Jeter/308 25.00
19 Randy Johnson/336 8.00
20 Greg Maddux/202 20.00
21 Pedro Martinez/298 10.00
22 Cal Ripken Jr./276 25.00
23 Ivan Rodriguez/232 8.00
24 Matt Williams/299 4.00
25 Javy Lopez/333 2.50
26 Tim Salmon/179 4.00
27 Raul Mondesi/295 2.50
28 Todd Helton/310 8.00
29 Magglio Ordonez/173 4.00
30 Sean Casey/269 2.50
31 Jeromy Burnitz/294 2.50
32 Jeff Kent/193 5.00
33 Jim Edmonds/294 5.00
34 Jim Thome/163 4.00
35 Dante Bichette/300 2.50
36 Larry Walker/225 8.00
37 Will Clark/302 6.00
38 Omar Vizquel/196 4.00
39 Mike Mussina/118 10.00
40 Eric Karros/177 4.00
41 Kenny Lofton/311 2.50
42 David Justice/214 5.00
43 Craig Biggio/318 2.50
44 J.D. Drew/35 25.00
45 Rickey Henderson/ 283 6.00
46 Bernie Williams/213 6.00
47 Brian Giles/157 4.00
48 Paul O'Neill/223 5.00
49 Orlando Hernandez/ 313 2.50
50 Jason Giambi/73 15.00
51 Curt Schilling/336 2.50
52 Scott Rolen/220 5.00
53 Mark Grace/310 6.00
54 Moises Alou/201 3.00
55 Jason Kendall/308 2.50
56 Ray Lankford/225 3.00
57 Kerry Wood/233 3.00
58 Gary Sheffield/202 5.00
59 Ruben Mateo/384 2.50
60 Darin Erstad/179 8.00
61 Troy Glaus/218 10.00
62 Jose Canseco/296 6.00
63 Wade Boggs/329 8.00
64 Tom Glavine/331 5.00
66 Juan Gonzalez/301 8.00
67 Rafael Palmeiro/314 5.00
68 Richie Sexson/308 2.50
69 Carl Everett/209 3.00
70 David Wells/124 5.00
71 Carlos Delgado/333 6.00
72 Eric Davis/342 2.50
73 Shawn Green/77 15.00
74 Andres Galarraga/364 4.00
75 Edgar Martinez/318 4.00
76 Roberto Alomar/302 6.00
77 John Olerud/301 2.50
78 Luis Gonzalez/237 3.00
79 Kevin Brown/330 2.50
80 Roger Clemens/295 12.00
82 Alfonso Soriano/113 15.00
83 Alex Escobar/181 10.00
84 Pat Burrell/303 12.00
85 Eric Chavez/314 2.50
86 Erubiel Durazo/147 5.00
87 Abraham Nunez/106 15.00
88 Carlos Pena/46 25.00
89 Nick Johnson/259 6.00
90 Eric Munson/392 6.00
91 Corey Patterson/117 15.00
92 Wily Mo Pena/247 8.00
93 Rafael Furcal/137 20.00
94 Eric Valent/53 10.00
95 Mark Mulder/340 4.00
97 Freddy Garcia/397 6.00
98 Tim Hudson/17 50.00
99 Rick Ankiel/222 10.00
100 Kip Wells/371 2.50

1999 Retro Stat Line Season

NM/M

Cards #1-80 print run 251-400: 2-3X
(1-80) p/r 151-250: 2-4X
(1-80) p/r 101-150: 3-6X
(1-80) p/r 76-100: 4-8X
(1-80) p/r 51-75: 5-10X
(1-80) p/r 30-50: 8-15X
1 Ken Griffey Jr./56 70.00
2 Nomar Garciaparra/35 100.00
3 Alex Rodriguez/42 100.00
4 Mark McGwire/70 80.00
5 Sammy Sosa/66 40.00
6 Chipper Jones/123 30.00
7 Mike Piazza/111 50.00
8 Barry Larkin/166 8.00
9 Andruw Jones/31 30.00
10 Albert Belle/49 8.00
11 Jeff Bagwell/164 12.00
12 Tony Gwynn/148 25.00
13 Manny Ramirez/145 20.00
14 Mo Vaughn/40 10.00
15 Barry Bonds/120 25.00
16 Frank Thomas/155 15.00
17 Vladimir Guerrero/38 40.00
18 Derek Jeter/127 60.00
19 Randy Johnson/19 75.00
21 Pedro Martinez/19 80.00
22 Cal Ripken Jr./163 40.00
23 Ivan Rodriguez/186 12.00
24 Matt Williams/136 8.00
25 Javy Lopez/106 6.00
26 Tim Salmon/139 5.00
27 Raul Mondesi/162 4.00
28 Todd Helton/25 60.00
29 Magglio Ordonez/151 4.00
30 Sean Casey/82 8.00
31 Jeromy Burnitz/125 5.00
32 Jeff Kent/128 8.00
33 Jim Edmonds/115 12.00
34 Jim Thome/129 6.00
35 Dante Bichette/122 5.00
36 Larry Walker/113 15.00
37 Will Clark/169 10.00
38 Omar Vizquel/166 4.00
39 Mike Mussina/175 10.00
40 Eric Karros/150 5.00
41 Kenny Lofton/54 10.00
42 David Justice/151 6.00
43 Craig Biggio/51 10.00
45 Rickey Henderson/66 25.00
46 Bernie Williams/26 30.00
47 Brian Giles/94 6.00
48 Paul O'Neill/116 10.00
49 Orlando Hernandez/12 35.00
50 Jason Giambi/166 10.00
51 Curt Schilling/15 40.00
52 Scott Rolen/31 30.00
53 Mark Grace/92 15.00
54 Moises Alou/124 5.00
55 Jason Kendall/175 4.00
56 Ray Lankford/156 4.00
57 Kerry Wood/13 50.00
58 Gary Sheffield/132 10.00
59 Ruben Mateo/134 5.00
60 Darin Erstad/159 10.00
62 Jose Canseco/46 30.00
63 Wade Boggs/122 15.00
64 Tom Glavine/20 50.00
65 Gabe Kapler/25 20.00
66 Juan Gonzalez/50 30.00
67 Rafael Palmeiro/121 10.00
69 Carl Everett/138 5.00
70 David Wells/163 4.00
71 Carlos Delgado/155 10.00
72 Eric Davis/148 5.00
73 Shawn Green/100 12.00
74 Andres Galarraga/44 20.00
75 Edgar Martinez/102 10.00
76 Roberto Alomar/166 15.00
77 John Olerud/22 20.00
78 Luis Gonzalez/146 5.00
79 Kevin Brown/18 25.00
80 Roger Clemens/20 120.00
81 Josh Beckett/178 10.00
83 Alex Escobar/27 40.00
85 Eric Chavez/33 15.00
86 Erubiel Durazo/19 20.00
87 Abraham Nunez/95 10.00
88 Carlos Pena/319 6.00
89 Nick Johnson/17 50.00
90 Eric Munson/16 40.00
91 Corey Patterson/22 40.00
93 Rafael Furcal/88 20.00
95 Mark Mulder/113 6.00
96 Chad Hutchinson/51 6.00
98 Tim Hudson/152 15.00
99 Rick Ankiel/12 40.00
100 Kip Wells/135 2.50

2000 Retro

NM/M

Complete Set (100): 90.00
Common Player: .25
Common (81-100): 3.00
Production 2,000
1 Vladimir Guerrero 1.00
2 Alex Rodriguez 4.00
3 Ken Griffey Jr. 2.50
4 Nomar Garciaparra 1.00
5 Mike Piazza 1.50
6 Mark McGwire 2.00
7 Sammy Sosa 1.50
8 Chipper Jones 1.00
9 Jim Edmonds .50
10 Tony Gwynn 1.00
11 Andruw Jones .75
12 Albert Belle .25
13 Jeff Bagwell .75
14 Manny Ramirez 1.00
15 Mo Vaughn .25
16 Barry Bonds 4.00
17 Frank Thomas 1.00
18 Ivan Rodriguez .75
19 Derek Jeter 4.00
20 Randy Johnson 1.00
21 Greg Maddux 1.00
22 Pedro Martinez 1.00
23 Cal Ripken Jr. 4.00
24 Mark Grace .50
25 Javy Lopez .25
26 Ray Durham .25
27 Todd Helton 1.00
28 Magglio Ordonez .75
29 Sean Casey .25
30 Darin Erstad .50
31 Barry Larkin .50
32 Will Clark .50
33 Jim Thome .50
34 Dante Bichette .25
35 Larry Walker .50
36 Ken Caminiti .25
37 Omar Vizquel .25
38 Miguel Tejada .50
39 Eric Karros .25
40 Gary Sheffield .75
41 Jeff Cirillo .25
42 Rondell White .25
43 Rickey Henderson .75

44 Bernie Williams .50
45 Brian Giles .25
46 Paul O'Neill .50
47 Orlando Hernandez .25
48 Ben Grieve .25
49 Jason Giambi .50
50 Curt Schilling 1.00
51 Scott Rolen 1.00
52 Bobby Abreu .50
53 Jason Kendall .25
54 Fernando Tatis .25
55 Jeff Kent .25
56 Mike Mussina .50
57 Troy Glaus .75
58 Jose Canseco .50
59 Wade Boggs 1.00
60 Fred McGriff .25
61 Juan Gonzalez .75
62 Rafael Palmeiro .75
63 Rusty Greer .25
64 Carl Everett .25
65 David Wells .25
66 Carlos Delgado .50
67 Shawn Green .40
68 David Justice .25
69 Edgar Martinez .25
70 Andres Galarraga .25
71 Roberto Alomar .50
72 Jermaine Dye .25
73 John Olerud .25
74 Luis Gonzalez .25
75 Craig Biggio .50
76 Kevin Millwood .25
77 Kevin Brown .25
78 John Smoltz .50
79 Roger Clemens 3.00
80 Mike Hampton .25
81 Tomas De La Rosa .25
82 C.C. Sabathia 1.00
83 Ryan Christenson .25
84 Pedro Feliz .50
85 Jose Ortiz .25
86 Xavier Nady .50
87 Julio Zuleta .25
88 Jason Hart .25
89 Keith Ginter .25
90 Brent Abernathy .25
91 Timo Perez .25
92 Juan Pierre .50
93 Tike Redman .25
94 Mike Lamb .50
95 Ben Sheets 1.00
96 Kazuhiro Sasaki .50
97 Barry Zito 1.00
98 Adam Bernero .25
99 Chad Durbin .25
100 Matt Ginter .25

2000 Diamond Kings

NM/M
Complete Set (5): 35.00
Common Player: 8.00
Production 2,500 Sets
Studio: 1-2X
Production 250 Sets
1 Frank Thomas 8.00
2 Greg Maddux 9.00
3 Alex Rodriguez 10.00
4 Jeff Bagwell 8.00
5 Manny Ramirez 8.00

2000 Retro Stat Line Career

NM/M
Cards #1-80 print run 251-400: 2-3X
1-80 p/r 151-250: 2-4X
1-80 p/r 101-150: 3-6X
1-80 p/r 76-100: 4-8X
1-80 p/r 51-75: 5-10X
1-80 p/r 31-50: 8-15X
1-80 p/r 21-30: 15-25X
Common (81-100) p/r 251-400: 1.00
Common (81-100) p/r 151-250: 1.00
Common (81-100) p/r 101-150: 2.00
Common (81-100) p/r 76-100: 2.00
Common (81-100) p/r 31-75 3.00

2000 Retro Stat Line Season

NM/M
Cards #1-80 print run 251-400: 2-3X
1-80 p/r 151-250: 2-4X
1-80 p/r 101-150: 3-6X
1-80 p/r 76-100: 4-8X
1-80 p/r 51-75: 5-10X
1-80 p/r 31-50: 8-15X
1-80 p/r 21-30: 15-25X
Common (81-100) p/r 151-200: 1.00
Common (81-100) p/r 81-150: 2.00
Common (81-100) p/r 51-80: 2.00

2001 Donruss Classics

NM/M
Common Player: .50

Common SP (101-150): 5.00
Production 585
Common SP (151-200): 3.00
Production 1,755
Pack (6): 12.00
Box (18): 180.00
1 Alex Rodriguez 3.00
2 Barry Bonds 3.00
3 Cal Ripken Jr. 4.00
4 Chipper Jones 2.00
5 Derek Jeter 3.00
6 Troy Glaus .75
7 Frank Thomas 1.00
8 Greg Maddux 2.00
9 Ivan Rodriguez 1.00
10 Jeff Bagwell 1.00
11 Cliff Floyd .50
12 Todd Helton 1.00
13 Ken Griffey Jr. 2.00
14 Manny Ramirez 1.00
15 Mark McGwire 3.00
16 Mike Piazza 2.00
17 Nomar Garciaparra 3.00
18 Pedro Martinez 1.50
19 Randy Johnson 1.50
20 Rick Ankiel .50
21 Rickey Henderson .75
22 Roger Clemens 3.00
23 Sammy Sosa 2.50
24 Tony Gwynn 1.50
25 Vladimir Guerrero 1.50
26 Kazuhiro Sasaki .50
27 Roberto Alomar .75
28 Barry Zito .75
29 Pat Burrell .75
30 Harold Baines .50
31 Carlos Delgado .75
32 J.D. Drew .50
33 Jim Edmonds .75
34 Darin Erstad .75
35 Jason Giambi 1.00
36 Tom Glavine .75
37 Juan Gonzalez 1.00
38 Mark Grace .75
39 Shawn Green .75
40 Tim Hudson .75
41 Andruw Jones .75
42 Jeff Kent .75
43 Barry Larkin .75
44 Rafael Furcal .50
45 Mike Mussina .75
46 Hideo Nomo .75
47 Rafael Palmeiro 1.00
48 Scott Rolen 1.00
49 Gary Sheffield .75
50 Bernie Williams .75
51 Bob Abreu .50
52 Edgardo Alfonzo .50
53 Edgar Martinez .50
54 Magglio Ordonez .75
55 Kerry Wood .75
56 Adrian Beltre .50
57 Lance Berkman .75
58 Kevin Brown .75
59 Sean Casey .50
60 Eric Chavez .75
61 Bartolo Colon .50
62 Johnny Damon .50
63 Jermaine Dye .50
64 Juan Encarnacion .50
65 Carl Everett .50
66 Brian Giles .75
67 Mike Hampton .50
68 Richard Hidalgo .50
69 Geoff Jenkins .50
70 Jacque Jones .50
71 Jason Kendall .50
72 Ryan Klesko .75
73 Chan Ho Park .50
74 Richie Sexson .75
75 Mike Sweeney .50
76 Fernando Tatis .50
77 Miguel Tejada .75
78 Jose Vidro .50
79 Larry Walker .75
80 Preston Wilson .50
81 Craig Biggio .75
82 Fred McGriff .75
83 Jim Thome 1.00
84 Garret Anderson .75
85 Russell Branyan .50
86 Tony Batista .50
87 Terrence Long .50
88 Brad Fullmer .50
89 Rusty Greer .50
90 Orlando Hernandez .50
91 Gabe Kapler .50
92 Paul Konerko .50
93 Carlos Lee .50
94 Kenny Lofton .75
95 Raul Mondesi .50
96 Jorge Posada .75
97 Tim Salmon .75
98 Greg Vaughn .50
99 Mo Vaughn .50
100 Omar Vizquel .50
101 Aubrey Huff 5.00
102 Jimmy Rollins 5.00
103 Cory Aldridge **RC** 5.00
104 Wilmy Caceres **RC** 5.00
105 Josh Beckett 6.00
106 Wilson Betemit **RC** 5.00
107 Timo Perez 5.00
108 Albert Pujols **RC** 240.00
109 Bud Smith **RC** 5.00
110 Jack Wilson **RC** 10.00
111 Alex Escobar 5.00
112 Johnny Estrada **RC** 10.00
113 Pedro Feliz 5.00
114 Nate Frese **RC** 5.00
115 Carlos Garcia **RC** 5.00
116 Brandon Larson **RC** 5.00
117 Alexis Gomez **RC** 5.00
118 Jason Hart 5.00
119 Adam Dunn 5.00
120 Marcus Giles 5.00
121 Christian Parker **RC** 5.00
122 Jackson Melian **RC** 5.00
123 Eric Chavez 5.00
124 Adrian Hernandez **RC** 5.00
125 Joe Kennedy **RC** 5.00
126 Jose Mieses **RC** 5.00
127 C.C. Sabathia 5.00
128 Eric Munson 5.00
129 Xavier Nady 5.00
130 Horacio Ramirez **RC** 10.00
131 Abraham Nunez 5.00
132 Jose Ortiz 5.00
133 Jeremy Owens **RC** 5.00
134 Claudio Vargas **RC** 5.00
135 Corey Patterson 5.00
136 Audres Torres 5.00
137 Ben Sheets 5.00
138 Joe Crede 5.00
139 Adam Pettyjohn **RC** 5.00
140 Elpidio Guzman **RC** 5.00
141 Jay Gibbons **RC** 10.00
142 Wilkin Ruan **RC** 5.00
143 Tsuyoshi Shinjo **RC** 10.00
144 Alfonso Soriano 5.00
145 Nick Johnson 5.00
146 Ichiro Suzuki **RC** 80.00
147 Juan Uribe **RC** 8.00
148 Jack Cust 5.00
149 Carlos Valderrama **RC** 5.00
150 Matt White **RC** 5.00
151 Hank Aaron 10.00
152 Ernie Banks 4.00
153 Johnny Bench 6.00
154 George Brett 10.00
155 Lou Brock 3.00
156 Rod Carew 3.00
157 Steve Carlton 3.00
158 Bob Feller 3.00
159 Bob Gibson 5.00
160 Reggie Jackson 5.00
161 Al Kaline 6.00
162 Sandy Koufax 600.00
163 Don Mattingly 10.00
164 Willie Mays 10.00
165 Willie McCovey 3.00
166 Joe Morgan 3.00
167 Stan Musial 8.00
168 Jim Palmer 3.00
169 Brooks Robinson 5.00
170 Frank Robinson 3.00
171 Nolan Ryan 15.00
172 Mike Schmidt 10.00
173 Tom Seaver 5.00
174 Warren Spahn 4.00
175 Robin Yount 5.00
176 Wade Boggs 4.00
177 Ty Cobb 10.00
178 Lou Gehrig 10.00
179 Luis Aparicio 3.00
180 Babe Ruth 15.00
181 Ryne Sandberg 10.00
182 Yogi Berra 5.00
183 Roberto Clemente 10.00
184 Eddie Murray 5.00
185 Robin Roberts 3.00
186 Duke Snider 5.00
187 Orlando Cepeda 3.00
188 Billy Williams 3.00
189 Juan Marichal 3.00
190 Harmon Killebrew 5.00
191 Kirby Puckett 8.00
192 Carlton Fisk 4.00
193 Dave Winfield 3.00
194 Whitey Ford 4.00
195 Paul Molitor 4.00
196 Tony Perez 3.00
197 Ozzie Smith 6.00
198 Ralph Kiner 3.00
199 Fergie Jenkins 3.00
200 Phil Rizzuto 4.00

Timeless Tributes

Stars (1-100): 4-8X
SP's (101-150): 1-1.5X
SP's (151-200): 1-2.5X
Production 100 Sets

Benchmarks

NM/M
Common Player: 5.00
Inserted 1:18
1 Todd Helton 5.00
2 Roberto Clemente 40.00
3 Mark McGwire 30.00
4 Barry Bonds 40.00
5 Bob Gibson 10.00
6 Ken Griffey Jr. 20.00
7 Frank Robinson 8.00
8 Greg Maddux 15.00
9 Reggie Jackson 10.00
10 Sammy Sosa 20.00
11 Willie Stargell 8.00
12 Vladimir Guerrero 8.00
13 Johnny Bench 15.00
14 Tony Gwynn 10.00
15 Mike Schmidt 17.50
16 Ivan Rodriguez 6.00
17 Jeff Bagwell 10.00
18 Cal Ripken Jr. 40.00
20 Kirby Puckett 15.00
21 Frank Thomas 8.00
22 Joe Morgan 5.00
23 Mike Piazza 20.00
25 Andruw Jones 5.00

Benchmarks Autographs

NM/M
5 Bob Gibson 60.00
7 Frank Robinson 50.00
9 Reggie Jackson 100.00
15 Mike Schmidt 100.00
22 Joe Morgan 50.00
25 Andruw Jones 60.00

Classic Combos

NM/M
Common Card: 20.00
1 Roberto Clemente 125.00
2 Willie Stargell 25.00
3 Babe Ruth 450.00
4 Lou Gehrig 300.00
5 Hank Aaron 100.00
6 Eddie Mathews 30.00
7 Johnny Bench 40.00
8 Joe Morgan 20.00
9 Robin Yount 40.00
10 Paul Molitor 35.00
11 Steve Carlton 25.00
12 Mike Schmidt 75.00
13 Stan Musial 75.00
14 Lou Brock 20.00
15 Yogi Berra 30.00
16 Phil Rizzuto 25.00
17 Ernie Banks 40.00
18 Billy Williams 20.00
19 Don Mattingly 70.00
60.00
21 Jackie Robinson 100.00
22 Duke Snider 30.00
23 Frank Robinson 25.00
24 Brooks Robinson 40.00
26 Willie McCovey 30.00
27 Ryne Sandberg 60.00
29 Harmon Killebrew 40.00
30 Rod Carew 40.00
31 Roberto Clemente, Willie Stargell 200.00
32 Babe Ruth, Lou Gehrig 1,000
33 Hank Aaron, Eddie Mathews 200.00
34 Johnny Bench, Joe Morgan 80.00
35 Robin Yount, Paul Molitor 100.00
36 Steve Carlton, Mike Schmidt 200.00
37 Stan Musial, Lou Brock 150.00
38 Phil Rizzuto, Yogi Berra 100.00
41 Jackie Robinson, Duke Snider 150.00
42 Brooks Robinson, Frank Robinson 75.00
43 Willie McCovey, Orlando Cepeda 60.00
45 Harmon Killebrew, Rod Carew 100.00

Classic Combos Autographs

No pricing due to scarcity.

Legendary Lumberjacks

NM/M
Common Player: 5.00
Inserted 1:18
1 Hack Wilson/244 75.00
2 Chipper Jones 10.00
3 Rogers Hornsby/SP/301 85.00
4 Nellie Fox 75.00
5 Ivan Rodriguez 10.00
6 Jimmie Foxx/300 120.00
7 Hank Aaron 40.00
8 Yogi Berra 15.00
9 Ernie Banks/SP/300 50.00
10 George Brett 25.00
11 Ty Cobb/SP/100 150.00
12 Roberto Clemente 125.00
13 Carlton Fisk 5.00
14 Reggie Jackson 10.00
15 Al Kaline 15.00
16 Harmon Killebrew 15.00
17 Ralph Kiner 5.00
18 Roger Maris/SP/275 120.00
19 Eddie Mathews 25.00
20 Ted Williams/SP/300 125.00
21 Willie McCovey 5.00
22 Eddie Murray 10.00
23 Joe Morgan/SP/268 20.00
24 Frank Robinson 10.00
25 Tony Perez 5.00
26 Mike Schmidt 20.00
27 Ryne Sandberg 25.00
28 Duke Snider/SP/300 25.00
30 Billy Williams 5.00
31 Dave Winfield 8.00
32 Robin Yount 10.00
33 Barry Bonds 30.00
34 Stan Musial/SP/300 35.00
35 Johnny Bench/SP/300 20.00
36 Orlando Cepeda 5.00
37 Jeff Bagwell 8.00
38 Frank Thomas 8.00
39 Juan Gonzalez 8.00
40 Cal Ripken Jr. 40.00
41 Rafael Palmeiro 8.00
42 Troy Glaus/SP/100 15.00
43 Manny Ramirez 8.00
44 Paul Molitor 15.00
45 Tony Gwynn 8.00
46 Rod Carew 8.00
47 Lou Brock 8.00
48 Wade Boggs 5.00
49 Babe Ruth/SP 225.00
50 Lou Gehrig/SP 150.00

Legendary Lumberjacks Autographs

NM/M
No pricing due to scarcity.
LL24 Frank Robinson 200.00

Significant Signatures

NM/M
Common Autograph: 5.00
Inserted 1:18
101 Aubrey Huff 6.00
103 Cory Aldridge 5.00
105 Josh Beckett/SP 30.00
106 Wilson Betemit 5.00

107 Timo Perez 5.00
108 Albert Pujols 600.00
110 Jack Wilson 10.00
111 Alex Escobar 5.00
112 Johnny Estrada 20.00
113 Pedro Feliz 5.00
114 Nate Frese 5.00
115 Carlos Garcia 5.00
116 Brandon Larson 8.00
118 Jason Hart 5.00
119 Adam Dunn/SP 25.00
120 Marcus Giles 8.00
121 Christian Parker 5.00
126 Jose Mieses 5.00
127 C.C. Sabathia 10.00
129 Xavier Nady 8.00
130 Horacio Ramirez 10.00
131 Abraham Nunez 5.00
132 Jose Ortiz 5.00
133 Jeremy Owens 5.00
134 Claudio Vargas 5.00
135 Corey Patterson/SP 20.00
136 Andres Torres 5.00
137 Ben Sheets/SP 25.00
138 Joe Crede 8.00
139 Adam Pettyjohn 5.00
140 Elpidio Guzman 5.00
141 Jay Gibbons 15.00
142 Wilkin Ruan 5.00
144 Alfonso Soriano/SP 40.00
145 Nick Johnson 10.00
147 Juan Uribe 10.00
149 Carlos Valderrama 5.00
151 Hank Aaron/SP 200.00
152 Ernie Banks 35.00
153 Johnny Bench/SP 100.00
154 George Brett/SP 150.00
155 Lou Brock 15.00
156 Rod Carew 25.00
157 Steve Carlton 25.00
158 Bob Feller 15.00
159 Bob Gibson 25.00
160 Reggie Jackson/SP 65.00
161 Al Kaline 40.00
162 Nolan Ryan/SP 150.00
163 Don Mattingly 80.00
164 Willie Mays/SP 160.00
165 Willie McCovey 20.00
166 Joe Morgan 10.00
167 Stan Musial/SP 85.00
168 Jim Palmer 15.00
169 Brooks Robinson 40.00
170 Frank Robinson 20.00
171 Nolan Ryan/SP 150.00
172 Mike Schmidt 75.00
173 Tom Seaver 30.00
174 Warren Spahn 40.00
175 Robin Yount/SP 100.00
176 Wade Boggs/SP 50.00
179 Luis Aparicio 10.00
181 Ryne Sandberg 75.00
182 Yogi Berra 30.00
184 Eddie Murray 50.00
185 Ron Santo 25.00
186 Duke Snider 25.00
187 Orlando Cepeda 10.00
188 Billy Williams 10.00
189 Juan Marichal 15.00
190 Harmon Killebrew 40.00
191 Kirby Puckett/SP 60.00
192 Carlton Fisk 20.00
193 Dave Winfield/SP 50.00
194 Whitey Ford 25.00
195 Paul Molitor/SP 50.00
196 Tony Perez 15.00
197 Ozzie Smith/SP 80.00
198 Ralph Kiner 25.00
199 Fergie Jenkins 10.00
200 Phil Rizzuto 40.00

Stadium Stars

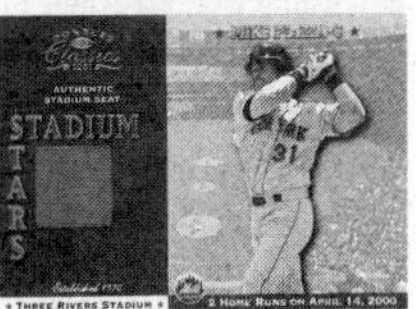

NM/M
Common Player: 4.00
Inserted 1:18
1 Babe Ruth 40.00
2 Cal Ripken Jr. 20.00
3 Brooks Robinson 8.00

4 Tony Gwynn 10.00
5 Ty Cobb 25.00
6 Vladimir Guerrero 8.00
7 Lou Gehrig 35.00
8 Nomar Garciaparra 12.00
9 Sammy Sosa 12.00
10 Reggie Jackson 8.00
11 Alex Rodriguez 12.00
12 Derek Jeter 20.00
13 Willie McCovey 4.00
14 Mark McGwire 15.00
15 Chipper Jones 10.00
16 Honus Wagner 10.00
17 Ken Griffey Jr. 12.00
18 Frank Robinson 8.00
19 Barry Bonds 20.00
20 Yogi Berra 8.00
21 Mike Piazza 12.00
22 Roger Clemens 10.00
23 Duke Snider 8.00
24 Frank Thomas 8.00
25 Andruw Jones 8.00

Stadium Stars Autographs

Common Autograph:

Timeless Treasures

NM/M

Inserted 1:420
1 Mark McGwire/Ball 200.00
2 Babe Ruth/Seat 60.00
3 Harmon Killebrew/Bat 30.00
4 Derek Jeter/Base 25.00
5 Barry Bonds/Ball 85.00

2001 Donruss Class of 2001 Samples

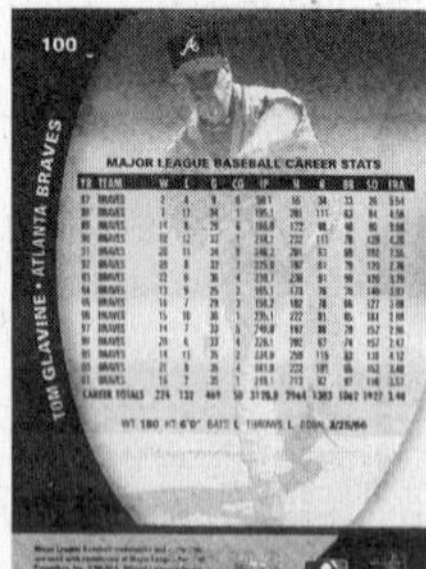

Each February 2002, issue of Beckett Baseball Card Monthly included a sample Donruss Class of 2001 card rubber-cemented inside. The cards differ from the issued version only in the appearance on back of a (usually) silver-foil "SAMPLE" notation. Some cards were produced with the overprint in gold-foil, in much more limited quantities. The number of different players' cards involved in the promotion is unknown.

NM/M

Common Player: .10
Stars: 1.5-2X
Gold: 20X

2001 Donruss Class of 2001

NM/M

Complete Set (300):
Common Player: .20
Common (101-200): 3.00
Production 1,875
Common (201-300): 3.00
Production 625
Pack (3): 6.00
Box (24 + Bobble Head): 125.00
1 Alex Rodriguez 2.00
2 Barry Bonds 2.50
3 Vladimir Guerrero .75
4 Jim Edmonds .20
5 Derek Jeter 2.50
6 Jose Canseco .40
7 Rafael Furcal .20
8 Cal Ripken Jr. 2.50
9 Brad Radke .20
10 Miguel Tejada .40
11 Pat Burrell .50
12 Ken Griffey Jr. 1.50
13 Cliff Floyd .20
14 Luis Gonzalez .20
15 Frank Thomas .75
16 Mike Sweeney .20
17 Paul LoDuca .20
18 Lance Berkman .20
19 Tony Gwynn 1.00
20 Chipper Jones 1.00
21 Eric Chavez .40
22 Kerry Wood .35
23 Jorge Posada .40
24 J.D. Drew .50
25 Garret Anderson .20
26 Mike Piazza 1.50
27 Kenny Lofton .20
28 Mike Mussina .40
29 Paul Konerko .20
30 Bernie Williams .20
31 Eric Milton .20
32 Shawn Green .40
33 Paul O'Neill .20
34 Juan Gonzalez .35
35 Andres Galarraga .20
36 Gary Sheffield .40
37 Ben Grieve .20
38 Scott Rolen .60
39 Mark Grace .20
40 Hideo Nomo .35
41 Barry Zito .50
42 Edgar Martinez .20
43 Jarrod Washburn .20
44 Greg Maddux 1.00
45 Mark Buehrle .20
46 Larry Walker .20
47 Trot Nixon .20
48 Nomar Garciaparra 1.50
49 Robert Fick .20
50 Sean Casey .40
51 Joe Mays .20
52 Roger Clemens 1.50
53 Chan Ho Park .20
54 Carlos Delgado .50
55 Phil Nevin .20
56 Jason Giambi .50
57 Raul Mondesi .20
58 Roberto Alomar .35
59 Ryan Klesko .20
60 Andruw Jones .75
61 Gabe Kapler .20
62 Darin Erstad .35
63 Cristian Guzman .20
64 Kazuhiro Sasaki .20
65 Doug Mientkiewicz .20
66 Sammy Sosa 1.50
67 Mike Hampton .20
68 Rickey Henderson .75
69 Mark Mulder .30
70 Mark McGwire 2.00
71 Freddy Garcia .20
72 Ivan Rodriguez .60
73 Terrence Long .20
74 Jeff Bagwell .75
75 Moises Alou .20
76 Todd Helton .65
77 Preston Wilson .20
78 Pedro Martinez .75
79 Bobby Abreu .20
80 Manny Ramirez .75
81 Jose Vidro .20
82 Randy Johnson .75
83 Richie Sexson .20
84 Troy Glaus .65
85 Kevin Brown .20
86 Carlos Lee .20
87 Adrian Beltre .30
88 Brian Giles .20
89 Jermaine Dye .20
90 Craig Biggio .20
91 Richard Hidalgo .20
92 Magglio Ordonez .20
93 Aramis Ramirez .20
94 Jeff Kent .20
95 Curt Schilling .50
96 Tim Hudson .40
97 Fred McGriff .20
98 Barry Larkin .20
99 Jim Thome .60
100 Tom Glavine .40
101 Sean Douglass **RC** 3.00
102 Rob Mackowiak **RC** 3.00
103 Jeremy Fikac **RC** 3.00
104 Henry Mateo **RC** 3.00
105 Geronimo Gil **RC** 3.00
106 Ramon Vazquez **RC** 5.00
107 Pedro Santana **RC** 3.00
108 Ryan Jensen **RC** 3.00
109 Paul Phillips **RC** 3.00
110 Saul Rivera **RC** 3.00
111 Larry Bigbie 3.00
112 Josh Phelps 3.00
113 Justin Kaye **RC** 3.00
114 Kris Keller **RC** 3.00
115 Adam Bernero 3.00
116 Victor Zambrano **RC** 3.00
117 Felipe Lopez 3.00
118 Brian Roberts **RC** 10.00
119 Kurt Ainsworth 3.00
120 George Perez **RC** 3.00
121 Wilson Guzman **RC** 3.00
122 Derrick Lewis **RC** 3.00
123 Nate Teut **RC** 3.00
124 Martin Vargas **RC** 3.00
125 Brandon Inge 3.00
126 Travis Phelps **RC** 3.00
127 Les Walrond **RC** 3.00
128 Justin Atchley **RC** 3.00
129 Stubby Clapp **RC** 3.00
130 Bret Prinz **RC** 3.00
131 Bert Snow **RC** 3.00
132 Joe Crede 3.00
133 Nick Punto **RC** 3.00
134 Carlos Hernandez **RC** 3.00
135 Ken Vining **RC** 3.00
136 Luis Pineda **RC** 3.00
137 Winston Abreu **RC** 3.00
138 Matt Ginter 3.00
139 Jason Smith **RC** 3.00
140 Gene Altman **RC** 3.00
141 Brian Rogers **RC** 3.00
142 Michael Cuddyer 3.00
143 Mike Penney **RC** 3.00
144 Scott Podsednik **RC** 10.00
145 Esix Snead **RC** 3.00
146 Steve Watkins **RC** 3.00
147 Orlando Woodards **RC** 3.00
148 Mike Young 3.00
149 Chris George 3.00
150 Blaine Neal **RC** 3.00
151 Ben Sheets 3.00
152 Scott Stewart **RC** 3.00
153 Mike Koplove **RC** 3.00
154 Kyle Lohse **RC** 8.00
155 Dee Brown 3.00
156 Aubrey Huff 3.00
157 Pablo Ozuna 3.00
158 Bill Ortega 3.00
159 Toby Hall 3.00
160 Kevin Olsen **RC** 3.00
161 Will Ohman **RC** 3.00
162 Nate Cornejo 3.00
163 Jack Cust 3.00
164 Juan Rivera 3.00
165 Jerrod Riggan **RC** 3.00
166 Dustan Mohr **RC** 3.00
167 Doug Nickle **RC** 3.00
168 Craig Monroe **RC** 3.00
169 Jason Jennings 3.00
170 Bart Miadich **RC** 3.00
171 Luis Rivas 3.00
172 Tim Christman **RC** 3.00
173 Luke Hudson **RC** 3.00
174 Brett Jodie **RC** 3.00
175 Jorge Julio **RC** 4.00
176 David Espinosa 3.00
177 Mike Maroth **RC** 3.00
178 Keith Ginter 3.00
179 Juan Moreno **RC** 3.00
180 Brandon Knight **RC** 3.00
181 Steve Lomasney 3.00
182 John Grabow **RC** 3.00
183 Steve Green **RC** 3.00
184 Jason Karnuth **RC** 3.00
185 Bob File **RC** 3.00
186 Brent Abernathy 3.00
187 Morgan Ensberg **RC** 10.00
188 Wily Mo Pena 3.00
189 Ken Harvey 3.00
190 Josh Pearce **RC** 3.00
191 Cesar Izturis 3.00
192 Eric Hinske **RC** 5.00
193 Joe Beimel **RC** 3.00
194 Timo Perez 3.00
195 Troy Mattes **RC** 3.00
196 Eric Valent 3.00
197 Ed Rogers **RC** 3.00
198 Grant Balfour **RC** 3.00
199 Brandon Baez **RC** 3.00
200 Vernon Wells 3.00
201 Joe Kennedy **RC** 4.00
202 Wilson Betemit **RC** 8.00
203 Christian Parker **RC** 3.00
204 Jay Gibbons **RC** 10.00
205 Carlos Garcia **RC** 4.00
206 Jack Wilson **RC** 4.00
207 Johnny Estrada **RC** 10.00
208 Wilkin Ruan **RC** 3.00
209 Brandon Duckworth **RC** 5.00
210 Willie Harris **RC** 5.00
211 Marlon Byrd **RC** 10.00
212 C.C. Sabathia 3.00
213 Dennis Tankersley **RC** 5.00
214 Brandon Larson **RC** 5.00
215 Alexis Gomez **RC** 4.00
216 Bill Hall **RC** 10.00
217 Antonio Perez **RC** 3.00
218 Jeremy Affeldt **RC** 4.00
219 Junior Spivey **RC** 8.00
220 Casey Fossum **RC** 8.00
221 Brandon Lyon **RC** 4.00
222 Angel Santos **RC** 4.00
223 Lance Davis **RC** 3.00
224 Zach Day **RC** 4.00
225 David Williams **RC** 3.00
226 Cesar Crespo **RC** 3.00
227 Jose Acevedo **RC** 3.00
228 Travis Hafner **RC** 20.00
229 Orlando Hudson **RC** 10.00
230 Jose Mieses **RC** 3.00
231 Ricardo Rodriguez **RC** 3.00
232 Alfonso Soriano 3.00
233 Jason Hart 3.00
234 Endy Chavez **RC** 3.00
235 Delvin James **RC** 3.00
236 Ryan Drese **RC** 3.00
237 Jeremy Owens **RC** 3.00
238 Brad Voyles **RC** 3.00
239 Nate Frese 3.00
240 Josh Beckett 3.00
241 Roy Oswalt 3.00
242 Juan Uribe **RC** 5.00
243 Cory Aldridge **RC** 3.00
244 Adam Dunn 3.00
245 Bud Smith **RC** 3.00
246 Adrian Hernandez **RC** 3.00
247 Matt Guerrier **RC** 3.00
248 Jimmy Rollins 3.00
249 Wilmy Caceres **RC** 3.00
250 Jason Michaels **RC** 3.00
251 Ichiro Suzuki **RC** 60.00
252 John Buck **RC** 3.00
253 Andres Torres **RC** 3.00
254 Alfredo Amezaga **RC** 3.00
255 Corky Miller **RC** 3.00
256 Rafael Soriano **RC** 10.00
257 Donaldo Mendez **RC** 3.00
258 Victor Martinez **RC** 50.00
259 Corey Patterson 3.00
260 Horacio Ramirez **RC** 8.00
261 Elpidio Guzman **RC** 3.00
262 Juan Diaz **RC** 3.00
263 Mike Rivera **RC** 3.00
264 Brian Lawrence **RC** 3.00
265 Josue Perez **RC** 3.00
266 Jose Nunez 3.00
267 Erik Bedard **RC** 20.00
268 Albert Pujols **RC** 200.00
269 Duaner Sanchez **RC** 3.00
270 Cody Ransom **RC** 3.00
271 Greg Miller **RC** 3.00
272 Adam Pettyjohn **RC** 3.00
273 Tsuyoshi Shinjo **RC** 3.00
274 Claudio Vargas **RC** 3.00
275 Justin Duchscherer **RC** 5.00
276 Tim Spooneybarger **RC** 3.00
277 Rick Bauer **RC** 3.00
278 Josh Fogg **RC** 5.00
279 Brian Reith **RC** 3.00
280 Scott MacRae **RC** 3.00
281 Ryan Ludwick **RC** 5.00
282 Erick Almonte **RC** 3.00
283 Josh Towers **RC** 8.00
284 Juan Pena 3.00
285 David Brous **RC** 3.00
286 Erik Hiljus **RC** 3.00
287 Nick Neugebauer 3.00
288 Jackson Melian **RC** 3.00
289 Billy Sylvester **RC** 3.00
290 Carlos Valderrama **RC** 3.00
291 Jose Cueto **RC** 3.00
292 Matt White **RC** 3.00
293 Nick Maness **RC** 3.00
294 Jason Lane **RC** 10.00
295 Brandon Berger **RC** 3.00
296 Angel Berroa **RC** 6.00
297 Juan Cruz **RC** 4.00
298 Dewon Brazelton **RC** 3.00
299 Mark Prior **RC** 15.00
300 Mark Teixeira **RC** 40.00

First Class

Stars (1-100): 5-10X
Production 100
SP's (101-300): 1-30X
Production 50

First Class Autographs

NM/M

Common Player:
10 Miguel Tejada/75 50.00
17 Paul LoDuca/100 20.00
21 Eric Chavez/100 20.00
41 Barry Zito/100 30.00
45 Mark Buehrle/100 25.00
49 Robert Fick/100 15.00
50 Sean Casey/100 25.00
51 Joe Mays/100 15.00
59 Ryan Klesko/50 20.00
69 Mark Mulder/100 25.00
73 Terrence Long/100 15.00
81 Jose Vidro/100 15.00
83 Richie Sexson/100 25.00
84 Troy Glaus/100 25.00
89 Jermaine Dye/100 20.00
91 Richard Hidalgo/100 15.00
93 Aramis Ramirez/100 20.00
96 Tim Hudson/100 25.00

Rookie Autographs

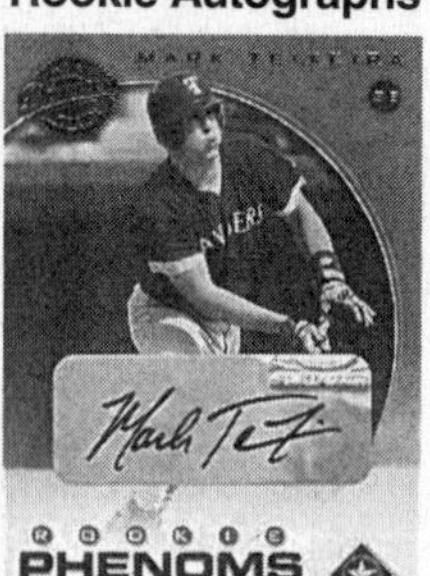

NM/M

Common Autograph: 8.00
109 Paul Phillips/250 8.00
114 Kris Keller/250 8.00
115 Adam Bernero/250 8.00
120 George Perez/250 8.00
123 Nate Teut/250 8.00
124 Martin Vargas/250 8.00
127 Les Walrond/250 8.00
132 Joe Crede/250 10.00
137 Winston Abreu/250 8.00
138 Matt Ginter/250 8.00
140 Gene Altman/250 8.00
142 Michael Cuddyer/250 8.00
143 Mike Penney/250 8.00
145 Esix Snead/250 8.00
147 Orlando Woodards/250 8.00
148 Jeff Deardorff/100 8.00
150 Blaine Neal/250 8.00
156 Aubrey Huff/250 10.00
157 Pablo Ozuna/250 8.00
158 Bill Ortega/250 8.00
160 Kevin Olsen/250 8.00
161 Will Ohman/250 8.00
163 Jack Cust/250 10.00
168 Craig Monroe/250 8.00
169 Jason Jennings/250 8.00
171 Luis Rivas/250 8.00
173 Luke Hudson/250 12.00
176 David Espinosa/250 8.00
177 Mike Maroth/250 8.00
178 Keith Ginter/250 8.00
181 Steve Lomasney/250 8.00
182 John Grabow/250 8.00
184 Jason Karnuth/250 8.00
186 Brent Abernathy/250 8.00
188 Wily Mo Pena/250 15.00
191 Cesar Izturis/250 8.00
192 Eric Hinske/250 10.00
194 Timo Perez/100 8.00
196 Eric Valent/250 8.00
201 Joe Kennedy/100 8.00
202 Wilson Betemit/100 15.00
203 Christian Parker/100 8.00
204 Jay Gibbons/100 20.00
205 Carlos Garcia/200 8.00
206 Jack Wilson/100 15.00
207 Johnny Estrada/200 20.00
208 Wilkin Ruan/200 8.00
209 Brandon Duckworth/100 8.00
211 Marlon Byrd/100 20.00
213 Dennis Tankersley/100 10.00
214 Brandon Larson/200 8.00
215 Alexis Gomez/200 10.00
216 Bill Hall/100 50.00
217 Antonio Perez/100 8.00
218 Jeremy Affeldt/100 10.00
220 Casey Fossum/200 10.00
224 Zach Day/200 8.00
225 David Williams/200 8.00
227 Jose Acevedo/200 8.00
229 Orlando Hudson/100 25.00
230 Jose Mieses/200 8.00
231 Ric Rodriguez/200 8.00
232 Alfonso Soriano/100 40.00
233 Jason Hart/100 8.00
234 Endy Chavez/200 8.00
235 Delvin James/100 8.00
237 Jeremy Owens/200 8.00
238 Brad Voyles/200 8.00
239 Nate Frese/200 8.00
240 Josh Beckett/25 80.00
241 Roy Oswalt/100 25.00
242 Juan Uribe/150 10.00
243 Cory Aldridge/200 8.00
244 Adam Dunn/100 30.00
245 Bud Smith/100 8.00
246 Adrian Hernandez/100 8.00
249 Wilmy Caceres/200 8.00
250 Jason Michaels/200 8.00
252 John Buck/100 15.00
253 Andres Torres/100 8.00
255 Corky Miller/100 8.00
256 Rafael Soriano/200 10.00
257 Donaldo Mendez/200 8.00
259 Corey Patterson/100 15.00
260 Horacio Ramirez/200 10.00
261 Elpidio Guzman/200 8.00
262 Juan Diaz/200 8.00
264 Brian Lawrence/200 10.00
265 Josue Perez/200 8.00
266 Jose Nunez/200 8.00
268 Albert Pujols/100 500.00
269 Duaner Sanchez/200 8.00
271 Greg Miller/200 8.00
272 Adam Pettyjohn/200 8.00
274 Claudio Vargas/200 8.00
279 Brian Reith/200 8.00
283 Josh Towers/100 8.00
285 David Brous/200 8.00
287 Nick Neugebauer/100 8.00
289 Billy Sylvester/200 8.00
290 Carlos Valderrama/200 8.00
292 Matt White/200 8.00
293 Nick Maness/200 8.00
296 Angel Berroa/100 15.00
297 Juan Cruz/100 8.00
298 Dewon Brazelton/100 8.00
299 Mark Prior/100 100.00
300 Mark Teixeira/100 250.00

Aces

NM/M

Complete Set (20): 70.00
Common Player: 3.00
Inserted 1:30
1 Roger Clemens 12.00
2 Randy Johnson 7.50
3 Freddy Garcia 3.00
4 Greg Maddux 10.00
5 Tim Hudson 5.00
6 Curt Schilling 5.00
7 Mark Buehrle 3.00
8 Matt Morris 3.00
9 Joe Mays 3.00
10 Javier Vazquez 3.00
11 Mark Mulder 4.00
12 Wade Miller 3.00
13 Barry Zito 5.00
14 Pedro Martinez 7.50
15 Al Leiter 3.00
16 Chan Ho Park 3.00
17 John Burkett 3.00
18 C.C. Sabathia 3.00
19 Jamie Moyer 3.00
20 Mike Mussina 5.00

Diamond Aces

NM/M

Common Player: 5.00
Varying quantities produced

1 Roger Clemens/200 30.00
2 Randy Johnson/750 10.00
3 Freddy Garcia/350 5.00
4 Greg Maddux/750 20.00
5 Tim Hudson/550 8.00
6 Curt Schilling/525 8.00
7 Mark Buehrle/750 5.00
9 Joe Mays/750 5.00
10 Javier Vazquez/500 5.00
11 Mark Mulder/300 6.00
12 Wade Miller/525 5.00
13 Barry Zito/550 8.00
14 Pedro Martinez/550 15.00
15 Al Leiter/525 5.00
16 Chan Ho Park/400 5.00
17 John Burkett/700 5.00
18 C.C. Sabathia/550 5.00
19 Jamie Moyer/700 5.00

Bobblehead

NM/M

Common Bobblehead: 10.00
One per box.
1 Ichiro Suzuki 40.00
2 Cal Ripken Jr. 40.00
3 Derek Jeter 35.00
4 Mark McGwire 35.00
5 Albert Pujols 40.00
6 Ken Griffey Jr. 20.00
7 Nomar Garciaparra 20.00
8 Mike Piazza 20.00
9 Alex Rodriguez 20.00
10 Manny Ramirez 10.00
11 Tsuyoshi Shinjo 10.00
12 Hideo Nomo 10.00
13 Chipper Jones 15.00
14 Sammy Sosa 20.00
15 Roger Clemens 17.50
16 Tony Gwynn 15.00
17 Barry Bonds 35.00
18 Kazuhiro Sasaki 10.00
19 Pedro Martinez 10.00
20 Jeff Bagwell 10.00
21 Ichiro Suzuki ROY 40.00
22 Albert Pujols ROY 40.00

Bobblehead Cards

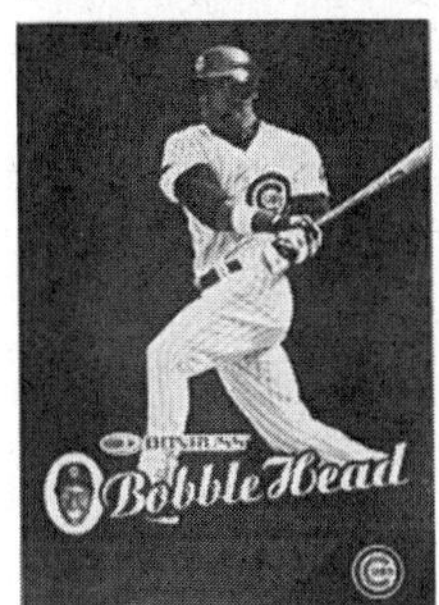

NM/M

Common Player: 4.00
1-20 2,000 Produced
21-22 1,000 Produced
1 Ichiro Suzuki 15.00
2 Cal Ripken Jr. 12.00
3 Derek Jeter 12.00
4 Mark McGwire 10.00
5 Albert Pujols 10.00
6 Ken Griffey Jr. 8.00
7 Nomar Garciaparra 8.00
8 Mike Piazza 8.00
9 Alex Rodriguez 8.00
10 Manny Ramirez 5.00
11 Tsuyoshi Shinjo 4.00
12 Hideo Nomo 4.00
13 Chipper Jones 6.00
14 Sammy Sosa 8.00
15 Roger Clemens 7.00
16 Tony Gwynn 6.00
17 Barry Bonds 15.00
18 Kazuhiro Sasaki 4.00
19 Pedro Martinez 5.00
20 Jeff Bagwell 5.00
21 Ichiro Suzuki 15.00
22 Albert Pujols 15.00

Crusade

NM/M

Complete Set (25): 125.00
Common Player: 3.00
1 Roger Clemens/275 15.00
2 Luis Gonzalez/275 3.00
3 Troy Glaus/275 6.00
4 Freddy Garcia/300 3.00
5 Sean Casey/285 5.00
6 Bobby Abreu/300 3.00
7 Matt Morris/300 3.00
8 Cal Ripken Jr./275 25.00
9 Miguel Tejada/285 5.00
10 Vladimir Guerrero/275 8.00
11 Mark Buehrle/100 5.00
12 Mike Sweeney/300 3.00
13 Ivan Rodriguez/275 8.00
14 Jeff Bagwell/275 8.00
15 Joe Mays/250 3.00
16 Cliff Floyd/300 3.00
17 Lance Berkman/300 3.00
18 Aramis Ramirez/100 5.00
19 Tony Gwynn/300 10.00
20 Shannon Stewart/100 5.00
21 Todd Helton/275 8.00
22 Chipper Jones/275 12.00
23 Javier Vazquez/100 5.00
24 Shawn Green/275 5.00
25 Barry Bonds/300 25.00

Rookie Crusade

NM/M

Complete Set (25): 110.00
Common Player: 3.00
26 Albert Pujols/250 30.00
27 Wilson Betemit/100 3.00
28 C.C. Sabathia/290 3.00
29 Roy Oswalt/100 4.00
30 Johnny Estrada/100 3.00
31 Nick Johnson/100 4.00
32 Aubrey Huff/100 3.00
33 Corey Patterson/200 4.00
34 Jay Gibbons/100 4.00
35 Marcus Giles/100 3.00
36 Juan Cruz/100 3.00
37 Tsuyoshi Shinjo/300 3.00
38 Ben Sheets/285 3.00
39 Bud Smith/100 3.00
40 Alex Escobar/100 3.00
41 Joe Kennedy/100 3.00
42 Alexis Gomez/100 3.00
43 Jimmy Rollins/300 3.00
44 Josh Towers/100 3.00
45 Joe Crede/100 3.00
46 Brandon Duckworth/100 3.00
47 Ichiro Suzuki/300 40.00
48 Jose Ortiz/100 3.00
49 Casey Fossum/100 3.00
50 Adam Dunn/200 5.00

Crusade Autographs

NM/M

Common Player:
11 Mark Buehrle/200 10.00
15 Joe Mays/50 10.00
18 Aramis Ramirez/200 8.00
20 Shannon Stewart/200 8.00
23 Javier Vazquez/200 10.00
26 Albert Pujols/50 750.00
27 Wilson Betemit/200 10.00
29 Roy Oswalt/200 12.00
30 Johnny Estrada/200 8.00
31 Nick Johnson/200 12.00
32 Aubrey Huff/200 8.00
33 Corey Patterson/200 10.00
34 Jay Gibbons/200 20.00
35 Marcus Giles/200 8.00
36 Juan Cruz/200 8.00
39 Bud Smith/200 8.00
40 Alex Escobar/200 8.00
41 Joe Kennedy/200 8.00
42 Alexis Gomez/200 10.00
44 Josh Towers/200 8.00
45 Joe Crede/200 10.00
46 Brandon Duckworth/200 12.00
48 Jose Ortiz/200 8.00
49 Casey Fossum/200 12.00
50 Adam Dunn/100 30.00

Dominators

NM/M

Complete Set (30): 90.00
Common Player: 2.00
Inserted 1:20
1 Manny Ramirez 4.00
2 Lance Berkman 2.00
3 Juan Gonzalez 4.00
4 Albert Pujols 10.00
5 Jason Giambi 3.00
6 Mike Sweeney 2.00
7 Rafael Palmeiro 4.00
8 Luis Gonzalez 2.00
9 Ichiro Suzuki 10.00
10 Cliff Floyd 2.00
11 Roberto Alomar 4.00
12 Paul LoDuca 2.00
13 Shannon Stewart 2.00
14 Barry Bonds 10.00
15 Larry Walker 2.00
16 Shawn Green 3.00
17 Moises Alou 2.00
18 Cal Ripken Jr. 10.00
19 Brian Giles 2.00
20 Magglio Ordonez 3.00
21 Jose Vidro 2.00
22 Edgar Martinez 2.00
23 Aramis Ramirez 2.00
24 Tony Gwynn 5.00
25 Richie Sexson 2.00
26 Todd Helton 4.00
27 Garret Anderson 2.00
28 Chipper Jones 5.00
29 Troy Glaus 4.00
30 Jeff Bagwell 4.00

Diamond Dominators

NM/M

Common Player: 4.00
Varying quantities produced
1 Manny Ramirez/725 8.00
2 Lance Berkman/725 4.00
3 Juan Gonzalez/500 6.00
4 Albert Pujols/125 65.00
5 Jason Giambi/250 8.00
6 Mike Sweeney/325 4.00
7 Rafael Palmeiro/550 8.00
8 Luis Gonzalez/725 4.00
10 Cliff Floyd/725 4.00
11 Roberto Alomar/200 8.00
12 Paul LoDuca/600 4.00
13 Shannon Stewart/725 6.00
14 Barry Bonds/250 30.00
15 Larry Walker/725 6.00
16 Shawn Green/500 6.00
17 Moises Alou/550 4.00
18 Cal Ripken/250 50.00
19 Brian Giles/725 5.00
20 Magglio Ordonez/725 5.00
21 Jose Vidro/725 4.00
22 Edgar Martinez/200 6.00
23 Aramis Ramirez/200 5.00
24 Tony Gwynn/500 10.00
25 Richie Sexson/725 6.00
26 Todd Helton/725 8.00
27 Garret Anderson/725 6.00
28 Chipper Jones/725 12.00
29 Troy Glaus/200 8.00
30 Jeff Bagwell/325 8.00

Rewards

NM/M

Common Player: 5.00
Inserted 1:212
1 Jason Giambi 7.50
2 Ichiro Suzuki 40.00
3 Roger Clemens 20.00
4 Freddy Garcia 5.00
5 Ichiro Suzuki 40.00
6 Albert Pujols 30.00
7 Barry Bonds 30.00
8 Albert Pujols 30.00
9 Randy Johnson 10.00
10 Matt Morris 5.00

Final Rewards

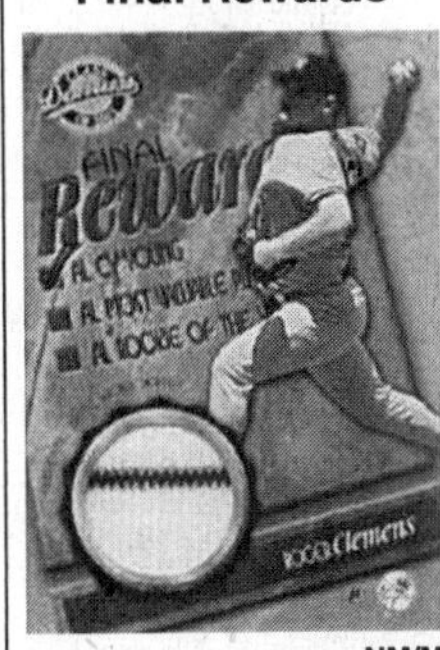

NM/M

Common Player: 5.00
Varying quantities produced
1 Jason Giambi/250 10.00
2 Ichiro Suzuki/50 120.00
3 Roger Clemens/200 30.00
4 Freddy Garcia/250 5.00
5 Ichiro Suzuki/50 120.00
6 Albert Pujols/125 60.00
7 Barry Bonds/200 40.00
8 Albert Pujols/125 60.00
9 Randy Johnson/250 15.00

Rookie Team

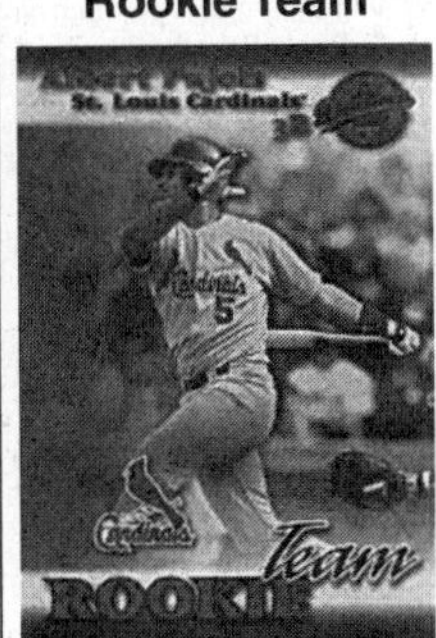

NM/M

Complete Set (15): 65.00
Common Player: 3.00
Inserted 1:83
1 Jay Gibbons 5.00
2 Alfonso Soriano 6.00
3 Jimmy Rollins 3.00
4 Wilson Betemit 3.00
5 Albert Pujols 20.00
6 Johnny Estrada 3.00
7 Ichiro Suzuki 15.00
8 Tsuyoshi Shinjo 4.00
9 Adam Dunn 5.00
10 C.C. Sabathia 3.00
11 Ben Sheets 3.00
12 Roy Oswalt 4.00
13 Bud Smith 3.00
14 Josh Towers 3.00
15 Juan Cruz 3.00

Rookie Team Materials

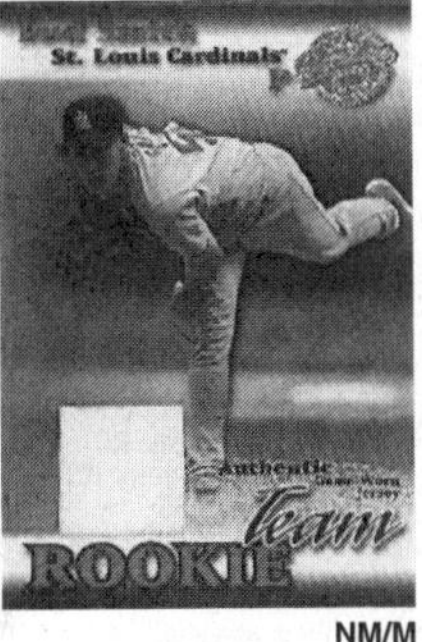

NM/M

Common Player: 5.00
Varying quantities produced
1 Jay Gibbons/100 8.00
2 Alfonso Soriano/100 15.00
3 Jimmy Rollins/200 5.00
5 Albert Pujols/100 65.00
6 Johnny Estrada/100 5.00
7 Ichiro Suzuki/50 120.00
8 Tsuyoshi Shinjo/200 10.00
9 Adam Dunn/200 8.00
10 C.C. Sabathia/200 5.00
11 Ben Sheets/200 5.00
13 Bud Smith/250 5.00
14 Josh Towers/200 5.00
15 Juan Cruz/200 5.00

Yearbook

NM/M

Complete Set (25): 85.00
Common Player: 2.00
Inserted 1:24
1 Barry Bonds 12.00
2 Mark Mulder 3.00
3 Luis Gonzalez 2.00
4 Lance Berkman 2.00
5 Matt Morris 2.00
6 Roy Oswalt 2.50
7 Todd Helton 3.00
8 Tsuyoshi Shinjo 2.00
9 C.C. Sabathia 2.00
10 Curt Schilling 3.00
11 Rickey Henderson 3.00
12 Jamie Moyer 2.00
13 Shawn Green 3.00
14 Randy Johnson 4.00
15 Jim Thome 2.00
16 Larry Walker 2.00
17 Jimmy Rollins 2.00
18 Kazuhiro Sasaki 2.00
19 Hideo Nomo 3.00
20 Roger Clemens 7.50
21 Bud Smith 2.00
22 Ichiro Suzuki 10.00
23 Albert Pujols 15.00
24 Cal Ripken Jr. 15.00
25 Tony Gwynn 5.00

Yearbook Scrapbook

NM/M

Common Player: 4.00
Varying quantities produced
1 Barry Bonds/525 30.00
2 Mark Mulder/500 6.00
3 Luis Gonzalez/500 4.00
4 Lance Berkman/525 4.00
6 Roy Oswalt/150 6.00
7 Todd Helton/525 6.00
8 Tsuyoshi Shinjo/75 15.00
9 C.C. Sabathia/500 4.00
10 Curt Schilling/525 6.00
11 Rickey Henderson/200 15.00
12 Jamie Moyer/500 4.00
13 Shawn Green/525 5.00
14 Randy Johnson/500 8.00
15 Jim Thome/400 4.00
16 Larry Walker/500 4.00
18 Kazuhiro Sasaki/500 4.00
19 Hideo Nomo/150 50.00
20 Roger Clemens/475 20.00
21 Bud Smith/525 4.00
22 Ichiro Suzuki/75 80.00
23 Albert Pujols/150 50.00
24 Cal Ripken/525 30.00
25 Tony Gwynn/500 10.00

2001 Donruss Elite

NM/M

Complete Set (200):
Common Player: .25
Common (151-200): 5.00
Production 900
Common 201-250: 4.00
(#201-250 available by redemption)
Pack (5): 12.00
Box (18): 200.00
1 Alex Rodriguez 2.00
2 Barry Bonds 2.50
3 Cal Ripken Jr. 2.50
4 Chipper Jones 1.50
5 Derek Jeter 2.50
6 Troy Glaus .75
7 Frank Thomas 1.00
8 Greg Maddux 1.50
9 Ivan Rodriguez .75
10 Jeff Bagwell 1.00
11 Jose Canseco .50
12 Todd Helton .75
13 Ken Griffey Jr. 1.75
14 Manny Ramirez 1.00
15 Mark McGwire 2.00
16 Mike Piazza 1.75
17 Nomar Garciaparra 1.50
18 Pedro Martinez 1.00
19 Randy Johnson 1.00
20 Rick Ankiel .25
21 Ricky Henderson 1.00
22 Roger Clemens 1.75
23 Sammy Sosa 1.50
24 Tony Gwynn 1.50
25 Vladimir Guerrero 1.00
26 Eric Davis .25
27 Roberto Alomar .35
28 Mark Mulder .35
29 Pat Burrell .50
30 Harold Baines .25
31 Carlos Delgado .60
32 J.D. Drew .40
33 Jim Edmonds .25
34 Darin Erstad .35
35 Jason Giambi .50
36 Tom Glavine .50
37 Juan Gonzalez .50
38 Mark Grace .25
39 Shawn Green .40
40 Tim Hudson .40
41 Andruw Jones 1.00
42 David Justice .25
43 Jeff Kent .25
44 Barry Larkin .25
45 Pokey Reese .25
46 Mike Mussina .40
47 Hideo Nomo .50
48 Rafael Palmeiro .65
49 Adam Piatt .25
50 Scott Rolen .65
51 Gary Sheffield .40
52 Bernie Williams .25
53 Bob Abreu .25
54 Edgardo Alfonzo .25
55 Jermaine Clark **RC** .25
56 Albert Belle .25
57 Craig Biggio .25
58 Andres Galarraga .25
59 Edgar Martinez .25
60 Fred McGriff .25
61 Magglio Ordonez .25
62 Jim Thome .65

63 Matt Williams .25
64 Kerry Wood .50
65 Moises Alou .25
66 Brady Anderson .25
67 Garret Anderson .25
68 Tony Armas Jr. .25
69 Tony Batista .25
70 Jose Cruz Jr. .25
71 Carlos Beltran .50
72 Adrian Beltre .40
73 Kris Benson .25
74 Lance Berkman .25
75 Kevin Brown .25
76 Jay Buhner .25
77 Jeromy Burnitz .25
78 Ken Caminiti .25
79 Sean Casey .40
80 Luis Castillo .25
81 Eric Chavez .40
82 Jeff Cirillo .25
83 Bartolo Colon .25
84 David Cone .25
85 Freddy Garcia .25
86 Johnny Damon .50
87 Ray Durham .25
88 Jermaine Dye .25
89 Juan Encarnacion .25
90 Terrence Long .25
91 Carl Everett .25
92 Steve Finley .25
93 Cliff Floyd .25
94 Brad Fulmer .25
95 Brian Giles .25
96 Luis Gonzalez .25
97 Rusty Greer .25
98 Jeffrey Hammonds .25
99 Mike Hampton .25
100 Orlando Hernandez .35
101 Richard Hidalgo .25
102 Geoff Jenkins .25
103 Jacque Jones .25
104 Brian Jordan .25
105 Gabe Kapler .25
106 Eric Karros .25
107 Jason Kendall .25
108 Adam Kennedy .25
109 Byung-Hyun Kim .25
110 Ryan Klesko .25
111 Chuck Knoblauch .25
112 Paul Konerko .25
113 Carlos Lee .25
114 Kenny Lofton .25
115 Javy Lopez .25
116 Tino Martinez .25
117 Ruben Mateo .25
118 Kevin Millwood .25
119 Ben Molina .25
120 Raul Mondesi .25
121 Trot Nixon .25
122 John Olerud .25
123 Paul O'Neill .25
124 Chan Ho Park .25
125 Andy Pettitte .40
126 Jorge Posada .35
127 Mark Quinn .25
128 Aramis Ramirez .25
129 Mariano Rivera .35
130 Tim Salmon .25
131 Curt Schilling .40
132 Richie Sexson .25
133 John Smoltz .25
134 J.T. Snow .25
135 Jay Payton .25
136 Shannon Stewart .25
137 B.J. Surhoff .25
138 Mike Sweeney .25
139 Fernando Tatis .25
140 Miguel Tejada .40
141 Jason Varitek .25
142 Greg Vaughn .25
143 Mo Vaughn .25
144 Robin Ventura .25
145 Jose Vidro .25
146 Omar Vizquel .25
147 Larry Walker .25
148 David Wells .25
149 Rondell White .25
150 Preston Wilson .25
151 Brent Abernathy 5.00
152 Cory Aldridge **RC** 5.00
153 Gene Altman **RC** 5.00
154 Josh Beckett 6.00
155 Wilson Betemit **RC** 5.00
156 Albert Pujols **RC** 400.00
157 Joe Crede 5.00
158 Jack Cust 5.00
159 Ben Sheets 5.00
160 Alex Escobar 5.00
161 Adrian Hernandez **RC** 5.00
162 Pedro Feliz 5.00
163 Nate Frese **RC** 5.00
164 Carlos Garcia **RC** 5.00
165 Marcus Giles 5.00
166 Alexis Gomez **RC** 5.00
167 Jason Hart 5.00
168 Aubrey Huff 5.00
169 Cesar Izturis 5.00
170 Nick Johnson 5.00
171 Jack Wilson **RC** 10.00
172 Brian Lawrence **RC** 5.00
173 Christian Parker **RC** 5.00
174 Nick Maness **RC** 5.00
175 Jose Mieses **RC** 5.00
176 Greg Miller **RC** 5.00
177 Eric Munson 5.00
178 Xavier Nady 5.00
179 Blaine Neal **RC** 5.00
180 Abraham Nunez 5.00
181 Jose Ortiz 5.00
182 Jeremy Owens **RC** 5.00
183 Jay Gibbons **RC** 10.00
184 Corey Patterson 5.00
185 Carlos Pena 5.00
186 C.C. Sabathia 5.00
187 Timo Perez 5.00
188 Adam Pettyjohn **RC** 5.00
189 Donaldo Mendez **RC** 5.00
190 Jackson Melian **RC** 5.00
191 Wilken Ruan **RC** 5.00
192 Duaner Sanchez **RC** 5.00
193 Alfonso Soriano 5.00
194 Rafael Soriano **RC** 10.00
195 Ichiro Suzuki **RC** 150.00
196 Billy Sylvester **RC** 5.00
197 Juan Uribe **RC** 5.00
198 Tsuyoshi Shinjo **RC** 10.00
199 Carlos Valderrama **RC** 5.00
200 Matt White **RC** 5.00
201 Adam Dunn 6.00
202 Joe Kennedy 4.00
203 Mike Rivera 4.00
204 Erick Almonte 4.00
205 Brandon Duckworth 4.00
206 Victor Martinez **RC** 100.00
207 Rick Bauer 4.00
208 Jeff Deardorff 4.00
209 Antonio Perez 4.00
210 Bill Hall 30.00
211 Dennis Tankersley 6.00
212 Jeremy Affeldt 8.00
213 Junior Spivey 8.00
214 Casey Fossum 6.00
215 Brandon Lyon 4.00
216 Angel Santos 4.00
217 Cody Ransom 4.00
218 Jason Lane 35.00
219 David Williams 4.00
220 Alex Herrera 4.00
221 Ryan Drese 4.00
222 Travis Hafner 40.00
223 Bud Smith 4.00
224 Johnny Estrada 25.00
225 Ricardo Rodriguez 4.00
226 Brandon Berger 4.00
227 Claudio Vargas 4.00
228 Luis Garcia 4.00
229 Marlon Byrd 20.00
230 Hee Seop Choi 20.00
231 Corky Miller 4.00
232 Justin Duchscherer 6.00
233 Tim Spooneybarger 4.00
234 Roy Oswalt 4.00
235 Willie Harris 4.00
236 Josh Towers 4.00
237 Juan Pena 4.00
238 Alfredo Amezaga 4.00
239 Geronimo Gil 4.00
240 Juan Cruz 4.00
241 Ed Rogers 4.00
242 Joe Thurston 4.00
243 Orlando Hudson **RC** 10.00
244 John Buck **RC** 8.00
245 Martin Vargas 4.00
246 David Brous 4.00
247 Dewon Brazelton 4.00
248 Mark Prior 50.00
249 Angel Berroa 10.00
250 Mark Teixeira 100.00

Aspirations

Cards 1-150 print run
76-100: 5-10X
1-150 p/r 51-75: 8-15X
1-150 p/r 26-50: 10-25X
Cards 151-200 print run
76-100: 1X
151-200 p/r 51-75: 1.5X
151-200 p/r 26-50: 1.5-2X
Varying quantities produced

Status

Cards 1-150 print run
76-100: 5-10X
1-150 p/r 51-75: 8-15X
1-150 p/r 26-50: 10-25X
Cards 151-200 print run
76-100: 1X
151-200 p/r 51-75: 1.5X
151-200 p/r 26-50: 1.5-2X
Varying quantities produced

Back 2 Back Jacks

NM/M
Common Player: 15.00
Singles production 100.
Doubles production 50.
SP print runs listed.
1 Ernie Banks/75 20.00
2 Ryne Sandberg/75 40.00
3 Babe Ruth 200.00
4 Lou Gehrig 150.00
5 Eddie Matthews 25.00
6 Troy Glaus 15.00
7 Don Mattingly/50 50.00
8 Todd Helton 20.00
9 Wade Boggs 15.00
10 Tony Gwynn 25.00
11 Robin Yount 25.00
12 Paul Molitor/50 25.00
13 Mike Schmidt/50 40.00
14 Scott Rolen/75 20.00
15 Reggie Jackson 20.00
16 Dave Winfield 15.00
17 Johnny Bench/50 40.00
18 Joe Morgan 15.00
19 Brooks Robinson/50 40.00
20 Cal Ripken Jr. 50.00
21 Ty Cobb 100.00
22 Al Kaline/50 40.00
23 Frank Robinson/50 25.00
24 Frank Thomas 20.00
25 Roberto Clemente 80.00
26 Vladimir Guerrero/50 25.00
27 Harmon Killebrew/50 25.00
28 Kirby Puckett 20.00
29 Yogi Berra/75 35.00
30 Phil Rizzuto/75 30.00
31 Ernie Banks, Ryne Sandberg 80.00
32 Babe Ruth, Lou Gehrig 350.00
33 Troy Glaus, Eddie Matthews 40.00
34 Don Mattingly, Todd Helton 100.00
35 Tony Gwynn, Wade Boggs 75.00
36 Paul Molitor, Robin Yount 50.00
37 Mike Schmidt, Scott Rolen 80.00
38 Dave Winfield, Reggie Jackson 40.00
39 Joe Morgan, Johnny Bench 50.00
40 Brooks Robinson, Cal Ripken Jr. 100.00
41 Al Kaline, Ty Cobb 175.00
42 Frank Robinson, Frank Thomas 40.00
43 Roberto Clemente, Vladimir Guerrero 100.00
44 Harmon Killebrew, Kirby Puckett 50.00
45 Phil Rizzuto, Yogi Berra/25 100.00

Back 2 Back Jacks Autograph

NM/M
Common Autograph: 60.00
Print runs listed.
1 Ernie Banks/25 200.00
2 Ryne Sandberg/25 250.00
6 Troy Glaus/50 50.00
7 Don Mattingly/50 200.00
12 Paul Molitor/50 75.00
13 Mike Schmidt/50 150.00
14 Scott Rolen/25 60.00
17 Johnny Bench/50 100.00
19 Brooks Robinson/50 75.00
22 Al Kaline/50 100.00
23 Frank Robinson/50 50.00
26 Vladimir Guerrero/50 100.00
27 Harmon Killebrew/50 100.00
29 Yogi Berra/25 125.00
30 Phil Rizzuto/25 125.00
45 Phil Rizzuto, Yogi Berra/25 200.00

2001 Donruss Elite Passing the Torch

NM/M
Common Player: 4.00
Singles production 1,000.
Doubles production 500.
1 Stan Musial 8.00
2 Tony Gwynn 6.00
3 Willie Mays 10.00
4 Barry Bonds 15.00
5 Mike Schmidt 10.00
6 Scott Rolen 4.00
7 Cal Ripken Jr. 15.00
8 Alex Rodriguez 10.00
9 Hank Aaron 10.00
10 Andruw Jones 4.00
11 Nolan Ryan 15.00
12 Pedro Martinez 5.00
13 Wade Boggs 6.00
14 Nomar Garciaparra 8.00
15 Don Mattingly 10.00
16 Todd Helton 5.00
17 Stan Musial, Tony Gwynn 10.00
18 Barry Bonds, Willie Mays 20.00
19 Mike Schmidt, Scott Rolen 15.00
20 Alex Rodriguez, Cal Ripken Jr. 25.00
21 Andruw Jones, Hank Aaron 15.00
22 Nolan Ryan, Pedro Martinez 25.00
23 Nomar Garciaparra, Wade Boggs 15.00
24 Don Mattingly, Todd Helton 15.00

Passing the Torch Autographs

NM/M
Common Player: 30.00
Singles production 100.
Doubles production 50.
1 Stan Musial 100.00
2 Tony Gwynn 75.00
3 Willie Mays 200.00
4 Barry Bonds 275.00
5 Mike Schmidt 100.00
6 Scott Rolen 50.00
7 Cal Ripken Jr. 150.00
8 Alex Rodriguez 120.00
9 Hank Aaron 200.00
10 Andruw Jones 30.00
11 Nolan Ryan 125.00
12 Pedro Martinez 75.00
13 Wade Boggs 30.00
14 Nomar Garciaparra 125.00
15 Don Mattingly 100.00
16 Todd Helton 40.00
17 Stan Musial, Tony Gwynn 175.00
18 Barry Bonds, Willie Mays 900.00
19 Mike Schmidt, Scott Rolen 150.00
20 Alex Rodriguez, Cal Ripken Jr. 400.00
21 Andruw Jones, Hank Aaron 250.00
22 Nolan Ryan, Pedro Martinez 300.00
22 Nolan Ryan, Roger Clemens FB redemp. 375.00
23 Wade Boggs FB Redemp. 25.00
24 Don Mattingly, Todd Helton 200.00

Primary Colors

NM/M
Complete Set (40): 100.00
Common Player: 1.00
Production 975 Sets
Red Die-Cut: 3-5X
Production 25
Blues: 1-1.5X
Production 200
Blue Die-Cut: 1.5-3X
Production 50
Yellows: 3-5X
Production 25
Yellow Die-Cut: 1.5-2X
Production 75
1 Alex Rodriguez 8.00
2 Barry Bonds 10.00
3 Cal Ripken Jr. 10.00
4 Chipper Jones 5.00
5 Derek Jeter 10.00
6 Troy Glaus 4.00
7 Frank Thomas 4.00
8 Greg Maddux 5.00
9 Ivan Rodriguez 2.50
10 Jeff Bagwell 4.00
11 Todd Helton 4.00
12 Ken Griffey Jr. 6.00
13 Manny Ramirez 4.00
14 Mark McGwire 8.00
15 Mike Piazza 6.00
16 Nomar Garciaparra 6.00
17 Pedro Martinez 4.00
18 Randy Johnson 4.00
19 Rick Ankiel 1.25
20 Roger Clemens 5.50
21 Sammy Sosa 6.00
22 Tony Gwynn 5.00
23 Vladimir Guerrero 4.00
24 Carlos Delgado 2.00
25 Jason Giambi 2.50
26 Andruw Jones 4.00
27 Bernie Williams 1.50
28 Roberto Alomar 1.50
29 Shawn Green 1.50
30 Barry Larkin 1.00
31 Scott Rolen 3.00
32 Gary Sheffield 2.00
33 Rafael Palmeiro 3.00
34 Albert Belle 1.00
35 Magglio Ordonez 1.50
36 Jim Thome 1.00
37 Jim Edmonds 1.00
38 Darin Erstad 2.00
39 Kris Benson 1.00
40 Sean Casey 1.50

Prime Numbers

NM/M
Print runs listed.
1a Alex Rodriguez/300 8.00
1b Alex Rodriguez/308 8.00
1c Alex Rodriguez/350 8.00
2a Ken Griffey Jr./400 6.00
2b Ken Griffey Jr./408 6.00
2c Ken Griffey Jr./430 6.00
3a Mark McGwire/500 8.00
3b Mark McGwire/504 8.00
3c Mark McGwire/550 8.00
4a Cal Ripken Jr./400 10.00
4b Cal Ripken Jr./407 10.00
4c Cal Ripken Jr./410 10.00
5a Derek Jeter/300 10.00
5b Derek Jeter/302 10.00
5c Derek Jeter/320 10.00
6a Mike Piazza/300 6.00
6b Mike Piazza/302 6.00
6c Mike Piazza/360 6.00
7a Nomar Garciaparra/300 6.00
7b Nomar Garciaparra/302 6.00
7c Nomar Garciaparra/370 6.00
8a Sammy Sosa/300 6.00
8b Sammy Sosa/306 6.00
8c Sammy Sosa/380 6.00
9a Vladimir Guerrero/300 4.00
9b Vladimir Guerrero/305 4.00
9c Vladimir Guerrero/340 4.00
10a Tony Gwynn/300 4.00
10b Tony Gwynn/304 4.00
10c Tony Gwynn/390 4.00

Prime Numbers Die-Cut

NM/M
Print runs listed.
1a Alex Rodriguez/58 25.00
1b Alex Rodriguez/50 25.00
2a Ken Griffey Jr./38 20.00
2b Ken Griffey Jr./30 20.00
3a Mark McGwire/54 25.00
3b Mark McGwire/50 25.00
5a Derek Jeter/22 75.00
5b Derek Jeter/20 75.00
6a Mike Piazza/62 15.00
6b Mike Piazza/60 15.00
7a Nomar Garciaparra/72 15.00
7b Nomar Garciaparra/70 15.00
8a Sammy Sosa/86 15.00
8b Sammy Sosa/80 15.00
9a Vladimir Guerrero/45 10.00
9b Vladimir Guerrero/40 10.00
10a Tony Gwynn/94 10.00
10b Tony Gwynn/90 10.00

Throwback Threads

NM/M
Common Player: 15.00
Singles production 100.
Doubles production 50.
SP production listed.
1 Stan Musial/75 50.00
2 Tony Gwynn/75 25.00
3 Willie McCovey 15.00
4 Barry Bonds 50.00
5 Babe Ruth 250.00
6 Lou Gehrig 200.00
7 Mike Schmidt/75 40.00
8 Scott Rolen 20.00
9 Harmon Killebrew/75 30.00
10 Kirby Puckett 20.00
11 Al Kaline/75 40.00
12 Eddie Matthews 25.00
13 Hank Aaron/75 60.00
14 Andruw Jones/50 20.00
15 Lou Brock 40.00
16 Ozzie Smith 25.00
17 Ernie Banks/75 35.00
18 Ryne Sandberg 50.00
19 Roberto Clemente 100.00
20 Vladimir Guerrero/50 30.00
21 Frank Robinson/50 25.00
22 Frank Thomas 15.00
23 Brooks Robinson/50 25.00
24 Cal Ripken Jr. 50.00
25 Roger Clemens 30.00
26 Pedro Martinez 20.00
27 Reggie Jackson 15.00
28 Dave Winfield 15.00
29 Don Mattingly/50 60.00
30 Todd Helton 15.00
31 Stan Musial, Tony Gwynn/25 120.00
32 Barry Bonds, Willie McCovey 85.00
33 Babe Ruth, Lou Gehrig 500.00
34 Mike Schmidt, Scott Rolen/25 150.00
35 Harmon Killebrew, Kirby Puckett 50.00
36 Al Kaline, Eddie Matthews 50.00
37 Andruw Jones, Hank Aaron 85.00
38 Lou Brock, Ozzie Smith 50.00
39 Ernie Banks, Ryne Sandberg/25 125.00
40 Roberto Clemente, Vladimir Guerrero 90.00
41 Frank Robinson, Frank Thomas 40.00
42 Brooks Robinson, Cal Ripken Jr. 85.00
43 Pedro Martinez, Roger Clemens 60.00
44 Dave Winfield, Reggie Jackson 30.00
45 Don Mattingly, Todd Helton 75.00

Throwback Threads Autograph

NM/M
Production Listed
Football Exchange for 21 & 22 will be redeemed for #'s listed for 21 & 22.
1 Stan Musial/25 150.00
2 Tony Gwynn/25 100.00
7 Mike Schmidt/25 200.00
9 Harmon Killebrew/25 125.00
11 Al Kaline/25 120.00
13 Hank Aaron/25 150.00
14 Andruw Jones/50 50.00
17 Ernie Banks/25 150.00
20 Vladimir Guerrero/50 75.00
21 Frank Robinson/50 FB Redemp 40.00
22 Frank Thomas/50 FB redemp 50.00
23 Brooks Robinson/50 100.00
29 Don Mattingly/50 150.00
31 Stan Musial, Tony Gwynn/25 225.00

34	Mike Schmidt, Scott Rolen/25	225.00
39	Ernie Banks, Ryne Sandberg/25	250.00

Title Waves

		NM/M
	Common Player:	1.00
	Numbered to title year.	
	Holofoil:	2-3X
	Production 100 Sets	
1	Tony Gwynn/1994	5.00
2	Todd Helton/2000	4.00
3	Nomar Garciaparra/2000	6.00
4	Frank Thomas/1997	4.00
5	Alex Rodriguez/1996	8.00
6	Jeff Bagwell/1994	4.00
7	Mark McGwire/1998	8.00
8	Sammy Sosa/2000	6.00
9	Ken Griffey Jr./1997	6.00
10	Albert Belle/1995	1.00
11	Barry Bonds/1993	10.00
12	Jose Canseco/1991	2.00
13	Manny Ramirez/1999	4.00
14	Sammy Sosa/1998	6.00
15	Andres Galarraga/1996	1.00
16	Todd Helton/2000	4.00
17	Ken Griffey Jr./1997	6.00
18	Jeff Bagwell/1994	4.00
19	Mike Piazza/1995	6.00
20	Alex Rodriguez/1995	8.00
21	Jason Giambi/2000	2.00
22	Ivan Rodriguez/1999	2.50
23	Greg Maddux/1997	5.00
24	Pedro Martinez/1994	4.00
25	Derek Jeter/2000	10.00
26	Bernie Williams/1998	1.50
27	Roger Clemens/1999	8.00
28	Chipper Jones/1995	4.00
29	Mark McGwire/1990	8.00
30	Cal Ripken Jr./1983	10.00

Turn of the Century Autographs

		NM/M
	Common Autograph:	8.00
	Production 100 Sets	
	Redemp. deadline 5/01/03.	
151	Brent Abernathy	8.00
152	Cory Aldridge	8.00
153	Gene Altman	8.00
154	Josh Beckett	80.00
155	Wilson Betemit	25.00
156	Albert Pujols	900.00
157	Joe Crede	30.00
158	Jack Cust	10.00
159	Ben Sheets	30.00
160	Alex Escobar	8.00
161	Adrian Hernandez	8.00
162	Pedro Feliz	8.00
163	Nate Frese	8.00
164	Carlos Garcia	8.00
165	Marcus Giles	20.00
166	Alexis Gomez	10.00
167	Jason Hart	8.00
168	Aubrey Huff	20.00
169	Cesar Izturis	10.00
170	Nick Johnson	20.00
171	Jack Wilson	15.00
172	Brian Lawrence	10.00
173	Christian Parker	8.00
174	Nick Maness	8.00
175	Jose Mieses	10.00
176	Greg Miller	8.00
177	Eric Munson	10.00
178	Xavier Nady	15.00
179	Blaine Neal	8.00
180	Abraham Nunez	10.00
181	Jose Ortiz	10.00
182	Jeremy Owens	10.00
183	Jay Gibbons	25.00
184	Corey Patterson	20.00
185	Carlos Pena	25.00
186	C.C. Sabathia	30.00
187	Timoniel Perez	8.00
188	Adam Pettyjohn	8.00
189	Donaldo Mendez	8.00
190	Jackson Melian	8.00
191	Wilken Ruan	8.00
192	Duaner Sanchez	8.00
193	Alfonso Soriano	60.00
194	Rafael Soriano	10.00
196	Billy Sylvester	8.00
197	Juan Uribe	20.00
199	Carlos Valderrama	10.00
200	Matt White	10.00

2001 Donruss Signature Series

		NM/M
	Complete Set (311):	
	Common Player:	.50
	Common (111-165):	8.00
	Auto. print run 330	
	Common (166-311):	4.00
	Production 800	
	Box:	100.00
1	Alex Rodriguez	3.00
2	Barry Bonds	4.00
3	Cal Ripken Jr.	4.00
4	Chipper Jones	2.00
5	Derek Jeter	4.00
6	Troy Glaus	1.50
7	Frank Thomas	1.50
8	Greg Maddux	2.00
9	Ivan Rodriguez	1.00
10	Jeff Bagwell	1.50
11	John Olerud	.50
12	Todd Helton	1.50
13	Ken Griffey Jr.	2.50
14	Manny Ramirez	1.50
15	Mark McGwire	3.00
16	Mike Piazza	2.50
17	Nomar Garciaparra	2.50
18	Moises Alou	.50
19	Aramis Ramirez	.50
20	Curt Schilling	.75
21	Pat Burrell	.75
22	Doug Mientkiewicz	.50
23	Carlos Delgado	.75
24	J.D. Drew	.50
25	Cliff Floyd	.50
26	Freddy Garcia	.50
27	Roberto Alomar	.75
28	Barry Zito	.75
29	Juan Encarnacion	.50
30	Paul Konerko	.50
31	Mark Mulder	.75
32	Andy Pettitte	.75
33	Jim Edmonds	.50
34	Darin Erstad	1.00
35	Jason Giambi	1.00
36	Tom Glavine	.75
37	Juan Gonzalez	1.50
38	Fred McGriff	.50
39	Shawn Green	.75
40	Tim Hudson	.75
41	Andruw Jones	1.50
42	Jeff Kent	.50
43	Barry Larkin	.50
44	Brad Radke	.50
45	Mike Mussina	.75
46	Hideo Nomo	.75
47	Rafael Palmeiro	1.50
48	Scott Rolen	1.50
49	Gary Sheffield	.75
50	Bernie Williams	.75
51	Bobby Abreu	.50
52	Edgardo Alfonzo	.50
53	Edgar Martinez	.50
54	Magglio Ordonez	.75
55	Kerry Wood	.75
56	Adrian Beltre	.75
57	Lance Berkman	.50
58	Kevin Brown	.65
59	Sean Casey	.65
60	Eric Chavez	.75
61	Bartolo Colon	.50
62	Sammy Sosa	2.50
63	Jermaine Dye	.50
64	Tony Gwynn	2.00
65	Carl Everett	.50
66	Brian Giles	.50
67	Mike Hampton	.50
68	Richard Hidalgo	.50
69	Geoff Jenkins	.50
70	Tony Clark	.50
71	Roger Clemens	2.25
72	Ryan Klesko	.50
73	Chan Ho Park	.50
74	Richie Sexson	.50
75	Mike Sweeney	.50
76	Kazuhiro Sasaki	.50
77	Miguel Tejada	.75
78	Jose Vidro	.50
79	Larry Walker	.50
80	Preston Wilson	.50
81	Craig Biggio	.50
82	Andres Galarraga	.50
83	Jim Thome	.50
84	Vladimir Guerrero	1.50
85	Rafael Furcal	.50
86	Cristian Guzman	.50
87	Terrence Long	.50
88	Bret Boone	.50
89	Wade Miller	.50
90	Eric Milton	.50
91	Gabe Kapler	.50
92	Johnny Damon	.75
93	Carlos Lee	.50
94	Kenny Lofton	.50
95	Raul Mondesi	.50
96	Jorge Posada	.65
97	Mark Grace	.65
98	Robert Fick	.50
99	Joe Mays	.50
100	Aaron Sele	.50
101	Ben Grieve	.50
102	Luis Gonzalez	.65
103	Ray Durham	.50
104	Mark Quinn	.50
105	Jose Canseco	1.00
106	David Justice	.50
107	Pedro Martinez	1.50
108	Randy Johnson	1.50
109	Phil Nevin	.50
110	Ricky Henderson	1.50
111	Alex Escobar/Auto.	8.00
112	Johnny Estrada/Auto. **RC**	15.00
113	Pedro Feliz/Auto.	8.00
114	Nate Frese/Auto.	8.00
115	Ricardo Rodriguez/Auto. **RC**	8.00
116	Brandon Larson/Auto. **RC**	8.00
117	Alexis Gomez/Auto. **RC**	8.00
118	Jason Hart/Auto.	8.00
119	C.C. Sabathia/Auto.	15.00
120	Endy Chavez/Auto. **RC**	8.00
121	Christian Parker/Auto. **RC**	8.00
122	Jackson Melian **RC**	8.00
123	Joe Kennedy/Auto. **RC**	10.00
124	Adrian Hernandez Auto. **RC**	8.00
125	Cesar Izturis/Auto.	10.00
126	Jose Mieses/Auto. **RC**	8.00
127	Roy Oswalt/Auto.	30.00
128	Eric Munson/Auto.	8.00
129	Xavier Nady/Auto.	8.00
130	Horacio Ramirez/Auto. **RC**	15.00
131	Abraham Nunez/Auto.	8.00
132	Jose Ortiz/Auto.	8.00
133	Jeremy Owens/Auto. **RC**	8.00
134	Claudio Vargas/Auto. **RC**	8.00
135	Corey Patterson/Auto.	15.00
136	Carlos Pena	15.00
137	Bud Smith/Auto. **RC**	8.00
138	Adam Dunn/Auto.	25.00
139	Adam Pettyjohn/Auto.	8.00
140	Elpidio Guzman/Auto. **RC**	8.00
141	Jay Gibbons/Auto. **RC**	15.00
142	Wilken Ruan/Auto. **RC**	8.00
143	Tsuyoshi Shinjo **RC**	8.00
144	Alfonso Soriano/Auto.	30.00
145	Marcus Giles/Auto.	10.00
146	Ichiro Suzuki **RC**	75.00
147	Juan Uribe/Auto.	10.00
148	David Williams/Auto. **RC**	8.00
149	Carlos Valderrama/Auto. **RC**	8.00
150	Matt White/Auto. **RC**	8.00
151	Albert Pujols/Auto. **RC**	700.00
152	Donaldo Mendez/Auto. **RC**	8.00
153	Cory Aldridge/Auto. **RC**	8.00
154	Brandon Duckworth/Auto. **RC**	8.00
155	Josh Beckett/Auto.	30.00
156	Wilson Betemit/Auto. **RC**	15.00
157	Ben Sheets/Auto.	25.00
158	Andres Torres/Auto. **RC**	8.00
159	Aubrey Huff/Auto.	15.00
160	Jack Wilson/Auto. **RC**	15.00
161	Rafael Soriano/Auto. **RC**	8.00
162	Nick Johnson/Auto.	12.00
163	Carlos Garcia/Auto. **RC**	8.00
164	Josh Towers/Auto. **RC**	10.00
165	Jason Michaels/Auto. **RC**	8.00
166	Ryan Drese **RC**	4.00
167	Dewon Brazelton **RC**	4.00
168	Kevin Olsen **RC**	4.00
169	Benito Baez **RC**	4.00
170	Mark Prior **RC**	20.00
171	Wilmy Caceres **RC**	4.00
172	Mark Teixeira **RC**	35.00
173	Willie Harris **RC**	4.00
174	Mike Koplove **RC**	4.00
175	Brandon Knight **RC**	4.00
176	John Grabow **RC**	4.00
177	Jeremy Affeldt **RC**	4.00
178	Brandon Inge	4.00
179	Casey Fossum **RC**	6.00
180	Scott Stewart **RC**	4.00
181	Luke Hudson **RC**	4.00
182	Ken Vining **RC**	4.00
183	Toby Hall	4.00
184	Eric Knott **RC**	4.00
185	Kris Foster **RC**	4.00
186	David Brous **RC**	4.00
187	Roy Smith **RC**	4.00
188	Grant Balfour **RC**	4.00
189	Jeremy Fikac **RC**	4.00
190	Morgan Ensberg **RC**	10.00
191	Ryan Freel **RC**	6.00
192	Ryan Jensen **RC**	4.00
193	Lance Davis **RC**	4.00
194	Delvin James **RC**	4.00
195	Timo Perez	4.00
196	Michael Cuddyer	4.00
197	Bob File **RC**	4.00
198	Martin Vargas **RC**	4.00
199	Kris Keller **RC**	4.00
200	Tim Spooneybarger **RC**	4.00
201	Adam Everett	4.00
202	Josh Fogg **RC**	6.00
203	Kip Wells	4.00
204	Rick Bauer **RC**	4.00
205	Brent Abernathy	4.00
206	Erick Almonte **RC**	4.00
207	Pedro Santana **RC**	4.00
208	Ken Harvey	4.00
209	Jerrod Riggan **RC**	4.00
210	Nick Punto **RC**	4.00
211	Steve Green **RC**	4.00
212	Nick Neugebauer	4.00
213	Chris George	4.00
214	Mike Penny	4.00
215	Bret Prinz **RC**	4.00
216	Tim Christman **RC**	4.00
217	Sean Douglass **RC**	4.00
218	Brett Jodie **RC**	4.00
219	Juan Diaz **RC**	4.00
220	Carlos Hernandez **RC**	4.00
221	Alex Cintron	4.00
222	Juan Cruz **RC**	4.00
223	Larry Bigbie	4.00
224	Junior Spivey **RC**	8.00
225	Luis Rivas	4.00
226	Brandon Lyon **RC**	4.00
227	Tony Cogan **RC**	4.00
228	Justin Duchscherer **RC**	6.00
229	Tike Redman	4.00
230	Jimmy Rollins	5.00
231	Scott Podsednik **RC**	15.00
232	Jose Acevedo **RC**	4.00
233	Luis Pineda **RC**	4.00
234	Josh Phelps	4.00
235	Paul Phillips **RC**	4.00
236	Brian Roberts **RC**	10.00
237	Orlando Woodwards	4.00
238	Bart Miadich **RC**	4.00
239	Les Walrond **RC**	4.00
240	Brad Voyles **RC**	4.00
241	Joe Crede	8.00
242	Juan Moreno **RC**	4.00
243	Matt Ginter	4.00
244	Brian Rogers **RC**	4.00
245	Pablo Ozuna	4.00
246	Geronimo Gil **RC**	4.00
247	Mike Maroth **RC**	4.00
248	Josue Perez **RC**	4.00
249	Dee Brown	4.00
250	Victor Zambrano **RC**	4.00
251	Nick Maness **RC**	4.00
252	Kyle Lohse **RC**	6.00
253	Greg Miller **RC**	4.00
254	Henry Mateo **RC**	4.00
255	Duaner Sanchez **RC**	4.00
256	Rob Mackowiak **RC**	6.00
257	Steve Lomasney	4.00
258	Angel Santos **RC**	4.00
259	Winston Abreu **RC**	4.00
260	Brandon Berger **RC**	4.00
261	Tomas De La Rosa	4.00
262	Ramon Vazquez **RC**	4.00
263	Mickey Callaway	4.00
264	Corky Miller **RC**	4.00
265	Keith Ginter	4.00
266	Cody Ransom **RC**	4.00
267	Doug Nickle **RC**	4.00
268	Derrick Lewis **RC**	4.00
269	Eric Hinske **RC**	6.00
270	Travis Phelps **RC**	4.00
271	Eric Valent	4.00
272	Michael Rivera **RC**	4.00
273	Esix Snead **RC**	4.00
274	Troy Mattes **RC**	4.00
275	Jermaine Clark	4.00
276	Nate Cornejo	4.00
277	George Perez **RC**	4.00
278	Juan Rivera	4.00
279	Justin Atchley **RC**	4.00
280	Adam Johnson	4.00
281	Gene Altman **RC**	4.00
282	Jason Jennings	4.00
283	Scott MacRae **RC**	4.00
284	Craig Monroe **RC**	6.00
285	Bert Snow **RC**	4.00
286	Stubby Clapp **RC**	4.00
287	Jack Cust	4.00
288	Will Ohman **RC**	4.00
289	Wily Mo Pena	4.00
290	Joe Beimel **RC**	4.00
291	Jason Karnuth **RC**	4.00
292	Bill Ortega	4.00
293	Nate Teut **RC**	4.00
294	Erik Hiljus **RC**	4.00
295	Jason Smith **RC**	4.00
296	Juan Pena	4.00
297	David Espinosa	4.00
298	Tim Redding	4.00
299	Brian Lawrence **RC**	4.00
300	Brian Reith **RC**	4.00
301	Chad Durbin	4.00
302	Kurt Ainsworth	4.00
303	Blaine Neal **RC**	4.00
304	Jorge Julio **RC**	4.00
305	Adam Bernero	4.00
306	Travis Hafner **RC**	20.00
307	Dustan Mohr **RC**	4.00
308	Cesar Crespo **RC**	4.00
309	Billy Sylvester **RC**	4.00
310	Zach Day **RC**	6.00
311	Angel Berroa **RC**	8.00

Signature Proofs

Stars (1-110):	2-3X
Production 175	
Cards (111-311) Production 25	

Award Winning Signatures

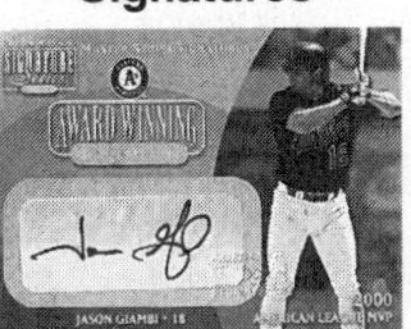

	NM/M
Common Player:	20.00
Jeff Bagwell/94	65.00
Carlos Beltran/99	40.00
Johnny Bench/68	75.00
Yogi Berra/55	50.00
Craig Biggio/97	25.00
Barry Bonds/93	200.00
Rod Carew/77	50.00
Orlando Cepeda/67	20.00
Andre Dawson/77	20.00
Dennis Eckersley/92	25.00
Dennis Eckersley/92	25.00
Whitey Ford/61	50.00
Jason Giambi/100	20.00
Bob Gibson/68	40.00
Juan Gonzalez/96	35.00
Orel Hershiser/88	25.00
Al Kaline/67	75.00
Fred Lynn/75	15.00
Fred Lynn/75	15.00
Jim Palmer/76	25.00
Cal Ripken/83	150.00
Phil Rizzuto/50	40.00
Brooks Robinson/64	40.00
Scott Rolen/97	30.00
Ryne Sandberg/84	90.00
Warren Spahn/57	50.00
Frank Thomas/94	35.00
Billy Williams/61	20.00
Kerry Wood/98	40.00
Robin Yount/89	60.00

Century Marks

	NM/M
Common Autograph:	5.00
Brent Abernathy/184	5.00
Roberto Alomar/102	40.00
Rick Ankiel/119	8.00
Lance Berkman/121	15.00
Mark Buehrle/224	10.00
Wilmy Caceres/194	5.00
Eric Chavez/170	10.00
Joe Crede/154	5.00
Jack Cust/178	10.00
Brandon Duckworth/183	5.00
David Espinosa/199	5.00
Johnny Estrada/198	5.00
Pedro Feliz/180	5.00
Robert Fick/232	5.00
Cliff Floyd/146	8.00
Casey Fossum/100	10.00
Jay Gibbons/175	15.00
Keith Ginter/163	5.00
Troy Glaus/144	20.00
Luis Gonzalez/101	10.00
Vladimir Guerrero/187	30.00
Richard Hidalgo/173	5.00
Tim Hudson/145	25.00
Adam Johnson/130	5.00
Gabe Kapler/150	8.00
Joe Kennedy/219	5.00
Ryan Klesko/176	10.00
Carlos Lee/179	8.00
Terrence Long/180	5.00
Edgar Martinez/110	20.00
Joe Mays/209	5.00
Greg Miller/194	5.00
Wade Miller/180	5.00
Mark Mulder/203	20.00
Xavier Nady/180	5.00
Magglio Ordonez/104	10.00
Jose Ortiz/187	5.00
Roy Oswalt/192	20.00
Wily Mo Pena/203	10.00
Brad Penny/198	5.00
Aramis Ramirez/241	20.00
Luis Rivas/163	5.00
Alex Rodriguez/110	120.00
Scott Rolen/106	30.00
Mike Sweeney/99	10.00
Eric Valent/163	5.00
Kip Wells/223	5.00
Kerry Wood/109	25.00

Milestone Marks

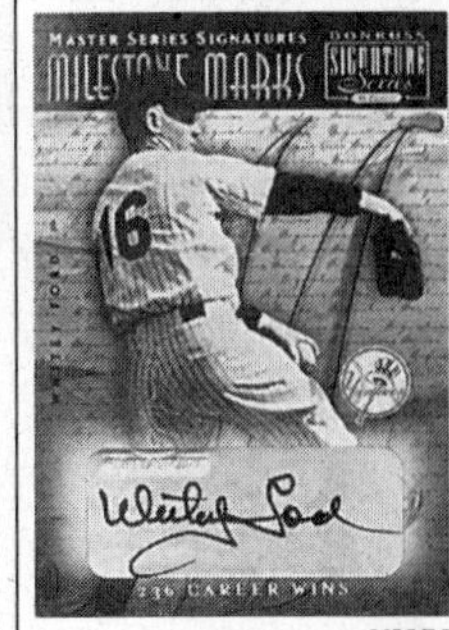

	NM/M
Common Player:	10.00
Ernie Banks/285	35.00
Yogi Berra/120	50.00
Wade Boggs/98	60.00
Barry Bonds/25	200.00
George Brett/27	150.00
George Brett/23	150.00
Lou Brock/83	25.00
Rod Carew/110	30.00
Steve Carlton/75	35.00
Gary Carter/213	20.00
Bobby Doerr/192	15.00
Bob Feller/202	15.00
Whitey Ford/186	25.00
Steve Garvey/175	10.00
Tony Gwynn/99	50.00
Fergie Jenkins/149	15.00
Al Kaline/149	40.00
Harmon Killebrew/127	40.00
Ralph Kiner/105	20.00
Willie McCovey/20	75.00
Paul Molitor/96	40.00
Eddie Murray/46	70.00
Stan Musial/109	75.00
Phil Niekro/300	10.00
Tony Perez/146	15.00
Cal Ripken/25	200.00
Frank Robinson/136	20.00
Mike Schmidt/40	125.00
Mike Schmidt/23	150.00
Enos Slaughter/117	20.00
Warren Spahn/300	40.00
Alan Trammell/154	25.00
Hoyt Wilhelm/227	10.00
Dave Winfield/31	50.00
Dave Winfield/15	80.00

Notable Nicknames

	NM/M
Common Player:	30.00
Production 100	
Ernie Banks	75.00
Orlando Cepeda	40.00
Will Clark	80.00
Roger Clemens/50	250.00
Andre Dawson	30.00
Bob Feller	50.00
Carlton Fisk	70.00
Andres Galarraga	40.00
Luis Gonzalez	30.00
Reggie Jackson	75.00
Harmon Killebrew	80.00
Stan Musial	120.00
Brooks Robinson	80.00
Nolan Ryan	250.00
Ryne Sandberg	150.00
Enos Slaughter	60.00
Duke Snider	75.00
Frank Thomas	100.00

Signature Stats

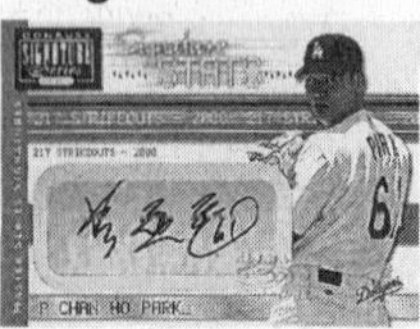

	NM/M
Quantity produced listed	
Roberto Alomar/120	40.00
Moises Alou/124	6.00
Luis Aparicio/313	10.00
Lance Berkman/297	15.00
Wade Boggs/51	75.00
Lou Brock/118	15.00
Gary Carter/32	50.00
Joe Carter/121	10.00
Sean Casey/103	10.00
Darin Erstad/100	15.00
Bob Feller/26	50.00
Cliff Floyd/45	15.00
Whitey Ford/72	40.00
Andres Galarraga/150	8.00
Bob Gibson/112	25.00
Brian Giles/123	10.00
Troy Glaus/102	20.00
Luis Gonzalez/114	10.00
Vladimir Guerrero/131	30.00
Richard Hidalgo/314	6.00
Bo Jackson/32	85.00
Al Kaline/128	45.00
Gabe Kapler/302	6.00
Ralph Kiner/54	30.00
Carlos Lee/261	10.00
Kenny Lofton/210	6.00
Edgar Martinez/145	20.00
Joe Mays/115	6.00
Paul Molitor/41	50.00
Mark Mulder/88	25.00
Maggio Ordonez/126	10.00
Rafael Palmeiro/47	40.00
Kirby Puckett/31	100.00
Manny Ramirez/45	60.00
Alex Rodriguez/132	85.00
Ivan Rodriguez/113	30.00
Shannon Stewart/319	6.00
Mike Sweeney/144	6.00
Miguel Tejada/115	35.00
Joe Torre/230	25.00
Javier Vazquez/405	6.00
Jose Vidro/330	6.00
Hoyt Wilhelm/243	6.00

Team Trademarks

	NM/M
Rick Ankiel/179	10.00
Ernie Banks/180	50.00
Johnny Bench/20	75.00
Yogi Berra/124	40.00
Wade Boggs/89	75.00
Barry Bonds/77	200.00
Lou Brock/29	35.00
Steve Carlton/174	25.00
Sean Casey/123	15.00
Orlando Cepeda/100	20.00
Roger Clemens/30 (Red Sox)	125.00
Roger Clemens/21 (Yankees)	150.00
Andre Dawson/176	15.00
Bobby Doerr/193	20.00
Whitey Ford/94	40.00
Steve Garvey/182	20.00
Bob Gibson/98	30.00
Juan Gonzalez/70	40.00
Shawn Green/109	20.00
Orel Hershiser/210	25.00
Reggie Jackson/73	50.00
Fergie Jenkins/213	15.00
Chipper Jones/74	50.00
Pedro Martinez/27	85.00
Don Mattingly/72	125.00
Willie Mays/197	125.00
Willie McCovey/26	70.00
Joe Morgan/33	80.00
Eddie Murray/45	75.00
Stan Musial/65	90.00
Mike Mussina/85 (Orioles)	40.00
Mike Mussina/95 (Yankees)	50.00
Phil Niekro/187	10.00
Rafael Palmeiro/99	30.00
Jim Palmer/142	15.00
Tony Perez/73	15.00
Manny Ramirez/57	50.00
Cal Ripken Jr./47	200.00
Phil Rizzuto/98	40.00
Brooks Robinson/146	25.00
Frank Robinson/118 (Orioles)	25.00
Frank Robinson/116 (Reds)	25.00
Alex Rodriguez/100	100.00
Ivan Rodriguez/62	50.00
Scott Rolen/39	40.00
Nolan Ryan/153	100.00
Ryne Sandberg/52	100.00
Curt Schilling/163	40.00
Mike Schmidt/107	75.00
Tom Seaver/25	125.00
Gary Sheffield/194	20.00
Enos Slaughter/215	20.00
Duke Snider/47	50.00
Warren Spahn/140	40.00
Joe Torre/90	40.00
Billy Williams/194	10.00
Kerry Wood/52	40.00

Hawaii

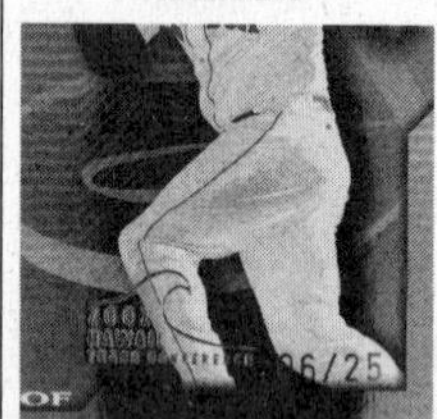

As part of its participation in the 2002 Hawaii Trade Conference, Donruss created special gold-foil enhanced versions of many of the base cards, inserts, parallels and autographs of its Signature Series issues. Cards all carry individual serial numbers from editions as low as 1-of-1 and as high as 25. Because of their scarcity and widely fluctuating demand, values cannot be quoted.

2001 Donruss Studio

		NM/M
Complete Set (200):		
Common Player:		.25
Common SP (151-200):		4.00
Production 700		
Pack (6):		8.00
Box (18) + 5x7 Auto.		140.00
1	Alex Rodriguez	2.00
2	Barry Bonds	2.50
3	Cal Ripken Jr.	2.50
4	Chipper Jones	1.00
5	Derek Jeter	2.50
6	Troy Glaus	.65
7	Frank Thomas	.75
8	Greg Maddux	1.00
9	Ivan Rodriguez	.65
10	Jeff Bagwell	.75
11	Mark Quinn	.25
12	Todd Helton	.65
13	Ken Griffey Jr.	1.50
14	Manny Ramirez	.75
15	Mark McGwire	2.00
16	Mike Piazza	1.50
17	Nomar Garciaparra	1.00
18	Robin Ventura	.25
19	Aramis Ramirez	.25
20	J.T. Snow	.25
21	Pat Burrell	.60
22	Curt Schilling	.50
23	Carlos Delgado	.50
24	J.D. Drew	.40
25	Cliff Floyd	.25
26	Brian Jordan	.25
27	Roberto Alomar	.35
28	Barry Zito	.40
29	Harold Baines	.25
30	Brad Penny	.25
31	Jose Cruz	.25
32	Andy Pettitte	.40
33	Jim Edmonds	.25
34	Darin Erstad	.35
35	Jason Giambi	.60
36	Tom Glavine	.50
37	Juan Gonzalez	.35
38	Mark Grace	.25
39	Shawn Green	.50
40	Tim Hudson	.50
41	Andruw Jones	.75
42	Jeff Kent	.25
43	Barry Larkin	.25
44	Rafael Furcal	.25
45	Mike Mussina	.50
46	Hideo Nomo	.50
47	Rafael Palmeiro	.65
48	Scott Rolen	.60
49	Gary Sheffield	.50
50	Bernie Williams	.25
51	Bobby Abreu	.25
52	Edgardo Alfonzo	.25
53	Edgar Martinez	.25
54	Magglio Ordonez	.25
55	Kerry Wood	.50
56	Matt Morris	.25
57	Lance Berkman	.25
58	Kevin Brown	.25
59	Sean Casey	.40
60	Eric Chavez	.40
61	Bartolo Colon	.25
62	Johnny Damon	.50
63	Jermaine Dye	.25
64	Juan Encarnacion	.25
65	Carl Everett	.25
66	Brian Giles	.25
67	Mike Hampton	.25
68	Richard Hidalgo	.25
69	Geoff Jenkins	.25
70	Jacque Jones	.25
71	Jason Kendall	.25
72	Ryan Klesko	.25
73	Chan Ho Park	.25
74	Richie Sexson	.25
75	Mike Sweeney	.25
76	Fernando Tatis	.25
77	Miguel Tejada	.50
78	Jose Vidro	.25
79	Larry Walker	.25
80	Preston Wilson	.25
81	Craig Biggio	.25
82	Fred McGriff	.25
83	Jim Thome	.65
84	Garret Anderson	.25
85	Mark Mulder	.40
86	Tony Batista	.25
87	Terrence Long	.25
88	Brad Fullmer	.25
89	Rusty Greer	.25
90	Orlando Hernandez	.25
91	Gabe Kapler	.25
92	Paul Konerko	.25
93	Carlos Lee	.25
94	Kenny Lofton	.25
95	Raul Mondesi	.25
96	Jorge Posada	.40
97	Tim Salmon	.25
98	Greg Vaughn	.25
99	Mo Vaughn	.25
100	Omar Vizquel	.25
101	Ben Grieve	.25
102	Luis Gonzalez	.25
103	Ray Durham	.25
104	Ryan Dempster	.25
105	Eric Karros	.25
106	David Justice	.25
107	Pedro Martinez	.75
108	Randy Johnson	.75
109	Rick Ankiel	.25
110	Rickey Henderson	.75
111	Roger Clemens	1.25
112	Sammy Sosa	1.00
113	Tony Gwynn	1.00
114	Vladimir Guerrero	.75
115	Kazuhiro Sasaki	.25
116	Phil Nevin	.25
117	Ruben Mateo	.25
118	Shannon Stewart	.25
119	Matt Williams	.25
120	Tino Martinez	.25
121	Ken Caminiti	.25
122	Edgar Renteria	.25
123	Charles Johnson	.25
124	Aaron Sele	.25
125	Javy Lopez	.25
126	Mariano Rivera	.35
127	Shea Hillenbrand	.25
128	Jeff D'Amico	.25
129	Brady Anderson	.25
130	Kevin Millwood	.25
131	Trot Nixon	.25
132	Mike Lieberthal	.25
133	Juan Pierre	.25
134	Russ Ortiz	.25
135	Jose Macias	.25
136	John Smoltz	.25
137	Jason Varitek	.25
138	Dean Palmer	.25
139	Jeff Cirillo	.25
140	Paul O'Neill	.25
141	Andres Galarraga	.25
142	David Wells	.25
143	Brad Radke	.25
144	Wade Miller	.25
145	John Olerud	.25
146	Moises Alou	.25
147	Carlos Beltran	.50
148	Jeromy Burnitz	.25
149	Steve Finley	.25
150	Joe Mays	.25
151	Alex Escobar	4.00
152	Johnny Estrada **RC**	8.00
153	Pedro Feliz	4.00
154	Nate Frese **RC**	4.00
155	Dee Brown	4.00
156	Brandon Larson **RC**	5.00
157	Alexis Gomez **RC**	4.00
158	Jason Hart	4.00
159	C.C. Sabathia	4.00
160	Josh Towers **RC**	6.00
161	Christian Parker **RC**	4.00
162	Jackson Melian **RC**	4.00
163	Joe Kennedy **RC**	4.00
164	Adrian Hernandez **RC**	4.00
165	Jimmy Rollins	4.00
166	Jose Mieses **RC**	4.00
167	Roy Oswalt	5.00
168	Eric Munson	4.00
169	Xavier Nady	4.00
170	Horacio Ramirez **RC**	8.00
171	Abraham Nunez	4.00
172	Jose Ortiz	4.00
173	Jeremy Owens **RC**	4.00
174	Claudio Vargas **RC**	4.00
175	Corey Patterson	4.00
176	Carlos Pena	4.00
177	Bud Smith **RC**	4.00
178	Adam Dunn	4.00
179	Adam Pettyjohn **RC**	4.00
180	Elpidio Guzman **RC**	4.00
181	Jay Gibbons **RC**	10.00
182	Wilkin Ruan **RC**	4.00
183	Tsuyoshi Shinjo **RC**	4.00
184	Alfonso Soriano	6.00
185	Marcus Giles	4.00
186	Ichiro Suzuki **RC**	85.00
187	Juan Uribe **RC**	6.00
188	David Williams **RC**	4.00
189	Carlos Valderrama **RC**	4.00
190	Matt White **RC**	4.00
191	Albert Pujols **RC**	240.00
192	Donaldo Mendez **RC**	4.00
193	Cory Aldridge **RC**	4.00
194	Endy Chavez **RC**	4.00
195	Josh Beckett	4.00
196	Wilson Betemit **RC**	4.00
197	Ben Sheets	4.00
198	Andres Torres **RC**	4.00
199	Aubrey Huff	4.00
200	Jack Wilson **RC**	8.00

Proofs

This parallel insert has a metallic holo-foil seal on front and is serially numbered to 25 each.

Values Undetermined
Production 25 Sets

Diamond Collection

		NM/M
Common Player:		5.00
1	Vladimir Guerrero	10.00
2	Barry Bonds	30.00
3	Cal Ripken Jr.	30.00
4	Nomar Garciaparra	20.00
5	Greg Maddux	15.00
6	Frank Thomas	10.00
7	Roger Clemens	20.00
8	Luis Gonzalez/SP	6.00
9	Tony Gwynn	15.00
10	Carlos Lee/SP	6.00
11	Troy Glaus	8.00
12	Randy Johnson	10.00
13	Manny Ramirez/SP	15.00
14	Pedro Martinez	10.00
15	Todd Helton	10.00
16	Jeff Bagwell	10.00
17	Rickey Henderson	10.00
18	Kazuhiro Sasaki	5.00
19	Albert Pujols/SP	50.00
20	Ivan Rodriguez	8.00
21	Darin Erstad	6.00
22	Andruw Jones	8.00
23	Roberto Alomar	6.00
25	Juan Gonzalez	10.00
26	Shawn Green	7.50
27	Lance Berkman	5.00
28	Scott Rolen	9.00
29	Rafael Palmeiro	8.00
30	J.D. Drew	5.00
31	Kerry Wood	8.00
32	Jim Edmonds	5.00
33	Tom Glavine/SP	8.00
34	Hideo Nomo/SP	50.00
36	Tim Hudson	5.00
37	Miguel Tejada	5.00
38	Chipper Jones	15.00
39	Edgar Martinez/SP	8.00
40	Chan Ho Park	5.00
41	Magglio Ordonez	5.00
42	Sean Casey	5.00
43	Larry Walker	5.00
45	Cliff Floyd	5.00
46	Mike Sweeney	5.00
47	Kevin Brown	5.00
48	Richie Sexson	5.00
49	Jermaine Dye	5.00
50	Craig Biggio	5.00

Leather & Lumber

		NM/M
Common Player:		5.00
Combos:		No Pricing
Production 25 Sets		
1	Barry Bonds	25.00
2	Cal Ripken Jr.	25.00
3	Miguel Tejada	5.00
5	Frank Thomas	8.00
6	Greg Maddux	10.00
7	Ivan Rodriguez	8.00
8	Jeff Bagwell/SP	10.00
9	Sean Casey/SP	6.00
10	Todd Helton	8.00
11	Cliff Floyd	5.00
12	Hideo Nomo	40.00
13	Chipper Jones	10.00
14	Rickey Henderson	8.00
15	Richard Hidalgo	5.00
16	Mike Piazza	15.00
17	Larry Walker	5.00
18	Tony Gwynn	10.00
19	Vladimir Guerrero	8.00
20	Rafael Furcal	5.00
21	Roberto Alomar/SP	8.00
23	Albert Pujols	60.00
24	Raul Mondesi	5.00
25	J.D. Drew	5.00
26	Jim Edmonds	5.00
27	Darin Erstad/SP	6.00
28	Craig Biggio	5.00
29	Kenny Lofton	5.00
30	Juan Gonzalez	8.00
31	John Olerud	5.00
32	Shawn Green	5.00
33	Andruw Jones/SP	8.00
34	Moises Alou	5.00
35	Jeff Kent	5.00
36	Ryan Klesko	5.00
37	Luis Gonzalez	5.00
38	Rafael Palmeiro	8.00
40	Scott Rolen	8.00
41	Carlos Lee	5.00
42	Bobby Abreu	5.00
43	Edgardo Alfonzo	5.00
44	Bernie Williams	5.00
45	Brian Giles	5.00
46	Jermaine Dye	5.00
47	Lance Berkman	5.00
48	Edgar Martinez	5.00
49	Richie Sexson	5.00
50	Magglio Ordonez	5.00

Masterstokes

		NM/M
Common Player:		8.00
Production 200 Sets		
1	Tony Gwynn	25.00
2	Ivan Rodriguez	10.00
3	J.D. Drew	8.00
4	Cal Ripken Jr.	60.00
5	Hideo Nomo	50.00
6	Darin Erstad	8.00
7	Frank Thomas	12.00
8	Andruw Jones	12.00
9	Roberto Alomar	8.00
10	Larry Walker	8.00
11	Vladimir Guerrero	12.00
12	Barry Bonds	65.00
14	Luis Gonzalez	8.00
16	Juan Gonzalez	12.00
17	Todd Helton	12.00
18	Jeff Bagwell	12.00
19	Albert Pujols	75.00
20	Shawn Green	8.00
21	Magglio Ordonez	8.00
22	Scott Rolen	12.00
23	Rafael Palmeiro	10.00
24	Sean Casey	8.00
25	Jim Edmonds	8.00
26	Chipper Jones	20.00
27	Cliff Floyd	8.00
28	Carlos Lee	8.00
29	Edgar Martinez	8.00
30	Lance Berkman	8.00

Private Signings

		NM/M
Common Player:		8.00
Inserted 1:Hobby Box		
1	Alex Rodriguez	80.00
2	Miguel Tejada	25.00
3	Ben Sheets	15.00
4	Tony Gwynn/SP/190	60.00
5	Wilson Betemit	8.00
6	Rick Ankiel	20.00
7	Ivan Rodriguez/SP/150	30.00
8	Ryan Klesko	8.00

9 Jason Giambi/SP/250 15.00
10 Brad Penny 8.00
11 Gabe Kapler 8.00
12 Vladimir Guerrero 30.00
13 Alex Escobar 8.00
14 Edgar Martinez 15.00
15 Cal Ripken/SP/50 200.00
16 Brian Giles 8.00
17 Todd Helton/SP/125 25.00
18 Mike Sweeney 8.00
19 Cliff Floyd 8.00
20 Corey Patterson 12.00
21 Alfonso Soriano 40.00
22 Bobby Abreu 8.00
23 Shawn Green/SP/190 20.00
24 C.C. Sabathia 8.00
25 Luis Gonzalez 8.00
26 Barry Bonds/SP/95 200.00
27 Rafael Palmeiro/SP/250 30.00
28 Mike Mussina/SP/144 40.00
29 Roger Clemens/SP/200 100.00
30 Greg Maddux/SP/200 80.00
31 Troy Glaus 20.00
32 Kerry Wood 15.00
33 Roberto Alomar/SP/200 30.00
34 Tom Glavine 40.00
35 Frank Thomas 20.00
36 Carlos Lee 8.00
37 Scott Rolen 20.00
38 Andruw Jones/SP/250 20.00
39 Manny Ramirez/SP/115 40.00
40 Magglio Ordonez 12.00
41 Lance Berkman 8.00
42 Josh Beckett 30.00
43 Adam Dunn 15.00
44 Albert Pujols/SP/50 600.00
45 Darin Erstad 12.00
46 Curt Schilling 40.00
47 Barry Zito 12.00
48 Sean Casey 8.00

Round Trip Tickets

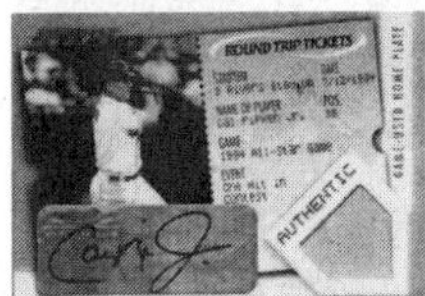

No Pricing
Production 25 Sets

Warning Track

NM/M
Common Player: 4.00
1 Andruw Jones 8.00
2 Rafael Palmeiro 7.00
3 Gary Sheffield 5.00
4 Larry Walker 4.00
5 Shawn Green 4.00
6 Mike Piazza 12.00
7 Barry Bonds 20.00
8 J.D. Drew 4.00
9 Magglio Ordonez 4.00
10 Todd Helton 8.00
11 Juan Gonzalez 8.00
12 Pat Burrell 5.00
13 Mark McGwire 15.00
14 Frank Robinson 4.00
15 Manny Ramirez 8.00
16 Lance Berkman 4.00
18 Johnny Bench 10.00
19 Chipper Jones 10.00
20 Mike Schmidt 15.00
21 Vladimir Guerrero 8.00
22 Sammy Sosa 12.00
23 Cal Ripken Jr. 20.00
24 Roberto Alomar 4.00
25 Willie Stargell 4.00
27 Scott Rolen 7.00
28 Roberto Clemente/SP 50.00
29 Tony Gwynn 10.00
30 Ivan Rodriguez 5.00
31 Sean Casey 4.00
32 Frank Thomas 8.00
33 Jeff Bagwell 8.00
34 Jeff Kent 4.00
35 Reggie Jackson 8.00

2001 Donruss The Rookies

NM/M
Complete Set (105): 80.00
Complete Factory Set (106): 100.00

Common Player: .25
1 Adam Dunn .50
2 Ryan Drese **RC** .40
3 Bud Smith **RC** .25
4 Tsuyoshi Shinjo **RC** .50
5 Roy Oswalt .50
6 Wilmy Caceres **RC** .25
7 Willie Harris **RC** .25
8 Andres Torres **RC** .25
9 Brandon Knight **RC** .25
10 Horacio Ramirez **RC** .75
11 Benito Baez **RC** .25
12 Jeremy Affeldt **RC** .25
13 Ryan Jensen **RC** .25
14 Casey Fossum **RC** .50
15 Ramon Vazquez **RC** .50
16 Dustan Mohr **RC** .25
17 Saul Rivera **RC** .25
18 Zach Day **RC** .50
19 Erik Hiljus **RC** .25
20 Cesar Crespo **RC** .25
21 Wilson Guzman **RC** .25
22 Travis Hafner **RC** 6.00
23 Grant Balfour **RC** .25
24 Johnny Estrada **RC** 1.50
25 Morgan Ensberg **RC** 1.00
26 Jack Wilson **RC** 1.50
27 Aubrey Huff .25
28 Endy Chavez **RC** .50
29 Delvin James **RC** .25
30 Michael Cuddyer .25
31 Jason Michaels **RC** .25
32 Martin Vargas **RC** .25
33 Donaldo Mendez **RC** .25
34 Jorge Julio **RC** .25
35 Tim Spooneybarger **RC** .25
36 Kurt Ainsworth .25
37 Josh Fogg **RC** .50
38 Brian Reith **RC** .25
39 Rick Baurer **RC** .25
40 Tim Redding .25
41 Erick Almonte **RC** .50
42 Juan Pena .25
43 Ken Harvey .25
44 David Brous **RC** .25
45 Kevin Olsen **RC** .25
46 Henry Mateo **RC** .25
47 Nick Neugebauer .25
48 Mike Penney **RC** .25
49 Jay Gibbons **RC** 1.00
50 Tim Christman **RC** .25
51 Brandon Duckworth **RC** .50
52 Brett Jodie **RC** .25
53 Christian Parker **RC** .25
54 Carlos Hernandez **RC** .25
55 Brandon Larson **RC** .50
56 Nick Punto **RC** .25
57 Elpidio Guzman **RC** .25
58 Joe Beimel **RC** .25
59 Junior Spivey **RC** .50
60 Will Ohman **RC** .25
61 Brandon Lyon **RC** .25
62 Stubby Clapp **RC** .25
63 Justin Duchscherer **RC** .50
64 Jimmy Rollins .40
65 David Williams **RC** .40
66 Craig Monroe **RC** .40
67 Jose Acevedo **RC** .25
68 Jason Jennings .25
69 Josh Phelps .25
70 Brian Roberts **RC** 2.00
71 Claudio Vargas **RC** .25
72 Adam Johnson .25
73 Bart Miadich **RC** .25
74 Juan Rivera .25
75 Brad Voyles **RC** .25
76 Nate Cornejo .25
77 Juan Moreno **RC** .25
78 Brian Rogers **RC** .25
79 Ricardo Rodriguez **RC** .40
80 Geronimo Gil **RC** .25
81 Joe Kennedy **RC** .40
82 Kevin Joseph **RC** .25
83 Josue Perez **RC** .25
84 Victor Zambrano **RC** .25
85 Josh Towers **RC** .40
86 Mike Rivera **RC** .25
87 Mark Prior **RC** 6.00
88 Juan Cruz **RC** .40
89 Dewon Brazelton **RC** .40
90 Angel Berroa **RC** 1.00
91 Mark Teixeira **RC** 15.00
92 Cody Ransom **RC** .25
93 Angel Santos **RC** .25
94 Corky Miller **RC** .40
95 Brandon Berger **RC** .40
96 Corey Patterson .25
97 Albert Pujols **RC** 60.00
98 Josh Beckett .50
99 C.C. Sabathia .25
100 Alfonso Soriano .75
101 Ben Sheets .25
102 Rafael Soriano **RC** .50
103 Wilson Betemit **RC** .50
104 Ichiro Suzuki **RC** 10.00
105 Jose Ortiz .25

Rookie Diamond Kings

NM/M
Complete Set (5): 40.00
Inserted 1:Rookies Set
106 C.C. Sabathia 5.00
107 Tsuyoshi Shinjo 8.00
108 Albert Pujols 25.00
109 Roy Oswalt 8.00
110 Ichiro Suzuki 12.00

2002 Donruss Samples

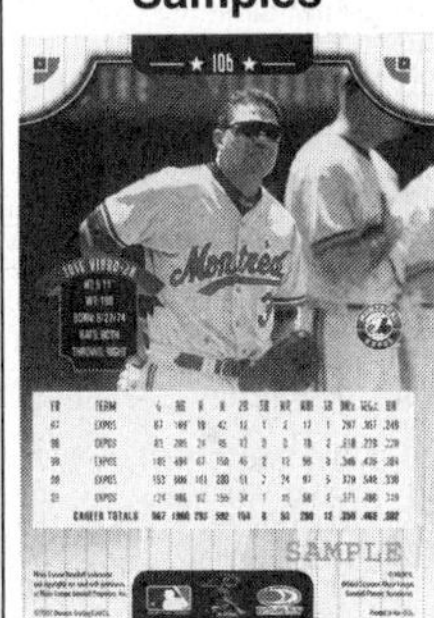

Each March, 2002, issue of Beckett Baseball Card Monthly included a sample 2002 Donruss card rubber-cemented inside. The cards differ from the issued version only in the appearance on back of a (usually) silver-foil silver-foil "SAMPLE" notation. Some cards were produced with the overprint in gold-foil, in much more limited quantities. The number of different players' cards involved in the promotion is unknown.

NM/M
Common Player: .10
Stars: 1.5-2X
Gold: 10X

2002 Donruss

NM/M
Complete Set (220): 100.00
Common Player: .15
Common (151-200): 1.00
Inserted 1:4
Common (201-220): 1.00
Inserted 1:8
Pack (5): 2.00
Box (24): 40.00
1 Alex Rodriguez 1.50
2 Barry Bonds 2.00
3 Derek Jeter 2.00
4 Robert Fick .15
5 Juan Pierre .20
6 Torii Hunter .25
7 Todd Helton .75
8 Cal Ripken Jr. 2.00
9 Manny Ramirez .75
10 Johnny Damon .25
11 Mike Piazza 1.25
12 Nomar Garciaparra 1.25
13 Pedro Martinez .75
14 Brian Giles .15
15 Albert Pujols 1.50
16 Roger Clemens 1.00
17 Sammy Sosa 1.25
18 Vladimir Guerrero .75
19 Tony Gwynn 1.00
20 Pat Burrell .35
21 Carlos Delgado .50
22 Tino Martinez .15
23 Jim Edmonds .15
24 Jason Giambi .50
25 Tom Glavine .30
26 Mark Grace .20
27 Tony Armas Jr. .15
28 Andruw Jones .75
29 Ben Sheets .15
30 Jeff Kent .15
31 Barry Larkin .15
32 Joe Mays .15
33 Mike Mussina .40
34 Hideo Nomo .60
35 Rafael Palmeiro .65
36 Scott Brosius .15
37 Scott Rolen .65
38 Gary Sheffield .35
39 Bernie Williams .35
40 Bobby Abreu .15
41 Edgardo Alfonzo .15
42 C.C. Sabathia .15
43 Jeremy Giambi .15
44 Craig Biggio .15
45 Andres Galarraga .15
46 Edgar Martinez .15
47 Fred McGriff .25
48 Magglio Ordonez .25
49 Jim Thome .15
50 Matt Williams .15
51 Kerry Wood .50
52 Moises Alou .15
53 Brady Anderson .15
54 Garret Anderson .15
55 Juan Gonzalez .75
56 Bret Boone .15
57 Jose Cruz Jr. .15
58 Carlos Beltran .50
59 Adrian Beltre .25
60 Joe Kennedy .15
61 Lance Berkman .15
62 Kevin Brown .25
63 Tim Hudson .35
64 Jeromy Burnitz .15
65 Jarrod Washburn .15
66 Sean Casey .20
67 Eric Chavez .25
68 Bartolo Colon .15
69 Freddy Garcia .15
70 Jermaine Dye .15
71 Terrence Long .15
72 Cliff Floyd .15
73 Luis Gonzalez .25
74 Ichiro Suzuki 1.50
75 Mike Hampton .15
76 Richard Hidalgo .15
77 Geoff Jenkins .15
78 Gabe Kapler .15
79 Ken Griffey Jr. 1.25
80 Jason Kendall .15
81 Josh Towers .15
82 Ryan Klesko .15
83 Paul Konerko .15
84 Carlos Lee .15
85 Kenny Lofton .15
86 Josh Beckett .40
87 Raul Mondesi .15
88 Trot Nixon .15
89 John Olerud .15
90 Paul O'Neill .15
91 Chan Ho Park .15
92 Andy Pettitte .35
93 Jorge Posada .30
94 Mark Quinn .15
95 Aramis Ramirez .15
96 Curt Schilling .40
97 Richie Sexson .15
98 John Smoltz .15
99 Wilson Betemit .15
100 Shannon Stewart .15
101 Alfonso Soriano .75
102 Mike Sweeney .15
103 Miguel Tejada .40
104 Greg Vaughn .15
105 Robin Ventura .15
106 Jose Vidro .15
107 Larry Walker .15
108 Preston Wilson .15
109 Corey Patterson .20
110 Mark Mulder .25
111 Tony Clark .15
112 Roy Oswalt .25
113 Jimmy Rollins .40
114 Kazuhiro Sasaki .15
115 Barry Zito .40
116 Javier Vazquez .15
117 Mike Cameron .15
118 Phil Nevin .15
119 Bud Smith .15
120 Cristian Guzman .15
121 Al Leiter .15
122 Brad Radke .15
123 Bobby Higginson .15
124 Robert Person .15
125 Adam Dunn .50
126 Ben Grieve .15
127 Rafael Furcal .15
128 Jay Gibbons .15
129 Paul LoDuca .15
130 Wade Miller .15
131 Tsuyoshi Shinjo .15
132 Eric Milton .15
133 Rickey Henderson .75
134 Roberto Alomar .40
135 Darin Erstad .50
136 J.D. Drew .35
137 Shawn Green .25
138 Randy Johnson .75
139 Mark McGwire 1.50
139 .15
140 Jose Canseco .40
141 Jeff Bagwell .75
142 Greg Maddux 1.00
143 Mark Buehrle .15
144 Ivan Rodriguez .65
145 Frank Thomas .75
146 Rich Aurilia .15
147 Troy Glaus .75
148 Ryan Dempster .15
149 Chipper Jones 1.00
150 Matt Morris .15
151 Marlon Byrd 2.00
152 Ben Howard **RC** 4.00
153 Brandon Backe **RC** 2.00
154 Jorge De La Rosa **RC** 2.00
155 Corky Miller 1.00
156 Dennis Tankersley 1.00
157 Kyle Kane **RC** 3.00
158 Justin Duchscherer 1.00
159 Brian Mallette **RC** 3.00
160 Chris Baker **RC** 3.00
161 Jason Lane 1.00
162 Hee Seop Choi 1.50
163 Juan Cruz 1.00
164 Rodrigo Rosario **RC** 2.00
165 Matt Guerrier 1.00
166 Anderson Machado **RC** 3.00
167 Geronimo Gil 1.00
168 Dewon Brazelton 1.00
169 Mark Prior 5.00
170 Bill Hall 1.00
171 Jorge Padilla **RC** 4.00
172 Jose Cueto 1.00
173 Allan Simpson **RC** 3.00
174 Doug DeVore **RC** 3.00
175 Josh Pearce 1.00
176 Angel Berroa 1.00
177 Steve Bechler **RC** 3.00
178 Antonio Perez 1.00
179 Mark Teixeira 3.00
180 Erick Almonte 1.00
181 Orlando Hudson 1.00
182 Mike Rivera 1.00
183 Raul Chavez **RC** 2.00
184 Juan Pena 1.00
185 Travis Hughes **RC** 2.00
186 Ryan Ludwick 1.00
187 Ed Rogers 1.00
188 Andy Pratt **RC** 2.00
189 Nick Neugebauer 1.00
190 Tom Shearn **RC** 3.00
191 Eric Cyr **RC** 3.00
192 Victor Martinez 1.00
193 Brandon Berger 1.00
194 Erik Bedard 1.00
195 Fernando Rodney 1.00
196 Joe Thurston 1.00
197 John Buck 1.00
198 Jeff Deardorff **RC** 2.00
199 Ryan Jamison **RC** 2.00
200 Alfredo Amezaga 1.00
201 Luis Gonzalez 1.00
202 Roger Clemens 4.00
203 Barry Zito 1.25
204 Bud Smith 1.00
205 Magglio Ordonez 1.25
206 Kerry Wood 1.50
207 Freddy Garcia 1.00
208 Adam Dunn 1.50
209 Curt Schilling 2.00
210 Lance Berkman 1.50
211 Rafael Palmeiro 2.00
212 Ichiro Suzuki 4.00
213 Bobby Abreu 1.00
214 Mark Mulder 1.00
215 Roy Oswalt 1.50
216 Mike Sweeney 1.00
217 Paul LoDuca 1.00
218 Aramis Ramirez 1.00
219 Randy Johnson 2.00
220 Albert Pujols 5.00

Stat Line Career

NM/M
Cards 1-150 print run 251-400: 2-4X
1-150 p/r 151-250: 3-6X
1-150 p/r 101-150: 4-8X
1-150 p/r 61-100: 5-10X
1-150 p/r 31-60: 8-20X
1-150 p/r 15-30: 15-30X
Common 151-200 p/r 251-400: 1.00
Common 151-200 p/r 151-250: 1.00

Common 151-200 p/r 76-150: 2.00
Common 151-200 p/r 30-75: 4.00

Stat Line Season

NM/M
Cards 1-150 print run 151-200: 3-6X
1-150 p/r 101-150: 4-8X
1-150 p/r 76-100: 5-10X
1-150 p/r 51-75: 6-12X
1-150 p/r 31-50: 8-20X
1-150 p/r 15-30: 15-30X
Comm. 151-200 p/r 151-200: 1.00
Comm. 151-200 p/r 101-150: 1.50
Comm. 151-200 p/r 76-100: 2.00
Comm. 151-200 p/r 30-75: 4.00

Autographs

NM/M
Common Autograph: 15.00
Varying quantities produced
203 Barry Zito/200 25.00
204 Bud Smith/200 15.00
205 Magglio Ordonez/200 20.00
206 Kerry Wood/200 30.00
207 Freddy Garcia/200 15.00
208 Adam Dunn/200 25.00
210 Lance Berkman/175 15.00
211 Rafael Palmeiro/25 20.00
213 Bobby Abreu/200 15.00
214 Mark Mulder/200 15.00
215 Roy Oswalt/200 15.00
216 Mike Sweeney/200 15.00
217 Paul LoDuca/200 15.00
218 Aramis Ramirez/200 15.00
220 Albert Pujols/200 75.00

All-Time Diamond Kings

NM/M
Complete Set (10): 80.00
Common Player: 5.00
Production 2,500 Sets
Studio Series: 2-3X
Production 250 Sets
1 Ted Williams 15.00
2 Cal Ripken Jr. 15.00
3 Lou Gehrig 10.00
4 Babe Ruth 15.00
5 Roberto Clemente 10.00
6 Don Mattingly 10.00
7 Kirby Puckett 8.00
8 Stan Musial 8.00
9 Yogi Berra 5.00
10 Ernie Banks 5.00

Bat Kings

NM/M
Quantities produced listed
Studio Series: 1.5-3X
Production 25 or 50
1 Jason Giambi/250 15.00
2 Alex Rodriguez/250 25.00
3 Mike Piazza/250 20.00
4 Roberto Clemente/125 100.00
5 Babe Ruth/125 220.00

Diamond Kings

NM/M
Complete Set (20): 80.00
Common Player: 2.00
Production 2,500 Sets
Studio Series: 2-3X

Production 250 Sets
1 Nomar Garciaparra 6.00
2 Shawn Green 2.00
3 Randy Johnson 4.00
4 Derek Jeter 7.50
5 Carlos Delgado 3.00
6 Roger Clemens 5.00
7 Jeff Bagwell 4.00
8 Vladimir Guerrero 4.00
9 Luis Gonzalez 2.00
10 Mike Piazza 6.00
11 Ichiro Suzuki 6.00
12 Pedro Martinez 4.00
13 Todd Helton 4.00
14 Sammy Sosa 6.00
15 Ivan Rodriguez 3.50
16 Barry Bonds 7.50
17 Albert Pujols 6.00
18 Jim Thome 2.00
19 Alex Rodriguez 6.00
20 Jason Giambi 3.00

Elite Series

NM/M
Complete Set (15): 30.00
Common Player: 2.00
Production 2,500 Sets
Autographs: No Pricing
Production 25
1 Barry Bonds 8.00
2 Lance Berkman 2.00
3 Jason Giambi 2.50
4 Nomar Garciaparra 6.00
5 Curt Schilling 2.50
6 Vladimir Guerrero 3.00
7 Shawn Green 2.00
8 Troy Glaus 2.00
9 Jeff Bagwell 3.00
10 Manny Ramirez 3.00
11 Eric Chavez 2.00
12 Carlos Delgado 2.50
13 Mike Sweeney 2.00
14 Todd Helton 3.00
15 Luis Gonzalez 2.00

Elite Series Legends

NM/M
Complete Set (5): 15.00
Common Player: 3.00
Production 2,500
16 Enos Slaughter 3.00
17 Frank Robinson 4.00
18 Bob Gibson 4.00
19 Warren Spahn 4.00
20 Whitey Ford 4.00

Elite Series Legends Autographs

NM/M
Production 250 Sets
16 Enos Slaughter 30.00
17 Frank Robinson 30.00
18 Bob Gibson 35.00
19 Warren Spahn 40.00
20 Whitey Ford 40.00

Jersey Kings

NM/M
Quantity produced listed
Studio Series: 1.5-3X
Production 25 or 50
1 Alex Rodriguez/250 15.00
2 Jason Giambi/250 10.00
3 Carlos Delgado/250 8.00
4 Barry Bonds/250 25.00
5 Randy Johnson/250 10.00
6 Jim Thome/250 8.00
7 Shawn Green/250 8.00
8 Pedro Martinez/250 10.00
9 Jeff Bagwell/250 10.00
10 Vladimir Guerrero/ 250 10.00
11 Ivan Rodriguez/250 10.00
12 Nomar Garciaparra/ 250 15.00
13 Don Mattingly/125 80.00
14 Ted Williams/125 125.00
15 Lou Gehrig/125 200.00

Longball Leaders

NM/M
Complete Set (20): 40.00
Common Player: 1.00
Production 1,000 Sets
Seasonal Sum Parallel: 2-4X
Parallel #'d to 2001 HR Total.
1 Barry Bonds 8.00
2 Sammy Sosa 6.00
3 Luis Gonzalez 1.00
4 Alex Rodriguez 6.00
5 Shawn Green 1.50
6 Todd Helton 3.00
7 Jim Thome 1.00
8 Rafael Palmeiro 2.50
9 Richie Sexson 1.00
10 Troy Glaus 3.00
11 Manny Ramirez 3.00
12 Phil Nevin 1.00
13 Jeff Bagwell 3.00
14 Carlos Delgado 2.00
15 Jason Giambi 2.00
16 Chipper Jones 4.00
17 Larry Walker 1.00
18 Albert Pujols 6.00
19 Brian Giles 1.00
20 Bret Boone 1.00

Production Line

NM/M
Common Card: 2.00
Numbered to category stat.
1 Barry Bonds/515 8.00
2 Jason Giambi/477 4.00
3 Larry Walker/449 2.50
4 Sammy Sosa/437 6.00
5 Todd Helton/432 3.00
6 Lance Berkman/430 2.00
7 Luis Gonzalez/429 2.00
8 Chipper Jones/427 6.00
9 Edgar Martinez/423 2.00
10 Gary Sheffield/417 2.00
11 Jim Thome/416 3.00
12 Roberto Alomar/415 3.00
13 J.D. Drew/414 2.00
14 Jim Edmonds/410 2.00
15 Carlos Delgado/408 3.00
16 Manny Ramirez/405 4.00
17 Brian Giles/404 2.00
18 Albert Pujols/403 8.00
19 John Olerud/401 2.00
20 Alex Rodriguez/399 8.00
21 Barry Bonds/863 6.00
22 Sammy Sosa/737 5.00
23 Luis Gonzalez/688 1.50
24 Todd Helton/685 2.00
25 Larry Walker/662 1.50
26 Jason Giambi/660 2.00
27 Jim Thome/624 2.00
28 Alex Rodriguez/620 5.00
29 Lance Berkman/620 1.50
30 J.D. Drew/613 1.50
31 Albert Pujols/610 5.00
32 Manny Ramirez/609 2.00
33 Chipper Jones/605 3.00
34 Shawn Green/598 1.50
35 Brian Giles/590 1.50
36 Juan Gonzalez/590 2.00
37 Phil Nevin/588 1.50
38 Gary Sheffield/583 1.50
39 Bret Boone/578 1.50
40 Cliff Floyd/578 1.50
41 Barry Bonds/1,378 5.00
42 Sammy Sosa/1,174 4.00
43 Jason Giambi/1,137 1.50
44 Todd Helton/1,117 1.50
45 Luis Gonzalez/1,117 1.00
46 Larry Walker/1,111 1.00
47 Lance Berkman/1,050 1.00
48 Jim Thome/1,040 1.50
49 Chipper Jones/1,032 2.50
50 J.D. Drew/1,027 1.00
51 Alex Rodriguez/1,021 4.00
52 Manny Ramirez/1,014 1.50
53 Albert Pujols/1,013 4.00
54 Gary Sheffield/1,000 1.50
55 Brian Giles/994 1.00
56 Phil Nevin/976 1.00
57 Jim Edmonds/974 1.50
58 Shawn Green/970 1.00
59 Cliff Floyd/968 1.00
60 Edgar Martinez/966 1.00

Recollection Collection

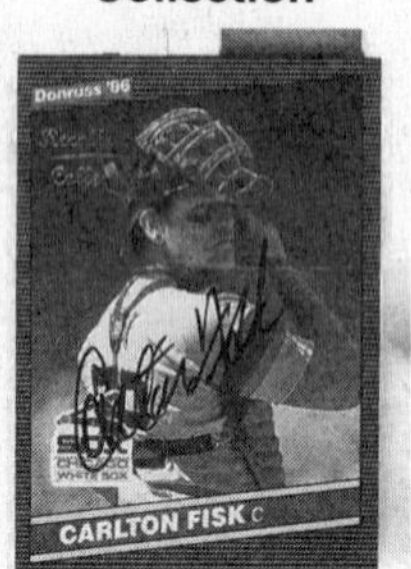

NM/M
Complete Set (47):
Common Player:
6 Steve Carlton 83/30 40.00
7 Steve Carlton 87/30 40.00
8 Gary Carter 87/100 25.00
9 Gary Carter 89/100 25.00
11 Joe Carter 87/45 20.00
13 Andre Dawson 81/50 20.00
14 Andre Dawson 83/50 20.00
16 Andre Dawson 87/45 20.00
17 Dennis Eckersley 81/45 20.00
24 Steve Garvey 87/75 20.00
26 Fergie Jenkins 81/40 25.00
46 Tom Seaver 87/60 60.00
47 Don Sutton 87/200 15.00

Rookie Year Materials - Bats

NM/M
Production 250 Sets
1 Barry Bonds 40.00
2 Cal Ripken Jr. 40.00
3 Kirby Puckett 15.00
4 Johnny Bench 15.00

Rookie Year Materials - Bats Autograph

NM/M
Numbered to debut year.
1 Barry Bonds/86 125.00
2 Cal Ripken Jr/81 140.00
3 Kirby Puckett/84 120.00
4 Johnny Bench/68 75.00

Rookie Year Materials - Jerseys

NM/M
Quantity produced listed
Parallel #'d to 25 or 50.
1 Nomar Garciaparra/ 250 20.00
2 Randy Johnson/250 10.00
3 Ivan Rodriguez/250 10.00
4 Vladimir Guerrero/ 250 15.00
5 Stan Musial/50 80.00
6 Yogi Berra/50 50.00

2002 Donruss Classics Samples

Each August, 2002, issue of Beckett Baseball Card Monthly included a sample Donruss Classics card rubber-cemented inside. The cards differ from the issued version only in the appearance on back of a (usually) silver-foil "SAMPLE" notation. Some cards were produced with the overprint in gold-foil, in much more limited quantities. Cards #1-100 from the set can be found in this Sample version.

NM/M
Common Player: .10
Stars: 1.5-2X
Gold: 10X

2002 Donruss Classics

NM/M
Complete Set (200):
Common Player: .50
Common (101-150): 3.00
Common (151-200): 2.00
Production 1,500
Pack (6): 5.00
Box (18): 70.00
1 Alex Rodriguez 3.00
2 Barry Bonds 4.00
3 C.C. Sabathia .50
4 Chipper Jones 2.00
5 Derek Jeter 4.00
6 Troy Glaus 1.50
7 Frank Thomas 1.50
8 Greg Maddux 2.00
9 Ivan Rodriguez 1.25
10 Jeff Bagwell 1.50
11 Mark Buehrle .50
12 Todd Helton 1.50
13 Ken Griffey Jr. 2.50
14 Manny Ramirez 1.50
15 Brad Penny .50
16 Mike Piazza 2.50
17 Nomar Garciaparra 2.50
18 Pedro J. Martinez 1.50
19 Randy Johnson 1.50
20 Bud Smith .50
21 Rickey Henderson 1.50
22 Roger Clemens 2.25
23 Sammy Sosa 2.50
24 Brandon Duckworth .50
25 Vladimir Guerrero 1.50
26 Kazuhiro Sasaki .50
27 Roberto Alomar .65
28 Barry Zito .75
29 Rich Aurilia .50
30 Ben Sheets .50
31 Carlos Delgado 1.00
32 J.D. Drew .75
33 Jermaine Dye .50
34 Darin Erstad .75
35 Jason Giambi 1.00
36 Tom Glavine .60
37 Juan Gonzalez 1.50
38 Luis Gonzalez .35
39 Shawn Green .75
40 Tim Hudson .65
41 Andruw Jones 1.50
42 Shannon Stewart .50
43 Barry Larkin .50
44 Wade Miller .50
45 Mike Mussina .65
46 Hideo Nomo 1.00
47 Rafael Palmeiro 1.25
48 Scott Rolen 1.00
49 Gary Sheffield .75
50 Bernie Williams .65
51 Bobby Abreu .50
52 Javier Vazquez .50
53 Edgar Martinez .50
54 Magglio Ordonez .75
55 Kerry Wood 1.00
56 Adrian Beltre .65
57 Lance Berkman .50
58 Kevin Brown .50
59 Sean Casey .50
60 Eric Chavez .75
61 Robert Person .50
62 Jeremy Giambi .50
63 Freddy Garcia .50
64 Alfonso Soriano 1.50
65 Doug Davis .50
66 Brian Giles .50
67 Moises Alou .50
68 Richard Hidalgo .50
69 Paul LoDuca .50
70 Aramis Ramirez .50
71 Andres Galarraga .50
72 Ryan Klesko .50
73 Chan Ho Park .50
74 Richie Sexson .50
75 Mike Sweeney .50
76 Aubrey Huff .50
77 Miguel Tejada .75
78 Jose Vidro .50
79 Larry Walker .50
80 Roy Oswalt .75
81 Craig Biggio .50
82 Juan Pierre .50
83 Jim Thome .50
84 Josh Towers .50
85 Alex Escobar .50
86 Cliff Floyd .50
87 Terrence Long .50
88 Curt Schilling .75
89 Carlos Beltran 1.00
90 Albert Pujols 2.50
91 Gabe Kapler .50
92 Mark Mulder .50
93 Carlos Lee .50
94 Robert Fick .50
95 Raul Mondesi .50
96 Ichiro Suzuki 2.50
97 Adam Dunn .75
98 Corey Patterson .75
99 Tsuyoshi Shinjo .50
100 Joe Mays .50
101 Juan Cruz 3.00
102 Marlon Byrd 5.00
103 Luis Garcia 3.00
104 Jorge Padilla **RC** 6.00
105 Dennis Tankersley 3.00
106 Josh Pearce 3.00
107 Ramon Vazquez 3.00
108 Chris Baker **RC** 5.00
109 Eric Cyr **RC** 3.00
110 Reed Johnson **RC** 5.00
111 Ryan Jamison **RC** 3.00
112 Antonio Perez 3.00
113 Satoru Komiyama **RC** 3.00
114 Austin Kearns 4.00
115 Juan Pena 3.00
116 Orlando Hudson 3.00
117 Kazuhisa Ishii **RC** 6.00
118 Eric Bedard 3.00
119 Luis Ugueto **RC** 3.00
120 Ben Howard **RC** 4.00
121 Morgan Ensberg 3.00
122 Doug DeVore **RC** 4.00
123 Josh Phelps 3.00
124 Angel Berroa 4.00
125 Ed Rogers 3.00
126 Takahito Nomura **RC** 3.00
127 John Ennis **RC** 3.00
128 Bill Hall 3.00
129 Dewon Brazelton 3.00
130 Hank Blalock 5.00
131 So Taguchi **RC** 5.00
132 Jorge De La Rosa **RC** 3.00
133 Matt Thornton 3.00
134 Brandon Backe **RC** 3.00
135 Jeff Deardorff **RC** 3.00
136 Steve Smyth 3.00
137 Anderson Machado **RC** 5.00
138 John Buck 3.00
139 Mark Prior 15.00
140 Sean Burroughs 3.00
141 Alex Herrera 3.00
142 Francis Beltran **RC** 3.00
143 Jason Romano 3.00
144 Michael Cuddyer 3.00
145 Steve Bechler **RC** 3.00
146 Alfredo Amezaga 3.00
147 Ryan Ludwick 3.00
148 Martin Vargas 3.00
149 Allan Simpson **RC** 3.00
150 Mark Teixeira 4.00
151 Hank Aaron 8.00
152 Ernie Banks 6.00
153 Johnny Bench 6.00
154 George Brett 10.00
155 Lou Brock 3.00
156 Rod Carew 3.00
157 Steve Carlton 4.00
158 Joe Torre 3.00
159 Dennis Eckersley 2.50
160 Reggie Jackson 5.00
161 Al Kaline 6.00
162 Dave Parker 2.00
163 Don Mattingly 10.00
164 Tony Gwynn 6.00
165 Willie McCovey 3.00
166 Joe Morgan 3.00
167 Stan Musial 8.00
168 Jim Palmer 3.00
169 Brooks Robinson 5.00
170 Bo Jackson 6.00
171 Nolan Ryan 15.00
172 Mike Schmidt 8.00
173 Tom Seaver 6.00
174 Cal Ripken Jr. 15.00
175 Robin Yount 6.00
176 Wade Boggs 5.00
177 Gary Carter 3.00
178 Ron Santo 2.00
179 Luis Aparicio 2.00
180 Bobby Doerr 3.00
181 Ryne Sandberg 6.00
182 Yogi Berra 5.00
183 Will Clark 5.00
184 Eddie Murray 4.00
185 Andre Dawson 3.00
186 Duke Snider 5.00
187 Orlando Cepeda 3.00
188 Billy Williams 2.00
189 Juan Marichal 4.00
190 Harmon Killebrew 5.00
191 Kirby Puckett 6.00
192 Carlton Fisk 4.00
193 Dave Winfield 3.00
194 Alan Trammell 3.00
195 Paul Molitor 6.00
196 Tony Perez 3.00
197 Ozzie Smith 6.00
198 Ralph Kiner 3.00
199 Fergie Jenkins 2.00
200 Phil Rizzuto 3.00

Timeless Tributes

Stars (1-100): 2-4X
SP's (101-150): 1-2X
SP's (151-200): 2-3X
Production 100 Sets

Classic Singles

NM/M
Common Player: 10.00
Some too scarce to price.
1 Cal Ripken Jr./Jsy/50 40.00
2 Eddie Murray/ Jsy/100 15.00
3 George Brett/Jsy/100 35.00
4 Bo Jackson/Jsy/100 20.00
5 Ted Williams/Bat/50 200.00
6 Jimmie Foxx/Bat/50 60.00
7 Reggie Jackson/ Jsy/100 15.00
8 Steve Carlton/Jsy/50 30.00
9 Mel Ott/Jsy/50 70.00
10 "Catfish" Hunter/ Jsy/100 10.00
11 Nolan Ryan/Jsy/100 40.00
12 Rickey Henderson/ Jsy/100 25.00
13 Robin Yount/Jsy/100 25.00
14 Orlando Cepeda/ Jsy/100 10.00
15 Ty Cobb/Bat/50 150.00
16 Babe Ruth/Bat/50 275.00
17 Dave Parker/Jsy/100 10.00
18 Willie Stargell/ Jsy/100 15.00
19 Ernie Banks/Bat/100 25.00
20 Mike Schmidt/ Jsy/100 35.00
21 Duke Snider/Jsy/50 25.00
22 Jackie Robinson/ Jsy/50 75.00
23 Rickey Henderson/ Bat/100 25.00
25 Lou Gehrig/Bat/50 175.00
26 Jimmie Foxx/Bat/50 65.00
28 Tony Gwynn/Bat/100 20.00
29 Bobby Doerr/Jsy/100 15.00
30 Joe Torre/Jsy/100 10.00

Classic Combos

Too scarce to price.

Legendary Hats

NM/M
50 Sets Produced
1 Don Mattingly/50 150.00
2 George Brett 150.00
3 Wade Boggs 30.00
5 Ryne Sandberg 120.00

Legendary Leather

NM/M
50 Sets Produced
1 Don Mattingly 125.00
2 Wade Boggs 30.00
4 Kirby Puckett 50.00
5 Mike Schmidt 80.00

Legendary Lumberjacks

NM/M
Varying quantities produced
1 Don Mattingly/500 20.00
2 George Brett/400 20.00
3 Stan Musial/100 35.00
4 Lou Gehrig/50 175.00
5 Mike Piazza/500 10.00
6 Mel Ott/50 75.00
7 Ted Williams/50 150.00
8 Bo Jackson/500 8.00
9 Kirby Puckett/500 15.00
10 Rafael Palmeiro/500 10.00
11 Andre Dawson/500 5.00
12 Ozzie Smith/500 15.00
13 Paul Molitor/500 15.00
14 Babe Ruth/50 220.00
15 Carlton Fisk/500 8.00
16 Rickey Henderson/ 500 10.00
17 Gary Carter/500 5.00
18 Cal Ripken Jr/100 40.00
19 Eddie Matthews/100 20.00
20 Luis Aparicio/500 5.00
21 Al Kaline/100 25.00
22 Eddie Murray/500 8.00
23 Yogi Berra/100 25.00
24 Alex Rodriguez/500 10.00
25 Tony Gwynn/500 10.00
26 Roberto Clemente/ 100 80.00
27 Mike Schmidt/400 20.00
28 Reggie Jackson/500 10.00
29 Ryne Sandberg/500 20.00
30 Joe Morgan/400 5.00
31 Joe Torre/500 5.00
32 Gary Sheffield/500 5.00
33 Nomar Garciaparra/ 500 10.00
34 Jeff Bagwell/500 8.00
35 Manny Ramirez/500 8.00

Legendary Spikes

NM/M
50 Sets Produced
1 Don Mattingly 125.00
2 Eddie Murray 30.00
3 Paul Molitor 50.00
4 Harmon Killebrew 40.00
5 Mike Schmidt 100.00

New Millennium Classics

		NM/M
Common Player:		4.00
Varying quantities produced		
All jerseys unless noted.		
1	Curt Schilling/500	6.00
2	Vladimir Guerrero/100	15.00
3	Jim Thome/500	8.00
4	Troy Glaus/400	6.00
5	Ivan Rodriguez/200	6.00
6	Todd Helton/400	8.00
7	Sean Casey/500	4.00
8	Scott Rolen/475	8.00
9	Ken Griffey Jr./150/Base	10.00
10	Hideo Nomo/100	25.00
11	Tom Glavine/350	5.00
12	Pedro Martinez/100	15.00
13	Cliff Floyd/500	4.00
14	Shawn Green/125	8.00
15	Rafael Palmeiro/250	8.00
16	Luis Gonzalez/100	5.00
17	Lance Berkman/100	6.00
18	Frank Thomas/500	8.00
19	Randy Johnson/400	8.00
20	Moises Alou/500	4.00
21	Chipper Jones/500	8.00
22	Larry Walker/300	4.00
23	Mike Sweeney/500	4.00
24	Juan Gonzalez/300	6.00
25	Roger Clemens/100	20.00
26	Albert Pujols/300/Base	15.00
27	Maggio Ordonez/500	5.00
28	Alex Rodriguez/400	10.00
29	Jeff Bagwell/125	10.00
30	Kazuhiro Sasaki/500	4.00
31	Barry Larkin/300	6.00
32	Andruw Jones/350	8.00
33	Kerry Wood/200	8.00
34	Rickey Henderson/100	10.00
35	Greg Maddux/100	15.00
36	Brian Giles/400	4.00
37	Craig Biggio/100	5.00
38	Roberto Alomar/400	6.00
39	Mike Piazza/400	10.00
40	Bernie Williams/100	10.00
41	Ichiro Suzuki 150/Ball	30.00
42	Kenny Lofton/450	4.00
43	Mark Mulder/500	4.00
44	Kazuhisa Ishii/100	15.00
45	Darin Erstad/500	4.00
46	Jose Vidro/500	4.00
47	Miguel Tejada/475	6.00
48	Roy Oswalt/500	5.00
50	Barry Zito/500	6.00
51	Manny Ramirez/400	8.00
52	Nomar Garciaparra/400	10.00
53	C.C. Sabathia/500	4.00
54	Carlos Delgado/500	8.00
55	Gary Sheffield/500	6.00
56	J.D. Drew/500	5.00
57	Barry Bonds/150/Ball	25.00
58	Derek Jeter/150/Ball	25.00
59	Edgar Martinez/400	5.00
60	Sammy Sosa/150/Ball	15.00

Significant Signatures

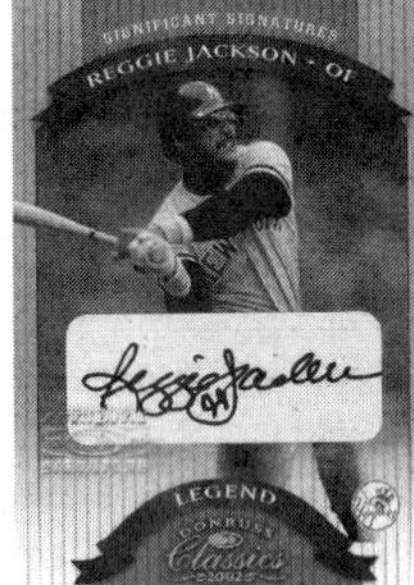

		NM/M
Common Prospect Autograph:		5.00
Varying quantities produced, many not priced due to scarcity.		
101	Juan Cruz/400	6.00
102	Marlon Byrd/500	10.00
103	Luis Garcia/500	6.00
104	Jorge Padilla/500	10.00
105	Dennis Tankersley/250	10.00
106	Josh Pearce/500	8.00
107	Ramon Vazquez/500	5.00
108	Chris Baker/500 **RC**	8.00
109	Eric Cyr/500	6.00
110	Reed Johnson/500	10.00
111	Ryan Jamison/500	5.00
112	Antonio Perez/500	5.00
113	Satoru Komiyama/50	40.00
114	Austin Kearns/500	15.00
115	Juan Pena/500	5.00
116	Orlando Hudson/400	10.00
117	Kazuhisa Ishii/50	40.00
118	Eric Bedard/500	15.00
119	Luis Ugueto/250	10.00
120	Ben Howard/500	8.00
121	Morgan Ensberg/500	10.00
122	Doug DeVore/500	8.00
123	Josh Phelps/500	8.00
124	Angel Berroa/500	10.00
125	Ed Rogers/500	5.00
127	John Ennis/500	5.00
128	Bill Hall/400	10.00
129	Dewon Brazelton/400	8.00
130	Hank Blalock/100	20.00
131	So Taguchi/150	30.00
132	Jorge De La Rosa/500	5.00
133	Matt Thornton/500	5.00
134	Brandon Backe/500	5.00
135	Jeff Deardorff/500	5.00
136	Steve Smyth/400	5.00
137	Anderson Machado/500	10.00
138	John Buck/500	5.00
139	Mark Prior/250	25.00
140	Sean Burroughs/50	10.00
141	Alex Herrera/500	5.00
142	Francis Beltran/500	5.00
143	Jason Romano/500	5.00
144	Michael Cuddyer/400	8.00
145	Steve Bechler/500	8.00
146	Alfredo Amezaga/500	5.00
147	Ryan Ludwick/500	8.00
148	Martin Vargas/500	5.00
149	Allan Simpson/500	5.00
150	Mark Teixeira/200	30.00
152	Ernie Banks/25	100.00
153	Johnny Bench/25	125.00
154	George Brett/25	260.00
155	Lou Brock/100	30.00
157	Steve Carlton/125	35.00
159	Dennis Eckersley/500	15.00
161	Al Kaline/125	35.00
162	Dave Parker/500	10.00
163	Don Mattingly/50	75.00
168	Jim Palmer/125	25.00
169	Brooks Robinson/125	40.00
177	Gary Carter/150	25.00
178	Ron Santo/500	20.00
179	Luis Aparicio/400	10.00
180	Bobby Doerr/500	15.00
182	Yogi Berra/25	80.00
184	Eddie Murray/25	60.00
185	Andre Dawson/200	20.00
186	Duke Snider/25	70.00
187	Orlando Cepeda/125	25.00
188	Billy Williams/200	15.00
189	Juan Marichal/500	15.00
190	Harmon Killebrew/100	50.00
194	Alan Trammell/200	25.00
195	Paul Molitor/25	60.00
196	Tony Perez/150	15.00
198	Ralph Kiner/125	20.00
199	Fergie Jenkins/200	15.00
200	Phil Rizzuto/125	40.00

Timeless Treasures

		NM/M
Some not priced.		
5	Ted Williams/Bat/42	140.00
6	Ted Williams/Bat/47	140.00
7	Ted Williams/Bat/46	140.00
8	Ted Williams/Bat/49	140.00
10	Cal Ripken Jr./Jsy/98	50.00
11	Cal Ripken Jr./Jsy/82	50.00
12	Cal Ripken Jr./Jsy/83	50.00
13	Cal Ripken Jr./Jsy/91	50.00

2002 Donruss Diamond Kings Samples

Each May and July 2002 issue of Beckett Baseball Card Monthly included a sample DK card rubber-cemented inside. The cards differ from the issued version only in the appearance on back of a (usually) silver-foil "SAMPLE" notation and, on some cards, the lack of silver-foil graphics on front. Some cards were produced with the back overprint in gold-foil in much more limited quantities. Cards #1-100 were issued in May, and 101-150 in July.

	NM/M
Common Player:	.25
Stars:	1.5-2X
Gold:	10X

2002 Donruss Diamond Kings

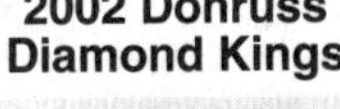

		NM/M
Complete Set (150):		150.00
Common Player:		.40
Common SP (101-150):		2.00
Inserted 1:3		
Pack (4):		4.50
Box (24):		80.00
1	Vladimir Guerrero	1.00
2	Adam Dunn	.75
3	Tsuyoshi Shinjo	.40
4	Adrian Beltre	.60
5	Troy Glaus	1.00
6	Albert Pujols	2.00
7	Trot Nixon	.40
8	Alex Rodriguez	2.50
9	Tom Glavine	.50
10	Alfonso Soriano	1.00
11	Todd Helton	1.00
12	Joe Torre	.40
13	Tim Hudson	.50
14	Andruw Jones	1.00
15	Shawn Green	.50
16	Aramis Ramirez	.40
17	Shannon Stewart	.40
18	Barry Bonds	3.00
19	Sean Casey	.40
20	Barry Larkin	.40
21	Scott Rolen	.75
22	Barry Zito	.50
23	Sammy Sosa	2.00
24	Bartolo Colon	.40
25	Ryan Klesko	.40
26	Ben Grieve	.40
27	Roy Oswalt	.50
28	Kazuhiro Sasaki	.40
29	Roger Clemens	1.75
30	Bernie Williams	.50
31	Roberto Alomar	.50
32	Bobby Abreu	.40
33	Robert Fick	.40
34	Bret Boone	.40
35	Rickey Henderson	1.00
36	Brian Giles	.40
37	Richie Sexson	.40
38	Bud Smith	.40
39	Richard Hidalgo	.40
40	C.C. Sabathia	.40
41	Rich Aurilia	.40
42	Carlos Beltran	.75
43	Raul Mondesi	.40
44	Carlos Delgado	.50
45	Randy Johnson	1.00
46	Chan Ho Park	.40
47	Rafael Palmeiro	.75
48	Chipper Jones	1.50
49	Phil Nevin	.40
50	Cliff Floyd	.40
51	Pedro Martinez	1.00
52	Craig Biggio	.40
53	Paul LoDuca	.40
54	Cristian Guzman	.40
55	Pat Burrell	.50
56	Curt Schilling	.50
57	Orlando Cabrera	.40
58	Darin Erstad	.65
59	Omar Vizquel	.40
60	Derek Jeter	3.00
61	Nomar Garciaparra	2.00
62	Edgar Martinez	.40
63	Moises Alou	.40
64	Eric Chavez	.50
65	Mike Sweeney	.40
66	Frank Thomas	1.00
67	Mike Piazza	2.00
68	Gary Sheffield	.50
69	Mike Mussina	.50
70	Greg Maddux	1.50
71	Juan Gonzalez	1.00
72	Hideo Nomo	.65
73	Miguel Tejada	.50
74	Ichiro Suzuki	2.00
75	Matt Morris	.40
76	Ivan Rodriguez	.75
77	Mark Mulder	.40
78	J.D. Drew	.40
79	Mark Grace	.50
80	Jason Giambi	.50
81	Mark Buehrle	.40
82	Jose Vidro	.40
83	Manny Ramirez	1.00
84	Jeff Bagwell	1.00
85	Magglio Ordonez	.50
86	Ken Griffey Jr.	2.00
87	Luis Gonzalez	.40
88	Jim Edmonds	.40
89	Larry Walker	.40
90	Jim Thome	.40
91	Lance Berkman	.40
92	Jorge Posada	.50
93	Kevin Brown	.40
94	Joe Mays	.40
95	Kerry Wood	.75
96	Mark Ellis	.40
97	Austin Kearns	.75
98	Jorge De La Rosa **RC**	.50
99	Brandon Berger	.40
100	Ryan Ludwick	.40
101	Marlon Byrd	2.00
102	Brandon Backe **RC**	2.00
103	Juan Cruz	2.00
104	Anderson Machado **RC**	3.00
105	So Taguchi **RC**	4.00
106	Dewon Brazelton	2.00
107	Josh Beckett	3.00
108	John Buck	2.00
109	Jorge Padilla **RC**	3.00
110	Hee Seop Choi	2.00
111	Angel Berroa	2.00
112	Mark Teixeira	3.00
113	Victor Martinez	2.00
114	Kazuhisa Ishii **RC**	6.00
115	Dennis Tankersley	2.00
116	Wilson Valdez **RC**	2.00
117	Antonio Perez	2.00
118	Ed Rogers	2.00
119	Wilson Betemit	2.00
120	Mike Rivera	2.00
121	Mark Prior	6.00
122	Roberto Clemente	6.00
123	Roberto Clemente	6.00
124	Roberto Clemente	6.00
125	Roberto Clemente	6.00
126	Roberto Clemente	6.00
127	Babe Ruth	10.00
128	Ted Williams	8.00
129	Andre Dawson	2.00
130	Eddie Murray	3.00
131	Juan Marichal	3.00
132	Kirby Puckett	5.00
133	Alan Trammell	2.00
134	Bobby Doerr	2.00
135	Carlton Fisk	3.00
136	Eddie Mathews	4.00
137	Mike Schmidt	6.00
138	Jim "Catfish" Hunter	2.00
139	Nolan Ryan	10.00
140	George Brett	6.00
141	Gary Carter	2.00
142	Paul Molitor	4.00
143	Lou Gehrig	8.00
144	Ryne Sandberg	5.00
145	Tony Gwynn	5.00
146	Ron Santo	2.00
147	Cal Ripken Jr.	10.00
148	Al Kaline	4.00
149	Bo Jackson	3.00
150	Don Mattingly	8.00

Bronze Foil

Cards 1-100:	1-2X
Cards 101-150:	.5X
Inserted 1:6	
Gold Foil (1-100):	4-8X
Gold Foil (101-150):	2-3X
Production 100 Sets	
Silver Foil (1-100):	3-4X
Silver Foil (101-150):	1-2X
Production 400 Sets	

Diamond Cut

		NM/M
Common Signature (1-30):		5.00
1	Vladimir Guerrero/400	30.00
2	Mark Prior/400	50.00
3	Victor Martinez/500	10.00
4	Marlon Byrd/500	15.00
5	Bud Smith/400	10.00
6	Joe Mays/500	10.00
7	Troy Glaus/500	20.00
8	Ron Santo/500	15.00
9	Roy Oswalt/500	20.00
10	Angel Berroa/500	10.00
11	Mark Buehrle/500	15.00
12	John Buck/500	10.00
13	Barry Larkin/250	40.00
14	Gary Carter/300	30.00
15	Mark Teixeira/300	25.00
16	Alan Trammell/500	20.00
17	Kazuhisa Ishii/100	65.00
18	Rafael Palmeiro/125	50.00
19	Austin Kearns/500	25.00
20	Joe Torre/125	40.00
21	J.D. Drew/400	20.00
22	So Taguchi/400	20.00
23	Juan Marichal/500	15.00
24	Bobby Doerr/500	20.00
25	Carlos Beltran/500	10.00
26	Robert Fick/500	10.00
27	Albert Pujols/200	70.00
28	Shannon Stewart/500	10.00
29	Antonio Perez/500	10.00
30	Wilson Betemit/500	10.00
Jerseys (31-80):		
31	Alex Rodriguez/500	15.00
32	Curt Schilling/500	8.00
33	George Brett/300	30.00
34	Hideo Nomo/100	40.00
35	Ivan Rodriguez/500	8.00
36	Don Mattingly/200	40.00
37	Joe Mays/500	5.00
38	Lance Berkman/400	5.00
39	Tony Gwynn/500	10.00
40	Darin Erstad/400	5.00
41	Adrian Beltre/400	5.00
42	Frank Thomas/500	8.00
43	Cal Ripken Jr./300	30.00
44	Jose Vidro/500	5.00
45	Randy Johnson/300	8.00
46	Carlos Delgado/500	6.00
47	Roger Clemens/400	20.00
48	Luis Gonzalez/500	5.00
49	Marlon Byrd/500	6.00
50	Carlton Fisk/500	8.00
51	Manny Ramirez/500	8.00
52	Vladimir Guerrero/500	8.00
53	Barry Larkin/500	8.00
54	Aramis Ramirez/500	5.00
55	Todd Helton/300	8.00
56	Carlos Beltran/250	5.00
57	Jeff Bagwell/250	8.00
58	Larry Walker/500	5.00
59	Al Kaline/200	25.00
60	Chipper Jones/500	8.00
61	Bernie Williams/500	6.00
62	Bud Smith/500	5.00
63	Edgar Martinez/500	5.00
64	Pedro Martinez/500	8.00
65	Andre Dawson/200	6.00
66	Mike Piazza/100	40.00
67	Barry Zito/500	6.00
68	Bo Jackson/300	8.00
69	Nolan Ryan/400	50.00
70	Troy Glaus/500	6.00
71	Jorge Posada/500	8.00
72	Ted Williams/100	200.00
73	Nomar Garciaparra/500	15.00
74	"Catfish" Hunter/100	25.00
75	Gary Carter/500	8.00
76	Craig Biggio/500	8.00
77	Andruw Jones/500	8.00
78	Rickey Henderson/250	30.00
79	Greg Maddux/400	15.00
80	Kerry Wood/500	10.00
Bats (81-100):		
81	Alex Rodriguez/500	20.00
82	Don Mattingly/425	30.00
83	Craig Biggio/500	5.00
84	Kazuhisa Ishii/375	8.00
85	Eddie Murray/500	8.00
86	Carlton Fisk/500	8.00
87	Tsuyoshi Shinjo/500	5.00
88	Bo Jackson/500	10.00
89	Eddie Mathews/100	30.00
90	Chipper Jones/500	8.00
91	Adam Dunn/375	6.00
92	Tony Gwynn/200	10.00
93	Kirby Puckett/500	15.00
94	Andre Dawson/500	5.00
95	Bernie Williams/500	6.00
96	Roberto Clemente/00	70.00
97	Babe Ruth/100	250.00
98	Roberto Alomar/500	8.00
99	Frank Thomas/500	8.00
100	So Taguchi/500	6.00

DK Originals

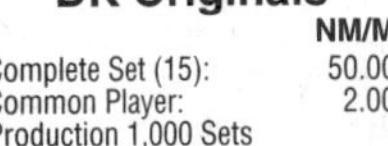

		NM/M
Complete Set (15):		50.00
Common Player:		2.00
Production 1,000 Sets		
1	Alex Rodriguez	7.00
2	Kazuhisa Ishii	2.00
3	Pedro Martinez	3.00
4	Nomar Garciaparra	6.00
5	Albert Pujols	6.00
6	Chipper Jones	5.00
7	So Taguchi	2.00
8	Jeff Bagwell	3.00
9	Vladimir Guerrero	3.00
10	Derek Jeter	8.00
11	Sammy Sosa	6.00
12	Ichiro Suzuki	6.00
13	Barry Bonds	8.00
14	Jason Giambi	3.00
15	Mike Piazza	6.00

Heritage Collection

		NM/M
Complete Set (25):		100.00
Common Player:		2.00
Inserted 1:23		
1	Lou Gehrig	8.00
2	Nolan Ryan	10.00
3	Ryne Sandberg	4.00
4	Ted Williams	8.00
5	Roberto Clemente	8.00
6	Mike Schmidt	6.00
7	Roger Clemens	5.00
8	Kirby Puckett	4.00
9	Andre Dawson	2.00
10	Carlton Fisk	2.00
11	Don Mattingly	8.00
12	Juan Marichal	2.00
13	George Brett	8.00
14	Bo Jackson	3.00
15	Eddie Mathews	3.00
16	Randy Johnson	3.00
17	Alan Trammell	2.00
18	Tony Gwynn	4.00
19	Paul Molitor	3.00
20	Barry Bonds	10.00
21	Eddie Murray	3.00
22	Jim "Catfish" Hunter	2.00
23	Rickey Henderson	3.00
24	Cal Ripken Jr.	10.00
25	Babe Ruth	10.00

Ramly T204

		NM/M
Complete Set (25):		120.00
Common Player:		3.00
Production 1,000 Sets		
1	Vladimir Guerrero	4.00
2	Jeff Bagwell	4.00
3	Barry Bonds	15.00
4	Rickey Henderson	4.00
5	Mike Piazza	8.00
6	Derek Jeter	15.00
7	Kazuhisa Ishii	3.00
8	Ichiro Suzuki	10.00
9	Chipper Jones	5.00
10	Sammy Sosa	8.00
11	Don Mattingly	10.00
12	Shawn Green	3.00
13	Nomar Garciaparra	10.00
14	Luis Gonzalez	3.00
15	Albert Pujols	8.00
16	Cal Ripken Jr.	15.00
17	Todd Helton	4.00
18	Hideo Nomo	3.00
19	Alex Rodriguez	10.00
20	So Taguchi	3.00
21	Lance Berkman	3.00
22	Tony Gwynn	5.00
23	Roger Clemens	6.00
24	Jason Giambi	4.00
25	Ken Griffey Jr.	8.00

Recollection Collection

NM/M
Common Player:
22 Fred Lynn 87 DK/28 15.00
30 Roy Oswalt 01 RDK Black/48 20.00
47 Alan Trammell 88 DK/110 30.00

Timeline

NM/M
Complete Set (10): 60.00
Common Card: 3.00
Inserted 1:60
1 Lou Gehrig, Don Mattingly 10.00
2 Hideo Nomo, Ichiro Suzuki 6.00
3 Cal Ripken Jr., Alex Rodriguez 10.00
4 Mike Schmidt, Scott Rolen 8.00
5 Ichiro Suzuki, Albert Pujols 8.00
6 Curt Schilling, Randy Johnson 5.00
7 Chipper Jones, Eddie Mathews 5.00
8 Lou Gehrig, Cal Ripken Jr. 10.00
9 Derek Jeter, Roger Clemens 10.00
10 Kazuhiko Ishimine, So Taguchi 3.00

LCS Programs

A perforated sheet of Diamond King cards was inserted into some of the programs sold for the American and National League Championship Series. The 8-1/2" x 11" sheet features eight player cards and a header card advertising the brand. Each 2-1/2" x 3-1/2" card is perforated on all sides and differs from the regularly issued version only in the card number on back. Sheet cards have either an "ALCS-" or "NLCS-" prefix to the number. Other programs could be found with similar sheets of Donruss Originals, Donruss Studio or Playoff Piece of the Game cards.

NM/M
Complete Sheet Set (2): 20.00
Common Player: .50
ALCS SHEET 10.00
1 Cal Ripken Jr. 3.00
2 Nomar Garciaparra 1.50
3 Roger Clemens 1.25
4 Alex Rodriguez 2.00
5 Troy Glaus 1.00
6 Miguel Tejada .50
7 Alfonso Soriano 1.00
8 Ted Williams 2.50
-- Header Card .10
NLCS SHEET 10.00
1 Randy Johnson 1.00
2 Josh Beckett .75
3 Mike Piazza 1.50
4 Greg Maddux 1.25
5 Lance Berkman .50
6 Mark Prior 2.00
7 Adam Dunn 1.00
8 Tony Gwynn 1.25
-- Header Card .10

2002 Donruss Elite Samples

Each June 2002 issue of Beckett Baseball Card Monthly included a sample Elite Series card rubber-cemented inside. The cards differ from the issued version only in the appearance on back of a (usually) silver-foil "SAMPLE" notation. Some cards were produced with the overprint in gold-foil, in much more limited quantities. Cards #1-100 from the set can be found in this Sample version.

NM/M
Common Player: .25
Stars: 1.5-2X
Gold: 10X

2002 Donruss Elite

NM/M
Complete Set (200):
Common Player: .25
Common (101-150): 2.00
Inserted 1:10
Common (151-200): 3.00
Production 1,500
Pack (5): 3.00
Box (20): 50.00
1 Vladimir Guerrero .75
2 Bernie Williams .35
3 Ichiro Suzuki 1.50
4 Roger Clemens 1.25
5 Greg Maddux 1.00
6 Fred McGriff .25
7 Jermaine Dye .25
8 Ken Griffey Jr. 1.50
9 Todd Helton .75
10 Torii Hunter .40
11 Pat Burrell .40
12 Chipper Jones 1.00
13 Ivan Rodriguez .50
14 Roy Oswalt .40
15 Shannon Stewart .25
16 Magglio Ordonez .40
17 Lance Berkman .25
18 Mark Mulder .25
19 Al Leiter .25
20 Sammy Sosa 1.50
21 Scott Rolen .75
22 Aramis Ramirez .25
23 Alfonso Soriano .75
24 Phil Nevin .25
25 Barry Bonds 2.50
26 Joe Mays .25
27 Jeff Kent .25
28 Mark Quinn .25
29 Adrian Beltre .25
30 Freddy Garcia .25
31 Pedro J. Martinez .75
32 Darryl Kile .25
33 Mike Cameron .25
34 Frank Catalanotto .25
35 Jose Vidro .25
36 Jim Thome .25
37 Javy Lopez .25
38 Paul Konerko .25
39 Jeff Bagwell .75
40 Curt Schilling .40
41 Miguel Tejada .40
42 Jim Edmonds .25
43 Ellis Burks .25
44 Mark Grace .35
45 Robb Nen .25
46 Jeff Conine .25
47 Derek Jeter 2.50
48 Mike Lowell .25
49 Javier Vazquez .25
50 Manny Ramirez .75
51 Bartolo Colon .25
52 Carlos Beltran .50
53 Tim Hudson .40
54 Rafael Palmeiro .65
55 Jimmy Rollins .50
56 Andruw Jones .75
57 Orlando Cabrera .25
58 Dean Palmer .25
59 Bret Boone .25
60 Carlos Febles .25
61 Ben Grieve .25
62 Richie Sexson .25
63 Alex Rodriguez 2.00
64 Juan Pierre .25
65 Bobby Higginson .25
66 Barry Zito .40
67 Raul Mondesi .25
68 Albert Pujols 2.00
69 Omar Vizquel .25
70 Bobby Abreu .25
71 Corey Koskie .25
72 Tom Glavine .40
73 Paul LoDuca .25
74 Terrence Long .25
75 Matt Morris .25
76 Andy Pettitte .40
77 Rich Aurilia .25
78 Todd Walker .25
79 John Olerud .25
80 Mike Sweeney .25
81 Ray Durham .25
82 Fernando Vina .25
83 Nomar Garciaparra 1.50
84 Mariano Rivera .35
85 Mike Piazza 1.50
86 Mark Buehrle .25
87 Adam Dunn .50
88 Luis Gonzalez .35
89 Richard Hidalgo .25
90 Brad Radke .25
91 Russ Ortiz .25
92 Brian Giles .25
93 Billy Wagner .25
94 Cliff Floyd .25
95 Eric Milton .25
96 Bud Smith .25
97 Wade Miller .25
98 Jon Lieber .25
99 Derrek Lee .25
100 Jose Cruz Jr. .25
101 Dmitri Young 2.00
102 Mo Vaughn 2.00
103 Tino Martinez 2.00
104 Larry Walker 2.50
105 Chuck Knoblauch 2.00
106 Troy Glaus 3.00
107 Jason Giambi 4.00
108 Travis Fryman 2.00
109 Josh Beckett 4.00
110 Edgar Martinez 2.00
111 Tim Salmon 2.00
112 C.C. Sabathia 2.00
113 Randy Johnson 5.00
114 Juan Gonzalez 4.00
115 Carlos Delgado 4.00
116 Hideo Nomo 4.00
117 Kerry Wood 4.00
118 Brian Jordan 2.00
119 Carlos Pena 2.00
120 Roger Cedeno 2.00
121 Chan Ho Park 2.00
122 Rafael Furcal 2.00
123 Frank Thomas 4.00
124 Mike Mussina 4.00
125 Rickey Henderson 5.00
126 Sean Casey 2.00
127 Barry Larkin 2.00
128 Kazuhiro Sasaki 2.00
129 Moises Alou 2.00
130 Jeff Cirillo 2.00
131 Jason Kendall 2.00
132 Gary Sheffield 3.00
133 Ryan Klesko 2.00
134 Kevin Brown 2.00
135 Darin Erstad 2.00
136 Roberto Alomar 3.00
137 Brad Fullmer 2.00
138 Eric Chavez 2.00
139 Ben Sheets 2.00
140 Trot Nixon 2.00
141 Garret Anderson 2.00
142 Shawn Green 2.50
143 Troy Percival 2.00
144 Craig Biggio 2.50
145 Jorge Posada 2.50
146 J.D. Drew 3.00
147 Johnny Damon 2.00
148 Jeromy Burnitz 2.00
149 Robin Ventura 2.00
150 Aaron Sele 2.00
151 Cam Esslinger **RC** 3.00
152 Ben Howard **RC** 4.00
153 Brandon Backe **RC** 3.00
154 Jorge De La Rosa **RC** 3.00
155 Austin Kearns 5.00
156 Carlos Zambrano 3.00
157 Kyle Kane **RC** 3.00
158 So Taguchi **RC** 5.00
159 Brian Mallette **RC** 3.00
160 Brett Jodie 3.00
161 Elio Serrano **RC** 3.00
162 Joe Thurston 3.00
163 Kevin Olsen 3.00
164 Rodrigo Rosario **RC** 4.00
165 Matt Guerrier 3.00
166 Anderson Machado **RC** 5.00
167 Bert Snow 3.00
168 Franklyn German **RC** 3.00
169 Brandon Claussen 3.00
170 Jason Romano 3.00
171 Jorge Padilla **RC** 5.00
172 Jose Cueto 3.00
173 Allan Simpson **RC** 3.00
174 Doug DeVore **RC** 3.00
175 Justin Duchscherer 3.00
176 Josh Pearce 3.00
177 Steve Bechler **RC** 3.00
178 Josh Phelps 3.00
179 Juan Diaz 3.00
180 Victor Alvarez **RC** 3.00
181 Ramon Vazquez 3.00
182 Mike Rivera 3.00
183 Kazuhisa Ishii **RC** 6.00
184 Henry Mateo 3.00
185 Travis Hughes **RC** 5.00
186 Zach Day 3.00
187 Brad Voyles 3.00
188 Sean Douglass 3.00
189 Nick Neugebauer 3.00
190 Tom Shearn **RC** 3.00
191 Eric Cyr **RC** 3.00
192 Adam Johnson 3.00
193 Michael Cuddyer 3.00
194 Erik Bedard 3.00
195 Mark Ellis 3.00
196 Carlos Hernandez 3.00
197 Deivi Santos 3.00
198 Morgan Ensberg 3.00
199 Ryan Jamison **RC** 3.00
200 Cody Ransom 3.00

Aspirations

1-100 print run 26-50: 15-30X
1-100 p/r 51-80: 8-15X
101-150 p/r 26-50: 1.5-3X
101-150 p/r 51-99: 1-2X

Status

1-100 print run 36-70: 10-20X
1-100 p/r 71-100: 5-10X
101-150 p/r 36-70: 1-2X
101-150 p/r 71-100: 1X

All-Star Salutes

NM/M
Common Player: 1.00
Century: 1-2X
Production 100
1 Ichiro Suzuki 5.00
2 Tony Gwynn 4.00
3 Magglio Ordonez 1.50
4 Cal Ripken Jr. 8.00
5 Tony Gwynn 4.00
6 Kazuhiro Sasaki 1.00
7 Freddy Garcia 1.00
8 Luis Gonzalez 1.00
9 Lance Berkman 1.00
10 Derek Jeter 8.00
11 Chipper Jones 4.00
12 Randy Johnson 3.00
13 Andruw Jones 3.00
14 Pedro J. Martinez 3.00
15 Jim Thome 1.00
16 Rafael Palmeiro 2.50
17 Barry Larkin 1.00
18 Ivan Rodriguez 2.50
19 Omar Vizquel 1.00
20 Edgar Martinez 1.00
21 Larry Walker 1.00
22 Javy Lopez 1.00
23 Mariano Rivera 1.25
24 Frank Thomas 3.00
25 Greg Maddux 4.00

Back to the Future

NM/M
Complete Set (24): 75.00
Common Player: 2.00
Duals 500 produced, singles 1,000.
1 Scott Rolen, Marlon Byrd 5.00
2 Joe Crede, Frank Thomas 6.00
3 Lance Berkman, Jeff Bagwell 6.00
4 Marcus Giles, Chipper Jones 10.00
5 Shawn Green, Paul LoDuca 4.00
7 Kerry Wood, Juan Cruz 4.00
8 Vladimir Guerrero, Orlando Cabrera 6.00
9 Scott Rolen 3.00
10 Marlon Byrd 2.00
11 Frank Thomas 4.00
12 Joe Crede 2.00
13 Jeff Bagwell 4.00
14 Lance Berkman 2.00
15 Chipper Jones 6.00
16 Marcus Giles 2.00
17 Shawn Green 2.50
18 Paul LoDuca 2.00
19 Jim Edmonds 2.00
21 Kerry Wood 3.00
22 Juan Cruz 2.00
23 Vladimir Guerrero 4.00
24 Orlando Cabrera 2.00

Back to the Future Threads

NM/M
Common Card: 10.00
Duals 50 produced, singles 100.
1 Scott Rolen, Marlon Byrd 30.00
2 Joe Crede, Frank Thomas 40.00
3 Lance Berkman, Jeff Bagwell 40.00
4 Marcus Giles, Chipper Jones 50.00
5 Shawn Green, Paul LoDuca 30.00
7 Kerry Wood, Juan Cruz 35.00
8 Vladimir Guerrero, Orlando Cabrera 40.00
9 Scott Rolen 15.00
10 Marlon Byrd 20.00
11 Frank Thomas 25.00
12 Joe Crede 10.00
13 Jeff Bagwell 25.00
14 Lance Berkman 15.00
15 Chipper Jones 25.00
16 Marcus Giles 10.00
17 Shawn Green 15.00
18 Paul LoDuca 10.00
19 Jim Edmonds 10.00
20 So Taguchi 50.00
21 Kerry Wood 15.00
22 Juan Cruz 10.00
23 Vladimir Guerrero 25.00
24 Orlando Cabrera 10.00

Back 2 Back Jacks

NM/M
Common Card: 10.00
Dual Production 75
Single Production 150
1 Ivan Rodriguez, Alex Rodriguez 40.00
2 Kirby Puckett, Dave Winfield 50.00
3 Ted Williams, Nomar Garciaparra 150.00
4 Jeff Bagwell, Craig Biggio 25.00
5 Eddie Murray, Cal Ripken Jr. 125.00
6 Andruw Jones, Chipper Jones 25.00
7 Roberto Clemente, Willie Stargell 120.00
8 Lou Gehrig, Don Mattingly 180.00
9 Larry Walker, Todd Helton 20.00
10 Manny Ramirez, Trot Nixon 25.00
11 Alex Rodriguez 30.00
12 Ivan Rodriguez 15.00
13 Kirby Puckett 40.00
14 Dave Winfield 15.00
15 Ted Williams 100.00
16 Nomar Garciaparra 40.00
17 Jeff Bagwell 15.00
18 Craig Biggio 10.00
19 Eddie Murray 20.00
20 Cal Ripken Jr. 60.00
21 Andruw Jones 10.00
22 Chipper Jones 20.00
23 Roberto Clemente 80.00
25 Lou Gehrig 160.00
26 Don Mattingly 65.00
27 Larry Walker 10.00
28 Todd Helton 15.00
29 Manny Ramirez 20.00
30 Trot Nixon 10.00

Career Bests

NM/M
Common Player: 2.00
1 Albert Pujols/1,013 8.00
2 Alex Rodriguez/52 20.00
3 Alex Rodriguez/135 15.00
4 Andruw Jones/104 6.00
5 Barry Bonds/73 25.00
6 Barry Bonds/1,379 10.00
7 Barry Bonds/177 20.00
8 C.C. Sabathia/171 4.00
9 Carlos Beltran/876 2.00
10 Chipper Jones/330 6.00
11 Derek Jeter/900 15.00
12 Eric Chavez/114 4.00
13 Frank Catalanotto/330 2.00
14 Ichiro Suzuki/838 10.00
15 Ichiro Suzuki/127 15.00
17 J.D. Drew/27 20.00
18 J.D. Drew/1,027 2.00
19 Jason Giambi/660 5.00
20 Jim Thome/49 25.00
21 Jim Thome/624 4.00
22 Jorge Posada/95 8.00
23 Jose Cruz Jr/856 2.00
24 Kazuhiro Sasaki/45 15.00
25 Kerry Wood/336 5.00
26 Lance Berkman/1,050 3.00
27 Magglio Ordonez/382 3.00
28 Mark Mulder/345 2.00
29 Pat Burrell/27 20.00
30 Pat Burrell/469 3.00
31 Randy Johnson/372 6.00
33 Richie Sexson/547 3.00
34 Roberto Alomar/956 3.00
35 Sammy Sosa/160 12.00
36 Sammy Sosa/1,174 6.00
37 Shawn Green/125 4.00
39 Trot Nixon/150 3.00
40 Troy Glaus/108 5.00

Passing the Torch

NM/M
Common Card: 4.00
Dual 500, single 1,000 produced.
1 Fergie Jenkins, Mark Prior 10.00
2 Nolan Ryan, Roy Oswalt 25.00
3 Ozzie Smith, J.D. Drew 8.00
4 George Brett, Carlos Beltran 15.00
5 Kirby Puckett, Michael Cuddyer 10.00
6 Johnny Bench, Adam Dunn 8.00
7 Duke Snider, Paul LoDuca 6.00
8 Tony Gwynn, Xavier Nady 10.00
9 Fergie Jenkins 4.00
10 Mark Prior 8.00
11 Nolan Ryan 15.00
12 Roy Oswalt 5.00
13 Ozzie Smith 6.00
14 J.D. Drew 4.00
15 George Brett 10.00
16 Carlos Beltran 6.00

17 Kirby Puckett 6.00
18 Michael Cuddyer 4.00
19 Johnny Bench 6.00
20 Adam Dunn 6.00
21 Duke Snider 6.00
22 Paul LoDuca 4.00
23 Tony Gwynn 6.00
24 Xavier Nady 4.00

Passing the Torch Autographs

NM/M
Common Autograph: 15.00
1 Ferguson Jenkins, Mark Prior/50 100.00
2 Nolan Ryan, Roy Oswalt/50 180.00
3 Ozzie Smith, J.D. Drew/50 125.00
4 George Brett, Carlos Beltran/25 300.00
5 Kirby Puckett, Michael Cuddyer/50 100.00
6 Johnny Bench, Adam Dunn/50 100.00
7 Duke Snider, Paul LoDuca/50 80.00
8 Tony Gwynn, Xavier Nady/50 120.00
9 Fergie Jenkins/50 40.00
10 Mark Prior/100 80.00
11 Nolan Ryan/100 125.00
12 Roy Oswalt/100 25.00
13 Ozzie Smith/25 160.00
14 J.D. Drew/100 30.00
15 George Brett/25 300.00
16 Carlos Beltran/100 40.00
17 Kirby Puckett/25 150.00
18 Michael Cuddyer/100 15.00
19 Johnny Bench/100 50.00
20 Adam Dunn/50 40.00
21 Duke Snider/100 30.00
22 Paul LoDuca/100 15.00
23 Tony Gwynn/100 50.00
24 Xavier Nady/100 15.00

Recollection Collection

NM/M
Common Player:
2 Alfredo Amezaga 01/50 15.00
13 Orlando Hudson 01/50 20.00
18 Antonio Perez 01/50 15.00
20 Mike Rivera 01/50 15.00
22 Claudio Vargas 01/50 15.00
23 Martin Vargas 01/50 15.00

Throwback Threads

NM/M
Common Card: 15.00
Dual 50, single 100 produced.
1 Manny Ramirez, Ted Williams 125.00
2 Mike Piazza, Carlton Fisk 50.00
3 George Brett, Bo Jackson 125.00
4 Randy Johnson, Curt Schilling 40.00
5 Don Mattingly, Lou Gehrig 250.00
6 Bernie Williams, Dave Winfield 25.00
7 Rickey Henderson 75.00
8 Paul Molitor, Robin Yount 75.00
9 J.D. Drew, Stan Musial 100.00
10 Andre Dawson, Ryne Sandberg 100.00
11 Babe Ruth, Reggie Jackson 325.00
12 Brooks Robinson, Cal Ripken Jr. 120.00
13 Ted Williams, Nomar Garciaparra 125.00
14 Shawn Green, Jackie Robinson 80.00
15 Tony Gwynn, Cal Ripken Jr. 120.00
16 Ted Williams 75.00
17 Manny Ramirez 20.00
18 Carlton Fisk 25.00
19 Mike Piazza 20.00
20 Bo Jackson 20.00
21 George Brett 50.00
22 Curt Schilling 20.00
23 Randy Johnson 20.00
24 Don Mattingly 50.00
25 Lou Gehrig 200.00
26 Bernie Williams 15.00
27 Dave Winfield 15.00
29 Rickey Henderson 40.00
30 Robin Yount 30.00
31 Paul Molitor 25.00
32 Stan Musial 65.00
33 J.D. Drew 15.00
34 Andre Dawson 15.00
35 Ryne Sandberg 50.00
36 Babe Ruth 250.00
37 Reggie Jackson 25.00
38 Brooks Robinson 25.00
39 Cal Ripken Jr. 75.00
40 Nomar Garciaparra 40.00
41 Jackie Robinson 80.00
42 Shawn Green 15.00
43 Pedro J. Martinez 20.00
44 Nolan Ryan 80.00
45 Kazuhiro Sasaki 15.00
46 Tony Gwynn 25.00
47 Carlton Fisk 20.00
48 Cal Ripken Jr. 75.00
49 Rod Carew 20.00
50 Nolan Ryan 80.00
51 Alex Rodriguez 25.00
52 Greg Maddux 25.00
53 Pedro J. Martinez 20.00
54 Rickey Henderson 30.00
55 Rod Carew 20.00
56 Roberto Clemente 100.00
57 Hideo Nomo 40.00
58 Rickey Henderson 40.00
59 Dave Parker 15.00
60 Eddie Mathews 25.00
61 Eddie Murray 20.00
62 Nolan Ryan 80.00
63 Tom Seaver 25.00
64 Roger Clemens 40.00
65 Rickey Henderson 40.00

Throwback Threads Autographs

Production 5-25

Turn of the Century

NM/M
Common Player: 8.00
154 Jorge De La Rosa/50 8.00
156 Carlos Zambrano/50 8.00
157 Kyle Kane/50 8.00
158 So Taguchi/25 15.00
159 Brian Mallette/50 8.00
160 Brett Jodie/50 8.00
165 Matt Guerrier/50 8.00
168 Franklyn German/50 8.00
169 Brandon Claussen/50 15.00
171 Jorge Padilla/50 10.00
172 Jose Cueto/50 8.00
176 Josh Pearce/50 8.00
177 Steve Bechler/50 8.00
178 Josh Phelps/50 8.00
180 Victor Alvarez/50 8.00
182 Michael Rivera/50 8.00
183 Kazuhisa Ishii/125 20.00
184 Henry Mateo/50 8.00
186 Zach Day/50 8.00
189 Nick Neugebauer/100 8.00
192 Adam Johnson/125 8.00
193 Michael Cuddyer/50 8.00
195 Mark Ellis/25 10.00
196 Carlos Hernandez/150 8.00
198 Morgan Ensberg/50 8.00
200 Cody Ransom/150 8.00

Turn of the Century Autographs

NM/M
Common Autograph: 10.00
151 Cam Esslinger/150 10.00
152 Ben Howard/150 10.00
153 Brandon Backe/150 15.00
154 Jorge De La Rosa/100 10.00
155 Austin Kearns/150 15.00
156 Carlos Zambrano/100 20.00
157 Kyle Kane/100 10.00
158 So Taguchi/125 20.00
159 Brian Mallette/100 10.00
160 Brett Jodie/100 10.00
161 Elio Serrano/150 10.00
162 Joe Thurston/150 10.00
163 Kevin Olsen/150 10.00
164 Rodrigo Rosario/150 10.00
165 Matt Guerrier/100 10.00
166 Anderson Machado/150 10.00
167 Bert Snow/150 10.00
168 Franklyn German/100 10.00
169 Brandon Claussen/100 15.00
170 Jason Romano/150 10.00
171 Jorge Padilla/100 15.00
172 Jose Cueto/100 10.00
173 Allan Simpson/150 10.00
174 Doug DeVore/150 15.00
175 Justin Duchscherer/150 10.00
176 Josh Pearce/100 10.00
177 Steve Bechler/100 10.00
178 Josh Phelps/100 15.00
179 Juan Diaz/150 10.00
180 Victor Alvarez/100 10.00
181 Ramon Vazquez/150 10.00
182 Michael Rivera/100 10.00
183 Kazuhisa Ishii/25 150.00
184 Henry Mateo/100 10.00
185 Travis Hughes/150 10.00
186 Zach Day/100 10.00
187 Brad Voyles/150 10.00
188 Sean Douglass/150 10.00
189 Nick Neugebauer/50 10.00
190 Tom Shearn/150 10.00
191 Eric Cyr/150 10.00
192 Adam Johnson/25 10.00
193 Michael Cuddyer/100 10.00
194 Erik Bedard/150 20.00
195 Mark Ellis/125 10.00
197 Deivis Santos/150 10.00
198 Morgan Ensberg/100 10.00
199 Ryan Jamison/150 10.00

2002 Donruss Fan Club

NM/M
Complete Set (300):
Common Player: .25
Common (201-260): 3.00
Production 1,350
Common (261-300): 2.00
Production 2,025
Pack (5): 3.50
Box (20): 60.00
1 Alex Rodriguez 2.00
2 Pedro Martinez .75
3 Vladimir Guerrero .75
4 Jim Edmonds .25
5 Derek Jeter 2.50
6 Johnny Damon .40
7 Rafael Furcal .25
8 Cal Ripken Jr. 2.50
9 Brad Radke .25
10 Bret Boone .25
11 Pat Burrell .50
12 Roy Oswalt .50
13 Cliff Floyd .25
14 Robin Ventura .25
15 Frank Thomas .75
16 Mariano Rivera .35
17 Paul LoDuca .25
18 Geoff Jenkins .25
19 Tony Gwynn 1.00
20 Chipper Jones 1.00
21 Eric Chavez .40
22 Kerry Wood .60
23 Jorge Posada .35
24 J.D. Drew .40
25 Garret Anderson .25
26 Javier Vazquez .25
27 Kenny Lofton .25
28 Mike Mussina .45
29 Paul Konerko .25
30 Bernie Williams .45
31 Eric Milton .25
32 Craig Wilson .25
33 Paul O'Neill .25
34 Dmitri Young .25
35 Andres Galarraga .25
36 Gary Sheffield .40
37 Ben Grieve .25
38 Scott Rolen .75
39 Mark Grace .35
40 Albert Pujols 2.00
41 Barry Zito .40
42 Edgar Martinez .25
43 Jarrod Washburn .25
44 Juan Pierre .25
45 Mark Buehrle .25
46 Larry Walker .25
47 Trot Nixon .25
48 Wade Miller .25
49 Robert Fick .25
50 Sean Casey .40
51 Joe Mays .25
52 Brad Fullmer .25
53 Chan Ho Park .25
54 Carlos Delgado .50
55 Phil Nevin .25
56 Mike Cameron .25
57 Raul Mondesi .25
58 Roberto Alomar .40
59 Ryan Klesko .25
60 Andruw Jones .75
61 Gabe Kapler .25
62 Darin Erstad .65
63 Cristian Guzman .25
64 Kazuhiro Sasaki .25
65 Doug Mientkiewicz .25
66 Sammy Sosa 1.50
67 Mike Hampton .25
68 Rickey Henderson .75
69 Mark Mulder .35
70 Jeff Conine .25
71 Freddy Garcia .25
72 Ivan Rodriguez .65
73 Terrence Long .25
74 Adam Dunn .50
75 Moises Alou .25
76 Todd Helton .75
77 Preston Wilson .25
78 Roger Cedeno .25
79 Tony Armas Jr. .25
80 Manny Ramirez .75
81 Jose Vidro .25
82 Randy Johnson .75
83 Richie Sexson .25
84 Troy Glaus .75
85 Kevin Brown .35
86 Woody Williams .25
87 Adrian Beltre .40
88 Brian Giles .25
89 Jermaine Dye .25
90 Craig Biggio .25
91 Richard Hidalgo .25
92 Magglio Ordonez .40
93 Al Leiter .25
94 Jeff Kent .25
95 Curt Schilling .50
96 Tim Hudson .50
97 Fred McGriff .25
98 Barry Larkin .25
99 Jim Thome .25
100 Tom Glavine .40
101 Alfonso Soriano .75
102 Jamie Moyer .25
103 Vinny Castilla .25
104 Rich Aurilia .25
105 Matt Morris .25
106 Rafael Palmeiro .65
107 Joe Crede .25
108 Barry Bonds 2.50
109 Robert Person .25
110 Nomar Garciaparra 1.50
111 Brandon Duckworth .25
112 Russ Ortiz .25
113 Jeff Weaver .25
114 Carlos Beltran .50
115 Ellis Burks .25
116 Jeremy Giambi .25
117 Carlos Lee .25
118 Ken Griffey Jr. 1.50
119 Torii Hunter .40
120 Andy Petitte .40
121 Jose Canseco .40
122 Charles Johnson .25
123 Nick Johnson .25
124 Luis Gonzalez .35
125 Rondell White .25
126 Miguel Tejada .50
127 Jose Cruz Jr. .25
128 Brent Abernathy .25
129 Scott Brosius .25
130 Jon Lieber .25
131 John Smoltz .25
132 Mike Sweeney .25
133 Shannon Stewart .25
134 Derrek Lee .25
135 Brian Jordan .25
136 Rusty Greer .25
137 Mike Piazza 1.50
138 Billy Wagner .25
139 Shawn Green .35
140 Orlando Cabrera .25
141 Jeff Bagwell .75
142 Aaron Sele .25
143 Hideo Nomo .75
144 Marlon Anderson .25
145 Todd Walker .25
146 Bobby Higginson .25
147 Ichiro Suzuki 2.00
148 Juan Uribe .25
149 Jason Kendall .25
150 Mark Quinn .25
151 Ben Sheets .25
152 Paul Abbott .25
153 Aubrey Huff .25
154 Greg Maddux 1.00
155 Darryl Kile .25
156 John Burkett .25
157 Juan Gonzalez .75
158 Javy Lopez .25
159 Aramis Ramirez .25
160 Lance Berkman .25
161 David Cone .25
162 Edgar Renteria .25
163 Roger Clemens 1.25
164 Frank Catalanotto .25
165 Bartolo Colon .25
166 Mark McGwire 2.00
167 Jay Gibbons .25
168 Tony Clark .25
169 Tsuyoshi Shinjo .25
170 Brad Penny .25
171 Marcus Giles .25
172 Matt Williams .25
173 Bud Smith .25
174 Tino Martinez .25
175 Ryan Dempster .25
176 Jimmy Rollins .40
177 Edgardo Alfonzo .25
178 Jason Giambi .50
179 Aaron Boone .25
180 Matt Dunigan .25
181 Mike Lowell .25
182 Jose Ortiz .25
183 Johnny Estrada .25
184 Shane Reynolds .25
185 Joe Kennedy .25
186 Corey Patterson .25
187 Jeromy Burnitz .25
188 C.C. Sabathia .25
189 Doug Davis .25
190 Omar Vizquel .25
191 John Olerud .25
192 Dee Brown .25
193 Kip Wells .25
194 A.J. Burnett .25
195 Josh Towers .25
196 Jason Varitek .25
197 Jason Isringhausen .25
198 Fernando Vina .25
199 Ramon Ortiz .25
200 Bobby Abreu .25
201 Willie Harris 3.00
202 Angel Santos 3.00
203 Corky Miller 3.00
204 Mike Rivera 3.00
205 Justin Duchscherer 3.00
206 Rick Bauer 3.00
207 Angel Berroa 3.00
208 Juan Cruz 3.00
209 Dewon Brazelton 3.00
210 Mark Prior 10.00
211 Mark Teixeira 8.00
212 Geronimo Gil 3.00
213 Casey Fossum 3.00
214 Ken Harvey 3.00
215 Michael Cuddyer 3.00
216 Wilson Betemit 3.00
217 David Brous 3.00
218 Juan Pena 3.00
219 Travis Hafner 4.00
220 Erick Almonte 3.00
221 Morgan Ensberg 3.00
222 Martin Vargas 3.00
223 Brandon Berger 3.00
224 Zach Day 3.00
225 Brad Voyles 3.00
226 Jeremy Affeldt 3.00
227 Nick Neugebauer 3.00
228 Tim Redding 3.00
229 Adam Johnson 3.00
230 Doug DeVore **RC** 4.00
231 Cody Ransom 3.00
232 Marlon Byrd 3.00
233 Delvin James 3.00
234 Eric Munson 3.00
235 Dennis Tankersley 3.00
236 Josh Beckett 8.00
237 Bill Hall 3.00
238 Kevin Olsen 3.00
239 Francis Beltran **RC** 5.00
240 Antonio Perez 3.00
241 Orlando Hudson 3.00
242 Anderson Machado **RC** 6.00
243 Tom Shearn **RC** 5.00
244 Brian Mallette **RC** 4.00
245 Raul Chavez **RC** 4.00
246 Andy Pratt **RC** 4.00
247 Jorge De La Rosa **RC** 4.00
248 Jeff Deardorff **RC** 4.00
249 Ben Howard **RC** 4.00
250 Brandon Backe **RC** 4.00
251 Ed Rogers 3.00
252 Travis Hughes **RC** 5.00
253 Rodrigo Rosario **RC** 5.00
254 Alfredo Amezaga 3.00
255 Jorge Padilla **RC** 5.00
256 Victor Martinez 4.00
257 Steve Bechler **RC** 4.00
258 Chris Baker **RC** 4.00
259 Ryan Freel 3.00
260 Allan Simpson **RC** 3.00
261 Alex Rodriguez 6.00
262 Vladimir Guerrero 3.00
263 Bud Smith 2.00
264 Miguel Tejada 2.00
265 Craig Biggio 2.00
266 Luis Gonzalez 2.00
267 Ivan Rodriguez 3.00
268 C.C. Sabathia 2.00
269 Jeff Bagwell 3.00
270 Aramis Ramirez 2.00
271 Bobby Abreu 2.00
272 Rich Aurilia 2.00
273 Jason Giambi 3.00
274 Rickey Henderson 3.00
275 Wade Miller 2.00
276 Andruw Jones 3.00
277 Troy Glaus 3.00
278 Roy Oswalt 2.00
279 Tony Gwynn 3.00
280 Adam Dunn 3.00
281 Larry Walker 2.00
282 Jose Canseco 3.00
283 Todd Helton 3.00
284 Lance Berkman 2.00
285 Cal Ripken Jr. 10.00
286 Albert Pujols 8.00
287 Alfonso Soriano 3.00
288 Mark Mulder 2.00
289 Mike Hampton 2.00
290 Andres Galarraga 2.00
291 Barry Bonds 8.00
292 Ben Sheets 2.00
293 Ichiro Suzuki 6.00
294 J.D. Drew 2.00
295 Jose Ortiz 2.00
296 Kerry Wood 3.00
297 Mark McGwire 8.00
298 Mike Sweeney 2.00
299 Pat Burrell 3.00
300 Tim Hudson 3.00

Autographs

NM/M
Common Player: 5.00
Varying quantities produced
201 Willie Harris/500 5.00
203 Corky Miller/500 5.00
205 Justin Duchscherer/500 8.00
207 Angel Berroa/100 15.00
208 Juan Cruz/175 8.00
209 Dewon Brazelton/52 15.00
210 Mark Prior/425 40.00
211 Mark Teixeira/425 25.00
213 Casey Fossum/100 10.00
215 Michael Cuddyer/52 15.00
216 Wilson Betemit/500 8.00
217 David Brous/500 5.00
218 Juan A. Pena/188 8.00
219 Travis Hafner/375 10.00
221 Morgan Ensberg/52 15.00
222 Martin Vargas/500 5.00
223 Brandon Berger/500 5.00
224 Zach Day/500 5.00
225 Brad Voyles/500 5.00
226 Jeremy Affeldt/250 5.00
227 Nick Neugebauer/225 8.00
228 Tim Redding/500 8.00
229 Adam Johnson/425 5.00
230 Doug DeVore/300 8.00
231 Cody Ransom/500 5.00
232 Marlon Byrd/475 15.00
233 Delvin James/375 5.00
234 Eric Munson/325 8.00
235 Dennis Tankersley/500 5.00
238 Kevin Olsen/325 5.00
240 Antonio Perez/525 5.00
241 Orlando Hudson/525 10.00
248 Jeff Deardorff/475 5.00
251 Ed Rogers/400 5.00
255 Jorge Padilla/450 15.00
260 Allan Simpson/475 8.00
278 Roy Oswalt/75 35.00

Artist

NM/M
Complete Set (14): 60.00
Common Player: 3.00
Production 300 Sets
1 Pedro Martinez 8.00
2 Curt Schilling 6.00
3 Kevin Brown 3.00
4 Tim Hudson 5.00
5 Kerry Wood 7.50
6 Barry Zito 4.00
7 Hideo Nomo 6.00
8 Randy Johnson 8.00
9 Greg Maddux 10.00
10 Roger Clemens 15.00
11 Kazuhiro Sasaki 3.00
12 Joe Mays 3.00
13 Mark Mulder 3.00
14 Javier Vazquez 3.00

Master Artists

NM/M
Common Player: 5.00
Production 150 Sets
1 Pedro Martinez 15.00
2 Curt Schilling 10.00
3 Kevin Brown 5.00
4 Tim Hudson 6.00
5 Kerry Wood 5.00
6 Barry Zito 8.00
7 Hideo Nomo 15.00
8 Randy Johnson 15.00
9 Greg Maddux 15.00
10 Roger Clemens 20.00
11 Kazuhiro Sasaki 5.00
12 Joe Mays 5.00
13 Mark Mulder 5.00
14 Javier Vazquez 5.00

Artist Autographs

NM/M
Production 15-100
6 Barry Zito/100 35.00

Craftsmen

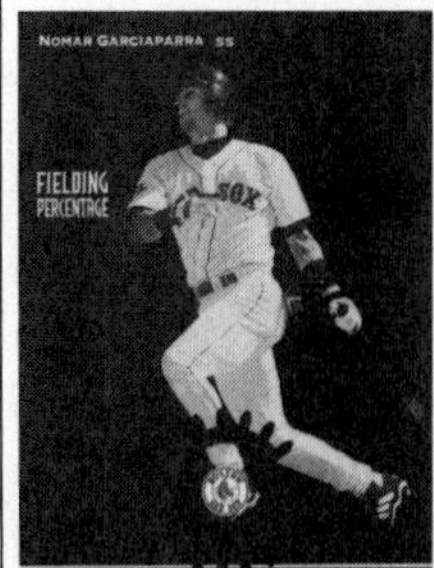

NM/M
Complete Set (18): 80.00
Common Player: 3.00
Production 300 Sets
1 Ichiro Suzuki 10.00
2 Todd Helton 5.00
3 Manny Ramirez 5.00
4 Luis Gonzalez 3.00
5 Roberto Alomar 3.50
6 Moises Alou 3.00
7 Darin Erstad 3.00
8 Mike Piazza 10.00
9 Edgar Martinez 3.00
10 Vladimir Guerrero 6.00
11 Juan Gonzalez 5.00
12 Nomar Garciaparra 10.00
13 Tony Gwynn 6.00
14 Jeff Bagwell 5.00
15 Albert Pujols 15.00
16 Larry Walker 3.00
17 Paul LoDuca 3.00
18 Lance Berkman 3.00

Master Craftsmen

NM/M
Common Player: 5.00
Production 150 Sets/H
1 Ichiro Suzuki/Ball/51 75.00
2 Todd Helton 10.00
3 Manny Ramirez 10.00
4 Luis Gonzalez 8.00
5 Roberto Alomar 8.00
6 Moises Alou 8.00
7 Darin Erstad 8.00
8 Mike Piazza 15.00
9 Edgar Martinez 8.00
10 Vladimir Guerrero 15.00
11 Juan Gonzalez 8.00
12 Nomar Garciaparra 20.00
13 Tony Gwynn/175 20.00
14 Jeff Bagwell 10.00
15 Albert Pujols/175 25.00
16 Larry Walker/175 5.00
17 Paul LoDuca/175 5.00
18 Lance Berkman 8.00

Craftsmen Autographs

NM/M
Common Player:
17 Paul LoDuca/100 20.00

Double Features

NM/M
Complete Set (10): 80.00
Common Card: 8.00
Production 125 Sets
1 Larry Walker, Todd Helton 10.00
2 Jose Vidro, Vladimir Guerrero 10.00
3 Jason Giambi, Jeremy Giambi 8.00
4 Nomar Garciaparra, Manny Ramirez 15.00
5 Troy Glaus, Darin Erstad 8.00
6 Shawn Green, Paul LoDuca 8.00
7 Jeff Bagwell, Craig Biggio 10.00
8 Pedro Martinez, Hideo Nomo 12.00
9 Curt Schilling, Randy Johnson 10.00
10 Andruw Jones, Chipper Jones 12.50

Double Features Game-Used

NM/M
Common Card: 10.00
Production 50 Sets
1 Larry Walker, Todd Helton 15.00
2 Jose Vidro, Vladimir Guerrero 20.00
3 Jason Giambi, Jeremy Giambi 15.00
4 Nomar Garciaparra, Manny Ramirez 30.00
5 Troy Glaus, Darin Erstad 15.00
6 Shawn Green, Paul LoDuca 10.00
7 Jeff Bagwell, Craig Biggio 15.00
8 Pedro Martinez, Hideo Nomo 30.00
9 Curt Schilling, Randy Johnson 20.00
10 Andruw Jones, Chipper Jones 20.00

Franchise Features

NM/M
Complete Set (40): 180.00
Common Player: 3.00
Production 300 Sets
1 Cliff Floyd 3.00
2 Mike Piazza 12.00
3 Cal Ripken Jr. 25.00
4 Mike Sweeney 3.00
5 Curt Schilling 5.00
6 Aramis Ramirez 3.00
7 Vladimir Guerrero 8.00
8 Andruw Jones 8.00

9 Tim Hudson 3.00
10 Bernie Williams 3.00
11 Pedro Martinez 8.00
12 Roberto Alomar 3.00
13 Joe Mays 3.00
14 Jason Giambi 5.00
15 Kazuhiro Sasaki 3.00
16 Magglio Ordonez 3.00
17 Nomar Garciaparra 12.00
18 Juan Gonzalez 8.00
19 Carlos Beltran 5.00
20 Javier Vazquez 3.00
21 Miguel Tejada 3.00
22 Luis Gonzalez 3.00
23 Greg Maddux 10.00
24 Rafael Palmeiro 6.00
25 Freddy Garcia 3.00
26 Barry Zito 4.00
27 Paul LoDuca 3.00
28 Robert Fick 3.00
29 Roger Clemens 10.00
30 Eric Chavez 3.00
31 Ivan Rodriguez 6.00
32 Chipper Jones 10.00
33 Kerry Wood 6.00
34 Randy Johnson 8.00
35 Alex Rodriguez 12.00
36 Manny Ramirez 8.00
37 Mark Buehrle 3.00
38 Mark Mulder 3.00
39 Ichiro Suzuki 15.00
40 Troy Glaus 4.00

Franchise Features Autographs

NM/M
Production 15-100
6 Aramis Ramirez/100 20.00
9 Tim Hudson/50 25.00
13 Joe Mays/75 10.00
19 Carlos Beltran/100 20.00
25 Freddy Garcia/100 20.00
26 Barry Zito/100 30.00
27 Paul LoDuca/100 15.00
28 Robert Fick/100 15.00
30 Eric Chavez/50 20.00
37 Mark Buehrle/100 15.00

Franchise Features Game-Used

NM/M
Common Player: 4.00
Production 150 Sets
All Jerseys unless noted.
1 Cliff Floyd 4.00
2 Mike Piazza 15.00
3 Cal Ripken Jr. 30.00
4 Mike Sweeney 4.00
5 Curt Schilling 8.00
6 Aramis Ramirez 6.00
7 Vladimir Guerrero 8.00
8 Andruw Jones 8.00
9 Tim Hudson 6.00
10 Bernie Williams 6.00
11 Pedro Martinez 10.00
12 Roberto Alomar 6.00
13 Joe Mays 4.00
14 Jason Giambi 8.00
15 Kazuhiro Sasaki 5.00
16 Magglio Ordonez 6.00
17 Nomar Garciaparra 20.00
18 Juan Gonzalez 8.00
19 Carlos Beltran 8.00
20 Javier Vazquez 4.00
21 Miguel Tejada 8.00
22 Luis Gonzalez 5.00
23 Greg Maddux 15.00
24 Rafael Palmeiro 10.00
25 Freddy Garcia 4.00
26 Barry Zito 8.00
27 Paul LoDuca 4.00
28 Robert Fick 4.00
29 Roger Clemens 20.00
30 Eric Chavez/bat 4.00
31 Ivan Rodriguez 8.00
32 Chipper Jones 8.00
33 Kerry Wood 10.00
34 Randy Johnson 10.00
35 Alex Rodriguez 15.00
36 Manny Ramirez 8.00
37 Mark Buehrle 4.00
38 Mark Mulder 6.00
39 Ichiro Suzuki/Ball 80.00
40 Troy Glaus 6.00

League Leaders

NM/M
Common Player: 3.00
Production 300 Sets
1 Roger Clemens 12.00
2 Curt Schilling 5.00
3 Matt Morris 3.00
4 Randy Johnson 6.00
5 Mark Mulder 4.00
6 Curt Schilling 5.00
7 Mike Mussina 4.00
8 Joe Mays 3.00
9 Matt Morris 3.00
10 Tim Hudson 4.00
11 Mark Buehrle 3.00
12 Greg Maddux 10.00
13 Freddy Garcia 3.00
14 Randy Johnson 6.00
15 Curt Schilling 5.00
16 Chan Ho Park 3.00
17 Roger Clemens 12.00
18 Mike Mussina 4.00
19 Javier Vazquez 3.00
20 Kerry Wood 8.00
21 Randy Johnson 6.00
22 Barry Zito 4.00
23 Hideo Nomo 8.00
24 Ichiro Suzuki 10.00
25 Todd Helton 6.00
26 Albert Pujols 20.00
27 Alex Rodriguez 12.00
28 Shannon Stewart 3.00
29 Luis Gonzalez 3.00
30 Alex Rodriguez 12.00
31 Barry Bonds 20.00
32 Sammy Sosa 15.00
33 Luis Gonzalez 3.00
34 Todd Helton 6.00
35 Jim Thome 3.00
36 Shawn Green 4.00
37 Jeff Bagwell 7.50
38 Todd Helton 5.00
39 Luis Gonzalez 3.00
40 Lance Berkman 3.00
41 Juan Gonzalez 6.00
42 Larry Walker 3.00
43 Ichiro Suzuki 10.00
44 Lance Berkman 3.00
45 Todd Helton 5.00

League Leaders Autographs

NM/M
Production 15-100
5 Mark Mulder/100 20.00
11 Mark Buehrle/100 15.00
13 Freddy Garcia/100 15.00
19 Javier Vazquez/100 15.00
26 Albert Pujols/100 150.00
28 Shannon Stewart/100 15.00

League Leaders Game-Used

NM/M
Common Player: 4.00
Production 150 or 175
1 Roger Clemens 20.00
2 Curt Schilling 10.00
4 Randy Johnson 8.00
5 Mark Mulder 6.00
6 Curt Schilling 10.00
7 Mike Mussina/Shoe/50 25.00
8 Joe Mays 4.00
10 Tim Hudson 6.00
11 Mark Buehrle 4.00
12 Greg Maddux 15.00
13 Freddy Garcia 4.00
14 Randy Johnson 8.00
15 Curt Schilling 10.00
16 Chan Ho Park 4.00
17 Roger Clemens 20.00
18 Mike Mussina/Shoe/50 25.00
19 Javier Vazquez 4.00
20 Kerry Wood 10.00
21 Randy Johnson 8.00
22 Barry Zito 6.00
23 Hideo Nomo 15.00
24 Ichiro Suzuki/Ball/51 75.00
25 Todd Helton 8.00
26 Albert Pujols 20.00
27 Alex Rodriguez 15.00
28 Shannon Stewart 4.00
29 Luis Gonzalez 5.00
30 Alex Rodriguez 15.00
31 Barry Bonds 25.00
32 Sammy Sosa 15.00
33 Luis Gonzalez 4.00
34 Todd Helton 8.00
35 Jim Thome 10.00
36 Shawn Green 5.00
37 Jeff Bagwell 8.00
38 Todd Helton 8.00
39 Luis Gonzalez 4.00
40 Lance Berkman 4.00
41 Juan Gonzalez 6.00
42 Larry Walker 4.00
43 Ichiro Suzuki/Ball/51 75.00
44 Lance Berkman 4.00
45 Todd Helton 8.00

Pure Power

NM/M
Complete Set (18): 65.00
Common Player: 2.00
Production 300 Sets
1 Sammy Sosa 8.00
2 Lance Berkman 2.00
3 Chipper Jones 6.00
4 Troy Glaus 4.00
5 Barry Bonds 12.00
6 Todd Helton 4.00
7 Manny Ramirez 4.00
8 Jason Giambi 3.00
9 Juan Gonzalez 4.00
10 Albert Pujols 10.00
11 Jim Thome 2.00
12 Mike Piazza 8.00
13 Frank Thomas 4.00
14 Richie Sexson 2.00
15 Jeff Bagwell 4.00
16 Rafael Palmeiro 3.00
17 Luis Gonzalez 2.00
18 Shawn Green 2.50

Pure Power Masters

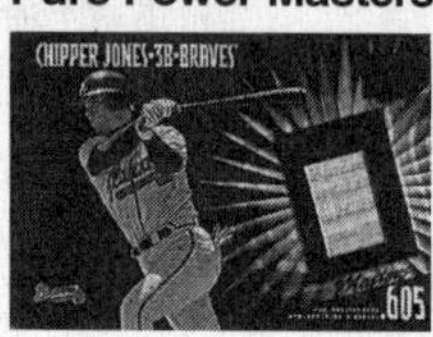

NM/M
Complete Set (18) 125.00
Common Player: 5.00
Production 150
1 Sammy Sosa 15.00
2 Lance Berkman 5.00
3 Chipper Jones 10.00
4 Troy Glaus 8.00
5 Barry Bonds 25.00
6 Todd Helton 8.00
7 Manny Ramirez 8.00
8 Jason Giambi 6.00
9 Juan Gonzalez 8.00
10 Albert Pujols 20.00
11 Jim Thome 5.00
12 Mike Piazza 15.00
13 Frank Thomas 8.00
14 Richie Sexson 5.00
15 Jeff Bagwell 8.00
16 Rafael Palmeiro 6.00
17 Luis Gonzalez 5.00
18 Shawn Green 6.00

Pure Power Autographs

NM/M
Varying quantities produced
14 Richie Sexson/100 20.00

Records

NM/M
Complete Set (5): 50.00
Common Player: 8.00
Production 300
1 Barry Bonds 15.00
2 Barry Bonds 15.00
3 Barry Bonds 15.00
4 Rickey Henderson 8.00
5 Rickey Henderson 8.00

Records Game-Used

NM/M
Production 150
1 Barry Bonds 40.00
2 Barry Bonds 40.00
3 Barry Bonds 40.00
4 Rickey Henderson 20.00
5 Rickey Henderson 20.00

2002 Donruss Originals Samples

Each November 2002 issue of Beckett Baseball Card Monthly included a sample '02 Donruss Originals card rubber-cemented inside. The cards differ from the issued version only in the appearance on back of a (usually) silver-foil silver-foil "SAMPLE" notation. Some cards were produced with the overprint in gold-foil, in much more limited quantities. The number of different players' cards involved in the promotion is unknown.

Common Player:
Stars: 1.5-2X
Gold: 10X

2002 Donruss Originals

NM/M
Complete Set (400): 75.00
Common Player: .10
Common Rated Rookie: .50
Pack (5): 2.00
Hobby Box (24): 40.00
1 So Taguchi/RR **RC** .75
2 Allan Simpson/RR **RC** .50
3 Brian Mallette/RR **RC** .50
4 Ben Howard/RR **RC** .50
5 Kazuhisa Ishii/RR **RC** 2.00
6 Francis Beltran/RR **RC** .50
7 Jorge Padilla/RR **RC** .50
8 Brandon Puffer/RR **RC** .50
9 Oliver Perez /RR **RC** 1.50
10 Kirk Saarloos/RR .50
11 Travis Driskill/RR **RC** .50
12 Jeremy Lambert/RR **RC** .50
13 John Foster/RR **RC** .50
14 Steve Kent/RR **RC** .50
15 Shawn Sedlacek/RR **RC** .50
16 Alex Rodriguez 1.25
17 Lance Berkman .10
18 Kevin Brown .10
19 Garret Anderson .10
20 Bobby Abreu .10
21 Richard Hidalgo .10
22 Matt Morris .10
23 Manny Ramirez .60
24 Derek Jeter 1.50
25 Kerry Wood .50
26 Mark Grace .15
27 Edgar Martinez .10
28 Nomar Garciaparra 1.00
29 Roberto Alomar .25
30 Jason Giambi .50
31 Juan Gonzalez .60
32 Albert Pujols 1.00
33 Juan Cruz .10
34 Troy Glaus .60
35 Greg Maddux .75
36 Adam Dunn .40
37 J.D. Drew .25
38 Tsuyoshi Shinjo .10
39 Vladimir Guerrero .60
40 Barry Bonds 1.50
41 Carlos Delgado .40
42 Ken Griffey Jr. 1.00
43 Carlos Pena .10
44 Jeff Kent .10
45 Roger Clemens .75
46 Frank Thomas .60
47 Larry Walker .10
48 Pedro J. Martinez .60
49 Moises Alou .10
50 Andruw Jones .60
51 Luis Gonzalez .25
52 Adrian Beltre .10
53 Bobby Hill .10
54 Roy Oswalt .20
55 Tim Hudson .20
56 Trot Nixon .10
57 Jeff Bagwell .60
58 Bernie Williams .30
59 Magglio Ordonez .25
60 Bartolo Colon .10
61 Shawn Green .20
62 Mark Buehrle .10
63 Sean Casey .10
64 Rickey Henderson .60
65 Aramis Ramirez .10
66 Ichiro Suzuki 1.00
67 Cliff Floyd .10
68 Darin Erstad .40
69 Paul LoDuca .10
70 Ivan Rodriguez .50
71 Mo Vaughn .10
72 Todd Helton .60
73 Raul Mondesi .10
74 Sammy Sosa 1.00
75 Cristian Guzman .10
76 Jimmy Rollins .25
77 Hideo Nomo .50
78 C.C. Sabathia .10
79 Wade Miller .10
80 Drew Henson .20
81 Chipper Jones .75
82 Miguel Tejada .25
83 Freddy Garcia .10
84 Richie Sexson .10
85 Robin Ventura .10
86 Jose Vidro .10
87 Rich Aurilia .10
88 Scott Rolen .60
89 Carlos Beltran .40
90 Austin Kearns .25
91 Kazuhiro Sasaki .10
92 Carlos Hernandez .10
93 Randy Johnson .60
94 Jim Thome .10
95 Curt Schilling .40
96 Alfonso Soriano .50
97 Barry Larkin .10
98 Rafael Palmeiro .50
99 Tom Glavine .25
100 Barry Zito .20
101 Craig Biggio .10
102 Mike Piazza 1.00
103 Ben Sheets .20
104 Mark Mulder .20
105 Mike Mussina .25
106 Jim Edmonds .10
107 Paul Konerko .10
108 Pat Burrell .25
109 Chan Ho Park .10
110 Mike Sweeney .10
111 Phil Nevin .10
112 Brian Giles .10
113 Eric Chavez .20
114 Corey Patterson .20
115 Gary Sheffield .25
116 Kazuhisa Ishii/RR 2.00
117 Kyle Kane/RR **RC** .50
118 Eric Junge/RR **RC** .50
119 Luis Ugueto/RR **RC** .50
120 Cam Esslinger/RR **RC** .50
121 Earl Snyder/RR **RC** .50
122 Oliver Perez/RR 1.50
123 Victor Alvarez/RR **RC** .50
124 Tom Shearn/RR **RC** .50
125 Corey Thurman/RR **RC** .50
126 Satoru Komiyama/RR **RC** .60
127 Hansel Izquierdo/RR **RC** .50
128 Elio Serrano/RR **RC** .50
129 Michael Crudale/RR **RC** .50
130 Chris Snelling/RR **RC** 1.50
131 Nomar Garciaparra 1.00
132 Roger Clemens .75
133 Hank Blalock .25
134 Eric Chavez .20
135 Corey Patterson .20
136 Richie Sexson .10
137 Freddy Garcia .10
138 Miguel Tejada .25
139 Alex Rodriguez/SP 1.50
140 Adrian Beltre .10
141 Bobby Abreu .10
142 Bret Boone .10
143 Tim Hudson .20
144 Roy Oswalt .20
145 Derek Jeter 1.50
146 Rich Aurilia .10
147 Mark Grace .15
148 Kerry Wood/SP 1.00
149 Geronimo Gil .10
150 Mark Buehrle .10
151 Jim Edmonds .10
152 Ichiro Suzuki 1.00
153 Juan Gonzalez .60
154 Darin Erstad .40
155 Barry Bonds/SP 2.50
156 Greg Maddux .75
157 Adam Dunn .40
158 Todd Helton .60
159 Roberto Alomar .25
160 Sammy Sosa 1.00
161 Sean Burroughs .10
162 Albert Pujols 1.00
163 Carlos Delgado .25
164 Frank Thomas .60
165 Ken Griffey Jr. 1.00
166 Jason Giambi/SP 1.00
167 Chipper Jones .75
168 Ivan Rodriguez .50
169 Pedro Martinez/SP 1.00
170 Gary Sheffield .25
171 Andruw Jones .60
172 Luis Gonzalez .25
173 Raul Mondesi .10
174 Jose Vidro .10
175 Garret Anderson/SP .50
176 Scott Rolen .60
177 Kazuhiro Sasaki .10
178 Jeff Bagwell .60
179 Manny Ramirez .60
180 Jim Thome .10
181 Ben Sheets .20
182 Randy Johnson .60
183 Lance Berkman .10
184 Shawn Green .20
185 Rickey Henderson .60
186 Edgar Martinez .10
187 Barry Larkin .10
188 Bernie Williams .30
189 Luis Aparicio .10
190 Troy Glaus/SP .50
191 Mike Mussina .30
192 Pee Wee Reese .20
193 Craig Biggio .10

194 Vladimir Guerrero .60
195 J.D. Drew .20
196 Jeff Kent .10
197 Dewon Brazelton .10
198 Tsuyoshi Shinjo/SP .40
199 Sean Casey .10
200 Hideo Nomo .50
201 C.C. Sabathia .10
202 Larry Walker .10
203 Mark Teixeira .20
204 Mike Sweeney .10
205 Moises Alou .10
206 Mark Prior .75
207 Javier Vazquez .10
208 Phil Nevin .10
209 Harmon Killebrew .50
210 Brian Giles .10
211 Carlos Beltran .40
212 Don Drysdale .40
213 Matt Morris .10
214 Trot Nixon .10
215 Magglio Ordonez .25
216 Curt Schilling/SP .75
217 Mark Mulder .20
218 Alfonso Soriano 1.00
219 Rafael Palmeiro/SP .75
220 Tom Glavine .25
221 Barry Zito .25
222 Mike Piazza 1.00
223 Bartolo Colon .10
224 Cliff Floyd .10
225 Paul LoDuca .10
226 Cristian Guzman .10
227 Mo Vaughn .10
228 Aramis Ramirez .10
229 Pat Burrell .25
230 Chan Ho Park .10
231 Satoru Komiyama/RR .50
232 Brandon Backe/RR **RC** .50
233 Anderson Machado/RR **RC** .50
234 Doug DeVore/RR **RC** .50
235 Steve Bechler/RR **RC** .50
236 John Ennis/RR **RC** .50
237 Rodrigo Rosario/RR **RC** .50
238 Jorge Sosa/RR **RC** .50
239 Ken Huckaby/RR **RC** .50
240 Mike Moriarty/RR **RC** .50
241 Kirk Saarloos/RR 1.00
242 Kevin Frederick/RR **RC** .50
243 Aaron Guiel/RR **RC** .50
244 Jose Rodriguez/RR .50
245 So Taguchi/RR 1.00
246 Albert Pujols 1.00
247 Derek Jeter 1.50
248 Brian Giles .10
249 Mike Cameron .10
250 Josh Beckett .25
251 Ken Griffey Jr./SP 1.50
252 Aramis Ramirez .10
253 Miguel Tejada .25
254 Carlos Delgado .25
255 Pedro J. Martinez .60
256 Raul Mondesi .10
257 Roger Clemens .75
258 Gary Sheffield .25
259 Jose Vidro .10
260 Alex Rodriguez 1.25
261 Larry Walker .10
262 Mark Mulder .20
263 Scott Rolen .60
264 Tim Hudson .20
265 Manny Ramirez .60
266 Rich Aurilia .10
267 Roy Oswalt .20
268 Mark Grace .15
269 Lance Berkman .10
270 Nomar Garciaparra 1.00
271 Barry Bonds 1.50
272 Ryan Klesko .10
273 Ichiro Suzuki 1.00
274 Shawn Green .20
275 Darin Erstad .40
276 Bernie Williams .30
277 Greg Maddux/SP 1.00
278 Eric Hinske .10
279 Randy Johnson .60
280 Todd Helton .60
281 Sammy Sosa/SP 1.50
282 Nick Johnson .10
283 Jose Cruz Jr. .10
284 Frank Thomas .60
285 Tsuyoshi Shinjo .10
286 Troy Glaus .60
287 Jason Giambi .50
288 Chipper Jones/SP 1.00
289 Roberto Alomar .30
290 Bobby Hill .10
291 Garret Anderson .10
292 Andruw Jones .60
293 Luis Gonzalez .15
294 Mike Mussina .30
295 Ivan Rodriguez/SP .75
296 Barry Larkin .10
297 Kazuhiro Sasaki .10
298 Alfonso Soriano .50
299 Jeff Bagwell/SP .75
300 Bobby Abreu .10
301 Ben Sheets .20
302 Curt Schilling .40
303 Jim Thome .10
304 Kerry Wood .50
305 Mark Buehrle .10
306 Rickey Henderson .60
307 Rafael Palmeiro .50
308 Jim Edmonds .10
309 Mike Piazza 1.00
310 Edgar Martinez .10
311 Tom Glavine .25
312 Adrian Beltre .10
313 Adam Dunn .40
314 Craig Biggio .10
315 Vladimir Guerrero/SP 1.00
316 Bret Boone .10
317 Hideo Nomo/SP .75
318 Jeff Kent .10
319 Juan Gonzalez .60
320 Sean Casey .10
321 C.C. Sabathia .10
322 J.D. Drew .20
323 Torii Hunter/SP .40
324 Chan Ho Park .10
325 Mike Sweeney .10
326 Javier Vazquez .10
327 Jorge Posada .25
328 Barry Zito .25
329 Willie McCovey .10
330 Kevin Brown .20
331 Mo Vaughn .10
332 Carlos Beltran .40
333 Bobby Doerr .10
334 Matt Morris .10
335 Trot Nixon .10
336 Magglio Ordonez .25
337 Paul LoDuca .10
338 Phil Nevin .10
339 Eric Chavez .20
340 Corey Patterson .20
341 Richie Sexson .10
342 Pat Burrell .25
343 Freddy Garcia .10
344 Bartolo Colon .10
345 Cliff Floyd .10
346 Deivis Santos/RR .50
347 Felix Escalona/RR **RC** .50
348 Miguel Asencio/RR **RC** .50
349 Takahito Nomura RR **RC** .50
350 Jorge Padilla/RR .50
351 Vladimir Guerrero .60
352 Ichiro Suzuki 1.00
353 Jay Gibbons .10
354 Alfonso Soriano .50
355 Mark Buehrle .10
356 Shawn Green .20
357 Barry Larkin .10
358 Josh Fogg .10
359 Shannon Stewart .10
360 Andruw Jones .60
361 Juan Gonzalez .60
362 Ken Griffey Jr. 1.00
363 Tim Hudson .20
364 Roy Oswalt/SP .50
365 Carlos Delgado .40
366 Albert Pujols/SP 2.00
367 Willie Stargell .25
368 Roger Clemens .75
369 Luis Gonzalez .25
370 Barry Zito .25
371 Alex Rodriguez 1.25
372 Troy Glaus .60
373 Vladimir Guerrero .60
374 Jeff Bagwell .60
375 Randy Johnson .60
376 Manny Ramirez .60
377 Derek Jeter/SP 2.00
378 C.C. Sabathia .10
379 Rickey Henderson .60
380 J.D. Drew .20
381 Nomar Garciaparra 1.00
382 Darin Erstad .40
383 Ben Sheets .20
384 Frank Thomas .60
385 Barry Bonds 1.50
386 Pedro J. Martinez .60
387 Mark Mulder .20
388 Greg Maddux .75
389 Todd Helton .60
390 Lance Berkman .10
391 Sammy Sosa 1.00
392 Mike Piazza 1.00
393 Chipper Jones .75
394 Adam Dunn .40
395 Jason Giambi .50
396 Eric Chavez .20
397 Bobby Abreu .10
398 Aramis Ramirez .10
399 Paul LoDuca .10
400 Miguel Tejada .25

Aqueous Glossy

Stars (1-400): 3-5X
Average of 1:Box

All-Stars

NM/M
Complete Set (25): 90.00
Common Player: 2.00
Inserted 1:30
1 George Brett 8.00
2 Rickey Henderson 4.00
3 Mike Schmidt 6.00
4 Vladimir Guerrero 3.00
5 Tony Gwynn 3.00
6 Curt Schilling 2.00
7 Don Mattingly 8.00
8 Roberto Alomar 2.00
9 Cal Ripken Jr. 8.00
10 Carlton Fisk 2.00
11 Roger Clemens 5.00
12 Jeff Bagwell 3.00
13 Kirby Puckett 8.00
14 Nolan Ryan 10.00
15 Ryne Sandberg 5.00
16 Ivan Rodriguez 2.00
17 Sammy Sosa 5.00
18 Greg Maddux 5.00
19 Alex Rodriguez 8.00
20 Todd Helton 2.00
21 Randy Johnson 3.00
22 Troy Glaus 2.00
23 Ichiro Suzuki 6.00
24 Barry Bonds 8.00
25 Derek Jeter 10.00

Champions

NM/M
Complete Set (25): 75.00
Common Player: 2.00
Production 800 Sets
1 Nolan Ryan 10.00
2 George Brett 6.00
3 Edgar Martinez 2.00
4 Mike Schmidt 6.00
5 Randy Johnson 3.00
6 Tony Gwynn 4.00
7 John Smoltz 2.00
8 Roger Clemens 4.00
9 Mel Ott 2.00
10 Todd Helton 3.00
11 Bernie Williams 2.00
12 Troy Glaus 3.00
13 Steve Carlton 2.00
14 Ryne Sandberg 4.00
15 Ted Williams 8.00
16 Alex Rodriguez 8.00
17 Lou Boudreau 2.00
18 Luis Gonzalez 2.00
19 Rickey Henderson 3.00
20 Jose Canseco 2.00
21 Stan Musial 5.00
22 Randy Johnson 3.00
23 Don Mattingly 6.00
24 Nomar Garciaparra 5.00
25 Wade Boggs 4.00

Champions Materials

NM/M
Common Player: 8.00
Varying quantities produced
1 Nolan Ryan/78 65.00
2 George Brett/80 30.00
3 Edgar Martinez/92 10.00
4 Mike Schmidt/80 40.00
5 Randy Johnson/94 15.00
6 Tony Gwynn/84 20.00
7 John Smoltz/96 8.00
8 Roger Clemens/88 20.00
10 Todd Helton/100 10.00
11 Bernie Williams/98 10.00
12 Troy Glaus/100 10.00
13 Steve Carlton/80 15.00
14 Ryne Sandberg/90 40.00
15 Ted Williams/42 200.00
16 Alex Rodriguez/96 20.00
17 Lou Boudreau/44 15.00
18 Luis Gonzalez/99 8.00
19 Rickey Henderson/82 20.00
21 Stan Musial/50 60.00
22 Randy Johnson/88 15.00
23 Don Mattingly/84 60.00
24 Nomar Garciaparra/100 30.00
25 Wade Boggs/88 15.00

Gamers

NM/M
Common Player: 3.00
Varying quantities produced
1 Alfonso Soriano/400 8.00
2 Shawn Green/500 5.00
3 Curt Schilling/250 8.00
4 Hideo Nomo/100 20.00
5 Toby Hall/500 4.00
6 Andruw Jones/500 8.00
7 Cliff Floyd/500 3.00
8 Mark Ellis/500 4.00
9 Gabe Kapler/500 3.00
10 Andres Galarraga/500 3.00
11 Freddy Garcia/500 3.00
12 Tsuyoshi Shinjo/200 4.00
13 Robin Ventura/500 3.00
14 Paul LoDuca/500 3.00
15 Manny Ramirez/500 8.00
16 Garret Anderson/250 5.00
17 Joe Kennedy/500 3.00
18 Roger Clemens/500 15.00
19 Gary Sheffield/500 6.00
20 Vernon Wells/500 4.00
22 Hideo Nomo/100 40.00
23 Tim Hudson/500 6.00
24 Larry Bigbie/500 4.00
25 Larry Walker/500 4.00
27 John Olerud/500 3.00
28 Chipper Jones/500 8.00
29 Tony Gwynn/500 10.00
30 Juan Gonzalez/500 8.00
31 Jacque Jones/500 5.00
32 Frank Thomas/500 8.00
33 Luis Gonzalez/500 4.00
34 Geoff Jenkins/500 6.00
35 J.D. Drew/500 5.00
36 Edgardo Alfonzo/500 3.00
37 Todd Helton/500 8.00
38 Brad Penny/500 4.00
39 Robert Fick/500 3.00
40 Will Clark/500 15.00
41 Tony Armas Jr./500 4.00
42 Nick Johnson/400 3.00
43 Ben Grieve/500 3.00
44 Vladimir Guerrero/500 8.00
45 Jason Jennings/500 3.00
46 Carlos Lee/500 3.00
47 Carlos Delgado/500 6.00
48 Chan Ho Park/500 3.00
49 Juan Diaz/500 3.00
50 Alex Rodriguez/400 15.00

Hit List

NM/M
Complete Set (20): 40.00
Common Player: 1.00
Production 1,500 Sets
1 Ichiro Suzuki 4.00
2 Shawn Green 1.00
3 Alex Rodriguez 5.00
4 Nomar Garciaparra 4.00
5 Derek Jeter 6.00
6 Barry Bonds 6.00
7 Mike Piazza 4.00
8 Albert Pujols 4.00
9 Chipper Jones 3.00
10 Sammy Sosa 4.00
11 Rickey Henderson 2.00
12 Frank Thomas 2.00
13 Jeff Bagwell 2.00
14 Vladimir Guerrero 2.00
15 Todd Helton 2.00
16 Adam Dunn 1.00
17 Rafael Palmeiro 1.00
18 Manny Ramirez 2.00
19 Lance Berkman 1.00
20 Jason Giambi 1.50

Hit List Total Bases

NM/M
Common Player: 5.00
Numbered to career high total bases.
1 Ichiro Suzuki/Base/316 15.00
2 Shawn Green/Bat/370 5.00
3 Alex Rodriguez/Bat/393 15.00
4 Nomar Garciaparra/Bat/365 10.00
5 Derek Jeter/346/Base 20.00
6 Barry Bonds/Base/411 20.00
7 Mike Piazza/Bat/355 10.00
8 Albert Pujols/Base/360 10.00
9 Chipper Jones/Bat/359 8.00
10 Sammy Sosa/Base/425 10.00
11 Rickey Henderson/Bat/285 10.00
12 Frank Thomas/Bat/364 8.00
13 Jeff Bagwell/Bat/363 8.00
14 Vladimir Guerrero/Bat/379 8.00
15 Todd Helton/Bat/405 8.00
16 Adam Dunn/Bat/141 8.00
17 Rafael Palmeiro/Bat/356 8.00
18 Manny Ramirez/Bat/346 8.00
19 Lance Berkman/Bat/358 5.00
20 Jason Giambi/Base/343 6.00

Making History

NM/M
Complete Set (10): 30.00
Common Player: 2.00
Production 800 Sets
1 Rafael Palmeiro 2.00
2 Roger Clemens 5.00
3 Greg Maddux 4.00
4 Randy Johnson 3.00
5 Barry Bonds 8.00
6 Mike Piazza 6.00
7 Roberto Alomar 2.00
8 Rickey Henderson 2.00
9 Sammy Sosa 6.00
10 Tom Glavine 2.00

Making History Materials

NM/M
Production 100 Sets
1 Rafael Palmeiro 15.00
2 Roger Clemens 20.00
3 Greg Maddux 15.00
4 Randy Johnson 10.00
5 Barry Bonds/Base 20.00
6 Mike Piazza 15.00
7 Roberto Alomar 8.00
8 Rickey Henderson 25.00
9 Sammy Sosa/Base 15.00
10 Tom Glavine 10.00

Mound Marvels

NM/M
Complete Set (15): 30.00
Common Player: 1.00
Inserted 1:40
1 Roger Clemens 6.00
2 Matt Morris 1.00
3 Pedro J. Martinez 5.00
4 Randy Johnson 5.00
5 Wade Miller 1.00
6 Tim Hudson 1.50
7 Mike Mussina 3.00
8 C.C. Sabathia 1.00
9 Kazuhiro Sasaki 1.00
10 Curt Schilling 4.00
11 Hideo Nomo 2.50
12 Roger Clemens 6.00
13 Mark Buehrle 1.00
14 Barry Zito 1.50
15 Roy Oswalt 1.50

Mound Marvels High Heat

NM/M
Production 100 Sets
1 Roger Clemens 25.00
2 Matt Morris 10.00
3 Pedro J. Martinez 20.00
4 Randy Johnson 15.00
5 Wade Miller 8.00
6 Tim Hudson 10.00
7 Mike Mussina 15.00
8 C.C. Sabathia 10.00
9 Kazuhiro Sasaki 10.00
10 Curt Schilling 15.00
11 Hideo Nomo 40.00
12 Roger Clemens 25.00
13 Mark Buehrle 8.00
14 Barry Zito 10.00
15 Roy Oswalt 8.00

Nifty Fifty Bats

NM/M
Common Player: 5.00
Production 50 Sets
1 Alex Rodriguez 20.00
2 Kerry Wood 15.00
3 Ivan Rodriguez 15.00
4 Geronimo Gil 5.00
5 Vladimir Guerrero 15.00
6 Corky Miller 5.00
7 Todd Helton 12.00
8 Rickey Henderson 15.00
9 Andruw Jones 10.00
10 Barry Bonds/Ball 30.00
11 Tom Glavine 10.00
12 Mark Teixeira 10.00
13 Mike Piazza 15.00
14 Austin Kearns 8.00
15 Rickey Henderson 15.00
16 Derek Jeter/Ball 20.00
17 Barry Larkin 8.00
18 Jeff Bagwell 10.00
19 Bernie Williams 10.00
20 Frank Thomas 10.00
21 Lance Berkman 8.00
22 Marlon Byrd 6.00
23 Randy Johnson 15.00
24 Ichiro Suzuki/Ball 40.00
25 Darin Erstad 8.00
26 Jason Lane 5.00
27 Roberto Alomar 10.00
28 Ken Griffey Jr./Ball 20.00
29 Tsuyoshi Shinjo 8.00
30 Pedro Martinez 15.00
31 Rickey Henderson 15.00
32 Albert Pujols/Ball 20.00
33 Nomar Garciaparra 15.00
34 Troy Glaus 10.00
35 Chipper Jones 15.00
36 Adam Dunn 8.00
37 Jason Giambi/Ball 10.00
38 Greg Maddux 20.00
39 Mike Piazza 15.00
40 So Taguchi 8.00
41 Manny Ramirez 10.00
42 Scott Rolen 15.00
43 Sammy Sosa/Ball 15.00
44 Shawn Green 8.00
45 Rickey Henderson 15.00
46 Alex Rodriguez 20.00
47 Hideo Nomo 30.00
48 Kazuhisa Ishii 8.00
49 Luis Gonzalez 8.00
50 Jim Thome 15.00

Nifty Fifty Jersey

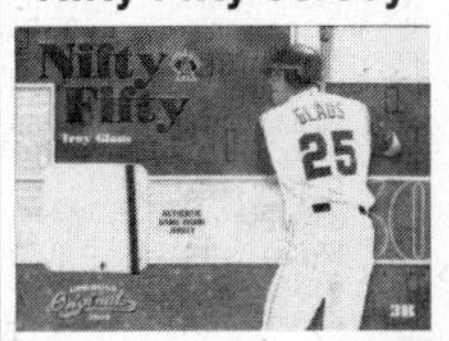

NM/M
Common Player: 5.00
Production 50 Sets
2 Kerry Wood 15.00
3 Ivan Rodriguez 15.00
4 Geronimo Gil 5.00
5 Vladimir Guerrero 15.00
6 Corky Miller 5.00
7 Todd Helton 12.00
8 Rickey Henderson 15.00
9 Andruw Jones 10.00
11 Tom Glavine 10.00
12 Mark Teixeira 10.00
13 Mike Piazza 15.00
14 Austin Kearns 8.00
15 Rickey Henderson 15.00
16 Derek Jeter/Base 20.00
17 Barry Larkin 8.00
18 Jeff Bagwell 10.00
19 Bernie Williams 10.00
20 Frank Thomas 10.00
21 Lance Berkman 8.00
22 Marlon Byrd 8.00
23 Randy Johnson 15.00
24 Ichiro Suzuki/Base 40.00
25 Darin Erstad 8.00
26 Jason Lane 5.00
27 Roberto Alomar 10.00
28 Ken Griffey Jr./Base 20.00
29 Tsuyoshi Shinjo 8.00
30 Pedro Martinez 15.00
31 Rickey Henderson 15.00
32 Albert Pujols/Base 20.00
33 Nomar Garciaparra 20.00
34 Troy Glaus 10.00
35 Chipper Jones 15.00
36 Adam Dunn 8.00
37 Jason Giambi/Base 10.00
38 Greg Maddux 20.00
39 Mike Piazza 15.00
40 So Taguchi 8.00
41 Manny Ramirez 10.00
42 Scott Rolen 15.00
43 Sammy Sosa/Base 15.00
44 Shawn Green 8.00
45 Rickey Henderson 15.00
46 Alex Rodriguez 20.00
47 Hideo Nomo 30.00
48 Kazuhisa Ishii 8.00
49 Luis Gonzalez 8.00
50 Jim Thome 15.00

Nifty Fifty Combos

NM/M
Production 50 Sets

All bat & jerseys unless noted.
1 Alex Rodriguez 30.00
2 Kerry Wood 20.00
3 Ivan Rodriguez 20.00
4 Geronimo Gil 10.00
5 Vladimir Guerrero 20.00
6 Corky Miller 10.00
7 Todd Helton 20.00
8 Rickey Henderson 25.00
9 Andruw Jones 15.00
10 Barry Bonds/Base/Ball 40.00
11 Tom Glavine 20.00
12 Mark Teixeira 20.00
13 Mike Piazza 25.00
14 Austin Kearns 15.00
15 Rickey Henderson 25.00
16 Derek Jeter/Base/Ball 30.00
17 Barry Larkin 15.00
18 Jeff Bagwell 20.00
19 Bernie Williams 20.00
20 Frank Thomas 20.00
21 Lance Berkman 15.00
22 Marlon Byrd 15.00
23 Randy Johnson 20.00
24 Ichiro Suzuki/Base/Ball 60.00
25 Darin Erstad 15.00
26 Jason Lane 10.00
27 Roberto Alomar 15.00
28 Ken Griffey Jr./Base/Ball 25.00
29 Tsuyoshi Shinjo 10.00
30 Pedro Martinez 20.00
31 Rickey Henderson 25.00
32 Albert Pujols/Base/Ball 50.00
33 Nomar Garciaparra 30.00
34 Troy Glaus 15.00
35 Chipper Jones 20.00
36 Adam Dunn 15.00
37 Jason Giambi 20.00
38 Greg Maddux 25.00
39 Mike Piazza 25.00
40 So Taguchi 15.00
41 Manny Ramirez 20.00
42 Scott Rolen 20.00
43 Sammy Sosa/Base/Ball 25.00
44 Shawn Green 10.00
45 Rickey Henderson 25.00
46 Alex Rodriguez 30.00
47 Hideo Nomo 30.00
48 Kazuhisa Ishii 15.00
49 Luis Gonzalez 10.00
50 Jim Thome 20.00

On The Record

NM/M
Complete Set (15): 60.00
Common Player: 3.00
Production 800 Sets
1 Ty Cobb 6.00
2 Jimmie Foxx 4.00
3 Lou Gehrig 10.00
4 Dale Murphy 5.00
5 Steve Carlton 3.00
6 Randy Johnson 4.00
7 Greg Maddux 6.00
8 Roger Clemens 8.00
9 Yogi Berra 5.00
10 Don Mattingly 8.00
11 Rickey Henderson 4.00
12 Stan Musial 6.00
13 Jackie Robinson 6.00
14 Roberto Clemente 10.00
15 Mike Schmidt 6.00

On the Record Materials

NM/M
Varying quantities produced
3 Lou Gehrig/34 220.00
4 Dale Murphy/83 10.00
5 Steve Carlton/72 10.00
6 Randy Johnson/100 10.00
7 Greg Maddux/93 15.00
8 Roger Clemens/87 20.00
9 Yogi Berra/51 12.00
10 Don Mattingly/85 25.00
11 Rickey Henderson/90 15.00
13 Jackie Robinson/49 50.00
14 Roberto Clemente/66 75.00
15 Mike Schmidt/80 25.00

Power Alley

NM/M
Complete Set (15): 30.00
Common Player: 1.00
Production 1,500 Sets
Die-Cut Parallel: 1.5-2X
Production 100 Sets
1 Barry Bonds 6.00
2 Sammy Sosa 3.00
3 Lance Berkman 1.00
4 Luis Gonzalez 1.00
5 Alex Rodriguez 5.00
6 Troy Glaus 2.00
7 Vladimir Guerrero 2.00
8 Jason Giambi 1.50
9 Mike Piazza 3.00
10 Todd Helton 2.00
11 Mike Schmidt 4.00
12 Don Mattingly 4.00
13 Andre Dawson 1.50
14 Reggie Jackson 2.00
15 Dale Murphy 1.50

Recollection Collection

No Pricing

Signature Marks

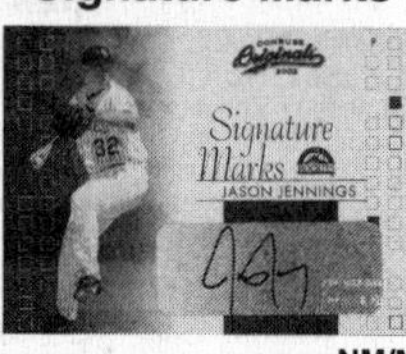

NM/M
Common Autograph: 5.00
Varying quantities produced
Many not priced, lack of market info.
2 Eric Hinske/200 8.00
3 Cesar Izturis/200 5.00
4 Roy Oswalt/100 20.00
5 Jack Cust/200 8.00
6 Nick Johnson/200 8.00
7 Jason Hart/200 6.00
8 Mark Prior/100 30.00
9 Luis Garcia/200 5.00
10 Jay Gibbons/200 10.00
11 Corky Miller/200 8.00
12 Antonio Perez/100 8.00
13 Andres Torres/200 5.00
14 Brandon Claussen/200 8.00
15 Ed Rogers/200 5.00
16 Jorge Padilla/200 10.00
17 Francis Beltran/200 5.00
18 Kip Wells/200 6.00
19 Ryan Ludwick/200 8.00
20 Juan Cruz/100 8.00
21 Juan Diaz/200 5.00
22 Marcus Giles/200 10.00
23 Joe Kennedy/200 10.00
24 Wade Miller/100 10.00
25 Corey Patterson/100 10.00
26 Angel Berroa/200 10.00
27 Ricardo Rodriguez/200 5.00
28 Toby Hall/200 8.00
29 Carlos Pena/50 10.00
30 Jason Jennings/200 8.00
31 Rafael Soriano/200 10.00
32 Marlon Byrd/100 10.00
33 Rodrigo Rosario/200 5.00
35 Brent Abernathy/200 5.00
36 Bill Hall/200 15.00
37 Fernando Rodney/200 10.00
38 Josh Pearce/200 8.00
39 Brian Lawrence/200 8.00
40 Tim Redding/200 5.00
42 Jeremy Giambi/200 5.00
43 Victor Martinez/200 25.00
44 Hank Blalock/50 25.00
46 Geronimo Gil/200 5.00
47 So Taguchi/50 25.00
48 Austin Kearns/200 15.00
49 Alfonso Soriano/50 40.00

What If - Rookies

NM/M
Complete Set (23): 75.00
Common Player: 1.50
Inserted 1:12
1 Wade Boggs 6.00
2 Ryne Sandberg 6.00
3 Cal Ripken Jr. 12.50
4 Tony Gwynn 6.00
5 Don Mattingly 10.00
6 Wade Boggs 6.00
7 Roger Clemens 7.50
8 Kirby Puckett 6.00
9 Eric Davis 1.50
10 Dwight Gooden 1.50
11 Eric Davis 1.50
12 Roger Clemens 7.50
13 Kirby Puckett 6.00
14 Dwight Gooden 1.50
15 Barry Bonds 12.50
16 Will Clark 1.50
17 Barry Larkin 1.50
18 Greg Maddux 6.00
19 Rafael Palmeiro 4.00
20 Craig Biggio 1.50
21 Gary Sheffield 1.50
22 Randy Johnson 5.00
23 Curt Schilling 3.00

What If -'78

NM/M
Complete Set (27): 75.00
Common Player: 1.50
Inserted 1:12
1 Paul Molitor 4.00
2 Alan Trammell 1.50
3 Ozzie Smith 6.00
4 George Brett 10.00
5 Johnny Bench 6.00
6 Rod Carew 2.00
7 Carlton Fisk 1.50
8 Reggie Jackson 5.00
9 Dale Murphy 2.00
10 Joe Morgan 1.50
11 Eddie Murray 4.00
12 Jim Palmer 2.00
13 Tom Seaver 4.00
14 Willie Stargell 2.00
15 Dave Winfield 2.00
16 Dave Parker 1.50
17 Mike Schmidt 8.00
18 Eddie Mathews 4.00
19 Lou Brock 1.50
20 Willie McCovey 1.50
21 Andre Dawson 1.50
22 Dennis Eckersley 4.00
23 Robin Yount 4.00
24 Nolan Ryan 15.00
25 Steve Carlton 1.50
26 Paul Molitor 4.00
27 Ozzie Smith 6.00

What If -'80

NM/M
Complete Set (25): 75.00
Common Player: 1.50
Inserted 1:12
1 Rickey Henderson 3.00
2 Johnny Bench 6.00
3 George Brett 10.00
4 Steve Carlton 2.50
5 Rod Carew 2.00
6 Gary Carter 1.50
7 Carlton Fisk 1.50
8 Reggie Jackson 5.00
9 Dave Parker 1.50
10 Dale Murphy 3.00
11 Paul Molitor 4.00
12 Mike Schmidt 8.00
13 Alan Trammell 1.50
14 Dave Winfield 1.50
15 Robin Yount 4.00
16 Joe Morgan 1.50
17 Jim Palmer 1.50
18 Nolan Ryan 15.00
19 Tom Seaver 4.00
20 Ozzie Smith 6.00
21 Willie McCovey 1.50
22 Andre Dawson 1.50
23 Eddie Murray 2.00
24 Al Kaline 5.00
25 Duke Snider 4.00

LCS Programs

A perforated sheet of Donruss Originals cards was inserted into some of the programs sold for the American and National League Championship Series. The 8-1/2" x 11" sheet features eight player cards and a header card advertising the brand. Each 2-1/2" x 3-1/2" card is perforated on all sides and differs from the regularly issued version only in the card number on back. Sheet cards have either an "ALCS-" or "NLCS-" prefix to the number. Other programs could be found with similar sheets of Donruss Diamond Kings, Donruss Studio or Playoff Piece of the Game cards.

NM/M
Complete Sheet Set (2): 16.00
Common Player: .50
ALCS SHEET 8.00
9 Manny Ramirez (1986 style) 1.00
10 Nolan Ryan/AS 2.50
11 Roger Clemens (Champions) 1.50
12 Alex Rodriguez/AS 2.00
13 Paul Konerko (1982 style) .50
14 Don Mattingly/AS 1.50
15 Miguel Tejada (1984 style) .50
16 Rickey Henderson (Making History) .50
--- Header Card .10
NLCS SHEET 8.00
25 Mike Schmidt (Champions) 2.00
26 Andruw Jones (1986 style) 1.00
27 Lance Berkman (Power Alley) .50
28 Vladimir Guerrero/AS 1.00
29 Roberto Clemente (On The Record) 3.00
30 Austin Kearns (1982 style) .50
31 Curt Schilling/AS .50
32 Kazuhisa Ishii (1984 style) 1.00
--- Header Card .10

2002 Donruss Studio Samples

Each issue of the September 2002 Beckett Baseball Card Monthly included a sample 2002 Donruss Studio card rubber-cemented inside. The cards differ from the issued version only in the appearance on back of a (usually) silver-foil "SAMPLE" notation. Some cards were produced with the overprint in gold-foil, in much more limited quantities. The number of different players' cards involved in the promotion is unknown.

NM/M
Common Player: .10
Stars: 1.5-2X
Gold: 10X

2002 Donruss Studio

NM/M
Complete Set (250): 150.00
Common Player: .25
Common (201-250): 3.00
Production 1,500
Pack (5): 3.00
Box (18): 45.00
1 Vladimir Guerrero .75
2 Chipper Jones 1.00
3 Bobby Abreu .25
4 Barry Zito .40
5 Larry Walker .25
6 Miguel Tejada .40
7 Mike Sweeney .25
8 Shannon Stewart .25
9 Sammy Sosa 1.50
10 Bud Smith .25
11 Wilson Betemit .25
12 Kevin Brown .35
13 Ellis Burks .25
14 Pat Burrell .40
15 Cliff Floyd .25
16 Marcus Giles .25
17 Troy Glaus .75
18 Barry Larkin .25
19 Carlos Lee .25
20 Brian Lawrence .25
21 Paul LoDuca .25
22 Ben Grieve .25
23 Shawn Green .40
24 Mike Cameron .25
25 Roger Clemens 1.25
26 Joe Crede .25
27 Jose Cruz .25
28 Jeremy Affeldt .25
29 Adrian Beltre .25
30 Josh Beckett .50
31 Roberto Alomar .40
32 Toby Hall .25
33 Mike Hampton .25
34 Eric Milton .25
35 Eric Munson .25
36 Trot Nixon .25
37 Roy Oswalt .40
38 Chan Ho Park .25
39 Charles Johnson .25
40 Nick Johnson .25
41 Tim Hudson .40
42 Cristian Guzman .25
43 Drew Henson .25
44 Mark Grace .35
45 Luis Gonzalez .35
46 Pedro J. Martinez .75
47 Joe Mays .25
48 Jorge Posada .40
49 Aramis Ramirez .25
50 Kip Wells .25
51 Moises Alou .25
52 Omar Vizquel .25
53 Ichiro Suzuki 1.50
54 Jimmy Rollins .40
55 Freddy Garcia .25
56 Steve Green .25
57 Brian Jordan .25
58 Paul Konerko .35
59 Jack Cust .25
60 Sean Casey .25
61 Bret Boone .25
62 Hideo Nomo .60
63 Magglio Ordonez .40
64 Frank Thomas .75
65 Josh Towers .25
66 Javier Vazquez .25
67 Robin Ventura .25
68 Aubrey Huff .25
69 Richard Hidalgo .25
70 Brandon Claussen .25
71 Bartolo Colon .25
72 John Buck .25
73 Dee Brown .25
74 Barry Bonds 2.00
75 Jason Giambi .50
76 Erick Almonte .25
77 Ryan Dempster .25
78 Jim Edmonds .25
79 Jay Gibbons .25
80 Shigetoshi Hasegawa .25
81 Todd Helton .75
82 Erik Bedard .25
83 Carlos Beltran .50
84 Rafael Soriano .25
85 Gary Sheffield .40
86 Richie Sexson .25
87 Mike Rivera .25
88 Jose Ortiz .25
89 Abraham Nunez .25
90 Dave Williams .25
91 Preston Wilson .25
92 Jason Jennings .25
93 Juan Diaz .25
94 Steve Smyth .25
95 Phil Nevin .25
96 John Olerud .25
97 Brad Penny .25
98 Andy Pettitte .40
99 Juan Pierre .25
100 Manny Ramirez .75
101 Edgardo Alfonzo .25
102 Michael Cuddyer .25
103 Johnny Damon .40
104 Carlos Zambrano .35
105 Jose Vidro .25
106 Tsuyoshi Shinjo .25
107 Ed Rogers .25
108 Scott Rolen .75
109 Mariano Rivera .35
110 Tim Redding .25
111 Josh Phelps .25
112 Gabe Kapler .25
113 Edgar Martinez .25
114 Fred McGriff .25
115 Raul Mondesi .25
116 Wade Miller .25
117 Mike Mussina .40
118 Rafael Palmeiro .65
119 Adam Johnson .25
120 Rickey Henderson .75
121 Bill Hall .25
122 Ken Griffey Jr. 1.50
123 Geronimo Gil .25
124 Robert Fick .25
125 Darin Erstad .50
126 Brandon Duckworth .25
127 Garret Anderson .25
128 Pedro Feliz .25
129 Jeff Cirillo .25
130 Brian Giles .25
131 Craig Biggio .25
132 Willie Harris .25
133 Doug Davis .25
134 Jeff Kent .25
135 Terrence Long .25
136 Carlos Delgado .50
137 Tino Martinez .25
138 Donaldo Mendez .25
139 Sean Douglass .25
140 Eric Chavez .40
141 Rick Ankiel .25
142 Jeremy Giambi .25
143 Juan Pena .25
144 Bernie Williams .40
145 Craig Wilson .25
146 Ricardo Rodriguez .25
147 Albert Pujols 1.50
148 Antonio Perez .25
149 Russ Ortiz .25
150 Corky Miller .25
151 Rich Aurilia .25
152 Kerry Wood .50
153 Joe Thurston .25
154 Jeff Deardorff **RC** .25
155 Jermaine Dye .25
156 Andruw Jones .75
157 Victor Martinez .25
158 Nick Neugebauer .25
159 Matt Morris .25
160 Casey Fossum .50
161 J.D. Drew .40
162 Matt Childers **RC** .50
163 Mark Buehrle .25
164 Jeff Bagwell .75
165 Kazuhiro Sasaki .25
166 Ben Sheets .50
167 Alex Rodriguez 1.50
168 Adam Pettyjohn .25
169 Chris Snelling **RC** .50
170 Robert Person .25
171 Juan Uribe .25
172 Mo Vaughn .25
173 Alfredo Amezaga .25
174 Ryan Drese .25
175 Corey Thurman **RC** .25
176 Jim Thome .25
177 Orlando Cabrera .25
178 Eric Cyr **RC** .50
179 Greg Maddux 1.00
180 Earl Snyder **RC** .25
181 C.C. Sabathia .25
182 Mark Mulder .40
183 Jose Mieses .25
184 Joe Kennedy .25
185 Randy Johnson .75
186 Tom Glavine .40
187 Eric Junge **RC** .25
188 Mike Piazza 1.50
189 Corey Patterson .40
190 Carlos Pena .25
191 Curt Schilling .40
192 Nomar Garciaparra 1.50
193 Lance Berkman .25
194 Ryan Klesko .25
195 Ivan Rodriguez .65
196 Alfonso Soriano .75
197 Derek Jeter 2.00
198 David Justice .25
199 Juan Gonzalez .75
200 Adam Dunn .50
201 Victor Alvarez **RC** 3.00
202 Miguel Asencio **RC** 3.00
203 Brandon Backe **RC** 3.00
204 Chris Baker **RC** 4.00
205 Steve Bechler **RC** 4.00
206 Francis Beltran **RC** 4.00
207 Angel Berroa 3.00
208 Hank Blalock 4.00
209 Dewon Brazelton 3.00
210 Sean Burroughs 3.00
211 Marlon Byrd 3.00
212 Raul Chavez **RC** 4.00
213 Juan Cruz 3.00
214 Jorge De La Rosa **RC** 3.00
215 Doug DeVore **RC** 3.00
216 John Ennis **RC** 3.00
217 Felix Escalona **RC** 3.00
218 Morgan Ensberg 3.00
219 Cam Esslinger **RC** 3.00
220 Kevin Frederick **RC** 3.00
221 Franklyn German **RC** 3.00
222 Eric Hinske 4.00
223 Ben Howard **RC** 3.00
224 Orlando Hudson 3.00
225 Travis Hughes **RC** 5.00
226 Kazuhisa Ishii **RC** 6.00
227 Ryan Jamison **RC** 3.00
228 Reed Johnson **RC** 4.00
229 Kyle Kane **RC** 3.00
230 Austin Kearns 3.00
231 Satoru Komiyama **RC** 4.00
232 Jason Lane 3.00
233 Jeremy Lambert **RC** 3.00
234 Anderson Machado **RC** 4.00
235 Brian Mallette **RC** 3.00
236 Takahito Nomura **RC** 3.00
237 Jorge Padilla **RC** 4.00
238 Luis Ugueto **RC** 3.00
239 Mark Prior 10.00
240 Rene Reyes **RC** 3.00
241 Deivis Santos 3.00
242 Elio Serrano **RC** 3.00
243 Tom Shearn **RC** 3.00
244 Allan Simpson **RC** 3.00
245 So Taguchi **RC** 5.00
246 Dennis Tankersley 3.00
247 Mark Teixeira 6.00
248 Matt Thornton 3.00
249 Bobby Hill 3.00
250 Ramon Vazquez 3.00

Proof

Proofs (1-200): 4-8X
Proofs (201-250): 1-2X
Production 100 Sets

Private Signings

		NM/M
	Common Autograph:	5.00
	Varying quantities produced	
1	Vladimir Guerrero/25	75.00
2	Chipper Jones/15	150.00
3	Bobby Abreu/50	20.00
4	Barry Zito/25	25.00
6	Miguel Tejada/50	25.00
7	Mike Sweeney/50	15.00
8	Shannon Stewart/100	10.00
10	Bud Smith/100	5.00
11	Wilson Betemit/250	8.00
12	Kevin Brown/25	25.00
15	Cliff Floyd/50	15.00
16	Marcus Giles/250	10.00
17	Troy Glaus/50	25.00
18	Barry Larkin/25	50.00
19	Carlos Lee/25	20.00
20	Brian Lawrence/250	8.00
21	Paul LoDuca/50	15.00
25	Roger Clemens/15	175.00
26	Joe Crede/250	8.00
28	Jeremy Affeldt/250	8.00
29	Adrian Beltre/25	20.00
30	Josh Beckett/25	40.00
31	Roberto Alomar/25	50.00
32	Toby Hall/250	8.00
37	Roy Oswalt/50	20.00
40	Nick Johnson/250	8.00
43	Drew Henson/150	15.00
45	Luis Gonzalez/15	25.00
47	Joe Mays/100	8.00
49	Aramis Ramirez/50	20.00
50	Kip Wells/250	8.00
51	Moises Alou/15	25.00
55	Freddy Garcia/50	10.00
56	Steve Green/250	5.00
59	Jack Cust/250	10.00
60	Sean Casey/50	10.00
63	Magglio Ordonez/15	40.00
65	Josh Towers/250	8.00
66	Javier Vazquez/100	15.00
68	Aubrey Huff/250	10.00
69	Richard Hidalgo/25	15.00
70	Brandon Claussen/250	10.00
72	John Buck/250	5.00
73	Dee Brown/250	5.00
76	Erick Almonte/250	8.00
79	Jay Gibbons/250	15.00
81	Todd Helton/15	85.00
82	Erik Bedard/250	15.00
84	Rafael Soriano/250	10.00
85	Gary Sheffield/15	40.00
86	Richie Sexson/50	20.00
87	Mike Rivera/250	5.00
88	Jose Ortiz/250	8.00
89	Abraham Nunez/250	5.00
90	Dave Williams/250	5.00
92	Jason Jennings/250	8.00
93	Juan Diaz/250	5.00
94	Steve Smyth/250	5.00
97	Brad Penny/80	10.00
99	Juan Pierre/100	15.00
100	Manny Ramirez/15	75.00
102	Michael Cuddyer/250	10.00
104	Carlos Zambrano/250	15.00
105	Jose Vidro/100	10.00
107	Ed Rogers/250	8.00
110	Tim Redding/250	5.00
111	Josh Phelps/250	8.00
112	Gabe Kapler/100	10.00
113	Edgar Martinez/50	40.00
116	Wade Miller/250	10.00
118	Rafael Palmeiro/25	40.00
121	Bill Hall/250	10.00
123	Geronimo Gil/250	8.00
124	Robert Fick/150	10.00
126	Brandon Duckworth/250	8.00
128	Pedro Feliz/250	8.00
130	Brian Giles/15	25.00
131	Craig Biggio/15	40.00
132	Willie Harris/250	5.00
133	Doug Davis/250	8.00
135	Terrence Long/150	10.00
138	Donaldo Mendez/250	5.00
139	Sean Douglass/250	5.00
140	Eric Chavez/15	25.00
141	Rick Ankiel/250	15.00
142	Jeremy Giambi/100	6.00
143	Juan Pena/250	8.00
144	Bernie Williams/15	75.00
145	Craig Wilson/250	10.00
146	Ricardo Rodriguez/250	10.00
147	Albert Pujols/25	200.00
148	Antonio Perez/250	5.00
150	Corky Miller/250	8.00
151	Rich Aurilia/25	15.00
152	Kerry Wood/25	30.00
153	Joe Thurston/250	5.00
154	Jeff Deardorff/250	8.00
155	Jermaine Dye/15	25.00
157	Victor Martinez/250	15.00
158	Nick Neugebauer/150	5.00
160	Casey Fossum/250	8.00
161	J.D. Drew/25	25.00
162	Matt Childers/250	5.00
163	Mark Buehrle/150	10.00
166	Ben Sheets/100	15.00
167	Alex Rodriguez/15	165.00
168	Adam Pettyjohn/250	5.00
169	Chris Snelling/250	10.00
170	Robert Person/250	5.00
171	Juan Uribe/250	10.00
173	Alfredo Amezaga/250	5.00
175	Corey Thurman/250	5.00
178	Eric Cyr/250	5.00
179	Greg Maddux/15	200.00
180	Earl Snyder/250	5.00
181	C.C. Sabathia/50	20.00
182	Mark Mulder/50	15.00
183	Jose Mieses/250	5.00
184	Joe Kennedy/250	5.00
187	Eric Junge/250	5.00
189	Corey Patterson/205	20.00
190	Carlos Pena/250	10.00
191	Curt Schilling/15	80.00
195	Ivan Rodriguez/15	50.00
196	Alfonso Soriano/50	40.00
201	Victor Alvarez/250	5.00
203	Brandon Backe/250	5.00
204	Chris Baker/250	5.00
205	Steve Bechler/250	8.00
206	Francis Beltran/250	5.00
207	Angel Berroa/250	10.00
208	Hank Blalock/100	20.00
209	Dewon Brazelton/200	5.00
210	Sean Burroughs/50	20.00
211	Marlon Byrd/200	10.00
212	Raul Chavez/250	5.00
213	Juan Cruz/50	15.00
214	Jorge De La Rosa/250	5.00
215	Doug DeVore/250	5.00
216	John Ennis/250	5.00
217	Felix Escalona/250	5.00
218	Morgan Ensberg/250	10.00
219	Cam Esslinger/250	5.00
220	Kevin Frederick/250	5.00
221	Franklyn German/250	5.00
222	Eric Hinske/250	8.00
223	Ben Howard/250	8.00
224	Orlando Hudson/250	10.00
225	Travis Hughes/250	10.00
226	Kazuhisa Ishii/50	25.00
227	Ryan Jamison/250	5.00
228	Reed Johnson/250	10.00
229	Kyle Kane/250	5.00
230	Austin Kearns/250	20.00
231	Satoru Komiyama/50	10.00
232	Jason Lane/200	5.00
233	Jeremy Lambert/250	5.00
234	Anderson Machado/200	10.00
235	Brian Mallette/250	5.00
236	Takahito Nomura/100	20.00
237	Jorge Padilla/200	10.00
238	Luis Ugueto/250	5.00
239	Mark Prior/100	30.00
240	Rene Reyes/250	5.00
241	Deivis Santos/250	5.00
242	Elio Serrano/250	5.00
243	Tom Shearn/250	5.00
244	Allan Simpson/250	5.00
245	So Taguchi/100	15.00
246	Dennis Tankersley/100	10.00
247	Mark Teixeira/50	40.00
248	Matt Thornton/250	5.00
249	Bobby Hill/100	10.00
250	Ramon Vazquez/250	5.00

Classic Studio

		NM/M
	Complete Set (25):	90.00
	Common Player:	3.00
	Production 1,000 Sets	
	First Ballot:	3-4X
	Print run based on HOF year.	
1	Kirby Puckett	5.00
2	George Brett	8.00
3	Nolan Ryan	10.00
4	Mike Schmidt	8.00
5	Steve Carlton	3.00
6	Reggie Jackson	5.00
7	Tom Seaver	3.00
8	Joe Morgan	3.00
9	Jim Palmer	3.00
10	Johnny Bench	5.00
11	Willie McCovey	3.00
12	Brooks Robinson	4.00
13	Al Kaline	5.00
14	Stan Musial	6.00
15	Ozzie Smith	6.00
16	Dave Winfield	3.00
17	Robin Yount	5.00
18	Rod Carew	3.00
19	Willie Stargell	3.00
20	Lou Brock	3.00
21	Ernie Banks	5.00
22	Ted Williams	10.00
23	Jackie Robinson	8.00
24	Roberto Clemente	10.00
25	Lou Gehrig	10.00

Classic Studio Autograph

Production 15-20

Diamond Collection

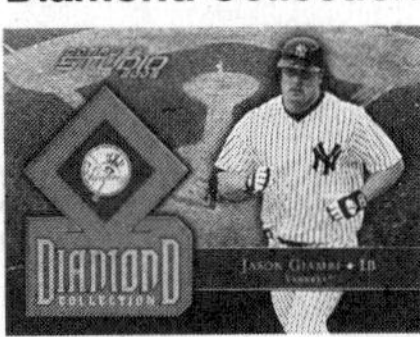

		NM/M
	Complete Set (25):	65.00
	Common Player:	1.50
	Inserted 1:17	
1	Todd Helton	3.00
2	Chipper Jones	4.00
3	Lance Berkman	1.50
4	Derek Jeter	8.00
5	Hideo Nomo	3.00
6	Kazuhisa Ishii	1.50
7	Barry Bonds	8.00
8	Alex Rodriguez	6.00
9	Ichiro Suzuki	5.00
10	Mike Piazza	5.00
11	Jim Thome	1.50
12	Greg Maddux	4.00
13	Jeff Bagwell	3.00
14	Vladimir Guerrero	3.00
15	Ken Griffey Jr.	5.00
16	Jason Giambi	2.50
17	Nomar Garciaparra	5.00
18	Albert Pujols	6.00
19	Manny Ramirez	3.00
20	Pedro J. Martinez	3.00
21	Roger Clemens	4.50
22	Randy Johnson	3.00
23	Mark Prior	2.00
24	So Taguchi	1.50
25	Sammy Sosa	5.00

Diamond Collection Artist's Proof

		NM/M
	Common Jersey Card:	4.00
	Varying quantities produced	
1	Todd Helton/200	8.00
2	Chipper Jones/150	10.00
3	Lance Berkman/200	6.00
4	Derek Jeter/200/Base	20.00
5	Hideo Nomo/150	25.00
6	Kazuhisa Ishii/150	8.00
7	Barry Bonds/200/Base	25.00
8	Alex Rodriguez/150	15.00
9	Ichiro Suzuki/200/Base	25.00
10	Mike Piazza/150	15.00
11	Jim Thome/150	10.00
12	Greg Maddux/150	15.00
13	Jeff Bagwell/150	8.00
14	Vladimir Guerrero/200	8.00
15	Ken Griffey Jr./200/Base	10.00
16	Jason Giambi/200/Base	6.00
17	Nomar Garciaparra/150	15.00
18	Albert Pujols/Base/200	10.00
19	Manny Ramirez/150	8.00
20	Pedro Martinez/150	8.00
21	Roger Clemens/150	15.00
22	Randy Johnson/150	8.00
24	So Taguchi/200	5.00
25	Sammy Sosa/200/Base	15.00

Hats Off

		NM/M
	Common Player:	8.00
	Production 100	
	MLB Logo:	No Pricing
	Production One Set	
10	Carlos Lee	10.00
14	Mark Buehrle	10.00
16	Paul LoDuca	10.00
22	Brandon Duckworth	10.00
26	J.D. Drew	12.00
28	Wade Miller	10.00
30	Brian Giles	10.00
31	Lance Berkman	10.00
32	Shannon Stewart	10.00
33	Kazuhisa Ishii/50	20.00
35	Rafael Palmeiro	20.00
36	Roy Oswalt	15.00
37	Jason Lane	10.00
38	Andruw Jones	15.00
39	Brad Penny	10.00
40	Bud Smith	8.00
41	Carlos Beltran	15.00
42	Magglio Ordonez	20.00
43	Craig Biggio	10.00
45	Jeff Bagwell	25.00
47	Juan Cruz	8.00
48	Kerry Wood	25.00
49	Brandon Berger	8.00
50	Juan Pierre	8.00

Leather & Lumber

		NM/M
	Common Player:	5.00
	Production 200 unless noted.	
	Artist's Proofs:	1.5-2X
	Production 50	
1	Nomar Garciaparra	15.00
2	Jeff Bagwell/150	8.00
3	Alex Rodriguez	15.00
4	Vladimir Guerrero/100	10.00
5	Luis Gonzalez	5.00
6	Chipper Jones	10.00
7	Shawn Green	5.00
8	Kirby Puckett/100	15.00
9	Juan Gonzalez	8.00
10	Troy Glaus	8.00
11	Don Mattingly/100	30.00
12	Todd Helton	8.00
13	Jim Thome	10.00
14	Rickey Henderson	15.00
15	Mike Schmidt/100	35.00
16	Adam Dunn/100	10.00
17	Ivan Rodriguez	10.00
18	Manny Ramirez/150	10.00
19	Tsuyoshi Shinjo	8.00
20	Andruw Jones/150	10.00
21	Roberto Alomar	8.00
22	Lance Berkman	5.00
23	Derek Jeter/50/Ball	30.00
24	Ichiro Suzuki/50/Ball	60.00
25	Mike Piazza	15.00

Masterstrokes

		NM/M
	Complete Set (25):	50.00
	Common Player:	1.50
	Inserted 1:17	
1	Vladimir Guerrero	3.00
2	Frank Thomas	3.00
3	Alex Rodriguez	6.00
4	Manny Ramirez	3.00
5	Jeff Bagwell	3.00
6	Jim Thome	1.50
7	Ichiro Suzuki	5.00
8	Andruw Jones	3.00
9	Troy Glaus	3.00
10	Chipper Jones	4.00
11	Juan Gonzalez	3.00
12	Lance Berkman	1.50
13	Mike Piazza	5.00
14	Darin Erstad	2.00
15	Albert Pujols	6.00
16	Kazuhisa Ishii	1.50
17	Shawn Green	1.50
18	Rafael Palmeiro	2.00
19	Todd Helton	3.00
20	Carlos Delgado	1.50
21	Ivan Rodriguez	2.00
22	Luis Gonzalez	1.50
23	Derek Jeter	8.00
24	Nomar Garciaparra	5.00
15	J.D. Drew	1.50

Masterstrokes Artist's Proof

		NM/M
	All Jersey/bat unless noted.	
	Varying quantities produced	
1	Vladimir Guerrero/200	15.00
2	Frank Thomas/200	15.00
3	Alex Rodriguez/100	25.00
4	Manny Ramirez/200	10.00
5	Jeff Bagwell/150	10.00
6	Jim Thome/200	15.00
7	Ichiro Suzuki/100/Ball/Base	50.00
8	Andruw Jones/200	10.00
9	Troy Glaus/200	10.00
10	Chipper Jones/200	15.00
11	Juan Gonzalez/200	10.00
12	Lance Berkman/200	8.00
13	Mike Piazza/200	25.00
14	Darin Erstad/200	10.00
15	Albert Pujols/100/Ball/Base	30.00
16	Kazuhisa Ishii/150	15.00
17	Shawn Green/200	10.00
18	Rafael Palmeiro/200	20.00
19	Todd Helton/200	15.00
20	Carlos Delgado/200	10.00
21	Ivan Rodriguez/200	15.00
22	Luis Gonzalez/200	10.00
23	Derek Jeter/100/Ball/Base	35.00
24	Nomar Garciaparra/150	25.00
25	J.D. Drew/150	8.00

Spirit of the Game

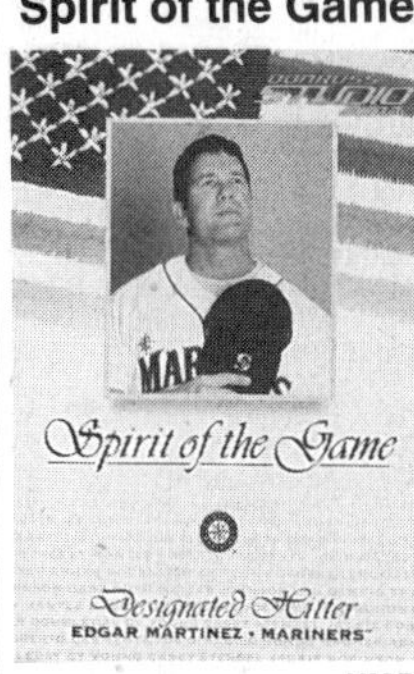

		NM/M
	Complete Set (50):	60.00
	Common Player:	1.00
	Inserted 1:9	
1	Alex Rodriguez	5.00
2	Curt Schilling	1.50
3	Hideo Nomo	2.00
4	Derek Jeter	6.00
5	Mike Sweeney	1.00
6	Mike Piazza	4.00
7	Roger Clemens	3.00
8	Shawn Green	1.50
9	Vladimir Guerrero	2.00
10	Carlos Lee	1.00
11	Edgar Martinez	1.00
12	Albert Pujols	5.00
13	Mark Prior	2.00
14	Mark Buehrle	1.00
15	Chipper Jones	3.00
16	Paul LoDuca	1.00
17	Frank Thomas	2.00
18	Randy Johnson	2.00
19	Cliff Floyd	1.00
20	Todd Helton	2.00
21	Luis Gonzalez	1.00
22	Brandon Duckworth	1.00
23	Jason Giambi	1.50
24	Juan Uribe	1.00
25	Dewon Brazelton	1.00
26	J.D. Drew	1.00
27	Troy Glaus	2.00
28	Wade Miller	1.00
29	Darin Erstad	1.50
30	Brian Giles	1.00
31	Lance Berkman	1.00
32	Shannon Stewart	1.00
33	Kazuhisa Ishii	1.00
34	Corey Patterson	1.00
35	Rafael Palmeiro	1.50
36	Roy Oswalt	1.00
37	Jason Lane	1.00
38	Andruw Jones	2.00
39	Brad Penny	1.00
40	Bud Smith	1.00
41	Carlos Beltran	1.50
42	Magglio Ordonez	1.50
43	Craig Biggio	1.00
44	Hank Blalock	1.50
45	Jeff Bagwell	2.00
46	Josh Beckett	1.50
47	Juan Cruz	1.00
48	Kerry Wood	1.50
49	Brandon Berger	1.00
50	Juan Pierre	1.00

Studio Stars

		NM/M
	Complete Set (50):	60.00
	Common Player:	1.00
	Production 700 Sets	
	Golds:	1.5-2X
	Production 250 Sets	
	Platinums:	3-5X
	Production 50 Sets	
1	Mike Piazza	3.00
2	Ivan Rodriguez	1.50
3	Albert Pujols	4.00
4	Scott Rolen	2.00
5	Alex Rodriguez	4.00
6	Curt Schilling	1.50
7	Vladimir Guerrero	2.00
8	Jim Thome	1.00
9	Derek Jeter	5.00
10	C.C. Sabathia	1.00
11	Sammy Sosa	3.00
12	Adam Dunn	1.50
13	Bernie Williams	1.00
14	Ichiro Suzuki	4.00
15	Barry Bonds	5.00
16	Rickey Henderson	2.00
17	Ken Griffey Jr.	3.00
18	Kazuhisa Ishii	1.00
19	Kerry Wood	1.50
20	Todd Helton	1.50
21	Hideo Nomo	2.00
22	Frank Thomas	2.00
23	Manny Ramirez	2.00
24	Luis Gonzalez	1.00
25	Rafael Palmeiro	1.50
26	Mike Mussina	1.50
27	Roy Oswalt	1.00
28	Darin Erstad	1.00
29	Barry Larkin	1.00
30	Randy Johnson	2.00
31	Tom Glavine	1.00
32	Lance Berkman	1.00
33	Juan Gonzalez	2.00
34	Shawn Green	1.00
35	Nomar Garciaparra	3.00
36	Troy Glaus	2.00
37	Tim Hudson	1.00
38	Carlos Delgado	1.50
39	Jason Giambi	1.50
40	Andruw Jones	2.00
41	Roberto Alomar	1.00
42	Greg Maddux	2.50
43	Pedro J. Martinez	2.00
44	Tony Gwynn	3.00
45	Alfonso Soriano	1.50
46	Chipper Jones	2.50
47	J.D. Drew	1.00
48	Roger Clemens	2.75
49	Barry Zito	1.00
50	Jeff Bagwell	1.50

LCS Programs

A perforated sheet of Donruss Studio cards was inserted into some of the programs sold for the American and National League Championship Series. The 8-1/2" x 11" sheet features eight player cards and a header card advertising the brand. Each 2-1/2" x 3-1/2" card is perforated on all sides and differs from the regularly issued version only in the card number on back. Sheet cards have either an "ALCS-" or "NLCS-" prefix to the number. Other programs could be found with similar sheets of Donruss Diamond Kings, Donruss Originals or Playoff Piece of the Game cards.

		NM/M
	Complete Sheet Set (2):	16.00
	Common Player:	.50
	ALCS SHEET	8.00
25	Eric Hinske	.50
26	Edgar Martinez (Spirit/Game)	.50
27	Pedro Martinez	.75
28	Roger Clemens (Spirit/Game)	1.75
29	Alex Rodriguez (Spirit/Game)	2.50
30	George Brett (Classic)	2.00
31	Dewon Brazelton (Spirit/Game)	.50
32	Barry Zito	.60
---	Header Card	.10
	NLCS SHEET	8.00
17	J.D. Drew (Spirit/Game)	.60
18	Randy Johnson	.75
19	Mike Piazza (Spirit/Game)	2.00
20	Ozzie Smith (Classic)	1.50
21	Jeff Kent	.50
22	Roy Oswalt (Spirit/Game)	.60
23	Pat Burrell	.60
24	Todd Helton (Spirit/Game)	.75
---	Header Card	.10

2002 Donruss The Rookies

	NM/M
Complete Set (110):	20.00

Common Player: .15
Common Rookie: .25
Pack (5): 2.00
Box (24): 40.00
1 Kazuhisa Ishii RC 1.00
2 P.J. Bevis RC .25
3 Jason Simontacchi RC .50
4 John Lackey .15
5 Travis Driskill RC .25
6 Carl Sadler RC .25
7 Tim Kalita RC .25
8 Nelson Castro RC .25
9 Francis Beltran RC .25
10 So Taguchi RC .50
11 Ryan Bukvich RC .25
12 Brian Fitzgerald .15
13 Kevin Frederick RC .25
14 Chone Figgins RC .75
15 Marlon Byrd .15
16 Ron Calloway RC .25
17 Jason Lane .15
18 Satoru Komiyama RC .25
19 John Ennis RC .25
20 Juan Brito RC .25
21 Gustavo Chacin RC .50
22 Josh Bard RC .50
23 Brett Myers .15
24 Mike Smith RC .25
25 Eric Hinske .15
26 Jake Peavy .15
27 Todd Donovan RC .25
28 Luis Ugueto RC .25
29 Corey Thurman RC .25
30 Takahito Nomura RC .25
31 Andy Shibilo RC .25
32 Mike Crudale RC .25
33 Earl Snyder RC .25
34 Brian Tallet .50
35 Miguel Asencio RC .25
36 Felix Escalona RC .25
37 Drew Henson .40
38 Steve Kent RC .25
39 Rene Reyes RC .25
40 Edwin Almonte RC .25
41 Chris Snelling RC .75
42 Franklyn German RC .25
43 Jeriome Robertson RC .25
44 Colin Young RC .25
45 Jeremy Lambert RC .25
46 Kirk Saarloos .75
47 Matt Childers RC .25
48 Justin Wayne .15
49 Jose Valverde RC .25
50 Wily Mo Pena .15
51 Victor Alvarez RC .25
52 Julius Matos RC .25
53 Aaron Cook RC .40
54 Jeff Austin RC .25
55 Adrian Burnside RC .25
56 Brandon Puffer RC .25
57 Jeremy Hill RC .25
58 Jaime Cerda RC .25
59 Aaron Guiel RC .25
60 Ron Chiavacci .15
61 Kevin Cash RC .25
62 Elio Serrano .15
63 Julio Mateo RC .25
64 Cam Esslinger RC .25
65 Ken Huckaby RC .25
66 Wiki Nieves RC .25
67 Luis Martinez RC .25
68 Scotty Layfield RC .25
69 Jeremy Guthrie RC .75
70 Hansel Izquierdo RC .25
71 Shane Nance RC .25
72 Jeff Baker RC .50
73 Clifford Bartosh RC .25
74 Mitch Wylie RC .25
75 Oliver Perez RC .75
76 Matt Thornton .15
77 John Foster RC .25
78 Joe Borchard .15
79 Eric Junge RC .25
80 Jorge Sosa RC .25
81 Runelvys Hernandez RC .25
82 Kevin Mench .15
83 Ben Kozlowski RC .25
84 Trey Hodges RC .40
85 Reed Johnson RC .25
86 Eric Eckenstahler RC .25
87 Franklin Nunez RC .25
88 Victor Martinez .50
89 Kevin Gryboski RC .25
90 Jason Jennings .15
91 Jim Rushford RC .25
92 Jeremy Ward RC .25
93 Adam Walker RC .25
94 Freddy Sanchez RC .50
95 Wilson Valdez RC .25
96 Lee Gardner .15
97 Eric Good RC .25
98 Hank Blalock .50
99 Mark Corey .15
100 Jason Davis RC .40
101 Mike Gonzalez RC .25
102 David Ross RC .25
103 Tyler Yates RC .25
104 Cliff Lee RC .50
105 Mike Moriarty RC .25
106 Josh Hancock RC .25
107 Jason Beverlin RC .25
108 Clay Condrey RC .25
109 Shawn Sedlacek RC .25
110 Sean Burroughs .15

Donruss Originals
401 Runelvys Hernandez RC .50
402 Wilson Valdez RC .25
403 Brian Tallet 1.00
404 Chone Figgins RC .25
405 Jeriome Robertson RC .50
406 Shane Nance RC .25
407 Aaron Cook RC .75
408 Trey Hodges RC .75
409 Matt Childers RC .40
410 Mitch Wylie RC .25
411 Rene Reyes RC .25
412 Mike Smith .25
413 Jason Simontacchi RC .75
414 Luis Martinez .40
415 Kevin Cash RC .40
416 Todd Donovan .25
417 Scotty Layfield .25
418 Joe Borchard .25
419 Adrian Burnside .25
420 Ben Kozlowski .25
421 Clay Condrey .25
422 Cliff Lee 1.00
423 Josh Bard .25
424 Freddy Sanchez 1.00
425 Ron Calloway .25

Donruss Studio
Common Studio RC: 3.00
Production 1,500
251 Freddy Sanchez RC 5.00
252 Josh Bard RC 3.00
253 Trey Hodges RC 5.00
254 Jorge Sosa RC 3.00
255 Ben Kozlowski RC 3.00
256 Eric Good RC 3.00
257 Brian Tallet 5.00
258 P.J. Bevis RC 3.00
259 Rodrigo Rosario RC 3.00
260 Kirk Saarloos 5.00
261 Runelvys Hernandez RC 4.00
262 Josh Hancock RC 3.00
263 Tim Kalita RC 3.00
264 Jason Simontacchi RC 5.00
265 Clay Condrey RC 3.00
266 Cliff Lee RC 8.00
267 Aaron Guiel RC 4.00
268 Andy Pratt RC 4.00
269 Wilson Valdez RC 3.00
270 Oliver Perez RC 6.00
271 Joe Borchard 3.00
272 Jeriome Robertson RC 4.00
273 Aaron Cook RC 5.00
274 Kevin Cash RC 3.00
275 Chone Figgins RC 3.00

Best of Fan Club
Common Best of Fan Club RC: 3.00
Production 1,350
Best of Fan Club Spotlights: 1.5-3X
Production 100 Sets
201 Kirk Saarloos 4.00
202 Oliver Perez RC 5.00
203 So Taguchi RC 6.00
204 Runelvys Hernandez RC 5.00
205 Freddy Sanchez RC 5.00
206 Cliff Lee RC 8.00
207 Kazuhisa Ishii RC 8.00
208 Kevin Cash RC 5.00
209 Trey Hodges RC 6.00
210 Wilson Valdez RC 3.00
211 Satoru Komiyama RC 3.00
212 Luis Ugueto RC 3.00
213 Joe Borchard 3.00
214 Brian Tallet 4.00
215 Jeriome Robertson RC 5.00
216 Eric Junge RC 4.00
217 Aaron Cook RC 4.00
218 Jason Simontacchi RC 3.00
219 Miguel Asencio RC 3.00
220 Josh Bard RC 3.00
221 Earl Snyder RC 3.00
222 Felix Escalona RC 3.00
223 Rene Reyes RC 3.00
224 Chone Figgins RC 3.00
225 Chris Snelling RC 5.00

Fan Club
Inserted 1:4 Retail
201 Kirk Saarloos 1.50
202 Oliver Perez RC 3.00
203 So Taguchi RC 2.00
204 Runelvys Hernandez RC 1.50
205 Freddy Sanchez RC 2.00
206 Cliff Lee 3.00
207 Kazuhisa Ishii RC 3.00
208 Kevin Cash 1.00
209 Trey Hodges 1.50
210 Wilson Valdez 1.00
211 Satoru Komiyama RC 1.00
212 Luis Ugueto RC 1.50
213 Joe Borchard 2.00
214 Brian Tallet 3.00
215 Jeriome Robertson RC 1.50
216 Eric Junge 1.50
217 Aaron Cook 1.50
218 Jason Simontacchi 1.50
219 Miguel Asencio 1.50
220 Josh Bard 1.50
221 Earl Snyder RC 1.50
222 Felix Escalona 1.00
223 Rene Reyes 1.00
224 Chone Figgins 1.00
225 Chris Snelling RC 4.00

Elite
Common Elite RC: 4.00
Production 1,000
Elite Turn of the Century: 1-2.5X
Production 100 Sets
201 Chris Snelling RC 5.00
202 Satoru Komiyama RC 5.00
203 Jason Simontacchi RC 8.00
204 Tim Kalita RC 4.00
205 Runelvys Hernandez RC 5.00
206 Kirk Saarloos 4.00
207 Aaron Cook RC 6.00
208 Luis Ugueto RC 5.00
209 Gustavo Chacin RC 5.00
210 Francis Beltran RC 5.00
211 Takahito Nomura RC 5.00
212 Oliver Perez RC 8.00
213 Miguel Asencio RC 4.00
214 Rene Reyes RC 5.00
215 Jeff Baker RC 15.00
216 Jon Adkins RC 5.00
217 Carlos Rivera RC 5.00
218 Corey Thurman RC 5.00
219 Earl Snyder RC 5.00
220 Felix Escalona RC 5.00
221 Jeremy Guthrie RC 15.00
222 Josh Hancock RC 5.00
223 Ben Kozlowski RC 5.00
224 Eric Good RC 5.00
225 Eric Junge RC 5.00
226 Andy Pratt RC 5.00
227 Matt Thornton 5.00
228 Jorge Sosa RC 5.00
229 Mike Smith 5.00
230 Mitch Wylie RC 5.00
231 John Ennis RC 5.00
232 Reed Johnson RC 5.00
233 Joe Borchard 8.00
234 Ron Calloway RC 5.00
235 Brian Tallet 5.00
236 Chris Baker RC 5.00
237 Cliff Lee RC 15.00
238 Matt Childers RC 5.00
239 Freddy Sanchez RC 5.00
240 Chone Figgins RC 8.00
241 Kevin Cash RC 5.00
242 Josh Bard RC 5.00
243 Jeriome Robertson RC 5.00
244 Jeremy Hill RC 5.00
245 Shane Nance RC 5.00
246 Wes Obermueller RC 5.00
247 Trey Hodges RC 5.00
248 Eric Eckenstahler RC 5.00
249 Jim Rushford RC 5.00
250 Jose Castillo RC 10.00
251 Garrett Atkins RC 20.00
252 Alexis Rios RC 100.00
253 Ryan Church RC 10.00
254 Jimmy Gobble RC 8.00
255 Corwin Malone 6.00
257 Nic Jackson RC 6.00
258 Tommy Whiteman RC 8.00
259 Mario Ramos 5.00
260 Rob Bowen RC 8.00
261 Josh Wilson RC 5.00
262 Tim Hummel RC 5.00
264 Gerald Laird RC 15.00
265 Vinnie Chulk RC 5.00
266 Jesus Medrano RC 5.00
272 Adam LaRoche RC 20.00
273 Adam Morrissey RC 5.00
274 Henri Stanley RC 5.00
275 Walter Young RC 10.00

Donruss Classics
Common Classics RC: 3.00
Production 1,500
Classics Timeless Tributes: 1.5-3X
Production 100 Sets
201 Oliver Perez RC 5.00
202 Aaron Cook RC 5.00
203 Eric Junge RC 3.00
204 Freddy Sanchez RC 5.00
205 Cliff Lee RC 5.00
206 Runelvys Hernandez RC 5.00
207 Chone Figgins RC 3.00
208 Rodrigo Rosario RC 3.00
209 Kevin Cash RC 3.00
210 Josh Bard RC 3.00
211 Felix Escalona RC 3.00
212 Jeriome Robertson RC 5.00
213 Jason Simontacchi RC 5.00
214 Shane Nance RC 3.00
215 Ben Kozlowski RC 3.00
216 Brian Tallet 5.00
217 Earl Snyder RC 3.00
218 Andy Pratt RC 3.00
219 Trey Hodges RC 5.00
220 Kirk Saarloos 5.00
221 Rene Reyes RC 3.00
222 Joe Borchard 3.00
223 Wilson Valdez RC 3.00
224 Miguel Asencio RC 3.00
225 Chris Snelling RC 5.00

Diamond Kings
Common DK RC: 3.00
Inserted 1:10
151 Chris Snelling RC 4.00
152 Satoru Komiyama RC 3.00
153 Oliver Perez RC 4.00
154 Kirk Saarloos 3.00
155 Rene Reyes RC 3.00
156 Runelvys Hernandez RC 3.00
157 Rodrigo Rosario RC 3.00
158 Jason Simontacchi RC 3.00
159 Miguel Asencio RC 3.00
160 Aaron Cook RC 3.00

Autographs

NM/M
Production 15-100 5.00
Print runs listed.
2 P.J. Bevis/50 20.00
9 Francis Beltran/100 5.00
13 Kevin Frederick/100 5.00
14 Chone Figgins/100 20.00
15 Marlon Byrd/100 10.00
17 Jason Lane/100 8.00
19 John Ennis/100 10.00
22 Josh Bard/100 10.00
25 Eric Hinske/100 10.00
28 Luis Ugueto/100 5.00
29 Corey Thurman/100 5.00
30 Takahito Nomura/100 20.00
33 Earl Snyder/100 10.00
34 Brian Tallet/100 15.00
37 Drew Henson/50 20.00
39 Rene Reyes/50 15.00
40 Edwin Almonte/50 15.00
41 Chris Snelling/50 20.00
42 Franklyn German/100 5.00
45 Jeremy Lambert/100 5.00
46 Kirk Saarloos/50 10.00
47 Matt Childers/100 5.00
50 Wily Mo Pena/100 15.00
51 Victor Alvarez/100 10.00
61 Kevin Cash/100 8.00
62 Elio Serrano/100 5.00
64 Cam Esslinger/100 5.00
69 Jeremy Guthrie/100 15.00
71 Shane Nance/100 8.00
72 Jeff Baker/100 20.00
76 Matt Thornton/100 10.00
78 Joe Borchard/100 10.00
82 Kevin Mench/100 10.00
83 Ben Kozlowski/100 8.00
84 Trey Hodges/100 10.00
85 Reed Johnson/100 15.00
88 Victor Martinez/100 25.00
90 Jason Jennings/100 8.00
95 Wilson Valdez/100 10.00
97 Eric Good/100 10.00
98 Hank Blalock/100 20.00
104 Cliff Lee/100 25.00
110 Sean Burroughs/50 10.00

Donruss Classics Signatures

NM/M
Print runs listed.
203 Eric Junge/50 10.00
205 Cliff Lee/100 30.00
207 Chone Figgins/100 10.00
208 Rodrigo Rosario/250 10.00
209 Kevin Cash/100 10.00
210 Josh Bard/100 10.00
214 Shane Nance/200 10.00
215 Ben Kozlowski/200 10.00
216 Brian Tallet/100 15.00
217 Earl Snyder/100 10.00
218 Andy Pratt/250 10.00
219 Trey Hodges/250 15.00
220 Kirk Saarloos/100 20.00
221 Rene Reyes/50 10.00
222 Joe Borchard/100 10.00
223 Wilson Valdez/100 10.00
225 Chris Snelling/100 25.00

Donruss Studio Private Signing

NM/M
Print runs listed.
252 Josh Bard/100 10.00
253 Trey Hodges/250 10.00
255 Ben Kozlowski/200 5.00
257 Brian Tallet/100 15.00
258 P.J. Bevis/50 15.00
259 Rodrigo Rosario/250 5.00
260 Kirk Saarloos/100 10.00
263 Tim Kalita/50 8.00
266 Cliff Lee/100 25.00
268 Andy Pratt/250 8.00
269 Wilson Valdez/200 5.00
271 Joe Borchard/100 15.00
274 Kevin Cash/100 8.00
275 Chone Figgins/100 8.00

Elite Turn of the Century Autographs

NM/M
Common Autograph:
Print runs listed.
201 Chris Snelling/50 30.00
206 Kirk Saarloos/50 20.00
215 Jeff Baker/100 40.00
216 Jon Adkins/100 10.00
217 Carlos Rivera/100 15.00
221 Jeremy Guthrie/100 25.00
223 Ben Kozlowski/100 10.00
224 Eric Good/100 10.00
240 Chone Figgins/100 30.00
241 Kevin Cash/100 10.00
247 Trey Hodges/100 15.00
251 Garrett Atkins/100 50.00
253 Ryan Church/100 35.00
254 Jimmy Gobble/100 10.00
255 Corwin Malone/100 15.00
258 Tom Whiteman/100 15.00
259 Mario Ramos/100 10.00
260 Rob Bowen/100 15.00
261 Josh Wilson/100 15.00
262 Tim Hummel/100 10.00
264 Gerald Laird/100 25.00
266 Jesus Medrano/100 10.00
272 Adam LaRoche/100 60.00
273 Adam Morrissey/100 15.00
274 Henri Stanley/100 15.00

Fan Club Autograph

NM/M
Common Autograph:
Print runs listed.
201 Kirk Saarloos/100 10.00
208 Kevin Cash/50 8.00
209 Trey Hodges/100 10.00
210 Wilson Valdez/50 10.00
212 Luis Ugueto/75 10.00
213 Joe Borchard/50 15.00
214 Brian Tallet/50 15.00
220 Josh Bard/50 8.00
221 Earl Snyder/100 8.00
223 Rene Reyes/50 8.00
224 Chone Figgins/100 8.00

Best of Fan Club Autograph

NM/M
Production 10-100
Print runs listed.
201 Kirk Saarloos/100 10.00
208 Kevin Cash/50 10.00
209 Trey Hodges/100 10.00
210 Wilson Valdez/50 10.00
212 Luis Ugueto/75 10.00
213 Joe Borchard/50 15.00
214 Brian Tallet/50 15.00
220 Josh Bard/50 8.00
221 Earl Snyder/100 8.00
223 Rene Reyes/50 8.00
224 Chone Figgins/100 8.00
225 Chris Snelling/50 15.00

Phenoms

NM/M
Common Player: 3.00
Production 1,000 Sets
1 Kazuhisa Ishii 5.00
2 Eric Hinske 3.00
3 Jason Lane 3.00
4 Victor Martinez 5.00
5 Mark Prior 6.00
6 Antonio Perez 3.00
7 John Buck 3.00
8 Joe Borchard 3.00
9 Alexis Gomez 3.00
10 Sean Burroughs 3.00
11 Carlos Pena 3.00
12 Bill Hall 3.00

13 Alfredo Amezaga 3.00
14 Ed Rogers 3.00
15 Mark Teixeira 5.00
16 Chris Snelling 4.00
17 Nick Johnson 3.00
18 Angel Berroa 3.00
19 Orlando Hudson 3.00
20 Drew Henson 3.00
21 Austin Kearns 3.00
22 Dewon Brazelton 3.00
23 Dennis Tankersley 3.00
24 Josh Beckett 4.00
25 Marlon Byrd 4.00

Phenoms Autographs

NM/M
Common Autograph: 5.00
Print runs listed.
2 Eric Hinske/500 10.00
3 Jason Lane/500 5.00
4 Victor Martinez/225 10.00
5 Mark Prior/100 50.00
6 Antonio Perez/500 5.00
7 John Buck/100 8.00
8 Joe Borchard/100 10.00
9 Alexis Gomez/400 5.00
10 Sean Burroughs/150 10.00
11 Carlos Pena/150 8.00
12 Bill Hall/200 8.00
13 Alfredo Amezaga/500 5.00
14 Ed Rogers/500 5.00
15 Mark Teixeira/100 20.00
16 Chris Snelling/100 15.00
17 Nick Johnson/250 8.00
18 Angel Berroa/500 8.00
19 Orlando Hudson/400 15.00
20 Drew Henson/500 25.00
21 Austin Kearns/75 20.00
22 Dewon Brazelton/350 5.00
23 Dennis Tankersley/100 8.00
24 Josh Beckett/125 30.00
25 Marlon Byrd/500 10.00

Rookie Crusade

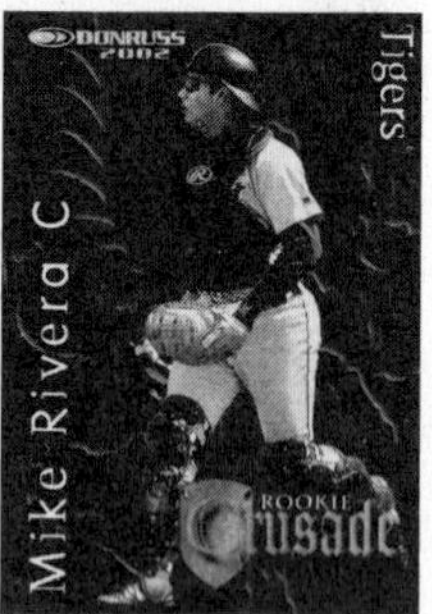

NM/M
Common Player: 3.00
Production 1,500 Sets
1 Corky Miller 3.00
2 Jack Cust 3.00
3 Erik Bedard 3.00
4 Andres Torres 3.00
5 Geronimo Gil 3.00
6 Rafael Soriano 3.00
7 Johnny Estrada 3.00
8 Steve Bechler 3.00
9 Adam Johnson 3.00
10 So Taguchi 3.00
11 Dee Brown 3.00
12 Kevin Frederick 3.00
13 Allan Simpson 3.00
14 Ricardo Rodriguez 3.00
15 Jason Hart 3.00
16 Matt Childers 3.00
17 Jason Jennings 3.00
18 Anderson Machado 3.00
19 Fernando Rodney 3.00
20 Brandon Larson 3.00
21 Satoru Komiyama 3.00
22 Francis Beltran 3.00
23 Joe Thurston 3.00
24 Josh Pearce 3.00
25 Carlos Hernandez 3.00
26 Ben Howard 3.00
27 Wilson Valdez 3.00
28 Victor Alvarez 3.00
29 Cesar Izturis 3.00

30 Endy Chavez 3.00
31 Michael Cuddyer 4.00
32 Bobby Hill 3.00
33 Willie Harris 3.00
34 Joe Crede 3.00
35 Jorge Padilla 3.00
36 Brandon Backe 3.00
37 Franklyn German 3.00
38 Xavier Nady 3.00
39 Raul Chavez 3.00
40 Shane Nance 3.00
41 Brandon Claussen 4.00
42 Tom Shearn 3.00
43 Freddy Sanchez 3.00
44 Chone Figgins 3.00
45 Cliff Lee 4.00
46 Brian Mallette 3.00
47 Mike Rivera 3.00
48 Elio Serrano 3.00
49 Rodrigo Rosario 3.00
50 Earl Snyder 3.00

Rookie Crusade Autograph

NM/M
Common Autograph: 5.00
Print runs listed.
1 Corky Miller/500 5.00
2 Jack Cust/500 6.00
3 Erik Bedard/100 10.00
4 Andres Torres/500 5.00
5 Geronimo Gil/500 5.00
6 Rafael Soriano/500 8.00
7 Johnny Estrada/400 5.00
8 Steve Bechler/500 6.00
9 Adam Johnson/500 5.00
11 Dee Brown/500 5.00
12 Kevin Frederick/150 5.00
13 Allan Simpson/150 5.00
14 Ricardo Rodriguez/500 5.00
15 Jason Hart/500 5.00
16 Matt Childers/150 5.00
17 Jason Jennings/500 5.00
18 Anderson Machado/500 8.00
19 Fernando Rodney/500 5.00
20 Brandon Larson/400 5.00
22 Francis Beltran/500 5.00
23 Joe Thurston/500 5.00
24 Josh Pearce/500 5.00
25 Carlos Hernandez/500 5.00
26 Ben Howard/500 6.00
27 Wilson Valdez/500 5.00
28 Victor Alvarez/500 5.00
29 Cesar Izturis/500 8.00
30 Endy Chavez/500 5.00
31 Michael Cuddyer/375 10.00
32 Bobby Hill/250 5.00
33 Willie Harris/300 5.00
34 Joe Crede/100 8.00
35 Jorge Padilla/475 10.00
36 Brandon Backe/350 5.00
37 Franklyn German/500 5.00
38 Xavier Nady/500 8.00
39 Raul Chavez/500 5.00
40 Shane Nance/500 5.00
41 Brandon Claussen/150 10.00
42 Tom Shearn/500 5.00
44 Chone Figgins/500 5.00
45 Cliff Lee/500 10.00
46 Brian Mallette/150 5.00
47 Mike Rivera/400 5.00
48 Elio Serrano/500 5.00
49 Rodrigo Rosario/100 10.00
50 Earl Snyder/100 10.00

2003 Donruss Samples

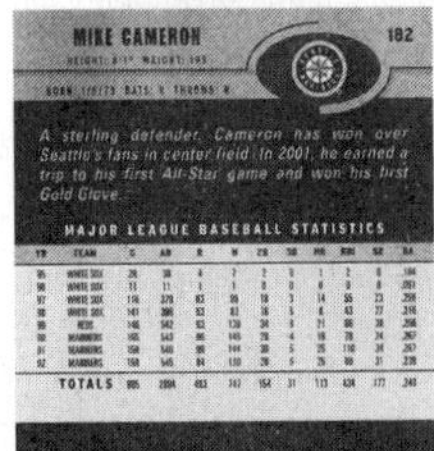

Each issue of the Jan., 2003, Beckett Baseball Card Monthly included a sample 2003 Donruss card rubber-cemented inside. The cards differ from the issued version only in the appearance on back of a (usually) silver-foil "SAMPLE" notation. Some cards were produced with the over-print in gold-foil, in much more limited quantities. The number of different players' cards involved in the promotion is unknown.

NM/M
Common Player: .10
Stars: 1.5-2X
Gold: 10X

2003 Donruss

NM/M
Complete Set (400): 40.00
Common Player: .15
Pack (13): 1.50
Box (24): 30.00
1 Vladimir Guerrero .75
2 Derek Jeter 2.00
3 Adam Dunn .50
4 Greg Maddux 1.00
5 Lance Berkman .40
6 Ichiro Suzuki 2.00
7 Mike Piazza 1.00
8 Alex Rodriguez 2.00
9 Tom Glavine .25
10 Randy Johnson .75
11 Nomar Garciaparra 1.00
12 Jason Giambi .50
13 Sammy Sosa 1.00
14 Barry Zito .25
15 Chipper Jones 1.00
16 Magglio Ordonez .25
17 Larry Walker .25
18 Alfonso Soriano .75
19 Curt Schilling .50
20 Barry Bonds 2.00
21 Joe Borchard .15
22 Chris Snelling .15
23 Brian Tallet .15
24 Cliff Lee .15
25 Freddy Sanchez .15
26 Chone Figgins .15
27 Kevin Cash .15
28 Josh Bard .15
29 Jeriome Robertson .15
30 Jeremy Hill .15
31 Shane Nance .15
32 Jake Peavy Padres .15
33 Trey Hodges .15
34 Eric Eckenstahler .15
35 Jim Rushford .15
36 Oliver Perez .15
37 Kirk Saarloos .15
38 Hank Blalock .50
39 Francisco Rodriguez .25
40 Runelvys Hernandez .15
41 Aaron Cook .15
42 Josh Hancock .15
43 P.J. Bevis .15
44 Jon Adkins .15
45 Tim Kalita .15
46 Nelson Castro .15
47 Colin Young .15
48 Adrian Burnside .15
49 Luis Martinez .15
50 Peter Zamora .15
51 Todd Donovan .15
52 Jeremy Ward .15
53 Wilson Valdez .15
54 Eric Good .15
55 Jeff Baker .15
56 Mitch Wylie .15
57 Ron Calloway .15
58 Jose Valverde .15
59 Jason Davis .15
60 Scotty Layfield .15
61 Matt Thornton .15
62 Adam Walker .15
63 Gustavo Chacin .15
64 Ron Chiavacci .15
65 Wiki Nieves .15
66 Clifford Bartosh .15
67 Mike Gonzalez .15
68 Justin Wayne .15
69 Eric Junge .15
70 Ben Kozlowski .15
71 Darin Erstad .25
72 Garret Anderson .40
73 Troy Glaus .40
74 David Eckstein .15
75 Adam Kennedy .15
76 Kevin Appier .15
77 Jarrod Washburn .15
78 Scott Spiezio .15
79 Tim Salmon .25
80 Ramon Ortiz .15
81 Bengie Molina .15
82 Brad Fullmer .15
83 Troy Percival .15
84 David Segui .15
85 Jay Gibbons .15
86 Tony Batista .15
87 Scott Erickson .15
88 Jeff Conine .15
89 Melvin Mora .15
90 Buddy Groom .15
91 Rodrigo Lopez .15
92 Marty Cordova .15
93 Geronimo Gil .15
94 Kenny Lofton .15
95 Shea Hillenbrand .15
96 Manny Ramirez .50
97 Pedro Martinez .75
98 Nomar Garciaparra 1.00
99 Rickey Henderson .40
100 Johnny Damon .25
101 Trot Nixon .15
102 Derek Lowe .15
103 Hee Seop Choi .15
104 Mark Teixeira .40
105 Tim Wakefield .15
106 Jason Varitek .25
107 Frank Thomas .50
108 Joe Crede .15
109 Magglio Ordonez .25
110 Ray Durham .15
111 Mark Buehrle .15
112 Paul Konerko .25
113 Jose Valentin .15
114 Carlos Lee .15
115 Royce Clayton .15
116 C.C. Sabathia .15
117 Ellis Burks .15
118 Omar Vizquel .25
119 Jim Thome .75
120 Matt Lawton .15
121 Travis Fryman .15
122 Earl Snyder .15
123 Ricky Gutierrez .15
124 Einar Diaz .15
125 Danys Baez .15
126 Robert Fick .15
127 Bobby Higginson .15
128 Steve Sparks .15
129 Mike Rivera .15
130 Wendell Magee .15
131 Randall Simon .15
132 Carlos Pena .15
133 Mark Redman .15
134 Juan Acevedo .15
135 Mike Sweeney .15
136 Aaron Guiel .15
137 Carlos Beltran .40
138 Joe Randa .15
139 Paul Byrd .15
140 Shawn Sedlacek .15
141 Raul Ibanez .15
142 Michael Tucker .15
143 Torii Hunter .40
144 Jacque Jones .15
145 David Ortiz .40
146 Corey Koskie .15
147 Brad Radke .15
148 Doug Mientkiewicz .15
149 A.J. Pierzynski .15
150 Dustan Mohr .15
151 Michael Cuddyer .15
152 Eddie Guardado .15
153 Cristian Guzman .15
154 Derek Jeter 2.00
155 Bernie Williams .50
156 Roger Clemens 1.50
157 Mike Mussina .50
158 Jorge Posada .40
159 Alfonso Soriano .75
160 Jason Giambi .50
161 Robin Ventura .25
162 Andy Pettitte .25
163 David Wells .15
164 Nick Johnson .15
165 Jeff Weaver .15
166 Raul Mondesi .15
167 Rondell White .15
168 Tim Hudson .25
169 Barry Zito .40
170 Mark Mulder .25
171 Miguel Tejada .40
172 Eric Chavez .25
173 Billy Koch .15
174 Jermaine Dye .15
175 Scott Hatteberg .15
176 Terrence Long .15
177 David Justice .25
178 Ramon Hernandez .15
179 Ted Lilly .15
180 Ichiro Suzuki 1.50
181 Edgar Martinez .25
182 Mike Cameron .15
183 John Olerud .15
184 Bret Boone .25
185 Dan Wilson .15
186 Freddy Garcia .15
187 Jamie Moyer .15
188 Carlos Guillen .15
189 Ruben Sierra .15
190 Kazuhiro Sasaki .15
191 Mark McLemore .15
192 Chris Snelling .15
193 Joel Pineiro .15
194 Jeff Cirillo .15
195 Rafael Soriano .15
196 Ben Grieve .15
197 Aubrey Huff .15
198 Steve Cox .15
199 Toby Hall .15
200 Randy Winn .15
201 Brent Abernathy .15
202 Chris Gomez .15
203 John Flaherty .15
204 Paul Wilson .15
205 Chan Ho Park .15
206 Alex Rodriguez 2.00
207 Juan Gonzalez .50
208 Rafael Palmeiro .50
209 Ivan Rodriguez .50
210 Rusty Greer .15
211 Kenny Rogers .15
212 Ismael Valdes .15
213 Frank Catalanotto .15
214 Hank Blalock .50
215 Michael Young .15
216 Kevin Mench .15
217 Herbert Perry .15
218 Gabe Kapler .25
219 Carlos Delgado .25
220 Shannon Stewart .15
221 Eric Hinske .15
222 Roy Halladay .25
223 Felipe Lopez .15
224 Vernon Wells .15
225 Josh Phelps .15
226 Jose Cruz .15
227 Curt Schilling .50
228 Randy Johnson .75
229 Luis Gonzalez .25
230 Mark Grace .40
231 Junior Spivey .15
232 Tony Womack .15
233 Matt Williams .25
234 Steve Finley .15
235 Byung-Hyun Kim .15
236 Craig Counsell .15
237 Greg Maddux 1.00
238 Tom Glavine .40
239 John Smoltz .25
240 Chipper Jones 1.00
241 Gary Sheffield .25
242 Andruw Jones .40
243 Vinny Castilla .15
244 Damian Moss .15
245 Rafael Furcal .15
246 Javy Lopez .25
247 Kevin Millwood .15
248 Kerry Wood .75
249 Fred McGriff .25
250 Sammy Sosa 1.00
251 Alex Gonzalez .15
252 Corey Patterson .25
253 Moises Alou .25
254 Juan Cruz .15
255 Jon Lieber .15
256 Matt Clement .15
257 Mark Prior .75
258 Ken Griffey Jr. 1.00
259 Barry Larkin .25
260 Adam Dunn .50
261 Sean Casey .15
262 Jose Rijo .15
263 Elmer Dessens .15
264 Austin Kearns .25
265 Corky Miller .15
266 Todd Walker .15
267 Chris Reitsma .15
268 Ryan Dempster .15
269 Aaron Boone .15
270 Danny Graves .15
271 Brandon Larson .15
272 Larry Walker .25
273 Todd Helton .50
274 Juan Uribe .15
275 Juan Pierre .15
276 Mike Hampton .15
277 Todd Zeile .15
278 Todd Hollandsworth .15
279 Jason Jennings .15
280 Josh Beckett .40
281 Mike Lowell .25
282 Derrek Lee .25
283 A.J. Burnett .15
284 Luis Castillo .15
285 Tim Raines .15
286 Preston Wilson .15
287 Juan Encarnacion .15
288 Charles Johnson .15
289 Jeff Bagwell .50
290 Craig Biggio .25
291 Lance Berkman .40
292 Daryle Ward .15
293 Roy Oswalt .40
294 Richard Hidalgo .15
295 Octavio Dotel .15
296 Wade Miller .15
297 Julio Lugo .15
298 Billy Wagner .15
299 Shawn Green .40
300 Adrian Beltre .25
301 Paul LoDuca .15
302 Eric Karros .15
303 Kevin Brown .15
304 Hideo Nomo .40
305 Odalis Perez .15
306 Eric Gagne .40
307 Brian Jordan .15
308 Cesar Izturis .15
309 Mark Grudzielanek .15
310 Kazuhisa Ishii .15
311 Geoff Jenkins .15
312 Richie Sexson .40
313 Jose Hernandez .15
314 Ben Sheets .25
315 Ruben Quevedo .15
316 Jeffrey Hammonds .15
317 Alex Sanchez .15
318 Eric Young .15
319 Takahito Nomura .15
320 Vladimir Guerrero .75
321 Jose Vidro .15
322 Orlando Cabrera .15
323 Michael Barrett .15
324 Javier Vazquez .15
325 Tony Armas Jr. .15
326 Andres Galarraga .15
327 Tomokazu Ohka .15
328 Bartolo Colon .15
329 Fernando Tatis .15
330 Brad Wilkerson .15
331 Masato Yoshii .15
332 Mike Piazza 1.00
333 Jeromy Burnitz .15
334 Roberto Alomar .50
335 Mo Vaughn .15
336 Al Leiter .25
337 Pedro Astacio .15
338 Edgardo Alfonzo .15
339 Armando Benitez .15
340 Timoniel Perez .15
341 Jay Payton .15
342 Roger Cedeno .15
343 Rey Ordonez .15
344 Steve Trachsel .15
345 Satoru Komiyama .15
346 Scott Rolen .75
347 Pat Burrell .40
348 Bobby Abreu .25
349 Mike Lieberthal .15
350 Brandon Duckworth .15
351 Jimmy Rollins .25
352 Marlon Anderson .15
353 Travis Lee .15
354 Vicente Padilla .15
355 Randy Wolf .15
356 Jason Kendall .15
357 Brian Giles .25
358 Aramis Ramirez .40
359 Pokey Reese .15
360 Kip Wells .15
361 Josh Fogg .15
362 Mike Williams .15
363 Jack Wilson .15
364 Craig Wilson .15
365 Kevin Young .15
366 Ryan Klesko .15
367 Phil Nevin .15
368 Brian Lawrence .15
369 Mark Kotsay .15
370 Brett Tomko .15
371 Trevor Hoffman .15
372 Deivi Cruz .15
373 Bubba Trammell .15
374 Sean Burroughs .15
375 Barry Bonds 2.00
376 Jeff Kent .25
377 Rich Aurilia .15
378 Tsuyoshi Shinjo .15
379 Benito Santiago .15
380 Kirk Rueter .15
381 Livan Hernandez .15
382 Russ Ortiz .15
383 David Bell .15
384 Jason Schmidt .40
385 Reggie Sanders .15
386 J.T. Snow .15
387 Robb Nen .15
388 Ryan Jensen .15
389 Jim Edmonds .40
390 J.D. Drew .25
391 Albert Pujols 1.50
392 Fernando Vina .15
393 Tino Martinez .15
394 Edgar Renteria .40
395 Matt Morris .15
396 Woody Williams .15
397 Jason Isringhausen .15
398 Placido Polanco .15
399 Eli Marrero .15
400 Jason Simontacchi .15

Stat Line Career

Cards serial numbered 251-400: 3-6X
Print run 151-250: 4-8X
Print run 101-150: 5-10X
Print run 61-100: 8-15X
Print run 31-60: 10-20X
Numbered to career stat.

Stat Line Season

Cards serial numbered 151-200: 4-8X
Print run 101-150: 5-10X
Print run 61-100: 8-15X
Print run 31-60: 10-20X
Numbered to 2002 stat.

All-Stars

NM/M
Complete Set (10): 25.00
Common Player: 1.50
Retail only.
1 Ichiro Suzuki 5.00
2 Alex Rodriguez 6.00
3 Nomar Garciaparra 3.00
4 Derek Jeter 6.00
5 Manny Ramirez 2.00
6 Barry Bonds 6.00
7 Adam Dunn 1.50
8 Mike Piazza 3.00
9 Sammy Sosa 4.00
10 Todd Helton 1.50

Anniversary 1983

NM/M
Complete Set (20): 50.00
Common Player: 1.50
Inserted 1:12
1 Dale Murphy 2.00
2 Jim Palmer 2.00
3 Nolan Ryan 6.00
4 Ozzie Smith 4.00
5 Tom Seaver 4.00
6 Mike Schmidt 5.00
7 Steve Carlton 2.00
8 Robin Yount 3.00
9 Ryne Sandberg 4.00
10 Cal Ripken Jr. 8.00
11 Fernando Valenzuela 1.50
12 Andre Dawson 2.00
13 George Brett 6.00
14 Eddie Murray 3.00
15 Dave Winfield 2.00
16 Johnny Bench 4.00
17 Wade Boggs 2.00
18 Tony Gwynn 4.00
19 San Diego Chicken 1.50
20 Ty Cobb 5.00

Bat Kings

NM/M
Common Player: 10.00
Studio Series: 1.5-3X
Production 25 or 50
1 Scott Rolen/250 20.00
2 Frank Thomas/250 15.00
3 Chipper Jones/250 20.00
4 Ivan Rodriguez/250 15.00
5 Stan Musial/100 40.00
6 Nomar Garciaparra/250 25.00
7 Vladimir Guerrero/250 15.00
8 Adam Dunn/250 15.00
9 Lance Berkman/250 10.00
10 Magglio Ordonez/250 10.00
11 Ernie Banks/50 40.00
12 Manny Ramirez/100 25.00
13 Mike Piazza/100 40.00
14 Alex Rodriguez/100 25.00
15 Todd Helton/100 20.00
16 Andre Dawson/100 20.00
17 Cal Ripken Jr/100 60.00
18 Tony Gwynn/100 25.00
19 Don Mattingly/100 60.00
20 Ryne Sandberg/100 45.00

Diamond Kings

NM/M
Complete Set (20): 120.00

Common Player:		2.00
Production 2,500 Sets		
Studio Series:		1.5-3X
Production 250 Sets		
1	Vladimir Guerrero	5.00
2	Derek Jeter	15.00
3	Adam Dunn	5.00
4	Greg Maddux	8.00
5	Lance Berkman	3.00
6	Ichiro Suzuki	10.00
7	Mike Piazza	10.00
8	Alex Rodriguez	10.00
9	Tom Glavine	3.00
10	Randy Johnson	8.00
11	Nomar Garciaparra	10.00
12	Jason Giambi	5.00
13	Sammy Sosa	8.00
14	Barry Zito	3.00
15	Chipper Jones	8.00
16	Magglio Ordonez	2.00
17	Larry Walker	2.00
18	Alfonso Soriano	8.00
19	Curt Schilling	4.00
20	Barry Bonds	15.00

Elite Series

		NM/M
Complete Set (15):		50.00
Common Player:		2.00
Production 2,500 Sets		
Dominators:		No Pricing
Production 25 Sets		
1	Alex Rodriguez	8.00
2	Barry Bonds	10.00
3	Ichiro Suzuki	8.00
4	Vladimir Guerrero	4.00
5	Randy Johnson	4.00
6	Pedro Martinez	4.00
7	Adam Dunn	3.00
8	Sammy Sosa	6.00
9	Jim Edmonds	2.00
10	Greg Maddux	6.00
11	Kazuhisa Ishii	2.00
12	Jason Giambi	3.00
13	Nomar Garciaparra	6.00
14	Tom Glavine	2.00
15	Todd Helton	3.00

Elite Dominators

No Pricing
25 sets produced.

Jersey Kings

		NM/M
Common Player:		10.00
Studio Series:		1.5-3X
Production 25 or 50		
1	Juan Gonzalez/250	15.00
2	Greg Maddux/250	20.00
3	Nomar Garciaparra/ 250	20.00
4	Troy Glaus/250	10.00
5	Reggie Jackson/100	20.00
6	Alex Rodriguez/250	25.00
7	Alfonso Soriano/250	15.00
8	Curt Schilling/250	12.00
9	Vladimir Guerrero/ 250	15.00
10	Adam Dunn/250	15.00
11	Mark Grace/100	25.00
12	Roger Clemens/100	30.00
13	Jeff Bagwell/100	25.00
14	Tom Glavine/100	20.00
15	Mike Piazza/100	25.00
16	Rod Carew/100	20.00
17	Rickey Henderson/ 100	25.00
18	Mike Schmidt/100	40.00
19	Cal Ripken Jr./100	60.00
20	Dale Murphy/100	15.00

Longball Leaders

		NM/M
Complete Set (10):		30.00
Common Player:		1.50
Production 1,000 Sets		
Seasonal Sum:		4-6X
Numbered to 2002 HR total.		
1	Alex Rodriguez	6.00
2	Alfonso Soriano	4.00
3	Rafael Palmeiro	2.00
4	Jim Thome	3.00
5	Jason Giambi	3.00
6	Sammy Sosa	5.00
7	Barry Bonds	8.00
8	Lance Berkman	2.00
9	Shawn Green	1.50
10	Vladimir Guerrero	4.00

Production Line

		NM/M
Complete Set (30):		120.00
Common Player:		2.00
Numbered to selected stat.		
Die-Cuts:		1-30X
Production 100 Sets		
1	Alex Rodriguez/1,015	6.00
2	Jim Thome/1,122	3.00
3	Lance Berkman/982	2.00
4	Barry Bonds/1,381	8.00
5	Sammy Sosa/993	5.00
6	Vladimir Guerrero/ 1,010	3.00
7	Barry Bonds/582	10.00
8	Jason Giambi/435	6.00
9	Vladimir Guerrero/417	4.00
10	Adam Dunn/400	3.00
11	Chipper Jones/435	6.00
12	Todd Helton/429	3.00
13	Rafael Palmeiro/571	2.00
14	Sammy Sosa/594	6.00
15	Alex Rodriguez/623	8.00
16	Larry Walker/602	2.00
17	Lance Berkman/578	2.00
18	Alfonso Soriano/547	5.00
19	Ichiro Suzuki/321	8.00
20	Mike Sweeney/340	2.00
21	Manny Ramirez/349	4.00
22	Larry Walker/338	2.00
23	Barry Bonds/370	12.00
24	Jim Edmonds/311	2.00
25	Alfonso Soriano/300	6.00
26	Jason Giambi/335	6.00
27	Miguel Tejada/336	4.00
28	Brian Giles/309	3.00
29	Vladimir Guerrero/364	5.00
30	Pat Burrell/319	8.00

Timber and Threads

		NM/M
Common Player:		6.00
1	Al Kaline/Bat/125	25.00
2	Alex Rodriguez/ Bat/350	20.00
3	Carlos Delgado/ Bat/250	8.00
4	Cliff Floyd/Bat/250	8.00
5	Eddie Mathews/ Bat/125	25.00
6	Edgar Martinez/ Bat/125	10.00
7	Ernie Banks/Bat/50	40.00
8	Ivan Rodriguez/ Bat/125	15.00
9	J.D. Drew/Bat/125	8.00
10	Jorge Posada/ Bat/300	10.00
11	Lou Brock/Bat/125	20.00
12	Mike Piazza/Bat/125	25.00
13	Mike Schmidt/ Bat/125	50.00
14	Reggie Jackson/ Bat/125	20.00
15	Rickey Henderson/ Bat/125	25.00
16	Robin Yount/Bat/125	35.00
17	Rod Carew/Bat/125	25.00
18	Scott Rolen/Bat/125	20.00
19	Shawn Green/Bat/200	8.00
20	Willie Stargell/ Bat/125	15.00
21	Alex Rodriguez/ Jsy/175	20.00
22	Andruw Jones/ Jsy/275	8.00
23	Brooks Robinson/ Jsy/150	25.00
24	Chipper Jones/ Jsy/150	20.00
25	Greg Maddux/ Jsy/175	20.00
26	Hideo Nomo/Jsy/300	40.00
27	Ivan Rodriguez/ Jsy/225	10.00
28	Jack Morris/Jsy/150	8.00
29	J.D. Drew/Jsy/150	8.00
30	Jeff Bagwell/Jsy/500	15.00
31	Jim Thome/Jsy/200	15.00
32	John Smoltz/Jsy/175	8.00
33	John Olerud/Jsy/450	8.00
34	Kerry Wood/Jsy/200	15.00
35	Harmon Killebrew/ Jsy/50	60.00
36	Larry Walker/Jsy/500	6.00
37	Magglio Ordonez/ Jsy/150	10.00
38	Manny Ramirez/ Jsy/500	15.00
39	Mike Piazza/Jsy/300	15.00
40	Mike Sweeney/ Jsy/200	8.00
41	Nomar Garciaparra/ Jsy/200	25.00
42	Paul Konerko/ Jsy/500	10.00
43	Pedro Martinez/ Jsy/175	15.00
44	Randy Johnson/ Jsy/175	15.00
45	Roger Clemens/ Jsy/350	20.00
46	Shawn Green/Jsy/250	8.00
47	Todd Helton/Jsy/175	8.00
48	Tom Glavine/Jsy/225	12.00
49	Tony Gwynn/Jsy/150	25.00
50	Vladimir Guerrero/ Jsy/450	15.00

Champions Samples

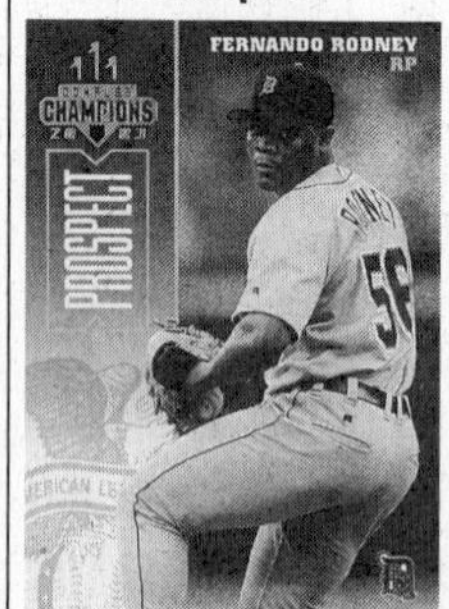

Each issue of the May 2003 Beckett Baseball Card Monthly included a sample 2003 Donruss Champions card rubber-cemented inside. The cards differ from the issued version only in the appearance on back of a (usually) silver-foil "SAMPLE" notation. Some cards were produced with the overprint in gold-foil, in much more limited quantities. The number of different players' cards involved in the promotion is unknown.

	NM/M
Common Player:	.10
Stars:	1.5-2X
Gold:	10X

2003 Donruss Champions

		NM/M
Complete Set (300):		40.00
Common Player:		.15
Pack (8):		2.00
Box (24):		40.00
1	Adam Kennedy	.15
2	Alfredo Amezaga	.15
3	Chone Figgins	.15
4	Darin Erstad	.25
5	David Eckstein	.15
6	Garret Anderson	.40
7	Jarrod Washburn	.15
8	Nolan Ryan	2.00
9	Tim Salmon	.25
10	Troy Glaus	.40
11	Troy Percival	.15
12	Curt Schilling	.50
13	Junior Spivey	.15
14	Luis Gonzalez	.25
15	Mark Grace	.50
16	Randy Johnson	1.00
17	Steve Finley	.15
18	Andruw Jones	.40
19	Chipper Jones	.75
20	Dale Murphy	.50
21	Gary Sheffield	.40
22	Greg Maddux	1.00
23	John Smoltz	.25
24	Andy Pratt	.15
25	Adam LaRoche	.15
26	Trey Hodges	.15
27	Warren Spahn	.75
28	Cal Ripken Jr.	3.00
29	Ed Rogers	.15
30	Brian Roberts	.15
31	Geronimo Gil	.15
32	Jay Gibbons	.15
33	Josh Towers	.15
34	Casey Fossum	.15
35	Cliff Floyd	.15
36	Derek Lowe	.15
37	Fred Lynn	.15
38	Freddy Sanchez	.15
39	Manny Ramirez	.50
40	Nomar Garciaparra	1.00
41	Pedro J. Martinez	.75
42	Rickey Henderson	.50
43	Shea Hillenbrand	.15
44	Trot Nixon	.15
45	Bobby Hill	.15
46	Corey Patterson	.25
47	Fred McGriff	.25
48	Hee Seop Choi	.15
49	Juan Cruz	.15
50	Kerry Wood	.75
51	Mark Prior	1.00
52	Moises Alou	.25
53	Nic Jackson	.15
54	Ryne Sandberg	1.00
55	Sammy Sosa	1.50
56	Carlos Lee	.15
57	Corwin Malone	.15
58	Frank Thomas	.50
59	Joe Borchard	.15
60	Joe Crede	.15
61	Magglio Ordonez	.25
62	Mark Buehrle	.15
63	Paul Konerko	.25
64	Tim Hummel	.15
65	Jon Adkins	.15
66	Adam Dunn	.50
67	Austin Kearns	.25
68	Barry Larkin	.40
69	Jose Acevedo	.15
70	Corky Miller	.15
71	Eric Davis	.15
72	Ken Griffey Jr.	1.00
73	Sean Casey	.15
74	Wily Mo Pena	.25
75	Bob Feller	.50
76	Brian Tallet	.15
77	C.C. Sabathia	.15
78	Cliff Lee	.15
79	Earl Snyder	.15
80	Ellis Burks	.15
81	Jeremy Guthrie	.15
82	Travis Hafner	.25
83	Luis Garcia	.15
84	Omar Vizquel	.25
85	Ricardo Rodriguez	.15
86	Ryan Church	.15
87	Victor Martinez	.15
88	Brandon Phillips	.15
89	Jack Cust	.15
90	Jason Jennings	.15
91	Jeff Baker	.15
92	Garrett Atkins	.15
93	Juan Uribe	.15
94	Larry Walker	.25
95	Rene Reyes	.15
96	Todd Helton	.50
97	Alan Trammell	.25
98	Fernando Rodney	.15
99	Carlos Pena	.15
100	Jack Morris	.15
101	Bobby Higginson	.15
102	Mike Maroth	.15
103	Robert Fick	.15
104	Jesus Medrano	.15
105	Josh Beckett	.40
106	Luis Castillo	.15
107	Mike Lowell	.25
108	Juan Pierre	.15
109	Josh Wilson	.15
110	Tim Redding	.15
111	Carlos Hernandez	.15
112	Craig Biggio	.25
113	Henri Stanley	.15
114	Jason Lane	.15
115	Jeff Bagwell	.50
116	John Buck	.15
117	Kirk Saarloos	.15
118	Lance Berkman	.75
119	Nolan Ryan	2.00
120	Richard Hidalgo	.15
121	Rodrigo Rosario	.15
122	Roy Oswalt	.25
123	Tommy Whiteman **RC**	.15
124	Wade Miller	.15
125	Alexis Gomez	.15
126	Angel Berroa	.15
127	Brandon Berger	.15
128	Carlos Beltran	.40
129	George Brett	2.00
130	Jimmy Gobble	.15
131	Dee Brown	.15
132	Mike Sweeney	.15
133	Raul Ibanez	.15
134	Runelvys Hernandez	.15
135	Adrian Beltre	.40
136	Brian Jordan	.15
137	Cesar Izturis	.15
138	Victor Alvarez	.15
139	Hideo Nomo	.50
140	Joe Thurston	.15
141	Kazuhisa Ishii	.15
142	Kevin Brown	.25
143	Odalis Perez	.15
144	Paul LoDuca	.15
145	Shawn Green	.25
146	Ben Sheets	.25
147	Bill Hall	.15
148	Nick Neugebauer	.15
149	Richie Sexson	.40
150	Robin Yount	1.00
151	Shane Nance	.15
152	Takahito Nomura	.15
153	A.J. Pierzynski	.15
154	Joe Mays	.15
155	Kirby Puckett	1.00
156	Adam Johnson	.15
157	Rob Bowen	.15
158	Torii Hunter	.40
159	Andres Galarraga	.15
160	Endy Chavez	.15
161	Javier Vazquez	.15
162	Jose Vidro	.15
163	Vladimir Guerrero	.75
164	Dwight Gooden	.15
165	Mike Piazza	1.00
166	Roberto Alomar	.40
167	Tom Glavine	.40
168	Alfonso Soriano	.75
169	Bernie Williams	.40
170	Brandon Claussen	.15
171	Derek Jeter	2.00
172	Don Mattingly	1.50
173	Drew Henson	.15
174	Jason Giambi	.50
175	Joe Torre	.25
176	Jorge Posada	.40
177	Mike Mussina	.50
178	Nick Johnson	.15
179	Roger Clemens	1.50
180	Whitey Ford	.75
181	Adam Morrissey	.15
182	Barry Zito	.40
183	David Justice	.15
184	Eric Chavez	.40
185	Jermaine Dye	.15
186	Mark Mulder	.25
187	Miguel Tejada	.40
188	Reggie Jackson	.75
189	Terrence Long	.15
190	Tim Hudson	.25
191	Anderson Machado	.15
192	Bobby Abreu	.40
193	Brandon Duckworth	.15
194	Jim Thome	.75
195	Eric Junge	.15
196	Jeremy Giambi	.15
197	Johnny Estrada	.15
198	Jorge Padilla	.15
199	Marlon Byrd	.15
200	Mike Schmidt	1.50
201	Pat Burrell	.50
202	Steve Carlton	.25
203	Aramis Ramirez	.25
204	Brian Giles	.25
205	Carlos Rivera	.15
206	Craig Wilson	.15
207	Dave Williams	.15
208	Jack Wilson	.15
209	Jose Castillo	.15
210	Kip Wells	.15
211	Roberto Clemente	1.50
212	Walter Young	.15
213	Ben Howard	.15
214	Brian Lawrence	.15
215	Clifford Bartosh	.15
216	Dennis Tankersley	.15
217	Oliver Perez	.15
218	Phil Nevin	.15
219	Ryan Klesko	.25
220	Sean Burroughs	.15
221	Tony Gwynn	.75
222	Xavier Nady	.15
223	Mike Rivera	.15
224	Barry Bonds	2.00
225	Benito Santiago	.15
226	Jason Schmidt	.40
227	Jeff Kent	.25
228	Kenny Lofton	.15
229	Rich Aurilia	.15
230	Robb Nen	.15
231	Tsuyoshi Shinjo	.15
232	Bret Boone	.15
233	Chris Snelling	.15
234	Edgar Martinez	.25
235	Freddy Garcia	.15
236	Ichiro Suzuki	1.50
237	John Olerud	.25
238	Kazuhiro Sasaki	.15
239	Mike Cameron	.15
240	Rafael Soriano	.15
241	Albert Pujols	1.50
242	J.D. Drew	.40
243	Jim Edmonds	.40
244	Ozzie Smith	1.00
245	Scott Rolen	.75
246	So Taguchi	.15
247	Stan Musial	1.00
248	Antonio Perez	.15
249	Aubrey Huff	.15
250	Dewon Brazelton	.15
251	Delvin James	.15
252	Joe Kennedy	.15
253	Toby Hall	.15
254	Alex Rodriguez	2.00
255	Ben Kozlowski	.15
256	Gerald Laird	.15
257	Hank Blalock	.50
258	Ivan Rodriguez	.50
259	Juan Gonzalez	.50
260	Kevin Mench	.15
261	Mario Ramos	.15
262	Mark Teixeira	.25
263	Nolan Ryan	2.00
264	Rafael Palmeiro	.50
265	Alexis Rios	.15
266	Carlos Delgado	.40
267	Eric Hinske	.15
268	Josh Phelps	.15
269	Kevin Cash	.15
270	Orlando Hudson	.15
271	Roy Halladay	.15
272	Shannon Stewart	.15
273	Vernon Wells	.15
274	Vinnie Chulk	.15
275	Jason Anderson	.15
276	Craig Brazell **RC**	.50
277	Terrmel Sledge **RC**	.50
278	Ryan Cameron **RC**	.50
279	Clint Barmes **RC**	.50
280	Jhonny Peralta	.50
281	Todd Wellemeyer **RC**	.50
282	Jon Leicester **RC**	.40
283	Brandon Webb **RC**	1.00
284	Tim Olson **RC**	.50
285	Matt Kata **RC**	.75
286	Rob Hammock **RC**	.50
287	Pete LaForest **RC**	.50
288	Nook Logan **RC**	.50
289	Prentice Redman **RC**	.40
290	Joe Valentine **RC**	.40
291	Jose Contreras **RC**	1.00
292	Josh Stewart **RC**	.40
293	Mike Nicolas **RC**	.40
294	Marshall McDougall	.15
295	Travis Chapman	.15
296	Jose Morban	.15
297	Michael Hessman **RC**	.40
298	Buddy Hernandez **RC**	.40
299	Shane Victorino **RC**	.40
300	Jason Dubois	.15
301	Hideki Matsui **RC**	3.00

Metalized

Stars:	4-8X
RC's:	1-30X
Production 100 Sets	
Holofoils:	No Pricing
Production 25 Sets	

Autographs

		NM/M
Common Autograph:		5.00
2	Alfredo Amezaga/325	8.00
3	Chone Figgins/375	10.00
13	Junior Spivey/45	10.00
24	Andy Pratt/475	8.00
25	Adam LaRoche/400	10.00
26	Trey Hodges/305	5.00
29	Ed Rogers/305	5.00
30	Brian Roberts/500	35.00
31	Geronimo Gil/150	8.00
32	Jay Gibbons/475	8.00
33	Josh Towers/500	10.00
34	Casey Fossum/160	5.00
35	Cliff Floyd/70	20.00
37	Fred Lynn/80	20.00
38	Freddy Sanchez/400	15.00
46	Corey Patterson/100	15.00
49	Juan Cruz/250	8.00
51	Mark Prior/50	30.00

53 Nic Jackson/100 10.00
57 Corwin Malone/400 8.00
59 Joe Borchard/215 8.00
64 Tim Hummel/400 5.00
65 Jon Adkins/400 5.00
66 Adam Dunn/100 30.00
67 Austin Kearns/50 20.00
69 Jose Acevedo/315 5.00
70 Corky Miller/295 5.00
71 Eric Davis/45 25.00
74 Wily Mo Pena/450 15.00
76 Brian Tallet/250 8.00
78 Cliff Lee/330 10.00
79 Earl Snyder/225 8.00
81 Jeremy Guthrie/400 8.00
83 Luis Garcia/395 5.00
86 Ryan Church/395 10.00
87 Victor Martinez/250 25.00
88 Brandon Phillips/375 10.00
89 Jack Cust/498 10.00
90 Jason Jennings/375 8.00
91 Jeff Baker/400 8.00
92 Garrett Atkins/400 8.00
95 Rene Reyes/350 8.00
98 Fernando Rodney/500 8.00
100 Jack Morris/50 20.00
102 Mike Maroth/400 8.00
104 Jesus Medrano/500 8.00
109 Josh Wilson/400 8.00
110 Tim Redding/375 8.00
111 Carlos Hernandez/250 8.00
113 Henri Stanley/390 5.00
114 Jason Lane/250 10.00
117 Kirk Saarloos/149 8.00
120 Richard Hidalgo/120 10.00
121 Rodrigo Rosario/500 10.00
122 Roy Oswalt/100 20.00
124 Wade Miller/125 10.00
126 Angel Berroa/400 10.00
127 Brandon Berger/325 8.00
130 Jimmy Gobble/400 8.00
131 Dee Brown/500 8.00
132 Mike Sweeney/45 20.00
134 Runelvys Hernandez/400 5.00
138 Victor Alvarez/308 8.00
144 Paul LoDuca/45 20.00
146 Ben Sheets/50 20.00
147 Bill Hall/450 10.00
148 Nick Neugebauer/375 5.00
151 Shane Nance/150 8.00
152 Takahito Nomura/50 20.00
153 A.J. Pierzynski/250 10.00
156 Adam Johnson/500 8.00
157 Rob Bowen/375 8.00
158 Torii Hunter/45 20.00
160 Endy Chavez/280 10.00
161 Javier Vazquez/50 15.00
162 Jose Vidro/45 15.00
164 Dwight Gooden/45 30.00
170 Brandon Claussen/475 10.00
178 Nick Johnson/500 8.00
181 Adam Morrissey/395 8.00
185 Jermaine Dye/125 15.00
189 Terrence Long/250 10.00
191 Anderson Machado/500 8.00
193 Brandon Duckworth/100 10.00
195 Eric Junge/279 8.00
196 Jeremy Giambi/195 8.00
205 Carlos Rivera/400 8.00
206 Craig Wilson/245 10.00
207 Dave Williams/265 8.00
208 Jack Wilson/500 15.00
212 Walter Young/400 8.00
213 Ben Howard/500 8.00
214 Brian Lawrence/500 8.00
215 Clifford Bartosh/400 8.00
222 Xavier Nady/250 8.00
223 Mike Rivera/90 8.00
233 Chris Snelling/200 8.00
240 Rafael Soriano/500 8.00
248 Antonio Perez/500 8.00
249 Aubrey Huff/475 15.00
250 Dewon Brazelton/50 15.00
251 Delvin James/400 8.00
252 Joe Kennedy/250 8.00
253 Toby Hall/500 8.00
255 Ben Kozlowski/400 8.00
256 Gerald Laird/450 8.00
257 Hank Blalock/50 25.00
260 Kevin Mench/475 10.00
261 Mario Ramos/475 5.00
262 Mark Teixeira/40 40.00
265 Alexis Rios/400 20.00
267 Eric Hinske/390 10.00
269 Kevin Cash/375 8.00
274 Vinnie Chulk/100 10.00
275 Jason Anderson/493 15.00
276 Craig Brazell/500 15.00
277 Terrmel Sledge/500 10.00
278 Ryan Cameron/475 8.00
279 Clint Barmes/475 15.00
280 Jhonny Peralta/500 15.00
281 Todd Wellemeyer/477 10.00
282 Jon Leicester/480 8.00
283 Brandon Webb/500 30.00
284 Tim Olson/500 10.00
285 Matt Kata/487 10.00
286 Rob Hammock/486 10.00
287 Pete LaForest/500 10.00
288 Nook Logan/500 10.00
289 Prentice Redman/488 10.00
290 Joe Valentine/475 8.00
291 Jose Contreras/100 25.00
292 Josh Stewart/485 10.00
293 Mike Nicolas/500 10.00
295 Travis Chapman/100 15.00
296 Jose Morban/475 8.00
297 Michael Hessman/500 8.00
298 Buddy Hernandez/500 8.00
299 Shane Victorino/480 8.00
300 Jason Dubois/480 10.00
302 Ryan Wagner/100 15.00
303 Adam Loewen/100 10.00
304 Chien-Ming Wang/100 200.00
305 Hong-Chih Kuo/100 80.00
307 Dan Haren/100 25.00
309 Ramon Nivar/100 15.00

Call to the Hall

NM/M
Complete Set (10): 30.00
Common Player: 2.00
Metalized: 2-4X
Production 100 Sets
Holofoils: No Pricing
Production 25 Sets
1 Nolan Ryan/2,490 10.00
2 Tom Seaver/2,490 4.00
3 Phil Rizzuto/2,500 4.00
4 Orlando Cepeda/2,500 2.00
5 Al Kaline/2,500 5.00
6 Hoyt Wilhelm/2,500 2.00
7 Luis Aparicio/2,500 2.00
8 Billy Williams/2,500 2.00
9 Jim Palmer/2,500 2.00
10 Mike Schmidt/2,500 6.00

Call to the Hall Autographs

No Pricing
Quantity produced listed

Grand Champions

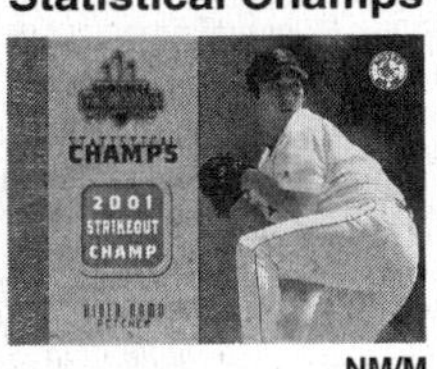

NM/M
Complete Set (25): 80.00
Common Player: 2.00
Inserted 1:18
Metalized: 2-4X
Production 100 Sets
Holo Foils: No Pricing
Production 25 Sets
1 Stan Musial 6.00
2 Bob Feller 2.00
3 Reggie Jackson 3.00
4 George Brett 8.00
5 Jim Palmer 2.00
6 Harmon Killebrew 4.00
7 Ernie Banks 4.00
8 Frank Robinson 2.00
9 Greg Maddux 4.00
10 Whitey Ford 4.00
11 Bob Gibson 4.00
12 Mike Schmidt 6.00
13 Nolan Ryan 10.00
14 Warren Spahn 4.00
15 Rod Carew 3.00
16 Hoyt Wilhelm 2.00
17 Duke Snider 4.00
18 Tom Seaver 4.00
19 Steve Carlton 3.00
20 Yogi Berra 4.00
21 Cal Ripken Jr. 10.00
22 Tony Gwynn 4.00
23 Wade Boggs 2.00
24 Rickey Henderson 3.00
25 Roger Clemens 8.00

Grand Champions Autographs

No Pricing

Numbers Game

NM/M
Quantity produced listed
1 Vladimir Guerrero/Jsy/200 10.00
2 Nomar Garciaparra/Jsy/200 20.00
3 Magglio Ordonez/Jsy/100 8.00
4 Garret Anderson/Jsy/50 15.00
5 Derek Jeter/Base/200 20.00
6 Jim Thome/Jsy/200 8.00
7 Torii Hunter/Jsy/200 10.00
8 Todd Helton/Jsy/200 10.00
9 Andruw Jones/Jsy/200 6.00
11 Luis Gonzalez/Jsy/200 5.00
12 Manny Ramirez/Jsy/200 12.00
13 Paul Konerko/Jsy/200 6.00
14 Alex Rodriguez/Jsy/200 20.00
15 Carlos Beltran/Jsy/200 4.00
16 Bernie Williams/Jsy/200 8.00
17 Barry Bonds/Base/200 20.00
18 Miguel Tejada/Jsy/50 15.00
19 Jason Giambi/Base/200 8.00
20 Ichiro Suzuki/Base/200 25.00
21 Ivan Rodriguez/Jsy/100 15.00
22 Rafael Palmeiro/Jsy/200 10.00
23 Carlos Delgado/Jsy/200 5.00
24 Vernon Wells/Jsy/200 4.00
25 Sammy Sosa/Jsy/200 20.00
26 Chipper Jones/Jsy/200 12.00
27 Adam Dunn/Jsy/44 25.00
28 Larry Walker/Jsy/200 8.00
29 Shawn Green/Jsy/100 10.00
30 Richie Sexson/Jsy/200 6.00
31 Jose Vidro/Jsy/200 4.00
32 Mike Piazza/Jsy/50 40.00
33 Roberto Alomar/Jsy/100 15.00
34 Bobby Abreu/Jsy/200 5.00
35 Pat Burrell/Jsy/200 8.00
36 Brian Giles/Jsy/200 6.00
37 Albert Pujols/Base/200 15.00
38 Lance Berkman/Jsy/50 15.00
39 Ryan Klesko/Jsy/200 6.00
40 Jeff Kent/Jsy/200 4.00

Statistical Champs

NM/M
Complete Set (30): 40.00
Common Player: 1.00
Inserted 1:10
1 Alex Rodriguez 5.00
2 Alfonso Soriano 2.00
3 Curt Schilling 1.50
4 Eddie Mathews 2.00
5 Fred Lynn 1.00
6 Harmon Killebrew 2.00
7 Hideo Nomo 1.00
8 Jim Thome 1.50
9 Kirby Puckett 3.00
10 Luis Gonzalez 1.00
11 Manny Ramirez 1.50
12 Jason Giambi 1.00
13 Mike Schmidt 4.00
14 Nomar Garciaparra 4.00
15 Lou Brock 1.50
16 Randy Johnson 2.00
17 Reggie Jackson 2.00
18 Rickey Henderson 1.50
19 Roberto Clemente 5.00
20 Barry Zito 1.50
21 Todd Helton 1.50
22 Tom Seaver 3.00
23 Tony Gwynn 2.00
24 Torii Hunter 1.00
25 Troy Glaus 1.00
26 Wade Boggs 1.50
27 Rod Carew 1.50
28 Juan Gonzalez 1.50
29 Sammy Sosa 3.00
30 Warren Spahn 2.00

Statistical Champs Materials

NM/M
Quantity produced listed
1 Alex Rodriguez/Jsy/250 20.00
3 Curt Schilling/Jsy/225 8.00
4 Eddie Mathews/Jsy/200 20.00
6 Harmon Killebrew/Jsy/250 20.00
7 Hideo Nomo/Jsy/110 50.00
8 Jim Thome/Jsy/250 8.00
9 Kirby Puckett/Jsy/250 20.00
10 Luis Gonzalez/Jsy/250 5.00
11 Manny Ramirez/Jsy/155 10.00
12 Jason Giambi/Jsy/250 10.00
13 Mike Schmidt/Jsy/250 35.00
14 Nomar Garciaparra/Jsy/99 30.00
15 Lou Brock/Jsy/250 15.00
16 Randy Johnson/Jsy/100 15.00
17 Reggie Jackson/Jsy/200 15.00
18 Rickey Henderson/Jsy/184 15.00
20 Barry Zito/Jsy/100 10.00
21 Todd Helton/Jsy/250 10.00
22 Tom Seaver/Jsy/100 30.00
23 Tony Gwynn/Jsy/200 15.00
24 Torii Hunter/Jsy/250 10.00
25 Troy Glaus/Jsy/125 10.00
26 Wade Boggs/Jsy/250 15.00
27 Rod Carew/Hat/150 15.00
28 Juan Gonzalez/Jsy/250 8.00
29 Sammy Sosa/Jsy/250 20.00
30 Warren Spahn/Jsy/150 30.00

Team Colors

NM/M
Complete Set (30): 60.00
Common Player: 1.00
Inserted 1:10
1 Miguel Tejada 1.50
2 Mike Schmidt 5.00
3 George Brett 6.00
4 Magglio Ordonez 1.00
5 Ryne Sandberg 4.00
6 Adam Dunn 1.50
7 Mark Prior 2.00
8 Tony Gwynn 2.00
9 Troy Glaus 1.50
10 Stan Musial 4.00
11 Kirby Puckett 3.00
12 Don Mattingly 5.00
13 Bobby Abreu 1.00
14 Ichiro Suzuki 4.00
15 Cal Ripken Jr. 8.00
16 Chipper Jones 3.00
17 Carlos Beltran 1.50
18 Alfonso Soriano 2.00
19 Albert Pujols 5.00
20 Andruw Jones 1.50
21 Bernie Williams 1.50
22 Todd Helton 1.50
23 Roberto Clemente 6.00
24 Jim Thome 1.50
25 Carlos Delgado 1.00
26 Derek Jeter 6.00
27 Garret Anderson 1.00
28 Nomar Garciaparra 4.00
29 Torii Hunter 1.00
30 Vladimir Guerrero 2.00

Team Colors Materials

NM/M
Quantity produced listed
1 Miguel Tejada/Jsy/50 15.00
2 Mike Schmidt/Jsy/200 35.00
3 George Brett/Jsy/200 35.00
4 Magglio Ordonez/Jsy/100 8.00
5 Ryne Sandberg/Jsy/200 30.00
6 Adam Dunn/Jsy/44 20.00
7 Mark Prior/Jsy/200 8.00
8 Tony Gwynn/Jsy/200 15.00
9 Troy Glaus/Jsy/200 8.00
10 Stan Musial/Jsy/200 35.00
11 Kirby Puckett/Jsy/200 15.00
12 Don Mattingly/Jsy/200 40.00
13 Bobby Abreu/Jsy/200 5.00
14 Ichiro Suzuki/Base/200 25.00
15 Cal Ripken Jr./Jsy/200 40.00
16 Chipper Jones/Jsy/200 12.00
17 Carlos Beltran/Jsy/200 8.00
19 Albert Pujols/Base/200 15.00
20 Andruw Jones/Jsy/200 6.00
21 Bernie Williams/Jsy/200 8.00
22 Todd Helton/Jsy/200 10.00
23 Roberto Clemente/Jsy/200 80.00
24 Jim Thome/Jsy/200 8.00
25 Carlos Delgado/Jsy/200 5.00
26 Derek Jeter/Base/200 20.00
27 Garret Anderson/Jsy/50 12.00
28 Nomar Garciaparra/Jsy/200 20.00
29 Torii Hunter/Jsy/200 10.00
30 Vladimir Guerrero/Jsy/200 10.00

Total Game

NM/M
Complete Set (40): 60.00
Common Player: 1.00
Inserted 1:9
1 Vladimir Guerrero 2.00
2 Nomar Garciaparra 4.00
3 Magglio Ordonez 1.00
4 Garret Anderson 1.00
5 Derek Jeter 6.00
6 Jim Thome 1.50
7 Torii Hunter 1.50
8 Todd Helton 1.50
9 Andruw Jones 1.50
10 Alfonso Soriano 2.00
11 Luis Gonzalez 1.00
12 Manny Ramirez 1.50
13 Paul Konerko 1.00
14 Alex Rodriguez 5.00
15 Carlos Beltran 1.00
16 Bernie Williams 1.50
17 Barry Bonds 6.00
18 Miguel Tejada 1.00
19 Jason Giambi 1.00
20 Ichiro Suzuki 4.00
21 Ivan Rodriguez 1.50
22 Rafael Palmeiro 1.50
23 Carlos Delgado 1.00
24 Vernon Wells 1.00
25 Sammy Sosa 4.00
26 Chipper Jones 2.00
27 Adam Dunn 1.50
28 Larry Walker 1.00
29 Shawn Green 1.00
30 Richie Sexson 1.00
31 Jose Vidro 1.00
32 Mike Piazza 3.00
33 Roberto Alomar 1.50
34 Bobby Abreu 1.00
35 Pat Burrell 1.00
36 Brian Giles 1.00
37 Albert Pujols 5.00
38 Lance Berkman 1.00
39 Ryan Klesko 1.00
40 Jeff Kent 1.00

World Series Champions

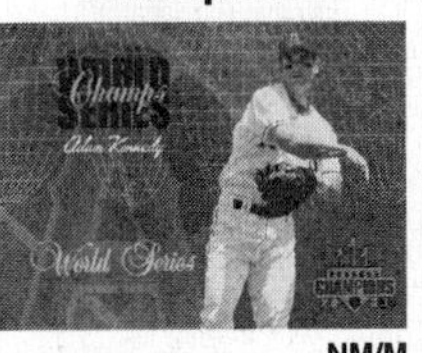

NM/M
Complete Set (15): 20.00
Common Player: 1.50
Production 2,002 Sets
Metalized: 2-3X
Production 100 Sets
Holo Foil: No Pricing
Production 25 Sets
1 Troy Glaus 3.00
2 Jarrod Washburn 1.50
3 Darin Erstad 2.50
4 Troy Percival 1.50
5 David Eckstein 1.50
6 Francisco Rodriguez 2.00
7 Garret Anderson 2.50
8 John Lackey 1.50
9 Tim Salmon 2.00
10 Chone Figgins 1.50
11 Adam Kennedy 1.50
12 Scott Spiezio 1.50
13 Ben Molina 1.50
14 Brad Fullmer 1.50
15 Troy Glaus MVP 3.00

World Series Champions Autograph

No Pricing

2003 Donruss Classics Samples

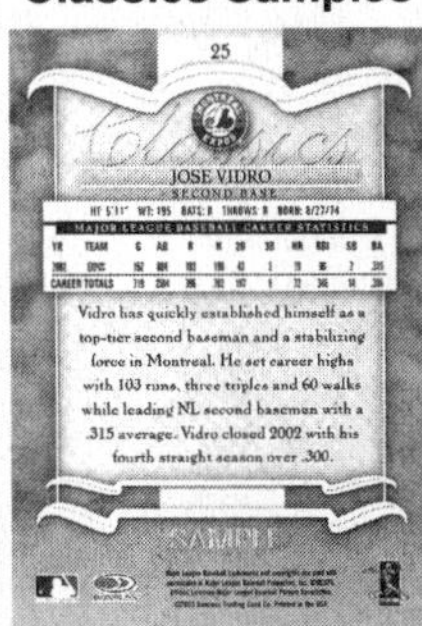

Each issue of the June, 2003, Beckett Baseball Card Monthly included a sample 2003 Donruss Classics card rubber-cemented inside. The cards differ from the issued version only in the appearance on back of a (usually) silver-foil "SAMPLE" notation. Some cards were produced with the overprint in gold-foil, in much more limited quantities. The number of different players' cards involved in the promotion is unknown.

NM/M
Common Player: .10
Stars: 1.5-2X
Gold: 10X

2003 Donruss Classics

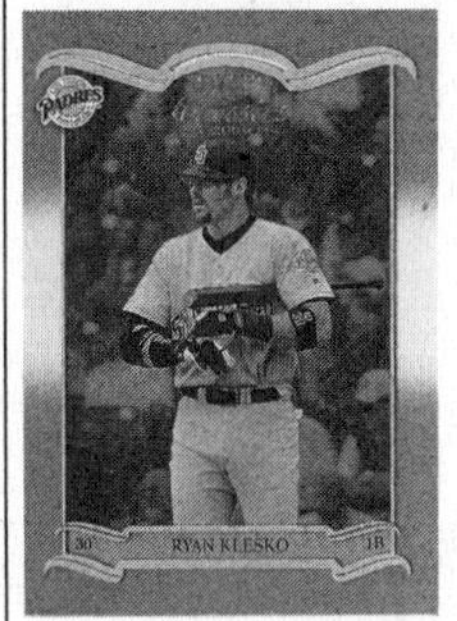

NM/M
Complete Set (200):
Common Player: .40
Common Legends (101-150): 3.00
Production 1,500
Common Prospect (151-200): 3.00
Production 1,500
Pack (7): 4.50
Box (18): 70.00
1 Troy Glaus .50
2 Barry Bonds 3.00
3 Miguel Tejada .50
4 Randy Johnson 1.00
5 Eric Hinske .40
6 Barry Zito .50
7 Jason Jennings .40
8 Derek Jeter 3.00
9 Vladimir Guerrero 1.00
10 Corey Patterson .50
11 Manny Ramirez .75
12 Edgar Martinez .50
13 Roy Oswalt .50
14 Andruw Jones .75
15 Alex Rodriguez 3.00
16 Mark Mulder .50
17 Kazuhisa Ishii .40
18 Gary Sheffield .50
19 Jay Gibbons .40
20 Roberto Alomar .50
21 A.J. Pierzynski .40
22 Eric Chavez .50
23 Roger Clemens 2.00
24 C.C. Sabathia .40
25 Jose Vidro .40
26 Shannon Stewart .40
27 Mark Teixeira .50
28 Joe Thurston .40

29 Josh Beckett .75
30 Jeff Bagwell .75
31 Geronimo Gil .40
32 Curt Schilling .75
33 Frank Thomas .75
34 Lance Berkman .50
35 Adam Dunn .75
36 Christian Parker .40
37 Jim Thome 1.00
38 Shawn Green .50
39 Drew Henson .40
40 Chipper Jones 1.00
41 Kevin Mench .40
42 Hideo Nomo .50
43 Andres Galarraga .40
44 Doug Davis .40
45 Mark Prior 1.00
46 Sean Casey .40
47 Magglio Ordonez .50
48 Tom Glavine .50
49 Marlon Byrd .40
50 Albert Pujols 2.00
51 Mark Buehrle .40
52 Aramis Ramirez .50
53 Pat Burrell .50
54 Craig Biggio .50
55 Alfonso Soriano 1.00
56 Kerry Wood 1.00
57 Wade Miller .40
58 Hank Blalock .75
59 Cliff Floyd .40
60 Jason Giambi .50
61 Carlos Beltran .50
62 Brian Roberts .40
63 Paul LoDuca .40
64 Tim Redding .40
65 Sammy Sosa 2.00
66 Joe Borchard .40
67 Ryan Klesko .40
68 Richie Sexson .50
69 Carlos Lee .40
70 Rickey Henderson .75
71 Brian Tallet .40
72 Luis Gonzalez .50
73 Satoru Komiyama .40
74 Tim Hudson .50
75 Ken Griffey Jr. 1.50
76 Adam Johnson .40
77 Bobby Abreu .60
78 Adrian Beltre .40
79 Rafael Palmeiro .75
80 Ichiro Suzuki 2.00
81 Kenny Lofton .40
82 Brian Giles .50
83 Barry Larkin .50
84 Robert Fick .40
85 Ben Sheets .50
86 Scott Rolen 1.00
87 Nomar Garciaparra 1.50
88 Brandon Phillips .40
89 Ben Kozlowski .40
90 Bernie Williams .75
91 Pedro J. Martinez 1.00
92 Todd Helton .75
93 Jermaine Dye .40
94 Carlos Delgado .50
95 Mike Piazza 1.50
96 Junior Spivey .40
97 Torii Hunter .50
98 Mike Sweeney .40
99 Ivan Rodriguez .75
100 Greg Maddux 1.50
101 Ernie Banks 5.00
102 Steve Garvey 3.00
103 George Brett 8.00
104 Lou Brock 3.00
105 Hoyt Wilhelm 3.00
106 Steve Carlton 4.00
107 Joe Torre 3.00
108 Dennis Eckersley 4.00
109 Reggie Jackson 5.00
110 Al Kaline 8.00
111 Harold Reynolds 3.00
112 Don Mattingly 8.00
113 Tony Gwynn 5.00
114 Willie McCovey 4.00
115 Joe Morgan 3.00
116 Stan Musial 8.00
117 Jim Palmer 3.00
118 Brooks Robinson 5.00
119 Don Sutton 3.00
120 Nolan Ryan 10.00
121 Mike Schmidt 6.00
122 Tom Seaver 5.00
123 Cal Ripken Jr. 8.00
124 Robin Yount 5.00
125 Bob Feller 3.00
126 Joe Carter 3.00
127 Jack Morris 3.00
128 Luis Aparicio 3.00
129 Bobby Doerr 3.00
130 Dave Parker 3.00
131 Yogi Berra 5.00
132 Will Clark 3.00
133 Fred Lynn 3.00
134 Andre Dawson 3.00
135 Duke Snider 4.00
136 Orlando Cepeda 3.00
137 Billy Williams 3.00
138 Dale Murphy 4.00
139 Harmon Killebrew 5.00
140 Kirby Puckett 6.00
141 Carlton Fisk 3.00
142 Eric Davis 3.00
143 Alan Trammell 3.00
144 Paul Molitor 5.00
145 Jose Canseco 3.00
146 Ozzie Smith 5.00
147 Ralph Kiner 3.00
148 Dwight Gooden 3.00
149 Phil Rizzuto 5.00
150 Lenny Dykstra 3.00
151 Adam LaRoche 4.00
152 Tim Hummel 3.00
153 Matt Kata **RC** 4.00
154 Jeff Baker 3.00
155 Josh Stewart **RC** 3.00
156 Marshall McDougall 4.00
157 Jhonny Peralta 4.00
158 Mike Nicolas **RC** 3.00
159 Jeremy Guthrie 3.00
160 Craig Brazell **RC** 4.00
161 Joe Valentine **RC** 4.00
162 Buddy Hernandez 3.00
163 Freddy Sanchez 4.00
164 Shane Victorino **RC** 4.00
165 Corwin Malone 4.00
166 Jason Dubois 3.00
167 Josh Wilson 3.00
168 Tim Olson **RC** 3.00
169 Clifford Bartosh 3.00
170 Michael Hessman **RC** 4.00
171 Ryan Church 5.00
172 Garrett Atkins 4.00
173 Jose Morban 3.00
174 Ryan Cameron **RC** 4.00
175 Todd Wellemeyer **RC** 4.00
176 Travis Chapman 3.00
177 Jason Anderson 4.00
178 Adam Morrissey 3.00
179 Jose Contreras **RC** 5.00
180 Nic Jackson 3.00
181 Rob Hammock **RC** 4.00
182 Carlos Rivera 3.00
183 Vinnie Chulk 3.00
184 Pete LaForest **RC** 3.00
185 Jon Leicester **RC** 4.00
186 Terrmel Sledge **RC** 3.00
187 Jose Castillo 3.00
188 Gerald Laird 3.00
189 Nook Logan **RC** 4.00
190 Clint Barmes **RC** 5.00
191 Jesus Medrano 3.00
192 Henri Stanley 4.00
193 Hideki Matsui **RC** 10.00
194 Walter Young 3.00
195 Jon Adkins 3.00
196 Tommy Whiteman **RC** 4.00
197 Rob Bowen 3.00
198 Brandon Webb **RC** 5.00
199 Prentice Redman **RC** 4.00
200 Jimmy Gobble 3.00

Dress Code

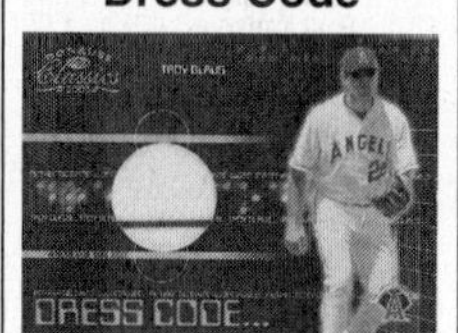

NM/M

Common Player: 4.00
Quantity produced listed
1 Roger Clemens/Jsy/500 15.00
2 M. Tejada/Jsy/Hat/Bat/250 20.00
3 V. Guerrero/Jsy/425 8.00
4 Kazuhisa Ishii/Jsy/250 10.00
5 Chipper Jones/Jsy/425 10.00
6 Troy Glaus/Jsy/425 8.00
7 Rafael Palmeiro/Jsy/425 8.00
8 Rickey Henderson/Jsy/250 10.00
9 Pedro Martinez/Jsy/425 8.00
10 Andruw Jones/Jsy/425 6.00
11 Nomar Garciaparra/Jsy/500 12.00
12 Carlos Delgado/Jsy/500 5.00
13 R.Henderson/Jsy/Hat/250 20.00
14 K. Wood/Jsy/Hat/250 20.00
15 L. Berkman/Jsy/Hat/50 20.00
16 Tony Gwynn/Quad/100 65.00
17 Mark Mulder/Jsy/425 8.00
18 Jim Thome/Jsy/500 8.00
19 Mike Piazza/Jsy/500 15.00
20 Mike Mussina/Jsy/500 10.00
21 Luis Gonzalez/Jsy/500 5.00
22 Ryan Klesko/Jsy/500 5.00
23 Richie Sexson/Jsy/500 6.00
24 Curt Schilling/Jsy/200 10.00
25 A. Rodriguez/Jsy/500 12.00
26 B. Williams/Jsy/425 8.00
27 Cal Ripken Jr/Jsy/500 35.00
28 C.C. Sabathia/Jsy/500 4.00
29 M. Piazza/Bat/Jsy/200 30.00
30 Rickey Henderson/Hat/Jsy/250 15.00
31 Torii Hunter/Jsy/425 8.00
32 Mark Teixeira/Jsy/425 8.00
33 D. Murphy/Jsy/Bat/300 15.00
34 Todd Helton/Jsy/425 8.00
35 Eric Chavez/Jsy/425 8.00
36 Vernon Wells/Jsy/425 5.00
37 J. Bagwell/Jsy/Hat/100 25.00
38 Nick Johnson/Jsy/425 5.00
39 Tim Hudson/Jsy/Hat/250 10.00
40 Shawn Green/Jsy/425 5.00
41 Mark Buehrle/Jsy/500 5.00
42 Garret Anderson/Jsy/100 5.00
43 Alex Rodriguez/Jsy/500 12.00
44 Jason Giambi/Jsy/500 8.00
45 Carlos Beltran/Jsy/500 5.00
46 Adam Dunn/Jsy/Hat/100 30.00
47 Jorge Posada/Jsy/425 8.00
48 Roy Oswalt/Jsy/Hat/200 15.00
49 Rich Aurilia/Jsy/500 5.00
50 Jason Jennings/Quad/250 15.00
51 Mark Prior/Quad/250 40.00
52 Jim Edmonds/Jsy/500 8.00
53 Fred McGriff/Jsy/500 8.00
54 A. Soriano/Jsy/Shoe/100 15.00
55 Jeff Kent/Jsy/425 5.00
56 Hideo Nomo/Jsy/200 30.00
57 Manny Ramirez/Jsy/425 8.00
58 J. Canseco/Jsy/Bat/350 15.00
59 M. Ordonez/Jsy/500 6.00
60 A. Trammell/Jsy/Bat/250 10.00
61 Bobby Abreu/Jsy/500 6.00
62 R.Henderson/Dual Jsy/200 20.00
63 Josh Beckett/Jsy/500 6.00
64 Barry Larkin/Jsy/500 8.00
65 Randy Johnson/Jsy/200 10.00
66 Juan Gonzalez/Jsy/500 8.00
67 Barry Zito/Jsy/Hat/125 15.00
68 Roger Clemens/Jsy/500 15.00
69 Rickey Henderson/Hat/Jsy/100 25.00
70 Hideo Nomo/Jsy/100 50.00
71 Paul Konerko/Jsy/400 6.00
72 Pat Burrell/Jsy/400 8.00
73 F.Thomas/Jsy/Pants/250 15.00
74 Sammy Sosa/Jsy/500 15.00
75 G. Maddux/Glove/Jsy/50 60.00

Legendary Hats

NM/M

Varying quantities produced
1 Roberto Clemente/80 100.00
2 Kirby Puckett/50 50.00
3 Mike Schmidt/50 75.00
4 Tony Gwynn/50 50.00
5 Rickey Henderson/50 60.00

Legendary Leather

NM/M

Varying quantities produced
1 Nolan Ryan/80 110.00

Legendary Lumberjacks

NM/M

Common Player: 10.00
Varying quantities produced
1 Babe Ruth/100 180.00
2 Lou Gehrig/80 125.00
3 George Brett/250 25.00
4 Duke Snider/250 20.00
5 Roberto Clemente/25 165.00
6 Ryne Sandberg/400 35.00
7 Robin Yount/300 25.00
8 Harmon Killebrew/250 25.00
9 Al Kaline/250 25.00
10 Eddie Mathews/225 20.00
11 Brooks Robinson/400 15.00
13 Kirby Puckett/375 20.00
14 Jose Canseco/400 15.00
15 Nellie Fox/325 20.00
16 Don Mattingly/400 35.00
17 Joe Torre/250 10.00
18 Cal Ripken Jr./250 40.00
19 Richie Ashburn/250 20.00
20 Mike Schmidt/250 30.00
21 Dale Murphy/250 25.00
22 Thurman Munson/400 15.00
23 Tony Gwynn/400 10.00
24 Orlando Cepeda/225 10.00
25 Ty Cobb/25 225.00
26 Paul Molitor/325 10.00
27 Ralph Kiner/200 10.00
28 Frank Robinson/225 20.00
29 Yogi Berra/50 50.00
30 Reggie Jackson/375 15.00
31 Rod Carew/325 15.00
32 Carlton Fisk/325 15.00
33 Rogers Hornsby/50 60.00
34 Mel Ott/125 30.00
35 Jimmie Foxx/50 60.00

Legendary Spikes

NM/M

Production 50 Sets
1 Kirby Puckett 60.00
2 Tony Gwynn 50.00
3 Don Mattingly 125.00
4 Frank Robinson 35.00
5 Gary Carter 30.00

Legends of the Fall

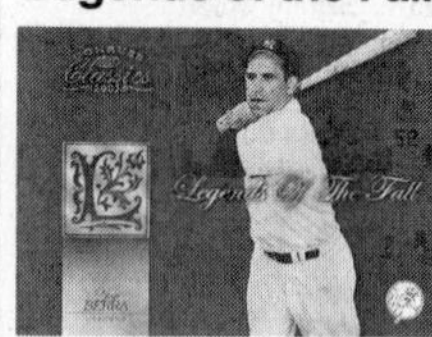

NM/M

Complete Set (10): 40.00
Common Player: 3.00
Production 2,500 Sets
1 Reggie Jackson 4.00
2 Duke Snider 4.00
3 Roberto Clemente 8.00
4 Mel Ott 5.00
5 Yogi Berra 5.00
6 Jackie Robinson 6.00
7 Enos Slaughter 3.00
8 Willie Stargell 4.00
9 Bobby Doerr 3.00
10 Thurman Munson 5.00

Legends of the Fall Fabrics

NM/M

Quantity produced listed 3.00
1 Reggie Jackson/100 20.00
3 Roberto Clemente/50 120.00
6 Jackie Robinson/50 80.00
8 Willie Stargell/100 20.00
9 Bobby Doerr/100 20.00

Membership

NM/M

Complete Set (15): 65.00
Common Player: 3.00
Production 2,500 Sets
1 Babe Ruth 10.00
2 Steve Carlton 3.00
3 Honus Wagner 6.00
4 Warren Spahn 5.00
5 Eddie Mathews 5.00
6 Nolan Ryan 10.00
7 Rogers Hornsby 5.00
8 Ernie Banks 5.00
9 Harmon Killebrew 5.00
10 Tom Seaver 5.00
11 Jimmie Foxx 6.00
12 Ty Cobb 6.00
13 Frank Robinson 4.00
14 Mel Ott 5.00
15 Lou Gehrig 8.00

Membership VIP Memorabilia

NM/M

Varying quantities produced
1 Babe Ruth/Bat/29 325.00
2 Steve Carlton/Jsy/81 25.00
4 Warren Spahn/Jsy/61 50.00
5 Eddie Mathews/Bat/67 60.00
6 Nolan Ryan/Jsy/80 75.00
7 R. Hornsby/Bat/31 75.00
8 Ernie Banks/Jsy/70 35.00
9 H. Killebrew/Jsy/71 60.00
10 Tom Seaver/Jsy/81 30.00
11 Jimmie Foxx/Bat/40 60.00
13 F. Robinson/Jsy/71 25.00
14 Mel Ott/Jsy/45 50.00

Significant Signatures

NM/M

Common Autograph: 8.00
#'s 201-211 exclusive to Donruss Rookies
5 Eric Hinske/250 15.00
6 Barry Zito/25 40.00
7 Jason Jennings/250 10.00
10 Corey Patterson/100 15.00
13 Roy Oswalt/100 20.00
16 Mark Mulder/100 25.00
19 Jay Gibbons/250 10.00
21 A.J. Pierzynski/75 20.00
22 Eric Chavez/20 40.00
25 Jose Vidro/75 15.00
27 Mark Teixeira/50 40.00
31 Geronimo Gil/50 10.00
35 Adam Dunn/100 40.00
36 Christian Parker/250 10.00
39 Drew Henson/100 20.00
41 Kevin Mench/250 10.00
45 Mark Prior/50 30.00
56 Kerry Wood/15 60.00
57 Wade Miller/200 10.00
58 Hank Blalock/50 25.00
62 Brian Roberts/250 25.00
63 Paul LoDuca/100 15.00
64 Tim Redding/250 8.00
66 Joe Borchard/100 15.00
68 Richie Sexson/20 40.00
69 Carlos Lee/25 20.00
73 Satoru Komiyama/124 20.00
76 Adam Johnson/200 8.00
84 Robert Fick/50 10.00
88 Brandon Phillips/250 10.00
89 Ben Kozlowski/150 8.00
93 Jermaine Dye/100 20.00
96 Junior Spivey/100 15.00
97 Torii Hunter/50 25.00
102 Steve Garvey/100 20.00
108 Dennis Eckersley/50 30.00
111 Harold Reynolds/50 25.00
119 Don Sutton/100 20.00
120 Nolan Ryan/50 200.00
123 Cal Ripken Jr/50 220.00
126 Joe Carter/100 25.00
127 Jack Morris/100 20.00
128 Luis Aparicio/50 20.00
132 Will Clark/20 125.00
133 Fred Lynn/50 15.00
134 Andre Dawson/50 30.00
136 Orlando Cepeda/100 20.00
137 Billy Williams/100 15.00
142 Eric Davis/50 25.00
143 Alan Trammell/50 35.00
148 Dwight Gooden/50 40.00
149 Phil Rizzuto/20 75.00
150 Lenny Dykstra/50 25.00
151 Adam LaRoche/250 15.00
152 Tim Hummel/500 8.00
153 Matt Kata/500 15.00
154 Jeff Baker/500 10.00
155 Josh Stewart/177 10.00
156 Marshall McDougall/500 10.00
157 Jhonny Peralta/500 20.00
158 Mike Nicolas/500 8.00
159 Jeremy Guthrie/500 10.00
160 Craig Brazell/500 15.00
161 Joe Valentine/172 10.00
162 Buddy Hernandez/500 8.00
163 Freddy Sanchez/500 10.00
164 Shane Victorino/351 8.00
165 Corwin Malone/500 8.00
166 Jason Dubois/500 12.00
167 Josh Wilson/500 8.00
168 Tim Olson/500 8.00
169 Clifford Bartosh/500 8.00
170 Michael Hessman/427 8.00
171 Ryan Church/500 10.00
172 Garrett Atkins/500 8.00
173 Jose Morban/500 8.00
174 Ryan Cameron/500 10.00
175 Todd Wellemeyer/500 10.00
176 Travis Chapman/477 10.00
177 Jason Anderson/500 15.00
178 Adam Morrissey/500 8.00
179 Jose Contreras/100 20.00
180 Nic Jackson/500 8.00
181 Rob Hammock/500 10.00
182 Carlos Rivera/500 8.00
183 Vinnie Chulk/500 8.00
184 Pete LaForest/177 10.00
185 Jon Leicester/500 8.00
186 Terrmel Sledge/500 8.00
187 Jose Castillo/500 10.00
188 Gerald Laird/500 8.00
189 Nook Logan/427 8.00
190 Clint Barmes/100 20.00
191 Jesus Medrano/500 8.00
192 Henri Stanley/500 8.00
194 Walter Young/500 10.00
195 Jon Adkins/500 8.00
196 Tommy Whiteman/500 8.00
197 Rob Bowen/500 8.00
198 Brandon Webb/500 30.00
199 Prentice Redman/127 10.00
200 Jimmy Gobble/500 10.00
201 Jeremy Bonderman/100 50.00
202 Adam Loewen/100 10.00
203 Chien-Ming Wang/50 220.00
205 Ryan Wagner/100 10.00
206 Dan Haren/100 40.00
209 Ramon Nivar/100 15.00

Singles

NM/M

Common Player: 10.00
Varying quantities produced
1 Babe Ruth/Jsy/100 275.00
2 Lou Gehrig/Jsy/80 200.00
3 Jackie Robinson/Jsy/80 75.00
5 Bobby Doerr/Jsy/100 15.00
6 Fred Lynn/Jsy/100 12.00
7 Honus Wagner/Seat/100 35.00
8 Roberto Clemente/Jsy/80 100.00
9 Kirby Puckett/Jsy/100 40.00
10 Torii Hunter/Jsy/100 10.00
11 Sammy Sosa/Jsy/100 25.00
12 Ryne Sandberg/Jsy/100 40.00
13 Hideo Nomo/Jsy/50 90.00
14 Kazuhisa Ishii/Jsy/50 15.00
15 Mike Schmidt/Jsy/100 45.00
16 Steve Carlton/Jsy/100 15.00
17 Robin Yount/Jsy/100 30.00
18 Paul Molitor/Jsy/100 20.00
19 Mike Piazza/Jsy/100 25.00
20 Duke Snider/Jsy/50 35.00
21 Al Kaline/Jsy/50 50.00
23 Don Mattingly/Jsy/100 60.00
24 Jason Giambi/Jsy/100 10.00
26 Ozzie Smith/Jsy/100 40.00
27 Roger Clemens/Jsy/100 25.00
28 Pedro Martinez/Jsy/100 20.00
29 Thurman Munson/Jsy/50 50.00
30 Yogi Berra/Jsy/25 70.00

Combos

NM/M

Varying quantities produced
CC1 Babe Ruth, Lou Gehrig/50 475.00
CC2 Jackie Robinson, Pee Wee Reese/50 80.00
CC3 Bobby Doerr, Fred Lynn/25 65.00
CC4 Honus Wagner, Roberto Clemente/50 150.00
CC5 Kirby Puckett, Torii Hunter/25 75.00
CC6 Sammy Sosa, Ryne Sandberg/25 100.00
CC7 Hideo Nomo, Kazuhisa Ishii/25 75.00
CC8 Mike Schmidt, Steve Carlton/25 150.00
CC9 Robin Yount, Paul Molitor/25 100.00
CC12 Don Mattingly, Jason Giambi/25 150.00
CC13 Stan Musial, Ozzie Smith/25 100.00

Timeless Treasures

NM/M

Varying quantities produced

1 Tony Gwynn, Stan Musial/50 100.00
3 Vladimir Guerrero, Roberto Clemente/50 125.00
5 Jason Giambi, Don Mattingly/50 100.00

2003 Donruss Diamond Kings Samples

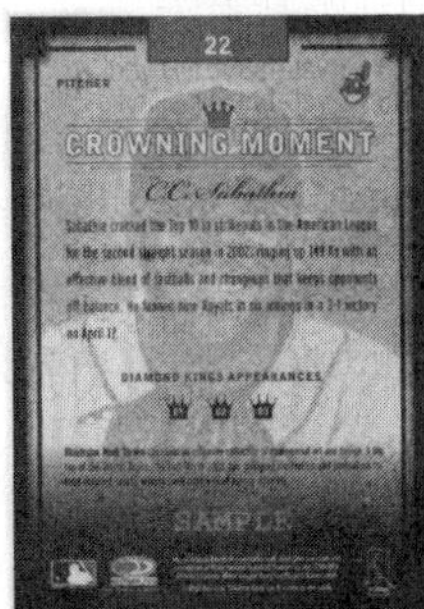

Each April, 2003, issue of Beckett Baseball Card Monthly included a sample DK card rubber-cemented inside. The cards differ from the issued version only in the appearance on back of a (usually) silver-foil "SAMPLE" notation and, on some cards, the lack of silver-foil graphics on front. Some cards were produced with the back overprint in gold-foil in much more limited quantities.

NM/M
Common Player: .25
Stars: 1.5-2X
Gold: 10X

2003 Donruss Diamond Kings

NM/M
Complete Set (176): 90.00
Common Player: .40
Common (151-176): 1.00
Pack (5): 4.00
Box (24): 75.00
1 Darin Erstad .50
2 Garret Anderson .50
3 Troy Glaus .50
4 David Eckstein .40
5 Jarrod Washburn .40
6 Adam Kennedy .40
7 Jay Gibbons .40
8 Tony Batista .40
9 Melvin Mora .40
10 Rodrigo Lopez .40
11 Manny Ramirez .75
12 Pedro J. Martinez 1.00
13 Nomar Garciaparra 1.50
14 Rickey Henderson .60
15 Johnny Damon .50
16 Derek Lowe .40
17 Cliff Floyd .40
18 Frank Thomas .75
19 Magglio Ordonez .50
20 Paul Konerko .40
21 Mark Buehrle .40
22 C.C. Sabathia .40
23 Omar Vizquel .40
24 Jim Thome .75
25 Ellis Burks .40
26 Robert Fick .40
27 Bobby Higginson .40
28 Randall Simon .40
29 Carlos Pena .40
30 Carlos Beltran .75
31 Paul Byrd .40
32 Raul Ibanez .40
33 Mike Sweeney .50
34 Torii Hunter .50
35 Corey Koskie .40
36 A.J. Pierzynski .40
37 Cristian Guzman .40
38 Jacque Jones .40
39 Derek Jeter 3.00
40 Bernie Williams .60
41 Roger Clemens 2.00
42 Mike Mussina .60
43 Jorge Posada .50
44 Alfonso Soriano 1.00
45 Jason Giambi .50
46 Robin Ventura .40
47 David Wells .40
48 Tim Hudson .50
49 Barry Zito .50
50 Mark Mulder .50
51 Miguel Tejada .50
52 Eric Chavez .50
53 Jermaine Dye .40
54 Ichiro Suzuki 2.00
55 Edgar Martinez .50
56 John Olerud .40
57 Dan Wilson .40
58 Joel Pineiro .40
59 Kazuhiro Sasaki .40
60 Freddy Garcia .40
61 Aubrey Huff .40
62 Steve Cox .40
63 Randy Winn .40
64 Alex Rodriguez 2.50
65 Juan Gonzalez .50
66 Rafael Palmeiro .75
67 Ivan Rodriguez .75
68 Kenny Rogers .40
69 Carlos Delgado .50
70 Eric Hinske .40
71 Roy Halladay .40
72 Vernon Wells .40
73 Shannon Stewart .40
74 Curt Schilling .75
75 Randy Johnson 1.00
76 Luis Gonzalez .40
77 Mark Grace .50
78 Junior Spivey .40
79 Greg Maddux 1.50
80 Tom Glavine .50
81 John Smoltz .40
82 Chipper Jones 1.00
83 Gary Sheffield .40
84 Andruw Jones .50
85 Kerry Wood 1.00
86 Fred McGriff .40
87 Sammy Sosa 1.50
88 Mark Prior 1.00
89 Ken Griffey Jr. 1.50
90 Barry Larkin .50
91 Adam Dunn .75
92 Sean Casey .40
93 Austin Kearns .50
94 Aaron Boone .40
95 Larry Walker .40
96 Todd Helton .75
97 Jason Jennings .40
98 Jay Payton .40
99 Josh Beckett .50
100 Mike Lowell .40
101 A.J. Burnett .40
102 Jeff Bagwell .75
103 Craig da Luz .40
104 Lance Berkman .50
105 Roy Oswalt .40
106 Wade Miller .40
107 Shawn Green .50
108 Adrian Beltre .50
109 Hideo Nomo .50
110 Kazuhisa Ishii .40
111 Odalis Perez .40
112 Paul LoDuca .40
113 Ben Sheets .40
114 Richie Sexson .50
115 Jose Hernandez .40
116 Vladimir Guerrero 1.00
117 Jose Vidro .40
118 Tomokazu Ohka .40
119 Andres Galarraga .40
120 Bartolo Colon .40
121 Mike Piazza 1.50
122 Roberto Alomar .50
123 Mo Vaughn .40
124 Al Leiter .40
125 Edgardo Alfonzo .40
126 Pat Burrell .75
127 Bobby Abreu .50
128 Mike Lieberthal .40
129 Vicente Padilla .40
130 Marlon Byrd .40
131 Jason Kendall .40
132 Brian Giles .40
133 Aramis Ramirez .50
134 Kip Wells .40
135 Ryan Klesko .40
136 Phil Nevin .40
137 Brian Lawrence .40
138 Sean Burroughs .40
139 Mark Kotsay .40
140 Barry Bonds 3.00
141 Jeff Kent .40
142 Benito Santiago .40
143 Kirk Reuter .40
144 Jason Schmidt .50
145 Jim Edmonds .50
146 J.D. Drew .50
147 Albert Pujols 2.00
148 Tino Martinez .40
149 Matt Morris .40
150 Scott Rolen 1.00
151 Joe Borchard 2.00
152 Cliff Lee 1.00
153 Brian Tallet 1.00
154 Freddy Sanchez 1.00
155 Chone Figgins 1.00
156 Kevin Cash 1.00
157 Justin Wayne 1.00
158 Ben Kozlowski 1.00
159 Babe Ruth 6.00
160 Jackie Robinson 4.00
161 Ozzie Smith 4.00
162 Lou Gehrig 5.00
163 Stan Musial 4.00
164 Mike Schmidt 5.00
165 Carlton Fisk 2.00
166 George Brett 6.00
167 Dale Murphy 4.00
168 Cal Ripken Jr. 8.00
169 Tony Gwynn 3.00
170 Don Mattingly 6.00
171 Jack Morris 2.00
172 Ty Cobb 5.00
173 Nolan Ryan 6.00
174 Ryne Sandberg 5.00
175 Thurman Munson 4.00
176 Jose Contreras **RC** 8.00

Framed Portraits Bronze

Cards (1-150): 1-2.5X
Cards (151-176): .75-1.5X
Silvers (1-150): 3-5X
Silvers (151-176): 2-3X
Production 400 Sets
Golds (1-150): 5-10X
Golds (151-176): 3-6X
Production 100 Sets

Diamond Cut

NM/M
Common Signature (1-25): 10.00
Quantity produced listed
1 Barry Zito/75 50.00
2 Edgar Martinez/125 50.00
3 Jay Gibbons/150 25.00
4 Joe Borchard/150 20.00
5 Marlon Byrd/150 20.00
6 Adam Dunn/150 40.00
7 Torii Hunter/150 40.00
8 Vladimir Guerrero/25 150.00
9 Wade Miller/150 25.00
10 Alfonso Soriano/100 60.00
11 Brian Lawrence/150 10.00
12 Cliff Floyd/100 25.00
13 Dale Murphy/75 75.00
14 Jack Morris/150 25.00
15 Eric Hinske/150 25.00
16 Jason Jennings/150 20.00
17 Mark Buehrle/150 30.00
18 Mark Prior/150 40.00
19 Mark Mulder/150 30.00
20 Mike Sweeney/150 25.00
21 Nolan Ryan/50 200.00
22 Don Mattingly/75 100.00
23 Andruw Jones/75 40.00
24 Aubrey Huff/150 20.00
Common Jerseys (26-75): 5.00
26 Nolan Ryan/250 50.00
27 Ozzie Smith/400 15.00
28 Rickey Henderson/300 10.00
29 Jack Morris/500 5.00
30 George Brett/350 25.00
31 Cal Ripken Jr./300 40.00
32 Ryne Sandberg/450 20.00
33 Don Mattingly/400 25.00
34 Tony Gwynn/400 15.00
35 Dale Murphy/350 10.00
36 Carlton Fisk/400 10.00
38 Lou Gehrig/50 240.00
39 Garret Anderson/450 8.00
40 Pedro J. Martinez/400 10.00
41 Nomar Garciaparra/350 15.00
42 Magglio Ordonez/450 8.00
43 C.C. Sabathia/500 5.00
44 Omar Vizquel/250 8.00
45 Jim Thome/500 10.00
46 Torii Hunter/500 8.00
47 Roger Clemens/500 15.00
48 Alfonso Soriano/400 10.00
49 Tim Hudson/500 8.00
50 Barry Zito/350 6.00
51 Mark Mulder/500 6.00
52 Miguel Tejada/400 8.00
53 John Olerud/350 5.00
54 Alex Rodriguez/500 15.00
55 Rafael Palmeiro/500 8.00
56 Curt Schilling/500 8.00
57 Randy Johnson/400 10.00
58 Greg Maddux/350 12.00
59 John Smoltz/400 6.00
60 Chipper Jones/450 10.00
61 Andruw Jones/500 8.00
62 Kerry Wood/500 10.00
63 Mark Prior/500 10.00
64 Adam Dunn/350 10.00
65 Larry Walker/500 5.00
66 Todd Helton/500 8.00
67 Jeff Bagwell/500 10.00
68 Roy Oswalt/500 8.00
69 Hideo Nomo/150 15.00
70 Kazuhisa Ishii/250 5.00
71 Vladimir Guerrero/500 10.00
72 Mike Piazza/500 15.00
73 Joe Borchard/500 5.00
74 Ryan Klesko/500 5.00
75 Shawn Green/500 6.00
Common Bat (76-105): 5.00
76 George Brett/350 25.00
77 Ozzie Smith/450 15.00
78 Cal Ripken Jr/150 50.00
79 Don Mattingly/400 25.00
80 Babe Ruth/50 200.00
81 Dale Murphy/350 10.00
82 Rickey Henderson/500 10.00
83 Ivan Rodriguez/500 8.00
84 Marlon Byrd/500 5.00
85 Eric Chavez/500 8.00
86 Nomar Garciaparra/500 15.00
87 Alex Rodriguez/500 15.00
88 Vladimir Guerrero/500 10.00
89 Paul LoDuca/500 5.00
90 Richie Sexson/500 6.00
91 Mike Piazza/350 15.00
92 J.D. Drew/500 8.00
93 Juan Gonzalez/500 8.00
94 Pat Burrell/500 8.00
95 Adam Dunn/250 15.00
96 Mike Schmidt/500 20.00
97 Ryne Sandberg/500 20.00
98 Edgardo Alfonzo/500 5.00
99 Andruw Jones/500 8.00
100 Carlos Beltran/500 6.00
101 Jeff Bagwell/500 10.00
102 Lance Berkman/500 8.00
103 Luis Gonzalez/500 5.00
104 Carlos Delgado/500 6.00
105 Jim Edmonds/250 8.00
Combos (106-110):
Some combos & autos. not priced.
106 Alfonso Soriano/75 40.00
107 Greg Maddux/Jsy/Auto./50 140.00
109 Adam Dunn/Bat/Auto./50 60.00
110 Rickey Henderson/Jsy/Bat/50 20.00

DK Evolution

NM/M
Complete Set (25): 85.00
Common Player: 2.00
Inserted 1:18
1 Cal Ripken Jr. 10.00
2 Ichiro Suzuki 6.00
3 Randy Johnson 4.00
4 Pedro J. Martinez 4.00
5 Nolan Ryan 10.00
6 Derek Jeter 10.00
7 Kerry Wood 4.00
8 Alex Rodriguez 8.00
9 Magglio Ordonez 2.00
10 Greg Maddux 5.00
11 Todd Helton 3.00
12 Sammy Sosa 5.00
13 Lou Gehrig 8.00
14 Lance Berkman 2.00
15 Barry Zito 2.00
16 Barry Bonds 10.00
17 Tom Glavine 2.00
18 Shawn Green 2.00
19 Roger Clemens 8.00
20 Nomar Garciaparra 6.00
21 Tony Gwynn 4.00
22 Vladimir Guerrero 3.00
23 Albert Pujols 8.00
24 Chipper Jones 4.00
25 Alfonso Soriano 4.00

Hall of Fame Heroes

NM/M
Complete Set (10): 40.00
Common Player: 3.00
Inserted 1:43
1 Bob Feller 3.00
2 Al Kaline 6.00
3 Lou Boudreau 3.00
4 Duke Snider 4.00
5 Jackie Robinson 6.00
6 Early Wynn 3.00
7 Yogi Berra 4.00
8 Stan Musial 6.00
9 Ty Cobb 6.00
10 Ted Williams 8.00

HOF Heroes Materials

NM/M
Common Player: 30.00
Production 50 Sets
1 Bob Feller/Jsy 70.00
2 Al Kaline/Bat 45.00
3 Lou Boudreau/Jsy 40.00
4 Duke Snider/Bat 30.00
7 Yogi Berra/Bat 40.00
8 Stan Musial/Bat 100.00
9 Ty Cobb/Bat 110.00
10 Ted Williams/Jsy 175.00

Heritage Collection

NM/M
Complete Set (25): 100.00
Common Player: 2.00
Inserted 1:23
1 Ozzie Smith 5.00
2 Lou Gehrig 8.00
3 Stan Musial 6.00
4 Mike Schmidt 6.00
5 Carlton Fisk 2.00
6 George Brett 10.00
7 Dale Murphy 4.00
8 Cal Ripken Jr. 10.00
9 Tony Gwynn 4.00
10 Don Mattingly 8.00
11 Jack Morris 2.00
12 Ty Cobb 8.00
13 Nolan Ryan 12.00
14 Ryne Sandberg 6.00
15 Thurman Munson 4.00
16 Ichiro Suzuki 6.00
17 Derek Jeter 10.00
18 Greg Maddux 5.00
19 Sammy Sosa 5.00
20 Pedro J. Martinez 4.00
21 Alex Rodriguez 8.00
22 Roger Clemens 5.00
23 Barry Bonds 10.00
24 Lance Berkman 2.00
25 Vladimir Guerrero 3.00

Recollection

Production 2-15

Recollection Autographs

NM/M
Common Player:
1 Adrian Beltre/40 15.00
2 Brandon Berger/99 10.00
9 Mark Buehrle/73 10.00
15 Andre Dawson/24 25.00
16 Andre Dawson/50 20.00
17 Andre Dawson/28 25.00
19 Jorge De La Rosa/148 5.00
24 Rob Fick/150 8.00
37 Tim Hudson/50 15.00
42 Ryan Ludwick/130 8.00
55 Roy Oswalt/65 15.00
56 Roy Oswalt/100 15.00
70 Bud Smith/114 5.00
72 Shannon Stewart/50 8.00

Team Timelines

NM/M
Complete Set (10): 85.00
Common Card: 4.00
Production 1,000 Sets
1 Nolan Ryan, Roy Oswalt 15.00
2 Dale Murphy, Chipper Jones 8.00
3 Stan Musial, Jim Edmonds 10.00
4 George Brett, Mike Sweeney 12.00
5 Tony Gwynn, Ryan Klesko 6.00
6 Carlton Fisk, Magglio Ordonez 4.00
7 Mike Schmidt, Pat Burrell 12.00
8 Don Mattingly, Bernie Williams 12.00
9 Ryne Sandberg, Kerry Wood 10.00
10 Lou Gehrig, Alfonso Soriano 10.00

Team Timelines Materials

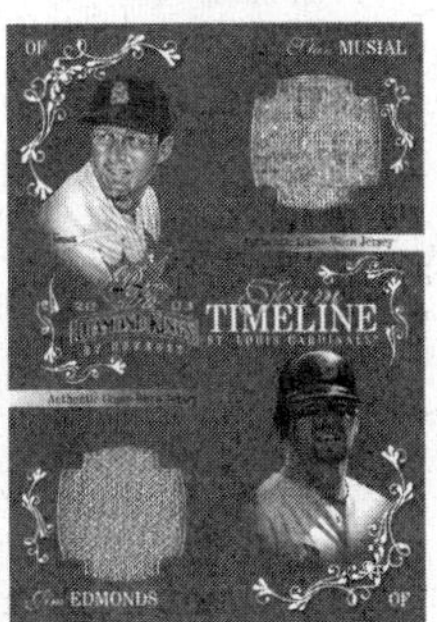

NM/M
Common Card: 30.00
Production 100 unless noted.
1 Nolan Ryan, Roy Oswalt 120.00
2 Dale Murphy, Chipper Jones 40.00
3 Stan Musial, Jim Edmonds 45.00
4 George Brett, Mike Sweeney 65.00
5 Tony Gwynn, Ryan Klesko 40.00
6 Carlton Fisk, Magglio Ordonez 30.00
7 Mike Schmidt, Pat Burrell 90.00
8 Don Mattingly, Bernie Williams 70.00
9 Ryne Sandberg, Kerry Wood 60.00
10 Lou Gehrig, Alfonso Soriano/50 200.00

2003 Donruss Diamond Kings Inserts Hawaii

At an invitation-only Donruss/Playoff reception during the SCD Hawaii Trade Conference, attendees were given a three-card pack with each card embossed with the show logo on front and gold-foil serial numbered on back. The packs had one each of the Diamond Kings inserts Heritage Collection (numbered to 20), Hall of Fame Heroes (50) and Team Timelines (50).

NM/M
Common Player: 4.00
1 Ozzie Smith 25.00
2 Lou Gehrig 35.00
3 Stan Musial 25.00
4 Mike Schmidt 35.00
5 Carlton Fisk 20.00
6 George Brett 60.00
7 Dale Murphy 15.00
8 Cal Ripken Jr. 75.00
9 Tony Gwynn 45.00
10 Don Mattingly 45.00
11 Jack Morris 6.00
12 Ty Cobb 35.00

13 Nolan Ryan 75.00
14 Ryne Sandberg 55.00
15 Thurman Munson 15.00
16 Ichiro Suzuki 75.00
17 Derek Jeter 75.00
18 Greg Maddux 25.00
19 Sammy Sosa 45.00
20 Pedro Martinez 9.00
21 Alex Rodriguez 60.00
22 Roger Clemens 25.00
23 Barry Bonds 75.00
24 Lance Berkman 6.00
25 Vladimir Guerrero 9.00
1 Bob Feller 6.00
2 Al Kaline 15.00
3 Lou Boudreau 4.00
4 Duke Snider 10.00
5 Jackie Robinson 15.00
6 Early Wynn 4.00
7 Yogi Berra 10.00
8 Stan Musial 15.00
9 Ty Cobb 9.00
10 Ted Williams 15.00
1 Nolan Ryan, Roy Oswalt 35.00
2 Dale Murphy, Chipper Jones 15.00
3 Stan Musial, Jim Edmonds 10.00
4 George Brett, Mike Sweeney 30.00
5 Tony Gwynn, Ryan Klesko 15.00
6 Carlton Fisk, Magglio Ordonez 10.00
7 Mike Schmidt, Pat Burrell 20.00
8 Don Mattingly, Bernie Williams 25.00
9 Ryne Sandberg, Kerry Wood 25.00
10 Lou Gehrig, Alfonso Soriano 20.00

2003 Donruss Elite

NM/M
Complete Set (200):
Common Player: .25
Common Rookie (181-200): 3.00
Production 1,750
Pack (5): 3.50
Box (20): 60.00
1 Darin Erstad .40
2 David Eckstein .40
3 Garret Anderson .40
4 Jarrod Washburn .25
5 Tim Salmon .40
6 Troy Glaus .50
7 Marty Cordova .25
8 Melvin Mora .25
9 Rodrigo Lopez .25
10 Tony Batista .25
11 Derek Lowe .25
12 Johnny Damon .40
13 Manny Ramirez .50
14 Nomar Garciaparra 1.50
15 Pedro J. Martinez .75
16 Shea Hillenbrand .25
17 Carlos Lee .25
18 Joe Crede .25
19 Frank Thomas .50
20 Magglio Ordonez .40
21 Mark Buehrle .25
22 Paul Konerko .25
23 C.C. Sabathia .25
24 Ellis Burks .25
25 Omar Vizquel .40
26 Brian Tallet .25
27 Bobby Higginson .25
28 Carlos Pena .25
29 Mark Redman .25
30 Steve Sparks .25
31 Carlos Beltran .50
32 Joe Randa .25
33 Mike Sweeney .25
34 Raul Ibanez .25
35 Runelvys Hernandez .25
36 Brad Radke .25
37 Corey Koskie .25
38 Cristian Guzman .25
39 David Ortiz .50
40 Doug Mientkiewicz .25
41 Jacque Jones .25
42 Torii Hunter .40
43 Alfonso Soriano .75
44 Andy Pettitte .40
45 Bernie Williams .50
46 David Wells .25
47 Derek Jeter 2.00
48 Jason Giambi .40
49 Jeff Weaver .25
50 Jorge Posada .40
51 Mike Mussina .40
52 Roger Clemens 1.50
53 Barry Zito .40
54 Eric Chavez .40
55 Jermaine Dye .25
56 Mark Mulder .40
57 Miguel Tejada .40
58 Tim Hudson .40
59 Bret Boone .25
60 Chris Snelling .25
61 Edgar Martinez .40
62 Freddy Garcia .25
63 Ichiro Suzuki 1.50
64 Jamie Moyer .25
65 John Olerud .25
66 Kazuhiro Sasaki .25
67 Aubrey Huff .25
68 Joe Kennedy .25
69 Paul Wilson .25
70 Alex Rodriguez 1.50
71 Chan Ho Park .25
72 Hank Blalock .50
73 Juan Gonzalez .50
74 Kevin Mench .25
75 Rafael Palmeiro .50
76 Carlos Delgado .40
77 Eric Hinske .25
78 Josh Phelps .25
79 Roy Halladay .40
80 Shannon Stewart .25
81 Vernon Wells .25
82 Curt Schilling .50
83 Junior Spivey .25
84 Luis Gonzalez .40
85 Mark Grace .50
86 Randy Johnson .75
87 Steve Finley .25
88 Andruw Jones .50
89 Chipper Jones .75
90 Gary Sheffield .50
91 Greg Maddux 1.00
92 John Smoltz .40
93 Corey Patterson .40
94 Kerry Wood .75
95 Mark Prior 1.00
96 Moises Alou .40
97 Sammy Sosa 1.50
98 Adam Dunn .50
99 Austin Kearns .40
100 Barry Larkin .40
101 Ken Griffey Jr. 1.00
102 Sean Casey .25
103 Jason Jennings .25
104 Jay Payton .25
105 Larry Walker .40
106 Todd Helton .50
107 A.J. Burnett .25
108 Josh Beckett .50
109 Juan Encarnacion .25
110 Mike Lowell .25
111 Craig Biggio .40
112 Daryle Ward .25
113 Jeff Bagwell .50
114 Lance Berkman .40
115 Roy Oswalt .40
116 Jason Lane .25
117 Adrian Beltre .50
118 Hideo Nomo .50
119 Kazuhisa Ishii .25
120 Kevin Brown .40
121 Odalis Perez .25
122 Paul LoDuca .25
123 Shawn Green .40
124 Ben Sheets .40
125 Jeffrey Hammonds .25
126 Jose Hernandez .25
127 Richie Sexson .50
128 Bartolo Colon .25
129 Brad Wilkerson .25
130 Javier Vazquez .25
131 Jose Vidro .25
132 Michael Barrett .25
133 Vladimir Guerrero .75
134 Al Leiter .25
135 Mike Piazza 1.00
136 Mo Vaughn .25
137 Pedro Astacio .25
138 Roberto Alomar .40
139 Pat Burrell .40
140 Vicente Padilla .25
141 Jimmy Rollins .40
142 Bobby Abreu .40
143 Marlon Byrd .25
144 Brian Giles .40
145 Jason Kendall .40
146 Aramis Ramirez .40
147 Josh Fogg .25
148 Ryan Klesko .40
149 Phil Nevin .25
150 Sean Burroughs .25
151 Mark Kotsay .25
152 Barry Bonds 2.00
153 Damian Moss .25
154 Jason Schmidt .50
155 Benito Santiago .25
156 Rich Aurilia .25
157 Scott Rolen .75
158 J.D. Drew .40
159 Jim Edmonds .40
160 Matt Morris .40
161 Tino Martinez .25
162 Albert Pujols 1.50
163 Russ Ortiz .25
164 Rey Ordonez .25
165 Paul Byrd .25
166 Kenny Lofton .25
167 Kenny Rogers .25
168 Rickey Henderson .50
169 Fred McGriff .40
170 Charles Johnson .25
171 Mike Hampton .25
172 Jim Thome .75
173 Travis Hafner .25
174 Ivan Rodriguez .50
175 Ray Durham .25
176 Jeremy Giambi .25
177 Jeff Kent .40
178 Cliff Floyd .25
179 Kevin Millwood .25
180 Tom Glavine .50
181 Hideki Matsui **RC** 10.00
182 Jose Contreras **RC** 5.00
183 Terrmel Sledge **RC** 3.00
184 Lew Ford **RC** 6.00
185 Jhonny Peralta 4.00
186 Alexis Rios 4.00
187 Jeff Baker 3.00
188 Jeremy Guthrie 3.00
189 Jose Castillo 3.00
190 Garrett Atkins 3.00
191 Jeremy Bonderman 8.00
192 Adam LaRoche 3.00
193 Vinnie Chulk 3.00
194 Walter Young 3.00
195 Jimmy Gobble 3.00
196 Prentice Redman **RC** 4.00
197 Jason Anderson 3.00
198 Nic Jackson 3.00
199 Travis Chapman 3.00
200 Shane Victorino **RC** 3.00

Aspirations

NM/M
Stars print run 25-50: 10-15X
Rookies (181-200)
p/r 25-50: 1-30X
Stars p/r 51-99: 5-10X
Serial numbered to jersey number.
Gold One-of-One's exist.
181 Hideki Matsui/45 125.00

Status

NM/M
Stars print run 25-50: 10-15X
Rookies (181-200)
p/r 25-50: 1-30X
Stars p/r 51-99: 5-10X
Gold Status: No Pricing
Production 24 Sets
181 Hideki Matsui/55 120.00

All-Time Career Best

NM/M
Complete Set (45): 120.00
Common Player: 2.00
Inserted 1:9
Gold print run 25-50: 4-8X
Gold print run 51-100: 3-5X
Gold p/r 101-239: 1.5-3X
Numbered to career stat.
1 Babe Ruth 6.00
2 Ty Cobb 4.00
3 Jackie Robinson 4.00
4 Lou Gehrig 5.00
5 Thurman Munson 2.00
6 Nolan Ryan 8.00
7 Mike Schmidt 4.00
8 Don Mattingly 5.00
9 Yogi Berra 3.00
10 Rod Carew 3.00
11 Reggie Jackson 3.00
12 Al Kaline 4.00
13 Harmon Killebrew 4.00
14 Eddie Mathews 3.00
15 Stan Musial 4.00
16 Jim Palmer 2.00
17 Phil Rizzuto 2.00
18 Brooks Robinson 3.00
19 Tom Seaver 3.00
20 Robin Yount 4.00
21 Carlton Fisk 3.00
22 Dale Murphy 4.00
23 Cal Ripken Jr. 8.00
24 Tony Gwynn 4.00
25 Andre Dawson 2.00
26 Derek Jeter 6.00
27 Ken Griffey Jr. 4.00
28 Albert Pujols 4.00
29 Sammy Sosa 4.00
30 Jason Giambi 3.00
31 Randy Johnson 3.00
32 Greg Maddux 4.00
33 Rickey Henderson 3.00
34 Pedro Martinez 3.00
35 Jeff Bagwell 3.00
36 Alex Rodriguez 5.00
37 Vladimir Guerrero 3.00
38 Chipper Jones 3.00
39 Shawn Green 2.00
40 Tom Glavine 2.00
41 Curt Schilling 2.00
42 Todd Helton 2.00
43 Roger Clemens 4.00
44 Lance Berkman 2.00
45 Nomar Garciaparra 5.00

All-Time Career Best Materials

NM/M
Common Player: 5.00
Varying quantities produced
1 Babe Ruth/Bat/25 250.00
2 Ty Cobb/Bat/25 150.00
3 Jackie Robinson/Jsy/50 50.00
4 Lou Gehrig/Bat/100 100.00
5 Thurman Munson/Bat/200 15.00
6 Nolan Ryan/Jsy/400 40.00
7 Mike Schmidt/Jsy/400 30.00
8 Don Mattingly/Jsy/250 40.00
9 Yogi Berra/Bat/100 25.00
10 Rod Carew/Bat/400 10.00
11 Reggie Jackson/Bat/400 10.00
12 Al Kaline/Bat/400 20.00
13 Harmon Killebrew/Jsy/400 15.00
14 Eddie Mathews/Bat/200 25.00
15 Stan Musial/Bat/100 40.00
16 Jim Palmer/Jsy/200 10.00
17 Phil Rizzuto/Bat/400 10.00
18 Brooks Robinson/Bat/400 15.00
19 Tom Seaver/Jsy/400 15.00
20 Robin Yount/Bat/400 15.00
21 Carlton Fisk/Bat/400 10.00
22 Dale Murphy/Bat/400 10.00
23 Cal Ripken Jr./Bat/400 35.00
24 Tony Gwynn/Jsy/400 12.00
25 Andre Dawson/Bat/400 5.00
26 Derek Jeter/Base/400 15.00
27 Ken Griffey Jr./Base/400 10.00
28 Albert Pujols/Base/400 15.00
29 Sammy Sosa/Bat/400 12.00
30 Jason Giambi/Bat/400 8.00
31 Randy Johnson/Jsy/400 8.00
32 Greg Maddux/Jsy/400 10.00
33 Rickey Henderson/Bat/400 10.00
34 Pedro Martinez/Jsy/400 10.00
35 Jeff Bagwell/Jsy/400 8.00
36 Alex Rodriguez/Bat/400 12.00
37 Vladimir Guerrero/Bat/400 8.00
38 Chipper Jones/Bat/400 10.00
39 Shawn Green/Bat/400 5.00
40 Tom Glavine/Jsy/400 5.00
41 Curt Schilling/Jsy/400 8.00
42 Todd Helton/Bat/400 8.00
43 Roger Clemens/Jsy/400 20.00
44 Lance Berkman/Bat/400 5.00
45 Nomar Garciaparra/Bat/400 15.00

All-Time Career Best Materials Gold

NM/M
Numbered to career stat.
Some not priced yet.
1 Babe Ruth/60 125.00
4 Lou Gehrig/49 125.00
5 Thurman Munson/105 25.00
7 Mike Schmidt/48 50.00
8 Don Mattingly/53 60.00
9 Yogi Berra/30 50.00
10 Rod Carew/239 10.00
11 Reggie Jackson/39 25.00
12 Al Kaline/29 50.00
13 Harmon Killebrew/140 20.00
14 Eddie Mathews/31 50.00
15 Stan Musial/39 60.00
18 Brooks Robinson/118 20.00
20 Robin Yount/49 40.00
21 Carlton Fisk/107 15.00
22 Dale Murphy/44 40.00
23 Cal Ripken Jr./211 40.00
24 Tony Gwynn/220 10.00
25 Andre Dawson/49 15.00
27 Ken Griffey Jr./56 25.00
28 Albert Pujols/37 30.00
29 Sammy Sosa/66 35.00
30 Jason Giambi/137 10.00
33 Rickey Henderson/130 20.00
35 Jeff Bagwell/47 15.00
36 Alex Rodriguez/393 10.00
37 Vladimir Guerrero/44 25.00
38 Chipper Jones/45 20.00
39 Shawn Green/49 15.00
41 Curt Schilling/35 20.00
42 Todd Helton/59 15.00
44 Lance Berkman/55 15.00
45 Nomar Garciaparra/35 50.00

Back to the Future

NM/M
Complete Set (15): 35.00
Common Card: 2.00
#'s 1-10 production 1,000:
#'s 11-15 production 500
1 Kerry Wood 4.00
2 Mark Prior 4.00
3 Magglio Ordonez 2.50
4 Joe Borchard 2.00
5 Lance Berkman 3.00
6 Jason Lane 2.00
7 Rafael Palmeiro 3.00
8 Mark Teixeira 3.00
9 Carlos Delgado 3.00
10 Josh Phelps 2.00
11 Kerry Wood, Mark Prior 4.00
12 Joe Borchard, Magglio Ordonez 2.50
13 Jason Lane, Lance Berkman 3.00
14 Mark Teixeira, Rafael Palmeiro 3.00
15 Carlos Delgado, Josh Phelps 3.00

Back to the Future Threads

NM/M
Common Card: 4.00
Singles production 250:
Doubles production 125:
1 Kerry Wood 10.00
2 Mark Prior 12.00
3 Magglio Ordonez 5.00
4 Joe Borchard 5.00
5 Lance Berkman 6.00
6 Jason Lane 4.00
7 Rafael Palmeiro 8.00
8 Mark Teixeira 10.00
9 Carlos Delgado 8.00
10 Josh Phelps 6.00
11 Kerry Wood, Mark Prior 20.00
12 Joe Borchard, Magglio Ordonez 8.00
13 Jason Lane, Lance Berkman 8.00
14 Mark Teixeira, Rafael Palmeiro 15.00
15 Carlos Delgado, Josh Phelps 8.00

Back 2 Back Jacks

NM/M
Common Player:
1 Adam Dunn/250 10.00
2 Alex Rodriguez/250 15.00
3 Alfonso Soriano/250 10.00
4 Andruw Jones/250 8.00
5 Chipper Jones/250 10.00
6 Jason Giambi/250 8.00
7 Jeff Bagwell/250 8.00
8 Jim Thome/250 8.00
9 Juan Gonzalez/250 8.00
10 Lance Berkman/250 6.00
11 Magglio Ordonez/250 4.00
12 Manny Ramirez/250 8.00
13 Miguel Tejada/250 6.00
14 Mike Piazza/250 15.00
15 Nomar Garciaparra/250 15.00
16 Rafael Palmeiro/250 8.00
17 Rickey Henderson/250 10.00
18 Sammy Sosa/250 15.00
19 Scott Rolen/250 8.00
20 Shawn Green/250 6.00
21 Todd Helton/250 8.00
22 Vladimir Guerrero/250 8.00
23 Ivan Rodriguez/250 8.00
24 Eric Chavez/250 6.00
25 Larry Walker/250 6.00
26 Troy Glaus/250, Garret Anderson 8.00
27 Adam Dunn, Austin Kearns/125 20.00
28 Alex Rodriguez, Rafael Palmeiro/125 20.00
29 Eric Chavez, Miguel Tejada/125 10.00
30 Frank Thomas, Magglio Ordonez/125 15.00
31 Jeff Bagwell, Lance Berkman/125 15.00
32 Manny Ramirez, Nomar Garciaparra/125 30.00
33 Jose Vidro, Vladimir Guerrero/125 15.00
34 Mike Piazza, Roberto Alomar/125 20.00
35 Larry Walker, Todd Helton/125 15.00
36 Babe Ruth/100 150.00
37 Cal Ripken Jr./100 65.00
38 Don Mattingly/100 50.00
39 Kirby Puckett/100 20.00
40 Roberto Clemente/100 75.00
41 Alfonso Soriano, Phil Rizzuto/75 25.00
42 Andre Dawson, Sammy Sosa/75 40.00
43 Ozzie Smith, Scott Rolen/75 60.00
44 Don Mattingly, Jason Giambi/75 75.00
45 Rickey Henderson, Ty Cobb/75 125.00
46 Joe Morgan, Johnny Bench/50 35.00
47 Brooks Robinson, Cal Ripken Jr./50 100.00
48 Bo Jackson, George Brett/50 100.00
49 Babe Ruth, Lou Gehrig/50 375.00
50 Thurman Munson, Yogi Berra/50 60.00

Career Best

NM/M
Common Player: 3.00
Numbered to statistic.
3 Garret Anderson/56 6.00
4 Andruw Jones/83 6.00
6 Magglio Ordonez/38 6.00
7 Magglio Ordonez/135 4.00
8 Adam Dunn/26 15.00
10 Lance Berkman/42 6.00
11 Lance Berkman/128 3.00
12 Shawn Green/385 3.00
13 Alfonso Soriano/39 12.00
14 Alfonso Soriano/300 5.00
15 Jason Giambi/120 5.00
16 Derek Jeter/32 30.00
17 Vladimir Guerrero/40 12.00
18 Vladimir Guerrero/417 5.00
19 Barry Zito/23 8.00
20 Miguel Tejada/34 8.00
21 Barry Bonds/198 15.00
22 Barry Bonds/370 15.00
23 Ichiro Suzuki/308 8.00
24 Alex Rodriguez/57 15.00
25 Alex Rodriguez/142 10.00

Career Best Materials

NM/M
Common Player: 4.00
Production 500 Sets
1 Randy Johnson/Jsy 8.00
2 Curt Schilling/Jsy 8.00
3 Garret Anderson/Bat 4.00
4 Andruw Jones/Bat 6.00
5 Kerry Wood/Shoe 10.00
6 Magglio Ordonez/Bat 4.00
7 Magglio Ordonez/Bat 4.00
8 Adam Dunn/Bat 6.00
9 Roy Oswalt/Jsy 5.00
10 Lance Berkman/Bat 5.00
11 Lance Berkman/Bat 5.00
12 Shawn Green/Bat 4.00
13 Alfonso Soriano/Bat 10.00
14 Alfonso Soriano/Bat 10.00
15 Jason Giambi/Bat 8.00
16 Derek Jeter/Base 15.00
17 Vladimir Guerrero/Bat 8.00
18 Vladimir Guerrero/Bat 8.00
19 Barry Zito/Jsy 6.00
20 Miguel Tejada/Bat 6.00
21 Barry Bonds/Base 15.00
22 Barry Bonds/Base 15.00
23 Ichiro Suzuki/Base 15.00
24 Alex Rodriguez/Jsy 10.00
25 Alex Rodriguez/Jsy 10.00

Career Best Materials Autograph

NM/M
Quantity produced listed
3 Garret Anderson/Bat/75 35.00
8 Adam Dunn/Bat/100 50.00
9 Roy Oswalt/Jsy/250 30.00
17 Vladimir Guerrero/Bat/50 75.00
18 Vladimir Guerrero/Bat/50 75.00
19 Barry Zito/Jsy/75 40.00

Highlights

NM/M
Production 500 Sets
1 Sammy Sosa 10.00
2 Rafael Palmeiro 8.00
3 Hideki Matsui 10.00
4 Jose Contreras 4.00
5 Kevin Millwood 4.00

Highlights Autographs

NM/M
Production 50 Sets
2 Rafael Palmeiro 75.00
4 Jose Contreras 25.00

Passing the Torch

NM/M
Complete Set (15): 50.00
Common Player: 1.50
1 Stan Musial 6.00
2 Jim Edmonds 2.00
3 Dale Murphy 3.00
4 Andruw Jones 3.00
5 Roger Clemens 8.00
6 Mark Prior 3.00
7 Tom Seaver 3.00
8 Tom Glavine 1.50
9 Mike Schmidt 8.00
10 Pat Burrell 2.00
11 Jim Edmonds, Stan Musial 8.00
12 Andruw Jones, Dale Murphy 5.00
13 Mark Prior, Roger Clemens 8.00
14 Tom Glavine, Tom Seaver 5.00
15 Mike Schmidt, Pat Burrell 10.00

Passing the Torch Autograph

NM/M
Common Auto. (1-10): 30.00
#'s 1-10 Production 50
#'s 11-15 Production 25
No pricing for #'s 11-15.
1 Stan Musial 80.00
2 Jim Edmonds 40.00
3 Dale Murphy 50.00
4 Andruw Jones 30.00
5 Roger Clemens 125.00
6 Mark Prior 40.00
7 Tom Seaver 60.00
8 Tom Glavine 50.00
9 Mike Schmidt 100.00
10 Pat Burrell 30.00

Recollection Autographs

NM/M
Some not priced due to scarcity.
1 Jeremy Affeldt/75 15.00
2 Erick Almonte/75 8.00
4 Adrian Beltre/36 30.00
7 Brandon Berger/83 8.00
8 Angel Berroa/28 25.00
13 Jeff Deardorff/53 8.00
14 Ryan Drese/100 25.00
21 Luis Garcia/28 15.00
22 Geronimo Gil/75 8.00
28 Travis Hafner/Black/52 30.00
30 Bill Hall/27 15.00
35 Gerald Laird/46 30.00
36 Jason Lane/27 15.00
44 Victor Martinez/52 100.00
46 Roy Oswalt/Black/61 20.00
51 Ricardo Rodriguez/75 8.00
55 Bud Smith/50 10.00
56 Bud Smith/28 10.00
58 Junior Spivey/45 20.00
59 Tim Spooneybarger/100 8.00
61 Shannon Stewart/35 20.00
64 Claudio Vargas/51 8.00

Throwback Threads

NM/M
Common Player: 4.00
1 Randy Johnson/Jsy 8.00
2 Randy Johnson/Hat 10.00
3 Roger Clemens/Jsy 20.00
4 Roger Clemens/Jsy 20.00
5 Manny Ramirez/Jsy 8.00
6 Greg Maddux/Jsy 15.00
7 Jason Giambi/Jsy 6.00
8 Jason Giambi/Jsy 6.00
9 Alex Rodriguez/Jsy 10.00
10 Alex Rodriguez/Jsy 10.00
11 Miguel Tejada/Jsy 6.00
12 Alfonso Soriano/Jsy 8.00
13 Nomar Garciaparra/Jsy 15.00
14 Pedro J. Martinez/Jsy 8.00
15 Pedro J. Martinez/Jsy 8.00
16 Andruw Jones/Jsy 6.00
17 Chipper Jones/Jsy 8.00
18 Barry Zito/Jsy 8.00
19 Mark Mulder/Jsy 4.00
20 Lance Berkman/Jsy 6.00
21 Maggio Ordonez/Jsy 4.00
22 Mike Piazza/Jsy 15.00
23 Mike Piazza/Jsy 15.00
24 Rickey Henderson/Jsy 8.00
25 Rickey Henderson/Jsy 8.00
26 Rickey Henderson/Jsy 8.00
27 Sammy Sosa/Jsy 15.00
28 Shawn Green/Jsy 5.00
29 Troy Glaus/Jsy 6.00
30 Vladimir Guerrero/Jsy 8.00
31 Adam Dunn/Jsy 8.00
32 Jeff Bagwell/Jsy 8.00
33 Curt Schilling/Jsy 8.00
34 Hideo Nomo/Jsy 20.00
35 Hideo Nomo/Jsy 20.00
36 Hideo Nomo/Jsy 20.00
37 Kerry Wood/Jsy 10.00
38 Mark Prior/Jsy 8.00
39 Roberto Alomar/Jsy 6.00
40 Todd Helton/Jsy 8.00
41 Jim Thome/Jsy 8.00
42 Rafael Palmeiro/Jsy 8.00
43 Juan Gonzalez/Jsy 8.00
44 Vernon Wells/Jsy 4.00
45 Torii Hunter/Jsy 6.00
46 Randi Johnson/Jsy 15.00
47 Roger Clemens/Jsy 30.00
48 Jason Giambi/Jsy 10.00
49 Alex Rodriguez/Jsy 25.00
50 Pedro J. Martinez/Jsy 20.00
51 Mike Piazza/Jsy 25.00
52 Rickey Henderson 20.00
53 Rickey Henderson 20.00
54 Rickey Henderson/Hat, Rickey Henderson/Jsy 20.00
55 Hideo Nomo/Jsy 40.00
56 Randy Johnson/Jsy 15.00
57 Curt Schilling, Randy Johnson/Jsy 15.00
58 Alfonso Soriano, Jason Giambi 20.00
59 Barry Zito, Mark Mulder 15.00
60 Andruw Jones, Chipper Jones/Tom Glavine 40.00
62 Jeff Bagwell, Lance Berkman/Jsy 15.00
63 Mark Prior, Roger Clemens/Jsy 20.00
64 Alex Rodriguez, Rafael Palmeiro/Jsy 20.00
65 Jim Thome, Roberto Alomar/Jsy 20.00
66 Mike Piazza, Roberto Alomar/Jsy 20.00
67 Mark Grace, Sammy Sosa/Jsy 25.00
68 Larry Walker, Todd Helton/Jsy 20.00
69 Adam Dunn, Austin Kearns/Jsy 20.00
70 Alex Rodriguez, Ivan Rodriguez/Jsy 20.00
71 Bobby Abreu, Marlon Byrd/Jsy 15.00
72 Eric Chavez, Miguel Tejada/Jsy 15.00
73 Greg Maddux, John Smoltz/Jsy 30.00
74 Kerry Wood, Mark Prior/Jsy 10.00
75 Barry Zito, Tim Hudson/Jsy 10.00
76 Babe Ruth 250.00
77 Ty Cobb 100.00
78 Jackie Robinson 75.00
79 Lou Gehrig 125.00
80 Thurman Munson 30.00
81 Nolan Ryan 40.00
82 Don Mattingly 50.00
83 Mike Schmidt 40.00
84 Reggie Jackson 20.00
85 George Brett 40.00
86 Cal Ripken Jr. 50.00
87 Tony Gwynn 15.00
88 Yogi Berra 25.00
89 Stan Musial 40.00
90 Jim Palmer 10.00
91 Thurman Munson 50.00
92 Chipper Jones, Dale Murphy 50.00
93 Don Mattingly, Jason Giambi 80.00
94 Andre Dawson, Sammy Sosa 40.00
95 Mark Prior, Nolan Ryan 50.00
96 Babe Ruth, Lou Gehrig 475.00
97 Joe Morgan, Tom Seaver 40.00
98 Harmon Killebrew, Rod Carew 40.00
99 Nolan Ryan 90.00
100 Reggie Jackson 35.00

Throwback Threads Autograph

NM/M
Production 5-75 4.00
30 Vladimir Guerrero/50 75.00
31 Adam Dunn/50 75.00
37 Kerry Wood/50 75.00
38 Mark Prior/75 50.00
39 Roberto Alomar/50 75.00

Turn of the Century Autographs

NM/M
Common Autograph: 10.00
Production 50 Sets
182 Jose Contreras 40.00
183 Terrmel Sledge 15.00
184 Lew Ford 20.00
185 Jhonny Peralta 35.00
186 Alexis Rios 40.00
187 Jeff Baker 15.00
188 Jeremy Guthrie 15.00
189 Jose Castillo 15.00
190 Garrett Atkins 20.00
191 Jeremy Bonderman 75.00
192 Adam LaRoche 15.00
193 Vinnie Chulk 15.00
194 Walter Young 15.00
195 Jimmy Gobble 10.00
196 Prentice Redman 15.00
197 Jason Anderson 15.00
198 Nic Jackson 15.00
199 Travis Chapman 10.00
200 Shane Victorino 10.00

Montreal Expos

Over the course of the season in a series of stadium give-aways, fans attending selected games at Olympic Stadium received a cello-wrapped pack of specially designed Donruss cards featuring many of the team's most popular players since entering the National League in 1969. Cards are the standard 2-1/2" x 3-1/2" format with either black-and-white or color photos on front, bordered in white with red and blue graphics. Backs have a dark blue background with personal data, a line of career stats and highlights.

NM/M
Complete Set (59): 25.00
Common Player: .25
Series 1, April 25 4.00
1 Claude Raymond .75
2 Javier Vasquez 1.50
3 John Boccabella .75
4 Bill Stoneman .75
5 Carl Morton .75
6 Ron Fairly .75
Series 2, May 9 4.00
7 Bob Bailey .25
8 Steve Renko .25
9 Mike Marshall .25
10 Ron Hunt .25
11 Ken Singleton .25
12 Pedro Martinez 3.00
Series 3, May 23 1.50
13 Tim Foli .25
14 Mike Jorgensen .25
15 Steve Rogers .25
16 Willie Davis .25
17 Larry Parrish .25
18 Jerry White .25
Series 4, June 20 8.00
19 Ellis Valentine .25
20 Woody Fryman .25
21 Andre Dawson 2.00
22 Warren Cromartie .25
23 Vladimir Guerrero 4.00
24 Tony Perez 2.00
Series 5, July 11 1.50
25 Chris Speier .25
26 Dan Schatzeder .25
27 Ross Grimsley .25
28 Scott Sanderson .25
29 Tim Wallach .25
30 Dave Cash .25
Series 6, July 25 2.00
31 Bill Gullickson .25
32 Tim Raines 1.00
33 Rodney Scott .25
34 Ron LeFlore .25
35 Charlie Lea .25
36 Bill Lee .25
Series 7, Aug. 1 3.00
37 Jeff Reardon .25
38 Bryn Smith .25
39 Al Oliver .75
40 Hubie Brooks .25
41 Terry Francona .25
42 Gary Carter 2.00
Series 8, Aug. 15 4.00
43 Spike Owen .25
44 Tim Burke .25
45 Andres Galarraga .50
46 Marquis Grissom .50
47 Larry Walker 2.00
48 Moises Alou .50
49 Dennis Martinez .50
Series 9, Sept. 12 3.50
50 Denis Boucher .25
51 Rondell White .25
52 Mel Rojas .25
53 Henry Rodriguez .25
54 David Segui .25
55 Ugueth Urbina .25
56 Jose Vidro 1.00
57 Darrin Fletcher .25
58 Orlando Cabrera 1.00
59 John Wetteland .25

2003 Donruss Rookie & Traded

NM/M
Complete Set (65): 8.00
Common Player: .25
Pack (8): 8.00
Box (24): 150.00
1 Jeremy Bonderman 1.00
2 Adam Loewen .50
3 Dan Haren .50
4 Jose Contreras **RC** .50
5 Hideki Matsui **RC** 2.00
6 Arnie Munoz .25
7 Miguel Cabrera .25
8 Andrew Brown **RC** .25
9 Josh Hall **RC** .25
10 Josh Stewart **RC** .25
11 Clint Barmes **RC** .25
12 Luis Ayala **RC** .25
13 Brandon Webb **RC** .75
14 Greg Aquino .25
15 Chien-Ming Wang **RC** 2.00
16 Rickie Weeks **RC** 1.50
17 Edgar Gonzalez **RC** .25
18 Dontrelle Willis .25
19 Bo Hart **RC** .25
20 Rosman Garcia **RC** .25
21 Jeremy Griffiths .25
22 Craig Brazell **RC** .50
23 Daniel Cabrera **RC** .50
24 Fernando Cabrera **RC** .25
25 Termel Sledge **RC** .25
26 Ramon Nivar .25
27 Rob Hammock **RC** .25
28 Francisco Rosario **RC** .25
29 Cory Stewart .25
30 Felix Sanchez .25
31 Jorge Cordova .25
32 Rocco Baldelli .50
33 Beau Kemp **RC** .25
34 Micheal Nakamura **RC** .25
35 Rett Johnson **RC** .25
36 Guillermo Quiroz **RC** .25
37 Hong-Chih Kuo **RC** 1.00
38 Ian Ferguson **RC** .25
39 Franklin Perez .25
40 Tim Olson **RC** .25
41 Jerome Williams .25
42 Rich Fischer .25
43 Phil Seibel **RC** .25
44 Aaron Looper **RC** .25
45 Jae Weong Seo .25
46 Chad Gaudin **RC** .25
47 Matt Kata **RC** .25
48 Ryan Wagner **RC** .25
49 Michel Hernandez **RC** .25
50 Diegomar Markwell .25
51 Doug Waechter .25
52 Mike Nicolas .25
53 Prentice Redman **RC** .25
54 Shane Bazzell .25
55 Delmon Young **RC** 2.00
56 Brian Stokes .25
57 Matt Bruback .25
58 Nook Logan **RC** .25
59 Oscar Villarreal **RC** .25
60 Pete LaForest **RC** .25
61 Shea Hillenbrand .25
62 Aramis Ramirez .40
63 Aaron Boone .25
64 Roberto Alomar .50
65 Rickey Henderson .50

Team Heroes
Common Player (541-548): .25
Team Heroes Glossy: 1-2X
541 Rickie Weeks **RC** 1.00
542 Hideki Matsui **RC** 1.50
543 Ramon Nivar .25
544 Adam Loewen **RC** .25
545 Brandon Webb **RC** .75
546 Dan Haren .50
547 Delmon Young **RC** 2.00
548 Ryan Wagner **RC** .25

Champions
Common Player (302-309): .25
Metalized: 4-8X
Production 100
302 Ryan Wagner **RC** .25
303 Adam Loewen **RC** .25
304 Chien-Ming Wang **RC** 2.50
305 Hong-Chih Kuo **RC** 1.00
306 Delmon Young **RC** 2.00
307 Dan Haren .50
308 Rickie Weeks **RC** 1.50
309 Ramon Nivar .25

Leaf
Common Player (321-329): .25
Leaf Red Press Proofs: 4-8X
Production 100
Leaf Blue Press Proofs: 5-10X
Production 50
321 Hideki Matsui **RC** 1.50
322 Ramon Nivar .25
323 Adam Loewen **RC** .25
324 Brandon Webb **RC** .75
325 Chien-Ming Wang **RC** 2.50
326 Delmon Young **RC** 2.00
327 Ryan Wagner **RC** .25
328 Dan Haren .50
329 Rickie Weeks **RC** 1.50

Playoff Prestige .25
Common Player (201-210):
Prestige X-Tra Points: 5-10X
Production 50
201 Jeremy Bonderman 1.00
202 Brandon Webb **RC** .75
203 Adam Loewen **RC** .25
204 Chien-Ming Wang **RC** 2.50
205 Hong-Chih Kuo **RC** 1.00
206 Delmon Young **RC** 2.00
207 Ryan Wagner **RC** .25
208 Dan Haren .50
209 Rickie Weeks **RC** 1.50
210 Ramon Nivar .25

Classics
Common Player (201-211): 4.00
Production 1,000
Classics Timeless Tributes: .75-1.5X
Production 100
201 Jeremy Bonderman 8.00
202 Adam Loewen **RC** 6.00
203 Chien-Ming Wang **RC** 25.00
204 Hong-Chih Kuo **RC** 8.00
205 Ryan Wagner **RC** 4.00
206 Dan Haren 6.00
207 Dontrelle Willis 4.00
208 Rickie Weeks **RC** 8.00
209 Ramon Nivar 4.00
210 Chad Gaudin **RC** 4.00
211 Delmon Young **RC** 10.00

Studio
Common Player (201-211): 3.00
Production 1,500
Studio Proof: 1-1.5X
Production 100
201 Adam Loewen **RC** 3.00
202 Jeremy Bonderman 6.00
203 Brandon Webb **RC** 8.00
204 Chien-Ming Wang **RC** 25.00
205 Chad Gaudin **RC** 3.00
206 Ryan Wagner **RC** 3.00
207 Hong-Chih Kuo **RC** 8.00
208 Dan Haren 6.00
209 Rickie Weeks **RC** 8.00
210 Ramon Nivar 3.00
211 Delmon Young **RC** 10.00

Diamond Kings
Common Player (177-201): 3.00
Inserted 1:30
DK Portraits Bronze: .5-1X
DK Portraits Silver: 1-1.5X
Production 100
DK Portraits Gold: 1-2X
Production 50
177 Hideki Matsui **RC** 10.00
178 Jeremy Bonderman 8.00
179 Brandon Webb **RC** 8.00
180 Adam Loewen **RC** 4.00
181 Chien-Ming Wang **RC** 15.00
182 Hong-Chih Kuo **RC** 6.00
183 Clint Barmes **RC** 3.00
184 Guillermo Quiroz **RC** 4.00
185 Edgar Gonzalez **RC** 3.00
186 Todd Wellemeyer **RC** 3.00
187 Dan Haren 4.00
188 Dustin McGowan 5.00
189 Preston Larrison 3.00
191 Kevin Youkilis 8.00
192 Bubba Nelson 3.00
193 Chris Burke 3.00
194 J.D. Durbin 4.00
195 Ryan Howard 30.00
196 Jason Kubel **RC** 6.00
197 Brendan Harris 6.00
198 Brian Bruney 3.00
199 Ramon Nivar 3.00
200 Rickie Weeks **RC** 8.00
201 Delmon Young **RC** 10.00

Leaf Certified Materials
Mirror Red Signature: .75-1.5X
Production 100 or 50
Mirror Blue Signature: 1-1.5X
Mirror Gold Signature: No Pricing
Mirror Emerald Signature: No Pricing
Mirror Reds: .2-.4X
Production 100
Mirror Blues: .4-.6X
Production 50
Mirror Golds: No Pricing
Production 25
251 Adam Loewen/Auto./250 **RC** 15.00
252 Dan Haren/Auto./250 30.00
253 Dontrelle Willis/Auto./250 25.00
254 Ramon Nivar/Auto./250 10.00
255 Chad Gaudin/Auto./250 20.00
256 Kevin Correia/Auto./250 **RC** 10.00
257 Rickie Weeks/Auto./100 **RC** 80.00
258 Ryan Wagner/Auto./250 **RC** 15.00
259 Delmon Young/Auto./100 **RC** 150.00

Playoff Absolute
Common Player (201-208): 4.00
Production 1,000
Spectrum: 1-2X
Production 100
201 Adam Loewen **RC** 4.00
202 Ramon Nivar 4.00
203 Dan Haren 5.00
204 Dontrelle Willis 4.00
205 Chad Gaudin 4.00
206 Rickie Weeks **RC** 8.00
207 Ryan Wagner **RC** 4.00
208 Delmon Young **RC** 12.00

Elite Extra Edition
Common Player (1-58): 4.00
Production 900
Elite Status: 1-30X
Numbered to Jersey Number
Elite Aspirations: 1-2X
Varying quantities produced
Turn of Century Non-Auto: 1-2X
Production 100
Elite Gold Status: No Pricing
Production 24
1 Adam Loewen **RC** 4.00
2 Brandon Webb **RC** 10.00
3 Chien-Ming Wang **RC** 30.00
4 Hong-Chih Kuo **RC** 20.00
5 Clint Barmes **RC** 4.00
6 Guillermo Quiroz **RC** 3.00
7 Edgar Gonzalez **RC** 3.00
8 Todd Wellemeyer **RC** 4.00
9 Alfredo Gonzalez **RC** 3.00
10 Craig Brazell **RC** 3.00
11 Tim Olson **RC** 3.00
12 Rich Fischer 3.00
13 Daniel Cabrera **RC** 5.00
14 Francisco Rosario **RC** 4.00
15 Francisco Cruceta **RC** 4.00
16 Alejandro Machado 4.00
17 Andrew Brown **RC** 4.00
18 Rob Hammock **RC** 4.00
19 Arnie Munoz 4.00
20 Felix Sanchez 4.00
21 Nook Logan **RC** 4.00
22 Cory Stewart 4.00
23 Michel Hernandez **RC** 4.00
24 Rett Johnson **RC** 4.00
25 Josh Hall **RC** 4.00
26 Doug Waechter 4.00
27 Matt Kata **RC** 4.00
28 Dan Haren 8.00
29 Dontrelle Willis 4.00
30 Ramon Nivar 4.00
31 Chad Gaudin **RC** 5.00
32 Rickie Weeks **RC** 10.00
33 Ryan Wagner **RC** 4.00

34 Kevin Correia **RC** 4.00
35 Bo Hart **RC** 4.00
36 Oscar Villarreal **RC** 4.00
37 Josh Willingham **RC** 5.00
38 Jeff Duncan **RC** 6.00
39 David DeJesus **RC** 6.00
40 Dustin McGowan **RC** 5.00
41 Preston Larrison 4.00
43 Kevin Youkilis 8.00
44 Bubba Nelson 4.00
45 Chris Burke 6.00
46 J.D. Durbin 4.00
47 Ryan Howard 80.00
48 Jason Kubel **RC** 8.00
49 Brendan Harris 6.00
50 Brian Bruney 4.00
52 Byron Gettis 4.00
53 Edwin Jackson **RC** 4.00
55 Daniel Garcia 4.00
57 Chad Cordero **RC** 4.00
58 Delmon Young **RC** 20.00
Common Leaf Limited Phenom:
Silver Spotlights: 1X
Production 50
Gold Spotlights: No Pricing
Production 10 or 25
201 Delmon Young/ Auto./99 **RC** 180.00
202 Rickie Weeks/ Auto./99 **RC** 80.00
203 Edwin Jackson/ Auto./99 **RC** 20.00
204 Dan Haren/Auto./99 40.00
Signature Series:
151 Delmon Young/ Auto./200 **RC** 100.00
152 Rickie Weeks/ Auto./200 **RC** 50.00
153 Edwin Jackson/ Auto./200 15.00

Autographs

NM/M
Common Autograph: 5.00
1 Jeremy Bonderman/ 50 50.00
2 Adam Loewen/500 10.00
3 Dan Haren/100 30.00
4 Jose Contreras/100 25.00
6 Arnie Munoz/584 5.00
7 Miguel Cabrera/50 50.00
8 Andrew Brown/584 5.00
9 Josh Hall/1000 10.00
10 Josh Stewart/300 5.00
11 Clint Barmes/129 15.00
12 Luis Ayala/1000 5.00
13 Brandon Webb/100 35.00
14 Greg Aquino/1000 5.00
15 Chien-Ming Wang/ 100 200.00
17 Edgar Gonzalez/400 5.00
19 Bo Hart/150 5.00
20 Rosman Garcia/250 5.00
21 Jeremy Griffiths/812 5.00
22 Craig Brazell/205 5.00
23 Daniel Cabrera/383 15.00
24 Fernando Cabrera/ 1,000 5.00
25 Terrmel Sledge/250 5.00
26 Ramon Nivar/100 5.00
27 Rob Hammock/201 10.00
29 Cory Stewart/1,000 5.00
30 Felix Sanchez/1,000 5.00
31 Jorge Cordova/1,000 5.00
33 Beau Kemp/1,000 5.00
34 Micheal Nakamura/ 1,000 5.00
35 Rett Johnson/1,000 8.00
36 Guillermo Quiroz/90 15.00
37 Hong-Chih Kuo/50 150.00
38 Ian Ferguson/1,000 5.00
39 Franklin Perez/1,000 5.00
40 Tim Olson/150 5.00
41 Jerome Williams/50 10.00
42 Rich Fischer/734 5.00
43 Phil Seibel/1000 5.00
44 Aaron Looper/513 5.00
45 Jae Weong Seo/50 30.00
47 Matt Kata/203 10.00
48 Ryan Wagner/100 10.00
50 Diegomar Markwell/ 1,000 5.00
51 Doug Waechter/583 5.00
52 Mike Nicolas/1,000 5.00
53 Prentice Redman/425 5.00
54 Shane Bazell/1,000 5.00
55 Delmon Young/75 125.00
56 Brian Stokes/1000 5.00
57 Matt Bruback/513 5.00
58 Nook Logan/150 5.00
59 Oscar Villarreal/150 5.00
60 Pete LaForest/250 5.00

Gamers

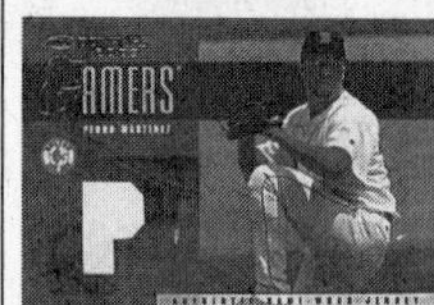

NM/M
Common Player: 4.00
Production 500
Position: 1-2X
Production 100
Number: 1-2X
Production 100
Patch: No Pricing
Production 25
Rewards: No Pricing
Production 10
1 Nomar Garciaparra 8.00
2 Alex Rodriguez 8.00
3 Mike Piazza 8.00
4 Greg Maddux 8.00
5 Roger Clemens 10.00
6 Sammy Sosa 8.00
7 Randy Johnson 8.00
8 Albert Pujols 15.00
9 Alfonso Soriano 8.00
10 Chipper Jones 8.00
11 Mark Prior 6.00
12 Hideo Nomo 6.00
13 Adam Dunn 6.00
14 Juan Gonzalez 5.00
15 Vladimir Guerrero 8.00
16 Pedro J. Martinez 8.00
17 Jim Thome 6.00
18 Brandon Webb/200 6.00
19 Mike Mussina 6.00
20 Mark Teixeira 5.00
21 Barry Larkin 5.00
22 Ivan Rodriguez 8.00
23 Hank Blalock 6.00
24 Rafael Palmeiro 6.00
25 Curt Schilling 6.00
26 Troy Glaus 5.00
27 Bernie Williams 6.00
28 Scott Rolen 6.00
29 Torii Hunter 5.00
30 Nick Johnson 4.00
31 Kazuhisa Ishii 4.00
32 Shawn Green 5.00
33 Jeff Bagwell 6.00
34 Lance Berkman 4.00
35 Roy Oswalt 4.00
36 Kerry Wood 4.00
37 Todd Helton 6.00
38 Manny Ramirez 8.00
39 Andruw Jones 5.00
40 Frank Thomas 8.00
41 Gary Sheffield 5.00
42 Maggio Ordonez 5.00
43 Mike Sweeney 4.00
44 Carlos Beltran 6.00
45 Richie Sexson 5.00
46 Jeff Kent 5.00
47 Carlos Delgado 5.00
48 Vernon Wells 4.00
49 Dontrelle Willis 8.00
50 Jae Weong Seo 4.00

Gamers Autograph

NM/M
Production 5-50 4.00
Many not priced due to scarcity.
20 Mark Teixeira/50 30.00
23 Hank Blalock/50 30.00
29 Torii Hunter/50 20.00
35 Roy Oswalt/50 20.00
43 Mike Sweeney/50 15.00
48 Vernon Wells/30 20.00
49 Dontrelle Willis/50 25.00

Playoff Prestige Autograph

NM/M
Quantity produced listed
201 Jeremy Bonderman/100 50.00
202 Brandon Webb/100 30.00
203 Adam Loewen/100 10.00
204 Chien-Ming Wang/ 50 300.00
205 Hong-Chih Kuo/100 150.00
207 Ryan Wagner/100 10.00
208 Dan Haren/100 25.00
210 Ramon Nivar/100 15.00

Recollection Autographs

NM/M
Common Player:
7 Jack McDowell 88/75 20.00

Stat Line Season/Career

Cards serial #'d from 101-150: 1-2X
Cards serial #'d from 50-100:2-3X
Cards serial #'d from 26-49: 3-4X
Cards numbered under 25 not priced.

Elite Turn of the Century Autograph

NM/M
Common Player: 10.00
Production 100
Aspirations: .75-1.5X
Varying quantities produced
1 Adam Loewen 15.00
2 Brandon Webb 80.00
3 Chien-Ming Wang 300.00
4 Hong-Chih Kuo 150.00
5 Clint Barmes 25.00
6 Guillermo Quiroz 20.00
7 Edgar Gonzalez 10.00
8 Todd Wellemeyer 10.00
9 Alfredo Gonzalez 10.00
10 Craig Brazell 10.00
11 Tim Olson 10.00
12 Rich Fischer 10.00
13 Daniel Cabrera 30.00
14 Francisco Rosario 10.00
15 Francisco Cruceta 10.00
16 Alejandro Machado 10.00
17 Andrew Brown 10.00
18 Rob Hammock 10.00
19 Arnie Munoz 10.00
20 Felix Sanchez 10.00
21 Nook Logan 10.00
22 Cory Stewart 10.00
23 Michel Hernandez 10.00
24 Rett Johnson 10.00
25 Josh Hall 15.00
26 Doug Waechter 10.00
27 Matt Kata 10.00
28 Dan Haren 60.00
29 Dontrelle Willis/25 60.00
30 Ramon Nivar 10.00
31 Chad Gaudin 20.00
32 Rickie Weeks/25 120.00
33 Ryan Wagner 10.00
35 Bo Hart 10.00
36 Oscar Villarreal 10.00
37 Josh Willingham 30.00
38 Jeff Duncan 15.00
40 Dustin McGowan 25.00
41 Preston Larrison 10.00
43 Kevin Youkilis 50.00
44 Bubba Nelson 15.00
45 Chris Burke 40.00
46 J.D. Durbin 15.00
47 Ryan Howard 1,100
48 Jason Kubel 40.00
49 Brendan Harris 20.00
50 Brian Bruney 10.00
52 Byron Gettis 10.00
53 Edwin Jackson 10.00
55 Daniel Garcia 10.00
58 Delmon Young 250.00

2003 Donruss Signature Series

NM/M
Complete Set (150): 150.00
Common Player: .50
Common Rk (101-150): 1.00
Inserted 1:Tin
Tin: 35.00
1 Garret Anderson .75
2 Tim Salmon .75
3 Troy Glaus .75
4 Curt Schilling 1.00
5 Luis Gonzalez .75
6 Mark Grace .75
7 Matt Williams .50
8 Randy Johnson 1.50
9 Andruw Jones 1.00
10 Chipper Jones 1.50
11 Gary Sheffield 1.00
12 Greg Maddux 2.00
13 Johnny Damon .75
14 Manny Ramirez 1.00
15 Nomar Garciaparra 2.50
16 Pedro J. Martinez 1.50
17 Corey Patterson .75
18 Kerry Wood 1.50
19 Mark Prior 2.00
20 Sammy Sosa 2.50
21 Bartolo Colon .50
22 Frank Thomas 1.00
23 Magglio Ordonez .50
24 Paul Konerko .50
25 Adam Dunn 1.00
26 Austin Kearns .75
27 Barry Larkin .75
28 Ken Griffey Jr. 2.00
29 C.C. Sabathia .50
30 Omar Vizquel .50
31 Larry Walker .50
32 Todd Helton 1.00
33 Ivan Rodriguez 1.00
34 Josh Beckett .75
35 Craig Biggio .75
36 Jeff Bagwell 1.00
37 Jeff Kent .50
38 Lance Berkman .75
39 Richard Hidalgo .50
40 Roy Oswalt .75
41 Carlos Beltran 1.00
42 Mike Sweeney .50
43 Runelvys Hernandez .50
44 Hideo Nomo .75
45 Kazuhisa Ishii .50
46 Paul LoDuca .50
47 Shawn Green .75
48 Ben Sheets .75
49 Richie Sexson .75
50 A.J. Pierzynski .50
51 Torii Hunter .75
52 Javier Vazquez .50
53 Jose Vidro .50
54 Vladimir Guerrero 1.50
55 Cliff Floyd .50
56 David Cone .50
57 Mike Piazza 2.00
58 Roberto Alomar .75
59 Tom Glavine .75
60 Alfonso Soriano 1.50
61 Derek Jeter 4.00
62 Drew Henson .50
63 Jason Giambi .75
64 Mike Mussina 1.00
65 Nick Johnson .50
66 Roger Clemens 3.00
67 Barry Zito .75
68 Eric Chavez .75
69 Mark Mulder .75
70 Miguel Tejada .75
71 Tim Hudson .75
72 Bobby Abreu .75
73 Jim Thome 1.00
74 Kevin Millwood .50
75 Pat Burrell .50
76 Brian Giles .50
77 Jason Kendall .50
78 Kenny Lofton .50
79 Phil Nevin .50
80 Ryan Klesko .50
81 Andres Galarraga .50
82 Barry Bonds 4.00
83 Rich Aurilia .50
84 Edgar Martinez .50
85 Freddy Garcia .50
86 Ichiro Suzuki 2.50
87 Albert Pujols 3.00
88 Jim Edmonds .75
89 Scott Rolen 1.50
90 So Taguchi .50
91 Rocco Baldelli .50
92 Alex Rodriguez 3.00
93 Hank Blalock 1.00
94 Juan Gonzalez 1.00
95 Mark Teixeira .75
96 Rafael Palmeiro 1.00
97 Carlos Delgado 1.00
98 Eric Hinske .50
99 Roy Halladay .75
100 Vernon Wells .50
101 Hideki Matsui **RC** 10.00
102 Jose Contreras **RC** 3.00
103 Jeremy Bonderman **RC** 4.00
104 Bernie Castro **RC** 1.00
105 Alfredo Gonzalez **RC** 1.00
106 Arnie Munoz **RC** 1.00
107 Andrew Brown **RC** 1.50
108 Josh Hall **RC** 1.50
109 Josh Stewart **RC** 1.50
110 Clint Barmes **RC** 1.50
111 Brandon Webb **RC** 2.50
112 Chien-Ming Wang **RC** 15.00
113 Edgar Gonzalez **RC** 1.00
114 Alejandro Machado **RC** 1.00
115 Jeremy Griffiths 1.00
116 Craig Brazell **RC** 1.50
117 Shane Bazell **RC** 1.50
118 Fernando Cabrera **RC** 1.50
119 Terrmel Sledge **RC** 1.50
120 Rob Hammock **RC** 1.50
121 Francisco Rosario **RC** 1.50
122 Francisco Cruceta **RC** 1.50
123 Rett Johnson **RC** 1.50
124 Guillermo Quiroz **RC** 2.00
125 Hong-Chih Kuo **RC** 2.00
126 Ian Ferguson **RC** 1.50
127 Tim Olson **RC** 1.50
128 Todd Wellemeyer **RC** 1.50
129 Richard Fischer **RC** 1.00
130 Phil Seibel **RC** 1.00
131 Joe Valentine **RC** 1.00
132 Matt Kata **RC** 1.50
133 Michael Hessman **RC** 1.00
134 Michel Hernandez **RC** 1.00
135 Doug Waechter **RC** 1.50
136 Prentice Redman **RC** 1.50
137 Nook Logan **RC** 1.00
138 Oscar Villarreal **RC** 1.00
139 Pete LaForest **RC** 1.00
140 Matt Bruback **RC** 1.00
141 Dontrelle Willis 1.50
142 Greg Aquino **RC** 1.00
143 Lew Ford **RC** 4.00
144 Jeff Duncan **RC** 2.00
145 Dan Haren 2.00
146 Miguel Ojeda **RC** 1.00
147 Rosman Garcia **RC** 1.00
148 Felix Sanchez **RC** 1.00
149 Jon Leicester **RC** 1.00
150 Roger Deago **RC** 1.00

Century Proofs

Stars (1-100): 2-4X
Century (101-150): 1-2X
Production 100 Sets

Decade Proofs

Production 10 Sets
No pricing due to scarcity.

Authentic Cuts

Quantity produced listed

Autographs

NM/M
Common Auto.: 8.00
Some not priced due to scarcity.
1 Garret Anderson 15.00
6 Mark Grace/141 50.00
7 Matt Williams 10.00
8 Randy Johnson/50 60.00
10 Chipper Jones/50 45.00
14 Manny Ramirez/50 40.00
17 Barry Larkin/159 25.00
33 Ivan Rodriguez/50 35.00
38 Lance Berkman/75 15.00
39 Richard Hidalgo 8.00
40 Roy Oswalt/150 15.00
42 Mike Sweeney 8.00
50 A.J. Pierzynski 8.00
51 Torii Hunter 10.00
53 Jose Vidro 6.00
54 Vladimir Guerrero 20.00
55 Cliff Floyd 8.00
56 David Cone/35 20.00
58 Roberto Alomar/50 40.00
65 Nick Johnson 10.00
67 Barry Zito/150 15.00
68 Eric Chavez 10.00
69 Mark Mulder/50 20.00
72 Bobby Abreu 10.00
78 Kenny Lofton/229 10.00
80 Ryan Klesko/150 10.00
81 Andres Galarraga 8.00
83 Rich Aurilia/122 8.00
84 Edgar Martinez 15.00
89 Scott Rolen/200 25.00
90 So Taguchi/220 10.00
95 Mark Teixeira/150 20.00
100 Vernon Wells 10.00
102 Jose Contreras 20.00
141 Dontrelle Willis/150 25.00

Century

NM/M
Common Auto.: 15.00
Production 100 Sets
Decades: No Pricing
Production 10 Sets
1 Garret Anderson 15.00
7 Matt Williams 15.00
27 Barry Larkin 30.00
39 Richard Hidalgo 15.00
42 Mike Sweeney 15.00
50 A.J. Pierzynski 15.00
51 Torii Hunter 20.00
53 Jose Vidro 15.00
54 Vladimir Guerrero 30.00
55 Cliff Floyd 15.00
62 Drew Henson 15.00
65 Nick Johnson 15.00
69 Mark Mulder 25.00
72 Bobby Abreu 20.00
78 Kenny Lofton 15.00
81 Andres Galarraga 15.00
84 Edgar Martinez 25.00
89 Scott Rolen 30.00
90 So Taguchi 15.00
100 Vernon Wells 15.00
102 Jose Contreras 25.00

Century Notations

NM/M
Production 100 Sets
Decade Notations: No Pricing
Production 10 Sets
1 Garret Anderson 20.00
7 Matt Williams 15.00
50 A.J. Pierzynski 15.00
68 Eric Chavez 15.00
78 Kenny Lofton 15.00
84 Edgar Martinez 25.00

INKredible - Three

NM/M
Production 50 Sets
1 Barry Zito, Mark Mulder, Tim Hudson 300.00
2 Andruw Jones, Chipper Jones, Greg Maddux 325.00
3 Ernie Banks, Kerry Wood, Mark Prior 300.00
4 Harmon Killebrew, Kirby Puckett, Torii Hunter 175.00
5 Javier Vazquez, Jose Vidro, Vladimir Guerrero 90.00

INKredible - Four

NM/M
Production 25 Sets
Limited pricing due to scarcity.
4 Brooks Robinson, Cal Ripken Jr., Frank Robinson, Jim Palmer 500.00
6 Bo Jackson, Carlos Beltran, George Brett, Mike Sweeney 225.00
7 Curt Schilling, Junior Spivey, Mark Grace, Randy Johnson 475.00
10 Joe Carter, Roberto Alomar, Ryan Klesko, Tony Gwynn 200.00

INKredible - Six

NM/M
Production 10 Sets
Limited pricing due to scarcity.
3 Andre Dawson, Ernie Banks, Kerry Wood, Mark Grace, Mark Prior, Ryne Sandberg 1,500
5 Alex Rodriguez, Don Mattingly, George Brett, Hideo Nomo, Nolan Ryan, Roger Clemens 3,100

Legends of Summer

NM/M
Complete Set (40): 125.00
Common Player: 3.00
Production 250 Sets
Century: 1X
Production 100 Sets
Decades: No Pricing
Production 10 Sets
1 Al Kaline 5.00
2 Alan Trammell 3.00
3 Andre Dawson 3.00
4 Babe Ruth 10.00
5 Billy Williams 3.00
6 Bo Jackson 4.00
7 Bob Feller 3.00
8 Bobby Doerr 3.00
9 Brooks Robinson 5.00
10 Dale Murphy 5.00
11 Dennis Eckersley 3.00
12 Don Mattingly 8.00
13 Duke Snider 3.00
14 Eric Davis 3.00
15 Frank Robinson 3.00
16 Fred Lynn 3.00
17 Gary Carter 3.00
18 Harmon Killebrew 5.00
19 Jack Morris 3.00
20 Jim Palmer 3.00
21 Jim Abbott 3.00
22 Joe Morgan 3.00
23 Joe Torre 3.00
24 Johnny Bench 5.00
25 Jose Canseco 3.00
26 Kirby Puckett 5.00
27 Lenny Dykstra 3.00
28 Lou Brock 3.00
29 Ralph Kiner 3.00
30 Mike Schmidt 6.00
31 Nolan Ryan 10.00
32 Nolan Ryan 10.00
33 Orel Hershiser 3.00
34 Phil Rizzuto 3.00
35 Orlando Cepeda 3.00
36 Ryne Sandberg 8.00
37 Stan Musial 6.00
38 Steve Garvey 3.00
39 Tony Perez 3.00
40 Ty Cobb 6.00

Legends of Summer Autographs

NM/M
Common Autograph: 8.00
1 Al Kaline 20.00
2 Alan Trammell 10.00
3 Andre Dawson 10.00
5 Billy Williams 8.00
6 Bo Jackson/100 50.00
7 Bob Feller 15.00

8 Bobby Doerr 15.00
9 Brooks Robinson 25.00
10 Dale Murphy/75 40.00
11 Dennis Eckersley 10.00
12 Don Mattingly/50 75.00
13 Duke Snider/225 20.00
14 Eric Davis 8.00
15 Frank Robinson 10.00
16 Fred Lynn 8.00
17 Gary Carter 10.00
18 Harmon Killebrew/171 20.00
19 Jack Morris 8.00
20 Jim Palmer 10.00
21 Jim Abbott 8.00
22 Joe Morgan/125 15.00
23 Joe Torre 10.00
24 Johnny Bench/75 30.00
25 Jose Canseco/75 30.00
26 Kirby Puckett/75 35.00
27 Lenny Dykstra 10.00
28 Lou Brock 15.00
29 Ralph Kiner 10.00
30 Mike Schmidt/75 60.00
31 Nolan Ryan/75 110.00
33 Orel Hershiser 20.00
34 Phil Rizzuto 15.00
35 Orlando Cepeda 15.00
36 Ryne Sandberg/75 60.00
37 Stan Musial/200 40.00
38 Steve Garvey 10.00
39 Tony Perez 10.00

Legends of Summer Century

NM/M
Production 100 Sets
Decades: No Pricing
Production 10 Sets
1 Al Kaline 25.00
2 Alan Trammell 20.00
3 Andre Dawson 15.00
5 Billy Williams 15.00
6 Bo Jackson 50.00
7 Bob Feller 25.00
8 Bobby Doerr 20.00
9 Brooks Robinson 30.00
11 Dennis Eckersley 15.00
12 Don Mattingly 65.00
14 Eric Davis 15.00
15 Frank Robinson 15.00
16 Fred Lynn 15.00
17 Gary Carter 20.00
19 Jack Morris 15.00
20 Jim Palmer 20.00
21 Jim Abbott 15.00
23 Joe Torre 15.00
27 Lenny Dykstra 15.00
28 Lou Brock 25.00
29 Ralph Kiner 15.00
33 Orel Hershiser 60.00
34 Phil Rizzuto 30.00
35 Orlando Cepeda 20.00
36 Ryne Sandberg 65.00
37 Stan Musial 60.00
38 Steve Garvey 15.00
39 Tony Perez 15.00

Legends of Summer Notations

NM/M
Common Autograph: 8.00
1 Al Kaline/200 20.00
2 Alan Trammell/250 10.00
3 Andre Dawson/165 10.00
3 Andre Dawson/250 10.00
5 Billy Williams/250 8.00
5 Billy Williams/150 8.00
7 Bob Feller/250 15.00
7 Bob Feller/200 15.00
8 Bobby Doerr/250 10.00
9 Brooks Robinson/150 20.00
9 Brooks Robinson/50 40.00
10 Dale Murphy/50 45.00
11 Dennis Eckersley/250 10.00
14 Eric Davis/250 8.00
14 Eric Davis/150 8.00
14 Eric Davis/200 8.00
16 Fred Lynn/240 10.00
16 Fred Lynn/250 10.00
18 Harmon Killebrew/75 40.00
18 Harmon Killebrew/50 40.00
18 Harmon Killebrew/125 30.00
19 Jack Morris/250 10.00
20 Jim Palmer/190 10.00
20 Jim Palmer/140 10.00
20 Jim Palmer/50 20.00
21 Jim Abbott/200 10.00
21 Jim Abbott/100 15.00
21 Jim Abbott/75 15.00
21 Jim Abbott/50 20.00
27 Lenny Dykstra/226 10.00
28 Lou Brock/50 35.00
29 Ralph Kiner/200 15.00
29 Ralph Kiner/100 15.00
29 Ralph Kiner/150 15.00
35 Orlando Cepeda/75 35.00
35 Orlando Cepeda/40 25.00
38 Steve Garvey/150 10.00
38 Steve Garvey/50 20.00
38 Steve Garvey/75 15.00
39 Tony Perez/250 10.00
39 Tony Perez/125 15.00
39 Tony Perez/75 20.00
39 Tony Perez/175 10.00

Notable Nicknames

NM/M
Complete Set (20): 75.00
Common Player: 3.00
Production 750 Sets
Century: 1-1.5X
Production 100 Sets
Decade: No Pricing
Production 10 Sets
1 Andre Dawson 3.00
2 Torii Hunter 3.00
3 Brooks Robinson 5.00
4 Carlton Fisk 3.00
5 Mike Mussina 4.00
6 Don Mattingly 8.00
7 Duke Snider 4.00
8 Eric Davis 3.00
9 Frank Thomas 4.00
10 Randy Johnson 5.00
11 Lenny Dykstra 3.00
12 Ivan Rodriguez 3.00
13 Nolan Ryan 10.00
14 Phil Rizzuto 3.00
15 Reggie Jackson 4.00
16 Roger Clemens 8.00
17 Ryne Sandberg 8.00
18 Stan Musial 6.00
19 Luis Gonzalez 3.00
20 Will Clark 4.00

Notable Nicknames Autograph

NM/M
Quantity produced listed
Decades: No Pricing
Production 10 Sets
1 Andre "The Hawk" Dawson/100 30.00
2 Torii "Spiderman" Hunter/100 30.00
3 Brooks "Hoover" Robinson 60.00
4 Carlton "Pudge" Fisk/100 50.00
5 Mike "Moose" Mussina/100 80.00
6 Don "Donnie Baseball" Mattingly/100 100.00
7 Duke "Duke of Flatbush" Snider/100 60.00
8 Eric "The Red" Davis/40 50.00
9 Frank "The Big Hurt" Thomas/100 60.00
10 Randy "Big Unit" Johnson/100 100.00
11 Lenny "Nails" Dykstra/100 20.00
12 Ivan "Pudge" Rodriguez/75 50.00
14 Phil "Scooter" Rizzuto/100 50.00
15 Reggie "Mr. October" Jackson/100 60.00
16 Roger "The Rocket" Clemens/100 150.00
17 Ryne "Ryno" Sandberg/100 75.00
18 Stan "The Man" Musial/100 85.00
19 Luis "Gonzo" Gonzalez/100 25.00
20 Will "The Thrill" Clark/100 60.00

Notations

NM/M
Varying quantities produced
Many not priced due to scarcity.
1 Garret Anderson/75 20.00
7 Matt Williams/250 10.00
7 Matt Williams/50 20.00
45 Kazuhisa Ishii/35 35.00
50 A.J. Pierzynski/200 10.00
53 Jose Vidro/40 15.00
62 Drew Henson/73 20.00
68 Eric Chavez/50 20.00
78 Kenny Lofton/150 10.00
80 Ryan Klesko/75 20.00
83 Rich Aurilia/61 15.00
84 Edgar Martinez/250 10.00
84 Edgar Martinez/60 20.00
100 Vernon Wells/75 15.00

Players Collection Autographs

NM/M
Quantity produced listed
Roberto Alomar/75 30.00
Adrian Beltre/104 30.00
Lance Berkman/50 20.00
Craig Biggio/26 35.00
Joe Borchard/53 10.00
J.D. Drew/52 20.00
Jim Edmonds/52 25.00
Todd Helton/50 40.00
Jason Jennings/49 10.00
Chipper Jones/51 50.00
Paul LoDuca/227 8.00
Magglio Ordonez/102 20.00
Mark Prior/27 100.00
Ivan Rodriguez/52 35.00
Richie Sexson/50 20.00
Matt Williams/482 8.00

Signature Cuts

NM/M
Some not priced due to scarcity.
Decades: No Pricing
Production 10 Sets
8 Randy Johnson/40 60.00
33 Ivan Rodriguez/122 30.00
54 Vladimir Guerrero/34 35.00
58 Roberto Alomar/100 30.00
64 Mike Mussina/82 40.00
73 Jim Thome/127 30.00
80 Ryan Klesko/35 20.00
81 Andres Galarraga/51 20.00
89 Scott Rolen/36 40.00

Team Trademarks

NM/M
Complete Set (40): 150.00
Common Player: 3.00
Production 100 Sets
Century: 1X
Production 100 Sets
Decade: No Pricing
Production 10 Sets
1 Adam Dunn 3.00
2 Andre Dawson 3.00
3 Babe Ruth 10.00
4 Barry Bonds 10.00
5 Brooks Robinson 4.00
6 Cal Ripken Jr. 10.00
7 Derek Jeter 8.00
8 Don Mattingly 8.00
9 Frank Robinson 3.00
10 Fred Lynn 3.00
11 Gary Carter 3.00
12 George Brett 6.00
13 Greg Maddux 5.00
14 Ichiro Suzuki 6.00
15 Jim Palmer 3.00
16 Jose Contreras 3.00
17 Kerry Wood 4.00
18 Lou Gehrig 8.00
19 Magglio Ordonez 3.00
20 Mark Grace 3.00
21 Mike Schmidt 8.00
22 Nolan Ryan 10.00
23 Nolan Ryan 10.00
24 Reggie Jackson 4.00
25 Rickey Henderson 3.00
26 Roberto Clemente 6.00
27 Roger Clemens 6.00
28 Roger Clemens 6.00
29 Ryne Sandberg 6.00
30 Sammy Sosa 6.00
31 Stan Musial 6.00
32 Steve Carlton 3.00
33 Tim Hudson 3.00
34 Tom Glavine 3.00
35 Tom Seaver 4.00
36 Tony Gwynn 4.00
37 Torii Hunter 3.00
38 Ty Cobb 6.00
39 Vladimir Guerrero 4.00
40 Will Clark 4.00

Team Trademarks Century

NM/M
Production 100 Sets
Decade: No Pricing
Production 10 Sets
2 Andre Dawson 15.00
5 Brooks Robinson 30.00
9 Frank Robinson 15.00
10 Fred Lynn 15.00
11 Gary Carter 20.00
15 Jim Palmer 15.00
16 Jose Contreras 25.00
20 Mark Grace 60.00
29 Ryne Sandberg 65.00
31 Stan Musial 65.00
32 Steve Carlton 25.00
34 Tom Glavine 25.00
37 Steve Hunter 15.00
39 Vladimir Guerrero 25.00

Team Trademarks Autograph

NM/M
Quantity produced listed
1 Adam Dunn/50 35.00
2 Andre Dawson/250 10.00
5 Brooks Robinson/250 20.00
6 Cal Ripken Jr./50 200.00
8 Don Mattingly/75 85.00
10 Fred Lynn/250 8.00
11 Gary Carter/250 10.00
12 George Brett/50 100.00
13 Greg Maddux/50 85.00
16 Jose Contreras/250 15.00
17 Kerry Wood/50 40.00
19 Magglio Ordonez/75 15.00
20 Mark Grace/25 90.00
23 Nolan Ryan/50 110.00
24 Reggie Jackson/75 25.00
25 Rickey Henderson/50 100.00
27 Roger Clemens/50 110.00
28 Roger Clemens/50 110.00
29 Ryne Sandberg/100 60.00
31 Stan Musial/200 50.00
32 Steve Carlton/150 20.00
33 Tim Hudson/100 35.00
34 Tom Glavine/50 35.00
35 Tom Seaver/50 35.00
36 Tony Gwynn/50 60.00
37 Torii Hunter/250 10.00
39 Vladimir Guerrero/250 20.00
40 Will Clark/125 30.00

Team Trademarks Notations

NM/M
Quantity produced listed
2 Andre Dawson/250 10.00
2 Andre Dawson/150 10.00
5 Brooks Robinson/75 35.00
5 Brooks Robinson/125 30.00
10 Fred Lynn/50 20.00
15 Jim Palmer/32 25.00
15 Jim Palmer/128 15.00
15 Jim Palmer/150 15.00
29 Ryne Sandberg/40 80.00
29 Ryne Sandberg/55 75.00
32 Steve Carlton/50 35.00
33 Tim Hudson/50 45.00
40 Will Clark/52 60.00

2003 Donruss Studio Samples

Each August 2003 issue of Beckett Baseball Card Monthly included a sample Donruss Studio card rubber-cemented inside. The cards differ from the issued version only in the appearance on back of a (usually) silver-foil "SAMPLE" notation. Some cards were produced with the back overprint in gold-foil in much more limited quantities. The number of different players' cards involved in the promotion is unknown.

NM/M
Common Player: .10
Stars: 1.5X
Gold: 20X

2003 Donruss Studio

NM/M
Complete Set (200): 35.00
Common Player: .25
Pack (6): 4.00
Box (20): 60.00
1 Darin Erstad .40
2 David Eckstein .25
3 Garret Anderson .50
4 Jarrod Washburn .25
5 Tim Salmon .50
6 Troy Glaus .50
7 Jay Gibbons .25
8 Melvin Mora .25
9 Rodrigo Lopez .25
10 Tony Batista .25
11 Freddy Sanchez .25
12 Derek Lowe .25
13 Johnny Damon .40
14 Manny Ramirez .75
15 Nomar Garciaparra 1.50
16 Pedro J. Martinez 1.00
17 Rickey Henderson .50
18 Shea Hillenbrand .25
19 Carlos Lee .25
20 Frank Thomas .75
21 Magglio Ordonez .40
22 Bartolo Colon .25
23 Paul Konerko .25
24 Josh Stewart **RC** .50
25 C.C. Sabathia .25
26 Jeremy Guthrie .25
27 Ellis Burks .25
28 Omar Vizquel .40
29 Victor Martinez .25
30 Cliff Lee .25
31 Jhonny Peralta .50
32 Brian Tallet .25
33 Bobby Higginson .25
34 Carlos Pena .25
35 Nook Logan **RC** .25
36 Steve Sparks .25
37 Travis Chapman .25
38 Carlos Beltran .75
39 Joe Randa .25
40 Mike Sweeney .25
41 Jimmy Gobble .25
42 Michael Tucker .25
43 Runelvys Hernandez .25
44 Brad Radke .25
45 Corey Koskie .25
46 Cristian Guzman .25
47 J.C. Romero .25
48 Doug Mientkiewicz .25
49 Lew Ford **RC** 1.50
50 Jacque Jones .40
51 Torii Hunter .50
52 Alfonso Soriano .75
53 Nick Johnson .25
54 Bernie Williams .50
55 Jose Contreras **RC** 1.50
56 Derek Jeter 3.00
57 Jason Giambi .50
58 Brandon Claussen .25
59 Jorge Posada .50
60 Mike Mussina .50
61 Roger Clemens 2.00
62 Hideki Matsui **RC** 5.00
63 Barry Zito .50
64 Adam Morrissey .25
65 Eric Chavez .40
66 Jermaine Dye .25
67 Mark Mulder .40
68 Miguel Tejada .50
69 Joe Valentine **RC** .25
70 Tim Hudson .50
71 Bret Boone .40
72 Chris Snelling .25
73 Edgar Martinez .25
74 Freddy Garcia .25
75 Ichiro Suzuki 2.00
76 Jamie Moyer .25
77 John Olerud .40
78 Kazuhiro Sasaki .25
79 Aubrey Huff .25
80 Joe Kennedy .25
81 Dewon Brazelton .25
82 Pete LaForest **RC** .25
83 Alex Rodriguez 2.50
84 Chan Ho Park .25
85 Hank Blalock .75
86 Juan Gonzalez .75
87 Kevin Mench .25
88 Rafael Palmeiro .75
89 Carlos Delgado .50
90 Eric Hinske .25
91 Josh Phelps .25
92 Roy Halladay .40
93 Shannon Stewart .25
94 Vernon Wells .40
95 Vinnie Chulk .25
96 Curt Schilling .75
97 Junior Spivey .25
98 Luis Gonzalez .50
99 Mark Grace .50
100 Randy Johnson 1.00
101 Andruw Jones .75
102 Chipper Jones 1.00
103 Gary Sheffield .50
104 Greg Maddux 1.50
105 John Smoltz .50
106 Mike Hampton .25
107 Adam LaRoche .25
108 Michael Hessman **RC** .50
109 Corey Patterson .40
110 Kerry Wood 1.00
111 Mark Prior 1.00
112 Moises Alou .50
113 Sammy Sosa 1.50
114 Adam Dunn .75
115 Austin Kearns .40
116 Barry Larkin .40
117 Ken Griffey Jr. 1.50
118 Sean Casey .25
119 Jason Jennings .25
120 Jay Payton .25
121 Larry Walker .40
122 Todd Helton .75
123 Jeff Baker .25
124 Clint Barmes **RC** 1.00
125 Ivan Rodriguez .75
126 Josh Beckett .50
127 Juan Encarnacion .25
128 Mike Lowell .25
129 Craig Biggio .40
130 Jason Lane .25
131 Jeff Bagwell .75
132 Lance Berkman .50
133 Roy Oswalt .40
134 Jeff Kent .40
135 Hideo Nomo .50
136 Kazuhisa Ishii .25
137 Kevin Brown .40
138 Odalis Perez .25
139 Paul LoDuca .25
140 Shawn Green .50
141 Adrian Beltre .50
142 Ben Sheets .40
143 Bill Hall .25
144 Jeffrey Hammonds .25
145 Richie Sexson .50
146 Termel Sledge **RC** .75
147 Brad Wilkerson .25
148 Javier Vazquez .25
149 Jose Vidro .25
150 Michael Barrett .25
151 Vladimir Guerrero .75
152 Al Leiter .25
153 Mike Piazza 2.00
154 Mo Vaughn .25
155 Cliff Floyd .25
156 Roberto Alomar .50
157 Roger Cedeno .25
158 Tom Glavine .50
159 Prentice Redman **RC** .50
160 Bobby Abreu .50
161 Jimmy Rollins .40
162 Mike Lieberthal .25
163 Pat Burrell .50
164 Vicente Padilla .25
165 Jim Thome .75
166 Kevin Millwood .40
167 Aramis Ramirez .50
168 Brian Giles .40
169 Jason Kendall .40
170 Josh Fogg .25
171 Kip Wells .25
172 Jose Castillo .25
173 Mark Kotsay .25
174 Oliver Perez .25
175 Phil Nevin .25
176 Ryan Klesko .40
177 Sean Burroughs .25
178 Brian Lawrence .25
179 Shane Victorino **RC** .25
180 Barry Bonds 3.00
181 Benito Santiago .25
182 Ray Durham .25
183 Rich Aurilia .25
184 Damian Moss .25
185 Albert Pujols 2.00
186 J.D. Drew .25
187 Jim Edmonds .50
188 Matt Morris .40
189 Tino Martinez .25
190 Scott Rolen .75
191 Troy Glaus, Tim Salmon .50
192 Sean Casey, Corky Miller .25
193 Carlos Lee, Frank Thomas .50
194 Lance Berkman, Jeff Kent .25
195 Jose Contreras, Mariano Rivera 1.00
196 Alex Rodriguez, Juan Gonzalez 1.00
197 Andy Pettitte, David Wells .25
198 Shawn Green, Dave Roberts .25
199 Mike Lieberthal, Jimmy Rollins .40
200 Mike Mussina, Hideki Matsui 2.00

Proofs

Stars (1-200): 4-8X
Rookies (1-200): 2-3X
Production 100 Sets

Private Signings

NM/M
7 Jay Gibbons/100 10.00
11 Freddy Sanchez/150 25.00
24 Josh Stewart/200 8.00
26 Jeremy Guthrie/125 8.00
29 Victor Martinez/200 20.00
30 Cliff Lee/150 10.00
31 Jhonny Peralta/200 20.00
35 Nook Logan/100 8.00
37 Travis Chapman/150 8.00
41 Jimmy Gobble/200 8.00
47 J.C. Romero/200 8.00
49 Lew Ford/200 15.00
51 Torii Hunter/50 20.00
53 Nick Johnson/100 10.00
55 Jose Contreras/100 25.00
58 Brandon Claussen/200 10.00
69 Joe Valentine/200 8.00
79 Aubrey Huff/50 20.00
81 Dewon Brazelton/75 10.00
82 Pete LaForest/200 10.00
85 Hank Blalock/50 20.00
87 Kevin Mench/200 8.00
90 Eric Hinske/125 8.00

95 Vinnie Chulk/100 8.00
97 Junior Spivey/50 10.00
107 Adam LaRoche/200 15.00
108 Michael Hessman/200 8.00
111 Mark Prior/50 30.00
119 Jason Jennings/50 10.00
123 Jeff Baker/75 10.00
124 Clint Barmes/200 10.00
130 Jason Lane/100 10.00
139 Paul LoDuca/75 15.00
143 Bill Hall/50 20.00
146 Terrmel Sledge/125 10.00
149 Jose Vidro/50 15.00
159 Prentice Redman/200 10.00
160 Bobby Abreu/50 20.00
171 Kip Wells/100 10.00
172 Jose Castillo/175 8.00
178 Brian Lawrence/100 10.00
179 Shane Victorino/200 10.00
201 Adam Loewen/100 20.00
202 Jeremy Bonderman/50 40.00
203 Brandon Webb/100 35.00
204 Chien-Ming Wang/50 250.00
206 Ryan Wagner/100 10.00
207 Hong-Chih Kuo/25 175.00
208 Dan Haren/100 25.00
210 Ramon Nivar/100 15.00

Big League Challenge

NM/M
Complete Set (50): 125.00
Common Player: 1.50
Production 400 Sets
Proofs 4-8X
Production 25 Sets
1 Jose Canseco 2.00
2 Magglio Ordonez 1.50
3 Alex Rodriguez 5.00
4 Lance Berkman 1.50
5 Rafael Palmeiro 3.00
6 Nomar Garciaparra 5.00
7 Nomar Garciaparra 5.00
8 Nomar Garciaparra 5.00
9 Troy Glaus 2.00
10 Mark McGwire 6.00
11 Mark McGwire 6.00
12 Mark McGwire 6.00
13 Jim Thome 3.00
14 Chipper Jones 3.00
15 Shawn Green 1.50
16 Alex Rodriguez 5.00
17 Alex Rodriguez 5.00
18 Alex Rodriguez 5.00
19 Alex Rodriguez 5.00
20 Jason Giambi 2.00
21 Pat Burrell 1.50
22 Mike Piazza 4.00
23 Mike Piazza 4.00
24 Mike Piazza 4.00
25 Frank Thomas 2.00
26 Rafael Palmeiro 2.00
27 Todd Helton 2.00
28 Jose Canseco 2.00
29 Albert Pujols 5.00
30 Troy Glaus 2.00
31 Barry Bonds 6.00
32 Barry Bonds 6.00
33 Barry Bonds 6.00
34 Todd Helton 3.00
35 Rafael Palmeiro 3.00
36 Jim Thome 3.00
37 Ozzie Smith 3.00
38 Troy Glaus 2.00
39 Shawn Green 1.50
40 Barry Bonds 6.00
41 Barry Bonds 6.00
42 Barry Bonds 6.00
43 Magglio Ordonez 1.50
44 Alex Rodriguez 5.00
45 Alex Rodriguez 5.00
46 Alex Rodriguez 5.00
47 Lance Berkman 1.50
48 Rafael Palmeiro 3.00
49 Pat Burrell 1.50
50 Albert Pujols 5.00

Big League Challenge Materials

NM/M
Common Player: 4.00
Inserted 1:20
2 Magglio Ordonez/Jsy 4.00
3 Alex Rodriguez/Jsy 10.00
4 Lance Berkman/Jsy 4.00
15 Shawn Green/Jsy 4.00
29 Albert Pujols/Jsy 15.00
36 Jim Thome/Jsy 6.00
39 Shawn Green/Pants 4.00
40 Barry Bonds/Base 10.00
41 Barry Bonds/Base 10.00
42 Barry Bonds/Base 10.00
43 Magglio Ordonez/Jsy 4.00
45 Alex Rodriguez/Jsy 10.00
46 Alex Rodriguez/Pants 10.00
47 Lance Berkman/Jsy 4.00
48 Rafael Palmeiro/Jsy 6.00
50 Albert Pujols/Pants 10.00

Big League Challenge Prime Material

NM/M
Common Player: 10.00
2 Magglio Ordonez/100 10.00
3 Alex Rodriguez/100 25.00
15 Shawn Green/50 15.00
29 Albert Pujols/100 25.00
36 Jim Thome/50 20.00
45 Alex Rodriguez/100 25.00
48 Rafael Palmeiro/100 15.00

Enshrinement

NM/M
Complete Set (50): 180.00
Common Player: 3.00
Production 750 Sets
Proofs: 5-10X
Production 20 or 21
1 Gary Carter 4.00
2 Ozzie Smith 10.00
3 Kirby Puckett 6.00
4 Carlton Fisk 4.00
5 Tony Perez 3.00
6 Nolan Ryan 15.00
7 George Brett 12.00
8 Robin Yount 10.00
9 Orlando Cepeda 3.00
10 Phil Niekro 3.00
11 Mike Schmidt 10.00
12 Richie Ashburn 6.00
13 Steve Carlton 4.00
14 Phil Rizzuto 4.00
15 Reggie Jackson 6.00
16 Tom Seaver 5.00
17 Rollie Fingers 3.00
18 Rod Carew 5.00
19 Gaylord Perry 3.00
20 Fergie Jenkins 3.00
21 Jim Palmer 3.00
22 Joe Morgan 3.00
23 Johnny Bench 6.00
24 Willie Stargell 4.00
25 Billy Williams 3.00
26 Jim "Catfish" Hunter 3.00
27 Willie McCovey 3.00
28 Bobby Doerr 3.00
29 Lou Brock 4.00
30 Enos Slaughter 3.00
31 Hoyt Wilhelm 3.00
32 Harmon Killebrew 6.00
33 Pee Wee Reese 3.00
34 Luis Aparicio 3.00
35 Brooks Robinson 6.00
36 Juan Marichal 4.00
37 Frank Robinson 5.00
38 Bob Gibson 4.00
39 Al Kaline 6.00
40 Duke Snider 6.00
41 Eddie Mathews 5.00
42 Robin Roberts 3.00
43 Ralph Kiner 3.00
44 Whitey Ford 5.00
45 Roberto Clemente 10.00
46 Warren Spahn 4.00
47 Yogi Berra 5.00
48 Early Wynn 3.00
49 Stan Musial 6.00
50 Bob Feller 4.00

Enshrinement Autographs

NM/M
Varying quantities produced
1 Gary Carter/50 30.00
5 Tony Perez/50 50.00
9 Orlando Cepeda/50 25.00
10 Phil Niekro/50 20.00
13 Steve Carlton/50 40.00
14 Phil Rizzuto/15 50.00
20 Fergie Jenkins/50 20.00
21 Jim Palmer/25 35.00
22 Joe Morgan/10 50.00
28 Bobby Doerr/100 20.00
31 Hoyt Wilhelm/50 25.00
34 Luis Aparicio/100 15.00
35 Brooks Robinson/25 65.00
37 Frank Robinson/25 50.00
43 Ralph Kiner/25 40.00
50 Bob Feller/100 25.00

Leather & Lumber

NM/M
Common Player: 5.00
1 Adam Dunn/400 10.00
2 Alex Rodriguez/250 12.00
3 Alfonso Soriano/250 10.00
4 Andruw Jones/400 8.00
5 Austin Kearns/400 8.00
6 Chipper Jones/400 10.00
7 Derek Jeter/100 35.00
8 Don Mattingly/100 40.00
9 Edgar Martinez 10.00
10 Frank Thomas/400 8.00
11 Fred McGriff/400 8.00
13 Greg Maddux/150 15.00
14 Hideki Matsui/Ball/100 40.00
15 Hideo Nomo/150 15.00
16 Ichiro Suzuki/Ball/100 40.00
17 Ivan Rodriguez/250 8.00
18 Jason Giambi/400 8.00
19 Jeff Bagwell/400 8.00
20 Jim Edmonds/150 8.00
21 Jim Thome/400 10.00
22 Juan Gonzalez/400 8.00
23 Kerry Wood/250 10.00
24 Kirby Puckett/100 25.00
25 Lance Berkman/400 5.00
26 Magglio Ordonez/400 5.00
27 Manny Ramirez/250 10.00
28 Mark Prior/400 8.00
29 Miguel Tejada/200 5.00
30 Mike Piazza/400 10.00
31 Mike Schmidt/200 25.00
32 Nomar Garciaparra/400 15.00
33 Pat Burrell/400 8.00
34 Pedro Martinez/150 10.00
36 Randy Johnson/250 10.00
37 Rickey Henderson/175 10.00
38 Sammy Sosa/300 10.00
39 Shawn Green/400 5.00
40 Vladimir Guerrero/400 8.00

Leather & Lumber Dual

NM/M
Common Player:
Those without bat & ball are noted.
1 Adam Dunn/50 25.00
2 Alex Rodriguez/50 30.00
4 Andruw Jones/50 25.00
5 Austin Kearns/Shoe/50 25.00
6 Chipper Jones/25 45.00
8 Don Mattingly/25 80.00
10 Frank Thomas/50 30.00
13 Greg Maddux/hoe/50 35.00
17 Ivan Rodriguez/50 25.00
19 Jeff Bagwell/25 35.00
23 Kerry Wood/50 35.00
24 Kirby Puckett/25 50.00
25 Lance Berkman/50 12.00
28 Mark Prior/Shoe/25 50.00
29 Miguel Tejada/25 15.00
33 Pat Burrell/25 20.00
36 Randy Johnson/25 40.00
38 Sammy Sosa/Shoe/25 60.00

Masterstrokes

NM/M
Complete Set (25): 50.00
Common Player: 1.00
Production 1,000 Sets
1 Adam Dunn 2.00
2 Albert Pujols 3.00
3 Alex Rodriguez 3.00
4 Alfonso Soriano 3.00
5 Andruw Jones 1.50
6 Chipper Jones 3.00
7 Derek Jeter 6.00
8 Greg Maddux 3.00
9 Hideki Matsui 8.00
10 Hideo Nomo 1.50
11 Ivan Rodriguez 2.00
12 Jason Giambi 1.50
13 Jeff Bagwell 2.00
14 Juan Gonzalez 1.50
15 Ken Griffey Jr. 3.00
16 Lance Berkman 1.00
17 Magglio Ordonez 1.00
18 Manny Ramirez 2.00
19 Mark Prior 2.00
20 Miguel Tejada 1.00
21 Mike Piazza 4.00
22 Nomar Garciaparra 4.00
23 Pat Burrell 1.50
24 Sammy Sosa 4.00
25 Vladimir Guerrero 1.50

Masterstrokes Artist's Proof

NM/M
Common Player: 15.00
Production 50 Sets
1 Adam Dunn 25.00
2 Albert Pujols 50.00
3 Alex Rodriguez 50.00
4 Alfonso Soriano 25.00
5 Andruw Jones 20.00
6 Chipper Jones 30.00
7 Derek Jeter 50.00
8 Greg Maddux 25.00
9 Hideki Matsui 75.00
10 Hideo Nomo 100.00
11 Ivan Rodriguez 20.00
12 Jason Giambi 15.00
13 Jeff Bagwell 25.00
14 Juan Gonzalez 25.00
15 Ken Griffey Jr. 30.00
16 Lance Berkman 15.00
17 Magglio Ordonez 15.00
18 Manny Ramirez 20.00
19 Mark Prior 20.00
20 Miguel Tejada 15.00
21 Mike Piazza 35.00
22 Nomar Garciaparra 40.00
23 Pat Burrell 15.00
24 Sammy Sosa 40.00
25 Vladimir Guerrero 25.00

Players Collection

NM/M
Common Player: 4.00
Production 300 Sets
1 Adam Dunn 8.00
2 Adrian Beltre 6.00
3 Alex Rodriguez 10.00
4 Alfonso Soriano 8.00
5 Andruw Jones 6.00
6 Andy Pettitte 4.00
7 Barry Larkin 6.00
8 Barry Zito 4.00
9 Ben Grieve 4.00
10 Bernie Williams 8.00
11 Cal Ripken Jr. 30.00
12 Carlos Delgado 5.00
13 C.C. Sabathia 4.00
14 Chipper Jones 10.00
15 Craig Biggio 4.00
16 Curt Schilling 6.00
17 Alex Rodriguez 10.00
18 Frank Thomas 8.00
19 Freddy Garcia 4.00
20 Jay Bell 4.00
21 Roger Clemens 12.00
22 Tony Gwynn 10.00
23 Ivan Rodriguez 6.00
24 Jason Giambi 6.00
25 Jason Jennings 4.00
26 Jay Payton 4.00
27 J.D. Drew 4.00
28 Jeff Bagwell 8.00
29 Jeromy Burnitz 4.00
30 Jim Edmonds 6.00
31 Jim Thome 8.00
32 Joe Borchard 4.00
33 Joe Mays 4.00
34 John Olerud 4.00
35 David Wells 4.00
36 Juan Gonzalez 6.00
37 Kazuhiro Sasaki 4.00
38 Chan Ho Park 4.00
39 Kerry Wood 8.00
40 Kevin Brown 5.00
41 Lance Berkman 4.00
42 Larry Walker 4.00
43 Bret Boone 4.00
44 Magglio Ordonez 4.00
45 Manny Ramirez 6.00
46 Mark Mulder 4.00
47 Mark Prior 8.00
48 Matt Williams 4.00
49 Miguel Tejada 6.00
50 Mike Piazza 10.00
51 Nomar Garciaparra 10.00
52 Doug Davis 4.00
53 Paul Konerko 4.00
54 Paul LoDuca 4.00
55 Pedro J. Martinez 8.00
56 Preston Wilson 4.00
57 Rafael Palmeiro 8.00
58 Marlon Byrd 4.00
59 Reggie Sanders 4.00
60 Richie Sexson 5.00
61 Rickey Henderson 10.00
62 Rickey Henderson 10.00
63 Robert Person 4.00
64 Jeff Bagwell 8.00
65 Roger Clemens 12.00
66 Roy Oswalt 4.00
67 Ryan Klesko 4.00
68 Sammy Sosa 12.00
69 Shawn Green 5.00
70 Steve Finley 4.00
71 Terrence Long 4.00
72 Tim Hudson 5.00
73 Toby Hall 4.00
74 Todd Helton 8.00
75 Travis Lee 4.00
76 Troy Glaus 6.00
77 Tsuyoshi Shinjo 4.00
78 Vernon Wells 4.00
79 Vladimir Guerrero 8.00
80 Wes Helms 4.00
81 Alex Rodriguez 10.00
82 Alfonso Soriano 8.00
83 Barry Larkin 6.00
84 Roberto Alomar 6.00
85 Ivan Rodriguez 6.00
86 Jason Giambi 6.00
87 Jeff Bagwell 8.00
88 Juan Gonzalez 6.00
89 Larry Walker 4.00
90 Luis Gonzalez 4.00
91 Magglio Ordonez 4.00
92 Manny Ramirez 8.00
93 Marlon Byrd 4.00
94 Mike Piazza 10.00
95 Pat Burrell 8.00
96 Todd Helton 8.00
97 Rickey Henderson 10.00
98 Andruw Jones 6.00
99 Craig Biggio 4.00
100 Mark Prior 8.00

Recollection Autographs 5x7

NM/M
3 Sean Casey/125 15.00
5 Troy Glaus/82 20.00
8 Vladimir Guerrero/125 35.00
10 Todd Helton/55 35.00
12 Ryan Klesko/75 15.00
18 Ivan Rodriguez/50 40.00
19 C.C. Sabathia/50 20.00
20 Curt Schilling/75 30.00
23 Mike Sweeney/42 15.00
24 Miguel Tejada/44 30.00
26 Kerry Wood/200 25.00
27 Barry Zito/200 15.00

Spirit of the Game

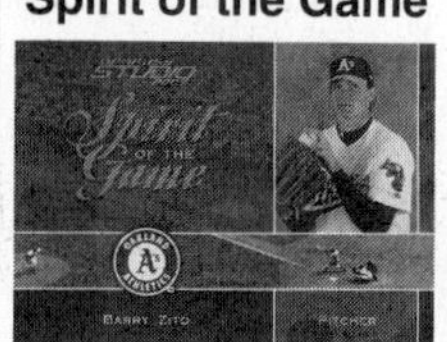

NM/M
Complete Set (35): 60.00
Common Player: 1.00
Production 1,250 Sets
1 Garret Anderson 1.00
2 Nomar Garciaparra 3.00
3 Pedro J. Martinez 2.00
4 Rickey Henderson 1.50
5 Magglio Ordonez 1.00
6 Torii Hunter 1.50
7 Alfonso Soriano 2.00
8 Jose Contreras 1.00
9 Derek Jeter 5.00
10 Jason Giambi 1.50
11 Roger Clemens 4.00
12 Hideki Matsui 6.00
13 Barry Zito 1.50
14 Ichiro Suzuki 3.00
15 Alex Rodriguez 4.00
16 Curt Schilling 2.00
17 Randy Johnson 2.00
18 Andruw Jones 1.50
19 Chipper Jones 2.00
20 Greg Maddux 3.00
21 Sammy Sosa 3.00
22 Adam Dunn 2.00
23 Ken Griffey Jr. 3.00
24 Todd Helton 2.00
25 Ivan Rodriguez 2.00
26 Lance Berkman 1.00
27 Hideo Nomo 1.50
28 Shawn Green 1.00
29 Vladimir Guerrero 2.00
30 Mike Piazza 3.00
31 Roberto Alomar 1.50
32 Jim Thome 2.00
33 Barry Bonds 5.00
34 Albert Pujols 3.00
35 Scott Rolen 2.00

Stars

NM/M
Complete Set (50): 65.00
Common Player: 1.00
Inserted 1:5
Golds: 3-5X
Production 100 Sets

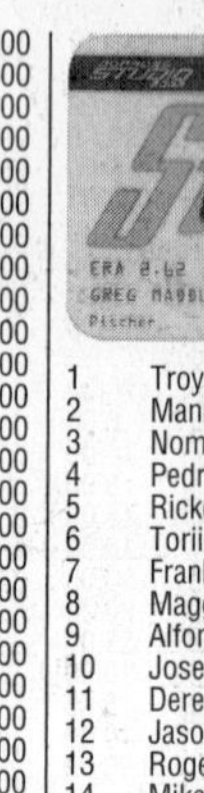

1 Troy Glaus 1.50
2 Manny Ramirez 2.00
3 Nomar Garciaparra 3.00
4 Pedro J. Martinez 2.00
5 Rickey Henderson 1.50
6 Torii Hunter 1.50
7 Frank Thomas 1.50
8 Magglio Ordonez 1.00
9 Alfonso Soriano 2.00
10 Jose Contreras 1.00
11 Derek Jeter 5.00
12 Jason Giambi 1.50
13 Roger Clemens 4.00
14 Mike Mussina 1.50
15 Barry Zito 1.50
16 Miguel Tejada 1.00
17 Ichiro Suzuki 4.00
18 Alex Rodriguez 1.00
19 Juan Gonzalez 1.00
20 Rafael Palmeiro 2.00
21 Hank Blalock 2.00
22 Curt Schilling 2.00
23 Randy Johnson 2.00
24 Junior Spivey 1.00
25 Andruw Jones 1.50
26 Chipper Jones 2.00
27 Greg Maddux 3.00
28 Kerry Wood 2.00
29 Mark Prior 1.50
30 Sammy Sosa 3.00
31 Adam Dunn 2.00
32 Ken Griffey Jr. 3.00
33 Austin Kearns 1.50
34 Larry Walker 1.00
35 Todd Helton 2.00
36 Ivan Rodriguez 2.00
37 Jeff Bagwell 2.00
38 Lance Berkman 1.00
39 Craig Biggio 1.00
40 Hideo Nomo 1.50
41 Shawn Green 1.00
42 Vladimir Guerrero 2.00
43 Mike Piazza 3.00
44 Tom Glavine 1.50
45 Roberto Alomar 1.50
46 Pat Burrell 1.50
47 Jim Thome 2.00
48 Barry Bonds 5.00
49 Albert Pujols 4.00
50 Scott Rolen 2.00

2003 Donruss Team Heroes Samples

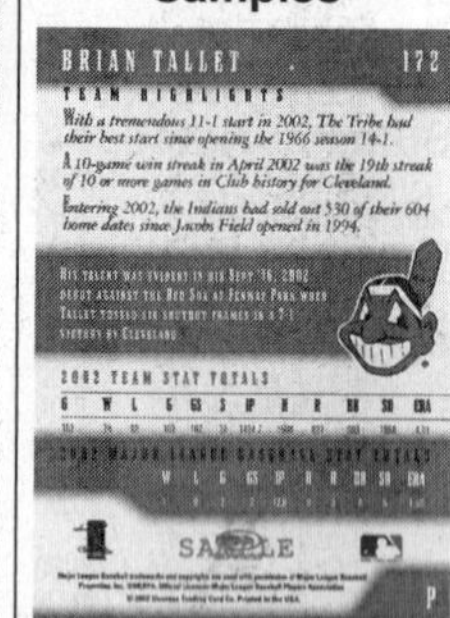

NM/M
Common Player: .10
Stars: 1.5-2X
Gold: 10X

2003 Donruss Team Heroes

Each issue of the February 2003 Beckett Baseball Card Monthly included a sample 2003 Donruss Team Heroes card rubber-cemented inside. The cards differ from the issued version only in the appearance on back of a (usually) silver-foil "SAMPLE" notation. Some cards were produced with the overprint in gold-foil, in much more limited quantities. The number of different players' cards involved in the promotion is unknown.

NM/M
Complete Set (540): 55.00
Common Player: .15
Pack (13): 1.50
Box (24): 25.00
1 Adam Kennedy .15
2 Steve Green .15
3 Rod Carew .40
4 Alfredo Amezaga .15
5 Reggie Jackson .50
6 Jarrod Washburn .15
7 Nolan Ryan 3.00
8 Tim Salmon .25
9 Garret Anderson .25
10 Darin Erstad .25
11 Elpidio Guzman .15
12 David Eckstein .15
13 Troy Percival .15
14 Troy Glaus .75
15 Doug DeVore .15
16 Tony Womack .15
17 Matt Williams .25
18 Junior Spivey .15
19 Mark Grace .50
20 Curt Schilling .75
21 Erubiel Durazo .15
22 Craig Counsell .15
23 Byung-Hyun Kim .15
24 Randy Johnson 1.00
25 Luis Gonzalez .40
26 John Smoltz .15
27 Tim Spooneybarger .15
28 Dale Murphy .50
29 Warren Spahn .50
30 Jason Marquis .15
31 Kevin Millwood .15
32 Javy Lopez .15
33 Vinny Castilla .15
34 Julio Franco .15
35 Trey Hodges .15
36 Chipper Jones 1.50
37 Gary Sheffield .25
38 Billy Sylvester .15
39 Tom Glavine .40
40 Rafael Furcal .15
41 Cory Aldridge .15
42 Greg Maddux 1.50
43 John Ennis .15
44 Wes Helms .15
45 Horacio Ramirez .15
46 Derrick Lewis .15
47 Marcus Giles .15
48 Eddie Mathews .75
49 Wilson Betemit .15
50 Andruw Jones .50
51 Josh Towers .15
52 Ed Rogers .15
53 Kris Foster .15
54 Brooks Robinson .75
55 Cal Ripken Jr. 3.00
56 Brian Roberts .15
57 Luis Rivera .15
58 Rodrigo Lopez .15
59 Geronimo Gil .15
60 Erik Bedard .15
61 Jim Palmer .40
62 Jay Gibbons .15
63 Travis Driskill .15
64 Larry Bigbie .15
65 Eddie Murray .40
66 Hoyt Wilhelm .15
67 Bobby Doerr .15
68 Pedro J. Martinez 1.00
69 Roger Clemens 1.50
70 Nomar Garciaparra 2.00
71 Trot Nixon .15
72 Dennis Eckersley .40
73 John Burkett .15
74 Tim Wakefield .15
75 Wade Boggs .40
76 Cliff Floyd .15
77 Casey Fossum .15
78 Johnny Damon .15
79 Fred Lynn .15
80 Rickey Henderson .40
81 Juan Diaz .15
82 Manny Ramirez .75
83 Carlton Fisk .50
84 Jorge De La Rosa .15
85 Shea Hillenbrand .15
86 Derek Lowe .15
87 Jason Varitek .15
88 Carlos Baerga .15
89 Freddy Sanchez .15
90 Ugueth Urbina .15
91 Rey Sanchez .15
92 Josh Hancock .15
93 Tony Clark .15
94 Dustin Hermanson .15
95 Ryne Sandberg 1.50
96 Fred McGriff .25
97 Alex Gonzalez .15
98 Mark Belhorn .15
99 Fergie Jenkins .25
100 Jon Lieber .15
101 Francis Beltran .15
102 Greg Maddux 1.50
103 Nate Frese .15
104 Andre Dawson .25
105 Carlos Zambrano .15
106 Steve Smyth .15
107 Ernie Banks 1.00
108 Will Ohman .15
109 Kerry Wood .50
110 Bobby Hill .15
111 Moises Alou .15
112 Hee Seop Choi .15
113 Corey Patterson .15
114 Sammy Sosa 1.50
115 Mark Prior .50
116 Juan Cruz .15
117 Ron Santo .15
118 Billy Williams .15
119 Antonio Alfonseca .15
120 Matt Clement .15
121 Carlton Fisk .50
122 Joe Crede .15
123 Magglio Ordonez .40
124 Frank Thomas .75
125 Joe Borchard .15
126 Royce Clayton .15
127 Luis Aparicio .15
128 Willie Harris .15
129 Kyle Kane .15
130 Paul Konerko .25
131 Matt Ginter .15
132 Carlos Lee .15
133 Mark Buehrle .15
134 Adam Dunn .75
135 Eric Davis .15
136 Johnny Bench 1.00
137 Joe Morgan .25
138 Austin Kearns .40
139 Barry Larkin .40
140 Ken Griffey Jr. 2.00
141 Luis Pineda .15
142 Corky Miller .15
143 Brandon Larson .15
144 Wily Mo Pena .15
145 Lance Davis .15
146 Tom Seaver 1.00
147 Luke Hudson .15
148 Sean Casey .15
149 Tony Perez .15
150 Todd Walker .15
151 Aaron Boone .15
152 Jose Rijo .15
153 Ryan Dempster .15
154 Danny Graves .15
155 Matt Lawton .15
156 Cliff Lee .15
157 Ryan Drese .15
158 Danys Baez .15
159 Einar Diaz .15
160 Milton Bradley .15
161 Earl Snyder .15
162 Ellis Burks .15
163 Lou Boudreau .15
164 Bob Feller .15
165 Ricardo Rodriguez .15
166 Victor Martinez .15
167 Alex Herrera .15
168 Omar Vizquel .15
169 David Elder .15
170 C.C. Sabathia .15
171 Alex Escobar .15
172 Brian Tallet .15
173 Jim Thome .75
174 Rene Reyes .15
175 Juan Uribe .15
176 Jason Romano .15
177 Juan Pierre .15
178 Jason Jennings .15
179 Jose Ortiz .15
180 Larry Walker .25
181 Cam Esslinger .15
182 Todd Helton .50
183 Aaron Cook .15
184 Jack Cust .15
185 Jack Morris .15
186 Mike Rivera .15
187 Bobby Higginson .15
188 Fernando Rodney .15
189 Al Kaline 1.00
190 Carlos Pena .15
191 Alan Trammell .15
192 Mike Maroth .15
193 Adam Pettyjohn .15
194 David Espinosa .15
195 Adam Bernero .15
196 Franklyn German .15
197 Robert Fick .15
198 Andres Torres .15
199 Luis Castillo .15
200 Preston Wilson .15
201 Pablo Ozuna .15
202 Brad Penny .15
203 Josh Beckett .15
204 Charles Johnson .15
205 Wilson Valdez .15
206 A.J. Burnett .15
207 Abraham Nunez .15
208 Mike Lowell .15
209 Jose Cueto .15
210 Jeriome Robertson .15
211 Jeff Bagwell .75
212 Kirk Saarloos .15
213 Craig Biggio .25
214 Rodrigo Rosario .15
215 Roy Oswalt .25
216 John Buck .15
217 Tim Redding .15
218 Morgan Ensberg .15
219 Richard Hidalgo .15
220 Wade Miller .15
221 Lance Berkman .50
222 Raul Chavez .15
223 Carlos Hernandez .15
224 Greg Miller .15
225 Tom Shearn .15
226 Jason Lane .15
227 Nolan Ryan 3.00
228 Billy Wagner .15
229 Octavio Dotel .15
230 Shane Reynolds .15
231 Julio Lugo .15
232 Daryle Ward .15
233 Mike Sweeney .15
234 Angel Berroa .15
235 George Brett 1.50
236 Brad Voyles .15
237 Brandon Berger .15
238 Chad Durbin .15
239 Alexis Gomez .15
240 Jeremy Affeldt .15
241 Bo Jackson .75
242 Dee Brown .15
243 Tony Cogan .15
244 Carlos Beltran .15
245 Joe Randa .15
246 Pee Wee Reese .25
247 Andy Ashby .15
248 Cesar Izturis .15
249 Duke Snider .50
250 Mark Grudzielanek .15
251 Chin-Feng Chen .15
252 Brian Jordan .15
253 Steve Garvey .15
254 Odalis Perez .15
255 Hideo Nomo .50
256 Kevin Brown .15
257 Eric Karros .15
258 Joe Thurston .15
259 Carlos Garcia .15
260 Shawn Green .40
261 Paul LoDuca .15
262 Kazuhisa Ishii .15
263 Victor Alvarez .15
264 Eric Gagne .15
265 Don Sutton .15
266 Orel Hershiser .15
267 Dave Roberts .15
268 Adrian Beltre .15
269 Don Drysdale .50
270 Jackie Robinson 1.50
271 Tyler Houston .15
272 Omar Daal .15
273 Marquis Grissom .15
274 Paul Quantrill .15
275 Paul Molitor .50
276 Jose Hernandez .15
277 Takahito Nomura .15
278 Nick Neugebauer .15
279 Jose Mieses .15
280 Richie Sexson .40
281 Matt Childers .15
282 Bill Hall .15
283 Ben Sheets .15
284 Brian Mallette .15
285 Geoff Jenkins .15
286 Robin Yount .75
287 Jeff Deardorff .15
288 Luis Rivas .15
289 Harmon Killebrew .50
290 Michael Cuddyer .15
291 Torii Hunter .15
292 Kevin Frederick .15
293 Adam Johnson .15
294 Jack Morris .15
295 Rod Carew .40
296 Kirby Puckett 1.50
297 Joe Mays .15
298 Jacque Jones .15
299 Cristian Guzman .15
300 Kyle Lohse .15
301 Eric Milton .15
302 Brad Radke .15
303 Doug Mientkiewicz .15
304 Corey Koskie .15
305 Jose Vidro .15
306 Claudio Vargas .15
307 Gary Carter .15
308 Andre Dawson .25
309 Henry Mateo .15
310 Andres Galarraga .15
311 Zach Day .15
312 Bartolo Colon .15
313 Endy Chavez .15
314 Javier Vazquez .15
315 Michael Barrett .15
316 Vladimir Guerrero 1.00
317 Orlando Cabrera .15
318 Al Leiter .15
319 Timoniel Perez .15
320 Rey Ordonez .15
321 Gary Carter .15
322 Armando Benitez .15
323 Dwight Gooden .15
324 Pedro Astacio .15
325 Roberto Alomar .50
326 Edgardo Alfonzo .15
327 Nolan Ryan 3.00
328 Mo Vaughn .25
329 Ryan Jamison .15
330 Satoru Komiyama .15
331 Mike Piazza 2.50
332 Tom Seaver 1.00
333 Jorge Posada .40
334 Derek Jeter 2.50
335 Babe Ruth 3.00
336 Lou Gehrig 2.50
337 Andy Pettitte .40
338 Mariano Rivera .25
339 Robin Ventura .15
340 Yogi Berra 1.00
341 Phil Rizzuto .50
342 Bernie Williams .50
343 Alfonso Soriano 1.50
344 Drew Henson .15
345 Erick Almonte .15
346 Rondell White .15
347 Christian Parker .15
348 Joe Torre .25
349 Nick Johnson .15
350 Raul Mondesi .15
351 Brandon Claussen .15
352 Reggie Jackson .50
353 Roger Clemens 1.50
354 Don Mattingly 2.00
355 Jason Giambi 1.50
356 Adrian Hernandez .15
357 Jeff Weaver .15
358 Mike Mussina .50
359 Brett Jodie .15
360 David Wells .15
361 Enos Slaughter .15
362 Whitey Ford .50
363 Eric Chavez .25
364 Miguel Tejada .40
365 Barry Zito .25
366 Bert Snow .15
367 Rickey Henderson .50
368 Juan A. Pena .15
369 Terrence Long .15
370 Dennis Eckersley .40
371 Mark Ellis .15
372 Tim Hudson .25
373 Jose Canseco .50
374 Reggie Jackson .50
375 Mark Mulder .15
376 David Justice .25
377 Jermaine Dye .15
378 Brett Myers .15
379 Lenny Dykstra .15
380 Vicente Padilla .15
381 Bobby Abreu .15
382 Pat Burrell .50
383 Jorge Padilla .15
384 Jeremy Giambi .15
385 Mike Lieberthal .15
386 Anderson Machado .15
387 Marlon Byrd .15
388 Bud Smith .15
389 Eric Valent .15
390 Elio Serrano .15
391 Jimmy Rollins .25
392 Brandon Duckworth .15
393 Robin Roberts .15
394 Marlon Anderson .15
395 Robert Person .15
396 Johnny Estrada .15
397 Mike Schmidt 1.00
398 Eric Junge .15
399 Jason Michaels .15
400 Steve Carlton .40
401 Placido Polanco .15
402 John Grabow .15
403 Tomas De La Rosa .15
404 Tike Redman .15
405 Willie Stargell .40
406 Dave Williams .15
407 John Candelaria .15
408 Jack Wilson .15
409 Matt Guerrier .15
410 Jason Kendall .15
411 Josh Fogg .15
412 Aramis Ramirez .15
413 Dave Parker .15
414 Roberto Clemente 2.00
415 Kip Wells .15
416 Brian Giles .25
417 Honus Wagner 1.50
418 Ramon Vazquez .15
419 Oliver Perez .15
420 Ryan Klesko .15
421 Brian Lawrence .15
422 Ben Howard .15
423 Ozzie Smith 1.00
424 Dennis Tankersley .15
425 Tony Gwynn 1.00
426 Sean Burroughs .15
427 Xavier Nady .15
428 Phil Nevin .15
429 Trevor Hoffman .15
430 Jake Peavy .15
431 Cody Ransom .15
432 Kenny Lofton .15
433 Mel Ott .50
434 Tsuyoshi Shinjo .15
435 Deivis Santos .15
436 Rich Aurilia .15
437 Will Clark .50
438 Pedro Feliz .15
439 J.T. Snow .15
440 Robb Nen .15
441 Carlos Valderrama .15
442 Willie McCovey .15
443 Jeff Kent .25
444 Orlando Cepeda .15
445 Barry Bonds 2.50
446 Alex Rodriguez 2.50
447 Allan Simpson .15
448 Antonio Perez .15
449 Edgar Martinez .15
450 Freddy Garcia .15
451 Chris Snelling .15
452 Matt Thornton .15
453 Kazuhiro Sasaki .15
454 Harold Reynolds .15
455 Randy Johnson 1.00
456 Bret Boone .15
457 Rafael Soriano .15
458 Luis Ugueto .15
459 Ken Griffey Jr. 2.00
460 Ichiro Suzuki 2.00
461 Jamie Moyer .15
462 Joel Pineiro .15
463 Jeff Cirillo .15
464 John Olerud .15
465 Mike Cameron .15
466 Ruben Sierra .15
467 Mark McLemore .15
468 Carlos Guillen .15
469 Dan Wilson .15
470 Shigetoshi Hasegawa .15
471 Ben Davis .15
472 Ozzie Smith 1.00
473 Matt Morris .15
474 Edgar Renteria .15
475 Les Walrond .15
476 Albert Pujols 1.00
477 Stan Musial 1.50
478 J.D. Drew .15
479 Josh Pearce .15
480 Enos Slaughter .15
481 Jason Simontacchi .15
482 Jeremy Lambert .15
483 Tino Martinez .15
484 Rogers Hornsby .50
485 Rick Ankiel .15
486 Jim Edmonds .25
487 Scott Rolen .50
488 Kevin Joseph .15
489 Fernando Vina .15
490 Jason Isringhausen .15
491 Lou Brock .40
492 Joe Torre .25
493 Bob Gibson .50
494 Chuck Finley .15
495 So Taguchi .15
496 Ben Grieve .15
497 Toby Hall .15
498 Brent Abernathy .15
499 Brandon Backe .15
500 Felix Escalona .15
501 Matt White .15
502 Randy Winn .15
503 Carl Crawford .15
504 Dewon Brazelton .15
505 Joe Kennedy .15
506 Wade Boggs .50
507 Aubrey Huff .15
508 Alex Rodriguez 2.50
509 Ivan Rodriguez .50
510 Will Clark .75
511 Hank Blalock .15
512 Travis Hughes .15
513 Travis Hafner .15
514 Ryan Ludwick .15
515 Doug Davis .15
516 Juan Gonzalez .50
517 Jason Hart .15
518 Mark Teixeira .40
519 Nolan Ryan 3.00
520 Rafael Palmeiro .50
521 Kevin Mench .15
522 Chan Ho Park .15
523 Kenny Rogers .15
524 Rusty Greer .15
525 Michael Young .15
526 Carlos Delgado .40
527 Vernon Wells .15
528 Orlando Hudson .15
529 Shannon Stewart .15
530 Joe Carter .15
531 Chris Baker .15
532 Eric Hinske .15
533 Corey Thurman .15
534 Josh Phelps .15
535 Reed Johnson .15
536 Brian Bowles .15
537 Roy Halladay .15
538 Jose Cruz Jr. .15
539 Kelvim Escobar .15
540 Chris Carpenter .15

Glossy

Stars: 1-2.5X
Inserted 1:1

Stat Line

Cards serial numbered 151-250: 4-8X
Print run 101-150: 5-10X
Print run 51-100: 8-15X
Print run 26-50: 10-20X

Autographs

NM/M
Common Player: 6.00
Some not priced due to scarcity.
4 Alfredo Amezaga/250 6.00
11 Elpidio Guzman/100 10.00
15 Doug DeVore/122 10.00
35 Trey Hodges/250 8.00
38 Billy Sylvester/250 6.00
41 Cory Aldridge/250 8.00
45 Horacio Ramirez/200 8.00
46 Derrick Lewis/250 6.00
47 Marcus Giles/200 8.00
49 Wilson Betemit/75 10.00
51 Josh Towers/110 10.00
52 Ed Rogers/250 6.00
53 Kris Foster/250 6.00
56 Brian Roberts/250 35.00
59 Geronimo Gil/60 10.00
60 Erik Bedard/250 8.00
62 Jay Gibbons/181 10.00
64 Larry Bigbie/100 10.00
77 Casey Fossum/250 6.00
79 Fred Lynn/50 20.00
81 Juan Diaz/250 6.00
84 Jorge De La Rosa/250 6.00
99 Fergie Jenkins/50 25.00
101 Francis Beltran/250 8.00
103 Nate Frese/250 6.00
105 Carlos Zambrano/150 20.00
108 Will Ohman/50 10.00
110 Bobby Hill/150 8.00
115 Mark Prior/50 40.00
116 Juan Cruz/50 10.00
122 Joe Crede/50 10.00
125 Joe Borchard/250 10.00
127 Luis Aparicio/50 20.00
128 Willie Harris/129 8.00
129 Kyle Kane/100 10.00
131 Matt Ginter/250 6.00
132 Carlos Lee/50 15.00
133 Mark Buehrle/50 20.00
135 Eric Davis/75 20.00
138 Austin Kearns/71 20.00
142 Corky Miller/250 6.00
143 Brandon Larson/143 10.00
144 Wily Mo Pena/250 15.00
147 Luke Hudson/50 12.00
149 Tony Perez/50 20.00
156 Cliff Lee/250 10.00
161 Earl Snyder/250 8.00
165 Ricardo Rodriguez/250 8.00
166 Victor Martinez/200 25.00
167 Alex Herrera/250 6.00
171 Alex Escobar/125 10.00
172 Brian Tallet/250 10.00
174 Rene Reyes/250 6.00
176 Jason Romano/50 15.00
177 Juan Pierre/66 15.00
178 Jason Jennings/250 10.00
179 Jose Ortiz/250 8.00
181 Cam Esslinger/250 6.00
184 Jack Cust/250 10.00
185 Jack Morris/50 20.00
186 Mike Rivera/250 6.00
188 Fernando Rodney/250 6.00
190 Carlos Pena/96 12.00
192 Mike Maroth/250 6.00
193 Adam Pettyjohn/250 6.00
194 David Espinosa/250 6.00
195 Adam Bernero/250 6.00
196 Franklyn German/250 8.00
197 Robert Fick/50 10.00
198 Andres Torres/250 6.00
201 Pablo Ozuna/250 6.00
205 Wilson Valdez/250 6.00
207 Abraham Nunez/250 8.00
212 Kirk Saarloos/250 8.00
214 Rodrigo Rosario/250 6.00
215 Roy Oswalt/50 20.00
217 Tim Redding/250 6.00
218 Morgan Ensberg/250 6.00
219 Richard Hidalgo/100 10.00
220 Wade Miller/200 10.00
222 Raul Chavez/125 15.00
223 Carlos Hernandez/250 10.00
224 Greg Miller/90 10.00
226 Jason Lane/250 10.00
234 Angel Berroa/200 10.00
236 Brad Voyles/200 10.00
237 Brandon Berger/250 8.00
238 Chad Durbin/250 8.00
239 Alexis Gomez/165 10.00
240 Jeremy Affeldt/250 6.00
242 Dee Brown/50 12.00
243 Tony Cogan/250 6.00
248 Cesar Izturis/200 10.00
253 Steve Garvey/75 30.00
258 Joe Thurston/108 10.00
259 Carlos Garcia/100 8.00
261 Paul LoDuca/50 20.00
263 Victor Alvarez/250 6.00
265 Don Sutton/50 20.00
277 Takahito Nomura/100 20.00
279 Jose Mieses/50 15.00
281 Matt Childers/50 12.00
283 Ben Sheets/100 20.00
284 Brian Mallette/250 6.00
287 Jeff Deardorff/100 6.00
288 Luis Rivas/200 8.00
290 Michael Cuddyer/250 10.00
291 Torii Hunter/100 25.00
294 Jack Morris/50 20.00
305 Jose Vidro/50 15.00

306 Claudio Vargas/150 6.00
309 Henry Mateo/250 6.00
311 Zach Day/250 6.00
313 Endy Chavez/250 6.00
314 Javier Vazquez/50 15.00
323 Dwight Gooden/75 25.00
344 Drew Henson/50 25.00
345 Erick Almonte/250 6.00
347 Christian Parker/200 6.00
351 Brandon Claussen/250 6.00
356 Adrian Hernandez/200 6.00
359 Brett Jodie/250 8.00
366 Bert Snow/250 6.00
368 Juan Pena/250 8.00
371 Mark Ellis/150 6.00
379 Lenny Dykstra/75 25.00
383 Jorge Padilla/250 8.00
384 Jeremy Giambi/100 10.00
386 Anderson Machado/250 6.00
387 Marlon Byrd/200 10.00
388 Bud Smith/125 10.00
389 Eric Valent/100 8.00
390 Elio Serrano/250 8.00
392 Brandon Duckworth/100 10.00
395 Robert Person/100 10.00
396 Johnny Estrada/209 15.00
398 Eric Junge/250 8.00
399 Jason Michaels/221 6.00
402 John Grabow/250 6.00
406 Dave Williams/250 6.00
407 John Candelaria/100 10.00
408 Jack Wilson/250 6.00
409 Matt Guerrier/200 6.00
412 Aramis Ramirez/50 30.00
413 Dave Parker/50 20.00
415 Kip Wells/250 8.00
418 Ramon Vazquez/200 6.00
419 Oliver Perez/150 15.00
421 Brian Lawrence/250 8.00
422 Ben Howard/250 6.00
427 Xavier Nady/50 15.00
431 Cody Ransom/100 10.00
435 Deivis Santos/100 10.00
438 Pedro Feliz/50 15.00
441 Carlos Valderrama/250 6.00
447 Allan Simpson/250 6.00
448 Antonio Perez/250 6.00
451 Chris Snelling/100 10.00
452 Matt Thornton/200 6.00
454 Harold Reynolds/100 15.00
457 Rafael Soriano/250 6.00
458 Luis Ugueto/50 10.00
475 Les Walrond/50 12.00
479 Josh Pearce/200 6.00
497 Toby Hall/200 8.00
498 Brent Abernathy/250 6.00
499 Brandon Backe/250 8.00
500 Felix Escalona/50 10.00
504 Dewon Brazelton/100 10.00
505 Joe Kennedy/200 6.00
507 Aubrey Huff/100 15.00
512 Travis Hughes/200 6.00
514 Ryan Ludwick/250 6.00
515 Doug Davis/250 6.00
517 Jason Hart/123 10.00
518 Mark Teixeira/50 40.00
521 Kevin Mench/250 10.00
528 Orlando Hudson/120 10.00
531 Chris Baker/200 6.00
532 Eric Hinske/250 10.00
533 Corey Thurman/250 8.00
534 Josh Phelps/150 10.00
535 Reed Johnson/250 6.00
536 Brian Bowles/250 6.00
543 Ramon Nivar/100 15.00
544 Adam Loewen/100 10.00
545 Brandon Webb/100 30.00
546 Dan Haren/100 25.00
548 Ryan Wagner/100 15.00

Timeline Threads

NM/M

Common Player:
Quantity produced listed
1 Bobby Doerr/39 20.00
2 Phil Rizzuto/47 30.00
3 Yogi Berra/47 35.00
4 Pee Wee Reese/58 15.00
6 Al Kaline/64 40.00
7 Orlando Cepeda/65 15.00
8 Eddie Mathews/66 40.00
9 Lou Brock/66 15.00
10 Juan Marichal/67 15.00
11 Ernie Banks/68 40.00
12 Willie Stargell/68 15.00
13 Jim Palmer/69 15.00
14 Luis Aparicio/69 15.00
15 Tom Seaver/69 30.00
16 Harmon Killebrew/71 50.00
17 Joe Morgan/74 15.00
18 Brooks Robinson/76 30.00
19 Mike Schmidt/81 65.00
20 Willie McCovey/77 15.00
21 Robin Yount/78 40.00
22 Reggie Jackson/79 20.00
23 Rod Carew/85 25.00
24 Nolan Ryan/91 80.00
25 Tony Gwynn/98 25.00
26 Alex Rodriguez/100 25.00
27 Carlos Delgado/101 10.00
28 Lance Berkman/102 10.00
29 Randy Johnson/100 20.00
30 Josh Beckett/101 15.00
31 Eric Davis/89 10.00
32 Todd Helton/100 15.00
33 Jose Canseco/89 25.00
34 Mike Piazza/101 25.00
35 Fred Lynn/75 10.00
36 Mike Sweeney/101 10.00
37 Miguel Tejada/101 15.00
38 Curt Schilling/101 15.00
39 Dale Murphy/87 40.00
40 Jim Thome/101 20.00
41 Adam Dunn/102 15.00
42 Nomar Garciaparra/100 25.00
43 Vladimir Guerrero/100 15.00
44 Alfonso Soriano/102 20.00
45 Wade Boggs/90 15.00
46 Randy Johnson/89 20.00
47 Hal Newhouser/55 15.00
48 Chipper Jones/93 20.00
49 Andruw Jones/96 15.00
50 Frank Thomas/94 15.00

Hawaii

The base set and, it is believed, all inserts including autographs from the Team Heroes issue were produced in a special edition for attendees at the 2003 SCD Hawaii Trade Conference. Each card is gold-foil stamped with a show logo and "1/1" notation. Because of their unique nature, no catalog values are assigned.

2003 Donruss Timeless Treasures

NM/M

Complete Set (100):
Common Player: 2.00
Production 900 Sets
Tin (4): 100.00
1 Adam Dunn 3.00
2 Al Kaline 5.00
3 Alan Trammell 2.00
4 Albert Pujols 8.00
5 Alex Rodriguez 8.00
6 Alfonso Soriano 4.00
7 Andre Dawson 2.00
8 Andruw Jones 3.00
9 Austin Kearns 2.00
10 Babe Ruth 10.00
11 Barry Bonds 10.00
12 Barry Larkin 2.00
13 Barry Zito 3.00
14 Bernie Williams 4.00
15 Bo Jackson 4.00
16 Brooks Robinson 4.00
17 Cal Ripken Jr. 10.00
18 Carlton Fisk 2.00
19 Chipper Jones 4.00
20 Curt Schilling 3.00
21 Dale Murphy 2.00
22 Derek Jeter 10.00
23 Don Mattingly 10.00
24 Duke Snider 3.00
25 Eddie Mathews 4.00
26 Frank Robinson 3.00
27 Frank Thomas 4.00
28 Garret Anderson 2.00
29 Gary Carter 2.00
30 George Brett 8.00
31 Greg Maddux 6.00
32 Harmon Killebrew 4.00
33 Hideki Matsui **RC** 10.00
34 Hideo Nomo 3.00
35 Ichiro Suzuki 6.00
36 Ivan Rodriguez 4.00
37 Jackie Robinson 6.00
38 Jason Giambi 3.00
39 Jeff Bagwell 4.00
40 Jim Edmonds 3.00
41 Jim Palmer 3.00
42 Jim Thome 4.00
43 Joe Morgan 2.00
44 Jorge Posada 3.00
45 Jose Contreras **RC** 5.00
46 Juan Gonzalez 3.00
47 Kazuhisa Ishii 2.00
48 Ken Griffey Jr. 5.00
49 Kerry Wood 3.00
50 Kirby Puckett 5.00
51 Lance Berkman 2.00
52 Larry Walker 2.00
53 Lou Brock 3.00
54 Lou Gehrig 8.00
55 Magglio Ordonez 2.00
56 Mark Prior 4.00
57 Miguel Tejada 3.00
58 Mike Mussina 3.00
59 Mike Piazza 6.00
60 Mike Schmidt 8.00
61 Nolan Ryan 10.00
62 Nomar Garciaparra 6.00
63 Ozzie Smith 5.00
64 Pat Burrell 2.00
65 Pedro J. Martinez 4.00
66 Pee Wee Reese 2.00
67 Phil Rizzuto 4.00
68 Rafael Palmeiro 3.00
69 Randy Johnson 5.00
70 Reggie Jackson 4.00
71 Richie Ashburn 2.00
72 Rickey Henderson 3.00
73 Roberto Alomar 3.00
74 Roberto Clemente 8.00
75 Robin Yount 4.00
76 Rod Carew 3.00
77 Roger Clemens 8.00
78 Rogers Hornsby 4.00
79 Roy Oswalt 2.00
80 Ryan Klesko 2.00
81 Ryne Sandberg 6.00
82 Sammy Sosa 6.00
83 Scott Rolen 4.00
84 Shawn Green 3.00
85 Stan Musial 6.00
86 Steve Carlton 3.00
87 Thurman Munson 5.00
88 Todd Helton 4.00
89 Tom Glavine 2.00
90 Tom Seaver 4.00
91 Tony Gwynn 4.00
92 Tony Perez 2.00
93 Torii Hunter 2.00
94 Troy Glaus 3.00
95 Ty Cobb 6.00
96 Vernon Wells 2.00
97 Vladimir Guerrero 4.00
98 Warren Spahn 4.00
99 Willie McCovey 3.00
100 Yogi Berra 5.00

Silver

Stars (1-100): 3-5X
Production 50 Sets
Golds: No Pricing
Production 10 Sets
Platinum 1-of-1's exist.

Award Materials

NM/M

Quantity produced listed
1 Ivan Rodriguez/100 10.00
2 Mike Schmidt/50 60.00
3 Roberto Clemente/50 80.00
4 Roger Clemens/50 25.00
5 Randy Johnson/100 15.00
6 Pedro J. Martinez/100 15.00
7 Ivan Rodriguez/100 10.00
8 Jeff Bagwell/100 15.00
9 Frank Thomas/100 15.00
10 Cal Ripken Jr./75 50.00
11 Tom Seaver/50 25.00

Award Prime Materials

NM/M

Quantity produced listed
6 Pedro J. Martinez/50 30.00
9 Frank Thomas/50 25.00

Award Materials Autographs

Complete Set (1):

Award Winning MLB Logos

Complete Set (2):
Common Player:

Classic Combos

NM/M

Quantity produced listed
1 Jason Giambi/100 15.00
2 Adrian Beltre/100 10.00
3 Alex Rodriguez/100 25.00
4 Alfonso Soriano/100 30.00
5 Andruw Jones/100 15.00
6 Andre Dawson/100 15.00
7 Barry Larkin/100 10.00
8 Barry Zito/100 15.00
9 Cal Ripken Jr./100 60.00
10 Chipper Jones/100 20.00
11 Don Mattingly/10 50.00
12 Eric Chavez/100 10.00
13 Frank Thomas/100 15.00
14 Greg Maddux/100 25.00
15 Ivan Rodriguez/100 15.00
16 Jeff Bagwell/100 15.00
17 Jim Thome/100 15.00
18 Juan Gonzalez/100 15.00
19 Kazuhisa Ishii/100 10.00
20 Kerry Wood/100 15.00
21 Lance Berkman/100 10.00
22 Magglio Ordonez/100 10.00
23 Manny Ramirez/100 15.00
24 Miguel Tejada/100 10.00
25 Mike Piazza/100 20.00
26 Nomar Garciaparra/100 20.00
27 Pedro J. Martinez/100 20.00
28 Randy Johnson/100 15.00
29 Rickey Henderson/100 20.00
30 Ryne Sandberg/100 30.00
32 Shawn Green/100 10.00
33 Todd Helton/100 10.00
34 Tony Gwynn/100 20.00
35 Vladimir Guerrero/100 15.00

Classic Prime Combos

NM/M

Quantity produced listed
6 Andre Dawson/25 40.00
11 Don Mattingly/25 75.00
16 Jeff Bagwell/25 50.00

Classic Combos Autograph

NM/M

Quantity produced listed
8 Barry Zito/25 100.00
22 Magglio Ordonez/25 65.00
34 Tony Gwynn/25 100.00

Game Day Materials

NM/M

Quantity produced listed
1 Tony Gwynn/100 15.00
2 Magglio Ordonez/100 8.00
3 George Brett/100 40.00
4 Rickey Henderson/100 15.00
5 Billy Williams/100 10.00
6 Frank Thomas/100 10.00
7 Tony Gwynn/75 20.00
10 Ryne Sandberg/100 30.00
11 Miguel Tejada/100 10.00

Game Day Materials Autographs

Quantity produced listed

HOF Cuts

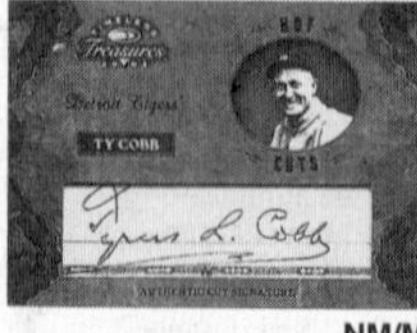

NM/M

Production One Set
Ty Cobb (8/03 Auction) 6,500

HOF Combos

NM/M

Quantity produced listed
1 Al Kaline/50 50.00
4 Kirby Puckett/75 40.00
6 Mike Schmidt/100 50.00
7 Nolan Ryan/50 100.00
8 Phil Rizzuto/50 30.00
9 Reggie Jackson/25 40.00
11 Rod Carew/100 25.00
14 George Brett/50 85.00
15 Carlton Fisk/100 20.00

HOF Prime Combos

Quantity produced listed

HOF Combos Autographs

Quantity produced listed

HOF Induction Year Combos

NM/M

Production 25 Sets
6 Enos Slaughter, Lou Brock/25 60.00
8 Phil Rizzuto, Steve Carlton/25 45.00
10 George Brett, Robin Yount/25 185.00

HOF Letters

Quantity produced listed

HOF Logos

NM/M

Quantity produced listed
29 Eddie Mathews/35 65.00
36 Nolan Ryan/35 100.00
37 Nolan Ryan/35 100.00
38 Nolan Ryan/35 100.00
43 Robin Yount/35 50.00

HOF Materials

NM/M

Quantity produced listed
1 Al Kaline 25.00
2 Babe Ruth/75 140.00
3 Carlton Fisk/100 15.00
4 Eddie Mathews/100 20.00
5 Gary Carter/100 15.00
6 George Brett/100 35.00
7 Harmon Killebrew/100 25.00
8 Joe Morgan/100 10.00
9 Kirby Puckett/100 20.00
10 Lou Gehrig/100 110.00
11 Luis Aparicio/100 10.00
12 Mike Schmidt/100 25.00
13 Ozzie Smith/100 25.00
14 Phil Rizzuto/100 10.00
15 Reggie Jackson/100 15.00
16 Richie Ashburn/100 15.00
17 Roberto Clemente/100 60.00
18 Robin Yount/100 20.00
19 Rod Carew/100 15.00
20 Rogers Hornsby/100 45.00
21 Stan Musial/100 35.00
22 Ty Cobb/100 120.00
23 Willie McCovey/100 10.00
24 Yogi Berra/100 30.00
25 Al Kaline/100 25.00
26 Babe Ruth/50 300.00
27 Bobby Doerr/100 15.00
28 Brooks Robinson/100 15.00
29 Eddie Mathews/100 20.00
30 Harmon Killebrew/100 25.00
31 Ty Cobb/50 150.00
32 Joe Morgan/100 10.00
33 Lou Brock/100 10.00
34 Lou Gehrig/50 225.00
35 Mike Schmidt/100 25.00
36 Nolan Ryan/100 40.00
37 Nolan Ryan/100 40.00
38 Nolan Ryan/100 40.00
39 Phil Rizzuto/100 10.00
40 Reggie Jackson/25 25.00
41 Reggie Jackson/100 15.00
42 Roberto Clemente/50 90.00
43 Robin Yount/100 20.00
44 Rod Carew/100 15.00
45 Stan Musial/100 35.00
46 Tom Seaver/100 20.00
47 Steve Carlton/100 15.00
48 Carlton Fisk/100 15.00
49 Pee Wee Reese/100 15.00
50 Jackie Robinson/50 85.00

HOF Materials Autographs

NM/M

Quantity produced listed
7 Harmon Killebrew/25 80.00
12 Mike Schmidt/15 180.00
24 Yogi Berra/15 150.00
28 Brooks Robinson/25 75.00
30 Harmon Killebrew/50 75.00
39 Phil Rizzuto/25 65.00
43 Robin Yount/25 175.00

HOF Numbers

NM/M

Quantity produced listed
35 Mike Schmidt/50 40.00
36 Nolan Ryan/35 100.00
43 Robin Yount/35 50.00
47 Steve Carlton/40 20.00
48 Carlton Fisk/35 45.00

Home Run Materials

NM/M

Quantity produced listed
1 Harmon Killebrew/100 20.00
2 Harmon Killebrew/100 20.00
3 Jose Canseco/100 15.00
4 Magglio Ordonez/100 8.00
5 Rafael Palmeiro/100 15.00
6 Rafael Palmeiro/100 15.00
7 Rafael Palmeiro/100 15.00
8 Alex Rodriguez/100 15.00
9 Alex Rodriguez/100 15.00
10 Alex Rodriguez/100 15.00
11 Alex Rodriguez/20 75.00
12 Adam Dunn/100 15.00

Home Run Materials Autographs

NM/M

Quantity produced listed
1 Harmon Killebrew/25 80.00
3 Jose Canseco/25 100.00

Material Ink

NM/M

Quantity produced listed
1 Adam Dunn/50 45.00
2 Alan Trammell/100 30.00
3 Alex Rodriguez/25 150.00
5 Andre Dawson/100 30.00
6 Barry Zito/100 45.00
7 Bo Jackson/100 60.00
8 Bob Feller/25 70.00
9 Bobby Doerr/50 45.00
11 Cal Ripken Jr./50 200.00
12 Cal Ripken Jr./50 200.00
13 Cal Ripken Jr./25 225.00
14 Dale Murphy/50 45.00
15 Dave Parker/75 35.00
16 David Cone/100 30.00
17 Don Mattingly/100 85.00
18 Duke Snider/25 75.00
19 Edgar Martinez/50 50.00
20 Gary Carter/100 30.00
21 Harmon Killebrew/75 70.00
22 Jim Edmonds/25 55.00
23 Jim Thome/50 50.00
24 Joe Carter/100 30.00
25 Jose Canseco/50 50.00
26 Jose Vidro/100 20.00
27 Kazuhisa Ishii/100 40.00
28 Kerry Wood/50 60.00
29 Lance Berkman/50 40.00
30 Mark Mulder/25 65.00
32 Mike Schmidt/25 90.00
33 Nick Johnson/100 25.00
34 Nolan Ryan/25 225.00
35 Nolan Ryan/25 225.00
36 Nolan Ryan/25 225.00
37 Paul LoDuca/100 25.00
38 Paul Molitor/50 45.00
40 Reggie Jackson/40 85.00
41 Roberto Alomar/50 50.00
42 Roberto Alomar/100 40.00
43 Robin Yount/50 75.00
47 Ryan Klesko/75 25.00
48 Ryne Sandberg/25 140.00
50 Stan Musial/25 150.00
51 Steve Carlton/100 35.00
52 Steve Carlton/100 35.00
53 Todd Helton/50 60.00
54 Tom Seaver/50 50.00
55 Tony Gwynn/25 100.00

56 Torii Hunter/100 40.00
57 Vladimir Guerrero/100 40.00
58 Will Clark/50 85.00

Material MLB Logo Ink

Complete Set (22):
Common Player:

Milestone Materials

NM/M
Quantity produced listed
3 Rickey Henderson/100 15.00

Past and Present

NM/M
Production 100 Sets
1 Alex Rodriguez/100 20.00
2 Hideo Nomo/100 25.00
3 Jason Giambi/100 20.00
4 Juan Gonzalez/100 15.00
5 Mike Piazza/100 20.00
6 Pedro J. Martinez/100 15.00
7 Randy Johnson/100 15.00
8 Rickey Henderson/100 20.00
9 Roberto Alomar/100 15.00
10 Roger Clemens/100 20.00
11 Sammy Sosa/100 35.00

Past & Present Letters

NM/M
Quantity produced listed
1 Alex Rodriguez/75 30.00
2 Hideo Nomo/25 90.00
4 Juan Gonzalez/50 25.00
6 Pedro J. Martinez/75 35.00
7 Randy Johnson/75 40.00

Past and Present Logos

NM/M
Quantity produced listed
2 Hideo Nomo/25 90.00
3 Jason Giambi/75 40.00
5 Mike Piazza/50 40.00

Past & Present Numbers

NM/M
Quantity produced listed
2 Hideo Nomo/25 75.00
3 Jason Giambi/75 40.00
6 Pedro J. Martinez/50 40.00
7 Randy Johnson/50 40.00

Past & Present Patches

Quantity produced listed

Post Season Materials

Quantity produced listed

Post Season Prime Material

NM/M
No Pricing
1 Ozzie Smith/75 50.00

Post Season Materials Autographs

NM/M
Quantity produced listed
1 Ozzie Smith/15 125.00

Prime Materials

NM/M
Quantity produced listed
1 Tony Gwynn/100 15.00
2 Magglio Ordonez/100 8.00
4 Rickey Henderson/100 15.00
6 Frank Thomas/100 10.00
7 Tony Gwynn/75 20.00
10 Ryne Sandberg/100 30.00
11 Miguel Tejada/100 10.00

Prime Material Ink

NM/M
Quantity produced listed
2 Alan Trammell/50 50.00
5 Andre Dawson/25 60.00
7 Bo Jackson/50 100.00
20 Gary Carter/50 50.00
24 Joe Carter/50 50.00
26 Jose Vidro/25 40.00
27 Kazuhisa Ishii/50 50.00
33 Nick Johnson/50 45.00
53 Steve Carlton/50 50.00
58 Torii Hunter/50 50.00
59 Vladimir Guerrero/50 70.00
60 Will Clark/25 180.00

Rookie Year Combos

NM/M
Quantity produced listed
6 Mark Prior/50 40.00
7 Albert Pujols/50 80.00

Rookie Year Materials

NM/M
Common Player: 8.00
1 Cal Ripken Jr./100 50.00
2 Mike Schmidt/50 40.00
3 Rafael Palmeiro/100 15.00
4 Nomar Garciaparra/100 20.00
6 Stan Musial/42 70.00
7 Yogi Berra/100 30.00
9 Ivan Rodriguez/100 10.00
12 Vladimir Guerrero/100 15.00
14 Ivan Rodriguez/91 10.00
15 Andruw Jones/96 15.00
16 Andruw Jones/100 15.00
17 Fred Lynn/100 10.00
18 Jeff Kent/100 8.00
19 Gary Sheffield/100 10.00
20 Ron Santo/100 15.00
21 Juan Gonzalez/100 15.00
22 Alfonso Soriano/100 25.00
23 Ryan Klesko/92 10.00
24 Adam Dunn/100 12.00
25 Hideo Nomo/100 25.00
26 Mark Prior/100 15.00
27 Pat Burrell/99 10.00
28 Magglio Ordonez/100 8.00
29 Kirby Puckett/84 25.00
30 Albert Pujols/100 30.00
31 Albert Pujols/100 30.00

R.Y. Materials Autographs

NM/M
Quantity produced listed
7 Yogi Berra/15 150.00
26 Mark Prior/25 150.00
28 Magglio Ordonez/25 50.00

Rookie Year Materials Lett

NM/M
Quantity produced listed
4 Nomar Garciaparra/35 40.00
9 Ivan Rodriguez/35 20.00
12 Vladimir Guerrero/35 25.00
15 Andruw Jones/25 35.00
30 Albert Pujols/25 90.00

R.Y. Materials Logos

NM/M
Quantity produced listed
12 Vladimir Guerrero/50 25.00
15 Andruw Jones/50 25.00
17 Fred Lynn/25 25.00
18 Jeff Kent/50 20.00
19 Gary Sheffield/50 25.00
22 Alfonso Soriano/20 60.00
23 Ryan Klesko/50 15.00
30 Albert Pujols/50 75.00

R.Y. Materials Numbers

NM/M
Quantity produced listed
12 Vladimir Guerrero/50 25.00
15 Andruw Jones/15 25.00
17 Fred Lynn/30 25.00
18 Jeff Kent/25 20.00
19 Gary Sheffield/25 30.00
21 Juan Gonzalez/30 30.00
22 Alfonso Soriano/35 50.00
23 Ryan Klesko/35 20.00
26 Mark Prior/35 40.00
30 Albert Pujols/25 90.00

R.Y. Materials Patches

Quantity produced listed

Playoff Babe Ruth Special Edition

Fifteen swatches from the jersey purchased in May 2003 for $265,000 were inserted into a special edition serially numbered card. Card No. 1 was given to Ruth's daughter. Some of the cards were reportedly given to Donruss/Playoff employees as year-end awards.

NM/M
Babe Ruth 2,100

Team Timeline

NM/M
Complete Set (19): 65.00
Common Duo: 2.00
Inserted 1:29
1 Deion Sanders, Andruw Jones 2.00
2 Rickie Weeks, Robin Yount 3.00
3 Don Mattingly, Whitey Ford 8.00
4 Chipper Jones, Dale Murphy 4.00
5 Nomar Garciaparra, Bobby Doerr 5.00
6 Mark Prior, Sammy Sosa 5.00
7 Hideo Nomo, Kazuhisa Ishii 2.00
8 Andre Dawson, Mark Grace 3.00
9 Roger Clemens, Carl Yastrzemski 6.00
10 Mike Mussina, Cal Ripken Jr. 8.00
11 Stan Musial, Albert Pujols 6.00
12 Jim Palmer, Mike Mussina 2.00
13 Marty Marion, Stan Musial 4.00
14 George Brett, Mike Sweeney 6.00
15 Roger Clemens, Roger Maris 6.00
16 Duke Snider, Shawn Green 3.00
17 Jim Thome, Mike Schmidt 4.00
18 Nolan Ryan, Alex Rodriguez 8.00
19 Roy Campanella, Mike Piazza 4.00

Gallery of Stars

NM/M
Complete Set (15): 50.00
Common Player: 2.00
Inserted 1:37
1 Nolan Ryan 8.00
2 Cal Ripken Jr. 8.00
3 George Brett 6.00
4 Don Mattingly 6.00
5 Deion Sanders 2.00
6 Mike Piazza 4.00
7 Hideo Nomo 2.00
8 Rickey Henderson 2.00
9 Roger Clemens 6.00
10 Greg Maddux 4.00
11 Albert Pujols 6.00
12 Alex Rodriguez 6.00
13 Dale Murphy 3.00
14 Mark Prior 4.00
15 Dontrelle Willis 2.00

Heritage Collection

NM/M
Complete Set (25): 75.00
Common Player: 2.00
Inserted 1:22
1 Dale Murphy 3.00
2 Cal Ripken Jr. 8.00
3 Carl Yastrzemski 4.00
4 Don Mattingly 6.00
5 Jim Palmer 2.00
6 Andre Dawson 2.00
7 Roy Campanella 3.00
8 George Brett 6.00
9 Duke Snider 3.00
10 Marty Marion 2.00
11 Deion Sanders 2.00
12 Whitey Ford 3.00
13 Stan Musial 5.00
14 Nolan Ryan 8.00
15 Steve Carlton 2.00
16 Robin Yount 3.00
17 Albert Pujols 6.00
18 Alex Rodriguez 6.00
19 Mike Piazza 4.00
20 Roger Clemens 6.00
21 Hideo Nomo 2.00
22 Mark Prior 4.00
23 Roger Maris 5.00
24 Greg Maddux 4.00
25 Mark Grace 2.00

2004 Donruss

NM/M
Complete Set (400): 75.00
Common Player: .10
Pack (10): 3.50
Box (24): 65.00
1 Derek Jeter 2.00
2 Greg Maddux 1.00
3 Albert Pujols 1.50
4 Ichiro Suzuki 1.00
5 Alex Rodriguez 1.50
6 Roger Clemens 1.50
7 Andruw Jones .50
8 Barry Bonds 2.00
9 Jeff Bagwell .50
10 Randy Johnson .75
12 Scott Rolen .50
13 Lance Berkman .40
14 Barry Zito .25
15 Manny Ramirez .50
16 Carlos Delgado .50
17 Alfonso Soriano .75
18 Todd Helton .50
19 Mike Mussina .50
20 Nomar Garciaparra 1.50
21 Chipper Jones 1.00
22 Mark Prior 2.00
23 Jim Thome .50
24 Vladimir Guerrero .75
25 Pedro Martinez .75
26 Sergio Mitre .10
27 Adam Loewen .10
28 Alfredo Gonzalez .10
29 Miguel Ojeda .10
30 Rosman Garcia .10
31 Arnie Munoz .10
32 Andrew Brown .10
33 Josh Hall .10
34 Josh Stewart .10
35 Clint Barmes .10
36 Brandon Webb .10
37 Chien-Ming Wang .40
38 Edgar Gonzalez .10
39 Alejandro Machado .10
40 Jeremy Griffiths .10
41 Craig Brazell .10
42 Daniel Cabrera .10
43 Fernando Cabrera .10
44 Terrmel Sledge .10
45 Rob Hammock .10
46 Francisco Rosario .10
47 Francisco Cruceta .10
48 Rett Johnson .10
49 Guillermo Quiroz .10
50 Hong-Chih Kuo .10
51 Ian Ferguson .10
52 Tim Olson .10
53 Todd Wellemeyer .10
54 Rich Fischer .10
55 Phil Seibel .10
56 Joe Valentine .10
57 Matt Kata .10
58 Michael Hessman .10
59 Michel Hernandez .10
60 Doug Waechter .10
61 Prentice Redman .10
62 Nook Logan .10
63 Oscar Villarreal .10
64 Pete LaForest .10
65 Matt Bruback .10
66 Dan Haren .10
67 Greg Aquino .10
68 Lew Ford .10
69 Jeff Duncan .10
70 Ryan Wagner .10
71 Bengie Molina .10
72 Brad Fullmer .10
73 Darin Erstad .25
74 David Eckstein .10
75 Garret Anderson .25
76 Jarrod Washburn .10
77 Kevin Appier .10
78 Scott Spiezio .10
79 Tim Salmon .25
80 Troy Glaus .40
81 Troy Percival .10
82 Jason Johnson .10
83 Jay Gibbons .25
84 Melvin Mora .10
85 Sidney Ponson .10
86 Tony Batista .10
87 Bill Mueller .10
88 Byung-Hyun Kim .10
89 David Ortiz .25
90 Derek Lowe .25
91 Johnny Damon .25
92 Casey Fossum .10
93 Manny Ramirez .50
94 Nomar Garciaparra 1.50
95 Pedro J. Martinez .75
96 Todd Walker .10
97 Trot Nixon .10
98 Bartolo Colon .25
99 Carlos Lee .10
100 D'Angelo Jimenez .10
101 Esteban Loaiza .10
102 Frank Thomas .50
103 Joe Crede .10
104 Jose Valentin .10
105 Magglio Ordonez .25
106 Mark Buehrle .10
107 Paul Konerko .10
108 Brandon Phillips .10
109 C.C. Sabathia .10
110 Ellis Burks .10
111 Jeremy Guthrie .10
112 Josh Bard .10
113 Matt Lawton .10
114 Milton Bradley .10
115 Omar Vizquel .20
116 Travis Hafner .10
117 Bobby Higginson .10
118 Carlos Pena .10
119 Dmitri Young .20
120 Eric Munson .10
121 Jeremy Bonderman .10
122 Nate Cornejo .10
123 Omar Infante .10
124 Ramon Santiago .10
125 Angel Berroa .10
126 Carlos Beltran .25
127 Desi Relaford .10
128 Jeremy Affeldt .10
129 Joe Randa .10
130 Ken Harvey .10
131 Mike MacDougal .10
132 Michael Tucker .10
133 Mike Sweeney .20
134 Raul Ibanez .20
135 Runelvys Hernandez .10
136 A.J. Pierzynski .10
137 Brad Radke .10
138 Corey Koskie .10
139 Cristian Guzman .10
140 Doug Mientkiewicz .10
141 Dustan Mohr .10
142 Jacque Jones .10
143 Kenny Rogers .10
144 Bobby Kielty .10
145 Kyle Lohse .10
146 Luis Rivas .10
147 Torii Hunter .25
148 Alfonso Soriano .75
149 Andy Pettitte .40
150 Bernie Williams .40
151 David Wells .10
152 Derek Jeter 2.00
153 Hideki Matsui 2.00
154 Jason Giambi .75
155 Jorge Posada .50
156 Jose Contreras .40
157 Mike Mussina .50
158 Nick Johnson .10
159 Robin Ventura .20
160 Roger Clemens 1.50
161 Barry Zito .25
162 Chris Singleton .10
163 Eric Byrnes .10
164 Eric Chavez .25
165 Erubiel Durazo .10
166 Keith Foulke .10
167 Mark Ellis .10
168 Miguel Tejada .40
169 Mark Mulder .25
170 Ramon Hernandez .10
171 Ted Lilly .10
172 Terrence Long .10
173 Tim Hudson .25
174 Bret Boone .25
175 Carlos Guillen .10
176 Dan Wilson .10
177 Edgar Martinez .25
178 Freddy Garcia .10
179 Gil Meche .10
180 Ichiro Suzuki 1.00
181 Jamie Moyer .10
182 Joel Pineiro .10
183 John Olerud .20
184 Mike Cameron .10
185 Randy Winn .10
186 Ryan Franklin .10
187 Kazuhiro Sasaki .10
188 Aubrey Huff .10
189 Carl Crawford .10
190 Joe Kennedy .10
191 Marlon Anderson .10
192 Rey Ordonez .10
193 Rocco Baldelli .25
194 Toby Hall .10
195 Travis Lee .10
196 Alex Rodriguez 1.50
197 Carl Everett .10
198 Chan Ho Park .10
199 Einar Diaz .10
200 Hank Blalock .50
201 Ismael Valdes .10
202 Juan Gonzalez .50
203 Mark Teixeira .40
204 Mike Young .10
205 Rafael Palmeiro .50
206 Carlos Delgado .50
207 Kelvim Escobar .10
208 Eric Hinske .10
209 Frank Catalanotto .10
210 Josh Phelps .10
211 Orlando Hudson .10
212 Roy Halladay .25
213 Shannon Stewart .10
214 Vernon Wells .25
215 Carlos Baerga .10
216 Curt Schilling .40
217 Junior Spivey .10
218 Luis Gonzalez .25
219 Lyle Overbay .10
220 Mark Grace .25
221 Matt Williams .20
222 Randy Johnson .75
223 Shea Hillenbrand .10
224 Steve Finley .10
225 Andruw Jones .50
226 Chipper Jones 1.00
227 Gary Sheffield .40
228 Greg Maddux 1.00
229 Javy Lopez .25
230 John Smoltz .25
231 Marcus Giles .20
232 Mike Hampton .10
233 Rafael Furcal .25
234 Robert Fick .10
235 Russ Ortiz .10
236 Alex Gonzalez .10
237 Carlos Zambrano .10
238 Corey Patterson .10
239 Hee Seop Choi .10
240 Kerry Wood .50
241 Mark Belhorn .10
242 Mark Prior 1.50
243 Moises Alou .25
244 Sammy Sosa 1.50
245 Aaron Boone .10
246 Adam Dunn .40
247 Austin Kearns .40
248 Barry Larkin .25
249 Felipe Lopez .10
250 Jose Guillen .10
251 Ken Griffey Jr. 1.00
252 Jason LaRue .10
253 Scott Williamson .10
254 Sean Casey .20
255 Shawn Chacon .10
256 Chris Stynes .10
257 Jason Jennings .10
258 Jay Payton .20
259 Jose Hernandez .10
260 Larry Walker .25
261 Preston Wilson .20
262 Ronnie Belliard .10
263 Todd Helton .50
264 A.J. Burnett .10
265 Alex Gonzalez .10
266 Brad Penny .10
267 Derrek Lee .10
268 Ivan Rodriguez .50
269 Josh Beckett .50
270 Juan Encarnacion .10
271 Juan Pierre .10
272 Luis Castillo .10
273 Mike Lowell .10
274 Todd Hollandsworth .10
275 Billy Wagner .25
276 Brad Ausmus .10
277 Craig Biggio .25
278 Jeff Bagwell .50
279 Jeff Kent .25
280 Lance Berkman .25
281 Richard Hidalgo .10
282 Roy Oswalt .25
283 Wade Miller .10
284 Adrian Beltre .10
285 Brian Jordan .10
286 Cesar Izturis .10
287 Dave Roberts .10
288 Eric Gagne .25
289 Fred McGriff .25
290 Hideo Nomo .40
291 Kazuhisa Ishii .10
292 Kevin Brown .25
293 Paul LoDuca .10
294 Shawn Green .40
295 Ben Sheets .25
296 Geoff Jenkins .25
297 Rey Sanchez .10
298 Richie Sexson .40
299 Wes Helms .10
300 Brad Wilkerson .10
301 Claudio Vargas .10
302 Endy Chavez .10
303 Fernando Tatis .10
304 Javier Vazquez .25
305 Jose Vidro .10
306 Michael Barrett .10
307 Orlando Cabrera .20
308 Tony Armas Jr. .10
309 Vladimir Guerrero .75
310 Zach Day .10
311 Al Leiter .10
312 Cliff Floyd .10
313 Jae Weong Seo .10
314 Jeromy Burnitz .10
315 Mike Piazza 1.00
316 Mo Vaughn .10
317 Roberto Alomar .40
318 Roger Cedeno .10
319 Tom Glavine .25
320 Jose Reyes .40
321 Bobby Abreu .20
322 Brett Myers .10
323 David Bell .10
324 Jim Thome .50
325 Jimmy Rollins .25
326 Kevin Millwood .25
327 Marlon Byrd .10
328 Mike Lieberthal .10

329 Pat Burrell .40
330 Randy Wolf .10
331 Aramis Ramirez .10
332 Brian Giles .25
333 Jason Kendall .20
334 Kenny Lofton .20
335 Kip Wells .10
336 Kris Benson .10
337 Randall Simon .10
338 Reggie Sanders .10
339 Albert Pujols 2.00
340 Edgar Renteria .10
341 Fernando Vina .10
342 J.D. Drew .10
343 Jim Edmonds .25
344 Matt Morris .10
345 Mike Matheny .10
346 Scott Rolen .50
347 Tino Martinez .10
348 Woody Williams .10
349 Brian Lawrence .10
350 Mark Kotsay .10
351 Mark Loretta .10
352 Ramon Vazquez .10
353 Rondell White .10
354 Ryan Klesko .25
355 Sean Burroughs .10
356 Trevor Hoffman .10
357 Xavier Nady .10
358 Andres Galarraga .10
359 Barry Bonds 2.00
360 Benito Santiago .10
361 Deivi Cruz .10
362 Edgardo Alfonzo .10
363 J.T. Snow .10
364 Jason Schmidt .10
365 Kirk Rueter .10
366 Kurt Ainsworth .10
367 Marquis Grissom .10
368 Ray Durham .10
369 Rich Aurilia .10
370 Tim Worrell .10
371 Troy Glaus .20
372 Melvin Mora .10
373 Nomar Garciaparra .75
374 Magglio Ordonez .20
375 Omar Vizquel .10
376 Dmitri Young .10
377 Mike Sweeney .10
378 Torii Hunter .20
379 Derek Jeter 1.00
380 Barry Zito .20
381 Ichiro Suzuki .50
382 Rocco Baldelli .20
383 Alex Rodriguez .75
384 Carlos Delgado .25
385 Randy Johnson .40
386 Greg Maddux .50
387 Sammy Sosa .75
388 Ken Griffey Jr. .50
389 Todd Helton .25
390 Ivan Rodriguez .25
391 Jeff Bagwell .25
392 Hideo Nomo .20
393 Richie Sexson .20
394 Vladimir Guerrero .40
395 Mike Piazza .50
396 Jim Thome .25
397 Jason Kendall .10
398 Albert Pujols 1.00
399 Ryan Klesko .10
400 Barry Bonds 1.00

Black Press Proofs

No pricing due to scarcity.
Production 10 Sets
Hot Pack exclusive.

Career Stat Line

Cards Serial #'d from 251-500: 3-5X
Print run 101-250: 4-6X
Print run 61-100: 4-8X
Print run 26-60: 8-15X
No pricing for P/R 25 or less.
Numbered to career statistic.

Season Stat Line

Print run 101-261: 4-6X
Print run 61-100: 4-8X
Print run 26-60: 8-15X
No pricing for P/R 25 or less.
Numbered to 2003 statistic.

All-Stars

NM/M
Complete Set (20): 40.00
Common Player: 1.50

Production 1,000 Sets
Black: 1-2X
Production 250 Sets
1 Alex Rodriguez 5.00
2 Roger Clemens 5.00
3 Ichiro Suzuki 3.00
4 Barry Zito 1.50
5 Garret Anderson 1.50
6 Derek Jeter 5.00
7 Manny Ramirez 2.00
8 Pedro J. Martinez 2.00
9 Alfonso Soriano 2.50
10 Carlos Delgado 1.50
11 Barry Bonds 5.00
12 Andruw Jones 2.00
13 Scott Rolen 2.00
14 Austin Kearns 1.50
15 Mark Prior 4.00
16 Vladimir Guerrero 2.00
17 Jeff Bagwell 2.00
18 Mike Piazza 3.00
19 Albert Pujols 5.00
20 Randy Johnson 2.50

Bat Kings

NM/M
Common Player: 5.00
Studio Current Player: 1.5X
Production 50
Studio Retired: No Pricing
Production 25
1 Alex Rodriguez/250 10.00
2 Albert Pujols/250 15.00
3 Chipper Jones/250 12.00
4 Lance Berkman/250 5.00
5 Cal Ripken Jr./100 50.00
6 George Brett/100 30.00
7 Don Mattingly/100 40.00
8 Roberto Clemente/100 75.00

Craftsmen

NM/M
Complete Set (15): 40.00
Common Player: 2.00
Production 2,000 Sets
Black: 1-2X
Production 275 Sets
Master Craftsmen: 1-2X
Production 150 Sets
1 Alex Rodriguez 5.00
2 Mark Prior 4.00
3 Ichiro Suzuki 3.00
4 Barry Bonds 5.00
5 Ken Griffey Jr. 3.00
6 Alfonso Soriano 3.00
7 Mike Piazza 3.00
8 Chipper Jones 3.00
9 Derek Jeter 5.00
10 Randy Johnson 2.50
11 Sammy Sosa 4.00
12 Roger Clemens 4.00
13 Nomar Garciaparra 4.00
14 Greg Maddux 3.00
15 Albert Pujols 5.00

Insert

NM/M
Complete Set (25): 80.00
Common Player: 2.00
Production 2,500 Sets
Studio Series: 1-2X
Production 250 Sets
Black: 1.5-2X
Production 100 Sets
1 Derek Jeter 8.00

2 Greg Maddux 6.00
3 Albert Pujols 8.00
4 Ichiro Suzuki 6.00
5 Alex Rodriguez 6.00
6 Roger Clemens 6.00
7 Andruw Jones 3.00
8 Barry Bonds 8.00
9 Jeff Bagwell 3.00
10 Randy Johnson 3.00
11 Scott Rolen 3.00
12 Lance Berkman 2.00
13 Barry Zito 2.00
14 Manny Ramirez 3.00
15 Carlos Delgado 2.50
16 Alfonso Soriano 4.00
17 Todd Helton 3.00
18 Mike Mussina 2.00
19 Austin Kearns 2.00
20 Nomar Garciaparra 6.00
21 Chipper Jones 4.00
22 Mark Prior 4.00
23 Jim Thome 3.00
24 Vladimir Guerrero 3.00
25 Pedro J. Martinez 3.00

Elite Series

NM/M
Complete Set (15): 60.00
Common Player: 2.00
Production 1,500 Sets
Black: 1-2X
Production 150 Sets
Dominators: No Pricing
Production 25 Sets
1 Albert Pujols 8.00
2 Barry Zito 3.00
3 Gary Sheffield 3.00
4 Mike Mussina 3.00
5 Lance Berkman 2.00
6 Alfonso Soriano 4.00
7 Randy Johnson 3.00
8 Nomar Garciaparra 8.00
9 Austin Kearns 3.00
10 Manny Ramirez 3.00
11 Mark Prior 6.00
12 Alex Rodriguez 6.00
13 Derek Jeter 8.00
14 Barry Bonds 8.00
15 Roger Clemens 6.00

Inside View

NM/M
Complete Set (25): 50.00
Common Player: 1.00
Production 1,250 Sets
1 Derek Jeter 5.00
2 Greg Maddux 3.00
3 Albert Pujols 5.00
4 Ichiro Suzuki 3.00
5 Alex Rodriguez 4.00
6 Roger Clemens 5.00
7 Andruw Jones 1.50
8 Barry Bonds 5.00
9 Jeff Bagwell 2.00
10 Randy Johnson 2.00
11 Scott Rolen 2.00
12 Lance Berkman 1.00
13 Barry Zito 1.50
14 Manny Ramirez 2.00
15 Carlos Delgado 1.50
16 Alfonso Soriano 2.00
17 Todd Helton 2.00
18 Mike Mussina 1.50
19 Austin Kearns 1.50
20 Nomar Garciaparra 4.00
21 Chipper Jones 3.00
22 Mark Prior 4.00
23 Jim Thome 2.00
24 Vladimir Guerrero 2.00
25 Pedro J. Martinez 2.50

Jersey Kings

NM/M
Quantity produced listed
Studio Current Player: 1.5X
Production 50
Studio Retired: No Pricing
Production 25
1 Alfonso Soriano/250 10.00
2 Sammy Sosa/250 15.00
3 Roger Clemens/250 15.00
4 Nomar Garciaparra/250 12.00
5 Mark Prior/250 10.00
6 Vladimir Guerrero/250 8.00
7 Don Mattingly/100 40.00
8 Roberto Clemente/100 80.00
9 George Brett/100 35.00
10 Nolan Ryan/100 40.00
11 Cal Ripken Jr./100 55.00
12 Mike Schmidt/100 40.00

Longball Leaders

NM/M
Complete Set (10): 20.00
Common Player: 1.50
Production 1,500 Sets
Black: 1-2X
Production 250 Sets
Die-Cuts: 1.5-3X
Production 50 Sets
1 Barry Bonds 5.00
2 Alfonso Soriano 3.00
3 Adam Dunn 1.50
4 Alex Rodriguez 5.00
5 Jim Thome 2.00
6 Garret Anderson 1.50
7 Juan Gonzalez 2.00
8 Jeff Bagwell 2.00
9 Gary Sheffield 1.50
10 Sammy Sosa 4.00

Mound Marvels

NM/M
Complete Set (15): 20.00
Common Player: 1.00
Production 750 Sets
Black: 1-2X
Production 175 Sets
1 Mark Prior 4.00
2 Curt Schilling 1.50
3 Mike Mussina 1.50
4 Kevin Brown 1.50
5 Pedro J. Martinez 2.50
6 Mark Mulder 1.00
7 Kerry Wood 1.50
8 Greg Maddux 3.00
9 Kevin Millwood 1.00
10 Barry Zito 1.50
11 Roger Clemens 5.00
12 Randy Johnson 2.50
13 Hideo Nomo 1.50
14 Tim Hudson 1.50
15 Tom Glavine 1.50

Power Alley Red

NM/M
Complete Set (20): 50.00
Common Player: 2.00
Production 2,500 Sets
Red Die-Cut: 1-2X
Production 250 Sets

Blues: 1X
Production 1,000 Sets
Blue Die-Cuts: 1.5-2X
Production 100 Sets
Purples: 1-2X
Production 250 Sets
Purple Die-Cuts: No Pricing
Production 25 Sets
Yellows: 1.5-2X
Production 100 Sets
Yellow Die-Cuts: No Pricing
Production 10 Sets
Greens: No Pricing
Production 25 Sets
Green Die-Cuts: No Pricing
Production Five Sets
1 Albert Pujols 8.00
2 Mike Piazza 5.00
3 Carlos Delgado 2.00
4 Barry Bonds 8.00
5 Jim Edmonds 2.00
6 Nomar Garciaparra 6.00
7 Alfonso Soriano 4.00
8 Alex Rodriguez 6.00
9 Lance Berkman 2.00
10 Scott Rolen 3.00
11 Manny Ramirez 3.00
12 Rafael Palmeiro 3.00
13 Sammy Sosa 6.00
14 Adam Dunn 2.00
15 Andruw Jones 2.00
16 Jim Thome 3.00
17 Jason Giambi 3.00
18 Jeff Bagwell 3.00
19 Juan Gonzalez 3.00
20 Austin Kearns 2.00

Production Line Average

NM/M
Complete Set (10): 35.00
Common Player:
Die-Cuts: 1-2X
Production 100 Sets
Black: 2-3X
Production 35 Sets
1 Gary Sheffield/330 2.00
2 Ichiro Suzuki/312 5.00
3 Todd Helton/358 3.00
4 Manny Ramirez/325 3.00
5 Garret Anderson/315 2.00
6 Barry Bonds/341 8.00
7 Albert Pujols/359 8.00
8 Derek Jeter/324 8.00
9 Nomar Garciaparra/301 6.00
10 Hank Blalock/300 3.00

Production Line OBP

NM/M
Complete Set (10): 25.00
Common Player: 2.00
Die-Cuts: 1-2X
Production 100 Sets
Black: 2-3X
Production 40 Sets
1 Todd Helton/458 3.00
2 Albert Pujols/439 6.00
3 Larry Walker/422 2.00
4 Barry Bonds/529 6.00
5 Chipper Jones/402 4.00
6 Manny Ramirez/427 3.00
7 Gary Sheffield/419 2.00
8 Lance Berkman/412 2.00
9 Alex Rodriguez/396 6.00
10 Jason Giambi/412 3.00

Production Line OPS

NM/M
Complete Set (10): 25.00
Varying quantities produced
Black: 1-2X
Production 125 Sets
Die-Cuts: 1-2X
Production 100 Sets
1 Albert Pujols/1,106 5.00
2 Barry Bonds/1,278 5.00
3 Gary Sheffield/1,023 1.50
4 Todd Helton/1,088 2.00
5 Scott Rolen/910 3.00
6 Manny Ramirez/1,014 3.00
7 Alex Rodriguez/995 5.00
8 Jim Thome/958 3.00
9 Jason Giambi/939 3.00
10 Frank Thomas/952 3.00

Production Line Slugging

NM/M
Complete Set (10): 25.00
Varying quantities produced
Black: 1-2X
Production 75 Sets
Die-Cuts: 1-2X
Production 100 Sets
1 Alex Rodriguez/604 6.00
2 Frank Thomas/562 3.00
3 Garret Anderson/541 2.00
4 Albert Pujols/667 6.00
5 Sammy Sosa/553 5.00
6 Gary Sheffield/604 2.00
7 Manny Ramirez/587 3.00
8 Jim Edmonds/617 2.00
9 Barry Bonds/688 6.00
10 Todd Helton/630 3.00

Timber & Threads

NM/M
Common Player: 4.00
Inserted 1:40
Studio Series: 1.5X
Production 50 Sets
1 Adam Dunn 6.00
2 Alex Rodriguez/Blue 10.00
3 Alex Rodriguez/White 10.00
4 Andruw Jones 6.00
5 Austin Kearns 6.00
6 Carlos Beltran 4.00
7 Carlos Lee 4.00
8 Frank Thomas 8.00
9 Greg Maddux 10.00
10 Hideo Nomo 10.00
11 Jeff Bagwell 8.00
12 Lance Berkman 4.00
13 Magglio Ordonez 4.00
14 Mike Sweeney 4.00
15 Randy Johnson 8.00
16 Rocco Baldelli 10.00
17 Roger Clemens 12.00
18 Sammy Sosa 12.00
19 Shawn Green 4.00
20 Tom Glavine 6.00
21 Adam Dunn 6.00
22 Andruw Jones 6.00
23 Bobby Abreu 4.00
24 Hank Blalock 6.00
25 Ivan Rodriguez 6.00
26 Jim Edmonds 6.00
27 Josh Phelps 4.00
28 Juan Gonzalez 6.00
29 Lance Berkman 4.00
30 Larry Walker 4.00
31 Magglio Ordonez 4.00
32 Manny Ramirez 8.00
33 Mike Piazza 10.00
34 Nomar Garciaparra 10.00
35 Paul LoDuca 4.00
36 Roberto Alomar 6.00
37 Rocco Baldelli 10.00
38 Sammy Sosa 12.00
39 Vernon Wells 4.00
40 Vladimir Guerrero 8.00

2004 Donruss Classics

NM/M
Complete Set (213):
Common Player: .40
Common (151-210): 3.00
Production 1,999
Pack (6): 6.00
Box (18): 90.00
1 Albert Pujols 2.50
2 Derek Jeter 3.00
3 Hank Blalock .50
4 Shannon Stewart .40
5 Jason Giambi 1.00
6 Carlos Lee .40

7 Trot Nixon .40
8 Bret Boone .50
9 Mark Mulder .40
10 Mariano Rivera .50
11 Scott Podsednik .75
12 Jim Edmonds .50
13 Mike Lowell .50
14 Robin Ventura .40
15 Brian Giles .50
16 Jose Vidro .40
17 Manny Ramirez .75
18 Alex Rodriquez 2.50
19 Carlos Beltran .50
20 Hideki Matsui 2.50
21 Johan Santana .40
22 Richie Sexson .50
23 Chipper Jones 1.00
24 Steve Finley .40
25 Mark Prior 1.50
26 Alexis Rios .40
27 Rafael Palmeiro .75
28 Jorge Posada .50
29 Barry Zito .50
30 Jamie Moyer .40
31 Preston Wilson .40
32 Miguel Cabrera .75
33 Pedro Martinez 1.00
34 Curt Schilling .75
35 Hee Seop Choi .40
36 Dontrelle Willis .50
37 Rafael Soriano .40
38 Richard Fischer .40
39 Brian Tallet .40
40 Jose Castillo .40
41 Wade Miller .40
42 Jose Contreras .40
43 Runelvys Hernandez .40
44 Joe Borchard .40
45 Kazuhisa Ishii .40
46 Jose Reyes .50
47 Adam Dunn .50
48 Randy Johnson 1.00
49 Brandon Phillips .40
50 Scott Rolen 1.00
51 Ken Griffey Jr. 1.50
52 Tom Glavine .50
53 Cliff Lee .40
54 Chien-Ming Wang .50
55 Roy Oswalt .50
56 Austin Kearns .50
57 Jhonny Peralta .40
58 Greg Maddux 1.50
59 Mark Grace .50
60 Jae Weong Seo .40
61 Nic Jackson .40
62 Roger Clemens 2.50
63 Jimmy Gobble .40
64 Travis Hafner .40
65 Paul Konerko .40
66 Jerome Williams .40
67 Ryan Klesko .50
68 Alexis Gomez .40
69 Omar Vizquel .50
70 Zach Day .40
71 Rickey Henderson .50
72 Morgan Ensberg .40
73 Josh Beckett .75
74 Garrett Atkins .40
75 Sean Casey .40
76 Julio Franco .40
77 Lyle Overbay .40
78 Josh Phelps .40
79 Juan Gonzalez .75
80 Rich Harden .40
81 Bernie Williams .50
82 Torii Hunter .50
83 Angel Berroa .40
84 Jody Gerut .40
85 Roberto Alomar .50
86 Byung-Hyun Kim .40
87 Jay Gibbons .40
88 Chone Figgins .40
89 Fred McGriff .50
90 Rich Aurilia .40
91 Xavier Nady .40
92 Marlon Byrd .40
93 Mike Piazza 1.50
94 Vladimir Guerrero 1.00
95 Shawn Green .50
96 Jeff Kent .50
97 Ivan Rodriguez .75
98 Jay Payton .40
99 Barry Larkin .50
100 Mike Sweeney .40
101 Adrian Beltre .40
102 Robby Hammock .40
103 Orlando Hudson .40
104 Mark Teixeira .50
105 Hong-Chih Kuo .40
106 Eric Chavez .50
107 Nick Johnson .40
108 Jacque Jones .40
109 Ken Harvey .40
110 Aramis Ramirez .40
111 Victor Martinez .40
112 Joe Crede .40
113 Jason Varitek .40
114 Troy Glaus .50
115 Billy Wagner .40
116 Kerry Wood 1.00
117 Hideo Nomo .50
118 Brandon Webb .40
119 Craig Biggio .40
120 Orlando Cabrera .40
121 Sammy Sosa 2.00
122 Bobby Abreu .50
123 Andruw Jones .75
124 Jeff Bagwell .75
125 Jim Thome 1.00
126 Javy Lopez .50
127 Luis Castillo .40
128 Todd Helton .75
129 Roy Halladay .50
130 Mike Mussina .50
131 Eric Byrnes .40
132 Eric Hinske .40
133 Nomar Garciaparra 2.00
134 Edgar Martinez .50
135 Rocco Baldelli .50
136 Miguel Tejada .50
137 Alfonso Soriano 1.00
138 Carlos Delgado .75
139 Rafael Furcal .50
140 Ichiro Suzuki 2.00
141 Aubrey Huff .40
142 Garret Anderson .50
143 Vernon Wells .40
144 Magglio Ordonez .50
145 Brett Myers .40
146 Luis Gonzalez .40
147 Lance Berkman .50
148 Frank Thomas .75
149 Gary Sheffield .50
150 Tim Hudson .50
151 Duke Snider 3.00
152 Carl Yastrzemski 4.00
153 Whitey Ford 3.00
154 Cal Ripken Jr. 8.00
155 Dwight Gooden 2.00
156 Warren Spahn 4.00
157 Bob Gibson 3.00
158 Don Mattingly 6.00
159 Jack Morris 2.00
160 Jim Bunning 2.00
161 Fergie Jenkins 2.00
162 Brooks Robinson 3.00
163 George Kell 2.00
164 Darryl Strawberry 2.00
165 Robin Roberts 2.00
166 Monte Irvin 2.00
167 Ernie Banks 4.00
168 Wade Boggs 3.00
169 Gaylord Perry 2.00
170 Keith Hernandez 2.00
171 Lou Brock 3.00
172 Frank Robinson 3.00
173 Nolan Ryan 8.00
174 Stan Musial 5.00
175 Eddie Murray 3.00
176 Byron Gettis 3.00
177 Merkin Valdez **RC** 5.00
178 Rickie Weeks 4.00
179 Akinori Otsuka **RC** 3.00
180 Brian Bruney 3.00
181 Freddy Guzman **RC** 3.00
182 Brendan Harris 3.00
183 John Gall **RC** 3.00
184 Jason Kubel 3.00
185 Delmon Young 4.00
186 Ryan Howard 3.00
187 Adam Loewen 3.00
188 J.D. Durbin 3.00
189 Dan Haren 3.00
190 Dustin McGowan 3.00
191 Chad Gaudin 3.00
192 Preston Larrison 3.00
193 Ramon Nivar 3.00
194 Ronald Belisario **RC** 3.00
195 Mike Gosling 3.00
196 Kevin Youkilis 3.00
197 Ryan Wagner 3.00
198 Bubba Nelson 3.00
199 Edwin Jackson 3.00
200 Chris Burke 3.00
201 Carlos Hines **RC** 3.00
202 Greg Dobbs **RC** 3.00
203 Jamie Brown **RC** 3.00
204 David Crouthers 3.00
205 Ian Snell **RC** 5.00
206 Gary Carter 3.00
207 Dale Murphy 3.00
208 Ryne Sandberg 5.00
209 Phil Niekro 2.00
210 Don Sutton 2.00
211 Alex Rodriguez/Yankees/SP 5.00
212 Alfonso Soriano/Rangers/SP 1.00
213 Greg Maddux/Cubs/SP 3.00

Timeless Tributes Green

Cards (1-150): 4-6X
Cards (151-210): 1-2X
Production 50 Sets

Timeless Tributes Red

Red (1-150): 2-4X
Red (151-210): 1-1.5X
Production 100 Sets

Timeless Tributes Platinum

No Pricing
Production One Set

Classic Singles Bat

NM/M

Quantity produced listed
1 Babe Ruth/15 250.00
3 Stan Musial/25 30.00
4 Ted Williams/25 100.00
5 Lou Gehrig/50 125.00
6 Eddie Murray/50 15.00
7 Roy Campanella/50 20.00
8 Robin Yount/50 20.00
9 Roberto Clemente/25 70.00
10 Don Mattingly/50 25.00
12 Carl Yastrzemski/50 20.00
13 Mark Grace/50 15.00
15 Rickey Henderson/50 15.00
16 Reggie Jackson/50 15.00
17 Pee Wee Reese/50 15.00
20 Roger Maris/25 40.00
21 Cal Ripken Jr./50 60.00
23 Willie Stargell/50 15.00
24 Paul Molitor/50 20.00
26 Alan Trammell/50 12.00
27 Sammy Sosa/50 20.00
28 Bobby Doerr/50 8.00
29 Rod Carew/50 15.00
30 Yogi Berra/25 20.00
32 George Brett/50 30.00

Classic Singles Jersey

NM/M

Quantity produced listed
Prime: No Pricing
Production One Set
2 Nolan Ryan/50 35.00
3 Stan Musial/15 50.00
6 Eddie Murray/100 10.00
7 Roy Campanella/Pants/50 20.00
8 Robin Yount/100 15.00
9 Roberto Clemente/25 75.00
10 Don Mattingly/100 20.00
11 Bob Gibson/15 25.00
12 Carl Yastrzemski/50 20.00
13 Mark Grace/25 20.00
14 Jack Morris/100 6.00
15 Rickey Henderson/25 20.00
16 Reggie Jackson/50 15.00
17 Pee Wee Reese/25 25.00
18 Marty Marion/100 6.00
19 Tommy John/100 6.00
20 Roger Maris/25 50.00
21 Cal Ripken Jr./25 75.00
22 Red Schoendienst/25 10.00
23 Willie Stargell/100 15.00
24 Paul Molitor/100 10.00
25 Whitey Ford/50 25.00
26 Alan Trammell/100 10.00
27 Sammy Sosa/50 20.00
28 Bobby Doerr/50 8.00
29 Rod Carew/100 10.00
30 Yogi Berra/15 35.00
31 Phil Rizzuto/25 20.00
32 George Brett/25 40.00

Classic Singles Jersey-Bat

NM/M

Quantity produced listed
Prime: No Pricing
Production One Set
2 Nolan Ryan/25 50.00
3 Stan Musial/15 45.00
6 Eddie Murray/25 25.00
7 Roy Campanella/Pants/25 35.00
8 Robin Yount/25 40.00
9 Roberto Clemente/25 125.00
10 Don Mattingly/25 40.00
12 Carl Yastrzemski/25 50.00
13 Mark Grace/25 20.00
15 Rickey Henderson/25 25.00
16 Reggie Jackson/25 25.00
17 Pee Wee Reese/25 25.00
20 Roger Maris/15 75.00
21 Cal Ripken Jr./25 75.00
23 Willie Stargell/25 20.00
24 Paul Molitor/25 25.00
26 Alan Trammell/25 20.00
27 Sammy Sosa/25 25.00
28 Bobby Doerr/25 25.00
29 Rod Carew/25 30.00
30 Yogi Berra/15 40.00
32 George Brett/25 50.00

Classic Combos Bat

NM/M

Quantity produced listed
1 Babe Ruth, Lou Gehrig/25 375.00
2 Roy Campanella, Pee Wee Reese/50 25.00
3 Ted Williams, Carl Yastrzemski/25 125.00
4 Roberto Clemente, Willie Stargell/25 100.00
5 Eddie Murray, Cal Ripken Jr./50 50.00
6 Roger Maris, Yogi Berra/25 65.00
10 Nolan Ryan, Rod Carew/50 35.00
11 Don Mattingly, Rickey Henderson/50 40.00
15 Robin Yount, Paul Molitor/50 40.00
16 Mark Grace, Sammy Sosa/50 30.00
17 Ted Williams, Bobby Doerr/25 80.00
18 Reggie Jackson, Rod Carew/50 25.00

Classic Combos Jersey

NM/M

Quantity produced listed
Prime: No Pricing
Production One Set
1 Babe Ruth/Pants, Lou Gehrig/Pants/15 500.00
2 Roy Campanella/Pants, Pee Wee Reese/25 30.00
3 Ted Williams, Carl Yastrzemski/15 200.00
4 Roberto Clemente, Willie Stargell/25 85.00
5 Eddie Murray, Cal Ripken Jr./25 75.00
6 Roger Maris, Yogi Berra/25 65.00
8 Whitey Ford, Yogi Berra/25 30.00
9 Marty Marion, Stan Musial/25 40.00
10 Nolan Ryan, Rod Carew/25 40.00
11 Don Mattingly, Rickey Henderson/50 40.00
12 Jack Morris, Alan Trammell/50 15.00
13 Whitey Ford, Phil Rizzuto/25 30.00
14 Marty Marion, Red Schoendienst/25 15.00
15 Robin Yount, Paul Molitor/50 40.00
16 Mark Grace, Sammy Sosa/50 30.00
17 Ted Williams, Bobby Doerr/15 150.00
18 Reggie Jackson, Rod Carew/50 25.00

Classic Combos Quad

NM/M

Quantity produced listed
Prime: No Pricing
Production One Set
2 Roy Campanella/Pants, Pee Wee Reese/25 50.00
3 Ted Williams, Carl Yastrzemski/15 250.00
4 Roberto Clemente, Willie Stargell/25 200.00
5 Eddie Murray, Cal Ripken Jr./25 125.00
6 Roger Maris, Yogi Berra/15 150.00
10 Nolan Ryan, Rod Carew/25 70.00
11 Don Mattingly, Rickey Henderson/25 80.00
15 Robin Yount, Paul Molitor/25 75.00
16 Mark Grace, Sammy Sosa/25 60.00
17 Ted Williams, Bobby Doerr/15 200.00
18 Reggie Jackson, Rod Carew/25 40.00

Dress Code Bat

NM/M

Common Player: 5.00
Production 50 Sets
Combo Material: 1-1.5X
Production 50 Sets
1 Derek Jeter 25.00
2 Kerry Wood 15.00
3 Nomar Garciaparra 15.00
4 Jacque Jones 5.00
5 Mark Teixeira 6.00
6 Troy Glaus 8.00
7 Todd Helton 10.00
8 Miguel Tejada 6.00
9 Mike Piazza 12.00
11 Mike Sweeney 5.00
12 Albert Pujols 20.00
13 Rickey Henderson 10.00
14 Chipper Jones 10.00
15 Don Mattingly 25.00
16 Shawn Green 5.00
17 Mark Grace 10.00
18 Jason Giambi 8.00
19 Barry Zito 8.00
20 Sammy Sosa 15.00
22 Rafael Palmeiro 10.00
23 Frank Thomas 10.00
24 Manny Ramirez 8.00
25 Mike Mussina 10.00
26 Magglio Ordonez 6.00
27 Rocco Baldelli 12.00
28 Andruw Jones 8.00
29 Torii Hunter 6.00
30 Ivan Rodriguez 10.00
31 Jeff Bagwell 10.00
32 Mark Mulder 6.00
33 Trot Nixon 10.00
34 Cal Ripken Jr. 60.00
35 Dontrelle Willis 8.00
36 Hank Blalock 8.00
37 Brandon Webb 8.00
38 Miguel Cabrera 10.00
39 Hideo Nomo 10.00
41 Tim Hudson 8.00
42 Pedro Martinez 12.00
43 Hee Seop Choi 6.00
44 Randy Johnson 10.00
45 Tony Gwynn 15.00
46 Mark Prior 10.00
47 Eric Chavez 8.00
48 Alex Rodriguez 15.00
50 Alfonso Soriano 12.00

Dress Code Jersey

NM/M

Common Player: 4.00
Production 100 Sets
Number: 1X
Production 100 Sets
Prime: 2X
Production 25 Sets
1 Derek Jeter 25.00
2 Kerry Wood 15.00
3 Nomar Garciaparra 10.00
4 Jacque Jones 4.00
5 Mark Teixeira 5.00
6 Troy Glaus 6.00
7 Todd Helton 6.00
8 Miguel Tejada 6.00
9 Mike Piazza 10.00
11 Mike Sweeney 4.00
12 Albert Pujols 15.00
13 Rickey Henderson 8.00
14 Chipper Jones 8.00
15 Don Mattingly 25.00
16 Shawn Green 5.00
17 Mark Grace 10.00
18 Jason Giambi 8.00
19 Barry Zito 8.00
20 Sammy Sosa 12.00
21 Jay Gibbons 4.00
22 Rafael Palmeiro 8.00
23 Frank Thomas 8.00
24 Manny Ramirez 6.00
25 Mike Mussina 8.00
26 Magglio Ordonez 6.00
27 Rocco Baldelli 6.00
28 Andruw Jones 8.00
29 Torii Hunter 6.00
30 Ivan Rodriguez 8.00
31 Jeff Bagwell 8.00
32 Mark Mulder 6.00
33 Trot Nixon 5.00
34 Cal Ripken Jr./25 80.00
35 Dontrelle Willis 6.00
36 Hank Blalock 5.00
37 Brandon Webb 4.00
38 Miguel Cabrera 12.00
39 Hideo Nomo 8.00
40 Shannon Stewart 4.00
41 Tim Hudson 6.00
42 Pedro Martinez 8.00
43 Hee Seop Choi 4.00
44 Randy Johnson 8.00
45 Tony Gwynn 10.00
46 Mark Prior 10.00
47 Eric Chavez 6.00
48 Alex Rodriguez 10.00
49 Johan Santana 4.00
50 Alfonso Soriano 8.00

Dress Code Combos Signature

NM/M

Quantity produced listed
Prime: No Pricing
Production One Set
4 Jacque Jones/Jsy/25 15.00
21 Jay Gibbons/Jsy/25 25.00
32 Mark Mulder/Jsy/25 35.00
33 Trot Nixon/Jsy/25 50.00
35 Dontrelle Willis/Jsy/25 40.00
38 Miguel Cabrera/Jsy/25 70.00
40 Shannon Stewart/Jsy/25 20.00
49 Johan Santana/Jsy/25 40.00

Famous Foursomes

NM/M

Production 99 Sets
1 Roy Campanella, Pee Wee Reese, Jackie Robinson, Duke Snider 15.00
2 Stan Musial, Bob Gibson, Red Schoendienst, Clete Boyer 15.00

Famous Foursomes Jersey

No Pricing
Production 10 Sets
Prime: No Pricing
Production One Set

Legendary Hats Material

NM/M

Quantity produced listed
2 Mike Schmidt/25 50.00
6 George Brett/25 60.00
14 Cal Ripken Jr./25 100.00
16 Kirby Puckett/25 30.00
20 Reggie Jackson/Yanks/25 25.00
22 Ernie Banks/25 35.00
29 Dave Winfield/25 15.00
40 Wade Boggs/25 25.00
42 Rickey Henderson/A'S/25 20.00
49 Reggie Jackson/Angels/25 25.00
51 Rafael Palmeiro/25 20.00
52 Sammy Sosa/25 30.00
55 Steve Carlton/25 15.00
56 Rod Carew/Angels/25 20.00
60 R Henderson/Angels/25 20.00

Legendary Jackets Material

NM/M

Production 100 Sets
2 Mike Schmidt 15.00
8 Reggie Jackson A's 15.00
17 Don Mattingly 20.00
32 Gary Carter 5.00
54 Nolan Ryan 30.00
56 Rod Carew Angels 10.00

Legendary Jerseys Material

NM/M

Quantity produced listed
Number: 1X
Production 3-50

No pricing for production 15 or less.
Prime: No Pricing
Production One Set
1 Tony Gwynn/50 20.00
2 Mike Schmidt/25 35.00
3 Johnny Bench/50 15.00
6 George Brett/25 50.00
7 Carlton Fisk/50 10.00
8 Reggie Jackson/25 30.00
9 Joe Morgan/25 15.00
10 Bo Jackson/25 50.00
12 Andre Dawson/50 10.00
13 R Henderson/25 20.00
14 Cal Ripken Jr./25 85.00
15 Dale Murphy/25 30.00
16 Kirby Puckett/50 15.00
17 Don Mattingly/50 25.00
18 Brooks Robinson/50 20.00
19 Orlando Cepeda/50 8.00
20 Reggie Jackson/25 25.00
21 Roberto Clemente/25 75.00
23 Frank Robinson/50 10.00
24 Harmon Killebrew/50 15.00
25 Willie Stargell/50 20.00
27 Carl Yastrzemski/50 25.00
29 Dave Winfield/50 10.00
30 Eddie Murray/50 20.00
31 Eddie Mathews/25 25.00
32 Gary Carter/50 8.00
33 Rod Carew/25 20.00
36 Paul Molitor/50 15.00
39 Robin Yount/50 25.00
40 Wade Boggs/50 15.00
42 Rickey Henderson/25 25.00
44 Yogi Berra/15 35.00
46 Luis Aparicio/50 8.00
47 Phil Rizzuto/25 20.00
48 Roger Maris/25 40.00
49 Reggie Jackson/50 15.00
51 Rafael Palmeiro/50 10.00
52 Sammy Sosa/50 20.00
53 Roger Clemens/50 25.00
p4 Nolan Ryan/50 30.00
55 Steve Carlton/50 8.00
56 Rod Carew/50 15.00
57 Whitey Ford/25 35.00

Legendary Leather Material

NM/M
Quantity produced listed
16 Kirby Puckett/ Fld Glv/25 40.00
32 Gary Carter/ Fld Glv/25 35.00
51 Rafael Palmeiro/ Fld Glv/25 25.00
52 Sammy Sosa/ Btg Glv/25 50.00
55 Steve Carlton/ Fld Glv/25 15.00
58 Fergie Jenkins/ Fld Glv/25 15.00

Legendary Lumberjacks

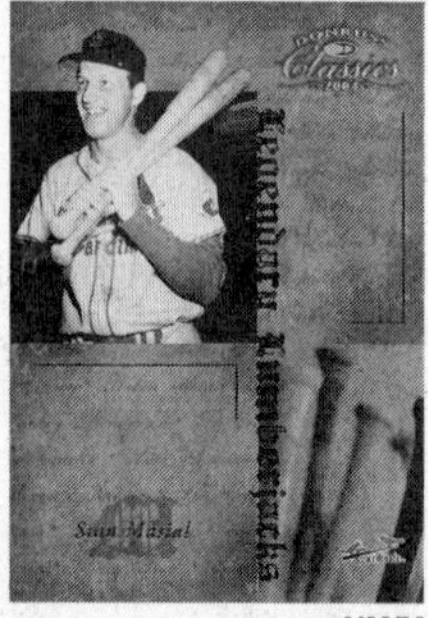

NM/M
Common Player: 2.00
Production 1,000 Sets
Spikes: 1-2X
Production 100 Sets
Hats: 2-3X
Production 50 Sets
Jackets: 2-3X
Production 50 Sets
Jerseys: 1X
Production 500 Sets
Leather: 1-2X
Production 100 Sets
Pants: 2-3X
Production 50 Sets
1 Tony Gwynn 3.00
2 Mike Schmidt 5.00
3 Johnny Bench 4.00
4 Roger Maris 5.00
5 Ted Williams 8.00
6 George Brett 6.00
7 Carlton Fisk 2.00
8 Reggie Jackson 3.00
9 Joe Morgan 2.00
10 Bo Jackson 3.00
11 Stan Musial 4.00
12 Andre Dawson 2.00
13 Rickey Henderson 2.00
14 Cal Ripken Jr. 8.00
15 Dale Murphy 2.00
16 Kirby Puckett 4.00
17 Don Mattingly 5.00
18 Brooks Robinson 3.00
19 Orlando Cepeda 2.00
20 Reggie Jackson 3.00
21 Roberto Clemente 6.00
22 Ernie Banks 4.00
23 Frank Robinson 3.00
24 Harmon Killebrew 3.00
25 Willie Stargell 3.00
26 Al Kaline 4.00
27 Carl Yastrzemski 4.00
28 Duke Snider 3.00
29 Dave Winfield 2.00
30 Eddie Murray 3.00
31 Eddie Matthews 3.00
32 Gary Carter 2.00
33 Rod Carew 3.00
34 Jimmie Foxx 4.00
35 Mel Ott 3.00
36 Paul Molitor 3.00
37 Thurman Munson 4.00
38 Rogers Hornsby 3.00
39 Robin Yount 4.00
40 Wade Boggs 3.00
41 Jackie Robinson 5.00
42 Rickey Henderson 2.00
43 Ty Cobb 5.00
44 Yogi Berra 3.00
45 Roy Campanella 3.00
46 Luis Aparicio 2.00
47 Phil Rizzuto 3.00
48 Roger Maris 5.00
49 Reggie Jackson 3.00
50 Lou Gehrig 6.00
51 Rafael Palmeiro 3.00
52 Sammy Sosa 5.00
53 Roger Clemens 6.00
54 Nolan Ryan 8.00
55 Steve Carlton 3.00
56 Rod Carew 3.00
57 Whitey Ford 3.00
58 Fergie Jenkins 2.00
59 Babe Ruth 8.00
60 R Henderson 2.00

Legendary Lumberjacks Material

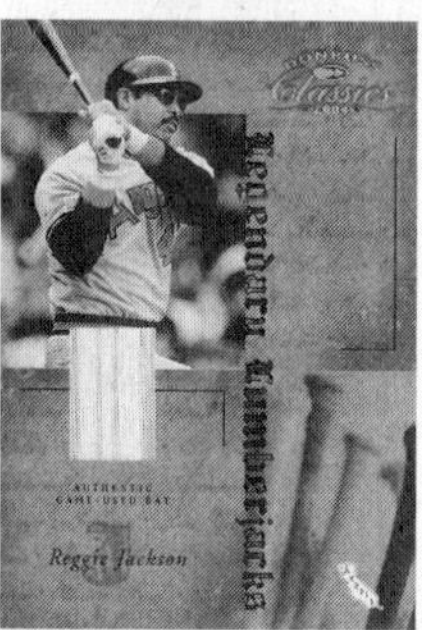

NM/M
Quantity produced listed
1 Tony Gwynn/100 15.00
2 Mike Schmidt/100 15.00
3 Johnny Bench/100 12.00
4 Roger Maris /25 40.00
5 Ted Williams/25 100.00
6 George Brett/100 25.00
7 Carlton Fisk/100 10.00
8 Reggie Jackson /100 12.00
9 Joe Morgan/100 5.00
10 Bo Jackson/100 15.00
11 Stan Musial/25 35.00
12 Andre Dawson/100 5.00
13 R Henderson/100 10.00
14 Cal Ripken Jr./100 40.00
15 Dale Murphy/100 12.00
16 Kirby Puckett/100 15.00
17 Don Mattingly/100 20.00
18 Brooks Robinson/ 100 15.00
19 Orlando Cepeda/100 5.00
20 Reggie Jackson/100 12.00
21 Roberto Clemente/25 65.00
22 Ernie Banks/100 15.00
23 Frank Robinson/100 15.00
24 Harmon Killebrew/ 100 20.00
25 Willie Stargell/100 15.00
26 Al Kaline/100 15.00
27 Carl Yastrzemski/100 15.00
29 Dave Winfield/100 5.00
30 Eddie Murray/100 15.00
31 Eddie Mathews/50 20.00
32 Gary Carter/100 8.00
33 Rod Carew/100 10.00
35 Mel Ott/25 35.00
36 Paul Molitor/100 10.00
37 Thurman Munson/50 20.00
38 Rogers Hornsby/25 50.00
39 Robin Yount/100 15.00
40 Wade Boggs/100 10.00
42 Rickey Henderson/50 10.00
44 Yogi Berra/25 40.00
45 Roy Campanella/25 30.00
46 Luis Aparicio/100 8.00
48 Roger Maris/25 40.00
49 Reggie Jackson/100 15.00
50 Lou Gehrig/25 125.00
51 Rafael Palmeiro/100 8.00
52 Sammy Sosa/100 15.00
56 Rod Carew/100 8.00
60 R Henderson/100 10.00

Legendary Pants Material

NM/M
Quantity produced listed
1 Tony Gwynn/25 25.00
12 Andre Dawson/25 10.00
24 Harmon Killebrew/50 20.00
26 Al Kaline/50 20.00
45 Roy Campanella/25 25.00
46 Luis Aparicio/50 10.00
47 Phil Rizzuto/50 15.00
48 Roger Maris A's/25 30.00
51 Rafael Palmeiro/25 20.00
56 Rod Carew/Angels/50 15.00
57 Whitey Ford/25 25.00
58 Fergie Jenkins/25 20.00

Legendary Spikes Material

NM/M
Quantity produced listed
13 R Henderson/ Yanks/25 30.00
17 Don Mattingly/50 40.00
29 Dave Winfield/50 15.00
42 Rickey Henderson/ A's/25 30.00
51 Rafael Palmeiro/25 25.00
52 Sammy Sosa/50 30.00
60 R Henderson/ Angels/25 30.00

Membership

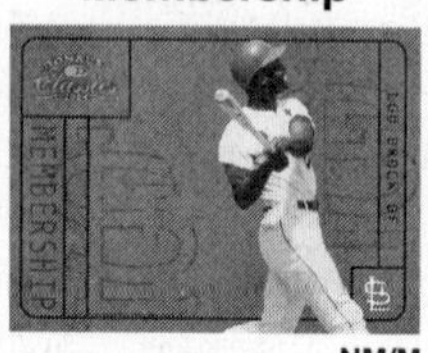

NM/M
Complete Set (25): 70.00
Common Player: 2.00
Production 2,499 Sets
1 Stan Musial 4.00
2 Ted Williams 5.00
3 Early Wynn 2.00
4 Roberto Clemente 5.00
5 Al Kaline 4.00
6 Bob Gibson 3.00
7 Lou Brock 2.00
8 Carl Yastrzemski 4.00
9 Gaylord Perry 2.00
10 Fergie Jenkins 2.00
11 Steve Carlton 2.00
12 Reggie Jackson 3.00
13 Rod Carew 3.00
14 Bert Blyleven 2.00
15 Mike Schmidt 4.00
16 Nolan Ryan 6.00
17 Robin Yount 4.00
18 George Brett 6.00
19 Eddie Murray 3.00
20 Tony Gwynn 3.00
21 Cal Ripken Jr. 8.00
22 Randy Johnson 4.00
23 Sammy Sosa 5.00
24 Rafael Palmeiro 3.00
25 Roger Clemens 5.00

Membership VIP Bat

NM/M
Quantity produced listed
1 Stan Musial/25 40.00
2 Ted Williams/25 100.00
4 Roberto Clemente/25 65.00
5 Al Kaline/25 20.00
7 Lou Brock/25 20.00
8 Carl Yastrzemski/25 25.00
11 Steve Carlton/25 15.00
12 Reggie Jackson/25 25.00
13 Rod Carew/25 20.00
15 Mike Schmidt/25 30.00
17 Robin Yount/25 25.00
19 Eddie Murray/25 25.00
20 Tony Gwynn/25 25.00
22 Randy Johnson/25 20.00
23 Sammy Sosa/25 30.00
24 Rafael Palmeiro/25 20.00
25 Roger Clemens/25 25.00

Membership VIP Jersey

NM/M
Quantity produced listed
Prime: No Pricing
Production One Set
1 Stan Musial/15 40.00
4 Roberto Clemente/25 75.00
5 Al Kaline/Pants/25 20.00
8 Carl Yastrzemski/25 30.00
9 Gaylord Perry/25 10.00
10 Fergie Jenkins/ Pants/25 15.00
11 Steve Carlton/25 15.00
12 Reggie Jackson/25 25.00
13 Rod Carew/25 20.00
14 Bert Blyleven/25 10.00
15 Mike Schmidt/25 30.00
16 Nolan Ryan/25 35.00
17 Robin Yount/25 25.00
18 George Brett/25 40.00
19 Eddie Murray/25 25.00
20 Tony Gwynn/25 25.00
21 Cal Ripken Jr./25 85.00
22 Randy Johnson/25 20.00
23 Sammy Sosa/25 30.00
24 Rafael Palmeiro/25 20.00
25 Roger Clemens/25 25.00

Membership VIP Signatures

NM/M
Quantity produced listed
5 Al Kaline/20 50.00
9 Gaylord Perry/50 15.00
10 Fergie Jenkins/50 20.00
11 Steve Carlton/20 30.00
14 Bert Blyleven/50 10.00

Membership VIP Combos Material

NM/M
Quantity produced listed
Prime: No Pricing
Production One Set
1 Stan Musial/ Bat-Jsy/15 40.00
4 Roberto Clemente/ Bat-Jsy/25 100.00
5 Al Kaline/ Bat-Pants/25 30.00
8 Carl Yastrzemski/ Bat-Jsy/25 50.00
10 Fergie Jenkins/ Fld Glv-Pants/25 15.00
11 Steve Carlton/ Bat-Jsy/25 15.00
12 Reggie Jackson/ Bat-Jsy/25 30.00
13 Rod Carew/ Bat-Pants/25 25.00
15 Mike Schmidt/ Bat-Jsy/25 40.00
16 Nolan Ryan/ Bat-Jsy/25 50.00
17 Robin Yount/ Bat-Jsy/25 40.00
18 George Brett/ Bat-Jsy/25 50.00
19 Eddie Murray/ Bat-Jsy/25 30.00
20 Tony Gwynn/ Bat-Jsy/25 40.00
21 Cal Ripken Jr./ Bat-Jsy/25 80.00
22 Randy Johnson/ Bat-Jsy/25 25.00
23 Sammy Sosa/ Bat-Jsy/25 35.00
24 Rafael Palmeiro/ Bat-Jsy/25 25.00
25 Roger Clemens/ Bat-Jsy/25 30.00

Membership VIP Combos Signature

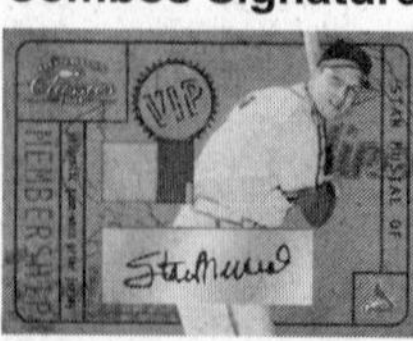

NM/M
Quantity produced listed
Prime: No Pricing
Production One Set
5 Al Kaline/Pants/25 50.00
9 Gaylord Perry/Jsy/50 15.00
10 Fergie Jenkins/ Pants/50 20.00
11 Steve Carlton/Jsy/25 40.00
14 Bert Blyleven/Jsy/50 15.00

National Trading Card Day

As part of its participation in NTCD on April 3, Donruss-Playoff issued a foil pack with four baseball player cards and

two football, plus a header. Only the baseball players are listed here. Fronts have game-action photos on a ghosted background; backs have recent stats, biographical data and career highlights. The NTCD logo appears on front.

NM/M
Unopened Pack: 3.00
Common Player: .25
DP-1 Albert Pujols .50
DP-2 Roger Clemens .25
DP-3 Mike Piazza .25
DP-4 Alfonso Soriano .25

October Heroes

NM/M
Production 2,499 Sets
1 Reggie Jackson 3.00
2 Bob Gibson 3.00
3 Carlton Fisk 2.00
4 Whitey Ford 2.00
5 George Brett 5.00
6 Roberto Clemente 5.00
7 Roy Campanella 3.00
8 Babe Ruth 6.00

October Heroes Bat

NM/M
Quantity produced listed
1 Reggie Jackson/25 25.00
3 Carlton Fisk/25 25.00
6 Roberto Clemente/25 65.00
7 Roy Campanella/25 25.00

October Heroes Fabric

NM/M
Quantity produced listed
2 Bob Gibson/Jsy/15 30.00
3 Carlton Fisk/Jsy/25 20.00
4 Whitey Ford/Jsy/25 20.00
5 George Brett/Jsy/25 40.00
7 Roy Campanella/ Pants/25 20.00

October Heroes Signature

NM/M
Quantity produced listed
4 Whitey Ford/50 40.00

October Heroes Combos Material

NM/M
Quantity produced listed
1 Reggie Jackson/ Bat-Hat/25 40.00
3 Carlton Fisk/ Bat-Jsy/25 30.00
5 George Brett/ Bat-Jsy/25 50.00
7 Roy Campanella/ Bat-Pants/25 35.00

October Heroes Combos Signature

NM/M
Quantity produced listed
4 Whitey Ford/Jsy/50 45.00

Significant Signatures Green

NM/M
Quantity produced listed
3 Hank Blalock/25 40.00
4 Shannon Stewart/50 10.00
7 Trot Nixon/25 30.00
13 Mike Lowell/25 25.00
14 Robin Ventura/25 15.00
19 Carlos Beltran/25 50.00
21 Johan Santana/50 35.00
24 Steve Finley/25 25.00
26 Alexis Rios/100 25.00
32 Miguel Cabrera/50 50.00
36 Dontrelle Willis/25 25.00
37 Rafael Soriano/100 6.00
38 Richard Fischer/100 6.00
39 Brian Tallet/100 6.00
40 Jose Castillo/100 6.00
41 Wade Miller/25 20.00
43 Runelvys Hernandez/ 20 10.00
44 Joe Borchard/50 8.00
47 Adam Dunn/25 30.00
49 Brandon Phillips/50 6.00
53 Cliff Lee/50 10.00
54 Chien-Ming Wang/ 50 150.00
57 Jhonny Peralta/100 6.00
60 Jae Weong Seo/50 15.00
61 Nic Jackson/100 8.00
63 Jimmy Gobble/45 10.00
64 Travis Hafner/50 12.00
66 Jerome Williams/50 20.00
68 Alexis Gomez/50 6.00
70 Zach Day/50 8.00
72 Morgan Ensberg/50 8.00
74 Garrett Atkins/99 6.00
77 Lyle Overbay/100 15.00
78 Josh Phelps/25 10.00
79 Juan Gonzalez/25 45.00
80 Rich Harden/50 15.00
84 Jody Gerut/50 15.00
87 Jay Gibbons/50 15.00
88 Chone Figgins/50 10.00
98 Jay Payton/50 10.00
99 Barry Larkin/25 40.00
102 Robby Hammock/50 6.00
103 Orlando Hudson/50 8.00
105 Hong-Chih Kuo/50 30.00
106 Eric Chavez/25 35.00
108 Jacque Jones/50 10.00
109 Ken Harvey/100 8.00
110 Aramis Ramirez/50 20.00
111 Victor Martinez/50 20.00
112 Joe Crede/50 10.00
113 Jason Varitek/25 40.00
118 Brandon Webb/25 15.00
121 Sammy Sosa/21 150.00
127 Luis Castillo/25 10.00
134 Edgar Martinez/25 40.00
145 Brett Myers/50 8.00
149 Gary Sheffield/25 25.00
151 Duke Snider/25 35.00
153 Whitey Ford/25 40.00
155 Dwight Gooden/50 20.00
158 Don Mattingly/25 100.00
159 Jack Morris/50 10.00
160 Jim Bunning/25 25.00
161 Fergie Jenkins/50 15.00
163 George Kell/50 15.00
164 Darryl Strawberry/50 20.00
165 Robin Roberts/25 30.00
166 Monte Irvin/25 20.00
167 Ernie Banks/25 60.00
168 Wade Boggs/25 40.00
169 Gaylord Perry/50 10.00
170 Keith Hernandez/50 20.00
172 Frank Robinson/25 30.00
173 Nolan Ryan/25 120.00
174 Stan Musial/25 70.00
175 Eddie Murray/25 50.00
176 Byron Gettis/100 6.00
177 Merkin Valdez/100 20.00
178 Rickie Weeks/25 50.00
180 Brian Bruney/100 6.00
181 Freddy Guzman/100 6.00
182 Brendan Harris/100 6.00
183 John Gall/100 8.00
184 Jason Kubel/100 12.00
185 Delmon Young/50 30.00
186 Ryan Howard/100 80.00
187 Adam Loewen/100 15.00
188 J.D. Durbin/100 8.00
189 Dan Haren/100 10.00
190 Dustin McGowan/100 10.00
191 Chad Gaudin/100 6.00
192 Preston Larrison/100 6.00
193 Ramon Nivar/100 6.00
195 Mike Gosling/100 6.00
196 Kevin Youkilis/100 15.00
197 Ryan Wagner/100 10.00
198 Bubba Nelson/100 8.00
199 Edwin Jackson/100 10.00
200 Chris Burke/100 6.00
201 Carlos Hines/100 10.00
202 Greg Dobbs/50 6.00
203 Jamie Brown/100 8.00
204 David Crouthers/100 6.00
205 Ian Snell/100 30.00
206 Gary Carter/50 25.00
207 Dale Murphy/50 40.00
208 Ryne Sandberg/50 75.00
209 Phil Niekro/50 20.00
210 Don Sutton/50 15.00

Significant Signatures Red

NM/M
Quantity produced listed
3 Hank Blalock/50 30.00
4 Shannon Stewart/100 8.00
6 Carlos Lee/25 20.00
7 Trot Nixon/50 20.00

9 Mark Mulder/25 30.00
12 Jim Edmonds/25 30.00
13 Mike Lowell/50 20.00
14 Robin Ventura/50 10.00
16 Jose Vidro/25 20.00
19 Carlos Beltran/25 50.00
21 Johan Santana/100 30.00
24 Steve Finley/100 20.00
26 Alexis Rios/250 25.00
27 Rafael Palmeiro/25 65.00
28 Jorge Posada/25 45.00
32 Miguel Cabrera/100 40.00
36 Dontrelle Willis/100 25.00
37 Rafael Soriano/250 6.00
38 Richard Fischer/250 6.00
39 Brian Tallet/250 6.00
40 Jose Castillo/250 6.00
41 Wade Miller/92 15.00
42 Jose Contreras/25 25.00
43 Runelvys Hernandez/50 8.00
44 Joe Borchard/250 6.00
47 Adam Dunn/25 30.00
49 Brandon Phillips/70 6.00
50 Scott Rolen/25 35.00
53 Cliff Lee/100 8.00
54 Chien-Ming Wang/250 100.00
55 Roy Oswalt/25 30.00
56 Austin Kearns/25 20.00
57 Jhonny Peralta/250 6.00
60 Jae Weong Seo/100 10.00
61 Nic Jackson/250 8.00
63 Jimmy Gobble/200 10.00
64 Travis Hafner/100 12.00
65 Paul Konerko/25 15.00
66 Jerome Williams/250 20.00
68 Alexis Gomez/100 6.00
70 Zach Day/100 8.00
72 Morgan Ensberg/100 8.00
74 Garrett Atkins/245 6.00
76 Julio Franco/25 20.00
77 Lyle Overbay/250 15.00
78 Josh Phelps/50 8.00
79 Juan Gonzalez/25 45.00
80 Rich Harden/150 10.00
82 Torii Hunter/25 30.00
84 Jody Gerut/100 15.00
87 Jay Gibbons/100 15.00
88 Chone Figgins/100 10.00
90 Rich Aurilia/25 15.00
92 Marlon Byrd/25 15.00
98 Jay Payton/100 8.00
99 Barry Larkin/25 40.00
102 Robby Hammock/150 6.00
103 Orlando Hudson/100 8.00
105 Hong-Chih Kuo/100 30.00
106 Eric Chavez/25 35.00
107 Nick Johnson/25 15.00
108 Jacque Jones/100 10.00
109 Ken Harvey/250 8.00
110 Aramis Ramirez/100 20.00
111 Victor Martinez/99 20.00
112 Joe Crede/250 10.00
113 Jason Varitek/50 35.00
114 Troy Glaus/25 30.00
118 Brandon Webb/50 15.00
119 Craig Biggio/25 30.00
120 Orlando Cabrera/50 10.00
121 Sammy Sosa/25 150.00
122 Bobby Abreu/25 15.00
123 Andruw Jones/25 30.00
124 Jeff Bagwell/25 65.00
127 Luis Castillo/50 10.00
131 Eric Byrnes/25 10.00
132 Eric Hinske/25 15.00
134 Edgar Martinez/50 30.00
135 Rocco Baldelli/25 40.00
143 Vernon Wells/25 15.00
144 Magglio Ordonez/25 30.00
145 Brett Myers/100 8.00
149 Gary Sheffield/50 20.00
150 Tim Hudson/25 40.00
151 Duke Snider/50 30.00
153 Whitey Ford/50 40.00
155 Dwight Gooden/100 20.00
156 Warren Spahn/25 45.00
158 Don Mattingly/25 100.00
159 Jack Morris/100 10.00
160 Jim Bunning/100 20.00
161 Fergie Jenkins/100 15.00
163 George Kell/100 15.00
164 Darryl Strawberry/100 20.00
165 Robin Roberts/100 15.00
166 Monte Irvin/100 15.00
167 Ernie Banks/50 50.00
168 Wade Boggs/50 30.00
169 Gaylord Perry/100 10.00
170 Keith Hernandez/100 20.00
171 Lou Brock/25 30.00
172 Frank Robinson/50 25.00
173 Nolan Ryan/50 85.00
174 Stan Musial/50 60.00
175 Eddie Murray/50 50.00
176 Byron Gettis/250 6.00
177 Merkin Valdez/250 15.00
178 Rickie Weeks/250 40.00
180 Brian Bruney/250 6.00
181 Freddy Guzman/250 6.00
182 Brendan Harris/250 6.00
183 John Gall/250 8.00
184 Jason Kubel/250 10.00
185 Delmon Young/100 30.00
186 Ryan Howard/250 70.00
187 Adam Loewen/250 15.00
188 J.D. Durbin/250 8.00
189 Dan Haren/250 10.00
190 Dustin McGowan/250 10.00
191 Chad Gaudin/250 6.00
192 Preston Larrison/250 6.00
193 Ramon Nivar/250 6.00
195 Mike Gosling/250 6.00
196 Kevin Youkilis/250 15.00
197 Ryan Wagner/250 10.00
198 Bubba Nelson/250 8.00
199 Edwin Jackson/250 10.00
200 Chris Burke/250 6.00
201 Carlos Hines/250 10.00
202 Greg Dobbs/100 6.00
203 Jamie Brown/250 8.00
204 David Crouthers/250 6.00
205 Ian Snell/250 25.00
206 Gary Carter/100 20.00
207 Dale Murphy/50 40.00
208 Ryne Sandberg/25 85.00
209 Phil Niekro/100 15.00
210 Don Sutton/100 15.00

Team Colors Bat

NM/M

Quantity produced listed
2 Steve Garvey/50 10.00
3 Eric Davis/25 15.00
4 Al Oliver/50 8.00
6 Bobby Doerr/25 20.00
7 Paul Molitor/50 15.00
8 Dale Murphy/50 20.00
11 Jose Canseco/50 20.00
12 Jim Rice/50 12.00
13 Will Clark/50 25.00
14 Alan Trammell/50 12.00
16 Dwight Evans/50 15.00
18 Dave Parker/Pirates/25 10.00
21 Andre Dawson/Expos/50 10.00
22 Darryl Strawberry/Dgr/50 10.00
23 George Foster/50 8.00
26 Bo Jackson/50 30.00
27 Cal Ripken Jr./50 50.00
28 Deion Sanders/25 15.00
29 Don Mattingly/Jkt/50 25.00
30 Mark Grace/50 15.00
31 Fred Lynn/50 8.00
33 Ernie Banks/25 30.00
34 Gary Carter/50 12.00
35 Roger Maris/25 40.00
36 Ron Santo/50 12.00
38 Tony Gwynn/50 15.00
40 Red Schoendienst/25 15.00
41 Steve Carlton/25 15.00
42 Wade Boggs/25 25.00
44 Luis Aparicio/25 10.00
46 Andre Dawson/Cubs/25 12.00
48 Darryl Strawberry/Mets/50 10.00
49 Dave Parker/Reds/50 8.00

Team Colors Jersey

NM/M

Quantity produced listed
Prime: No Pricing
Production One Set
1 Lenny Dykstra/Mets/Fld Glv/25 15.00
2 Steve Garvey/100 6.00
3 Eric Davis/25 15.00
5 Nolan Ryan/50 30.00
6 Bobby Doerr/25 20.00
7 Paul Molitor/100 10.00
8 Dale Murphy/50 20.00
9 Harold Baines/100 8.00
10 Dwight Gooden/50 10.00
11 Jose Canseco/100 15.00
12 Jim Rice/100 8.00
13 Will Clark/50 25.00
14 Alan Trammell/100 8.00
15 Lee Smith/100 5.00
16 Dwight Evans/50 15.00
17 Tony Oliva/100 8.00
18 Dave Parker/Pirates/25 10.00
19 Jack Morris/100 5.00
20 Luis Tiant/100 6.00
21 Andre Dawson/Expos/100 6.00
22 Darryl Strawberry/Dgr/100 8.00
23 George Foster/100 5.00
24 Marty Marion/50 6.00
25 Dennis Eckersley/100 6.00
26 Bo Jackson/50 30.00
27 Cal Ripken Jr./100 35.00
28 Deion Sanders/50 8.00
29 Don Mattingly/Jkt/100 20.00
30 Mark Grace/50 15.00
31 Fred Lynn/50 8.00
33 Ernie Banks/25 30.00
34 Gary Carter/Jkt/100 8.00
37 Keith Hernandez/25 15.00
38 Tony Gwynn/50 15.00
39 Jim Palmer/25 15.00
40 Red Schoendienst/25 15.00
41 Steve Carlton/25 15.00
42 Wade Boggs/25 25.00
43 Tommy John/100 5.00
44 Luis Aparicio/25 10.00
46 Andre Dawson/Cubs/25 15.00
47 Bert Blyleven/100 5.00
48 Darryl Strawberry/Mets/100 8.00
49 Dave Parker/Reds/100 5.00

Team Colors Signatures

NM/M

Quantity produced listed
1 Lenny Dykstra/Mets/50 15.00
2 Steve Garvey/50 25.00
3 Eric Davis/50 20.00
4 Al Oliver/50 15.00
6 Bobby Doerr/50 20.00
9 Harold Baines/50 25.00
10 Dwight Gooden/50 20.00
12 Jim Rice/50 20.00
14 Alan Trammell/50 20.00
15 Lee Smith/50 15.00
16 Dwight Evans/50 15.00
17 Tony Oliva/50 20.00
18 Dave Parker/Pirates/50 15.00
19 Jack Morris/50 10.00
20 Luis Tiant/50 15.00
21 Andre Dawson/Expos/25 25.00
22 Darryl Strawberry/Dgr/50 20.00
23 George Foster/50 15.00
24 Marty Marion/50 15.00
25 Dennis Eckersley/50 25.00
31 Fred Lynn/50 15.00
34 Gary Carter/20 35.00
37 Keith Hernandez/25 35.00
39 Jim Palmer/20 20.00
40 Red Schoendienst/50 15.00
41 Steve Carlton/20 35.00
43 Tommy John/50 15.00
44 Luis Aparicio/50 20.00
45 Bob Feller/50 20.00
46 Andre Dawson/Cubs/25 25.00
47 Bert Blyleven/50 12.00
48 Darryl Strawberry/Mets/50 20.00
49 Dave Parker/Reds/50 15.00
50 Lenny Dykstra/Phils/50 15.00

Team Colors Combos Material

NM/M

Production 25 Sets
Prime: No Pricing
Production One Set
2 Steve Garvey/Bat-Jsy 15.00
3 Eric Davis/Bat-Jsy 20.00
5 Nolan Ryan/Bat-Jsy 50.00
6 Bobby Doerr/Bat-Jsy 25.00
7 Paul Molitor/Bat-Jsy 25.00
8 Dale Murphy/Bat-Jsy 25.00
11 Jose Canseco/Bat-Jsy 30.00
12 Jim Rice/Bat-Jsy 25.00
13 Will Clark/Bat-Jst 40.00
14 Alan Trammell/Bat-Jsy 30.00
16 Dwight Evans/Bat-Jsy 25.00
18 Dave Parker/Pirates/Bat-Jsy 20.00
21 Andre Dawson/Expos/Bat-Jsy 15.00
22 Darryl Strawberry/Dgr/Bat-Jsy 20.00
23 George Foster/Bat-Jsy 10.00
26 Bo Jackson/Bat-Jsy 40.00
27 Cal Ripken Jr./Bat-Jsy 65.00
28 Deion Sanders/Bat-Jsy 25.00
29 Don Mattingly/Bat-Jsy 45.00
30 Mark Grace Bat-Jsy 25.00
33 Ernie Banks/Bat-Jsy 45.00
34 Gary Carter/Bat-Jkt 25.00
38 Tony Gwynn/Bat-Jsy 40.00
40 Red Schoendienst/Bat-Jsy 15.00
41 Steve Carlton/Bat-Jsy 20.00
42 Wade Boggs/Bat-Jsy 25.00
44 Luis Aparicio/Bat-Jsy 15.00
46 Andre Dawson/Cubs/Bat-Jsy 15.00
48 Darryl Strawberry/Mets/Bat-Jsy 20.00
49 Dave Parker/Reds/Bat-Jsy 20.00

Team Colors Combos Signature

NM/M

Quantity produced listed
Prime: No Pricing
Production One Set
1 Lenny Dykstra/Mets/Fld Glv/100 15.00
2 Steve Garvey/Jsy/100 15.00
3 Eric Davis/Jsy/100 25.00
4 Al Oliver/Bat/100 20.00
6 Bobby Doerr/Jsy/100 20.00
9 Harold Baines/Jsy/100 20.00
10 Dwight Gooden/Jsy/100 25.00
12 Jim Rice/Jsy/100 25.00
14 Alan Trammell/Jsy/100 25.00
15 Lee Smith/Jsy/100 20.00
16 Dwight Evans/Jsy/100 25.00
17 Tony Oliva/Jsy/100 20.00
18 Dave Parker/Pirates Jsy/100 15.00
19 Jack Morris/Jsy/100 20.00
20 Luis Tiant/Jsy/100 20.00
21 Andre Dawson/Expos/Jsy/50 25.00
22 Darryl Strawberry/Dgr/Jsy/100 25.00
23 George Foster/Jsy/100 20.00
24 Marty Marion/Jsy/100 20.00
25 Dennis Eckersley/Jsy/100 25.00
31 Fred Lynn Jsy/100 20.00
33 Ernie Banks Jsy/25 90.00
34 Gary Carter/Jkt/50 40.00
36 Ron Santo Bat/25 50.00
37 Keith Hernandez/Jsy/25 45.00
39 Jim Palmer/Jsy/50 35.00
40 Red Schoendienst/Jsy/100 15.00
41 Steve Carlton/Jsy/50 40.00
43 Tommy John/Jsy/100 20.00
44 Luis Aparicio/Jsy/100 15.00
46 Andre Dawson/Cubs/Jsy/50 25.00
47 Bert Blyleven/Jsy/100 25.00
48 Darryl Strawberry/Mets/Jsy/100 25.00
49 Dave Parker/Reds/Jsy/100 15.00
50 Lenny Dykstra/Phils/Btg Glv/30 25.00

Timeless Triples

NM/M

Complete Set (6): 40.00
Common Player:
Production 500 Sets
1 Ted Williams, Carl Yastrzemski, Carlton Fisk 10.00
2 Lou Gehrig, Roger Maris, Thurman Munson 8.00
3 Brooks Robinson, Frank Robinson, Cal Ripken Jr. 10.00
4 Roger Clemens, Andy Pettitte, Roy Oswalt 6.00
5 Greg Maddux, Mark Prior, Kerry Wood 8.00
6 Alex Rodriguez, Derek Jeter, Gary Sheffield 10.00

Timeless Triples Bat

NM/M

Production 25 Sets
1 Ted Williams, Carl Yastrzemski, Carlton Fisk 185.00
2 Lou Gehrig, Roger Maris, Thurman Munson 200.00
3 Brooks Robinson, Frank Robinson, Cal Ripken Jr. 140.00

Timeless Triples Jersey

NM/M

Quantity produced listed
Prime: No Pricing
Production One Set

3 Brooks Robinson, Frank Robinson, Cal Ripken Jr./25 140.00

2004 Donruss Diamond Kings

NM/M

Complete Set (175): 75.00
Common Player: .25
Common (151-175): 1.50
Pack (5): 7.50
Box (12): 80.00
1 Alex Rodriguez 2.50
2 Andruw Jones .75
3 Nomar Garciaparra 2.00
4 Kerry Wood .75
5 Magglio Ordonez .50
6 Victor Martinez .25
7 Jeremy Bonderman .25
8 Josh Beckett .75
9 Jeff Kent .40
10 Carlos Beltran .50
11 Hideo Nomo .50
12 Richie Sexson .50
13 Jose Vidro .25
14 Jae Weong Seo .25
15 Alfonso Soriano 1.00
16 Barry Zito .50
17 Brett Myers .25
18 Brian Giles .40
19 Edgar Martinez .40
20 Jim Edmonds .50
21 Rocco Baldelli .75
22 Mark Teixeira .50
23 Carlos Delgado .75
24 Julius Matos .25
25 Jose Reyes .50
26 Marlon Byrd .25
27 Albert Pujols 2.50
28 Vernon Wells .40
29 Garret Anderson .50
30 Jerome Williams .25
31 Chipper Jones 1.00
32 Rich Harden .25
33 Manny Ramirez .75
34 Derek Jeter 3.00
35 Brandon Webb .25
36 Mark Prior 1.50
37 Roy Halladay .50
38 Frank Thomas .75
39 Rafael Palmeiro .75
40 Adam Dunn .50
41 Aubrey Huff .25
42 Todd Helton .75
43 Matt Morris .40
44 Dontrelle Willis .40
45 Lance Berkman .50
46 Mike Sweeney .25
47 Kazuhisa Ishii .25
48 Torii Hunter .50
49 Vladimir Guerrero 1.00
50 Mike Piazza 1.50
51 Alexis Rios .25
52 Shannon Stewart .25
53 Eric Hinske .25
54 Jason Jennings .25
55 Jason Giambi 1.00
56 Brandon Claussen .25
57 Joe Thurston .25
58 Ramon Nivar .25
59 Jay Gibbons .25
60 Eric Chavez .50
61 Jimmy Gobble .25
62 Walter Young .25
63 Mark Grace .50
64 Austin Kearns .50
65 Bobby Abreu .25
66 Hee Seop Choi .25
67 Brandon Phillips .25
68 Rickie Weeks .50
69 Luis Gonzalez .50
70 Mariano Rivera .50
71 Jason Lane .25
72 Xavier Nady .25
73 Runelvys Hernandez .25
74 Aramis Ramirez .25
75 Ichiro Suzuki 2.00
76 Cliff Lee .25
77 Chris Snelling .25
78 Ryan Wagner .25
79 Miguel Tejada .50
80 Juan Gonzalez .75
81 Joe Borchard .25
82 Gary Sheffield .50
83 Wade Miller .25
84 Jeff Bagwell .75
85 Ryan Church .25
86 Adrian Beltre .25
87 Jeff Baker .25
88 Adam Loewen .25
89 Bernie Williams .50
90 Pedro J. Martinez 1.00
91 Carlos Rivera .25
92 Junior Spivey .25
93 Tim Hudson .50
94 Troy Glaus .50
95 Ken Griffey Jr. 1.50
96 Alexis Gomez .25
97 Antonio Perez .25
98 Dan Haren .25
99 Ivan Rodriguez .75
100 Randy Johnson 1.00
101 Lyle Overbay .25
102 Oliver Perez .25
103 Miguel Cabrera .75
104 Scott Rolen 1.00
105 Roger Clemens 2.00
106 Brian Tallet .25
107 Nic Jackson .25
108 Angel Berroa .25
109 Hank Blalock .50
110 Ryan Klesko .40
111 Jose Castillo .25
112 Paul Konerko .25
113 Greg Maddux 1.50
114 Mark Mulder .50
115 Pat Burrell .50
116 Garrett Atkins .25
117 Jeremy Guthrie .25
118 Orlando Cabrera .25
119 Nick Johnson .25
120 Tom Glavine .50
121 Morgan Ensberg .25
122 Sean Casey .25
123 Orlando Hudson .25
124 Hideki Matsui 2.50
125 Craig Biggio .25
126 Adam LaRoche .25
127 Hong-Chih Kuo .25
128 Paul LoDuca .25
129 Shawn Green .50
130 Luis Castillo .25
131 Joe Crede .25
132 Ken Harvey .25
133 Freddy Sanchez .25
134 Roy Oswalt .50
135 Curt Schilling .75
136 Alfredo Amezaga .25
137 Chien-Ming Wang .50
138 Barry Larkin .50
139 Trot Nixon .25
140 Jim Thome 1.00
141 Bret Boone .40
142 Jacque Jones .25
143 Travis Hafner .25
144 Sammy Sosa 2.00
145 Mike Mussina .50
146 Vinnie Chulk .25
147 Chad Gaudin .25
148 Delmon Young .50
149 Mike Lowell .40
150 Rickey Henderson .50
151 Roger Clemens 4.00
152 Mark Grace 2.00
153 Rickey Henderson 2.00
154 Alex Rodriguez 5.00
155 Rafael Palmeiro 2.00
156 Greg Maddux 3.00
157 Mike Piazza 3.00
158 Mike Mussina 1.50
159 Dale Murphy 1.50
160 Cal Ripken Jr. 6.00
161 Carl Yastrzemski 2.00
162 Marty Marion 1.50
163 Don Mattingly 4.00
164 Robin Yount 2.00
165 Andre Dawson 1.50
166 Jim Palmer 1.50
167 George Brett 5.00
168 Whitey Ford 2.00
169 Roy Campanella 2.00
170 Roger Maris 4.00
171 Duke Snider 2.00
172 Steve Carlton 2.00
173 Stan Musial 3.00
174 Nolan Ryan 6.00
175 Deion Sanders 1.50

Bronze

Bronze (1-150): 4-6X
Bronze (151-175): 2-3X
Production 100 Sets
Bronze Sepia: 2-3X
Production 100

Framed Bronze

Framed Bronze (1-150): 2-3X
Framed Bronze (151-175): 1-2X
Framed Bronze Sepia: 1-2X
Inserted 1:6

Silver

Silver (1-150): 5-10X

Silver (151-175): 2-4X
Production 50 Sets
Silver Sepia: 2-4X
Production 50

Framed Silver

Framed Silver (1-150): 4-8X
Framed Silver (151-175): 2-3X
Production 100 Sets
Framed Silver Sepia: 2-3X
Production 100

Platinum

Platinum: No Pricing
Production One Set
Platinum Sepia: No Pricing
Production One Set

Framed Platinum

Framed Platinum: No Pricing
Production One Set

Diamond Cut Bat

NM/M
Common Player: 6.00
Production 100 unless noted.
1 Alex Rodriguez 15.00
2 Nomar Garciaparra 12.00
3 Hideo Nomo 8.00
4 Alfonso Soriano 10.00
6 Edgar Martinez 8.00
7 Rocco Baldelli 10.00
8 Mark Teixeira 10.00
9 Albert Pujols 20.00
10 Vernon Wells 8.00
11 Garret Anderson 8.00
14 Brandon Webb 6.00
15 Mark Prior 15.00
16 Rafael Palmeiro 10.00
17 Adam Dunn 10.00
18 Dontrelle Willis 8.00
19 Kazuhisa Ishii 6.00
20 Torii Hunter 8.00
21 Vladimir Guerrero 10.00
22 Mike Piazza 15.00
23 Jason Giambi 10.00
26 Bobby Abreu 6.00
27 Hee Seop Choi 6.00
28 Rickie Weeks 12.00
30 Troy Glaus 8.00
31 Ivan Rodriguez 10.00
32 Hank Blalock 10.00
33 Greg Maddux 15.00
34 Nick Johnson 6.00
35 Shawn Green 8.00
36 Sammy Sosa 15.00
37 Dale Murphy/50 15.00
38 Cal Ripken Jr./50 50.00
39 Carl Yastrzemski 15.00
41 Don Mattingly 25.00
43 George Brett/50 40.00
46 Steve Carlton/50 15.00
47 Stan Musial/25 40.00
48 Nolan Ryan/50 35.00
49 Deion Sanders/50 15.00
50 Roberto Clemente/ 25 120.00

Diamond Cut Jersey

NM/M
Common Player: 6.00
Production 100 unless noted.
1 Alex Rodriguez 15.00
2 Nomar Garciaparra 15.00
3 Hideo Nomo/50 15.00
4 Alfonso Soriano 10.00
5 Brett Myers/50 10.00
6 Edgar Martinez 8.00
7 Rocco Baldelli 12.00
8 Mark Teixeira 10.00
9 Albert Pujols 20.00
10 Vernon Wells 8.00
11 Garret Anderson/50 8.00
12 Jerome Williams 8.00
13 Rich Harden 8.00
14 Brandon Webb 6.00
15 Mark Prior 15.00
16 Rafael Palmeiro 10.00
17 Adam Dunn 10.00
18 Dontrelle Willis 8.00
19 Kazuhisa Ishii 6.00
20 Torii Hunter 8.00
21 Vladimir Guerrero/50 15.00
22 Mike Piazza 15.00
23 Jason Giambi 10.00
25 Ramon Nivar 6.00
26 Bobby Abreu 6.00
27 Hee Seop Choi 6.00
30 Troy Glaus 8.00
31 Ivan Rodriguez 10.00
32 Hank Blalock 10.00
33 Greg Maddux 15.00
34 Nick Johnson 6.00
35 Shawn Green 8.00
36 Sammy Sosa 15.00
37 Dale Murphy/50 20.00
38 Cal Ripken Jr./50 50.00
39 Carl Yastrzemski 20.00
40 Marty Marion/50 15.00
41 Don Mattingly 25.00
42 Jim Palmer/25 20.00
43 George Brett/50 35.00
44 Whitey Ford/25 25.00
46 Steve Carlton/50 15.00
48 Nolan Ryan/50 40.00
49 Deion Sanders/50 15.00

Diamond Cut Signature

NM/M
Many not priced due to scarcity.
7 Rocco Baldelli/25 45.00
8 Mark Teixeira/25 30.00
13 Rich Harden/50 25.00
14 Brandon Webb/50 25.00
20 Torii Hunter/25 30.00
24 Ryan Wagner/50 20.00
25 Ramon Nivar/50 10.00
28 Rickie Weeks/50 40.00
29 Adam Loewen/50 20.00
32 Hank Blalock/25 30.00
40 Marty Marion/25 25.00
41 Don Mattingly/23 110.00
42 Jim Palmer/22 45.00
46 Steve Carlton/32 35.00
48 Nolan Ryan/34 125.00

Diamond Cut Combo

NM/M
Common Player: 10.00
Production 50 unless noted.
1 Alex Rodriguez 30.00
2 Nomar Garciaparra 25.00
3 Hideo Nomo/25 30.00
4 Alfonso Soriano 15.00
6 Edgar Martinez/25 15.00
7 Rocco Baldelli/25 25.00
8 Mark Teixeira/25 20.00
9 Albert Pujols 40.00
10 Vernon Wells/25 15.00
11 Garret Anderson/25 15.00
14 Brandon Webb/25 15.00
15 Mark Prior 20.00
16 Rafael Palmeiro/25 20.00
17 Adam Dunn/25 15.00
18 Dontrelle Willis/25 20.00
19 Kazuhisa Ishii/25 15.00
20 Torii Hunter/25 15.00
21 Vladimir Guerrero/25 25.00
22 Mike Piazza 20.00
23 Jason Giambi/25 25.00
26 Bobby Abreu 10.00
27 Hee Seop Choi 10.00
30 Troy Glaus/25 20.00
31 Ivan Rodriguez/25 20.00
32 Hank Blalock/25 20.00
33 Greg Maddux 25.00
34 Nick Johnson/25 12.00
35 Shawn Green/25 15.00
36 Sammy Sosa 25.00
41 Don Mattingly/23 50.00
42 Jim Palmer/22 20.00
46 Steve Carlton/32 20.00
48 Nolan Ryan/34 50.00
49 Deion Sanders/24 25.00
50 Roberto Clemente/ 21 150.00

Diamond Cut Signature Combo

NM/M
Varying quantities produced
40 Marty Marion/25 30.00
46 Steve Carlton/32 45.00

DK Combos Bronze

NM/M
Varying quantities produced
26 Marlon Byrd/ Bat-Jsy/30 20.00
32 Rich Harden/ Jsy-Jsy/15 50.00
53 Eric Hinske/ Bat-Jsy/30 20.00
57 Joe Thurston/ Bat-Jsy/25 15.00
59 Jay Gibbons/ Jsy-Jsy/15 35.00
65 Bob Abreu/ Bat-Jsy/15 25.00
74 Aramis Ramirez/ Bat-Bat/15 25.00
92 Junior Spivey/ Bat-Jsy/15 30.00
101 Lyle Overbay/ Bat-Jsy/30 15.00
103 Miguel Cabrera/ Bat-Jsy/30 35.00
108 Angel Berroa/ Bat-Pants/30 15.00
109 Hank Blalock/ Bat-Jsy/30 35.00
111 Jose Castillo/ Bat-Bat/15 15.00
121 Morgan Ensberg/ Bat-Jsy/30 15.00
123 Orlando Hudson/ Bat-Jsy/30 15.00
126 Adam LaRoche/ Bat-Bat/30 15.00
130 Luis Castillo/ Bat-Jsy/30 15.00
143 Travis Hafner/ Bat-Jsy/30 12.00
147 Chad Gaudin/ Jsy-Jsy/25 12.00

DK Combos Framed Bronze

NM/M
Varying quantities produced
26 Marlon Byrd/ Bat-Jsy/25 12.00
35 Brandon Webb/ Bat-Jsy/25 25.00
53 Eric Hinske/ Bat-Jsy/25 15.00
57 Joe Thurston/ Bat-Jsy/25 12.00
59 Jay Gibbons/ Jsy-Jsy/25 15.00
62 Walter Young/ Bat-Bat/25 12.00
65 Bobby Abreu/ Bat-Jsy/25 15.00
71 Jason Lane/ Bat-Hat/25 15.00
74 Aramis Ramirez/ Bat-Bat/25 20.00
77 Chris Snelling/ Bat-Bat/25 12.00
81 Joe Borchard/ Bat-Jsy/25 10.00
92 Junior Spivey/ Bat-Jsy/25 12.00
97 Antonio Perez/ Bat-Pants/25 12.00
98 Dan Haren/ Bat-Jsy/25 15.00
101 Lyle Overbay/ Bat-Jsy/25 10.00
103 Miguel Cabrera/ Bat-Jsy/25 40.00
107 Nic Jackson/ Bat-Bat/25 10.00
108 Angel Derroa/ Bat-Pants/25 12.00
109 Hank Blalock/ Bat-Jsy/25 30.00
110 Ryan Klesko/ Bat-Jsy/15 20.00
111 Jose Castillo/ Bat-Bat/25 10.00
121 Morgan Ensberg/ Bat-Jsy/25 15.00
123 Orlando Hudson/ Bat-Jsy/25 12.00
126 Adam LaRoche/ Bat-Bat/25 15.00
127 Hong-Chih Kuo/ Bat-Bat/25 10.00
130 Luis Castillo/ Bat-Jsy/25 12.00
136 Alfredo Amezaga/ Bat-Jsy/15 15.00
143 Travis Hafner/ Bat-Jsy/15 15.00
147 Chad Gaudin/ Jsy-Jsy/25 10.00

DK Combos Silver

NM/M
Varying quantities produced
26 Marlon Byrd/ Bat-Jsy/15 15.00
101 Lyle Overbay/ Bat-Jsy/15 15.00
102 Miguel Cabrera/ Bat-Jsy/15 50.00
108 Angel Berroa/ Bat-Pants/15 20.00
109 Hank Blalock/ Bat-Jsy/15 50.00
121 Morgan Ensberg/ Bat-Jsy/15 20.00
123 Orlando Hudson/ Bat-Jsy/15 15.00
126 Adam LaRoche/ Bat-Bat/15 20.00

DK Combos Framed Silver

Framed Silver: No Pricing
Production 1-15
Framed Silver Sepia: No Pricing
Production 1-5

DK Combos Gold

Gold Combos: No Pricing
Production 1-5
Gold Combos Sepia: No Pricing
Production One Set

DK Combos Framed Gold

Framed Gold Combos: No Pricing
Production 1-5
Framed Gold Sepia: No Pricing
Production 1-5

DK Combos Platinum

Platinum Combos: No Pricing
Production One Set
Platinum Combos Sepia: No Pricing
Production One Set

DK Combos Framed Platinum

Framed Platinum: No Pricing
Production One Set

DK Materials Bronze

NM/M
Common Player:
No pricing for production 15 or less.
Framed Bronze: 1-1.5X
Production 5-100
Framed Bronze Sepia: 1.5-2X
Production 5-50
Silver: 1-2X
Production 5-50
Silver Sepia: 1.5-2X
Production 1-30
Framed Silver: 1-2X
Production 5-75
Framed Silver Sepia: 1.5-2X
Production 1-30
Gold: 1.5-2X
Production 1-50
Gold Sepia: No Pricing
Production 1-15
Framed Gold: 1.5-2X
Production 5-50
Framed Gold Sepia: No Pricing
Production 1-15
Platinums: No Pricing
All Platinums limited to one set.
1 Alex Rodriguez/ Bat-Jsy/150 20.00
2 Andruw Jones/ Bat-Jsy/150 8.00
3 Nomar Garciaparra/ Bat-Jsy/150 15.00
4 Kerry Wood/ Dat-Jsy/150 15.00
5 Magglio Ordonez/ Bat-Jsy/150 8.00
6 Victor Martinez/ Bat-Bat/100 6.00
7 Jeremy Bonderman/ Jsy-Jsy/30 10.00
8 Josh Beckett/ Bat-Jsy/150 10.00
9 Jeff Kent/Bat-Jsy/150 8.00
10 Carlos Beltran/ Bat-Jsy/150 8.00
11 Hideo Nomo/ Bat-Jsy/150 10.00
12 Richie Sexson/ Bat-Jsy/150 10.00
13 Jose Vidro/Bat-Jsy/50 8.00
14 Jae Weong Seo/ Jsy-Jsy/100 8.00
15 Alfonso Soriano/ Bat-Jsy/150 10.00
16 Barry Zito/ Bat-Jsy/100 10.00
17 Brett Myers/ Jsy-Jsy/30 10.00
18 Brian Giles/ Bat-Bat/100 8.00
19 Edgar Martinez/ Bat-Jsy/150 8.00
20 Jim Edmonds/ Bat-Jsy/150 8.00
21 Rocco Baldelli/ Bat-Jsy/100 12.00
22 Mark Teixeira/ Bat-Jsy/150 8.00
23 Carlos Delgado/ Bat-Jsy/150 8.00
25 Jose Reyes/ Bat-Jsy/100 8.00
26 Marlon Byrd/ Bat-Jsy/100 8.00
27 Albert Pujols/ Bat-Jsy/150 25.00
28 Vernon Wells/ Bat-Jsy/150 8.00
29 Garret Anderson/ Bat-Jsy/15 20.00
30 Jerome Williams/ Jsy-Jsy/100 8.00
31 Chipper Jones/ Bat-Jsy/150 12.00
32 Rich Harden/ Jsy-Jsy/100 8.00
33 Manny Ramirez/ Bat-Jsy/150 10.00
34 Derek Jeter/ Base-Base/100 20.00
35 Brandon Webb/ Bat-Jsy/100 8.00
36 Mark Prior/ Bat-Jsy/100 15.00
37 Roy Halladay/ Jsy-Jsy/100 8.00
38 Frank Thomas/ Bat-Jsy/150 12.00
39 Rafael Palmeiro/ Bat-Jsy/150 10.00
40 Adam Dunn/ Bat-Jsy/150 8.00
41 Aubrey Huff/ Bat-Jsy/30 10.00
42 Todd Helton/ Bat-Jsy/150 10.00
43 Matt Morris/ Jsy-Jsy/100 8.00
44 Dontrelle Willis/ Bat-Jsy/100 10.00
45 Lance Berkman/ Bat-Jsy/150 6.00
46 Mike Sweeney/ Bat-Jsy/100 8.00
47 Kazuhisa Ishii/ Bat-Jsy/100 8.00
48 Torii Hunter/ Bat-Jsy/100 8.00
49 Vladimir Guerrero/ Bat-Jsy/100 15.00
50 Mike Piazza/ Bat-Jsy/150 15.00
51 Alexis Rios/ Bat-Bat/150 12.00
52 Shannon Stewart/ Bat-Bat/100 6.00
53 Eric Hinske/ Bat-Jsy/100 6.00
54 Jason Jennings/ Bat-Jsy/150 6.00
55 Jason Giambi/ Bat-Jsy/150 10.00
57 Joe Thurston/ Bat-Jsy/150 6.00
58 Ramon Nivar/ Bat-Jsy/100 6.00
59 Jay Gibbons/ Jsy-Jsy/100 8.00
60 Eric Chavez/ Bat-Jsy/150 8.00
62 Walter Young/ Bat-Bat/100 6.00
63 Mark Grace/ Bat-Jsy/150 10.00
64 Austin Kearns/ Bat-Jsy/150 8.00
65 Bob Abreu/ Bat-Jsy/150 6.00
66 Hee Seop Choi/ Bat-Jsy/100 6.00
67 Brandon Phillips/ Bat-Bat/100 6.00
68 Rickie Weeks/ Bat-Bat/100 15.00
69 Luis Gonzalez/ Bat-Jsy/150 6.00
70 Mariano Rivera/ Jsy-Jsy/100 10.00
71 Jason Lane 15.00
73 Runelvys Hernandez/ Jsy-Jsy/30 8.00
75 Ichiro Suzuki/ Ball-Base/15 50.00
77 Chris Snelling/ Bat-Bat/30 8.00
79 Miguel Tejada/ Bat-Jsy/150 8.00
80 Juan Gonzalez/ Bat-Jsy/150 8.00
82 Gary Sheffield/ Bat-Jsy/150 8.00
83 Wade Miller/ Bat-Jsy/50 6.00
84 Jeff Bagwell/ Bat-Jsy/150 15.00
86 Adrian Beltre/ Bat-Jsy/100 6.00
87 Jeff Baker/Bat-Bat/100 6.00
89 Bernie Williams/ Bat-Jsy/150 10.00
90 Pedro J. Martinez/ Bat-Jsy/100 15.00
92 Junior Spivey/ Bat-Jsy/100 8.00
93 Tim Hudson/ Bat-Jsy/150 8.00
94 Troy Glaus/ Bat-Jsy/100 8.00
95 Ken Griffey Jr./ Base-Base/100 15.00
96 Alexis Gomez/ Bat-Bat/30 10.00
97 Antonio Perez/ Bat-Pants/100 6.00
98 Dan Haren/ Bat-Jsy/100 6.00
99 Ivan Rodriguez/ Bat-Jsy/150 10.00
100 Randy Johnson/ Bat-Jsy/100 12.00
101 Lyle Overbay/ Bat-Jsy/100 6.00
103 Miguel Cabrera/ Bat-Jsy/100 15.00
104 Scott Rolen/ Bat-Jsy/100 10.00
105 Roger Clemens/ Bat-Jsy/100 20.00
107 Nic Jackson/ Bat-Bat/100 6.00
108 Angel Berroa/ Bat-Pants/30 10.00
109 Hank Blalock/ Bat-Jsy/100 10.00
110 Ryan Klesko/ Bat-Jsy/100 8.00
111 Jose Castillo/ Bat-Bat/100 6.00
112 Paul Konerko/ Bat-Jsy/100 6.00
113 Greg Maddux/ Bat-Jsy/100 15.00
114 Mark Mulder/ Bat-Jsy/100 8.00
115 Pat Burrell/ Bat-Jsy/100 8.00
116 Garrett Atkins/ Jsy-Jsy/100 6.00
118 Orlando Cabrera/ Bat-Jsy/100 8.00
119 Nick Johnson/ Bat-Jsy/100 6.00
120 Tom Glavine/ Bat-Jsy/100 10.00
121 Morgan Ensberg/ Bat-Jsy/100 6.00
123 Orlando Hudson/ Bat-Jsy/100 6.00
124 Hideki Matsui/ Ball-Base/15 70.00
125 Craig Biggio/ Bat-Jsy/100 8.00
126 Adam LaRoche/ Bat-Bat/100 8.00
127 Hong-Chih Kuo/ Bat-Bat/100 6.00
128 Paul LoDuca/ Bat-Jsy/100 6.00
129 Shawn Green/ Bat-Jsy/100 8.00
130 Luis Castillo/ Bat-Jsy/100 6.00
132 Ken Harvey/ Bat-Bat/100 6.00
133 Freddy Sanchez/ Bat-Bat/100 6.00
134 Roy Oswalt/ Bat-Jsy/100 8.00
135 Curt Schilling/ Bat-Jsy/100 8.00
136 Alfredo Amezaga/ Bat-Jsy/15 15.00
139 Trot Nixon/ Bat-Bat/100 10.00
140 Jim Thome/ Bat-Jsy/100 15.00
141 Bret Boone/ Bat-Jsy/100 8.00
142 Jacque Jones/ Bat-Jsy/100 8.00
143 Todd Hafner/ Bat-Jsy/100 8.00
144 Sammy Sosa/ Bat-Jsy/100 20.00
145 Mike Mussina/ Bat-Jsy/100 12.00
147 Chad Gaudin/ Jsy-Jsy/100 6.00
149 Mike Lowell/ Bat-Jsy/100 8.00
150 Rickey Henderson/ Bat-Jsy/100 15.00
151 Roger Clemens/ FB Bat-Jsy/100 20.00
153 Rickey Henderson/ FB Bat-Jsy/30 30.00
154 Alex Rodriguez/ FB Bat-Jsy/100 20.00
155 Rafael Palmeiro/ FB Bat-Jsy/100 10.00
156 Greg Maddux/ FB Bat-Bat/100 15.00
157 Mike Piazza/ FB Bat-Jsy/100 15.00
158 Mike Mussina/ FB Bat-Jsy/100 12.00
159 Dale Murphy/ LGD Bat-Jsy/30 20.00
160 Cal Ripken Jr./ LGD Bat-Jsy/100 50.00
161 Carl Yastrzemski/ LGD Bat-Jsy/100 25.00
162 Marty Marion/ LGD Jsy-Jsy/30 10.00
163 Don Mattingly/ LGD Bat-Jsy/100 25.00
164 Robin Yount/ LGD Bat-Jsy/100 25.00
165 Andre Dawson/ LGD Bat-Jsy/30 15.00
167 George Brett/ LGD Bat-Jsy/30 50.00
168 Whitey Ford/ LGD Jsy-Pants/30 20.00
172 Steve Carlton/ LGD Bat-Jsy/100 15.00
173 Stan Musial/ LGD Bat-Jsy/30 25.00
174 Nolan Ryan/ LGD Bat-Jsy/30 50.00
175 Deion Sanders/ LGD Bat-Jsy/100 12.00

DK Signatures Bronze

NM/M
No Pricing For Prod. less than 15.
Framed Bronze: 1X
Production 1-50
Bronze Sepia: No Pricing
Production 1-15
6 Victor Martinez/200 10.00
13 Jose Vidro/200 10.00
14 Jae Weong Seo/200 15.00
17 Brett Myers/200 10.00

19 Edgar Martinez/25 40.00
26 Marlon Byrd/200 10.00
32 Rich Harden/200 15.00
35 Brandon Webb/25 30.00
41 Aubrey Huff/100 12.00
48 Torii Hunter/100 20.00
51 Alexis Rios/200 20.00
52 Shannon Stewart/200 10.00
53 Eric Hinske/25 20.00
56 Brandon Claussen/200 10.00
57 Joe Thurston/200 8.00
58 Ramon Nivar/100 10.00
59 Jay Gibbons/25 25.00
61 Jimmy Gobble/100 15.00
62 Walter Young/200 8.00
67 Brandon Phillips/100 6.00
68 Rickie Weeks/30 40.00
71 Jason Lane/200 8.00
73 Runelvys Hernandez/50 10.00
74 Aramis Ramirez/100 15.00
76 Cliff Lee/200 10.00
77 Chris Snelling/200 8.00
78 Ryan Wagner/100 15.00
81 Joe Borchard/200 8.00
85 Ryan Church/200 8.00
87 Jeff Baker/100 10.00
88 Adam Loewen/100 20.00
91 Carlos Rivera/100 8.00
92 Junior Spivey/25 20.00
96 Alexis Gomez/200 8.00
97 Antonio Perez/46 10.00
98 Dan Haren/100 12.00
101 Lyle Overbay/200 8.00
102 Oliver Perez/200 8.00
103 Miguel Cabrera/100 35.00
106 Brian Tallet/200 8.00
107 Nic Jackson/200 8.00
108 Angel Berroa/25 15.00
109 Hank Blalock/25 35.00
111 Jose Castillo/200 8.00
114 Mark Mulder/25 30.00
116 Garrett Atkins/100 8.00
117 Jeremy Guthrie/200 8.00
118 Orlando Cabrera/75 12.00
121 Morgan Ensberg/200 10.00
123 Orlando Hudson/100 10.00
126 Adam LaRoche/100 15.00
127 Hong-Chih Kuo/25 75.00
130 Luis Castillo/25 20.00
131 Joe Crede/100 8.00
132 Ken Harvey/200 8.00
133 Freddy Sanchez/50 10.00
136 Alfredo Amezaga/90 8.00
137 Chien-Ming Wang/25 125.00
142 Jacque Jones/25 20.00
143 Travis Hafner/200 10.00
146 Vinnie Chulk/200 8.00
147 Chad Gaudin/100 8.00
149 Mike Lowell/25 20.00

DK Signatures Silver

NM/M

No pricing for prod. less than 15.
Framed Silver: 1.5-2X
Production 1-25
Silver Sepia: No Pricing
Production 1-10
6 Victor Martinez/49 15.00
13 Jose Vidro/20 20.00
14 Jae Weong Seo/80 20.00
17 Brett Myers/90 15.00
26 Marlon Byrd/100 10.00
32 Rich Harden/100 15.00
35 Brandon Webb/15 35.00
41 Aubrey Huff/40 15.00
51 Alexis Rios/100 20.00
52 Shannon Stewart/30 15.00
56 Brandon Claussen/100 10.00
57 Joe Thurston/100 8.00
58 Ramon Nivar/30 15.00
61 Jimmy Gobble/30 20.00
62 Walter Young/100 8.00
67 Brandon Phillips/30 10.00
68 Rickie Weeks/20 50.00
71 Jason Lane/100 8.00
73 Runelvys Hernandez/30 10.00
74 Aramis Ramirez/30 25.00
76 Cliff Lee/100 10.00
77 Chris Snelling/100 8.00
78 Ryan Wagner/30 20.00
81 Joe Borchard/100 8.00
85 Ryan Church/100 8.00
87 Jeff Baker/30 15.00
88 Adam Loewen/30 25.00
96 Alexis Gomez/100 8.00
98 Dan Haren/30 15.00
101 Lyle Overbay/100 8.00
102 Oliver Perez/100 8.00
103 Miguel Cabrera/30 40.00
106 Brian Tallet/100 8.00
107 Nic Jackson/100 8.00
109 Hank Blalock/30 35.00
111 Jose Castillo/100 8.00
116 Garrett Atkins/30 10.00
117 Jeremy Guthrie/30 15.00
121 Morgan Ensberg/50 15.00
123 Orlando Hudson/30 15.00
126 Adam LaRoche/30 20.00
131 Joe Crede/35 12.00
132 Ken Harvey/30 15.00
136 Alfredo Amezaga/30 10.00
143 Travis Hafner/30 15.00
146 Vinnie Chulk/100 8.00
147 Chad Gaudin/30 10.00

DK Signatures Gold

NM/M

Many not priced due to scarcity.
Framed Gold: No Pricing
Production 1-5
Gold Sepia: No Pricing
Production 1-5
32 Rich Harden/50 20.00
51 Alexis Rios/50 25.00
56 Brandon Claussen/50 15.00
57 Joe Thurston/50 10.00
62 Walter Young/50 10.00
71 Jason Lane/40 15.00
77 Chris Snelling/50 10.00
81 Joe Borchard/50 15.00
85 Ryan Church/50 10.00
96 Alexis Gomez/50 10.00
101 Lyle Overbay/50 10.00
102 Oliver Perez/50 10.00
106 Brian Tallet/50 10.00
107 Nic Jackson/50 15.00
121 Morgan Ensberg/48 15.00
146 Vinnie Chulk/50 10.00

DK Signatures Platinum

No Pricing
Production One Set
Framed Platinum: No Pricing
Platinum Sepia: No Pricing
Production One Set

Gallery of Stars

NM/M

Complete Set (15): 50.00
Common Player: 2.00
Inserted 1:37
1 Nolan Ryan 8.00
2 Cal Ripken Jr. 8.00
3 George Brett 6.00
4 Don Mattingly 6.00
5 Deion Sanders 2.00
6 Mike Piazza 4.00
7 Hideo Nomo 2.00
8 Rickey Henderson 2.00
9 Roger Clemens 6.00
10 Greg Maddux 4.00
11 Albert Pujols 6.00
12 Alex Rodriguez 6.00
13 Dale Murphy 3.00
14 Mark Prior 4.00
15 Dontrelle Willis 2.00

Heritage Collection

NM/M

Complete Set (25): 75.00
Common Player: 2.00
Inserted 1:22
1 Dale Murphy 3.00
2 Cal Ripken Jr. 8.00
3 Carl Yastrzemski 4.00
4 Don Mattingly 6.00
5 Jim Palmer 2.00
6 Andre Dawson 2.00
7 Roy Campanella 3.00
8 George Brett 6.00
9 Duke Snider 3.00
10 Marty Marion 2.00
11 Deion Sanders 2.00
12 Whitey Ford 3.00
13 Stan Musial 5.00
14 Nolan Ryan 8.00
15 Steve Carlton 2.00
16 Robin Yount 3.00
17 Albert Pujols 6.00
18 Alex Rodriguez 6.00
19 Mike Piazza 4.00
20 Roger Clemens 6.00
21 Hideo Nomo 2.00
22 Mark Prior 4.00
23 Roger Maris 5.00
24 Greg Maddux 4.00
25 Mark Grace 2.00

Heritage Collection Autograph

No Pricing

Heritage Collection Bat

NM/M

Production 50 unless noted.
1 Dale Murphy 20.00
2 Cal Ripken Jr. 40.00
3 Carl Yastrzemski 20.00
4 Don Mattingly 30.00
6 Andre Dawson/25 20.00
7 Roy Campanella/25 30.00
8 George Brett/25 40.00
11 Deion Sanders 10.00
13 Stan Musial/25 35.00
14 Nolan Ryan/25 40.00
15 Steve Carlton/25 20.00
16 Robin Yount 20.00
17 Albert Pujols 25.00
18 Alex Rodriguez 25.00
19 Mike Piazza 15.00
20 Roger Clemens 25.00
21 Hideo Nomo 15.00
22 Mark Prior 15.00
23 Roger Maris/25 50.00
24 Greg Maddux 15.00
25 Mark Grace 10.00

Heritage Collection Jersey

NM/M

Production 50 unless noted.
1 Dale Murphy 15.00
2 Cal Ripken Jr. 40.00
3 Carl Yastrzemski 20.00
4 Don Mattingly 30.00
6 Andre Dawson/25 20.00
7 Roy Campanella/25 30.00
8 George Brett/25 40.00
10 Marty Marion 10.00
11 Deion Sanders 10.00
12 Whitey Ford/25 25.00
14 Nolan Ryan/25 40.00
15 Steve Carlton/25 20.00
16 Robin Yount 20.00
17 Albert Pujols 25.00
18 Alex Rodriguez 25.00
19 Mike Piazza 15.00
20 Roger Clemens 25.00
21 Hideo Nomo 15.00
22 Mark Prior 15.00
23 Roger Maris/25 50.00
24 Greg Maddux 15.00
25 Mark Grace 10.00

HOF Heroes

NM/M

Common Player: 2.50
1 George Brett/1,000 6.00
2 George Brett/500 8.00
3 George Brett/250 12.00
4 Mike Schmidt/1,000 5.00
5 Mike Schmidt/250 8.00
6 Nolan Ryan/1,000 8.00
7 Nolan Ryan/500 10.00
8 Nolan Ryan/250 15.00
9 Roberto Clemente/1,000 6.00
10 Roberto Clemente/500 10.00
11 Roberto Clemente/250 15.00
12 Roberto Clemente/100 20.00
13 Carl Yastrzemski/1,000 4.00
14 Robin Yount/1,000 4.00
15 Whitey Ford/1,000 4.00
16 Duke Snider/1,000 4.00
17 Duke Snider/1,000 8.00
18 Carlton Fisk/1,000 3.00
19 Ozzie Smith/1,000 5.00
20 Kirby Puckett/1,000 4.00
21 Bobby Doerr/1,000 2.50
22 Frank Robinson/1,000 3.00
23 Ralph Kiner/1,000 2.50
24 Al Kaline/1,000 4.00
25 Bob Feller/1,000 3.00
26 Yogi Berra/1,000 4.00
27 Stan Musial/1,000 5.00
28 Stan Musial/500 8.00
29 Stan Musial/250 10.00
30 Jim Palmer/1,000 2.50
31 Johnny Bench/1,000 4.00
32 Steve Carlton/1,000 3.00
33 Gary Carter/1,000 3.00
34 Roy Campanella/1,000 3.00
35 Roy Campanella/250 8.00

HOF Heroes Bat

NM/M

Production 25 unless noted.
1 George Brett 35.00
2 George Brett 35.00
3 George Brett 35.00
4 Mike Schmidt 35.00
5 Mike Schmidt 35.00
6 Nolan Ryan 40.00
7 Nolan Ryan 40.00
8 Nolan Ryan 40.00
13 Carl Yastrzemski 30.00
14 Robin Yount 35.00
18 Carlton Fisk 25.00
19 Ozzie Smith 30.00
20 Kirby Puckett 30.00
21 Bobby Doerr 20.00
23 Ralph Kiner 15.00
24 Al Kaline 25.00
31 Johnny Bench 25.00
32 Steve Carlton 20.00
33 Gary Carter 20.00
34 Roy Campanella 30.00
35 Roy Campanella 30.00

HOF Heroes Jersey

NM/M

Production 25 unless noted.
1 George Brett 35.00
2 George Brett 35.00
3 George Brett 35.00
4 Mike Schmidt 35.00
5 Mike Schmidt 35.00
6 Nolan Ryan 40.00
7 Nolan Ryan 40.00
8 Nolan Ryan 40.00
13 Carl Yastrzemski 30.00
14 Robin Yount 35.00
15 Whitey Ford 30.00
18 Carlton Fisk 25.00
19 Ozzie Smith 30.00
20 Kirby Puckett 30.00
21 Bobby Doerr 20.00
24 Al Kaline 25.00
32 Steve Carlton 20.00
33 Gary Carter 20.00
34 Roy Campanella 30.00
35 Roy Campanella 30.00

HOF Heroes Combo

NM/M

Production 25 unless noted.
1 George Brett 50.00
2 George Brett 50.00
3 George Brett 50.00
4 Mike Schmidt 40.00
5 Mike Schmidt 40.00
6 Nolan Ryan 50.00
7 Nolan Ryan 50.00
8 Nolan Ryan 50.00
13 Carl Yastrzemski 40.00
14 Robin Yount 40.00
15 Whitey Ford 30.00
18 Carlton Fisk 30.00
19 Ozzie Smith 40.00
20 Kirby Puckett 40.00
21 Bobby Doerr 25.00
23 Ralph Kiner 20.00
24 Al Kaline 35.00
32 Steve Carlton 30.00
33 Gary Carter 25.00
34 Roy Campanella 40.00
35 Roy Campanella 40.00

HOF Heroes Signature

NM/M

Many not priced.
14 Robin Yount/19 70.00
15 Whitey Ford/16 50.00
22 Frank Robinson/20 50.00
25 Bob Feller/19 40.00
30 Jim Palmer/22 40.00
32 Steve Carlton/32 35.00

Recollection Autographs

NM/M

Varying quantities produced
6 Clint Barmes/03 DK Black/82 10.00
7 Clint Barmes/03 DK Blue/72 10.00
8 Carlos Beltran/02 DK/23 20.00
9 Carlos Beltran/03 DK/99 15.00
10 Adrian Beltre/02 DK/40 10.00
19 Chris Burke/03 DK/150 10.00
20 Marlon Byrd/02 DK/23 15.00
21 Marlon Byrd/03 DK Murphy 10.00
24 Kevin Cash/03 DK/103 10.00
25 Jose Cruz/85 DK/59 10.00
26 J.D. Durbin/03 DK/151 10.00
27 Jim Edmonds/03 DK/24 25.00
32 Julio Franco/87 DK/25 20.00
33 Freddy Garcia/03 DK/50 20.00
34 Jay Gibbons/03 DK/100 12.00
39 Brendan Harris/03 DK/150 8.00
42 Runelvys Hernandez/02 DK/100 8.00
43 Eric Hinske/03 DK/20 20.00
44 Tim Hudson/02 DK/25 30.00
45 Tim Hudson/03 DK/25 30.00
46 Aubrey Huff/03 DK/99 15.00
49 Jason Jennings/03 DK/50 10.00
50 Tommy John/88 DK Black/62 15.00
52 Howard Johnson/90 DK/52 10.00
54 Austin Kearns/02 DK/25 30.00
55 Austin Kearns/03 DK/25 30.00
59 Preston Larrison/03 DK Black/74 10.00
60 Preston Larrison/03 DK Blue/77 10.00
67 Dustin McGowan/03 DK/159 8.00
69 Melvin Mora/03 DK/101 8.00
71 Jack Morris/03 DK/60 10.00
72 Jack Morris/03 DK Her/19 20.00
74 Dale Murphy/03 DK Blue/47 30.00
82 Magglio Ordonez/03 DK/25 30.00
85 Dave Parker/82 DK/20 30.00
86 Dave Parker/90 DK/18 30.00
88 Jorge Posada/02 DK/25 50.00
89 Mark Prior/03 DK/25 100.00
92 Mike Rivera/02 DK/24 15.00
97 Ivan Rodriguez/03 DK/22 40.00
100 Rodrigo Rosario/02 DK/50 8.00
105 Ron Santo/02 DK/29 35.00
106 Richie Sexson/02 DK/25 25.00
107 Richie Sexson/03 DK/25 25.00
109 Chris Snelling/02 DK/46 12.00
119 Shannon Stewart/02 DK/50 15.00
120 Shannon Stewart/03 DK Black/92 12.00
126 Gorman Thomas/82 DK Black/22 20.00
127 Gorman Thomas/82 DK Blue/20 20.00
128 Alan Trammell/02 DK/29 30.00
129 Alan Trammell/02 DK Her/25 30.00
130 Robin Ventura/03 DK/25 20.00
131 Jose Vidro/03 DK/25 20.00
132 Rickie Weeks/3 DK/52 50.00
133 Kevin Youkilis/03 DK/153 15.00

Timeline

NM/M

Common Player: 3.00
Inserted 1:92
1 Roger Clemens 6.00
2 Mark Grace 3.00
3 Mike Mussina 3.00
4 Mike Piazza 4.00
5 Nolan Ryan 8.00
6 Rickey Henderson 3.00

Team Timeline

NM/M

Complete Set (19): 65.00
Common Duo: 2.00
Inserted 1:29
1 Deion Sanders, Andruw Jones 2.00
2 Rickie Weeks, Robin Yount 3.00
3 Don Mattingly, Whitey Ford 8.00
4 Chipper Jones, Dale Murphy 4.00
5 Nomar Garciaparra, Bobby Doerr 5.00
6 Mark Prior, Sammy Sosa 5.00
7 Hideo Nomo, Kazuhisa Ishii 2.00
8 Andre Dawson, Mark Grace 3.00
9 Roger Clemens, Carl Yastrzemski 6.00
10 Mike Mussina, Cal Ripken Jr. 8.00
11 Stan Musial, Albert Pujols 6.00
12 Jim Palmer, Mike Mussina 2.00
13 Marty Marion, Stan Musial 4.00
14 George Brett, Mike Sweeney 6.00
15 Roger Clemens, Roger Maris 6.00
16 Duke Snider, Shawn Green 3.00
17 Jim Thome, Mike Schmidt 4.00
18 Nolan Ryan, Alex Rodriguez 8.00
19 Roy Campanella, Mike Piazza 4.00

Team Timeline Bat

NM/M

Production 25 unless noted.
1 Deion Sanders, Andruw Jones 15.00
2 Rickie Weeks, Robin Yount 40.00
3 Don Mattingly, Whitey Ford 60.00
4 Chipper Jones, Dale Murphy 35.00
5 Nomar Garciaparra, Bobby Doerr 30.00
6 Mark Prior, Sammy Sosa 40.00
7 Hideo Nomo, Kazuhisa Ishii 40.00
8 Andre Dawson, Mark Grace 20.00
9 Roger Clemens, Carl Yastrzemski 50.00
10 Mike Mussina, Cal Ripken Jr. 75.00
11 Stan Musial, Albert Pujols 65.00
12 Jim Palmer, Mike Mussina 25.00
14 George Brett, Mike Sweeney 30.00
15 Roger Clemens, Roger Maris 60.00
17 Jim Thome, Mike Schmidt 40.00
18 Nolan Ryan, Alex Rodriguez 60.00
19 Roy Campanella, Mike Piazza 40.00

Team Timeline Jersey

NM/M

Production 25 Sets
Prime: No Pricing
Production One Set
1 Deion Sanders, Andruw Jones 15.00
2 Rickie Weeks, Robin Yount 40.00
3 Don Mattingly, Whitey Ford 60.00
4 Chipper Jones, Dale Murphy 35.00
5 Nomar Garciaparra, Bobby Doerr 30.00
6 Mark Prior, Sammy Sosa 40.00
7 Hideo Nomo, Kazuhisa Ishii 40.00
8 Andre Dawson, Mark Grace 20.00

9 Roger Clemens, Carl Yastrzemski 50.00
10 Mike Mussina, Cal Ripken Jr. 75.00
14 George Brett, Mike Sweeney 30.00
15 Roger Clemens, Roger Maris 60.00
17 Jim Thome, Mike Schmidt 40.00
18 Nolan Ryan, Alex Rodriguez 60.00
19 Roy Campanella, Mike Piazza 40.00

2004 Donruss Elite

NM/M
Complete Set (205):
Common Player: .25
Common Auto. (151-180): 5.00
Production 250-1,000
Common (181-200): 2.00
Production 1,000
Pack (5): 5.00
Box (24): 100.00
1 Troy Glaus .40
2 Darin Erstad .25
3 Garret Anderson .40
4 Tim Salmon .40
5 Bartolo Colon .40
6 Jose Guillen .25
7 Miguel Tejada .40
8 Adam Loewen .25
9 Jay Gibbons .25
10 Melvin Mora .25
11 Javy Lopez .40
12 Pedro J. Martinez .75
13 Curt Schilling .50
14 David Ortiz .50
15 Keith Foulke .25
16 Nomar Garciaparra 1.00
17 Magglio Ordonez .40
18 Frank Thomas .50
19 Carlos Lee .40
20 Paul Konerko .40
21 Mark Buehrle .25
22 Jody Gerut .25
23 Victor Martinez .25
24 C.C. Sabathia .25
25 Ellis Burks .25
26 Bobby Higginson .25
27 Jeremy Bonderman .25
28 Fernando Vina .25
29 Carlos Pena .25
30 Dmitri Young .25
31 Carlos Beltran .50
32 Benito Santiago .25
33 Mike Sweeney .25
34 Angel Berroa .25
35 Runelvys Hernandez .25
36 Johan Santana .25
37 Doug Mientkiewicz .25
38 Shannon Stewart .25
39 Torii Hunter .40
40 Derek Jeter 2.00
41 Jason Giambi .50
42 Bernie Williams .40
43 Alfonso Soriano .50
44 Gary Sheffield .40
45 Mike Mussina .50
46 Jorge Posada .40
47 Hideki Matsui 1.00
48 Kevin Brown .40
49 Javier Vazquez .40
50 Mariano Rivera .40
51 Eric Chavez .40
52 Tim Hudson .40
53 Mark Mulder .40
54 Barry Zito .40
55 Ichiro Suzuki 1.00
56 Edgar Martinez .40
57 Bret Boone .40
58 John Olerud .40
59 Scott Spiezio .25
60 Aubrey Huff .40
61 Rocco Baldelli .40
62 Jose Cruz Jr. .25
63 Delmon Young .40
64 Mark Teixeira .40
65 Hank Blalock .50
66 Michael Young .40
67 Alex Rodriguez 2.00
68 Carlos Delgado .50
69 Eric Hinske .25
70 Roy Halladay .40
71 Vernon Wells .25
72 Randy Johnson .75
73 Richie Sexson .50
74 Brandon Webb .25
75 Luis Gonzalez .40
76 Steve Finley .25
77 Chipper Jones .75
78 Andruw Jones .50
79 Marcus Giles .25
80 Rafael Furcal .25
81 J.D. Drew .40
82 Sammy Sosa 1.50
83 Kerry Wood .75
84 Mark Prior 1.00
85 Derrek Lee .40
86 Moises Alou .40
87 Corey Patterson .40
88 Ken Griffey Jr. 1.00
89 Austin Kearns .40
90 Adam Dunn .50
91 Barry Larkin .40
92 Todd Helton .50
93 Larry Walker .40
94 Preston Wilson .25
95 Charles Johnson .25
96 Luis Castillo .25
97 Josh Beckett .40
98 Mike Lowell .40
99 Miguel Cabrera .75
100 Juan Pierre .25
101 Dontrelle Willis .40
102 Andy Pettitte .40
103 Wade Miller .25
104 Jeff Bagwell .50
105 Craig Biggio .40
106 Lance Berkman .40
107 Jeff Kent .40
108 Roy Oswalt .40
109 Hideo Nomo .40
110 Adrian Beltre .25
111 Paul LoDuca .25
112 Shawn Green .40
113 Fred McGriff .40
114 Eric Gagne .40
115 Geoff Jenkins .40
116 Rickie Weeks .40
117 Scott Podsednik .40
118 Nick Johnson .25
119 Orlando Cabrera .25
120 Jose Vidro .25
121 Kazuo Matsui **RC** 5.00
122 Tom Glavine .40
123 Al Leiter .25
124 Mike Piazza 1.00
125 Jose Reyes .50
126 Mike Cameron .25
127 Pat Burrell .40
128 Jim Thome .75
129 Mike Lieberthal .25
130 Bobby Abreu .40
131 Kip Wells .25
132 Jack Wilson .40
133 Pokey Reese .25
134 Brian Giles .40
135 Sean Burroughs .25
136 Ryan Klesko .40
137 Trevor Hoffman .25
138 Jason Schmidt .40
139 J.T. Snow .25
140 A.J. Pierzynski .25
141 Ray Durham .25
142 Jim Edmonds .40
143 Albert Pujols 1.50
144 Edgar Renteria .40
145 Scott Rolen .75
146 Matt Morris .25
147 Ivan Rodriguez .50
148 Vladimir Guerrero .75
149 Greg Maddux 1.00
150 Kevin Millwood .40
151 Hector Gimenez/ AU/750 **RC** 5.00
152 Willy Taveras/ AU/750 **RC** 15.00
153 Ruddy Yan/AU/750 5.00
154 Graham Koonce/ AU/750 8.00
155 Jose Capellan/ AU/750 **RC** 15.00
156 Onil Joseph/ AU/750 **RC** 5.00
157 John Gall/ AU/1000 **RC** 10.00
158 Carlos Hines/ AU/750 **RC** 5.00
159 Jerry Gil/AU/750 **RC** 5.00
160 Mike Gosling/AU/750 5.00
161 Jason Frasor/ AU/750 **RC** 5.00
162 Justin Knoedler/ AU/750 **RC** 5.00
163 Merkin Valdez/ AU/500 **RC** 10.00
164 Angel Chavez/ AU/1000 **RC** 5.00
165 Ivan Ochoa/ AU/750 **RC** 10.00
166 Greg Dobbs/ AU/750 **RC** 5.00
167 Ronald Belisario/ AU/750 **RC** 5.00
168 Aarom Baldiris/ AU/750 **RC** 10.00
170 David Crouthers/ AU/750 5.00
171 Freddy Guzman/ AU/750 **RC** 10.00
172 Akinori Otsuka/ AU/250 **RC** 25.00
173 Ian Snell/AU/750 **RC** 30.00
174 Nick Regilio/ AU/1000 **RC** 5.00
175 Jamie Brown/ AU/750 **RC** 5.00
176 Jerome Gamble/ AU/750 **RC** 5.00
177 Roberto Novoa/ AU/1000 **RC** 5.00
178 Sean Henn/AU/1000 10.00
179 Ramon Ramirez/ AU/1000 **RC** 10.00
180 Jason Bartlett/ AU/1000 **RC** 10.00
181 Bob Gibson/RET 2.00
182 Cal Ripken Jr./RET 8.00
183 Carl Yastrzemski/RET 4.00
184 Dale Murphy/RET 3.00
185 Don Mattingly/RET 6.00
186 Eddie Murray/RET 2.00
187 George Brett/RET 6.00
188 Jackie Robinson/RET 4.00
189 Jim Palmer/RET 2.00
190 Lou Gehrig/RET 5.00
191 Mike Schmidt/RET 5.00
192 Ozzie Smith/RET 5.00
193 Nolan Ryan/RET 8.00
194 Reggie Jackson/RET 3.00
195 Roberto Clemente/RET 6.00
196 Robin Yount/RET 4.00
197 Stan Musial/RET 5.00
198 Ted Williams/RET 8.00
199 Tony Gwynn/RET 3.00
200 Ty Cobb/RET 5.00
201 James Gandolfini/FG 3.00
202 Freddy Adu/FG 3.00
203 Summer Sanders/FG 1.50
204 Janet Evans/FG 1.50
205 Brandi Chastain/FG 1.50

Aspirations

Cards (1-150) print run 61-99: 4-8X
(1-150) p/r 41-60: 6-10X
(1-150) p/r 21-40: 8-15X
Autos (151-180): .75-1.5X
(181-200): 2-3X
Production 19-99

Status

Cards (1-150) print run 61-81: 4-8X
(1-150) p/r 41-60: 6-10X
(1-150) p/r 21-40: 8-15X
Autos (151-180): .75-1X
(181-200): 3-4X
Production 1-81

Status Gold

Gold (1-150): 10-20X
Gold (151-180): No Pricing
Gold (181-200): 3-6X
Production 24 Sets

Back to the Future

NM/M
#1-6
Production 500
#6-9
Production 250
Black: 1-2X
Production 25 or 50
Gold: .75-1.5X
Production 50 or 100
Red: 1X
Production 125 or 250
1 Tim Hudson 2.00
2 Rich Harden 1.50
3 Alex Rodriguez/Rgr 5.00
4 Hank Blalock 3.00
5 Sammy Sosa 5.00
6 Hee Seop Choi 1.50
7 Tim Hudson, Rich Harden 3.00
8 Alex Rodriguez, Hank Blalock 6.00
9 Sammy Sosa, Hee Seop Choi 6.00

Back to the Future Bats

NM/M
#1-6
Production 200
#8-9
Production 100
1 Tim Hudson 4.00
3 Alex Rodriguez 10.00
4 Hank Blalock 6.00
5 Sammy Sosa 10.00
6 Hee Seop Choi 4.00
8 Alex Rodriguez, Hank Blalock 12.00
9 Sammy Sosa, Hee Seop Choi 12.00

Back to the Future Jerseys

NM/M
#1-6
Production 200
#7-9
Production 100
Prime: 1.5-2X
Production 25 or 50
1 Tim Hudson 4.00
2 Rich Harden 4.00
3 Alex Rodriguez/Rgr 10.00
4 Hank Blalock 6.00
5 Sammy Sosa 10.00
6 Hee Seop Choi 4.00
7 Tim Hudson, Rich Harden 8.00
8 Alex Rodriguez, Hank Blalock 12.00
9 Sammy Sosa, Hee Seop Choi 12.00

2 Back 2 Back Jacks

NM/M
Singles Production 25-125
Duals Production 25-50
1 Albert Pujols/125 15.00
2 Alex Rodriguez/125 10.00
3 Alfonso Soriano/125 8.00
4 Andruw Jones/125 5.00
5 Chipper Jones/125 8.00
6 Derek Jeter/125 20.00
7 Frank Thomas/125 8.00
8 Miguel Cabrera/125 8.00
9 Jason Giambi/125 8.00
10 Jim Thome/125 8.00
11 Mike Piazza/125 10.00
12 Nomar Garciaparra/ 25 35.00
13 Sammy Sosa/125 10.00
14 Shawn Green/125 4.00
15 Vladimir Guerrero/125 8.00
16 Andruw Jones, Chipper Jones/50 20.00
17 Alfonso Soriano, Derek Jeter/50 30.00
18 Jeff Bagwell, Lance Berkman/50 15.00
19 Alex Rodriguez, Rafael Palmeiro/50 20.00
20 Adam Dunn, Austin Kearns/25 20.00
21 Al Kaline/100 15.00
22 Babe Ruth/50 140.00
23 Cal Ripken Jr./100 40.00
24 Dale Murphy/100 10.00
25 Don Mattingly/100 15.00
26 George Brett/100 20.00
27 Lou Gehrig/100 85.00
28 Mike Schmidt/100 15.00
29 Roberto Clemente/ 100 50.00
30 Roy Campanella/100 15.00
31 Babe Ruth, Roger Maris/25 200.00
32 Harmon Killebrew, Kirby Puckett/50 35.00
33 Paul Molitor, Robin Yount/50 40.00
34 Reggie Jackson/50 15.00
35 Lou Gehrig, Ty Cobb/50 200.00
36 Don Mattingly, Jason Giambi/50 25.00
37 Ted Williams, Nomar Garciaparra/ 50 75.00
38 Andre Dawson, Sammy Sosa/50 25.00
39 Dale Murphy, Chipper Jones/50 15.00
40 Stan Musial, Jim Edmonds/50 25.00

Back 2 Back Jacks Combos

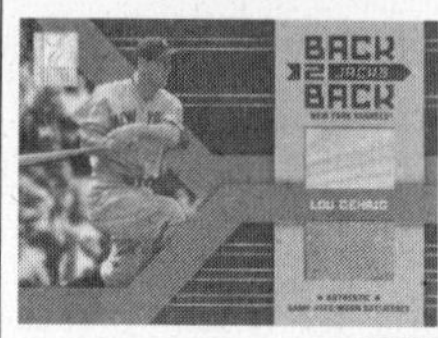

NM/M
Singles Production 25-50
Duals Production 10-25
1 Albert Pujols/ Bat-Jsy/50 30.00
2 Alex Rodriguez/ Bat-Jsy/50 20.00
3 Alfonso Soriano/ Bat-Jsy/50 15.00
4 Andruw Jones/ Bat-Jsy/50 8.00
5 Chipper Jones/ Bat-Jsy/50 12.00
6 Derek Jeter/ Bat-Jsy/50 35.00
7 Frank Thomas/ Bat-Jsy/50 15.00
8 Miguel Cabrera/ Bat-Jsy/50 15.00
9 Jason Giambi/ Bat-Jsy/50 15.00
10 Jim Thome/ Bat-Jsy/50 15.00
11 Mike Piazza/ Bat-Jsy/50 20.00
12 Nomar Garciaparra/ Bat-Jsy/50 20.00
13 Sammy Sosa/ Bat-Jsy/50 20.00
14 Shawn Green/ Bat-Jsy/50 6.00
15 Vladimir Guerrero/ Bat-Jsy/50 15.00
16 Andruw Jones, Chipper Jones/25 30.00
17 Alfonso Soriano, Lance Berkman/25 50.00
18 Jeff Bagwell, Lance Berkman/25 20.00
19 Alex Rodriguez, Rafael Palmeiro/25 30.00
20 Adam Dunn, Austin Kearns/25 20.00
21 Al Kaline/ Bat-Jsy/50 25.00
22 Babe Ruth/ Bat-Jsy/25 350.00
23 Cal Ripken Jr./ Bat-Jsy/50 60.00
24 Dale Murphy/ Bat-Jsy/50 15.00
25 Don Mattingly/ Bat-Jsy/50 25.00
26 George Brett/ Bat-Jsy/50 30.00
27 Lou Gehrig/ Bat-Jsy/25 150.00
28 Mike Schmidt/ Bat-Jsy/25 30.00
29 Roberto Clemente/ Bat-Jsy/50 80.00
30 Roy Campanella/ Bat-Jsy/50 25.00
31 Babe Ruth, Roger Maris/10 185.00
32 Harmon Killebrew, Kirby Puckett/25 50.00
33 Paul Molitor, Robin Yount/25 50.00
34 Reggie Jackson/25 25.00
35 Lou Gehrig, Ty Cobb/25 350.00
36 Don Mattingly, Jason Giambi/25 35.00
37 Ted Williams, Nomar Garciaparra 140.00
38 Andre Dawson, Sammy Sosa 40.00
39 Dale Murphy, Chipper Jones 20.00
40 Stan Musial, Jim Edmonds 35.00

Career Best

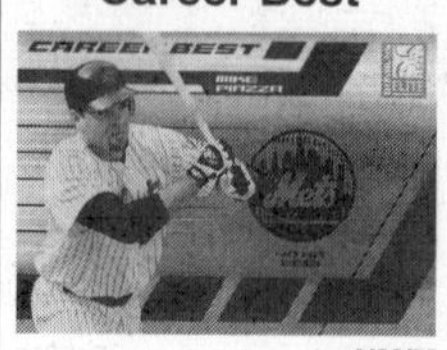

NM/M
Common Player: 1.00
Production 1,000 Sets
Black: 2X
Production 100 Sets
Gold Print Run 200-390: 1.5X
Gold P/R 101-200: 2X
Gold P/R 50-100: 3X
Gold P/R 26-50: 3-5X
Gold P/R 15-25: 5-8X
1 Albert Pujols 3.00
2 Alex Rodriguez 3.00
3 Alfonso Soriano 1.50
4 Andruw Jones 1.00
5 Barry Zito 1.00
6 Cal Ripken Jr. 5.00
7 Chipper Jones 1.50
8 Curt Schilling 1.00
9 Derek Jeter 4.00
10 Don Mattingly 4.00
11 Dontrelle Willis 1.00
12 Doc Gooden 1.00
13 Eddie Murray 1.50
14 Frank Thomas 1.50
15 Gary Sheffield 1.00
16 George Brett 4.00
17 Greg Maddux 2.00
18 Hideo Nomo 1.00
19 Ichiro Suzuki 2.00
20 Ivan Rodriguez 1.50
21 Jason Giambi 1.50
22 Jeff Bagwell 1.50
23 Jim Thome 1.50
24 Kerry Wood 1.50
25 Lance Berkman 1.00
26 Magglio Ordonez 1.00
27 Mark Prior 2.00
28 Mike Piazza 2.00
29 Mike Schmidt 3.00
30 Nomar Garciaparra 2.50
31 Pedro J. Martinez 2.00
32 Randy Johnson 2.00
33 Roger Clemens 3.00
34 Sammy Sosa 2.50
35 Tony Gwynn 1.50

Career Best Bats

NM/M
Production 100 Or 200
Combo Print Run 50: 1-2X
Combo P/R 25: 2X
Production 25 or 50
1 Albert Pujols/200 15.00
2 Alex Rodriguez/200 10.00
3 Alfonso Soriano/200 8.00
4 Andruw Jones/200 5.00
5 Barry Zito/200 4.00
6 Cal Ripken Jr./200 25.00
7 Chipper Jones/200 8.00
8 Curt Schilling/200 5.00
9 Derek Jeter/200 15.00
10 Don Mattingly/200 15.00
11 Dontrelle Willis/100 6.00
12 Doc Gooden/200 6.00
13 Eddie Murray/200 4.00
14 Frank Thomas/200 8.00
15 Gary Sheffield/200 5.00
16 George Brett/200 15.00
17 Greg Maddux/100 10.00
18 Hideo Nomo/100 8.00
20 Ivan Rodriguez/200 8.00
21 Jason Giambi/200 8.00
22 Jeff Bagwell/200 6.00
23 Jim Thome/200 8.00
24 Kerry Wood/100 10.00
25 Lance Berkman/200 4.00
26 Magglio Ordonez/200 4.00
27 Mark Prior/100 8.00
28 Mike Piazza/200 10.00
29 Mike Schmidt/200 10.00
30 Nomar Garciaparra/ 200 10.00
31 Pedro J. Martinez/200 8.00
32 Randy Johnson/200 8.00
33 Roger Clemens/200 15.00
34 Sammy Sosa/200 10.00
35 Tony Gwynn/200 8.00

Career Best Jerseys

NM/M
Quantity produced listed
Prime: 1.5-2X
Production 25-50
1 Albert Pujols/200 15.00
2 Alex Rodriguez/200 10.00
3 Alfonso Soriano/200 8.00
4 Andruw Jones/200 5.00
5 Barry Zito/200 4.00
6 Cal Ripken Jr./50 40.00
7 Chipper Jones/200 8.00
8 Curt Schilling/200 5.00
9 Derek Jeter/200 15.00
10 Don Mattingly/50 20.00

11 Dontrelle Willis/200 6.00
12 Doc Gooden/200 6.00
13 Eddie Murray/200 6.00
14 Frank Thomas/200 8.00
15 Gary Sheffield/200 5.00
16 George Brett/50 25.00
17 Greg Maddux/200 10.00
18 Hideo Nomo/200 8.00
20 Ivan Rodriguez/200 8.00
21 Jason Giambi/200 8.00
22 Jeff Bagwell/200 6.00
23 Jim Thome/200 8.00
24 Kerry Wood/200 10.00
25 Lance Berkman/200 4.00
26 Magglio Ordonez/200 4.00
27 Mark Prior/200 8.00
28 Mike Piazza/200 10.00
29 Mike Schmidt/100 10.00
30 Nomar Garciaparra/ 200 10.00
31 Pedro J. Martinez/200 8.00
32 Randy Johnson/200 8.00
33 Roger Clemens/200 15.00
34 Sammy Sosa/200 10.00
35 Tony Gwynn/50 15.00

Passing the Torch

NM/M

#1-30
Production 1,000
#31-45
Production 500
Black: 1-2X
Production 50 or 100
Blue: 1X
Production 125 or 250
Gold: 1.5-3X
Production 25 or 50
Green: .75-1X
Production 250 or 500
1 Whitey Ford 3.00
2 Andy Pettitte 1.50
3 Willie McCovey 2.00
4 Will Clark 3.00
5 Stan Musial 4.00
6 Albert Pujols 5.00
7 Andre Dawson 2.00
8 Vladimir Guerrero 2.00
9 Dale Murphy 2.00
10 Chipper Jones 2.00
11 Joe Morgan 1.50
12 Barry Larkin 1.50
13 Jim "Catfish" Hunter 1.50
14 Tim Hudson 1.50
15 Jim Rice 1.50
16 Manny Ramirez 2.00
17 Greg Maddux 2.50
18 Mark Prior 2.00
19 Don Mattingly 4.00
20 Jason Giambi 2.00
21 Roy Campanella 2.00
22 Mike Piazza 3.00
23 Ozzie Smith 2.00
24 Scott Rolen 2.00
25 Roger Clemens 4.00
26 Mike Mussina 2.00
27 Babe Ruth 6.00
28 Roger Maris 4.00
29 Nolan Ryan 6.00
30 Roy Oswalt 1.50
31 Whitey Ford, Andy Pettitte 3.00
32 Willie McCovey, Will Clark 3.00
33 Stan Musial, Albert Pujols 6.00
34 Andre Dawson, Vladimir Guerrero 3.00
35 Dale Murphy, Chipper Jones 3.00
36 Joe Morgan, Barry Larkin 3.00
37 Jim "Catfish," Hunter, Tim Hudson 2.00
38 Jim Rice, Manny Ramirez 3.00
39 Greg Maddux, Mark Prior 4.00
40 Don Mattingly, Jason Giambi 8.00
41 Roy Campanella, Mike Piazza 5.00
42 Ozzie Smith, Scott Rolen 5.00
43 Roger Clemens, Mike Mussina 5.00
44 Babe Ruth, Roger Maris 10.00
45 Nolan Ryan, Roy Oswalt 8.00

Passing the Torch Autographs

NM/M

Quantity produced listed
Many not priced due to scarcity.
4 Will Clark/15 100.00
7 Andre Dawson/50 15.00
9 Dale Murphy/50 30.00
11 Joe Morgan/15 25.00
14 Tim Hudson/15 45.00
15 Jim Rice/50 15.00
18 Mark Prior/15 80.00
24 Scott Rolen/15 50.00
30 Roy Oswalt/50 15.00

Passing the Torch Bats

NM/M

Quantity produced listed
2 Andy Pettitte/200 4.00
3 Willie McCovey/100 6.00
4 Will Clark/100 10.00
5 Stan Musial/100 25.00
6 Albert Pujols/200 15.00
7 Andre Dawson/100 8.00
8 Vladimir Guerrero/200 8.00
9 Dale Murphy/100 10.00
10 Chipper Jones/200 8.00
11 Joe Morgan/200 4.00
12 Barry Larkin/200 5.00
14 Tim Hudson/200 5.00
15 Jim Rice/200 5.00
16 Manny Ramirez/200 8.00
17 Greg Maddux/200 10.00
18 Mark Prior/200 8.00
19 Don Mattingly/100 15.00
20 Jason Giambi/200 8.00
21 Roy Campanella/50 30.00
22 Mike Piazza/200 10.00
23 Ozzie Smith/200 15.00
24 Scott Rolen/200 8.00
25 Roger Clemens/200 15.00
26 Mike Mussina/200 8.00
27 Babe Ruth/25 150.00
28 Roger Maris/50 50.00
29 Nolan Ryan/100 25.00
30 Roy Oswalt/200 4.00
32 Willie McCovey, Will Clark/50 20.00
33 Stan Musial, Albert Pujols/50 50.00
34 Andre Dawson, Vladimir Guerrero/50 20.00
35 Dale Murphy, Chipper Jones/50 20.00
36 Joe Morgan, Barry Larkin/50 15.00
38 Jim Rice, Manny Ramirez/50 20.00
39 Greg Maddux, Mark Prior/50 25.00
40 Don Mattingly, Jason Giambi/50 35.00
41 Roy Campanella, Mike Piazza/25 35.00
42 Ozzie Smith, Scott Rolen/50 30.00
43 Roger Clemens, Mike Mussina/50 30.00
44 Babe Ruth, Roger Maris/25 200.00
45 Nolan Ryan, Roy Oswalt/50 35.00

Passing the Torch Jerseys

NM/M

Quantity produced listed
1 Whitey Ford/100 15.00
2 Andy Pettitte/200 4.00
3 Willie McCovey/100 6.00
4 Will Clark/100 10.00
5 Stan Musial/100 25.00
6 Albert Pujols/200 15.00
7 Andre Dawson/200 8.00
8 Vladimir Guerrero/200 8.00
9 Dale Murphy/100 10.00
10 Chipper Jones/200 8.00
11 Joe Morgan/100 4.00
12 Barry Larkin/200 5.00
13 Jim "Catfish" Hunter/ 100 5.00
14 Tim Hudson/200 5.00
15 Jim Rice/200 5.00
16 Manny Ramirez/200 8.00
18 Mark Prior/200 8.00
19 Don Mattingly/100 15.00
20 Jason Giambi/200 8.00
21 Roy Campanella/50 30.00
22 Mike Piazza/200 10.00
23 Ozzie Smith/100 12.00
24 Scott Rolen/200 8.00
25 Roger Clemens/200 15.00
26 Mike Mussina/200 8.00
27 Babe Ruth/25 300.00
28 Roger Maris/50 50.00
29 Nolan Ryan/100 25.00
30 Roy Oswalt/200 4.00
31 Whitey Ford, Andy Pettitte/50 20.00
32 Willie McCovey, Will Clark/50 20.00
33 Stan Musial, Albert Pujols/50 50.00
34 Andre Dawson, Vladimir Guerrero/50 20.00
35 Dale Murphy, Chipper Jones/50 20.00
36 Joe Morgan, Barry Larkin/50 15.00
37 Jim "Catfish" Hunter, Tim Hudson/50 15.00
38 Jim Rice, Manny Ramirez/50 20.00
40 Don Mattingly, Jason Giambi/50 35.00
41 Roy Campanella, Mike Piazza 35.00
42 Ozzie Smith, Scott Rolen/50 30.00
43 Roger Clemens, Mike Mussina/50 30.00
45 Nolan Ryan, Roy Oswalt/50 35.00

Recollection Autographs

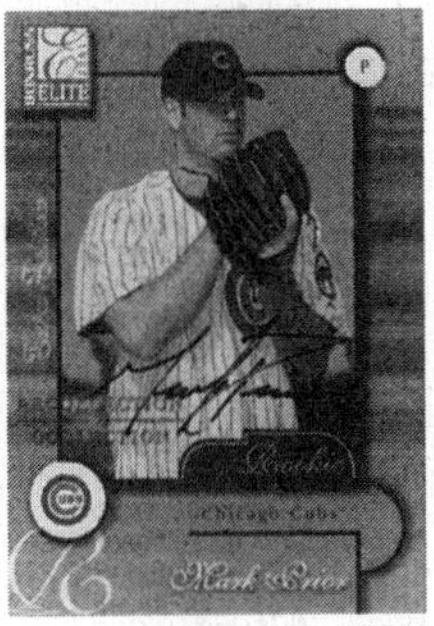

NM/M

Common Autograph: 8.00
1 Jeremy Affeldt/01/25 15.00
2 Erick Almonte/01/26 10.00
4 Jeff Baker/02/25 30.00
5 Brandon Berger/01/25 8.00
6 Marlon Byrd/01/24 25.00
8 Ryan Drese/02/45 8.00
9 Brandon Duckworth/ 01/16 15.00
10 Casey Fossum/01/23 15.00
11 Geronimo Gil/01/25 8.00
13 Jeremy Guthrie/ 02/25 20.00
14 Nic Jackson/02/95 8.00
21 Ricardo Rodriguez/ 01/25 8.00
23 Bud Smith/01/25 8.00
25 Junior Spivey/01/20 20.00
26 Tim Spooneybarger/ 01/25 10.00
28 Martin Vargas/01/37 8.00

Team

NM/M

Production 1,500 Sets
Black: 1X-2X
Production 150 Sets
Gold: 1-1.5X
Production 250 Sets
1 Cal Ripken Jr., Eddie Murray, im Palmer 8.00
2 Derek Jeter, Roger Clemens, Bernie Williams, Andy Pettitte 4.00
3 Johnny Bench, Tony Perez, George Foster, Dave Concepcion 4.00
4 Josh Beckett, Dontrelle Willis, Ivan Rodriguez 2.00
5 Randy Johnson, Curt Schilling, Luis Gonzalez, Mark Grace 2.00
6 Derek Jeter, Wade Boggs, Darryl Strawberry 5.00
7 Chipper Jones, Tom Glavine, Greg Maddux, Ryan Klesko 4.00
8 Dwight Gooden, Gary Carter, Darryl Strawberry 2.00
9 Jackie Robinson, Roy Campanella, Duke Snider 3.00
10 Phil Rizzuto, Yogi Berra, Whitey Ford 2.00
11 Stan Musial, Curt Schilling, Marty Marion, Enos Slaughter 4.00

Team Bats

NM/M

Production 100 Sets
2 Derek Jeter, Roger Clemens, Bernie Williams, Andy Pettitte 30.00
3 Johnny Bench, Tony Perez, George Foster, Dave Concepcion 50.00
4 Josh Beckett, Dontrelle Willis, Ivan Rodriguez 15.00
5 Randy Johnson, Curt Schilling, Luis Gonzalez, Mark Grace 25.00
6 Derek Jeter, Wade Boggs, Darryl Strawberry 30.00
7 Chipper Jones, Tom Glavine, Greg Maddux, Ryan Klesko 25.00
8 Dwight Gooden, Gary Carter, Darryl Strawberry 20.00

Team Jerseys

NM/M

Production 100 unless noted.
1 Cal Ripken Jr., Eddie Murray, Jim Palmer 50.00
2 Derek Jeter, Roger Clemens, Bernie Williams, Andy Pettitte 40.00
4 Josh Beckett, Dontrelle Willis, Ivan Rodriguez 15.00
5 Randy Johnson, Curt Schilling, Luis Gonzalez, Mark Grace 25.00
6 Derek Jeter, Wade Boggs, Darryl Strawberry 30.00
7 Chipper Jones, Tom Glavine, Greg Maddux, Ryan Klesko 25.00
9 Jackie Robinson, Roy Campanella, Duke Snider 75.00
10 Phil Rizzuto, Yogi Berra, Whitey Ford 35.00
11 Stan Musial, Curt Schilling, Marty Marion, Enos Slaughter 50.00

Throwback Threads

NM/M

Quantity produced listed
Prime: 1.5-3X
Prime Singles Production 10-25
Prime Duals Production 5-15
1 Albert Pujols/150 60.00
2 Alex Rodriguez/ Rgr/150 125.00
3 Alfonso Soriano/ 150 175.00
4 Chipper Jones/150 120.00
5 Derek Jeter/150 15.00
6 Greg Maddux/150 10.00
7 Hideo Nomo/150 8.00
8 Miguel Cabrera/150 8.00
9 Ivan Rodriguez/150 8.00
10 Jason Giambi/150 8.00
11 Jeff Bagwell/150 8.00
12 Lance Berkman/150 4.00
13 Mark Prior/150 8.00
14 Mike Piazza/150 10.00
15 Nomar Garciaparra/ 150 10.00
16 Pedro J. Martinez/150 8.00
17 Randy Johnson/150 8.00
18 Sammy Sosa/150 10.00
19 Shawn Green/150 4.00
20 Vladimir Guerrero/150 8.00
21 Adam Dunn, Austin Kearns/75 20.00
22 Barry Zito, Mark Mulder/75 10.00
23 Curt Schilling/75 10.00
24 Derek Jeter, Jason Giambi/75 25.00
25 Dontrelle Willis, Josh Beckett/75 15.00
26 Frank Thomas, Magglio Ordonez/75 15.00
27 Jim Thome/75 15.00
28 Kerry Wood, Mark Prior/75 25.00
29 Hank Blalock, Mark Teixeira/75 15.00
30 Albert Pujols, Scott Rolen/75 40.00
31 Babe Ruth/50 280.00
32 Cal Ripken Jr./100 40.00
33 Carl Yastrzemski/100 20.00
34 Deion Sanders/100 10.00
35 Don Mattingly/100 20.00
36 George Brett/100 20.00
37 Jim Palmer/100 8.00
38 Kirby Puckett/100 15.00
39 Lou Gehrig/100 125.00
40 Mark Grace/100 10.00
41 Mike Schmidt/100 20.00
42 Nolan Ryan/100 25.00
43 Ozzie Smith/100 20.00
44 Reggie Jackson/100 10.00
45 Rickey Henderson/ 100 10.00
46 Roberto Clemente/ 100 75.00
47 Roger Clemens/100 15.00
48 Roger Maris/100 40.00
49 Roy Campanella/ Pants/100 20.00
50 Tony Gwynn/100 15.00
51 Babe Ruth, Lou Gehrig/25 400.00
52 Cal Ripken Jr., Eddie Murray/50 50.00
53 Ted Williams, Carl Yastrzemski/50 85.00
54 Andre Dawson, Gary Carter/50 20.00
55 Reggie Jackson, Rod Carew/50 20.00
56 Derek Jeter, Phil Rizzuto/50 40.00
57 Nolan Ryan, Roy Oswalt/50 40.00
58 Roger Clemens, Mike Mussina/50 25.00
59 Albert Pujols, Stan Musial/50 40.00
60 Nomar Garciaparra, Stan Musial/50 85.00

Threads Autographs

NM/M

Production 25 Sets
Prime: No Pricing
Production 5-10
9 Ivan Rodriguez/25 60.00
13 Mark Prior/25 80.00
18 Sammy Sosa/25 175.00
35 Don Mattingly/25 120.00
37 Jim Palmer/25 40.00

Throwback Threads Prime

Quantity produced listed

Turn of the Century

Stars (1-150): 2-3X
Production 750
Stars (181-200): 1X
Production 250

2004 Donruss Elite Extra Edition

NM/M

Complete Set (288):
Common (1-150): .25
Common (206-215): 2.00
Production 1,000
Common Auto.(216-355): 6.00
Common No Auto. (234-254): 3.00
No Auto. Production 1,000
Pack (5): 14.00
Box (12): 150.00
Note: Cards 151-205 do not exist.
1 Troy Glaus .40
2 John Lackey .25
3 Garret Anderson .40
4 Francisco Rodriguez .25
5 Casey Kotchman .25
6 Jose Guillen .25
7 Miguel Tejada .50
8 Rafael Palmeiro .50
9 Jay Gibbons .25
10 Melvin Mora .25
11 Javy Lopez .25
12 Pedro Martinez .75
13 Curt Schilling .75
14 David Ortiz .75
15 Manny Ramirez .75
16 Nomar Garciaparra 1.00
17 Magglio Ordonez .25
18 Frank Thomas .75
19 Esteban Loaiza .25
20 Paul Konerko .50
21 Mark Buehrle .25
22 Jody Gerut .25
23 Victor Martinez .40
24 C.C. Sabathia .25
25 Travis Hafner .50
26 Cliff Lee .25
27 Jeremy Bonderman .40
28 Dallas McPherson .25
29 Jermaine Dye .25
30 Carlos Guillen .25
31 Carlos Beltran .50
32 Ken Harvey .25
33 Mike Sweeney .25
34 Angel Berroa .25
35 Joe Nathan .25
36 Johan Santana .50
37 Jacque Jones .25
38 Shannon Stewart .25
39 Torii Hunter .40
40 Derek Jeter 2.00
41 Jason Giambi .50
42 Danny Graves .25
43 Alfonso Soriano .75
44 Gary Sheffield .50
45 Mike Mussina .50
46 Jorge Posada .50
47 Hideki Matsui 1.00
48 Francisco Cordero .25
49 Javier Vazquez .25
50 Mariano Rivera .40
51 Eric Chavez .40
52 Tim Hudson .40
53 Mark Mulder .40
54 Barry Zito .40
55 Ichiro Suzuki 1.50
56 Edgar Martinez .25
57 Bret Boone .25
58 Lew Ford .25
59 B.J. Upton .40
60 Aubrey Huff .25
61 Rocco Baldelli .25
62 Carl Crawford .40
63 Delmon Young .40
64 Mark Teixeira .40
65 Hank Blalock .50
66 Michael Young .25
67 Alex Rodriguez 1.50
68 Carlos Delgado .40
69 Milton Bradley .25
70 Roy Halladay .40
71 Vernon Wells .25
72 Randy Johnson .75
73 Bobby Crosby .75
74 Lyle Overbay .25
75 Luis Gonzalez .25
76 Steve Finley .25
77 Chipper Jones .75
78 Andruw Jones .40

79 Marcus Giles .25
80 Rafael Furcal .25
81 J.D. Drew .40
82 Sammy Sosa 1.00
83 Kerry Wood .40
84 Mark Prior .75
85 Derrek Lee .50
86 Moises Alou .40
87 Carlos Zambrano .40
88 Ken Griffey Jr. 1.00
89 Austin Kearns .40
90 Adam Dunn .50
91 Barry Larkin .40
92 Todd Helton .50
93 Larry Walker .40
94 Preston Wilson .25
95 Sean Casey .25
96 Luis Castillo .25
97 Josh Beckett .25
98 Mike Lowell .25
99 Miguel Cabrera .75
100 Brad Penny .25
101 Dontrelle Willis .25
102 Andy Pettitte .40
103 Wade Miller .25
104 Jeff Bagwell .50
105 Craig Biggio .40
106 Lance Berkman .40
107 Jeff Kent .25
108 Roy Oswalt .40
109 Hideo Nomo .40
110 Adrian Beltre .40
111 Paul LoDuca .25
112 Shawn Green .40
113 Roger Clemens 2.00
114 Eric Gagne .40
115 Danny Kolb .25
116 Rickie Weeks .25
117 Scott Podsednik .25
118 Livan Hernandez .25
119 Orlando Cabrera .25
120 Jose Vidro .25
121 David Wright 1.50
122 Tom Glavine .40
123 Al Leiter .25
124 Mike Piazza 1.00
125 Jose Reyes .50
126 Richard Hidalgo .25
127 Eric Milton .25
128 Jim Thome .75
129 Mike Lieberthal .25
130 Bobby Abreu .40
131 Kip Wells .25
132 Jack Wilson .25
133 Jason Bay .40
134 Brian Giles .25
135 Sean Burroughs .25
136 Khalil Greene .25
137 Jake Peavy .40
138 Jason Schmidt .40
139 J.T. Snow .25
140 Craig Wilson .25
141 Chase Utley .50
142 Jim Edmonds .40
143 Albert Pujols 2.00
144 Edgar Renteria .40
145 Scott Rolen .75
146 Matt Morris .25
147 Ivan Rodriguez .50
148 Vladimir Guerrero .75
149 Greg Maddux 1.00
150 Ben Sheets .40
206 Will Clark 2.00
207 Nolan Ryan 8.00
208 Bob Feller 2.00
209 Red Schoendienst 2.00
210 Brooks Robinson 3.00
211 Al Kaline 3.00
212 Ozzie Smith 4.00
213 Maury Wills 2.00
214 Steve Carlton 2.00
215 Duke Snider 3.00
216 Scott Lewis/Auto./603 **RC** 15.00
217 Josh Johnson/Auto./597 **RC** 10.00
218 Jeff Fiorentino/Auto./597 **RC** 15.00
219 Grant Hansen/Auto./599 **RC** 6.00
220 Yovani Gallardo/Auto./803 **RC** 75.00
221 Eddie Prasch/Auto./603 **RC** 10.00
222 Danny Hill/Auto./603 **RC** 6.00
223 Chuck Lofgren/Auto./803 **RC** 25.00
224 Blake Johnson/Auto./811 **RC** 10.00
225 Cory Dunlap/Auto./599 **RC** 15.00
226 Carlos Vasquez/Auto./869 **RC** 8.00
227 Jesse Crain/Auto./1000 **RC** 10.00
228 Yhency Brazoban/Auto./1000 **RC** 6.00
229 Abe Alvarez/Auto./1000 **RC** 8.00
230 Scott Kazmir/Auto./350 50.00
231 J.A. Happ/Auto./1195 **RC** 8.00
232 Mark Jecmen/Auto./1047 **RC** 6.00
234 Kameron Loe/1000 **RC** 3.00
235 Ervin Santana/1000 **RC** 5.00
239 Josh Karp/1000 **RC** 3.00
242 Alberto Callaspo/1000 **RC** 3.00
243 Jesse Hoover/Auto./1191 **RC** 8.00
246 Justin Hoyman/Auto./1124 **RC** 8.00
247 Juan Cedeno/1000 **RC** 3.00
250 Jake Dittler/1000 4.00
252 Benjamin Zobrist/Auto./1178 **RC** 10.00
253 Jeff Salazar/1000 **RC** 3.00
254 Fausto Carmona/1000 **RC** 4.00
256 Jorge Vasquez/Auto./1000 **RC** 6.00
257 Rafael Gonzalez/Auto./603 **RC** 6.00
258 Andrew Dobies/Auto./601 **RC** 10.00
259 Colby Miller/Auto./997 **RC** 6.00
260 K.C. Herren/Auto./735 **RC** 10.00
261 Ryan Meaux/Auto./546 **RC** 6.00
262 Dustin Pedroia/Auto./1114 **RC** 75.00
263 Fernando Nieve/Auto./1000 **RC** 10.00
264 Mariano Gomez/Auto./1000 **RC** 6.00
265 Eric Campbell/Auto./260 **RC** 60.00
266 Billy Killian/Auto./703 **RC** 6.00
267 Mike Rouse/Auto./999 6.00
268 Kyle Bono/Auto./1203 **RC** 8.00
269 Mitch Einertson/Auto./1047 **RC** 10.00
270 Scott Proctor/Auto./1000 **RC** 8.00
271 Tim Bittner/Auto./1000 **RC** 6.00
272 Christian Garcia/Auto./799 **RC** 10.00
273 Yadier Molina/Auto./1000 **RC** 20.00
275 Charles Thomas/Auto./907 **RC** 8.00
276 Travis Blackley/Auto./1000 **RC** 8.00
277 Frankie Francisco/Auto./1000 **RC** 6.00
278 Dioner Navarro/Auto./1000 **RC** 10.00
279 Joey Gathright/Auto./1000 **RC** 8.00
280 Kazuhito Tadano/Auto./1000 **RC** 15.00
281 Matt Bush/Auto./1100 **RC** 20.00
282 David Haehnel/Auto./865 **RC** 8.00
283 Tommy Hottovy/Auto./825 **RC** 8.00
284 Chris Carter/Auto./973 **RC** 25.00
285 Mark Rogers/Auto./578 **RC** 20.00
286 Jeremy Sowers/Auto./537 **RC** 25.00
287 Homer Bailey/Auto./1571 **RC** 50.00
288 Mike Butia/Auto./825 **RC** 8.00
289 Chris Nelson/Auto./465 **RC** 30.00
290 Thomas Diamond/Auto./1055 **RC** 15.00
291 Neil Walker/Auto./1343 **RC** 25.00
292 Sean Gamble/Auto./1229 **RC** 8.00
293 Bill Bray/Auto./1073 **RC** 6.00
294 Reid Brignac/Auto./522 **RC** 60.00
295 Ryan Klosterman/Auto./865 **RC** 6.00
296 David Purcey/Auto./1485 **RC** 8.00
297 Scott Elbert/Auto./1617 **RC** 30.00
298 Josh Fields/Auto./961 **RC** 30.00
299 Chris Lambert/Auto./954 **RC** 8.00
300 Trevor Plouffe/Auto./1329 **RC** 15.00
301 Greg Golson/Auto./1334 **RC** 15.00
302 Josh Baker/Auto./525 **RC** 8.00
303 Phillip Hughes/Auto./1485 **RC** 80.00
304 Matt Macri/Auto./979 **RC** 10.00
305 Kyle Waldrop/Auto./823 **RC** 10.00
306 Richie Robnett/Auto./1575 **RC** 15.00
307 Taylor Tankersley/Auto./1073 **RC** 8.00
308 Blake DeWitt/Auto./1562 **RC** 25.00
309 Daryl Jones/Auto./575 **RC** 15.00
310 Eric Hurley/Auto./1021 **RC** 30.00
311 J.P. Howell/Auto./1453 **RC** 10.00
312 Zach Jackson/Auto./1069 **RC** 8.00
313 Justin Orenduff/Auto./473 **RC** 10.00
314 Tyler Lumsden/Auto./473 **RC** 10.00
315 Matt Fox/Auto./473 **RC** 12.00
316 Danny Putnam/Auto./473 **RC** 10.00
317 Jon Poterson/Auto./464 **RC** 15.00
318 Gio Gonzalez/Auto./473 **RC** 30.00
319 Jay Rainville/Auto./823 **RC** 12.00
320 Huston Street/Auto./709 **RC** 30.00
321 Jeff Marquez/Auto./493 **RC** 20.00
322 Eric Beattie/Auto./930 **RC** 8.00
323 B.J. Szymanski/Auto./1327 **RC** 8.00
324 Seth Smith/Auto./1065 **RC** 20.00
325 Robert Johnson/Auto./790 **RC** 8.00
326 Wes Whisler/Auto./473 **RC** 8.00
327 Billy Buckner/Auto./673 **RC** 8.00
328 Jon Zeringue/Auto./473 **RC** 15.00
329 Curtis Thigpen/Auto./673 **RC** 10.00
330 Donny Lucy/Auto./573 **RC** 6.00
331 Mike Ferris/Auto./558 **RC** 10.00
332 Anthony Swarzak/Auto./370 **RC** 25.00
333 Jason Jaramillo/Auto./573 **RC** 8.00
334 Hunter Pence/Auto./672 **RC** 150.00
335 Mike Rozier/Auto./628 **RC** 8.00
336 Kurt Suzuki/Auto./473 **RC** 20.00
337 Jason Vargas/Auto./621 **RC** 20.00
338 Brian Bixler/Auto./665 **RC** 10.00
340 Dexter Fowler/Auto./623 **RC** 50.00
341 Mark Trumbo/Auto./1321 **RC** 15.00
342 Jeff Frazier/Auto./423 **RC** 15.00
343 Steven Register/Auto./673 **RC** 8.00
344 Michael Schlact/Auto./477 **RC** 8.00
345 Garrett Mock/Auto./471 **RC** 12.00
346 Eric Haberer/Auto./473 **RC** 8.00
347 Matt Tuiasosopo/Auto./473 **RC** 25.00
348 Jason Windsor/Auto./473 **RC** 15.00
349 Grant Johnson/Auto./815 **RC** 10.00
350 J.C. Holt/Auto./673 **RC** 10.00
351 Joseph Bauserman/Auto./472 **RC** 8.00
352 Jamar Walton/Auto./481 **RC** 15.00
353 Eric Patterson/Auto.1571 **RC** 20.00
354 Tyler Johnson/Auto./775 **RC** 15.00
355 Nick Adenhart/Auto./653 **RC** 80.00

Aspirations

1-150 print run 61-99: 4-8X
1-150 p/r 41-60: 6-12X
1-150 p/r 26-40: 8-15X
1-150 p/r 25 or less: No Pricing
206-355 p/r 51-99: 1-2X No auto.
216-355 p/r 61-99: .4-1X Auto.
216-355 p/r 41-60: .5-1X Auto.
216-355 p/r 26-40: .75-1X Auto.
No Pricing print run 25 or less.

Aspirations Gold

Gold (1-150): 10-20X
Gold (206-215): 3-6X
Gold (216-355): No Pricing
Production 25 Sets

Status

1-150 print run 61-99: 4-8X
1-150 p/r 41-60: 6-12X
1-150 p/r 26-40: 8-15X
1-150 p/r 25 or less: No Pricing
206-355 p/r 51-99: 1-2X No Auto.
216-355 p/r 61-99: .4-1X Auto.
216-355 p/r 41-60: .5-1X Auto.
216-355 p/r 26-40: .75-1X Auto.
No pricing print run 25 or less.

Status Gold

No Pricing
Production 10 Sets

Turn of the Century

(1-150): 3-5X
Production 250 Sets
(206-215): 2-3X
(216-355 No Auto.): .5-1X
(216-355 Auto.): .2-.5X
206-355 production 100

Back to Back Picks Signature

NM/M

Quantity produced listed
1 Delmon Young, Rickie Weeks/25 50.00
3 Adam Dunn, Austin Kearns/25 50.00
5 Michael Young, Vernon Wells/25 35.00
6 Brian Roberts, Larry Bigbie/50 30.00
7 Ron Cey, Steve Garvey/50 35.00
8 Bill Madlock, Dave Parker/50 40.00
9 Derrek Lee, Torii Hunter, Trot Nixon/50 50.00
11 Chris Nelson, Matt Bush, Reid Brignac/250 65.00
12 B.J. Szymanski, Greg Golson, Jeff Frazier/250 40.00
13 Mark Trumbo, Nick Adenhart, Tyler Johnson/100 50.00
14 Chris Carter, Danny Putnam, Mark Jecmen/100 40.00
15 Billy Killian, Daryl Jones, Matt Bush/100 40.00
16 Blake DeWitt, Justin Orenduff, Scott Elbert/250 40.00
17 Jay Rainville, Kyle Waldrop, Trevor Plouffe/250 40.00
18 Jeff Marquez, Jon Poterson, Phillip Hughes/100 80.00
19 Wes Whisler, Tyler Lumsden, Wes Whisler/100 40.00
20 Curtis Thigpen, David Purcey, Zach Jackson/100 40.00

Career Best All-Stars

NM/M

Common Player: 2.00
Production 500 Sets
1 Randy Johnson 3.00
2 David Ortiz 3.00
3 Edgar Renteria 2.00
4 Victor Martinez 2.00
5 Albert Pujols 6.00
6 Hideki Matsui 5.00
7 Mariano Rivera 2.00
8 Carlos Zambrano 2.00
9 Hank Blalock 2.00
10 Michael Young 2.00
11 Mike Piazza 4.00
12 Alfonso Soriano 3.00
13 Carl Crawford 2.00
14 Scott Rolen 3.00
15 Vladimir Guerrero 3.00
16 Lance Berkman 2.00
17 Todd Helton 3.00
18 Curt Schilling 3.00
19 Francisco Cordero 2.00
20 Mark Mulder 2.00
21 Sammy Sosa 4.00
22 Roger Clemens 6.00
23 Miguel Cabrera 3.00
24 Manny Ramirez 3.00
25 Jim Thome 3.00

Career Best A-S Jersey

NM/M

Production 50 Sets
Prime: 1X-2X
Production 5-25
No pricing 15 or less.
1 Randy Johnson 15.00
2 David Ortiz 15.00
3 Edgar Renteria 8.00
4 Victor Martinez 8.00
5 Albert Pujols 25.00
6 Hideki Matsui 40.00
7 Mariano Rivera 10.00
8 Carlos Zambrano 8.00
9 Hank Blalock 10.00
10 Michael Young 8.00
11 Mike Piazza 20.00
12 Alfonso Soriano 15.00
13 Carl Crawford 8.00
14 Scott Rolen 15.00
15 Vladimir Guerrero 15.00
16 Lance Berkman 8.00
17 Todd Helton 10.00
18 Curt Schilling 15.00
19 Francisco Cordero 8.00
20 Mark Mulder 8.00
21 Sammy Sosa 20.00
22 Roger Clemens 20.00
23 Miguel Cabrera 12.00
24 Manny Ramirez 15.00
25 Jim Thome 15.00

Career Best A-S Jersey Prime

NM/M

2 David Ortiz/25 25.00
4 Victor Martinez/25 15.00
5 Albert Pujols/25 40.00
6 Hideki Matsui/25 75.00
8 Carlos Zambrano/25 15.00
9 Hank Blalock/25 20.00
10 Michael Young/25 15.00
11 Mike Piazza/25 30.00
12 Alfonso Soriano/25 25.00
13 Carl Crawford/25 15.00
14 Scott Rolen/25 25.00
15 Vladimir Guerrero/25 25.00
16 Lance Berkman/25 15.00
17 Todd Helton/25 20.00
18 Curt Schilling/25 25.00
20 Mark Mulder/25 15.00
21 Sammy Sosa/25 30.00
22 Roger Clemens/25 40.00
23 Miguel Cabrera/25 20.00
24 Manny Ramirez/25 25.00
25 Jim Thome/25 25.00

Career Best A-S Signature Black

No Pricing
Production 1-5

Career Best A-S Signature Gold

No Pricing
Production 1-10

Career Best A-S Signature Jersey Go

NM/M

Production 1-25
2 David Ortiz/25 75.00
3 Edgar Renteria/25 40.00
4 Victor Martinez/25 40.00
8 Carlos Zambrano/25 40.00
10 Michael Young/25 35.00
13 Carl Crawford/25 30.00
19 Francisco Cordero/25 20.00

Career Best A-S Signature Jersey Prime

No Pricing
Production 1-10

Draft Class

NM/M

Common Duo: 2.00
Production 500 Sets
1 Johnny Bench, Nolan Ryan 10.00
2 Bert Blyleven, Dwight Evans 2.00
3 Jim Rice, Keith Hernandez 2.00
4 Dennis Eckersley, Gary Carter 3.00
5 Fred Lynn, Robin Yount 5.00
6 Andre Dawson, Lee Smith 2.00
7 Alan Trammell, Jack Morris 2.00
8 Harold Baines, Paul Molitor 3.00
9 Cal Ripken Jr., Kirk Gibson 10.00
10 Don Mattingly, Orel Hershiser 6.00
11 Darryl Strawberry, Eric Davis 2.00
12 Dwight Gooden, Jose Canseco 3.00
13 Rafael Palmeiro, Randy Johnson 4.00
14 Curt Schilling, Gary Sheffield 3.00
15 Mike Piazza, Robin Ventura 4.00
16 Frank Thomas, Jeff Bagwell 3.00
17 Chipper Jones, Mike Mussina 3.00
18 Garret Anderson, Jorge Posada 2.00
19 Scott Rolen, Torii Hunter 3.00
20 Kerry Wood, Todd Helton 3.00
21 Eric Chavez, Roy Oswalt 2.00
22 Johnny Estrada, Vernon Wells 2.00
23 Lance Berkman, Tim Hudson 2.00
24 Mark Buehrle, Mark Mulder 2.00
25 C.C. Sabathia, Sean Burroughs 2.00
26 Albert Pujols, Barry Zito 6.00
27 Rich Harden, Rocco Baldelli 2.00
28 Bobby Crosby, Mark Teixeira 2.00
29 Casey Kotchman, Mark Prior 3.00
30 Dewon Brazelton, Jeremy Bonderman 2.00
31 J.C. Holt, Jon Zeringue 3.00
32 Kyle Bono, Matt Fox 3.00
33 Dexter Fowler, Mike Rozier 3.00
34 Huston Street, J.P. Howell 3.00
35 Grant Johnson, Matt Macri 3.00
36 Eric Beattie, Jeff Frazier 3.00
37 Jason Windsor, Kurt Suzuki 5.00
38 Josh Fields, Matt Tuiasosopo 6.00
39 Joseph Bauserman, K.C. Herren 3.00
40 Chris Lambert, Eric Haberer, Matt Tuiasosopo 3.00

Passing the Torch

NM/M

Common Duo: 3.00
Production 500 Sets
1 Dennis Eckersley, Huston Street 4.00
2 Matt Bush, Tony Gwynn 6.00
3 Homer Bailey, Tom Seaver 4.00
4 Bob Feller, Jeremy Sowers 3.00
5 Josh Fields, Robin Ventura 3.00
6 Nolan Ryan, Thomas Diamond 8.00
7 Eric Patterson, Ryne Sandberg 6.00
8 Richie Robnett, Rickey Henderson 4.00
9 Mike Ferris, Stan Musial 5.00
10 Bobby Doerr, Dustin Pedroia 3.00

Passing the Torch Autograph Black

No Pricing
Production 5-10 Sets

Passing the Torch Autograph Gold

NM/M

Production 5-25
2 Matt Bush, Tony Gwynn/25 90.00
4 Bob Feller, Jeremy Sowers/25 60.00
10 Bobby Doerr, Dustin Pedroia/25 75.00

Round Numbers

NM/M

Common Player: 2.00
Production 500 Sets
1 Ozzie Smith 4.00
2 Derek Jeter 6.00
3 Alex Rodriguez 5.00
4 Paul Molitor 3.00
5 George Brett 6.00
6 Delmon Young 2.00
7 Dontrelle Willis 2.00
8 Gary Carter 2.00
9 Reggie Jackson 3.00
10 Andre Dawson 2.00
11 Neil Walker 2.00
12 Laynce Nix 2.00
13 Matt Bush 6.00
14 Lyle Overbay 2.00
15 Carlos Beltran 3.00
16 Todd Helton 3.00
17 Mark Grace 2.00
18 Fred Lynn 2.00

19 Robin Yount 4.00
20 Mike Schmidt 6.00
21 Roger Clemens 6.00
22 Will Clark 3.00
23 Don Mattingly 5.00
24 Blake DeWitt 2.00
25 Rafael Palmeiro 3.00
26 Wade Boggs 3.00
27 Mark Rogers 5.00
28 Billy Buckner 3.00
29 Jeff Baker 2.00
30 Nolan Ryan 8.00
31 Mike Piazza 4.00
32 Alexis Rios 2.00
33 Eddie Murray 3.00
34 Jose Canseco 3.00
35 Mike Mussina 3.00
36 Eric Beattie 3.00
37 Keith Hernandez 2.00
38 Michael Young 2.00
39 Dwight Evans 2.00
40 Scott Elbert 3.00
41 Adrian Gonzalez 2.00
42 Johnny Bench 3.00
43 Dennis Eckersley 2.00
44 Dale Murphy 3.00
45 Ryne Sandberg 4.00
46 David Wright 3.00
47 Hank Blalock 3.00
48 Orel Hershiser 2.00
49 Sean Casey 2.00
50 Albert Pujols 6.00

Round Numbers Signature

NM/M

Production 5-250
1 Ozzie Smith/25 65.00
4 Paul Molitor/25 35.00
6 Delmon Young/50 25.00
7 Dontrelle Willis/25 20.00
8 Gary Carter/50 20.00
10 Andre Dawson/50 20.00
11 Neil Walker/250 20.00
12 Laynce Nix/50 20.00
13 Matt Bush/100 40.00
14 Lyle Overbay/50 15.00
15 Carlos Beltran/25 50.00
17 Mark Grace/25 35.00
18 Fred Lynn/50 15.00
20 Mike Schmidt/25 85.00
22 Will Clark/20 60.00
23 Don Mattingly/25 80.00
24 Blake DeWitt/250 30.00
27 Mark Rogers/100 40.00
28 Billy Buckner/100 15.00
32 Alexis Rios/50 15.00
34 Jose Canseco/25 50.00
36 Eric Beattie/100 10.00
37 Keith Hernandez/50 20.00
38 Michael Young/50 20.00
39 Dwight Evans/50 25.00
40 Scott Elbert/250 15.00
41 Adrian Gonzalez/50 10.00
43 Dennis Eckersley/50 30.00
44 Dale Murphy/50 30.00
46 David Wright/25 75.00
47 Hank Blalock/25 20.00
49 Sean Casey/25 15.00

Signature

NM/M

Production 1-50
132 Jack Wilson/25 25.00
133 Jason Bay/25 25.00
231 J.A. Happ/50 10.00
233 Mark Jecmen/50 8.00
234 Kameron Loe/50 20.00
235 Ervin Santana/50 40.00
239 Josh Karp/50 15.00
243 Jesse Hoover/50 10.00
246 Justin Hoyman/50 15.00
247 Juan Cedeno/50 15.00
252 Benjamin Zobrist/50 10.00
253 Jeff Salazar/50 30.00
254 Fausto Carmona/50 20.00

Signature Aspirations

NM/M

Production 1-100
Golds: No Pricing
Production 1-25
216 Scott Lewis/50 15.00
217 Josh Johnson/50 15.00
218 Jeff Fiorentino/50 25.00
219 Grant Hansen/50 8.00
220 Yovani Gallardo/50 150.00
221 Eddie Prasch/50 10.00
222 Danny Hill/50 8.00
223 Chuck Lofgren/50 40.00
224 Blake Johnson/50 15.00
225 Cory Dunlap/50 20.00
226 Carlos Vasquez/50 10.00
227 Jesse Crain/50 15.00
228 Yhency Brazoban/50 10.00
229 Abe Alvarez/50 10.00
256 Jorge Vasquez/50 8.00
257 Rafael Gonzalez/50 8.00
258 Andrew Dobies/50 15.00
259 Colby Miller/49 10.00
260 K.C. Herren/50 15.00
261 Ryan Meaux/50 10.00
262 Dustin Pedroia/50 100.00
263 Fernando Nieve/50 8.00
264 Mariano Gomez/50 8.00
266 Billy Killian/50 8.00
267 Mike Rouse/50 10.00
268 Kyle Bono/50 10.00
269 Mitch Einertson/50 25.00
270 Scott Proctor/50 15.00
271 Tim Bittner/50 8.00
272 Christian Garcia/50 10.00
273 Yadier Molina/50 30.00
274 Justin Leone/50 15.00
275 Charles Thomas/50 15.00
276 Travis Blackley/50 10.00
277 Frankie Francisco/50 10.00
278 Dioner Navarro/50 15.00
279 Joey Gathright/50 10.00
280 Kazuhito Tadano/50 20.00
281 Matt Bush/100 30.00
282 David Haehnel/100 10.00
283 Tommy Hottovy/100 10.00
284 Chris Carter/100 30.00
286 Jeremy Sowers/100 40.00
287 Homer Bailey/100 75.00
288 Mike Butia/100 10.00
289 Chris Nelson/100 40.00
290 Thomas Diamond/100 30.00
291 Neil Walker/100 30.00
292 Sean Gamble/100 10.00
293 Bill Bray/100 8.00
294 Reid Brignac/50 80.00
295 Ryan Klosterman/100 8.00
296 David Purcey/100 10.00
297 Scott Elbert/100 50.00
298 Josh Fields/100 40.00
299 Chris Lambert/100 10.00
300 Trevor Plouffe/100 25.00
301 Greg Golson/100 20.00
302 Josh Baker/100 10.00
303 Phillip Hughes/100 125.00
304 Matt Macri/50 12.00
305 Kyle Waldrop/100 25.00
306 Richie Robnett/100 25.00
307 Taylor Tankersley/100 10.00
308 Blake DeWitt/100 50.00
309 Daryl Jones/50 25.00
310 Eric Hurley/100 40.00
311 J.P. Howell/100 10.00
312 Zach Jackson/100 20.00
313 Justin Orenduff/100 20.00
314 Tyler Lumsden/100 15.00
315 Matt Fox/100 15.00
316 Danny Putnam/100 15.00
317 Jon Poterson/100 20.00
318 Gio Gonzalez/100 40.00
319 Jay Rainville/100 25.00
320 Huston Street/100 50.00
321 Jeff Marquez/100 15.00
322 Eric Beattie/100 10.00
323 B.J. Szymanski/100 10.00
324 Seth Smith/100 30.00
325 Robert Johnson/100 10.00
326 Wes Whisler/50 10.00
327 Billy Buckner/50 10.00
328 Jon Zeringue/100 30.00
329 Curtis Thigpen/50 12.00
330 Donny Lucy/50 10.00
331 Mike Ferris/100 12.00
333 Jason Jaramillo/100 10.00
334 Hunter Pence/50 160.00
335 Mike Rozier/50 10.00
336 Kurt Suzuki/100 25.00
337 Jason Vargas/50 50.00
338 Brian Bixler/50 10.00
340 Dexter Fowler/50 80.00
341 Mark Trumbo/50 15.00
342 Jeff Frazier/100 20.00
343 Steven Register/50 10.00
344 Michael Schlact/50 10.00
345 Garrett Mock/50 15.00
346 Eric Haberer/50 10.00
347 Matt Tuiasosopo/100 30.00
348 Jason Windsor/50 20.00
349 Grant Johnson/50 10.00
350 J.C. Holt/50 10.00
351 Joseph Bauserman/50 10.00
352 Jamar Walton/50 10.00
353 Eric Patterson/100 35.00
354 Tyler Johnson/50 25.00
355 Nick Adenhart/100 125.00

Signature Status

NM/M

Production 1-50
Golds: No Pricing
Production 1-10
221 Eddie Prasch/25 15.00
224 Blake Johnson/25 20.00
229 Abe Alvarez/25 15.00
257 Rafael Gonzalez/25 10.00
268 Kyle Bono/25 15.00
272 Christian Garcia/25 15.00
276 Travis Blackley/25 15.00
281 Matt Bush/50 40.00
282 David Haehnel/50 15.00
283 Tommy Hottovy/50 15.00
284 Chris Carter/50 40.00
286 Jeremy Sowers/50 40.00
287 Homer Bailey/50 125.00
288 Mike Butia/50 15.00
289 Chris Nelson/50 40.00
290 Thomas Diamond/50 40.00
291 Neil Walker/50 40.00
292 Sean Gamble/50 15.00
293 Bill Bray/50 10.00
294 Reid Brignac/50 80.00
295 Ryan Klosterman/50 10.00
296 David Purcey/50 15.00
297 Scott Elbert/50 75.00
298 Josh Fields/50 50.00
299 Chris Lambert/50 15.00
300 Trevor Plouffe/50 25.00
301 Greg Golson/50 35.00
302 Josh Baker/50 15.00
303 Phillip Hughes/50 160.00
304 Matt Macri/50 15.00
305 Kyle Waldrop/50 25.00
306 Richie Robnett/50 25.00
307 Taylor Tankersley/50 15.00
308 Blake DeWitt/50 40.00
309 Daryl Jones/50 30.00
310 Eric Hurley/50 50.00
311 J.P. Howell/50 20.00
312 Zach Jackson/50 15.00
313 Justin Orenduff/50 20.00
314 Tyler Lumsden/50 20.00
315 Matt Fox/50 20.00
316 Danny Putnam/50 20.00
317 Jon Poterson/50 20.00
318 Gio Gonzalez/50 50.00
319 Jay Rainville/50 35.00
320 Huston Street/50 60.00
321 Jeff Marquez/50 20.00
322 Eric Beattie/50 15.00
323 B.J. Szymanski/50 15.00
324 Seth Smith/50 40.00
325 Robert Johnson/50 15.00
326 Wes Whisler/50 15.00
327 Billy Buckner/50 15.00
328 Jon Zeringue/50 35.00
329 Curtis Thigpen/50 12.00
330 Donny Lucy/50 15.00
331 Mike Ferris/50 15.00
333 Jason Jaramillo/50 15.00
334 Hunter Pence/50 160.00
335 Mike Rozier/50 15.00
336 Kurt Suzuki/50 25.00
337 Jason Vargas/50 50.00
338 Brian Bixler/50 15.00
340 Dexter Fowler/50 80.00
341 Mark Trumbo/50 25.00
342 Jeff Frazier/50 20.00
343 Steven Register/50 10.00
344 Michael Schlact/50 10.00
345 Garrett Mock/50 15.00
346 Eric Haberer/50 10.00
347 Matt Tuiasosopo/50 40.00
348 Jason Windsor/50 20.00
349 Grant Johnson/50 10.00
350 J.C. Holt/50 10.00
351 Joseph Bauserman/50 10.00
352 Jamar Walton/50 25.00
353 Eric Patterson/50 35.00
354 Tyler Johnson/50 15.00
355 Nick Adenhart/50 150.00

Signature Turn of Century

NM/M

216 Scott Lewis/100 12.00
217 Josh Johnson/100 12.00
218 Jeff Fiorentino/100 10.00
219 Grant Hansen/100 8.00
220 Yovani Gallardo/100 125.00
221 Eddie Prasch/100 10.00
222 Danny Hill/100 8.00
223 Chuck Lofgren/100 35.00
224 Blake Johnson/100 20.00
225 Cory Dunlap/100 20.00
226 Carlos Vasquez/100 10.00
227 Jesse Crain/100 15.00
228 Yhency Brazoban/100 10.00
229 Abe Alvarez/100 10.00
246 Justin Hoyman/250 10.00
252 Benjamin Zobrist/150 10.00
256 Jorge Vasquez/100 8.00
257 Rafael Gonzalez/100 8.00
258 Andrew Dobies/100 15.00
259 Colby Miller/100 10.00
260 K.C. Herren/100 15.00
261 Ryan Meaux/100 10.00
262 Dustin Pedroia/100 75.00
263 Fernando Nieve/100 10.00
264 Mariano Gomez/100 10.00
266 Billy Killian/100 15.00
267 Mike Rouse/100 10.00
268 Kyle Bono/100 10.00
269 Mitch Einertson/100 15.00
270 Scott Proctor/100 10.00
271 Tim Bittner/100 8.00
272 Christian Garcia/100 10.00
273 Yadier Molina/100 30.00
274 Justin Leone/100 15.00
275 Charles Thomas/100 15.00
276 Travis Blackley/100 10.00
277 Frankie Francisco/100 10.00
278 Dioner Navarro/100 15.00
279 Joey Gathright/100 15.00
280 Kazuhito Tadano/100 15.00
281 Matt Bush/250 20.00
282 David Haehnel/250 8.00
283 Tommy Hottovy/250 8.00
284 Chris Carter/250 30.00
285 Mark Rogers/100 30.00
286 Jeremy Sowers/250 30.00
287 Homer Bailey/250 75.00
288 Mike Butia/250 8.00
289 Chris Nelson/100 30.00
290 Thomas Diamond/250 25.00
291 Neil Walker/242 25.00
292 Sean Gamble/250 8.00
293 Bill Bray/250 8.00
294 Reid Brignac/100 60.00
295 Ryan Klosterman/250 8.00
296 David Purcey/250 8.00
297 Scott Elbert/250 50.00
298 Josh Fields/250 40.00
299 Chris Lambert/250 15.00
300 Trevor Plouffe/250 15.00
301 Greg Golson/250 20.00
302 Josh Baker/100 10.00
303 Phillip Hughes/250 100.00
304 Matt Macri/250 15.00
305 Kyle Waldrop/250 15.00
306 Richie Robnett/250 15.00
307 Taylor Tankersley/250 10.00
308 Blake DeWitt/250 25.00
309 Daryl Jones/250 15.00
310 Eric Hurley/250 30.00
311 J.P. Howell/250 10.00
312 Zach Jackson/250 10.00
313 Justin Orenduff/100 15.00
314 Tyler Lumsden/250 10.00
315 Matt Fox/250 12.00
316 Danny Putnam/250 12.00
317 Jon Poterson/238 12.00
318 Gio Gonzalez/250 35.00
319 Jay Rainville/250 20.00
320 Huston Street/250 30.00
321 Jeff Marquez/250 10.00
322 Eric Beattie/250 8.00
323 B.J. Szymanski/250 8.00
324 Seth Smith/250 20.00
325 Robert Johnson/100 10.00
326 Wes Whisler/100 8.00
327 Billy Buckner/100 10.00
328 Jon Zeringue/250 20.00
329 Curtis Thigpen/100 10.00
330 Donny Lucy/100 8.00
331 Mike Ferris/250 10.00
332 Anthony Swarzak/100 25.00
333 Jason Jaramillo/250 8.00
334 Hunter Pence/200 180.00
335 Mike Rozier/250 8.00
336 Kurt Suzuki/250 20.00
337 Jason Vargas/200 20.00
338 Brian Bixler/200 8.00
340 Dexter Fowler/250 40.00
341 Mark Trumbo/250 20.00
342 Jeff Frazier/50 20.00
343 Steven Register/200 8.00
344 Michael Schlact/200 8.00
345 Garrett Mock/200 15.00
346 Eric Haberer/100 8.00
347 Matt Tuiasosopo/250 25.00
348 Jason Windsor/100 15.00
349 Grant Johnson/250 8.00
350 J.C. Holt/100 8.00
351 Joseph Bauserman/100 8.00
352 Jamar Walton/200 12.00
353 Eric Patterson/250 25.00
354 Tyler Johnson/250 15.00
355 Nick Adenhart/100 12.00

Throwback Threads

NM/M

Production 50 Sets
1 Roger Maris 60.00
2 Ted Williams 80.00
3 Cal Ripken Jr. 75.00
4 Duke Snider 20.00
5 George Brett 40.00

Throwback Threads Autograph

No Pricing

2004 Donruss Leather & Lumber

NM/M

Complete Set (175):
Common Player (1-150): .25
Common Auto. (151-173): 6.00
Production 500
Pack (5): 5.00
Box (24): 100.00
1 Bartolo Colon .25
2 Garret Anderson .50
3 Tim Salmon .50
4 Troy Glaus .50
5 Vladimir Guerrero 1.00
6 Brandon Webb .25
7 Luis Gonzalez .40
8 Randy Johnson 1.00
9 Richie Sexson .50
10 Shea Hillenbrand .25
11 Adam LaRoche .25
12 Andruw Jones .50
13 Chipper Jones 1.00
14 Dale Murphy .75
15 J.D. Drew .50
16 Marcus Giles .25
17 Rafael Furcal .25
18 Cal Ripken Jr. 3.00
19 Javy Lopez .50
20 Jay Gibbons .25
21 Luis Matos .25
22 Miguel Tejada .50
23 Rafael Palmeiro .75
24 Curt Schilling .75
25 Jason Varitek .40
26 Manny Ramirez .75
27 Nomar Garciaparra 1.50
28 Pedro J. Martinez 1.00
29 Trot Nixon .25
30 Greg Maddux 1.50
31 Kerry Wood 1.00
32 Mark Prior 1.00
33 Ryne Sandberg 1.50
34 Sammy Sosa 2.00
35 Carlos Lee .25
36 Frank Thomas .75
37 Magglio Ordonez .40
38 Paul Konerko .25
39 Adam Dunn .75
40 Austin Kearns .25
41 Barry Larkin .50
42 Ken Griffey Jr. 1.50
43 Ryan Wagner .25
44 C.C. Sabathia .25
45 Jody Gerut .25
46 Omar Vizquel .25
47 Larry Walker .40
48 Preston Wilson .25
49 Todd Helton .75
50 Alan Trammell .25
51 Ivan Rodriguez .75
52 Jeremy Bonderman .25
53 Dontrelle Willis .25
54 Josh Beckett .50
55 Luis Castillo .25
56 Miguel Cabrera 1.00
57 Mike Lowell .25
58 Andy Pettitte .40
59 Craig Biggio .40
60 Jeff Bagwell .75
61 Jeff Kent .40
62 Lance Berkman .40
63 Roger Clemens 2.50
64 Roy Oswalt .40
65 Angel Berroa .25
66 Carlos Beltran .75
67 George Brett 2.00
68 Juan Gonzalez .50
69 Mike Sweeney .25
70 Eric Gagne .50
71 Hideo Nomo .50
72 Kazuhisa Ishii .25
73 Paul LoDuca .25
74 Shawn Green .50
75 Geoff Jenkins .25
76 Junior Spivey .25
77 Rickie Weeks .25
78 Robin Yount .75
79 Scott Podsednik .25
80 Jacque Jones .25
81 Johan Santana .50
82 Shannon Stewart .25
83 Torii Hunter .40
84 Andre Dawson .50
85 Chad Cordero .25
86 Jose Vidro .25
87 Nick Johnson .25
88 Orlando Cabrera .40
89 Gary Carter .50
90 Jae Weong Seo .25
91 Jose Reyes .50
92 Mike Piazza 1.50
93 Tom Glavine .50
94 Alex Rodriguez 2.50
95 Bernie Williams .50
96 Derek Jeter 2.50
97 Don Mattingly 2.00
98 Gary Sheffield .50
99 Hideki Matsui 1.50
100 Jason Giambi .50
101 Jorge Posada .50
102 Mike Mussina .50
103 Barry Zito .50
104 Bobby Crosby .25
105 Eric Chavez .40
106 Jermaine Dye .25
107 Mark Mulder .40
108 Rich Harden .25
109 Rickey Henderson .25
110 Tim Hudson .40
111 Bobby Abreu .40
112 Brett Myers .25
113 Jim Thome 1.00
114 Kevin Millwood .25
115 Marlon Byrd .25
116 Mike Schmidt 2.00
117 Pat Burrell .25
118 Dave Parker .25
119 Jason Bay .25
120 Jason Kendall .25
121 Brian Giles .25
122 Jay Payton .25
123 Ryan Klesko .25
124 Tony Gwynn 1.00
125 Edgardo Alfonzo .25
126 Jason Schmidt .50
127 Jerome Williams .25
128 Bret Boone .25
129 Edgar Martinez .25
130 Ichiro Suzuki 2.00
131 Jamie Moyer .25
132 John Olerud .25
133 Albert Pujols 2.00
134 Edgar Renteria .40
135 Jim Edmonds .50
136 Matt Morris .25
137 Scott Rolen 1.00
138 Aubrey Huff .25
139 Carl Crawford .25
140 Delmon Young .25
141 Rocco Baldelli .25
142 Alfonso Soriano 1.00
143 Hank Blalock .75
144 Mark Teixeira .50
145 Michael Young .25
146 Nolan Ryan 2.50
147 Carlos Delgado .50
148 Eric Hinske .25
149 Roy Halladay .25
150 Vernon Wells .25
151 Andres Blanco **RC** 8.00
152 Kevin Cave **RC** 6.00
153 Ryan Meaux **RC** 6.00
154 Tim Bausher **RC** 6.00
155 Jesse Harper **RC** 6.00
156 Mike Wuertz **RC** 8.00
157 Colby Miller **RC** 8.00
158 Donald Kelly **RC** 6.00
159 Edwin Moreno **RC** 8.00
160 Mike Johnston **RC** 6.00
161 Orlando Rodriguez **RC** 6.00
162 Phil Stockman **RC** 8.00
163 Yadier Molina **RC** 8.00
164 Jorge Vasquez **RC** 6.00
165 Scott Proctor **RC** 8.00
166 Jake Woods 6.00
167 Aarom Baldiris **RC** 8.00
168 Jason Bartlett **RC** 6.00
169 Casey Daigle **RC** 6.00
170 Dennis Sarfate **RC** 6.00
171 Edwardo Sierra **RC** 8.00
172 Merkin Valdez **RC** 8.00
173 Eddy Rodriguez **RC** 8.00
174 Kazuo Matsui **RC** 8.00
175 David Aardsma **RC** 4.00

Silver

Stars (1-150): 4-8X
SP's (151-175): .5X
Production 100 Sets

Gold

Stars (1-150): 10-15X
SP's (151-175): No Pricing
Production 25 Sets

Platinum

No Pricing
Production One Set

B/W

NM/M

Common Player: 1.50
Production 1,000 Sets
Gold B/W: 4-6X
Production 25 Sets
Silver B/W: 2-3X
Production 100 Sets
Platinum B/W: No Pricing
Production One Set
13 Chipper Jones 2.00
14 Dale Murphy 1.50
18 Cal Ripken Jr. 8.00
27 Nomar Garciaparra 3.00
30 Greg Maddux 2.50
32 Mark Prior 1.50
33 Ryne Sandberg 3.00
34 Sammy Sosa 3.00
63 Roger Clemens 4.00
67 George Brett 4.00
78 Robin Yount 3.00
89 Gary Carter 1.50
92 Mike Piazza 3.00
94 Alex Rodriguez 5.00
96 Derek Jeter 5.00
97 Don Mattingly 4.00
99 Hideki Matsui 3.00
109 Rickey Henderson 1.50
116 Mike Schmidt 3.00
124 Tony Gwynn 2.00
130 Ichiro Suzuki 4.00
133 Albert Pujols 4.00
142 Alfonso Soriano 2.00
146 Nolan Ryan 5.00
174 Kazuo Matsui 6.00

Bat-Spikes

NM/M

Bat/Glove: .75-1.5X
Production 1-50
Bat/Ball: .75-1.5X
Production 5-25
No pricing 15 or less.
Barrel/Jersey: No Pricing
Production 1-5
1 Andruw Jones/25 15.00
3 Angel Berroa/25 10.00
6 Barry Zito/25 15.00
7 Ben Sheets/50 10.00

8 Brad Penny/50 8.00
9 Brian Giles/50 8.00
10 Carlos Lee/50 8.00
11 Corey Patterson/50 15.00
13 Don Mattingly/25 40.00
15 Gary Carter/50 12.00
17 Ivan Rodriguez/50 15.00
18 Jack Cust/50 8.00
19 Jason Jennings/50 8.00
21 Jim Edmonds/50 10.00
22 Joe Borchard/50 8.00
23 Joe Crede/50 8.00
24 Josh Beckett/25 15.00
25 Josh Phelps/50 8.00
26 Juan Pierre/50 8.00
27 Kenny Lofton/50 8.00
29 Lance Berkman/25 15.00
30 Magglio Ordonez/25 10.00
31 Marcus Giles/50 10.00
32 Mark Buehrle/50 8.00
33 Mark Prior/25 20.00
34 Mark Teixeira/25 15.00
35 Marlon Byrd/50 8.00
38 Nick Johnson/25 10.00
39 Orlando Hudson/50 8.00
40 Paul LoDuca/25 10.00
41 Rafael Palmeiro/25 20.00
43 Roy Oswalt/25 15.00
44 Ryan Klesko/50 10.00
46 Sean Casey/50 10.00
48 Travis Hafner/50 15.00
49 Victor Martinez/50 10.00
50 Wade Miller/50 10.00

Cuts

NM/M
Common Player:
1 Adam Dunn/192 20.00
2 Al Kaline/192 35.00
3 Alfonso Soriano/160 40.00
4 Andre Dawson/224 15.00
5 Angel Berroa/224 10.00
6 Harmon Killebrew/192 35.00
7 Bob Gibson/96 30.00
8 Brooks Robinson/192 30.00
9 Cal Ripken Jr./32 200.00
10 Dale Murphy/224 25.00
11 Darryl Strawberry/224 15.00
12 Delmon Young/192 20.00
13 Don Mattingly/96 65.00
14 Duke Snider/96 30.00
15 Dwight Gooden/224 15.00
16 Ozzie Smith/96 60.00
18 Garret Anderson/224 15.00
19 Gary Carter/160 20.00
20 George Kell/224 15.00
21 Hank Blalock/224 20.00
22 Jim Palmer/192 20.00
23 Kirk Gibson/160 15.00
24 Lou Brock/192 25.00
25 Ryne Sandberg/160 50.00
26 Mark Prior/160 40.00
27 Miguel Cabrera/224 25.00
28 Mike Lowell/160 15.00
29 Nolan Ryan/96 100.00
30 Luis Aparicio/224 15.00
31 Paul Molitor/160 30.00
32 Red Schoendienst/224 25.00
33 Rickie Weeks/224 15.00
34 Ron Santo/224 25.00
35 Roy Oswalt/224 20.00
36 Stan Musial/96 60.00
37 Steve Carlton/192 20.00
38 Tony Gwynn/192 35.00
39 Vernon Wells/160 10.00
40 Will Clark/192 35.00
41 Bob Feller/224 25.00
42 Bobby Doerr/224 20.00
44 Ralph Kiner/224 30.00
45 Torii Hunter/224 15.00
46 Rollie Fingers/224 15.00
47 Steve Garvey/224 15.00
48 Alan Trammell/224 15.00
49 Maury Wills/224 15.00
50 Gaylord Perry/224 15.00

Cuts Glove

NM/M
Quantity produced listed
1 Adam Dunn/192 20.00
2 Al Kaline/192 35.00
3 Alfonso Soriano/160 40.00
4 Andre Dawson/224 15.00
5 Angel Berroa/224 10.00
6 Harmon Killebrew/192 35.00
7 Bob Gibson/96 30.00
8 Brooks Robinson/192 30.00
9 Cal Ripken Jr./32 200.00
10 Dale Murphy/224 25.00
11 Darryl Strawberry/224 15.00
12 Delmon Young/192 20.00
13 Don Mattingly/96 65.00
14 Duke Snider/96 30.00
15 Dwight Gooden/224 15.00
16 Ozzie Smith/96 60.00
18 Garret Anderson/224 15.00
19 Gary Carter/160 20.00
20 George Kell/224 15.00
21 Hank Blalock/224 20.00
22 Jim Palmer/192 20.00
23 Kirk Gibson/160 15.00
24 Lou Brock/192 25.00
25 Ryne Sandberg/160 50.00
26 Mark Prior/160 40.00
27 Miguel Cabrera/224 25.00
28 Mike Lowell/160 15.00
29 Nolan Ryan/96 100.00
30 Luis Aparicio/224 15.00
31 Paul Molitor/160 30.00
32 Red Schoendienst/224 25.00
33 Rickie Weeks/224 15.00
34 Ron Santo/224 25.00
35 Roy Oswalt/224 20.00
36 Stan Musial/96 60.00
37 Steve Carlton/192 20.00
38 Tony Gwynn/192 35.00
39 Vernon Wells/160 10.00
40 Will Clark/192 35.00
41 Bob Feller/224 25.00
42 Bobby Doerr/224 20.00
44 Ralph Kiner/224 30.00
45 Torii Hunter/224 15.00
46 Rollie Fingers/224 15.00
47 Steve Garvey/224 15.00
48 Alan Trammell/224 15.00
49 Maury Wills/224 15.00
50 Gaylord Perry/224 15.00

Hall of Fame

NM/M
Common Player: 2.00
Quantity produced listed
Silver: 1-2X
Production 100 Sets
1 Carl Yastrzemski/1989 4.00
2 Carlton Fisk/2000 2.00
3 George Brett/1999 5.00
4 Johnny Bench/1989 4.00
5 Mike Schmidt/1995 5.00
6 Nolan Ryan/1999 6.00
7 Ozzie Smith/2002 4.00
8 Robin Yount/1999 4.00
9 Rod Carew/1991 3.00
10 Tom Seaver/1992 3.00

Hall of Fame Materials

NM/M
Quantity produced listed
1 Carl Yastrzemski/Jsy/250 15.00
2 Carlton Fisk/Jsy/250 10.00
3 George Brett/Jsy/250 15.00
4 Johnny Bench/Jsy/100 15.00
5 Mike Schmidt/Jkt/250 15.00
6 Nolan Ryan/Pants/100 25.00
7 Ozzie Smith/Jsy/100 20.00
8 Robin Yount/Jsy/250 12.00
9 Rod Carew/Jkt/250 10.00
10 Tom Seaver/Jsy/200 15.00

Leather Cuts Ball

No Pricing
Production 5-10

Leather in Leather

NM/M
Common Player:
Production 2,499 Sets

Silver: 1-2X
Production 100 Sets
1 Garret Anderson/BB 1.50
2 Albert Pujols/BB 5.00
3 John Smoltz/BB 1.50
4 Cal Ripken Jr./BB 8.00
5 Ichiro Suzuki/BB 5.00
6 Pedro J. Martinez/BB 2.00
7 Shawn Green/BB 1.50
8 Juan Gonzalez/BB 1.50
9 Mariano Rivera/BB 1.50
10 Jason Giambi/BB 1.50
11 Dave Parker/BG 1.50
12 Dwight Gooden/BG 1.50
13 Eric Munson/BG 1.50
14 Frank Thomas/BG 2.00
15 Joe Carter/BG 1.50
16 Jose Canseco/BG 2.00
17 Paul O'Neill/BG 1.50
18 Tony Gwynn/BG 3.00
19 Wade Boggs/BG 2.00
20 Xavier Nady/BG 1.50
21 Albert Pujols/FG 5.00
22 Alex Rodriguez/FG 6.00
23 Chipper Jones/FG 3.00
24 Derek Jeter/FG 6.00
25 Jack Wilson/FG 1.50
26 Lenny Dykstra/FG 1.50
27 Mark Grace/FG 2.00
28 Steve Carlton/FG 2.00
29 Tony Perez/FG 2.00
30 Vladimir Guerrero/FG 3.00
31 Bernie Williams/SH 2.00
32 Eddie Murray/SH 3.00
33 Frank Robinson/SH 3.00
34 Greg Maddux/SH 4.00
35 Harmon Killebrew/SH 3.00
36 Manny Ramirez/SH 2.00
37 Mike Piazza/SH 4.00
38 Paul Molitor/SH 3.00
39 Sammy Sosa/SH 4.00
40 Tim Hudson/SH 2.00

Leather Materials

NM/M
Quantity produced listed
1 Garret Anderson/Ball/50 8.00
2 Albert Pujols/Ball/50 25.00
3 John Smoltz/Ball/50 20.00
4 Cal Ripken Jr./Ball/50 75.00
5 Ichiro Suzuki/Ball/50 60.00
6 Pedro J. Martinez/Ball/50 15.00
7 Shawn Green/Ball/50 8.00
8 Juan Gonzalez/Ball/50 10.00
9 Mariano Rivera/Ball/50 10.00
10 Jason Giambi/Ball/50 10.00
11 Dave Parker/Btg Glv/25 20.00
12 Dwight Gooden/Btg Glv/25 20.00
13 Eric Munson/Btg Glv/50 8.00
14 Frank Thomas/Btg Glv/50 20.00
15 Joe Carter/Btg Glv/50 10.00
16 Jose Canseco/Btg Glv/50 20.00
17 Paul O'Neill/Btg Glv/50 20.00
18 Tony Gwynn/Btg Glv/50 30.00
19 Wade Boggs/Btg Glv/25 20.00
20 Xavier Nady/Btg Glv/50 8.00
22 Alex Rodriguez/Fld Glv/25 35.00
23 Chipper Jones/Fld Glv/25 30.00
24 Derek Jeter/Fld Glv/25 50.00
25 Jack Wilson/Fld Glv/50 8.00
26 Lenny Dykstra/Fld Glv/50 10.00
27 Mark Grace/Fld Glv/50 15.00
28 Steve Carlton/Fld Glv/50 12.00
29 Tony Perez/Fld Glv/25 15.00
31 Bernie Williams/Spikes/50 10.00
32 Eddie Murray/Spikes/50 30.00
33 Frank Robinson/Spikes/50 10.00
34 Greg Maddux/Spikes/25 30.00
35 Harmon Killebrew/Spikes/25 35.00

Materials Bat B/W

NM/M
Production 100 unless noted.
13 Chipper Jones 8.00
14 Dale Murphy 10.00
18 Cal Ripken Jr. 30.00
27 Nomar Garciaparra 10.00
30 Greg Maddux 10.00
32 Mark Prior 8.00
33 Ryne Sandberg/50 30.00
34 Sammy Sosa 12.00
63 Roger Clemens/50 20.00
67 George Brett 15.00
78 Robin Yount 12.00
89 Gary Carter 8.00
92 Mike Piazza 10.00
94 Alex Rodriguez 10.00
96 Derek Jeter 20.00
97 Don Mattingly 20.00
109 Rickey Henderson 10.00
116 Mike Schmidt 15.00
124 Tony Gwynn 10.00
133 Albert Pujols 20.00
142 Alfonso Soriano 8.00
146 Nolan Ryan/25 65.00
174 Kazuo Matsui 20.00

Materials Jersey

NM/M
Common Jersey: 4.00
Quantity produced listed
MLB Logo: No Pricing
Production One Set
Prime: 1-1.25X
Production 1-25
No pricing 15 or less.
Barrel: No Pricing
Production 1-5
2 Garret Anderson/50 8.00
3 Tim Salmon/250 4.00
4 Troy Glaus/200 4.00
6 Brandon Webb/100 4.00
7 Luis Gonzalez/250 4.00
8 Randy Johnson/100 10.00
12 Andruw Jones/250 4.00
13 Chipper Jones/250 8.00
14 Dale Murphy/250 10.00
16 Marcus Giles/250 4.00
17 Rafael Furcal/250 4.00
18 Cal Ripken Jr./100 30.00
19 Javy Lopez/150 4.00
20 Jay Gibbons/250 4.00
21 Luis Matos/250 4.00
22 Miguel Tejada/250 6.00
23 Rafael Palmeiro/250 8.00
25 Jason Varitek/250 8.00
26 Manny Ramirez/250 8.00
28 Pedro J. Martinez/250 8.00
29 Trot Nixon/25 10.00
30 Greg Maddux/100 10.00
31 Kerry Wood/250 10.00
32 Mark Prior/250 8.00
33 Ryne Sandberg/50 30.00
34 Sammy Sosa/250 10.00
35 Carlos Lee/250 4.00
36 Frank Thomas/250 8.00
37 Magglio Ordonez/250 4.00
38 Paul Konerko/250 4.00
39 Adam Dunn/250 8.00
40 Austin Kearns/250 4.00
41 Barry Larkin/250 6.00
44 C.C. Sabathia/250 4.00
45 Jody Gerut/250 4.00
46 Omar Vizquel/250 4.00
47 Larry Walker/250 4.00
48 Preston Wilson/250 4.00
49 Todd Helton 8.00
50 Alan Trammell/50 10.00
51 Ivan Rodriguez/100 10.00
52 Jeremy Bonderman/150 4.00
53 Dontrelle Willis/100 4.00
54 Josh Beckett/250 4.00
55 Luis Castillo/250 4.00
56 Miguel Cabrera/50 15.00
57 Mike Lowell/25 10.00
58 Andy Pettitte/25 15.00
59 Craig Biggio/250 4.00
60 Jeff Bagwell/250 8.00
61 Jeff Kent/250 4.00
62 Lance Berkman/250 4.00
64 Roy Oswalt/250 4.00
65 Angel Berroa/50 6.00
66 Carlos Beltran/250 6.00
67 George Brett/50 15.00
69 Mike Sweeney/100 4.00
71 Hideo Nomo/250 6.00
72 Kazuhisa Ishii/250 4.00
73 Paul LoDuca/250 4.00
74 Shawn Green/250 4.00
75 Geoff Jenkins/250 4.00
78 Robin Yount/250 10.00
80 Jacque Jones/250 10.00
81 Johan Santana/250 8.00
82 Shannon Stewart/250 4.00
83 Torii Hunter/250 4.00
84 Andre Dawson/50 10.00
86 Jose Vidro/100 4.00
88 Orlando Cabrera/100 4.00
89 Gary Carter/250 8.00
90 Jae Weong Seo/100 4.00
91 Jose Reyes/250 6.00
92 Mike Piazza/250 10.00
93 Tom Glavine/250 6.00
95 Bernie Williams/250 6.00
96 Derek Jeter/150 20.00
97 Don Mattingly/250 15.00
99 Hideki Matsui/250 20.00
100 Jason Giambi/250 4.00
101 Jorge Posada/50 10.00
102 Mike Mussina/100 8.00
103 Barry Zito/250 4.00
105 Eric Chavez/100 4.00
107 Mark Mulder/250 4.00
108 Rich Harden/50 8.00
109 Rickey Henderson/100 10.00
110 Tim Hudson/250 4.00
111 Bobby Abreu/250 4.00
112 Brett Myers/250 4.00
113 Jim Thome/250 8.00
114 Kevin Millwood/250 4.00
115 Marlon Byrd/250 4.00
116 Mike Schmidt/50 25.00
117 Pat Burrell/250 4.00
118 Dave Parker/250 8.00
120 Jason Kendall/50 6.00
123 Ryan Klesko/250 4.00
124 Tony Gwynn/100 12.00
127 Jerome Williams/200 4.00
129 Edgar Martinez/250 6.00
131 Jamie Moyer/250 4.00
132 John Olerud/150 4.00
133 Albert Pujols/250 15.00
134 Edgar Renteria/100 6.00
135 Jim Edmonds/250 4.00
136 Matt Morris/250 4.00
137 Scott Rolen/250 8.00
138 Aubrey Huff/100 4.00
139 Carl Crawford/250 4.00
141 Rocco Baldelli/250 4.00
143 Hank Blalock/250 6.00
146 Nolan Ryan/100 30.00
147 Carlos Delgado/250 4.00
148 Eric Hinske/100 4.00
149 Roy Halladay/100 4.00
150 Vernon Wells/250 4.00

Materials Jersey B/W

NM/M
Common Player: 5.00
Jersey Prime B/W: No Pricing
Production 1-25
13 Chipper Jones/250 8.00
14 Dale Murphy/250 8.00
18 Cal Ripken Jr./100 35.00
30 Greg Maddux/100 10.00
32 Mark Prior/250 8.00
33 Ryne Sandberg/50 30.00
34 Sammy Sosa/250 12.00
67 George Brett/250 15.00
78 Robin Yount/150 10.00
89 Gary Carter/250 5.00
92 Mike Piazza/250 10.00
96 Derek Jeter/100 20.00
97 Don Mattingly/250 15.00
99 Hideki Matsui/250 20.00
109 Rickey Henderson/250 8.00
116 Mike Schmidt/50 25.00
124 Tony Gwynn/100 10.00
133 Albert Pujols/250 15.00
146 Nolan Ryan/100 25.00
174 Kazuo Matsui/50 25.00

Naturals

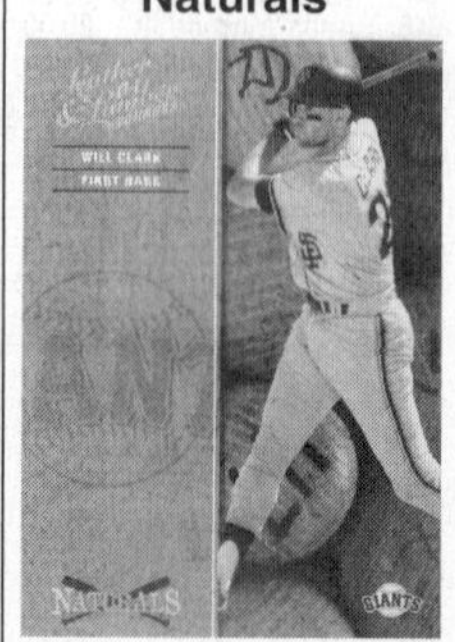

NM/M
Common Player: 1.50
Production 1,499 Sets
Silver: 1-2X
Production 100 Sets
1 Eric Chavez 1.50
2 Garret Anderson 1.50
3 Lance Berkman 1.50
4 Paul Molitor 3.00
5 Rafael Palmeiro 2.00
6 Ralph Kiner 3.00
7 Todd Helton 2.00
8 Tony Gwynn 4.00
9 Wade Boggs 2.00
10 Will Clark 2.00

Naturals Materials Bat

NM/M
Barrel: No Pricing
Production 1-5
1 Eric Chavez/20 12.00
2 Garret Anderson/250 5.00
3 Lance Berkman/250 5.00
4 Paul Molitor/250 8.00
5 Rafael Palmeiro/250 8.00
6 Ralph Kiner/250 10.00
7 Todd Helton/250 8.00
8 Tony Gwynn/250 12.00
9 Wade Boggs/250 8.00
10 Will Clark/250 10.00

Pennants/ Pinstripes

NM/M
Common Player: 1.50
Production 1,499 Sets
Gold: 1-2X
Production 100 Sets
1 Reggie Jackson 2.50
2 Mike Schmidt 5.00
3 Steve Carlton 2.00
4 Dwight Gooden 1.50
5 Darryl Strawberry 1.50
6 Roger Clemens 5.00
7 Curt Schilling 2.00
8 Mark Grace 2.00
9 Ivan Rodriguez 2.00
10 Josh Beckett 1.50

Pennants/ Pinstripes Materials

NM/M
Quantity produced listed
1 Reggie Jackson/Pants/100 10.00
2 Mike Schmidt/Jsy/25 35.00
3 Steve Carlton/Jsy/100 8.00
4 Dwight Gooden/Jsy/250 8.00
5 Darryl Strawberry/Pants/250 5.00
6 Roger Clemens/Jsy/250 10.00
7 Curt Schilling/Jsy/250 6.00
8 Mark Grace/Jsy/250 8.00
9 Ivan Rodriguez/Jsy/250 8.00
10 Josh Beckett/Jsy/100 5.00

Rivals

NM/M
Common Duo:
Production 1,499 Sets
Silver: 1-2X
Production 100 Sets
1 Derek Jeter, Nomar Garciaparra 6.00
2 Mark Prior, Albert Pujols 4.00
3 Warren Spahn, Stan Musial 4.00
4 Don Sutton, Reggie Jackson 2.00
5 Roger Clemens, Mike Piazza 4.00
6 Dennis Eckersley, M. Williams 1.50
7 Kerry Wood, Frank Thomas 3.00
8 Jim Palmer, Willie Stargell 2.00
9 Tom Seaver, Mike Schmidt 5.00
10 Jack Morris, George Brett 5.00
11 Randy Johnson, Todd Helton 2.00
12 Tommy John, Rod Carew 2.00
13 Pedro J. Martinez, Jason Giambi 2.00
14 Dwight Gooden, Wade Boggs 1.50
15 Bob Gibson, Ernie Banks 3.00

No.	Player	Price
16	Hideo Nomo, Barry Larkin	1.50
17	Roy Halladay, Vladimir Guerrero	2.00
18	Greg Maddux, Jeff Bagwell	3.00
19	Barry Zito, Alex Rodriguez	5.00
20	Steve Carlton, Andre Dawson	1.50
21	Mariano Rivera, Chipper Jones	2.00
22	Tom Glavine, Manny Ramirez	2.00
23	Whitey Ford, Harmon Killebrew	2.00
24	Carl Yastrzemski, Jim "Catfish" Hunter	2.00
25	Nolan Ryan, Robin Ventura	5.00
26	Carlton Fisk, Joe Morgan	1.50
27	Phil Rizzuto, Duke Snider	2.00
28	Fergie Jenkins, Lou Brock	1.50
29	Jose Canseco, Will Clark	1.50
30	Mike Mussina, Josh Beckett	1.50
31	Rickey Henderson, Ivan Rodriguez	2.00
32	Don Mattingly, Eddie Murray	5.00
33	Troy Glaus, Eric Chavez	1.50
34	Ryne Sandberg, Steve Garvey	3.00
35	Bob Gibson, Roger Maris	4.00
36	Roger Clemens, Cal Ripken Jr.	8.00
37	Orel Hershiser, Darryl Strawberry	1.50
38	Curt Schilling, Paul Molitor	2.00
39	Ichiro Suzuki, Hideki Matsui	5.00
40	Sammy Sosa, Jim Thome	4.00

Rivals Materials

		NM/M
	Quantity produced listed	
1	Derek Jeter/Jsy, Nomar Garciaparra/Bat/250	25.00
2	Mark Prior/Jsy, Albert Pujols/Jsy/250	20.00
3	Warren Spahn/Pants, Stan Musial/Jsy/100	30.00
5	Roger Clemens/Jsy, Mike Piazza/Jsy/250	20.00
7	Kerry Wood/Jsy, Frank Thomas/Jsy/250	10.00
8	Jim Palmer/Jsy, Willie Stargell/Jsy/250	12.00
9	Tom Seaver/Jsy, Mike Schmidt/Jsy/250	20.00
10	Jack Morris/Jsy, George Brett/Jsy/250	15.00
11	Randy Johnson/Jsy, Todd Helton/Jsy/250	12.00
12	Tommy John/Pants, Rod Carew/Jkt/250	12.00
13	Pedro J. Martinez/Jsy, Jason Giambi/Jsy/250	12.00
14	Dwight Gooden/Jsy, Wade Boggs/Jsy/250	10.00
15	Bob Gibson/Jsy, Ernie Banks/Pants/100	20.00
16	Hideo Nomo/Jsy, Barry Larkin/Jsy/250	10.00
17	Roy Halladay/Jsy, Vladimir Guerrero/Jsy/250	10.00
18	Greg Maddux/Jsy, Jeff Bagwell/Jsy/250	15.00
19	Barry Zito/Jsy, Alex Rodriguez/Jsy/250	15.00
20	Steve Carlton/Jsy, Andre Dawson/Jsy/250	10.00
22	Tom Glavine/Jsy, Manny Ramirez/Jsy/250	10.00
23	Whitey Ford/Pants, Harmon Killebrew/Jsy/100	35.00
24	Carl Yastrzemski/Jsy, Jim "Catfish" Hunter/Jsy/250	20.00
25	Nolan Ryan/Pants, Robin Ventura/Jsy/250	25.00
26	Carlton Fisk/Jsy, Joe Morgan/Jsy/250	10.00
28	Fergie Jenkins/Pants, Lou Brock/Jsy/100	20.00
29	Jose Canseco/Bat, Will Clark/Bat/250	15.00
30	Mike Mussina/Jsy, Josh Beckett/Jsy/250	10.00
31	Rickey Henderson/Jsy, Ivan Rodriguez/Jsy/250	10.00
32	Don Mattingly/Pants, Eddie Murray/Jsy/250	20.00
33	Troy Glaus/Jsy, Eric Chavez/Jsy/250	8.00
34	Ryne Sandberg/Jsy, Steve Garvey/Jsy/250	20.00
35	Bob Gibson/Jsy, Roger Maris/Jsy/100	40.00
36	Roger Clemens/Jsy, Cal Ripken Jr./Pants/250	30.00
38	Curt Schilling/Jsy, Paul Molitor/Bat/250	12.00
39	Ichiro Suzuki/Base, Hideki Matsui/Base/250	40.00
40	Sammy Sosa/Jsy, Jim Thome/Jsy/250	12.00

Signatures Bronze

		NM/M
	Quantity produced listed	8.00
2	Garret Anderson/25	25.00
10	Shea Hillenbrand/100	10.00
11	Adam LaRoche/100	10.00
14	Dale Murphy/25	35.00
16	Marcus Giles/50	15.00
17	Rafael Furcal/25	20.00
20	Jay Gibbons/100	10.00
21	Luis Matos/100	10.00
35	Carlos Lee/100	10.00
39	Adam Dunn/25	30.00
44	C.C. Sabathia/100	15.00
48	Preston Wilson/50	15.00
50	Alan Trammell/50	20.00
52	Jeremy Bonderman/100	10.00
56	Miguel Cabrera/50	30.00
65	Angel Berroa/100	10.00
66	Carlos Beltran/100	25.00
79	Scott Podsednik/100	10.00
80	Jacque Jones/100	10.00
81	Johan Santana/100	40.00
82	Shannon Stewart/100	10.00
83	Torii Hunter/50	15.00
84	Andre Dawson/100	15.00
85	Chad Cordero/100	8.00
86	Jose Vidro/100	10.00
88	Orlando Cabrera/100	10.00
104	Bobby Crosby/100	20.00
106	Jermaine Dye/100	15.00
108	Rich Harden/50	20.00
115	Marlon Byrd/25	15.00
119	Jason Bay/100	15.00
122	Jay Payton/50	10.00
138	Aubrey Huff/50	15.00
139	Carl Crawford/50	20.00
145	Michael Young/100	15.00
151	Andres Blanco/50	10.00
152	Kevin Cave/50	10.00
153	Ryan Meaux/50	10.00
154	Tim Bausher/50	10.00
155	Jesse Harper/50	10.00
156	Mike Wuertz/50	10.00
158	Donald Kelly/50	8.00
159	Edwin Moreno/50	8.00
160	Mike Johnston/50	8.00
161	Orlando Rodriguez/50	8.00
164	Jorge Vasquez/50	10.00
166	Jake Woods/50	10.00
167	Aarom Baldiris/50	10.00
170	Dennis Sarfate/50	8.00
173	Eddy Rodriguez/50	10.00

Signatures Bronze B/W

No Pricing
Production 1-25

Signatures Silver

		NM/M
	Quantity produced listed	
2	Garret Anderson/50	20.00
10	Shea Hillenbrand/50	15.00
11	Adam LaRoche/50	15.00
14	Dale Murphy/50	25.00
16	Marcus Giles/50	15.00
17	Rafael Furcal/50	15.00
20	Jay Gibbons/50	10.00
21	Luis Matos/50	10.00
29	Trot Nixon/25	35.00
32	Mark Prior/25	40.00
35	Carlos Lee/50	10.00
39	Adam Dunn/25	30.00
40	Austin Kearns/25	20.00
43	Ryan Wagner/50	10.00
44	C.C. Sabathia/50	15.00
45	Jody Gerut/50	15.00
48	Preston Wilson/50	15.00
50	Alan Trammell/50	20.00
52	Jeremy Bonderman/50	10.00
56	Miguel Cabrera/50	30.00
65	Angel Berroa/50	10.00
66	Carlos Beltran/50	30.00
73	Paul LoDuca/25	20.00
79	Scott Podsednik/50	15.00
80	Jacque Jones/50	15.00
81	Johan Santana/50	40.00
82	Shannon Stewart/50	15.00
83	Torii Hunter/50	15.00
84	Andre Dawson/50	15.00
85	Chad Cordero/50	8.00
86	Jose Vidro/50	10.00
88	Orlando Cabrera/50	12.00
104	Bobby Crosby/50	25.00
106	Jermaine Dye/50	15.00
107	Mark Mulder/25	20.00
108	Rich Harden/50	20.00
115	Marlon Byrd/50	10.00
119	Jason Bay/50	20.00
122	Jay Payton/50	10.00
138	Aubrey Huff/50	15.00
139	Carl Crawford/50	20.00
143	Hank Blalock/50	25.00
145	Michael Young/50	20.00
150	Vernon Wells/50	15.00
151	Andres Blanco/100	10.00
152	Kevin Cave/100	10.00
153	Ryan Meaux/100	8.00
154	Tim Bausher/100	8.00
155	Jesse Harper/100	8.00
156	Mike Wuertz/100	10.00
158	Donald Kelly/100	6.00
159	Edwin Moreno/100	6.00
160	Mike Johnston/100	6.00
161	Orlando Rodriguez/100	6.00
164	Jorge Vasquez/100	8.00
166	Jake Woods/100	8.00
167	Aarom Baldiris/100	8.00
170	Dennis Sarfate/100	6.00
173	Eddy Rodriguez/100	8.00

Signatures Silver B/W

No Pricing
Production 1-25

Signatures Gold

		NM/M
	Quantity produced listed	
2	Garret Anderson/25	25.00
10	Shea Hillenbrand/25	20.00
11	Adam LaRoche/25	15.00
14	Dale Murphy/25	35.00
16	Marcus Giles/25	20.00
17	Rafael Furcal/25	20.00
20	Jay Gibbons/25	15.00
21	Luis Matos/25	15.00
35	Carlos Lee/25	15.00
39	Adam Dunn/25	30.00
44	C.C. Sabathia/25	20.00
45	Jody Gerut/25	20.00
48	Preston Wilson/25	20.00
50	Alan Trammell/25	25.00
52	Jeremy Bonderman/25	15.00
56	Miguel Cabrera/25	35.00
65	Angel Berroa/25	10.00
66	Carlos Beltran/25	40.00
79	Scott Podsednik/25	20.00
80	Jacque Jones/25	20.00
81	Johan Santana/25	50.00
82	Shannon Stewart/25	20.00
83	Torii Hunter/25	20.00
84	Andre Dawson/25	20.00
85	Chad Cordero/25	10.00
86	Jose Vidro/25	15.00
88	Orlando Cabrera/25	15.00
104	Bobby Crosby/25	30.00
106	Jermaine Dye/25	20.00
115	Marlon Byrd/25	15.00
119	Jason Bay/25	25.00
122	Jay Payton/25	15.00
138	Aubrey Huff/25	20.00
139	Carl Crawford/25	25.00
145	Michael Young/25	30.00
151	Andres Blanco/50	10.00
152	Kevin Cave/50	10.00
153	Ryan Meaux/50	10.00
154	Tim Bausher/50	10.00
155	Jesse Harper/50	10.00
156	Mike Wuertz/50	10.00
158	Donald Kelly/50	8.00
159	Edwin Moreno/50	8.00
160	Mike Johnston/50	8.00
161	Orlando Rodriguez/50	8.00
164	Jorge Vasquez/50	10.00
166	Jake Woods/50	10.00
167	Aarom Baldiris/50	10.00
168	Jason Bartlett/50	12.00
170	Dennis Sarfate/50	8.00
173	Eddy Rodriguez/50	10.00

Signatures Gold B/W

No Pricing
Production 1-25

Signatures Platinum

No Pricing
Production One Set

Signatures Platinum B/W

No Pricing
Production One Set

2004 Donruss Studio

		NM/M
	Complete Set (220):	
	Common Player:	.15
	Common SP (201-221):	6.00
	Production 400-800:	
	Pack (6):	4.00
	Box (24):	75.00
1	Bartolo Colon	.15
2	Garret Anderson	.40
3	Tim Salmon	.25
4	Troy Glaus	.40
5	Vladimir Guerrero	.75
6	Brandon Webb	.15
7	Brian Bruney	.15
8	Casey Fossum	.15
9	Luis Gonzales	.25
10	Randy Johnson	1.00
11	Richie Sexson	.40
12	Robby Hammock	.15
13	Roberto Alomar	.40
14	Shea Hillenbrand	.15
15	Steve Finley	.15
16	Adam LaRoche	.15
17	Andruw Jones	.50
18	Bubba Nelson	.15
19	Chipper Jones	.75
20	Dale Murphy	.50
21	J.D. Drew	.25
22	Marcus Giles	.15
23	Michael Hessman	.15
24	Rafael Furcal	.25
25	Warren Spahn	.50
26	Adam Loewen	.15
27	Cal Ripken Jr.	3.00
28	Javy Lopez	.40
29	Jay Gibbons	.15
30	Luis Matos	.15
31	Miguel Tejada	.40
32	Rafael Palmeiro	.50
33	Curt Schilling	.50
34	Jason Varitek	.25
35	Kevin Youkilis	.15
36	Manny Ramirez	.50
37	Nomar Garciaparra	1.50
38	Pedro Martinez	.75
39	Trot Nixon	.25
40	Aramis Ramirez	.40
41	Brendan Harris	.15
42	Derrek Lee	.25
43	Ernie Banks	1.00
44	Greg Maddux	1.00
45	Kerry Wood	.75
46	Mark Prior	1.00
47	Ryne Sandberg	1.00
48	Sammy Sosa	1.50
49	Todd Wellemeyer	.15
50	Carlos Lee	.15
51	Edwin Almonte	.15
52	Frank Thomas	.50
53	Joe Borchard	.15
54	Joe Crede	.15
55	Magglio Ordonez	.25
56	Adam Dunn	.50
57	Austin Kearns	.25
58	Barry Larkin	.40
59	Brandon Larson	.15
60	Ken Griffey Jr.	1.00
61	Ryan Wagner	.15
62	Sean Casey	.25
63	Brian Tallet	.15
64	C.C. Sabathia	.15
65	Jeremy Guthrie	.15
66	Jody Gerut	.15
67	Travis Hafner	.25
68	Clint Barmes	.15
69	Jeff Baker	.15
70	Joe Kennedy	.15
71	Larry Walker	.25
72	Preston Wilson	.15
73	Todd Helton	.50
74	Dmitri Young	.15
75	Ivan Rodriguez	.50
76	Jeremy Bonderman	.15
77	Preston Larrison	.15
78	Dontrelle Willis	.15
79	Josh Beckett	.50
80	Juan Pierre	.15
81	Luis Castillo	.15
82	Miguel Cabrera	.75
83	Mike Lowell	.25
84	Andy Pettitte	.25
85	Chris Burke	.15
86	Craig Biggio	.25
87	Jeff Bagwell	.50
88	Jeff Kent	.25
89	Lance Berkman	.25
90	Morgan Ensberg	.15
91	Richard Hidalgo	.15
92	Roger Clemens	1.50
93	Roy Oswalt	.25
94	Wade Miller	.15
95	Angel Berroa	.25
96	Byron Gettis	.15
97	Carlos Beltran	.25
98	Juan Gonzalez	.50
99	Mike Sweeney	.15
100	Duke Snider	.50
101	Edwin Jackson	.15
102	Eric Gagne	.50
103	Hideo Nomo	.40
104	Hong-Chih Kuo	.15
105	Kazuhisa Ishii	.15
106	Paul Lo Duca	.15
107	Robin Ventura	.15
108	Shawn Green	.25
109	Junior Spivey	.15
110	Lyle Overbay	.25
111	Rickie Weeks	.25
112	Scott Podsednik	.25
113	J.D. Durbin	.15
114	Jacque Jones	.15
115	Jason Kubel	.15
116	Johan Santana	.15
117	Shannon Stewart	.15
118	Torii Hunter	.25
119	Brad Wilkerson	.15
120	Jose Vidro	.15
121	Nick Johnson	.15
122	Orlando Cabrera	.15
123	Zach Day	.15
124	Gary Carter	.40
125	Jae Weong Seo	.15
126	Kazuo Matsui **RC**	5.00
127	Mike Piazza	1.00
128	Tom Glavine	.40
129	Alex Rodriguez	2.00
130	Bernie Williams	.40
131	Chien-Ming Wang	.50
132	Derek Jeter	2.00
133	Don Mattingly	2.00
134	Gary Sheffield	.40
135	Hideki Matsui	1.00
136	Jason Giambi	.50
137	Javier Vazquez	.25
138	Jorge Posada	.40
139	Jose Contreras	.15
140	Kevin Brown	.25
141	Mariano Rivera	.40
142	Mike Mussina	.40
143	Whitey Ford	.50
144	Barry Zito	.25
145	Eric Chavez	.25
146	Mark Mulder	.25
147	Rich Harden	.15
148	Tim Hudson	.25
149	Bobby Abreu	.25
150	Jim Thome	.75
151	Kevin Millwood	.25
152	Marlon Byrd	.15
153	Mike Schmidt	1.00
154	Ryan Howard	.75
155	Jack Wilson	.15
156	Jason Kendall	.15
157	Akinori Otsuka **RC**	1.00
158	Brian Giles	.25
159	David Wells	.15
160	Jay Payton	.15
161	Phil Nevin	.15
162	Ryan Klesko	.15
163	Sean Burroughs	.15
164	A.J. Pierzynski	.15
165	J.T. Snow	.15
166	Jason Schmidt	.25
167	Jerome Williams	.15
168	Merkin Valdez **RC**	1.00
169	Will Clark	.50
170	Bret Boone	.25
171	Chris Snelling	.15
172	Edgar Martinez	.25
173	Ichiro Suzuki	1.00
174	Jamie Moyer	.15
175	Randy Winn	.15
176	Rich Aurilia	.15
177	Shigetoshi Hasegawa	.15
178	Albert Pujols	1.50
179	Dan Haren	.15
180	Edgar Renteria	.25
181	Jim Edmonds	.25
182	Matt Morris	.25
183	Scott Rolen	.75
184	Stan Musial	1.00
185	Aubrey Huff	.15
186	Chad Gaudin	.15
187	Delmon Young	.15
188	Fred McGriff	.25
189	Rocco Baldelli	.25
190	Alfonso Soriano	.75
191	Hank Blalock	.50
192	Mark Teixeira	.50
193	Nolan Ryan	2.50
194	Alexis Rios	.15
195	Carlos Delgado	.50
196	Dustin McGowan	.15
197	Guillermo Quiroz	.15
198	Josh Phelps	.15
199	Roy Halladay	.25
200	Vernon Wells	.25
201	Mike Gosling/AU/400	8.00
202	Ronny Cedeno/AU/76 **RC**	8.00
203	Ronald Belisario/AU/400 **RC**	8.00
204	Justin Hampson/AU/800 **RC**	6.00
205	Carlos Vasquez/AU/800 **RC**	6.00
206	Lincoln Holdzkom/AU/800 **RC**	6.00
207	Casey Daigle/AU/550 **RC**	6.00
208	Jason Bartlett/AU/700 **RC**	6.00
209	Mariano Gomez/AU/800 **RC**	8.00
210	Mike House/AU/800 **RC**	6.00
211	Chris Shelton/AU/800 **RC**	25.00
212	Dennis Sarfate/AU/800 **RC**	8.00
213	Shingo Takatsu/AU/400 **RC**	35.00
214	Justin Leone/AU/800 **RC**	15.00
215	Cory Sullivan/AU/800 **RC**	8.00
216	Mike Wuertz/AU/800 **RC**	8.00
217	Tim Bausher/AU/800 **RC**	8.00
218	Jesse Harper/AU/800 **RC**	8.00
219	Ryan Meaux/AU/800 **RC**	8.00
221	Kevin Cave/AU/800 **RC**	8.00

Proofs Silver

Silver (1-200): 3-6X
Silver (201-225): .25X
#220, 222-225 exist only in parallel set.
Production 100 Sets

Proofs Gold

Gold (1-200): 5-10X
Gold (201-225): .5X
#220, 222-225 exist only in parallel set.
Production 50 Sets

Proofs Platinum

No Pricing
Production 10 Sets

Big League Challenge

		NM/M
	Production 999 Sets	6.00
	Die-Cut:	1X
	Production 500 Sets	
1	Albert Pujols/Left	6.00
2	Albert Pujols/Right	6.00
3	Alex Rodriguez/Rgr Left	5.00
4	Alex Rodriguez/Rgr Right	5.00
5	Magglio Ordonez	2.00
6	Rafael Palmeiro	3.00
7	Troy Glaus/Follow	2.00
8	Troy Glaus/Start	2.00
9	Albert Pujols/Bat Up	6.00
10	Alex Rodriguez/Rgr Bat Up	5.00

Big League Challenge Material

		NM/M
	Production 100 Sets	15.00
	Combo:	1-2X
	Production 50 Sets	
1	Albert Pujols/Jsy	15.00
2	Alex Pujols/Pants	15.00
3	Alex Rodriguez/Rgr Jsy	10.00

4 Alex Rodriguez/ Rgr Pants 10.00
5 Magglio Ordonez/Jsy 5.00
6 Rafael Palmeiro/Jsy 8.00
7 Troy Glaus/Jsy 6.00
8 Troy Glaus/Pants 6.00
9 Albert Pujols/Hat 20.00
10 Alex Rodriguez/ Rgr Hat 15.00

Diamond Cuts Combo Material

NM/M
Quantity produced listed 15.00
1 Derek Jeter/ Bat-Jsy/50 40.00
2 Greg Maddux/ Bat-Jsy/50 25.00
4 Miguel Cabrera/ Bat-Jsy/50 20.00
5 Mark Mulder/ Bat-Jsy/50 15.00
6 Rafael Furcal/ Bat-Jsy/50 10.00
7 Mark Prior/ Bat-Jsy/50 20.00
8 Roy Oswalt/ Bat-Jsy/50 10.00
9 Dontrelle Willis/ Bat-Jsy/25 15.00
10 Jay Gibbons/ Bat-Jsy/50 10.00
11 Josh Beckett/ Bat-Jsy/50 15.00
12 Angel Berroa/ Bat-Jsy/50 10.00
13 Adam Dunn/ Bat-Jsy/50 15.00
14 Hank Blalock/ Bat-Jsy/50 15.00
15 Carlos Beltran/ Bat-Jsy/50 15.00
16 Shannon Stewart/ Bat-Jsy/50 10.00
17 Aubrey Huff/ Bat-Jsy/50 10.00
18 Jeff Bagwell/ Bat-Jsy/50 20.00
19 Trot Nixon/ Bat-Jsy/50 15.00
20 Nolan Ryan/ Jkt-Jsy/50 40.00
21 Tony Gwynn/ Bat-Jsy/50 30.00
22 Andre Dawson/ Bat-Jsy/50 15.00
23 Don Mattingly/ Bat-Jkt/50 40.00
24 Dale Murphy/ Bat-Jsy/50 20.00
25 Gary Carter/ Bat-Jsy/50 15.00

Diamond Cuts Combo Material Signature

Production 1-5 Sets

Diamond Cuts Material Bat

NM/M
Quantity produced listed 8.00
1 Derek Jeter/100 25.00
2 Greg Maddux/100 10.00
3 Nomar Garciaparra/ 200 10.00
4 Miguel Cabrera/200 8.00
5 Mark Mulder/200 6.00
6 Rafael Furcal/200 4.00
7 Mark Prior/200 8.00
8 Roy Oswalt/200 4.00
9 Dontrelle Willis/100 6.00
10 Jay Gibbons/200 4.00
11 Josh Beckett/200 6.00
12 Angel Berroa/200 4.00
13 Adam Dunn/200 8.00
14 Hank Blalock/200 8.00
15 Carlos Beltran/200 6.00
16 Shannon Stewart/200 4.00
17 Aubrey Huff/200 4.00
18 Jeff Bagwell/200 8.00
19 Trot Nixon/200 6.00
21 Tony Gwynn/200 10.00
22 Andre Dawson/200 6.00
23 Don Mattingly/200 15.00
24 Dale Murphy/200 10.00
25 Gary Carter/200 6.00

Diamond Cuts Material Jersey

NM/M
Production 250 Sets 8.00
1 Derek Jeter 20.00
2 Greg Maddux 10.00
3 Nomar Garciaparra 10.00
4 Miguel Cabrera 8.00
5 Mark Mulder 6.00
6 Rafael Furcal 4.00
7 Mark Prior 8.00
8 Roy Oswalt 4.00
9 Dontrelle Willis 6.00
10 Jay Gibbons 4.00
11 Josh Beckett 6.00
12 Angel Berroa 4.00
13 Adam Dunn 8.00
14 Hank Blalock 8.00
15 Carlos Beltran 6.00
16 Shannon Stewart 4.00
17 Aubrey Huff 4.00
18 Jeff Bagwell 8.00
19 Trot Nixon 6.00
20 Nolan Ryan/Jkt 25.00
21 Tony Gwynn 10.00
22 Andre Dawson 6.00
23 Don Mattingly/Jkt 15.00
24 Dale Murphy 10.00
25 Gary Carter 6.00

Game Day Souvenirs Number

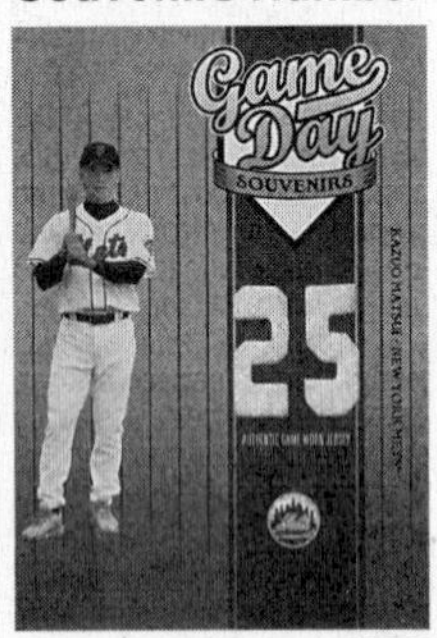

NM/M
Quantity produced listed 4.00
Position: .5-1X
Production 25-300
1 Garret Anderson/ Jsy/300 4.00
2 Troy Glaus/ Jsy/300 6.00
3 Vladimir Guerrero/ Jsy/300 8.00
4 Steve Finley/Jsy/250 4.00
5 Luis Gonzalez/Jsy/25 4.00
6 Richie Sexson/ Jsy/250 6.00
7 Andruw Jones/ Jsy/300 6.00
8 Chipper Jones/ Jsy/250 8.00
9 Rafael Furcal/Jsy/250 4.00
13 Curt Schilling/Jsy/300 6.00
14 Pedro Martinez/ Jsy/300 8.00
15 David Ortiz/Jsy/300 8.00
16 Sammy Sosa/ Jsy/300 10.00
17 Corey Patterson/ Jsy/250 6.00
18 Moises Alou/Jsy/300 6.00
19 Magglio Ordonez/ Jsy/250 4.00
20 Paul Konerko/Jsy/300 4.00
21 Frank Thomas/Jsy/300 8.00
22 Austin Kearns/Jsy/50 8.00
23 Sean Casey/Jsy/200 6.00
24 Adam Dunn/Jsy/200 10.00
25 Omar Vizquel/Jsy/250 4.00
26 C.C. Sabathia/Jsy/300 4.00
27 Jody Gerut/Jsy/250 4.00
28 Todd Helton/Jsy/300 8.00
29 Vinny Castilla/Jsy/300 4.00
30 Jeromy Burnitz/ Jsy/300 4.00
31 Fernando Vina/ Jsy/150 4.00
32 Ivan Rodriguez/ Jsy/300 8.00
33 Jeremy Bonderman/ Jsy/300 4.00
34 Mike Lowell/Jsy/225 4.00
35 Luis Castillo/Jsy/250 4.00
36 Miguel Cabrera/ Jsy/250 8.00
37 Roger Clemens/ Jsy/300 10.00
38 Andy Pettitte/Jsy/300 6.00
39 Jeff Bagwell/Jsy/300 6.00
40 Mike Sweeney/Jsy/150 4.00
41 Carlos Beltran/Jsy/200 6.00
42 Angel Berroa/Jsy/100 6.00
43 Paul Lo Duca/Jsy/75 6.00
44 Shawn Green/Jsy/300 4.00
45 Adrian Beltre/Jsy/150 4.00
46 Ben Sheets/Jsy/300 6.00
47 Geoff Jenkins/Jsy/250 4.00
48 Junior Spivey/Jsy/300 4.00
49 Doug Mientkiewicz/ Jsy/100 4.00
50 Shannon Stewart/ Jsy/100 4.00
51 Torii Hunter/Jsy/300 6.00
52 Livan Hernandez/ Jsy/300 4.00
53 Jose Vidro/Jsy/200 4.00
54 Orlando Cabrera/ Jsy/300 4.00
55 Mike Piazza/Jsy/250 8.00
56 Mike Cameron/ Jsy/250 4.00
57 Kazuo Matsui/ Jsy/200 30.00
58 Derek Jeter/Jsy/50 30.00
59 Jason Giambi/Jsy/50 10.00
61 Barry Zito/Jsy/200 6.00
62 Eric Chavez/Jsy/150 4.00
63 Eric Byrnes/Jsy/150 4.00
65 Jim Thome/Jsy/300 8.00
66 Jimmy Rollins/ Jsy/250 4.00
67 Jason Kendall/Jsy/250 4.00
68 Craig Wilson/Jsy/250 4.00
69 Jack Wilson/Jsy/250 4.00
70 Ryan Klesko/Jsy/300 4.00
71 Brian Giles/Jsy/300 4.00
72 Sean Burroughs/ Jsy/300 4.00
73 A.J. Pierzynski/ Jsy/300 4.00
74 J.T. Snow/Jsy/300 4.00
75 Michael Tucker/ Jsy/300 4.00
77 Edgar Martinez/ Jsy/50 10.00
79 Scott Rolen/Jsy/300 8.00
80 Albert Pujols/Jsy/300 15.00
81 Jim Edmonds/Jsy/300 6.00
82 Aubrey Huff/Jsy/100 4.00
83 Tino Martinez/Jsy/100 4.00
84 Rocco Baldelli/ Jsy/100 6.00
85 Alfonso Soriano/ Jsy/200 8.00
86 Michael Young/ Jsy/250 6.00
87 Hank Blalock/Jsy/200 6.00
88 Eric Hinske/Jsy/200 4.00
89 Carlos Delgado/ Jsy/300 4.00
90 Vernon Wells/Jsy/250 4.00

Game Day Souvenirs Signature Number

Production Five Sets

Heritage

NM/M
Production 999 Sets 4.00
Die-Cut: 2-3X
Production 100 Sets
1 George Brett 6.00
2 Nolan Ryan 8.00
3 Cal Ripken Jr. 8.00
4 Mike Schmidt 5.00
5 Roberto Clemente 6.00
6 Don Mattingly 5.00
7 Dale Murphy 4.00
8 Ryne Sandberg 5.00
9 Harmon Killebrew 4.00
10 Stan Musial 5.00

Heritage Material Bat

NM/M
Production 50 Sets 15.00
1 George Brett 30.00
3 Cal Ripken Jr. 40.00
4 Mike Schmidt 20.00
5 Roberto Clemente 60.00
6 Don Mattingly 30.00
7 Dale Murphy 15.00
8 Ryne Sandberg 30.00
9 Harmon Killebrew 15.00
10 Stan Musial 35.00

Heritage Material Jersey

NM/M
Quantity produced listed 15.00
1 George Brett/200 15.00
2 Nolan Ryan/Jkt/200 20.00
3 Cal Ripken Jr./200 30.00
4 Mike Schmidt/ Pants/200 15.00
5 Roberto Clemente/50 60.00
6 Don Mattingly/ Jkt/200 15.00
7 Dale Murphy/200 8.00
8 Ryne Sandberg/200 20.00
9 Harmon Killebrew/ Pants/200 15.00
10 Stan Musial/100 20.00

Heritage Signature Material Jersey

Production Five Sets

Heroes of the Hall

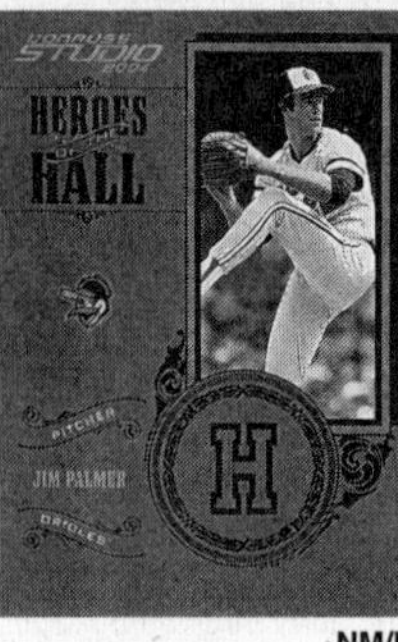

NM/M
Production 999 Sets 4.00
Die-cut: 1X
Production 500 Sets
1 Fergie Jenkins 3.00
2 Gary Carter 3.00
3 Gaylord Perry 3.00
4 George Brett 6.00
5 Jim Palmer 3.00
6 Nolan Ryan 8.00
7 Paul Molitor 4.00
8 Rod Carew 4.00
9 Steve Carlton 3.00
10 Robin Yount 5.00

Heroes of the Hall Material Bat

NM/M
Production 100 Sets 8.00
2 Gary Carter 8.00
4 George Brett 20.00
7 Paul Molitor 10.00
8 Rod Carew 8.00
9 Steve Carlton 8.00
10 Robin Yount 15.00

Heroes of the Hall Material Jersey

NM/M
Production 200 Unless Noted
Prime: No Pricing
Production 10 Sets
1 Fergie Jenkins Pants 8.00
2 Gary Carter 8.00
3 Gaylord Perry/100 8.00
4 George Brett 15.00
5 Jim Palmer 8.00
6 Nolan Ryan 25.00
7 Paul Molitor 10.00
8 Rod Carew 10.00
9 Steve Carlton 8.00
10 Robin Yount 15.00

Heroes of the Hall Material Signature

No Pricing
Production 1-10

Masterstrokes Material Bat

NM/M
Production 200 Sets 6.00
1 Todd Helton 8.00
2 Jose Vidro 4.00
3 Edgar Renteria 6.00
4 Mike Lowell 4.00
5 Gary Sheffield 6.00
6 Albert Pujols 15.00
7 Javy Lopez 6.00
8 Carlos Delgado 6.00
9 Bret Boone 4.00
10 Alex Rodriguez 10.00
11 Vernon Wells 4.00
12 Manny Ramirez 6.00
13 Jorge Posada 6.00
14 Edgar Martinez 4.00
15 Bernie Williams 6.00
16 Magglio Ordonez 4.00
17 Garret Anderson 4.00
18 Eric Chavez 4.00
19 Alfonso Soriano 8.00
20 Jason Giambi 6.00
21 Jeff Kent 4.00
22 Scott Rolen 8.00
23 Vladimir Guerrero 8.00
24 Sammy Sosa 10.00
25 Mike Piazza 8.00

Masterstrokes Material Jersey

NM/M
Prime: No Pricing
Production Five Sets
1 Todd Helton/250 8.00
2 Jose Vidro/250 4.00
3 Edgar Renteria/250 6.00
4 Mike Lowell/250 4.00
5 Gary Sheffield/250 6.00
6 Albert Pujols/250 15.00
7 Javy Lopez/250 6.00
8 Carlos Delgado/250 6.00
9 Bret Boone/250 4.00
10 Alex Rodriguez/250 10.00
11 Vernon Wells/250 4.00
12 Manny Ramirez/250 6.00
13 Jorge Posada/250 6.00
14 Edgar Martinez/250 4.00
15 Bernie Williams/250 6.00
16 Magglio Ordonez/250 4.00
17 Garret Anderson/250 4.00
18 Eric Chavez/250 4.00
19 Alfonso Soriano/150 8.00
20 Jason Giambi/250 6.00
21 Jeff Kent/250 4.00
22 Scott Rolen/250 8.00
23 Vladimir Guerrero/250 8.00
24 Sammy Sosa/250 10.00
25 Mike Piazza/250 8.00

Masterstrokes Combo Material

NM/M
Production 50 Sets 10.00
1 Todd Helton/ Bat-Jsy/50 15.00
2 Jose Vidro/Bat-Jsy/50 8.00
3 Edgar Renteria/ Bat-Jsy/50 10.00
4 Mike Lowell/ Bat-Jsy/50 10.00
5 Gary Sheffield/ Bat-Jsy/50 10.00
6 Albert Pujols/ Bat-Jsy/50 30.00
7 Javy Lopez/ Bat-Jsy/50 10.00
8 Carlos Delgado/ Bat-Jsy/50 10.00
9 Bret Boone/Bat-Jsy/50 8.00
10 Alex Rodriguez/ Rgr/Bat-Jsy/50 20.00
11 Vernon Wells/ Bat-Jsy/50 8.00
12 Manny Ramirez/ Bat-Jsy/50 10.00
13 Jorge Posada/ Bat-Jsy/50 10.00
14 Edgar Martinez/ Bat-Jsy/50 10.00
15 Bernie Williams/ Bat-Jsy/50 10.00
16 Magglio Ordonez/ Bat-Jsy/50 8.00
17 Garret Anderson/ Bat-Jsy/50 8.00
18 Eric Chavez/Bat-Jsy/50 8.00
19 Alfonso Soriano/ Bat-Jsy/50 15.00
20 Jason Giambi/ Bat-Jsy/50 10.00
21 Jeff Kent/Bat-Jsy/50 8.00
22 Scott Rolen/ Bat-Jsy/50 20.00
23 Vladimir Guerrero/ Bat-Jsy/50 20.00
24 Sammy Sosa/ Bat-Jsy/50 25.00
25 Mike Piazza/ Bat-Jsy/50 20.00

Masterstrokes Combo Material Signature

No Pricing
Production 1-10

Players Collection Jersey

NM/M
Common Jersey:
Production 150 Sets
Platinum: 1-2X
Production 50 Sets
1 Adam Dunn/AS 6.00
2 Adam Dunn/Gray 6.00

3 Adam Dunn/White 6.00
4 Alex Rodriguez 10.00
5 Alex Rodriguez/AS 10.00
6 Alex Rodriguez/Blue 10.00
7 Alex Rodriguez/White 10.00
8 Andruw Jones/Home 6.00
9 Andruw Jones/Road 6.00
10 Austin Kearns 6.00
11 Brandon Webb 4.00
12 C.C. Sabathia 4.00
13 Cal Ripken Jr. 25.00
14 Carlos Beltran 6.00
15 Carlos Delgado 6.00
16 Carlos Lee 4.00
17 Chipper Jones/Home 8.00
18 Chipper Jones/Road 8.00
19 Craig Biggio 6.00
20 Curt Schilling 6.00
21 David Wells 4.00
22 Don Mattingly 20.00
23 Dontrelle Willis 6.00
24 Frank Thomas/Black 8.00
25 Frank Thomas/White 8.00
26 Fred McGriff 4.00
27 Garret Anderson/AS 6.00
28 Gary Sheffield 6.00
29 Gary Sheffield 6.00
30 Greg Maddux/Gray 8.00
31 Hank Blalock/Home 6.00
32 Hank Blalock/Road 6.00
33 Hee Seop Choi 6.00
34 Hideo Nomo 6.00
35 Hideo Nomo/Gray 6.00
36 Hideo Nomo/White 6.00
37 Ivan Rodriguez 6.00
38 Ivan Rodriguez 6.00
39 Jason Giambi/Home 6.00
40 Jim Edmonds 6.00
41 Jim Thome 8.00
42 John Olerud 4.00
43 John Smoltz 6.00
44 Josh Beckett 6.00
45 Josh Phelps 4.00
46 Juan Gonzalez 6.00
47 Juan Gonzalez 6.00
48 Kazuhisa Ishii 6.00
49 Lance Berkman 6.00
50 Larry Walker/Home 4.00
51 Larry Walker/Road 4.00
52 Luis Gonzalez/AS 4.00
53 Magglio Ordonez/ Home 4.00
54 Magglio Ordonez/ Road 4.00
55 Manny Ramirez 8.00
56 Manny Ramirez/AS 8.00
57 Mark Prior Home 8.00
58 Mark Prior Road 8.00
59 Mark Teixeira 6.00
60 Mike Mussina 6.00
61 Mike Piazza/AS 8.00
62 Mike Piazza/Black 8.00
63 Mike Piazza/White 8.00
64 Nomar Garciaparra/ Gray 8.00
65 Nomar Garciaparra/ White 8.00
66 Pat Burrell 6.00
67 Paul Konerko 4.00
68 Paul Lo Duca 4.00
69 Pedro Martinez 8.00
70 Rafael Furcal 4.00
71 Rafael Palmeiro/Blue 6.00
72 Rafael Palmeiro/Gray 6.00
73 Ramon Hernandez 4.00
74 Rickey Henderson 6.00
75 Rickey Henderson/ Black 6.00
76 Rickey Henderson/ White 6.00
77 Roberto Alomar 6.00
78 Roberto Alomar 6.00
79 Robin Ventura/AS 4.00
80 Roger Clemens/Away 10.00
81 Roger Clemens/ Home 10.00
82 Roy Halladay 6.00
83 Sammy Sosa/AS 12.00
84 Sammy Sosa/Gray 12.00
85 Sammy Sosa/White 12.00
86 Scott Rolen 8.00
87 Shannon Stewart 4.00
88 Shawn Green/Blue 4.00
89 Shawn Green/Gray 4.00
90 Shawn Green/White 4.00
91 Terrence Long 4.00
92 Tim Hudson 6.00
93 Todd Helton/Away 8.00

94 Todd Helton/Home 8.00
95 Tom Glavine 6.00
96 Tom Glavine 6.00
97 Torii Hunter 6.00
98 Vernon Wells 4.00
99 Vladimir Guerrero 8.00
100 Vladimir Guerrero/AS 8.00

Private Signings Silver

NM/M
2 Garret Anderson/25 25.00
6 Brandon Webb/25 15.00
7 Brian Bruney/200 5.00
8 Casey Fossum/63 8.00
14 Shea Hillenbrand/25 20.00
16 Adam LaRoche/26 15.00
18 Bubba Nelson/250 8.00
22 Marcus Giles/25 30.00
24 Rafael Furcal/25 25.00
26 Adam Loewen/25 20.00
29 Jay Gibbons/50 15.00
30 Luis Matos/250 10.00
35 Kevin Youkilis/250 20.00
39 Trot Nixon/25 50.00
40 Aramis Ramirez/25 25.00
41 Brendan Harris/100 8.00
43 Ernie Banks/25 75.00
48 Sammy Sosa/21 150.00
50 Carlos Lee/25 20.00
51 Edwin Almonte/227 5.00
53 Joe Borchard/100 5.00
59 Brandon Larson/100 5.00
61 Ryan Wagner/50 10.00
63 Brian Tallet/250 5.00
65 Jeremy Guthrie/89 8.00
66 Jody Gerut/100 10.00
67 Travis Hafner/100 15.00
68 Clint Barmes/100 8.00
70 Joe Kennedy/100 5.00
72 Preston Wilson/25 25.00
77 Preston Larrison/100 8.00
81 Luis Castillo/25 15.00
82 Miguel Cabrera/25 60.00
85 Chris Burke/100 5.00
90 Morgan Ensberg/50 15.00
96 Byron Gettis/250 10.00
97 Carlos Beltran/50 35.00
100 Duke Snider/50 40.00
101 Edwin Jackson/100 15.00
104 Hong-Chih Kuo/250 30.00
10.00
106 Paul Lo Duca/25 25.00
107 Robin Ventura/25 30.00
109 Junior Spivey/50 15.00
112 Scott Podsednik/100 20.00
113 J.D. Durbin/250 5.00
114 Jacque Jones/50 20.00
115 Jason Kubel/100 15.00
116 Johan Santana/25 25.00
117 Shannon Stewart/25 15.00
120 Jose Vidro/15 30.00
122 Orlando Cabrera/15 25.00
124 Gary Carter/50 25.00
131 Chien-Ming Wang/243 100.00
133 Don Mattingly/25 75.00
134 Gary Sheffield/25 25.00
147 Rich Harden/200 15.00
154 Ryan Howard/250 65.00
160 Jay Payton/50 10.00
167 Jerome Williams/57 25.00
168 Merkin Valdez/250 10.00
169 Will Clark/25 75.00
171 Chris Snelling/200 5.00
177 Shigetoshi Hasegawa/25 75.00
179 Dan Haren/250 8.00
184 Stan Musial/25 80.00
185 Aubrey Huff/250 10.00
186 Chad Gaudin/100 5.00
187 Delmon Young/25 40.00
192 Mark Teixeira/23 25.00
193 Nolan Ryan/34 100.00
194 Alexis Rios/250 15.00
196 Dustin McGowan/115 10.00
197 Guillermo Quiroz/120 8.00

Private Signings Gold

NM/M
2 Garret Anderson/16 35.00
6 Brandon Webb/55 10.00
7 Brian Bruney/100 5.00
14 Shea Hillenbrand/28 25.00

16 Adam LaRoche/25 15.00
18 Bubba Nelson/100 10.00
22 Marcus Giles/25 30.00
23 Michael Hessman/25 15.00
29 Jay Gibbons/25 20.00
30 Luis Matos/100 10.00
35 Kevin Youkilis/100 25.00
40 Aramis Ramirez/16 35.00
41 Brendan Harris/75 10.00
49 Todd Wellemeyer/50 10.00
50 Carlos Lee/45 15.00
51 Edwin Almonte/56 10.00
53 Joe Borchard/25 10.00
54 Joe Crede/24 15.00
57 Austin Kearns/28 25.00
59 Brandon Larson/16 15.00
61 Ryan Wagner/38 10.00
63 Brian Tallet/50 10.00
65 Jeremy Guthrie/67 8.00
66 Jody Gerut/25 20.00
67 Travis Hafner/34 25.00
68 Clint Barmes/36 10.00
69 Jeff Baker/62 10.00
70 Joe Kennedy/37 15.00
73 Todd Helton/17 50.00
77 Preston Larrison/56 10.00
78 Dontrelle Willis/35 40.00
82 Miguel Cabrera/24 60.00
85 Chris Burke/46 8.00
89 Lance Berkman/17 50.00
90 Morgan Ensberg/25 15.00
96 Byron Gettis/100 8.00
97 Carlos Beltran/25 50.00
98 Juan Gonzalez/22 35.00
100 Duke Snider/25 50.00
101 Edwin Jackson/50 20.00
104 Hong-Chih Kuo/100 40.00
105 Kazuhisa Ishii/17 50.00
106 Paul Lo Duca/16 30.00
107 Robin Ventura/25 30.00
108 Shawn Green/15 30.00
109 Junior Spivey/37 15.00
112 Scott Podsednik/20 25.00
113 J.D. Durbin/31 15.00
114 Jacque Jones/25 25.00
116 Johan Santana/57 25.00
117 Shannon Stewart/23 15.00
121 Nick Johnson/21 15.00
122 Orlando Cabrera/18 25.00
124 Gary Carter/25 30.00
125 Jae Weong Seo/25 25.00
131 Chien-Ming Wang/100 125.00
147 Rich Harden/53 20.00
152 Marlon Byrd/29 15.00
154 Ryan Howard/100 75.00
160 Jay Payton/17 20.00
167 Jerome Williams/50 25.00
168 Merkin Valdez/100 15.00
171 Chris Snelling/32 10.00
177 Shigetoshi Hasegawa/17 75.00
179 Dan Haren/100 10.00
184 Stan Musial/15 80.00
185 Aubrey Huff/19 25.00
186 Chad Gaudin/100 5.00
187 Delmon Young/73 20.00
192 Mark Teixeira/25 25.00
194 Alexis Rios/50 20.00
196 Dustin McGowan/50 10.00
198 Josh Phelps/17 15.00

Private Signings Platinum

No Pricing
Production 1-10

Rally Caps

NM/M
Production 999 Sets
Die-cut: 1X
Production 500 Sets
1 Adam Dunn 2.00
2 Adrian Beltre 1.50
3 Albert Pujols 5.00
4 Alex Rodriguez 5.00
5 Andruw Jones 2.00
6 Angel Berroa 1.50
7 Aubrey Huff 1.50
8 Austin Kearns 1.50
9 Ben Sheets 2.00
10 Brad Penny 1.50
11 Carlos Beltran 2.00
12 Carlos Lee 1.50
13 Casey Fossum 1.50
14 Eric Hinske 1.50
15 Geoff Jenkins 1.50
16 Jack Wilson 1.50
17 Jason Jennings 1.50
18 Joe Kennedy 1.50
19 Lance Berkman 1.50
20 Magglio Ordonez 1.50
21 Kerry Wood 3.00
22 Mark Buehrle 1.50
23 Mark Prior 3.00
24 Mark Teixeira 2.00
25 Michael Cuddyer 1.50
26 Jeff Conine 1.50
27 Mike Mussina 2.50
28 Mike Piazza 4.00
29 Jose Reyes 2.00
30 Paul Lo Duca 1.50
31 Pedro Martinez 2.00
32 Roy Oswalt 2.00
33 Ryan Klesko 1.50
34 Sammy Sosa 4.00
35 Tim Hudson 1.50
36 Todd Helton 2.00
37 Torii Hunter 2.00
38 Vernon Wells 1.50
39 Craig Wilson 1.50
40 Edgar Renteria 1.50

Spirit of the Game

NM/M
Production 999 Sets
Die-Cut: 1X
Production 500 Sets
1 Sammy Sosa 4.00
2 Alex Rodriguez Rgr 4.00
3 Nomar Garciaparra 4.00
4 Derek Jeter 6.00
5 Albert Pujols 5.00
6 Roger Clemens 5.00
7 Mark Prior 3.00
8 Randy Johnson 2.00
9 Pedro Martinez 2.00
10 Vladimir Guerrero 2.00
11 Todd Helton 2.00
12 Jeff Bagwell 2.00
13 Mike Mussina 1.50
14 Josh Beckett 1.50
15 Hideo Nomo 1.50
16 Mike Piazza 4.00
17 Don Mattingly 5.00
18 George Brett 5.00
19 Nolan Ryan 8.00
20 Cal Ripken Jr. 8.00

Spirit of the Game Material Bat

NM/M
1 Sammy Sosa/100 15.00
2 Alex Rodriguez/Rgr/100 10.00
3 Nomar Garciaparra/100 10.00
4 Derek Jeter/100 20.00
5 Albert Pujols/100 15.00
6 Roger Clemens/50 20.00
7 Mark Prior/100 8.00
8 Randy Johnson/100 10.00
10 Vladimir Guerrero/100 10.00
11 Todd Helton/100 10.00
12 Jeff Bagwell/100 8.00
13 Mike Mussina/50 10.00
14 Josh Beckett/100 8.00
15 Hideo Nomo/100 10.00
16 Mike Piazza/100 10.00
17 Don Mattingly/100 20.00
18 George Brett/100 20.00
20 Cal Ripken Jr./50 50.00

Spirit of the Game Material Jersey

NM/M
Prime: No Pricing
Production 1-5
1 Sammy Sosa/200 10.00
2 Alex Rodriguez/200 10.00
3 Nomar Garciaparra/100 10.00
4 Derek Jeter/200 20.00
5 Albert Pujols/100 20.00
7 Mark Prior/200 8.00
8 Randy Johnson/100 10.00
9 Pedro Martinez/200 10.00
11 Todd Helton/100 10.00
12 Jeff Bagwell/200 8.00
13 Mike Mussina/200 8.00
14 Josh Beckett/200 8.00
15 Hideo Nomo/200 8.00
16 Mike Piazza/200 12.00
17 Don Mattingly/Jkt/200 15.00
18 George Brett/200 15.00
19 Nolan Ryan/100 40.00
20 Cal Ripken Jr./100 40.00

Spirit of the Game Material Signature Jersey

No Pricing
Production 1-5

Stars

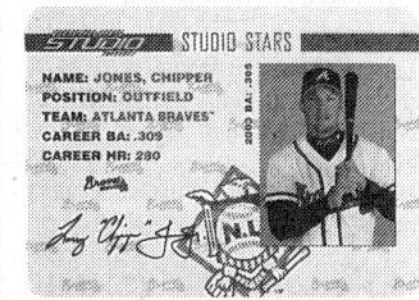

NM/M
Inserted 1:5
Gold: 1.5-3X
Production 100 Sets
Platinum: 3-5X
Production 25 Sets
1 Albert Pujols 3.00
2 Alex Rodriguez 4.00
3 Alfonso Soriano 1.50
4 Andy Pettitte .50
5 Angel Berroa .50
6 Aubrey Huff .50
7 Austin Kearns .75
8 Barry Zito .75
9 Brian Giles .75
10 Carlos Delgado .75
11 Chipper Jones 1.50
12 Craig Biggio .75
13 Curt Schilling 1.00
14 Derek Jeter 4.00
15 Edgar Martinez .50
16 Eric Gagne 1.00
17 Frank Thomas 1.00
18 Hank Blalock 1.00
19 Hideki Matsui 3.00
20 Hideo Nomo .75
21 Ichiro Suzuki 2.00
22 Ivan Rodriguez 1.00
23 Jason Kendall .50
24 Jason Schmidt .75
25 Jeff Bagwell 1.00
26 Jim Edmonds 1.00
27 Jim Thome 1.50
28 Josh Beckett .75
29 Kazuo Matsui 4.00
30 Ken Griffey Jr. 2.50
31 Larry Walker .50
32 Magglio Ordonez .50
33 Manny Ramirez 1.00
34 Mark Mulder .75
35 Mark Prior 2.00
36 Mark Teixeira 1.00
37 Miguel Tejada 1.00
38 Mike Mussina 1.00
39 Mike Piazza 2.50
40 Pedro Martinez 1.50
41 Randy Johnson 1.50
42 Roger Clemens 3.00
43 Roy Halladay .50
44 Russ Ortiz .50
45 Sammy Sosa 3.00
46 Scott Podsednik .50
47 Tim Hudson .75
48 Todd Helton 1.50
49 Vernon Wells .50
50 Vladimir Guerrero 2.00

2004 Donruss Team Heroes

NM/M
Complete Set (465): 75.00
Common Player: .25
Common SP (441-465): .50
Pack (8): 2.00
Box (24): 40.00
1 Troy Glaus .40
2 Garret Anderson .40
3 John Lackey .25
4 Jarrod Washburn .25
5 Bengie Molina .25
6 Adam Kennedy .25
7 Francisco Rodriguez .25
8 Darin Erstad .25
9 Ramon Ortiz .25
10 Chone Figgins .25
11 Rich Fischer .25
12 David Eckstein .25
13 Troy Percival .25
14 Tim Salmon .40
15 Nolan Ryan Angels 2.00
16 Luis Gonzalez .40
17 Matt Kata .25
18 Randy Johnson .75
19 Oscar Villarreal .25
20 Tim Olson .25
21 Rob Hammock .25
22 Alex Cintron .25
23 Brian Bruney .25
24 Brandon Webb .25
25 Greg Aquino .25
26 Shea Hillenbrand .25
27 Steve Finley .25
28 Rod Barajas .25
29 Mike Hampton .25
30 Adam LaRoche .25
31 Russ Ortiz .25
32 Chipper Jones .75
33 John Smoltz .40
34 Andruw Jones .50
35 Bubba Nelson .25
36 Johnny Estrada .25
37 Marcus Giles .25
38 Rafael Furcal .25
39 Horacio Ramirez .25
40 Dale Murphy .40
41 Gaylord Perry/Braves .25
42 Mark DeRosa .25
43 Adam Loewen .25
44 Jerry Hairston Jr. .25
45 Jose Morban .25
46 Daniel Cabrera .25
47 Jay Gibbons .25
48 Larry Bigbie .25
49 Luis Matos .25
50 Rodrigo Lopez .25
51 Melvin Mora .25
52 Cal Ripken Jr. 2.50
53 Geronimo Gil .25
54 Tony Batista .25
55 Jason Johnson .25
56 Jason Varitek .25
57 Bill Mueller .25
58 Todd Walker .25
59 Trot Nixon .40
60 Tim Wakefield .25
61 Kevin Youkilis .25
62 David Ortiz .50
63 Johnny Damon .40
64 Derek Lowe .25
65 Pedro J. Martinez .75
66 Carl Yastrzemski .75
67 Bobby Doerr .25
68 Matt Clement .25
69 Sammy Sosa 1.50
70 Randall Simon .25
71 Nate Frese .25
72 Carlos Zambrano .40
73 Moises Alou .40
74 Mark Prior 1.00
75 Jason Dubois .25
76 Nic Jackson .25
77 Corey Patterson .40
78 John Webb .25
79 Kerry Wood .75
80 Aramis Ramirez .40
81 Brendan Harris .25
82 Kenny Lofton .40
83 Alex Gonzalez .25
84 Gary Matthews Sr. .25
85 Mark Grace .40
86 Mark Grudzielanek .25
87 Joe Borowski .25
88 Joe Crede .25
89 Mark Buehrle .25
90 Paul Konerko .40
91 Magglio Ordonez .40
92 Corwin Malone .25
93 Frank Thomas .50
94 Jose Valentin .25
95 Miguel Olivo .25
96 Esteban Loaiza .25
97 Carlos Lee .40
98 Harold Baines .25
99 Jason LaRue .25
100 Sean Casey .40
101 Adam Dunn .50
102 Josh Hall .25
103 Danny Graves .25
104 Barry Larkin .40
105 Ken Griffey Jr. 1.00
106 Brandon Claussen .25
107 Austin Kearns .40
108 D'Angelo Jimenez .25
109 Ryan Wagner .25
110 Tim Hummel .25
111 Johnny Bench 1.00
112 Eric Davis .25
113 Jose Rijo .25
114 Travis Hafner .40
115 Jody Gerut .25
116 Fernando Cabrera .25
117 Jhonny Peralta .25
118 Ryan Church .25
119 Francisco Cruceta .25
120 Omar Vizquel .40
121 Jason Davis .25
122 Jeremy Guthrie .25
123 C.C. Sabathia .25
124 Milton Bradley .25
125 Cliff Lee .25
126 Victor Martinez .25
127 Bob Feller .50
128 Casey Blake .25
129 Josh Bard .25
130 Billy Traber .25
131 Coco Crisp .25
132 Larry Walker .40
133 Jason Jennings .25
134 Garrett Atkins .25
135 Rene Reyes .25
136 Chin-Hui Tsao .25
137 Preston Wilson .25
138 Jeff Baker .25
139 Charles Johnson .25
140 Shawn Chacon .25
141 Todd Helton .50
142 Jay Payton .25
143 Omar Infante .25
144 Bobby Higginson .25
145 Dmitri Young .25
146 Jorge Cordova .25
147 Jeremy Bonderman .25
148 Brandon Inge .25
149 Franklyn German .25
150 Nook Logan .25
151 Alex Sanchez .25
152 Craig Monroe .25
153 Preston Larrison .25
154 Carlos Pena .25
155 Alan Trammell .50
156 Jack Morris .25
157 Eric Munson .25
158 Mike Maroth .25
159 Josh Beckett .40
160 Josh Willingham .25
161 Mike Lowell .40
162 Luis Castillo .25
163 Wilson Valdez .25
164 Miguel Cabrera .75
165 Alex Gonzalez .25
166 Carl Pavano .25
167 Dontrelle Willis .40
168 Juan Pierre .25
169 Juan Encarnacion .25
170 Brad Penny .25
171 Ivan Rodriguez/Marlins .50
172 Josh Wilson .25
173 Jeff Conine .25
174 Mark Redman .25
175 A.J. Burnett .25
176 Jeff Bagwell .50
177 Octavio Dotel .25
178 Craig Biggio .40
179 John Buck .25
180 Rodrigo Rosario .25
181 Tommy Whiteman .25
182 Kirk Saarloos .25
183 Jason Lane .25
184 Wade Miller .25
185 Lance Berkman .40
186 Roy Oswalt .40
187 Tim Redding .25
188 Jeff Kent .40
189 Chris Burke .25
190 Morgan Ensberg .25
191 Nolan Ryan/Astros 2.00
192 Geoff Blum .25
193 Jeremy Affeldt .25
194 Mike Sweeney .25
195 Angel Berroa .25
196 Jimmy Gobble .25
197 Ken Harvey .25
198 Carlos Beltran .50
199 Alexis Gomez .25
200 Byron Gettis .25
201 Mike MacDougal .25
202 David DeJesus .25
203 Runelvys Hernandez .25
204 George Brett 1.50
205 Amos Otis .25
206 Joe Randa .25
207 Aaron Guiel .25
208 Eric Gagne .40
209 Shawn Green .40
210 Kevin Brown .40
211 Cesar Izturis .25
212 Kazuhisa Ishii .25
213 Joe Thurston .25
214 Odalis Perez .25
215 Rickey Henderson .50
216 Hideo Nomo .40
217 Hong-Chih Kuo .25
218 Edwin Jackson .25
219 Paul LoDuca .25
220 Adrian Beltre .40
221 Duke Snider .75
222 Steve Garvey .50
223 Rickie Weeks .40
224 Bill Hall .25
225 Doug Davis .25
226 Geoff Jenkins .40
227 Matt Childers .25
228 Dan Kolb .25
229 Scott Podsednik .40

230 Pedro Liriano .25
231 Ben Sheets .40
232 Robin Yount .75
233 Gorman Thomas .25
234 Ben Oglivie .25
235 Matt LeCroy .25
236 Cristian Guzman .25
237 Lew Ford .25
238 J.C. Romero .25
239 Rob Bowen .25
240 Corey Koskie .25
241 Jacque Jones .25
242 Brad Radke .25
243 Shannon Stewart .25
244 J.D. Durbin .25
245 Doug Mientkiewicz .25
246 Jason Kubel .25
247 Torii Hunter .40
248 Johan Santana .25
249 Kirby Puckett .75
250 Luis Rivas .25
251 Orlando Cabrera .25
252 Tony Armas Jr. .25
253 Brad Wilkerson .25
254 Endy Chavez .25
255 Jose Vidro .25
256 Zach Day .25
257 Livan Hernandez .25
258 Terrmel Sledge .25
259 Michael Barrett .25
260 Gary Carter .50
261 Andre Dawson .50
262 Craig Brazell .25
263 Mike Piazza 1.00
264 Jeff Duncan .25
265 Jason Anderson .25
266 Tom Glavine .40
267 Danny Garcia .25
268 Ty Wigginton .25
269 Al Leiter .25
270 Jeremy Griffiths .25
271 Jose Reyes .40
272 Prentice Redman .25
273 Cliff Floyd .25
274 Jae Weong Seo .25
275 Nolan Ryan Mets 2.00
276 Keith Hernandez .25
277 Jason Phillips .25
278 Kazuo Matsui **RC** 3.00
279 Jose Contreras .25
280 Aaron Boone .25
281 Mike Mussina .40
282 Jason Giambi .50
283 Hideki Matsui 1.00
284 Derek Jeter 2.00
285 Mariano Rivera .40
286 Chien-Ming Wang .40
287 Bernie Williams .40
288 Alfonso Soriano/Yanks .50
289 Jorge Posada .40
290 Michel Hernandez .25
291 Erick Almonte .25
292 Don Mattingly 1.50
293 Roger Clemens/Yanks 1.50
294 Gaylord Perry/Rgr .25
295 Tommy John .25
296 Tim Hudson .40
297 Rich Harden .25
298 Eric Chavez .40
299 Adam Morrissey .25
300 Mark Mulder .40
301 Eric Byrnes .25
302 Jermaine Dye .25
303 Barry Zito .40
304 Erubiel Durazo .25
305 Mark Ellis .25
306 Bobby Crosby .25
307 Shane Bazzell .25
308 Mario Ramos .25
309 Jose Canseco .50
310 Placido Polanco .25
311 Jimmy Rollins .25
312 Jim Thome .75
313 Brett Myers .25
314 Jason Michaels .25
315 Vicente Padilla .25
316 Bobby Abreu .40
317 Ryan Howard .50
318 Chase Utley .50
319 Pat Burrell .40
320 Randy Wolf .25
321 Franklin Perez .25
322 Marlon Byrd .25
323 Kevin Millwood .40
324 Mike Lieberthal .25
325 Anderson Machado .25
326 Travis Chapman .25
327 Steve Carlton .50
328 Greg Luzinski .25
329 David Bell .25
330 Craig Wilson .40
331 Kris Benson .25
332 Jose Castillo .25
333 Josh Fogg .25
334 Jason Kendall .25
335 Walter Young .25
336 Oliver Perez .25
337 Jason Bay .25
338 Duaner Sanchez .25
339 Jack Wilson .40
340 Carlos Rivera .25
341 Kip Wells .25
342 Freddy Sanchez .25
343 Roberto Clemente 2.00
344 Al Oliver .25
345 Phil Nevin .25
346 Trevor Hoffman .25
347 Ryan Klesko .40
348 Khalil Greene .25
349 Freddy Guzman **RC** .25
350 Brian Giles .40
351 Brian Lawrence .25
352 Sean Burroughs .25
353 Ben Howard .25
354 Xavier Nady .25
355 Mark Loretta .25
356 Ramon Vazquez .25
357 Tony Gwynn .75
358 Adam Eaton .25
359 Merkin Valdez **RC** .75
360 Kevin Correia .25
361 Edgardo Alfonzo .25
362 Mike Cameron .25
363 Ray Durham .25
364 Jesse Foppert .25
365 Robb Nen .25
366 Marquis Grissom .25
367 Jerome Williams .25
368 Jason Schmidt .40
369 Will Clark .50
370 Bret Boone .40
371 Freddy Garcia .25
372 Dan Wilson .25
373 Rett Johnson .25
374 Kazuhiro Sasaki .25
375 Ichiro Suzuki 1.00
376 Edgar Martinez .40
377 Jamie Moyer .25
378 Joel Pineiro .25
379 Carlos Guillen .25
380 Randy Winn .25
381 J.J. Putz .25
382 John Olerud .40
383 Matt Thornton .25
384 Rafael Soriano .25
385 Gil Meche .25
386 Albert Pujols 1.50
387 Woody Williams .25
388 Dan Haren .25
389 Matt Morris .40
390 Jim Edmonds .40
391 Edgar Renteria .40
392 Scott Rolen .75
393 J.D. Drew .40
394 Bo Hart .25
395 Stan Musial 1.00
396 Red Schoendienst .25
397 Terry Pendleton .25
398 Mike Matheny .25
399 Dewon Brazelton .25
400 Chad Gaudin .25
401 Aubrey Huff .25
402 Victor Zambrano .25
403 Antonio Perez .25
404 Carl Crawford .25
405 Joe Kennedy .25
406 Pete LaForest .25
407 Delmon Young .40
408 Rocco Baldelli .40
409 Doug Waechter .25
410 Brian Stokes .25
411 Edwin Almonte .25
412 Toby Hall .25
413 Lance Carter .25
414 Greg Maddux/Braves 1.00
415 Hank Blalock .50
416 Colby Lewis .25
417 Mark Teixeira .40
418 Gerald Laird .25
419 Ricardo Rodriguez .25
420 Ben Kozlowski .25
421 Kevin Mench .25
422 Michael Young .25
423 Ramon Nivar .25
424 Laynce Nix .25
425 Nolan Ryan Rgr 2.00
426 Einar Diaz .25
427 Carlos Delgado .40
428 Eric Hinske .25
429 Dustin McGowan .25
430 Frank Catalanotto .25
431 Kevin Cash .25
432 Roy Halladay .40
433 Orlando Hudson .25
434 Francisco Rosario .25
435 Guillermo Quiroz .25
436 Vernon Wells .25
437 Josh Phelps .25
438 Alexis Rios .25
439 Reed Johnson .25
440 Chris Woodward .25
441 Bartolo Colon/SP .50
442 Richie Sexson/SP .75
443 Greg Maddux/Cubs/SP 2.00
444 Javy Lopez/SP .75
445 Gary Sheffield/SP .75
446 Curt Schilling/SP 1.00
447 Nomar Garciaparra/SP 2.50
448 Manny Ramirez/SP 1.50
449 Derrek Lee/SP .75
450 Roberto Alomar/SP .75
451 Ivan Rodriguez/Tigers/SP 1.50
452 Junior Spivey/SP .50
453 Alfonso Soriano/Rgr/SP 1.00
454 Vladimir Guerrero/SP 1.50
455 Nick Johnson/SP .50
456 Javier Vazquez/SP .50
457 Andy Pettitte/SP .75
458 Miguel Tejada/SP .75
459 Rich Aurilia/SP .50
460 A.J. Pierzynski/SP .50
461 Raul Ibanez/SP .50
462 Roger Clemens/Astros/SP 3.00
463 Juan Gonzalez/SP 1.00
464 Rafael Palmeiro/SP 1.00
465 Alex Rodriguez/Yanks/SP 4.00

Showdown Bronze

Bronze (1-440): 3-5X
Bronze (441-465): 2-3X
Production 150 Sets

Showdown Silver

Silver (1-440): 5-10X
Silver (441-465): 3-5X
Production 50 Sets

Showdown Gold

No Pricing
Production 10 Sets

Autographs

NM/M
Inserted 1:24
10 Chone Figgins 10.00
11 Rich Fischer 5.00
17 Matt Kata 5.00
19 Oscar Villarreal 5.00
20 Tim Olson 5.00
21 Rob Hammock/57 10.00
23 Brian Bruney 5.00
25 Greg Aquino 5.00
35 Bubba Nelson 5.00
45 Jose Morban 5.00
46 Daniel Cabrera 5.00
61 Kevin Youkilis/50 15.00
71 Nate Frese 5.00
75 Jason Dubois 5.00
76 Nic Jackson 5.00
78 John Webb 5.00
81 Brendan Harris 10.00
84 Gary Matthews Sr. 10.00
92 Corwin Malone 5.00
102 Josh Hall/25 15.00
106 Brandon Claussen 10.00
110 Tim Hummel 5.00
116 Francisco Cabrera 5.00
117 Jhonny Peralta 8.00
118 Ryan Church 5.00
119 Francisco Cruceta/75 8.00
146 Jorge Cordova 5.00
149 Franklyn German 5.00
150 Nook Logan 5.00
153 Preston Larrison 8.00
160 Josh Willingham 8.00
163 Wilson Valdez 5.00
172 Josh Wilson 5.00
180 Rodrigo Rosario 8.00
181 Tommy Whiteman 5.00
187 Tim Redding/22 10.00
189 Chris Burke 5.00
197 Ken Harvey 15.00
200 Byron Gettis 8.00
205 Amos Otis 10.00
211 Cesar Izturis 8.00
225 Doug Davis 8.00
227 Matt Childers 5.00
230 Pedro Liriano 10.00
233 Gorman Thomas 15.00
234 Ben Oglivie/86 15.00
237 Lew Ford 10.00
238 J.C. Romero 5.00
239 Rob Bowen 5.00
246 Jason Kubel/50 15.00
258 Terrmel Sledge 5.00
262 Craig Brazell 5.00
264 Jeff Duncan 8.00
265 Jason Anderson 5.00
267 Danny Garcia 5.00
270 Jeremy Griffiths 8.00
272 Prentice Redman 8.00
291 Erick Almonte/66 8.00
307 Shane Bazzell 5.00
308 Mario Ramos 5.00
314 Jason Michaels/42 8.00
321 Franklin Perez 5.00
325 Anderson Machado/50 10.00
326 Travis Chapman 5.00
328 Greg Luzinski 15.00
331 Kris Benson 10.00
335 Walter Young/67 10.00
338 Duaner Sanchez 5.00
353 Ben Howard 5.00
359 Merkin Valdez/50 20.00
360 Kevin Correia 5.00
373 Rett Johnson/76 8.00
381 J.J. Putz 5.00
383 Matt Thornton/50 8.00
384 Rafael Soriano 8.00
406 Pete LaForest 5.00
410 Brian Stokes 5.00
411 Edwin Almonte 5.00
419 Ricardo Rodriguez 5.00
420 Ben Kozlowski 5.00
431 Kevin Cash 5.00
434 Francisco Rosario/48 8.00

2004 Donruss Throwback Threads

NM/M
Complete Set (250):
Common Player: .15
Common (201-225): 1.50
Common (226-250): 3.00
Production 1,000
Hobby Pack (5): 5.00
Hobby Box (24): 90.00
1 Bartolo Colon .15
2 Darin Erstad .25
3 David Eckstein .15
4 Garret Anderson .25
5 Tim Salmon .25
6 Troy Glaus .25
7 Vladimir Guerrero .75
8 Brandon Webb .15
9 Luis Gonzalez .25
10 Randy Johnson .75
11 Richie Sexson .40
12 Roberto Alomar .50
13 Shea Hillenbrand .15
14 Steve Finley .15
15 Adam LaRoche .15
16 Andruw Jones .50
17 Chipper Jones .75
18 J.D. Drew .25
19 John Smoltz .25
20 Rafael Furcal .25
21 Russ Ortiz .15
22 Javy Lopez .25
23 Jay Gibbons .15
24 Larry Bigbie .15
25 Luis Matos .15
26 Melvin Mora .15
27 Miguel Tejada .40
28 Rafael Palmeiro .50
29 Curt Schilling .50
30 David Ortiz .75
31 Derek Lowe .15
32 Jason Varitek .15
33 Johnny Damon .25
34 Manny Ramirez .50
35 Nomar Garciaparra 1.00
36 Pedro J. Martinez .75
37 Trot Nixon .25
38 Aramis Ramirez .40
39 Corey Patterson .25
40 Derrek Lee .25
41 Greg Maddux 1.00
42 Kerry Wood .75
43 Mark Prior .75
44 Sammy Sosa 1.50
45 Carlos Lee .15
46 Esteban Loaiza .15
47 Frank Thomas .50
48 Joe Borchard .15
49 Magglio Ordonez .25
50 Mark Buehrle .15
51 Paul Konerko .15
52 Adam Dunn .50
53 Austin Kearns .25
54 Barry Larkin .40
55 Brandon Larson .15
56 Ken Griffey Jr. 1.00
57 Ryan Wagner .15
58 Sean Casey .15
59 C.C. Sabathia .15
60 Jody Gerut .15
61 Omar Vizquel .15
62 Travis Hafner .25
63 Victor Martinez .25
64 Charles Johnson .15
65 Garrett Atkins .15
66 Jason Jennings .15
67 Joe Kennedy .15
68 Larry Walker .25
69 Preston Wilson .15
70 Todd Helton .50
71 Ivan Rodriguez .50
72 Jeremy Bonderman .15
73 A.J. Burnett .15
74 Brad Penny .15
75 Dontrelle Willis .25
76 Josh Beckett .50
77 Juan Pierre .15
78 Luis Castillo .15
79 Miguel Cabrera .75
80 Mike Lowell .25
81 Andy Pettitte .25
82 Craig Biggio .25
83 Jeff Bagwell .50
84 Jeff Kent .25
85 Lance Berkman .25
86 Morgan Ensberg .15
87 Richard Hidalgo .15
88 Roger Clemens 1.50
89 Roy Oswalt .25
90 Wade Miller .15
91 Angel Berroa .15
92 Carlos Beltran .50
93 Juan Gonzalez .40
94 Ken Harvey .15
95 Mike Sweeney .15
96 Runelvys Hernandez .15
97 Adrian Beltre .40
98 Edwin Jackson .15
99 Eric Gagne .40
100 Hideo Nomo .25
101 Hong-Chih Kuo .15
102 Kazuhisa Ishii .15
103 Paul LoDuca .15
104 Shawn Green .25
105 Ben Sheets .25
106 Geoff Jenkins .15
107 Junior Spivey .15
108 Rickie Weeks .25
109 Scott Podsednik .25
110 Corey Koskie .15
111 Doug Mientkiewicz .15
112 Jacque Jones .15
113 Joe Mays .15
114 Johan Santana .25
115 Shannon Stewart .15
116 Torii Hunter .25
117 Brad Wilkerson .15
118 Carl Everett .15
119 Chad Cordero .15
120 Jose Vidro .15
121 Nick Johnson .15
122 Orlando Cabrera .25
123 Al Leiter .15
124 Cliff Floyd .15
125 Jae Weong Seo .15
126 Jose Reyes .25
127 Mike Cameron .15
128 Mike Piazza 1.00
129 Tom Glavine .25
130 Alex Rodriguez 2.00
131 Bernie Williams .40
132 Chien-Ming Wang .40
133 Derek Jeter 2.00
134 Gary Sheffield .50
135 Hideki Matsui 1.00
136 Jason Giambi .25
137 Javier Vazquez .15
138 Jorge Posada .25
139 Jose Contreras .15
140 Kevin Brown .15
141 Mariano Rivera .25
142 Mike Mussina .40
143 Barry Zito .25
144 Bobby Crosby .15
145 Eric Chavez .25
146 Erubiel Durazo .15
147 Jermaine Dye .15
148 Mark Kotsay .15
149 Mark Mulder .25
150 Rich Harden .15
151 Tim Hudson .25
152 Billy Wagner .15
153 Bobby Abreu .25
154 Brett Myers .15
155 Jim Thome .75
156 Jimmy Rollins .25
157 Kevin Millwood .25
158 Marlon Byrd .15
159 Pat Burrell .25
160 Jason Bay .15
161 Jason Kendall .15
162 Brian Giles .25
163 Jay Payton .15
164 Ryan Klesko .15
165 Edgardo Alfonzo .15
166 Jason Schmidt .40
167 Jerome Williams .15
168 Todd Linden .15
169 Bret Boone .15
170 Edgar Martinez .25
171 Freddy Garcia .15
172 Ichiro Suzuki 1.50
173 Jamie Moyer .15
174 John Olerud .15
175 Shigetoshi Hasegawa .15
176 Albert Pujols 1.50
177 Dan Haren .15
178 Edgar Renteria .25
179 Jim Edmonds .25
180 Matt Morris .25
181 Scott Rolen .75
182 Aubrey Huff .15
183 Carl Crawford .15
184 Chad Gaudin .15
185 Delmon Young .25
186 Dewon Brazelton .15
187 Fred McGriff .25
188 Rocco Baldelli .15
189 Alfonso Soriano .75
190 Hank Blalock .50
191 Laynce Nix .15
192 Mark Teixeira .25
193 Michael Young .15
194 Carlos Delgado .40
195 Eric Hinske .15
196 Frank Catalanotto .15
197 Josh Phelps .15
198 Orlando Hudson .15
199 Roy Halladay .15
200 Vernon Wells .15
201 Dale Murphy 2.00
202 Cal Ripken Jr. 10.00
203 Fred Lynn 1.50
204 Wade Boggs 2.00
205 Nolan Ryan 6.00
206 Rod Carew 2.00
207 Andre Dawson 1.50
208 Ernie Banks 3.00
209 Ryne Sandberg 5.00
210 Bo Jackson 3.00
211 Carlton Fisk 3.00
212 Dave Concepcion 1.50
213 Alan Trammell 1.50
214 George Brett 5.00
215 Robin Yount 4.00
216 Gary Carter 1.50
217 Darryl Strawberry 1.50
218 Dwight Gooden 1.50
219 Babe Ruth 6.00
220 Don Mattingly 5.00
221 Reggie Jackson 3.00
222 Mike Schmidt 6.00
223 Tony Gwynn 4.00
224 Keith Hernandez 2.00
225 Hector Gimenez **RC** 3.00
226 Graham Koonce 3.00
227 John Gall **RC** 5.00
228 Jerry Gil **RC** 3.00
229 Jason Frasor **RC** 3.00
230 Justin Knoedler **RC** 3.00
231 Ivan Ochoa **RC** 3.00
232 Greg Dobbs **RC** 3.00
233 Ronald Belisario **RC** 3.00
234 Jerome Gamble **RC** 3.00
235 Roberto Novoa **RC** 3.00
236 Sean Henn 4.00
237 Willy Taveras **RC** 3.00
238 Ramon Ramirez **RC** 3.00
239 Kazuo Matsui **RC** 8.00
240 Akinori Otsuka **RC** 4.00
241 Jason Bartlett **RC** 5.00
242 Fernando Nieve **RC** 3.00
243 Freddy Guzman **RC** 3.00
244 Aarom Baldiris **RC** 5.00
245 Merkin Valdez **RC** 5.00
246 Mike Gosling 3.00
247 Shingo Takatsu **RC** 8.00
248 William Bergolla **RC** 3.00
249 Shawn Hill **RC** 3.00
250 Justin Germano **RC** 3.00

Blast From the Past

NM/M
Common Player: 1.50
Production 1,500 Sets
Spectrum: 2-3X
Production 100 Sets
1 Albert Pujols 5.00
2 Alex Rodriguez 4.00
3 Babe Ruth 6.00
4 Cal Ripken Jr. 8.00
5 Carlton Fisk 2.00
6 Eddie Mathews 3.00
7 Eddie Murray 2.00
8 Ernie Banks 3.00
9 Frank Robinson 2.00
10 George Foster 1.50

11 Harmon Killebrew 3.00
12 Jim Rice 1.50
13 Jim Thome 2.00
14 Johnny Bench 3.00
15 Jose Canseco 2.00
16 Juan Gonzalez 2.00
17 Ken Griffey Jr. 3.00
18 Mike Piazza 4.00
19 Mike Schmidt 5.00
20 Reggie Jackson 2.00
21 Roger Maris 3.00
22 Sammy Sosa 4.00
23 Stan Musial 4.00
24 Willie McCovey 2.00
25 Willie Stargell 2.00

Blast From the Past Bat

NM/M
Production 250 unless noted.
1 Albert Pujols 15.00
2 Alex Rodriguez 10.00
3 Babe Ruth/50 150.00
4 Cal Ripken Jr. 25.00
5 Carlton Fisk 8.00
6 Eddie Mathews 10.00
7 Eddie Murray 8.00
8 Ernie Banks 10.00
9 Frank Robinson 8.00
10 George Foster 6.00
11 Harmon Killebrew 10.00
12 Jim Rice 8.00
13 Jim Thome 8.00
14 Johnny Bench 10.00
15 Jose Canseco/100 10.00
16 Juan Gonzalez 8.00
18 Mike Piazza 10.00
19 Mike Schmidt 15.00
20 Reggie Jackson 8.00
21 Roger Maris 30.00
22 Sammy Sosa 10.00
23 Stan Musial 15.00
24 Willie McCovey 8.00
25 Willie Stargell 8.00

Century Collection Material

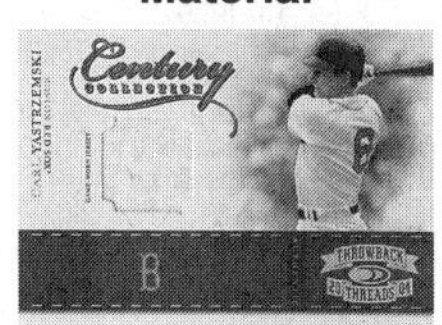

NM/M
All Jersey unless noted.
Prime: 1.5-3X
Production 10-25
Combo: .75-2X
Production 5-50
Combo Prime: 2-3X
Production 5-25
No pricing 15 or less.
1 Alan Trammell/250 8.00
2 Alex Rodriguez/250 10.00
3 Alfonso Soriano/250 8.00
4 Andre Dawson/250 6.00
5 Andy Pettitte/250 6.00
6 Bert Blyleven/250 6.00
7 Bo Jackson/250 12.00
8 Bobby Doerr/250 8.00
9 Brooks Robinson/25 30.00
10 Carl Yastrzemski/250 15.00
11 Carlos Delgado/250 4.00
12 Carlton Fisk Jkt/250 8.00
13 Curt Schilling/250 6.00
14 Darryl Strawberry/250 6.00
15 Dave Concepcion/250 6.00
16 Dave Parker/100 8.00
17 Dennis Eckersley/250 8.00
18 Don Sutton/250 6.00
19 Duke Snider/250 10.00
20 Dwight Gooden/250 6.00
21 Eddie Mathews/25 25.00
22 Enos Slaughter/100 8.00
23 Ernie Banks/ Pants/250 15.00
24 Frankie Frisch/ Jkt/250 12.00
25 Frank Robinson/50 10.00
26 Frank Thomas/250 10.00
27 Garret Anderson/250 6.00
28 Gary Carter/250 6.00
29 Gary Sheffield/250 6.00
30 Harmon Killebrew/50 25.00
31 Harold Baines/250 6.00
32 Hideo Nomo/250 8.00
33 Jack Morris/250 6.00
34 Jason Giambi/250 6.00
35 Jeff Kent/250 4.00
36 Jim "Catfish" Hunter/ 250 6.00
37 Jim Palmer/50 10.00
38 Jim Rice/250 8.00
39 Jim Thome/250 10.00
40 John Smoltz/250 8.00
41 Johnny Mize/ Pants/250 8.00
42 Jose Canseco/250 8.00
43 Juan Gonzalez/250 6.00
44 Juan Marichal/250 8.00
45 Keith Hernandez/250 8.00
46 Kerry Wood/250 10.00
47 Kevin Brown/250 4.00
48 Lance Berkman/250 6.00
49 Larry Walker/250 6.00
50 Lee Smith/250 6.00
51 Lenny Dykstra/ Bat/250 6.00
52 Luis Tiant/250 6.00
53 Magglio Ordonez/250 4.00
54 Manny Ramirez/250 8.00
55 Mariano Rivera/100 8.00
56 Mark Grace/250 8.00
57 Mark Mulder/250 6.00
58 Mark Teixeira/150 6.00
59 Marty Marion/25 15.00
60 Mike Mussina/ Pants/250 8.00
61 Mike Piazza/250 10.00
62 Nellie Fox Bat/250 15.00
63 Nolan Ryan Jkt/250 20.00
65 Ozzie Smith/250 12.00
66 Pedro J. Martinez/250 8.00
67 Pee Wee Reese/ Bat/250 8.00
68 Phil Niekro/250 8.00
69 Phil Rizzuto/ Pants/250 10.00
70 Rafael Palmeiro/250 8.00
71 Ralph Kiner/Bat/250 8.00
72 Randy Johnson/250 10.00
73 Reggie Jackson/ Jkt/250 8.00
74 Rickey Henderson/ 250 10.00
75 Roberto Alomar/250 8.00
76 Robin Ventura/250 4.00
77 Rod Carew/250 10.00
78 Roger Clemens/250 15.00
79 Ron Santo Bat/250 10.00
80 Scott Rolen/250 10.00
81 Shawn Green/250 6.00
82 Steve Garvey/250 6.00
83 Tim Hudson/250 4.00
84 Tom Glavine/250 6.00
85 Tom Seaver/25 30.00
86 Adam Dunn/250 8.00
87 Tommy John/250 6.00
88 Tommy Lasorda/250 6.00
89 Tony Oliva/250 8.00
90 Tony Perez Bat/250 8.00
91 Torii Hunter/250 4.00
92 Troy Glaus/250 4.00
93 Vernon Wells/250 4.00
94 Vladimir Guerrero/250 8.00
95 Wade Boggs/250 8.00
96 Warren Spahn/100 20.00
97 Will Clark Bat/250 10.00
98 Willie McCovey/250 8.00
99 Willie Stargell/250 8.00
100 George Foster/250 8.00

Century Collection Signature Material

NM/M
All Jersey unless noted.
Prime: No Pricing
Production 5-10
Combo: .75-1.5X
Production 5-25
No pricing 15 or less.
Combo Prime: No Pricing
Production 5-10
1 Alan Trammell/50 25.00
3 Alfonso Soriano/50 40.00
4 Andre Dawson/50 25.00
6 Bert Blyleven/50 20.00
8 Bobby Doerr/50 25.00
14 Darryl Strawberry/50 25.00
15 Dave Concepcion/50 25.00
16 Dave Parker/50 20.00
17 Dennis Eckersley/50 40.00
18 Don Sutton/50 20.00
19 Duke Snider/25 40.00
20 Dwight Gooden/50 25.00
27 Garret Anderson/50 25.00
28 Gary Carter/50 25.00
29 Gary Sheffield/25 30.00
31 Harold Baines/50 20.00
33 Jack Morris/50 15.00
37 Jim Palmer/25 25.00
38 Jim Rice/50 20.00
42 Jose Canseco/25 50.00
44 Juan Marichal/50 25.00
45 Keith Hernandez/50 25.00
50 Lee Smith/50 15.00
51 Lenny Dykstra/ Bat/50 20.00
52 Luis Tiant/50 15.00
53 Magglio Ordonez/50 25.00
56 Mark Grace/50 40.00
57 Mark Mulder/25 25.00
58 Mark Teixeira/25 40.00
59 Marty Marion/50 25.00
68 Phil Niekro/50 25.00
71 Ralph Kiner Bat/50 40.00
75 Roberto Alomar/25 50.00
76 Robin Ventura/50 20.00
82 Steve Garvey/50 25.00
87 Tommy John/50 15.00
90 Tony Perez/Bat/25 40.00
91 Torii Hunter/25 30.00
93 Vernon Wells/25 25.00
94 Vladimir Guerrero/50 40.00
100 George Foster/50 20.00

Century Stars

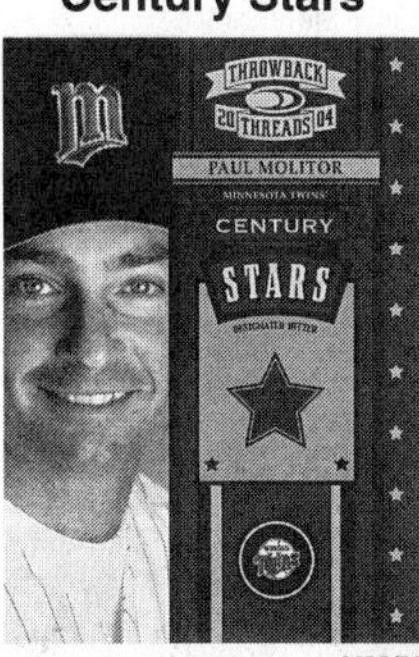

NM/M
Common Player: 1.50
Production 1,500 Sets
Spectrum: 1.5-3X
Production 100 Sets
1 Al Kaline 2.00
2 Albert Pujols 5.00
3 Alex Rodriguez 4.00
4 Barry Larkin 2.00
5 Barry Zito 1.50
6 Billy Williams 1.50
7 Bob Feller 1.50
8 Bob Gibson 3.00
9 Cal Ripken Jr. 8.00
10 Chipper Jones 3.00
11 Curt Schilling 2.00
12 Dale Murphy 2.00
13 Dave Parker 1.50
14 Derek Jeter 6.00
15 Don Drysdale 1.50
16 Don Mattingly 5.00
17 Eddie Murray 2.00
18 Fergie Jenkins 2.00
19 Gary Carter 2.00
20 George Brett 5.00
21 Greg Maddux 3.00
22 Ivan Rodriguez 2.00
23 Jeff Bagwell 2.00
24 Joe Morgan 2.00
25 Johnny Bench 3.00
26 Kirby Puckett 3.00
27 Lou Boudreau 1.50
28 Lou Brock 1.50
29 Luis Aparicio 1.50
30 Manny Ramirez 2.00
31 Mark Prior 2.00
32 Miguel Tejada 2.00
33 Mike Mussina 2.00
34 Mike Piazza 4.00
35 Mike Schmidt 5.00
36 Nolan Ryan 6.00
37 Nomar Garciaparra 4.00
38 Ozzie Smith 4.00
39 Paul Molitor 3.00
40 Pedro J. Martinez 3.00
41 Rafael Palmeiro 2.00
42 Randy Johnson 3.00
43 Red Schoendienst 1.50
44 Reggie Jackson 3.00
45 Rickey Henderson 2.00
46 Roberto Alomar 2.00
47 Roberto Clemente 5.00
48 Robin Yount 3.00
49 Rod Carew 2.00
50 Roger Clemens 5.00
51 Ryne Sandberg 4.00
52 Sammy Sosa 4.00
53 Stan Musial 4.00
54 Steve Carlton 2.00
55 Todd Helton 2.00
56 Tom Glavine 2.00
57 Tom Seaver 3.00
58 Tony Gwynn 3.00
59 Wade Boggs 2.00
60 Whitey Ford 3.00

Century Stars Material

NM/M
All Jersey unless noted.
Prime: No Pricing
Production Five Sets
1 Al Kaline/Pants/25 30.00
2 Albert Pujols/50 25.00
4 Barry Larkin/50 10.00
5 Barry Zito/50 6.00
6 Billy Williams/50 8.00
8 Bob Gibson/25 20.00
9 Cal Ripken Jr./50 60.00
10 Chipper Jones/50 10.00
11 Curt Schilling/50 8.00
12 Dale Murphy/50 12.00
13 Dave Parker/50 8.00
14 Derek Jeter/50 35.00
15 Don Drysdale/50 12.00
16 Don Mattingly/Jkt/50 20.00
17 Eddie Murray/50 15.00
18 Fergie Jenkins/ Pants/25 12.00
19 Gary Carter/Pants/50 8.00
20 George Brett/50 25.00
21 Greg Maddux/50 15.00
22 Ivan Rodriguez/50 12.00
23 Jeff Bagwell/50 10.00
24 Joe Morgan/25 10.00
25 Johnny Bench/50 20.00
26 Kirby Puckett/50 15.00
27 Lou Boudreau/50 8.00
28 Lou Brock/25 20.00
29 Luis Aparicio/Pants/50 8.00
30 Manny Ramirez/50 10.00
31 Mark Prior/50 8.00
32 Miguel Tejada/50 8.00
33 Mike Mussina/50 10.00
34 Mike Piazza/50 20.00
35 Mike Schmidt/50 20.00
36 Nolan Ryan/50 35.00
37 Nomar Garciaparra/50 15.00
38 Ozzie Smith/50 25.00
40 Pedro J. Martinez/50 10.00
41 Rafael Palmeiro/25 15.00
42 Randy Johnson/50 12.00
43 Red Schoendienst/50 8.00
44 Reggie Jackson/ Pants/50 15.00
45 Rickey Henderson/50 15.00
46 Roberto Alomar/50 12.00
48 Robin Yount/50 20.00
49 Rod Carew Jkt/50 10.00
50 Roger Clemens/50 15.00
51 Ryne Sandberg/50 20.00
52 Sammy Sosa/50 15.00
54 Steve Carlton/25 15.00
55 Todd Helton/50 12.00
56 Tom Glavine/50 10.00
57 Tom Seaver/50 15.00
58 Tony Gwynn/50 15.00
59 Wade Boggs/50 10.00

Century Stars Signature

NM/M
Signature Material: No Pricing
Production Five Sets
Sig. Material Prime: No Pricing
Production Five Sets
1 Al Kaline/25 50.00
6 Billy Williams/25 35.00
7 Bob Feller/25 30.00
8 Bob Gibson/25 35.00
12 Dale Murphy/25 40.00
13 Dave Parker/25 20.00
18 Fergie Jenkins/25 25.00
19 Gary Carter/25 25.00
24 Joe Morgan/25 30.00
28 Lou Brock/25 35.00
29 Luis Aparicio/25 20.00
35 Mike Schmidt/25 60.00
38 Ozzie Smith/25 75.00
53 Stan Musial/25 75.00

Threads Dynasty

NM/M
Common Player: 3.00
Production 1,500 Sets
Spectrum: 2-3X
Production 100 Sets
1 Phil Rizzuto, Whitey Ford 3.00
2 Pee Wee Reese, Duke Snider, Tom Lasorda 3.00
3 Jim "Catfish" Hunter, Reggie Jackson 3.00
4 Roger Maris, Whitey Ford 5.00
5 Enos Slaughter, Shawn Marion, Stan Musial 5.00
6 Dwight Gooden, Gary Carter, Darryl Strawberry, Keith Hernandez 3.00
7 Johnny Bench, Tony Perez, Joe Morgan, George Foster 3.00
8 Derek Jeter, Jorge Posada, Bernie Williams, Andy Pettitte 6.00
9 Frank Robinson, Brooks Robinson, Jim Palmer 3.00
10 Willie Stargell, Dave Parker, Bill Madlock 3.00
11 Bob Gibson, Lou Brock, Ken Boyer 3.00
12 Rickey Henderson, Paul Molitor, Joe Carter, Roberto Alomar 3.00

Dynasty Material

NM/M
Quantity produced listed
Prime: No Pricing
Production Five Sets
3 Jim "Catfish" Hunter, Reggie Jackson/25 25.00
6 Dwight Gooden, Gary Carter, Darryl Strawberry, Keith Hernandez/50 35.00
7 Johnny Bench, Tony Perez, Joe Morgan, George Foster/25 80.00
8 Derek Jeter, Jorge Posada, Bernie Williams, Andy Pettitte/50 50.00
10 Willie Stargell, Dave Parker, Bill Madlock/25 30.00
11 Bob Gibson, Lou Brock, Ken Boyer/25 35.00
12 Rickey Henderson, Paul Molitor, Joe Carter, Roberto Alomar/25 60.00

Generations

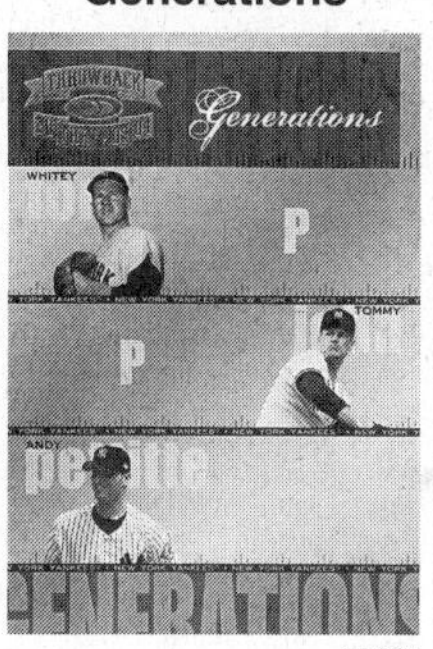

NM/M
Common Duo: 1.50
Production 1,500 Sets
Spectrum: 2-3X
Production 100 Sets
1 George Brett, Albert Pujols 5.00
2 Wade Boggs, Aubrey Huff 2.00
3 Jim "Catfish" Hunter, Tim Hudson 2.00
4 Steve Garvey, Shawn Green 1.50
5 Tony Gwynn, Garret Anderson 4.00
6 Fergie Jenkins, Mark Prior 2.00
7 Robin Yount, Rickie Weeks 4.00
8 Warren Spahn, Greg Maddux 4.00
9 Brooks Robinson, Cal Ripken Jr., Miguel Tejada 8.00
10 Bobby Doerr, Carl Yastrzemski, Manny Ramirez 5.00
11 Al Kaline, Alan Trammell, Ivan Rodriguez 2.50
12 Tom Seaver, Dwight Gooden, Tom Glavine 3.00
13 Stan Musial, Lou Brock, Jim Edmonds 4.00
14 George Foster, Dave Parker, Austin Kearns 1.50
15 Ed Mathews, Dale Murphy, Chipper Jones 3.00
16 Don Sutton, Nolan Ryan, Roger Clemens 8.00
17 Bernie Williams, Andre Dawson, Sammy Sosa 4.00
18 Whitey Ford, Tommy John, Andy Pettitte 2.00
19 Carlton Fisk, Roger Clemens, Nomar Garciaparra 5.00
20 Shawn Marion, Ozzie Smith, Edgar Renteria 4.00
21 Reggie Jackson, Rickey Henderson, Eric Chavez 2.00
22 Babe Ruth, Don Mattingly, Derek Jeter 8.00
23 Roberto Clemente Jr., Reggie Jackson, Sammy Sosa 6.00
24 Bob Feller, Tom Seaver, Roger Clemens 5.00
25 Ernie Banks, Cal Ripken Jr., Alex Rodriguez 8.00
26 Pee Wee Reese, Ozzie Smith, Derek Jeter 6.00
27 Harmon Killebrew, Mike Schmidt, Alex Rodriguez 5.00
28 Bob Gibson, Dwight Gooden, Josh Beckett 2.00

Generations Material

NM/M
Quantity produced listed
Prime: No Pricing
Production Five Sets
1 George Brett, Albert Pujols/50 40.00
2 Wade Boggs, Aubrey Huff/50 10.00
3 Jim "Catfish" Hunter, Tim Hudson/25 20.00
5 Tony Gwynn, Garret Anderson/50 20.00
6 Fergie Jenkins, Mark Prior/25 15.00
7 Robin Yount, Rickie Weeks/Bat/50 20.00
8 Warren Spahn, Greg Maddux/25 40.00
11 Al Kaline, Alan Trammell, Ivan Rodriguez/ Bat/25 40.00
14 George Foster, Dave Parker, Austin Kearns/25 20.00
16 Don Sutton, Nolan Ryan, Roger Clemens/ Bat/50 50.00
17 Billy Williams, Andre Dawson, Sammy Sosa/50 30.00
18 Whitey Ford, Tommy John, Andy Pettitte/25 40.00
19 Carlton Fisk, Roger Clemens, Nomar Garciaparra 40.00
20 Marty Marion, Ozzie Smith, Edgar Renteria/25 40.00
21 Reggie Jackson, Rickey Henderson, Eric Chavez/50 30.00
24 Bob Feller, Tom Seaver, Roger Clemens/25 40.00
25 Ernie Banks, Cal Ripken Jr., Alex Rodriguez 65.00
26 Pee Wee Reese, Ozzie Smith, Derek Jeter/25 50.00
27 Harmon Killebrew, Mike Schmidt, Alex Rodriguez/ Bat/25 50.00
28 Bob Gibson, Dwight Gooden, Josh Beckett/25 30.00

Material

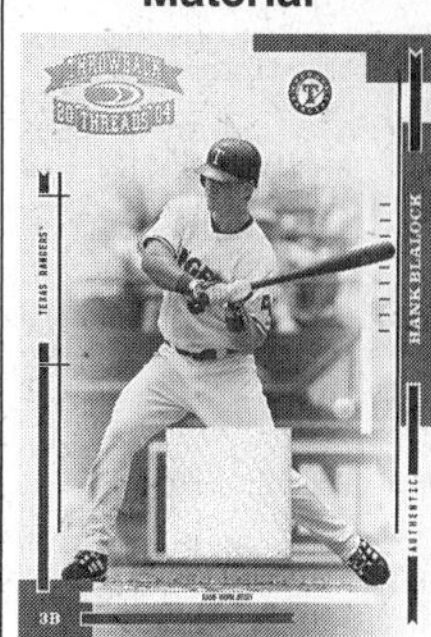

NM/M
Common Player: 4.00
2 Darin Erstad/Jsy/100 6.00
4 Garret Anderson/ Jsy/100 6.00
5 Tim Salmon/Jsy/100 6.00
6 Troy Glaus/Jsy/100 6.00
7 Vladimir Guerrero/ Bat/100 10.00

8 Brandon Webb/Pants/100 4.00
9 Luis Gonzalez/Jsy/100 4.00
10 Randy Johnson/Jsy/100 10.00
11 Richie Sexson/Bat/50 8.00
12 Roberto Alomar/Bat/100 8.00
14 Steve Finley/Jsy/100 4.00
15 Adam LaRoche/Bat/100 4.00
16 Andruw Jones/Jsy/100 6.00
17 Chipper Jones/Jsy/100 8.00
18 J.D. Drew Bat/100 6.00
19 John Smoltz/Jsy/100 8.00
20 Rafael Furcal/Jsy/100 4.00
22 Javy Lopez/Bat/100 6.00
23 Jay Gibbons/Jsy/100 4.00
24 Larry Bigbie/Jsy/100 4.00
25 Luis Matos/Jsy/100 4.00
26 Melvin Mora/Jsy/100 4.00
27 Miguel Tejada/Bat/100 6.00
28 Rafael Palmeiro/Jsy/100 8.00
29 Curt Schilling Bat/100 6.00
30 David Ortiz/Bat/100 10.00
32 Jason Varitek/Jsy/100 8.00
33 Johnny Damon/Bat/100 6.00
34 Manny Ramirez/Jsy/100 8.00
35 Nomar Garciaparra/Jsy/100 8.00
36 Pedro J. Martinez/Jsy/100 8.00
37 Trot Nixon/Bat/100 4.00
38 Aramis Ramirez/Jsy/100 6.00
39 Corey Patterson/Pants/100 6.00
41 Greg Maddux/Bat/100 10.00
42 Kerry Wood/Pants/100 10.00
43 Mark Prior/Jsy/100 6.00
44 Sammy Sosa/Jsy/100 12.00
45 Carlos Lee/Jsy/100 4.00
47 Frank Thomas/Pants/100 8.00
48 Joe Borchard/Jsy/100 4.00
49 Magglio Ordonez/Jsy/100 4.00
50 Mark Buehrle/Jsy/100 4.00
51 Paul Konerko/Jsy/100 4.00
52 Adam Dunn/Jsy/100 8.00
53 Austin Kearns/Jsy/100 6.00
54 Barry Larkin/Jsy/100 6.00
55 Brandon Larson/Fld Glv/100 4.00
58 Sean Casey Jsy/100 4.00
59 C.C. Sabathia Jsy/100 4.00
60 Jody Gerut Jsy/100 4.00
61 Omar Vizquel/Jsy/100 4.00
62 Travis Hafner/Jsy/100 4.00
63 Victor Martinez/Bat/100 6.00
64 Charles Johnson/Bat/100 4.00
65 Garrett Atkins/Jsy/100 4.00
66 Jason Jennings/Jsy/100 4.00
67 Joe Kennedy/Bat/100 4.00
68 Larry Walker/Jsy/100 6.00
69 Preston Wilson/Jsy/100 4.00
70 Todd Helton/Jsy/100 8.00
71 Ivan Rodriguez/Bat/100 8.00
72 Jeremy Bonderman/Jsy/100 4.00
73 A.J. Burnett/Jsy/100 4.00
74 Brad Penny/Jsy/100 4.00
75 Dontrelle Willis/Jsy/100 4.00
76 Josh Beckett/Jsy/100 6.00
77 Juan Pierre/Bat/100 4.00
78 Luis Castillo/Jsy/100 4.00
79 Miguel Cabrera/Jsy/100 8.00
80 Mike Lowell/Jsy/50 8.00
81 Andy Pettitte/Bat/100 6.00
82 Craig Biggio/Jsy/100 6.00
83 Jeff Bagwell/Jsy/100 8.00
84 Jeff Kent/Jsy/100 4.00
85 Lance Berkman/Jsy/100 4.00
86 Morgan Ensberg/Jsy/100 4.00
87 Richard Hidalgo/Pants/100 4.00
88 Roger Clemens/Bat/50 15.00
89 Roy Oswalt/Jsy/100 4.00
90 Wade Miller/Jsy/100 4.00
91 Angel Berroa/Pants/100 4.00
92 Carlos Beltran/Jsy/100 8.00
93 Juan Gonzalez/Bat/100 8.00
94 Ken Harvey/Bat/100 4.00
95 Mike Sweeney/Jsy/100 4.00
96 Runelvys Hernandez/Jsy/100 4.00
97 Adrian Beltre/Jsy/100 6.00
98 Edwin Jackson/Jsy/100 4.00
100 Hideo Nomo/Jsy/100 8.00
101 Hong-Chih Kuo/Bat/100 8.00
102 Kazuhisa Ishii/Jsy/100 4.00
103 Paul LoDuca/Jsy/100 4.00
104 Shawn Green/Jsy/100 6.00
105 Ben Sheets/Jsy/100 6.00
106 Geoff Jenkins/Jsy/100 4.00
107 Junior Spivey/Bat/50 4.00
108 Rickie Weeks/Bat/50 8.00
111 Doug Mientkiewicz/Bat/100 4.00
112 Jacque Jones/Jsy/100 4.00
113 Joe Mays/Jsy/100 4.00
114 Johan Santana/Jsy/100 8.00
115 Shannon Stewart/Jsy/100 4.00
116 Torii Hunter/Jsy/100 6.00
117 Brad Wilkerson/Bat/100 4.00
118 Carl Everett/Bat/100 4.00
120 Jose Vidro/Jsy/100 4.00
121 Nick Johnson/Bat/100 4.00
122 Orlando Cabrera/Jsy/100 4.00
123 Al Leiter/Jsy/100 4.00
124 Cliff Floyd/Bat/100 4.00
125 Jae Weong Seo/Jsy/100 4.00
126 Jose Reyes/Jsy/100 8.00
128 Mike Piazza/Jsy/100 10.00
129 Tom Glavine/Jsy/100 6.00
130 Alex Rodriguez/Bat/100 10.00
131 Bernie Williams/Jsy/100 6.00
133 Derek Jeter/Jsy/100 20.00
134 Gary Sheffield/Bat/100 6.00
135 Hideki Matsui/Jsy/100 20.00
136 Jason Giambi/Jsy/100 6.00
138 Jorge Posada/Jsy/100 6.00
141 Mariano Rivera/Jsy/50 15.00
142 Mike Mussina/Jsy/100 6.00
143 Barry Zito Jsy/100 4.00
145 Eric Chavez Jsy/100 4.00
146 Erubiel Durazo/Bat/100 4.00
147 Jermaine Dye/Bat/100 4.00
149 Mark Mulder/Jsy/100 6.00
150 Rich Harden/Jsy/100 4.00
151 Tim Hudson/Jsy/100 6.00
153 Bobby Abreu/Jsy/100 6.00
154 Brett Myers/Jsy/100 4.00
155 Jim Thome/Jsy/100 8.00
157 Kevin Millwood/Jsy/100 4.00
158 Marlon Byrd/Jsy/100 4.00
159 Pat Burrell Jsy/100 6.00
161 Jason Kendall Jsy/100 4.00
162 Brian Giles/Bat/100 4.00
164 Ryan Klesko/Jsy/100 4.00
165 Edgardo Alfonzo/Bat/100 4.00
167 Jerome Williams/Jsy/100 4.00
170 Edgar Martinez/Jsy/100 8.00
171 Freddy Garcia/Jsy/100 4.00
173 Jamie Moyer/Jsy/100 4.00
174 John Olerud/Jsy/100 4.00
176 Albert Pujols/Jsy/100 20.00
177 Dan Haren/Jsy/100 4.00
178 Edgar Renteria/Jsy/100 6.00
179 Jim Edmonds/Jsy/100 6.00
180 Matt Morris/Jsy/100 4.00
181 Scott Rolen/Jsy/100 8.00
182 Aubrey Huff/Jsy/100 4.00
183 Carl Crawford/Jsy/100 4.00
184 Chad Gaudin/Jsy/100 4.00
185 Delmon Young/Bat/100 6.00
186 Dewon Brazelton/Jsy/100 4.00
187 Fred McGriff/Jsy/100 6.00
188 Rocco Baldelli/Jsy/100 4.00
189 Alfonso Soriano/Bat/100 8.00
190 Hank Blalock/Jsy/100 6.00
191 Laynce Nix/Bat/100 4.00
192 Mark Teixeira/Jsy/23 15.00
193 Michael Young/Bat/100 6.00
194 Carlos Delgado/Jsy/100 6.00
195 Eric Hinske/Jsy/100 4.00
196 Frank Catalanotto/Jsy/100 4.00
197 Josh Phelps/Jsy/100 4.00
198 Orlando Hudson/Jsy/100 4.00
199 Roy Halladay/Jsy/100 4.00
200 Vernon Wells/Jsy/100 4.00
201 Dale Murphy/Jsy/100 12.00
202 Cal Ripken Jr./Jsy/100 30.00
203 Fred Lynn/Bat/100 8.00
204 Wade Boggs/Jsy/100 8.00
205 Nolan Ryan/Jkt/100 25.00
206 Rod Carew/Jkt/100 8.00
207 Andre Dawson/Pants/100 6.00
208 Ernie Banks/Pants/50 20.00
209 Ryne Sandberg/Jsy/50 25.00
210 Bo Jackson/Jsy/100 12.00
211 Carlton Fisk/Jkt/100 10.00
212 Dave Concepcion/Jsy/100 8.00
213 Alan Trammell/Bat/100 8.00
214 George Brett/Jsy/100 15.00
215 Robin Yount/Jsy/100 15.00
216 Gary Carter/Jsy/100 8.00
217 Darryl Strawberry/Pants/100 8.00
218 Dwight Gooden/Jsy/50 8.00
219 Babe Ruth/Jsy/25 400.00
220 Don Mattingly/Jkt/100 15.00
221 Reggie Jackson/Jkt/100 10.00
222 Mike Schmidt/Jkt/100 15.00
223 Tony Gwynn/Jsy/100 10.00
224 Keith Hernandez/Jsy/100 8.00

Player Threads

NM/M
Common Player: 4.00
Production 250 Sets
Prime: 2-3X
Production 10-25
No pricing 15 or less.
1 Aaron Boone 4.00
2 Alex Rodriguez/M's-Rgr 15.00
3 Andres Galarraga/Braves-Giants-Rgr 10.00
4 Aramis Ramirez 4.00
5 Bartolo Colon 4.00
6 Ben Grieve/A's-D'Rays 4.00
7 Brad Fullmer 4.00
8 Bret Boone/Braves-M's 4.00
9 Brian Giles 4.00
10 Brian Jordan 4.00
11 Byung-Hyun Kim 4.00
12 Casey Fossum 4.00
13 Cesar Izturis 4.00
14 Chan Ho Park 4.00
15 Charles Johnson 4.00
16 Cliff Floyd 4.00
17 Darryl Strawberry/Dgr-Met-Ynk 10.00
18 David Ortiz 10.00
19 David Wells/Jays-Yanks 4.00
20 Derrek Lee 6.00
21 Dmitri Young 4.00
22 Edgardo Alfonzo 4.00
23 Ellis Burks 4.00
24 Gary Sheffield/Braves-Brew-Dgr 8.00
25 Hee Seop Choi 4.00
26 Ivan Rodriguez/Marlins-Rgr 10.00
27 J.D. Drew 6.00
28 Javier Vazquez 4.00
29 Jay Payton 4.00
30 Jeff Kent/Astros-Giants-Jays 4.00
31 Jeromy Burnitz 4.00
32 Jim Thome/Indians-Phils 10.00
33 Joe Kennedy 4.00
34 Joe Torre 8.00
35 Jose Cruz Jr. 4.00
36 Juan Encarnacion 4.00
37 Juan Gonzalez/Indians-Rgr 8.00
38 Juan Pierre 4.00
39 Junior Spivey 4.00
40 Kenny Lofton/Brave-Tribe 8.00
41 Kevin Millwood 6.00
42 Manny Ramirez/Indians-Sox 12.00
43 Mark Grace/Cubs-D'backs 10.00
44 Mike Hampton 4.00
45 Mike Piazza/Dgr-Marlins-Mets 20.00
46 Milton Bradley 4.00
47 Moises Alou 6.00
48 Nick Johnson 4.00
49 Nolan Ryan/Ang/Jkt-Ast Jkt-Rgr 50.00
50 Preston Wilson/Marlins-Rockies 6.00
51 Rafael Palmeiro/O's-Rgr 10.00
52 Ray Durham 4.00
53 Reggie Jackson/A's-Ang-Yank 15.00
54 Reggie Sanders 4.00
55 Rich Aurilia 4.00
56 Richie Sexson 6.00
57 Rickey Henderson/A's-M's-Yanks/25 50.00
58 Rickey Henderson/Dgr-Mets-Padres 20.00
59 Robert Fick 4.00
60 Roberto Alomar/Mets-Sox 8.00
61 Roberto Alomar/Indians-O's 8.00
62 Robin Ventura/Mets-Sox-Yanks 10.00
63 Rondell White/Cubs-Expos 6.00
64 Ryan Klesko/Braves-Padres 6.00
65 Sean Casey 6.00
66 Shannon Stewart/Jays-Twins 6.00
67 Shawn Green/Jays-Dgr 8.00
68 Shea Hillenbrand 4.00
69 Steve Carlton/Giants-Sox 8.00
70 Terrence Long 4.00
71 Tony Batista 4.00
72 Travis Hafner/Indians-Rgr 6.00
73 Travis Lee 4.00
74 Vladimir Guerrero 8.00
75 Wes Helms 4.00

Player Threads Signature

NM/M
Quantity produced listed
4 Aramis Ramirez/25 30.00
17 Darryl Strawberry/Dgr-Met-Ynk/25 40.00
24 Gary Sheffield/Brave-Brw-Dgr/25 40.00
28 Javier Vazquez/25 20.00
29 Jay Payton/25 15.00
37 Juan Gonzalez Indians-Rgr/25 40.00
39 Junior Spivey/25 15.00
50 Preston Wilson Marlins-Rockies/25 25.00
55 Rich Aurilia/25 15.00
62 Robin Ventura Mets-Sox-Yanks/25 40.00
68 Shea Hillenbrand/25 20.00
74 Vladimir Guerrero/25 60.00

Signature Marks

NM/M
Common Autograph: 8.00
4 Garret Anderson/25 25.00
8 Brandon Webb/50 10.00
13 Shea Hillenbrand/50 15.00
14 Adam LaRoche/50 10.00
20 Rafael Furcal/25 25.00
23 Jay Gibbons/50 10.00
24 Larry Bigbie/50 20.00
25 Luis Matos/50 10.00
26 Melvin Mora/50 15.00
30 David Ortiz/25 40.00
37 Trot Nixon/25 30.00
40 Derrek Lee/25 30.00
43 Mark Prior/25 40.00
45 Carlos Lee/50 10.00
46 Esteban Loaiza/50 12.00
48 Joe Borchard/25 10.00
50 Mark Buehrle/25 25.00
53 Austin Kearns/25 20.00
55 Brandon Larson/25 15.00
60 Jody Gerut/50 20.00
62 Travis Hafner/50 20.00
63 Victor Martinez/50 25.00
69 Preston Wilson/50 15.00
74 Brad Penny/50 10.00
79 Miguel Cabrera/25 40.00
80 Mike Lowell/25 20.00
86 Morgan Ensberg/50 12.00
89 Roy Oswalt/25 25.00
91 Angel Berroa/25 12.00
92 Carlos Beltran/25 35.00
98 Edwin Jackson/50 15.00
101 Hong-Chih Kuo/50 30.00
109 Scott Podsednik/50 15.00
112 Jacque Jones/50 15.00
114 Johan Santana/25 50.00
115 Shannon Stewart/25 20.00
116 Torii Hunter/25 25.00
119 Chad Cordero/50 8.00
120 Jose Vidro/25 15.00
122 Orlando Cabrera/50 15.00
132 Chien-Ming Wang/25 100.00
147 Jermaine Dye/50 12.00
160 Jason Bay/50 20.00
163 Jay Payton/50 15.00
168 Todd Linden/50 15.00
175 Shigetoshi Hasegawa/25 50.00
177 Dan Haren/50 15.00
181 Scott Rolen/25 50.00
182 Aubrey Huff/50 15.00
184 Chad Gaudin/50 10.00
186 Dewon Brazelton/50 10.00
187 Fred McGriff/25 40.00
189 Alfonso Soriano/25 50.00
193 Michael Young/50 20.00
203 Fred Lynn/50 15.00
207 Andre Dawson/50 20.00
216 Gary Carter/25 25.00
217 Darryl Strawberry/50 20.00
218 Dwight Gooden/50 15.00
224 Keith Hernandez/50 20.00
225 Hector Gimenez/100 8.00
226 Graham Koonce/100 8.00
228 Jerry Gil/100 8.00
229 Jason Frasor/100 8.00
230 Justin Knoedler/50 10.00
233 Ronald Belisario/200 8.00
234 Jerome Gamble/200 8.00
235 Roberto Novoa/200 8.00
236 Sean Henn/200 10.00
237 Willy Taveras/100 8.00
238 Ramon Ramirez/200 10.00
241 Jason Bartlett/25 20.00
242 Fernando Nieve/25 12.00
243 Freddy Guzman/25 20.00
248 William Bergolla/100 10.00
249 Shawn Hill/100 8.00
250 Justin Germano/100 8.00

2004 Donruss Timeless Treasures

NM/M
Complete Set (100): 200.00
Common Player: 1.50
Production 999 Sets
Tin (4): 125.00
1 Albert Pujols 6.00
2 Garret Anderson 2.00
3 Randy Johnson 3.00
4 Alex Rodriguez Yanks 8.00
5 Manny Ramirez 3.00
6 Mark Prior 4.00
7 Roberto Alomar 2.00
8 Barry Larkin 2.00
9 Todd Helton 2.50
10 Ivan Rodriguez 3.00
11 Jacque Jones 1.50
12 Jeff Kent 2.00
13 Mike Sweeney 1.50
14 Shawn Green 2.00
15 Richie Sexson 2.00
16 Mike Piazza 5.00
17 Vladimir Guerrero 4.00
18 Mike Mussina 2.00
19 Barry Zito 2.00
20 Don Mattingly 6.00
21 Ichiro Suzuki 5.00
22 Rocco Baldelli 2.00
23 Rafael Palmeiro 3.00
24 Carlos Delgado 2.00
25 Roger Clemens 6.00
26 Luis Gonzalez 2.00
27 Gary Sheffield 2.00
28 Jay Gibbons 1.50
29 Nomar Garciaparra 5.00
30 Aramis Ramirez 2.00
31 Frank Thomas 3.00
32 Ryan Wagner 1.50
33 Preston Wilson 1.50
34 Hideki Matsui 4.00
35 Roy Oswalt 2.00
36 Angel Berroa 1.50
37 Kazuhisa Ishii 1.50
38 Scott Podsednik 2.00
39 Torii Hunter 2.00
40 Tom Glavine 2.00
41 Jason Giambi 3.00
42 Eric Chavez 2.00
43 Jim Thome 3.00
44 Tony Gwynn 3.00
45 Edgar Martinez 2.00
46 Jim Edmonds 2.00
47 Delmon Young 2.00
48 Hank Blalock 2.00
49 Vernon Wells 1.50
50 Curt Schilling 2.50
51 Chipper Jones 3.00
52 Cal Ripken Jr. 8.00
53 Jason Varitek 1.50
54 Kerry Wood 3.00
55 Magglio Ordonez 2.00
56 Adam Dunn 2.00
57 Jay Payton 1.50
58 Josh Beckett 2.00
59 Jeff Bagwell 3.00
60 Carlos Beltran 2.00
61 Hideo Nomo 2.00
62 Rickie Weeks 2.00
63 Alfonso Soriano 2.50
64 Miguel Tejada 2.00
65 Bret Boone 2.00
66 Scott Rolen 3.00
67 Aubrey Huff 1.50
68 Juan Gonzalez 2.50
69 Roy Halladay 2.50
70 Brandon Webb 1.50
71 Andruw Jones 2.50
72 Pedro J. Martinez 3.00
73 Carlos Lee 1.50
74 Lance Berkman 2.00
75 Paul LoDuca 1.50
76 Jorge Posada 2.00
77 Tim Hudson 2.00
78 Stan Musial 4.00
79 Mark Teixeira 2.00
80 Trot Nixon 1.50
81 Fred McGriff 1.50
82 Nick Johnson 1.50
83 Nolan Ryan 8.00
84 Ken Griffey Jr. 4.00
85 Mariano Rivera 2.00
86 Mark Mulder 2.00
87 Bob Gibson 2.50
88 Dale Murphy UER 2.50
89 Bernie Williams 2.00
90 Carl Yastrzemski 3.00
91 Sammy Sosa 5.00
92 Miguel Cabrera 4.00
93 Craig Biggio 2.00
94 George Brett 6.00
95 Rickey Henderson 3.00
96 Derek Jeter 8.00
97 Greg Maddux 4.00
98 Bob Abreu 2.00
99 Troy Glaus 2.00
100 Dontrelle Willis 2.00

Bronze

Bronze: 1-2X
Production 100 Sets

Silver

Silver: 2-4X
Production 25 Sets

Gold

Gold: No Pricing
Production 10 Sets

Platinum

Platinum: No Pricing
Production One Set

Award Materials

NM/M
Common Player: 10.00
Quantity produced listed
Prime: 1-2X
Production 1-25
No Pricing 10 or less.
Number: .75-1.5X
Production 3-51
No Pricing 15 or less.
2 Stan Musial/Jsy/43 25.00
3 Lou Boudreau/Jsy/19 15.00
4 Roger Maris/Pants/61 40.00
5 Roger Maris/Bat/61 40.00
6 Roberto Clemente/Bat/66 60.00
7 Bob Gibson/68 CY Jsy/68 20.00
8 Bob Gibson/68 MVP/Jsy/68 20.00
9 Tom Seaver/Jsy/19 20.00
10 Fred Lynn/Jsy/75 8.00
11 Jim Rice/Jsy/78 10.00
12 Mike Schmidt/80 MVP Jsy/80 15.00
13 Mike Schmidt/80 MVP Pants/80 15.00
14 Mike Schmidt/80 MVP Stir/80 15.00
15 Mike Schmidt/81 MVP Jsy/81 15.00
16 Mike Schmidt/81 MVP Bat/81 15.00
17 Dale Murphy/Jsy/82 10.00
18 Mike Schmidt/86 MVP Hat/19 35.00
19 Mike Schmidt/86 MVP Shoe/19 35.00
20 Mike Schmidt/86 MVP Bat/86 15.00
21 Mike Schmidt/86 MVP Stir/19 35.00
22 Jose Canseco/Jsy/88 10.00
23 Frank Thomas/93 MVP Bat/93 10.00
24 Frank Thomas/93 MVP Jsy/93 10.00
25 Jeff Bagwell/Pants/94 10.00
26 Frank Thomas/94 MVP Jsy/94 10.00
27 Frank Thomas/94 MVP Pants/94 10.00
28 Jeff Bagwell/Bat/94 10.00
29 Pedro J. Martinez/97 CY Jsy/97 10.00

30 Ivan Rodriguez/ Bat/99 10.00
31 Randy Johnson/ 00 CY Jsy/25 20.00
32 Pedro J. Martinez/ 00 CY Jsy/25 20.00
33 Roger Clemens/ Jsy/50 20.00
34 Randy Johnson/ 02 CY Jsy/25 20.00
35 Miguel Tejada Jsy/25 15.00

Award Materials Combos

NM/M
Prime: .75-1.5X
Production 19 Sets
4 Roger Maris/ Bat-Pants/25 70.00
12 Mike Schmidt/ 80M Jsy-Pants/25 40.00
13 Mike Schmidt/ 80M Pant-Stir/50 30.00
14 Mike Schmidt/ 80M Jsy-Stir/50 30.00
15 Mike Schmidt/ 81M Bat-Jsy/25 40.00
16 Mike Schmidt/ 81M Bat-Stir/50 30.00
18 Mike Schmidt/ 86M Hat-Shoe/50 30.00
19 Mike Schmidt/ 86M Hat-Bat/50 30.00
20 Mike Schmidt/ 86M Hat-Stir/50 30.00
21 Mike Schmidt/ 86M Bat-Shoe/50 30.00
23 Frank Thomas/ 93M Bat-Jsy/25 25.00
25 Jeff Bagwell/ Bat-Jsy/25 25.00
26 Frank Thomas/ 94M Bat-Jsy/25 25.00
35 Miguel Tejada/ Bat-Jsy/25 15.00

Award Materials Combo Prime

Production 19 Sets

Award Materials Combo Signature

No Pricing
Production Five Sets
Prime: No Pricing
Production One Set

Award Materials Number

Production 3-45

Award Materials Signature Number

No Pricing

Award Materials Prime

Production 1-25

Award Materials Signature Prime

No Pricing

Award Materials Signature

NM/M
Common Autograph:
Quantity produced listed
Number: 1-2X
Production 1-19
No Pricing 10 or less.
Prime: No Pricing
7 Bob Gibson/ 68 CY Jsy/19 50.00
8 Bob Gibson/ 68 MVP Jsy/19 50.00
10 Fred Lynn/Jsy/75 15.00
11 Jim Rice/Jsy/78 30.00

Game Day Materials

NM/M
Quantity produced listed
1 Nellie Fox/Bat/58 40.00
2 Frank Robinson/ Bat/61 10.00
3 George Brett/Bat/77 20.00
4 George Brett/Hat/82 30.00
5 Nolan Ryan/Hat/19 80.00
6 Cal Ripken Jr./Hat/85 50.00
7 Rod Carew/Hat/19 25.00
8 Ryne Sandberg/ Bat/91 20.00
9 Kirby Puckett/Bat/92 15.00
10 Frank Thomas/Bat/93 10.00
12 Tony Gwynn/ Pants/99 20.00
13 Vladimir Guerrero/ Bat/99 15.00
14 Tony Gwynn/Hat/99 20.00
15 Magglio Ordonez/ Hat/15 15.00
16 Rickey Henderson/ Bat/50 10.00

Game Day Material Signature

NM/M
Many not priced due to scarcity.
2 Frank Robinson/ Bat/25 40.00
15 Magglio Ordonez/ Hat/25 30.00

HOF Materials Barrel

Production One Set

HOF Materials Bat

NM/M
1 Al Kaline/25 25.00
2 Babe Ruth/50 200.00
4 Bobby Doerr/25 10.00
5 Brooks Robinson/25 30.00
6 Carl Yastrzemski/25 30.00
7 Carlton Fisk/25 20.00
8 Dave Winfield/25 15.00
10 Eddie Murray/25 25.00
11 Ernie Banks/25 30.00
13 Frank Robinson/25 15.00
18 Joe Morgan/25 15.00
19 Johnny Bench/25 30.00
21 Kirby Puckett/25 30.00
22 Lou Brock/25 20.00
23 Lou Gehrig/50 125.00
24 Luis Aparicio/25 10.00
25 Mel Ott/25 40.00
26 Orlando Cepeda/25 15.00
27 Pee Wee Reese/25 15.00
28 Phil Rizzuto/25 15.00
29 Red Schoendienst/25 10.00
30 Roberto Clemente/25 65.00
31 Roy Campanella/25 25.00
32 Paul Molitor/25 20.00
33 Ty Cobb/25 100.00
35 Willie McCovey/25 15.00
36 Willie Stargell/25 15.00

HOF Materials Bat Signature

NM/M
1 Al Kaline/50 40.00
4 Bobby Doerr/50 35.00
5 Brooks Robinson/50 40.00
11 Ernie Banks/25 75.00
13 Frank Robinson/50 35.00
18 Joe Morgan/25 40.00
19 Johnny Bench/25 60.00
22 Lou Brock/50 30.00
24 Luis Aparicio/50 20.00
26 Orlando Cepeda/50 25.00
28 Phil Rizzuto/50 35.00
29 Red Schoendienst/50 25.00
32 Paul Molitor/25 50.00

HOF Material Combo Bat-Jersey

NM/M
Quantity produced listed
Prime: No Pricing
Production 1-5
1 Al Kaline/25 40.00
2 Babe Ruth/25 500.00
4 Bobby Doerr/25 15.00
5 Brooks Robinson/50 30.00
6 Carl Yastrzemski/50 40.00
7 Carlton Fisk/50 20.00
8 Dave Winfield/50 15.00
10 Eddie Murray/50 35.00
13 Frank Robinson/50 20.00
18 Joe Morgan/50 15.00
21 Kirby Puckett/50 30.00
22 Lou Brock/50 15.00
23 Lou Gehrig/25 220.00
24 Luis Aparicio/25 20.00
25 Mel Ott/25 60.00
27 Pee Wee Reese/50 20.00
28 Phil Rizzuto/50 20.00
29 Red Schoendienst/25 15.00
30 Roberto Clemente/50 80.00
32 Paul Molitor/50 20.00
35 Willie McCovey/50 15.00
36 Willie Stargell/50 20.00

HOF Material Combo Bat-Jersey Signature

NM/M
Quantity produced listed
Prime: No Pricing
Production 1-5
4 Bobby Doerr/25 30.00
5 Brooks Robinson/25 80.00
11 Ernie Banks/25 80.00
13 Frank Robinson/25 65.00
18 Joe Morgan/25 40.00
22 Lou Brock/25 40.00
24 Luis Aparicio/25 40.00
29 Red Schoendienst/25 40.00
32 Paul Molitor/25 60.00

HOF Material Bat-Jersey Signature Prime

No Pricing

HOF Material Combo Bat-Pant

NM/M
Production 25 Sets
1 Al Kaline/25 35.00
2 Babe Ruth/25 350.00
12 Fergie Jenkins/ Fld Glv-Pants/25 15.00
23 Lou Gehrig/25 200.00
24 Luis Aparicio/25 15.00
25 Mel Ott/25 60.00
31 Roy Campanella/25 40.00
33 Ty Cobb/25 200.00

HOF Mat Combo Bat-Pant Signature

NM/M
1 Al Kaline/25 75.00
12 Fergie Jenkins/ Fld Glv-Pants/25 35.00
24 Luis Aparicio/25 25.00

HOF Material Combo Jersey-Pant

NM/M
2 Babe Ruth/25 500.00
23 Lou Gehrig/25 220.00
24 Luis Aparicio/25 15.00

HOF Material Combo Jersey-Pant Signature

NM/M
Prime: No Pricing
Production 1-5
24 Luis Aparicio/25 25.00

HOF Material Combo Jersey-Pant Prime

No Pricing

HOF Materials Jersey

NM/M
Quantity produced listed
Prime: No Pricing
Production 1-10
Jersey Number: .75-1.5X
Production 1-44
No Pricing 15 or less.
2 Babe Ruth/25 500.00
3 Bob Feller/10 10.00
4 Bobby Doerr/25 15.00
5 Brooks Robinson/50 15.00
6 Carl Yastrzemski/50 25.00
7 Carlton Fisk/50 15.00
8 Dave Winfield/50 10.00
10 Eddie Murray/25 25.00
13 Frank Robinson/25 20.00
14 Hal Newhouser/50 10.00
15 Hoyt Wilhelm/50 10.00
17 Jim Palmer/50 10.00
18 Joe Morgan/50 10.00
20 Juan Marichal/50 10.00
21 Kirby Puckett/50 20.00
22 Lou Brock/25 15.00
23 Lou Gehrig/25 140.00
24 Luis Aparicio/25 10.00
25 Mel Ott/25 40.00
27 Pee Wee Reese/50 15.00
28 Phil Rizzuto/50 15.00
29 Red Schoendienst/25 15.00
30 Roberto Clemente/50 60.00
32 Paul Molitor/50 15.00
34 Warren Spahn/50 20.00
35 Willie McCovey/50 10.00
36 Willie Stargell/50 15.00

HOF Materials Jersey Signature

NM/M
Quantity produced listed
Prime: No Pricing
Production 1-10
Number: 1X
Production 10-25
1 Al Kaline/25 50.00
4 Bobby Doerr/50 30.00
5 Brooks Robinson/25 60.00
13 Frank Robinson/50 35.00
15 Hoyt Wilhelm/25 25.00
17 Jim Palmer/50 30.00
18 Joe Morgan/25 30.00
20 Juan Marichal/50 35.00
22 Lou Brock/50 30.00
24 Luis Aparicio/50 25.00
26 Orlando Cepeda/25 25.00
28 Phil Rizzuto/50 40.00
29 Red Schoendienst/50 20.00
32 Paul Molitor/50 30.00
34 Warren Spahn/25 65.00

HOF Material Jsy Number

NM/M
16 Jackie Robinson/42 50.00

HOF Materials Jsy Prime

No Pricing

HOF Materials Pants

NM/M
1 Al Kaline/25 30.00
2 Babe Ruth/50 200.00
12 Fergie Jenkins/25 15.00
23 Lou Gehrig/50 125.00
24 Luis Aparicio/25 15.00
25 Mel Ott/25 40.00
31 Roy Campanella/25 30.00
33 Ty Cobb/25 125.00

HOF Material Pants Signature

NM/M
Production 25 Sets
1 Al Kaline 50.00
12 Fergie Jenkins 30.00
24 Luis Aparicio 25.00
28 Phil Rizzuto 40.00

HOF Materials Signature

NM/M
Quantity produced listed
Prime: No Pricing
Production 1-10
1 Al Kaline/25 50.00
3 Bob Feller/25 25.00
5 Brooks Robinson/25 50.00
7 Carlton Fisk/27 50.00
9 Duke Snider/25 40.00
11 Ernie Banks/25 60.00
12 Fergie Jenkins/31 30.00
13 Frank Robinson/20 40.00
15 Hoyt Wilhelm/25 25.00
17 Jim Palmer/22 30.00
20 Juan Marichal/27 30.00
21 Kirby Puckett/34 60.00
22 Lou Brock/20 40.00
26 Orlando Cepeda/30 30.00
28 Phil Rizzuto/25 40.00
29 Red Schoendienst/25 30.00
32 Paul Molitor/25 50.00
34 Warren Spahn/21 50.00
35 Willie McCovey/25 40.00

HOF Material Jersey Signature Number

No Pricing

HOF Material Jersey Signature Prime

NM/M
23 Lou Gehrig/1 (7/04 Auction) 4,950

Home Away Gamers

NM/M
Quantity produced listed
Prime: No Pricing
Production 3-5
1 Babe Ruth/ Jsy-Jsy/25 600.00
3 Wade Boggs/ Jsy-Jsy/50 15.00
4 Tony Gwynn/ Jsy-Jsy/50 30.00
5 Steve Carlton/ Jsy-Jsy/50 15.00
7 Ryne Sandberg/ Jsy-Jsy/50 35.00
8 Rod Carew/ Jsy-Jsy/50 15.00
9 Rickey Henderson/ Jsy-Jsy/50 25.00
11 Ted Williams/ Jsy-Jsy/100 85.00
12 Ozzie Smith/ Jsy-Jsy/50 25.00
13 Mike Schmidt/ Jsy-Jsy/50 30.00
14 Harmon Killebrew/ Jsy-Jsy/50 30.00
15 George Brett/ Jsy-Jsy/100 30.00
16 Don Mattingly/ Jsy-Jsy/50 35.00
17 Dale Murphy/ Jsy-Jsy/50 15.00
18 Cal Ripken Jr./ Jsy-Jsy/100 50.00
19 Lou Gehrig/ Jsy-Jsy/50 200.00
20 Nolan Ryan/ Jsy-Jsy/100 40.00

Home Away Gamers Signature

NM/M
5 Steve Carlton/ Jsy-Jsy/25 40.00
13 Mike Schmidt/ Jsy-Jsy/20 100.00
14 Harmon Killebrew/ Jsy-Jsy/25 90.00
16 Don Mattingly/ Jsy-Jsy/25 120.00
17 Dale Murphy/ Jsy-Jsy/25 70.00
19 Lou Gehrig/ Jsy-Jsy/1 (5/04 Auction) 7,100

Home Away Gamers Prime

No Pricing

Home Away Gamers Combos

NM/M
Quantity produced listed
Prime: No Pricing
Production 3-10
1 Babe Ruth/25 800.00
3 Wade Boggs/50 25.00
4 Tony Gwynn/50 40.00
5 Steve Carlton/50 25.00
6 Stan Musial/25 85.00
7 Ryne Sandberg/50 40.00
8 Rod Carew/50 25.00
9 Rickey Henderson/50 35.00
11 Ted Williams/100 150.00
12 Ozzie Smith/50 40.00
13 Mike Schmidt/50 50.00
14 Harmon Killebrew/25 40.00
15 George Brett/100 50.00
16 Don Mattingly/50 60.00
17 Dale Murphy/50 25.00
18 Cal Ripken Jr./100 65.00
19 Lou Gehrig/25 400.00
20 Nolan Ryan/100 65.00

Home Away Gamer Combo Signature

No Pricing
Production 1-5
Prime: No Pricing
Production One Set

Home Away Gamer Combo Prime

No Pricing

Home Run Materials

NM/M
1 Roger Maris/Bat/61 40.00
3 Harmon Killebrew/ HR 570 Bat/75 20.00
4 Harmon Killebrew/ HR 565 Bat/75 20.00
5 Jose Canseco/Bat/96 10.00
6 Alex Rodriguez/ Bat/100 15.00
7 Sammy Sosa/ Jsy/100 15.00
8 Rafael Palmeiro/ Jsy/25 20.00
9 Ivan Rodriguez/ Jsy/25 20.00

Home Run Material Signature

No Pricing

Material Ink Bat

NM/M
1 Adam Dunn/25 40.00
2 Alan Trammell/25 35.00
4 Andre Dawson/25 35.00
5 Bo Jackson/25 60.00
7 Dale Murphy/25 40.00
12 Don Mattingly/50 65.00
20 Mark Prior/25 80.00
25 Paul O'Neill/25 40.00
29 Ron Santo/50 35.00
30 Ryne Sandberg/25 85.00
32 Tony Gwynn/25 80.00
34 Will Clark/25 45.00

Material Ink Combos

NM/M
Quantity produced listed
Prime: No Pricing
Production 1-10
1 Adam Dunn/ Bat-Jsy/25 40.00
2 Alan Trammell/ Bat-Jsy/25 35.00
4 Andre Dawson/ Bat-Jsy/25 35.00
5 Bo Jackson/ Bat-Jsy/25 60.00
7 Dale Murphy/ Bat-Jsy/25 40.00
12 Don Mattingly/ Bat-Jsy/25 100.00
17 Jose Canseco/ Bat-Jsy/25 50.00
30 Ryne Sandberg/ Bat-Jsy/25 85.00
32 Tony Gwynn/ Bat-Jsy/25 80.00
34 Will Clark/Bat-Jsy/50 40.00

Material Ink Combo Prime

Quantity produced listed
No Pricing

Material Ink Jersey

NM/M
Quantity produced listed
Number: .75-1X
Production 1-100
No Pricing 15 or less.
Prime: .75-1.5X
Production 1-25
No Pricing 15 or less.
1 Adam Dunn/25 40.00
2 Alan Trammell/100 20.00
4 Andre Dawson/100 25.00
5 Bo Jackson/25 60.00
7 Dale Murphy/50 35.00
8 Darryl Strawberry/ 100 25.00
9 Dave Parker/25 20.00
11 Doc Gooden/100 20.00
12 Don Mattingly/50 65.00
13 Dontrelle Willis/25 40.00
15 Ivan Rodriguez/25 50.00
16 Joe Carter/25 30.00
17 Jose Canseco/25 50.00
20 Mark Prior/50 60.00
21 Mark Teixeira/25 30.00
22 Marty Marion/25 25.00
26 Rocco Baldelli/25 40.00
30 Ryne Sandberg/50 75.00
31 Ernie Banks/25 75.00
33 Vladimir Guerrero/25 60.00
34 Will Clark/50 40.00

Material Ink Jersey Number

NM/M
Quantity produced listed
1 Adam Dunn/25 40.00
2 Alan Trammell/100 20.00
4 Andre Dawson/100 20.00
5 Bo Jackson/25 75.00
7 Dale Murphy/50 30.00
8 Darryl Strawberry/ 100 20.00
9 Dave Parker/25 30.00
11 Doc Gooden/100 15.00
12 Don Mattingly/50 75.00
13 Dontrelle Willis/25 40.00
16 Joe Carter/25 30.00
19 Mark Grace/25 40.00
21 Mark Teixeira/25 40.00
22 Marty Marion/25 20.00
26 Rocco Baldelli/25 25.00
31 Ernie Banks/25 65.00
33 Vladimir Guerrero/25 50.00
34 Will Clark/50 25.00

Milestone Materials

Quantity produced listed
Number: .75-1.5X
Production 9-36
Prime: 1-2X
Production 25 Sets

Milestone Material Signature

NM/M
4 Gaylord Perry/Jsy/82 20.00

Milestone Material Number

No Pricing

Milestone Material Signature Number

NM/M
4 Gaylord Perry/Jsy/82 20.00

Milestone Material Prime

No Pricing

Milestone Material Signature Prime

NM/M

Quantity produced listed
- 4 Gaylord Perry/Jsy/19 30.00

No-Hitters Quad Signature

No Pricing
Production One Set

Rookie Year Materials

NM/M

Quantity produced listed
Prime: No Pricing
Production 5-10
Number: .75-1.5X
Production 3-51
No Pricing 15 or less.
- 1 Stan Musial/Jsy/19 60.00
- 2 Yogi Berra Stripe/Jsy/19 40.00
- 3 Yogi Berra/Grey/Jsy/47 25.00
- 4 Whitey Ford/Jsy/50 20.00
- 5 Jim "Catfish" Hunter/Jsy/65 10.00
- 6 Johnny Bench/Bat/68 15.00
- 7 Mike Schmidt/Bat/72 15.00
- 8 Gary Carter/Jsy/74 8.00
- 9 Robin Yount/Jsy/74 20.00
- 11 Cal Ripken Jr./Bat/81 40.00
- 12 Kirby Puckett/Bat/84 10.00
- 13 Roger Clemens/Jsy/84 20.00
- 15 Gary Sheffield/Jsy/89 8.00
- 16 Juan Gonzalez/Jsy/89 10.00
- 17 Randy Johnson/Jsy/89 10.00
- 18 Ivan Rodriguez/Jsy/91 10.00
- 20 Pedro J. Martinez/Jsy/92 10.00
- 21 Mike Piazza/Jsy/93 10.00
- 22 Hideo Nomo/Jsy/95 10.00
- 23 Hideo Nomo/Pants/95 10.00
- 24 Alex Rodriguez/Jsy/95 15.00
- 26 Scott Rolen/Jsy/96 10.00
- 27 Andruw Jones/Jsy/96 8.00
- 28 Nomar Garciaparra/Jsy/97 10.00
- 29 Vladimir Guerrero/Jsy/97 10.00
- 31 Alfonso Soriano/Jsy/100 10.00
- 32 Albert Pujols/White/Jsy/100 20.00
- 33 Albert Pujols/Grey/Jsy/100 20.00
- 34 Albert Pujols/Bat/100 20.00
- 36 Mark Prior/Blue Jsy/100 10.00
- 37 Mark Prior/Grey Jsy/100 10.00
- 38 Dontrelle Willis/Jsy/35 15.00

Rookie Year Material Signature

NM/M

Quantity produced listed
Prime: 1X
Production 1-35
Number: 1X
No Pricing 15 or less.
- 1 Stan Musial/Jsy/9 125.00
- 3 Yogi Berra/Grey Jsy/19 100.00
- 4 Whitey Ford/Jsy/19 85.00
- 8 Gary Carter/Jsy/19 35.00
- 10 Fred Lynn/Jsy/75 15.00
- 14 Lenny Dykstra/Fld Glv/85 20.00
- 16 Juan Gonzalez/Jsy/19 40.00
- 25 Garret Anderson/Jsy/95 20.00
- 30 Shannon Stewart/Jsy/97 15.00
- 36 Mark Prior/Blue Jsy/22 80.00
- 37 Mark Prior/Grey Jsy/22 80.00
- 38 Dontrelle Willis/Jsy/35 40.00
- 39 Rocco Baldelli/Jsy/19 40.00

Rookie Year Material Combo

NM/M

Quantity produced listed
- 2 Yogi Berra/Jsy-Jsy/8 60.00
- 22 Hideo Nomo/Jsy-Pants/16 30.00
- 36 Mark Prior/Jsy-Jsy/22 30.00
- 38 Dontrelle Willis/Jsy-Jsy/35 10.00

R.Y. Materials Combos Signature

NM/M

Quantity produced listed
- 36 Mark Prior/Jsy-Jsy/22 100.00
- 38 Dontrelle Willis/Jsy-Jsy/35 40.00

R.Y. Material Combos Prime

NM/M

Quantity produced listed
- 36 Mark Prior/Jsy-Jsy/22 30.00
- 38 Dontrelle Willis/Jsy-Jsy/35 10.00

R.Y. Mat. Combo Signature Prime

NM/M

Quantity produced listed
- 36 Mark Prior/Jsy-Jsy/22 100.00
- 38 Dontrelle Willis/Jsy-Jsy/35 40.00

Rookie Year Material Dual

NM/M

Production 25 Sets
Prime: No Pricing
Production 10 Sets
- 40 Roger Clemens/Jsy, Nomar Garciaparra/Jsy 40.00
- 41 Pedro J. Martinez/Jsy, Mike Piazza/Jsy 35.00
- 42 Mike Piazza/Jsy, Hideo Nomo/Jsy 35.00
- 43 Pedro J. Martinez/Jsy, Hideo Nomo/Jsy 20.00
- 44 Yogi Berra/Jsy, Whitey Ford/Jsy 50.00
- 45 Mike Schmidt Bat, Scott Rolen Jsy 40.00
- 46 Stan Musial Jsy, Albert Pujols Jsy 75.00
- 47 Juan Gonzalez Jsy, Ivan Rodriguez Jsy 15.00

Rookie Year Material Dual Signature

No Pricing
Production Five Sets

Rookie Year Material Dual Prime

No Pricing
Production 10 Sets

Rookie Year Material Number

Quantity produced listed

Rookie Year Material Signature Number

Quantity produced listed

Rookie Year Material Prime

Quantity produced listed

Rookie Year Material Signature Prime

Quantity produced listed

Signature Bronze

NM/M
- 1 Albert Pujols/25 125.00
- 2 Garret Anderson/16 30.00
- 4 Alex Rodriguez/25 100.00
- 5 Manny Ramirez/24 40.00
- 6 Mark Prior/50 50.00
- 8 Barry Larkin/25 30.00
- 9 Todd Helton/17 40.00
- 14 Shawn Green/15 30.00
- 17 Vladimir Guerrero 50.00
- 20 Don Mattingly/50 60.00
- 23 Rafael Palmeiro/25 45.00
- 27 Gary Sheffield/50 25.00
- 37 Kazuhisa Ishii/17 40.00
- 40 Tom Glavine/25 30.00
- 42 Eric Chavez/25 25.00
- 44 Tony Gwynn/50 40.00
- 46 Jim Edmonds/15 35.00
- 47 Delmon Young/73 20.00
- 49 Vernon Wells/25 20.00
- 50 Curt Schilling/38 40.00
- 53 Jason Varitek/33 30.00
- 56 Adam Dunn/25 30.00
- 58 Josh Beckett/21 30.00
- 59 Jeff Bagwell/25 50.00
- 60 Carlos Beltran/15 40.00
- 68 Juan Gonzalez/25 40.00
- 71 Andruw Jones/25 30.00
- 76 Jorge Posada/25 40.00
- 78 Stan Musial/50 75.00
- 79 Mark Teixeira/23 35.00
- 83 Nolan Ryan/50 90.00
- 87 Bob Gibson/25 40.00
- 88 Dale Murphy/50 35.00
- 90 Carl Yastrzemski/25 60.00
- 91 Sammy Sosa/50 125.00
- 92 Miguel Cabrera/24 50.00
- 94 George Brett/25 100.00
- 95 Rickey Henderson/25 25.00
- 97 Greg Maddux/31 75.00
- 100 Dontrelle Willis/35 30.00

Signature Silver

NM/M

Quantity produced listed
- 2 Garret Anderson/10 10.00
- 6 Mark Prior/22 50.00
- 17 Vladimir Guerrero/27 50.00
- 20 Don Mattingly/23 90.00
- 27 Gary Sheffield/25 35.00
- 44 Tony Gwynn/19 75.00
- 47 Delmon Young/25 30.00
- 68 Juan Gonzalez/22 35.00
- 76 Jorge Posada/20 40.00
- 78 Stan Musial/25 75.00
- 83 Nolan Ryan/34 120.00
- 88 Dale Murphy/25 40.00
- 91 Sammy Sosa/21 125.00

Signature Gold

No Pricing
Production 1-11

Statistical Champions

NM/M

Number: .75-1.5X
Production 1-51
No Pricing 15 or less.
Prime: No Pricing
Production 5-10
- 2 Stan Musial/43 BA Jsy/19 40.00
- 3 Ralph Kiner/Bat/49 10.00
- 4 Stan Musial/57 BA Jsy/57 30.00
- 5 Ted Williams Jsy/25 90.00
- 6 Warren Spahn/Jsy/25 30.00
- 7 Eddie Mathews/Jsy/19 40.00
- 8 Roger Maris/61 HR Bat/61 40.00
- 9 Roger Maris/61 HR Pants/61 40.00
- 10 Roger Maris/61 RBI Bat/61 40.00
- 11 Roger Maris/61 RBI Pants/61 40.00
- 12 Roberto Clemente/Jsy/19 100.00
- 13 Frank Robinson/Bat/66 10.00
- 14 Bob Gibson/68 ERA Jsy/68 15.00
- 15 Bob Gibson/68 K Jsy/68 15.00
- 16 Tom Seaver/Jsy/19 25.00
- 18 Harmon Killebrew/Pants/71 15.00
- 19 Mike Schmidt/Jsy/74 15.00
- 20 Reggie Jackson/Jsy/19 20.00
- 22 Rod Carew/Hat/78 15.00
- 23 Jim Rice/78 HR Jsy/78 10.00
- 24 Jim Rice/78 RBI Jsy/78 10.00
- 25 Reggie Jackson/Hat/80 15.00
- 26 Dale Murphy/82 RBI Jsy/82 15.00
- 27 Steve Carlton/Jsy/83 10.00
- 28 Dale Murphy/85 HR Jsy/85 15.00
- 29 Wade Boggs/86 BA Jsy/86 15.00
- 30 Wade Boggs/87 BA Jsy/87 15.00
- 31 Will Clark/Jsy/88 15.00
- 32 Nolan Ryan/89 K Jsy/89 20.00
- 33 Nolan Ryan/90 K Jsy/90 20.00
- 34 Nolan Ryan/90 K Pants/90 20.00
- 35 Ryne Sandberg/Jsy/90 20.00
- 36 Roger Clemens/90 K Jsy/90 20.00
- 37 George Brett/Jsy/90 20.00
- 38 Roger Clemens/92 ERA Jsy/100 20.00
- 39 Roger Clemens/96 K Jsy/100 20.00
- 40 Tony Gwynn/Jsy/25 35.00
- 41 Pedro Martinez/Expos Jsy/25 20.00
- 42 Greg Maddux/Jsy/100 10.00
- 43 Juan Gonzalez/Pants/25 20.00
- 44 Manny Ramirez/Bat/25 15.00
- 45 Nomar Garciaparra/99 BA Jsy/100 10.00
- 47 Nomar Garciaparra/00 BA Jsy/100 10.00
- 48 Todd Helton/00 BA Jsy/25 15.00
- 49 Todd Helton/00 RBI Jsy/25 15.00
- 50 Troy Glaus/Jsy/25 10.00
- 51 Randy Johnson/00 K Jsy/25 15.00
- 52 Tom Glavine/Jsy/25 10.00
- 53 Sammy Sosa/00 HR Jsy/100 15.00
- 54 Alex Rodriguez/01 HR Bat/100 15.00
- 55 Curt Schilling Jsy/25 10.00
- 56 Pedro J. Martinez/99 K Jsy/25 20.00
- 57 Alex Rodriguez/01 HR Jsy/100 15.00
- 58 Mark Mulder Jsy/25 10.00
- 59 Sammy Sosa/01 RBI Jsy/100 15.00
- 60 Manny Ramirez/Jsy/25 15.00
- 61 Lance Berkman/Jsy/25 10.00
- 62 Randy Johnson/02 W Jsy/25 15.00
- 63 Alex Rodriguez/02 HR Jsy/100 15.00
- 64 Alex Rodriguez/02 RBI Jsy/100 15.00
- 65 Alex Rodriguez/02 HR Bat/100 15.00
- 66 Alex Rodriguez/02 RBI Bat/100 15.00
- 67 Pedro J. Martinez/02 K Jsy/25 20.00
- 68 Pedro J. Martinez/02 ERA Jsy/25 20.00
- 69 Sammy Sosa/02 HR Jsy/100 15.00
- 70 Jim Thome/Jsy/25 15.00
- 71 Alex Rodriguez/03 HR Bat/100 15.00
- 72 Albert Pujols/Bat/100 20.00
- 73 Alex Rodriguez/03 HR Jsy/100 15.00
- 74 Albert Pujols/Jsy/100 20.00

Statistical Champions Signature

NM/M

Quantity produced listed
Number: .5-1.5X
Production 1-47
Prime: No Pricing
Production 1-10
- 3 Ralph Kiner/Bat/49 35.00
- 6 Warren Spahn/Jsy/25 75.00
- 13 Frank Robinson/Bat/66 40.00
- 14 Bob Gibson/68 ERA Jsy/25 50.00
- 15 Bob Gibson/68 K Jsy/25 50.00
- 17 Harmon Killebrew/Jsy/71 50.00
- 18 Harmon Killebrew/Pants/71 50.00
- 19 Mike Schmidt/Jsy/25 75.00
- 20 Reggie Jackson/Jsy/25 65.00
- 21 Phil Niekro/Jsy/50 30.00
- 22 Rod Carew/Hat/25 40.00
- 23 Jim Rice/78 HR Jsy/78 30.00
- 24 Jim Rice/78 RBI Jsy/78 30.00
- 25 Reggie Jackson/Hat/25 65.00
- 26 Dale Murphy/82 RBI Jsy/25 50.00
- 27 Steve Carlton/Jsy/25 50.00
- 28 Dale Murphy/85 HR Jsy/25 50.00
- 29 Wade Boggs/86 BA Jsy/25 40.00
- 30 Wade Boggs/87 BA Jsy/25 40.00
- 31 Will Clark/Jsy/88 30.00
- 32 Nolan Ryan/89 K Jsy/25 120.00
- 33 Nolan Ryan/90 K Jsy/25 120.00
- 34 Nolan Ryan/90 K Pants/25 120.00
- 35 Ryne Sandberg/Jsy/25 80.00
- 40 Tony Gwynn/Jsy/25 70.00
- 43 Juan Gonzalez/Pants/19 40.00
- 50 Troy Glaus/Jsy/25 35.00
- 52 Tom Glavine/Jsy/20 40.00
- 53 Sammy Sosa/00 HR Jsy/25 150.00
- 55 Curt Schilling/Jsy/25 40.00
- 58 Mark Mulder/Jsy/25 30.00
- 59 Sammy Sosa/01 RBI Jsy/25 150.00
- 61 Lance Berkman/Jsy/20 40.00
- 69 Sammy Sosa/02 HR Jsy/25 150.00

Statistical Champions Number

No Pricing

Statistical Champions Signature Number

No Pricing

Statistical Champions Prime

No Pricing

Statistical Champions Signature Prime

No Pricing

World Series Materials

NM/M

Quantity produced listed
- 1 Frank Robinson/Bat/61 15.00
- 2 Ozzie Smith/Jsy/87 15.00
- 3 Rickey Henderson/Bat/93 15.00
- 4 Tom Glavine/Jsy/96 10.00
- 5 Roger Clemens/Jsy/100 15.00

World Series Materials Signature

NM/M

Quantity produced listed
Prime: No Pricing
Production 9-10
- 1 Frank Robinson/Bat/19 50.00
- 4 Tom Glavine/Jsy/19 40.00

World Series Materials Prime

NM/M

Quantity produced listed
- 2 Ozzie Smith/Jsy/19 25.00
- 4 Tom Glavine/Jsy/19 20.00
- 5 Roger Clemens/Jsy/20 30.00

2004 Donruss Timelines

NM/M

Complete Set (50): 40.00
Common Player: .75
Pack (5): 40.00
Box (4): 120.00
- 1 Adam Dunn .75
- 2 Albert Pujols 3.00
- 3 Alex Rodriguez 3.00
- 4 Alfonso Soriano 1.50
- 5 Andruw Jones 1.00
- 6 Austin Kearns .75
- 7 Miguel Cabrera 1.00
- 8 Barry Zito .75
- 9 Carlos Beltran .75
- 10 Carlos Delgado 1.00
- 11 Chipper Jones 2.00
- 12 Curt Schilling 1.00
- 13 Derek Jeter 4.00
- 14 Frank Thomas 1.00
- 15 Garret Anderson .75
- 16 Gary Sheffield .75
- 17 Greg Maddux 2.00
- 18 Hank Blalock .75
- 19 Hideki Matsui 3.00
- 20 Hideo Nomo .75
- 21 Ichiro Suzuki 2.00
- 22 Ivan Rodriguez 1.00
- 23 Jason Giambi 1.50
- 24 Jeff Bagwell 1.00
- 25 Jim Thome 1.50
- 26 Juan Gonzalez .75
- 27 Ken Griffey Jr. 2.00
- 28 Kevin Brown .75
- 29 Kerry Wood 1.00
- 30 Lance Berkman .75
- 31 Magglio Ordonez .75
- 32 Manny Ramirez 1.00
- 33 Mark Prior 3.00
- 34 Mike Mussina 1.00
- 35 Mike Piazza 2.00
- 36 Nomar Garciaparra 3.00
- 37 Pedro J. Martinez 1.50
- 38 Rafael Palmeiro 1.00
- 39 Randy Johnson 1.50
- 40 Richie Sexson .75
- 41 Roger Clemens 3.00
- 42 Roy Halladay .75
- 43 Sammy Sosa 2.50
- 44 Scott Rolen 1.50
- 45 Shawn Green .75
- 46 Tim Hudson .75
- 47 Todd Helton 1.00
- 48 Torii Hunter .75
- 49 Vernon Wells .75
- 50 Vladimir Guerrero 1.50

Silver

Cards (1-50): 2X
Production 100 Sets

Gold

Cards (1-50): 4-6X
Production 25 Sets

Gold Autographs

NM/M

Production 25 Sets 30.00
- 1 Adam Dunn 40.00
- 7 Miguel Cabrera 80.00
- 9 Carlos Beltran 40.00
- 15 Garret Anderson 30.00
- 18 Hank Blalock 35.00
- 22 Ivan Rodriguez 60.00
- 26 Juan Gonzalez 50.00
- 31 Magglio Ordonez 40.00
- 33 Mark Prior 50.00
- 44 Scott Rolen 45.00
- 48 Torii Hunter 35.00
- 49 Vernon Wells 30.00
- 50 Vladimir Guerrero 70.00

Platinum

No Pricing
Production One Set

Platinum Autographs

No Pricing
Production One Set

Boys of Summer

NM/M

Complete Set (25): 75.00
Common Player: 3.00
Production 250 Sets
Silver 1-1.5x
Production 100 Sets
Gold: 3-4X
Production 25 Sets
Platinum: No Pricing
Production One Set
- 1 Alan Trammell 5.00
- 2 Marty Marion 3.00
- 3 Andre Dawson 3.00
- 4 Bo Jackson 5.00
- 5 Cal Ripken Jr. 10.00
- 6 Steve Garvey 3.00
- 7 Dale Murphy 3.00
- 8 Darren Daulton 3.00
- 9 Darryl Strawberry 3.00
- 10 Dave Parker 3.00
- 11 Doc Gooden 3.00
- 12 Don Mattingly 6.00
- 13 Eric Davis 3.00
- 14 Dwight Evans 3.00
- 15 Fred Lynn 3.00
- 16 Graig Nettles 3.00
- 17 Jay Buhner 3.00
- 18 Jim Rice 3.00
- 19 Jose Canseco 3.00
- 20 Keith Hernandez 3.00
- 21 Rickey Henderson 3.00
- 22 Jack Morris 3.00
- 23 Tony Gwynn 4.00
- 24 Vida Blue 3.00
- 25 Will Clark 3.00

Boys of Summer Autographs

		NM/M
	Common Autograph:	10.00
2	Marty Marion	10.00
3	Andre Dawson	15.00
6	Steve Garvey	12.00
8	Darren Daulton	10.00
9	Darryl Strawberry	15.00
10	Dave Parker	10.00
11	Doc Gooden	15.00
13	Eric Davis	10.00
15	Fred Lynn	12.00
16	Graig Nettles	15.00
17	Jay Buhner	15.00
20	Keith Hernandez	12.00
22	Jack Morris	12.00
24	Vida Blue	12.00

Boys of Summer Silver Autograph

		NM/M
	Common Autograph:	12.00
	Production 100	
2	Marty Marion	12.00
3	Andre Dawson	15.00
6	Steve Garvey	20.00
8	Darren Daulton	12.00
9	Darryl Strawberry	18.00
10	Dave Parker	12.00
11	Doc Gooden	20.00
12	Don Mattingly	65.00
13	Eric Davis	12.00
15	Fred Lynn	15.00
16	Graig Nettles	15.00
18	Jim Rice	20.00
20	Keith Hernandez	15.00
22	Jack Morris	15.00
24	Vida Blue	15.00

Boys of Summer Gold Autographs

		NM/M
	Common Autograph:	20.00
	Production 25	
1	Alan Trammell	35.00
2	Marty Marion	20.00
3	Andre Dawson	20.00
6	Steve Garvey	20.00
8	Darren Daulton	20.00
9	Darryl Strawberry	20.00
10	Dave Parker	20.00
11	Doc Gooden	20.00
12	Don Mattingly	75.00
13	Eric Davis	20.00
14	Dwight Evans	25.00
15	Fred Lynn	25.00
16	Graig Nettles	20.00
17	Jay Buhner	25.00
18	Jim Rice	25.00
20	Keith Hernandez	20.00
22	Jack Morris	20.00
24	Vida Blue	20.00
25	Will Clark	100.00

Boys of Summer Platinum Auto.

No Pricing
Production One Set

Boys of Summer Materials

		NM/M
	Common Player:	5.00
	Combos:	1-2X
	Production 100 Sets	
	Prime:	1-2X
	Production 100 Sets	
3	Andre Dawson	5.00
4	Bo Jackson	10.00
5	Cal Ripken Jr.	20.00
7	Dale Murphy	6.00
9	Darryl Strawberry	5.00
11	Doc Gooden	5.00
12	Don Mattingly	15.00
19	Jose Canseco	6.00
21	Rickey Henderson	8.00
22	Jack Morris	5.00
23	Tony Gwynn	8.00
25	Will Clark	8.00

Boys of Summer Combo Materials

		NM/M
	Production 100 Sets	
3	Andre Dawson	10.00
4	Bo Jackson	15.00
5	Cal Ripken Jr.	30.00
7	Dale Murphy	10.00
12	Don Mattingly	25.00
19	Jose Canseco	10.00
21	Rickey Henderson	15.00
23	Tony Gwynn	10.00
25	Will Clark	10.00

Boys of Summer Material Autos.

		NM/M
	Varying quantities produced	
3	Andre Dawson/50	25.00
9	Darryl Strawberry/150	25.00
11	Doc Gooden/100	25.00
12	Don Mattingly/25	80.00
22	Jack Morris/150	12.00

Boys of Summer Prime Materials

		NM/M
	Common Player:	8.00
	Production 100 Sets	
3	Andre Dawson	8.00
4	Bo Jackson	15.00
5	Cal Ripken Jr.	30.00
9	Darryl Strawberry	8.00
11	Doc Gooden	8.00
12	Don Mattingly	25.00
21	Rickey Henderson	15.00
23	Tony Gwynn	12.00
25	Will Clark	12.00

Boys/Summer Prime Materials Autographs

No Pricing
Production One Set

Call to the Hall

		NM/M
	Complete Set (25):	80.00
	Common Player:	3.00
	Production 250 Sets	
	Silver:	1X
	Production 100 Sets	
	Gold:	3-4X
	Production 25 Sets	
	Platinum:	No Pricing
	Production One Set	
1	Babe Ruth	10.00
2	Billy Williams	3.00
3	Bob Feller	3.00
4	Bobby Doerr	3.00
5	Carlton Fisk	3.00
6	Gary Carter	3.00
7	George Brett	8.00
8	Carl Yastrzemski	5.00
9	Harmon Killebrew	5.00
10	Jim Palmer	3.00
11	Joe Morgan	3.00
12	Johnny Bench	5.00
13	Kirby Puckett	5.00
14	Gaylord Perry	3.00
15	Mike Schmidt	6.00
16	Nolan Ryan	10.00
17	Ozzie Smith	5.00
18	Phil Rizzuto	3.00
19	Reggie Jackson	4.00
20	Roberto Clemente	6.00
21	Robin Yount	4.00
22	Rod Carew	3.00
23	Rollie Fingers	3.00
24	Steve Carlton	3.00
25	Tom Seaver	4.00

Call to the Hall Autographs

		NM/M
	Common Autograph:	15.00
	Silver Autos.:	1X
	Production 100	
3	Bob Feller	15.00
4	Bobby Doerr	15.00
14	Gaylord Perry	15.00
23	Rollie Fingers	15.00

Call to the Hall Gold Autographs

		NM/M
	Production 25 Sets	
2	Billy Williams	25.00
3	Bob Feller	40.00
6	Gary Carter	40.00
10	Jim Palmer	30.00
18	Phil Rizzuto	40.00
24	Steve Carlton	40.00

Call to the Hall Platinum Autograph

NM/M
No Pricing
Production One Set

Call to the Hall Materials

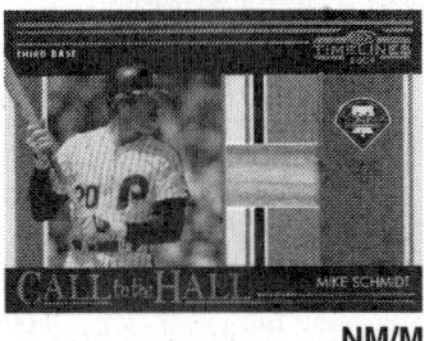

		NM/M
	Common Player:	6.00
1	Babe Ruth/50	575.00
4	Bobby Doerr	6.00
6	Gary Carter	8.00
7	George Brett	12.00
8	Carl Yastrzemski	12.00
13	Kirby Puckett	10.00
15	Mike Schmidt	12.00
16	Nolan Ryan	20.00
17	Ozzie Smith	8.00
19	Reggie Jackson	8.00
20	Roberto Clemente/100	50.00

Call to the Hall Combo Materials

		NM/M
	Production 125 Sets	
6	Gary Carter	12.00
7	George Brett	25.00
13	Kirby Puckett	20.00
15	Mike Schmidt	25.00
16	Nolan Ryan	35.00
19	Reggie Jackson	20.00

Call to the Hall Material Autograph

		NM/M
	Varying quantities produced	
4	Bobby Doerr/100	25.00
6	Gary Carter/25	45.00
19	Reggie Jackson/25	50.00

Materials

		NM/M
	Common Player:	5.00
	Combos:	1-2X
	Production 125	
	Primes:	1-2X
	Production 125	
1	Adam Dunn	5.00
2	Albert Pujols	12.00
3	Alex Rodriguez	10.00
4	Alfonso Soriano	8.00
5	Andruw Jones	5.00
7	Miguel Cabrera/SP	10.00
10	Carlos Delgado	5.00
11	Chipper Jones	8.00
14	Frank Thomas	8.00
17	Greg Maddux	8.00
20	Hideo Nomo	6.00
22	Ivan Rodriguez	6.00
23	Jason Giambi	6.00
24	Jeff Bagwell	6.00
25	Jim Thome	8.00
26	Juan Gonzalez	6.00
30	Lance Berkman	5.00
33	Mark Prior	10.00
35	Mike Piazza	8.00
36	Nomar Garciaparra	10.00
37	Pedro J. Martinez	8.00
39	Randy Johnson	6.00
41	Roger Clemens	10.00
43	Sammy Sosa	10.00
45	Shawn Green	5.00
47	Todd Helton	6.00
49	Vernon Wells	5.00

Materials Autographs

		NM/M
	Varying quantities produced	
7	Miguel Cabrera/25	85.00
22	Ivan Rodriguez/25	65.00
33	Mark Prior/50	75.00
49	Vernon Wells/25	25.00

Materials Combo

		NM/M
	Common Player:	8.00
	Production 125 Sets	
1	Adam Dunn	8.00
2	Albert Pujols	20.00
3	Alex Rodriguez	15.00
4	Alfonso Soriano	10.00
5	Andruw Jones	8.00
7	Miguel Cabrera	20.00
11	Chipper Jones	15.00
14	Frank Thomas	12.00
17	Greg Maddux	15.00
20	Hideo Nomo	10.00
25	Jim Thome	12.00
30	Lance Berkman	8.00
33	Mark Prior	20.00
35	Mike Piazza	15.00
36	Nomar Garciaparra	15.00
37	Pedro J. Martinez	12.00
39	Randy Johnson	10.00
41	Roger Clemens	15.00
43	Sammy Sosa	15.00
45	Shawn Green	10.00
47	Todd Helton	10.00

Materials Prime

		NM/M
	Common Player:	8.00
	Production 125 Sets	
1	Adam Dunn	8.00
2	Albert Pujols	20.00
3	Alex Rodriguez	20.00
4	Alfonso Soriano	10.00
5	Andruw Jones	8.00
7	Miguel Cabrera	20.00
10	Carlos Delgado	8.00
11	Chipper Jones	15.00
14	Frank Thomas	12.00
17	Greg Maddux	15.00
20	Hideo Nomo	10.00
25	Jim Thome	12.00
30	Lance Berkman	8.00
33	Mark Prior	20.00
35	Mike Piazza	15.00
36	Nomar Garciaparra	15.00
37	Pedro J. Martinez	12.00
39	Randy Johnson	10.00
41	Roger Clemens	15.00
43	Sammy Sosa	15.00
45	Shawn Green	10.00
47	Todd Helton	10.00
49	Vernon Wells	8.00

Materials Prime Autograph

No Pricing
Production One Set

Recollection Autographs

Complete Set (1576):
Common Player:

2004 Donruss World Series

		NM/M
	Complete Set (200):	
	Common Player:	.15
	Common SP (176-200):	8.00
	Pack (6):	6.00
	Box (24):	120.00
1	Bartolo Colon	.15
2	Darin Erstad	.25
3	Garret Anderson	.25
4	Tim Salmon	.25
5	Troy Glaus	.25
6	Vladimir Guerrero	.75
7	Brandon Webb	.15
8	Luis Gonzalez	.15
9	Randy Johnson	.75
10	Roberto Alomar	.40
11	Shea Hillenbrand	.15
12	Steve Finley	.15
13	Andruw Jones	.40
14	Chipper Jones	.75
15	J.D. Drew	.25
16	Marcus Giles	.15
17	Rafael Furcal	.25
18	Javy Lopez	.25
19	Jay Gibbons	.15
20	Luis Matos	.15
21	Melvin Mora	.15
22	Miguel Tejada	.40
23	Rafael Palmeiro	.50
24	Curt Schilling	.75
25	Dwight Evans	.15
26	Fred Lynn	.15
27	Jason Varitek	.25
28	Jim Rice	.25
29	Johnny Damon	.40
30	Luis Tiant	.15
31	Manny Ramirez	.50
32	Nomar Garciaparra	1.00
33	Pedro Martinez	.75
34	Trot Nixon	.15
35	Aramis Ramirez	.25
36	Corey Patterson	.25
37	Derrek Lee	.25
38	Greg Maddux	1.00
39	Kerry Wood	.75
40	Mark Prior	.75
41	Moises Alou	.25
42	Sammy Sosa	1.50
43	Carlos Lee	.15
44	Frank Thomas	.50
45	Luis Aparicio	.15
46	Magglio Ordonez	.25
47	Mark Buehrle	.15
48	Paul Konerko	.25
49	Adam Dunn	.50
50	Austin Kearns	.15
51	Barry Larkin	.25
52	Dave Concepcion	.15
53	George Foster	.15
54	Joe Morgan	.15
55	Sean Casey	.25
56	Tony Perez	.15
57	C.C. Sabathia	.15
58	Jody Gerut	.15
59	Omar Vizquel	.15
60	Victor Martinez	.15
61	Charles Johnson	.15
62	Jeromy Burnitz	.15
63	Larry Walker	.25
64	Preston Wilson	.15
65	Todd Helton	.50
66	Alan Trammell	.15
67	Dmitri Young	.15
68	Ivan Rodriguez	.50
69	Jeremy Bonderman	.15
70	A.J. Burnett	.15
71	Brad Penny	.15
72	Dontrelle Willis	.15
73	Josh Beckett	.40
74	Juan Pierre	.15
75	Luis Castillo	.15
76	Miguel Cabrera	.75
77	Mike Lowell	.25
78	Andy Pettitte	.25
79	Craig Biggio	.25
80	Jeff Bagwell	.50
81	Jeff Kent	.25
82	Lance Berkman	.25
83	Roger Clemens	2.00
84	Roy Oswalt	.25
85	Wade Miller	.15
86	Angel Berroa	.15
87	Carlos Beltran	.50
88	Juan Gonzalez	.40
89	Ken Harvey	.15
90	Mike Sweeney	.15
91	Adrian Beltre	.40
92	Hideo Nomo	.40
93	Kazuhisa Ishii	.15
94	Milton Bradley	.15
95	Orel Hershiser	.15
96	Paul LoDuca	.15
97	Shawn Green	.25
98	Ben Sheets	.25
99	Geoff Jenkins	.15
100	Junior Spivey	.15
101	Rickie Weeks	.15
102	Scott Podsednik	.15
103	Jack Morris	.15
104	Jacque Jones	.15
105	Johan Santana	.50
106	Shannon Stewart	.15
107	Torii Hunter	.25
108	Jose Vidro	.15
109	Orlando Cabrera	.25
110	Al Leiter	.25
111	Darryl Strawberry	.25
112	Dwight Gooden	.15
113	Jose Reyes	.25
114	Kazuo Matsui **RC**	2.00
115	Keith Hernandez	.15
116	Lenny Dykstra	.15
117	Mike Piazza	1.00
118	Tom Glavine	.40
119	Alex Rodriguez	2.00
120	Bernie Williams	.40
121	Derek Jeter	2.00
122	Gary Sheffield	.50
123	Jason Giambi	.25
124	Javier Vazquez	.25
125	Jorge Posada	.25
126	Kenny Lofton	.15
127	Kevin Brown	.25
128	Mariano Rivera	.25
129	Mike Mussina	.40
130	Barry Zito	.25
131	Eric Chavez	.25
132	Jermaine Dye	.15
133	Mark Mulder	.25
134	Rich Harden	.25
135	Tim Hudson	.25
136	Brett Myers	.15
137	Jim Thome	.75
138	Kevin Millwood	.15
139	Marlon Byrd	.15
140	Mike Lieberthal	.15
141	Pat Burrell	.15
142	Steve Carlton	.25
143	Dave Parker	.15
144	Jason Kendall	.15
145	Brian Giles	.15
146	Jay Payton	.15
147	Ryan Klesko	.15
148	J.T. Snow	.15
149	Jason Schmidt	.25
150	Bret Boone	.15
151	Edgar Martinez	.25
152	Jamie Moyer	.15
153	Rich Aurilia	.15
154	Shigetoshi Hasegawa	.15
155	Albert Pujols	2.00
156	Dan Haren	.15
157	Edgar Renteria	.25
158	Fernando Vina	.15
159	Jim Edmonds	.40
160	Matt Morris	.15
161	Scott Rolen	.75
162	Aubrey Huff	.15
163	Carl Crawford	.15
164	Dewon Brazelton	.15
165	Fred McGriff	.25
166	Rocco Baldelli	.15
167	Alfonso Soriano	.75
168	Hank Blalock	.50
169	Kenny Rogers	.15
170	Mark Teixeira	.25
171	Michael Young	.15
172	Carlos Delgado	.40
173	Eric Hinske	.15
174	Roy Halladay	.15
175	Vernon Wells	.15
176	Ivan Ochoa/ Auto./487 **RC**	8.00
177	Jason Bartlett/ Auto./1000 **RC**	8.00
178	Josh Labandeira/ Auto./703 **RC**	8.00
179	Phil Stockman/ Auto./1000 **RC**	8.00
180	Ronny Cedeno/ Auto./715 **RC**	8.00
181	Shawn Camp/ Auto./1000 **RC**	8.00
182	Ruddy Yan/ Auto./1000	8.00
183	Roberto Novoa/ Auto./568 **RC**	10.00
184	Justin Knoedler/ Auto./1000 **RC**	8.00
185	Jesse Harper/ Auto./1000 **RC**	8.00
186	Jason Szuminski/ Auto./1000 **RC**	8.00
187	Jamie Brown/ Auto./800 **RC**	8.00
188	Eddy Rodriguez/ Auto./1000 **RC**	8.00
189	Dennis Sarfate/ Auto./1000 **RC**	8.00
190	Ryan Meaux/ Auto./1000 **RC**	8.00
191	Charles Thomas/ Auto./1000 **RC**	10.00

192 Frank Francisco/ Auto./1000 **RC** 8.00
193 Orlando Rodriguez/ Auto./500 **RC** 8.00
194 Joey Gathright/ Auto./1000 **RC** 10.00
195 Renyel Pinto/ Auto./1000 **RC** 10.00
196 Justin Leone/ Auto./1000 **RC** 10.00
197 Tim Bausher/ Auto./834 **RC** 8.00
198 Travis Blackley/ Auto./1000 **RC** 10.00
199 Yadier Molina/ Auto./500 **RC** 15.00
200 Brad Halsey/ Auto./500 **RC** 10.00

HoloFoil 10

No Pricing
Production 10 Sets

HoloFoil 25

HoloFoil (1-175): 10-20X
HoloFoil (176-200): No Pricing
Production 25 Sets

HoloFoil 50

HoloFoil (1-175): 6-12X
HoloFoil (176-200): .75X
Production 50 Sets

HoloFoil 100

HoloFoil (1-175): 4-8X
HoloFoil (176-200): .5X
Production 100 Sets

Champions

NM/M
Complete Boxed Set (25): 25.00
Common Player: .50
201 Curt Schilling 3.00
202 Pedro Martinez 3.00
203 Derek Lowe .50
204 Tim Wakefield .50
205 Bronson Arroyo .50
206 Mike Timlin .50
207 Curt Leskanic .50
208 Mike Myers .50
209 Alan Embree .50
210 Keith Foulke .50
211 Jason Varitek 2.00
212 Doug Mirabelli .50
213 Doug Mientkiewicz .50
214 Mark Bellhorn .50
215 Pokey Reese .50
216 Orlando Cabrera 1.00
217 Bill Mueller .50
218 Kevin Youkilis .50
219 Manny Ramirez 3.00
220 Johnny Damon 3.00
221 Dave Roberts .50
222 Trot Nixon .50
223 Gabe Kapler .50
224 David Ortiz 3.00

Champions Box Topper

NM/M
Inserted 1:Set
WS1 World Series Champions 2.00

Blue

NM/M
Complete Set (100): 50.00
Common Player: .50
Inserted 1:1
HoloFoil 100: 2-4X
Production 100 Sets
HoloFoil 50: 4-6X
Production 50 Sets
HoloFoil 25: 6-10X
Production 25 Sets
HoloFoil 10: No Pricing
Production 10 Sets
1 Josh Beckett .50
2 Miguel Cabrera 1.00
3 Derrek Lee .50
4 Mike Lowell .50
5 Brad Penny .50
6 Ivan Rodriguez 1.00
7 Dontrelle Willis .50
8 Luis Castillo .50
9 Garret Anderson .75
10 Troy Glaus .75
11 John Lackey .50
12 Chone Figgins .50
13 Tim Salmon .50
14 Darin Erstad .50
15 Troy Percival .50
16 Steve Finley .50
17 Mark Grace .75
18 Randy Johnson 1.00
19 Curt Schilling 1.00
20 Luis Gonzalez .50
21 Andy Pettitte .75
22 Bernie Williams .75
23 Jorge Posada .75
24 Mariano Rivera .75
25 Roger Clemens 3.00
26 Jose Canseco 1.00
27 David Justice .50
28 Paul O'Neill .75
29 Darryl Strawberry .50
30 David Wells .50
31 Wade Boggs .75
32 Charles Johnson .50
33 Cliff Floyd .50
34 Moises Alou .50
35 Edgar Renteria .75
36 Chipper Jones 1.50
37 Tom Glavine .75
38 John Smoltz .75
39 Greg Maddux 1.50
40 Ryan Klesko .50
41 Javy Lopez .50
42 Fred McGriff .50
43 Roberto Alomar .75
44 Joe Carter .50
45 Rickey Henderson .50
46 Paul Molitor 1.00
47 Jack Morris .50
48 Jack Morris .50
49 Kirby Puckett 1.50
50 Eric Davis .50
51 Barry Larkin .75
52 Paul O'Neill .75
53 Dennis Eckersley .75
54 Jose Canseco 1.00
55 Rickey Henderson .75
56 Dave Parker .50
57 Orel Hershiser .50
58 Kirk Gibson .50
59 Bert Blyleven .50
60 Dwight Gooden .50
61 Gary Carter .50
62 Lenny Dykstra .50
63 Keith Hernandez .50
64 Darryl Strawberry .50
65 George Brett 3.00
66 Kirk Gibson .50
67 Alan Trammell .50
68 Jim Palmer .75
69 Eddie Murray .75
70 Cal Ripken Jr. 5.00
71 Keith Hernandez .50
72 Ozzie Smith 1.50
73 Steve Garvey .50
74 Steve Carlton 1.00
75 Mike Schmidt 4.00
76 John Candelaria .50
77 Bert Blyleven .50
78 Dave Parker .50
79 Willie Stargell 1.00
80 Reggie Jackson 1.00
81 Johnny Bench 2.00
82 Dave Concepcion .50
83 George Foster .50
84 Joe Morgan .50
85 Tony Perez .50
86 Rollie Fingers .50
87 Jim "Catfish" Hunter .50
88 Reggie Jackson 1.00
89 Al Oliver .50
90 Roberto Clemente 3.00
91 Willie Stargell .75
92 Brooks Robinson 1.00
93 Frank Robinson .75
94 Nolan Ryan 4.00
95 Tom Seaver 1.50
96 Al Kaline 1.00
97 Bob Gibson 1.00
98 Lou Brock .75
99 Orlando Cepeda .50
100 Duke Snider 1.00

Blue Material Bat

NM/M
Common Player: 5.00
Production 50 Sets
1 Josh Beckett 8.00
2 Miguel Cabrera 12.00
3 Derrek Lee 8.00
4 Mike Lowell 5.00
5 Brad Penny 5.00
6 Ivan Rodriguez 12.00
8 Luis Castillo 5.00
9 Garret Anderson 5.00
10 Troy Glaus 8.00
13 Tim Salmon 5.00
14 Darin Erstad 5.00
17 Mark Grace 12.00
19 Curt Schilling 12.00
20 Luis Gonzalez 5.00
21 Andy Pettitte 5.00
22 Bernie Williams 8.00
23 Jorge Posada 10.00
25 Roger Clemens 20.00
27 David Justice 5.00
28 Paul O'Neill 10.00
29 Darryl Strawberry 10.00
31 Wade Boggs 15.00
32 Charles Johnson 5.00
33 Cliff Floyd 5.00
34 Moises Alou 8.00
35 Edgar Renteria 8.00
36 Chipper Jones 15.00
37 Tom Glavine 10.00
39 Greg Maddux 20.00
40 Ryan Klesko 5.00
41 Javy Lopez 5.00
42 Fred McGriff 8.00
43 Roberto Alomar 8.00
44 Joe Carter 5.00
45 Rickey Henderson 15.00
46 Paul Molitor 15.00
49 Kirby Puckett 15.00
50 Eric Davis 5.00
51 Barry Larkin 8.00
52 Paul O'Neill 8.00
55 Rickey Henderson 15.00
56 Dave Parker 8.00
58 Kirk Gibson 10.00
60 Dwight Gooden 8.00
61 Gary Carter 8.00
62 Lenny Dykstra 5.00
63 Keith Hernandez 5.00
64 Darryl Strawberry 5.00
65 George Brett 25.00
66 Kirk Gibson 8.00
67 Alan Trammell 8.00
69 Eddie Murray 20.00
70 Cal Ripken Jr. 70.00
71 Keith Hernandez 8.00
72 Ozzie Smith 20.00
73 Steve Garvey 5.00
74 Steve Carlton 10.00
75 Mike Schmidt 25.00
78 Dave Parker 8.00
79 Willie Stargell 15.00
80 Reggie Jackson 15.00
81 Johnny Bench 20.00
82 Dave Concepcion 5.00
83 George Foster 5.00
84 Joe Morgan 8.00
85 Tony Perez 8.00
88 Reggie Jackson 15.00
89 Al Oliver 5.00
90 Roberto Clemente 60.00
91 Willie Stargell 15.00
92 Brooks Robinson 15.00
93 Frank Robinson 10.00
96 Al Kaline 15.00
98 Lou Brock 15.00
99 Orlando Cepeda 10.00

Blue Material Fabric

NM/M
Common Player: 4.00
Quantity produced listed
1 Josh Beckett/Jsy/103 4.00
2 Miguel Cabrera/ Jsy/103 8.00
3 Derrek Lee/Jsy/103 6.00
4 Mike Lowell/Jsy/103 4.00
5 Brad Penny/Jsy/103 4.00
6 Ivan Rodriguez/ Jsy/103 8.00
7 Dontrelle Willis/ Jsy/103 4.00
9 Garret Anderson/ Jsy/102 4.00
10 Troy Glaus/Jsy/102 4.00
13 Tim Salmon/Jsy/102 4.00
14 Darin Erstad/Jsy/102 4.00
15 Tony Percival/Jsy/102 4.00
16 Steve Finley/Jsy/101 4.00
18 Randy Johnson/ Pants/101 8.00
19 Curt Schilling/Jsy/101 8.00
20 Luis Gonzalez/Jsy/101 4.00
21 Andy Pettitte/Jsy/100 6.00
22 Bernie Williams/ Jsy/100 6.00
24 Mariano Rivera/ Jsy/100 6.00
25 Roger Clemens/ Jsy/100 12.00
29 Darryl Strawberry/ Jsy/99 6.00
30 David Wells/Jsy/99 4.00
31 Wade Boggs/Jsy/96 8.00
32 Charles Johnson/ Jsy/97 4.00
33 Cliff Floyd/Jsy/97 4.00
36 Chipper Jones/Jsy/95 8.00
37 Tom Glavine/Jsy/95 6.00
39 Greg Maddux/Jsy/95 10.00
40 Ryan Klesko/Jsy/95 4.00
41 Javy Lopez/Jsy/95 4.00
51 Barry Larkin/Jsy/90 8.00
54 Jose Canseco/Jsy/89 10.00
55 Rickey Henderson/ Jsy/89 12.00
57 Orel Hershiser/Jsy/88 8.00
59 Bert Blyleven/Jsy/87 6.00
60 Dwight Gooden/ Jsy/86 6.00
61 Gary Carter/Jkt/86 6.00
64 Darryl Strawberry/ Jsy/86 6.00
65 George Brett/Jsy/85 20.00
68 Jim Palmer/Pants/83 8.00
69 Eddie Murray/Jsy/83 15.00
70 Cal Ripken Jr./Jsy/83 40.00
71 Keith Hernandez/ Jsy/82 6.00
74 Steve Carlton/Jsy/80 6.00
75 Mike Schmidt/Jkt/80 15.00
78 Dave Parker/Jsy/79 6.00
79 Willie Stargell/Jsy/79 8.00
80 Reggie Jackson/ Jsy/78 8.00
81 Johnny Bench/Jsy/75 12.00
82 Dave Concepcion/ Jsy/75 4.00
83 George Foster/Jsy/75 4.00
86 Rollie Fingers/Jsy/74 4.00
87 Jim "Catfish" Hunter/ Jsy/74 8.00
88 Reggie Jackson/Jkt/73 8.00
91 Willie Stargell/Jsy/71 8.00
98 Lou Brock/Jkt/67 8.00
100 Duke Snider/ Pants/55 10.00

Blue Material Fabric AL/NL

NM/M
Common Player: 4.00
Quantity produced listed
1 Josh Beckett/Jsy/100 4.00
2 Miguel Cabrera/ Jsy/100 8.00
3 Derrek Lee/Jsy/100 4.00
4 Mike Lowell/Jsy/100 4.00
5 Brad Penny/Jsy/103 4.00
6 Ivan Rodriguez/ Jsy/100 8.00
7 Dontrelle Willis/ Jsy/100 4.00
9 Garret Anderson/ Jsy/100 4.00
10 Troy Glaus/Jsy/100 4.00
13 Tim Salmon/Jsy/100 4.00
14 Darin Erstad/Jsy/100 4.00
15 Tony Percival/Jsy/100 4.00
16 Steve Finley/Jsy/100 4.00
18 Randy Johnson/ Pants/100 8.00
19 Curt Schilling/Jsy/100 8.00
20 Luis Gonzalez/Jsy/100 4.00
21 Andy Pettitte/Jsy/100 6.00
22 Bernie Williams/ Jsy/100 6.00
24 Mariano Rivera/ Jsy/100 6.00
25 Roger Clemens/ Jsy/100 15.00
29 Darryl Strawberry/ Jsy/100 4.00
30 David Wells/Jsy/10 4.00
31 Wade Boggs/Jsy/100 8.00
32 Charles Johnson/ Jsy/100 4.00
33 Cliff Floyd/Jsy/100 4.00
36 Chipper Jones/Jsy/100 8.00
37 Tom Glavine/Jsy/100 6.00
39 Greg Maddux/ Jsy/100 10.00
40 Ryan Klesko/Jsy/100 4.00
41 Javy Lopez/Jsy/10 4.00
51 Barry Larkin/Jsy/100 8.00
54 Jose Canseco/ Jsy/100 10.00
55 Rickey Henderson/ Jsy/100 10.00
57 Orel Hershiser/ Jsy/100 8.00
59 Bert Blyleven/Jsy/50 8.00
60 Dwight Gooden/ Jsy/100 6.00
61 Gary Carter/Jkt/100 6.00
64 Darryl Strawberry/ Jsy/100 6.00
65 George Brett/Jsy/50 25.00
68 Jim Palmer/Pants/50 8.00
69 Eddie Murray/Jsy/50 15.00
70 Cal Ripken Jr./ Jsy/50 65.00
71 Keith Hernandez/ Jsy/50 8.00
74 Steve Carlton/Jsy/50 8.00
75 Mike Schmidt/Jkt/50 25.00
78 Dave Parker/Jsy/50 8.00
79 Willie Stargell/Jsy/50 15.00
80 Reggie Jackson/ Jsy/50 15.00
82 Dave Concepcion/ Jsy/50 8.00
83 George Foster/Jsy/50 8.00
86 Rollie Fingers/Jsy/50 8.00
87 Jim "Catfish" Hunter/ Jsy/50 15.00
88 Reggie Jackson/ Jkt/50 15.00
91 Willie Stargell/Jsy/50 15.00
98 Lou Brock/Jkt/50 15.00
100 Duke Snider/ Pants/50 15.00

Blue Signature

NM/M
Quantity produced listed
2 Miguel Cabrera/25 40.00
3 Derrek Lee/25 30.00
5 Brad Penny/25 15.00
9 Garret Anderson/25 20.00
11 John Lackey/50 10.00
12 Chone Figgins/25 15.00
16 Steve Finley/25 20.00
29 Darryl Strawberry/25 20.00
42 Fred McGriff/25 40.00
47 Jack Morris/25 20.00
48 Jack Morris/25 20.00
50 Eric Davis/25 25.00
53 Dennis Eckersley/25 40.00
56 Dave Parker/25 20.00
59 Bert Blyleven/25 25.00
60 Dwight Gooden/25 25.00
62 Lenny Dykstra/25 25.00
63 Keith Hernandez/25 25.00
64 Darryl Strawberry/25 25.00
67 Alan Trammell/25 25.00
68 Jim Palmer/25 25.00
71 Keith Hernandez/25 25.00
76 John Candelaria/25 25.00
77 Bert Blyleven/25 25.00
78 Dave Parker/25 20.00
82 Dave Concepcion/25 20.00
83 George Foster/25 20.00
85 Tony Perez/25 35.00
86 Rollie Fingers/25 25.00
89 Al Oliver/25 25.00

Face Off

NM/M
Complete Set (20): 75.00
Common Duo: 2.00
Production 500 Sets
HoloFoil: 2-4X
Production 25 Sets
1 Roger Clemens, Mike Piazza 6.00
2 Mike Mussina, Ivan Rodriguez 3.00
3 Mark Grace, Jorge Posada 4.00
4 Greg Maddux, Jim Thome 5.00
5 Rickey Henderson, Curt Schilling 4.00
6 Kirby Puckett, Tom Glavine 4.00
7 Dennis Eckersley, Will Clark 3.00
8 Bernie Williams, Randy Johnson 4.00
9 Cal Ripken Jr., Steve Carlton 12.00
10 Tom Seaver, Reggie Jackson 4.00
11 Mike Schmidt, George Brett 8.00
12 Wade Boggs, Keith Hernandez 3.00
13 Dwight Gooden, Dwight Evans 2.00
14 Johnny Bench, Jim "Catfish" Hunter 4.00
15 Jim Palmer, Dave Parker 4.00
16 Bob Gibson, Al Kaline 4.00
17 Carl Yastrzemski, Lou Brock 6.00
18 Duke Snider, Whitey Ford 4.00
19 Carlton Fisk, Tony Perez 4.00
20 Roberto Clemente, Frank Robinson 8.00

Face Off Material

NM/M
Common Duo: 10.00
Quantity produced listed
1 Roger Clemens/Jsy, Mike Piazza/Jsy/100 25.00
2 Mike Mussina/Jsy, Ivan Rodriguez/ Jsy/100 20.00
4 Greg Maddux/Jsy, Jim Thome/Jsy/25 35.00
5 Rickey Henderson/Jsy, Curt Schilling/ Jsy/100 15.00
6 Kirby Puckett/Jsy, Tom Glavine/Jsy/100 25.00
8 Bernie Williams/Jsy, Randy Johnson/ Pants/100 20.00
9 Cal Ripken Jr./Jsy, Steve Carlton/Jsy/50 75.00
11 Mike Schmidt/Jkt, George Brett/Jsy/50 40.00
13 Dwight Gooden/Jsy, Dwight Evans/Jsy/50 25.00
15 Jim Palmer/Jsy, Dave Parker/Jsy/50 10.00
17 Carl Yastrzemski/Jsy, Lou Brock/Jkt/50 40.00
18 Duke Snider/Pants, Whitey Ford/Jsy/50 25.00
19 Carlton Fisk/Jsy, Tony Perez/ Fld Glv/50 20.00

Legends of the Fall

NM/M
Complete Set (20): 75.00
Common Player: 3.00
Production 500 Sets
HoloFoil: 2-4X
Production 25 Sets
1 Bob Gibson 4.00
2 Brooks Robinson 4.00
3 Cal Ripken Jr. 12.00
4 Carl Yastrzemski 6.00
5 Carlton Fisk 4.00
6 Derek Jeter 8.00
7 Duke Snider 4.00
8 Eddie Murray 4.00
9 Frank Robinson 3.00
10 Gary Carter 3.00
11 George Brett 8.00
12 Jim Palmer 3.00
13 Johnny Bench 4.00
14 Marco Rivera 3.00
15 Mike Schmidt 8.00
16 Phil Rizzuto 3.00
17 Red Schoendienst 3.00
18 Reggie Jackson 4.00
19 Rickey Henderson 3.00
20 Whitey Ford 4.00

Legends of the Fall Material

NM/M
Common Player: 5.00
Quantity produced listed
1 Bob Gibson/Jsy/50 12.00
2 Brooks Robinson/ Bat/100 10.00
3 Cal Ripken Jr./ Jkt/100 40.00
4 Carl Yastrzemski/ Bat/50 10.00
5 Carlton Fisk/Bat/50 10.00
7 Duke Snider/ Pants/50 15.00
8 Eddie Murray/Jsy/50 15.00
9 Frank Robinson/ Bat/100 5.00
10 Gary Carter/Jkt/100 5.00
11 George Brett/Bat/50 25.00
12 Jim Palmer/Pants/25 12.00
13 Johnny Bench/ Bat/100 12.00
14 Marco Rivera/Jsy/100 8.00
15 Mike Schmidt/Jkt/50 25.00
16 Phil Rizzuto/Pants/50 10.00
17 Red Schoendienst/ Bat/100 5.00
18 Reggie Jackson/ Bat/100 10.00
19 Rickey Henderson/ Bat/100 10.00

Legends of the Fall Signature

NM/M
Common Player:
2 Brooks Robinson/25 30.00
9 Frank Robinson/25 35.00
10 Gary Carter/25 25.00
12 Jim Palmer/25 25.00
16 Phil Rizzuto/25 30.00
17 Red Schoendienst/50 20.00

Legends of the Fall Signature Material

NM/M
Quantity produced listed
1 Bob Gibson/Jsy/25 40.00
2 Brooks Robinson/ Bat/50 35.00

7 Duke Snider/ Pants/50 35.00
9 Frank Robinson/ Bat/50 30.00
10 Gary Carter/Jkt/50 25.00
12 Jim Palmer/Pants/25 25.00
13 Johnny Bench/Bat/25 70.00
16 Phil Rizzuto/ Pants/50 35.00
17 Red Schoendienst/ Bat/100 20.00

Material Bat

NM/M
Common Player: 4.00
Production 100 Sets
2 Darin Erstad 4.00
3 Garret Anderson 4.00
4 Tim Salmon 4.00
5 Troy Glaus 4.00
6 Vladimir Guerrero 8.00
8 Luis Gonzalez 4.00
13 Andruw Jones 6.00
14 Chipper Jones 8.00
15 J.D. Drew 4.00
16 Marcus Giles 4.00
17 Rafael Furcal 4.00
18 Javy Lopez 4.00
19 Jay Gibbons 4.00
22 Miguel Tejada 6.00
23 Rafael Palmeiro 8.00
25 Dwight Evans 4.00
26 Fred Lynn 4.00
27 Jason Varitek 8.00
28 Jim Rice 6.00
29 Johnny Damon 10.00
31 Manny Ramirez 8.00
32 Nomar Garciaparra 10.00
33 Pedro Martinez 8.00
34 Trot Nixon 4.00
35 Aramis Ramirez 6.00
37 Derrek Lee 6.00
40 Mark Prior 6.00
41 Moises Alou 4.00
42 Sammy Sosa 12.00
43 Carlos Lee 4.00
44 Frank Thomas 8.00
45 Luis Aparicio 4.00
46 Magglio Ordonez 4.00
47 Mark Buehrle 4.00
48 Paul Konerko 4.00
49 Adam Dunn Jsy 8.00
50 Austin Kearns 4.00
51 Barry Larkin 8.00
52 Dave Concepcion 4.00
53 George Foster 4.00
54 Joe Morgan 6.00
55 Sean Casey 4.00
56 Tony Perez 4.00
59 Omar Vizquel 4.00
60 Victor Martinez 4.00
61 Charles Johnson 4.00
63 Larry Walker 8.00
64 Preston Wilson 4.00
65 Todd Helton 8.00
66 Alan Trammell 4.00
68 Ivan Rodriguez 8.00
71 Brad Penny 4.00
73 Josh Beckett 6.00
74 Juan Pierre 4.00
75 Luis Castillo 4.00
76 Miguel Cabrera 8.00
77 Mike Lowell 4.00
78 Andy Pettitte 6.00
79 Craig Biggio 6.00
80 Jeff Bagwell 8.00
81 Jeff Kent 4.00
82 Lance Berkman 4.00
83 Roger Clemens 15.00
84 Roy Oswalt 4.00
86 Angel Berroa 4.00
87 Carlos Beltran 8.00
88 Juan Gonzalez 6.00
89 Ken Harvey 4.00
90 Mike Sweeney 4.00
91 Adrian Beltre 6.00
93 Kazuhisa Ishii 4.00
96 Paul LoDuca 4.00
97 Shawn Green 4.00
98 Ben Sheets 4.00
99 Geoff Jenkins 4.00
104 Jacque Jones 4.00
106 Shannon Stewart 4.00
107 Torii Hunter 6.00
108 Jose Vidro 4.00
109 Orlando Cabrera 6.00
111 Darryl Strawberry 6.00
112 Dwight Gooden 6.00
113 Jose Reyes 6.00
114 Kazuo Matsui 10.00
115 Keith Hernandez 6.00
116 Lenny Dykstra 4.00
118 Tom Glavine 8.00
122 Gary Sheffield 8.00
123 Jason Giambi 4.00
125 Jorge Posada 8.00
126 Kenny Lofton 4.00
127 Kevin Brown 4.00
129 Mike Mussina 8.00
131 Eric Chavez 4.00
132 Jermaine Dye 4.00
133 Mark Mulder 4.00
135 Tim Hudson 6.00
137 Jim Thome 8.00
139 Marlon Byrd 4.00
141 Pat Burrell 4.00
142 Steve Carlton 6.00
143 Dave Parker 4.00
145 Brian Giles 4.00
147 Ryan Klesko 4.00
151 Edgar Martinez 4.00
153 Rich Aurilia 4.00
155 Albert Pujols 15.00
156 Dan Haren 4.00
157 Edgar Renteria 6.00
159 Jim Edmonds 6.00
161 Scott Rolen 8.00
162 Aubrey Huff 4.00
165 Fred McGriff 4.00
166 Rocco Baldelli 4.00
167 Alfonso Soriano 8.00
168 Hank Blalock 8.00
170 Mark Teixeira 6.00
171 Michael Young 4.00
172 Carlos Delgado 4.00
175 Vernon Wells 4.00

Material Fabric AL/NL

NM/M
Common Player: 4.00
Production 250 unless noted.
2 Darin Erstad/Jsy 4.00
3 Garret Anderson/Jsy 4.00
4 Tim Salmon/Jsy 4.00
5 Troy Glaus/Jsy 4.00
6 Vladimir Guerrero/Jsy 8.00
7 Brandon Webb/Pants 4.00
8 Luis Gonzalez/Jsy 4.00
9 Randy Johnson/ Pants/100 10.00
12 Steve Finley/Jsy 4.00
13 Andruw Jones/Jsy 6.00
14 Chipper Jones/Jsy 8.00
16 Marcus Giles/Jsy 4.00
17 Rafael Furcal/Jsy 4.00
19 Jay Gibbons/Jsy 4.00
20 Luis Matos/Jsy 4.00
21 Melvin Mora/Jsy 4.00
22 Miguel Tejada/Jsy 6.00
23 Rafael Palmeiro/ Jsy/100 8.00
25 Dwight Evans/Jsy 4.00
26 Fred Lynn/Jsy 4.00
28 Jim Rice/Jsy 6.00
31 Manny Ramirez/Jsy 8.00
33 Pedro Martinez/Jsy 8.00
35 Aramis Ramirez/Jsy 6.00
38 Greg Maddux/ Jsy/100 12.00
39 Kerry Wood/Pants 8.00
40 Mark Prior/Jsy 6.00
42 Sammy Sosa/Jsy 10.00
43 Carlos Lee/Jsy 4.00
44 Frank Thomas/Jsy 8.00
47 Mark Buehrle/Jsy 4.00
48 Paul Konerko/Jsy 4.00
49 Adam Dunn/Jsy 8.00
50 Austin Kearns/Jsy 4.00
52 Dave Concepcion/Jsy 4.00
57 C.C. Sabathia/Jsy 4.00
58 Jody Gerut/Jsy 4.00
59 Omar Vizquel/Jsy 4.00
60 Victor Martinez/Jsy 4.00
63 Larry Walker/Jsy 8.00
64 Preston Wilson/Jsy 4.00
65 Todd Helton/Jsy 8.00
70 A.J. Burnett/Jsy 4.00
71 Brad Penny/Jsy 4.00
72 Dontrelle Willis/Jsy 4.00
73 Josh Beckett/Jsy 6.00
76 Miguel Cabrera/Jsy 8.00
77 Mike Lowell/Jsy 4.00
79 Craig Biggio/Jsy 6.00
80 Jeff Bagwell/Pants 8.00
81 Jeff Kent/Jsy 4.00
82 Lance Berkman/Jsy 4.00
86 Angel Berroa/Pants 4.00
90 Mike Sweeney/Jsy 4.00
91 Adrian Beltre/Jsy 6.00
92 Hideo Nomo/Jsy 8.00
93 Kazuhisa Ishii/Jsy 4.00
95 Orel Hershiser/ Jsy/100 6.00
96 Paul LoDuca/Jsy 4.00
97 Shawn Green/Jsy 6.00
98 Ben Sheets/Pants 4.00
99 Geoff Jenkins/Jsy 4.00
104 Jacque Jones/Jsy 4.00
105 Johan Santana/Jsy 8.00
106 Shannon Stewart/Jsy 4.00
110 Al Leiter/Jsy 4.00
111 Darryl Strawberry/Jsy 4.00
117 Mike Piazza/Jsy 10.00
118 Tom Glavine/Jsy 8.00
120 Bernie Williams/Jsy 6.00
123 Jason Giambi/Jsy 4.00
128 Mariano Rivera/Jsy 6.00
129 Mike Mussina/Jsy 8.00
130 Barry Zito/Jsy 4.00
131 Eric Chavez/Jsy 4.00
133 Mark Mulder/Jsy 4.00
135 Tim Hudson/Jsy 4.00
136 Brett Myers/Jsy 4.00
137 Jim Thome/Jsy 8.00
138 Kevin Millwood/Jsy 4.00
139 Marlon Byrd/Jsy 4.00
141 Pat Burrell/Jsy 4.00
142 Steve Carlton/Jsy/100 6.00
143 Dave Parker/Jsy/100 4.00
147 Ryan Klesko/Jsy 4.00
152 Jamie Moyer/Jsy 4.00
155 Albert Pujols/Jsy/100 15.00
156 Dan Haren/Jsy 4.00
159 Jim Edmonds/Jsy 6.00
161 Scott Rolen/Jsy 8.00
162 Aubrey Huff/Jsy 4.00
163 Carl Crawford/Jsy 4.00
164 Dewon Brazelton/Jsy 4.00
165 Fred McGriff/Jsy 4.00
166 Rocco Baldelli/Jsy 4.00
168 Hank Blalock/Jsy 8.00
174 Roy Halladay/Jsy 4.00
175 Vernon Wells/Jsy 4.00

Material Fabric Number

NM/M
Common Player:
5 Troy Glaus/Jsy/25 10.00
6 Vladimir Guerrero/ Jsy/27 20.00
7 Brandon Webb/ Pants/55 6.00
8 Luis Gonzalez/Jsy/20 8.00
9 Randy Johnson/ Pants/51 15.00
13 Andruw Jones/Jsy/25 10.00
16 Marcus Giles/Jsy/22 8.00
19 Jay Gibbons/Jsy/31 8.00
23 Rafael Palmeiro/ Jsy/25 15.00
25 Dwight Evans/Jsy/24 15.00
26 Fred Lynn/Jsy/19 10.00
30 Luis Tiant/Jsy/23 8.00
31 Manny Ramirez/ Jsy/24 20.00
33 Pedro Martinez/ Jsy/45 15.00
38 Greg Maddux/Jsy/31 20.00
39 Kerry Wood/Pants/34 20.00
40 Mark Prior/Jsy/22 15.00
42 Sammy Sosa/Jsy/21 25.00
43 Carlos Lee/Jsy/45 6.00
44 Frank Thomas/Jsy/35 15.00
46 Magglio Ordonez/ Jsy/30 8.00
47 Mark Buehrle/Jsy/56 6.00
49 Adam Dunn/Jsy/44 12.00
50 Austin Kearns/Jsy/28 10.00
57 C.C. Sabathia/Jsy/52 6.00
60 Victor Martinez/Jsy/41 8.00
63 Larry Walker/Jsy/33 10.00
64 Preston Wilson/Jsy/44 6.00
65 Todd Helton/Jsy/17 25.00
70 A.J. Burnett/Jsy/34 6.00
71 Brad Penny/Jsy/31 6.00
72 Dontrelle Willis/Jsy/35 6.00
73 Josh Beckett/Jsy/21 15.00
76 Miguel Cabrera/ Jsy/24 20.00
90 Mike Sweeney/Jsy/29 10.00
91 Adrian Beltre/Jsy/29 15.00
95 Orel Hershiser/Jsy/55 8.00
105 Johan Santana/ Jsy/57 15.00
106 Shannon Stewart/ Jsy/23 8.00
107 Torii Hunter/Jsy/48 10.00
110 Al Leiter/Jsy/22 10.00
117 Mike Piazza/Jsy/31 20.00
118 Tom Glavine/Jsy/47 12.00
120 Bernie Williams/ Jsy/51 12.00
123 Jason Giambi/Jsy/25 10.00
125 Jorge Posada/Jsy/20 15.00
128 Mariano Rivera/ Jsy/42 10.00
129 Mike Mussina/Jsy/35 15.00
130 Barry Zito/Jsy/75 8.00
133 Mark Mulder/Jsy/20 15.00
136 Brett Myers/Jsy/39 6.00
137 Jim Thome/Jsy/25 20.00
138 Kevin Millwood/Jsy/34 8.00
139 Marlon Byrd/Jsy/29 8.00
142 Steve Carlton/Jsy/32 12.00
143 Dave Parker/Jsy/39 8.00
147 Ryan Klesko/Jsy/30 10.00
152 Jamie Moyer/Jsy/50 6.00
156 Dan Haren/Jsy/55 6.00
159 Jim Edmonds/Jsy/15 15.00
161 Scott Rolen/Jsy/27 25.00
164 Dewon Brazelton/ Jsy/45 6.00
165 Fred McGriff/Jsy/29 15.00
174 Roy Halladay/Jsy/32 8.00

MVP

NM/M
Complete Set (15): 35.00

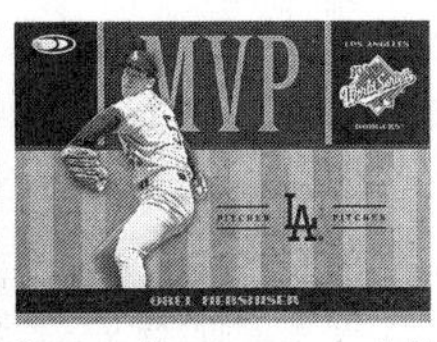

Common Player: 2.00
Production 1,000 Sets
HoloFoil: 2-4X
Production 50 Sets
1 Whitey Ford 3.00
2 Bob Gibson 3.00
3 Frank Robinson 2.00
4 Brooks Robinson 3.00
5 Roberto Clemente 6.00
6 Reggie Jackson 3.00
7 Rollie Fingers 2.00
8 Johnny Bench 4.00
9 Reggie Jackson 3.00
10 Mike Schmidt 6.00
11 Alan Trammell 2.00
12 Orel Hershiser 2.00
13 Jack Morris 2.00
14 Paul Molitor 4.00
15 Tom Glavine 3.00

MVP Material

NM/M
Quantity produced listed
1 Whitey Ford/Jsy/50 10.00
2 Bob Gibson/Jsy/50 10.00
3 Frank Robinson/ Jsy/25 12.00
6 Reggie Jackson/ Jkt/100 10.00
7 Rollie Fingers/Jsy/100 5.00
9 Reggie Jackson/ Jsy/25 20.00
10 Mike Schmidt/Jsy/50 25.00
12 Orel Hershiser/ Jsy/100 5.00
15 Tom Glavine/Jsy/100 8.00

MVP Signature

NM/M
Quantity produced listed
11 Alan Trammell/25 20.00
13 Jack Morris/25 20.00

MVP Signature Material

NM/M
Quantity produced listed
2 Bob Gibson/Jsy/50 35.00
3 Frank Robinson/ Shoe/50 40.00
7 Rollie Fingers/ Jsy/100 15.00
12 Orel Hershiser/ Jsy/25 25.00

October Heroes

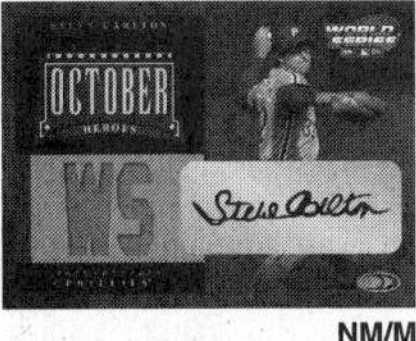

NM/M
Complete Set (20): 40.00
Common Player: 2.00
Production 500 Sets
HoloFoil: 2-4X
Production 25 Sets
1 Alan Trammell 2.00
2 Andy Pettitte 3.00
3 Jim "Catfish" Hunter 2.00
4 Chipper Jones 4.00
5 Dave Concepcion 2.00
6 David Wells 2.00
7 Jack Morris 2.00
8 Joe Morgan 3.00
9 Josh Beckett 2.00
10 Kirby Puckett 4.00
11 Kirk Gibson 2.00
12 Marty Marion 2.00
13 Miguel Cabrera 4.00
14 Paul Molitor 4.00
15 Paul O'Neill 2.00
16 Randy Johnson 4.00
17 Roger Clemens 6.00
18 Steve Carlton 3.00
19 Steve Garvey 2.00
20 Wade Boggs 3.00

October Heroes Material

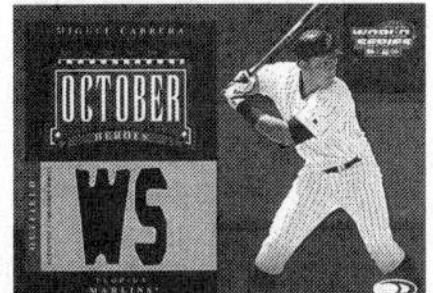

NM/M
Common Player: 4.00
1 Alan Trammell/ Jsy/25 10.00
2 Andy Pettite/ Jsy/100 4.00
3 Jim "Catfish" Hunter/ Jsy/25 15.00
4 Chipper Jones/ Jsy/100 8.00
5 Dave Concepcion/ Jsy/100 4.00
6 David Wells/ Jsy/25 8.00
9 Josh Beckett/ Jsy/100 4.00
10 Kirby Puckett/Jsy/25 25.00
12 Marty Marion/Jsy/25 10.00
13 Miguel Cabrera/ Jsy/100 8.00
16 Randy Johnson/ Pants/50 12.00
17 Roger Clemens/ Jsy/100 12.00
18 Steve Carlton/Jsy/100 6.00
19 Steve Garvey/Jsy/100 4.00
20 Wade Boggs/Jsy/100 8.00

October Heroes Signatures

NM/M
Quantity produced listed
1 Alan Trammell/25 25.00
5 Dave Concepcion/25 20.00
7 Jack Morris/25 20.00
12 Marty Marion/25 20.00
13 Miguel Cabrera/25 40.00
18 Steve Carlton/25 35.00
19 Steve Garvey/25 20.00

October Heroes Signature Material

NM/M
Quantity produced listed
1 Alan Trammell/ Jsy/100 20.00
5 Dave Concepcion/ Jsy/100 15.00
12 Marty Marion/ Jsy/100 15.00
13 Miguel Cabrera/ Jsy/100 30.00
18 Steve Carlton/ Jsy/50 35.00
19 Steve Garvey/ Jsy/100 15.00

October Legends

NM/M
Complete Set (20): 60.00
Common Player: 2.00
Production 500 Sets
HoloFoil: 2-4X
Production 25 Sets
1 Bob Gibson 4.00
2 Cal Ripken Jr. 10.00
3 Carl Yastrzemski 6.00
4 Carlton Fisk 3.00
5 Duke Snider 4.00
6 Eddie Murray 4.00
7 Frank Robinson 3.00
8 George Brett 8.00
9 Joe Morgan 2.00
10 Johnny Bench 4.00
11 Lou Brock 3.00
12 Mike Schmidt 8.00
13 Paul Molitor 4.00
14 Phil Rizzuto 3.00
15 Reggie Jackson 4.00
16 Robin Yount 4.00
17 Stan Musial 6.00
18 Steve Carlton 2.00
19 Whitey Ford 3.00
20 Willie McCovey 2.00

October Legends Materials

NM/M
Common Player: 5.00
Quantity produced listed
1 Bob Gibson/Jsy/50 10.00
2 Cal Ripken Jr./Jsy/50 50.00
3 Carl Yastrzemski/ Jsy/50 20.00
4 Carlton Fisk/Jsy/100 8.00
5 Duke Snider/Jsy/25 20.00
6 Eddie Murray/ Jsy/100 10.00
7 Frank Robinson/ Jsy/50 8.00
8 George Brett/Jsy/50 25.00
10 Johnny Bench/Jsy/50 15.00
11 Lou Brock/Jkt/100 8.00
12 Mike Schmidt/ Jkt/100 15.00
14 Phil Rizzuto/Pants/25 15.00
15 Reggie Jackson/ Jkt/100 8.00
16 Robin Yount/Jsy/100 10.00
18 Steve Carlton/Jsy/100 5.00
19 Whitey Ford/Pants/25 15.00
20 Willie McCovey/ Jsy/25 15.00

October Legends Signature

NM/M
Quantity produced listed
11 Lou Brock/25 35.00
14 Phil Rizzuto/25 35.00
18 Steve Carlton/25 30.00

October Legends Signature Material

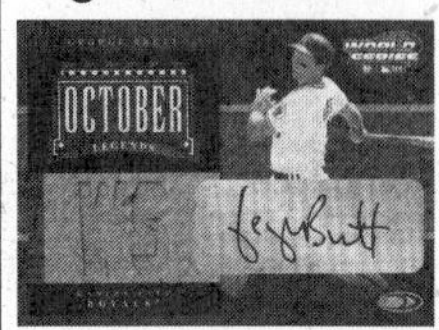

NM/M
Quantity produced listed
1 Bob Gibson/Jsy/50 40.00
5 Duke Snider Jsy/50 40.00
7 Frank Robinson/ Jsy/50 30.00
11 Lou Brock/Jkt/100 25.00
13 Paul Molitor/Jsy/25 40.00
14 Phil Rizzuto/Pants/50 30.00
16 Robin Yount/Jsy/25 65.00
17 Stan Musial/Jsy/25 90.00
18 Steve Carlton/ Jsy/100 25.00
19 Whitey Ford/Pants/25 40.00
20 Willie McCovey/ Jsy/25 40.00

Playoff All-Stars

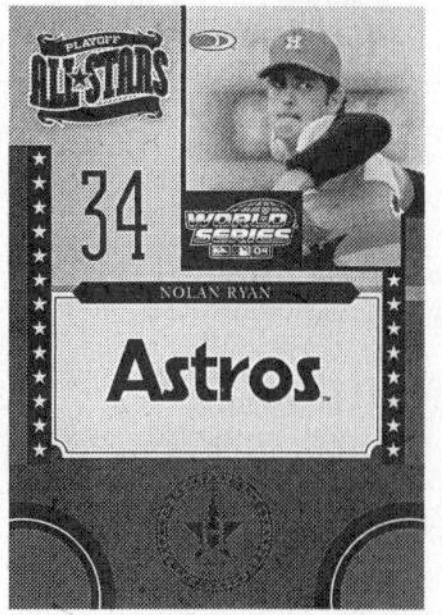

NM/M
Complete Set (20): 50.00
Common Player: 2.00
Production 500 Sets
HoloFoil: 2-4X
Production 25 Sets
1 Mark Prior 3.00
2 Sammy Sosa 6.00
3 Steve Finley 2.00
4 David Ortiz 4.00
5 Mike Piazza 5.00
6 Edgar Martinez 2.00
7 Roy Oswalt 2.00
8 Johan Santana 3.00
9 Jacque Jones 2.00
10 Will Clark 4.00
11 Albert Pujols 8.00
12 Andre Dawson 3.00
13 Nolan Ryan 10.00
14 Fred Lynn 2.00
15 Jim Rice 2.00
16 Dwight Evans 2.00
17 Harmon Killebrew 4.00
18 Maury Wills 2.00
19 Mark Mulder 2.00
20 Frank Thomas 4.00

Playoff All-Stars Material 1

NM/M
Quantity produced listed
1 Mark Prior/Jsy/100 6.00
2 Sammy Sosa/ Jsy/100 10.00
3 Steve Finley/Jsy/100 4.00
4 David Ortiz/Jsy/100 10.00
5 Mike Piazza/Jsy/100 10.00
6 Edgar Martinez/Jsy/50 6.00
7 Roy Oswalt/Jsy/100 4.00
8 Johan Santana/ Jsy/100 8.00
9 Jacque Jones/Jsy/100 4.00
10 Will Clark/Bat/100 10.00
11 Albert Pujols/Jsy/100 20.00

12 Andre Dawson/Jsy/100 6.00
13 Nolan Ryan/Jsy/100 25.00
14 Fred Lynn/Jsy/50 6.00
15 Jim Rice/Jsy/50 6.00
16 Dwight Evans/Jsy/50 6.00
17 Harmon Killebrew/Jsy/50 20.00
19 Mark Mulder/Jsy/50 6.00
20 Frank Thomas/Jsy/100 8.00

Playoff All-Stars Material 2

NM/M
Common Dual: 6.00
1 Mark Prior/Jsy-Jsy/100 8.00
2 Sammy Sosa/Jsy-Jsy/100 15.00
3 Steve Finley/Jsy-Jsy/100 6.00
4 David Ortiz/Bat-Jsy/100 20.00
5 Mike Piazza/Bat-Jsy/100 15.00
6 Edgar Martinez/Bat-Jsy/50 10.00
7 Roy Oswalt/Bat-Jsy/100 6.00
8 Johan Santana/Jsy-Jsy/100 10.00
9 Jacque Jones/Bat-Jsy/100 6.00
11 Albert Pujols/Jsy-Jsy/100 25.00
12 Andre Dawson/Bat-Jsy/100 8.00
13 Nolan Ryan/Jkt-Jsy/50 40.00
14 Fred Lynn/Bat-Jsy/50 8.00
15 Jim Rice/Bat-Jsy/50 10.00
16 Dwight Evans/Bat-Jsy/50 6.00
17 Harmon Killebrew/Bat-Jsy/50 25.00
19 Mark Mulder/Bat-Jsy/100 6.00
20 Frank Thomas/Bat-Jsy/100 12.00

Playoff All-Stars Material 3

NM/M
Common Triple: 10.00
1 Mark Prior/Bat-Hat-Jsy/100 15.00
2 Sammy Sosa/Bat-Jsy-Jsy/100 20.00
3 Steve Finley/Jsy-Jsy-Jsy/100 10.00
4 David Ortiz/Bat-Jsy-Jsy/100 25.00
5 Mike Piazza/Bat-Jsy-Jsy/100 20.00
6 Edgar Martinez/Bat-Jsy-Jsy/50 10.00
7 Roy Oswalt/Bat-Fld Glv-Jsy/50 10.00
9 Jacque Jones/Bat-Jsy-Jsy/50 10.00
11 Albert Pujols/Bat-Jsy-Jsy/100 40.00
12 Andre Dawson/Bat-Hat-Jsy/100 10.00
13 Nolan Ryan/Bat-Jkt-Jsy/50 65.00
15 Jim Rice/Bat-Jsy-Jsy/100 10.00
16 Dwight Evans/Bat-Hat-Jsy/100 10.00
17 Harmon Killebrew/Bat-Jsy-Shoe/25 50.00
20 Frank Thomas/Jsy-Jsy-Pants/100 20.00

Playoff All-Stars Signature

NM/M
Quantity produced listed
1 Mark Prior/25 40.00
3 Steve Finley/25 20.00
4 David Ortiz/25 60.00
7 Roy Oswalt/25 20.00
8 Johan Santana/25 40.00
9 Jacque Jones/25 20.00
10 Will Clark/25 50.00
12 Andre Dawson/25 20.00
13 Nolan Ryan/25 125.00
14 Fred Lynn/25 20.00
15 Jim Rice/25 25.00
16 Dwight Evans/25 30.00
18 Maury Wills/25 20.00

Playoff All-Stars Signature Material 1

NM/M
Quantity produced listed
Material 2: .75-1.5X
Production 5-100
Material 3: .75-1.5X
Production 5-100
3 Steve Finley/Jsy/100 15.00
4 David Ortiz/Jsy/100 50.00
6 Edgar Martinez/Jsy/50 30.00
7 Roy Oswalt/Jsy/100 15.00
8 Johan Santana/Jsy/100 35.00
9 Jacque Jones/Jsy/100 15.00
10 Will Clark/Bat/25 65.00
12 Andre Dawson/Jsy/100 20.00
14 Fred Lynn/Jsy/25 20.00
15 Jim Rice/Jsy/25 25.00
16 Dwight Evans/Jsy/50 30.00
19 Mark Mulder/Jsy/25 30.00
20 Frank Thomas/Jsy/25 50.00

Records

NM/M
Complete Set (5): 10.00
Common Player: 3.00
Production 1,000 Sets
HoloFoil: 2-4X
Production 50 Sets
1 Lou Brock 3.00
2 Yogi Berra 4.00
3 Reggie Jackson 3.00
4 Bob Gibson 3.00
5 Whitey Ford 3.00

Records Material

NM/M
Quantity produced listed
1 Lou Brock/Bat/100 10.00
2 Yogi Berra/Bat/50 20.00
3 Reggie Jackson/Bat/100 10.00
5 Whitey Ford/Pants/25 20.00

Records Signature

NM/M
Common Player:
1 Lou Brock/25 30.00

Records Signature Material

NM/M
Quantity produced listed
1 Lou Brock/Bat/100 25.00
3 Reggie Jackson/Bat/20 40.00

Signature

NM/M
Common Autograph: 10.00
201-222 Exclusive to Red Sox Champs Sets
3 Garret Anderson/25 25.00
7 Brandon Webb/25 10.00
11 Shea Hillenbrand/25 20.00
12 Steve Finley/25 15.00
16 Marcus Giles/25 15.00
17 Rafael Furcal/25 20.00
19 Jay Gibbons/25 10.00
20 Luis Matos/25 10.00
21 Melvin Mora/25 20.00
25 Dwight Evans/25 30.00
26 Fred Lynn/25 20.00
28 Jim Rice/25 25.00
30 Luis Tiant/25 20.00
34 Trot Nixon/25 25.00
35 Aramis Ramirez/25 35.00
37 Derrek Lee/25 30.00
40 Mark Prior/25 40.00
43 Carlos Lee/25 10.00
45 Luis Aparicio/25 20.00
46 Magglio Ordonez/25 20.00
47 Mark Buehrle/25 20.00
49 Adam Dunn/25 40.00
50 Austin Kearns/25 20.00
52 Dave Concepcion/25 15.00
53 George Foster/25 15.00
56 Tony Perez/25 35.00
57 C.C. Sabathia/25 20.00
58 Jody Gerut/25 10.00
60 Victor Martinez/25 25.00
64 Preston Wilson/25 15.00
66 Alan Trammell/25 25.00
69 Jeremy Bonderman/25 10.00
71 Brad Penny/25 10.00
76 Miguel Cabrera/25 40.00
84 Roy Oswalt/25 20.00
85 Wade Miller/25 10.00
86 Angel Berroa/25 10.00
87 Carlos Beltran/25 50.00
89 Ken Harvey/25 10.00
94 Milton Bradley/25 20.00
96 Paul LoDuca/25 25.00
101 Rickie Weeks/25 25.00
102 Scott Podsednik/25 20.00
103 Jack Morris/25 20.00
104 Jacque Jones/25 15.00
105 Johan Santana/25 50.00
106 Shannon Stewart/25 15.00
107 Torii Hunter/25 25.00
108 Jose Vidro/25 15.00
109 Orlando Cabrera/25 40.00
111 Darryl Strawberry/25 25.00
112 Dwight Gooden/25 25.00
115 Keith Hernandez/25 25.00
116 Lenny Dykstra/25 20.00
132 Jermaine Dye/25 20.00
133 Mark Mulder/25 25.00
134 Rich Harden/25 25.00
139 Marlon Byrd/25 10.00
142 Steve Carlton/25 35.00
143 Dave Parker/25 25.00
146 Jay Payton/25 10.00
148 J.T. Snow/25 15.00
154 Shigetoshi Hasegawa/25 40.00
156 Dan Haren/25 15.00
162 Aubrey Huff/25 20.00
163 Carl Crawford/25 20.00
164 Dewon Brazelton/25 10.00
168 Hank Blalock/25 25.00
170 Mark Teixeira/25 35.00
171 Michael Young/25 20.00

Signature Trio

NM/M
Quantity produced listed
2 Derek Lee, Brad Penny, Mike Lowell/25 40.00
3 Garret Anderson, John Lackey, Chone Figgins/25 75.00
8 Roberto Alomar, Paul Molitor, Jack Morris/25 125.00
9 Eric Davis, Barry Larkin, Paul O'Neill/25 100.00
10 Dennis Eckersley, Jose Canseco, Dave Parker/25 125.00
11 Keith Hernandez, Dwight Gooden, Gary Carter/25 75.00
12 Lenny Dykstra, George Foster, Darryl Strawberry/25 65.00
13 Alan Trammell, Kirk Gibson, Jack Morris/25 100.00
15 Bert Blyleven, John Candelaria, Dave Parker/25 75.00

Souvenirs Playoff

NM/M
Common Player: 5.00
Production 100 Sets
1 Chipper Jones/Ball 10.00
2 Randy Johnson/Ball 10.00
3 Albert Pujols/Ball 20.00
4 Jason Schmidt/Ball 8.00
5 Gary Sheffield/Ball 8.00
6 Miguel Tejada/Ball 8.00
7 J.D. Drew/Ball 5.00
8 John Smoltz/Ball 10.00
9 Eric Milton/Ball 5.00
10 Mark Grace/Ball 10.00
11 Tim Hudson/Ball 5.00
12 Jeff Bagwell/Ball 10.00
13 Jim Edmonds/Ball 8.00
14 Sammy Sosa/Ball 15.00
15 Albert Pujols/Ball 20.00

Souvenirs World Series

NM/M
Common Player: 5.00
Production 100 Sets
1 Jason Schmidt/Ball 8.00
2 Troy Glaus/Base 5.00
3 Reggie Sanders/Base 5.00
4 Tim Salmon/Base 5.00
5 Garret Anderson/Base 5.00
6 Francisco Rodriguez/Base 5.00
7 Rich Aurilia/Ball 5.00
8 Jeff Kent/Ball 5.00
9 Darin Erstad/Base 5.00
10 Troy Glaus/Base 5.00
11 Jeff Kent/Ball 5.00
12 Scott Spiezio/Base 5.00
13 Tony Percival/Base 5.00
14 Garret Anderson/Base 5.00
15 Darin Erstad/Base 5.00

Triple Threads

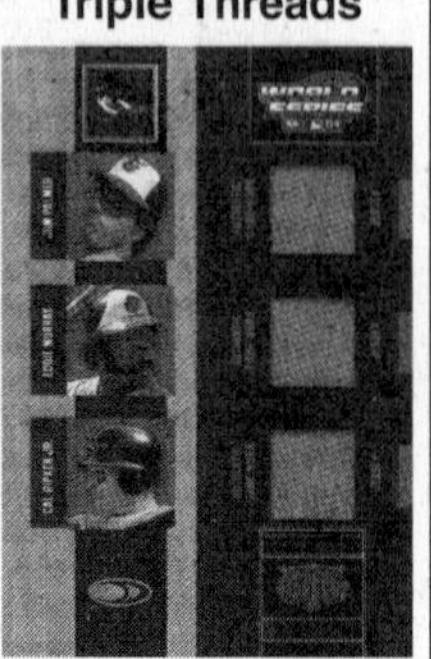

NM/M
Common Player: 10.00
1 Josh Beckett, Miguel Cabrera, Mike Lowell/100 15.00
2 Luis Castillo, Ivan Rodriguez, Dontrelle Willis/100 20.00
3 Garret Anderson, Troy Glaus, Tim Salmon/100 20.00
4 Curt Schilling, Mark Grace, Randy Johnson/50 25.00
5 Jorge Posada, Bernie Williams, Roger Clemens/50 25.00
6 Andy Pettitte, Wade Boggs, Mariano Rivera/50 20.00
7 Charles Johnson, Cliff Floyd, Moises Alou/100 10.00
8 Chipper Jones, Tom Glavine, Greg Maddux/100 30.00
9 Joe Carter, Rickey Henderson, David Wells/100 25.00
10 Eric Davis, Barry Larkin, Paul O'Neill/100 20.00
11 Dwight Gooden, Gary Carter, Darryl Strawberry/100 20.00
12 Frank White, Willie Wilson, George Brett/100 30.00
13 Jim Palmer, Eddie Murray, Cal Ripken Jr./50 125.00
14 Willie Stargell, Dave Parker, Bill Madlock/100 20.00
15 Johnny Bench, Joe Morgan, Tony Perez/100 35.00
16 Dave Concepcion, George Foster, Johnny Bench/50 40.00
17 Al Oliver, Roberto Clemente, Willie Stargell/50 80.00
18 Jim Palmer, Frank Robinson, Brooks Robinson/50 25.00
19 Bob Gibson, Lou Brock, Orlando Cepeda/50 25.00
20 Stan Musial, Red Schoendienst, Marty Marion/50 40.00

2005 Donruss

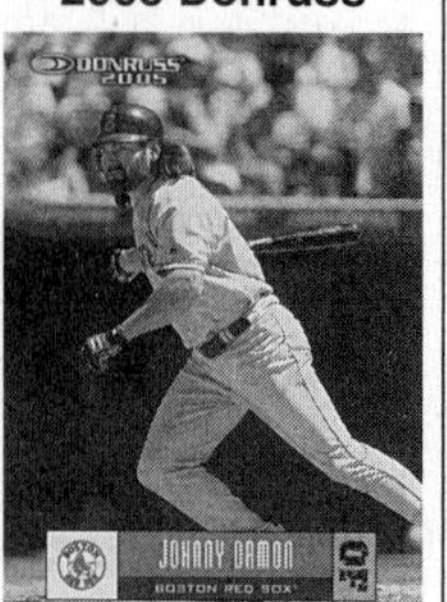

NM/M
Complete Set (400): 120.00
Common Player: .15
Common SP (1-70, 371-400): 1.00
Inserted 1:6
Pack (10): 2.50
Box (24): 50.00
1 Garret Anderson 1.00
2 Vladimir Guerrero 2.00
3 Manny Ramirez 2.00
4 Kerry Wood 2.00
5 Sammy Sosa 3.00
6 Magglio Ordonez 1.00
7 Adam Dunn 1.50
8 Todd Helton 1.50
9 Josh Beckett 1.00
10 Miguel Cabrera 2.00
11 Lance Berkman 1.00
12 Carlos Beltran 1.50
13 Shawn Green 1.00
14 Roger Clemens 4.00
15 Mike Piazza 2.50
16 Alex Rodriguez 3.00
17 Derek Jeter 4.00
18 Mark Mulder 1.00
19 Jim Thome 2.00
20 Albert Pujols 3.00
21 Scott Rolen 2.00
22 Aubrey Huff 1.00
23 Alfonso Soriano 2.00
24 Hank Blalock 1.50
25 Vernon Wells 1.00
26 Kazuo Matsui 1.50
27 B.J. Upton 1.50
28 Charles Thomas 1.00
29 Akinori Otsuka 1.00
30 David Aardsma 1.00
31 Travis Blackley 1.00
32 Brad Halsey 1.00
33 David Wright 5.00
34 Kazuhito Tadano 1.00
35 Casey Kotchman 1.00
36 Khalil Greene 2.00
37 Adrian Gonzalez 1.00
38 Zack Greinke 1.00
39 Chad Cordero 1.00
40 Scott Kazmir 4.00
41 Jeremy Guthrie 1.00
42 Noah Lowry 1.00
43 Chase Utley 1.00
44 Billy Traber 1.00
45 Aarom Baldiris 1.00
46 Abe Alvarez 1.00
47 Angel Chavez 1.00
48 Joe Mauer 1.00
49 Joey Gathright 1.00
50 John Gall 1.00
51 Ronald Belisario 1.00
52 Ryan Wing 1.00
53 Scott Proctor 1.00
54 Yadier Molina 1.00
55 Carlos Hines 1.00
56 Frankie Francisco 1.00
57 Graham Koonce 1.00
58 Jake Woods 1.00
59 Jason Bartlett 1.00
60 Mike Rouse 1.00
61 Phil Stockman 1.00
62 Renyel Pinto 1.00
63 Roberto Novoa 1.00
64 Ryan Meaux 1.00
65 David Crouthers 1.00
66 Justin Knoedler 1.00
67 Justin Leone 1.00
68 Nick Regilio 1.00
69 Mike Gosling 1.00
70 Onil Joseph 1.00
71 Bartolo Colon .15
72 Brad Fullmer .15
73 Chone Figgins .15
74 Darin Erstad .25
75 Francisco Rodriguez .15
76 Garret Anderson .25
77 Jarrod Washburn .15
78 John Lackey .15
79 Jose Guillen .15
80 Robb Quinlan .15
81 Tim Salmon .25
82 Troy Glaus .25
83 Troy Percival .15
84 Vladimir Guerrero .50
85 Brandon Webb .15
86 Casey Fossum .15
87 Luis Gonzalez .25
88 Randy Johnson .50
89 Richie Sexson .25
90 Robby Hammock .15
91 Roberto Alomar .25
92 Adam LaRoche .15
93 Andruw Jones .25
94 Bubba Nelson .15
95 Chipper Jones .50
96 J.D. Drew .25
97 John Smoltz .25
98 Johnny Estrada .15
99 Marcus Giles .15
100 Mike Hampton .15
101 Nick Green .15
102 Rafael Furcal .15
103 Russ Ortiz .15
104 Adam Loewen .15
105 Brian Roberts .15
106 Javy Lopez .25
107 Jay Gibbons .15
108 Larry Bigbie .15
109 Luis Matos .15
110 Melvin Mora .15
111 Miguel Tejada .40
112 Rafael Palmeiro .40
113 Rodrigo Lopez .15
114 Sidney Ponson .15
115 Bill Mueller .15
116 Byung-Hyun Kim .15
117 Curt Schilling .40
118 David Ortiz .40
119 Derek Lowe .15
120 Doug Mientkiewicz .15
121 Jason Varitek .25
122 Johnny Damon .25
123 Keith Foulke .15
124 Kevin Youkilis .15
125 Manny Ramirez .50
126 Orlando Cabrera .25
127 Pedro J. Martinez .50
128 Trot Nixon .15
129 Aramis Ramirez .25
130 Carlos Zambrano .25
131 Corey Patterson .25
132 Derrek Lee .25
133 Greg Maddux .75
134 Kerry Wood .50
135 Mark Prior .50
136 Matt Clement .15
137 Moises Alou .25
138 Nomar Garciaparra 1.00
139 Sammy Sosa 1.00
140 Todd Walker .15
141 Angel Guzman .15
142 Billy Koch .15
143 Carlos Lee .15
144 Frank Thomas .40
145 Magglio Ordonez .25
146 Mark Buehrle .25
147 Paul Konerko .25
148 Wilson Valdez .15
149 Adam Dunn .40
150 Austin Kearns .15
151 Barry Larkin .25
152 Benito Santiago .15
153 Jason LaRue .15
154 Ken Griffey Jr. .75
155 Ryan Wagner .15
156 Sean Casey .15
157 Brandon Phillips .15
158 Brian Tallet .15
159 C.C. Sabathia .15
160 Cliff Lee .15
161 Jeremy Guthrie .15
162 Jody Gerut .15
163 Matt Lawton .15
164 Omar Vizquel .15
165 Travis Hafner .15
166 Victor Martinez .25
167 Charles Johnson .15
168 Garrett Atkins .15
169 Jason Jennings .15
170 Jay Payton .15
171 Jeromy Burnitz .15
172 Joe Kennedy .15
173 Larry Walker .25
174 Preston Wilson .15
175 Todd Helton .40
176 Vinny Castilla .15
177 Bobby Higginson .15
178 Brandon Inge .15
179 Carlos Guillen .15
180 Carlos Pena .15
181 Craig Monroe .15
182 Dmitri Young .15
183 Eric Munson .15
184 Fernando Vina .15
185 Ivan Rodriguez .40
186 Jeremy Bonderman .15
187 Rondell White .15
188 A.J. Burnett .15
189 Dontrelle Willis .25
190 Guillermo Mota .15
191 Hee Seop Choi .15
192 Jeff Conine .15
193 Josh Beckett .25
194 Juan Encarnacion .15
195 Juan Pierre .15
196 Luis Castillo .15
197 Miguel Cabrera .50
198 Mike Lowell .15
199 Paul LoDuca .15
200 Andy Pettitte .25
201 Brad Ausmus .15
202 Carlos Beltran .40
203 Chris Burke .15
204 Craig Biggio .25
205 Jeff Bagwell .40
206 Jeff Kent .25
207 Lance Berkman .25
208 Morgan Ensberg .15
209 Octavio Dotel .15
210 Roger Clemens 1.50
211 Roy Oswalt .25
212 Tim Redding .15
213 Angel Berroa .15
214 Juan Gonzalez .25
215 Ken Harvey .15
216 Mike Sweeney .15
217 Adrian Beltre .25
218 Brad Penny .15
219 Eric Gagne .25
220 Hideo Nomo .25
221 Hong-Chih Kuo .15
222 Jeff Weaver .15
223 Kazuhisa Ishii .15
224 Milton Bradley .15
225 Shawn Green .25
226 Steve Finley .15
227 Danny Kolb .15
228 Geoff Jenkins .15
229 Junior Spivey .15
230 Lyle Overbay .15
231 Rickie Weeks .15
232 Scott Podsednik .15
233 Brad Radke .15
234 Corey Koskie .15
235 Cristian Guzman .15
236 Dustan Mohr .15
237 Eddie Guardado .15
238 J.D. Durbin .15
239 Jacque Jones .15
240 Joe Nathan .15
241 Johan Santana .40
242 Lew Ford .15
243 Michael Cuddyer .15
244 Shannon Stewart .15
245 Torii Hunter .15
246 Brad Wilkerson .15
247 Carl Everett .15
248 Jeff Fassero .15
249 Jose Vidro .15
250 Livan Hernandez .15
251 Michael Barrett .15
252 Tony Batista .15
253 Zach Day .15
254 Al Leiter .15
255 Cliff Floyd .15
256 Jae Weong Seo .15
257 John Olerud .15
258 Jose Reyes .40
259 Mike Cameron .15
260 Mike Piazza 1.00
261 Richard Hidalgo .15
262 Tom Glavine .25
263 Vance Wilson .15
264 Alex Rodriguez 1.50
265 Armando Benitez .15
266 Bernie Williams .25
267 Bubba Crosby .15
268 Chien-Ming Wang .40
269 Derek Jeter 1.50
270 Esteban Loaiza .15
271 Gary Sheffield .25
272 Hideki Matsui 1.00
273 Jason Giambi .25
274 Javier Vazquez .15

275 Jorge Posada .25
276 Jose Contreras .25
277 Kenny Lofton .15
278 Kevin Brown .15
279 Mariano Rivera .25
280 Mike Mussina .25
281 Barry Zito .25
282 Bobby Crosby .15
283 Eric Byrnes .15
284 Eric Chavez .25
285 Erubiel Durazo .15
286 Jermaine Dye .15
287 Mark Kotsay .15
288 Mark Mulder .25
289 Rich Harden .15
290 Tim Hudson .15
291 Billy Wagner .15
292 Bobby Abreu .25
293 Brett Myers .15
294 Eric Milton .15
295 Jim Thome .50
296 Jimmy Rollins .25
297 Kevin Millwood .15
298 Marlon Byrd .15
299 Mike Lieberthal .15
300 Pat Burrell .15
301 Randy Wolf .15
302 Craig Wilson .15
303 Jack Wilson .15
304 Jacob Cruz .15
305 Jason Bay .15
306 Jason Kendall .15
307 Jose Castillo .15
308 Kip Wells .15
309 Brian Giles .15
310 Brian Lawrence .15
311 Chris Oxspring .15
312 David Wells .15
313 Freddy Guzman .15
314 Jake Peavy .15
315 Mark Loretta .15
316 Ryan Klesko .15
317 Sean Burroughs .15
318 Trevor Hoffman .15
319 Xavier Nady .15
320 A.J. Pierzynski .15
321 Edgardo Alfonzo .15
322 J.T. Snow .15
323 Jason Schmidt .25
324 Jerome Williams .15
325 Kirk Rueter .15
326 Bret Boone .15
327 Bucky Jacobsen .15
328 Edgar Martinez .15
329 Freddy Garcia .15
330 Ichiro Suzuki 1.00
331 Jamie Moyer .15
332 Joel Pineiro .15
333 Scott Spiezio .15
334 Shigetoshi Hasegawa .15
335 Albert Pujols 1.50
336 Edgar Renteria .25
337 Jason Isringhausen .15
338 Jim Edmonds .25
339 Matt Morris .15
340 Mike Matheny .15
341 Reggie Sanders .15
342 Scott Rolen .50
343 Woody Williams .15
344 Jeff Suppan .15
345 Aubrey Huff .15
346 Carl Crawford .15
347 Chad Gaudin .15
348 Delmon Young .15
349 Dewon Brazelton .15
350 Jose Cruz Jr. .15
351 Rocco Baldelli .25
352 Tino Martinez .15
353 Toby Hall .15
354 Alfonso Soriano .40
355 Brian Jordan .15
356 Francisco Cordero .15
357 Hank Blalock .40
358 Kenny Rogers .15
359 Kevin Mench .15
360 Laynce Nix .15
361 Mark Teixeira .25
362 Michael Young .15
363 Alex Gonzalez .15
364 Alexis Rios .15
365 Carlos Delgado .25
366 Eric Hinske .15
367 Frank Catalanotto .15
368 Josh Phelps .15
369 Roy Halladay .15
370 Vernon Wells .15
371 Vladimir Guerrero 2.00
372 Randy Johnson 2.00
373 Chipper Jones 2.00
374 Miguel Tejada 1.50
375 Pedro Martinez 2.00
376 Sammy Sosa 3.00
377 Frank Thomas 1.50
378 Ken Griffey Jr. 3.00
379 Victor Martinez 1.00
380 Todd Helton 1.50
381 Ivan Rodriguez 1.50
382 Miguel Cabrera 2.00
383 Roger Clemens 4.00
384 Ken Harvey 1.00
385 Eric Gagne 1.50
386 Lyle Overbay 1.00
387 Shannon Stewart 1.00
388 Brad Wilkerson 1.00
389 Mike Piazza 2.50
390 Alex Rodriguez 3.00
391 Mark Mulder 1.00
392 Jim Thome 2.00
393 Jack Wilson 1.00
394 Khalil Greene 1.50
395 Jason Schmidt 1.00
396 Ichiro Suzuki 3.00
397 Albert Pujols 4.00
398 Rocco Baldelli 1.00
399 Alfonso Soriano 1.50
400 Vernon Wells 1.00

Press Proofs Black

No Pricing
Production 10 Sets

Press Proofs Blue

Blue (71-370): 4-8X
Blue SP's: 2-3X
Production 100 Sets

Press Proofs Gold

Gold (71-370): 10-20X
Gold SP's: 3-6X
Production 25 Sets

Press Proofs Red

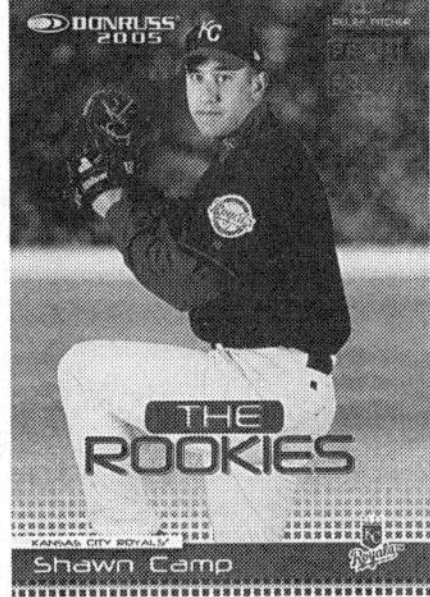

Red (71-370): 2-4X
Red SP's: .75-1.5X
Production 200 Sets

Stat Line Career

#71-370 print run 201-400: 2-4X
71-370 p/r 101-200: 3-6X
71-370 p/r 51-100: 4-8X
71-370 p/r 26-50: 6-12X
71-370 p/r 25 or less: No Pricing
SP's print run 200 or more: 1-2X
SP's p/r 101-200: 1.5-2X
SP's p/r 51-100: 2-4X
SP's p/r 26-50: 3-5X
SP's p/r 25 or less: No Pricing
Cards are numbered to career statistic.

Stat Line Season

#71-370 print run 101-200: 3-6X
71-370 p/r 51-100: 4-8X
71-370 p/r 26-50: 6-12X
71-370 p/r 25 or less: No Pricing
SP's p/r 101 or more 1.5-2X
SP's p/r 51-100: 2-4X
SP's p/r 26-50: 3-5X
SP's p/r 25 or less: No Pricing
Cards are numbered to season statistic.

25th Anniversary

Stars: 10-20X
SP's (1-70, 371-400): 3-6X
Production 25 Sets

All-Stars AL

NM/M
Common Player: 2.00
Production 1,000 Sets
Gold: 1-2X
Production 100 Sets
1 Alex Rodriguez 6.00
2 Alfonso Soriano 3.00
3 Curt Schilling 2.00
4 Derek Jeter 8.00
5 Hank Blalock 2.00
6 Hideki Matsui 6.00
7 Ichiro Suzuki 6.00
8 Ivan Rodriguez 3.00
9 Jason Giambi 2.00
10 Manny Ramirez 3.00
11 Mark Mulder 2.00
12 Michael Young 2.00
13 Tim Hudson 2.00
14 Victor Martinez 2.00
15 Vladimir Guerrero 3.00

All-Stars NL

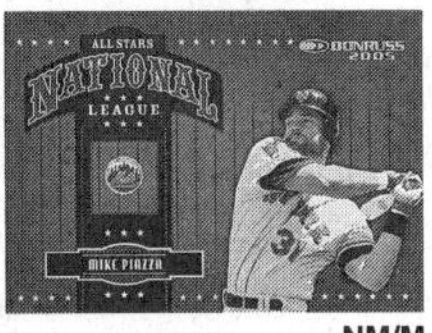

NM/M
Common Player: 2.00
Production 1,000 Sets
Gold: 1-2X
Production 100 Sets
1 Albert Pujols 8.00
2 Ben Sheets 2.00
3 Edgar Renteria 2.00
4 Eric Gagne 2.00
5 Jack Wilson 2.00
6 Jason Schmidt 2.00
7 Jeff Kent 2.00
8 Jim Thome 3.00
9 Ken Griffey Jr. 4.00
10 Mike Piazza 4.00
11 Roger Clemens 8.00
12 Sammy Sosa 5.00
13 Scott Rolen 3.00
14 Sean Casey 2.00
15 Todd Helton 2.00

Autographs

No Pricing

Bat Kings

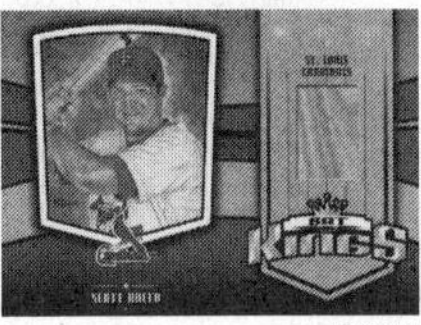

NM/M
Common Player: 5.00
Quantity produced listed
1 Garret Anderson/250 5.00
2 Vladimir Guerrero/250 8.00
3 Cal Ripken Jr./100 50.00
4 Manny Ramirez/250 8.00
5 Kerry Wood/250 8.00
6 Sammy Sosa/250 12.00
7 Magglio Ordonez/250 5.00
8 Adam Dunn/250 8.00
9 Todd Helton/250 8.00
10 Josh Beckett/250 5.00
11 Miguel Cabrera/250 8.00
12 Lance Berkman/250 5.00
13 Carlos Beltran/250 8.00
14 Shawn Green/250 5.00
15 Roger Clemens/100 15.00
16 Mike Piazza/250 12.00
17 Nolan Ryan/100 50.00
18 Mark Mulder/250 5.00
19 Jim Thome/250 10.00
20 Albert Pujols/250 20.00
21 Scott Rolen/250 10.00
22 Aubrey Huff/250 5.00
23 Alfonso Soriano/250 8.00

Bat Kings Signatures

No Pricing
Production 5 or 10

Craftsmen

NM/M
Complete Set (30): 40.00
Common Player: 1.00
Production 1,000 Sets
Black: 1.5-2X
Production 100 Sets
Master: 1-2X
Production 250 Sets
Master Black: No Pricing
Production 10 Sets
1 Albert Pujols 5.00
2 Alex Rodriguez 4.00
3 Alfonso Soriano 2.00
4 Andruw Jones 1.00
5 Carlos Beltran 1.50
6 Derek Jeter 5.00
7 Greg Maddux 2.50
8 Hank Blalock 1.50
9 Ichiro Suzuki 4.00
10 Jeff Bagwell 1.50
11 Jim Thome 2.00
12 Josh Beckett 1.00
13 Ken Griffey Jr. 2.50
14 Manny Ramirez 2.00
15 Mark Mulder 1.00
16 Mark Prior 2.00
17 Mark Teixeira 1.00
18 Miguel Tejada 1.50
19 Mike Mussina 1.50
20 Mike Piazza 2.50
21 Nomar Garciaparra 3.00
22 Pedro Martinez 2.00
23 Rafael Palmeiro 1.50
24 Randy Johnson 2.00
25 Roger Clemens 5.00
26 Sammy Sosa 3.00
27 Scott Rolen 2.00
28 Tim Hudson 1.00
29 Vernon Wells 1.00
30 Vladimir Guerrero 2.00

Kings Inserts

NM/M
Complete Set (25): 40.00
Common Player: 1.50
Production 2,005 Sets
Studio: 1.5-2X
Production 250 Sets
Studio Black: 1.5-3X
Production 100 Sets
1 Garret Anderson 1.50
2 Vladimir Guerrero 2.00
3 Manny Ramirez 2.00
4 Kerry Wood 1.50
5 Sammy Sosa 4.00
6 Magglio Ordonez 1.50
7 Adam Dunn 1.50
8 Todd Helton 1.50
9 Josh Beckett 1.50
10 Miguel Cabrera 2.00
11 Lance Berkman 1.50
12 Carlos Beltran 2.00
13 Shawn Green 1.50
14 Roger Clemens 6.00
15 Mike Piazza 3.00
16 Alex Rodriguez 5.00
17 Derek Jeter 6.00
18 Mark Mulder 1.50
19 Jim Thome 2.00
20 Albert Pujols 6.00
21 Scott Rolen 2.00
22 Aubrey Huff 1.50
23 Alfonso Soriano 2.00
24 Hank Blalock 1.50
25 Vernon Wells 1.50

Elite Series

NM/M
Complete Set (25): 50.00
Common Player: 2.00
Production 1,500 Sets
Black: 1-2X
Production 100 Sets
Dominator: 1-1.5X
Production 250 Sets
Dominator Black: 3-5X
Production 25 Sets
1 Albert Pujols 6.00
2 Alex Rodriguez 5.00
3 Alfonso Soriano 2.00
4 Derek Jeter 6.00
5 Hank Blalock 1.50
6 Ichiro Suzuki 5.00
7 Ivan Rodriguez 2.00
8 Jim Thome 2.00
9 Ken Griffey Jr. 3.00
10 Manny Ramirez 2.00
11 Mark Mulder 1.50
12 Mark Prior 2.00
13 Michael Young 1.50
14 Miguel Cabrera 2.00
15 Miguel Tejada 2.00
16 Mike Piazza 3.00
17 Nomar Garciaparra 4.00
18 Rafael Palmeiro 2.00
19 Randy Johnson 2.00
20 Roger Clemens 6.00
21 Sammy Sosa 4.00
22 Scott Rolen 2.00
23 Tim Hudson 1.50
24 Todd Helton 1.50
25 Vladimir Guerrero 2.00

Fans of the Game

NM/M
Complete Set (5): 10.00
1 Jesse Ventura 3.00
2 John C. McGinley 2.00
3 Susie Essman 2.00
4 Dean Cain 2.00
5 Meat Loaf 3.00

Fans of the Game Signatures

NM/M
1 Jesse Ventura 50.00
2 John C. McGinley/SP/300 50.00
3 Susie Essman 60.00
4 Dean Cain/SP/250 90.00
5 Meat Loaf 60.00

Jersey Kings

NM/M
Common Player: 5.00
1 Garret Anderson/250 5.00
2 Vladimir Guerrero/250 8.00
3 Cal Ripken Jr./100 50.00
4 Manny Ramirez/250 8.00
5 Kerry Wood/250 10.00
6 Sammy Sosa/250 12.00
7 Magglio Ordonez/250 5.00
8 Adam Dunn/250 8.00
9 Todd Helton/250 8.00
10 Josh Beckett/250 5.00
11 Miguel Cabrera/250 8.00
12 Lance Berkman/250 5.00
13 Carlos Beltran/250 8.00
14 Shawn Green/250 5.00
15 Roger Clemens/250 15.00
16 Mike Piazza/250 10.00
17 Nolan Ryan/100 50.00
18 Mark Mulder/250 5.00
19 Jim Thome/250 8.00
20 Albert Pujols/250 20.00
21 Scott Rolen/250 10.00
22 Aubrey Huff/250 5.00
23 Alfonso Soriano/250 8.00
24 Hank Blalock/250 8.00
25 Vernon Wells/250 5.00

Jersey Kings Signatures

No Pricing
Production 5 or 10

Longball Leaders

NM/M
Complete Set (15): 30.00
Common Player: 2.00
Black: 1-2X
Production 250 Sets
Die-Cut: 2-3X
Production 50 Sets
Black Die-Cut: No Pricing
Production 10 Sets
1 Adam Dunn 3.00
2 Adrian Beltre 3.00
3 Albert Pujols 6.00
4 Alex Rodriguez 5.00
5 David Ortiz 3.00
6 Hank Blalock 3.00
7 J.D. Drew 2.00
8 Jeromy Burnitz 2.00
9 Jim Edmonds 2.50
10 Jim Thome 3.00
11 Manny Ramirez 3.00
12 Mark Teixeira 2.00
13 Moises Alou 2.00
14 Paul Konerko 2.00
15 Steve Finley 2.00

Mound Marvels

NM/M
Complete Set (15): 40.00
Common Player: 2.00
Production 1,000 Sets
Black: No Pricing
Production 10 Sets
1 Curt Schilling 4.00
2 Dontrelle Willis 2.00
3 Eric Gagne 4.00
4 Greg Maddux 6.00
5 John Smoltz 3.00
6 Kenny Rogers 2.00
7 Kerry Wood 4.00
8 Mariano Rivera 3.00
9 Mark Mulder 2.00
10 Mark Prior 4.00
11 Mike Mussina 3.00
12 Pedro Martinez 4.00
13 Randy Johnson 4.00
14 Roger Clemens 8.00
15 Tim Hudson 2.00

Power Alley Red

NM/M
Common Player: 1.50
Production 2,500 Sets
Black: No Pricing
Production 10 Sets
Black Die-Cut: No Pricing
Production Five Sets
Blue: 1X
Production 1,000 Sets
Blue Die-Cut: 2-3X
Production 100 Sets
Green: 3-5X
Production 25 Sets
Green Die-Cut: No Pricing
Production 10 Sets
Purple: 1-2X
Production 250 Sets
Purple Die-Cut: 2-3X
Production 50 Sets
Red Die-Cut: 1-2X
Production 250 Sets
Yellow: 2-3X
Production 100 Sets
Yellow Die-Cut: 3-5X
Production 25 Sets
1 Adam Dunn 2.00
2 Adrian Beltre 2.00
3 Albert Pujols 6.00
4 Alex Rodriguez 5.00
5 Alfonso Soriano 3.00
6 Gary Sheffield 2.00
7 Hank Blalock 2.00
8 Hideki Matsui 4.00
9 J.D. Drew 1.50
10 Jeromy Burnitz 1.50
11 Jim Edmonds 2.00
12 Jim Thome 3.00
13 Ken Griffey Jr. 3.00
14 Manny Ramirez 2.00
15 Mark Teixeira 1.50
16 Miguel Cabrera 2.00
17 Miguel Tejada 2.00
18 Mike Lowell 1.50
19 Mike Piazza 3.00
20 Moises Alou 1.50
21 Paul Konerko 1.50
22 Sammy Sosa 4.00
23 Scott Rolen 3.00
24 Todd Helton 2.00
25 Vladimir Guerrero 3.00

Production Line BA

NM/M
Common Player: 3.00
Black: 2-3X
Production 25 Sets
Die-Cut: 1X

Production 100 Sets
Black Die-Cut: No Pricing
Production 10 Sets
1 Ichiro Suzuki/372 8.00
2 Ivan Rodriguez/334 5.00
3 Juan Pierre/326 3.00
4 Adrian Beltre/334 5.00
5 Albert Pujols/331 10.00
6 Mark Loretta/335 3.00
7 Melvin Mora/340 3.00
8 Sean Casey/324 3.00
9 Todd Helton/347 5.00
10 Vladimir Guerrero/337 5.00

Production Line OBP

NM/M
Common Player: 3.00
Black: 2-3X
Production 25 Sets
Die-Cut: 1X
Production 100 Sets
Black Die-Cut: No Pricing
Production 10 Sets
1 Albert Pujols/415 8.00
2 Bobby Abreu/428 3.00
3 Lance Berkman/450 3.00
4 J.D. Drew/436 3.00
5 Jorge Posada/400 4.00
6 Ichiro Suzuki/414 8.00
7 Manny Ramirez/397 4.00
8 Melvin Mora/419 3.00
9 Todd Helton/469 4.00
10 Travis Hafner/410 3.00

Production Line OPS

NM/M
Common Player: 3.00
Black: 1.5-2X
Production 50 Sets
Die-Cut: 1X
Production 100 Sets
Black Die-Cut: 2-3X
Production 25 Sets
1 Albert Pujols/1072 8.00
2 Bobby Abreu/983 4.00
3 Lance Berkman/1017 4.00
4 J.D. Drew/1006 3.00
5 Jorge Posada/977 4.00
6 Ichiro Suzuki/1016 3.00
7 Manny Ramirez/1009 4.00
8 Melvin Mora/1007 4.00
9 Todd Helton/1088 4.00
10 Travis Hafner/993 3.00

Production Line Slugging

NM/M
Common Player: 3.00
Black: 1.5-2X
Production 50 Sets
Die-Cut: 1X
Production 100 Sets
Black Die-Cut: 2-3X
Production 25 Sets
1 Adrian Beltre/629 4.00
2 Albert Pujols/657 8.00
3 Todd Helton/620 4.00
4 J.D. Drew/569 3.00
5 Jim Edmonds/643 3.00
6 Jim Thome/581 4.00
7 Vladimir Guerrero/598 4.00
8 Manny Ramirez/613 4.00
9 Scott Rolen/598 4.00
10 Travis Hafner/583 3.00

Recollection Autographs

No Pricing
Production 1-5

Rookies

NM/M
Common Player: 2.00
Inserted 1:23
Black: No Pricing
Production 10 Sets
Blue: 1X
Production 100 Sets
Gold: 2-3X
Production 25 Sets
Red: .75-1X
Production 200 Sets
1 Fernando Nieve 2.00
2 Frankie Francisco 2.00
3 Jorge Vasquez 2.00
4 Travis Blackley 2.00
5 Joey Gathright 4.00
6 Kazuhito Tadano 2.00
7 Edwin Moreno 2.00
8 Lance Cormier 2.00
9 Justin Knoedler 2.00
10 Orlando Rodriguez 2.00
11 Renyel Pinto 2.00
12 Justin Leone 2.00
13 Dennis Sarfate 2.00
14 Sam Narron 2.00
15 Yadier Molina 4.00
16 Carlos Vasquez 2.00
17 Ryan Wing 2.00
18 Brad Halsey 2.00
19 Ryan Meaux 2.00
20 Mike Wuertz 2.00
21 Shawn Camp 2.00
22 Ruddy Yan 2.00
23 Donald Kelly 2.00
24 Jake Woods 2.00
25 Colby Miller 2.00
26 Abe Alvarez 2.00
27 Mike Rouse 2.00
28 Phil Stockman 2.00
29 Kevin Cave 2.00
30 Chris Shelton 4.00
31 Tim Bittner 2.00
32 Mariano Gomez 2.00
33 Angel Chavez 2.00
34 Carlos Hines 2.00
35 Aarom Baldiris 2.00
36 Kazuo Matsui 5.00
37 Nick Regilio 2.00
38 Ivan Ochoa 2.00
39 Graham Koonce 2.00
40 Merkin Valdez 3.00
41 Greg Dobbs 2.00
42 Chris Oxspring 2.00
43 David Crouthers 2.00
44 Freddy Guzman 2.00
45 Akinori Otsuka 3.00
46 Jesse Crain 2.00
47 Casey Daigle 2.00
48 Roberto Novoa 2.00
49 Eddy Rodriguez 2.00
50 Jason Bartlett 2.00

Rookies Stat Line Career

Print run 201-316: 1X
Print run 101-200: 1X
Print run 51-100: 1-1.5X
Print run 26-50: 1-2X
Print run 25 or less: No Pricing
Cards are numbered to career statistic.

Rookies Stat Line Season

Print run 101-200: 1X
Print run 51-100: 1-1.5X
Print run 26-50: 1-2X
Print run 25 or less: No Pricing
Cards are numbered to season statistic.

Rookies Autographs

NM/M
Common Autographs: 5.00
1 Fernando Nieve 5.00
2 Frankie Francisco 5.00
3 Jorge Vasquez 5.00
4 Travis Blackley 5.00
5 Joey Gathright 8.00
7 Edwin Moreno 5.00
8 Lance Cormier 5.00
9 Justin Knoedler 5.00
10 Orlando Rodriguez 5.00
11 Renyel Pinto 5.00
13 Dennis Sarfate 5.00
15 Yadier Molina 10.00
16 Carlos Vasquez 8.00
17 Ryan Wing/SP 10.00
18 Brad Halsey 8.00
19 Ryan Meaux 5.00
20 Mike Wuertz 5.00
22 Ruddy Yan 5.00
23 Donald Kelly 5.00
24 Jake Woods 5.00
25 Colby Miller 5.00
26 Abe Alvarez 8.00
27 Mike Rouse/SP 8.00
28 Phil Stockman 5.00
29 Kevin Cave 5.00
30 Chris Shelton/SP 10.00
31 Tim Bittner 5.00
32 Mariano Gomez 5.00
33 Angel Chavez 5.00
34 Carlos Hines 5.00
35 Aarom Baldiris 5.00
37 Nick Regilio 5.00
38 Ivan Ochoa 5.00
39 Graham Koonce 5.00
42 Chris Oxspring 5.00
43 David Crouthers 5.00
48 Roberto Novoa 5.00
49 Eddy Rodriguez 5.00
50 Jason Bartlett 5.00

Timber and Threads Bat

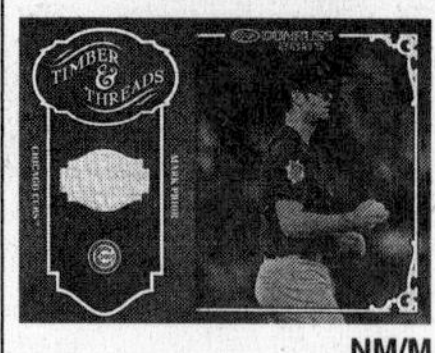

NM/M
Common Player: 5.00
1 Albert Pujols 15.00
2 Alfonso Soriano 8.00
3 Andre Dawson 8.00
4 Austin Kearns 5.00
5 Brad Penny 5.00
6 Carlos Beltran 8.00
7 Carlos Lee 5.00
8 Chipper Jones 8.00
9 Dale Murphy 8.00
10 Don Mattingly 20.00
11 Frank Thomas 8.00
12 Garret Anderson 5.00
13 Gary Carter 8.00
14 Hank Blalock 8.00
15 Jacque Jones 5.00
17 Jay Gibbons 5.00
18 Jeff Bagwell 8.00
20 Jermaine Dye 5.00
21 Jim Thome 8.00
22 Jose Vidro 5.00
23 Lance Berkman 5.00
24 Laynce Nix 5.00
25 Magglio Ordonez 5.00
26 Marcus Giles 5.00
27 Mark Prior 10.00
28 Mark Teixeira 5.00
29 Melvin Mora 5.00
30 Michael Young 5.00
31 Miguel Cabrera 8.00
32 Mike Lowell 5.00
33 Roy Oswalt 5.00
34 Sammy Sosa 10.00
35 Scott Rolen 10.00
36 Sean Burroughs 5.00
37 Sean Casey 5.00
38 Shannon Stewart 5.00
39 Torii Hunter 5.00
40 Travis Hafner 5.00

Timber and Threads Bat Signature

No Pricing
Production 5 or 10

Timber and Threads Combo

NM/M
1 Albert Pujols/Bat-Jsy 25.00
2 Alfonso Soriano/at-Jsy 10.00
3 Andre Dawson/Bat-Jsy 8.00
4 Austin Kearns/Bat-Jsy 8.00
5 Brad Penny/Bat-Jsy 6.00
6 Carlos Beltran/Bat-Jsy 12.00
7 Carlos Lee/Bat-Jsy 6.00
8 Chipper Jones/Bat-Jsy 12.00
9 Dale Murphy/Bat-Jsy 10.00
10 Don Mattingly/Bat-Jsy 25.00
11 Frank Thomas/Bat-Jsy 12.00
12 Garret Anderson/Bat-Jsy 8.00
13 Gary Carter/Bat-Jsy 10.00
14 Hank Blalock/Bat-Jsy 10.00
15 Jacque Jones/Bat-Jsy 6.00
17 Jay Gibbons/Bat-Jsy 6.00
18 Jeff Bagwell/Bat-Jsy 12.00
20 Jermaine Dye/Bat-Jsy 6.00
21 Jim Thome/Bat-Jsy 12.00
22 Jose Vidro/Bat-Jsy 6.00
23 Lance Berkman/Bat-Jsy 6.00
24 Laynce Nix/Bat-Jsy 6.00
25 Magglio Ordonez/Bat-Jsy 8.00
26 Marcus Giles/Bat-Jsy 6.00
27 Mark Prior/Bat-Jsy 15.00
28 Mark Teixeira/Bat-Jsy 8.00
29 Melvin Mora/Bat-Jsy 6.00
30 Michael Young/Bat-Jsy 8.00
31 Miguel Cabrera/Bat-Jsy 12.00
32 Mike Lowell/Bat-Jsy 8.00
33 Roy Oswalt/Bat-Jsy 8.00
34 Sammy Sosa/Bat-Jsy 15.00
35 Scott Rolen/Bat-Jsy 15.00
36 Sean Burroughs/Bat-Jsy 6.00
37 Sean Casey/Bat-Jsy 6.00
38 Shannon Stewart/at-Jsy 6.00
39 Torii Hunter/Bat-Jsy 8.00
40 Travis Hafner/Bat-Jsy 8.00

Timber and Threads Combo Signture

No Pricing
Production 5 or 10

Timber and Threads Jersey

NM/M
Common Player: 5.00
1 Albert Pujols 15.00
2 Alfonso Soriano 8.00
4 Austin Kearns 5.00
5 Brad Penny 5.00
6 Carlos Beltran 8.00
7 Carlos Lee 5.00
9 Dale Murphy 8.00
10 Don Mattingly 25.00
11 Frank Thomas 8.00
12 Garret Anderson 5.00
13 Gary Carter 5.00
14 Hank Blalock 8.00
15 Jacque Jones 5.00
17 Jay Gibbons 5.00
18 Jeff Bagwell 8.00
19 Jeremy Bonderman 5.00
20 Jermaine Dye 5.00
21 Jim Thome 8.00
22 Jose Vidro 5.00
23 Lance Berkman 5.00
24 Laynce Nix 5.00
25 Magglio Ordonez 5.00
26 Marcus Giles 5.00
27 Mark Prior 10.00
28 Mark Teixeira 5.00
29 Melvin Mora 5.00
30 Michael Young 5.00
31 Miguel Cabrera 8.00
32 Mike Lowell 5.00
33 Roy Oswalt 5.00
34 Sammy Sosa 10.00
35 Scott Rolen 10.00
36 Sean Burroughs 5.00
37 Sean Casey 5.00
38 Shannon Stewart 5.00
39 Torii Hunter 5.00
40 Travis Hafner 5.00

Timber and Threads Jersey Signature

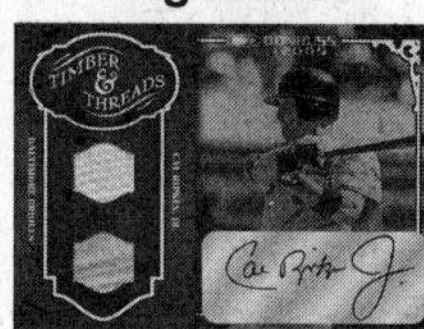

No Pricing
Production 5 or 10

'85 Reprints

NM/M
Complete Set (12): 40.00
Common Player: 2.00
Production 1,985 Sets
1 Eddie Murray 3.00
2 George Brett 6.00
3 Nolan Ryan 8.00
4 Mike Schmidt 6.00
5 Tony Gwynn 3.00
7 Cal Ripken Jr. 10.00
8 Dwight Gooden 2.00
9 Roger Clemens 8.00
10 Don Mattingly 6.00
11 Kirby Puckett 4.00
12 Orel Hershiser 2.00

'85 Reprints Material

NM/M
Production 85 Sets
1 Eddie Murray/Jsy 20.00
2 George Brett/Jsy 35.00
3 Nolan Ryan/Jkt 40.00
4 Mike Schmidt/Jkt 35.00
5 Tony Gwynn/Jsy 20.00
7 Cal Ripken Jr./Jsy 50.00
9 Roger Clemens/Jsy 40.00
10 Don Mattingly/Jsy 35.00
11 Kirby Puckett/Jsy 20.00
12 Orel Hershiser/Jsy 10.00

1965 Minnesota Twins 40th Anniversary

To commemorate the 40th anniversary of the team's 1965 American League championship, this set was produced by Donruss as a stadium giveaway. Fifteen-card cello packs containing cards #1-15 were distributed on August 18. Cards #19-30 were given away the next day. Fronts have black-and-white photos bordered in blue.

NM/M
Complete Set (30): 15.00
Common Player: .25
1 Dave Boswell .25
2 Jim Kaat .50
3 Jim Merritt .25
4 Mel Nelson .25
5 Bill Pleis .25
6 Dick Stigman .25
7 Earl Battey .25
8 Jerry Kindall .25
9 Frank Quilici .25
10 Zoilo Versalles .50
11 Bob Allison .50
12 Joe Nossek .25
13 Tony Oliva 3.00
14 Sam Mele .25
15 John Sain .25
16 Jim "Mudcat" Grant .35
17 Johnny Klippstein .25
18 Camilo Pascual .40
19 Jim Perry .35
20 Al Worthington .25
21 John Sevcik .25
22 Jerry Zimmerman .25
23 Harmon Killebrew 5.00
24 Don Mincher .25
25 Rich Rollins .25
26 Billy Martin 2.00
27 Jimmie Hall .25
28 Sandy Valdespino .25
29 Hal Naragon .25
30 Jim Lemon .25

2005 Donruss Classics

NM/M
Complete Set (250):
Common Player (1-200): .25
Common Auto. (201-225): 6.00
Common SP (226-250): 3.00
Production 1,000
Pack (5): 8.00
Box (18): 120.00
1 Scott Rolen 1.00
2 Derek Jeter 3.00
3 Jose Vidro .25
4 Johnny Damon 1.00
5 Nomar Garciaparra 2.00
6 Jose Guillen .25
7 Trot Nixon .25
8 Mark Loretta .25
9 Jody Gerut .25
10 Miguel Tejada .75
11 Barry Larkin .50
12 Jeff Kent .40
13 Carl Crawford .25
14 Paul Konerko .40
15 Jim Edmonds .50
16 Garret Anderson .40
17 Jay Gibbons .25
18 Moises Alou .40
19 Mike Lowell .25
20 Mark Mulder .40
21 Josh Beckett .50
22 Tim Salmon .25
23 Shannon Stewart .25
24 Miguel Cabrera 1.00
25 Jim Thome 1.00
26 Kevin Youkilis .25
27 Justin Morneau .75
28 Austin Kearns .25
29 Cliff Lee .25
30 Ken Griffey Jr. 1.50
31 Mike Piazza 1.50
32 Roy Halladay .40
33 Larry Walker .50
34 David Ortiz 1.00
35 Dontrelle Willis .50
36 Craig Wilson .25
37 Jeff Suppan .25
38 Curt Schilling 1.00
39 Larry Bigbie .25
40 Rich Harden .40
41 Victor Martinez .40
42 Jorge Posada .50
43 Joey Gathright .25
44 Adam Dunn .75
45 Pedro Martinez 1.00
46 Dallas McPherson .50
47 Tom Glavine .40
48 Torii Hunter .40
49 Angel Berroa .25
50 Mark Prior 1.00
51 Ichiro Suzuki 2.00
52 C.C. Sabathia .25
53 Bobby Abreu .50
54 Shigetoshi Hasegawa .25
55 Brandon Webb .50
56 Mark Buehrle .50
57 Johan Santana .75
58 Francisco Rodriguez .25
59 Roy Oswalt .50
60 Mike Sweeney .25
61 Jake Peavy .50
62 Akinori Otsuka .25
63 Dioner Navarro .25
64 Kazuhito Tadano .25
65 Ryan Wagner .25
66 Abe Alvarez .25
67 Mark Teixeira .75
68 Jermaine Dye .25
69 Todd Walker .25
70 Octavio Dotel .25
71 Frank Thomas .75
72 Javy Lopez .50
73 Scott Podsednik .25
74 B.J. Upton .25
75 Barry Zito .40
76 Raul Ibanez .25
77 Orlando Cabrera .25
78 Sean Burroughs .25
79 Esteban Loaiza .25
80 Jason Schmidt .50
81 Vinny Castilla .25
82 Shingo Takatsu .25
83 Juan Pierre .25
84 David Dellucci .25
85 Travis Blackley .25
86 Brad Penny .25
87 Nick Johnson .25
88 Brian Roberts .50
89 Kazuo Matsui .25
90 Mike Lieberthal .25
91 Craig Biggio .40
92 Sean Casey .25
93 Andy Pettitte .50
94 Milton Bradley .40
95 Rocco Baldelli .25
96 Adrian Gonzalez .25
97 Chad Tracy .25
98 Chad Cordero .25
99 Albert Pujols 3.00
100 Jason Kubel .25
101 Rafael Furcal .25
102 Jack Wilson .25
103 Eric Chavez .40
104 Casey Kotchman .25
105 Jeff Bagwell .75
106 Melvin Mora .25
107 Bobby Crosby .25
108 Preston Wilson .25
109 Hank Blalock .75
110 Vernon Wells .40
111 Francisco Cordero .25
112 Steve Finley .25
113 Omar Vizquel .25
114 Eric Byrnes .25
115 Tim Hudson .50
116 Aramis Ramirez .50
117 Lance Berkman .40
118 Shea Hillenbrand .25
119 Aubrey Huff .25
120 Lew Ford .25
121 Sammy Sosa 2.00
122 Marcus Giles .25
123 Rickie Weeks .25
124 Manny Ramirez 1.00
125 Jason Giambi .40
126 Adam LaRoche .25
127 Vladimir Guerrero 1.00
128 Ken Harvey .25
129 Adrian Beltre .50
130 Magglio Ordonez .25
131 Greg Maddux 1.50
132 Russ Ortiz .25
133 Jason Varitek .75
134 Kerry Wood 1.00
135 Mike Mussina .75
136 Joe Nathan .25
137 Troy Glaus .50
138 Carlos Zambrano .50
139 Ben Sheets .50
140 Jae Weong Seo .25

141 Derrek Lee .50
142 Carlos Beltran .50
143 John Lackey .25
144 Aaron Rowand .25
145 Dewon Brazelton .25
146 Jason Bay .25
147 Alfonso Soriano 1.00
148 Travis Hafner .25
149 Ryan Church .25
150 Bret Boone .25
151 Bernie Williams .50
152 Wade Miller .25
153 Zack Greinke .25
154 Scott Kazmir .25
155 Hideki Matsui 2.00
156 Livan Hernandez .25
157 Jose Capellan .25
158 David Wright 1.00
159 Chone Figgins .25
160 Jeremy Reed .25
161 J.D. Drew .40
162 Hideo Nomo .50
163 Merkin Valdez .25
164 Shawn Green .40
165 Alexis Rios .25
166 Johnny Estrada .25
167 Danny Graves .25
168 Carlos Lee .25
169 John Van Benschoten .25
170 Randy Johnson 1.00
171 Randy Wolf .25
172 Luis Gonzalez .40
173 Chipper Jones 1.00
174 Delmon Young .50
175 Edwin Jackson .25
176 Carlos Delgado .50
177 Matt Clement .25
178 Jacque Jones .25
179 Gary Sheffield .50
180 Layne Nix .25
181 Tom Gordon .25
182 Jose Castillo .25
183 Andruw Jones .50
184 Brian Giles .40
185 Paul LoDuca .25
186 Roger Clemens 3.00
187 Todd Helton .75
188 Keith Foulke .25
189 Jeremy Bonderman .25
190 Troy Percival .25
191 Michael Young .25
192 Carlos Guillen .25
193 Rafael Palmeiro .75
194 Brett Myers .25
195 Carl Pavano .40
196 Alex Rodriguez 2.50
197 Lyle Overbay .25
198 Ivan Rodriguez .75
199 Khalil Greene .40
200 Edgar Renteria .40
201 Justin Verlander/ AU/400 **RC** 40.00
202 Miguel Negron/ AU/1300 **RC** 6.00
204 Paul Reynoso/ AU/1200 **RC** 8.00
205 Colter Bean/ AU/1200 **RC** 8.00
206 Raul Tablado/ AU/1200 **RC** 8.00
207 Mark McLemore/ AU/1500 **RC** 8.00
208 Russel Rohlicek/ AU/1200 **RC** 8.00
210 Chris Seddon/ AU/785 **RC** 8.00
213 Mike Morse/ AU/1200 **RC** 6.00
215 Randy Messenger/ AU/1200 **RC** 8.00
217 Carlos Ruiz/ AU/1200 **RC** 8.00
218 Chris Roberson/ AU/1200 **RC** 8.00
219 Ryan Speier/ AU/1200 **RC** 8.00
221 Ambiorix Burgos/ AU/750 **RC** 8.00
223 David Gassner/ AU/1200 **RC** 6.00
224 Sean Tracey/ AU/1200 **RC** 8.00
225 Casey Rogowski/ AU/1500 **RC** 8.00
226 Billy Williams 3.00
227 Ralph Kiner 3.00
228 Ozzie Smith 5.00
229 Rod Carew 3.00
230 Nolan Ryan 8.00
231 Fergie Jenkins 3.00
232 Paul Molitor 4.00
233 Carlton Fisk 4.00
234 Rollie Fingers 3.00
235 Lou Brock 3.00
236 Gaylord Perry 3.00
237 Don Mattingly 6.00
238 Maury Wills 3.00
239 Luis Aparicio 3.00
240 George Brett 8.00
241 Mike Schmidt 6.00
242 Joe Morgan 3.00
243 Dennis Eckersley 3.00
244 Reggie Jackson 4.00
245 Bobby Doerr 3.00
246 Bob Feller 3.00
247 Cal Ripken Jr. 10.00
248 Harmon Killebrew 4.00
249 Frank Robinson 4.00
250 Stan Musial 5.00

Timeless Tributes Gold

Gold (1-200): 4-8X
Gold (201-225): .4-.75X
Gold (226-250): 2-4X
Production 50 Sets

Timeless Tributes Silver

Gold (1-200): 2-4X
Gold (201-225): .25X
Gold (226-250): 1-2X
Production 100 Sets

Timeless Tributes Platinum

No Pricing
Production One Set

Classic Combos

NM/M
Common Combo: 4.00
Production 400 Sets
Gold: 2-4X
Production 25 Sets
Platinum: No Pricing
Production One Set
33 Babe Ruth, Ted Williams 10.00
34 Roberto Clemente, Vladimir Guerrero 8.00
35 Willie Mays, Willie McCovey 8.00
36 Yogi Berra, Mike Piazza 6.00
37 Sandy Koufax, Nolan Ryan 30.00
38 Harmon Killebrew, Mike Schmidt 8.00
39 Whitey Ford, Randy Johnson 4.00
40 Cal Ripken Jr., George Brett 15.00
41 Hank Aaron, Stan Musial 8.00
42 Carl Yastrzemski, Frank Robinson 6.00
43 Bob Feller, Roger Clemens 6.00
44 Bob Gibson, Tom Seaver 4.00
45 Roger Maris, Jim Thome 4.00
46 Albert Pujols, Don Mattingly 8.00
47 Duke Snider, Sammy Sosa 4.00
48 Rickey Henderson, Bo Jackson 4.00
49 Ernie Banks, Reggie Jackson 4.00
50 Burleigh Grimes, Greg Maddux 6.00

Classic Combos Bat

No Pricing
Production Five Sets

Classic Combos Jersey

NM/M
Production 5-50
Prime: No Pricing
Production 1-5
38 Harmon Killebrew, Mike Schmidt/50 30.00
39 Whitey Ford, Randy Johnson/25 25.00
40 Cal Ripken Jr., George Brett/50 50.00
45 Roger Maris, Jim Thome/25 50.00
46 Albert Pujols, Don Mattingly/50 40.00
47 Duke Snider, Sammy Sosa/25 30.00
48 Rickey Henderson, Bo Jackson/50 25.00

Classic Combos Materials

NM/M
Production 1-25
Prime: No Pricing
Production Five Sets
46 Albert Pujols, Don Mattingly/25 50.00
48 Rickey Henderson, Bo Jackson/25 30.00

Classic Combos Materials HR

NM/M
Production 1-25
46 Albert Pujols, Don Mattingly/25 50.00
48 Rickey Henderson, Bo Jackson/25 30.00

Classic Combos Signature

No Pricing
Production One Set

Classic Combos Signature Bat

No Pricing
Production One Set

Classic Combos Signature Jersey

No Pricing
Production 1-5

Classic Combos Signature Material

No Pricing
Production One Set

Classic Combos Signature Materials HR

No Pricing
Production One Set

Classic Singles

NM/M
Complete Set (32): 120.00
Common Player: 3.00
Production 400 Sets
Gold: 2-4X
Production 25 Sets
Platinum: No Pricing
Production One Set
1 Hank Aaron 8.00
2 Tom Seaver 4.00
3 Harmon Killebrew 4.00
4 Paul Molitor 4.00
5 Brooks Robinson 4.00
6 Stan Musial 5.00
7 Bobby Doerr 3.00
8 Cal Ripken Jr. 12.00
9 Phil Niekro 3.00
10 Eddie Murray 4.00
11 Randy Johnson 4.00
12 Steve Carlton 3.00
13 Rickey Henderson 3.00
14 Ernie Banks 4.00
15 Curt Schilling 4.00
16 Whitey Ford 4.00
17 Al Kaline 4.00
18 Gary Carter 3.00
19 Robin Yount 4.00
20 Johnny Bench 4.00
21 Bob Feller 3.00
22 Jim Palmer 3.00
23 Don Mattingly 6.00
24 Willie Mays 6.00
25 Dave Righetti 3.00
26 Roger Clemens 6.00
27 Juan Marichal 3.00
28 Tony Gwynn 4.00
29 Nolan Ryan 8.00
30 Carlton Fisk 3.00
31 Greg Maddux 5.00
32 Sandy Koufax 25.00

Classic Singles Bat

NM/M
Production 25-50
1 Hank Aaron/25 50.00
2 Tom Seaver/50 15.00
4 Paul Molitor/50 15.00
5 Brooks Robinson/50 15.00
6 Stan Musial/25 30.00
7 Bobby Doerr/25 10.00
8 Cal Ripken Jr./25 70.00
9 Phil Niekro/50 8.00
10 Eddie Murray/50 15.00
11 Randy Johnson/25 20.00
12 Steve Carlton/25 10.00
13 Rickey Henderson/50 15.00
14 Ernie Banks/50 20.00
17 Al Kaline/25 25.00
18 Gary Carter/50 8.00
19 Robin Yount/50 15.00
20 Johnny Bench/25 20.00
23 Don Mattingly/25 30.00
24 Willie Mays/25 50.00
28 Tony Gwynn/50 15.00
29 Nolan Ryan/25 40.00
30 Carlton Fisk/50 15.00

Classic Singles Jersey

NM/M
Production 10-100
Prime: No Pricing
Production 1-5
2 Tom Seaver/25 20.00
3 Harmon Killebrew/25 20.00
4 Paul Molitor/50 15.00
5 Brooks Robinson/50 15.00
7 Bobby Doerr/ Pants/100 10.00
8 Cal Ripken Jr./25 70.00
9 Phil Niekro/50 8.00
10 Eddie Murray/50 15.00
11 Randy Johnson/100 12.00
12 Steve Carlton/25 12.00
13 Rickey Henderson/ 100 12.00
14 Ernie Banks/25 25.00
15 Curt Schilling/100 15.00
16 Whitey Ford/25 20.00
18 Gary Carter/100 8.00
19 Robin Yount/50 15.00
20 Johnny Bench/50 15.00
21 Bob Feller/Pants/25 20.00
22 Jim Palmer/100 8.00
23 Don Mattingly/100 25.00
24 Willie Mays/25 50.00
25 Dave Righetti/50 8.00
26 Roger Clemens/25 25.00
27 Juan Marichal/50 10.00
28 Tony Gwynn/100 15.00
29 Nolan Ryan/50 30.00
30 Carlton Fisk/25 15.00
31 Greg Maddux/100 15.00
32 Sandy Koufax/25 375.00

Classic Singles Materials

NM/M
Production 10-25
Prime: No Pricing
Production 10-25
2 Tom Seaver/ Bat-Jsy/25 20.00
3 Harmon Killebrew/ Bat-Jys/25 25.00
4 Paul Molitor/ Bat-Jsy/25 20.00
5 Brooks Robinson/ Bat-Jsy/25 20.00
7 Bobby Doerr/ Bat-Pants/25 10.00
11 Randy Johnson/ Bat-Jsy/25 20.00
12 Steve Carlton/ Bat-Jsy/25 15.00
13 Rickey Henderson/ Bat-Jsy/25 30.00
18 Gary Carter/ Bat-Jsy/25 15.00
19 Robin Yount/ Bat-Jsy/25 25.00
20 Johnny Bench/ Bat-Jsy/25 25.00
23 Don Mattingly/ Bat-Jsy/25 35.00
28 Tony Gwynn/ Bat-Jsy/25 25.00
29 Nolan Ryan/ Bat-Jsy/25 40.00
30 Carlton Fisk/ Bat-Jsy/25 15.00

Classic Singles Materials HR

NM/M
Production 10-25
2 Tom Seaver/ Bat-Jsy/25 20.00
3 Harmon Killebrew/ Bat-Jsy/25 25.00
4 Paul Molitor/ Bat-Jsy/25 20.00
5 Brooks Robinson/ Bat-Jsy/25 20.00
7 Bobby Doerr/ Bat-Pants/25 10.00
11 Randy Johnson/ Bat-Jsy/25 20.00
12 Steve Carlton/ Bat-Pants/25 15.00
13 Rickey Henderson/ Bat-Jsy/25 30.00
18 Gary Carter/ Bat-Jsy/25 15.00
19 Robin Yount/ Bat-Jsy/25 25.00
20 Johnny Bench/ Bat-Jsy/25 25.00
23 Don Mattingly/ Bat-Jsy/25 35.00
28 Tony Gwynn/ Bat-Jsy/25 25.00

Classic Singles Signature

No Pricing
Production 1-5

Classic Singles Signature Bat

No Pricing
Production 1-10

Classic Singles Signature Jersey

No Pricing
Production 1-5

Classic Singles Signature Materials

No Pricing
Production 1-10

Classic Singles Signature Materials HR

No Pricing
Production 1-10

Dress Code Bat

NM/M
Production 50-100
1 Albert Pujols/100 25.00
2 Bernie Williams/50 10.00
4 Carlos Beltran/100 10.00
5 Chipper Jones/100 10.00
7 David Ortiz/100 12.00
8 Hank Blalock/100 6.00
9 Hideki Matsui/100 30.00
10 Jim Edmonds/100 8.00
11 Jim Thome/100 10.00
14 Mark Prior/50 8.00
15 Mark Teixeira/100 6.00
16 Miguel Cabrera/100 8.00
17 Miguel Tejada/100 6.00
18 Mike Piazza/100 12.00
22 Sammy Sosa/100 12.00
23 Scott Rolen/100 10.00
26 Torii Hunter/100 6.00
30 Vladimir Guerrero/ 100 10.00

Dress Code Jersey Number

NM/M
Production 5-57
2 Bernie Williams/51 10.00
4 Carlos Beltran/15 20.00
6 Curt Schilling/38 15.00
7 David Ortiz/34 20.00
9 Hideki Matsui/55 30.00
11 Jim Thome/25 15.00
12 Johan Santana/57 12.00
13 Mark Mulder/20 10.00
14 Mark Prior/22 15.00
15 Mark Teixeira/23 10.00
16 Miguel Cabrera/24 15.00
18 Mike Piazza/31 20.00
19 Pedro J. Martinez/45 10.00
20 Randy Johnson/ Pants/51 12.00
21 Roger Clemens/23 25.00
22 Sammy Sosa/21 20.00
23 Scott Rolen/27 15.00
26 Torii Hunter/48 6.00
27 Travis Hafner/48 6.00
29 Victor Martinez/51 8.00
30 Vladimir Guerrero/27 20.00

Dress Code Jersey Prime

NM/M
Production 25 Sets
1 Albert Pujols 75.00
2 Bernie Williams 20.00
3 Carl Crawford 12.00
4 Carlos Beltran 25.00
5 Chipper Jones 30.00
6 Curt Schilling 30.00
7 David Ortiz 30.00
8 Hank Blalock 20.00
10 Jim Edmonds 20.00
11 Jim Thome 25.00
12 Johan Santana 30.00
13 Mark Mulder 20.00
14 Mark Prior 20.00
15 Mark Teixeira 15.00
16 Miguel Cabrera 25.00
17 Miguel Tejada 25.00
18 Mike Piazza 30.00
19 Pedro J. Martinez 25.00
20 Randy Johnson 30.00
21 Roger Clemens 50.00
22 Sammy Sosa 30.00
23 Scott Rolen 30.00
24 Tim Hudson 20.00
25 Todd Helton 20.00
26 Torii Hunter 15.00
27 Travis Hafner 10.00
28 Vernon Wells 10.00
29 Victor Martinez 15.00
30 Vladimir Guerrero 30.00

Dress Code Materials

NM/M
Production 5-100
Prime: No Pricing
Production Five Sets
1 Albert Pujols/ Bat-Jsy/100 25.00
2 Bernie Williams/ Bat-Jsy/50 10.00
4 Carlos Beltran/ Bat-Bat/Jsy/100 10.00
5 Chipper Jones/ Bat-Jsy/100 12.00
6 Curt Schilling/ Bat-Jsy/50 15.00
7 David Ortiz/ Bat-Hat/100 15.00
8 Hank Blalock/ Bat-Jsy/100 8.00
9 Hideki Matsui/ Bat-Jsy/100 30.00
10 Jim Edmonds 10.00
11 Jim Thome/ Jsy-Jsy/100 12.00
15 Mark Teixeira/ Bat-Jsy/100 8.00
16 Miguel Cabrera/ Jsy-Jsy/100 10.00
17 Miguel Tejada/ Bat-Jsy/100 8.00
18 Mike Piazza/ Bat-Jsy/100 12.00
19 Pedro J. Martinez/ Bat-Jsy/100 12.00
22 Sammy Sosa/ Bat-Jsy/100 12.00
23 Scott Rolen/ Bat-Jsy/100 12.00
25 Todd Helton/ Jsy-Jsy/50 12.00
26 Torii Hunter/ Bat-Jsy/100 8.00
27 Travis Hafner/ Jsy-Shoes/50 8.00
28 Vernon Wells/ Jsy-Jsy/50 8.00
29 Victor Martinez/ Jsy-Jsy/50 8.00
30 Vladimir Guerrero/ Bat-Jsy/100 12.00

Dress Code Signature Bat

NM/M
Production 1-25
7 David Ortiz/25 50.00
8 Hank Blalock/25 30.00
16 Miguel Cabrera/25 50.00
26 Torii Hunter/25 30.00
27 Travis Hafner/25 25.00
28 Vernon Wells/25 25.00

Dress Code Signature Jersey

NM/M
Production 5-25
7 David Ortiz/25 50.00
8 Hank Blalock/25 30.00
12 Johan Santana/25 50.00
16 Miguel Cabrera/25 50.00
26 Torii Hunter/25 30.00
27 Travis Hafner/25 25.00
28 Vernon Wells/25 25.00
29 Victor Martinez/25 25.00

Dress Code Signature Jersey Number

NM/M
Production 1-25
Prime: No Pricing
Production 1-5
7 David Ortiz/25 50.00
8 Hank Blalock/25 30.00
12 Johan Santana/25 50.00
26 Torii Hunter/25 30.00
27 Travis Hafner/25 25.00
29 Victor Martinez/25 25.00

Dress Code Signature Materials

No Pricing
Production 1-5

Home Run Heroes

NM/M
Complete Set (50): 90.00
Common Player: 1.50
Production 1,000 Sets
Gold: 2-4X
Production 50 Sets
Platinum: No Pricing
Production One Set
1 Mike Schmidt 4.00
2 Ken Griffey Jr. 4.00
3 Babe Ruth 6.00
4 Duke Snider 2.00
5 Johnny Bench 3.00
6 Stan Musial 3.00
7 Willie McCovey 2.00
8 Willie Stargell 2.00
9 Ted Williams 5.00
10 Frank Thomas 2.00
11 Gary Sheffield 2.00
12 Jim Thome 2.00
13 Harmon Killebrew 2.00
14 Ernie Banks 3.00
15 George Foster 1.50
16 Albert Pujols 5.00
17 Tony Perez 1.50
18 Richie Sexson 1.50
19 Juan Gonzalez 1.50
20 Frank Robinson 2.00
21 Sammy Sosa 3.00
22 Jeff Bagwell 1.50
23 Mark Teixeira 1.50
24 Willie Mays 5.00
25 Rafael Palmeiro 2.00
26 Billy Williams 1.50
27 Vladimir Guerrero 2.00
28 Gary Carter 2.00
29 Fred McGriff 1.50
30 Orlando Cepeda 1.50
31 Dave Winfield 2.00
32 Shawn Green 1.50
33 Jose Canseco 1.50
34 Hideki Matsui 4.00
35 Roger Maris 4.00
36 Andre Dawson 2.00
37 Paul Konerko 1.50
38 Darryl Strawberry 1.50
39 Dave Parker 1.50
40 Adam Dunn 2.00
41 Ralph Kiner 2.00
42 Miguel Tejada 2.00
43 Dale Murphy 2.00
44 Hank Aaron 6.00
45 Mike Piazza 3.00
46 Reggie Jackson 2.00
47 Adrian Beltre 2.00
48 Cal Ripken Jr. 8.00
49 Manny Ramirez 3.00
50 Alex Rodriguez 5.00

Home Run Heroes Jersey HR

NM/M
Production 1-66
Prime: No Pricing
Production One Set
1 Mike Schmidt/48 25.00
3 Babe Ruth/25 165.00
5 Johnny Bench/45 15.00
7 Willie McCovey/23 15.00
8 Willie Stargell/48 15.00
9 Ted Williams/43 60.00
10 Frank Thomas/43 12.00
11 Gary Sheffield/36 8.00
12 Jim Thome/47 15.00
13 Harmon Killebrew/49 20.00
14 Ernie Banks/Pants/47 20.00
15 Gene Foster/25 10.00
16 Albert Pujols/46 35.00
18 Richie Sexson/45 8.00
19 Juan Gonzalez/47 8.00
21 Sammy Sosa/66 12.00
22 Jeff Bagwell/47 10.00
23 Mark Teixeira/38 8.00
24 Willie Mays/51 50.00
25 Rafael Palmeiro/47 10.00
26 Billy Williams/26 10.00
27 Vladimir Guerrero/44 12.00
28 Gary Carter/31 10.00
29 Fred McGriff/32 12.00
30 Orlando Cepeda/Pants/46 8.00
31 Dave Winfield/34 10.00
32 Shawn Green/49 8.00
33 Jose Canseco/44 10.00
34 Hideki Matsui/Pants/31 40.00
35 Roger Maris/Pants/19 50.00
36 Andre Dawson/49 8.00
38 Darryl Strawberry/24 10.00
39 Dave Parker/34 8.00
40 Adam Dunn/46 10.00
42 Miguel Tejada/34 10.00
43 Dale Murphy/44 12.00
44 Hank Aaron/47 50.00
45 Mike Piazza/40 15.00
46 Reggie Jackson/39 12.00
47 Adrian Beltre/48 8.00
48 Cal Ripken Jr./34 50.00
49 Manny Ramirez/43 12.00

Home Run Heroes Materials

NM/M
Production 1-66
Prime: No Pricing
Production One Set
1 Mike Schmidt/Bat-Jsy/48 30.00
3 Babe Ruth/Bat-Jsy/25 300.00
5 Johnny Bench/Bat-Jsy/45 20.00
7 Willie McCovey/Bat-Jsy/23 20.00
8 Willie Stargell/Bat-Jsy/48 20.00
9 Ted Williams/Bat-Jsy/43 85.00
10 Frank Thomas/Jsy-Jsy/43 15.00
11 Gary Sheffield/Bat-Jsy/36 10.00
12 Jim Thome/Bat-Jsy/47 15.00
13 Harmon Killebrew/Bat-Jsy/49 25.00
14 Ernie Banks/Bat-Pants/47 25.00
15 George Foster/Bat-Jsy/52 10.00
16 Albert Pujols/Jsy-Jsy/46 40.00
17 Tony Perez/Bat-Fld Glv/24 15.00
18 Richie Sexson/Bat-Jsy/45 10.00
19 Juan Gonzalez/Bat-Jsy/47 10.00
21 Sammy Sosa/Bat-Jsy/66 15.00
22 Jeff Bagwell/Bat-Jsy/47 12.00
23 Mark Teixeira/Bat-Jsy/38 10.00
24 Willie Mays/Bat-Jsy/51 50.00
25 Rafael Palmeiro/Bat-Jsy/47 12.00
26 Billy Williams/Bat-Jsy/26 10.00
27 Vladimir Guerrero/Bat-Jsy/44 15.00
28 Gary Carter/Bat-Jsy/31 12.00
29 Fred McGriff/Bat-Jsy/32 15.00
30 Orlando Cepeda/Bat-Pants/34 12.00
31 Dave Winfield/Bat-Jsy/34 15.00
32 Shawn Green/Bat-Jsy/49 10.00
33 Jose Canseco/Hat-Jsy/44 12.00
34 Hideki Matsui/Bat-Pants/31 60.00
35 Roger Maris/Bat-Pants/19 50.00
36 Andre Dawson/Bat-Jsy/49 10.00
38 Darryl Strawberry/Jsy-Pants/24 12.00
39 Dave Parker/Bat-Jsy/34 12.00
40 Adam Dunn/Bat-Jsy/46 15.00
42 Miguel Tejada/Bat-Jsy/34 15.00
43 Dale Murphy/Jsy-Jsy/44 15.00
44 Hank Aaron/Bat-Jsy/47 50.00
45 Mike Piazza/Jsy-Jsy/40 15.00
46 Reggie Jackson/Bat-Jsy/39 15.00
47 Adrian Beltre/Bat-Jsy/48 12.00
48 Cal Ripken Jr./Bat-Jsy/34 60.00
49 Manny Ramirez/Jsy-Jsy/43 15.00

Home Run Heroes Signature

No Pricing
Production 1-10

Home Run Heroes Signature Materials

No Pricing
Production 1-10

Legendary Lumberjacks

NM/M
Common Player: 2.00
Production 400 Sets
Gold: 2-4X
Production 50 Sets
Platinum: No Pricing
Production One Set
1 Al Kaline 4.00
2 Babe Ruth 8.00
3 Billy Williams 2.00
4 Bob Feller 3.00
5 Bob Gibson 3.00
6 Brooks Robinson 4.00
7 Cal Ripken Jr. 10.00
8 Carlton Fisk 3.00
9 Dennis Eckersley 2.00
10 Don Mattingly 6.00
11 Duke Snider 3.00
12 Eddie Murray 3.00
13 Ernie Banks 4.00
14 Fergie Jenkins 2.00
15 Frank Robinson 4.00
16 Gaylord Perry 2.00
17 George Brett 6.00
18 George Kell 2.00
19 Harmon Killebrew 4.00
20 Jim Palmer 2.00
21 Joe Morgan 2.00
22 Johnny Bench 5.00
23 Juan Marichal 2.00
24 Lou Brock 3.00
25 Maury Wills 2.00
26 Mike Schmidt 6.00
27 Nolan Ryan 8.00
28 Ozzie Smith 4.00
29 Paul Molitor 3.00
30 Pee Wee Reese 2.00
31 Phil Niekro 2.00
32 Phil Rizzuto 3.00
33 Ralph Kiner 2.00
34 Reggie Jackson 3.00
35 Rickey Henderson 3.00
36 Roberto Clemente 8.00
37 Robin Yount 4.00
38 Rod Carew 2.00
39 Roger Maris 5.00
40 Stan Musial 5.00
41 Steve Carlton 2.00
42 Ted Williams 8.00
43 Tom Seaver 3.00
44 Tony Gwynn 3.00
45 Tony Perez 2.00
46 Wade Boggs 3.00
47 Warren Spahn 4.00
48 Whitey Ford 4.00
49 Willie McCovey 3.00
50 Yogi Berra 4.00

Legendary Lumberjacks Bat

NM/M
Production 1-50
2 Babe Ruth/25 200.00
6 Brooks Robinson/50 15.00
7 Cal Ripken Jr./50 50.00
8 Carlton Fisk/50 10.00
10 Don Mattingly/50 25.00
12 Eddie Murray/50 15.00
13 Ernie Banks/50 15.00
15 Frank Robinson/50 15.00
17 George Brett/50 20.00
19 Harmon Killebrew/50 15.00
21 Joe Morgan/50 10.00
22 Johnny Bench/50 15.00
24 Lou Brock/50 10.00
26 Mike Schmidt/50 20.00
28 Ozzie Smith/50 15.00
29 Paul Molitor/50 12.00
30 Pee Wee Reese/50 10.00
34 Reggie Jackson/50 12.00
35 Rickey Henderson/50 12.00
36 Roberto Clemente/50 50.00
37 Robin Yount/50 15.00
38 Rod Carew/50 10.00
39 Roger Maris/25 40.00
40 Stan Musial/25 25.00
42 Ted Williams/25 60.00
44 Tony Gwynn/50 15.00
46 Wade Boggs/50 12.00
49 Willie McCovey/50 12.00
50 Yogi Berra/25 25.00

Legendary Lumberjacks Jersey

NM/M
Production 1-50
3 Billy Williams/25 12.00
6 Brooks Robinson/25 20.00
7 Cal Ripken Jr./50 50.00
8 Carlton Fisk/25 15.00
10 Don Mattingly/50 25.00
12 Eddie Murray/50 15.00
13 Ernie Banks/25 20.00
19 Harmon Killebrew/25 20.00
22 Johnny Bench/25 20.00
24 Lou Brock/25 12.00
25 Maury Wills/25 12.00
26 Mike Schmidt/25 25.00
28 Ozzie Smith/25 20.00
29 Paul Molitor/50 12.00
34 Reggie Jackson/25 15.00
35 Rickey Henderson/50 12.00
37 Robin Yount/50 15.00
38 Rod Carew/50 10.00

Legendary Lumberjacks Jersey HR

NM/M
Production 1-25
6 Brooks Robinson/25 20.00
7 Cal Ripken Jr./25 60.00
10 Don Mattingly/25 30.00
12 Eddie Murray/25 20.00
29 Paul Molitor/25 20.00
35 Rickey Henderson/25 20.00
37 Robin Yount/25 20.00
38 Rod Carew/25 15.00
44 Tony Gwynn/25 20.00
45 Tony Perez/25 15.00
46 Wade Boggs/25 15.00
49 Willie McCovey/25 15.00

Legendary Lumberjacks Materials

NM/M
Production 1-50
2 Babe Ruth/Bat-Jsy/25 300.00
6 Brooks Robinson/Bat-Jsy/50 20.00
7 Cal Ripken Jr./Bat-Jsy/50 60.00
8 Carlton Fisk/Bat-Jsy/25 15.00
10 Don Mattingly/Bat-Jsy/50 30.00
12 Eddie Murray/Bat-Jsy/50 20.00
13 Ernie Banks/Bat-Jsy/25 25.00
19 Harmon Killebrew/Bat-Jsy/25 20.00
22 Johnny Bench/Bat-Jsy/25 20.00
24 Lou Brock/Bat-Jsy/50 12.00
26 Mike Schmidt/Bat-Jsy/50 25.00
29 Paul Molitor/Bat-Jsy/50 15.00
34 Reggie Jackson/Bat-Jsy/25 20.00
35 Rickey Henderson/Bat-Jsy/50 15.00
37 Robin Yount/Bat-Jsy/50 20.00
38 Rod Carew/Bat-Jsy/50 15.00
44 Tony Gwynn/Bat-Jsy/50 20.00
46 Wade Boggs/Bat-Jsy/50 15.00
49 Willie McCovey/Bat-Jsy/44 15.00

Legendary Players

NM/M
Common Player: 1.50
Production 800 Sets
Gold: 2-3X
Production 75 Sets
Platinum: No Pricing
Production One Set
1 Al Kaline 3.00
2 Babe Ruth 6.00
3 Billy Williams 1.50
4 Bob Feller 2.00
5 Bob Gibson 2.00
6 Brooks Robinson 3.00
7 Cal Ripken Jr. 8.00
8 Carlton Fisk 2.00
9 Dennis Eckersley 2.00
10 Don Mattingly 5.00
11 Duke Snider 2.00
12 Eddie Murray 2.00
13 Ernie Banks 3.00
14 Fergie Jenkins 1.50
15 Frank Robinson 3.00
16 Gaylord Perry 1.50
17 George Brett 5.00
18 George Kell 1.50
19 Harmon Killebrew 3.00
20 Jim Palmer 1.50
21 Joe Morgan 1.50
22 Johnny Bench 4.00
23 Juan Marichal 1.50
24 Lou Brock 2.00
25 Maury Wills 1.50
26 Mike Schmidt 5.00
27 Nolan Ryan 6.00
28 Ozzie Smith 3.00
29 Paul Molitor 2.00
30 Pee Wee Reese 1.50
31 Phil Niekro 1.50
32 Phil Rizzuto 2.00
33 Ralph Kiner 1.50
34 Reggie Jackson 2.00
35 Rickey Henderson 2.00
36 Roberto Clemente 6.00
37 Robin Yount 3.00
38 Rod Carew 2.00
39 Roger Maris 4.00
40 Stan Musial 4.00
41 Steve Carlton 1.50
42 Ted Williams 6.00
43 Tom Seaver 2.00
44 Tony Gwynn 2.00
45 Tony Perez 1.50
46 Wade Boggs 2.00
47 Warren Spahn 3.00
48 Whitey Ford 3.00
49 Willie McCovey 2.00
50 Yogi Berra 3.00

Legendary Players Hat

NM/M
Production 1-25
10 Don Mattingly/25 30.00
13 Ernie Banks/25 20.00
17 George Brett/25 30.00
20 Jim Palmer/25 10.00
26 Mike Schmidt/25 30.00
28 Ozzie Smith/25 25.00
37 Robin Yount/25 25.00
44 Tony Gwynn/25 20.00

Legendary Players Jacket

NM/M
Production 25 Sets
7 Cal Ripken Jr. 60.00
8 Carlton Fisk 12.00
10 Don Mattingly 40.00
24 Lou Brock 15.00
26 Mike Schmidt 35.00
27 Nolan Ryan 50.00
34 Reggie Jackson 15.00
35 Rickey Henderson 20.00
38 Rod Carew 20.00
42 Ted Williams 85.00

Legendary Players Jersey Number

NM/M
Production 1-44
Prime: No Pricing
Production One Set
3 Billy Williams/26 10.00
8 Carlton Fisk/72 10.00
9 Dennis Eckersley/43 10.00
10 Don Mattingly/23 30.00
12 Eddie Murray/33 15.00
16 Gaylord Perry/36 8.00
20 Jim Palmer/22 10.00
23 Juan Marichal/27 10.00
24 Lou Brock/20 15.00
25 Maury Wills/30 8.00
26 Mike Schmidt/20 30.00
27 Nolan Ryan/34 40.00
31 Phil Niekro/35 8.00
35 Rickey Henderson/24 15.00
37 Robin Yount/19 25.00
38 Rod Carew/29 15.00
41 Steve Carlton/32 10.00
43 Tom Seaver/41 15.00
44 Tony Gwynn/19 20.00
45 Tony Perez/24 10.00
46 Wade Boggs/26 15.00
47 Warren Spahn/24 20.00
49 Willie McCovey/44 12.00

Legendary Players Leather

NM/M
Production 10-25
10 Don Mattingly/Btg Glv/25 40.00
14 Fergie Jenkins/Fld Glv/25 15.00
26 Mike Schmidt/Fld Glv/25 40.00
35 Rickey Henderson/Btg Glv/25 25.00
41 Steve Carlton/Fld Glv/25 15.00
44 Tony Gwynn/Btg Glv/25 30.00
45 Tony Perez/Fld Glv/25 15.00

Legendary Players Pants

NM/M
Production 1-25
4 Bob Feller/19 20.00
7 Cal Ripken Jr./25 60.00
11 Duke Snider/25 20.00
12 Eddie Murray/25 20.00
14 Fergie Jenkins/25 10.00
20 Jim Palmer/25 10.00
23 Juan Marichal/25 10.00
28 Ozzie Smith/25 25.00
29 Paul Molitor/25 15.00
35 Rickey Henderson/25 20.00
38 Rod Carew/25 15.00
39 Roger Maris/25 50.00
43 Tom Seaver/25 15.00
44 Tony Gwynn/25 20.00
47 Warren Spahn/24 20.00
49 Willie McCovey/25 15.00

Legendary Players Signature

No Pricing
Production 1-10

Legendary Players Spikes

NM/M
Production 1-25
15 Frank Robinson/25 20.00
44 Tony Gwynn/25 30.00

Membership

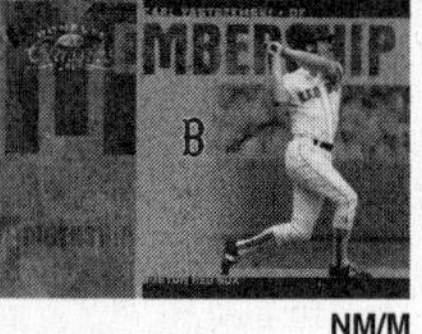

NM/M
Common Player: 1.50
Production 1,000 Sets
Gold: 2-4X
Production 50 Sets
Platinum: No Pricing
Production One Set
1 Bobby Doerr 1.50
2 Tom Seaver 2.00
3 Cal Ripken Jr. 8.00
4 Paul Molitor 2.00
5 Brooks Robinson 2.00
6 Al Kaline 4.00
7 Steve Carlton 2.00
8 Carl Yastrzemski 4.00
9 Bob Feller 2.00
10 Fred Lynn 1.50
11 Luis Aparicio 1.50
12 Hank Aaron 6.00
13 Willie Mays 6.00
14 Bob Gibson 3.00
15 Joe Morgan 2.00
16 Whitey Ford 3.00
17 Don Sutton 1.50
18 Harmon Killebrew 3.00
19 Tony Gwynn 3.00
20 Lou Brock 1.50
21 Dennis Eckersley 1.50
22 Jim Palmer 1.50
23 Don Mattingly 5.00
24 Carlton Fick 2.00
25 Gaylord Perry 1.50
26 Mike Schmidt 5.00
27 Nolan Ryan 6.00
28 Sandy Koufax 10.00
29 Rod Carew 2.00
30 Maury Wills 1.50

Membership VIP Bat

NM/M
Production 25 Sets
1 Bobby Doerr 10.00
2 Tom Seaver 20.00
3 Cal Ripken Jr. 60.00
4 Paul Molitor 15.00
5 Brooks Robinson 15.00
6 Al Kaline 20.00
7 Steve Carlton 10.00
8 Carl Yastrzemski 20.00
10 Fred Lynn 8.00
11 Luis Aparicio 8.00
12 Hank Aaron 40.00
13 Willie Mays 50.00
15 Joe Morgan 10.00
18 Harmon Killebrew 20.00
19 Tony Gwynn 20.00
20 Lou Brock 15.00
23 Don Mattingly 30.00
24 Carlton Fisk 15.00
29 Rod Carew 12.00

Membership VIP Jersey

NM/M
Production 5-50
Prime: No Pricing
Production One Set
7 Steve Carlton/25 10.00
10 Fred Lynn/25 10.00
11 Luis Aparicio/25 10.00
15 Joe Morgan/25 10.00
17 Don Sutton/25 8.00
19 Tony Gwynn/50 15.00
20 Lou Brock/25 15.00
21 Dennis Eckersley/50 8.00
22 Jim Palmer/25 10.00
23 Don Mattingly/25 30.00
24 Carlton Fisk/25 15.00
25 Gaylord Perry/50 8.00
26 Mike Schmidt/50 20.00
27 Nolan Ryan/25 40.00
29 Rod Carew/50 10.00

Membership VIP Materials

NM/M
Production 5-25
Prime: No Pricing
Production One Set
1 Bobby Doerr/Bat-Pants/25 10.00
2 Tom Seaver/Bat-Jsy/25 20.00

3 Cal Ripken Jr./ Bat-Jsy/25 75.00
4 Paul Molitor/ Bat-Jsy/25 20.00
5 Brooks Robinson/ Bat-Jsy/25 25.00
7 Steve Carlton/ Bat-Jsy/25 15.00
10 Fred Lynn/Bat-Jsy/25 10.00
11 Luis Aparicio/ Bat-Jsy/25 10.00
15 Joe Morgan/ Bat-Jsy/25 12.00
18 Harmon Killebrew/ Bat-Jsy/25 25.00
19 Tony Gwynn/ Bat-Jsy/25 25.00
20 Lou Brock/ Bat-Jsy/25 25.00
23 Don Mattingly/ Bat-Jsy/25 35.00
27 Nolan Ryan/ Bat-Jsy/25 50.00
29 Rod Carew/ Bat-Jsy/25 20.00

Membership VIP Materials Awards

No Pricing
Production 5-10

Membership VIP Materials HOF

No Pricing
Production 10 Sets

Membership VIP Materials HR

NM/M
Production 6-49
1 Bobby Doerr/ Jsy-Pants/27 15.00
3 Cal Ripken Jr./ Jsy-Pants/34 60.00
4 Paul Molitor/ Bat-Jsy/22 15.00
8 Carl Yastrzemski/ Bat-Jsy/44 25.00
10 Fred Lynn/Bat-Jsy/39 8.00
12 Hank Aaron/ Bat-Jsy/47 50.00
15 Joe Morgan/ Bat-Jsy/27 12.00
18 Harmon Killebrew/ Bat-Jsy/49 20.00
20 Lou Brock/Bat-Jsy/21 15.00
23 Don Mattingly/ Bat-Jsy/35 40.00
24 Carlton Fisk/ Bat-Jsy/37 15.00
26 Mike Schmidt/ Bat-Jsy/48 25.00

Membership VIP Materials Stats

No Pricing
Production 10 Sets

Membership VIP Signature

No Pricing
Production 1-5

Membership VIP Signature Bat

No Pricing
Production 1-10

Membership VIP Signature Jersey

No Pricing
Production 1-10

Membership VIP Signature Material

NM/M
Production 1-25
Prime: No Pricing
Production One Set
1 Bobby Doerr/ Bat-Pants/25 35.00
10 Fred Lynn/ Bat-Jsy/25 30.00
11 Luis Aparicio/ Bat-Jsy/25 30.00
20 Lou Brock/ Bat-Jsy/25 50.00

Membership VIP Signature Material Awards

No Pricing
Production 1-10

Membership VIP Signature Materials HOF

No Pricing
Production 1-10

Membership VIP Signature Materials HR

No Pricing
Production 1-10

Membership VIP Signature Material Stats

No Pricing
Production 5-10

Significant Signatures Silver

NM/M
Production 1-200
Gold: .75-1.5X
Production 1-100
No pricing 20 or less.
Platinum: No Pricing
Production One Set
17 Jay Gibbons/25 15.00
22 Tim Salmon/100 15.00
26 Kevin Youkilis/25 12.00
29 Cliff Lee/200 8.00
37 Jeff Suppan/200 10.00
39 Larry Bigbie/100 15.00
40 Rich Harden/100 15.00
41 Victor Martinez/25 20.00
43 Joey Gathright/100 8.00
61 Jake Peavy/25 40.00
63 Dioner Navarro/100 15.00
64 Kazuhito Tadano/100 15.00
65 Ryan Wagner/50 10.00
66 Abe Alvarez/100 15.00
68 Jermaine Dye/25 15.00
69 Todd Walker/25 15.00
70 Octavio Dotel/25 15.00
73 Scott Podsednik/25 20.00
76 Raul Ibanez/50 10.00
77 Orlando Cabrera/25 20.00
79 Esteban Loaiza/50 15.00
84 David Dellucci/50 20.00
85 Travis Blackley/200 8.00
86 Brad Penny/25 15.00
88 Brian Roberts/100 35.00
90 Mike Lieberthal/25 15.00
94 Milton Bradley/100 15.00
96 Adrian Gonzalez/200 12.00
97 Chad Tracy/100 10.00
98 Chad Cordero/100 8.00
100 Jason Kubel/200 12.00
102 Jack Wilson/100 10.00
104 Casey Kotchman/100 12.00
106 Melvin Mora/100 15.00
107 Bobby Crosby/100 15.00
111 Francisco Cordero/50 15.00
114 Eric Byrnes/50 10.00
118 Shea Hillenbrand/25 15.00
119 Aubrey Huff/25 20.00
120 Lew Ford/25 20.00
126 Adam LaRoche/25 15.00
128 Ken Harvey/50 10.00
132 Russ Ortiz/25 15.00
133 Jason Varitek 10.00
136 Joe Nathan/100 20.00
138 Carlos Zambrano/25 35.00
143 John Lackey/200 10.00
145 Dewon Brazelton/200 10.00
146 Jason Bay/25 25.00
148 Travis Hafner/100 12.00
152 Wade Miller/50 12.00
154 Scott Kazmir/25 35.00
156 Livan Hernandez/25 15.00
158 David Wright/25 85.00
159 Chone Figgins/50 12.00
163 Merkin Valdez/200 10.00
165 Alexis Rios/50 15.00
166 Johnny Estrada/200 10.00
167 Danny Graves/50 15.00
168 Carlos Lee/25 25.00
171 Randy Wolf/25 15.00
175 Edwin Jackson/25 12.00
178 Jacque Jones/25 15.00
180 Laynce Nix/200 10.00
181 Tom Gordon/25 15.00
182 Jose Castillo/100 12.00
188 Keith Foulke/25 60.00
189 Jeremy Bonderman/50 20.00
190 Troy Percival/25 15.00
194 Brett Myers/50 15.00
197 Lyle Overbay/25 20.00
202 Miguel Negron/100 8.00
204 Paulino Reynoso/100 8.00
205 Colter Bean/100 10.00
206 Raul Tablado/100 8.00
207 Mark McLemore/100 8.00
208 Russel Rohlicek/100 8.00
210 Chris Seddon/100 8.00
213 Mike Morse/100 20.00
217 Carlos Ruiz/100 15.00
218 Chris Roberson/100 8.00
219 Ryan Speier/100 8.00
221 Ambiorix Burgos/100 8.00
223 David Gassner/100 10.00
224 Sean Tracey/100 8.00
225 Casey Rogowski/100 8.00
236 Gaylord Perry/ LGD/25 25.00
245 Bobby Doerr/LGD/25 25.00
246 Bob Feller/LGD/25 30.00

Stars of Summer

NM/M
Common Player: 1.50
Production 1,000 Sets
Gold: 2-4X
Production 50 Sets
Platinum: No Pricing
Production One Set
1 Andre Dawson 2.00
2 Bert Blyleven 2.00
3 Bill Madlock 1.50
4 Dale Murphy 3.00
5 Darryl Strawberry 2.00
6 Dave Parker 2.00
7 Dave Righetti 2.00
8 Dwight Evans 2.00
9 Dwight Gooden 2.00
10 Fred Lynn 1.50
11 George Foster 2.00
12 Harold Baines 2.00
13 Jack Morris 1.50
14 Jim Rice 3.00
15 Keith Hernandez 2.00
16 Kirk Gibson 2.00
17 Luis Aparicio 2.00
18 Mark Grace 2.00
19 Marty Marion 1.50
20 Orel Hershiser 2.00
21 Ron Guidry 3.00
22 Ron Santo 2.00
23 Steve Garvey 2.00
24 Tony Oliva 2.00
25 Will Clark 3.00

Stars of Summer Material

NM/M
Production 100-250
1 Andre Dawson/ Jsy/250 8.00
2 Bert Blyleven/Jsy/150 8.00
3 Bill Madlock/Bat/250 5.00
4 Dale Murphy/Jsy/100 12.00
5 Darryl Strawberry/ Jsy/250 8.00
6 Dave Parker/Jsy/100 10.00
7 Dave Righetti/Jsy/150 8.00
8 Dwight Evans/Bat/250 8.00
9 Dwight Gooden/ Bat/150 8.00
10 Fred Lynn/Jsy/100 5.00
11 George Foster/Bat/250 5.00
12 Harold Baines/Jsy/250 5.00
13 Jack Morris/Jsy/100 5.00
14 Jim Rice/Pants/250 8.00
15 Keith Hernandez/ Bat/100 5.00
16 Kirk Gibson/Jsy/250 8.00
17 Luis Aparicio/Bat/250 8.00
18 Mark Grace/Bat/250 10.00
22 Ron Santo/Bat/150 10.00
23 Steve Garvey/Jsy/250 8.00
24 Tony Oliva/Jsy/250 8.00
25 Will Clark/Bat/250 10.00

Stars of Summer Signature Material

NM/M
Production 25-100
1 Andre Dawson/ Jsy/100 20.00
2 Bert Blyleven/Jsy/50 20.00
3 Bill Madlock/Bat/100 20.00
4 Dale Murphy/Jsy/25 40.00
6 Dave Parker/Jsy/50 20.00
7 Dave Righetti/Jsy/50 20.00
8 Dwight Evans/Jsy/50 30.00
9 Dwight Gooden/ Bat/25 25.00
10 Fred Lynn/Jsy/100 15.00
11 George Foster/ Bat/50 20.00
12 Harold Baines/ Jsy/100 25.00
13 Jack Morris/Jsy/100 15.00
14 Jim Rice/Pants/50 25.00
15 Keith Hernandez/ Jsy/50 20.00
16 Kirk Gibson/Jsy/25 40.00
17 Luis Aparicio/Bat/50 20.00
18 Mark Grace/Bat/25 40.00
22 Ron Santo/Bat/50 35.00
23 Steve Garvey/Jsy/50 20.00
24 Tony Oliva/Jsy/50 20.00
25 Will Clark/Bat/25 40.00

Team Colors

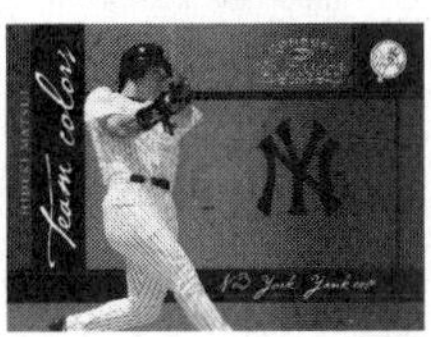

NM/M
Common Player: 1.50
Production 800 Sets
Gold: 2-4X
Production 50 Sets
Platinum: No Pricing
Production One Set
1 Adam Dunn 2.00
2 Albert Pujols 6.00
3 Andruw Jones 2.00
4 Aramis Ramirez 2.00
5 Aubrey Huff 1.50
6 Bobby Abreu 2.00
7 Cal Ripken Jr. 8.00
8 Carlos Lee 1.50
9 Craig Biggio 2.00
10 Derrek Lee 2.00
11 Garret Anderson 2.00
12 Gary Carter 2.00
13 Geoff Jenkins 1.50
14 Greg Maddux 4.00
15 Hank Blalock 2.00
16 Hideki Matsui 5.00
17 Jake Peavy 2.00
18 Jim Edmonds 2.00
19 Jim Palmer 2.00
20 Jose Guillen 1.50
21 Jose Vidro 1.50
22 Juan Pierre 1.50
23 Lew Ford 1.50
24 Lyle Overbay 1.50
25 Manny Ramirez 3.00
26 Mark Loretta 1.50
27 Mark Teixeira 3.00
28 Melvin Mora 1.50
29 Michael Young 2.00
30 Miguel Cabrera 4.00
31 Mike Lowell 1.50
32 Mike Mussina 2.00
33 Milton Bradley 2.00
34 Randy Johnson 4.00
35 Roger Clemens 6.00
36 Sean Casey 2.00
37 Shawn Green 2.00
38 Steve Carlton 2.00
39 Todd Helton 2.00
40 Travis Hafner 1.50

Team Colors Bat

NM/M
Production 100 Sets
1 Adam Dunn 8.00
2 Albert Pujols 20.00
3 Andruw Jones 5.00
4 Aramis Ramirez 8.00
7 Cal Ripken Jr. 30.00
9 Craig Biggio 8.00
10 Derrek Lee 8.00
11 Garret Anderson 5.00
12 Gary Carter 5.00
15 Hank Blalock 8.00
16 Hideki Matsui 30.00
18 Jim Edmonds 10.00
21 Jose Vidro 5.00
22 Juan Pierre 5.00
23 Lew Ford 5.00
27 Mark Teixeira 8.00
28 Melvin Mora 5.00
29 Michael Young 5.00
30 Miguel Cabrera 10.00
31 Mike Lowell 5.00
36 Sean Casey 5.00
37 Shawn Green 5.00

Team Colors Materials

NM/M
Production 25-100
Prime: No Pricing
Production Five Sets
1 Adam Dunn/ Bat-Jsy/100 10.00
2 Albert Pujols/ Bat-Jsy/100 25.00
3 Andruw Jones/ Bat-Jsy/100 8.00
4 Aramis Ramirez/ Bat-Jsy/100 10.00
6 Bobby Abreu/ Jsy-Jsy/100 10.00
7 Cal Ripken Jr./ Bat-Jsy/100 40.00
8 Carlos Lee/ Jsy-Jsy/100 8.00
9 Craig Biggio/ Bat-Jsy/100 10.00
11 Garret Anderson/ Bat-Jsy/50 8.00
12 Gary Carter/ Bat-Jsy/50 8.00
13 Geoff Jenkins/ Jsy-Pants/100 8.00
15 Hank Blalock/ Bat-Jsy/100 10.00
16 Hideki Matsui/ Bat-Jsy/50 45.00
18 Jim Edmonds/ Bat-Jkt/100 12.00
19 Jim Palmer/ Jsy-Pants/25 12.00
21 Jose Vidro/Bat-Jsy/50 8.00
23 Lew Ford/Bat-Jsy/100 8.00
25 Manny Ramirez/ Jsy-Jsy/100 15.00
27 Mark Teixeira/ Bat-Jsy/100 10.00
28 Melvin Mora/ Bat-Jsy/50 8.00
29 Michael Young/ Bat-Jsy/100 8.00
30 Miguel Cabrera/ Bat-Jsy/100 15.00
31 Mike Lowell/ Bat-Jsy/100 8.00
36 Sean Casey/ Bat-Jsy/100 8.00
37 Shawn Green/ Bat-Jsy/100 8.00
39 Todd Helton/ Jsy-Jsy/50 10.00

Team Colors Signature

NM/M
Production 1-25
4 Aramis Ramirez/25 40.00
5 Aubrey Huff/25 20.00
8 Carlos Lee/25 25.00
17 Jake Peavy/25 40.00
20 Jose Guillen/25 25.00
21 Jose Vidro/25 20.00
23 Lew Ford/25 20.00
24 Lyle Overbay/25 25.00
26 Mark Loretta/25 25.00
28 Melvin Mora/25 25.00
33 Milton Bradley/25 25.00
40 Travis Hafner/25 20.00

Team Colors Signature Bat

NM/M
Production 5-25
1 Adam Dunn/25 40.00
4 Aramis Ramirez/25 40.00
5 Aubrey Huff/25 20.00
10 Derrek Lee/25 35.00
11 Garret Anderson/25 25.00
15 Hank Blalock/25 30.00
21 Jose Vidro/25 20.00
23 Lew Ford/25 20.00
29 Michael Young/25 20.00

Team Colors Signature Jersey

NM/M
Production 1-25
Prime: No Pricing
Production One Set
1 Adam Dunn/25 40.00
4 Aramis Ramirez/25 40.00
5 Aubrey Huff/25 20.00
8 Carlos Lee/25 25.00
11 Garret Anderson/25 25.00
12 Gary Carter/25 25.00
15 Hank Blalock/25 30.00
21 Jose Vidro/25 20.00
23 Lew Ford/25 20.00
24 Lyle Overbay/25 25.00
28 Melvin Mora/25 25.00
29 Michael Young/25 20.00
40 Travis Hafner/25 20.00

Team Colors Signature Materials

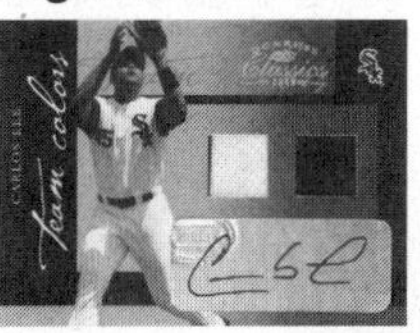

NM/M
Production 5-25
Prime: No Pricing
Production One Set
4 Aramis Ramirez/ Bat-Jsy/25 50.00
5 Aubrey Huff/ Jsy-Jsy/25 25.00
8 Carlos Lee/ Jsy-Jsy/25 30.00
11 Garret Anderson/ Bat-Jsy/25 30.00
15 Hank Blalock/ Bat-Jsy/25 40.00
21 Jose Vidro/ Bat-Jsy/25 25.00
23 Lew Ford/Bat-Jsy/25 25.00
28 Melvin Mora/ Bat-Jsy/25 30.00
29 Michael Young/ Bat-Jsy/25 30.00
40 Travis Hafner/ Jsy-Jsy/25 25.00

Texas Rangers Hall of Fame

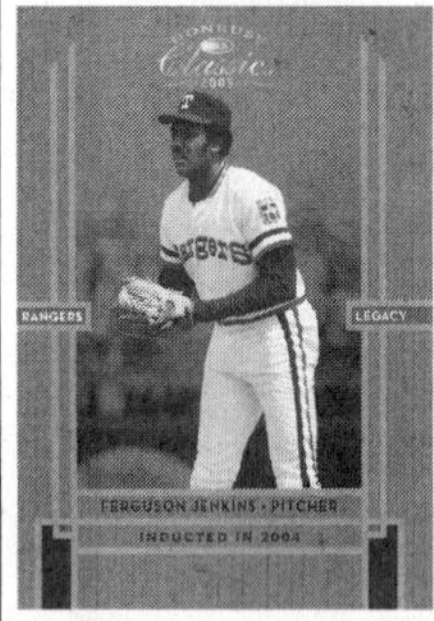

This cello-wrapped set was a stadium giveaway.

NM/M
Complete Set (9): 7.00
Common Player: .25
(1) Buddy Bell .50
(2) Mark Holtz (Broadcaster) .25
(3) Charlie Hough .50
(4) Ferguson Jenkins .50
(5) Johnny Oates .50
(6) Nolan Ryan 5.00
(7) Jim Sundberg .50
(8) Tom Vandergriff (Broadcaster) .25
(9) John Wetteland .50

2005 Donruss Diamond Kings

NM/M
Complete Set (300): 85.00
Complete Update Set (150): 40.00
Common Player: .25
Pack (5): 8.00
Box (12): 75.00
Update Pack (5): 5.00
Update Box (16): 75.00
1 Garret Anderson .40
2 Vladimir Guerrero .75
3 Jose Guillen .40
4 Troy Glaus .40
5 Tim Salmon .25
6 Casey Kotchman .25
7 Chone Figgins .25
8 Robb Quinlan .25
9 Francisco Rodriguez .25
10 Troy Percival .25
11 Randy Johnson .75
12 Brandon Webb .25
13 Richie Sexson .40
14 Shea Hillenbrand .25
15 Chad Tracy .25
16 Alex Cintron .25
17 Luis Gonzalez .25
18 Rafael Furcal .25
19 Andruw Jones .50
20 Marcus Giles .25
21 John Smoltz .50
22 Adam LaRoche .25
23 Russ Ortiz .25

No.	Player	Price
24	J.D. Drew	.25
25	Chipper Jones	.75
26	Nick Green	.25
27	Rafael Palmeiro	.50
28	Miguel Tejada	.50
29	Javy Lopez	.25
30	Luis Matos	.25
31	Larry Bigbie	.25
32	Rodrigo Lopez	.25
33	Brian Roberts	.25
34	Melvin Mora	.25
35	Adam Loewen	.25
36	Manny Ramirez	.75
37	Jason Varitek	.50
38	Trot Nixon	.25
39	Curt Schilling	.75
40	Keith Foulke	.25
41	Pedro Martinez	.75
42	Johnny Damon	.75
43	Kevin Youkilis	.25
44	Orlando Cabrera	.25
45	Abe Alvarez	.25
46	David Ortiz	.75
47	Kerry Wood	.75
48	Mark Prior	.75
49	Aramis Ramirez	.50
50	Greg Maddux	1.00
51	Carlos Zambrano	.40
52	Derrek Lee	.50
53	Corey Patterson	.40
54	Moises Alou	.40
55	Matt Clement	.25
56	Sammy Sosa	1.50
57	Nomar Garciaparra	1.00
58	Todd Walker	.25
59	Angel Guzman	.25
60	Magglio Ordonez	.25
61	Carlos Lee	.25
62	Joe Crede	.25
63	Paul Konerko	.25
64	Shingo Takatsu	.25
65	Frank Thomas	.50
66	Freddy Garcia	.25
67	Aaron Rowand	.25
68	Jose Contreras	.25
69	Adam Dunn	.50
70	Austin Kearns	.25
71	Barry Larkin	.40
72	Ken Griffey Jr.	1.00
73	Ryan Wagner	.25
74	Sean Casey	.25
75	Danny Graves	.25
76	C.C. Sabathia	.25
77	Jody Gerut	.25
78	Omar Vizquel	.25
79	Victor Martinez	.40
80	Matt Lawton	.25
81	Jake Westbrook	.25
82	Kazuhito Tadano	.25
83	Travis Hafner	.25
84	Todd Helton	.50
85	Preston Wilson	.25
86	Matt Holiday	.25
87	Jeromy Burnitz	.25
88	Vinny Castilla	.25
89	Jeremy Bonderman	.25
90	Ivan Rodriguez	.50
91	Carlos Guillen	.25
92	Brandon Inge	.25
93	Rondell White	.25
94	Dontrelle Willis	.25
95	Miguel Cabrera	.75
96	Josh Beckett	.40
97	Mike Lowell	.25
98	Luis Castillo	.25
99	Juan Pierre	.25
100	Paul LoDuca	.25
101	Guillermo Mota	.25
102	Craig Biggio	.25
103	Lance Berkman	.25
104	Roy Oswalt	.25
105	Roger Clemens	2.00
106	Jeff Kent	.25
107	Morgan Ensberg	.25
108	Jeff Bagwell	.50
109	Carlos Beltran	.50
110	Angel Berroa	.25
111	Mike Sweeney	.25
112	Jeremy Affeldt	.25
113	Zack Greinke	.25
114	Juan Gonzalez	.25
115	Andres Blanco	.25
116	Shawn Green	.25
117	Milton Bradley	.25
118	Adrian Beltre	.50
119	Hideo Nomo	.50
120	Steve Finley	.25
121	Eric Gagne	.25
122	Brad Penny	.25
123	Scott Podsednik	.25
124	Ben Sheets	.40
125	Lyle Overbay	.25
126	Junior Spivey	.25
127	Bill Hall	.25
128	Rickie Weeks	.25
129	Jacque Jones	.25
130	Torii Hunter	.40
131	Johan Santana	.50
132	Lew Ford	.25
133	Joe Mauer	.75
134	Justin Morneau	.50
135	Jason Kubel	.25
136	Jose Vidro	.25
137	Chad Cordero	.25
138	Brad Wilkerson	.25
139	Nick Johnson	.25
140	Livan Hernandez	.25
141	Tom Glavine	.40
142	Jae Weong Seo	.25
143	Jose Reyes	.50
144	Al Leiter	.25
145	Mike Piazza	1.00
146	Kazuo Matsui	.25
147	Richard Hidalgo	.25
148	David Wright	.75
149	Mariano Rivera	.50
150	Mike Mussina	.50
151	Alex Rodriguez	1.50
152	Derek Jeter	2.00
153	Jorge Posada	.50
154	Jason Giambi	.25
155	Gary Sheffield	.50
156	Bubba Crosby	.25
157	Javier Vazquez	.25
158	Kevin Brown	.25
159	Tom Gordon	.25
160	Esteban Loaiza	.25
161	Hideki Matsui	1.50
162	Eric Chavez	.40
163	Mark Mulder	.40
164	Barry Zito	.40
165	Tim Hudson	.40
166	Jermaine Dye	.25
167	Octavio Dotel	.25
168	Bobby Crosby	.25
169	Mark Kotsay	.25
170	Scott Hatteberg	.25
171	Jim Thome	.75
172	Bobby Abreu	.40
173	Kevin Millwood	.25
174	Mike Lieberthal	.25
175	Jimmy Rollins	.50
176	Chase Utley	.50
177	Randy Wolf	.25
178	Craig Wilson	.25
179	Jason Kendall	.25
180	Jack Wilson	.25
181	Jose Castillo	.25
182	Robert Mackowiak	.25
183	Oliver Perez	.25
184	Oliver Perez	.25
185	Sean Burroughs	.25
186	Jay Payton	.25
187	Brian Giles	.25
188	Akinori Otsuka	.25
189	Jake Peavy	.25
190	Phil Nevin	.25
191	Mark Loretta	.25
192	Khalil Greene	.40
193	Trevor Hoffman	.25
194	Freddy Guzman	.25
195	Jerome Williams	.25
196	Jason Schmidt	.40
197	Todd Linden	.25
198	Merkin Valdez	.25
199	J.T. Snow	.25
200	A.J. Pierzynski	.25
201	Edgar Martinez	.40
202	Ichiro Suzuki	1.50
203	Raul Ibanez	.25
204	Bret Boone	.25
205	Shigetoshi Hasegawa	.25
206	Miguel Olivo	.25
207	Bucky Jacobsen	.25
208	Jamie Moyer	.25
209	Jim Edmonds	.50
210	Scott Rolen	.75
211	Edgar Renteria	.50
212	Dan Haren	.25
213	Matt Morris	.25
214	Albert Pujols	2.00
215	Larry Walker	.40
216	Jason Isringhausen	.25
217	Chris Carpenter	.25
218	Jason Marquis	.25
219	Jeff Suppan	.25
220	Aubrey Huff	.25
221	Carl Crawford	.25
222	Rocco Baldelli	.25
223	Fred McGriff	.25
224	Dewon Brazelton	.25
225	B.J. Upton	.40
226	Joey Gathright	.25
227	Scott Kazmir	.40
228	Hank Blalock	.50
229	Mark Teixeira	.50
230	Michael Young	.25
231	Adrian Gonzalez	.25
232	Laynce Nix	.25
233	Alfonso Soriano	.75
234	Rafael Palmeiro	.50
235	Kevin Mench	.25
236	David Dellucci	.25
237	Francisco Cordero	.25
238	Kenny Rogers	.25
239	Roy Halladay	.25
240	Carlos Delgado	.40
241	Alexis Rios	.25
242	Vernon Wells	.25
243	Yadier Molina	.25
244	Rene Rivera	.25
245	Logan Kensing	.25
246	Gavin Floyd	.25
247	Russ Adams	.25
248	Dioner Navarro	.25
249	Ryan Howard	1.00
250	Ryan Church	.25
251	Jeff Francis	.25
252	John Van Benschoten	.25
253	Yhency Brazoban	.25
254	David Krynzel	.25
255	Victor Diaz	.25
256	Jairo Garcia	.25
257	Scott Proctor	.25
258	Shawn Hill	.25
259	Jeff Baker	.25
260	Matt Peterson	.25
261	Josh Kroeger	.25
262	Grady Sizemore	.40
263	Clint Nageotte	.25
264	Andy Green	.25
265	Justin Verlander **RC**	2.00
266	Jim Thome	.75
267	Larry Walker	.40
268	Ivan Rodriguez	.50
269	Brad Penny	.25
270	Carlos Beltran	.50
271	Paul LoDuca	.25
272	Orlando Cabrera	.25
273	Nomar Garciaparra	1.00
274	Esteban Loaiza	.25
275	Richard Hidalgo	.25
276	John Olerud	.25
277	Greg Maddux	1.00
278	Roger Clemens	2.00
279	Alfonso Soriano	.75
280	Dale Murphy	.50
281	Cal Ripken Jr.	4.00
282	Dwight Evans	.25
283	Ron Santo	.25
284	Andre Dawson	.50
285	Harold Baines	.25
286	Jack Morris	.25
287	Kirk Gibson	.25
288	Bo Jackson	.75
289	Orel Hershiser	.25
290	Maury Wills	.25
291	Tony Oliva	.25
292	Darryl Strawberry	.25
293	Roger Maris	1.00
294	Don Mattingly	2.00
295	Rickey Henderson	.50
296	Dave Stewart	.25
297	Dave Parker	.25
298	Steve Garvey	.25
299	Matt Williams	.25
300	Keith Hernandez	.25
301	John Lackey	.25
302	Vladimir Guerrero	.75
303	Garret Anderson	.25
304	Dallas McPherson	.25
305	Orlando Cabrera	.25
306	Steve Finley	.25
307	Luis Gonzalez	.25
308	Randy Johnson	.75
309	Scott Hairston	.25
310	Shawn Green	.25
311	Troy Glaus	.40
312	Javier Vazquez	.25
313	Russ Ortiz	.25
314	Chipper Jones	.75
315	Johnny Estrada	.25
316	Andruw Jones	.50
317	Tim Hudson	.50
318	Danny Kolb	.25
319	Jay Gibbons	.25
320	Melvin Mora	.25
321	Rafael Palmeiro	.50
322	Val Majewski	.25
323	David Ortiz	.75
324	Manny Ramirez	.75
325	Edgar Renteria	.25
326	Matt Clement	.25
327	Curt Schilling	.75
328	Sammy Sosa	1.00
329	Mark Prior	.75
330	Greg Maddux	1.00
331	Nomar Garciaparra	1.00
332	Frank Thomas	.50
333	Mark Buehrle	.25
334	Jermaine Dye	.25
335	Scott Podsednik	.25
336	Sean Casey	.25
337	Adam Dunn	.50
338	Ken Griffey Jr.	1.00
339	Travis Hafner	.25
340	Victor Martinez	.25
341	Cliff Lee	.25
342	Todd Helton	.50
343	Preston Wilson	.25
344	Ivan Rodriguez	.50
345	Dmitri Young	.25
346	Nate Robertson	.25
347	Miguel Cabrera	.75
348	Jeff Bagwell	.40
349	Andy Pettitte	.40
350	Roger Clemens	2.00
351	Ken Harvey	.25
352	Danny Bautista	.25
353	Hideo Nomo	.50
354	Kazuhisa Ishii	.25
355	Edwin Jackson	.25
356	J.D. Drew	.25
357	Jeff Kent	.25
358	Geoff Jenkins	.25
359	Carlos Lee	.25
360	Shannon Stewart	.25
361	Joe Nathan	.25
362	Johan Santana	.50
363	Mike Piazza	1.00
364	Hideki Matsui	1.50
365	Carlos Beltran	.50
366	Pedro Martinez	.75
367	Ambiorix Concepcion **RC**	.40
368	Hideki Matsui	1.50
369	Bernie Williams	.40
370	Gary Sheffield	.50
371	Randy Johnson	.75
372	Jaret Wright	.25
373	Carl Pavano	.25
374	Derek Jeter	2.00
375	Alex Rodriguez	1.50
376	Eric Byrnes	.25
377	Rich Harden	.25
378	Mark Mulder	.40
379	Nick Swisher	.25
380	Eric Chavez	.25
381	Jason Kendall	.25
382	Marlon Byrd	.25
383	Pat Burrell	.25
384	Brett Myers	.25
385	Jim Thome	.50
386	Jason Bay	.25
387	Jake Peavy	.25
388	Moises Alou	.25
389	Omar Vizquel	.25
390	Travis Blackley	.25
391	Jose Lopez	.25
392	Jeremy Reed	.25
393	Adrian Beltre	.25
394	Richie Sexson	.25
395	Wladimir Balentien **RC**	1.50
396	Ichiro Suzuki	1.50
397	Albert Pujols	2.00
398	Scott Rolen	.75
399	Mark Mulder	.40
400	David Eckstein	.25
401	Delmon Young	.25
402	Aubrey Huff	.25
403	Alfonso Soriano	.50
404	Hank Blalock	.25
405	Richard Hidalgo	.25
406	Vernon Wells	.25
407	Orlando Hudson	.25
408	Alexis Rios	.25
409	Shea Hillenbrand	.25
410	Jose Guillen	.25
411	Vinny Castilla	.25
412	Jose Vidro	.25
413	Nick Johnson	.25
414	Livan Hernandez	.25
415	Miguel Tejada	.50
416	Gary Sheffield	.50
417	Curt Schilling	.75
418	Rafael Palmeiro	.50
419	Scott Rolen	.75
420	Aramis Ramirez	.40
421	Vladimir Guerrero	.75
422	Steve Finley	.25
423	Roger Clemens	2.00
424	Mike Piazza	1.00
425	Ivan Rodriguez	.50
426	David Justice	.25
427	Mark Grace	.40
428	Alan Trammell	.25
429	Bert Blyleven	.25
430	Dwight Gooden	.25
431	Deion Sanders	.25
432	Joe Torre	.25
433	Jose Canseco	.40
434	Tony Gwynn	.75
435	Will Clark	.40
436	Marty Marion	.25
437	Nolan Ryan	3.00
438	Billy Martin	.25
439	Carlos Delgado	.25
440	Magglio Ordonez	.25
441	Sammy Sosa	1.00
442	Keiichi Yabu **RC**	.50
443	Yuniesky Betancourt **RC**	1.00
444	Jeff Niemann **RC**	1.50
445	Brandon McCarthy **RC**	1.50
446	Philip Humber **RC**	1.50
447	Tadahito Iguchi **RC**	2.00
448	Cal Ripken Jr.	4.00
449	Ryne Sandberg	2.00
450	Willie Mays	2.00

Non-Canvas

No Pricing
Production 20 Sets

Bronze

Stars: 3-5X
Production 100 Sets
Update Bronze (301-450): 3-5X
Production 50

Silver

Silvers: 4-8X
Production 50 Sets
Update (301-450): No Pricing
Production 25 Sets

Silver B/W

Silvers: 4-8X
Production 50 Sets

Gold

Golds: 5-10X
Production 25 Sets
Gold Update (301-450):No Pricing
Production 10 Sets

Platinum

No Pricing
Production One Set
Framed Platinums: No Pricing
Production One Set

Framed Black

Stars: 5-10X
Production 25 Sets

Framed Blue

Stars: 5-10X
Production 25 Sets

Framed Green

Stars: 4-8X
Production 50 Sets

Framed Red

Stars: 1-30X
Inserted 1:3

Diamond Cuts Bat

		NM/M
	Common Player:	4.00
1	Adam Dunn/200	8.00
2	Adrian Beltre/200	6.00
3	Alfonso Soriano/50	8.00
4	Andruw Jones/200	4.00
5	Andy Pettitte/50	6.00
6	Aramis Ramirez/100	6.00
7	Brian Giles/200	4.00
10	Carlos Beltran/200	8.00
12	Craig Wilson/200	4.00
13	Curt Schilling/50	10.00
14	Darin Erstad/200	4.00
16	Derrek Lee/200	6.00
17	Fred McGriff/100	4.00
19	Ivan Rodriguez/200	8.00
20	Jason Bay/200	4.00
21	Jason Giambi/100	4.00
22	Jay Gibbons/200	4.00
23	Jeff Kent/200	4.00
24	John Olerud/200	4.00
25	Juan Gonzalez/200	4.00
27	Kazuhisa Ishii/50	6.00
28	Kevin Brown/100	4.00
29	Larry Walker/200	6.00
31	Mark Teixeira/200	6.00
32	Melvin Mora/50	6.00
33	Michael Young/200	4.00
34	Miguel Tejada/100	8.00
35	Mike Mussina/50	8.00
36	Paul LoDuca/200	4.00
37	Preston Wilson/200	4.00
38	Randy Johnson/50	10.00
39	Richie Sexson/200	6.00
40	Roger Clemens/50	15.00
41	Scott Rolen/100	8.00
42	Sean Burroughs/200	4.00
43	Sean Casey/200	4.00
44	Shannon Stewart/200	4.00
45	Shawn Green/200	4.00
47	Tim Salmon/200	4.00
48	Tom Glavine/200	6.00
49	Torii Hunter/200	6.00

Diamond Cuts Jersey

		NM/M
	Common Player:	4.00
	Prime:	No Pricing
	Production One Set	
1	Adam Dunn/50	10.00
2	Adrian Beltre/200	6.00
3	Alfonso Soriano/50	8.00
4	Andruw Jones/200	4.00
5	Andy Pettitte/100	6.00
6	Aramis Ramirez/200	6.00
7	Brian Giles/200	4.00
8	C.C. Sabathia/200	4.00
9	Carl Crawford/200	4.00
10	Carlos Beltran/200	8.00
11	Carlos Lee/200	4.00
12	Craig Wilson/200	4.00
13	Curt Schilling/50	10.00
14	Darin Erstad/200	4.00
17	Fred McGriff/200	4.00
18	Greg Maddux/50	12.00
19	Ivan Rodriguez/200	8.00
20	Jason Bay/200	4.00
21	Jason Giambi/200	4.00
22	Jay Gibbons/100	4.00
23	Jeff Kent/200	4.00
24	John Olerud/200	4.00
25	Juan Gonzalez/Pants/200	4.00
26	Junior Spivey/200	4.00
27	Kazuhisa Ishii/200	6.00
28	Kevin Brown/200	4.00
29	Larry Walker/Rockies/200	6.00
30	Lyle Overbay/200	4.00
31	Mark Teixeira/100	6.00
32	Melvin Mora/200	4.00
33	Michael Young/200	4.00
34	Miguel Tejada/200	8.00
35	Mike Mussina/100	8.00
36	Paul LoDuca/50	6.00
37	Preston Wilson/200	4.00
38	Randy Johnson/200	8.00
39	Richie Sexson/200	6.00
40	Roger Clemens/50	15.00
41	Scott Rolen/50	10.00
42	Sean Burroughs/200	4.00
43	Sean Casey/200	4.00
44	Shannon Stewart/100	4.00
45	Shawn Green/200	4.00
46	Steve Finley/200	4.00
48	Tom Glavine/200	6.00
50	Travis Hafner/100	4.00

Diamond Cuts Combos

		NM/M
	Common Player:	6.00
	Prime:	No Pricing
	Production One Set	
1	Adam Dunn/Bat-Jsy/100	10.00
2	Adrian Beltre/Bat-Jsy/100	8.00
3	Alfonso Soriano/Bat-Jsy/100	10.00
4	Andruw Jones/Bat-Jsy/100	8.00
5	Andy Pettitte/Jsy-Jsy/100	10.00
6	Aramis Ramirez/Bat-Jsy/100	8.00
7	Brian Giles/Bat-Jsy/100	6.00
10	Carlos Beltran/Bat-Jsy/50	15.00
11	Carlos Lee/Jsy-Jsy/100	6.00
12	Craig Wilson/Bat-Jsy/100	6.00
13	Curt Schilling/Bat-Jsy/100	12.00
14	Darin Erstad/Bat-Jsy/100	6.00
17	Fred McGriff/Bat-Jsy/100	6.00
19	Ivan Rodriguez/Bat-Jsy/100	10.00
21	Jason Giambi/Bat-Jsy/50	8.00
22	Jay Gibbons/Bat-Jsy/50	8.00
23	Jeff Kent/Bat-Jsy/100	6.00
24	John Olerud/Bat-Jsy/200	6.00
25	Juan Gonzalez/Bat-Pants/100	8.00
27	Kazuhisa Ishii/Bat-Jsy/100	8.00
28	Kevin Brown/Bat-Jsy/100	6.00
29	Larry Walker/Bat-Jsy/100	8.00
31	Mark Teixeira/Bat-Jsy/100	10.00
34	Miguel Tejada/Jsy-Jsy/100	10.00
35	Mike Mussina/Bat-Pants/50	12.00
36	Paul LoDuca/Bat-Jsy/50	8.00
37	Preston Wilson/Bat-Jsy/100	6.00
38	Randy Johnson/Bat-Jsy/50	15.00
40	Roger Clemens/Bat-Jsy/50	20.00
44	Shannon Stewart/Bat-Jsy/100	6.00
45	Shawn Green/Bat-Jsy/100	6.00
48	Tom Glavine/Bat-Jsy/100	8.00
49	Torii Hunter/Bat-Jsy/25	8.00

Diamond Cuts Signature

		NM/M
	Production 1-100	
8	C.C. Sabathia/25	20.00
9	Carl Crawford/50	20.00
11	Carlos Lee/100	15.00
12	Craig Wilson/100	15.00
20	Jason Bay/100	15.00
22	Jay Gibbons/100	10.00

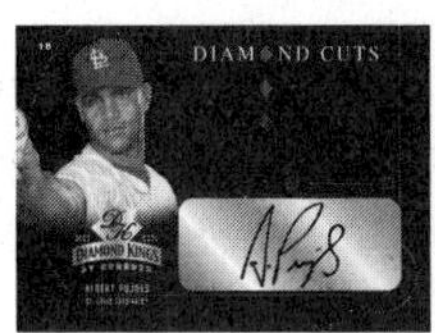

30 Lyle Overbay/100 15.00
32 Melvin Mora/50 15.00
44 Shannon Stewart/25 20.00
47 Tim Salmon/100 20.00
50 Travis Hafner/100 15.00

Diamond Cuts Signature Bat

NM/M
Production 5-100
1 Adam Dunn/25 40.00
2 Adrian Beltre/50 35.00
6 Aramis Ramirez/100 30.00
10 Carlos Beltran/50 40.00
12 Craig Wilson/100 15.00
16 Derrek Lee/100 20.00
17 Fred McGriff/25 50.00
22 Jay Gibbons/100 10.00
31 Mark Teixeira/25 40.00
33 Michael Young/100 20.00
36 Paul LoDuca/25 25.00
43 Sean Casey/25 25.00
44 Shannon Stewart/25 20.00
49 Torii Hunter/25 25.00

Diamond Cuts Signature Jersey

NM/M
Production 5-100
Prime: No Pricing
Production One Set
2 Adrian Beltre/100 25.00
6 Aramis Ramirez/100 30.00
8 C.C. Sabathia/100 15.00
9 Carl Crawford/50 20.00
11 Carlos Lee/100 15.00
12 Craig Wilson/100 15.00
30 Lyle Overbay/100 15.00
31 Mark Teixeira/25 40.00
32 Melvin Mora/50 15.00
33 Michael Young/100 20.00
36 Paul LoDuca/25 25.00
42 Sean Burroughs/50 10.00
43 Sean Casey/25 25.00
44 Shannon Stewart/25 20.00
46 Steve Finley/25 25.00
50 Travis Hafner/50 20.00
57 Mark Mulder/25 25.00
60 Victor Martinez/25 20.00

Diamond Cuts Signature Combos

NM/M
Production 1-100
Prime: No Pricing
Production One Set
1 Adam Dunn/Bat-Jsy/25 40.00
2 Adrian Beltre/Bat-Bat/25 40.00
6 Aramis Ramirez/Bat-Jsy/100 30.00
8 C.C. Sabathia/Jsy-Jsy/50 25.00
11 Carlos Lee/Jsy-Jsy/50 20.00
12 Craig Wilson/Bat-Bat/100 15.00
17 Fred McGriff/Bat-Jsy/25 50.00
22 Jay Gibbons/Bat-Bat/50 10.00
25 Juan Gonzalez/Bat-Jsy/100 25.00
27 Kazuhisa Ishii/Bat-Jsy/25 50.00
31 Mark Teixeira/Bat-Bat/25 40.00
33 Michael Young/Bat-Jsy/50 25.00
36 Paul LoDuca/Bat-Bat/25 25.00
43 Sean Casey/Bat-Jsy/25 25.00
44 Shannon Stewart/Bat-Jsy/25 20.00
49 Torii Hunter/Bat-Jsy/25 25.00
50 Travis Hafner/Bat-Jsy/25 25.00
51 Aramis Ramirez/Jsy/24 25.00
60 Victor Martinez/25 20.00

Heritage Collection

NM/M
Common Player: 1.50
Inserted 1:21
#26-35 inserted 1:76
#26-35 are DK Update exclusive
1 Andre Dawson 1.50
2 Bob Gibson 2.50
3 Cal Ripken Jr. 8.00
4 Dale Murphy 2.00

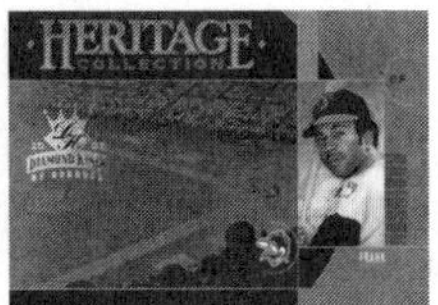

5 Darryl Strawberry 1.50
6 Dennis Eckersley 1.50
7 Don Mattingly 6.00
8 Duke Snider 3.00
9 Dwight Gooden 1.50
10 Eddie Murray 3.00
11 Frank Robinson 3.00
12 Gary Carter 2.00
13 George Brett 6.00
14 Harmon Killebrew 3.00
15 Jack Morris 1.50
16 Jim Palmer 1.50
17 Lou Brock 2.00
18 Mike Schmidt 6.00
19 Nolan Ryan 8.00
20 Ozzie Smith 4.00
21 Phil Niekro 1.50
22 Rod Carew 2.00
23 Rollie Fingers 1.50
24 Steve Carlton 1.50
25 Tony Gwynn 3.00
26 Curt Schilling 3.00
27 Bobby Doerr 1.50
28 Edgar Martinez 1.50
29 Jim Thorpe 4.00
30 Mark Grace 1.50
31 Matt Williams 1.50
32 Paul Molitor 2.50
33 Robin Yount 4.00
34 Ryne Sandberg 5.00
35 Will Clark 2.00

Heritage Collection Bat

NM/M
Production 50-100
1 Andre Dawson/50 8.00
3 Cal Ripken Jr./100 40.00
4 Dale Murphy/100 10.00
5 Darryl Strawberry/50 8.00
7 Don Mattingly/100 20.00
9 Dwight Gooden/100 5.00
10 Eddie Murray/100 15.00
11 Frank Robinson/50 8.00
12 Gary Carter/100 5.00
13 George Brett/100 15.00
14 Harmon Killebrew/100 10.00
17 Lou Brock/100 8.00
18 Mike Schmidt/100 20.00
19 Nolan Ryan/50 30.00
20 Ozzie Smith/100 15.00
21 Phil Niekro/50 8.00
22 Rod Carew/100 8.00
24 Steve Carlton/100 5.00
25 Tony Gwynn/100 10.00

Heritage Collection Jersey

NM/M
Production 25-100
Prime: No Pricing
Production One Set
1 Andre Dawson/100 8.00
2 Bob Gibson/50 10.00
3 Cal Ripken Jr./100 40.00
4 Dale Murphy/100 10.00
5 Darryl Strawberry/25 10.00
6 Dennis Eckersley/100 5.00
7 Don Mattingly/100 20.00
8 Duke Snider/50 15.00
9 Dwight Gooden/100 5.00
10 Eddie Murray/100 15.00
12 Gary Carter/100 5.00
13 George Brett/50 20.00
14 Harmon Killebrew/100 10.00
15 Jack Morris/100 5.00
16 Jim Palmer/100 5.00
17 Lou Brock/100 8.00
18 Mike Schmidt/Jkt/100 20.00
19 Nolan Ryan/100 25.00
20 Ozzie Smith/Pants/100 15.00
21 Phil Niekro/50 8.00
22 Rod Carew/100 8.00
23 Rollie Fingers/50 8.00
24 Steve Carlton/50 8.00
25 Tony Gwynn/100 10.00

Heritage Collection Combos

NM/M
Production 25-100
Prime: No Pricing
Production One Set
1 Andre Dawson/Bat-Jsy/50 8.00
3 Cal Ripken Jr./Bat-Jsy/50 60.00
4 Dale Murphy/Bat-Jsy/25 20.00
7 Don Mattingly/Bat-Jkt/100 25.00
8 Duke Snider/Jsy-Pants/25 20.00
9 Dwight Gooden/Bat-Jsy/50 10.00
10 Eddie Murray/Bat-Jsy/100 20.00
14 Harmon Killebrew/Bat-Jsy/100 15.00
16 Jim Palmer/Jsy-Pants/100 10.00
17 Lou Brock/Bat-Jkt/50 10.00
18 Mike Schmidt/Bat-Jsy/100 25.00
19 Nolan Ryan/Jsy-Pants/50 40.00
20 Ozzie Smith/Bat-Pants/100 20.00
21 Phil Niekro/Bat-Jsy/50 10.00
22 Rod Carew/Bat-Jsy/100 10.00
24 Steve Carlton/Bat-Jsy/100 8.00
25 Tony Gwynn/Bat-Jsy/50 15.00

Heritage Collection Signature

NM/M
Production 1-50
1 Andre Dawson/50 25.00
5 Darryl Strawberry/50 25.00
9 Dwight Gooden/25 25.00
15 Jack Morris/50 20.00
23 Rollie Fingers/25 40.00

Heritage Collection Signature Bat

NM/M
Production 5-100
#26-35 are DK Update exclusive
1 Andre Dawson/50 25.00
4 Dale Murphy/25 40.00
7 Don Mattingly/25 75.00
9 Dwight Gooden/100 25.00
11 Frank Robinson/25 40.00
14 Harmon Killebrew/50 50.00
17 Lou Brock/50 35.00
20 Ozzie Smith/25 65.00
21 Phil Niekro/20 30.00
22 Rod Carew/25 40.00
24 Steve Carlton/25 40.00
25 Tony Gwynn/25 50.00
28 Edgar Martinez/25 40.00
31 Matt Williams/25 35.00
35 Will Clark/25 40.00

Heritage Collection Signature Jersey

NM/M
Production 5-100
#26-35 are DK Update exclusive
Prime: No Pricing
Production One Set
1 Andre Dawson/100 25.00
2 Bob Gibson/25 40.00
4 Dale Murphy/50 40.00
5 Darryl Strawberry/Pants/100 20.00
6 Dennis Eckersley/50 25.00
7 Don Mattingly/25 85.00
8 Duke Snider/50 35.00
9 Dwight Gooden/100 20.00
11 Frank Robinson/25 40.00
12 Gary Carter/50 25.00
14 Harmon Killebrew/50 50.00
15 Jack Morris/100 15.00
16 Jim Palmer/25 35.00
17 Lou Brock/50 35.00
20 Ozzie Smith/25 60.00
21 Phil Niekro/25 30.00
22 Rod Carew/25 40.00
23 Rollie Fingers/25 30.00
24 Steve Carlton/25 40.00
27 Bobby Doerr/25 25.00
28 Edgar Martinez/25 35.00
31 Matt Williams/25 35.00
35 Will Clark/25 40.00

Heritage Collection Signature Combos

NM/M
Production 5-100
#26-35 are DK Update exclusive
Prime: No Pricing
Production One Set
1 Andre Dawson/Bat-Jsy/50 25.00
4 Dale Murphy/Bat-Jsy/25 40.00
6 Dennis Eckersley/Jsy-Jsy/50 25.00
7 Don Mattingly/Bat-Jkt/25 80.00
9 Dwight Gooden/Bat-Jsy/100 25.00
12 Gary Carter/Jkt-Jsy/50 25.00
14 Harmon Killebrew/Bat-Bat/25 50.00
15 Jack Morris/Jsy-Jsy/25 30.00
16 Jim Palmer/Jsy-Pants/25 30.00
17 Lou Brock/Bat-Jsy/50 40.00
21 Phil Niekro/Bat-Jsy/50 25.00
22 Rod Carew/Bat-Jkt/25 40.00
24 Steve Carlton/Bat-Jsy/25 40.00
25 Tony Gwynn/Bat-Jsy/25 50.00
27 Bobby Doerr/Jsy/Pants/25 25.00
28 Edgar Martinez/Bat/Jsy/25 40.00
31 Matt Williams/Bat/Jsy/25 35.00
35 Will Clark/Bat/Jsy/25 40.00

HOF Heroes

NM/M
#51-100 are DK Update exclusive
Common Player: 1.50
Inserted 1:5
Non Canvas: No Pricing
Production 20 Sets
Bronze: 1-2X
Production 100 Sets
Gold: 3-5X
Production 25 Sets
Platinum: No Pricing
Production One Set
Silver: 2-4X
Production 50 Sets
Frame Black: 3-5X
Production 25 Sets
Frame Blue: 1-2X
Production 100 Sets
Frame Green: 2-4X
Production 50 Sets
Frame Red: 1X
Inserted 1:18
1 Phil Niekro 1.50
2 Brooks Robinson 2.00
3 Jim Palmer 2.00
4 Carl Yastrzemski 3.00
5 Ted Williams 5.00
6 Duke Snider 3.00
7 Burleigh Grimes 1.50
8 Don Sutton 1.50
9 Nolan Ryan 6.00
10 Fergie Jenkins 1.50
11 Carlton Fisk 2.00
12 Tom Seaver 2.00
13 Bob Feller 2.00
14 Nolan Ryan 6.00
15 George Brett 5.00
16 Warren Spahn 3.00
17 Paul Molitor 3.00
18 Rod Carew 3.00
19 Harmon Killebrew 3.00
20 Monte Irvin 2.00
21 Gary Carter 1.50
22 Phil Rizzuto 2.00
23 Babe Ruth 6.00
24 Reggie Jackson 2.00
25 Mike Schmidt 5.00
26 Roberto Clemente 5.00
27 Juan Marichal 1.50
28 Willie McCovey 2.00
29 Stan Musial 4.00
30 Ozzie Smith 3.00
31 Dennis Eckersley 1.50
32 Phil Niekro 1.50
33 Jim Palmer 2.00
34 Carl Yastrzemski 3.00
35 Duke Snider 3.00
36 Don Sutton 1.50
37 Nolan Ryan 6.00
38 Carlton Fisk 2.00
39 Tom Seaver 2.00
40 Bob Feller 2.00
41 Nolan Ryan 6.00
42 George Brett 5.00
43 Harmon Killebrew 3.00
44 Gary Carter 1.50
45 Mike Schmidt 5.00
46 Stan Musial 4.00
47 Ozzie Smith 3.00
48 Dennis Eckersley 1.50
49 Fergie Jenkins 1.50
50 Brooks Robinson 2.00
51 Eddie Murray 2.00
52 Frank Robinson 2.00
53 Carlton Fisk 1.50
54 Ted Williams 5.00
55 Rod Carew 2.00
56 Ernie Banks 3.00
57 Luis Aparicio 1.50
58 Johnny Bench 3.00
59 Al Kaline 2.00
60 George Kell 1.50
61 Robin Yount 3.00
62 Nolan Ryan 6.00
63 Whitey Ford 1.50
64 Reggie Jackson 2.00
65 Babe Ruth 6.00
66 Rollie Fingers 1.50
67 Steve Carlton 1.50
68 Robin Roberts 1.50
69 Ralph Kiner 1.50
70 Willie Stargell 2.00
71 Roberto Clemente 5.00
72 Gaylord Perry 1.50
73 Bob Gibson 2.00
74 Lou Brock 1.50
75 Frankie Frisch 1.50
76 Eddie Murray 2.00
77 Frank Robinson 2.00
78 Carlton Fisk 1.50
79 Ted Williams 5.00
80 Rod Carew 2.00
81 Ernie Banks 3.00
82 Luis Aparicio 1.50
83 Johnny Bench 3.00
84 Al Kaline 2.00
85 Willie Mays 5.00
86 Robin Yount 3.00
87 Nolan Ryan 5.00
88 Whitey Ford 2.00
89 Reggie Jackson 2.00
90 Babe Ruth 6.00
91 Rollie Fingers 1.50
92 Steve Carlton 1.50
93 Wade Boggs 2.00
94 Wade Boggs 2.00
95 Willie Stargell 2.00
96 Roberto Clemente 5.00
97 Gaylord Perry 1.50
98 Bob Gibson 2.00
99 Lou Brock 1.50
100 Frankie Frisch 1.50

HOF Heroes Materials Bronze

NM/M
Production 1-100
No pricing 20 or less.
Gold: .75-1.5X
Production 1-25
Silver: .75-1.5X
Production 10-50
Framed Black: No Pricing
Production 1-10
Framed Blue: .75-1.5X
Production 1-25
Framed Red: .75-1.5X
Production 10-50
1 Phil Niekro/Bat-Jsy/100 8.00
2 Brooks Robinson/Bat-Jsy/100 12.00
3 Jim Palmer/Jsy-Pants/100 8.00
4 Carl Yastrzemski/Bat-Pants/50 20.00
6 Duke Snider/Jsy-Pants/50 15.00
7 Burleigh Grimes/Pants-Pants/25 75.00
8 Don Sutton/Jsy-Jsy/100 8.00
9 Nolan Ryan/Bat-Jkt/50 40.00
10 Fergie Jenkins/Pants-Pants/100 8.00
11 Carlton Fisk/Bat-Jkt/100 12.00
12 Tom Seaver/Jsy-Pants/50 15.00
13 Bob Feller/Pants-Pants/25 20.00
14 Nolan Ryan/Bat-Jsy/50 40.00
15 George Brett/Bat-Bat/25 40.00
16 Warren Spahn/Jsy-Pants/25 30.00
17 Paul Molitor/Bat-Jsy/100 15.00
18 Rod Carew/Bat-Jsy/50 15.00
19 Harmon Killebrew/Bat-Jsy/50 20.00
21 Gary Carter/Bat-Jsy/100 8.00
23 Babe Ruth/Bat-Pants/25 300.00
24 Reggie Jackson/Bat-Jkt/100 15.00
25 Mike Schmidt/Bat-Jkt/50 30.00
26 Roberto Clemente/Bat-Bat/50 60.00
27 Juan Marichal/Pants-Pants/25 12.00
28 Willie McCovey/Jsy-Pants/100 10.00
29 Stan Musial/Bat-Bat/25 30.00
30 Ozzie Smith/Bat-Pants/100 20.00
31 Dennis Eckersley/Jsy-Jsy/100 8.00
32 Phil Niekro/Bat-Jsy/100 8.00
33 Jim Palmer/Jsy-Pants/25 12.00
34 Carl Yastrzemski/Bat-Pants/25 30.00
35 Duke Snider/Jsy-Pants 20.00
36 Don Sutton/Jsy-Jsy/100 8.00
37 Nolan Ryan/Bat-Jkt/25 50.00
38 Carlton Fisk/Bat-Jkt/100 12.00
39 Tom Seaver/Bat-Jsy/25 20.00
40 Bob Feller/Pants-Pants/25 20.00
41 Nolan Ryan/Bat-Jkt/25 50.00
42 George Brett/Bat-Bat/25 40.00
43 Harmon Killebrew/at-Jsy/25 25.00
44 Gary Carter/Bat-Jsy/100 8.00
45 Mike Schmidt/Bat-Jsy/25 40.00
46 Stan Musial/Bat-Bat/25 30.00
47 Ozzie Smith/Bat-Pants/100 20.00
48 Dennis Eckersley/Jsy-Jsy/100 8.00
49 Fergie Jenkins/Pants-Pants/25 12.00
50 Brooks Robinson/Bat-Jsy/25 20.00
51 Eddie Murray/Bat/Pants/50 12.00
52 Frank Robinson/Bat/Bat/50 12.00
53 Carlton Fisk/Bat/Bat/50 10.00
55 Rod Carew/Bat/Jsy/50 12.00
56 Ernie Banks/Bat/Pants/50 15.00
57 Luis Aparicio/Bat/Bat/50 8.00
58 Johnny Bench/Bat/Jsy/50 15.00
59 Al Kaline/Bat/Bat/25 20.00
61 Robin Yount/Bat/Jsy/50 15.00
62 Nolan Ryan/Bat/Jsy/25 50.00
63 Whitey Ford/Jsy/Jsy/25 25.00
64 Reggie Jackson/Jsy/Jsy/50 15.00
66 Rollie Fingers/Jsy/Jsy/50 8.00
67 Steve Carlton/Bat/Jsy/50 10.00
70 Willie Stargell/Bat/Jsy/50 15.00
72 Gaylord Perry/Jsy/Jsy/50 8.00
73 Bob Gibson/Jsy/Jsy/25 15.00
74 Lou Brock/Bat/Jsy/50 12.00
76 Eddie Murray/Bat/Bat/50 12.00
77 Frank Robinson/Bat/Bat/50 12.00
78 Carlton Fisk/Bat/Bat/50 12.00
80 Rod Carew/Bat/Jkt/50 12.00
81 Ernie Banks/Bat/Jsy/25 15.00
82 Luis Aparicio/Bat/Bat/50 8.00
83 Johnny Bench/Bat/Jsy/50 15.00
86 Robin Yount/Bat/Jsy/50 15.00
87 Nolan Ryan/Bat/Jsy/25 40.00
88 Whitey Ford/Jsy/Jsy/25 25.00
89 Reggie Jackson/Jsy/Jsy/50 15.00
91 Rollie Fingers/Jsy/Jsy/50 8.00
92 Steve Carlton/Bat/Jsy/50 10.00
95 Willie Stargell/Jsy/Jsy/50 15.00
97 Gaylord Perry/Jsy/Jsy/50 8.00
99 Lou Brock/Bat/Jsy/50 10.00

HOF Heroes Signatures Bronze

NM/M
Production 1-25
No pricing 20 or less.
Gold: No Pricing
Production 1-10
Platinum: No Pricing
Production One Set
Silver: 1X
Production 1-25

Framed Blue: No Pricing
Production One Set
Framed Black: No Pricing
Production One Set
Framed Green: No Pricing
Production 1-10
Framed Red: No Pricing
Production 1-25
Cards #52-99 are seeded in DK Update
13 Bob Feller/25 35.00
40 Bob Feller/25 35.00
52 Frank Robinson/25 35.00
57 Luis Aparicio/25 15.00
59 Al Kaline/25 40.00
60 George Kell/25 20.00
66 Rollie Fingers/25 15.00
67 Steve Carlton/25 20.00
68 Robin Roberts/25 20.00
69 Ralph Kiner/25 35.00
72 Gaylord Perry/15 15.00
74 Lou Brock/25 35.00
82 Luis Aparicio/25 15.00
84 Al Kaline/25 40.00
91 Rollie Fingers/25 15.00
92 Steve Carlton/25 20.00
93 Wade Boggs/ Yanks/25 30.00
94 Wade Boggs/Sox/25 30.00
97 Gaylord Perry/25 15.00
99 Lou Brock/25 35.00

Signature Materials Bronze

NM/M
Production 5-50
No pricing 20 or less.
Gold: .75-1.5X
Production 5-25
Platinum: No Pricing
Production One Set
Silver: .75-1X
Production 5-50
Framed Black: No Pricing
Production 5-10
Framed Blue: .75-1.5X
Production 5-25
Framed Green: No Pricing
Production 1-10
Framed Red: .75-1.5X
Production 1-25
#53-99 are found in DK Update
2 Brooks Robinson/ Bat-Jsy/25 50.00
3 Jim Palmer/ Jsy-Pants/25 40.00
6 Duke Snider/ Jsy-Pants/25 40.00
8 Don Sutton/ Jsy-Jsy/25 30.00
10 Fergie Jenkins/ Pants-Pants/25 30.00
13 Bob Feller/ Pants-Pants/50 35.00
18 Rod Carew/ Bat-Jsy/50 40.00
19 Harmon Killebrew/ Bat-Jsy/25 50.00
21 Gary Carter/ Bat-Jsy/50 25.00
27 Juan Marichal/ Pants-Pants/25 40.00
28 Willie McCovey/ Jsy-Pants/25 50.00
29 Stan Musial/ Bat-Bat/25 85.00
30 Ozzie Smith/ Bat-Pants/25 75.00
31 Dennis Eckersley/ Jsy-Jsy/25 35.00
32 Phil Niekro/ Bat-Jsy/25 30.00
33 Jim Palmer/ Jsy-Pants/25 40.00
35 Duke Snider/ Jsy-Pants/25 40.00
36 Don Sutton/ Jsy-Jsy/25 30.00
40 Bob Feller/ Pants-Pants/50 35.00
43 Harmon Killebrew/ Bat-Jsy/50 40.00
44 Gary Carter/ Bat-Jsy/50 25.00
47 Ozzie Smith/ Bat-Pants/25 75.00
48 Dennis Eckersley/ Jsy-Jsy/50 25.00
49 Fergie Jenkins/ Pants-Pants/50 30.00
50 Brooks Robinson/ Bat-Jsy/25 50.00
61 Robin Yount/ Bat-Jsy/25 50.00
66 Rollie Fingers/ Jsy-Jsy/50 15.00
72 Gaylord Perry/ Jsy-Jsy/50 15.00
74 Lou Brock/ Jsy-Jsy/50 30.00
80 Rod Carew/ Bat-Jsy/50 25.00
99 Lou Brock/ Bat-Jsy/25 40.00

Materials Bronze

NM/M
Production 10-200
No pricing 20 or less.
Gold: .75-1.5X
Production 25-50
Silver: .75-1.5X
Production 25-100
Platinum: No Pricing
Production One Set
Framed Black: No Pricing
Production 10 Sets
Framed Blue: .75-1.5X
Production 50 Sets
Framed Green:
Production 25 Sets
Framed Red: .75-1.5X
Production 25-100
#302-450 are found in DK Update
1 Garret Anderson/ Bat-Jsy/200 5.00
2 Vladimir Guerrero/ Bat-Jsy/200 10.00
4 Troy Glaus/ Bat-Jsy/200 5.00
5 Tim Salmon/ Bat-Jsy/200 5.00
7 Chone Figgins/ Bat-Jsy/200 5.00
10 Tony Percival/ Jsy-Jsy/200 5.00
12 Brandon Webb/ Bat-Pants/200 5.00
13 Richie Sexson/ Bat-Bat/200 8.00
17 Luis Gonzalez/ Jsy-Jsy/200 5.00
18 Rafael Furcal/ Bat-Jsy/200 5.00
19 Andruw Jones/ Bat-Jsy/200 8.00
21 John Smoltz/ Jsy-Jsy/200 8.00
24 J.D. Drew/Bat-Bat/200 5.00
25 Chipper Jones/ Bat-Jsy/200 10.00
27 Rafael Palmeiro/ Bat-Jsy/200 8.00
28 Miguel Tejada/ Bat-Jsy/200 10.00
29 Javy Lopez/ Bat-Jsy/25 10.00
30 Luis Matos/ Jsy-Jsy/100 5.00
31 Larry Bigbie/ Jsy-Jsy/200 5.00
32 Rodrigo Lopez/ Jsy-Jsy/200 5.00
34 Melvin Mora/ Bat-Jsy/200 5.00
36 Manny Ramirez/ Bat-Jsy/200 10.00
38 Trot Nixon/ Bat-Bat/200 10.00
39 Curt Schilling/ Bat-Jsy/200 10.00
41 Pedro Martinez/ Bat-Jsy/200 10.00
42 Johnny Damon/ Bat-Bat/200 15.00
43 Kevin Youkilis/ Bat-Bat/200 5.00
46 David Ortiz/ Bat-Jsy/200 10.00
47 Kerry Wood/ Jsy-Pants/200 10.00
48 Mark Prior/ Bat-Jsy/200 8.00
49 Aramis Ramirez/ Bat-Jsy/200 8.00
50 Greg Maddux/ Bat-Jsy/100 15.00
51 Carlos Zambrano/ Jsy-Jsy/200 8.00
52 Derrek Lee/ Bat-Bat/200 8.00
54 Moises Alou/ Bat-Bat/200 8.00
56 Sammy Sosa/ Bat-Jsy/200 10.00
57 Nomar Garciaparra/ Bat-Bat/200 10.00
60 Magglio Ordonez/ Bat-Jsy/200 5.00
61 Carlos Lee/ Bat-Jsy/200 5.00
62 Joe Crede/Bat-Bat/200 5.00
65 Frank Thomas/ Bat-Jsy/200 8.00
69 Adam Dunn/ Bat-Jsy/200 8.00
70 Austin Kearns/ Bat-Bat/200 5.00
74 Sean Casey/ Jsy-Pants/200 5.00
76 C.C. Sabathia/ Jsy-Jsy/200 5.00
77 Jody Gerut/ Bat-Jsy/200 5.00
78 Omar Vizquel/ Bat-Jsy/200 5.00
79 Victor Martinez/ Bat-Jsy/200 5.00
80 Matt Lawton/ Bat-Bat/200 5.00
84 Todd Helton/ Bat-Jsy/200 8.00
85 Preston Wilson/ Bat-Jsy/200 5.00
90 Ivan Rodriguez/ Bat-Jsy/200 8.00
92 Brandon Inge/ Bat-Jsy/200 5.00
94 Dontrelle Willis/ Jsy-Jsy/200 5.00
95 Miguel Cabrera/ Bat-Jsy/200 10.00
96 Josh Beckett/ Bat-Bat/100 5.00
97 Mike Lowell/ Bat-Jsy/100 5.00
98 Luis Castillo/ Bat-Bat/200 5.00
99 Juan Pierre/ Bat-Bat/200 5.00
100 Paul LoDuca/ Bat-Bat/200 5.00
102 Craig Biggio/ Bat-Pants/200 5.00
103 Lance Berkman/ Bat-Jsy/200 5.00
104 Roy Oswalt/ Jsy-Jsy/200 5.00
105 Roger Clemens/ Bat-Jsy/200 15.00
106 Jeff Kent/Bat-Jsy/100 5.00
108 Jeff Bagwell/ Bat-Jsy/200 8.00
109 Carlos Beltran/ Bat-Jsy/200 8.00
110 Angel Berroa/ Bat-Bat/200 5.00
111 Mike Sweeney/ Bat-Jsy/200 5.00
112 Jeremy Affeldt/ Pants-Pants/200 5.00
114 Juan Gonzalez/ Bat-Jsy/200 8.00
116 Shawn Green/ Bat-Jsy/200 5.00
118 Adrian Beltre/ Bat-Jsy/200 8.00
119 Hideo Nomo/B at-Jsy/200 8.00
123 Scott Podsednik/ Jsy-Jsy/200 5.00
124 Ben Sheets/ Bat-Pants/200 8.00
125 Lyle Overbay/ Jsy-Jsy/200 5.00
126 Junior Spivey/ Jsy-Jsy/200 5.00
127 Bill Hall/Bat-Jsy/200 5.00
129 Jacque Jones/ Bat-Jsy/200 5.00
130 Torii Hunter/ Bat-Jsy/200 5.00
131 Johan Santana/ Jsy-Jsy/200 10.00
132 Lew Ford/Bat-Jsy/200 5.00
136 Jose Vidro/ Bat-Jsy/200 5.00
138 Brad Wilkerson/ Bat-Bat/100 5.00
139 Nick Johnson/ Bat-Bat/100 5.00
140 Livan Hernandez/ Jsy-Jsy/25 5.00
141 Tom Glavine/ Bat-Bat/200 8.00
143 Jose Reyes/ Bat-Jsy/200 6.00
144 Al Leiter/Jsy-Jsy/200 5.00
145 Mike Piazza/ Jsy-Jsy/100 15.00
146 Kazuo Matsui/ Bat-Jsy/200 8.00
147 Richard Hidalgo/ Bat-Bat/200 5.00
149 Mariano Rivera/ Jsy-Jsy/100 8.00
150 Mike Mussina/ Bat-Jsy/200 8.00
153 Jorge Posada/ Bat-Jsy/200 8.00
154 Jason Giambi/ Bat-Jsy/200 5.00
155 Gary Sheffield/ Bat-Jsy/200 8.00
158 Kevin Brown/ Bat-Bat/100 5.00
160 Esteban Loaiza/ Bat-Bat/100 5.00
161 Hideki Matsui/ Jsy-Pants/200 20.00
162 Eric Chavez/ Bat-Jsy/200 5.00
163 Mark Mulder/ Bat-Bat/25 10.00
164 Barry Zito/Bat-Jsy/200 5.00
165 Tim Hudson/ Bat-Jsy/200 8.00
166 Jermaine Dye/ Bat-Jsy/200 5.00
168 Bobby Crosby/ Jsy-Jsy/200 8.00
171 Jim Thome/ Bat-Jsy/200 8.00
172 Bobby Abreu/ Jsy-Jsy/200 8.00
173 Kevin Millwood/ Jsy-Jsy/200 5.00
178 Craig Wilson/ Bat-Jsy/200 5.00
180 Jack Wilson/ Bat-Bat/200 5.00
181 Jose Castillo/ Bat-Bat/200 5.00
184 Jason Bay/B at-Jsy/200 5.00
185 Sean Burroughs/ Bat-Jsy/200 8.00
187 Brian Giles/ Bat-Bat/100 5.00
193 Trevor Hoffman/ Jsy-Jsy/200 5.00
199 J.T. Snow/Jsy-Jsy/25 5.00
200 A.J. Pierzynski/ Jsy-Jsy/100 5.00
201 Edgar Martinez/ Bat-Bat/200 5.00
204 Bret Boone/ Jsy-Jsy/200 5.00
208 Jamie Moyer/ Jsy-Jsy/50 5.00
209 Jim Edmonds/ Bat-Jsy/200 8.00
210 Scott Rolen/ Bat-Jsy/200 10.00
211 Edgar Renteria/ Bat-Jsy/200 8.00
212 Dan Haren/ Bat-Jsy/100 5.00
213 Matt Morris/ Jsy-Jsy/100 5.00
214 Albert Pujols/ Jsy-Jsy/200 20.00
215 Larry Walker/ Bat-Bat/200 8.00
220 Aubrey Huff/ Bat-Bat/100 5.00
221 Carl Crawford/ Jsy-Jsy/200 5.00
222 Rocco Baldelli/ Bat-Jsy/200 5.00
223 Fred McGriff/ Bat-Jsy/200 5.00
224 Dewon Brazelton/ Jsy-Jsy/200 5.00
225 B.J. Upton/ Bat-Bat/200 8.00
226 Joey Gathright/ Bat-Jsy/200 5.00
228 Hank Blalock/ Bat-Jsy/100 8.00
229 Mark Teixeira/ Bat-Jsy/200 8.00
230 Michael Young/ Bat-Jsy/200 5.00
232 Laynce Nix/B at-Jsy/200 5.00
233 Alfonso Soriano/ Bat-Jsy/200 8.00
234 Rafael Palmeiro/ Bat-Jsy/200 8.00
235 Kevin Mench/ Bat-Jsy/200 5.00
236 David Dellucci/ Jsy-Jsy/200 8.00
237 Francisco Cordero/ Jsy-Jsy/200 5.00
239 Roy Halladay/ Jsy-Jsy/200 5.00
240 Carlos Delgado/ Bat-Jsy/200 5.00
242 Vernon Wells/ Bat-Jsy/200 5.00
267 Larry Walker/ Jsy-Jsy/200 8.00
268 Ivan Rodriguez/ Jsy-Jsy/200 8.00
269 Brad Penny/ Bat-Jsy/200 5.00
270 Carlos Beltran/ Bat-Jsy/200 8.00
271 Paul LoDuca/ Bat-Jsy/200 5.00
273 Nomar Garciaparra/ Bat-Bat/100 10.00
274 Esteban Loiaza/ Bat-Bat/100 5.00
275 Richard Hidalgo/ Jkt-Pants/200 5.00
276 John Olerud/ Bat-Jsy/200 5.00
277 Greg Maddux/ Jsy-Jsy/200 12.00
278 Roger Clemens/ Bat-Jsy/200 15.00
279 Alfonso Soriano/ Bat-Jsy/200 8.00
280 Dale Murphy/ Jsy-Jsy/200 8.00
281 Cal Ripken Jr./ Bat-Jsy/200 30.00
282 Dwight Evans/ Bat-Jsy/200 8.00
283 Ron Santo/ Bat-Bat/200 10.00
284 Andre Dawson/ Bat-Jsy/100 8.00
285 Harold Baines/ Bat-Jsy/200 8.00
286 Jack Morris/ Jsy-Jsy/100 8.00
287 Kirk Gibson/ Bat-Jsy/200 5.00
288 Bo Jackson/ Bat-Jsy/200 10.00
289 Orel Hershiser/ Jsy-Jsy/50 8.00
291 Tony Oliva/ Bat-Jsy/200 10.00
292 Darryl Strawberry/ Bat-Jsy/100 8.00
293 Roger Maris/ Bat-Jsy/100 50.00
294 Don Mattingly/ Bat-Jsy/100 25.00
295 Rickey Henderson/ Bat-Jsy/100 10.00
297 Dave Parker/ Bat-Jsy/200 8.00
298 Steve Garvey/ Bat-Jsy/200 8.00
299 Matt Williams/ Jsy-Jsy/200 8.00
300 Keith Hernandez/ Bat-Jsy/200 8.00
302 Vladimir Guerrero/ Jsy-Jsy/200 10.00
303 Garret Anderson/ Bat-Jsy/200 5.00
307 Luis Gonzalez/ Jsy-Jsy/200 5.00
310 Shawn Green/ Bat-Bat/200 5.00
311 Troy Glaus/ Bat-Bat/200 5.00
314 Chipper Jones/ Jsy-Jsy/100 10.00
315 Johnny Estrada/ Jsy-Jsy/200 5.00
316 Andruw Jones/ Bat-Jsy/200 8.00
319 Jay Gibbons/ Bat-Bat/200 5.00
320 Melvin Mora/ Jsy-Jsy/200 5.00
321 Rafael Palmeiro/ Bat-Jsy/200 8.00
323 David Ortiz/ Bat-Jsy/200 10.00
324 Manny Ramirez/ Bat-Jsy/200 10.00
327 Curt Schilling/ Jsy-Jsy/200 10.00
328 Sammy Sosa/ Bat-Jsy/100 10.00
329 Mark Prior/ Bat-Jsy/200 8.00
330 Greg Maddux/ Jsy-Jsy/25 15.00
332 Frank Thomas/ Bat-Pants/200 10.00
333 Mark Buehrle/ Bat-Jsy/200 5.00
336 Sean Casey/ Bat-Jsy/200 5.00
337 Adam Dunn/ Bat-Jsy/200 8.00
339 Travis Hafner/ Jsy-Jsy/100 5.00
340 Victor Martinez/ Bat-Jsy/100 5.00
341 Cliff Lee/Jsy-Jsy/200 5.00
342 Todd Helton/ Bat-Jsy/25 8.00
343 Preston Wilson/ Jsy-Jsy/200 5.00
344 Ivan Rodriguez/ Bat-Jsy/200 8.00
347 Miguel Cabrera/ Bat-Jsy/200 10.00
348 Jeff Bagwell/ Bat-Jsy/200 8.00
349 Andy Pettitte/ Bat-Jsy/200 8.00
350 Roger Clemens/ Bat-Jsy/100 15.00
351 Ken Harvey/ Jsy-Jsy/200 5.00
353 Hideo Nomo/ Bat-Jsy/200 8.00
354 Kazuhisa Ishii/ Jsy-Jsy/200 5.00
355 Edwin Jackson/ Jsy-Jsy/200 5.00
356 J.D. Drew/Bat-Bat/200 5.00
357 Jeff Kent/Bat-Bat/25 5.00
358 Geoff Jenkins/ Jsy-Pants/200 5.00
359 Carlos Lee/ Bat-Bat/200 5.00
360 Shannon Stewart/ Jsy-Jsy/200 5.00
362 Johan Santana/ Jsy-Jsy/100 10.00
363 Mike Piazza/ Jsy-Jsy/100 12.00
364 Kazuo Matsui/ Jsy-Jsy/100 5.00
366 Pedro Martinez/ Bat-Bat/100 10.00
368 Hideki Matsui/ Bat-Jsy/100 20.00
369 Bernie Williams/ Bat-Jsy/200 8.00
370 Gary Sheffield/ Bat-Jsy/100 8.00
371 Randy Johnson/ Bat-Bat/25 10.00
378 Mark Mulder/ Bat-Bat/50 8.00
380 Eric Chavez/ Jsy-Jsy/100 5.00
382 Marlon Byrd/ Bat-Jsy/200 5.00
383 Pat Burrell/ Jsy-Jsy/200 5.00
385 Jim Thome/ Bat-Bat/200 8.00
388 Moises Alou/ Bat-Bat/200 5.00
393 Adrian Beltre/ Bat-Bat/50 5.00
394 Richie Sexson/ Bat-Bat/200 5.00
397 Albert Pujols/ Bat-Jsy/200 20.00
398 Scott Rolen/ Bat-Jsy/200 10.00
401 Delmon Young/ Bat-Bat/200 5.00
402 Aubrey Huff/B at-Bat/50 5.00
403 Alfonso Soriano/ Bat-Jsy/200 8.00
404 Hank Blalock/ Bat-Jsy/200 5.00
405 Richard Hidalgo/ Bat-Bat/200 5.00
406 Vernon Wells/ Jsy-Jsy/200 5.00
407 Orlando Hudson/ Bat-Bat/200 5.00
412 Jose Vidro/Bat-Jsy/5 5.00
415 Miguel Tejada/ Jsy-Jsy/100 8.00
416 Gary Sheffield/ Bat-Bat/200 8.00
417 Curt Schilling/ Jsy-Jsy/200 10.00
418 Rafael Palmeiro/ Bat-Pants/50 8.00
419 Scott Rolen/ Bat-Jsy/200 10.00
420 Aramis Ramirez/ Jsy-Jsy/200 8.00
421 Vladimir Guerrero/ Bat-Bat/200 10.00
422 Steve Finley/ Jsy-Jsy/200 5.00
423 Roger Clemens/ Bat-Jsy/200 15.00
424 Mike Piazza/ Jsy-Jsy/200 12.00
425 Ivan Rodriguez/ Bat-Jsy/200 8.00
426 David Justice/ Jsy-Jsy/200 5.00
427 Mark Grace/ Bat-Jsy/25 8.00
428 Alan Trammell/ Bat-Jsy/100 5.00
430 Dwight Gooden/ Bat-Jsy/200 5.00
431 Deion Sanders/ Bat-Jsy/200 8.00
432 Joe Torre/Bat-Bat/100 5.00
433 Jose Canseco/ Jsy-Jsy/100 8.00
434 Tony Gwynn/ Bat-Pants/200 10.00
435 Will Clark/Bat-Jsy/100 8.00
437 Nolan Ryan/ Bat-Jsy/50 15.00
438 Billy Martin/ Jsy-Pants/200 10.00
439 Carlos Delgado/ Bat-Bat/100 5.00
440 Magglio Ordonez/ Bat-Bat/200 5.00
441 Sammy Sosa/ Bat-Bat/25 10.00
449 Ryne Sandberg/ Bat-Jsy/100 10.00

Recollection Autographs Gold

No Pricing
Production One Set
Silver: No Pricing
Production One Set
Platinum: No Pricing
Production One Set

Signature Bronze

NM/M
Production 1-100
No pricing 20 or less.
Black: No Pricing
Production One Set
Gold: .75-1.5X
Production 1-50
Silver: .75-1.5X
Production 1-100
Platinum: No Pricing
Production One Set
Framed Blue: .75-1.5X
Production 1-50
Framed Green: .75-1.5X
Production 1-25
Framed Red: .75-1.5X
Production 1-100
#303-450 found in DK Update
3 Jose Guillen/100 15.00
5 Tim Salmon/100 20.00
6 Casey Kotchman/100 15.00
7 Chone Figgins/100 15.00
8 Robb Quinlan/100 8.00
9 Francisco Rodriguez/50 40.00
10 Troy Percival/50 15.00

14 Shea Hillenbrand/100 10.00
15 Chad Tracy/100 10.00
16 Alex Cintron/100 8.00
22 Adam LaRoche/50 10.00
23 Russ Ortiz/50 12.00
26 Nick Green/100 8.00
30 Luis Matos/100 10.00
31 Larry Bigbie/100 10.00
32 Rodrigo Lopez/100 15.00
33 Brian Roberts/100 25.00
34 Melvin Mora/100 15.00
40 Keith Foulke/50 40.00
43 Kevin Youkilis/100 10.00
44 Orlando Cabrera/50 20.00
45 Abe Alvarez/100 8.00
51 Carlos Zambrano/50 30.00
58 Todd Walker/50 15.00
59 Angel Guzman/100 15.00
61 Carlos Lee/100 15.00
73 Ryan Wagner/100 10.00
75 Danny Graves/100 12.00
76 C.C. Sabathia/50 20.00
77 Jody Gerut/100 8.00
79 Victor Martinez/50 20.00
82 Kazuhito Tadano/100 20.00
83 Travis Hafner/100 15.00
89 Jeremy Bonderman/100 15.00
92 Brandon Inge/100 10.00
101 Guillermo Mota/50 10.00
107 Morgan Ensberg/100 10.00
112 Jeremy Affeldt/100 10.00
117 Milton Bradley/100 15.00
122 Brad Penny/100 10.00
123 Scott Podsednik/50 15.00
125 Lyle Overbay/100 12.00
127 Bill Hall/100 8.00
132 Lew Ford/100 15.00
135 Jason Kubel/100 15.00
137 Chad Cordero/100 10.00
140 Livan Hernandez/25 15.00
156 Bubba Crosby/100 10.00
159 Tom Gordon/25 20.00
160 Esteban Loaiza/100 10.00
166 Jermaine Dye/50 15.00
167 Octavio Dotel/50 15.00
168 Bobby Crosby/100 20.00
174 Mike Lieberthal/100 12.00
177 Randy Wolf/100 10.00
178 Craig Wilson/100 10.00
180 Jack Wilson/100 12.00
181 Jose Castillo/100 10.00
184 Jason Bay/100 15.00
186 Jay Payton/50 10.00
189 Jake Peavy/50 30.00
194 Freddy Guzman/100 8.00
197 Todd Linden/50 10.00
198 Merkin Valdez/100 10.00
203 Raul Ibanez/100 10.00
206 Miguel Olivo/100 8.00
207 Bucky Jacobsen/100 12.00
208 Jamie Moyer/50 15.00
212 Dan Haren/100 12.00
219 Jeff Suppan/100 10.00
220 Aubrey Huff/50 15.00
221 Carl Crawford/25 20.00
224 Dewon Brazelton/100 8.00
226 Joey Gathright/100 10.00
227 Scott Kazmir/25 25.00
230 Michael Young/50 20.00
231 Adrian Gonzalez/100 10.00
232 Laynce Nix/100 15.00
236 David Dellucci/100 20.00
237 Francisco Cordero/100 15.00
241 Alexis Rios/100 15.00
248 Dioner Navarro/100 15.00
253 Yhency Brazoban/100 10.00
257 Scott Proctor/100 8.00
260 Matt Peterson/100 8.00
269 Brad Penny/50 10.00
272 Orlando Cabrera/50 15.00
274 Esteban Loaiza/100 10.00
284 Andre Dawson/50 20.00
285 Harold Baines/100 15.00
286 Jack Morris/100 10.00
290 Maury Wills/100 15.00
292 Darryl Strawberry/100 15.00
297 Dave Parker/100 20.00
299 Matt Williams/25 25.00
303 Garret Anderson/50 15.00
304 Dallas McPherson/100 10.00
305 Orlando Cabrera/25 10.00
306 Steve Finley/50 10.00
313 Russ Ortiz/50 10.00
315 Johnny Estrada/100 8.00
318 Danny Kolb/100 8.00
319 Jay Gibbons/50 8.00
320 Melvin Mora/50 10.00
325 Edgar Renteria/50 15.00
333 Mark Buehrle/50 20.00
336 Sean Casey/25 15.00
339 Travis Hafner/50 15.00
340 Victor Martinez/50 10.00
341 Cliff Lee/100 10.00
343 Preston Wilson/50 15.00
351 Ken Harvey/100 8.00
355 Edwin Jackson/100 8.00
359 Carlos Lee/100 10.00
360 Shannon Stewart/25 15.00
361 Joe Nathan/100 15.00
376 Eric Byrnes/100 8.00
377 Rich Harden/100 15.00
378 Mark Mulder/25 20.00
380 Eric Chavez/25 15.00
382 Marlon Byrd/100 8.00
384 Brett Myers/100 10.00
386 Jason Bay/50 15.00
387 Jake Peavy/50 25.00
402 Aubrey Huff/50 15.00
407 Orlando Hudson/25 10.00
410 Jose Guillen/25 15.00
429 Bert Blyleven/50 10.00
430 Dwight Gooden/50 15.00
436 Marty Marion/50 15.00

Signature Materials Bronze

NM/M

Production 1-200
No pricing 20 or less.
Platinum: No Pricing
Production One Set
Framed Black: No Pricing
Production 1-10
Framed Blue: No Pricing
Production 1-50
Framed Green: 1-2X
Production 1-25
Framed Red: .75-1.5X
Production 1-100

1 Garret Anderson/Bat-Jsy/50 25.00
7 Chone Figgins/Bat-Jsy/200 15.00
18 Rafael Furcal/Bat-Jsy/50 20.00
19 Andruw Jones/Bat-Jsy/25 35.00
31 Larry Bigbie/Jsy-Jsy/200 15.00
32 Rodrigo Lopez/Jsy-Jsy/200 15.00
38 Trot Nixon/Jsy-Jsy/100 30.00
46 David Ortiz/Bat-Jsy/100 50.00
48 Mark Prior/Bat-Jsy/25 40.00
49 Aramis Ramirez/Bat-Jsy/100 25.00
51 Carlos Zambrano/Jsy-Jsy/200 25.00
52 Derrek Lee/Bat-Bat/100 20.00
61 Carlos Lee/Bat-Jsy/100 10.00
76 C.C. Sabathia/Jsy-Jsy/100 20.00
78 Omar Vizquel/Jsy-Jsy/25 40.00
95 Miguel Cabrera/Bat-Jsy/25 50.00
109 Carlos Beltran/Bat-Jsy/50 40.00
112 Jeremy Affeldt/Pants-Pants/100 10.00
127 Bill Hall/Bat-Bat/100 10.00
129 Jacque Jones/Bat-Jsy/50 20.00
131 Johan Santana/Jsy-Jsy/50 40.00
132 Lew Ford/Bat-Jsy/200 15.00
139 Nick Johnson/Bat-Bat/50 12.00
153 Jorge Posada/Bat-Jsy/25 40.00
162 Eric Chavez/Bat-Jsy/25 25.00
178 Craig Wilson/Bat-Jsy/200 15.00
185 Sean Burroughs/Bat-Jsy/100 10.00
201 Edgar Martinez/Bat-Bat/25 40.00
211 Edgar Renteria/Bat-Jsy/50 30.00
221 Carl Crawford/Jsy-Jsy/200 15.00
229 Mark Teixeira/Bat-Jsy/25 40.00
230 Michael Young/Bat-Jsy/100 20.00
232 Laynce Nix/Bat-Jsy/200 12.00
233 Alfonso Soriano/Bat-Jsy/25 50.00
239 Roy Halladay/Jsy-Jsy/25 25.00
269 Brad Penny/Bat-Jsy/100 10.00
280 Dale Murphy/Jsy-Jsy/50 35.00
282 Dwight Evans/Bat-Jsy/50 25.00
283 Ron Santo/Bat-Bat/100 35.00
284 Andre Dawson/Bat-Jsy/100 25.00
286 Jack Morris/Jsy-Jsy/100 20.00
287 Kirk Gibson/Bat-Jsy/25 40.00
289 Orel Hershiser/Jsy-Jsy/25 35.00
291 Tony Oliva/Bat-Jsy/100 25.00
294 Don Mattingly/Bat-Jsy/25 90.00
297 Dave Parker/Bat-Jsy/100 25.00
298 Steve Garvey/Bat-Jsy/50 25.00
300 Keith Hernandez/Bat-Jsy/100 20.00
303 Garret Anderson/Bat-Jsy/50 20.00
315 Johnny Estrada/Jsy-Jsy/50 12.00
319 Jay Gibbons/Bat-Bat/50 12.00
320 Melvin Mora/Jsy-Jsy/50 15.00
323 David Ortiz/Jsy-Jsy/25 50.00
333 Mark Buehrle/Jsy-Jsy/25 25.00
339 Travis Hafner/Jsy-Jsy/25 25.00
340 Victor Martinez/Jsy-Jsy/25 20.00
341 Cliff Lee/Jsy-Jsy/25 15.00
343 Preston Wilson/Bat-Jsy/25 20.00
351 Ken Harvey/Jsy-Jsy/25 12.00
382 Marlon Byrd/Bat-Jsy/50 12.00
401 Delmon Young/Bat-Bat/25 25.00
407 Orlando Hudson/Bat-Bat/25 12.00
419 Scott Rolen/Bat-Jsy/25 30.00
428 Alan Trammell/Bat-Jsy/25 25.00
430 Dwight Gooden/Bat-Jsy/25 25.00
434 Tony Gwynn/Bat-Jsy/25 40.00

Signature Materials Silver

NM/M

Production 1-100

7 Chone Figgins/Bat-Jsy/100 15.00
18 Rafael Furcal/Bat-Jsy/25 30.00
31 Larry Bigbie/Jsy-Jsy/100 15.00
32 Rodrigo Lopez/Jsy-Jsy/100 15.00
46 David Ortiz/Bat-Jsy/50 60.00
49 Aramis Ramirez/Bat-Jsy/50 35.00
51 Carlos Zambrano/Jsy-Jsy/100 30.00
61 Carlos Lee/Bat-Jsy/100 10.00
76 C.C. Sabathia/Jsy-Jsy/100 20.00
104 Roy Oswalt/Jsy-Jsy/50 30.00
112 Jeremy Affeldt/Pants-Pants/100 10.00
127 Bill Hall/Bat-Bat/100 10.00
129 Jacque Jones/Bat-Jsy/50 20.00
132 Lew Ford/Bat-Jsy/100 15.00
178 Craig Wilson/Bat-Jsy/100 15.00
221 Carl Crawford/Jsy-Jsy/100 15.00
230 Michael Young/Bat-Jsy/50 25.00
232 Laynce Nix/Bat-Jsy/100 15.00
269 Brad Penny/Bat-Jsy/50 15.00
280 Dale Murphy/Jsy-Jsy/25 50.00
282 Dwight Evans/Bat-Jsy/25 30.00
283 Ron Santo/Bat-Bat/50 45.00
284 Andre Dawson/Bat-Jsy/50 30.00
285 Harold Baines/Bat-Jsy/50 25.00
286 Jack Morris/Jsy-Jsy/50 25.00
291 Tony Oliva/Bat-Jsy/50 30.00
297 Dave Parker/Bat-Jsy/50 30.00
298 Steve Garvey/Bat-Jsy/25 30.00
299 Matt Williams/Jsy-Jsy/25 35.00
300 Keith Hernandez/Bat-Jsy/50 25.00

Signature Materials Gold

NM/M

Production 1-50

7 Chone Figgins/Bat-Jsy/50 20.00
18 Rafael Furcal/Bat-Jsy/25 30.00
31 Larry Bigbie/Jsy-Jsy/50 20.00
32 Rodrigo Lopez/Jsy-Jsy/50 20.00
46 David Ortiz/Bat-Jsy/50 60.00
49 Aramis Ramirez/Bat-Jsy/50 35.00
51 Carlos Zambrano/Jsy-Jsy/50 35.00
76 C.C. Sabathia/Jsy-Jsy/50 25.00
104 Roy Oswalt/Jsy-Jsy/50 30.00
112 Jeremy Affeldt/Pants-Pants/50 15.00
127 Bill Hall/Bat-Bat/50 15.00
129 Jacque Jones/Bat-Jsy/50 20.00
132 Lew Ford/Bat-Jsy/50 20.00
178 Craig Wilson/Bat-Jsy/50 20.00
221 Carl Crawford/Jsy-Jsy/50 20.00
230 Michael Young/Bat-Jsy/50 25.00
269 Brad Penny/Bat-Jsy/50 15.00
280 Dale Murphy/Jsy-Jsy/25 50.00
282 Dwight Evans/Bat-Jsy/25 30.00
283 Ron Santo/Bat-Bat/50 45.00
284 Andre Dawson/Bat-Jsy/50 30.00
285 Harold Baines/Bat-Jsy/50 25.00
286 Jack Morris/Jsy-Jsy/50 25.00
291 Tony Oliva/Bat-Jsy/50 30.00
297 Dave Parker/Bat-Jsy/50 30.00
299 Matt Williams/Jsy-Jsy/25 35.00

Team Timeline

NM/M

Complete Set (25): 65.00
Common Duo: 1.50
Inserted 1:21
#26-30 found in DK Update

1 Albert Pujols, Scott Rolen 6.00
2 Roger Clemens, Andy Pettitte 6.00
3 Tim Hudson, Mark Mulder 1.50
4 Hank Blalock, Mark Teixeira 2.00
5 Miguel Cabrera, Mike Lowell 2.00
6 Greg Maddux, Sammy Sosa 4.00
7 Miguel Tejada, Cal Ripken Jr. 8.00
8 Vladimir Guerrero, Reggie Jackson 3.00
9 Mike Schmidt, Jim Thome 4.00
10 Chipper Jones, Greg Maddux 4.00
11 George Brett, Ken Harvey 5.00
12 Don Mattingly, Hideki Matsui 5.00
13 Torii Hunter, Johan Santana 2.00
14 Carlos Delgado, Vernon Wells 1.50
15 Todd Helton, Larry Walker 2.00
16 Duke Snider, Adrian Beltre 2.00
17 Al Kaline, Ivan Rodriguez 3.00
18 Rafael Palmeiro, Eddie Murray 2.00
19 Manny Ramirez, Carl Yastrzemski 3.00
20 Ralph Kiner, Jason Bay 1.50
21 Johnny Bench, Adam Dunn 3.00
22 Robin Yount, Lyle Overbay 4.00
23 Nolan Ryan, Randy Johnson 8.00
24 Gary Carter, Mike Piazza 4.00
25 Carlton Fisk, Frank Thomas 3.00
26 Nolan Ryan, Mike Piazza 8.00
27 Roger Clemens, Jeff Bagwell 8.00
28 Cal Ripken Jr., Sammy Sosa 8.00
29 Willie Mays, Jim Thorpe 8.00
30 Albert Pujols, Stan Musial 8.00

Team Timeline Materials Bat

NM/M

Production 25-100

2 Roger Clemens, Andy Pettitte/50 25.00
5 Miguel Cabrera, Mike Lowell/100 15.00
8 Vladimir Guerrero, Reggie Jackson/75 20.00
9 Mike Schmidt, Jim Thome/50 30.00
12 Don Mattingly, Hideki Matsui/50 50.00
15 Todd Helton, Larry Walker/100 10.00
17 Al Kaline, Ivan Rodriguez/25 30.00
18 Rafael Palmeiro, Eddie Murray/100 15.00
21 Johnny Bench, Adam Dunn/100 15.00
22 Robin Yount, Lyle Overbay/100 20.00
23 Nolan Ryan, Randy Johnson/25 40.00

Teams Timeline Materials Jersey

NM/M

Common Duo: 8.00
Production 100 Sets
Prime: No Pricing
Production One Set
#26-30 found in DK Update

1 Albert Pujols, Scott Rolen 40.00
2 Roger Clemens, Andy Pettitte 25.00
3 Tim Hudson, Mark Mulder 8.00
4 Hank Blalock, Mark Teixeira 10.00
7 Miguel Tejada, Cal Ripken Jr. 40.00
8 Vladimir Guerrero, Reggie Jackson 15.00
9 Mike Schmidt Jkt, Jim Thome 30.00
10 Chipper Jones, Greg Maddux 20.00
12 Don Mattingly Jkt, Hideki Matsui 50.00
14 Carlos Delgado, Vernon Wells 8.00
15 Todd Helton, Larry Walker 10.00
16 Duke Snider, Adrian Beltre 10.00
18 Rafael Palmeiro, Eddie Murray 15.00
19 Manny Ramirez, Carl Yastrzemski 25.00
21 Johnny Bench, Adam Dunn 15.00
22 Robin Yount, Lyle Overbay 15.00
24 Gary Carter, Mike Piazza 15.00
25 Carlton Fisk, Frank Thomas 15.00
26 Nolan Ryan, Mike Piazza 30.00
27 Roger Clemens, Jeff Bagwell 20.00
30 Albert Pujols, Stan Musial 40.00

Timeline

NM/M

Complete Set (25): 50.00
Common Player: 1.50
Inserted 1:21
#26-30 found in DK Update

1 Roger Clemens 6.00
2 Nolan Ryan 8.00
3 Carlos Beltran 3.00
4 Ivan Rodriguez 3.00
5 Jim Thome 3.00
6 Mike Piazza 4.00
7 Miguel Tejada 3.00
8 Rafael Palmeiro 2.00
9 Greg Maddux 4.00
10 Tom Glavine 1.50
11 Vladimir Guerrero 3.00
12 Curt Schilling 3.00
13 Mike Mussina 2.00
14 Rickey Henderson 2.00
15 Scott Rolen 3.00
16 Alfonso Soriano 2.00
17 Gary Sheffield 2.00
18 Carlton Fisk 2.00
19 Aramis Ramirez 2.00
20 Mark Grace 1.50
21 Jason Giambi 1.50
22 Juan Gonzalez 1.50
23 Brad Penny 1.50
24 Nomar Garciaparra 4.00
25 Larry Walker 2.00
26 Curt Schilling 2.00
27 Reggie Jackson 2.00
28 Gary Carter 1.50
29 Roger Clemens 6.00
30 Nolan Ryan 8.00

Timeline Materials Bat

NM/M

Production 25-100

1 Roger Clemens 30.00
2 Nolan Ryan 50.00
3 Carlos Beltran 10.00
4 Ivan Rodriguez 10.00
5 Jim Thome 20.00
8 Rafael Palmeiro 10.00
9 Greg Maddux 30.00
10 Tom Glavine 10.00
11 Vladimir Guerrero 15.00
12 Curt Schilling 20.00
13 Mike Mussina 10.00
14 Rickey Henderson 10.00
15 Scott Rolen 20.00
17 Gary Sheffield 10.00
18 Carlton Fisk 10.00
19 Aramis Ramirez 10.00
20 Mark Grace 10.00
22 Juan Gonzalez 10.00
25 Larry Walker 10.00

Timeline Materials Jersey

NM/M

Production 50-200
Prime: No Pricing
Production One Set
#26-30 found in DK Update

1 Roger Clemens 15.00
2 Nolan Ryan 25.00
3 Carlos Beltran 10.00
4 Ivan Rodriguez 8.00
6 Mike Piazza 15.00
7 Miguel Tejada 10.00
8 Rafael Palmeiro 10.00
9 Greg Maddux 15.00
11 Vladimir Guerrero 15.00
12 Curt Schilling 10.00
13 Mike Mussina 10.00
14 Rickey Henderson 10.00
15 Scott Rolen 15.00
16 Alfonso Soriano 10.00
18 Carlton Fisk 10.00
19 Aramis Ramirez 10.00
21 Jason Giambi 8.00
22 Juan Gonzalez 8.00
26 Curt Schilling 10.00
27 Reggie Jackson 10.00
28 Gary Carter 8.00
29 Roger Clemens 15.00
30 Nolan Ryan 25.00

Update B/W

B/W: 1X
Inserted 1:2

Update Gallery of Stars

NM/M

Complete Set (25): 30.00
Common Player: 1.50
Inserted 1:8

1 Andre Dawson 1.50
2 Bob Feller 2.00
3 Bobby Doerr 1.50
4 C.C. Sabathia 1.50
5 Carl Crawford 1.50
6 Dale Murphy 2.00
7 Danny Kolb 1.50
8 Darryl Strawberry 1.50
9 Dave Parker 1.50
10 David Ortiz 3.00
11 Dwight Gooden 1.50
12 Garret Anderson 1.50
13 Jack Morris 1.50
14 Jacque Jones 1.50
15 Jim Palmer 2.00
16 Johan Santana 3.00
17 Ken Harvey 1.50
18 Lyle Overbay 1.50
19 Marty Marion 1.50
20 Melvin Mora 1.50
21 Michael Young 1.50
22 Miguel Cabrera 3.00
23 Preston Wilson 1.50
24 Sean Casey 1.50
25 Victor Martinez 1.50

Update Gallery of Stars Autograph

NM/M

Production 5-100

1 Andre Dawson/100 15.00
2 Bob Feller/100 25.00
3 Bobby Doerr/100 15.00
4 C.C. Sabathia/25 20.00
5 Carl Crawford/100 12.00
6 Dale Murphy/100 20.00
7 Danny Kolb/100 10.00
8 Darryl Strawberry/100 15.00
9 Dave Parker/100 12.00
11 Dwight Gooden/100 15.00
13 Jack Morris/100 12.00
14 Jacque Jones/50 10.00
17 Ken Harvey/100 8.00
18 Lyle Overbay/50 10.00

19 Marty Marion/25 20.00
20 Melvin Mora/100 12.00
25 Victor Martinez/100 12.00

Update Gallery of Stars Bat

NM/M

Production 50-200
1 Andre Dawson/50 8.00
3 Bobby Doerr/100 4.00
6 Dale Murphy/100 8.00
8 Darryl Strawberry/100 4.00
9 Dave Parker/200 4.00
10 David Ortiz/200 10.00
11 Dwight Gooden/100 4.00
12 Garret Anderson/100 4.00
18 Lyle Overbay/50 4.00
21 Michael Young/200 4.00
22 Miguel Cabrera/100 8.00
23 Preston Wilson/200 4.00
24 Sean Casey/200 4.00

Update Gallery of Stars Bat Autograph

NM/M

Production 5-200
1 Andre Dawson/25 25.00
3 Bobby Doerr/200 15.00
9 Dave Parker/200 15.00
11 Dwight Gooden/100 20.00
12 Garret Anderson/100 15.00
14 Jacque Jones/100 15.00
17 Ken Harvey/25 12.00
21 Michael Young/100 15.00
22 Miguel Cabrera/50 35.00
24 Sean Casey/50 20.00

Update Gallery of Stars Jersey

NM/M

Production 25-100
Prime: No Pricing
Production One Set
1 Andre Dawson/100 6.00
2 Bob Feller/50 8.00
3 Bobby Doerr/100 6.00
4 C.C. Sabathia/100 4.00
5 Carl Crawford/100 4.00
6 Dale Murphy/100 8.00
8 Darryl Strawberry/25 6.00
9 Dave Parker/100 4.00
10 David Ortiz/100 8.00
11 Dwight Gooden/25 4.00
12 Garret Anderson/50 4.00
13 Jack Morris/100 4.00
14 Jacque Jones/100 4.00
15 Jim Palmer/50 6.00
17 Ken Harvey/100 4.00
18 Lyle Overbay/100 4.00
20 Melvin Mora/100 4.00
21 Michael Young/100 4.00
22 Miguel Cabrera/100 8.00
23 Preston Wilson/100 4.00
24 Sean Casey/100 4.00
25 Victor Martinez/25 6.00

Update Gallery of Stars Jersey Autograph

NM/M

Production 25-100
Prime: No Pricing
Production One Set
1 Andre Dawson/25 25.00
2 Bob Feller/50 30.00
3 Bobby Doerr/100 15.00
4 C.C. Sabathia/100 15.00
5 Carl Crawford/50 15.00
6 Dale Murphy/50 25.00
9 Dave Parker/100 15.00
10 David Ortiz/50 40.00
11 Dwight Gooden/50 20.00
12 Garret Anderson/50 20.00
13 Jack Morris/50 15.00
14 Jacque Jones/25 20.00
15 Jim Palmer/25 25.00
17 Ken Harvey/100 8.00
18 Lyle Overbay/100 10.00
19 Marty Marion/25 20.00
20 Melvin Mora/100 15.00
24 Sean Casey/25 20.00
25 Victor Martinez/100 20.00

Update Gallery of Star Combo

NM/M

Production 50-200 5.00
Prime: No Pricing
Production One Set
1 Andre Dawson/100 10.00
3 Bobby Doerr/100 8.00
4 C.C. Sabathia/100 5.00
6 Dale Murphy/100 10.00
9 Dave Parker/200 5.00
10 David Ortiz/200 12.00
11 Dwight Gooden/100 5.00
12 Garret Anderson/100 6.00
14 Jacque Jones/50 5.00
15 Jim Palmer/50 8.00
18 Lyle Overbay/50 5.00
21 Michael Young/200 5.00
22 Miguel Cabrera/200 10.00
23 Preston Wilson/200 5.00
24 Sean Casey/200 5.00

Update Gallery of Stars Combo Autograph

NM/M

Production 25-200
Prime: No Pricing
Production One Set
1 Andre Dawson/50 25.00
3 Bobby Doerr/200 20.00
6 Dale Murphy/50 30.00
9 Dave Parker/100 15.00
10 David Ortiz/50 40.00
11 Dwight Gooden/100 20.00
12 Garret Anderson/50 20.00
14 Jacque Jones/50 20.00
15 Jim Palmer/25 25.00
17 Ken Harvey/25 15.00
21 Michael Young/50 20.00
22 Miguel Cabrera/50 35.00
24 Sean Casey/25 20.00
25 Victor Martinez/100 20.00

Update HOF Sluggers

NM/M

Common Player: 2.00
1 Duke Snider 2.00
2 Eddie Murray 2.00
3 Frank Robinson 2.00
4 George Brett 5.00
5 Harmon Killebrew 3.00
6 Mike Schmidt 5.00
7 Reggie Jackson 3.00
8 Roberto Clemente 6.00
9 Stan Musial 4.00
10 Willie Mays 5.00

Update HOF Sluggers Jersey

NM/M

Production 5-50
1 Duke Snider/Pants/25 10.00
2 Eddie Murray/50 10.00
5 Harmon Killebrew/25 15.00
6 Mike Schmidt/50 15.00
7 Reggie Jackson/Pants/50 8.00
9 Stan Musial/Pants/25 20.00
10 Willie Mays/Pants/50 25.00

Update Masters of the Game

NM/M

Common Player: 2.00
1 Albert Pujols 4.00
2 Cal Ripken Jr. 6.00
3 Don Mattingly 4.00
4 Greg Maddux 3.00
5 Jim Thorpe 4.00
6 Nolan Ryan 5.00
7 Randy Johnson 2.00
8 Roberto Clemente 6.00
9 Roger Clemens 4.00
10 Willie Mays 4.00

Update Masters of the Game Jersey

NM/M

Production 25-50
1 Albert Pujols/50 20.00
2 Cal Ripken Jr./50 30.00
3 Don Mattingly/25 20.00
4 Greg Maddux/50 10.00
5 Jim Thorpe/25 250.00
6 Nolan Ryan/50 20.00
7 Randy Johnson/25 10.00
9 Roger Clemens/50 10.00
10 Willie Mays/Pants/25 30.00

2005 Donruss Elite

NM/M

Complete Set (200):
Common Player (1-150): .25
Common SP (151-170): 3.00
Production 1,250
Common Auto. (171-200): 8.00
Production 500 to 1,500

Pack (5): 5.00
Box (20): 90.00
1 Bartolo Colon .25
2 Casey Kotchman .25
3 Chone Figgins .25
4 Darin Erstad .25
5 Garret Anderson .40
6 Jose Guillen .25
7 Vladimir Guerrero .75
8 Luis Gonzalez .25
9 Randy Johnson .75
10 Troy Glaus .40
11 Andruw Jones .40
12 Chipper Jones .75
13 J.D. Drew .25
14 John Smoltz .40
15 Johnny Estrada .25
16 Marcus Giles .25
17 Rafael Furcal .25
18 Javy Lopez .40
19 Jay Gibbons .25
20 Melvin Mora .25
21 Miguel Tejada .50
22 Rafael Palmeiro .50
23 Sidney Ponson .25
24 Curt Schilling .75
25 David Ortiz .75
26 Derek Lowe .25
27 Jason Varitek .40
28 Johnny Damon .75
29 Manny Ramirez .75
30 Pedro Martinez .75
31 Aramis Ramirez .40
32 Carlos Zambrano .40
33 Corey Patterson .25
34 Derrek Lee .50
35 Greg Maddux 1.00
36 Kerry Wood .50
37 Mark Prior .75
38 Moises Alou .40
39 Nomar Garciaparra 1.00
40 Sammy Sosa 1.00
41 Carlos Lee .25
42 Frank Thomas .50
43 Jermaine Dye .25
44 Magglio Ordonez .25
45 Mark Buehrle .25
46 Paul Konerko .25
47 Adam Dunn .50
48 Austin Kearns .25
49 Barry Larkin .40
50 Ken Griffey Jr. 1.00
51 Sean Casey .25
52 C.C. Sabathia .25
53 Cliff Lee .25
54 Travis Hafner .25
55 Victor Martinez .25
56 Jeromy Burnitz .25
57 Preston Wilson .25
58 Todd Helton .50
59 Brandon Inge .25
60 Ivan Rodriguez .50
61 Jeremy Bonderman .25
62 Troy Percival .25
63 Dontrelle Willis .40
64 Josh Beckett .40
65 Juan Pierre .25
66 Miguel Cabrera .75
67 Mike Lowell .25
68 Paul LoDuca .25
69 Andy Pettitte .40
70 Brad Ausmus .25
71 Carlos Beltran .50
72 Craig Biggio .40
73 Jeff Bagwell .50
74 Lance Berkman .40
75 Roger Clemens 2.00
76 Roy Oswalt .25
77 Juan Gonzalez .25
78 Mike Sweeney .25
79 Zack Greinke .25
80 Adrian Beltre .25
81 Hideo Nomo .25
82 Jeff Kent .25
83 Milton Bradley .25
84 Shawn Green .25
85 Steve Finley .25
86 Ben Sheets .25
87 Lyle Overbay .25
88 Scott Podsednik .25
89 Lew Ford .25
90 Shannon Stewart .25
91 Torii Hunter .25
92 David Wright .75
93 Jose Reyes .50
94 Kazuo Matsui .25
95 Mike Piazza 1.00
96 Tom Glavine .40
97 Alex Rodriguez 1.50
98 Bernie Williams .40
99 Derek Jeter 2.00
100 Gary Sheffield .50
101 Hideki Matsui 1.50
102 Jason Giambi .25
103 Kevin Brown .25
104 Mike Mussina .40
105 Barry Zito .25
106 Bobby Crosby .40
107 Eric Chavez .40
108 Jason Kendall .25
109 Mark Mulder .40
110 Bobby Abreu .40
111 Jim Thome .75
112 Kevin Millwood .25
113 Pat Burrell .25
114 Craig Wilson .25
115 Jack Wilson .25
116 Jason Bay .40
117 Brian Giles .25
118 Khalil Greene .40
119 Mark Loretta .25
120 Ryan Klesko .25
121 Sean Burroughs .25
122 Edgardo Alfonzo .25
123 J.T. Snow .25
124 Jason Schmidt .25
125 Omar Vizquel .25
126 Ichiro Suzuki 1.50
127 Jamie Moyer .25
128 Bret Boone .25
129 Richie Sexson .40
130 Albert Pujols 2.00
131 Edgar Renteria .40
132 Jeff Suppan .25
133 Jim Edmonds .40
134 Larry Walker .40
135 Scott Rolen .75
136 Aubrey Huff .25
137 B.J. Upton .25
138 Carl Crawford .25
139 Rocco Baldelli .25
140 Alfonso Soriano .75
141 Hank Blalock .40
142 Kenny Rogers .25
143 Laynce Nix .25
144 Mark Teixeira .50
145 Michael Young .25
146 Carlos Delgado .40
147 Eric Hinske .25
148 Roy Halladay .25
149 Vernon Wells .25
150 Jose Vidro .25
151 Bob Gibson 3.00
152 Brooks Robinson 3.00
153 Cal Ripken Jr. 10.00
154 Carl Yastrzemski 4.00
155 Don Mattingly 5.00
156 Eddie Murray 3.00
157 Ernie Banks 4.00
158 Frank Robinson 3.00
159 George Brett 5.00
160 Harmon Killebrew 4.00
161 Johnny Bench 4.00
162 Mike Schmidt 5.00
163 Nolan Ryan 6.00
164 Paul Molitor 4.00
165 Stan Musial 5.00
166 Steve Carlton 3.00
167 Tony Gwynn 4.00
168 Warren Spahn 4.00
169 Willie Mays 6.00
170 Willie McCovey 3.00
171 Miguel Negron/AU/1500 **RC** 8.00
172 Mike Morse/AU/1000 **RC** 15.00
173 Wladimir Balentien/AU/1500 **RC** 10.00
174 Alberto Concepcion/AU/651 **RC** 10.00
175 Ubaldo Jimenez/AU/500 **RC** 10.00
176 Justin Verlander/AU/500 **RC** 50.00
177 Ryan Speier/AU/1000 **RC** 8.00
178 Geovany Soto/AU/500 **RC** 15.00
179 Mark McLemore/AU/1200 **RC** 8.00
180 Ambiorix Burgos/AU/599 **RC** 8.00
181 Chris Roberson/AU/1000 **RC** 10.00
182 Colter Bean/AU/625 **RC** 10.00
183 Erick Threets/AU/500 **RC** 8.00
184 Carlos Ruiz/AU/1000 **RC** 15.00
186 Jared Gothreaux/AU/1500 **RC** 10.00
187 Luis Hernandez/AU/1000 **RC** 8.00
188 Agustin Montero/1000 **RC** 2.00
189 Paulino Reynoso/1000 **RC** 2.00
190 Garrett Jones/AU/500 **RC** 8.00
191 Sean Thompson/AU/500 **RC** 8.00
192 Matt Lindstrom/AU/1500 **RC** 8.00
193 Nate McLouth/AU/500 **RC** 10.00
194 Luke Scott/AU/671 **RC** 25.00
195 Keith Hattig/AU/500 10.00
196 Jason Hammel/AU/1500 **RC** 10.00
197 Danny Rueckel/AU/671 **RC** 8.00
198 Justin Wechsler/AU/500 **RC** 8.00
199 Chris Resop/AU/500 **RC** 15.00
200 Jeff Miller/AU/500 **RC** 10.00

Aspirations

Cards (1-150) print run 61-99: 4-8X
(1-150) p/r 41-60: 6-10X
(1-150) p/r 21-40: 8-15X
(151-170) p/r 36-80: 1.5-3X
Autos (171-200) p/r 40-99: .5-1.5X
No pricing production 20 or less.
Production 15-99

Status

Cards (1-150) print run 61-81: 4-8X
(1-150) p/r 41-60: 6-10X
(1-150) p/r 21-40: 8-15X
(151-170) p/r 36-81: 1.5-3X
Autos (171-200) p/r 40-81: .5-1.5X
No pricing production 20 or less.
Production 1-81

Status Gold

Gold (1-150): 10-20X
Gold (151-170): 3-5X
Gold (171-200): No Pricing
Production 24 Sets

Turn of the Century

Stars (1-150): 2-3X
Production 750
(151-170): 1X
Production 250
Rookies (171-200): .25-1X
Production 500

Back 2 Back Jacks

NM/M

Production 25-200
1 Adam Dunn/200 8.00
3 Albert Pujols/100 15.00
4 Babe Ruth/50 160.00
5 Cal Ripken Jr./100 30.00
6 David Ortiz/200 10.00
7 Eddie Murray/150 8.00
8 Ernie Banks/50 15.00
9 Frank Robinson/50 8.00
10 Gary Sheffield/200 5.00
11 George Foster/125 5.00
12 Don Mattingly/10 15.00
13 Hideki Matsui/25 30.00
14 Jason Giambi/50 5.00
16 Jim Rice/125 8.00
17 Jim Thome/200 8.00
18 Johnny Bench/125 10.00
19 Lance Berkman/200 5.00
20 Manny Ramirez/200 8.00
21 Mike Piazza/200 10.00
22 Mike Schmidt/125 15.00
23 Rafael Palmeiro/200 8.00
24 Reggie Jackson/125 10.00
25 Sammy Sosa/100 10.00
26 Scott Rolen/200 8.00
27 Stan Musial/125 15.00
28 Willie Mays/50 40.00
29 Kirk Gibson/125 5.00
30 Will Clark/125 5.00
31 Willie Mays, Sammy Sosa/50 50.00
32 Eddie Murray, Mike Piazza/50 20.00
33 Mike Schmidt, Jim Thome/50 30.00
34 Rafael Palmeiro, Kirk Gibson/50 10.00
35 Jim Rice, Manny Ramirez/50 15.00
36 Adrian Beltre, Will Clark/50 15.00
37 Reggie Jackson, David Ortiz/50 15.00
38 Johnny Bench, Adam Dunn/50 20.00

Back 2 Back Jacks Combos

NM/M

1 Adam Dunn/Bat-Jsy/100 10.00
2 Adrian Beltre/Bat-Jsy/100 8.00
5 Cal Ripken Jr./Bat-Jsy/50 40.00
6 David Ortiz/Bat-Jsy/50 12.00
7 Eddie Murray/Bat-Jsy/50 10.00
8 Ernie Banks/Bat-Jsy/10 20.00
10 Gary Sheffield/Bat-Jsy/100 8.00
11 George Foster/Bat-Jsy/50 8.00
12 Don Mattingly/Bat-Jsy/50 20.00
13 Hideki Matsui/Bat-Jsy/25 40.00
14 Jason Giambi/Bat-Jsy/50 8.00
15 Jim Edmonds/Bat-Jsy/100 10.00
17 Jim Thome/Bat-Jsy/100 8.00
18 Johnny Bench/Bat-Jsy/50 15.00
19 Lance Berkman/Bat-Jsy/100 8.00
20 Manny Ramirez/Bat-Jsy/100 12.00
21 Mike Piazza/Bat-Jsy/50 15.00
22 Mike Schmidt/Bat-Jsy/50 20.00
23 Rafael Palmeiro/Bat-Jsy/50 10.00
24 Reggie Jackson/Bat-Jsy/50 15.00
25 Sammy Sosa/Bat-Jsy/100 15.00
26 Scott Rolen/Bat-Jsy/100 12.00
27 Stan Musial/Bat-Pants/50 25.00
28 Willie Mays/Bat-Jsy/50 60.00
29 Kirk Gibson/Bat-Jsy/50 10.00
30 Will Clark/Bat-Jsy/50 12.00
32 Eddie Murray, Mike Piazza/25 30.00
33 Mike Schmidt, Jim Thome/25 50.00
34 Rafael Palmeiro, Kirk Gibson/25 20.00
35 Jim Rice, Manny Ramirez/50 25.00
36 Adrian Beltre, Will Clark/50 15.00
37 Reggie Jackson, David Ortiz/25 30.00
38 Johnny Bench, Adam Dunn/25 30.00
40 Cal Ripken Jr., Albert Pujols/25 100.00

Career Best

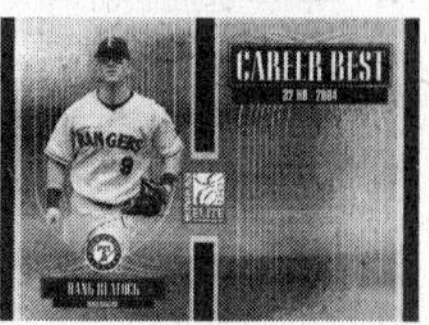

NM/M

Common Player: 1.00
Production 1,500 Sets
Black: 1-2X
Production 150 Sets
Blue: 1-2X
Production 250 Sets
Gold: 1-1.5X
Production 500 Sets
1 Adam Dunn 1.50
2 Adrian Beltre 1.00
3 Albert Pujols 4.00
4 Andruw Jones 1.50
5 Ben Sheets 1.00
6 Bo Jackson 2.00
7 Brooks Robinson 2.00
8 Cal Ripken Jr. 6.00
9 Dale Murphy 1.50
10 Don Mattingly 3.00
11 Eddie Murray 1.50
12 George Brett 3.00
13 Hank Blalock 1.50
14 Ichiro Suzuki 3.00
15 Jim Thome 1.50
16 Kerry Wood 1.50
17 Lance Berkman 1.00
18 Mark Prior 2.00
19 Mark Teixeira 1.50
20 Mike Schmidt 3.00
21 Pedro Martinez 2.00
22 Randy Johnson 2.00
23 Rickey Henderson 1.50
24 Sammy Sosa 3.00
25 Tony Gwynn 2.00

Career Best Bats

NM/M

Production 50-250
1 Adam Dunn/250 8.00
2 Adrian Beltre/250 5.00
3 Albert Pujols/250 15.00
4 Andruw Jones/250 5.00
5 Ben Sheets/250 5.00
6 Bo Jackson/250 10.00
7 Brooks Robinson/250 8.00
8 Cal Ripken Jr./150 25.00
9 Dale Murphy/150 10.00
10 Don Mattingly/250 12.00
11 Eddie Murray/250 8.00
12 George Brett/250 15.00
13 Hank Blalock/250 8.00

15 Jim Thome/100 8.00
16 Kerry Wood/100 8.00
17 Lance Berkman/250 5.00
18 Mark Prior/150 6.00
19 Mark Teixeira/250 8.00
20 Mike Schmidt/250 12.00
21 Pedro Martinez/100 10.00
22 Randy Johnson/100 10.00
23 Rickey Henderson/250 8.00
24 Sammy Sosa/100 10.00
25 Tony Gwynn/100 10.00

Career Best Jerseys

NM/M
Production 100-250
1 Adam Dunn/250 8.00
2 Adrian Beltre/250 5.00
3 Albert Pujols/250 15.00
4 Andruw Jones/250 5.00
5 Ben Sheets/250 5.00
6 Bo Jackson/250 10.00
7 Brooks Robinson/50 10.00
8 Cal Ripken Jr./150 25.00
9 Dale Murphy/100 10.00
10 Don Mattingly/150 12.00
11 Eddie Murray/100 8.00
12 George Brett/100 15.00
13 Hank Blalock/250 8.00
15 Jim Thome/250 8.00
16 Kerry Wood/250 8.00
17 Lance Berkman/250 5.00
18 Mark Prior/250 6.00
19 Mark Teixeira/250 8.00
20 Mike Schmidt/100 12.00
21 Pedro Martinez/250 8.00
22 Randy Johnson/100 10.00
23 Rickey Henderson/50 10.00
24 Sammy Sosa/250 10.00
25 Tony Gwynn/250 10.00

Career Best Combos

NM/M
Production 25-150 10.00
1 Adam Dunn/ Bat-Jsy/150 10.00
2 Adrian Beltre/ Bat-Jsy/150 8.00
3 Albert Pujols/ Bat-Jsy/150 20.00
4 Andruw Jones /Bat-Jsy/150 8.00
5 Ben Sheets/ Bat-Jsy/150 8.00
6 Bo Jackson/ Bat-Jsy/25 20.00
7 Brooks Robinson/ Bat-Jsy/25 20.00
8 Cal Ripken Jr./ Bat-Jsy/25 40.00
9 Dale Murphy/ Bat-Jsy/25 10.00
10 Don Mattingly/ Bat-Jsy/25 20.00
11 Eddie Murray/ Bat-Jsy/25 12.00
12 George Brett/ Bat-Jsy/25 25.00
13 Hank Blalock/ Bat-Jsy/150 10.00
15 Jim Thome/ Bat-Jsy/150 10.00
16 Kerry Wood/ Bat-Pants/150 10.00
17 Lance Berkman/ Bat-Jsy/150 8.00
18 Mark Prior/ Bat-Jsy/150 8.00
19 Mark Teixeira/ Bat-Jsy/150 12.00
21 Pedro Martinez/ Bat-Jsy/125 10.00
23 Rickey Henderson/ Bat-Jsy/25 15.00
24 Sammy Sosa/ Bat-Jsy/150 12.00
25 Tony Gwynn/ Bat-Jsy/25 15.00

Face 2 Face

NM/M
Complete Set (20): 35.00
Common Duo:
Production 1,500 Sets
Black: 1-1.5X
Production 500 Sets
Gold: 1-2X
Production 250 Sets
Red: 1X
Production 750 Sets
1 Roger Clemens, Scott Rolen 3.00
2 Greg Maddux, Jeff Bagwell 3.00
3 Mark Prior, Mike Piazza 3.00
4 Mike Mussina, Ivan Rodriguez 2.00
5 Josh Beckett, Sammy Sosa 2.00
6 Roy Oswalt, Miguel Cabrera 2.00
7 Roger Clemens, Albert Pujols 4.00
8 Pedro Martinez, Vladimir Guerrero 2.00
9 Randy Johnson, Jim Edmonds 2.00
10 Curt Schilling, Derek Jeter 4.00
11 Kerry Wood, Lance Berkman 1.50
12 Tim Hudson, Garret Anderson 1.00
13 Pedro Martinez, Gary Sheffield 2.00
14 Barry Zito, Magglio Ordonez 1.00
15 Kerry Wood, Shawn Green 1.50
16 Mike Mussina, Miguel Tejada 2.00
17 Randy Johnson, Albert Pujols 4.00
18 Nolan Ryan, George Brett 4.00
19 Tom Seaver, Mike Schmidt 3.00
20 Jim Palmer, Harmon Killebrew 2.00

Face 2 Face Bats

NM/M
Production 25-150
3 Mark Prior, Mike Piazza/10 8.00
4 Mike Mussina, Ivan Rodriguez/100 8.00
5 Josh Beckett, Sammy Sosa/50 10.00
6 Roy Oswalt, Miguel Cabrera/100 10.00
8 Pedro Martinez, Vladimir Guerrero/50 10.00
9 Randy Johnson, Jim Edmonds/50 10.00
11 Kerry Wood, Lance Berkman/150 8.00
12 Tim Hudson, Garret Anderson/150 8.00
13 Pedro Martinez, Gary Sheffield/150 10.00
14 Barry Zito, Magglio Ordonez/50 8.00
15 Kerry Wood, Shawn Green/150 8.00
18 Nolan Ryan, George Brett/100 25.00
19 Tom Seaver, Mike Schmidt/150 15.00

Face 2 Face Jerseys

NM/M
Production 25-200
1 Roger Clemens, Scott Rolen/200 15.00
2 Greg Maddux, Jeff Bagwell/75 10.00
3 Mark Prior, Mike Piazza/200 8.00
4 Mike Mussina, Ivan Rodriguez/200 8.00
5 Josh Beckett, Sammy Sosa/200 12.00
6 Roy Oswalt, Miguel Cabrera/200 8.00
7 Roger Clemens, Albert Pujols/200 20.00
8 Pedro Martinez, Vladimir Guerrero/75 10.00
11 Kerry Wood, Lance Berkman/200 8.00
12 Tim Hudson, Garret Anderson/75 8.00
13 Pedro Martinez, Gary Sheffield/75 10.00
14 Barry Zito, Magglio Ordonez/200 8.00
15 Kerry Wood, Shawn Green/200 8.00
16 Mike Mussina, Miguel Tejada/200 10.00
17 Randy Johnson, Albert Pujols/75 20.00
19 Tom Seaver, Mike Schmidt/50 20.00

Face 2 Face Combos

NM/M
Production 25-250
1 Roger Clemens/Jsy, Scott Rolen/Bat/100 15.00
2 Greg Maddux/Jsy, Jeff Bagwell/Bat/100 10.00
3 Mark Prior/Jsy, Mike Piazza/Bat/250 8.00
4 Mike Mussina/Jsy, Ivan Rodriguez/ Bat/250 8.00
5 Josh Beckett/Jsy, Sammy Sosa/Bat/250 10.00
6 Roy Oswalt Jsy, Miguel Cabrera/ Bat/250 8.00
8 Pedro Martinez/Jsy, Vladimir Guerrero/ Bat/75 10.00
11 Kerry Wood/Bat, Lance Berkman/ Jsy/250 8.00
12 Tim Hudson/Jsy, Garret Anderson/ Bat/100 8.00
13 Pedro Martinez/Bat, Gary Sheffield/Jsy/75 12.00
14 Barry Zito/Jsy, Magglio Ordonez/ Bat/250 8.00
15 Kerry Wood/Jsy, Shawn Green/Bat/250 8.00
16 Mike Mussina/Jsy, Miguel Tejada/ Bat/250 10.00
19 Tom Seaver Jsy, Mike Schmidt Bat/50 20.00

Passing the Torch

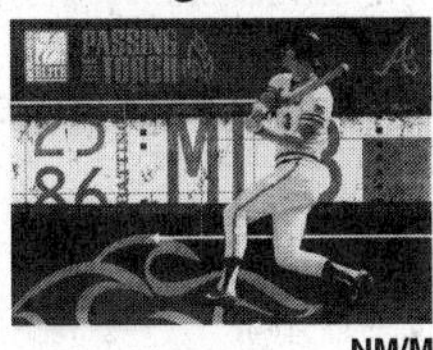

NM/M
Common Player: 1.50
1-30 Production 1,000
31-45 Production 500
Black: 2-3X
1-30 Production 50
31-45 Production 25
Gold: 1-2X
1-30 Production 100
31-45 Production 50
Green: 1-1.5X
1-30 Production 250
31-45 Production 125
Red: 1X
1-30 Production 500
31-45 Production 250
1 Adrian Beltre 1.50
2 Albert Pujols 5.00
3 Alex Rodriguez 4.00
4 Andruw Jones 1.50
5 Babe Ruth 6.00
6 Ben Sheets 1.50
7 Brooks Robinson 2.00
8 Cal Ripken Jr. 8.00
9 Carl Yastrzemski 3.00
10 Dale Murphy 2.00
11 David Ortiz 2.00
12 Derek Jeter 5.00
13 Don Mattingly 4.00
14 George Brett 4.00
15 Greg Maddux 3.00
16 Hank Blalock 1.50
17 Jeff Bagwell 1.50
18 Johnny Bench 3.00
19 Magglio Ordonez 1.50
20 Mark Prior 2.00
21 Mark Teixeira 2.00
22 Miguel Cabrera 2.00
23 Mike Schmidt 3.00
24 Nolan Ryan 6.00
25 Pedro Martinez 2.00
26 Sammy Sosa 3.00
27 Scott Rolen 2.00
28 Tom Seaver 2.00
29 Vladimir Guerrero 2.00
30 Willie Mays 4.00
31 Carlton Fisk, Magglio Ordonez 3.00
32 Nolan Ryan, Ben Sheets 8.00
33 Babe Ruth, Alex Rodriguez 8.00
34 Cal Ripken Jr., B.J. Upton 10.00
35 Willie Mays, Andruw Jones 5.00
36 George Brett, Hank Blalock 5.00
37 Greg Maddux, Whitey Ford 4.00
38 Harmon Killebrew, Mark Prior 3.00
39 Tom Seaver, Mark Prior 3.00
40 Don Mattingly, Mark Teixeira 5.00
41 Stan Musial, Carlos Beltran 5.00
42 Dale Murphy, Lance Berkman 3.00
43 Willie McCovey, Jeff Bagwell 3.00
44 Andre Dawson, Miguel Cabrera 3.00
45 Brooks Robinson, Scott Rolen 4.00

Passing the Torch Autographs

NM/M
Production 5-100
1 Adrian Beltre/75 15.00
6 Ben Sheets/75 15.00
7 Brooks Robinson/ 100 25.00
10 Dale Murphy/100 20.00
13 Don Mattingly/50 50.00
18 Johnny Bench/25 50.00
19 Magglio Ordonez/75 10.00
20 Mark Prior/25 40.00
21 Mark Teixeira/75 25.00
22 Miguel Cabrera/75 25.00
23 Mike Schmidt/25 50.00
27 Scott Rolen/25 40.00
28 Tom Seaver/25 50.00
31 Carlton Fisk, Magglio Ordonez/25 50.00
44 Andre Dawson, Miguel Cabrera/25 50.00
45 Brooks Robinson, Scott Rolen/25 75.00

Passing the Torch Bats

NM/M
Production 25-250
1 Adrian Beltre/250 4.00
2 Albert Pujols/250 15.00
4 Andruw Jones/250 4.00
6 Ben Sheets/250 4.00
7 Brooks Robinson/ 150 10.00
8 Cal Ripken Jr./150 25.00
9 Carl Yastrzemski/150 10.00
10 Dale Murphy/150 6.00
11 David Ortiz/250 8.00
13 Don Mattingly/150 10.00
14 George Brett/150 10.00
16 Hank Blalock/250 4.00
17 Jeff Bagwell/250 6.00
18 Johnny Bench/150 10.00
19 Magglio Ordonez/250 4.00
20 Mark Prior/50 10.00
21 Mark Teixeira/250 6.00
22 Miguel Cabrera/250 8.00
23 Mike Schmidt/150 10.00
24 Nolan Ryan/50 20.00
25 Pedro Martinez/150 8.00
26 Sammy Sosa/250 8.00
27 Scott Rolen/250 8.00
28 Tom Seaver/150 8.00
29 Vladimir Guerrero/250 8.00
30 Willie Mays/50 30.00
31 Carlton Fisk, Magglio Ordonez/250 6.00
32 Nolan Ryan, Ben Sheets/50 35.00
34 Cal Ripken Jr., B.J. Upton/50 50.00
35 Willie Mays, Andruw Jones/50 35.00
36 George Brett, Hank Blalock/150 15.00
39 Tom Seaver, Mark Prior/25 20.00
40 Don Mattingly, Mark Teixeira/150 15.00
42 Dale Murphy, Lance Berkman/50 12.00
43 Willie McCovey, Jeff Bagwell/25 20.00
44 Andre Dawson, Miguel Cabrera/150 10.00
45 Brooks Robinson, Scott Rolen/150 15.00

Passing the Torch Jerseys

NM/M
Production 25-250
1 Adrian Beltre/250 4.00
2 Albert Pujols/250 15.00
4 Andruw Jones/250 4.00
6 Ben Sheets/250 4.00
8 Cal Ripken Jr./250 20.00
9 Carl Yastrzemski/ Pants/50 10.00
10 Dale Murphy/250 6.00
11 David Ortiz/250 8.00
13 Don Mattingly/150 10.00
14 George Brett/50 12.00
15 Greg Maddux/250 10.00
16 Hank Blalock/250 4.00
17 Jeff Bagwell/250 6.00
18 Johnny Bench/ Pants/150 10.00
19 Magglio Ordonez/250 4.00
20 Mark Prior/250 8.00
21 Mark Teixeira/250 6.00
22 Miguel Cabrera/250 8.00
23 Mike Schmidt/150 10.00
24 Nolan Ryan/50 20.00
25 Pedro Martinez/250 8.00
26 Sammy Sosa/250 8.00
27 Scott Rolen/250 8.00
28 Tom Seaver/150 8.00
29 Vladimir Guerrero/250 8.00
31 Carlton Fisk, Magglio Ordonez/50 8.00
32 Nolan Ryan, Ben Sheets/50 35.00
34 Cal Ripken Jr., B.J. Upton/50 50.00
35 Willie Mays, Andruw Jones/50 35.00
36 George Brett, Hank Blalock/50 15.00
39 Tom Seaver, Mark Prior/25 20.00
40 Don Mattingly, Mark Teixeira/100 15.00
42 Dale Murphy, Lance Berkman/150 10.00
43 Willie McCovey, Jeff Bagwell/50 15.00
44 Andre Dawson, Miguel Cabrera/150 10.00

Recollection Autographs

Production 10-25

Teams

NM/M
Common Card:
Production 1,500 Sets
Black: 1X-2X
Production 250 Sets
Blue: 1X
Production 1,000 Sets
Gold: 2X-3X
Production 100 Sets
Green: 1X-1.5X
Production 750 Sets
Red: 1X-1.5X
Production 500 Sets
1 Manny Ramirez, Pedro Martinez, David Ortiz 4.00
2 Albert Pujols, Scott Rolen, Jim Edmonds 4.00
3 Roger Clemens, Jeff Bagwell, Lance Berkman, Craig Biggio 4.00
4 Miguel Cabrera, Josh Beckett, Mike Lowell 2.00
5 Kerry Wood, Mark Prior, Sammy Sosa, Greg Maddux 4.00
6 Adrian Beltre, Shawn Green, Hideo Nomo, Kazuhisa Ishii 2.00
7 Cal Ripken Jr., Eddie Murray, Jim Palmer 8.00
8 George Brett, Bo Jackson, Frank White 4.00
9 Roger Clemens, Mike Mussina, Alfonso Soriano, Bernie Williams 4.00
10 Tom Glavine, Greg Maddux, Ryan Klesko, David Justice 4.00

Teams Bats

NM/M
Production 50-100
1 Manny Ramirez, Pedro Martinez, David Ortiz/100 20.00
2 Albert Pujols, Scott Rolen, Jim Edmonds/100 40.00
3 Roger Clemens, Jeff Bagwell, Lance Berkman, Craig Biggio/50 35.00
4 Miguel Cabrera, Josh Beckett, Mike Lowell/100 10.00
6 Adrian Beltre, Shawn Green, Hideo Nomo, Kazuhisa Ishii/50 20.00
8 George Brett, Bo Jackson, Frank White/100 25.00

Teams Jerseys

NM/M
Production 50-150
1 Manny Ramirez, Pedro Martinez, David Ortiz/150 20.00
2 Albert Pujols, Scott Rolen, Jim Edmonds/150 30.00
3 Roger Clemens, Jeff Bagwell, Lance Berkman, Craig Biggio/150 25.00
4 Miguel Cabrera, Josh Beckett, Mike Lowell/50 15.00
5 Kerry Wood, Mark Prior, Sammy Sosa, Greg Maddux/150 25.00
6 Adrian Beltre, Shawn Green, Hideo Nomo, Kazuhisa Ishii/50 20.00
7 Cal Ripken Jr., Eddie Murray, Jim Palmer/100 35.00
9 Roger Clemens, Mike Mussina, Alfonso Soriano, Bernie Williams/100 25.00
10 Tom Glavine, Greg Maddux, Ryan Klesko, David Justice/100 30.00

Throwback Threads

NM/M
Production 10-200
1 Albert Pujols/200 15.00
3 Bert Blyleven/200 4.00
4 Bobby Doerr/ Pants/200 6.00
6 Cal Ripken Jr./150 25.00
7 Carl Yastrzemski/ Pants/150 12.00
8 Dale Murphy/150 8.00
9 Dennis Eckersley/50 8.00
10 Don Mattingly/200 10.00
11 Don Sutton/100 4.00
13 Early Wynn/50 6.00
14 Eddie Murray/100 8.00
16 Greg Maddux/150 8.00
17 Harmon Killebrew/100 8.00
18 Hoyt Wilhelm/150 6.00
19 Jim Edmonds/200 8.00
21 Lou Boudreau/100 8.00
22 Lou Brock/100 8.00
23 Miguel Cabrera/200 8.00
24 Mike Mussina/150 8.00
25 Mike Piazza/150 8.00
26 Mike Schmidt/150 15.00
27 Nolan Ryan/50 20.00
28 Phil Niekro/100 6.00
29 Randy Johnson/150 8.00
30 Rickey Henderson/150 8.00
31 Sammy Sosa/150 8.00
32 Scott Rolen/200 8.00
34 Steve Carlton/100 8.00
36 Tommy John/150 6.00
37 Vladimir Guerrero/200 8.00
38 Whitey Ford/25 15.00
39 Willie Mays/50 40.00
40 Willie McCovey/150 8.00
46 Lou Brock, Rickey Henderson/ 100 15.00
49 Bo Jackson, Deion Sanders/150 15.00
50 Nolan Ryan, Curt Schilling/100 25.00
51 Don Sutton, Greg Maddux/100 15.00
52 Harmon Killebrew, Rafael Palmeiro/100 15.00
53 Dale Murphy, Dwight Evans/150 12.00
55 Carl Yastrzemski, Vladimir Guerrero/50 15.00
56 Eddie Murray, Mike Piazza/100 12.00
57 Johnny Bench, Ivan Rodriguez/50 12.00
58 Jim Palmer, Tim Hudson/50 10.00
59 Cal Ripken Jr., Hank Blalock/50 35.00
60 Jim Rice, Manny Ramirez/100 12.00

Throwback Threads Autographs

NM/M
Production 5-100
Prime: No Pricing
Production 1-10
3 Bert Blyleven/100 15.00
4 Bobby Doerr/ Pants/100 20.00

5 Brooks Robinson/50 30.00
8 Dale Murphy/100 25.00
9 Dennis Eckersley/75 20.00
11 Don Sutton/50 20.00
17 Harmon Killebrew/75 30.00
20 Jim Palmer/75 15.00
22 Lou Brock Jkt/75 30.00
23 Miguel Cabrera/75 30.00

Throwback Threads Prime

Production 1-25

2005 Donruss Greats

NM/M
Complete Set (150): 50.00
Common Player: .50
Pack (5): 9.00
Box (15): 120.00
1 Al Kaline .75
2 Alan Trammell .50
3 Andre Dawson .50
4 Barry Larkin .75
5 Bert Blyleven .50
6 Billy Williams .50
7 Bo Jackson 1.00
8 Bob Feller .75
9 Bobby Doerr .50
10 Brooks Robinson 1.00
11 Cal Ripken Jr. 4.00
12 Dale Murphy .50
13 Darryl Strawberry .50
14 Dave Parker .50
15 Dave Stewart .50
16 David Cone .50
17 Dennis Eckersley .50
18 Don Larsen .50
19 Don Mattingly 2.00
20 Don Sutton .50
21 Duke Snider 1.00
22 Dwight Evans .50
23 Dwight Gooden .50
24 Earl Weaver .50
25 Fergie Jenkins .50
26 Frank Robinson 1.00
27 Fred Lynn .50
28 Gary Carter .50
29 Gaylord Perry .50
30 George Brett 2.50
31 George Foster .50
32 George Kell .50
33 Harmon Killebrew 1.50
34 Harold Baines .50
35 Harold Reynolds .50
36 Jack Morris .50
37 Jim Abbott .50
38 Jim Bunning .50
39 Jim Palmer .50
40 Jim Rice .50
41 Jim Leyritz .50
42 Joe Morgan .50
43 John Kruk .50
44 Johnny Bench 2.00
45 Johnny Podres .50
46 Jose Canseco 1.00
47 Juan Marichal .50
48 Keith Hernandez .50
49 Kent Hrbek .50
50 Kirby Puckett 2.00
51 Lee Smith .50
52 Lenny Dykstra .50
53 Luis Aparicio .50
54 Luis Tiant .50
55 Mark Grace .50
56 Marty Marion .50
57 Matt Williams .50
58 Maury Wills .50
59 Mike Schmidt 2.00
60 Minnie Minoso .50
61 Nolan Ryan 3.00
62 Ozzie Smith 1.00
63 Paul Molitor .75
64 Phil Rizzuto .75
65 Ralph Kiner .50
66 Randy Jones .50
67 Red Schoendienst .50
68 Rich "Goose" Gossage .50
69 Rob Dibble .50
70 Robin Roberts .50
71 Rod Carew .50
72 Rollie Fingers .50
73 Ron Guidry .50
74 Ron Santo .50
75 Ryne Sandberg 2.00
76 Stan Musial 2.00
77 Steve Carlton .50
78 Steve Garvey .50
79 Steve Stone .50
80 Terry Pendleton .50
81 Terry Steinbach .50
82 Tom Seaver 1.00
83 Tommy John .50
84 Tony Gwynn 1.00
85 Tony Oliva .50
86 Whitey Ford 1.00
87 Will Clark .75
88 Willie Mays 3.00
89 Willie McCovey 1.00
90 Roberto Clemente 2.50
91 Roger Maris 2.00
92 Bob Gibson .75
93 Carl Yastrzemski 1.50
94 Jim "Catfish" Hunter .50
95 Warren Spahn 1.00
96 Reggie Jackson 1.00
97 Lou Brock .75
98 Joe Morgan .50
99 Carlton Fisk .50
100 Eddie Murray .50
101 Roger Clemens 3.00
102 Greg Maddux 2.00
103 Derek Jeter 3.00
104 Albert Pujols 3.00
105 Ken Griffey Jr. 2.00
106 Alex Rodriguez 3.00
107 Mike Piazza 1.50
108 Manny Ramirez 1.00
109 Sammy Sosa 1.00
110 Rafael Palmeiro .75
111 Randy Johnson 1.00
112 Vladimir Guerrero 1.00
113 Ichiro Suzuki 2.00
114 David Ortiz 1.00
115 Miguel Cabrera 1.00
116 Frank Thomas 1.00
117 Pedro Martinez 1.00
118 Chipper Jones 1.00
119 Todd Helton .75
120 Alfonso Soriano 1.00
121 Ivan Rodriguez .75
122 Carlos Delgado .75
123 Carlos Beltran .75
124 Jeff Kent .50
125 Curt Schilling .75
126 Derrek Lee .75
127 Jason Bay .50
128 Mark Teixeira .75
129 Craig Biggio .50
130 Miguel Tejada .50
131 Johan Santana .75
132 Jim Thome .75
133 Tim Hudson .50
134 Barry Zito .50
135 Mark Mulder .50
136 Hideki Matsui 2.00
137 John Smoltz .50
138 Mark Prior .75
139 Andruw Jones .75
140 Adam Dunn .75
141 Prince Fielder 4.00
142 Tadahito Iguchi **RC** 2.00
143 Randy Johnson 1.00
144 Pedro Martinez 1.00
145 Alex Rodriguez 3.00
146 Roger Clemens 3.00
147 Vladimir Guerrero 1.00
148 Greg Maddux 2.00
149 Ken Griffey Jr. 2.00
150 Roger Clemens 3.00

Gold Holofoil

Gold Holofoil: 3-4X
Production 100 Sets

Platinum Holofoil

Platinum Holofoil: 3-5X
Production 50 Sets

Silver Holofoil

Silver Holofoil: 1-2X
Inserted 1:3

Dodger Blues Brooklyn Material

NM/M
Common Player: 10.00
Prime: No Pricing
Production 10
1 Sandy Koufax/43 140.00
2 Duke Snider/27 40.00
3 Burleigh Grimes 40.00
4 Tommy Lasorda 10.00

Dodger Blues Brooklyn Signature Material

NM/M
1 Sandy Koufax/37 300.00

Dodger Blues LA Material

NM/M
Common Player: 10.00
Prime: No Pricing
Production 1-10
1 Sandy Koufax/43 140.00
2 Duke Snider/55 35.00
4 Tommy Lasorda 10.00
5 Orel Hershiser 10.00
6 Don Sutton 10.00

Dodger Blues LA Signature Material

NM/M
Production 10-37
Prime: No Pricing
Production 1-5
1 Sandy Koufax/37 300.00

Hall of Fame Souvenirs

NM/M
Common Player: 2.00
1 Willie Mays/Giants 4.00
2 Hank Aaron/Mil. 4.00
3 Hank Aaron/Atl. 4.00
4 Willie Mays/Mets 4.00
5 Nolan Ryan 6.00
6 Roberto Clemente/ Kneeling 4.00
7 Nellie Fox 2.00
8 Pee Wee Reese 3.00
9 Babe Ruth 6.00
10 Bobby Doerr 2.00
11 Brooks Robinson 3.00
12 Carlton Fisk 3.00
13 Eddie Murray 3.00
14 Ernie Banks 4.00
15 Frank Robinson 3.00
16 Gary Carter 2.00
17 Hack Wilson 2.00
18 Harmon Killebrew 4.00
19 Joe Morgan 2.00
20 Kirby Puckett 4.00
21 Lou Brock 3.00
22 Orlando Cepeda 2.00
23 Red Schoendienst 2.00
24 Richie Ashburn 2.00
25 Stan Musial 5.00
26 Roberto Clemente/ Standing 6.00
27 Wade Boggs/Sox 3.00
28 Wade Boggs/Yanks. 3.00

Hall of Fame Souvenirs Material Bat

NM/M
Common Player: 10.00
1 Willie Mays 25.00
2 Hank Aaron 25.00
3 Hank Aaron 25.00
4 Willie Mays 25.00
5 Nolan Ryan/30 25.00
6 Roberto Clemente 40.00
7 Nellie Fox 10.00
8 Pee Wee Reese 10.00
9 Babe Ruth 140.00
11 Brooks Robinson 10.00
12 Carlton Fisk 10.00
13 Eddie Murray 10.00
14 Ernie Banks 15.00
15 Frank Robinson 8.00
16 Gary Carter 8.00
17 Hack Wilson 30.00
18 Harmon Killebrew 10.00
19 Joe Morgan 8.00
20 Kirby Puckett 10.00
21 Lou Brock 8.00
22 Orlando Cepeda 8.00
23 Red Schoendienst 8.00
24 Richie Ashburn 8.00
25 Stan Musial 20.00
26 Roberto Clemente 40.00
27 Wade Boggs 10.00
28 Wade Boggs 10.00

HOF Souvenirs Material Combo

NM/M
Common Combo: 10.00
1 Willie Mays Giants 50.00
2 Hank Aaron Mil 50.00
3 Hank Aaron Atl 50.00
4 Willie Mays/25 50.00
5 Nolan Ryan/25 40.00
8 Pee Wee Reese/38 25.00
9 Babe Ruth/50 300.00
10 Bobby Doerr 10.00
11 Brooks Robinson/29 20.00
12 Carlton Fisk 10.00
13 Eddie Murray 10.00
14 Ernie Banks 20.00
16 Gary Carter 10.00
18 Harmon Killebrew 15.00
23 Red Schoendienst 10.00
26 Roberto Clemente 75.00
27 Wade Boggs 15.00
28 Wade Boggs 25.00

HOF Souvenirs Material Jersey

NM/M
Common Player: 10.00
1 Willie Mays/25 40.00
2 Hank Aaron/25 40.00
3 Hank Aaron/25 40.00
4 Willie Mays/25 40.00
5 Nolan Ryan/25 25.00
9 Babe Ruth/25 225.00
10 Bobby Doerr 10.00
12 Carlton Fisk 10.00
24 Richie Ashburn 10.00
25 Stan Musial 25.00
27 Wade Boggs 12.00

Hall of Fame Souvenirs Signature

No Pricing

HOF Souvenirs Signature Material Bat

NM/M
No pricing production 22 or less.
10 Bobby Doerr 20.00
11 Brooks Robinson 30.00
12 Carlton Fisk 30.00
15 Frank Robinson 20.00
16 Gary Carter 20.00
18 Harmon Killebrew 30.00
19 Joe Morgan 20.00
20 Kirby Puckett/52 90.00
21 Lou Brock 25.00
22 Orlando Cepeda 20.00
23 Red Schoendienst 25.00
25 Stan Musial/50 60.00

HOF Souvenirs Signature Material Combo

NM/M
Common Signature: 20.00
10 Bobby Doerr 20.00
11 Brooks Robinson 40.00
12 Carlton Fisk/50 40.00
15 Frank Robinson/39 30.00
16 Gary Carter 20.00
18 Harmon Killebrew 30.00
19 Joe Morgan/23 25.00
20 Kirby Puckett/45 125.00
22 Orlando Cepeda 25.00
25 Stan Musial 80.00
27 Wade Boggs/50 40.00
28 Wade Boggs/31 40.00

HOF Souvenirs Signature Material Jersey

NM/M
Common Signature: 20.00
10 Bobby Doerr 20.00
11 Brooks Robinson 40.00
12 Carlton Fisk 30.00
15 Frank Robinson 30.00
16 Gary Carter/63 20.00
18 Harmon Killebrew 30.00
22 Orlando Cepeda/68 20.00
23 Red Schoendienst 25.00
25 Stan Musial 65.00
27 Wade Boggs/50 40.00
28 Wade Boggs/3 40.00

Redbirds Material

NM/M
Common Player: 8.00
Prime: No Pricing
Production 1-25
1 Stan Musial/ w/Glove Jsy T2 35.00
2 Ozzie Smith/Jkt T4 20.00
3 Enos Slaughter/ Jsy T4 15.00
4 Frankie Frisch/Jkt T3 20.00
5 Lou Brock/Jsy T2 15.00
6 Bob Gibson/Jsy T2 20.00
7 Ken Boyer/Jsy T3 25.00
8 Lee Smith/Jsy T4 8.00
9 Albert Pujols/ Jsy T2 30.00
10 Stan Musial/ w/Bant Pants T2 35.00

Redbirds Signature Material

NM/M
Production 5-50
Prime: No Pricing
Production 1-5
8 Lee Smith/50 20.00

Signature Gold HoloFoil

NM/M
Tier 1 Production 1-50
Tier 2 Production 51-100
Tier 3 Production 101-250
Tier 4 Production 251-800
Tier 5 Production 801-1200
Tier 6 Production 1201-2000
Cards are not serial numbered.
1 Al Kaline/T2 30.00
2 Alan Trammell/T3 15.00
3 Andre Dawson/T5 10.00
4 Barry Larkin/T2/55 30.00
5 Bert Blyleven/T4 10.00
6 Billy Williams/T2/55 15.00
7 Bo Jackson/T1/35 50.00
8 Bob Feller/T6 15.00
9 Bobby Doerr/T5 20.00
10 Brooks Robinson/T2 30.00
11 Cal Ripken Jr./T3 120.00
12 Dale Murphy/T3 20.00
13 Darryl Strawberry/T6 15.00
14 Dave Parker/T3 10.00
15 Dave Stewart/T4 10.00
16 David Cone/T2 15.00
17 Dennis Eckersley/T2 20.00
18 Don Larsen/T4 20.00
19 Don Mattingly/T1/45 75.00
20 Don Sutton/T3 15.00
21 Duke Snider/T2/55 25.00
22 Dwight Evans/T3 15.00
23 Dwight Gooden/T4 15.00
24 Earl Weaver/T4 15.00
25 Fergie Jenkins/T3 15.00
26 Frank Robinson/T2 25.00
27 Fred Lynn/T4 10.00
28 Gary Carter/T2/55 15.00
29 Gaylord Perry/T3 15.00
30 George Brett/T1/35 75.00
31 George Foster/T5 10.00
32 George Kell/T6 15.00
33 Harmon Killebrew/ T2/55 30.00
34 Harold Baines/T4 10.00
35 Harold Reynolds/T4 10.00
36 Jack Morris/T5 10.00
37 Jim Abbott/T4 10.00
38 Jim Bunning/T2 25.00
39 Jim Palmer/T3 15.00
40 Jim Rice/T2 20.00
41 Jim Leyritz/T3 10.00
42 Joe Morgan/T1/35 20.00
43 John Kruk/T2 20.00
44 Johnny Bench/T1/35 50.00
45 Johnny Podres/T6 10.00
46 Jose Canseco/T1/45 35.00
47 Juan Marichal/T2 20.00
48 Keith Hernandez/T5 15.00
49 Kent Hrbek/T5 10.00
50 Kirby Puckett/T1/35 85.00
51 Lee Smith/T5 10.00
52 Lenny Dykstra/T4 10.00
53 Luis Aparicio/T3 15.00
54 Luis Tiant/T3 15.00
55 Mark Grace/T1/45 25.00
56 Marty Marion/T4 15.00
57 Matt Williams/T5 15.00
58 Maury Wills/T4 15.00
59 Mike Schmidt/T1/35 50.00
60 Minnie Minoso/T5 15.00
61 Nolan Ryan/T2/75 80.00
62 Ozzie Smith/T2/55 40.00
63 Paul Molitor/T2/55 30.00
64 Phil Rizzuto/T2/55 30.00
65 Ralph Kiner/T5 25.00
66 Randy Jones/T4 10.00
67 Red Schoendienst/T3 10.00
68 Rich "Goose" Gossage/T3 10.00
69 Rob Dibble/T4 30.00
70 Robin Roberts/T2 30.00
71 Rod Carew/T2/55 25.00
72 Rollie Fingers/T3 15.00
73 Ron Guidry/T3 25.00
74 Ron Santo/T3 20.00
75 Ryne Sandberg/ T1/35 60.00
76 Stan Musial 20.00
77 Steve Carlton/T2 15.00
78 Steve Garvey/T3 15.00
79 Steve Stone/T5 15.00
81 Terry Steinbach/T3 10.00
82 Tom Seaver/T1/35 40.00
83 Tommy John/T6 10.00
84 Tony Gwynn/T1/45 40.00
85 Tony Oliva/T5 15.00
86 Whitey Ford/T1/35 40.00
87 Will Clark/T2/55 25.00
88 Willie Mays/T2 150.00
89 Willie McCovey/ T1/45 35.00

Signature Platinum HoloFoil

NM/M
Production 1-50
Cards are not serial #'d.
3 Andre Dawson 15.00
5 Bert Blyleven 15.00
8 Bob Feller 25.00
9 Bobby Doerr 20.00
13 Darryl Strawberry 15.00
14 Dave Parker 15.00
18 Don Larsen 30.00
23 Dwight Gooden 20.00
25 Fergie Jenkins 25.00
27 Fred Lynn 15.00
31 George Foster 15.00
32 George Kell 25.00
34 Harold Baines 20.00
35 Harold Reynolds 15.00
36 Jack Morris 15.00
39 Jim Palmer 25.00
45 Johnny Podres 20.00
48 Keith Hernandez 15.00
49 Kent Hrbek 20.00
51 Lee Smith 20.00
52 Lenny Dykstra 20.00
54 Luis Tiant 20.00
56 Marty Marion 25.00
57 Matt Williams 20.00
58 Maury Wills 20.00
60 Minnie Minoso 25.00
65 Ralph Kiner 40.00
66 Randy Jones 15.00
67 Red Schoendienst 25.00
69 Rob Dibble 15.00
74 Ron Santo 30.00
79 Steve Stone 20.00
81 Terry Steinbach 15.00
83 Tommy John 15.00
85 Tony Oliva 20.00

Souvenirs

NM/M
Common Player: 2.00
1 Jim Thorpe 4.00
2 Joe Carter 2.00
3 Will Clark 3.00
4 Cal Ripken Jr. 6.00
5 Dwight Evans 2.00
6 George Foster 2.00
7 Steve Garvey 2.00
8 Don Mattingly 4.00
9 Deion Sanders 3.00
10 Ron Santo 3.00
11 Alan Trammell 2.00
12 Robin Ventura 2.00
13 Matt Williams 3.00

Souvenirs Material Bat

NM/M
Common Player: 5.00
2 Joe Carter 5.00
3 Will Clark 8.00
5 Dwight Evans 5.00
6 George Foster 5.00
7 Steve Garvey 5.00
8 Don Mattingly 15.00
9 Deion Sanders 8.00
10 Ron Santo 8.00
11 Alan Trammell 8.00
12 Robin Ventura 5.00
13 Matt Williams 5.00

Souvenirs Material Combo

NM/M
Common Combo:
2 Joe Carter/50 10.00
3 Will Clark 12.00
9 Deion Sanders 12.00
11 Alan Trammell 10.00
13 Matt Williams 10.00

Souvenirs Material Jersey

NM/M
Common Player: 5.00
1 Jim Thorpe 120.00
3 Will Clark 10.00
4 Cal Ripken Jr. 25.00
9 Deion Sanders 10.00
11 Alan Trammell/68 10.00
12 Robin Ventura/48 5.00
13 Matt Williams 8.00

Souvenirs Signature

NM/M
Common Auto.: 15.00
3 Will Clark 25.00
5 Dwight Evans/25 20.00
7 Steve Garvey 15.00
10 Ron Santo 25.00
11 Alan Trammell 20.00

Souvenirs Signature Material Bat

NM/M
Common Player: 15.00
3 Will Clark 25.00
5 Dwight Evans 20.00
7 Steve Garvey 15.00
10 Ron Santo 25.00
11 Alan Trammell 20.00
12 Robin Ventura 15.00

Souvenirs Signature Material Combo

NM/M
Common Player: 20.00
3 Will Clark 30.00
7 Steve Garvey 20.00
11 Alan Trammell 20.00

Souvenirs Signature Material Jersey

NM/M
Common Player: 15.00
3 Will Clark 25.00
5 Dwight Evans 25.00
7 Steve Garvey 15.00
11 Alan Trammell 20.00

Sox Nation Material

NM/M
Common Player: 10.00
Prime: No Pricing
Production 1-10
1 Ted Williams 75.00
2 Bobby Doerr 20.00
3 Roger Clemens/55 40.00
4 Carl Yastrzemski 25.00
5 Carl Yastrzemski 25.00
6 Jim Rice 15.00
7 Jim Rice 15.00
8 Joe Cronin 15.00
9 Joe Cronin 15.00
10 Carlton Fisk 20.00
11 Fred Lynn 10.00
12 Wade Boggs 25.00
13 Wade Boggs/55 25.00

Sox Nation Signature Material

NM/M
Prime: No Pricing
Production 1-5
2 Bobby Doerr/50 25.00
6 Jim Rice/50 25.00
7 Jim Rice/50 25.00
11 Fred Lynn/50 15.00

Yankee Clippings Material

NM/M
Common Player: 8.00
Prime: No Pricing
Production 1-33
2 Babe Ruth 300.00
3 Billy Martin 40.00
4 Billy Martin 40.00
5 Bobby Murcer 15.00
6 Bucky Dent 10.00
7 Jim "Catfish" Hunter 15.00
8 Jim "Catfish" Hunter 15.00
9 Darryl Strawberry 8.00
10 Dave Righetti 8.00
11 Dave Winfield 10.00
12 Deion Sanders 15.00
13 Deion Sanders 15.00
14 Don Mattingly 35.00
15 Elston Howard 15.00
16 Graig Nettles 10.00
17 Roger Clemens/43 50.00
18 Luis Tiant 8.00
19 Mickey Rivers 15.00
20 Phil Rizzuto 15.00
21 Reggie Jackson 20.00
22 Rickey Henderson 15.00
23 Roger Maris 50.00
24 Roger Maris 50.00
25 Ron Guidry 15.00
26 Sparky Lyle 8.00
27 Phil Niekro 20.00
28 Tommy John 20.00
29 Whitey Ford 40.00
30 Yogi Berra 60.00

Yankee Clippings Signature Material

NM/M
Prime: No Pricing
Production 1-5
9 Darryl Strawberry/25 30.00
18 Luis Tiant/50 30.00
20 Phil Rizzuto/25 60.00
25 Ron Guidry/25 50.00
28 Tommy John/25 30.00

2005 Donruss Leather & Lumber

NM/M
Complete Set (177):
Common Player (1-150): .25
Common Auto. (151-175): 8.00
Production 256
Card #176 doesn't exist.
Pack (5): 7.00
Box (18): 100.00
1 Adam Dunn .50
2 Adrian Beltre .40
3 Akinori Otsuka .25
4 Al Leiter .25
5 Albert Pujols 2.00
6 Alex Rodriguez 1.50
7 Alfonso Soriano .75
8 Andy Pettitte .40
9 Aramis Ramirez .40
10 Aubrey Huff .25
11 Austin Kearns .25
12 Barry Larkin .40
13 Barry Zito .40
14 Bartolo Colon .25
15 Bernie Williams .40
16 Bobby Abreu .40
17 Bobby Crosby .40
18 Brad Penny .25
19 Brian Giles .25
20 C.C. Sabathia .25
21 Carl Crawford .25
22 Carl Pavano .25
23 Carlos Beltran .50
24 Carlos Delgado .40
25 Carlos Lee .40
26 Carlos Zambrano .40
27 Casey Kotchman .25
28 Chipper Jones .75
29 Chone Figgins .25
30 Craig Biggio .40
31 Craig Monroe .25
32 Cristian Guzman .25
33 Curt Schilling .75
34 Danny Haren .25
35 Darin Erstad .25
36 David Dellucci .25
37 David Ortiz .75
38 David Wells .25
39 Derek Jeter 2.00
40 Dontrelle Willis .40
41 Edgar Renteria .40
42 Eric Gagne .40
43 Frank Thomas .50
44 Garret Anderson .40
45 Gary Sheffield .50
46 Geoff Jenkins .25
47 Greg Maddux 1.50
48 Hideo Nomo .40
49 Ichiro Suzuki 1.50
50 Ivan Rodriguez .50
51 J.D. Drew .25
52 Jake Peavy .40
53 Jamie Moyer .25
54 Jason Giambi .40
55 Jason Kendall .25
56 Jason Schmidt .40
57 Jason Varitek .40
58 Javy Lopez .40
59 Jay Gibbons .25
60 Jeff Bagwell .50
61 Jeff Bagwell .25
62 Jeremy Bonderman .25
63 Jermaine Dye .25
64 Jim Edmonds .40
65 Jim Thome .50
66 Joe Nathan .25
67 Johan Santana .50
68 John Olerud .25
69 John Smoltz .40
70 Johnny Damon .75
71 Johnny Estrada .25
72 Jose Reyes .50
73 Jose Vidro .25
74 Josh Beckett .40
75 Juan Pierre .25
76 Junior Spivey .25
77 Justin Morneau .40
78 Kazuhisa Ishii .25
79 Kazuo Matsui .25
80 Ken Griffey Jr. 1.50
81 Kerry Wood .40
82 Kevin Brown .25
83 Kevin Millwood .25
84 Khalil Greene .40
85 Lance Berkman .25
86 Larry Walker .40
87 Laynce Nix .25
88 Lyle Overbay .25
89 Magglio Ordonez .25
90 Manny Ramirez .50
91 Marcus Giles .25
92 Mark Loretta .25
93 Mark Mulder .40
94 Mark Prior .50
95 Mark Teixeira .40
96 Melvin Mora .25
97 Michael Young .25
98 Miguel Tejada .50
99 Mike Lieberthal .25
100 Mike Lowell .25
101 Mike Mussina .40
102 Mike Piazza 1.00
103 Milton Bradley .25
104 Moises Alou .40
105 Morgan Ensberg .25
106 Nomar Garciaparra 1.00
107 Omar Vizquel .25
108 Paul Konerko .40
109 Paul LoDuca .25
110 Pedro Martinez .75
111 Rafael Furcal .25
112 Rafael Palmeiro .40
113 Randy Johnson .75
114 Richie Sexson .40
115 Rocco Baldelli .25
116 Roger Clemens 2.00
117 Roy Halladay .40
118 Sammy Sosa .75
119 Scott Podsednik .25
120 Scott Rolen .75
121 Sean Burroughs .25
122 Sean Casey .25
123 Shannon Stewart .25
124 Shawn Green .25
125 Steve Finley .25
126 Tim Hudson .40
127 Tim Salmon .25
128 Todd Helton .50
129 Tom Glavine .40
130 Torii Hunter .40
131 Travis Hafner .40
132 Troy Glaus .40
133 Troy Percival .25
134 Vernon Wells .25
135 Victor Martinez .25
136 Vladimir Guerrero .75
137 Andre Dawson .40
138 Brooks Robinson .75
139 Cal Ripken Jr. 3.00
140 Dale Murphy .50
141 Darryl Strawberry .40
142 George Brett 2.00
143 Harmon Killebrew 1.00
144 Jim Palmer .50
145 Lou Brock .75
146 Mike Schmidt 2.00
147 Nolan Ryan 2.00
148 Steve Carlton .50
149 Tony Gwynn 1.00
150 Willie Mays 2.00
151 Agustin Montero **RC** 10.00
152 Carlos Ruiz **RC** 15.00
153 Casey Rogowski **RC** 8.00
154 Chris Resop **RC** 15.00
155 Chris Roberson **RC** 15.00
156 Colter Bean **RC** 15.00
157 Danny Rueckel **RC** 8.00
158 David Gassner **RC** 10.00
159 Geovany Soto **RC** 15.00
160 John Hattig Jr. **RC** 8.00
161 Justin Wechsler **RC** 10.00
162 Luke Scott **RC** 25.00
163 Mark McLemore **RC** 10.00
164 Miguel Negron **RC** 8.00
165 Mike Morse **RC** 20.00
166 Nate McLouth **RC** 8.00
167 Philip Humber **RC** 20.00
168 Randy Messenger **RC** 8.00
169 Raul Tablado **RC** 8.00
170 Russel Rohlicek **RC** 8.00
171 Ryan Speier **RC** 8.00
172 Scott Munter **RC** 10.00
173 Sean Thompson **RC** 10.00
174 Sean Tracey **RC** 10.00
175 Wladimir Balentien **RC** 25.00
177 Norihiro Nakamura/128 **RC** 75.00

Silver

Silver (1-150): 3-5X
Production 100 Sets

Gold

Gold (1-150): 4-8X
Production 50 Sets

Platinum

Platinum: No Pricing
Production One Set

Big Bang

NM/M
Common Player: 1.50
Production 2,000 Sets
Gold: 1-2X
Production 100 Sets
Silver: 1-2X
Production 200 Sets
Platinum: No Pricing
Production One Set
1 Adam Dunn 2.00
2 Adrian Beltre 1.50
3 Albert Pujols 6.00
4 Alex Rodriguez 5.00
5 Chipper Jones 2.00
6 Dale Murphy 2.00
7 Darryl Strawberry 1.50
8 Dave Parker 1.50
9 David Ortiz 2.00
10 Duke Snider 2.00
11 Frank Robinson 2.00
12 Gary Sheffield 1.50
13 George Foster 1.50
14 Harmon Killebrew 3.00
15 Jim Edmonds 2.00
16 Jim Rice 1.50
17 Jim Thome 2.00
18 Ken Griffey Jr. 4.00
19 Manny Ramirez 2.00
20 Matt Williams 1.50
21 Mike Piazza 3.00
22 Mike Schmidt 5.00
23 Rafael Palmeiro 2.00
24 Sammy Sosa 3.00
25 Ted Williams 5.00

Big Bang Bat

NM/M
Production 50-250
3 Albert Pujols/250 15.00
8 Dave Parker/250 4.00
9 David Ortiz/250 8.00
11 Frank Robinson/100 8.00
13 George Foster/250 4.00
16 Jim Rice/50 6.00
19 Manny Ramirez/250 8.00
22 Mike Schmidt/100 15.00
23 Rafael Palmeiro/250 6.00
24 Sammy Sosa/250 8.00
25 Ted Williams/100 60.00

Big Bang Jersey

NM/M
Production 25-250
Prime: No Pricing
Production Five Sets
1 Adam Dunn/250 6.00
3 Albert Pujols/250 15.00
5 Chipper Jones/250 8.00
6 Dale Murphy/250 8.00
7 Darryl Strawberry/Pants/250 6.00
8 Dave Parker/250 4.00
9 David Ortiz/250 8.00
10 Duke Snider/25 12.00
12 Gary Sheffield/250 6.00
14 Harmon Killebrew/100 10.00
15 Jim Edmonds/250 6.00
16 Jim Rice Pants/250 6.00
17 Jim Thome/250 8.00
19 Manny Ramirez/100 8.00
20 Matt Williams/250 6.00
21 Mike Piazza/250 10.00
22 Mike Schmidt/100 15.00
23 Rafael Palmeiro/Pants/250 6.00
24 Sammy Sosa/250 8.00
25 Ted Williams/Jkt/250 40.00

Big Bang Combos

NM/M
Production 25-100
Prime: No Pricing
Production Five Sets
1 Adam Dunn/Bat-Jsy/25 12.00
2 Adrian Beltre/Bat-Jsy/25 8.00
3 Albert Pujols/Bat-Jsy/100 25.00
7 Darryl Strawberry/Jsy-Pants/100 8.00
8 Dave Parker/Bat-Jsy/100 8.00
9 David Ortiz/Bat-Jsy/100 15.00
15 Jim Edmonds/Jsy-Jsy/100 10.00
16 Jim Rice/Jsy-Jsy/100 10.00
19 Manny Ramirez/Bat-Jsy/100 12.00
20 Matt Williams/Jsy-Jsy/100 8.00
21 Mike Piazza/Bat-Jsy/50 15.00
22 Mike Schmidt/Bat-Jsy/100 20.00
23 Rafael Palmeiro/Bat-Jsy/100 10.00
24 Sammy Sosa/Bat-Jsy/100 12.00

Big Bang Signatures

No Pricing
Production 1-10

Game Ball Signatures

NM/M
Production 1-50
1 Ben Grieve/50 10.00
3 Eli Marrero/24 12.00
4 Jeff Fassero/24 25.00
5 Jose Guillen/47 25.00
7 Mark Grudzielanek/23 30.00
9 Paul Konerko/45 25.00

Great Gloves

NM/M
Common Player: 1.50
Production 2,000 Sets
Gold: 2-3X
Production 50 Sets
Silver: 1-2X
Production 100 Sets
Platinum: No Pricing
Production One Set
1 Austin Kearns 1.50
2 Gary Carter 2.00
3 Ivan Rodriguez 2.00
4 Mark Grace 2.00
5 Mark Teixeira 2.00
6 Mike Schmidt 5.00
7 Omar Vizquel 1.50
8 Scott Rolen 3.00
9 Tony Gwynn 3.00
10 Willie Mays 5.00

Great Gloves Fielding Glove

NM/M
Production 25 Sets
1 Austin Kearns/25 10.00
2 Gary Carter/25 20.00
3 Ivan Rodriguez/25 15.00
4 Mark Grace/25 20.00
5 Mark Teixeira/25 15.00
6 Mike Schmidt/25 40.00
9 Tony Gwynn/25 20.00

Great Gloves Jersey

NM/M
Production 25-50
Prime: No Pricing
Production Five Sets
1 Austin Kearns/50 8.00
2 Gary Carter/50 8.00
3 Ivan Rodriguez/50 8.00
4 Mark Grace/50 10.00
5 Mark Teixeira/50 8.00
6 Mike Schmidt/50 20.00
7 Omar Vizquel/50 8.00
8 Scott Rolen/50 10.00
9 Tony Gwynn/50 12.00
10 Willie Mays/25 40.00

Hitters Inc.

NM/M
Common Player: 1.50
Production 2,000 Sets
Gold: 2-3X
Production 50 Sets
Silver: 1-2X
Production 100 Sets
Platinum: No Pricing
Production One Set
1 Albert Pujols 6.00
2 Alfonso Soriano 2.00
3 Cal Ripken Jr. 8.00
4 Don Mattingly 5.00
5 Dwight Evans 1.50
6 George Brett 5.00
7 Hank Blalock 1.50
8 Ichiro Suzuki 5.00
9 Ivan Rodriguez 2.00
10 Jack Wilson 1.50
11 Keith Hernandez 1.50
12 Larry Walker 2.00
13 Lou Brock 2.00
14 Lyle Overbay 1.50
15 Michael Young 1.50
16 Paul Molitor 2.00
17 Rod Carew 2.00
18 Sean Casey 1.50
19 Steve Garvey 1.50
20 Todd Helton 2.00
21 Tony Gwynn 3.00
22 Travis Hafner 1.50
23 Ted Williams 6.00
24 Wade Boggs 2.00
25 Willie Mays 5.00

Hitters Inc. Bat

NM/M
Production 25-100
1 Albert Pujols/100 15.00
2 Alfonso Soriano/50 6.00
3 Cal Ripken Jr./100 25.00
4 Don Mattingly/100 15.00
5 Dwight Evans/100 6.00
6 George Brett/50 15.00
7 Hank Blalock/50 6.00
9 Ivan Rodriguez/100 6.00
10 Jack Wilson/100 4.00
12 Larry Walker/100 6.00
13 Lou Brock/100 8.00
15 Michael Young/100 4.00
16 Paul Molitor/100 8.00
17 Rod Carew/100 8.00
18 Sean Casey/100 4.00
19 Steve Garvey/100 6.00
21 Tony Gwynn/100 10.00
23 Ted Williams/25 60.00
24 Wade Boggs/100 8.00
25 Willie Mays/25 40.00

Hitters Inc. Signature Bat

NM/M
Production 5-25
5 Dwight Evans/25 20.00
7 Hank Blalock/25 25.00
10 Jack Wilson/25 15.00
13 Lou Brock/25 30.00
15 Michael Young/25 20.00
18 Sean Casey/25 15.00
19 Steve Garvey/25 30.00

Hitters Inc. Jersey

NM/M
Production 25-100
1 Albert Pujols/100 15.00
2 Alfonso Soriano/100 6.00
3 Cal Ripken Jr./100 25.00
4 Don Mattingly/100 15.00
5 Dwight Evans/100 6.00
7 Hank Blalock/100 4.00
9 Ivan Rodriguez/100 6.00
10 Jack Wilson/100 4.00
12 Larry Walker/100 6.00
13 Lou Brock/50 8.00
14 Lyle Overbay/100 4.00
16 Paul Molitor/100 8.00
17 Rod Carew/100 8.00
18 Sean Casey/100 4.00
19 Steve Garvey/100 6.00
20 Todd Helton/100 8.00
21 Tony Gwynn/100 10.00
22 Travis Hafner/100 4.00
23 Ted Williams/Jkt/100 40.00
24 Wade Boggs/100 8.00
25 Willie Mays/25 40.00

Hitters Inc. Signature Jersey

NM/M
Production 5-25
5 Dwight Evans/25 20.00
7 Hank Blalock/25 25.00
10 Jack Wilson/25 15.00
13 Lou Brock/25 30.00
14 Lyle Overbay/25 15.00
18 Sean Casey/25 15.00
19 Steve Garvey/25 30.00
22 Travis Hafner/25 20.00

Hitters Inc. Signatures

No Pricing
Production 5-10

Leather Cuts

NM/M
Production 1-128
2 Andre Dawson/128 15.00
3 Bert Blyleven/128 15.00
4 Lee Smith/32 15.00
5 Billy Williams/64 15.00
6 Bob Feller/128 25.00
7 Joe Pepitone/128 20.00
8 Bobby Doerr/128 15.00
9 Juan Marichal/112 20.00
12 Dale Murphy/96 25.00
13 Darryl Strawberry/128 15.00
14 Johnny Podres/128 20.00
18 Duke Snider/128 25.00
20 Dwight Gooden/128 15.00
21 Fergie Jenkins/96 15.00
23 Fred Lynn/128 15.00
24 Justin Morneau/128 20.00
25 Gaylord Perry/128 15.00
27 George Foster/128 15.00
28 Harmon Killebrew/64 30.00
29 Jack Morris/128 15.00
30 Jim Palmer/128 15.00
31 Jim Rice/128 15.00
33 John Kruk/128 20.00
34 Randy Jones/128 15.00
35 Keith Hernandez/128 15.00
36 Lenny Dykstra/128 15.00
37 Lou Brock/64 35.00
38 Luis Aparicio/128 15.00
39 Lyle Overbay/128 10.00
40 Maury Wills/128 15.00
41 Earl Weaver/128 15.00
42 Miguel Cabrera/64 40.00
44 Monte Irvin/96 20.00
47 Red Schoendienst/128 15.00
48 Rich "Goose" Gossage/128 20.00
50 Minnie Minoso/128 20.00
51 Sean Casey/64 15.00
54 Steve Stone/128 15.00
55 Tommy John/128 15.00
57 Victor Martinez/128 15.00
61 Lee Smith/128 15.00

Leather Cuts Bat

NM/M
Production 6-128
1 Al Kaline/58 40.00
10 Cal Ripken Jr./60 125.00
13 Darryl Strawberry/96 20.00
19 Dwight Evans/128 25.00
20 Dwight Gooden/128 15.00
22 Frank Robinson/40 25.00
23 Fred Lynn/96 15.00
27 George Foster/128 15.00
31 Jim Rice/32 25.00
36 Lenny Dykstra/128 15.00
37 Lou Brock/128 30.00
38 Luis Aparicio/128 15.00
39 Lyle Overbay/128 10.00
51 Sean Casey/32 15.00
55 Tommy John/128 15.00
57 Victor Martinez/128 15.00

Leather Cuts Jersey

NM/M
Production 1-128
2 Andre Dawson/128 20.00
3 Bert Blyleven/128 15.00
4 Lee Smith/96 15.00
8 Bobby Doerr/Pants/128 20.00
9 Juan Marichal/112 20.00
10 Cal Ripken Jr./60 125.00
12 Dale Murphy/96 25.00
13 Darryl Strawberry/96 20.00
15 Dave Righetti/48 20.00
16 David Cone/128 15.00
19 Dwight Evans/44 30.00
20 Dwight Gooden/128 15.00
21 Fergie Jenkins/Pants/96 15.00
23 Fred Lynn/96 15.00
25 Gaylord Perry/128 15.00
28 Harmon Killebrew/32 40.00
29 Jack Morris/64 15.00
31 Jim Rice Pants/128 20.00
33 John Kruk/128 20.00
35 Keith Hernandez/32 20.00
36 Lenny Dykstra/128 15.00
38 Luis Aparicio/128 15.00
39 Lyle Overbay/128 10.00
42 Miguel Cabrera/64 40.00
51 Sean Casey/32 15.00
55 Tommy John/128 15.00
57 Victor Martinez/128 15.00

Lumber Cuts

NM/M
Production 1-128
2 Andre Dawson/128 15.00
3 Bert Blyleven/128 15.00
4 Lee Smith/32 20.00
5 Billy Williams/64 20.00
6 Bob Feller/128 25.00
7 Joe Pepitone/128 20.00
8 Bobby Doerr/128 20.00
9 Juan Marichal/112 20.00
12 Dale Murphy/96 25.00

13 Darryl Strawberry/128 15.00
14 Johnny Podres/128 15.00
18 Duke Snider/128 25.00
20 Dwight Gooden/128 15.00
21 Fergie Jenkins/96 15.00
23 Fred Lynn/128 15.00
24 Justin Morneau/128 20.00
25 Gaylord Perry/128 15.00
27 George Foster/128 10.00
28 Harmon Killebrew/64 30.00
29 Jack Morris/128 15.00
30 Jim Palmer/128 15.00
31 Jim Rice/128 15.00
33 John Kruk/128 20.00
34 Randy Jones/128 15.00
35 Keith Hernandez/128 15.00
36 Lenny Dykstra/128 15.00
37 Lou Brock/64 35.00
38 Luis Aparicio/128 15.00
39 Lyle Overbay/128 10.00
40 Maury Wills/128 15.00
41 Earl Weaver/128 15.00
42 Miguel Cabrera/64 40.00
44 Monte Irvin/96 20.00
46 Kent Hrbek/128 15.00
47 Red Schoendienst/128 20.00
48 Rich "Goose" Gossage/128 15.00
50 Minnie Minoso/128 20.00
51 Sean Casey/64 15.00
54 Steve Stone/128 15.00
55 Tommy John/128 15.00
57 Victor Martinez/128 15.00
61 Lee Smith/128 15.00

Lumber Cuts Bat

NM/M

Production 6-128
1 Al Kaline 40.00
10 Cal Ripken Jr./60 125.00
13 Darryl Strawberry/96 20.00
19 Dwight Evans/128 25.00
20 Dwight Gooden/128 15.00
22 Frank Robinson/40 25.00
23 Fred Lynn/96 15.00
27 George Foster/128 15.00
31 Jim Rice/32 25.00
36 Lenny Dykstra/128 15.00
37 Lou Brock/128 30.00
38 Luis Aparicio/128 15.00
39 Lyle Overbay/128 10.00
51 Sean Casey/32 15.00
55 Tommy John/128 15.00
57 Victor Martinez/128 15.00

Lumber Cuts Jersey

NM/M

Production 7-128
2 Andre Dawson/128 20.00
3 Bert Blyleven/128 15.00
4 Lee Smith/96 15.00
8 Bobby Doerr/Pants/128 20.00
9 Juan Marichal/112 20.00
10 Cal Ripken Jr./60 125.00
12 Dale Murphy/96 25.00
13 Darryl Strawberry/96 20.00
15 Dave Righetti/48 20.00
16 David Cone/120 15.00
19 Dwight Evans/44 30.00
20 Dwight Gooden/128 15.00
21 Fergie Jenkins/Pants/96 15.00
23 Fred Lynn/96 15.00
25 Gaylord Perry/128 15.00
28 Harmon Killebrew/32 40.00
29 Jack Morris/64 15.00
31 Jim Rice Pants/128 20.00
33 John Kruk/128 20.00
35 Keith Hernandez/32 20.00
36 Lenny Dykstra/128 15.00
38 Luis Aparicio/128 15.00
39 Lyle Overbay/128 10.00
42 Miguel Cabrera/64 40.00
51 Sean Casey/32 15.00
55 Tommy John/128 15.00
57 Victor Martinez/128 15.00

Lumber/Leather

NM/M

Common Player: 1.50
Production 2,000 Sets
Gold: 2-3X
Production 50 Sets
Silver: 1-2X
Production 100 Sets
Platinum: No Pricing
Production One Set
1 Albert Pujols 6.00
2 Alex Rodriguez 5.00
3 Alfonso Soriano 2.00
4 Cal Ripken Jr. 8.00
5 Carlos Lee 2.00
6 Derek Jeter 6.00
7 Don Mattingly 5.00
8 Ichiro Suzuki 4.00
9 Ivan Rodriguez 2.00
10 Jack Wilson 1.50
11 Josh Beckett 1.50
12 Ken Griffey Jr. 4.00
13 Lance Berkman 1.50
14 Magglio Ordonez 1.50
15 Mark Grace 2.00
16 Mark Prior 2.00
17 Mark Teixeira 2.00
18 Mike Schmidt 4.00
19 Nolan Ryan 6.00
20 Nomar Garciaparra 3.00
21 Paul LoDuca 1.50
22 Rafael Palmeiro 2.00
23 Randy Johnson 2.00
24 Richie Sexson 2.00
25 Rickey Henderson 2.00
26 Roger Clemens 6.00
27 Ryan Klesko 1.50
28 Stan Musial 3.00
29 Steve Carlton 2.00
30 Tim Hudson 2.00
31 Tony Gwynn 2.00
32 Travis Hafner 1.50
33 Victor Martinez 1.50
34 Wade Boggs 2.00
35 Willie Mays 5.00

Lumber/Leather Barrel

No Pricing
Production One Set

L/L Barrel-Jersey

No Pricing
Production One Set

L/L Bat-Btg Glove

NM/M

Production 1-25
3 Alfonso Soriano/25 15.00
5 Carlos Lee/25 12.00
7 Don Mattingly/25 40.00
9 Ivan Rodriguez/25 15.00
13 Lance Berkman/25 15.00
14 Magglio Ordonez/25 10.00
18 Mike Schmidt/25 40.00
21 Paul LoDuca/25 10.00
22 Rafael Palmeiro/25 15.00
24 Richie Sexson/25 15.00
25 Rickey Henderson/25 20.00
27 Ryan Klesko/25 10.00
31 Tony Gwynn/25 20.00

L/L Bat-Fld Glove

NM/M

Production 5-25
5 Carlos Lee/25 12.00
9 Ivan Rodriguez/25 15.00
10 Jack Wilson/25 10.00
13 Lance Berkman/25 15.00
15 Mark Grace/25 20.00
16 Mark Prior/25 20.00
18 Mike Schmidt/25 40.00
21 Paul LoDuca/25 10.00
22 Rafael Palmeiro/25 15.00
24 Richie Sexson/25 15.00
27 Ryan Klesko/25 10.00
29 Steve Carlton/25 15.00
30 Tim Hudson/25 15.00
31 Tony Gwynn/25 20.00

Lumber/Leather Bat-Spikes

NM/M

Production 1-25
1 Albert Pujols/25 40.00
5 Carlos Lee/25 12.00
9 Ivan Rodriguez/25 15.00
11 Josh Beckett/25 12.00
13 Lance Berkman/25 15.00
14 Magglio Ordonez/25 10.00
16 Mark Prior/25 20.00
21 Paul LoDuca/25 10.00
22 Rafael Palmeiro/25 15.00
24 Richie Sexson/25 15.00
25 Rickey Henderson/25 20.00
27 Ryan Klesko/25 10.00
30 Tim Hudson/25 15.00
31 Tony Gwynn/25 20.00

Materials Barrel

No Pricing
Production 1-4

Materials Bat

NM/M

Production 25-250
1 Adam Dunn/250 6.00
2 Adrian Beltre/100 4.00
5 Albert Pujols/250 15.00
7 Alfonso Soriano/100 6.00
8 Andy Pettitte/100 6.00
9 Aramis Ramirez/100 6.00
10 Aubrey Huff/250 4.00
11 Austin Kearns/100 4.00
12 Barry Larkin/200 6.00
13 Barry Zito/25 8.00
15 Bernie Williams/250 6.00
18 Brad Penny/75 4.00
19 Brian Giles/50 6.00
23 Carlos Beltran/100 8.00
24 Carlos Delgado/250 4.00
25 Carlos Lee/150 4.00
27 Casey Kotchman/250 4.00
29 Chone Figgins/250 4.00
30 Craig Biggio/250 6.00
31 Craig Monroe/250 4.00
33 Curt Schilling/100 8.00
35 Darin Erstad/250 4.00
37 David Ortiz/250 8.00
40 Dontrelle Willis/250 6.00
43 Frank Thomas/50 8.00
44 Garret Anderson/250 4.00
46 Geoff Jenkins/50 4.00
47 Greg Maddux/250 10.00
51 J.D. Drew/250 4.00
57 Jason Varitek/100 6.00
58 Javy Lopez/250 4.00
59 Jay Gibbons/250 4.00
60 Jeff Bagwell/250 6.00
61 Jeff Kent/250 4.00
68 John Olerud/250 4.00
72 Jose Reyes/250 6.00
73 Jose Vidro/250 4.00
75 Juan Pierre/250 4.00
81 Kerry Wood/100 6.00
82 Kevin Brown/100 4.00
85 Lance Berkman/250 4.00
87 Laynce Nix/250 4.00
89 Magglio Ordonez/250 4.00
90 Manny Ramirez/100 8.00
94 Mark Prior/100 6.00
97 Michael Young/250 4.00
104 Moises Alou/250 4.00
106 Nomar Garciaparra/100 8.00
109 Paul LoDuca/250 4.00
111 Rafael Furcal/250 4.00
112 Rafael Palmeiro/250 6.00
114 Richie Sexson/250 4.00
115 Rocco Baldelli/250 8.00
118 Sammy Sosa/100 8.00
122 Sean Casey/100 4.00
123 Shannon Stewart/50 4.00
124 Shawn Green/250 4.00
126 Tim Hudson/50 6.00
127 Tim Salmon/250 4.00
129 Tom Glavine/250 4.00
130 Torii Hunter/250 4.00
132 Troy Glaus/250 4.00
138 Brooks Robinson/100 8.00
139 Cal Ripken Jr./50 30.00
145 Lou Brock/100 8.00
146 Mike Schmidt/50 15.00
147 Nolan Ryan/50 25.00
149 Tony Gwynn/100 10.00
150 Willie Mays/25 40.00

Materials Jersey

NM/M

Production 20-250
1 Adam Dunn/150 6.00
5 Albert Pujols/250 15.00
7 Alfonso Soriano/150 6.00
8 Andy Pettitte/150 6.00
9 Aramis Ramirez/250 4.00
10 Aubrey Huff/250 4.00
12 Barry Larkin/250 6.00
13 Barry Zito/150 4.00
15 Bernie Williams/150 6.00
16 Bobby Abreu/250 4.00
17 Bobby Crosby/150 4.00
20 C.C. Sabathia/250 4.00
21 Carl Crawford/200 4.00
26 Carlos Zambrano/250 6.00
27 Casey Kotchman/140 4.00
28 Chipper Jones/250 8.00
29 Chone Figgins/200 4.00
30 Craig Biggio/200 6.00
33 Curt Schilling/250 8.00
35 Darin Erstad/150 4.00
36 David Dellucci/250 4.00
37 David Ortiz/250 8.00
40 Dontrelle Willis/250 4.00
43 Frank Thomas/Pants/150 8.00
44 Garret Anderson/250 4.00
45 Gary Sheffield/250 6.00
46 Geoff Jenkins/250 4.00
47 Greg Maddux/25 15.00
48 Hideo Nomo/250 6.00
50 Ivan Rodriguez/150 6.00
53 Jamie Moyer/50 6.00
54 Jason Giambi/250 4.00
57 Jason Varitek/100 10.00
58 Javy Lopez/150 4.00
59 Jay Gibbons/75 4.00
60 Jeff Bagwell/250 6.00
62 Jeremy Bonderman/150 4.00
64 Jim Edmonds/250 6.00
65 Jim Thome/150 6.00
67 Johan Santana/250 8.00
69 John Smoltz/250 6.00
70 Johnny Damon/250 8.00
71 Johnny Estrada/250 4.00
72 Jose Reyes/150 6.00
73 Jose Vidro/150 4.00
74 Josh Beckett/50 4.00
76 Junior Spivey/250 4.00
77 Justin Morneau/250 6.00
78 Kazuhisa Ishii/250 4.00
79 Kazuo Matsui/250 4.00
81 Kerry Wood/Pants/150 6.00
85 Lance Berkman/250 4.00
86 Larry Walker/250 4.00
87 Laynce Nix/250 4.00
88 Lyle Overbay/200 4.00
90 Manny Ramirez/250 8.00
91 Marcus Giles/150 4.00
94 Mark Prior/250 6.00
95 Mark Teixeira/250 6.00
96 Melvin Mora/100 4.00
97 Michael Young/25 8.00
98 Miguel Tejada/250 6.00
100 Mike Lowell/250 4.00
101 Mike Mussina/250 6.00
102 Mike Piazza/250 8.00
105 Morgan Ensberg/150 4.00
108 Paul Konerko/150 4.00
111 Rafael Furcal/150 4.00
112 Rafael Palmeiro/150 6.00
115 Rocco Baldelli/250 4.00
116 Roger Clemens/150 10.00
117 Roy Halladay/150 4.00
119 Scott Podsednik/250 4.00
120 Scott Rolen/250 6.00
121 Sean Burroughs/150 4.00
122 Sean Casey/250 4.00
123 Shannon Stewart/150 4.00
128 Todd Helton/250 6.00
130 Torii Hunter/250 4.00
131 Travis Hafner 6.00
134 Vernon Wells/250 4.00
135 Victor Martinez/150 4.00
136 Vladimir Guerrero/250 8.00
137 Andre Dawson/50 8.00
139 Cal Ripken Jr./250 20.00
140 Dale Murphy/250 6.00
141 Darryl Strawberry/Pants/150 4.00
143 Harmon Killebrew/100 8.00
145 Lou Brock Jkt/250 8.00
146 Mike Schmidt/50 15.00
147 Nolan Ryan/250 15.00
148 Steve Carlton/25 10.00
149 Tony Gwynn/250 8.00
150 Willie Mays Pants/25 40.00

Naturals

NM/M

Common Player: 1.50
Production 2,000 Sets
Gold: 2-3X
Production 50 Sets
Silver: 1-2X
Production 100 Sets
Platinum: No Pricing
Production One Set
1 Andruw Jones 2.00
2 Bernie Williams 1.50
3 Brooks Robinson 2.00
4 Cal Ripken Jr. 8.00
5 Casey Kotchman 1.50
6 Craig Biggio 2.00
7 Craig Wilson 1.50
8 David Ortiz 3.00
9 Eddie Murray 2.00
10 Javy Lopez 1.50
11 Jeff Bagwell 2.00
12 Lance Berkman 1.50
13 Magglio Ordonez 1.50
14 Michael Young 1.50
15 Rafael Palmeiro 2.00
16 Reggie Jackson 2.00
17 Rickey Henderson 2.00
18 Rocco Baldelli 1.50
19 Sammy Sosa 4.00
20 Shawn Green 1.50
21 Ted Williams 6.00
22 Tony Gwynn 3.00
23 Wade Boggs 2.00
24 Will Clark 2.00
25 Willie Mays 5.00

Naturals Barrel

No Pricing
Production 1-3

Naturals Bat

NM/M

Production 25-100
1 Andruw Jones/100 6.00
2 Bernie Williams/100 6.00
3 Brooks Robinson/100 8.00
4 Cal Ripken Jr./100 25.00
5 Casey Kotchman/100 4.00
6 Craig Biggio/100 6.00
7 Craig Wilson/100 4.00
8 David Ortiz/100 10.00
9 Eddie Murray/100 8.00
10 Javy Lopez/100 4.00
11 Jeff Bagwell/100 6.00
12 Lance Berkman/100 4.00
13 Magglio Ordonez/100 4.00
14 Michael Young/100 4.00
15 Rafael Palmeiro/100 6.00
16 Reggie Jackson/100 8.00
17 Rickey Henderson/100 8.00
18 Rocco Baldelli/100 4.00
19 Sammy Sosa/100 8.00
20 Shawn Green/100 4.00
21 Ted Williams/50 50.00
22 Tony Gwynn/100 10.00
23 Wade Boggs/100 8.00
24 Will Clark/100 8.00
25 Willie Mays/25 40.00

Naturals Jersey

NM/M

Production 25-100
Prime: No Pricing
Production Five Sets
1 Andruw Jones/100 6.00
2 Bernie Williams/100 6.00
4 Cal Ripken Jr./100 25.00
5 Casey Kotchman/100 4.00
6 Craig Biggio/100 6.00
7 Craig Wilson/100 4.00
8 David Ortiz/100 10.00
9 Eddie Murray/100 8.00
10 Javy Lopez/100 4.00
11 Jeff Bagwell/100 6.00
12 Lance Berkman/100 4.00
13 Magglio Ordonez/50 4.00
14 Michael Young/50 4.00
15 Rafael Palmeiro/100 6.00
16 Reggie Jackson/100 8.00
17 Rickey Henderson/Jkt/100 8.00
18 Rocco Baldelli/100 4.00
19 Sammy Sosa/100 8.00
20 Shawn Green/100 4.00
21 Ted Williams/Jkt/100 40.00
22 Tony Gwynn/100 10.00
23 Wade Boggs/100 8.00
24 Will Clark/50 8.00
25 Willie Mays/25 40.00

Naturals Combos

NM/M

Production 25-100
Prime: No Pricing
Production Five Sets
1 Andruw Jones/Bat-Jsy/100 8.00
2 Bernie Williams/Bat-Jsy/100 8.00
3 Brooks Robinson/Bat-Jsy/25 15.00
4 Cal Ripken Jr./Bat-Jsy/100 30.00
5 Casey Kotchman/Bat-Jsy/100 6.00
6 Craig Biggio/Bat-Jsy/100 8.00
7 Craig Wilson/Bat-Jsy/100 6.00
8 David Ortiz/Bat-Jsy/100 12.00
9 Eddie Murray/Bat-Jsy/100 10.00
10 Javy Lopez/Bat-Jsy/100 6.00
11 Jeff Bagwell/Bat-Jsy/100 8.00
12 Lance Berkman/Bat-Jsy/100 6.00
13 Magglio Ordonez/Bat-Jsy/25 8.00
14 Michael Young/Bat-Jsy/100 6.00
15 Rafael Palmeiro/Bat-Jsy/100 8.00
16 Reggie Jackson/Bat-Jsy/50 12.00
17 Rickey Henderson/Bat-Jkt/100 10.00
18 Rocco Baldelli/Bat-Jsy/100 6.00
19 Sammy Sosa/Bat-Jsy/100 10.00
20 Shawn Green/Bat-Jsy/100 6.00
21 Ted Williams/Bat-Jkt/50 60.00
22 Tony Gwynn/Bat-Jsy/100 12.00
23 Wade Boggs/Bat-Jsy/100 10.00
24 Will Clark/Bat-Jsy/50 10.00
25 Willie Mays/Bat-Jsy/25 50.00

Rivals

NM/M

Common Duo: 1.50
Production 2,000 Sets
Gold: 2-3X
Production 50 Sets
Silver: 1-2X
Production 100 Sets
Platinum: No Pricing
Production One Set
1 Ichiro Suzuki, Hideki Matsui 5.00
2 Mark Mulder, Vladimir Guerrero 2.00
3 Tim Hudson, Mark Teixeira 2.00
4 Roger Clemens, Albert Pujols 6.00
5 Greg Maddux, Jeff Bagwell 4.00
6 Randy Johnson, Adrian Beltre 3.00
7 Kerry Wood, Larry Walker 2.00
8 Mike Mussina, Manny Ramirez 2.00
9 C.C. Sabathia, Torii Hunter 1.50
10 Josh Beckett, Chipper Jones 2.00
11 Derek Jeter, Miguel Tejada 6.00
12 Alex Rodriguez, Hank Blalock 5.00
13 Carlos Beltran, Sammy Sosa 3.00
14 Mark Prior, Jim Thome 2.00
15 Miguel Cabrera, Andruw Jones 2.00
16 Johan Santana, Magglio Ordonez 2.00
17 Josh Beckett, Craig Biggio 2.00
18 Adam Dunn, Shawn Green 2.00
19 J. Morris, Rod Carew 2.00
20 Jim Palmer, Paul Molitor 2.00
21 Mike Schmidt, George Brett 5.00
22 Cal Ripken Jr., Don Mattingly 8.00
23 Bob Gibson, Ernie Banks 4.00
24 Eddie Murray, Bert Blyleven 3.00
25 Warren Spahn, Willie Mays 6.00

Rivals Bat

NM/M

Production 50-100
3 Tim Hudson, Mark Teixeira/50 10.00
4 Roger Clemens, Albert Pujols/100 25.00
5 Greg Maddux, Jeff Bagwell/100 15.00
7 Kerry Wood, Larry Walker/100 15.00
10 Josh Beckett, Chipper Jones/50 15.00
13 Carlos Beltran, Sammy Sosa/100 15.00
14 Mark Prior, Jim Thome/50 15.00
18 Adam Dunn, Shawn Green/100 10.00
21 Mike Schmidt, George Brett/100 20.00
22 Cal Ripken Jr., Don Mattingly/100 30.00

Rivals Jersey

NM/M

Production 50-250
Prime: No Pricing
Production Five Sets
2 Mark Mulder, Vladimir Guerrero/100 10.00
3 Tim Hudson, Mark Teixeira/250 10.00
4 Roger Clemens, Albert Pujols/100 20.00
5 Greg Maddux, Jeff Bagwell/250 10.00
7 Kerry Wood, Larry Walker/250 8.00
9 C.C. Sabathia, Torii Hunter/150 6.00
10 Josh Beckett Pants, Chipper Jones/150 10.00
13 Carlos Beltran, Sammy Sosa/250 10.00
14 Mark Prior, Jim Thome/250 10.00
15 Miguel Cabrera, Andruw Jones/250 10.00
16 Johan Santana, Magglio Ordonez/100 10.00
18 Adam Dunn, Shawn Green/100 10.00
19 J. Morris, Rod Carew/250 10.00
21 Mike Schmidt, George Brett/100 15.00
22 Cal Ripken Jr., Don Mattingly/100 40.00
23 Bob Gibson, Ernie Banks/50 15.00
24 Eddie Murray, Bert Blyleven 10.00
25 Warren Spahn/Pant, Willie Mays/Pant/50 60.00

Signatures Gold

NM/M

Production 5-100
Platinum: No Pricing
Production One Set
1 Adam Dunn/25 35.00
2 Adrian Beltre/25 25.00
3 Akinori Otsuka/50 30.00
10 Aubrey Huff/50 15.00
11 Austin Kearns/25 15.00
17 Bobby Crosby/100 15.00
18 Brad Penny/100 10.00
25 Carlos Lee/100 15.00
26 Carlos Zambrano/100 25.00
27 Casey Kotchman/100 10.00
29 Chone Figgins/100 15.00
31 Craig Monroe/100 10.00
34 Danny Haren/100 10.00
36 David Dellucci/100 15.00
52 Jake Peavy/100 25.00
53 Jamie Moyer/100 15.00
59 Jay Gibbons/100 10.00

62 Jeremy Bonderman/100 10.00
63 Jermaine Dye/100 12.00
66 Joe Nathan/100 15.00
71 Johnny Estrada/50 10.00
87 Laynce Nix/100 10.00
88 Lyle Overbay/100 10.00
92 Mark Loretta/100 15.00
99 Mike Lieberthal/100 10.00
103 Milton Bradley/100 12.00
105 Morgan Ensberg/100 12.00
108 Paul Konerko/25 20.00
111 Rafael Furcal/50 15.00
117 Roy Halladay/25 25.00
119 Scott Podsednik/50 15.00
121 Sean Burroughs/100 8.00
122 Sean Casey/25 15.00
123 Shannon Stewart/100 8.00
125 Steve Finley/50 15.00
126 Tim Hudson/25 30.00
127 Tim Salmon/100 15.00
130 Torii Hunter/25 20.00
131 Travis Hafner/100 12.00
133 Troy Percival/50 15.00
134 Vernon Wells/25 15.00
135 Victor Martinez/100 15.00
137 Andre Dawson/100 15.00
138 Brooks Robinson/25 30.00
140 Dale Murphy/50 25.00
141 Darryl Strawberry/100 15.00
143 Harmon Killebrew/50 30.00
144 Jim Palmer/25 20.00
145 Lou Brock/25 30.00
146 Mike Schmidt/25 60.00
148 Steve Carlton/50 25.00
149 Tony Gwynn/25 50.00

Signatures Lumber Cuts

NM/M
Production 256 Sets
151 Agustin Montero 8.00
152 Carlos Ruiz 8.00
153 Casey Rogowski 10.00
154 Chris Resop 15.00
155 Chris Roberson 10.00
156 Colter Bean 10.00
157 Danny Rueckel 8.00
158 David Gassner 8.00
159 Geovany Soto 15.00
160 John Hattig Jr. 8.00
161 Justin Wechsler 8.00
162 Luke Scott 15.00
163 Mark McLemore 8.00
164 Miguel Negron 8.00
165 Mike Morse 40.00
166 Nate McLouth/254 10.00
167 Philip Humber 20.00
168 Randy Messenger 8.00
169 Raul Tablado 8.00
170 Russel Rohlicek 8.00
171 Ryan Speier 8.00
172 Scott Munter 12.00
173 Sean Thompson 10.00
174 Sean Tracey 10.00
175 Wladimir Balentien 20.00
177 Norihiro Nakamura/128 75.00

2005 Donruss Cal Ripken 10th Anniversary

This card marking the 10th anniversary of Ripken's 2,131st consecutive game was issued in the September 4 issue of the Baltimore Sun newspaper.

NM/M
Cal Ripken Jr. 4.00

2005 Donruss Studio

NM/M
Complete Set (300):
Common Player: .25
Pack (6): 4.00
Box (24): 90.00
1 Casey Kotchman .25
2 Chone Figgins .25
3 Dallas McPherson .25
4 Darin Erstad .25
5 Ervin Santana .25
6 Garret Anderson .40
7 Norihiro Nakamura **RC** 2.00
8 John Lackey .25
9 Orlando Cabrera .25
10 Robb Quinlan .25
11 Steve Finley .25
12 Tim Salmon .25
13 Vladimir Guerrero .75
14 Brandon Webb .25
15 Craig Counsell .25
16 Javier Vazquez .25
17 Luis Gonzalez .25
18 Tony Pena **RC** .40
19 Russ Ortiz .25
20 Scott Hairston .25
21 Shawn Green .25
22 Jose Cruz Jr. .25
23 Troy Glaus .40
24 Adam LaRoche .25
25 Andruw Jones .50
26 Chipper Jones .75
27 Danny Kolb .25
28 John Smoltz .40
29 Johnny Estrada .25
30 Marcus Giles .25
31 Nick Green .25
32 Rafael Furcal .25
33 Tim Hudson .40
34 Brian Roberts .25
35 Javy Lopez .25
36 Jay Gibbons .25
37 Melvin Mora .25
38 Miguel Tejada .50
39 Rafael Palmeiro .50
40 Rodrigo Lopez .25
41 Sidney Ponson .25
42 Abe Alvarez .25
43 Bill Mueller .25
44 Curt Schilling .75
45 David Ortiz .75
46 David Wells .25
47 Edgar Renteria .25
48 Jason Varitek .50
49 Jay Payton .25
50 Johnny Damon .75
51 Juan Cedeno .25
52 Manny Ramirez .75
53 Matt Clement .25
54 Trot Nixon .25
55 Wade Miller .25
56 Aramis Ramirez .40
57 Carlos Zambrano .40
58 Corey Patterson .25
59 Derrek Lee .50
60 Greg Maddux 1.50
61 Kerry Wood .40
62 Mark Prior .75
63 Nomar Garciaparra .75
64 Sammy Sosa 1.00
65 Todd Walker .25
66 A.J. Pierzynski .25
67 Aaron Rowand .25
68 Frank Thomas .50
69 Freddy Garcia .25
70 Jermaine Dye .25
71 Mark Buehrle .40
72 Paul Konerko .40
73 Tadahito Iguchi **RC** 3.00
74 Pedro Lopez **RC** .40
75 Scott Podsednik .25
76 Shingo Takatsu .25
77 Adam Dunn .50
78 Austin Kearns .25
79 Barry Larkin .50
80 Bubba Nelson .25
81 Danny Graves .25
82 Eric Milton .25
83 Ken Griffey Jr. 1.50
84 Ryan Wagner .25
85 Sean Casey .25
86 C.C. Sabathia .25
87 Cliff Lee .25
88 Fausto Carmona .25
89 Grady Sizemore .40
90 Jake Westbrook .25
91 Jody Gerut .25
92 Juan Gonzalez .40
93 Kazuhito Tadano .25
94 Travis Hafner .25
95 Victor Martinez .25
96 Charles Johnson .25
97 Clint Barmes .25
98 Cory Sullivan .25
99 Jeff Baker .25
100 Jeff Francis .25
101 Jeff Salazar .25
102 Jeromy Burnitz .25
103 Joe Kennedy .25
104 Matt Holliday .50
105 Preston Wilson .25
106 Todd Helton .50
107 Ubaldo Jimenez **RC** .40
108 Brandon Inge .25
109 Carlos Guillen .25
110 Carlos Pena .25
111 Craig Monroe .25
112 Ivan Rodriguez .50
113 Jeremy Bonderman .25
114 Justin Verlander **RC** 2.00
115 Magglio Ordonez .25
116 Troy Percival .25
117 Vance Wilson .25
118 A.J. Burnett .25
119 Al Leiter .25
120 Dontrelle Willis .40
121 Josh Beckett .40
122 Juan Pierre .25
123 Miguel Cabrera .75
124 Mike Lowell .25
125 Paul LoDuca .25
126 Randy Messenger **RC** .40
127 Yorman Bazardo **RC** .40
128 Andy Pettitte .40
129 Brad Lidge .25
130 Chris Burke .25
131 Craig Biggio .40
132 Fernando Nieve .25
133 Jason Lane .25
134 Jeff Bagwell .50
135 Lance Berkman .40
136 Morgan Ensberg .25
137 Roger Clemens 2.00
138 Roy Oswalt .25
139 Ambiorix Burgos **RC** .40
140 David DeJesus .25
141 Jeremy Affeldt .25
142 Jose Lima .25
143 Ken Harvey .25
144 Mike MacDougal .25
145 Mike Sweeney .25
146 Terrence Long .25
147 Zack Greinke .25
148 Brad Penny .25
149 Derek Lowe .25
150 Dioner Navarro .25
151 Edwin Jackson .25
152 Eric Gagne .25
153 Hee Seop Choi .25
154 Hideo Nomo .50
155 J.D. Drew .40
156 Jeff Kent .25
157 Jeff Weaver .25
158 Milton Bradley .25
159 Yhency Brazoban .25
160 Ben Sheets .40
161 Bill Hall .25
162 Carlos Lee .25
163 Gustavo Chacin .25
164 Geoff Jenkins .25
165 Jose Capellan .25
166 Lyle Overbay .25
167 Rickie Weeks .40
168 Jacque Jones .25
169 Joe Mauer .50
170 Joe Nathan .25
171 Johan Santana .50
172 Justin Morneau .40
173 Lew Ford .25
174 Michael Cuddyer .25
175 Shannon Stewart .25
176 Torii Hunter .25
177 Brad Radke .25
178 Ambiorix Concepcion **RC** .40
179 Carlos Beltran .50
180 David Wright .75
181 Jose Reyes .50
182 Kazuo Matsui .25
183 Kris Benson .25
184 Mike Piazza 1.00
185 Pedro Martinez .75
186 Philip Humber **RC** 1.00
187 Tom Glavine .40
188 Alex Rodriguez 1.50
189 Carl Pavano .25
190 Derek Jeter 2.00
191 Yuniesky Betancourt **RC** 1.00
192 Hideki Matsui 1.50
193 Jorge Posada .40
194 Kevin Brown .25
195 Mariano Rivera .40
196 Mike Mussina .40
197 Randy Johnson .75
198 Scott Proctor .25
199 Tom Gordon .25
200 Barry Zito .40
201 Bobby Crosby .40
202 Danny Haren .25
203 Eric Chavez .40
204 Keiichi Yabu **RC** .40
205 Jason Kendall .25
206 Joe Blanton .25
207 Mark Kotsay .25
208 Nick Swisher .25
209 Octavio Dotel .25
210 Rich Harden .40
211 Billy Wagner .25
212 Bobby Abreu .40
213 Chase Utley .50
214 Gavin Floyd .25
215 Jim Thome .50
216 Jimmy Rollins .50
217 Jon Lieber .25
218 Kenny Lofton .25
219 Mike Lieberthal .25
220 Pat Burrell .25
221 Randy Wolf .25
222 Craig Wilson .25
223 Jack Wilson .25
224 Jason Bay .25
225 John Van Benschoten .25
226 Jose Castillo .25
227 Kip Wells .25
228 Matt Lawton .25
229 Akinori Otsuka .25
230 Brian Giles .25
231 Freddy Guzman .25
232 Jake Peavy .40
233 Khalil Greene .40
234 Mark Loretta .25
235 Sean Burroughs .25
236 Trevor Hoffman .25
237 Woody Williams .25
238 Armando Benitez .25
239 Edgardo Alfonzo .25
240 Erick Threets **RC** .40
241 Jason Schmidt .40
242 Marquis Grissom .25
243 Merkin Valdez .25
244 Michael Tucker .25
245 Moises Alou .40
246 Omar Vizquel .25
247 Adrian Beltre .40
248 Bret Boone .25
249 Bucky Jacobsen .25
250 Clint Nageotte .25
251 Ichiro Suzuki 1.50
252 J.J. Putz .25
253 Jeremy Reed .25
254 Miguel Olivo .25
255 Mike Morse **RC** 2.00
256 Richie Sexson .40
257 Wladimir Balentien **RC** 1.00
258 Albert Pujols 2.00
259 Jason Isringhausen .25
260 Jeff Suppan .25
261 Jim Edmonds .40
262 Larry Walker .40
263 Mark Mulder .40
264 Rick Ankiel .25
265 Scott Rolen .75
266 Yadier Molina .25
267 Aubrey Huff .25
268 B.J. Upton .25
269 Carl Crawford .25
270 Chris Seddon **RC** .40
271 Delmon Young .25
272 Dewon Brazelton .25
273 Jeff Niemann **RC** 1.00
274 Rocco Baldelli .25
275 Scott Kazmir .25
276 Adrian Gonzalez .25
277 Alfonso Soriano .75
278 Francisco Cordero .25
279 Hank Blalock .40
280 Kameron Loe .25
281 Kenny Rogers .25
282 Laynce Nix .25
283 Mark Teixeira .40
284 Michael Young .25
285 Corey Koskie .25
286 David Bush .25
287 Frank Catalanotto .25
288 Gabe Gross .25
289 Raul Tablado **RC** .40
290 Roy Halladay .40
291 Shea Hillenbrand .25
292 Vernon Wells .25
293 Chad Cordero .25
294 Cristian Guzman .25
295 Jose Guillen .25
296 Jose Vidro .25
297 Josh Karp .25
298 Livan Hernandez .25
299 Nick Johnson .25
300 Vinny Castilla .25

Proofs Silver

Stars: 3-5X
Production 100 Sets

Proofs Gold

Stars: 8-12X
Production 25 Sets

Proofs Platinum

No Pricing
Production 10 Sets

Autographs

No Pricing

Diamond Cuts

NM/M
Common Player: 1.00
Production 1,250 Sets
Die-Cut: 1-1.5X
Production 250 Sets
Die-Cut Gold: 1.5-3X
Production 75 Sets
1 Roger Clemens 4.00
2 Manny Ramirez 1.50
3 Francisco Rodriguez 1.00
4 Brian Roberts 1.00
5 Javy Lopez 1.00
6 Vernon Wells 1.00
7 Johan Santana 1.50
8 Torii Hunter 1.00
9 Mike Mussina 1.50
10 Sammy Sosa 2.50
11 Ryan Wagner 1.00
12 Jack Wilson 1.00
13 Ichiro Suzuki 3.00
14 Greg Maddux 3.00
15 Albert Pujols 4.00
16 Jeremy Bonderman 1.00
17 Johnny Estrada 1.00
18 Mark Buehrle 1.00
19 Jorge Posada 1.00
20 Carl Crawford 1.00
21 Paul Konerko 1.00
22 Victor Martinez 1.00
23 Jose Vidro 1.00
24 Jim Thome 1.50
25 Andruw Jones 1.50

Diamond Cuts Bat

NM/M
Production 5-300
1 Roger Clemens/50 15.00
2 Manny Ramirez/200 8.00
5 Javy Lopez/300 4.00
8 Torii Hunter/300 4.00
10 Sammy Sosa/25 15.00
12 Jack Wilson/300 4.00
14 Greg Maddux/225 10.00
15 Albert Pujols/300 15.00
21 Paul Konerko/50 6.00
22 Victor Martinez/300 4.00
23 Jose Vidro/300 4.00
25 Andruw Jones/300 6.00

Diamond Cuts Jersey

NM/M
Production 15-250
Prime: No Pricing
Production 5-10
1 Roger Clemens/125 10.00
2 Manny Ramirez/250 8.00
3 Francisco Rodriguez/250 4.00
4 Brian Roberts/250 6.00
5 Javy Lopez/250 4.00
6 Vernon Wells/250 4.00
7 Johan Santana/175 8.00
8 Torii Hunter/250 4.00
9 Mike Mussina/250 6.00
10 Sammy Sosa/250 8.00
11 Ryan Wagner/250 4.00
14 Greg Maddux/250 8.00
15 Albert Pujols/250 20.00
16 Jeremy Bonderman/250 4.00
17 Johnny Estrada/250 4.00
18 Mark Buehrle/250 4.00
19 Jorge Posada/250 4.00
20 Carl Crawford/250 4.00
21 Paul Konerko/250 4.00
22 Victor Martinez/250 4.00
23 Jose Vidro/175 4.00
24 Jim Thome/250 6.00
25 Andruw Jones/250 6.00

Diamond Cuts Combo

NM/M
Production 5-50
Prime: No Pricing
Production 10 Sets
1 Roger Clemens/Bat-Jsy/50 20.00
2 Manny Ramirez/Bat-Jsy/50 12.00
3 Freddy Rodriguez/Jsy-Jsy/50 10.00
5 Javy Lopez/Bat-Jsy/50 8.00
6 Vernon Wells/Jsy-Jsy/50 8.00
8 Torii Hunter/Bat-Jsy/50 8.00
10 Sammy Sosa/Jsy-Jsy/50 12.00
11 Ryan Wagner/Jsy-Jsy/50 8.00
12 Jack Wilson/Bat-Jsy/50 8.00
14 Greg Maddux/Bat-Jsy/50 15.00
15 Albert Pujols/Bat-Jsy/50 30.00
17 Johnny Estrada/Fld Glve-Jsy/50 10.00
21 Paul Konerko/Jsy-Jsy/50 10.00
22 Victor Martinez/Bat-Jsy/50 10.00
23 Jose Vidro/Bat-Jsy/50 8.00
24 Jim Thome/Jsy-Jsy/45 12.00
25 Andruw Jones/Bat-Jsy/50 10.00

Diamond Cuts Signature Combo

NM/M
Production 25-50
Prime: No Pricing
Production 10 Sets
3 Freddy Rodriguez/Jsy-Jsy/25 40.00
6 Vernon Wells/Jsy-Jsy/25 25.00
8 Torii Hunter/Bat-Jsy/50 20.00
11 Ryan Wagner/Jsy-Jsy/50 15.00
12 Jack Wilson/Bat-Jsy/50 20.00
16 Jeremy Bonderman/Jsy-Jsy/50 20.00
17 Johnny Estrada/Fld Glv-Jsy/50 15.00
21 Paul Konerko/Jsy-Jsy/25 25.00

Heritage

NM/M
Common Player: 1.00
Production 1,000 Sets
Die-cut: 1-1.5X
Production 200 Sets
Die-cut Gold: 2-3X
Production 50 Sets
1 Rickey Henderson 1.50
2 Jeff Bagwell 1.50
3 Steve Garvey 1.00
4 Albert Pujols 5.00
5 Don Mattingly 4.00
6 Frank Thomas 1.50
7 Tony Gwynn 2.00
8 Gary Sheffield 1.50
9 Dale Murphy 1.50
10 Kerry Wood 1.50
11 Cal Ripken Jr. 6.00
12 Miguel Cabrera 2.00
13 Dwight Gooden 1.00
14 Barry Zito 1.00
15 Darryl Strawberry 1.00

Heritage Bat

NM/M
Production 150 Sets
1 Rickey Henderson 8.00
2 Jeff Bagwell 6.00
3 Steve Garvey 4.00
4 Albert Pujols 15.00
5 Don Mattingly 10.00
6 Frank Thomas 6.00
7 Tony Gwynn 8.00
8 Gary Sheffield 6.00
9 Dale Murphy 6.00
11 Cal Ripken Jr. 20.00
12 Miguel Cabrera 6.00
13 Dwight Gooden 4.00
15 Darryl Strawberry 4.00

Heritage Jersey

NM/M
Production 50-250
Prime: No Pricing
Production 10 Sets
1 Rickey Henderson/250 8.00
2 Jeff Bagwell/250 6.00
3 Steve Garvey/250 4.00
4 Albert Pujols/250 15.00
5 Don Mattingly/250 12.00
6 Frank Thomas/250 6.00
7 Tony Gwynn/250 8.00
9 Dale Murphy/250 6.00
10 Kerry Wood/250 6.00
11 Cal Ripken Jr./250 20.00
12 Miguel Cabrera/50 8.00
13 Dwight Gooden/250 4.00
14 Barry Zito/250 4.00
15 Darryl Strawberry/250 4.00

Heritage Combo

NM/M
Production 10-50
Prime: No Pricing
Production 10 Sets
1 Rickey Henderson/Bat-Jsy/50 15.00
2 Jeff Bagwell/Bat-Jsy/50 10.00
3 Steve Garvey/Bat-Jsy/50 10.00
4 Albert Pujols/Bat-Jsy/50 25.00
5 Don Mattingly/Bat-Jsy/50 20.00
6 Frank Thomas/Bat-Jsy/50 10.00
7 Tony Gwynn/Bat-Jsy/50 15.00
8 Gary Sheffield/Bat-Jsy/50 10.00
9 Dale Murphy/Bat-Jsy/50 12.00
10 Kerry Wood/Jsy-Pants/25 10.00
11 Cal Ripken Jr./Bat-Jsy/50 4.00
12 Miguel Cabrera/Bat-Jsy/50 12.00
13 Dwight Gooden/Bat-Jsy/50 10.00
15 Darryl Strawberry/Bat-Jsy/50 10.00

Heritage Signature Combo

NM/M
Production 10-50
Prime: No Pricing
Production 5-10

3 Steve Garvey/ Bat-Jsy/50 25.00
5 Don Mattingly/ Bat-Jsy/25 75.00
9 Dale Murphy/ Bat-Jsy/25 40.00
11 Cal Ripken Jr./ Bat-Jsy/50 160.00
12 Miguel Cabrera/ Bat-Jsy/25 50.00
13 Dwight Gooden/ Bat-Jsy/25 25.00
15 Darryl Strawberry/ Bat-Jsy/25 25.00

Heroes of the Hall

NM/M
Common Player: 2.00
Production 350 Sets
Die-Cut: 1-1.5X
Production 75 Sets
Die-Cut Gold: 2-3X
Production 25 Sets
1 Luis Aparicio 2.00
2 Dennis Eckersley 2.00
3 Brooks Robinson 4.00
4 Carlton Fisk 4.00
5 Tom Seaver 4.00
6 Paul Molitor 4.00
7 Rod Carew 3.00
8 George Brett 6.00
9 Nolan Ryan 8.00
10 Mike Schmidt 6.00
11 Willie Mays 6.00
12 Gary Carter 2.00
13 Lou Brock 2.00
14 Steve Carlton 2.00
15 Harmon Killebrew 4.00

Heroes of the Hall Bat

NM/M
Production 100-150
1 Luis Aparicio/150 4.00
3 Brooks Robinson/150 8.00
4 Carlton Fisk/150 6.00
6 Paul Molitor/150 8.00
8 George Brett/150 12.00
10 Mike Schmidt/125 15.00
11 Willie Mays/100 35.00
12 Gary Carter/125 6.00
13 Lou Brock/150 6.00
15 Harmon Killebrew/150 8.00

Heroes of the Hall Jersey

NM/M
Production 50-150
Prime: No Pricing
Production 5-10
1 Luis Aparicio/150 4.00
2 Dennis Eckersley/150 6.00
3 Brooks Robinson/50 10.00
4 Carlton Fisk/150 6.00
5 Tom Seaver/150 8.00
6 Paul Molitor/150 8.00
7 Rod Carew/150 6.00
8 George Brett/150 12.00
9 Nolan Ryan/100 20.00
10 Mike Schmidt/100 15.00
11 Willie Mays/50 40.00
12 Gary Carter/150 6.00
14 Steve Carlton/150 4.00
15 Harmon Killebrew/150 8.00

Heroes of the Hall Combo

NM/M
Production 25-50
Prime: No Pricing
Production 5-10
1 Luis Aparicio/ Bat-Jsy/50 10.00
2 Dennis Eckersley/ Jsy-Pants/50 10.00
3 Brooks Robinson/ Bat-Jsy/25 15.00
4 Carlton Fisk/ Bat-Jsy/50 12.00
5 Tom Seaver/ Jsy-Pants/50 15.00
6 Paul Molitor/ Bat-Jsy/50 15.00
7 Rod Carew/ Bat-Jsy/50 12.00
8 George Brett/ Bat-Jsy/50 20.00
9 Nolan Ryan/ Bat-Jsy/50 25.00
10 Mike Schmidt/ Bat-Jsy/50 20.00
11 Willie Mays/ Bat-Jsy/25 60.00
12 Gary Carter/ Jsy-Pants/50 10.00
13 Lou Brock/Bat-Jkt/50 15.00
15 Harmon Killebrew/ Bat-Jsy/50 15.00

Heroes of the Hall Signature Combo

NM/M
Production 5-50

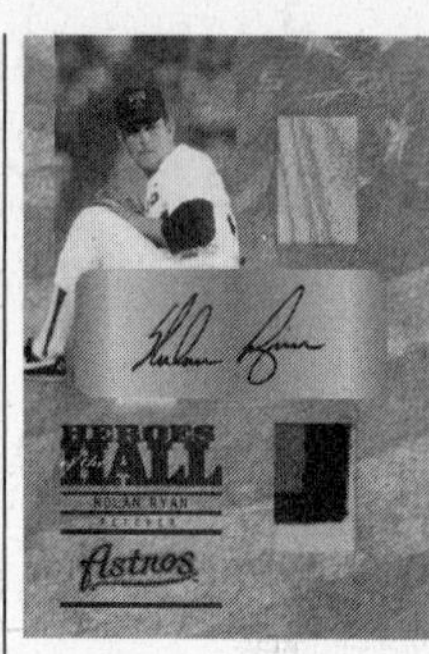

Prime: No Pricing
Production 5-10
1 Luis Aparicio/ Bat-Jsy/50 20.00
2 Dennis Eckersley/ Jsy-Pants/25 30.00
4 Carlton Fisk/ Bat-Jsy/25 40.00
6 Paul Molitor/ Bat-Jsy/25 35.00
14 Steve Carlton/ Bat-Jsy/25 35.00
15 Harmon Killebrew/ Bat-Jsy/25 40.00

Masterstrokes

NM/M
Common Player: 1.50
Production 750 Sets
Die-Cut: 1-1.5X
Production 150 Sets
Die-Cut Gold: 1.5-2X
Production 50 Sets
1 Hideki Matsui 6.00
2 David Ortiz 3.00
3 Aramis Ramirez 2.00
4 Lance Berkman 1.50
5 Ichiro Suzuki 6.00
6 Mike Piazza 4.00
7 Ivan Rodriguez 2.00
8 Hideo Nomo 2.00
9 Jeff Bagwell 2.00
10 Travis Hafner 1.50
11 Casey Kotchman 1.50
12 Jim Edmonds 2.00
13 Michael Young 1.50
14 Lyle Overbay 1.50
15 Eric Chavez 2.00
16 Jason Bay 1.50
17 Hank Blalock 2.00
18 Frank Thomas 2.00
19 Craig Biggio 2.00
20 Miguel Cabrera 3.00
21 Vladimir Guerrero 3.00
22 Sammy Sosa 4.00
23 Chipper Jones 3.00
24 Rafael Palmeiro 2.00
25 Adam Dunn 2.00

Masterstrokes Bat

NM/M
Production 25-250
1 Hideki Matsui/25 30.00
2 David Ortiz/250 8.00
3 Aramis Ramirez/35 8.00
4 Lance Berkman/250 4.00
6 Mike Piazza/100 10.00
7 Ivan Rodriguez/250 6.00
9 Jeff Bagwell/250 6.00
10 Travis Hafner/250 4.00
11 Casey Kotchman/250 4.00
13 Michael Young/250 4.00
14 Lyle Overbay/250 4.00
16 Jason Bay/250 4.00
17 Hank Blalock/50 6.00
18 Frank Thomas/250 6.00
19 Craig Biggio/250 6.00
20 Miguel Cabrera/250 6.00
21 Vladimir Guerrero/250 8.00
22 Sammy Sosa/200 8.00
23 Chipper Jones/250 6.00
25 Adam Dunn/250 6.00

Masterstrokes Jersey

NM/M
Production 40-250
Prime: No Pricing
Production 10 Sets
1 Hideki Matsui/250 20.00
2 David Ortiz/250 8.00
3 Aramis Ramirez/250 6.00
4 Lance Berkman/250 4.00
6 Mike Piazza/250 8.00
7 Ivan Rodriguez/250 6.00
8 Hideo Nomo/250 6.00
9 Jeff Bagwell/250 6.00
10 Travis Hafner/200 4.00
11 Casey Kotchman/250 4.00
12 Jim Edmonds/250 6.00
13 Michael Young/150 4.00
14 Lyle Overbay/250 4.00
15 Eric Chavez/250 4.00
16 Jason Bay/150 4.00
17 Hank Blalock/250 4.00
18 Frank Thomas/250 6.00
19 Craig Biggio/250 6.00
20 Miguel Cabrera/250 6.00
21 Vladimir Guerrero/50 10.00
22 Sammy Sosa/250 8.00
23 Chipper Jones/225 6.00
24 Rafael Palmeiro/40 8.00
25 Adam Dunn/250 6.00

Masterstrokes Combo

NM/M
Production 15-50
Prime: No Pricing
Production 10 Sets
2 David Ortiz/ Bat-Jsy/50 15.00
3 Aramis Ramirez/ Jsy-Jsy/50 10.00
4 Lance Berkman/ Bat-Jsy/50 8.00
6 Mike Piazza/ Jsy-Jsy/50 15.00
7 Ivan Rodriguez/ Bat-Jsy/50 10.00
8 Hideo Nomo/ Jsy-Jsy/50 12.00
9 Jeff Bagwell/ Bat-Jsy/50 10.00
10 Travis Hafner/ Bat-Jsy/50 8.00
11 Casey Kotchman/ Bat-Jsy/50 8.00
12 Jim Edmonds/ Jsy-Jsy/50 10.00
13 Michael Young/ Bat-Jsy/50 10.00
14 Lyle Overbay/ Bat-Jsy/50 8.00
15 Eric Chavez/ Bat-Jsy/50 10.00
16 Jason Bay/Bat-Jsy/50 8.00
17 Hank Blalock/ Jsy-Jsy/50 10.00
18 Frank Thomas/ Bat-Jsy/50 12.00
19 Craig Biggio/ Bat-Jsy/50 10.00
20 Miguel Cabrera/ Bat-Jsy/50 15.00
21 Vladimir Guerrero/ Bat-Jsy/50 15.00
22 Sammy Sosa/ Bat-Jsy/50 15.00
23 Chipper Jones/ Bat-Jsy/50 12.00
24 Rafael Palmeiro/ Bat-Pants/50 12.00
25 Adam Dunn/ Bat-Jsy/50 10.00

Masterstrokes Signature Combo

NM/M
Production 5-50
Prime: No Pricing
Production 5-10
10 Travis Hafner/ Bat-Jsy/50 25.00
11 Casey Kotchman/ Bat-Jsy/50 20.00
14 Lyle Overbay/ Bat-Jsy/50 12.00
15 Eric Chavez/ Bat-Jsy/25 25.00
16 Jason Bay/ Bat-Jsy/50 25.00
17 Hank Blalock/ Jsy-Jsy/25 30.00
20 Miguel Cabrera/ Bat-Jsy/25 50.00

Portraits Zenith White

NM/M
Common Player: 2.00
Production 70 Sets
Parallel #'d 40-60: .75-1X
Parallel #'d 20-35: .75-1.5X
No pricing 15 or less.
1 Ozzie Smith 6.00
2 Derek Jeter 8.00
3 Eric Chavez 2.00
4 Duke Snider 4.00
5 Albert Pujols 8.00
6 Stan Musial 6.00
7 Ivan Rodriguez 3.00
8 Cal Ripken Jr. 15.00
9 Hank Blalock 2.00
10 Chipper Jones 3.00
11 Gary Sheffield 2.00
12 Alfonso Soriano 3.00
13 Carl Crawford 2.00
14 Lou Brock 4.00
15 Jim Edmonds 3.00
16 Bo Jackson 4.00
17 Todd Helton 3.00
18 Javy Lopez 2.00
19 Tony Gwynn 5.00
20 Mark Mulder 2.00
21 Sammy Sosa 4.00
22 Roger Clemens 6.00
23 Don Mattingly 8.00
24 Willie Mays 8.00
25 Andruw Jones 3.00
26 Steve Garvey 2.00
27 Scott Rolen 3.00
28 George Brett 8.00
29 Rod Carew 4.00
30 Ken Griffey Jr. 6.00
31 Mike Piazza 5.00
32 Steve Carlton 3.00
33 Larry Walker 3.00
34 Kerry Wood 2.00
35 Frank Thomas 3.00
36 Lance Berkman 2.00
37 Nomar Garciaparra 4.00
38 Curt Schilling 3.00
39 Carl Yastrzemski 6.00
40 Mark Grace 3.00
41 Tom Seaver 4.00
42 Mariano Rivera 3.00
43 Carlos Beltran 3.00
44 Reggie Jackson 4.00
45 Pedro Martinez 4.00
46 Richie Sexson 2.00
47 Tom Glavine 2.00
48 Torii Hunter 2.00
49 Ron Guidry 2.00
50 Michael Young 2.00
51 Ichiro Suzuki 6.00
52 C.C. Sabathia 2.00
53 Johnny Bench 4.00
54 Mark Teixeira 3.00
55 Hideki Matsui 6.00
56 Mike Mussina 3.00
57 Johan Santana 3.00
58 Fergie Jenkins 2.00
59 Hideo Nomo 3.00
60 Nolan Ryan 10.00
61 Whitey Ford 4.00
62 Jim Thome 3.00
63 Gary Carter 3.00
64 Randy Johnson 3.00
65 Vladimir Guerrero 3.00
66 Harmon Killebrew 4.00
67 Tim Hudson 3.00
68 Josh Beckett 2.00
69 Eddie Murray 4.00
70 Greg Maddux 5.00
71 J.D. Drew 2.00
72 Bob Feller 4.00
73 Adrian Beltre 2.00
74 Wade Boggs 4.00
75 Barry Zito 2.00
76 David Ortiz 3.00
77 Mike Schmidt 8.00
78 Miguel Cabrera 4.00
79 Carlos Delgado 2.00
80 Andre Dawson 2.00
81 Garret Anderson 2.00
82 Rickey Henderson 3.00
83 Shawn Green 2.00
84 Dale Murphy 3.00
85 Alex Rodriguez 6.00
86 Mark Prior 3.00
87 Paul Molitor 4.00
88 Jeff Bagwell 3.00
89 Eric Gagne 2.00
90 Troy Glaus 2.00
91 Robin Yount 4.00
92 Miguel Tejada 3.00
93 Kirk Gibson 2.00
94 Manny Ramirez 3.00
95 Rafael Palmeiro 3.00
96 Maury Wills 2.00
97 Craig Biggio 2.00
98 Jim Palmer 3.00
99 Adam Dunn 3.00
100 Carlton Fisk 3.00

Private Signings Silver

NM/M
Common Autograph: 8.00
Production 100 Sets
1 Casey Kotchman 15.00
2 Chone Figgins 8.00
5 Ervin Santana 8.00
9 Orlando Cabrera 12.00
12 Tim Salmon 12.00
18 Tony Pena 8.00
19 Russ Ortiz 8.00
24 Adam LaRoche 10.00
27 Danny Kolb 8.00
31 Nick Green 8.00
34 Brian Roberts 15.00
36 Jay Gibbons 8.00
49 Jay Payton 8.00
51 Juan Cedeno 8.00
55 Wade Miller 8.00
57 Carlos Zambrano 20.00
65 Todd Walker 10.00
70 Jermaine Dye 12.00
80 Bubba Nelson 8.00
81 Danny Graves 8.00
84 Ryan Wagner 8.00
87 Cliff Lee 8.00
88 Fausto Carmona 8.00
91 Jody Gerut 8.00
94 Travis Hafner 12.00
98 Cory Sullivan 8.00
101 Jeff Salazar 8.00
103 Joe Kennedy 8.00
108 Brandon Inge 8.00
111 Craig Monroe 8.00
113 Jeremy Bonderman 12.00
117 Vance Wilson 8.00
127 Yorman Bazardo 8.00
127 Yorman Bazardo 8.00
133 Jason Lane 8.00
136 Morgan Ensberg 12.00
141 Jeremy Affeldt 8.00
143 Ken Harvey 8.00
150 Dioner Navarro 12.00
151 Edwin Jackson 8.00
158 Milton Bradley 10.00
159 Yhency Brazoban 8.00
161 Bill Hall 8.00
162 Carlos Lee 12.00
166 Lyle Overbay 8.00
170 Joe Nathan 10.00
173 Lew Ford 8.00
191 Yuniesky Betancourt 25.00
198 Scott Proctor 8.00
201 Bobby Crosby 10.00
202 Danny Haren 8.00
209 Octavio Dotel 8.00
210 Rich Harden 12.00
219 Mike Lieberthal 12.00
221 Randy Wolf 8.00
222 Craig Wilson 8.00
223 Jack Wilson 8.00
224 Jason Bay 10.00
226 Jose Castillo 8.00
231 Freddy Guzman 8.00
232 Jake Peavy 25.00
234 Mark Loretta 10.00
250 Clint Nageotte 8.00
252 J.J. Putz 8.00
260 Jeff Suppan 10.00
276 Adrian Gonzalez 8.00
278 Francisco Cordero 8.00
280 Kameron Loe 8.00
282 Laynce Nix 8.00
291 Shea Hillenbrand 10.00
293 Chad Cordero 10.00
295 Jose Guillen 10.00
297 Josh Karp 8.00
298 Livan Hernandez 12.00

Private Signings Gold

NM/M
Common Autograph: 8.00
Production 50 Sets
1 Casey Kotchman 20.00
2 Chone Figgins 10.00
5 Ervin Santana 10.00
6 Garret Anderson 15.00
9 Orlando Cabrera 15.00
10 Robb Quinlan 8.00
11 Steve Finley 15.00
12 Tim Salmon 15.00
14 Brandon Webb 10.00
18 Tony Pena 10.00
19 Russ Ortiz 10.00
24 Adam LaRoche 12.00
27 Danny Kolb 10.00
29 Johnny Estrada 10.00
31 Nick Green 8.00
32 Rafael Furcal 15.00
34 Brian Roberts 20.00
36 Jay Gibbons 10.00
40 Rodrigo Lopez 10.00
47 Edgar Renteria 25.00
49 Jay Payton 10.00
51 Juan Cedeno 8.00
53 Matt Clement 30.00
54 Trot Nixon 20.00
55 Wade Miller 10.00
57 Carlos Zambrano 25.00
59 Derrek Lee 40.00
65 Todd Walker 12.00
70 Jermaine Dye 15.00
71 Mark Buehrle 25.00
72 Paul Konerko 15.00
76 Shingo Takatsu 20.00
78 Austin Kearns 10.00
80 Bubba Nelson 8.00
81 Danny Graves 8.00
84 Ryan Wagner 8.00
87 Cliff Lee 10.00
88 Fausto Carmona 8.00
91 Jody Gerut 10.00
93 Kazuhito Tadano 15.00
94 Travis Hafner 15.00
98 Cory Sullivan 8.00
101 Jeff Salazar 8.00
103 Joe Kennedy 8.00
108 Brandon Inge 10.00
111 Craig Monroe 10.00
113 Jeremy Bonderman 15.00
116 Troy Percival 15.00
117 Vance Wilson 8.00
123 Miguel Cabrera 35.00
127 Yorman Bazardo 10.00
133 Jason Lane 10.00
136 Morgan Ensberg 15.00
141 Jeremy Affeldt 8.00
143 Ken Harvey 8.00
148 Brad Penny 10.00
150 Dioner Navarro 15.00
151 Edwin Jackson 10.00
158 Milton Bradley 12.00
159 Yhency Brazoban 8.00
161 Bill Hall 10.00
162 Carlos Lee 15.00
166 Lyle Overbay 8.00
168 Jacque Jones 8.00
170 Joe Nathan 12.00
173 Lew Ford 10.00
175 Shannon Stewart 10.00
191 Yuniesky Betancourt 30.00
198 Scott Proctor 10.00
199 Tom Gordon 12.00
201 Bobby Crosby 20.00
202 Danny Haren 10.00
209 Octavio Dotel 10.00
210 Rich Harden 15.00
219 Mike Lieberthal 15.00
221 Randy Wolf 8.00
222 Craig Wilson 8.00
223 Jack Wilson 10.00
224 Jason Bay 15.00
226 Jose Castillo 10.00
229 Akinori Otsuka 20.00
231 Freddy Guzman 8.00
232 Jake Peavy 30.00
234 Mark Loretta 12.00
235 Sean Burroughs 8.00
243 Merkin Valdez 10.00
246 Omar Vizquel 8.00
249 Bucky Jacobsen 10.00
250 Clint Nageotte 15.00
252 J.J. Putz 15.00
254 Miguel Olivo 8.00
260 Jeff Suppan 12.00
266 Yadier Molina 12.00
267 Aubrey Huff 12.00
268 B.J. Upton 20.00
269 Carl Crawford 20.00
271 Delmon Young 25.00
272 Dewon Brazelton 10.00
276 Adrian Gonzalez 10.00
278 Francisco Cordero 10.00
280 Kameron Loe 10.00
282 Laynce Nix 10.00
284 Michael Young 15.00
291 Shea Hillenbrand 12.00
293 Chad Cordero 12.00
295 Jose Guillen 12.00
297 Josh Karp 8.00
298 Livan Hernandez 15.00
299 Nick Johnson 15.00

Spirit of the Game

NM/M
Common Player: 1.50
Production 600 Sets
Die-Cut: 1-1.5X
Production 125 Sets
Die-Cut Gold: 2-4X
Production 25 Sets
1 Mark Prior 3.00
2 Sean Casey 1.50
3 Ichiro Suzuki 6.00
4 Andruw Jones 2.00
5 Francisco Cordero 1.50
6 Ben Sheets 2.00
7 Rocco Baldelli 1.50
8 Rafael Furcal 1.50
9 Angel Berroa 1.50
10 Roy Oswalt 1.50
11 Jose Reyes 1.50
12 Shannon Stewart 1.50
13 Greg Maddux 5.00
14 Alfonso Soriano 3.00
15 Curt Schilling 3.00
16 Jody Gerut 1.50
17 Brandon Webb 1.50
18 Josh Beckett 2.00
19 Laynce Nix 1.50
20 Scott Rolen 3.00

Spirit of the Game Bat

NM/M
Production 75-300
1 Mark Prior/300 6.00
4 Andruw Jones/300 6.00
6 Ben Sheets/300 4.00
7 Rocco Baldelli/300 4.00
8 Rafael Furcal/300 4.00
9 Angel Berroa/300 4.00
11 Jose Reyes/300 4.00
12 Shannon Stewart/75 4.00
13 Greg Maddux/300 8.00
14 Alfonso Soriano/225 6.00
16 Jody Gerut/300 4.00
17 Brandon Webb/300 4.00
19 Laynce Nix/300 4.00

Spirit of the Game Jersey

NM/M
Production 125-250
Prime: No Pricing
Production 10 Sets
1 Mark Prior/250 6.00
2 Sean Casey/250 4.00
4 Andruw Jones/250 6.00
5 Francisco Cordero/250 4.00
6 Ben Sheets/250 4.00
7 Rocco Baldelli/250 4.00
8 Rafael Furcal/250 4.00
10 Roy Oswalt/250 4.00
11 Jose Reyes/250 4.00
12 Shannon Stewart/250 4.00
13 Greg Maddux/250 8.00
14 Alfonso Soriano/250 6.00
15 Curt Schilling/250 6.00
16 Jody Gerut/125 4.00
18 Josh Beckett/250 4.00
19 Laynce Nix/250 4.00
20 Scott Rolen/250 6.00

Spirit of the Game Combo

NM/M
Production 50 Sets
Prime: No Pricing
Production 10 Sets
1 Mark Prior/Bat-Jsy 12.00

2 Sean Casey/Jsy-Jsy 6.00
4 Andruw Jones/Bat-Jsy 8.00
6 Ben Sheets/Bat-Jsy 8.00
7 Rocco Baldelli/Bat-Jsy 6.00
8 Rafael Furcal/Bat-Jsy 6.00
10 Roy Oswalt/Bat-Jsy 8.00
11 Jose Reyes/Bat-Jsy 8.00
12 Shannon Stewart/ Jsy-Jsy 6.00
13 Greg Maddux/ Bat-Jsy 15.00
14 Alfonso Soriano/ Jsy-Jsy 12.00
15 Curt Schilling/Bat-Jsy 12.00
16 Jody Gerut/Bat-Jsy 6.00
19 Laynce Nix/Bat-Jsy 6.00
20 Scott Rolen/Jsy-Jsy 12.00

Spirit of the Game Signature Combo

NM/M
Production 10-25
Prime: No Pricing
Production 5-10
2 Sean Casey/ Jsy-Jsy/25 20.00
8 Rafael Furcal/ Bat-Jsy/25 25.00
12 Shannon Stewart/ Jsy-Jsy/25 20.00
16 Jody Gerut/ Bat-Jsy/25 15.00
19 Laynce Nix/ Bat-Jsy/25 15.00

Stars

NM/M
Common Player: 1.00
Inserted 1:6
Gold: 1-2X
Production 500 Sets
Platinum: 2-4X
Production 50 Sets
1 Carlos Beltran 1.50
2 Sean Casey 1.00
3 Ichiro Suzuki 3.00
4 Vladimir Guerrero 1.50
5 Tim Hudson 1.50
6 Alex Rodriguez 4.00
7 Miguel Tejada 1.50
8 Curt Schilling 1.50
9 Roger Clemens 4.00
10 Ben Sheets 1.00
11 Todd Helton 1.50
12 Mark Mulder 1.00
13 Scott Podsednik 1.00
14 Victor Martinez 1.00
15 Mark Prior 1.50
16 Ivan Rodriguez 1.50
17 Dontrelle Willis 1.00
18 Andy Pettitte 1.00
19 Khalil Greene 1.50
20 Jeff Kent 1.00
21 Paul Konerko 1.00
22 Joe Mauer 1.50
23 Bobby Crosby 1.00
24 Pedro Martinez 2.00
25 John Smoltz 1.00
26 Derek Jeter 4.00
27 Moises Alou 1.00
28 Rich Harden 1.00
29 Jim Thome 1.50
30 Jason Bay 2.00
31 Aramis Ramirez 3.00
32 Carlos Lee 1.00
33 B.J. Upton 1.00
34 Nomar Garciaparra 1.00
35 Ken Griffey Jr. 1.00
36 Darin Erstad 1.00
37 Larry Walker 1.00
38 Jose Vidro 1.00
39 Zack Greinke 1.00
40 Michael Young 1.00
41 David Wright 2.00
42 Albert Pujols 4.00
43 Vernon Wells 1.00
44 Mark Teixeira 1.50
45 Jacque Jones 1.00
46 Brian Giles 1.00
47 Austin Kearns 1.00
48 Omar Vizquel 1.00
49 Randy Johnson 1.50
50 Jason Varitek 1.50

2005 Donruss Team Heroes

NM/M
Complete Set (440): 80.00
Common Player: .15
Pack (8): 1.75
Box (24): 35.00
1 Adam Kennedy .15
2 Bartolo Colon .15
3 Bengie Molina .15
4 Casey Kotchman .15
5 Chone Figgins .15
6 Dallas McPherson .25
7 Darin Erstad .15
8 David Eckstein .15
9 Francisco Rodriguez .15
10 Garret Anderson .25
11 Jarrod Washburn .15
12 John Lackey .15
13 Jose Guillen .25
14 Robb Quinlan .15
15 Tim Bittner .15
16 Tim Salmon .15
17 Vladimir Guerrero .25
18 Alex Cintron .15
19 Craig Counsell .15
20 Brandon Webb .15
21 Chad Tracy .15
22 Doug DeVore .15
23 Luis Gonzalez .25
24 Mark Grace .25
25 Randy Johnson .75
26 Scott Hairston .15
27 Shea Hillenbrand .15
28 Tim Olson .15
29 Adam LaRoche .15
30 Andruw Jones .40
31 Charles Thomas .15
32 Chipper Jones .75
33 Dale Murphy .50
34 John Smoltz .25
35 Johnny Estrada .15
36 Jose Capellan .15
37 Marcus Giles .15
38 Nick Green .15
39 Phil Niekro .15
40 Rafael Furcal .25
41 Brian Roberts .50
42 Cal Ripken Jr. 4.00
43 Javy Lopez .25
44 Jay Gibbons .15
45 Larry Bigbie .15
46 Luis Matos .15
47 Melvin Mora .15
48 Miguel Tejada .50
49 Rafael Palmeiro .50
50 Rodrigo Lopez .15
51 Sidney Ponson .15
52 Abe Alvarez .15
53 Bill Mueller .15
54 Curt Schilling .75
55 David Ortiz .75
56 Doug Mientkiewicz .15
57 Dwight Evans .15
58 Fred Lynn .15
59 Jim Rice .40
60 Johnny Damon .75
61 Keith Foulke .15
62 Kevin Youkilis .15
63 Manny Ramirez .75
64 Tim Wakefield .15
65 Trot Nixon .15
66 Angel Guzman .15
67 Aramis Ramirez .40
68 Carlos Zambrano .40
69 Corey Patterson .40
70 Derrek Lee .40
71 Greg Maddux 1.00
72 Kerry Wood .75
73 Lee Smith .15
74 Mark Prior .75
75 Sammy Sosa 1.50
76 Aaron Rowand .15
77 Carlos Lee .25
78 Frank Thomas .50
79 Freddy Garcia .15
80 Harold Baines .15
81 Jose Contreras .15
82 Juan Uribe .15
83 Mark Buehrle .15
84 Paul Konerko .15
85 Shingo Takatsu .15
86 Adam Dunn .50
87 Austin Kearns .15
88 Danny Graves .15
89 Eric Davis .15
90 Jacob Cruz .15
91 Jason LaRue .15
92 Ken Griffey Jr. 1.50
93 Ryan Wagner .15
94 Sean Casey .25
95 Casey Blake .15
96 C.C. Sabathia .15
97 Cliff Lee .15
98 Grady Sizemore .25
99 Jake Westbrook .15
100 Jody Gerut .15
101 Kazuhito Tadano .15
102 Matt Lawton .15
103 Travis Hafner .15
104 Victor Martinez .15
105 Charles Johnson .15
106 Clint Barmes .25
107 Garrett Atkins .15
108 Jason Jennings .15
109 Jeff Francis .15
110 Joe Kennedy .15
111 Matt Holliday .25
112 Preston Wilson .15
113 Todd Helton .50
114 Alan Trammell .40
115 Bobby Higginson .15
116 Brandon Inge .15
117 Carlos Guillen .15
118 Carlos Pena .15
119 Craig Monroe .15
120 Dmitri Young .15
121 Eric Munson .15
122 Ivan Rodriguez .50
123 Jeremy Bonderman .15
124 Roberto Novoa .15
125 A.J. Burnett .15
126 Alex Gonzalez .15
127 Dontrelle Willis .40
128 Guillermo Mota .15
129 Josh Beckett .40
130 Juan Pierre .15
131 Luis Castillo .15
132 Miguel Cabrera .75
133 Paul LoDuca .15
134 Adam Everett .15
135 Andy Pettitte .25
136 Brad Ausmus .15
137 Chris Burke .15
138 Craig Biggio .25
139 Jeff Bagwell .50
140 Lance Berkman .15
141 Morgan Ensberg .15
142 Nolan Ryan 3.00
143 Roger Clemens 2.00
144 Roy Oswalt .25
145 Tim Redding .15
146 Wade Miller .15
147 Andres Blanco .15
148 Angel Berroa .15
149 Benito Santiago .15
150 Byron Gettis .15
151 George Brett 2.00
152 Jeremy Affeldt .15
153 Ken Harvey .15
154 Mike MacDougal .15
155 Mike Sweeney .15
156 Shawn Camp .15
157 Zack Greinke .15
158 Brad Penny .15
159 Cesar Izturis .15
160 Edwin Jackson .15
161 Eric Gagne .40
162 Jerry Hairston .15
163 Jeff Weaver .15
164 Kazuhisa Ishii .15
165 Milton Bradley .15
166 Orel Hershiser .15
167 Shawn Green .25
168 Steve Garvey .15
169 Tommy John .15
170 Yhency Brazoban .15
171 Ben Sheets .25
172 Bill Hall .15
173 Danny Kolb .15
174 Lyle Overbay .15
175 Paul Molitor .50
176 Robin Yount 1.00
177 Rollie Fingers .15
178 Rickie Weeks .15
179 Scott Podsednik .15
180 Jack Morris .15
181 Jacque Jones .15
182 Jason Kubel .15
183 Joe Mauer .50
184 Joe Nathan .15
185 Johan Santana .50
186 Justin Morneau .25
187 Lew Ford .15
188 Matthew LeCroy .15
189 Rod Carew .50
190 Shannon Stewart .15
191 Torii Hunter .25
192 Aarom Baldiris .15
193 Cliff Floyd .15
194 Darryl Strawberry .15
195 Dwight Gooden .15
196 David Wright .75
197 Victor Zambrano .15
198 Jose Reyes .25
199 Kazuo Matsui .15
200 Keith Hernandez .15
201 Mike Piazza 1.00
202 Tom Glavine .40
203 Vance Wilson .15
204 Tom Seaver .75
205 Alex Rodriguez 1.50
206 Bernie Williams .40
207 Chien-Ming Wang .40
208 Derek Jeter 2.00
209 Dioner Navarro .15
210 Don Mattingly 1.50
211 Gary Sheffield .50
212 Hideki Matsui 1.50
213 Jason Giambi .25
214 Javier Vazquez .15
215 Jim Leyritz .15
216 Jorge Posada .40
217 Kevin Brown .15
218 Mariano Rivera .40
219 Mike Mussina .40
220 Scott Proctor .15
221 Tom Gordon .15
222 Barry Zito .25
223 Bobby Crosby .25
224 Dave Stewart .15
225 Dennis Eckersley .50
226 Eric Byrnes .15
227 Eric Chavez .25
228 Erubiel Durazo .15
229 Mark Kotsay .15
230 Mark Mulder .40
231 Octavio Dotel .15
232 Rich Harden .40
233 Tim Hudson .40
234 Billy Wagner .15
235 Bobby Abreu .40
236 Brett Myers .15
237 Chase Utley .25
238 Jim Thome .75
239 Jimmy Rollins .25
240 Lenny Dykstra .15
241 Marlon Byrd .15
242 Mike Lieberthal .15
243 Mike Schmidt 1.50
244 Pat Burrell .25
245 Randy Wolf .15
246 Ryan Howard .75
247 Steve Carlton .40
248 Bert Blyleven .15
249 Bill Madlock .15
250 Dave Parker .40
251 Craig Wilson .15
252 Jack Wilson .15
253 Jason Bay .25
254 Jason Kendall .15
255 Jose Castillo .15
256 Kip Wells .15
257 Akinori Otsuka .15
258 Brian Giles .25
259 Brian Lawrence .15
260 Freddy Guzman .15
261 Gaylord Perry .15
262 Jake Peavy .40
263 Jay Payton .15
264 Khalil Greene .25
265 Mark Loretta .15
266 Phil Nevin .15
267 Ryan Klesko .15
268 Sean Burroughs .15
269 Tony Gwynn .75
270 Trevor Hoffman .15
271 A.J. Pierzynski .15
272 Dustan Mohr .15
273 Edgardo Alfonzo .15
274 Jason Schmidt .40
275 Jerome Williams .15
276 Matt Williams .40
277 Merkin Valdez .15
278 Todd Linden .15
279 Will Clark .50
280 Bret Boone .15
281 Bucky Jacobsen .15
282 Clint Nageotte .15
283 Ichiro Suzuki 1.50
284 J.J. Putz .15
285 Jamie Moyer .15
286 Bobby Madritsch .15
287 Mike Morse **RC** .25
288 Joel Pineiro .15
289 Shigetoshi Hasegawa .15
290 Travis Blackley .15
291 Albert Pujols 2.00
292 Dan Haren .15
293 Jason Isringhausen .15
294 Jason Marquis .15
295 Jeff Suppan .15
296 Jim Edmonds .40
297 Larry Walker .40
298 Reggie Sanders .15
299 Scott Rolen .75
300 Yadier Molina .15
301 Aubrey Huff .15
302 B.J. Upton .15
303 Carl Crawford .15
304 Chad Gaudin .15
305 Delmon Young .40
306 Dewon Brazelton .15
307 Joey Gathright .15
308 Jose Cruz Jr. .15
309 Rocco Baldelli .15
310 Wade Boggs .50
311 Adrian Gonzalez .15
312 Alfonso Soriano .75
313 Francisco Cordero .15
314 Frankie Francisco .15
315 Hank Blalock .50
316 Kenny Rogers .15
317 Laynce Nix .15
318 Mark Teixeira .50
319 Michael Young .15
320 Alexis Rios .15
321 David Bush .15
322 Eric Hinske .15
323 Frank Catalanotto .15
324 Gabe Gross .15
325 Guillermo Quiroz .15
326 Rickey Henderson .50
327 Orlando Hudson .15
328 Roy Halladay .40
329 Ted Lilly .15
330 Vernon Wells .15
331 Alberto Callaspo .15
332 Jeff Mathis .15
333 Ervin Santana .15
334 Troy Percival .15
335 Troy Glaus .40
336 Greg Aquino .15
337 Tony Pena **RC** .25
338 Luis Terrero .15
339 J.D. Drew .15
340 Jon Lieber .15
341 Russ Ortiz .15
342 Daniel Cabrera .15
343 Kenny Lofton .15
344 Val Majewski .15
345 Orlando Cabrera .15
346 Hanley Ramirez .25
347 Jason Varitek .50
348 Pedro Martinez .75
349 Derek Lowe .15
350 Juan Cedeno .15
351 Todd Walker .15
352 Matt Clement .25
353 Moises Alou .25
354 Nomar Garciaparra 1.00
355 Michael Barrett .15
356 Todd Hollandsworth .15
357 Jose Valentin .15
358 Magglio Ordonez .15
359 Pedro Lopez **RC** .25
360 Barry Larkin .25
361 Jaret Wright .15
362 Elizardo Ramirez .15
363 Omar Vizquel .15
364 Fausto Carmona .15
365 Jake Dittler .15
366 Jeff Salazar .15
367 Jeromy Burnitz .15
368 Jayson Nix .15
369 Ubaldo Jimenez **RC** .25
370 Vinny Castilla .15
371 Justin Verlander **RC** .75
372 Armando Benitez .15
373 Carl Pavano .25
374 Chris Aguila .15
375 Logan Kensing .15
376 Mike Lowell .15
377 Yorman Bazardo **RC** .25
378 Willy Taveras .15
379 Jeff Kent .25
380 Carlos Beltran .50
381 Kevin Millwood .15
382 Juan Gonzalez .25
383 Steve Finley .15
384 Hideo Nomo .40
385 Adrian Beltre .40
386 David Krynzel .15
387 Richie Sexson .40
388 Jesse Crain .15
389 Brad Radke .15
390 Jason Lane .15
391 Corey Koskie .15
392 Cristian Guzman .15
393 Brad Wilkerson .15
394 Brendan Harris .15
395 Chad Cordero .15
396 Endy Chavez .15
397 Jose Vidro .15
398 Josh Karp .15
399 Livan Hernandez .15
400 Nick Johnson .15
401 Ryan Church .15
402 Terrmel Sledge .15
403 Philip Humber **RC** 1.50
404 Ambiorix Concepcion **RC** .25
405 Al Leiter .15
406 Richard Hidalgo .15
407 Kris Benson .15
408 Mike Cameron .15
409 Victor Diaz .15
410 Tony Womack .15
411 Ferdin Tejeda .15
412 Nick Swisher .15
413 Jairo Garcia .15
414 Jermaine Dye .15
415 Joe Blanton .15
416 Eric Milton .15
417 Gavin Floyd .15
418 John Van Benschoten .15
419 Matt Peterson .15
420 David Wells .15
421 J.T. Snow .15
422 Willie Mays 2.00
423 Jeremy Reed .15
424 Jose Lopez .15
425 Raul Ibanez .15
426 Wladimir Balentien **RC** 1.50
427 Matt Morris .15
428 Mike Matheny .15
429 Edgar Renteria .25
430 Woody Williams .15
431 Jeff Niemann **RC** 4.00
432 Scott Kazmir .15
433 Tino Martinez .15
434 Chris Young **RC** .50
435 David Dellucci .15
436 Kameron Loe .15
437 Nolan Ryan 3.00
438 John-Ford Griffin .15
439 Carlos Delgado .40
440 Russ Adams .15

Autographs

NM/M
4 Casey Kotchman/SP 20.00
14 Robb Quinlan 8.00
15 Tim Bittner 5.00
18 Alex Cintron/SP 8.00
22 Doug DeVore 5.00
28 Tim Olson 5.00
38 Nick Green 5.00
44 Jay Gibbons/SP 12.00
50 Rodrigo Lopez/SP 8.00
66 Angel Guzman 12.00
90 Jacob Cruz 5.00
97 Cliff Lee/SP 10.00
101 Kazuhito Tadano 20.00
104 Victor Martinez/SP 20.00
110 Joe Kennedy 5.00
116 Brandon Inge 10.00
119 Craig Monroe 8.00
124 Roberto Novoa 5.00
150 Byron Gettis/SP 8.00
152 Jeremy Affeldt 5.00
156 Shawn Camp 5.00
170 Yhency Brazoban 8.00
172 Bill Hall/SP 8.00
182 Jason Kubel/SP 12.00
192 Aarom Baldiris/SP 10.00
203 Vance Wilson 5.00
220 Scott Proctor 8.00
277 Merkin Valdez 5.00
278 Todd Linden/SP 25.00
281 Bucky Jacobsen 5.00
282 Clint Nageotte 5.00
290 Travis Blackley 5.00
292 Dan Haren/SP 12.00
295 Jeff Suppan 10.00
300 Yadier Molina/SP 15.00
306 Dewon Brazelton 8.00
307 Joey Gathright/SP 10.00
311 Adrian Gonzalez 10.00
313 Francisco Cordero/ SP 10.00
314 Frankie Francisco 5.00
317 Laynce Nix 8.00
333 Ervin Santana 10.00
337 Tony Pena 8.00
346 Hanley Ramirez 15.00
350 Juan Cedeno 8.00
359 Pedro Lopez 15.00
364 Fausto Carmona 5.00
365 Jake Dittler 5.00
366 Jeff Salazar 10.00
368 Jayson Nix 5.00
377 Yorman Bazardo 8.00
378 Willy Taveras/SP 15.00
398 Josh Karp 5.00
411 Ferdin Tejeda 5.00
419 Matt Peterson 5.00
435 David Dellucci/SP 20.00
436 Kameron Loe 5.00

Movie Gallery

NM/M
1 Cal Ripken Jr. 1.00

Showdown Blue

Blue: 3-5X

Showdown Bronze

Bronze: 4-6X
Production 100 Sets

Showdown Gold

Gold: No Pricing
Production 10 Sets

Showdown Red

Red: 1.5-3X

Showdown Silver

Silver: 6-8X
Production 50 Sets

National Convention

These cello-wrapped team sets were available at the National Sports Collectors Convention to persons who redeemed a free coupon available at Wal-Mart. Cards share the basic design of Donruss Team Heroes but have a National Convention logo on front and are numbered "X of 6" on back.

NM/M
Complete Set (12): 5.00
Common Player: .25
Chicago Cubs Team Heroes (6) 3.00
1 Kerry Wood .50
2 Aramis Ramirez .25
3 Mark Prior .50
4 Nomar Garciaparra .50
5 Greg Maddux .50
6 Derrek Lee 1.00
Chicago White Sox Team Heroes (6) 2.00
1 Frank Thomas 1.00
2 Shingo Takatsu .25
3 Aaron Rowand .25
4 Paul Konerko .25
5 Jermaine Dye .25
6 Mark Buehrle .25

2005 Donruss Throwback Threads

NM/M
Complete Set (300):
Common Player: .20
Pack (5): 3.00
Box (24): 65.00
1 Luis Castillo .20
2 Derek Jeter 1.50
3 Eric Chavez .20
4 Angel Berroa .20
5 Jeff Bagwell .40
6 J.T. Snow .20
7 Craig Biggio .30
8 Michael Barrett .20
9 Hank Blalock .40
10 Chipper Jones .50
11 Jacque Jones .20

12 Mark Teixeira .50
13 Omar Vizquel .20
14 Paul LoDuca .30
15 Jim Edmonds .30
16 Aramis Ramirez .30
17 Lance Berkman .30
18 Javy Lopez .30
19 Adam LaRoche .20
20 Jorge Posada .40
21 Sean Casey .20
22 Mark Prior .40
23 Phil Nevin .20
24 Manny Ramirez .50
25 Andruw Jones .40
26 Matt Lawton .20
27 Vladimir Guerrero .50
28 Austin Kearns .20
29 John Smoltz .40
30 Ken Griffey Jr. 1.00
31 Mike Piazza .75
32 Jason Jennings .20
33 Jason Varitek .40
34 David Ortiz .50
35 Mike Mussina .40
36 Joe Nathan .20
37 Kenny Rogers .20
38 Carlos Zambrano .30
39 Eric Byrnes .20
40 Clint Barmes .20
41 Danny Kolb .20
42 Mariano Rivera .40
43 Joey Gathright .20
44 Adam Dunn .40
45 Carlos Lee .20
46 Yhency Brazoban .20
47 Roy Oswalt .30
48 Torii Hunter .20
49 Scott Podsednik .20
50 Jason Hammel **RC** .40
51 Ichiro Suzuki 1.00
52 C.C. Sabathia .20
53 Bobby Abreu .40
54 Jon Garland .20
55 Brandon Webb .30
56 Mark Buehrle .20
57 Johan Santana .50
58 Mike Sweeney .20
59 Tadahito Iguchi **RC** 1.50
60 Edgar Renteria .20
61 Aaron Rowand .20
62 Craig Wilson .20
63 J.D. Drew .30
64 Bobby Crosby .40
65 Justin Morneau .50
66 Scott Rolen .50
67 Jose Vidro .20
68 Carlos Beltran .40
69 Jeff Weaver .20
70 Jason Schmidt .30
71 Brad Wilkerson .20
72 Yuniesky
Betancourt **RC** 1.50
73 Octavio Dotel .20
74 Mike Cameron .20
75 Barry Zito .40
76 Woody Williams .20
77 Russel Rohlicek **RC** .40
78 Mark Kotsay .20
79 Jeff Suppan .20
80 Eric Gagne .40
81 Tim Salmon .20
82 Troy Glaus .40
83 Kevin Mench .20
84 Ivan Rodriguez .40
85 Sean Burroughs .20
86 Dallas McPherson .20
87 Jamie Moyer .20
88 Orlando Cabrera .20
89 Wladimir Balentien **RC** 1.00
90 Philip Humber **RC** 1.00
91 Francisco Cordero .20
92 Danny Graves .20
93 Bucky Jacobsen .20
94 Cliff Lee .20
95 Oliver Perez .20
96 Jake Peavy .30
97 Doug Mientkiewicz .20
98 Brad Radke .20
99 Jeremy Reed .20
100 Garret Anderson .30
101 Rafael Furcal .20
102 Jack Wilson .20
103 Bernie Williams .20
104 Josh Beckett .20
105 Albert Pujols 1.50
106 Ubaldo Jimenez **RC** .40
107 Richard Hidalgo .20
108 Luke Scott **RC** 1.00
109 Hideo Nomo .40
110 Vernon Wells .30
111 Richie Sexson .40
112 Chad Cordero .20
113 Alex Rodriguez 1.50
114 Paul Konerko .30
115 Carlos Guillen .20
116 Francisco Rodriguez .20
117 Johnny Damon .50
118 David Wright 1.00
119 Lyle Overbay .20
120 Brian Roberts .20
121 Sammy Sosa 1.00
122 Roger Clemens 1.50
123 Rickie Weeks .50
124 Larry Bigbie .20
125 Rafael Palmeiro .40
126 Jason Giambi .30
127 Hideki Matsui 1.00
128 Brad Lidge .20
129 Jeremy Affeldt .20
130 Mike MacDougal .20
131 Troy Percival .20
132 Matt Morris .20
133 David Gassner **RC** .40
134 Kerry Wood .40
135 Dontrelle Willis .40
136 Michael Young .30
137 Andy Pettitte .40
138 Kris Benson .20
139 Miguel Negron **RC** .40
140 Rich Harden .40
141 Bret Boone .20
142 Danny Rueckel **RC** .40
143 Jeff Niemann **RC** 1.00
144 Randy Messenger **RC** .40
145 Pedro Martinez .50
146 Kazuhisa Ishii .20
147 Carlos Delgado .30
148 Tom Glavine .30
149 Russ Ortiz .20
150 Gavin Floyd .20
151 Randy Johnson .50
152 Prince Fielder 10.00
153 Nomar Garciaparra .75
154 Pat Burrell .30
155 Melvin Mora .20
156 Jose Reyes .50
157 Trot Nixon .20
158 B.J. Upton .20
159 Jody Gerut .20
160 Juan Pierro .20
161 Miguel Tejada .40
162 Barry Larkin .40
163 Carl Crawford .20
164 Ben Sheets .30
165 Tim Hudson .40
166 Darin Erstad .20
167 Todd Helton .40
168 Luis Gonzalez .30
169 Mark Mulder .30
170 David Dellucci .20
171 Marcus Giles .20
172 Shannon Stewart .20
173 Zack Greinke .20
174 Miguel Cabrera .50
175 Nick Johnson .20
176 Derrek Lee .50
177 Jim Thome .40
178 Ken Harvey .20
179 Ambiorix
Concepcion **RC** .40
180 Roy Halladay .40
181 Larry Walker .40
182 Greg Maddux 1.00
183 Frank Thomas .50
184 Travis Hafner .30
185 Matt Holliday .20
186 Victor Martinez .20
187 Jason Isringhausen .20
188 Bill Mueller .20
189 Dewon Brazelton .20
190 Adrian Beltre .40
191 Tim Wakefield .20
192 Alexis Rios .20
193 Alfonso Soriano .50
194 Fernando Vina .20
195 Armando Benitez .20
196 Bartolo Colon .30
197 A.J. Burnett .20
198 Milton Bradley .20
199 Brad Penny .20
200 Rocco Baldelli .20
201 Curt Schilling .50
202 Ryan Wagner .20
203 Preston Wilson .20
204 Akinori Otsuka .20
205 Bill McCarthy **RC** .40
206 Edgardo Alfonzo .20
207 Mike Lieberthal .20
208 Shea Hillenbrand .20
209 Tom Gordon .20
210 Kip Wells .20
211 Frank Catalanotto .20
212 Casey Kotchman .20
213 Justin Verlander **RC** 1.50
214 Brandon Inge .20
215 Termel Sledge .20
216 Gary Sheffield .40
217 Steve Finley .20
218 Kenny Lofton .20
219 Chris Carpenter .30
220 Danny Haren .20
221 Brett Myers .20
222 Joe Mauer .50
223 David Wells .20
224 Brian Giles .20
225 Moises Alou .30
226 Casey Rogowski **RC** .40
227 Chase Utley .50
228 Corey Koskie .20
229 Derek Lowe .20
230 Erick Threets **RC** .40
231 Grady Sizemore .40
232 Jason Lane .20
233 Jeremy Bonderman .20
234 Livan Hernandez .20
235 Ryan Klesko .20
236 Sidney Ponson .20
237 Jimmy Rollins .40
238 Eric Milton .20
239 Shingo Takatsu .20
240 Scott Kazmir .20
241 Shawn Green .30
242 Nick Swisher .20
243 Shawn Chacon .20
244 Javier Vazquez .20
245 Mark Loretta .20
246 Dmitri Young .20
247 Charles Johnson .20
248 Magglio Ordonez .30
249 Sean Thompson **RC** .40
250 Jared Gothreaux **RC** .40
251 Kevin Millwood .20
252 Mike Lowell .20
253 Cristian Guzman .20
254 Nate McLouth **RC** .40
255 Delmon Young .40
256 Jeromy Burnitz .20
257 Garrett Atkins .20
258 Junior Spivey .20
259 Morgan Ensberg .20
260 Chone Figgins .20
261 Hayden Penn **RC** .50
262 Jason Bay .40
263 Jose Cruz Jr. .20
264 Khalil Greene .40
265 Ray Durham .20
266 Juan Gonzalez .40
267 Jeff Kent .20
268 Dioner Navarro .20
269 Rodrigo Lopez .20
270 Geoff Jenkins .20
271 Jermaine Dye .20
272 Orlando Hudson .20
273 Jose Lima .20
274 Jeff Francis .20
275 Luis Matos .20
276 Jason Kendall .20
277 Mike Hampton .20
278 Al Kaline .75
279 Bert Blyleven .20
280 Bill Madlock .20
281 Cal Ripken Jr. 3.00
282 Dale Murphy .50
283 Gary Carter .50
284 George Brett 2.00
285 Harmon Killebrew 1.00
286 Harold Baines .30
287 John Kruk .50
288 Keith Hernandez .40
289 Willie Mays 3.00
290 Matt Williams .20
291 Nolan Ryan 2.50
292 Paul Molitor .50
293 Reggie Jackson .75
294 Rickey Henderson .50
295 Ron Cey .50
296 Ryne Sandberg 1.00
297 Ted Williams 2.50
298 Tom Seaver .50
299 Tony Gwynn .75
300 Babe Ruth/SP 20.00

Century Proof Blue

Blue (1-299): 3-6X
Production 150 Sets

Century Proof Green

Green (1-299): 3-6X

Century Proof Gold

Gold (1-299): 3-6X
Production 100 Sets

Century Stars

NM/M
Common Player: 1.00
Spectrum: 1.5-3X
Production 100 Sets
1 Bobby Doerr 1.00
2 Derek Jeter 4.00
3 Harmon Killebrew 1.50
4 Paul Molitor 1.50
5 Brooks Robinson 1.50
6 Steve Garvey 1.00
7 Ivan Rodriguez 1.00
8 Carl Yastrzemski 2.50
9 Nomar Garciaparra 2.00
10 Miguel Tejada 1.00
11 Edgar Martinez 1.00
12 Kevin Brown 1.00
13 Alex Rodriguez 3.00
14 Carlton Fisk 1.00
15 Craig Biggio 1.00
16 Dwight Gooden 1.00
17 Jim Palmer 1.00
18 Ken Griffey Jr. 2.00
19 Bob Feller 1.50
20 Don Sutton 1.00
21 Al Kaline 1.50
22 Roger Clemens 4.00
23 Kirk Gibson 1.00
24 Willie Mays 3.00
25 Frank Robinson 1.00
26 Randy Johnson 1.50
27 Jim "Catfish" Hunter 1.00
28 Austin Kearns 1.00
29 John Smoltz 1.00
30 Nolan Ryan 4.00
31 Duke Snider 1.50
32 Bernie Williams 1.00
33 David Wells 1.00
34 Bo Jackson 1.50
35 Mike Mussina 1.00
36 Gaylord Perry 1.00
37 Andre Dawson 1.00
38 Curt Schilling 1.50
39 Darryl Strawberry 1.00
40 Willie McCovey 1.00
41 Tom Seaver 1.50
42 Mariano Rivera 1.00
43 Dennis Eckersley 1.00
44 David Cone 1.00
45 Bret Boone 1.00
46 Will Clark 1.00
47 Jack Morris 1.00
48 Ichiro Suzuki 3.00
49 Alan Trammell 1.00
50 Cal Ripken Jr. 4.00

Century Stars Material

NM/M
Common Player: 4.00
Production 20-50
Prime: No Pricing
Production Five Sets
1 Bobby Doerr/
Pants/50 8.00
3 Harmon Killebrew/
Jsy/50 15.00
4 Paul Molitor/Jsy/50 10.00
5 Brooks Robinson/
Bat/50 10.00
6 Steve Garvey/Jsy/50 4.00
7 Ivan Rodriguez/Jsy/50 8.00
8 Carl Yastrzemski/
Jsy/50 15.00
10 Miguel Tejada/Jsy/50 6.00
11 Edgar Martinez/
Jsy/50 6.00
12 Kevin Brown/Jsy/50 4.00
14 Carlton Fisk/Jsy/50 8.00
15 Craig Biggio/Jsy/50 8.00
16 Dwight Gooden/
Jsy/50 4.00
17 Jim Palmer/Jsy/50 6.00
20 Don Sutton/Jsy/50 4.00
21 Al Kaline/Bat/50 15.00
22 Roger Clemens/
Jsy/50 15.00
23 Kirk Gibson/Jsy/50 4.00
25 Frank Robinson/
Bat/50 6.00
26 Randy Johnson/
Jsy/50 8.00
28 Austin Kearns/Jsy/50 4.00
29 John Smoltz/Jsy/50 8.00
30 Nolan Ryan/Jkt/50 25.00
32 Bernie Williams/
Jsy/50 6.00
33 David Wells/Jsy/50 4.00
34 Bo Jackson/Jsy/50 10.00
35 Mike Mussina/Jsy/50 8.00
36 Gaylord Perry/Jsy/50 6.00
37 Andre Dawson/Jsy/50 6.00
38 Curt Schilling/Jsy/50 8.00
39 Darryl Strawberry/
Jsy/50 6.00
40 Willie McCovey/
Jsy/50 8.00
42 Mariano Rivera/
Jsy/50 10.00
43 Dennis Eckersley/
Jsy/50 6.00
44 David Cone/Jsy/50 4.00
45 Bret Boone/Jsy/50 4.00
47 Jack Morris/Jsy/50 4.00
49 Alan Trammell/Jsy/50 6.00
50 Cal Ripken Jr./
Jsy/50 30.00

Century Stars Signature Material

No Pricing
Production 10 Sets
Prime: No Pricing
Production Five Sets

Dynasty

NM/M
Common Trio: 2.00
Spectrum: 1.25X
Production 100 Sets
1 Reggie Jackson,
Jim "Catfish" Hunter,
Sparky Lyle 2.00
2 Cal Ripken Jr., Jim Palmer,
Eddie Murray 8.00
3 Dwight Gooden,
Gary Carter,
Darryl Strawberry 2.00
4 Rickey Henderson,
Dennis Eckersley,
Jose Canseco 2.00
5 Chipper Jones,
Greg Maddux,
David Justice 3.00
6 Roger Clemens,
Alfonso Soriano,
Bernie Williams 6.00
7 Randy Johnson,
Curt Schilling,
Matt Williams 3.00
8 Troy Glaus,
Garret Anderson,
Francisco Rodriguez 2.00
9 Josh Beckett,
Miguel Cabrera,
Mike Lowell 2.00
10 Curt Schilling,
Manny Ramirez,
Jason Varitek 8.00

Dynasty Material

NM/M
Production 20-50
Prime: No Pricing
Production Five Sets
1 Reggie Jackson/Pants,
Jim "Catfish" Hunter/Pants,
Sparky Lyle/Pants/50 20.00
2 Cal Ripken Jr./Jsy,
Jim Palmer/Jsy,
Eddie Murray/Jsy/50 40.00
3 Dwight Gooden/Jsy,
Gary Carter/Jsy,
Darryl Strawberry/
Pants/20 15.00
4 Rickey Henderson/Jsy,
Dennis Eckersley/Pants,
Jose Canseco/Jsy/50 35.00
5 Chipper Jones/Jsy,
Greg Maddux/Jsy,
David Justice/Jsy/50 25.00
6 Roger Clemens/Jsy,
Alfonso Soriano/Jsy,
Bernie Williams/
Jsy/50 30.00
7 Randy Johnson/Jsy,
Curt Schilling/Jsy,
Matt Williams/Jsy/50 20.00
8 Troy Glaus/Jsy,
Garret Anderson/Jsy,
Francisco Rodriguez/
Jsy/50 15.00
10 Curt Schilling/Jsy,
Manny Ramirez/Jsy,
Jason Varitek/Jsy/50 40.00

Generations

NM/M
Common Player: 2.00
Spectrum: 1-2.5X
Production 100 Sets
1 Duke Snider,
Reggie Jackson,
Sammy Sosa 2.00
2 Rod Carew, John Kruk,
Eric Chavez 2.00
3 Bo Jackson,
Deion Sanders,
Brian Jordan 3.00
4 Brett George, Tony Gwynn,
Todd Helton 4.00
5 Babe Ruth, Ted Williams,
Willie Mays 5.00
6 Rickey Henderson,
Lenny Dykstra,
Ichiro Suzuki 3.00
7 Keith Hernandez,
Don Mattingly,
Casey Kotchman 3.00
8 Wade Boggs, Mark Grace,
Hank Blalock 2.00
9 Gary Carter,
Ivan Rodriguez,
Victor Martinez 2.00
10 Gaylord Perry, Morris,
Greg Maddux 2.00
11 Joe Morgan,
Ryne Sandberg,
Alfonso Soriano 3.00
12 Juan Marichal, Luis Tiant,
Pedro Martinez 2.00
13 Stan Musial,
Carl Yastrzemski,
Lance Berkman 3.00
14 Johnny Bench,
Carlton Fisk,
Mike Piazza 3.00
15 Harmon Killebrew,
Cal Ripken Jr.,
Albert Pujols 5.00
16 Frank Robinson,
Andre Dawson,
Gary Sheffield 2.00
17 Bob Feller, Roger Clemens,
Kerry Wood 4.00
18 Steve Carlton,
Tom Glavine,
Barry Zito 2.00
19 Murray, Rafael Palmeiro,
Mark Teixeira 2.00
20 Brooks Robinson,
Mike Schmidt,
Scott Rolen 3.00
21 Luis Aparicio,
Omar Vizquel,
Rafael Furcal 2.00
22 Don Sutton, David Cone,
Roy Oswalt 2.00
23 Fred Lynn, Dale Murphy,
Jim Edmonds 2.00
24 Ozzie, Barry Larkin,
B.J. Upton 3.00
25 Gibson, Nolan Ryan,
Mark Prior 4.00

Generations Material

NM/M
Production 20-50
Prime: No Pricing
Production 10 Sets
2 Rod Carew/Jsy,
John Kruk/Jsy,
Eric Chavez/Jsy/50 15.00
3 Bo Jackson/Jsy,
Deion Sanders/Jsy,
Brian Jordan/Jsy/50 25.00
4 Brett George/Jsy,
Tony Gwynn/Jsy,
Todd Helton/Jsy/50 25.00
7 Keith Hernandez/Jsy,
Don Mattingly/Pants,
Casey Kotchman/
Jsy/20 30.00
8 Wade Boggs/Jsy,
Mark Grace/Jsy,
Hank Blalock/Jsy/50 15.00
9 Gary Carter/Jsy,
Ivan Rodriguez/Jsy,
Victor Martinez/
Jsy/50 15.00
10 Gaylord Perry/Jsy,
Morris/Jsy,
Greg Maddux/Jsy/50 25.00
11 Joe Morgan/Jsy,
Ryne Sandberg/Jsy,
Alfonso Soriano/
Jsy/50 35.00
12 Juan Marichal/Pants,
Luis Tiant/Pants,
Pedro Martinez/
Jsy/50 20.00
14 Johnny Bench/Pants,
Carlton Fisk/Jsy,
Mike Piazza/Jsy/50 20.00
15 Harmon Killebrew/Jsy,
Cal Ripken Jr./Jsy,
Albert Pujols/Jsy/50 50.00
16 Frank Robinson/Bat,
Andre Dawson/Jsy,
Gary Sheffield/Jsy/20 15.00
17 Bob Feller/Pants,
Roger Clemens/Jsy,
Kerry Wood/Jsy/20 50.00
18 Steve Carlton/Jsy,
Tom Glavine/Jsy,
Barry Zito/Jsy/50 20.00
19 Murray/Jsy,
Rafael Palmeiro/Jsy,
Mark Teixeira/Jsy/50 20.00

Material Bat

NM/M
Common Player: 4.00
Production 5-250
1 Luis Castillo/250 4.00
4 Angel Berroa/250 4.00
5 Jeff Bagwell/250 6.00
7 Craig Biggio/250 6.00
14 Paul LoDuca/250 4.00
17 Lance Berkman/250 4.00
18 Javy Lopez/250 4.00
21 Sean Casey/50 6.00
25 Andruw Jones/250 6.00
26 Matt Lawton/250 4.00
28 Austin Kearns/250 4.00
32 Jason Jennings/250 4.00
33 Jason Varitek/50 12.00
34 David Ortiz/250 8.00
43 Joey Gathright/250 4.00
48 Torii Hunter/250 4.00
55 Brandon Webb/250 4.00
58 Mike Sweeney/250 4.00
62 Craig Wilson/250 4.00
63 J.D. Drew/250 4.00
67 Jose Vidro/250 4.00
68 Carlos Beltran/250 6.00
81 Tim Salmon/250 4.00
82 Troy Glaus/250 4.00
83 Kevin Mench/250 4.00
101 Rafael Furcal/150 4.00
102 Jack Wilson/25 4.00
103 Bernie Williams/250 4.00
107 Richard Hidalgo/250 4.00
111 Richie Sexson/100 6.00
121 Sammy Sosa/50 8.00
123 Rickie Weeks/25 6.00
125 Rafael Palmeiro/250 6.00
135 Dontrelle Willis/50 6.00
136 Michael Young/250 4.00
141 Bret Boone/50 4.00
147 Carlos Delgado/250 4.00
148 Tom Glavine/250 4.00
153 Nomar
Garciaparra/150 8.00
154 Pat Burrell/150 4.00
156 Jose Reyes/50 6.00
158 B.J. Upton/250 6.00
159 Jody Gerut/250 4.00

160 Juan Pierre/250 4.00
162 Barry Larkin/100 6.00
164 Ben Sheets/250 4.00
165 Tim Hudson/50 6.00
166 Darin Erstad/250 4.00
168 Luis Gonzalez/25 6.00
169 Mark Mulder/35 6.00
174 Miguel Cabrera/50 10.00
175 Nick Johnson/250 4.00
176 Derrek Lee/50 8.00
192 Alex Rios/50 4.00
197 A.J. Burnett/250 4.00
200 Rocco Baldelli/250 4.00
203 Preston Wilson/150 4.00
206 Edgardo Alfonzo/250 4.00
212 Casey Kotchman/250 4.00
215 Terrmel Sledge/250 4.00
218 Kenny Lofton/150 4.00
224 Brian Giles/35 6.00
225 Moises Alou/250 6.00
232 Jason Lane/250 4.00
235 Ryan Klesko/25 4.00
241 Shawn Green/250 4.00
247 Charles Johnson/250 4.00
248 Magglio Ordonez/250 4.00
252 Mike Lowell/50 4.00
255 Delmon Young/250 4.00
259 Morgan Ensberg/25 6.00
260 Chone Figgins/250 4.00
262 Jason Bay/175 6.00
265 Ray Durham/200 4.00
266 Juan Gonzalez/250 6.00
267 Jeff Kent/250 4.00
272 Orlando Hudson/250 4.00
280 Bill Madlock/100 4.00
281 Cal Ripken Jr./150 25.00
283 Gary Carter/25 8.00
284 George Brett/25 25.00
286 Harold Baines/50 6.00
288 Keith Hernandez/25 8.00
289 Willie Mays/25 35.00
291 Nolan Ryan/50 25.00
292 Paul Molitor/150 6.00
293 Reggie Jackson/25 10.00
294 Rickey Henderson/250 8.00
296 Ryne Sandberg/50 15.00
297 Ted Williams/25 50.00
299 Tony Gwynn/50 10.00
300 Babe Ruth/25 180.00

Material Jersey

NM/M
Common Player: 4.00
Production 5-250
Prime: 1-2X
Production 10-100
No pricing 20 or less.
1 Luis Castillo/45 4.00
3 Eric Chavez/250 4.00
5 Jeff Bagwell/250 6.00
6 J.T. Snow/250 4.00
7 Craig Biggio/50 6.00
9 Hank Blalock/25 6.00
10 Chipper Jones/250 8.00
11 Jacque Jones/250 4.00
12 Mark Teixeira/150 6.00
15 Jim Edmonds/250 6.00
16 Aramis Ramirez/250 6.00
17 Lance Berkman/250 4.00
18 Javy Lopez/250 4.00
20 Jorge Posada/250 6.00
21 Sean Casey/250 4.00
22 Mark Prior/50 8.00
23 Phil Nevin/50 4.00
24 Manny Ramirez/250 8.00
25 Andruw Jones/250 6.00
27 Vladimir Guerrero/250 8.00
28 Austin Kearns/250 4.00
29 John Smoltz/250 8.00
31 Mike Piazza/250 8.00
32 Jason Jennings/250 4.00
34 David Ortiz/250 10.00
35 Mike Mussina/250 6.00
38 Carlos Zambrano/250 6.00
42 Mariano Rivera/50 8.00
43 Joey Gathright/100 4.00
44 Adam Dunn/250 6.00
47 Roy Oswalt/250 4.00
48 Torii Hunter/100 4.00
52 C.C. Sabathia/250 4.00
53 Bobby Abreu/250 4.00
56 Mark Buehrle/250 4.00
57 Johan Santana/250 6.00
58 Mike Sweeney/75 4.00
62 Craig Wilson/250 4.00
64 Bobby Crosby/100 6.00
66 Scott Rolen/250 6.00
67 Jose Vidro/75 4.00
74 Mike Cameron/250 4.00
75 Barry Zito/250 4.00
83 Kevin Mench/250 4.00
84 Ivan Rodriguez/250 6.00
87 Jamie Moyer/50 4.00
91 Francisco Cordero/250 4.00
94 Cliff Lee/250 4.00
98 Brad Radke/250 4.00
100 Garret Anderson/50 6.00
101 Rafael Furcal/100 4.00
103 Bernie Williams/250 6.00
104 Josh Beckett/25 6.00
105 Albert Pujols/250 15.00
109 Hideo Nomo/250 8.00
110 Vernon Wells/250 4.00
114 Paul Konerko/250 4.00
116 Francisco Rodriguez/250 4.00
117 Johnny Damon/250 8.00
118 David Wright/250 10.00
119 Lyle Overbay/250 4.00
120 Brian Roberts/100 4.00
122 Roger Clemens/100 12.00
124 Larry Bigbie/200 4.00
125 Rafael Palmeiro/250 6.00
126 Jason Giambi/250 6.00
127 Hideki Matsui/250 15.00
134 Kerry Wood/250 6.00
135 Dontrelle Willis/250 6.00
136 Michael Young/250 4.00
137 Andy Pettitte/250 6.00
141 Bret Boone/250 4.00
146 Kazuhisa Ishii/250 4.00
147 Carlos Delgado/250 4.00
148 Tom Glavine/250 4.00
154 Pat Burrell/250 4.00
155 Melvin Mora/250 4.00
156 Jose Reyes/200 6.00
157 Trot Nixon/250 4.00
158 B.J. Upton/250 4.00
159 Jody Gerut/100 4.00
161 Miguel Tejada/35 8.00
162 Barry Larkin/40 8.00
163 Carl Crawford/40 4.00
164 Ben Sheets/250 6.00
166 Darin Erstad/25 6.00
167 Todd Helton/150 6.00
168 Luis Gonzalez/250 4.00
170 David Dellucci/150 4.00
172 Shannon Stewart/250 4.00
174 Miguel Cabrera/100 8.00
176 Derrek Lee/250 8.00
177 Jim Thome/250 6.00
178 Ken Harvey/150 4.00
180 Roy Halladay/250 4.00
182 Greg Maddux/250 8.00
186 Victor Martinez/250 4.00
189 Dewon Brazelton/250 4.00
190 Adrian Beltre/250 4.00
193 Alfonso Soriano/250 8.00
197 A.J. Burnett/250 4.00
200 Rocco Baldelli/250 4.00
201 Curt Schilling/250 8.00
202 Ryan Wagner/250 4.00
203 Preston Wilson/250 4.00
211 Frank Catalanotto/250 4.00
212 Casey Kotchman/250 4.00
214 Brandon Inge/250 4.00
221 Brett Myers/50 4.00
232 Jason Lane/95 4.00
233 Jeremy Bonderman/250 4.00
234 Livan Hernandez/250 4.00
235 Ryan Klesko/250 4.00
237 Jimmy Rollins/35 6.00
252 Mike Lowell/250 4.00
257 Garrett Atkins/250 4.00
258 Junior Spivey/250 4.00
259 Morgan Ensberg/150 4.00
260 Chone Figgins/250 4.00
262 Jason Bay/250 6.00
269 Rodrigo Lopez/250 4.00
270 Geoff Jenkins/250 4.00
275 Luis Matos/250 4.00
279 Bert Blyleven/50 6.00
281 Cal Ripken Jr./50 30.00
282 Dale Murphy/25 10.00
283 Gary Carter/50 8.00
284 George Brett/50 15.00
285 Harmon Killebrew/25 15.00
286 Harold Baines/50 6.00
287 John Kruk/50 8.00
289 Willie Mays Pants/25 40.00
290 Matt Williams/50 8.00
291 Nolan Ryan/50 25.00
292 Paul Molitor/50 10.00
293 Reggie Jackson/25 8.00
294 Rickey Henderson/50 10.00
295 Ron Cey/50 6.00
296 Ryne Sandberg/50 15.00
297 Ted Williams/25 60.00
298 Tom Seaver/25 15.00
299 Tony Gwynn/50 12.00
300 Babe Ruth/25 200.00

Material Combo

NM/M
Common Player: 6.00
Production 10-100
Prime: 1-2X
Production 5-40
No pricing 20 or less.
1 Luis Castillo/Bat-Jsy/90 6.00
3 Eric Chavez/Bat-Jsy/25 8.00
5 Jeff Bagwell/Bat-Jsy/100 8.00
7 Craig Biggio/Bat-Jsy/25 10.00
12 Mark Teixeira/Bat-Jsy/25 10.00
17 Lance Berkman/Bat-Jsy/100 6.00
21 Sean Casey/Bat-Jsy/100 6.00
22 Mark Prior/Bat-Jsy/25 10.00
25 Andruw Jones/Bat-Jsy/100 8.00
32 Jason Jennings/Bat-Jsy/100 6.00
34 David Ortiz/Bat-Jsy/25 20.00
43 Joey Gathright/Bat-Jsy/50 6.00
55 Brandon Webb/Bat-Pants/100 6.00
58 Mike Sweeney/Bat-Jsy/65 6.00
62 Craig Wilson/Bat-Jsy/100 6.00
67 Jose Vidro/Bat-Jsy/100 6.00
83 Kevin Mench/Bat-Jsy/100 6.00
101 Rafael Furcal/Bat-Jsy/50 6.00
103 Bernie Williams/Bat-Jsy/50 8.00
104 Josh Beckett/Bat-Jsy/25 8.00
110 Vernon Wells/Hat-Jsy/100 6.00
124 Larry Bigbie/Jsy-Jsy/100 6.00
126 Jason Giambi/Jsy-Jsy/100 8.00
136 Michael Young/Bat-Jsy/50 8.00
146 Kazuhisa Ishii/Hat-Jsy/25 10.00
154 Pat Burrell/Bat-Jsy/50 8.00
156 Jose Reyes/Bat-Jsy/25 8.00
157 Trot Nixon/Bat-Jsy/25 10.00
160 Juan Pierre/Bat-Fld Glv/95 6.00
164 Ben Sheets/Bat-Jsy/100 8.00
168 Luis Gonzalez/Jsy-Jsy/100 6.00
171 Marcus Giles/Hat-Jsy/50 6.00
172 Shannon Stewart/Jsy-Jsy/30 6.00
174 Miguel Cabrera/Bat-Jsy/25 12.00
180 Roy Halladay/Jsy-Jsy/85 8.00
183 Frank Thomas/Hat-Jsy/25 15.00
186 Victor Martinez/Fld Glv-Jsy/40 8.00
197 A.J. Burnett/Bat-Jsy/100 6.00
200 Rocco Baldelli/Bat-Jsy/100 6.00
201 Curt Schilling/Bat-Jsy/25 12.00
202 Ryan Wagner/Jsy-Jsy/100 6.00
203 Preston Wilson/Bat-Jsy/85 6.00
212 Casey Kotchman/Bat-Jsy/50 6.00
218 Kenny Lofton/Bat-Fld Glv/100 6.00
232 Jason Lane/Bat-Hat/50 6.00
235 Ryan Klesko/Hat-Jsy/100 6.00
252 Mike Lowell/Bat-Jsy/100 6.00
257 Garrett Atkins/Jsy-Jsy/100 6.00
259 Morgan Ensberg/Hat-Jsy/100 8.00
260 Chone Figgins/Bat-Jsy/50 6.00
262 Jason Bay/Bat-Jsy/40 8.00
272 Orlando Hudson/Bat-Jsy/40 6.00
275 Luis Matos/Jsy-Jsy/50 6.00
281 Cal Ripken Jr./Bat-Jsy/50 40.00
283 Gary Carter/Jsy-Pants/25 15.00
284 George Brett/Bat-Jsy/25 30.00
286 Harold Baines/Bat-Jsy/50 10.00
288 Keith Hernandez/Bat-Jsy/25 10.00
289 Willie Mays/Bat-Pants/25 50.00
291 Nolan Ryan/Bat-Jsy/50 25.00
292 Paul Molitor/Bat-Jsy/50 15.00
293 Reggie Jackson/Bat-Jsy/25 15.00
294 Rickey Henderson/Bat-Jsy/50 15.00
296 Ryne Sandberg/Bat-Jsy/50 25.00
297 Ted Williams/Bat-Jsy/25 75.00
298 Tom Seaver/Jsy-Pants/25 15.00
299 Tony Gwynn/Jsy-Pants/50 15.00
300 Babe Ruth/Bat-Jsy/25 375.00

Player Timelines

NM/M
Common Player: 1.00
Spectrum: 1-2.5X
Production 100 Sets
1 Dale Murphy 2.00
2 Greg Maddux 3.00
3 Tom Glavine 2.00
4 David Ortiz 3.00
5 Bo Jackson 2.00
6 Lyle Overbay 1.00
7 Tommy John 1.00
8 Shawn Green 1.00
9 Aramis Ramirez 1.50
10 Javy Lopez 1.00
11 Vladimir Guerrero 3.00
12 Travis Hafner 1.00
13 Junior Spivey 1.00
14 Alfonso Soriano 2.00
15 Andre Dawson 1.00
16 Sammy Sosa 3.00
17 Andy Pettitte 1.50
18 Jim Edmonds 1.50
19 Willie McCovey 2.00
20 Scott Rolen 2.00
21 Jermaine Dye 1.00
22 Pedro Martinez 2.50
23 Don Sutton 1.00
24 Randy Johnson 2.00
25 Nolan Ryan 3.00
26 Dennis Eckersley 1.00
27 Reggie Jackson 2.00
28 Deion Sanders 1.00
29 Curt Schilling 2.00
30 Rickey Henderson 1.00
31 Mike Piazza 2.00
32 Gary Carter 1.00
33 Roberto Alomar 1.00
34 Hideo Nomo 1.00
35 Andres Galarraga 1.00
36 Juan Gonzalez 1.00
37 Roger Clemens 4.00
38 Jeff Kent 1.00
39 Steve Carlton 1.00
40 Wade Boggs 1.50

Player Timeline Material

NM/M
Production 25-250
1 Dale Murphy/50 10.00
2 Greg Maddux/100 10.00
3 Tom Glavine/50 8.00
4 David Ortiz/250 10.00
5 Bo Jackson/100 12.00
6 Lyle Overbay/250 4.00
7 Tommy John/Pants/250 4.00
8 Shawn Green/100 4.00
9 Aramis Ramirez/250 6.00
10 Javy Lopez/100 4.00
11 Vladimir Guerrero/25 15.00
12 Travis Hafner/25 8.00
13 Junior Spivey/250 4.00
14 Alfonso Soriano/100 6.00
16 Sammy Sosa/250 8.00
17 Andy Pettitte/100 8.00
18 Jim Edmonds/100 8.00
19 Willie McCovey/Pants/50 12.00
20 Scott Rolen/50 10.00
21 Jermaine Dye/100 4.00
22 Pedro Martinez/50 12.00
23 Don Sutton/25 10.00
24 Randy Johnson/50 15.00
25 Nolan Ryan/Jkt/50 40.00
27 Reggie Jackson/Pants/50 15.00
28 Deion Sanders/25 15.00
29 Curt Schilling/50 10.00
30 Rickey Henderson/Pants/100 15.00
31 Mike Piazza/50 15.00
32 Gary Carter/Pants/50 10.00
33 Roberto Alomar/250 8.00
34 Hideo Nomo/50 15.00
35 Andres Galarraga/250 6.00
36 Juan Gonzalez/25 8.00
37 Roger Clemens/25 30.00
38 Jeff Kent/50 6.00

Player Timelines Signature Material

NM/M
Production 5-50
Prime: No Pricing
Production 5-10
1 Dale Murphy/50 30.00
6 Lyle Overbay/50 12.00
7 Tommy John/Pants/50 15.00
12 Travis Hafner/25 20.00
13 Junior Spivey/50 12.00
15 Andre Dawson/25 25.00
21 Jermaine Dye/50 15.00
23 Don Sutton/25 20.00
32 Gary Carter/Pants/50 20.00
36 Juan Gonzalez/25 40.00

Polo Grounds 85 HIT Long Fly

NM/M
Common Player: 1.50
Production 85 Sets
Parallel #'d 40-75: .75-1.5X
Parallel #'d 20-35: 1-2X
No pricing 15 or less.
1 Ken Griffey Jr. 4.00
2 Roger Clemens 6.00
3 Barry Zito 2.00
4 Alex Rodriguez 5.00
5 Melvin Mora 1.50
6 Kevin Brown 1.50
7 Chipper Jones 3.00
8 Scott Kazmir 2.00
9 Kip Wells 1.50
10 Khalil Greene 2.00
11 Kevin Millwood 1.50
12 Kerry Wood 2.00
13 Mark Kotsay 1.50
14 Jeff Bagwell 2.00
15 Hank Blalock 2.00
16 Scott Rolen 2.00
17 Lance Berkman 2.00
18 Mike Mussina 2.00
19 Jim Edmonds 2.00
20 Jorge Posada 2.00
21 Curt Schilling 3.00
22 Vernon Wells 1.50
23 Pedro Martinez 3.00
24 Jeremy Reed 1.50
25 Hideki Matsui 4.00
26 Steve Finley 1.50
27 Gavin Floyd 1.50
28 Darin Erstad 1.50
29 Bernie Williams 2.00
30 Mark Mulder 2.00
31 Rafael Palmeiro 2.00
32 Andruw Jones 2.00
33 Roy Halladay 2.00
34 Dontrelle Willis 2.00
35 Bret Boone 1.50
36 Andy Pettitte 2.00
37 Vladimir Guerrero 3.00
38 Randy Johnson 3.00
39 Michael Young 2.00
40 Frank Thomas 2.00
41 Todd Helton 2.00
42 Johan Santana 3.00
43 Mark Teixeira 2.00
44 Justin Morneau 1.50
45 Brad Radke 1.50
46 Dallas McPherson 1.50
47 Tim Hudson 2.00
48 Carl Crawford 1.50
49 Eric Gagne 2.00
50 Mark Prior 3.00
51 Tom Glavine 2.00
52 Craig Biggio 2.00
53 John Smoltz 2.00
54 Manny Ramirez 3.00
55 Ivan Rodriguez 2.00
56 Gary Sheffield 2.00
57 Josh Beckett 2.00
58 Miguel Tejada 2.00
59 Bobby Abreu 2.00
60 Ichiro Suzuki 4.00
61 Sammy Sosa 2.50
62 Garret Anderson 2.00
63 Sean Casey 1.50
64 Troy Glaus 2.00
65 Larry Walker 2.00
66 Alfonso Soriano 2.00
67 Luis Gonzalez 2.00
68 Eric Chavez 2.00
69 Adrian Beltre 2.00
70 Miguel Cabrera 3.00
71 Carlos Beltran 2.00
72 Jim Thome 2.00
73 David Ortiz 3.00
74 Adam Dunn 2.00
75 Jacque Jones 1.50
76 Shawn Green 1.50
77 Victor Martinez 1.50
78 Torii Hunter 1.50
79 Cliff Lee 1.50
80 C.C. Sabathia 1.50
81 Joe Mauer 2.00
82 Kris Benson 1.50
83 Zack Greinke 1.50
84 Greg Maddux 4.00
85 David Wright 4.00
86 Mike Piazza 4.00
87 Johnny Damon 3.00
88 Derek Jeter 6.00
89 B.J. Upton 1.50
90 Albert Pujols 6.00
91 Cal Ripken Jr. 6.00
92 Nolan Ryan 5.00
93 George Brett 5.00
94 Don Mattingly 4.00
95 Ryne Sandberg 4.00
96 Rickey Henderson 3.00
97 Robin Yount 3.00
98 Mike Schmidt 4.00
99 Tony Gwynn 3.00
100 Willie Mays 5.00

Signature Marks

NM/M
Production 5-1,000
4 Angel Berroa/25 12.00
19 Adam LaRoche/50 20.00
36 Joe Nathan/25 20.00
38 Carlos Zambrano/25 30.00
39 Eric Byrnes/50 10.00
41 Danny Kolb/25 10.00
45 Carlos Lee/25 20.00
49 Scott Podsednik/20 20.00
52 C.C. Sabathia/25 15.00
56 Mark Buehrle/25 30.00
62 Craig Wilson/50 10.00
64 Bobby Crosby/100 15.00
67 Jose Vidro/25 12.00
73 Octavio Dotel/25 12.00
77 Russel Rohlicek/250 5.00
81 Tim Salmon/50 20.00
85 Sean Burroughs/25 10.00
87 Jamie Moyer/25 15.00
88 Orlando Cabrera/25 20.00
90 Philip Humber/50 20.00
91 Francisco Cordero/50 10.00
92 Danny Graves/25 10.00
93 Bucky Jacobsen/64 8.00
94 Cliff Lee/50 10.00
96 Jake Peavy/25 35.00
101 Rafael Furcal/25 20.00
102 Jack Wilson/100 10.00
108 Luke Scott/250 15.00
110 Vernon Wells/25 15.00
112 Chad Cordero/25 15.00
114 Paul Konerko/25 20.00
116 Francisco Rodriguez/25 20.00
118 David Wright/25 85.00
119 Lyle Overbay/25 10.00
120 Brian Roberts/100 15.00
124 Larry Bigbie/25 8.00
129 Jeremy Affeldt/50 8.00
131 Troy Percival/25 15.00
133 David Gassner/1000 5.00
136 Michael Young/25 20.00
139 Miguel Negron/250 5.00
140 Rich Harden/50 25.00
142 Danny Rueckel/250 5.00
144 Randy Messenger/500 5.00
149 Russ Ortiz/25 15.00
157 Trot Nixon/25 25.00
158 B.J. Upton/25 20.00
159 Jody Gerut/25 10.00
170 David Dellucci/50 15.00
172 Shannon Stewart/25 15.00
175 Nick Johnson/25 15.00
176 Derrek Lee/25 40.00
178 Ken Harvey/50 8.00
179 Ambiorix Concepcion/500 8.00
184 Travis Hafner/50 15.00
189 Dewon Brazelton/66 8.00
192 Alexis Rios/25 15.00
198 Milton Bradley/100 12.00
199 Brad Penny/25 10.00
202 Ryan Wagner/25 10.00
204 Akinori Otsuka/25 20.00
207 Mike Lieberthal/25 10.00
208 Shea Hillenbrand/25 20.00
209 Tom Gordon/25 20.00
212 Casey Kotchman/100 10.00
213 Justin Verlander/50 40.00
220 Danny Haren/25 20.00
226 Casey Rogowski/250 5.00
230 Erick Threets/500 5.00
232 Jason Lane/25 10.00
233 Jeremy Bonderman/50 15.00
234 Livan Hernandez/25 15.00
239 Shingo Takatsu/25 20.00
245 Mark Loretta/25 20.00
250 Jared Gothreaux/1000 5.00
254 Nate McLouth/1000 8.00
258 Junior Spivey/25 10.00
259 Morgan Ensberg/25 20.00
260 Chone Figgins/50 10.00
262 Jason Bay/186 15.00
268 Dioner Navarro/75 8.00
271 Jermaine Dye/25 15.00
272 Orlando Hudson/100 8.00
275 Luis Matos/50 10.00
279 Bert Blyleven/25 15.00
280 Bill Madlock/50 15.00
281 Cal Ripken Jr./25 150.00
282 Dale Murphy/25 30.00
286 Harold Baines/25 15.00
288 Keith Hernandez/25 15.00
290 Matt Williams/25 30.00

Throwback Collection

NM/M
Common Player: 1.00
Spectrum: 1-2.5X
Production 100 Sets
1 Billy Martin 2.00
2 Tony Gwynn 2.00
3 Babe Ruth 4.00
4 Angel Berroa 1.00
5 Jeff Bagwell 1.50
6 Tony Oliva 1.00
7 Ivan Rodriguez 1.50
8 Gary Carter 1.50
9 Ted Williams 4.00
10 Chipper Jones 2.00
11 Al Oliver 1.00
12 Roberto Alomar 1.00
13 Omar Vizquel 1.00
14 Ernie Banks 2.00
15 Carlos Beltran 1.50
16 Garret Anderson 1.00
17 Mark Grace 1.00
18 Jason Giambi 1.00
19 Dave Righetti 1.00
20 Mike Schmidt 3.00
21 Roger Clemens 4.00
22 Juan Gonzalez 1.50
23 Carlos Delgado 1.00
24 Manny Ramirez 2.00
25 Jim Thome 1.50
26 Wade Boggs 2.00
27 Luis Tiant 1.00
28 Kerry Wood 1.50
29 Rod Carew 1.50
30 Dwight Evans 1.00
31 Mike Piazza 2.00
32 Billy Williams 1.00
33 Larry Walker 1.00
34 Nolan Ryan 4.00
35 Edgar Renteria 1.00
36 Greg Maddux 2.50
37 Gaylord Perry 1.00
38 Curt Schilling 2.00
39 Dave Parker 1.00
40 Andruw Jones 1.50
41 Orlando Cepeda 1.50
42 Fergie Jenkins 1.00
43 Kirby Puckett 2.00
44 Reggie Jackson 2.00
45 Bob Gibson 2.00
46 Rickey Henderson 2.00
47 Lee Smith 1.00
48 Lou Brock 1.50
49 Fred Lynn 1.00
50 Lance Berkman 1.00
51 Shawn Green 1.00
52 Hoyt Wilhelm 1.00
53 Sammy Sosa 2.50
54 Tim Hudson 1.50
55 Matt Williams 1.00
56 Marty Marion 1.00
57 Eric Chavez 1.00
58 Rafael Palmeiro 1.50
59 Randy Johnson 2.00
60 David Ortiz 2.00
61 Hank Blalock 1.00
62 Jim Rice 1.00
63 Mark Mulder 1.50
64 Kazuo Matsui 1.00
65 Pedro Martinez 2.00
66 Sean Casey 1.00
67 Carlos Lee 1.00
68 Stan Musial 3.00
69 Fred McGriff 1.00
70 Darryl Strawberry 1.00
71 Tommy John 1.00
72 Hideo Nomo 1.00
73 Johnny Bench 2.00
74 Cal Ripken Jr. 5.00
75 Harold Baines 1.00

Throwback Collection Material

NM/M
Production 5-500
Prime: 1-2X
Production 5-25
No pricing 20 or less.
1 Billy Martin/Pants/250 8.00
2 Tony Gwynn/Jsy/250 8.00
4 Angel Berroa/Pants/100 4.00
5 Jeff Bagwell/Jsy/250 6.00
6 Tony Oliva/Jsy/250 4.00
7 Ivan Rodriguez/Jsy/500 6.00
8 Gary Carter/Pants/250 4.00
10 Chipper Jones/Jsy/250 6.00
11 Al Oliver/Jsy/250 4.00
12 Roberto Alomar/Jsy/500 6.00
13 Omar Vizquel/Jsy/500 4.00
15 Carlos Beltran/Jsy/100 6.00
16 Garret Anderson/Jsy/50 4.00
17 Mark Grace/Jsy/250 6.00
18 Jason Giambi/Jsy/500 4.00
19 Dave Righetti/Jsy/250 4.00
21 Roger Clemens/Jsy/250 10.00
22 Juan Gonzalez/Jsy/150 4.00
23 Carlos Delgado/Jsy/150 4.00
24 Manny Ramirez/Jsy/50 10.00
25 Jim Thome/Jsy/500 4.00
26 Wade Boggs/Jsy/250 6.00
27 Luis Tiant/Pants/500 4.00
28 Kerry Wood/Jsy/50 4.00
29 Rod Carew/Jkt/250 6.00
30 Dwight Evans/Jsy/50 6.00
31 Mike Piazza/Jsy/250 8.00
32 Billy Williams/Jsy/100 4.00
33 Larry Walker/Jsy/500 4.00
34 Nolan Ryan/Pants/100 15.00
35 Edgar Renteria/Jsy/500 4.00
36 Greg Maddux/Jsy/375 8.00
37 Gaylord Perry/Jsy/250 4.00
38 Curt Schilling/Jsy/500 4.00
39 Dave Parker/Jsy/50 4.00
40 Andruw Jones/Jsy/500 4.00
41 Orlando Cepeda/Pants/250 4.00
42 Fergie Jenkins/Jsy/250 4.00
43 Kirby Puckett/Jsy/400 6.00
44 Reggie Jackson/Jsy/250 6.00
45 Bob Gibson/Jsy/100 8.00
46 Rickey Henderson/Jsy/500 6.00
47 Lee Smith/Jsy/250 4.00
49 Fred Lynn/Jsy/250 4.00
50 Lance Berkman/Jsy/500 4.00
51 Shawn Green/Jsy/500 4.00
52 Hoyt Wilhelm/Jsy/250 4.00
53 Sammy Sosa/Jsy/500 8.00
54 Tim Hudson/Jsy/500 4.00
55 Matt Williams/Jsy/250 4.00
57 Eric Chavez/Jsy/500 4.00
58 Rafael Palmeiro/Jsy/500 6.00
59 Randy Johnson/Jsy/250 6.00
60 David Ortiz/Jsy/500 8.00
61 Hank Blalock/Jsy/50 4.00
62 Jim Rice/Pants/250 4.00
63 Mark Mulder/Jsy/100 4.00
64 Kazuo Matsui/Jsy/500 4.00
65 Pedro Martinez/Jsy/250 6.00
66 Sean Casey/Jsy/500 4.00
67 Carlos Lee/Jsy/500 4.00
68 Stan Musial/Pants/100 20.00
69 Fred McGriff/Jsy/500 4.00
70 Darryl Strawberry/Jsy/250 4.00
71 Tommy John/Jsy/250 4.00
72 Hideo Nomo/Jsy/500 6.00
73 Johnny Bench/Pants/100 8.00
74 Cal Ripken Jr./Jsy/250 20.00
75 Harold Baines/Jsy/250 4.00

Throwback Collection Material Combo

NM/M
Production 5-100
1 Billy Martin/Jsy-Pants/100 10.00
2 Tony Gwynn/Jsy-Pants/100 12.00
4 Angel Berroa/Bat-Pants/100 4.00
5 Jeff Bagwell/Jsy-Pants/100 8.00
6 Tony Oliva/Bat-Jsy/100 6.00
7 Ivan Rodriguez/Chest Prot-Jsy/100 8.00
8 Gary Carter/Jsy-Pants/100 4.00
10 Chipper Jones/Bat-Jsy/100 8.00
11 Al Oliver/Bat-Jsy/100 6.00
12 Roberto Alomar/Bat-Jsy/100 8.00
13 Omar Vizquel/Bat-Jsy/100 6.00
15 Carlos Beltran/Bat-Jsy/100 8.00
17 Mark Grace/Bat-Jsy/50 10.00
18 Jason Giambi/Jsy-Jsy/100 6.00
19 Dave Righetti/Jsy-Jsy/100 6.00
21 Roger Clemens/Jsy-Jsy/100 15.00
22 Juan Gonzalez/Bat-Jsy/100 6.00
23 Carlos Delgado/Bat-Jsy/100 4.00
26 Wade Boggs/Bat-Jsy/100 10.00
29 Rod Carew/Jkt-Jsy/100 10.00
33 Larry Walker/Jsy-Jsy/100 6.00
34 Nolan Ryan/Bat-Pants/100 20.00
36 Greg Maddux/Jsy-Jsy/100 12.00
38 Curt Schilling/Jsy-Jsy/100 6.00
40 Andruw Jones/Bat-Jsy/100 8.00
41 Orlando Cepeda/Bat-Pants/100 8.00
43 Kirby Puckett/Bat-Jsy/100 12.00
44 Reggie Jackson/Bat-Jsy/100 10.00
46 Rickey Henderson/Bat-Jsy/100 10.00
47 Lee Smith/Jsy-Jsy/100 6.00
49 Fred Lynn/Bat-Jsy/100 4.00
50 Lance Berkman/Bat-Jsy/100 4.00
51 Shawn Green/Bat-Jsy/100 4.00
52 Hoyt Wilhelm/Jsy-Jsy/100 4.00
53 Sammy Sosa/Hat-Jsy/100 8.00
54 Tim Hudson/Jsy-Jsy/100 4.00
57 Eric Chavez/Jsy-Jsy/50 6.00
58 Rafael Palmeiro/Bat-Jsy/100 8.00
59 Randy Johnson/Jsy-Pants/100 10.00
60 David Ortiz/Bat-Jsy/100 10.00
61 Hank Blalock/Jsy-Jsy/50 6.00
62 Jim Rice/Jsy-Pants/100 6.00
64 Kazuo Matsui/Bat-Jsy/100 4.00
65 Pedro Martinez/Jsy-Jsy/100 8.00
66 Sean Casey/Jsy-Pants/100 4.00
67 Carlos Lee/Hat-Jsy/100 4.00
69 Fred McGriff/Bat-Jsy/100 8.00
70 Darryl Strawberry/Jsy-Jsy/100 6.00
71 Tommy John/Bat-Jsy/100 4.00
72 Hideo Nomo/Jsy-Jsy/100 10.00
73 Johnny Bench/Bat-Pants/100 12.00
74 Cal Ripken Jr./Bat-Jsy/100 30.00
75 Harold Baines/B at-Jsy/100 4.00

Throwback Collection Signature Material

NM/M
Production 5-50
2 Tony Gwynn/Jsy/50 40.00
4 Angel Berroa/Pants/50 10.00
6 Tony Oliva/Jsy/50 20.00
8 Gary Carter/Pants/50 20.00
12 Roberto Alomar/Jsy/50 30.00
13 Omar Vizquel/Jsy/50 30.00
15 Carlos Beltran/Jsy/50 30.00
17 Mark Grace/Jsy/50 30.00
19 Dave Righetti/Jsy/50 20.00
26 Wade Boggs/Jsy/50 35.00
27 Luis Tiant/Pants/50 20.00
29 Rod Carew/Jkt/50 30.00
30 Dwight Evans/Jsy/25 25.00
32 Billy Williams/Jsy/50 20.00
35 Edgar Renteria/Jsy/50 20.00
37 Gaylord Perry/Jsy/50 15.00
39 Dave Parker/Jsy/50 20.00
41 Orlando Cepeda/Pants/25 25.00
42 Fergie Jenkins/Jsy/50 20.00
44 Reggie Jackson/Jsy/25 50.00
45 Bob Gibson/Jsy/25 40.00
49 Fred Lynn/Jsy/50 20.00
54 Tim Hudson/Jsy/25 25.00
55 Matt Williams/Jsy/50 30.00
57 Eric Chavez/Jsy/50 20.00
62 Jim Rice/Pants/50 25.00
63 Mark Mulder/Jsy/50 20.00
66 Sean Casey/Jsy/50 20.00
67 Carlos Lee/Jsy/50 20.00
68 Stan Musial/Pants/25 75.00
70 Darryl Strawberry/Jsy/50 20.00
71 Tommy John/Jsy/50 15.00
75 Harold Baines/Jsy/50 15.00

Throwback Collection Signature Material Combo

NM/M
Production 5-25
2 Tony Gwynn/Jsy-Pants/25 50.00
4 Angel Berroa/Bat-Pants/25 15.00
6 Tony Oliva/Bat-Jsy/25 25.00
8 Gary Carter/Jsy-Pants/25 25.00
12 Roberto Alomar/Bat-Jsy/25 40.00
15 Carlos Beltran/Bat-Jsy/25 35.00
17 Mark Grace/Bat-Jsy/25 35.00
19 Dave Righetti/Jsy-Jsy/25 25.00
26 Wade Boggs/Bat-Jsy/25 40.00
29 Rod Carew/Jkt-Jsy/25 40.00
44 Reggie Jackson/Bat-Jsy/25 50.00
49 Fred Lynn/Bat-Jsy/25 25.00
62 Jim Rice/Jsy-Pants/25 30.00
67 Carlos Lee/Hat-Jsy/25 25.00
68 Stan Musial/Bat-Pants/25 75.00
70 Darryl Strawberry/Jsy-Jsy/25 20.00
75 Harold Baines/Bat-Jsy/25 20.00

2005 Donruss Timeless Treasures

NM/M
Complete Set (100):
Common Player: 1.50
Production 799 Sets
Tin (4): 100.00
1 David Ortiz 3.00
2 Derek Jeter 8.00
3 Edgar Renteria 2.00
4 Paul Molitor 3.00
5 Jeff Bagwell 2.00
6 Melvin Mora 1.50
7 Bobby Crosby 1.50
8 Cal Ripken Jr. 10.00
9 Hank Blalock 2.00
10 Hideo Nomo 2.00
11 Gary Sheffield 2.00
12 Alfonso Soriano 3.00
13 Carl Crawford 1.50
14 Paul Konerko 1.50
15 Jim Edmonds 2.00
16 Garret Anderson 2.00
17 Lance Berkman 1.50
18 Javy Lopez 1.50
19 Tony Gwynn 3.00
20 Mark Mulder 1.50
21 Sammy Sosa 5.00
22 Roger Clemens 8.00
23 Mark Teixeira 2.00
24 Miguel Cabrera 3.00
25 Jim Thome 3.00
26 Mike Piazza 4.00
27 Vladimir Guerrero 3.00
28 Austin Kearns 1.50
29 Rod Carew 3.00
30 Ken Griffey Jr. 5.00
31 Mike Piazza 4.00
32 David Wright 3.00
33 Jason Varitek 2.00
34 Kerry Wood 3.00
35 Frank Thomas 2.00
36 Mark Prior 3.00
37 Mike Mussina 2.00
38 Curt Schilling 3.00
39 Greg Maddux 4.00
40 Miguel Tejada 3.00
41 Tom Seaver 3.00
42 Mariano Rivera 2.00
43 Jason Giambi 1.50
44 Roy Oswalt 1.50
45 Pedro Martinez 3.00
46 Jeff Niemann **RC** 5.00
47 Tom Glavine 1.50
48 Torii Hunter 1.50
49 Scott Rolen 3.00
50 Curt Schilling 3.00
51 Randy Johnson 3.00
52 C.C. Sabathia 1.50
53 Rafael Palmeiro 2.00
54 Jake Peavy 2.00
55 Hideki Matsui 6.00
56 Ichiro Suzuki 6.00
57 Johan Santana 3.00
58 Todd Helton 2.00
59 Justin Verlander **RC** 8.00
60 Kazuo Matsui 1.50
61 Rafael Palmeiro 2.00
62 Sean Casey 1.50
63 Nolan Ryan 8.00
64 Magglio Ordonez 1.50
65 Craig Biggio 2.00
66 Vernon Wells 1.50
67 Manny Ramirez 3.00
68 Aramis Ramirez 2.00
69 Omar Vizquel 1.50
70 Eric Gagne 1.50
71 Troy Glaus 2.00
72 Carlton Fisk 2.00
73 Victor Martinez 1.50
74 Adrian Beltre 2.00
75 Barry Zito 1.50
76 Josh Beckett 2.00
77 Michael Young 1.50
78 Eric Chavez 1.50
79 Hideo Nomo 2.00
80 Andruw Jones 2.00
81 Ivan Rodriguez 2.00
82 Don Mattingly 6.00
83 Larry Walker 2.00
84 Philip Humber **RC** 5.00
85 Juan Gonzalez 1.50
86 Tim Hudson 2.00
87 Alex Rodriguez 6.00
88 Greg Maddux 4.00
89 J.D. Drew 2.00
90 Shawn Green 1.50
91 Roger Clemens 8.00
92 Nomar Garciaparra 4.00
93 Andy Pettitte 2.00
94 Khalil Greene 1.50
95 Mike Schmidt 5.00
96 Carlos Beltran 2.00
97 Mike Mussina 2.00
98 Ben Sheets 1.50
99 Chipper Jones 3.00
100 Albert Pujols 8.00

Bronze

Bronze: 1-2X
Production 100 Sets

Silver

Gold: 2-3X
Production 50 Sets

Gold

Gold: 3-5X
Production 25 Sets

Platinum

No Pricing
Production One Set

Award Materials Number

NM/M
Production 1-29
Prime: No Pricing
Production 1-5
9 Jim Palmer/Pants/22 12.00
10 Rod Carew/Jsy/29 15.00
12 Mike Schmidt/Jsy/20 25.00
13 Robin Yount/Jsy/19 25.00
15 Roger Clemens/Jsy/21 25.00

Award Material Signature Number

No Pricing
Production 1-5

Award Materials Year

NM/M
Production 1-99
1 Lou Boudreau/Jsy/48 20.00
2 Roger Maris/Pants/61 40.00
6 Johnny Bench/Jsy/72 15.00
9 Jim Palmer/Pants/76 10.00
10 Rod Carew/Jsy/77 10.00
12 Mike Schmidt/Jsy/81 20.00
13 Robin Yount/Jsy/89 15.00
14 Dale Murphy/Jsy/83 10.00
15 Roger Clemens/Jsy/86 20.00
16 Cal Ripken Jr./Jsy/91 40.00
17 Tom Glavine/Jsy/91 8.00
18 Frank Thomas/Jsy/94 10.00
19 Jeff Bagwell/Pants/94 8.00
20 Randy Johnson/Jsy/95 10.00
21 Pedro Martinez/Jsy/97 10.00
22 Ivan Rodriguez/Jsy/99 10.00

Award Material Signature Year

NM/M
Production 1-25
Prime: No Pricing
Production 1-5
6 Johnny Bench/Jsy/25 60.00
9 Jim Palmer/Pants/25 35.00
10 Rod Carew/Jsy/25 50.00
12 Mike Schmidt/Jsy/25 75.00
14 Dale Murphy/Jsy/25 50.00

Game Day Materials

NM/M
Production 5-100
1 Rod Carew/Hat/25 20.00
2 Kirby Puckett/Bat/100 15.00
5 Nellie Fox/Bat/25 60.00
6 Vladimir Guerrero/Fld Glv/25 15.00
7 Tony Gwynn/Jsy/100 15.00
8 Rickey Henderson/Bat/100 10.00
9 David Ortiz/Hat/100 15.00
10 Carlos Beltran/Jsy/50 10.00

Game Day Material Signature

NM/M
Production 3-25
7 Tony Gwynn/Jsy/25 50.00

Gamers NY

NM/M
Production 25 Sets
1 Jim Thorpe/Jsy-Jsy/25 450.00
2 Willie Mays/Jsy-Pants/25 75.00
3 Nolan Ryan/Bat-Jsy/25 65.00

Gamers NY Signatures

NM/M
Production 25 Sets
2 Willie Mays/Jsy-Pants/25 250.00
3 Nolan Ryan/Bat-Jsy/25 125.00

HOF Cuts

No Pricing
Production 1-10

HOF Cuts Materials

No Pricing
Production 1-10

HOF Materials Barrel

Production One Set

HOF Materials Bat

NM/M
Production 5-50
1 Pee Wee Reese/25 20.00
3 Harmon Killebrew/25 20.00
4 Hack Wilson/50 65.00
5 Brooks Robinson/50 20.00
6 Stan Musial/50 30.00
8 Carl Yastrzemski/50 20.00
9 Ted Williams/50 50.00
11 Luis Aparicio/25 15.00
12 Bobby Doerr/25 15.00
14 Ernie Banks/50 20.00
15 Ralph Kiner/25 20.00
20 Mike Schmidt/50 20.00
21 Roberto Clemente/50 75.00
24 Willie Mays/50 40.00
25 Willie Stargell/25 25.00
26 Frank Robinson/50 10.00
28 Reggie Jackson/50 15.00
30 Orlando Cepeda/50 10.00
34 Nolan Ryan/50 30.00
35 George Brett/50 25.00
39 Nellie Fox/50 40.00
43 Johnny Bench/50 20.00
44 Hank Aaron/50 40.00
50 Al Kaline/50 20.00

HOF Material Signature Bat

NM/M
Production 1-25
3 Harmon Killebrew/25 50.00
5 Brooks Robinson/25 50.00
6 Stan Musial/25 85.00
11 Luis Aparicio/25 25.00
12 Bobby Doerr/25 25.00
15 Ralph Kiner/25 50.00
20 Mike Schmidt/25 75.00
24 Willie Mays/25 240.00
26 Frank Robinson/25 40.00
30 Orlando Cepeda/25 25.00
34 Nolan Ryan/25 120.00
43 Johnny Bench/25 60.00
50 Al Kaline/25 50.00

HOF Materials Hat

No Pricing

HOF Materials Signature Hat
Production 5-10

HOF Materials Jersey
NM/M
Production 1-100
Prime: No Pricing
Production 1-5
3 Harmon Killebrew/100 15.00
5 Brooks Robinson/50 15.00
6 Stan Musial/100 25.00
8 Carl Yastrzemski/100 15.00
9 Ted Williams/100 60.00
14 Ernie Banks/100 15.00
16 Whitey Ford/100 15.00
17 Duke Snider/25 20.00
18 Willie McCovey/25 20.00
20 Mike Schmidt/50 25.00
22 Jim Palmer/25 12.00
23 Enos Slaughter/50 15.00
24 Willie Mays/100 40.00
25 Willie Stargell/50 20.00
28 Reggie Jackson/25 25.00
29 Warren Spahn/25 25.00
31 Hoyt Wilhelm/50 10.00
32 Sandy Koufax/25 250.00
33 Hal Newhouser/50 10.00
34 Nolan Ryan/50 30.00
35 George Brett/50 25.00
37 Jim "Catfish" Hunter/25 15.00
38 Frankie Frisch Jkt/50 15.00
40 Lou Boudreau/25 15.00
43 Johnny Bench/50 15.00
44 Hank Aaron/100 40.00
45 Joe Cronin/50 20.00
49 Early Wynn/50 15.00

HOF Material Signature Jersey
NM/M
Production 1-25
Prime: No Pricing
Production 1-5
3 Harmon Killebrew/25 50.00
5 Brooks Robinson/25 50.00
6 Stan Musial/25 85.00
17 Duke Snider/25 40.00
18 Willie McCovey/25 50.00
20 Mike Schmidt/25 75.00
22 Jim Palmer/25 40.00
24 Willie Mays/25 240.00
34 Nolan Ryan/25 120.00
43 Johnny Bench/25 60.00

HOF Material Jersey Number
NM/M
Production 1-44
18 Willie McCovey/44 15.00
20 Mike Schmidt/20 30.00
22 Jim Palmer/22 12.00
24 Willie Mays/24 65.00
28 Reggie Jackson/44 15.00
29 Warren Spahn/21 25.00
31 Hoyt Wilhelm/31 10.00
32 Sandy Koufax/32 250.00
34 Nolan Ryan/34 30.00
37 Jim "Catfish" Hunter/29 15.00
44 Hank Aaron/44 50.00
49 Early Wynn/24 15.00

HOF Materials Signature Jersey Number
NM/M
Production 1-44
18 Willie McCovey/44 50.00
20 Mike Schmidt/20 75.00
22 Jim Palmer/22 40.00
24 Willie Mays/24 240.00
34 Nolan Ryan/34 120.00

HOF Materials Combos
NM/M
Production 1-25
Prime: No Pricing
Production 1-5
3 Harmon Killebrew/Bat-Jsy/25 25.00
5 Brooks Robinson/Bat-Jsy/25 30.00
6 Stan Musial/Bat-Jsy/25 40.00
8 Carl Yastrzemski/Bat-Jsy/25 30.00
9 Ted Williams/Bat-Jsy/25 85.00
12 Bobby Doerr/Bat-Pants/25 15.00
14 Ernie Banks/Bat-Jsy/25 25.00
18 Willie McCovey/Jsy-Pants/25 25.00
20 Mike Schmidt/Bat-Jsy/25 30.00
24 Willie Mays/Bat-Jsy/25 75.00
25 Willie Stargell/Bat-Jsy/25 30.00
28 Reggie Jackson/Bat-Jsy/25 30.00
29 Warren Spahn/Jsy-Pants/25 30.00
34 Nolan Ryan/Jsy-Pants/25 50.00
35 George Brett/Bat-Jsy/25 30.00
43 Johnny Bench/Bat-Jsy/25 25.00
44 Hank Aaron/Bat-Jsy/25 60.00

HOF Material Signature Combos
NM/M
Production 1-25
Prime: No Pricing
Production 1-5
3 Harmon Killebrew/Bat-Jsy/25 65.00
5 Brooks Robinson/Bat-Jsy/25 65.00
6 Stan Musial/Bat-Jsy/25 100.00
12 Bobby Doerr/Bat-Pants/25 30.00
18 Willie McCovey/Jsy-Pants/25 60.00
20 Mike Schmidt/Bat-Jsy/25 85.00
24 Willie Mays/Bat-Jsy/25 250.00
30 Orlando Cepeda/Bat-Pants/25 30.00
34 Nolan Ryan/Jsy-Pants/25 120.00
43 Johnny Bench/Bat-Jsy/25 60.00

HOF Materials Pants
NM/M
Production 1-50
6 Stan Musial/50 30.00
8 Carl Yastrzemski/50 20.00
12 Bobby Doerr/50 10.00
17 Duke Snider/25 20.00
18 Willie McCovey/50 15.00
19 Bob Feller/25 20.00
22 Jim Palmer/25 10.00
24 Willie Mays/50 40.00
29 Warren Spahn/25 25.00
30 Orlando Cepeda/50 10.00
34 Nolan Ryan/50 25.00
42 Burleigh Grimes/50 75.00
43 Johnny Bench/50 15.00
45 Joe Cronin/50 20.00
46 Fergie Jenkins/50 10.00

HOF Material Signature Pants
NM/M
Production 1-50
6 Stan Musial/25 85.00
12 Bobby Doerr/50 25.00
17 Duke Snider/25 40.00
18 Willie McCovey/25 50.00
22 Jim Palmer/25 40.00
24 Willie Mays/25 240.00
30 Orlando Cepeda/25 25.00
34 Nolan Ryan/25 120.00
43 Johnny Bench/25 60.00
46 Fergie Jenkins/25 30.00

HOF Silver
NM/M
Common Player: 4.00
Production 500 Sets
Gold: 2-4X
Production 25 Sets
Platinum: No Pricing
Production One Set
1 Pee Wee Reese 4.00
2 Red Schoendienst 4.00
3 Harmon Killebrew 5.00
4 Hack Wilson 5.00
5 Brooks Robinson 5.00
6 Stan Musial 6.00
7 Al Simmons 4.00
8 Carl Yastrzemski 5.00
9 Ted Williams 8.00
10 Phil Rizzuto 4.00
11 Luis Aparicio 4.00
12 Bobby Doerr 4.00
13 Bob Lemon 4.00
14 Ernie Banks 5.00
15 Ralph Kiner 4.00
16 Whitey Ford 4.00
17 Duke Snider 4.00
18 Willie McCovey 4.00
19 Bob Feller 4.00
20 Mike Schmidt 6.00
21 Roberto Clemente 8.00
22 Jim Palmer 4.00
23 Enos Slaughter 4.00
24 Willie Mays 8.00
25 Willie Stargell 4.00
26 Frank Robinson 4.00
27 Carl Hubbell 4.00
28 Reggie Jackson 4.00
29 Warren Spahn 5.00
30 Orlando Cepeda 4.00
31 Hoyt Wilhelm 4.00
32 Sandy Koufax 15.00
33 Hal Newhouser 4.00
34 Nolan Ryan 8.00
35 George Brett 6.00
36 Bill Dickey 4.00
37 Jim "Catfish" Hunter 4.00
38 Frankie Frisch 4.00
39 Nellie Fox 4.00
40 Lou Boudreau 4.00
41 Hank Greenberg 5.00
42 Burleigh Grimes 4.00
43 Johnny Bench 5.00
44 Hank Aaron 8.00
45 Joe Cronin 4.00
46 Fergie Jenkins 4.00
47 Luke Appling 4.00
48 Yogi Berra 5.00
49 Early Wynn 4.00
50 Al Kaline 5.00

Home Road Gamers Duos
NM/M
Production 1-100
Prime: No Pricing
Production 1-10
3 Babe Ruth/Jsy-Jsy/25 450.00
4 Paul Molitor/Jsy-Pants/100 15.00
7 Ivan Rodriguez/Jsy-Jsy/100 10.00
9 Ted Williams/Jsy-Jsy/25 85.00
10 Andre Dawson/Jsy-Jsy/25 15.00
11 Darryl Strawberry/Jsy-Jsy/25 12.00
14 Ernie Banks/Jsy-Jsy/25 30.00
15 Jim Edmonds/Jsy-Jsy/25 15.00
16 Bo Jackson/Jsy-Jsy/25 20.00
17 Mark Grace/Jsy-Jsy/100 15.00
18 Albert Pujols/Jsy-Jsy/100 25.00
19 Tony Gwynn/Jsy-Jsy/100 15.00
20 Cal Ripken Jr./Jsy-Jsy/100 40.00
21 Chipper Jones/Jsy-Jsy/50 15.00
23 Don Mattingly/Jsy-Jsy/100 25.00
24 Willie Mays/Jsy-Jsy/25 80.00
25 Tony Oliva/Jsy-Jsy/50 10.00
28 Reggie Jackson/Jsy-Jsy/100 15.00
29 Rod Carew/Jsy-Jsy/100 15.00
30 Harmon Killebrew/Jsy-Jsy/25 25.00
32 Nolan Ryan/Jsy-Jsy/100 30.00
33 Eddie Murray/Jsy-Pants/100 15.00
35 Rickey Henderson/Jsy-Jsy/50 15.00
36 Jim Rice/Jsy-Jsy/50 12.00
37 Hoyt Wilhelm/Jsy-Jsy/50 10.00
38 Curt Schilling/Jsy-Jsy/100 10.00
42 Greg Maddux/Jsy-Jsy/100 15.00
43 Dennis Eckersley/Jsy-Jsy/50 10.00
44 Willie McCovey/Jsy-Pants/100 15.00
45 Willie Stargell/Jsy-Jsy/50 20.00
46 Mike Mussina/Jsy-Pants/50 15.00
47 Gary Carter/Jsy-Jsy/50 15.00
48 Dale Murphy/Jsy-Jsy/50 15.00
49 Mike Piazza/Jsy-Jsy/50 20.00
50 Jim Palmer/Jsy-Pants/100 10.00

Home Road Gamers Signature Duos
NM/M
Production 1-25
4 Paul Molitor/Jsy-Pants/25 60.00
11 Darryl Strawberry/Jsy-Jsy/25 30.00
17 Mark Grace/Jsy-Jsy/25 50.00
19 Tony Gwynn/Jsy-Jsy/25 50.00
23 Don Mattingly/Jsy-Jsy/25 80.00
25 Tony Oliva/Jsy-Jsy/25 30.00
29 Rod Carew/Jsy-Jsy/25 50.00
30 Harmon Killebrew/Jsy-Jsy/25 50.00
36 Jim Rice/Jsy-Jsy/25 35.00
43 Dennis Eckersley/Jsy-Jsy/25 30.00
44 Willie McCovey/Jsy-Pants/25 50.00
47 Gary Carter/Jsy-Jsy/25 30.00
48 Dale Murphy/Jsy-Jsy/25 50.00
50 Jim Palmer/Jsy-Pants/25 40.00

Home Road Gamer Signature Trios
NM/M
Production 1-25
Prime: No Pricing
Production 1-5
4 Paul Molitor/Bat-Jsy-Pants/25 75.00
11 Darryl Strawberry/Fld Glv-Jsy-Jsy/25 40.00
17 Mark Grace/Bat-Jsy-Jsy/25 60.00
19 Tony Gwynn/Jsy-Jsy-Jsy/25 70.00
23 Don Mattingly/Bat-Jsy-Jsy/25 90.00
25 Tony Oliva/Bat-Jsy-Jsy/25 35.00
29 Rod Carew/Bat-Jsy-Jsy/25 60.00
30 Harmon Killebrew/Bat-Jsy-Jsy/25 70.00
36 Jim Rice/Bat-Jsy-Jsy/25 40.00

Home Road Gamers Trios
NM/M
Production 1-100
Prime: No Pricing
Production 1-10
4 Paul Molitor/Bat-Jsy-Pants/100 25.00
7 Ivan Rodriguez/Jsy-Jsy-Jsy/100 15.00
9 Ted Williams/Bat-Jsy-Jsy/25 120.00
11 Darryl Strawberry/Fld Glv-Jsy-Jsy/25 20.00
14 Ernie Banks/Bat-Jsy-Jsy/25 40.00
15 Jim Edmonds/Bat-Jsy-Jsy/25 25.00
17 Mark Grace/Bat-Jsy-Jsy/100 20.00
18 Albert Pujols/Bat-Jsy-Jsy/100 40.00
19 Tony Gwynn/Jsy-Jsy-Jsy/100 25.00
20 Cal Ripken Jr./Jsy-Jsy-Jsy/100 60.00
21 Chipper Jones/Bat-Jsy-Jsy/25 20.00
23 Don Mattingly/Bat-Jsy-Jsy/100 30.00
24 Willie Mays/Bat-Jsy-Jsy/25 75.00
25 Tony Oliva/Bat-Jsy-Jsy/25 20.00
28 Reggie Jackson/Bat-Jsy-Jsy/100 20.00
29 Rod Carew/Bat-Jsy-Jsy/100 20.00
30 Harmon Killebrew/Bat-Jsy-Jsy/25 35.00
32 Nolan Ryan/Jkt-Jsy-Jsy/100 35.00
33 Eddie Murray/Jsy-Jsy-Pants/100 20.00
35 Rickey Henderson/Bat-Jsy-Jsy/100 20.00
36 Jim Rice/Bat-Jsy-Jsy/25 20.00
38 Curt Schilling/Bat-Jsy-Jsy/50 15.00
44 Willie McCovey/Bat-Jsy-Pants/100 20.00
45 Willie Stargell/Bat-Jsy-Jsy/50 25.00
46 Mike Mussina/Bat-Jsy-Pants/25 35.00
47 Gary Carter/Bat-Jsy-Jsy/50 25.00
48 Dale Murphy/Bat-Jsy-Jsy/25 30.00
49 Mike Piazza/Jsy-Jsy-Jsy/25 35.00

Home Run Materials
NM/M
Production 1-100
1 Ernie Banks/Bat/60 15.00
2 Roger Maris/Bat/61 50.00
4 Johnny Bench/Pants/71 10.00
5 Harmon Killebrew/Bat/75 10.00
6 Jose Canseco/Bat/25 15.00
8 Sammy Sosa/Jsy/100 10.00
9 Jim Thome/Jsy/50 10.00
10 Rafael Palmeiro/Jsy/50 8.00

Home Run Materials Signature
NM/M
Production 3-25
1 Ernie Banks/Bat/25 60.00
4 Johnny Bench/Pants/25 60.00
5 Harmon Killebrew/Bat/25 50.00

Material Ink Bat
No Pricing
Production 1-10

Material Ink Jersey
NM/M
Production 1-50
2 Fred Lynn/50 15.00
3 Dale Murphy/50 30.00
4 Paul Molitor/50 30.00
5 Alan Trammell/50 15.00
8 Gary Carter/50 20.00
10 Andre Dawson/50 20.00
11 Luis Aparicio/50 15.00
14 Darryl Strawberry/50 15.00
18 Kirk Gibson/50 20.00
20 Don Sutton/25 20.00
23 Don Mattingly Jkt/25 75.00
24 Tony Perez/50 25.00
27 Carlton Fisk/25 40.00
29 Fred McGriff/25 40.00
30 John Kruk/25 50.00
32 Dwight Evans/50 25.00
33 Gary Sheffield/25 50.00
34 Bo Jackson/25 65.00
36 Gaylord Perry/50 20.00
39 Dave Parker/25 20.00
42 Harmon Killebrew/50 50.00
43 Dennis Eckersley/25 25.00
44 Willie McCovey/25 50.00
46 Luis Tiant/50 20.00
48 Mark Grace/25 40.00

Material Ink Jersey Number
NM/M
Production 1-44
2 Fred Lynn/19 30.00
14 Darryl Strawberry/44 20.00
20 Don Sutton/20 25.00
22 Mark Prior/22 50.00
23 Don Mattingly/Jkt/23 80.00
24 Tony Perez/34 30.00
27 Carlton Fisk/27 40.00
29 Fred McGriff/29 40.00
30 John Kruk/29 50.00
32 Dwight Evans/24 35.00
36 Gaylord Perry/36 20.00
40 Mark Teixeira/23 40.00
43 Dennis Eckersley/43 20.00
44 Willie McCovey/44 40.00
46 Luis Tiant/27 25.00

Material Ink Combos
NM/M
Production 1-25
Prime: No Pricing
Production 1-5
2 Fred Lynn/Bat-Jsy/25 35.00
8 Gary Carter/Bat-Jsy/25 30.00
10 Andre Dawson/Bat-Jsy/25 30.00
11 Luis Aparicio/Bat-Jsy/25 30.00
14 Darryl Strawberry/Bat-Jsy/25 30.00
27 Carlton Fisk/Bat-Jsy/25 40.00
37 Miguel Cabrera/Bat-Jsy/25 50.00
39 Dave Parker/Bat-Jsy/25 25.00
48 Mark Grace/Bat-Jsy/25 40.00

Milestone Material Number
NM/M
Production 1-31
2 Nolan Ryan/Jsy/30 35.00
10 Greg Maddux/Jsy/31 20.00

Milestone Materials Signature Number
No Pricing
Production 1-10

Milestone Material Year
NM/M
Production 10-25
Prime: No Pricing
Production 1-10
1 Roger Maris/Pants/25 40.00
2 Nolan Ryan/Jsy/25 30.00
5 Steve Garvey/Jsy/25 10.00
6 Wade Boggs/Jsy/25 20.00
7 Tony Gwynn/Jsy/25 20.00
8 Sammy Sosa/Jsy/25 20.00
9 Randy Johnson/Jsy/25 15.00
10 Greg Maddux/Jsy/25 20.00

Milestone Materials Signature Year
NM/M
Production 1-25
Prime: No Pricing
Production 1-10
2 Nolan Ryan/Jsy/25 120.00
5 Steve Garvey/Jsy/25 25.00
7 Tony Gwynn/Jsy/25 40.00

No-Hitters
NM/M
Production 3-25
7 Dennis Eckersley, Bert Blyleven/25 35.00
8 Juan Marichal, Gaylord Perry/25 35.00
9 Jim Palmer, Bob Gibson/25 40.00

Rookie Year Materials Number
NM/M
Production 1-44
1 Rod Carew/Jsy/29 20.00
6 Juan Marichal/Jsy/27 12.00
8 Jim Palmer/Hat/22 15.00
16 Kirk Gibson/Hat/23 15.00
18 Roger Clemens/Jsy/21 25.00
20 David Cone/Jsy/44 8.00
23 Deion Sanders/Jsy/21 20.00
24 Dwight Gooden/Jsy/16 15.00
28 Mike Piazza/Jsy/31 20.00
33 Andruw Jones/Jsy/25 10.00
34 Vladimir Guerrero/Jsy/27 15.00
37 Kerry Wood/Jsy/34 15.00
38 Magglio Ordonez/Jsy/30 8.00
40 Mark Mulder/Jsy/20 10.00
41 Lance Berkman/Jsy/17 10.00
42 Alfonso Soriano/Jsy/33 10.00
46 Mark Prior/Jsy/22 10.00
47 Mark Teixeira/Jsy/23 10.00
48 Miguel Cabrera/Jsy/20 15.00
50 Victor Martinez/Jsy/41 8.00

Rookie Year Material Signature Number
NM/M
Production 1-30
1 Rod Carew/Jsy/29 35.00
4 Duke Snider/Jsy/25 40.00
6 Juan Marichal/Jsy/25 25.00
11 Gary Carter/Jsy/25 30.00
12 Robin Yount/Jsy/19 65.00
13 Keith Hernandez/Jsy/18 35.00
15 Ozzie Smith/Jsy/25 50.00
20 David Cone/Jsy/25 25.00
21 Gary Sheffield/Jsy/25 40.00
24 Dwight Gooden/Jsy/25 25.00
38 Magglio Ordonez/Jsy/30 20.00
46 Mark Prior/Jsy/22 40.00
47 Mark Teixeira/Jsy/23 40.00
48 Miguel Cabrera/Jsy/20 50.00
50 Victor Martinez/Jsy/25 20.00

Rookie Year Materials Year
NM/M
Production 1-100
Prime: No Pricing
Production Five Sets
1 Rod Carew/Jsy/100 12.00
4 Duke Snider/Jsy/100 12.00
6 Juan Marichal/Jsy/100 10.00
11 Gary Carter/Jsy/100 8.00
12 Robin Yount/Jsy/100 15.00
13 Keith Hernandez/Jsy/25 10.00

15 Ozzie Smith/Jsy/25 20.00
17 Dave Righetti/Jsy/25 10.00
18 Roger Clemens/ Jsy/100 15.00
19 Greg Maddux/Jsy/25 25.00
20 David Cone/Jsy/100 8.00
21 Gary Sheffield/ Jsy/100 10.00
22 Randy Johnson/ Jsy/100 10.00
23 Deion Sanders/ Jsy/100 10.00
24 Dwight Gooden/ Jsy/25 10.00
25 Ivan Rodriguez/ Jsy/100 8.00
26 Jeff Bagwell/P ants/100 8.00
27 Pedro Martinez/ Jsy/100 10.00
28 Mike Piazza/Jsy/100 12.00
29 Chipper Jones/ Jsy/100 10.00
30 Hideo Nomo/Jsy/100 12.00
32 Scott Rolen/Jsy/100 10.00
33 Andruw Jones/ Jsy/100 8.00
34 Vladimir Guerrero/ Jsy/100 10.00
35 Sean Casey/Jsy/25 10.00
36 Paul LoDuca/Jsy/25 8.00
37 Kerry Wood/Jsy/100 12.00
38 Magglio Ordonez/ Jsy/25 8.00
39 Vernon Wells/Jsy/25 8.00
40 Mark Mulder/Jsy/100 8.00
41 Lance Berkman/ Jsy/100 8.00
42 Alfonso Soriano/ Jsy/100 8.00
43 Albert Pujols/ Jsy/100 20.00
44 Ben Sheets/Jsy/25 10.00
45 Roy Oswalt/Jsy/25 10.00
46 Mark Prior/Jsy/100 8.00
47 Mark Teixeira/Jsy/100 8.00
48 Miguel Cabrera/ Jsy/100 10.00
49 Travis Hafner/Jsy/25 10.00
50 Victor Martinez/ Jsy/25 10.00

Rookie Year Materials Signature Year

NM/M
Production 1-25
Prime: No Pricing
Production 1-5
1 Rod Carew/Jsy/25 35.00
4 Duke Snider/Jsy/25 40.00
6 Juan Marichal/Jsy/25 25.00
11 Gary Carter/Jsy/25 30.00
12 Robin Yount/Jsy/25 65.00
13 Keith Hernandez/ Jsy/25 30.00
15 Ozzie Smith/Jsy/25 50.00
17 Dave Righetti/Jsy/25 20.00
20 David Cone/Jsy/25 25.00
21 Gary Sheffield/ Jsy/25 40.00
24 Dwight Gooden/ Jsy/25 25.00
32 Scott Rolen/Jsy/25 50.00
35 Sean Casey/Jsy/25 20.00
36 Paul LoDuca/Jsy/25 20.00
38 Magglio Ordonez/ Jsy/25 20.00
39 Vernon Wells/Jsy/25 20.00
40 Mark Mulder/Jsy/25 25.00
42 Alfonso Soriano/ Jsy/25 35.00
44 Ben Sheets/Jsy/25 25.00
46 Mark Prior/Jsy/25 40.00
47 Mark Teixeira/Jsy/25 40.00
48 Miguel Cabrera/ Jsy/25 50.00
49 Travis Hafner/Jsy/25 20.00
50 Victor Martinez/ Jsy/25 20.00

Salutations Signature

NM/M
Production 1-24
1 Al Kaline/24 70.00
5 Dale Murphy/24 50.00
7 Duke Snider/24 50.00
11 Johnny Bench/24 60.00
19 Steve Carlton/24 40.00

Signature Bronze

NM/M
Production 10-100
Platinum: No Pricing
Production One Set
3 Edgar Renteria/50 30.00
4 Paul Molitor/100 25.00
7 Bobby Crosby/25 25.00
8 Cal Ripken Jr./25 200.00
9 Hank Blalock/50 20.00
11 Gary Sheffield/50 35.00
12 Alfonso Soriano/50 25.00
14 Paul Konerko/50 20.00
15 Jim Edmonds/50 30.00
16 Garret Anderson/50 20.00
19 Tony Gwynn/100 40.00
20 Mark Mulder/100 20.00
23 Mark Teixeira/50 30.00
24 Miguel Cabrera/50 30.00
28 Austin Kearns/50 15.00
29 Rod Carew/100 25.00
32 David Wright/25 75.00
34 Kerry Wood/50 35.00
36 Mark Prior/100 40.00
41 Tom Seaver/100 40.00
44 Roy Oswalt/25 20.00
46 Jeff Niemann/100 35.00
48 Torii Hunter/50 20.00
49 Scott Rolen/50 40.00
52 C.C. Sabathia/25 25.00
53 Rafael Palmeiro/25 50.00
57 Johan Santana/50 40.00
59 Justin Verlander/100 30.00
61 Rafael Palmeiro/25 50.00
62 Sean Casey/25 20.00
63 Nolan Ryan/100 85.00
64 Magglio Ordonez/50 15.00
65 Craig Biggio/50 30.00
66 Vernon Wells/25 20.00
67 Manny Ramirez/25 50.00
69 Omar Vizquel/50 40.00
72 Carlton Fisk/100 25.00
73 Victor Martinez/50 15.00
74 Adrian Beltre/50 25.00
75 Barry Zito/50 20.00
76 Josh Beckett/25 35.00
77 Michael Young/50 20.00
78 Eric Chavez/50 15.00
82 Don Mattingly/100 60.00
84 Philip Humber/100 25.00
85 Juan Gonzalez/50 25.00
86 Tim Hudson/50 30.00
90 Shawn Green/25 30.00
95 Mike Schmidt/100 50.00
98 Ben Sheets/25 25.00
99 Chipper Jones/25 60.00

Signature Silver

NM/M
Production 5-50
3 Edgar Renteria/25 40.00
4 Paul Molitor/50 30.00
9 Hank Blalock/25 25.00
11 Gary Sheffield/25 40.00
12 Alfonso Soriano/25 35.00
14 Paul Konerko/25 25.00
15 Jim Edmonds/25 35.00
16 Garret Anderson/25 25.00
19 Tony Gwynn/50 60.00
20 Mark Mulder/50 25.00
23 Mark Teixeira/25 40.00
24 Miguel Cabrera/25 40.00
28 Austin Kearns/25 20.00
29 Rod Carew/50 30.00
34 Kerry Wood/25 40.00
36 Mark Prior/50 40.00
41 Tom Seaver/50 50.00
46 Jeff Niemann/50 40.00
48 Torii Hunter/25 25.00
49 Scott Rolen/25 50.00
57 Johan Santana/25 50.00
59 Justin Verlander/50 35.00
63 Nolan Ryan/50 100.00
64 Magglio Ordonez/25 20.00
65 Craig Biggio/25 35.00
69 Omar Vizquel/25 40.00
72 Carlton Fisk/50 25.00
73 Victor Martinez/25 20.00
74 Adrian Beltre/25 25.00
75 Barry Zito/25 20.00
77 Michael Young/25 20.00
78 Eric Chavez/25 20.00
82 Don Mattingly/50 60.00
84 Philip Humber/50 30.00
85 Juan Gonzalez/25 30.00
86 Tim Hudson/25 40.00
95 Mike Schmidt/50 65.00

Signature Gold

NM/M
Production 3-25
4 Paul Molitor/25 35.00
19 Tony Gwynn/25 50.00
20 Mark Mulder/25 30.00
29 Rod Carew/25 35.00
36 Mark Prior/25 50.00
41 Tom Seaver/25 60.00
63 Nolan Ryan/25 120.00
72 Carlton Fisk/25 35.00
82 Don Mattingly/25 80.00
95 Mike Schmidt/25 85.00

Statistical Champions Material Number

NM/M
Production 1-47
1 Nolan Ryan/Jsy/34 30.00
2 Lee Smith/Jsy/47 8.00
4 Kerry Wood/Jsy/34 12.00
6 Curt Schilling/Jsy/38 10.00
20 Mark Mulder/Jsy/20 10.00
21 Roger Clemens/ Jsy/21 25.00
22 Will Clark/Jsy/22 20.00
23 Don Mattingly/Jsy/23 25.00
24 Manny Ramirez/ Jsy/24 12.00
25 Billy Williams/Jsy/26 10.00
26 Wade Boggs/Jsy/26 15.00
27 Kevin Brown/Jsy/27 8.00
29 Adrian Beltre/Jsy/29 8.00
32 Sandy Koufax/ Jsy/32 250.00
33 Jose Canseco/Jsy/33 12.00
34 Kirby Puckett/Jsy/34 15.00
35 Rickey Henderson/ Jsy/35 15.00
38 Curt Schilling/Jsy/38 10.00
41 Nolan Ryan/Jsy/34 30.00
44 Roy Oswalt/Jsy/44 8.00

Statistical Champion Materials Signature Number

NM/M
Production 1-34
1 Nolan Ryan/Jsy/34 120.00
19 Tony Gwynn/Jsy/19 75.00
20 Mark Mulder/Jsy/20 25.00
22 Will Clark/Jsy/22 40.00
23 Don Mattingly/Jsy/23 75.00
26 Wade Boggs/Jsy/26 40.00
29 Adrian Beltre/Jsy/29 35.00
39 Don Sutton/Jsy/20 30.00
41 Nolan Ryan/Jsy/34 120.00

Statistical Champions Materials Year

NM/M
Production 1-100
Prime: No Pricing
Production 1-5
1 Nolan Ryan/Jsy/100 25.00
2 Lee Smith/Jsy/25 10.00
3 Harmon Killebrew/ sy/100 12.00
4 Kerry Wood/Jsy/100 12.00
5 Albert Pujols/Jsy/100 20.00
6 Curt Schilling/Jsy/100 8.00
7 Joe Cronin/Pants/100 12.00
8 Cal Ripken Jr./ Jsy/100 30.00
9 Barry Zito/Jsy/100 8.00
10 Miguel Tejada/ Jsy/100 10.00
11 Edgar Martinez/Jsy/25 8.00
14 Andre Dawson/ Jsy/25 10.00
17 Todd Helton/Jsy/100 8.00
19 Tony Gwynn/Jsy/100 12.00
20 Mark Mulder/Jsy/100 5.00
21 Roger Clemens/ Jsy/100 15.00
22 Will Clark/Jsy/25 20.00
23 Don Mattingly/ Jsy/100 20.00
24 Manny Ramirez/ Jsy/25 10.00
25 Billy Williams/Jsy/100 8.00
26 Wade Boggs/Jsy/100 10.00
27 Kevin Brown/Jsy/25 8.00
28 George Brett/Jsy/100 20.00
29 Adrian Beltre/Jsy/25 10.00
30 Lance Berkman/ Jsy/100 5.00
31 Sammy Sosa/ Jsy/100 10.00
32 Sandy Koufax/ Jsy/25 250.00
33 Jose Canseco/Jsy/25 15.00
34 Kirby Puckett/ Jsy/100 10.00
35 Rickey Henderson/ Jsy/100 12.00
36 Juan Gonzalez/ Jsy/100 8.00
38 Curt Schilling/Jsy/100 8.00
39 Don Sutton/Jsy/100 8.00
40 Johan Santana/ Jsy/100 10.00
41 Nolan Ryan/Jsy/100 25.00
43 Lou Brock/Jsy/100 10.00
44 Roy Oswalt/Jsy/25 8.00
45 Dale Murphy/Jsy/100 10.00

Statistical Champions Materials Signature Year

NM/M
Production 1-50
Prime: No Pricing
Production 1-5
1 Nolan Ryan/Jsy/50 100.00
3 Harmon Killebrew/ Jsy/50 40.00
4 Kerry Wood/Jsy/25 40.00
8 Cal Ripken Jr./ Jsy/25 175.00
9 Barry Zito/Jsy/25 25.00
11 Edgar Martinez/ Jsy/25 40.00
19 Tony Gwynn/Jsy/50 60.00
20 Mark Mulder/Jsy/25 25.00
22 Will Clark/Jsy/25 40.00
23 Don Mattingly/ Jsy/50 60.00
26 Wade Boggs/Jsy/25 40.00
29 Adrian Beltre/Jsy/25 35.00
39 Don Sutton/Jsy/25 30.00
40 Johan Santana/ Jsy/25 60.00
41 Nolan Ryan/Jsy/50 100.00
43 Lou Brock/Jsy/50 40.00
45 Dale Murphy/Jsy/50 30.00

World Series Materials

NM/M
Production 1-100
1 Frank Robinson/ Bat/100 10.00
3 Carl Yastrzemski/ Bat/100 25.00
4 Jack Morris/Jsy/50 8.00
5 Wade Boggs/Bat/100 12.00
8 Andruw Jones/ Jsy/100 8.00
10 Darryl Strawberry/ Jsy/25 10.00

World Series Materials Signatures

NM/M
Production 1-25
Prime: No Pricing
Production 1-10
4 Jack Morris/Jsy/25 25.00
5 Wade Boggs/Bat/25 40.00
10 Darryl Strawberry/ Jsy/25 25.00

2005 Donruss Zenith Promos

This 7-1/2" x 10" Dufex foil-technology card was distributed as a wrapper redemption at the National Sports Collectors Convention in Chicago. The back has a promo overprint.

NM/M
32 Sandy Koufax 12.00

2005 Donruss Zenith

NM/M
Complete Set (250): 50.00
Common Player: .25
Hobby Pack (5): 5.00
Hobby Box (18): 80.00
1 Curt Schilling .50
2 Jim Edmonds .40
3 Ichiro Suzuki 1.50
4 Jody Gerut .25
5 Carlos Beltran .50
6 Miguel Tejada .50
7 Ted Lilly .25
8 Bobby Abreu .40
9 Mark Teixeira .50
10 Manny Ramirez .75
11 Eric Gagne .40
12 Adrian Beltre .40
13 Dmitri Young .25
14 Alfonso Soriano .50
15 Vladimir Guerrero .75
16 Carl Crawford .25
17 David Ortiz .75
18 Jose Guillen .25
19 Miguel Cabrera .75
20 Alex Rodriguez 2.00
21 Brad Lidge .25
22 Francisco Rodriguez .25
23 Carlos Lee .25
24 Ben Sheets .40
25 Jason Schmidt .25
26 Cesar Izturis .25
27 Corey Patterson .25
28 Marcus Giles .25
29 Melvin Mora .25
30 Yadier Molina .25
31 Juan Pierre .25
32 Aubrey Huff .25
33 Rafael Furcal .25
34 David Dellucci .25
35 Jake Peavy .40
36 Aramis Ramirez .40
37 Javy Lopez .40
38 Aaron Rowand .25
39 Raul Ibanez .25
40 Jason Bay .40
41 Michael Young .25
42 Ivan Rodriguez .50
43 Derrek Lee .50
44 Adam Dunn .50
45 Eric Chavez .40
46 Pedro Martinez .75
47 Roy Oswalt .40
48 Kevin Millwood .25
49 Carlos Delgado .40
50 Derek Jeter 2.00
51 Johnny Damon .50
52 Richie Sexson .40
53 Nomar Garciaparra .75
54 Edgar Renteria .25
55 Carl Pavano .25
56 Tim Wakefield .25
57 Michael Barrett .25
58 Johnny Estrada .25
59 Jeff Kent .25
60 Mark Loretta .25
61 Greg Maddux 1.00
62 Hank Blalock .40
63 Moises Alou .40
64 Brad Radke .25
65 Brad Wilkerson .25
66 Sean Casey .25
67 Oliver Perez .40
68 Scott Hatteberg .25
69 Mike Lowell .25
70 Kazuo Matsui .25
71 Mark Prior .50
72 Hideki Matsui 1.50
73 Geoff Jenkins .25
74 Gary Sheffield .50
75 A.J. Burnett .25
76 Vernon Wells .25
77 Kenny Rogers .25
78 Jose Reyes .50
79 Victor Martinez .25
80 Jorge Posada .40
81 Rich Harden .25
82 Travis Hafner .25
83 Bret Boone .25
84 Chipper Jones .75
85 Bartolo Colon .25
86 Scott Podsednik .25
87 Coco Crisp .25
88 Luis Castillo .25
89 John Smoltz .40
90 Andruw Jones .50
91 Milton Bradley .25
92 Torii Hunter .25
93 Shawn Green .40
94 Paul Konerko .40
95 David Wells .25
96 Scott Rolen .50
97 Rodrigo Lopez .25
98 Garret Anderson .40
99 Tim Hudson .40
100 Sammy Sosa .75
101 Jason Varitek .50
102 Lance Berkman .40
103 Troy Glaus .40
104 Carlos Guillen .25
105 Jeff Bagwell .50
106 Phil Nevin .25
107 Freddy Garcia .25
108 Jake Westbrook .25
109 Marquis Grissom .25
110 Johan Santana .75
111 Kerry Wood .40
112 Jose Vidro .25
113 Mike Mussina .40
114 Josh Beckett .40
115 Matt Lawton .25
116 Craig Biggio .40
117 Reggie Sanders .25
118 Jason Kendall .25
119 Larry Walker .40
120 Roger Clemens 2.00
121 C.C. Sabathia .25
122 Javier Vazquez .25
123 Barry Zito .40
124 Jon Lieber .25
125 Kris Benson .25
126 Jacque Jones .25
127 Ray Durham .25
128 Mark Kotsay .25
129 Jack Wilson .25
130 Bobby Crosby .25
131 Todd Helton .50
132 Lyle Overbay .25
133 Jon Garland .25
134 Roy Halladay .40
135 Orlando Cabrera .25
136 Danny Kolb .25
137 Austin Kearns .25
138 Paul LoDuca .25
139 Magglio Ordonez .40
140 Rafael Palmeiro .50
141 Omar Vizquel .25
142 Mike Piazza 1.00
143 Mark Mulder .40
144 Dontrelle Willis .40
145 Tom Glavine .40
146 Khalil Greene .40
147 Ken Griffey Jr. 1.50
148 Mike Sweeney .25
149 Trot Nixon .25
150 Randy Johnson .75
151 Doug Mientkiewicz .25
152 Jeromy Burnitz .25
153 Brandon Webb .25
154 Kevin Brown .25
155 Carlos Zambrano .40
156 Shingo Takatsu .25
157 Erubiel Durazo .25
158 Jason Isringhausen .25
159 Corey Koskie .25
160 Aaron Boone .25
161 Joe Nathan .25
162 Nick Johnson .25
163 Michael Tucker .25
164 Chris Carpenter .25
165 Preston Wilson .25
166 J.T. Snow .25
167 Hideo Nomo .40
168 Miguel Olivo .25
169 Jarrod Washburn .25
170 Derek Lowe .25
171 Eric Milton .25
172 Andy Pettitte .40
173 Jason Giambi .40
174 Richard Hidalgo .25
175 Jayson Werth .25
176 Juan Gonzalez .25
177 Rocco Baldelli .25
178 Steve Finley .25
179 Frank Thomas .40
180 Kenny Lofton .25
181 Randy Winn .25
182 Brandon McCarthy **RC** 1.50
183 Lew Ford .25
184 Mike Cameron .25
185 Carlos Pena .25
186 Brian Roberts .25
187 Jeremy Bonderman .25
188 Luis Gonzalez .25
189 J.D. Drew .25
190 Frank Catalanotto .25
191 John Buck .25
192 Pat Burrell .25
193 Ryan Klesko .25
194 Jermaine Dye .25
195 Mariano Rivera .40
196 Angel Berroa .25
197 Carlos Zambrano .25
198 Joel Pineiro .25
199 Jay Gibbons .25
200 Albert Pujols 2.00
201 Billy Wagner .25
202 Darin Erstad .25
203 Jim Thome .50
204 Adam LaRoche .25
205 Cliff Floyd .25
206 Grady Sizemore .50
207 Garrett Atkins .25
208 Philip Humber **RC** 1.00
209 Zack Greinke .25
210 Wladimir Balentien **RC** 1.00
211 Ubaldo Jimenez **RC** .50
212 Dallas McPherson .25
213 Justin Verlander **RC** 3.00
214 Justin Morneau .50
215 Chase Utley .50
216 Casey Kotchman .25
217 Tadahito Iguchi **RC** 3.00
218 Hanley Ramirez .50
219 Scott Kazmir .25
220 J.J. Hardy .25
221 Ambiorix Concepcion **RC** .50
222 Jeff Niemann **RC** 1.00
223 David Wright 1.00
224 Joe Mauer .50
225 Rickie Weeks .25
226 Yuniesky Betancourt **RC** 1.00
227 Brady Clark .25
228 Keiichi Yabu **RC** .50
229 Delmon Young .50
230 Nick Swisher .50
231 George Brett 1.00
232 Ryne Sandberg 1.00
233 Mike Schmidt 1.00
234 Tony Gwynn .75
235 Rickey Henderson .50
236 Ozzie Smith 1.00
237 Reggie Jackson .75
238 Steve Carlton .40
239 Robin Yount 1.00
240 Tom Seaver .50
241 Ted Williams 1.50
242 Don Mattingly 1.00
243 Mark Grace .40
244 Rod Carew .40
245 Willie Mays 1.50
246 Gary Carter .40
247 Wade Boggs .50
248 Dale Murphy .40
249 Nolan Ryan 2.00
250 Cal Ripken Jr. 3.00

Artist's Proofs Silver

Silver AP (1-250): 3-5X
Inserted 1:16

Artist's Proofs Gold

Gold AP (1-250): 5-10X
Production 50 Sets

Museum Collection

Museum (1-250): 2-3X
Inserted 1:3

Epix Orange Play

NM/M
Common Player: 1.50
Production 750 Sets
Black Game: 1-2X
Production 75 Sets
Black Moment: 2-3X
Production 25 Sets
Black Play: 1X
Production 100 Sets
Black Season: 1-2X
Production 50 Sets
Blue Game: 1X
Production 350
Blue Moment: 1X
Production 150 Sets
Blue Play: 1X
Production 500 Sets
Blue Season: 1X
Production 250 Sets
Emerald Game: 1X
Production 100 Sets
Emerald Moment: 1-2X
Production 50 Sets
Emerald Play: 1X
Production 150 Sets
Emerald Season: 1X
Production 75 Sets
Orange Game: 1X
Production 500 Sets
Orange Moment: 1X
Production 250 Sets
Orange Season: 1X
Production 350 Sets
Purple Game: 1X
Production 250 Sets
Purple Moment: 1X
Production 100 Sets
Purple Play: 1X
Production 350 Sets
Purple Season: 1X
Production 150 Sets
Red Game: 1X
Production 150 Sets
Red Moment: 1-2X
Production 50 Sets
Red Play: 1X
Production 250 Sets
Red Season: 1X
Production 100 Sets
1 Vladimir Guerrero 3.00
2 Alex Rodriguez 6.00
3 Johan Santana 3.00
4 Todd Helton 2.00
5 Mark Teixeira 2.00
6 Manny Ramirez 3.00
7 Scott Rolen 2.00
8 Gary Sheffield 2.00
9 Miguel Cabrera 3.00
10 Jim Thome 2.00
11 Eric Chavez 1.50
12 Roger Clemens 6.00
13 Pedro Martinez 3.00
14 Roy Oswalt 1.50
15 Carlos Delgado 1.50
16 Nomar Garciaparra 2.00
17 Hideki Matsui 5.00
18 Shawn Green 1.50
19 Greg Maddux 4.00
20 Ted Williams 6.00
21 Don Mattingly 5.00
22 Cal Ripken Jr. 10.00
23 George Brett 6.00
24 Nolan Ryan 8.00
25 Willie Mays 6.00

Mozaics

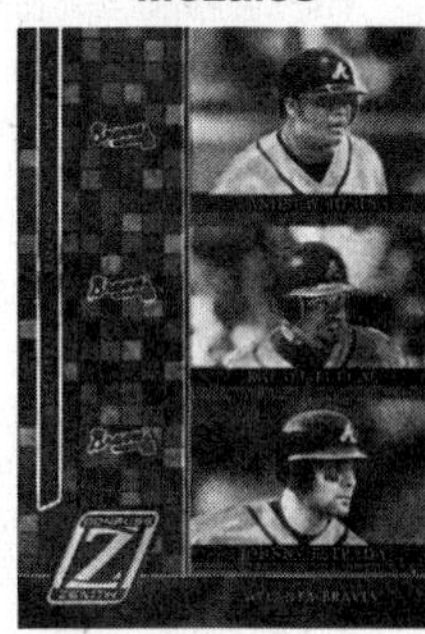

NM/M
Common Trio: 1.00
Inserted 1:8
1 Pedro Martinez, Carlos Beltran, Tom Glavine 2.00
2 Albert Pujols, Jim Edmonds, Mark Mulder 5.00
3 Sammy Sosa, Miguel Tejada, Rafael Palmeiro 2.00
4 Mark Teixeira, Hank Blalock, Michael Young 2.00
5 Andruw Jones, Rafael Furcal, Johnny Estrada 1.50
6 Bobby Crosby, Eric Chavez, Barry Zito 1.00
7 Shawn Green, Troy Glaus, Luis Gonzalez 1.00
8 Austin Kearns, Adam Dunn, Sean Casey 1.00
9 Jim Thome, Bobby Abreu, Pat Burrell 1.50
10 Lance Berkman, Jeff Bagwell, Craig Biggio 1.50
11 Orlando Cabrera, Steve Finley, Darin Erstad 1.00
12 J.D. Drew, Jeff Kent, Milton Bradley 1.00
13 Dontrelle Willis, Mike Lowell, A.J. Burnett 1.00
14 Adrian Beltre, Jeremy Reed, Richie Sexson 1.00
15 Joe Mauer, Justin Morneau, Jacque Jones 1.00
16 Gary Sheffield, Hideki Matsui, Mike Mussina 4.00

Mozaics Materials Single

NM/M
Common Player: 4.00
1 Pedro Martinez/Jsy 6.00
2 Albert Pujols/Bat 15.00
3 Miguel Tejada/Jsy 6.00
4 Mark Teixeira/Bat 6.00
5 Andruw Jones/Bat 6.00
7 Luis Gonzalez/Bat 4.00
8 Adam Dunn/Bat 6.00
9 Bobby Abreu/Jsy 4.00
10 Craig Biggio/Bat 4.00
11 Darin Erstad/Bat 4.00
12 J.D. Drew/Bat 4.00
13 A.J. Burnett/Bat 4.00
14 Richie Sexson/Bat 4.00
15 Jacque Jones/Bat 4.00
16 Gary Sheffield/Fld Glv 6.00

Mozaics Materials Triple Jerseys

NM/M
Production 5-100
Prime: No Pricing
Production 5-10
4 Mark Teixeira, Hank Blalock, Michael Young/100 10.00
6 Bobby Crosby, Eric Chavez, Barry Zito/25 10.00
8 Austin Kearns, Adam Dunn, Sean Casey/100 10.00
9 Jim Thome, Bobby Abreu, Pat Burrell/100 10.00
10 Lance Berkman, Jeff Bagwell, Craig Biggio/100 10.00
16 Gary Sheffield, Hideki Matsui, Mike Mussina/50 25.00

Positions

NM/M
Common Card:
Inserted 1:21
Gold: 1X-2X
Production 100 Sets
1 Randy Johnson, Mark Prior, Roger Clemens 4.00
2 Ivan Rodriguez, Mike Piazza, Victor Martinez 2.00
3 Albert Pujols, Todd Helton, David Ortiz 5.00
4 Marcus Giles, Mark Loretta, Bret Boone 1.00
5 Scott Rolen, Aramis Ramirez, Chipper Jones 2.00
6 Kazuo Matsui, Miguel Tejada, Michael Young 1.50
7 Brian Giles, Manny Ramirez, Shannon Stewart 2.00
8 Rocco Baldelli, Andruw Jones, Vernon Wells 1.50
9 Miguel Cabrera, Lance Berkman, Vladimir Guerrero 2.00

Positions Materials Single

NM/M
Common Player: 4.00
1 Mark Prior/Bat 6.00
2 Ivan Rodriguez/Bat 6.00
3 Albert Pujols/Bat 15.00
4 Bret Boone/Jsy 4.00
5 Chipper Jones/Bat 6.00
6 Kazuo Matsui/Jsy 4.00
7 Manny Ramirez/Bat 6.00
8 Andruw Jones/Bat 6.00
9 Lance Berkman/Bat 4.00

Positions Materials Triple Jersey

NM/M
Production 5-100
2 Ivan Rodriguez, Mike Piazza, Victor Martinez/50 15.00
3 Albert Pujols, Todd Helton, David Ortiz/50 25.00
5 Scott Rolen, Aramis Ramirez, Chipper Jones/100 15.00
6 Kazuo Matsui, Miguel Tejada, Michael Young/75 10.00
8 Rocco Baldelli, Andruw Jones, Vernon Wells/100 10.00
9 Miguel Cabrera, Lance Berkman, Vladimir Guerrero/100 15.00

Positions Material Triple Jersey Prime

NM/M
Production 5-25
2 Ivan Rodriguez, Mike Piazza, Victor Martinez/25 35.00
5 Scott Rolen, Aramis Ramirez, Chipper Jones/25 35.00
6 Kazuo Matsui, Miguel Tejada, Michael Young/25 25.00
7 Brian Giles, Manny Ramirez, Shannon Stewart/25 20.00
8 Rocco Baldelli, Andruw Jones, Vernon Wells/25 25.00
9 Miguel Cabrera, Lance Berkman, Vladimir Guerrero/25 35.00

Red Hot

NM/M
Common Player:
Inserted 1:16
1 Scott Rolen 1.50
2 Johan Santana 1.50
3 Josh Beckett 1.00
4 Aubrey Huff 1.00
5 Alfonso Soriano 1.50
6 Jeff Bagwell 1.50
7 Ted Williams 5.00
8 Mark Prior 1.50
9 Todd Helton 1.50
10 Vladimir Guerrero 2.00

Red Hot Bats

NM/M
Production 50-150
1 Scott Rolen/150 6.00
4 Aubrey Huff/150 4.00
5 Alfonso Soriano/150 6.00
6 Jeff Bagwell/150 6.00
7 Ted Williams/50 40.00
8 Mark Prior/150 6.00
9 Todd Helton/150 6.00
10 Vladimir Guerrero/150 8.00

Red Hot Jerseys

NM/M
Production 25-300
1 Scott Rolen/150 6.00
2 Johan Santana/150 6.00
3 Josh Beckett/300 4.00
4 Aubrey Huff/25 6.00
5 Alfonso Soriano/150 6.00
6 Jeff Bagwell/300 6.00
7 Ted Williams/25 60.00
8 Mark Prior/250 6.00
9 Todd Helton/165 6.00
10 Vladimir Guerrero/150 8.00

Red Hot Jerseys Prime

NM/M
Production 1-25
1 Scott Rolen/25 20.00
2 Johan Santana/25 20.00
3 Josh Beckett/25 15.00
4 Aubrey Huff/25 10.00
5 Alfonso Soriano/25 15.00
6 Jeff Bagwell/25 20.00
8 Mark Prior/25 20.00
9 Todd Helton/25 20.00
10 Vladimir Guerrero/25 25.00

White Hot

NM/M
Common Player:
Inserted 1:65
1 Scott Rolen 2.00
2 Johan Santana 2.00
3 Josh Beckett 1.50
4 Aubrey Huff 1.50
5 Alfonso Soriano 2.00
6 Jeff Bagwell 2.00
7 Ted Williams 6.00
8 Mark Prior 2.00
9 Todd Helton 2.00
10 Vladimir Guerrero 2.00

White Hot Bats

NM/M
Production 50 Sets
1 Scott Rolen/50 8.00
4 Aubrey Huff/50 4.00
5 Alfonso Soriano/50 6.00
6 Jeff Bagwell/50 6.00
7 Ted Williams/50 40.00
8 Mark Prior/50 8.00
9 Todd Helton/50 6.00
10 Vladimir Guerrero/50 8.00

White Hot Jerseys

NM/M
Production 1-200
Prime: No Pricing
Production 1-10
1 Scott Rolen/50 8.00
2 Johan Santana/50 8.00
3 Josh Beckett/185 4.00
5 Alfonso Soriano/50 6.00
6 Jeff Bagwell/200 6.00
8 Mark Prior/200 6.00
9 Todd Helton/151 6.00
10 Vladimir Guerrero/50 8.00

Roll Call Autographs

NM/M
Inserted 1:24
1 Hanley Ramirez 20.00
2 Sean Tracey 8.00
3 Justin Wechsler 8.00
4 Matt Lindstrom 6.00
5 Garrett Jones 8.00
6 Ambiorix Concepcion 8.00
7 Casey Rogowski 8.00
8 Kelly Shoppach 6.00
9 Sean Thompson 8.00
10 Jeff Miller 6.00
11 Chris Resop 10.00
12 Justin Verlander 25.00
13 Geovany Soto 8.00
14 Paulino Reynoso 6.00
15 Chris Roberson 8.00
16 Justin Leone 6.00
17 Jeff Niemann 15.00
18 Mark Woodyard 6.00
19 Raul Tablado 8.00
20 Norihiro Nakamura 40.00
21 Tony Pena 8.00
22 Wladimir Balentien 10.00
23 Miguel Negron 6.00
24 Eude Brito 8.00
25 Ubaldo Jimenez 6.00
26 Mike Morse 10.00
27 Devon Lowery 6.00
28 Philip Humber 12.00
29 Nate McLouth 10.00
30 Jason Hammel 8.00

Spellbound

NM/M
Common Maddux (1-4): 3.00
Common Clemens (5-9): 4.00
Common A-Rod (10-13): 4.00
Common Pujols (14-19): 4.00
Inserted 1:11
1 Greg Maddux/G 3.00
2 Greg Maddux/R 3.00
3 Greg Maddux/E 3.00
4 Greg Maddux/G 3.00
5 Roger Clemens/R 4.00
6 Roger Clemens/O 4.00
7 Roger Clemens/G 4.00
8 Roger Clemens/E 4.00
9 Roger Clemens/R 4.00
10 Alex Rodriguez/A 4.00
11 Alex Rodriguez/L 4.00
12 Alex Rodriguez/E 4.00
13 Alex Rodriguez/X 4.00
14 Albert Pujols/A 4.00
15 Albert Pujols/L 4.00
16 Albert Pujols/B 4.00
17 Albert Pujols/E 4.00
18 Albert Pujols/R 4.00
19 Albert Pujols/T 4.00

Spellbound Jerseys

NM/M
Production 150-250
1 Greg Maddux/G/150 12.00
2 Greg Maddux/R/150 12.00
3 Greg Maddux/E/150 12.00
4 Greg Maddux/G/150 12.00
5 Roger Clemens/R/150 15.00
6 Roger Clemens/O/150 15.00
7 Roger Clemens/G/150 15.00
8 Roger Clemens/E/150 15.00
9 Roger Clemens/R/150 15.00
14 Albert Pujols/A/250 15.00
15 Albert Pujols/L/250 15.00
16 Albert Pujols/B/250 15.00
17 Albert Pujols/E/250 15.00
18 Albert Pujols/R/250 15.00
19 Albert Pujols/T/250 15.00

Spellbound Jerseys Prime

NM/M
Production 10-25
5 Roger Clemens R/25 40.00
6 Roger Clemens O/25 40.00
7 Roger Clemens G/25 40.00
8 Roger Clemens E/25 40.00
9 Roger Clemens R/25 40.00

Team Zenith

NM/M
Common Player:
Inserted 1:31
Gold: 1-2X
Production 100 Sets
1 Ichiro Suzuki 5.00
2 Jim Edmonds 2.00
3 Hideki Matsui 5.00
4 Alex Rodriguez 5.00
5 Derek Jeter 6.00
6 Alfonso Soriano 2.00
7 Jim Thome 2.00
8 Jorge Posada 1.50
9 Barry Zito 1.50
10 Curt Schilling 2.00
11 Willie Mays 4.00

Team Zenith Bats

NM/M
Production 15-25
3 Hideki Matsui/50 25.00
7 Jim Thome/150 6.00
8 Jorge Posada/25 8.00
11 Willie Mays/25 70.00

Team Zenith Jerseys

NM/M
Production 15-300
3 Hideki Matsui/165 20.00
7 Jim Thome/175 6.00
8 Jorge Posada/300 6.00
9 Barry Zito/150 4.00
10 Curt Schilling/150 6.00
11 Willie Mays/175 30.00

Team Zenith Jerseys Prime

NM/M
Production 25 Sets
2 Jim Edmonds/25 15.00
6 Alfonso Soriano/25 15.00
7 Jim Thome/25 20.00
8 Jorge Posada/25 15.00
9 Barry Zito/25 15.00
10 Curt Schilling/25 20.00

Z-Graphs

NM/M
Production 1-250
1 Danny Haren/250 10.00
2 Dallas McPherson/250 12.00
5 Jeremy Bonderman/200 15.00
7 Craig Wilson/250 8.00
8 Adam LaRoche/250 12.00
9 Nick Johnson/250 10.00
11 Dontrelle Willis/25 25.00
15 Morgan Ensberg/250 10.00
17 Trot Nixon/100 20.00
19 B.J. Upton/50 20.00
20 Brian Roberts/250 15.00
21 Omar Vizquel/100 20.00
22 Shannon Stewart/100 10.00
24 Angel Berroa/100 8.00

26 Brandon Webb/100 10.00
29 Magglio Ordonez/100 12.00
30 Cal Ripken Jr./100 90.00
31 Johnny Estrada/50 10.00
32 Austin Kearns/100 10.00
33 Nolan Ryan/34 80.00
34 Orlando Cabrera/25 10.00
35 Roy Oswalt/100 15.00
36 Roy Halladay/50 20.00
38 Bobby Crosby/50 20.00
39 Jack Wilson/25 10.00
40 Jacque Jones/100 12.00
41 Eric Byrnes/250 8.00
44 Tony Gwynn/25 40.00
52 Paul Molitor/25 30.00
55 Ryne Sandberg/25 50.00
57 Casey Kotchman/100 12.00
60 Paul Konerko/100 20.00
62 David Wright/100 60.00
63 Milton Bradley/100 12.00
67 Rich Harden/250 15.00
68 Travis Hafner/250 10.00
69 Victor Martinez/25 20.00
70 Vernon Wells/25 15.00
72 Francisco Rodriguez/100 20.00
73 Mark Prior/25 40.00
75 Sean Casey/50 15.00
77 Carlos Zambrano/50 20.00
80 Livan Hernandez/100 12.00
84 Mark Buehrle/100 15.00
85 Keith Foulke/100 20.00
86 Edgar Renteria/50 15.00
88 Derrek Lee/100 25.00
89 Joe Nathan/100 10.00
90 Michael Young/50 15.00
91 Dale Murphy/100 20.00
93 Francisco Cordero/100 8.00
94 Jake Peavy/100 20.00
95 Aubrey Huff/100 10.00
96 Ben Sheets/50 20.00
97 Carlos Lee/25 15.00
98 Miguel Cabrera/25 40.00
99 Mark Teixeira/25 40.00

Z-Bats

NM/M
Common Player: 4.00
3 Rickey Henderson 8.00
4 Andy Pettitte 4.00
7 Craig Wilson 4.00
9 Nick Johnson 4.00
10 Bernie Williams 6.00
11 Dontrelle Willis 6.00
12 Kenny Lofton 4.00
13 Tom Glavine 4.00
14 Kazuo Matsui/SP 6.00
15 Morgan Ensberg/SP 6.00
16 Mike Piazza 8.00
17 Trot Nixon/SP 8.00
18 Ryan Klesko/SP 6.00
19 B.J. Upton 4.00
21 Omar Vizquel 4.00
22 Shannon Stewart 4.00
23 Preston Wilson 4.00
24 Angel Berroa 4.00
26 Brandon Webb 4.00
27 Rafael Palmeiro 6.00
28 Mike Sweeney 4.00
29 Magglio Ordonez 4.00
30 Cal Ripken Jr. 25.00
31 Johnny Estrada 4.00
32 Austin Kearns 4.00
33 Nolan Ryan 20.00
34 Orlando Cabrera 4.00
35 Roy Oswalt 4.00
37 Lyle Overbay 4.00
39 Jack Wilson 4.00
40 Jacque Jones 4.00
44 Tony Gwynn 8.00
46 Geoff Jenkins 4.00
47 Bo Jackson 8.00
48 Luis Gonzalez 4.00
50 Craig Biggio 4.00
51 Josh Beckett 4.00
52 Paul Molitor 6.00
55 Ryne Sandberg 10.00
56 Jeff Bagwell 6.00
57 Casey Kotchman 4.00
58 Chipper Jones 6.00
60 Paul Konerko 6.00
61 Kevin Mench 4.00
62 David Wright 10.00
64 Andruw Jones 6.00
65 Garret Anderson 4.00
66 Jorge Posada 6.00
68 Travis Hafner 4.00

69 Victor Martinez 4.00
70 Vernon Wells 4.00
71 A.J. Burnett 4.00
73 Mark Prior 6.00
74 Mike Lowell 4.00
76 Brad Wilkerson 4.00
79 Moises Alou 4.00
81 Hank Blalock 4.00
82 J.D. Drew 4.00
83 Reggie Jackson/SP 8.00
84 Mark Buehrle/SP 6.00
87 Adam Dunn 6.00
88 Derrek Lee 6.00
90 Michael Young 4.00
91 Dale Murphy 6.00
92 Aramis Ramirez 4.00
95 Aubrey Huff 4.00
96 Ben Sheets 4.00
97 Carlos Lee 4.00
98 Miguel Cabrera 6.00
99 Mark Teixeira 6.00
100 Albert Pujols 15.00

Z-Batgraphs

NM/M
Production 1-100
7 Craig Wilson/100 12.00
9 Nick Johnson/100 15.00
11 Dontrelle Willis/25 40.00
24 Angel Berroa/100 8.00
29 Magglio Ordonez/100 10.00
39 Jack Wilson/25 15.00
44 Tony Gwynn/25 50.00
52 Paul Molitor/25 40.00
55 Ryne Sandberg/25 65.00
57 Casey Kotchman/50 20.00
59 Chone Figgins/50 20.00
69 Victor Martinez/25 25.00
73 Mark Prior/25 50.00
90 Michael Young/100 15.00
91 Dale Murphy/100 20.00
97 Carlos Lee/50 20.00
99 Mark Teixeira/25 40.00

Z-Jerseys

NM/M
Common Player: 4.00
1 Danny Haren 6.00
3 Rickey Henderson 8.00
4 Andy Pettitte 4.00
5 Jeremy Bonderman 4.00
6 Pat Burrell 4.00
7 Craig Wilson 4.00
10 Bernie Williams 4.00
11 Dontrelle Willis 6.00
13 Tom Glavine 4.00
14 Kazuo Matsui 4.00
16 Mike Piazza 8.00
17 Trot Nixon 4.00
18 Ryan Klesko 4.00
19 B.J. Upton 4.00
20 Brian Roberts 4.00
21 Omar Vizquel 4.00
22 Shannon Stewart 4.00
23 Preston Wilson 4.00
25 Garrett Atkins 4.00
27 Rafael Palmeiro 6.00
28 Mike Sweeney 4.00
29 Magglio Ordonez 4.00
30 Cal Ripken Jr. 25.00
32 Austin Kearns 4.00
33 Nolan Ryan 20.00
34 Orlando Cabrera 4.00
35 Roy Oswalt 4.00
36 Roy Halladay 6.00
37 Lyle Overbay 4.00
39 Jack Wilson 4.00
40 Jacque Jones 4.00
41 Eric Byrnes 4.00
42 Barry Zito 4.00
43 C.C. Sabathia 4.00
44 Tony Gwynn 8.00
45 Mike Cameron 4.00
46 Geoff Jenkins 4.00
47 Bo Jackson 8.00
48 Luis Gonzalez 4.00
49 Johnny Damon 6.00
50 Craig Biggio 6.00
51 Josh Beckett 4.00
52 Paul Molitor 8.00
53 Kerry Wood 4.00
54 Lew Ford 4.00
55 Ryne Sandberg 10.00
56 Jeff Bagwell 6.00
57 Casey Kotchman 4.00
58 Chipper Jones 8.00
59 Chone Figgins 4.00
60 Paul Konerko 6.00
61 Kevin Mench 4.00
62 David Wright 10.00
64 Andruw Jones 6.00
65 Garret Anderson 4.00
66 Jorge Posada 6.00
68 Travis Hafner 4.00
69 Victor Martinez 4.00
70 Vernon Wells 4.00
71 A.J. Burnett 4.00
72 Francisco Rodriguez 4.00
73 Mark Prior 6.00
74 Mike Lowell 4.00
75 Sean Casey 4.00
77 Carlos Zambrano 4.00
78 Brad Radke 4.00
79 Moises Alou 4.00
80 Livan Hernandez 4.00
81 Hank Blalock 4.00
82 J.D. Drew 4.00
83 Reggie Jackson 8.00
84 Mark Buehrle 6.00
86 Edgar Renteria 4.00
87 Adam Dunn 6.00
88 Derrek Lee 6.00
90 Michael Young 4.00
91 Dale Murphy 6.00
92 Aramis Ramirez 4.00
93 Francisco Cordero 4.00
95 Aubrey Huff 4.00
96 Ben Sheets 4.00
97 Carlos Lee 4.00
98 Miguel Cabrera 8.00
99 Mark Teixeira 8.00
100 Albert Pujols 15.00

Z-Jerseygraphs

NM/M
Production 1-100
5 Jeremy Bonderman/100 20.00
7 Craig Wilson/100 10.00
11 Dontrelle Willis/25 35.00
15 Morgan Ensberg/25 20.00
17 Trot Nixon/50 25.00
19 B.J. Upton/50 25.00
20 Brian Roberts/100 20.00
22 Shannon Stewart/100 15.00
31 Johnny Estrada/100 10.00
35 Roy Oswalt/20 25.00
36 Roy Halladay/25 25.00
37 Lyle Overbay/25 15.00
38 Bobby Crosby/25 25.00
40 Jacque Jones/100 15.00
44 Tony Gwynn/25 50.00
52 Paul Molitor/25 35.00
55 Ryne Sandberg/25 65.00
57 Casey Kotchman/50 20.00
59 Chone Figgins/50 20.00
60 Paul Konerko/25 35.00
68 Travis Hafner/50 20.00
69 Victor Martinez/25 25.00
70 Vernon Wells/25 20.00
72 Francisco Rodriguez/100 25.00
73 Mark Prior/25 50.00
75 Sean Casey/25 20.00
80 Livan Hernandez/100 15.00
84 Mark Buehrle/100 20.00
88 Derrek Lee/100 30.00
90 Michael Young/100 20.00
91 Dale Murphy/100 25.00
93 Francisco Cordero/100 12.00
96 Ben Sheets/25 25.00
99 Mark Teixeira/25 50.00

Z-Jerseys Prime

NM/M
Production 1-150
3 Rickey Henderson/150 15.00
4 Andy Pettitte/100 10.00
5 Jeremy Bonderman/150 8.00
6 Pat Burrell/150 8.00
7 Craig Wilson/150 8.00
10 Bernie Williams/50 10.00
11 Dontrelle Willis/100 10.00
14 Kazuo Matsui/150 8.00
17 Trot Nixon/25 12.00
18 Ryan Klesko/150 8.00
19 B.J. Upton/50 10.00
20 Brian Roberts/50 10.00
22 Shannon Stewart/150 8.00
23 Preston Wilson/150 8.00
25 Garrett Atkins/150 8.00
27 Rafael Palmeiro/150 10.00
28 Mike Sweeney/150 8.00
30 Cal Ripken Jr./25 50.00
31 Johnny Estrada/100 8.00
32 Austin Kearns/150 8.00
33 Nolan Ryan/100 30.00
35 Roy Oswalt/100 10.00
36 Roy Halladay/150 10.00
37 Lyle Overbay/100 8.00
40 Jacque Jones/100 8.00
41 Eric Byrnes/50 8.00
42 Barry Zito/150 10.00
43 C.C. Sabathia/150 8.00
44 Tony Gwynn/150 15.00
45 Mike Cameron/150 8.00
46 Geoff Jenkins/50 10.00
47 Bo Jackson/100 20.00
48 Luis Gonzalez/150 8.00
49 Johnny Damon/25 20.00
51 Josh Beckett/150 10.00
52 Paul Molitor/70 15.00
54 Lew Ford/150 8.00
55 Ryne Sandberg/50 25.00
56 Jeff Bagwell/150 12.00
57 Casey Kotchman/50 10.00
58 Chipper Jones/150 15.00
60 Paul Konerko/150 10.00
61 Kevin Mench/150 8.00
64 Andruw Jones/150 12.00
65 Garret Anderson/25 12.00
66 Jorge Posada/50 12.00
68 Travis Hafner/100 10.00
69 Victor Martinez/25 12.00
70 Vernon Wells/150 10.00
71 A.J. Burnett/150 10.00
72 Francisco Rodriguez/100 8.00
73 Mark Prior/50 15.00
74 Mike Lowell/150 8.00
75 Sean Casey/150 8.00
77 Carlos Zambrano/100 10.00
78 Brad Radke/150 8.00
80 Livan Hernandez/50 10.00
81 Hank Blalock/100 10.00
83 Reggie Jackson/150 15.00
84 Mark Buehrle/50 12.00
87 Adam Dunn/150 10.00
88 Derrek Lee/50 15.00
90 Michael Young/50 10.00
91 Dale Murphy/50 20.00
92 Aramis Ramirez/100 10.00
93 Francisco Cordero/50 10.00
95 Aubrey Huff/150 8.00
96 Ben Sheets/150 10.00
98 Miguel Cabrera/150 15.00
99 Mark Teixeira/100 15.00

Z-Jerseygraphs Prime

NM/M
Production 1-25
5 Jeremy Bonderman/25 35.00
7 Craig Wilson/25 20.00
11 Dontrelle Willis/25 50.00
17 Trot Nixon/25 40.00
19 B.J. Upton/25 35.00
20 Brian Roberts/25 40.00
22 Shannon Stewart/25 25.00
24 Angel Berroa/25 20.00
31 Johnny Estrada/25 20.00
32 Austin Kearns/25 20.00
35 Roy Oswalt/25 35.00
36 Roy Halladay/25 45.00
40 Jacque Jones/25 25.00
41 Eric Byrnes/25 20.00
44 Tony Gwynn/25 65.00
52 Paul Molitor/25 50.00
55 Ryne Sandberg/25 80.00
57 Casey Kotchman/25 30.00
60 Paul Konerko/25 50.00
68 Travis Hafner/25 35.00
69 Victor Martinez/25 35.00
70 Vernon Wells/25 30.00
72 Francisco Rodriguez/25 40.00
73 Mark Prior/25 60.00
75 Sean Casey/25 30.00
77 Carlos Zambrano/25 30.00
80 Livan Hernandez/25 25.00
84 Mark Buehrle/25 30.00
88 Derrek Lee/25 50.00
90 Michael Young/25 30.00
91 Dale Murphy/25 40.00
93 Francisco Cordero/25 20.00
95 Aubrey Huff/25 25.00
96 Ben Sheets/25 35.00
98 Miguel Cabrera/25 50.00
99 Mark Teixeira/25 60.00

Z-Combos

NM/M
Production 1-150
Cards are bat/jsy unless noted.
3 Rickey Henderson/100 12.00
7 Craig Wilson/150 6.00
10 Bernie Williams/150 8.00
11 Dontrelle Willis/25 10.00
14 Kazuo Matsui/50 8.00
19 B.J. Upton/25 10.00
24 Angel Berroa/Bat-Pants/100 6.00
26 Brandon Webb/Bat-Pants/100 6.00
30 Cal Ripken Jr./100 30.00
33 Nolan Ryan/25 40.00
44 Tony Gwynn/100 12.00
47 Bo Jackson/100 12.00
50 Craig Biggio/50 10.00
52 Paul Molitor/50 12.00
53 Kerry Wood/25 10.00
54 Lew Ford/25 8.00
55 Ryne Sandberg/100 20.00
56 Jeff Bagwell/50 10.00
57 Casey Kotchman/50 8.00
58 Chipper Jones/100 10.00
59 Chone Figgins/100 6.00
61 Kevin Mench/100 6.00
64 Andruw Jones/100 10.00
69 Victor Martinez/100 8.00
71 A.J. Burnett/100 6.00
73 Mark Prior/100 10.00
81 Hank Blalock/100 8.00
87 Adam Dunn/25 10.00
88 Derrek Lee/25 12.00
90 Michael Young/100 6.00
91 Dale Murphy/100 10.00
99 Mark Teixeira/Bat-Hat/100 12.00

Z-Combos Prime

NM/M
Production 1-25
All are bat/patch.
3 Rickey Henderson/25 25.00
7 Craig Wilson/25 10.00
10 Bernie Williams/25 15.00
11 Dontrelle Willis/25 15.00
14 Kazuo Matsui/25 10.00
19 B.J. Upton/25 15.00
27 Rafael Palmeiro/25 15.00
30 Cal Ripken Jr./25 65.00
33 Nolan Ryan/25 50.00
44 Tony Gwynn/25 25.00
47 Bo Jackson/25 25.00
55 Ryne Sandberg/25 35.00
56 Jeff Bagwell/25 15.00
57 Casey Kotchman/25 15.00
58 Chipper Jones/25 20.00
61 Kevin Mench/25 10.00
64 Andruw Jones/25 20.00
65 Garret Anderson/25 15.00
69 Victor Martinez/25 15.00
71 A.J. Burnett/25 10.00
73 Mark Prior/25 20.00
74 Mike Lowell/25 15.00
81 Hank Blalock/25 15.00
87 Adam Dunn/25 15.00
88 Derrek Lee/25 20.00
90 Michael Young/25 15.00
91 Dale Murphy/25 20.00
96 Ben Sheets/25 15.00
99 Mark Teixeira/25 25.00

Z-Team

NM/M
Common Player:
Inserted 1:11
Gold: 1-2X
Production 100 Sets
1 Albert Pujols 5.00
2 Carlos Beltran 1.50
3 Randy Johnson 2.00
4 Miguel Tejada 1.50
5 Ichiro Suzuki 4.00
6 Eric Gagne 1.00
7 Adrian Beltre 1.00
8 Alfonso Soriano 1.50
9 Jim Edmonds 1.50
10 David Ortiz 2.00
11 Curt Schilling 2.00
12 Mariano Rivera 1.50
13 Derek Jeter 5.00
14 Ivan Rodriguez 1.50
15 Johnny Damon 2.00
16 Mark Prior 1.50
17 Vernon Wells 1.00
18 Chipper Jones 2.00
19 Torii Hunter 1.00
20 Tim Hudson 1.50
21 Lance Berkman 1.00
22 Troy Glaus 1.00
23 Mike Piazza 2.50
24 Mark Mulder 1.00
25 Ken Griffey Jr. 3.00

2007 Donruss Elite Extra Edition

NM/M
Common (1-92): .25
Common Auto. (93-142): 8.00
Pack (5): 6.00
Box (20): 110.00
1 Andrew Brackman 1.00
2 Austin Gallagher .50
3 Brett Cecil 1.00
4 Darwin Barney 1.00
5 David Price 2.00
6 J.P. Arencibia 1.00
7 Josh Donaldson .25
8 Brandon Hicks .25
9 Brian Rike .25
10 Bryan Morris .25
11 Cale Iorg .50
12 Casey Weathers .25
13 Corey Kluber .25
14 Daniel Moskos 1.00
15 Danny Payne .25
16 David Kopp .50
17 Dellin Betances .25
18 Derrick Robinson .25
19 Drew Stubbs .50
20 Eric Eiland .50
21 Francisco Pena .25
22 Greg Reynolds .25
23 Jeff Samardzija 1.00
24 Jess Todd .25
25 John Tolisano .50
26 Jordan Zimmerman .50
27 Julian Sampson .25
28 Luke Hochevar 1.00
29 Mat Latos .50
30 Matt Mangini .25
31 Matt Spencer .50
32 Matthew Sweeney .25
33 Max Scherzer 1.00
34 Mitch Canham .50
35 Nick Schmidt .25
36 Paul Kelly .25
37 Ryan Pope .75
38 Sam Runion .50
39 Steven Souza .50
40 Travis Mattair .75
41 Trystan Magnuson 1.00
42 Willie Middlebrooks 1.00
43 Zack Cozart .50
44 James Adkins .50
45 Cory Luebke .25
46 Aaron Poreda .50
47 Clayton Mortensen .50
48 Bradley Suttle 1.00
49 Tony Butler .50
50 Zach Britton .50
51 Scott Cousins .25
52 Wendell Fairley 1.00
53 Eric Sogard .50
54 Jonathan Lucroy .50
55 Lars Davis .25
56 Demetris Nichols .25
57 Aaron Gray .25
58 Daequan Cook .25
59 Derrick Byars .25
60 Reyshawn Terry .25
61 Taurean Green .25
62 Don Haskins .25
63 Jerry Tarkanian .50
64 Rick Majerus .25
65 Rollie Massimino .25
66 Ara Parseghian .25
67 Dale Brown .25
68 Dean Smith .50
69 Eddie Sutton .25
70 Frank Broyles .25
71 Gene Keady .25
72 Jim Boeheim .50
73 Norm Stewart .25
74 Steve Spurrier .25
75 Tom Osborne .25
76 Vince Dooley .25
77 Jennie Finch .50
78 Amanda Beard .50
79 Mike Powell .25
80 Rebecca Lobo .25
81 Brandi Chastain .25
82 Clint Dolezel .25
83 Elvin Hayes .50
84 Cobi Jones .25
85 Bill Walton .50
86 Sidney Moncrief .25
87 Dominique Wilkins .50
88 Summer Sanders .25
89 Michelle Akers .25
90 Muggsy Bogues .25
91 Charlie Culberson .50
92 Jacob Smolinski 1.00
93 Blake Beaven/Auto./719 15.00
94 Brad Chalk/Auto./613 8.00
95 Brett Anderson/Auto./549 20.00
96 Chris Withrow/Auto./700 20.00
97 Clay Fuller/Auto./674 8.00
98 Damon Sublett/Auto./674 25.00
99 Devin Mesoraco/Auto./674 15.00
100 Drew Cumberland/Auto./744 15.00
101 Jack McGeary/Auto./674 20.00
102 Jake Arrieta/Auto./949 15.00
103 James Simmons/Auto./624 15.00
104 Jarrod Parker/Auto./499 40.00
105 Jason Dominguez/Auto./744 8.00
106 Jason Heyward/Auto./750 50.00
107 Joe Savery/Auto./750 15.00
108 Jon Gilmore/Auto./819 15.00
109 Jordan Walden/Auto./794 25.00
110 Josh Smoker/Auto./719 20.00
111 Josh Vitters/Auto./769 50.00
112 Julio Borbon/Auto./594 15.00
113 Justin Jackson/Auto./850 10.00
114 Kellen Kulbacki/Auto./549 20.00
115 Kevin Ahrens/Auto./794 20.00
116 Kyle Lotzkar/Auto./611 15.00
117 Madison Bumgarner/Auto./794 25.00
118 Matt Dominguez/Auto./769 25.00
119 Matt LaPorta/Auto./594 50.00
120 Matt Wieters/Auto./799 60.00
121 Michael Burgess/Auto./672 25.00
122 Michael Main/Auto./794 15.00
123 Michael Moustakas/Auto./999 75.00
124 Nathan Vineyard/Auto./700 10.00
125 Neil Ramirez/Auto./774 10.00
126 Nick Hagadone/Auto./544 20.00
127 Peter Kozma/Auto./719 15.00
128 Phillippe Aumont/Auto./674 25.00
129 Preston Mattingly/Auto./519 30.00
130 Mystery Redemption 80.00
131 Ross Detwiler/Auto./650 15.00
132 Tim Alderson/Auto./719 20.00
15 Todd Frazier/Auto./774 .25
134 Wes Roemer/Auto./694 15.00
135 Ben Revere/Auto./700 10.00
136 D.J. Strawberry/Auto./374 10.00
137 Alando Tucker/Auto./494 10.00
138 Jared Jordan/Auto./474 8.00
139 Marc Gasol/Auto./474 8.00
140 Stephane Lasme/Auto./674 8.00
141 Austin Jackson/Auto./794 80.00
142 Beau Mills/Auto./624 20.00

Aspirations

Aspirations (1-92): 4-8X
Non Auto. Aspir. (93-142): .2-.25X
Production 100 Sets

Black Status Autographs

Production One Set

Status

Status (1-92): 6-10X
Non Auto. Status (93-142): .2-.3X
Production 50 Sets
Gold Status (1-92): 8-15X
Non Auto. Gold Status: No Pricing
Production 25 Sets

College Ties

NM/M
Common Duo: 2.00
Production 1,500 Sets
Gold: 1X
Production 500 Sets
Red: 1.5-3X
Production 100 Sets
1 Daniel Moskos, David Kopp 2.00
2 Jess Todd, Nick Schmidt 2.00
3 J.P. Arencibia, Julio Borbon 2.00
4 Casey Weathers, David Price 3.00
5 Matt LaPorta, Taurean Green 3.00
6 Amanda Beard, Jennie Finch 3.00
7 Demetris Nichols, Jim Boeheim 2.00
8 Danny Payne, Matt Wieters 2.00
9 Darwin Barney, Mitch Canham 2.00
10 James Adkins, Luke Hochevar 2.00
11 Cory Luebke, Daequan Cook 2.00
12 Brett Cecil, D.J. Strawberry 2.00

College Ties Autograph

NM/M
Production 50 or 100
1 Daniel Moskos, David Kopp/100 15.00
2 Jess Todd, Nick Schmidt/100 15.00
3 J.P. Arencibia, Julio Borbon/100 15.00
4 Casey Weathers, David Price/100 30.00
5 Matt LaPorta, Taurean Green/100 30.00
6 Amanda Beard, Jennie Finch/50 60.00
7 Demetris Nichols, Jim Boeheim/50 15.00
8 Danny Payne, Matt Wieters/100 40.00
9 Darwin Barney, Mitch Canham/100 30.00
10 James Adkins, Luke Hochevar/50 30.00
11 Cory Luebke, Daequan Cook/100 20.00
12 Brett Cecil, D.J. Strawberry/50 10.00

College Ties Jerseys

NM/M
Production 50-500
Prime: No Pricing
Production 5-50
1 Daniel Moskos, David Kopp/75 8.00
6 Amanda Beard, Jennie Finch/50 20.00
9 Darwin Barney, Mitch Canham/500 10.00

Collegiate Patches Autograph

NM/M
Production 25-250
1 Amanda Beard/100 40.00
2 Ara Parseghian/250 30.00
4 Burt Reynolds/25 100.00
5 Dale Brown/250 200.00
6 Dean Smith/250 60.00
7 Eddie Sutton/250 30.00
8 Frank Broyles/250 20.00
9 Gene Keady/250 20.00
10 Jennie Finch/249 50.00
11 Jim Boeheim/250 25.00
12 Sheryl Swoopes/250 20.00
14 Rebecca Lobo/250 20.00
15 Ron Howard/25 75.00
16 Steve Spurrier/ S.Carolina/100 40.00
17 Tom Osborne/249 40.00
18 Vince Dooley/250 25.00
19 Josh Donaldson/250 20.00
20 Cobi Jones/97 25.00
21 Bill Walton/50 40.00
22 Sidney Moncrief/250 20.00
23 Dominique Wilkins/100 40.00
24 Steve Spurrier/ Florida/100 40.00
25 Drew Stubbs/250 20.00
26 Andrew Brackman/250 30.00
27 Casey Weathers/250 20.00
28 Daniel Moskos/250 20.00
29 David Price/250 50.00
30 Greg Reynolds/250 15.00
31 J.P. Arencibia/249 20.00
32 Jeff Samardzija/150 50.00
33 Julio Borbon/250 15.00
34 Luke Hochevar/100 25.00
35 Matt LaPorta/250 50.00
36 Matt Mangini/250 20.00
37 Matt Wieters/250 50.00
38 Max Scherzer/182 40.00
39 Mitch Canham/250 25.00
40 Nick Schmidt/250 20.00
41 James Adkins/250 15.00
42 Demetris Nichols/250 10.00
43 Aaron Gray/250 15.00
44 Daequan Cook/250 20.00
45 Derrick Byars/250 10.00
46 Reyshawn Terry/250 15.00
47 Taurean Green/250 15.00
48 Summer Sanders/ 250 25.00
49 Bobby Hurley/250 20.00
50 Muggsy Bogues/250 20.00
51 Jerry Tarkanian/250 20.00
52 Cale Iorg/250 20.00
53 Lynette Woodard/249 15.00
54 Nick Hagadone/250 20.00
55 Trystan Magnuson/ 248 15.00
64 Matt Spencer/249 15.00
65 Darwin Barney/250 20.00
67 Connie Mack III/100 15.00
68 Mike Powell/99 25.00

School Colors

NM/M
Common Card: 2.00
Production 1,500 Sets
1 David Price 3.00
2 Daniel Moskos 2.00
3 Greg Reynolds 2.00
4 Matt LaPorta 3.00
5 Matt Wieters 3.00
6 Luke Hochevar 2.00
7 Max Scherzer 2.00
8 Alando Tucker 2.00
9 Daequan Cook 2.00
10 Eddie Sutton 2.00
11 Dean Smith 3.00
12 Steve Spurrier 2.00
13 Tom Osborne 2.00
14 Don Haskins 2.00
15 Jerry Tarkanian 2.00
16 Rick Majerus 2.00
17 Rollie Massimino 2.00
18 Ara Parseghian 2.00
19 Dale Brown 2.00
20 Frank Broyles 2.00
21 Gene Keady 2.00
22 Jim Boeheim 2.00
23 Norm Stewart 2.00
24 Vince Dooley 2.00
25 Bill Walton 3.00
26 Nick Schmidt 2.00
27 Burt Reynolds 3.00
28 Ron Howard 2.00
29 Beau Mills 3.00
30 James Simmons 2.00
31 Joe Savery 2.00
32 Ross Detwiler 2.00
33 J.P. Arencibia 2.00
34 Drew Stubbs 2.00

School Colors Autographs

NM/M
Production 10-50
1 David Price/50 60.00
2 Daniel Moskos/50 15.00
3 Greg Reynolds/50 20.00
4 Matt LaPorta/50 80.00
5 Matt Wieters/50 75.00
6 Luke Hochevar/50 20.00
7 Max Scherzer/50 40.00
8 Alando Tucker/50 15.00
9 Daequan Cook/50 20.00
10 Eddie Sutton/25 30.00
12 Steve Spurrier/25 40.00
13 Tom Osborne/25 40.00
14 Don Haskins/25 20.00
15 Jerry Tarkanian/25 25.00
16 Rick Majerus/25 20.00
18 Ara Parseghian/25 30.00
19 Dale Brown/25 20.00
20 Frank Broyles/25 20.00
21 Gene Keady/25 20.00
22 Jim Boeheim/25 30.00
23 Norm Stewart/25 20.00
24 Vince Dooley/25 25.00
25 Bill Walton/25 30.00
26 Nick Schmidt/50 15.00
29 Beau Mills/50 25.00
30 James Simmons/50 15.00
31 Joe Savery/50 30.00
32 Ross Detwiler/50 15.00
33 J.P. Arencibia/50 15.00
34 Drew Stubbs/50 25.00

Signature Aspirations

NM/M
Production 5-100
1 Andrew Brackman/100 50.00
2 Austin Gallagher/100 20.00
3 Brett Cecil/100 20.00
4 Darwin Barney/100 15.00
5 David Price/100 80.00
6 J.P. Arencibia/100 15.00
7 Josh Donaldson/100 20.00
8 Brandon Hicks/100 20.00
9 Brian Rike/100 20.00
10 Bryan Morris/100 15.00
11 Cale Iorg/100 20.00
12 Casey Weathers/100 20.00
13 Corey Kluber/100 10.00
14 Daniel Moskos/100 15.00
15 Danny Payne/50 15.00
16 David Kopp/36 15.00
17 Dellin Betances/50 40.00
18 Derrick Robinson/ 100 15.00
19 Drew Stubbs/100 20.00
20 Eric Eiland/100 15.00
21 Francisco Pena/100 20.00
22 Greg Reynolds/100 20.00
24 Jess Todd/50 25.00
25 John Tolisano/100 25.00
26 Jordan Zimmerman/75 25.00
27 Julian Sampson/50 15.00
29 Mat Latos/34 40.00
30 Matt Mangini/80 15.00
31 Matt Spencer/30 20.00
32 Matthew Sweeney/ 100 20.00
34 Mitch Canham/25 40.00
35 Nick Schmidt/25 20.00
36 Paul Kelly/100 15.00
37 Ryan Pope/100 25.00
38 Sam Runion/50 20.00
39 Steven Souza/100 20.00
40 Travis Mattair/50 25.00
41 Trystan Magnuson/ 50 20.00
42 Willie Middlebrooks/25 50.00
43 Zack Cozart/25 20.00
44 James Adkins/100 20.00
45 Cory Luebke/100 15.00
46 Aaron Poreda/100 20.00
47 Clayton Mortensen/ 100 10.00
48 Bradley Suttle/100 25.00
49 Tony Butler/100 20.00
50 Zach Britton/100 20.00
51 Scott Cousins/50 15.00
52 Wendell Fairley/100 35.00
53 Eric Sogard/100 10.00
54 Jonathan Lucroy/100 25.00
55 Lars Davis/100 15.00
56 Demetris Nichols/100 10.00
57 Aaron Gray/100 10.00
58 Daequan Cook/50 20.00
59 Derrick Byars/100 10.00
60 Reyshawn Terry/100 10.00
61 Taurean Green/75 15.00
62 Don Haskins/100 15.00
63 Jerry Tarkanian/50 15.00
64 Rick Majerus/100 15.00
66 Ara Parseghian/100 15.00
67 Dale Brown/25 15.00
69 Eddie Sutton/50 20.00
70 Frank Broyles/100 15.00
71 Gene Keady/50 15.00
72 Jim Boeheim/100 20.00
74 Steve Spurrier/25 40.00
75 Tom Osborne/100 30.00
76 Vince Dooley/50 25.00
77 Jennie Finch/50 50.00
79 Mike Powell/100 20.00
80 Rebecca Lobo/100 30.00
81 Brandi Chastain/50 50.00
82 Clint Dolezel/100 10.00
83 Elvin Hayes/100 20.00
84 Cobi Jones/100 20.00
85 Bill Walton/100 25.00
86 Sidney Moncrief/50 15.00
87 Dominique Wilkins/50 20.00
88 Summer Sanders/50 20.00
89 Michelle Akers/100 15.00
90 Muggsy Bogues/100 15.00
91 Charlie Culberson/ 100 30.00
92 Jacob Smolinski/100 25.00
93 Blake Beaven/100 25.00
94 Brad Chalk/100 15.00
95 Brett Anderson/100 30.00
96 Chris Withrow/100 30.00
97 Clay Fuller/100 15.00
98 Damon Sublett/50 35.00
99 Devin Mesoraco/100 20.00
100 Drew Cumberland/ 100 20.00
101 Jack McGeary/100 25.00
102 Jake Arrieta/100 15.00
103 James Simmons/50 15.00
104 Jarrod Parker/50 75.00
105 Jason Dominguez/ 100 10.00
106 Jason Heyward/100 60.00
107 Joe Savery/100 20.00
108 Jon Gilmore/100 25.00
109 Jordan Walden/50 40.00
110 Josh Smoker/100 35.00
111 Josh Vitters/100 80.00
112 Julio Borbon/100 20.00
113 Justin Jackson/50 25.00
114 Kellen Kulbacki/100 20.00
115 Kevin Ahrens/50 25.00
116 Kyle Lotzkar/100 15.00
117 Madison Bumgarner/50 40.00
118 Matt Dominguez/50 40.00
119 Matt LaPorta/100 60.00
120 Matt Wieters/50 100.00
121 Michael Burgess/50 40.00
122 Michael Main/50 30.00
123 Michael Moustakas/ 100 150.00
124 Nathan Vineyard/100 15.00
125 Neil Ramirez/100 15.00
126 Nick Hagadone/50 30.00
127 Peter Kozma/100 20.00
128 Phillippe Aumont/100 40.00
129 Preston Mattingly/50 40.00
131 Ross Detwiler/100 25.00
132 Tim Alderson/100 25.00
133 Todd Frazier/100 20.00
134 Wes Roemer/100 15.00
135 Ben Revere/100 20.00
136 D.J. Strawberry/50 15.00
137 Alando Tucker/50 15.00
138 Jared Jordan/50 10.00
139 Marc Gasol/50 15.00
140 Stephane Lasme/100 10.00
141 Austin Jackson/50 100.00
142 Beau Mills/50 40.00

Signature Status

NM/M
Production 1-50
Gold Status: No Pricing
Production 1-10
1 Andrew Brackman/ 50 60.00
2 Austin Gallagher/50 25.00
3 Brett Cecil/50 25.00
4 Darwin Barney/50 20.00
5 David Price/50 100.00
6 J.P. Arencibia/50 20.00
7 Josh Donaldson/50 25.00
8 Brandon Hicks/50 25.00
9 Brian Rike/50 25.00
10 Bryan Morris/50 20.00
11 Cale Iorg/50 25.00
12 Casey Weathers/50 25.00
13 Corey Kluber/50 10.00
14 Daniel Moskos/50 20.00
15 Danny Payne/25 20.00
16 David Kopp/25 15.00
17 Dellin Betances/25 50.00
18 Derrick Robinson/50 20.00
19 Drew Stubbs/50 25.00
20 Eric Eiland/50 20.00
21 Francisco Pena/50 25.00
22 Greg Reynolds/50 25.00
24 Jess Todd/25 30.00
25 John Tolisano/50 30.00
26 Jordan Zimmerman/25 35.00
27 Julian Sampson/25 20.00
29 Mat Latos/25 40.00
30 Matt Mangini/50 20.00
32 Matthew Sweeney/ 50 25.00
36 Paul Kelly/50 20.00
37 Ryan Pope/50 30.00
38 Sam Runion/25 25.00
39 Steven Souza/50 25.00
40 Travis Mattair/25 30.00
41 Trystan Magnuson/25 25.00
44 James Adkins/50 25.00
45 Cory Luebke/50 20.00
46 Aaron Poreda/50 25.00
47 Clayton Mortensen/ 50 15.00
48 Bradley Suttle/50 30.00
49 Tony Butler/50 25.00
50 Zach Britton/50 25.00
52 Wendell Fairley/50 40.00
53 Eric Sogard/50 15.00
54 Jonathan Lucroy/50 30.00
55 Lars Davis/50 20.00
56 Demetris Nichols/50 15.00
57 Aaron Gray/50 15.00
58 Daequan Cook/25 20.00
59 Derrick Byars/50 10.00
60 Reyshawn Terry/50 10.00
61 Taurean Green/29 20.00
62 Don Haskins/50 20.00
63 Jerry Tarkanian/25 20.00
64 Rick Majerus/50 20.00
66 Ara Parseghian/50 20.00
69 Eddie Sutton/25 25.00
70 Frank Broyles/50 20.00
71 Gene Keady/25 20.00
72 Jim Boeheim/50 25.00
75 Tom Osborne/50 40.00
76 Vince Dooley/25 30.00
77 Jennie Finch/25 60.00
79 Mike Powell/50 25.00
80 Rebecca Lobo/50 40.00
81 Brandi Chastain/25 50.00
82 Clint Dolezel/50 10.00
83 Elvin Hayes/50 25.00
84 Cobi Jones/50 25.00
85 Bill Walton/50 30.00
86 Sidney Moncrief/25 20.00
87 Dominique Wilkins/25 25.00
88 Summer Sanders/25 25.00
89 Michelle Akers/50 15.00
90 Muggsy Bogues/50 15.00
91 Charlie Culberson/50 35.00
92 Jacob Smolinski/50 30.00
93 Blake Beaven/50 30.00
94 Brad Chalk/50 20.00
95 Brett Anderson/50 35.00
96 Chris Withrow/50 35.00
97 Clay Fuller/50 20.00
98 Damon Sublett/25 40.00
99 Devin Mesoraco/50 25.00
100 Drew Cumberland/50 25.00
101 Jack McGeary/50 30.00
102 Jake Arrieta/50 20.00
103 James Simmons/25 20.00
104 Jarrod Parker/25 100.00
105 Jason Dominguez/50 15.00
106 Jason Heyward/50 90.00
107 Joe Savery/50 25.00
108 Jon Gilmore/50 30.00
109 Jordan Walden/25 50.00
110 Josh Smoker/50 40.00
111 Josh Vitters/50 100.00
112 Julio Borbon/50 25.00
113 Justin Jackson/25 30.00
114 Kellen Kulbacki/50 25.00
115 Kevin Ahrens/25 30.00
116 Kyle Lotzkar/50 20.00
117 Madison Bumgarner/25 50.00
118 Matt Dominguez/25 50.00
119 Matt LaPorta/50 75.00
120 Matt Wieters/25 120.00
121 Michael Burgess/25 50.00
122 Michael Main/25 40.00
123 Michael Moustakas/50 250.00
124 Nathan Vineyard/50 20.00
125 Neil Ramirez/50 20.00
126 Nick Hagadone/25 40.00
127 Peter Kozma/50 25.00
128 Phillippe Aumont/50 20.00
129 Preston Mattingly/25 50.00
131 Ross Detwiler/50 30.00
132 Tim Alderson/50 30.00
133 Todd Frazier/50 30.00
134 Wes Roemer/50 20.00
135 Ben Revere/50 25.00
136 D.J. Strawberry/25 20.00
137 Alando Tucker/25 20.00
138 Jared Jordan/25 15.00
139 Marc Gasol/25 15.00
340 Stephane Lasme/50 10.00
141 Austin Jackson/25 125.00
142 Beau Mills/25 50.00

Signature Turn of the Century

NM/M
Production 10-500
1 Andrew Brackman/ 500 35.00
2 Austin Gallagher/500 20.00
3 Brett Cecil/500 20.00
4 Darwin Barney/500 15.00
5 David Price/500 50.00
6 J.P. Arencibia/500 15.00
7 Josh Donaldson/500 20.00
8 Brandon Hicks/419 20.00
9 Brian Rike/500 20.00
10 Bryan Morris/500 15.00
11 Cale Iorg/397 20.00
12 Casey Weathers/500 20.00
13 Corey Kluber/419 8.00
14 Daniel Moskos/500 15.00
15 Danny Payne/394 10.00
16 David Kopp/449 10.00
17 Dellin Betances/494 30.00
18 Derrick Robinson/ 500 15.00
19 Drew Stubbs/494 20.00
20 Eric Eiland/419 15.00
21 Francisco Pena/396 20.00
22 Greg Reynolds/500 20.00
23 Jeff Samardzija/219 30.00
24 Jess Todd/394 20.00
25 John Tolisano/419 20.00
26 Jordan Zimmerman/ 469 20.00
27 Julian Sampson/494 10.00
28 Luke Hochevar/158 25.00
29 Mat Latos/499 25.00
30 Matt Mangini/500 15.00
31 Matt Spencer/500 10.00
32 Matthew Sweeney/ 500 20.00
33 Max Scherzer/250 40.00
34 Mitch Canham/250 25.00
35 Nick Schmidt/209 10.00
36 Paul Kelly/500 15.00
37 Ryan Pope/500 20.00
38 Sam Runion/494 15.00
39 Steven Souza/500 15.00
40 Travis Mattair/494 20.00
41 Trystan Magnuson/ 246 15.00
42 Willie Middlebrooks/ 409 30.00
43 Zack Cozart/409 10.00
44 James Adkins/500 15.00
45 Cory Luebke/469 10.00
46 Aaron Poreda/500 15.00
47 Clayton Mortensen/ 500 8.00
48 Bradley Suttle/500 20.00
49 Tony Butler/419 15.00
50 Zach Britton/437 15.00
51 Scott Cousins/500 8.00
52 Wendell Fairley/500 30.00
53 Eric Sogard/500 8.00
54 Jonathan Lucroy/500 20.00
55 Lars Davis/500 10.00
56 Demetris Nichols/500 8.00
57 Aaron Gray/500 8.00
58 Daequan Cook/494 10.00
59 Derrick Byars/300 8.00
60 Reyshawn Terry/300 8.00
61 Taurean Green/500 10.00
62 Don Haskins/194 15.00
63 Jerry Tarkanian/144 15.00
64 Rick Majerus/194 15.00
66 Ara Parseghian/69 15.00
67 Dale Brown/89 15.00
69 Eddie Sutton/144 15.00
70 Frank Broyles/69 15.00
71 Gene Keady/144 15.00
74 Steve Spurrier/59 25.00
75 Tom Osborne/320 25.00
76 Vince Dooley/91 20.00
77 Jennie Finch/119 50.00
79 Mike Powell/119 20.00
80 Rebecca Lobo/234 25.00
81 Brandi Chastain/94 40.00
82 Clint Dolezel/243 8.00
83 Elvin Hayes/344 15.00
84 Cobi Jones/247 15.00
86 Sidney Moncrief/169 15.00
88 Summer Sanders/ 169 15.00
89 Michelle Akers/344 10.00
90 Muggsy Bogues/94 15.00
91 Charlie Culberson/ 500 25.00
92 Jacob Smolinski/500 20.00
93 Blake Beaven/100 25.00
94 Brad Chalk/100 15.00
95 Brett Anderson/145 30.00
96 Chris Withrow/168 30.00
97 Clay Fuller/145 15.00
98 Damon Sublett/220 30.00
99 Devin Mesoraco/145 20.00
100 Drew Cumberland/ 125 20.00
101 Jack McGeary/145 25.00
102 Jake Arrieta/145 15.00
103 James Simmons/100 15.00
104 Jarrod Parker/55 75.00
105 Jason Dominguez/ 100 10.00
106 Jason Heyward/169 60.00
107 Joe Savery/119 20.00
108 Jon Gilmore/100 25.00
109 Jordan Walden/100 30.00
110 Josh Smoker/200 30.00
111 Josh Vitters/150 80.00
112 Julio Borbon/100 20.00
113 Justin Jackson/100 20.00
114 Kellen Kulbacki/145 20.00
115 Kevin Ahrens/100 20.00
116 Kyle Lotzkar/100 15.00
117 Madison Bumgarner/100 40.00
118 Matt Dominguez/100 30.00
119 Matt LaPorta/100 60.00
120 Matt Wieters/100 80.00
121 Michael Burgess/100 30.00
122 Michael Main/100 25.00
123 Michael Moustakas/ 345 80.00
124 Nathan Vineyard/119 15.00
125 Neil Ramirez/145 15.00
126 Nick Hagadone/100 25.00
127 Peter Kozma/100 20.00
128 Phillippe Aumont/120 40.00
129 Preston Mattingly/ 100 35.00
131 Ross Detwiler/119 25.00
132 Tim Alderson/100 25.00
133 Todd Frazier/145 20.00
134 Wes Roemer/100 15.00
135 Ben Revere/119 20.00
136 D.J. Strawberry/100 10.00
137 Alando Tucker/100 10.00
138 Jared Jordan/100 10.00
139 Marc Gasol/100 10.00
140 Stephane Lasme/145 10.00
141 Austin Jackson/100 75.00
142 Beau Mills/100 30.00

Throwback Threads

NM/M
Common Player: 5.00
Production 500 unless noted.
Prime: No Pricing
Production 3-50
1 Brandi Chastain 20.00
2 Amanda Beard/44 15.00
3 Drew Stubbs 5.00
4 Drew Cumberland 5.00
5 Clint Dolezel 5.00
6 Mat Latos 5.00
7 Brett Cecil 5.00
8 Vince Dooley 8.00
9 Brett Anderson 5.00
10 Casey Weathers/75 5.00
11 Daniel Moskos 5.00
12 Darwin Barney 5.00
13 Kellen Kulbacki 5.00
14 Matt Dominguez 8.00
15 Matt Mangini 5.00
16 Mitch Canham 5.00
18 Willie Middlebrooks 8.00
19 Mike Powell 5.00
20 Steve Spurrier 5.00
21 Dale Brown 5.00
22 Don Haskins 5.00
23 Nick Schmidt 5.00
24 Zack Cozart 5.00

Throwback Threads Autograph

NM/M
Production 50 or 100
Prime Auto.: No Pricing
Production 1-25
1 Brandi Chastain/100 50.00
2 Amanda Beard/50 40.00
3 Drew Stubbs/100 15.00
4 Drew Cumberland/ 100 15.00
5 Clint Dolezel/100 15.00
6 Mat Latos/100 25.00
9 Brett Anderson/100 15.00
10 Casey Weathers/100 15.00
11 Daniel Moskos/100 15.00
12 Darwin Barney/100 25.00
13 Kellen Kulbacki/100 20.00
14 Matt Dominguez/100 30.00
15 Matt Mangini/100 15.00
16 Mitch Canham/100 20.00
18 Willie Middlebrooks/ 100 25.00
19 Mike Powell/100 25.00
20 Steve Spurrier/50 40.00
21 Dale Brown/50 25.00
22 Don Haskins/100 15.00
23 Nick Schmidt/100 20.00
24 Zack Cozart/100 15.00

2007 Donruss Americana

NM/M
Complete Set (100): 40.00
Common Player: .25
1 John Travolta 1.00
2 Stacy Keibler 2.00
3 Burt Reynolds 1.00
4 Steve Guttenberg .25
5 William Shatner 1.00
6 Lee Majors .50
7 Gretchen Wilson .25
8 Ultimate Warrior .50
9 Barbara Eden .50
10 Carrie Fisher .50
11 Lori Petty .25
12 Morgan Fairchild .50
13 Vince Neil .50
14 Gail Kim .25
15 Cedric the Entertainer .50
16 Corin Nemec .25
17 Billy Dee Williams .50
18 Jim Furyk .50
19 Dick Van Patten .25
20 Debbie Reynolds .25
21 William Fichtner .25
22 Bob Eubanks .25
23 Mike Huckabee 1.00
24 Jack Hanna .25
25 Elliott Gould .25
26 Lou Gossett Jr. .50
27 Catherine Bach .50
28 Tippi Hedren .25
29 Walter Koenig .50
30 Ernest Borgnine .25
31 Cindy Williams .25
32 Cindy Morgan .25
33 Giovanni Ribisi .25
34 Story Musgrave .25
35 Esther Williams .25
36 Connie Mack III .25
37 Gilbert Gottfried .25
38 Burt Ward .50
39 Josh Duhamel .25
40 Larry Hagman .50
41 Catherine Hicks .25
42 Karen Lynn Gorney .25
43 Larry King .50
44 Autumn Reeser .25
45 Mickey Rooney .50

46 Aidan Quinn .25
47 Martin Klebba .25
48 Michael Pare' .25
49 Hugh O'Brian .25
50 Molly Shannon .25
51 Dee Snider .75
52 Melissa Jo Hunter .25
53 Jennie Finch 1.00
54 Henry Winkler .50
55 Neil Patrick Harris .25
56 Val Kilmer .25
57 Peter Marshall .25
58 Clint Howard .25
59 Buzz Aldrin .50
60 Heather Cox .25
61 Angela Simmons .25
62 Richard Kiel .25
63 Leonard Nimoy .50
64 Jan Rooney .25
65 Shirley Jones .25
66 Bruce Jenner .50
67 Tom Green .25
68 Dom DeLuise .25
69 Bobby Allison .50
70 Tony Curtis .25
71 Shawnee Smith .25
72 Wink Martindale .25
73 Tara Conner .25
74 Sheryl Swoopes .25
75 Wayne Newton .50
76 Justine Simmons .25
77 Keiko Agena .25
78 Tom Savini .25
79 David Faustino .25
80 Adam West .50
81 Gina Phillips .25
82 Dawn Wells .25
83 George Allen .25
84 Chris Sarandon .25
85 Amanda Beard .50
86 Katey Sagal .50
87 Ed O'Neill .50
88 Dina Meyer .50
89 Ron Howard .25
90 Randy Owen .25
91 Yunjin Kim .25
92 Chuck Woolery .25
93 Ed McMahon .25
94 Stephanie Powers .25
95 Warwick Davis .25
96 Scott Baio .25
97 Russell Johnson .25
98 Michael Berryman .25
99 Bernie Mac .50
100 Ashley Judd 1.00

Cinema Stars

NM/M
Common Card: 4.00
Production 500 Sets
1 John Travolta 5.00
2 Burt Reynolds 5.00
3 William Shatner 5.00
4 Carrie Fisher 5.00
5 Ron Howard 5.00
6 Elliott Gould 4.00
7 Lou Gossett Jr. 4.00
8 Ernest Borgnine 4.00
9 Giovanni Ribisi 4.00
10 Quentin Tarantino 4.00
11 Shirley Jones 4.00
12 Dom DeLuise 4.00
13 Adam West 4.00
14 Bernie Mac 4.00
15 Ashley Judd 5.00
16 Josh Duhamel 4.00
17 Catherine Bach 4.00
18 Cindy Morgan 4.00
19 Karen Lynn Gorney 4.00
20 Larry Hagman 4.00
21 Lee Majors 4.00
22 Morgan Fairchild 4.00
23 Richard Kiel 4.00
24 Tippi Hedren 4.00
25 Walter Koenig 4.00
26 Burt Ward 4.00
27 Barbara Eden 4.00
28 Cedric the Entertainer 5.00
29 Billy Dee Williams 4.00
30 Leonard Nimoy 5.00

Cinema Stars Directors Cut Signature

NM/M
Production 10-100
2 Burt Reynolds/25 250.00
3 William Shatner/25 150.00
5 Ron Howard/25 125.00
11 Shirley Jones/25 80.00
12 Dom DeLuise/25 60.00
16 Josh Duhamel/25 80.00
17 Catherine Bach/50 100.00
18 Cindy Morgan/100 40.00
19 Karen Lynn Gorney/50 40.00
20 Larry Hagman/25 100.00
22 Morgan Fairchild/50 60.00
23 Richard Kiel/25 75.00
24 Tippi Hedren/25 100.00
25 Walter Koenig/25 100.00
27 Barbara Eden/25 125.00
29 Billy Dee Williams/25 150.00
30 Leonard Nimoy/25 200.00

Cinema Stars Materials

NM/M
Common Card: 8.00
Production 100-500
Golden Era: 1-1.5X
Production 5-50
Silver Screen: 1-1.5X
Production 25-100
Super Stars: 2-3X
Production 5-25
No pricing production 20 or less.
1 John Travolta/Jkt/500 20.00
2 Burt Reynolds/Shirt/500 15.00
3 William Shatner/Shirt/500 15.00
4 Carrie Fisher/Shirt/250 20.00
6 Elliott Gould/Sweater/500 8.00
7 Lou Gossett Jr./Shirt/500 8.00
8 Ernest Borgnine/Shirt/500 10.00
9 Giovanni Ribisi/Shirt/380 8.00
11 Shirley Jones/Skirt/500 10.00
13 Adam West Shirt/500 15.00
15 Ashley Judd/Shirt/400 20.00
16 Josh Duhamel/Shirt/350 8.00
17 Catherine Bach/Shirt/500 15.00
18 Cindy Morgan/Shirt/500 8.00
20 Larry Hagman/Shirt/350 10.00
21 Lee Majors/Pajamas/500 10.00
22 Morgan Fairchild/Shirt/100 20.00
24 Tippi Hedren/Dress/500 10.00
26 Burt Ward/Shirt/400 10.00
27 Barbara Eden/Shirt/195 20.00
30 Leonard Nimoy/Shirt/400 15.00

Cinema Stars Signatures

NM/M
Production 10-100
Signature Materials: 1-1.5X
Production 4-25
2 Burt Reynolds/25 80.00
3 William Shatner/25 140.00
4 Carrie Fisher/50 150.00
5 Ron Howard/75 75.00
6 Elliott Gould/100 25.00
7 Lou Gossett/50 30.00
8 Ernest Borgnine/50 60.00
9 Giovanni Ribisi/50 25.00
11 Shirley Jones/50 50.00
12 Dom DeLuise/50 40.00
13 Adam West/50 60.00
14 Bernie Mac/50 50.00
15 Ashley Judd/50 160.00
16 Josh Duhamel/50 50.00
17 Catherine Bach/25 75.00
18 Cindy Morgan/25 25.00
19 Karen Lynn Gorney/25 25.00
20 Larry Hagman/50 75.00
21 Lee Majors/25 60.00
22 Morgan Fairchild/25 60.00
23 Richard Kiel/50 25.00
24 Tippi Hedren/25 75.00
25 Walter Koenig/75 50.00
26 Burt Ward/50 50.00
27 Barbara Eden/50 75.00
28 Cedric the Entertainer/50 30.00
29 Billy Dee Williams/50 50.00
30 Leonard Nimoy/25 120.00

Co-Stars Materials

NM/M
Production 50 unless noted.
Golden Era: No Pricing
Production 10 Sets
Silver Screen: 1-1.5X
Production 25 Sets
1 Marilyn Monroe/Skirt, Bette Davis/Dress 150.00
2 Humphrey Bogart/Shirt, Ingrid Bergman/Dress 100.00
3 James Dean/Robe, Natalie Wood/Dress 100.00
4 Burt Reynolds/Shirt, Jackie Gleason/Coat/100 50.00
5 William Shatner/Shirt, Leonard Nimoy/Shirt/100 50.00
6 Adam West/Shirt, Burt Ward/Shirt/100 40.00
7 Rock Hudson/Jkt, James Dean/Robe 100.00
8 Ed O'Neill/Shirt, Katey Sagal/Blouse/100 30.00
9 Dawn Wells/Shirt, Russell Johnson/Shirt/100 40.00
10 Ernest Borgnine/Shirt, Debbie Reynolds/H'chief 40.00

Co-Stars Signatures

NM/M
Production 50 unless noted.
1 S. Smith, D. Meyer 100.00
2 Barbara Eden, Larry Hagman 200.00
3 William Shatner, Leonard Nimoy/25 300.00
4 Adam West, Burt Ward 150.00
5 Ed O'Neill, Katey Sagal 150.00
6 Burt Reynolds, Dom DeLuise/25 150.00
7 Ron Howard, Henry Winkler/25 200.00
8 Billy Dee Williams, Carrie Fisher/25 200.00
9 Mickey Rooney, Jan Rooney/25 150.00
10 Dawn Wells, Russell Johnson 150.00

Hollywood Legends

NM/M
Common Card:
Production 500 Sets
1 James Dean 8.00
2 Ingrid Bergman 4.00
3 Gloria Swanson 4.00
4 Rock Hudson 4.00
5 Bette Davis 6.00
6 Jayne Mansfield 8.00
7 Greta Garbo 4.00
8 Ava Gardner 4.00
9 Mae West 4.00
10 Steve McQueen 4.00
11 Audrey Hepburn 6.00
12 Jean Harlow 4.00
13 Lillian Gish 4.00
14 Carole Lombard 4.00
15 James Cagney 4.00
16 Marilyn Monroe 10.00
17 Mary Pickford 4.00
18 Debbie Reynolds 4.00
19 Ginger Rogers 4.00
20 Glenn Ford 4.00
21 Eleanor Powell 4.00
22 Gene Tierney 4.00
23 Lana Turner 4.00
24 Esther Williams 4.00
25 Natalie Wood 4.00
26 Loretta Young 4.00
27 Humphrey Bogart 4.00
28 Marlon Brando 6.00
29 Dorothy Lamour 4.00
30 Tony Curtis 4.00
31 Bob Denver 4.00
32 Errol Flynn 4.00
33 Peter Sellers 4.00
34 Patricia Neal 4.00
35 Mickey Rooney 4.00
36 Marlene Dietrich 4.00
37 Jimmy Stewart 6.00
38 Yvonne De Carlo 4.00
39 Rudolph Valentino 4.00
40 Bing Crosby 4.00

Hollywood Legends Directors Cut Signatures

NM/M
Production 1-25
24 Esther Williams/25 200.00
34 Patricia Neal/25 150.00

Hollywood Legends Materials

NM/M
Common Card:
Production 25-350
Golden Era: 1-1.5X
Production 5-50
Silver Screen: 1-1.5X
Production 10-100
Super Stars: 2-3X
Production 1-25
1 James Dean/Robe/155 100.00
2 Ingrid Bergman/Dress/250 35.00
3 Gloria Swanson/Dress/350 25.00
4 Rock Hudson/Jkt/250 25.00
5 Bette Davis/Dress/250 35.00
6 Jayne Mansfield/Shirt/325 40.00
7 Greta Garbo/Dress/350 35.00
8 Ava Gardner/Dress/325 35.00
9 Mae West/Coat/350 30.00
10 Steve McQueen/Jkt/350 30.00
11 Audrey Hepburn/Dress/325 50.00
12 Jean Harlow/Coat/325 35.00
13 Lillian Gish/Coat/325 30.00
14 Carole Lombard/Dress/350 30.00
15 James Cagney/Coat/350 35.00
16 Marilyn Monroe/Skirt/250 125.00
17 Mary Pickford/Dress/350 25.00
18 Debbie Reynolds/Handkerchief/25 40.00
19 Ginger Rogers/Coat/325 30.00
20 Glenn Ford/Shirt/350 20.00
21 Eleanor Powell/Tights/350 25.00
22 Gene Tierney/Dress/325 25.00
23 Lana Turner/Dress/325 30.00
24 Esther Williams/Bathing Suit/100 25.00
25 Natalie Wood/Dress/250 40.00
26 Loretta Young/Coat/350 25.00
27 Humphrey Bogart/Shirt/350 50.00
28 Marlon Brando/Pants/325 30.00
29 Dorothy Lamour/Dress/325 30.00
30 Tony Curtis/Shirt/325 20.00
31 Bob Denver/Shirt/350 20.00
32 Errol Flynn/Jkt/325 40.00
33 Peter Sellers/Jkt/325 25.00
34 Patricia Neal/Shawl/350 30.00
35 Mickey Rooney/Shirt/325 25.00
36 Marlene Dietrich/Coat/350 30.00
37 Jimmy Stewart/Coat/325 50.00
38 Yvonne De Carlo/Coat/350 25.00
40 Bing Crosby/Shoes/25 200.00

Hollywood Legends Signatures

NM/M
Production 25 Sets
Signature Materials: 1-1.5X
Production 25 Sets
18 Debbie Reynolds 100.00
24 Esther Williams 100.00
30 Tony Curtis 100.00
35 Mickey Rooney 100.00

Private Signings

NM/M
Production 5-1,250 40.00
1 John Travolta/25 180.00
2 Stacy Keibler/250 50.00
4 Steve Guttenberg/300 20.00
5 William Shatner/25 120.00
7 Gretchen Wilson/200 60.00
8 Ultimate Warrior/250 50.00
9 Barbara Eden/25 75.00
10 Carrie Fisher/25 150.00
11 Lori Petty/200 15.00
12 Morgan Fairchild/150 50.00
13 Vince Neil/250 30.00
14 Gail Kim/250 30.00
15 Cedric the Entertainer/135 30.00
16 Corin Nemec/200 15.00
17 Billy Dee Williams/85 50.00
18 Jim Furyk/100 50.00
19 Dick Van Patten 25.00
21 William Fichtner/100 15.00
22 Bob Eubanks/50 25.00
23 Mike Huckabee/275 50.00
24 Jack Hanna/400 20.00
25 Elliott Gould/200 25.00
26 Lou Gossett Jr./50 30.00
28 Tippi Hedren 40.00
29 Walter Koenig/60 50.00
30 Ernest Borgnine/50 50.00
31 Cindy Williams/25 40.00
32 Cindy Morgan/330 15.00
33 Giovanni Ribisi/100 20.00
34 Story Musgrave/250 25.00
35 Esther Williams/50 75.00
36 Connie Mack III/150 10.00
37 Gilbert Gottfried/450 15.00
38 Burt Ward/25 75.00
39 Josh Duhamel/50 50.00
40 Larry Hagman/50 65.00
41 Catherine Hicks/350 20.00
42 Karen Lynn Gorney/418 10.00
43 Larry King/200 30.00
44 Autumn Reeser/364 25.00
45 Mickey Rooney/25 80.00
46 Aidan Quinn/168 15.00
47 Martin Klebba/1,250 10.00
48 Michael Pare'/1,250 10.00
49 Hugh O'Brian/70 25.00
50 Molly Shannon/250 25.00
51 Dee Snider 25.00
52 Melissa Jo Hunter/1,250 10.00
53 Jennie Finch/500 40.00
54 Henry Winkler/50 80.00
55 Neil Patrick Harris/100 30.00
56 Val Kilmer/100 40.00
57 Peter Marshall/200 15.00
58 Clint Howard/100 25.00
59 Buzz Aldrin/50 150.00
60 Heather Cox/500 25.00
61 Angela Simmons/159 15.00
62 Richard Kiel/100 50.00
63 Leonard Nimoy/25 125.00
64 Jan Rooney/175 20.00
66 Bruce Jenner/250 25.00
67 Tom Green/200 20.00
68 Dom DeLuise/105 40.00
69 Bobby Allison/100 25.00
70 Tony Curtis/25 80.00
71 Shawnee Smith 40.00
72 Wink Martindale/95 15.00
73 Tara Conner/150 40.00
74 Sheryl Swoopes/375 20.00
75 Wayne Newton/110 50.00
76 Justine Simmons/250 10.00
77 Keiko Agena/130 15.00
78 Tom Savini/364 15.00
79 David Faustino/150 20.00
80 Adam West/50 60.00
81 Gina Phillips/350 20.00
82 Dawn Wells/100 50.00
83 George Allen/224 15.00
84 Chris Sarandon/312 10.00
86 Katey Sagal/100 40.00
87 Ed O'Neill/100 50.00
88 Dina Meyer/100 40.00
89 Ron Howard/60 80.00
90 Randy Owen/200 25.00
91 Yunjin Kim/400 30.00
92 Chuck Woolery/100 15.00
93 Ed McMahon/470 25.00
94 Stephanie Powers/100 50.00
95 Warwick Davis/250 10.00
96 Scott Baio/200 25.00
97 Russell Johnson/100 40.00
98 Michael Berryman/314 15.00
99 Bernie Mac/85 40.00
100 Ashley Judd/50 180.00

Promos

Sports Legends

NM/M
Common Card: 4.00
Production 500 Sets
1 Willie Mays 8.00
2 Jackie Robinson 8.00
3 Walt Frazier 4.00
4 Lou Gehrig 10.00
5 Jim Courier 4.00
6 Tony Esposito 4.00
7 Martina Navratilova 4.00
8 Stan Musial 8.00
9 Patrick Roy 8.00
10 Larry Bird 8.00

Sports Legends Materials

NM/M
Production 25-500
1 Willie Mays/Jsy/100 40.00
2 Jackie Robinson/Jkt/100 50.00
3 Walt Frazier/Jsy/500 10.00
4 Lou Gehrig/Jsy/100 150.00
5 Jim Courier/Shirt/500 10.00
6 Tony Esposito/Jsy/500 10.00
8 Stan Musial/Jsy/25 40.00

Sports Legends Signatures

NM/M
Production 25-50
Signature Materials: 1X
Production 25-50
1 Willie Mays/25 200.00
3 Walt Frazier/25 50.00
5 Jim Courier/50 40.00
6 Tony Esposito/25 50.00
7 Martina Navratilova/50 75.00
8 Stan Musial/25 75.00
9 Patrick Roy/25 125.00
10 Larry Bird/25 125.00

Stars Materials

NM/M
Common Card: 5.00
Production 10-250 .25
1 John Travolta/Jkt/250 15.00
2 Stacy Keibler/Shirt/195 20.00
3 Burt Reynolds/Shirt/250 15.00
4 Steve Guttenberg/Shirt/250 5.00
5 William Shatner/Shirt/250 15.00
6 Lee Majors/Pajamas/250 10.00
8 Ultimate Warrior/Trunks/95 20.00
9 Barbara Eden/Shirt/50 25.00
10 Carrie Fisher/Shirt/50 25.00
11 Lori Petty/Shirt/250 8.00
12 Morgan Fairchild/Shirt/50 25.00
13 Vince Neil/Shirt/250 10.00
16 Corin Nemec/Shirt/250 8.00
18 Jim Furyk/Shirt/250 15.00
19 Dick Van Patten/Shirt/250 8.00
20 Debbie Reynolds/Handkerchief/25 40.00
21 William Fichtner/Shirt/250 5.00
22 Bob Eubanks/Shirt/250 8.00
23 Mike Huckabee/Shirt/250 10.00
25 Elliott Gould/Sweater/250 8.00
26 Lou Gossett Jr./Shirt/250 8.00
27 Catherine Bach/Shirt/250 15.00
28 Tippi Hedren/Dress/250 15.00
30 Ernest Borgnine/Shirt/100 10.00
31 Cindy Williams/Shirt/100 5.00
32 Cindy Morgan/Shirt/190 8.00
33 Giovanni Ribisi/Shirt/250 8.00
35 Esther Williams/Bathing Suit/100 25.00
36 Connie Mack III/Shirt/250 5.00
37 Gilbert Gottfried/Shirt/100 10.00
38 Burt Ward/Shirt/100 15.00
39 Josh Duhamel/Shirt/100 10.00
40 Larry Hagman/Shirt/100 15.00
45 Mickey Rooney/Shirt/80 25.00
46 Aidan Quinn/Pants/250 5.00
47 Martin Klebba/Shirt/250 5.00
49 Hugh O'Brian/Shirt/250 8.00
52 Melissa Jo Hunter/Shirt/25 25.00
55 Neil Patrick Harris/Shirt/250 8.00
63 Leonard Nimoy/Shirt/100 15.00
65 Shirley Jones/Shirt/100 5.00
66 Bruce Jenner/Shirt/250 8.00
67 Tom Green/Pants/250 5.00
69 Bobby Allison/Shirt/250 8.00
70 Tony Curtis/Shirt/85 20.00
72 Wink Martindale/Shirt/250 5.00
73 Tara Conner/Shirt/100 20.00
77 Keiko Agena/Shirt/250 5.00
79 David Faustino/Shirt/250 8.00
80 Adam West/Shirt/100 20.00
82 Dawn Wells/Shirt/100 15.00
83 George Allen/Pants/250 5.00
85 Amanda Beard/Bathing Suit/25 30.00
86 Katey Sagal/Blouse/250 10.00
87 Ed O'Neill Shirt/250 10.00
88 Dina Meyer Shirt/55 15.00
92 Chuck Woolery/Pants/250 5.00
96 Scott Baio/Shirt/250 8.00
97 Russell Johnson/Shirt/100 15.00
100 Ashley Judd/Shirt/100 25.00

Stars Signature Materials

NM/M
Production 10-250
1 John Travolta/Jkt/25 180.00

2	Stacy Keibler/Shirt/250	60.00
3	Burt Reynolds/Shirt/25	80.00
5	William Shatner/Shirt/25	120.00
6	Lee Majors/Pajamas/25	60.00
8	Ultimate Warrior/Trunks/50	75.00
9	Barbara Eden/Shirt/100	60.00
10	Carrie Fisher/Shirt/25	160.00
11	Lori Petty/Shirt/200	15.00
12	Morgan Fairchild/Shirt/150	50.00
13	Vince Neil/Shirt/250	30.00
14	Gail Kim/Trunks/150	30.00
16	Corin Nemec/Shirt/200	15.00
18	Jim Furyk/Shirt/100	50.00
19	Dick Van Patten/Shirt/200	20.00
20	Debbie Reynolds/Handerkerchief/25	100.00
21	William Fichtner/Shirt/250	15.00
22	Bob Eubanks/Shirt/150	20.00
23	Mike Huckabee/Shirt/225	50.00
26	Lou Gossett Jr./Shirt/50	30.00
27	Catherine Bach/Shirt/22	100.00
28	Tippi Hedren/Dress/25	80.00
30	Ernest Borgnine/Shirt/100	50.00
31	Cindy Williams/Shirt/200	25.00
33	Giovanni Ribisi/Shirt/200	20.00
35	Esther Williams/Bathing Suit/50	80.00
36	Connie Mack III/Shirt/250	10.00
38	Burt Ward/Shirt/100	50.00
45	Mickey Rooney/Shirt/50	80.00
46	Aidan Quinn/Pants/200	15.00
47	Martin Klebba/Shirt/250	15.00
49	Hugh O'Brian/Shirt/200	30.00
52	Melissa Jo Hunter/Shirt/250	15.00
55	Neil Patrick Harris/Shirt/100	25.00
56	Val Kilmer/Coat/100	35.00
63	Leonard Nimoy/Shirt/25	125.00
65	Shirley Jones/Skirt/50	50.00
66	Bruce Jenner/Shirt/250	25.00
67	Tom Green/Pants/200	20.00
69	Bobby Allison/Shirt/100	25.00
70	Tony Curtis/Shirt/50	75.00
72	Wink Martindale/Shirt/150	20.00
73	Tara Conner/Shirt/100	50.00
77	Keiko Agena/Shirt/250	15.00
79	David Faustino/Shirt/200	20.00
80	Adam West/Shirt/50	60.00
82	Dawn Wells/Shirt/100	50.00
83	George Allen/Pants/250	15.00
86	Katey Sagal/Blouse/100	40.00
87	Ed O'Neill Shirt/100	50.00
88	Dina Meyer/Shirt/100	50.00
92	Chuck Woolery/Pants/100	15.00
94	Stephanie Powers/Handkerchief/25	60.00
96	Scott Baio Shirt/100	20.00
97	Russell Johnson/Shirt/100	40.00
100	Ashley Judd/Shirt/50	160.00

1986 Dorman's Cheese

Found in specially-marked packages of Dorman's American Cheese Singles, this set consists of 10 two-card panels of baseball superstars. Labeled "Super Star Limited Edition," the panels measure 2" x 1-1/2" and have a perforation line in the center. Fronts have a color photo along with the Dorman's logo and the player's name, team and position. Due to a lack of MLB licensing, all team insignias have been airbrushed from the players' caps. Backs contain brief player statistics. The unnumbered panels and cards are listed here alphabetically by the player on the left.

		NM/M
Complete Panel Set (10):		5.00
Complete Singles Set (20):		4.00
Common Panel:		.50
Common Player:		.20
Panel 1		1.00
(1)	George Brett	.75
(2)	Jack Morris	.20
Panel 2		1.50
(3)	Gary Carter	.40
(4)	Cal Ripken Jr.	1.00
Panel 3		.65
(5)	Dwight Gooden	.20
(6)	Kent Hrbek	.20
Panel 4		1.00
(7)	Rickey Henderson	.40
(8)	Mike Schmidt	.75
Panel 5		.75
(9)	Keith Hernandez	.20
(10)	Dale Murphy	.25
Panel 6		1.00
(11)	Reggie Jackson	.60
(12)	Eddie Murray	.40
Panel 7		1.25
(13)	Don Mattingly	.75
(14)	Ryne Sandberg	.60
Panel 8		1.00
(15)	Willie McGee	.20
(16)	Robin Yount	.40
Panel 9		1.00
(17)	Rick Sutcliff (Sutcliffe)	.20
(18)	Wade Boggs	.60
Panel 10		1.00
(19)	Dave Winfield	.40
(20)	Jim Rice	.25

1981 Drake's

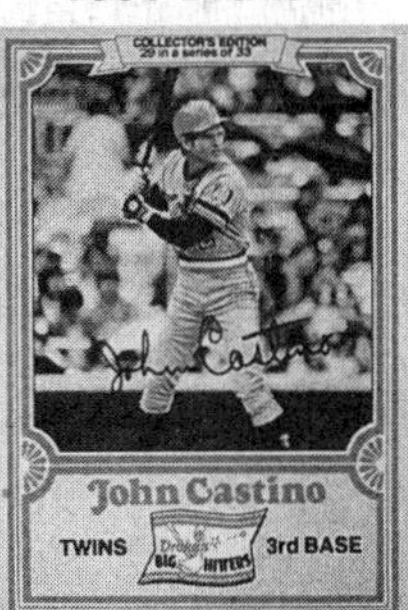

Producing its first baseball card set since 1950, Drake Bakeries, in conjunction with Topps, issued a 33-card set entitled "Big Hitters." The cards, in standard 2-1/2" x 3-1/2" size, feature 19 American League and 14 National League sluggers. Full-color action photos, containing a facsimile autograph, are positioned in red frames for A.L. players and blue frames for N.L. hitters. The player's name, team, position, and Drake's logo are also on front. Backs, which are similar to the regular 1981 Topps issue, contain the card number, statistical and biographical information, and the Drake's logo.

		NM/M
Complete Set (33):		6.00
Common Player:		.25
1	Carl Yastrzemski	1.50
2	Rod Carew	1.00
3	Pete Rose	3.00
4	Dave Parker	.25
5	George Brett	2.00
6	Eddie Murray	1.00
7	Mike Schmidt	2.00
8	Jim Rice	.50
9	Fred Lynn	.25
10	Reggie Jackson	1.50
11	Steve Garvey	.50
12	Ken Singleton	.25
13	Bill Buckner	.25
14	Dave Winfield	1.00
15	Jack Clark	.25
16	Cecil Cooper	.25
17	Bob Horner	.25
18	George Foster	.25
19	Dave Kingman	.25
20	Cesar Cedeno	.25
21	Joe Charboneau	.75
22	George Hendrick	.25
23	Gary Carter	1.00
24	Al Oliver	.25
25	Bruce Bochte	.25
26	Jerry Mumphrey	.25
27	Steve Kemp	.25
28	Bob Watson	.25
29	John Castino	.25
30	Tony Armas	.25
31	John Mayberry	.25
32	Carlton Fisk	1.00
33	Lee Mazzilli	.25

1982 Drake's

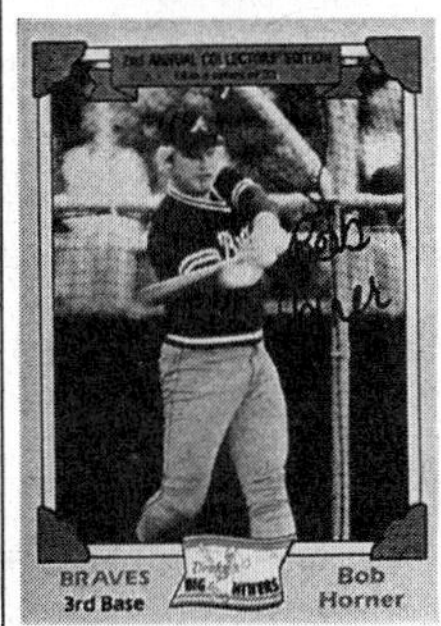

Drake Bakeries produced, in conjunction with Topps, a "2nd Annual Collectors' Edition" in 1982. Thirty-three standard-size cards (2-1/2" x 3-1/2") make up the set. Like the previous year, the set is entitled "Big Hitters" and is comprised of 19 American League players and 14 from the National League. Fronts have a mounted photo appearance and contain a facsimile autograph. The player's name, team, position, and the Drake's logo also are on front. Backs, other than being numbered 1-33 and containing a Drake's copyright line, are identical to the regular 1982 Topps.

		NM/M
Complete Set (33):		5.00
Common Player:		.25
1	Tony Armas	.25
2	Buddy Bell	.25
3	Johnny Bench	.50
4	George Brett	1.00
5	Bill Buckner	.25
6	Rod Carew	.50
7	Gary Carter	.50
8	Jack Clark	.25
9	Cecil Cooper	.25
10	Jose Cruz	.25
11	Dwight Evans	.25
12	Carlton Fisk	.50
13	George Foster	.25
14	Steve Garvey	.40
15	Kirk Gibson	.25
16	Mike Hargrove	.25
17	George Hendrick	.25
18	Bob Horner	.25
19	Reggie Jackson	.75
20	Terry Kennedy	.25
21	Dave Kingman	.25
22	Greg Luzinski	.25
23	Bill Madlock	.25
24	John Mayberry	.25
25	Eddie Murray	.50
26	Graig Nettles	.25
27	Jim Rice	.40
28	Pete Rose	2.00
29	Mike Schmidt	1.00
30	Ken Singleton	.25
31	Dave Winfield	.50
32	Butch Wynegar	.25
33	Richie Zisk	.25

1983 Drake's

Seventeen American League and 16 National League "Big Hitters" make up the 33-card "3rd Annual Collectors' Edition" set issued by Drake Bakeries in 1983. The Topps-produced cards measure 2-1/2" x 3-1/2". Fronts are somewhat similar in design to the previous year's set. Backs are identical to the 1983 Topps regular issue

except for being numbered 1-33 and containing a Drake's logo and copyright line.

		NM/M
Complete Set (33):		5.00
Common Player:		.25
1	Don Baylor	.25
2	Bill Buckner	.25
3	Rod Carew	.60
4	Gary Carter	.60
5	Jack Clark	.25
6	Cecil Cooper	.25
7	Dwight Evans	.25
8	George Foster	.25
9	Pedro Guerrero	.25
10	George Hendrick	.25
11	Bob Horner	.25
12	Reggie Jackson	.75
13	Steve Kemp	.25
14	Dave Kingman	.25
15	Bill Madlock	.25
16	Gary Matthews	.25
17	Hal McRae	.25
18	Dale Murphy	.40
19	Eddie Murray	.60
20	Ben Oglivie	.25
21	Al Oliver	.25
22	Jim Rice	.40
23	Cal Ripken, Jr.	3.00
24	Pete Rose	2.00
25	Mike Schmidt	1.50
26	Ken Singleton	.25
27	Gorman Thomas	.25
28	Jason Thompson	.25
29	Mookie Wilson	.25
30	Willie Wilson	.25
31	Dave Winfield	.60
32	Carl Yastrzemski	.75
33	Robin Yount	.60

1984 Drake's

For the fourth year in a row, Drake Bakeries issued a 33-card "Big Hitters" set. The 1984 edition, produced again by Topps, includes 17 National League players and 16 from the American League. As in all previous years, card fronts feature the player in a batting pose. Backs are identical to the 1984 Topps regular issue except for being numbered 1-33 and carrying the Drake's logo and copyright line. The cards are the standard 2-1/2" x 3-1/2".

		NM/M
Complete Set (33):		4.00
Common Player:		.25
1	Don Baylor	.25
2	Wade Boggs	.75
3	George Brett	1.00
4	Bill Buckner	.25
5	Rod Carew	.50
6	Gary Carter	.50
7	Ron Cey	.25
8	Cecil Cooper	.25
9	Andre Dawson	.35
10	Steve Garvey	.35
11	Pedro Guerrero	.25
12	George Hendrick	.25
13	Keith Hernandez	.25
14	Bob Horner	.25
15	Reggie Jackson	.75
16	Steve Kemp	.25
17	Ron Kittle	.25
18	Greg Luzinski	.25
19	Fred Lynn	.25
20	Bill Madlock	.25
21	Gary Matthews	.25
22	Dale Murphy	.35
23	Eddie Murray	.50
24	Al Oliver	.25
25	Jim Rice	.25
26	Cal Ripken, Jr.	2.00
27	Pete Rose	1.25
28	Mike Schmidt	1.00
29	Darryl Strawberry	.25
30	Alan Trammell	.25
31	Mookie Wilson	.25
32	Dave Winfield	.50
33	Robin Yount	.50

1985 Drake's

The "5th Annual Collectors' Edition" set produced by Topps for Drake Bakeries consists of 33 "Big Hitters" and 11 "Super Pitchers." The new "Super Pitchers" feature increased the set's size from the usual 33 cards to 44. The 2-1/2" x 3-1/2" cards show the player in a game-action photo. Backs differ from the regular 1985 Topps issue only in that they are numbered 1-44 and carry the Drake's logo.

		NM/M
Complete Set (44):		3.00
Common Player:		.15
1	Tony Armas	.15
2	Harold Baines	.15
3	Don Baylor	.15
4	George Brett	.75
5	Gary Carter	.40
6	Ron Cey	.15
7	Jose Cruz	.15
8	Alvin Davis	.15
9	Chili Davis	.15
10	Dwight Evans	.15
11	Steve Garvey	.25
12	Kirk Gibson	.15
13	Pedro Guerrero	.15
14	Tony Gwynn	.50
15	Keith Hernandez	.15
16	Kent Hrbek	.15
17	Reggie Jackson	.50
18	Gary Matthews	.15
19	Don Mattingly	.75
20	Dale Murphy	.25
21	Eddie Murray	.40
22	Dave Parker	.15
23	Lance Parrish	.15
24	Tim Raines	.15
25	Jim Rice	.25
26	Cal Ripken, Jr.	1.50
27	Juan Samuel	.15
28	Ryne Sandberg	.50
29	Mike Schmidt	.75
30	Darryl Strawberry	.15
31	Alan Trammell	.15
32	Dave Winfield	.40
33	Robin Yount	.40
34	Mike Boddicker	.15
35	Steve Carlton	.40
36	Dwight Gooden	.15
37	Willie Hernandez	.15
38	Mark Langston	.15
39	Dan Quisenberry	.15
40	Dave Righetti	.15
41	Tom Seaver	.40
42	Bob Stanley	.15
43	Rick Sutcliffe	.15
44	Bruce Sutter	.30

1986 Drake's

For the sixth consecutive year, Drake Bakeries issued a baseball card set. The 1986 set was the first in that sequence not produced by Topps. Cards were available only by buying the snack products on whose boxes the cards were printed. Cards, measuring 2-1/2" x 3-1/2", were

issued in either two-, three-, or four-card panels. Fourteen panels, consisting of 37 different players, comprise the set. The players who make up the set are tabbed as either "Big Hitters" or "Super Pitchers." Logos of various Drake's products can be found on the panel backs. The value of the set is higher when collected in either panel or complete box form.

		NM/M
Complete Panel Set (14):		20.00
Complete Singles Set (37):		12.00
Common Panel:		1.00
Common Player:		.25
Panel (1)		.75
1	Gary Carter	.40
2	Dwight Evans	.25
Panel (2)		1.00
3	Reggie Jackson	.50
4	Dave Parker	.25
Panel (3)		1.50
5	Rickey Henderson	.40
6	Pedro Guerrero	.25
Panel (4)		3.00
7	Don Mattingly	.75
8	Mike Marshall	.25
9	Keith Moreland	.25
Panel (5)		4.00
10	Keith Hernandez	.25
11	Cal Ripken Jr.	2.50
Panel (6)		2.50
12	Dale Murphy	.35
13	Jim Rice	.35
Panel (7)		3.00
14	George Brett	.75
15	Tim Raines	.25
Panel (8)		1.50
16	Darryl Strawberry	.25
17	Bill Buckner	.25
Panel (9)		3.00
18	Dave Winfield	.40
19	Ryne Sandberg	.50
20	Steve Balboni	.25
21	Tommy Herr	.25
Panel (10)		3.00
22	Pete Rose	1.50
23	Willie McGee	.25
24	Harold Baines	.25
25	Eddie Murray	.40
Panel (11)		3.00
26	Mike Schmidt	.75
27	Wade Boggs	.50
28	Kirk Gibson	.25
Panel (12)		1.50
29	Bret Saberhagen	.25
30	John Tudor	.25
31	Orel Hershiser	.25
Panel (13)		4.00
32	Ron Guidry	.25
33	Nolan Ryan	2.50
34	Dave Steib	.25
Panel (14)		1.50
35	Dwight Gooden	.25
36	Fernando Valenzuela	.25
37	Tom Browning	.25

1987 Drake's

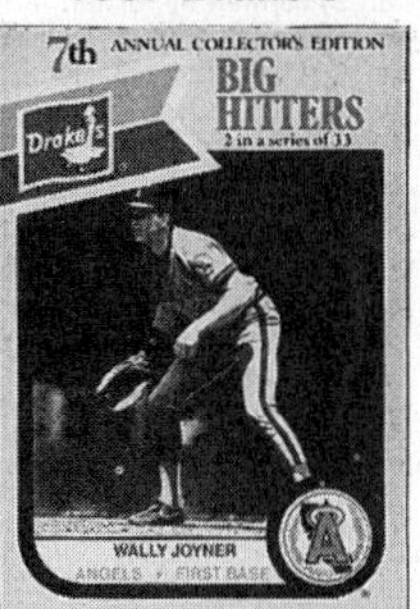

For the seventh consecutive season, Drake Bakeries produced a baseball card set. The 2-1/2" x 3-1/2" cards were printed in either two-, three-, or four-card panels on boxes of various snack products distributed in the eastern U.S. The set is comprised of 33 cards, with 25 players branded as "Big Hitters" and eight as "Super Pitchers." Fronts carry a game-action photo and the Drake's logo surrounded by a brown and yellow border. Backs have the player's complete major league record.

		NM/M
Complete Panel Set (12):		20.00
Complete Singles Set (33):		12.00
Common Panel:		1.50
Common Single Player:		.25
Panel (1)		1.00
1	Darryl Strawberry	.25
2	Wally Joyner	.25
Panel (2)		1.00
3	Von Hayes	.25
4	Jose Canseco	.40
Panel (3)		5.00
5	Dave Winfield	.60
6	Cal Ripken Jr.	2.50
7	Keith Moreland	.25
Panel (4)		2.50
8	Don Mattingly	1.00
9	Willie McGee	.25
Panel (5)		2.00
10	Keith Hernandez	.25
11	Tony Gwynn	.75
Panel (6)		3.00
12	Rickey Henderson	.60
13	Dale Murphy	.35
14	George Brett	1.00
15	Jim Rice	.35
Panel (7)		5.00
16	Wade Boggs	.75
17	Kevin Bass	.25
18	Dave Parker	.25
19	Kirby Puckett	.75
Panel (8)		2.00
20	Gary Carter	.60
21	Ryne Sandberg	.75
22	Harold Baines	.25
Panel (9)		3.00
23	Mike Schmidt	1.00
24	Eddie Murray	.60
25	Steve Sax	.25
Panel (10)		1.00
26	Dwight Gooden	.25
27	Jack Morris	.25
Panel (11)		.75
28	Ron Darling	.25
29	Fernando Valenzuela	.25
30	John Tudor	.25
Panel (12)		7.50
31	Roger Clemens	1.00
32	Nolan Ryan	2.50
33	Mike Scott	.25

1988 Drake's

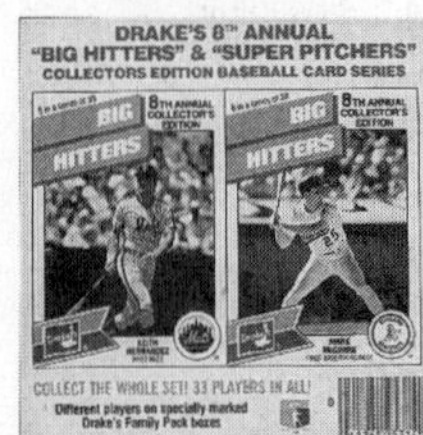

The 8th annual edition of this set includes 33 glossy full-color cards printed on cut-out panels of two, three of four cards on Drake's dessert snack boxes. Card fronts have white borders with a large red and blue "Super Pitchers" (6 cards) or "Big Hitters" (27 cards) caption upper-left, beside the "8th Annual Collector's Edition" label. Backs are printed in black and include the card number, personal data, batting/pitching record and sponsor logos.

		NM/M
Complete Panel Set (12):		20.00
Complete Singles Set (33):		10.00
Common Panel:		1.50
Common Player:		.25
Panel (1)		2.00
1	Don Mattingly	1.00
2	Tim Raines	.25
Panel (2)		1.00
3	Darryl Strawberry	.25
4	Wade Boggs	.75
Panel (3)		6.00
5	Keith Hernandez	.25
6	Mark McGwire	1.50
Panel (4)		3.00
7	Rickey Henderson	.60
8	Mike Schmidt	1.00
9	Dwight Evans	.25
Panel (5)		2.00
10	Gary Carter	.60
11	Paul Molitor	.60
Panel (6)		3.50
12	Dave Winfield	.60
13	Alan Trammell	.25
14	Tony Gwynn	.75
Panel (7)		2.50
15	Dale Murphy	.35
16	Andre Dawson	.35
17	Von Hayes	.25
18	Willie Randolph	.25
Panel (8)		3.50
19	Kirby Puckett	.75
20	Juan Samuel	.25
21	Eddie Murray	.60
Panel (9)		1.00
22	George Bell	.25
23	Larry Sheets	.25
24	Eric Davis	.25
Panel (10)		5.00
25	Cal Ripken Jr.	2.00
26	Pedro Guerrero	.25
27	Will Clark	.25
Panel (11)		1.00
28	Dwight Gooden	.25
29	Frank Viola	.25
Panel (12)		3.00
30	Roger Clemens	1.00
31	Rick Sutcliffe	.25
32	Jack Morris	.25
33	John Tudor	.25

1989 Dubuque Braves

Given away at Sunday home games to correspond with player appearances at a stadium autograph booth, these 2-3/8" x 3-1/2" cards were sponsored by the Braves hot dog concessionaire, Dubuque Meats. Cards have player photos centered within a dark blue border. A Braves cap is at upper-left, the hot dog company's logo at lower-left. The player's name, team and position are in white. Backs, printed in black on white, have the Braves logo, a few personal facts and figures and previous year/career stats. Because only 15,000 of each card were distributed over the course of the season, compilation of complete sets is extremely challenging. The checklist here is arranged in alphabetical order.

		NM/M
Complete Set (33):		40.00
Common Player:		.50
(1)	Paul Assenmacher	.50
(2)	Jim Acker	.50
(3)	Jose Alvarez	.50
(4)	Bruce Benedict	.50
(5)	Geronimo Berroa/SP	8.00
(6)	Jeff Blauser	.50
(7)	Joe Boever	.50
(8)	Marty Clary	.50
(9)	Bruce dal Canton	.50
(10)	Jody Davis	.50
(11)	Mark Eichhorn	.50
(12)	Ron Gant	1.50
(13)	Tom Glavine	5.00
(14)	Tommy Gregg	.50
(15)	Dion James/SP	4.00
(16)	Clarence Jones	.50
(17)	Derek Lilliquist	.50
(18)	Roy Majtyka	.50
(19)	Oddibe McDowell	.50
(20)	Dale Murphy	6.00
(21)	Russ Nixon	.50
(22)	Gerald Perry	.50
(23)	John Russell	.50
(24)	Lonnie Smith	.50
(25)	Pete Smith	.50
(26)	Zane Smith	.50
(27)	John Smoltz	4.00
(28)	Brian Snitker	.50
(29)	Andres Thomas	.50
(30)	Jeff Treadway	.50
(31)	Jeff Wetherby	.50
(32)	Ed Whited	.50
(33)	Bobby Wine	.50

1990 Dubuque Braves

For a second season, the Braves' hot dog vendor, Dubuque Meats, sponsored this season-long promotion. Up to four different player cards were given out at Sunday home games, corresponding with player appearances at an autograph booth. Some player cards were distributed more than once, while others, such as Dale Murphy, who was traded, were only given out one day. Players were added to the set right up through the final Sunday home game of the season. Complete sets are extremely difficult to assemble. The player photo on these 2-3/8" x 3-1/2" cards have a white border. A red banner beneath the photo has the player's name, uniform number and position printed in black. Backs are printed in dark blue and feature full minor and major league stats. The checklist here is arranged alphabetically.

		NM/M
Complete Set (35):		25.00
Common Player:		.50
(1)	Steve Avery	.50
(2)	Jeff Blauser	.50
(3)	Joe Boever	.50
(4)	Francisco Cabrera	.50
(5)	Pat Corrales	.50
(6)	Bobby Cox	.50
(7)	Nick Esasky	.50
(8)	Ron Gant	1.50
(9)	Tom Glavine	4.00
(10)	Mark Grant	.50
(11)	Tommy Gregg	.50
(12)	Dwayne Henry	.50
(13)	Alexis Infante	.50
(14)	Clarence Jones	.50
(15)	Dave Justice	4.50
(16)	Jimmy Kremers	.50
(17)	Charlie Leibrandt	.50
(18)	Mark Lemke	.50
(19)	Roy Majtyka	.50
(20)	Leo Mazzone	.50
(21)	Oddibe McDowell	.50
(22)	Dale Murphy	5.00
(23)	Phil Niekro	3.00
(24)	Greg Olson	.50
(25)	Jim Presley	.50
(26)	Lonnie Smith	.50
(27)	Pete Smith	.50
(28)	John Smoltz	1.50
(29)	Brian Snitker	.50
(30)	Andres Thomas	.50
(31)	Jeff Treadway	.50
(32)	Ernie Whitt	.50
(33)	Jimy Williams	.50
(34)	Homer the Brave (Mascot)	.50
(35)	Rally (Mascot)	.50

Team Photo Set

This three-panel team set was given away at an early-season game, commemorating the Braves 25th season in Atlanta. The sheet measures 11" x 28-1/2". The top panel is a team photo. The two lower panels contain 30 individual cards, 2-1/2" x 3-1/4", perforated to allow them to be separated. Backs are printed in red and blue. The perforated team set is much more common than the Dubuque cards given out a few at a time during Sunday home games. The checklist below is arranged according to uniform numbers which appear on the front of each card.

		NM/M
Complete Panel:		9.00
Common Player:		.25
1	Oddibe McDowell	.25
2	Russ Nixon	.25
3	Dale Murphy	3.00
4	Jeff Blauser	.25
5	Ron Gant	.50
10	Greg Olson	.25
12	Ernie Whitt	.25
14	Andres Thomas	.25
15	Jeff Treadway	.25
16	Tommy Gregg	.25
17	Nick Esasky	.25
18	Jim Presley	.25
19	Francisco Cabrera	.25
20	Mark Lemke	.25
23	Dave Justice	2.00
24	Derek Lilliquist	.25
25	Pete Smith	.25
27	Lonnie Smith	.25
29	John Smoltz	1.00
30	Mike Stanton	.25
36	Tony Castillo	.25
37	Joe Boever	.25
40	Charlie Kerfeld	.25
45	Charlie Leibrandt	.25
46	Dwayne Henry	.25
47	Tom Glavine	1.50
48	Marty Clary	.25
49	Rick Luecken	.25
58a	Joe Hesketh	.25
58b	Alexis Infante	.25

1991 Dubuque Braves

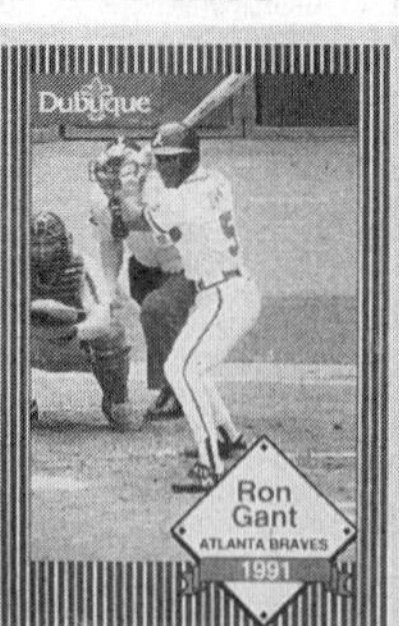

At each Sunday home game the Braves distributed some 15,000 of each of three to six player cards to kids under 14. The cards corresponded to appearances by those players at an autograph session. That method of distribution makes accumulation of complete sets very difficult. Sponsor of the set for the third straight year was the stadium's hot dog concessionaire, Dubuque Meats. Their logo appears in the upper-left corner of the player photo. At lower-right on the 2-1/4" x 3-1/2" cards is a baseball diamond figure with the team and player name and the year of issue. There is a white outer border on the card, with the photo framed in white-pinstriped dark blue. Backs are printed in dark blue, with logos, complete stats, biographical information and the player's uniform number. Cards are checklisted here in alphabetical order.

		NM/M
Complete Set (41):		25.00
Common Player:		.50
(1)	Steve Avery	.50
(2)	Jim Beauchamp	.50
(3)	Mike Bell	.50
(4)	Rafael Belliard	.50
(5)	Juan Berenguer	.50
(6)	Jeff Blauser	.50
(7)	Sid Bream	.50
(8)	Francisco Cabrera	.50
(9)	Jim Clancy	.50
(10)	Pat Corrales	.50
(11)	Bobby Cox	.50
(12)	Nick Esasky	.50
(13)	Marvin Freeman	.50
(14)	Ron Gant	1.00
(15)	Tom Glavine	3.00
(16)	Mark Grant	.50
(17)	Tommy Gregg	.50
(18)	Mike Heath	.50
(19)	Brian Hunter	.50
(20)	Clarence Jones	.50
(21)	David Justice	2.00
(22)	Charlie Leibrandt	.50
(23)	Mark Lemke	.50
(24)	Leo Mazzone	.50
(25)	Kent Mercker	.50
(26)	Keith Mitchell	.50
(27)	Otis Nixon	.50
(28)	Greg Olson	.50
(29)	Jeff Parrett	.50
(30)	Terry Pendleton	.50
(31)	Armando Reynoso	.50
(32)	Deion Sanders	3.00
(33)	Lonnie Smith	.50
(34)	Pete Smith	.50
(35)	John Smoltz	1.50
(36)	Mike Stanton	.50
(37)	Jeff Treadway	.50
(38)	Jimy Williams	.50
(39)	Ned Yost	.50
(40)	Homer the Brave (Mascot)	.50
(41)	Rally (Mascot)	.50

Team Photo Set

This team photo/player card triptych was an early season give-away. Each of the three fold-out panels measures about 9-1/2" x 10-1/2". The 30 individual player cards have perforated edges for easy removal from the sheet. The 2-1/8" x 3-1/8" cards have a player portrait photo at center, with blue diamond designs at the corners. A red box below the photo has the player's name and uniform number. Blue Braves and Dubuque logos appear at the lower corners of the white border. Backs are printed in red and blue and include full stats and a facsimile autograph, plus a few biographical details. The team sheet cards are considered much more common than the other Braves baseball card promotional giveaways, especially in complete sets. Cards are checklisted here alphabetically.

		NM/M
Complete Panel:		15.00
Common Player:		.50
(1)	Steve Avery	.50
(2)	Rafael Belliard	.50
(3)	Juan Berenguer	.50
(4)	Jeff Blauser	.50
(5)	Sid Bream	.50
(6)	Francisco Cabrera	.50
(7)	Bobby Cox	.50
(8)	Nick Esasky	.50
(9)	Marvin Freeman	.50
(10)	Ron Gant	.75
(11)	Tom Glavine	3.00
(12)	Mark Grant	.50
(13)	Tommy Gregg	.50
(14)	Mike Heath	.50
(15)	Danny Heep	.50
(16)	David Justice	2.00
(17)	Charlie Leibrandt	.50
(18)	Mark Lemke	.50
(19)	Kent Mercker	.50
(20)	Otis Nixon	.50
(21)	Greg Olson	.50
(22)	Jeff Parrett	.50
(23)	Terry Pendleton	.50
(24)	Deion Sanders	2.00
(25)	Doug Sisk	.50
(26)	Lonnie Smith	.50
(27)	Pete Smith	.50
(28)	John Smoltz	1.50
(29)	Mike Stanton	.50
(30)	Jeff Treadway	.50

1992 Dunkin' Donuts Red Sox

The 1992 Boston Red Sox were the subject of a set of 30 cards, including the manager and coaches. Co-sponsored by Dunkin Donuts and WVIT-TV and released in May in Connecticut, the set was sold as an uncut, perforated sheet of 30 cards, measuring about 9-1/2" x 10-3/4". Individual perforated cards could be removed from the sheet; they measure 2-1/8" x 3-1/8". Fronts have a player photo framed in black on a white background. In the border beneath the photo are the player's name, position, uniform number and sponsors' logos. Backs have complete major and minor league stats. The cards are checklisted here by uniform number, which appears on the card front.

		NM/M
Complete Panel:		7.50
Common Player:		.25
2	Luis Rivera	.25
3	Jody Reed	.25
6	Tony Pena	.25
7	Rick Burleson	.25
11	Tim Naehring	.25
12	Ellis Burks	.25
16	Frank Viola	.25
17	Butch Hobson	.25
18	Carlos Quintana	.25
20	John Marzano	.25
21	Roger Clemens	6.00
23	Tom Brunansky	.25
25	Jack Clark	.25
26	Wade Boggs	3.00
27	Greg Harris	.25
29	Phil Plantier	.25
30	Matt Young	.25
32	Gary Allenson	.25
34	Don Zimmer	.25
35	Rich Gale	.25
37	Al Bumbry	.25
39	Mike Greenwell	.25
41	Jeff Reardon	.25
42	Mo Vaughn	.35
43	Kevin Morton	.25
44	Danny Darwin	.25
47	Mike Gardiner	.25
48	Tony Fossas	.25
50	Tom Bolton	.25
55	Joe Hesketh	.25

1993 Duracell Power Players

The Duracell battery company issued a 48-card set in 1993 that was presented in two 24-card series. The cards were available through the mail with proofs of purchase from selected Duracell products. Cards feature a Duracell logo at top, with a black and orange border surrounding a color photo of the player. The player's name is printed in yellow with team and position in white on top of a green background. Because the set was not licensed to use major league uniform logos, they were airbrushed off the photos. Backs have a player portrait photo, a facsimile autograph, recent stats and a few biographical and career details printed over a ballpark scene. Series I cards are number "X of 24;" Series II cards are so indicated beneath the card number.

		NM/M
Complete Set (48):		4.00
Common Player:		.10
Series 1		2.00
1	Roger Clemens	.60
2	Frank Thomas	.40
3	Andre Dawson	.25
4	Orel Hershiser	.10
5	Kirby Puckett	.50
6	Edgar Martinez	.10
7	Craig Biggio	.10
8	Terry Pendleton	.10
9	Mark McGwire	.75
10	Dave Stewart	.10
11	Ozzie Smith	.50
12	Doug Drabek	.10
13	Dwight Gooden	.10
14	Tony Gwynn	.50
15	Carlos Baerga	.10
16	Robin Yount	.40
17	Barry Bonds	1.00
18	Bip Roberts	.10
19	Don Mattingly	.60
20	Nolan Ryan	1.00
21	Tom Glavine	.25
22	Will Clark	.10
23	Cecil Fielder	.10
24	Dave Winfield	.40
Series 2		2.00
1	Cal Ripken, Jr.	1.00
2	Melido Perez	.10
3	John Kruk	.10
4	Charlie Hayes	.10
5	George Brett	.60
6	Ruben Sierra	.10
7	Deion Sanders	.15
8	Andy Van Slyke	.10
9	Fred McGriff	.10
10	Benito Santiago	.10
11	Charles Nagy	.10
12	Greg Maddux	.50
13	Ryne Sandberg	.50
14	Dennis Martinez	.10
15	Ken Griffey Jr.	.75
16	Jim Abbott	.10
17	Barry Larkin	.10
18	Gary Sheffield	.30
19	Jose Canseco	.25
20	Jack McDowell	.10
21	Darryl Strawberry	.10
22	Delino DeShields	.10
23	Dennis Eckersley	.40
24	Paul Molitor	.40

E

2003 Easton Gloves

A set of standard-format cards featuring members of the Easton Advisory Staff was issued as a premium for the purchase of youth model baseball gloves. The cards were distributed in four-card cello packs. Fronts have black borders, game-action photos, a facimile autograph, player identification and Easton logos. Backs have a smaller photo, personal data and recent stats.

		NM/M
Complete Set (12):		20.00
Common Player:		2.00
1	Bobby Abreu	2.00
2	Luis Castillo	2.00
3	Eric Chavez	2.00
4	Eric Gagne	2.00
5	Luis Gonzalez	2.00
6	Eddie Guardado	2.00
7	Jeff Kent	2.00
8	Javy Lopez	2.00
9	John Olerud	2.00
10	Vicente Padilla	2.00
11	Sammy Sosa	7.50
12	Mike Williams	2.00

2005 Easton Gloves

A set of standard-format cards featuring members of the Easton Advisory Staff was issued as a premium for the purchase of youth model baseball gloves. Card fronts have game-action photos, a facimile autograph and player identification. Backs have a smaller photo, personal data and recent stats.

		NM/M
Complete Set (12):		8.00
Common Player:		1.00
1	Sammy Sosa	2.50
2	Orlando Cabrera	1.00
3	Eric Chavez	1.00
4	Luis Gonzalez	1.00
5	Jeff Kent	1.00
6	Javy Lopez	1.00
7	Aramis Ramirez	1.00
8	Edgar Renteria	1.00
9	Luis Castillo	1.00
10	Eric Gagne	1.00
11	Michael Barrett	1.00
12	Bobby Abreu	1.00

1990 Eclipse Stars of the Negro Leagues

Better known in the field of comic books than baseball cards, Eclipse of California produced this set of cards honoring stars of the defunct Negro Leagues. The 2-1/2" x 3-1/2" cards have water color paintings (by Mark Chiarello) of the players on front. Well-written (by Jack Morelli) career summaries on back give a real flavor for this brand of pro ball and its era. Copyright

lines for all parties are at bottom back. The issue was sold only as a boxed set.

		NM/M
Complete Set (36):		16.00
Common Player:		.50
1	Header Card	.25
2a	Josh Gibson (Wrong picture, "H" on cap.)	4.00
2b	Josh Gibson (Correct picture, "G" on cap.)	4.00
3	Cannonball Redding	.50
4	Biz Mackey	2.00
5	Pop Lloyd	1.00
6	Bingo DeMoss	1.00
7	Willard Brown	2.00
8	John Donaldson	.50
9	Monte Irvin	1.50
10	Ben Taylor	2.00
11	Willie Wells	1.25
12	Dave Brown	.50
13	Leon Day	1.00
14	Ray Dandridge	1.00
15	Turkey Stearnes	1.00
16	Rube Foster	1.00
17	Oliver Marcelle	.50
18	Judy Johnson	1.00
19	Christobel Torrienti	2.00
20	Satchel Paige	4.00
21	Mule Suttles	2.00
22	John Beckwith	.50
23	Martin Dihigo	1.00
24	Willie Foster	.50
25	Dick Lundy	.50
26	Buck Leonard	1.00
27	Smokey Joe Williams	1.00
28	Cool Papa Bell	1.00
29	Bullet Rogan	1.00
30	Newt Allen	.75
31	Bruce Petway	.50
32	Jose Mendez	2.00
33	Louis Santop	2.00
34	Jud Wilson	2.00
35	Sammy Hughes	.50
36a	Oscar Charleston (Wrong picture, "G" on cap.)	1.00
36b	Oscar Charleston (Correct picture, "H" on cap.)	1.00

1992 Eclipse Negro League BPA - Paul Lee

Four Negro League baseball cards were handed out to the first 50,000 fans attending Negro League Baseball Players Association night at Shea Stadium on June 2. Cards feature the artwork of Paul Lee on front. Backs have a career summary and biographical details, along with the Mets and Eclipse logos.

		NM/M
Complete Set (4):		4.00
Common Player:		1.50
1	Monte Irvin	1.50
2	"Buck" Leonard	1.00
3	Josh Gibson	3.00
4	Ray Dandridge	1.00

1992 Eclipse Negro League BPA - John Clapp

Sponsored by Kraft, and produced by Eclipse, 15,000 sets of these cards were made for distribution at The Negro League Baseball Players Association night, August 9 at Lackawanna County Stadium, home of the Scranton Wilkes-Barre Red Barons. The 2-1/2" x 3-1/2" cards have watercolor player pictures on front, by artist John Clapp. Backs have career summaries, sponsor and issuer logos and copyright information.

		NM/M
Complete Set (18):		6.00
Common Player:		.50
1	Leon Day	1.50
2	Clinton (Casey) Jones	.50
3	Lester Lockett	.50
4	Monte Irvin	2.00
5	Armando Vazquez	.50
6	Jimmie Crutchfield	.50
7	Ted Radcliffe	.50
8	Albert Haywood	.50
9	Artie Wilson	1.50
10	Sam Jethroe	1.25
11	Edsall Walker	.50
12	Bill Wright	.50
13	Jim Cohen	.50
14	Andy Porter	.50
15	Tommy Sampson	.50
16	Buck Leonard	1.50
17	Josh Gibson	2.00
18	Martinez Jackson	1.50

1990 Elite Senior League

This 126-card set features the players of the first Senior League season. Cards are printed on high quality stock with full-color photos. The card backs feature statistics. Earl Weaver and Mike Easler cards were distributed as promo cards. Original retail price was about $12 per boxed set, the only manner of distribution.

		NM/M
Complete Set (126):		4.00
Common Player:		.05
1	Curt Flood	.15
2	Bob Tolan	.05
3	Dick Bosman	.05
4	Ivan DeJesus	.05
5	Dock Ellis	.05
6	Roy Howell	.05
7	Lamar Johnson	.05
8	Steve Kemp	.05
9	Ken Landreaux	.05
10	Randy Lerch	.05
11	Jon Matlack	.05
12	Gary Rajsich	.05
13	Lenny Randle	.05
14	Elias Sosa	.05
15	Ozzie Virgil	.05
16	Milt Wilcox	.05
17	Steve Henderson	.05
18	Ray Burris	.05
19	Mike Easler	.05
20	Juan Eichelberger	.05
21	Rollie Fingers	.50
22	Toby Harrah	.05
23	Randy Johnson	.05
24	Dave Kingman	.15
25	Lee Lacy	.05
26	Tito Landrum	.05
27	Paul Mirabella	.05
28	Mickey Rivers	.10
29	Rodney Scott	.05
30	Tim Stoddard	.05
31	Ron Washington	.05
32	Jerry White	.05
33	Dick Williams	.05
34	Clete Boyer	.10
35	Steve Dillard	.05
36	Garth Iorg	.05
37	Bruce Kison	.05
38	Wayne Krenchicki	.05
39	Ron LeFlore	.10
40	Tippy Martinez	.05
41	Omar Moreno	.05
42	Jim Morrison	.05
43	Graig Nettles	.15
44	Jim Nettles	.05
45	Wayne Nordhagen	.05
46	Al Oliver	.15
47	Jerry Royster	.05
48	Sammy Stewart	.05
49	Randy Bass	.05
50	Vida Blue	.10
51	Bruce Bochy	.05
52	Doug Corbett	.05
53	Jose Cruz	.05
54	Jamie Easterly	.05
55	Pete Falcone	.05
56	Bob Galasso	.05
57	Johnny Grubb	.05
58	Bake McBride	.05
59	Dyar Miller	.05
60	Tom Paciorek	.05
61	Ken Reitz	.05
62	U.L. Washington	.05
63	Alan Ashby	.05
64	Pat Dobson	.05
65	Doug Bird	.05
66	Marty Castillo	.05
67	Dan Driessen	.05
68	Wayne Garland	.05
69	Tim Ireland	.05
70	Ron Jackson	.05
71	Bobby Jones	.05
72	Dennis Leonard	.05
73	Rick Manning	.05
74	Amos Otis	.05
75	Pat Putnam	.05
76	Eric Rasmussen	.05
77	Paul Blair	.05
78	Bert Campaneris	.05
79	Cesar Cedeno	.10
80	Ed Figueroa	.05
81	Ross Grimsley	.05
82	George Hendrick	.05
83	Cliff Johnson	.05
84	Mike Kekich	.05
85	Rafael Landestoy	.05
86	Larry Milbourne	.05
87	Bobby Molinaro	.05
88	Sid Monge	.05
89	Rennie Stennett	.05
90	Derrell Thomas	.05
91	Earl Weaver	.30
92	Gary Allenson	.05
93	Pedro Borbon	.05
94	Al Bumbry	.05
95	Bill Campbell	.05
96	Bernie Carbo	.05
97	Ferguson Jenkins	.50
98	Pete LaCock	.05
99	Bill Lee	.05
100	Tommy McMillan	.05
101	Joe Pittman	.05
102	Gene Richards	.05
103	Leon Roberts	.05
104	Tony Scott	.05
105	Doug Simunic	.05
106	Rick Wise	.05
107	Willie Aikens	.05
108	Juan Beniquez	.05
109	Bobby Bonds	.10
110	Sergio Ferrer	.05
111	Chuck Ficks	.05
112	George Foster	.10
113	Dave Hilton	.05
114	Al Holland	.05
115	Clint Hurdle	.05
116	Bill Madlock	.10
117	Steve Ontiveros	.05
118	Roy Thomas	.05
119	Luis Tiant	.10
120	Walt Williams	.05
121	Vida Blue	.10
122	Bobby Bonds	.10
123	Rollie Fingers	.50
124	George Foster	.10
125	Fergie Jenkins	.50
126	Dave Kingman	.10

2003 El Nueva Dia Montreal Expos

To commemorate the series played by the Expos in Puerto Rico, a local newspaper

El Nuevo Día

En la Isla Sosa con los Cachorros

Gran expectativa en la fanaticada boricua ante la presencia del estelar bateador

sponsored this set given away to fans at Hiram Bithorn Stadium on September 11 at the final San Juan "home" game. The cello-wrapped set has nine colorful 4-3/4" x 5-5/8" blank-back cards arranged like a newspaper page. At top is the sponsor's logo and the logo created for the historic series of games throughout the 2003 season. At bottom are one or two color photos with captions. In between are a headline and story summary about one of the series. All text is in Spanish. Each player named or prominently pictured on the card is listed.

		NM/M
Complete Set (9):		12.50
Common Card:		.60
1	Montreal pisa el 'home' (Jose Vidro, Wilfredo Cordero, Mark Grudzielanek)	1.25
2	Ovacion a Robero Alomar (Roberto Alomar)	2.50
3	Abuso casero de los Expos (Javier Vazquez, Javier Lopez, Marcus Giles)	1.25
4	Javy Lopez carga a los Bravos (Henry Mateo, Rocky Biddle, Javy Lopez, Andruw Jones)	.60
5	Reaccion por todo lo alto (Javier Vazquez, Brian Schneider)	1.25
6	Recibe el Bithorn a los campeones (Bengie Molina, Jose Molina)	.60
7	Puerto Rico (Juan Gonzalez)	2.50
8	Card' (Dontrelle Willis, Ivan Rodriguez, Braden Looper)	1.25
9	En la Isla Sosa con los Cachorros (Sammy Sosa)	5.00

1983 English's Chicken Baltimore Orioles Lids

The World Champion O's were featured on this set of fried chicken bucket lids. Printed on thick cardboard discs with the blank backs heavily waxed, the lids come in two sizes, 8-3/8" diameter and 7-1/4". The design is the same on each, with a black, white and orange player portrait at center, flanked by some personal data and '83 stats. His name is in orange below, with his position and team in black beneath that. In the wide orange border is "English's Salutes / 1983 Champions". The player's union logo is at right of the portrait, but cap logos are missing because the issue was not licensed through MLB. The lids are not numbered.

		NM/M
Complete Set (13):		45.00
Common Player:		2.00
(1)	Mike Boddicker	2.00
(2)	Rich Dauer	2.00
(3)	Storm Davis	2.00
(4)	Mike Flanagan	2.00
(5)	John Lowenstein	2.00
(6)	Tippy Martinez	2.00
(7)	Gary Roenicke	2.00
(8)	Ken Singleton	2.00
(9)	Rick Dempsey	2.00
(10)	Scott McGregor	2.00
(11)	Eddie Murray	6.00
(12)	Jim Palmer	6.00
(13)	Cal Ripken, Jr.	30.00

1991 Enor Kevin Maas Story

This 20-card set was produced by one of the hobby's leading manufacturers of plastic supplies. Not surprisingly, the set was housed in a 6" x 8-1/4" plastic album with eight four-card plastic sheets inside. Besides the cards and album, the set came with a biographical brochure on the 1990 A.L. Rookie of the Year runner-up. Each of the 2-1/2" x 3-1/2" cards features one or more color photos of the player on front. A series of red stripes at the top of the card features the player's name in the uppermost stripe. Backs have the same stripe motif at top and include career information or stats at center. The logos of MLB, the Yankees and Enor appear at the bottom.

	NM/M
Complete Set w/Album (20):	4.00
Single Card:	.10

1981 Family Fun Centers Padres

Six Padres players or staff are featured on these 13" x 10" coupon sheets. At the right end of each glossy paper sheet is a group of coupons and advertising for the recreation centers, printed in black, yellow and green. At left are six photos. Each of the 3" x 4" photos has a color player pose. At either top or bottom, depending on placement on the sheet, is the player name in black, "FAMILY FUN CENTER" in green and a red building logo. Backs are blank and the sheets are not perforated.

		NM/M
Complete Set (5):		110.00
Common Sheet:		10.00
(1)	Randy Bass, Frank Howard, Gary Lucas, Gene Richards, Ozzie Smith, Jerry Turner	60.00
(2)	Kurt Bevacqua, Dave Cash, Paul Dade, Rollie Fingers, Don Williams, Dave Winfield	25.00
(3)	Dan Boone, Chuck Estrada, Joe Lefebvre, Tim Lollar, Ed Stevens, Steve Swisher	10.00
(4)	John Curtis, Barry Evans, Tim Flannery, Terry Kennedy, Steve Mura, Bob Tolan	10.00
(5)	Von Joshua, Fred Kendall, Dennis Kinney, Jerry Mumphrey, Steve Mura, Dick Phillips	10.00

1994 FanFest Roberto Clemente Commemorative

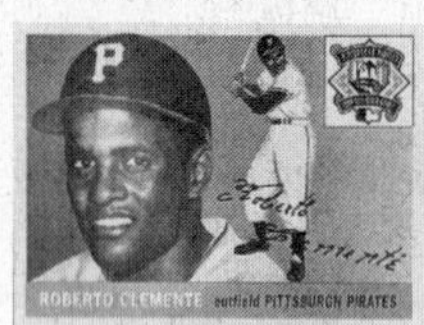

In an unprecdented show of co-operation, the five Major League Baseball trading card licensees created this set of Roberto Clemente commemorative cards for distribution at the All-Star Fan Fest. Cards were available at participating manufacturers' booths, making complete sets somewhat difficult to assemble. Topps an Fleer based their commemorative cards on their companies' respective 1955 and 1963 Clemente cards. Donruss had artist Dick Perez create a Diamond King card of Clemente, while Upper Deck and Score Select created new designs. It is believed fewer than 10,000 of each card exist.

		NM/M
Complete Set (5):		30.00
Common Card:		6.00
1	Roberto Clemente (Donruss Diamond King)	6.00
2	Roberto Clemente (Fleer 1963 reprint)	6.00
3	Roberto Clemente (Score Select)	6.00
4	Roberto Clemente (Topps 1955 reprint)	10.00
5	Roberto Clemente (Upper Deck)	6.00

1995 FanFest Nolan Ryan Commemorative

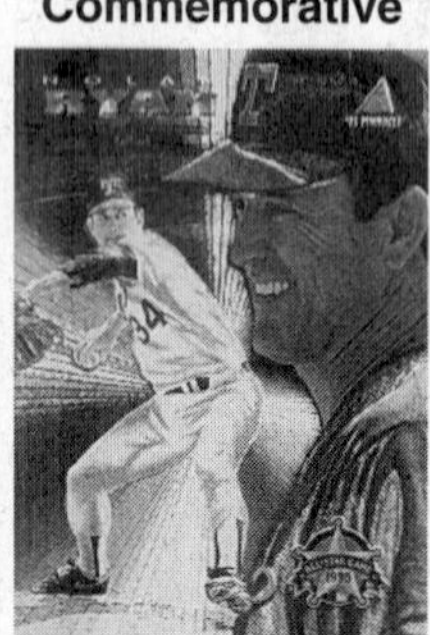

At the July 7-11,1995, FanFest, held in Dallas, Texas, site of the All-Star Game, five of Major League Baseball's principal licensees combined on a wrapper redemption program which offered Nolan Ryan Tribute cards. With 3,000 of the cards pegged as each day's maximum giveaway, only 15,000 total sets were available. Most of the companies opted for gold-leaf and/or foil-print extravaganzas, while Topps chose to recreate a single-player 1968-style Nolan Ryan rookie card with full career stats on back.

		NM/M
Complete Set (5):		16.00
Common Card:		4.00
1	Nolan Ryan (Upper Deck)	4.00
2	Nolan Ryan (Topps)	4.50
3	Nolan Ryan (Pinnacle)	4.00
4	Nolan Ryan (Fleer Ultra)	4.00
5	Nolan Ryan (Donruss)	4.00

1996 FanFest Steve Carlton Commemorative

Philadelphia's most famous Lefty (before Rocky Balboa) was chosen as the subject of the '96 All-Star FanFest multi-company card tribute. Each of the five largest baseball card licensees produced a Carlton card for use in a wrapper redemption promotion at the annual show. Each of the cards featured the Liberty Bell All-Star Game logo along with such bells and whistles as embossing, metallic-foil highlights, etc.

		NM/M
Complete Set (5):		12.50
Common Card:		3.00
1	Steve Carlton (Donruss)	3.00
2	Steve Carlton (Fleer Ultra)	3.00
3	Steve Carlton (Pinnacle)	3.00
4	Steve Carlton (Topps)	4.00
5	Steve Carlton (Upper Deck)	3.00

1997 FanFest Jackie Robinson Commemorative

In conjunction with FanFest in Cleveland, July 4-8, preceding the All-Star Game, five of the major card companies combined to create a card set honoring Jackie Robinson. Each company made its card available at the show in a wrapper redemption exchange. In most cases the tribute cards showcased the respective companies' technical expertise. Production of each card was limited to 15,000.

		NM/M
Complete Set (5):		12.00
Common Card:		2.50
1	Jackie Robinson (Pinnacle Dufex)	2.50
2	Jackie Robinson (Topps Finest '52 reprint)	3.00
3	Jackie Robinson (Upper Deck)	2.50
4	Jackie Robinson (Donruss - 1948 Leaf reprint)	2.50
5	Jackie Robinson (Fleer)	2.50

1998 FanFest Lou Brock Commemorative

In the years before the Rockies joined the National League, Denver's "home team" was the St. Louis Cardinals. One of that team's greatest players of the 1960s and 1970s, Hall of Famer Lou Brock, was selected to be honored in the annual All-Star FanFest commemorative series used by the card companies as a wrapper redemption premium (five wrappers for each card). Card fronts include the All-Star Game logo, backs have the Cooperstown Collection logo. Topps' card is a chromium version reproduction of Brock's 1962 rookie card, which depicts him as a Cub.

		NM/M
Complete Set (5):		3.00
Common Card:		.50
1	Lou Brock (Topps)	2.00
2	Lou Brock (Pinnacle)	1.00
3	Lou Brock (Fleer)	.50
4	Lou Brock (Donruss DK)	1.00
5	Lou Brock (Upper Deck)	.50

1999 FanFest Carl Yastrzemski Commemorative

One of the modern Red Sox most popular players of the of the 1960s-1980s, Hall of Famer Carl Yastrzemski, was selected to be honored in the 1999 Boston All-Star FanFest commemorative series used by the card companies as a wrapper redemption premium (five wrappers for each card). Card fronts include the All-Star Game logo.

		NM/M
Complete Set (4):		7.50
Common Card:		2.00
1	Carl Yastrzemski (Topps)	2.75
2	Carl Yastrzemski (Ultra)	2.00
3	Carl Yastrzemski (Upper Deck)	2.00
4	Carl Yastrzemski (Pacific)	2.00

2000 FanFest Hank Aaron Commemorative

As in past years, each of Major League Baseball's major card licensees produced a special card in conjunction with FanFest in Atlanta prior to the All-Star Game. Visitors to the Collector's Showcase area of FanFest could obtain one card from each company's booth via a wrapper redemption.

		NM/M
Complete Set (4):		7.50
Common Card:		2.50
1	Hank Aaron (Topps)	2.50
2	Hank Aaron (Fleer)	2.50
3	Hank Aaron (Upper Deck)	2.50
4	Hank Aaron (Pacific)	2.50

2000 FanFest Hank Aaron Rookie Reprint

It has been reported that Topps originally intended to use this rookie reprint as its redemption card at FanFest, but later switched to a version of the Aaron card which appeared in 2000 Topps. It is said the rookie version was only distributed to a few of the vendors. Like the other cards in the redemption program, the '54 Topps reprint has the event logo on front. It is numbered "1 of 4" on back.

		NM/M
1	Hank Aaron (1954 Topps reprint)	4.00

2001 FanFest Seattle Mariners

A multi-manufacturer wrapper-redemption promotion at the July 6-10 All-Star FanFest in Seattle allowed collectors to acquire a special set of nine cards featuring current and former M's stars. Cards were generally available by visiting the booth of each manufacturer and opening five packs of that company's 2001 baseball cards. Original artwork, and metallic-foil

highlights were featured on some cards. Production was 10,000 of each card.

		NM/M
Complete Set (9):		20.00
Common Player:		2.00
1	Ken Griffey Jr. (Upper Deck)	4.00
2	Alex Rodriguez (Donruss Diamond Kings)	5.00
3	Ichiro Suzuki (Fleer)	7.50
4	Edgar Martinez (Topps Gallery)	2.00
5	John Olerud (Topps Gallery)	2.00
6	Jay Buhner (Fleer)	2.00
7	Randy Johnson (Donruss Diamond Kings)	3.50
8	Lou Piniella (Upper Deck)	2.00
9	Alvin Davis, Harold Reynolds (Tuff Stuff)	2.00

2002 FanFest

All of the major baseball card licensees participated in a wrapper redemption program at the 2002 FanFest in Milwaukee. Each company produced one card of a Brewers star and one from another team. Five wrappers from selected products could be traded in for one of the cards. Wrappers from super-premium brands could be exchanged for cards featuring game-used base swatches. All cards carry special All-Star Game logos.

		NM/M
Complete Set (8):		10.00
Common Player:		2.00
1	Derek Jeter (Fleer)	3.00
2	Ichiro (Upper Deck)	4.00
3a	Sammy Sosa (Topps Finest)	2.50
3b	Sammy Sosa (Topps Finest Refractor)	12.00
4	Barry Bonds (Donruss Studio)	3.00
5	Robin Yount (Donruss Studio)	2.00
6	Geoff Jenkins (Topps Finest)	2.00
7	Ben Sheets (Upper Deck)	2.00
8	Richie Sexson (Fleer)	2.00

2002 FanFest Game-Used Base Cards

All of the major baseball card licensees participated in a wrapper redemption program at the 2002 FanFest in Milwaukee. Each company produced one card of a Brewers star and one from another team. Five wrappers from se-

lected products could be traded in for one of the cards. Wrappers from super-premium brands could be exchanged for cards featuring game-used base swatches. All cards carry special All-Star Game logos.

		NM/M
	Complete Set GU Base Cards (4):	35.00
	Common Player:	5.00
GU1a	Derek Jeter (Fleer,First Base)	6.00
GU1b	Derek Jeter (Fleer, Second Base)	6.00
GU2	Ichiro (Upper Deck)	20.00
GU3	Sammy Sosa (Topps)	5.00
GU4	Barry Bonds (Donruss Studio)	7.50

2003 FanFest

By opening packs of specified brands at various card companies' FanFest booths, collectors could receive one of eight redemption cards. Low-priced card wrappers could be redeemed for base brand-type cards while opening high-priced packs would net a game-used base card. Cards feature the All-Star Game logo and are numbered within the edition of eight.

		NM/M
	Complete Set (8):	35.00
	Common Player:	2.00
1	Hideki Matsui (Upper Deck, g-u base)	7.50
2	Barry Bonds (Topps, g-u base)	10.00
3	Derek Jeter (Fleer, g-u base)	10.00
4	Sammy Sosa (Donruss, g-u base)	7.50
5	Frank Thomas (Upper Deck)	3.00
6	Bartolo Colon (Topps)	2.00
7	Paul Konerko (Fleer)	2.00
8	Magglio Ordonez (Donruss)	2.00

2004 FanFest

By opening packs of specified brands at various card companies' FanFest booths at the All-Star related event in Houston, collectors could receive one of 12 redemption cards featuring current and former (Ryan) Astros players. Low-priced card wrappers could be redeemed for base brand-type cards while opening high-priced packs would net a game-used base card. Ten thousand of each of the regular redemption and Ryan-Clemens cards were produced; the game-used cards were in an edition of 1,000 each. Cards feature the All-Star Game and FanFest logos and are numbered within the edition of 12.

		NM/M
	Complete Set (12):	45.00
	Common Player:	2.00
1	Roger Clemens (Fleer GU)	10.00
2	Andy Pettitte (Upper Deck GU)	5.00
3	Jeff Bagwell (Donruss GU)	7.50
4	Lance Berkman (Topps GU)	5.00
5	Roy Oswalt (Topps)	2.00
6	Craig Biggio (Donruss)	2.00
7	Jeff Kent (Upper Deck)	2.00
8	Adam Everett (Fleer)	2.00
9	Roger Clemens, Nolan Ryan (Fleer)	5.00
10	Roger Clemens, Nolan Ryan (Upper Deck)	5.00
11	Roger Clemens, Nolan Ryan (Donruss)	5.00
12	Roger Clemens, Nolan Ryan (Topps)	5.00

2005 FanFest

By opening packs of specified brands at various card companies' FanFest booths at the All-Star related event in Detroit, collectors could receive one of nine redemption cards. Low-priced card wrappers could be redeemed for base brand-type cards while opening high-priced packs would net a game-used jersey card. Ten thousand of each of the regular redemption and dual-player cards were produced; the game-used cards were in an edition of 1,000 each. Cards feature the All-Star Game and FanFest logos.

		NM/M
	Complete Set (9):	25.00
	Common Player:	1.00
1	Ivan Rodriguez (Topps jersey)	12.50
2	Jeremy Bonderman (UD jersey)	6.00
3	Dmitri Young (Donruss jersey)	6.00
4	Derek Jeter (UD)	3.00
5	Alex Rodriguez (Topps)	3.00
6	Albert Pujols (Donruss)	3.00
7	Al Kaline, Ivan Rodriguez (UD)	1.00
8	Al Kaline, Ivan Rodriguez (Donruss)	1.00
9	Al Kaline, Ivan Rodriguez (Topps)	1.00

1988 Fantastic Sam's

This set of color player discs (2-1/2" diameter) was distributed during a Superstar Sweepstakes sponsored by Fantastic Sam's Family Haircutters' 1,800 stores nationwide. Each card consists of two connected discs (bright orange fronts, white backs) perforated for easy separation. One disc features the baseball player photo, the other carries the sweepstakes logo and a list of prizes. Player discs carry a Fantastic Sam's Baseball Superstars header curved above the photo, with player name, team and position printed in black. Backs are black-and-white and include personal info, card number and 1987 stats. Sweepstakes discs list contest prizes (Grand Prize was 4 tickets to a 1988 Championship game) on the front and an entry form on the flipside. Below the prize list is a silver scratch-off rectangle which may reveal an instant prize.

		NM/M
	Complete Set (20):	4.00
	Uncut Sheet:	10.00
	Common Player:	.10
1	Kirby Puckett	.50
2	George Brett	.75
3	Mark McGwire	1.00
4	Wally Joyner	.10
5	Paul Molitor	.45
6	Alan Trammell	.10
7	George Bell	.10
8	Wade Boggs	.50
9	Don Mattingly	.75
10	Julio Franco	.10
11	Ozzie Smith	.50
12	Will Clark	.10
13	Dale Murphy	.15
14	Eric Davis	.10
15	Andre Dawson	.25
16	Tim Raines	.10
17	Darryl Strawberry	.10
18	Tony Gwynn	.50
19	Mike Schmidt	.75
20	Pedro Guerrero	.10

1984 Farmer Jack Detroit Tigers

Though there is no indication on the picutres themselves, this issue was a promotion by the Farmer Jack grocery store chain. Printed on semi-gloss paper, the color photos are bordered in white and measure 6" x 9". A facsimile autograph is printed on front. The unnumbered pictures are blank-backed and are checklisted here in alphabetical order.

		NM/M
	Complete Set (16):	15.00
	Common Player:	.50
(1)	Dave Bergman	.50
(2)	Darrell Evans	1.25
(3)	Barbaro Garbey	.50
(4)	Kirk Gibson	1.00
(5)	John Grubb	.50
(6)	Willie Hernandez	.50
(7)	Larry Herndon	.50
(8)	Howard Johnson	.90
(9)	Chet Lemon	.75
(10)	Jack Morris	.90
(11)	Lance Parrish	1.00
(12)	Dan Petry	.50
(13)	Dave Rozema	.50
(14)	Alan Trammell	4.00
(15)	Lou Whitaker	2.50
(16)	Milt Wilcox	.50

1987 Farmland Dairies Mets

The New York Mets and Farmland Dairies produced a nine-card panel of baseball cards for members of the Junior Mets Club. Members of the club, kids 14 years of age and younger, received the perforated panel as part of a package featuring gifts and special

privileges. The cards are the standard 2-1/2" x 3-1/2" with fronts containing a full-color photo encompassed by a blue border. The backs are designed on a vertical format and have player statistics and career highlights. The Farmland Dairies and Junior Mets Club logos are also carried on the card backs.

		NM/M
	Complete Panel Set:	4.50
	Complete Singles Set (9):	3.00
	Common Single Player:	.25
1	Mookie Wilson	.35
4	Lenny Dykstra	.35
8	Gary Carter	1.50
12	Ron Darling	.25
18	Darryl Strawberry	.35
19	Bob Ojeda	.25
22	Kevin McReynolds	.25
42	Roger McDowell	.25
---	Team Card	.25

1988 Farmland Dairies Mets

Part of the Junior Mets Fan Club membership package, this set of nine standard size cards was printed on a single panel. Card fronts feature full-color action shots framed in orange and blue. A white player name runs across the top border, with a large team logo, uniform number and position printed below the photo. Card backs are blue on brown and include personal data, stats and 1987 season highlights. The set was offered to fans 14 years and younger for a $6 fan club membership fee, with a $1 discount for those who sent in two proofs of purchase from Farmland Dairies milk cartons.

		NM/M
	Complete Panel Set:	4.50
	Complete Singles Set (9):	2.50
	Common Single Player:	.25
8	Gary Carter	1.50
16	Dwight Gooden	.25
17	Keith Hernandez	.40
18	Darryl Strawberry	.25
20	Howard Johnson	.25
21	Kevin Elster	.25
42	Roger McDowell	.25
48	Randy Myers	.25
50	Sid Fernandez	.25

1989 Farmland Dairies Mets

For the third consecutive year in 1989, Farmland Dairies sponsored the Junior Mets fan club. One of the club's membership benefits was a nine-

card set issued on a 7-1/2" x 10-1/2" perforated sheet. Individual cards measure the standard 2-1/2" x 3-1/2" with team-color borders of blue and gold. Backs have the Junior Mets and Farmland logos along with 1988 highlights and stats, career stats and some biographical data. The checklist is by uniform number as shown on the cards' front.

		NM/M
	Complete Set, Sheet	3.50
	Complete Set, Singles (9):	3.00
	Common Player:	.50
8	Gary Carter	1.50
9	Gregg Jefferies	.50
16	Dwight Gooden	.25
18	Darryl Strawberry	.25
22	Kevin McReynolds	.25
25	Keith Miller	.25
42	Roger McDowell	.25
44	David Cone	.50
---	1988 Eastern Division Champs (Team Photo)	.25

1993 Fax Pax

Titled "Fax Pax World of Sports," this 40-card set was issued in Great Britain and features top athletes from many sports around the world. The 2-1/2" x 3-1/2" cards have borderless color action photos on front. A white strip near the bottom carries the player's name and the flag of his nation. Black, white and red backs have biographical data, stats and a career summary. Only the baseball players are listed here.

		NM/M
	Common Player:	1.00
1	Roger Clemens	1.50
2	Ken Griffey Jr.	2.00
3	John Olerud	1.00
4	Nolan Ryan	3.00

1982 FBI Foods Discs

This set was issued in the form of a pair of 2-7/8" diameter discs printed on the bottoms of six-pack cartons of Canadian soft drinks. The discs have black-and-white player portrait photos at center, with cap logos airbrushed off. At top is a green and orange FBI logo. Player identification flanks the photo. The copyright and logo of the Players Association appear at right. The initials of the set's producer, Mike Schechter Associates, appear at lower-left. The unnumbered discs are checklisted here in alphabetical order. Because of their appearance on the bottom of a cardboard box, many cards suffer scuffing on the front, or show indentations from the soda cans. A premium of 25-50 percent attaches to intact boxes or panels.

		NM/M
	Complete Set, Singles (30):	650.00
	Common Player:	10.00
(1)	Vida Blue	10.00
(2)	George Brett	100.00
(3)	Rod Carew	25.00
(4)	Steve Carlton	30.00
(5)	Gary Carter	30.00
(6)	Warren Cromartie	10.00
(7)	Andre Dawson	15.00
(8)	Rollie Fingers	20.00
(9)	Carlton Fisk	30.00
(10)	Steve Garvey	15.00
(11)	Goose Gossage	10.00
(12)	Bill Gullickson	10.00
(13)	Steve Henderson	10.00
(14)	Keith Hernandez	10.00
(15)	John Mayberry	10.00
(16)	Al Oliver	10.00
(17)	Dave Parker	10.00
(18)	Tim Raines	10.00
(19)	Jim Rice	15.00
(20)	Steve Rogers	10.00
(21)	Pete Rose	150.00
(22)	Nolan Ryan	150.00
(23)	Mike Schmidt	100.00
(24)	Tom Seaver	30.00
(25)	Ken Singleton	10.00
(26)	Dave Steib	10.00
(27)	Bruce Sutter	20.00
(28)	Ellis Valentine	10.00
(29)	Fernando Valenzuela	10.00
(30)	Dave Winfield	30.00

1993 Finest Promos

Debuting at the 1993 National Convention in Chicago, this three-card set introduced the hobby to the Topps Finest baseball issue. While the promos are identical in high-tech format to the regular Finest cards issued later, including the same card numbers, there are differences in the promos; some subtle, some glaring. For instance, the Ryan and Alomar cards were issued in promo form in the "gray" style of the basic set. In the regularly issued set, those cards were in the green All-Star format. Each of the promos is overprinted in red on the back, "Promotional Sample 1 of 5000". Of considerably greater rarity are refractor versions of these promo cards, with production numbers unknown.

		NM/M
	Complete Set (3):	25.00
	Complete Set, Refractors (3):	1,500
88	Roberto Alomar	3.50
88r	Roberto Alomar (Refractor)	300.00
98	Don Mattingly	10.00
98r	Don Mattingly (Refractor)	500.00
107	Nolan Ryan	15.00
107r	Nolan Ryan (Refractor)	750.00

1993 Finest

This 199-card set uses a process of multi-color metallization; this chromium technology adds depth and dimension to the card. The set has a 33-card subset of All-Stars; a parallel version of these cards (Refractors) were also created with refracting foil using the metallization enhancement process. There is one refracting foil card in every nine packs. Packs have five cards. Each 18-count box contains a 5" x 7" version of one of the 33 All-Star players in the set.

		NM/M
Complete Set (199):		75.00
Common Player:		.50
Refractors:		40-50X
Pack (6):		15.00
Wax Box (18):		300.00
1	Dave Justice	.50
2	Lou Whitaker	.50
3	Bryan Harvey	.50
4	Carlos Garcia	.50
5	Sid Fernandez	.50
6	Brett Butler	.50
7	Scott Cooper	.50
8	B.J. Surhoff	.50
9	Steve Finley	.50
10	Curt Schilling	2.00
11	Jeff Bagwell	4.00
12	Alex Cole	.50
13	John Olerud	.50
14	John Smiley	.50
15	Bip Roberts	.50
16	Albert Belle	.50
17	Duane Ward	.50
18	Alan Trammell	.50
19	Andy Benes	.50
20	Reggie Sanders	.50
21	Todd Zeile	.50
22	Rick Aguilera	.50
23	Dave Hollins	.50
24	Jose Rijo	.50
25	Matt Williams	.50
26	Sandy Alomar	.50
27	Alex Fernandez	.50
28	Ozzie Smith	6.00
29	Ramon Martinez	.50
30	Bernie Williams	.50
31	Gary Sheffield	1.00
32	Eric Karros	.50
33	Frank Viola	.50
34	Kevin Young	.50
35	Ken Hill	.50
36	Tony Fernandez	.50
37	Tim Wakefield	.50
38	John Kruk	.50
39	Chris Sabo	.50
40	Marquis Grissom	.50
41	Glenn Davis	.50
42	Jeff Montgomery	.50
43	Kenny Lofton	.50
44	John Burkett	.50
45	Darryl Hamilton	.50
46	Jim Abbott	.50
47	Ivan Rodriguez	3.00
48	Eric Young	.50
49	Mitch Williams	.50
50	Harold Reynolds	.50
51	Brian Harper	.50
52	Rafael Palmeiro	3.00
53	Bret Saberhagen	.50
54	Jeff Conine	.50
55	Ivan Calderon	.50
56	Juan Guzman	.50
57	Carlos Baerga	.50
58	Charles Nagy	.50
59	Wally Joyner	.50
60	Charlie Hayes	.50
61	Shane Mack	.50
62	Pete Harnisch	.50
63	George Brett	8.00
64	Lance Johnson	.50
65	Ben McDonald	.50
66	Bobby Bonilla	.50
67	Terry Steinbach	.50
68	Ron Gant	.50
69	Doug Jones	.50
70	Paul Molitor	4.00
71	Brady Anderson	.50
72	Chuck Finley	.50
73	Mark Grace	.75
74	Mike Devereaux	.50
75	Tony Phillips	.50
76	Chuck Knoblauch	.50
77	Tony Gwynn	6.00
78	Kevin Appier	.50
79	Sammy Sosa	6.00
80	Mickey Tettleton	.50
81	Felix Jose	.50
82	Mark Langston	.50
83	Gregg Jefferies	.50
84	Andre Dawson/AS	1.00
85	Greg Maddux/AS	6.00
86	Rickey Henderson/AS	4.00
87	Tom Glavine/AS	2.50
88	Roberto Alomar/AS	1.00
89	Darryl Strawberry/AS	.50
90	Wade Boggs/AS	6.00
91	Bo Jackson/AS	1.00
92	Mark McGwire/AS	6.00
93	Robin Ventura/AS	.50
94	Joe Carter/AS	.50
95	Lee Smith/AS	.50
96	Cal Ripken, Jr./AS	10.00
97	Larry Walker/AS	.50
98	Don Mattingly/AS	8.00
99	Jose Canseco/AS	2.50
100	Dennis Eckersley/AS	3.00
101	Terry Pendleton/AS	.50
102	Frank Thomas/AS	4.00
103	Barry Bonds/AS	10.00
104	Roger Clemens/AS	8.00
105	Ryne Sandberg/AS	6.00
106	Fred McGriff/AS	.50
107	Nolan Ryan/AS	10.00
108	Will Clark/AS	.50
109	Pat Listach/AS	.50
110	Ken Griffey Jr./AS	6.00
111	Cecil Fielder/AS	.50
112	Kirby Puckett/AS	6.00
113	Dwight Gooden/AS	.50
114	Barry Larkin/AS	.50
115	David Cone/AS	.50
116	Juan Gonzalez/AS	2.50
117	Kent Hrbek	.50
118	Tim Wallach	.50
119	Craig Biggio	.50
120	Bobby Kelly	.50
121	Greg Olson	.50
122	Eddie Murray	4.00
123	Wil Cordero	.50
124	Jay Buhner	.50
125	Carlton Fisk	4.00
126	Eric Davis	.50
127	Doug Drabek	.50
128	Ozzie Guillen	.50
129	John Wetteland	.50
130	Andres Galarraga	.50
131	Ken Caminiti	.50
132	Tom Candiotti	.50
133	Pat Borders	.50
134	Kevin Brown	.50
135	Travis Fryman	.50
136	Kevin Mitchell	.50
137	Greg Swindell	.50
138	Benny Santiago	.50
139	Reggie Jefferson	.50
140	Chris Bosio	.50
141	Deion Sanders	.60
142	Scott Erickson	.50
143	Howard Johnson	.50
144	Orestes Destrade	.50
145	Jose Guzman	.50
146	Chad Curtis	.50
147	Cal Eldred	.50
148	Willie Greene	.50
149	Tommy Greene	.50
150	Erik Hanson	.50
151	Bob Welch	.50
152	John Jaha	.50
153	Harold Baines	.50
154	Randy Johnson	4.00
155	Al Martin	.50
156	J.T. Snow **RC**	1.50
157	Mike Mussina	2.50
158	Ruben Sierra	.50
159	Dean Palmer	.50
160	Steve Avery	.50
161	Julio Franco	.50
162	Dave Winfield	4.00
163	Tim Salmon	.50
164	Tom Henke	.50
165	Mo Vaughn	.50
166	John Smoltz	.50
167	Danny Tartabull	.50
168	Delino DeShields	.50
169	Charlie Hough	.50
170	Paul O'Neill	.50
171	Darren Daulton	.50
172	Jack McDowell	.50
173	Junior Felix	.50
174	Jimmy Key	.50
175	George Bell	.50
176	Mike Stanton	.50
177	Len Dykstra	.50
178	Norm Charlton	.50
179	Eric Anthony	.50
180	Bob Dibble	.50
181	Otis Nixon	.50
182	Randy Myers	.50
183	Tim Raines	.50
184	Orel Hershiser	.50
185	Andy Van Slyke	.50
186	Mike Lansing **RC**	1.00
187	Ray Lankford	.50
188	Mike Morgan	.50
189	Moises Alou	.50
190	Edgar Martinez	.50
191	John Franco	.50
192	Robin Yount	5.00
193	Bob Tewksbury	.50
194	Jay Bell	.50
195	Luis Gonzalez	.50
196	Dave Fleming	.50
197	Mike Greenwell	.50
198	David Nied	.50
199	Mike Piazza	10.00

Refractors

This parallel insert set comprises each of the 199 cards from the regular Topps Finest set recreated with refracting foil using the metallization enhancement process. One refractor card was inserted in every nine packs, on average. Estimated production was about 250 of each card, though short-prints are known. In the mid 2000s large quantities of the refractors began appearing in the market, fueling speculation that some form of unissued remainder inventory had been released from the printer.

		NM/M
Common Player:		15.00
1	Dave Justice	15.00
2	Lou Whitaker	15.00
3	Bryan Harvey/SP	45.00
4	Carlos Garcia	15.00
5	Sid Fernandez	15.00
6	Brett Butler	15.00
7	Scott Cooper	15.00
8	B.J. Surhoff	15.00
9	Steve Finley	15.00
10	Curt Schilling	50.00
11	Jeff Bagwell	100.00
12	Alex Cole	15.00
13	John Olerud	15.00
14	John Smiley	15.00
15	Bip Roberts	15.00
16	Albert Belle	15.00
17	Duane Ward	15.00
18	Alan Trammell	15.00
19	Andy Benes	15.00
20	Reggie Sanders	15.00
21	Todd Zeile	15.00
22	Rick Aguilera	15.00
23	Dave Hollins	15.00
24	Jose Rijo	15.00
25	Matt Williams	15.00
26	Sandy Alomar	15.00
27	Alex Fernandez	15.00
28	Ozzie Smith	100.00
29	Ramon Martinez	15.00
30	Bernie Williams	15.00
31	Gary Sheffield	40.00
32	Eric Karros	15.00
33	Frank Viola	15.00
34	Kevin Young	15.00
35	Ken Hill	15.00
36	Tony Fernandez	15.00
37	Tim Wakefield	15.00
38	John Kruk	15.00
39	Chris Sabo/SP	75.00
40	Marquis Grissom	15.00
41	Glenn Davis/SP	50.00
42	Jeff Montgomery	15.00
43	Kenny Lofton	15.00
44	John Burkett	15.00
45	Darryl Hamilton	15.00
46	Jim Abbott	15.00
47	Ivan Rodriguez	150.00
48	Eric Young	15.00
49	Mitch Williams	15.00
50	Harold Reynolds	15.00
51	Brian Harper	15.00
52	Rafael Palmeiro	75.00
53	Bret Saberhagen	15.00
54	Jeff Conine	15.00
55	Ivan Calderon	15.00
56	Juan Guzman	15.00
57	Carlos Baerga	15.00
58	Charles Nagy	15.00
59	Wally Joyner	15.00
60	Charlie Hayes	15.00
61	Shane Mack	15.00
62	Pete Harnisch	15.00
63	George Brett	125.00
64	Lance Johnson	15.00
65	Ben McDonald	15.00
66	Bobby Bonilla	15.00
67	Terry Steinbach	15.00
68	Ron Gant	15.00
69	Doug Jones	15.00
70	Paul Molitor	100.00
71	Brady Anderson	15.00
72	Chuck Finley	15.00
73	Mark Grace	15.00
74	Mike Devereaux	15.00
75	Tony Phillips	15.00
76	Chuck Knoblauch	15.00
77	Tony Gwynn	100.00
78	Kevin Appier	15.00
79	Sammy Sosa	150.00
80	Mickey Tettleton	15.00
81	Felix Jose	15.00
82	Mark Langston	15.00
83	Gregg Jefferies	15.00
84	Andre Dawson/AS	35.00
85	Greg Maddux/AS	150.00
86	Rickey Henderson/AS	125.00
87	Tom Glavine/AS	50.00
88	Roberto Alomar/AS	45.00
89	Darryl Strawberry/AS	15.00
90	Wade Boggs/AS	100.00
91	Bo Jackson/AS	60.00
92	Mark McGwire/AS	200.00
93	Robin Ventura/AS	15.00
94	Joe Carter/AS/SP	50.00
95	Lee Smith/AS	15.00
96	Cal Ripken, Jr./AS	500.00
97	Larry Walker/AS/SP	100.00
98	Don Mattingly/AS	100.00
99	Jose Canseco/AS	50.00
100	Dennis Eckersley/AS	75.00
101	Terry Pendleton/AS	15.00
102	Frank Thomas/AS/SP	200.00
103	Barry Bonds/AS	300.00
104	Roger Clemens/AS	200.00
105	Ryne Sandberg/AS	125.00
106	Fred McGriff/AS	15.00
107	Nolan Ryan/AS	500.00
108	Will Clark/AS/SP	75.00
109	Pat Listach/AS	15.00
110	Ken Griffey Jr./AS	450.00
111	Cecil Fielder/AS	15.00
112	Kirby Puckett/AS	100.00
113	Dwight Gooden/AS	15.00
114	Barry Larkin/AS	15.00
115	David Cone/AS	15.00
116	Juan Gonzalez/AS/SP	150.00
117	Kent Hrbek	15.00
118	Tim Wallach	15.00
119	Craig Biggio	15.00
120	Bobby Kelly	15.00
121	Greg Olson	15.00
122	Eddie Murray	100.00
123	Wil Cordero	15.00
124	Jay Buhner	15.00
125	Carlton Fisk	75.00
126	Eric Davis	15.00
127	Doug Drabek	15.00
128	Ozzie Guillen	15.00
129	John Wetteland	15.00
130	Andres Galarraga	15.00
131	Ken Caminiti	15.00
132	Tom Candiotti	15.00
133	Pat Borders	15.00
134	Kevin Brown	15.00
135	Travis Fryman	15.00
136	Kevin Mitchell	15.00
137	Greg Swindell	15.00
138	Benny Santiago	15.00
139	Reggie Jefferson	15.00
140	Chris Bosio	15.00
141	Deion Sanders	15.00
142	Scott Erickson	15.00
143	Howard Johnson	15.00
144	Orestes Destrade	15.00
145	Jose Guzman	15.00
146	Chad Curtis	15.00
147	Cal Eldred	15.00
148	Willie Greene/SP	75.00
149	Tommy Greene	15.00
150	Erik Hanson	15.00
151	Bob Welch	15.00
152	John Jaha	15.00
153	Harold Baines	15.00
154	Randy Johnson	100.00
155	Al Martin	15.00
156	J.T. Snow	15.00
157	Mike Mussina	45.00
158	Ruben Sierra	15.00
159	Dean Palmer	15.00
160	Steve Avery	15.00
161	Julio Franco	15.00
162	Dave Winfield	100.00
163	Tim Salmon/SP	50.00
164	Tom Henke	15.00
165	Mo Vaughn	15.00
166	John Smoltz	15.00
167	Danny Tartabull	15.00
168	Delino DeShields	15.00
169	Charlie Hough	15.00
170	Paul O'Neill	15.00
171	Darren Daulton	15.00
172	Jack McDowell	15.00
173	Junior Felix	15.00
174	Jimmy Key	15.00
175	George Bell	15.00
176	Mike Stanton	15.00
177	Len Dykstra	15.00
178	Norm Charlton	15.00
179	Eric Anthony	15.00
180	Bob Dibble	15.00
181	Otis Nixon	15.00
182	Randy Myers	15.00
183	Tim Raines	15.00
184	Orel Hershiser	15.00
185	Andy Van Slyke	15.00
186	Mike Lansing	15.00
187	Ray Lankford	15.00
188	Mike Morgan	15.00
189	Moises Alou	15.00
190	Edgar Martinez	15.00
191	John Franco	15.00
192	Robin Yount	90.00
193	Bob Tewksbury	15.00
194	Jay Bell	15.00
195	Luis Gonzalez	15.00
196	Dave Fleming	15.00
197	Mike Greenwell	15.00
198	David Nied	15.00
199	Mike Piazza	250.00

Jumbo All-Stars

These 4-1/2" x 6" cards were produced using the chromium metallization process. Each 18-pack Finest box contains one of the All-Star jumbo cards. Based on '93 Finest production, it is estimated fewer than 1,500 of each were issued.

		NM/M
Complete Set (33):		185.00
Common Player:		2.00
84	Andre Dawson	2.50
85	Greg Maddux	10.00
86	Rickey Henderson	7.50
87	Tom Glavine	3.00
88	Roberto Alomar	3.00
89	Darryl Strawberry	2.00
90	Wade Boggs	10.00
91	Bo Jackson	2.00
92	Mark McGwire	20.00
93	Robin Ventura	2.00
94	Joe Carter	2.00
95	Lee Smith	2.00
96	Cal Ripken, Jr.	30.00
97	Larry Walker	2.00
98	Don Mattingly	12.00
99	Jose Canseco	3.50
100	Dennis Eckersley	6.00
101	Terry Pendleton	2.00
102	Frank Thomas	7.50
103	Barry Bonds	30.00
104	Roger Clemens	12.00
105	Ryne Sandberg	10.00
106	Fred McGriff	2.00
107	Nolan Ryan	30.00
108	Will Clark	2.50
109	Pat Listach	2.00
110	Ken Griffey Jr.	15.00
111	Cecil Fielder	2.00
112	Kirby Puckett	10.00
113	Dwight Gooden	2.00
114	Barry Larkin	2.00
115	David Cone	2.00
116	Juan Gonzalez	7.50

1994 Finest Pre-Production

Forty cards premiering the upcoming 1994 Topps Finest set were issued as a random insert in packs of Topps Series 2 regular-issue cards. The promos are in the same format as the regular-issue Finest cards and share the same card numbers. On back there is a red "Pre-Production" notice printed diagonally over the statistics.

		NM/M
Complete Set (40):		35.00
Common Player:		1.00
22	Deion Sanders	1.00
23	Jose Offerman	1.00
26	Alex Fernandez	1.00
31	Steve Finley	1.00
35	Andres Galarraga	1.00
43	Reggie Sanders	1.00
47	Dave Hollins	1.00
52	David Cone	1.00
59	Dante Bichette	1.00
61	Orlando Merced	1.00
62	Brian McRae	1.00
66	Mike Mussina	2.50
76	Mike Stanley	1.00
78	Mark McGwire	6.00
79	Pat Listach	1.00
82	Dwight Gooden	1.00
84	Phil Plantier	1.00
90	Jeff Russell	1.00
92	Gregg Jefferies	1.00
93	Jose Guzman	1.00
100	John Smoltz	1.00
102	Jim Thome	3.00
121	Moises Alou	1.00
125	Devon White	1.00
126	Ivan Rodriguez	3.00
130	Dave Magadan	1.00
136	Ozzie Smith	4.00
141	Chris Hoiles	1.00
149	Jim Abbott	1.00
151	Bill Swift	1.00
154	Edgar Martinez	1.00
157	J.T. Snow	1.00
159	Alan Trammell	1.00
163	Roberto Kelly	1.00
166	Scott Erickson	1.00
168	Scott Cooper	1.00
169	Rod Beck	1.00
177	Dean Palmer	1.00
182	Todd Van Poppel	1.00
185	Paul Sorrento	1.00

1994 Finest

The 1994 Finest set comprises two series of 220 cards each; subsets of 20 superstars and 20 top rookies are featured in each series. Each card has a metallic look to it, using Topps Finest technology. Backs picture the player on the top half and statistics on the bottom. Baseball's Finest was limited to 4,000 cases and available to dealers through an allocation process, based on their sales the previous year. Along with the regular-issue set, there was a parallel set, called Refractors, of 440 cards and a 4 x 6-inch version of the 80 subset cards.

		NM/M
Complete Set (440):		40.00
Common Player:		.15
Refractors:		3X
Series 1 or 2 Pack (7):		1.50
Series 1 or 2 Box (24):		25.00
1	Mike Piazza	3.00
2	Kevin Stocker	.15
3	Greg McMichael	.15
4	Jeff Conine	.15
5	Rene Arocha	.15
6	Aaron Sele	.15
7	Brent Gates	.15
8	Chuck Carr	.15
9	Kirk Rueter	.15

10	Mike Lansing	.15
11	Al Martin	.15
12	Jason Bere	.15
13	Troy Neel	.15
14	Armando Reynoso	.15
15	Jeromy Burnitz	.15
16	Rich Amaral	.15
17	David McCarty	.15
18	Tim Salmon	.15
19	Steve Cooke	.15
20	Wil Cordero	.15
21	Kevin Tapani	.15
22	Deion Sanders	.15
23	Jose Offerman	.15
24	Mark Langston	.15
25	Ken Hill	.15
26	Alex Fernandez	.15
27	Jeff Blauser	.15
28	Royce Clayton	.15
29	Brad Ausmus	.15
30	Ryan Bowen	.15
31	Steve Finley	.15
32	Charlie Hayes	.15
33	Jeff Kent	.15
34	Mike Henneman	.15
35	Andres Galarraga	.15
36	Wayne Kirby	.15
37	Joe Oliver	.15
38	Terry Steinbach	.15
39	Ryan Thompson	.15
40	Luis Alicea	.15
41	Randy Velarde	.15
42	Bob Tewksbury	.15
43	Reggie Sanders	.15
44	Brian Williams	.15
45	Joe Orsulak	.15
46	Jose Lind	.15
47	Dave Hollins	.15
48	Graeme Lloyd	.15
49	Jim Gott	.15
50	Andre Dawson	.40
51	Steve Buechele	.15
52	David Cone	.15
53	Ricky Gutierrez	.15
54	Lance Johnson	.15
55	Tino Martinez	.15
56	Phil Hiatt	.15
57	Carlos Garcia	.15
58	Danny Darwin	.15
59	Dante Bichette	.15
60	Scott Kamieniecki	.15
61	Orlando Merced	.15
62	Brian McRae	.15
63	Pat Kelly	.15
64	Tom Henke	.15
65	Jeff King	.15
66	Mike Mussina	.75
67	Tim Pugh	.15
68	Robby Thompson	.15
69	Paul O'Neill	.15
70	Hal Morris	.15
71	Ron Karkovice	.15
72	Joe Girardi	.15
73	Eduardo Perez	.15
74	Raul Mondesi	.15
75	Mike Gallego	.15
76	Mike Stanley	.15
77	Kevin Roberson	.15
78	Mark McGwire	4.00
79	Pat Listach	.15
80	Eric Davis	.15
81	Mike Bordick	.15
82	Dwight Gooden	.15
83	Mike Moore	.15
84	Phil Plantier	.15
85	Darren Lewis	.15
86	Rick Wilkins	.15
87	Darryl Strawberry	.15
88	Rob Dibble	.15
89	Greg Vaughn	.15
90	Jeff Russell	.15
91	Mark Lewis	.15
92	Gregg Jefferies	.15
93	Jose Guzman	.15
94	Kenny Rogers	.15
95	Mark Lemke	.15
96	Mike Morgan	.15
97	Andujar Cedeno	.15
98	Orel Hershiser	.15
99	Greg Swindell	.15
100	John Smoltz	.15
101	Pedro Martinez	.15
102	Jim Thome	1.00
103	David Segui	.15
104	Charles Nagy	.15
105	Shane Mack	.15
106	John Jaha	.15
107	Tom Candiotti	.15
108	David Wells	.15
109	Bobby Jones	.15
110	Bob Hamelin	.15
111	Bernard Gilkey	.15
112	Chili Davis	.15
113	Todd Stottlemyre	.15
114	Derek Bell	.15
115	Mark McLemore	.15
116	Mark Whiten	.15
117	Mike Devereaux	.15
118	Terry Pendleton	.15
119	Pat Meares	.15
120	Pete Harnisch	.15
121	Moises Alou	.15
122	Jay Buhner	.15
123	Wes Chamberlain	.15
124	Mike Perez	.15
125	Devon White	.15
126	Ivan Rodriguez	1.25
127	Don Slaught	.15
128	John Valentin	.15
129	Jaime Navarro	.15
130	Dave Magadan	.15
131	Brady Anderson	.15
132	Juan Guzman	.15
133	John Wetteland	.15
134	Dave Stewart	.15
135	Scott Servais	.15
136	Ozzie Smith	2.50
137	Darrin Fletcher	.15
138	Jose Mesa	.15
139	Wilson Alvarez	.15
140	Pete Incaviglia	.15
141	Chris Hoiles	.15
142	Darryl Hamilton	.15
143	Chuck Finley	.15
144	Archi Cianfrocco	.15
145	Bill Wegman	.15
146	Joey Cora	.15
147	Darrell Whitmore	.15
148	David Hulse	.15
149	Jim Abbott	.15
150	Curt Schilling	.40
151	Bill Swift	.15
152	Tommy Greene	.15
153	Roberto Mejia	.15
154	Edgar Martinez	.15
155	Roger Pavlik	.15
156	Randy Tomlin	.15
157	J.T. Snow	.15
158	Bob Welch	.15
159	Alan Trammell	.15
160	Ed Sprague	.15
161	Ben McDonald	.15
162	Derrick May	.15
163	Roberto Kelly	.15
164	Bryan Harvey	.15
165	Ron Gant	.15
166	Scott Erickson	.15
167	Anthony Young	.15
168	Scott Cooper	.15
169	Rod Beck	.15
170	John Franco	.15
171	Gary DiSarcina	.15
172	Dave Fleming	.15
173	Wade Boggs	2.50
174	Kevin Appier	.15
175	Jose Bautista	.15
176	Wally Joyner	.15
177	Dean Palmer	.15
178	Tony Phillips	.15
179	John Smiley	.15
180	Charlie Hough	.15
181	Scott Fletcher	.15
182	Todd Van Poppel	.15
183	Mike Blowers	.15
184	Willie McGee	.15
185	Paul Sorrento	.15
186	Eric Young	.15
187	Bret Barberie	.15
188	Manuel Lee	.15
189	Jeff Branson	.15
190	Jim Deshaies	.15
191	Ken Caminiti	.15
192	Tim Raines	.15
193	Joe Grahe	.15
194	Hipolito Pichardo	.15
195	Denny Neagle	.15
196	Jeff Gardner	.15
197	Mike Benjamin	.15
198	Milt Thompson	.15
199	Bruce Ruffin	.15
200	Chris Hammond	.15
201	Tony Gwynn	2.50
202	Robin Ventura	.15
203	Frank Thomas	1.50
204	Kirby Puckett	2.50
205	Roberto Alomar	.30
206	Dennis Eckersley	1.25
207	Joe Carter	.15
208	Albert Belle	.15
209	Greg Maddux	2.50
210	Ryne Sandberg	2.50
211	Juan Gonzalez	.75
212	Jeff Bagwell	1.50
213	Randy Johnson	1.50
214	Matt Williams	.15
215	Dave Winfield	1.50
216	Larry Walker	.15
217	Roger Clemens	2.75
218	Kenny Lofton	.15
219	Cecil Fielder	.15
220	Darren Daulton	.15
221	John Olerud	.15
222	Jose Canseco	.75
223	Rickey Henderson	1.50
224	Fred McGriff	.15
225	Gary Sheffield	.50
226	Jack McDowell	.15
227	Rafael Palmeiro	1.25
228	Travis Fryman	.15
229	Marquis Grissom	.15
230	Barry Bonds	5.00
231	Carlos Baerga	.15
232	Ken Griffey Jr.	3.00
233	Dave Justice	.15
234	Bobby Bonilla	.15
235	Cal Ripken	5.00
236	Sammy Sosa	2.50
237	Len Dykstra	.15
238	Will Clark	.15
239	Paul Molitor	1.50
240	Barry Larkin	.15
241	Bo Jackson	.35
242	Mitch Williams	.15
243	Ron Darling	.15
244	Darryl Kile	.15
245	Geronimo Berroa	.15
246	Gregg Olson	.15
247	Brian Harper	.15
248	Rheal Cormier	.15
249	Rey Sanchez	.15
250	Jeff Fassero	.15
251	Sandy Alomar	.15
252	Chris Bosio	.15
253	Andy Stankiewicz	.15
254	Harold Baines	.15
255	Andy Ashby	.15
256	Tyler Green	.15
257	Kevin Brown	.15
258	Mo Vaughn	.15
259	Mike Harkey	.15
260	Dave Henderson	.15
261	Kent Hrbek	.15
262	Darrin Jackson	.15
263	Bob Wickman	.15
264	Spike Owen	.15
265	Todd Jones	.15
266	Pat Borders	.15
267	Tom Glavine	.45
268	Dave Nilsson	.15
269	Rich Batchelor	.15
270	Delino DeShields	.15
271	Felix Fermin	.15
272	Orestes Destrade	.15
273	Mickey Morandini	.15
274	Otis Nixon	.15
275	Ellis Burks	.15
276	Greg Gagne	.15
277	John Doherty	.15
278	Julio Franco	.15
279	Bernie Williams	.15
280	Rick Aguilera	.15
281	Mickey Tettleton	.15
282	David Nied	.15
283	Johnny Ruffin	.15
284	Dan Wilson	.15
285	Omar Vizquel	.15
286	Willie Banks	.15
287	Erik Pappas	.15
288	Cal Eldred	.15
289	Bobby Witt	.15
290	Luis Gonzalez	.15
291	Greg Pirkl	.15
292	Alex Cole	.15
293	Ricky Bones	.15
294	Denis Boucher	.15
295	John Burkett	.15
296	Steve Trachsel	.15
297	Ricky Jordan	.15
298	Mark Dewey	.15
299	Jimmy Key	.15
300	Mike MacFarlane	.15
301	Tim Belcher	.15
302	Carlos Reyes	.15
303	Greg Harris	.15
304	Brian Anderson **RC**	.15
305	Terry Mulholland	.15
306	Felix Jose	.15
307	Darren Holmes	.15
308	Jose Rijo	.15
309	Paul Wagner	.15
310	Bob Scanlan	.15
311	Mike Jackson	.15
312	Jose Vizcaino	.15
313	Rob Butler	.15
314	Kevin Seitzer	.15
315	Geronimo Pena	.15
316	Hector Carrasco	.15
317	Eddie Murray	1.50
318	Roger Salkeld	.15
319	Todd Hundley	.15
320	Danny Jackson	.15
321	Kevin Young	.15
322	Mike Greenwell	.15
323	Kevin Mitchell	.15
324	Chuck Knoblauch	.15
325	Danny Tartabull	.15
326	Vince Coleman	.15
327	Marvin Freeman	.15
328	Andy Benes	.15
329	Mike Kelly	.15
330	Karl Rhodes	.15
331	Allen Watson	.15
332	Damion Easley	.15
333	Reggie Jefferson	.15
334	Kevin McReynolds	.15
335	Arthur Rhodes	.15
336	Brian Hunter	.15
337	Tom Browning	.15
338	Pedro Munoz	.15
339	Billy Ripken	.15
340	Gene Harris	.15
341	Fernando Vina	.15
342	Sean Berry	.15
343	Pedro Astacio	.15
344	B.J. Surhoff	.15
345	Doug Drabek	.15
346	Jody Reed	.15
347	Ray Lankford	.15
348	Steve Farr	.15
349	Eric Anthony	.15
350	Pete Smith	.15
351	Lee Smith	.15
352	Mariano Duncan	.15
353	Doug Strange	.15
354	Tim Bogar	.15
355	Dave Weathers	.15
356	Eric Karros	.15
357	Randy Myers	.15
358	Chad Curtis	.15
359	Steve Avery	.15
360	Brian Jordan	.15
361	Tim Wallach	.15
362	Pedro Martinez	1.50
363	Bip Roberts	.15
364	Lou Whitaker	.15
365	Luis Polonia	.15
366	Benny Santiago	.15
367	Brett Butler	.15
368	Shawon Dunston	.15
369	Kelly Stinnett	.15
370	Chris Turner	.15
371	Ruben Sierra	.15
372	Greg Harris	.15
373	Xavier Hernandez	.15
374	Howard Johnson	.15
375	Duane Ward	.15
376	Roberto Hernandez	.15
377	Scott Leius	.15
378	Dave Valle	.15
379	Sid Fernandez	.15
380	Doug Jones	.15
381	Zane Smith	.15
382	Craig Biggio	.15
383	Rick White	.15
384	Tom Pagnozzi	.15
385	Chris James	.15
386	Bret Boone	.15
387	Jeff Montgomery	.15
388	Chad Kreuter	.15
389	Greg Hibbard	.15
390	Mark Grace	.15
391	Phil Leftwich	.15
392	Don Mattingly	2.75
393	Ozzie Guillen	.15
394	Gary Gaetti	.15
395	Erik Hanson	.15
396	Scott Brosius	.15
397	Tom Gordon	.15
398	Bill Gullickson	.15
399	Matt Mieske	.15
400	Pat Hentgen	.15
401	Walt Weiss	.15
402	Greg Blosser	.15
403	Stan Javier	.15
404	Doug Henry	.15
405	Ramon Martinez	.15
406	Frank Viola	.15
407	Mike Hampton	.15
408	Andy Van Slyke	.15
409	Bobby Ayala	.15
410	Todd Zeile	.15
411	Jay Bell	.15
412	Denny Martinez	.15
413	Mark Portugal	.15
414	Bobby Munoz	.15
415	Kirt Manwaring	.15
416	John Kruk	.15
417	Trevor Hoffman	.15
418	Chris Sabo	.15
419	Bret Saberhagen	.15
420	Chris Nabholz	.15
421	James Mouton	.15
422	Tony Tarasco	.15
423	Carlos Delgado	.75
424	Rondell White	.15
425	Javier Lopez	.15
426	Chan Ho Park **RC**	1.00
427	Cliff Floyd	.15
428	Dave Staton	.15
429	J.R. Phillips	.15
430	Manny Ramirez	1.50
431	Kurt Abbott	.15
432	Melvin Nieves	.15
433	Alex Gonzalez	.15
434	Rick Helling	.15
435	Danny Bautista	.15
436	Matt Walbeck	.15
437	Ryan Klesko	.15
438	Steve Karsay	.15
439	Salomon Torres	.15
440	Scott Ruffcorn	.15

Refractors

It takes an experienced eye and good light to detect a Refractor parallel card from a regular-issue Topps Finest. The Refractor utilizes a variation of the Finest metallic printing process to produce rainbow-effect highlights on the card front. The Refractors share the checklist with the regular-issue Finest and were inserted at a rate of about one per 10 packs.

	NM/M
Complete Set (440):	300.00
Common Player:	1.00
Stars/Rookies:	3X

Superstar Jumbos

Identical in format to the Superstars subset in the Finest issue, these cards measure about 4" x 5-1/2" and were distributed one per box in Finest foil packs. Backs carry a card number under the banner with the player's name and position. There were 20 rookies and 20 superstars from both Series 1 and Series 2.

		NM/M
Complete Set (80):		140.00
Common Player:		1.00
1	Mike Piazza	12.50
2	Kevin Stocker	1.00
3	Greg McMichael	1.00
4	Jeff Conine	1.00
5	Rene Arocha	1.00
6	Aaron Sele	1.00
7	Brent Gates	1.00
8	Chuck Carr	1.00
9	Kirk Rueter	1.00
10	Mike Lansing	1.00
11	Al Martin	1.00
12	Jason Bere	1.00
13	Troy Neel	1.00
14	Armando Reynoso	1.00
15	Jeromy Burnitz	1.00
16	Rich Amaral	1.00
17	David McCarty	1.00
18	Tim Salmon	1.00
19	Steve Cooke	1.00
20	Wil Cordero	1.00
201	Tony Gwynn	7.50
202	Robin Ventura	1.00
203	Frank Thomas	6.00
204	Kirby Puckett	7.50
205	Roberto Alomar	2.00
206	Dennis Eckersley	5.00
207	Joe Carter	1.00
208	Albert Belle	1.00
209	Greg Maddux	7.50
210	Ryne Sandberg	7.50
211	Juan Gonzalez	3.00
212	Jeff Bagwell	6.00
213	Randy Johnson	6.00
214	Matt Williams	1.00
215	Dave Winfield	6.00
216	Larry Walker	1.00
217	Roger Clemens	10.00
218	Kenny Lofton	1.00
219	Cecil Fielder	1.00
220	Darren Daulton	1.00
221	John Olerud	1.00
222	Jose Canseco	4.00
223	Rickey Henderson	6.00
224	Fred McGriff	1.00
225	Gary Sheffield	2.00
226	Jack McDowell	1.00
227	Rafael Palmeiro	5.00
228	Travis Fryman	1.00
229	Marquis Grissom	1.00
230	Barry Bonds	20.00
231	Carlos Baerga	1.00
232	Ken Griffey Jr.	12.50
233	Dave Justice	1.00
234	Bobby Bonilla	1.00
235	Cal Ripken	20.00
236	Sammy Sosa	7.50
237	Len Dykstra	1.00
238	Will Clark	1.00
239	Paul Molitor	6.00
240	Barry Larkin	1.00
421	James Mouton	1.00
422	Tony Tarasco	1.00
423	Carlos Delgado	3.00
424	Rondell White	1.00
425	Javier Lopez	1.00
426	Chan Ho Park	1.00
427	Cliff Floyd	1.00
428	Dave Staton	1.00
429	J.R. Phillips	1.00
430	Manny Ramirez	6.00
431	Kurt Abbott	1.00
432	Melvin Nieves	1.00
433	Alex Gonzalez	1.00
434	Rick Helling	1.00
435	Danny Bautista	1.00
436	Matt Walbeck	1.00
437	Ryan Klesko	1.00
438	Steve Karsay	1.00
439	Salomon Torres	1.00
440	Scott Ruffcorn	1.00

Superstar Sampler

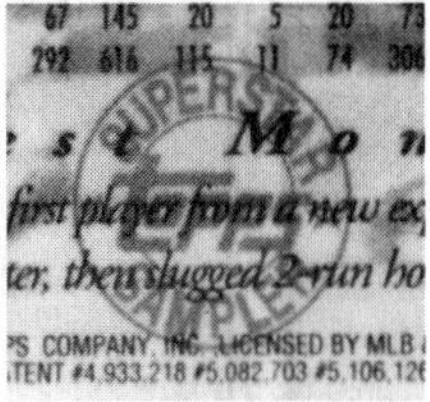

This special version of 45 of the biggest-name stars from the 1994 Topps Finest set was issued in a three-card cello pack with the same player's '94 Bowman and Stadium Club cards. The packs were available only in 1994 Topps retail factory sets. Cards are identical to the regular-issue Finest cards except for a round, red "Topps Superstar Sampler" logo printed at bottom center on back.

		NM/M
Complete Set (45):		400.00
Common Player:		4.00
1	Mike Piazza	35.00
18	Tim Salmon	4.00
35	Andres Galarraga	4.00
74	Raul Mondesi	4.00
92	Gregg Jefferies	4.00
201	Tony Gwynn	20.00
203	Frank Thomas	15.00
204	Kirby Puckett	20.00
205	Roberto Alomar	6.00
207	Joe Carter	4.00
208	Albert Belle	4.00
209	Greg Maddux	20.00
210	Ryne Sandberg	20.00
211	Juan Gonzalez	7.50
212	Jeff Bagwell	15.00
213	Randy Johnson	15.00
214	Matt Williams	4.00
216	Larry Walker	4.00
217	Roger Clemens	30.00
219	Cecil Fielder	4.00
220	Darren Daulton	4.00
221	John Olerud	4.00
222	Jose Canseco	7.50
224	Fred McGriff	4.00
225	Gary Sheffield	6.00
226	Jack McDowell	4.00
227	Rafael Palmeiro	12.00
229	Marquis Grissom	4.00
230	Barry Bonds	65.00
231	Carlos Baerga	4.00
232	Ken Griffey Jr.	35.00
233	Dave Justice	4.00
234	Bobby Bonilla	4.00
235	Cal Ripken Jr.	65.00
237	Len Dykstra	4.00
238	Will Clark	4.00
239	Paul Molitor	15.00
240	Barry Larkin	4.00
258	Mo Vaughn	4.00
267	Tom Glavine	7.50
390	Mark Grace	4.00
392	Don Mattingly	30.00
408	Andy Van Slyke	4.00
427	Cliff Floyd	4.00
430	Manny Ramirez	15.00

Bronze

This three-card set was included as part of the purchase of a 1994 Topps Stadium Club Members Only set, but was also made available on a limited basis via newspaper ads. The cards feature a version of Topps' Finest technology with the multi-colored front design laminated to a bronze base by a heavy lucite overlay. Backs are engraved in black on bronze and contain complete major and minor league stats and a few personal data. The Finest bronze cards are slightly larger than current standard suze, measuring 2-3/4" x 3-3/4".

		NM/M
Complete Set (3):		40.00
Common Player:		10.00
1	Barry Bonds	20.00
2	Ken Griffey Jr.	15.00
3	Frank Thomas	10.00

1995 Finest

In its third year Finest baseball was reduced to a 220-card base set. All cards feature the chrome-printing technology associated with the Finest logo and include a peel-off plastic protector on the card front. Backgrounds are green with gold pinstripes. Behind the action photo at center is a large diamond with each corner intersected by a silver semi-circle. On the Finest Rookies subset which makes up the first 30 cards of the issue, the diamond has a graduated pink to orange center, with flecks of red throughout. Veterans cards have a graduated blue to purple center of the diamond. On the rookies cards there is a teal brand name at top, while the vets show a gold "FINEST". Backs repeat the front background motif in shades of green. There is a player photo at right, with biographical data, 1994 and career stats, and a "Finest Moment" career highlight at left. Finest was sold in seven-card packs with a suggested retail price of $4.99.

		NM/M
Complete Set (220):		75.00
Common Player:		.25
Refractors:		5X
Series 1 or 2 Pack (7):		2.00
Series 1 or 2 Wax Box (24):		30.00
1	Raul Mondesi (Rookie Theme)	.25
2	Kurt Abbott (Rookie Theme)	.25
3	Chris Gomez (Rookie Theme)	.25
4	Manny Ramirez (Rookie Theme)	1.50
5	Rondell White (Rookie Theme)	.25
6	William Van Landingham (Rookie Theme)	.25
7	Jon Lieber (Rookie Theme)	.25
8	Ryan Klesko (Rookie Theme)	.25
9	John Hudek (Rookie Theme)	.25
10	Joey Hamilton (Rookie Theme)	.25
11	Bob Hamelin (Rookie Theme)	.25
12	Brian Anderson (Rookie Theme)	.25
13	Mike Lieberthal (Rookie Theme)	.25
14	Rico Brogna (Rookie Theme)	.25
15	Rusty Greer (Rookie Theme)	.25
16	Carlos Delgado (Rookie Theme)	1.00
17	Jim Edmonds (Rookie Theme)	.65
18	Steve Trachsel (Rookie Theme)	.25
19	Matt Walbeck (Rookie Theme)	.25
20	Armando Benitez (Rookie Theme)	.25
21	Steve Karsay (Rookie Theme)	.25
22	Jose Oliva (Rookie Theme)	.25
23	Cliff Floyd (Rookie Theme)	.25
24	Kevin Foster (Rookie Theme)	.25
25	Javier Lopez (Rookie Theme)	.25
26	Jose Valentin (Rookie Theme)	.25
27	James Mouton (Rookie Theme)	.25
28	Hector Carrasco (Rookie Theme)	.25
29	Orlando Miller (Rookie Theme)	.25
30	Garret Anderson (Rookie Theme)	.25
31	Marvin Freeman	.25
32	Brett Butler	.25
33	Roberto Kelly	.25
34	Rod Beck	.25
35	Jose Rijo	.25
36	Edgar Martinez	.25
37	Jim Thome	.65
38	Rick Wilkins	.25
39	Wally Joyner	.25
40	Wil Cordero	.25
41	Tommy Greene	.25
42	Travis Fryman	.25
43	Don Slaught	.25
44	Brady Anderson	.25
45	Matt Williams	.25
46	Rene Arocha	.25
47	Rickey Henderson	1.50
48	Mike Mussina	.75
49	Greg McMichael	.25
50	Jody Reed	.25
51	Tino Martinez	.25
52	Dave Clark	.25
53	John Valentin	.25
54	Bret Boone	.25
55	Walt Weiss	.25
56	Kenny Lofton	.25
57	Scott Leius	.25
58	Eric Karros	.25
59	John Olerud	.25
60	Chris Hoiles	.25
61	Sandy Alomar	.25
62	Tim Wallach	.25
63	Cal Eldred	.25
64	Tom Glavine	.50
65	Mark Grace	.25
66	Rey Sanchez	.25
67	Bobby Ayala	.25
68	Dante Bichette	.25
69	Andres Galarraga	.25
70	Chuck Carr	.25
71	Bobby Witt	.25
72	Steve Avery	.25
73	Bobby Jones	.25
74	Delino DeShields	.25
75	Kevin Tapani	.25
76	Randy Johnson	1.50
77	David Nied	.25
78	Pat Hentgen	.25
79	Tim Salmon	.25
80	Todd Zeile	.25
81	John Wetteland	.25
82	Albert Belle	.25
83	Ben McDonald	.25
84	Bobby Munoz	.25
85	Bip Roberts	.25
86	Mo Vaughn	.25
87	Chuck Finley	.25
88	Chuck Knoblauch	.25
89	Frank Thomas	1.50
90	Danny Tartabull	.25
91	Dean Palmer	.25
92	Len Dykstra	.25
93	J.R. Phillips	.25
94	Tom Candiotti	.25
95	Marquis Grissom	.25
96	Barry Larkin	.25
97	Bryan Harvey	.25
98	Dave Justice	.25
99	David Cone	.25
100	Wade Boggs	2.50
101	Jason Bere	.25
102	Hal Morris	.25
103	Fred McGriff	.25
104	Bobby Bonilla	.25
105	Jay Buhner	.25
106	Allen Watson	.25
107	Mickey Tettleton	.25
108	Kevin Appier	.25
109	Ivan Rodriguez	1.00
110	Carlos Garcia	.25
111	Andy Benes	.25
112	Eddie Murray	1.50
113	Mike Piazza	3.50
114	Greg Vaughn	.25
115	Paul Molitor	1.50
116	Terry Steinbach	.25
117	Jeff Bagwell	1.50
118	Ken Griffey Jr.	3.50
119	Gary Sheffield	.75
120	Cal Ripken Jr.	5.00
121	Jeff Kent	.25
122	Jay Bell	.25
123	Will Clark	.25
124	Cecil Fielder	.25
125	Alex Fernandez	.25
126	Don Mattingly	3.00
127	Reggie Sanders	.25
128	Moises Alou	.25
129	Craig Biggio	.25
130	Eddie Williams	.25
131	John Franco	.25
132	John Kruk	.25
133	Jeff King	.25
134	Royce Clayton	.25
135	Doug Drabek	.25
136	Ray Lankford	.25
137	Roberto Alomar	.50
138	Todd Hundley	.25
139	Alex Cole	.25
140	Shawon Dunston	.25
141	John Roper	.25
142	Mark Langston	.25
143	Tom Pagnozzi	.25
144	Wilson Alvarez	.25
145	Scott Cooper	.25
146	Kevin Mitchell	.25
147	Mark Whiten	.25
148	Jeff Conine	.25
149	Chili Davis	.25
150	Luis Gonzalez	.25
151	Juan Guzman	.25
152	Mike Greenwell	.25
153	Mike Henneman	.25
154	Rick Aguilera	.25
155	Dennis Eckersley	1.00
156	Darrin Fletcher	.25
157	Darren Lewis	.25
158	Juan Gonzalez	.75
159	Dave Hollins	.25
160	Jimmy Key	.25
161	Roberto Hernandez	.25
162	Randy Myers	.25
163	Joe Carter	.25
164	Darren Daulton	.25
165	Mike MacFarlane	.25
166	Bret Saberhagen	.25
167	Kirby Puckett	2.50
168	Lance Johnson	.25
169	Mark McGwire	4.00
170	Jose Canseco	.75
171	Mike Stanley	.25
172	Lee Smith	.25
173	Robin Ventura	.25
174	Greg Gagne	.25
175	Brian McRae	.25
176	Mike Bordick	.25
177	Rafael Palmeiro	1.00
178	Kenny Rogers	.25
179	Chad Curtis	.25
180	Devon White	.25
181	Paul O'Neill	.25
182	Ken Caminiti	.25
183	Dave Nilsson	.25
184	Tim Naehring	.25
185	Roger Clemens	3.00
186	Otis Nixon	.25
187	Tim Raines	.25
188	Dennis Martinez	.25
189	Pedro Martinez	1.50
190	Jim Abbott	.25
191	Ryan Thompson	.25
192	Barry Bonds	5.00
193	Joe Girardi	.25
194	Steve Finley	.25
195	John Jaha	.25
196	Tony Gwynn	2.50
197	Sammy Sosa	2.50
198	John Burkett	.25
199	Carlos Baerga	.25
200	Ramon Martinez	.25
201	Aaron Sele	.25
202	Eduardo Perez	.25
203	Alan Trammell	.25
204	Orlando Merced	.25
205	Deion Sanders	.35
206	Robb Nen	.25
207	Jack McDowell	.25
208	Ruben Sierra	.25
209	Bernie Williams	.25
210	Kevin Seitzer	.25
211	Charles Nagy	.25
212	Tony Phillips	.25
213	Greg Maddux	2.50
214	Jeff Montgomery	.25
215	Larry Walker	.25
216	Andy Van Slyke	.25
217	Ozzie Smith	2.50
218	Geronimo Pena	.25
219	Gregg Jefferies	.25
220	Lou Whitaker	.25

Refractors

A parallel set with a counterpart to each of the 220 cards in the regular Finest emission, the Refractors are printed in a version of the Finest chrome technology that produces a rainbow effect when viewed at the proper angle. The relatively open spaces of the 1995 Finest design make the Refractors easier to spot than the previous years' versions, but just to assist the identification process, Topps placed a small black "REFRACTOR" in the dark green background on the cards' backs, as well. Advertised rate of insertion for the Refractors was about one per 12 packs.

	NM/M
Complete Set (220):	400.00
Common Player:	1.00
Stars:	5X

Flame Throwers

The scarcest of the Finest inserts is the nine-card set of baseball's hardest throwing pitchers. Flame Throwers cards are found at an average rate of one per 48 packs. Fronts have a central photo of a pitcher bringing his best heat. Behind the photo is the Flame Throwers typographic logo in tones of red, yellow and orange. Backs have another photo and a bar graph rating the pitcher's skill levels.

		NM/M
Complete Set (9):		20.00
Common Player:		1.50
1	Jason Bere	1.50
2	Roger Clemens	8.00
3	Juan Guzman	1.50
4	John Hudek	1.50
5	Randy Johnson	5.00
6	Pedro Martinez	4.00
7	Jose Rijo	1.50
8	Bret Saberhagen	1.50
9	John Wetteland	1.50

Power Kings

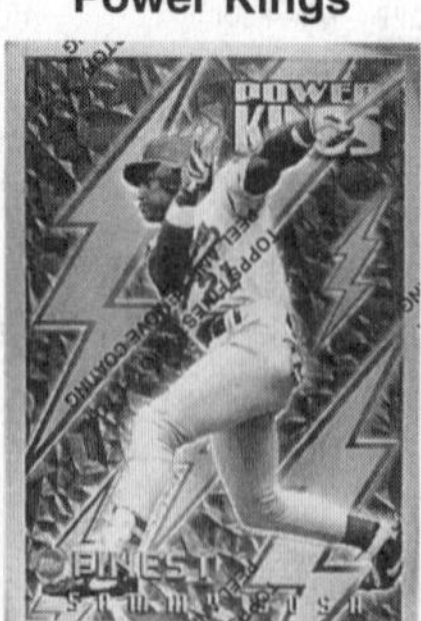

The emphasis is on youth in this chase set of baseball's top distance threats. Found at a rate of one per 24 packs, on average, the Power Kings inserts have a central photo of the player in batting action. The background, in shades of blue, features lightning strokes. Backs feature another pair of player photos and a bar graph charting the hitter's power skills.

		NM/M
Complete Set (18):		35.00
Common Player:		.75
1	Bob Hamelin	.75
2	Raul Mondesi	.75
3	Ryan Klesko	.75
4	Carlos Delgado	1.50
5	Manny Ramirez	3.00
6	Mike Piazza	5.00
7	Jeff Bagwell	3.00
8	Mo Vaughn	.75
9	Frank Thomas	3.00
10	Ken Griffey Jr.	5.00
11	Albert Belle	.75
12	Sammy Sosa	4.00
13	Dante Bichette	.75
14	Gary Sheffield	.75
15	Matt Williams	.75
16	Fred McGriff	.75
17	Barry Bonds	7.50
18	Cecil Fielder	.75

Update

Players who changed teams through trades or free agent signings and more of the season's rookie player crop are included in the Finest Update series of 110 cards. The cards are numbered contiguously with the base Finest set and share the same design. Once again, Refractor cards were found on an average of once per 12 packs. Finest Update was sold in seven-card packs with a suggested retail price of $4.99.

		NM/M
Complete Set (110):		20.00
Common Player:		.25
Refractors:		5X
Wax Pack (7):		1.25
Wax Box (24):		20.00
221	Chipper Jones	2.50
222	Benji Gil	.25
223	Tony Phillips	.25
224	Trevor Wilson	.25
225	Tony Tarasco	.25
226	Roberto Petagine	.25
227	Mike MacFarlane	.25
228	Hideo Nomo **RC**	3.00
229	Mark McLemore	.25
230	Ron Gant	.25
231	Andujar Cedeno	.25
232	Mike Mimbs **RC**	.25
233	Jim Abbott	.25
234	Ricky Bones	.25
235	Marty Cordova	.25
236	Mark Johnson	.25
237	Marquis Grissom	.25
238	Tom Henke	.25
239	Terry Pendleton	.25
240	John Wetteland	.25
241	Lee Smith	.25
242	Jaime Navarro	.25
243	Luis Alicea	.25
244	Scott Cooper	.25
245	Gary Gaetti	.25
246	Edgardo Alfonzo	.25
247	Brad Clontz	.25
248	Dave Mlicki	.25
249	Dave Winfield	1.50
250	Mark Grudzielanek **RC**	.50
251	Alex Gonzalez	.25
252	Kevin Brown	.25
253	Esteban Loaiza	.25
254	Vaughn Eshelman	.25
255	Bill Swift	.25
256	Brian McRae	.25
257	Bobby Higginson **RC**	.50
258	Jack McDowell	.25
259	Scott Stahoviak	.25
260	Jon Nunnally	.25
261	Charlie Hayes	.25
262	Jacob Brumfield	.25
263	Chad Curtis	.25
264	Heathcliff Slocumb	.25
265	Mark Whiten	.25
266	Mickey Tettleton	.25
267	Jose Mesa	.25
268	Doug Jones	.25
269	Trevor Hoffman	.25
270	Paul Sorrento	.25
271	Shane Andrews	.25
272	Brett Butler	.25
273	Curtis Goodwin	.25
274	Larry Walker	.25
275	Phil Plantier	.25
276	Ken Hill	.25
277	Vinny Castilla	.25
278	Billy Ashley	.25
279	Derek Jeter	6.00
280	Bob Tewksbury	.25
281	Jose Offerman	.25
282	Glenallen Hill	.25
283	Tony Fernandez	.25
284	Mike Devereaux	.25
285	John Burkett	.25
286	Geronimo Berroa	.25
287	Quilvio Veras	.25
288	Jason Bates	.25
289	Lee Tinsley	.25
290	Derek Bell	.25
291	Jeff Fassero	.25
292	Ray Durham	.25
293	Chad Ogea	.25
294	Bill Pulsipher	.25
295	Phil Nevin	.25
296	Carlos Perez **RC**	.25
297	Roberto Kelly	.25
298	Tim Wakefield	.25
299	Jeff Manto	.25
300	Brian Hunter	.25
301	C.J. Nitkowski	.25
302	Dustin Hermanson	.25
303	John Mabry	.25
304	Orel Hershiser	.25
305	Ron Villone	.25
306	Sean Bergman	.25
307	Tom Goodwin	.25
308	Al Reyes	.25
309	Todd Stottlemyre	.25
310	Rich Becker	.25
311	Joey Cora	.25
312	Ed Sprague	.25
313	John Smoltz	.25
314	Frank Castillo	.25
315	Chris Hammond	.25
316	Ismael Valdes	.25
317	Pete Harnisch	.25
318	Bernard Gilkey	.25
319	John Kruk	.25
320	Marc Newfield	.25
321	Brian Johnson	.25
322	Mark Portugal	.25
323	David Hulse	.25
324	Luis Ortiz	.25
325	Mike Benjamin	.25
326	Brian Jordan	.25
327	Shawn Green	.75
328	Joe Oliver	.25
329	Felipe Lira	.25
330	Andre Dawson	.75

Update Refractors

The special version of Topps' chromium printing process which creates a rainbow effect was applied to a limited number of each card in the Finest Update set to create a parallel Refractor edition. To assist in identification, a small black "REFRACTOR" is printed on the cards' backs, as well. Refractors are found on average once every 12 packs of Finest Update.

	NM/M
Complete Set (110):	100.00
Common Player:	1.00
Stars:	5X

Bronze League Leaders

Available only by mail directly from Topps, this set features N.L. and A.L. leaders in various batting categories for the 1994 season. Fronts employ Topps' Finest technology with a stained-glass effect in the background, overlaid with a heavy layer of resin. Backs are bronze and feature 1994 stats and highlights embossed in blue. The cards are oversized, measuring 2-3/4" x 3-3/4".

NM/M
Complete Set (6): 20.00
Common Player: 2.50
1 Matt Williams 2.50
2 Tony Gwynn 6.50
3 Jeff Bagwell 5.00
4 Ken Griffey Jr. 9.00
5 Paul O'Neill 2.50
6 Frank Thomas 5.00

1996 Finest

Utilizing three levels of base-card scarcity, the 359-card Finest set comprises 220 Commons (Bronze), 91 Uncommons (Silver) and 49 Rares (Gold). Cards were somewhat randomly assigned a status. Uncommon cards are found one in four packs; Rare cards are seeded one per 24 packs. The set has eight themes. Series 1 themes are Phenoms, Intimidators, Gamers and Sterling, the latter of which consists of star players already included within the first three themes. Series 2 themes are Franchise, Additions, Prodigies and Sterling. Regular-issue cards are not only numbered from 1-359 in the set as a whole, but also numbered within each subset. Finest Refractor parallel cards were also made. Rare Refractor cards are found one every 288 packs (fewer than 150 of each produced), while Uncommon Refractors are found one per 48 packs. Common Refractors are seeded 1:12.

NM/M
Complete Set (359): 300.00
Bronze Set (220): 60.00
Common Bronze: .15
Silver Set (91): 90.00
Typical Silver: .50
Gold Set (47): 200.00
Typical Gold: 2.00
Series 1 Pack (6): 1.50
Series 1 Wax Box (24): 30.00
Series 2 Pack (6): 1.50
Series 2 Wax Box (24): 30.00
1 Greg Maddux/S (Intimidators) 3.00
2 Bernie Williams/S (Gamers) .50
3 Ivan Rodriguez/S (Intimidators) 1.50
4 Marty Cordova/G (Phenoms) 2.00
5 Roberto Hernandez (Intimidators) .15
6 Tony Gwynn/G (Gamers) 7.50
7 Barry Larkin/S (Sterling) .50
8 Terry Pendleton (Gamers) .15
9 Albert Belle/G (Sterling) 2.00
10 Ray Lankford/S (Gamers) .50
11 Mike Piazza/S (Sterling) 4.00
12 Ken Caminiti (Gamers) .15
13 Larry Walker/S (Intimidators) .50
14 Matt Williams/S (Intimidators) .50
15 Dan Miceli (Phenoms) .15
16 Chipper Jones (Sterling) 2.00
17 John Wetteland (Intimidators) .15
18 Kirby Puckett/G (Sterling) 7.50
19 Tim Naehring (Gamers) .15
20 Karim Garcia/G (Phenoms) 2.00
21 Eddie Murray (Gamers) 1.25
22 Tim Salmon/S (Intimidators) .50
23 Kevin Appier (Intimidators) .15
24 Ken Griffey Jr. (Sterling) 3.00
25 Cal Ripken Jr./G (Gamers) 15.00
26 Brian McRae (Gamers) .15
27 Pedro Martinez (Intimidators) 1.25
28 Brian Jordan (Gamers) .15
29 Mike Fetters (Intimidators) .15
30 Carlos Delgado (Phenoms) .65
31 Shane Reynolds (Intimidators) .15
32 Terry Steinbach (Gamers) .15
33 Hideo Nomo/G (Sterling) 2.50
34 Mark Leiter (Gamers) .15
35 Edgar Martinez/S (Intimidators) .50
36 David Segui (Gamers) .15
37 Gregg Jefferies/S (Gamers) .50
38 Bill Pulsipher/S (Phenoms) .50
39 Ryne Sandberg/G (Gamers) 7.50
40 Fred McGriff (Intimidators) .15
41 Shawn Green/S (Phenoms) .75
42 Jeff Bagwell/G (Sterling) 5.00
43 Jim Abbott/S (Gamers) .50
44 Glenallen Hill (Intimidators) .15
45 Brady Anderson (Gamers) .15
46 Roger Clemens/S (Intimidators) 3.50
47 Jim Thome (Gamers) .60
48 Frank Thomas (Sterling) 1.25
49 Chuck Knoblauch (Gamers) .15
50 Lenny Dykstra (Gamers) .15
51 Jason Isringhausen/G (Phenoms) 2.00
52 Rondell White/S (Phenoms) .50
53 Tom Pagnozzi (Gamers) .15
54 Dennis Eckersley/S (Intimidators) 1.50
55 Ricky Bones (Gamers) .15
56 David Justice (Intimidators) .15
57 Steve Avery (Gamers) .15
58 Robby Thompson (Gamers) .15
59 Hideo Nomo/S (Phenoms) 1.00
60 Gary Sheffield/S (Intimidators) .75
61 Tony Gwynn (Sterling) 2.00
62 Will Clark/S (Gamers) .50
63 Denny Neagle (Gamers) .15
64 Mo Vaughn/G (Intimidators) 2.00
65 Bret Boone/S (Gamers) .50
66 Dante Bichette/G (Sterling) 2.00
67 Robin Ventura (Gamers) .15
68 Rafael Palmeiro/S (Intimidators) 1.50
69 Carlos Baerga/S (Gamers) .50
70 Kevin Seitzer (Gamers) .15
71 Ramon Martinez (Intimidators) .15
72 Tom Glavine/S (Gamers) 1.00
73 Garret Anderson/S (Phenoms) .50
74 Mark McGwire/G (Intimidators) 12.00
75 Brian Hunter (Phenoms) .15
76 Alan Benes (Phenoms) .15
77 Randy Johnson/S (Intimidators) 2.00
78 Jeff King/S (Gamers) .50
79 Kirby Puckett/S (Intimidators) 3.00
80 Ozzie Guillen (Gamers) .15
81 Kenny Lofton/G (Intimidators) 2.00
82 Benji Gil (Phenoms) .15
83 Jim Edmonds/G (Gamers) 2.00
84 Cecil Fielder/S (Intimidators) .50
85 Todd Hundley (Gamers) .15
86 Reggie Sanders/S (Intimidators) .50
87 Pat Hentgen (Gamers) .15
88 Ryan Klesko/S (Intimidators) .50
89 Chuck Finley (Gamers) .15
90 Mike Mussina/G (Intimidators) 2.50
91 John Valentin/S (Intimidators) .50
92 Derek Jeter (Phenoms) 4.00
93 Paul O'Neill (Intimidators) .15
94 Darrin Fletcher (Gamers) .15
95 Manny Ramirez/S (Phenoms) 2.00
96 Delino DeShields (Gamers) .15
97 Tim Salmon (Sterling) .15
98 John Olerud (Gamers) .15
99 Vinny Castilla/S (Intimidators) .50
100 Jeff Conine/G (Gamers) 2.00
101 Tim Wakefield (Gamers) .15
102 Johnny Damon/G (Phenoms) 3.50
103 Dave Stevens (Gamers) .15
104 Orlando Merced (Gamers) .15
105 Barry Bonds/G (Sterling) 15.00
106 Jay Bell (Gamers) .15
107 John Burkett (Gamers) .15
108 Chris Hoiles (Gamers) .15
109 Carlos Perez/S (Phenoms) .50
110 Dave Nilsson (Gamers) .15
111 Rod Beck (Intimidators) .15
112 Craig Biggio/S (Gamers) .50
113 Mike Piazza (Intimidators) 3.00
114 Mark Langston (Gamers) .15
115 Juan Gonzalez/S (Intimidators) 1.00
116 Rico Brogna (Gamers) .15
117 Jose Canseco/G (Intimidators) 3.00
118 Tom Goodwin (Gamers) .15
119 Bryan Rekar (Phenoms) .15
120 David Cone (Intimidators) .15
121 Ray Durham/S (Phenoms) .50
122 Andy Pettitte (Phenoms) .40
123 Chili Davis (Intimidators) .15
124 John Smoltz (Gamers) .15
125 Heathcliff Slocumb (Intimidators) .15
126 Dante Bichette (Intimidators) .15
127 C.J. Nitkowski/S (Phenoms) .50
128 Alex Gonzalez (Phenoms) .15
129 Jeff Montgomery (Intimidators) .15
130 Raul Mondesi/S (Intimidators) .50
131 Denny Martinez (Gamers) .15
132 Mel Rojas (Intimidators) .15
133 Derek Bell (Gamers) .15
134 Trevor Hoffman (Intimidators) .15
135 Ken Griffey Jr./G (Intimidators) 9.00
136 Darren Daulton (Gamers) .15
137 Pete Schourek (Gamers) .15
138 Phil Nevin (Phenoms) .15
139 Andres Galarraga (Intimidators) .15
140 Chad Fonville (Phenoms) .15
141 Chipper Jones/G (Phenoms) 7.50
142 Lee Smith/S (Intimidators) .50
143 Joe Carter/S (Gamers) .50
144 J.T. Snow (Gamers) .15
145 Greg Maddux/G (Sterling) 7.50
146 Barry Bonds (Intimidators) 4.00
147 Orel Hershiser (Gamers) .15
148 Quilvio Veras (Phenoms) .15
149 Will Clark (Sterling) .15
150 Jose Rijo (Gamers) .15
151 Mo Vaughn/S (Sterling) .50
152 Travis Fryman (Gamers) .15
153 Frank Rodriguez/S (Phenoms) .50
154 Alex Fernandez (Gamers) .15
155 Wade Boggs (Gamers) 2.00
156 Troy Percival (Phenoms) .15
157 Moises Alou (Gamers) .15
158 Javy Lopez (Gamers) .15
159 Jason Giambi (Phenoms) .50
160 Steve Finley/S (Gamers) .50
161 Jeff Bagwell/S (Intimidators) 2.00
162 Mark McGwire (Sterling) 3.50
163 Eric Karros (Gamers) .15
164 Jay Buhner/G (Intimidators) 2.00
165 Cal Ripken Jr./S (Sterling) 6.00
166 Mickey Tettleton (Intimidators) .15
167 Barry Larkin (Intimidators) .15
168 Lyle Mouton/S (Phenoms) .50
169 Ruben Sierra (Intimidators) .15
170 Bill Swift (Gamers) .15
171 Sammy Sosa/S (Intimidators) 3.00
172 Chad Curtis (Gamers) .15
173 Dean Palmer (Gamers) .15
174 John Franco/S (Gamers) .50
175 Bobby Bonilla (Intimidators) .15
176 Greg Colbrunn (Gamers) .15
177 Jose Mesa (Intimidators) .15
178 Mike Greenwell (Gamers) .15
179 Greg Vaughn/S (Intimidators) .50
180 Mark Wohlers/S (Intimidators) .50
181 Doug Drabek (Gamers) .15
182 Paul O'Neill/S (Sterling) .50
183 Wilson Alvarez (Gamers) .15
184 Marty Cordova (Sterling) .15
185 Hal Morris (Gamers) .15
186 Frank Thomas/G (Intimidators) 6.00
187 Carlos Garcia (Gamers) .15
188 Albert Belle/S (Intimidators) .50
189 Mark Grace/S (Gamers) .50
190 Marquis Grissom (Gamers) .15
191 Checklist .15
192 Chipper Jones/G 7.50
193 Will Clark .15
194 Paul Molitor 1.25
195 Kenny Rogers .15
196 Reggie Sanders .15
197 Roberto Alomar/G 2.50
198 Dennis Eckersley/G 4.00
199 Raul Mondesi .15
200 Lance Johnson .15
201 Alvin Morman .15
202 George Arias/G 2.00
203 Jack McDowell .15
204 Randy Myers .15
205 Harold Baines .15
206 Marty Cordova .15
207 Rich Hunter **RC** .15
208 Al Leiter .15
209 Greg Gagne .15
210 Ben McDonald .15
211 Ernie Young/S .50
212 Terry Adams .15
213 Paul Sorrento .15
214 Albert Belle .15
215 Mike Blowers .15
216 Jim Edmonds .15
217 Felipe Crespo .15
218 Fred McGriff/S .50
219 Shawon Dunston .15
220 Jimmy Haynes .15
221 Jose Canseco .50
222 Eric Davis .15
223 Kimera Bartee/S .50
224 Tim Raines .15
225 Tony Phillips .15
226 Charlie Hayes .15
227 Eric Owens .15
228 Roberto Alomar .30
229 Rickey Henderson/S 2.00
230 Sterling Hitchcock/S .50
231 Bernard Gilkey/S .50
232 Hideo Nomo/G 2.50
233 Kenny Lofton .15
234 Ryne Sandberg/S 3.00
235 Greg Maddux/S 3.00
236 Mark McGwire 3.50
237 Jay Buhner .15
238 Craig Biggio .15
239 Todd Stottlemyre/S .50
240 Barry Bonds 4.00
241 Jason Kendall/S .50
242 Paul O'Neill/S .50
243 Chris Snopek/G 2.00
244 Ron Gant .15
245 Paul Wilson .15
246 Todd Hollandsworth .15
247 Todd Zeile .15
248 David Justice .15
249 Tim Salmon/G 2.00
250 Moises Alou .15
251 Bob Wolcott .15
252 David Wells .15
253 Juan Gonzalez .65
254 Andres Galarraga .15
255 Dave Hollins .15
256 Devon White/S .50
257 Sammy Sosa 2.00
258 Ivan Rodriguez .75
259 Bip Roberts .15
260 Tino Martinez .15
261 Chuck Knoblauch/S .50
262 Mike Stanley .15
263 Wally Joyner/S .50
264 Butch Huskey .15
265 Jeff Conine .15
266 Matt Williams/G 2.00
267 Mark Grace .15
268 Jason Schmidt .15
269 Otis Nixon .15
270 Randy Johnson/G 5.00
271 Kirby Puckett 2.00
272 Andy Fox/S **RC** .50
273 Andy Benes .15
274 Sean Berry/S .50
275 Mike Piazza 3.00
276 Rey Ordonez .15
277 Benito Santiago/S .50
278 Gary Gaetti .15
279 Paul Molitor/G 5.00
280 Robin Ventura .15
281 Cal Ripken Jr. 4.00
282 Carlos Baerga .15
283 Roger Cedeno .15
284 Chad Mottola/S .50
285 Terrell Wade .15
286 Kevin Brown .15
287 Rafael Palmeiro 1.00
288 Mo Vaughn .15
289 Dante Bichette/S .50
290 Cecil Fielder/G 2.00
291 Doc Gooden/S .50
292 Bob Tewksbury .15
293 Kevin Mitchell/S .50
294 Livan Hernandez/G **RC** 2.00
295 Russ Davis/S .50
296 Chan Ho Park/S .50
297 T.J. Mathews .15
298 Manny Ramirez 1.25
299 Jeff Bagwell 1.25
300 Marty Janzen/G **RC** 2.00
301 Wade Boggs 2.00
302 Larry Walker/S .50
303 Steve Gibralter .15
304 B.J. Surhoff .15
305 Ken Griffey Jr./S 4.00
306 Royce Clayton .15
307 Sal Fasano .15
308 Ron Gant/G 2.00
309 Gary Sheffield .40
310 Ken Hill .15
311 Joe Girardi .15
312 Matt Lawton **RC** .15
313 Billy Wagner/S .50
314 Julio Franco .15
315 Joe Carter .15
316 Brooks Kieschnick .15
317 Mike Grace/S **RC** .50
318 Heathcliff Slocumb .15
319 Barry Larkin .15
320 Tony Gwynn 2.00
321 Ryan Klesko/G 2.00
322 Frank Thomas 1.25
323 Edgar Martinez .15
324 Jermaine Dye/G 2.00
325 Henry Rodriguez .15
326 Marvin Benard **RC** .50
327 Kenny Lofton/S .50
328 Derek Bell/S .50
329 Ugueth Urbina .15
330 Jason Giambi/G 3.00
331 Roger Salkeld .15
332 Edgar Renteria .15
333 Ryan Klesko .15
334 Ray Lankford .15
335 Edgar Martinez/G 2.00
336 Justin Thompson .15
337 Gary Sheffield/S .75
338 Rey Ordonez/G 2.00
339 Mark Clark .15
340 Ruben Rivera .15
341 Mark Grace/S .50
342 Matt Williams .15
343 Francisco Cordova **RC** .25
344 Cecil Fielder .15
345 Andres Galarraga/S .50
346 Brady Anderson/S .50
347 Sammy Sosa/G 7.50
348 Mark Grudzielanek .15
349 Ron Coomer .15
350 Derek Jeter/S 6.00
351 Rich Aurilia .15
352 Jose Herrera .15
353 Jay Buhner/S .50
354 Juan Gonzalez/G 2.50
355 Craig Biggio/G 2.00
356 Tony Clark .15
357 Tino Martinez/S .50
358 Dan Naulty **RC** .15
359 Checklist .15

Refractors

Finest Refractor cards were created as a parallel set to Topps' 1996 Finest set. Rare Refractor cards are found about one per 288 packs (less than 150 of these sets were produced), while Uncommon Refractors are found one every 48 packs. Common Refractors are seeded one every 12 packs.

NM/M
Complete Set (359): 900.00
Bronze Set (220): 300.00
Common Bronze: 1.00
Bronze Stars: 4X
Silver Set (91): 250.00
Typical Silver: 2.00
Silver Stars: 2.5X
Gold Set (48): 600.00
Typical Gold: 6.00
Gold Stars: 2X

1997 Finest Samples

Many of the subsets included in the 1997 Finest issue were previewed with a cello-wrapped pack of five cards distributed to hobby dealers. Cards are virtually identical to the issued versions and are designated a Refractor on back. Overprinted on back is a red notice, "PROMOTIONAL SAMPLE / NOT FOR RESALE."

NM/M
Complete Set (5): 15.00
Common Player: 2.50
1 Barry Bonds 3.50
15 Derek Jeter 3.50
30 Mark McGwire 3.00
143 Hideo Nomo 2.50
159 Jeff Bagwell 2.50

1997 Finest

Finest returned for 1997 in its three-tiered format from 1996, but added several new twists. Issued in two series of 175 cards each, cards numbered 1-100 and 176-275 are bronze; 101-150 and 276-325 are silver and 151-175 and 326-350 are gold. All cards are designated among one of five different subsets per series. In Series 1 they are: Warriors, Blue Chips, Power, Hurlers and Masters. Series 2 subsets are: Power, Masters, Blue Chips, Competitors and Acquisitions. The bronze cards are the "common" card, while silvers are found every four packs and golds every 24 packs. Each card has a parallel Refractor version: bronze (1:12), silver (1:48) and gold (1:288). In addition, silver and gold cards have an additional parallel set. Silvers are found in an embossed version (1:16) and embossed Refractor version (1:192), while golds are found in a die-cut embossed version (1:96) and a die-cut embossed Refractor (1:1152).

	NM/M
Complete Set (350):	200.00
Bronze Set (200):	15.00
Common Bronze:	.15
Silver Set (100):	75.00
Typical Silver:	.50
Embossed Silvers:	2X
Gold Set (50):	150.00
Typical Gold:	2.00
Embossed Die-Cut Golds:	1.5X
Series 1 or 2 Pack (6):	1.50
Series 1 or 2 Wax Box (24):	25.00

#	Player	NM/M
1	Barry Bonds/B	2.00
2	Ryne Sandberg/B	.75
3	Brian Jordan/B	.15
4	Rocky Coppinger/B	.15
5	Dante Bichette/B	.15
6	Al Martin/B	.15
7	Charles Nagy/B	.15
8	Otis Nixon/B	.15
9	Mark Johnson/B	.15
10	Jeff Bagwell/B	.60
11	Ken Hill/B	.15
12	Willie Adams/B	.15
13	Raul Mondesi/B	.15
14	Reggie Sanders/B	.15
15	Derek Jeter/B	2.00
16	Jermaine Dye/B	.15
17	Edgar Renteria/B	.15
18	Travis Fryman/B	.15
19	Roberto Hernandez/B	.15
20	Sammy Sosa/B	.75
21	Garret Anderson/B	.15
22	Rey Ordonez/B	.15
23	Glenallen Hill/B	.15
24	Dave Nilsson/B	.15
25	Kevin Brown/B	.15
26	Brian McRae/B	.15
27	Joey Hamilton/B	.15
28	Jamey Wright/B	.15
29	Frank Thomas/B	.60
30	Mark McGwire/B	1.50
31	Ramon Martinez/B	.15
32	Jaime Bluma/B	.15
33	Frank Rodriguez/B	.15
34	Andy Benes/B	.15
35	Jay Buhner/B	.15
36	Justin Thompson/B	.15
37	Darin Erstad/B	.30
38	Gregg Jefferies/B	.15
39	Jeff D'Amico/B	.15
40	Pedro Martinez/B	.60
41	Nomar Garciaparra/B	.75
42	Jose Valentin/B	.15
43	Pat Hentgen/B	.15
44	Will Clark/B	.15
45	Bernie Williams/B	.15
46	Luis Castillo/B	.15
47	B.J. Surhoff/B	.15
48	Greg Gagne/B	.15
49	Pete Schourek/B	.15
50	Mike Piazza/B	1.00
51	Dwight Gooden/B	.15
52	Javy Lopez/B	.15
53	Chuck Finley/B	.15
54	James Baldwin/B	.15
55	Jack McDowell/B	.15
56	Royce Clayton/B	.15
57	Carlos Delgado/B	.35
58	Neifi Perez/B	.15
59	Eddie Taubensee/B	.15
60	Rafael Palmeiro/B	.50
61	Marty Cordova/B	.15
62	Wade Boggs/B	.75
63	Rickey Henderson/B	.60
64	Mike Hampton/B	.15
65	Troy Percival/B	.15
66	Barry Larkin/B	.15
67	Jermaine Allensworth/B	.15
68	Mark Clark/B	.15
69	Mike Lansing/B	.15
70	Mark Grudzielanek/B	.15
71	Todd Stottlemyre/B	.15
72	Juan Guzman/B	.15
73	John Burkett/B	.15
74	Wilson Alvarez/B	.15
75	Ellis Burks/B	.15
76	Bobby Higginson/B	.15
77	Ricky Bottalico/B	.15
78	Omar Vizquel/B	.15
79	Paul Sorrento/B	.15
80	Denny Neagle/B	.15
81	Roger Pavlik/B	.15
82	Mike Lieberthal/B	.15
83	Devon White/B	.15
84	John Olerud/B	.15
85	Kevin Appier/B	.15
86	Joe Girardi/B	.15
87	Paul O'Neill/B	.15
88	Mike Sweeney/B	.15
89	John Smiley/B	.15
90	Ivan Rodriguez/B	.50
91	Randy Myers/B	.15
92	Bip Roberts/B	.15
93	Jose Mesa/B	.15
94	Paul Wilson/B	.15
95	Mike Mussina/B	.30
96	Ben McDonald/B	.15
97	John Mabry/B	.15
98	Tom Goodwin/B	.15
99	Edgar Martinez/B	.15
100	Andruw Jones/B	.60
101	Jose Canseco/S	.75
102	Billy Wagner/S	.50
103	Dante Bichette/S	.50
104	Curt Schilling/S	1.00
105	Dean Palmer/S	.50
106	Larry Walker/S	.50
107	Bernie Williams/S	.50
108	Chipper Jones/S	2.00
109	Gary Sheffield/S	1.00
110	Randy Johnson/S	1.50
111	Roberto Alomar/S	.75
112	Todd Walker/S	.50
113	Sandy Alomar/S	.50
114	John Jaha/S	.50
115	Ken Caminiti/S	.50
116	Ryan Klesko/S	.50
117	Mariano Rivera/S	.75
118	Jason Giambi/S	1.00
119	Lance Johnson/S	.50
120	Robin Ventura/S	.50
121	Todd Hollandsworth/S	.50
122	Johnny Damon/S	.75
123	William Van Landingham/S	.50
124	Jason Kendall/S	.50
125	Vinny Castilla/S	.50
126	Harold Baines/S	.50
127	Joe Carter/S	.50
128	Craig Biggio/S	.50
129	Tony Clark/S	.50
130	Ron Gant/S	.50
131	David Segui/S	.50
132	Steve Trachsel/S	.50
133	Scott Rolen/S	1.00
134	Mike Stanley/S	.50
135	Cal Ripken Jr./S	5.00
136	John Smoltz/S	.50
137	Bobby Jones/S	.50
138	Manny Ramirez/S	1.50
139	Ken Griffey Jr./S	3.00
140	Chuck Knoblauch/S	.50
141	Mark Grace/S	.50
142	Chris Snopek/S	.50
143	Hideo Nomo/S	.75
144	Tim Salmon/S	.50
145	David Cone/S	.50
146	Eric Young/S	.50
147	Jeff Brantley/S	.50
148	Jim Thome/S	1.00
149	Trevor Hoffman/S	.50
150	Juan Gonzalez/S	.75
151	Mike Piazza/G	8.00
152	Ivan Rodriguez/G	4.00
153	Mo Vaughn/G	2.00
154	Brady Anderson/G	2.00
155	Mark McGwire/G	8.00
156	Rafael Palmeiro/G	4.00
157	Barry Larkin/G	2.00
158	Greg Maddux/G	7.50
159	Jeff Bagwell/G	5.00
160	Frank Thomas/G	6.00
161	Ken Caminiti/G	2.00
162	Andruw Jones/G	5.00
163	Dennis Eckersley/G	4.00
164	Jeff Conine/G	2.00
165	Jim Edmonds/G	2.00
166	Derek Jeter/G	12.00
167	Vladimir Guerrero/G	6.00
168	Sammy Sosa/G	5.00
169	Tony Gwynn/G	6.00
170	Andres Galarraga/G	2.00
171	Todd Hundley/G	2.00
172	Jay Buhner/G	2.00
173	Paul Molitor/G	6.00
174	Kenny Lofton/G	2.00
175	Barry Bonds/G	12.00
176	Gary Sheffield/B	.35
177	Dmitri Young/B	.15
178	Jay Bell/B	.15
179	David Wells/B	.15
180	Walt Weiss/B	.15
181	Paul Molitor/B	.60
182	Jose Guillen/B	.15
183	Al Leiter/B	.15
184	Mike Fetters/B	.15
185	Mark Langston/B	.15
186	Fred McGriff/B	.15
187	Darrin Fletcher/B	.15
188	Brant Brown/B	.15
189	Geronimo Berroa/B	.15
190	Jim Thome/B	.50
191	Jose Vizcaino/B	.15
192	Andy Ashby/B	.15
193	Rusty Greer/B	.15
194	Brian Hunter/B	.15
195	Chris Hoiles/B	.15
196	Orlando Merced/B	.15
197	Brett Butler/B	.15
198	Derek Bell/B	.15
199	Bobby Bonilla/B	.15
200	Alex Ochoa/B	.15
201	Wally Joyner/B	.15
202	Mo Vaughn/B	.15
203	Doug Drabek/B	.15
204	Tino Martinez/B	.15
205	Roberto Alomar/B	.30
206	Brian Giles/B **RC**	.75
207	Todd Worrell/B	.15
208	Alan Benes/B	.15
209	Jim Leyritz/B	.15
210	Darryl Hamilton/B	.15
211	Jimmy Key/B	.15
212	Juan Gonzalez/B	.35
213	Vinny Castilla/B	.15
214	Chuck Knoblauch/B	.15
215	Tony Phillips/B	.15
216	Jeff Cirillo/B	.15
217	Carlos Garcia/B	.15
218	Brooks Kieschnick/B	.15
219	Marquis Grissom/B	.15
220	Dan Wilson/B	.15
221	Greg Vaughn/B	.15
222	John Wetteland/B	.15
223	Andres Galarraga/B	.15
224	Ozzie Guillen/B	.15
225	Kevin Elster/B	.15
226	Bernard Gilkey/B	.15
227	Mike MacFarlane/B	.15
228	Heathcliff Slocumb/B	.15
229	Wendell Magee Jr./B	.15
230	Carlos Baerga/B	.15
231	Kevin Seitzer/B	.15
232	Henry Rodriguez/B	.15
233	Roger Clemens/B	1.00
234	Mark Wohlers/B	.15
235	Eddie Murray/B	.60
236	Todd Zeile/B	.15
237	J.T. Snow/B	.15
238	Ken Griffey Jr./B	1.00
239	Sterling Hitchcock/B	.15
240	Albert Belle/B	.15
241	Terry Steinbach/B	.15
242	Robb Nen/B	.15
243	Mark McLemore/B	.15
244	Jeff King/B	.15
245	Tony Clark/B	.15
246	Tim Salmon/B	.15
247	Benito Santiago/B	.15
248	Robin Ventura/B	.15
249	Bubba Trammell/B **RC**	.15
250	Chili Davis/B	.15
251	John Valentin/B	.15
252	Cal Ripken Jr./B	2.00
253	Matt Williams/B	.15
254	Jeff Kent/B	.15
255	Eric Karros/B	.15
256	Ray Lankford/B	.15
257	Ed Sprague/B	.15
258	Shane Reynolds/B	.15
259	Jaime Navarro/B	.15
260	Eric Davis/B	.15
261	Orel Hershiser/B	.15
262	Mark Grace/B	.15
263	Rod Beck/B	.15
264	Ismael Valdes/B	.15
265	Manny Ramirez/B	.60
266	Ken Caminiti/B	.15
267	Tim Naehring/B	.15
268	Jose Rosado/B	.15
269	Greg Colbrunn/B	.15
270	Dean Palmer/B	.15
271	David Justice/B	.15
272	Scott Spiezio/B	.15
273	Chipper Jones/B	.75
274	Mel Rojas/B	.15
275	Bartolo Colon/B	.15
276	Darin Erstad/S	1.00
277	Sammy Sosa/S	2.00
278	Rafael Palmeiro/S	1.00
279	Frank Thomas/S	1.50
280	Ruben Rivera/S	.50
281	Hal Morris/S	.50
282	Jay Buhner/S	.50
283	Kenny Lofton/S	.50
284	Jose Canseco/S	.75
285	Alex Fernandez/S	.50
286	Todd Helton/S	1.25
287	Andy Pettitte/S	1.00
288	John Franco/S	.50
289	Ivan Rodriguez/S	1.25
290	Ellis Burks/S	.50
291	Julio Franco/S	.50
292	Mike Piazza/S	3.00
293	Brian Jordan/S	.50
294	Greg Maddux/S	2.00
295	Bob Abreu/S	.50
296	Rondell White/S	.50
297	Moises Alou/S	.50
298	Tony Gwynn/S	2.00
299	Deion Sanders/S	.50
300	Jeff Montgomery/S	.50
301	Ray Durham/S	.50
302	John Wasdin/S	.50
303	Ryne Sandberg/S	2.00
304	Delino DeShields/S	.50
305	Mark McGwire/S	4.00
306	Andruw Jones/S	1.50
307	Kevin Orie/S	.50
308	Matt Williams/S	.50
309	Karim Garcia/S	.50
310	Derek Jeter/S	5.00
311	Mo Vaughn/S	.50
312	Brady Anderson/S	.50
313	Barry Bonds/S	5.00
314	Steve Finley/S	.50
315	Vladimir Guerrero/S	1.50
316	Matt Morris/S	.50
317	Tom Glavine/S	1.00
318	Jeff Bagwell/S	1.50
319	Albert Belle/S	.50
320	Hideki Irabu/S **RC**	1.00
321	Andres Galarraga/S	.50
322	Cecil Fielder/S	.50
323	Barry Larkin/S	.50
324	Todd Hundley/S	.50
325	Fred McGriff/S	.50
326	Gary Sheffield/G	3.00
327	Craig Biggio/G	2.00
328	Raul Mondesi/G	2.00
329	Edgar Martinez/G	2.00
330	Chipper Jones/G	8.00
331	Bernie Williams/G	2.00
332	Juan Gonzalez/G	3.00
333	Ron Gant/G	2.00
334	Cal Ripken Jr./G	12.00
335	Larry Walker/G	2.00
336	Matt Williams/G	2.00
337	Jose Cruz Jr./G	2.00
338	Joe Carter/G	2.00
339	Wilton Guerrero/G	2.00
340	Cecil Fielder/G	2.00
341	Todd Walker/G	2.00
342	Ken Griffey Jr./G	10.00
343	Ryan Klesko/G	2.00
344	Roger Clemens/G	10.00
345	Hideo Nomo/G	3.00
346	Dante Bichette/G	2.00
347	Albert Belle/G	2.00
348	Randy Johnson/G	6.00
349	Manny Ramirez/G	6.00
350	John Smoltz/G	2.00

Embossed

Each Uncommon (silver) and Rare (gold) card in both Series 1 and 2 Finest was also issued in a parallel Embossed version. The Embossed Silver were a 1:16 find, while the die-cut Embossed Gold were found on average of just one per 96 packs.

	NM/M
Common Embossed Silver:	1.00
Embossed Silver Stars:	2X
Common Embossed Gold:	3.00
Embossed/Die-Cut Gold Stars:	1.5X

Refractors

Every card in '97 Finest - both regular and embossed parallel - has a Refractor version. The Uncommon parallel set of Refractors features a mosaic pattern in the background while the Rare embossed die-cut parallel set of Refractors are produced with a hyper-plaid foil design. The number of cards and the insertion ratios for each level of Refractors is as follows: Common (200 cards, 1:12 packs), Uncommon (100, 1:48), Rare (50, 1:288), Embossed Uncommon (100, 1:192), Embossed Die-cut Rare (50, 1:1152).

	NM/M
Common Bronze:	2.00
Bronze Stars:	6X
Typical Silver:	3.00
Silver Stars:	3X
Typical Gold:	8.00
Gold Stars:	2X
Typical Embossed Silver:	7.50
Embossed Silver Stars:	7X
Typical Embossed Gold:	20.00
Embossed Gold Stars:	5X

1998 Finest Pre-Production

Five-card cello packs of '98 Finest were distributed in the hobby market to preview the always-popular issue. The cards are virtually identical to the issued versions except for the card number, which bears a "PP" prefix.

		NM/M
Complete Set (5):		8.00
Common Player:		2.00
1	Nomar Garciaparra	2.25
2	Mark McGwire	3.00
3	Ivan Rodriguez	2.00
4	Ken Griffey Jr.	2.50
5	Roger Clemens	2.25

1998 Finest

Finest dropped its three-tiered format in 1998 and produced a 275-card set on a thicker 26-point stock, with 150 cards in Series 1 and 125 in Series 2. The catch in 1998 was that each card arrived in Protector, No-Protector, Protector Refractor and No-Protector Refractor versions. Six-card packs sold for a suggested retail price of $5. Finest also included insert sets for the first time since 1995. Included in Series 1 packs were Centurions, Mystery Finest and Power Zone inserts. Series 2 had Mystery Finest, Stadium Stars and The Man. Throughout both series, Finest Protector cards are considered base cards, while No-Protector are inserted one per two packs (HTA odds 1:1), No-Protector Refractors are seeded 1:24 packs (HTA odds 1:10) and Finest Refractors are seeded 1:12 packs (HTA odds 1:5).

		NM/M
Complete Set (275):		30.00
Common Player:		.15
No-Protector:		2.5X
Refractors:		4X
No-Protector Refractor:		8X
Pack (6):		1.50
Wax Box (24):		25.00
Jumbo Pack (13):		2.50
Jumbo Box (12):		25.00
1	Larry Walker	.15
2	Andruw Jones	.75
3	Ramon Martinez	.15
4	Geronimo Berroa	.15
5	David Justice	.15
6	Rusty Greer	.15
7	Chad Ogea	.15
8	Tom Goodwin	.15
9	Tino Martinez	.15
10	Jose Guillen	.15
11	Jeffrey Hammonds	.15
12	Brian McRae	.15
13	Jeremi Gonzalez	.15
14	Craig Counsell	.15
15	Mike Piazza	1.50
16	Greg Maddux	1.00
17	Todd Greene	.15
18	Rondell White	.15
19	Kirk Rueter	.15
20	Tony Clark	.15
21	Brad Radke	.15
22	Jaret Wright	.15
23	Carlos Delgado	.50
24	Dustin Hermanson	.15
25	Gary Sheffield	.40
26	Jose Canseco	.35
27	Kevin Young	.15
28	David Wells	.15
29	Mariano Rivera	.25
30	Reggie Sanders	.15
31	Mike Cameron	.15
32	Bobby Witt	.15
33	Kevin Orie	.15
34	Royce Clayton	.15
35	Edgar Martinez	.15
36	Neifi Perez	.15
37	Kevin Appier	.15
38	Darryl Hamilton	.15
39	Michael Tucker	.15
40	Roger Clemens	1.25
41	Carl Everett	.15
42	Mike Sweeney	.15
43	Pat Meares	.15
44	Brian Giles	.15
45	Matt Morris	.15
46	Jason Dickson	.15
47	Rich Loiselle	.15
48	Joe Girardi	.15
49	Steve Trachsel	.15
50	Ben Grieve	.15
51	Jose Vizcaino	.15
52	Hideki Irabu	.15
53	J.T. Snow	.15
54	Mike Hampton	.15
55	Dave Nilsson	.15
56	Alex Fernandez	.15
57	Brett Tomko	.15
58	Wally Joyner	.15
59	Kelvim Escobar	.15
60	Roberto Alomar	.30
61	Todd Jones	.15
62	Paul O'Neill	.15
63	Jamie Moyer	.15
64	Mark Wohlers	.15
65	Jose Cruz Jr.	.15
66	Troy Percival	.15
67	Rick Reed	.15
68	Will Clark	.15
69	Jamey Wright	.15
70	Mike Mussina	.35
71	David Cone	.15
72	Ryan Klesko	.15
73	Scott Hatteberg	.15
74	James Baldwin	.15
75	Tony Womack	.15
76	Carlos Perez	.15
77	Charles Nagy	.15
78	Jeromy Burnitz	.15
79	Shane Reynolds	.15
80	Cliff Floyd	.15
81	Jason Kendall	.15
82	Chad Curtis	.15
83	Matt Karchner	.15
84	Ricky Bottalico	.15
85	Sammy Sosa	1.00
86	Javy Lopez	.15
87	Jeff Kent	.15
88	Shawn Green	.25
89	Devon White	.15
90	Tony Gwynn	1.00
91	Bob Tewksbury	.15
92	Derek Jeter	2.50
93	Eric Davis	.15
94	Jeff Fassero	.15
95	Denny Neagle	.15
96	Ismael Valdes	.15
97	Tim Salmon	.15
98	Mark Grudzielanek	.15
99	Curt Schilling	.35
100	Ken Griffey Jr.	1.50
101	Edgardo Alfonzo	.15
102	Vinny Castilla	.15
103	Jose Rosado	.15
104	Scott Erickson	.15
105	Alan Benes	.15
106	Shannon Stewart	.15
107	Delino DeShields	.15
108	Mark Loretta	.15
109	Todd Hundley	.15
110	Chuck Knoblauch	.15
111	Quinton McCracken	.15
112	F.P. Santangelo	.15
113	Gerald Williams	.15
114	Omar Vizquel	.15
115	John Valentin	.15
116	Damion Easley	.15
117	Matt Lawton	.15
118	Jim Thome	.60
119	Sandy Alomar	.15
120	Albert Belle	.15
121	Chris Stynes	.15
122	Butch Huskey	.15
123	Shawn Estes	.15
124	Terry Adams	.15
125	Ivan Rodriguez	.60
126	Ron Gant	.15
127	John Mabry	.15
128	Jeff Shaw	.15
129	Jeff Montgomery	.15
130	Justin Thompson	.15
131	Livan Hernandez	.15
132	Ugueth Urbina	.15
133	Doug Glanville	.15

No.	Player	NM/M
134	Troy O'Leary	.15
135	Cal Ripken Jr.	2.50
136	Quilvio Veras	.15
137	Pedro Astacio	.15
138	Willie Greene	.15
139	Lance Johnson	.15
140	Nomar Garciaparra	1.00
141	Jose Offerman	.15
142	Scott Rolen	.60
143	Derek Bell	.15
144	Johnny Damon	.35
145	Mark McGwire	2.00
146	Chan Ho Park	.15
147	Edgar Renteria	.15
148	Eric Young	.15
149	Craig Biggio	.15
150	Checklist 1-150	.15
151	Frank Thomas	.75
152	John Wetteland	.15
153	Mike Lansing	.15
154	Pedro Martinez	.75
155	Rico Brogna	.15
156	Kevin Brown	.15
157	Alex Rodriguez	2.00
158	Wade Boggs	1.00
159	Richard Hidalgo	.15
160	Mark Grace	.15
161	Jose Mesa	.15
162	John Olerud	.15
163	Tim Belcher	.15
164	Chuck Finley	.15
165	Brian Hunter	.15
166	Joe Carter	.15
167	Stan Javier	.15
168	Jay Bell	.15
169	Ray Lankford	.15
170	John Smoltz	.15
171	Ed Sprague	.15
172	Jason Giambi	.50
173	Todd Walker	.15
174	Paul Konerko	.15
175	Rey Ordonez	.15
176	Dante Bichette	.15
177	Bernie Williams	.15
178	Jon Nunnally	.15
179	Rafael Palmeiro	.60
180	Jay Buhner	.15
181	Devon White	.15
182	Jeff D'Amico	.15
183	Walt Weiss	.15
184	Scott Spiezio	.15
185	Moises Alou	.15
186	Carlos Baerga	.15
187	Todd Zeile	.15
188	Gregg Jefferies	.15
189	Mo Vaughn	.15
190	Terry Steinbach	.15
191	Ray Durham	.15
192	Robin Ventura	.15
193	Jeff Reed	.15
194	Ken Caminiti	.15
195	Eric Karros	.15
196	Wilson Alvarez	.15
197	Gary Gaetti	.15
198	Andres Galarraga	.15
199	Alex Gonzalez	.15
200	Garret Anderson	.15
201	Andy Benes	.15
202	Harold Baines	.15
203	Ron Coomer	.15
204	Dean Palmer	.15
205	Reggie Jefferson	.15
206	John Burkett	.15
207	Jermaine Allensworth	.15
208	Bernard Gilkey	.15
209	Jeff Bagwell	.75
210	Kenny Lofton	.15
211	Bobby Jones	.15
212	Bartolo Colon	.15
213	Jim Edmonds	.15
214	Pat Hentgen	.15
215	Matt Williams	.15
216	Bob Abreu	.15
217	Jorge Posada	.15
218	Marty Cordova	.15
219	Ken Hill	.15
220	Steve Finley	.15
221	Jeff King	.15
222	Quinton McCracken	.15
223	Matt Stairs	.15
224	Darin Erstad	.35
225	Fred McGriff	.15
226	Marquis Grissom	.15
227	Doug Glanville	.15
228	Tom Glavine	.35
229	John Franco	.15
230	Darren Bragg	.15
231	Barry Larkin	.15
232	Trevor Hoffman	.15
233	Brady Anderson	.15
234	Al Martin	.15
235	B.J. Surhoff	.15
236	Ellis Burks	.15
237	Randy Johnson	.75
238	Mark Clark	.15
239	Tony Saunders	.15
240	Hideo Nomo	.40
241	Brad Fullmer	.15
242	Chipper Jones	1.00
243	Jose Valentin	.15
244	Manny Ramirez	.75
245	Derrek Lee	.50
246	Jimmy Key	.15
247	Tim Naehring	.15
248	Bobby Higginson	.15
249	Charles Johnson	.15
250	Chili Davis	.15
251	Tom Gordon	.15
252	Mike Lieberthal	.15
253	Billy Wagner	.15
254	Juan Guzman	.15
255	Todd Stottlemyre	.15
256	Brian Jordan	.15
257	Barry Bonds	2.50
258	Dan Wilson	.15
259	Paul Molitor	.75
260	Juan Gonzalez	.40
261	Francisco Cordova	.15
262	Cecil Fielder	.15
263	Travis Lee	.15
264	Kevin Tapani	.15
265	Raul Mondesi	.15
266	Travis Fryman	.15
267	Armando Benitez	.15
268	Pokey Reese	.15
269	Rick Aguilera	.15
270	Andy Pettitte	.35
271	Jose Vizcaino	.15
272	Kerry Wood	.40
273	Vladimir Guerrero	.75
274	John Smiley	.15
275	Checklist 151-275	.15

Refractors

All 275 cards from Finest Series 1 and 2 are available in a Refractor version. seeded one per 12 packs. Besides the refractive quality of the printing of front, Refractors are designated with an "R" suffix to the card number on back.

	NM/M
Complete Set (275):	200.00
Common Player:	1.00
Stars/Rookies:	4X

No-Protector

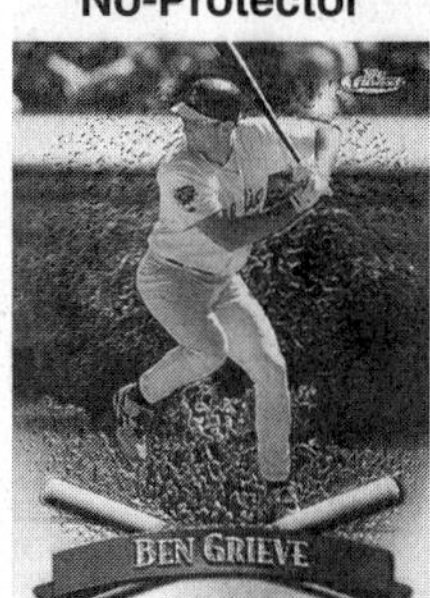

This parallel to the 275-card base set foregoes the peel-off front protector and adds Finest technology to the back of the card. Stated insertion rates were one per two packs or one per pack in Home Team Advantage (HTA) boxes.

	NM/M
Complete Set (275):	150.00
Common Player:	.50
Stars/Rookies:	2.5X

No-Protector Refractor

A Refractor parallel to the 275 No-Protector parallel cards was a 1:24 pack insert. In Series 1, only the refractive quality of the front and back printing reveals this insert. Series 2 No-Protector Refractors have an "R" suffix to the card number on back.

	NM/M
Complete Set (275):	400.00
Common Player:	2.00
Stars/Rookies:	8X

Centurions

Centurions is a 20-card insert found only Series 1 hobby (1:153) and Home Team Advantage packs (1:71). The theme of the insert to top players who will lead the game into the next century. Each card is sequentially numbered on the back to 500, while Refractor versions are numbered to 75.

No.	Player	NM/M
	Complete Set (20):	75.00
	Common Player:	1.50
	Production 500 Sets	
	Refractors (75 Sets):	4X
C1	Andruw Jones	4.50
C2	Vladimir Guerrero	4.50
C3	Nomar Garciaparra	6.00
C4	Scott Rolen	3.50
C5	Ken Griffey Jr.	8.00
C6	Jose Cruz Jr.	1.50
C7	Barry Bonds	12.00
C8	Mark McGwire	10.00
C9	Juan Gonzalez	2.50
C10	Jeff Bagwell	4.50
C11	Frank Thomas	4.50
C12	Paul Konerko	2.00
C13	Alex Rodriguez	10.00
C14	Mike Piazza	8.00
C15	Travis Lee	1.50
C16	Chipper Jones	6.00
C17	Larry Walker	1.50
C18	Mo Vaughn	1.50
C19	Livan Hernandez	1.50
C20	Jaret Wright	1.50

Mystery Finest

This 50-card insert was seeded one per 36 Series 1 packs and one per 15 HTA packs. The set includes 20 top players, each matched on a double-sided card with three other players and once with himself. Each side of the card is printed on a chromium finish and arrives with a black opaque protector. Mystery Finest inserts are numbered with an "M" prefix. Refractor versions were seeded one per 64 packs (HTA odds 1:15).

		NM/M
	Complete Set (50):	125.00
	Common Player:	1.50
	Refractors:	4X
M1	Frank Thomas, Ken Griffey Jr.	3.00
M2	Frank Thomas, Mike Piazza	3.00
M3	Frank Thomas, Mark McGwire	4.00
M4	Frank Thomas, Frank Thomas	2.00
M5	Ken Griffey Jr., Mike Piazza	3.00
M6	Ken Griffey Jr., Mark McGwire	4.00
M7	Ken Griffey Jr., Ken Griffey Jr.	4.00
M8	Mike Piazza, Mark McGwire	4.00
M9	Mike Piazza, Mike Piazza	4.00
M10	Mark McGwire, Mark McGwire	6.00
M11	Nomar Garciaparra, Jose Cruz Jr.	2.50
M12	Nomar Garciaparra, Derek Jeter	5.00
M13	Nomar Garciaparra, Andruw Jones	2.50
M14	Nomar Garciaparra, Nomar Garciaparra	3.00
M15	Jose Cruz Jr., Derek Jeter	5.00
M16	Jose Cruz Jr., Andruw Jones	1.50
M17	Jose Cruz Jr., Jose Cruz Jr.	1.50
M18	Derek Jeter, Andruw Jones	5.00
M19	Derek Jeter, Derek Jeter	7.50
M20	Andruw Jones, Andruw Jones	2.00
M21	Cal Ripken Jr., Tony Gwynn	5.00
M22	Cal Ripken Jr., Barry Bonds	5.00
M23	Cal Ripken Jr., Greg Maddux	5.00
M24	Cal Ripken Jr., Cal Ripken Jr.	7.50
M25	Tony Gwynn, Barry Bonds	5.00
M26	Tony Gwynn, Greg Maddux	2.50
M27	Tony Gwynn, Tony Gwynn	3.00
M28	Barry Bonds, Greg Maddux	5.00
M29	Barry Bonds, Barry Bonds	7.50
M30	Greg Maddux, Greg Maddux	3.00
M31	Juan Gonzalez, Larry Walker	1.50
M32	Juan Gonzalez, Andres Galarraga	1.50
M33	Juan Gonzalez, Chipper Jones	2.50
M34	Juan Gonzalez, Juan Gonzalez	1.50
M35	Larry Walker, Andres Galarraga	1.50
M36	Larry Walker, Chipper Jones	2.50
M37	Larry Walker, Larry Walker	1.50
M38	Andres Galarraga, Chipper Jones	2.50
M39	Andres Galarraga, Andres Galarraga	1.50
M40	Chipper Jones, Chipper Jones	3.00
M41	Gary Sheffield, Sammy Sosa	3.00
M42	Gary Sheffield, Jeff Bagwell	1.50
M43	Gary Sheffield, Tino Martinez	1.50
M44	Gary Sheffield, Gary Sheffield	2.00
M45	Sammy Sosa, Jeff Bagwell	3.00
M46	Sammy Sosa, Tino Martinez	3.00
M47	Sammy Sosa, Sammy Sosa	3.00
M48	Jeff Bagwell, Tino Martinez	1.50
M49	Jeff Bagwell, Jeff Bagwell	2.00
M50	Tino Martinez, Tino Martinez	1.50

Mystery Finest 2

Forty more Mystery Finest inserts were seeded in Series 2 packs at a rate of one per 36 packs (HTA odds 1:15), with Refrators every 1:144 packs (HTA odds 1:64). As with Series 1, 20 players are in the checklist; some players are found with another player on the back or by himself on each side. Each side is printed in Finest technology with an opaque black protector.

		NM/M
	Complete Set (40):	100.00
	Common Player:	1.50
	Refractors:	4X
M1	Nomar Garciaparra, Frank Thomas	3.50
M2	Nomar Garciaparra, Albert Belle	3.50
M3	Nomar Garciaparra, Scott Rolen	3.50
M4	Frank Thomas, Albert Belle	2.50
M5	Frank Thomas, Scott Rolen	2.50
M6	Albert Belle, Scott Rolen	1.50
M7	Ken Griffey Jr., Jose Cruz	4.00
M8	Ken Griffey Jr., Alex Rodriguez	6.00
M9	Ken Griffey Jr., Roger Clemens	4.50
M10	Jose Cruz, Alex Rodriguez	6.00
M11	Jose Cruz, Roger Clemens	3.00
M12	Alex Rodriguez, Roger Clemens	6.00
M13	Mike Piazza, Barry Bonds	6.00
M14	Mike Piazza, Derek Jeter	6.00
M15	Mike Piazza, Bernie Williams	5.00
M16	Barry Bonds, Derek Jeter	6.50
M17	Barry Bonds, Bernie Williams	4.00
M18	Derek Jeter, Bernie Williams	6.00
M19	Mark McGwire, Jeff Bagwell	4.50
M20	Mark McGwire, Mo Vaughn	5.00
M21	Mark McGwire, Jim Thome	5.00
M22	Jeff Bagwell, Mo Vaughn	2.00
M23	Jeff Bagwell, Jim Thome	1.50
M24	Mo Vaughn, Jim Thome	1.50
M25	Juan Gonzalez, Travis Lee	1.50
M26	Juan Gonzalez, Ben Grieve	1.50
M27	Juan Gonzalez, Fred McGriff	1.50
M28	Travis Lee, Ben Grieve	1.50
M29	Travis Lee, Fred McGriff	1.50
M30	Ben Grieve, Fred McGriff	1.50
M31	Albert Belle, Albert Belle	1.50
M32	Scott Rolen, Scott Rolen	2.00
M33	Alex Rodriguez, Alex Rodriguez	6.00
M34	Roger Clemens, Roger Clemens	4.00
M35	Bernie Williams, Bernie Williams	1.50
M36	Mo Vaughn, Mo Vaughn	1.50
M37	Jim Thome, Jim Thome	2.00
M38	Travis Lee, Travis Lee	1.50
M39	Fred McGriff, Fred McGriff	1.50
M40	Ben Grieve, Ben Grieve	1.50

Mystery Finest Jumbo

Series 2 Home Team Advantage (HTA) boxes were the exclusive venue for these large-format (3" x 5") versions of Mystery Finest. Regular cards were found one per six boxes of HTA, while Refractor versions were a 1:12 seed.

		NM/M
	Complete Set (3):	12.50
	Common Card:	4.00
	Refractor:	1.5X
1	Ken Griffey Jr., Alex Rodriguez	4.00
2	Derek Jeter, Bernie Williams	5.00
3	Mark McGwire, Jeff Bagwell	4.00

Power Zone

This Series 1 insert features Topps' new "Flop Inks" technology which changes the color of the card depending at what angle it is viewed. They are inserted one per 72 hobby packs (HTA odds 1:32). Cards are numbered with a "P" prefix.

No.	Player	NM/M
	Complete Set (20):	25.00
	Common Player:	.50
1	Ken Griffey Jr.	3.00
2	Jeff Bagwell	2.00
3	Jose Cruz Jr.	.50
4	Barry Bonds	5.00
5	Mark McGwire	4.00
6	Jim Thome	1.50
7	Mo Vaughn	.50
8	Gary Sheffield	1.00
9	Andres Galarraga	.50
10	Nomar Garciaparra	2.50
11	Rafael Palmeiro	1.50
12	Sammy Sosa	2.50
13	Jay Buhner	.50
14	Tony Clark	.50
15	Mike Piazza	3.00
16	Larry Walker	.50
17	Albert Belle	.50
18	Tino Martinez	.50
19	Juan Gonzalez	1.25
20	Frank Thomas	2.00

Stadium Stars

Stadium Stars is a 24-card insert that features Topps' new lenticular holographic chromium technology. These are exclusive to Series 2 packs and carried an insertion rate of one per 72 packs (HTA odds 1:32).

No.	Player	NM/M
	Complete Set (24):	95.00
	Common Player:	1.00
SS1	Ken Griffey Jr.	8.00
SS2	Alex Rodriguez	10.00
SS3	Mo Vaughn	1.00
SS4	Nomar Garciaparra	6.00
SS5	Frank Thomas	4.50
SS6	Albert Belle	1.00
SS7	Derek Jeter	12.00
SS8	Chipper Jones	6.00
SS9	Cal Ripken Jr.	12.00
SS10	Jim Thome	3.00
SS11	Mike Piazza	8.00
SS12	Juan Gonzalez	2.50
SS13	Jeff Bagwell	4.50

SS14	Sammy Sosa	6.00
SS15	Jose Cruz Jr.	1.00
SS16	Gary Sheffield	2.00
SS17	Larry Walker	1.00
SS18	Tony Gwynn	6.00
SS19	Mark McGwire	10.00
SS20	Barry Bonds	12.00
SS21	Tino Martinez	1.00
SS22	Manny Ramirez	4.50
SS23	Ken Caminiti	1.00
SS24	Andres Galarraga	1.00

The Man

This 20-card insert features the top players in baseball and was exlusively found in Series 2 packs. Regular versions are sequentially numbered to 500 and inserted one per 119 packs, while Refractor versions are numbered to 75 and inserted one per 793 packs.

		NM/M
Complete Set (20):		125.00
Common Player:		1:50
Refractors:		3X
TM1	Ken Griffey Jr.	10.00
TM2	Barry Bonds	15.00
TM3	Frank Thomas	6.00
TM4	Chipper Jones	7.50
TM5	Cal Ripken Jr.	15.00
TM6	Nomar Garciaparra	7.50
TM7	Mark McGwire	12.50
TM8	Mike Piazza	10.00
TM9	Derek Jeter	15.00
TM10	Alex Rodriguez	12.50
TM11	Jose Cruz Jr.	1.50
TM12	Larry Walker	1.50
TM13	Jeff Bagwell	6.00
TM14	Tony Gwynn	7.50
TM15	Travis Lee	2.00
TM16	Juan Gonzalez	6.00
TM17	Scott Rolen	4.50
TM18	Randy Johnson	6.00
TM19	Roger Clemens	9.00
TM20	Greg Maddux	7.50

Jumbo

Eight oversized cards were inserted into both Series 1 and Series 2 boxes as box toppers. The cards measure 3" x 5" and are inserted one per three boxes, with Refractor versions every six boxes. The oversized cards are similar to the regular-issue cards except for the numbering which designates each "X of 8."

		NM/M
Complete Set (16):		30.00
Common Player:		1.00
Refractors:		1.5X
1	Mark McGwire	4.00
2	Cal Ripken Jr.	5.00
3	Nomar Garciaparra	2.00
4	Mike Piazza	3.00
5	Greg Maddux	2.00
6	Jose Cruz Jr.	1.00
7	Roger Clemens	2.50
8	Ken Griffey Jr.	3.00
1	Frank Thomas	1.50
2	Bernie Williams	1.00
3	Randy Johnson	1.50
4	Chipper Jones	1.25
5	Manny Ramirez	1.50
6	Barry Bonds	5.00
7	Juan Gonzalez	1.25
8	Jeff Bagwell	1.50

1999 Finest

Released in two series, with each consisting of 100 regular and 50 subset cards divided into three categories: Gems, Sensations and Rookies in Series 1, and Sterling, Gamers and Rookies in the second series. The subset cards are short-printed, seeded one per pack. Cards are printed on 27 point stock utilizing chromium technology. There are two parallels: Refractors and die-cut Gold Refractors. Refractors are seeded 1:12 packs, while Gold Refractors are numbered to 100 sets. Six-cards packs carried an SRP of $4.99.

		NM/M
Complete Set (300):		80.00
Complete Series 1 (150):		30.00
Complete Series 2 (150):		50.00
Common Player:		.15
Common SP (101-150, 251-300):		.50
Star Refractors:		6X
SP Refractors:		3X
Star Gold Refractors:		15X
SP Gold Refractors:		10X
Pack (6):		1.50
Wax Box (24):		30.00
1	Darin Erstad	.35
2	Javy Lopez	.15
3	Vinny Castilla	.15
4	Jim Thome	.60
5	Tino Martinez	.15
6	Mark Grace	.15
7	Shawn Green	.40
8	Dustin Hermanson	.15
9	Kevin Young	.15
10	Tony Clark	.15
11	Scott Brosius	.15
12	Craig Biggio	.15
13	Brian McRae	.15
14	Chan Ho Park	.15
15	Manny Ramirez	1.00
16	Chipper Jones	1.50
17	Rico Brogna	.15
18	Quinton McCracken	.15
19	J.T. Snow Jr.	.15
20	Tony Gwynn	1.50
21	Juan Guzman	.15
22	John Valentin	.15
23	Rick Helling	.15
24	Sandy Alomar	.15
25	Frank Thomas	1.00
26	Jorge Posada	.15
27	Dmitri Young	.15
28	Rick Reed	.15
29	Kevin Tapani	.15
30	Troy Glaus	.75
31	Kenny Rogers	.15
32	Jeromy Burnitz	.15
33	Mark Grudzielanek	.15
34	Mike Mussina	.50
35	Scott Rolen	.75
36	Neifi Perez	.15
37	Brad Radke	.15
38	Darryl Strawberry	.15
39	Robb Nen	.15
40	Moises Alou	.15
41	Eric Young	.15
42	Livan Hernandez	.15
43	John Wetteland	.15
44	Matt Lawton	.15
45	Ben Grieve	.15
46	Fernando Tatis	.15
47	Travis Fryman	.15
48	David Segui	.15
49	Bob Abreu	.15
50	Nomar Garciaparra	1.50
51	Paul O'Neill	.15
52	Jeff King	.15
53	Francisco Cordova	.15
54	John Olerud	.15
55	Vladimir Guerrero	1.00
56	Fernando Vina	.15
57	Shane Reynolds	.15
58	Chuck Finley	.15
59	Rondell White	.15
60	Greg Vaughn	.15
61	Ryan Minor	.15
62	Tom Gordon	.15
63	Damion Easley	.15
64	Ray Durham	.15
65	Orlando Hernandez	.15
66	Bartolo Colon	.15
67	Jaret Wright	.15
68	Royce Clayton	.15
69	Tim Salmon	.15
70	Mark McGwire	2.50
71	Alex Gonzalez	.15
72	Tom Glavine	.40
73	David Justice	.15
74	Omar Vizquel	.15
75	Juan Gonzalez	.50
76	Bobby Higginson	.15
77	Todd Walker	.15
78	Dante Bichette	.15
79	Kevin Millwood	.15
80	Roger Clemens	1.75
81	Kerry Wood	.50
82	Cal Ripken Jr.	3.00
83	Jay Bell	.15
84	Barry Bonds	3.00
85	Alex Rodriguez	2.50
86	Doug Glanville	.15
87	Jason Kendall	.15
88	Sean Casey	.25
89	Aaron Sele	.15
90	Derek Jeter	3.00
91	Andy Ashby	.15
92	Rusty Greer	.15
93	Rod Beck	.15
94	Matt Williams	.15
95	Mike Piazza	2.00
96	Wally Joyner	.15
97	Barry Larkin	.15
98	Eric Milton	.15
99	Gary Sheffield	.50
100	Greg Maddux	1.50
101	Ken Griffey Jr. (Gem)	4.00
102	Frank Thomas (Gem)	2.00
103	Nomar Garciaparra (Gem)	3.00
104	Mark McGwire (Gem)	5.00
105	Alex Rodriguez (Gem)	5.00
106	Tony Gwynn (Gem)	3.00
107	Juan Gonzalez (Gem)	.75
108	Jeff Bagwell (Gem)	2.00
109	Sammy Sosa (Gem)	3.00
110	Vladimir Guerrero (Gem)	2.00
111	Roger Clemens (Gem)	3.50
112	Barry Bonds (Gem)	6.00
113	Darin Erstad (Gem)	.50
114	Mike Piazza (Gem)	4.00
115	Derek Jeter (Gem)	6.00
116	Chipper Jones (Gem)	3.00
117	Larry Walker (Gem)	.50
118	Scott Rolen (Gem)	1.50
119	Cal Ripken Jr. (Gem)	6.00
120	Greg Maddux (Gem)	3.00
121	Troy Glaus (Sensations)	1.50
122	Ben Grieve (Sensations)	.50
123	Ryan Minor (Sensations)	.50
124	Kerry Wood (Sensations)	.50
125	Travis Lee (Sensations)	.50
126	Adrian Beltre (Sensations)	.50
127	Brad Fullmer (Sensations)	.50
128	Aramis Ramirez (Sensations)	.50
129	Eric Chavez (Sensations)	.50
130	Todd Helton (Sensations)	1.50
131	Pat Burrell **RC** (Finest Rookies)	4.00
132	Ryan Mills **RC** (Finest Rookies)	.50
133	Austin Kearns **RC** (Finest Rookies)	3.00
134	Josh McKinley **RC** (Finest Rookies)	.50
135	Adam Everett **RC** (Finest Rookies)	.75
136	Marlon Anderson	.50
137	Bruce Chen	.50
138	Matt Clement	.50
139	Alex Gonzalez	.50
140	Roy Halladay	.50
141	Calvin Pickering	.50
142	Randy Wolf	.50
143	Ryan Anderson	.50
144	Ruben Mateo	.50
145	Alex Escobar **RC**	.50
146	Jeremy Giambi	.50
147	Lance Berkman	.50
148	Michael Barrett	.50
149	Preston Wilson	.50
150	Gabe Kapler	.50
151	Roger Clemens	1.75
152	Jay Buhner	.15
153	Brad Fullmer	.15
154	Ray Lankford	.15
155	Jim Edmonds	.15
156	Jason Giambi	.60
157	Bret Boone	.15
158	Jeff Cirillo	.15
159	Rickey Henderson	1.00
160	Edgar Martinez	.15
161	Ron Gant	.15
162	Mark Kotsay	.15
163	Trevor Hoffman	.15
164	Jason Schmidt	.15
165	Brett Tomko	.15
166	David Ortiz	.50
167	Dean Palmer	.15
168	Hideki Irabu	.15
169	Mike Cameron	.15
170	Pedro Martinez	1.00
171	Tom Goodwin	.15
172	Brian Hunter	.15
173	Al Leiter	.15
174	Charles Johnson	.15
175	Curt Schilling	.50
176	Robin Ventura	.15
177	Travis Lee	.15
178	Jeff Shaw	.15
179	Ugueth Urbina	.15
180	Roberto Alomar	.30
181	Cliff Floyd	.15
182	Adrian Beltre	.25
183	Tony Womack	.15
184	Brian Jordan	.15
185	Randy Johnson	1.00
186	Mickey Morandini	.15
187	Todd Hundley	.15
188	Jose Valentin	.15
189	Eric Davis	.15
190	Ken Caminiti	.15
191	David Wells	.15
192	Ryan Klesko	.15
193	Garret Anderson	.15
194	Eric Karros	.15
195	Ivan Rodriguez	.75
196	Aramis Ramirez	.15
197	Mike Lieberthal	.15
198	Will Clark	.15
199	Rey Ordonez	.15
200	Ken Griffey Jr.	2.00
201	Jose Guillen	.15
202	Scott Erickson	.15
203	Paul Konerko	.15
204	Johnny Damon	.40
205	Larry Walker	.15
206	Denny Neagle	.15
207	Jose Offerman	.15
208	Andy Pettitte	.30
209	Bobby Jones	.15
210	Kevin Brown	.15
211	John Smoltz	.15
212	Henry Rodriguez	.15
213	Tim Belcher	.15
214	Carlos Delgado	.50
215	Andruw Jones	1.00
216	Andy Benes	.15
217	Fred McGriff	.15
218	Edgar Renteria	.15
219	Miguel Tejada	.25
220	Bernie Williams	.15
221	Justin Thompson	.15
222	Marty Cordova	.15
223	Delino DeShields	.15
224	Ellis Burks	.15
225	Kenny Lofton	.15
226	Steve Finley	.15
227	Eric Chavez	.25
228	Jose Cruz Jr.	.15
229	Marquis Grissom	.15
230	Jeff Bagwell	1.00
231	Jose Canseco	.50
232	Edgardo Alfonzo	.15
233	Richie Sexson	.15
234	Jeff Kent	.15
235	Rafael Palmeiro	.75
236	David Cone	.15
237	Gregg Jefferies	.15
238	Mike Lansing	.15
239	Mariano Rivera	.25
240	Albert Belle	.15
241	Chuck Knoblauch	.15
242	Derek Bell	.15
243	Pat Hentgen	.15
244	Andres Galarraga	.15
245	Mo Vaughn	.15
246	Wade Boggs	1.50
247	Devon White	.15
248	Todd Helton	.75
249	Raul Mondesi	.15
250	Sammy Sosa	1.50
251	Nomar Garciaparra (Sterling)	3.00
252	Mark McGwire (Sterling)	5.00
253	Alex Rodriguez (Sterling)	5.00
254	Juan Gonzalez (Sterling)	.75
255	Vladimir Guerrero (Sterling)	2.00
256	Ken Griffey Jr. (Sterling)	4.00
257	Mike Piazza (Sterling)	4.00
258	Derek Jeter (Sterling)	6.00
259	Albert Belle (Sterling)	.50
260	Greg Vaughn (Sterling)	.50
261	Sammy Sosa (Sterling)	3.00
262	Greg Maddux (Sterling)	3.00
263	Frank Thomas (Sterling)	2.00
264	Mark Grace (Sterling)	.50
265	Ivan Rodriguez (Sterling)	1.25
266	Roger Clemens (Gamers)	3.50
267	Mo Vaughn (Gamers)	.50
268	Jim Thome (Gamers)	.75
269	Darin Erstad (Gamers)	.65
270	Chipper Jones (Gamers)	2.50
271	Larry Walker (Gamers)	.50
272	Cal Ripken Jr. (Gamers)	6.00
273	Scott Rolen (Gamers)	1.25
274	Randy Johnson (Gamers)	2.00
275	Tony Gwynn (Gamers)	2.50
276	Barry Bonds (Gamers)	6.00
277	Sean Burroughs **RC**	1.50
278	J.M. Gold **RC**	.50
279	Carlos Lee	.50
280	George Lombard	.50
281	Carlos Beltran	1.50
282	Fernando Seguignol	.50
283	Eric Chavez	.65
284	Carlos Pena **RC**	3.00
285	Corey Patterson **RC**	2.00
286	Alfonso Soriano **RC**	12.00
287	Nick Johnson **RC**	2.00
288	Jorge Toca **RC**	.50
289	A.J. Burnett **RC**	1.00
290	Andy Brown **RC**	.50
291	Doug Mientkiewicz **RC**	1.00
292	Bobby Seay **RC**	.50
293	Chip Ambres **RC**	.50
294	C.C. Sabathia **RC**	2.50
295	Choo Freeman **RC**	1.00
296	Eric Valent **RC**	.50
297	Matt Belisle **RC**	.50
298	Jason Tyner **RC**	.50
299	Masao Kida **RC**	.50
300	Hank Aaron, Mark McGwire (Homerun Kings)	3.00

Refractors

Inserted at the rate of one card per 12 packs, Refractors use special technology to impart a more colorful sheen to the card fronts. To eliminate doubt, the backs have the word "REFRACTOR" printed to the right of the card number at top.

	NM/M
Complete Set (300):	750.00
Common Player:	1.00
Stars:	6X
SP's:	3X

Gold Refractors

At the top of Finest's chase-card line-up for 1999 are the Gold Refractors. Fronts have an overall gold tone in the background. Backs are individually serial numbered in gold foil with an edition of 100 each, and have the words "GOLD REFRACTOR" printed at top, to the right of the card number. The Gold Refractors are die-cut along the edges to create a deckled effect. Stated pack insertion rates were between 1:26 and 1:82 depending on series and type.

	NM/M
Common Player:	3.00
Stars:	15X
SP's:	10X

Complements

This Series 2 insert set pairs two players on a "split-screen" card front. There are three different versions for each card, Non-Refractor/Refractor (1:56), Refractor/Non-Refractor (1:56) and Refractor/Refractor (1:168). Each card is numbered with a "C" prefix. Values shown are for cards with either the left- or right-side player as Refractor; dual-refractor cards valued at 2X.

		NM/M
Complete Set (7):		25.00
Common Player:		2.50
Inserted 1:56		
Dual-Refractors:		2X
Inserted 1:168		
1	Mike Piazza, Ivan Rodriguez	4.00
2	Tony Gwynn, Wade Boggs	3.00
3	Kerry Wood, Roger Clemens	3.50
4	Juan Gonzalez, Sammy Sosa	3.00
5	Derek Jeter, Nomar Garciaparra	6.00
6	Mark McGwire, Frank Thomas	5.00
7	Vladimir Guerrero, Andruw Jones	2.50

Double Feature

Similar to Finest Complements, this Series 2 set utilizes split-screen fronts to accomodate two players on a horizontal format. Each card has three versions: Non-Refractor/Refractor (1:56), Refractor/Non-Refractor (1:56) and Refractor/Refractor (1:168). Card numbers have a "DF" prefix. Values shown are for cards with either left- or right-side Refractor; Dual-Refractor cards are valued at 2X.

		NM/M
Complete Set (7):		30.00
Common Player:		2.00
Dual-Refractors:		2X
1	Ken Griffey Jr., Alex Rodriguez	10.00
2	Chipper Jones, Andruw Jones	6.00
3	Darin Erstad, Mo Vaughn	2.00
4	Craig Biggio, Jeff Bagwell	4.00
5	Ben Grieve, Eric Chavez	2.00
6	Albert Belle, Cal Ripken Jr.	10.00
7	Scott Rolen, Pat Burrell	3.00

Franchise Records

This Series 2 insert set focuses on players who led their teams in various statistical categories. They are randomly seeded in 1:129 packs, while a parallel Refractor version is inserted 1:378. Card numbers have a "FR" prefix.

	NM/M
Complete Set (10):	35.00

Common Player:		2.00
Refractors:		3X
1	Frank Thomas	2.50
2	Ken Griffey Jr.	5.00
3	Mark McGwire	6.00
4	Juan Gonzalez	2.00
5	Nomar Garciaparra	3.00
6	Mike Piazza	5.00
7	Cal Ripken Jr.	7.50
8	Sammy Sosa	3.00
9	Barry Bonds	7.50
10	Tony Gwynn	3.00

Future's Finest

This Series 2 insert focuses on up-and-coming players who are primed to emerge as superstars. These are seeded 1:171 packs and limited to 500 numbered sets. Card numbers have a "FF" prefix.

		NM/M
Complete Set (10):		35.00
Common Player:		2.00
1	Pat Burrell	10.00
2	Troy Glaus	12.50
3	Eric Chavez	3.00
4	Ryan Anderson	2.00
5	Ruben Mateo	2.00
6	Gabe Kapler	2.00
7	Alex Gonzalez	2.00
8	Michael Barrett	2.00
9	Lance Berkman	2.00
10	Fernando Seguignol	2.00

Hank Aaron Award Contenders

This insert set focuses on nine players who had the best chance to win baseball's newest award. Production varies from card to card, with nine times as many of card #9 as of card #1, and so on. Insertion odds thus vary greatly, from 1:12 to 1:216. Refractor versions are found at odds which vary from 1:96 to 1:1728. Card numbers have an "HA" prefix.

		NM/M
Complete Set (9):		20.00
Common Player:		2.00
Refractors:		3X
1	Juan Gonzalez	2.00
2	Vladimir Guerrero	2.50
3	Nomar Garciaparra	3.00
4	Albert Belle	2.00
5	Frank Thomas	2.50
6	Sammy Sosa	3.00
7	Alex Rodriguez	5.00
8	Ken Griffey Jr.	4.00
9	Mark McGwire	5.00

Leading Indicators

Utilizing a heat-sensitive, thermal ink technology, these cards highlight the 1998 home run totals of 10 players. Touching the left, right or center field portion of the card behind each player's image reveals his 1998 season home run total in that specific direction. These are seeded in Series 1 packs.

		NM/M
Complete Set (10):		20.00
Common Player:		.50
Inserted 1:24		
L1	Mark McGwire	5.00
L2	Sammy Sosa	3.00
L3	Ken Griffey Jr.	4.00
L4	Greg Vaughn	.50
L5	Albert Belle	.50
L6	Juan Gonzalez	.75
L7	Andres Galarraga	.50
L8	Alex Rodriguez	5.00
L9	Barry Bonds	6.00
L10	Jeff Bagwell	1.50

Milestones

This Series 2 insert set is fractured into four subsets, each focusing on a statistical category: Hits, Home Runs, RBIs and Doubles. The Hits category is limited to 3,000 numbered sets. Home Runs are limited to 500 numbered sets. RBIs are limited to 1,400 numbered sets and Doubles is limited to 500 numbered sets. Each card number carries an "M" prefix.

		NM/M
Complete Set (40):		125.00
Common Hits (1-10):		.50
Common Homeruns (11-20):		2.00
Common RBI (21-30):		1.00
Common Doubles (31-40):		2.00
1	Tony Gwynn (Hits)	1.50
2	Cal Ripken Jr. (Hits)	3.00
3	Wade Boggs (Hits)	1.50
4	Ken Griffey Jr. (Hits)	2.00
5	Frank Thomas (Hits)	1.00
6	Barry Bonds (Hits)	3.00
7	Travis Lee (Hits)	.50
8	Alex Rodriguez (Hits)	2.50
9	Derek Jeter (Hits)	3.00
10	Vladimir Guerrero (Hits)	1.00
11	Mark McGwire (Home Runs)	8.00
12	Ken Griffey Jr. (Home Runs)	7.00
13	Vladimir Guerrero (Home Runs)	4.00
14	Alex Rodriguez (Home Runs)	8.00
15	Barry Bonds (Home Runs)	10.00
16	Sammy Sosa (Home Runs)	5.00
17	Albert Belle (Home Runs)	2.00
18	Frank Thomas (Home Runs)	4.00
19	Jose Canseco (Home Runs)	3.00
20	Mike Piazza (Home Runs)	7.00
21	Jeff Bagwell (RBI)	2.00
22	Barry Bonds (RBI)	6.00
23	Ken Griffey Jr. (RBI)	4.00
24	Albert Belle (RBI)	1.00
25	Juan Gonzalez (RBI)	1.50
26	Vinny Castilla (RBI)	1.00
27	Mark McGwire (RBI)	5.00
28	Alex Rodriguez (RBI)	5.00
29	Nomar Garciaparra (RBI)	3.00
30	Frank Thomas (RBI)	2.50
31	Barry Bonds (Doubles)	10.00
32	Albert Belle (Doubles)	2.00
33	Ben Grieve (Doubles)	2.00
34	Craig Biggio (Doubles)	2.00
35	Vladimir Guerrero (Doubles)	4.00
36	Nomar Garciaparra (Doubles)	5.00
37	Alex Rodriguez (Doubles)	7.00
38	Derek Jeter (Doubles)	10.00
39	Ken Griffey Jr. (Doubles)	7.00
40	Brad Fullmer (Doubles)	2.00

Peel & Reveal

This Series 1 insert offers 20 players produced in varying levels of scarcity designated by background design: Sparkle is common, Hyperplaid is uncommon and Stadium Stars is rare. Each card has a peel-off opaque protective coating on both front and back. Stated insertion odds are: Sparkle 1:30; Hyperplaid 1:60, and Stadium Stars 1:120. Home Team Advantage (HTA) boxes have odds which are twice as good.

		NM/M
Complete Set (20):		40.00
Common Player:		1.00
Hyperplaid:		1.5X
Stadium Stars:		2.5X
1	Kerry Wood	1.50
2	Mark McGwire	5.00
3	Sammy Sosa	3.00
4	Ken Griffey Jr.	4.00
5	Nomar Garciaparra	3.00
6	Greg Maddux	3.00
7	Derek Jeter	6.00
8	Andres Galarraga	1.00
9	Alex Rodriguez	5.00
10	Frank Thomas	2.00
11	Roger Clemens	3.50
12	Juan Gonzalez	1.50
13	Ben Grieve	1.00
14	Jeff Bagwell	2.00
15	Todd Helton	2.00
16	Chipper Jones	3.00
17	Barry Bonds	6.00
18	Travis Lee	1.00
19	Vladimir Guerrero	2.00
20	Pat Burrell	1.50

Prominent Figures

Fifty cards on Refractor technology highlight superstars chasing the all-time records in five different statistical categories: Home Runs, Slugging Percentage, Batting Average, RBIs and Total Bases. Ten players are featured in each category, each sequentially numbered to the all-time single season record statistic for that category. Home Run category is numbered to 70, Slugging Percentage to 847, Batting Average to 424, RBIs to 190 and Total Bases to 457.

		NM/M
Complete Set (50):		250.00
Common Home Runs (1-10); #d to 70:		3.00
Common Slugging % (11-20); #d to 847:		1.00
Common Batting Ave. (21-30); #d to 424:		1.75
Common RBIs (31-40); #d to 190:		2.00
Common Total Bases (41-50); #d to 457:		1.75
1	Mark McGwire (HR)	25.00
2	Sammy Sosa (HR)	10.00
3	Ken Griffey Jr. (HR)	15.00
4	Mike Piazza (HR)	15.00
5	Juan Gonzalez (HR)	5.00
6	Greg Vaughn (HR)	3.00
7	Alex Rodriguez (HR)	25.00
8	Manny Ramirez (HR)	7.50
9	Jeff Bagwell (HR)	7.50
10	Andres Galarraga (HR)	3.00
11	Mark McGwire (S%)	6.00
12	Sammy Sosa (S%)	5.00
13	Juan Gonzalez (S%)	2.50
14	Ken Griffey Jr. (S%)	5.00
15	Barry Bonds (S%)	7.50
16	Greg Vaughn (S%)	1.00
17	Larry Walker (S%)	1.00
18	Andres Galarraga (S%)	1.00
19	Jeff Bagwell (S%)	2.50
20	Albert Belle (S%)	1.00
21	Tony Gwynn (BA)	5.00
22	Mike Piazza (BA)	6.00
23	Larry Walker (BA)	1.75
24	Alex Rodriguez (BA)	7.50
25	John Olerud (BA)	1.75
26	Frank Thomas (BA)	3.50
27	Bernie Williams (BA)	1.75
28	Chipper Jones (BA)	5.00
29	Jim Thome (BA)	2.50
30	Barry Bonds (BA)	9.00
31	Juan Gonzalez (RBI)	3.00
32	Sammy Sosa (RBI)	9.00
33	Mark McGwire (RBI)	20.00
34	Albert Belle (RBI)	2.00
35	Ken Griffey Jr. (RBI)	15.00
36	Jeff Bagwell (RBI)	6.00
37	Chipper Jones (RBI)	9.00
38	Vinny Castilla (RBI)	2.00
39	Alex Rodriguez (RBI)	20.00
40	Andres Galarraga (RBI)	2.00
41	Sammy Sosa (TB)	6.00
42	Mark McGwire (TB)	7.50
43	Albert Belle (TB)	1.75
44	Ken Griffey Jr. (TB)	6.00
45	Jeff Bagwell (TB)	3.50
46	Juan Gonzalez (TB)	3.50
47	Barry Bonds (TB)	9.00
48	Vladimir Guerrero (TB)	3.50
49	Larry Walker (TB)	1.75
50	Alex Rodriguez (TB)	7.50

Split Screen

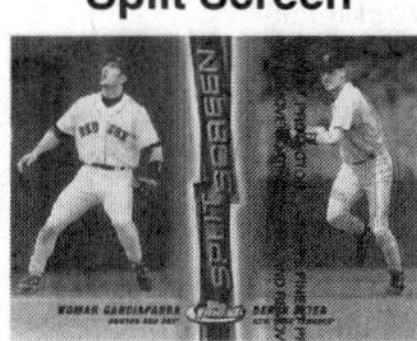

Players who share a common bond are highlighted in this Series 1 insert set which includes 14 paired players. Each card is available in three variations: Non-Refractor/Refractor (1:28), Refractor/Non-Refractor (1:28) and Refractor/Refractor (1:84). Values shown are for a card with either left- or right-side Refractor; dual-Refractor cards are worth 2X.

		NM/M
Complete Set (14):		30.00
Common Card:		1.00
Dual-Refractor:		2X
1	Mark McGwire, Sammy Sosa	4.00
2	Ken Griffey Jr., Alex Rodriguez	4.00
3	Nomar Garciaparra, Derek Jeter	5.00
4	Barry Bonds, Albert Belle	4.00
5	Cal Ripken Jr., Tony Gwynn	4.00
6	Manny Ramirez, Juan Gonzalez	1.50
7	Frank Thomas, Andres Galarraga	1.50
8	Scott Rolen, Chipper Jones	2.00
9	Ivan Rodriguez, Mike Piazza	3.00
10	Kerry Wood, Roger Clemens	2.50
11	Greg Maddux, Tom Glavine	2.00
12	Troy Glaus, Eric Chavez	1.50
13	Ben Grieve, Todd Helton	1.00
14	Travis Lee, Pat Burrell	2.50

Team Finest

The first 10 cards are showcased in Series 1 while the last 10 cards showcased in Series 2. Team Finest are available in three colors: Blue, Red and Gold (Red and Gold are only available in Home Team Advantage packs). All Team Finest are serially numbered as follows: Blue, numbered to 1,500; Blue Refractors to 150; Red to 500; Red Refractors to 50; Gold to 250 and Gold Refractors to 25. Cards have a TF prefix to the card number.

		NM/M
Complete Set (20):		25.00
Common Blue:		1.00
Production 1,500 Sets		
Blue Refractors:		3X
Production 150 Sets		
Reds:		1.5X
Production 500 Sets		
Red Refractors:		7X
Production 50 Sets		
Golds:		2X
Production 250 Sets		
Gold Refractors:		10X
Production 25 Sets		
1	Greg Maddux	2.50
2	Mark McGwire	4.50
3	Sammy Sosa	2.50
4	Juan Gonzalez	1.25
5	Alex Rodriguez	4.50
6	Travis Lee	1.00
7	Roger Clemens	2.75
8	Darin Erstad	1.25
9	Todd Helton	1.75
10	Mike Piazza	3.50
11	Kerry Wood	1.25
12	Ken Griffey Jr.	3.50
13	Frank Thomas	2.00
14	Jeff Bagwell	2.00
15	Nomar Garciaparra	2.50
16	Derek Jeter	6.00
17	Chipper Jones	2.50
18	Barry Bonds	6.00
19	Tony Gwynn	2.50
20	Ben Grieve	1.00

2000 Finest

The 286-card base set has the traditional chromium finish with the Topps Finest logo in the upper left portion on the front. Also in the upper left portion is a partial image of a baseball with seams in the background of the player photo. Card backs have a small photo with '99 stats and career totals. The rookies from Series 1 are serial numbered to 2,000 and in Series 2 to 3,000.

		NM/M
Complete Set (286):		250.00
Complete Series 1 (147)		175.00
Complete Series 2 (140):		125.00
Common Player:		.25
Common Rookie (101-120):		4.00
Production 2,000		
Common Rookie (247-266)		4.00
Production 3,000		
Common Counterpart (267-276)		.75
Inserted 1:8		
Common Gem (136-145):		1.50
Inserted 1:24		
Pack (6):		2.00
Series 1 & 2 Box (24):		40.00
1	Nomar Garciaparra	2.00
2	Chipper Jones	1.50
3	Erubiel Durazo	.25
4	Robin Ventura	.25
5	Garret Anderson	.25
6	Dean Palmer	.25
7	Mariano Rivera	.35
8	Rusty Greer	.25
9	Jim Thome	.25
10	Jeff Bagwell	1.00
11	Jason Giambi	.75
12	Jeromy Burnitz	.25
13	Mark Grace	.35
14	Russ Ortiz	.25
15	Kevin Brown	.25
16	Kevin Millwood	.25
17	Scott Williamson	.25
18	Orlando Hernandez	.25
19	Todd Walker	.25
20	Carlos Beltran	.50
21	Ruben Rivera	.25
22	Curt Schilling	.40
23	Brian Giles	.25
24	Eric Karros	.25
25	Preston Wilson	.25
26	Al Leiter	.25
27	Juan Encarnacion	.25
28	Tim Salmon	.40
29	B.J. Surhoff	.25
30	Bernie Williams	.45
31	Lee Stevens	.25
32	Pokey Reese	.25
33	Mike Sweeney	.25
34	Corey Koskie	.25
35	Roberto Alomar	.40
36	Tim Hudson	.40
37	Tom Glavine	.40
38	Jeff Kent	.25
39	Mike Lieberthal	.25
40	Barry Larkin	.25
41	Paul O'Neill	.25
42	Rico Brogna	.25
43	Brian Daubach	.25
44	Rich Aurilia	.25
45	Vladimir Guerrero	1.00
46	Luis Castillo	.25
47	Bartolo Colon	.25
48	Kevin Appier	.25
49	Mo Vaughn	.25
50	Alex Rodriguez	2.50
51	Randy Johnson	1.00
52	Kris Benson	.25
53	Tony Clark	.25
54	Chad Allen	.25
55	Larry Walker	.25
56	Freddy Garcia	.25
57	Paul Konerko	.35
58	Edgardo Alfonzo	.25
59	Brady Anderson	.25
60	Derek Jeter	3.00
61	Mike Hampton	.25
62	Jeff Cirillo	.25

63 Shannon Stewart .25
64 Greg Maddux 1.50
65 Mark McGwire 2.50
66 Gary Sheffield .50
67 Kevin Young .25
68 Tony Gwynn 1.50
69 Rey Ordonez .25
70 Cal Ripken Jr. 3.00
71 Todd Helton 1.00
72 Brian Jordan .25
73 Jose Canseco .50
74 Luis Gonzalez .40
75 Barry Bonds 3.00
76 Jermaine Dye .25
77 Jose Offerman .25
78 Magglio Ordonez .40
79 Fred McGriff .25
80 Ivan Rodriguez .60
81 Josh Hamilton (Prospects) .50
82 Vernon Wells (Prospects) .25
83 Mark Mulder (Prospects) .35
84 John Patterson (Prospects) .25
85 Nick Johnson (Prospects) .50
86 Pablo Ozuna (Prospects) .25
87 A.J. Burnett (Prospects) .25
88 Jack Cust (Prospects) .25
89 Adam Piatt (Prospects) .25
90 Rob Ryan (Prospects) .25
91 Sean Burroughs (Prospects) .35
92 D'Angelo Jimenez (Prospects) .25
93 Chad Hermansen (Prospects) .25
94 Rob Fick (Prospects) .25
95 Ruben Mateo (Prospects) .25
96 Alex Escobar (Prospects) .25
97 Willi Mo Pena (Prospects) .25
98 Corey Patterson (Prospects) .50
99 Eric Munson (Prospects) .25
100 Pat Burrell (Prospects) .75
101 Michael Tejera **RC** 4.00
102 Bobby Bradley **RC** 4.00
103 Larry Bigbie **RC** 6.00
104 B.J. Garbe **RC** 4.00
105 Josh Kalinowski **RC** 4.00
106 Brett Myers **RC** 15.00
107 Chris Mears **RC** 4.00
108 Aaron Rowand **RC** 10.00
109 Corey Myers **RC** 4.00
110 John Sneed **RC** 4.00
111 Ryan Christensen **RC** 4.00
112 Kyle Snyder **RC** 4.00
113 Mike Paradis **RC** 4.00
114 Chance Caple **RC** 4.00
115 Ben Christiansen **RC** 4.00
116 Brad Baker **RC** 4.00
117 Rob Purvis **RC** 4.00
118 Rick Asadoorian **RC** 4.00
119 Ruben Salazar **RC** 4.00
120 Julio Zuleta **RC** 4.00
121 Ken Griffey Jr., Alex Rodriguez (Features) 4.00
122 Nomar Garciaparra, Derek Jeter (Features) 5.00
123 Mark McGwire, Sammy Sosa (Features) 4.00
124 Randy Johnson, Pedro Martinez (Features) 2.00
125 Mike Piazza, Ivan Rodriguez (Features) 3.00
126 Manny Ramirez, Roberto Alomar (Features) 2.00
127 Chipper Jones, Andruw Jones (Features) 3.00
128 Cal Ripken Jr., Tony Gwynn (Features) 5.00
129 Jeff Bagwell, Craig Biggio (Features) 1.50
130 Vladimir Guerrero, Barry Bonds (Features) 5.00
131 Alfonso Soriano, Nick Johnson (Features) 2.00
132 Josh Hamilton, Pat Burrell (Features) 1.50
133 Corey Patterson, Ruben Mateo (Features) .75
134 Larry Walker, Todd Helton (Features) 1.50
135 Edgardo Alfonzo, Rey Ordonez (Features) .75
136 Derek Jeter (Gems) 10.00
137 Alex Rodriguez (Gems) 8.00
138 Chipper Jones (Gems) 5.00
139 Mike Piazza (Gems) 6.00
140 Mark McGwire (Gems) 8.00
141 Ivan Rodriguez (Gems) 2.00
142 Cal Ripken Jr. (Gems) 10.00
143 Vladimir Guerrero (Gems) 3.00
144 Randy Johnson (Gems) 3.00
145 Jeff Bagwell (Gems) 3.00
146 Ken Griffey Jr./Field 1.50
146a Ken Griffey Jr./Press 1.50
147 Andruw Jones 1.00
148 Kerry Wood .50
149 Jim Edmonds .25
150 Pedro Martinez 1.00
151 Warren Morris .25
152 Trevor Hoffman .25
153 Eric Young .25
154 Andy Pettitte .40
155 Frank Thomas 1.00
156 Damion Easley .25
157 Cliff Floyd .25
158 Ben Davis .25
159 John Valentin .25
160 Rafael Palmeiro .65
161 Andy Ashby .25
162 J.D. Drew .40
163 Jay Bell .25
164 Adam Kennedy .25
165 Manny Ramirez 1.00
166 John Halama .25
167 Octavio Dotel .25
168 Darin Erstad .40
169 Jose Lima .25
170 Andres Galarraga .25
171 Scott Rolen .75
172 Delino DeShields .25
173 J.T. Snow Jr. .25
174 Tony Womack .25
175 John Olerud .25
176 Jason Kendall .25
177 Carlos Lee .25
178 Eric Milton .25
179 Jeff Cirillo .25
180 Gabe Kapler .25
181 Greg Vaughn .25
182 Denny Neagle .25
183 Tino Martinez .25
184 Doug Mientkiewicz .25
185 Juan Gonzalez 1.00
186 Ellis Burks .25
187 Mike Hampton .25
188 Royce Clayton .25
189 Mike Mussina .50
190 Carlos Delgado .50
191 Ben Grieve .25
192 Fernando Tatis .25
193 Matt Williams .25
194 Rondell White .25
195 Shawn Green .50
196 Justin Thompson .25
197 Troy Glaus 1.00
198 Roger Cedeno .25
199 Ray Lankford .25
200 Sammy Sosa 2.00
201 Kenny Lofton .25
202 Edgar Martinez .25
203 Mark Kotsay .25
204 David Wells .25
205 Craig Biggio .25
206 Ray Durham .25
207 Troy O'Leary .25
208 Rickey Henderson .75
209 Bob Abreu .25
210 Neifi Perez .25
211 Carlos Febles .25
212 Chuck Knoblauch .25
213 Moises Alou .25
214 Omar Vizquel .25
215 Vinny Castilla .25
216 Javy Lopez .25
217 Johnny Damon .40
218 Roger Clemens 1.75
219 Miguel Tejada .40
220 Deion Sanders .35
221 Matt Lawton .25
222 Albert Belle .25
223 Adrian Beltre .50
224 Dante Bichette .25
225 Raul Mondesi .25
226 Mike Piazza 2.00
227 Brad Penny (Prospects) .25
228 Kip Wells (Prospects) .25
229 Adam Everett (Prospects) .25
230 Eddie Yarnall (Prospects) .25
231 Matt LeCroy (Prospects) .25
232 Ryan Anderson (Prospects) .25
233 Rick Ankiel (Prospects) .25
234 Daryle Ward (Prospects) .25
235 Rafael Furcal (Prospects) .25
236 Dee Brown (Prospects) .25
237 Travis Dawkins (Prospects) .25
238 Eric Valent (Prospects) .25
239 Peter Bergeron (Prospects) .25
240 Alfonso Soriano (Prospects) 1.50
241 John Patterson (Prospects) .25
242 Jorge Toca (Prospects) .25
243 Ryan Anderson (Prospects) .25
244 Jason Dallaero (Prospects) .25
245 Jason Grilli (Prospects) .25
246 Chad Hermansen (Prospects) .25
247 Scott Downs **RC** 4.00
248 Keith Reed **RC** 4.00
249 Edgar Cruz **RC** 4.00
250 Wes Anderson **RC** 4.00
251 Lyle Overbay **RC** 10.00
252 Mike Lamb **RC** 4.00
253 Vince Faison **RC** 4.00
254 Chad Alexander **RC** 4.00
255 Chris Wakeland 4.00
256 Aaron McNeal **RC** 4.00
257 Tomokazu Ohka **RC** 4.00
258 Ty Howington **RC** 6.00
259 Javier Colina **RC** 4.00
260 Jason Jennings 4.00
261 Ramon Santiago **RC** 4.00
262 Johan Santana **RC** 150.00
263 Quincey Foster **RC** 4.00
264 Junior Brignac **RC** 4.00
265 Rico Washington **RC** 4.00
266 Scott Sobkowiak **RC** 4.00
267 Pedro Martinez, Rick Ankiel (Counterparts) 2.00
268 Manny Ramirez, Vladimir Guerrero (Counterparts) 2.00
269 A.J. Burnett, Mark Mulder (Counterparts) .75
270 Mike Piazza, Eric Munson (Counterparts) 2.50
271 Josh Hamilton, Corey Patterson (Counterparts) 1.00
272 Ken Griffey Jr., Sammy Sosa (Counterparts) 3.00
273 Derek Jeter, Alfonso Soriano (Counterparts) 5.00
274 Mark McGwire, Pat Burrell (Counterparts) 4.00
275 Chipper Jones, Cal Ripken Jr. (Counterparts) 5.00
276 Nomar Garciaparra, Alex Rodriguez (Counterparts) 4.00
277 Pedro Martinez (Gems) 3.00
278 Tony Gwynn (Gems) 5.00
279 Barry Bonds (Gems) 10.00
280 Juan Gonzalez (Gems) 3.00
281 Larry Walker (Gems) 1.50
282 Nomar Garciaparra (Gems) 8.00
283 Ken Griffey Jr. (Gems) 6.00
284 Manny Ramirez (Gems) 3.00
285 Shawn Green (Gems) 2.00
286 Sammy Sosa (Gems) 6.00

Refractor

These are a parallel to the base set and have a mirror like sheen. Card backs have "refractor" written underneath the card number.

Stars (1-100): 5-10X
Inserted 1:24
Rookies (101-120,247-266):.5-1X
Production 500 Sets
Features (121-135): 2-3X
Inserted 1:96
Counterparts (267-276): 2-3X
Inserted 1:96
Gems (136-145,277-286): 2-3X
Inserted 1:288

Gold Refractor

A parallel to the base set, these have the usual mirror like appearance with a deckle edged border. Regular cards are seeded 1:240 packs, Rookies are limited to 100 serial numbered sets, Features and Counterparts subsets (1:960) and Gems (1:2,880).

Stars (1-100): 20-40X
Inserted 1:240
Rookies (101-120, 247-266):1-2X
Production 100 Sets
Features: 4-8X
Inserted 1:960
Counterparts: 4-8X
Inserted 1:960
Gems: 5-10X
Inserted 1:2,880

Ballpark Bounties

Seeded across both Series 1 and 2 these inserts use Serigraph Fresnal technology and have a metallic looking image of a baseball in the background of the player photo. Card backs are numbered with a "BB" prefix.

	NM/M
Complete Set (30):	85.00
Complete Series 1 (15):	45.00
Complete Series 2 (15):	45.00
Common Player:	1.50
Inserted 1:24	
1 Chipper Jones	5.00
2 Mike Piazza	6.00
3 Vladimir Guerrero	3.00
4 Sammy Sosa	6.00
5 Nomar Garciaparra	6.00
6 Manny Ramirez	3.00
7 Jeff Bagwell	3.00
8 Scott Rolen	2.00
9 Carlos Beltran	2.50
10 Pedro Martinez	3.00
11 Greg Maddux	5.00
12 Josh Hamilton	2.00
13 Adam Piatt	1.50
14 Pat Burrell	2.00
15 Alfonso Soriano	3.00
16 Alex Rodriguez	8.00
17 Derek Jeter	10.00
18 Cal Ripken Jr.	10.00
19 Larry Walker	1.50
20 Barry Bonds	10.00
21 Ken Griffey Jr.	6.00
22 Mark McGwire	8.00
23 Ivan Rodriguez	2.00
24 Andruw Jones	2.50
25 Todd Helton	2.50
26 Randy Johnson	3.00
27 Ruben Mateo	1.50
28 Corey Patterson	1.50
29 Sean Burroughs	1.50
30 Eric Munson	1.50

Dream Cast

These inserts are found exclusively in Series 2 packs and utilize Duflex technology. The card fronts try to portray a "dream sequence" with sky and clouds in the background. They are numbered with a "DC" prefix on the card back.

	NM/M
Complete Set (10):	40.00
Common Player:	2.00
Inserted 1:36	
1 Mark McGwire	8.00
2 Roberto Alomar	2.00
3 Chipper Jones	5.00
4 Derek Jeter	10.00
5 Barry Bonds	10.00
6 Ken Griffey Jr.	6.00
7 Sammy Sosa	6.00
8 Mike Piazza	6.00
9 Pedro Martinez	3.00
10 Randy Johnson	3.00

Finest Moments

This four-card set pays tribute to milestone achievements accomplished during the 1999 season. They are numbered with a "FM" prefix. A Refractor parallel version is seeded 1:20 packs.

	NM/M
Complete Set (4):	6.00
Common Player:	1.00
Inserted 1:9	
Refractor:	1-2X
Inserted 1:20	
1 Chipper Jones	3.00
2 Ivan Rodriguez	1.50
3 Tony Gwynn	3.00
4 Wade Boggs	3.00

Moments Autographs

An autographed version of the four-card set, these were seeded 1:425 packs.

	NM/M
Common Autograph:	25.00
Inserted 1:425	
1 Chipper Jones	50.00
2 Ivan Rodriguez	25.00
3 Tony Gwynn	50.00
4 Wade Boggs	25.00

For The Record

Printed on Finest Clear Card technology, each of the 10 players featured has three cards. Each card sequentially numbered to the distance of the outfield wall in their home ballpark (left, center and right). Combining all three cards forms a panaromic view of the stadium.

	NM/M
Complete Set (30):	300.00
Common Player:	8.00
1A Derek Jeter/318	20.00
1B Derek Jeter/408	20.00
1C Derek Jeter/314	20.00
2A Mark McGwire/330	15.00
2B Mark McGwire/402	15.00
2C Mark McGwire/330	15.00
3A Ken Griffey Jr./331	10.00
3B Ken Griffey Jr./405	10.00
3C Ken Griffey Jr./327	10.00
4A Alex Rodriguez/331	15.00
4B Alex Rodriguez/405	15.00
4C Alex Rodriguez/327	15.00
5A Nomar Garciaparra/310	10.00
5B Nomar Garciaparra/390	10.00
5C Nomar Garciaparra/302	10.00
6A Cal Ripken Jr./333	20.00
6B Cal Ripken Jr./410	20.00
6C Cal Ripken Jr./318	20.00
7A Sammy Sosa/355	10.00
7B Sammy Sosa/400	10.00
7C Sammy Sosa/353	10.00
8A Manny Ramirez/325	8.00
8B Manny Ramirez/410	8.00
8C Manny Ramirez/325	8.00
9A Mike Piazza/338	10.00
9B Mike Piazza/410	10.00
9C Mike Piazza/338	10.00
10A Chipper Jones/335	9.00
10B Chipper Jones/401	9.00
10C Chipper Jones/330	9.00

Gems Oversized

Each of the 10 Gems subset cards in series 1 and 2 were also done on an oversized format. The oversized cards were added as a box topper to each box. Home Team Advantage stores received Refractor versions of the Gems Oversized cards as a box topper.

	NM/M
Complete Set (20):	50.00
Common Player:	1.00
Inserted 1:Box	
1 Derek Jeter	6.00
2 Alex Rodriguez	5.00
3 Chipper Jones	3.00
4 Mike Piazza	4.00
5 Mark McGwire	5.00
6 Ivan Rodriguez	1.25
7 Cal Ripken Jr.	6.00
8 Vladimir Guerrero	2.00
9 Randy Johnson	2.00
10 Jeff Bagwell	2.00
11 Nomar Garciaparra	4.00
12 Ken Griffey Jr.	4.00
13 Manny Ramirez	2.00
14 Shawn Green	1.50
15 Sammy Sosa	4.00
16 Pedro Martinez	2.00
17 Tony Gwynn	2.00
18 Barry Bonds	6.00
19 Juan Gonzalez	1.50
20 Larry Walker	1.00

Going the Distance

This 12-card set highlights the top hitters in baseball, utilizing Photopolymer hologram technology. Card backs are numbered with a "GTD" prefix.

	NM/M
Complete Set (12):	45.00
Common Player:	3.00
Inserted 1:24	
1 Tony Gwynn	3.50
2 Alex Rodriguez	6.00
3 Derek Jeter	8.00
4 Chipper Jones	3.50
5 Nomar Garciaparra	4.00

6 Sammy Sosa 4.00
7 Ken Griffey Jr. 4.00
8 Vladimir Guerrero 3.00
9 Mark McGwire 6.00
10 Mike Piazza 4.00
11 Manny Ramirez 3.00
12 Cal Ripken Jr. 8.00

2001 Finest

NM/M
Complete Set (140): 250.00
Common Player: .25
Common Standout Veteran (1-10): 5.00
Production 1999
Common Rookie (111-140): 4.00
Production 999
Pack (6): 8.00
Box (20): 140.00
1 Mike Piazza/SV 10.00
2 Andruw Jones 1.00
3 Jason Giambi .75
4 Fred McGriff .25
5 Vladimir Guerrero/SV 6.00
6 Adrian Gonzalez .25
7 Pedro Martinez 1.00
8 Mike Lieberthal .25
9 Warren Morris .25
10 Juan Gonzalez 1.00
11 Jose Canseco .50
12 Jose Valentin .25
13 Jeff Cirillo .25
14 Pokey Reese .25
15 Scott Rolen .75
16 Greg Maddux 1.50
17 Carlos Delgado .50
18 Rick Ankiel .25
19 Steve Finley .25
20 Shawn Green .40
21 Orlando Cabrerra .25
22 Roberto Alomar .45
23 John Olerud .25
24 Albert Belle .35
25 Edgardo Alfonzo .25
26 Rafael Palmeiro .75
27 Mike Sweeney .25
28 Bernie Williams .35
29 Larry Walker .25
30 Barry Bonds/SV 15.00
31 Orlando Hernandez .25
32 Randy Johnson 1.00
33 Shannon Stewart .25
34 Mark Grace .35
35 Alex Rodriguez/SV 12.00
36 Tino Martinez .25
37 Carlos Febles .25
38 Al Leiter .25
39 Omar Vizquel .25
40 Chuck Knoblauch .25
41 Tim Salmon .40
42 Brian Jordan .25
43 Edgar Renteria .25
44 Preston Wilson .25
45 Mariano Rivera .40
46 Gabe Kapler .25
47 Jason Kendall .25
48 Rickey Henderson .75
49 Luis Gonzalez .40
50 Tom Glavine .40
51 Jeromy Burnitz .25
52 Garret Anderson .25
53 Craig Biggio .25
54 Vinny Castilla .25
55 Jeff Kent .25
56 Gary Sheffield .50
57 Jorge Posada .40
58 Sean Casey .40
59 Johnny Damon .40
60 Dean Palmer .25
61 Todd Helton 1.00
62 Barry Larkin .25
63 Robin Ventura .25
64 Kenny Lofton .25
65 Sammy Sosa/SV 10.00
66 Rafael Furcal .25
67 Jay Bell .25
68 J.T. Snow Jr. .25
69 Jose Vidro .25
70 Ivan Rodriguez .75
71 Jermaine Dye .25
72 Chipper Jones/SV 8.00
73 Fernando Vina .25
74 Ben Grieve .25
75 Mark McGwire/SV 12.00
76 Matt Williams .25
77 Mark Grudzielanek .25
78 Mike Hampton .25
79 Brian Giles .25
80 Tony Gwynn 1.50
81 Carlos Beltran .50
82 Ray Durham .25
83 Brad Radke .25
84 David Justice .25
85 Frank Thomas 1.00
86 Todd Zeile .25
87 Pat Burrell .75
88 Jim Thome .25
89 Greg Vaughn .25
90 Ken Griffey Jr./SV 10.00
91 Mike Mussina .40
92 Magglio Ordonez .40
93 Bobby Abreu .25
94 Alex Gonzalez .25
95 Kevin Brown .25
96 Jay Buhner .25
97 Roger Clemens 2.00
98 Nomar Garciaparra/SV 10.00
99 Derek Lee .25
100 Derek Jeter/SV 15.00
101 Adrian Beltre .45
102 Geoff Jenkins .25
103 Javy Lopez .25
104 Raul Mondesi .25
105 Troy Glaus 1.00
106 Jeff Bagwell 1.00
107 Eric Karros .25
108 Mo Vaughn .25
109 Cal Ripken Jr. 3.00
110 Manny Ramirez 1.00
111 Scott Heard 4.00
112 Luis Montanez **RC** 5.00
113 Ben Diggins 4.00
114 Shaun Boyd **RC** 4.00
115 Sean Burnett 4.00
116 Carmen Cali **RC** 4.00
117 Derek Thompson 4.00
118 David Parrish **RC** 4.00
119 Dominic Rich **RC** 4.00
120 Chad Petty **RC** 4.00
121 Steve Smyth **RC** 4.00
122 John Lackey 4.00
123 Matt Galante **RC** 4.00
124 Danny Borrell **RC** 4.00
125 Bob Keppel **RC** 4.00
126 Justin Wayne **RC** 8.00
127 J.R. House 4.00
128 Brian Sellier **RC** 4.00
129 Dan Moylan **RC** 4.00
130 Scott Pratt **RC** 4.00
131 Victor Hall **RC** 4.00
132 Joel Pineiro 8.00
133 Josh Axelson **RC** 4.00
134 Jose Reyes **RC** 200.00
135 Greg Runser **RC** 4.00
136 Bryan Hebson **RC** 4.00
137 Sammy Serrano **RC** 4.00
138 Kevin Joseph **RC** 4.00
139 Juan Richardson **RC** 8.00
140 Mark Fischer **RC** 4.00

Refractors

Stars (1-110): 4-8X
Production 499
SP's: .5-1.5X
Production 399
Cards (111-140): 1-2X
Production 241

All-Stars

NM/M
Complete Set (10): 30.00
Common Player: 2.00
Inserted 1:10
Refractors: 1.5-2X
Inserted 1:40
1 Mark McGwire 5.00
2 Derek Jeter 6.00
3 Alex Rodriguez 5.00
4 Chipper Jones 3.00
5 Nomar Garciaparra 4.00
6 Sammy Sosa 4.00
7 Mike Piazza 4.00
8 Barry Bonds 6.00
9 Vladimir Guerrero 2.00
10 Ken Griffey Jr. 4.00

Autographed

NM/M
Common Player: 5.00
Inserted 1:22
MB Milton Bradley 10.00
SB Sean Burnett 5.00
BKC Brian Cole 5.00
JC Joe Crede 6.00
BC Brad Creese 5.00
BD Ben Diggins 5.00
CD Chad Durham 5.00
TF Troy Farnsworth 5.00
RF Rafael Furcal 8.00
KG Keith Ginter 5.00
AG Adrian Gonzalez 15.00
JHH Josh Hamilton 40.00
JH Jason Hart 5.00
JRH J.R. House 5.00
AH Adam Hyzdu 5.00
DKC David Kelton 5.00
AK Adam Kennedy 5.00
DK David Krynzel 8.00
ML Mike Lamb 5.00
TL Terrence Long 5.00
KM Kevin Mench 5.00
BM Ben Molina 5.00
JM Justin Morneau 100.00
CM Chad Mottola 5.00
JO Jose Ortiz 5.00
DP David Parrish 5.00
DCP Corey Patterson 15.00
JP Jay Payton 6.00
CP Carlos Pena 8.00
AP Albert Pujols 400.00
MQ Mark Quinn 5.00
MR Mark Redman 5.00
BS Ben Sheets 15.00
JS Juan Silvestre 5.00
JNS Jamal Strong 5.00
BZ Barry Zito 20.00

Moments

NM/M
Complete Set (25): 45.00
Common Player: 1.00
Inserted 1:12
Refractors: 1.5-2X
Inserted 1:40
1 Pat Burrell 2.00
2 Adam Kennedy 1.00
3 Mike Lamb 1.00
4 Rafael Furcal 1.00
5 Terrence Long 1.00
6 Jay Payton 1.00
7 Mark Quinn 1.00
8 Ben Molina 1.00
9 Kazuhiro Sasaki 1.00
10 Mark Redman 1.00
11 Barry Bonds 8.00
12 Alex Rodriguez 6.00
13 Roger Clemens 5.00
14 Jim Edmonds 1.00
15 Jason Giambi 2.00
16 Todd Helton 2.50
17 Troy Glaus 2.50
18 Carlos Delgado 2.00
19 Darin Erstad 2.00
20 Cal Ripken Jr. 8.00
21 Paul Molitor 3.00
22 Robin Yount 2.50
23 George Brett 5.00
24 Dave Winfield 2.50
25 Wade Boggs 3.00

Moments Autographs

NM/M
Inserted 1:250
BB Barry Bonds 180.00
GB George Brett 75.00
JG Jason Giambi 25.00
TG Troy Glaus 20.00
TH Todd Helton 30.00
PM Paul Molitor 30.00
EM Eddie Murray 20.00
CR Cal Ripken Jr. 125.00
DW Dave Winfield 20.00
RY Robin Yount 50.00

Origins

NM/M
Complete Set (15): 18.00
Common Player: 1.00
Inserted 1:7
Refractors: 1.5-2X
Inserted 1:40
1 Derek Jeter 5.00
2 Jason Kendall 1.00
3 Jose Vidro 1.00
4 Preston Wilson 1.00
5 Jim Edmonds 1.00
6 Vladimir Guerrero 2.00
7 Andruw Jones 1.50
8 Scott Rolen 1.50
9 Edgardo Alfonzo 1.00
10 Mike Sweeney 1.00
11 Alex Rodriguez 4.00
12 Jermaine Dye 1.00
13 Charles Johnson 1.00
14 Darren Dreifort 1.00
15 Neifi Perez 1.00

2002 Finest

NM/M
Complete Set (110): 125.00
Common Player: .25
Common SP Auto. (101-110): 8.00
Pack (5): 4.00
Box (18): 60.00
1 Mike Mussina .50
2 Steve Sparks .25
3 Randy Johnson 1.00
4 Orlando Cabrera .25
5 Jeff Kent .25
6 Carlos Delgado .75
7 Ivan Rodriguez .75
8 Jose Cruz .25
9 Jason Giambi .75
10 Brad Penny .25
11 Moises Alou .25
12 Mike Piazza 2.00
13 Ben Grieve .25
14 Derek Jeter 3.00
15 Roy Oswalt .40
16 Pat Burrell .65
17 Preston Wilson .25
18 Kevin Brown .25
19 Barry Bonds 3.00
20 Phil Nevin .25
21 Juan Gonzalez 1.00
22 Carlos Beltran .60
23 Chipper Jones 1.50
24 Curt Schilling .50
25 Jorge Posada .40
26 Alfonso Soriano 1.00
27 Cliff Floyd .25
28 Rafael Palmeiro .75
29 Terrence Long .25
30 Ken Griffey Jr. 2.00
31 Jason Kendall .25
32 Jose Vidro .25
33 Jermaine Dye .25
34 Bobby Higginson .25
35 Albert Pujols 2.50
36 Miguel Tejada .40
37 Jim Edmonds .25
38 Barry Zito .40
39 Jimmy Rollins .50
40 Rafael Furcal .25
41 Omar Vizquel .25
42 Kazuhiro Sasaki .25
43 Brian Giles .25
44 Darin Erstad .50
45 Mariano Rivera .40
46 Troy Percival .25
47 Mike Sweeney .25
48 Vladimir Guerrero 1.00
49 Troy Glaus 1.00
50 Hideo Nomo .65
51 Edgardo Alfonzo .25
52 Roger Clemens 1.75
53 Eric Chavez .40
54 Alex Rodriguez 2.50
55 Cristian Guzman .25
56 Jeff Bagwell 1.00
57 Bernie Williams .40
58 Kerry Wood .60
59 Ryan Klesko .25
60 Ichiro Suzuki 2.00
61 Larry Walker .25
62 Nomar Garciaparra 2.00
63 Craig Biggio .25
64 J.D. Drew .40
65 Juan Pierre .25
66 Roberto Alomar .50
67 Luis Gonzalez .40
68 Bud Smith .25
69 Magglio Ordonez .50
70 Scott Rolen 1.00
71 Tsuyoshi Shinjo .25
72 Reggie Sanders .25
73 Garret Anderson .25
74 Tim Hudson .40
75 Adam Dunn .75
76 Gary Sheffield .50
77 Johnny Damon .40
78 Todd Helton 1.00
79 Geoff Jenkins .25
80 Shawn Green .40
81 C.C. Sabathia .25
82 Kazuhisa Ishii **RC** 3.00
83 Rich Aurilia .25
84 Mike Hampton .25
85 Ben Sheets .25
86 Andruw Jones 1.00
87 Richie Sexson .25
88 Jim Thome .25
89 Sammy Sosa 2.00
90 Greg Maddux 1.50
91 Pedro Martinez 1.00
92 Jeromy Burnitz .25
93 Raul Mondesi .25
94 Bret Boone .25
95 Jerry Hairston Jr. .25
96 Carlos Pena .25
97 Juan Cruz .25
98 Morgan Ensberg .25
99 Nathan Haynes .25
100 Xavier Nady .25
101 Nic Jackson/Auto. **RC** 10.00
102 Mauricio Lara/Auto. **RC** 8.00
103 Freddy Sanchez/Auto. **RC** 20.00
104 Clint Nageotte/Auto. **RC** 15.00
105 Beltran Perez/Auto. **RC** 8.00
106 Garrett Gentry/Auto. **RC** 8.00
107 Chad Qualls/Auto. **RC** 8.00
108 Jason Bay/Auto. **RC** 65.00
109 Michael Hill/Auto. **RC** 8.00
110 Brian Tallet/Auto. 10.00

Refractors

Star Refractors: 2-5X
Numbered to 499
X-Fractors: 3-6X
Numbered to 299
X-Fractor Protector: 5-10X
X-Fract. Protector (101-110): 1-2X
Numbered to 99

Moments Autographs

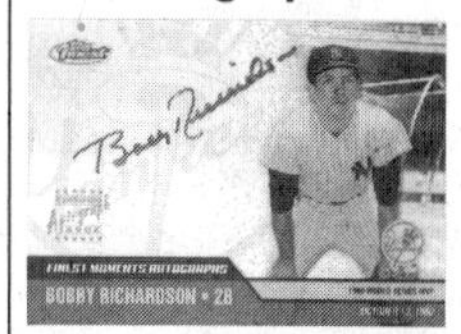

NM/M
Common Autograph: 10.00
Inserted 1:18
LA Luis Aparicio 15.00
YB Yogi Berra 30.00
JB Jim Bunning 10.00
BG Bob Gibson 25.00
GG Rich "Goose" Gossage 10.00
FJ Fergie Jenkins 15.00
DL Don Larsen 15.00
DM Don Mattingly 75.00
GP Gaylord Perry 10.00
BR Bobby Richardson 10.00
BRO Brooks Robinson 35.00
JS Johnny Sain 10.00
MS Mike Schmidt 50.00
RS Red Schoendienst 10.00
BT Bobby Thomson 15.00

Bat Relics

NM/M
Common Player: 5.00
Inserted 1:72
BB Barry Bonds 25.00
BBO Bret Boone 5.00
NG Nomar Garciaparra 15.00
LG Luis Gonzalez 5.00
TG Tony Gwynn 10.00
TH Todd Helton 8.00
AJ Andruw Jones 5.00
CJ Chipper Jones 10.00
MP Mike Piazza 10.00
AP Albert Pujols 20.00
AR Alex Rodriguez 10.00
IR Ivan Rodriguez 8.00
TS Tsuyoshi Shinjo 5.00
AS Alfonso Soriano 8.00
BW Bernie Williams 8.00

Team Topps Legends

Common Autograph

Uniform Relics

NM/M
Common Player: 5.00
Inserted 1:24
RA Roberto Alomar 8.00
JB Jeff Bagwell 8.00
BB Barry Bonds 20.00
BBO Bret Boone 5.00
CD Carlos Delgado 8.00
LG Luis Gonzalez 5.00
MG Mark Grace 8.00
SG Shawn Green 5.00
TG Tony Gwynn 10.00
TH Todd Helton 8.00
RH Rickey Henderson 15.00
AJ Andruw Jones 8.00
CJ Chipper Jones 10.00
GM Greg Maddux 10.00
PM Pedro Martinez 10.00

HN	Hideo Nomo	20.00
RP	Rafael Palmeiro	10.00
MP	Mike Piazza	10.00
AR	Alex Rodriguez	10.00
IR	Ivan Rodriguez	8.00
CS	Curt Schilling	10.00
TS	Tsuyoshi Shinjo	5.00
FT	Frank Thomas	8.00
LW	Larry Walker	5.00

2003 Finest

		NM/M
Complete Set (110):		
Common Player:		.25
Common Auto. (101-110):		10.00
Pack (5):		5.00
Box (18):		75.00
1	Sammy Sosa	2.00
2	Paul Konerko	.25
3	Todd Helton	.75
4	Mike Lowell	.25
5	Lance Berkman	.25
6	Kazuhisa Ishii	.25
7	A.J. Pierzynski	.25
8	Jose Vidro	.25
9	Roberto Alomar	.40
10	Derek Jeter	3.00
11	Barry Zito	.50
12	Jimmy Rollins	.50
13	Brian Giles	.25
14	Ryan Klosko	.25
15	Rich Aurilia	.25
16	Jim Edmonds	.25
17	Aubrey Huff	.25
18	Ivan Rodriguez	.65
19	Eric Hinske	.25
20	Barry Bonds	3.00
21	Darin Erstad	.60
22	Curt Schilling	.50
23	Andruw Jones	.75
24	Jay Gibbons	.25
25	Nomar Garciaparra	1.50
26	Kerry Wood	.60
27	Magglio Ordonez	.50
28	Austin Kearns	.50
29	Jason Jennings	.25
30	Jason Giambi	.50
31	Tim Hudson	.40
32	Edgar Martinez	.25
33	Carl Crawford	.25
34	Hee Seop Choi	15.00
35	Vladimir Guerrero	.75
36	Jeff Kent	.25
37	John Smoltz	.25
38	Frank Thomas	.75
39	Cliff Floyd	.25
40	Mike Piazza	1.50
41	Mark Prior	.75
42	Tim Salmon	.40
43	Shawn Green	.50
44	Bernie Williams	.40
45	Jim Thome	.25
46	John Olerud	.25
47	Orlando Hudson	.25
48	Mark Teixeira	.75
49	Gary Sheffield	.50
50	Ichiro Suzuki	2.00
51	Tom Glavine	.40
52	Torii Hunter	.25
53	Craig Biggio	.25
54	Carlos Beltran	.75
55	Bartolo Colon	.25
56	Jorge Posada	.35
57	Pat Burrell	.65
58	Edgar Renteria	.25
59	Rafael Palmeiro	.65
60	Alfonso Soriano	.75
61	Brandon Phillips	.25
62	Luis Gonzalez	.40
63	Manny Ramirez	.75
64	Garret Anderson	.25
65	Ken Griffey Jr.	1.50
66	A.J. Burnett	.25
67	Mike Sweeney	.25
68	Doug Mientkiewicz	.25
69	Eric Chavez	.50
70	Adam Dunn	.75
71	Shea Hillenbrand	.25
72	Troy Glaus	.75
73	Rodrigo Lopez	.25
74	Moises Alou	.25
75	Chipper Jones	1.00
76	Bobby Abreu	.25
77	Mark Mulder	.40
78	Kevin Brown	.25
79	Josh Beckett	.50
80	Larry Walker	.25
81	Randy Johnson	.75
82	Greg Maddux	1.00
83	Johnny Damon	.40
84	Omar Vizquel	.25
85	Jeff Bagwell	.75
86	Carlos Pena	.25
87	Roy Oswalt	.40
88	Richie Sexson	.25
89	Roger Clemens	1.25
90	Miguel Tejada	.40
91	Vicente Padilla	.25
92	Phil Nevin	.25
93	Edgardo Alfonzo	.25
94	Bret Boone	.25
95	Albert Pujols	2.00
96	Carlos Delgado	.50
97	Marlon Byrd	.25
98	Scott Rolen	.75
99	Pedro J. Martinez	.75
100	Alex Rodriguez	2.00
101	Adam LaRoche	15.00
102	Andy Marte **RC**	40.00
103	Daryl Clark **RC**	10.00
104	J.D. Durbin **RC**	10.00
105	Craig Brazell **RC**	15.00
106	Brian Burgamy **RC**	10.00
107	Tyler Johnson **RC**	10.00
108	Joey Gomes	10.00
109	Bryan Bullington **RC**	15.00
110	Byron Gettis **RC**	10.00

Refractors

Stars (1-100): 2-4X
Rookie Autos. (101-110): .75-1.5X
Inserted 1:6

X-Fractors

Stars (1-100): 5-10X
Rookie Autos (101-110): 1-2.5X
Production 99 Sets
X-Factor Golds (1-100): 3-6X
Golds Rk Autos. (101-110): 1-2X
Production 199 Sets

Bat Relics

		NM/M
Common Player:		8.00
Inserted 1:6		
JB	Jeff Bagwell	8.00
LB	Lance Berkman	8.00
WB	Wade Boggs	8.00
BB	Barry Bonds	20.00
RC	Rod Carew	10.00
RCL	Roger Clemens	15.00
AD	Adam Dunn	8.00
NG	Nomar Garciaparra	20.00
TH	Todd Helton	8.00
RH	Rickey Henderson	10.00
CJ	Chipper Jones	10.00
AK	Austin Kearns	8.00
GM	Greg Maddux	15.00
PM	Paul Molitor	8.00
DM	Dale Murphy	15.00
RP	Rafael Palmeiro	8.00
MP	Mike Piazza	15.00
KP	Kirby Puckett	15.00
AP	Albert Pujols	15.00
MR	Manny Ramirez	8.00
CR	Cal Ripken Jr.	35.00
AR	Alex Rodriguez	12.00
IR	Ivan Rodriguez	8.00
MS	Mike Schmidt	20.00
AS	Alfonso Soriano	10.00
MT	Miguel Tejada	8.00
JT	Jim Thome	10.00

Moments Autographs

		NM/M
Common Player:		10.00
EB	Ernie Banks	60.00
PB	Paul Blair	10.00
LB	Lou Brock	25.00
GC	Gary Carter	15.00
OC	Orlando Cepeda	15.00
GF	George Foster	15.00
GG	Rich "Goose" Gossage	15.00
KH	Keith Hernandez	15.00
DL	Don Larsen	15.00
WMA	Willie Mays	150.00
JP	Jim Palmer	15.00
GP	Gaylord Perry	15.00
JS	Johnny Sain	10.00

Team Topps Legends Autograph

	NM/M
Common Autograph:	10.00
Luis Aparicio	15.00
Paul Blair	10.00
Lou Brock	25.00
Rich "Goose" Gossage	15.00
Al Kaline	35.00
Don Larsen	20.00
Vern Law	12.00
Stan Musial	75.00

Uniform Relics

		NM/M
Common Player:		5.00
BB	Barry Bonds	20.00
EC	Eric Chavez	5.00
AD	Adam Dunn	10.00
LG	Luis Gonzalez	5.00
TH	Todd Helton	8.00
RJ	Randy Johnson	8.00
AJ	Andruw Jones	8.00
CJ	Chipper Jones	10.00
GM	Greg Maddux	12.00
WM	Willie Mays	30.00
MM	Mark Mulder	6.00
RO	Roy Oswalt	5.00
RP	Rafael Palmeiro	8.00
MP	Mike Piazza	12.00
AP	Albert Pujols	15.00
MR	Manny Ramirez	8.00
AR	Alex Rodriguez	15.00
CS	Curt Schilling	5.00
AS	Alfonso Soriano	10.00
SS	Sammy Sosa	15.00
MSW	Mike Sweeney	5.00
LW	Larry Walker	5.00

2004 Finest

		NM/M
Complete Set (122):		
Common Player:		.40
Common Star Relic (101-110):		8.00
Inserted 1:42		
Common FYP Autograph (111-122):		10.00
Inserted 1:18		
Pack (5):		6.00
Box (18):		85.00
Mini-Box (6):		30.00
1	Juan Pierre	.40
2	Derek Jeter	3.00
3	Garret Anderson	.50
4	Javy Lopez	.50
5	Corey Patterson	.50
6	Todd Helton	.75
7	Roy Oswalt	.50
8	Shawn Green	.50
9	Vladimir Guerrero	1.00
10	Jorge Posada	.50
11	Jason Kendall	.40
12	Scott Rolen	1.00
13	Randy Johnson	1.00
14	Bill Mueller	.40
15	Magglio Ordonez	.50
16	Larry Walker	.50
17	Lance Berkman	.50
18	Richie Sexson	.75
19	Orlando Cabrera	.40
20	Alfonso Soriano	1.00
21	Kevin Millwood	.50
22	Edgar Martinez	.50
23	Aubrey Huff	.40
24	Carlos Delgado	.75
25	Vernon Wells	.40
26	Mark Teixeira	.40
27	Troy Glaus	.50
28	Jeff Kent	.50
29	Hideo Nomo	.50
30	Torii Hunter	.50
31	Hank Blalock	.50
32	Brandon Webb	.40
33	Tony Batista	.40
34	Bret Boone	.50
35	Ryan Klesko	.50
36	Barry Zito	.50
37	Aaron Boone	.40
38	Geoff Jenkins	.50
39	Jeff Bagwell	.75
40	Dontrelle Willis	.50
41	Adam Dunn	.75
42	Mark Buehrle	.40
43	Esteban Loaiza	.40
44	Angel Berroa	.40
45	Ivan Rodriguez	.75
46	Jose Vidro	.40
47	Mark Mulder	.50
48	Marlon Byrd	.40
49	Jim Edmonds	.50
50	Eric Gagne	.50
51	Marcus Giles	.40
52	Curt Schilling	.75
53	Ken Griffey Jr.	1.50
54	Jason Schmidt	.50
55	Miguel Tejada	.50
56	Dmitri Young	.40
57	Mike Lowell	.50
58	Mike Sweeney	.40
59	Scott Podsednik	.75
60	Miguel Cabrera	1.00
61	Johan Santana	.40
62	Bernie Williams	.50
63	Eric Chavez	.50
64	Bobby Abreu	.50
65	Brian Giles	.50
66	Michael Young	.40
67	Paul LoDuca	.40
68	Austin Kearns	.40
69	Jody Gerut	.40
70	Kerry Wood	1.00
71	Luis Matos	.40
72	Greg Maddux	1.50
73	Alex Rodriguez	4.00
74	Mike Lieberthal	.40
75	Jim Thome	1.00
76	Javier Vazquez	.40
77	Bartolo Colon	.50
78	Manny Ramirez	.75
79	Jacque Jones	.40
80	Johnny Damon	.40
81	Carlos Beltran	.75
82	C.C. Sabathia	.40
83	Preston Wilson	.40
84	Luis Castillo	.40
85	Kevin Brown	.50
86	Shannon Stewart	.40
87	Cliff Floyd	.40
88	Mike Mussina	.50
89	Rafael Furcal	.40
90	Roy Halladay	.50
91	Frank Thomas	.75
92	Melvin Mora	.40
93	Andruw Jones	.75
94	Luis Gonzalez	.50
95	David Ortiz	.75
96	Gary Sheffield	.50
97	Tim Hudson	.50
98	Phil Nevin	.40
99	Ichiro Suzuki	2.00
100	Albert Pujols	2.50
101	Nomar Garciaparra	15.00
102	Sammy Sosa	15.00
103	Josh Beckett	8.00
104	Jason Giambi	8.00
105	Rocco Baldelli	8.00
106	Jose Reyes	8.00
107	Chipper Jones	10.00
108	Pedro J. Martinez	10.00
109	Mike Piazza	8.00
110	Mark Prior	8.00
111	Craig Ansman **RC**	10.00
112	Jeff Allison	15.00
113	David Murphy	20.00
114	Jason Hirsh	20.00
115	Matt Moses	20.00
116	Estee Harris **RC**	10.00
117	Logan Kensing **RC**	10.00
118	Lastings Milledge	40.00
119	Merkin Valdez **RC**	15.00
120	Travis Blackley **RC**	15.00
121	Vito Chiaravalloti **RC**	15.00
122	Dioner Navarro **RC**	25.00

Refractor

Refractor (1-100): 2-4X
Inserted 1:6
Refractor (101-110): 1-2X
Inserted 1:156
Refractor (111-122): 1-2X
Inserted 1:132

Gold Refractor

Gold Refractor (1-100): 6-12X
Gold Refr. (101-110): 1.5-2X
Gold Refr. (111-122): 2-4X
Production 50 Sets

Uncirculated X-Fractor

Stars (1-100): 4-8X
Relics (101-110): 1-2X
Autographs (111-122): 1-2X

Inserted as a box topper.
Production 139 Sets

Moments Autographs

		NM/M
Common Autograph:		10.00
JA	Jim Abbott	15.00
VB	Vida Blue	12.00
OC	Orlando Cepeda	12.00
LD	Lenny Dykstra	10.00
GS	George Foster	10.00
EK	Ed Kranepool	10.00
WM	Willie Mays	100.00
JP	Johnny Podres	10.00
DS	Duke Snider	40.00
RY	Robin Yount	75.00

Relics

		NM/M
Common Player:		4.00
JB	Jeff Bagwell	8.00
RB1	Rocco Baldelli/Jsy	6.00
RB3	Rocco Baldelli/Jsy	6.00
JPB1	Josh Beckett	8.00
LB1	Lance Berkman/Bat	5.00
LB2	Lance Berkman/Jsy	5.00
AB	Angel Berroa	4.00
HB1	Hank Blalock/Bat	8.00
HB2	Hank Blalock/Jsy	8.00
PB	Pat Burrell	10.00
SB	Sean Burroughs	5.00
MB	Marlon Byrd	4.00
MC	Miguel Cabrera	10.00
EC	Eric Chavez	6.00
AD	Adam Dunn	8.00
DE	Darin Erstad	4.00
NG	Nomar Garciaparra	12.00
TG	Troy Glaus	6.00
AG	Adrian Gonzalez	4.00
LG	Luis Gonzalez	4.00
SG	Shawn Green	6.00
VG	Vladimir Guerrero	8.00
CG	Cristian Guzman	4.00
RH	Rich Harden	5.00
TH1	Todd Helton/Bat	8.00
TH2	Todd Helton/Jsy	8.00
TH	Tim Hudson	5.00
TKH1	Torii Hunter/Bat	6.00
TKH2	Torii Hunter/Jsy	6.00
KI	Kazuhisa Ishii	4.00
RJ	Randy Johnson	8.00
AJ	Andruw Jones	6.00
JL	Javy Lopez	6.00
DL	Derek Lowe	6.00
ML1	Mike Lowell/Jsy	5.00
ML2	Mike Lowell/Jsy	5.00
GM	Greg Maddux	10.00
KM	Kevin Millwood	6.00
MM	Mark Mulder	4.00
BM1	Brett Myers/Jsy	4.00
BM2	Brett Myers/Jsy	4.00
MO1	Magglio Ordonez/Jsy	6.00
MO2	Magglio Ordonez/Bat	6.00
RP1	Rafael Palmeiro/Bat	8.00
RP2	Rafael Palmeiro/Jsy	8.00
RP3	Rafael Palmeiro/Jsy	8.00
AP	Andy Pettitte	6.00
JP	Juan Pierre	4.00
MP	Mark Prior	10.00
AP1	Albert Pujols/Jsy	15.00
AP2	Albert Pujols/Bat	15.00
JR1	Jose Reyes/Jsy	8.00
JR2	Jose Reyes/Bat	8.00
JR3	Jose Reyes/Jsy	8.00
MR	Mariano Rivera	10.00
AR1	Alex Rodriguez/ Rangers	10.00
AR2	Alex Rodriguez/ Yankees	20.00
IR1	Ivan Rodriguez/Jsy	4.00
IR2	Ivan Rodriguez/Jsy	8.00
IR3	Ivan Rodriguez/Bat	8.00
SR	Scott Rolen	8.00
CCS	C.C. Sabathia	6.00
KS	Kazuhiro Sasaki	4.00
CS	Curt Schilling	6.00
GS	Gary Sheffield	6.00
JS	John Smoltz	8.00
AS	Alfonso Soriano	8.00
SS	Sammy Sosa	12.00
MT1	Miguel Tejada/Bat	6.00
MT2	Miguel Tejada/Jsy	6.00
FT	Frank Thomas	8.00
JT	Jim Thome	10.00
LW	Larry Walker	4.00
VW	Vernon Wells	5.00
BW	Bernie Williams	6.00
DW	Dontrelle Willis	6.00
PW	Preston Wilson	4.00
KW1	Kerry Wood/Jsy	10.00
KW2	Kerry Wood/Bat	10.00
DY	Delmon Young	8.00
BZ	Barry Zito	8.00

2005 Finest

		NM/M
Complete Set (166):		
Common Player:		.40
Common Auto. (141-156):		10.00
Production 970, unless noted.		
Pack (5):		10.00
Box (18):		150.00
1	Alexis Rios	.40
2	Hank Blalock	.50
3	Bobby Abreu	.50
4	Curt Schilling	1.00
5	Albert Pujols	3.00
6	Aaron Rowand	.40
7	B.J. Upton	.50
8	Andruw Jones	.75
9	Jeff Francis	.40
10	Sammy Sosa	1.50
11	Aramis Ramirez	.75
12	Carl Pavano	.40
13	Bartolo Colon	.40
14	Greg Maddux	2.00
15	Scott Kazmir	.50
16	Melvin Mora	.40
17	Brandon Backe	.40
18	Bobby Crosby	.40
19	Carlos Lee	.50
20	Carl Crawford	.50
21	Brian Giles	.40
22	Jeff Bagwell	.75
23	J.D. Drew	.50
24	C.C. Sabathia	.40
25	Alfonso Soriano	1.00
26	Chipper Jones	1.00
27	Austin Kearns	.40
28	Carlos Delgado	.75
29	Jack Wilson	.40
30	Dmitri Young	.40
31	Carlos Guillen	.40
32	Jim Thome	1.00
33	Eric Chavez	.50
34	Jason Schmidt	.50
35	Brad Radke	.40
36	Frank Thomas	.75
37	Darin Erstad	.40
38	Javier Vazquez	.40
39	Garret Anderson	.50
40	David Ortiz	1.00

41 Javy Lopez .40
42 Geoff Jenkins .40
43 Jose Vidro .40
44 Aubrey Huff .40
45 Bernie Williams .50
46 Dontrelle Willis .50
47 Jim Edmonds .50
48 Ivan Rodriguez .75
49 Gary Sheffield .50
50 Alex Rodriguez 2.50
51 John Buck .40
52 Andy Pettitte .50
53 Ichiro Suzuki 2.50
54 Johnny Estrada .40
55 Jake Peavy .50
56 Carlos Zambrano .50
57 Jose Reyes .75
58 Bret Boone .40
59 Jason Bay .50
60 David Wright 1.50
61 Jeromy Burnitz .40
62 Corey Patterson .50
63 Juan Pierre .40
64 Zack Greinke .40
65 Mike Lowell .40
66 Ken Griffey Jr. 2.00
67 Marcus Giles .40
68 Edgar Renteria .50
69 Ken Harvey .40
70 Pedro Martinez 1.00
71 Johnny Damon 1.00
72 Lyle Overbay .50
73 Mike Maroth .40
74 Jorge Posada .50
75 Carlos Beltran .75
76 Mark Buehrle .50
77 Khalil Greene .40
78 Josh Beckett .50
79 Mark Loretta .40
80 Rafael Palmeiro .75
81 Justin Morneau .75
82 Rocco Baldelli .50
83 Ben Sheets .50
84 Kerry Wood .50
85 Miguel Tejada .75
86 Magglio Ordonez .50
87 Livan Hernandez .40
88 Kazuo Matsui .40
89 Manny Ramirez 1.00
90 Hideki Matsui 2.00
91 Jeff Kent .50
92 Matt Lawton .40
93 Richie Sexson .50
94 Mike Mussina .75
95 Adam Dunn .75
96 Johan Santana .75
97 Nomar Garciaparra 1.50
98 Michael Young .40
99 Victor Martinez .50
100 Barry Bonds 3.00
101 Oliver Perez .40
102 Randy Johnson 1.00
103 Mark Mulder .50
104 Pat Burrell .40
105 Mike Sweeney .40
106 Mark Teixeira .75
107 Paul LoDuca .40
108 Jon Lieber .40
109 Mike Piazza 1.50
110 Roger Clemens 3.00
111 Rafael Furcal .50
112 Troy Glaus .50
113 Miguel Cabrera 1.00
114 Randy Wolf .40
115 Lance Berkman .75
116 Mark Prior .75
117 Rich Harden .50
118 Preston Wilson .40
119 Roy Oswalt .50
120 Luis Gonzalez .40
121 Ronnie Belliard .40
122 Sean Casey .50
123 Barry Zito .50
124 Larry Walker .50
125 Derek Jeter 3.00
126 Tim Hudson .50
127 Tom Glavine .50
128 Scott Rolen 1.00
129 Torii Hunter .50
130 Paul Konerko .75
131 Shawn Green .40
132 Travis Hafner .50
133 Vernon Wells .50
134 Sidney Ponson .40
135 Vladimir Guerrero 1.00
136 Mark Kotsay .40
137 Todd Helton .75
138 Adrian Beltre .50
139 Wily Mo Pena .40
140 Joe Mauer .75
141 Brian Stavisky **RC** 10.00
142 Nate McLouth **RC** 15.00
143 Glen Perkins/375 **RC** 20.00
144 Chip Cannon **RC** 15.00
145 Shane Costa **RC** 10.00
146 Wes Swackhamer **RC** 10.00
147 Kevin Melillo **RC** 15.00
148 Billy Butler **RC** 60.00
149 Landon Powell **RC** 15.00
150 Scott Mathieson **RC** 10.00
151 Chris Roberson **RC** 10.00
152 Chad Orvella/375 **RC** 15.00
153 Eric Nielsen **RC** 10.00
154 Matt Campbell **RC** 10.00
155 Mike Rogers **RC** 10.00
156 Melky Cabrera **RC** 40.00
157 Nolan Ryan 4.00
158 Bo Jackson 1.00
159 Wade Boggs 1.00
160 Andre Dawson .75
161 Dave Winfield 1.00
162 Reggie Jackson 1.00
163 David Justice .50
164 Dale Murphy 1.00
165 Paul O'Neill .75
166 Tom Seaver 1.50

Refractors

Refrac. (1-140, 157-166): 2-4X
Autograph (141-156): .5-1X
Production 399 Sets

Refractors Black

Refrac. (1-140, 157-166): 4-8X
Autograph (141-156): 1-2X
Production 99 Sets

Refractors Blue

Refrac. (1-140, 157-166): 2-4X
Autograph (141-156): .5-1X
Production 299 Sets

Refractors Gold

Refrac. (1-140, 157-166): 5-10X
Autograph (141-156): 2-4X
Production 49 Sets

Refractors Green

Refrac. (1-140, 157-166): 2-4X
Autograph (141-156): .5-1.5X
Production 199 Sets

Refractors White Framed

No Pricing
Production One Set

Super Fractor

No Pricing
Production One Set

X-Fractor

Refrac. (1-140, 157-166): 2-4X
Autograph (141-156): .5-1X
Production 250 Sets

X-Fractor Black

Refrac. (1-140, 157-166): 8-15X
Autograph (141-156): No Pricing
Production 25 Sets

X-Fractor Blue

Refrac. (1-140, 157-166): 3-5X
Autograph (141-156): .5-1.5X
Production 150 Sets

X-Fractor Gold

No Pricing
Production 10 Sets

X-Fractor Green

Refrac. (1-140, 157-166): 5-10X
Autograph (141-156): 1.5-3X
Production 50 Sets

X-Fractor White Framed

No Pricing
Production One Set

Autographs

NM/M
X-Fractor: 1.5-2X
Production 25 Sets
JB Jason Bay 25.00
CB Carlos Beltran 30.00
BB Barry Bonds 280.00
MB Milton Bradley 15.00
EC Eric Chavez 20.00
JE Johnny Estrada 15.00
EG Eric Gagne 30.00
KM Kevin Millar 35.00
DO David Ortiz 50.00
MR Mariano Rivera 60.00
JS Johan Santana 40.00
GS Gary Sheffield 30.00
AS Alfonso Soriano 30.00
JST Jacob Stevens 10.00
DW David Wright 80.00

2005 Finest Finest Moment Autographs

No Pricing
Production 50

Printing Plates

No Pricing
Production one set for each color.

Alex Rodriguez Finest Moments

NM/M
A-Rod 1-49: 10.00
Production 190 Sets

Alex Rodriguez Finest Moments Autograph

NM/M
Production 13 Sets
A-Rod Auto. 1-49: 150.00

2 of a Kind Autographs

No Pricing
Production 13

2006 Finest

NM/M
Complete Set (155):
Common Player: .40
Common Auto. (141-155): 10.00
Pack (5): 9.00
Box (18): 150.00
1 Vladimir Guerrero 1.00
2 Troy Glaus .50
3 Andruw Jones 1.00
4 Miguel Tejada .75
5 Manny Ramirez 1.00
6 Curt Schilling 1.00
7 Mark Prior .75
8 Kerry Wood .50
9 Tadahito Iguchi .40
10 Freddy Garcia .40
11 Ryan Howard 1.50
12 Mark Buehrle .50
13 Wily Mo Pena .40
14 C.C. Sabathia .40
15 Garret Anderson .40
16 Shawn Green .40
17 Rafael Furcal .40
18 Jeff Francoeur .40
19 Ken Griffey Jr. 2.00
20 Derrek Lee .75
21 Paul Konerko .75
22 Rickie Weeks .50
23 Magglio Ordonez .40
24 Juan Pierre .40
25 Felix Hernandez 1.00
26 Roger Clemens 3.00
27 Zack Greinke .40
28 Johan Santana 1.00
29 Jose Reyes .75
30 Bobby Crosby .40
31 Jason Schmidt .40
32 Khalil Greene .40
33 Richie Sexson .50
34 Mark Mulder .50
35 Mark Teixeira .75
36 Nick Johnson .40
37 Vernon Wells .50
38 Scott Kazmir .40
39 Jim Edmonds .50
40 Adrian Beltre .40
41 Dan Johnson .40
42 Carlos Lee .50
43 Lance Berkman .75
44 Josh Beckett .50
45 Morgan Ensberg .40
46 Garrett Atkins .40
47 Chase Utley .50
48 Joe Mauer .75
49 Travis Hafner .75
50 Alex Rodriguez 3.00
51 Austin Kearns .40
52 Scott Podsednik .50
53 Jose Contreras .40
54 Greg Maddux 2.00
55 Hideki Matsui 2.00
56 Matt Clement .40
57 Javy Lopez .40
58 Tim Hudson .50
59 Luis Gonzalez .40
60 Bartolo Colon .50
61 Marcus Giles .40
62 Justin Morneau .75
63 Nomar Garciaparra 1.00
64 Robinson Cano 1.00
65 Ervin Santana .40
66 Brady Clark .40
67 Edgar Renteria .50
68 Jon Garland .40
69 Felipe Lopez .40
70 Ivan Rodriguez .75
71 Dontrelle Willis .50
72 Carlos Guillen .40
73 J.D. Drew .40
74 Rich Harden .40
75 Albert Pujols 3.00
76 Livan Hernandez .40
77 Roy Halladay .50
78 Hank Blalock .50
79 David Wright 1.50
80 Jimmy Rollins .50
81 John Smoltz .50
82 Miguel Cabrera 1.00
83 David DeJesus .40
84 Torii Hunter .50
85 Adam Dunn .75
86 Randy Johnson 1.00
87 Roy Oswalt .50
88 Bobby Abreu .50
89 Rocco Baldelli .40
90 Ichiro Suzuki 2.00
91 Jorge Cantu .40
92 Jack Wilson .40
93 Jose Vidro .40
94 Kevin Millwood .50
95 David Ortiz 1.00
96 Victor Martinez .50
97 Jeremy Bonderman .40
98 Todd Helton .75
99 Carlos Beltran .75
100 Barry Bonds 3.00
101 Jeff Kent .50
102 Mike Sweeney .40
103 Ben Sheets .50
104 Melvin Mora .40
105 Gary Sheffield .75
106 Craig Wilson .40
107 Chris Carpenter .75
108 Michael Young .40
109 Gustavo Chacin .40
110 Chipper Jones 1.00
111 Mark Loretta .40
112 Andy Pettitte .50
113 Carlos Delgado .75
114 Pat Burrell .50
115 Jason Bay .50
116 Brian Roberts .50
117 Joe Crede .40
118 Jake Peavy .50
119 Aubrey Huff .40
120 Pedro Martinez 1.00
121 Jorge Posada .50
122 Barry Zito .50
123 Scott Rolen .75
124 Brett Myers .40
125 Derek Jeter 3.00
126 Eric Chavez .50
127 Carl Crawford .50
128 Jim Thome 1.00
129 Johnny Damon 1.00
130 Alfonso Soriano .75
131 Clint Barmes .40
132 Dustin Nippert **(RC)** 1.00
133 Hanley Ramirez **(RC)** 2.00
134 Matt Capps **(RC)** 1.00
135 Miguel Perez **(RC)** 1.00
136 Tom Gorzelanny **(RC)** 1.00
137 Charlton Jimerson **(RC)** 1.00
138 Bryan Bullington **(RC)** 1.00
139 Kenji Johjima **RC** 4.00
140 Craig Hansen **RC** 3.00
141 Craig Breslow **RC** 15.00
142 Adam Wainwright **(RC)** 20.00
143 Joey Devine **RC** 15.00
144 Hong-Chih Kuo **(RC)** 40.00
145 Jason Botts **(RC)** 15.00
146 Josh Johnson **(RC)** 15.00
147 Jason Bergmann **RC** 15.00
148 Scott Olsen **(RC)** 15.00
149 Darrell Rasner **(RC)** 15.00
150 Daniel Ortmeier **(RC)** 15.00
151 Chuck James **(RC)** 20.00
152 Ryan Garko **(RC)** 20.00
153 Nelson Cruz **(RC)** 15.00
154 Anthony Lerew **(RC)** 10.00
155 Francisco Liriano **(RC)** 35.00

SuperFractor

No Pricing
Production One Set

Gold Refractor

Stars (1-140): 6-12X
Autos. (141-155): 2-3X
Production 49 Sets

Black Refractor

Stars (1-140): 4-8X
Autos. (141-155): 1-2X
Production 99 Sets

Green Refractor

Stars (1-140): 2-5X
Autos. (141-155): .75-1.5X
Production 199 Sets

Blue Refractor

Stars (1-140): 2-5X
Autos. (141-155): .75-1X
Production 299 Sets

Refractor

Stars (1-140): 2-4X
Autos. (141-155): .5-1X
Production 399 Sets

White Framed Refractor

No Pricing
Production One Set

Gold X-Fractor

No Pricing
Production 10 Sets

Black X-Fractor

Stars (1-140): 8-15X
Autos. (141-155): No Pricing
Production 25 Sets

Green X-Fractor

Stars (1-140): 6-12X
Autos. (141-155): 2-3X
Production 50 Sets

Blue X-Fractor

Stars (1-140): 3-5X
Autos. (141-155): 1-1.5X
Production 150 Sets

X-Fractor

Stars (1-140): 2-5X
Autos. (141-155): .75-1X
Production 250 Sets

Mickey Mantle Finest Moments

NM/M
Common Mantle: 10.00
Production 850 Sets
Refractor: 1X
Production 399 Sets
Blue Refractor: 1-1.5X
Production 299 Sets
Green Refractor: 1-2X
Production 199 Sets
Black Refractor: 1.5-3X

Production 99 Sets
Gold Refractor: 3-4X
Production 49 Sets
X-Fractor: 1-1.5X
Production 250 Sets
Blue X-Fractor: 1-2X
Production 150 Sets
Green X-Fractor: 3-4X
Production 50 Sets
Black X-Fractor: 4-6X
Production 25 Sets
Gold X-Fractor: No Pricing
Production 10 Sets
1-20 Mickey Mantle 10.00

Autographs

NM/M
JB Jason Bay 25.00
MC Miguel Cabrera 40.00
RC Robinson Cano 50.00
EC Eric Chavez 20.00
MG Marcus Giles 15.00
VG Vladimir Guerrero 50.00
JG Jose Guillen 12.00
RH Rich Harden 20.00
KJ Kenji Johjima 80.00
AJ Andruw Jones 40.00
CJ Chipper Jones 60.00
DL Derrek Lee 30.00
RO Roy Oswalt 25.00
AR Alex Rodriguez 160.00
GS Gary Sheffield 30.00
DWI Dontrelle Willis 25.00
CW Craig Wilson 10.00
DW David Wright 60.00

Barry Bonds Finest Moments Autographs

No Pricing

Barry Bonds Finest Moments

NM/M
Common Bonds: 10.00
Production 425 Sets
Gold Refractor: 1-2X
Production 199 Sets
1-25 Barry Bonds 10.00

Mickey Mantle Finest Moments Cut Signature

No Pricing
Production One Set

2007 Finest

NM/M
Complete Set (165):
Common Player (1-135): .25
Common RC (136-150): 1.00
Common RC Auto. (151-165): 10.00
Pack (5): 8.00
Box (18): 125.00
1 David Wright 2.00
2 Jered Weaver .50
3 Chipper Jones 1.00
4 Magglio Ordonez .25
5 Ben Sheets .50
6 Nick Johnson .25
7 Melvin Mora .25
8 Chien-Ming Wang 1.00

9 Andre Ethier .50
10 Carlos Beltran 1.00
11 Ryan Zimmerman 1.00
12 Troy Glaus .50
13 Hanley Ramirez .75
14 Mark Buehrle .50
15 Dan Uggla .50
16 Richie Sexson .75
17 Scott Kazmir .50
18 Garrett Atkins .25
19 Matt Cain .50
20 Jorge Posada .50
21 Brett Myers .25
22 Jeff Francoeur .50
23 Scott Rolen 1.00
24 Derrek Lee .75
25 Manny Ramirez 1.00
26 Johnny Damon 1.00
27 Mark Teixeira 1.00
28 Mark Prior .75
29 Victor Martinez .50
30 Greg Maddux 2.00
31 Prince Fielder 1.50
32 Jeremy Bonderman .50
33 Paul LoDuca .25
34 Brandon Webb .50
35 Robinson Cano 1.00
36 Josh Beckett .50
37 David DeJesus .25
38 Kenny Rogers .25
39 Jim Thome 1.00
40 Brian McCann .50
41 Lance Berkman .50
42 Adam Dunn .75
43 Rocco Baldelli .50
44 Brian Roberts .50
45 Vladimir Guerrero 1.00
46 Dontrelle Willis .50
47 Eric Chavez .50
48 Carlos Zambrano .50
49 Ivan Rodriguez 1.00
50 Alex Rodriguez 3.00
51 Curt Schilling 1.00
52 Carlos Delgado .75
53 Matt Holliday .75
54 Mark Teahen .25
55 Frank Thomas 1.00
56 Grady Sizemore .75
57 Aramis Ramirez .50
58 Rafael Furcal .50
59 David Ortiz 1.00
60 Paul Konerko .50
61 Barry Zito .50
62 Travis Hafner .50
63 Nick Swisher .50
64 Johan Santana 1.00
65 Miguel Tejada .75
66 Carl Crawford .50
67 Kenji Johjima .50
68 Derek Jeter 3.00
69 Francisco Liriano .50
70 Ken Griffey Jr. 2.00
71 Pat Burrell .50
72 Adrian Gonzalez .25
73 Miguel Cabrera 1.00
74 Albert Pujols 3.00
75 Justin Verlander .75
76 Carlos Lee .50
77 John Smoltz .50
78 Orlando Hudson .25
79 Joe Mauer .50
80 Freddy Sanchez .25
81 Bobby Abreu .50
82 Pedro Martinez 1.00
83 Vernon Wells .50
84 Justin Morneau .50
85 Bill Hall .50
86 Jason Schmidt .50
87 Michael Young .50
88 Tadahito Iguchi .25
89 Kevin Millwood .50
90 Randy Johnson 1.00
91 Roy Halladay .50
92 Mike Lowell .25
93 Jake Peavy .50
94 Jason Varitek .75
95 Todd Helton .75
96 Mark Loretta .25
97 Gary Matthews .25
98 Ryan Howard 2.00
99 Jose Reyes 1.00
100 Chris Carpenter .50
101 Hideki Matsui 2.00
102 Brian Giles .25
103 Torii Hunter .50
104 Rich Harden .25
105 Ichiro Suzuki 2.00
106 Chase Utley 1.00
107 Nicholas Markakis .50
108 Marcus Giles .25
109 Gary Sheffield .75
110 Jim Edmonds .50
111 Brandon Phillips .25
112 Roy Oswalt .50
113 Jeff Kent .50
114 Jason Bay .50
115 Raul Ibanez .25
116 Stephen Drew .50
117 Hank Blalock .50
118 Tom Glavine .50
119 Andruw Jones .75
120 Alfonso Soriano 1.00
121 Mariano Rivera .50
122 Garret Anderson .25
123 Erik Bedard .50
124 Huston Street .25
125 Austin Kearns .50
126 Jermaine Dye .25
127 C.C. Sabathia .25
128 Joe Nathan .25
129 Craig Monroe .25
130 Aubrey Huff .25
131 Billy Wagner .25
132 Jorge Cantu .25
133 Trevor Hoffman .25
134 Ronnie Belliard .25
135 B.J. Ryan .25
136 Adam Lind **(RC)** 1.00
137 Hector Gimenez **(RC)** 1.00
138 Shawn Riggans **(RC)** 1.00
139 Joaquin Arias **(RC)** 1.00
140 Drew Anderson **(RC)** 1.00
141 Mike Rabelo **RC** 1.00
142 Chris Narveson **(RC)** 1.00
143 Ryan Feierabend **(RC)** 1.00
144 Vinny Rottino **(RC)** 2.00
145 Jon Knott **(RC)** 1.00
146 Oswaldo Navarro **RC** 1.00
147 Brian Stokes **(RC)** 1.00
148 Glen Perkins **(RC)** 1.00
149 Mitch Maier **(RC)** 1.00
150 Delmon Young **(RC)** 2.00
151 Andrew Miller **RC** 50.00
152 Troy Tulowitzki **(RC)** 40.00
153 Philip Humber **(RC)** 20.00
154 Kevin Kouzmanoff **(RC)** 20.00
155 Michael Bourn **(RC)** 15.00
156 Miguel Montero **(RC)** 15.00
157 David Murphy **(RC)** 15.00
158 Ryan Sweeney **(RC)** 15.00
159 Jeff Baker **(RC)** 10.00
160 Jeff Salazar **(RC)** 10.00
161 Jose Garcia **(RC)** 10.00
162 Josh Fields **(RC)** 20.00
163 Delwyn Young **(RC)** 15.00
164 Fred Lewis **(RC)** 10.00
165 Scott Moore **(RC)** 15.00

Printing Plates

Production one set per color.

SuperFractor

Production One Set

X-Fractor

X-Fractor (1-135): 10-20X
RC Autos.: No Pricing
Production 25 Sets

Gold Refractor

Gold Refractor (1-150): 5-10X
Production 50
RC Autos.: 2X
Production 49

Black Refractor

Black Refractor (1-150): 4-8X
RC Autos.: 1.5X
Production 99 Sets

Green Refractor

Green Refractor (1-150): 2-5X
RC Autos.: 1-1.5X
Production 199 Sets

Blue Refractor

Blue Refractor (1-150): 2-5X
Production 399 Sets
RC Autos.: .75-1X
Production 299

Refractor

Refractor (1-150): 2-4X
RC Autographs: .5-1X
Production 399 only autos serial #'d.

Rookies Finest Moments Autograph

NM/M
Common Autograph: 10.00
Refractors: No Pricing
Production 25 Sets
DO David Ortiz 50.00
DW David Wright 75.00
JN Joe Nathan 10.00
AR Alex Rodriguez 125.00
TH Travis Hafner 20.00
RH Ryan Howard 100.00
AS Anibal Sanchez 20.00
BP Brandon Phillips 10.00
CH Cole Hamels 40.00
DWW Dontrelle Willis 20.00
LM Lastings Milledge 25.00
RC Robinson Cano 50.00
MN Michael Napoli 20.00
DU Dan Uggla 15.00
BW Brad Wilkerson 10.00
MC Melky Cabrera 35.00
AW Adam Wainwright 30.00
CQ Carlos Quentin 15.00
RJH Rich Hill 30.00
YP Yusmeiro Petit 15.00
FC Fausto Carmona 15.00
CJ Chuck James 20.00
JM Justin Morneau 25.00
RZ Ryan Zimmerman 35.00
RM Russell Martin 15.00
JP Jonathan Papelbon 50.00
HR Hanley Ramirez 20.00
MTC Matt Cain 25.00
DY Delmon Young 30.00

Dual Rookies Finest Moments Autograph

NM/M
Refractors: No Pricing
Production 25 Sets
VR Justin Verlander, Hanley Ramirez 60.00
US Dan Uggla, Anibal Sanchez 25.00
RP Mariano Rivera, Jorge Posada 80.00
OP Roy Oswalt, Mark Prior 40.00
UW Chase Utley, David Wright 100.00
CY Robinson Cano, Michael Young 50.00
HR Travis Hafner, Manny Ramirez 40.00
WW Chien-Ming Wang, Brandon Webb 175.00
JH Chuck James, Cole Hamels 40.00
MNA Russell Martin, Michael Napoli 20.00
PO Yusmeiro Petit, Scott Olsen 20.00
PP Jonathan Papelbon, Dustin Pedroia 75.00
CC Eric Chavez, Miguel Cabrera 40.00
UG Dan Uggla, Marcus Giles 15.00
CK Nelson Cruz, Matthew Kemp 25.00
HJ Rich Hill, Josh Johnson 30.00
HM Cole Hamels, Brett Myers 60.00
MC Lastings Milledge, Melky Cabrera 35.00
CR Matt Cain, Anthony Reyes 25.00
ZC Joel Zumaya, Fausto Carmona 20.00
BM Jason Bay, Justin Morneau 35.00
MG Russell Martin, Ryan Garko 25.00
MN Kendry Morales, Michael Napoli 25.00
MK Lastings Milledge, Matthew Kemp 30.00
RU Hanley Ramirez, Dan Uggla 40.00

A-Rod Road to 500

NM/M
Common A-Rod (26-50): 2.00
Inserted 2:Box

Ryan Howard HR History

NM/M
Common Howard (1-58): 4.00
Inserted 2:Box
Production 459 Sets
Refractor: 1.5-2X
Production 149 Sets
X-Fractor: 2-4X
Production 50 Sets
Gold Refractor: No Pricing
Production One Set

Mantle Cut Signature

Production One

Rookies Finest Moments

NM/M
Common Player: .50
Refractor: 2-3X
Blue Refractor: 2-4X
Production 299 Sets
Green Refractor: 2-4X
Production 199 Sets
Black Refractor: 4-6X
Production 99 Sets
Gold Refractor: 4-8X
Production 50 Sets
X-Fractor: 10-15X
Production 25 Sets
AD Adam Dunn 1.00
AJ Andruw Jones 1.50
AP Albert Pujols 4.00
AR Alex Rodriguez 4.00
CB Carlos Beltran 1.50
CC Carl Crawford .50
CJ Chipper Jones 1.50
DJ Derek Jeter 4.00
DL Derrek Lee 1.50
DO David Ortiz 1.50
DW David Wright 2.50
DWW Dontrelle Willis .50
HM Hideki Matsui 2.50
IS Ichiro Suzuki 2.50
JB Jason Bay 1.00
JM Joe Mauer 1.00
JR Jose Reyes 2.00
KG Ken Griffey Jr. 3.00
MC Miguel Cabrera 1.50
MP Mike Piazza 2.00
MR Manny Ramirez 1.50
MT Miguel Tejada 1.00
NG Nomar Garciaparra 1.50
RH Ryan Howard 3.00
VG Vladimir Guerrero 1.50
AS Anibal Sanchez .50
JP Jonathan Papelbon 1.50
DU Dan Uggla .50
HR Hanley Ramirez 1.00
JV Justin Verlander 1.00
FL Francisco Liriano 1.00
SD Stephen Drew 1.00
JW Jered Weaver 1.00
JS Jeremy Sowers .50
KJ Kenji Johjima 1.00
MCA Melky Cabrera 1.00
NM Nicholas Markakis 1.00
PF Prince Fielder 2.00
RM Russell Martin .50
AE Andre Ethier 1.00
MK Matthew Kemp 1.00
JH Jason Hirsh .50
CH Cole Hamels 2.00
JBA Josh Barfield .50
IK Ian Kinsler .50
AW Adam Wainwright 1.00
JST Brian Stokes .50
MN Michael Napoli .50
CQ Carlos Quentin 1.00
NC Nelson Cruz .50

Rookie Redemption

NM/M
Complete Set (10):
Common card:
Inserted 1:3 Mini Box
1 Hideki Okajima **RC** 15.00
2 Elijah Dukes **RC** 10.00
3 Akinori Iwamura **RC** 20.00
4 Tim Lincecum **RC** 40.00
5 Daisuke Matsuzaka **RC** 40.00
6 Ryan Braun **(RC)** 25.00
7 Daisuke Matsuzaka, Hideki Okajima 15.00
8 Justin Upton **RC** 30.00
9 Phil Hughes **(RC)** 25.00
10 Joba Chamberlain/ Auto. **RC** 140.00

2008 Finest

NM/M
Common Player (1-125): .25
Common RC (126-150): 1.00
Common RC Auto. (151-166): 10.00
Pack (5): 10.00
Box (15): 140.00
1 Daisuke Matsuzaka 2.00
2 Justin Upton 1.00
3 Andruw Jones .50
4 John Lackey .50
5 Brandon Phillips .50
6 Ryan Zimmerman .50
7 Tim Lincecum .75
8 Johnny Damon .75
9 Garrett Atkins .50
10 Magglio Ordonez .50
11 Tom Gorzelanny .25
12 Eric Chavez .25
13 Troy Tulowitzki 1.00
14 Mike Lowell .50
15 Brandon Webb .50
16 Chipper Jones 1.00
17 Alex Gordon .75
18 Ken Griffey Jr. 2.00
19 Roy Oswalt .50
20 Miguel Cabrera 1.00
21 Chase Utley 1.00
22 Scott Kazmir .50
23 Kenji Johjima .25
24 Frank Thomas 1.00
25 Ryan Braun 1.50
26 Carlos Pena .50
27 Robinson Cano .75
28 Ben Sheets .50
29 Russell Martin .50
30 Joe Mauer .50
31 Gary Sheffield .50
32 Carlos Zambrano .50
33 Jermaine Dye .25
34 Dan Uggla .25
35 Erik Bedard .50
36 Tim Hudson .50
37 David Ortiz 1.00
38 Tom Glavine .50
39 Adrian Gonzalez .50
40 Jorge Posada .50
41 Noah Lowry .25
42 Vernon Wells .50
43 Johan Santana 1.00
44 Dmitri Young .25
45 Manny Ramirez 1.00
46 Jim Edmonds .25
47 Roy Halladay .50
48 Delmon Young .50
49 Nick Swisher .25
50 David Wright 1.50
51 Paul Konerko .50
52 Curt Schilling .75
53 Torii Hunter .50
54 Gary Matthews Jr. .25
55 Derrek Lee .75
56 John Smoltz .50
57 Adam Dunn .75
58 C.C. Sabathia .50
59 Chris Young .50
60 Jake Peavy .50
61 Joba Chamberlain 1.50
62 Jason Bay .50
63 Chris Carpenter .50
64 Jimmy Rollins .75
65 Grady Sizemore .75
66 Joe Blanton .25
67 Justin Morneau .50
68 Lance Berkman .50
69 Jeff Francis .25
70 Nicholas Markakis .50
71 Orlando Cabrera .50
72 Barry Zito .25
73 Eric Byrnes .50
74 Brian McCann .50
75 Albert Pujols 3.00
76 Josh Beckett .75
77 Jim Thome .75
78 Fausto Carmona .50
79 Brad Hawpe .25
80 Prince Fielder 1.00
81 Justin Verlander .75
82 Billy Butler .25
83 J.J. Hardy .25
84 Hideki Matsui 1.50
85 Matt Holliday .75
86 Bobby Crosby .25
87 Orlando Hudson .25
88 Ichiro Suzuki 2.00
89 Troy Glaus .50
90 Hanley Ramirez 1.00
91 Carlos Beltran .75
92 Mark Buehrle .25
93 Andy Pettitte .50
94 Mark Teixeira .75
95 Curtis Granderson .75
96 Cole Hamels .50
97 Jarrod Saltalamacchia .25
98 Carl Crawford .50
99 Dontrelle Willis .25
100 Alex Rodriguez 3.00
101 Brad Penny .25
102 Michael Young .25
103 Greg Maddux 1.50
104 Brian Roberts .50
105 Hunter Pence .75
106 Aaron Harang .25
107 Ivan Rodriguez .50
108 Danny Haren .50
109 Freddy Sanchez .25
110 Alfonso Soriano 1.00
111 Hank Blalock .50
112 Chien-Ming Wang 1.00
113 Carlos Delgado .50
114 Aramis Ramirez .50
115 Jose Reyes 1.00
116 Victor Martinez .50
117 Carlos Lee .50
118 Jeff Kent .25
119 Miguel Tejada .50
120 Vladimir Guerrero 1.00
121 Travis Hafner .50
122 Todd Helton .50
123 Chris Young .50
124 Derek Jeter 3.00
125 Ryan Howard 1.50
126 Alberto Gonzalez **RC** 1.00
127 Felipe Paulino **RC** 1.00
128 Donny Lucy **RC** 1.00
129 Nick Blackburn **RC** 4.00
130 Luke Hochevar **RC** 3.00
131 Bronson Sardinha **RC** 1.00
132 Heath Phillips **RC** 1.00
133 Bryan Bullington **RC** 1.00
134 Jeff Clement **RC** 4.00
135 Josh Banks **RC** 1.00
136 Emilio Bonifacio **RC** 1.00
137 Ryan Hanigan **RC** 1.00
138 Erick Threets **RC** 1.00
139 Seth Smith **RC** 1.00
140 Billy Buckner **RC** 1.00
141 Bill Murphy **RC** 1.00
142 Radhames Liz **RC** 1.00
143 Joey Votto **RC** 2.00
144 Mel Stocker **RC** 2.00
145 Dan Meyer **RC** 1.00
146 Rob Johnson **RC** 1.00
147 Josh Newman **RC** 1.00
148 Daniel Giese **RC** 1.00
149 Luis Mendoza **RC** 1.00
150 Wladimir Balentien **RC** 2.00
151 Brandon Jones/ Auto. **RC** 15.00
152 Rich Thompson/ Auto. **RC** 10.00
153 Chin-Lung Hu/ Auto. **RC** 50.00
154 Chris Seddon/ Auto. **RC** 10.00
155 Steve Pearce/ Auto. **RC** 20.00
156 Lance Broadway/ Auto. **RC** 10.00
157 Nyjer Morgan/ Auto. **RC** 15.00
158 Jonathan Meloan/ Auto. **RC** 10.00
159 Josh Anderson/ Auto. **RC** 10.00
160 Clay Buchholz/ Auto. **RC** 40.00
161 Joe Koshansky/ Auto. **RC** 10.00
162 Clint Sammons/ Auto. **RC** 15.00
163 Daric Barton/ Auto. **RC** 15.00
164 Ross Detwiler/ Auto. **RC** 20.00
165 Sam Fuld/Auto. **RC** 15.00
166 Justin Ruggiano/ Auto. **RC** 10.00

Moments Autographs

NM/M
Common Auto.: 10.00
Red Refractor: No Pricing
Production 25 Sets
RH Ryan Howard 60.00
BP Brandon Phillips 20.00
JC Jack Cust 15.00
JR Jose Reyes 50.00
HR Hanley Ramirez 25.00
RB Ryan Braun 40.00
ME Mark Ellis 10.00
JD Justin Duchscherer 10.00
MR Mark Reynolds 15.00
AS Andrew Sonnanstine 10.00
DW David Wright 60.00
NM Nicholas Markakis 30.00
MC Miguel Cabrera 30.00
BPB Brian Bannister 15.00
CH Cole Hamels 30.00
JA Jeremy Accardo 10.00
PH Phil Hughes 40.00
JS Jarrod Saltalamacchia 15.00
CMW Chien-Ming Wang 125.00
CG Curtis Granderson 30.00
RZ Ryan Zimmerman 25.00
JH Josh Hamilton 15.00
FC Fausto Carmona 15.00
VG Vladimir Guerrero 35.00

Refractor

Refractor (1-150): 2-4X
RC Autographs: 1X
Production 499 only autos. serial #'d.

Blue Refractor

Blue Refractor (1-150): 2-5X
Production 299 Sets
RC Autos.: .75-1X
Production 399
Green Refractor
Green Refractor (1-150): 2-5X
RC Autos.: 1-1.5X
Production 199 Sets

Black Refractor

Black Refractor (1-150): 4-8X
RC Autos.: 1.5X
Production 99 Sets

Gold Refractor

Gold Refractor (1-150): 5-10X
RC Autos.: 2X
Production 50 Sets

Red Refractor

Red Refractor (1-150): 8-15X
RC Autos.: 3-4X
Production 25 Sets

White X-Fractor

Production One Set

Moments

NM/M
Common Player: .50
Refractor: 2-3X
Blue Refractor: 2-4X
Production 299 Sets
Green Refractor: 2-4X
Production 199 Sets
Black Refractor: 4-6X
Production 99 Sets
Gold Refractor: 4-8X
Production 50 Sets
Red Refractor: 8-15X
Production 25 Sets
AR Alex Rodriguez 3.00
JT Jim Thome 1.00
SS Sammy Sosa 1.00
TG Tom Glavine 1.00
TH Trevor Hoffman .50
RA Rick Ankiel 1.00
MB Mark Buehrle .50
JV Justin Verlander 1.00
CB Clay Buchholz 1.00
FT Frank Thomas 1.00
CG Curtis Granderson 1.00
DW David Wright 2.00
RH Ryan Howard 2.00
PM Pedro Martinez 1.00
ROH Roy Halladay 1.00
TT Troy Tulowitzki 1.00
JS John Smoltz 1.00
PF Prince Fielder 2.00
IS Ichiro Suzuki 2.00
CP Carlos Pena 1.00
DJ Derek Jeter 3.00
JR Jose Reyes 2.00
AP Andy Pettitte .50
TOH Todd Helton 1.00
ISS Ichiro Suzuki 2.00

DO	David Ortiz	2.00
BP	Brandon Phillips	1.00
JSA	Jarrod Saltalamacchia	.50
BW	Brandon Webb	1.00
APU	Albert Pujols	3.00
CF	Chone Figgins	.50
MH	Matt Holliday	1.50
DH	Danny Haren	.50
FH	Felix Hernandez	1.00
EB	Eric Byrnes	.50
AG	Adrian Gonzalez	.75
VG	Vladimir Guerrero	1.00
RB	Ryan Braun	1.50
HP	Hunter Pence	1.00
FC	Fausto Carmona	.50
HR	Hanley Ramirez	1.50
AS	Andrew Sonnanstine	.50
CH	Cole Hamels	1.00
JAS	Johan Santana	1.50
MR	Mark Reynolds	.50
JMC	Miguel Cabrera	1.50
BPB	Brian Bannister	.50
DL	Derrek Lee	1.00
ME	Mark Ellis	.50
CS	C.C. Sabathia	1.00

2008 Finest Topps Team Favorites Autographs

		NM/M
	Production 100 Sets	
	Red Refractor:	No Pricing
	Production 25 Sets	
JR	Jose Reyes	50.00
DW	David Wright	60.00
MC	Melky Cabrera	30.00
RC	Robinson Cano	40.00
AS	Alfonso Soriano	30.00
FP	Felix Pie	15.00
EC	Eric Chavez	10.00
BC	Bobby Crosby	10.00

Topps Team Favorites

		NM/M
	Complete Set (8):	10.00
	Common Player:	1.00
	Refractors:	2-4X
JR	Jose Reyes	3.00
DW	David Wright	4.00
MC	Melky Cabrera	1.50
RC	Robinson Cano	2.00
AS	Alfonso Soriano	2.00
FP	Felix Pie	1.50
EC	Eric Chavez	1.00
BC	Bobby Crosby	1.00

Topps Team Favorites Dual Autographs

		NM/M
	Production 74 Sets	
	Red Refractor:	No Pricing
	Production 25 Sets	
RW	Jose Reyes, David Wright	180.00
CC	Melky Cabrera, Robinson Cano	80.00
SP	Alfonso Soriano, Felix Pie	50.00
EB	Eric Chavez, Bobby Crosby	25.00

Printing Plates

Production one set per color.

Topps Team Favorites Cut Signatures

Production One Set

Topps Team Favorites Dual

		NM/M
	Common Duo:	2.00
	Red Refractor:	No Pricing
	Production 25 Sets	
RW	Jose Reyes, David Wright	4.00
CC	Melky Cabrera, Robinson Cano	3.00
SP	Alfonso Soriano, Felix Pie	2.00
EB	Eric Chavez, Bobby Crosby	2.00

Rookie Redemption

Common Redemption:
Inserted 1:15

1993 Flair Promos

Among the scarcest modern baseball promo cards are those produced to introduce Fleer's new premium product for 1993, Flair. Basically similar to the issued versions, the promo cards have "000" in place of the card number on back. The promos are checklisted here in alphabetical order.

		NM/M
	Complete Set (8):	200.00
	Common Player:	10.00
(1)	Will Clark	10.00
(2)	Darren Daulton	10.00
(3)	Andres Galarraga	10.00
(4)	Bryan Harvey	10.00
(5)	David Justice	10.00
(6)	Jody Reed	10.00
(7)	Nolan Ryan	100.00
(8)	Sammy Sosa	60.00

1993 Flair

Designed as Fleer's super-premium card brand, this 300-card set contains extra-thick cards which feature gold-foil highlights and UV coating front and back. Portrait and action photos are combined in a high-tech front picture and there is a muted photo on the back, as well.

		NM/M
	Complete Set (300):	15.00
	Common Player:	.10
	Pack (10):	1.50
	Wax Box (24):	20.00
1	Steve Avery	.10
2	Jeff Blauser	.10
3	Ron Gant	.10
4	Tom Glavine	.25
5	Dave Justice	.10
6	Mark Lemke	.10
7	Greg Maddux	1.00
8	Fred McGriff	.10
9	Terry Pendleton	.10
10	Deion Sanders	.15
11	John Smoltz	.10
12	Mike Stanton	.10
13	Steve Buechele	.10
14	Mark Grace	.10
15	Greg Hibbard	.10
16	Derrick May	.10
17	Chuck McElroy	.10
18	Mike Morgan	.10
19	Randy Myers	.10
20	Ryne Sandberg	1.00
21	Dwight Smith	.10
22	Sammy Sosa	1.00
23	Jose Vizcaino	.10
24	Tim Belcher	.10
25	Rob Dibble	.10
26	Roberto Kelly	.10
27	Barry Larkin	.10
28	Kevin Mitchell	.10
29	Hal Morris	.10
30	Joe Oliver	.10
31	Jose Rijo	.10
32	Bip Roberts	.10
33	Chris Sabo	.10
34	Reggie Sanders	.10
35	Dante Bichette	.10
36	Willie Blair	.10
37	Jerald Clark	.10
38	Alex Cole	.10
39	Andres Galarraga	.10
40	Joe Girardi	.10
41	Charlie Hayes	.10
42	Chris Jones	.10
43	David Nied	.10
44	Eric Young	.10
45	Alex Arias	.10
46	Jack Armstrong	.10
47	Bret Barberie	.10
48	Chuck Carr	.10
49	Jeff Conine	.10
50	Orestes Destrade	.10
51	Chris Hammond	.10
52	Bryan Harvey	.10
53	Benito Santiago	.10
54	Gary Sheffield	.35
55	Walt Weiss	.10
56	Eric Anthony	.10
57	Jeff Bagwell	.75
58	Craig Biggio	.10
59	Ken Caminiti	.10
60	Andujar Cedeno	.10
61	Doug Drabek	.10
62	Steve Finley	.10
63	Luis Gonzalez	.10
64	Pete Harnisch	.10
65	Doug Jones	.10
66	Darryl Kile	.10
67	Greg Swindell	.10
68	Brett Butler	.10
69	Jim Gott	.10
70	Orel Hershiser	.10
71	Eric Karros	.10
72	Pedro Martinez	.75
73	Ramon Martinez	.10
74	Roger McDowell	.10
75	Mike Piazza	1.50
76	Jody Reed	.10
77	Tim Wallach	.10
78	Moises Alou	.10
79	Greg Colbrunn	.10
80	Wil Cordero	.10
81	Delino DeShields	.10
82	Jeff Fassero	.10
83	Marquis Grissom	.10
84	Ken Hill	.10
85	Mike Lansing **RC**	.25
86	Dennis Martinez	.10
87	Larry Walker	.10
88	John Wetteland	.10
89	Bobby Bonilla	.10
90	Vince Coleman	.10
91	Dwight Gooden	.10
92	Todd Hundley	.10
93	Howard Johnson	.10
94	Eddie Murray	.75
95	Joe Orsulak	.10
96	Bret Saberhagen	.10
97	Darren Daulton	.10
98	Mariano Duncan	.10
99	Len Dykstra	.10
100	Jim Eisenreich	.10
101	Tommy Greene	.10
102	Dave Hollins	.10
103	Pete Incaviglia	.10
104	Danny Jackson	.10
105	John Kruk	.10
106	Terry Mulholland	.10
107	Curt Schilling	.25
108	Mitch Williams	.10
109	Stan Belinda	.10
110	Jay Bell	.10
111	Steve Cooke	.10
112	Carlos Garcia	.10
113	Jeff King	.10
114	Al Martin	.10
115	Orlando Merced	.10
116	Don Slaught	.10
117	Andy Van Slyke	.10
118	Tim Wakefield	.10
119	Rene Arocha **RC**	.10
120	Bernard Gilkey	.10
121	Gregg Jefferies	.10
122	Ray Lankford	.10
123	Donovan Osborne	.10
124	Tom Pagnozzi	.10
125	Erik Pappas	.10
126	Geronimo Pena	.10
127	Lee Smith	.10
128	Ozzie Smith	1.00
129	Bob Tewksbury	.10
130	Mark Whiten	.10
131	Derek Bell	.10
132	Andy Benes	.10
133	Tony Gwynn	1.00
134	Gene Harris	.10
135	Trevor Hoffman	.10
136	Phil Plantier	.10
137	Rod Beck	.10
138	Barry Bonds	2.50
139	John Burkett	.10
140	Will Clark	.10
141	Royce Clayton	.10
142	Mike Jackson	.10
143	Darren Lewis	.10
144	Kirt Manwaring	.10
145	Willie McGee	.10
146	Bill Swift	.10
147	Robby Thompson	.10
148	Matt Williams	.10
149	Brady Anderson	.10
150	Mike Devereaux	.10
151	Chris Hoiles	.10
152	Ben McDonald	.10
153	Mark McLemore	.10
154	Mike Mussina	.40
155	Gregg Olson	.10
156	Harold Reynolds	.10
157	Cal Ripken, Jr.	2.50
158	Rick Sutcliffe	.10
159	Fernando Valenzuela	.10
160	Roger Clemens	1.25
161	Scott Cooper	.10
162	Andre Dawson	.30
163	Scott Fletcher	.10
164	Mike Greenwell	.10
165	Greg Harris	.10
166	Billy Hatcher	.10
167	Jeff Russell	.10
168	Mo Vaughn	.10
169	Frank Viola	.10
170	Chad Curtis	.10
171	Chili Davis	.10
172	Gary DiSarcina	.10
173	Damion Easley	.10
174	Chuck Finley	.10
175	Mark Langston	.10
176	Luis Polonia	.10
177	Tim Salmon	.10
178	Scott Sanderson	.10
179	J.T. Snow **RC**	.50
180	Wilson Alvarez	.10
181	Ellis Burks	.10
182	Joey Cora	.10
183	Alex Fernandez	.10
184	Ozzie Guillen	.10
185	Roberto Hernandez	.10
186	Bo Jackson	.20
187	Lance Johnson	.10
188	Jack McDowell	.10
189	Frank Thomas	.75
190	Robin Ventura	.10
191	Carlos Baerga	.10
192	Albert Belle	.10
193	Wayne Kirby	.10
194	Derek Lilliquist	.10
195	Kenny Lofton	.10
196	Carlos Martinez	.10
197	Jose Mesa	.10
198	Eric Plunk	.10
199	Paul Sorrento	.10
200	John Doherty	.10
201	Cecil Fielder	.10
202	Travis Fryman	.10
203	Kirk Gibson	.10
204	Mike Henneman	.10
205	Chad Kreuter	.10
206	Scott Livingstone	.10
207	Tony Phillips	.10
208	Mickey Tettleton	.10
209	Alan Trammell	.10
210	David Wells	.10
211	Lou Whitaker	.10
212	Kevin Appier	.10
213	George Brett	1.25
214	David Cone	.10
215	Tom Gordon	.10
216	Phil Hiatt	.10
217	Felix Jose	.10
218	Wally Joyner	.10
219	Jose Lind	.10
220	Mike Macfarlane	.10
221	Brian McRae	.10
222	Jeff Montgomery	.10
223	Cal Eldred	.10
224	Darryl Hamilton	.10
225	John Jaha	.10
226	Pat Listach	.10
227	Graeme Lloyd **RC**	.10
228	Kevin Reimer	.10
229	Bill Spiers	.10
230	B.J. Surhoff	.10
231	Greg Vaughn	.10
232	Robin Yount	.75
233	Rick Aguilera	.10
234	Jim Deshaies	.10
235	Brian Harper	.10
236	Kent Hrbek	.10
237	Chuck Knoblauch	.10
238	Shane Mack	.10
239	David McCarty	.10
240	Pedro Munoz	.10
241	Mike Pagliarulo	.10
242	Kirby Puckett	1.00
243	Dave Winfield	.75
244	Jim Abbott	.10
245	Wade Boggs	1.00
246	Pat Kelly	.10
247	Jimmy Key	.10
248	Jim Leyritz	.10
249	Don Mattingly	1.25
250	Matt Nokes	.10
251	Paul O'Neill	.10
252	Mike Stanley	.10
253	Danny Tartabull	.10
254	Bob Wickman	.10
255	Bernie Williams	.10
256	Mike Bordick	.10
257	Dennis Eckersley	.60
258	Brent Gates	.10
259	Goose Gossage	.10
260	Rickey Henderson	.75
261	Mark McGwire	2.00
262	Ruben Sierra	.10
263	Terry Steinbach	.10
264	Bob Welch	.10
265	Bobby Witt	.10
266	Rich Amaral	.10
267	Chris Bosio	.10
268	Jay Buhner	.10
269	Norm Charlton	.10
270	Ken Griffey Jr.	1.50
271	Erik Hanson	.10
272	Randy Johnson	.75
273	Edgar Martinez	.10
274	Tino Martinez	.10
275	Dave Valle	.10
276	Omar Vizquel	.10
277	Kevin Brown	.10
278	Jose Canseco	.45
279	Julio Franco	.10
280	Juan Gonzalez	.40
281	Tom Henke	.10
282	David Hulse	.10
283	Rafael Palmeiro	.65
284	Dean Palmer	.10
285	Ivan Rodriguez	.65
286	Nolan Ryan	2.50
287	Roberto Alomar	.25
288	Pat Borders	.10
289	Joe Carter	.10
290	Juan Guzman	.10
291	Pat Hentgen	.10
292	Paul Molitor	.75
293	John Olerud	.10
294	Ed Sprague	.10
295	Dave Stewart	.10
296	Duane Ward	.10
297	Devon White	.10
298	Checklist	.05
299	Checklist	.05
300	Checklist	.05

Wave of the Future

The game's top prospects are featured in this insert issue randomly packaged in Flair packs. Cards #19-20, Darrell Whitmore and Nigel Wilson, were printed with each other's back; no corrected version was made.

		NM/M
	Complete Set (20):	6.00
	Common Player:	.15
1	Jason Bere	.15
2	Jeremy Burnitz	.15
3	Russ Davis	.15
4	Jim Edmonds	.25
5	Cliff Floyd	.15
6	Jeffrey Hammonds	.15
7	Trevor Hoffman	.15
8	Domingo Jean	.15
9	David McCarty	.15
10	Bobby Munoz	.15
11	Brad Pennington	.15
12	Mike Piazza	3.00
13	Manny Ramirez	2.00
14	John Roper	.15
15	Tim Salmon	.25
16	Aaron Sele	.15
17	Allen Watson	.15
18	Rondell White	.15
19	Darell Whitmore	.15
20	Nigel Wilson	.15

1994 Flair

One of the success stories of 1993 returned with the release of Fleer Flair for 1994. At $4 per pack this was pricey stuff, but collectors apparently liked the look that includes an extremely thick card stock, full-bleed photos and gold-foil graphics on both sides with a protective polyester laminate described as "far beyond mere UV coating." In addition to the 250 regular-issue cards, there are three 10-card, insert sets; Wave of the Future, Outfield Power and Hot Numbers in Series 1, the last with players' images printed on 100 percent etched foil. Series 2 has 200 base cards and Hot Glove, Infield Power and 10 more Wave of the Future insert cards.

		NM/M
	Complete Set (450):	60.00
	Common Player:	.10
	Series 1 Pack (10):	1.50
	Series 1 Box (24):	20.00
	Series 2 Pack (10):	3.00
	Series 2 Box (24):	50.00
1	Harold Baines	.10
2	Jeffrey Hammonds	.10
3	Chris Hoiles	.10
4	Ben McDonald	.10
5	Mark McLemore	.10
6	Jamie Moyer	.10
7	Jim Poole	.10
8	Cal Ripken, Jr.	3.00
9	Chris Sabo	.10
10	Scott Bankhead	.10
11	Scott Cooper	.10
12	Danny Darwin	.10
13	Andre Dawson	.30
14	Billy Hatcher	.10
15	Aaron Sele	.10
15a	Aaron Sele/OPS	2.00
16	John Valentin	.10
17	Dave Valle	.10
18	Mo Vaughn	.10
19	Brian Anderson **RC**	.50
20	Gary DiSarcina	.10
21	Jim Edmonds	.10
22	Chuck Finley	.10
23	Bo Jackson	.20
24	Mark Leiter	.10
25	Greg Myers	.10
26	Eduardo Perez	.10
27	Tim Salmon	.10
28	Wilson Alvarez	.10
29	Jason Bere	.10
30	Alex Fernandez	.10
31	Ozzie Guillen	.10
32	Joe Hall	.10
33	Darrin Jackson	.10
34	Kirk McCaskill	.10
35	Tim Raines	.10
36	Frank Thomas	1.00
37	Carlos Baerga	.10
38	Albert Belle	.10
39	Mark Clark	.10
40	Wayne Kirby	.10
41	Dennis Martinez	.10
42	Charles Nagy	.10
43	Manny Ramirez	1.00
44	Paul Sorrento	.10
45	Jim Thome	.65
46	Eric Davis	.10
47	John Doherty	.10
48	Junior Felix	.10
49	Cecil Fielder	.10
50	Kirk Gibson	.10
51	Mike Moore	.10
52	Tony Phillips	.10
53	Alan Trammell	.10
54	Kevin Appier	.10
55	Stan Belinda	.10
56	Vince Coleman	.10
57	Greg Gagne	.10
58	Bob Hamelin	.10
59	Dave Henderson	.10
60	Wally Joyner	.10
61	Mike Macfarlane	.10
62	Jeff Montgomery	.10
63	Ricky Bones	.10
64	Jeff Bronkey	.10
65	Alex Diaz	.10
66	Cal Eldred	.10
67	Darryl Hamilton	.10
68	John Jaha	.10
69	Mark Kiefer	.10
70	Kevin Seitzer	.10
71	Turner Ward	.10
72	Rich Becker	.10
73	Scott Erickson	.10
74	Keith Garagozzo	.10
75	Kent Hrbek	.10
76	Scott Leius	.10
77	Kirby Puckett	1.50
78	Matt Walbeck	.10
79	Dave Winfield	1.00
80	Mike Gallego	.10
81	Xavier Hernandez	.10
82	Jimmy Key	.10
83	Jim Leyritz	.10
84	Don Mattingly	1.75
85	Matt Nokes	.10
86	Paul O'Neill	.10
87	Melido Perez	.10
88	Danny Tartabull	.10
89	Mike Bordick	.10
90	Ron Darling	.10
91	Dennis Eckersley	.75
92	Stan Javier	.10
93	Steve Karsay	.10
94	Mark McGwire	2.50
95	Troy Neel	.10
96	Terry Steinbach	.10
97	Bill Taylor	.10
98	Eric Anthony	.10
99	Chris Bosio	.10
100	Tim Davis	.10
101	Felix Fermin	.10
102	Dave Fleming	.10

#	Player	Price
103	Ken Griffey Jr.	2.00
104	Greg Hibbard	.10
105	Reggie Jefferson	.10
106	Tino Martinez	.10
107	Jack Armstrong	.10
108	Will Clark	.10
109	Juan Gonzalez	.50
110	Rick Helling	.10
111	Tom Henke	.10
112	David Hulse	.10
113	Manuel Lee	.10
114	Doug Strange	.10
115	Roberto Alomar	.25
116	Joe Carter	.10
117	Carlos Delgado	.50
118	Pat Hentgen	.10
119	Paul Molitor	1.00
120	John Olerud	.10
121	Dave Stewart	.10
122	Todd Stottlemyre	.10
123	Mike Timlin	.10
124	Jeff Blauser	.10
125	Tom Glavine	.30
126	Dave Justice	.10
127	Mike Kelly	.10
128	Ryan Klesko	.10
129	Javier Lopez	.10
130	Greg Maddux	1.50
131	Fred McGriff	.10
132	Kent Mercker	.10
133	Mark Wohlers	.10
134	Willie Banks	.10
135	Steve Buechele	.10
136	Shawon Dunston	.10
137	Jose Guzman	.10
138	Glenallen Hill	.10
139	Randy Myers	.10
140	Karl Rhodes	.10
141	Ryne Sandberg	1.50
142	Steve Trachsel	.10
143	Bret Boone	.10
144	Tom Browning	.10
145	Hector Carrasco	.10
146	Barry Larkin	.10
147	Hal Morris	.10
148	Jose Rijo	.10
149	Reggie Sanders	.10
150	John Smiley	.10
151	Dante Bichette	.10
152	Ellis Burks	.10
153	Joe Girardi	.10
154	Mike Harkey	.10
155	Roberto Mejia	.10
156	Marcus Moore	.10
157	Armando Reynoso	.10
158	Bruce Ruffin	.10
159	Eric Young	.10
160	Kurt Abbott **RC**	.10
161	Jeff Conine	.10
162	Orestes Destrade	.10
163	Chris Hammond	.10
164	Bryan Harvey	.10
165	Dave Magadan	.10
166	Gary Sheffield	.40
167	David Weathers	.10
168	Andujar Cedeno	.10
169	Tom Edens	.10
170	Luis Gonzalez	.10
171	Pete Harnisch	.10
172	Todd Jones	.10
173	Darryl Kile	.10
174	James Mouton	.10
175	Scott Servais	.10
176	Mitch Williams	.10
177	Pedro Astacio	.10
178	Orel Hershiser	.10
179	Raul Mondesi	.10
180	Jose Offerman	.10
181	Chan Ho Park **RC**	1.00
182	Mike Piazza	2.00
183	Cory Snyder	.10
184	Tim Wallach	.10
185	Todd Worrell	.10
186	Sean Berry	.10
187	Wil Cordero	.10
188	Darrin Fletcher	.10
189	Cliff Floyd	.10
190	Marquis Grissom	.10
191	Rod Henderson	.10
192	Ken Hill	.10
193	Pedro Martinez	1.00
194	Kirk Rueter	.10
195	Jeromy Burnitz	.10
196	John Franco	.10
197	Dwight Gooden	.10
198	Todd Hundley	.10
199	Bobby Jones	.10
200	Jeff Kent	.10
201	Mike Maddux	.10
202	Ryan Thompson	.10
203	Jose Vizcaino	.10
204	Darren Daulton	.10
205	Len Dykstra	.10
206	Jim Eisenreich	.10
207	Dave Hollins	.10
208	Danny Jackson	.10
209	Doug Jones	.10
210	Jeff Juden	.10
211	Ben Rivera	.10
212	Kevin Stocker	.10
213	Milt Thompson	.10
214	Jay Bell	.10
215	Steve Cooke	.10
216	Mark Dewey	.10
217	Al Martin	.10
218	Orlando Merced	.10
219	Don Slaught	.10
220	Zane Smith	.10
221	Rick White	.10
222	Kevin Young	.10
223	Rene Arocha	.10
224	Rheal Cormier	.10
225	Brian Jordan	.10
226	Ray Lankford	.10
227	Mike Perez	.10
228	Ozzie Smith	1.50
229	Mark Whiten	.10
230	Todd Zeile	.10
231	Derek Bell	.10
232	Archi Cianfrocco	.10
233	Ricky Gutierrez	.10
234	Trevor Hoffman	.10
235	Phil Plantier	.10
236	Dave Staton	.10
237	Wally Whitehurst	.10
238	Todd Benzinger	.10
239	Barry Bonds	3.00
240	John Burkett	.10
241	Royce Clayton	.10
242	Bryan Hickerson	.10
243	Mike Jackson	.10
244	Darren Lewis	.10
245	Kirt Manwaring	.10
246	Mark Portugal	.10
247	Salomon Torres	.10
248	Checklist	.10
249	Checklist	.10
250	Checklist	.10
251	Brady Anderson	.10
252	Mike Devereaux	.10
253	Sid Fernandez	.10
254	Leo Gomez	.10
255	Mike Mussina	.40
256	Mike Oquist	.10
257	Rafael Palmeiro	.75
258	Lee Smith	.10
259	Damon Berryhill	.10
260	Wes Chamberlain	.10
261	Roger Clemens	1.75
262	Gar Finnvold	.10
263	Mike Greenwell	.10
264	Tim Naehring	.10
265	Otis Nixon	.10
266	Ken Ryan	.10
267	Chad Curtis	.10
268	Chili Davis	.10
269	Damion Easley	.10
270	Jorge Fabregas	.10
271	Mark Langston	.10
272	Phil Leftwich	.10
273	Harold Reynolds	.10
274	J.T. Snow	.10
275	Joey Cora	.10
276	Julio Franco	.10
277	Roberto Hernandez	.10
278	Lance Johnson	.10
279	Ron Karkovice	.10
280	Jack McDowell	.10
281	Robin Ventura	.10
282	Sandy Alomar Jr.	.10
283	Kenny Lofton	.10
284	Jose Mesa	.10
285	Jack Morris	.10
286	Eddie Murray	1.00
287	Chad Ogea	.10
288	Eric Plunk	.10
289	Paul Shuey	.10
290	Omar Vizquel	.10
291	Danny Bautista	.10
292	Travis Fryman	.10
293	Greg Gohr	.10
294	Chris Gomez	.10
295	Mickey Tettleton	.10
296	Lou Whitaker	.10
297	David Cone	.10
298	Gary Gaetti	.10
299	Tom Gordon	.10
300	Felix Jose	.10
301	Jose Lind	.10
302	Brian McRae	.10
303	Mike Fetters	.10
304	Brian Harper	.10
305	Pat Listach	.10
306	Matt Mieske	.10
307	Dave Nilsson	.10
308	Jody Reed	.10
309	Greg Vaughn	.10
310	Bill Wegman	.10
311	Rick Aguilera	.10
312	Alex Cole	.10
313	Denny Hocking	.10
314	Chuck Knoblauch	.10
315	Shane Mack	.10
316	Pat Meares	.10
317	Kevin Tapani	.10
318	Jim Abbott	.10
319	Wade Boggs	1.00
320	Sterling Hitchcock	.10
321	Pat Kelly	.10
322	Terry Mulholland	.10
323	Luis Polonia	.10
324	Mike Stanley	.10
325	Bob Wickman	.10
326	Bernie Williams	.10
327	Mark Acre	.10
328	Geronimo Berroa	.10
329	Scott Brosius	.10
330	Brent Gates	.10
331	Rickey Henderson	1.00
332	Carlos Reyes	.10
333	Ruben Sierra	.10
334	Bobby Witt	.10
335	Bobby Ayala	.10
336	Jay Buhner	.10
337	Randy Johnson	1.00
338	Edgar Martinez	.10
339	Bill Risley	.10
340	Alex Rodriguez **RC**	40.00
341	Roger Salkeld	.10
342	Dan Wilson	.10
343	Kevin Brown	.10
344	Jose Canseco	.45
345	Dean Palmer	.10
346	Ivan Rodriguez	.75
347	Kenny Rogers	.10
348	Pat Borders	.10
349	Juan Guzman	.10
350	Ed Sprague	.10
351	Devon White	.10
352	Steve Avery	.10
353	Roberto Kelly	.10
354	Mark Lemke	.10
355	Greg McMichael	.10
356	Terry Pendleton	.10
357	John Smoltz	.10
358	Mike Stanton	.10
359	Tony Tarasco	.10
360	Mark Grace	.10
361	Derrick May	.10
362	Rey Sanchez	.10
363	Sammy Sosa	1.50
364	Rick Wilkins	.10
365	Jeff Brantley	.10
366	Tony Fernandez	.10
367	Chuck McElroy	.10
368	Kevin Mitchell	.10
369	John Roper	.10
370	Johnny Ruffin	.10
371	Deion Sanders	.15
372	Marvin Freeman	.10
373	Andres Galarraga	.10
374	Charlie Hayes	.10
375	Nelson Liriano	.10
376	David Nied	.10
377	Walt Weiss	.10
378	Bret Barberie	.10
379	Jerry Browne	.10
380	Chuck Carr	.10
381	Greg Colbrunn	.10
382	Charlie Hough	.10
383	Kurt Miller	.10
384	Benito Santiago	.10
385	Jeff Bagwell	1.00
386	Craig Biggio	.10
387	Ken Caminiti	.10
388	Doug Drabek	.10
389	Steve Finley	.10
390	John Hudek	.10
391	Orlando Miller	.10
392	Shane Reynolds	.10
393	Brett Butler	.10
394	Tom Candiotti	.10
395	Delino DeShields	.10
396	Kevin Gross	.10
397	Eric Karros	.10
398	Ramon Martinez	.10
399	Henry Rodriguez	.10
400	Moises Alou	.10
401	Jeff Fassero	.10
402	Mike Lansing	.10
403	Mel Rojas	.10
404	Larry Walker	.10
405	John Wetteland	.10
406	Gabe White	.10
407	Bobby Bonilla	.10
408	Josias Manzanillo	.10
409	Bret Saberhagen	.10
410	David Segui	.10
411	Mariano Duncan	.10
412	Tommy Greene	.10
413	Billy Hatcher	.10
414	Ricky Jordan	.10
415	John Kruk	.10
416	Bobby Munoz	.10
417	Curt Schilling	.30
418	Fernando Valenzuela	.10
419	David West	.10
420	Carlos Garcia	.10
421	Brian Hunter	.10
422	Jeff King	.10
423	Jon Lieber	.10
424	Ravelo Manzanillo	.10
425	Denny Neagle	.10
426	Andy Van Slyke	.10
427	Bryan Eversgerd	.10
428	Bernard Gilkey	.10
429	Gregg Jefferies	.10
430	Tom Pagnozzi	.10
431	Bob Tewksbury	.10
432	Allen Watson	.10
433	Andy Ashby	.10
434	Andy Benes	.10
435	Donnie Elliott	.10
436	Tony Gwynn	1.50
437	Joey Hamilton	.10
438	Tim Hyers	.10
439	Luis Lopez	.10
440	Bip Roberts	.10
441	Scott Sanders	.10
442	Rod Beck	.10
443	Dave Burba	.10
444	Darryl Strawberry	.10
445	Bill Swift	.10
446	Robby Thompson	.10
447	William Van Landingham **RC**	.10
448	Matt Williams	.10
449	Checklist	.10
450	Checklist	.10

Hot Gloves

Hot Glove is a 10-card Series 2 insert set. It focuses on players with outstanding de-

fensive ability. Cards feature a die-cut design, with the player photo in front of a baseball glove. Player identification and a "Hot Glove" logo are in gold foil in the lower-left corner.

		NM/M
Complete Set (10):		40.00
Common Player:		2.00
1	Barry Bonds	10.00
2	Will Clark	2.00
3	Ken Griffey Jr.	7.50
4	Kenny Lofton	2.00
5	Greg Maddux	5.00
6	Don Mattingly	6.50
7	Kirby Puckett	5.00
8	Cal Ripken, Jr.	10.00
9	Tim Salmon	2.00
10	Matt Williams	2.00

Hot Numbers

Hot Numbers is an insert set found in Series 1 packs at an average rate of 1:24. Each card is printed on 100 percent etched foil and displays the player in the forefront with a background made up of floating numbers. The player's name is in gold foil across the bottom-right side and a large foil "Hot Numbers" and that player's uniform number are in a square at bottom-left.

		NM/M
Complete Set (10):		15.00
Common Player:		.50
1	Roberto Alomar	1.00
2	Carlos Baerga	.50
3	Will Clark	.50
4	Fred McGriff	.50
5	Paul Molitor	3.00
6	John Olerud	.50
7	Mike Piazza	4.50
8	Cal Ripken, Jr.	6.00
9	Ryne Sandberg	4.00
10	Frank Thomas	3.00

Infield Power

Infield Power is a horizontally formatted insert set. Cards show the player batting on one half and in the field on the other half of the card, divided by a black, diagonal strip that reads "Infield Power" and the player's name. The set spotlights infielders that often hit the longball. Infield Power was inserted into Series 2 packs at an average rate of 1:5.

		NM/M
Complete Set (10):		5.00
Common Player:		.25
1	Jeff Bagwell	.75
2	Will Clark	.25
3	Darren Daulton	.25
4	Don Mattingly	1.25
5	Fred McGriff	.25
6	Rafael Palmeiro	.65
7	Mike Piazza	1.50
8	Cal Ripken, Jr.	2.50
9	Frank Thomas	.75
10	Matt Williams	.25

Outfield Power

Flair's Outfield Power was randomly inserted in Series 1 packs at a 1:5 rate. This vertically formatted card shows the player in the field on top, while the bottom half shows the player at the plate. The photos divided by a black strip with "Outfield Power" and the player's name on it.

		NM/M
Complete Set (10):		5.00
Common Player:		.30
1	Albert Belle	.30
2	Barry Bonds	2.00
3	Joe Carter	.30
4	Len Dykstra	.30
5	Juan Gonzalez	.45
6	Ken Griffey Jr.	1.50
7	Dave Justice	.30
8	Kirby Puckett	1.00
9	Tim Salmon	.30
10	Dave Winfield	.75

Wave of the Future 1

Series 1 Wave of the Future is horizontally formatted and depicts 10 outstanding 1994 rookies who have the potential to become superstars. Each player is featured on a colorful wavelike background. A Wave of the Future gold-foil stamp is placed in the bottom-right corner with the player name in gold foil starting in the opposite bottom corner and running across the bottom. Advertised insertion rate was 1:5.

		NM/M
Complete Set (10):		6.00
Common Player:		.25
1	Kurt Abbott	.25
2	Carlos Delgado	5.00
3	Steve Karsay	.25
4	Ryan Klesko	.25
5	Javier Lopez	.25
6	Raul Mondesi	.25
7	James Mouton	.25
8	Chan Ho Park	.25
9	Dave Staton	.25
10	Rick White	.25

Wave of the Future 2

Series 2 Flair also has a Wave of the Future insert set. Unlike the earlier series, this 10-card set is vertically formated. The Wave of the Future logo appears in the bottom-left with the player's name stretching across the rest of

the bottom. The background has a swirling water effect, on which the player is superimposed. Insertion rate is one per five packs.

		NM/M
Complete Set (10):		22.50
Common Player:		.50
1	Mark Acre	.50
2	Chris Gomez	.50
3	Joey Hamilton	.50
4	John Hudek	.50
5	Jon Lieber	.50
6	Matt Mieske	.50
7	Orlando Miller	.50
8	Alex Rodriguez	20.00
9	Tony Tarasco	.50
10	Bill VanLandingham	.50

1995 Flair

There's no mistaking that 1995 Flair is Fleer's super-premium brand. Cards are printed on double-thick cardboard with a background of etched metallic foil: Gold for National Leaguers, silver for American. A portrait and an action photo are featured on the horizontal front design. Backs are vertically formatted with a borderless action photo, several years worth of stats and foil trim. The basic set was issued in two series of 216 basic cards each, along with several insert sets exclusive to each series. Cards were sold in a hard pack of nine with a suggested retail price of $5.

		NM/M
Complete Set (432):		30.00
Common Player:		.10
Series 1 or 2 Pack (9):		1.00
Series 1 or 2 Wax Box (24):		15.00
1	Brady Anderson	.10
2	Harold Baines	.10
3	Leo Gomez	.10
4	Alan Mills	.10
5	Jamie Moyer	.10
6	Mike Mussina	.40
7	Mike Oquist	.10
8	Arthur Rhodes	.10
9	Cal Ripken Jr.	3.00
10	Roger Clemens	1.75
11	Scott Cooper	.10
12	Mike Greenwell	.10
13	Aaron Sele	.10
14	John Valentin	.10
15	Mo Vaughn	.10
16	Chad Curtis	.10
17	Gary DiSarcina	.10
18	Chuck Finley	.10
19	Andrew Lorraine	.10
20	Spike Owen	.10
21	Tim Salmon	.10
22	J.T. Snow	.10
23	Wilson Alvarez	.10
24	Jason Bere	.10
25	Ozzie Guillen	.10
26	Mike LaValliere	.10
27	Frank Thomas	1.00
28	Robin Ventura	.10
29	Carlos Baerga	.10
30	Albert Belle	.10
31	Jason Grimsley	.10
32	Dennis Martinez	.10
33	Eddie Murray	1.00
34	Charles Nagy	.10
35	Manny Ramirez	1.00
36	Paul Sorrento	.10
37	John Doherty	.10

#	Player	NM/M
38	Cecil Fielder	.10
39	Travis Fryman	.10
40	Chris Gomez	.10
41	Tony Phillips	.10
42	Lou Whitaker	.10
43	David Cone	.10
44	Gary Gaetti	.10
45	Mark Gubicza	.10
46	Bob Hamelin	.10
47	Wally Joyner	.10
48	Rusty Meacham	.10
49	Jeff Montgomery	.10
50	Ricky Bones	.10
51	Cal Eldred	.10
52	Pat Listach	.10
53	Matt Mieske	.10
54	Dave Nilsson	.10
55	Greg Vaughn	.10
56	Bill Wegman	.10
57	Chuck Knoblauch	.10
58	Scott Leius	.10
59	Pat Mahomes	.10
60	Pat Meares	.10
61	Pedro Munoz	.10
62	Kirby Puckett	1.50
63	Wade Boggs	1.00
64	Jimmy Key	.10
65	Jim Leyritz	.10
66	Don Mattingly	1.75
67	Paul O'Neill	.10
68	Melido Perez	.10
69	Danny Tartabull	.10
70	John Briscoe	.10
71	Scott Brosius	.10
72	Ron Darling	.10
73	Brent Gates	.10
74	Rickey Henderson	1.00
75	Stan Javier	.10
76	Mark McGwire	2.50
77	Todd Van Poppel	.10
78	Bobby Ayala	.10
79	Mike Blowers	.10
80	Jay Buhner	.10
81	Ken Griffey Jr.	2.00
82	Randy Johnson	1.00
83	Tino Martinez	.10
84	Jeff Nelson	.10
85	Alex Rodriguez	2.50
86	Will Clark	.10
87	Jeff Frye	.10
88	Juan Gonzalez	.50
89	Rusty Greer	.10
90	Darren Oliver	.10
91	Dean Palmer	.10
92	Ivan Rodriguez	.75
93	Matt Whiteside	.10
94	Roberto Alomar	.25
95	Joe Carter	.10
96	Tony Castillo	.10
97	Juan Guzman	.10
98	Pat Hentgen	.10
99	Mike Huff	.10
100	John Olerud	.10
101	Woody Williams	.10
102	Roberto Kelly	.10
103	Ryan Klesko	.10
104	Javier Lopez	.10
105	Greg Maddux	1.50
106	Fred McGriff	.10
107	Jose Oliva	.10
108	John Smoltz	.10
109	Tony Tarasco	.10
110	Mark Wohlers	.10
111	Jim Bullinger	.10
112	Shawon Dunston	.10
113	Derrick May	.10
114	Randy Myers	.10
115	Karl Rhodes	.10
116	Rey Sanchez	.10
117	Steve Trachsel	.10
118	Eddie Zambrano	.10
119	Bret Boone	.10
120	Brian Dorsett	.10
121	Hal Morris	.10
122	Jose Rijo	.10
123	John Roper	.10
124	Reggie Sanders	.10
125	Pete Schourek	.10
126	John Smiley	.10
127	Ellis Burks	.10
128	Vinny Castilla	.10
129	Marvin Freeman	.10
130	Andres Galarraga	.10
131	Mike Munoz	.10
132	David Nied	.10
133	Bruce Ruffin	.10
134	Walt Weiss	.10
135	Eric Young	.10
136	Greg Colbrunn	.10
137	Jeff Conine	.10
138	Jeremy Hernandez	.10
139	Charles Johnson	.10
140	Robb Nen	.10
141	Gary Sheffield	.40
142	Dave Weathers	.10
143	Jeff Bagwell	1.00
144	Craig Biggio	.10
145	Tony Eusebio	.10
146	Luis Gonzalez	.10
147	John Hudek	.10
148	Darryl Kile	.10
149	Dave Veres	.10
150	Billy Ashley	.10
151	Pedro Astacio	.10
152	Rafael Bournigal	.10
153	Delino DeShields	.10
154	Raul Mondesi	.10
155	Mike Piazza	2.00
156	Rudy Seanez	.10
157	Ismael Valdes	.10
158	Tim Wallach	.10
159	Todd Worrell	.10
160	Moises Alou	.10
161	Cliff Floyd	.10
162	Gil Heredia	.10
163	Mike Lansing	.10
164	Pedro Martinez	1.00
165	Kirk Rueter	.10
166	Tim Scott	.10
167	Jeff Shaw	.10
168	Rondell White	.10
169	Bobby Bonilla	.10
170	Rico Brogna	.10
171	Todd Hundley	.10
172	Jeff Kent	.10
173	Jim Lindeman	.10
174	Joe Orsulak	.10
175	Bret Saberhagen	.10
176	Toby Borland	.10
177	Darren Daulton	.10
178	Lenny Dykstra	.10
179	Jim Eisenreich	.10
180	Tommy Greene	.10
181	Tony Longmire	.10
182	Bobby Munoz	.10
183	Kevin Stocker	.10
184	Jay Bell	.10
185	Steve Cooke	.10
186	Ravelo Manzanillo	.10
187	Al Martin	.10
188	Denny Neagle	.10
189	Don Slaught	.10
190	Paul Wagner	.10
191	Rene Arocha	.10
192	Bernard Gilkey	.10
193	Jose Oquendo	.10
194	Tom Pagnozzi	.10
195	Ozzie Smith	1.50
196	Allen Watson	.10
197	Mark Whiten	.10
198	Andy Ashby	.10
199	Donnie Elliott	.10
200	Bryce Florie	.10
201	Tony Gwynn	1.50
202	Trevor Hoffman	.10
203	Brian Johnson	.10
204	Tim Mauser	.10
205	Bip Roberts	.10
206	Rod Beck	.10
207	Barry Bonds	3.00
208	Royce Clayton	.10
209	Darren Lewis	.10
210	Mark Portugal	.10
211	Kevin Rogers	.10
212	William Van Landingham	.10
213	Matt Williams	.10
214	Checklist	.10
215	Checklist	.10
216	Checklist	.10
217	Bret Barberie	.10
218	Armando Benitez	.10
219	Kevin Brown	.10
220	Sid Fernandez	.10
221	Chris Hoiles	.10
222	Doug Jones	.10
223	Ben McDonald	.10
224	Rafael Palmeiro	.75
225	Andy Van Slyke	.10
226	Jose Canseco	.40
227	Vaughn Eshelman	.10
228	Mike Macfarlane	.10
229	Tim Naehring	.10
230	Frank Rodriguez	.10
231	Lee Tinsley	.10
232	Mark Whiten	.10
233	Garret Anderson	.10
234	Chili Davis	.10
235	Jim Edmonds	.10
236	Mark Langston	.10
237	Troy Percival	.10
238	Tony Phillips	.10
239	Lee Smith	.10
240	Jim Abbott	.10
241	James Baldwin	.10
242	Mike Devereaux	.10
243	Ray Durham	.10
244	Alex Fernandez	.10
245	Roberto Hernandez	.10
246	Lance Johnson	.10
247	Ron Karkovice	.10
248	Tim Raines	.10
249	Sandy Alomar Jr.	.10
250	Orel Hershiser	.10
251	Julian Tavarez	.10
252	Jim Thome	.65
253	Omar Vizquel	.10
254	Dave Winfield	1.00
255	Chad Curtis	.10
256	Kirk Gibson	.10
257	Mike Henneman	.10
258	Bob Higginson **RC**	.25
259	Felipe Lira	.10
260	Rudy Pemberton	.10
261	Alan Trammell	.10
262	Kevin Appier	.10
263	Pat Borders	.10
264	Tom Gordon	.10
265	Jose Lind	.10
266	Jon Nunnally	.10
267	Dilson Torres	.10
268	Michael Tucker	.10
269	Jeff Cirillo	.10
270	Darryl Hamilton	.10
271	David Hulse	.10
272	Mark Kiefer	.10
273	Graeme Lloyd	.10
274	Joe Oliver	.10
275	Al Reyes	.10
276	Kevin Seitzer	.10
277	Rick Aguilera	.10
278	Marty Cordova	.10
279	Scott Erickson	.10
280	LaTroy Hawkins	.10
281	Brad Radke	.10
282	Kevin Tapani	.10
283	Tony Fernandez	.10
284	Sterling Hitchcock	.10
285	Pat Kelly	.10
286	Jack McDowell	.10
287	Andy Pettitte	.30
288	Mike Stanley	.10
289	John Wetteland	.10
290	Bernie Williams	.10
291	Mark Acre	.10
292	Geronimo Berroa	.10
293	Dennis Eckersley	.75
294	Steve Ontiveros	.10
295	Ruben Sierra	.10
296	Terry Steinbach	.10
297	Dave Stewart	.10
298	Todd Stottlemyre	.10
299	Darren Bragg	.10
300	Joey Cora	.10
301	Edgar Martinez	.10
302	Bill Risley	.10
303	Ron Villone	.10
304	Dan Wilson	.10
305	Benji Gil	.10
306	Wilson Heredia	.10
307	Mark McLemore	.10
308	Otis Nixon	.10
309	Kenny Rogers	.10
310	Jeff Russell	.10
311	Mickey Tettleton	.10
312	Bob Tewksbury	.10
313	David Cone	.10
314	Carlos Delgado	.50
315	Alex Gonzalez	.10
316	Shawn Green	.40
317	Paul Molitor	1.00
318	Ed Sprague	.10
319	Devon White	.10
320	Steve Avery	.10
321	Jeff Blauser	.10
322	Brad Clontz	.10
323	Tom Glavine	.30
324	Marquis Grissom	.10
325	Chipper Jones	1.50
326	Dave Justice	.10
327	Mark Lemke	.10
328	Kent Mercker	.10
329	Jason Schmidt	.10
330	Steve Buechele	.10
331	Kevin Foster	.10
332	Mark Grace	.10
333	Brian McRae	.10
334	Sammy Sosa	1.50
335	Ozzie Timmons	.10
336	Rick Wilkins	.10
337	Hector Carrasco	.10
338	Ron Gant	.10
339	Barry Larkin	.10
340	Deion Sanders	.15
341	Benito Santiago	.10
342	Roger Bailey	.10
343	Jason Bates	.10
344	Dante Bichette	.10
345	Joe Girardi	.10
346	Bill Swift	.10
347	Mark Thompson	.10
348	Larry Walker	.10
349	Kurt Abbott	.10
350	John Burkett	.10
351	Chuck Carr	.10
352	Andre Dawson	.30
353	Chris Hammond	.10
354	Charles Johnson	.10
355	Terry Pendleton	.10
356	Quilvio Veras	.10
357	Derek Bell	.10
358	Jim Dougherty	.10
359	Doug Drabek	.10
360	Todd Jones	.10
361	Orlando Miller	.10
362	James Mouton	.10
363	Phil Plantier	.10
364	Shane Reynolds	.10
365	Todd Hollandsworth	.10
366	Eric Karros	.10
367	Ramon Martinez	.10
368	Hideo Nomo **RC**	3.00
369	Jose Offerman	.10
370	Antonio Osuna	.10
371	Todd Williams	.10
372	Shane Andrews	.10
373	Wil Cordero	.10
374	Jeff Fassero	.10
375	Darrin Fletcher	.10
376	Mark Grudzielanek **RC**	.50
377	Carlos Perez **RC**	.25
378	Mel Rojas	.10
379	Tony Tarasco	.10
380	Edgardo Alfonzo	.10
381	Brett Butler	.10
382	Carl Everett	.10
383	John Franco	.10
384	Pete Harnisch	.10
385	Bobby Jones	.10
386	Dave Mlicki	.10
387	Jose Vizcaino	.10
388	Ricky Bottalico	.10
389	Tyler Green	.10
390	Charlie Hayes	.10
391	Dave Hollins	.10
392	Gregg Jefferies	.10
393	Michael Mimbs **RC**	.10
394	Mickey Morandini	.10
395	Curt Schilling	.30
396	Heathcliff Slocumb	.10
397	Jason Christiansen	.10
398	Midre Cummings	.10
399	Carlos Garcia	.10
400	Mark Johnson	.10
401	Jeff King	.10
402	Jon Lieber	.10
403	Esteban Loaiza	.10
404	Orlando Merced	.10
405	Gary Wilson **RC**	.10
406	Scott Cooper	.10
407	Tom Henke	.10
408	Ken Hill	.10
409	Danny Jackson	.10
410	Brian Jordan	.10
411	Ray Lankford	.10
412	John Mabry	.10
413	Todd Zeile	.10
414	Andy Benes	.10
415	Andres Berumen	.10
416	Ken Caminiti	.10
417	Andujar Cedeno	.10
418	Steve Finley	.10
419	Joey Hamilton	.10
420	Dustin Hermanson	.10
421	Melvin Nieves	.10
422	Roberto Petagine	.10
423	Eddie Williams	.10
424	Glenallen Hill	.10
425	Kirt Manwaring	.10
426	Terry Mulholland	.10
427	J.R. Phillips	.10
428	Joe Rosselli	.10
429	Robby Thompson	.10
430	Checklist	.10
431	Checklist	.10
432	Checklist	.10

Cal Ripken, Jr. Enduring Flair

The career of Cal Ripken, Jr., is traced in this insert set found in Series 2 Flair at the average rate of once per dozen packs. Each card has a vintage photo on front, with a large silver-foil "ENDURING" logo toward bottom. Backs have another color photo, a quote and other information about the milestone. The series was extended by a special mail-in offer for five additional cards which chronicled Ripken's record-breaking 1995 season.

		NM/M
Complete Set (15):		40.00
Common Card:		4.00
1	Rookie Of The Year	4.00
2	1st MVP Season	4.00
3	World Series Highlight	4.00
4	Family Tradition	4.00
5	8,243 Consecutive Innings	4.00
6	95 Consecutive Errorless Games	4.00
7	All-Star MVP	4.00
8	1,000th RBI	4.00
9	287th Home Run	4.00
10	2,000th Consecutive Game	4.00
11	Record-tying Game	6.00
12	Record-breaking Game	6.00
13	Defensive Prowess	6.00
14	Literacy Work	6.00
15	2,153 and Counting	6.00

Hot Gloves

The cream of the crop among Series 2 Flair inserts is this set featuring fine fielders. Cards have a background of an embossed gold-foil glove, with a color player photo centered in front. Silver foil comprises the card title and player name

at bottom and the Flair logo at top. Backs have a white background, a photo of a glove with a career summary overprinted and a player portrait photo in a lower corner. These inserts are found at the average rate of once per 25 packs.

		NM/M
Complete Set (12):		35.00
Common Player:		1.25
1	Roberto Alomar	2.00
2	Barry Bonds	10.00
3	Ken Griffey Jr.	7.50
4	Marquis Grissom	1.25
5	Barry Larkin	1.25
6	Darren Lewis	1.25
7	Kenny Lofton	1.25
8	Don Mattingly	6.00
9	Cal Ripken Jr.	10.00
10	Ivan Rodriguez	2.50
11	Devon White	1.25
12	Matt Williams	1.25

Hot Numbers

These Series 1 inserts are a 1:9 find. Gold metallic-foil background with 1994 seasonal stat numbers are the background for a color action photo on front. Horizontal backs have a ghosted portrait photo at right and career highlights at left.

		NM/M
Complete Set (10):		10.00
Common Player:		.50
1	Jeff Bagwell	1.00
2	Albert Belle	.50
3	Barry Bonds	2.25
4	Ken Griffey Jr.	2.00
5	Kenny Lofton	.50
6	Greg Maddux	1.25
7	Mike Piazza	2.00
8	Cal Ripken Jr.	2.25
9	Frank Thomas	1.00
10	Matt Williams	.50

Infield Power

Power rays and waves eminating from the player's bat in an action photo are the front design of this Series 2 chase set. The card title, name and team at bottom, and the Flair logo at top are in silver foil. Backs repeat the wave theme with a player photo on one end and a career summary at the other. These inserts are seeded at the average rate of one per five packs.

		NM/M
Complete Set (10):		4.00
Common Player:		.25
1	Jeff Bagwell	.75
2	Darren Daulton	.25
3	Cecil Fielder	.25
4	Andres Galarraga	.25
5	Fred McGriff	.25
6	Rafael Palmeiro	.65
7	Mike Piazza	1.50
8	Frank Thomas	1.00
9	Mo Vaughn	.25
10	Matt Williams	.25

Outfield Power

Laser-like colored rays are the background to the action photo on front and portrait on back of this series. The card title, player identification and Flair logo on front are in silver foil. Backs are horizontal, silver-foil enhanced and include a career summary. This chase set is seeded at the average rate of one card per six packs of Series 1 Flair.

		NM/M
Complete Set (10):		4.00
Common Player:		.25
1	Albert Belle	.25
2	Dante Bichette	.25
3	Barry Bonds	2.00
4	Jose Canseco	.50
5	Joe Carter	.25
6	Juan Gonzalez	.50
7	Ken Griffey Jr.	1.00
8	Kirby Puckett	.75
9	Gary Sheffield	.50
10	Ruben Sierra	.25

Today's Spotlight

The premier insert set in Flair Series I, found once every 30 packs or so, this die-cut issue has the player action photo spotlighted in a 2-3/8" bright spot, with the rest of the photo muted in gray and dark gray. The card title, Flair logo, player name and team are in silver foil. The horizontal backs have a portrait photo in the spotlight and career summary on the side.

		NM/M
Complete Set (12):		15.00
Common Player:		1.00
1	Jeff Bagwell	3.00
2	Jason Bere	1.00
3	Cliff Floyd	1.00

4 Chuck Knoblauch 1.00
5 Kenny Lofton 1.00
6 Javier Lopez 1.00
7 Raul Mondesi 1.00
8 Mike Mussina 1.50
9 Mike Piazza 5.00
10 Manny Ramirez 3.00
11 Tim Salmon 1.00
12 Frank Thomas 3.00

Wave Of The Future

The cream of baseball's rookie crop is featured in this Series 2 insert set, found once per eight packs on average. Fronts have a graduated color background with a baseball/wave morph, which is repeated at the bottom in silver foil, along with the player name. A color action photo is at center. The player's name, team and "Wave of the Future" are repeated in horizontal rows behind the photo. Horizontal backs repeat the wave logo, have another player photo and a career summary.

NM/M
Complete Set (10): 7.50
Common Player: .35
1 Jason Bates .25
2 Armando Benitez .25
3 Marty Cordova .25
4 Ray Durham .25
5 Vaughn Eshelman .25
6 Carl Everett .25
7 Shawn Green 1.50
8 Dustin Hermanson .25
9 Chipper Jones 4.00
10 Hideo Nomo 1.50

1996 Flair Promotional Sheet

Three samples of Flair's 1996 issue and an information card are included on this 5" x 7" promotional sheet. Sheets are found with either a gold or silver finish.

NM/M
Complete Sheet: 5.00

1996 Flair

Fleer's 1996 Flair baseball set has 400 cards, a parallel set and four insert types. Regular card fronts have two photos of the featured player; backs have a photo and career statistics. All cards have a silver-foil version and a gold-foil version, with each version appearing in equal numbers. Seven-card packs carried an issue price of $4.99.

NM/M
Complete Set (400): 50.00
Common Player: .15
Pack (9): 3.00
Wax Box (18): 40.00
1 Roberto Alomar .30
2 Brady Anderson .15
3 Bobby Bonilla .15
4 Scott Erickson .15
5 Jeffrey Hammonds .15
6 Jimmy Haynes .15
7 Chris Hoiles .15
8 Kent Mercker .15
9 Mike Mussina .50
10 Randy Myers .15
11 Rafael Palmeiro .75
12 Cal Ripken Jr. 3.00
(12p) Cal Ripken Jr./OPS (No card #.) 3.00
13 B.J. Surhoff .15
14 David Wells .15
15 Jose Canseco .50
16 Roger Clemens 1.75
17 Wil Cordero .15
18 Tom Gordon .15
19 Mike Greenwell .15
20 Dwayne Hosey .15
21 Jose Malave .15
22 Tim Naehring .15
23 Troy O'Leary .15
24 Aaron Sele .15
25 Heathcliff Slocumb .15
26 Mike Stanley .15
27 Jeff Suppan .15
28 John Valentin .15
29 Mo Vaughn .15
30 Tim Wakefield .15
31 Jim Abbott .15
32 Garret Anderson .15
33 George Arias .15
34 Chili Davis .15
35 Gary DiSarcina .15
36 Jim Edmonds .15
37 Chuck Finley .15
38 Todd Greene .15
39 Mark Langston .15
40 Troy Percival .15
41 Tim Salmon .15
42 Lee Smith .15
43 J.T. Snow .15
44 Randy Velarde .15
45 Tim Wallach .15
46 Wilson Alvarez .15
47 Harold Baines .15
48 Jason Bere .15
49 Ray Durham .15
50 Alex Fernandez .15
51 Ozzie Guillen .15
52 Roberto Hernandez .15
53 Ron Karkovice .15
54 Darren Lewis .15
55 Lyle Mouton .15
56 Tony Phillips .15
57 Chris Snopek .15
58 Kevin Tapani .15
59 Danny Tartabull .15
30 Frank Thomas 1.00
61 Robin Ventura .15
62 Sandy Alomar .15
63 Carlos Baerga .15
64 Albert Belle .15
65 Julio Franco .15
66 Orel Hershiser .15
67 Kenny Lofton .15
68 Dennis Martinez .15
69 Jack McDowell .15
70 Jose Mesa .15
71 Eddie Murray 1.00
72 Charles Nagy .15
73 Tony Pena .15
74 Manny Ramirez 1.00
75 Julian Tavarez .15
76 Jim Thome .65
77 Omar Vizquel .15
78 Chad Curtis .15
79 Cecil Fielder .15
80 Travis Fryman .15
81 Chris Gomez .15
82 Bob Higginson .15
83 Mark Lewis .15
84 Felipe Lira .15
85 Alan Trammell .15
86 Kevin Appier .15
87 Johnny Damon .50
88 Tom Goodwin .15
89 Mark Gubicza .15
90 Bob Hamelin .15
91 Keith Lockhart .15
92 Jeff Montgomery .15
93 Jon Nunnally .15
94 Bip Roberts .15
95 Michael Tucker .15
96 Joe Vitiello .15
97 Ricky Bones .15
98 Chuck Carr .15
99 Jeff Cirillo .15
100 Mike Fetters .15
101 John Jaha .15
102 Mike Matheny .15
103 Ben McDonald .15
104 Matt Mieske .15
105 Dave Nilsson .15
106 Kevin Seitzer .15
107 Steve Sparks .15
108 Jose Valentin .15
109 Greg Vaughn .15
110 Rick Aguilera .15
111 Rich Becker .15
112 Marty Cordova .15
113 LaTroy Hawkins .15
114 Dave Hollins .15
115 Roberto Kelly .15
116 Chuck Knoblauch .15
117 Matt Lawton **RC** .50
118 Pat Meares .15
119 Paul Molitor 1.00
120 Kirby Puckett 1.50
121 Brad Radke .15
122 Frank Rodriguez .15
123 Scott Stahoviak .15
124 Matt Walbeck .15
125 Wade Boggs 1.00
126 David Cone .15
127 Joe Girardi .15
128 Dwight Gooden .15
129 Derek Jeter 3.00
130 Jimmy Key .15
131 Jim Leyritz .15
132 Tino Martinez .15
133 Paul O'Neill .15
134 Andy Pettitte .40
135 Tim Raines .15
136 Ruben Rivera .15
137 Kenny Rogers .15
138 Ruben Sierra .15
139 John Wetteland .15
140 Bernie Williams .15
141 Tony Batista **RC** .60
142 Allen Battle .15
143 Geronimo Berroa .15
144 Mike Bordick .15
145 Scott Brosius .15
146 Steve Cox .15
147 Brent Gates .15
148 Jason Giambi .65
149 Doug Johns .15
150 Mark McGwire 2.50
151 Pedro Munoz .15
152 Ariel Prieto .15
153 Terry Steinbach .15
154 Todd Van Poppel .15
155 Bobby Ayala .15
156 Chris Bosio .15
157 Jay Buhner .15
158 Joey Cora .15
159 Russ Davis .15
160 Ken Griffey Jr. 2.00
161 Sterling Hitchcock .15
162 Randy Johnson 1.00
163 Edgar Martinez .15
164 Alex Rodriguez 2.50
165 Paul Sorrento .15
166 Dan Wilson .15
167 Will Clark .15
168 Benji Gil .15
169 Juan Gonzalez .50
170 Rusty Greer .15
171 Kevin Gross .15
172 Darryl Hamilton .15
173 Mike Henneman .15
174 Ken Hill .15
175 Mark McLemore .15
176 Dean Palmer .15
177 Roger Pavlik .15
178 Ivan Rodriguez .75
179 Mickey Tettleton .15
180 Bobby Witt .15
181 Joe Carter .15
182 Felipe Crespo .15
183 Alex Gonzalez .15
184 Shawn Green .40
185 Juan Guzman .15
186 Erik Hanson .15
187 Pat Hentgen .15
188 Sandy Martinez **RC** .15
189 Otis Nixon .15
190 John Olerud .15
191 Paul Quantrill .15
192 Bill Risley .15
193 Ed Sprague .15
194 Steve Avery .15
195 Jeff Blauser .15
196 Brad Clontz .15
197 Jermaine Dye .15
198 Tom Glavine .40
199 Marquis Grissom .15
200 Chipper Jones 1.50
201 David Justice .15
202 Ryan Klesko .15
203 Mark Lemke .15
204 Javier Lopez .15
205 Greg Maddux 1.50
206 Fred McGriff .15
207 Greg McMichael .15
208 Wonderful Monds .15
209 Jason Schmidt .15
210 John Smoltz .15
211 Mark Wohlers .15
212 Jim Bullinger .15
213 Frank Castillo .15
214 Kevin Foster .15
215 Luis Gonzalez .15
216 Mark Grace .15
217 Robin Jennings **RC** .15
218 Doug Jones .15
219 Dave Magadan .15
220 Brian McRae .15
221 Jaime Navarro .15
222 Rey Sanchez .15
223 Ryne Sandberg 1.50
224 Scott Servais .15
225 Sammy Sosa 1.50
226 Ozzie Timmons .15
227 Bret Boone .15
228 Jeff Branson .15
229 Jeff Brantley .15
230 Dave Burba .15
231 Vince Coleman .15
232 Steve Gibralter .15
233 Mike Kelly .15
234 Barry Larkin .15
235 Hal Morris .15
236 Mark Portugal .15
237 Jose Rijo .15
238 Reggie Sanders .15
239 Pete Schourek .15
240 John Smiley .15
241 Eddie Taubensee .15
242 Jason Bates .15
243 Dante Bichette .15
244 Ellis Burks .15
245 Vinny Castilla .15
246 Andres Galarraga .15
247 Darren Holmes .15
248 Curt Leskanic .15
249 Steve Reed .15
250 Kevin Ritz .15
251 Bret Saberhagen .15
252 Bill Swift .15
253 Larry Walker .15
254 Walt Weiss .15
255 Eric Young .15
256 Kurt Abbott .15
257 Kevin Brown .15
258 John Burkett .15
259 Greg Colbrunn .15
260 Jeff Conine .15
261 Andre Dawson .40
262 Chris Hammond .15
263 Charles Johnson .15
264 Al Leiter .15
265 Robb Nen .15
266 Terry Pendleton .15
267 Pat Rapp .15
268 Gary Sheffield .50
269 Quilvio Veras .15
270 Devon White .15
271 Bob Abreu .15
272 Jeff Bagwell 1.00
273 Derek Bell .15
274 Sean Berry .15
275 Craig Biggio .15
276 Doug Drabek .15
277 Tony Eusebio .15
278 Richard Hidalgo .15
279 Brian Hunter .15
280 Todd Jones .15
281 Derrick May .15
282 Orlando Miller .15
283 James Mouton .15
284 Shane Reynolds .15
285 Greg Swindell .15
286 Mike Blowers .15
287 Brett Butler .15
288 Tom Candiotti .15
289 Roger Cedeno .15
290 Delino DeShields .15
291 Greg Gagne .15
292 Karim Garcia .15
293 Todd Hollandsworth .15
294 Eric Karros .15
295 Ramon Martinez .15
296 Raul Mondesi .15
297 Hideo Nomo .50
298 Mike Piazza 2.00
299 Ismael Valdes .15
300 Todd Worrell .15
301 Moises Alou .15
302 Shane Andrews .15
303 Yamil Benitez .15
304 Jeff Fassero .15
305 Darrin Fletcher .15
306 Cliff Floyd .15
307 Mark Grudzielanek .15
308 Mike Lansing .15
309 Pedro Martinez 1.00
310 Ryan McGuire .15
311 Carlos Perez .15
312 Mel Rojas .15
313 David Segui .15
314 Rondell White .15
315 Edgardo Alfonzo .15
316 Rico Brogna .15
317 Carl Everett .15
318 John Franco .15
319 Bernard Gilkey .15
320 Todd Hundley .15
321 Jason Isringhausen .15
322 Lance Johnson .15
323 Bobby Jones .15
324 Jeff Kent .15
325 Rey Ordonez .15
326 Bill Pulsipher .15
327 Jose Vizcaino .15
328 Paul Wilson .15
329 Ricky Bottalico .15
330 Darren Daulton .15
331 David Doster **RC** .15
332 Lenny Dykstra .15
333 Jim Eisenreich .15
334 Sid Fernandez .15
335 Gregg Jefferies .15
336 Mickey Morandini .15
337 Benito Santiago .15
338 Curt Schilling .40
339 Kevin Stocker .15
340 David West .15
341 Mark Whiten .15
342 Todd Zeile .15
343 Jay Bell .15
344 John Ericks .15
345 Carlos Garcia .15
346 Charlie Hayes .15
347 Jason Kendall .15
348 Jeff King .15
349 Mike Kingery .15
350 Al Martin .15
351 Orlando Merced .15
352 Dan Miceli .15
353 Denny Neagle .15
354 Alan Benes .15
355 Andy Benes .15
356 Royce Clayton .15
357 Dennis Eckersley .75
358 Gary Gaetti .15
359 Ron Gant .15
360 Brian Jordan .15
361 Ray Lankford .15
362 John Mabry .15
363 T.J. Mathews .15
364 Mike Morgan .15
365 Donovan Osborne .15
366 Tom Pagnozzi .15
367 Ozzie Smith 1.50
368 Todd Stottlemyre .15
369 Andy Ashby .15
370 Brad Ausmus .15
371 Ken Caminiti .15
372 Andujar Cedeno .15
373 Steve Finley .15
374 Tony Gwynn 1.50
375 Joey Hamilton .15
376 Rickey Henderson 1.00
377 Trevor Hoffman .15
378 Wally Joyner .15
379 Marc Newfield .15
380 Jody Reed .15
381 Bob Tewksbury .15
382 Fernando Valenzuela .15
383 Rod Beck .15
384 Barry Bonds 3.00
385 Mark Carreon .15
386 Shawon Dunston .15
387 Osvaldo Fernandez **RC** .40
388 Glenallen Hill .15
389 Stan Javier .15
390 Mark Leiter .15
391 Kirt Manwaring .15
392 Robby Thompson .15
393 William Van Landingham .15
394 Allen Watson .15
395 Matt Williams .15
396 Checklist .15
397 Checklist .15
398 Checklist .15
399 Checklist .15
400 Checklist .15

Diamond Cuts

Ten of the game's top stars are showcased on these 1996 Flair inserts. They are seeded one per 20 packs. Fronts have a textured background rainbow metallic foil and silver glitter.

NM/M
Complete Set (12): 25.00
Common Player: 1.00
1 Jeff Bagwell 2.50
2 Albert Belle 1.00
3 Barry Bonds 6.00
4 Juan Gonzalez 1.25
5 Ken Griffey Jr. 4.00
6 Greg Maddux 3.00
7 Eddie Murray 2.50
8 Mike Piazza 4.00
9 Cal Ripken Jr. 6.00
10 Frank Thomas 2.50
11 Mo Vaughn 1.00
12 Matt Williams 1.00

Hot Gloves

Ten top defensive players are highlighted on these die-cut insert cards, a design first made popular in 1994. Hot Gloves can only be found in hobby packs, at a rate of one per every 90 packs.

NM/M
Complete Set (10): 60.00
Common Player: 3.00
1 Roberto Alomar 4.00
2 Barry Bonds 15.00
3 Will Clark 3.00
4 Ken Griffey Jr. 10.00
5 Kenny Lofton 3.00
6 Greg Maddux 7.50
7 Mike Piazza 10.00
8 Cal Ripken Jr. 15.00
9 Ivan Rodriguez 6.00
10 Matt Williams 3.00

Powerline

Ten of baseball's top sluggers are featured on these Flair inserts. They are the easiest of the Flair inserts to obtain; seeded one per six packs. Fronts combine yellow-green artwork with the player photo. Backs have a vertical color photo and career information.

NM/M
Complete Set (10): 6.00
Common Player: .25
1 Albert Belle .25
2 Barry Bonds 2.00
3 Juan Gonzalez .35
4 Ken Griffey Jr. .75
5 Mark McGwire 1.00
6 Mike Piazza .75
7 Manny Ramirez .50
8 Sammy Sosa .65
9 Frank Thomas .50
10 Matt Williams .25

Wave of the Future

These inserts feature up-and-coming young talent in baseball. Twenty 1996 rookies and prospects are printed on lenticular cards. They are seeded one per every 72 packs.

		NM/M
Complete Set (20):		30.00
Common Player:		2.00
1	Bob Abreu	3.00
2	George Arias	2.00
3	Tony Batista	2.00
4	Alan Benes	2.00
5	Yamil Benitez	2.00
6	Steve Cox	2.00
7	David Doster	2.00
8	Jermaine Dye	2.00
9	Osvaldo Fernandez	2.00
10	Karim Garcia	3.00
11	Steve Gibralter	2.00
12	Todd Greene	2.00
13	Richard Hidalgo	2.00
14	Robin Jennings	2.00
15	Jason Kendall	2.00
16	Jose Malave	2.00
17	Wonderful Monds	2.00
18	Rey Ordonez	2.00
19	Ruben Rivera	2.00
20	Paul Wilson	2.00

1997 Flair Showcase Promo Strip

The concept of Flair Showcase's Style-Grace-Showcase set composition is debuted on this 7-1/2" x 3-1/2" strip featuring three cards of Alex Rodriguez. The cards are overprinted in gold on front and black on back with "PROMOTIONAL SAMPLE."

	NM/M
Complete Strip (3):	5.00

1997 Flair Showcase Row 2 (Style)

The 1997 Flair issue is actually three different versions of a 180-player set printed on a super-glossy thick stock. The most common version, Style, is designated Row 2 on back. Fronts have a color action photo with a black-and-white portrait image in the background, all printed on silver foil. Cards #1-60 are designated "Showtime" on back; #61-120 are "Showpiece" and #121-180 are labeled "Showstopper" and were inserted in varying ratios: Showtime - 1.5:1; Showpiece 1:1.5 and Showstopper 1:1. Cards were sold exclusively at hobby shops in five-card packs for $4.99.

		NM/M
Complete Set (180):		15.00
Common Showtime (1-60):		.15
Common Showpiece (61-120):		.25
Common Showstopper (121-180):		.20
A-Rod Glove Exchange:		125.00
Pack (5):		2.00
Wax Box (24):		35.00
1	Andruw Jones	1.25
2	Derek Jeter	3.00
3	Alex Rodriguez	2.25
4	Paul Molitor	1.25
5	Jeff Bagwell	1.25
6	Scott Rolen	1.00
7	Kenny Lofton	.15
8	Cal Ripken Jr.	3.00
9	Brady Anderson	.15
10	Chipper Jones	1.50
11	Todd Greene	.15
12	Todd Walker	.15
13	Billy Wagner	.15
14	Craig Biggio	.15
15	Kevin Orie	.15
16	Hideo Nomo	.65
17	Kevin Appier	.15
18	Bubba Trammell **RC**	.25
19	Juan Gonzalez	.65
20	Randy Johnson	1.25
21	Roger Clemens	1.75
22	Johnny Damon	.35
23	Ryne Sandberg	1.50
24	Ken Griffey Jr.	2.00
25	Barry Bonds	3.00
26	Nomar Garciaparra	1.50
27	Vladimir Guerrero	1.25
28	Ron Gant	.15
29	Joe Carter	.15
30	Tim Salmon	.15
31	Mike Piazza	2.00
32	Barry Larkin	.15
33	Manny Ramirez	1.25
34	Sammy Sosa	1.50
35	Frank Thomas	1.25
36	Melvin Nieves	.15
37	Tony Gwynn	1.50
38	Gary Sheffield	.35
39	Darin Erstad	.50
40	Ken Caminiti	.15
41	Jermaine Dye	.15
42	Mo Vaughn	.15
43	Raul Mondesi	.15
44	Greg Maddux	1.50
45	Chuck Knoblauch	.15
46	Andy Pettitte	.50
47	Deion Sanders	.25
48	Albert Belle	.15
49	Jamey Wright	.15
50	Rey Ordonez	.15
51	Bernie Williams	.15
52	Mark McGwire	2.25
53	Mike Mussina	.50
54	Bob Abreu	.20
55	Reggie Sanders	.15
56	Brian Jordan	.15
57	Ivan Rodriguez	1.00
58	Roberto Alomar	.30
59	Tim Naehring	.15
60	Edgar Renteria	.15
61	Dean Palmer	.25
62	Benito Santiago	.25
63	David Cone	.25
64	Carlos Delgado	.75
65	Brian Giles **RC**	.75
66	Alex Ochoa	.25
67	Rondell White	.25
68	Robin Ventura	.25
69	Eric Karros	.25
70	Jose Valentin	.25
71	Rafael Palmeiro	1.00
72	Chris Snopek	.25
73	David Justice	.25
74	Tom Glavine	.45
75	Rudy Pemberton	.25
76	Larry Walker	.25
77	Jim Thome	.75
78	Charles Johnson	.25
79	Dante Powell	.25
80	Derrek Lee	.75
81	Jason Kendall	.25
82	Todd Hollandsworth	.25
83	Bernard Gilkey	.25
84	Mel Rojas	.25
85	Dmitri Young	.25
86	Bret Boone	.25
87	Pat Hentgen	.25
88	Bobby Bonilla	.25
89	John Wetteland	.25
90	Todd Hundley	.25
91	Wilton Guerrero	.25
92	Geronimo Berroa	.25
93	Al Martin	.25
94	Danny Tartabull	.25
95	Brian McRae	.25
96	Steve Finley	.25
97	Todd Stottlemyre	.25
98	John Smoltz	.25
99	Matt Williams	.25
100	Eddie Murray	1.25
101	Henry Rodriguez	.25
102	Marty Cordova	.25
103	Juan Guzman	.25
104	Chili Davis	.25
105	Eric Young	.25
106	Jeff Abbott	.25
107	Shannon Stewart	.25
108	Rocky Coppinger	.25
109	Jose Canseco	.65
110	Dante Bichette	.25
111	Dwight Gooden	.25
112	Scott Brosius	.25
113	Steve Avery	.25
114	Andres Galarraga	.25
115	Sandy Alomar Jr.	.25
116	Ray Lankford	.25
117	Jorge Posada	.25
118	Ryan Klesko	.25
119	Jay Buhner	.25
120	Jose Guillen	.25
121	Paul O'Neill	.20
122	Jimmy Key	.20
123	Hal Morris	.20
124	Travis Fryman	.20
125	Jim Edmonds	.20
126	Jeff Cirillo	.20
127	Fred McGriff	.20
128	Alan Benes	.20
129	Derek Bell	.20
130	Tony Graffanino	.20
131	Shawn Green	.40
132	Denny Neagle	.20
133	Alex Fernandez	.20
134	Mickey Morandini	.20
135	Royce Clayton	.20
136	Jose Mesa	.20
137	Edgar Martinez	.20
138	Curt Schilling	.40
139	Lance Johnson	.20
140	Andy Benes	.20
141	Charles Nagy	.20
142	Mariano Rivera	.40
143	Mark Wohlers	.20
144	Ken Hill	.20
145	Jay Bell	.20
146	Bob Higginson	.20
147	Mark Grudzielanek	.20
148	Ray Durham	.20
149	John Olerud	.20
150	Joey Hamilton	.20
151	Trevor Hoffman	.20
152	Dan Wilson	.20
153	J.T. Snow	.20
154	Marquis Grissom	.20
155	Yamil Benitez	.20
156	Rusty Greer	.20
157	Darryl Kile	.20
158	Ismael Valdes	.20
159	Jeff Conine	.20
160	Darren Daulton	.20
161	Chan Ho Park	.20
162	Troy Percival	.20
163	Wade Boggs	1.50
164	Dave Nilsson	.20
165	Vinny Castilla	.20
166	Kevin Brown	.20
167	Dennis Eckersley	1.00
168	Wendell Magee Jr.	.20
169	John Jaha	.20
170	Garret Anderson	.20
171	Jason Giambi	.75
172	Mark Grace	.15
173	Tony Clark	.20
174	Moises Alou	.20
175	Brett Butler	.20
176	Cecil Fielder	.20
177	Chris Widger	.20
178	Doug Drabek	.20
179	Ellis Burks	.20
180	Shigetosi Hasegawa	.20

Showcase Row 1 (Grace)

The second level of '97 Flair scarcity is represented by the Row 1/Grace cards (so designated on back). These are visually differentiated on front by the use of a full background to the action photo, and the addition of a color portrait. Row 1/Grace cards are further broken down by their designation on back as: "Showstopper" (#1-60; seeded 1:2.5 packs), "Showtime" (#61-120; 1:2) and "Showpiece" (#121-180; 1:3) with varying insertion rates as shown.

	NM/M
Complete Set (180):	50.00
Common Showstopper (1-60):	.35
Stars:	1.5X
Common Showtime (#61-120):	.25
Stars:	1X
Common Showpiece (#121-180):	.60
Stars:	1.5X

Showcase Row 0 (Showcase)

The scarcest level of '97 Flair is the Row 0/Showcase cards (so designated on front and back). These are identifiable on front by the use of a color portrait in the foreground, with a large action photo behind, printed on a gold-flecked metallic background. Row 0/Showcase cards are further broken down by their designation on back as: "Showpiece" (#1-60; seeded 1:24 packs), "Showstopper" (#61-120; 1:12) and "Showtime" (#121-180; 1:5) with varying insertion rates as shown.

	NM/M
Complete Set (180):	200.00
Common Showpiece (1-60):	1.50
Stars:	2X
Common Showstopper (61-120):	.75
Stars:	4X
Common Showtime (121-180):	.35
Stars:	3X

Showcase Legacy Collection

This 540-card parallel set is printed on matte-finish stock rather than the high-gloss of the regular cards. Front graphic highlights are in blue foil, as is the serial number on back from within each card's edition of just 100. Stated odds of insertion are one per 30 packs. Because all Legacies are printed in identical numbers, there is no premium for cards of different rows.

	NM/M
Common Player:	10.00
Stars:	25X

Showcase Legacy Masterpiece

The insert card chase reached its inevitable zenith with the creation of this series of one-of-a-kind inserts. Each of the 180 players' three cards (Row 2/Style, Row 1/Grace, Row 0/Showcase) in the '97 Flair Legacy Collection was also produced in an edition of one card and inserted at a rate of about one per 3,000 packs. Instead of the blue metallic foil highlights on front and back of the regular Legacy cards, the one-of-a-kind Masterpieces are highlighted in purple and carry a notation on back, "The Only 1 of 1 Masterpiece." Because of the unique nature of each card, value depends solely on demand, thus presentation of meaningful "catalog" values is not possible.

	NM/M
Common Player:	100.00

Showcase Diamond Cuts

This 20-card insert, found 1:20 packs, features a die-cut design with an action photo of the player appearing above a baseball diamond in the lower background.

		NM/M
Complete Set (20):		55.00
Common Player:		1.50
1	Jeff Bagwell	3.00
2	Albert Belle	1.50
3	Ken Caminiti	1.50
4	Juan Gonzalez	2.00
5	Ken Griffey Jr.	4.50
6	Tony Gwynn	4.00
7	Todd Hundley	1.50
8	Andruw Jones	3.00
9	Chipper Jones	4.00
10	Greg Maddux	4.00
11	Mark McGwire	5.00
12	Mike Piazza	4.50
13	Derek Jeter	6.00
14	Manny Ramirez	3.00
15	Cal Ripken Jr.	6.00
16	Alex Rodriguez	5.00
17	Frank Thomas	3.00
18	Mo Vaughn	1.50
19	Bernie Williams	1.50
20	Matt Williams	1.50

Showcase Hot Gloves

Inserted 1:90 packs, Hot Gloves features 15 cards with a die-cut "flaming glove" design printed in thermally active inks and saluting some of baseball's best defensive players.

		NM/M
Complete Set (15):		125.00
Common Player:		2.50
1	Roberto Alomar	3.00
2	Barry Bonds	20.00
3	Juan Gonzalez	6.00
4	Ken Griffey Jr.	15.00
5	Marquis Grissom	2.50
6	Derek Jeter	20.00
7	Chipper Jones	12.00
8	Barry Larkin	2.50
9	Kenny Lofton	2.50
10	Greg Maddux	12.00
11	Mike Piazza	15.00
12	Cal Ripken Jr.	20.00
13	Alex Rodriguez	17.50
14	Ivan Rodriguez	7.50
15	Frank Thomas	10.00

Wave of the Future

This insert focuses on some of the up-and-coming young stars in the game. Cards

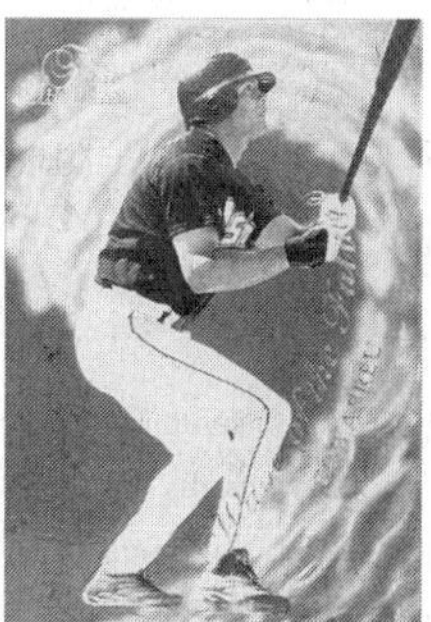

were seeded 1:4 packs. A large ocean wave makes up the background of each card front.

		NM/M
Complete Set (27):		10.00
Common Player:		.25
1	Todd Greene	.25
2	Andruw Jones	1.50
3	Randall Simon	.25
4	Wady Almonte	.25
5	Pat Cline	.25
6	Jeff Abbott	.25
7	Justin Towle	.25
8	Richie Sexson	.25
9	Bubba Trammell	.25
10	Bob Abreu	.35
11	David Arias (Last name actually Ortiz.)	9.00
12	Todd Walker	.25
13	Orlando Cabrera	.25
14	Vladimir Guerrero	1.50
15	Ricky Ledee	.25
16	Jorge Posada	.25
17	Ruben Rivera	.25
18	Scott Spiezio	.25
19	Scott Rolen	1.00
20	Emil Brown	.25
21	Jose Guillen	.25
22	T.J. Staton	.25
23	Elieser Marrero	.25
24	Fernando Tatis	.25
25	Ryan Jones	.25
WF1	Hideki Irabu	.25
WF2	Jose Cruz Jr.	.25

1998 Flair Showcase Promo Strip

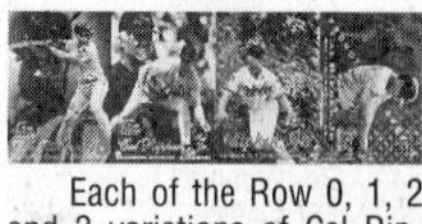

Each of the Row 0, 1, 2 and 3 variations of Cal Ripken's cards are featured on this 10" x 3-1/2" promo strip. The front of each card has "PROMOTIONAL SAMPLE" printed diagonally in gold; on the back the notice is printed in black-and-white.

	NM/M
Complete Promo Strip:	5.00

1998 Flair Showcase Row 3

Row 3, or Flair, cards are considered the base cards of '98 Showcase. They feature a close-up black-and-white portrait photo in the background and an action shot in front, overprinted on a silver-foil background. Flair/Showtime (#1-30) cards are inserted 1:.9 packs, Flair/Showstopper (#31-60) are found 1:1.1 packs, Flair/Showdown (#61-90) cards are inserted 1:1.5

packs and Flair/Showdown (#91-120) cards are inserted 1:2 packs.

NM/M
Complete Set (120): 20.00
Common Player (1-30): .25
Common Player (31-60): .25
Common Player (61-90): .35
Common Player (91-120): .45
Pack (5): 2.50
Wax Box (24): 45.00
1 Ken Griffey Jr. 2.00
2 Travis Lee .25
3 Frank Thomas 1.25
4 Ben Grieve .25
5 Nomar Garciaparra 1.50
6 Jose Cruz Jr. .25
7 Alex Rodriguez 2.50
8 Cal Ripken Jr. 3.00
9 Mark McGwire 2.50
10 Chipper Jones 1.50
11 Paul Konerko .40
12 Todd Helton 1.00
13 Greg Maddux 1.50
14 Derek Jeter 3.00
15 Jaret Wright .25
16 Livan Hernandez .25
17 Mike Piazza 2.00
18 Juan Encarnacion .25
19 Tony Gwynn 1.50
20 Scott Rolen 1.00
21 Roger Clemens 1.75
22 Tony Clark .25
23 Albert Belle .25
24 Mo Vaughn .25
25 Andruw Jones 1.25
26 Jason Dickson .25
27 Fernando Tatis .25
28 Ivan Rodriguez .75
29 Ricky Ledee .25
30 Darin Erstad .50
31 Brian Rose .25
32 Magglio Ordonez **RC** 3.00
33 Larry Walker .25
34 Bobby Higginson .25
35 Chili Davis .25
36 Barry Bonds 3.00
37 Vladimir Guerrero 1.25
38 Jeff Bagwell 1.25
39 Kenny Lofton .25
40 Ryan Klesko .25
41 Mike Cameron .25
42 Charles Johnson .25
43 Andy Pettitte .40
44 Juan Gonzalez 1.25
45 Tim Salmon .25
46 Hideki Irabu .25
47 Paul Molitor 1.25
48 Edgar Renteria .25
49 Manny Ramirez 1.25
50 Jim Edmonds .25
51 Bernie Williams .25
52 Roberto Alomar .40
53 David Justice .25
54 Rey Ordonez .25
55 Ken Caminiti .25
56 Jose Guillen .25
57 Randy Johnson 1.25
58 Brady Anderson .25
59 Hideo Nomo .50
60 Tino Martinez .25
61 John Smoltz .35
62 Joe Carter .35
63 Matt Williams .35
64 Robin Ventura .35
65 Barry Larkin .35
66 Dante Bichette .35
67 Travis Fryman .35
68 Gary Sheffield .60
69 Eric Karros .35
70 Matt Stairs .35
71 Al Martin .35
72 Jay Buhner .35
73 Ray Lankford .35
74 Carlos Delgado .65
75 Edgardo Alfonzo .35
76 Rondell White .35
77 Chuck Knoblauch .35
78 Raul Mondesi .35
79 Johnny Damon .60
80 Matt Morris .35
81 Tom Glavine .60
82 Kevin Brown .35
83 Garret Anderson .35
84 Mike Mussina .40
85 Pedro Martinez 1.25
86 Craig Biggio .35
87 Darryl Kile .35
88 Rafael Palmeiro .75
89 Jim Thome .60
90 Andres Galarraga .35
91 Sammy Sosa 1.50
92 Willie Greene .45
93 Vinny Castilla .45
94 Justin Thompson .45
95 Jeff King .45
96 Jeff Cirillo .45
97 Mark Grudzielanek .45
98 Brad Radke .45
99 John Olerud .45
100 Curt Schilling .65
101 Steve Finley .45
102 J.T. Snow .45
103 Edgar Martinez .45
104 Wilson Alvarez .45
105 Rusty Greer .45
106 Pat Hentgen .45
107 David Cone .45
108 Fred McGriff .45
109 Jason Giambi .75
110 Tony Womack .45
111 Bernard Gilkey .45
112 Alan Benes .45
113 Mark Grace .45
114 Reggie Sanders .45
115 Moises Alou .45
116 John Jaha .45
117 Henry Rodriguez .45
118 Dean Palmer .45
119 Mike Lieberthal .45
120 Shawn Estes .45

Showcase Row 2

Row 2, or Style (as they are designated on front) cards in Flair Showcase are the second easiest type of card to pull from packs. Fronts are similar to Row 3 base cards, but include the entire background of the action photo and have a color portrait photo. Cards #1-30 are inserted one per three packs, #31-60 are found 1:2.5 packs, #61-90 cards are 1:4 and #91-120 are inserted one per three packs.

NM/M
Complete Set (120): 40.00
Common Player: .50
Stars: 1.5-2X

Showcase Row 1

Row 1, also referred to as Grace, was the second most difficult type of card to pull from Flair Showcase. The front design has an action photo overprinted on a large portrait which is printed on a rainbow metallic-foil background. Cards #1-30 are seeded one per 16 packs, #31-60 are 1:24, #61-90 are 1:6 and #91-120 are 1:10.

NM/M
Complete Set (1-120): 100.00
Commons (1-30): 1.00
Stars: 2X
Commons (31-60): 1.25
Stars: 3X
Commons (61-90): .35
Stars: 1X
Commons (91-120): .75
Stars: 1.5X

Showcase Row 0

Row 0 is the most difficult of the four tiers to obtain from packs. Two action photos are combined on a horizontal format with one in a prismatic foil background. The first 30 cards are serially numbered to 250, cards #30-60 are numbered to 500, #61-90 are numbered to 1,000 and #91-120 are numbered within an edition of 2,000.

NM/M
Complete Set (120): 350.00
Common Player (1-30): 5.00
Stars: 10X
Common Player (31-60): 3.00
Stars: 8X
Common Player (61-90): 2.00
Stars: 6X
Common Player (91-120): 1.00
Stars: 4X

Showcase Legacy Collection

Legacy Collection parallels all 480 cards in the Flair Showcase set. Each Legacy Collection card displays the player's name in black plate laminated on the back, with the card's sequential numbering to 100 in gold foil.

NM/M
Common Player: 7.50
Stars: 25X

Showcase Legacy Masterpiece

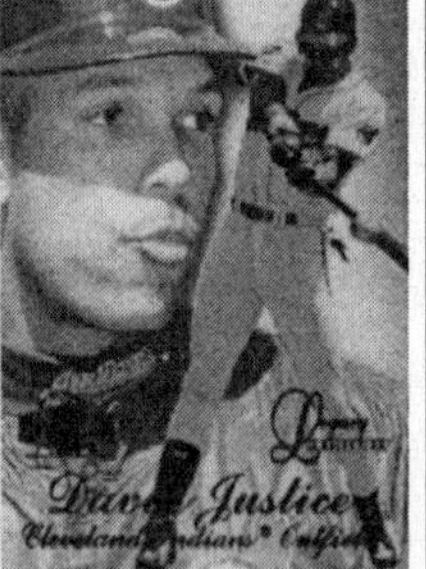

Each of the 120 players' four cards (Rows 3, 2, 1 and 0) in the '98 Flair Legacy Collection was also produced in an edition of one card and inserted at a rate of about one per 3,000 packs. The one-of-a-kind cards carry a notation on back: "The Only 1 of 1 Masterpiece". With supply a fixed quantity, value depends on demand at any particular time, thus it is not possible to present meaningful "catalog" values.

NM/M
Common Player: 50.00

Showcase Perfect 10

Perfect 10 features the game's most popular players on a silk-screen technology design. The cards were serial numbered to 10 on the back and were inserted into packs of Flair Showcase.

NM/M
Complete Set (10): 1,600
Common Player: 100.00

1 Ken Griffey Jr. 200.00
2 Cal Ripken Jr. 300.00
3 Frank Thomas 125.00
4 Mike Piazza 200.00
5 Greg Maddux 150.00
6 Nomar Garciaparra 150.00
7 Mark McGwire 250.00
8 Scott Rolen 100.00
9 Alex Rodriguez 250.00
10 Roger Clemens 175.00

Showcase Wave of the Future

Twelve up-and-coming players with hot minor league stats and Major League potential are displayed in Wave of the Future. The cards contain a clear acetate card inside a plastic covering that is filled with vegetable oil and glitter. These were inserted one per 20 packs and are numbered with a "WF" prefix.

NM/M
Complete Set (12): 10.00
Common Player: .50
WF1 Travis Lee .50
WF2 Todd Helton 5.00
WF3 Ben Grieve .50
WF4 Juan Encarnacion .50
WF5 Brad Fullmer .50
WF6 Ruben Rivera .50
WF7 Paul Konerko .75
WF8 Derrek Lee 1.50
WF9 Mike Lowell .50
WF10 Magglio Ordonez 2.00
WF11 Rich Butler .50
WF12 Eli Marrero .50

1999 Flair Showcase Row 3 (Power)

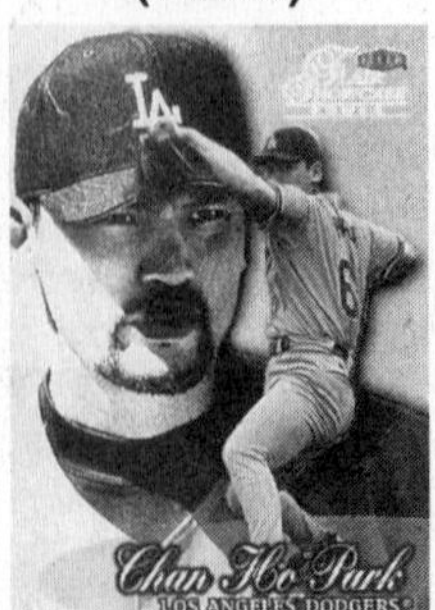

Power is one of three tiers in 1999 Showcase. The front on this base-level version is rainbow holofoil including the large portrait photo in the background. In the foreground is a color action photo. Matte textured silver spot embossing is printed over the player's name and team at lower-right. All three Rows of Showcase can be found with three different back designs. Showtime presents traditional annual and career stats. Horizontally formatted Showpiece cards have a black-and-white player photo as a "Classic Matchup" of the player's stats to those of a past star. Showdown backs have a color action photo on a brightly-colored wave-pattern background. A stat box at center offers career numbers in four unique categories like day-night, grass-turf, etc. Each of these three back-design levels of scarcity has a different advertised insertion rate. Within Row 3/Power, these vary only between one card in .9 packs, and one card in 1.2 packs, thus there is no practical value differential. Five-card packs of Flair Showcase had a $4.99 SRP.

NM/M
Complete Set (144): 25.00
Common Player: .25
Pack (5): 3.00
Wax Box (24): 45.00
1 Mark McGwire 2.50
2 Sammy Sosa 1.50
3 Ken Griffey Jr. 2.00
4 Chipper Jones 1.50
5 Ben Grieve .25
6 J.D. Drew .75
7 Jeff Bagwell 1.00
8 Cal Ripken Jr. 3.00
9 Tony Gwynn 1.50
10 Nomar Garciaparra 1.50
11 Travis Lee .35
12 Troy Glaus .75
13 Mike Piazza 2.00
14 Alex Rodriguez 2.50
15 Kevin Brown .25
16 Darin Erstad .50
17 Scott Rolen .50
18 Micah Bowie **RC** .25
19 Juan Gonzalez .50
20 Kerry Wood .50
21 Roger Clemens 1.75
22 Derek Jeter 3.00
23 Pat Burrell **RC** 3.00
24 Tim Salmon .25
25 Barry Bonds 3.00
26 Roosevelt Brown **RC** .25
27 Vladimir Guerrero 1.00
28 Randy Johnson 1.00
29 Mo Vaughn .25
30 Fernando Seguignol .25
31 Greg Maddux 1.50
32 Tony Clark .25
33 Eric Chavez .40
34 Kris Benson .25
35 Frank Thomas 1.00
36 Mario Encarnacion .25
37 Gabe Kapler .25
38 Jeremy Giambi .25
39 Peter Tucci **RC** .25
40 Manny Ramirez 1.00
41 Albert Belle .25
42 Warren Morris .25
43 Michael Barrett .25
44 Andruw Jones 1.00
45 Carlos Delgado .60
46 Jaret Wright .25
47 Juan Encarnacion .25
48 Scott Hunter .25
49 Tino Martinez .25
50 Craig Biggio .25
51 Jim Thome .60
52 Vinny Castilla .25
53 Tom Glavine .40
54 Bob Higginson .25
55 Moises Alou .25
56 Robin Ventura .25
57 Bernie Williams .25
58 Pedro J. Martinez 1.00
59 Greg Vaughn .25
60 Ray Lankford .25
61 Jose Canseco .40
62 Ivan Rodriguez .75
63 Shawn Green .40
64 Rafael Palmeiro .75
65 Ellis Burks .25
66 Jason Kendall .25
67 David Wells .25
68 Rondell White .25
69 Gary Sheffield .40
70 Ken Caminiti .25
71 Cliff Floyd .25
72 Larry Walker .25
73 Bartolo Colon .25
74 Barry Larkin .25
75 Calvin Pickering .25
76 Jim Edmonds .25
77 Henry Rodriguez .25
78 Roberto Alomar .40
79 Andres Galarraga .25
80 Richie Sexson .25
81 Todd Helton .75
82 Damion Easley .25
83 Livan Hernandez .25
84 Carlos Beltran .60
85 Todd Hundley .25
86 Todd Walker .25
87 Scott Brosius .25
88 Bob Abreu .25
89 Corey Koskie .25
90 Ruben Rivera .25
91 Edgar Renteria .25
92 Quinton McCracken .25
93 Bernard Gilkey .25
94 Shannon Stewart .25
95 Dustin Hermanson .25
96 Mike Caruso .25
97 Alex Gonzalez .25
98 Raul Mondesi .25
99 David Cone .25
100 Curt Schilling .40
101 Brian Giles .25
102 Edgar Martinez .25
103 Rolando Arrojo .25
104 Derek Bell .25
105 Denny Neagle .25
106 Marquis Grissom .25
107 Bret Boone .25
108 Mike Mussina .50
109 John Smoltz .25
110 Brett Tomko .25
111 David Justice .25
112 Andy Pettitte .40
113 Eric Karros .25
114 Dante Bichette .25
115 Jeromy Burnitz .25
116 Paul Konerko .40
117 Steve Finley .25
118 Ricky Ledee .25
119 Edgardo Alfonzo .25
120 Dean Palmer .25
121 Rusty Greer .25
122 Luis Gonzalez .25
123 Randy Winn .25
124 Jeff Kent .25
125 Doug Glanville .25
126 Justin Thompson .25
127 Bret Saberhagen .25
128 Wade Boggs 1.50
129 Al Leiter .25
130 Paul O'Neill .25
131 Chan Ho Park .25
132 Johnny Damon .60
133 Darryl Kile .25
134 Reggie Sanders .25
135 Kevin Millwood .25
136 Charles Johnson .25
137 Ray Durham .25
138 Rico Brogna .25
139 Matt Williams .25
140 Sandy Alomar .25
141 Jeff Cirillo .25
142 Devon White .25
143 Andy Benes .25
144 Mike Stanley .25
Checklist Card .05

Showcase Row 2 (Passion)

The metallic-foil background in the second level of Flair Showcase - Row 2/Passion - has an action photo printed in front of large textured numerals representing the player's uniform number. In the foreground is another action shot. Backs have the same three designs as Row 3, but only vary in insertion rate from one card per 1.3 packs to one card per three packs.

NM/M
Complete Set (144): 65.00
Common Player: .25
Showdown (1-48): 2X
Showpiece (49-96): 1X
Showtime (97-144): 1X

Showcase Row 1 (Showcase)

Showcase level - Row 1 - presents two portraits and an action photo and the player's uniform number on a plastic

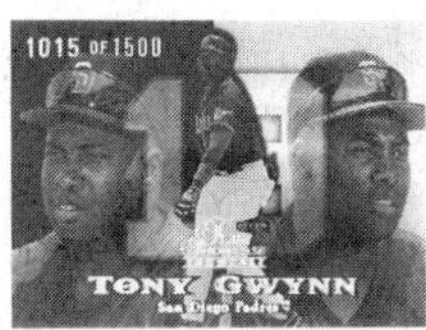

laminate in a horizontal format. A gold-foil serial number is stamped into the upper-left corner in one of three levels of scarcity: Showpiece (#1-48) is limited to 1,500 numbered sets, Showtime (#49-96) is limited to 3,000 sets and Showdown (#97-144) is numbered to 6,000 sets.

		NM/M
Complete Set (144):		300.00
Common Showpiece (1-48):		2.00
Showpiece Stars:		5X
Common Showtime (49-96):		1.00
Showtime Stars:		3X
Common Showdown (97-144):		.50
Showdown Stars:		2X

Showcase Legacy /Masterpiece

Each of the 432 total cards in Flair Showcase was also produced in a pair of extremely limited parallels. The blue-foil enhanced Legacy Collection cards are serially numbered within an edition of just 99. The presence of purple foil on front signifies a Legacy Masterpiece card, which is identified on front by the notation, "The Only 1 of 1 Masterpiece." Because of their unique nature, determination of a "book value" for Masterpiece cards is not possible.

	NM/M
Common Legacy:	6.00
Legacy Stars:	20X
Common Masterpiece:	50.00

Showcase Measure of Greatness

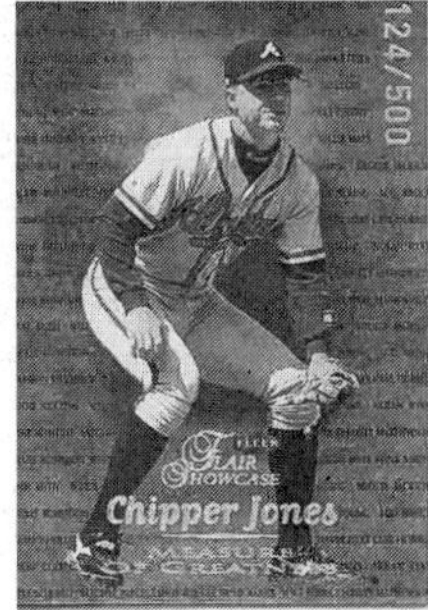

This 15-card set captures baseball's top superstars who were closing in on milestones during the 1999 season. Each card is sequentially numbered to 500.

		NM/M
Complete Set (15):		100.00
Common Player:		3.00
Production 500 Sets		
1	Roger Clemens	7.50
2	Nomar Garciaparra	6.50
3	Juan Gonzalez	3.00
4	Ken Griffey Jr.	9.00
5	Vladimir Guerrero	5.00
6	Tony Gwynn	6.50
7	Derek Jeter	15.00
8	Chipper Jones	6.50
9	Mark McGwire	12.50
10	Mike Piazza	9.00
11	Manny Ramirez	5.00
12	Cal Ripken Jr.	15.00
13	Alex Rodriguez	12.50
14	Sammy Sosa	6.50
15	Frank Thomas	5.00

Showcase Wave of the Future

This insert set spotlights young stars on the rise and is limited to 1,000 serial numbered sets.

		NM/M
Complete Set (15):		40.00
Common Player:		1.50
Production 1,000 Sets		
1	Kerry Wood	4.00
2	Ben Grieve	1.50
3	J.D. Drew	4.00
4	Juan Encarnacion	1.50
5	Travis Lee	2.00
6	Todd Helton	7.50
7	Troy Glaus	7.50
8	Ricky Ledee	1.50
9	Eric Chavez	2.00
10	Ben Davis	1.50
11	George Lombard	1.50
12	Jeremy Giambi	1.50
13	Roosevelt Brown	1.50
14	Pat Burrell	6.00
15	Preston Wilson	1.50

2003 Flair

		NM/M
Complete Set (125):		
Common Player:		.25
Common SP (91-125):		4.00
Production 500		
Pack (5):		3.50
Box (20):		50.00
1	Hideo Nomo	.60
2	Derek Jeter	3.00
3	Junior Spivey	.25
4	Rich Aurilia	.25
5	Luis Gonzalez	.35
6	Sean Burroughs	.25
7	Pedro J. Martinez	1.00
8	Randy Winn	.25
9	Carlos Delgado	.50
10	Pat Burrell	.50
11	Barry Larkin	.25
12	Roberto Alomar	.40
13	Tony Batista	.25
14	Barry Bonds	3.00
15	Craig Biggio	.25
16	Ivan Rodriguez	.65
17	Javier Vazquez	.25
18	Joe Borchard	.25
19	Josh Phelps	.25
20	Omar Vizquel	.25
21	Tom Glavine	.40
22	Darin Erstad	.50
23	Hee Seop Choi	.25
24	Roger Clemens	1.75
25	Michael Cuddyer	.25
26	Mike Sweeney	.25
27	Phil Nevin	.25
28	Torii Hunter	.25
29	Vladimir Guerrero	1.00
30	Ellis Burks	.25
31	Jimmy Rollins	.50
32	Ken Griffey Jr.	2.00
33	Magglio Ordonez	.40
34	Mark Prior	1.00
35	Mike Lieberthal	.25
36	Jorge Posada	.30
37	Rodrigo Lopez	.25
38	Todd Helton	1.00
39	Adam Kennedy	.25
40	Curt Schilling	.40
41	Jim Thome	.25
42	Josh Beckett	.25
43	Carlos Pena	.25
44	Jason Kendall	.25
45	Sammy Sosa	2.00
46	Scott Rolen	.75
47	Alex Rodriguez	2.50
48	Aubrey Huff	.25
49	Bobby Abreu	.25
50	Jeff Kent	.25
51	Joe Randa	.25
52	Lance Berkman	.25
53	Orlando Cabrera	.25
54	Richie Sexson	.25
55	Albert Pujols	2.00
56	Alfonso Soriano	.50
57	Greg Maddux	1.50
58	Jason Giambi	.75
59	Jeff Bagwell	1.00
60	Kerry Wood	.50
61	Manny Ramirez	1.00
62	Eric Chavez	.40
63	Preston Wilson	.25
64	Shawn Green	.50
65	Shea Hillenbrand	.25
66	Austin Kearns	.75
67	Cliff Floyd	.25
68	Edgardo Alfonzo	.25
69	J.D. Drew	.40
70	Larry Walker	.25
71	Mike Piazza	2.00
72	Andruw Jones	.75
73	Ben Grieve	.25
74	Eric Hinske	.25
75	Geoff Jenkins	.25
76	Kazuhiro Sasaki	.25
77	Matt Morris	.25
78	Miguel Tejada	.40
79	Aramis Ramirez	.25
80	Troy Glaus	1.00
81	Ichiro Suzuki	2.00
82	Mark Teixeira	.50
83	Nomar Garciaparra	2.00
84	Chipper Jones	1.50
85	Frank Thomas	1.00
86	Paul LoDuca	.25
87	Bernie Williams	.35
88	Adam Dunn	.75
89	Randy Johnson	1.00
90	Barry Zito	.40
91	Lew Ford **RC**	8.00
92	Joe Valentine **RC**	3.00
93	Jhonny Peralta	4.00
94	Hideki Matsui **RC**	20.00
95	Francisco Rosario **RC**	3.00
96	Adam LaRoche	4.00
97	Josh Hall **RC**	6.00
98	Chien-Ming Wang **RC**	25.00
99	Josh Willingham **RC**	6.00
100	Guillermo Quiroz **RC**	6.00
101	Terrmel Sledge **RC**	3.00
102	Prentice Redman **RC**	3.00
103	Matt Bruback **RC**	6.00
104	Alejandro Machado **RC**	3.00
105	Shane Victorino **RC**	6.00
106	Chris Waters **RC**	3.00
107	Jose Contreras **RC**	8.00
108	Pete LaForest **RC**	3.00
109	Nook Logan **RC**	3.00
110	Hector Luna **RC**	8.00
111	Daniel Cabrera **RC**	6.00
112	Matt Kata **RC**	6.00
113	Rontrez Johnson **RC**	6.00
114	Josh Stewart **RC**	8.00
115	Michael Hessman **RC**	3.00
116	Felix Sanchez **RC**	3.00
117	Michel Hernandez **RC**	3.00
118	Arnaldo Munoz **RC**	3.00
119	Ian Ferguson **RC**	3.00
120	Clint Barmes **RC**	6.00
121	Brian Stokes **RC**	3.00
122	Craig Brazell **RC**	6.00
123	John Webb	3.00
124	Tim Olson **RC**	6.00
125	Jeremy Bonderman	10.00

Row 1

Stars (1-90):	5-10X
Rookies (91-125):	.75-1.5X
Production 150 Sets	
Row 2:	No Pricing
Production 25 Sets	

Diamond Cuts

		NM/M
Common Player:		4.00
Inserted 1:10		
Golds:		1-2X
Production 100 Sets		
1DC	Alex Rodriguez	12.00
2DC	Roberto Alomar	4.00
3DC	Scott Rolen	5.00
4DC	Alfonso Soriano	6.00
5DC	Chipper Jones	7.50
6DC	Pat Burrell	5.00
7DC	Derek Jeter	15.00
8DC	Mike Piazza	10.00
9DC	J.D. Drew	4.00
10DC	Vladimir Guerrero	6.00
11DC	Greg Maddux	7.50
12DC	Barry Zito	4.00
13DC	Troy Glaus	5.00
14DC	Roy Oswalt	4.00
15DC	Roger Clemens	9.00

Hot Numbers

		NM/M
Common Player:		15.00
Production 100 Sets		
1HN	Alex Rodriguez	35.00
2HN	Roberto Alomar	20.00
3HN	Scott Rolen	30.00
4HN	Alfonso Soriano	30.00
5HN	Chipper Jones	25.00
6HN	Pat Burrell	25.00
7HN	Derek Jeter	40.00
8HN	Mike Piazza	30.00
9HN	J.D. Drew	15.00
10HN	Vladimir Guerrero	20.00
11HN	Greg Maddux	30.00
12HN	Barry Zito	15.00
13HN	Troy Glaus	15.00
14HN	Roy Oswalt	15.00

Hot Numbers Dual

Production 25 Sets: No Pricing

Power Tools

		NM/M
Common Player:		5.00
Production 500 Sets		
Golds:		1-1.5X
Production 100 Sets		
1PT	Nomar Garciaparra	15.00
2PT	Derek Jeter	25.00
3PT	Sammy Sosa	12.00
4PT	Miguel Tejada	5.00
5PT	Austin Kearns	10.00
6PT	Jason Giambi	8.00
7PT	Adam Dunn	8.00
8PT	Jim Thome	8.00
9PT	Lance Berkman	6.00
10PT	Alfonso Soriano	15.00
12PT	Alex Rodriguez	15.00
13PT	Mike Piazza	10.00
14PT	Bernie Williams	10.00
15PT	Jeff Bagwell	8.00
16PT	Andruw Jones	5.00
17PT	Scott Rolen	12.00
19PT	Juan Gonzalez	6.00

Power Tools - Dual

		NM/M
Common Duo:		
Production 200 Sets		
1PTD	Nomar Garciaparra, Derek Jeter	40.00
3PTD	Adam Dunn, Austin Kearns	25.00
4PTD	Jim Thome, Sammy Sosa	15.00
5PTD	Alex Rodriguez, Nomar Garciaparra	20.00
6PTD	Jason Giambi, Bernie Williams	15.00
7PTD	Derek Jeter, Alfonso Soriano	25.00
8PTD	Lance Berkman, Jeff Bagwell	10.00
9PTD	Miguel Tejada, Alex Rodriguez	20.00
10PTD	Jason Giambi, Mike Piazza	20.00

Sweet Swatch

	NM/M
Common Player:	5.00
Production 250 Sets	
Derek Jeter	20.00
Sammy Sosa	15.00
Hideo Nomo	20.00
Vladimir Guerrero	6.00
Jason Giambi	8.00
Nomar Garciaparra	15.00
Randy Johnson	12.00
Miguel Tejada	5.00
Pedro J. Martinez	10.00
Adam Dunn	8.00
Roger Clemens	15.00
Mark Prior	10.00
Chipper Jones	10.00
Alex Rodriguez	15.00
Bernie Williams	6.00
Lance Berkman	6.00
Kazuhiro Sasaki	6.00
Alfonso Soriano	12.00

Sweet Swatch Oversized

	NM/M
Common Player:	6.00
1:Hobby Box	
Masterpiece One-of-One's exist.	
Derek Jeter/150	20.00
Sammy Sosa/279	15.00
Hideo Nomo/970	12.00
Jason Giambi/350	15.00
Nomar Garciaparra/727	15.00
Randy Johnson/274	15.00
Miguel Tejada/518	6.00
Pedro Martinez/1,480	10.00
Adam Dunn/1,090	8.00
Roger Clemens/97	25.00
Mark Prior/1,195	10.00
Chipper Jones/80	15.00
Alex Rodriguez/150	15.00
Bernie Williams/1,420	8.00
Lance Berkman/1,465	6.00
Kazuhiro Sasaki/505	10.00

Sweet Swatch Autograph Oversized

	NM/M
Common Player:	
Golds:	1.5-2X
Production 25, Jeter 50	
Masterpiece One-of-Ones exist.	
Derek Jeter/312	90.00
Randy Johnson/218	60.00
Adam Dunn/218	30.00
Jeff Bagwell/218	40.00

Sweet Swatch Patch

	NM/M
Common Player:	15.00
Production 50 Sets	
Sammy Sosa	50.00
Hideo Nomo	50.00
Jason Giambi	20.00
Nomar Garciaparra	45.00
Randy Johnson	40.00
Miguel Tejada	15.00
Pedro J. Martinez	40.00
Adam Dunn	35.00
Roger Clemens	50.00
Mark Prior	25.00
Alex Rodriguez	45.00
Bernie Williams	20.00
Kazuhiro Sasaki	30.00
Alfonso Soriano	35.00

Sweet Swatch Patch Oversized

	NM/M
Common Player:	15.00
Derek Jeter/35	75.00
Sammy Sosa/190	40.00
Hideo Nomo/114	50.00
Vladimir Guerrero/290	35.00
Nomar Garciaparra/124	40.00
Miguel Tejada/183	15.00
Pedro Martinez/185	40.00
Adam Dunn/130	30.00
Mark Prior/290	25.00
Chipper Jones/284	25.00
Alex Rodriguez/298	40.00
Bernie Williams/123	25.00
Lance Berkman/287	25.00
Kazuhiro Sasaki/90	40.00

Sweet Swatch Dual Oversized

Production 25 Sets: No Pricing

Wave of the Future

		NM/M
Common Player:		3.00
Production 500 Sets		
Golds:		1-2X
Production 100 Sets		
1WOF	Francisco Rodriguez	3.00
2WOF	Carl Crawford	4.00
3WOF	Austin Kearns	10.00
4WOF	Hank Blalock	8.00
5WOF	Marlon Byrd	3.00
6WOF	Michael Restovich	3.00
7WOF	Joe Borchard	3.00
8WOF	Sean Burroughs	4.00
9WOF	Aubrey Huff	3.00
10WOF	Josh Phelps	5.00

Greats of the Game

		NM/M
Complete Set (95):		35.00
Common Player:		.40
Pack (5):		6.00
Box (20):		100.00
1	Ozzie Smith	1.00
2	Red Schoendienst	.40
3	Harmon Killebrew	1.50
4	Ralph Kiner	.40
5	Johnny Bench	2.00
6	Al Kaline	1.00
7	Bobby Doerr	.40
8	Cal Ripken Jr.	4.00
9	Enos Slaughter	.40
10	Phil Rizzuto	1.00
11	Luis Aparicio	.40
12	Pee Wee Reese	.40
13	Richie Ashburn	.40
14	Ernie Banks	2.00
15	Earl Weaver	.40
16	Whitey Ford	1.50
17	Brooks Robinson	1.00
18	Lou Boudreau	.40
19	Robin Yount	1.00
20	Mike Schmidt	2.50
21	Bob Lemon	.40
22	Stan Musial	2.50
23	Joe Morgan	.60
24	Early Wynn	.40
25	Willie Stargell	.75
26	Yogi Berra	2.00
27	Juan Marichal	.40
28	Rick Ferrell	.40
29	Rod Carew	.75
30	Jim Bunning	.40
31	Ferguson Jenkins	.40
32	Steve Carlton	.75
33	Larry Doby	.40
34	Nolan Ryan	4.00
35	Phil Niekro	.40
36	Billy Williams	.40
37	Hal Newhouser	.40
38	Bob Feller	.75
39	Lou Brock	.75
40	Monte Irvin	.75
41	Eddie Mathews	1.00
42	Rollie Fingers	.40
43	Gaylord Perry	.40
44	Reggie Jackson	1.50
45	Bob Gibson	1.00
46	Robin Roberts	.40
47	Tom Seaver	1.00
48	Willie McCovey	.40
49	Hoyt Wilhelm	.40
50	George Kell	.40
51	Warren Spahn	1.00
52	Jim "Catfish" Hunter	.40
53	Dom DiMaggio	.40
54	Joe Medwick	.40
55	Johnny Pesky	.40
56	Steve Garvey	.40
57	Harry Heilmann	.40
58	Dave Winfield	.75
59	Andre Dawson	.40
60	Jimmie Foxx	1.00
61	Buddy Bell	.40
62	Gabby Hartnett	.40
63	Babe Ruth	4.00
64	Dizzy Dean	1.50
65	Hank Greenberg	.40
66	Don Drysdale	.75
67	Gary Carter	.40
68	Wade Boggs	.75
69	Tony Perez	.40
70	Mickey Cochrane	.75
71	Bill Dickey	.40
72	George Brett	3.00
73	Honus Wagner	3.00
74	George Sisler	1.00

75 Walter Johnson 2.00
76 Ron Santo .40
77 Roy Campanella 1.00
78 Roger Maris 2.50
79 Kirby Puckett 2.50
80 Alan Trammell .40
81 Don Mattingly 4.00
82 Ty Cobb 3.00
83 Lou Gehrig 3.00
84 Jackie Robinson 3.00
85 Billy Martin .75
86 Paul Molitor .75
87 Duke Snider 1.00
88 Thurman Munson 1.50
89 Luke Appling .40
90 Ernie Lombardi .40
91 Rube Waddell .40
92 Travis Jackson .40
93 Joe Sewell .40
94 King Kelly .40
95 Heinie Manush .40
Common Home Team (96-133): 2.00
96HT Bobby Doerr 2.00
97HT Johnny Pesky 2.00
98HT Wade Boggs 3.00
99HT Tony Conigliaro 2.00
100HT Carlton Fisk 3.00
101HT Rico Petrocelli 2.00
102HT Jim Rice 2.00
103HT Al Lopez 2.00
104HT Pee Wee Reese 2.00
105HT Tommy Lasorda 2.00
106HT Gil Hodges 3.00
107HT Jackie Robinson 6.00
108HT Duke Snider 4.00
109HT Don Drysdale 4.00
110HT Steve Garvey 2.00
111HT Hoyt Wilhelm 2.00
112HT Juan Marichal 3.00
113HT Monte Irvin 3.00
114HT Willie McCovey 3.00
115HT Travis Jackson 2.00
116HT Bobby Bonds 2.00
117HT Orlando Cepeda 2.00
118HT Whitey Ford 4.00
119HT Phil Rizzuto 4.00
120HT Reggie Jackson 4.00
121HT Yogi Berra 5.00
122HT Roger Maris 6.00
123HT Don Mattingly 10.00
124HT Babe Ruth 10.00
125HT Dave Winfield 3.00
126HT Bob Gibson 4.00
127HT Enos Slaughter 2.00
128HT Joe Medwick 2.00
129HT Lou Brock 3.00
130HT Ozzie Smith 5.00
131HT Stan Musial 6.00
132HT Steve Carlton 3.00
133HT Dizzy Dean 4.00

Greats of the Game Ballpark Heroes

NM/M
Complete Set (9): 25.00
Common Player: 2.00
Inserted 1:10
1BH Nolan Ryan 5.00
2BH Babe Ruth 5.00
3BH Honus Wagner 3.00
4BH Ty Cobb 4.00
5BH Ernie Banks 3.00
6BH Mike Schmidt 3.00
7BH Duke Snider 2.00
8BH Cal Ripken Jr. 5.00
9BH Stan Musial 3.00

Greats of the Game Bat Rack Triple

NM/M
Common Card: 15.00
Production 300
Eddie Murray, Cal Ripken Jr., Brooks Robinson 75.00
Ryne Sandberg, Ron Santo, Billy Williams 45.00
Johnny Bench, Joe Morgan, Tony Perez 35.00
Eddie Mathews, Paul Molitor, Robin Yount 40.00
Tommie Agee, Jerry Grote, Bud Harrelson 15.00
Reggie Jackson, Don Mattingly, Dave Winfield 45.00
Dave Parker, Willie Stargell 20.00

Greats of the Game Bat Rack Quad

NM/M
Common Card: 50.00
Numbered to 150.
Don Mattingly, Joe Morgan, Cal Ripken Jr., Brooks Robinson 90.00
Ryne Sandberg, Ron Santo, Billy Williams, Andre Dawson 60.00
Dave Winfield, Cal Ripken Jr., Paul Molitor, Robin Yount 80.00
Eddie Murray, Eddie Mathews, Reggie Jackson, Willie McCovey 50.00

Greats of the Game Classic Numbers

NM/M
Complete Set (13): 50.00
Common Player: 3.00
Inserted 1:20
1CN Jackie Robinson 6.00
2CN Willie McCovey 3.00
3CN Brooks Robinson 5.00
4CN Reggie Jackson 6.00
5CN Ozzie Smith 6.00
6CN Johnny Bench 6.00
7CN Yogi Berra 6.00
8CN Cal Ripken Jr. 10.00
9CN George Brett 8.00
10CN Thurman Munson 5.00
11CN Joe Morgan 3.00
12CN Nolan Ryan 10.00
13CN Steve Carlton 3.00

Greats of the Game Classic Numbers Game-Used

NM/M
Common Player: 10.00
Inserted 1:24
Willie McCovey 12.00
George Brett 20.00
Joe Morgan 10.00
Yogi Berra 20.00
Cal Ripken Jr. 25.00
Nolan Ryan 35.00
Ozzie Smith 15.00
Johnny Bench 15.00
Ryne Sandberg 25.00
Thurman Munson 20.00
Steve Carlton 10.00

Greats of the Game Classic Numbers Dual-side

NM/M
Common Card: 25.00
Production 250 Sets
Yogi Berra, Thurman Munson 45.00
Nolan Ryan, Steve Carlton 65.00
Johnny Bench, Thurman Munson 35.00
Cal Ripken Jr., Ozzie Smith 60.00
Joe Morgan, Ryne Sandberg 35.00
Willie McCovey, Johnny Bench 25.00
Yogi Berra, Cal Ripken Jr. 50.00
George Brett, Nolan Ryan 75.00

Greats of the Game Cut of History

NM/M
Common Player: 5.00
Inserted 1:10
Paul O'Neill 5.00
Dennis Eckersley 8.00
Jim Palmer 6.00
Graig Nettles 8.00
Frank Baker 30.00
Wade Boggs 8.00
Roger Maris 60.00
Jim "Catfish" Hunter 8.00
Alan Trammell 12.00
Eddie Murray 20.00
Steve Carlton 10.00
Tom Seaver 8.00
Gary Carter 8.00
Phil Niekro 6.00
Luis Aparicio 8.00
Reggie Jackson 12.00
Fergie Jenkins 8.00
Kirby Puckett 15.00
Billy Martin 15.00
Joe Medwick 25.00
Buddy Bell 5.00
Early Wynn 10.00
Cal Ripken Jr. 25.00
Hoyt Wilhelm 8.00
Willie McCovey 10.00

Greats of the Game Cut of History Autograph

NM/M
Common Player:
Alan Trammell/211 25.00
Steve Carlton/506 30.00
Cal Ripken Jr./155 150.00
Johnny Bench/161 50.00

Greats of the Game Greats of the Grain

NM/M
Production 50 Sets
1GOG Ty Cobb 100.00
2GOG Mike Schmidt 50.00
3GOG Babe Ruth 140.00
4GOG Lou Gehrig 80.00
5GOG George Brett 160.00
6GOG Stan Musial 75.00
7GOG Don Mattingly 110.00
8GOG Cal Ripken Jr. 100.00
9GOG Eddie Mathews 75.00

Greats of the Game HOF Postmark

NM/M
Production 2,002
Ozzie Smith 20.00
Ozzie Smith/Auto./202 100.00

Greats of the Game Home Team Cut

NM/M
Common Player: 8.00
Patch: 2-5X
Production 25 Sets
Wade Boggs 15.00
Carlton Fisk 20.00
Jim Rice 15.00
Pee Wee Reese 15.00
Duke Snider 20.00
Steve Garvey 10.00
Tommy Lasorda 15.00
Juan Marichal 10.00
Bobby Bonds 8.00
Willie McCovey 10.00
Billy Martin 15.00
Roger Maris 65.00
Reggie Jackson 15.00
Dave Winfield 12.00
Red Schoendienst 8.00
Ozzie Smith 35.00
Joe Medwick 25.00

Greats of the Game Sweet Swatch Bat

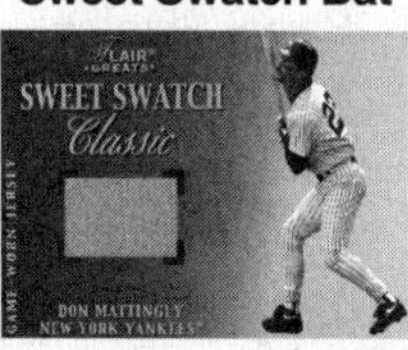

NM/M
Common Player: 15.00
Cal Ripken Jr./305 40.00
George Brett/320 30.00
Johnny Bench/175 20.00
Reggie Jackson/155 20.00
Don Mattingly/340 40.00
Willie McCovey/155 15.00
Jose Canseco/175 25.00
Kirby Puckett/251 30.00
Orlando Cepeda/165 15.00
Eddie Mathews/185 40.00
Pee Wee Reese/165 30.00
Andre Dawson/310 15.00

Greats of the Game Sweet Swatch Jersey

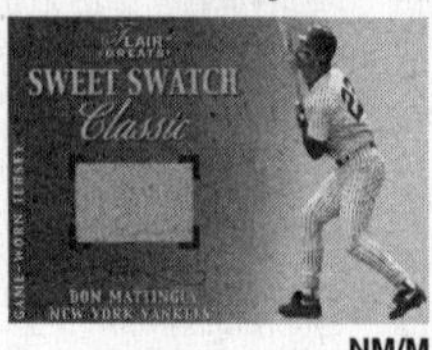

NM/M
Common Player: 15.00
Jerry Coleman/528 20.00
Ryne Sandberg/374 25.00
Johnny Bench/410 20.00
Paul Molitor/592 15.00
Cal Ripken Jr./557 45.00
Gil Hodges/545 20.00
Carlton Fisk/1,200 15.00
Nolan Ryan/590 40.00
Tom Seaver/385 20.00
Don Mattingly/880 35.00
Jose Canseco/1,329 15.00
George Brett/384 30.00
Jim Palmer/335 15.00
Kirby Puckett/445 20.00
Juan Marichal/385 15.00
Robin Yount/340 25.00
Andre Dawson/335 15.00

Greats of the Game Sweet Swatch Jersey Autograph

NM/M
Common Autograph:
Cal Ripken Jr/40 240.00
Johnny Bench/40 130.00
Alan Trammell/40 75.00

Poland Springs Yankees Greats

The "Official Bottled Water of the N.Y. Yankees" sponsored this stadium giveaway card set. The first 18,000 youngsters through the gates at the May 14 game received five-card cello packs which included four player cards and a sponsor's card. The player cards are virtually identical to the regular-issue versions except for the addition on a Poland Springs logo on front and, in the case of Berra, a card number change on back.

NM/M
Complete Set (5): 6.00
Common Player: 1.50
8 Yogi Berra 2.00
10 Phil Rizzuto 1.50
16 Whitey Ford 2.00
44 Reggie Jackson 2.00
--- Sponsor's Card .10

2006 Flair Showcase

NM/M
Complete Set (200):
Common Player (1-100): .50
Common Player (101-150): 1.50
Inserted 1:4 Hobby
Common Player (151-200): 2.00

Inserted 1:8 Hobby
Pack (5): 5.00
Box (18): 80.00
1 Jeremy Hermida **(RC)** .50
2 Albert Pujols 3.00
3 Ryan Shealy **(RC)** .50
4 Mark Prior .75
5 Chuck James **(RC)** 1.00
6 Shawn Green .50
7 Rickie Weeks .50
8 Roy Halladay .75
9 Luis Gonzalez .50
10 David Ortiz 1.50
11 Josh Beckett .50
12 Gary Sheffield .75
13 Jose Reyes .75
14 Brandon Watson **(RC)** .50
15 Tadahito Iguchi .50
16 Rich Harden .50
17 Skip Schumaker **(RC)** .50
18 Vladimir Guerrero 1.00
19 Chris Carpenter .75
20 Brian Roberts .50
21 Roy Oswalt .50
22 Ben Johnson **(RC)** .50
23 Todd Helton .75
24 Wilbert Nieves **(RC)** .50
25 Michael Young .50
26 A.J. Burnett .50
27 J.D. Drew .50
28 Adrian Beltre .50
29 Tim Hudson .50
30 Jake Peavy .50
31 Magglio Ordonez .50
32 Brad Wilkerson .50
33 Ryan Freel .50
34 Javier Vazquez .50
35 Tom Glavine .50
36 Jason Bergmann **RC** 1.00
37 Marcus Giles .50
38 Jim Thome 1.00
39 Ichiro Suzuki 2.00
40 Jeff Harris **RC** .75
41 Miguel Cabrera 1.00
42 Nomar Garciaparra 1.00
43 Brian Giles .50
44 Jeremy Accardo **RC** 1.00
45 Taylor Buchholz **(RC)** .50
46 Mike Jacobs .50
47 Chris Denorfia **(RC)** .50
48 Ivan Rodriguez .75
49 Mike Piazza 1.50
50 Curt Schilling 1.00
51 Kelly Stoppach **(RC)** .50
52 Jason Kubel **(RC)** .50
53 Craig Biggio .50
54 Livan Hernandez .50
55 Joe Mauer .75
56 Scott Feldman **RC** 1.00
57 Garret Anderson .50
58 Steve Stemle **RC** 1.00
59 Boof Bonser **(RC)** .50
60 Jose Guillen .50
61 Rafael Furcal .50
62 John Van Benschoten **(RC)** .50
63 Dontrelle Willis .75
64 Jose Vidro .50
65 David Wright 2.00
66 Alfonso Soriano 1.00
67 Scott Podsednik .50
68 Felix Hernandez .75
69 Richie Sexson .75
70 Jeff Francoeur .50
71 Conor Jackson .50
72 Javy Lopez .50
73 Jonathan Papelbon **(RC)** 6.00
74 Frank Thomas .75
75 Greg Maddux 2.00
76 Josh Rupe **(RC)** .50
77 Eric Chavez .50
78 Ben Sheets .50
79 Chase Utley .75
80 Derrek Lee .75
81 Manny Ramirez 1.00
82 Pedro Martinez 1.00
83 Hideki Matsui 2.00
84 Jeremy Bonderman .50
85 Ronny Cedeno .50
86 Trevor Hoffman .50
87 Mark Buehrle .50
88 Jason Bay .75
89 Reggie Sanders .50
90 Brian Anderson **(RC)** .50
91 Travis Hafner .75
92 Carlos Beltran .75
93 Cody Ross **(RC)** .50
94 Melvin Mora .50
95 Chris Duffy .50
96 Vernon Wells .50
97 Bartolo Colon .50
98 Aubrey Huff .50
99 Paul Konerko .50
100 Cesar Izturis .50
101 Josh Willingham **(RC)** 1.50
102 Matt Cain **(RC)** 2.00
103 Macay McBride **(RC)** 1.50
104 Jeff Mathis 1.50
105 Alex Rodriguez 8.00
106 Justin Morneau 2.00
107 Felipe Lopez 1.50
108 Justin Verlander **(RC)** 8.00
109 Ryan Howard 5.00
110 Mike Sweeney 1.50
111 Scott Rolen 3.00
112 Hank Blalock 1.50
113 Kerry Wood 1.50
114 B.J. Ryan 1.50
115 Garrett Atkins 1.50
116 Carlos Delgado 2.50
117 Zack Greinke 1.50
118 Chad Cordero 1.50
119 Julio Lugo 1.50
120 Bobby Crosby 1.50
121 Barry Zito 2.00
122 Jhonny Peralta 1.50
123 Miguel Tejada 2.50
124 Grady Sizemore 2.00
125 Derek Jeter 10.00
126 Cliff Lee 1.50
127 Khalil Greene 1.50
128 Lance Berkman 2.00
129 Huston Street 1.50
130 Jermaine Dye 2.00
131 Chone Figgins 1.50
132 Torii Hunter 2.00
133 Jorge Cantu 1.50
134 Jason Giambi 3.00
135 Johan Santana 3.00
136 Chad Tracy 1.50
137 Troy Glaus 2.00
138 Moises Alou 2.00
139 Jason Schmidt 2.00
140 Ken Griffey Jr. 8.00
141 Jason Varitek 3.00
142 John Smoltz 2.50
143 Andy Pettitte 2.00
144 Jeff Kent 2.00
145 Coco Crisp 2.00
146 Jonny Gomes 1.50
147 Aaron Rowand 1.50
148 Mike Mussina 2.50
149 Johnny Damon 4.00
150 Edgar Renteria 1.50
151 Scott Kazmir 2.00
152 Lyle Overbay 2.00
153 Placido Polanco 2.00
154 Mariano Rivera 3.00
155 Hanley Ramirez **(RC)** 3.00
156 Morgan Ensberg 2.00
157 Kenny Rogers 2.00
158 Brad Lidge 2.00
159 A.J. Pierzynski 2.00
160 Aramis Ramirez 3.00
161 Mark Teixeira 3.00
162 Carl Crawford 3.00
163 Ryan Zimmerman **(RC)** 10.00
164 Adam Dunn 3.00
165 Joe Nathan 2.00
166 Juan Pierre 2.00
167 Pat Burrell 3.00
168 Carlos Lee 3.00
169 Billy Wagner 2.00
170 Prince Fielder **(RC)** 10.00
171 Randy Johnson 4.00
172 Andruw Jones 4.00
173 Francisco Rodriguez 2.00
174 Robinson Cano 3.00
175 Matt Holliday 2.00
176 Jim Edmonds 3.00
177 Josh Barfield **(RC)** 2.00
178 Chipper Jones 4.00
179 Bobby Jenks 2.00
180 Carlos Zambrano 3.00
181 Bobby Abreu 3.00
182 Brandon Webb 2.00
183 Kevin Millwood 2.00
184 Zachary Duke 2.00
185 Randy Winn 2.00
186 Eric Gagne 2.00
187 Kenji Johjima **RC** 10.00
188 John Patterson 2.00
189 Mark Loretta 2.00
190 Anderson Hernandez **(RC)** 2.00
191 Chris Resop **(RC)** 2.00
192 Ian Kinsler **(RC)** 2.00
193 Francisco Liriano **(RC)** 8.00
194 Noah Lowry 2.00
195 Brett Myers 2.00
196 Rocco Baldelli 2.00
197 Cliff Floyd 2.00
198 Sean Casey 2.00
199 Geoff Jenkins 2.00
200 Clint Barmes 2.00

Showcase Printing Plates

No Pricing
Production one set per color.

Showcase Legacy Blue

Blue (1-100):	2-4X
Blue (101-150):	1-1.5X
Blue (151-200):	1X

Production 150 Sets

Showcase Legacy Emerald

Emerald (1-100):	2-4X
Emerald (101-150):	1-1.5X
Emerald (151-200):	1X

Production 150 Sets

Showcase Autographics

		NM/M
Common Autograph:		8.00
BA	Bronson Arroyo	20.00
JB	Jason Bay	20.00
HB	Hank Blalock	10.00
BO	Jeremy Bonderman	20.00
SC	Sean Casey/SP	15.00
GC	Gustavo Chacin	10.00
BC	Brandon Claussen	10.00
CH	Chad Cordero	8.00
CO	Craig Counsell	10.00
CA	Carl Crawford	15.00
CC	Coco Crisp	25.00
KG	Ken Griffey Jr./SP	75.00
JG	Jose Guillen	8.00
TH	Travis Hafner/SP	15.00
AH	Aaron Harang	15.00
LH	Livan Hernandez	8.00
CI	Cesar Izturis	8.00
MK	Mark Kotsay	8.00
CL	Cliff Lee	8.00
JM	Justin Morneau	20.00
XN	Xavier Nady	10.00
RO	Roy Oswalt/SP	20.00
WP	Wily Mo Pena	15.00
JH	Jhonny Peralta	10.00
JP	Joel Pineiro	10.00
RA	Aramis Ramirez	15.00
AR	Aaron Rowand	15.00
CU	Chase Utley/SP/100	25.00
JV	Javier Vazquez/SP	8.00
OV	Omar Vizquel	30.00
RZ	Ryan Zimmerman	50.00

Showcase Fresh Ink

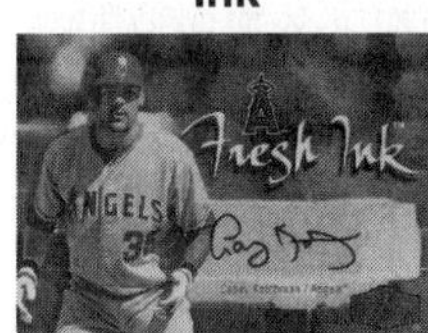

		NM/M
Common Auto.:		10.00
GA	Garrett Atkins	10.00
CB	Clint Barmes/SP	10.00
JB	Joe Blanton	15.00
MC	Miguel Cabrera/SP	25.00
MA	Matt Cain/SP	25.00
BC	Bobby Crosby	10.00
DD	David DeJesus	15.00
GF	Gavin Floyd	10.00
JG	Jonny Gomes	15.00
KG	Khalil Greene/SP	25.00
ZG	Zack Greinke	10.00
HA	Rich Harden	15.00
DH	Danny Haren	10.00
RH	Rich Hill	30.00
TI	Tadahito Iguchi	40.00
SK	Scott Kazmir	15.00
CK	Casey Kotchman	10.00
NL	Noah Lowry	20.00
VM	Victor Martinez	15.00
BM	Brandon McCarthy	10.00
OP	Odalis Perez	10.00
RE	Jeremy Reed	10.00
BR	Brian Roberts	15.00
ES	Ervin Santana	15.00
JS	Johan Santana/SP	50.00
CS	Chris Shelton	15.00
HS	Huston Street	15.00
MT	Mark Teahen	10.00
DW	Dontrelle Willis	15.00
WR	David Wright/ SP/100	60.00
KY	Kevin Youkilis	15.00
MY	Michael Young/ SP/100	20.00

Showcase Hot Gloves

		NM/M
Common Player:		10.00
Inserted 1:108 Hobby		
1	Derrek Lee	15.00
2	Andruw Jones	15.00
3	Bobby Abreu	10.00
4	Luis Castillo	10.00
5	Mike Matheny	10.00
6	Cesar Izturis	10.00
7	Craig Biggio	15.00
8	Darin Erstad	10.00
9	Derek Jeter	40.00
10	Eric Chavez	10.00
11	Greg Maddux	40.00
12	Ichiro Suzuki	35.00
13	Ivan Rodriguez	15.00
14	J.T. Snow	10.00
15	Jim Edmonds	15.00
16	Steve Finley	10.00
17	Kenny Rogers	10.00
18	Jason Varitek	20.00
19	Ken Griffey Jr.	40.00
20	Mark Teixeira	15.00
21	Orlando Hudson	10.00
22	Mike Hampton	10.00
23	Mike Mussina	15.00
24	Vernon Wells	10.00
25	Omar Vizquel	15.00
26	Alex Rodriguez	40.00
27	Mike Cameron	15.00
28	Scott Rolen	25.00
29	Todd Helton	15.00
30	Torii Hunter	15.00

Showcase Hot Numbers

		NM/M
Common Player:		1.50
Inserted 1:6 Hobby		
1	Albert Pujols	8.00
2	Alex Rodriguez	8.00
3	Andruw Jones	3.00
4	Bobby Abreu	1.50
5	Chipper Jones	3.00
6	Curt Schilling	3.00
7	David Ortiz	3.00
8	David Wright	5.00
9	Derek Jeter	8.00
10	Derrek Lee	3.00
11	Eric Gagne	1.50
12	Greg Maddux	5.00
13	Hideki Matsui	5.00
14	Ichiro Suzuki	5.00
15	Ivan Rodriguez	2.00
16	Johan Santana	2.00
17	Johnny Damon	3.00
18	Ken Griffey Jr.	5.00
19	Manny Ramirez	3.00
20	Mark Prior	2.00
21	Mark Teixeira	2.00
22	Miguel Cabrera	3.00
23	Miguel Tejada	2.00
24	Pedro Martinez	3.00
25	Randy Johnson	3.00
26	Rickie Weeks	1.50
27	Roger Clemens	6.00
28	Todd Helton	2.00
29	Torii Hunter	1.50
30	Vladimir Guerrero	3.00

Showcase Lettermen

No Pricing
Production 3-9

Showcase Showcase Signatures

		NM/M
Production 35 Sets		
JE	Jeremy Bonderman	30.00
SC	Sean Casey	20.00
CD	Chad Cordero	10.00
JG	Jose Guillen	10.00
AH	Aaron Harang	20.00
HA	Rich Harden	30.00
CI	Cesar Izturis	10.00
XN	Xavier Nady	20.00
RO	Roy Oswalt	20.00
WM	Wily Mo Pena	20.00
PE	Jhonny Peralta	15.00
BR	Brian Roberts	30.00
CS	Chris Shelton	20.00
KY	Kevin Youkilis	20.00
RZ	Ryan Zimmerman	65.00

Showcase Stitches

		NM/M
Common Player:		4.00
Inserted 1:9		
BA	Bobby Abreu	4.00
MA	Moises Alou	6.00
RB	Rocco Baldelli	6.00
JO	Josh Beckett	6.00
CB	Carlos Beltran	8.00
AB	Adrian Beltre	4.00
LB	Lance Berkman	4.00
HB	Hank Blalock	6.00
BO	Jeremy Bonderman	6.00
MB	Mark Buehrle	4.00
MC	Miguel Cabrera	10.00
RC	Robinson Cano	12.00
JC	Jorge Cantu	6.00
EC	Eric Chavez	6.00
CO	Michael Collins	4.00
CA	Carl Crawford	4.00
BC	Bobby Crosby	4.00
JD	Johnny Damon	10.00
CD	Carlos Delgado	6.00
DR	J.D. Drew	6.00
AD	Adam Dunn	6.00
JE	Jim Edmonds	6.00
RF	Rafael Furcal	6.00
EG	Eric Gagne	6.00
FG	Freddy Garcia	4.00
JG	Jason Giambi	8.00
BG	Brian Giles	4.00
TG	Tom Glavine	8.00
LG	Luis Gonzalez	4.00
GR	Khalil Greene	4.00
KG	Ken Griffey Jr.	10.00
VG	Vladimir Guerrero	8.00
TR	Travis Hafner	8.00
RH	Roy Halladay	6.00
RI	Rich Harden	6.00
HA	J.J. Hardy	4.00
TH	Todd Helton	8.00
HO	Trevor Hoffman	4.00
MH	Matt Holliday	8.00
HU	Tim Hudson	6.00
TO	Torii Hunter	6.00
DJ	Derek Jeter	20.00
RJ	Randy Johnson	8.00
AJ	Andruw Jones	6.00
CJ	Chipper Jones	8.00
JJ	Jacque Jones	4.00
SK	Scott Kazmir	6.00
JK	Jeff Kent	6.00
CL	Carlos Lee	4.00
DL	Derrek Lee	8.00
PL	Paul LoDuca	6.00
JL	Javy Lopez	4.00
GM	Greg Maddux	10.00
PM	Pedro Martinez	10.00
KM	Kazuo Matsui	6.00
DM	Daisuke Matsuzaka	125.00
JM	Joe Mauer	8.00
KE	Kevin Millwood	4.00
MM	Mike Mussina	8.00
TN	Trot Nixon	8.00
DO	David Ortiz	10.00
JP	Jake Peavy	6.00
AN	Andy Pettitte	6.00
MI	Mike Piazza	10.00
MP	Mark Prior	6.00
AP	Albert Pujols	20.00
AR	Aramis Ramirez	6.00
MR	Manny Ramirez	8.00
RE	Jeremy Reed	4.00
JR	Jose Reyes	10.00
BR	Brian Roberts	4.00
FR	Francisco Rodriguez	4.00
IR	Ivan Rodriguez	8.00
SR	Scott Rolen	8.00
CC	C.C. Sabathia	4.00
JS	Johan Santana	8.00
CS	Curt Schilling	8.00
JA	Jason Schmidt	6.00
RS	Richie Sexson	6.00
BS	Ben Sheets	4.00
GS	Gary Sheffield	6.00
SM	John Smoltz	8.00
AS	Alfonso Soriano	8.00
SW	Mike Sweeney	4.00
MT	Mark Teixeira	8.00
TE	Miguel Tejada	8.00
FT	Frank Thomas	10.00
JT	Jim Thome	8.00
JU	Juan Uribe	4.00
JV	Jason Varitek	10.00
OV	Omar Vizquel	6.00
RW	Rickie Weeks	6.00
VW	Vernon Wells	6.00
DW	Dontrelle Willis	6.00
PW	Preston Wilson	4.00
KW	Kerry Wood	6.00
WR	David Wright	15.00
MY	Michael Young	6.00
BZ	Barry Zito	4.00

Showcase Wave of the Future

		NM/M
Common Player:		1.00
Inserted 1:2		
WF-1	Jeremy Hermida	1.00
WF-2	Kelly Stoppach	1.00
WF-3	Adam Wainwright	1.00
WF-4	Ryan Zimmerman	4.00
WF-5	Josh Willingham	1.00
WF-6	Brandon McCarthy	1.00
WF-7	Conor Jackson	1.00
WF-8	Grady Sizemore	1.50
WF-9	Curtis Granderson	1.00
WF-10	Jose Capellan	1.00
WF-11	Mike Jacobs	1.00
WF-12	Gavin Floyd	1.00
WF-13	Hanley Ramirez	1.50
WF-14	Jason Kubel	1.00
WF-15	Nate McLouth	1.00
WF-16	Felix Hernandez	1.50
WF-17	Jeff Francoeur	1.00
WF-18	Wilbert Nieves	1.00
WF-19	Cody Ross	1.00
WF-20	Justin Verlander	5.00
WF-21	Ben Johnson	1.00
WF-22	Guillermo Quiroz	1.00
WF-23	Jonathan Papelbon	4.00
WF-24	Prince Fielder	4.00
WF-25	Rickie Weeks	1.50
WF-26	Robinson Cano	2.00
WF-27	Kenji Johjima	4.00
WF-28	Anderson Hernandez	1.00
WF-29	Yuniesky Betancourt	1.00
WF-30	Zachary Duke	1.00

Showcase WBC Classic Moments

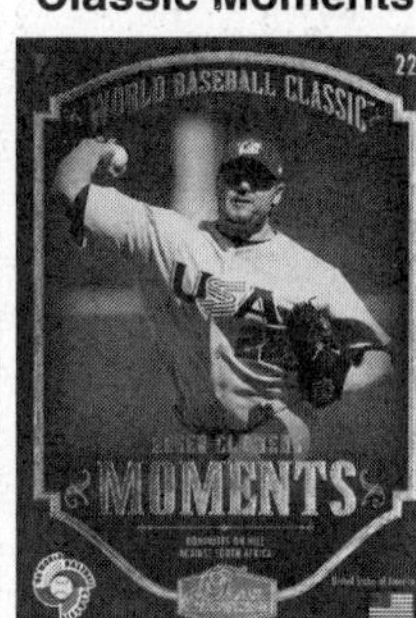

		NM/M
Common Player:		1.50
Inserted 1:8		
CM-1	Adam Stern	1.50
CM-2	Jason Bay	2.00
CM-3	Wei Wang	1.50
CM-4	Yung-Chi Chen	3.00
CM-5	Pedro Luis Lazo	2.00
CM-6	Yoandy Garlobo	1.50
CM-7	Ormari Romero	1.50
CM-8	Frederich Cepeda	1.50
CM-9	Yulieski Gourriel	1.50
CM-10	Yadel Marti	1.50
CM-11	David Ortiz	2.50
CM-12	Albert Pujols	5.00
CM-13	Adrian Beltre	1.50
CM-14	Alberto Castillo	1.50
CM-15	Odalis Perez	1.50
CM-16	Jason Grilli	1.50
CM-17	Daisuke Matsuzaka	5.00
CM-18	Sadaharu Oh	10.00
CM-19	Nobuhiko Matsunaka	3.00
CM-20	Ichiro Suzuki	5.00
CM-21	Akinori Otsuka	3.00
CM-22	Koji Uehara	3.00
CM-23	Kosuke Fukudome	3.00
CM-24	Daisuke Matsuzaka	5.00
CM-25	Ichiro Suzuki	5.00
CM-26	Seung-Yeop Lee	2.00
CM-27	Seung-Yeop Lee	2.00
CM-28	Jong Beom Lee	1.50
CM-29	Jae Weong Seo	1.50
CM-30	Chan Ho Park	1.50
CM-31	Hee Seop Choi	1.50
CM-32	Jorge Cantu	1.50
CM-33	Oliver Perez	1.50
CM-34	Vinny Castilla	1.50
CM-35	Esteban Loaiza	1.50
CM-36	Shairon Martis	1.50
CM-37	Bernie Williams	2.00
CM-38	Javier Vazquez	1.50
CM-39	Carlos Beltran	2.00
CM-40	Bernie Williams	2.00
CM-41	Roger Clemens	5.00
CM-42	Ken Griffey Jr.	5.00
CM-43	Alex Rodriguez	5.00
CM-44	Derrek Lee	2.00
CM-45	Derek Jeter	5.00
CM-46	Chipper Jones	2.00
CM-47	Miguel Cabrera	2.00
CM-48	Francisco Rodriguez	1.50
CM-49	Victor Martinez	1.50
CM-50	Freddy Garcia	1.50

1981 Fleer

For the first time in 18 years, Fleer issued a baseball card set featuring current players. The 660-card effort included numerous errors in the first print run which were subsequently corrected. The 2-1/2" x 3-1/2" cards are numbered by team in order of the previous season's finish. Card fronts feature a full-color photo inside a border which is color-coded by team. Backs are printed in black, gray and yellow on white stock and carry full player statistical information. The player's batting average or earned run average is located in a circle in the upper-right corner of the back. The complete set price in the checklist that follows does not include the higher priced variations.

		NM/M
Complete Set (660):		30.00
Common Player:		.05
Wax Pack (17):		1.75
Wax Box (38):		50.00
Vending Box (500):		20.00
1	Pete Rose	3.00
2	Larry Bowa	.05
3	Manny Trillo	.05
4	Bob Boone	.05
5a	Mike Schmidt/Portrait	2.50
5b	Mike Schmidt/Btg	2.00
6a	Steve Carlton ("Lefty" on front.)	1.00
6b	Steve Carlton (Pitcher of the Year on front, date 1066 on back.)	2.00
6c	Steve Carlton (Pitcher of the Year on front, date 1966 on back.)	2.50
7a	Tug McGraw (Game Saver on front.)	.50
7b	Tug McGraw (Pitcher on front.)	.05
8	Larry Christenson	.05
9	Bake McBride	.05
10	Greg Luzinski	.05
11	Ron Reed	.05
12	Dickie Noles	.05
13	Keith Moreland **RC**	.15
14	Bob Walk **RC**	.05
15	Lonnie Smith	.05
16	Dick Ruthven	.05
17	Sparky Lyle	.05
18	Greg Gross	.05
19	Garry Maddox	.05
20	Nino Espinosa	.05
21	George Vukovich	.05
22	John Vukovich	.05
23	Ramon Aviles	.05
24a	Kevin Saucier (Ken Saucier on back.)	.10
24b	Kevin Saucier (Kevin Saucier on back.)	.50
25	Randy Lerch	.05
26	Del Unser	.05
27	Tim McCarver	.15
28a	George Brett/Btg	2.00
28b	George Brett/Portrait	2.00
29a	Willie Wilson/Portrait	.50
29b	Willie Wilson/Btg	.15
30	Paul Splittorff	.05
31	Dan Quisenberry	.05
32a	Amos Otis/Btg	.50
32b	Amos Otis/Portrait	.10
33	Steve Busby	.05
34	U.L. Washington	.05
35	Dave Chalk	.05
36	Darrell Porter	.05
37	Marty Pattin	.05
38	Larry Gura	.05
39	Renie Martin	.05
40	Rich Gale	.05
41a	Hal McRae (Dark blue "Royals" on front.)	.40
41b	Hal McRae (Light blue "Royals" on front.)	.10
42	Dennis Leonard	.05
43	Willie Aikens	.05
44	Frank White	.05
45	Clint Hurdle	.05
46	John Wathan	.05
47	Pete LaCock	.05
48	Rance Mulliniks	.05
49	Jeff Twitty	.05
50	Jamie Quirk	.05
51	Art Howe	.05
52	Ken Forsch	.05
53	Vern Ruhle	.05
54	Joe Niekro	.05
55	Frank LaCorte	.05
56	J.R. Richard	.05
57	Nolan Ryan	4.00
58	Enos Cabell	.05
59	Cesar Cedeno	.05
60	Jose Cruz	.05
61	Bill Virdon	.05
62	Terry Puhl	.05
63	Joaquin Andujar	.05
64	Alan Ashby	.05
65	Joe Sambito	.05
66	Denny Walling	.05
67	Jeff Leonard	.05
68	Luis Pujols	.05
69	Bruce Bochy	.05
70	Rafael Landestoy	.05
71	Dave Smith **RC**	.05
72	Danny Heep **RC**	.05
73	Julio Gonzalez	.05
74	Craig Reynolds	.05
75	Gary Woods	.05
76	Dave Bergman	.05
77	Randy Niemann	.05
78	Joe Morgan	1.00
79a	Reggie Jackson/ Portrait	2.50
79b	Reggie Jackson/Btg	2.00
80	Bucky Dent	.10
81	Tommy John	.10
82	Luis Tiant	.05
83	Rick Cerone	.05
84	Dick Howser	.05
85	Lou Piniella	.10
86	Ron Davis	.05
87a	Graig Nettles (Craig on back.)	4.50
87b	Graig Nettles (Graig on back.)	.15
88	Ron Guidry	.10
89	Rich Gossage	.10
90	Rudy May	.05
91	Gaylord Perry	.75
92	Eric Soderholm	.05
93	Bob Watson	.05
94	Bobby Murcer	.10
95	Bobby Brown	.05
96	Jim Spencer	.05
97	Tom Underwood	.05
98	Oscar Gamble	.05
99	Johnny Oates	.05
100	Fred Stanley	.05
101	Ruppert Jones	.05
102	Dennis Werth	.05
103	Joe Lefebvre	.05
104	Brian Doyle	.05
105	Aurelio Rodriguez	.05
106	Doug Bird	.05
107	Mike Griffin	.05
108	Tim Lollar	.05
109	Willie Randolph	.05
110	Steve Garvey	.30
111	Reggie Smith	.05
112	Don Sutton	.75
113	Burt Hooton	.05
114a	Davy Lopes (Davey) (No finger on back.)	.05
114b	Davy Lopes (Davey) (Small finger on back.)	.50
115	Dusty Baker	.05
116	Tom Lasorda	.10
117	Bill Russell	.05
118	Jerry Reuss	.05
119	Terry Forster	.05

120a Bob Welch (Bob on back.) .10
120b Bob Welch (Robert) .50
121 Don Stanhouse .05
122 Rick Monday .05
123 Derrel Thomas .05
124 Joe Ferguson .05
125 Rick Sutcliffe .10
126a Ron Cey (No finger on back.) .05
126b Ron Cey (Small finger on back.) .50
127 Dave Goltz .05
128 Jay Johnstone .05
129 Steve Yeager .05
130 Gary Weiss .05
131 Mike Scioscia **RC** .50
132 Vic Davalillo .05
133 Doug Rau .05
134 Pepe Frias .05
135 Mickey Hatcher .05
136 Steve Howe **RC** .10
137 Robert Castillo .05
138 Gary Thomasson .05
139 Rudy Law .05
140 Fernando Valenzuela **RC** 1.50
141 Manny Mota .05
142 Gary Carter 1.00
143 Steve Rogers .05
144 Warren Cromartie .05
145 Andre Dawson .40
146 Larry Parrish .05
147 Rowland Office .05
148 Ellis Valentine .05
149 Dick Williams .05
150 Bill Gullickson **RC** .15
151 Elias Sosa .05
152 John Tamargo .05
153 Chris Speier .05
154 Ron LeFlore .05
155 Rodney Scott .05
156 Stan Bahnsen .05
157 Bill Lee .05
158 Fred Norman .05
159 Woodie Fryman .05
160 Dave Palmer .05
161 Jerry White .05
162 Roberto Ramos .05
163 John D'Acquisto .05
164 Tommy Hutton .05
165 Charlie Lea **RC** .15
166 Scott Sanderson .05
167 Ken Macha .05
168 Tony Bernazard .05
169 Jim Palmer 1.00
170 Steve Stone .10
171 Mike Flanagan .05
172 Al Bumbry .05
173 Doug DeCinces .05
174 Scott McGregor .05
175 Mark Belanger .05
176 Tim Stoddard .05
177a Rick Dempsey (No finger on front.) .05
177b Rick Dempsey (Small finger on front.) .50
178 Earl Weaver .25
179 Tippy Martinez .05
180 Dennis Martinez .05
181 Sammy Stewart .05
182 Rich Dauer .05
183 Lee May .05
184 Eddie Murray 1.00
185 Benny Ayala .05
186 John Lowenstein .05
187 Gary Roenicke .05
188 Ken Singleton .05
189 Dan Graham .05
190 Terry Crowley .05
191 Kiko Garcia .05
192 Dave Ford .05
193 Mark Corey .05
194 Lenn Sakata .05
195 Doug DeCinces .05
196 Johnny Bench 1.00
197 Dave Concepcion .05
198 Ray Knight .05
199 Ken Griffey .10
200 Tom Seaver 1.00
201 Dave Collins .05
202 George Foster .05
203 Junior Kennedy .05
204 Frank Pastore .05
205 Dan Driessen .05
206 Hector Cruz .05
207 Paul Moskau .05
208 Charlie Leibrandt **RC** .25
209 Harry Spilman .05
210 Joe Price **RC** .05
211 Tom Hume .05
212 Joe Nolan .05
213 Doug Bair .05
214 Mario Soto .05
215a Bill Bonham (No finger on back.) .05
215b Bill Bonham (Small finger on back.) .50
216a George Foster (Slugger on front.) .25
216b George Foster (Outfield on front.) .15
217 Paul Householder .05
218 Ron Oester .05
219 Sam Mejias .05
220 Sheldon Burnside .05
221 Carl Yastrzemski 1.00
222 Jim Rice .40
223 Fred Lynn .05
224 Carlton Fisk 1.00
225 Rick Burleson .05
226 Dennis Eckersley .75
227 Butch Hobson .05
228 Tom Burgmeier .05
229 Garry Hancock .05
230 Don Zimmer .05
231 Steve Renko .05
232 Dwight Evans .05
233 Mike Torrez .05
234 Bob Stanley .05
235 Jim Dwyer .05
236 Dave Stapleton .05
237 Glenn Hoffman .05
238 Jerry Remy .05
239 Dick Drago .05
240 Bill Campbell .05
241 Tony Perez .75
242 Phil Niekro .75
243 Dale Murphy .30
244 Bob Horner .05
245 Jeff Burroughs .05
246 Rick Camp .05
247 Bob Cox .25
248 Bruce Benedict .05
249 Gene Garber .05
250 Jerry Royster .05
251a Gary Matthews (No finger on back.) .05
251b Gary Matthews (Small finger on back.) .50
252 Chris Chambliss .05
253 Luis Gomez .05
254 Bill Nahorodny .05
255 Doyle Alexander .05
256 Brian Asselstine .05
257 Biff Pocoroba .05
258 Mike Lum .05
259 Charlie Spikes .05
260 Glenn Hubbard .05
261 Tommy Boggs .05
262 Al Hrabosky .05
263 Rick Matula .05
264 Preston Hanna .05
265 Larry Bradford .05
266 Rafael Ramirez **RC** .05
267 Larry McWilliams .05
268 Rod Carew 1.00
269 Bobby Grich .05
270 Carney Lansford .05
271 Don Baylor .05
272 Joe Rudi .05
273 Dan Ford .05
274 Jim Fregosi .05
275 Dave Frost .05
276 Frank Tanana .05
277 Dickie Thon .05
278 Jason Thompson .05
279 Rick Miller .05
280 Bert Campaneris .05
281 Tom Donohue .05
282 Brian Downing .05
283 Fred Patek .05
284 Bruce Kison .05
285 Dave LaRoche .05
286 Don Aase .05
287 Jim Barr .05
288 Alfredo Martinez .05
289 Larry Harlow .05
290 Andy Hassler .05
291 Dave Kingman .05
292 Bill Buckner .05
293 Rick Reuschel .05
294 Bruce Sutter .75
295 Jerry Martin .05
296 Scot Thompson .05
297 Ivan DeJesus .05
298 Steve Dillard .05
299 Dick Tidrow .05
300 Randy Martz .05
301 Lenny Randle .05
302 Lynn McGlothen .05
303 Cliff Johnson .05
304 Tim Blackwell .05
305 Dennis Lamp .05
306 Bill Caudill .05
307 Carlos Lezcano .05
308 Jim Tracy .05
309 Doug Capilla .05
310 Willie Hernandez .05
311 Mike Vail .05
312 Mike Krukow .05
313 Barry Foote .05
314 Larry Biittner .05
315 Mike Tyson .05
316 Lee Mazzilli .05
317 John Stearns .05
318 Alex Trevino .05
319 Craig Swan .05
320 Frank Taveras .05
321 Steve Henderson .05
322 Neil Allen .05
323 Mark Bomback .05
324 Mike Jorgensen .05
325 Joe Torre .25
326 Elliott Maddox .05
327 Pete Falcone .05
328 Ray Burris .05
329 Claudell Washington .05
330 Doug Flynn .05
331 Joel Youngblood .05
332 Bill Almon .05
333 Tom Hausman .05
334 Pat Zachry .05
335 Jeff Reardon **RC** 2.00
336 Wally Backman **RC** .15
337 Dan Norman .05
338 Jerry Morales .05
339 Ed Farmer .05
340 Bob Molinaro .05
341 Todd Cruz .05
342a Britt Burns **RC** (No finger on front.) .10
342b Britt Burns **RC** (Small finger on front.) .50
343 Kevin Bell .05
344 Tony LaRussa .25
345 Steve Trout .05
346 Harold Baines **RC** 3.00
347 Richard Wortham .05
348 Wayne Nordhagen .05
349 Mike Squires .05
350 Lamar Johnson .05
351 Rickey Henderson 2.50
352 Francisco Barrios .05
353 Thad Bosley .05
354 Chet Lemon .05
355 Bruce Kimm .05
356 Richard Dotson **RC** .05
357 Jim Morrison .05
358 Mike Proly .05
359 Greg Pryor .05
360 Dave Parker .05
361 Omar Moreno .05
362a Kent Tekulve (1071 Waterbury on back) .15
362b Kent Tekulve (1971 Waterbury on back) .50
363 Willie Stargell 1.00
364 Phil Garner .05
365 Ed Ott .05
366 Don Robinson .05
367 Chuck Tanner .05
368 Jim Rooker .05
369 Dale Berra .05
370 Jim Bibby .05
371 Steve Nicosia .05
372 Mike Easler .05
373 Bill Robinson .05
374 Lee Lacy .05
375 John Candelaria .05
376 Manny Sanguillen .05
377 Rick Rhoden .05
378 Grant Jackson .05
379 Tim Foli .05
380 Rod Scurry **RC** .05
381 Bill Madlock .05
382a Kurt Bevacqua (Photo reversed, backwards "P" on cap.) .15
382b Kurt Bevacqua (Correct photo.) .50
383 Bert Blyleven .10
384 Eddie Solomon .05
385 Enrique Romo .05
386 John Milner .05
387 Mike Hargrove .05
388 Jorge Orta .05
389 Toby Harrah .05
390 Tom Veryzer .05
391 Miguel Dilone .05
392 Dan Spillner .05
393 Jack Brohamer .05
394 Wayne Garland .05
395 Sid Monge .05
396 Rick Waits .05
397 Joe Charboneau **RC** .50
398 Gary Alexander .05
399 Jerry Dybzinski .05
400 Mike Stanton .05
401 Mike Paxton .05
402 Gary Gray .05
403 Rick Manning .05
404 Bo Diaz .05
405 Ron Hassey .05
406 Ross Grimsley .05
407 Victor Cruz .05
408 Len Barker .05
409 Bob Bailor .05
410 Otto Velez .05
411 Ernie Whitt .05
412 Jim Clancy .05
413 Barry Bonnell .05
414 Dave Stieb .05
415 Damaso Garcia **RC** .10
416 John Mayberry .05
417 Roy Howell .05
418 Dan Ainge **RC** 3.00
419a Jesse Jefferson (Pirates on back.) .10
419b Jesse Jefferson (Blue Jays on back.) .50
420 Joey McLaughlin .05
421 Lloyd Moseby **RC** .10
422 Al Woods .05
423 Garth Iorg .05
424 Doug Ault .05
425 Ken Schrom **RC** .05
426 Mike Willis .05
427 Steve Braun .05
428 Bob Davis .05
429 Jerry Garvin .05
430 Alfredo Griffin .05
431 Bob Mattick .05
432 Vida Blue .05
433 Jack Clark .05
434 Willie McCovey 1.00
435 Mike Ivie .05
436a Darrel Evans (Darrel on front.) .15
436b Darrell Evans (Darrell on front.) .50
437 Terry Whitfield .05
438 Rennie Stennett .05
439 John Montefusco .05
440 Jim Wohlford .05
441 Bill North .05
442 Milt May .05
443 Max Venable .05
444 Ed Whitson .05
445 Al Holland **RC** .05
446 Randy Moffitt .05
447 Bob Knepper .05
448 Gary Lavelle .05
449 Greg Minton .05
450 Johnnie LeMaster .05
451 Larry Herndon .05
452 Rich Murray .05
453 Joe Pettini .05
454 Allen Ripley .05
455 Dennis Littlejohn .05
456 Tom Griffin .05
457 Alan Hargesheimer .05
458 Joe Strain .05
459 Steve Kemp .05
460 Sparky Anderson .25
461 Alan Trammell .05
462 Mark Fidrych .25
463 Lou Whitaker .05
464 Dave Rozema .05
465 Milt Wilcox .05
466 Champ Summers .05
467 Lance Parrish .05
468 Dan Petry .05
469 Pat Underwood .05
470 Rick Peters .05
471 Al Cowens .05
472 John Wockenfuss .05
473 Tom Brookens .05
474 Richie Hebner .05
475 Jack Morris .05
476 Jim Lentine .05
477 Bruce Robbins .05
478 Mark Wagner .05
479 Tim Corcoran .05
480a Stan Papi (Pitcher on front.) .15
480b Stan Papi (Shortstop on front.) .50
481 Kirk Gibson **RC** 5.00
482 Dan Schatzeder .05
483 Amos Otis .05
484 Dave Winfield 1.00
485 Rollie Fingers .75
486 Gene Richards .05
487 Randy Jones .05
488 Ozzie Smith 2.00
489 Gene Tenace .05
490 Bill Fahey .05
491 John Curtis .05
492 Dave Cash .05
493a Tim Flannery (Photo reversed, batting righty.) .15
493b Tim Flannery (Photo correct, batting lefty.) .50
494 Jerry Mumphrey .05
495 Bob Shirley .05
496 Steve Mura .05
497 Eric Rasmussen .05
498 Broderick Perkins .05
499 Barry Evans .05
500 Chuck Baker .05
501 Luis Salazar **RC** .05
502 Gary Lucas .05
503 Mike Armstrong .05
504 Jerry Turner .05
505 Dennis Kinney .05
506 Willy Montanez (Willie) .05
507 Gorman Thomas .05
508 Ben Oglivie .05
509 Larry Hisle .05
510 Sal Bando .05
511 Robin Yount 1.00
512 Mike Caldwell .05
513 Sixto Lezcano .05
514a Jerry Augustine (Billy Travers photo.) .15
514b Billy Travers (Correct name with photo.) .50
515 Paul Molitor 1.00
516 Moose Haas .05
517 Bill Castro .05
518 Jim Slaton .05
519 Lary Sorensen .05
520 Bob McClure .05
521 Charlie Moore .05
522 Jim Gantner .05
523 Reggie Cleveland .05
524 Don Money .05
525 Billy Travers .05
526 Buck Martinez .05
527 Dick Davis .05
528 Ted Simmons .05
529 Garry Templeton .05
530 Ken Reitz .05
531 Tony Scott .05
532 Ken Oberkfell .05
533 Bob Sykes .05
534 Keith Smith .05
535 John Littlefield .05
536 Jim Kaat .05
537 Bob Forsch .05
538 Mike Phillips .05
539 Terry Landrum **RC** .05
540 Leon Durham **RC** .10
541 Terry Kennedy .05
542 George Hendrick .05
543 Dane Iorg .05
544 Mark Littell (Photo actually Jeff Little.) .05
545 Keith Hernandez .05
546 Silvio Martinez .05
547a Pete Vuckovich (Photo actually Don Hood.) .15
547b Don Hood (Correct name with photo.) .50
548 Bobby Bonds .10
549 Mike Ramsey .05
550 Tom Herr .05
551 Roy Smalley .05
552 Jerry Koosman .05
553 Ken Landreaux .05
554 John Castino .05
555 Doug Corbett .05
556 Bombo Rivera .05
557 Ron Jackson .05
558 Butch Wynegar .05
559 Hosken Powell .05
560 Pete Redfern .05
561 Roger Erickson .05
562 Glenn Adams .05
563 Rick Sofield .05
564 Geoff Zahn .05
565 Pete Mackanin .05
566 Mike Cubbage .05
567 Darrell Jackson .05
568 Dave Edwards .05
569 Rob Wilfong .05
570 Sal Butera .05
571 Jose Morales .05
572 Rick Langford .05
573 Mike Norris .05
574 Rickey Henderson 2.50
575 Tony Armas .05
576 Dave Revering .05
577 Jeff Newman .05
578 Bob Lacey .05
579 Brian Kingman (Photo actually Alan Wirth.) .05
580 Mitchell Page .05
581 Billy Martin .25
582 Rob Picciolo .05
583 Mike Heath .05
584 Mickey Klutts .05
585 Orlando Gonzalez .05
586 Mike Davis **RC** .05
587 Wayne Gross .05
588 Matt Keough .05
589 Steve McCatty .05
590 Dwayne Murphy .05
591 Mario Guerrero .05
592 Dave McKay .05
593 Jim Essian .05
594 Dave Heaverlo .05
595 Maury Wills .10
596 Juan Beniquez .05
597 Rodney Craig .05
598 Jim Anderson .05
599 Floyd Bannister .05
600 Bruce Bochte .05
601 Julio Cruz .05
602 Ted Cox .05
603 Dan Meyer .05
604 Larry Cox .05
605 Bill Stein .05
606 Steve Garvey .30
607 Dave Roberts .05
608 Leon Roberts .05
609 Reggie Walton .05
610 Dave Edler .05
611 Larry Milbourne .05
612 Kim Allen .05
613 Mario Mendoza .05
614 Tom Paciorek .05
615 Glenn Abbott .05
616 Joe Simpson .05
617 Mickey Rivers .05
618 Jim Kern .05
619 Jim Sundberg .05
620 Richie Zisk .05
621 Jon Matlack .05
622 Fergie Jenkins .75
623 Pat Corrales .05
624 Ed Figueroa .05
625 Buddy Bell .05
626 Al Oliver .05
627 Doc Medich .05
628 Bump Wills .05
629 Rusty Staub .05
630 Pat Putnam .05
631 John Grubb .05
632 Danny Darwin .05
633 Ken Clay .05
634 Jim Norris .05
635 John Butcher .05
636 Dave Roberts .05
637 Billy Sample .05
638 Carl Yastrzemski 1.00
639 Cecil Cooper .05
640 Mike Schmidt 2.00
641a Checklist 1-50 (41 Hal McRae) .10
641b Checklist 1-50 (41 Hal McRae Double Threat) .10
642 Checklist 51-109 .05
643 Checklist 110-168 .05
644a Checklist 169-220 (202 George Foster) .10
644b Checklist 169-220 (202 George Foster "Slugger") .10
(645a) Triple Threat (Larry Bowa, Pete Rose, Mike Schmidt (No number on back.)) 2.00
645b Triple Threat (Pete Rose, Larry Bowa, Mike Schmidt (Number on back.)) 2.00
646 Checklist 221-267 .05
647 Checklist 268-315 .05
648 Checklist 316-359 .05
649 Checklist 360-408 .05
650 Reggie Jackson 2.00
651 Checklist 409-458 .05
652a Checklist 459-509 (483 Aurelio Lopez) .10
652b Checklist 459-506 (No 483.) .10
653 Willie Wilson .05
654a Checklist 507-550 (514 Jerry Augustine) .10
654b Checklist 507-550 (514 Billy Travers) .10
655 George Brett 3.00
656 Checklist 551-593 .05
657 Tug McGraw .05
658 Checklist 594-637 .05
659a Checklist 640-660 (Last number on front is 551.) .10
659b Checklist 640-660 (Last number on front is 483.) .15
660a Steve Carlton (Date 1066 on back.) 1.00
660b Steve Carlton (Date 1966 on back.) 2.00

All Star Game/ Team Logo Stickers

Highlights of previous All-Star Games are presented in Robert Laughlin cartoons on the cardboard backings of these stickers which feature team logos, caps or patches. Though none of the players are named on the cards, many are identifiable by the pictures, uniform numbers and/or game-action descriptions on the cards. Where a specific player is clearly depicted, his name is listed.

NM/M

Complete Set (47): 15.00
Common Card: .50
1933 AL wins newsman's first "Dream Game" (Babe Ruth) 1.00
1934 out (Carl Hubbell, Babe Ruth, Lou Gehrig, Jimmie Foxx, Al Simmons, Joe Cronin) .50
1935 in row (Mel Harder, Lefty Gomez) .60
1936 first time (Dizzy Dean) .75
1937 lineup (Lou Gehrig) .75
1938 gets strong pitching (Johnny VanderMeer) .60
1939 in World's Fair city (Joe DiMaggio) .75
1940 shutout (Paul Derringer) .50
1941 Two-out homer in 9th wins for AL (Ted Williams) .65
1942 victory (Lou Boudreau, Rudy York) .50
1943 anyway .50
1944 easiest win .50
1946 most lopsided win .50
1947 AL pinch hits break up pitchers' battle .50
1948 AL wins despite stars on injury list .50
1949 gains 12-4 series lead (George Kell, Johnny Mize) .50
1950 park .50
1951 NL bombs rivals with four homers (Ralph Kiner) .60
1952 Two NL homers win rain-shortened game (Jackie Robinson, Hank Sauer) .65
1953 first eight innings (Red Schoendienst, Minnie Minoso) .50
1954 slugfest (Al Rosen) .50
1955 in 12th (Stan Musial) .65
1956 NL scores in five straight innings (Ted Williams) .75
1957 in ninth (Mickey Mantle) 1.00
1958 of no extra-base hits (Nellie Fox) .65
1959 two games (Frank Robinson, Al Kaline) .60
1960 NL wins both games in AL parks .50
1961 for only tie (Stu Miller) .50

1962 year of two games is split .50
1963 NL is outhit 11-6 but wins anyway .50
1964 All-Star series .50
1965 All-Star series (Willie Mays) .75
1966 NL takes pitchers' battle in 10th (Juan Marichal, Denny McLain) .60
1967 30 batters fan in 15-inning marathon .50
1968 AL scoreless streak reaches 18 innings .50
1969 runaway (Willie McCovey) .60
1970 12th (Bud Harrelson) .50
1971 triumph from 1963 to 1980 (Reggie Jackson, Harmon Killebrew, Frank Robinson) .65
1972 games (Hank Aaron) .75
1973 they win again .50
1974 Dodgers are heroes in easy NL victory .50
1975 9th .50
1976 NL breezes .50
1977 win again .50
1978 with four in 8th .50
1979 row to win seesaw 50th game .50
1980 series lead of 32-18 (1 tie) .50

Star Stickers

The 128-card 1981 Fleer Star Sticker set was designed to allow the card fronts to be peeled away from the cardboard backs. Fronts feature color photos with blue and yellow trim. Backs are identical in design to the regular 1981 Fleer set except for color and numbering. The set contains three unnumbered checklist cards whose fronts depict Reggie Jackson, George Brett and Mike Schmidt. The sticker-cards, which are the standard 2-1/2" x 3-1/2", were issued in gum wax packs.

NM/M
Complete Set (128): 15.00
Common Player: .15
Wax Pack (5): 1.25
Wax Box (36): 15.00
1 Steve Garvey .40
2 Ron LeFlore .15
3 Ron Cey .15
4 Dave Revering .15
5 Tony Armas .15
6 Mike Norris .15
7 Steve Kemp .15
8 Bruce Bochte .15
9 Mike Schmidt 2.00
10 Scott McGregor .15
11 Buddy Bell .15
12 Carney Lansford .15
13 Carl Yastrzemski 1.00
14 Ben Oglivie .15
15 Willie Stargell 1.00
16 Cecil Cooper .15
17 Gene Richards .15
18 Jim Kern .15
19 Jerry Koosman .15
20 Larry Bowa .15
21 Kent Tekulve .15
22 Dan Driessen .15
23 Phil Niekro .75
24 Dan Quisenberry .15
25 Dave Winfield 1.00
26 Dave Parker .15
27 Rick Langford .15
28 Amos Otis .15
29 Bill Buckner .15
30 Al Bumbry .15
31 Bake McBride .15
32 Mickey Rivers .15
33 Rick Burleson .15
34 Dennis Eckersley .75
35 Cesar Cedeno .15
36 Enos Cabell .15
37 Johnny Bench 1.00
38 Robin Yount 1.00
39 Mark Belanger .15
40 Rod Carew 1.00
41 George Foster .15
42 Lee Mazzilli .15
43 Triple Threat (Larry Bowa, Pete Rose, Mike Schmidt) 2.00
44 J.R. Richard .15
45 Lou Piniella .15
46 Ken Landreaux .15
47 Rollie Fingers .75
48 Joaquin Andujar .15
49 Tom Seaver 1.00
50 Bobby Grich .15
51 Jon Matlack .15
52 Jack Clark .15
53 Jim Rice .15
54 Rickey Henderson 3.00
55 Roy Smalley .15
56 Mike Flanagan .15
57 Steve Rogers .15
58 Carlton Fisk 1.00
59 Don Sutton .75
60 Ken Griffey .15
61 Burt Hooton .15
62 Dusty Baker .15
63 Vida Blue .15
64 Al Oliver .15
65 Jim Bibby .15
66 Tony Perez .75
67 Davy Lopes (Davey) .15
68 Bill Russell .15
69 Larry Parrish .15
70 Garry Maddox .15
71 Phil Garner .15
72 Graig Nettles .20
73 Gary Carter 1.00
74 Pete Rose 3.00
75 Greg Luzinski .15
76 Ron Guidry .15
77 Gorman Thomas .15
78 Jose Cruz .15
79 Bob Boone .15
80 Bruce Sutter .75
81 Chris Chambliss .15
82 Paul Molitor 1.00
83 Tug McGraw .15
84 Ferguson Jenkins .75
85 Steve Carlton 1.00
86 Miguel Dilone .15
87 Reggie Smith .15
88 Rick Cerone .15
89 Alan Trammell .15
90 Doug DeCinces .15
91 Sparky Lyle .15
92 Warren Cromartie .15
93 Rick Reuschel .15
94 Larry Hisle .15
95 Paul Splittorff .15
96 Manny Trillo .15
97 Frank White .15
98 Fred Lynn .15
99 Bob Horner .15
100 Omar Moreno .15
101 Dave Concepcion .15
102 Larry Gura .15
103 Ken Singleton .15
104 Steve Stone .15
105 Richie Zisk .15
106 Willie Wilson .15
107 Willie Randolph .15
108 Nolan Ryan 3.00
109 Joe Morgan 1.00
110 Bucky Dent .20
111 Dave Kingman .15
112 John Castino .15
113 Joe Rudi .15
114 Ed Farmer .15
115 Reggie Jackson 2.50
116 George Brett 2.00
117 Eddie Murray 1.00
118 Rich Gossage .20
119 Dale Murphy .40
120 Ted Simmons .15
121 Tommy John .20
122 Don Baylor .15
123 Andre Dawson .60
124 Jim Palmer 1.00
125 Garry Templeton .15
---- Checklist 1-42 (Reggie Jackson) .50
---- Checklist 43-83 (George Brett) .50
---- Checklist 84-125 (Mike Schmidt) .50

Superstar Stickers

While these small (about 1-1/2" x 2") stickers carry the Fleer name and were, indeed, produced by Fleer, they are more akin to collectors' issues than a legitimate product. Wrappers of 1981 Fleer Star Stickers offered the opportunity to put one's own photo, or the photo of someone else, on 24 stickers for a couple of dollars and proofs of purchase. Some enterprising hobbyists sent in several different pictures of Mickey Mantle and pictures of then-current stars and had them made into stickers. Because they are unauthorized by Mantle, or the other players seen (Boggs, Mattingly, Yaz, etc.), there is no collector value.

1982 Fleer

Fleer's 1982 set did not match the quality of the previous year's effort. Many of the card photos are blurred and have muddied backgrounds. The 2-1/2" x 3-1/2" cards feature color photos bordered by a frame which is color-coded by team. Backs are blue, white, and yellow and contain the player's team logo plus the logos of Major League Baseball and the Major League Baseball Players Association. Due to a lawsuit by Topps, Fleer was forced to issue the set with team logo stickers rather than gum. The complete set price does not include the higher priced variations.

NM/M
Complete Set (660): 45.00
Common Player: .05
Wax Pack (15): 3.00
Wax Box (36): 85.00
Cello Pack (28): 4.00
Cello Box (24): 85.00
Vending Box (500): 40.00
1 Dusty Baker .05
2 Robert Castillo .05
3 Ron Cey .05
4 Terry Forster .05
5 Steve Garvey .30
6 Dave Goltz .05
7 Pedro Guerrero .05
8 Burt Hooton .05
9 Steve Howe .05
10 Jay Johnstone .05
11 Ken Landreaux .05
12 Davey Lopes .05
13 Mike Marshall **RC** .15
14 Bobby Mitchell .05
15 Rick Monday .05
16 Tom Niedenfuer **RC** .05
17 Ted Power **RC** .05
18 Jerry Reuss .05
19 Ron Roenicke .05
20 Bill Russell .05
21 Steve Sax **RC** .45
22 Mike Scioscia .05
23 Reggie Smith .05
24 Dave Stewart **RC** 1.50
25 Rick Sutcliffe .05
26 Derrel Thomas .05
27 Fernando Valenzuela .10
28 Bob Welch .05
29 Steve Yeager .05
30 Bobby Brown .05
31 Rick Cerone .05
32 Ron Davis .05
33 Bucky Dent .10
34 Barry Foote .05
35 George Frazier .05
36 Oscar Gamble .05
37 Rich Gossage .10
38 Ron Guidry .10
39 Reggie Jackson 1.50
40 Tommy John .10
41 Rudy May .05
42 Larry Milbourne .05
43 Jerry Mumphrey .05
44 Bobby Murcer .10
45 Gene Nelson **RC** .05
46 Graig Nettles .10
47 Johnny Oates .05
48 Lou Piniella .10
49 Willie Randolph .05
50 Rick Reuschel .05
51 Dave Revering .05
52 Dave Righetti **RC** .45
53 Aurelio Rodriguez .05
54 Bob Watson .05
55 Dennis Werth .05
56 Dave Winfield 1.00
57 Johnny Bench 1.00
58 Bruce Berenyi .05
59 Larry Biittner .05
60 Scott Brown .05
61 Dave Collins .05
62 Geoff Combe .05
63 Dave Concepcion .05
64 Dan Driessen .05
65 Joe Edelen .05
66 George Foster .05
67 Ken Griffey .05
68 Paul Householder .05
69 Tom Hume .05
70 Junior Kennedy .05
71 Ray Knight .05
72 Mike LaCoss .05
73 Rafael Landestoy .05
74 Charlie Leibrandt .05
75 Sam Mejias .05
76 Paul Moskau .05
77 Joe Nolan .05
78 Mike O'Berry .05
79 Ron Oester .05
80 Frank Pastore .05
81 Joe Price .05
82 Tom Seaver 1.00
83 Mario Soto .05
84 Mike Vail .05
85 Tony Armas .05
86 Shooty Babitt .05
87 Dave Beard .05
88 Rick Bosetti .05
89 Keith Drumright .05
90 Wayne Gross .05
91 Mike Heath .05
92 Rickey Henderson 1.00
93 Cliff Johnson .05
94 Jeff Jones .05
95 Matt Keough .05
96 Brian Kingman .05
97 Mickey Klutts .05
98 Rick Langford .05
99 Steve McCatty .05
100 Dave McKay .05
101 Dwayne Murphy .05
102 Jeff Newman .05
103 Mike Norris .05
104 Bob Owchinko .05
105 Mitchell Page .05
106 Rob Picciolo .05
107 Jim Spencer .05
108 Fred Stanley .05
109 Tom Underwood .05
110 Joaquin Andujar .05
111 Steve Braun .05
112 Bob Forsch .05
113 George Hendrick .05
114 Keith Hernandez .05
115 Tom Herr .05
116 Dane Iorg .05
117 Jim Kaat .10
118 Tito Landrum .05
119 Sixto Lezcano .05
120 Mark Littell .05
121 John Martin .05
122 Silvio Martinez .05
123 Ken Oberkfell .05
124 Darrell Porter .05
125 Mike Ramsey .05
126 Orlando Sanchez .05
127 Bob Shirley .05
128 Lary Sorensen .05
129 Bruce Sutter .75
130 Bob Sykes .05
131 Garry Templeton .05
132 Gene Tenace .05
133 Jerry Augustine .05
134 Sal Bando .05
135 Mark Brouhard .05
136 Mike Caldwell .05
137 Reggie Cleveland .05
138 Cecil Cooper .05
139 Jamie Easterly .05
140 Marshall Edwards .05
141 Rollie Fingers .75
142 Jim Gantner .05
143 Moose Haas .05
144 Larry Hisle .05
145 Roy Howell .05
146 Rickey Keeton .05
147 Randy Lerch .05
148 Paul Molitor 1.00
149 Don Money .05
150 Charlie Moore .05
151 Ben Oglivie .05
152 Ted Simmons .05
153 Jim Slaton .05
154 Gorman Thomas .05
155 Robin Yount 1.00
156 Pete Vukovich .05
157 Benny Ayala .05
158 Mark Belanger .05
159 Al Bumbry .05
160 Terry Crowley .05
161 Rich Dauer .05
162 Doug DeCinces .05
163 Rick Dempsey .05
164 Jim Dwyer .05
165 Mike Flanagan .05
166 Dave Ford .05
167 Dan Graham .05
168 Wayne Krenchicki .05
169 John Lowenstein .05
170 Dennis Martinez .05
171 Tippy Martinez .05
172 Scott McGregor .05
173 Jose Morales .05
174 Eddie Murray 1.00
175 Jim Palmer 1.00
176 Cal Ripken, Jr. **RC** 40.00
177 Gary Roenicke .05
178 Lenn Sakata .05
179 Ken Singleton .05
180 Sammy Stewart .05
181 Tim Stoddard .05
182 Steve Stone .05
183 Stan Bahnsen .05
184 Ray Burris .05
185 Gary Carter 1.00
186 Warren Cromartie .05
187 Andre Dawson .50
188 Terry Francona **RC** .05
189 Woodie Fryman .05
190 Bill Gullickson .05
191 Grant Jackson .05
192 Wallace Johnson .05
193 Charlie Lea .05
194 Bill Lee .05
195 Jerry Manuel .05
196 Brad Mills .05
197 John Milner .05
198 Rowland Office .05
199 David Palmer .05
200 Larry Parrish .05
201 Mike Phillips .05
202 Tim Raines .25
203 Bobby Ramos .05
204 Jeff Reardon .05
205 Steve Rogers .05
206 Scott Sanderson .05
207 Rodney Scott (Photo actually Tim Raines.) .10
208 Elias Sosa .05
209 Chris Speier .05
210 Tim Wallach **RC** 1.00
211 Jerry White .05
212 Alan Ashby .05
213 Cesar Cedeno .05
214 Jose Cruz .05
215 Kiko Garcia .05
216 Phil Garner .05
217 Danny Heep .05
218 Art Howe .05
219 Bob Knepper .05
220 Frank LaCorte .05
221 Joe Niekro .05
222 Joe Pittman .05
223 Terry Puhl .05
224 Luis Pujols .05
225 Craig Reynolds .05
226 J.R. Richard .05
227 Dave Roberts .05
228 Vern Ruhle .05
229 Nolan Ryan 3.00
230 Joe Sambito .05
231 Tony Scott .05
232 Dave Smith .05
233 Harry Spilman .05
234 Don Sutton .75
235 Dickie Thon .05
236 Denny Walling .05
237 Gary Woods .05
238 Luis Aguayo **RC** .05
239 Ramon Aviles .05
240 Bob Boone .05
241 Larry Bowa .05
242 Warren Brusstar .05
243 Steve Carlton 1.00
244 Larry Christenson .05
245 Dick Davis .05
246 Greg Gross .05
247 Sparky Lyle .05
248 Garry Maddox .05
249 Gary Matthews .05
250 Bake McBride .05
251 Tug McGraw .05
252 Keith Moreland .05
253 Dickie Noles .05
254 Mike Proly .05
255 Ron Reed .05
256 Pete Rose 2.50
257 Dick Ruthven .05
258 Mike Schmidt 2.00
259 Lonnie Smith .05
260 Manny Trillo .05
261 Del Unser .05
262 George Vukovich .05
263 Tom Brookens .05
264 George Cappuzzello .05
265 Marty Castillo .05
266 Al Cowens .05
267 Kirk Gibson .05
268 Richie Hebner .05
269 Ron Jackson .05
270 Lynn Jones .05
271 Steve Kemp .05
272 Rick Leach **RC** .25
273 Aurelio Lopez .05
274 Jack Morris .05
275 Kevin Saucier .05
276 Lance Parrish .05
277 Rick Peters .05
278 Dan Petry .05
279 David Rozema .05
280 Stan Papi .05
281 Dan Schatzeder .05
282 Champ Summers .05
283 Alan Trammell .05
284 Lou Whitaker .05
285 Milt Wilcox .05
286 John Wockenfuss .05
287 Gary Allenson .05
288 Tom Burgmeier .05
289 Bill Campbell .05
290 Mark Clear .05
291 Steve Crawford .05
292 Dennis Eckersley .75
293 Dwight Evans .05
294 Rich Gedman **RC** .10
295 Garry Hancock .05
296 Glenn Hoffman .05
297 Bruce Hurst .05
298 Carney Lansford .05
299 Rick Miller .05
300 Reid Nichols .05
301 Bob Ojeda **RC** .25
302 Tony Perez .75
303 Chuck Rainey .05
304 Jerry Remy .05
305 Jim Rice .50
306 Joe Rudi .05
307 Bob Stanley .05
308 Dave Stapleton .05
309 Frank Tanana .05
310 Mike Torrez .05
311 John Tudor .05
312 Carl Yastrzemski 1.00
313 Buddy Bell .05
314 Steve Comer .05
315 Danny Darwin .05
316 John Ellis .05
317 John Grubb .05
318 Rick Honeycutt .05
319 Charlie Hough .05
320 Fergie Jenkins .75
321 John Henry Johnson .05
322 Jim Kern .05
323 Jon Matlack .05
324 Doc Medich .05
325 Mario Mendoza .05
326 Al Oliver .05
327 Pat Putnam .05
328 Mickey Rivers .05
329 Leon Roberts .05
330 Billy Sample .05
331 Bill Stein .05
332 Jim Sundberg .05
333 Mark Wagner .05
334 Bump Wills .05
335 Bill Almon .05
336 Harold Baines .05
337 Ross Baumgarten .05
338 Tony Bernazard .05
339 Britt Burns .05
340 Richard Dotson .05
341 Jim Essian .05
342 Ed Farmer .05
343 Carlton Fisk 1.00
344 Kevin Hickey .05
345 Lamarr Hoyt (LaMarr) .05
346 Lamar Johnson .05
347 Jerry Koosman .05
348 Rusty Kuntz .05
349 Dennis Lamp .05
350 Ron LeFlore .05
351 Chet Lemon .05
352 Greg Luzinski .05
353 Bob Molinaro .05
354 Jim Morrison .05
355 Wayne Nordhagen .05
356 Greg Pryor .05
357 Mike Squires .05
358 Steve Trout .05
359 Alan Bannister .05
360 Len Barker .05
361 Bert Blyleven .10
362 Joe Charboneau .10
363 John Denny .05
364 Bo Diaz .05
365 Miguel Dilone .05
366 Jerry Dybzinski .05
367 Wayne Garland .05
368 Mike Hargrove .05
369 Toby Harrah .05
370 Ron Hassey .05
371 Von Hayes **RC** .25
372 Pat Kelly .05
373 Duane Kuiper .05
374 Rick Manning .05
375 Sid Monge .05
376 Jorge Orta .05
377 Dave Rosello .05
378 Dan Spillner .05
379 Mike Stanton .05
380 Andre Thornton .05
381 Tom Veryzer .05
382 Rick Waits .05
383 Doyle Alexander .05
384 Vida Blue .05
385 Fred Breining .05
386 Enos Cabell .05
387 Jack Clark .05
388 Darrell Evans .05
389 Tom Griffin .05

390 Larry Herndon .05
391 Al Holland .05
392 Gary Lavelle .05
393 Johnnie LeMaster .05
394 Jerry Martin .05
395 Milt May .05
396 Greg Minton .05
397 Joe Morgan 1.00
398 Joe Pettini .05
399 Alan Ripley .05
400 Billy Smith .05
401 Rennie Stennett .05
402 Ed Whitson .05
403 Jim Wohlford .05
404 Willie Aikens .05
405 George Brett 2.00
406 Ken Brett .05
407 Dave Chalk .05
408 Rich Gale .05
409 Cesar Geronimo .05
410 Larry Gura .05
411 Clint Hurdle .05
412 Mike Jones .05
413 Dennis Leonard .05
414 Renie Martin .05
415 Lee May .05
416 Hal McRae .05
417 Darryl Motley .05
418 Rance Mulliniks .05
419 Amos Otis .05
420 Ken Phelps **RC** .05
421 Jamie Quirk .05
422 Dan Quisenberry .05
423 Paul Splittorff .05
424 U.L. Washington .05
425 John Wathan .05
426 Frank White .05
427 Willie Wilson .05
428 Brian Asselstine .05
429 Bruce Benedict .05
430 Tom Boggs .05
431 Larry Bradford .05
432 Rick Camp .05
433 Chris Chambliss .05
434 Gene Garber .05
435 Preston Hanna .05
436 Bob Horner .05
437 Glenn Hubbard .05
438a Al Hrabosky (All Hrabosky, 5'1" on back.) 4.50
438b Al Hrabosky (Al Hrabosky, 5'1" on back.) 1.00
438c Al Hrabosky (Al Hrabosky, 5'10" on back.) .25
439 Rufino Linares .05
440 Rick Mahler **RC** .05
441 Ed Miller .05
442 John Montefusco .05
443 Dale Murphy .50
444 Phil Niekro .75
445 Gaylord Perry .75
446 Biff Pocoroba .05
447 Rafael Ramirez .05
448 Jerry Royster .05
449 Claudell Washington .05
450 Don Aase .05
451 Don Baylor .05
452 Juan Beniquez .05
453 Rick Burleson .05
454 Bert Campaneris .05
455 Rod Carew 1.00
456 Bob Clark .05
457 Brian Downing .05
458 Dan Ford .05
459 Ken Forsch .05
460 Dave Frost .05
461 Bobby Grich .05
462 Larry Harlow .05
463 John Harris .05
464 Andy Hassler .05
465 Butch Hobson .05
466 Jesse Jefferson .05
467 Bruce Kison .05
468 Fred Lynn .05
469 Angel Moreno .05
470 Ed Ott .05
471 Fred Patek .05
472 Steve Renko .05
473 Mike Witt **RC** .10
474 Geoff Zahn .05
475 Gary Alexander .05
476 Dale Berra .05
477 Kurt Bevacqua .05
478 Jim Bibby .05
479 John Candelaria .05
480 Victor Cruz .05
481 Mike Easler .05
482 Tim Foli .05
483 Lee Lacy .05
484 Vance Law .05
485 Bill Madlock .05
486 Willie Montanez .05
487 Omar Moreno .05
488 Steve Nicosia .05
489 Dave Parker .05
490 Tony Pena .05
491 Pascual Perez .05
492 Johnny Ray **RC** .05
493 Rick Rhoden .05
494 Bill Robinson .05
495 Don Robinson .05
496 Enrique Romo .05
497 Rod Scurry .05
498 Eddie Solomon .05
499 Willie Stargell 1.00
500 Kent Tekulve .05
501 Jason Thompson .05
502 Glenn Abbott .05
503 Jim Anderson .05
504 Floyd Bannister .05
505 Bruce Bochte .05
506 Jeff Burroughs .05
507 Bryan Clark .05
508 Ken Clay .05
509 Julio Cruz .05
510 Dick Drago .05
511 Gary Gray .05
512 Dan Meyer .05
513 Jerry Narron .05
514 Tom Paciorek .05
515 Casey Parsons .05
516 Lenny Randle .05
517 Shane Rawley .05
518 Joe Simpson .05
519 Richie Zisk .05
520 Neil Allen .05
521 Bob Bailor .05
522 Hubie Brooks .05
523 Mike Cubbage .05
524 Pete Falcone .05
525 Doug Flynn .05
526 Tom Hausman .05
527 Ron Hodges .05
528 Randy Jones .05
529 Mike Jorgensen .05
530 Dave Kingman .05
531 Ed Lynch .05
532 Mike Marshall .05
533 Lee Mazzilli .05
534 Dyar Miller .05
535 Mike Scott .05
536 Rusty Staub .05
537 John Stearns .05
538 Craig Swan .05
539 Frank Taveras .05
540 Alex Trevino .05
541 Ellis Valentine .05
542 Mookie Wilson .05
543 Joel Youngblood .05
544 Pat Zachry .05
545 Glenn Adams .05
546 Fernando Arroyo .05
547 John Verhoeven .05
548 Sal Butera .05
549 John Castino .05
550 Don Cooper .05
551 Doug Corbett .05
552 Dave Engle .05
553 Roger Erickson .05
554 Danny Goodwin .05
555a Darrell Jackson (Black cap.) .65
555b Darrell Jackson (Red cap w/speck of white.) 3.00
555c Darrell Jackson (Red cap w/white T.) .10
556 Pete Mackanin .05
557 Jack O'Connor .05
558 Hosken Powell .05
559 Pete Redfern .05
560 Roy Smalley .05
561 Chuck Baker .05
562 Gary Ward .05
563 Rob Wilfong .05
564 Al Williams .05
565 Butch Wynegar .05
566 Randy Bass .05
567 Juan Bonilla .05
568 Danny Boone .05
569 John Curtis .05
570 Juan Eichelberger .05
571 Barry Evans .05
572 Tim Flannery .05
573 Ruppert Jones .05
574 Terry Kennedy .05
575 Joe Lefebvre .05
576a John Littlefield (Pitching lefty.) 80.00
576b John Littlefield (Pitching righty.) .05
577 Gary Lucas .05
578 Steve Mura .05
579 Broderick Perkins .05
580 Gene Richards .05
581 Luis Salazar .05
582 Ozzie Smith 1.50
583 John Urrea .05
584 Chris Welsh .05
585 Rick Wise .05
586 Doug Bird .05
587 Tim Blackwell .05
588 Bobby Bonds .10
589 Bill Buckner .05
590 Bill Caudill .05
591 Hector Cruz .05
592 Jody Davis **RC** .10
593 Ivan DeJesus .05
594 Steve Dillard .05
595 Leon Durham .05
596 Rawly Eastwick .05
597 Steve Henderson .05
598 Mike Krukow .05
599 Mike Lum .05
600 Randy Martz .05
601 Jerry Morales .05
602 Ken Reitz .05
603a Lee Smith **RC** (Cubs logo reversed on back.) 2.50
603b Lee Smith **RC** (corrected) 2.50
604 Dick Tidrow .05
605 Jim Tracy .05
606 Mike Tyson .05
607 Ty Waller .05
608 Danny Ainge .50
609 Jorge Bell **RC** 1.00
610 Mark Bomback .05
611 Barry Bonnell .05
612 Jim Clancy .05
613 Damaso Garcia .05
614 Jerry Garvin .05
615 Alfredo Griffin .05
616 Garth Iorg .05
617 Luis Leal .05
618 Ken Macha .05
619 John Mayberry .05
620 Joey McLaughlin .05
621 Lloyd Moseby .05
622 Dave Stieb .05
623 Jackson Todd .05
624 Willie Upshaw **RC** .05
625 Otto Velez .05
626 Ernie Whitt .05
627 Al Woods .05
628 1981 All-Star Game .05
629 All-Star Infielders (Bucky Dent, Frank White) .05
630 Big Red Machine (Dave Concepcion, Dan Driessen, George Foster) .10
631 Top N.L. Relief Pitcher (Bruce Sutter) .30
632 Steve & Carlton (Steve Carlton, Carlton Fisk) .25
633 3000th Game, May 25, 1981 (Carl Yastrzemski) .35
634 Dynamic Duo (Johnny Bench, Tom Seaver) .30
635 West Meets East (Gary Carter, Fernando Valenzuela) .20
636a N.L. Strikeout King (Fernando Valenzuela ("...led the National League...")) .50
636b N.L. Strikeout King (Fernando Valenzuela ("... led the National League...")) .25
637 Home Run King (Mike Schmidt) .50
638 N.L. All-Stars (Gary Carter, Dave Parker) .25
639 Perfect Game! (Len Barker, Bo Diaz) .05
640 Pete Rose, Pete Rose, Jr. (Re-Pete) 2.00
641 Phillies' Finest (Steve Carlton, Mike Schmidt, Lonnie Smith) .50
642 Red Sox Reunion (Dwight Evans, Fred Lynn) .10
643 Most Hits and Runs (Rickey Henderson) 1.00
644 Most Saves 1981 A.L. (Rollie Fingers) .15
645 Most 1981 Wins (Tom Seaver) .25
646a Yankee Powerhouse (Reggie Jackson, Dave Winfield (Comma after "outfielder" on back.) 1.50
646b Yankee Powerhouse (Reggie Jackson, Dave Winfield (No comma.) 2.00
647 Checklist 1-56 .05
648 Checklist 57-109 .05
649 Checklist 110-156 .05
650 Checklist 157-211 .05
651 Checklist 212-262 .05
652 Checklist 263-312 .05
653 Checklist 313-358 .05
654 Checklist 359-403 .05
655 Checklist 404-449 .05
656 Checklist 450-501 .05
657 Checklist 502-544 .05
658 Checklist 545-585 .05
659 Checklist 586-627 .05
660 Checklist 628-646 .05

Proofs

More than two dozen proof cards which differ significantly from the issued versions in 1982 Fleer are known, though the quantities in which they have made their way into the hobby market are not known. Blank-backed and hand-cut from press sheets, the proofs include a number of Hall of Famers and high-demand stars. The manner in which the proof card differs from the issued version is listed parenthetically.

NM/M

--- Dave Patterson (No issued version.) 75.00
4 Terry Forster (Green photo border.) 50.00
31 Rick Cerone/Catching (Game-action.) 75.00
37 Rich Gossage (Pose to knees.) 75.00
48 Lou Piniella/Trotting (Game-action.) 75.00
49 Willie Randolph/Btg (Game-action.) 75.00
61 Dave Collins/Btg (Game-action.) 50.00
67 Ken Griffey (Home uniform.) 60.00
82 Tom Seaver/Pitching (Game-action.) 600.00
312 Carl Yastrzemski (Misspelled "Yastremski.") 350.00
395 Milt May (Ed Whitson photo.) 60.00
402 Ed Whitson (Milt May photo.) 60.00
416 Hal McRae (Position: OF.) 25.00
427 Willie Wilson (Pose, no microphone.) 50.00
449 Claudell Washington/Btg (Game-action.) 50.00
503 Jim Anderson (Incorrect name: Mike.) 25.00
555 Darrell Jackson (Pictures unidentifed pitcher.) 45.00
629 All-Star Infielders (Captioned: "Dent & White.") 25.00
632 Steve & Carlton (Captioned: "Carlton & Steve / FISK & CARLTON.") 40.00
635 West Meets East (Captioned: "East Meets West.") 25.00
638 N.L. All Stars (Captioned: "Parker & Carter.") 25.00
644 Most Saves 1981 (Captioned: "A.L. Most Saves in 1981.") 25.00
646 Yankee Powerhouse (Captioned: "Winfield & Jackson.") 45.00
652 Checklist (Lists #275 as Stan Papi.) 15.00
655 Checklist (McRae's position: OF.) 15.00
660 Checklist (White border, incorrect captions as above.) 15.00

Test Cards

To test a proposed cardboard stock from International Paper Co., a run of 100 sheets of test cards was printed and delivered to Fleer officials. The cards on the sheet include various combinations of correct picture/name combinations, incorrect picture/name combinations and cards with no player identification. All cards have the words "TEST CARD" overprinted in black in the player identification area at bottom center, along with the letters "o," "n" or both vertically at the left end of the oblong. Backs are blank. At least half of the 132-card test sheets have made their way into the hobby where they are offered both as complete sheets and as hand-cut single cards or panels. A number of the photos seen on the test cards did not appear in Fleer's 1982 card set. The checklist here is arranged by row and card number on the sheets. Player names are as printed, if the photo is not that player it is identified in parentheses. Each of the 66 cards is double-printed on the sheet.

NM/M

Complete Sheet (132): 1,500
Complete Set (66): 900.00
Common Card: 10.00
1-1 Jon Matlack (Steve Christmas) 10.00
1-2 Wayne Gross (Jose Brito) 10.00
1-3 Mario Mendoza (John Lickert) 10.00
1-4 Mike Heath (Daryl Sconiers) 10.00
1-5 Bump Wills (Lee Mazzilli) 10.00
1-6 Steve McCatty (Jose Rodriguez) 10.00
1-7 Steve Stone 25.00
1-8 No identification (Brian Harper) 10.00
1-9 Dennis Martinez (Cubs player) 15.00
1-10 No identification (Julio Valdez) 10.00
1-11 Jim Palmer (Del Unser) 25.00
2-1 Billy Sample (Bill Doran) 10.00
2-2 Tony Armas (Tony Armas) 10.00
2-3 Rick Honeycutt (Rick Honeycutt) 10.00
2-4 Cliff Jackson (Tim Ireland) 10.00
2-5 John Ellis (Floyd Rayford) 10.00
2-6 Dave McKay (Jim Wright) 10.00
2-7 Ken Singleton (Larry Milbourne) 10.00
2-8 No identification (Steve Balboni) 10.00
2-9 John Lowenstein (Mickey Mahler) 10.00
2-10 No identification (Ty Waller) 10.00
2-11 Doug DeCinces (Mike Patterson) 10.00
3-1 Mickey Rivers (Pat Putnam) 10.00
3-2 Rickey Henderson (Mike Norris) 25.00
3-3 Jim Sundberg (Jim Kern) 10.00
3-4 Bob Owchinko (Fred Stanley) 10.00
3-5 Buddy Bell (Danny Darwin) 10.00
3-6 Shooty Babbitt (Rick Langford) 10.00
3-7 Sammy Stewart (Tippy Martinez) 10.00
3-8 No identification (Juan Eichelberger) 10.00
3-9 Lenn Sakata (Eddie Murray) 25.00
3-10 No identification (Juan Bonilla) 10.00
3-11 Benny Ayala (Terry Crowley) 10.00
4-1 Al Oliver (Bill Stein) 10.00
4-2 Dwayne Murphy (Matt Keough) 10.00
4-3 Leon Roberts (John Grubb) 10.00
4-4 Rob Picciolo (Brian Kingman) 10.00
4-5 Mark Wagner (Steve Comer) 10.00
4-6 Jeff Jones (Jeff Neumann) 10.00
4-7 Tim Stoddard (Mike Flanagan) 10.00
4-8 No identification (John Urrea) 10.00
4-9 Rick Dempsey (Mark Belanger) 10.00
4-10 No identification (Luis Salazar) 10.00
4-11 Dave Ford (Cal Ripken Jr.) 250.00
5-1 Pat Putnam 15.00
5-2 Mike Norris 15.00
5-3 Jim Kern 15.00
5-4 Fred Stanley 15.00
5-5 Danny Darwin 15.00
5-6 Rick Langford 15.00
5-7 Tippy Martinez 15.00
5-8 No identification (Juan Eichelberger) 10.00
5-9 Eddie Murray 30.00
5-10 No identification (Juan Bonilla) 10.00
5-11 Terry Crowley 15.00
6-1 Bill Stein 15.00
6-2 Matt Keough 15.00
6-3 John Grubb 15.00
6-4 Brian Kingman 15.00
6-5 Steve Comer 15.00
6-6 Jeff Neumann 15.00
6-7 Mike Flanagan 15.00
6-8 No identification (John Urrea) 10.00
6-9 Mark Belanger 15.00
6-10 No identification (Luis Salazar) 10.00
6-11 Cal Ripken, Jr. 400.00

Stamps

Issued by Fleer in 1982, this set consists of 242 player stamps, each measuring 1-13/16" x 2-1/2". Originally issued in perforated strips of 10, the full-color stamps are numbered in the lower-left corner and were designed to be placed in an album. Six stamps feature two players each.

NM/M

Complete Set (242): 10.00
Common Player: .05
Stamp Album: 1.50
Wax Pack (10): .35
Wax Box (60): 12.50
1 Fernando Valenzuela .05
2 Rick Monday .05
3 Ron Cey .05
4 Dusty Baker .05
5 Burt Hooton .05
6 Pedro Guerrero .05
7 Jerry Reuss .05
8 Bill Russell .05
9 Steve Garvey .15
10 Davey Lopes .05
11 Tom Seaver .25
12 George Foster .05
13 Frank Pastore .05
14 Dave Collins .05
15 Dave Concepcion .05
16 Ken Griffey .05
17 Johnny Bench .25
18 Ray Knight .05
19 Mario Soto .05
20 Ron Oester .05
21 Ken Oberkfell .05
22 Bob Forsch .05
23 Keith Hernandez .05
24 Dane Iorg .05
25 George Hendrick .05
26 Gene Tenace .05
27 Garry Templeton .05
28 Bruce Sutter .20
29 Darrell Porter .05
30 Tom Herr .05
31 Tim Raines .05
32 Chris Speier .05
33 Warren Cromartie .05
34 Larry Parrish .05
35 Andre Dawson .25
36 Steve Rogers .05
37 Jeff Reardon .05
38 Rodney Scott .05
39 Gary Carter .25
40 Scott Sanderson .05
41 Cesar Cedeno .05
42 Nolan Ryan 1.00
43 Don Sutton .20
44 Terry Puhl .05
45 Joe Niekro .05
46 Tony Scott .05
47 Joe Sambito .05
48 Art Howe .05
49 Bob Knepper .05
50 Jose Cruz .05
51 Pete Rose .50
52 Dick Ruthven .05
53 Mike Schmidt .35
54 Steve Carlton .25
55 Tug McGraw .05
56 Larry Bowa .05
57 Garry Maddox .05
58 Gary Matthews .05
59 Manny Trillo .05
60 Lonnie Smith .05
61 Vida Blue .05
62 Milt May .05
63 Joe Morgan .25
64 Enos Cabell .05
65 Jack Clark .05
66 Claudell Washington .05
67 Gaylord Perry .20
68 Phil Niekro .20

69 Bob Horner .05
70 Chris Chambliss .05
71 Dave Parker .05
72 Tony Pena .05
73 Kent Tekulve .05
74 Mike Easler .05
75 Tim Foli .05
76 Willie Stargell .25
77 Bill Madlock .05
78 Jim Bibby .05
79 Omar Moreno .05
80 Lee Lacy .05
81 Hubie Brooks .05
82 Rusty Staub .05
83 Ellis Valentine .05
84 Neil Allen .05
85 Dave Kingman .05
86 Mookie Wilson .05
87 Doug Flynn .05
88 Pat Zachry .05
89 John Stearns .05
90 Lee Mazzilli .05
91 Ken Reitz .05
92 Mike Krukow .05
93 Jerry Morales .05
94 Leon Durham .05
95 Ivan DeJesus .05
96 Bill Buckner .05
97 Jim Tracy .05
98 Steve Henderson .05
99 Dick Tidrow .05
100 Mike Tyson .05
101 Ozzie Smith .35
102 Ruppert Jones .05
103 Broderick Perkins .05
104 Gene Richrds .05
105 Terry Kennedy .05
106 Jim Bibby, Willie Stargell .10
107 Larry Bowa, Pete Rose .25
108 Warren Spahn, Fernando Valenzuela .10
109 Dave Concepcion, Pete Rose .25
110 Reggie Jackson, Dave Winfield .20
111 Tom Lasorda, Fernando Valenzuela .20
112 Reggie Jackson .35
113 Dave Winfield .25
114 Lou Piniella .10
115 Tommy John .10
116 Rich Gossage .10
117 Ron Davis .05
118 Rick Cerone .05
119 Graig Nettles .05
120 Ron Guidry .05
121 Willie Randolph .05
122 Dwayne Murphy .05
123 Rickey Henderson .25
124 Wayne Gross .05
125 Mike Norris .05
126 Rick Langford .05
127 Jim Spencer .05
128 Tony Armas .05
129 Matt Keough .05
130 Jeff Jones .05
131 Steve McCatty .05
132 Rollie Fingers .20
133 Jim Gantner .05
134 Gorman Thomas .05
135 Robin Yount .25
136 Paul Molitor .25
137 Ted Simmons .05
138 Ben Oglivie .05
139 Moose Haas .05
140 Cecil Cooper .05
141 Pete Vuckovich .05
142 Doug DeCinces .05
143 Jim Palmer .25
144 Steve Stone .05
145 Mike Flanagan .05
146 Rick Dempsey .05
147 Al Bumbry .05
148 Mark Belanger .05
149 Scott McGregor .05
150 Ken Singleton .05
151 Eddie Murray .25
152 Lance Parrish .05
153 David Rozema .05
154 Champ Summers .05
155 Alan Trammell .05
156 Lou Whitaker .05
157 Milt Wilcox .05
158 Kevin Saucier .05
159 Jack Morris .05
160 Steve Kemp .05
161 Kirk Gibson .05
162 Carl Yastrzemski .25
163 Jim Rice .20
164 Carney Lansford .05
165 Dennis Eckersley .20
166 Mike Torrez .05
167 Dwight Evans .05
168 Glenn Hoffman .05
169 Bob Stanley .05
170 Tony Perez .20
171 Jerry Remy .05
172 Buddy Bell .05
173 Ferguson Jenkins .20
174 Mickey Rivers .05
175 Bump Wills .05
176 Jon Matlack .05
177 Steve Comer .05
178 Al Oliver .05
179 Bill Stein .05
180 Pat Putnam .05
181 Jim Sundberg .05
182 Ron LeFlore .05
183 Carlton Fisk .25
184 Harold Baines .05
185 Bill Almon .05
186 Richard Dotson .05
187 Greg Luzinski .05
188 Mike Squires .05
189 Britt Burns .05
190 Lamarr Hoyt .05
191 Chet Lemon .05
192 Joe Charboneau .10
193 Toby Harrah .05
194 John Denny .05
195 Rick Manning .05
196 Miguel Dilone .05
197 Bo Diaz .05
198 Mike Hargrove .05
199 Bert Blyleven .05
200 Len Barker .05
201 Andre Thornton .05
202 George Brett .35
203 U.L. Washington .05
204 Dan Quisenberry .05
205 Larry Gura .05
206 Willie Aikens .05
207 Willie Wilson .05
208 Dennis Leonard .05
209 Frank White .05
210 Hal McRae .05
211 Amos Otis .05
212 Don Aase .05
213 Butch Hobson .05
214 Fred Lynn .05
215 Brian Downing .05
216 Dan Ford .05
217 Rod Carew .25
218 Bobby Grich .05
219 Rick Burleson .05
220 Don Baylor .05
221 Ken Forsch .05
222 Bruce Bochte .05
223 Richie Zisk .05
224 Tom Paciorek .05
225 Julio Cruz .05
226 Jeff Burroughs .05
227 Doug Corbett .05
228 Roy Smalley .05
229 Gary Ward .05
230 John Castino .05
231 Rob Wilfong .05
232 Dave Stieb .05
233 Otto Velez .05
234 Damaso Garcia .05
235 John Mayberry .05
236 Alfredo Griffin .05
237 Ted Williams, Carl Yastrzemski .50
238 Rick Cerone, Graig Nettles .05
239 Buddy Bell, George Brett .15
240 Steve Carlton, Jim Kaat .10
241 Steve Carlton, Dave Parker .10
242 Ron Davis, Nolan Ryan .40

1983 Fleer Promo Sheet

The consumer, rather than dealer, was the target audience for this sheet premiering '83 Fleer. Six player cards, identical to the issued versions, appear on the 9-5/8" x 7-1/2" sheet, along with advertising messages on front and back. Versions of the sheet can be found with the name of hobby publications which inserted the sample into their issues.

	NM/M
Uncut Sheet:	5.00

1983 Fleer

The 1983 Fleer set features color photos set inside a light brown border. The cards are standard 2-1/2" x 3-1/2". A team logo is located at the card bottom and the word "Fleer" is found at the top. The card backs are designed on a vertical format and include a small

black and white photo of the player along with biographical and statistical information. The reverses are done in two shades of brown on white stock. The set was issued with team logo stickers.

	NM/M
Complete Set (660):	40.00
Common Player:	.05
Wax Pack (15):	3.00
Wax Box (38):	100.00
Cello Pack (28):	4.00
Cello Box (24):	80.00
Vending Box (500):	35.00

1 Joaquin Andujar .05
2 Doug Bair .05
3 Steve Braun .05
4 Glenn Brummer .05
5 Bob Forsch .05
6 David Green .05
7 George Hendrick .05
8 Keith Hernandez .05
9 Tom Herr .05
10 Dane Iorg .05
11 Jim Kaat .10
12 Jeff Lahti .05
13 Tito Landrum .05
14 Dave LaPoint **RC** .05
15 Willie McGee **RC** 1.50
16 Steve Mura .05
17 Ken Oberkfell .05
18 Darrell Porter .05
19 Mike Ramsey .05
20 Gene Roof .05
21 Lonnie Smith .05
22 Ozzie Smith 1.50
23 John Stuper .05
24 Bruce Sutter .65
25 Gene Tenace .05
26 Jerry Augustine .05
27 Dwight Bernard .05
28 Mark Brouhard .05
29 Mike Caldwell .05
30 Cecil Cooper .05
31 Jamie Easterly .05
32 Marshall Edwards .05
33 Rollie Fingers .65
34 Jim Gantner .05
35 Moose Haas .05
36 Roy Howell .05
37 Peter Ladd .05
38 Bob McClure .05
39 Doc Medich .05
40 Paul Molitor .75
41 Don Money .05
42 Charlie Moore .05
43 Ben Oglivie .05
44 Ed Romero .05
45 Ted Simmons .05
46 Jim Slaton .05
47 Don Sutton .65
48 Gorman Thomas .05
49 Pete Vuckovich .05
50 Ned Yost .05
51 Robin Yount .75
52 Benny Ayala .05
53 Bob Bonner .05
54 Al Bumbry .05
55 Terry Crowley .05
56 Storm Davis **RC** .10
57 Rich Dauer .05
58 Rick Dempsey .05
59 Jim Dwyer .05
60 Mike Flanagan .05
61 Dan Ford .05
62 Glenn Gulliver .05
63 John Lowenstein .05
64 Dennis Martinez .05
65 Tippy Martinez .05
66 Scott McGregor .05
67 Eddie Murray .75
68 Joe Nolan .05
69 Jim Palmer .75
70 Cal Ripken, Jr. 6.00
71 Gary Roenicke .05
72 Lenn Sakata .05
73 Ken Singleton .05
74 Sammy Stewart .05
75 Tim Stoddard .05
76 Don Aase .05
77 Don Baylor .05
78 Juan Beniquez .05
79 Bob Boone .05
80 Rick Burleson .05
81 Rod Carew .75
82 Bobby Clark .05
83 Doug Corbett .05
84 John Curtis .05
85 Doug DeCinces .05
86 Brian Downing .05
87 Joe Ferguson .05
88 Tim Foli .05
89 Ken Forsch .05
90 Dave Goltz .05
91 Bobby Grich .05
92 Andy Hassler .05
93 Reggie Jackson 1.50
94 Ron Jackson .05
95 Tommy John .10
96 Bruce Kison .05
97 Fred Lynn .05
98 Ed Ott .05
99 Steve Renko .05
100 Luis Sanchez .05
101 Rob Wilfong .05
102 Mike Witt .05
103 Geoff Zahn .05
104 Willie Aikens .05
105 Mike Armstrong .05
106 Vida Blue .05
107 Bud Black **RC** .50
108 George Brett 2.00
109 Bill Castro .05
110 Onix Concepcion .05
111 Dave Frost .05
112 Cesar Geronimo .05
113 Larry Gura .05
114 Steve Hammond .05
115 Don Hood .05
116 Dennis Leonard .05
117 Jerry Martin .05
118 Lee May .05
119 Hal McRae .05
120 Amos Otis .05
121 Greg Pryor .05
122 Dan Quisenberry .05
123 Don Slaught **RC** .20
124 Paul Splittorff .05
125 U.L. Washington .05
126 John Wathan .05
127 Frank White .05
128 Willie Wilson .05
129 Steve Bedrosian .05
130 Bruce Benedict .05
131 Tommy Boggs .05
132 Brett Butler .05
133 Rick Camp .05
134 Chris Chambliss .05
135 Ken Dayley .05
136 Gene Garber .05
137 Terry Harper .05
138 Bob Horner .05
139 Glenn Hubbard .05
140 Rufino Linares .05
141 Rick Mahler .05
142 Dale Murphy .50
143 Phil Niekro .65
144 Pascual Perez .05
145 Biff Pocoroba .05
146 Rafael Ramirez .05
147 Jerry Royster .05
148 Ken Smith .05
149 Bob Walk .05
150 Claudell Washington .05
151 Bob Watson .05
152 Larry Whisenton .05
153 Porfirio Altamirano .05
154 Marty Bystrom .05
155 Steve Carlton .75
156 Larry Christenson .05
157 Ivan DeJesus .05
158 John Denny .05
159 Bob Dernier .05
160 Bo Diaz .05
161 Ed Farmer .05
162 Greg Gross .05
163 Mike Krukow .05
164 Garry Maddox .05
165 Gary Matthews .05
166 Tug McGraw .05
167 Bob Molinaro .05
168 Sid Monge .05
169 Ron Reed .05
170 Bill Robinson .05
171 Pete Rose 3.00
172 Dick Ruthven .05
173 Mike Schmidt 2.00
174 Manny Trillo .05
175 Ozzie Virgil .05
176 George Vukovich .05
177 Gary Allenson .05
178 Luis Aponte .05
179 Wade Boggs **RC** 10.00
180 Tom Burgmeier .05
181 Mark Clear .05
182 Dennis Eckersley .65
183 Dwight Evans .05
184 Rich Gedman .05
185 Glenn Hoffman .05
186 Bruce Hurst .05
187 Carney Lansford .05
188 Rick Miller .05
189 Reid Nichols .05
190 Bob Ojeda .05
191 Tony Perez .65
192 Chuck Rainey .05
193 Jerry Remy .05
194 Jim Rice .35
195 Bob Stanley .05
196 Dave Stapleton .05
197 Mike Torrez .05
198 John Tudor .05
199 Julio Valdez .05
200 Carl Yastrzemski .75
201 Dusty Baker .05
202 Joe Beckwith .05
203 Greg Brock **RC** .05
204 Ron Cey .05
205 Terry Forster .05
206 Steve Garvey .30
207 Pedro Guerrero .05
208 Burt Hooton .05
209 Steve Howe .05
210 Ken Landreaux .05
211 Mike Marshall .05
212 Candy Maldonado **RC** .05
213 Rick Monday .05
214 Tom Niedenfuer .05
215 Jorge Orta .05
216 Jerry Reuss .05
217 Ron Roenicke .05
218 Vicente Romo .05
219 Bill Russell .05
220 Steve Sax .05
221 Mike Scioscia .05
222 Dave Stewart .05
223 Derrel Thomas .05
224 Fernando Valenzuela .05
225 Bob Welch .05
226 Ricky Wright .05
227 Steve Yeager .05
228 Bill Almon .05
229 Harold Baines .05
230 Salome Barojas .05
231 Tony Bernazard .05
232 Britt Burns .05
233 Richard Dotson .05
234 Ernesto Escarrega .05
235 Carlton Fisk .75
236 Jerry Hairston Sr. .05
237 Kevin Hickey .05
238 LaMarr Hoyt .05
239 Steve Kemp .05
240 Jim Kern .05
241 Ron Kittle **RC** .25
242 Jerry Koosman .05
243 Dennis Lamp .05
244 Rudy Law .05
245 Vance Law .05
246 Ron LeFlore .05
247 Greg Luzinski .05
248 Tom Paciorek .05
249 Aurelio Rodriguez .05
250 Mike Squires .05
251 Steve Trout .05
252 Jim Barr .05
253 Dave Bergman .05
254 Fred Breining .05
255 Bob Brenly .05
256 Jack Clark .05
257 Chili Davis .05
258 Darrell Evans .05
259 Alan Fowlkes .05
260 Rich Gale .05
261 Atlee Hammaker .05
262 Al Holland .05
263 Duane Kuiper .05
264 Bill Laskey .05
265 Gary Lavelle .05
266 Johnnie LeMaster .05
267 Renie Martin .05
268 Milt May .05
269 Greg Minton .05
270 Joe Morgan .75
271 Tom O'Malley .05
272 Reggie Smith .05
273 Guy Sularz .05
274 Champ Summers .05
275 Max Venable .05
276 Jim Wohlford .05
277 Ray Burris .05
278 Gary Carter .75
279 Warren Cromartie .05
280 Andre Dawson .40
281 Terry Francona .05
282 Doug Flynn .05
283 Woody Fryman .05
284 Bill Gullickson .05
285 Wallace Johnson .05
286 Charlie Lea .05
287 Randy Lerch .05
288 Brad Mills .05
289 Dan Norman .05
290 Al Oliver .05
291 David Palmer .05
292 Tim Raines .05
293 Jeff Reardon .05
294 Steve Rogers .05
295 Scott Sanderson .05
296 Dan Schatzeder .05
297 Bryn Smith .05
298 Chris Speier .05
299 Tim Wallach .05
300 Jerry White .05
301 Joel Youngblood .05
302 Ross Baumgarten .05
303 Dale Berra .05
304 John Candelaria .05
305 Dick Davis .05
306 Mike Easler .05
307 Richie Hebner .05
308 Lee Lacy .05
309 Bill Madlock .05
310 Larry McWilliams .05
311 John Milner .05
312 Omar Moreno .05
313 Jim Morrison .05
314 Steve Nicosia .05
315 Dave Parker .05
316 Tony Pena .05
317 Johnny Ray .05
318 Rick Rhoden .05
319 Don Robinson .05
320 Enrique Romo .05
321 Manny Sarmiento .05
322 Rod Scurry .05
323 Jim Smith .05
324 Willie Stargell .75
325 Jason Thompson .05
326 Kent Tekulve .05
327a Tom Brookens (Narrow (1/4") brown box at bottom on back.) .45
327b Tom Brookens (Wide (1-1/4") brown box at bottom on back.) .05
328 Enos Cabell .05
329 Kirk Gibson .05
330 Larry Herndon .05
331 Mike Ivie .05
332 Howard Johnson **RC** 1.00
333 Lynn Jones .05
334 Rick Leach .05
335 Chet Lemon .05
336 Jack Morris .05
337 Lance Parrish .05
338 Larry Pashnick .05
339 Dan Petry .05
340 Dave Rozema .05
341 Dave Rucker .05
342 Elias Sosa .05
343 Dave Tobik .05
344 Alan Trammell .05
345 Jerry Turner .05
346 Jerry Ujdur .05
347 Pat Underwood .05
348 Lou Whitaker .05
349 Milt Wilcox .05
350 Glenn Wilson **RC** .05
351 John Wockenfuss .05
352 Kurt Bevacqua .05
353 Juan Bonilla .05
354 Floyd Chiffer .05
355 Luis DeLeon .05
356 Dave Dravecky **RC** .30
357 Dave Edwards .05
358 Juan Eichelberger .05
359 Tim Flannery .05
360 Tony Gwynn **RC** 15.00
361 Ruppert Jones .05
362 Terry Kennedy .05
363 Joe Lefebvre .05
364 Sixto Lezcano .05
365 Tim Lollar .05
366 Gary Lucas .05
367 John Montefusco .05
368 Broderick Perkins .05
369 Joe Pittman .05
370 Gene Richards .05
371 Luis Salazar .05
372 Eric Show **RC** .05
373 Garry Templeton .05
374 Chris Welsh .05
375 Alan Wiggins .05
376 Rick Cerone .05
377 Dave Collins .05
378 Roger Erickson .05
379 George Frazier .05
380 Oscar Gamble .05
381 Goose Gossage .10
382 Ken Griffey .05
383 Ron Guidry .10
384 Dave LaRoche .05
385 Rudy May .05
386 John Mayberry .05
387 Lee Mazzilli .05
388 Mike Morgan .05
389 Jerry Mumphrey .05
390 Bobby Murcer .10
391 Graig Nettles .10
392 Lou Piniella .10
393 Willie Randolph .05
394 Shane Rawley .05
395 Dave Righetti .05
396 Andre Robertson .05
397 Roy Smalley .05
398 Dave Winfield .75
399 Butch Wynegar .05
400 Chris Bando .05
401 Alan Bannister .05
402 Len Barker .05
403 Tom Brennan .05
404 Carmelo Castillo **RC** .05
405 Miguel Dilone .05
406 Jerry Dybzinski .05
407 Mike Fischlin .05
408 Ed Glynn (Photo actually Bud Anderson.) .05
409 Mike Hargrove .05
410 Toby Harrah .05
411 Ron Hassey .05
412 Von Hayes .05
413 Rick Manning .05
414 Bake McBride .05
415 Larry Milbourne .05
416 Bill Nahorodny .05
417 Jack Perconte .05
418 Larry Sorensen .05
419 Dan Spillner .05
420 Rick Sutcliffe .05
421 Andre Thornton .05
422 Rick Waits .05
423 Eddie Whitson .05
424 Jesse Barfield .05
425 Barry Bonnell .05
426 Jim Clancy .05
427 Damaso Garcia .05
428 Jerry Garvin .05
429 Alfredo Griffin .05

430	Garth Iorg	.05
431	Roy Lee Jackson	.05
432	Luis Leal	.05
433	Buck Martinez	.05
434	Joey McLaughlin	.05
435	Lloyd Moseby	.05
436	Rance Mulliniks	.05
437	Dale Murray	.05
438	Wayne Nordhagen	.05
439	Gene Petralli **RC**	.05
440	Hosken Powell	.05
441	Dave Stieb	.05
442	Willie Upshaw	.05
443	Ernie Whitt	.05
444	Al Woods	.05
445	Alan Ashby	.05
446	Jose Cruz	.05
447	Kiko Garcia	.05
448	Phil Garner	.05
449	Danny Heep	.05
450	Art Howe	.05
451	Bob Knepper	.05
452	Alan Knicely	.05
453	Ray Knight	.05
454	Frank LaCorte	.05
455	Mike LaCoss	.05
456	Randy Moffitt	.05
457	Joe Niekro	.05
458	Terry Puhl	.05
459	Luis Pujols	.05
460	Craig Reynolds	.05
461	Bert Roberge	.05
462	Vern Ruhle	.05
463	Nolan Ryan	4.00
464	Joe Sambito	.05
465	Tony Scott	.05
466	Dave Smith	.05
467	Harry Spilman	.05
468	Dickie Thon	.05
469	Denny Walling	.05
470	Larry Andersen	.05
471	Floyd Bannister	.05
472	Jim Beattie	.05
473	Bruce Bochte	.05
474	Manny Castillo	.05
475	Bill Caudill	.05
476	Bryan Clark	.05
477	Al Cowens	.05
478	Julio Cruz	.05
479	Todd Cruz	.05
480	Gary Gray	.05
481	Dave Henderson	.05
482	Mike Moore **RC**	.05
483	Gaylord Perry	.65
484	Dave Revering	.05
485	Joe Simpson	.05
486	Mike Stanton	.05
487	Rick Sweet	.05
488	Ed Vande Berg **RC**	.05
489	Richie Zisk	.05
490	Doug Bird	.05
491	Larry Bowa	.05
492	Bill Buckner	.05
493	Bill Campbell	.05
494	Jody Davis	.05
495	Leon Durham	.05
496	Steve Henderson	.05
497	Willie Hernandez	.05
498	Fergie Jenkins	.65
499	Jay Johnstone	.05
500	Junior Kennedy	.05
501	Randy Martz	.05
502	Jerry Morales	.05
503	Keith Moreland	.05
504	Dickie Noles	.05
505	Mike Proly	.05
506	Allen Ripley	.05
507	Ryne Sandberg **RC**	10.00
508	Lee Smith	1.00
509	Pat Tabler	.05
510	Dick Tidrow	.05
511	Bump Wills	.05
512	Gary Woods	.05
513	Tony Armas	.05
514	Dave Beard	.05
515	Jeff Burroughs	.05
516	John D'Acquisto	.05
517	Wayne Gross	.05
518	Mike Heath	.05
519	Rickey Henderson	.75
520	Cliff Johnson	.05
521	Matt Keough	.05
522	Brian Kingman	.05
523	Rick Langford	.05
524	Davey Lopes	.05
525	Steve McCatty	.05
526	Dave McKay	.05
527	Dan Meyer	.05
528	Dwayne Murphy	.05
529	Jeff Newman	.05
530	Mike Norris	.05
531	Bob Owchinko	.05
532	Joe Rudi	.05
533	Jimmy Sexton	.05
534	Fred Stanley	.05
535	Tom Underwood	.05
536	Neil Allen	.05
537	Wally Backman	.05
538	Bob Bailor	.05
539	Hubie Brooks	.05
540	Carlos Diaz	.05
541	Pete Falcone	.05
542	George Foster	.05
543	Ron Gardenhire	.05
544	Brian Giles	.05
545	Ron Hodges	.05
546	Randy Jones	.05
547	Mike Jorgensen	.05
548	Dave Kingman	.05
549	Ed Lynch	.05
550	Jesse Orosco	.05
551	Rick Ownbey	.05
552	Charlie Puleo **RC**	.05
553	Gary Rajsich	.05
554	Mike Scott	.05
555	Rusty Staub	.05
556	John Stearns	.05
557	Craig Swan	.05
558	Ellis Valentine	.05
559	Tom Veryzer	.05
560	Mookie Wilson	.05
561	Pat Zachry	.05
562	Buddy Bell	.05
563	John Butcher	.05
564	Steve Comer	.05
565	Danny Darwin	.05
566	Bucky Dent	.05
567	John Grubb	.05
568	Rick Honeycutt	.05
569	Dave Hostetler	.05
570	Charlie Hough	.05
571	Lamar Johnson	.05
572	Jon Matlack	.05
573	Paul Mirabella	.05
574	Larry Parrish	.05
575	Mike Richardt	.05
576	Mickey Rivers	.05
577	Billy Sample	.05
578	Dave Schmidt **RC**	.05
579	Bill Stein	.05
580	Jim Sundberg	.05
581	Frank Tanana	.05
582	Mark Wagner	.05
583	George Wright	.05
584	Johnny Bench	.75
585	Bruce Berenyi	.05
586	Larry Biittner	.05
587	Cesar Cedeno	.05
588	Dave Concepcion	.05
589	Dan Driessen	.05
590	Greg Harris	.05
591	Ben Hayes	.05
592	Paul Householder	.05
593	Tom Hume	.05
594	Wayne Krenchicki	.05
595	Rafael Landestoy	.05
596	Charlie Leibrandt	.05
597	Eddie Milner **RC**	.05
598	Ron Oester	.05
599	Frank Pastore	.05
600	Joe Price	.05
601	Tom Seaver	.75
602	Bob Shirley	.05
603	Mario Soto	.05
604	Alex Trevino	.05
605	Mike Vail	.05
606	Duane Walker	.05
607	Tom Brunansky	.05
608	Bobby Castillo	.05
609	John Castino	.05
610	Ron Davis	.05
611	Lenny Faedo	.05
612	Terry Felton	.05
613	Gary Gaetti **RC**	.35
614	Mickey Hatcher	.05
615	Brad Havens	.05
616	Kent Hrbek	.05
617	Randy S. Johnson	.05
618	Tim Laudner	.05
619	Jeff Little	.05
620	Bob Mitchell	.05
621	Jack O'Connor	.05
622	John Pacella	.05
623	Pete Redfern	.05
624	Jesus Vega	.05
625	Frank Viola **RC**	1.00
626	Ron Washington	.05
627	Gary Ward	.05
628	Al Williams	.05
629	Red Sox All-Stars (Mark Clear, Dennis Eckersley, Carl Yastrzemski)	.25
630	300 Career Wins (Terry Bulling, Gaylord Perry)	.10
631	Pride of Venezuela (Dave Concepcion, Manny Trillo)	.10
632	All-Star Infielders (Buddy Bell, Robin Yount)	.20
633	Mr. Vet & Mr. Rookie (Kent Hrbek, Dave Winfield)	.25
634	Fountain of Youth (Pete Rose, Willie Stargell)	.40
635	Big Chiefs (Toby Harrah, Andre Thornton)	.05
636	"Smith Bros." (Lonnie Smith, Ozzie Smith)	.15
637	Base Stealers' Threat (Gary Carter, Bo Diaz)	.10
638	All-Star Catchers (Gary Carter, Carlton Fisk)	.15
639	Rickey Henderson/IA	.50
640	Home Run Threats (Reggie Jackson, Ben Oglivie)	.25
641	Two Teams - Same Day (Joel Youngblood)	.05
642	Last Perfect Game (Len Barker, Ron Hassey)	.05
643	Blue (Vida Blue)	.05
644	Black & (Bud Black)	.05
645	Power (Reggie Jackson)	.30
646	Speed & (Rickey Henderson)	.30
647	Checklist 1-51	.05
648	Checklist 52-103	.05
649	Checklist 104-152	.05
650	Checklist 153-200	.05
651	Checklist 201-251	.05
652	Checklist 252-301	.05
653	Checklist 302-351	.05
654	Checklist 352-399	.05
655	Checklist 400-444	.05
656	Checklist 445-489	.05
657	Checklist 490-535	.05
658	Checklist 536-583	.05
659	Checklist 584-628	.05
660	Checklist 629-646	.05

Star Stamps

72
WHAT ATL. BRAVE STARTED AS CATCHER AND IS NOW A NL ALL-STAR OUTFIELDER?

The 1983 Fleer Stamp set consists of 288 stamps, including 224 player stamps and 64 team logo stamps. They were originally issued on four different sheets of 72 stamps each (checklisted below) and in "Vend-A-Stamp" dispensers of 18 stamps each. Sixteen different dispenser strips were needed to complete the set (strips 1-4 comprise Sheet 1; strips 5-8 comprise Sheet 2; strips 9-12 comprise Sheet 3; and strips 13-16 comprise Sheet 4.) Stamps measure 1-1/4" x 1-13/16".

		NM/M
	Complete Sheet Set (4):	5.00
	Complete Vend-A-Stamp Set (288):	5.00
	Common Sheet:	2.50
	Common Stamp Dispenser:	.35
	Common Single Stamp:	.01
1	Sheet 1 (A's Logo, Angels Logo, Willie Upshaw, Fernando Valenzuela, U.L. Washington, Bump Wills, Dave Winfield, Robin Yount, Pat Zachry, Astros Logo, Cardinals Logo, Cubs Logo, Dodgers Logo, Expos Logo, Giants Logo, Indians Logo, Mets Logo, Orioles Logo, Phillies Logo, Pirates Logo, Red Sox Logo, Twins Logo, White Sox Logo, Neil Allen, Harold Baines, Buddy Bell, Dale Berra, Wade Boggs, George Brett, Bill Buckner, Jack Clark, Dave Concepcion, Warren Cromar)	2.50
2	Sheet 2 (Angels Logo, Astros Logo, Gorman Thomas, Jason Thompson, Tom Underwood, Mookie Wilson, Willie Wilson, John Wockenfuss, Carl Yastrzemski, Braves Logo, Cardinals logo, Dodgers Logo, Expos Logo, Indians Logo, Mariners Logo, Mets Logo, Phillies Logo, Pirates Logo, Rangers Logo, Reds Logo, Royals Logo, Tigers Logo, Yankees Logo, Willie Aikens, Bob Bailor, Dusty Baker, Floyd Bannister, Len Barker, Hubie Brooks, Tom Brunansky, Chris Chambliss, Mark Clea)	2.50
3	Sheet 3 (A's Logo, Angels Logo, Andre Thornton, Manny Trillo, John Tudor, Ed Vande Berg, Bob Watson, Frank White, Milt Wilcox, Blue Jays Logo, Braves Logo, Brewers Logo, Dodgers Logo, Giants Logo, Indians Logo, Mariners Logo, Orioles Logo, Padres Logo, Reds Logo, Royals Logo, Tigers Logo, Twins Logo, White Sox Logo, Alan Ashby, Dave Beard, Jim Beattie, Johnny Bench, Larry Biittner, Bob Boone, Rod Carew, Gary Carter, Bobby Castillo, Bill Caudill, Cecil Coo)	2.50
4	Sheet 4 (Blue Jays Logo, Braves logo, Ellis Valentine, Pete Vuckovich, Gary Ward, Claudell Washington, Lou Whitaker, Al Williams, Richie Zisk, Brewers Logo, Cubs Logo, Expos Logo, Giants Logo, Padres Logo, Phillies Logo, Pirates Logo, Rangers Logo, Red Sox Logo, Reds Logo, Royals Logo, Twins Logo, White Sox Logo, Yankees Logo, Joaquin Andujar, Don Baylor, Vida Blue, Bruce Bochte, Larry Bowa, Al Bumbry, Jeff Burroughs, Enos Cabell, Steve Carlton, Cesar Ced)	2.50

Star Stamps Poster

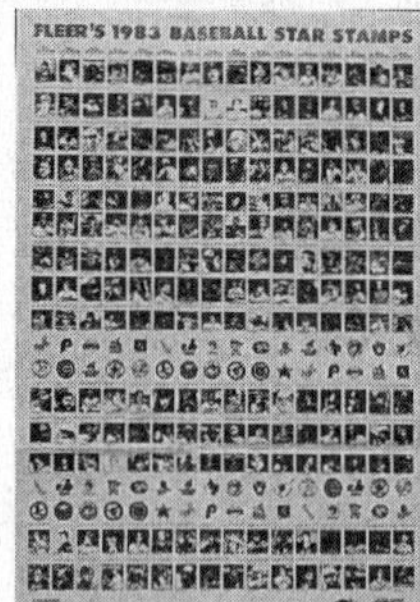

Available via a wrapper redemption offer, this huge (31-3/4" x 21-3/4") poster is printed in red and blue on glossy white paper stock. Besides blue-tone photos of each stamp, the poster has trivia questions and the logos of each team, league, MLB and the players' association. Sheets were folded to 9-1/2" x 12-1/2" for mailing.

	NM/M
Star Stamp Poster	10.00

Stickers

This 270-sticker set consists of both player stickers and team logo stickers, all measuring 1-13/16" x 2-1/2". The player stickers are numbered on the back. The front features a full-color photo surrounded by a blue border with two stars at the top. The stickers were issued in strips of 10 player stickers plus two team

logo stickers. The 26 logo stickers have been assigned numbers 271 through 296.

		NM/M
	Complete Set (296):	10.00
	Common Player:	.05
	Wax Pack (12):	.30
	Wax Box (48):	10.00
1	Bruce Sutter	.20
2	Willie McGee	.05
3	Darrell Porter	.05
4	Lonnie Smith	.05
5	Dane Iorg	.05
6	Keith Hernandez	.05
7	Joaquin Andujar	.05
8	Ken Oberkfell	.05
9	John Stuper	.05
10	Ozzie Smith	.40
11	Bob Forsch	.05
12	Jim Gantner	.05
13	Rollie Fingers	.20
14	Pete Vuckovich	.05
15	Ben Oglivie	.05
16	Don Sutton	.20
17	Bob McClure	.05
18	Robin Yount	.25
19	Paul Molitor	.25
20	Gorman Thomas	.05
21	Mike Caldwell	.05
22	Ted Simmons	.05
23	Cecil Cooper	.05
24	Steve Renko	.05
25	Tommy John	.10
26	Rod Carew	.25
27	Bruce Kison	.05
28	Ken Forsch	.05
29	Geoff Zahn	.05
30	Doug DiCinces	.05
31	Fred Lynn	.05
32	Reggie Jackson	.40
33	Don Baylor	.05
34	Bob Boone	.05
35	Brian Downing	.05
36	Goose Gossage	.05
37	Roy Smalley	.05
38	Graig Nettles	.05
39	Dave Winfield	.25
40	Lee Mazzilli	.05
41	Jerry Mumphrey	.05
42	Dave Collins	.05
43	Rick Cerone	.05
44	Willie Randolph	.05
45	Lou Piniella	.10
46	Ken Griffey	.05
47	Ron Guidry	.05
48	Jack Clark	.05
49	Reggie Smith	.05
50	Atlee Hammaker	.05
51	Fred Breining	.05
52	Gary Lavelle	.05
53	Chili Davis	.05
54	Greg Minton	.05
55	Joe Morgan	.25
56	Al Holland	.05
57	Bill Laskey	.05
58	Duane Kuiper	.05
59	Tom Burgmeier	.05
60	Carl Yastrzemski	.25
61	Mark Clear	.05
62	Mike Torrez	.05
63	Dennis Eckersley	.20
64	Wade Boggs	.50
65	Bob Stanley	.05
66	Jim Rice	.15
67	Carney Lansford	.05
68	Jerry Remy	.05
69	Dwight Evans	.05
70	John Candelaria	.05
71	Bill Madlock	.05
72	Dave Parker	.05
73	Kent Tekulve	.05
74	Tony Pena	.05
75	Manny Sarmiento	.05
76	Johnny Ray	.05
77	Dale Berra	.05
78	Lee Lacy	.05
79	Jason Thompson	.05
80	Mike Easler	.05
81	Willie Stargell	.25
82	Rick Camp	.05
83	Bob Watson	.05
84	Bob Horner	.05
85	Rafael Ramirez	.05
86	Chris Chambliss	.05
87	Gene Garber	.05
88	Claudell Washington	.05
89	Steve Bedrosian	.05
90	Dale Murphy	.15
91	Phil Niekro	.20
92	Jerry Royster	.05
93	Bob Walk	.05
94	Frank White	.05
95	Dennis Leonard	.05
96	Vida Blue	.05
97	U.L. Washington	.05
98	George Brett	.45
99	Amos Otis	.05
100	Dan Quisenberry	.05
101	Willie Aikens	.05
102	Hal McRae	.05
103	Larry Gura	.05
104	Willie Wilson	.05
105	Damaso Garcia	.05
106	Hosken Powell	.05
107	Joey McLaughlin	.05
108	Jim Clancy	.05
109	Barry Bonnell	.05
110	Garth Lorg	.05
111	Dave Stieb	.05
112	Fernando Valenzuela	.05
113	Steve Garvey	.10
114	Rick Monday	.05
115	Burt Hooton	.05
116	Bill Russell	.05
117	Pedro Guerrero	.05
118	Steve Sax	.05
119	Steve Howe	.05
120	Ken Landreaux	.05
121	Dusty Baker	.05
122	Ron Cey	.05
123	Jerry Reuss	.05
124	Bump Wills	.05
125	Keith Moreland	.05
126	Dick Tidrow	.05
127	Bill Campbell	.05
128	Larry Bowa	.05
129	Randy Martz	.05
130	Ferguson Jenkins	.20
131	Leon Durham	.05
132	Bill Buckner	.05
133	Ron Davis	.05
134	Jack O'Connor	.05
135	Kent Hrbek	.05
136	Gary Ward	.05
137	Al Williams	.05
138	Tom Brunansky	.05
139	Bobby Castillo	.05
140	Dusty Baker, Dale Murphy	.10
141	Nolan Ryan	.65
142	Lee Lacey (Lacy), Omar Moreno	.05
143	Al Oliver, Pete Rose	.25
144	Rickey Henderson	.25
145	Ray Knight, Pete Rose, Mike Schmidt	.30
146	Hal McRae, Ben Oglivie	.05
147	Tom Hume, Ray Knight	.05
148	Buddy Bell, Carlton Fisk	.05
149	Steve Kemp	.05
150	Rudy Law	.05
151	Ron LeFlore	.05
152	Jerry Koosman	.05
153	Carlton Fisk	.25
154	Salome Barojas	.05
155	Harold Baines	.05
156	Britt Burns	.05
157	Tom Paciorek	.05
158	Greg Luzinski	.05
159	LaMarr Hoyt	.05
160	George Wright	.05
161	Danny Darwin	.05
162	Lamar Johnson	.05
163	Charlie Hough	.05
164	Buddy Bell	.05
165	John Matlack (Jon)	.05
166	Billy Sample	.05
167	John Grubb	.05
168	Larry Parrish	.05
169	Ivan DeJesus	.05
170	Mike Schmidt	.45
171	Tug McGraw	.05
172	Ron Reed	.05
173	Garry Maddox	.05
174	Pete Rose	.50
175	Manny Trillo	.05
176	Steve Carlton	.25
177	Bo Diaz	.05
178	Gary Matthews	.05
179	Bill Caudill	.05
180	Ed Vande Berg	.05
181	Gaylord Perry	.20
182	Floyd Bannister	.05
183	Richie Zisk	.05
184	Al Cowens	.05
185	Bruce Bochte	.05
186	Jeff Burroughs	.05
187	Dave Beard	.05
188	Davey Lopes	.05
189	Dwayne Murphy	.05
190	Rick Langford	.05
191	Tom Underwood	.05
192	Rickey Henderson	.25
193	Mike Flanagan	.05
194	Scott McGregor	.05
195	Ken Singleton	.05
196	Rich Dauer	.05
197	John Lowenstein	.05
198	Cal Ripken, Jr.	1.00
199	Dennis Martinez	.05
200	Jim Palmer	.25
201	Tippy Martinez	.05
202	Eddie Murray	.25
203	Al Bumbry	.05
204	Dickie Thon	.05

205 Phil Garner .05
206 Jose Cruz .05
207 Nolan Ryan .65
208 Ray Knight .05
209 Terry Puhl .05
210 Joe Niekro .05
211 Art Howe .05
212 Alan Ashby .05
213 Tom Hume .05
214 Johnny Bench .25
215 Larry Biittner .05
216 Mario Soto .05
217 Dan Driessen .05
218 Tom Seaver .25
219 Dave Concepcion .05
220 Wayne Krenchicki .05
221 Cesar Cedeno .05
222 Ruppert Jones .05
223 Terry Kennedy .05
224 Luis DeLeon .05
225 Eric Show .05
226 Tim Flannery .05
227 Garry Templeton .05
228 Tim Lollar .05
229 Sixto Lezcano .05
230 Bob Bailor .05
231 Craig Swan .05
232 Dave Kingman .05
233 Mookie Wilson .05
234 John Stearns .05
235 Ellis Valentine .05
236 Neil Allen .05
237 Pat Zachry .05
238 Rusty Staub .05
239 George Foster .05
240 Rick Sutcliffe .05
241 Andre Thornton .05
242 Mike Hargrove .05
243 Dan Spillner .05
244 Lary Sorensen .05
245 Len Barker .05
246 Rick Manning .05
247 Toby Harrah .05
248 Milt Wilcox .05
249 Lou Whitaker .05
250 Tom Brookens .05
251 Chet Lemon .05
252 Jack Morris .05
253 Alan Trammell .05
254 John Wockenfuss .05
255 Lance Parrish .05
256 Larry Herndon .05
257 Chris Speier .05
258 Woody Fryman .05
259 Scott Sanderson .05
260 Steve Rogers .05
261 Warren Cromartie .05
262 Gary Carter .25
263 Bill Gullickson .05
264 Andre Dawson .15
265 Tim Raines .05
266 Charlie Lea .05
267 Jeff Reardon .05
268 Al Oliver .05
269 George Hendrick .05
270 John Montefusco .05
(271) A's Logo .05
(272) Angels Logo .05
(273) Astros Logo .05
(274) Blue Jays Logo .05
(275) Braves Logo .05
(276) Brewers Logo .05
(277) Cardinals Logo .05
(278) Cubs Logo .05
(279) Dodgers Logo .05
(280) Expos Logo .05
(281) Giants Logo .05
(282) Indians Logo .05
(283) Mariners Logo .05
(284) Mets Logo .05
(285) Orioles Logo .05
(286) Padres Logo .05
(287) Phillies Logo .05
(288) Pirates Logo .05
(289) Rangers Logo .05
(290) Red Sox Logo .05
(291) Reds Logo .05
(292) Royals Logo .05
(293) Tigers Logo .05
(294) Twins Logo .05
(295) Yankees Logo .05
(296) White Sox Logo .05

1984 Fleer Sample Sheet

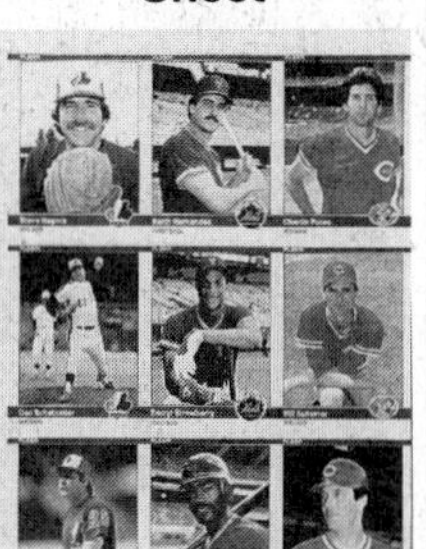

Reportedly available only as an insert in a trade magazine for the grocery industry, this full-color 7-7/8" x 10-7/8" sheet is printed on glossy paper rather than cardboard. The full-color front reproduces nine cards from the forthcoming '84 Fleer issue. The black and red back has details of the cards and ordering informartion.

NM/M

Sample Sheet: George Foster, Keith Hernandez, Ron Oester, Charlie Puleo, Steve Rogers, Dan Schatzeder, Bill Scherrer, Bryn Smith, Darryl Strawberry 10.00

1984 Fleer

The 1984 Fleer set contained 660 cards for the fourth consecutive year. The 2-1/2" x 3-1/2" cards feature a color photo surrounded by white borders and horizontal dark blue stripes. The top stripe contains the word "Fleer" with the lower carrying the player's name. Backs have a small black-and-white player photo and are done in blue ink on white stock. The set was issued with team logo stickers.

NM/M

Complete Set (660): 40.00
Common Player: .05
Wax Pack (15): 2.50
Wax Box (36): 75.00
Cello Pack (28): 4.50
Cello Box (24): 85.00
Vending Box (500): 40.00

1 Mike Boddicker **RC** .05
2 Al Bumbry .05
3 Todd Cruz .05
4 Rich Dauer .05
5 Storm Davis .05
6 Rick Dempsey .05
7 Jim Dwyer .05
8 Mike Flanagan .05
9 Dan Ford .05
10 John Lowenstein .05
11 Dennis Martinez .05
12 Tippy Martinez .05
13 Scott McGregor .05
14 Eddie Murray 1.00
15 Joe Nolan .05
16 Jim Palmer 1.00
17 Cal Ripken, Jr. 4.00
18 Gary Roenicke .05
19 Lenn Sakata .05
20 John Shelby **RC** .05
21 Ken Singleton .05
22 Sammy Stewart .05
23 Tim Stoddard .05
24 Marty Bystrom .05
25 Steve Carlton 1.00
26 Ivan DeJesus .05
27 John Denny .05
28 Bob Dernier .05
29 Bo Diaz .05
30 Kiko Garcia .05
31 Greg Gross .05
32 Kevin Gross **RC** .05
33 Von Hayes .05
34 Willie Hernandez .05
35 Al Holland .05
36 Charles Hudson **RC** .05
37 Joe Lefebvre .05
38 Sixto Lezcano .05
39 Garry Maddox .05
40 Gary Matthews .05
41 Len Matuszek .05
42 Tug McGraw .05
43 Joe Morgan 1.00
44 Tony Perez .75
45 Ron Reed .05
46 Pete Rose 3.00
47 Juan Samuel **RC** .25
48 Mike Schmidt 2.50
49 Ozzie Virgil .05
50 Juan Agosto **RC** .05
51 Harold Baines .05
52 Floyd Bannister .05
53 Salome Barojas .05
54 Britt Burns .05
55 Julio Cruz .05
56 Richard Dotson .05
57 Jerry Dybzinski .05
58 Carlton Fisk 1.00
59 Scott Fletcher **RC** .05
60 Jerry Hairston Sr. .05
61 Kevin Hickey .05
62 Marc Hill .05
63 LaMarr Hoyt .05
64 Ron Kittle .05
65 Jerry Koosman .05
66 Dennis Lamp .05
67 Rudy Law .05
68 Vance Law .05
69 Greg Luzinski .05
70 Tom Paciorek .05
71 Mike Squires .05
72 Dick Tidrow .05
73 Greg Walker **RC** .05
74 Glenn Abbott .05
75 Howard Bailey .05
76 Doug Bair .05
77 Juan Berenguer .05
78 Tom Brookens .05
79 Enos Cabell .05
80 Kirk Gibson .05
81 John Grubb .05
82 Larry Herndon .05
83 Wayne Krenchicki .05
84 Rick Leach .05
85 Chet Lemon .05
86 Aurelio Lopez .05
87 Jack Morris .05
88 Lance Parrish .05
89 Dan Petry .05
90 Dave Rozema .05
91 Alan Trammell .05
92 Lou Whitaker .05
93 Milt Wilcox .05
94 Glenn Wilson .05
95 John Wockenfuss .05
96 Dusty Baker .05
97 Joe Beckwith .05
98 Greg Brock .05
99 Jack Fimple .05
100 Pedro Guerrero .05
101 Rick Honeycutt .05
102 Burt Hooton .05
103 Steve Howe .05
104 Ken Landreaux .05
105 Mike Marshall .05
106 Rick Monday .05
107 Jose Morales .05
108 Tom Niedenfuer .05
109 Alejandro Pena **RC** .05
110 Jerry Reuss .05
111 Bill Russell .05
112 Steve Sax .05
113 Mike Scioscia .05
114 Derrel Thomas .05
115 Fernando Valenzuela .05
116 Bob Welch .05
117 Steve Yeager .05
118 Pat Zachry .05
119 Don Baylor .05
120 Bert Campaneris .05
121 Rick Cerone .05
122 Ray Fontenot **RC** .05
123 George Frazier .05
124 Oscar Gamble .05
125 Goose Gossage .10
126 Ken Griffey .05
127 Ron Guidry .10
128 Jay Howell **RC** .05
129 Steve Kemp .05
130 Matt Keough .05
131 Don Mattingly **RC** 20.00
132 John Montefusco .05
133 Omar Moreno .05
134 Dale Murray .05
135 Graig Nettles .05
136 Lou Piniella .10
137 Willie Randolph .05
138 Shane Rawley .05
139 Dave Righetti .05
140 Andre Robertson .05
141 Bob Shirley .05
142 Roy Smalley .05
143 Dave Winfield 1.00
144 Butch Wynegar .05
145 Jim Acker **RC** .05
146 Doyle Alexander .05
147 Jesse Barfield .05
148 George Bell .05
149 Barry Bonnell .05
150 Jim Clancy .05
151 Dave Collins .05
152 Tony Fernandez **RC** .50
153 Damaso Garcia .05
154 Dave Geisel .05
155 Jim Gott **RC** .05
156 Alfredo Griffin .05
157 Garth Iorg .05
158 Roy Lee Jackson .05
159 Cliff Johnson .05
160 Luis Leal .05
161 Buck Martinez .05
162 Joey McLaughlin .05
163 Randy Moffitt .05
164 Lloyd Moseby .05
165 Rance Mulliniks .05
166 Jorge Orta .05
167 Dave Stieb .05
168 Willie Upshaw .05
169 Ernie Whitt .05
170 Len Barker .05
171 Steve Bedrosian .05
172 Bruce Benedict .05
173 Brett Butler .05
174 Rick Camp .05
175 Chris Chambliss .05
176 Ken Dayley .05
177 Pete Falcone .05
178 Terry Forster .05
179 Gene Garber .05
180 Terry Harper .05
181 Bob Horner .05
182 Glenn Hubbard .05
183 Randy Johnson .05
184 Craig McMurtry **RC** .05
185 Donnie Moore **RC** .05
186 Dale Murphy .60
187 Phil Niekro .75
188 Pascual Perez .05
189 Biff Pocoroba .05
190 Rafael Ramirez .05
191 Jerry Royster .05
192 Claudell Washington .05
193 Bob Watson .05
194 Jerry Augustine .05
195 Mark Brouhard .05
196 Mike Caldwell .05
197 Tom Candiotti **RC** .25
198 Cecil Cooper .05
199 Rollie Fingers .75
200 Jim Gantner .05
201 Bob L. Gibson .05
202 Moose Haas .05
203 Roy Howell .05
204 Pete Ladd .05
205 Rick Manning .05
206 Bob McClure .05
207 Paul Molitor 1.00
208 Don Money .05
209 Charlie Moore .05
210 Ben Oglivie .05
211 Chuck Porter .05
212 Ed Romero .05
213 Ted Simmons .05
214 Jim Slaton .05
215 Don Sutton .75
216 Tom Tellmann .05
217 Pete Vuckovich .05
218 Ned Yost .05
219 Robin Yount 1.00
220 Alan Ashby .05
221 Kevin Bass **RC** .05
222 Jose Cruz .05
223 Bill Dawley **RC** .05
224 Frank DiPino .05
225 Bill Doran **RC** .05
226 Phil Garner .05
227 Art Howe .05
228 Bob Knepper .05
229 Ray Knight .05
230 Frank LaCorte .05
231 Mike LaCoss .05
232 Mike Madden .05
233 Jerry Mumphrey .05
234 Joe Niekro .05
235 Terry Puhl .05
236 Luis Pujols .05
237 Craig Reynolds .05
238 Vern Ruhle .05
239 Nolan Ryan 4.00
240 Mike Scott .05
241 Tony Scott .05
242 Dave Smith .05
243 Dickie Thon .05
244 Denny Walling .05
245 Dale Berra .05
246 Jim Bibby .05
247 John Candelaria .05
248 Jose DeLeon **RC** .05
249 Mike Easler .05
250 Cecilio Guante **RC** .05
251 Richie Hebner .05
252 Lee Lacy .05
253 Bill Madlock .05
254 Milt May .05
255 Lee Mazzilli .05
256 Larry McWilliams .05
257 Jim Morrison .05
258 Dave Parker .05
259 Tony Pena .05
260 Johnny Ray .05
261 Rick Rhoden .05
262 Don Robinson .05
263 Manny Sarmiento .05
264 Rod Scurry .05
265 Kent Tekulve .05
266 Gene Tenace .05
267 Jason Thompson .05
268 Lee Tunnell **RC** .05
269 Marvell Wynne **RC** .05
270 Ray Burris .05
271 Gary Carter 1.00
272 Warren Cromartie .05
273 Andre Dawson .30
274 Doug Flynn .05
275 Terry Francona .05
276 Bill Gullickson .05
277 Bob James .05
278 Charlie Lea .05
279 Bryan Little .05
280 Al Oliver .05
281 Tim Raines .05
282 Bobby Ramos .05
283 Jeff Reardon .05
284 Steve Rogers .05
285 Scott Sanderson .05
286 Dan Schatzeder .05
287 Bryn Smith .05
288 Chris Speier .05
289 Manny Trillo .05
290 Mike Vail .05
291 Tim Wallach .05
292 Chris Welsh .05
293 Jim Wohlford .05
294 Kurt Bevacqua .05
295 Juan Bonilla .05
296 Bobby Brown .05
297 Luis DeLeon .05
298 Dave Dravecky .05
299 Tim Flannery .05
300 Steve Garvey .25
301 Tony Gwynn 2.00
302 Andy Hawkins **RC** .10
303 Ruppert Jones .05
304 Terry Kennedy .05
305 Tim Lollar .05
306 Gary Lucas .05
307 Kevin McReynolds **RC** .25
308 Sid Monge .05
309 Mario Ramirez .05
310 Gene Richards .05
311 Luis Salazar .05
312 Eric Show .05
313 Elias Sosa .05
314 Garry Templeton .05
315 Mark Thurmond **RC** .05
316 Ed Whitson .05
317 Alan Wiggins .05
318 Neil Allen .05
319 Joaquin Andujar .05
320 Steve Braun .05
321 Glenn Brummer .05
322 Bob Forsch .05
323 David Green .05
324 George Hendrick .05
325 Tom Herr .05
326 Dane Iorg .05
327 Jeff Lahti .05
328 Dave LaPoint .05
329 Willie McGee .05
330 Ken Oberkfell .05
331 Darrell Porter .05
332 Jamie Quirk .05
333 Mike Ramsey .05
334 Floyd Rayford .05
335 Lonnie Smith .05
336 Ozzie Smith 2.00
337 John Stuper .05
338 Bruce Sutter .75
339 Andy Van Slyke **RC** 1.00
340 Dave Von Ohlen .05
341 Willie Aikens .05
342 Mike Armstrong .05
343 Bud Black .05
344 George Brett 2.50
345 Onix Concepcion .05
346 Keith Creel .05
347 Larry Gura .05
348 Don Hood .05
349 Dennis Leonard .05
350 Hal McRae .05
351 Amos Otis .05
352 Gaylord Perry .75
353 Greg Pryor .05
354 Dan Quisenberry .05
355 Steve Renko .05
356 Leon Roberts .05
357 Pat Sheridan **RC** .05
358 Joe Simpson .05
359 Don Slaught .05
360 Paul Splittorff .05
361 U.L. Washington .05
362 John Wathan .05
363 Frank White .05
364 Willie Wilson .05
365 Jim Barr .05
366 Dave Bergman .05
367 Fred Breining .05
368 Bob Brenly .05
369 Jack Clark .05
370 Chili Davis .05
371 Mark Davis **RC** .05
372 Darrell Evans .05
373 Atlee Hammaker .05
374 Mike Krukow .05
375 Duane Kuiper .05
376 Bill Laskey .05
377 Gary Lavelle .05
378 Johnnie LeMaster .05
379 Jeff Leonard .05
380 Randy Lerch .05
381 Renie Martin .05
382 Andy McGaffigan .05
383 Greg Minton .05
384 Tom OMalley .05
385 Max Venable .05
386 Brad Wellman .05
387 Joel Youngblood .05
388 Gary Allenson .05
389 Luis Aponte .05
390 Tony Armas .05
391 Doug Bird .05
392 Wade Boggs 2.00
393 Dennis Boyd **RC** .05
394 Mike Brown .05
395 Mark Clear .05
396 Dennis Eckersley .75
397 Dwight Evans .05
398 Rich Gedman .05
399 Glenn Hoffman .05
400 Bruce Hurst .05
401 John Henry Johnson .05
402 Ed Jurak .05
403 Rick Miller .05
404 Jeff Newman .05
405 Reid Nichols .05
406 Bob Ojeda .05
407 Jerry Remy .05
408 Jim Rice .05
409 Bob Stanley .05
410 Dave Stapleton .05
411 John Tudor .05
412 Carl Yastrzemski 1.50
413 Buddy Bell .05
414 Larry Biittner .05
415 John Butcher .05
416 Danny Darwin .05
417 Bucky Dent .05
418 Dave Hostetler .05
419 Charlie Hough .05
420 Bobby Johnson .05
421 Odell Jones .05
422 Jon Matlack .05
423 Pete O'Brien **RC** .05
424 Larry Parrish .05
425 Mickey Rivers .05
426 Billy Sample .05
427 Dave Schmidt .05
428 Mike Smithson **RC** .05
429 Bill Stein .05
430 Dave Stewart .05
431 Jim Sundberg .05
432 Frank Tanana .05
433 Dave Tobik .05
434 Wayne Tolleson **RC** .05
435 George Wright .05
436 Bill Almon .05
437 Keith Atherton **RC** .05
438 Dave Beard .05
439 Tom Burgmeier .05
440 Jeff Burroughs .05
441 Chris Codiroli **RC** .05
442 Tim Conroy **RC** .05
443 Mike Davis .05
444 Wayne Gross .05
445 Garry Hancock .05
446 Mike Heath .05
447 Rickey Henderson 1.00
448 Don Hill **RC** .05
449 Bob Kearney .05
450 Bill Krueger .05
451 Rick Langford .05
452 Carney Lansford .05
453 Davey Lopes .05
454 Steve McCatty .05
455 Dan Meyer .05
456 Dwayne Murphy .05
457 Mike Norris .05
458 Ricky Peters .05
459 Tony Phillips .05
460 Tom Underwood .05
461 Mike Warren .05
462 Johnny Bench 1.50
463 Bruce Berenyi .05
464 Dann Bilardello .05
465 Cesar Cedeno .05
466 Dave Concepcion .05
467 Dan Driessen .05
468 Nick Esasky **RC** .05
469 Rich Gale .05
470 Ben Hayes .05
471 Paul Householder .05
472 Tom Hume .05
473 Alan Knicely .05
474 Eddie Milner .05
475 Ron Oester .05
476 Kelly Paris .05
477 Frank Pastore .05
478 Ted Power .05
479 Joe Price .05
480 Charlie Puleo .05
481 Gary Redus **RC** .05
482 Bill Scherrer .05
483 Mario Soto .05
484 Alex Trevino .05
485 Duane Walker .05
486 Larry Bowa .05
487 Warren Brusstar .05
488 Bill Buckner .05
489 Bill Campbell .05
490 Ron Cey .05
491 Jody Davis .05
492 Leon Durham .05
493 Mel Hall **RC** .05
494 Fergie Jenkins .75
495 Jay Johnstone .05
496 Craig Lefferts **RC** .10
497 Carmelo Martinez **RC** .05
498 Jerry Morales .05
499 Keith Moreland .05
500 Dickie Noles .05
501 Mike Proly .05
502 Chuck Rainey .05
503 Dick Ruthven .05
504 Ryne Sandberg 2.00
505 Lee Smith .05
506 Steve Trout .05
507 Gary Woods .05
508 Juan Beniquez .05
509 Bob Boone .05
510 Rick Burleson .05
511 Rod Carew 1.00
512 Bobby Clark .05
513 John Curtis .05
514 Doug DeCinces .05
515 Brian Downing .05
516 Tim Foli .05
517 Ken Forsch .05
518 Bobby Grich .05
519 Andy Hassler .05
520 Reggie Jackson 1.50

521 Ron Jackson .05
522 Tommy John .10
523 Bruce Kison .05
524 Steve Lubratich .05
525 Fred Lynn .05
526 Gary Pettis **RC** .05
527 Luis Sanchez .05
528 Daryl Sconiers .05
529 Ellis Valentine .05
530 Rob Wilfong .05
531 Mike Witt .05
532 Geoff Zahn .05
533 Bud Anderson .05
534 Chris Bando .05
535 Alan Bannister .05
536 Bert Blyleven .10
537 Tom Brennan .05
538 Jamie Easterly .05
539 Juan Eichelberger .05
540 Jim Essian .05
541 Mike Fischlin .05
542 Julio Franco .05
543 Mike Hargrove .05
544 Toby Harrah .05
545 Ron Hassey .05
546 Neal Heaton **RC** .05
547 Bake McBride .05
548 Broderick Perkins .05
549 Lary Sorensen .05
550 Dan Spillner .05
551 Rick Sutcliffe .05
552 Pat Tabler .05
553 Gorman Thomas .05
554 Andre Thornton .05
555 George Vukovich .05
556 Darrell Brown .05
557 Tom Brunansky .05
558 Randy Bush **RC** .05
559 Bobby Castillo .05
560 John Castino .05
561 Ron Davis .05
562 Dave Engle .05
563 Lenny Faedo .05
564 Pete Filson .05
565 Gary Gaetti .05
566 Mickey Hatcher .05
567 Kent Hrbek .05
568 Rusty Kuntz .05
569 Tim Laudner .05
570 Rick Lysander .05
571 Bobby Mitchell .05
572 Ken Schrom .05
573 Ray Smith .05
574 Tim Teufel **RC** .05
575 Frank Viola .05
576 Gary Ward .05
577 Ron Washington .05
578 Len Whitehouse .05
579 Al Williams .05
580 Bob Bailor .05
581 Mark Bradley .05
582 Hubie Brooks .05
583 Carlos Diaz .05
584 George Foster .05
585 Brian Giles .05
586 Danny Heep .05
587 Keith Hernandez .05
588 Ron Hodges .05
589 Scott Holman .05
590 Dave Kingman .05
591 Ed Lynch .05
592 Jose Oquendo **RC** .05
593 Jesse Orosco .05
594 Junior Ortiz **RC** .05
595 Tom Seaver 1.00
596 Doug Sisk **RC** .05
597 Rusty Staub .05
598 John Stearns .05
599 Darryl Strawberry .25
600 Craig Swan .05
601 Walt Terrell **RC** .05
602 Mike Torrez .05
603 Mookie Wilson .05
604 Jamie Allen .05
605 Jim Beattie .05
606 Tony Bernazard .05
607 Manny Castillo .05
608 Bill Caudill .05
609 Bryan Clark .05
610 Al Cowens .05
611 Dave Henderson .05
612 Steve Henderson .05
613 Orlando Mercado .05
614 Mike Moore .05
615 Ricky Nelson .05
616 Spike Owen **RC** .10
617 Pat Putnam .05
618 Ron Roenicke .05
619 Mike Stanton .05
620 Bob Stoddard .05
621 Rick Sweet .05
622 Roy Thomas .05
623 Ed Vande Berg .05
624 Matt Young **RC** .05
625 Richie Zisk .05
626 '83 All-Star Game Record Breaker (Fred Lynn) .05
627 '83 All-Star Game Record Breaker (Manny Trillo) .05
628 N.L. Iron Man (Steve Garvey) .10
629 A.L. Batting Runner-Up (Rod Carew) .15
630 A.L. Batting Champion (Wade Boggs) .50
631 Letting Go Of The Raines (Tim Raines) .10
632 Double Trouble (Al Oliver) .05
633 All-Star Second Base (Steve Sax) .05
634 All-Star Shortstop (Dickie Thon) .05
635 Ace Firemen (Tippy Martinez, Dan Quisenberry) .05
636 Reds Reunited (Joe Morgan, Tony Perez, Pete Rose) .75
637 Backstop Stars (Bob Boone, Lance Parrish) .05
638 The Pine Tar Incident, 7/24/83 (George Brett, Gaylord Perry) .25
639 1983 No-Hitters (Bob Forsch, Dave Righetti, Mike Warren) .05
640 Retiring Superstars (Johnny Bench, Carl Yastrzemski) .50
641 Going Out In Style (Gaylord Perry) .05
642 300 Club & Strikeout Record (Steve Carlton) .10
643 The Managers (Joe Altobelli, Paul Owens) .05
644 The MVP (Rick Dempsey) .05
645 The Rookie Winner (Mike Boddicker) .05
646 The Clincher (Scott McGregor) .05
647 Checklist: Orioles/Royals (Joe Altobelli) .05
648 Checklist: Phillies/Giants (Paul Owens) .05
649 Checklist: White Sox/Red Sox (Tony LaRussa) .05
650 Checklist: Tigers/Rangers (Sparky Anderson) .10
651 Checklist: Dodgers/A's (Tommy Lasorda) .10
652 Checklist: Yankees/Reds (Billy Martin) .05
653 Checklist: Blue Jays/Cubs (Bobby Cox) .10
654 Checklist: Braves/Angels (Joe Torre) .10
655 Checklist: Brewers/Indians (Rene Lacheman) .05
656 Checklist: Astros/Twins (Bob Lillis) .05
657 Checklist: Pirates/Mets (Chuck Tanner) .05
658 Checklist: Expos/Mariners (Bill Virdon) .05
659 Checklist: Padres/Specials (Dick Williams) .05
660 Checklist: Cardinals/Specials (Whitey Herzog) .05

Update

Following the lead of Topps, Fleer issued near the end of the baseball season a 132-card set to update player trades and include rookies not depicted in the regular issue. The cards are identical in design to the regular issue but are numbered U-1 through U-132. Available only as a boxed set through hobby dealers, the set was printed in limited quantities. Sets were not factory sealed.

NM/M
Complete Set (132): 250.00
Common Player: .25
1 Willie Aikens .25
2 Luis Aponte .25
3 Mark Bailey .25
4 Bob Bailor .25
5 Dusty Baker .25
6 Steve Balboni .25
7 Alan Bannister .25
8 Marty Barrett .25
9 Dave Beard .25
10 Joe Beckwith .25
11 Dave Bergman .25
12 Tony Bernazard .25
13 Bruce Bochte .25
14 Barry Bonnell .25
15 Phil Bradley .25
16 Fred Breining .25
17 Mike Brown .25
18 Bill Buckner .25
19 Ray Burris .25
20 John Butcher .25
21 Brett Butler .25
22 Enos Cabell .25
23 Bill Campbell .25
24 Bill Caudill .25
25 Bobby Clark .25
26 Bryan Clark .25
27 Roger Clemens **RC** 200.00
28 Jaime Cocanower .25
29 Ron Darling **RC** 1.00
30 Alvin Davis **RC** .25
31 Bob Dernier .25
32 Carlos Diaz .25
33 Mike Easler .25
34 Dennis Eckersley 4.00
35 Jim Essian .25
36 Darrell Evans .25
37 Mike Fitzgerald .25
38 Tim Foli .25
39 John Franco **RC** 3.00
40 George Frazier .25
41 Rich Gale .25
42 Barbaro Garbey .25
43 Dwight Gooden **RC** 7.50
44 Goose Gossage .40
45 Wayne Gross .25
46 Mark Gubicza 1.00
47 Jackie Gutierrez .25
48 Toby Harrah .25
49 Ron Hassey .25
50 Richie Hebner .25
51 Willie Hernandez .25
52 Ed Hodge .25
53 Ricky Horton .25
54 Art Howe .25
55 Dane Iorg .25
56 Brook Jacoby .25
57 Dion James **RC** .25
58 Mike Jeffcoat **RC** .25
59 Ruppert Jones .25
60 Bob Kearney .25
61 Jimmy Key **RC** 1.00
62 Dave Kingman .25
63 Brad Komminsk **RC** .25
64 Jerry Koosman .25
65 Wayne Krenchicki .25
66 Rusty Kuntz .25
67 Frank LaCorte .25
68 Dennis Lamp .25
69 Tito Landrum .25
70 Mark Langston **RC** 4.00
71 Rick Leach .25
72 Craig Lefferts .25
73 Gary Lucas .25
74 Jerry Martin .25
75 Carmelo Martinez .25
76 Mike Mason **RC** .25
77 Gary Matthews .25
78 Andy McGaffigan .25
79 Joey McLaughlin .25
80 Joe Morgan 5.00
81 Darryl Motley .25
82 Graig Nettles .40
83 Phil Niekro 3.00
84 Ken Oberkfell .25
85 Al Oliver .25
86 Jorge Orta .25
87 Amos Otis .25
88 Bob Owchinko .25
89 Dave Parker .25
90 Jack Perconte .25
91 Tony Perez 3.00
92 Gerald Perry .25
93 Kirby Puckett **RC** 75.00
94 Shane Rawley .25
95 Floyd Rayford .25
96 Ron Reed .25
97 R.J. Reynolds .25
98 Gene Richards .25
99 Jose Rijo **RC** 1.00
100 Jeff Robinson .25
101 Ron Romanick .25
102 Pete Rose 10.00
103 Bret Saberhagen **RC** 5.00
104 Scott Sanderson .25
105 Dick Schofield **RC** .25
106 Tom Seaver 7.50
107 Jim Slaton .25
108 Mike Smithson .25
109 Lary Sorensen .25
110 Tim Stoddard .25
111 Jeff Stone .25
112 Champ Summers .25
113 Jim Sundberg .25
114 Rick Sutcliffe .35
115 Craig Swan .25
116 Derrel Thomas .25
117 Gorman Thomas .25
118 Alex Trevino .25
119 Manny Trillo .25
120 John Tudor .25
121 Tom Underwood .25
122 Mike Vail .25
123 Tom Waddell .25
124 Gary Ward .25
125 Terry Whitfield .25
126 Curtis Wilkerson .25
127 Frank Williams .25
128 Glenn Wilson .25
129 John Wockenfuss .25
130 Ned Yost .25
131 Mike Young **RC** .25
132 Checklist 1-132 .10

Stickers

This set was designed to be housed in a special collector's album that was organized according to various league leader categories, resulting in some players being pictured on more than one sticker. Each full-color sticker measures 1-15/16" x 2-1/2" and is framed with a beige border. The stickers, which were sold in packs of six, are numbered on the back.

NM/M
Complete Set (126): 9.00
Common Player: .05
Sticker Album: 1.00
Wax Box (100): 12.00
1 Dickie Thon .05
2 Ken Landreaux .05
3 Darrell Evans .05
4 Harold Baines .05
5 Dave Winfield .25
6 Bill Madlock .05
7 Lonnie Smith .05
8 Jose Cruz .05
9 George Hendrick .05
10 Ray Knight .05
11 Wade Boggs .30
12 Rod Carew .25
13 Lou Whitaker .05
14 Alan Trammell .05
15 Cal Ripken, Jr. .50
16 Mike Schmidt .40
17 Dale Murphy .20
18 Andre Dawson .15
19 Pedro Guerrero .05
20 Jim Rice .15
21 Tony Armas .05
22 Ron Kittle .05
23 Eddie Murray .25
24 Jose Cruz .05
25 Andre Dawson .15
26 Rafael Ramirez .05
27 Al Oliver .05
28 Wade Boggs .30
29 Cal Ripken, Jr. .50
30 Lou Whitaker .05
31 Cecil Cooper .05
32 Dale Murphy .20
33 Andre Dawson .15
34 Pedro Guerrero .05
35 Mike Schmidt .40
36 George Brett .40
37 Jim Rice .15
38 Eddie Murray .25
39 Carlton Fisk .25
40 Rusty Staub .05
41 Duane Walker .05
42 Steve Braun .05
43 Kurt Bevacqua .05
44 Hal McRae .05
45 Don Baylor .05
46 Ken Singleton .05
47 Greg Luzinski .05
48 Mike Schmidt .40
49 Keith Hernandez .05
50 Dale Murphy .20
51 Tim Raines .05
52 Wade Boggs .30
53 Rickey Henderson .25
54 Rod Carew .25
55 Ken Singleton .05
56 John Denny .05
57 John Candelaria .05
58 Larry McWilliams .05
59 Pascual Perez .05
60 Jesse Orosco .05
61 Moose Haas .05
62 Richard Dotson .05
63 Mike Flanagan .05
64 Scott McGregor .05
65 Atlee Hammaker .05
66 Rick Honeycutt .05
67 Lee Smith .05
68 Al Holland .05
69 Greg Minton .05
70 Bruce Sutter .20
71 Jeff Reardon .05
72 Frank DiPino .05
73 Dan Quisenberry .05
74 Bob Stanley .05
75 Ron Davis .05
76 Bill Caudill .05
77 Peter Ladd .05
78 Steve Carlton .25
79 Mario Soto .05
80 Larry McWilliams .05
81 Fernando Valenzuela .05
82 Nolan Ryan .75
83 Jack Morris .05
84 Floyd Bannister .05
85 Dave Stieb .05
86 Dave Righetti .05
87 Rick Sutcliffe .05
88 Tim Raines .05
89 Alan Wiggins .05
90 Steve Sax .05
91 Mookie Wilson .05
92 Rickey Henderson .25
93 Rudy Law .05
94 Willie Wilson .05
95 Julio Cruz .05
96 Johnny Bench .30
97 Carl Yastrzemski .25
98 Gaylord Perry .15
99 Pete Rose .45
100 Joe Morgan .25
101 Steve Carlton .25
102 Jim Palmer .25
103 Rod Carew .25
104 Darryl Strawberry .20
105 Craig McMurtry .05
106 Mel Hall .05
107 Lee Tunnell .05
108 Bill Dawley .05
109 Ron Kittle .05
110 Mike Boddicker .05
111 Julio Franco .05
112 Daryl Sconiers .05
113 Neal Heaton .05
114 John Shelby .05
115 Rick Dempsey .05
116 John Lowenstein .05
117 Jim Dwyer .05
118 Bo Diaz .05
119 Pete Rose .45
120 Joe Morgan .25
121 Gary Matthews .05
122 Garry Maddox .05
123 Paul Owens .05
124 Tom Lasorda .05
125 Joe Altobelli .05
126 Tony LaRussa .05

1985 Fleer

The 1985 Fleer set consists of 660 cards, each measuring 2-1/2" x 3-1/2". Card fronts feature a color photo plus the player's team logo and the word "Fleer." The photos have a color-coded frame which corresponds to the player's team. A gray border surrounds the frame. Backs are similar in design to previous years, but have two shades of red and black ink on white stock. For the fourth consecutive year, Fleer included special cards and team checklists in the set. Also incorporated in a set for the first time were 10 "Major League Prospect" cards, each featuring two rookie hopefuls. The set was issued with team logo stickers.

NM/M
Unopened Factory Set (660): 50.00
Complete Set (660): 40.00
Common Player: .05
Wax Pack (15): 4.50
Wax Box (36): 150.00
Cello Pack (28): 6.00
Cello Box (24): 150.00
Rack Pack (45): 8.00
Vending Box (500): 35.00
1 Doug Bair .05
2 Juan Berenguer .05
3 Dave Bergman .05
4 Tom Brookens .05
5 Marty Castillo .05
6 Darrell Evans .05
7 Barbaro Garbey .05
8 Kirk Gibson .05
9 John Grubb .05
10 Willie Hernandez .05
11 Larry Herndon .05
12 Howard Johnson .05
13 Ruppert Jones .05
14 Rusty Kuntz .05
15 Chet Lemon .05
16 Aurelio Lopez .05
17 Sid Monge .05
18 Jack Morris .05
19 Lance Parrish .05
20 Dan Petry .05
21 Dave Rozema .05
22 Bill Scherrer .05
23 Alan Trammell .05
24 Lou Whitaker .05
25 Milt Wilcox .05
26 Kurt Bevacqua .05
27 Greg Booker **RC** .05
28 Bobby Brown .05
29 Luis DeLeon .05
30 Dave Dravecky .05
31 Tim Flannery .05
32 Steve Garvey .40
33 Goose Gossage .10
34 Tony Gwynn 2.00
35 Greg Harris .05
36 Andy Hawkins .05
37 Terry Kennedy .05
38 Craig Lefferts .05
39 Tim Lollar .05
40 Carmelo Martinez .05
41 Kevin McReynolds .05
42 Graig Nettles .05
43 Luis Salazar .05
44 Eric Show .05
45 Garry Templeton .05
46 Mark Thurmond .05
47 Ed Whitson .05
48 Alan Wiggins .05
49 Rich Bordi .05
50 Larry Bowa .05
51 Warren Brusstar .05
52 Ron Cey .05
53 Henry Cotto **RC** .05
54 Jody Davis .05
55 Bob Dernier .05
56 Leon Durham .05
57 Dennis Eckersley .75
58 George Frazier .05
59 Richie Hebner .05
60 Dave Lopes .05
61 Gary Matthews .05
62 Keith Moreland .05
63 Rick Reuschel .05
64 Dick Ruthven .05
65 Ryne Sandberg 2.00
66 Scott Sanderson .05
67 Lee Smith .05
68 Tim Stoddard .05
69 Rick Sutcliffe .05
70 Steve Trout .05
71 Gary Woods .05
72 Wally Backman .05
73 Bruce Berenyi .05
74 Hubie Brooks .05
75 Kelvin Chapman .05
76 Ron Darling .05
77 Sid Fernandez **RC** .05
78 Mike Fitzgerald .05
79 George Foster .05
80 Brent Gaff .05
81 Ron Gardenhire .05
82 Dwight Gooden .25
83 Tom Gorman .05
84 Danny Heep .05
85 Keith Hernandez .05
86 Ray Knight .05
87 Ed Lynch .05
88 Jose Oquendo .05
89 Jesse Orosco .05
90 Rafael Santana **RC** .05
91 Doug Sisk .05
92 Rusty Staub .05
93 Darryl Strawberry .10
94 Walt Terrell .05
95 Mookie Wilson .05
96 Jim Acker .05
97 Willie Aikens .05
98 Doyle Alexander .05
99 Jesse Barfield .05
100 George Bell .05
101 Jim Clancy .05
102 Dave Collins .05
103 Tony Fernandez .05
104 Damaso Garcia .05
105 Jim Gott .05
106 Alfredo Griffin .05
107 Garth Iorg .05
108 Roy Lee Jackson .05
109 Cliff Johnson .05
110 Jimmy Key .05
111 Dennis Lamp .05
112 Rick Leach .05
113 Luis Leal .05
114 Buck Martinez .05
115 Lloyd Moseby .05
116 Rance Mulliniks .05
117 Dave Stieb .05
118 Willie Upshaw .05
119 Ernie Whitt .05
120 Mike Armstrong .05

121 Don Baylor .05
122 Marty Bystrom .05
123 Rick Cerone .05
124 Joe Cowley **RC** .05
125 Brian Dayett **RC** .05
126 Tim Foli .05
127 Ray Fontenot .05
128 Ken Griffey .05
129 Ron Guidry .10
130 Toby Harrah .05
131 Jay Howell .05
132 Steve Kemp .05
133 Don Mattingly 2.50
134 Bobby Meacham .05
135 John Montefusco .05
136 Omar Moreno .05
137 Dale Murray .05
138 Phil Niekro .75
139 Mike Pagliarulo **RC** .20
140 Willie Randolph .05
141 Dennis Rasmussen **RC** .05
142 Dave Righetti .05
143 Jose Rijo .05
144 Andre Robertson .05
145 Bob Shirley .05
146 Dave Winfield 1.00
147 Butch Wynegar .05
148 Gary Allenson .05
149 Tony Armas .05
150 Marty Barrett .05
151 Wade Boggs 2.00
152 Dennis Boyd .05
153 Bill Buckner .05
154 Mark Clear .05
155 Roger Clemens 30.00
156 Steve Crawford .05
157 Mike Easler .05
158 Dwight Evans .05
159 Rich Gedman .05
160 Jackie Gutierrez .05
161 Bruce Hurst .05
162 John Henry Johnson .05
163 Rick Miller .05
164 Reid Nichols .05
165 Al Nipper **RC** .05
166 Bob Ojeda .05
167 Jerry Remy .05
168 Jim Rice .25
169 Bob Stanley .05
170 Mike Boddicker .05
171 Al Bumbry .05
172 Todd Cruz .05
173 Rich Dauer .05
174 Storm Davis .05
175 Rick Dempsey .05
176 Jim Dwyer .05
177 Mike Flanagan .05
178 Dan Ford .05
179 Wayne Gross .05
180 John Lowenstein .05
181 Dennis Martinez .05
182 Tippy Martinez .05
183 Scott McGregor .05
184 Eddie Murray 1.00
185 Joe Nolan .05
186 Floyd Rayford .05
187 Cal Ripken, Jr. 4.00
188 Gary Roenicke .05
189 Lenn Sakata .05
190 John Shelby .05
191 Ken Singleton .05
192 Sammy Stewart .05
193 Bill Swaggerty .05
194 Tom Underwood .05
195 Mike Young .05
196 Steve Balboni .05
197 Joe Beckwith .05
198 Bud Black .05
199 George Brett 2.50
200 Onix Concepcion .05
201 Mark Gubicza **RC** .50
202 Larry Gura .05
203 Mark Huismann **RC** .05
204 Dane Iorg .05
205 Danny Jackson **RC** .05
206 Charlie Leibrandt .05
207 Hal McRae .05
208 Darryl Motley .05
209 Jorge Orta .05
210 Greg Pryor .05
211 Dan Quisenberry .05
212 Bret Saberhagen .25
213 Pat Sheridan .05
214 Don Slaught .05
215 U.L. Washington .05
216 John Wathan .05
217 Frank White .05
218 Willie Wilson .05
219 Neil Allen .05
220 Joaquin Andujar .05
221 Steve Braun .05
222 Danny Cox **RC** .05
223 Bob Forsch .05
224 David Green .05
225 George Hendrick .05
226 Tom Herr .05
227 Ricky Horton **RC** .05
228 Art Howe .05
229 Mike Jorgensen .05
230 Kurt Kepshire .05
231 Jeff Lahti .05
232 Tito Landrum .05
233 Dave LaPoint .05
234 Willie McGee .05
235 Tom Nieto **RC** .05
236 Terry Pendleton **RC** 1.00
237 Darrell Porter .05
238 Dave Rucker .05
239 Lonnie Smith .05
240 Ozzie Smith 2.00
241 Bruce Sutter .75
242 Andy Van Slyke .05
243 Dave Von Ohlen .05
244 Larry Andersen .05
245 Bill Campbell .05
246 Steve Carlton 1.00
247 Tim Corcoran .05
248 Ivan DeJesus .05
249 John Denny .05
250 Bo Diaz .05
251 Greg Gross .05
252 Kevin Gross .05
253 Von Hayes .05
254 Al Holland .05
255 Charles Hudson .05
256 Jerry Koosman .05
257 Joe Lefebvre .05
258 Sixto Lezcano .05
259 Garry Maddox .05
260 Len Matuszek .05
261 Tug McGraw .05
262 Al Oliver .05
263 Shane Rawley .05
264 Juan Samuel .05
265 Mike Schmidt 2.50
266 Jeff Stone **RC** .05
267 Ozzie Virgil .05
268 Glenn Wilson .05
269 John Wockenfuss .05
270 Darrell Brown .05
271 Tom Brunansky .05
272 Randy Bush .05
273 John Butcher .05
274 Bobby Castillo .05
275 Ron Davis .05
276 Dave Engle .05
277 Pete Filson .05
278 Gary Gaetti .05
279 Mickey Hatcher .05
280 Ed Hodge .05
281 Kent Hrbek .05
282 Houston Jimenez .05
283 Tim Laudner .05
284 Rick Lysander .05
285 Dave Meier .05
286 Kirby Puckett 8.00
287 Pat Putnam .05
288 Ken Schrom .05
289 Mike Smithson .05
290 Tim Teufel .05
291 Frank Viola .05
292 Ron Washington .05
293 Don Aase .05
294 Juan Beniquez .05
295 Bob Boone .05
296 Mike Brown .05
297 Rod Carew 1.00
298 Doug Corbett .05
299 Doug DeCinces .05
300 Brian Downing .05
301 Ken Forsch .05
302 Bobby Grich .05
303 Reggie Jackson 2.00
304 Tommy John .10
305 Curt Kaufman .05
306 Bruce Kison .05
307 Fred Lynn .05
308 Gary Pettis .05
309 Ron Romanick **RC** .05
310 Luis Sanchez .05
311 Dick Schofield .05
312 Daryl Sconiers .05
313 Jim Slaton .05
314 Derrel Thomas .05
315 Rob Wilfong .05
316 Mike Witt .05
317 Geoff Zahn .05
318 Len Barker .05
319 Steve Bedrosian .05
320 Bruce Benedict .05
321 Rick Camp .05
322 Chris Chambliss .05
323 Jeff Dedmon **RC** .05
324 Terry Forster .05
325 Gene Garber .05
326 Albert Hall **RC** .05
327 Terry Harper .05
328 Bob Horner .05
329 Glenn Hubbard .05
330 Randy Johnson .05
331 Brad Komminsk .05
332 Rick Mahler .05
333 Craig McMurtry .05
334 Donnie Moore .05
335 Dale Murphy .40
336 Ken Oberkfell .05
337 Pascual Perez .05
338 Gerald Perry .05
339 Rafael Ramirez .05
340 Jerry Royster .05
341 Alex Trevino .05
342 Claudell Washington .05
343 Alan Ashby .05
344 Mark Bailey **RC** .05
345 Kevin Bass .05
346 Enos Cabell .05
347 Jose Cruz .05
348 Bill Dawley .05
349 Frank DiPino .05
350 Bill Doran .05
351 Phil Garner .05
352 Bob Knepper .05
353 Mike LaCoss .05
354 Jerry Mumphrey .05
355 Joe Niekro .05
356 Terry Puhl .05
357 Craig Reynolds .05
358 Vern Ruhle .05
359 Nolan Ryan 4.00
360 Joe Sambito .05
361 Mike Scott .05
362 Dave Smith .05
363 Julio Solano **RC** .05
364 Dickie Thon .05
365 Denny Walling .05
366 Dave Anderson .05
367 Bob Bailor .05
368 Greg Brock .05
369 Carlos Diaz .05
370 Pedro Guerrero .05
371 Orel Hershiser **RC** 3.00
372 Rick Honeycutt .05
373 Burt Hooton .05
374 Ken Howell **RC** .05
375 Ken Landreaux .05
376 Candy Maldonado .05
377 Mike Marshall .05
378 Tom Niedenfuer .05
379 Alejandro Pena .05
380 Jerry Reuss .05
381 R.J. Reynolds **RC** .05
382 German Rivera .05
383 Bill Russell .05
384 Steve Sax .05
385 Mike Scioscia .05
386 Franklin Stubbs **RC** .05
387 Fernando Valenzuela .05
388 Bob Welch .05
389 Terry Whitfield .05
390 Steve Yeager .05
391 Pat Zachry .05
392 Fred Breining .05
393 Gary Carter 1.00
394 Andre Dawson .25
395 Miguel Dilone .05
396 Dan Driessen .05
397 Doug Flynn .05
398 Terry Francona .05
399 Bill Gullickson .05
400 Bob James .05
401 Charlie Lea .05
402 Bryan Little .05
403 Gary Lucas .05
404 David Palmer .05
405 Tim Raines .05
406 Mike Ramsey .05
407 Jeff Reardon .05
408 Steve Rogers .05
409 Dan Schatzeder .05
410 Bryn Smith .05
411 Mike Stenhouse .05
412 Tim Wallach .05
413 Jim Wohlford .05
414 Bill Almon .05
415 Keith Atherton .05
416 Bruce Bochte .05
417 Tom Burgmeier .05
418 Ray Burris .05
419 Bill Caudill .05
420 Chris Codiroli .05
421 Tim Conroy .05
422 Mike Davis .05
423 Jim Essian .05
424 Mike Heath .05
425 Rickey Henderson 1.00
426 Donnie Hill .05
427 Dave Kingman .05
428 Bill Krueger .05
429 Carney Lansford .05
430 Steve McCatty .05
431 Joe Morgan 1.00
432 Dwayne Murphy .05
433 Tony Phillips .05
434 Lary Sorensen .05
435 Mike Warren .05
436 Curt Young **RC** .05
437 Luis Aponte .05
438 Chris Bando .05
439 Tony Bernazard .05
440 Bert Blyleven .10
441 Brett Butler .05
442 Ernie Camacho .05
443 Joe Carter .25
444 Carmelo Castillo .05
445 Jamie Easterly .05
446 Steve Farr **RC** .05
447 Mike Fischlin .05
448 Julio Franco .05
449 Mel Hall .05
450 Mike Hargrove .05
451 Neal Heaton .05
452 Brook Jacoby .05
453 Mike Jeffcoat **RC** .05
454 Don Schulze **RC** .05
455 Roy Smith .05
456 Pat Tabler .05
457 Andre Thornton .05
458 George Vukovich .05
459 Tom Waddell .05
460 Jerry Willard .05
461 Dale Berra .05
462 John Candelaria .05
463 Jose DeLeon .05
464 Doug Frobel .05
465 Cecilio Guante .05
466 Brian Harper .05
467 Lee Lacy .05
468 Bill Madlock .05
469 Lee Mazzilli .05
470 Larry McWilliams .05
471 Jim Morrison .05
472 Tony Pena .05
473 Johnny Ray .05
474 Rick Rhoden .05
475 Don Robinson .05
476 Rod Scurry .05
477 Kent Tekulve .05
478 Jason Thompson .05
479 John Tudor .05
480 Lee Tunnell .05
481 Marvell Wynne .05
482 Salome Barojas .05
483 Dave Beard .05
484 Jim Beattie .05
485 Barry Bonnell .05
486 Phil Bradley **RC** .05
487 Al Cowens .05
488 Alvin Davis .05
489 Dave Henderson .05
490 Steve Henderson .05
491 Bob Kearney .05
492 Mark Langston .15
493 Larry Milbourne .05
494 Paul Mirabella .05
495 Mike Moore .05
496 Edwin Nunez **RC** .05
497 Spike Owen .05
498 Jack Perconte .05
499 Ken Phelps .05
500 Jim Presley **RC** .05
501 Mike Stanton .05
502 Bob Stoddard .05
503 Gorman Thomas .05
504 Ed Vande Berg .05
505 Matt Young .05
506 Juan Agosto .05
507 Harold Baines .05
508 Floyd Bannister .05
509 Britt Burns .05
510 Julio Cruz .05
511 Richard Dotson .05
512 Jerry Dybzinski .05
513 Carlton Fisk 1.00
514 Scott Fletcher .05
515 Jerry Hairston Sr. .05
516 Marc Hill .05
517 LaMarr Hoyt .05
518 Ron Kittle .05
519 Rudy Law .05
520 Vance Law .05
521 Greg Luzinski .05
522 Gene Nelson .05
523 Tom Paciorek .05
524 Ron Reed .05
525 Bert Roberge .05
526 Tom Seaver 1.00
527 Roy Smalley .05
528 Dan Spillner .05
529 Mike Squires .05
530 Greg Walker .05
531 Cesar Cedeno .05
532 Dave Concepcion .05
533 Eric Davis **RC** 2.00
534 Nick Esasky .05
535 Tom Foley .05
536 John Franco .05
537 Brad Gulden .05
538 Tom Hume .05
539 Wayne Krenchicki .05
540 Andy McGaffigan .05
541 Eddie Milner .05
542 Ron Oester .05
543 Bob Owchinko .05
544 Dave Parker .05
545 Frank Pastore .05
546 Tony Perez .75
547 Ted Power .05
548 Joe Price .05
549 Gary Redus .05
550 Pete Rose 3.00
551 Jeff Russell **RC** .05
552 Mario Soto .05
553 Jay Tibbs **RC** .05
554 Duane Walker .05
555 Alan Bannister .05
556 Buddy Bell .05
557 Danny Darwin .05
558 Charlie Hough .05
559 Bobby Jones .05
560 Odell Jones .05
561 Jeff Kunkel **RC** .05
562 Mike Mason **RC** .05
563 Pete O'Brien .05
564 Larry Parrish .05
565 Mickey Rivers .05
566 Billy Sample .05
567 Dave Schmidt .05
568 Donnie Scott .05
569 Dave Stewart .05
570 Frank Tanana .05
571 Wayne Tolleson .05
572 Gary Ward .05
573 Curtis Wilkerson .05
574 George Wright .05
575 Ned Yost .05
576 Mark Brouhard .05
577 Mike Caldwell .05
578 Bobby Clark .05
579 Jaime Cocanower .05
580 Cecil Cooper .05
581 Rollie Fingers .75
582 Jim Gantner .05
583 Moose Haas .05
584 Dion James .05
585 Pete Ladd .05
586 Rick Manning .05
587 Bob McClure .05
588 Paul Molitor 1.00
589 Charlie Moore .05
590 Ben Oglivie .05
591 Chuck Porter .05
592 Randy Ready **RC** .05
593 Ed Romero .05
594 Bill Schroeder **RC** .05
595 Ray Searage .05
596 Ted Simmons .05
597 Jim Sundberg .05
598 Don Sutton .75
599 Tom Tellmann .05
600 Rick Waits .05
601 Robin Yount 1.00
602 Dusty Baker .05
603 Bob Brenly .05
604 Jack Clark .05
605 Chili Davis .05
606 Mark Davis .05
607 Dan Gladden **RC** .25
608 Atlee Hammaker .05
609 Mike Krukow .05
610 Duane Kuiper .05
611 Bob Lacey .05
612 Bill Laskey .05
613 Gary Lavelle .05
614 Johnnie LeMaster .05
615 Jeff Leonard .05
616 Randy Lerch .05
617 Greg Minton .05
618 Steve Nicosia .05
619 Gene Richards .05
620 Jeff Robinson **RC** .05
621 Scot Thompson .05
622 Manny Trillo .05
623 Brad Wellman .05
624 Frank Williams **RC** .05
625 Joel Youngblood .05
626 Cal Ripken, Jr./IA 1.00
627 Mike Schmidt/IA .50
628 Giving the Signs (Sparky Anderson) .05
629 A.L. Pitcher's Nightmare (Rickey Henderson, Dave Winfield) .50
630 N.L. Pitcher's Nightmare (Ryne Sandberg, Mike Schmidt) 1.00
631 N.L. All-Stars (Gary Carter, Steve Garvey, Ozzie Smith, Darryl Strawberry) .25
632 All-Star Game Winning Battery (Gary Carter, Charlie Lea) .10
633 N.L. Pennant Clinchers (Steve Garvey, Goose Gossage) .10
634 N.L. Rookie Phenoms (Dwight Gooden, Juan Samuel) .05
635 Toronto's Big Guns (Willie Upshaw) .05
636 Toronto's Big Guns (Lloyd Moseby) .05
637 Holland (Al Holland) .05
638 Tunnell (Lee Tunnell) .05
639 Reggie Jackson/IA .50
640 Pete Rose/IA .75
641 Father & Son (Cal Ripken, Jr., Cal Ripken, Sr.) 1.00
642 Cubs team .10
643 1984's Two Perfect Games & One No-Hitter (Jack Morris, David Palmer, Mike Witt) .05
644 Major League Prospect (Willie Lozado, Vic Mata) .05
645 Major League Prospect (Kelly Gruber **RC**, Randy O'Neal **RC**) .15
646 Major League Prospect (Jose Roman **RC**, Joel Skinner **RC**) .05
647 Major League Prospect (Steve Kiefer **RC**, Danny Tartabull **RC**) .50
648 Major League Prospect (Rob Deer **RC**, Alejandro Sanchez **RC**) .25
649 Major League Prospect (Shawon Dunston **RC**, Bill Hatcher **RC**) 1.00
650 Major League Prospect (Mike Bielecki **RC**, Ron Robinson **RC**) .10
651 Major League Prospect (Zane Smith **RC**, Paul Zuvella **RC**) .10
652 Major League Prospect (Glenn Davis **RC**, Joe Hesketh **RC**) .20
653 Major League Prospect (Steve Jeltz **RC**, John Russell **RC**) .10
654 Checklist 1-95 .05
655 Checklist 96-195 .05
656 Checklist 196-292 .05
657 Checklist 293-391 .05
658 Checklist 392-481 .05
659 Checklist 482-575 .05
660 Checklist 576-660 .05

Update

For the second straight year, Fleer issued a 132-card update set. Cards portray traded players on their new teams and also include rookies not de-

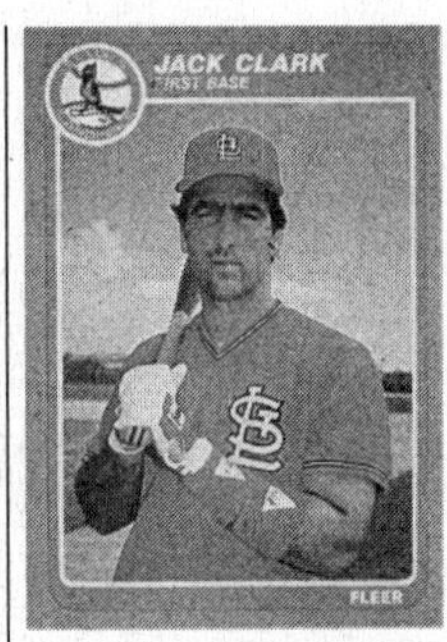

picted in the regular issue. The cards are identical in design to the 1985 Fleer set but are numbered U-1 through U-132. The set was issued with team logo stickers in a specially designed box and was available only through hobby dealers.

		NM/M
Complete Set (132):		5.00
Common Player:		.10
1	Don Aase	.10
2	Bill Almon	.10
3	Dusty Baker	.10
4	Dale Berra	.10
5	Karl Best **RC**	.10
6	Tim Birtsas **RC**	.10
7	Vida Blue	.10
8	Rich Bordi	.10
9	Daryl Boston **RC**	.10
10	Hubie Brooks	.10
11	Chris Brown **RC**	.10
12	Tom Browning **RC**	.10
13	Al Bumbry	.10
14	Tim Burke **RC**	.10
15	Ray Burris	.10
16	Jeff Burroughs	.10
17	Ivan Calderon **RC**	.10
18	Jeff Calhoun	.10
19	Bill Campbell	.10
20	Don Carman **RC**	.10
21	Gary Carter	.50
22	Bobby Castillo	.10
23	Bill Caudill	.10
24	Rick Cerone	.10
25	Jack Clark	.10
26	Pat Clements **RC**	.10
27	Stewart Cliburn **RC**	.10
28	Vince Coleman **RC**	.10
29	Dave Collins	.10
30	Fritz Connally	.10
31	Henry Cotto **RC**	.10
32	Danny Darwin	.10
33	Darren Daulton **RC**	1.00
34	Jerry Davis	.10
35	Brian Dayett	.10
36	Ken Dixon **RC**	.10
37	Tommy Dunbar	.10
38	Mariano Duncan **RC**	.10
39	Bob Fallon	.10
40	Brian Fisher **RC**	.10
41	Mike Fitzgerald	.10
42	Ray Fontenot	.10
43	Greg Gagne **RC**	.10
44	Oscar Gamble	.10
45	Jim Gott	.10
46	David Green	.10
47	Alfredo Griffin	.10
48	Ozzie Guillen **RC**	2.00
49	Toby Harrah	.10
50	Ron Hassey	.10
51	Rickey Henderson	3.00
52	Steve Henderson	.10
53	George Hendrick	.10
54	Teddy Higuera **RC**	.10
55	Al Holland	.10
56	Burt Hooton	.10
57	Jay Howell	.10
58	LaMarr Hoyt	.10
59	Tim Hulett **RC**	.10
60	Bob James	.10
61	Cliff Johnson	.10
62	Howard Johnson	.10
63	Ruppert Jones	.10
64	Steve Kemp	.10
65	Bruce Kison	.10
66	Mike LaCoss	.10
67	Lee Lacy	.10
68	Dave LaPoint	.10
69	Gary Lavelle	.10
70	Vance Law	.10
71	Manny Lee **RC**	.10
72	Sixto Lezcano	.10
73	Tim Lollar	.10
74	Urbano Lugo **RC**	.10
75	Fred Lynn	.10
76	Steve Lyons **RC**	.10
77	Mickey Mahler	.10
78	Ron Mathis **RC**	.10
79	Len Matuszek	.10
80	Oddibe McDowell **RC**	.10
81	Roger McDowell **RC**	.10
82	Donnie Moore	.10
83	Ron Musselman	.10
84	Al Oliver	.10
85	Joe Orsulak **RC**	.10

86	Dan Pasqua **RC**	.10
87	Chris Pittaro **RC**	.10
88	Rick Reuschel	.10
89	Earnie Riles **RC**	.10
90	Jerry Royster	.10
91	Dave Rozema	.10
92	Dave Rucker	.10
93	Vern Ruhle	.10
94	Mark Salas **RC**	.10
95	Luis Salazar	.10
96	Joe Sambito	.10
97	Billy Sample	.10
98	Alex Sanchez	.10
99	Calvin Schiraldi **RC**	.10
100	Rick Schu **RC**	.10
101	Larry Sheets **RC**	.10
102	Ron Shepherd	.10
103	Nelson Simmons **RC**	.10
104	Don Slaught	.10
105	Roy Smalley	.10
106	Lonnie Smith	.10
107	Nate Snell **RC**	.10
108	Lary Sorensen	.10
109	Chris Speier	.10
110	Mike Stenhouse	.10
111	Tim Stoddard	.10
112	John Stuper	.10
113	Jim Sundberg	.10
114	Bruce Sutter	.40
115	Don Sutton	.50
116	Bruce Tanner **RC**	.10
117	Kent Tekulve	.10
118	Walt Terrell	.10
119	Mickey Tettleton **RC**	1.00
120	Rich Thompson	.10
121	Louis Thornton **RC**	.10
122	Alex Trevino	.10
123	John Tudor	.10
124	Jose Uribe **RC**	.10
125	Dave Valle **RC**	.10
126	Dave Von Ohlen	.10
127	Curt Wardle	.10
128	U.L. Washington	.10
129	Ed Whitson	.10
130	Herm Winningham **RC**	.10
131	Rich Yett **RC**	.10
132	Checklist	.10

Limited Edition

The 1985 Fleer Limited Edition boxed set was distributed through several chains of retail stores. The cards, which are the standard 2-1/2" x 3-1/2", have full-color photos inside a red and yellow frame. The backs are set in black type against two different shades of yellow and contain the player's personal and statistical information. The set was issued in a specially designed box which carried the complete checklist for the set on the back. Six team logo stickers were also included with the set.

		NM/M
Complete Set (44):		4.00
Common Player:		.10
1	Buddy Bell	.10
2	Bert Blyleven	.15
3	Wade Boggs	.60
4	George Brett	.75
5	Rod Carew	.50
6	Steve Carlton	.50
7	Alvin Davis	.10
8	Andre Dawson	.25
9	Steve Garvey	.15
10	Goose Gossage	.15
11	Tony Gwynn	.60
12	Keith Hernandez	.10
13	Kent Hrbek	.10
14	Reggie Jackson	.60
15	Dave Kingman	.10
16	Ron Kittle	.10
17	Mark Langston	.10
18	Jeff Leonard	.10
19	Bill Madlock	.10
20	Don Mattingly	.75
21	Jack Morris	.10
22	Dale Murphy	.15
23	Eddie Murray	.50
24	Tony Pena	.10
25	Dan Quisenberry	.10
26	Tim Raines	.10
27	Jim Rice	.25
28	Cal Ripken, Jr.	1.00
29	Pete Rose	.85
30	Nolan Ryan	1.00
31	Ryne Sandberg	.60
32	Steve Sax	.10
33	Mike Schmidt	.75
34	Tom Seaver	.50
35	Ozzie Smith	.60
36	Mario Soto	.10
37	Dave Stieb	.10
38	Darryl Strawberry	.10
39	Rick Sutcliffe	.10
40	Alan Trammell	.10
41	Willie Upshaw	.10
42	Fernando Valenzuela	.10
43	Dave Winfield	.50
44	Robin Yount	.50

Star Stickers

The 1985 Fleer sticker set consists of 126 player stickers, each measuring 1-15/16" x 2-1/2". Numbered on the back, the stickers were designed to be put in a special album. Distributed in packs of six, the 1985 stickers are the scarcest of all Fleer baseball sticker issues.

		NM/M
Complete Set (126):		12.50
Common Player:		.05
Sticker Album:		1.25
Wax Pack (6):		.25
Wax Box (100):		16.00
1	Pete Rose	1.00
2	Pete Rose	1.00
3	Pete Rose	1.00
4	Don Mattingly	1.50
5	Dave Winfield	.40
6	Wade Boggs	.50
7	Buddy Bell	.10
8	Tony Gwynn	.40
9	Lee Lacy	.05
10	Chili Davis	.05
11	Ryne Sandberg	.50
12	Tony Armas	.05
13	Jim Rice	.15
14	Dave Kingman	.05
15	Alvin Davis	.05
16	Gary Carter	.25
17	Mike Schmidt	1.00
18	Dale Murphy	.20
19	Ron Cey	.05
20	Eddie Murray	.40
21	Harold Baines	.05
22	Kirk Gibson	.05
23	Jim Rice	.15
24	Gary Matthews	.05
25	Keith Hernandez	.05
26	Gary Carter	.25
27	George Hendrick	.05
28	Tony Armas	.05
29	Dave Kingman	.05
30	Dwayne Murphy	.05
31	Lance Parrish	.05
32	Andre Thornton	.05
33	Dale Murphy	.20
34	Mike Schmidt	1.00
35	Gary Carter	.25
36	Darryl Strawberry	.05
37	Don Mattingly	1.50
38	Larry Parrish	.05
39	George Bell	.05
40	Dwight Evans	.05
41	Cal Ripken, Jr.	2.00
42	Tim Raines	.05
43	Johnny Ray	.05
44	Juan Samuel	.05
45	Ryne Sandberg	.50
46	Mike Easler	.05
47	Andre Thornton	.05
48	Dave Kingman	.05
49	Don Baylor	.05
50	Rusty Staub	.05
51	Steve Braun	.05
52	Kevin Bass	.05
53	Greg Gross	.05
54	Rickey Henderson	.40
55	Dave Collins	.05
56	Brett Butler	.05
57	Gary Pettis	.05
58	Tim Raines	.05
59	Juan Samuel	.05
60	Alan Wiggins	.05
61	Lonnie Smith	.05
62	Eddie Murray	.05
63	Eddie Murray	.05
64	Eddie Murray	.05
65	Eddie Murray	.05
66	Eddie Murray	.05
67	Eddie Murray	.05
68	Tom Seaver	.05
69	Tom Seaver	.05
70	Tom Seaver	.05
71	Tom Seaver	.05
72	Tom Seaver	.05
73	Tom Seaver	.05
74	Mike Schmidt	.25
75	Mike Schmidt	.25
76	Mike Schmidt	.25
77	Mike Schmidt	.25
78	Mike Schmidt	.25
79	Mike Schmidt	.25
80	Mike Boddicker	.05
81	Bert Blyleven	.05
82	Jack Morris	.05
83	Dan Petry	.05
84	Frank Viola	.05
85	Joaquin Andujar	.05
86	Mario Soto	.05
87	Dwight Gooden	.05
88	Joe Niekro	.05
89	Rick Sutcliffe	.05
90	Mike Boddicker	.05
91	Dave Stieb	.05
92	Bert Blyleven	.05
93	Phil Niekro	.25
94	Alejandro Pena	.05
95	Dwight Gooden	.05
96	Orel Hershiser	.15
97	Rick Rhoden	.05
98	John Candelaria	.05
99	Dan Quisenberry	.05
100	Bill Caudill	.05
101	Willie Hernandez	.05
102	Dave Righetti	.05
103	Ron Davis	.05
104	Bruce Sutter	.20
105	Lee Smith	.05
106	Jesse Orosco	.05
107	Al Holland	.05
108	Goose Gossage	.05
109	Mark Langston	.05
110	Dave Stieb	.05
111	Mike Witt	.05
112	Bert Blyleven	.05
113	Dwight Gooden	.05
114	Fernando Valenzuela	.05
115	Nolan Ryan	2.00
116	Mario Soto	.05
117	Ron Darling	.05
118	Dan Gladden	.05
119	Jeff Stone	.05
120	John Franco	.05
121	Barbaro Garbey	.05
122	Kirby Puckett	1.50
123	Roger Clemens	7.50
124	Bret Saberhagen	.05
125	Sparky Anderson	.05
126	Dick Williams	.05

1986 Fleer

The 1986 Fleer set contains 660 color cards measuring 2-1/2" x 3-1/2". The card fronts feature a player photo enclosed by a dark blue border. The card backs are minus the black-and-white photo that was included in past Fleer efforts. Player biographical and statistical information appear in black and yellow on white stock. As in 1985, Fleer devoted 10 cards, entitled "Major League Prospects," to 20 promising rookie players. The 1986 set, as in the previous four years was issued with team logo stickers.

		NM/M
Unopened Fact. Set (660):		30.00
Complete Set (660):		25.00
Common Player:		.05
Wax Pack (15):		1.50
Wax Box (36):		45.00
Cello Pack (28):		2.00
Cello Box (24):		40.00
Rack Pack (45):		4.00
Rack Box (24):		65.00
1	Steve Balboni	.05
2	Joe Beckwith	.05
3	Buddy Biancalana	.05
4	Bud Black	.05
5	George Brett	2.00
6	Onix Concepcion	.05
7	Steve Farr	.05
8	Mark Gubicza	.05
9	Dane Iorg	.05
10	Danny Jackson	.05
11	Lynn Jones	.05
12	Mike Jones	.05
13	Charlie Leibrandt	.05
14	Hal McRae	.05
15	Omar Moreno	.05
16	Darryl Motley	.05
17	Jorge Orta	.05
18	Dan Quisenberry	.05
19	Bret Saberhagen	.05
20	Pat Sheridan	.05
21	Lonnie Smith	.05
22	Jim Sundberg	.05
23	John Wathan	.05
24	Frank White	.05
25	Willie Wilson	.05
26	Joaquin Andujar	.05
27	Steve Braun	.05
28	Bill Campbell	.05
29	Cesar Cedeno	.05
30	Jack Clark	.05
31	Vince Coleman	.05
32	Danny Cox	.05
33	Ken Dayley	.05
34	Ivan DeJesus	.05
35	Bob Forsch	.05
36	Brian Harper	.05
37	Tom Herr	.05
38	Ricky Horton	.05
39	Kurt Kepshire	.05
40	Jeff Lahti	.05
41	Tito Landrum	.05
42	Willie McGee	.05
43	Tom Nieto	.05
44	Terry Pendleton	.05
45	Darrell Porter	.05
46	Ozzie Smith	1.50
47	John Tudor	.05
48	Andy Van Slyke	.05
49	Todd Worrell **RC**	.25
50	Jim Acker	.05
51	Doyle Alexander	.05
52	Jesse Barfield	.05
53	George Bell	.05
54	Jeff Burroughs	.05
55	Bill Caudill	.05
56	Jim Clancy	.05
57	Tony Fernandez	.05
58	Tom Filer	.05
59	Damaso Garcia	.05
60	Tom Henke **RC**	.05
61	Garth Iorg	.05
62	Cliff Johnson	.05
63	Jimmy Key	.05
64	Dennis Lamp	.05
65	Gary Lavelle	.05
66	Buck Martinez	.05
67	Lloyd Moseby	.05
68	Rance Mulliniks	.05
69	Al Oliver	.05
70	Dave Stieb	.05
71	Louis Thornton	.05
72	Willie Upshaw	.05
73	Ernie Whitt	.05
74	Rick Aguilera **RC**	.75
75	Wally Backman	.05
76	Gary Carter	1.00
77	Ron Darling	.05
78	Len Dykstra **RC**	2.00
79	Sid Fernandez	.05
80	George Foster	.05
81	Dwight Gooden	.05
82	Tom Gorman	.05
83	Danny Heep	.05
84	Keith Hernandez	.05
85	Howard Johnson	.05
86	Ray Knight	.05
87	Terry Leach	.05
88	Ed Lynch	.05
89	Roger McDowell	.05
90	Jesse Orosco	.05
91	Tom Paciorek	.05
92	Ronn Reynolds	.05
93	Rafael Santana	.05
94	Doug Sisk	.05
95	Rusty Staub	.05
96	Darryl Strawberry	.05
97	Mookie Wilson	.05
98	Neil Allen	.05
99	Don Baylor	.05
100	Dale Berra	.05
101	Rich Bordi	.05
102	Marty Bystrom	.05
103	Joe Cowley	.05
104	Brian Fisher **RC**	.05
105	Ken Griffey	.05
106	Ron Guidry	.10
107	Ron Hassey	.05
108	Rickey Henderson	1.00
109	Don Mattingly	2.00
110	Bobby Meacham	.05
111	John Montefusco	.05
112	Phil Niekro	.75
113	Mike Pagliarulo	.05
114	Dan Pasqua	.05
115	Willie Randolph	.05
116	Dave Righetti	.05
117	Andre Robertson	.05
118	Billy Sample	.05
119	Bob Shirley	.05
120	Ed Whitson	.05
121	Dave Winfield	1.00
122	Butch Wynegar	.05
123	Dave Anderson	.05
124	Bob Bailor	.05
125	Greg Brock	.05
126	Enos Cabell	.05
127	Bobby Castillo	.05
128	Carlos Diaz	.05
129	Mariano Duncan	.05
130	Pedro Guerrero	.05
131	Orel Hershiser	.05
132	Rick Honeycutt	.05
133	Ken Howell	.05
134	Ken Landreaux	.05
135	Bill Madlock	.05
136	Candy Maldonado	.05
137	Mike Marshall	.05
138	Len Matuszek	.05
139	Tom Niedenfuer	.05
140	Alejandro Pena	.05
141	Jerry Reuss	.05
142	Bill Russell	.05
143	Steve Sax	.05
144	Mike Scioscia	.05
145	Fernando Valenzuela	.05
146	Bob Welch	.05
147	Terry Whitfield	.05
148	Juan Beniquez	.05
149	Bob Boone	.05
150	John Candelaria	.05
151	Rod Carew	1.00
152	Stewart Cliburn **RC**	.05
153	Doug DeCinces	.05
154	Brian Downing	.05
155	Ken Forsch	.05
156	Craig Gerber	.05
157	Bobby Grich	.05
158	George Hendrick	.05
159	Al Holland	.05
160	Reggie Jackson	1.50
161	Ruppert Jones	.05
162	Urbano Lugo **RC**	.05
163	Kirk McCaskill **RC**	.25
164	Donnie Moore	.05
165	Gary Pettis	.05
166	Ron Romanick	.05
167	Dick Schofield	.05
168	Daryl Sconiers	.05
169	Jim Slaton	.05
170	Don Sutton	.75
171	Mike Witt	.05
172	Buddy Bell	.05
173	Tom Browning	.05
174	Dave Concepcion	.05
175	Eric Davis	.05
176	Bo Diaz	.05
177	Nick Esasky	.05
178	John Franco	.05
179	Tom Hume	.05
180	Wayne Krenchicki	.05
181	Andy McGaffigan	.05
182	Eddie Milner	.05
183	Ron Oester	.05
184	Dave Parker	.05
185	Frank Pastore	.05
186	Tony Perez	.75
187	Ted Power	.05
188	Joe Price	.05
189	Gary Redus	.05
190	Ron Robinson	.05
191	Pete Rose	2.50
192	Mario Soto	.05
193	John Stuper	.05
194	Jay Tibbs	.05
195	Dave Van Gorder	.05
196	Max Venable	.05
197	Juan Agosto	.05
198	Harold Baines	.05
199	Floyd Bannister	.05
200	Britt Burns	.05
201	Julio Cruz	.05
202	Joel Davis **RC**	.05
203	Richard Dotson	.05
204	Carlton Fisk	1.00
205	Scott Fletcher	.05
206	Ozzie Guillen	.05
207	Jerry Hairston Sr.	.05
208	Tim Hulett	.05
209	Bob James	.05
210	Ron Kittle	.05
211	Rudy Law	.05
212	Bryan Little	.05
213	Gene Nelson	.05
214	Reid Nichols	.05
215	Luis Salazar	.05
216	Tom Seaver	1.00
217	Dan Spillner	.05
218	Bruce Tanner	.05
219	Greg Walker	.05
220	Dave Wehrmeister	.05
221	Juan Berenguer	.05
222	Dave Bergman	.05
223	Tom Brookens	.05
224	Darrell Evans	.05
225	Barbaro Garbey	.05
226	Kirk Gibson	.05
227	John Grubb	.05
228	Willie Hernandez	.05
229	Larry Herndon	.05
230	Chet Lemon	.05
231	Aurelio Lopez	.05
232	Jack Morris	.05
233	Randy O'Neal	.05
234	Lance Parrish	.05
235	Dan Petry	.05
236	Alex Sanchez	.05
237	Bill Scherrer	.05
238	Nelson Simmons	.05
239	Frank Tanana	.05
240	Walt Terrell	.05
241	Alan Trammell	.05
242	Lou Whitaker	.05
243	Milt Wilcox	.05
244	Hubie Brooks	.05
245	Tim Burke **RC**	.05
246	Andre Dawson	.35
247	Mike Fitzgerald	.05
248	Terry Francona	.05
249	Bill Gullickson	.05
250	Joe Hesketh	.05
251	Bill Laskey	.05
252	Vance Law	.05
253	Charlie Lea	.05
254	Gary Lucas	.05
255	David Palmer	.05
256	Tim Raines	.05
257	Jeff Reardon	.05
258	Bert Roberge	.05
259	Dan Schatzeder	.05
260	Bryn Smith	.05
261	Randy St. Claire **RC**	.05
262	Scot Thompson	.05
263	Tim Wallach	.05
264	U.L. Washington	.05
265	Mitch Webster **RC**	.05
266	Herm Winningham **RC**	.05
267	Floyd Youmans **RC**	.05
268	Don Aase	.05
269	Mike Boddicker	.05
270	Rich Dauer	.05
271	Storm Davis	.05
272	Rick Dempsey	.05
273	Ken Dixon	.05
274	Jim Dwyer	.05
275	Mike Flanagan	.05
276	Wayne Gross	.05
277	Lee Lacy	.05
278	Fred Lynn	.05
279	Tippy Martinez	.05
280	Dennis Martinez	.05
281	Scott McGregor	.05
282	Eddie Murray	1.00
283	Floyd Rayford	.05
284	Cal Ripken, Jr.	3.00
285	Gary Roenicke	.05
286	Larry Sheets	.05
287	John Shelby	.05
288	Nate Snell	.05
289	Sammy Stewart	.05
290	Alan Wiggins	.05
291	Mike Young	.05
292	Alan Ashby	.05
293	Mark Bailey	.05
294	Kevin Bass	.05
295	Jeff Calhoun	.05
296	Jose Cruz	.05
297	Glenn Davis	.05
298	Bill Dawley	.05
299	Frank DiPino	.05
300	Bill Doran	.05
301	Phil Garner	.05
302	Jeff Heathcock **RC**	.05
303	Charlie Kerfeld **RC**	.05
304	Bob Knepper	.05
305	Ron Mathis	.05
306	Jerry Mumphrey	.05
307	Jim Pankovits	.05
308	Terry Puhl	.05
309	Craig Reynolds	.05
310	Nolan Ryan	3.00
311	Mike Scott	.05
312	Dave Smith	.05
313	Dickie Thon	.05
314	Denny Walling	.05
315	Kurt Bevacqua	.05
316	Al Bumbry	.05
317	Jerry Davis	.05
318	Luis DeLeon	.05
319	Dave Dravecky	.05
320	Tim Flannery	.05
321	Steve Garvey	.30
322	Goose Gossage	.05
323	Tony Gwynn	1.50
324	Andy Hawkins	.05
325	LaMarr Hoyt	.05
326	Roy Lee Jackson	.05
327	Terry Kennedy	.05
328	Craig Lefferts	.05
329	Carmelo Martinez	.05
330	Lance McCullers **RC**	.05
331	Kevin McReynolds	.05
332	Graig Nettles	.05
333	Jerry Royster	.05
334	Eric Show	.05
335	Tim Stoddard	.05
336	Garry Templeton	.05
337	Mark Thurmond	.05
338	Ed Wojna	.05
339	Tony Armas	.05
340	Marty Barrett	.05
341	Wade Boggs	1.50
342	Dennis Boyd	.05
343	Bill Buckner	.05
344	Mark Clear	.05
345	Roger Clemens	2.00
346	Steve Crawford	.05
347	Mike Easler	.05
348	Dwight Evans	.05
349	Rich Gedman	.05
350	Jackie Gutierrez	.05
351	Glenn Hoffman	.05
352	Bruce Hurst	.05
353	Bruce Kison	.05

No.	Player	NM/M
354	Tim Lollar	.05
355	Steve Lyons	.05
356	Al Nipper	.05
357	Bob Ojeda	.05
358	Jim Rice	.30
359	Bob Stanley	.05
360	Mike Trujillo	.05
361	Thad Bosley	.05
362	Warren Brusstar	.05
363	Ron Cey	.05
364	Jody Davis	.05
365	Bob Dernier	.05
366	Shawon Dunston	.05
367	Leon Durham	.05
368	Dennis Eckersley	.75
369	Ray Fontenot	.05
370	George Frazier	.05
371	Bill Hatcher	.05
372	Dave Lopes	.05
373	Gary Matthews	.05
374	Ron Meredith	.05
375	Keith Moreland	.05
376	Reggie Patterson	.05
377	Dick Ruthven	.05
378	Ryne Sandberg	1.50
379	Scott Sanderson	.05
380	Lee Smith	.05
381	Lary Sorensen	.05
382	Chris Speier	.05
383	Rick Sutcliffe	.05
384	Steve Trout	.05
385	Gary Woods	.05
386	Bert Blyleven	.10
387	Tom Brunansky	.05
388	Randy Bush	.05
389	John Butcher	.05
390	Ron Davis	.05
391	Dave Engle	.05
392	Frank Eufemia	.05
393	Pete Filson	.05
394	Gary Gaetti	.05
395	Greg Gagne	.05
396	Mickey Hatcher	.05
397	Kent Hrbek	.05
398	Tim Laudner	.05
399	Rick Lysander	.05
400	Dave Meier	.05
401	Kirby Puckett	1.50
402	Mark Salas	.05
403	Ken Schrom	.05
404	Roy Smalley	.05
405	Mike Smithson	.05
406	Mike Stenhouse	.05
407	Tim Teufel	.05
408	Frank Viola	.05
409	Ron Washington	.05
410	Keith Atherton	.05
411	Dusty Baker	.05
412	Tim Birtsas **RC**	.05
413	Bruce Bochte	.05
414	Chris Codiroli	.05
415	Dave Collins	.05
416	Mike Davis	.05
417	Alfredo Griffin	.05
418	Mike Heath	.05
419	Steve Henderson	.05
420	Donnie Hill	.05
421	Jay Howell	.05
422	Tommy John	.10
423	Dave Kingman	.05
424	Bill Krueger	.05
425	Rick Langford	.05
426	Carney Lansford	.05
427	Steve McCatty	.05
428	Dwayne Murphy	.05
429	Steve Ontiveros **RC**	.05
430	Tony Phillips	.05
431	Jose Rijo	.05
432	Mickey Tettleton	.05
433	Luis Aguayo	.05
434	Larry Andersen	.05
435	Steve Carlton	1.00
436	Don Carman **RC**	.05
437	Tim Corcoran	.05
438	Darren Daulton	.05
439	John Denny	.05
440	Tom Foley	.05
441	Greg Gross	.05
442	Kevin Gross	.05
443	Von Hayes	.05
444	Charles Hudson	.05
445	Garry Maddox	.05
446	Shane Rawley	.05
447	Dave Rucker	.05
448	John Russell	.05
449	Juan Samuel	.05
450	Mike Schmidt	2.00
451	Rick Schu	.05
452	Dave Shipanoff	.05
453	Dave Stewart	.05
454	Jeff Stone	.05
455	Kent Tekulve	.05
456	Ozzie Virgil	.05
457	Glenn Wilson	.05
458	Jim Beattie	.05
459	Karl Best	.05
460	Barry Bonnell	.05
461	Phil Bradley	.05
462	Ivan Calderon **RC**	.05
463	Al Cowens	.05
464	Alvin Davis	.05
465	Dave Henderson	.05
466	Bob Kearney	.05
467	Mark Langston	.05
468	Bob Long	.05
469	Mike Moore	.05
470	Edwin Nunez	.05
471	Spike Owen	.05
472	Jack Perconte	.05
473	Jim Presley	.05
474	Donnie Scott	.05
475	Bill Swift **RC**	.05
476	Danny Tartabull	.05
477	Gorman Thomas	.05
478	Roy Thomas	.05
479	Ed Vande Berg	.05
480	Frank Wills	.05
481	Matt Young	.05
482	Ray Burris	.05
483	Jaime Cocanower	.05
484	Cecil Cooper	.05
485	Danny Darwin	.05
486	Rollie Fingers	.75
487	Jim Gantner	.05
488	Bob Gibson	.05
489	Moose Haas	.05
490	Teddy Higuera **RC**	.05
491	Paul Householder	.05
492	Pete Ladd	.05
493	Rick Manning	.05
494	Bob McClure	.05
495	Paul Molitor	1.00
496	Charlie Moore	.05
497	Ben Oglivie	.05
498	Randy Ready	.05
499	Earnie Riles **RC**	.05
500	Ed Romero	.05
501	Bill Schroeder	.05
502	Ray Searage	.05
503	Ted Simmons	.05
504	Pete Vuckovich	.05
505	Rick Waits	.05
506	Robin Yount	1.00
507	Len Barker	.05
508	Steve Bedrosian	.05
509	Bruce Benedict	.05
510	Rick Camp	.05
511	Rick Cerone	.05
512	Chris Chambliss	.05
513	Jeff Dedmon	.05
514	Terry Forster	.05
515	Gene Garber	.05
516	Terry Harper	.05
517	Bob Horner	.05
518	Glenn Hubbard	.05
519	Joe Johnson **RC**	.05
520	Brad Komminsk	.05
521	Rick Mahler	.05
522	Dale Murphy	.30
523	Ken Oberkfell	.05
524	Pascual Perez	.05
525	Gerald Perry	.05
526	Rafael Ramirez	.05
527	Steve Shields **RC**	.05
528	Zane Smith	.05
529	Bruce Sutter	.75
530	Milt Thompson **RC**	.05
531	Claudell Washington	.05
532	Paul Zuvella	.05
533	Vida Blue	.05
534	Bob Brenly	.05
535	Chris Brown **RC**	.05
536	Chili Davis	.05
537	Mark Davis	.05
538	Rob Deer	.05
539	Dan Driessen	.05
540	Scott Garrelts	.05
541	Dan Gladden	.05
542	Jim Gott	.05
543	David Green	.05
544	Atlee Hammaker	.05
545	Mike Jeffcoat	.05
546	Mike Krukow	.05
547	Dave LaPoint	.05
548	Jeff Leonard	.05
549	Greg Minton	.05
550	Alex Trevino	.05
551	Manny Trillo	.05
552	Jose Uribe **RC**	.05
553	Brad Wellman	.05
554	Frank Williams	.05
555	Joel Youngblood	.05
556	Alan Bannister	.05
557	Glenn Brummer	.05
558	Steve Buechele **RC**	.05
559	Jose Guzman **RC**	.05
560	Toby Harrah	.05
561	Greg Harris	.05
562	Dwayne Henry **RC**	.05
563	Burt Hooton	.05
564	Charlie Hough	.05
565	Mike Mason	.05
566	Oddibe McDowell **RC**	.05
567	Dickie Noles	.05
568	Pete O'Brien	.05
569	Larry Parrish	.05
570	Dave Rozema	.05
571	Dave Schmidt	.05
572	Don Slaught	.05
573	Wayne Tolleson	.05
574	Duane Walker	.05
575	Gary Ward	.05
576	Chris Welsh	.05
577	Curtis Wilkerson	.05
578	George Wright	.05
579	Chris Bando	.05
580	Tony Bernazard	.05
581	Brett Butler	.05
582	Ernie Camacho	.05
583	Joe Carter	.05
584	Carmello Castillo (Carmelo)	.05
585	Jamie Easterly	.05
586	Julio Franco	.05
587	Mel Hall	.05
588	Mike Hargrove	.05
589	Neal Heaton	.05
590	Brook Jacoby	.05
591	Otis Nixon **RC**	.25
592	Jerry Reed	.05
593	Vern Ruhle	.05
594	Pat Tabler	.05
595	Rich Thompson	.05
596	Andre Thornton	.05
597	Dave Von Ohlen	.05
598	George Vukovich	.05
599	Tom Waddell	.05
600	Curt Wardle	.05
601	Jerry Willard	.05
602	Bill Almon	.05
603	Mike Bielecki	.05
604	Sid Bream	.05
605	Mike Brown	.05
606	Pat Clements **RC**	.05
607	Jose DeLeon	.05
608	Denny Gonzalez	.05
609	Cecilio Guante	.05
610	Steve Kemp	.05
611	Sam Khalifa	.05
612	Lee Mazzilli	.05
613	Larry McWilliams	.05
614	Jim Morrison	.05
615	Joe Orsulak **RC**	.25
616	Tony Pena	.05
617	Johnny Ray	.05
618	Rick Reuschel	.05
619	R.J. Reynolds	.05
620	Rick Rhoden	.05
621	Don Robinson	.05
622	Jason Thompson	.05
623	Lee Tunnell	.05
624	Jim Winn	.05
625	Marvell Wynne	.05
626	Dwight Gooden/IA	.05
627	Don Mattingly/IA	.50
628	Pete Rose (4,192 Hits)	1.00
629	Rod Carew (3,000 Hits)	.25
630	Phil Niekro, Tom Seaver (300 Wins)	.25
631	Ouch! (Don Baylor)	.05
632	Instant Offense (Tim Raines, Darryl Strawberry)	.05
633	Shortstops Supreme (Cal Ripken, Jr., Alan Trammell)	1.00
634	Boggs & "Hero" (Wade Boggs, George Brett)	1.00
635	Braves Dynamic Duo (Bob Horner, Dale Murphy)	.25
636	Cardinal Ignitors (Vince Coleman, Willie McGee)	.25
637	Terror on the Basepaths (Vince Coleman)	.05
638	Charlie Hustle & Dr. K (Dwight Gooden, Pete Rose)	.50
639	1984 and 1985 A.L. Batting Champs (Wade Boggs, Don Mattingly)	1.00
640	N.L. West Sluggers (Steve Garvey, Dale Murphy, Dave Parker)	.25
641	Staff Aces (Dwight Gooden, Fernando Valenzuela)	.10
642	Blue Jay Stoppers (Jimmy Key, Dave Stieb)	.05
643	A.L. All-Star Backstops (Carlton Fisk, Rich Gedman)	.10
644	Major League Prospect (Benito Santiago **RC**, Gene Walter **RC**)	1.00
645	Major League Prospect (Colin Ward **RC**, Mike Woodard **RC**)	.10
646	Major League Prospect (Kal Daniels **RC**, Paul O'Neill **RC**)	2.00
647	Major League Prospect (Andres Galarraga **RC**, Fred Toliver **RC**)	3.00
648	Major League Prospect (Curt Ford **RC**, Bob Kipper **RC**)	.10
649	Major League Prospect (Jose Canseco **RC**, Eric Plunk **RC**)	5.00
650	Major League Prospect (Mark McLemore **RC**, Gus Polidor **RC**)	.75
651	Major League Prospect (Mickey Brantley **RC**, Rob Woodward **RC**)	.10
652	Major League Prospect (Mark Funderburk **RC**, Billy Joe Robidoux **RC**)	.10
653	Major League Prospect (Cecil Fielder **RC**, Cory Snyder **RC**)	1.50
654	Checklist 1-97	.05
655	Checklist 98-196	.05
656	Checklist 197-291	.05
657	Checklist 292-385	.05
658	Checklist 386-482	.05
659	Checklist 483-578	.05
660	Checklist 579-660	.05

All Stars

Fleer's choices for a major league All-Star team make up this 12-card set. The cards were randomly inserted in 35¢ wax packs and 59¢ cello packs. The card fronts have a color photo set against a bright red background for A.L. players or a bright blue background for N.L. players. Backs feature the player's career highlights on a red and blue background.

		NM/M
Complete Set (12):		7.50
Common Player:		.10
1	Don Mattingly	2.00
2	Tom Herr	.10
3	George Brett	2.00
4	Gary Carter	.75
5	Cal Ripken, Jr.	4.00
6	Dave Parker	.10
7	Rickey Henderson	.75
8	Pedro Guerrero	.10
9	Dan Quisenberry	.10
10	Dwight Gooden	.10
11	Gorman Thomas	.10
12	John Tudor	.10

Future Hall Of Famers

The 1986 Future Hall of Famers set is comprised of six players Fleer felt would gain eventual entrance into the Baseball Hall of Fame. The cards are the standard 2-1/2" x 3-1/2" and were randomly inserted in three-pack rack packs. Card fronts feature a player photo set against a blue background with horizontal light blue stripes. Backs are printed in black on blue and feature career highlights in narrative form.

		NM/M
Complete Set (6):		5.00
Common Player:		.75
1	Pete Rose	2.00
2	Steve Carlton	.75
3	Tom Seaver	.75
4	Rod Carew	.75
5	Nolan Ryan	3.00
6	Reggie Jackson	1.00

Box Panels

Picking up on a Donruss idea, Fleer issued eight cards in panels of four on the bottoms of the wax and cello pack boxes. The cards are numbered C-1 through C-8 and are 2-1/2" x 3-1/2", with a complete panel measuring 5" x 7-1/8". Included in the eight cards are six players and two team logo/checklist cards.

		NM/M
Complete Panel Set (2):		4.00
Complete Singles Set (8):		4.00
Common Single Player:		.20
Panel		2.50
1	Royals Logo/Checklist	.05
2	George Brett	2.00
3	Ozzie Guillen	.20
4	Dale Murphy	.40
Panel		1.50
5	Cardinals Logo/Checklist	.05
6	Tom Browning	.20
7	Gary Carter	1.00
8	Carlton Fisk	1.00

Update

Issued near the end of the baseball season, the 1986 Fleer Update set consists of cards numbered U-1 through U-132. The 2-1/2" x 3-1/2" cards are identical in design to the regular 1986 Fleer set. The purpose of the set is to update player trades and include rookies not depicted in the regular issue. The set was issued with team logo stickers in a specially designed box and was available only through hobby dealers.

		NM/M
Unopened Fact. Set (132):		40.00
Complete Set (132):		30.00
Common Player:		.05
1	Mike Aldrete **RC**	.05
2	Andy Allanson **RC**	.05
3	Neil Allen	.05
4	Joaquin Andujar	.05
5	Paul Assenmacher **RC**	.05
6	Scott Bailes **RC**	.05
7	Jay Baller **RC**	.05
8	Scott Bankhead **RC**	.05
9	Bill Bathe **RC**	.05
10	Don Baylor	.05
11	Billy Beane **RC**	.05
12	Steve Bedrosian	.05
13	Juan Beniquez	.05
14	Barry Bonds **RC**	25.00
15	Bobby Bonilla **RC**	1.00
16	Rich Bordi	.05
17	Bill Campbell	.05
18	Tom Candiotti	.05
19	John Cangelosi **RC**	.05
20	Jose Canseco	4.00
21	Chuck Cary **RC**	.05
22	Juan Castillo **RC**	.05
23	Rick Cerone	.05
24	John Cerutti **RC**	.05
25	Will Clark **RC**	1.00
26	Mark Clear	.05
27	Darnell Coles **RC**	.05
28	Dave Collins	.05
29	Tim Conroy	.05
30	Ed Correa **RC**	.05
31	Joe Cowley	.05
32	Bill Dawley	.05
33	Rob Deer	.05
34	John Denny	.05
35	Jim DeShaies	.05
36	Doug Drabek **RC**	1.00
37	Mike Easler	.05
38	Mark Eichhorn **RC**	.05
39	Dave Engle	.05
40	Mike Fischlin	.05
41	Scott Fletcher	.05
42	Terry Forster	.05
43	Terry Francona	.05
44	Andres Galarraga	.50
45	Lee Guetterman **RC**	.05
46	Bill Gullickson	.05
47	Jackie Gutierrez	.05
48	Moose Haas	.05
49	Billy Hatcher	.05
50	Mike Heath	.05
51	Guy Hoffman **RC**	.05
52	Tom Hume	.05
53	Pete Incaviglia **RC**	.50
54	Dane Iorg	.05
55	Chris James **RC**	.05
56	Stan Javier **RC**	.05
57	Tommy John	.15
58	Tracy Jones **RC**	.05
59	Wally Joyner **RC**	1.00
60	Wayne Krenchicki	.05
61	John Kruk **RC**	1.00
62	Mike LaCoss	.05
63	Pete Ladd	.05
64	Dave LaPoint	.05
65	Mike LaValliere **RC**	.05
66	Rudy Law	.05
67	Dennis Leonard	.05
68	Steve Lombardozzi **RC**	.05
69	Aurelio Lopez	.05
70	Mickey Mahler	.05
71	Candy Maldonado	.05
72	Roger Mason **RC**	.05
73	Greg Mathews **RC**	.05
74	Andy McGaffigan	.05
75	Joel McKeon **RC**	.05
76	Kevin Mitchell **RC**	.50
77	Bill Mooneyham **RC**	.05
78	Omar Moreno	.05
79	Jerry Mumphrey	.05
80	Al Newman **RC**	.05
81	Phil Niekro	.50
82	Randy Niemann	.05
83	Juan Nieves **RC**	.05
84	Bob Ojeda	.05
85	Rick Ownbey	.05
86	Tom Paciorek	.05
87	David Palmer	.05
88	Jeff Parrett **RC**	.05
89	Pat Perry **RC**	.05
90	Dan Plesac **RC**	.05
91	Darrell Porter	.05
92	Luis Quinones **RC**	.05
93	Rey Quinonez **RC**	.05
94	Gary Redus	.05
95	Jeff Reed **RC**	.05
96	Bip Roberts **RC**	.05
97	Billy Joe Robidoux	.05
98	Gary Roenicke	.05
99	Ron Roenicke	.05
100	Angel Salazar	.05
101	Joe Sambito	.05
102	Billy Sample	.05
103	Dave Schmidt	.05
104	Ken Schrom	.05
105	Ruben Sierra **RC**	.75
106	Ted Simmons	.05
107	Sammy Stewart	.05
108	Kurt Stillwell **RC**	.05
109	Dale Sveum **RC**	.05
110	Tim Teufel	.05
111	Bob Tewksbury **RC**	.05
112	Andres Thomas **RC**	.05
113	Jason Thompson	.05
114	Milt Thompson	.05
115	Rob Thompson **RC**	.05
116	Jay Tibbs	.05
117	Fred Toliver	.05
118	Wayne Tolleson	.05
119	Alex Trevino	.05
120	Manny Trillo	.05
121	Ed Vande Berg	.05
122	Ozzie Virgil	.05
123	Tony Walker **RC**	.05
124	Gene Walter	.05
125	Duane Ward **RC**	.05
126	Jerry Willard	.05
127	Mitch Williams **RC**	.05
128	Reggie Williams **RC**	.05
129	Bobby Witt **RC**	.05
130	Marvell Wynne	.05
131	Steve Yeager	.05
132	Checklist	.05

Baseball's Best

The 1986 Fleer Baseball's Best set was produced for the McCrory's retail chain and its affiliated stores. Subtitled "Sluggers vs. Pitchers," the set contains 22 each of the game's best hitters and pitchers. The 2-1/2" x 3-1/2" cards have color action photos on front. Backs are done in blue and red and carry players' personal and statistical data. The sets were issued in a specially designed box with six team logo stickers.

		NM/M
Complete Set (44):		4.00
Common Player:		.10
1	Bert Blyleven	.25
2	Wade Boggs	.75
3	George Brett	1.00
4	Tom Browning	.10
5	Jose Canseco	.60
6	Will Clark	.15
7	Roger Clemens	1.00
8	Alvin Davis	.10
9	Julio Franco	.10
10	Kirk Gibson	.10
11	Dwight Gooden	.10
12	Goose Gossage	.10
13	Pedro Guerrero	.10
14	Ron Guidry	.10
15	Tony Gwynn	.75
16	Orel Hershiser	.10
17	Kent Hrbek	.10
18	Reggie Jackson	.75
19	Wally Joyner	.15
20	Charlie Leibrandt	.10
21	Don Mattingly	1.00
22	Willie McGee	.10
23	Jack Morris	.10
24	Dale Murphy	.25
25	Eddie Murray	.50
26	Jeff Reardon	.10
27	Rick Reuschel	.10
28	Cal Ripken, Jr.	2.00
29	Pete Rose	1.50
30	Nolan Ryan	2.00
31	Bret Saberhagen	.10
32	Ryne Sandberg	.75
33	Mike Schmidt	1.00
34	Tom Seaver	.50
35	Bryn Smith	.10
36	Mario Soto	.10
37	Dave Stieb	.10
38	Darryl Strawberry	.10
39	Rick Sutcliffe	.10
40	John Tudor	.10
41	Fernando Valenzuela	.10
42	Bobby Witt	.10
43	Mike Witt	.10
44	Robin Yount	.50

League Leaders

Fleer's 1986 "League Leaders" set features 44 of the game's top players and was issued through the Walgreen's drug store chain. Fronts contain a color photo and feature player name, team and position in a blue band near the bottom of the card. The words "League Leaders" appear in a red band at the top of the card. The background for the card fronts is alternating blue and white stripes. The card backs are printed in blue, red and white and carry statistical information and team logo. Cards are the standard 2-1/2" x 3-1/2". The set was issued in a special cardboard box, along with six team logo stickers.

		NM/M
Complete Set (44):		4.00
Common Player:		.10
1	Wade Boggs	.60
2	George Brett	.75
3	Jose Canseco	.60
4	Rod Carew	.40
5	Gary Carter	.40
6	Jack Clark	.10
7	Vince Coleman	.10
8	Jose Cruz	.10
9	Alvin Davis	.10
10	Mariano Duncan	.10
11	Leon Durham	.10
12	Carlton Fisk	.40
13	Julio Franco	.10
14	Scott Garrelts	.10
15	Steve Garvey	.25
16	Dwight Gooden	.10
17	Ozzie Guillen	.10
18	Willie Hernandez	.10
19	Bob Horner	.10
20	Kent Hrbek	.10
21	Charlie Leibrandt	.10
22	Don Mattingly	.75
23	Oddibe McDowell	.10
24	Willie McGee	.10
25	Keith Moreland	.10
26	Lloyd Moseby	.10
27	Dale Murphy	.25
28	Phil Niekro	.35
29	Joe Orsulak	.10
30	Dave Parker	.10
31	Lance Parrish	.10
32	Kirby Puckett	.60
33	Tim Raines	.10
34	Earnie Riles	.10
35	Cal Ripken, Jr.	1.50
36	Pete Rose	1.00
37	Bret Saberhagen	.10
38	Juan Samuel	.10
39	Ryne Sandberg	.60
40	Tom Seaver	.40
41	Lee Smith	.10
42	Ozzie Smith	.60
43	Dave Stieb	.10
44	Robin Yount	.40

Limited Edition

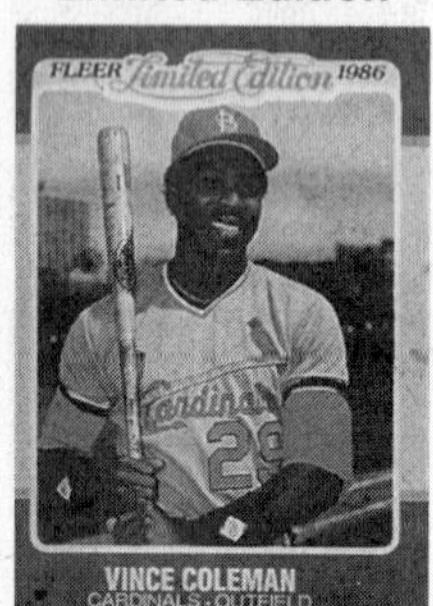

Produced for the McCrory's store chain and its affiliates for the second year in a row, the Limited Edition set contains 44 cards. In standard 2-1/2" x 3-1/2" size, cards have color photos enclosed by green, red and yellow trim. Backs carry black print on two shades of red. The set was issued in a special cardboard box, along with six team logo stickers.

		NM/M
Complete Set (44):		4.00
Common Player:		.10
1	Doyle Alexander	.10
2	Joaquin Andujar	.10
3	Harold Baines	.10
4	Wade Boggs	.60
5	Phil Bradley	.10
6	George Brett	.75
7	Hubie Brooks	.10
8	Chris Brown	.10
9	Tom Brunansky	.10
10	Gary Carter	.50
11	Vince Coleman	.10
12	Cecil Cooper	.10
13	Jose Cruz	.10
14	Mike Davis	.10
15	Carlton Fisk	.50
16	Julio Franco	.10
17	Damaso Garcia	.10
18	Rich Gedman	.10
19	Kirk Gibson	.10
20	Dwight Gooden	.10
21	Pedro Guerrero	.10
22	Tony Gwynn	.60
23	Rickey Henderson	.50
24	Orel Hershiser	.10
25	LaMarr Hoyt	.10
26	Reggie Jackson	.60
27	Don Mattingly	.75
28	Oddibe McDowell	.10
29	Willie McGee	.10
30	Paul Molitor	.50
31	Dale Murphy	.20
32	Eddie Murray	.50
33	Dave Parker	.10
34	Tony Pena	.10
35	Jeff Reardon	.10
36	Cal Ripken, Jr.	1.50
37	Pete Rose	1.00
38	Bret Saberhagen	.10
39	Juan Samuel	.10
40	Ryne Sandberg	.60
41	Mike Schmidt	.75
42	Lee Smith	.10
43	Don Sutton	.40
44	Lou Whitaker	.10

Mini

Fleer's 1986 "Classic Miniatures" set contains 120 cards that measure 1-13/16" x 2-9/16". The design of the high-gloss cards is identical to the regular 1986 Fleer set but the player photos are entirely different. The set, which was issued in a specially designed box along with 18 team logo stickers, was available only through hobby dealers.

		NM/M
Complete Set (120):		3.50
Common Player:		.05
1	George Brett	.65
2	Dan Quisenberry	.05
3	Bret Saberhagen	.05
4	Lonnie Smith	.05
5	Willie Wilson	.05
6	Jack Clark	.05
7	Vince Coleman	.05
8	Tom Herr	.05
9	Willie McGee	.05
10	Ozzie Smith	.50
11	John Tudor	.05
12	Jesse Barfield	.05
13	George Bell	.05
14	Tony Fernandez	.05
15	Damaso Garcia	.05
16	Dave Stieb	.05
17	Gary Carter	.40
18	Ron Darling	.05
19	Dwight Gooden	.05
20	Keith Hernandez	.05
21	Darryl Strawberry	.05
22	Ron Guidry	.05
23	Rickey Henderson	.40
24	Don Mattingly	.65
25	Dave Righetti	.05
26	Dave Winfield	.40
27	Mariano Duncan	.05
28	Pedro Guerrero	.05
29	Bill Madlock	.05
30	Mike Marshall	.05
31	Fernando Valenzuela	.05
32	Reggie Jackson	.50
33	Gary Pettis	.05
34	Ron Romanick	.05
35	Don Sutton	.30
36	Mike Witt	.05
37	Buddy Bell	.05
38	Tom Browning	.05
39	Dave Parker	.05
40	Pete Rose	.75
41	Mario Soto	.05
42	Harold Baines	.05
43	Carlton Fisk	.40
44	Ozzie Guillen	.05
45	Ron Kittle	.05
46	Tom Seaver	.40
47	Kirk Gibson	.05
48	Jack Morris	.05
49	Lance Parrish	.05
50	Alan Trammell	.05
51	Lou Whitaker	.05
52	Hubie Brooks	.05
53	Andre Dawson	.25
54	Tim Raines	.05
55	Bryn Smith	.05
56	Tim Wallach	.05
57	Mike Boddicker	.05
58	Eddie Murray	.40
59	Cal Ripken, Jr.	1.25
60	John Shelby	.05
61	Mike Young	.05
62	Jose Cruz	.05
63	Glenn Davis	.05
64	Phil Garner	.05
65	Nolan Ryan	1.25
66	Mike Scott	.05
67	Steve Garvey	.15
68	Goose Gossage	.05
69	Tony Gwynn	.50
70	Andy Hawkins	.05
71	Garry Templeton	.05
72	Wade Boggs	.50
73	Roger Clemens	.65
74	Dwight Evans	.05
75	Rich Gedman	.05
76	Jim Rice	.25
77	Shawon Dunston	.05
78	Leon Durham	.05
79	Keith Moreland	.05
80	Ryne Sandberg	.50
81	Rick Sutcliffe	.05
82	Bert Blyleven	.05
83	Tom Brunansky	.05
84	Kent Hrbek	.05
85	Kirby Puckett	.50
86	Bruce Bochte	.05
87	Jose Canseco	.40
88	Mike Davis	.05
89	Jay Howell	.05
90	Dwayne Murphy	.05
91	Steve Carlton	.40
92	Von Hayes	.05
93	Juan Samuel	.05
94	Mike Schmidt	.65
95	Glenn Wilson	.05
96	Phil Bradley	.05
97	Alvin Davis	.05
98	Jim Presley	.05
99	Danny Tartabull	.05
100	Cecil Cooper	.05
101	Paul Molitor	.40
102	Earnie Riles	.05
103	Robin Yount	.40
104	Bob Horner	.05
105	Dale Murphy	.20
106	Bruce Sutter	.30
107	Claudell Washington	.05
108	Chris Brown	.05
109	Chili Davis	.05
110	Scott Garrelts	.05
111	Oddibe McDowell	.05
112	Pete O'Brien	.05
113	Gary Ward	.05
114	Brett Butler	.05
115	Julio Franco	.05
116	Brook Jacoby	.05
117	Mike Brown	.05
118	Joe Orsulak	.05
119	Tony Pena	.05
120	R.J. Reynolds	.05

Star Stickers

Fleer's 1986 sticker-card set again measures 2-1/2" x 3-1/2" and features color photos inside dark maroon borders. Backs are identical to the 1986 baseball card issue except for the 1-132 numbering system and blue ink instead of yellow. Card #132 is a multi-player card featuring Dwight Gooden and Dale Murphy on the front and a complete checklist for the set on the reverse. The cards were sold in wax packs with team logo stickers.

		NM/M
Complete Set (132):		7.00
Common Player:		.05
Wax Pack (5):		1.00
Wax Box (36):		12.00
1	Harold Baines	.05
2	Jesse Barfield	.05
3	Don Baylor	.05
4	Juan Beniquez	.05
5	Tim Birtsas	.05
6	Bert Blyleven	.10
7	Bruce Bochte	.05
8	Wade Boggs	.50
9	Dennis Boyd	.05
10	Phil Bradley	.05
11	George Brett	.65
12	Hubie Brooks	.05
13	Chris Brown	.05
14	Tom Browning	.05
15	Tom Brunansky	.05
16	Bill Buckner	.05
17	Britt Burns	.05
18	Brett Butler	.05
19	Jose Canseco	.40
20	Rod Carew	.40
21	Steve Carlton	.40
22	Don Carman	.05
23	Gary Carter	.40
24	Jack Clark	.05
25	Vince Coleman	.05
26	Cecil Cooper	.05
27	Jose Cruz	.05
28	Ron Darling	.05
29	Alvin Davis	.05
30	Jody Davis	.05
31	Mike Davis	.05
32	Andre Dawson	.25
33	Mariano Duncan	.05
34	Shawon Dunston	.05
35	Leon Durham	.05
36	Darrell Evans	.05
37	Tony Fernandez	.05
38	Carlton Fisk	.40
39	John Franco	.05
40	Julio Franco	.05
41	Damaso Garcia	.05
42	Scott Garrelts	.05
43	Steve Garvey	.15
44	Rich Gedman	.05
45	Kirk Gibson	.05
46	Dwight Gooden	.05
47	Pedro Guerrero	.05
48	Ron Guidry	.05
49	Ozzie Guillen	.05
50	Tony Gwynn	.50
51	Andy Hawkins	.05
52	Von Hayes	.05
53	Rickey Henderson	.40
54	Tom Henke	.05
55	Keith Hernandez	.05
56	Willie Hernandez	.05
57	Tom Herr	.05
58	Orel Hershiser	.05
59	Teddy Higuera	.05
60	Bob Horner	.05
61	Charlie Hough	.05
62	Jay Howell	.05
63	LaMarr Hoyt	.05
64	Kent Hrbek	.05
65	Reggie Jackson	.50
66	Bob James	.05
67	Dave Kingman	.05
68	Ron Kittle	.05
69	Charlie Leibrandt	.05
70	Fred Lynn	.05
71	Mike Marshall	.05
72	Don Mattingly	.65
73	Oddibe McDowell	.05
74	Willie McGee	.05
75	Scott McGregor	.05
76	Paul Molitor	.40
77	Donnie Moore	.05
78	Keith Moreland	.05
79	Jack Morris	.05
80	Dale Murphy	.15
81	Eddie Murray	.40
82	Phil Niekro	.35
83	Joe Orsulak	.05
84	Dave Parker	.05
85	Lance Parrish	.05
86	Larry Parrish	.05
87	Tony Pena	.05
88	Gary Pettis	.05
89	Jim Presley	.05
90	Kirby Puckett	.50
91	Dan Quisenberry	.05
92	Tim Raines	.05
93	Johnny Ray	.05
94	Jeff Reardon	.05
95	Rick Reuschel	.05
96	Jim Rice	.25
97	Dave Righetti	.05
98	Earnie Riles	.05
99	Cal Ripken, Jr.	1.25
100	Ron Romanick	.05
101	Pete Rose	.85
102	Nolan Ryan	1.25
103	Bret Saberhagen	.05
104	Mark Salas	.05
105	Juan Samuel	.05
106	Ryne Sandberg	.50
107	Mike Schmidt	.65
108	Mike Scott	.05
109	Tom Seaver	.40
110	Bryn Smith	.05
111	Dave Smith	.05
112	Lee Smith	.05
113	Ozzie Smith	.50
114	Mario Soto	.05
115	Dave Stieb	.05
116	Darryl Strawberry	.05
117	Bruce Sutter	.35
118	Garry Templeton	.05
119	Gorman Thomas	.05
120	Andre Thornton	.05
121	Alan Trammell	.05
122	John Tudor	.05
123	Fernando Valenzuela	.05
124	Frank Viola	.05
125	Gary Ward	.05
126	Lou Whitaker	.05
127	Frank White	.05
128	Glenn Wilson	.05
129	Willie Wilson	.05
130	Dave Winfield	.40
131	Robin Yount	.40
132	Dwight Gooden, Dale Murphy	.10

Star Stickers Box Panels

Four cards, numbered S-1 through S-4, were placed on the bottoms of 1986 Fleer Star Stickers wax pack boxes. The cards are nearly identical in format to the regular issue

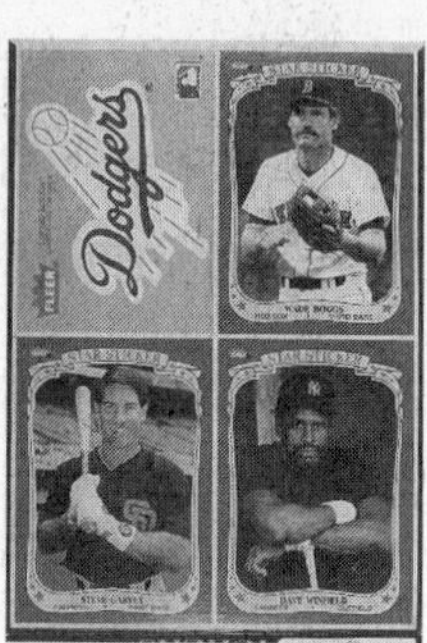

sticker cards. Individual cards measure 2-1/2" x 3-1/2" in size, while a complete panel of four measures 5" x 7-1/8".

		NM/M
Complete Panel Set:		2.00
Complete Singles Set (4):		2.00
Common Single Player:		.30
1	Dodgers Logo	.05
2	Wade Boggs	1.25
3	Steve Garvey	.30
4	Dave Winfield	1.00

1987 Fleer

The 1987 Fleer set consists of 660 cards. Fronts feature a graduated blue-to-white border design. The player's name and position appear in the upper-left corner of the card; his team logo is located in the lower-right. Backs are done in blue, red and white and contain an innovative "Pro Scouts Report" feature which rates the player's batting or pitching skills. For the third year in a row, Fleer included its "Major League Prospects" subset. Fleer produced a glossy-finish Collectors Edition set which came housed in a specially-designed tin box. After experiencing a dramatic hike in price during 1987, the glossy set now sells for only a few dollars more than the regular issue.

		NM/M
Unopened Fact. Set (672):		65.00
Complete Set (660):		50.00
Common Player:		.05
Wax Pack (15/17):		3.00
Wax Box (36):		100.00
Cello Pack (28):		5.00
Cello Box (24):		100.00
Rack Pack (51):		8.00
Rack Box (24):		160.00
1	Rick Aguilera	.05
2	Richard Anderson	.05
3	Wally Backman	.05
4	Gary Carter	.75
5	Ron Darling	.05
6	Len Dykstra	.05
7	Kevin Elster **RC**	.15
8	Sid Fernandez	.05
9	Dwight Gooden	.05
10	Ed Hearn **RC**	.05
11	Danny Heep	.05
12	Keith Hernandez	.05
13	Howard Johnson	.05
14	Ray Knight	.05
15	Lee Mazzilli	.05
16	Roger McDowell	.05
17	Kevin Mitchell	.05
18	Randy Niemann	.05
19	Bob Ojeda	.05
20	Jesse Orosco	.05
21	Rafael Santana	.05
22	Doug Sisk	.05
23	Darryl Strawberry	.05
24	Tim Teufel	.05

25 Mookie Wilson .05
26 Tony Armas .05
27 Marty Barrett .05
28 Don Baylor .05
29 Wade Boggs 1.00
30 Oil Can Boyd .05
31 Bill Buckner .05
32 Roger Clemens 2.00
33 Steve Crawford .05
34 Dwight Evans .05
35 Rich Gedman .05
36 Dave Henderson .05
37 Bruce Hurst .05
38 Tim Lollar .05
39 Al Nipper .05
40 Spike Owen .05
41 Jim Rice .30
42 Ed Romero .05
43 Joe Sambito .05
44 Calvin Schiraldi .05
45 Tom Seaver .75
46 Jeff Sellers **RC** .05
47 Bob Stanley .05
48 Sammy Stewart .05
49 Larry Andersen .05
50 Alan Ashby .05
51 Kevin Bass .05
52 Jeff Calhoun .05
53 Jose Cruz .05
54 Danny Darwin .05
55 Glenn Davis .05
56 Jim Deshaies **RC** .10
57 Bill Doran .05
58 Phil Garner .05
59 Billy Hatcher .05
60 Charlie Kerfeld .05
61 Bob Knepper .05
62 Dave Lopes .05
63 Aurelio Lopez .05
64 Jim Pankovits .05
65 Terry Puhl .05
66 Craig Reynolds .05
67 Nolan Ryan 3.00
68 Mike Scott .05
69 Dave Smith .05
70 Dickie Thon .05
71 Tony Walker .05
72 Denny Walling .05
73 Bob Boone .05
74 Rick Burleson .05
75 John Candelaria .05
76 Doug Corbett .05
77 Doug DeCinces .05
78 Brian Downing .05
79 Chuck Finley **RC** 1.00
80 Terry Forster .05
81 Bobby Grich .05
82 George Hendrick .05
83 Jack Howell **RC** .05
84 Reggie Jackson 1.00
85 Ruppert Jones .05
86 Wally Joyner .05
87 Gary Lucas .05
88 Kirk McCaskill .05
89 Donnie Moore .05
90 Gary Pettis .05
91 Vern Ruhle .05
92 Dick Schofield .05
93 Don Sutton .65
94 Rob Wilfong .05
95 Mike Witt .05
96 Doug Drabek .05
97 Mike Easler .05
98 Mike Fischlin .05
99 Brian Fisher .05
100 Ron Guidry .10
101 Rickey Henderson .75
102 Tommy John .10
103 Ron Kittle .05
104 Don Mattingly 2.00
105 Bobby Meacham .05
106 Joe Niekro .05
107 Mike Pagliarulo .05
108 Dan Pasqua .05
109 Willie Randolph .05
110 Dennis Rasmussen .05
111 Dave Righetti .05
112 Gary Roenicke .05
113 Rod Scurry .05
114 Bob Shirley .05
115 Joel Skinner .05
116 Tim Stoddard .05
117 Bob Tewksbury **RC** .35
118 Wayne Tolleson .05
119 Claudell Washington .05
120 Dave Winfield .75
121 Steve Buechele .05
122 Ed Correa **RC** .05
123 Scott Fletcher .05
124 Jose Guzman .05
125 Toby Harrah .05
126 Greg Harris .05
127 Charlie Hough .05
128 Pete Incaviglia .05
129 Mike Mason .05
130 Oddibe McDowell .05
131 Dale Mohorcic **RC** .05
132 Pete O'Brien .05
133 Tom Paciorek .05
134 Larry Parrish .05
135 Geno Petralli .05
136 Darrell Porter .05
137 Jeff Russell .05
138 Ruben Sierra .05
139 Don Slaught .05
140 Gary Ward .05
141 Curtis Wilkerson .05
142 Mitch Williams **RC** .10
143 Bobby Witt **RC** .10
144 Dave Bergman .05
145 Tom Brookens .05
146 Bill Campbell .05
147 Chuck Cary **RC** .05
148 Darnell Coles .05
149 Dave Collins .05
150 Darrell Evans .05
151 Kirk Gibson .05
152 John Grubb .05
153 Willie Hernandez .05
154 Larry Herndon .05
155 Eric King **RC** .05
156 Chet Lemon .05
157 Dwight Lowry .05
158 Jack Morris .05
159 Randy O'Neal .05
160 Lance Parrish .05
161 Dan Petry .05
162 Pat Sheridan .05
163 Jim Slaton .05
164 Frank Tanana .05
165 Walt Terrell .05
166 Mark Thurmond .05
167 Alan Trammell .05
168 Lou Whitaker .05
169 Luis Aguayo .05
170 Steve Bedrosian .05
171 Don Carman .05
172 Darren Daulton .05
173 Greg Gross .05
174 Kevin Gross .05
175 Von Hayes .05
176 Charles Hudson .05
177 Tom Hume .05
178 Steve Jeltz .05
179 Mike Maddux **RC** .05
180 Shane Rawley .05
181 Gary Redus .05
182 Ron Roenicke .05
183 Bruce Ruffin **RC** .10
184 John Russell .05
185 Juan Samuel .05
186 Dan Schatzeder .05
187 Mike Schmidt 2.00
188 Rick Schu .05
189 Jeff Stone .05
190 Kent Tekulve .05
191 Milt Thompson .05
192 Glenn Wilson .05
193 Buddy Bell .05
194 Tom Browning .05
195 Sal Butera .05
196 Dave Concepcion .05
197 Kal Daniels .05
198 Eric Davis .05
199 John Denny .05
200 Bo Diaz .05
201 Nick Esasky .05
202 John Franco .05
203 Bill Gullickson .05
204 Barry Larkin **RC** 2.00
205 Eddie Milner .05
206 Rob Murphy **RC** .05
207 Ron Oester .05
208 Dave Parker .05
209 Tony Perez .65
210 Ted Power .05
211 Joe Price .05
212 Ron Robinson .05
213 Pete Rose 2.50
214 Mario Soto .05
215 Kurt Stillwell **RC** .05
216 Max Venable .05
217 Chris Welsh .05
218 Carl Willis **RC** .05
219 Jesse Barfield .05
220 George Bell .05
221 Bill Caudill .05
222 John Cerutti **RC** .05
223 Jim Clancy .05
224 Mark Eichhorn **RC** .10
225 Tony Fernandez .05
226 Damaso Garcia .05
227 Kelly Gruber .05
228 Tom Henke .05
229 Garth Iorg .05
230 Cliff Johnson .05
231 Joe Johnson .05
232 Jimmy Key .05
233 Dennis Lamp .05
234 Rick Leach .05
235 Buck Martinez .05
236 Lloyd Moseby .05
237 Rance Mulliniks .05
238 Dave Stieb .05
239 Willie Upshaw .05
240 Ernie Whitt .05
241 Andy Allanson **RC** .05
242 Scott Bailes **RC** .05
243 Chris Bando .05
244 Tony Bernazard .05
245 John Butcher .05
246 Brett Butler .05
247 Ernie Camacho .05
248 Tom Candiotti .05
249 Joe Carter .05
250 Carmen Castillo .05
251 Julio Franco .05
252 Mel Hall .05
253 Brook Jacoby .05
254 Phil Niekro .65
255 Otis Nixon .05
256 Dickie Noles .05
257 Bryan Oelkers .05
258 Ken Schrom .05
259 Don Schulze .05
260 Cory Snyder .05
261 Pat Tabler .05
262 Andre Thornton .05
263 Rich Yett **RC** .05
264 Mike Aldrete **RC** .05
265 Juan Berenguer .05
266 Vida Blue .05
267 Bob Brenly .05
268 Chris Brown .05
269 Will Clark .05
270 Chili Davis .05
271 Mark Davis .05
272 Kelly Downs **RC** .05
273 Scott Garrelts .05
274 Dan Gladden .05
275 Mike Krukow .05
276 Randy Kutcher **RC** .05
277 Mike LaCoss .05
278 Jeff Leonard .05
279 Candy Maldonado .05
280 Roger Mason .05
281 Bob Melvin **RC** .05
282 Greg Minton .05
283 Jeff Robinson .05
284 Harry Spilman .05
285 Rob Thompson **RC** .05
286 Jose Uribe .05
287 Frank Williams .05
288 Joel Youngblood .05
289 Jack Clark .05
290 Vince Coleman .05
291 Tim Conroy .05
292 Danny Cox .05
293 Ken Dayley .05
294 Curt Ford .05
295 Bob Forsch .05
296 Tom Herr .05
297 Ricky Horton .05
298 Clint Hurdle .05
299 Jeff Lahti .05
300 Steve Lake .05
301 Tito Landrum .05
302 Mike LaValliere **RC** .05
303 Greg Mathews **RC** .05
304 Willie McGee .05
305 Jose Oquendo .05
306 Terry Pendleton .05
307 Pat Perry .05
308 Ozzie Smith 1.50
309 Ray Soff .05
310 John Tudor .05
311 Andy Van Slyke .05
312 Todd Worrell .05
313 Dann Bilardello .05
314 Hubie Brooks .05
315 Tim Burke .05
316 Andre Dawson .35
317 Mike Fitzgerald .05
318 Tom Foley .05
319 Andres Galarraga .05
320 Joe Hesketh .05
321 Wallace Johnson .05
322 Wayne Krenchicki .05
323 Vance Law .05
324 Dennis Martinez .05
325 Bob McClure .05
326 Andy McGaffigan .05
327 Al Newman **RC** .05
328 Tim Raines .05
329 Jeff Reardon .05
330 Luis Rivera **RC** .05
331 Bob Sebra **RC** .05
332 Bryn Smith .05
333 Jay Tibbs .05
334 Tim Wallach .05
335 Mitch Webster .05
336 Jim Wohlford .05
337 Floyd Youmans .05
338 Chris Bosio **RC** .25
339 Glenn Braggs **RC** .05
340 Rick Cerone .05
341 Mark Clear .05
342 Bryan Clutterbuck **RC** .05
343 Cecil Cooper .05
344 Rob Deer .05
345 Jim Gantner .05
346 Ted Higuera .05
347 John Henry Johnson .05
348 Tim Leary **RC** .05
349 Rick Manning .05
350 Paul Molitor .75
351 Charlie Moore .05
352 Juan Nieves .05
353 Ben Oglivie .05
354 Dan Plesac **RC** .10
355 Ernest Riles .05
356 Billy Joe Robidoux .05
357 Bill Schroeder .05
358 Dale Sveum **RC** .05
359 Gorman Thomas .05
360 Bill Wegman **RC** .05
361 Robin Yount .75
362 Steve Balboni .05
363 Scott Bankhead **RC** .05
364 Buddy Biancalana .05
365 Bud Black .05
366 George Brett 2.00
367 Steve Farr .05
368 Mark Gubicza .05
369 Bo Jackson .75
370 Danny Jackson .05
371 Mike Kingery **RC** .05
372 Rudy Law .05
373 Charlie Leibrandt .05
374 Dennis Leonard .05
375 Hal McRae .05
376 Jorge Orta .05
377 Jamie Quirk .05
378 Dan Quisenberry .05
379 Bret Saberhagen .05
380 Angel Salazar .05
381 Lonnie Smith .05
382 Jim Sundberg .05
383 Frank White .05
384 Willie Wilson .05
385 Joaquin Andujar .05
386 Doug Bair .05
387 Dusty Baker .05
388 Bruce Bochte .05
389 Jose Canseco .65
390 Chris Codiroli .05
391 Mike Davis .05
392 Alfredo Griffin .05
393 Moose Haas .05
394 Donnie Hill .05
395 Jay Howell .05
396 Dave Kingman .05
397 Carney Lansford .05
398 David Leiper **RC** .05
399 Bill Mooneyham **RC** .05
400 Dwayne Murphy .05
401 Steve Ontiveros .05
402 Tony Phillips .05
403 Eric Plunk .05
404 Jose Rijo .05
405 Terry Steinbach **RC** .50
406 Dave Stewart .05
407 Mickey Tettleton .05
408 Dave Von Ohlen .05
409 Jerry Willard .05
410 Curt Young .05
411 Bruce Bochy .05
412 Dave Dravecky .05
413 Tim Flannery .05
414 Steve Garvey .25
415 Goose Gossage .10
416 Tony Gwynn 1.50
417 Andy Hawkins .05
418 LaMarr Hoyt .05
419 Terry Kennedy .05
420 John Kruk .05
421 Dave LaPoint .05
422 Craig Lefferts .05
423 Carmelo Martinez .05
424 Lance McCullers .05
425 Kevin McReynolds .05
426 Graig Nettles .05
427 Bip Roberts .05
428 Jerry Royster .05
429 Benito Santiago .05
430 Eric Show .05
431 Bob Stoddard .05
432 Garry Templeton .05
433 Gene Walter .05
434 Ed Whitson .05
435 Marvell Wynne .05
436 Dave Anderson .05
437 Greg Brock .05
438 Enos Cabell .05
439 Mariano Duncan .05
440 Pedro Guerrero .05
441 Orel Hershiser .05
442 Rick Honeycutt .05
443 Ken Howell .05
444 Ken Landreaux .05
445 Bill Madlock .05
446 Mike Marshall .05
447 Len Matuszek .05
448 Tom Niedenfuer .05
449 Alejandro Pena .05
450 Dennis Powell **RC** .05
451 Jerry Reuss .05
452 Bill Russell .05
453 Steve Sax .05
454 Mike Scioscia .05
455 Franklin Stubbs .05
456 Alex Trevino .05
457 Fernando Valenzuela .05
458 Ed Vande Berg .05
459 Bob Welch .05
460 Reggie Williams **RC** .05
461 Don Aase .05
462 Juan Beniquez .05
463 Mike Boddicker .05
464 Juan Bonilla .05
465 Rich Bordi .05
466 Storm Davis .05
467 Rick Dempsey .05
468 Ken Dixon .05
469 Jim Dwyer .05
470 Mike Flanagan .05
471 Jackie Gutierrez .05
472 Brad Havens .05
473 Lee Lacy .05
474 Fred Lynn .05
475 Scott McGregor .05
476 Eddie Murray .75
477 Tom O'Malley .05
478 Cal Ripken, Jr. 3.00
479 Larry Sheets .05
480 John Shelby .05
481 Nate Snell .05
482 Jim Traber **RC** .05
483 Mike Young .05
484 Neil Allen .05
485 Harold Baines .05
486 Floyd Bannister .05
487 Daryl Boston .05
488 Ivan Calderon .05
489 John Cangelosi **RC** .05
490 Steve Carlton .75
491 Joe Cowley .05
492 Julio Cruz .05
493 Bill Dawley .05
494 Jose DeLeon .05
495 Richard Dotson .05
496 Carlton Fisk .75
497 Ozzie Guillen .05
498 Jerry Hairston Sr. .05
499 Ron Hassey .05
500 Tim Hulett .05
501 Bob James .05
502 Steve Lyons .05
503 Joel McKeon **RC** .05
504 Gene Nelson .05
505 Dave Schmidt .05
506 Ray Searage .05
507 Bobby Thigpen **RC** .15
508 Greg Walker .05
509 Jim Acker .05
510 Doyle Alexander .05
511 Paul Assenmacher **RC** .05
512 Bruce Benedict .05
513 Chris Chambliss .05
514 Jeff Dedmon .05
515 Gene Garber .05
516 Ken Griffey .05
517 Terry Harper .05
518 Bob Horner .05
519 Glenn Hubbard .05
520 Rick Mahler .05
521 Omar Moreno .05
522 Dale Murphy .35
523 Ken Oberkfell .05
524 Ed Olwine .05
525 David Palmer .05
526 Rafael Ramirez .05
527 Billy Sample .05
528 Ted Simmons .05
529 Zane Smith .05
530 Bruce Sutter .65
531 Andres Thomas **RC** .05
532 Ozzie Virgil .05
533 Allan Anderson **RC** .05
534 Keith Atherton .05
535 Billy Beane .05
536 Bert Blyleven .10
537 Tom Brunansky .05
538 Randy Bush .05
539 George Frazier .05
540 Gary Gaetti .05
541 Greg Gagne .05
542 Mickey Hatcher .05
543 Neal Heaton .05
544 Kent Hrbek .05
545 Roy Lee Jackson .05
546 Tim Laudner .05
547 Steve Lombardozzi .05
548 Mark Portugal **RC** .10
549 Kirby Puckett 1.50
550 Jeff Reed .05
551 Mark Salas .05
552 Roy Smalley .05
553 Mike Smithson .05
554 Frank Viola .05
555 Thad Bosley .05
556 Ron Cey .05
557 Jody Davis .05
558 Ron Davis .05
559 Bob Dernier .05
560 Frank DiPino .05
561 Shawon Dunston .05
562 Leon Durham .05
563 Dennis Eckersley .65
564 Terry Francona .05
565 Dave Gumpert .05
566 Guy Hoffman .05
567 Ed Lynch .05
568 Gary Matthews .05
569 Keith Moreland .05
570 Jamie Moyer **RC** .05
571 Jerry Mumphrey .05
572 Ryne Sandberg 1.00
573 Scott Sanderson .05
574 Lee Smith .05
575 Chris Speier .05
576 Rick Sutcliffe .05
577 Manny Trillo .05
578 Steve Trout .05
579 Karl Best .05
580 Scott Bradley **RC** .05
581 Phil Bradley .05
582 Mickey Brantley .05
583 Mike Brown .05
584 Alvin Davis .05
585 Lee Guetterman **RC** .05
586 Mark Huismann .05
587 Bob Kearney .05
588 Pete Ladd .05
589 Mark Langston .05
590 Mike Moore .05
591 Mike Morgan .05
592 John Moses .05
593 Ken Phelps .05
594 Jim Presley .05
595 Rey Quinonez (Quinones) **RC** .05
596 Harold Reynolds .05
597 Billy Swift .05
598 Danny Tartabull .05
599 Steve Yeager .05
600 Matt Young .05
601 Bill Almon .05
602 Rafael Belliard **RC** .05
603 Mike Bielecki .05
604 Barry Bonds 40.00
605 Bobby Bonilla .05
606 Sid Bream .05
607 Mike Brown .05
608 Pat Clements .05
609 Mike Diaz **RC** .05
610 Cecilio Guante .05
611 Barry Jones **RC** .05
612 Bob Kipper .05
613 Larry McWilliams .05
614 Jim Morrison .05
615 Joe Orsulak .05
616 Junior Ortiz .05
617 Tony Pena .05
618 Johnny Ray .05
619 Rick Reuschel .05
620 R.J. Reynolds .05
621 Rick Rhoden .05
622 Don Robinson .05
623 Bob Walk .05
624 Jim Winn .05
625 Youthful Power (Jose Canseco, Pete Incaviglia) .15
626 300 Game Winners (Phil Niekro, Don Sutton) .25
627 A.L. Firemen (Don Aase, Dave Righetti) .05
628 Rookie All-Stars (Jose Canseco, Wally Joyner) .15
629 Magic Mets (Gary Carter, Dwight Gooden, Keith Hernandez, Darryl Strawberry) .15
630 N.L. Best Righties (Mike Krukow, Mike Scott) .05
631 Sensational Southpaws (John Franco, Fernando Valenzuela) .05
632 Count 'Em (Bob Horner) .05
633 A.L. Pitcher's Nightmare (Jose Canseco, Kirby Puckett, Jim Rice) .25
634 All Star Battery (Gary Carter, Roger Clemens) .50
635 4,000 Strikeouts (Steve Carlton) .15
636 Big Bats At First Sack (Glenn Davis, Eddie Murray) .15
637 On Base (Wade Boggs, Keith Hernandez) .25
638 Sluggers From Left Side (Don Mattingly, Darryl Strawberry) .50
639 Former MVP's (Dave Parker, Ryne Sandberg) .25
640 Dr. K. & Super K (Roger Clemens, Dwight Gooden) .50
641 A.L. West Stoppers (Charlie Hough, Mike Witt) .05
642 Doubles & Triples (Tim Raines, Juan Samuel) .05
643 Outfielders With Punch (Harold Baines, Jesse Barfield) .05
644 Major League Prospects (Dave Clark **RC**, Greg Swindell **RC**) .35
645 Major League Prospects (Ron Karkovice **RC**, Russ Morman **RC**) .25
646 Major League Prospects (Willie Fraser **RC**, Devon White **RC**) 1.00
647 Major League Prospects (Jerry Browne **RC**, Mike Stanley **RC**) .25
648 Major League Prospects (Phil Lombardi **RC**, Dave Magadan **RC**) .20
649 Major League Prospects (Ralph Bryant **RC**, Jose Gonzalez **RC**) .10
650 Major League Prospects (Randy Asadoor **RC**, Jimmy Jones **RC**) .10
651 Major League Prospects (Marvin Freeman **RC**, Tracy Jones **RC**) .10
652 Major League Prospects (Kevin Seitzer **RC**, John Stefero **RC**) .25
653 Major League Prospects (Steve Fireovid **RC**, Rob Nelson **RC**) .10
654 Checklist 1-95 .05
655 Checklist 96-192 .05
656 Checklist 193-288 .05
657 Checklist 289-384 .05
658 Checklist 385-483 .05
659 Checklist 484-578 .05
660 Checklist 579-660 .05

All Stars

As in 1986, Fleer All Star Team cards were randomly inserted in wax and cello packs. Twelve cards, measuring the standard 2-1/2" x 3-1/2", comprise the set. Fronts feature a full-color player photo set against a gray background for American League players and a black background for National Leaguers. Backs are printed in black, red and white and feature a lengthy player biography. Fleer's choices for a major league All-Star team is once again the theme for the set.

		NM/M
Complete Set (12):		8.00
Common Player:		.25
1	Don Mattingly	2.00
2	Gary Carter	1.00
3	Tony Fernandez	.25
4	Steve Sax	.25
5	Kirby Puckett	1.50
6	Mike Schmidt	2.00
7	Mike Easler	.25
8	Todd Worrell	.25
9	George Bell	.25
10	Fernando Valenzuela	.25
11	Roger Clemens	2.00
12	Tim Raines	.25

Headliners

A continuation of the 1986 Future Hall of Famers idea, Fleer encountered legal problems with using the Hall of Fame name and abated them by entitling the set "Headliners." The cards were randomly inserted in three-pack rack packs. Fronts feature a player photo set against a beige background with bright red stripes. Backs are printed in black, red and gray and offer a brief biography with an emphasis on the player's performance during the 1986 season.

		NM/M
Complete Set (6):		4.00
Common Player:		.50
1	Wade Boggs	1.50
2	Jose Canseco	1.00
3	Dwight Gooden	.50
4	Rickey Henderson	1.00
5	Keith Hernandez	.50
6	Jim Rice	.75

'86 World Series

Fleer issued a set of 12 cards highlighting the 1986 World Series between the Boston Red Sox and New York Mets. The sets were available only with Fleer factory sets, both regular and glossy. The cards, 2-1/2" x 3-1/2", have either horizontal or vertical formats. The fronts are bordered in red, white and blue stars and stripes with a thin gold frame around the photo. Backs are printed in red and blue on white stock and include information regarding the photo on the card fronts.

		NM/M
Complete Set, Regular (12):		6.00
Complete Set, Glossy (12):		6.00
Common Card:		.25
1	Left-Hand Finesse Beats Mets (Bruce Hurst)	.25
2	Wade Boggs, Keith Hernandez	1.25
3	Roger Clemens	4.00
4	Gary Carter	1.00
5	Ron Darling	.25
6	.433 Series Batting Average (Marty Barrett)	.25
7	Dwight Gooden	.50
8	Strategy At Work	.25
9	Dewey! (Dwight Evans)	.25
10	One Strike From Boston Victory (Dave Henderson, Spike Owen)	.25
11	Ray Knight, Darryl Strawberry	.25
12	Series M.V.P. (Ray Knight)	.25

Box Panels

For the second straight year, Fleer produced a special set of cards designed to stimulate sales of their wax and cello pack boxes. In 1987, Fleer issued 16 cards in panels of four on the bottoms of retail boxes. The cards are numbered C-1 through C-16 and are 2-1/2" x 3-1/2" in size. The cards have the same design as the regular issue set with the player photos and card numbers being different.

		NM/M
Complete Panel Set (4):		6.00
Complete Singles Set (16):		6.00
Common Panel:		1.50
Common Single Player:		.15
Panel		1.50
1	Mets Logo	.05
6	Keith Hernandez	.25
8	Dale Murphy	.45
14	Ryne Sandberg	1.00
Panel		2.50
2	Jesse Barfield	.15
3	George Brett	1.50
5	Red Sox Logo	.05
11	Kirby Puckett	1.00
Panel		1.50
4	Dwight Gooden	.15
9	Astros Logo	.05
10	Dave Parker	.15
15	Mike Schmidt	1.50
Panel		1.00
7	Wally Joyner	.25
12	Dave Righetti	.15
13	Angels Logo	.05
16	Robin Yount	.75

Glossy Tin

The three-year run of limited edition, glossy collectors' issues by Fleer from 1987-89 has become known to the hobby as "tins" for the colorful lithographed metal boxes in which complete sets were sold. In their debut year a reported 100,000 sets were made, each serial numbered on a sticker attached to the shrink-wrapped tin box. While the glossy version of the 1987 Fleer set once enjoyed a significant premium over regular cards, today that premium has evaporated and, indeed, it can be harder to find a buyer for the glossy version.

	NM/M
Unopened Set (672):	75.00
Complete Set (672):	50.00
Common Player:	.10

Update

The 1987 update edition brings the regular Fleer set up to date by including traded players and hot rookies. The cards measure 2-1/2" x 3-1/2" and are housed in a specially designed box with 25 team logo stickers. A glossy-coated Fleer Collectors Edition set was also produced.

		NM/M
Complete Set (132):		9.00
Common Player:		.05
1	Scott Bankhead	.05
2	Eric Bell **RC**	.05
3	Juan Beniquez	.05
4	Juan Berenguer	.05
5	Mike Birkbeck **RC**	.05
6	Randy Bockus **RC**	.05
7	Rod Booker **RC**	.05
8	Thad Bosley	.05
9	Greg Brock	.05
10	Bob Brower **RC**	.05
11	Chris Brown	.05
12	Jerry Browne	.05
13	Ralph Bryant	.05
14	DeWayne Buice **RC**	.05
15	Ellis Burks **RC**	.05
16	Casey Candaele **RC**	.05
17	Steve Carlton	.50
18	Juan Castillo	.05
19	Chuck Crim **RC**	.05
20	Mark Davidson **RC**	.05
21	Mark Davis	.05
22	Storm Davis	.05
23	Bill Dawley	.05
24	Andre Dawson	.30
25	Brian Dayett	.05
26	Rick Dempsey	.05
27	Ken Dowell **RC**	.05
28	Dave Dravecky	.05
29	Mike Dunne **RC**	.05
30	Dennis Eckersley	.40
31	Cecil Fielder	.05
32	Brian Fisher	.05
33	Willie Fraser	.05
34	Ken Gerhart **RC**	.05
35	Jim Gott	.05
36	Dan Gladden	.05
37	Mike Greenwell **RC**	.05
38	Cecilio Guante	.05
39	Albert Hall	.05
40	Atlee Hammaker	.05
41	Mickey Hatcher	.05
42	Mike Heath	.05
43	Neal Heaton	.05
44	Mike Henneman **RC**	.05
45	Guy Hoffman	.05
46	Charles Hudson	.05
47	Chuck Jackson **RC**	.05
48	Mike Jackson **RC**	.05
49	Reggie Jackson	.75
50	Chris James	.05
51	Dion James	.05
52	Stan Javier	.05
53	Stan Jefferson **RC**	.05
54	Jimmy Jones	.05
55	Tracy Jones	.05
56	Terry Kennedy	.05
57	Mike Kingery	.05
58	Ray Knight	.05
59	Gene Larkin **RC**	.05
60	Mike LaValliere	.05
61	Jack Lazorko **RC**	.05
62	Terry Leach	.05
63	Rick Leach	.05
64	Craig Lefferts	.05
65	Jim Lindeman **RC**	.05
66	Bill Long **RC**	.05
67	Mike Loynd **RC**	.05
68	Greg Maddux **RC**	8.00
69	Bill Madlock	.05
70	Dave Magadan	.05
71	Joe Magrane **RC**	.05
72	Fred Manrique **RC**	.05
73	Mike Mason	.05
74	Lloyd McClendon **RC**	.05
75	Fred McGriff **RC**	.05
76	Mark McGwire	3.00
77	Mark McLemore	.05
78	Kevin McReynolds	.05
79	Dave Meads **RC**	.05
80	Greg Minton	.05
81	John Mitchell **RC**	.05
82	Kevin Mitchell	.05
83	John Morris	.05
84	Jeff Musselman **RC**	.05
85	Randy Myers **RC**	.05
86	Gene Nelson	.05
87	Joe Niekro	.05
88	Tom Nieto	.05
89	Reid Nichols	.05
90	Matt Nokes **RC**	.05
91	Dickie Noles	.05
92	Edwin Nunez	.05
93	Jose Nunez **RC**	.05
94	Paul O'Neill	.05
95	Jim Paciorek **RC**	.05
96	Lance Parrish	.05
97	Bill Pecota **RC**	.05
98	Tony Pena	.05
99	Luis Polonia **RC**	.05
100	Randy Ready	.05
101	Jeff Reardon	.05
102	Gary Redus	.05
103	Rick Rhoden	.05
104	Wally Ritchie **RC**	.05
105	Jeff Robinson **RC**	.05
106	Mark Salas	.05
107	Dave Schmidt	.05
108	Kevin Seitzer	.05
109	John Shelby	.05
110	John Smiley **RC**	.05
111	Lary Sorenson	.05
112	Chris Speier	.05
113	Randy St. Claire	.05
114	Jim Sundberg	.05
115	B.J. Surhoff **RC**	.05
116	Greg Swindell	.05
117	Danny Tartabull	.05
118	Dorn Taylor **RC**	.05
119	Lee Tunnell	.05
120	Ed Vande Berg	.05
121	Andy Van Slyke	.05
122	Gary Ward	.05
123	Devon White	.05
124	Alan Wiggins	.05
125	Bill Wilkinson **RC**	.05
126	Jim Winn	.05
127	Frank Williams	.05
128	Ken Williams **RC**	.05
129	Matt Williams **RC**	1.00
130	Herm Winningham	.05
131	Matt Young	.05
132	Checklist 1-132	.05

Update Glossy Tin

The 1987 Fleer glossy tin update set is identical to the regular-issue updates, except for the high-gloss coating on the cards' fronts and the lithographed metal box in which the sets were sold. Production was estimated at 100,000. Because of perceived overproduction, the glossy tin update set and singles currently carry little, if any, premium over the regular-issue updates.

	NM/M
Unopened Set (132):	12.00
Complete Set (132):	7.50
Common Player:	.10

Award Winners

The 1987 Fleer Award Winners boxed set was prepared for distribution by 7-Eleven stores. The 2-1/2" x 3-1/2" cards feature players who have won various major league awards during their careers. Fronts contain full-color photos surrounded by a yellow border. The name of the award the player won is printed at the bottom of the card in an oval-shaped band designed to resemble a metal nameplate on a trophy. Backs are printed in red, black and white, and include lifetime major and minor league statistics along with typical personal information. Each boxed set contained six team logo stickers.

		NM/M
Complete Set (44):		5.00
Common Player:		.10
1	Marty Barrett	.10
2	George Bell	.10
3	Bert Blyleven	.20
4	Bob Boone	.10
5	John Candelaria	.10
6	Jose Canseco	.45
7	Gary Carter	.50
8	Joe Carter	.10
9	Roger Clemens	1.00
10	Cecil Cooper	.10
11	Eric Davis	.10
12	Tony Fernandez	.10
13	Scott Fletcher	.10
14	Bob Forsch	.10
15	Dwight Gooden	.10
16	Ron Guidry	.10
17	Ozzie Guillen	.10
18	Bill Gullickson	.10
19	Tony Gwynn	.75
20	Bob Knepper	.10
21	Ray Knight	.10
22	Mark Langston	.10
23	Candy Maldonado	.10
24	Don Mattingly	1.00
25	Roger McDowell	.10
26	Dale Murphy	.20
27	Dave Parker	.10
28	Lance Parrish	.10
29	Gary Pettis	.10
30	Kirby Puckett	.75
31	Johnny Ray	.10
32	Dave Righetti	.10
33	Cal Ripken, Jr.	1.50
34	Bret Saberhagen	.10
35	Ryne Sandberg	.75
36	Mike Schmidt	1.00
37	Mike Scott	.10
38	Ozzie Smith	.75
39	Robbie Thompson	.10
40	Fernando Valenzuela	.10
41	Mitch Webster	.10
42	Frank White	.10
43	Mike Witt	.10
44	Todd Worrell	.10

Baseball All Stars

Produced by Fleer for exclusive distribution through Ben Franklin stores, the "Baseball All Stars" set is comprised of 44 cards in the standard 2-1/2" x 3-1/2" format. Cards have full-color photos surrounded by a bright red border with white pinstripes at the top and bottom. Backs are printed in blue, white and dark red and include complete major and minor league statistics. The set was issued in a special cardboard box with a handful of team logo stickers.

		NM/M
Complete Set (44):		5.00
Common Player:		.10
1	Harold Baines	.10
2	Jesse Barfield	.10
3	Wade Boggs	.65
4	Dennis "Oil Can" Boyd	.10
5	Scott Bradley	.10
6	Jose Canseco	.40
7	Gary Carter	.50
8	Joe Carter	.10
9	Mark Clear	.10
10	Roger Clemens	.85
11	Jose Cruz	.10
12	Chili Davis	.10
13	Jody Davis	.10
14	Rob Deer	.10
15	Brian Downing	.10
16	Sid Fernandez	.10
17	John Franco	.10
18	Andres Galarraga	.10
19	Dwight Gooden	.10
20	Tony Gwynn	.65
21	Charlie Hough	.10
22	Bruce Hurst	.10
23	Wally Joyner	.10
24	Carney Lansford	.10
25	Fred Lynn	.10
26	Don Mattingly	.85
27	Willie McGee	.10
28	Jack Morris	.10
29	Dale Murphy	.20
30	Bob Ojeda	.10
31	Tony Pena	.10
32	Kirby Puckett	.65
33	Dan Quisenberry	.10
34	Tim Raines	.10
35	Willie Randolph	.10
36	Cal Ripken, Jr.	1.50
37	Pete Rose	1.00
38	Nolan Ryan	1.50
39	Juan Samuel	.10
40	Mike Schmidt	.85
41	Ozzie Smith	.65
42	Andres Thomas	.10
43	Fernando Valenzuela	.10
44	Mike Witt	.10

Baseball's Best

For a second straight baseball card season, Fleer produced for McCrory's stores and their affiliates a 44-card "Baseball's Best" set. Subtitled "Sluggers vs. Pitchers," 28 everyday players and 16 pitchers are featured. The card design is nearly identical to the previous year's effort. The cards were sold in a specially designed box along with six team logo stickers.

		NM/M
Complete Set (44):		4.00
Common Player:		.10
1	Kevin Bass	.10
2	Jesse Barfield	.10
3	George Bell	.10
4	Wade Boggs	.65
5	Sid Bream	.10
6	George Brett	.85
7	Ivan Calderon	.10
8	Jose Canseco	.50
9	Jack Clark	.10
10	Roger Clemens	.85
11	Eric Davis	.10
12	Andre Dawson	.25
13	Sid Fernandez	.10
14	John Franco	.10
15	Dwight Gooden	.10
16	Pedro Guerrero	.10
17	Tony Gwynn	.65
18	Rickey Henderson	.60
19	Tom Henke	.10
20	Ted Higuera	.10
21	Pete Incaviglia	.10
22	Wally Joyner	.10
23	Jeff Leonard	.10
24	Joe Magrane	.10
25	Don Mattingly	.85

26	Mark McGwire	1.00
27	Jack Morris	.10
28	Dale Murphy	.20
29	Dave Parker	.10
30	Ken Phelps	.10
31	Kirby Puckett	.65
32	Tim Raines	.10
33	Jeff Reardon	.10
34	Dave Righetti	.10
35	Cal Ripken, Jr.	1.50
36	Bret Saberhagen	.10
37	Mike Schmidt	.85
38	Mike Scott	.10
39	Kevin Seitzer	.10
40	Darryl Strawberry	.10
41	Rick Sutcliffe	.10
42	Pat Tabler	.10
43	Fernando Valenzuela	.10
44	Mike Witt	.10

Best Box Bottom

These special cards were printed on the bottom of retail boxes of Fleer's "Baseball's Best" boxed sets. The box-bottom cards are in the same format as the boxed cards, with red, white and blue borders and a yellow title strip at top. Backs are also similar in design to the regular-issue cards, carrying player data and stats. Cards are numbered with a "M" prefix.

		NM/M
Complete Panel:		3.00
Complete Set (6):		3.00
Common Player:		.50
1	Steve Bedrosian	.50
2	Will Clark	1.00
3	Vince Coleman	.50
4	Bo Jackson	2.00
5	Cory Snyder	.50
---	K.C. Royals Logo	.10

Exciting Stars

Another entry into the Fleer lineup of individual boxed sets, the "Baseball's Exciting Stars" set was produced for Cumberland Farms stores. The card fronts feature a red, white and blue border with the words "Exciting Stars" printed in yellow at the top. The backs are printed in red and blue and carry complete major and minor league statistics. Included with the boxed set of 44 cards were six team logo stickers.

		NM/M
Complete Set (44):		4.00
Common Player:		.10
1	Don Aase	.10
2	Rick Aguilera	.10
3	Jesse Barfield	.10
4	Wade Boggs	.65
5	Dennis "Oil Can" Boyd	.10
6	Sid Bream	.10
7	Jose Canseco	.45
8	Steve Carlton	.50
9	Gary Carter	.50
10	Will Clark	.50
11	Roger Clemens	.85
12	Danny Cox	.10
13	Alvin Davis	.10
14	Eric Davis	.10
15	Rob Deer	.10
16	Brian Downing	.10
17	Gene Garber	.10
18	Steve Garvey	.20
19	Dwight Gooden	.10
20	Mark Gubicza	.10
21	Mel Hall	.10
22	Terry Harper	.10
23	Von Hayes	.10
24	Rickey Henderson	.50
25	Tom Henke	.10
26	Willie Hernandez	.10
27	Ted Higuera	.10
28	Rick Honeycutt	.10
29	Kent Hrbek	.08
30	Wally Joyner	.10
31	Charlie Kerfeld	.10
32	Fred Lynn	.10
33	Don Mattingly	.85
34	Tim Raines	.10
35	Dennis Rasmussen	.10
36	Johnny Ray	.10
37	Jim Rice	.25
38	Pete Rose	1.00
39	Lee Smith	.10
40	Cory Snyder	.10
41	Darryl Strawberry	.10
42	Kent Tekulve	.10
43	Willie Wilson	.10
44	Bobby Witt	.10

Game Winners

The 1987 Fleer "Baseball's Game Winners" boxed set was produced for distribution through Bi-Mart Discount Drug, Pay'n-Save, Mott's 5 & 10, M.E. Moses, and Winn's stores. Cards have a light blue border with the player's name and game winning RBI or games-won statistics in a yellow oval band at the top. Backs are similar to the regular-issue 1987 Fleer, with full professional stats. Included with the boxed set were six team logo stickers.

		NM/M
Complete Set (44):		4.00
Common Player:		.10
1	Harold Baines	.10
2	Don Baylor	.10
3	George Bell	.10
4	Tony Bernazard	.10
5	Wade Boggs	.75
6	George Brett	.85
7	Hubie Brooks	.10
8	Jose Canseco	.50
9	Gary Carter	.60
10	Roger Clemens	.85
11	Eric Davis	.10
12	Glenn Davis	.10
13	Shawon Dunston	.10
14	Mark Eichhorn	.10
15	Gary Gaetti	.10
16	Steve Garvey	.15
17	Kirk Gibson	.10
18	Dwight Gooden	.10
19	Von Hayes	.10
20	Willie Hernandez	.10
21	Ted Higuera	.10
22	Wally Joyner	.10
23	Bob Knepper	.10
24	Mike Krukow	.10
25	Jeff Leonard	.10
26	Don Mattingly	.85
27	Kirk McCaskill	.10
28	Kevin McReynolds	.10
29	Jim Morrison	.10
30	Dale Murphy	.15
31	Pete O'Brien	.10
32	Bob Ojeda	.10
33	Larry Parrish	.10
34	Ken Phelps	.10
35	Dennis Rasmussen	.10
36	Ernest Riles	.10
37	Cal Ripken, Jr.	1.00
38	Ron Robinson	.10
39	Steve Sax	.10
40	Mike Schmidt	.85
41	John Tudor	.10
42	Fernando Valenzuela	.10
43	Mike Witt	.10
44	Curt Young	.10

Hottest Stars

The "Baseball's Hottest Stars" set was produced by Fleer for the Revco Drug Store chain. Measuring the standard 2-1/2" x 3-1/2", the cards feature full-color photos surrounded by a red, white and blue border. Card backs are printed in red, white and black and contain the player's lifetime professional statistics. The set was sold in a special cardboard box with six team logo stickers.

		NM/M
Unopened Set (44):		45.00
Complete Set (44):		25.00
Common Player:		.10
1	Joaquin Andujar	.10
2	Harold Baines	.10
3	Kevin Bass	.10
4	Don Baylor	.10
5	Barry Bonds	20.00
6	George Brett	1.00
7	Tom Brunansky	.10
8	Brett Butler	.10
9	Jose Canseco	.60
10	Roger Clemens	1.00
11	Ron Darling	.10
12	Eric Davis	.10
13	Andre Dawson	.25
14	Doug DeCinces	.10
15	Leon Durham	.10
16	Mark Eichhorn	.10
17	Scott Garrelts	.10
18	Dwight Gooden	.10
19	Dave Henderson	.10
20	Rickey Henderson	.60
21	Keith Hernandez	.10
22	Ted Higuera	.10
23	Bob Horner	.10
24	Pete Incaviglia	.10
25	Wally Joyner	.10
26	Mark Langston	.10
27	Don Mattingly	1.00
28	Dale Murphy	.20
29	Kirk McCaskill	.10
30	Willie McGee	.10
31	Dave Righetti	.10
32	Pete Rose	1.50
33	Bruce Ruffin	.10
34	Steve Sax	.10
35	Mike Schmidt	1.00
36	Larry Sheets	.10
37	Eric Show	.10
38	Dave Smith	.10
39	Cory Snyder	.10
40	Frank Tanana	.10
41	Alan Trammell	.10
42	Reggie Williams	.10
43	Mookie Wilson	.10
44	Todd Worrell	.10

League Leaders

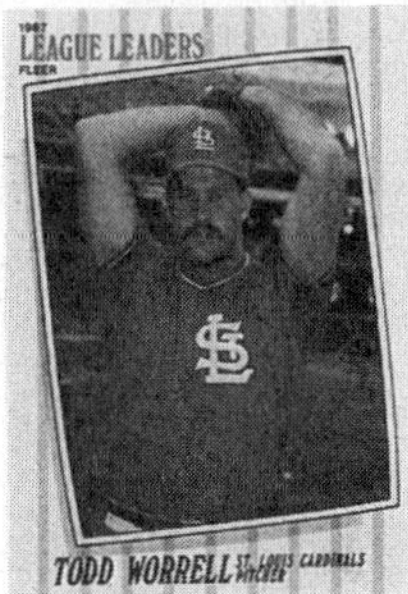

For a second year, Fleer produced a 44- card "League Leaders" set for Walgreens. The card fronts feature a border style which is identical to that used in 1986. However, a trapezoidal shaped full-color player photo is placed diagonally on the front. "1987 Fleer League Leaders" appears in the upper left corner of the front although nowhere on the card does it state in which pitching, hitting or fielding department was the player a league leader. Backs are printed in red and blue on white stock. The cards in the boxed set are the standard 2-1/2" x 3-1/2" size.

		NM/M
Complete Set (44):		4.00
Common Player:		.10
1	Jesse Barfield	.10
2	Mike Boddicker	.10
3	Wade Boggs	.65
4	Phil Bradley	.10
5	George Brett	.85
6	Hubie Brooks	.10
7	Chris Brown	.10
8	Jose Canseco	.50
9	Joe Carter	.10
10	Roger Clemens	.85
11	Vince Coleman	.10
12	Joe Cowley	.10
13	Kal Daniels	.10
14	Glenn Davis	.10
15	Jody Davis	.10
16	Darrell Evans	.10
17	Dwight Evans	.10
18	John Franco	.10
19	Julio Franco	.10
20	Dwight Gooden	.10
21	Goose Gossage	.10
22	Tom Herr	.10
23	Ted Higuera	.10
24	Bob Horner	.10
25	Pete Incaviglia	.10
26	Wally Joyner	.10
27	Dave Kingman	.10
28	Don Mattingly	.85
29	Willie McGee	.10
30	Donnie Moore	.10
31	Keith Moreland	.10
32	Eddie Murray	.60
33	Mike Pagliarulo	.10
34	Larry Parrish	.10
35	Tony Pena	.10
36	Kirby Puckett	.65
37	Pete Rose	1.00
38	Juan Samuel	.10
39	Ryne Sandberg	.65
40	Mike Schmidt	.85
41	Darryl Strawberry	.10
42	Greg Walker	.10
43	Bob Welch	.10
44	Todd Worrell	.10

Limited Edition

For the third straight year, Fleer produced a Limited Edition set for the McCrory's store chain and its affiliates. The cards are the standard 2-1/2" x 3-1/2" and feature light blue borders at the top and bottom and a diagonal red and white border running along both sides. The set was issued in a specially prepared cardboard box, along with six team logo stickers.

		NM/M
Complete Set (44):		4.00
Common Player:		.10
1	Floyd Bannister	.10
2	Marty Barrett	.10
3	Steve Bedrosian	.10
4	George Bell	.10
5	George Brett	.85
6	Jose Canseco	.40
7	Joe Carter	.10
8	Will Clark	.10
9	Roger Clemens	.85
10	Vince Coleman	.10
11	Glenn Davis	.10
12	Mike Davis	.10
13	Len Dykstra	.10
14	John Franco	.10
15	Julio Franco	.10
16	Steve Garvey	.25
17	Kirk Gibson	.10
18	Dwight Gooden	.10
19	Tony Gwynn	.65
20	Keith Hernandez	.10
21	Teddy Higuera	.10
22	Kent Hrbek	.10
23	Wally Joyner	.10
24	Mike Krukow	.10
25	Mike Marshall	.10
26	Don Mattingly	.85
27	Oddibe McDowell	.10
28	Jack Morris	.10
29	Lloyd Moseby	.10
30	Dale Murphy	.20
31	Eddie Murray	.50
32	Tony Pena	.10
33	Jim Presley	.10
34	Jeff Reardon	.10
35	Jim Rice	.25
36	Pete Rose	1.00
37	Mike Schmidt	.85
38	Mike Scott	.10
39	Lee Smith	.10
40	Lonnie Smith	.10
41	Gary Ward	.10
42	Dave Winfield	.50
43	Todd Worrell	.10
44	Robin Yount	.50

Limited Edition Box Bottom

These special cards were printed on the bottom of retail boxes of Fleer's "Limited Edition" boxed sets. The box-bottom cards are in the same format as the boxed cards, with red, white and blue borders. Backs are also similar in design to the regular-issue cards, carrying player data and stats.

		NM/M
Complete Panel:		2.00
Complete Set (6):		2.00
Common Player:		.50
C1	Ron Darling	.50
C2	Bill Buckner	.50
C3	John Candelaria	.50
C4	Jack Clark	.50
C5	Bret Saberhagen	.50
C6	Houston Astros Logo	.25

Mini

Continuing with an idea originated the previous year, the Fleer "Classic Miniatures" set consists of 120 cards that measure 1-13/16" x 2-9/16". The cards are identical in design to the regular-issue set, but use completely different photos. The set was issued in a specially prepared collectors box along with 18 team logo stickers. The mini set was available only through hobby dealers.

		NM/M
Complete Set (120):		4.00
Common Player:		.05
1	Don Aase	.05
2	Joaquin Andujar	.05
3	Harold Baines	.05
4	Jesse Barfield	.05
5	Kevin Bass	.05
6	Don Baylor	.05
7	George Bell	.05
8	Tony Bernazard	.05
9	Bert Blyleven	.05
10	Wade Boggs	.65
11	Phil Bradley	.05
12	Sid Bream	.05
13	George Brett	.85
14	Hubie Brooks	.05
15	Chris Brown	.05
16	Tom Candiotti	.05
17	Jose Canseco	.40
18	Gary Carter	.50
19	Joe Carter	.05
20	Roger Clemens	.85
21	Vince Coleman	.05
22	Cecil Cooper	.05
23	Ron Darling	.05
24	Alvin Davis	.05
25	Chili Davis	.05
26	Eric Davis	.05
27	Glenn Davis	.05
28	Mike Davis	.05
29	Doug DeCinces	.05
30	Rob Deer	.05
31	Jim Deshaies	.05
32	Bo Diaz	.05
33	Richard Dotson	.05
34	Brian Downing	.05
35	Shawon Dunston	.05
36	Mark Eichhorn	.05
37	Dwight Evans	.05
38	Tony Fernandez	.05
39	Julio Franco	.05
40	Gary Gaetti	.05
41	Andres Galarraga	.05
42	Scott Garrelts	.05
43	Steve Garvey	.15
44	Kirk Gibson	.05
45	Dwight Gooden	.05
46	Ken Griffey	.05
47	Mark Gubicza	.05
48	Ozzie Guillen	.05
49	Bill Gullickson	.05
50	Tony Gwynn	.65
51	Von Hayes	.05
52	Rickey Henderson	.50
53	Keith Hernandez	.05
54	Willie Hernandez	.05
55	Ted Higuera	.05
56	Charlie Hough	.05
57	Kent Hrbek	.05
58	Pete Incaviglia	.05
59	Wally Joyner	.05
60	Bob Knepper	.05
61	Mike Krukow	.05
62	Mark Langston	.05
63	Carney Lansford	.05
64	Jim Lindeman	.05
65	Bill Madlock	.05
66	Don Mattingly	.85
67	Kirk McCaskill	.05
68	Lance McCullers	.05
69	Keith Moreland	.05
70	Jack Morris	.05
71	Jim Morrison	.05
72	Lloyd Moseby	.05
73	Jerry Mumphrey	.05
74	Dale Murphy	.15
75	Eddie Murray	.50
76	Pete O"Brien	.05
77	Bob Ojeda	.05
78	Jesse Orosco	.05
79	Dan Pasqua	.05
80	Dave Parker	.05
81	Larry Parrish	.05
82	Jim Presley	.05
83	Kirby Puckett	.65
84	Dan Quisenberry	.05
85	Tim Raines	.05
86	Dennis Rasmussen	.05
87	Johnny Ray	.05
88	Jeff Reardon	.05
89	Jim Rice	.25
90	Dave Righetti	.05
91	Earnest Riles	.05
92	Cal Ripken, Jr.	1.50
93	Ron Robinson	.05
94	Juan Samuel	.05
95	Ryne Sandberg	.65
96	Steve Sax	.05
97	Mike Schmidt	.85
98	Ken Schrom	.05
99	Mike Scott	.05
100	Ruben Sierra	.05
101	Lee Smith	.05
102	Ozzie Smith	.65
103	Cory Snyder	.05
104	Kent Tekulve	.05
105	Andres Thomas	.05
106	Rob Thompson	.05
107	Alan Trammell	.05
108	John Tudor	.05
109	Fernando Valenzuela	.05
110	Greg Walker	.05
111	Mitch Webster	.05
112	Lou Whitaker	.05
113	Frank White	.05
114	Reggie Williams	.05
115	Glenn Wilson	.05
116	Willie Wilson	.05
117	Dave Winfield	.50
118	Mike Witt	.05
119	Todd Worrell	.05
120	Floyd Youmans	.05

Record Setters

Produced by Fleer for the Eckerd Drug chain, the Record Setters set contains 44 cards in standard 2-1/2" x 3-1/2" size. Although the set is titled "Record Setters," the actual records the players have set is not specified anywhere on the cards. Given that several players included in the set were young prospects, a better title for those cards might have been "Possible Record Set-

ters". The set came housed in a special cardboard box with six team logo stickers.

		NM/M
Complete Set (44):		4.00
Common Player:		.10
1	George Brett	.85
2	Chris Brown	.10
3	Jose Canseco	.40
4	Roger Clemens	.85
5	Alvin Davis	.10
6	Shawon Dunston	.10
7	Tony Fernandez	.10
8	Carlton Fisk	.45
9	Gary Gaetti	.10
10	Gene Garber	.10
11	Rich Gedman	.10
12	Dwight Gooden	.10
13	Ozzie Guillen	.10
14	Bill Gullickson	.10
15	Billy Hatcher	.10
16	Orel Hershiser	.10
17	Wally Joyner	.10
18	Ray Knight	.10
19	Craig Lefferts	.10
20	Don Mattingly	.85
21	Kevin Mitchell	.10
22	Lloyd Moseby	.10
23	Dale Murphy	.15
24	Eddie Murray	.45
25	Phil Niekro	.30
26	Ben Oglivie	.10
27	Jesse Orosco	.10
28	Joe Orsulak	.10
29	Larry Parrish	.10
30	Tim Raines	.10
31	Shane Rawley	.10
32	Dave Righetti	.10
33	Pete Rose	1.00
34	Steve Sax	.10
35	Mike Schmidt	.85
36	Mike Scott	.10
37	Don Sutton	.30
38	Alan Trammell	.10
39	John Tudor	.10
40	Gary Ward	.10
41	Lou Whitaker	.10
42	Willie Wilson	.10
43	Todd Worrell	.10
44	Floyd Youmans	.10

Star Stickers

The 1987 Fleer Star Stickers set contains 132 cards which become stickers if the back is bent and peeled off. As in the previous year, the card backs are identical, save the numbering system, to the regular-issue cards. The cards measure 2-1/2" x 3-1/2" and were sold in wax packs with team logo stickers. The fronts have a green border with a red and white banner wrapped across the upper left corner and the sides. The backs are printed in green and yellow.

		NM/M
Complete Set (132):		6.00
Common Player:		.05
Wax Pack (5):		.50
Wax Box (36):		12.00
1	Don Aase	.05
2	Harold Baines	.05
3	Floyd Bannister	.05
4	Jesse Barfield	.05
5	Marty Barrett	.05
6	Kevin Bass	.05
7	Don Baylor	.05
8	Steve Bedrosian	.05
9	George Bell	.05
10	Bert Blyleven	.05
11	Mike Boddicker	.05
12	Wade Boggs	.65
13	Phil Bradley	.05
14	Sid Bream	.05
15	George Brett	.85
16	Hubie Brooks	.05
17	Tom Brunansky	.05
18	Tom Candiotti	.05
19	Jose Canseco	.40
20	Gary Carter	.50
21	Joe Carter	.05
22	Will Clark	.05
23	Mark Clear	.05
24	Roger Clemens	.85
25	Vince Coleman	.05
26	Jose Cruz	.05
27	Ron Darling	.05
28	Alvin Davis	.05
29	Chili Davis	.05
30	Eric Davis	.05
31	Glenn Davis	.05
32	Mike Davis	.05
33	Andre Dawson	.25
34	Doug DeCinces	.05
35	Brian Downing	.05
36	Shawon Dunston	.05
37	Mark Eichhorn	.05
38	Dwight Evans	.05
39	Tony Fernandez	.05
40	Bob Forsch	.05
41	John Franco	.05
42	Julio Franco	.05
43	Gary Gaetti	.05
44	Gene Garber	.05
45	Scott Garrelts	.05
46	Steve Garvey	.20
47	Kirk Gibson	.05
48	Dwight Gooden	.05
49	Ken Griffey	.05
50	Ozzie Guillen	.05
51	Bill Gullickson	.05
52	Tony Gwynn	.65
53	Mel Hall	.05
54	Greg Harris	.05
55	Von Hayes	.05
56	Rickey Henderson	.50
57	Tom Henke	.05
58	Keith Hernandez	.05
59	Willie Hernandez	.05
60	Ted Higuera	.05
61	Bob Horner	.05
62	Charlie Hough	.05
63	Jay Howell	.05
64	Kent Hrbek	.05
65	Bruce Hurst	.05
66	Pete Incaviglia	.05
67	Bob James	.05
68	Wally Joyner	.05
69	Mike Krukow	.05
70	Mark Langston	.05
71	Carney Lansford	.05
72	Fred Lynn	.05
73	Bill Madlock	.05
74	Don Mattingly	.85
75	Kirk McCaskill	.05
76	Lance McCullers	.05
77	Oddibe McDowell	.05
78	Paul Molitor	.50
79	Keith Moreland	.05
80	Jack Morris	.05
81	Jim Morrison	.05
82	Jerry Mumphrey	.05
83	Dale Murphy	.20
84	Eddie Murray	.50
85	Ben Oglivie	.05
86	Bob Ojeda	.05
87	Jesse Orosco	.05
88	Dave Parker	.05
89	Larry Parrish	.05
90	Tony Pena	.05
91	Jim Presley	.05
92	Kirby Puckett	.65
93	Dan Quisenberry	.05
94	Tim Raines	.05
95	Dennis Rasmussen	.05
96	Shane Rawley	.05
97	Johnny Ray	.05
98	Jeff Reardon	.05
99	Jim Rice	.25
100	Dave Righetti	.05
101	Cal Ripken, Jr.	2.00
102	Pete Rose	1.00
103	Nolan Ryan	2.00
104	Juan Samuel	.05
105	Ryne Sandberg	.65
106	Steve Sax	.05
107	Mike Schmidt	.85
108	Mike Scott	.05
109	Dave Smith	.05
110	Lee Smith	.05
111	Lonnie Smith	.05
112	Ozzie Smith	.65
113	Cory Snyder	.05
114	Darryl Strawberry	.05
115	Don Sutton	.45
116	Kent Tekulve	.05
117	Gorman Thomas	.05
118	Alan Trammell	.05
119	John Tudor	.05
120	Fernando Valenzuela	.05
121	Bob Welch	.05
122	Lou Whitaker	.05
123	Frank White	.05
124	Reggie Williams	.05
125	Willie Wilson	.05
126	Dave Winfield	.50
127	Mike Witt	.05
128	Todd Worrell	.05
129	Curt Young	.05
130	Robin Yount	.50
131	Checklist (Jose Canseco, Don Mattingly)	.25
132	Checklist (Bo Jackson, Eric Davis)	.05

Star Stickers Box Panels

Fleer issued on the bottoms of its Fleer Star Stickers wax pack boxes six player cards plus two team logo/checklist cards. The cards, which measure 2-1/2" x 3-1/2", are numbered S-1 through S-8, and are identical in design to the Star Stickers.

		NM/M
Complete Panel Set (2):		2.50
Complete Singles Set (8):		2.50
Common Single Player:		.10
Panel		2.00
2	Wade Boggs	.75
3	Bert Blyleven	.10
6	Phillies Logo	.05
8	Don Mattingly	1.50
Panel		1.00
1	Tigers Logo	.05
4	Jose Cruz	.10
5	Glenn Davis	.10
7	Bob Horner	.10

1988 Fleer

A clean, uncluttered look was featured in the 1988 Fleer set. Cards in the standard 2-1/2" x 3-1/2" format feature blue and red diagonal lines on a white background. Player identification and team logo appears at top. Backs include personal information and career statistics, plus a new feature called "At Their Best." This feature graphically shows a player's pitching or hitting statistics for home and road games and how he fared during day games as opposed to night contests. The set includes 19 special cards (#622-640) and 12 "Major League Prospects" cards.

		NM/M
Retail Factory Set (672):		12.00
Hobby Factory Set (672):		10.00
Complete Set (660):		8.00
Common Player:		.05
Wax Pack (15):		.75
Wax Box (36):		12.00
Cello Pack (28):		1.25
Cello Box (24):		16.00
1	Keith Atherton	.05
2	Don Baylor	.05
3	Juan Berenguer	.05
4	Bert Blyleven	.10
5	Tom Brunansky	.05
6	Randy Bush	.05
7	Steve Carlton	.50
8	Mark Davidson **RC**	.05
9	George Frazier	.05
10	Gary Gaetti	.05
11	Greg Gagne	.05
12	Dan Gladden	.05
13	Kent Hrbek	.05
14	Gene Larkin **RC**	.05
15	Tim Laudner	.05
16	Steve Lombardozzi	.05
17	Al Newman	.05
18	Joe Niekro	.05
19	Kirby Puckett	.65
20	Jeff Reardon	.05
21a	Dan Schatzader (Incorrect spelling.)	.10
21b	Dan Schatzeder (Correct spelling.)	.05
22	Roy Smalley	.05
23	Mike Smithson	.05
24	Les Straker **RC**	.05
25	Frank Viola	.05
26	Jack Clark	.05
27	Vince Coleman	.05
28	Danny Cox	.05
29	Bill Dawley	.05
30	Ken Dayley	.05
31	Doug DeCinces	.05
32	Curt Ford	.05
33	Bob Forsch	.05
34	David Green	.05
35	Tom Herr	.05
36	Ricky Horton	.05
37	Lance Johnson **RC**	.25
38	Steve Lake	.05
39	Jim Lindeman	.05
40	Joe Magrane **RC**	.10
41	Greg Mathews	.05
42	Willie McGee	.05
43	John Morris	.05
44	Jose Oquendo	.05
45	Tony Pena	.05
46	Terry Pendleton	.05
47	Ozzie Smith	.65
48	John Tudor	.05
49	Lee Tunnell	.05
50	Todd Worrell	.05
51	Doyle Alexander	.05
52	Dave Bergman	.05
53	Tom Brookens	.05
54	Darrell Evans	.05
55	Kirk Gibson	.05
56	Mike Heath	.05
57	Mike Henneman	.05
58	Willie Hernandez	.05
59	Larry Herndon	.05
60	Eric King	.05
61	Chet Lemon	.05
62	Scott Lusader **RC**	.05
63	Bill Madlock	.05
64	Jack Morris	.05
65	Jim Morrison	.05
66	Matt Nokes	.05
67	Dan Petry	.05
68a	Jeff Robinson **RC** (Born 12-13-60 on back.)	.25
68b	Jeff Robinson **RC** (Born 12/14/61 on back.)	.10
69	Pat Sheridan	.05
70	Nate Snell	.05
71	Frank Tanana	.05
72	Walt Terrell	.05
73	Mark Thurmond	.05
74	Alan Trammell	.05
75	Lou Whitaker	.05
76	Mike Aldrete	.05
77	Bob Brenly	.05
78	Will Clark	.05
79	Chili Davis	.05
80	Kelly Downs	.05
81	Dave Dravecky	.05
82	Scott Garrelts	.05
83	Atlee Hammaker	.05
84	Dave Henderson	.05
85	Mike Krukow	.05
86	Mike LaCoss	.05
87	Craig Lefferts	.05
88	Jeff Leonard	.05
89	Candy Maldonado	.05
90	Ed Milner	.05
91	Bob Melvin	.05
92	Kevin Mitchell	.05
93	Jon Perlman **RC**	.05
94	Rick Reuschel	.05
95	Don Robinson	.05
96	Chris Speier	.05
97	Harry Spilman	.05
98	Robbie Thompson	.05
99	Jose Uribe	.05
100	Mark Wasinger **RC**	.05
101	Matt Williams	.05
102	Jesse Barfield	.05
103	George Bell	.05
104	Juan Beniquez	.05
105	John Cerutti	.05
106	Jim Clancy	.05
107	Rob Ducey **RC**	.05
108	Mark Eichhorn	.05
109	Tony Fernandez	.05
110	Cecil Fielder	.05
111	Kelly Gruber	.05
112	Tom Henke	.05
113	Garth Iorg (Iorg)	.05
114	Jimmy Key	.05
115	Rick Leach	.05
116	Manny Lee	.05
117	Nelson Liriano **RC**	.05
118	Fred McGriff	.05
119	Lloyd Moseby	.05
120	Rance Mulliniks	.05
121	Jeff Musselman	.05
122	Jose Nunez **RC**	.05
123	Dave Stieb	.05
124	Willie Upshaw	.05
125	Duane Ward **RC**	.05
126	Ernie Whitt	.05
127	Rick Aguilera	.05
128	Wally Backman	.05
129	Mark Carreon **RC**	.10
130	Gary Carter	.50
131	David Cone **RC**	.05
132	Ron Darling	.05
133	Len Dykstra	.05
134	Sid Fernandez	.05
135	Dwight Gooden	.05
136	Keith Hernandez	.05
137	Gregg Jefferies **RC**	.50
138	Howard Johnson	.05
139	Terry Leach	.05
140	Barry Lyons **RC**	.05
141	Dave Magadan	.05
142	Roger McDowell	.05
143	Kevin McReynolds	.05
144	Keith Miller **RC**	.05
145	John Mitchell **RC**	.05
146	Randy Myers	.05
147	Bob Ojeda	.05
148	Jesse Orosco	.05
149	Rafael Santana	.05
150	Doug Sisk	.05
151	Darryl Strawberry	.05
152	Tim Teufel	.05
153	Gene Walter	.05
154	Mookie Wilson	.05
155	Jay Aldrich **RC**	.05
156	Chris Bosio	.05
157	Glenn Braggs	.05
158	Greg Brock	.05
159	Juan Castillo	.05
160	Mark Clear	.05
161	Cecil Cooper	.05
162	Chuck Crim **RC**	.05
163	Rob Deer	.05
164	Mike Felder	.05
165	Jim Gantner	.05
166	Ted Higuera	.05
167	Steve Kiefer	.05
168	Rick Manning	.05
169	Paul Molitor	.50
170	Juan Nieves	.05
171	Dan Plesac	.05
172	Earnest Riles	.05
173	Bill Schroeder	.05
174	Steve Stanicek **RC**	.05
175	B.J. Surhoff	.05
176	Dale Sveum	.05
177	Bill Wegman	.05
178	Robin Yount	.50
179	Hubie Brooks	.05
180	Tim Burke	.05
181	Casey Candaele	.05
182	Mike Fitzgerald	.05
183	Tom Foley	.05
184	Andres Galarraga	.05
185	Neal Heaton	.05
186	Wallace Johnson	.05
187	Vance Law	.05
188	Dennis Martinez	.05
189	Bob McClure	.05
190	Andy McGaffigan	.05
191	Reid Nichols	.05
192	Pascual Perez	.05
193	Tim Raines	.05
194	Jeff Reed	.05
195	Bob Sebra	.05
196	Bryn Smith	.05
197	Randy St. Claire	.05
198	Tim Wallach	.05
199	Mitch Webster	.05
200	Herm Winningham	.05
201	Floyd Youmans	.05
202	Brad Arnsberg **RC**	.05
203	Rick Cerone	.05
204	Pat Clements	.05
205	Henry Cotto	.05
206	Mike Easler	.05
207	Ron Guidry	.10
208	Bill Gullickson	.05
209	Rickey Henderson	.50
210	Charles Hudson	.05
211	Tommy John	.10
212	Roberto Kelly **RC**	.25
213	Ron Kittle	.05
214	Don Mattingly	.75
215	Bobby Meacham	.05
216	Mike Pagliarulo	.05
217	Dan Pasqua	.05
218	Willie Randolph	.05
219	Rick Rhoden	.05
220	Dave Righetti	.05
221	Jerry Royster	.05
222	Tim Stoddard	.05
223	Wayne Tolleson	.05
224	Gary Ward	.05
225	Claudell Washington	.05
226	Dave Winfield	.50
227	Buddy Bell	.05
228	Tom Browning	.05
229	Dave Concepcion	.05
230	Kal Daniels	.05
231	Eric Davis	.05
232	Bo Diaz	.05
233	Nick Esasky	.05
234	John Franco	.05
235	Guy Hoffman	.05
236	Tom Hume	.05
237	Tracy Jones	.05
238	Bill Landrum **RC**	.05
239	Barry Larkin	.05
240	Terry McGriff **RC**	.05
241	Rob Murphy	.05
242	Ron Oester	.05
243	Dave Parker	.05
244	Pat Perry	.05
245	Ted Power	.05
246	Dennis Rasmussen	.05
247	Ron Robinson	.05
248	Kurt Stillwell	.05
249	Jeff Treadway **RC**	.05
250	Frank Williams	.05
251	Steve Balboni	.05
252	Bud Black	.05
253	Thad Bosley	.05
254	George Brett	.75
255	John Davis **RC**	.05
256	Steve Farr	.05
257	Gene Garber	.05
258	Jerry Gleaton	.05
259	Mark Gubicza	.05
260	Bo Jackson	.10
261	Danny Jackson	.05
262	Ross Jones **RC**	.05
263	Charlie Leibrandt	.05
264	Bill Pecota **RC**	.05
265	Melido Perez **RC**	.05
266	Jamie Quirk	.05
267	Dan Quisenberry	.05
268	Bret Saberhagen	.05
269	Angel Salazar	.05
270	Kevin Seitzer	.05
271	Danny Tartabull	.05
272	Gary Thurman **RC**	.05
273	Frank White	.05
274	Willie Wilson	.05
275	Tony Bernazard	.05
276	Jose Canseco	.30
277	Mike Davis	.05
278	Storm Davis	.05
279	Dennis Eckersley	.40
280	Alfredo Griffin	.05
281	Rick Honeycutt	.05
282	Jay Howell	.05
283	Reggie Jackson	.65
284	Dennis Lamp	.05
285	Carney Lansford	.05
286	Mark McGwire	.85
287	Dwayne Murphy	.05
288	Gene Nelson	.05
289	Steve Ontiveros	.05
290	Tony Phillips	.05
291	Eric Plunk	.05
292	Luis Polonia **RC**	.15
293	Rick Rodriguez **RC**	.05
294	Terry Steinbach	.05
295	Dave Stewart	.05
296	Curt Young	.05
297	Luis Aguayo	.05
298	Steve Bedrosian	.05
299	Jeff Calhoun	.05
300	Don Carman	.05
301	Todd Frohwirth **RC**	.05
302	Greg Gross	.05
303	Kevin Gross	.05
304	Von Hayes	.05
305	Keith Hughes **RC**	.05
306	Mike Jackson **RC**	.05
307	Chris James	.05
308	Steve Jeltz	.05
309	Mike Maddux	.05
310	Lance Parrish	.05
311	Shane Rawley	.05
312	Wally Ritchie **RC**	.05
313	Bruce Ruffin	.05
314	Juan Samuel	.05
315	Mike Schmidt	.75
316	Rick Schu	.05
317	Jeff Stone	.05
318	Kent Tekulve	.05
319	Milt Thompson	.05
320	Glenn Wilson	.05
321	Rafael Belliard	.05
322	Barry Bonds	1.00
323	Bobby Bonilla	.05
324	Sid Bream	.05
325	John Cangelosi	.05
326	Mike Diaz	.05
327	Doug Drabek	.05
328	Mike Dunne **RC**	.05
329	Brian Fisher	.05
330	Brett Gideon **RC**	.05
331	Terry Harper	.05
332	Bob Kipper	.05
333	Mike LaValliere	.05
334	Jose Lind **RC**	.15
335	Junior Ortiz	.05
336	Vicente Palacios **RC**	.05
337	Bob Patterson **RC**	.05
338	Al Pedrique **RC**	.05
339	R.J. Reynolds	.05
340	John Smiley	.05
341	Andy Van Slyke	.05
342	Bob Walk	.05
343	Marty Barrett	.05
344	Todd Benzinger **RC**	.05
345	Wade Boggs	.65
346	Tom Bolton **RC**	.05
347	Oil Can Boyd	.05
348	Ellis Burks	.05

349 Roger Clemens .75
350 Steve Crawford .05
351 Dwight Evans .05
352 Wes Gardner **RC** .05
353 Rich Gedman .05
354 Mike Greenwell .05
355 Sam Horn **RC** .05
356 Bruce Hurst .05
357 John Marzano **RC** .05
358 Al Nipper .05
359 Spike Owen .05
360 Jody Reed **RC** .15
361 Jim Rice .20
362 Ed Romero .05
363 Kevin Romine **RC** .05
364 Joe Sambito .05
365 Calvin Schiraldi .05
366 Jeff Sellers .05
367 Bob Stanley .05
368 Scott Bankhead .05
369 Phil Bradley .05
370 Scott Bradley .05
371 Mickey Brantley .05
372 Mike Campbell **RC** .05
373 Alvin Davis .05
374 Lee Guetterman .05
375 Dave Hengel **RC** .05
376 Mike Kingery .05
377 Mark Langston .05
378 Edgar Martinez **RC** 1.00
379 Mike Moore .05
380 Mike Morgan .05
381 John Moses .05
382 Donnell Nixon **RC** .05
383 Edwin Nunez .05
384 Ken Phelps .05
385 Jim Presley .05
386 Rey Quinones .05
387 Jerry Reed .05
388 Harold Reynolds .05
389 Dave Valle .05
390 Bill Wilkinson **RC** .05
391 Harold Baines .05
392 Floyd Bannister .05
393 Daryl Boston .05
394 Ivan Calderon .05
395 Jose DeLeon .05
396 Richard Dotson .05
397 Carlton Fisk .50
398 Ozzie Guillen .05
399 Ron Hassey .05
400 Donnie Hill .05
401 Bob James .05
402 Dave LaPoint .05
403 Bill Lindsey **RC** .05
404 Bill Long **RC** .05
405 Steve Lyons .05
406 Fred Manrique **RC** .05
407 Jack McDowell **RC** .25
408 Gary Redus .05
409 Ray Searage .05
410 Bobby Thigpen .05
411 Greg Walker .05
412 Kenny Williams **RC** .05
413 Jim Winn .05
414 Jody Davis .05
415 Andre Dawson .25
416 Brian Dayett .05
417 Bob Dernier .05
418 Frank DiPino .05
419 Shawon Dunston .05
420 Leon Durham .05
421 Les Lancaster **RC** .10
422 Ed Lynch .05
423 Greg Maddux .75
424 Dave Martinez **RC** .05
425a Keith Moreland/Bunting (Photo actually Jody Davis.) 2.00
425b Keith Moreland/Standing Upright (Correct photo.) .05
426 Jamie Moyer .05
427 Jerry Mumphrey .05
428 Paul Noce **RC** .05
429 Rafael Palmeiro .40
430 Wade Rowdon **RC** .05
431 Ryne Sandberg .65
432 Scott Sanderson .05
433 Lee Smith .05
434 Jim Sundberg .05
435 Rick Sutcliffe .05
436 Manny Trillo .05
437 Juan Agosto .05
438 Larry Andersen .05
439 Alan Ashby .05
440 Kevin Bass .05
441 Ken Caminiti **RC** .25
442 Rocky Childress **RC** .05
443 Jose Cruz .05
444 Danny Darwin .05
445 Glenn Davis .05
446 Jim Deshaies .05
447 Bill Doran .05
448 Ty Gainey .05
449 Billy Hatcher .05
450 Jeff Heathcock .05
451 Bob Knepper .05
452 Rob Mallicoat **RC** .05
453 Dave Meads **RC** .05
454 Craig Reynolds .05
455 Nolan Ryan 1.00
456 Mike Scott .05
457 Dave Smith .05
458 Denny Walling .05
459 Robbie Wine **RC** .05
460 Gerald Young **RC** .05
461 Bob Brower .05
462a Jerry Browne/White Player (Photo actually Bob Brower.) 2.00
462b Jerry Browne/Black Player (Correct photo.) .05
463 Steve Buechele .05
464 Edwin Correa .05
465 Cecil Espy **RC** .05
466 Scott Fletcher .05
467 Jose Guzman .05
468 Greg Harris .05
469 Charlie Hough .05
470 Pete Incaviglia .05
471 Paul Kilgus **RC** .05
472 Mike Loynd .05
473 Oddibe McDowell .05
474 Dale Mohorcic .05
475 Pete O'Brien .05
476 Larry Parrish .05
477 Geno Petralli .05
478 Jeff Russell .05
479 Ruben Sierra .05
480 Mike Stanley .05
481 Curtis Wilkerson .05
482 Mitch Williams .05
483 Bobby Witt .05
484 Tony Armas .05
485 Bob Boone .05
486 Bill Buckner .05
487 DeWayne Buice **RC** .05
488 Brian Downing .05
489 Chuck Finley .05
490 Willie Fraser .05
491 Jack Howell .05
492 Ruppert Jones .05
493 Wally Joyner .05
494 Jack Lazorko .05
495 Gary Lucas .05
496 Kirk McCaskill .05
497 Mark McLemore .05
498 Darrell Miller .05
499 Greg Minton .05
500 Donnie Moore .05
501 Gus Polidor .05
502 Johnny Ray .05
503 Mark Ryal **RC** .05
504 Dick Schofield .05
505 Don Sutton .40
506 Devon White .05
507 Mike Witt .05
508 Dave Anderson .05
509 Tim Belcher **RC** .05
510 Ralph Bryant .05
511 Tim Crews **RC** .15
512 Mike Devereaux **RC** .10
513 Mariano Duncan .05
514 Pedro Guerrero .05
515 Jeff Hamilton **RC** .05
516 Mickey Hatcher .05
517 Brad Havens .05
518 Orel Hershiser .05
519 Shawn Hillegas **RC** .05
520 Ken Howell .05
521 Tim Leary .05
522 Mike Marshall .05
523 Steve Sax .05
524 Mike Scioscia .05
525 Mike Sharperson **RC** .05
526 John Shelby .05
527 Franklin Stubbs .05
528 Fernando Valenzuela .05
529 Bob Welch .05
530 Matt Young .05
531 Jim Acker .05
532 Paul Assenmacher .05
533 Jeff Blauser **RC** .10
534 Joe Boever **RC** .05
535 Martin Clary **RC** .05
536 Kevin Coffman **RC** .05
537 Jeff Dedmon .05
538 Ron Gant **RC** .50
539 Tom Glavine **RC** 2.00
540 Ken Griffey .05
541 Al Hall .05
542 Glenn Hubbard .05
543 Dion James .05
544 Dale Murphy .20
545 Ken Oberkfell .05
546 David Palmer .05
547 Gerald Perry .05
548 Charlie Puleo .05
549 Ted Simmons .05
550 Zane Smith .05
551 Andres Thomas .05
552 Ozzie Virgil .05
553 Don Aase .05
554 Jeff Ballard **RC** .05
555 Eric Bell .05
556 Mike Boddicker .05
557 Ken Dixon .05
558 Jim Dwyer .05
559 Ken Gerhart .05
560 Rene Gonzales **RC** .05
561 Mike Griffin .05
562 John Habyan (Habyan) .05
563 Terry Kennedy .05
564 Ray Knight .05
565 Lee Lacy .05
566 Fred Lynn .05
567 Eddie Murray .50
568 Tom Niedenfuer .05
569 Bill Ripken **RC** .05
570 Cal Ripken, Jr. 1.00
571 Dave Schmidt .05
572 Larry Sheets .05
573 Pete Stanicek **RC** .05
574 Mark Williamson **RC** .05
575 Mike Young .05
576 Shawn Abner **RC** .05
577 Greg Booker .05
578 Chris Brown .05
579 Keith Comstock **RC** .05
580 Joey Cora **RC** .05
581 Mark Davis .05
582 Tim Flannery .05
583 Goose Gossage .05
584 Mark Grant .05
585 Tony Gwynn .65
586 Andy Hawkins .05
587 Stan Jefferson .05
588 Jimmy Jones .05
589 John Kruk .05
590 Shane Mack **RC** .10
591 Carmelo Martinez .05
592 Lance McCullers .05
593 Eric Nolte **RC** .05
594 Randy Ready .05
595 Luis Salazar .05
596 Benito Santiago .05
597 Eric Show .05
598 Garry Templeton .05
599 Ed Whitson .05
600 Scott Bailes .05
601 Chris Bando .05
602 Jay Bell **RC** .50
603 Brett Butler .05
604 Tom Candiotti .05
605 Joe Carter .05
606 Carmen Castillo .05
607 Brian Dorsett **RC** .05
608 John Farrell **RC** .05
609 Julio Franco .05
610 Mel Hall .05
611 Tommy Hinzo **RC** .05
612 Brook Jacoby .05
613 Doug Jones **RC** .10
614 Ken Schrom .05
615 Cory Snyder .05
616 Sammy Stewart .05
617 Greg Swindell .05
618 Pat Tabler .05
619 Ed Vande Berg .05
620 Eddie Williams **RC** .05
621 Rich Yett .05
622 Slugging Sophomores (Wally Joyner, Cory Snyder) .10
623 Dominican Dynamite (George Bell, Pedro Guerrero) .05
624 Oakland's Power Team (Jose Canseco, Mark McGwire) .50
625 Classic Relief (Dan Plesac, Dave Righetti) .05
626 All Star Righties (Jack Morris, Bret Saberhagen, Mike Witt) .05
627 Game Closers (Steve Bedrosian, John Franco) .05
628 Masters of the Double Play (Ryne Sandberg, Ozzie Smith) .50
629 Rookie Record Setter (Mark McGwire) .50
630 Changing the Guard in Boston (Todd Benzinger, Ellis Burks, Mike Greenwell) .10
631 N.L. Batting Champs (Tony Gwynn, Tim Raines) .20
632 Pitching Magic (Orel Hershiser, Mike Scott) .05
633 Big Bats At First (Mark McGwire, Pat Tabler) .50
634 Hitting King and the Thief (Tony Gwynn, Vince Coleman) .15
635 A.L. Slugging Shortstops (Tony Fernandez, Cal Ripken, Jr., Alan Trammell) .40
636 Tried and True Sluggers (Gary Carter, Mike Schmidt) .40
637 Crunch Time (Eric Davis) .05
638 A.L. All Stars (Matt Nokes, Kirby Puckett) .25
639 N.L. All Stars (Keith Hernandez, Dale Murphy) .10
640 The "O's" Brothers (Bill Ripken, Cal Ripken, Jr.) .50
641 Major League Prospects (Mark Grace **RC**, Darrin Jackson **RC**) 1.00
642 Major League Prospects (Damon Berryhill **RC**, Jeff Montgomery **RC**) .20
643 Major League Prospects (Felix Fermin **RC**, Jessie Reid **RC**) .05
644 Major League Prospects (Greg Myers **RC**, Greg Tabor **RC**) .05
645 Major League Prospects (Jim Eppard **RC**, Joey Meyer **RC**) .05
646 Major League Prospects (Adam Peterson **RC**, Randy Velarde **RC**) .10
647 Major League Prospects (Chris Gwynn **RC**, Peter Smith **RC**) .15
648 Major League Prospects (Greg Jelks **RC**, Tom Newell **RC**) .05
649 Major League Prospects (Mario Diaz **RC**, Clay Parker **RC**) .05
650 Major League Prospects (Jack Savage **RC**, Todd Simmons **RC**) .05
651 Major League Prospects (John Burkett **RC**, Kirt Manwaring **RC**) .30
652 Major League Prospects (Dave Otto **RC**, Walt Weiss **RC**) .25
653 Major League Prospects (Randell Byers (Randall) **RC**, Jeff King **RC**) .25
654a Checklist 1-101 (21 is Schatzader) .10
654b Checklist 1-101 (21 is Schatzeder) .05
655 Checklist 102-201 .05
656 Checklist 202-296 .05
657 Checklist 297-390 .05
658 Checklist 391-483 .05
659 Checklist 484-575 .05
660 Checklist 576-660 .05

All Stars

For the third consecutive year, Fleer randomly inserted All Star Team cards in its wax and cello packs. Twelve cards make up the set, with players chosen for the set being Fleer's idea of a major league All-Star team.

		NM/M
Complete Set (12):		3.00
Common Player:		.10
1	Matt Nokes	.10
2	Tom Henke	.10
3	Ted Higuera	.10
4	Roger Clemens	1.50
5	George Bell	.10
6	Andre Dawson	.25
7	Eric Davis	.10
8	Wade Boggs	.85
9	Alan Trammell	.10
10	Juan Samuel	.10
11	Jack Clark	.10
12	Paul Molitor	.75

Headliners

This six-card set was inserted in Fleer three-packs, sold by retail outlets and hobby dealers nationwide. The card fronts feature crisp full-color player cut-outs printed on a gray and white facsimile sports page. "Fleer Headliners 1988" is printed in black and red on a white banner across the top of the card, both front and back. A similar white banner across the card bottom bears the black and white National or American League logo and a red player/team name. Card backs are black on grey with red accents and include the card number and a narrative career summary.

		NM/M
Complete Set (6):		3.00
Common Player:		.25
1	Don Mattingly	1.50
2	Mark McGwire	2.00
3	Jack Morris	.15
4	Darryl Strawberry	.15
5	Dwight Gooden	.15
6	Tim Raines	.15

'87 World Series

Highlights of the 1987 Series are captured in this full-color insert set found only in Fleer's regular 660-card factory sets. This second World Series edition by Fleer features cards framed in red, with a blue and white starred bunting draped over the upper edges of the photo and a brief photo caption printed on a yellow band across the lower border. Numbered card backs are red, white and blue and include a description of the action pictured on the front, with stats for the Series.

		NM/M
Complete Set (12):		2.50
Common Player:		.25
1	"Grand" Hero In Game 1 (Dan Gladden)	.25
2	The Cardinals "Bush" Whacked (Randy Bush, Tony Pena)	.25
3	Masterful Performance Turns Momentum (John Tudor)	.25
4	Ozzie Smith	1.00
5	Throw Smoke! (Tony Pena, Todd Worrell)	.25
6	Cardinal Attack - Disruptive Speed (Vince Coleman)	.25
7	Herr's Wallop (Dan Driessen, Tom Herr)	.25
8	Kirby Puckett	1.00
9	Kent Hrbek	.25
10	Rich Hacker/Coach, Tom Herr, Lee Weyer/Umpire	.25
11	Game 7's Play At The Plate (Don Baylor, Dave Phillips/Umpire	.25
12	Frank Viola	.25

Box Panels

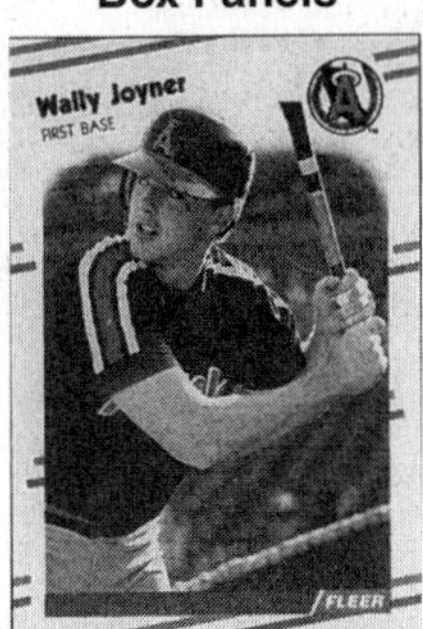

Fleer's third annual box-bottom issue once again included 16 full-color trading cards printed on the bottoms of four different wax and cello pack retail display boxes. Each box contains three player cards and one team logo card. Player cards follow the same design as the basic 1988 Fleer issue. Standard size, the cards are numbered C-1 through C-16.

		NM/M
Complete Panel Set (4):		4.00
Complete Singles Set (16):		4.00
Common Panel:		1.00
Common Single Player:		.10
Panel		1.50
1	Cardinals Logo	.05
11	Mike Schmidt	1.00
14	Dave Stewart	.10
15	Tim Wallach	.10
Panel		1.00
2	Dwight Evans	.10
8	Shane Rawley	.10
10	Ryne Sandberg	.75
13	Tigers Logo	.05
Panel		1.25
3	Andres Galarraga	.10
6	Dale Murphy	.45
9	Giants Logo	.05
12	Kevin Seitzer	.10
Panel		1.00
4	Wally Joyner	.10
5	Twins Logo	.05
7	Kirby Puckett	1.00
16	Todd Worrell	.10

Glossy Tin

In its second year of production, Fleer radically reduced production numbers on its glossy version of the 1988 baseball card set. With production estimates in the 60,000 set range, values of the '88 tin glossies are about double those of the regular issue cards. Once again the issue was sold only as complete sets in colorful lithographed metal boxes.

	NM/M
Complete Set (672):	20.00
Common Player:	.15

Update

This update set (numbered U-1 through U-132 are 2-1/2" x 3-1/2") features traded veterans and rookies in a mixture of full-color action shots and close-ups, framed by white borders with red and blue stripes. The backs are red, white and blue-gray and include personal info, along with yearly and "At Their Best" (day, night, home, road) stats charts. The set was packaged in white cardboard boxes with red and blue stripes. A glossy-coated edition of the update set was issued in its own box and is valued at two times the regular issue.

		NM/M
Complete Set (132):		5.00
Common Player:		.05
1	Jose Bautista **RC**	.05
2	Joe Orsulak	.05
3	Doug Sisk	.05
4	Craig Worthington **RC**	.05
5	Mike Boddicker	.05
6	Rick Cerone	.05
7	Larry Parrish	.05
8	Lee Smith	.10
9	Mike Smithson	.05
10	John Trautwein **RC**	.05
11	Sherman Corbett **RC**	.05
12	Chili Davis	.05
13	Jim Eppard	.05
14	Bryan Harvey **RC**	.05
15	John Davis	.05
16	Dave Gallagher **RC**	.05

17 Ricky Horton .05
18 Dan Pasqua .05
19 Melido Perez .05
20 Jose Segura **RC** .05
21 Andy Allanson .05
22 Jon Perlman .05
23 Domingo Ramos .05
24 Rick Rodriguez .05
25 Willie Upshaw .05
26 Paul Gibson **RC** .05
27 Don Heinkel **RC** .05
28 Ray Knight .05
29 Gary Pettis .05
30 Luis Salazar .05
31 Mike MacFarlane .05
32 Jeff Montgomery .05
33 Ted Power .05
34 Israel Sanchez **RC** .05
35 Kurt Stillwell .05
36 Pat Tabler .05
37 Don August **RC** .05
38 Darryl Hamilton **RC** .05
39 Jeff Leonard .05
40 Joey Meyer .05
41 Allan Anderson .05
42 Brian Harper .05
43 Tom Herr .05
44 Charlie Lea .05
45 John Moses .05
46 John Candelaria .05
47 Jack Clark .05
48 Richard Dotson .05
49 Al Leiter **RC** .05
50 Rafael Santana .05
51 Don Slaught .05
52 Todd Burns **RC** .05
53 Dave Henderson .05
54 Doug Jennings **RC** .05
55 Dave Parker .05
56 Walt Weiss .05
57 Bob Welch .05
58 Henry Cotto .05
59 Marion Diaz (Mario) .05
60 Mike Jackson .05
61 Bill Swift .05
62 Jose Cecena **RC** .05
63 Ray Hayward **RC** .05
64 Jim Steels **RC** .05
65 Pat Borders **RC** .05
66 Sil Campusano **RC** .05
67 Mike Flanagan .05
68 Todd Stottlemyre **RC** .05
69 David Wells **RC** .05
70 Jose Alvarez **RC** .05
71 Paul Runge .05
72 Cesar Jimenez **RC** (German) .05
73 Pete Smith .05
74 John Smoltz **RC** 1.50
75 Damon Berryhill .05
76 Goose Gossage .05
77 Mark Grace .10
78 Darrin Jackson .05
79 Vance Law .05
80 Jeff Pico **RC** .05
81 Gary Varsho **RC** .05
82 Tim Birtsas .05
83 Rob Dibble **RC** .05
84 Danny Jackson .05
85 Paul O'Neill .05
86 Jose Rijo .05
87 Chris Sabo **RC** .25
88 John Fishel **RC** .05
89 Craig Biggio **RC** 4.00
90 Terry Puhl .05
91 Rafael Ramirez .05
92 Louie Meadows **RC** .05
93 Kirk Gibson .05
94 Alfredo Griffin .05
95 Jay Howell .05
96 Jesse Orosco .05
97 Alejandro Pena .05
98 Tracy Woodson **RC** .05
99 John Dopson **RC** .05
100 Brian Holman **RC** .05
101 Rex Hudler **RC** .05
102 Jeff Parrett **RC** .05
103 Nelson Santovenia **RC** .05
104 Kevin Elster .05
105 Jeff Innis **RC** .05
106 Mackey Sasser **RC** .05
107 Phil Bradley .05
108 Danny Clay **RC** .05
109 Greg Harris .05
110 Ricky Jordan **RC** .05
111 David Palmer .05
112 Jim Gott .05
113 Tommy Gregg **RC** (Photo actually Randy Milligan.) .05
114 Barry Jones .05
115 Randy Milligan **RC** .05
116 Luis Alicea **RC** .05
117 Tom Brunansky .05
118 John Costello **RC** .05
119 Jose DeLeon .05
120 Bob Horner .05
121 Scott Terry **RC** .05
122 Roberto Alomar **RC** 1.50
123 Dave Leiper .05
124 Keith Moreland .05
125 Mark Parent **RC** .05
126 Dennis Rasmussen .05
127 Randy Bockus .05
128 Brett Butler .05
129 Donell Nixon .05
130 Earnest Riles .05
131 Roger Samuels **RC** .05
132 Checklist .05

Update Glossy Tin

The glossy version of the 1988 Fleer Update set differs from the regular-issue Update set only in the high-gloss finish applied to the cards' fronts and the lithographed metal box in which sets were sold.

NM/M
Complete Set (132): 9.00
Common Player: .15

Award Winners

This limited edition boxed set of 1987 award-winning player cards also includes six team logo sticker cards. Red, white, blue and yellow bands border the sharp, full-color player photos printed below a "Fleer Award Winners 1988" banner. The player's name and award are printed beneath the photo. Flip sides are red, white and blue and list personal information, career data, team logo and card number. This set was sold exclusively at 7-11 stores nationwide.

NM/M
Complete Set (44): 3.50
Common Player: .05
1 Steve Bedrosian .05
2 George Bell .05
3 Wade Boggs .65
4 Jose Canseco .30
5 Will Clark .05
6 Roger Clemens .75
7 Kal Daniels .05
8 Eric Davis .05
9 Andre Dawson .25
10 Mike Dunne .05
11 Dwight Evans .05
12 Carlton Fisk .50
13 Julio Franco .05
14 Dwight Gooden .05
15 Pedro Guerrero .05
16 Tony Gwynn .65
17 Orel Hershiser .05
18 Tom Henke .05
19 Ted Higuera .05
20 Charlie Hough .05
21 Wally Joyner .05
22 Jimmy Key .05
23 Don Mattingly .75
24 Mark McGwire 1.50
25 Paul Molitor .50
26 Jack Morris .05
27 Dale Murphy .20
28 Terry Pendleton .05
29 Kirby Puckett .65
30 Tim Raines .05
31 Jeff Reardon .05
32 Harold Reynolds .05
33 Dave Righetti .05
34 Benito Santiago .05
35 Mike Schmidt .75
36 Mike Scott .05
37 Kevin Seitzer .05
38 Larry Sheets .05
39 Ozzie Smith .65
40 Darryl Strawberry .05
41 Rick Sutcliffe .05
42 Danny Tartabull .05
43 Alan Trammell .05
44 Tim Wallach .05

Baseball All Stars

This limited edition boxed set features major league All-Stars. The standard-size cards feature a sporty bright blue and yellow striped background. Card backs feature a blue and white striped design with a yellow highlighted section at the top that contains the player name, card number, team, position and personal data, followed by lifetime career stats.

Fleer All Stars are cello-wrapped in blue and yellow striped boxes with checklist backs. The set includes six team logo sticker cards that feature black-and-white aerial shots of major league ballparks. The set was marketed exclusively by Ben Franklin stores.

NM/M
Complete Set (44): 4.00
Common Player: .05
1 George Bell .05
2 Wade Boggs .65
3 Bobby Bonilla .05
4 George Brett .85
5 Jose Canseco .35
6 Jack Clark .05
7 Will Clark .05
8 Roger Clemens .85
9 Eric Davis .05
10 Andre Dawson .25
11 Julio Franco .05
12 Dwight Gooden .05
13 Tony Gwynn .65
14 Orel Hershiser .05
15 Teddy Higuera .05
16 Charlie Hough .05
17 Kent Hrbek .05
18 Bruce Hurst .05
19 Wally Joyner .05
20 Mark Langston .05
21 Dave LaPoint .05
22 Candy Maldonado .05
23 Don Mattingly .85
24 Roger McDowell .05
25 Mark McGwire 1.00
26 Jack Morris .05
27 Dale Murphy .20
28 Eddie Murray .50
29 Matt Nokes .05
30 Kirby Puckett .65
31 Tim Raines .05
32 Willie Randolph .05
33 Jeff Reardon .05
34 Nolan Ryan 1.00
35 Juan Samuel .05
36 Mike Schmidt .85
37 Mike Scott .05
38 Kevin Seitzer .05
39 Ozzie Smith .65
40 Darryl Strawberry .05
41 Rick Sutcliffe .05
42 Alan Trammell .05
43 Tim Wallach .05
44 Dave Winfield .50

Baseball's Best

This boxed set of 44 standard-size cards (2-1/2" x 3-1/2") and six team logo stickers is the third annual issue from Fleer highlighting the best major league sluggers and pitchers. Five additional player cards were printed on retail display box bottoms, along with a checklist logo card (numbered C-1 through C-6). Full-color player photos are framed by a green border that fades to yellow. A red (slugger) or blue (pitcher) player name is printed beneath the photo. Backs are printed in green on a white background with yellow highlights. Card number, player name and personal info appear in a green vertical box on the left-hand side of the card back with a yellow cartoon-style team logo overprinted across a stats chart on the right. This set was produced by Fleer for exclusive distribution by McCrory's stores (McCrory, McClellan, J.J. Newberry, H.L. Green, TG&Y).

NM/M
Complete Set (44): 4.00
Common Player: .05
1 George Bell .05
2 Wade Boggs .65
3 Bobby Bonilla .05
4 Tom Brunansky .05
5 Ellis Burks .05
6 Jose Canseco .40
7 Joe Carter .05
8 Will Clark .05
9 Roger Clemens .85
10 Eric Davis .05
11 Glenn Davis .05
12 Andre Dawson .25
13 Dennis Eckersley .45
14 Andres Galarraga .05
15 Dwight Gooden .05
16 Pedro Guerrero .05
17 Tony Gwynn .65
18 Orel Hershiser .05
19 Ted Higuera .05
20 Pete Incaviglia .05
21 Danny Jackson .05
22 Doug Jennings .05
23 Mark Langston .05
24 Dave LaPoint .05
25 Mike LaValliere .05
26 Don Mattingly .85
27 Mark McGwire 1.00
28 Dale Murphy .20
29 Ken Phelps .05
30 Kirby Puckett .65
31 Johnny Ray .05
32 Jeff Reardon .05
33 Dave Righetti .05
34 Cal Ripkin, Jr. (Ripken) 1.50
35 Chris Sabo .05
36 Mike Schmidt .85
37 Mike Scott .05
38 Kevin Seitzer .05
39 Dave Stewart .05
40 Darryl Strawberry .05
41 Greg Swindell .05
42 Frank Tanana .05
43 Dave Winfield .50
44 Todd Worrell .05

Baseball's Best Box Panel

Six cards were placed on the bottoms of retail boxes of the Fleer Baseball's Best boxed sets in 1988. The cards, 2-1/2" x 3-1/2", are identical in design to cards found in the 44-card set. The cards are numbered C-1 through C-6 and were produced for distribution by McCrory stores and its affiliates.

NM/M
Complete Panel Set: 1.50
Complete Singles Set (6): 1.50
Common Single Player: .10
1 Ron Darling .10
2 Rickey Henderson .75
3 Carney Lansford .10
4 Rafael Palmeiro .60
5 Frank Viola .10
6 Minnesota Twins Logo .05

Exciting Stars

This boxed set showcases star major leaguers. Player photos are slanted upwards to the right, framed by a blue border with a red and white stripe across the middle. Card backs are numbered and printed in red, white and blue. The set

was packaged in a checklist box, with six team logo sticker cards featuring black-and-white stadium photos on the flip sides. Exciting Stars was distributed via Cumberland Farm stores throughout the northeastern U.S. and Florida.

NM/M
Complete Set (44): 3.00
Common Player: .05
1 Harold Baines .05
2 Kevin Bass .05
3 George Bell .05
4 Wade Boggs .65
5 Mickey Brantley .05
6 Sid Bream .05
7 Jose Canseco .30
8 Jack Clark .05
9 Will Clark .05
10 Roger Clemens .85
11 Vince Coleman .05
12 Eric Davis .05
13 Andre Dawson .25
14 Julio Franco .05
15 Dwight Gooden .05
16 Mike Greenwell .05
17 Tony Gwynn .65
18 Von Hayes .05
19 Tom Henke .05
20 Orel Hershiser .05
21 Teddy Higuera .05
22 Brook Jacoby .05
23 Wally Joyner .05
24 Jimmy Key .05
25 Don Mattingly .85
26 Mark McGwire 1.00
27 Jack Morris .05
28 Dale Murphy .20
29 Matt Nokes .05
30 Kirby Puckett .65
31 Tim Raines .05
32 Ryne Sandberg .65
33 Benito Santiago .05
34 Mike Schmidt .85
35 Mike Scott .05
36 Kevin Seitzer .05
37 Larry Sheets .05
38 Ruben Sierra .05
39 Darryl Strawberry .05
40 Rick Sutcliffe .05
41 Danny Tartabull .05
42 Alan Trammell .05
43 Fernando Valenzuela .05
44 Devon White .05

Hottest Stars

This boxed set of standard-size player cards and six team logo stickers was produced by Fleer for exclusive distribution at Revco drug stores nationwide. Card fronts feature full-color photos of players representing every major league team. Photos are framed in red, orange and yellow, with a blue-and-white player name printed at bottom. A flaming baseball logo bearing the words "Hottest Stars" appears in the lower-left corner of the photo. Card backs are red, white and blue. The player's name, position, card number and team logo are printed at top, followed by a stats box and personal data. The set also includes six team logo sticker cards with flipside stadium photos in black-and-white.

NM/M
Complete Set (44): 3.50
Common Player: .05
1 George Bell .05
2 Wade Boggs .65
3 Bobby Bonilla .05
4 George Brett .85
5 Jose Canseco .30
6 Will Clark .05
7 Roger Clemens .85
8 Eric Davis .05
9 Andre Dawson .25
10 Tony Fernandez .05
11 Julio Franco .05
12 Gary Gaetti .05
13 Dwight Gooden .05
14 Mike Greenwell .05
15 Tony Gwynn .65
16 Rickey Henderson .50
17 Keith Hernandez .05
18 Tom Herr .05
19 Orel Hershiser .05
20 Ted Higuera .05
21 Wally Joyner .05
22 Jimmy Key .05
23 Mark Langston .05
24 Don Mattingly .85
25 Jack McDowell .05
26 Mark McGwire 1.00
27 Kevin Mitchell .05
28 Jack Morris .05
29 Dale Murphy .20
30 Kirby Puckett .65
31 Tim Raines .05
32 Shane Rawley .05
33 Benito Santiago .05
34 Mike Schmidt .85
35 Mike Scott .05
36 Kevin Seitzer .05
37 Larry Sheets .05
38 Ruben Sierra .05
39 Dave Smith .05
40 Ozzie Smith .65
41 Darryl Strawberry .05
42 Rick Sutcliffe .05
43 Pat Tabler .05
44 Alan Trammell .05

League Leaders

This boxed set is the third annual limited edition set from Fleer highlighting leading players. The 1988 edition contains the same type of information, front and back, as the previous sets, with a new color scheme and design. Card fronts have bright blue borders, solid on the lower portion, striped on the upper, with a gold bar separating the two sections. The full-color player photo is centered above a yellow name banner. The numbered card backs are blue, pink and white, and contain player stats and personal notes. Six team logo sticker cards, with flipside black-and-white photos of ballparks, accompany this set which was marketed exclusively by Walgreen drug stores.

NM/M
Complete Set (44): 3.50
Common Player: .05
1 George Bell .05
2 Wade Boggs .65
3 Ivan Calderon .05
4 Jose Canseco .30
5 Will Clark .05
6 Roger Clemens .85

7 Vince Coleman .05
8 Eric Davis .05
9 Andre Dawson .25
10 Bill Doran .05
11 Dwight Evans .05
12 Julio Franco .05
13 Gary Gaetti .05
14 Andres Galarraga .05
15 Dwight Gooden .05
16 Tony Gwynn .65
17 Tom Henke .05
18 Keith Hernandez .05
19 Orel Hershiser .05
20 Ted Higuera .05
21 Kent Hrbek .05
22 Wally Joyner .05
23 Jimmy Key .05
24 Mark Langston .05
25 Don Mattingly .85
26 Mark McGwire 1.00
27 Paul Molitor .50
28 Jack Morris .05
29 Dale Murphy .20
30 Kirby Puckett .65
31 Tim Raines .05
32 Rick Rueschel .05
33 Bret Saberhagen .05
34 Benito Santiago .05
35 Mike Schmidt .85
36 Mike Scott .05
37 Kevin Seitzer .05
38 Larry Sheets .05
39 Ruben Sierra .05
40 Darryl Strawberry .05
41 Rick Sutcliffe .05
42 Alan Trammell .05
43 Andy Van Slyke .05
44 Todd Worrell .05

Mini

This third annual issue of miniatures (1-7/8" x 2-5/8") includes 120 high-gloss cards featuring new photos, not copies from the regular issue, although the card designs are identical. Card backs are red, white and blue and include personal data, yearly career stats and a stats breakdown of batting average, slugging percentage and on-base average, listed for day, night, home and road games. Card backs are numbered in alphabetical order by teams which are also listed alphabetically. The set includes 18 team logo stickers with black-and-white aerial stadium photos on the flip sides.

NM/M
Complete Set (120): 3.50
Common Player: .05
1 Eddie Murray .50
2 Dave Schmidt .05
3 Larry Sheets .05
4 Wade Boggs .65
5 Roger Clemens .85
6 Dwight Evans .05
7 Mike Greenwell .05
8 Sam Horn .05
9 Lee Smith .05
10 Brian Downing .05
11 Wally Joyner .05
12 Devon White .05
13 Mike Witt .05
14 Ivan Calderon .05
15 Ozzie Guillen .05
16 Jack McDowell .05
17 Kenny Williams .05
18 Joe Carter .05
19 Julio Franco .05
20 Pat Tabler .05
21 Doyle Alexander .05
22 Jack Morris .05
23 Matt Nokes .05
24 Walt Terrell .05
25 Alan Trammell .05
26 Bret Saberhagen .05
27 Kevin Seitzer .05
28 Danny Tartabull .05
29 Gary Thurman .05
30 Ted Higuera .05
31 Paul Molitor .50
32 Dan Plesac .05
33 Robin Yount .50
34 Gary Gaetti .05
35 Kent Hrbek .05
36 Kirby Puckett .65
37 Jeff Reardon .05
38 Frank Viola .05
39 Jack Clark .05
40 Rickey Henderson .50
41 Don Mattingly .85
42 Willie Randolph .05
43 Dave Righetti .05
44 Dave Winfield .50
45 Jose Canseco .30
46 Mark McGwire 1.00
47 Dave Parker .05
48 Dave Stewart .05
49 Walt Weiss .05
50 Bob Welch .05
51 Mickey Brantley .05
52 Mark Langston .05
53 Harold Reynolds .05
54 Scott Fletcher .05
55 Charlie Hough .05
56 Pete Incaviglia .05
57 Larry Parrish .05
58 Ruben Sierra .05
59 George Bell .05
60 Mark Eichhorn .05
61 Tony Fernandez .05
62 Tom Henke .05
63 Jimmy Key .05
64 Dion James .05
65 Dale Murphy .20
66 Zane Smith .05
67 Andre Dawson .25
68 Mark Grace .25
69 Jerry Mumphrey .05
70 Ryne Sandberg .65
71 Rick Sutcliffe .05
72 Kal Daniels .05
73 Eric Davis .05
74 John Franco .05
75 Ron Robinson .05
76 Jeff Treadway .05
77 Kevin Bass .05
78 Glenn Davis .05
79 Nolan Ryan 1.00
80 Mike Scott .05
81 Dave Smith .05
82 Kirk Gibson .05
83 Pedro Guerrero .05
84 Orel Hershiser .05
85 Steve Sax .05
86 Fernando Valenzuela .05
87 Tim Burke .05
88 Andres Galarraga .05
89 Neal Heaton .05
90 Tim Raines .05
91 Tim Wallach .05
92 Dwight Gooden .05
93 Keith Hernandez .05
94 Gregg Jefferies .10
95 Howard Johnson .05
96 Roger McDowell .05
97 Darryl Strawberry .05
98 Steve Bedrosian .05
99 Von Hayes .05
100 Shane Rawley .05
101 Juan Samuel .05
102 Mike Schmidt .85
103 Bobby Bonilla .05
104 Mike Dunne .05
105 Andy Van Slyke .05
106 Vince Coleman .05
107 Bob Horner .05
108 Willie McGee .05
109 Ozzie Smith .65
110 John Tudor .05
111 Todd Worrell .05
112 Tony Gwynn .65
113 John Kruk .05
114 Lance McCullers .05
115 Benito Santiago .05
116 Will Clark .05
117 Jeff Leonard .05
118 Candy Maldonado .05
119 Kirt Manwaring .05
120 Don Robinson .05

MVP

This boxed set of 44 standard-size cards and six team logo stickers was produced by Fleer for exclusive distribution at Toys "R" Us stores. This premiere edition features full-color player photos framed by a yellow and blue border. Card backs are yellow and blue on a white background. The player's team, position and personal data are followed by stats, logo and a blue banner bearing the player's name, team logo and card number. The six sticker cards feature black-and-white stadium photos on the backs.

NM/M
Complete Set (44): 3.50
Common Player: .05
1 George Bell .05
2 Wade Boggs .65
3 Jose Canseco .30
4 Ivan Calderon .05
5 Will Clark .05
6 Roger Clemens .85
7 Vince Coleman .05
8 Eric Davis .05
9 Andre Dawson .25
10 Dave Dravecky .05
11 Mike Dunne .05
12 Dwight Evans .05
13 Sid Fernandez .05
14 Tony Fernandez .05
15 Julio Franco .05
16 Dwight Gooden .05
17 Tony Gwynn .65
18 Ted Higuera .05
19 Charlie Hough .05
20 Wally Joyner .05
21 Mark Langston .05
22 Don Mattingly .85
23 Mark McGwire 1.00
24 Jack Morris .05
25 Dale Murphy .20
26 Kirby Puckett .65
27 Tim Raines .05
28 Willie Randolph .05
29 Ryne Sandberg .65
30 Benito Santiago .05
31 Mike Schmidt .85
32 Mike Scott .05
33 Kevin Seitzer .05
34 Larry Sheets .05
35 Ozzie Smith .65
36 Dave Stewart .05
37 Darryl Strawberry .05
38 Rick Sutcliffe .05
39 Alan Trammell .05
40 Fernando Valenzuela .05
41 Frank Viola .05
42 Tim Wallach .05
43 Dave Winfield .50
44 Robin Yount .50

Record Setters

For the second consecutive year, Fleer issued this set for exclusive distribution by Eckerd Drug stores. Cards are standard size with red and blue borders framing the full-color player photos. Card backs list personal information and career stats in red and blue on a white background. Each 44-card set comes cello-wrapped in a checklist box that contains six additional cards with peel-off team logo stickers. The sticker cards feature black-and-white aerial photos of major league ballparks, along with stadium statistics such as field size, seating capacity and date of the first game played.

NM/M
Complete Set (44): 3.50
Common Player: .05
1 Jesse Barfield .05
2 George Bell .05
3 Wade Boggs .65
4 Jose Canseco .35
5 Jack Clark .05
6 Will Clark .05
7 Roger Clemens .85
8 Alvin Davis .05
9 Eric Davis .05
10 Andre Dawson .25
11 Mike Dunne .05
12 John Franco .05
13 Julio Franco .05
14 Dwight Gooden .05
15 Mark Gubicza .05
16 Ozzie Guillen .05
17 Tony Gwynn .65
18 Orel Hershiser .05
19 Teddy Higuera .05
20 Howard Johnson .05
21 Wally Joyner .05
22 Jimmy Key .05
23 Jeff Leonard .05
24 Don Mattingly .85
25 Mark McGwire 1.00
26 Jack Morris .05
27 Dale Murphy .20
28 Larry Parrish .05
29 Kirby Puckett .65
30 Tim Raines .05
31 Harold Reynolds .05
32 Dave Righetti .05
33 Cal Ripken, Jr. 1.00
34 Benito Santiago .05
35 Mike Schmidt .85
36 Mike Scott .05
37 Kevin Seitzer .05
38 Ozzie Smith .65
39 Darryl Strawberry .05
40 Rick Sutcliffe .05
41 Alan Trammell .05
42 Frank Viola .05
43 Mitch Williams .05
44 Todd Worrell .05

Star Stickers

This set of 132 standard-size sticker cards (including a checklist card) features exclusive player photos, different from those in the Fleer regular issue. Card fronts have light gray borders sprinkled with multi-colored stars. Card backs are printed in red, gray and black on white and include personal data and a breakdown of pitching and batting stats into day, night, home and road categories. Cards were marketed in two different display boxes that feature six players and two team logos on the bottoms.

NM/M
Complete Set (132): 7.50
Common Player: .05
Wax Pack (5): .50
Wax Box (36): 10.00
1 Mike Boddicker .05
2 Eddie Murray .50
3 Cal Ripken, Jr. 1.50
4 Larry Sheets .05
5 Wade Boggs .65
6 Ellis Burks .05
7 Roger Clemens .85
8 Dwight Evans .05
9 Mike Greenwell .05
10 Bruce Hurst .05
11 Brian Downing .05
12 Wally Joyner .05
13 Mike Witt .05
14 Ivan Calderon .05
15 Jose DeLeon .05
16 Ozzie Guillen .05
17 Bobby Thigpen .05
18 Joe Carter .05
19 Julio Franco .05
20 Brook Jacoby .05
21 Cory Snyder .05
22 Pat Tabler .05
23 Doyle Alexander .05
24 Kirk Gibson .05
25 Mike Henneman .05
26 Jack Morris .05
27 Matt Nokes .05
28 Walt Terrell .05
29 Alan Trammell .05
30 George Brett .85
31 Charlie Leibrandt .05
32 Bret Saberhagen .05
33 Kevin Seitzer .05
34 Danny Tartabull .05
35 Frank White .05
36 Rob Deer .05
37 Ted Higuera .05
38 Paul Molitor .50
39 Dan Plesac .05
40 Robin Yount .50
41 Bert Blyleven .05
42 Tom Brunansky .05
43 Gary Gaetti .05
44 Kent Hrbek .05
45 Kirby Puckett .65
46 Jeff Reardon .05
47 Frank Viola .05
48 Don Mattingly .85
49 Mike Pagliarulo .05
50 Willie Randolph .05
51 Rick Rhoden .05
52 Dave Righetti .05
53 Dave Winfield .50
54 Jose Canseco .30
55 Carney Lansford .05
56 Mark McGwire 1.00
57 Dave Stewart .05
58 Curt Young .05
59 Alvin Davis .05
60 Mark Langston .05
61 Ken Phelps .05
62 Harold Reynolds .05
63 Scott Fletcher .05
64 Charlie Hough .05
65 Pete Incaviglia .05
66 Oddibe McDowell .05
67 Pete O'Brien .05
68 Larry Parrish .05
69 Ruben Sierra .05
70 Jesse Barfield .05
71 George Bell .05
72 Tony Fernandez .05
73 Tom Henke .05
74 Jimmy Key .05
75 Lloyd Moseby .05
76 Dion James .05
77 Dale Murphy .20
78 Zane Smith .05
79 Andre Dawson .25
80 Ryne Sandberg .65
81 Rick Sutcliffe .05
82 Kal Daniels .05
83 Eric Davis .05
84 John Franco .05
85 Kevin Bass .05
86 Glenn Davis .05
87 Bill Doran .05
88 Nolan Ryan 1.50
89 Mike Scott .05
90 Dave Smith .05
91 Pedro Guerrero .05
92 Orel Hershiser .05
93 Steve Sax .05
94 Fernando Valenzuela .05
95 Tim Burke .05
96 Andres Galarraga .05
97 Tim Raines .05
98 Tim Wallach .05
99 Mitch Webster .05
100 Ron Darling .05
101 Sid Fernandez .05
102 Dwight Gooden .05
103 Keith Hernandez .05
104 Howard Johnson .05
105 Roger McDowell .05
106 Darryl Strawberry .05
107 Steve Bedrosian .05
108 Von Hayes .05
109 Shane Rawley .05
110 Juan Samuel .05
111 Mike Schmidt .85
112 Milt Thompson .05
113 Sid Bream .05
114 Bobby Bonilla .05
115 Mike Dunne .05
116 Andy Van Slyke .05
117 Vince Coleman .05
118 Willie McGee .05
119 Terry Pendleton .05
120 Ozzie Smith .65
121 John Tudor .05
122 Todd Worrell .05
123 Tony Gwynn .65
124 John Kruk .05
125 Benito Santiago .05
126 Will Clark .05
127 Dave Dravecky .05
128 Jeff Leonard .05
129 Candy Maldonado .05
130 Rick Rueschel .05
131 Don Robinson .05
132 Checklist .05

Star Stickers Box Panels

This set of eight box-bottom cards was printed on two different retail display boxes. Six players and two team logo sticker cards are included in the set, three player photos and one team photo per box. The full-color player photos are exclusive to the Fleer Star Sticker set. The cards, which measure

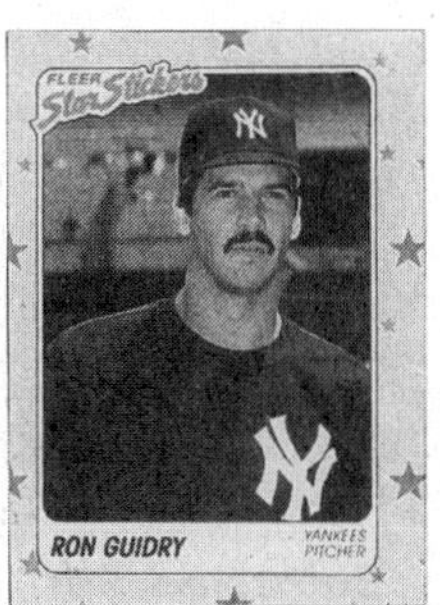

2-1/2" x 3-1/2", have a light gray border sprinkled with multi-color stars. The backs are printed in navy blue and red.

NM/M
Complete Panel Set (2): 1.50
Complete Singles Set (8): 1.50
Common Singles Player: .15
Panel 1.00
1 Eric Davis .10
3 Kevin Mitchell .10
5 Rickey Henderson .75
7 Tigers Logo .05
Panel 1.00
2 Gary Carter .75
4 Ron Guidry .10
6 Don Baylor .10
8 Giants Logo .05

Superstars

This is the fourth edition of Fleer boxed sets produced for distribution by McCrory's (1985-87 issues were titled "Fleer Limited Edition"). The Superstars standard-size card set features full-color player photos framed by red, white and blue striped top and bottom borders. Card fronts have a semi-glossy slightly textured finish. Card backs are red and blue on white and include card numbers, personal data and statistics. Six team logo sticker cards are also included in this set which was marketed in red, white and blue boxes with checklist backs. Boxed sets were sold exclusively at McCrory's stores and its affiliates.

NM/M
Complete Set (44): 5.00
Common Player: .10
1 Steve Bedrosian .10
2 George Bell .10
3 Wade Boggs .65
4 Barry Bonds 1.50
5 Jose Canseco .45
6 Joe Carter .10
7 Jack Clark .10
8 Will Clark .10
9 Roger Clemens .85
10 Alvin Davis .10
11 Eric Davis .10
12 Glenn Davis .10
13 Andre Dawson .25
14 Dwight Gooden .10
15 Orel Hershiser .10
16 Teddy Higuera .10
17 Kent Hrbek .10
18 Wally Joyner .10
19 Jimmy Key .10
20 John Kruk .10
21 Jeff Leonard .10
22 Don Mattingly .85
23 Mark McGwire 1.00
24 Kevin McReynolds .10
25 Dale Murphy .15
26 Matt Nokes .10
27 Terry Pendleton .10
28 Kirby Puckett .65

29 Tim Raines .10
30 Rick Rhoden .10
31 Cal Ripken, Jr. 1.50
32 Benito Santiago .10
33 Mike Schmidt .85
34 Mike Scott .10
35 Kevin Seitzer .10
36 Ruben Sierra .10
37 Cory Snyder .10
38 Darryl Strawberry .10
39 Rick Sutcliffe .10
40 Danny Tartabull .10
41 Alan Trammell .10
42 Ken Williams .10
43 Mike Witt .10
44 Robin Yount .50

Superstars Box Panel

Six cards were placed on the bottoms of retail boxes of the Fleer Superstars boxed sets. in 1988. The cards, 2-1/2" x 3-1/2", are identical in design to cards found in the 44-card set. The cards are numbered C-1 through C-6 and were produced for distribution by McCrory stores and its affiliates.

NM/M
Complete Panel: 2.50
Complete Set (6): 2.50
Common Player: .25
C1 Pete Incaviglia .15
C2 Rickey Henderson 1.00
C3 Tony Fernandez .15
C4 Shane Rawley .15
C5 Ryne Sandberg 1.50
C6 St. Louis Cardinals Logo/Checklist .10

1989 Fleer

This set includes 660 standard-size cards and was issued with 45 team logo stickers. Individual card fronts feature a gray and white striped background with full-color player photos framed by a bright line of color that slants upward to the right. The set also includes two subsets: 15 Major League Prospects and 12 SuperStar Specials. A special bonus set of 12 All-Star Team cards was randomly inserted in individual wax packs of 15 cards. The last seven cards in the set are checklists, with players listed alphabetically by teams.

NM/M
Retail Factory Set (660): 17.50
Hobby Factory Set (672): 20.00
Complete Set (660): 15.00
Common Player: .05
Wax Pack (15): 1.00
Wax Box (36): 25.00
Cello Pack (36): 1.50
Cello Box (24): 20.00
Rack Pack (42+1): 1.50
Rack Box (24): 25.00
1 Don Baylor .05
2 Lance Blankenship **RC** .05
3 Todd Burns **RC** .05
4 Greg Cadaret **RC** .05
5 Jose Canseco .35
6 Storm Davis .05
7 Dennis Eckersley .35
8 Mike Gallego **RC** .05
9 Ron Hassey .05
10 Dave Henderson .05
11 Rick Honeycutt .05
12 Glenn Hubbard .05
13 Stan Javier .05
14 Doug Jennings **RC** .05
15 Felix Jose **RC** .05
16 Carney Lansford .05
17 Mark McGwire .65
18 Gene Nelson .05
19 Dave Parker .05
20 Eric Plunk .05
21 Luis Polonia .05
22 Terry Steinbach .05
23 Dave Stewart .05
24 Walt Weiss .05
25 Bob Welch .05
26 Curt Young .05
27 Rick Aguilera .05
28 Wally Backman .05
29 Mark Carreon .05
30 Gary Carter .40
31 David Cone .05
32 Ron Darling .05
33 Len Dykstra .05
34 Kevin Elster .05
35 Sid Fernandez .05
36 Dwight Gooden .05
37 Keith Hernandez .05
38 Gregg Jefferies .05
39 Howard Johnson .05
40 Terry Leach .05
41 Dave Magadan .05
42 Bob McClure .05
43 Roger McDowell .05
44 Kevin McReynolds .05
45 Keith Miller .05
46 Randy Myers .05
47 Bob Ojeda .05
48 Mackey Sasser .05
49 Darryl Strawberry .05
50 Tim Teufel .05
51 Dave West **RC** .05
52 Mookie Wilson .05
53 Dave Anderson .05
54 Tim Belcher .05
55 Mike Davis .05
56 Mike Devereaux .05
57 Kirk Gibson .05
58 Alfredo Griffin .05
59 Chris Gwynn .05
60 Jeff Hamilton .05
61a Danny Heep (Home: San Antonio, TX) .25
61b Danny Heep (Home: Lake Hills, TX) .05
62 Orel Hershiser .05
63 Brian Holton **RC** .05
64 Jay Howell .05
65 Tim Leary .05
66 Mike Marshall .05
67 Ramon Martinez **RC** .25
68 Jesse Orosco .05
69 Alejandro Pena .05
70 Steve Sax .05
71 Mike Scioscia .05
72 Mike Sharperson .05
73 John Shelby .05
74 Franklin Stubbs .05
75 John Tudor .05
76 Fernando Valenzuela .05
77 Tracy Woodson .05
78 Marty Barrett .05
79 Todd Benzinger .05
80 Mike Boddicker .05
81 Wade Boggs .50
82 "Oil Can" Boyd .05
83 Ellis Burks .05
84 Rick Cerone .05
85 Roger Clemens .75
86 Steve Curry **RC** .05
87 Dwight Evans .05
88 Wes Gardner .05
89 Rich Gedman .05
90 Mike Greenwell .05
91 Bruce Hurst .05
92 Dennis Lamp .05
93 Spike Owen .05
94 Larry Parrish .05
95 Carlos Quintana **RC** .05
96 Jody Reed .05
97 Jim Rice .25
98a Kevin Romine (Batting follow-thru, photo actually Randy Kutcher.) .25
98b Kevin Romine (Arms crossed on chest, correct photo.) .25
99 Lee Smith .05
100 Mike Smithson .05
101 Bob Stanley .05
102 Allan Anderson .05
103 Keith Atherton .05
104 Juan Berenguer .05
105 Bert Blyleven .10
106 Eric Bullock **RC** .05
107 Randy Bush .05
108 John Christensen **RC** .05
109 Mark Davidson .05
110 Gary Gaetti .05
111 Greg Gagne .05
112 Dan Gladden .05
113 German Gonzalez **RC** .05
114 Brian Harper .05
115 Tom Herr .05
116 Kent Hrbek .05
117 Gene Larkin .05
118 Tim Laudner .05
119 Charlie Lea .05
120 Steve Lombardozzi .05
121a John Moses (Home: Phoenix, AZ) .25
121b John Moses (Home: Tempe, AZ) .05
122 Al Newman .05
123 Mark Portugal .05
124 Kirby Puckett .50
125 Jeff Reardon .05
126 Fred Toliver .05
127 Frank Viola .05
128 Doyle Alexander .05
129 Dave Bergman .05
130a Tom Brookens (Mike Heath stats on back.) .50
130b Tom Brookens (Correct stats on back.) .05
131 Paul Gibson **RC** .05
132a Mike Heath (Tom Brookens stats on back.) .50
132b Mike Heath (Correct stats on back.) .05
133 Don Heinkel **RC** .05
134 Mike Henneman .05
135 Guillermo Hernandez .05
136 Eric King .05
137 Chet Lemon .05
138 Fred Lynn .05
139 Jack Morris .05
140 Matt Nokes .05
141 Gary Pettis .05
142 Ted Power .05
143 Jeff Robinson .05
144 Luis Salazar .05
145 Steve Searcy **RC** .05
146 Pat Sheridan .05
147 Frank Tanana .05
148 Alan Trammell .05
149 Walt Terrell .05
150 Jim Walewander **RC** .05
151 Lou Whitaker .05
152 Tim Birtsas .05
153 Tom Browning .05
154 Keith Brown **RC** .05
155 Norm Charlton **RC** .15
156 Dave Concepcion .05
157 Kal Daniels .05
158 Eric Davis .05
159 Bo Diaz .05
160 Rob Dibble .05
161 Nick Esasky .05
162 John Franco .05
163 Danny Jackson .05
164 Barry Larkin .05
165 Rob Murphy .05
166 Paul O'Neill .05
167 Jeff Reed .05
168 Jose Rijo .05
169 Ron Robinson .05
170 Chris Sabo .05
171 Candy Sierra **RC** .05
172 Van Snider **RC** .05
173a Jeff Treadway (Blue "target" above head.) 75.00
173b Jeff Treadway (No "target.") .05
174 Frank Williams .05
175 Herm Winningham .05
176 Jim Adduci **RC** .05
177 Don August .05
178 Mike Birkbeck .05
179 Chris Bosio .05
180 Glenn Braggs .05
181 Greg Brock .05
182 Mark Clear .05
183 Chuck Crim .05
184 Rob Deer .05
185 Tom Filer .05
186 Jim Gantner .05
187 Darryl Hamilton .05
188 Ted Higuera .05
189 Odell Jones .05
190 Jeffrey Leonard .05
191 Joey Meyer .05
192 Paul Mirabella .05
193 Paul Molitor .40
194 Charlie O'Brien **RC** .05
195 Dan Plesac .05
196 Gary Sheffield **RC** 1.00
197 B.J. Surhoff .05
198 Dale Sveum .05
199 Bill Wegman .05
200 Robin Yount .40
201 Rafael Belliard .05
202 Barry Bonds .75
203 Bobby Bonilla .05
204 Sid Bream .05
205 Benny Distefano **RC** .05
206 Doug Drabek .05
207 Mike Dunne .05
208 Felix Fermin .05
209 Brian Fisher .05
210 Jim Gott .05
211 Bob Kipper .05
212 Dave LaPoint .05
213 Mike LaValliere .05
214 Jose Lind .05
215 Junior Ortiz .05
216 Vicente Palacios .05
217 Tom Prince **RC** .05
218 Gary Redus .05
219 R.J. Reynolds .05
220 Jeff Robinson .05
221 John Smiley .05
222 Andy Van Slyke .05
223 Bob Walk .05
224 Glenn Wilson .05
225 Jesse Barfield .05
226 George Bell .05
227 Pat Borders .05
228 John Cerutti .05
229 Jim Clancy .05
230 Mark Eichhorn .05
231 Tony Fernandez .05
232 Cecil Fielder .05
233 Mike Flanagan .05
234 Kelly Gruber .05
235 Tom Henke .05
236 Jimmy Key .05
237 Rick Leach .05
238 Manny Lee .05
239 Nelson Liriano .05
240 Fred McGriff .05
241 Lloyd Moseby .05
242 Rance Mulliniks .05
243 Jeff Musselman .05
244 Dave Stieb .05
245 Todd Stottlemyre **RC** .05
246 Duane Ward .05
247 David Wells .05
248 Ernie Whitt .05
249 Luis Aguayo .05
250a Neil Allen (Home: Sarasota, FL) .25
250b Neil Allen (Home: Syosset, NY) .05
251 John Candelaria .05
252 Jack Clark .05
253 Richard Dotson .05
254 Rickey Henderson .40
255 Tommy John .10
256 Roberto Kelly .05
257 Al Leiter .05
258 Don Mattingly .60
259 Dale Mohorcic .05
260 Hal Morris **RC** .25
261 Scott Nielsen **RC** .05
262 Mike Pagliarulo .05
263 Hipolito Pena **RC** .05
264 Ken Phelps .05
265 Willie Randolph .05
266 Rick Rhoden .05
267 Dave Righetti .05
268 Rafael Santana .05
269 Steve Shields **RC** .05
270 Joel Skinner .05
271 Don Slaught .05
272 Claudell Washington .05
273 Gary Ward .05
274 Dave Winfield .40
275 Luis Aquino **RC** .05
276 Floyd Bannister .05
277 George Brett .60
278 Bill Buckner .05
279 Nick Capra **RC** .05
280 Jose DeJesus **RC** .05
281 Steve Farr .05
282 Jerry Gleaton .05
283 Mark Gubicza .05
284 Tom Gordon **RC** .25
285 Bo Jackson .10
286 Charlie Leibrandt .05
287 Mike Macfarlane **RC** .10
288 Jeff Montgomery .05
289 Bill Pecota .05
290 Jamie Quirk .05
291 Bret Saberhagen .05
292 Kevin Seitzer .05
293 Kurt Stillwell .05
294 Pat Tabler .05
295 Danny Tartabull .05
296 Gary Thurman .05
297 Frank White .05
298 Willie Wilson .05
299 Roberto Alomar .20
300 Sandy Alomar, Jr. **RC** .25
301 Chris Brown .05
302 Mike Brumley **RC** .05
303 Mark Davis .05
304 Mark Grant .05
305 Tony Gwynn .50
306 Greg Harris **RC** .05
307 Andy Hawkins .05
308 Jimmy Jones .05
309 John Kruk .05
310 Dave Leiper .05
311 Carmelo Martinez .05
312 Lance McCullers .05
313 Keith Moreland .05
314 Dennis Rasmussen .05
315 Randy Ready .05
316 Benito Santiago .05
317 Eric Show .05
318 Todd Simmons .05
319 Garry Templeton .05
320 Dickie Thon .05
321 Ed Whitson .05
322 Marvell Wynne .05
323 Mike Aldrete .05
324 Brett Butler .05
325 Will Clark .05
326 Kelly Downs .05
327 Dave Dravecky .05
328 Scott Garrelts .05
329 Atlee Hammaker .05
330 Charlie Hayes **RC** .10
331 Mike Krukow .05
332 Craig Lefferts .05
333 Candy Maldonado .05
334 Kirt Manwaring .05
335 Bob Melvin .05
336 Kevin Mitchell .05
337 Donell Nixon .05
338 Tony Perezchica **RC** .05
339 Joe Price .05
340 Rick Reuschel .05
341 Earnest Riles .05
342 Don Robinson .05
343 Chris Speier .05
344 Robby Thompson .05
345 Jose Uribe .05
346 Matt Williams .05
347 Trevor Wilson **RC** .15
348 Juan Agosto .05
349 Larry Andersen .05
350a Alan Ashby ("Throws Right") .25
350b Alan Ashby ("Throws Right") .05
351 Kevin Bass .05
352 Buddy Bell .05
353 Craig Biggio .05
354 Danny Darwin .05
355 Glenn Davis .05
356 Jim Deshaies .05
357 Bill Doran .05
358 John Fishel **RC** .05
359 Billy Hatcher .05
360 Bob Knepper .05
361 Louie Meadows **RC** .05
362 Dave Meads .05
363 Jim Pankovits .05
364 Terry Puhl .05
365 Rafael Ramirez .05
366 Craig Reynolds .05
367 Mike Scott .05
368 Nolan Ryan .75
369 Dave Smith .05
370 Gerald Young .05
371 Hubie Brooks .05
372 Tim Burke .05
373 John Dopson **RC** .05
374 Mike Fitzgerald .05
375 Tom Foley .05
376 Andres Galarraga .05
377 Neal Heaton .05
378 Joe Hesketh .05
379 Brian Holman **RC** .05
380 Rex Hudler .05
381a Randy Johnson **RC** (Marlboro ad on scoreboard.) 40.00
381b Randy Johnson (Ad partially obscured.) 10.00
381c Randy Johnson **RC** (Ad completely blacked out.) 3.00
382 Wallace Johnson .05
383 Tracy Jones .05
384 Dave Martinez .05
385 Dennis Martinez .05
386 Andy McGaffigan .05
387 Otis Nixon .05
388 Johnny Paredes **RC** .05
389 Jeff Parrett .05
390 Pascual Perez .05
391 Tim Raines .05
392 Luis Rivera .05
393 Nelson Santovenia **RC** .05
394 Bryn Smith .05
395 Tim Wallach .05
396 Andy Allanson .05
397 Rod Allen **RC** .05
398 Scott Bailes .05
399 Tom Candiotti .05
400 Joe Carter .05
401 Carmen Castillo .05
402 Dave Clark .05
403 John Farrell .05
404 Julio Franco .05
405 Don Gordon .05
406 Mel Hall .05
407 Brad Havens .05
408 Brook Jacoby .05
409 Doug Jones .05
410 Jeff Kaiser **RC** .05
411 Luis Medina **RC** .05
412 Cory Snyder .05
413 Greg Swindell .05
414 Ron Tingley **RC** .05
415 Willie Upshaw .05
416 Ron Washington .05
417 Rich Yett .05
418 Damon Berryhill .05
419 Mike Bielecki .05
420 Doug Dascenzo **RC** .05
421 Jody Davis .05
422 Andre Dawson .25
423 Frank DiPino .05
424 Shawon Dunston .05
425 "Goose" Gossage .10
426 Mark Grace .05
427 Mike Harkey **RC** .05
428 Darrin Jackson .05
429 Les Lancaster .05
430 Vance Law .05
431 Greg Maddux .50
432 Jamie Moyer .05
433 Al Nipper .05
434 Rafael Palmeiro .35
435 Pat Perry .05
436 Jeff Pico **RC** .05
437 Ryne Sandberg .50
438 Calvin Schiraldi .05
439 Rick Sutcliffe .05
440a Manny Trillo ("Throws Rig") .35
440b Manny Trillo ("Throws Right") .05
441 Gary Varsho **RC** .05
442 Mitch Webster .05
443 Luis Alicea .05
444 Tom Brunansky .05
445 Vince Coleman .05
446 John Costello **RC** .05
447 Danny Cox .05
448 Ken Dayley .05
449 Jose DeLeon .05
450 Curt Ford .05
451 Pedro Guerrero .05
452 Bob Horner .05
453 Tim Jones **RC** .05
454 Steve Lake .05
455 Joe Magrane .05
456 Greg Mathews .05
457 Willie McGee .05
458 Larry McWilliams .05
459 Jose Oquendo .05
460 Tony Pena .05
461 Terry Pendleton .05
462 Steve Peters **RC** .05
463 Ozzie Smith .50
464 Scott Terry .05
465 Denny Walling .05
466 Todd Worrell .05
467 Tony Armas .05
468 Dante Bichette **RC** .25
469 Bob Boone .05
470 Terry Clark **RC** .05
471 Stew Cliburn **RC** .05
472 Mike Cook **RC** .05
473 Sherman Corbett **RC** .05
474 Chili Davis .05
475 Brian Downing .05
476 Jim Eppard .05
477 Chuck Finley .05
478 Willie Fraser .05
479 Bryan Harvey .05
480 Jack Howell .05
481 Wally Joyner .05
482 Jack Lazorko .05
483 Kirk McCaskill .05
484 Mark McLemore .05
485 Greg Minton .05
486 Dan Petry .05
487 Johnny Ray .05
488 Dick Schofield .05
489 Devon White .05
490 Mike Witt .05
491 Harold Baines .05
492 Daryl Boston .05
493 Ivan Calderon .05
494 Mike Diaz .05
495 Carlton Fisk .40
496 Dave Gallagher **RC** .05
497 Ozzie Guillen .05
498 Shawn Hillegas .05
499 Lance Johnson .05
500 Barry Jones .05
501 Bill Long .05
502 Steve Lyons .05
503 Fred Manrique .05
504 Jack McDowell .05
505 Donn Pall **RC** .05
506 Kelly Paris .05
507 Dan Pasqua .05
508 Ken Patterson **RC** .05
509 Melido Perez .05
510 Jerry Reuss .05
511 Mark Salas .05
512 Bobby Thigpen .05
513 Mike Woodard .05
514 Bob Brower .05
515 Steve Buechele .05
516 Jose Cecena **RC** .05
517 Cecil Espy .05
518 Scott Fletcher .05
519 Cecilio Guante .05
520 Jose Guzman .05
521 Ray Hayward .05
522 Charlie Hough .05
523 Pete Incaviglia .05
524 Mike Jeffcoat .05
525 Paul Kilgus .05
526 Chad Kreuter **RC** .15
527 Jeff Kunkel .05
528 Oddibe McDowell .05
529 Pete O'Brien .05
530 Geno Petralli .05
531 Jeff Russell .05
532 Ruben Sierra .05
533 Mike Stanley .05
534 Ed Vande Berg .05
535 Curtis Wilkerson .05
536 Mitch Williams .05
537 Bobby Witt .05
538 Steve Balboni .05
539 Scott Bankhead .05
540 Scott Bradley .05
541 Mickey Brantley .05
542 Jay Buhner .05
543 Mike Campbell .05
544 Darnell Coles .05
545 Henry Cotto .05
546 Alvin Davis .05
547 Mario Diaz .05
548 Ken Griffey Jr. **RC** 6.00
549 Erik Hanson **RC** .05
550 Mike Jackson .05
551 Mark Langston .05
552 Edgar Martinez .05
553 Bill McGuire **RC** .05

554	Mike Moore	.05
555	Jim Presley	.05
556	Rey Quinones	.05
557	Jerry Reed	.05
558	Harold Reynolds	.05
559	Mike Schooler **RC**	.05
560	Bill Swift	.05
561	Dave Valle	.05
562	Steve Bedrosian	.05
563	Phil Bradley	.05
564	Don Carman	.05
565	Bob Dernier	.05
566	Marvin Freeman	.05
567	Todd Frohwirth	.05
568	Greg Gross	.05
569	Kevin Gross	.05
570	Greg Harris	.05
571	Von Hayes	.05
572	Chris James	.05
573	Steve Jeltz	.05
574	Ron Jones **RC**	.05
575	Ricky Jordan **RC**	.05
576	Mike Maddux	.05
577	David Palmer	.05
578	Lance Parrish	.05
579	Shane Rawley	.05
580	Bruce Ruffin	.05
581	Juan Samuel	.05
582	Mike Schmidt	.60
583	Kent Tekulve	.05
584	Milt Thompson	.05
585	Jose Alvarez **RC**	.05
586	Paul Assenmacher	.05
587	Bruce Benedict	.05
588	Jeff Blauser	.05
589	Terry Blocker **RC**	.05
590	Ron Gant	.05
591	Tom Glavine	.30
592	Tommy Gregg	.05
593	Albert Hall	.05
594	Dion James	.05
595	Rick Mahler	.05
596	Dale Murphy	.25
597	Gerald Perry	.05
598	Charlie Puleo	.05
599	Ted Simmons	.05
600	Pete Smith	.05
601	Zane Smith	.05
602	John Smoltz	.50
603	Bruce Sutter	.35
604	Andres Thomas	.05
605	Ozzie Virgil	.05
606	Brady Anderson	.05
607	Jeff Ballard	.05
608	Jose Bautista **RC**	.05
609	Ken Gerhart	.05
610	Terry Kennedy	.05
611	Eddie Murray	.40
612	Carl Nichols **RC**	.05
613	Tom Niedenfuer	.05
614	Joe Orsulak	.05
615	Oswaldo Peraza **RC** ((Oswald))	.05
616a	Bill Ripken (Vulgarity on bat knob.)	8.00
616b	Bill Ripken (Scribble over vulgarity.)	6.00
616c	Bill Ripken (Black box over vulgarity.)	.10
616d	Bill Ripken (Vulgarity whited out. (Many fake "white out" cards exist, created by erasures.)	250.00
616e	Billy Ripken (Strip cut out of bottom of card.)	.10
617	Cal Ripken, Jr.	.75
618	Dave Schmidt	.05
619	Rick Schu	.05
620	Larry Sheets	.05
621	Doug Sisk	.05
622	Pete Stanicek	.05
623	Mickey Tettleton	.05
624	Jay Tibbs	.05
625	Jim Traber	.05
626	Mark Williamson	.05
627	Craig Worthington **RC**	.05
628	Speed and Power (Jose Canseco)	.20
629	Pitcher Perfect (Tom Browning)	.05
630	Like Father Like Sons (Roberto Alomar, Sandy Alomar, Jr.)	.20
631	N.L. All-Stars (Will Clark, Rafael Palmeiro)	.10
632	Homeruns Coast to Coast (Will Clark, Darryl Strawberry)	.05
633	Hot Corner's Hot Hitters (Wade Boggs, Carney Lansford)	.25
634	Triple A's (Jose Canseco, Mark McGwire, Terry Steinbach)	.40
635	Dual Heat (Mark Davis, Dwight Gooden)	.05
636	N.L. Pitching Power (David Cone, Danny Jackson)	.05
637	Cannon Arms (Bobby Bonilla, Chris Sabo)	.05
638	Double Trouble (Andres Galarraga, Gerald Perry)	.05
639	Power Center (Eric Davis)	.05
640	Major League Prospects (Cameron Drew **RC**, Steve Wilson **RC**)	.05
641	Major League Prospects (Kevin Brown, Kevin Reimer **RC**)	.30
642	Major League Prospects (Jerald Clark **RC**, Brad Pounders **RC**)	.05
643	Major League Prospects (Mike Capel **RC**, Drew Hall **RC**)	.05
644	Major League Prospects (Joe Girardi **RC**, Rolando Roomes **RC**)	.20
645	Major League Prospects (Marty Brown **RC**, Lenny Harris **RC**)	.15
646	Major League Prospects (Luis de los Santos **RC**, Jim Campbell **RC**)	.05
647	Major League Prospects (Miguel Garcia **RC**, Randy Kramer **RC**)	.05
648	Major League Prospects (Torey Lovullo **RC**, Robert Palacios **RC**)	.05
649	Major League Prospects (Jim Corsi **RC**, Bob Milacki **RC**)	.05
650	Major League Prospects (Grady Hall **RC**, Mike Rochford **RC**)	.05
651	Major League Prospects (Vance Lovelace **RC**, Terry Taylor **RC**)	.05
652	Major League Prospects (Dennis Cook **RC**, Ken Hill **RC**)	.20
653	Major League Prospects (Scott Service **RC**, Shane Turner **RC**)	.05
654	Checklist 1-101	.05
655	Checklist 102-200	.05
656	Checklist 201-298	.05
657	Checklist 299-395	.05
658	Checklist 396-490	.05
659	Checklist 491-584	.05
660	Checklist 585-660	.05

All-Star Team

This special 12-card set represents Fleer's choices for its 1989 Major League All-Star Team. For the fourth consecutive year, Fleer inserted the special cards randomly in wax and cello packs. The cards feature two player photos set against a green background with the "'89 Fleer All Star Team" logo bannered across the top, and the player's name, position and team in the lower left corner. The backs contain a narrative player profile.

		NM/M
Complete Set (12):		2.50
Common Player:		.25
1	Bobby Bonilla	.25
2	Jose Canseco	.75
3	Will Clark	.40
4	Dennis Eckersley	.50
5	Julio Franco	.25
6	Mike Greenwell	.25
7	Orel Hershiser	.25
8	Paul Molitor	1.00
9	Mike Scioscia	.25
10	Darryl Strawberry	.25
11	Alan Trammell	.25
12	Frank Viola	.25

For The Record

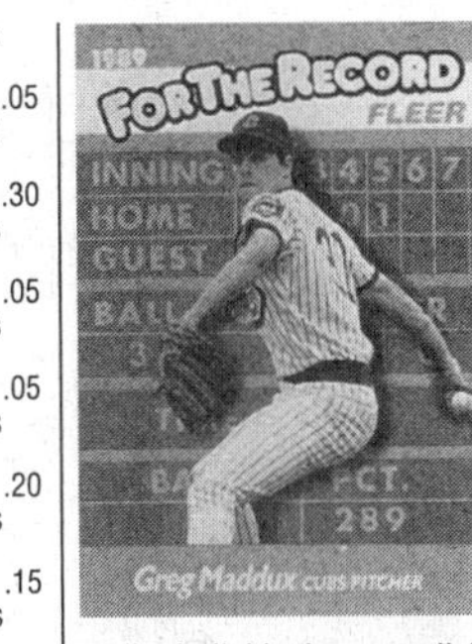

Fleer's "For the Record" set features six players and their achievements from 1988. Fronts of the standard 2-1/2" x 3-1/2" cards feature a photo of the player set against a red scoreboard background. Card backs are grey and describe individual accomplishments. The cards were distributed randomly in rack packs.

		NM/M
Complete Set (6):		2.50
Common Player:		.25
1	Wade Boggs	.75
2	Roger Clemens	1.00
3	Andres Galarraga	.25
4	Kirk Gibson	.25
5	Greg Maddux	.75
6	Don Mattingly	1.00

World Series

This 12-card set, which depicts highlights of the 1988 World Series, was included as a special sub-set with the regular and glossy factory-collated Fleer set. It was not available as individual cards in wax packs, cello packs or any other form.

		NM/M
Complete Set, Regular (12):		2.00
Common Card:		.10
1	Dodgers Secret Weapon (Mickey Hatcher)	.10
2	Rookie Starts Series (Tim Belcher)	.10
3	Jose Canseco	.25
4	Dramatic Comeback (Mike Scioscia)	.10
5	Kirk Gibson	.25
6	Orel Hershiser	.15
7	One Swings, Three RBIs (Mike Marshall)	.10
8	Mark McGwire	1.00
9	Sax's Speed Wins Game 4 (Steve Sax)	.10
10	Series Caps Award Winning Year (Walt Weiss)	.10
11	Orel Hershiser	.15
12	Dodger Blue, World Champs	.25

Box Panels

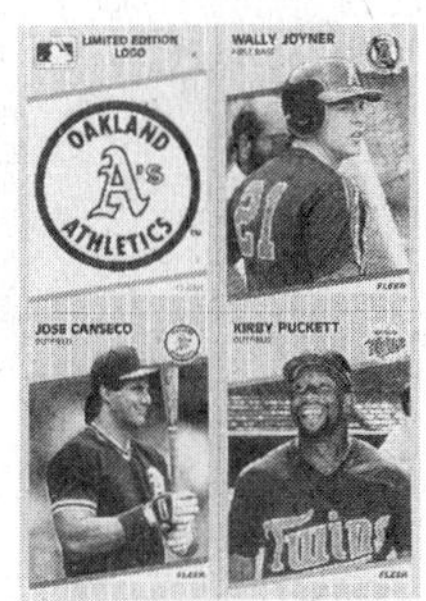

For the fourth consecutive year, Fleer issued a series of cards on the bottom panels of its regular 1989 wax pack boxes. The 28-card set includes 20 players and eight team logo cards, all designed in the identical style of the regular 1989 Fleer set. The box-bottom cards were randomly printed, four cards (three player cards and one team logo) on each bottom panel. Cards are numbered C-1 to C-28.

		NM/M
Complete Panel Set (7):		6.00
Complete Singles Set (28):		3.00
Common Single Player:		.15
1	Mets Logo	.05
2	Wade Boggs	.75
3	George Brett	1.25
4	Jose Canseco	.50
5	A's Logo	.05
6	Will Clark	.10
7	David Cone	.10
8	Andres Galarraga	.10
9	Dodgers Logo	.05
10	Kirk Gibson	.10
11	Mike Greenwell	.10
12	Tony Gwynn	.75
13	Tigers Logo	.05
14	Orel Hershiser	.10
15	Danny Jackson	.10
16	Wally Joyner	.10
17	Red Sox Logo	.05
18	Yankees Logo	.05
19	Fred McGriff	.10
20	Kirby Puckett	.75
21	Chris Sabo	.10
22	Kevin Seitzer	.10
23	Pirates logo	.05
24	Astros logo	.05
25	Darryl Strawberry	.10
26	Alan Trammell	.10
27	Andy Van Slyke	.10
28	Frank Viola	.10

Glossy Tin

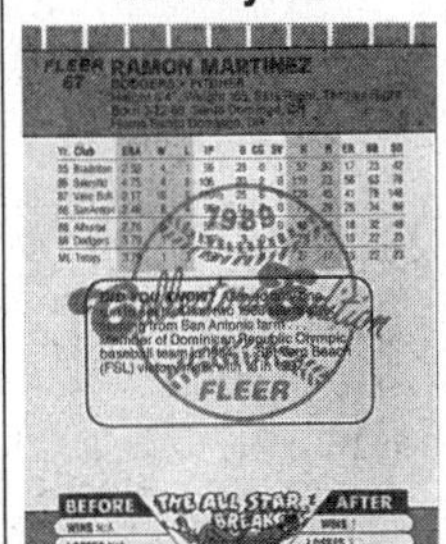

The last of the limited-edition, collector-version glossy tin sets is estimated to have been produced in an edition of 30,000-60,000, creating a significant premium over their counterparts in the regular Fleer set. The issue was sold only in complete-set form in a lithographed metal box. The 1989 glossies differ from the regular cards on back in the use of blue, rather than yellow ink, and the appearance at center of a large baseball logo with 1989 / Collector's Edition / Fleer at center. No glossy version of the '89 Update set was made. Fleer glossy sets were originally wholesaled at $40 each.

	NM/M
Unopened Set (672):	75.00
Complete Set (672):	50.00
Common Player:	.25

Update

Fleer produced its sixth consecutive "Update" set in 1989 to supplement the company's regular set. As in the past, the set consisted of 132 cards (numbered U-1 through U-132) that were sold by hobby dealers in special collector's boxes.

		NM/M
Complete Set (132):		6.00
Common Player:		.05
1	Phil Bradley	.05
2	Mike Devereaux	.05
3	Steve Finley **RC**	.05
4	Kevin Hickey	.05
5	Brian Holton	.05
6	Bob Milacki	.05
7	Randy Milligan	.05
8	John Dopson	.05
9	Nick Esasky	.05
10	Rob Murphy	.05
11	Jim Abbott **RC**	.05
12	Bert Blyleven	.10
13	Jeff Manto **RC**	.05
14	Bob McClure	.05
15	Lance Parrish	.05
16	Lee Stevens **RC**	.05
17	Claudell Washington	.05
18	Mark Davis	.05
19	Eric King	.05
20	Ron Kittle	.05
21	Matt Merullo **RC**	.05
22	Steve Rosenberg **RC**	.05
23	Robin Ventura **RC**	.25
24	Keith Atherton	.05
25	Joey (Albert) Belle **RC**	1.00
26	Jerry Browne	.05
27	Felix Fermin	.05
28	Brad Komminsk	.05
29	Pete O'Brien	.05
30	Mike Brumley	.05
31	Tracy Jones	.05
32	Mike Schwabe **RC**	.05
33	Gary Ward	.05
34	Frank Williams	.05
35	Kevin Appier **RC**	.25
36	Bob Boone	.05
37	Luis de los Santos	.05
38	Jim Eisenreich **RC**	.05
39	Jaime Navarro **RC**	.05
40	Bill Spiers **RC**	.05
41	Greg Vaughn **RC**	.25
42	Randy Veres **RC**	.05
43	Wally Backman	.05
44	Shane Rawley	.05
45	Steve Balboni	.05
46	Jesse Barfield	.05
47	Alvaro Espinoza **RC**	.05
48	Bob Geren **RC**	.05
49	Mel Hall	.05
50	Andy Hawkins	.05
51	Hensley Meulens **RC**	.05
52	Steve Sax	.05
53	Deion Sanders **RC**	.75
54	Rickey Henderson	.40
55	Mike Moore	.05
56	Tony Phillips	.05
57	Greg Briley	.05
58	Gene Harris	.05
59	Randy Johnson	2.00
60	Jeffrey Leonard	.05
61	Dennis Powell	.05
62	Omar Vizquel	.05
63	Kevin Brown	.05
64	Julio Franco	.05
65	Jamie Moyer	.05
66	Rafael Palmeiro	.35
67	Nolan Ryan	1.00
68	Francisco Cabrera **RC**	.05
69	Junior Felix **RC**	.05
70	Al Leiter	.05
71	Alex Sanchez **RC**	.05
72	Geronimo Berroa **RC**	.05
73	Derek Lilliquist **RC**	.05
74	Lonnie Smith	.05
75	Jeff Treadway	.05
76	Paul Kilgus	.05
77	Lloyd McClendon	.05
78	Scott Sanderson	.05
79	Dwight Smith **RC**	.05
80	Jerome Walton **RC**	.05
81	Mitch Williams	.05
82	Steve Wilson	.05
83	Todd Benzinger	.05
84	Ken Griffey	.05
85	Rick Mahler	.05
86	Rolando Roomes	.05
87	Scott Scudder **RC**	.05
88	Jim Clancy	.05
89	Rick Rhoden	.05
90	Dan Schatzeder	.05
91	Mike Morgan	.05
92	Eddie Murray	.40
93	Willie Randolph	.05
94	Ray Searage	.05
95	Mike Aldrete	.05
96	Kevin Gross	.05
97	Mark Langston	.05
98	Spike Owen	.05
99	Zane Smith	.05
100	Don Aase	.05
101	Barry Lyons	.05
102	Juan Samuel	.05
103	Wally Whitehurst **RC**	.05
104	Dennis Cook	.05
105	Len Dykstra	.05
106	Charlie Hayes **RC**	.05
107	Tommy Herr	.05
108	Ken Howell	.05
109	John Kruk	.05
110	Roger McDowell	.05
111	Terry Mulholland **RC**	.05
112	Jeff Parrett	.05
113	Neal Heaton	.05
114	Jeff King	.05
115	Randy Kramer	.05
116	Bill Landrum	.05
117	Cris Carpenter **RC**	.05
118	Frank DiPino	.05
119	Ken Hill	.05
120	Dan Quisenberry	.05
121	Milt Thompson	.05
122	Todd Zeile **RC**	.25
123	Jack Clark	.05
124	Bruce Hurst	.05
125	Mark Parent	.05
126	Bip Roberts	.05
127	Jeff Brantley **RC**	.05
128	Terry Kennedy	.05
129	Mike LaCoss	.05
130	Greg Litton **RC**	.05
131	Mike Schmidt	.65
132	Checklist	.05

Bill Ripken FF 'Test'

At the height of the furor over the vulgarity shown on the initial print run of Bill Ripken's card, when genuine examples were selling for as high as $125, this fantasy card surfaced to prey on collectors. In standard size, the card is printed in black-and-white on front and back, reproducing a genuine card. On the back, typography was also added to make the piece look like a test card. This fraudulent product has no collectible value.

Baseball All-Stars

This specially-boxed set was produced by Fleer for the Ben Franklin store chain. The full-color player photos are surrounded by a border of pink and yellow vertical bands. "Fleer Baseball All-Stars" appears along the top in red, white and blue. The set was sold in a box with a checklist on the back.

		NM/M
Complete Set (44):		4.00
Common Player:		.10
1	Doyle Alexander	.10
2	George Bell	.10
3	Wade Boggs	.65
4	Bobby Bonilla	.10
5	Jose Canseco	.40
6	Will Clark	.10
7	Roger Clemens	.75
8	Vince Coleman	.10
9	David Cone	.10
10	Mark Davis	.10
11	Andre Dawson	.25
12	Dennis Eckersley	.45
13	Andres Galarraga	.10

14	Kirk Gibson	.10
15	Dwight Gooden	.10
16	Mike Greenwell	.10
17	Mark Gubicza	.10
18	Ozzie Guillen	.10
19	Tony Gwynn	.65
20	Rickey Henderson	.50
21	Orel Hershiser	.10
22	Danny Jackson	.10
23	Doug Jones	.10
24	Ricky Jordan	.10
25	Bob Knepper	.10
26	Barry Larkin	.10
27	Vance Law	.10
28	Don Mattingly	.75
29	Mark McGwire	1.00
30	Paul Molitor	.50
31	Gerald Perry	.10
32	Kirby Puckett	.65
33	Johnny Ray	.10
34	Harold Reynolds	.10
35	Cal Ripken, Jr.	1.50
36	Don Robinson	.10
37	Ruben Sierra	.10
38	Dave Smith	.10
39	Darryl Strawberry	.10
40	Dave Steib	.10
41	Alan Trammell	.10
42	Andy Van Slyke	.10
43	Frank Viola	.10
44	Dave Winfield	.50

Exciting Stars

Sold exclusively in Cumberland Farm stores, this boxed set pictures the game's top stars. The card fronts feature a color player photo surrounded by a blue border with "Baseball's Exciting Stars" along the top. The cards were numbered alphabetically and packed in a special box with a complete checklist on the back.

		NM/M
Complete Set (44):		4.00
Common Player:		.10
1	Harold Baines	.10
2	Wade Boggs	.65
3	Jose Canseco	.50
4	Joe Carter	.10
5	Will Clark	.10
6	Roger Clemens	.75
7	Vince Coleman	.10
8	David Cone	.10
9	Eric Davis	.10
10	Glenn Davis	.10
11	Andre Dawson	.25
12	Dwight Evans	.10
13	Andres Galarraga	.10
14	Kirk Gibson	.10
15	Dwight Gooden	.10
16	Jim Gott	.10
17	Mark Grace	.10
18	Mike Greenwell	.10
19	Mark Gubicza	.10
20	Tony Gwynn	.65
21	Rickey Henderson	.60
22	Tom Henke	.10
23	Mike Henneman	.10
24	Orel Hershiser	.10
25	Danny Jackson	.10
26	Gregg Jefferies	.10
27	Ricky Jordan	.10
28	Wally Joyner	.10
29	Mark Langston	.10
30	Tim Leary	.10
31	Don Mattingly	.75
32	Mark McGwire	1.50
33	Dale Murphy	.15
34	Kirby Puckett	.65
35	Chris Sabo	.10
36	Kevin Seitzer	.10
37	Ruben Sierra	.10
38	Ozzie Smith	.65
39	Dave Stewart	.10
40	Darryl Strawberry	.10
41	Alan Trammell	.10
42	Frank Viola	.10
43	Dave Winfield	.60
44	Robin Yount	.60

Heroes of Baseball

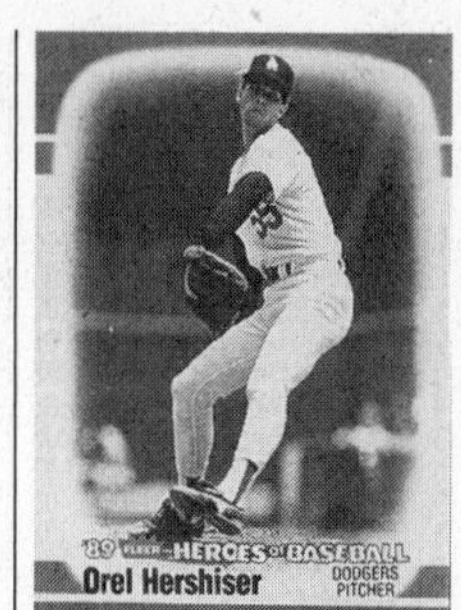

This boxed set was produced by Fleer for the Woolworth store chain. The fronts of the cards are designed in a red and blue color scheme and feature full-color photos that fade into a soft focus on all edges. The set is numbered alphabetically and was packaged in a special box with a checklist on the back.

		NM/M
Complete Set (44):		4.00
Common Player:		.10
1	George Bell	.10
2	Wade Boggs	.75
3	Barry Bonds	1.50
4	Tom Brunansky	.10
5	Jose Canseco	.40
6	Joe Carter	.10
7	Will Clark	.10
8	Roger Clemens	.85
9	David Cone	.10
10	Eric Davis	.10
11	Glenn Davis	.10
12	Andre Dawson	.25
13	Dennis Eckersley	.50
14	John Franco	.10
15	Gary Gaetti	.10
16	Andres Galarraga	.10
17	Kirk Gibson	.10
18	Dwight Gooden	.10
19	Mike Greenwell	.10
20	Tony Gwynn	.75
21	Bryan Harvey	.10
22	Orel Hershiser	.10
23	Ted Higuera	.10
24	Danny Jackson	.10
25	Ricky Jordan	.10
26	Don Mattingly	.85
27	Fred McGriff	.10
28	Mark McGwire	1.00
29	Kevin McReynolds	.10
30	Gerald Perry	.10
31	Kirby Puckett	.75
32	Johnny Ray	.10
33	Harold Reynolds	.10
34	Cal Ripken, Jr.	1.50
35	Ryne Sandberg	.75
36	Kevin Seitzer	.10
37	Ruben Sierra	.10
38	Darryl Strawberry	.10
39	Bobby Thigpen	.10
40	Alan Trammell	.10
41	Andy Van Slyke	.10
42	Frank Viola	.10
43	Dave Winfield	.65
44	Robin Yount	.65

League Leaders

Another of the various small, boxed sets issued by Fleer, "League Leaders" was produced for Walgreen stores. The standard-size cards feature color photos on the front surrounded by a red border with "Fleer League Leaders" across the top. The backs include player stats and data and the team logo. The cards are numbered alphabetically and packaged in a special box that includes the full checklist on the back.

		NM/M
Complete Set (44):		3.00
Common Player:		.10
1	Allan Anderson	.10
2	Wade Boggs	.75
3	Jose Canseco	.50
4	Will Clark	.10
5	Roger Clemens	.85
6	Vince Coleman	.10
7	David Cone	.10
8	Kal Daniels	.10
9	Chili Davis	.10
10	Eric Davis	.10
11	Glenn Davis	.10
12	Andre Dawson	.25
13	John Franco	.10
14	Andres Galarraga	.10
15	Kirk Gibson	.10
16	Dwight Gooden	.10
17	Mark Grace	.10
18	Mike Greenwell	.10
19	Tony Gwynn	.75
20	Orel Hershiser	.10
21	Pete Incaviglia	.10
22	Danny Jackson	.10
23	Gregg Jefferies	.10
24	Joe Magrane	.10
25	Don Mattingly	.85
26	Fred McGriff	.10
27	Mark McGwire	1.00
28	Dale Murphy	.15
29	Dan Plesac	.10
30	Kirby Puckett	.75
31	Harold Reynolds	.10
32	Cal Ripken, Jr.	1.50
33	Jeff Robinson	.10
34	Mike Scott	.10
35	Ozzie Smith	.75
36	Dave Stewart	.10
37	Darryl Strawberry	.10
38	Greg Swindell	.10
39	Bobby Thigpen	.10
40	Alan Trammell	.10
41	Andy Van Slyke	.10
42	Frank Viola	.10
43	Dave Winfield	.65
44	Robin Yount	.65

MVP

Filled with superstars, this boxed set was produced by Fleer in 1989 for the Toys "R" Us chain. The fronts of the cards are designed in a yellow and green color scheme and include a "Fleer Baseball MVP" logo above the color player photo. The backs are printed in shades of green and yellow and include biographical notes and stats. The set was issued in a special box with a checklist on the back.

		NM/M
Complete Set (44):		5.00
Common Player:		.10
1	Steve Bedrosian	.10
2	George Bell	.10
3	Wade Boggs	.75
4	George Brett	.85
5	Hubie Brooks	.10
6	Jose Canseco	.50
7	Will Clark	.10
8	Roger Clemens	.85
9	Eric Davis	.10
10	Glenn Davis	.10
11	Andre Dawson	.25
12	Andres Galarraga	.10
13	Kirk Gibson	.10
14	Dwight Gooden	.10
15	Mark Grace	.10
16	Mike Greenwell	.10
17	Tony Gwynn	.75
18	Bryan Harvey	.10
19	Orel Hershiser	.10
20	Ted Higuera	.10
21	Danny Jackson	.10
22	Mike Jackson	.10
23	Doug Jones	.10
24	Greg Maddux	.75
25	Mike Marshall	.10
26	Don Mattingly	.85
27	Fred McGriff	.10
28	Mark McGwire	1.50
29	Kevin McReynolds	.10
30	Jack Morris	.10
31	Gerald Perry	.10
32	Kirby Puckett	.75
33	Chris Sabo	.10
34	Mike Scott	.10
35	Ruben Sierra	.10
36	Darryl Strawberry	.10
37	Danny Tartabull	.10
38	Bobby Thigpen	.10
39	Alan Trammell	.10
40	Andy Van Slyke	.10
41	Frank Viola	.10
42	Walt Weiss	.10
43	Dave Winfield	.65
44	Todd Worrell	.10

Superstars

This boxed set was produced by Fleer for the McCrory store chain. The cards are standard 2-1/2" x 3-1/2" and the full-color player photos are outlined in red with a tan-and-white striped border. The backs carry yellow and white stripes and include the Fleer "SuperStars" logo, player stats and biographical information. The cards are numbered alphabetically and packaged in a special box that includes a checklist on the back.

		NM/M
Complete Set (44):		4.00
Common Player:		.10
1	Roberto Alomar	.35
2	Harold Baines	.10
3	Tim Belcher	.10
4	Wade Boggs	.65
5	George Brett	.85
6	Jose Canseco	.50
7	Gary Carter	.60
8	Will Clark	.10
9	Roger Clemens	.85
10	Kal Daniels	.10
11	Eric Davis	.10
12	Andre Dawson	.25
13	Tony Fernandez	.10
14	Scott Fletcher	.10
15	Andres Galarraga	.10
16	Kirk Gibson	.10
17	Dwight Gooden	.10
18	Jim Gott	.10
19	Mark Grace	.10
20	Mike Greenwell	.10
21	Tony Gwynn	.75
22	Rickey Henderson	.60
23	Orel Hershiser	.10
24	Ted Higuera	.10
25	Gregg Jefferies	.10
26	Wally Joyner	.10
27	Mark Langston	.10
28	Greg Maddux	.75
29	Don Mattingly	.85
30	Fred McGriff	.10
31	Mark McGwire	1.50
32	Dan Plesac	.10
33	Kirby Puckett	.75
34	Jeff Reardon	.10
35	Chris Sabo	.10
36	Mike Schmidt	.85
37	Mike Scott	.10
38	Cory Snyder	.10
39	Darryl Strawberry	.10
40	Alan Trammell	.10
41	Frank Viola	.10
42	Walt Weiss	.10
43	Dave Winfield	.60
44	Todd Worrell	.10

1990 Fleer

Fleer's 1990 set, its 10th annual baseball card offering, again consisted of 660 cards numbered by team. The front of the cards feature mostly action photos surrounded by one of several different color bands and a white border. The set includes various special cards, including a series of "Major League Prospects," Players of the Decade, team checklist cards and a series of

multi-player cards. The backs include complete career stats, player data, and a special "Vital Signs" section showing on-base percentage, slugging percentage, etc. for batters; and strikeout and walk ratios, opposing batting averages, etc. for pitchers.

		NM/M
Factory Hobby Set (672):		12.50
Retail Hobby Set (660):		12.00
Complete Set (660):		10.00
Common Player:		.05
Wax Pack (15):		.50
Wax Box (36):		10.00
Cello Pack (33):		1.00
Cello Box (24):		12.00
1	Lance Blankenship	.05
2	Todd Burns	.05
3	Jose Canseco	.30
4	Jim Corsi	.05
5	Storm Davis	.05
6	Dennis Eckersley	.35
7	Mike Gallego	.05
8	Ron Hassey	.05
9	Dave Henderson	.05
10	Rickey Henderson	.40
11	Rick Honeycutt	.05
12	Stan Javier	.05
13	Felix Jose	.05
14	Carney Lansford	.05
15	Mark McGwire	.65
16	Mike Moore	.05
17	Gene Nelson	.05
18	Dave Parker	.05
19	Tony Phillips	.05
20	Terry Steinbach	.05
21	Dave Stewart	.05
22	Walt Weiss	.05
23	Bob Welch	.05
24	Curt Young	.05
25	Paul Assenmacher	.05
26	Damon Berryhill	.05
27	Mike Bielecki	.05
28	Kevin Blankenship	.05
29	Andre Dawson	.25
30	Shawon Dunston	.05
31	Joe Girardi	.05
32	Mark Grace	.05
33	Mike Harkey	.05
34	Paul Kilgus	.05
35	Les Lancaster	.05
36	Vance Law	.05
37	Greg Maddux	.50
38	Lloyd McClendon	.05
39	Jeff Pico	.05
40	Ryne Sandberg	.50
41	Scott Sanderson	.05
42	Dwight Smith	.05
43	Rick Sutcliffe	.05
44	Jerome Walton **RC**	.05
45	Mitch Webster	.05
46	Curt Wilkerson	.05
47	Dean Wilkins **RC**	.05
48	Mitch Williams	.05
49	Steve Wilson	.05
50	Steve Bedrosian	.05
51	Mike Benjamin **RC**	.05
52	Jeff Brantley **RC**	.10
53	Brett Butler	.05
54	Will Clark	.05
55	Kelly Downs	.05
56	Scott Garrelts	.05
57	Atlee Hammaker	.05
58	Terry Kennedy	.05
59	Mike LaCoss	.05
60	Craig Lefferts	.05
61	Greg Litton **RC**	.05
62	Candy Maldonado	.05
63	Kirt Manwaring	.05
64	Randy McCament **RC**	.05
65	Kevin Mitchell	.05
66	Donell Nixon	.05
67	Ken Oberkfell	.05
68	Rick Reuschel	.05
69	Ernest Riles	.05
70	Don Robinson	.05
71	Pat Sheridan	.05
72	Chris Speier	.05
73	Robby Thompson	.05
74	Jose Uribe	.05
75	Matt Williams	.05
76	George Bell	.05
77	Pat Borders	.05
78	John Cerutti	.05
79	Junior Felix **RC**	.05
80	Tony Fernandez	.05
81	Mike Flanagan	.05
82	Mauro Gozzo **RC**	.05
83	Kelly Gruber	.05
84	Tom Henke	.05
85	Jimmy Key	.05
86	Manny Lee	.05
87	Nelson Liriano	.05
88	Lee Mazzilli	.05
89	Fred McGriff	.05
90	Lloyd Moseby	.05
91	Rance Mulliniks	.05
92	Alex Sanchez	.05
93	Dave Steib	.05
94	Todd Stottlemyre	.05
95	Duane Ward	.05
96	David Wells	.05
97	Ernie Whitt	.05
98	Frank Wills	.05
99	Mookie Wilson	.05
100	Kevin Appier	.05
101	Luis Aquino	.05
102	Bob Boone	.05
103	George Brett	.60
104	Jose DeJesus	.05
105	Luis de los Santos	.05
106	Jim Eisenreich	.05
107	Steve Farr	.05
108	Tom Gordon	.05
109	Mark Gubicza	.05
110	Bo Jackson	.10
111	Terry Leach	.05
112	Charlie Leibrandt	.05
113	Rick Luecken **RC**	.05
114	Mike Macfarlane	.05
115	Jeff Montgomery	.05
116	Bret Saberhagen	.05
117	Kevin Seitzer	.05
118	Kurt Stillwell	.05
119	Pat Tabler	.05
120	Danny Tartabull	.05
121	Gary Thurman	.05
122	Frank White	.05
123	Willie Wilson	.05
124	Matt Winters **RC**	.05
125	Jim Abbott	.05
126	Tony Armas	.05
127	Dante Bichette	.05
128	Bert Blyleven	.10
129	Chili Davis	.05
130	Brian Downing	.05
131	Mike Fetters **RC**	.05
132	Chuck Finley	.05
133	Willie Fraser	.05
134	Bryan Harvey	.05
135	Jack Howell	.05
136	Wally Joyner	.05
137	Jeff Manto **RC**	.05
138	Kirk McCaskill	.05
139	Bob McClure	.05
140	Greg Minton	.05
141	Lance Parrish	.05
142	Dan Petry	.05
143	Johnny Ray	.05
144	Dick Schofield	.05
145	Lee Stevens **RC**	.05
146	Claudell Washington	.05
147	Devon White	.05
148	Mike Witt	.05
149	Roberto Alomar	.20
150	Sandy Alomar, Jr.	.05
151	Andy Benes	.05
152	Jack Clark	.05
153	Pat Clements	.05
154	Joey Cora	.05
155	Mark Davis	.05
156	Mark Grant	.05
157	Tony Gwynn	.50
158	Greg Harris	.05
159	Bruce Hurst	.05
160	Darrin Jackson	.05
161	Chris James	.05
162	Carmelo Martinez	.05
163	Mike Pagliarulo	.05
164	Mark Parent	.05
165	Dennis Rasmussen	.05
166	Bip Roberts	.05
167	Benito Santiago	.05
168	Calvin Schiraldi	.05
169	Eric Show	.05
170	Garry Templeton	.05
171	Ed Whitson	.05
172	Brady Anderson	.05
173	Jeff Ballard	.05
174	Phil Bradley	.05
175	Mike Devereaux	.05
176	Steve Finley	.05
177	Pete Harnisch **RC**	.05
178	Kevin Hickey	.05
179	Brian Holton	.05
180	Ben McDonald **RC**	.15
181	Bob Melvin	.05
182	Bob Milacki	.05
183	Randy Milligan	.05
184	Gregg Olson **RC**	.05
185	Joe Orsulak	.05
186	Bill Ripken	.05
187	Cal Ripken, Jr.	.75
188	Dave Schmidt	.05
189	Larry Sheets	.05
190	Mickey Tettleton	.05
191	Mark Thurmond	.05
192	Jay Tibbs	.05
193	Jim Traber	.05
194	Mark Williamson	.05
195	Craig Worthington	.05
196	Don Aase	.05

197 Blaine Beatty **RC** .05
198 Mark Carreon .05
199 Gary Carter .40
200 David Cone .05
201 Ron Darling .05
202 Kevin Elster .05
203 Sid Fernandez .05
204 Dwight Gooden .05
205 Keith Hernandez .05
206 Jeff Innis **RC** .05
207 Gregg Jefferies .05
208 Howard Johnson .05
209 Barry Lyons .05
210 Dave Magadan .05
211 Kevin McReynolds .05
212 Jeff Musselman .05
213 Randy Myers .05
214 Bob Ojeda .05
215 Juan Samuel .05
216 Mackey Sasser .05
217 Darryl Strawberry .05
218 Tim Teufel .05
219 Frank Viola .05
220 Juan Agosto .05
221 Larry Anderson .05
222 Eric Anthony **RC** .10
223 Kevin Bass .05
224 Craig Biggio .05
225 Ken Caminiti .05
226 Jim Clancy .05
227 Danny Darwin .05
228 Glenn Davis .05
229 Jim Deshaies .05
230 Bill Doran .05
231 Bob Forsch .05
232 Brian Meyer .05
233 Terry Puhl .05
234 Rafael Ramirez .05
235 Rick Rhoden .05
236 Dan Schatzeder .05
237 Mike Scott .05
238 Dave Smith .05
239 Alex Trevino .05
240 Glenn Wilson .05
241 Gerald Young .05
242 Tom Brunansky .05
243 Cris Carpenter .05
244 Alex Cole **RC** .05
245 Vince Coleman .05
246 John Costello .05
247 Ken Dayley .05
248 Jose DeLeon .05
249 Frank DiPino .05
250 Pedro Guerrero .05
251 Ken Hill .05
252 Joe Magrane .05
253 Willie McGee .05
254 John Morris .05
255 Jose Oquendo .05
256 Tony Pena .05
257 Terry Pendleton .05
258 Ted Power .05
259 Dan Quisenberry .05
260 Ozzie Smith .50
261 Scott Terry .05
262 Milt Thompson .05
263 Denny Walling .05
264 Todd Worrell .05
265 Todd Zeile .05
266 Marty Barrett .05
267 Mike Boddicker .05
268 Wade Boggs .50
269 Ellis Burks .05
270 Rick Cerone .05
271 Roger Clemens .60
272 John Dopson .05
273 Nick Esasky .05
274 Dwight Evans .05
275 Wes Gardner .05
276 Rich Gedman .05
277 Mike Greenwell .05
278 Danny Heep .05
279 Eric Hetzel .05
280 Dennis Lamp .05
281 Rob Murphy .05
282 Joe Price .05
283 Carlos Quintana .05
284 Jody Reed .05
285 Luis Rivera .05
286 Kevin Romine .05
287 Lee Smith .05
288 Mike Smithson .05
289 Bob Stanley .05
290 Harold Baines .05
291 Kevin Brown .05
292 Steve Buechele .05
293 Scott Coolbaugh **RC** .05
294 Jack Daugherty **RC** .05
295 Cecil Espy .05
296 Julio Franco .05
297 Juan Gonzalez **RC** 2.00
298 Cecilio Guante .05
299 Drew Hall .05
300 Charlie Hough .05
301 Pete Incaviglia .05
302 Mike Jeffcoat .05
303 Chad Kreuter .05
304 Jeff Kunkel .05
305 Rick Leach .05
306 Fred Manrique .05
307 Jamie Moyer .05
308 Rafael Palmeiro .35
309 Geno Petralli .05
310 Kevin Reimer .05
311 Kenny Rogers **RC** .10
312 Jeff Russell .05
313 Nolan Ryan .75
314 Ruben Sierra .05
315 Bobby Witt .05
316 Chris Bosio .05
317 Glenn Braggs .05
318 Greg Brock .05
319 Chuck Crim .05
320 Rob Deer .05
321 Mike Felder .05
322 Tom Filer .05
323 Tony Fossas **RC** .05
324 Jim Gantner .05
325 Darryl Hamilton .05
326 Ted Higuera .05
327 Mark Knudson **RC** .05
328 Bill Krueger .05
329 Tim McIntosh **RC** .05
330 Paul Molitor .40
331 Jaime Navarro .05
332 Charlie O'Brien .05
333 Jeff Peterek **RC** .05
334 Dan Plesac .05
335 Jerry Reuss .05
336 Gary Sheffield .35
337 Bill Spiers **RC** .05
338 B.J. Surhoff .05
339 Greg Vaughn .05
340 Robin Yount .40
341 Hubie Brooks .05
342 Tim Burke .05
343 Mike Fitzgerald .05
344 Tom Foley .05
345 Andres Galarraga .05
346 Damaso Garcia .05
347 Marquis Grissom **RC** .50
348 Kevin Gross .05
349 Joe Hesketh .05
350 Jeff Huson **RC** .05
351 Wallace Johnson .05
352 Mark Langston .05
353a Dave Martinez (Yellow 90.) 6.00
353b Dave Martinez (Red 90.) .05
354 Dennis Martinez .05
355 Andy McGaffigan .05
356 Otis Nixon .05
357 Spike Owen .05
358 Pascual Perez .05
359 Tim Raines .05
360 Nelson Santovenia .05
361 Bryn Smith .05
362 Zane Smith .05
363 Larry Walker **RC** .75
364 Tim Wallach .05
365 Rick Aguilera .05
366 Allan Anderson .05
367 Wally Backman .05
368 Doug Baker **RC** .05
369 Juan Berenguer .05
370 Randy Bush .05
371 Carmen Castillo .05
372 Mike Dyer **RC** .05
373 Gary Gaetti .05
374 Greg Gagne .05
375 Dan Gladden .05
376 German Gonzalez .05
377 Brian Harper .05
378 Kent Hrbek .05
379 Gene Larkin .05
380 Tim Laudner .05
381 John Moses .05
382 Al Newman .05
383 Kirby Puckett .50
384 Shane Rawley .05
385 Jeff Reardon .05
386 Roy Smith .05
387 Gary Wayne **RC** .05
388 Dave West .05
389 Tim Belcher .05
390 Tim Crews .05
391 Mike Davis .05
392 Rick Dempsey .05
393 Kirk Gibson .05
394 Jose Gonzalez .05
395 Alfredo Griffin .05
396 Jeff Hamilton .05
397 Lenny Harris .05
398 Mickey Hatcher .05
399 Orel Hershiser .05
400 Jay Howell .05
401 Mike Marshall .05
402 Ramon Martinez .05
403 Mike Morgan .05
404 Eddie Murray .40
405 Alejandro Pena .05
406 Willie Randolph .05
407 Mike Scioscia .05
408 Ray Searage .05
409 Fernando Valenzuela .05
410 Jose Vizcaino **RC** .10
411 John Wetteland **RC** .20
412 Jack Armstrong .05
413 Todd Benzinger .05
414 Tim Birtsas .05
415 Tom Browning .05
416 Norm Charlton .05
417 Eric Davis .05
418 Rob Dibble .05
419 John Franco .05
420 Ken Griffey Sr. .05
421 Chris Hammond **RC** .15
422 Danny Jackson .05
423 Barry Larkin .05
424 Tim Leary .05
425 Rick Mahler .05
426 Joe Oliver **RC** .05
427 Paul O'Neill .05
428 Luis Quinones .05
429 Jeff Reed .05
430 Jose Rijo .05
431 Ron Robinson .05
432 Rolando Roomes .05
433 Chris Sabo .05
434 Scott Scudder **RC** .05
435 Herm Winningham .05
436 Steve Balboni .05
437 Jesse Barfield .05
438 Mike Blowers **RC** .05
439 Tom Brookens .05
440 Greg Cadaret .05
441 Alvaro Espinoza .05
442 Bob Geren **RC** .05
443 Lee Guetterman .05
444 Mel Hall .05
445 Andy Hawkins .05
446 Roberto Kelly .05
447 Don Mattingly .60
448 Lance McCullers .05
449 Hensley Meulens .05
450 Dale Mohorcic .05
451 Clay Parker .05
452 Eric Plunk .05
453 Dave Righetti .05
454 Deion Sanders .10
455 Steve Sax .05
456 Don Slaught .05
457 Walt Terrell .05
458 Dave Winfield .40
459 Jay Bell .05
460 Rafael Belliard .05
461 Barry Bonds .75
462 Bobby Bonilla .05
463 Sid Bream .05
464 Benny Distefano .05
465 Doug Drabek .05
466 Jim Gott .05
467 Billy Hatcher .05
468 Neal Heaton .05
469 Jeff King .05
470 Bob Kipper .05
471 Randy Kramer .05
472 Bill Landrum .05
473 Mike LaValliere .05
474 Jose Lind .05
475 Junior Ortiz .05
476 Gary Redus .05
477 Rick Reed **RC** .05
478 R.J. Reynolds .05
479 Jeff Robinson .05
480 John Smiley .05
481 Andy Van Slyke .05
482 Bob Walk .05
483 Andy Allanson .05
484 Scott Bailes .05
485 Albert Belle .05
486 Bud Black .05
487 Jerry Browne .05
488 Tom Candiotti .05
489 Joe Carter .05
490 David Clark .05
491 John Farrell .05
492 Felix Fermin .05
493 Brook Jacoby .05
494 Dion James .05
495 Doug Jones .05
496 Brad Komminsk .05
497 Rod Nichols .05
498 Pete O'Brien .05
499 Steve Olin **RC** .05
500 Jesse Orosco .05
501 Joel Skinner .05
502 Cory Snyder .05
503 Greg Swindell .05
504 Rich Yett .05
505 Scott Bankhead .05
506 Scott Bradley .05
507 Greg Briley .05
508 Jay Buhner .05
509 Darnell Coles .05
510 Keith Comstock .05
511 Henry Cotto .05
512 Alvin Davis .05
513 Ken Griffey Jr. .65
514 Erik Hanson .05
515 Gene Harris .05
516 Brian Holman .05
517 Mike Jackson .05
518 Randy Johnson .40
519 Jeffrey Leonard .05
520 Edgar Martinez .05
521 Dennis Powell .05
522 Jim Presley .05
523 Jerry Reed .05
524 Harold Reynolds .05
525 Mike Schooler .05
526 Bill Swift .05
527 David Valle .05
528 Omar Vizquel .05
529 Ivan Calderon .05
530 Carlton Fisk .40
531 Scott Fletcher .05
532 Dave Gallagher .05
533 Ozzie Guillen .05
534 Greg Hibbard **RC** .05
535 Shawn Hillegas .05
536 Lance Johnson .05
537 Eric King .05
538 Ron Kittle .05
539 Steve Lyons .05
540 Carlos Martinez .05
541 Tom McCarthy **RC** .05
542 Matt Merullo **RC** .05
543 Donn Pall .05
544 Dan Pasqua .05
545 Ken Patterson .05
546 Melido Perez .05
547 Steve Rosenberg .05
548 Sammy Sosa **RC** 5.00
549 Bobby Thigpen .05
550 Robin Ventura .05
551 Greg Walker .05
552 Don Carman .05
553 Pat Combs **RC** .05
554 Dennis Cook .05
555 Darren Daulton .05
556 Len Dykstra .05
557 Curt Ford .05
558 Charlie Hayes .05
559 Von Hayes .05
560 Tom Herr .05
561 Ken Howell .05
562 Steve Jeltz .05
563 Ron Jones .05
564 Ricky Jordan .05
565 John Kruk .05
566 Steve Lake .05
567 Roger McDowell .05
568 Terry Mulholland .05
569 Dwayne Murphy .05
570 Jeff Parrett .05
571 Randy Ready .05
572 Bruce Ruffin .05
573 Dickie Thon .05
574 Jose Alvarez .05
575 Geronimo Berroa .05
576 Jeff Blauser .05
577 Joe Boever .05
578 Marty Clary .05
579 Jody Davis .05
580 Mark Eichhorn .05
581 Darrell Evans .05
582 Ron Gant .05
583 Tom Glavine .25
584 Tommy Greene **RC** .05
585 Tommy Gregg .05
586 Dave Justice **RC** .40
587 Mark Lemke **RC** .05
588 Derek Lilliquist .05
589 Oddibe McDowell .05
590 Kent Mercker **RC** .05
591 Dale Murphy .20
592 Gerald Perry .05
593 Lonnie Smith .05
594 Pete Smith .05
595 John Smoltz .05
596 Mike Stanton **RC** .05
597 Andres Thomas .05
598 Jeff Treadway .05
599 Doyle Alexander .05
600 Dave Bergman .05
601 Brian Dubois **RC** .05
602 Paul Gibson .05
603 Mike Heath .05
604 Mike Henneman .05
605 Guillermo Hernandez .05
606 Shawn Holman **RC** .05
607 Tracy Jones .05
608 Chet Lemon .05
609 Fred Lynn .05
610 Jack Morris .05
611 Matt Nokes .05
612 Gary Pettis .05
613 Kevin Ritz **RC** .05
614 Jeff Robinson .05
615 Steve Searcy .05
616 Frank Tanana .05
617 Alan Trammell .05
618 Gary Ward .05
619 Lou Whitaker .05
620 Frank Williams .05
621a Players of the Decade - 1980 (George Brett (... 10 .390 hitting ...)) 1.00
621b Players of the Decade - 1980 (George Brett) .25
622 Players of the Decade - 1981 (Fernando Valenzuela) .05
623 Players of the Decade - 1982 (Dale Murphy) .05
624a Players of the Decade - 1983 (Cal Ripkin, Jr. (Ripken)) 1.50
624b Players of the Decade - 1983 (Cal Ripken, Jr.) .30
625 Players of the Decade - 1984 (Ryne Sandberg) .25
626 Players of the Decade - 1985 (Don Mattingly) .30
627 Players of the Decade - 1986 (Roger Clemens) .30
628 Players of the Decade - 1987 (George Bell) .05
629 Players of the Decade - 1988 (Jose Canseco) .10
630a Players of the Decade - 1989 (Will Clark (Total bases 32.)) .35
630b Players of the Decade - 1989 (Will Clark (Total bases 321.)) .05
631 Game Savers (Mark Davis, Mitch Williams) .05
632 Boston Igniters (Wade Boggs, Mike Greenwell) .15
633 Starter & Stopper (Mark Gubicza, Jeff Russell) .05
634 League's Best Shortstops (Tony Fernandez, Cal Ripken Jr.) .30
635 Human Dynamos (Kirby Puckett, Bo Jackson) .20
636 300 Strikeout Club (Mike Scott, Nolan Ryan) .30
637 The Dymanic Duo (Will Clark, Kevin Mitchell) .05
638 A.L. All-Stars (Don Mattingly, Mark McGwire) .65
639 N.L. East Rivals (Howard Johnson, Ryne Sandberg) .20
640 Major League Prospects (Rudy Seanez **RC**, Colin Charland **RC**) .05
641 Major League Prospects (George Canale **RC**, Kevin Maas **RC**) .10
642 Major League Prospects (Kelly Mann **RC**, Dave Hansen **RC**) .05
643 Major League Prospects (Greg Smith **RC**, Stu Tate **RC**) .05
644 Major League Prospects (Tom Drees **RC**, Dan Howitt **RC**) .05
645 Major League Prospects (Mike Roesler **RC**, Derrick May **RC**) .05
646 Major League Prospects (Scott Hemond **RC**, Mark Gardner **RC**) .10
647 Major League Prospects (John Orton **RC**, Scott Leius **RC**) .10
648 Major League Prospects (Rich Monteleone **RC**, Dana Williams **RC**) .05
649 Major League Prospects (Mike Huff **RC**, Steve Frey **RC**) .05
650 Major League Prospects (Chuck McElroy **RC**, Moises Alou **RC**) .50
651 Major League Prospects (Bobby Rose **RC**, Mike Hartley **RC**) .10
652 Major League Prospects (Matt Kinzer **RC**, Wayne Edwards **RC**) .05
653 Major League Prospects (Delino DeShields **RC**, Jason Grimsley **RC**) .15
654 Athletics, Cubs, Giants & Blue Jays (Checklist) .05
655 Royals, Angels, Padres & Orioles (Checklist) .05
656 Mets, Astros, Cardinals & Red Sox (Checklist) .05
657 Rangers, Brewers, Expos & Twins (Checklist) .05
658 Dodgers, Reds, Yankees & Pirates (Checklist) .05
659 Indians, Mariners, White Sox & Phillies (Checklist) .05
660 Braves, Tigers & Special Cards (Checklist) .05

All-Stars

The top players at each position, as selected by Fleer, are featured in this 12-card set inserted in cello packs and some wax packs. The cards measure 2-1/2" x 3-1/2" and feature a unique two-photo format on the card fronts.

		NM/M
Complete Set (12):		4.00
Common Player:		.20
1	Harold Baines	.20
2	Will Clark	.20
3	Mark Davis	.20
4	Howard Johnson	.20
5	Joe Magrane	.20
6	Kevin Mitchell	.20
7	Kirby Puckett	1.00
8	Cal Ripken	2.00
9	Ryne Sandberg	1.00
10	Mike Scott	.20
11	Ruben Sierra	.20
12	Mickey Tettleton	.20

League Standouts

Fleer's "League Standouts" are six of baseball's top players distributed randomly in Fleer rack packs. Fronts feature full color photos with a six-dimensional effect. A black and gold frame borders the photo. Backs are yellow and describe the player's accomplishments. The cards measure 2-1/2" x 3-1/2".

		NM/M
Complete Set (6):		3.00
Common Player:		.50
1	Barry Larkin	.50
2	Don Mattingly	1.50
3	Darryl Strawberry	.50
4	Jose Canseco	.75
5	Wade Boggs	1.00
6	Mark Grace	.50

Soaring Stars

Cards from this 12-card set could be found in 1990 Fleer jumbo cello packs. The cards are styled with a cartoon flavor, featuring astronomical graphics surrounding the player. Backs feature information about the promising young player.

		NM/M
Complete Set (12):		5.00
Common Player:		.10
1	Todd Zeile	.25
2	Mike Stanton	.25
3	Larry Walker	.50
4	Robin Ventura	.50
5	Scott Coolbaugh	.25
6	Ken Griffey Jr.	4.00
7	Tom Gordon	.25
8	Jerome Walton	.25
9	Junior Felix	.25
10	Jim Abbott	.25
11	Ricky Jordan	.25
12	Dwight Smith	.25

World Series

This 12-card set depicts highlights of the 1989 World Series and was included in the factory-collated Fleer set. Single World Series cards were discovered in cello and rack packs, but this was not intended to happen. Fronts of the 2-1/2" x 3-1/2" cards feature action photos set against a white background with a red and blue "'89 World Series" banner. Backs are pink and white and describe the events of the 1989 Fall Classic.

		NM/M
Complete Set (12):		1.50
Common Player:		.10
1	The Final Piece To The Puzzle (Mike Moore)	.10
2	Kevin Mitchell	.15
3	Game Two's Crushing Blow	.20
4	Will Clark	.15
5	Jose Canseco	.75
6	Great Leather in the Field	.10
7	Game One And A's Break Out On Top	.10
8	Dave Stewart	.10
9	Parker's Bat Produces Power (Dave Parker)	.25
10	World Series Record Book Game 3	.10
11	Rickey Henderson	.75
12	Oakland A's - Baseball's Best In '89	.25

Box Panels

For the fifth consecutive year, Fleer issued a series of cards on the bottom panels of its wax pack boxes. This 28-card set features both players and team logo cards. The cards were numbered C-1 to C-28.

		NM/M
Complete Set, Panels (7):		7.00
Complete Set, Singles (28):		7.00
Common Player:		.05
1	Giants Logo	.05
2	Tim Belcher	.05
3	Roger Clemens	1.00
4	Eric Davis	.05
5	Glenn Davis	.05
6	Cubs Logo	.05
7	John Franco	.05
8	Mike Greenwell	.05
9	Athletics logo	.05
10	Ken Griffey Jr.	2.00
11	Pedro Guerrero	.05
12	Tony Gwynn	.75
13	Blue Jays Logo	.05
14	Orel Hershiser	.05
15	Bo Jackson	.10
16	Howard Johnson	.05
17	Mets Logo	.05
18	Cardinals Logo	.05
19	Don Mattingly	1.00
20	Mark McGwire	2.00
21	Kevin Mitchell	.05
22	Kirby Puckett	.75
23	Royals Logo	.05
24	Orioles Logo	.05
25	Ruben Sierra	.05
26	Dave Stewart	.05
27	Jerome Walton	.05
28	Robin Yount	.60

Printed in Canada

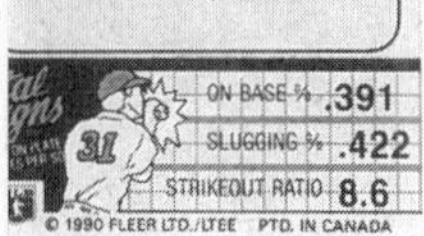

Whether these cards were printed for distribution in Canada or simply the work of a Canadian printer engaged by Fleer to meet U.S. demand is unknown. Each of the 660 cards in the 1990 Fleer issue can be found with a "1990 FLEER LTD./LTEE PTD. IN CANADA" copyright notice on back in the bottom border. Except for various superstar cards, little demand attaches to this variation.

	NM/M
Complete Set (660):	25.00
Common Player:	.25
Wax Pack (10):	1.50
Wax Box (48):	50.00

Update

Fleer produced its seventh consecutive "Update" set in 1990. As in the past, the set consists of 132 cards (numbered U-1 through U-132) that were sold by hobby dealers in special collectors boxes. The cards are designed in the same style as the regular issue. A special Nolan Ryan commemorative card is included in the set.

		NM/M
Complete Set (132):		3.00
Common Player:		.05
1	Steve Avery **RC**	.05
2	Francisco Cabrera	.05
3	Nick Esasky	.05
4	Jim Kremers **RC**	.05
5	Greg Olson **RC**	.05
6	Jim Presley	.05
7	Shawn Boskie **RC**	.05
8	Joe Kraemer **RC**	.05
9	Luis Salazar	.05
10	Hector Villanueva **RC**	.05
11	Glenn Braggs	.05
12	Mariano Duncan	.05
13	Billy Hatcher	.05
14	Tim Layana **RC**	.05
15	Hal Morris	.05
16	Javier Ortiz **RC**	.05
17	Dave Rohde **RC**	.05
18	Eric Yelding **RC**	.05
19	Hubie Brooks	.05
20	Kal Daniels	.05
21	Dave Hansen	.05
22	Mike Hartley	.05
23	Stan Javier	.05
24	Jose Offerman **RC**	.05
25	Juan Samuel	.05
26	Dennis Boyd	.05
27	Delino DeShields	.05
28	Steve Frey	.05
29	Mark Gardner	.05
30	Chris Nabholz **RC**	.05
31	Bill Sampen **RC**	.05
32	Dave Schmidt	.05
33	Daryl Boston	.05
34	Chuck Carr **RC**	.05
35	John Franco	.05
36	Todd Hundley **RC**	.25
37	Julio Machado **RC**	.05
38	Alejandro Pena	.05
39	Darren Reed **RC**	.05
40	Kelvin Torve **RC**	.05
41	Darrel Akerfelds **RC**	.05
42	Jose DeJesus	.05
43	Dave Hollins **RC**	.05
44	Carmelo Martinez	.05
45	Brad Moore **RC**	.05
46	Dale Murphy	.15
47	Wally Backman	.05
48	Stan Belinda **RC**	.05
49	Bob Patterson	.05
50	Ted Power	.05
51	Don Slaught	.05
52	Geronimo Pena **RC**	.05
53	Lee Smith	.05
54	John Tudor	.05
55	Joe Carter	.05
56	Tom Howard **RC**	.05
57	Craig Lefferts	.05
58	Rafael Valdez **RC**	.05
59	Dave Anderson	.05
60	Kevin Bass	.05
61	John Burkett	.05
62	Gary Carter	.40
63	Rick Parker **RC**	.05
64	Trevor Wilson	.05
65	Chris Hoiles **RC**	.05
66	Tim Hulett	.05
67	Dave Johnson **RC**	.05
68	Curt Schilling **RC**	.35
69	David Segui **RC**	.05
70	Tom Brunansky	.05
71	Greg Harris	.05
72	Dana Kiecker **RC**	.05
73	Tim Naehring **RC**	.05
74	Tony Pena	.05
75	Jeff Reardon	.05
76	Jerry Reed	.05
77	Mark Eichhorn	.05
78	Mark Langston	.05
79	John Orton	.05
80	Luis Polonia	.05
81	Dave Winfield	.40
82	Cliff Young **RC**	.05
83	Wayne Edwards	.05
84	Alex Fernandez **RC**	.05
85	Craig Grebeck **RC**	.05
86	Scott Radinsky **RC**	.05
87	Frank Thomas **RC**	2.00
88	Beau Allred **RC**	.05
89	Sandy Alomar, Jr.	.05
90	Carlos Baerga **RC**	.10
91	Kevin Bearse **RC**	.05
92	Chris James	.05
93	Candy Maldonado	.05
94	Jeff Manto	.05
95	Cecil Fielder	.05
96	Travis Fryman **RC**	.25
97	Lloyd Moseby	.05
98	Edwin Nunez	.05
99	Tony Phillips	.05
100	Larry Sheets	.05
101	Mark Davis	.05
102	Storm Davis	.05
103	Gerald Perry	.05
104	Terry Shumpert	.05
105	Edgar Diaz **RC**	.05
106	Dave Parker	.05
107	Tim Drummond **RC**	.05
108	Junior Ortiz	.05
109	Park Pittman **RC**	.05
110	Kevin Tapani **RC**	.05
111	Oscar Azocar **RC**	.05
112	Jim Leyritz **RC**	.05
113	Kevin Maas	.05
114	Alan Mills **RC**	.05
115	Matt Nokes	.05
116	Pascual Perez	.05
117	Ozzie Canseco **RC**	.05
118	Scott Sanderson	.05
119	Tino Martinez **RC**	.05
120	Jeff Schaefer **RC**	.05
121	Matt Young	.05
122	Brian Bohanon **RC**	.05
123	Jeff Huson	.05
124	Ramon Manon **RC**	.05
125	Gary Mielke **RC**	.05
126	Willie Blair **RC**	.05
127	Glenallen Hill **RC**	.05
128	John Olerud **RC**	.35
129	Luis Sojo **RC**	.05
130	Mark Whiten **RC**	.05
131	Three Decades of No Hitters (Nolan Ryan)	1.00
132	Checklist	.05

Award Winners

Hill's department stores and 7-Eleven outlets exclusively sold the 1990 Fleer "Award Winners." This 44-card boxed set includes baseball's statistical leaders of 1989. Card fronts feature a full-color player photo framed by a winner's cup design and blue border. Backs showcase player statistics in blue on a yellow and white background. The cards measure 2-1/2" x 3-1/2". The checklist provided on the back of each box is not correct. It incorrectly lists Bob Boone's team as the Angels and card #10 as Ron Darling. Darryl Strawberry (#38) is not checklisted and all cards #10-38 are off by a number. This is one of the scarcer Fleer box sets of the era.

		NM/M
Complete Set (44):		6.00
Common Player:		.05
1	Jeff Ballard	.05
2	Tim Belcher	.05
3	Bert Blyleven	.05
4	Wade Boggs	.75
5	Bob Boone	.05
6	Jose Canseco	.50
7	Will Clark	.05
8	Jack Clark	.05
9	Vince Coleman	.05
10	Eric Davis	.05
11	Jose DeLeon	.05
12	Tony Fernandez	.05
13	Carlton Fisk	.60
14	Scott Garrelts	.05
15	Tom Gordon	.05
16	Ken Griffey Jr.	1.50
17	Von Hayes	.05
18	Rickey Henderson	.60
19	Bo Jackson	.10
20	Howard Johnson	.05
21	Don Mattingly	1.00
22	Fred McGriff	.05
23	Kevin Mitchell	.05
24	Gregg Olson	.05
25	Gary Pettis	.05
26	Kirby Puckett	.75
27	Harold Reynolds	.05
28	Jeff Russell	.05
29	Nolan Ryan	2.00
30	Bret Saberhagen	.05
31	Ryne Sandberg	.75
32	Benito Santiago	.05
33	Mike Scott	.05
34	Ruben Sierra	.05
35	Lonnie Smith	.05
36	Ozzie Smith	.75
37	Dave Stewart	.05
38	Darryl Strawberry	.05
39	Greg Swindell	.05
40	Andy Van Slyke	.05
41	Tim Wallach	.05
42	Jerome Walton	.05
43	Mitch Williams	.05
44	Robin Yount	.60

Baseball All-Stars

Sold exclusively in Ben Franklin stores, this boxed set showcases the game's top players. Fronts feature a player photo surrounded by a pin-striped tan border. Backs have statistics and data printed in shades of red and dark blue. The cards measure 2-1/2" x 3-1/2" and are packed in a special box with a complete checklist on the back. Like other Fleer boxed sets, the cards are numbered alphabetically. All cards carry a "Printed in Canada" note on back.

		NM/M
Complete Set (44):		6.00
Common Player:		.05
1	Wade Boggs	.75
2	Bobby Bonilla	.05
3	Tim Burke	.05
4	Jose Canseco	.50
5	Will Clark	.05
6	Eric Davis	.05
7	Glenn Davis	.05
8	Julio Franco	.05
9	Tony Fernandez	.05
10	Gary Gaetti	.05
11	Scott Garrelts	.05
12	Mark Grace	.05
13	Mike Greenwell	.05
14	Ken Griffey Jr.	1.00
15	Mark Gubicza	.05
16	Pedro Guerrero	.05
17	Von Hayes	.05
18	Orel Hershiser	.05
19	Bruce Hurst	.05
20	Bo Jackson	.10
21	Howard Johnson	.05
22	Doug Jones	.05
23	Barry Larkin	.05
24	Don Mattingly	.85
25	Mark McGwire	1.00
26	Kevin McReynolds	.05
27	Kevin Mitchell	.05
28	Dan Plesac	.05
29	Kirby Puckett	.75
30	Cal Ripken, Jr.	1.50
31	Bret Saberhagen	.05
32	Ryne Sandberg	.75
33	Steve Sax	.05
34	Ruben Sierra	.05
35	Ozzie Smith	.75
36	John Smoltz	.05
37	Darryl Strawberry	.05
38	Terry Steinbach	.05
39	Dave Stewart	.05
40	Bobby Thigpen	.05
41	Alan Trammell	.05
42	Devon White	.05
43	Mitch Williams	.05
44	Robin Yount	.60

League Leaders

For the fifth consecutive year Fleer released a "League Leaders" boxed set of 44 top Major League players. Card number 42 (Jerome Walton) pictures a player other than Walton. The 2-1/2" x 3-1/2" cards display a full-color photo bordered by a blue frame. Backs feature complete statistics. The cards are numbered alphabetically and a complete checklist is displayed on the back of the box. The set was available at Walgreen drug stores. Cards carry a "Printed in Canada" notice on back.

		NM/M
Complete Set (44):		6.00
Common Player:		.10
1	Roberto Alomar	.25
2	Tim Belcher	.10
3	George Bell	.10
4	Wade Boggs	.75
5	Jose Canseco	.50
6	Will Clark	.10
7	David Cone	.10
8	Eric Davis	.10
9	Glenn Davis	.10
10	Nick Esasky	.10
11	Dennis Eckersley	.55
12	Mark Grace	.10
13	Mike Greenwell	.10
14	Ken Griffey Jr.	1.25
15	Mark Gubicza	.10
16	Pedro Guerrero	.10
17	Tony Gwynn	.75
18	Rickey Henderson	.60
19	Bo Jackson	.15
20	Doug Jones	.10
21	Ricky Jordan	.10
22	Barry Larkin	.10
23	Don Mattingly	.85
24	Fred McGriff	.10
25	Mark McGwire	1.25
26	Kevin Mitchell	.10
27	Jack Morris	.10
28	Gregg Olson	.10
29	Dan Plesac	.10
30	Kirby Puckett	.75
31	Nolan Ryan	1.50
32	Bret Saberhagen	.10
33	Ryne Sandberg	.75
34	Steve Sax	.10
35	Mike Scott	.10
36	Ruben Sierra	.10
37	Lonnie Smith	.10
38	Darryl Strawberry	.10
39	Bobby Thigpen	.10
40	Andy Van Slyke	.10
41	Tim Wallach	.10
42	Jerome Walton	.10
43	Devon White	.10
44	Robin Yount	.60

MVP

This 44-card boxed set was produced by Fleer for the Toys R Us chain. Fronts are designed

with graduating black-to-white borders, surrounding a color player photo. Backs contain individual data and career statistics. The back of each box carries a checklist of all the players in the set. Six peel-off team logo stickers featuring a baseball trivia quiz on the back are also included with each set. The cards are 2-1/2" x 3-1/2" and numbered alphabetically. All cards carry a "Printed in Canada" notation on the back at bottom.

		NM/M
Complete Set (44):		6.00
Common Player:		.10
1	George Bell	.10
2	Bert Blyleven	.10
3	Wade Boggs	.65
4	Bobby Bonilla	.10
5	George Brett	.85
6	Jose Canseco	.45
7	Will Clark	.10
8	Roger Clemens	.85
9	Eric Davis	.10
10	Glenn Davis	.10
11	Tony Fernandez	.10
12	Dwight Gooden	.10
13	Mike Greenwell	.10
14	Ken Griffey Jr.	1.25
15	Pedro Guerrero	.10
16	Tony Gwynn	.65
17	Rickey Henderson	.50
18	Tom Herr	.10
19	Orel Hershiser	.10
20	Kent Hrbek	.10
21	Bo Jackson	.15
22	Howard Johnson	.10
23	Don Mattingly	.85
24	Fred McGriff	.10
25	Mark McGwire	1.25
26	Kevin Mitchell	.10
27	Paul Molitor	.50
28	Dale Murphy	.25
29	Kirby Puckett	.65
30	Tim Raines	.10
31	Cal Ripken, Jr.	1.50
32	Bret Saberhagen	.10
33	Ryne Sandberg	.65
34	Ruben Sierra	.10
35	Dwight Smith	.10
36	Ozzie Smith	.65
37	Darryl Strawberry	.10
38	Dave Stewart	.10
39	Greg Swindell	.10
40	Bobby Thigpen	.10
41	Alan Trammell	.10
42	Jerome Walton	.10
43	Mitch Williams	.10
44	Robin Yount	.50

1991 Fleer Promo Strip

This three-card strip was issued to introduce Fleer's 1991 baseball card set. The cards on the 7-1/2" x 3-1/2" strip are identical to the players' regular issue cards.

	NM/M
Three-card Strip:	4.00

1991 Fleer

Fleer expanded its 1991 set to include 720 cards. The cards feature yellow borders surrounding full-color action photos. Backs feature a circular portrait photo, biographical information, complete statistics, and career highlights. Once again the cards are num-

bered alphabetically within team. Because Fleer used more than one printer, many minor variations in photo cropping and typography can be found. The most notable are included in the checklist here.

	NM/M
Unopened Factory Set (732):	12.00
Complete Set (720):	10.00
Common Player:	.05
Wax Pack (15):	.50
Wax Box (36):	12.50
Jumbo Wax Pack (53):	1.25
Jumbo Wax Box (24):	20.00
Cello Pack (30):	1.00
Cello Box (24):	16.00

1 Troy Afenir **RC** .05
2 Harold Baines .05
3 Lance Blankenship .05
4 Todd Burns .05
5 Jose Canseco .30
6 Dennis Eckersley .35
7 Mike Gallego .05
8 Ron Hassey .05
9 Dave Henderson .05
10 Rickey Henderson .40
11 Rick Honeycutt .05
12 Doug Jennings .05
13 Joe Klink **RC** .05
14 Carney Lansford .05
15 Darren Lewis **RC** .05
16 Willie McGee .05
17a Mark McGwire (Six-line career summary.) .65
17b Mark McGwire (Seven-line career summary.) .65
18 Mike Moore .05
19 Gene Nelson .05
20 Dave Otto .05
21 Jamie Quirk .05
22 Willie Randolph .05
23 Scott Sanderson .05
24 Terry Steinbach .05
25 Dave Stewart .05
26 Walt Weiss .05
27 Bob Welch .05
28 Curt Young .05
29 Wally Backman .05
30 Stan Belinda **RC** .05
31 Jay Bell .05
32 Rafael Belliard .05
33 Barry Bonds .75
34 Bobby Bonilla .05
35 Sid Bream .05
36 Doug Drabek .05
37 Carlos Garcia **RC** .10
38 Neal Heaton .05
39 Jeff King .05
40 Bob Kipper .05
41 Bill Landrum .05
42 Mike LaValliere .05
43 Jose Lind .05
44 Carmelo Martinez .05
45 Bob Patterson .05
46 Ted Power .05
47 Gary Redus .05
48 R.J. Reynolds .05
49 Don Slaught .05
50 John Smiley .05
51 Zane Smith .05
52 Randy Tomlin **RC** .10
53 Andy Van Slyke .05
54 Bob Walk .05
55 Jack Armstrong .05
56 Todd Benzinger .05
57 Glenn Braggs .05
58 Keith Brown .05
59 Tom Browning .05
60 Norm Charlton .05
61 Eric Davis .05
62 Rob Dibble .05
63 Bill Doran .05
64 Mariano Duncan .05
65 Chris Hammond .05
66 Billy Hatcher .05
67 Danny Jackson .05
68 Barry Larkin .05
69 Tim Layana **RC** .05
70 Terry Lee **RC** .05
71 Rick Mahler .05
72 Hal Morris .05
73 Randy Myers .05
74 Ron Oester .05
75 Joe Oliver .05
76 Paul O'Neill .05
77 Luis Quinones .05
78 Jeff Reed .05
79 Jose Rijo .05
80 Chris Sabo .05
81 Scott Scudder .05
82 Herm Winningham .05
83 Larry Andersen .05
84 Marty Barrett .05
85 Mike Boddicker .05
86 Wade Boggs .50
87 Tom Bolton .05
88 Tom Brunansky .05
89 Ellis Burks .05
90 Roger Clemens .55
91 Scott Cooper **RC** .05
92 John Dopson .05
93 Dwight Evans .05
94 Wes Gardner .05
95 Jeff Gray **RC** .05
96 Mike Greenwell .05
97 Greg Harris .05
98 Daryl Irvine **RC** .05
99 Dana Kiecker **RC** .05
100 Randy Kutcher .05
101 Dennis Lamp .05
102 Mike Marshall .05
103 John Marzano .05
104 Rob Murphy .05
105a Tim Naehring **RC** (Seven-line career summary.) .05
105b Tim Naehring **RC** (Nine-line career summary.) .05
106 Tony Pena .05
107 Phil Plantier **RC** .05
108 Carlos Quintana .05
109 Jeff Reardon .05
110 Jerry Reed .05
111 Jody Reed .05
112 Luis Rivera .05
113a Kevin Romine (One-line career summary.) .05
113b Kevin Romine (Two-line career summary.) .05
114 Phil Bradley .05
115 Ivan Calderon .05
116 Wayne Edwards .05
117 Alex Fernandez .05
118 Carlton Fisk .40
119 Scott Fletcher .05
120 Craig Grebeck **RC** .05
121 Ozzie Guillen .05
122 Greg Hibbard .05
123 Lance Johnson .05
124 Barry Jones .05
125a Ron Karkovice (Two-line career summary.) .05
125b Ron Karkovice (One-line career summary.) .05
126 Eric King .05
127 Steve Lyons .05
128 Carlos Martinez .05
129 Jack McDowell .05
130 Donn Pall .05
131 Dan Pasqua .05
132 Ken Patterson .05
133 Melido Perez .05
134 Adam Peterson .05
135 Scott Radinsky **RC** .05
136 Sammy Sosa .50
137 Bobby Thigpen .05
138 Frank Thomas .40
139 Robin Ventura .05
140 Daryl Boston .05
141 Chuck Carr **RC** .05
142 Mark Carreon .05
143 David Cone .05
144 Ron Darling .05
145 Kevin Elster .05
146 Sid Fernandez .05
147 John Franco .05
148 Dwight Gooden .05
149 Tom Herr .05
150 Todd Hundley .05
151 Gregg Jefferies .05
152 Howard Johnson .05
153 Dave Magadan .05
154 Kevin McReynolds .05
155 Keith Miller .05
156 Bob Ojeda .05
157 Tom O'Malley .05
158 Alejandro Pena .05
159 Darren Reed **RC** .05
160 Mackey Sasser .05
161 Darryl Strawberry .05
162 Tim Teufel .05
163 Kelvin Torve .05
164 Julio Valera .05
165 Frank Viola .05
166 Wally Whitehurst .05
167 Jim Acker .05
168 Derek Bell **RC** .10
169 George Bell .05
170 Willie Blair **RC** .05
171 Pat Borders .05
172 John Cerutti .05
173 Junior Felix .05
174 Tony Fernandez .05
175 Kelly Gruber .05
176 Tom Henke .05
177 Glenallen Hill .05
178 Jimmy Key .05
179 Manny Lee .05
180 Fred McGriff .05
181 Rance Mulliniks .05
182 Greg Myers .05
183 John Olerud .05
184 Luis Sojo .05
185 Dave Steib .05
186 Todd Stottlemyre .05
187 Duane Ward .05
188 David Wells .05
189 Mark Whiten **RC** .05
190 Ken Williams .05
191 Frank Wills .05
192 Mookie Wilson .05
193 Don Aase .05
194 Tim Belcher .05
195 Hubie Brooks .05
196 Dennis Cook .05
197 Tim Crews .05
198 Kal Daniels .05
199 Kirk Gibson .05
200 Jim Gott .05
201 Alfredo Griffin .05
202 Chris Gwynn .05
203 Dave Hansen .05
204 Lenny Harris .05
205 Mike Hartley .05
206 Mickey Hatcher .05
207 Carlos Hernandez **RC** .05
208 Orel Hershiser .05
209 Jay Howell .05
210 Mike Huff .05
211 Stan Javier .05
212 Ramon Martinez .05
213 Mike Morgan .05
214 Eddie Murray .40
215 Jim Neidlinger **RC** .05
216 Jose Offerman .05
217 Jim Poole **RC** .05
218 Juan Samuel .05
219 Mike Scioscia .05
220 Ray Searage .05
221 Mike Sharperson .05
222 Fernando Valenzuela .05
223 Jose Vizcaino .05
224 Mike Aldrete .05
225 Scott Anderson **RC** .05
226 Dennis Boyd .05
227 Tim Burke .05
228 Delino DeShields .05
229 Mike Fitzgerald .05
230 Tom Foley .05
231 Steve Frey .05
232 Andres Galarraga .05
233 Mark Gardner .05
234 Marquis Grissom .05
235 Kevin Gross .05
236 Drew Hall .05
237 Dave Martinez .05
238 Dennis Martinez .05
239 Dale Mohorcic .05
240 Chris Nabholz **RC** .05
241 Otis Nixon .05
242 Junior Noboa **RC** .05
243 Spike Owen .05
244 Tim Raines .05
245 Mel Rojas **RC** .10
246 Scott Ruskin **RC** .05
247 Bill Sampen **RC** .05
248 Nelson Santovenia .05
249 Dave Schmidt .05
250 Larry Walker .05
251 Tim Wallach .05
252 Dave Anderson .05
253 Kevin Bass .05
254 Steve Bedrosian .05
255 Jeff Brantley .05
256 John Burkett .05
257 Brett Butler .05
258 Gary Carter .40
259 Will Clark .05
260 Steve Decker **RC** .05
261 Kelly Downs .05
262 Scott Garrelts .05
263 Terry Kennedy .05
264 Mike LaCoss (Photo on back actually Ken Oberkfell.) .05
265 Mark Leonard **RC** .05
266 Greg Litton .05
267 Kevin Mitchell .05
268 Randy O'Neal **RC** .05
269 Rick Parker **RC** .05
270 Rick Reuschel .05
271 Ernest Riles .05
272 Don Robinson .05
273 Robby Thompson .05
274 Mark Thurmond .05
275 Jose Uribe .05
276 Matt Williams .05
277 Trevor Wilson .05
278 Gerald Alexander **RC** .05
279 Brad Arnsberg .05
280 Kevin Belcher **RC** .05
281 Joe Bitker **RC** .05
282 Kevin Brown .05
283 Steve Buechele .05
284 Jack Daugherty .05
285 Julio Franco .05
286 Juan Gonzalez .20
287 Bill Haselman **RC** .05
288 Charlie Hough .05
289 Jeff Huson .05
290 Pete Incaviglia .05
291 Mike Jeffcoat .05
292 Jeff Kunkel .05
293 Gary Mielke .05
294 Jamie Moyer .05
295 Rafael Palmeiro .35
296 Geno Petralli .05
297 Gary Pettis .05
298 Kevin Reimer .05
299 Kenny Rogers .05
300 Jeff Russell .05
301 John Russell .05
302a Nolan Ryan (First horizontal line between 1979/1980.) .75
302b Nolan Ryan (First horizontal line between 1980/1981.) .75
303 Ruben Sierra .05
304 Bobby Witt .05
305 Jim Abbott .05
306 Kent Anderson **RC** .05
307 Dante Bichette .05
308 Bert Blyleven .05
309 Chili Davis .05
310 Brian Downing .05
311 Mark Eichhorn .05
312 Mike Fetters .05
313 Chuck Finley .05
314 Willie Fraser .05
315 Bryan Harvey .05
316 Donnie Hill .05
317 Wally Joyner .05
318 Mark Langston .05
319 Kirk McCaskill .05
320 John Orton .05
321 Lance Parrish .05
322 Luis Polonia .05
323 Johnny Ray .05
324 Bobby Rose .05
325 Dick Schofield .05
326 Rick Schu .05
327a Lee Stevens (Six-line career summary.) .05
327b Lee Stevens (Seven-line career summary.) .05
328 Devon White .05
329 Dave Winfield .40
330 Cliff Young **RC** .05
331 Dave Bergman .05
332 Phil Clark **RC** .05
333 Darnell Coles .05
334 Milt Cuyler **RC** .05
335 Cecil Fielder .05
336 Travis Fryman .05
337 Paul Gibson .05
338 Jerry Don Gleaton .05
339 Mike Heath .05
340 Mike Henneman .05
341 Chet Lemon .05
342 Lance McCullers .05
343 Jack Morris .05
344 Lloyd Moseby .05
345 Edwin Nunez .05
346 Clay Parker .05
347 Dan Petry .05
348 Tony Phillips .05
349 Jeff Robinson .05
350 Mark Salas .05
351 Mike Schwabe **RC** .05
352 Larry Sheets .05
353 John Shelby .05
354 Frank Tanana .05
355 Alan Trammell .05
356 Gary Ward .05
357 Lou Whitaker .05
358 Beau Allred .05
359 Sandy Alomar,Jr. .05
360 Carlos Baerga .05
361 Kevin Bearse **RC** .05
362 Tom Brookens .05
363 Jerry Browne .05
364 Tom Candiotti .05
365 Alex Cole .05
366 John Farrell .05
367 Felix Fermin .05
368 Keith Hernandez .05
369 Brook Jacoby .05
370 Chris James .05
371 Dion James .05
372 Doug Jones .05
373 Candy Maldonado .05
374 Steve Olin .05
375 Jesse Orosco .05
376 Rudy Seanez .05
377 Joel Skinner .05
378 Cory Snyder .05
379 Greg Swindell .05
380 Sergio Valdez **RC** .05
381 Mike Walker **RC** .05
382 Colby Ward **RC** .05
383 Turner Ward **RC** .05
384 Mitch Webster .05
385 Kevin Wickander **RC** .05
386 Darrel Akerfelds .05
387 Joe Boever .05
388a Rod Booker (No 1981 stats.) .05
388b Rod Booker (1981 stats included) .05
389 Sil Campusano .05
390 Don Carman .05
391 Wes Chamberlain **RC** .05
392 Pat Combs .05
393 Darren Daulton .05
394 Jose DeJesus .05
395 Len Dykstra .05
396 Jason Grimsley .05
397 Charlie Hayes .05
398 Von Hayes .05
399 Dave Hollins **RC** .05
400 Ken Howell .05
401 Ricky Jordan .05
402 John Kruk .05
403 Steve Lake .05
404 Chuck Malone **RC** .05
405 Roger McDowell .05
406 Chuck McElroy .05
407 Mickey Morandini **RC** .05
408 Terry Mulholland .05
409 Dale Murphy .15
410 Randy Ready .05
411 Bruce Ruffin .05
412 Dickie Thon .05
413 Paul Assenmacher .05
414 Damon Berryhill .05
415 Mike Bielecki .05
416 Shawn Boskie **RC** .05
417 Dave Clark .05
418 Doug Dascenzo .05
419a Andre Dawson (No 1976 stats.) .25
419b Andre Dawson (1976 stats included) .25
420 Shawon Dunston .05
421 Joe Girardi .05
422 Mark Grace .05
423 Mike Harkey .05
424 Les Lancaster .05
425 Bill Long .05
426 Greg Maddux .50
427 Derrick May .05
428 Jeff Pico .05
429 Domingo Ramos .05
430 Luis Salazar .05
431 Ryne Sandberg .50
432 Dwight Smith .05
433 Greg Smith .05
434 Rick Sutcliffe .05
435 Gary Varsho .05
436 Hector Villanueva **RC** .05
437 Jerome Walton .05
438 Curtis Wilkerson .05
439 Mitch Williams .05
440 Steve Wilson .05
441 Marvell Wynne .05
442 Scott Bankhead .05
443 Scott Bradley .05
444 Greg Briley .05
445 Mike Brumley .05
446 Jay Buhner .05
447 Dave Burba **RC** .05
448 Henry Cotto .05
449 Alvin Davis .05
450 Ken Griffey Jr. .60
451 Erik Hanson .05
452 Gene Harris .05
453 Brian Holman .05
454 Mike Jackson .05
455 Randy Johnson .40
456 Jeffrey Leonard .05
457 Edgar Martinez .05
458 Tino Martinez .05
459 Pete O'Brien .05
460 Harold Reynolds .05
461 Mike Schooler .05
462 Bill Swift .05
463 David Valle .05
464 Omar Vizquel .05
465 Matt Young .05
466 Brady Anderson .05
467 Jeff Ballard .05
468 Juan Bell **RC** .05
469a Mike Devereaux ("Six" last word in career summary top line.) .05
469b Mike Devereaux ("Runs" last word in career summary top line.) .05
470 Steve Finley .05
471 Dave Gallagher .05
472 Leo Gomez **RC** .05
473 Rene Gonzales .05
474 Pete Harnisch .05
475 Kevin Hickey .05
476 Chris Hoiles **RC** .10
477 Sam Horn .05
478 Tim Hulett .05
479 Dave Johnson .05
480 Ron Kittle .05
481 Ben McDonald .05
482 Bob Melvin .05
483 Bob Milacki .05
484 Randy Milligan .05
485 John Mitchell **RC** .05
486 Gregg Olson .05
487 Joe Orsulak .05
488 Joe Price .05
489 Bill Ripken .05
490 Cal Ripken, Jr. .75
491 Curt Schilling .25
492 David Segui **RC** .10
493 Anthony Telford **RC** .05
494 Mickey Tettleton .05
495 Mark Williamson .05
496 Craig Worthington .05
497 Juan Agosto .05
498 Eric Anthony .05
499 Craig Biggio .05
500 Ken Caminiti .05
501 Casey Candaele .05
502 Andujar Cedeno **RC** .05
503 Danny Darwin .05
504 Mark Davidson .05
505 Glenn Davis .05
506 Jim Deshaies .05
507 Luis Gonzalez **RC** 1.00
508 Bill Gullickson .05
509 Xavier Hernandez **RC** .05
510 Brian Meyer .05
511 Ken Oberkfell .05
512 Mark Portugal .05
513 Rafael Ramirez .05
514 Karl Rhodes **RC** .10
515 Mike Scott .05
516 Mike Simms **RC** .05
517 Dave Smith .05
518 Franklin Stubbs .05
519 Glenn Wilson .05
520 Eric Yelding .05
521 Gerald Young .05
522 Shawn Abner .05
523 Roberto Alomar .20
524 Andy Benes .05
525 Joe Carter .05
526 Jack Clark .05
527 Joey Cora .05
528 Paul Faries **RC** .05
529 Tony Gwynn .50
530 Atlee Hammaker .05
531 Greg Harris .05
532 Thomas Howard **RC** .05
533 Bruce Hurst .05
534 Craig Lefferts .05
535 Derek Lilliquist .05
536 Fred Lynn .05
537 Mike Pagliarulo .05
538 Mark Parent .05
539 Dennis Rasmussen .05
540 Bip Roberts .05
541 Richard Rodriguez **RC** .05
542 Benito Santiago .05
543 Calvin Schiraldi .05
544 Eric Show .05
545 Phil Stephenson .05
546 Garry Templeton .05
547 Ed Whitson .05
548 Eddie Williams .05
549 Kevin Appier .05
550 Luis Aquino .05
551 Bob Boone .05
552 George Brett .55
553 Jeff Conine **RC** .30
554 Steve Crawford .05
555 Mark Davis .05
556 Storm Davis .05
557 Jim Eisenreich .05
558 Steve Farr .05
559 Tom Gordon .05
560 Mark Gubicza .05
561 Bo Jackson .10
562 Mike Macfarlane .05
563 Brian McRae **RC** .10
564 Jeff Montgomery .05
565 Bill Pecota .05
566 Gerald Perry .05
567 Bret Saberhagen .05
568 Jeff Schulz **RC** .05
569 Kevin Seitzer .05
570 Terry Shumpert **RC** .05
571 Kurt Stillwell .05
572 Danny Tartabull .05
573 Gary Thurman .05
574 Frank White .05
575 Willie Wilson .05
576 Chris Bosio .05
577 Greg Brock .05
578 George Canale .05
579 Chuck Crim .05
580 Rob Deer .05
581 Edgar Diaz **RC** .05
582 Tom Edens **RC** .05
583 Mike Felder .05
584 Jim Gantner .05
585 Darryl Hamilton .05
586 Ted Higuera .05
587 Mark Knudson .05
588 Bill Krueger .05
589 Tim McIntosh .05
590 Paul Mirabella .05
591 Paul Molitor .40
592 Jaime Navarro .05
593 Dave Parker .05
594 Dan Plesac .05
595 Ron Robinson .05
596 Gary Sheffield .30
597 Bill Spiers .05
598 B.J. Surhoff .05
599 Greg Vaughn .05
600 Randy Veres .05
601 Robin Yount .40
602a Rick Aguilera (Five-line career summary.) .05
602b Rick Aguilera (Four-line career summary.) .05
603 Allan Anderson .05
604 Juan Berenguer .05
605 Randy Bush .05
606 Carmen Castillo .05
607 Tim Drummond .05
608 Scott Erickson **RC** .10
609 Gary Gaetti .05
610a Greg Gagne (Horizontal lines under 82 Ft. Lauderdale, 84 Toledo and 87 Twins.) .05
610b Greg Gagne (Horizontal lines under 82 Orlando, 84 Twins and 88 Twins.) .05
611 Dan Gladden .05
612 Mark Guthrie **RC** .05
613 Brian Harper .05
614 Kent Hrbek .05
615 Gene Larkin .05
616 Terry Leach .05
617 Nelson Liriano .05
618 Shane Mack .05
619 John Moses .05
620 Pedro Munoz **RC** .05
621 Al Newman .05
622 Junior Ortiz .05
623 Kirby Puckett .50
624 Roy Smith .05
625 Kevin Tapani .05
626 Gary Wayne .05

#	Player	Price
627	David West	.05
628	Cris Carpenter	.05
629	Vince Coleman	.05
630	Ken Dayley	.05
631	Jose DeLeon	.05
632	Frank DiPino	.05
633	Bernard Gilkey **RC**	.25
634	Pedro Guerrero	.05
635	Ken Hill	.05
636	Felix Jose	.05
637	Ray Lankford **RC**	.25
638	Joe Magrane	.05
639	Tom Niedenfuer	.05
640	Jose Oquendo	.05
641	Tom Pagnozzi	.05
642	Terry Pendleton	.05
643	Mike Perez **RC**	.05
644	Bryn Smith	.05
645	Lee Smith	.05
646	Ozzie Smith	.50
647	Scott Terry	.05
648	Bob Tewksbury	.05
649	Milt Thompson	.05
650	John Tudor	.05
651	Denny Walling	.05
652	Craig Wilson **RC**	.05
653	Todd Worrell	.05
654	Todd Zeile	.05
655	Oscar Azocar **RC**	.05
656	Steve Balboni	.05
657	Jesse Barfield	.05
658	Greg Cadaret	.05
659	Chuck Cary	.05
660	Rick Cerone	.05
661	Dave Eiland **RC**	.05
662a	Alvaro Espinoza (No 1979-80 stats.)	.05
662b	Alvaro Espinoza (1979-80 stats included)	.05
663	Bob Geren	.05
664	Lee Guetterman	.05
665	Mel Hall	.05
666a	Andy Hawkins (No 1978 stats.)	.05
666b	Andy Hawkins (1978 stats included)	.05
667	Jimmy Jones	.05
668	Roberto Kelly	.05
669	Dave LaPoint	.05
670	Tim Leary	.05
671	Jim Leyritz **RC**	.10
672	Kevin Maas	.05
673	Don Mattingly	.60
674	Matt Nokes	.05
675	Pascual Perez	.05
676	Eric Plunk	.05
677	Dave Righetti	.05
678	Jeff Robinson	.05
679	Steve Sax	.05
680	Mike Witt	.05
681	Steve Avery	.05
682	Mike Bell	.05
683	Jeff Blauser	.05
684	Francisco Cabrera	.05
685	Tony Castillo **RC**	.05
686	Marty Clary	.05
687	Nick Esasky	.05
688	Ron Gant	.05
689	Tom Glavine	.25
690	Mark Grant	.05
691	Tommy Gregg	.05
692	Dwayne Henry	.05
693	Dave Justice	.05
694	Jimmy Kremers **RC**	.05
695	Charlie Leibrandt	.05
696	Mark Lemke	.05
697	Oddibe McDowell	.05
698	Greg Olson **RC**	.05
699	Jeff Parrett	.05
700	Jim Presley	.05
701	Victor Rosario **RC**	.05
702	Lonnie Smith	.05
703	Pete Smith	.05
704	John Smoltz	.05
705	Mike Stanton	.05
706	Andres Thomas	.05
707	Jeff Treadway	.05
708	Jim Vatcher **RC**	.05
709	Home Run Kings (Ryne Sandberg, Cecil Fielder)	.10
710	Second Generation Superstars (Barry Bonds, Ken Griffey Jr.)	.65
711	NLCS Team Leaders (Bobby Bonilla, Barry Larkin)	.05
712	Top Game Savers (Bobby Thigpen, John Franco)	.05
713	Chicago's 100 Club (Andre Dawson, Ryne Sandberg)	.10
714	Checklists (Athletics, Pirates, Reds, Red Sox)	.05
715	Dodgers	.05
716	Checklists (Expos, Giants, Rangers, Angels)	.05
717	Checklists (Tigers, Indians, Phillies, Cubs)	.05
718	Checklists (Mariners, Orioles, Astros, Padres)	.05
719	Checklists (Royals, Brewers, Twins, Cardinals)	.05
720	Checklists (Yankees, Braves, Super Stars)	.05

All-Stars

Three player photos are featured on each card in this special insert set. An action shot and portrait close-up are featured on the front, while a full-figure pose is showcased on the back. The cards were inserted into 1991 Fleer cello packs.

		NM/M
Complete Set (10):		5.00
Common Player:		.25
1	Ryne Sandberg	.75
2	Barry Larkin	.25
3	Matt Williams	.25
4	Cecil Fielder	.25
5	Barry Bonds	2.00
6	Rickey Henderson	.50
7	Ken Griffey Jr.	1.50
8	Jose Canseco	.25
9	Benito Santiago	.25
10	Roger Clemens	1.00

World Series

Once again Fleer released a set in honor of the World Series from the previous season. The 1991 issue features only eight cards compared to 12 in 1990. The cards feature white borders surrounding full-color action shots from the 1990 Fall Classic. The card backs feature an overview of the World Series action.

		NM/M
Complete Set (8):		1.50
Common Player:		.25
1	Eric Davis	.25
2	Billy Hatcher	.25
3	Jose Canseco	.35
4	Rickey Henderson	.45
5	Chris Sabo, Carney Lansford	.25
6	Dave Stewart	.25
7	Jose Rijo	.25
8	Reds Celebrate	.25

Box Panels

Unlike past box panel sets, the 1991 Fleer box panels feature a theme; 1990 no-hitters are celebrated on the three different boxes. The cards feature blank backs and are numbered in order of no-hitter on the front. A team logo was included on each box. The card fronts are styled after the 1991 Fleer cards. A special no-hitter logo appears in the lower left corner.

		NM/M
Complete Set, Singles (10):		3.00
Complete Set, Panels (3):		3.00
Common Player:		.10
1	Mark Langston, Mike Witt	.10
2	Randy Johnson	1.00
3	Nolan Ryan	2.00
4	Dave Stewart	.10
5	Fernando Valenzuela	.10
6	Andy Hawkins	.10
7	Melido Perez	.10
8	Terry Mulholland	.10
9	Dave Steib	.10
----	Team Logos	.05

Update

Fleer produced its eighth consecutive "Update" set in 1991 to supplement the company's regular set. As in the past, the set consists of 132 cards that were sold by hobby dealers in special collectors boxes. The cards are designed in the same style as the regular Fleer issue.

		NM/M
Complete Set (132):		3.00
Common Player:		.05
1	Glenn Davis	.05
2	Dwight Evans	.05
3	Jose Mesa **RC**	.05
4	Jack Clark	.05
5	Danny Darwin	.05
6	Steve Lyons	.05
7	Mo Vaughn **RC**	.05
8	Floyd Bannister	.05
9	Gary Gaetti	.05
10	Dave Parker	.05
11	Joey Cora	.05
12	Charlie Hough	.05
13	Matt Merullo	.05
14	Warren Newson **RC**	.05
15	Tim Raines	.05
16	Albert Belle	.05
17	Glenallen Hill	.05
18	Shawn Hillegas	.05
19	Mark Lewis **RC**	.05
20	Charles Nagy **RC**	.05
21	Mark Whiten	.05
22	John Cerutti	.05
23	Rob Deer	.05
24	Mickey Tettleton	.05
25	Warren Cromartie	.05
26	Kirk Gibson	.05
27	David Howard **RC**	.05
28	Brent Mayne **RC**	.05
29	Dante Bichette	.05
30	Mark Lee **RC**	.05
31	Julio Machado	.05
32	Edwin Nunez	.05
33	Willie Randolph	.05
34	Franklin Stubbs	.05
35	Bill Wegman	.05
36	Chili Davis	.05
37	Chuck Knoblauch **RC**	.05
38	Scott Leius	.05
39	Jack Morris	.05
40	Mike Pagliarulo	.05
41	Lenny Webster **RC**	.05
42	John Habyan **RC**	.05
43	Steve Howe	.05
44	Jeff Johnson **RC**	.05
45	Scott Kamieniecki **RC**	.05
46	Pat Kelly **RC**	.05
47	Hensley Meulens	.05
48	Wade Taylor **RC**	.05
49	Bernie Williams **RC**	.20
50	Kirk Dressendorfer **RC**	.05
51	Ernest Riles	.05
52	Rich DeLucia **RC**	.05
53	Tracy Jones	.05
54	Bill Krueger	.05
55	Alonzo Powell **RC**	.05
56	Jeff Schaefer	.05
57	Russ Swan **RC**	.05
58	John Barfield **RC**	.05
59	Rich Gossage	.10
60	Jose Guzman	.05
61	Dean Palmer **RC**	.05
62	Ivan Rodriguez **RC**	1.50
63	Roberto Alomar	.20
64	Tom Candiotti	.05
65	Joe Carter	.05
66	Ed Sprague **RC**	.05
67	Pat Tabler	.05
68	Mike Timlin **RC**	.05
69	Devon White	.05
70	Rafael Belliard	.05
71	Juan Berenguer	.05
72	Sid Bream	.05
73	Marvin Freeman	.05
74	Kent Mercker	.05
75	Otis Nixon	.05
76	Terry Pendleton	.05
77	George Bell	.05
78	Danny Jackson	.05
79	Chuck McElroy	.05
80	Gary Scott **RC**	.05
81	Heathcliff Slocumb **RC**	.05
82	Dave Smith	.05
83	Rick Wilkins **RC**	.05
84	Freddie Benavides **RC**	.05
85	Ted Power	.05
86	Mo Sanford **RC**	.05
87	Jeff Bagwell **RC**	2.00
88	Steve Finley	.05
89	Pete Harnisch	.05
90	Darryl Kile **RC**	.05
91	Brett Butler	.05
92	John Candelaria	.05
93	Gary Carter	.40
94	Kevin Gross	.05
95	Bob Ojeda	.05
96	Darryl Strawberry	.05
97	Ivan Calderon	.05
98	Ron Hassey	.05
99	Gilberto Reyes	.05
100	Hubie Brooks	.05
101	Rick Cerone	.05
102	Vince Coleman	.05
103	Jeff Innis	.05
104	Pete Schourek **RC**	.05
105	Andy Ashby **RC**	.05
106	Wally Backman	.05
107	Darrin Fletcher **RC**	.05
108	Tommy Greene	.05
109	John Morris	.05
110	Mitch Williams	.05
111	Lloyd McClendon	.05
112	Orlando Merced **RC**	.05
113	Vicente Palacios	.05
114	Gary Varsho	.05
115	John Wehner **RC**	.05
116	Rex Hudler	.05
117	Tim Jones	.05
118	Geronimo Pena **RC**	.05
119	Gerald Perry	.05
120	Larry Andersen	.05
121	Jerald Clark	.05
122	Scott Coolbaugh	.05
123	Tony Fernandez	.05
124	Darrin Jackson	.05
125	Fred McGriff	.05
126	Jose Mota **RC**	.05
127	Tim Teufel	.05
128	Bud Black	.05
129	Mike Felder	.05
130	Willie McGee	.05
131	Dave Righetti	.05
132	Checklist	.05

ProVisions

The illustrations of artist Terry Smith are showcased in this special set. Twelve fantasy portraits were produced for cards inserted into rack packs. Four other ProVision cards were inserted into factory sets. The rack pack cards feature black borders, while the factory set cards have white borders. Information on the card backs explains the manner in which Smith painted each player. Factory insert ProVisions are indicated by an "F" suffix in the checklist here.

		NM/M
Complete Set (12):		5.00
Common Player:		.15
Complete Factory Set (4):		5.00
Common Player:		.25
1	Kirby Puckett	.75
2	Will Clark	.15
3	Ruben Sierra	.15
4	Mark McGwire	1.50
5	Bo Jackson	.25
6	Jose Canseco	.50
7	Dwight Gooden	.15
8	Mike Greenwell	.15
9	Roger Clemens	1.00
10	Eric Davis	.15
11	Don Mattingly	1.00
12	Darryl Strawberry	.15
1F	Barry Bonds	3.50
2F	Rickey Henderson	.50
3F	Ryne Sandberg	1.00
4F	Dave Stewart	.25

1992 Fleer Promo

It has been reported that only 100 of this sample card were made for distribution at the 1991 FanFest event. The card differs from the issued Kirby Puckett card in the '92 Fleer set in the card number, the absence of 1991 stats and the overprinting of a sample card notice, all on the back.

		NM/M
123	Kirby Puckett	400.00

1992 Fleer

For the second consecutive year, Fleer produced a 720-card set. The standard card fronts feature full-color action photos bordered in green with the player's name, position and team logo on the right border. The backs feature another full-color action photo, biographical information and statistics. A special 12-card Roger Clemens subset is also included in the 1992 Fleer set. Three more Clemens cards were available through a mail-in offer, and 2,000 Roger Clemens autographed cards were inserted in 1992 packs. Once again the cards are numbered according to team. Subsets in the issue included Major League Propects (#652-680), Record Setters (#681-687), League Leaders (#688-697), Superstar Specials (#698-707) and ProVisions (#708-713), which for the first time were part of the regular numbered set rather than limited edition insert cards.

		NM/M
Unopened Factory Set (732):		17.50
Complete Set (720):		8.00
Common Player:		.05
Wax Pack (15):		.45
Wax Box (36):		10.00
Cello Pack (35):		1.00
Cello Box (24):		16.00
1	Brady Anderson	.05
2	Jose Bautista	.05
3	Juan Bell	.05
4	Glenn Davis	.05
5	Mike Devereaux	.05
6	Dwight Evans	.05
7	Mike Flanagan	.05
8	Leo Gomez	.05
9	Chris Hoiles	.05
10	Sam Horn	.05
11	Tim Hulett	.05
12	Dave Johnson	.05
13	Chito Martinez **RC**	.05
14	Ben McDonald	.05
15	Bob Melvin	.05
16	Luis Mercedes **RC**	.10
17	Jose Mesa	.05
18	Bob Milacki	.05
19	Randy Milligan	.05
20	Mike Mussina	.30
21	Gregg Olson	.05
22	Joe Orsulak	.05
23	Jim Poole	.05
24	Arthur Rhodes **RC**	.10
25	Billy Ripken	.05
26	Cal Ripken, Jr.	1.00
27	David Segui	.05
28	Roy Smith	.05
29	Anthony Telford	.05
30	Mark Williamson	.05
31	Craig Worthington	.05
32	Wade Boggs	.55
33	Tom Bolton	.05
34	Tom Brunansky	.05
35	Ellis Burks	.05
36	Jack Clark	.05
37	Roger Clemens	.60
38	Danny Darwin	.05
39	Mike Greenwell	.05
40	Joe Hesketh	.05
41	Daryl Irvine	.05
42	Dennis Lamp	.05
43	Tony Pena	.05
44	Phil Plantier	.05
45	Carlos Quintana	.05
46	Jeff Reardon	.05
47	Jody Reed	.05
48	Luis Rivera	.05
49	Mo Vaughn	.05
50	Jim Abbott	.05
51	Kyle Abbott	.05
52	Ruben Amaro Jr. **RC**	.05
53	Scott Bailes	.05
54	Chris Beasley **RC**	.05
55	Mark Eichhorn	.05
56	Mike Fetters	.05
57	Chuck Finley	.05
58	Gary Gaetti	.05
59	Dave Gallagher	.05
60	Donnie Hill	.05
61	Bryan Harvey	.05
62	Wally Joyner	.05
63	Mark Langston	.05
64	Kirk McCaskill	.05
65	John Orton	.05
66	Lance Parrish	.05
67	Luis Polonia	.05
68	Bobby Rose	.05
69	Dick Schofield	.05
70	Luis Sojo	.05
71	Lee Stevens	.05
72	Dave Winfield	.50
73	Cliff Young	.05
74	Wilson Alvarez	.05
75	Esteban Beltre **RC**	.05
76	Joey Cora	.05
77	Brian Drahman **RC**	.05
78	Alex Fernandez	.05
79	Carlton Fisk	.50
80	Scott Fletcher	.05
81	Craig Grebeck	.05
82	Ozzie Guillen	.05
83	Greg Hibbard	.05
84	Charlie Hough	.05
85	Mike Huff	.05
86	Bo Jackson	.10
87	Lance Johnson	.05
88	Ron Karkovice	.05
89	Jack McDowell	.05
90	Matt Merullo	.05
91	Warren Newson **RC**	.05
92	Donn Pall	.05
93	Dan Pasqua	.05
94	Ken Patterson	.05
95	Melido Perez	.05
96	Scott Radinsky	.05
97	Tim Raines	.05
98	Sammy Sosa	.55
99	Bobby Thigpen	.05
100	Frank Thomas	.50
101	Robin Ventura	.05
102	Mike Aldrete	.05
103	Sandy Alomar, Jr.	.05
104	Carlos Baerga	.05
105	Albert Belle	.05
106	Willie Blair	.05
107	Jerry Browne	.05
108	Alex Cole	.05
109	Felix Fermin	.05
110	Glenallen Hill	.05
111	Shawn Hillegas	.05
112	Chris James	.05
113	Reggie Jefferson **RC**	.05
114	Doug Jones	.05
115	Eric King	.05
116	Mark Lewis	.05
117	Carlos Martinez	.05
118	Charles Nagy	.05
119	Rod Nichols	.05
120	Steve Olin	.05
121	Jesse Orosco	.05
122	Rudy Seanez	.05
123	Joel Skinner	.05
124	Greg Swindell	.05
125	Jim Thome **RC**	.50
126	Mark Whiten	.05
127	Scott Aldred	.05
128	Andy Allanson	.05
129	John Cerutti	.05
130	Milt Cuyler	.05
131	Mike Dalton **RC**	.05
132	Rob Deer	.05
133	Cecil Fielder	.05
134	Travis Fryman	.05
135	Dan Gakeler **RC**	.05
136	Paul Gibson	.05
137	Bill Gullickson	.05

138 Mike Henneman .05
139 Pete Incaviglia .05
140 Mark Leiter **RC** .05
141 Scott Livingstone **RC** .10
142 Lloyd Moseby .05
143 Tony Phillips .05
144 Mark Salas .05
145 Frank Tanana .05
146 Walt Terrell .05
147 Mickey Tettleton .05
148 Alan Trammell .05
149 Lou Whitaker .05
150 Kevin Appier .05
151 Luis Aquino .05
152 Todd Benzinger .05
153 Mike Boddicker .05
154 George Brett .60
155 Storm Davis .05
156 Jim Eisenreich .05
157 Kirk Gibson .05
158 Tom Gordon .05
159 Mark Gubicza .05
160 David Howard **RC** .05
161 Mike Macfarlane .05
162 Brent Mayne .05
163 Brian McRae .05
164 Jeff Montgomery .05
165 Bill Pecota .05
166 Harvey Pulliam **RC** .05
167 Bret Saberhagen .05
168 Kevin Seitzer .05
169 Terry Shumpert .05
170 Kurt Stillwell .05
171 Danny Tartabull .05
172 Gary Thurman .05
173 Dante Bichette .05
174 Kevin Brown .05
175 Chuck Crim .05
176 Jim Gantner .05
177 Darryl Hamilton .05
178 Ted Higuera .05
179 Darren Holmes .05
180 Mark Lee .05
181 Julio Machado .05
182 Paul Molitor .50
183 Jaime Navarro .05
184 Edwin Nunez .05
185 Dan Plesac .05
186 Willie Randolph .05
187 Ron Robinson .05
188 Gary Sheffield .30
189 Bill Spiers .05
190 B.J. Surhoff .05
191 Dale Sveum .05
192 Greg Vaughn .05
193 Bill Wegman .05
194 Robin Yount .50
195 Rick Aguilera .05
196 Allan Anderson .05
197 Steve Bedrosian .05
198 Randy Bush .05
199 Larry Casian **RC** .05
200 Chili Davis .05
201 Scott Erickson .05
202 Greg Gagne .05
203 Dan Gladden .05
204 Brian Harper .05
205 Kent Hrbek .05
206 Chuck Knoblauch .05
207 Gene Larkin .05
208 Terry Leach .05
209 Scott Leius .05
210 Shane Mack .05
211 Jack Morris .05
212 Pedro Munoz **RC** .05
213 Denny Neagle **RC** .10
214 Al Newman .05
215 Junior Ortiz .05
216 Mike Pagliarulo .05
217 Kirby Puckett .55
218 Paul Sorrento .05
219 Kevin Tapani .05
220 Lenny Webster .05
221 Jesse Barfield .05
222 Greg Cadaret .05
223 Dave Eiland .05
224 Alvaro Espinoza .05
225 Steve Farr .05
226 Bob Geren .05
227 Lee Guetterman .05
228 John Habyan .05
229 Mel Hall .05
230 Steve Howe .05
231 Mike Humphreys **RC** .05
232 Scott Kamieniecki **RC** .10
233 Pat Kelly .05
234 Roberto Kelly .05
235 Tim Leary .05
236 Kevin Maas .05
237 Don Mattingly .60
238 Hensley Meulens .05
239 Matt Nokes .05
240 Pascual Perez .05
241 Eric Plunk .05
242 John Ramos **RC** .05
243 Scott Sanderson .05
244 Steve Sax .05
245 Wade Taylor **RC** .05
246 Randy Velarde .05
247 Bernie Williams .05
248 Troy Afenir .05
249 Harold Baines .05
250 Lance Blankenship .05
251 Mike Bordick **RC** .10
252 Jose Canseco .30
253 Steve Chitren .05
254 Ron Darling .05
255 Dennis Eckersley .45
256 Mike Gallego .05
257 Dave Henderson .05
258 Rickey Henderson .50
259 Rick Honeycutt .05
260 Brook Jacoby .05
261 Carney Lansford .05
262 Mark McGwire .75
263 Mike Moore .05
264 Gene Nelson .05
265 Jamie Quirk .05
266 Joe Slusarski **RC** .10
267 Terry Steinbach .05
268 Dave Stewart .05
269 Todd Van Poppel **RC** .05
270 Walt Weiss .05
271 Bob Welch .05
272 Curt Young .05
273 Scott Bradley .05
274 Greg Briley .05
275 Jay Buhner .05
276 Henry Cotto .05
277 Alvin Davis .05
278 Rich DeLucia .05
279 Ken Griffey Jr. .65
280 Erik Hanson .05
281 Brian Holman .05
282 Mike Jackson .05
283 Randy Johnson .50
284 Tracy Jones .05
285 Bill Krueger .05
286 Edgar Martinez .05
287 Tino Martinez .05
288 Rob Murphy .05
289 Pete O'Brien .05
290 Alonzo Powell .05
291 Harold Reynolds .05
292 Mike Schooler .05
293 Russ Swan .05
294 Bill Swift .05
295 Dave Valle .05
296 Omar Vizquel .05
297 Gerald Alexander .05
298 Brad Arnsberg .05
299 Kevin Brown .05
300 Jack Daugherty .05
301 Mario Diaz .05
302 Brian Downing .05
303 Julio Franco .05
304 Juan Gonzalez .25
305 Rich Gossage .10
306 Jose Guzman .05
307 Jose Hernandez **RC** .05
308 Jeff Huson .05
309 Mike Jeffcoat .05
310 Terry Mathews **RC** .05
311 Rafael Palmeiro .45
312 Dean Palmer .05
313 Geno Petralli .05
314 Gary Pettis .05
315 Kevin Reimer .05
316 Ivan Rodriguez .45
317 Kenny Rogers .05
318 Wayne Rosenthal **RC** .05
319 Jeff Russell .05
320 Nolan Ryan 1.00
321 Ruben Sierra .05
322 Jim Acker .05
323 Roberto Alomar .20
324 Derek Bell .05
325 Pat Borders .05
326 Tom Candiotti .05
327 Joe Carter .05
328 Rob Ducey .05
329 Kelly Gruber .05
330 Juan Guzman **RC** .25
331 Tom Henke .05
332 Jimmy Key .05
333 Manny Lee .05
334 Al Leiter .05
335 Bob MacDonald **RC** .05
336 Candy Maldonado .05
337 Rance Mulliniks .05
338 Greg Myers .05
339 John Olerud .05
340 Ed Sprague **RC** .10
341 Dave Stieb .05
342 Todd Stottlemyre .05
343 Mike Timlin **RC** .10
344 Duane Ward .05
345 David Wells .05
346 Devon White .05
347 Mookie Wilson .05
348 Eddie Zosky .05
349 Steve Avery .05
350 Mike Bell **RC** .05
351 Rafael Belliard .05
352 Juan Berenguer .05
353 Jeff Blauser .05
354 Sid Bream .05
355 Francisco Cabrera .05
356 Marvin Freeman .05
357 Ron Gant .05
358 Tom Glavine .30
359 Brian Hunter **RC** .05
360 Dave Justice .05
361 Charlie Leibrandt .05
362 Mark Lemke .05
363 Kent Mercker .05
364 Keith Mitchell **RC** .05
365 Greg Olson .05
366 Terry Pendleton .05
367 Armando Reynoso **RC** .05
368 Deion Sanders .10
369 Lonnie Smith .05
370 Pete Smith .05
371 John Smoltz .05
372 Mike Stanton .05
373 Jeff Treadway .05
374 Mark Wohlers **RC** .05
375 Paul Assenmacher .05
376 George Bell .05
377 Shawn Boskie .05
378 Frank Castillo **RC** .05
379 Andre Dawson .25
380 Shawon Dunston .05
381 Mark Grace .05
382 Mike Harkey .05
383 Danny Jackson .05
384 Les Lancaster .05
385 Cedric Landrum **RC** .05
386 Greg Maddux .55
387 Derrick May .05
388 Chuck McElroy .05
389 Ryne Sandberg .55
390 Heathcliff Slocumb **RC** .10
391 Dave Smith .05
392 Dwight Smith .05
393 Rick Sutcliffe .05
394 Hector Villanueva .05
395 Chico Walker **RC** .05
396 Jerome Walton .05
397 Rick Wilkins **RC** .15
398 Jack Armstrong .05
399 Freddie Benavides **RC** .05
400 Glenn Braggs .05
401 Tom Browning .05
402 Norm Charlton .05
403 Eric Davis .05
404 Rob Dibble .05
405 Bill Doran .05
406 Mariano Duncan .05
407 Kip Gross **RC** .05
408 Chris Hammond .05
409 Billy Hatcher .05
410 Chris Jones **RC** .05
411 Barry Larkin .05
412 Hal Morris .05
413 Randy Myers .05
414 Joe Oliver .05
415 Paul O'Neill .05
416 Ted Power .05
417 Luis Quinones .05
418 Jeff Reed .05
419 Jose Rijo .05
420 Chris Sabo .05
421 Reggie Sanders **RC** .05
422 Scott Scudder .05
423 Glenn Sutko .05
424 Eric Anthony .05
425 Jeff Bagwell .50
426 Craig Biggio .05
427 Ken Caminiti .05
428 Casey Candaele .05
429 Mike Capel .05
430 Andujar Cedeno .05
431 Jim Corsi .05
432 Mark Davidson .05
433 Steve Finley .05
434 Luis Gonzalez .05
435 Pete Harnisch .05
436 Dwayne Henry .05
437 Xavier Hernandez .05
438 Jimmy Jones .05
439 Darryl Kile **RC** .05
440 Rob Mallicoat **RC** .05
441 Andy Mota **RC** .05
442 Al Osuna .05
443 Mark Portugal .05
444 Scott Servais **RC** .10
445 Mike Simms .05
446 Gerald Young .05
447 Tim Belcher .05
448 Brett Butler .05
449 John Candelaria .05
450 Gary Carter .50
451 Dennis Cook .05
452 Tim Crews .05
453 Kal Daniels .05
454 Jim Gott .05
455 Alfredo Griffin .05
456 Kevin Gross .05
457 Chris Gwynn .05
458 Lenny Harris .05
459 Orel Hershiser .05
460 Jay Howell .05
461 Stan Javier .05
462 Eric Karros .05
463 Ramon Martinez .05
464 Roger McDowell .05
465 Mike Morgan .05
466 Eddie Murray .50
467 Jose Offerman .05
468 Bob Ojeda .05
469 Juan Samuel .05
470 Mike Scioscia .05
471 Darryl Strawberry .05
472 Bret Barberie **RC** .10
473 Brian Barnes .05
474 Eric Bullock .05
475 Ivan Calderon .05
476 Delino DeShields .05
477 Jeff Fassero **RC** .10
478 Mike Fitzgerald .05
479 Steve Frey .05
480 Andres Galarraga .05
481 Mark Gardner .05
482 Marquis Grissom .05
483 Chris Haney **RC** .05
484 Barry Jones .05
485 Dave Martinez .05
486 Dennis Martinez .05
487 Chris Nabholz .05
488 Spike Owen .05
489 Gilberto Reyes .05
490 Mel Rojas .05
491 Scott Ruskin .05
492 Bill Sampen .05
493 Larry Walker .05
494 Tim Wallach .05
495 Daryl Boston .05
496 Hubie Brooks .05
497 Tim Burke .05
498 Mark Carreon .05
499 Tony Castillo .05
500 Vince Coleman .05
501 David Cone .05
502 Kevin Elster .05
503 Sid Fernandez .05
504 John Franco .05
505 Dwight Gooden .05
506 Todd Hundley .05
507 Jeff Innis .05
508 Gregg Jefferies .05
509 Howard Johnson .05
510 Dave Magadan .05
511 Terry McDaniel **RC** .05
512 Kevin McReynolds .05
513 Keith Miller .05
514 Charlie O'Brien .05
515 Mackey Sasser .05
516 Pete Schourek **RC** .05
517 Julio Valera .05
518 Frank Viola .05
519 Wally Whitehurst .05
520 Anthony Young **RC** .05
521 Andy Ashby **RC** .10
522 Kim Batiste **RC** .05
523 Joe Boever .05
524 Wes Chamberlain .05
525 Pat Combs .05
526 Danny Cox .05
527 Darren Daulton .05
528 Jose DeJesus .05
529 Len Dykstra .05
530 Darrin Fletcher .05
531 Tommy Greene .05
532 Jason Grimsley .05
533 Charlie Hayes .05
534 Von Hayes .05
535 Dave Hollins .05
536 Ricky Jordan .05
537 John Kruk .05
538 Jim Lindeman .05
539 Mickey Morandini .05
540 Terry Mulholland .05
541 Dale Murphy .20
542 Randy Ready .05
543 Wally Ritchie .05
544 Bruce Ruffin .05
545 Steve Searcy .05
546 Dickie Thon .05
547 Mitch Williams .05
548 Stan Belinda .05
549 Jay Bell .05
550 Barry Bonds 1.00
551 Bobby Bonilla .05
552 Steve Buechele .05
553 Doug Drabek .05
554 Neal Heaton .05
555 Jeff King .05
556 Bob Kipper .05
557 Bill Landrum .05
558 Mike LaValliere .05
559 Jose Lind .05
560 Lloyd McClendon .05
561 Orlando Merced .05
562 Bob Patterson .05
563 Joe Redfield **RC** .05
564 Gary Redus .05
565 Rosario Rodriguez .05
566 Don Slaught .05
567 John Smiley .05
568 Zane Smith .05
569 Randy Tomlin .05
570 Andy Van Slyke .05
571 Gary Varsho .05
572 Bob Walk .05
573 John Wehner **RC** .05
574 Juan Agosto .05
575 Cris Carpenter .05
576 Jose DeLeon .05
577 Rich Gedman .05
578 Bernard Gilkey .05
579 Pedro Guerrero .05
580 Ken Hill .05
581 Rex Hudler .05
582 Felix Jose .05
583 Ray Lankford .05
584 Omar Olivares .05
585 Jose Oquendo .05
586 Tom Pagnozzi .05
587 Geronimo Pena .05
588 Mike Perez .05
589 Gerald Perry .05
590 Bryn Smith .05
591 Lee Smith .05
592 Ozzie Smith .55
593 Scott Terry .05
594 Bob Tewksbury .05
595 Milt Thompson .05
596 Todd Zeile .05
597 Larry Andersen .05
598 Oscar Azocar .05
599 Andy Benes .05
600 Ricky Bones **RC** .05
601 Jerald Clark .05
602 Pat Clements .05
603 Paul Faries .05
604 Tony Fernandez .05
605 Tony Gwynn .55
606 Greg Harris .05
607 Thomas Howard .05
608 Bruce Hurst .05
609 Darrin Jackson .05
610 Tom Lampkin .05
611 Craig Lefferts .05
612 Jim Lewis **RC** .05
613 Mike Maddux .05
614 Fred McGriff .05
615 Jose Melendez **RC** .05
616 Jose Mota **RC** .05
617 Dennis Rasmussen .05
618 Bip Roberts .05
619 Rich Rodriguez .05
620 Benito Santiago .05
621 Craig Shipley **RC** .05
622 Tim Teufel .05
623 Kevin Ward **RC** .05
624 Ed Whitson .05
625 Dave Anderson .05
626 Kevin Bass .05
627 Rod Beck **RC** .10
628 Bud Black .05
629 Jeff Brantley .05
630 John Burkett .05
631 Will Clark .05
632 Royce Clayton **RC** .05
633 Steve Decker .05
634 Kelly Downs .05
635 Mike Felder .05
636 Scott Garrelts .05
637 Eric Gunderson .05
638 Bryan Hickerson **RC** .05
639 Darren Lewis .05
640 Greg Litton .05
641 Kirt Manwaring .05
642 Paul McClellan **RC** .05
643 Willie McGee .05
644 Kevin Mitchell .05
645 Francisco Olivares .05
646 Mike Remlinger **RC** .10
647 Dave Righetti .05
648 Robby Thompson .05
649 Jose Uribe .05
650 Matt Williams .05
651 Trevor Wilson .05
652 Tom Goodwin **RC** (Prospects) .05
653 Terry Bross **RC** (Prospects) .05
654 Mike Christopher **RC** (Prospects) .05
655 Kenny Lofton (Prospects) .05
656 Chris Cron **RC** (Prospects) .05
657 Willie Banks **RC** (Prospects) .05
658 Pat Rice **RC** (Prospects) .05
659a Rob Mauer **RC** (Prospects) (Last name misspelled.) .75
659b Rob Maurer **RC** (Prospects) (Corrected)) .05
660 Don Harris **RC** (Prospects) .05
661 Henry Rodriguez (Prospects) .05
662 Cliff Brantley **RC** (Prospects) .05
663 Mike Linskey **RC** (Prospects) .05
664 Gary Disarcina **RC** (Prospects) .05
665 Gil Heredia **RC** (Prospects) .10
666 Vinny Castilla **RC** (Prospects) .50
667 Paul Abbott **RC** (Prospects) .05
668 Monty Fariss **RC** (Prospects) .05
669 Jarvis Brown **RC** (Prospects) .05
670 Wayne Kirby **RC** (Prospects) .05
671 Scott Brosius **RC** (Prospects) .05
672 Bob Hamelin (Prospects) .05
673 Joel Johnston **RC** (Prospects) .05
674 Tim Spehr **RC** (Prospects) .05
675 Jeff Gardner **RC** (Prospects) .05
676 Rico Rossy **RC** (Prospects) .05
677 Roberto Hernandez **RC** (Prospects) .20
678 Ted Wood **RC** (Prospects) .05
679 Cal Eldred (Prospects) .05
680 Sean Berry **RC** (Prospects) .05
681 Rickey Henderson (Stolen Base Record) .20
682 Nolan Ryan (Record 7th No-hitter) .25
683 Dennis Martinez (Perfect Game) .05
684 Wilson Alvarez (Rookie No-hitter) .05
685 Joe Carter (3 100 RBI Seasons) .05
686 Dave Winfield (400 Home Runs) .20
687 David Cone (Ties NL Record Strikeouts) .05
688 Jose Canseco (League Leaders) .15
689 Howard Johnson (League Leaders) .05
690 Julio Franco (League Leaders) .05
691 Terry Pendleton (League Leaders) .05
692 Cecil Fielder (League Leaders) .05
693 Scott Erickson (League Leaders) .05
694 Tom Glavine (League Leaders) .05
695 Dennis Martinez (League Leaders) .05
696 Bryan Harvey (League Leaders) .05
697 Lee Smith (League Leaders) .05
698 Super Siblings (Roberto & Sandy Alomar, Roberto & Sandy Alomar) .10
699 The Indispensables (Bobby Bonilla, Will Clark) .05
700 Teamwork (Mark Wohlers, Kent Mercker, Alejandro Pena) .05
701 Tiger Tandems (Chris Jones, Bo Jackson, Gregg Olson, Frank Thomas) .05
702 The Ignitors (Brett Butler, Paul Molitor) .10
703 The Indispensables II (Cal Ripken Jr., Joe Carter) .20
704 Power Packs (Barry Larkin, Kirby Puckett) .15
705 Today and Tomorrow (Mo Vaughn, Cecil Fielder) .05
706 Teenage Sensations (Ramon Martinez, Ozzie Guillen) .05
707 Designated Hitters (Harold Baines, Wade Boggs) .20
708 Robin Yount (ProVision) .35
709 Ken Griffey Jr. (ProVision) .60
710 Nolan Ryan (ProVision) .75
711 Cal Ripken, Jr. (ProVision) .75
712 Frank Thomas (ProVision) .50
713 Dave Justice (ProVision) .05
714 Checklist 1-101 .05
715 Checklist 102-194 .05
716 Checklist 195-296 .05
717 Checklist 297-397 .05
718 Checklist 398-494 .05
719 Checklist 495-596 .05
720a Checklist 597-720 (659 Rob Mauer) .05
720b Checklist 597-720 (659 Rob Maurer) .05

All-Stars

Black borders with gold highlights are featured on these special wax pack insert cards. The fronts feature glossy action photos with a portrait photo inset. Backs feature career highlights.

		NM/M
Complete Set (24):		8.00
Common Player:		.10
1	Felix Jose	.10
2	Tony Gwynn	1.25
3	Barry Bonds	3.00
4	Bobby Bonilla	.10
5	Mike LaValliere	.10
6	Tom Glavine	.40
7	Ramon Martinez	.10
8	Lee Smith	.10
9	Mickey Tettleton	.10
10	Scott Erickson	.10
11	Frank Thomas	.75
12	Danny Tartabull	.10
13	Will Clark	.10
14	Ryne Sandberg	1.25

15	Terry Pendleton	.10
16	Barry Larkin	.10
17	Rafael Palmeiro	.65
18	Julio Franco	.10
19	Robin Ventura	.10
20	Cal Ripken, Jr.	3.00
21	Joe Carter	.10
22	Kirby Puckett	1.25
23	Ken Griffey Jr.	2.25
24	Jose Canseco	.50

Roger Clemens

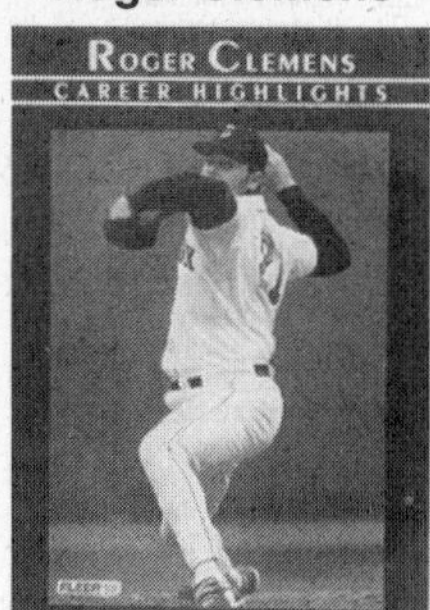

This set chronicles the career highlights of Roger Clemens. The initial 12 cards from the set were inserted in 1992 Fleer wax packs. A limited number of autographed cards were inserted as well. The additional three cards from the set were available through a mail-in offer. The card fronts feature black borders with metallic gold type. The flip side is yellow with black borders.

		NM/M
Complete Set (15):		6.00
Common Card:		.50
Autographed Card:		40.00
1	Quiet Storm	.50
2	Courted by the Mets and Twins	.50
3	The Show	.50
4	A Rocket Launched	.50
5	Time of Trial	.50
6	Break Through	.50
7	Play it Again Roger	.50
8	Business as Usual	.50
9	Heee's Back	.50
10	Blood, Sweat and Tears	.50
11	Prime of Life	.50
12	Man for Every Season	.50
13	Cooperstown Bound	1.50
14	The Heat of the Moment	1.50
15	Final Words	1.50

Lumber Co.

Baseball's top power hitters at each position are featured in this nine-card set. Fronts feature full-color action photos bordered in black. Backs feature posed player photos and career highlights. The set was included only in factory sets released to the hobby trade.

		NM/M
Complete Set (9):		5.00
Common Player:		.25
1	Cecil Fielder	.25
2	Mickey Tettleton	.25
3	Darryl Strawberry	.25
4	Ryne Sandberg	1.00
5	Jose Canseco	.40
6	Matt Williams	.25
7	Cal Ripken, Jr.	2.00
8	Barry Bonds	2.00
9	Ron Gant	.25

Rookie Sensations

This 20-card set features the top rookies of 1991 and rookie prospects from 1992. The card fronts feature blue borders with "Rookie Sensations" in gold along the top border. The flip sides feature background information on the player. The cards were randomly inserted in 1992 Fleer cello packs. This issue saw very high prices when initially released then suffered long-term declines as the hobby became inundated with more and more insert sets.

		NM/M
Complete Set (20):		13.50
Common Player:		.35
1	Frank Thomas	6.00
2	Todd Van Poppel	.35
3	Orlando Merced	.35
4	Jeff Bagwell	6.00
5	Jeff Fassero	.35
6	Darren Lewis	.35
7	Milt Cuyler	.35
8	Miko Timlin	.35
9	Brian McRae	.35
10	Chuck Knoblauch	.35
11	Rich DeLucia	.35
12	Ivan Rodriguez	4.50
13	Juan Guzman	.35
14	Steve Chitren	.35
15	Mark Wohlers	.35
16	Wes Chamberlain	.35
17	Ray Lankford	.35
18	Chito Martinez	.35
19	Phil Plantier	.35
20	Scott Leius	.35

Smoke 'N Heat

This 12-card set of top pitchers was included in factory sets designated for sale within the general retail trade. Card numbers have an "S" prefix.

		NM/M
Complete Set (12):		7.50
Common Player:		.25
1	Lee Smith	.25
2	Jack McDowell	.25
3	David Cone	.25
4	Roger Clemens	2.00
5	Nolan Ryan	3.00
6	Scott Erickson	.25
7	Tom Glavine	.50
8	Dwight Gooden	.25
9	Andy Benes	.25
10	Steve Avery	.25
11	Randy Johnson	1.00
12	Jim Abbott	.25

Team Leaders

White and green borders highlight this insert set from Fleer. The card fronts also feature a special gold-foil "team leaders" logo beneath the full-color player photo. The card backs feature player

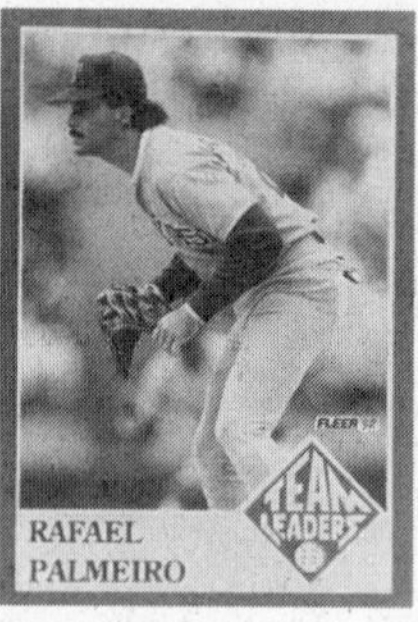

information. The cards were randomly inserted in 1992 Fleer rack packs.

		NM/M
Complete Set (20):		10.00
Common Player:		.50
1	Don Mattingly	2.00
2	Howard Johnson	.50
3	Chris Sabo	.50
4	Carlton Fisk	1.25
5	Kirby Puckett	1.50
6	Cecil Fielder	.50
7	Tony Gwynn	1.50
8	Will Clark	.50
9	Bobby Bonilla	.50
10	Len Dykstra	.50
11	Tom Glavine	.75
12	Rafael Palmeiro	1.00
13	Wade Boggs	1.50
14	Joe Carter	.50
15	Ken Griffey Jr.	2.50
16	Darryl Strawberry	.50
17	Cal Ripken, Jr.	3.00
18	Danny Tartabull	.50
19	Jose Canseco	.75
20	Andre Dawson	.50

Update

This 132-card set was released in boxed set form and features traded players, free agents and top rookies from 1992. The cards are styled after the regular 1992 Fleer and are numbered alphabetically according to team. This set marks the ninth year that Fleer has released an update set. The set includes four black-bordered "Headliner" cards.

		NM/M
Complete Set (136):		60.00
Common Player:		.05
H1	1992 All-Star Game MVP (Ken Griffey Jr.)	1.50
H2	3000 Career Hits (Robin Yount)	.50
H3	Major League Career Saves Record (Jeff Reardon)	.10
H4	Record RBI Performance (Cecil Fielder)	.05
1	Todd Frohwirth	.05
2	Alan Mills	.05
3	Rick Sutcliffe	.05
4	John Valentin **RC**	.25
5	Frank Viola	.05
6	Bob Zupcic **RC**	.05
7	Mike Butcher **RC**	.05
8	Chad Curtis **RC**	.50
9	Damion Easley **RC**	.25
10	Tim Salmon **RC**	.50
11	Julio Valera	.05
12	George Bell	.05
13	Roberto Hernandez **RC**	.05
14	Shawn Jeter **RC**	.05
15	Thomas Howard	.05
16	Jesse Levis **RC**	.05
17	Kenny Lofton	.05
18	Paul Sorrento	.05
19	Rico Brogna **RC**	.05
20	John Doherty **RC**	.05
21	Dan Gladden	.05
22	Buddy Groom **RC**	.05
23	Shawn Hare **RC**	.05
24	John Kiely **RC**	.05
25	Kurt Knudsen **RC**	.05
26	Gregg Jefferies	.05
27	Wally Joyner	.05
28	Kevin Koslofski **RC**	.05
29	Kevin McReynolds	.05
30	Rusty Meacham	.05
31	Keith Miller	.05
32	Hipolito Pichardo **RC**	.05
33	James Austin **RC**	.05
34	Scott Fletcher	.05
35	John Jaha **RC**	.05
36	Pat Listach **RC**	.05
37	Dave Nilsson **RC**	.05
38	Kevin Seitzer	.05
39	Tom Edens	.05
40	Pat Mahomes **RC**	.05
41	John Smiley	.05
42	Charlie Hayes	.05
43	Sam Militello **RC**	.05
44	Andy Stankiewicz **RC**	.05
45	Danny Tartabull	.05
46	Bob Wickman **RC**	.05
47	Jerry Browne	.05
48	Kevin Campbell **RC**	.05
49	Vince Horsman **RC**	.05
50	Troy Neel **RC**	.05
51	Ruben Sierra	.05
52	Bruce Walton **RC**	.05
53	Willie Wilson	.05
54	Bret Boone **RC**	.50
55	Dave Fleming **RC**	.05
56	Kevin Mitchell	.05
57	Jeff Nelson **RC**	.05
58	Shane Turner **RC**	.05
59	Jose Canseco	.65
60	Jeff Frye **RC**	.05
61	Damilo Leon **RC**	.05
62	Roger Pavlik **RC**	.05
63	David Cone	.05
64	Pat Hentgen **RC**	.05
65	Randy Knorr **RC**	.05
66	Jack Morris	.05
67	Dave Winfield	1.00
68	David Nied **RC**	.05
69	Otis Nixon	.05
70	Alejandro Pena	.05
71	Jeff Reardon	.05
72	Alex Arias **RC**	.05
73	Jim Bullinger **RC**	.05
74	Mike Morgan	.05
75	Rey Sanchez **RC**	.05
76	Bob Scanlan	.05
77	Sammy Sosa	3.00
78	Scott Bankhead	.05
79	Tim Belcher	.05
80	Steve Foster **RC**	.05
81	Willie Greene **RC**	.05
82	Bip Roberts	.05
83	Scott Ruskin	.05
84	Greg Swindell	.05
85	Juan Guerrero **RC**	.05
86	Butch Henry **RC**	.05
87	Doug Jones	.05
88	Brian Williams **RC**	.05
89	Tom Candiotti	.05
90	Eric Davis	.05
91	Carlos Hernandez **RC**	.05
92	Mike Piazza **RC**	45.00
93	Mike Sharperson	.05
94	Eric Young **RC**	.05
95	Moises Alou	.05
96	Greg Colbrunn	.05
97	Wil Cordero **RC**	.05
98	Ken Hill	.05
99	John Vander Wal **RC**	.05
100	John Wetteland	.05
101	Bobby Bonilla	.05
102	Eric Hilman **RC**	.05
103	Pat Howell **RC**	.05
104	Jeff Kent **RC**	15.00
105	Dick Schofield	.05
106	Ryan Thompson **RC**	.05
107	Chico Walker	.05
108	Juan Bell	.05
109	Mariano Duncan	.05
110	Jeff Grotewold **RC**	.05
111	Ben Rivera **RC**	.05
112	Curt Schilling	.65
113	Victor Cole **RC**	.05
114	Al Martin **RC**	.05
115	Roger Mason	.05
116	Blas Minor **RC**	.05
117	Tim Wakefield **RC**	4.00
118	Mark Clark **RC**	.05
119	Rheal Cormier **RC**	.05
120	Donovan Osborne **RC**	.05
121	Todd Worrell	.05
122	Jeremy Hernandez **RC**	.05
123	Randy Myers	.05
124	Frank Seminara **RC**	.05
125	Gary Sheffield	.75
126	Dan Walters **RC**	.05
127	Steve Hosey **RC**	.05
128	Mike Jackson	.05
129	Jim Pena **RC**	.05
130	Cory Snyder	.05
131	Bill Swift	.05
132	Checklist	.05

7-Eleven

The 1992 Performer Collection was a combined effort from Fleer and 7-11. Customers at 7-11 stores received a packet of five cards with gas-

oline purchases to build the 24-card set of major stars. The cards are standard size, with virtually the identical design to the regular issue Fleer set of 1992, with only the addition of "The Performer" logo on the front of the card and a pair of sponsors' logos on back.

		NM/M
Complete Set (24):		9.00
Common Player:		.20
1	Nolan Ryan	1.50
2	Frank Thomas	.65
3	Ryne Sandberg	.75
4	Ken Griffey Jr.	1.00
5	Cal Ripken, Jr.	1.50
6	Roger Clemens	.85
7	Cecil Fielder	.20
8	Dave Justice	.20
9	Wade Boggs	.75
10	Tony Gwynn	.75
11	Kirby Puckett	.75
12	Darryl Strawberry	.20
13	Jose Canseco	.50
14	Barry Larkin	.20
15	Terry Pendleton	.20
16	Don Mattingly	.85
17	Rickey Henderson	.65
18	Ruben Sierra	.20
19	Jeff Bagwell	.65
20	Tom Glavine	.45
21	Ramon Martinez	.20
22	Will Clark	.20
23	Barry Bonds	1.50
24	Roberto Alomar	.40

1993 Fleer

The card fronts feature silver borders with the player's name, team and position in a banner along the left side of the card. The backs feature an action photo of the player with his name in bold behind him. A box featuring biographical information, statistics and player information is located to the right of the action photo. The cards are numbered alphabetically by team. The basic Fleer issue for 1993 was issued in two series of 360 cards each. The 720-card set included a number of subsets and could be found in many different types of packaging with an unprecedented number of inserts sets to spice up each offering.

		NM/M
Complete Set (720):		10.00
Common Player:		.05
Series 1 or 2 Pack (15):		.50
Series 1 or 2 Box (36):		12.50
1	Steve Avery	.05
2	Sid Bream	.05
3	Ron Gant	.05
4	Tom Glavine	.25
5	Brian Hunter	.05
6	Ryan Klesko	.05
7	Charlie Leibrandt	.05
8	Kent Mercker	.05
9	David Nied	.05
10	Otis Nixon	.05
11	Greg Olson	.05
12	Terry Pendleton	.05
13	Deion Sanders	.10
14	John Smoltz	.05
15	Mike Stanton	.05
16	Mark Wohlers	.05
17	Paul Assenmacher	.05
18	Steve Buechele	.05
19	Shawon Dunston	.05
20	Mark Grace	.05
21	Derrick May	.05
22	Chuck McElroy	.05
23	Mike Morgan	.05
24	Rey Sanchez	.05
25	Ryne Sandberg	.60
26	Bob Scanlan	.05
27	Sammy Sosa	.60
28	Rick Wilkins	.05
29	Bobby Ayala **RC**	.05
30	Tim Belcher	.05
31	Jeff Branson **RC**	.05
32	Norm Charlton	.05
33	Steve Foster **RC**	.05
34	Willie Greene **RC**	.05
35	Chris Hammond	.05
36	Milt Hill **RC**	.05
37	Hal Morris	.05
38	Joe Oliver	.05
39	Paul O'Neill	.05
40	Tim Pugh **RC**	.05
41	Jose Rijo	.05
42	Bip Roberts	.05
43	Chris Sabo	.05
44	Reggie Sanders	.05
45	Eric Anthony	.05
46	Jeff Bagwell	.50
47	Craig Biggio	.05
48	Joe Boever	.05
49	Casey Candaele	.05
50	Steve Finley	.05
51	Luis Gonzalez	.05
52	Pete Harnisch	.05
53	Xavier Hernandez	.05
54	Doug Jones	.05
55	Eddie Taubensee	.05
56	Brian Williams	.05
57	Pedro Astacio **RC**	.10
58	Todd Benzinger	.05
59	Brett Butler	.05
60	Tom Candiotti	.05
61	Lenny Harris	.05
62	Carlos Hernandez	.05
63	Orel Hershiser	.05
64	Eric Karros	.05
65	Ramon Martinez	.05
66	Jose Offerman	.05
67	Mike Scioscia	.05
68	Mike Sharperson	.05
69	Eric Young **RC**	.10
70	Moises Alou	.05
71	Ivan Calderon	.05
72	Archi Cianfrocco **RC**	.05
73	Wil Cordero	.05
74	Delino DeShields	.05
75	Mark Gardner	.05
76	Ken Hill	.05
77	Tim Laker **RC**	.05
78	Chris Nabholz	.05
79	Mel Rojas	.05
80	John Vander Wal **RC**	.10
81	Larry Walker	.05
82	Tim Wallach	.05
83	John Wetteland	.05
84	Bobby Bonilla	.05
85	Daryl Boston	.05
86	Sid Fernandez	.05
87	Eric Hillman **RC**	.05
88	Todd Hundley	.05
89	Howard Johnson	.05
90	Jeff Kent	.05
91	Eddie Murray	.50
92	Bill Pecota	.05
93	Bret Saberhagen	.05
94	Dick Schofield	.05
95	Pete Schourek	.05
96	Anthony Young	.05
97	Ruben Amaro Jr.	.05
98	Juan Bell	.05
99	Wes Chamberlain	.05
100	Darren Daulton	.05
101	Mariano Duncan	.05
102	Mike Hartley	.05
103	Ricky Jordan	.05
104	John Kruk	.05
105	Mickey Morandini	.05
106	Terry Mulholland	.05
107	Ben Rivera **RC**	.05
108	Curt Schilling	.25
109	Keith Shepherd **RC**	.05
110	Stan Belinda	.05
111	Jay Bell	.05
112	Barry Bonds	1.00
113	Jeff King	.05
114	Mike LaValliere	.05
115	Jose Lind	.05
116	Roger Mason	.05
117	Orlando Merced	.05
118	Bob Patterson	.05
119	Don Slaught	.05
120	Zane Smith	.05
121	Randy Tomlin	.05
122	Andy Van Slyke	.05
123	Tim Wakefield **RC**	.10
124	Rheal Cormier	.05

125 Bernard Gilkey .05
126 Felix Jose .05
127 Ray Lankford .05
128 Bob McClure .05
129 Donovan Osborne .05
130 Tom Pagnozzi .05
131 Geronimo Pena .05
132 Mike Perez .05
133 Lee Smith .05
134 Bob Tewksbury .05
135 Todd Worrell .05
136 Todd Zeile .05
137 Jerald Clark .05
138 Tony Gwynn .60
139 Greg Harris .05
140 Jeremy Hernandez .05
141 Darrin Jackson .05
142 Mike Maddux .05
143 Fred McGriff .05
144 Jose Melendez .05
145 Rich Rodriguez .05
146 Frank Seminara .05
147 Gary Sheffield .35
148 Kurt Stillwell .05
149 Dan Walters **RC** .05
150 Rod Beck .05
151 Bud Black .05
152 Jeff Brantley .05
153 John Burkett .05
154 Will Clark .05
155 Royce Clayton .05
156 Mike Jackson .05
157 Darren Lewis .05
158 Kirt Manwaring .05
159 Willie McGee .05
160 Cory Snyder .05
161 Bill Swift .05
162 Trevor Wilson .05
163 Brady Anderson .05
164 Glenn Davis .05
165 Mike Devereaux .05
166 Todd Frohwirth .05
167 Leo Gomez .05
168 Chris Hoiles .05
169 Ben McDonald .05
170 Randy Milligan .05
171 Alan Mills .05
172 Mike Mussina .30
173 Gregg Olson .05
174 Arthur Rhodes .05
175 David Segui .05
176 Ellis Burks .05
177 Roger Clemens .65
178 Scott Cooper .05
179 Danny Darwin .05
180 Tony Fossas .05
181 Paul Quantrill **RC** .10
182 Jody Reed .05
183 John Valentin **RC** .10
184 Mo Vaughn .05
185 Frank Viola .05
186 Bob Zupcic .05
187 Jim Abbott .05
188 Gary DiSarcina .05
189 Damion Easley **RC** .10
190 Junior Felix .05
191 Chuck Finley .05
192 Joe Grahe .05
193 Bryan Harvey .05
194 Mark Langston .05
195 John Orton .05
196 Luis Polonia .05
197 Tim Salmon .05
198 Luis Sojo .05
199 Wilson Alvarez .05
200 George Bell .05
201 Alex Fernandez .05
202 Craig Grebeck .05
203 Ozzie Guillen .05
204 Lance Johnson .05
205 Ron Karkovice .05
206 Kirk McCaskill .05
207 Jack McDowell .05
208 Scott Radinsky .05
209 Tim Raines .05
210 Frank Thomas .50
211 Robin Ventura .05
212 Sandy Alomar Jr. .05
213 Carlos Baerga .05
214 Dennis Cook .05
215 Thomas Howard .05
216 Mark Lewis .05
217 Derek Lilliquist .05
218 Kenny Lofton .05
219 Charles Nagy .05
220 Steve Olin .05
221 Paul Sorrento .05
222 Jim Thome .40
223 Mark Whiten .05
224 Milt Cuyler .05
225 Rob Deer .05
226 John Doherty **RC** .05
227 Cecil Fielder .05
228 Travis Fryman .05
229 Mike Henneman .05
230 John Kiely **RC** .05
231 Kurt Knudsen **RC** .05
232 Scott Livingstone .05
233 Tony Phillips .05
234 Mickey Tettleton .05
235 Kevin Appier .05
236 George Brett .65
237 Tom Gordon .05
238 Gregg Jefferies .05
239 Wally Joyner .05
240 Kevin Koslofski **RC** .05
241 Mike Macfarlane .05
242 Brian McRae .05
243 Rusty Meacham .05
244 Keith Miller .05
245 Jeff Montgomery .05
246 Hipolito Pichardo **RC** .05
247 Ricky Bones .05
248 Cal Eldred .05
249 Mike Fetters .05
250 Darryl Hamilton .05
251 Doug Henry .05
252 John Jaha **RC** .05
253 Pat Listach .05
254 Paul Molitor .50
255 Jaime Navarro .05
256 Kevin Seitzer .05
257 B.J. Surhoff .05
258 Greg Vaughn .05
259 Bill Wegman .05
260 Robin Yount .50
261 Rick Aguilera .05
262 Chili Davis .05
263 Scott Erickson .05
264 Greg Gagne .05
265 Mark Guthrie .05
266 Brian Harper .05
267 Kent Hrbek .05
268 Terry Jorgensen .05
269 Gene Larkin .05
270 Scott Leius .05
271 Pat Mahomes .05
272 Pedro Munoz .05
273 Kirby Puckett .60
274 Kevin Tapani .05
275 Carl Willis .05
276 Steve Farr .05
277 John Habyan .05
278 Mel Hall .05
279 Charlie Hayes .05
280 Pat Kelly .05
281 Don Mattingly .65
282 Sam Militello .05
283 Matt Nokes .05
284 Melido Perez .05
285 Andy Stankiewicz .05
286 Danny Tartabull .05
287 Randy Velarde .05
288 Bob Wickman .05
289 Bernie Williams .05
290 Lance Blankenship .05
291 Mike Bordick .05
292 Jerry Browne .05
293 Dennis Eckersley .40
294 Rickey Henderson .50
295 Vince Horsman **RC** .05
296 Mark McGwire .85
297 Jeff Parrett .05
298 Ruben Sierra .05
299 Terry Steinbach .05
300 Walt Weiss .05
301 Bob Welch .05
302 Willie Wilson .05
303 Bobby Witt .05
304 Bret Boone .05
305 Jay Buhner .05
306 Dave Fleming .05
307 Ken Griffey Jr. .75
308 Erik Hanson .05
309 Edgar Martinez .05
310 Tino Martinez .05
311 Jeff Nelson .05
312 Dennis Powell .05
313 Mike Schooler .05
314 Russ Swan .05
315 Dave Valle .05
316 Omar Vizquel .05
317 Kevin Brown .05
318 Todd Burns .05
319 Jose Canseco .35
320 Julio Franco .05
321 Jeff Frye .05
322 Juan Gonzalez .30
323 Jose Guzman .05
324 Jeff Huson .05
325 Dean Palmer .05
326 Kevin Reimer .05
327 Ivan Rodriguez .40
328 Kenny Rogers .05
329 Dan Smith **RC** .05
330 Roberto Alomar .20
331 Derek Bell .05
332 Pat Borders .05
333 Joe Carter .05
334 Kelly Gruber .05
335 Tom Henke .05
336 Jimmy Key .05
337 Manuel Lee .05
338 Candy Maldonado .05
339 John Olerud .05
340 Todd Stottlemyre .05
341 Duane Ward .05
342 Devon White .05
343 Dave Winfield .50
344 Edgar Martinez (League Leaders) .05
345 Cecil Fielder (League Leaders) .05
346 Kenny Lofton (League Leaders) .05
347 Jack Morris (League Leaders) .05
348 Roger Clemens (League Leaders) .35
349 Fred McGriff (Round Trippers) .05
350 Barry Bonds (Round Trippers) .60
351 Gary Sheffield (Round Trippers) .05
352 Darren Daulton (Round Trippers) .05
353 Dave Hollins (Round Trippers) .05
354 Brothers In Blue (Pedro Martinez, Ramon Martinez) .25
355 Power Packs (Ivan Rodriguez, Kirby Puckett) .25
356 Triple Threats (Ryne Sandberg, Gary Sheffield) .20
357 Infield Trifecta (Roberto Alomar, Chuck Knoblauch, Carlos Baerga) .05
358 Checklist .05
359 Checklist .05
360 Checklist .05
361 Rafael Belliard .05
362 Damon Berryhill .05
363 Mike Bielecki .05
364 Jeff Blauser .05
365 Francisco Cabrera .05
366 Marvin Freeman .05
367 Dave Justice .05
368 Mark Lemke .05
369 Alejandro Pena .05
370 Jeff Reardon .05
371 Lonnie Smith .05
372 Pete Smith .05
373 Shawn Boskie .05
374 Jim Bullinger .05
375 Frank Castillo .05
376 Doug Dascenzo .05
377 Andre Dawson .25
378 Mike Harkey .05
379 Greg Hibbard .05
380 Greg Maddux .60
381 Ken Patterson .05
382 Jeff Robinson .05
383 Luis Salazar .05
384 Dwight Smith .05
385 Jose Vizcaino .05
386 Scott Bankhead .05
387 Tom Browning .05
388 Darnell Coles .05
389 Rob Dibble .05
390 Bill Doran .05
391 Dwayne Henry .05
392 Cesar Hernandez .05
393 Roberto Kelly .05
394 Barry Larkin .05
395 Dave Martinez .05
396 Kevin Mitchell .05
397 Jeff Reed .05
398 Scott Ruskin .05
399 Greg Swindell .05
400 Dan Wilson .05
401 Andy Ashby .05
402 Freddie Benavides .05
403 Dante Bichette .05
404 Willie Blair .05
405 Denis Boucher .05
406 Vinny Castilla .05
407 Braulio Castillo .05
408 Alex Cole .05
409 Andres Galarraga .05
410 Joe Girardi .05
411 Butch Henry .05
412 Darren Holmes .05
413 Calvin Jones .05
414 Steve Reed **RC** .05
415 Kevin Ritz .05
416 Jim Tatum **RC** .05
417 Jack Armstrong .05
418 Bret Barberie .05
419 Ryan Bowen .05
420 Cris Carpenter .05
421 Chuck Carr .05
422 Scott Chiamparino .05
423 Jeff Conine .05
424 Jim Corsi .05
425 Steve Decker .05
426 Chris Donnels .05
427 Monty Fariss .05
428 Bob Natal .05
429 Pat Rapp **RC** .05
430 Dave Weathers .05
431 Nigel Wilson **RC** .05
432 Ken Caminiti .05
433 Andujar Cedeno .05
434 Tom Edens .05
435 Juan Guerrero .05
436 Pete Incaviglia .05
437 Jimmy Jones .05
438 Darryl Kile .05
439 Rob Murphy .05
440 Al Osuna .05
441 Mark Portugal .05
442 Scott Servais .05
443 John Candelaria .05
444 Tim Crews .05
445 Eric Davis .05
446 Tom Goodwin .05
447 Jim Gott .05
448 Kevin Gross .05
449 Dave Hansen .05
450 Jay Howell .05
451 Roger McDowell .05
452 Bob Ojeda .05
453 Henry Rodriguez .05
454 Darryl Strawberry .05
455 Mitch Webster .05
456 Steve Wilson .05
457 Brian Barnes .05
458 Sean Berry .05
459 Jeff Fassero .05
460 Darrin Fletcher .05
461 Marquis Grissom .05
462 Dennis Martinez .05
463 Spike Owen .05
464 Matt Stairs .05
465 Sergio Valdez .05
466 Kevin Bass .05
467 Vince Coleman .05
468 Mark Dewey .05
469 Kevin Elster .05
470 Tony Fernandez .05
471 John Franco .05
472 Dave Gallagher .05
473 Paul Gibson .05
474 Dwight Gooden .05
475 Lee Guetterman .05
476 Jeff Innis .05
477 Dave Magadan .05
478 Charlie O'Brien .05
479 Willie Randolph .05
480 Mackey Sasser .05
481 Ryan Thompson .05
482 Chico Walker .05
483 Kyle Abbott .05
484 Bob Ayrault .05
485 Kim Batiste .05
486 Cliff Brantley .05
487 Jose DeLeon .05
488 Len Dykstra .05
489 Tommy Greene .05
490 Jeff Grotewold .05
491 Dave Hollins .05
492 Danny Jackson .05
493 Stan Javier .05
494 Tom Marsh .05
495 Greg Matthews .05
496 Dale Murphy .15
497 Todd Pratt **RC** .05
498 Mitch Williams .05
499 Danny Cox .05
500 Doug Drabek .05
501 Carlos Garcia .05
502 Lloyd McClendon .05
503 Denny Neagle .05
504 Gary Redus .05
505 Bob Walk .05
506 John Wehner .05
507 Luis Alicea .05
508 Mark Clark .05
509 Pedro Guerrero .05
510 Rex Hudler .05
511 Brian Jordan .05
512 Omar Olivares .05
513 Jose Oquendo .05
514 Gerald Perry .05
515 Bryn Smith .05
516 Craig Wilson .05
517 Tracy Woodson .05
518 Larry Andersen .05
519 Andy Benes .05
520 Jim Deshaies .05
521 Bruce Hurst .05
522 Randy Myers .05
523 Benito Santiago .05
524 Tim Scott .05
525 Tim Teufel .05
526 Mike Benjamin .05
527 Dave Burba .05
528 Craig Colbert .05
529 Mike Felder .05
530 Bryan Hickerson .05
531 Chris James .05
532 Mark Leonard .05
533 Greg Litton .05
534 Francisco Oliveras .05
535 John Patterson .05
536 Jim Pena .05
537 Dave Righetti .05
538 Robby Thompson .05
539 Jose Uribe .05
540 Matt Williams .05
541 Storm Davis .05
542 Sam Horn .05
543 Tim Hulett .05
544 Craig Lefferts .05
545 Chito Martinez .05
546 Mark McLemore .05
547 Luis Mercedes .05
548 Bob Milacki .05
549 Joe Orsulak .05
550 Billy Ripken .05
551 Cal Ripken, Jr. 1.00
552 Rick Sutcliffe .05
553 Jeff Tackett .05
554 Wade Boggs .60
555 Tom Brunansky .05
556 Jack Clark .05
557 John Dopson .05
558 Mike Gardiner .05
559 Mike Greenwell .05
560 Greg Harris .05
561 Billy Hatcher .05
562 Joe Hesketh .05
563 Tony Pena .05
564 Phil Plantier .05
565 Luis Rivera .05
566 Herm Winningham .05
567 Matt Young .05
568 Bert Blyleven .05
569 Mike Butcher .05
570 Chuck Crim .05
571 Chad Curtis **RC** .15
572 Tim Fortugno .05
573 Steve Frey .05
574 Gary Gaetti .05
575 Scott Lewis .05
576 Lee Stevens .05
577 Ron Tingley .05
578 Julio Valera .05
579 Shawn Abner .05
580 Joey Cora .05
581 Chris Cron .05
582 Carlton Fisk .50
583 Roberto Hernandez .05
584 Charlie Hough .05
585 Terry Leach .05
586 Donn Pall .05
587 Dan Pasqua .05
588 Steve Sax .05
589 Bobby Thigpen .05
590 Albert Belle .05
591 Felix Fermin .05
592 Glenallen Hill .05
593 Brook Jacoby .05
594 Reggie Jefferson .05
595 Carlos Martinez .05
596 Jose Mesa .05
597 Rod Nichols .05
598 Junior Ortiz .05
599 Eric Plunk .05
600 Ted Power .05
601 Scott Scudder .05
602 Kevin Wickander .05
603 Skeeter Barnes .05
604 Mark Carreon .05
605 Dan Gladden .05
606 Bill Gullickson .05
607 Chad Kreuter .05
608 Mark Leiter .05
609 Mike Munoz .05
610 Rich Rowland .05
611 Frank Tanana .05
612 Walt Terrell .05
613 Alan Trammell .05
614 Lou Whitaker .05
615 Luis Aquino .05
616 Mike Boddicker .05
617 Jim Eisenreich .05
618 Mark Gubicza .05
619 David Howard .05
620 Mike Magnante .05
621 Brent Mayne .05
622 Kevin McReynolds .05
623 Eddie Pierce **RC** .05
624 Bill Sampen .05
625 Steve Shifflett .05
626 Gary Thurman .05
627 Curtis Wilkerson .05
628 Chris Bosio .05
629 Scott Fletcher .05
630 Jim Gantner .05
631 Dave Nilsson .05
632 Jesse Orosco .05
633 Dan Plesac .05
634 Ron Robinson .05
635 Bill Spiers .05
636 Franklin Stubbs .05
637 Willie Banks .05
638 Randy Bush .05
639 Chuck Knoblauch .05
640 Shane Mack .05
641 Mike Pagliarulo .05
642 Jeff Reboulet .05
643 John Smiley .05
644 Mike Trombley **RC** .05
645 Gary Wayne .05
646 Lenny Webster .05
647 Tim Burke .05
648 Mike Gallego .05
649 Dion James .05
650 Jeff Johnson .05
651 Scott Kamieniecki .05
652 Kevin Maas .05
653 Rich Monteleone .05
654 Jerry Nielsen .05
655 Scott Sanderson .05
656 Mike Stanley .05
657 Gerald Williams .05
658 Curt Young .05
659 Harold Baines .05
660 Kevin Campbell .05
661 Ron Darling .05
662 Kelly Downs .05
663 Eric Fox .05
664 Dave Henderson .05
665 Rick Honeycutt .05
666 Mike Moore .05
667 Jamie Quirk .05
668 Jeff Russell .05
669 Dave Stewart .05
670 Greg Briley .05
671 Dave Cochrane .05
672 Henry Cotto .05
673 Rich DeLucia .05
674 Brian Fisher .05
675 Mark Grant .05
676 Randy Johnson .50
677 Tim Leary .05
678 Pete O'Brien .05
679 Lance Parrish .05
680 Harold Reynolds .05
681 Shane Turner .05
682 Jack Daugherty .05
683 David Hulse **RC** .05
684 Terry Mathews .05
685 Al Newman .05
686 Edwin Nunez .05
687 Rafael Palmeiro .40
688 Roger Pavlik .05
689 Geno Petralli .05
690 Nolan Ryan 1.00
691 David Cone .05
692 Alfredo Griffin .05
693 Juan Guzman .05
694 Pat Hentgen .05
695 Randy Knorr .05
696 Bob MacDonald .05
697 Jack Morris .05
698 Ed Sprague .05
699 Dave Stieb .05
700 Pat Tabler .05
701 Mike Timlin .05
702 David Wells .05
703 Eddie Zosky .05
704 Gary Sheffield (League Leaders) .05
705 Darren Daulton (League Leaders) .05
706 Marquis Grissom (League Leaders) .05
707 Greg Maddux (League Leaders) .10
708 Bill Swift (League Leaders) .05
709 Juan Gonzalez (Round Trippers) .15
710 Mark McGwire (Round Trippers) .50
711 Cecil Fielder (Round Trippers) .05
712 Albert Belle (Round Trippers) .05
713 Joe Carter (Round Trippers) .05
714 Power Brokers (Frank Thomas, Cecil Fielder) .10
715 Unsung Heroes (Larry Walker, Darren Daulton) .05
716 Hot Corner Hammers (Edgar Martinez, Robin Ventura) .05
717 Start to Finish (Roger Clemens, Dennis Eckersley) .25
718 Checklist .05
719 Checklist .05
720 Checklist .05

All-Stars

Horizontal-format All-Star cards comprised one of the many 1993 Fleer insert issues. Twelve cards of National League All-Stars were included in Series I wax packs, while a dozen American League All-Stars were found in Series II packs. They are among the more popular and valuable of the '93 Fleer inserts.

		NM/M
Complete Set A.L. (12):		6.00
Complete Set N.L. (12):		3.75
Common Player:		.15
AMERICAN LEAGUE		
1	Frank Thomas	.85
2	Roberto Alomar	.40
3	Edgar Martinez	.15
4	Pat Listach	.15
5	Cecil Fielder	.15
6	Juan Gonzalez	.40
7	Ken Griffey Jr.	2.00
8	Joe Carter	.15
9	Kirby Puckett	1.00
10	Brian Harper	.15
11	Dave Fleming	.15
12	Jack McDowell	.15
NATIONAL LEAGUE		
1	Fred McGriff	.15
2	Delino DeShields	.15
3	Gary Sheffield	.40
4	Barry Larkin	.15
5	Felix Jose	.15
6	Larry Walker	.15
7	Barry Bonds	2.50
8	Andy Van Slyke	.15
9	Darren Daulton	.15
10	Greg Maddux	.75
11	Tom Glavine	.25
12	Lee Smith	.15

Tom Glavine Career Highlights

This 15-card insert set spotlighted career highlights of Fleer's 1993 spokesman, Tom Glavine. Twelve cards were available in Series 1 and Series 2 packs; cards #13-15 could be obtained only via a special mail offer. A limited number of certified autograph cards were also inserted into packs. Cards #1-4 and 7-10

can each be found with two variations of the writeups on the back. The versions found in Series 2 packaging are the "correct" backs. Neither version carries a premium value.

		NM/M
Complete Set (15):		5.00
Common Card:		.50
Autographed Card:		30.00
1-15	Tom Glavine	.50

Golden Moments

Three cards of this insert set were available in both series of wax packs. Fronts feature black borders with gold-foil baseballs in the corners. The player's name appears in a "Golden Moments" banner at the bottom of the photo. Backs have a portrait photo of the player at top-center and a information on the highlight. The cards are unnumbered and are checklisted here alphabetically within series.

		NM/M
Complete Set (6):		4.00
Common Player:		.25
SERIES 1		2.00
(1)	George Brett	1.50
(2)	Mickey Morandini	.25
(3)	Dave Winfield	.50
SERIES 2		2.00
(1)	Dennis Eckersley	.40
(2)	Bip Roberts	.25
(3)	Frank Thomas, Juan Gonzalez	1.50

Major League Prospects

Yet another way to package currently hot rookies and future prospects to increase sales of the base product, there were 18 insert cards found in each series' wax packs. Fronts are bordered in black and have gold-foil highlights. Most of the depicted players were a few seasons away from everyday play in the major leagues.

		NM/M
Complete Set (36):		7.50
Common Player:		.15
SERIES 1		5.00
1	Melvin Nieves	.15
2	Sterling Hitchcock	.15
3	Tim Costo	.15
4	Manny Alexander	.15
5	Alan Embree	.15
6	Kevin Young	.15
7	J.T. Snow	.15
8	Russ Springer	.15
9	Billy Ashley	.15
10	Kevin Rogers	.15
11	Steve Hosey	.15
12	Eric Wedge	.15
13	Mike Piazza	3.50
14	Jesse Levis	.15
15	Rico Brogna	.15
16	Alex Arias	.15
17	Rod Brewer	.15
18	Troy Neel	.15
SERIES 2		2.50
1	Scooter Tucker	.15
2	Kerry Woodson	.15
3	Greg Colbrunn	.15
4	Pedro Martinez	1.50
5	Dave Silvestri	.15
6	Kent Bottenfield	.15
7	Rafael Bournigal	.15
8	J.T. Bruett	.15
9	Dave Mlicki	.15
10	Paul Wagner	.15
11	Mike Williams	.15
12	Henry Mercedes	.15
13	Scott Taylor	.15
14	Dennis Moeller	.15
15	Javier Lopez	.15
16	Steve Cooke	.15
17	Pete Young	.15
18	Ken Ryan	.15

ProVisions

This three-card insert set in Series I wax packs features the baseball art of Wayne Still. Black-bordered fronts feature a player-fantasy painting at center, with the player's name gold-foil stamped beneath. Backs are also bordered in black and have a white box with a career summary.

		NM/M
Complete Set (6):		3.00
Common Player:		.40
SERIES 1		2.00
1	Roberto Alomar	.65
2	Dennis Eckersley	1.00
3	Gary Sheffield	.75
SERIES 2		1.00
1	Andy Van Slyke	.40
2	Tom Glavine	.75
3	Cecil Fielder	.40

Rookie Sensations

Ten rookie sensations - some of whom had not been true rookies for several seasons - were featured in this insert issue packaged exclusively in Series 1 and Series 2 cello packs. Card fronts have a player photo set against a silver background and surrounded by a blue border. The player's name and other front printing are in gold foil. Backs are also printed in silver with a blue border. There is a player portrait photo and career summary.

		NM/M
Complete Set (20):		6.25
Common Player:		.25
SERIES 1		3.00
1	Kenny Lofton	.50
2	Cal Eldred	.25
3	Pat Listach	.25
4	Roberto Hernandez	.25
5	Dave Fleming	.25
6	Eric Karros	.25
7	Reggie Sanders	.25
8	Derrick May	.25
9	Mike Perez	.25
10	Donovan Osborne	.25
SERIES 2		2.00
1	Moises Alou	.50
2	Pedro Astacio	.25
3	Jim Austin	.25
4	Chad Curtis	.25
5	Gary DiSarcina	.25
6	Scott Livingstone	.25
7	Sam Militello	.25
8	Arthur Rhodes	.25
9	Tim Wakefield	.35
10	Bob Zupcic	.25

Team Leaders

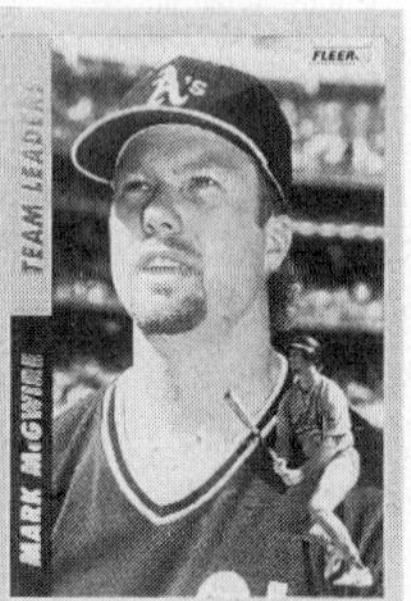

This 20-card insert issue was exclusive to Series 1 and 2 rack packs. Fronts have a portrait photo, with a small action photo superimposed. At the side is a colored bar with the player's name and "Team Leaders" printed vertically. On back is a career summary. Card borders are a light metallic green and both sides of the card are UV coated.

		NM/M
Complete Set (20):		12.50
Common Player:		.40
SERIES 1		10.00
1	Kirby Puckett	1.25
2	Mark McGwire	3.00
3	Pat Listach	.40
4	Roger Clemens	1.50
5	Frank Thomas	1.00
6	Carlos Baerga	.40
7	Brady Anderson	.40
8	Juan Gonzalez	.50
9	Roberto Alomar	.60
10	Ken Griffey Jr.	2.00
SERIES 2		4.00
1	Will Clark	.40
2	Terry Pendleton	.40
3	Ray Lankford	.40
4	Eric Karros	.40
5	Gary Sheffield	.75
6	Ryne Sandberg	1.25
7	Marquis Grissom	.40
8	John Kruk	.40
9	Jeff Bagwell	1.00
10	Andy Van Slyke	.40

Final Edition

This 310-card set was sold as a complete set in its own box. Card numbers have the prefix "F." The set also includes 10 Diamond Tribute cards, which are numbered DT1-DT10.

		NM/M
Complete Set (310):		7.50
Common Player:		.05
1	Steve Bedrosian	.05
2	Jay Howell	.05
3	Greg Maddux	.65
4	Greg McMichael **RC**	.05
5	Tony Tarasco **RC**	.05
6	Jose Bautista	.05
7	Jose Guzman	.05
8	Greg Hibbard	.05
9	Candy Maldonado	.05
10	Randy Myers	.05
11	Matt Walbeck **RC**	.05
12	Turk Wendell	.05
13	Willie Nelson	.05
14	Greg Cadaret	.05
15	Roberto Kelly	.05
16	Randy Milligan	.05
17	Kevin Mitchell	.05
18	Jeff Reardon	.05
19	John Roper	.05
20	John Smiley	.05
21	Andy Ashby	.05
22	Dante Bichette	.05
23	Willie Blair	.05
24	Pedro Castellano	.05
25	Vinny Castilla	.05
26	Jerald Clark	.05
27	Alex Cole	.05
28	Scott Fredrickson **RC**	.05
29	Jay Gainer **RC**	.05
30	Andres Galarraga	.05
31	Joe Girardi	.05
32	Ryan Hawblitzel	.05
33	Charlie Hayes	.05
34	Darren Holmes	.05
35	Chris Jones	.05
36	David Nied	.05
37	J. Owens **RC**	.05
38	Lance Painter **RC**	.05
39	Jeff Parrett	.05
40	Steve Reed **RC**	.05
41	Armando Reynoso	.05
42	Bruce Ruffin	.05
43	Danny Sheaffer **RC**	.05
44	Keith Shepherd	.05
45	Jim Tatum	.05
46	Gary Wayne	.05
47	Eric Young	.05
48	Luis Aquino	.05
49	Alex Arias	.05
50	Jack Armstrong	.05
51	Bret Barberie	.05
52	Geronimo Berroa	.05
53	Ryan Bowen	.05
54	Greg Briley	.05
55	Chris Carpenter	.05
56	Chuck Carr	.05
57	Jeff Conine	.05
58	Jim Corsi	.05
59	Orestes Destrade	.05
60	Junior Felix	.05
61	Chris Hammond	.05
62	Bryan Harvey	.05
63	Charlie Hough	.05
64	Joe Klink	.05
65	Richie Lewis **RC**	.05
66	Mitch Lyden **RC**	.05
67	Bob Natal	.05
68	Scott Pose **RC**	.05
69	Rich Renteria	.05
70	Benito Santiago	.05
71	Gary Sheffield	.15
72	Matt Turner **RC**	.05
73	Walt Weiss	.05
74	Darrell Whitmore **RC**	.05
75	Nigel Wilson	.05
76	Kevin Bass	.05
77	Doug Drabek	.05
78	Tom Edens	.05
79	Chris James	.05
80	Greg Swindell	.05
81	Omar Daal **RC**	.05
82	Raul Mondesi	.05
83	Jody Reed	.05
84	Cory Snyder	.05
85	Rick Trlicek	.05
86	Tim Wallach	.05
87	Todd Worrell	.05
88	Tavo Alvarez	.05
89	Frank Bolick	.05
90	Kent Bottenfield	.05
91	Greg Colbrunn	.05
92	Cliff Floyd	.05
93	Lou Frazier **RC**	.05
94	Mike Gardiner	.05
95	Mike Lansing **RC**	.25
96	Bill Risley	.05
97	Jeff Shaw	.05
98	Kevin Baez	.05
99	Tim Bogar **RC**	.05
100	Jeromy Burnitz	.05
101	Mike Draper	.05
102	Darrin Jackson	.05
103	Mike Maddux	.05
104	Joe Orsulak	.05
105	Doug Saunders	.05
106	Frank Tanana	.05
107	Dave Telgheder	.05
108	Larry Anderson	.05
109	Jim Eisenreich	.05
110	Pete Incaviglia	.05
111	Danny Jackson	.05
112	David West	.05
113	Al Martin	.05
114	Blas Minor	.05
115	Dennis Moeller	.05
116	Will Pennyfeather	.05
117	Rich Robertson	.05
118	Ben Shelton	.05
119	Lonnie Smith	.05
120	Freddie Toliver	.05
121	Paul Wagner	.05
122	Kevin Young	.05
123	Rene Arocha **RC**	.05
124	Gregg Jefferies	.05
125	Paul Kilgus	.05
126	Les Lancaster	.05
127	Joe Magrane	.05
128	Rob Murphy	.05
129	Erik Pappas	.05
130	Stan Royer	.05
131	Ozzie Smith	.65
132	Tom Urbani	.05
133	Mark Whiten	.05
134	Derek Bell	.05
135	Doug Brocail	.05
136	Phil Clark	.05
137	Mark Ettles **RC**	.05
138	Jeff Gardner	.05
139	Pat Gomez **RC**	.05
140	Ricky Gutierrez	.05
141	Gene Harris	.05
142	Kevin Higgins **RC**	.05
143	Trevor Hoffman	.05
144	Phil Plantier	.05
145	Kerry Taylor **RC**	.05
146	Guillermo Velasquez	.05
147	Wally Whitehurst	.05
148	Tim Worrell **RC**	.05
149	Todd Benzinger	.05
150	Barry Bonds	2.00
151	Greg Brummett	.05
152	Mark Carreon	.05
153	Dave Martinez	.05
154	Jeff Reed	.05
155	Kevin Rogers	.05
156	Harold Baines	.05
157	Damon Buford	.05
158	Paul Carey **RC**	.05
159	Jeffrey Hammonds	.05
160	Jamie Moyer	.05
161	Sherman Obando **RC**	.05
162	John O'Donoghue **RC**	.05
163	Brad Pennington	.05
164	Jim Poole	.05
165	Harold Reynolds	.05
166	Fernando Valenzuela	.05
167	Jack Voight **RC**	.05
168	Mark Williamson	.05
169	Scott Bankhead	.05
170	Greg Blosser	.05
171	Jim Byrd **RC**	.05
172	Ivan Calderon	.05
173	Andre Dawson	.25
174	Scott Fletcher	.05
175	Jose Melendez	.05
176	Carlos Quintana	.05
177	Jeff Russell	.05
178	Aaron Sele	.05
179	Rod Correia **RC**	.05
180	Chili Davis	.05
181	Jim Edmonds **RC**	3.00
182	Rene Gonzales	.05
183	Hilly Hathaway **RC**	.05
184	Torey Lovullo	.05
185	Greg Myers	.05
186	Gene Nelson	.05
187	Troy Percival	.05
188	Scott Sanderson	.05
189	Darryl Scott **RC**	.05
190	J.T. Snow **RC**	.50
191	Russ Springer	.05
192	Jason Bere	.05
193	Rodney Bolton	.05
194	Ellis Burks	.05
195	Bo Jackson	.15
196	Mike LaValliere	.05
197	Scott Ruffcorn	.05
198	Jeff Schwartz **RC**	.05
199	Jerry DiPoto	.05
200	Alvaro Espinoza	.05
201	Wayne Kirby	.05
202	Tom Kramer **RC**	.05
203	Jesse Levis	.05
204	Manny Ramirez	.50
205	Jeff Treadway	.05
206	Bill Wertz **RC**	.05
207	Cliff Young	.05
208	Matt Young	.05
209	Kirk Gibson	.05
210	Greg Gohr	.05
211	Bill Krueger	.05
212	Bob MacDonald	.05
213	Mike Moore	.05
214	David Wells	.05
215	Billy Brewer **RC**	.05
216	David Cone	.05
217	Greg Gagne	.05
218	Mark Gardner	.05
219	Chis Haney	.05
220	Phil Hiatt	.05
221	Jose Lind	.05
222	Juan Bell	.05
223	Tom Brunansky	.05
224	Mike Ignasiak	.05
225	Joe Kmak	.05
226	Tom Lampkin	.05
227	Graeme Lloyd **RC**	.05
228	Carlos Maldonado	.05
229	Matt Mieske	.05
230	Angel Miranda	.05
231	Troy O'Leary **RC**	.10
232	Kevin Reimer	.05
233	Larry Casian	.05
234	Jim Deshaies	.05
235	Eddie Guardado **RC**	.10
236	Chip Hale	.05
237	Mike Maksudian **RC**	.05
238	David McCarty	.05
239	Pat Meares **RC**	.05
240	George Tsamis **RC**	.05
241	Dave Winfield	.50
242	Jim Abbott	.05
243	Wade Boggs	.65
244	Andy Cook **RC**	.05
245	Russ Davis **RC**	.10
246	Mike Humphreys	.05
247	Jimmy Key	.05
248	Jim Leyritz	.05
249	Bobby Munoz	.05
250	Paul O'Neill	.05
251	Spike Owen	.05
252	Dave Silvestri	.05
253	Marcos Armas **RC**	.05
254	Brent Gates	.05
255	Goose Gossage	.25
256	Scott Lydy **RC**	.05
257	Henry Mercedes	.05
258	Mike Mohler **RC**	.05
259	Troy Neel	.05
260	Edwin Nunez	.05
261	Craig Paquette	.05
262	Kevin Seitzer	.05
263	Rich Amaral	.05
264	Mike Blowers	.05
265	Chris Bosio	.05
266	Norm Charlton	.05
267	Jim Converse **RC**	.05
268	John Cummings **RC**	.05
269	Mike Felder	.05
270	Mike Hampton	.05
271	Bill Haselman	.05
272	Dwayne Henry	.05
273	Greg Litton	.05
274	Mackey Sasser	.05
275	Lee Tinsley	.05
276	David Wainhouse	.05
277	Jeff Bronkey **RC**	.05
278	Benji Gil	.05
279	Tom Henke	.05
280	Charlie Leibrandt	.05
281	Robb Nen	.05
282	Bill Ripken	.05
283	Jon Shave **RC**	.05
284	Doug Strange	.05
285	Matt Whiteside **RC**	.05
286	Scott Drow **RC**	.05
287	Willie Canate **RC**	.05
288	Tony Castillo	.05
289	Domingo Cedeno **RC**	.05
290	Darnell Coles	.05
291	Danny Cox	.05
292	Mark Eichhorn	.05
293	Tony Fernandez	.05
294	Al Leiter	.05
295	Paul Molitor	.50
296	Dave Stewart	.05
297	Woody Williams **RC**	.05
298	Checklist	.05
299	Checklist	.05
300	Checklist	.05
1DT	Wade Boggs	.65
2DT	George Brett	.75
3DT	Andre Dawson	.25
4DT	Carlton Fisk	.50
5DT	Paul Molitor	.50
6DT	Nolan Ryan	2.00
7DT	Lee Smith	.05
8DT	Ozzie Smith	.65
9DT	Dave Winfield	.50
10DT	Robin Yount	.50

Atlantic

The Atlantic Collectors Edition set of 1993 features 24 of the top players in the game (plus one checklist) portrayed in a style matching the regular-issue Fleer set, with the addition of the Atlantic logo and a gold border. The cards were given away five at a time with gasoline purchases at gas stations in New York and Pennsylvania during the summer.

		NM/M
Complete Set (25):		3.50
Common Player:		.12
1	Roberto Alomar	.20
2	Barry Bonds	1.00
3	Bobby Bonilla	.10
4	Will Clark	.10
5	Roger Clemens	.60
6	Darren Daulton	.10
7	Dennis Eckersley	.30
8	Cecil Fielder	.10
9	Tom Glavine	.25
10	Juan Gonzalez	.25
11	Ken Griffey Jr.	.75
12	John Kruk	.10
13	Greg Maddux	.50
14	Don Mattingly	.60
15	Fred McGriff	.10
16	Mark McGwire	.85
17	Terry Pendleton	.10
18	Kirby Puckett	.50
19	Cal Ripken Jr.	1.00
20	Nolan Ryan	1.00
21	Ryne Sandberg	.50
22	Gary Sheffield	.25
23	Frank Thomas	.40
24	Andy Van Slyke	.10
25	Checklist	.05

Fruit of the Loom

Fruit of the Loom and Fleer combined to create a 66-card baseball set in 1993 that featured many of the top players in the game. The cards, with the same design as the regular-issue Fleer cards, also display the Fruit of the Loom logo in the upper-left corner. Three cards were inserted in specially marked packages of the company's products.

		NM/M
Complete Set (66):		30.00
Common Player:		.25
1	Roberto Alomar	.45
2	Brady Anderson	.25
3	Jeff Bagwell	1.00
4	Albert Belle	.25
5	Craig Biggio	.25
6	Barry Bonds	3.00
7	George Brett	1.75
8	Brett Butler	.25
9	Jose Canseco	.65
10	Joe Carter	.25
11	Will Clark	.25
12	Roger Clemens	1.75
13	Darren Daulton	.25
14	Andre Dawson	.40
15	Delino DeShields	.25
16	Rob Dibble	.25
17	Doug Drabek	.25
18	Dennis Eckersley	.85
19	Cecil Fielder	.25
20	Travis Fryman	.25
21	Tom Glavine	.45
22	Juan Gonzalez	.50
23	Dwight Gooden	.25
24	Mark Grace	.25
25	Ken Griffey Jr.	2.00
26	Marquis Grissom	.25
27	Juan Guzman	.25
28	Tony Gwynn	1.50
29	Rickey Henderson	1.00
30	David Justice	.25
31	Eric Karros	.25
32	Chuck Knoblauch	.25
33	John Kruk	.25
34	Ray Lankford	.25
35	Barry Larkin	.25
36	Pat Listach	.25
37	Kenny Lofton	.25
38	Shane Mack	.25
39	Greg Maddux	1.50
40	Dennis Martinez	.25
41	Edgar Martinez	.25
42	Ramon Martinez	.25
43	Don Mattingly	1.75
44	Jack McDowell	.25
45	Fred McGriff	.25
46	Mark McGwire	2.50
47	Jeff Montgomery	.25
48	Eddie Murray	1.00
49	Charles Nagy	.25
50	Tom Pagnozzi	.25
51	Terry Pendleton	.25
52	Kirby Puckett	1.50
53	Jose Rijo	.25
54	Cal Ripken, Jr.	3.00
55	Nolan Ryan	3.00
56	Ryne Sandberg	1.50
57	Gary Sheffield	.65
58	Bill Swift	.25
59	Danny Tartabull	.25
60	Mickey Tettleton	.25
61	Frank Thomas	1.00
62	Andy Van Slyke	.25
63	Robin Ventura	.25
64	Larry Walker	.25
65	Robin Yount	1.00
66	Checklist	.05

1994 Fleer "Highlights" Promo Sheet

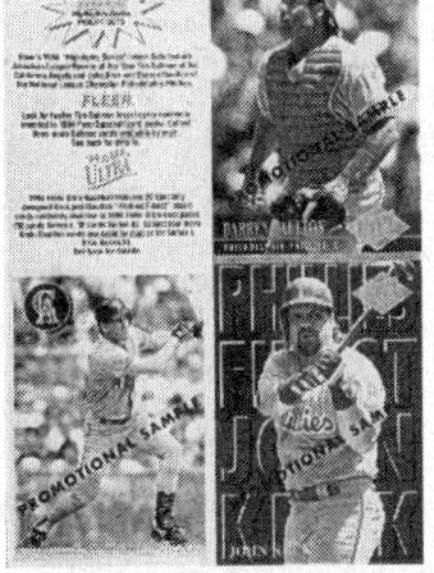

To introduce its special insert card series honoring 1993 A.L. Rookie of the Year Tim Salmon and Phillies stars John Kruk and Darren Daulton, Fleer issued this 5" x 7" promo sheet. The three player cards on the sheet are similar to the issued versions except they have black overprinting on front and back which reads, "PROMOTIONAL SAMPLE." The non-player segment of the sheet has details about the inserts and special mail-in offers for additional cards.

	NM/M
Sheet:	6.00

1994 Fleer

Fleer's 720-card 1994 set, released in one series, includes another 204 insert cards to be pursued by collectors. Every pack includes one of the cards, randomly inserted from among the 12 insert sets. Regular cards have action photos on front, with a team logo in one of the lower corners. The player's name and position is stamped in gold foil around the logo. On back, another color player photo is overprinted with color boxes, data and stats, leaving a clear image of the player's face, 1-1/2" x 1-3/4" in size. Cards are UV coated on both sides.

		NM/M
Complete Set (720):		12.50
Common Player:		.05
Pack (15):		.50
Wax Box (36):		12.50
1	Brady Anderson	.05
2	Harold Baines	.05
3	Mike Devereaux	.05
4	Todd Frohwirth	.05
5	Jeffrey Hammonds	.05
6	Chris Hoiles	.05
7	Tim Hulett	.05
8	Ben McDonald	.05
9	Mark McLemore	.05
10	Alan Mills	.05
11	Jamie Moyer	.05
12	Mike Mussina	.40
13	Gregg Olson	.05
14	Mike Pagliarulo	.05
15	Brad Pennington	.05
16	Jim Poole	.05
17	Harold Reynolds	.05
18	Arthur Rhodes	.05
19	Cal Ripken, Jr.	2.00
20	David Segui	.05
21	Rick Sutcliffe	.05
22	Fernando Valenzuela	.05
23	Jack Voigt	.05
24	Mark Williamson	.05
25	Scott Bankhead	.05
26	Roger Clemens	1.00
27	Scott Cooper	.05
28	Danny Darwin	.05
29	Andre Dawson	.25
30	Rob Deer	.05
31	John Dopson	.05
32	Scott Fletcher	.05
33	Mike Greenwell	.05
34	Greg Harris	.05
35	Billy Hatcher	.05
36	Bob Melvin	.05
37	Tony Pena	.05
38	Paul Quantrill	.05
39	Carlos Quintana	.05
40	Ernest Riles	.05
41	Jeff Russell	.05
42	Ken Ryan	.05
43	Aaron Sele	.05
44	John Valentin	.05
45	Mo Vaughn	.05
46	Frank Viola	.05
47	Bob Zupcic	.05
48	Mike Butcher	.05
49	Rod Correia	.05
50	Chad Curtis	.05
51	Chili Davis	.05
52	Gary DiSarcina	.05
53	Damion Easley	.05
54	Jim Edmonds	.05
55	Chuck Finley	.05
56	Steve Frey	.05
57	Rene Gonzales	.05
58	Joe Grahe	.05
59	Hilly Hathaway	.05
60	Stan Javier	.05
61	Mark Langston	.05
62	Phil Leftwich	.05
63	Torey Lovullo	.05
64	Joe Magrane	.05
65	Greg Myers	.05
66	Ken Patterson	.05
67	Eduardo Perez	.05
68	Luis Polonia	.05
69	Tim Salmon	.20
69a	Tim Salmon/OPS	2.00
70	J.T. Snow	.05
71	Ron Tingley	.05
72	Julio Valera	.05
73	Wilson Alvarez	.05
74	Tim Belcher	.05
75	George Bell	.05
76	Jason Bere	.05
77	Rod Bolton	.05
78	Ellis Burks	.05
79	Joey Cora	.05
80	Alex Fernandez	.05
81	Craig Grebeck	.05
82	Ozzie Guillen	.05
83	Roberto Hernandez	.05
84	Bo Jackson	.10
85	Lance Johnson	.05
86	Ron Karkovice	.05
87	Mike LaValliere	.05
88	Kirk McCaskill	.05
89	Jack McDowell	.05
90	Warren Newson	.05
91	Dan Pasqua	.05
92	Scott Radinsky	.05
93	Tim Raines	.05
94	Steve Sax	.05
95	Jeff Schwarz	.05
96	Frank Thomas	.75
97	Robin Ventura	.05
98	Sandy Alomar, Jr.	.05
99	Carlos Baerga	.05
100	Albert Belle	.05
101	Mark Clark	.05
102	Jerry DiPoto	.05
103	Alvaro Espinoza	.05
104	Felix Fermin	.05
105	Jeremy Hernandez	.05
106	Reggie Jefferson	.05
107	Wayne Kirby	.05
108	Tom Kramer	.05
109	Mark Lewis	.05
110	Derek Lilliquist	.05
111	Kenny Lofton	.05
112	Candy Maldonado	.05
113	Jose Mesa	.05
114	Jeff Mutis	.05
115	Charles Nagy	.05
116	Bob Ojeda	.05
117	Junior Ortiz	.05
118	Eric Plunk	.05
119	Manny Ramirez	.75
120	Paul Sorrento	.05
121	Jim Thome	.60
122	Jeff Treadway	.05
123	Bill Wertz	.05
124	Skeeter Barnes	.05
125	Milt Cuyler	.05
126	Eric Davis	.05
127	John Doherty	.05
128	Cecil Fielder	.05
129	Travis Fryman	.05
130	Kirk Gibson	.05
131	Dan Gladden	.05
132	Greg Gohr	.05
133	Chris Gomez	.05
134	Bill Gullickson	.05
135	Mike Henneman	.05
136	Kurt Knudsen	.05
137	Chad Kreuter	.05
138	Bill Krueger	.05
139	Scott Livingstone	.05
140	Bob MacDonald	.05
141	Mike Moore	.05
142	Tony Phillips	.05
143	Mickey Tettleton	.05
144	Alan Trammell	.05
145	David Wells	.05
146	Lou Whitaker	.05
147	Kevin Appier	.05
148	Stan Belinda	.05
149	George Brett	1.00
150	Billy Brewer	.05
151	Hubie Brooks	.05
152	David Cone	.05
153	Gary Gaetti	.05
154	Greg Gagne	.05
155	Tom Gordon	.05
156	Mark Gubicza	.05
157	Chris Gwynn	.05
158	John Habyan	.05
159	Chris Haney	.05
160	Phil Hiatt	.05
161	Felix Jose	.05
162	Wally Joyner	.05
163	Jose Lind	.05
164	Mike Macfarlane	.05
165	Mike Magnante	.05
166	Brent Mayne	.05
167	Brian McRae	.05
168	Kevin McReynolds	.05
169	Keith Miller	.05
170	Jeff Montgomery	.05
171	Hipolito Pichardo	.05
172	Rico Rossy	.05
173	Juan Bell	.05
174	Ricky Bones	.05
175	Cal Eldred	.05
176	Mike Fetters	.05
177	Darryl Hamilton	.05
178	Doug Henry	.05
179	Mike Ignasiak	.05
180	John Jaha	.05
181	Pat Listach	.05
182	Graeme Lloyd	.05
183	Matt Mieske	.05
184	Angel Miranda	.05
185	Jaime Navarro	.05
186	Dave Nilsson	.05
187	Troy O'Leary	.05
188	Jesse Orosco	.05
189	Kevin Reimer	.05
190	Kevin Seitzer	.05
191	Bill Spiers	.05
192	B.J. Surhoff	.05
193	Dickie Thon	.05
194	Jose Valentin	.05
195	Greg Vaughn	.05
196	Bill Wegman	.05
197	Robin Yount	.75
198	Rick Aguilera	.05
199	Willie Banks	.05
200	Bernardo Brito	.05
201	Larry Casian	.05
202	Scott Erickson	.05
203	Eddie Guardado	.05
204	Mark Guthrie	.05
205	Chip Hale	.05
206	Brian Harper	.05
207	Mike Hartley	.05
208	Kent Hrbek	.05
209	Terry Jorgensen	.05
210	Chuck Knoblauch	.05
211	Gene Larkin	.05
212	Shane Mack	.05
213	David McCarty	.05
214	Pat Meares	.05
215	Pedro Munoz	.05
216	Derek Parks	.05
217	Kirby Puckett	.85
218	Jeff Reboulet	.05
219	Kevin Tapani	.05
220	Mike Trombley	.05
221	George Tsamis	.05
222	Carl Willis	.05
223	Dave Winfield	.75
224	Jim Abbott	.05
225	Paul Assenmacher	.05
226	Wade Boggs	.85
227	Russ Davis	.05
228	Steve Farr	.05
229	Mike Gallego	.05
230	Paul Gibson	.05
231	Steve Howe	.05
232	Dion James	.05
233	Domingo Jean	.05
234	Scott Kamieniecki	.05
235	Pat Kelly	.05
236	Jimmy Key	.05
237	Jim Leyritz	.05
238	Kevin Maas	.05
239	Don Mattingly	1.00
240	Rich Monteleone	.05
241	Bobby Munoz	.05
242	Matt Nokes	.05
243	Paul O'Neill	.05
244	Spike Owen	.05
245	Melido Perez	.05
246	Lee Smith	.05
247	Mike Stanley	.05
248	Danny Tartabull	.05
249	Randy Velarde	.05
250	Bob Wickman	.05
251	Bernie Williams	.20
252	Mike Aldrete	.05
253	Marcos Armas	.05
254	Lance Blankenship	.05
255	Mike Bordick	.05
256	Scott Brosius	.05
257	Jerry Browne	.05
258	Ron Darling	.05
259	Kelly Downs	.05
260	Dennis Eckersley	.60
261	Brent Gates	.05
262	Goose Gossage	.05
263	Scott Hemond	.05
264	Dave Henderson	.05
265	Rick Honeycutt	.05
266	Vince Horsman	.05
267	Scott Lydy	.05
268	Mark McGwire	1.50
269	Mike Mohler	.05
270	Troy Neel	.05
271	Edwin Nunez	.05
272	Craig Paquette	.05
273	Ruben Sierra	.05
274	Terry Steinbach	.05
275	Todd Van Poppel	.05
276	Bob Welch	.05
277	Bobby Witt	.05
278	Rich Amaral	.05
279	Mike Blowers	.05
280	Bret Boone	.05
281	Chris Bosio	.05
282	Jay Buhner	.05
283	Norm Charlton	.05
284	Mike Felder	.05
285	Dave Fleming	.05
286	Ken Griffey Jr.	1.25
287	Erik Hanson	.05
288	Bill Haselman	.05
289	Brad Holman **RC**	.05
290	Randy Johnson	.75
291	Tim Leary	.05
292	Greg Litton	.05
293	Dave Magadan	.05
294	Edgar Martinez	.05
295	Tino Martinez	.05
296	Jeff Nelson	.05
297	Erik Plantenberg **RC**	.05
298	Mackey Sasser	.05
299	Brian Turang **RC**	.05
300	Dave Valle	.05
301	Omar Vizquel	.05
302	Brian Bohanon	.05
303	Kevin Brown	.05
304	Jose Canseco	.40
305	Mario Diaz	.05
306	Julio Franco	.05
307	Juan Gonzalez	.75
308	Tom Henke	.05
309	David Hulse	.05
310	Manuel Lee	.05
311	Craig Lefferts	.05
312	Charlie Leibrandt	.05
313	Rafael Palmeiro	.75
314	Dean Palmer	.05
315	Roger Pavlik	.05
316	Dan Peltier	.05
317	Geno Petralli	.05
318	Gary Redus	.05
319	Ivan Rodriguez	.65
320	Kenny Rogers	.05
321	Nolan Ryan	2.00
322	Doug Strange	.05
323	Matt Whiteside	.05
324	Roberto Alomar	.30
325	Pat Borders	.05
326	Joe Carter	.05
327	Tony Castillo	.05
328	Darnell Coles	.05
329	Danny Cox	.05
330	Mark Eichhorn	.05
331	Tony Fernandez	.05
332	Alfredo Griffin	.05
333	Juan Guzman	.05
334	Rickey Henderson	.75
335	Pat Hentgen	.05
336	Randy Knorr	.05
337	Al Leiter	.05
338	Paul Molitor	.75
339	Jack Morris	.05
340	John Olerud	.05
341	Dick Schofield	.05
342	Ed Sprague	.05
343	Dave Stewart	.05
344	Todd Stottlemyre	.05
345	Mike Timlin	.05
346	Duane Ward	.05
347	Turner Ward	.05
348	Devon White	.05
349	Woody Williams	.05
350	Steve Avery	.05
351	Steve Bedrosian	.05
352	Rafael Belliard	.05
353	Damon Berryhill	.05
354	Jeff Blauser	.05
355	Sid Bream	.05
356	Francisco Cabrera	.05
357	Marvin Freeman	.05
358	Ron Gant	.05
359	Tom Glavine	.25
360	Jay Howell	.05
361	Dave Justice	.05
362	Ryan Klesko	.05
363	Mark Lemke	.05
364	Javier Lopez	.05
365	Greg Maddux	.85
366	Fred McGriff	.05
367	Greg McMichael	.05
368	Kent Mercker	.05
369	Otis Nixon	.05
370	Greg Olson	.05
371	Bill Pecota	.05
372	Terry Pendleton	.05
373	Deion Sanders	.05
374	Pete Smith	.05
375	John Smoltz	.05
376	Mike Stanton	.05
377	Tony Tarasco	.05
378	Mark Wohlers	.05
379	Jose Bautista	.05
380	Shawn Boskie	.05
381	Steve Buechele	.05
382	Frank Castillo	.05
383	Mark Grace	.10
384	Jose Guzman	.05
385	Mike Harkey	.05
386	Greg Hibbard	.05
387	Glenallen Hill	.05
388	Steve Lake	.05
389	Derrick May	.05
390	Chuck McElroy	.05
391	Mike Morgan	.05
392	Randy Myers	.05
393	Dan Plesac	.05
394	Kevin Roberson	.05
395	Rey Sanchez	.05
396	Ryne Sandberg	.85
397	Bob Scanlan	.05
398	Dwight Smith	.05
399	Sammy Sosa	1.25
400	Jose Vizcaino	.05
401	Rick Wilkins	.05
402	Willie Wilson	.05
403	Eric Yelding	.05
404	Bobby Ayala	.05
405	Jeff Branson	.05
406	Tom Browning	.05
407	Jacob Brumfield	.05
408	Tim Costo	.05
409	Rob Dibble	.05
410	Willie Greene	.05
411	Thomas Howard	.05
412	Roberto Kelly	.05
413	Bill Landrum	.05
414	Barry Larkin	.05
415	Larry Luebbers **RC**	.05
416	Kevin Mitchell	.05
417	Hal Morris	.05
418	Joe Oliver	.05
419	Tim Pugh	.05
420	Jeff Reardon	.05
421	Jose Rijo	.05
422	Bip Roberts	.05
423	John Roper	.05
424	Johnny Ruffin	.05
425	Chris Sabo	.05
426	Juan Samuel	.05
427	Reggie Sanders	.05
428	Scott Service	.05
429	John Smiley	.05
430	Jerry Spradlin **RC**	.05
431	Kevin Wickander	.05
432	Freddie Benavides	.05
433	Dante Bichette	.05
434	Willie Blair	.05
435	Daryl Boston	.05
436	Kent Bottenfield	.05
437	Vinny Castilla	.05
438	Jerald Clark	.05
439	Alex Cole	.05
440	Andres Galarraga	.05
441	Joe Girardi	.05
442	Greg Harris	.05
443	Charlie Hayes	.05
444	Darren Holmes	.05
445	Chris Jones	.05
446	Roberto Mejia	.05
447	David Nied	.05
448	J. Owens	.05
449	Jeff Parrett	.05
450	Steve Reed	.05
451	Armando Reynoso	.05
452	Bruce Ruffin	.05
453	Mo Sanford	.05
454	Danny Sheaffer	.05
455	Jim Tatum	.05
456	Gary Wayne	.05
457	Eric Young	.05
458	Luis Aquino	.05
459	Alex Arias	.05
460	Jack Armstrong	.05
461	Bret Barberie	.05
462	Ryan Bowen	.05
463	Chuck Carr	.05
464	Jeff Conine	.05
465	Henry Cotto	.05

#	Player	NM/M
466	Orestes Destrade	.05
467	Chris Hammond	.05
468	Bryan Harvey	.05
469	Charlie Hough	.05
470	Joe Klink	.05
471	Richie Lewis	.05
472	Bob Natal **RC**	.05
473	Pat Rapp **RC**	.05
474	Rich Renteria **RC**	.10
475	Rich Rodriguez	.05
476	Benito Santiago	.05
477	Gary Sheffield	.35
478	Matt Turner	.05
479	David Weathers	.05
480	Walt Weiss	.05
481	Darrell Whitmore	.05
482	Eric Anthony	.05
483	Jeff Bagwell	.75
484	Kevin Bass	.05
485	Craig Biggio	.05
486	Ken Caminiti	.05
487	Andujar Cedeno	.05
488	Chris Donnels	.05
489	Doug Drabek	.05
490	Steve Finley	.05
491	Luis Gonzalez	.25
492	Pete Harnisch	.05
493	Xavier Hernandez	.05
494	Doug Jones	.05
495	Todd Jones	.05
496	Darryl Kile	.05
497	Al Osuna	.05
498	Mark Portugal	.05
499	Scott Servais	.05
500	Greg Swindell	.05
501	Eddie Taubensee	.05
502	Jose Uribe	.05
503	Brian Williams	.05
504	Billy Ashley	.05
505	Pedro Astacio	.05
506	Brett Butler	.05
507	Tom Candiotti	.05
508	Omar Daal	.05
509	Jim Gott	.05
510	Kevin Gross	.05
511	Dave Hansen	.05
512	Carlos Hernandez	.05
513	Orel Hershiser	.05
514	Eric Karros	.05
515	Pedro Martinez	.75
516	Ramon Martinez	.05
517	Roger McDowell	.05
518	Raul Mondesi	.05
519	Jose Offerman	.05
520	Mike Piazza	1.25
521	Jody Reed	.05
522	Henry Rodriguez	.05
523	Mike Sharperson	.05
524	Cory Snyder	.05
525	Darryl Strawberry	.05
526	Rick Trlicek	.05
527	Tim Wallach	.05
528	Mitch Webster	.05
529	Steve Wilson	.05
530	Todd Worrell	.05
531	Moises Alou	.05
532	Brian Barnes	.05
533	Sean Berry	.05
534	Greg Colbrunn	.05
535	Delino DeShields	.05
536	Jeff Fassero	.05
537	Darrin Fletcher	.05
538	Cliff Floyd	.05
539	Lou Frazier	.05
540	Marquis Grissom	.05
541	Butch Henry	.05
542	Ken Hill	.05
543	Mike Lansing	.05
544	Brian Looney **RC**	.05
545	Dennis Martinez	.05
546	Chris Nabholz	.05
547	Randy Ready	.05
548	Mel Rojas	.05
549	Kirk Rueter	.05
550	Tim Scott	.05
551	Jeff Shaw	.05
552	Tim Spehr	.05
553	John VanderWal	.05
554	Larry Walker	.05
555	John Wetteland	.05
556	Rondell White	.05
557	Tim Bogar	.05
558	Bobby Bonilla	.05
559	Jeromy Burnitz	.05
560	Sid Fernandez	.05
561	John Franco	.05
562	Dave Gallagher	.05
563	Dwight Gooden	.05
564	Eric Hillman	.05
565	Todd Hundley	.05
566	Jeff Innis	.05
567	Darrin Jackson	.05
568	Howard Johnson	.05
569	Bobby Jones	.05
570	Jeff Kent	.05
571	Mike Maddux	.05
572	Jeff McKnight	.05
573	Eddie Murray	.75
574	Charlie O'Brien	.05
575	Joe Orsulak	.05
576	Bret Saberhagen	.05
577	Pete Schourek	.05
578	Dave Telgheder	.05
579	Ryan Thompson	.05
580	Anthony Young	.05
581	Ruben Amaro	.05
582	Larry Andersen	.05
583	Kim Batiste	.05
584	Wes Chamberlain	.05
585	Darren Daulton	.05
586	Mariano Duncan	.05
587	Len Dykstra	.05
588	Jim Eisenreich	.05
589	Tommy Greene	.05
590	Dave Hollins	.05
591	Pete Incaviglia	.05
592	Danny Jackson	.05
593	Ricky Jordan	.05
594	John Kruk	.05
595	Roger Mason	.05
596	Mickey Morandini	.05
597	Terry Mulholland	.05
598	Todd Pratt	.05
599	Ben Rivera	.05
600	Curt Schilling	.25
601	Kevin Stocker	.05
602	Milt Thompson	.05
603	David West	.05
604	Mitch Williams	.05
605	Jay Bell	.05
606	Dave Clark	.05
607	Steve Cooke	.05
608	Tom Foley	.05
609	Carlos Garcia	.05
610	Joel Johnston	.05
611	Jeff King	.05
612	Al Martin	.05
613	Lloyd McClendon	.05
614	Orlando Merced	.05
615	Blas Minor	.05
616	Denny Neagle	.05
617	Mark Petkovsek **RC**	.05
618	Tom Prince	.05
619	Don Slaught	.05
620	Zane Smith	.05
621	Randy Tomlin	.05
622	Andy Van Slyke	.05
623	Paul Wagner	.05
624	Tim Wakefield	.05
625	Bob Walk	.05
626	Kevin Young	.05
627	Luis Alicea	.05
628	Rene Arocha	.05
629	Rod Brewer	.05
630	Rheal Cormier	.05
631	Bernard Gilkey	.05
632	Lee Guetterman	.05
633	Gregg Jefferies	.05
634	Brian Jordan	.05
635	Les Lancaster	.05
636	Ray Lankford	.05
637	Rob Murphy	.05
638	Omar Olivares	.05
639	Jose Oquendo	.05
640	Donovan Osborne	.05
641	Tom Pagnozzi	.05
642	Erik Pappas	.05
643	Geronimo Pena	.05
644	Mike Perez	.05
645	Gerald Perry	.05
646	Ozzie Smith	.85
647	Bob Tewksbury	.05
648	Allen Watson	.05
649	Mark Whiten	.05
650	Tracy Woodson	.05
651	Todd Zeile	.05
652	Andy Achby	.05
653	Brad Ausmus	.05
654	Billy Bean	.05
655	Derek Bell	.05
656	Andy Benes	.05
657	Doug Brocail	.05
658	Jarvis Brown	.05
659	Archi Cianfrocco	.05
660	Phil Clark	.05
661	Mark Davis	.05
662	Jeff Gardner	.05
663	Pat Gomez	.05
664	Ricky Gutierrez	.05
665	Tony Gwynn	.85
666	Gene Harris	.05
667	Kevin Higgins	.05
668	Trevor Hoffman	.05
669	Pedro A. Martinez **RC**	.05
670	Tim Mauser	.05
671	Melvin Nieves	.05
672	Phil Plantier	.05
673	Frank Seminara	.05
674	Craig Shipley	.05
675	Kerry Taylor	.05
676	Tim Teufel	.05
677	Guillermo Velasquez	.05
678	Wally Whitehurst	.05
679	Tim Worrell	.05
680	Rod Beck	.05
681	Mike Benjamin	.05
682	Todd Benzinger	.05
683	Bud Black	.05
684	Barry Bonds	2.00
685	Jeff Brantley	.05
686	Dave Burba	.05
687	John Burkett	.05
688	Mark Carreon	.05
689	Will Clark	.10
690	Royce Clayton	.05
691	Bryan Hickerson	.05
692	Mike Jackson	.05
693	Darren Lewis	.05
694	Kirt Manwaring	.05
695	Dave Martinez	.05
696	Willie McGee	.05
697	John Patterson	.05
698	Jeff Reed	.05
699	Kevin Rogers	.05
700	Scott Sanderson	.05
701	Steve Scarsone	.05
702	Billy Swift	.05
703	Robby Thompson	.05
704	Matt Williams	.05
705	Trevor Wilson	.05
706	"Brave New World" (Fred McGriff, Ron Gant, Dave Justice)	.10
707	"1-2 Punch" (Paul Molitor, John Olerud)	.10
708	"American Heat" (Mike Mussina, Jack McDowell)	.10
709	"Together Again" (Lou Whitaker, Alan Trammell)	.10
710	"Lone Star Lumber" (Rafael Palmeiro, Juan Gonzalez)	.20
711	"Batmen" (Brett Butler, Tony Gwynn)	.10
712	"Twin Peaks" (Kirby Puckett, Chuck Knoblauch)	.20
713	"Back to Back" (Mike Piazza, Eric Karros)	.25
714	Checklist	.05
715	Checklist	.05
716	Checklist	.05
717	Checklist	.05
718	Checklist	.05
719	Checklist	.05
720	Checklist	.05

All-Stars

Each league's 25 representatives for the 1993 All-Star Game are featured in this insert set. Fronts have a player action photo with a rippling American flag in the top half of the background. The '93 All-Star logo is featured at the bottom, along with a gold-foil impression of the player's name. The flag motif is repeated at top of the card back, along with a player portrait photo set against a red (American League) or blue (National League) background. Odds of finding one of the 50 All-Star inserts are one in every two 15-card foil packs.

		NM/M
Complete Set (50):		10.00
Common Player:		.10
1	Roberto Alomar	.20
2	Carlos Baerga	.10
3	Albert Belle	.10
4	Wade Boggs	.75
5	Joe Carter	.10
6	Scott Cooper	.10
7	Cecil Fielder	.10
8	Travis Fryman	.10
9	Juan Gonzalez	.60
10	Ken Griffey Jr.	1.50
11	Pat Hentgen	.10
12	Randy Johnson	.60
13	Jimmy Key	.10
14	Mark Langston	.10
15	Jack McDowell	.10
16	Paul Molitor	.60
17	Jeff Montgomery	.10
18	Mike Mussina	.40
19	John Olerud	.10
20	Kirby Puckett	.75
21	Cal Ripken, Jr.	2.00
22	Ivan Rodriguez	.50
23	Frank Thomas	.65
24	Greg Vaughn	.10
25	Duane Ward	.10
26	Steve Avery	.10
27	Rod Beck	.10
28	Jay Bell	.10
29	Andy Benes	.10
30	Jeff Blauser	.10
31	Barry Bonds	2.00
32	Bobby Bonilla	.10
33	John Burkett	.10
34	Darren Daulton	.10
35	Andres Galarraga	.10
36	Tom Glavine	.30
37	Mark Grace	.25
38	Marquis Grissom	.10
39	Tony Gwynn	.75
40	Bryan Harvey	.10
41	Dave Hollins	.10
42	Dave Justice	.10
43	Darryl Kile	.10
44	John Kruk	.10
45	Barry Larkin	.10
46	Terry Mulholland	.10
47	Mike Piazza	1.50
48	Ryne Sandberg	.75
49	Gary Sheffield	.30
50	John Smoltz	.10

Award Winners

The 1993 MVP, Cy Young and Rookie of the Year award winners from each league are featured in this insert set. Cards are UV coated on both sides. Three different croppings of the same player action photo are featured on the front, with the player's name and other printing in gold foil. Backs have a player portrait and short summary of his previous season's performance. According to the company, odds of finding one of these horizontal-format inserts were one in 37 packs.

		NM/M
Complete Set (6):		4.50
Common Player:		.25
1	Frank Thomas	.75
2	Barry Bonds	2.00
3	Jack McDowell	.25
4	Greg Maddux	1.00
5	Tim Salmon	.50
6	Mike Piazza	1.50

Golden Moments

Ten highlights from the 1993 Major League baseball season are commemorated in this insert set. Each of the cards has a title which summarizes the historical moment. These inserts were available exclusively in Fleer cards packaged for large retail outlets.

		NM/M
Complete Set (10):		5.00
Common Player:		.10
1	"Four in One" (Mark Whiten)	.10
2	"Left and Right" (Carlos Baerga)	.10
3	"3,000 Hit Club" (Dave Winfield)	.50
4	"Eight Straight" (Ken Griffey Jr.)	1.50
5	"Triumphant Return" (Bo Jackson)	.25
6	"Farewell to Baseball" (George Brett)	1.00
7	"Farewell to Baseball" (Nolan Ryan)	2.00
8	"Thirty Times Six" (Fred McGriff)	.10
9	"Enters 5th Dimension" (Frank Thomas)	.75
10	"The No-Hit Parade" (Chris Bosio, Jim Abbott, Darryl Kile)	.10

Golden Moments Super

Super-size (3-1/2" x 5") versions of the Golden Moments insert set were included in hobby cases at the rate of one set, in a specially-printed folder, per 20-box case. Each card carries a serial number designating its position in an edition of 10,000.

		NM/M
Complete Set (10):		7.50
Common Player:		.50
1	"Four in One" (Mark Whiten)	.50
2	"Left and Right" (Carlos Baerga)	.50
3	"3,000 Hit Club" (Dave Winfield)	.75
4	"Eight Straight" (Ken Griffey Jr.)	2.00
5	"Triumphant Return" (Bo Jackson)	.75
6	"Farewell to Baseball" (George Brett)	1.50
7	"Farewell to Baseball" (Nolan Ryan)	2.50
8	"Thirty Times Six" (Fred McGriff)	.50
9	"Enters 5th Dimension" (Frank Thomas)	1.00
10	"The No-Hit Parade" (Chris Bosio, Jim Abbott, Darryl Kile)	.50

League Leaders

Twelve players who led the major leagues in various statistical categories in 1993 are featured in this insert set. Cards are UV coated and have gold-foil stamping on both sides. Within a light metallic green border, card fronts feature a color action photo superimposed over a similar photo in black-and-white. The category in which the player led his league is printed down the right border. Other printing is gold-foil. On back is a color photo and details of the league-leading performance. Stated odds of finding a League Leaders card were one per 17 packs.

		NM/M
Complete Set (12):		3.00
Common Player:		.10
1	John Olerud	.10
2	Albert Belle	.10
3	Rafael Palmeiro	.75
4	Kenny Lofton	.10
5	Jack McDowell	.10
6	Kevin Appier	.10
7	Andres Galarraga	.10
8	Barry Bonds	2.00
9	Len Dykstra	.10
10	Chuck Carr	.10
11	Tom Glavine	.30
12	Greg Maddux	1.00

Lumber Co.

This insert set features the major leagues' top home run hitters. Inserted only in 21-card jumbo packs, odds of finding one were given as one per five packs. Card fronts feature player action photos against a background resembling the label area of a baseball bat. On back is a background photo of a row of bats on the dirt. A player write-up and close-up photo complete the design.

		NM/M
Complete Set (10):		7.50
Common Player:		.40
1	Albert Belle	.40
2	Barry Bonds	2.50
3	Ron Gant	.40
4	Juan Gonzalez	1.00
5	Ken Griffey Jr.	2.00
6	Dave Justice	.40
7	Fred McGriff	.40
8	Rafael Palmeiro	.75
9	Frank Thomas	1.25
10	Matt Williams	.40

Major League Prospects

Thirty-five of the game's promising young stars are featured in this insert set. A light green metallic border frames a player photo, with his team logo lightly printed over the background. Most of the printing is gold-foil stamped. Backs have a player photo against a pinstriped background. A light blue box contains career details. Given odds of finding a "Major League Prospects" card are one in six packs.

		NM/M
Complete Set (35):		4.00
Common Player:		.10
1	Kurt Abbott	.10
2	Brian Anderson	.10
3	Rich Aude	.10
4	Cory Bailey	.10
5	Danny Bautista	.10
6	Marty Cordova	.10
7	Tripp Cromer	.10
8	Midre Cummings	.10
9	Carlos Delgado	1.50
10	Steve Dreyer	.10
11	Steve Dunn	.10
12	Jeff Granger	.10
13	Tyrone Hill	.10
14	Denny Hocking	.10
15	John Hope	.10
16	Butch Huskey	.10
17	Miguel Jimenez	.10
18	Chipper Jones	2.50
19	Steve Karsay	.10
20	Mike Kelly	.10
21	Mike Lieberthal	.20
22	Albie Lopez	.10
23	Jeff McNeely	.10
24	Dan Miceli	.10
25	Nate Minchey	.10
26	Marc Newfield	.10
27	Darren Oliver	.10

28 Luis Ortiz .10
29 Curtis Pride .10
30 Roger Salkeld .10
31 Scott Sanders .10
32 Dave Staton .10
33 Salomon Torres .10
34 Steve Trachsel .10
35 Chris Turner .10

ProVisions

Nine players are featured in this insert set. Cards feature the fantasy artwork of Wayne Still in a format that produces one large image when all nine cards are properly arranged. Besides the art, card fronts feature the player's name in gold-foil. Backs have a background in several shades of red, with the player's name and team at the top in white. A short career summary is printed in black. Odds of finding this particular insert in a pack are one in 12.

		NM/M
Complete Set (9):		4.00
Common Player:		.25
1	Darren Daulton	.25
2	John Olerud	.25
3	Matt Williams	.25
4	Carlos Baerga	.25
5	Ozzie Smith	1.00
6	Juan Gonzalez	.75
7	Jack McDowell	.25
8	Mike Piazza	2.00
9	Tony Gwynn	1.00

Rookie Sensations

This insert set features the top rookies from 1993. These inserts were available only in 21-card jumbo packs, with stated odds of one in four packs. Full-bleed fronts have a pair of player photos - one highlighted by a neon outline - superimposed on a graduated background approximating the team colors. Team uniform logo details appear vertically at the right or left side. The player's name is gold-foil stamped in a banner at bottom. The Rookie Sensations and Fleer logos are also gold-imprinted. On back, the team uniform logo is repeated on a white background, along with another player photo and a short write-up.

		NM/M
Complete Set (20):		6.00
Common Player:		.25
1	Rene Arocha	.25
2	Jason Bere	.25
3	Jeromy Burnitz	.25
4	Chuck Carr	.25
5	Jeff Conine	.25
6	Steve Cooke	.25
7	Cliff Floyd	.25
8	Jeffrey Hammonds	.25
9	Wayne Kirby	.25
10	Mike Lansing	.25
11	Al Martin	.25
12	Greg McMichael	.25
13	Troy Neel	.25
14	Mike Piazza	4.00
15	Armando Reynoso	.25
16	Kirk Rueter	.25
17	Tim Salmon	1.00
18	Aaron Sele	.25
19	J.T. Snow	.25
20	Kevin Stocker	.25

Tim Salmon A.L. Rookie of the Year

The popular Angels Rookie of the Year is featured in a 15-card set produced in what Fleer terms "metallized" format. The first 12 cards in the set were inserted into foil packs at the rate of about one card per box. Three additional cards could be obtained by sending $1.50 and 10 '94 Fleer wrappers to a mail-in offer. On both front and back, the cards have a color player photo set against a metallic-image background.

	NM/M
Complete Set (15):	12.50
Common Card:	1.00
Autograph/2,000:	15.00
1-12 Tim Salmon	1.00
13-15 Tim Salmon	1.50

Smoke N' Heat

Among the scarcest of the '94 Fleer inserts, available at a stated rate of one per 30 packs, these feature 10 of the top strikeout pitchers in the major leagues. "Metallized" card fronts have a player photo set against an infernal background with large letters, "Smoke 'N Heat." The player's name is in gold foil at bottom. Backs have a similar chaotic hot-red background, a player photo and career summary.

		NM/M
Complete Set (12):		10.00
Common Player:		.20
1	Roger Clemens	4.00
2	David Cone	.25
3	Juan Guzman	.25
4	Pete Harnisch	.25
5	Randy Johnson	2.00
6	Mark Langston	.25
7	Greg Maddux	3.00
8	Mike Mussina	1.00
9	Jose Rijo	.25
10	Nolan Ryan	5.00
11	Curt Schilling	1.00
12	John Smoltz	.75

Team Leaders

A player from each major league team has been chosen for this 28-card insert set. Fronts feature a team logo against a backgound of graduated team colors. Player portrait and action photos are superimposed. At bottom is the player name, team and position, all in gold foil. Backs have a team logo and player photo set against a white background, with a short write-up justifying the player's selection as a "Team Leader." Odds of finding one of these inserts were given as one in eight packs.

		NM/M
Complete Set (28):		7.50
Common Player:		.10
1	Cal Ripken, Jr.	2.00
2	Mo Vaughn	.10
3	Tim Salmon	.15
4	Frank Thomas	.50
5	Carlos Baerga	.10
6	Cecil Fielder	.10
7	Brian McRae	.10
8	Greg Vaughn	.10
9	Kirby Puckett	.65
10	Don Mattingly	.75
11	Mark McGwire	1.50
12	Ken Griffey Jr.	1.00
13	Juan Gonzalez	.50
14	Paul Molitor	.50
15	Dave Justice	.10
16	Ryne Sandberg	.65
17	Barry Larkin	.10
18	Andres Galarraga	.10
19	Gary Sheffield	.25
20	Jeff Bagwell	.50
21	Mike Piazza	1.00
22	Marquis Grissom	.10
23	Bobby Bonilla	.10
24	Len Dykstra	.10
25	Jay Bell	.10
26	Gregg Jefferies	.10
27	Tony Gwynn	.65
28	Will Clark	.15

All-Rookie Team

Sharing the format of the basic 1994 Fleer issue, this nine-card set of rookies was available only by redemption of a trade card randomly inserted into foil packs. The exchange card expired Sept. 30, 1994. The cards are numbered with an "M" prefix.

		NM/M
Complete Set (9):		3.00
Common Player:		.25
Exchange Card:		.25
1	Kurt Abbott	.25
2	Rich Becker	.25
3	Carlos Delgado	2.00
4	Jorge Fabregas	.25
5	Bob Hamelin	.25
6	John Hudek	.25
7	Tim Hyers	.25
8	Luis Lopez	.25
9	James Mouton	.25

Update

Rookies, traded players and free agents who changed teams were included in the annual update issue. In the same format as the regular-issue '94 Fleer set, cards are numbered alphabetically within team. Ten special Diamond Tribute cards included in the Update set feature baseball's proven superstars.

		NM/M
Complete Set (210):		50.00
Common Player:		.05
1	Mark Eichhorn	.05
2	Sid Fernandez	.05
3	Leo Gomez	.05
4	Mike Oquist	.05
5	Rafael Palmeiro	.60
6	Chris Sabo	.05
7	Dwight Smith	.05
8	Lee Smith	.05
9	Damon Berryhill	.05
10	Wes Chamberlain	.05
11	Gar Finnvold	.05
12	Chris Howard	.05
13	Tim Naehring	.05
14	Otis Nixon	.05
15	Brian Anderson	.05
16	Jorge Fabregas	.05
17	Rex Hudler	.05
18	Bo Jackson	.15
19	Mark Leiter	.05
20	Spike Owen	.05
21	Harold Reynolds	.05
22	Chris Turner	.05
23	Dennis Cook	.05
24	Jose DeLeon	.05
25	Julio Franco	.05
26	Joe Hall	.05
27	Darrin Jackson	.05
28	Dane Johnson	.05
29	Norberto Martin	.05
30	Scott Sanderson	.05
31	Jason Grimsley	.05
32	Dennis Martinez	.05
33	Jack Morris	.05
34	Eddie Murray	.75
35	Chad Ogea	.05
36	Tony Pena	.05
37	Paul Shuey	.05
38	Omar Vizquel	.05
39	Danny Bautista	.05
40	Tim Belcher	.05
41	Joe Boever	.05
42	Storm Davis	.05
43	Junior Felix	.05
44	Mike Gardiner	.05
45	Buddy Groom	.05
46	Juan Samuel	.05
47	Vince Coleman	.05
48	Bob Hamelin	.05
49	Dave Henderson	.05
50	Rusty Meacham	.05
51	Terry Shumpert	.05
52	Jeff Bronkey	.05
53	Alex Diaz	.05
54	Brian Harper	.05
55	Jose Mercedes	.05
56	Jody Reed	.05
57	Bob Scanlan	.05
58	Turner Ward	.05
59	Rich Becker	.05
60	Alex Cole	.05
61	Denny Hocking	.05
62	Scott Leius	.05
63	Pat Mahomes	.05
64	Carlos Pulido	.05
65	Dave Stevens	.05
66	Matt Walbeck	.05
67	Xavier Hernandez	.05
68	Sterling Hitchcock	.05
69	Terry Mulholland	.05
70	Luis Polonia	.05
71	Gerald Williams	.05
72	Mark Acre	.05
73	Geronimo Berroa	.05
74	Rickey Henderson	.75
75	Stan Javier	.05
76	Steve Karsay	.05
77	Carlos Reyes	.05
78	Bill Taylor	.05
79	Eric Anthony	.05
80	Bobby Ayala	.05
81	Tim Davis	.05
82	Felix Fermin	.05
83	Reggie Jefferson	.05
84	Keith Mitchell	.05
85	Bill Risley	.05
86	Alex Rodriguez **RC**	40.00
87	Roger Salkeld	.05
88	Dan Wilson	.05
89	Cris Carpenter	.05
90	Will Clark	.10
91	Jeff Frye	.05
92	Rick Helling	.05
93	Chris James	.05
94	Oddibe McDowell	.05
95	Billy Ripken	.05
96	Carlos Delgado	.60
97	Alex Gonzalez	.05
98	Shawn Green	.50
99	Darren Hall	.05
100	Mike Huff	.05
101	Mike Kelly	.05
102	Roberto Kelly	.05
103	Charlie O'Brien	.05
104	Jose Oliva	.05
105	Gregg Olson	.05
106	Willie Banks	.05
107	Jim Bullinger	.05
108	Chuck Crim	.05
109	Shawon Dunston	.05
110	Karl Rhodes	.05
111	Steve Trachsel	.05
112	Anthony Young	.05
113	Eddie Zambrano	.05
114	Bret Boone	.05
115	Jeff Brantley	.05
116	Hector Carrasco	.05
117	Tony Fernandez	.05
118	Tim Fortugno	.05
119	Erik Hanson	.05
120	Chuck McElroy	.05
121	Deion Sanders	.05
122	Ellis Burks	.05
123	Marvin Freeman	.05
124	Mike Harkey	.05
125	Howard Johnson	.05
126	Mike Kingery	.05
127	Nelson Liriano	.05
128	Marcus Moore	.05
129	Mike Munoz	.05
130	Kevin Ritz	.05
131	Walt Weiss	.05
132	Kurt Abbott	.05
133	Jerry Browne	.05
134	Greg Colbrunn	.05
135	Jeremy Hernandez	.05
136	Dave Magadan	.05
137	Kurt Miller	.05
138	Robb Nen	.05
139	Jesus Taverez	.05
140	Sid Bream	.05
141	Tom Edens	.05
142	Tony Eusebio	.05
143	John Hudek	.05
144	Brian Hunter	.05
145	Orlando Miller	.05
146	James Mouton	.05
147	Shane Reynolds	.05
148	Rafael Bournigal	.05
149	Delino DeShields	.05
150	Garey Ingram	.05
151	Chan Ho Park	.05
152	Wil Cordero	.05
153	Pedro Martinez	.75
154	Randy Milligan	.05
155	Lenny Webster	.05
156	Rico Brogna	.05
157	Josias Manzanillo	.05
158	Kevin McReynolds	.05
159	Mike Remlinger	.05
160	David Segui	.05
161	Pete Smith	.05
162	Kelly Stinnett	.05
163	Jose Vizcaino	.05
164	Billy Hatcher	.05
165	Doug Jones	.05
166	Mike Lieberthal	.05
167	Tony Longmire	.05
168	Bobby Munoz	.05
169	Paul Quantrill	.05
170	Heathcliff Slocumb	.05
171	Fernando Valenzuela	.05
172	Mark Dewey	.05
173	Brian Hunter	.05
174	Jon Lieber	.05
175	Ravelo Manzanillo	.05
176	Dan Miceli	.05
177	Rick White	.05
178	Bryan Eversgerd	.05
179	John Habyan	.05
180	Terry McGriff	.05
181	Vicente Palacios	.05
182	Rich Rodriguez	.05
183	Rick Sutcliffe	.05
184	Donnie Elliott	.05
185	Joey Hamilton	.05
186	Tim Hyers	.05
187	Luis Lopez	.05
188	Ray McDavid	.05
189	Bip Roberts	.05
190	Scott Sanders	.05
191	Eddie Williams	.05
192	Steve Frey	.05
193	Pat Gomez	.05
194	Rich Monteleone	.05
195	Mark Portugal	.05
196	Darryl Strawberry	.05
197	Salomon Torres	.05
198	W. Van Landingham	.05
199	Checklist	.05
200	Checklist	.05
DIAMOND TRIBUTE		.05
DT1	Barry Bonds	2.00
DT2	Joe Carter	.05
DT3	Will Clark	.10
DT4	Roger Clemens	1.50
DT5	Tony Gwynn	1.00
DT6	Don Mattingly	1.50
DT7	Fred McGriff	.05
DT8	Eddie Murray	.75
DT9	Kirby Puckett	1.00
DT10	Cal Ripken Jr.	2.00

Atlantic

Five-card packs of this special Fleer set were given away with an eight-gallon premium gasoline purchase at Atlantic/Sunoco stations in the Eastern U.S. between June 1 and July 31. Many of the cards suffered damaged borders from the packaging process. Cards are in the basic 1994 Fleer format, though the name and position around the team logo at top are in white on these cards, rather than gold-foil. Different front and back photos are used in this set. Backs include the gas station logos at bottom.

		NM/M
Complete Set (25):		3.00
Common Player:		.10
1	Roberto Alomar	.20
2	Carlos Baerga	.10
3	Jeff Bagwell	.40
4	Jay Bell	.10
5	Barry Bonds	1.00
6	Joe Carter	.10
7	Roger Clemens	.60
8	Darren Daulton	.10
9	Lenny Dykstra	.10
10	Cecil Fielder	.10
11	Tom Glavine	.35
12	Juan Gonzalez	.40
13	Ken Griffey Jr.	.75
14	Dave Justice	.10
15	John Kruk	.10
16	Greg Maddux	.50
17	Don Mattingly	.60
18	Jack McDowell	.10
19	John Olerud	.10
20	Mike Piazza	.75
21	Kirby Puckett	.50
22	Tim Salmon	.25
23	Frank Thomas	.40
24	Andy Van Slyke	.10
25	Checklist	.05

Extra Bases

Extra Bases was a 400-card, oversized set, plus 80 insert cards in four different subsets. The cards, 4-11/16"

by 2-1/2", have a full-bleed photo on the front and back, as well as UV coating and color coding by team. As was the case in other Fleer products, Extra Bases contained an insert card in every pack. All 80 insert cards feature gold or silver foil stamping.

		NM/M
Complete Set (400):		15.00
Common Player:		.10
Wax Pack:		.45
Wax Box (36):		10.00
1	Brady Anderson	.10
2	Harold Baines	.10
3	Mike Devereaux	.10
4	Sid Fernandez	.10
5	Jeffrey Hammonds	.10
6	Chris Hoiles	.10
7	Ben McDonald	.10
8	Mark McLemore	.10
9	Mike Mussina	.40
10	Mike Oquist	.10
11	Rafael Palmeiro	.75
12	Cal Ripken, Jr.	2.50
13	Chris Sabo	.10
14	Lee Smith	.10
15	Wes Chamberlain	.10
16	Roger Clemens	1.25
17	Scott Cooper	.10
18	Danny Darwin	.10
19	Andre Dawson	.25
20	Mike Greenwell	.10
21	Tim Naehring	.10
22	Otis Nixon	.10
23	Jeff Russell	.10
24	Ken Ryan	.10
25	Aaron Sele	.10
26	John Valentin	.10
27	Mo Vaughn	.10
28	Frank Viola	.10
29	Brian Anderson **RC**	.15
30	Chad Curtis	.10
31	Chili Davis	.10
32	Gary DiSarcina	.10
33	Damion Easley	.10
34	Jim Edmonds	.10
35	Chuck Finley	.10
36	Bo Jackson	.15
37	Mark Langston	.10
38	Harold Reynolds	.10
39	Tim Salmon	.20
40	Wilson Alvarez	.10
41	James Baldwin	.10
42	Jason Bere	.10
43	Joey Cora	.10
44	Ray Durham **RC**	.50
45	Alex Fernandez	.10
46	Julio Franco	.10
47	Ozzie Guillen	.10
48	Darrin Jackson	.10
49	Lance Johnson	.10
50	Ron Karkovice	.10
51	Jack McDowell	.10
52	Tim Raines	.10
53	Frank Thomas	.75
54	Robin Ventura	.10
55	Sandy Alomar Jr.	.10
56	Carlos Baerga	.10
57	Albert Belle	.10
58	Mark Clark	.10
59	Wayne Kirby	.10
60	Kenny Lofton	.10
61	Dennis Martinez	.10
62	Jose Mesa	.10
63	Jack Morris	.10
64	Eddie Murray	.75
65	Charles Nagy	.10
66	Manny Ramirez	.75
67	Paul Shuey	.10
68	Paul Sorrento	.10
69	Jim Thome	.50
70	Omar Vizquel	.10
71	Eric Davis	.10
72	John Doherty	.10
73	Cecil Fielder	.10
74	Travis Fryman	.10
75	Kirk Gibson	.10
76	Gene Harris	.10
77	Mike Henneman	.10
78	Mike Moore	.10
79	Tony Phillips	.10
80	Mickey Tettleton	.10
81	Alan Trammell	.10
82	Lou Whitaker	.10
83	Kevin Appier	.10
84	Vince Coleman	.10
85	David Cone	.10
86	Gary Gaetti	.10
87	Greg Gagne	.10
88	Tom Gordon	.10
89	Jeff Granger	.10
90	Bob Hamelin	.10
91	Dave Henderson	.10
92	Felix Jose	.10
93	Wally Joyner	.10
94	Jose Lind	.10
95	Mike Macfarlane	.10
96	Brian McRae	.10
97	Jeff Montgomery	.10
98	Ricky Bones	.10
99	Jeff Bronkey	.10
100	Alex Diaz	.10
101	Cal Eldred	.10
102	Darryl Hamilton	.10
103	Brian Harper	.10
104	John Jaha	.10
105	Pat Listach	.10
106	Dave Nilsson	.10
107	Jody Reed	.10
108	Kevin Seitzer	.10
109	Greg Vaughn	.10
110	Turner Ward	.10
111	Wes Weger	.10
112	Bill Wegman	.10
113	Rick Aguilera	.10
114	Rich Becker	.10
115	Alex Cole	.10
116	Scott Erickson	.10
117	Kent Hrbek	.10
118	Chuck Knoblauch	.10
119	Scott Leius	.10
120	Shane Mack	.10
121	Pat Mahomes	.10
122	Pat Meares	.10
123	Kirby Puckett	1.00
124	Kevin Tapani	.10
125	Matt Walbeck	.10
126	Dave Winfield	.75
127	Jim Abbott	.10
128	Wade Boggs	1.00
129	Mike Gallego	.10
130	Xavier Hernandez	.10
131	Pat Kelly	.10
132	Jimmy Key	.10
133	Don Mattingly	1.25
134	Terry Mulholland	.10
135	Matt Nokes	.10
136	Paul O'Neill	.10
137	Melido Perez	.10
138	Luis Polonia	.10
139	Mike Stanley	.10
140	Danny Tartabull	.10
141	Randy Velarde	.10
142	Bernie Williams	.20
143	Mark Acre	.10
144	Geronimo Berroa	.10
145	Mike Bordick	.10
146	Scott Brosius	.10
147	Ron Darling	.10
148	Dennis Eckersley	.65
149	Brent Gates	.10
150	Rickey Henderson	.75
151	Stan Javier	.10
152	Steve Karsay	.10
153	Mark McGwire	2.00
154	Troy Neel	.10
155	Ruben Sierra	.10
156	Terry Steinbach	.10
157	Bill Taylor	.10
158	Rich Amaral	.10
159	Eric Anthony	.10
160	Bobby Ayala	.10
161	Chris Bosio	.10
162	Jay Buhner	.10
163	Tim Davis	.10
164	Felix Fermin	.10
165	Dave Fleming	.10
166	Ken Griffey Jr.	1.50
167	Reggie Jefferson	.10
168	Randy Johnson	.75
169	Edgar Martinez	.10
170	Tino Martinez	.10
171	Bill Risley	.10
172	Roger Salkeld	.10
173	Mac Suzuki **RC**	.20
174	Dan Wilson	.10
175	Kevin Brown	.10
176	Jose Canseco	.40
177	Will Clark	.15
178	Juan Gonzalez	.75
179	Rick Helling	.10
180	Tom Henke	.10
181	Chris James	.10
182	Manuel Lee	.10
183	Dean Palmer	.10
184	Ivan Rodriguez	.65
185	Kenny Rogers	.10
186	Roberto Alomar	.20
187	Pat Borders	.10
188	Joe Carter	.10
189	Carlos Delgado	.50
190	Juan Guzman	.10
191	Pat Hentgen	.10
192	Paul Molitor	.75
192a	Paul Molitor (Promotional sample.)	2.00
193	John Olerud	.10
194	Ed Sprague	.10
195	Dave Stewart	.10
196	Todd Stottlemyre	.10
197	Duane Ward	.10
198	Devon White	.10
199	Steve Avery	.10
200	Jeff Blauser	.10
201	Tom Glavine	.30
202	Dave Justice	.10
203	Mike Kelly	.10
204	Roberto Kelly	.10
205	Ryan Klesko	.10
206	Mark Lemke	.10
207	Javier Lopez	.10
208	Greg Maddux	1.00
209	Fred McGriff	.10
210	Greg McMichael	.10
211	Kent Mercker	.10
212	Terry Pendleton	.10
213	John Smoltz	.10
214	Tony Tarasco	.10
215	Willie Banks	.10
216	Steve Buechele	.10
217	Shawon Dunston	.10
218	Mark Grace	.15
219	Brooks Kieschnick **RC**	.10
220	Derrick May	.10
221	Randy Myers	.10
222	Karl Rhodes	.10
223	Rey Sanchez	.10
224	Sammy Sosa	1.50
225	Steve Traschel	.10
226	Rick Wilkins	.10
227	Bret Boone	.15
228	Jeff Brantley	.10
229	Tom Browning	.10
230	Hector Carrasco	.10
231	Rob Dibble	.10
232	Erik Hanson	.10
233	Barry Larkin	.10
234	Kevin Mitchell	.10
235	Hal Morris	.10
236	Joe Oliver	.10
237	Jose Rijo	.10
238	Johnny Ruffin	.10
239	Deion Sanders	.15
240	Reggie Sanders	.10
241	John Smiley	.10
242	Dante Bichette	.10
243	Ellis Burks	.10
244	Andres Galarraga	.10
245	Joe Girardi	.10
246	Greg Harris	.10
247	Charlie Hayes	.10
248	Howard Johnson	.10
249	Roberto Mejia	.10
250	Marcus Moore	.10
251	David Nied	.10
252	Armando Reynoso	.10
253	Bruce Ruffin	.10
254	Mark Thompson	.10
255	Walt Weiss	.10
256	Kurt Abbott **RC**	.20
257	Bret Barberie	.10
258	Chuck Carr	.10
259	Jeff Conine	.10
260	Chris Hammond	.10
261	Bryan Harvey	.10
262	Jeremy Hernandez	.10
263	Charlie Hough	.10
264	Dave Magadan	.10
265	Benito Santiago	.10
266	Gary Sheffield	.25
267	David Weathers	.10
268	Jeff Bagwell	.75
269	Craig Biggio	.10
270	Ken Caminiti	.10
271	Andujar Cedeno	.10
272	Doug Drabek	.10
273	Steve Finley	.10
274	Luis Gonzalez	.20
275	Pete Harnisch	.10
276	John Hudek	.10
277	Darryl Kile	.10
278	Orlando Miller	.10
279	James Mouton	.10
280	Shane Reynolds	.10
281	Scott Servais	.10
282	Greg Swindell	.10
283	Pedro Astacio	.10
284	Brett Butler	.10
285	Tom Candiotti	.10
286	Delino DeShields	.10
287	Kevin Gross	.10
288	Orel Hershiser	.10
289	Eric Karros	.10
290	Ramon Martinez	.10
291	Raul Mondesi	.10
292	Jose Offerman	.10
293	Chan Ho Park **RC**	.75
294	Mike Piazza	1.50
295	Henry Rodriguez	.10
296	Cory Snyder	.10
297	Tim Wallach	.10
298	Todd Worrell	.10
299	Moises Alou	.10
300	Sean Berry	.10
301	Wil Cordero	.10
302	Joey Eischen	.10
303	Jeff Fassero	.10
304	Darrin Fletcher	.10
305	Cliff Floyd	.10
306	Marquis Grissom	.10
307	Ken Hill	.10
308	Mike Lansing	.10
309	Pedro Martinez	.75
310	Mel Rojas	.10
311	Kirk Rueter	.10
312	Larry Walker	.10
313	John Wetteland	.10
314	Rondell White	.10
315	Bobby Bonilla	.10
316	John Franco	.10
317	Dwight Gooden	.10
318	Todd Hundley	.10
319	Bobby Jones	.10
320	Jeff Kent	.10
321	Kevin McReynolds	.10
322	Bill Pulsipher	.10
323	Bret Saberhagen	.10
324	David Segui	.10
325	Pete Smith	.10
326	Kelly Stinnett	.10
327	Ryan Thompson	.10
328	Jose Vizcaino	.10
329	Ricky Bottalico	.10
330	Darren Daulton	.10
331	Mariano Duncan	.10
332	Len Dykstra	.10
333	Tommy Greene	.10
334	Billy Hatcher	.10
335	Dave Hollins	.10
336	Pete Incaviglia	.10
337	Danny Jackson	.10
338	Doug Jones	.10
339	Ricky Jordan	.10
340	John Kruk	.10
341	Curt Schilling	.30
342	Kevin Stocker	.10
343	Jay Bell	.10
344	Steve Cooke	.10
345	Carlos Garcia	.10
346	Brian Hunter	.10
347	Jeff King	.10
348	Al Martin	.10
349	Orlando Merced	.10
350	Denny Neagle	.10
351	Don Slaught	.10
352	Andy Van Slyke	.10
353	Paul Wagner	.10
354	Rick White	.10
355	Luis Alicea	.10
356	Rene Arocha	.10
357	Rheal Cormier	.10
358	Bernard Gilkey	.10
359	Gregg Jefferies	.10
360	Ray Lankford	.10
361	Tom Pagnozzi	.10
362	Mike Perez	.10
363	Ozzie Smith	1.00
364	Bob Tewksbury	.10
365	Mark Whiten	.10
366	Todd Zeile	.10
367	Andy Ashby	.10
368	Brad Ausmus	.10
369	Derek Bell	.10
370	Andy Benes	.10
371	Archi Cianfrocco	.10
372	Tony Gwynn	1.00
373	Trevor Hoffman	.10
374	Tim Hyers	.10
375	Pedro Martinez	.10
376	Phil Plantier	.10
377	Bip Roberts	.10
378	Scott Sanders	.10
379	Dave Staton	.10
380	Wally Whitehurst	.10
381	Rod Beck	.10
382	Todd Benzinger	.10
383	Barry Bonds	2.50
384	John Burkett	.10
385	Royce Clayton	.10
386	Bryan Hickerson	.10
387	Mike Jackson	.10
388	Darren Lewis	.10
389	Kirt Manwaring	.10
390	Willie McGee	.10
391	Mark Portugal	.10
392	Bill Swift	.10
393	Robby Thompson	.10
394	Salomon Torres	.10
395	Matt Williams	.10
396	Checklist	.10
397	Checklist	.10
398	Checklist	.10
399	Checklist	.10
400	Checklist	.10

Extra Bases Game Breakers

Game Breakers featured 30 big-name stars from both leagues who have exhibited offensive firepower. This insert set was done in a horizontal format picturing the player in two different shots, one close-up and one slightly further away. The words "Game Breakers" is written across the bottom, with the player name and team in much smaller letters, printed under it.

		NM/M
Complete Set (30):		15.00
Common Player:		.25
1	Jeff Bagwell	.75
2	Rod Beck	.25
3	Albert Belle	.25
4	Barry Bonds	3.00
5	Jose Canseco	.65
6	Joe Carter	.25
7	Roger Clemens	1.50
8	Darren Daulton	.25
9	Len Dykstra	.25
10	Cecil Fielder	.25
11	Tom Glavine	.50
12	Juan Gonzalez	.75
13	Mark Grace	.35
14	Ken Griffey Jr.	2.00
15	Dave Justice	.25
16	Greg Maddux	1.25
17	Don Mattingly	1.50
18	Ben McDonald	.25
19	Fred McGriff	.25
20	Paul Molitor	.75
21	John Olerud	.25
22	Mike Piazza	2.00
23	Kirby Puckett	1.25
24	Cal Ripken, Jr.	3.00
25	Tim Salmon	.35
26	Gary Sheffield	.50
27	Frank Thomas	1.00
28	Mo Vaughn	.25
29	Matt Williams	.25
30	Dave Winfield	.75

Extra Bases Major League Hopefuls

Minor league standouts with impressive credentials were showcased in Major League Hopefuls. Each card in this insert set shows the player over a computer enhanced background, with three smaller photos running down the top half, on the left side of the card. The insert set title runs across the bottom and the player's name is just under it on a black strip.

		NM/M
Complete Set (10):		2.00
Common Player:		.25
1	James Baldwin	.25
2	Ricky Bottalico	.25
3	Ray Durham	.25
4	Joey Eischen	.25
5	Brooks Kieschnick	.25
6	Orlando Miller	.25
7	Bill Pulsipher	.25
8	Mac Suzuki	.25
9	Mark Thompson	.25
10	Wes Weger	.25

Extra Bases Rookie Standouts

Rookie Standouts highlights 20 of the best and brightest first-year players of the 1994 season. Cards picture the player on a baseball background, with a black, jagged-edged "aura" around the player. Names and teams were placed in the bottom-left corner, running up the side. The Rookie Standouts logo, which is a gold glove with a baseball in it and "Rookie Standouts" printed under it, was placed in the bottom-right corner and the Extra Bases logo appears in the upper-left.

		NM/M
Complete Set (20):		7.50
Common Player:		.25
1	Kurt Abbott	.25
2	Brian Anderson	.25
3	Hector Carrasco	.25
4	Tim Davis	.25
5	Carlos Delgado	2.50
6	Cliff Floyd	.25
7	Bob Hamelin	.25
8	Jeffrey Hammonds	.25
9	Rick Helling	.25
10	Steve Karsay	.25
11	Ryan Klesko	.25
12	Javier Lopez	.25
13	Raul Mondesi	.25
14	James Mouton	.25
15	Chan Ho Park	.25
16	Manny Ramirez	3.00
17	Tony Tarasco	.25
18	Steve Trachsel	.25
19	Rick White	.25
20	Rondell White	.25

Extra Bases Second Year Stars

Second-Year Stars contains 1993 rookies who were expected to have an even bigger impact in the 1994 season. Each card features five photos of the player. Four are in a filmstrip down the left side; the remaining two-thirds of the card contain a larger photo. "Second-Year Stars" is printed across the bottom, along with the player name and team. Backs repeat the film-strip motif.

		NM/M
Complete Set (20):		5.00
Common Player:		.25
1	Bobby Ayala	.25
2	Jason Bere	.25
3	Chuck Carr	.25
4	Jeff Conine	.25
5	Steve Cooke	.25
6	Wil Cordero	.25
7	Carlos Garcia	.25
8	Brent Gates	.25
9	Trevor Hoffman	.25
10	Wayne Kirby	.25
11	Al Martin	.25
12	Pedro Martinez	1.50
13	Greg McMichael	.25
14	Troy Neel	.25
15	David Nied	.25
16	Mike Piazza	3.00
17	Kirk Rueter	.25
18	Tim Salmon	.50
19	Aaron Sele	.25
20	Kevin Stocker	.25

Extra Bases Pitcher's Duel

Pitcher's Duel was available to collectors who mailed in 10 Extra Bases wrappers. The set features 20 of the top pitchers in baseball. Contained in the set were five American League and five National League cards, with two pitchers from the same league on each card. The front background pictures a wide-angle photo of a major league stadium, viewed from above the diamond, behind home plate. Backs have two more action photos set against a sepia-toned background photo of an Old West street to enhance the shootout theme of the set. Cards are numbered with an "M" prefix.

		NM/M
Complete Set (10):		7.50
Common Player:		.50
1	Roger Clemens, Jack McDowell	2.50
2	Ben McDonald, Randy Johnson	1.50
3	Jimmy Key, David Cone	.50
4	Mike Mussina, Aaron Sele	1.00
5	Chuck Finley, Wilson Alvarez	.50
6	Steve Avery, Curt Schilling	.75
7	Greg Maddux, Jose Rijo	2.00
8	Bret Saberhagen, Bob Tewksbury	.50
9	Tom Glavine, Bill Swift	.75
10	Doug Drabek, Orel Hershiser	.50

1995 Fleer Promos

This eight-player (plus a header card), cello-wrapped promo set was included in a special "Fleer" national newsstand magazine in early 1995. At first glance the cards seem identical to the regularly issued cards of the same players, but there are subtle differences on the back of each card.

		NM/M
Complete Set (9):		4.00
Common Player:		.50
26	Roger Clemens (1988 291 SO and 1992 2.41 ERA boxed)	2.00
78	Paul O'Neill (1991 boxed)	.50
155	David Cone (1990 233 SO boxed, white shadow on team names)	.50
235	Tim Salmon (No box on 1992 101 R.)	.50
285	Juan Gonzalez (Black stats, 1993 boxed.)	1.00
351	Marquis Grissom (No box on 1988 291 AB.)	.50
509	Ozzie Smith (Black stats, no box on 1986 Cardinals.)	1.50
514	Dante Bichette (Black stats.)	.50
--	Header Card "Different by Design"	.05

1995 Fleer

Fleer baseball in 1995 offered six different designs, one for each division. The basic set contains 600 cards and was sold in 12- and 18-card packs. National League West cards feature many smaller pictures in the background that are identical to the picture in the forefront, while AL West cards contain an action photo over top of a close-up on the right side and a water colored look on the left side. AL Central cards exhibit numbers pertinant to each player throughout the front design, with the player in the middle. NL East players appear in action on the left half of the card with a colorful, encripted look on the rest. National League Central and American League East feature more standard designs with the player in the forefront, with vital numbers and a color background.

		NM/M
Complete Set (600):		15.00
Common Player:		.05
Pack (12):		.75
Wax Box (36):		17.50
1	Brady Anderson	.05
2	Harold Baines	.05
3	Damon Buford	.05
4	Mike Devereaux	.05
5	Mark Eichhorn	.05
6	Sid Fernandez	.05
7	Leo Gomez	.05
8	Jeffrey Hammonds	.05
9	Chris Hoiles	.05
10	Rick Krivda	.05
11	Ben McDonald	.05
12	Mark McLemore	.05
13	Alan Mills	.05
14	Jamie Moyer	.05
15	Mike Mussina	.40
16	Mike Oquist	.05
17	Rafael Palmeiro	.65
18	Arthur Rhodes	.05
19	Cal Ripken, Jr.	2.50
20	Chris Sabo	.05
21	Lee Smith	.05
22	Jack Voight	.05
23	Damon Berryhill	.05
24	Tom Brunansky	.05
25	Wes Chamberlain	.05
26	Roger Clemens	1.25
27	Scott Cooper	.05
28	Andre Dawson	.25
29	Gar Finnvold	.05
30	Tony Fossas	.05
31	Mike Greenwell	.05
32	Joe Hesketh	.05
33	Chris Howard	.05
34	Chris Nabholz	.05
35	Tim Naehring	.05
36	Otis Nixon	.05
37	Carlos Rodriguez	.05
38	Rich Rowland	.05
39	Ken Ryan	.05
40	Aaron Sele	.05
41	John Valentin	.05
42	Mo Vaughn	.05
43	Frank Viola	.05
44	Danny Bautista	.05
45	Joe Boever	.05
46	Milt Cuyler	.05
47	Storm Davis	.05
48	John Doherty	.05
49	Junior Felix	.05
50	Cecil Fielder	.05
51	Travis Fryman	.05
52	Mike Gardiner	.05
53	Kirk Gibson	.05
54	Chris Gomez	.05
55	Buddy Groom	.05
56	Mike Henneman	.05
57	Chad Kreuter	.05
58	Mike Moore	.05
59	Tony Phillips	.05
60	Juan Samuel	.05
61	Mickey Tettleton	.05
62	Alan Trammell	.05
63	David Wells	.05
64	Lou Whitaker	.05
65	Jim Abbott	.05
66	Joe Ausanio	.05
67	Wade Boggs	1.00
68	Mike Gallego	.05
69	Xavier Hernandez	.05
70	Sterling Hitchcock	.05
71	Steve Howe	.05
72	Scott Kamieniecki	.05
73	Pat Kelly	.05
74	Jimmy Key	.05
75	Jim Leyritz	.05
76	Don Mattingly	1.25
77	Terry Mulholland	.05
78	Paul O'Neill	.05
79	Melido Perez	.05
80	Luis Polonia	.05
81	Mike Stanley	.05
82	Danny Tartabull	.05
83	Randy Velarde	.05
84	Bob Wickman	.05
85	Bernie Williams	.10
86	Gerald Williams	.05
87	Roberto Alomar	.10
88	Pat Borders	.05
89	Joe Carter	.05
90	Tony Castillo	.05
91	Brad Cornett	.05
92	Carlos Delgado	.50
93	Alex Gonzalez	.05
94	Shawn Green	.40
95	Juan Guzman	.05
96	Darren Hall	.05
97	Pat Hentgen	.05
98	Mike Huff	.05
99	Randy Knorr	.05
100	Al Leiter	.05
101	Paul Molitor	.75
102	John Olerud	.05
103	Dick Schofield	.05
104	Ed Sprague	.05
105	Dave Stewart	.05
106	Todd Stottlemyre	.05
107	Devon White	.05
108	Woody Williams	.05
109	Wilson Alvarez	.05
110	Paul Assenmacher	.05
111	Jason Bere	.05
112	Dennis Cook	.05
113	Joey Cora	.05
114	Jose DeLeon	.05
115	Alex Fernandez	.05
116	Julio Franco	.05
117	Craig Grabeck	.05
118	Ozzie Guillen	.05
119	Roberto Hernandez	.05
120	Darrin Jackson	.05
121	Lance Johnson	.05
122	Ron Karkovice	.05
123	Mike LaValliere	.05
124	Norberto Martin	.05
125	Kirk McCaskill	.05
126	Jack McDowell	.05
127	Tim Raines	.05
128	Frank Thomas	.75
129	Robin Ventura	.05
130	Sandy Alomar Jr.	.05
131	Carlos Baerga	.05
132	Albert Belle	.05
133	Mark Clark	.05
134	Alvaro Espinoza	.05
135	Jason Grimsley	.05
136	Wayne Kirby	.05
137	Kenny Lofton	.05
138	Albie Lopez	.05
139	Dennis Martinez	.05
140	Jose Mesa	.05
141	Eddie Murray	.75
142	Charles Nagy	.05
143	Tony Pena	.05
144	Eric Plunk	.05
145	Manny Ramirez	.75
146	Jeff Russell	.05
147	Paul Shuey	.05
148	Paul Sorrento	.05
149	Jim Thome	.65
150	Omar Vizquel	.05
151	Dave Winfield	.75
152	Kevin Appier	.05
153	Billy Brewer	.05
154	Vince Coleman	.05
155	David Cone	.05
156	Gary Gaetti	.05
157	Greg Gagne	.05
158	Tom Gordon	.05
159	Mark Gubicza	.05
160	Bob Hamelin	.05
161	Dave Henderson	.05
162	Felix Jose	.05
163	Wally Joyner	.05
164	Jose Lind	.05
165	Mike Macfarlane	.05
166	Mike Magnante	.05
167	Brent Mayne	.05
168	Brian McRae	.05
169	Rusty Meacham	.05
170	Jeff Montgomery	.05
171	Hipolito Pichardo	.05
172	Terry Shumpert	.05
173	Michael Tucker	.05
174	Ricky Bones	.05
175	Jeff Cirillo **RC**	.30
176	Alex Diaz	.05
177	Cal Eldred	.05
178	Mike Fetters	.05
179	Darryl Hamilton	.05
180	Brian Harper	.05
181	John Jaha	.05
182	Pat Listach	.05
183	Graeme Lloyd	.05
184	Jose Mercedes	.05
185	Matt Mieske	.05
186	Dave Nilsson	.05
187	Jody Reed	.05
188	Bob Scanlan	.05
189	Kevin Seitzer	.05
190	Bill Spiers	.05
191	B.J. Surhoff	.05
192	Jose Valentin	.05
193	Greg Vaughn	.05
194	Turner Ward	.05
195	Bill Wegman	.05
196	Rick Aguilera	.05
197	Rich Becker	.05
198	Alex Cole	.05
199	Marty Cordova	.05
200	Steve Dunn	.05
201	Scott Erickson	.05
202	Mark Guthrie	.05
203	Chip Hale	.05
204	LaTroy Hawkins	.05
205	Denny Hocking	.05
206	Chuck Knoblauch	.05
207	Scott Leius	.05
208	Shane Mack	.05
209	Pat Mahomes	.05
210	Pat Meares	.05
211	Pedro Munoz	.05
212	Kirby Puckett	1.00
213	Jeff Reboulet	.05
214	Dave Stevens	.05
215	Kevin Tapani	.05
216	Matt Walbeck	.05
217	Carl Willis	.05
218	Brian Anderson	.05
219	Chad Curtis	.05
220	Chili Davis	.05
221	Gary DiSarcina	.05
222	Damion Easley	.05
223	Jim Edmonds	.05
224	Chuck Finley	.05
225	Joe Grahe	.05
226	Rex Hudler	.05
227	Bo Jackson	.10
228	Mark Langston	.05
229	Phil Leftwich	.05
230	Mark Leiter	.05
231	Spike Owen	.05
232	Bob Patterson	.05
233	Troy Percival	.05
234	Eduardo Perez	.05
235	Tim Salmon	.10
236	J.T. Snow	.05
237	Chris Turner	.05
238	Mark Acre	.05
239	Geronimo Berroa	.05
240	Mike Bordick	.05
241	John Briscoe	.05
242	Scott Brosius	.05
243	Ron Darling	.05
244	Dennis Eckersley	.65
245	Brent Gates	.05
246	Rickey Henderson	.75
247	Stan Javier	.05
248	Steve Karsay	.05
249	Mark McGwire	2.00
250	Troy Neel	.05
251	Steve Ontiveros	.05
252	Carlos Reyes	.05
253	Ruben Sierra	.05
254	Terry Steinbach	.05
255	Bill Taylor	.05
256	Todd Van Poppel	.05
257	Bobby Witt	.05
258	Rich Amaral	.05
259	Eric Anthony	.05
260	Bobby Ayala	.05
261	Mike Blowers	.05
262	Chris Bosio	.05
263	Jay Buhner	.05
264	John Cummings	.05
265	Tim Davis	.05
266	Felix Fermin	.05
267	Dave Fleming	.05
268	Goose Gossage	.05
269	Ken Griffey Jr.	1.50
270	Reggie Jefferson	.05
271	Randy Johnson	.75
272	Edgar Martinez	.05
273	Tino Martinez	.05
274	Greg Pirkl	.05
275	Bill Risley	.05
276	Roger Salkeld	.05
277	Luis Sojo	.05
278	Mac Suzuki	.05
279	Dan Wilson	.05
280	Kevin Brown	.05
281	Jose Canseco	.40
282	Cris Carpenter	.05
283	Will Clark	.10
284	Jeff Frye	.05
285	Juan Gonzalez	.65
286	Rick Helling	.05
287	Tom Henke	.05
288	David Hulse	.05
289	Chris James	.05
290	Manuel Lee	.05
291	Oddibe McDowell	.05
292	Dean Palmer	.05
293	Roger Pavlik	.05
294	Bill Ripken	.05
295	Ivan Rodriguez	.65
296	Kenny Rogers	.05
297	Doug Strange	.05
298	Matt Whiteside	.05
299	Steve Avery	.05
300	Steve Bedrosian	.05
301	Rafael Belliard	.05
302	Jeff Blauser	.05
303	Dave Gallagher	.05
304	Tom Glavine	.30
305	Dave Justice	.05
306	Mike Kelly	.05
307	Roberto Kelly	.05
308	Ryan Klesko	.05
309	Mark Lemke	.05
310	Javier Lopez	.05
311	Greg Maddux	1.00
312	Fred McGriff	.05
313	Greg McMichael	.05
314	Kent Mercker	.05
315	Charlie O'Brien	.05
316	Jose Oliva	.05
317	Terry Pendleton	.05
318	John Smoltz	.05
319	Mike Stanton	.05
320	Tony Tarasco	.05
321	Terrell Wade	.05
322	Mark Wohlers	.05
323	Kurt Abbott	.05
324	Luis Aquino	.05
325	Bret Barberie	.05
326	Ryan Bowen	.05
327	Jerry Browne	.05
328	Chuck Carr	.05
329	Matias Carrillo	.05
330	Greg Colbrunn	.05
331	Jeff Conine	.05
332	Mark Gardner	.05
333	Chris Hammond	.05
334	Bryan Harvey	.05
335	Richie Lewis	.05
336	Dave Magadan	.05
337	Terry Mathews	.05
338	Robb Nen	.05
339	Yorkis Perez	.05
340	Pat Rapp	.05
341	Benito Santiago	.05
342	Gary Sheffield	.40
343	Dave Weathers	.05
344	Moises Alou	.05
345	Sean Berry	.05
346	Wil Cordero	.05
347	Joe Eischen	.05
348	Jeff Fassero	.05
349	Darrin Fletcher	.05
350	Cliff Floyd	.05
351	Marquis Grissom	.05
352	Butch Henry	.05
353	Gil Heredia	.05
354	Ken Hill	.05
355	Mike Lansing	.05
356	Pedro Martinez	.75
357	Mel Rojas	.05
358	Kirk Rueter	.05
359	Tim Scott	.05
360	Jeff Shaw	.05
361	Larry Walker	.05
362	Lenny Webster	.05
363	John Wetteland	.05
364	Rondell White	.05
365	Bobby Bonilla	.05
366	Rico Brogna	.05
367	Jeromy Burnitz	.05
368	John Franco	.05
369	Dwight Gooden	.05
370	Todd Hundley	.05
371	Jason Jacome	.05
372	Bobby Jones	.05
373	Jeff Kent	.05
374	Jim Lindeman	.05
375	Josias Manzanillo	.05
376	Roger Mason	.05
377	Kevin McReynolds	.05
378	Joe Orsulak	.05
379	Bill Pulsipher	.05
380	Bret Saberhagen	.05
381	David Segui	.05
382	Pete Smith	.05
383	Kelly Stinnett	.05
384	Ryan Thompson	.05
385	Jose Vizcaino	.05
386	Toby Borland	.05
387	Ricky Bettalico	.05
388	Darren Daulton	.05
389	Mariano Duncan	.05
390	Len Dykstra	.05
391	Jim Eisenreich	.05
392	Tommy Greene	.05
393	Dave Hollins	.05
394	Pete Incaviglia	.05
395	Danny Jackson	.05
396	Doug Jones	.05
397	Ricky Jordan	.05
398	John Kruk	.05
399	Mike Lieberthal	.05
400	Tony Longmire	.05
401	Mickey Morandini	.05
402	Bobby Munoz	.05
403	Curt Schilling	.25
404	Heathcliff Slocumb	.05
405	Kevin Stocker	.05
406	Fernando Valenzuela	.05
407	David West	.05
408	Willie Banks	.05
409	Jose Bautista	.05
410	Steve Buechele	.05
411	Jim Bullinger	.05
412	Chuck Crim	.05
413	Shawon Dunston	.05
414	Kevin Foster	.05
415	Mark Grace	.10
416	Jose Hernandez	.05
417	Glenallen Hill	.05
418	Brooks Kieschnick	.05
419	Derrick May	.05
420	Randy Myers	.05
421	Dan Plesac	.05
422	Karl Rhodes	.05
423	Rey Sanchez	.05
424	Sammy Sosa	1.50
425	Steve Trachsel	.05
426	Rick Wilkins	.05
427	Anthony Young	.05
428	Eddie Zambrano	.05
429	Bret Boone	.05
430	Jeff Branson	.05
431	Jeff Brantley	.05
432	Hector Carrasco	.05
433	Brian Dorsett	.05
434	Tony Fernandez	.05
435	Tim Fortugno	.05
436	Erik Hanson	.05
437	Thomas Howard	.05
438	Kevin Jarvis	.05
439	Barry Larkin	.05
440	Chuck McElroy	.05
441	Kevin Mitchell	.05
442	Hal Morris	.05
443	Jose Rijo	.05
444	John Roper	.05
445	Johnny Ruffin	.05
446	Deion Sanders	.05
447	Reggie Sanders	.05
448	Pete Schourek	.05
449	John Smiley	.05
450	Eddie Taubensee	.05
451	Jeff Bagwell	.75
452	Kevin Bass	.05
453	Craig Biggio	.05
454	Ken Caminiti	.05
455	Andujar Cedeno	.05
456	Doug Drabek	.05
457	Tony Eusebio	.05
458	Mike Felder	.05
459	Steve Finley	.05
460	Luis Gonzalez	.10
461	Mike Hampton	.05
462	Pete Harnisch	.05
463	John Hudek	.05
464	Todd Jones	.05
465	Darryl Kile	.05
466	James Mouton	.05
467	Shane Reynolds	.05
468	Scott Servais	.05
469	Greg Swindell	.05
470	Dave Veres	.05
471	Brian Williams	.05
472	Jay Bell	.05
473	Jacob Brumfield	.05
474	Dave Clark	.05
475	Steve Cooke	.05
476	Midre Cummings	.05
477	Mark Dewey	.05
478	Tom Foley	.05
479	Carlos Garcia	.05
480	Jeff King	.05
481	Jon Lieber	.05
482	Ravelo Manzanillo	.05
483	Al Martin	.05
484	Orlando Merced	.05
485	Danny Miceli	.05
486	Denny Neagle	.05
487	Lance Parrish	.05
488	Don Slaught	.05
489	Zane Smith	.05
490	Andy Van Slyke	.05
491	Paul Wagner	.05
492	Rick White	.05
493	Luis Alicea	.05
494	Rene Arocha	.05
495	Rheal Cormier	.05
496	Bryan Eversgerd	.05
497	Bernard Gilkey	.05
498	John Habyan	.05
499	Gregg Jefferies	.05
500	Brian Jordan	.05
501	Ray Lankford	.05
502	John Mabry	.05
503	Terry McGriff	.05
504	Tom Pagnozzi	.05
505	Vicente Palacios	.05
506	Geronimo Pena	.05
507	Gerald Perry	.05
508	Rich Rodriguez	.05
509	Ozzie Smith	1.00
510	Bob Tewksbury	.05
511	Allen Watson	.05
512	Mark Whiten	.05
513	Todd Zeile	.05
514	Dante Bichette	.05
515	Willie Blair	.05
516	Ellis Burks	.05
517	Marvin Freeman	.05
518	Andres Galarraga	.05
519	Joe Girardi	.05
520	Greg Harris	.05
521	Charlie Hayes	.05
522	Mike Kingery	.05
523	Nelson Liriano	.05
524	Mike Munoz	.05
525	David Nied	.05
526	Steve Reed	.05
527	Kevin Ritz	.05
528	Bruce Ruffin	.05
529	John Vander Wal	.05
530	Walt Weiss	.05
531	Eric Young	.05
532	Billy Ashley	.05
533	Pedro Astacio	.05
534	Rafael Bournigal	.05
535	Brett Butler	.05
536	Tom Candiotti	.05
537	Omar Daal	.05
538	Delino DeShields	.05
539	Darren Dreifort	.05
540	Kevin Gross	.05
541	Orel Hershiser	.05
542	Garey Ingram	.05
543	Eric Karros	.05
544	Ramon Martinez	.05
545	Raul Mondesi	.05
546	Chan Ho Park	.05
547	Mike Piazza	1.50
548	Henry Rodriguez	.05
549	Rudy Seanez	.05
550	Ismael Valdes	.05
551	Tim Wallach	.05
552	Todd Worrell	.05
553	Andy Ashby	.05
554	Brad Ausmus	.05
555	Derek Bell	.05
556	Andy Benes	.05

#	Player	NM/M
557	Phil Clark	.05
558	Donnie Elliott	.05
559	Ricky Gutierrez	.05
560	Tony Gwynn	1.00
561	Joey Hamilton	.05
562	Trevor Hoffman	.05
563	Luis Lopez	.05
564	Pedro Martinez	.05
565	Tim Mauser	.05
566	Phil Plantier	.05
567	Bip Roberts	.05
568	Scott Sanders	.05
569	Craig Shipley	.05
570	Jeff Tabaka	.05
571	Eddie Williams	.05
572	Rod Beck	.05
573	Mike Benjamin	.05
574	Barry Bonds	2.50
575	Dave Burba	.05
576	John Burkett	.05
577	Mark Carreon	.05
578	Royce Clayton	.05
579	Steve Frey	.05
580	Bryan Hickerson	.05
581	Mike Jackson	.05
582	Darren Lewis	.05
583	Kirt Manwaring	.05
584	Rich Monteleone	.05
585	John Patterson	.05
586	J.R. Phillips	.05
587	Mark Portugal	.05
588	Joe Rosselli	.05
589	Darryl Strawberry	.05
590	Bill Swift	.05
591	Robby Thompson	.05
592	William Van Landingham	.05
593	Matt Williams	.05
594	Checklist	.05
595	Checklist	.05
596	Checklist	.05
597	Checklist	.05
598	Checklist	.05
599	Checklist	.05
600	Checklist	.05

All-Stars

All-Stars is a horizontal, two-sided insert set consisting of 25 cards. A National League All-Star is on one side, while an American League All-Star is on the other, by position. All-Stars are the most common insert in Fleer 1995 baseball, with an insertion ratio of one per three packs.

#	Player	NM/M
	Complete Set (25):	8.00
	Common Card:	.20
1	Ivan Rodriguez, Mike Piazza	.75
2	Frank Thomas, Gregg Jefferies	.50
3	Roberto Alomar, Mariano Duncan	.40
4	Wade Boggs, Matt Williams	.65
5	Cal Ripken, Jr., Ozzie Smith	1.50
6	Joe Carter, Barry Bonds	1.50
7	Ken Griffey Jr., Tony Gwynn	.75
8	Kirby Puckett, Dave Justice	.65
9	Jimmy Key, Greg Maddux	.65
10	Chuck Knoblauch, Wil Cordero	.20
11	Scott Cooper, Ken Caminiti	.20
12	Will Clark, Carlos Garcia	.50
13	Paul Molitor, Jeff Bagwell	.50
14	Travis Fryman, Craig Biggio	.20
15	Mickey Tettleton, Fred McGriff	.20
16	Kenny Lofton, Moises Alou	.20
17	Albert Belle, Marquis Grissom	.20
18	Paul O'Neill, Dante Bichette	.20
19	David Cone, Ken Hill	.20
20	Mike Mussina, Doug Drabek	.50
21	Randy Johnson, John Hudek	.50
22	Pat Hentgen, Danny Jackson	.20
23	Wilson Alvarez, Rod Beck	.20
24	Lee Smith, Randy Myers	.20
25	Jason Bere, Doug Jones	.20

Award Winners

Fleer Award Winners contain Fleer's choices of baseball's most outstanding players. This six-card set was only inserted at a rate of one per 24 packs. Each card has an embossed gold foil design, with the gold strip running up the left side and containing the words "Fleer Award Winner" and the player name.

#	Player	NM/M
	Complete Set (6):	4.00
	Common Player:	.25
1	Frank Thomas	1.50
2	Jeff Bagwell	1.50
3	David Cone	.25
4	Greg Maddux	2.00
5	Bob Hamelin	.25
6	Raul Mondesi	.25

League Leaders

League Leaders feature players on a horizontal format from 10 statistical categories from both leagues. "League Leader" is placed in a blue strip down the left-side of the card, with their respective league and their name in it. These were inserted at a rate of one per 12 packs.

#	Player	NM/M
	Complete Set (10):	4.00
	Common Player:	.25
1	Paul O'Neill	.25
2	Ken Griffey Jr.	1.50
3	Kirby Puckett	.75
4	Jimmy Key	.25
5	Randy Johnson	.65
6	Tony Gwynn	.75
7	Matt Williams	.25
8	Jeff Bagwell	.50
9	Greg Maddux, Ken Hill	.75
10	Andy Benes	.25

Lumber Co.

Ten of the top longball hitters were featured in Lumber Co., which were inserted into every 24 12-card retailer packs. They show the power hitter in action, with a wood-grain Lumber Co. logo across the bottom, contain the player's name and team.

#	Player	NM/M
	Complete Set (10):	12.00
	Common Player:	.40
1	Jeff Bagwell	1.50
2	Albert Belle	.40
3	Barry Bonds	3.50
4	Jose Canseco	.75
5	Joe Carter	.40
6	Ken Griffey Jr.	2.50
7	Fred McGriff	.40
8	Kevin Mitchell	.40
9	Frank Thomas	1.75
10	Matt Williams	.40

Major League Prospects

Major League Prospects showcases 10 of 1995's most promising young players. The set title is repeatedly printed across the background, with the player's name and team in a gray strip across the bottom. These cards were inserted into one every six packs.

#	Player	NM/M
	Complete Set (10):	6.00
	Common Player:	.25
1	Garret Anderson	.50
2	James Baldwin	.25
3	Alan Benes	.25
4	Armando Benitez	.25
5	Ray Durham	.25
6	Brian Hunter	.25
7a	Derek Jeter (No licensor logos on back.)	4.00
7b	Derek Jeter (Licensor logos on back.)	4.00
8	Charles Johnson	.25
9	Orlando Miller	.25
10	Alex Rodriguez	3.00

Pro-Visions

Pro-Visions contain six interlocking cards that form one giant picture. These original art cards exhibit the player in a fantasy art background and are inserted into every nine packs.

#	Player	NM/M
	Complete Set (6):	2.00
	Common Player:	.25
1	Mike Mussina	.40
2	Raul Mondesi	.25
3	Jeff Bagwell	.75
4	Greg Maddux	1.00
5	Tim Salmon	.25
6	Manny Ramirez	.75

Rookie Sensations

A perenial favorite within Fleer products, Rookie Sensations cards were inserted in 18-card packs only, at a rate of one per 16 packs. This 20-card set featured the top rookies from the 1994 season. The player's name and team run up the right

side of the card, while the words "Rookie Sensations" appear in the bottom-left corner, separated by a colorful, zig-zagged image of a player.

#	Player	NM/M
	Complete Set (20):	5.00
	Common Player:	.25
1	Kurt Abbott	.25
2	Rico Brogna	.25
3	Hector Carrasco	.25
4	Kevin Foster	.25
5	Chris Gomez	.25
6	Darren Hall	.25
7	Bob Hamelin	.25
8	Joey Hamilton	.25
9	John Hudek	.25
10	Ryan Klesko	.25
11	Javier Lopez	.25
12	Matt Mieske	.25
13	Raul Mondesi	.25
14	Manny Ramirez	4.00
15	Shane Reynolds	.25
16	Bill Risley	.25
17	Johnny Ruffin	.25
18	Steve Trachsel	.25
19	William Van Landingham	.25
20	Rondell White	.25

Team Leaders

Team Leaders are two-player cards featuring the leading hitter and pitcher from each major league team, one on each side. Inserted at a rate of one per 24 packs, these are only found in 12-card hobby packs. Team Leaders consisted of 28 cards and included a Team Leader logo in the bottom-left corner.

#	Player	NM/M
	Complete Set (28):	50.00
	Common Card:	.50
1	Cal Ripken, Jr., Mike Mussina	7.50
2	Mo Vaughn, Roger Clemens	4.50
3	Tim Salmon, Chuck Finley	.75
4	Frank Thomas, Jack McDowell	2.50
5	Albert Belle, Dennis Martinez	.50
6	Cecil Fielder, Mike Moore	.50
7	Bob Hamelin, David Cone	.50
8	Greg Vaughn, Ricky Bones	.50
9	Kirby Puckett, Rick Aguilera	3.00
10	Don Mattingly, Jimmy Key	4.50
11	Ruben Sierra, Dennis Eckersley	1.50
12	Ken Griffey Jr., Randy Johnson	6.00
13	Jose Canseco, Kenny Rogers	1.00
14	Joe Carter, Pat Hentgen	.50
15	Dave Justice, Greg Maddux	3.00
16	Sammy Sosa, Steve Trachsel	5.00
17	Kevin Mitchell, Jose Rijo	.50
18	Dante Bichette, Bruce Ruffin	.50
19	Jeff Conine, Robb Nen	.50
20	Jeff Bagwell, Doug Drabek	2.50
21	Mike Piazza, Ramon Martinez	5.00
22	Moises Alou, Ken Hill	.50
23	Bobby Bonilla, Bret Saberhagen	.50
24	Darren Daulton, Danny Jackson	.50
25	Jay Bell, Zane Smith	.50
26	Gregg Jefferies, Bob Tewksbury	.50
27	Tony Gwynn, Andy Benes	3.00
28	Matt Williams, Rod Beck	.50

All-Fleer 9

Available only by mailing in 10 Fleer wrappers and $3, this set presents an all-star lineup in a unique design. Colored scribbles down one side of the card front offer a background for gold-foil printing of the card title, player name, position and team. Backs repeat the colored scribbles across virtually the entire surface, making it extremely difficult to read the career summary printed in white over it.

#	Player	NM/M
	Complete Set (9):	4.00
	Common Player:	.25
1	Mike Piazza	1.00
2	Frank Thomas	.50
3	Roberto Alomar	.40
4	Cal Ripken Jr.	2.50
5	Matt Williams	.25
6	Barry Bonds	2.50
7	Ken Griffey Jr.	1.00
8	Tony Gwynn	.65
9	Greg Maddux	.65

All-Rookies

This mail-in set was available by redeeming a randomly inserted trade card found in packs. The cards feature action player photos on a muted background, with the player ID in gold-foil beneath a huge rookie banner. Horizontal backs have a player photo at left and professional highlights at right. Cards have an "M" prefix to the card number.

#	Player	NM/M
	Complete Set (9):	1.50
	Common Player:	.25
	Trade card: 2X	.12
1	Edgardo Alfonzo	.25
2	Jason Bates	.25
3	Brian Boehringer	.25
4	Darren Bragg	.25
5	Brad Clontz	.25
6	Jim Dougherty	.25
7	Todd Hollandsworth	.25
8	Rudy Pemberton	.25
9	Frank Rodriguez	.25

Update

Fleer carried its "different by design" concept of six formats (one for each division in each league) from the regular set into its 1995 Update issue. The issue consists of 200 cards of 1995's traded, rookie and free agent players, plus five different insert sets. One insert card was found in each regular (12-card, $1.49) and jumbo (18-card, $2.29) pack. Cards are numbered with a "U" prefix.

#	Player	NM/M
	Complete Set (200):	7.00
	Common Player:	.05
	Pack (12):	.50
	Wax Box (36):	7.50
1	Manny Alexander	.05
2	Bret Barberie	.05
3	Armando Benitez	.05
4	Kevin Brown	.05
5	Doug Jones	.05
6	Sherman Obando	.05
7	Andy Van Slyke	.05
8	Stan Belinda	.05
9	Jose Canseco	.30
10	Vaughn Eshelman	.05
11	Mike Macfarlane	.05
12	Troy O'Leary	.05
13	Steve Rodriguez	.05
14	Lee Tinsley	.05
15	Tim Vanegmond	.05
16	Mark Whiten	.05
17	Sean Bergman	.05
18	Chad Curtis	.05
19	John Flaherty	.05
20	Bob Higginson **RC**	.15
21	Felipe Lira	.05
22	Shannon Penn	.05
23	Todd Steverson	.05
24	Sean Whiteside	.05
25	Tony Fernandez	.05
26	Jack McDowell	.05
27	Andy Petitte	.15
28	John Wetteland	.05
29	David Cone	.05
30	Mike Timlin	.05
31	Duane Ward	.05
32	Jim Abbott	.05
33	James Baldwin	.05
34	Mike Devereaux	.05
35	Ray Durham	.05
36	Tim Fortugno	.05
37	Scott Ruffcorn	.05
38	Chris Sabo	.05
39	Paul Assenmacher	.05
40	Bud Black	.05
41	Orel Hershiser	.05
42	Julian Tavarez	.05
43	Dave Winfield	.60
44	Pat Borders	.05
45	Melvin Bunch **RC**	.05
46	Tom Goodwin	.05
47	Jon Nunnally	.05
48	Joe Randa	.05
49	Dilson Torres **RC**	.05
50	Joe Vitiello	.05
51	David Hulse	.05
52	Scott Karl	.05
53	Mark Kiefer	.05
54	Derrick May	.05
55	Joe Oliver	.05
56	Al Reyes	.05
57	Steve Sparks **RC**	.05
58	Jerald Clark	.05
59	Eddie Guardado	.05
60	Kevin Maas	.05
61	David McCarty	.05
62	Brad Radke **RC**	.50
63	Scott Stahoviak	.05
64	Garret Anderson	.05
65	Shawn Boskie	.05
66	Mike James	.05
67	Tony Phillips	.05

68	Lee Smith	.05
69	Mitch Williams	.05
70	Jim Corsi	.05
71	Mark Harkey	.05
72	Dave Stewart	.05
73	Todd Stottlemyre	.05
74	Joey Cora	.05
75	Chad Kreuter	.05
76	Jeff Nelson	.05
77	Alex Rodriguez	2.00
78	Ron Villone	.05
79	Bob Wells **RC**	.05
80	Jose Alberro **RC**	.05
81	Terry Burrows	.05
82	Kevin Gross	.05
83	Wilson Heredia	.05
84	Mark McLemore	.05
85	Otis Nixon	.05
86	Jeff Russell	.05
87	Mickey Tettleton	.05
88	Bob Tewksbury	.05
89	Pedro Borbon	.05
90	Marquis Grissom	.05
91	Chipper Jones	.75
92	Mike Mordecai	.05
93	Jason Schmidt	.15
94	John Burkett	.05
95	Andre Dawson	.25
96	Matt Dunbar **RC**	.05
97	Charles Johnson	.05
98	Terry Pendleton	.05
99	Rich Scheid	.05
100	Quilvio Veras	.05
101	Bobby Witt	.05
102	Eddie Zosky	.05
103	Shane Andrews	.05
104	Reid Cornelius	.05
105	Chad Fonville **RC**	.05
106	Mark Grudzielanek **RC**	.25
107	Roberto Kelly	.05
108	Carlos Perez **RC**	.05
109	Tony Tarasco	.05
110	Brett Butler	.05
111	Carl Everett	.05
112	Pete Harnisch	.05
113	Doug Henry	.05
114	Kevin Lomon	.05
115	Blas Minor	.05
116	Dave Mlicki	.05
117	Ricky Otero **RC**	.05
118	Norm Charlton	.05
119	Tyler Green	.05
120	Gene Harris	.05
121	Charlie Hayes	.05
122	Gregg Jefferies	.05
123	Michael Mimbs **RC**	.05
124	Paul Quantrill	.05
125	Frank Castillo	.05
126	Brian McRae	.05
127	Jaime Navarro	.05
128	Mike Perez	.05
129	Tanyon Sturtze	.05
130	Ozzie Timmons	.05
131	John Courtright	.05
132	Ron Gant	.05
133	Xavier Hernandez	.05
134	Brian Hunter	.05
135	Benito Santiago	.05
136	Pete Smith	.05
137	Scott Sullivan	.05
138	Derek Bell	.05
139	Doug Brocail	.05
140	Ricky Gutierrez	.05
141	Pedro Martinez	.05
142	Orlando Miller	.05
143	Phil Plantier	.05
144	Craig Shipley	.05
145	Rich Aude	.05
146	Jason Christiansen **RC**	.05
147	Freddy Garcia **RC**	.25
148	Jim Gott	.05
149	Mark Johnson **RC**	.05
150	Esteban Loaiza	.05
151	Dan Plesac	.05
152	Gary Wilson **RC**	.05
153	Allen Battle	.05
154	Terry Bradshaw	.05
155	Scott Cooper	.05
156	Tripp Cromer	.05
157	John Frascatore	.05
158	John Habyan	.05
159	Tom Henke	.05
160	Ken Hill	.05
161	Danny Jackson	.05
162	Donovan Osborne	.05
163	Tom Urbani	.05
164	Roger Bailey	.05
165	Jorge Brito **RC**	.05
166	Vinny Castilla	.05
167	Darren Holmes	.05
168	Roberto Mejia	.05
169	Bill Swift	.05
170	Mark Thompson	.05
171	Larry Walker	.05
172	Greg Hansell	.05
173	Dave Hansen	.05
174	Carlos Hernandez	.05
175	Hideo Nomo **RC**	2.00
176	Jose Offerman	.05
177	Antonio Osuna	.05
178	Reggie Williams	.05
179	Todd Williams	.05
180	Andres Berumen	.05
181	Ken Caminiti	.05
182	Andujar Cedeno	.05
183	Steve Finley	.05
184	Bryce Florie	.05
185	Dustin Hermanson	.05
186	Ray Holbert	.05
187	Melvin Nieves	.05
188	Roberto Petagine	.05
189	Jody Reed	.05
190	Fernando Valenzuela	.05
191	Brian Williams	.05
192	Mark Dewey	.05
193	Glenallen Hill	.05
194	Chris Hook **RC**	.05
195	Terry Mulholland	.05
196	Steve Scarsone	.05
197	Trevor Wilson	.05
198	Checklist	.05
199	Checklist	.05
200	Checklist	.05

Update Diamond Tribute

Borderless action photos and gold-foil graphics are front features of this chase set honoring perhaps the 10 top names among baseball's veteran players. Backs have another photo and a few sentences describing what makes the player worthy of inclusion in such a set. The Diamond Tribute cards are found on the average of one per five packs.

		NM/M
Complete Set (10):		6.00
Common Player:		.25
1	Jeff Bagwell	.75
2	Albert Belle	.25
3	Barry Bonds	3.00
4	David Cone	.25
5	Dennis Eckersley	.50
6	Ken Griffey Jr.	1.50
7	Rickey Henderson	.60
8	Greg Maddux	1.00
9	Frank Thomas	.75
10	Matt Williams	.25

Update Headliners

The most common of the Fleer Update inserts are the Headliners cards found on average of one per three packs. Fronts have an action photo set against a collage of newspaper clippings. The graphics are gold-foil. Backs have another color photo and a "Fleer Times" newspaper background with career summary and/or quotes about the featured player.

		NM/M
Complete Set (20):		8.00
Common Player:		.10
1	Jeff Bagwell	.50
2	Albert Belle	.15
3	Barry Bonds	3.00
4	Jose Canseco	.40
5	Joe Carter	.15
6	Will Clark	.25
7	Roger Clemens	2.00
8	Lenny Dykstra	.15
9	Cecil Fielder	.15
10	Juan Gonzalez	.40
11	Ken Griffey Jr.	2.00
12	Kenny Lofton	.15
13	Greg Maddux	.75
14	Fred McGriff	.15
15	Mike Piazza	1.50
16	Kirby Puckett	.75
17	Tim Salmon	.15
18	Frank Thomas	.50
19	Mo Vaughn	.15
20	Matt Williams	.15

Update Rookie Update

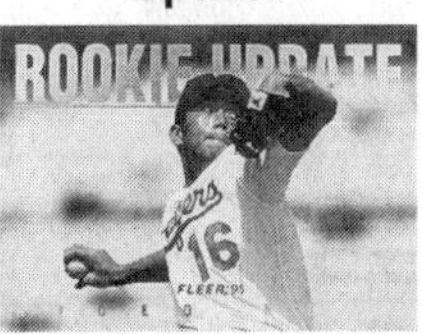

Ten of 1995's top rookies are featured in this horizontally formatted insert set. Fronts have an action photo with a large gold-foil "ROOKIE UPDATE" headline at top. Backs have another photo and career summary. Rookie Update chase cards are found on the average of one per four packs.

		NM/M
Complete Set (10):		4.00
Common Player:		.10
1	Shane Andrews	.10
2	Ray Durham	.10
3	Shawn Green	.40
4	Charles Johnson	.10
5	Chipper Jones	1.50
6	Esteban Loaiza	.10
7	Hideo Nomo	1.00
8	Jon Nunnally	.10
9	Alex Rodriguez	2.00
10	Julian Tavarez	.10

Update Smooth Leather

These inserts featuring top fielders were found only in pre-priced (magazine) foil packs, at an average rate of one card per 12 packs. Fronts are highlighted with gold-foil graphics. Backs have a glove in the background and explain the player's defensive abilities.

		NM/M
Complete Set (10):		7.50
Common Player:		.25
1	Roberto Alomar	.50
2	Barry Bonds	2.50
3	Ken Griffey Jr.	1.50
4	Marquis Grissom	.25
5	Darren Lewis	.25
6	Kenny Lofton	.25
7	Don Mattingly	1.00
8	Cal Ripken Jr.	2.50
9	Ivan Rodriguez	.75
10	Matt Williams	.25

Update Soaring Stars

A metallic foil-etched background behind the color player action photo identifies this chase set as the toughest among those in the 1995 Fleer Update issue. The Soaring Star cards are found at the average rate of one per box. Backs are conventionally printed and featured a colorful posterized version of the front background, along with another color photo and a career summary.

		NM/M
Complete Set (9):		3.50
Common Player:		.15
1	Moises Alou	.35
2	Jason Bere	.25
3	Jeff Conine	.25
4	Cliff Floyd	.25
5	Pat Hentgen	.25
6	Kenny Lofton	.25
7	Raul Mondesi	.25
8	Mike Piazza	3.00
9	Tim Salmon	.35

Panini Stickers

Following Fleer's purchase of the well-known Italian sticker company, Panini, it was no surprise to see the companies produce a 1995 baseball issue. Titled "Major League Baseball All-Stars," the set consists of 156 player and team logo stickers. A 36-page color album to house the stickers was sold for $1.19. Sold in six-sticker packs for about .50, the individual stickers measure 1-15/16" x 3". Borders are team color-coded and have the player name and team logo at bottom, with the position abbreviation in a diamond at top-right. Backs are printed in black-and-white and include a sticker number, copyright notice and large logos of the licensors and Fleer/Panini. Each sticker can be found with backs that do, or do not, include a promotional message beginning, "Collect all 156 . . ."

		NM/M
Complete Set (156):		3.00
Common Player:		.05
Album:		1.00
Wax Pack (6):		.25
Wax Box (100):		15.00
1	Tom Glavine	.15
2	Doug Drabek	.05
3	Rod Beck	.05
4	Pedro J. Martinez	.25
5	Danny Jackson	.05
6	Greg Maddux	.30
7	Bret Saberhagen	.05
8	Ken Hill	.05
9	Marvin Freeman	.05
10	Andy Benes	.05
11	Wilson Alvarez	.05
12	Jimmy Key	.05
13	Mike Mussina	.15
14	Roger Clemens	.35
15	Pat Hentgen	.05
16	Randy Johnson	.25
17	Lee Smith	.05
18	David Cone	.05
19	Jason Bere	.05
20	Dennis Martinez	.05
21	Darren Daulton	.05
22	Darrin Fletcher	.05
23	Tom Pagnozzi	.05
24	Mike Piazza	.40
25	Benito Santiago	.05
26	Sandy Alomar Jr.	.05
27	Chris Hoiles	.05
28	Ivan Rodriguez	.20
29	Mike Stanley	.05
30	Dave Nilsson	.05
31	Jeff Bagwell	.25
32	Mark Grace	.10
33	Gregg Jefferies	.05
34	Andres Galarraga	.05
35	Fred McGriff	.05
36	Will Clark	.10
37	Mo Vaughn	.05
38	Don Mattingly	.35
39	Frank Thomas	.25
40	Cecil Fielder	.05
41	Robby Thompson	.05
42	Delino DeShields	.05
43	Carlos Garcia	.05
44	Bret Boone	.05
45	Craig Biggio	.05
46	Roberto Alomar	.10
47	Chuck Knoblauch	.05
48	Jose Lind	.05
49	Carlos Baerga	.05
50	Lou Whitaker	.05
51	Bobby Bonilla	.05
52	Tim Wallach	.05
53	Todd Zeile	.05
54	Matt Williams	.05
55	Ken Caminiti	.05
56	Robin Ventura	.05
57	Wade Boggs	.30
58	Scott Cooper	.05
59	Travis Fryman	.05
60	Dean Palmer	.05
61	Jay Bell	.05
62	Barry Larkin	.05
63	Ozzie Smith	.30
64	Wil Cordero	.05
65	Royce Clayton	.05
66	Chris Gomez	.05
67	Ozzie Guillen	.05
68	Cal Ripken Jr.	.50
69	Omar Vizquel	.05
70	Gary DiSarcina	.05
71	Dante Bichette	.05
72	Lenny Dykstra	.05
73	Barry Bonds	.50
74	Gary Sheffield	.20
75	Larry Walker	.05
76	Raul Mondesi	.05
77	Dave Justice	.05
78	Moises Alou	.05
79	Tony Gwynn	.30
80	Deion Sanders	.05
81	Kenny Lofton	.05
82	Kirby Puckett	.30
83	Juan Gonzalez	.20
84	Jay Buhner	.05
85	Joe Carter	.05
86	Ken Griffey Jr.	.40
87	Ruben Sierra	.05
88	Tim Salmon	.05
89	Paul O'Neill	.05
90	Albert Belle	.05
91	Danny Tartabull	.05
92	Jose Canseco	.20
93	Harold Baines	.05
94	Kirk Gibson	.05
95	Chili Davis	.05
96	Eddie Murray	.25
97	Bob Hamelin	.05
98	Paul Molitor	.25
99	Raul Mondesi	.05
100	Ryan Klesko	.05
101	Cliff Floyd	.05
102	William Van Landingham	.05
103	Joey Hamilton	.05
104	John Hudek	.05
105	Manny Ramirez	.25
106	Bob Hamelin	.05
107	Rusty Greer	.05
108	Chris Gomez	.05
109	Greg Maddux	.20
110	Jeff Bagwell	.15
111	Raul Mondesi	.05
112	David Cone	.05
113	Frank Thomas	.25
114	Bob Hamelin	.05
115	Tony Gwynn	.20
116	Matt Williams	.05
117	Jeff Bagwell	.15
118	Craig Biggio	.05
119	Andy Benes	.05
120	Greg Maddux	.20
121	John Franco	.05
122	Paul O'Neill	.05
123	Ken Griffey Jr.	.35
124	Kirby Puckett	.20
125	Kenny Lofton	.05
126	Randy Johnson	.05
127	Jimmy Key	.05
128	Lee Smith	.05
129	San Francisco Giants Logo	.05
130	Montreal Expos Logo	.05
131	Cincinnati Reds Logo	.05
132	Los Angeles Dodgers Logo	.05
133	New York Mets Logo	.05
134	San Diego Padres Logo	.05
135	Colorado Rockies Logo	.05
136	Pittsburgh Pirates Logo	.05
137	Florida Marlins Logo	.05
138	Philadelphia Phillies Logo	.05
139	Atlanta Braves Logo	.05
140	Houston Astros Logo	.05
141	St. Louis Cardinals Logo	.05
142	Chicago Cubs Logo	.05
143	Cleveland Indians Logo	.05
144	New York Yankees Logo	.05
145	Kansas City Royals Logo	.05
146	Chicago White Sox Logo	.05
147	Baltimore Orioles Logo	.05
148	Seattle Mariners Logo	.05
149	Boston Red Sox Logo	.05
150	California Angels Logo	.05
151	Toronto Blue Jays Logo	.05
152	Detroit Tigers Logo	.05
153	Texas Rangers Logo	.05
154	Oakland A's Logo	.05
155	Milwaukee Brewers Logo	.05
156	Minnesota Twins Logo	.05

Revco Cleveland Indians

In the midst of their pennant winning season in 1995, the Cleveland Indians were the subject of a special "Update" set produced by Fleer and sold exclusively by Revco stores and the team itself. Seventeen of the 20 cards in the set are virtually identical to the regular-issue 1995 Fleer cards, except for a change in card number on the back, designating each card as "X of 20," and the use of silver foil on front, as opposed to the gold foil found on regular cards. The Dave Winfield card in the Update issue pictures him in an Indians uniform, instead of the Twins uniform in which he appears in the regular set. Logo and checklist cards were added to the team set. Cards were sold in 10-card foil packs.

		NM/M
Complete Set (20):		6.00
Common Player:		.10
1	Sandy Alomar Jr.	.10
2	Carlos Baerga	.10
3	Albert Belle	.10
4	Mark Clark	.10
5	Alvaro Espinoza	.10
6	Wayne Kirby	.10
7	Kenny Lofton	.10
8	Dennis Martinez	.10
9	Jose Mesa	.10
10	Eddie Murray	2.00
11	Charles Nagy	.10
12	Tony Pena	.10
13	Eric Plunk	.10
14	Manny Ramirez	2.00
15	Paul Sorrento	.10
16	Jim Thome	1.00
17	Omar Vizquel	.10
18	Dave Winfield	2.00
19	Indians/Fleer Logo Card	.05
20	Checklist/Indians Logo	.05

1996 Fleer

In a radical departure from the UV-coated standard for even base-brand baseball cards, Fleer's 1996 issue is printed on a matte surface. Fronts feature borderless game-action photos with minimal (player ID, Fleer logo) graphic enhancement in gold foil. Backs have a white background, a portrait photo, full pro stats and a few career highlights. The single-series set was sold in basic 11-card packs with one of nearly a dozen insert-set cards in each $1.49 pack. The set is arranged alphabetically by player within team and league. A glossy-surface Tiffany Collection parallel was included in each pack.

	NM/M
Complete Set (600):	20.00
Common Player:	.05
Complete Tiffany Set (600):	100.00
Tiffanies:	2X
Pack (11):	.75
Wax Box (36):	16.00

1 Manny Alexander .05
2 Brady Anderson .05
3 Harold Baines .05
4 Armando Benitez .05
5 Bobby Bonilla .05
6 Kevin Brown .05
7 Scott Erickson .05
8 Curtis Goodwin .05
9 Jeffrey Hammonds .05
10 Jimmy Haynes .05
11 Chris Hoiles .05
12 Doug Jones .05
13 Rick Krivda .05
14 Jeff Manto .05
15 Ben McDonald .05
16 Jamie Moyer .05
17 Mike Mussina .50
18 Jesse Orosco .05
19 Rafael Palmeiro .65
20 Cal Ripken Jr. 2.50
20(p) Cal Ripken Jr./OPS 2.50
21 Rick Aguilera .05
22 Luis Alicea .05
23 Stan Belinda .05
24 Jose Canseco .50
25 Roger Clemens 1.25
26 Vaughn Eshelman .05
27 Mike Greenwell .05
28 Erik Hanson .05
29 Dwayne Hosey .05
30 Mike Macfarlane .05
31 Tim Naehring .05
32 Troy O'Leary .05
33 Aaron Sele .05
34 Zane Smith .05
35 Jeff Suppan .05
36 Lee Tinsley .05
37 John Valentin .05
38 Mo Vaughn .05
39 Tim Wakefield .05
40 Jim Abbott .05
41 Brian Anderson .05
42 Garret Anderson .05
43 Chili Davis .05
44 Gary DiSarcina .05
45 Damion Easley .05
46 Jim Edmonds .05
47 Chuck Finley .05
48 Todd Greene .05
49 Mike Harkey .05
50 Mike James .05
51 Mark Langston .05
52 Greg Myers .05
53 Orlando Palmeiro .05
54 Bob Patterson .05
55 Troy Percival .05
56 Tony Phillips .05
57 Tim Salmon .10
58 Lee Smith .05
59 J.T. Snow .05
60 Randy Velarde .05
61 Wilson Alvarez .05
62 Luis Andujar **RC** .05
63 Jason Bere .05
64 Ray Durham .05
65 Alex Fernandez .05
66 Ozzie Guillen .05
67 Roberto Hernandez .05
68 Lance Johnson .05
69 Matt Karchner .05
70 Ron Karkovice .05
71 Norberto Martin .05
72 Dave Martinez .05
73 Kirk McCaskill .05
74 Lyle Mouton .05
75 Tim Raines .05
76 Mike Sirotka **RC** .05
77 Frank Thomas .75
78 Larry Thomas .05
79 Robin Ventura .05
80 Sandy Alomar Jr. .05
81 Paul Assenmacher .05
82 Carlos Baerga .05
83 Albert Belle .05
84 Mark Clark .05
85 Alan Embree .05
86 Alvaro Espinoza .05
87 Orel Hershiser .05
88 Ken Hill .05
89 Kenny Lofton .05
90 Dennis Martinez .05
91 Jose Mesa .05
92 Eddie Murray .75
93 Charles Nagy .05
94 Chad Ogea .05
95 Tony Pena .05
96 Herb Perry .05
97 Eric Plunk .05
98 Jim Poole .05
99 Manny Ramirez .75
100 Paul Sorrento .05
101 Julian Travarez .05
102 Jim Thome .60
103 Omar Vizquel .05
104 Dave Winfield .75
105 Danny Bautista .05
106 Joe Boever .05
107 Chad Curtis .05
108 John Doherty .05
109 Cecil Fielder .05
110 John Flaherty .05
111 Travis Fryman .05
112 Chris Gomez .05
113 Bob Higginson .05
114 Mark Lewis .05
115 Jose Lima .05
116 Felipe Lira .05
117 Brian Maxcy .05
118 C.J. Nitkowski .05
119 Phil Plantier .05
120 Clint Sodowsky .05
121 Alan Trammell .05
122 Lou Whitaker .05
123 Kevin Appier .05
124 Johnny Damon .35
125 Gary Gaetti .05
126 Tom Goodwin .05
127 Tom Gordon .05
128 Mark Gubicza .05
129 Bob Hamelin .05
130 David Howard .05
131 Jason Jacome .05
132 Wally Joyner .05
133 Keith Lockhart .05
134 Brent Mayne .05
135 Jeff Montgomery .05
136 Jon Nunnally .05
137 Juan Samuel .05
138 Mike Sweeney **RC** .50
139 Michael Tucker .05
140 Joe Vitiello .05
141 Ricky Bones .05
142 Chuck Carr .05
143 Jeff Cirillo .05
144 Mike Fetters .05
145 Darryl Hamilton .05
146 David Hulse .05
147 John Jaha .05
148 Scott Karl .05
149 Mark Kiefer .05
150 Pat Listach .05
151 Mark Loretta .05
152 Mike Matheny .05
153 Matt Mieske .05
154 Dave Nilsson .05
155 Joe Oliver .05
156 Al Reyes .05
157 Kevin Seitzer .05
158 Steve Sparks .05
159 B.J. Surhoff .05
160 Jose Valentin .05
161 Greg Vaughn .05
162 Fernando Vina .05
163 Rich Becker .05
164 Ron Coomer .05
165 Marty Cordova .05
166 Chuck Knoblauch .05
167 Matt Lawton **RC** .30
168 Pat Meares .05
169 Paul Molitor .75
170 Pedro Munoz .05
171 Jose Parra .05
172 Kirby Puckett 1.00
173 Brad Radke .05
174 Jeff Reboulet .05
175 Rich Robertson .05
176 Frank Rodriguez .05
177 Scott Stahoviak .05
178 Dave Stevens .05
179 Matt Walbeck .05
180 Wade Boggs 1.00
181 David Cone .05
182 Tony Fernandez .05
183 Joe Girardi .05
184 Derek Jeter 2.50
185 Scott Kamieniecki .05
186 Pat Kelly .05
187 Jim Leyritz .05
188 Tino Martinez .05
189 Don Mattingly 1.25
190 Jack McDowell .05
191 Jeff Nelson .05
192 Paul O'Neill .05
193 Melido Perez .05
194 Andy Pettitte .30
195 Mariano Rivera .15
196 Ruben Sierra .05
197 Mike Stanley .05
198 Darryl Strawberry .05
199 John Wetteland .05
200 Bob Wickman .05
201 Bernie Williams .10
202 Mark Acre .05
203 Geronimo Berroa .05
204 Mike Bordick .05
205 Scott Brosius .05
206 Dennis Eckersley .65
207 Brent Gates .05
208 Jason Giambi .60
209 Rickey Henderson .75
210 Jose Herrera .05
211 Stan Javier .05
212 Doug Johns .05
213 Mark McGwire 2.00
214 Steve Ontiveros .05
215 Craig Paquette .05
216 Ariel Prieto .05
217 Carlos Reyes .05
218 Terry Steinbach .05
219 Todd Stottlemyre .05
220 Danny Tartabull .05
221 Todd Van Poppel .05
222 John Wasdin .05
223 George Williams .05
224 Steve Wojciechowski .05
225 Rich Amaral .05
226 Bobby Ayala .05
227 Tim Belcher .05
228 Andy Benes .05
229 Chris Bosio .05
230 Darren Bragg .05
231 Jay Buhner .05
232 Norm Charlton .05
233 Vince Coleman .05
234 Joey Cora .05
235 Russ Davis .05
236 Alex Diaz .05
237 Felix Fermin .05
238 Ken Griffey Jr. 1.75
239 Sterling Hitchcock .05
240 Randy Johnson .75
241 Edgar Martinez .05
242 Bill Risley .05
243 Alex Rodriguez 2.00
244 Luis Sojo .05
245 Dan Wilson .05
246 Bob Wolcott .05
247 Will Clark .10
248 Jeff Frye .05
249 Benji Gil .05
250 Juan Gonzalez .65
251 Rusty Greer .05
252 Kevin Gross .05
253 Roger McDowell .05
254 Mark McLemore .05
255 Otis Nixon .05
256 Luis Ortiz .05
257 Mike Pagliarulo .05
258 Dean Palmer .05
259 Roger Pavlik .05
260 Ivan Rodriguez .65
261 Kenny Rogers .05
262 Jeff Russell .05
263 Mickey Tettleton .05
264 Bob Tewksbury .05
265 Dave Valle .05
266 Matt Whiteside .05
267 Roberto Alomar .10
268 Joe Carter .05
269 Tony Castillo .05
270 Domingo Cedeno .05
271 Timothy Crabtree .05
272 Carlos Delgado .60
273 Alex Gonzalez .05
274 Shawn Green .20
275 Juan Guzman .05
276 Pat Hentgen .05
277 Al Leiter .05
278 Sandy Martinez **RC** .05
279 Paul Menhart .05
280 John Olerud .05
281 Paul Quantrill .05
282 Ken Robinson .05
283 Ed Sprague .05
284 Mike Timlin .05
285 Steve Avery .05
286 Rafael Belliard .05
287 Jeff Blauser .05
288 Pedro Borbon .05
289 Brad Clontz .05
290 Mike Devereaux .05
291 Tom Glavine .25
292 Marquis Grissom .05
293 Chipper Jones 1.00
294 David Justice .05
295 Mike Kelly .05
296 Ryan Klesko .05
297 Mark Lemke .05
298 Javier Lopez .05
299 Greg Maddux 1.00
300 Fred McGriff .05
301 Greg McMichael .05
302 Kent Mercker .05
303 Mike Mordecai .05
304 Charlie O'Brien .05
305 Eduardo Perez .05
306 Luis Polonia .05
307 Jason Schmidt .05
308 John Smoltz .05
309 Terrell Wade .05
310 Mark Wohlers .05
311 Scott Bullett .05
312 Jim Bullinger .05
313 Larry Casian .05
314 Frank Castillo .05
315 Shawon Dunston .05
316 Kevin Foster .05
317 Matt Franco .05
318 Luis Gonzalez .10
319 Mark Grace .10
320 Jose Hernandez .05
321 Mike Hubbard .05
322 Brian McRae .05
323 Randy Myers .05
324 Jaime Navarro .05
325 Mark Parent .05
326 Mike Perez .05
327 Rey Sanchez .05
328 Ryne Sandberg 1.00
329 Scott Servais .05
330 Sammy Sosa 1.50
331 Ozzie Timmons .05
332 Steve Trachsel .05
333 Todd Zeile .05
334 Bret Boone .10
335 Jeff Branson .05
336 Jeff Brantley .05
337 Dave Burba .05
338 Hector Carrasco .05
339 Mariano Duncan .05
340 Ron Gant .05
341 Lenny Harris .05
342 Xavier Hernandez .05
343 Thomas Howard .05
344 Mike Jackson .05
345 Barry Larkin .05
346 Darren Lewis .05
347 Hal Morris .05
348 Eric Owens .05
349 Mark Portugal .05
350 Jose Rijo .05
351 Reggie Sanders .05
352 Benito Santiago .05
353 Pete Schourek .05
354 John Smiley .05
355 Eddie Taubensee .05
356 Jerome Walton .05
357 David Wells .05
358 Roger Bailey .05
359 Jason Bates .05
360 Dante Bichette .05
361 Ellis Burks .05
362 Vinny Castilla .05
363 Andres Galarraga .05
364 Darren Holmes .05
365 Mike Kingery .05
366 Curt Leskanic .05
367 Quinton McCracken .05
368 Mike Munoz .05
369 David Nied .05
370 Steve Reed .05
371 Bryan Rekar .05
372 Kevin Ritz .05
373 Bruce Ruffin .05
374 Bret Saberhagen .05
375 Bill Swift .05
376 John Vander Wal .05
377 Larry Walker .05
378 Walt Weiss .05
379 Eric Young .05
380 Kurt Abbott .05
381 Alex Arias .05
382 Jerry Browne .05
383 John Burkett .05
384 Greg Colbrunn .05
385 Jeff Conine .05
386 Andre Dawson .35
387 Chris Hammond .05
388 Charles Johnson .05
389 Terry Mathews .05
390 Robb Nen .05
391 Joe Orsulak .05
392 Terry Pendleton .05
393 Pat Rapp .05
394 Gary Sheffield .45
395 Jesus Tavarez .05
396 Marc Valdes .05
397 Quilvio Veras .05
398 Randy Veres .05
399 Devon White .05
400 Jeff Bagwell .75
401 Derek Bell .05
402 Craig Biggio .05
403 John Cangelosi .05
404 Jim Dougherty .05
405 Doug Drabek .05
406 Tony Eusebio .05
407 Ricky Gutierrez .05
408 Mike Hampton .05
409 Dean Hartgraves .05
410 John Hudek .05
411 Brian Hunter .05
412 Todd Jones .05
413 Darryl Kile .05
414 Dave Magadan .05
415 Derrick May .05
416 Orlando Miller .05
417 James Mouton .05
418 Shane Reynolds .05
419 Greg Swindell .05
420 Jeff Tabaka .05
421 Dave Veres .05
422 Billy Wagner .05
423 Donne Wall **RC** .05
424 Rick Wilkins .05
425 Billy Ashley .05
426 Mike Blowers .05
427 Brett Butler .05
428 Tom Candiotti .05
429 Juan Castro .05
430 John Cummings .05
431 Delino DeShields .05
432 Joey Eischen .05
433 Chad Fonville .05
434 Greg Gagne .05
435 Dave Hansen .05
436 Carlos Hernandez .05
437 Todd Hollandsworth .05
438 Eric Karros .05
439 Roberto Kelly .05
440 Ramon Martinez .05
441 Raul Mondesi .05
442 Hideo Nomo .65
443 Antonio Osuna .05
444 Chan Ho Park .05
445 Mike Piazza 1.75
446 Felix Rodriguez .05
447 Kevin Tapani .05
448 Ismael Valdes .05
449 Todd Worrell .05
450 Moises Alou .05
451 Shane Andrews .05
452 Yamil Benitez .05
453 Sean Berry .05
454 Wil Cordero .05
455 Jeff Fassero .05
456 Darrin Fletcher .05
457 Cliff Floyd .05
458 Mark Grudzielanek .05
459 Gil Heredia .05
460 Tim Laker .05
461 Mike Lansing .05
462 Pedro Martinez .75
463 Carlos Perez .05
464 Curtis Pride .05
465 Mel Rojas .05
466 Kirk Rueter .05
467 F.P. Santangelo **RC** .05
468 Tim Scott .05
469 David Segui .05
470 Tony Tarasco .05
471 Rondell White .05
472 Edgardo Alfonzo .05
473 Tim Bogar .05
474 Rico Brogna .05
475 Damon Buford .05
476 Paul Byrd .05
477 Carl Everett .10
478 John Franco .05
479 Todd Hundley .05
480 Butch Huskey .05
481 Jason Isringhausen .05
482 Bobby Jones .05
483 Chris Jones .05
484 Jeff Kent .10
485 Dave Mlicki .05
486 Robert Person .05
487 Bill Pulsipher .05
488 Kelly Stinnett .05
489 Ryan Thompson .05
490 Jose Vizcaino .05
491 Howard Battle .05
492 Toby Borland .05
493 Ricky Bottalico .05
494 Darren Daulton .05
495 Lenny Dykstra .05
496 Jim Eisenreich .05
497 Sid Fernandez .05
498 Tyler Green .05
499 Charlie Hayes .05
500 Gregg Jefferies .05
501 Kevin Jordan .05
502 Tony Longmire .05
503 Tom Marsh .05
504 Michael Mimbs .05
505 Mickey Morandini .05
506 Gene Schall .05
507 Curt Schilling .25
508 Heathcliff Slocumb .05
509 Kevin Stocker .05
510 Andy Van Slyke .05
511 Lenny Webster .05
512 Mark Whiten .05
513 Mike Williams .05
514 Jay Bell .05
515 Jacob Brumfield .05
516 Jason Christiansen .05
517 Dave Clark .05
518 Midre Cummings .05
519 Angelo Encarnacion .05
520 John Ericks .05
521 Carlos Garcia .05
522 Mark Johnson .05
523 Jeff King .05
524 Nelson Liriano .05
525 Esteban Loaiza .05
526 Al Martin .05
527 Orlando Merced .05
528 Dan Miceli .05
529 Ramon Morel .05
530 Denny Neagle .05
531 Steve Parris .05
532 Dan Plesac .05
533 Don Slaught .05
534 Paul Wagner .05
535 John Wehner .05
536 Kevin Young .05
537 Allen Battle .05
538 David Bell .05
539 Alan Benes .05
540 Scott Cooper .05
541 Tripp Cromer .05
542 Tony Fossas .05
543 Bernard Gilkey .05
544 Tom Henke .05
545 Brian Jordan .05
546 Ray Lankford .05
547 John Mabry .05
548 T.J. Mathews .05
549 Mike Morgan .05
550 Jose Oliva .05
551 Jose Oquendo .05
552 Donovan Osborne .05
553 Tom Pagnozzi .05
554 Mark Petkovsek .05
555 Danny Sheaffer .05
556 Ozzie Smith 1.00
557 Mark Sweeney .05
558 Allen Watson .05
559 Andy Ashby .05
560 Brad Ausmus .05
561 Willie Blair .05
562 Ken Caminiti .05
563 Andujar Cedeno .05
564 Glenn Dishman .05
565 Steve Finley .05
566 Bryce Florie .05
567 Tony Gwynn 1.00
568 Joey Hamilton .05
569 Dustin Hermanson .05
570 Trevor Hoffman .05
571 Brian Johnson .05
572 Marc Kroon .05
573 Scott Livingstone .05
574 Marc Newfield .05
575 Melvin Nieves .05
576 Jody Reed .05
577 Bip Roberts .05
578 Scott Sanders .05
579 Fernando Valenzuela .05
580 Eddie Williams .05
581 Rod Beck .05
582 Marvin Benard **RC** .10
583 Barry Bonds 2.50
584 Jamie Brewington .05
585 Mark Carreon .05
586 Royce Clayton .05
587 Shawn Estes .05
588 Glenallen Hill .05
589 Mark Leiter .05
590 Kirt Manwaring .05
591 David McCarty .05
592 Terry Mulholland .05
593 John Patterson .05
594 J.R. Phillips .05
595 Deion Sanders .05
596 Steve Scarsone .05
597 Robby Thompson .05
598 Sergio Valdez .05
599 William Van Landingham .05
600 Matt Williams .05

Tiffany

While Fleer's basic card set for 1996 feature matte-surface cards, a glossy version of each regular card was also issued as a parallel insert set. Other than the UV coating on front and back and the use of silver- rather than gold-foil typography on front, the cards are identical to the regular '96 Fleer player cards. One glossy version card is found in each pack.

	NM/M
Complete Set (600):	100.00
Common Player:	.15
Stars:	2X

Checklists

Checklist cards are treated as an insert set in 1996 Fleer, appearing on average once every six packs. Like all other Fleer hobby inserts in the baseball set, the checklists are UV-coated front and back, in contrast to the matte-finish regular issue cards. Checklists have borderless game-action photos on front, with gold-foil typography. Backs have a large Fleer logo and checklist data on a white background.

		NM/M
Complete Set (10):		5.00
Common Player:		.25
1	Barry Bonds	2.00
2	Ken Griffey Jr.	1.00
3	Chipper Jones	.75
4	Greg Maddux	.75
5	Mike Piazza	1.00
6	Manny Ramirez	.60
7	Cal Ripken Jr.	2.00
8	Frank Thomas	.60
9	Mo Vaughn	.25
10	Matt Williams	.25

Golden Memories

Some of the 1995 season's greatest moments are captured in this insert set, a one per 10 pack pick. Fronts have two photos of the player, one in full color in the foreground and one in monochrome as a backdrop. Typography is in prismatic foil vertically down one side. Backs have another color player photo, along with details of the milestone. Two of the cards feature multiple players.

		NM/M
Complete Set (10):		6.00
Common Player:		.10
1	Albert Belle	.10
2	Barry Bonds, Sammy Sosa	1.50
3	Greg Maddux	1.00
4	Edgar Martinez	.10
5	Ramon Martinez	.10
6	Mark McGwire	1.50
7	Eddie Murray	.75
8	Cal Ripken Jr.	2.00
9	Frank Thomas	.75
10	Alan Trammell, Lou Whitaker	.15

Lumber Co.

Once again for 1996, a Fleer "Lumber Company" chase set honors the game's top sluggers. The '96 version has a horizontal format with a rather small player action photo on a background resembling the trademark area of a bat. The "trademark" is actually the player and team name along with the "Lumber Company" ID, printed in textured glossy black ink. Backs repeat the trademark motif and also include a close-up player photo and a few words about his power-hitting numbers. Lumber Company cards are a one per nine pack pick, on average, found only in retail packs.

		NM/M
Complete Set (12):		12.50
Common Player:		.50
1	Albert Belle	.50
2	Dante Bichette	.50
3	Barry Bonds	3.00
4	Ken Griffey Jr.	1.50
5	Mark McGwire	2.00
6	Mike Piazza	1.50
7	Manny Ramirez	1.00
8	Tim Salmon	.60
9	Sammy Sosa	1.25
10	Frank Thomas	1.00
11	Mo Vaughn	.50
12	Matt Williams	.50

Post-Season Glory

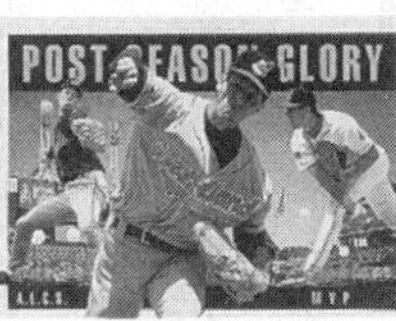

Highlights of the 1995 postseason are featured in this small chase card set. Against a stadium background are multiple photos of the featured player, arranged horizontally. The vertical backs have another player photo down one side, and a description of his play-off performance on the other. Stated odds of picking one of these cards are one per five packs.

		NM/M
Complete Set (5):		1.50
Common Player:		.15
1	Tom Glavine	.25
2	Ken Griffey Jr.	1.00
3	Orel Hershiser	.15
4	Randy Johnson	.50
5	Jim Thome	.50

Prospects

Minor leaguers who are expected to make it big in the big time are featured in this insert issue. Fronts feature large portrait photos against pastel backgrounds with player and set ID in prismatic foil. Backs have an action photo and repeat the front background color in a box which details the player's potential and career to date. Average odds of finding a Prospects card are one per six packs.

		NM/M
Complete Set (10):		1.00
Common Player:		.15
1	Yamil Benitez	.15
2	Roger Cedeno	.15
3	Tony Clark	.15
4	Micah Franklin	.15
5	Karim Garcia	.30
6	Todd Greene	.15
7	Alex Ochoa	.15
8	Ruben Rivera	.15
9	Chris Snopek	.15
10	Shannon Stewart	.15

Road Warriors

A black-and-white country highway photo is the background for the color player action photo on this insert set. Front typography is in silver foil. The players featured are those whose performance on the road is considered outstanding. Backs have a white background, portrait photo and stats bearing out the

away-game superiority. These inserts are found at an average pace of one per 13 packs.

		NM/M
Complete Set (10):		9.00
Common Player:		.40
1	Derek Bell	.40
2	Tony Gwynn	1.25
3	Greg Maddux	1.25
4	Mark McGwire	2.50
5	Mike Piazza	2.00
6	Manny Ramirez	1.00
7	Tim Salmon	.50
8	Frank Thomas	1.00
9	Mo Vaughn	.40
10	Matt Williams	.40

Rookie Sensations

Top rookies of the 1995 season are featured on this chase card set. Horizontally formatted, the cards have an action photo on one side and a large prismatic-foil end strip which displays the player name, team logo and card company identifiers. Backs have a portrait photo on a white background with a few sentences about the player's rookie season. Stated odds of finding one of these inserts is one per 11 packs, on average.

		NM/M
Complete Set (15):		5.00
Common Player:		.25
1	Garret Anderson	.40
2	Marty Cordova	.25
3	Johnny Damon	1.00
4	Ray Durham	.25
5	Carl Everett	.25
6	Shawn Green	.50
7	Brian Hunter	.25
8	Jason Isringhausen	.25
9	Charles Johnson	.25
10	Chipper Jones	2.00
11	John Mabry	.25
12	Hideo Nomo	.50
13	Troy Percival	.25
14	Andy Pettitte	.50
15	Quilvio Veras	.25

Smoke 'N Heat

Once more using the "Smoke 'N Heat" identifier for a chase set of the game's hardest throwers, Fleer presents these select pitchers in action photos against a black-and-flame background. Front typography is in gold foil. Backs have a large portrait photo, repeat the flame motif as background and have a description of the pitcher's prowess in a black box. The cards are found, on average, once per nine packs.

		NM/M
Complete Set (10):		4.00
Common Player:		.15
1	Kevin Appier	.15
2	Roger Clemens	1.50
3	David Cone	.15
4	Chuck Finley	.15
5	Randy Johnson	.75
6	Greg Maddux	1.00
7	Pedro Martinez	.75
8	Hideo Nomo	.50
9	John Smoltz	.30
10	Todd Stottlemyre	.15

Team Leaders

One player from each club has been selected for inclusion in the "Team Leaders" chase set. Fronts have action player photos on a background of metallic foil littered with multiple representations of the team logo. Gold-foil lettering identifies the player, team and chase set. Backs have a white background, portrait photo and description of the player's leadership role. Stated rate of insertion for this set is one card per nine packs, on average, found only in hobby packs.

		NM/M
Complete Set (28):		30.00
Common Player:		.50
1	Cal Ripken Jr.	6.00
2	Mo Vaughn	.50
3	Jim Edmonds	1.00
4	Frank Thomas	2.00
5	Kenny Lofton	.50
6	Travis Fryman	.50
7	Gary Gaetti	.50
8	B.J. Surhoff	.50
9	Kirby Puckett	2.50
10	Don Mattingly	3.00
11	Mark McGwire	4.00
12	Ken Griffey Jr.	3.00
13	Juan Gonzalez	1.00
14	Joe Carter	.50
15	Greg Maddux	2.50
16	Sammy Sosa	3.00
17	Barry Larkin	.50
18	Dante Bichette	.50
19	Jeff Conine	.50
20	Jeff Bagwell	2.00
21	Mike Piazza	3.00
22	Rondell White	.50
23	Rico Brogna	.50
24	Darren Daulton	.50
25	Jeff King	.50
26	Ray Lankford	.50
27	Tony Gwynn	2.50
28	Barry Bonds	6.00

Tomorrow's Legends

In this insert set the projected stars of tomorrow are featured in action poses on a busy multi-colored, quartered background of baseball symbols and the globe. Typography is in silver foil. Backs have a portrait photo and large team logo along with an early-career summary. Odds of finding a "Tomorrow's Legends" card are posted at one per 13 packs, on average.

		NM/M
Complete Set (10):		3.50
Common Player:		.25
1	Garret Anderson	.25
2	Jim Edmonds	.50
3	Brian Hunter	.25
4	Jason Isringhausen	.25
5	Charles Johnson	.25
6	Chipper Jones	2.00
7	Ryan Klesko	.25
8	Hideo Nomo	1.00
9	Manny Ramirez	1.50
10	Rondell White	.25

Zone

The toughest pull (one in 90 packs, average) among the '96 Fleer chase cards is this set evoking the "zone" that the game's great players seek in which their performance is at its peak. The cards have action photos with a background of prismatic foil. Backs are conventionally printed but simulate the foil background and include a player portrait photo plus quotes about the player.

		NM/M
Complete Set (12):		20.00
Common Player:		.75
1	Albert Belle	.75
2	Barry Bonds	6.00
3	Ken Griffey Jr.	4.00
4	Tony Gwynn	3.00
5	Randy Johnson	2.00
6	Kenny Lofton	.75
7	Greg Maddux	3.00
8	Edgar Martinez	.75
9	Mike Piazza	4.00
10	Frank Thomas	2.00
11	Mo Vaughn	.75
12	Matt Williams	.75

Update

Fleer Update Baseball has 250 cards, including more than 55 rookies, plus traded players and free agents in their new uniforms, 35 Encore subset cards and five checklists. Each card in the regular-issue set also has a parallel "Tiffany Collection" version, which has UV coating and holographic foil stamping in contrast to the matte finish and gold foil of the regular cards. Insert cards include Diamond Tribute, New Horizons, Smooth Leather and Soaring Stars. Each pack also contains a Fleer "Thanks a Million" scratch-off game card, redeemable for prizes. Cards are numbered with a "U" prefix.

		NM/M
Complete Set (250):		12.00
Common Player:		.05
Complete Tiffany Set (250):		40.00
Tiffany Stars:		2X
Pack (11):		1.00
Wax Box (24):		15.00
1	Roberto Alomar	.10
2	Mike Devereaux	.05
3	Scott McClain **RC**	.05
4	Roger McDowell	.05
5	Kent Mercker	.05
6	Jimmy Myers	.05
7	Randy Myers	.05
8	B.J. Surhoff	.05
9	Tony Tarasco	.05
10	David Wells	.05
11	Wil Cordero	.05
12	Tom Gordon	.05
13	Reggie Jefferson	.05
14	Jose Malave	.05
15	Kevin Mitchell	.05
16	Jamie Moyer	.05
17	Heathcliff Slocumb	.05
18	Mike Stanley	.05
19	George Arias	.05
20	Jorge Fabregas	.05
21	Don Slaught	.05
22	Randy Velarde	.05
23	Harold Baines	.05
24	Mike Cameron **RC**	.75
25	Darren Lewis	.05
26	Tony Phillips	.05
27	Bill Simas	.05
28	Chris Snopek	.05
29	Kevin Tapani	.05
30	Danny Tartabull	.05
31	Julio Franco	.05
32	Jack McDowell	.05
33	Kimera Bartee	.05
34	Mark Lewis	.05
35	Melvin Nieves	.05
36	Mark Parent	.05
37	Eddie Williams	.05
38	Tim Belcher	.05
39	Sal Fasano	.05
40	Chris Haney	.05
41	Mike Macfarlane	.05
42	Jose Offerman	.05
43	Joe Randa	.05
44	Bip Roberts	.05
45	Chuck Carr	.05
46	Bobby Hughes	.05
47	Graeme Lloyd	.05
48	Ben McDonald	.05
49	Kevin Wickander	.05
50	Rick Aguilera	.05
51	Mike Durant	.05
52	Chip Hale	.05
53	LaTroy Hawkins	.05
54	Dave Hollins	.05
55	Roberto Kelly	.05
56	Paul Molitor	.75
57	Dan Naulty **RC**	.05
58	Mariano Duncan	.05
59	Andy Fox **RC**	.05
60	Joe Girardi	.05
61	Dwight Gooden	.05
62	Jimmy Key	.05
63	Matt Luke **RC**	.05
64	Tino Martinez	.05
65	Jeff Nelson	.05
66	Tim Raines	.05
67	Ruben Rivera	.05
68	Kenny Rogers	.05
69	Gerald Williams	.05
70	Tony Batista **RC**	.50
71	Allen Battle	.05
72	Jim Corsi	.05
73	Steve Cox	.05
74	Pedro Munoz	.05
75	Phil Plantier	.05
76	Scott Spiezio	.05
77	Ernie Young	.05
78	Russ Davis	.05
79	Sterling Hitchcock	.05
80	Edwin Hurtado	.05
81	Raul Ibanez **RC**	.05
82	Mike Jackson	.05
83	Ricky Jordan	.05
84	Paul Sorrento	.05
85	Doug Strange	.05
86	Mark Brandenburg	.05
87	Damon Buford	.05
88	Kevin Elster	.05
89	Darryl Hamilton	.05
90	Ken Hill	.05
91	Ed Vosberg	.05
92	Craig Worthington	.05
93	Tilson Brito	.05
94	Giovanni Carrara	.05
95	Felipe Crespo	.05
96	Erik Hanson	.05
97	Marty Janzen **RC**	.05
98	Otis Nixon	.05
99	Charlie O'Brien	.05

100 Robert Perez .05
101 Paul Quantrill .05
102 Bill Risley .05
103 Juan Samuel .05
104 Jermaine Dye .05
105 Wonderful Monds .05
106 Dwight Smith .05
107 Jerome Walton .05
108 Terry Adams .05
109 Leo Gomez .05
110 Robin Jennings **RC** .05
111 Doug Jones .05
112 Brooks Kieschnick .05
113 Dave Magadan .05
114 Jason Maxwell **RC** .05
115 Rodney Myers .05
116 Eric Anthony .05
117 Vince Coleman .05
118 Eric Davis .05
119 Steve Gibralter .05
120 Curtis Goodwin .05
121 Willie Greene .05
122 Mike Kelly .05
123 Marcus Moore .05
124 Chad Mottola .05
125 Chris Sabo .05
126 Roger Salkeld .05
127 Pedro Castellano .05
128 Trenidad Hubbard .05
129 Jayhawk Owens .05
130 Jeff Reed .05
131 Kevin Brown .05
132 Al Leiter .05
133 Matt Mantei **RC** .05
134 Dave Weathers .05
135 Devon White .05
136 Bob Abreu .05
137 Sean Berry .05
138 Doug Brocail .05
139 Richard Hidalgo .05
140 Alvin Morman .05
141 Mike Blowers .05
142 Roger Cedeno .05
143 Greg Gagne .05
144 Karim Garcia .10
145 Wilton Guerrero **RC** .05
146 Israel Alcantara **RC** .05
147 Omar Daal .05
148 Ryan McGuire .05
149 Sherman Obando .05
150 Jose Paniagua .05
151 Henry Rodriguez .05
152 Andy Stankiewicz .05
153 Dave Veres .05
154 Juan Acevedo .05
155 Mark Clark .05
156 Bernard Gilkey .05
157 Pete Harnisch .05
158 Lance Johnson .05
159 Brent Mayne .05
160 Rey Ordonez .05
161 Kevin Roberson .05
162 Paul Wilson .05
163 David Doster **RC** .05
164 Mike Grace **RC** .05
165 Rich Hunter **RC** .05
166 Pete Incaviglia .05
167 Mike Lieberthal .05
168 Terry Mulholland .05
169 Ken Ryan .05
170 Benito Santiago .05
171 Kevin Sefcik **RC** .05
172 Lee Tinsley .05
173 Todd Zeile .05
174 Francisco Cordova **RC** .05
175 Danny Darwin .05
176 Charlie Hayes .05
177 Jason Kendall .05
178 Mike Kingery .05
179 Jon Lieber .05
180 Zane Smith .05
181 Luis Alicea .05
182 Cory Bailey .05
183 Andy Benes .05
184 Pat Borders .05
185 Mike Busby **RC** .05
186 Royce Clayton .05
187 Dennis Eckersley .65
188 Gary Gaetti .05
189 Ron Gant .05
190 Aaron Holbert .05
191 Willie McGee .05
192 Miguel Mejia **RC** .05
193 Jeff Parrett .05
194 Todd Stottlemyre .05
195 Sean Bergman .05
196 Archi Cianfrocco .05
197 Rickey Henderson .75
198 Wally Joyner .05
199 Craig Shipley .05
200 Bob Tewksbury .05
201 Tim Worrell .05
202 Rich Aurilia **RC** .05
203 Doug Creek .05
204 Shawon Dunston .05
205 Osvaldo Fernandez **RC** .05
206 Mark Gardner .05
207 Stan Javier .05
208 Marcus Jensen .05
209 Chris Singleton **RC** .05
210 Allen Watson .05
211 Jeff Bagwell (Encore) .75
212 Derek Bell (Encore) .05
213 Albert Belle (Encore) .05
214 Wade Boggs (Encore) 1.00
215 Barry Bonds (Encore) 2.00
216 Jose Canseco (Encore) .50
217 Marty Cordova (Encore) .05
218 Jim Edmonds (Encore) .05
219 Cecil Fielder (Encore) .05
220 Andres Galarraga (Encore) .05
221 Juan Gonzalez (Encore) .65
222 Mark Grace (Encore) .10
223 Ken Griffey Jr. (Encore) 1.50
224 Tony Gwynn (Encore) 1.00
225 Jason Isringhausen (Encore) .05
226 Derek Jeter (Encore) 2.00
227 Randy Johnson (Encore) .75
228 Chipper Jones (Encore) 1.00
229 Ryan Klesko (Encore) .05
230 Barry Larkin (Encore) .05
231 Kenny Lofton (Encore) .05
232 Greg Maddux (Encore) 1.00
233 Raul Mondesi (Encore) .05
234 Hideo Nomo (Encore) .65
235 Mike Piazza (Encore) 1.50
236 Manny Ramirez (Encore) .75
237 Cal Ripken Jr. (Encore) 2.00
238 Tim Salmon (Encore) .10
239 Ryne Sandberg (Encore) 1.00
240 Reggie Sanders (Encore) .05
241 Gary Sheffield (Encore) .30
242 Sammy Sosa (Encore) 1.25
243 Frank Thomas (Encore) .75
244 Mo Vaughn (Encore) .05
245 Matt Williams (Encore) .05
246 Checklist .05
247 Checklist .05
248 Checklist .05
249 Checklist .05
250 Checklist .05

Update Tiffany

NM/M
Complete Set (250): 45.00
Common Player: .15
Glossy Stars: 2X

Update Diamond Tribute

These insert cards are the most difficult to pull from 1996 Fleer Update packs; they are seeded one per every 100 packs. The 10-card set features cards of future Hall of Famers on stock utilizing two different holographic foils and a diamond design, similar to the "Zone" insert cards in Fleer Baseball.

NM/M
Complete Set (10): 50.00
Common Player: 4.00
1 Wade Boggs 6.00
2 Barry Bonds 10.00
3 Ken Griffey Jr. 7.50
4 Tony Gwynn 6.00
5 Rickey Henderson 4.00
6 Greg Maddux 6.00
7 Eddie Murray 4.00
8 Cal Ripken Jr. 10.00
9 Ozzie Smith 6.00
10 Frank Thomas 5.00

Update Headliners

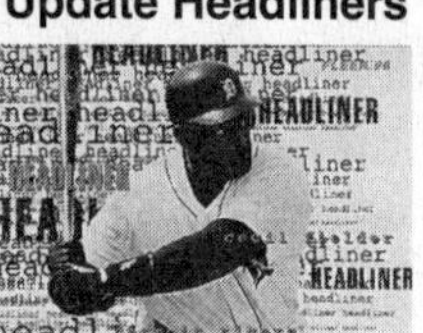

These 20 cards feature newsmakers from 1996. The cards were random inserts in 1996 Fleer Update packs, one per every five retail packs.

NM/M
Complete Set (20): 20.00
Common Player: .25
1 Roberto Alomar .50
2 Jeff Bagwell 1.00
3 Albert Belle .25
4 Barry Bonds 3.50
5 Cecil Fielder .25
6 Juan Gonzalez .75
7 Ken Griffey Jr. 2.25
8 Tony Gwynn 1.50
9 Randy Johnson 1.00
10 Chipper Jones 1.50
11 Ryan Klesko .25
12 Kenny Lofton .25
13 Greg Maddux 1.50
14 Hideo Nomo .75
15 Mike Piazza 2.25
16 Manny Ramirez 1.00
17 Cal Ripken Jr. 3.50
18 Tim Salmon .40
19 Frank Thomas 1.00
20 Matt Williams .25

Update New Horizons

These 1996 Fleer Update inserts feature 20 promising youngsters with bright futures in the majors. The cards were seeded one per every five hobby packs.

NM/M
Complete Set (20): 2.00
Common Player: .25
1 Bob Abreu .45
2 George Arias .25
3 Tony Batista .25
4 Steve Cox .25
5 David Doster .25
6 Jermaine Dye .25
7 Andy Fox .25
8 Mike Grace .25
9 Todd Greene .25
10 Wilton Guerrero .25
11 Richard Hidalgo .25
12 Raul Ibanez .25
13 Robin Jennings .25
14 Marcus Jensen .25
15 Jason Kendall .35
16 Brooks Kieschnick .25
17 Ryan McGuire .25
18 Miguel Mejia .25
19 Rey Ordonez .25
20 Paul Wilson .25

Update Smooth Leather

Ten of the game's top fielders are showcased on these 1996 Fleer Update insert cards. The cards were seeded one per every five packs.

NM/M
Complete Set (10): 7.00
Common Player: .40
1 Roberto Alomar .50
1p Roberto Alomar (Promo) 2.00
2 Barry Bonds 2.50
3 Will Clark .45
4 Ken Griffey Jr. 1.75
5 Kenny Lofton .40
6 Greg Maddux 1.00
7 Raul Mondesi .40
8 Rey Ordonez .40
9 Cal Ripken Jr. 2.50
9p Cal Ripken Jr. (Promo) 6.00
10 Matt Williams .40

Update Soaring Stars

Ten of the game's top players are spotlighted on these 1996 Fleer Update in-

serts. The cards were seeded one per every 11 packs.

NM/M
Complete Set (10): 6.00
Common Player: .25
1 Jeff Bagwell .75
2 Barry Bonds 2.00
3 Juan Gonzalez .75
4 Ken Griffey Jr. 1.50
5 Chipper Jones 1.00
6 Greg Maddux 1.00
7 Mike Piazza 1.50
8 Manny Ramirez .75
9 Frank Thomas .75
10 Matt Williams .25

Baseball '96

For a second consecutive year Fleer issued a special version of its Cleveland Indians cards for sale at Revco stores and Jacobs Field. Sold in 10-card packs with a suggested retail price of $1.49, the Revco version Indians team set differs from the regular Fleer cards in the application of UV coating on front and back, the use of silver- rather than gold-foil highlights and the numbering "X of 20." Following up on the Indians team-set issue, Fleer also issued 20-card sets for several other teams, distributed regionally. They were also sold in 10-card packs ($1.99 SRP) and feature UV coating, silver-foil graphics and special numbering. Some cards were updated and feature new photos reflecting trades, free agent signings, etc.

NM/M
Complete Set (180): 27.00
Common Player: .09

Atlanta Braves Team Set: 4.00
1 Steve Avery .10
2 Jeff Blauser .10
3 Brad Clontz .10
4 Tom Glavine .35
5 Marquis Grissom .10
6 Chipper Jones 1.25
7 David Justice .10
8 Ryan Klesko .10
9 Mark Lemke .10
10 Javier Lopez .10
11 Greg Maddux 1.25
12 Fred McGriff .10
13 Greg McMichael .10
14 Eddie Perez .10
15 Jason Schmidt .10
16 John Smoltz .10
17 Terrell Wade .10
18 Mark Wohlers .10
19 Logo Card .10
20 Checklist .10

Baltimore Orioles Team Set: 5.00
1 Roberto Alomar .20
2 Brady Anderson .10
3 Armando Benitez .10
4 Bobby Bonilla .10
5 Scott Erickson .10
6 Jeffrey Hammonds .10
7 Jimmy Haynes .10
8 Chris Hoiles .10
9 Rick Krivda .10
10 Kent Mercker .10
11 Mike Mussina .45
12 Randy Myers .10
13 Jesse Orosco .10
14 Rafael Palmeiro .75
15 Cal Ripken Jr. 2.50
16 B.J. Surhoff .10
17 Tony Tarasco .10
18 David Wells .10
19 Logo Card .10
20 Checklist .10

Boston Red Sox Team Set: 3.00
1 Stan Belinda .10
2 Jose Canseco .50
3 Roger Clemens 2.00
4 Wil Cordero .10
5 Vaughn Eshelman .10
6 Tom Gordon .10
7 Mike Greenwell .10
8 Dwayne Hosey .10
9 Kevin Mitchell .10
10 Tim Naehring .10
11 Troy O'Leary .10
12 Aaron Sele .10
13 Heathcliff Slocumb .10
14 Mike Stanley .10
15 Jeff Suppan .10
16 John Valentin .10
17 Mo Vaughn .10
18 Tim Wakefield .10
19 Logo Card .10
20 Checklist .10

Chicago Cubs Team Set: 4.00
1 Terry Adams .10
2 Jim Bullinger .10
3 Frank Castillo .10
4 Kevin Foster .10
5 Leo Gomez .10
6 Luis Gonzalez .20
7 Mark Grace .15
8 Jose Hernandez .10
9 Robin Jennings **RC** .10
10 Doug Jones .10
11 Brooks Kieschnick .10
12 Brian McRae .10
13 Jaime Navarro .10
14 Rey Sanchez .10
15 Ryne Sandberg 1.25
16 Scott Servais .10
17 Sammy Sosa 1.50
18 Steve Trachsel .10
19 Logo Card .10
20 Checklist .10

Chicago White Sox Team Set: 4.00
1 Wilson Alvarez .10
2 Harold Baines .10
3 Jason Bere .10
4 Ray Durham .10
5 Alex Fernandez .10
6 Ozzie Guillen .10
7 Roberto Hernandez .10
8 Matt Karchner .10
9 Ron Karkovice .10
10 Darren Lewis .10
11 Dave Martinez .10
12 Lyle Mouton .10
13 Tony Phillips .10
14 Chris Snopek .10
15 Kevin Tapani .10
16 Danny Tartabull .10
17 Frank Thomas 1.00
18 Robin Ventura .10
19 Logo Card .10
20 Checklist .10

Cleveland Indians Team Set: 4.00
1 Sandy Alomar Jr. .10
2 Paul Assenmacher .10
3 Carlos Baerga .10
4 Albert Belle .09
5 Orel Hershiser .10
6 Kenny Lofton .10
7 Dennis Martinez .10
8 Jose Mesa .10
9 Eddie Murray 1.00
10 Charles Nagy .10
11 Tony Pena .10
12 Herb Perry .10
13 Eric Plunk .10
14 Jim Poole .10
15 Manny Ramirez 1.00
16 Julian Tavarez .10
17 Jim Thome .75
18 Omar Vizquel .10
19 Logo Card .10
20 Checklist .10

Colorado Rockies Team Set: 2.75
1 Jason Bates .10
2 Dante Bichette .10
3 Ellis Burks .10
4 Vinny Castilla .10
5 Andres Galarraga .10
6 Darren Holmes .10
7 Curt Leskanic .10
8 Quinton McCracken .10
9 Mike Munoz .10
10 Jayhawk Owens .10
11 Steve Reed .10
12 Kevin Ritz .10
13 Bret Saberhagen .10
14 Bill Swift .10
15 John Vander Wal .10
16 Larry Walker .10
17 Walt Weiss .10
18 Eric Young .10
19 Logo Card .10
20 Checklist .10

L.A. Dodgers Team Set: 4.00
1 Mike Blowers .10
2 Brett Butler .10
3 Tom Candiotti .10
4 Roger Cedeno .10
5 Delino DeShields .10
6 Chad Fonville .10
7 Greg Gagne .10
8 Karim Garcia .15
9 Todd Hollandsworth .10
10 Eric Karros .10
11 Ramon Martinez .10
12 Raul Mondesi .10
13 Hideo Nomo .75
14 Antonio Osuna .10
15 Chan Ho Park .10
16 Mike Piazza 2.00
17 Ismael Valdes .10
18 Todd Worrell .10
19 Logo Card .10
20 Checklist .10

Texas Rangers Team Set: 2.75
1 Mark Brandenburg .10
2 Damon Buford .10
3 Will Clark .15
4 Kevin Elster .10
5 Benji Gil .10
6 Juan Gonzalez .75
7 Rusty Greer .10
8 Kevin Gross .10
9 Darryl Hamilton .10
10 Ken Hill .10
11 Mark McLemore .10
12 Dean Palmer .10
13 Roger Pavlik .10
14 Ivan Rodriguez .75
15 Mickey Tettleton .10
16 Dave Valle .10
17 Ed Vosberg .10
18 Matt Whiteside .10
19 Logo Card .10
20 Checklist .10

Panini Stickers

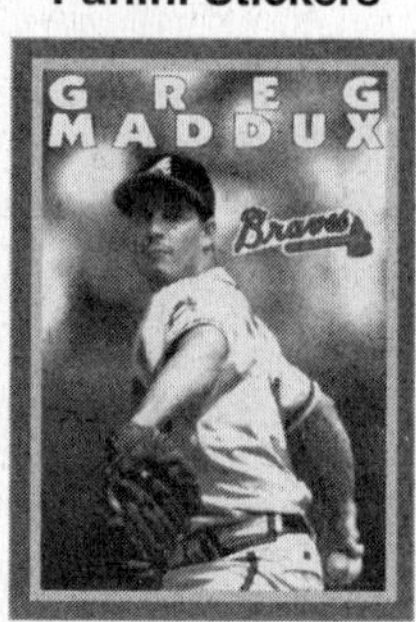

For the second year of distribution by Fleer/SkyBox, the annual baseball sticker set once again used Panini as the dominant brand identification. Printed in Italy, the stickers were sold in packs of six for 49 cents in the U.S., 69 cents in Canada. At 2-1/8" x 3", the basic player stickers have a green border around the color action photo; a second, ghosted, version of the photo appear in the background. Team logo and player ID are in a bat at bottom. Backs are printed in blue with the sticker number, Panini and licensor logos, along with copyright information. Team logo and special rookie stickers were printed on silver foil. A 60-page album was issued to house the set.

NM/M
Complete Set (246): 4.00
Common Player: .05
Album: .75
1 David Justice .05
2 Tom Glavine .20
3 Javier Lopez .05
4 Greg Maddux .45
5 Marquis Grissom .05
6 Braves Logo .05
7 Ryan Klesko .05
8 Chipper Jones .45
9 Quilvio Veras .05
10 Chris Hammond .05
11 Charles Johnson .05
12 John Burkett .05
13 Marlins Logo .05
14 Jeff Conine .05
15 Gary Sheffield .25
16 Greg Colbrunn .05
17 Moises Alou .05
18 Pedro J. Martinez .35

#	Card	Price
19	Rondell White	.05
20	Tony Tarasco	.05
21	Expos Logo	.05
22	Carlos Perez	.05
23	David Segui	.05
24	Wil Cordero	.05
25	Jason Isringhausen	.05
26	Rico Brogna	.05
27	Edgardo Alfonzo	.05
28	Todd Hundley	.05
29	Mets Logo	.05
30	Bill Pulsipher	.05
31	Carl Everett	.05
32	Jose Vizcaino	.05
33	Lenny Dykstra	.05
34	Charlie Hayes	.05
35	Heathcliff Slocumb	.05
36	Darren Daulton	.05
37	Phillies Logo	.05
38	Mickey Morandini	.05
39	Gregg Jefferies	.05
40	Jim Eisenreich	.05
41	Brian McRae	.05
42	Luis Gonzalez	.10
43	Randy Myers	.05
44	Shawon Dunston	.05
45	Cubs Logo	.05
46	Jaime Navarro	.05
47	Mark Grace	.10
48	Sammy Sosa	.50
49	Barry Larkin	.05
50	Pete Schourek	.05
51	John Smiley	.05
52	Reggie Sanders	.05
53	Reds Logo	.05
54	Hal Morris	.05
55	Ron Gant	.05
56	Bret Boone	.05
57	Craig Biggio	.05
58	Brian L. Hunter	.05
59	Jeff Bagwell	.35
60	Shane Reynolds	.05
61	Astros Logo	.05
62	Derek Bell	.05
63	Doug Drabek	.05
64	Orlando Miller	.05
65	Jay Bell	.05
66	Dan Miceli	.05
67	Orlando Merced	.05
68	Jeff King	.05
69	Carlos Garcia	.05
70	Pirates Logo	.05
71	Al Martin	.05
72	Denny Neagle	.05
73	Ray Lankford	.05
74	Ozzie Smith	.45
75	Bernard Gilkey	.05
76	John Mabry	.05
77	Cardinals Logo	.05
78	Brian Jordan	.05
79	Scott Cooper	.05
80	Allen Watson	.05
81	Dante Bichette	.05
82	Bret Saberhagen	.05
83	Walt Weiss	.05
84	Andres Galarraga	.05
85	Rockies Logo	.05
86	Larry Walker	.05
87	Bill Swift	.05
88	Vinny Castilla	.05
89	Raul Mondesi	.05
90	Roger Cedeno	.05
91	Chad Fonville	.05
92	Hideo Nomo	.30
93	Dodgers Logo	.05
94	Ramon Martinez	.05
95	Mike Piazza	.60
96	Eric Karros	.05
97	Tony Gwynn	.45
98	Brad Ausmus	.05
99	Trevor Hoffman	.05
100	Ken Caminiti	.05
101	Padres Logo	.05
102	Andy Ashby	.05
103	Steve Finley	.05
104	Joey Hamilton	.05
105	Matt Williams	.05
106	Rod Beck	.05
107	Barry Bonds	.75
108	William Van Landingham	.05
109	Giants Logo	.05
110	Deion Sanders	.05
111	Royce Clayton	.05
112	Glenallen Hill	.05
113	Tony Gwynn (League Leader - BA)	.20
114	Dante Bichette (League Leader - HR)	.05
115	Dante Bichette (League Leader - RBI)	.05
116	Quilvio Veras (League Leader - SB)	.05
117	Hideo Nomo (League Leader - K)	.15
118	Greg Maddux (League Leader - W)	.20
119	Randy Myers (League Leader - Saves)	.05
120	Edgar Martinez (League Leader - BA)	.05
121	Albert Belle (League Leader - HR)	.05
122	Mo Vaughn (League Leader - RBI)	.05
123	Kenny Lofton (League Leader - SB)	.05
124	Randy Johnson (League Leader - K)	.15
125	Mike Mussina (League Leader - W)	.10
126	Jose Mesa (League Leader - Saves)	.05
127	Mike Mussina	.20
128	Cal Ripken Jr.	.75
129	Rafael Palmeiro	.30
130	Ben McDonald	.05
131	Orioles Logo	.05
132	Chris Hoiles	.05
133	Bobby Bonilla	.05
134	Brady Anderson	.05
135	Jose Canseco	.20
136	Roger Clemens	.50
137	Mo Vaughn	.05
138	Mike Greenwell	.05
139	Red Sox Logo	.05
140	Tim Wakefield	.05
141	John Valentin	.05
142	Tim Naehring	.05
143	Travis Fryman	.05
144	Chad Curtis	.05
145	Felipe Lira	.05
146	Cecil Fielder	.05
147	Tigers Logo	.05
148	John Flaherty	.05
149	Chris Gomez	.05
150	Sean Bergman	.05
151	Don Mattingly	.50
152	Andy Pettitte	.15
153	Wade Boggs	.45
154	Paul O'Neill	.05
155	Yankees Logo	.05
156	Bernie Williams	.10
157	Jack McDowell	.05
158	David Cone	.05
159	Roberto Alomar	.10
160	Paul Molitor	.35
161	Shawn Green	.15
162	Joe Carter	.05
163	Blue Jays Logo	.05
164	Alex Gonzalez	.05
165	Al Leiter	.05
166	John Olerud	.05
167	Alex Fernandez	.05
168	Ray Durham	.05
169	Lance Johnson	.05
170	Ozzie Guillen	.05
171	White Sox Logo	.05
172	Robin Ventura	.05
173	Frank Thomas	.35
174	Tim Raines	.05
175	Albert Belle	.05
176	Manny Ramirez	.35
177	Eddie Murray	.35
178	Orel Hershiser	.05
179	Indians Logo	.05
180	Kenny Lofton	.05
181	Carlos Baerga	.05
182	Jose Mesa	.05
183	Gary Gaetti	.05
184	Tom Goodwin	.05
185	Kevin Appier	.05
186	Jon Nunnally	.05
187	Royals Logo	.05
188	Wally Joyner	.05
189	Jeff Montgomery	.05
190	Johnny Damon	.25
191	B.J. Surhoff	.05
192	Ricky Bones	.05
193	John Jaha	.05
194	Dave Nilsson	.05
195	Brewers Logo	.05
196	Greg Vaughn	.05
197	Kevin Seitzer	.05
198	Joe Oliver	.05
199	Chuck Knoblauch	.05
200	Kirby Puckett	.45
201	Marty Cordova	.05
202	Pat Meares	.05
203	Twins Logo	.05
204	Scott Stahoviak	.05
205	Matt Walbeck	.05
206	Pedro Munoz	.05
207	Garret Anderson	.05
208	Chili Davis	.05
209	Tim Salmon	.10
210	J.T. Snow	.05
211	Angels Logo	.05
212	Jim Edmonds	.05
213	Chuck Finley	.05
214	Mark Langston	.05
215	Dennis Eckersley	.30
216	Todd Stottlemyre	.05
217	Geronimo Berroa	.05
218	Mark McGwire	.65
219	A's Logo	.05
220	Brent Gates	.05
221	Terry Steinbach	.05
222	Rickey Henderson	.35
223	Ken Griffey Jr.	.60
224	Alex Rodriguez	.65
225	Tino Martinez	.05
226	Randy Johnson	.35
227	Mariners Logo	.05
228	Jay Buhner	.05
229	Vince Coleman	.05
230	Edgar Martinez	.05
231	Will Clark	.10
232	Juan Gonzalez	.35
233	Kenny Rogers	.05
234	Ivan Rodriguez	.30
235	Rangers Logo	.05
236	Mickey Tettleton	.05
237	Dean Palmer	.05
238	Otis Nixon	.05
239	Hideo Nomo (Rookie)	.20
240	Quilvio Veras (Rookie)	.05
241	Jason Isringhausen (Rookie)	.05
242	Andy Pettitte (Rookie)	.05
243	Chipper Jones (Rookie)	.25
244	Garret Anderson (Rookie)	.05
245	Charles Johnson (Rookie)	.05
246	Marty Cordova (Rookie)	.05

1997 Fleer

Fleer maintained its matte-finish coating for 1997 after it debuted in the 1996 product. The regular-issue Series 1 has 500 cards equipped with icons designating All-Stars, League Leaders and World Series cards. There were also 10 checklist cards in the regular-issue set, featuring stars on the front. Fleer arrived in 10-card packs and had a Tiffany Collection parallel set and six different insert sets, including Rookie Sensations, Golden Memories, Team Leaders, Night and Day, Zone and Lumber Company. Series 2 comprises 261 cards plus inserts Decade of Excellence, Bleacher Bashers, Diamond Tributes, Goudey Greats, Headliners, New Horizons and Soaring Stars.

	NM/M
Complete Set (761):	100.00
Complete Series 1 Set (500):	30.00
Complete Series 2 Set (261):	70.00
Common Player:	.05
Complete Tiffany Set (1-761):	500.00
Tiffany Stars/RC's:	8X
A. Jones Circa AU/200:	35.00
Series 2 Pack (10):	3.00
Series 2 Wax Box (36):	90.00

#	Card	Price
1	Roberto Alomar	.10
2	Brady Anderson	.05
3	Bobby Bonilla	.05
4	Rocky Coppinger	.05
5	Cesar Devarez	.05
6	Scott Erickson	.05
7	Jeffrey Hammonds	.05
8	Chris Hoiles	.05
9	Eddie Murray	1.00
10	Mike Mussina	.40
11	Randy Myers	.05
12	Rafael Palmeiro	.75
13	Cal Ripken Jr.	2.50
14	B.J. Surhoff	.05
15	David Wells	.05
16	Todd Zeile	.05
17	Darren Bragg	.05
18	Jose Canseco	.40
19	Roger Clemens	1.75
20	Wil Cordero	.05
21	Jeff Frye	.05
22	Nomar Garciaparra	1.75
23	Tom Gordon	.05
24	Mike Greenwell	.05
25	Reggie Jefferson	.05
26	Jose Malave	.05
27	Tim Naehring	.05
28	Troy O'Leary	.05
29	Heathcliff Slocumb	.05
30	Mike Stanley	.05
31	John Valentin	.05
32	Mo Vaughn	.05
33	Tim Wakefield	.05
34	Garret Anderson	.05
35	George Arias	.05
36	Shawn Boskie	.05
37	Chili Davis	.05
38	Jason Dickson	.05
39	Gary DiSarcina	.05
40	Jim Edmonds	.05
41	Darin Erstad	.10
42	Jorge Fabregas	.05
43	Chuck Finley	.05
44	Todd Greene	.05
45	Mike Holtz **RC**	.05
46	Rex Hudler	.05
47	Mike James	.05
48	Mark Langston	.05
49	Troy Percival	.05
50	Tim Salmon	.15
51	Jeff Schmidt	.05
52	J.T. Snow	.05
53	Randy Velarde	.05
54	Wilson Alvarez	.05
55	Harold Baines	.05
56	James Baldwin	.05
57	Jason Bere	.05
58	Mike Cameron	.05
59	Ray Durham	.05
60	Alex Fernandez	.05
61	Ozzie Guillen	.05
62	Roberto Hernandez	.05
63	Ron Karkovice	.05
64	Darren Lewis	.05
65	Dave Martinez	.05
66	Lyle Mouton	.05
67	Greg Norton	.05
68	Tony Phillips	.05
69	Chris Snopek	.05
70	Kevin Tapani	.05
71	Danny Tartabull	.05
72	Frank Thomas	1.00
73	Robin Ventura	.05
74	Sandy Alomar Jr.	.05
75	Albert Belle	.05
76	Mark Carreon	.05
77	Julio Franco	.05
78	Brian Giles **RC**	1.00
79	Orel Hershiser	.05
80	Kenny Lofton	.05
81	Dennis Martinez	.05
82	Jack McDowell	.05
83	Jose Mesa	.05
84	Charles Nagy	.05
85	Chad Ogea	.05
86	Eric Plunk	.05
87	Manny Ramirez	1.00
88	Kevin Seitzer	.05
89	Julian Tavarez	.05
90	Jim Thome	.65
91	Jose Vizcaino	.05
92	Omar Vizquel	.05
93	Brad Ausmus	.05
94	Kimera Bartee	.05
95	Raul Casanova	.05
96	Tony Clark	.05
97	John Cummings	.05
98	Travis Fryman	.05
99	Bob Higginson	.05
100	Mark Lewis	.05
101	Felipe Lira	.05
102	Phil Nevin	.05
103	Melvin Nieves	.05
104	Curtis Pride	.05
105	A.J. Sager	.05
106	Ruben Sierra	.05
107	Justin Thompson	.05
108	Alan Trammell	.05
109	Kevin Appier	.05
110	Tim Belcher	.05
111	Jaime Bluma	.05
112	Johnny Damon	.35
113	Tom Goodwin	.05
114	Chris Haney	.05
115	Keith Lockhart	.05
116	Mike Macfarlane	.05
117	Jeff Montgomery	.05
118	Jose Offerman	.05
119	Craig Paquette	.05
120	Joe Randa	.05
121	Bip Roberts	.05
122	Jose Rosado	.05
123	Mike Sweeney	.05
124	Michael Tucker	.05
125	Jeromy Burnitz	.05
126	Jeff Cirillo	.05
127	Jeff D'Amico	.05
128	Mike Fetters	.05
129	John Jaha	.05
130	Scott Karl	.05
131	Jesse Levis	.05
132	Mark Loretta	.05
133	Mike Matheny	.05
134	Ben McDonald	.05
135	Matt Mieske	.05
136	Marc Newfield	.05
137	Dave Nilsson	.05
138	Jose Valentin	.05
139	Fernando Vina	.05
140	Bob Wickman	.05
141	Gerald Williams	.05
142	Rick Aguilera	.05
143	Rich Becker	.05
144	Ron Coomer	.05
145	Marty Cordova	.05
146	Roberto Kelly	.05
147	Chuck Knoblauch	.05
148	Matt Lawton	.05
149	Pat Meares	.05
150	Travis Miller	.05
151	Paul Molitor	1.00
152	Greg Myers	.05
153	Dan Naulty	.05
154	Kirby Puckett	1.50
155	Brad Radke	.05
156	Frank Rodriguez	.05
157	Scott Stahoviak	.05
158	Dave Stevens	.05
159	Matt Walbeck	.05
160	Todd Walker	.05
161	Wade Boggs	1.50
162	David Cone	.05
163	Mariano Duncan	.05
164	Cecil Fielder	.05
165	Joe Girardi	.05
166	Dwight Gooden	.05
167	Charlie Hayes	.05
168	Derek Jeter	2.50
169	Jimmy Key	.05
170	Jim Leyritz	.05
171	Tino Martinez	.05
172	Ramiro Mendoza **RC**	.10
173	Jeff Nelson	.05
174	Paul O'Neill	.05
175	Andy Pettitte	.35
176	Mariano Rivera	.15
177	Ruben Rivera	.05
178	Kenny Rogers	.05
179	Darryl Strawberry	.05
180	John Wetteland	.05
181	Bernie Williams	.10
182	Willie Adams	.05
183	Tony Batista	.05
184	Geronimo Berroa	.05
185	Mike Bordick	.05
186	Scott Brosius	.05
187	Bobby Chouinard	.05
188	Jim Corsi	.05
189	Brent Gates	.05
190	Jason Giambi	.50
191	Jose Herrera	.05
192	Damon Mashore **RC**	.05
193	Mark McGwire	2.25
194	Mike Mohler	.05
195	Scott Spiezio	.05
196	Terry Steinbach	.05
197	Bill Taylor	.05
198	John Wasdin	.05
199	Steve Wojciechowski	.05
200	Ernie Young	.05
201	Rich Amaral	.05
202	Jay Buhner	.05
203	Norm Charlton	.05
204	Joey Cora	.05
205	Russ Davis	.05
206	Ken Griffey Jr.	2.00
207	Sterling Hitchcock	.05
208	Brian Hunter	.05
209	Raul Ibanez	.05
210	Randy Johnson	1.00
211	Edgar Martinez	.05
212	Jamie Moyer	.05
213	Alex Rodriguez	2.25
214	Paul Sorrento	.05
215	Matt Wagner	.05
216	Bob Wells	.05
217	Dan Wilson	.05
218	Damon Buford	.05
219	Will Clark	.10
220	Kevin Elster	.05
221	Juan Gonzalez	.75
222	Rusty Greer	.05
223	Kevin Gross	.05
224	Darryl Hamilton	.05
225	Mike Henneman	.05
226	Ken Hill	.05
227	Mark McLemore	.05
228	Darren Oliver	.05
229	Dean Palmer	.05
230	Roger Pavlik	.05
231	Ivan Rodriguez	.75
232	Mickey Tettleton	.05
233	Bobby Witt	.05
234	Jacob Brumfield	.05
235	Joe Carter	.05
236	Tim Crabtree	.05
237	Carlos Delgado	.50
238	Huck Flener	.05
239	Alex Gonzalez	.05
240	Shawn Green	.20
241	Juan Guzman	.05
242	Pat Hentgen	.05
243	Marty Janzen	.05
244	Sandy Martinez	.05
245	Otis Nixon	.05
246	Charlie O'Brien	.05
247	John Olerud	.05
248	Robert Perez	.05
249	Ed Sprague	.05
250	Mike Timlin	.05
251	Steve Avery	.05
252	Jeff Blauser	.05
253	Brad Clontz	.05
254	Jermaine Dye	.05
255	Tom Glavine	.30
256	Marquis Grissom	.05
257	Andruw Jones	1.00
258	Chipper Jones	1.50
259	David Justice	.05
260	Ryan Klesko	.05
261	Mark Lemke	.05
262	Javier Lopez	.05
263	Greg Maddux	1.50
264	Fred McGriff	.05
265	Greg McMichael	.05
266	Denny Neagle	.05
267	Terry Pendleton	.05
268	Eddie Perez	.05
269	John Smoltz	.05
270	Terrell Wade	.05
271	Mark Wohlers	.05
272	Terry Adams	.05
273	Brant Brown	.05
274	Leo Gomez	.05
275	Luis Gonzalez	.10
276	Mark Grace	.10
277	Tyler Houston	.05
278	Robin Jennings	.05
279	Brooks Kieschnick	.05
280	Brian McRae	.05
281	Jaime Navarro	.05
282	Ryne Sandberg	1.50
283	Scott Servais	.05
284	Sammy Sosa	1.75
285	Dave Swartzbaugh **RC**	.05
286	Amaury Telemaco	.05
287	Steve Trachsel	.05
288	Pedro Valdes **RC**	.05
289	Turk Wendell	.05
290	Bret Boone	.05
291	Jeff Branson	.05
292	Jeff Brantley	.05
293	Eric Davis	.05
294	Willie Greene	.05
295	Thomas Howard	.05
296	Barry Larkin	.05
297	Kevin Mitchell	.05
298	Hal Morris	.05
299	Chad Mottola	.05
300	Joe Oliver	.05
301	Mark Portugal	.05
302	Roger Salkeld	.05
303	Reggie Sanders	.05
304	Pete Schourek	.05
305	John Smiley	.05
306	Eddie Taubensee	.05
307	Dante Bichette	.05
308	Ellis Burks	.05
309	Vinny Castilla	.05
310	Andres Galarraga	.05
311	Curt Leskanic	.05
312	Quinton McCracken	.05
313	Neifi Perez	.05
314	Jeff Reed	.05
315	Steve Reed	.05
316	Armando Reynoso	.05
317	Kevin Ritz	.05
318	Bruce Ruffin	.05
319	Larry Walker	.05
320	Walt Weiss	.05
321	Jamey Wright	.05
322	Eric Young	.05
323	Kurt Abbott	.05
324	Alex Arias	.05
325	Kevin Brown	.05
326	Luis Castillo	.05
327	Greg Colbrunn	.05
328	Jeff Conine	.05
329	Andre Dawson	.25
330	Charles Johnson	.05
331	Al Leiter	.05
332	Ralph Milliard	.05
333	Robb Nen	.05
334	Pat Rapp	.05
335	Edgar Renteria	.05
336	Gary Sheffield	.35
337	Devon White	.05
338	Bob Abreu	.05
339	Jeff Bagwell	1.00
340	Derek Bell	.05
341	Sean Berry	.05
342	Craig Biggio	.05
343	Doug Drabek	.05
344	Tony Eusebio	.05
345	Ricky Gutierrez	.05
346	Mike Hampton	.05
347	Brian Hunter	.05
348	Todd Jones	.05
349	Darryl Kile	.05
350	Derrick May	.05
351	Orlando Miller	.05
352	James Mouton	.05
353	Shane Reynolds	.05
354	Billy Wagner	.05
355	Donne Wall	.05
356	Mike Blowers	.05
357	Brett Butler	.05
358	Roger Cedeno	.05
259	Chad Curtis	.05
360	Delino DeShields	.05
361	Greg Gagne	.05
362	Karim Garcia	.10
363	Wilton Guerrero	.05
364	Todd Hollandsworth	.05
365	Eric Karros	.05
366	Ramon Martinez	.05
367	Raul Mondesi	.05
368	Hideo Nomo	.75
369	Antonio Osuna	.05
370	Chan Ho Park	.05
371	Mike Piazza	2.00
372	Ismael Valdes	.05
373	Todd Worrell	.05
374	Moises Alou	.05
375	Shane Andrews	.05
376	Yamil Benitez	.05
377	Jeff Fassero	.05
378	Darrin Fletcher	.05
379	Cliff Floyd	.05
380	Mark Grudzielanek	.05
381	Mike Lansing	.05
382	Barry Manuel	.05
383	Pedro Martinez	1.00
384	Henry Rodriguez	.05
385	Mel Rojas	.05
386	F.P. Santangelo	.05
387	David Segui	.05
388	Ugueth Urbina	.05
389	Rondell White	.05
390	Edgardo Alfonzo	.05
391	Carlos Baerga	.05
392	Mark Clark	.05
393	Alvaro Espinoza	.05
394	John Franco	.05
395	Bernard Gilkey	.05
396	Pete Harnisch	.05
397	Todd Hundley	.05
398	Butch Huskey	.05

399 Jason Isringhausen .05
400 Lance Johnson .05
401 Bobby Jones .05
402 Alex Ochoa .05
403 Rey Ordonez .05
404 Robert Person .05
405 Paul Wilson .05
406 Matt Beech .05
407 Ron Blazier .05
408 Ricky Bottalico .05
409 Lenny Dykstra .05
410 Jim Eisenreich .05
411 Bobby Estalella .05
412 Mike Grace .05
413 Gregg Jefferies .05
414 Mike Lieberthal .05
415 Wendell Magee Jr. .05
416 Mickey Morandini .05
417 Ricky Otero .05
418 Scott Rolen .75
419 Ken Ryan .05
420 Benito Santiago .05
421 Curt Schilling .25
422 Kevin Sefcik .05
423 Jermaine Allensworth .05
424 Trey Beamon .05
425 Jay Bell .05
426 Francisco Cordova .05
427 Carlos Garcia .05
428 Mark Johnson .05
429 Jason Kendall .05
430 Jeff King .05
431 Jon Lieber .05
432 Al Martin .05
433 Orlando Merced .05
434 Ramon Morel .05
435 Matt Ruebel .05
436 Jason Schmidt .05
437 Marc Wilkins **RC** .05
438 Alan Benes .05
439 Andy Benes .05
440 Royce Clayton .05
441 Dennis Eckersley .65
442 Gary Gaetti .05
443 Ron Gant .05
444 Aaron Holbert .05
445 Brian Jordan .05
446 Ray Lankford .05
447 John Mabry .05
448 T.J. Mathews .05
449 Willie McGee .05
450 Donovan Osborne .05
451 Tom Pagnozzi .05
452 Ozzie Smith 1.50
453 Todd Stottlemyre .05
454 Mark Sweeney .05
455 Dmitri Young .05
456 Andy Ashby .05
457 Ken Caminiti .05
458 Archi Cianfrocco .05
459 Steve Finley .05
460 John Flaherty .05
461 Chris Gomez .05
462 Tony Gwynn 1.50
463 Joey Hamilton .05
464 Rickey Henderson 1.00
465 Trevor Hoffman .05
466 Brian Johnson .05
467 Wally Joyner .05
468 Jody Reed .05
469 Scott Sanders .05
470 Bob Tewksbury .05
471 Fernando Valenzuela .05
472 Greg Vaughn .05
473 Tim Worrell .05
474 Rich Aurilia .05
475 Rod Beck .05
476 Marvin Benard .05
477 Barry Bonds 2.50
478 Jay Canizaro .05
479 Shawon Dunston .05
480 Shawn Estes .05
481 Mark Gardner .05
482 Glenallen Hill .05
483 Stan Javier .05
484 Marcus Jensen .05
485 Bill Mueller **RC** 1.50
486 William Van Landingham .05
487 Allen Watson .05
488 Rick Wilkins .05
489 Matt Williams .05
489p Matt Williams ("PROMOTIONAL SAMPLE") 1.50
490 Desi Wilson .05
491 Checklist (Albert Belle) .05
492 Checklist (Ken Griffey Jr.) .85
493 Checklist (Andruw Jones) .40
494 Checklist (Chipper Jones) .60
495 Checklist (Mark McGwire) 1.00
496 Checklist (Paul Molitor) .45
497 Checklist (Mike Piazza) .85
498 Checklist (Cal Ripken Jr.) 1.25
499 Checklist (Alex Rodriguez) 1.00
500 Checklist (Frank Thomas) .45
501 Kenny Lofton .05
502 Carlos Perez .05
503 Tim Raines .05
504 Danny Patterson **RC** .05
505 Derrick May .05
506 Dave Hollins .05
507 Felipe Crespo .05
508 Brian Banks .05
509 Jeff Kent .05
510 Bubba Trammell **RC** .25
511 Robert Person .05
512 David Arias **RC** (Ortiz) 40.00
513 Ryan Jones .05
514 David Justice .05
515 Will Cunnane .05
516 Russ Johnson .05
517 John Burkett .05
518 Robinson Checo **RC** .05
519 Ricardo Rincon **RC** .05
520 Woody Williams .05
521 Rick Helling .05
522 Jorge Posada .05
523 Kevin Orie .05
524 Fernando Tatis **RC** .15
525 Jermaine Dye .05
526 Brian Hunter .05
527 Greg McMichael .05
528 Matt Wagner .05
529 Richie Sexson .05
530 Scott Ruffcorn .05
531 Luis Gonzalez .10
532 Mike Johnson .05
533 Mark Petkovsek .05
534 Doug Drabek .05
535 Jose Canseco .40
536 Bobby Bonilla .05
537 J.T. Snow .05
538 Shawon Dunston .05
539 John Ericks .05
540 Terry Steinbach .05
541 Jay Bell .05
542 Joe Borowski .05
543 David Wells .05
544 Justin Towle **RC** .10
545 Mike Blowers .05
546 Shannon Stewart .05
547 Rudy Pemberton .05
548 Bill Swift .05
549 Osvaldo Fernandez .05
550 Eddie Murray 1.00
551 Don Wengert .05
552 Brad Ausmus .05
553 Carlos Garcia .05
554 Jose Guillen .05
555 Rheal Cormier .05
556 Doug Brocail .05
557 Rex Hudler .05
558 Armando Benitez .05
559 Elieser Marrero .05
560 Ricky Ledee **RC** .25
561 Bartolo Colon .05
562 Quilvio Veras .05
563 Alex Fernandez .05
564 Darren Dreifort .05
565 Benji Gil .05
566 Kent Mercker .05
567 Glendon Rusch .05
568 Ramon Tatis **RC** .05
569 Roger Clemens 1.75
570 Mark Lewis .05
571 Emil Brown **RC** .05
572 Jaime Navarro .05
573 Sherman Obando .05
574 John Wasdin .05
575 Calvin Maduro .05
576 Todd Jones .05
577 Orlando Merced .05
578 Cal Eldred .05
579 Mark Gubicza .05
580 Michael Tucker .05
581 Tony Saunders **RC** .05
582 Garvin Alston .05
583 Joe Roa .05
584 Brady Raggio **RC** .05
585 Jimmy Key .05
586 Marc Sagmoen **RC** .05
587 Jim Bullinger .05
588 Yorkis Perez .05
589 Jose Cruz Jr. **RC** .75
590 Mike Stanton .05
591 Deivi Cruz **RC** .25
592 Steve Karsay .05
593 Mike Trombley .05
594 Doug Glanville .05
595 Scott Sanders .05
596 Thomas Howard .05
597 T.J. Staton .05
598 Garrett Stephenson .05
599 Rico Brogna .05
600 Albert Belle .05
601 Jose Vizcaino .05
602 Chili Davis .05
603 Shane Mack .05
604 Jim Eisenreich .05
605 Todd Zeile .05
606 Brian Boehringer .05
607 Paul Shuey .05
608 Kevin Tapani .05
609 John Wetteland .05
610 Jim Leyritz .05
611 Ray Montgomery .05
612 Doug Bochtler .05
613 Wady Almonte .05
614 Danny Tartabull .05
615 Orlando Miller .05
616 Bobby Ayala .05
617 Tony Graffanino .05
618 Marc Valdes .05
619 Ron Villone .05
620 Derrek Lee .05
621 Greg Colbrunn .05
622 Felix Heredia **RC** .10
623 Carl Everett .05
624 Mark Thompson .05
625 Jeff Granger .05
626 Damian Jackson .05
627 Mark Leiter .05
628 Chris Holt .05
629 Dario Veras **RC** .05
630 Dave Burba .05
631 Darryl Hamilton .05
632 Mark Acre .05
633 Fernando Hernandez .05
634 Terry Mulholland .05
635 Dustin Hermanson .05
636 Delino DeShields .05
637 Steve Avery .05
638 Tony Womack **RC** .10
639 Mark Whiten .05
640 Marquis Grissom .05
641 Xavier Hernandez .05
642 Eric Davis .05
643 Bob Tewksbury .05
644 Dante Powell .05
645 Carlos Castillo .05
646 Chris Widger .05
647 Moises Alou .05
648 Pat Listach .05
649 Edgar Ramos .05
650 Deion Sanders .05
651 John Olerud .05
652 Todd Dunwoody .05
653 Randall Simon **RC** .10
654 Dan Carlson .05
655 Matt Williams .05
656 Jeff King .05
657 Luis Alicea .05
658 Brian Moehler .05
659 Ariel Prieto .05
660 Kevin Elster .05
661 Mark Hutton .05
662 Aaron Sele .05
663 Graeme Lloyd .05
664 John Burke .05
665 Mel Rojas .05
666 Sid Fernandez .05
667 Pedro Astacio .05
668 Jeff Abbott .05
669 Darren Daulton .05
670 Mike Bordick .05
671 Sterling Hitchcock .05
672 Damion Easley .05
673 Armando Reynoso .05
674 Pat Cline .05
675 Orlando Cabrera **RC** .50
676 Alan Embree .05
677 Brian Bevil .05
678 David Weathers .05
679 Cliff Floyd .05
680 Joe Randa .05
681 Bill Haselman .05
682 Jeff Fassero .05
683 Matt Morris .05
684 Mark Portugal .05
685 Lee Smith .05
686 Pokey Reese .05
687 Benito Santiago .05
688 Brian Johnson .05
689 Brent Brede **RC** .05
690 Shigetosi Hasegawa .05
691 Julio Santana .05
692 Steve Kline .05
693 Julian Tavarez .05
694 John Hudek .05
695 Manny Alexander .05
696 Roberto Alomar (Encore) .10
697 Jeff Bagwell (Encore) .45
698 Barry Bonds (Encore) 1.25
699 Ken Caminiti (Encore) .05
700 Juan Gonzalez (Encore) .35
701 Ken Griffey Jr. (Encore) .85
702 Tony Gwynn (Encore) .60
703 Derek Jeter (Encore) 1.25
704 Andruw Jones (Encore) .45
705 Chipper Jones (Encore) .60
706 Barry Larkin (Encore) .05
707 Greg Maddux (Encore) .60
708 Mark McGwire (Encore) 1.00
709 Paul Molitor (Encore) .45
710 Hideo Nomo (Encore) .35
711 Andy Pettitte (Encore) .30
712 Mike Piazza (Encore) .85
713 Manny Ramirez (Encore) .45
714 Cal Ripken Jr. (Encore) 1.25
715 Alex Rodriguez (Encore) 1.00
716 Ryne Sandberg (Encore) .60
717 John Smoltz (Encore) .05
718 Frank Thomas (Encore) .50
719 Mo Vaughn (Encore) .05
720 Bernie Williams (Encore) .10
721 Checklist (Tim Salmon) .05
722 Checklist (Greg Maddux) .60
723 Checklist (Cal Ripken Jr.) 1.25
724 Checklist (Mo Vaughn) .05
725 Checklist (Ryne Sandberg) .45
726 Checklist (Frank Thomas) .50
727 Checklist (Barry Larkin) .05
728 Checklist (Manny Ramirez) .45
729 Checklist (Andres Galarraga) .05
730 Checklist (Tony Clark) .05
731 Checklist (Gary Sheffield) .20
732 Checklist (Jeff Bagwell) .40
733 Checklist (Kevin Appier) .05
734 Checklist (Mike Piazza) .85
735 Checklist (Jeff Cirillo) .05
736 Checklist (Paul Molitor) .40
737 Checklist (Henry Rodriguez) .05
738 Checklist (Todd Hundley) .05
739 Checklist (Derek Jeter) 1.25
740 Checklist (Mark McGwire) 1.00
741 Checklist (Curt Schilling) .15
742 Checklist (Jason Kendall) .05
743 Checklist (Tony Gwynn) .60
744 Checklist (Barry Bonds) 1.25
745 Checklist (Ken Griffey Jr.) .85
746 Checklist (Brian Jordan) .05
747 Checklist (Juan Gonzalez) .40
748 Checklist (Joe Carter) .05
749 Arizona Diamondbacks .05
750 Tampa Bay Devil Rays .05
751 Hideki Irabu **RC** .15
752 Jeremi Gonzalez **RC** .15
753 Mario Valdez **RC** .05
754 Aaron Boone .05
755 Brett Tomko .05
756 Jaret Wright **RC** 1.00
757 Ryan McGuire .05
758 Jason McDonald .05
759 Adrian Brown **RC** .05
760 Keith Foulke **RC** .25
761 Checklist .05

Tiffany

Insertion odds were considerably lengthened for the UV-coated Tiffany Collection parallels in 1997 Fleer - to one card per 20 packs.

	NM/M
Complete Set (761):	500.00
Common Player:	1.00
Stars/Rcs:	8X
512 David Arias (Ortiz)	140.00

Bleacher Blasters

This 10-card insert features some of the game's top power hitters and was found in retail packs only. Cards featured a die-cut "burst" pattern on an etched foil background. Backs have a portrait photo and career highlights. Cards were inserted 1:36 packs.

		NM/M
Complete Set (10):		40.00
Common Player:		1.50
1	Albert Belle	1.50
2	Barry Bonds	10.00
3	Juan Gonzalez	2.00
4	Ken Griffey Jr.	6.00
5	Mark McGwire	8.00
6	Mike Piazza	6.00
7	Alex Rodriguez	8.00
8	Frank Thomas	4.00
9	Mo Vaughn	1.50
10	Matt Williams	1.50

Decade of Excellence

A 12-card insert found 1:36 in hobby shop packs, cards are in a format similar to the 1987 Fleer set and feature vintage photos of players who started their careers no later than the '87 season. Ten percent of the press run

(1:360 packs) received a special foil treatment and designation as "Rare Traditions."

		NM/M
Complete Set (12):		35.00
Common Player:		1.50
Rare Tradition:		12X
1	Wade Boggs	4.50
2	Barry Bonds	9.00
3	Roger Clemens	6.00
4	Tony Gwynn	4.50
5	Rickey Henderson	3.00
6	Greg Maddux	4.50
7	Mark McGwire	6.00
8	Paul Molitor	3.00
9	Eddie Murray	3.00
10	Cal Ripken Jr.	9.00
11	Ryne Sandberg	4.50
12	Matt Williams	1.50

Diamond Tribute

Twelve of the game's top stars are highlighted in this set. Fronts feature an embossed rainbow prismatic foil background and gold lettering. Backs have an action photo and a few sentences about the player. They were inserted 1:288 packs.

		NM/M
Complete Set (12):		120.00
Common Player:		3.00
1	Albert Belle	3.00
2	Barry Bonds	20.00
3	Juan Gonzalez	5.00
4	Ken Griffey Jr.	12.50
5	Tony Gwynn	10.00
6	Greg Maddux	10.00
7	Mark McGwire	15.00
8	Eddie Murray	8.00
9	Mike Piazza	12.50
10	Cal Ripken Jr.	20.00
11	Alex Rodriguez	15.00
12	Frank Thomas	8.00

Golden Memories

Golden Memories captures 10 different highlights from the 1996 season, and is inserted one per 16 packs. Moments like Dwight Gooden's no hitter, Paul Molitor's 3000th hit and Eddie Murray's 500th home run are highlighted on a horizontal format.

		NM/M
Complete Set (10):		6.00
Common Player:		.25
1	Barry Bonds	2.00
2	Dwight Gooden	.25
3	Todd Hundley	.25
4	Mark McGwire	1.50
5	Paul Molitor	.75
6	Eddie Murray	.75
7	Hideo Nomo	.50
8	Mike Piazza	1.25
9	Cal Ripken Jr.	2.00
10	Ozzie Smith	1.00

Goudey Greats

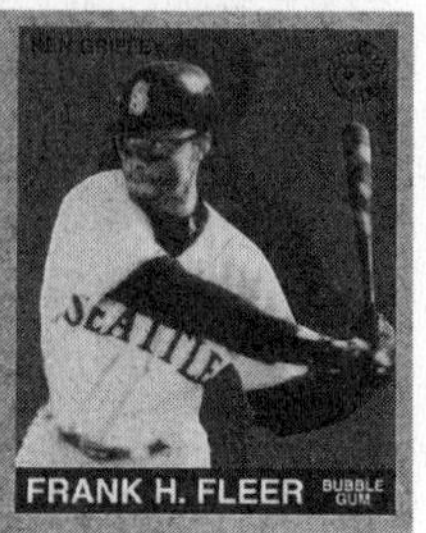

Using a 2-3/8" x 2-7/8" format reminiscent of 1933 Goudey cards, this 15-card insert offers today's top players in classic old-time design. Cards were inserted 1:8 packs. A limited number (1 percent of press run) of cards received a special gold-foil treatment and were found only in hobby packs.

		NM/M
Complete Set (15):		20.00
Common Player:		.50
Foils:		15X
1	Barry Bonds	4.00
2	Ken Griffey Jr.	3.00
3	Tony Gwynn	2.00
4	Derek Jeter	4.00
5	Chipper Jones	2.00
6	Kenny Lofton	.50
7	Greg Maddux	2.00
8	Mark McGwire	3.50
9	Eddie Murray	1.50
10	Mike Piazza	3.00
11	Cal Ripken Jr.	4.00
12	Alex Rodriguez	3.50
13	Ryne Sandberg	2.00
14	Frank Thomas	1.50
15	Mo Vaughn	.50

Headliners

This 20-card insert highlights the personal achievements of each of the players depicted. Cards were inserted 1:2 packs and feature multi-color foil stamping on the fronts and a newspaper-style account of the player's achievement on the back.

		NM/M
Complete Set (20):		5.00
Common Player:		.10
1	Jeff Bagwell	.25
2	Albert Belle	.10
3	Barry Bonds	1.00
4	Ken Caminiti	.10
5	Juan Gonzalez	.20
6	Ken Griffey Jr.	.60
7	Tony Gwynn	.40
8	Derek Jeter	1.00
9	Andruw Jones	.25
10	Chipper Jones	.40
11	Greg Maddux	.40
12	Mark McGwire	.75
13	Paul Molitor	.25
14	Eddie Murray	.25
15	Mike Piazza	.60
16	Cal Ripken Jr.	1.00
17	Alex Rodriguez	.75
18	Ryne Sandberg	.40
19	John Smoltz	.20
20	Frank Thomas	.25

Lumber Company

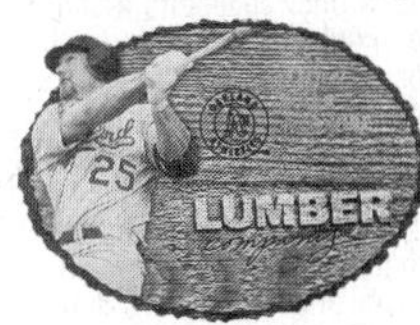

Lumber Company inserts were found every 48 retail packs. The cards were printed on a die-cut, spherical wood-like pattern, with the player imposed on the left side. Eighteen of the top power hitters in baseball are highlighted.

		NM/M
Complete Set (18):		45.00
Common Player:		1.00
1	Brady Anderson	1.00
2	Jeff Bagwell	3.00
3	Albert Belle	1.00
4	Barry Bonds	8.00
5	Jay Buhner	1.00
6	Ellis Burks	1.00
7	Andres Galarraga	1.00
8	Juan Gonzalez	2.00
9	Ken Griffey Jr.	5.00
10	Todd Hundley	1.00
11	Ryan Klesko	1.00
12	Mark McGwire	6.00
13	Mike Piazza	5.00
14	Alex Rodriguez	6.00
15	Gary Sheffield	2.00
16	Sammy Sosa	4.00
17	Frank Thomas	3.00
18	Mo Vaughn	1.00

1997-98 Fleer Million Dollar Moments

By assembling a complete set of 50 baseball "Million Dollar Moments" cards prior to July 31, 1998, a collector could win $50,000 a year through 2018. The catch, of course, is that cards #46-50 were printed in very limited quantities, with only one card #50. (Stated odds of winning the million were one in nearly 46,000,000.) The Moments cards have player action photos on front vignetted into a black border. The Fleer Million Dollar Moments logo is at top, with the player name and the date and details of his highlight at bottom in orange and white. Backs have the contest rules in fine print. Instant Win versions of some cards were also issued.

		NM/M
Complete Set (45):		2.00
Common Player:		.05
1	Checklist	.05
2	Derek Jeter	.45
3	Babe Ruth	.25
4	Barry Bonds	.45
5	Brooks Robinson	.05
6	Todd Hundley	.05
7	Johnny Vander Meer	.05
8	Cal Ripken Jr.	.45
9	Bill Mazeroski	.05
10	Chipper Jones	.25
11	Frank Robinson	.05
12	Roger Clemens	.35
13	Bob Feller	.05
14	Mike Piazza	.30
15	Joe Nuxhall	.05
16	Hideo Nomo	.15
17	Jackie Robinson	.25
18	Orel Hershiser	.05
19	Bobby Thomson	.05
20	Joe Carter	.05
21	Al Kaline	.05
22	Bernie Williams	.05
23	Don Larsen	.05
24	Rickey Henderson	.15
25	Maury Wills	.05
26	Andruw Jones	.15
27	Bobby Richardson	.05
28	Alex Rodriguez	.35
29	Jim Bunning	.05
30	Ken Caminiti	.05
31	Bob Gibson	.05
32	Frank Thomas	.20
33	Mickey Lolich	.05
34	John Smoltz	.05
35	Ron Swoboda	.05
36	Albert Belle	.05
37	Chris Chambliss	.05
38	Juan Gonzalez	.10
39	Ron Blomberg	.05
40	John Wetteland	.05
41	Carlton Fisk	.05
42	Mo Vaughn	.05
43	Bucky Dent	.05
44	Greg Maddux	.25
45	Willie Stargell	.05

New Horizons

Rookies and prospects expected to make an impact during the 1996 season were featured in this 15-card insert set. Card fronts feature a rainbow foil background with the words "New Horizon" featured prominently on the bottom under the player's name. Cards were inserted 1:4 packs.

		NM/M
Complete Set (15):		2.00
Common Player:		.05
1	Bob Abreu	.10
2	Jose Cruz Jr.	.05
3	Darin Erstad	.10
4	Nomar Garciaparra	.75
5	Vladimir Guerrero	.60
6	Wilton Guerrero	.05
7	Jose Guillen	.05
8	Hideki Irabu	.05
9	Andruw Jones	.60
10	Kevin Orie	.05
11	Scott Rolen	.50
12	Scott Spiezio	.05
13	Bubba Trammell	.05
14	Todd Walker	.05
15	Dmitri Young	.05

Night & Day

Night and Day spotlighted 10 stars with unusual prowess during night or day games. These lenticular cards carried the toughest insert ratios in Fleer Baseball at one per 288 packs.

		NM/M
Complete Set (10):		45.00
Common Player:		1.00
1	Barry Bonds	12.00
2	Ellis Burks	1.00
3	Juan Gonzalez	2.00
4	Ken Griffey Jr.	6.00
5	Mark McGwire	7.50
6	Mike Piazza	6.00
7	Manny Ramirez	4.00
8	Alex Rodriguez	8.00
9	John Smoltz	2.00
10	Frank Thomas	4.00

Rookie Sensations

Rookies Sensations showcased 20 of the top up-and-coming stars in baseball. Appearing every six packs, these inserts have the feaured player in the foreground, with the background look of painted brush strokes.

		NM/M
Complete Set (20):		6.00
Common Player:		.25
1	Jermaine Allensworth	.25
2	James Baldwin	.25
3	Alan Benes	.25
4	Jermaine Dye	.25
5	Darin Erstad	.50
6	Todd Hollandsworth	.25
7	Derek Jeter	2.50
8	Jason Kendall	.25
9	Alex Ochoa	.25
10	Rey Ordonez	.25
11	Edgar Renteria	.25
12	Bob Abreu	.50
13	Nomar Garciaparra	1.50
14	Wilton Guerrero	.25
15	Andruw Jones	1.00
16	Wendell Magee	.25
17	Neifi Perez	.25
18	Scott Rolen	.75
19	Scott Spiezio	.25
20	Todd Walker	.25

Soaring Stars

A 12-card insert found 1:12 packs designed to profile players with outstanding statistical performances early in their careers. Fronts have player action photos set against a background of rainbow holographic stars which appear, disappear and twinkle as the viewing angle is changed. Conventionally printed backs have another player photo and a few sentences about his career. A parallel version on which the background stars glow was issued at a greatly reduced rate.

		NM/M
Complete Set (12):		10.00
Common Player:		.25
Glowing:		6X
1	Albert Belle	.25
2	Barry Bonds	2.00
3	Juan Gonzalez	.50
4	Ken Griffey Jr.	1.25
5	Derek Jeter	2.00
6	Andruw Jones	.60
7	Chipper Jones	1.00
8	Greg Maddux	1.00
9	Mark McGwire	1.50
10	Mike Piazza	1.25
11	Alex Rodriguez	1.50
12	Frank Thomas	.75

Team Leaders

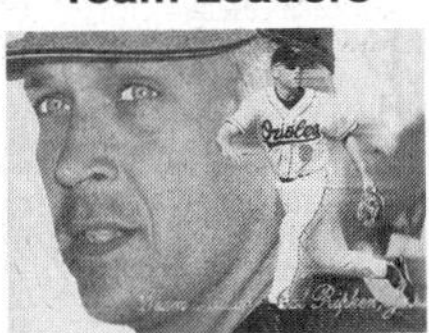

Team Leaders captured the statistical and/or inspirational leaders from all 28 teams. Inserted every 20 packs, these inserts were printed on a horizontal format, with the player's face die-cut in the perimeter of the card.

		NM/M
Complete Set (28):		25.00
Common Player:		.25
1	Cal Ripken Jr.	5.00
2	Mo Vaughn	.25
3	Jim Edmonds	.40
4	Frank Thomas	1.50
5	Albert Belle	.25
6	Bob Higginson	.25
7	Kevin Appier	.25
8	John Jaha	.25
9	Paul Molitor	1.50
10	Andy Pettitte	.65
11	Mark McGwire	4.00
12	Ken Griffey Jr.	3.00
13	Juan Gonzalez	.75
14	Pat Hentgen	.25
15	Chipper Jones	2.00
16	Mark Grace	.35
17	Barry Larkin	.25
18	Ellis Burks	.25
19	Gary Sheffield	.60
20	Jeff Bagwell	1.50
21	Mike Piazza	3.00
22	Henry Rodriguez	.25
23	Todd Hundley	.25
24	Curt Schilling	.60
25	Jeff King	.25
26	Brian Jordan	.25
27	Tony Gwynn	1.50
28	Barry Bonds	5.00

Zone

Twenty of the top hitters in baseball are featured on these holographic cards with the words Zone printed across the front. Zone inserts were found only in hobby packs at a rate of one per 80.

		NM/M
Complete Set (20):		80.00
Common Player:		1.50
1	Jeff Bagwell	5.00
2	Albert Belle	1.50
3	Barry Bonds	15.00
4	Ken Caminiti	1.50
5	Andres Galarraga	1.50
6	Juan Gonzalez	2.50
7	Ken Griffey Jr.	8.00
8	Tony Gwynn	6.00
9	Chipper Jones	6.00
10	Greg Maddux	6.00
11	Mark McGwire	10.00
12	Dean Palmer	1.50
13	Andy Pettitte	3.00
14	Mike Piazza	8.00
15	Alex Rodriguez	12.00
16	Gary Sheffield	2.50
17	John Smoltz	2.50
18	Frank Thomas	5.00
19	Jim Thome	4.00
20	Matt Williams	1.50

1998 Fleer

Fleer was issued in two series in 1998, with 350 cards in Series 1 and 250 in Series 2. Each card features a borderless color action shot, with backs containing player information. Subsets in Series 1 included Smoke 'N Heat (301-310), Golden Memories (311-320) and Tale of the Tape (321-340). Golden Memories (1:6 packs) and Tale of the Tape (1:4) were shortprinted. Series 2 subsets included 25 short-printed (1:4) Unforgetable Moments (571-595). Inserts in Series 1 were Vintage '63, Vintage '63 Classic, Decade of Excellence, Decade of Excellence Rare Traditions, Diamond Ink, Diamond Standouts, Lumber Company, Power Game, Rookie Sensations and Zone. Series 2 inserts include: Vintage '63, Vintage '63 Classic, Promising Forecast, In the Clutch, Mickey Mantle: Monumental Moments, Mickey Mantle: Monumental Moments Gold Edition, Diamond Tribute and Diamond Ink.

		NM/M
Complete Set (600):		65.00
Complete Series 1 (350):		40.00
Complete Series 2 (250):		25.00
Common Player:		.05
Series 1 or 2 Pack (10):		1.00
Series 1 or 2 Wax Box (36):		20.00
1	Ken Griffey Jr.	1.50
2	Derek Jeter	2.50
3	Gerald Williams	.05
4	Carlos Delgado	.50
5	Nomar Garciaparra	1.50
6	Gary Sheffield	.30
7	Jeff King	.05
8	Cal Ripken Jr.	2.50
9	Matt Williams	.05
10	Chipper Jones	1.00
11	Chuck Knoblauch	.05
12	Mark Grudzielanek	.05
13	Edgardo Alfonzo	.05
14	Andres Galarraga	.05
15	Tim Salmon	.15
16	Reggie Sanders	.05
17	Tony Clark	.05
18	Jason Kendall	.05
19	Juan Gonzalez	.65
20	Ben Grieve	.10
21	Roger Clemens	1.25
22	Raul Mondesi	.05
23	Robin Ventura	.05
24	Derrek Lee	.05
25	Mark McGwire	2.00
26	Luis Gonzalez	.10
27	Kevin Brown	.05
28	Kirk Rueter	.05
29	Bobby Estalella	.05
30	Shawn Green	.35
31	Greg Maddux	1.00
32	Jorge Velandia	.05
33	Larry Walker	.05
34	Joey Cora	.05
35	Frank Thomas	.85
36	Curtis King RC	.05
37	Aaron Boone	.05
38	Curt Schilling	.25
39	Bruce Aven	.05
40	Ben McDonald	.05
41	Andy Ashby	.05
42	Jason McDonald	.05
43	Eric Davis	.05
44	Mark Grace	.10
45	Pedro Martinez	.75
46	Lou Collier	.05
47	Chan Ho Park	.05
48	Shane Halter	.05
49	Brian Hunter	.05
50	Jeff Bagwell	.75
51	Bernie Williams	.10
52	J.T. Snow	.05
53	Todd Greene	.05
54	Shannon Stewart	.05
55	Darren Bragg	.05
56	Fernando Tatis	.05
57	Darryl Kile	.05
58	Chris Stynes	.05
59	Javier Valentin	.05
60	Brian McRae	.05
61	Tom Evans	.05
62	Randall Simon	.05
63	Darrin Fletcher	.05
64	Jaret Wright	.05
65	Luis Ordaz	.05
66	Jose Canseco	.40
67	Edgar Renteria	.05
68	Jay Buhner	.05
69	Paul Konerko	.10
70	Adrian Brown	.05
71	Chris Carpenter	.05
72	Mike Lieberthal	.05
73	Dean Palmer	.05
74	Jorge Fabregas	.05
75	Stan Javier	.05
76	Damion Easley	.05
77	David Cone	.05
78	Aaron Sele	.05
79	Antonio Alfonseca	.05
80	Bobby Jones	.05
81	David Justice	.05
82	Jeffrey Hammonds	.05
83	Doug Glanville	.05
84	Jason Dickson	.05
85	Brad Radke	.05
86	David Segui	.05
87	Greg Vaughn	.05
88	Mike Cather RC	.05
89	Alex Fernandez	.05
90	Billy Taylor	.05
91	Jason Schmidt	.05
92	Mike DeJean RC	.05
93	Domingo Cedeno	.05
94	Jeff Cirillo	.05
95	Manny Aybar RC	.10
96	Jaime Navarro	.05
97	Dennis Reyes	.05
98	Barry Larkin	.05
99	Troy O'Leary	.05
100	Alex Rodriguez	2.00
100p	Alex Rodriguez/OPS	2.00
101	Pat Hentgen	.05
102	Bubba Trammell	.05
103	Glendon Rusch	.05
104	Kenny Lofton	.05
105	Craig Biggio	.05
106	Kelvim Escobar	.05
107	Mark Kotsay	.05
108	Rondell White	.05
109	Darren Oliver	.05
110	Jim Thome	.65
111	Rich Becker	.05
112	Chad Curtis	.05
113	Dave Hollins	.05
114	Bill Mueller	.05
115	Antone Williamson	.05
116	Tony Womack	.05
117	Randy Myers	.05
118	Rico Brogna	.05
119	Pat Watkins	.05
120	Eli Marrero	.05
121	Jay Bell	.05
122	Kevin Tapani	.05
123	Todd Erdos RC	.10
124	Neifi Perez	.05
125	Todd Hundley	.05
126	Jeff Abbott	.05
127	Todd Zeile	.05
128	Travis Fryman	.05
129	Sandy Alomar	.05
130	Fred McGriff	.05
131	Richard Hidalgo	.05
132	Scott Spiezio	.05
133	John Valentin	.05
134	Quilvio Veras	.05
135	Mike Lansing	.05
136	Paul Molitor	.75
137	Randy Johnson	.75
138	Harold Baines	.05
139	Doug Jones	.05
140	Abraham Nunez	.05
141	Alan Benes	.05
142	Matt Perisho	.05
143	Chris Clemons	.05
144	Andy Pettitte	.30
145	Jason Giambi	.40
146	Moises Alou	.05
147	Chad Fox RC	.05
148	Felix Martinez	.05
149	Carlos Mendoza RC	.05
150	Scott Rolen	.65
151	Jose Cabrera RC	.05
152	Justin Thompson	.05
153	Ellis Burks	.05
154	Pokey Reese	.05
155	Bartolo Colon	.05
156	Ray Durham	.05
157	Ugueth Urbina	.05
158	Tom Goodwin	.05
159	David Dellucci RC	.25
160	Rod Beck	.05
161	Ramon Martinez	.05
162	Joe Carter	.05
163	Kevin Orie	.05
164	Trevor Hoffman	.05
165	Emil Brown	.05
166	Robb Nen	.05
167	Paul O'Neill	.05
168	Ryan Long	.05
169	Ray Lankford	.05
170	Ivan Rodriguez	.65
171	Rick Aguilera	.05
172	Deivi Cruz	.05
173	Ricky Bottalico	.05
174	Garret Anderson	.05
175	Jose Vizcaino	.05
176	Omar Vizquel	.05
177	Jeff Blauser	.05
178	Orlando Cabrera	.05

179 Russ Johnson .05
180 Matt Stairs .05
181 Will Cunnane .05
182 Adam Riggs .05
183 Matt Morris .05
184 Mario Valdez .05
185 Larry Sutton .05
186 Marc Pisciotta **RC** .05
187 Dan Wilson .05
188 John Franco .05
189 Darren Daulton .05
190 Todd Helton .75
191 Brady Anderson .05
192 Ricardo Rincon .05
193 Kevin Stocker .05
194 Jose Valentin .05
195 Ed Sprague .05
196 Ryan McGuire .05
197 Scott Eyre **RC** .05
198 Steve Finley .05
199 T.J. Mathews .05
200 Mike Piazza 1.50
201 Mark Wohlers .05
202 Brian Giles .05
203 Eduardo Perez .05
204 Shigetosi Hasegawa .05
205 Mariano Rivera .15
206 Jose Rosado .05
207 Michael Coleman .05
208 James Baldwin .05
209 Russ Davis .05
210 Billy Wagner .05
211 Sammy Sosa 1.50
212 Frank Catalanotto **RC** .15
213 Delino DeShields .05
214 John Olerud .05
215 Heath Murray .05
216 Jose Vidro .05
217 Jim Edmonds .05
218 Shawon Dunston .05
219 Homer Bush .05
220 Midre Cummings .05
221 Tony Saunders .05
222 Jeromy Burnitz .05
223 Enrique Wilson .05
224 Chili Davis .05
225 Jerry DiPoto .05
226 Dante Powell .05
227 Javier Lopez .05
228 Kevin Polcovich **RC** .10
229 Deion Sanders .05
230 Jimmy Key .05
231 Rusty Greer .05
232 Reggie Jefferson .05
233 Ron Coomer .05
234 Bobby Higginson .05
235 Magglio Ordonez **RC** 2.00
236 Miguel Tejada .25
237 Rick Gorecki .05
238 Charles Johnson .05
239 Lance Johnson .05
240 Derek Bell .05
241 Will Clark .10
242 Brady Raggio .05
243 Orel Hershiser .05
244 Vladimir Guerrero .75
245 John LeRoy .05
246 Shawn Estes .05
247 Brett Tomko .05
248 Dave Nilsson .05
249 Edgar Martinez .05
250 Tony Gwynn 1.00
251 Mark Bellhorn .05
252 Jed Hansen .05
253 Butch Huskey .05
254 Eric Young .05
255 Vinny Castilla .05
256 Hideki Irabu .05
257 Mike Cameron .05
258 Juan Encarnacion .05
259 Brian Rose .05
260 Brad Ausmus .05
261 Dan Serafini .05
262 Willie Greene .05
263 Troy Percival .05
264 Jeff Wallace **RC** .05
265 Richie Sexson .05
266 Rafael Palmeiro .65
267 Brad Fullmer .05
268 Jeremi Gonzalez .05
269 Rob Stanifer **RC** .05
270 Mickey Morandini .05
271 Andruw Jones .75
272 Royce Clayton .05
273 Takashi Kashiwada .05
274 Steve Woodard **RC** .10
275 Jose Cruz Jr. .05
276 Keith Foulke .05
277 Brad Rigby .05
278 Tino Martinez .05
279 Todd Jones .05
280 John Wetteland .05
281 Alex Gonzalez .05
282 Ken Cloude .05
283 Jose Guillen .05
284 Danny Clyburn .05
285 David Ortiz .05
286 John Thomson .05
287 Kevin Appier .05
288 Ismael Valdes .05
289 Gary DiSarcina .05
290 Todd Dunwoody .05
291 Wally Joyner .05
292 Charles Nagy .05
293 Jeff Shaw .05
294 Kevin Millwood **RC** 1.00
295 Rigo Beltran **RC** .05
296 Jeff Frye .05
297 Oscar Henriquez .05
298 Mike Thurman .05
299 Garrett Stephenson .05
300 Barry Bonds 2.50
301 Roger Clemens (Smoke 'N Heat) .75
302 David Cone (Smoke 'N Heat) .05
303 Hideki Irabu (Smoke 'N Heat) .05
304 Randy Johnson (Smoke 'N Heat) .40
305 Greg Maddux (Smoke 'N Heat) .50
306 Pedro Martinez (Smoke 'N Heat) .35
307 Mike Mussina (Smoke 'N Heat) .25
308 Andy Pettitte (Smoke 'N Heat) .15
309 Curt Schilling (Smoke 'N Heat) .10
310 John Smoltz (Smoke 'N Heat) .05
311 Roger Clemens (Golden Memories) 1.00
312 Jose Cruz Jr. (Golden Memories) .25
313 Nomar Garciaparra (Golden Memories) 1.00
314 Ken Griffey Jr. (Golden Memories) 1.00
315 Tony Gwynn (Golden Memories) .75
316 Hideki Irabu (Golden Memories) .25
317 Randy Johnson (Golden Memories) .60
318 Mark McGwire (Golden Memories) 1.50
319 Curt Schilling (Golden Memories) .35
320 Larry Walker (Golden Memories) .15
321 Jeff Bagwell (Tale of the Tape) .60
322 Albert Belle (Tale of the Tape) .15
323 Barry Bonds (Tale of the Tape) 1.50
324 Jay Buhner (Tale of the Tape) .15
325 Tony Clark (Tale of the Tape) .15
326 Jose Cruz Jr. (Tale of the Tape) .15
327 Andres Galarraga (Tale of the Tape) .15
328 Juan Gonzalez (Tale of the Tape) .30
329 Ken Griffey Jr. (Tale of the Tape) .85
330 Andruw Jones (Tale of the Tape) .60
331 Tino Martinez (Tale of the Tape) .15
332 Mark McGwire (Tale of the Tape) 1.00
333 Rafael Palmeiro (Tale of the Tape) .50
334 Mike Piazza (Tale of the Tape) .85
335 Manny Ramirez (Tale of the Tape) .65
336 Alex Rodriguez (Tale of the Tape) 1.00
337 Frank Thomas (Tale of the Tape) .65
338 Jim Thome (Tale of the Tape) .65
339 Mo Vaughn (Tale of the Tape) .15
340 Larry Walker (Tale of the Tape) .15
341 Checklist (Jose Cruz Jr.) .15
342 Checklist (Ken Griffey Jr.) .65
343 Checklist (Derek Jeter) 1.00
344 Checklist (Andruw Jones) .40
345 Checklist (Chipper Jones) .50
346 Checklist (Greg Maddux) .50
347 Checklist (Mike Piazza) .65
348 Checklist (Cal Ripken Jr.) 1.00
349 Checklist (Alex Rodriguez) .75
350 Checklist (Frank Thomas) .45
351 Mo Vaughn .05
352 Andres Galarraga .05
353 Roberto Alomar .10
354 Darin Erstad .10
355 Albert Belle .05
356 Matt Williams .05
357 Darryl Kile .05
358 Kenny Lofton .05
359 Orel Hershiser .05
360 Bob Abreu .05
361 Chris Widger .05
362 Glenallen Hill .05
363 Chili Davis .05
364 Kevin Brown .05
365 Marquis Grissom .05
366 Livan Hernandez .05
367 Moises Alou .05
368 Matt Lawton .05
369 Rey Ordonez .05
370 Kenny Rogers .05
371 Lee Stevens .05
372 Wade Boggs 1.00
373 Luis Gonzalez .05
374 Jeff Conine .05
375 Esteban Loaiza .05
376 Jose Canseco .40
377 Henry Rodriguez .05
378 Dave Burba .05
379 Todd Hollandsworth .05
380 Ron Gant .05
381 Pedro Martinez .75
382 Ryan Klesko .05
383 Derrek Lee .05
384 Doug Glanville .05
385 David Wells .05
386 Ken Caminiti .05
387 Damon Hollins .05
388 Manny Ramirez .75
389 Mike Mussina .45
390 Jay Bell .05
391 Mike Piazza 1.50
392 Mike Lansing .05
393 Mike Hampton .05
394 Geoff Jenkins .05
395 Jimmy Haynes .05
396 Scott Servais .05
397 Kent Mercker .05
398 Jeff Kent .05
399 Kevin Elster .05
400 Masato Yoshii **RC** .50
401 Jose Vizcaino .05
402 Javier Martinez .05
403 David Segui .05
404 Tony Saunders .05
405 Karim Garcia .05
406 Armando Benitez .05
407 Joe Randa .05
408 Vic Darensbourg .05
409 Sean Casey .20
410 Eric Milton .05
411 Trey Moore .05
412 Mike Stanley .05
413 Tom Gordon .05
414 Hal Morris .05
415 Braden Looper .05
416 Mike Kelly .05
417 John Smoltz .05
418 Roger Cedeno .05
419 Al Leiter .05
420 Chuck Knoblauch .05
421 Felix Rodriguez .05
422 Bip Roberts .05
423 Ken Hill .05
424 Jermaine Allensworth .05
425 Esteban Yan .05
426 Scott Karl .05
427 Sean Berry .05
428 Rafael Medina .05
429 Javier Vazquez .05
430 Rickey Henderson .75
431 Adam Butler **RC** .05
432 Todd Stottlemyre .05
433 Yamil Benitez .05
434 Sterling Hitchcock .05
435 Paul Sorrento .05
436 Bobby Ayala .05
437 Tim Raines .05
438 Chris Hoiles .05
439 Rod Beck .05
440 Donnie Sadler .05
441 Charles Johnson .05
442 Russ Ortiz .05
443 Pedro Astacio .05
444 Wilson Alvarez .05
445 Mike Blowers .05
446 Todd Zeile .05
447 Mel Rojas .05
448 F.P. Santangelo .05
449 Dmitri Young .05
450 Brian Anderson .05
451 Cecil Fielder .05
452 Roberto Hernandez .05
453 Todd Walker .05
454 Tyler Green .05
455 Jorge Posada .05
456 Geronimo Berroa .05
457 Jose Silva .05
458 Bobby Bonilla .05
459 Walt Weiss .05
460 Darren Dreifort .05
461 B.J. Surhoff .05
462 Quinton McCracken .05
463 Derek Lowe .05
464 Jorge Fabregas .05
465 Joey Hamilton .05
466 Brian Jordan .05
467 Allen Watson .05
468 John Jaha .05
469 Heathcliff Slocumb .05
470 Gregg Jefferies .05
471 Scott Brosius .05
472 Chad Ogea .05
473 A.J. Hinch .05
474 Bobby Smith .05
475 Brian Moehler .05
476 DaRond Stovall .05
477 Kevin Young .05
478 Jeff Suppan .05
479 Marty Cordova .05
480 John Halama **RC** .25
481 Bubba Trammell .05
482 Mike Caruso .05
483 Eric Karros .05
484 Jamey Wright .05
485 Mike Sweeney .05
486 Aaron Sele .05
487 Cliff Floyd .05
488 Jeff Brantley .05
489 Jim Leyritz .05
490 Denny Neagle .05
491 Travis Fryman .05
492 Carlos Baerga .05
493 Eddie Taubensee .05
494 Darryl Strawberry .05
495 Brian Johnson .05
496 Randy Myers .05
497 Jeff Blauser .05
498 Jason Wood .05
499 Rolando Arrojo **RC** .25
500 Johnny Damon .05
501 Jose Mercedes .05
502 Tony Batista .05
503 Mike Piazza 1.50
504 Hideo Nomo .65
505 Chris Gomez .05
506 Jesus Sanchez **RC** .05
507 Al Martin .05
508 Brian Edmondson .05
509 Joe Girardi .05
510 Shayne Bennett .05
511 Joe Carter .05
512 Dave Mlicki .05
513 Rich Butler **RC** .10
514 Dennis Eckersley .65
515 Travis Lee .10
516 John Mabry .05
517 Jose Mesa .05
518 Phil Nevin .05
519 Raul Casanova .05
520 Mike Fetters .05
521 Gary Sheffield .30
522 Terry Steinbach .05
523 Steve Trachsel .05
524 Josh Booty .05
525 Darryl Hamilton .05
526 Mark McLemore .05
527 Kevin Stocker .05
528 Bret Boone .05
529 Shane Andrews .05
530 Robb Nen .05
531 Carl Everett .05
532 LaTroy Hawkins .05
533 Fernando Vina .05
534 Michael Tucker .05
535 Mark Langston .05
536 Mickey Mantle 2.00
537 Bernard Gilkey .05
538 Francisco Cordova .05
539 Mike Bordick .05
540 Fred McGriff .05
541 Cliff Politte .05
542 Jason Varitek .05
543 Shawon Dunston .05
544 Brian Meadows .05
545 Pat Meares .05
546 Carlos Perez .05
547 Desi Relaford .05
548 Antonio Osuna .05
549 Devon White .05
550 Sean Runyan .05
551 Mickey Morandini .05
552 Dave Martinez .05
553 Jeff Fassero .05
554 Ryan Jackson **RC** .05
555 Stan Javier .05
556 Jaime Navarro .05
557 Jose Offerman .05
558 Mike Lowell **RC** .50
559 Darrin Fletcher .05
560 Mark Lewis .05
561 Dante Bichette .05
562 Chuck Finley .05
563 Kerry Wood .35
564 Andy Benes .05
565 Freddy Garcia .05
566 Tom Glavine .25
567 Jon Nunnally .05
568 Miguel Cairo .05
569 Shane Reynolds .05
570 Roberto Kelly .05
571 Checklist (Jose Cruz Jr.) .25
572 Checklist (Ken Griffey Jr.) .65
573 Checklist (Mark McGwire) .75
574 Checklist (Cal Ripken Jr.) 1.00
575 Checklist (Frank Thomas) .45
576 Jeff Bagwell (Unforgettable Moments) 1.00
577 Barry Bonds (Unforgettable Moments) 3.00
578 Tony Clark (Unforgettable Moments) .25
579 Roger Clemens (Unforgettable Moments) 2.00
580 Jose Cruz Jr. (Unforgettable Moments) .25
581 Nomar Garciaparra (Unforgettable Moments) 1.50
582 Juan Gonzalez (Unforgettable Moments) 1.00
583 Ben Grieve (Unforgettable Moments) .25
584 Ken Griffey Jr. (Unforgettable Moments) 2.00
585 Tony Gwynn (Unforgettable Moments) 1.50
586 Derek Jeter (Unforgettable Moments) 3.00
587 Randy Johnson (Unforgettable Moments) 1.00
588 Chipper Jones (Unforgettable Moments) 1.50
589 Greg Maddux (Unforgettable Moments) 1.50
590 Mark McGwire (Unforgettable Moments) 2.50
591 Andy Pettitte (Unforgettable Moments) .45
592 Paul Molitor (Unforgettable Moments) 1.00
593 Cal Ripken Jr. (Unforgettable Moments) 3.00
594 Alex Rodriguez (Unforgettable Moments) 2.50
595 Scott Rolen (Unforgettable Moments) .50
596 Curt Schilling (Unforgettable Moments) .50
597 Frank Thomas (Unforgettable Moments) 1.25
598 Jim Thome (Unforgettable Moments) .75
599 Larry Walker (Unforgettable Moments) .25
600 Bernie Williams (Unforgettable Moments) .30

Decade of Excellence

Decade of Excellence inserts were found in one per 72 Series 1 hobby packs of Fleer Tradition. The 12-card set features 1988 season photos in Fleer's 1988 card design. The set includes only those current players who have been in baseball for 10 years or more. The use of blue and red metallic foil stripes in the background differentiates a scarcer (1:720 hobby packs) "Rare Traditions" parallel to the insert.

		NM/M
Complete Set (12):		35.00
Common Player:		1.00
Inserted 1:72		
Rare Traditions:		3X
Inserted 1:720		
1	Roberto Alomar	1.50
2	Barry Bonds	8.00
3	Roger Clemens	5.00
4	David Cone	1.00
5	Andres Galarraga	1.00
6	Mark Grace	1.00
7	Tony Gwynn	4.00
8	Randy Johnson	3.00
9	Greg Maddux	4.00
10	Mark McGwire	6.00
11	Paul O'Neill	1.00
12	Cal Ripken Jr.	8.00

Diamond Ink

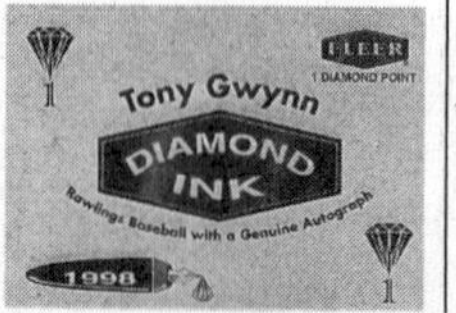

These one-per-pack inserts offer collectors a chance to acquire genuine autographed baseballs. Issued in denominations of 1, 5 and 10 points, the cards had to be accumulated to a total of 500 points of the same player to be redeemed for an autographed ball of that player. Cards are the standard 3-1/2" x 2-1/2" and are printed in black and purple on front and black and yellow on back. The point value of each card is embossed at center to prevent counterfeiting. The rules of the exchange program are printed on back. The deadline for redemption was Dec. 31, 1998. Values shown are for 1-pt. cards. The unnumbered players in the series are listed alphabetically.

		NM/M
Complete Set, 1 pt. (11):		1.00
Common Player, 1 pt.:		.05
5-pt. Cards:		5X
10-pt. Cards:		10X
(1)	Jay Buhner	.05
(2)	Roger Clemens	.20
(3)	Jose Cruz Jr.	.05
(4)	Nomar Garciaparra	.20
(5)	Tony Gwynn	.15
(6)	Roberto Hernandez	.05
(7)	Greg Maddux	.15
(8)	Cal Ripken Jr.	.30
(9)	Alex Rodriguez	.25
(10)	Scott Rolen	.10
(11)	Tony Womack	.05

Diamond Standouts

Diamond Standouts were inserted into Series I packs at a rate of one per 12. The 20-card insert set features players over a diamond design silver foil background.

		NM/M
Complete Set (20):		25.00
Common Player:		.50
1	Jeff Bagwell	1.00
2	Barry Bonds	4.00
3	Roger Clemens	2.00
4	Jose Cruz Jr.	.50
5	Andres Galarraga	.50
6	Nomar Garciaparra	2.00
7	Juan Gonzalez	.75
8	Ken Griffey Jr.	2.00
9	Derek Jeter	4.00
10	Randy Johnson	1.00
11	Chipper Jones	1.50
12	Kenny Lofton	.50
13	Greg Maddux	1.50
14	Pedro Martinez	1.00
15	Mark McGwire	3.00
16	Mike Piazza	2.00
17	Alex Rodriguez	3.00
18	Curt Schilling	.75
19	Frank Thomas	1.00
20	Larry Walker	.50

Diamond Tribute

This 10-card insert was exclusive to Series 2 packs and seeded one per 300 packs. Cards were printed on a leather- like laminated stock and had silver holofoil stamping.

	NM/M
Complete Set (10):	90.00

Common Player:		5.00
DT1	Jeff Bagwell	7.50
DT2	Roger Clemens	10.00
DT3	Nomar Garciaparra	10.00
DT4	Juan Gonzalez	5.00
DT5	Ken Griffey Jr.	12.00
DT6	Mark McGwire	15.00
DT7	Mike Piazza	12.00
DT8	Cal Ripken Jr.	20.00
DT9	Alex Rodriguez	15.00
DT10	Frank Thomas	7.50

Heroes For Kids Commemorative Card

More than two dozen nominees for Players Choice Awards are featured in action photos on both sides of this 11" x 8-1/2" card.

	NM/M
Commemorative Card:	3.00

In the Clutch

This Series 2 insert features stars who can stand up to pressure of big league ball. Fronts have embossed action photos on a prismatic metallic foil background. Backs have a portrait photo and a few words about the player. Stated insertion rate for the inserts was one per 20 packs on average.

		NM/M
Complete Set (15):		25.00
Common Player:		.40
IC1	Jeff Bagwell	1.00
IC2	Barry Bonds	5.00
IC3	Roger Clemens	2.00
IC4	Jose Cruz Jr.	.40
IC5	Nomar Garciaparra	2.00
IC6	Juan Gonzalez	.75
IC7	Ken Griffey Jr.	2.50
IC8	Tony Gwynn	1.50
IC9	Derek Jeter	5.00
IC10	Chipper Jones	1.50
IC11	Greg Maddux	1.50
IC12	Mark McGwire	4.00
IC13	Mike Piazza	2.50
IC14	Frank Thomas	1.00
IC15	Larry Walker	.40

Lumber Company

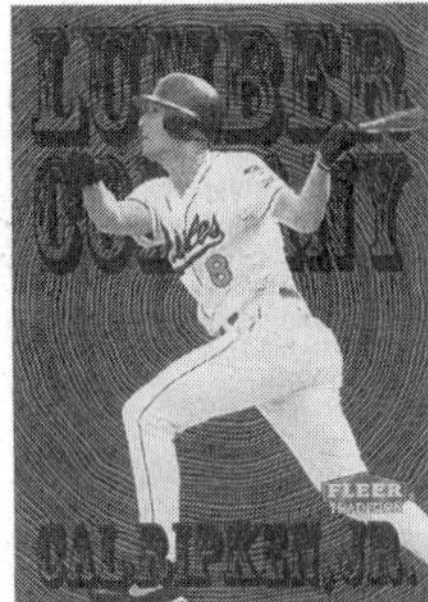

This 15-card set was exclusive to Series I retail packs and inserted one per 36 packs. It included power hitters and featured the insert name in large letters across the top.

		NM/M
Complete Set (15):		50.00
Common Player:		.75
Inserted 1:36 R		
1	Jeff Bagwell	2.50
2	Barry Bonds	8.00
3	Jose Cruz Jr.	.75
4	Nomar Garciaparra	4.00
5	Juan Gonzalez	1.50
6	Ken Griffey Jr.	5.00
7	Tony Gwynn	3.00
8	Chipper Jones	3.00
9	Tino Martinez	.75
10	Mark McGwire	6.00
11	Mike Piazza	5.00
12	Cal Ripken Jr.	8.00
13	Alex Rodriguez	6.00
14	Frank Thomas	2.50
15	Larry Walker	.75

Mickey Mantle Monumental Moments

This 10-card insert honors Hall of Famer Mickey Mantle's legendary career and was seeded one per 68 packs of Series 2. Fleer/SkyBox worked closely with Mantle's family with each photo in the set personally selected by them. A gold-enhanced version was issued with each card serially numbered to 51.

		NM/M
Complete Set (10):		40.00
Common Card:		5.00
Inserted 1:68		
Gold (51 Sets):		3X
1	Armed and Dangerous	5.00
2	Getting Ready in Spring Training	5.00
3	Mantle and Rizzuto Celebrate	5.00
4	Posed for Action	5.00
5	Signed, Sealed and Ready to Deliver	5.00
6	Triple Crown 1956 Season	5.00
7	Number 7 . . .	5.00
8	Mantle's Powerful Swing . . .	5.00
9	Old-Timers Day Introduction	5.00
10	Portrait of Determination	5.00

Promising Forecast

Potential future stars are showcased in this Series 2 insert. Both front and back have a background of a colorful weather map. Fronts have a glossy player action photo on a matte-finish background. Backs are all-glossy and have a second photo and a few words about the player's potential. Average odds of pulling a Promising Forecast card were stated as one per 12 packs.

		NM/M
Complete Set (20):		7.00
Common Player:		.25
Inserted 1:12		
PF1	Rolando Arrojo	.25
PF2	Sean Casey	.40
PF3	Brad Fullmer	.25
PF4	Karim Garcia	.35
PF5	Ben Grieve	.25
PF6	Todd Helton	3.00
PF7	Richard Hidalgo	.25
PF8	A.J. Hinch	.25
PF9	Paul Konerko	.35
PF10	Mark Kotsay	.25
PF11	Derrek Lee	1.00
PF12	Travis Lee	.35
PF13	Eric Milton	.25
PF14	Magglio Ordonez	.50
PF15	David Ortiz	.50
PF16	Brian Rose	.25
PF17	Miguel Tejada	.40
PF18	Jason Varitek	.35
PF19	Enrique Wilson	.25
PF20	Kerry Wood	1.00

Rookie Sensations

Rookie Sensations included 20 gray-bordered cards of the 1997 most promising players who were eligible for the Rookie of the Year award. Each card contained a multi-colored background and was inserted one per 18 packs.

		NM/M
Complete Set (20):		12.00
Common Player:		.50
Inserted 1:18		
1	Mike Cameron	.50
2	Jose Cruz Jr.	.50
3	Jason Dickson	.50
4	Kelvim Escobar	.50
5	Nomar Garciaparra	3.00
6	Ben Grieve	.50
7	Vladimir Guerrero	3.00
8	Wilton Guerrero	.50
9	Jose Guillen	.50
10	Todd Helton	2.00
11	Livan Hernandez	.50
12	Hideki Irabu	.50
13	Andruw Jones	3.00
14	Matt Morris	.50
15	Magglio Ordonez	1.00
16	Neifi Perez	.50
17	Scott Rolen	2.00
18	Fernando Tatis	.50
19	Brett Tomko	.50
20	Jaret Wright	.50

The Power Game

Pitchers and hitters are pictured over a purple metallic background with UV coating in this 20-card insert. Power Game inserts were exclusive to Series I and seeded one per 36 packs.

		NM/M
Complete Set (20):		30.00
Common Player:		.50
Inserted 1:36		
1	Jeff Bagwell	2.00
2	Albert Belle	.50
3	Barry Bonds	6.00
4	Tony Clark	.50
5	Roger Clemens	3.50
6	Jose Cruz Jr.	.50
7	Andres Galarraga	.50
8	Nomar Garciaparra	3.50
9	Juan Gonzalez	1.00
10	Ken Griffey Jr.	4.00
11	Randy Johnson	2.00
12	Greg Maddux	3.00
13	Pedro Martinez	2.00
14	Tino Martinez	.50
15	Mark McGwire	5.00
16	Mike Piazza	4.00
17	Curt Schilling	.75
18	Frank Thomas	2.00
19	Jim Thome	2.00
20	Larry Walker	.50

Vintage '63

Vintage featured 126 different players, with 63 in Series I and 63 in Series II, on the design of 1963 Fleer cards. The insert commemorated the 35th anniversary of Fleer and was seeded one per hobby pack. In addition, Series II featured Mickey Mantle on card No. 67, which completed the original 1963 Fleer set that ended at card No. 66 and wasn't able to include Mantle for licensing reasons. The Mantle card was printed in vintage looking stock and was purposely made to look and feel like the originals. Fleer also printed a Classic parallel version to this insert that contained gold foil on the front and was sequentially numbered to 63 with a "C" prefix on the back.

		NM/M
Complete Set (126):		20.00
Complete Series 1 (63):		10.00
Complete Series 2 (63):		10.00
Common Player:		.10
Classics (63 Sets):		20X
1	Jason Dickson	.10
2	Tim Salmon	.25
3	Andruw Jones	.75
4	Chipper Jones	1.00
5	Kenny Lofton	.10
6	Greg Maddux	1.00
7	Rafael Palmeiro	.65
8	Cal Ripken Jr.	2.50
9	Nomar Garciaparra	1.25
10	Mark Grace	.10
11	Sammy Sosa	1.25
12	Frank Thomas	.75
13	Deion Sanders	.10
14	Sandy Alomar	.10
15	David Justice	.10
16	Jim Thome	.75
17	Matt Williams	.10
18	Jaret Wright	.10
19	Vinny Castilla	.10
20	Andres Galarraga	.10
21	Todd Helton	.75
22	Larry Walker	.10
23	Tony Clark	.10
24	Moises Alou	.10
25	Kevin Brown	.10
26	Charles Johnson	.10
27	Edgar Renteria	.10
28	Gary Sheffield	.50
29	Jeff Bagwell	.75
30	Craig Biggio	.10
31	Raul Mondesi	.10
32	Mike Piazza	1.50
33	Chuck Knoblauch	.10
34	Paul Molitor	.75
35	Vladimir Guerrero	.75
36	Pedro Martinez	.75
37	Todd Hundley	.10
38	Derek Jeter	2.50
39	Tino Martinez	.10
40	Paul O'Neill	.10
41	Andy Pettitte	.35
42	Mariano Rivera	.20
43	Bernie Williams	.20
44	Ben Grieve	.10
45	Scott Rolen	.65
46	Curt Schilling	.45
47	Jason Kendall	.10
48	Tony Womack	.10
49	Ray Lankford	.10
50	Mark McGwire	2.00
51	Matt Morris	.10
52	Tony Gwynn	1.00
53	Barry Bonds	2.50
54	Jay Buhner	.10
55	Ken Griffey Jr.	1.50
56	Randy Johnson	.75
57	Edgar Martinez	.10
58	Alex Rodriguez	2.00
59	Juan Gonzalez	.65
60	Rusty Greer	.10
61	Ivan Rodriguez	.65
62	Roger Clemens	1.25
63	Jose Cruz Jr.	.10
	Checklist #1-63	.10
64	Darin Erstad	.20
65	Jay Bell	.10
66	Andy Benes	.10
67	Mickey Mantle	2.00
68	Karim Garcia	.10
69	Travis Lee	.10
70	Matt Williams	.10
71	Andres Galarraga	.10
72	Tom Glavine	.35
73	Ryan Klesko	.10
74	Denny Neagle	.10
75	John Smoltz	.10
76	Roberto Alomar	.20
77	Joe Carter	.10
78	Mike Mussina	.50
79	B.J. Surhoff	.10
80	Dennis Eckersley	.65
81	Pedro Martinez	.75
82	Mo Vaughn	.10
83	Jeff Blauser	.10
84	Henry Rodriguez	.10
85	Albert Belle	.10
86	Sean Casey	.25
87	Travis Fryman	.10
88	Kenny Lofton	.10
89	Darryl Kile	.10
90	Mike Lansing	.10
91	Bobby Bonilla	.10
92	Cliff Floyd	.10
93	Livan Hernandez	.10
94	Derrek Lee	.10
95	Moises Alou	.10
96	Shane Reynolds	.10
97	Jeff Conine	.10
98	Johnny Damon	.35
99	Eric Karros	.10
100	Hideo Nomo	.65
101	Marquis Grissom	.10
102	Matt Lawton	.10
103	Todd Walker	.10
104	Gary Sheffield	.50
105	Bernard Gilkey	.10
106	Rey Ordonez	.10
107	Chili Davis	.10
108	Chuck Knoblauch	.10
109	Charles Johnson	.10
110	Rickey Henderson	.75
111	Bob Abreu	.10
112	Doug Glanville	.10
113	Gregg Jefferies	.10
114	Al Martin	.10
115	Kevin Young	.10
116	Ron Gant	.10
117	Kevin Brown	.10
118	Ken Caminiti	.10
119	Joey Hamilton	.10
120	Jeff Kent	.10
121	Wade Boggs	1.00
122	Quinton McCracken	.10
123	Fred McGriff	.10
124	Paul Sorrento	.10
125	Jose Canseco	.50
126	Randy Myers	.10
	Checklist #64-126	.10

Vintage '63 Classic

DAVID JUSTICE
Cleveland Indians—OF
000 of 63 CLASSIC '63
15¢
MAJOR LEAGUE RECORD

Vintage '63 Classic paralleled all 126 Vintage '63 inserts throughout Series 1 and 2, plus the checklists. These cards feature gold-foil stamping on front, specifically around the diamond in the lower-left corner, and are sequentially numbered to 63 sets. Cards have a "C" suffix to the card number.

	NM/M
Complete Set (128):	650.00
Common Player:	4.00
Stars/RC's:	20X

Zone

Inserted in one per 288 packs of Series I Fleer Tradition, Zone featured 15 top players printed on rainbow foil and etching.

		NM/M
Complete Set (15):		130.00
Common Player:		4.00
Inserted 1:288		
1	Jeff Bagwell	7.50
2	Barry Bonds	25.00
3	Roger Clemens	10.00
4	Jose Cruz Jr.	4.00
5	Nomar Garciaparra	10.00
6	Juan Gonzalez	6.00
7	Ken Griffey Jr.	12.00
8	Tony Gwynn	9.00
9	Chipper Jones	9.00
10	Greg Maddux	9.00
11	Mark McGwire	15.00
12	Mike Piazza	12.00
13	Alex Rodriguez	20.00
14	Frank Thomas	7.50
15	Larry Walker	4.00

Update

Fleer's first Update set since 1994 is this 100-card boxed set. It arrived soon after the conclusion of the 1998 World Series and focused on rookies who made their major league debut in September and had not yet had a rookie card. The set had 70 rookies, including 15 making their major league debut, 20 traded players and free agents. There was one subset called Season's Highlights that focused on feats like Mark McGwire's 70th home run, Sammy Sosa's single-month home run record and Kerry Wood's 20 strikeout performance.

		NM/M
Complete Set (100):		12.50
Common Player:		.05
U1	Mark McGwire (Season Highlights)	.75
U2	Sammy Sosa (Season Highlights)	.45
U3	Roger Clemens (Season Highlights)	.45
U4	Barry Bonds (Season Highlights)	1.00
U5	Kerry Wood (Season Highlights)	.20
U6	Paul Molitor (Season Highlights)	.25

U7	Ken Griffey Jr. (Season Highlights)	.50
U8	Cal Ripken Jr. (Season Highlights)	1.00
U9	David Wells (Season Highlights)	.05
U10	Alex Rodriguez (Season Highlights)	.75
U11	Angel Pena **RC**	.25
U12	Bruce Chen	.05
U13	Craig Wilson	.05
U14	Orlando Hernandez **RC**	1.50
U15	Aramis Ramirez	.10
U16	Aaron Boone	.05
U17	Bob Henley	.05
U18	Juan Guzman	.05
U19	Darryl Hamilton	.05
U20	Jay Payton	.05
U21	Jeremy Powell **RC**	.05
U22	Ben Davis	.05
U23	Preston Wilson	.10
U24	Jim Parque **RC**	.15
U25	Odalis Perez **RC**	.25
U26	Ron Belliard	.05
U27	Royce Clayton	.05
U28	George Lombard	.05
U29	Tony Phillips	.05
U30	Fernando Seguignol **RC**	.15
U31	Armando Rios **RC**	.10
U32	Jerry Hairston Jr. **RC**	.25
U33	Justin Baughman **RC**	.05
U34	Seth Greisinger	.05
U35	Alex Gonzalez	.05
U36	Michael Barrett	.05
U37	Carlos Beltran	.35
U38	Ellis Burks	.05
U39	Jose Jimenez	.05
U40	Carlos Guillen	.05
U41	Marlon Anderson	.05
U42	Scott Elarton	.05
U43	Glenallen Hill	.05
U44	Shane Monahan	.05
U45	Dennis Martinez	.05
U46	Carlos Febles **RC**	.20
U47	Carlos Perez	.05
U48	Wilton Guerrero	.05
U49	Randy Johnson	.45
U50	Brian Simmons **RC**	.05
U51	Carlton Loewer	.05
U52	Mark DeRosa **RC**	.50
U53	Tim Young **RC**	.05
U54	Gary Gaetti	.05
U55	Eric Chavez	.25
U56	Carl Pavano	.15
U57	Mike Stanley	.05
U58	Todd Stottlemyre	.05
U59	Gabe Kapler **RC**	.50
U60	Mike Jerzembeck **RC**	.05
U61	Mitch Meluskey **RC**	.15
U62	Bill Pulsipher	.05
U63	Derrick Gibson	.05
U64	John Rocker **RC**	.75
U65	Calvin Pickering	.05
U66	Blake Stein	.05
U67	Fernando Tatis	.05
U68	Gabe Alvarez	.05
U69	Jeffrey Hammonds	.05
U70	Adrian Beltre	.25
U71	Ryan Bradley **RC**	.10
U72	Edgar Clemente **RC**	.05
U73	Rick Croushore **RC**	.05
U74	Matt Clement	.15
U75	Dermal Brown	.05
U76	Paul Bako	.05
U77	Placido Polanco **RC**	1.00
U78	Jay Tessmer	.05
U79	Jarrod Washburn	.05
U80	Kevin Witt	.05
U81	Mike Metcalfe	.05
U82	Daryle Ward	.05
U83	Benj Sampson **RC**	.05
U84	Mike Kinkade **RC**	.20
U85	Randy Winn	.05
U86	Jeff Shaw	.05
U87	Troy Glaus **RC**	4.00
U88	Hideo Nomo	.35
U89	Mark Grudzielanek	.05
U90	Mike Frank **RC**	.05
U91	Bobby Howry **RC**	.10
U92	Ryan Minor **RC**	.15
U93	Corey Koskie **RC**	1.00
U94	Matt Anderson **RC**	.20
U95	Joe Carter	.05
U96	Paul Konerko	.15
U97	Sidney Ponson	.05
U98	Jeremy Giambi **RC**	.25
U99	Jeff Kubenka **RC**	.05
U100	J.D. Drew **RC**	5.00

Diamond Skills Commemorative Sheet

In conjunction with its sponsorship of the Diamond Skills program, Fleer and its 2,500 direct dealers distributed this eight-player sheet to 7-14 year olds participating in the event. Participants could get a sheet by redeeming Fleer wrappers at a local card store. The 10" x 9" sheet features full size Fleer Tradition card reproductions. At top is a list of 1997 Diamond Skills winners.

	NM/M
Complete Sheet:	2.00

Mantle & Sons

As part of its participation in SportsFest in May, 1998, Fleer issued a promotional card featuring a vintage color photo of Mickey Mantle and his sons, David and Danny. The back of the card announced Fleer's first-ever inclusion of Mickey Mantle cards in some of its forthcoming releases.

	NM/M
Mickey Mantle, Danny Mantle, David Mantle	3.00

Mickey Mantle Promo Postcard

This 4-1/4" x 5-1/2" color postcard was sent to Fleer dealers to announce a Mickey Mantle commemorative series in its Series 2 product. The address side has the Fleer Tradition logo in black, blue and red. The picture side has a color photo of one of the Mantle cards to be issued in the format of the 1963 Fleer issue. Cards are individually serial numbered within an edition of 3,500.

	NM/M
Mickey Mantle	4.00

Mark McGwire 62nd HR 23K Gold Commemorative

Marketed as a retail-exclusive "Official 62nd HR 23 Kt. Gold Commemorative Card," this 2-1/2" x 3-1/2" card was sold in a colorful blister pack. Embossed in 23-karat gold foil is an image of McGwire in action. Also on front are a 62-HR logo and a facsimile autograph, along with the legend "Smashing the Record." On back is a small picture of McGwire with the large 9-8-98 date and the

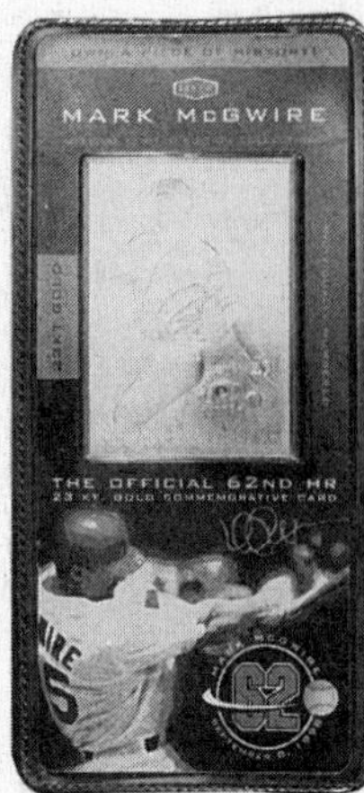

details of the record blast. There are appropriate licensing logos and a serial number from within an edition of 200,000.

	NM/M
Mark McGwire	5.00

National Convention Commemorative Set

In conjunction with its participation at the 19th National Sports Collectors Convention in Chicago in August, 1998 Fleer distributed this commemorative set to persons purchasing VIP admission packages. The set includes a specially numbered (NC1) Fleer Tradition Mickey Mantle card, a card picturing Mick with his sons, one of seven large-format (3-1/2" x 5") cards reproducing Mantle Monumental Moments inserts, and an unnumbered header card. The Monumental Moments reproductions are printed on a pinstriped-sky background.

		NM/M
Complete Set (8):		15.00
Common Card:		2.25
NC1	Mickey Mantle (Fleer Tradition)	2.25
NC2	Mickey Mantle (With sons.)	2.25
NC3	Mickey Mantle (Monumental Moments - accepting trophy.)	2.25
NC4	Mickey Mantle (Monumental Moments - making a throw.)	2.25
NC5	Mickey Mantle (Monumental Moments - in sliding pit.)	2.25
NC6	Mickey Mantle (Monumental Moments - batting.)	2.25
NC7	Mickey Mantle (Monumental Moments - number retired.)	2.25
	Header Card	.25

1999 Fleer

Released as a single series in 10-card packs with a suggested retail price of $1.59, the base set consists of 600 cards, including 10 checklists and a 15-card Fran-

chise Futures subset. Cards are UV coated, with borderless photos and gold-foil graphics. Backs have personal bio-information along with year-by-year career stats and a small photo. There are two parallels, Starting Nine, which are hobby-exclusive, numbered to nine sets with blue foil stamping and Warning Track. Found exclusively in retail packs, Warning Tracks can be identified by red foil stamping and a Warning Track logo.

		NM/M
Complete Set (600):		25.00
Common Player:		.05
Warning Track:		2X
Inserted 1:1 R		
Pack (10):		1.00
Wax Box (36):		25.00
1	Mark McGwire	2.00
2	Sammy Sosa	1.25
3	Ken Griffey Jr.	1.50
4	Kerry Wood	.30
5	Derek Jeter	2.50
6	Stan Musial	2.00
7	J.D. Drew	.65
7p	J.D. Drew/OPS	1.50
8	Cal Ripken Jr.	2.50
9	Alex Rodriguez	2.00
10	Travis Lee	.15
11	Andres Galarraga	.05
12	Nomar Garciaparra	1.25
13	Albert Belle	.05
14	Barry Larkin	.05
15	Dante Bichette	.05
16	Tony Clark	.05
17	Moises Alou	.05
18	Rafael Palmeiro	.65
19	Raul Mondesi	.05
20	Vladimir Guerrero	.75
21	John Olerud	.05
22	Bernie Williams	.10
23	Ben Grieve	.05
24	Scott Rolen	.65
25	Jeromy Burnitz	.05
26	Ken Caminiti	.05
27	Barry Bonds	2.50
28	Todd Helton	.75
29	Juan Gonzalez	.65
30	Roger Clemens	1.25
31	Andruw Jones	.75
32	Mo Vaughn	.05
33	Larry Walker	.05
34	Frank Thomas	.75
35	Manny Ramirez	.75
36	Randy Johnson	.75
37	Vinny Castilla	.05
38	Juan Encarnacion	.05
39	Jeff Bagwell	.75
40	Gary Sheffield	.50
41	Mike Piazza	1.50
42	Richie Sexson	.05
43	Tony Gwynn	1.00
44	Chipper Jones	1.00
45	Jim Thome	.65
46	Craig Biggio	.05
47	Carlos Delgado	.40
48	Greg Vaughn	.05
49	Greg Maddux	1.00
50	Troy Glaus	.65
51	Roberto Alomar	.10
52	Dennis Eckersley	.60
53	Mike Caruso	.05
54	Bruce Chen	.05
55	Aaron Boone	.05
56	Bartolo Colon	.05
57	Derrick Gibson	.05
58	Brian Anderson	.05
59	Gabe Alvarez	.05
60	Todd Dunwoody	.05
61	Rod Beck	.05
62	Derek Bell	.05
63	Francisco Cordova	.05
64	Johnny Damon	.25
65	Adrian Beltre	.15
66	Garret Anderson	.05
67	Armando Benitez	.05
68	Edgardo Alfonzo	.05
69	Ryan Bradley	.05
70	Eric Chavez	.30
71	Bobby Abreu	.05
72	Andy Ashby	.05
73	Ellis Burks	.05
74	Jeff Cirillo	.05
75	Jay Buhner	.05
76	Ron Gant	.05
77	Rolando Arrojo	.05
78	Will Clark	.10
79	Chris Carpenter	.05
80	Jim Edmonds	.05
81	Tony Batista	.05
82	Shane Andrews	.05
83	Mark DeRosa	.05
84	Brady Anderson	.05
85	Tony Gordon	.05
86	Brant Brown	.05
87	Ray Durham	.05
88	Ron Coomer	.05
89	Bret Boone	.05
90	Travis Fryman	.05
91	Darryl Kile	.05
92	Paul Bako	.05
93	Cliff Floyd	.05
94	Scott Elarton	.05
95	Jeremy Giambi	.05
96	Darren Dreifort	.05
97	Marquis Grissom	.05
98	Marty Cordova	.05
99	Fernando Seguignol	.05
100	Orlando Hernandez	.05
101	Jose Cruz Jr.	.05
102	Jason Giambi	.60
103	Damion Easley	.05
104	Freddy Garcia	.05
105	Marlon Anderson	.05
106	Kevin Brown	.05
107	Joe Carter	.05
108	Russ Davis	.05
109	Brian Jordan	.05
110	Wade Boggs	1.00
111	Tom Goodwin	.05
112	Scott Brosius	.05
113	Darin Erstad	.10
114	Jay Bell	.05
115	Tom Glavine	.25
116	Pedro Martinez	.75
117	Mark Grace	.10
118	Russ Ortiz	.05
119	Magglio Ordonez	.10
120	Sean Casey	.15
121	Rafael Roque **RC**	.05
122	Brian Giles	.05
123	Mike Lansing	.05
124	David Cone	.05
125	Alex Gonzalez	.05
126	Carl Everett	.05
127	Jeff King	.05
128	Charles Johnson	.05
129	Geoff Jenkins	.05
130	Corey Koskie	.05
131	Brad Fullmer	.05
132	Al Leiter	.05
133	Rickey Henderson	.75
134	Rico Brogna	.05
135	Jose Guillen	.05
136	Matt Clement	.05
137	Carlos Guillen	.05
138	Orel Hershiser	.05
139	Ray Lankford	.05
140	Miguel Cairo	.05
141	Chuck Finley	.05
142	Rusty Greer	.05
143	Kelvim Escobar	.05
144	Ryan Klesko	.05
145	Andy Benes	.05
146	Eric Davis	.05
147	David Wells	.05
148	Trot Nixon	.05
149	Jose Hernandez	.05
150	Mark Johnson	.05
151	Mike Frank	.05
152	Joey Hamilton	.05
153	David Justice	.05
154	Mike Mussina	.40
155	Neifi Perez	.05
156	Luis Gonzalez	.10
157	Livan Hernandez	.05
158	Dermal Brown	.05
159	Jose Lima	.05
160	Eric Karros	.05
161	Ronnie Belliard	.05
162	Matt Lawton	.05
163	Dustin Hermanson	.05
164	Brian McRae	.05
165	Mike Kinkade	.05
166	A.J. Hinch	.05
167	Doug Glanville	.05
168	Hideo Nomo	.65
169	Jason Kendall	.05
170	Steve Finley	.05
171	Jeff Kent	.05
172	Ben Davis	.05
173	Edgar Martinez	.05
174	Eli Marrero	.05
175	Quinton McCracken	.05
176	Rick Helling	.05
177	Tom Evans	.05
178	Carl Pavano	.10
179	Todd Greene	.05
180	Omar Daal	.05
181	George Lombard	.05
182	Ryan Minor	.05
183	Troy O'Leary	.05
184	Robb Nen	.05
185	Mickey Morandini	.05
186	Robin Ventura	.05
187	Pete Harnisch	.05
188	Kenny Lofton	.05
189	Eric Milton	.05
190	Bobby Higginson	.05
191	Jamie Moyer	.05
192	Mark Kotsay	.05
193	Shane Reynolds	.05
194	Carlos Febles	.05
195	Jeff Kubenka	.05
196	Chuck Knoblauch	.05
197	Kenny Rogers	.05
198	Bill Mueller	.05
199	Shane Monahan	.05
200	Matt Morris	.05
201	Fred McGriff	.05
202	Ivan Rodriguez	.65
203	Kevin Witt	.05
204	Troy Percival	.05
205	David Dellucci	.05
206	Kevin Millwood	.05
207	Jerry Hairston Jr.	.05
208	Mike Stanley	.05
209	Henry Rodriguez	.05
210	Trevor Hoffman	.05
211	Craig Wilson	.05
212	Reggie Sanders	.05
213	Carlton Loewer	.05
214	Omar Vizquel	.05
215	Gabe Kapler	.05
216	Derrek Lee	.05
217	Billy Wagner	.05
218	Dean Palmer	.05
219	Chan Ho Park	.05
220	Fernando Vina	.05
221	Roy Halladay	.05
222	Paul Molitor	.75
223	Ugueth Urbina	.05
224	Rey Ordonez	.05
225	Ricky Ledee	.05
226	Scott Spiezio	.05
227	Wendell Magee Jr.	.05
228	Aramis Ramirez	.05
229	Brian Simmons	.05
230	Fernando Tatis	.05
231	Bobby Smith	.05
232	Aaron Sele	.05
233	Shawn Green	.20
234	Mariano Rivera	.15
235	Tim Salmon	.10
236	Andy Fox	.05
237	Denny Neagle	.05
238	John Valentin	.05
239	Kevin Tapani	.05
240	Paul Konerko	.10
241	Robert Fick	.05
242	Edgar Renteria	.05
243	Brett Tomko	.05
244	Daryle Ward	.05
245	Carlos Beltran	.30
246	Angel Pena	.05
247	Steve Woodard	.05
248	David Ortiz	.05
249	Justin Thompson	.05
250	Rondell White	.05
251	Jaret Wright	.05
252	Ed Sprague	.05
253	Jay Payton	.05
254	Mike Lowell	.05
255	Orlando Cabrera	.05
256	Jason Schmidt	.05
257	David Segui	.05
258	Paul Sorrento	.05
259	John Wetteland	.05
260	Devon White	.05
261	Odalis Perez	.05
262	Calvin Pickering	.05
263	Alex Ramirez	.05
264	Preston Wilson	.05
265	Brad Radke	.05
266	Walt Weiss	.05
267	Tim Young	.05
268	Tino Martinez	.05
269	Matt Stairs	.05
270	Curt Schilling	.25
271	Tony Womack	.05
272	Ismael Valdes	.05
273	Wally Joyner	.05
274	Armando Rios	.05
275	Andy Pettitte	.25
276	Bubba Trammell	.05
277	Todd Zeile	.05
278	Shannon Stewart	.05
279	Matt Williams	.05
280	John Rocker	.05
281	B.J. Surhoff	.05
282	Eric Young	.05
283	Dmitri Young	.05
284	John Smoltz	.05
285	Todd Walker	.05
286	Paul O'Neill	.05
287	Blake Stein	.05
288	Kevin Young	.05
289	Quilvio Veras	.05
290	Kirk Rueter	.05
291	Randy Winn	.05
292	Miguel Tejada	.05
293	J.T. Snow	.05
294	Michael Tucker	.05
295	Jay Tessmer	.05
296	Scott Erickson	.05
297	Tim Wakefield	.05
298	Jeff Abbott	.05
299	Eddie Taubensee	.05
300	Darryl Hamilton	.05
301	Kevin Orie	.05
302	Jose Offerman	.05
303	Scott Karl	.05
304	Chris Widger	.05
305	Todd Hundley	.05
306	Desi Relaford	.05
307	Sterling Hitchcock	.05

308 Delino DeShields .05
309 Alex Gonzalez .05
310 Justin Baughman .05
311 Jamey Wright .05
312 Wes Helms .05
313 Dante Powell .05
314 Jim Abbott .05
315 Manny Alexander .05
316 Harold Baines .05
317 Danny Graves .05
318 Sandy Alomar .05
319 Pedro Astacio .05
320 Jermaine Allensworth .05
321 Matt Anderson .05
322 Chad Curtis .05
323 Antonio Osuna .05
324 Brad Ausmus .05
325 Steve Trachsel .05
326 Mike Blowers .05
327 Brian Bohanon .05
328 Chris Gomez .05
329 Valerio de los Santos .05
330 Rich Aurilia .05
331 Michael Barrett .05
332 Rick Aguilera .05
333 Adrian Brown .05
334 Bill Spiers .05
335 Matt Beech .05
336 David Bell .05
337 Juan Acevedo .05
338 Jose Canseco .50
339 Wilson Alvarez .05
340 Luis Alicea .05
341 Jason Dickson .05
342 Mike Bordick .05
343 Ben Ford .05
344 Keith Lockhart .05
345 Jason Christiansen .05
346 Darren Bragg .05
347 Doug Brocail .05
348 Jeff Blauser .05
349 James Baldwin .05
350 Jeffrey Hammonds .05
351 Ricky Bottalico .05
352 Russ Branyon .05
353 Mark Brownson .05
354 Dave Berg .05
355 Sean Bergman .05
356 Jeff Conine .05
357 Shayne Bennett .05
358 Bobby Bonilla .05
359 Bob Wickman .05
360 Carlos Baerga .05
361 Chris Fussell .05
362 Chili Davis .05
363 Jerry Spradlin .05
364 Carlos Hernandez .05
365 Roberto Hernandez .05
366 Marvin Benard .05
367 Ken Cloude .05
368 Tony Fernandez .05
369 John Burkett .05
370 Gary DiSarcina .05
371 Alan Benes .05
372 Karim Garcia .05
373 Carlos Perez .05
374 Damon Buford .05
375 Mark Clark .05
376 Edgard Clemente **RC** .05
377 Chad Bradford .05
378 Frank Catalanotto .05
379 Vic Darensbourg .05
380 Sean Berry .05
381 Dave Burba .05
382 Sal Fasano .05
383 Steve Parris .05
384 Roger Cedeno .05
385 Chad Fox .05
386 Wilton Guerrero .05
387 Dennis Cook .05
388 Joe Girardi .05
389 LaTroy Hawkins .05
390 Ryan Christenson .05
391 Paul Byrd .05
392 Lou Collier .05
393 Jeff Fassero .05
394 Jim Leyritz .05
395 Shawn Estes .05
396 Mike Kelly .05
397 Rich Croushore .05
398 Royce Clayton .05
399 Rudy Seanez .05
400 Darrin Fletcher .05
401 Shigetosi Hasegawa .05
402 Bernard Gilkey .05
403 Juan Guzman .05
404 Jeff Frye .05
405 Marino Santana .05
406 Alex Fernandez .05
407 Gary Gaetti .05
408 Dan Miceli .05
409 Mike Cameron .05
410 Mike Remlinger .05
411 Joey Cora .05
412 Mark Gardner .05
413 Aaron Ledesma .05
414 Jerry Dipoto .05
415 Ricky Gutierrez .05
416 John Franco .05
417 Mendy Lopez .05
418 Hideki Irabu .05
419 Mark Grudzielanek .05
420 Bobby Hughes .05
421 Pat Meares .05
422 Jimmy Haynes .05
423 Bob Henley .05
424 Bobby Estalella .05
425 Jon Lieber .05
426 Giomar Guevara **RC** .05
427 Jose Jimenez .05
428 Deivi Cruz .05
429 Jonathan Johnson .05
430 Ken Hill .05
431 Craig Grebeck .05
432 Jose Rosado .05
433 Danny Klassen .05
434 Bobby Howry .05
435 Gerald Williams .05
436 Omar Olivares .05
437 Chris Hoiles .05
438 Seth Greisinger .05
439 Scott Hatteberg .05
440 Jeremi Gonzalez .05
441 Wil Cordero .05
442 Jeff Montgomery .05
443 Chris Stynes .05
444 Tony Saunders .05
445 Einar Diaz .05
446 Laril Gonzalez .05
447 Ryan Jackson .05
448 Mike Hampton .05
449 Todd Hollandsworth .05
450 Gabe White .05
451 John Jaha .05
452 Bret Saberhagen .05
453 Otis Nixon .05
454 Steve Kline .05
455 Butch Huskey .05
456 Mike Jerzembeck .05
457 Wayne Gomes .05
458 Mike Macfarlane .05
459 Jesus Sanchez .05
460 Al Martin .05
461 Dwight Gooden .05
462 Ruben Rivera .05
463 Pat Hentgen .05
464 Jose Valentin .05
465 Vladimir Nunez .05
466 Charlie Hayes .05
467 Jay Powell .05
468 Raul Ibanez .05
469 Kent Mercker .05
470 John Mabry .05
471 Woody Williams .05
472 Roberto Kelly .05
473 Jim Mecir .05
474 Dave Hollins .05
475 Rafael Medina .05
476 Darren Lewis .05
477 Felix Heredia .05
478 Brian Hunter .05
479 Matt Mantei .05
480 Richard Hidalgo .05
481 Bobby Jones .05
482 Hal Morris .05
483 Ramiro Mendoza .05
484 Matt Luke .05
485 Esteban Loaiza .05
486 Mark Loretta .05
487 A.J. Pierzynski .05
488 Charles Nagy .05
489 Kevin Sefcik .05
490 Jason McDonald .05
491 Jeremy Powell .05
492 Scott Servais .05
493 Abraham Nunez .05
494 Stan Spencer .05
495 Stan Javier .05
496 Jose Paniagua .05
497 Gregg Jefferies .05
498 Gregg Olson .05
499 Derek Lowe .05
500 Willis Otanez .05
501 Brian Moehler .05
502 Glenallen Hill .05
503 Bobby Jones .05
504 Greg Norton .05
505 Mike Jackson .05
506 Kirt Manwaring .05
507 Eric Weaver .05
508 Mitch Meluskey .05
509 Todd Jones .05
510 Mike Matheny .05
511 Benj Sampson .05
512 Tony Phillips .05
513 Mike Thurman .05
514 Jorge Posada .05
515 Bill Taylor .05
516 Mike Sweeney .05
517 Jose Silva .05
518 Mark Lewis .05
519 Chris Peters .05
520 Brian Johnson .05
521 Mike Timlin .05
522 Mark McLemore .05
523 Dan Plesac .05
524 Kelly Stinnett .05
525 Sidney Ponson .05
526 Jim Parque .05
527 Tyler Houston .05
528 John Thomson .05
529 Mike Metcalfe .05
530 Robert Person .05
531 Marc Newfield .05
532 Javier Vazquez .05
533 Terry Steinbach .05
534 Turk Wendell .05
535 Tim Raines .05
536 Brian Meadows .05
537 Mike Lieberthal .05
538 Ricardo Rincon .05
539 Dan Wilson .05
540 John Johnstone .05
541 Todd Stottlemyre .05
542 Kevin Stocker .05
543 Ramon Martinez .05
544 Mike Simms .05
545 Paul Quantrill .05
546 Matt Walbeck .05
547 Turner Ward .05
548 Bill Pulsipher .05
549 Donnie Sadler .05
550 Lance Johnson .05
551 Bill Simas .05
552 Jeff Reed .05
553 Jeff Shaw .05
554 Joe Randa .05
555 Paul Shuey .05
556 Mike Redmond .05
557 Sean Runyan .05
558 Enrique Wilson .05
559 Scott Radinsky .05
560 Larry Sutton .05
561 Masato Yoshii .05
562 David Nilsson .05
563 Mike Trombley .05
564 Darryl Strawberry .05
565 Dave Mlicki .05
566 Placido Polanco .05
567 Yorkis Perez .05
568 Esteban Yan .05
569 Lee Stevens .05
570 Steve Sinclair .05
571 Jarrod Washburn .05
572 Lenny Webster .05
573 Mike Sirotka .05
574 Jason Varitek .05
575 Terry Mulholland .05
576 Adrian Beltre (Franchise Futures) .10
577 Eric Chavez (Franchise Futures) .20
578 J.D. Drew (Franchise Futures) .35
579 Juan Encarnacion (Franchise Futures) .05
580 Nomar Garciaparra (Franchise Futures) .65
581 Troy Glaus (Franchise Futures) .35
582 Ben Grieve (Franchise Futures) .05
583 Vladimir Guerrero (Franchise Futures) .40
584 Todd Helton (Franchise Futures) .35
585 Derek Jeter (Franchise Futures) 1.25
586 Travis Lee (Franchise Futures) .10
587 Alex Rodriguez (Franchise Futures) 1.00
588 Scott Rolen (Franchise Futures) .30
589 Richie Sexson (Franchise Futures) .05
590 Kerry Wood (Franchise Futures) .20
591 Ken Griffey Jr. (Checklist) .75
592 Chipper Jones (Checklist) .50
593 Alex Rodriguez (Checklist) 1.00
594 Sammy Sosa (Checklist) .65
595 Mark McGwire (Checklist) 1.00
596 Cal Ripken Jr. (Checklist) 1.25
597 Nomar Garciaparra (Checklist) .65
598 Derek Jeter (Checklist) 1.25
599 Kerry Wood (Checklist) .20
600 J.D. Drew (Checklist) .40

Starting Nine

This ultra-scarce, hobby-only parallel insert, found at the rate of about two cards per case, includes just nine cards of each player. Sharing the basic design of the Fleer Tradition set, the cards have blue metallic foil printing on front, including a "STARTING 9 NINE" logo at lower-right. At bottom right, the card's individual serial number from within the edition of nine is printed. Backs have an "S" suffix to the card number.

NM/M
Common Player: 20.00

Warning Track Collection

Each of the cards in '99 Fleer Tradition was paralleled in this retail-only issue found one per pack. Warning Track cards are distinguished by the use of red metallic foil on front for the player's name, team, position that are in gold-foil on the regular version. There is also a special "Warning Track Collection" logo in red foil at bottom-right. On back, WTC cards have a "W" suffix to the card number.

NM/M
Complete Set (600): 160.00
Common Player: .50
Stars: 2X

Date With Destiny

This 10-card set takes a look at what Hall of Fame plaques might look like for some of today's great players. These are serially numbered to 100 sets.

NM/M
Complete Set (10): 300.00
Common Player: 20.00
Production 100 Sets
1 Barry Bonds 60.00
2 Roger Clemens 35.00
3 Ken Griffey Jr. 40.00
4 Tony Gwynn 30.00
5 Greg Maddux 30.00
6 Mark McGwire 50.00
7 Mike Piazza 40.00
8 Cal Ripken Jr. 60.00
9 Alex Rodriguez 50.00
10 Frank Thomas 20.00

Diamond Magic

A multi-layer card, where collectors turn a "wheel" for a kaleidoscope effect behind the player image. These are seeded 1:96 packs.

NM/M
Complete Set (15): 50.00
Common Player: 1.00
Inserted 1:96
1 Barry Bonds 9.00
2 Roger Clemens 4.50
3 Nomar Garciaparra 4.50
4 Ken Griffey Jr. 5.00
5 Tony Gwynn 3.75
6 Orlando Hernandez 1.00
7 Derek Jeter 9.00
8 Randy Johnson 3.00
9 Chipper Jones 3.75
10 Greg Maddux 3.75
11 Mark McGwire 6.00
12 Alex Rodriguez 7.50
13 Sammy Sosa 4.50
14 Bernie Williams 1.50
15 Kerry Wood 2.00

Going Yard

This 15-card set features the top home run hitters from the '98 season. These 1:18 pack inserts unfold to be twice as wide as regular cards and takes an unorthodox look at how far the longest home runs went.

NM/M
Complete Set (15): 4.00
Common Player: .10
Inserted 1:18
1 Moises Alou .10
2 Albert Belle .10
3 Jose Canseco .30
4 Vinny Castilla .10
5 Andres Galarraga .10
6 Juan Gonzalez .20
7 Ken Griffey Jr. .75
8 Chipper Jones .50
9 Mark McGwire 1.00
10 Rafael Palmeiro .35
11 Mike Piazza .75
12 Alex Rodriguez 1.00
13 Sammy Sosa .65
14 Greg Vaughn .10
15 Mo Vaughn .10

Golden Memories

This 15-card set pays tribute to the great moments from the 1998 season including David Wells perfect game and McGwire's record breaking season. These are seeded 1:54 packs on an embossed frame design.

NM/M
Complete Set (15): 45.00
Common Player: .75
Inserted 1:54
1 Albert Belle .75
2 Barry Bonds 7.50
3 Roger Clemens 4.50
4 Nomar Garciaparra 4.50
5 Juan Gonzalez 1.50
6 Ken Griffey Jr. 3.75
7 Randy Johnson 2.75
8 Greg Maddux 3.25
9 Mark McGwire 5.00
10 Mike Piazza 3.75
11 Cal Ripken Jr. 7.50
12 Alex Rodriguez 6.00
13 Sammy Sosa 4.50
14 David Wells .75
15 Kerry Wood 2.00

Home Run Heroes

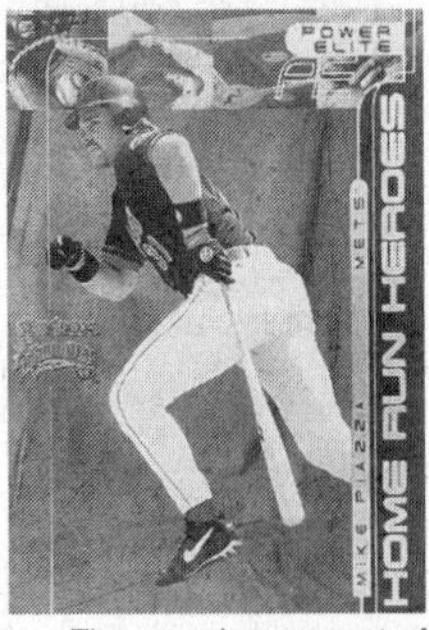

These cards were part of an unannounced multi-manufacturer (Fleer, Upper Deck, Topps, Pacific) insert program which was exclusive to Wal-Mart. Each company produced cards of Mark McGwire and Sammy Sosa, along with two other premier sluggers. Each company's cards share a "Power Elite" logo at top and "Home Run Heroes" logo vertically at right.

NM/M
Complete Set (4): 7.50
Common Player: 1.50
1 Mark McGwire (Tradition) 3.00
2 Sammy Sosa (Sports Illustrated) 2.00
3 Mike Piazza (SkyBox Thunder) 2.00
4 Nomar Garciaparra (SkyBox Thunder) 2.00

Stan Musial Monumental Moments

Great moments and insight from and about the St. Louis Cardinals great. This 10-card tribute set chronicles Musial's legendary career. These are seeded 1:36 packs with 500 autographed cards randomly seeded.

NM/M
Complete Set (10): 15.00
Common Musial: 2.00
Autographed Card: 60.00
1 Life in Donora 2.00
2 Values 2.00
3 In the Beginning 2.00
4 In the Navy 2.00
5 The 1948 Season (W/Red Schoendienst.) 2.00
6 Success Stories (W/Pres. Kennedy.) 2.00
7 Mr. Cardinal 2.00
8 Most Valuable Player 2.00
9 ... baseball's perfect knight 2.00
10 Hall of Fame 2.00

Rookie Flashback

This 15-card set features the impact rookies from the 1998 season. These are seed-

ed 1:6 packs and feature sculpture embossing.

		NM/M
Complete Set (15):		5.00
Common Player:		.25
Inserted 1:6		
1	Matt Anderson	.25
2	Rolando Arrojo	.25
3	Adrian Beltre	.50
4	Mike Caruso	.25
5	Eric Chavez	.40
6	J.D. Drew	.75
7	Juan Encarnacion	.25
8	Brad Fullmer	.25
9	Troy Glaus	1.50
10	Ben Grieve	.25
11	Todd Helton	1.50
12	Orlando Hernandez	.25
13	Travis Lee	.40
14	Richie Sexson	.25
15	Kerry Wood	.65

Vintage '61

This 50-card set takes the first 50 cards from the base set and showcases them in the 1961 Fleer "Baseball Greats" card design. These are seeded one per hobby pack.

		NM/M
Complete Set (50):		7.50
Common Player:		.05
Inserted 1:1		
1	Mark McGwire	.75
2	Sammy Sosa	.50
3	Ken Griffey Jr.	.60
4	Kerry Wood	.25
5	Derek Jeter	1.00
6	Stan Musial	.75
7	J.D. Drew	.30
8	Cal Ripken Jr.	1.00
9	Alex Rodriguez	.75
10	Travis Lee	.10
11	Andres Galarraga	.05
12	Nomar Garciaparra	.50
13	Albert Belle	.05
14	Barry Larkin	.05
15	Dante Bichette	.05
16	Tony Clark	.05
17	Moises Alou	.05
18	Rafael Palmeiro	.30
19	Raul Mondesi	.05
20	Vladimir Guerrero	.35
21	John Olerud	.05
22	Bernie Williams	.10
23	Ben Grieve	.05
24	Scott Rolen	.30
25	Jeromy Burnitz	.05
26	Ken Caminiti	.05
27	Barry Bonds	1.00
28	Todd Helton	.35
29	Juan Gonzalez	.25
30	Roger Clemens	.50
31	Andruw Jones	.35
32	Mo Vaughn	.05
33	Larry Walker	.05
34	Frank Thomas	.35
35	Manny Ramirez	.35
36	Randy Johnson	.35
37	Vinny Castilla	.05
38	Juan Encarnacion	.05
39	Jeff Bagwell	.35
40	Gary Sheffield	.25
41	Mike Piazza	.60
42	Richie Sexson	.05
43	Tony Gwynn	.45
44	Chipper Jones	.45
45	Jim Thome	.30
46	Craig Biggio	.05
47	Carlos Delgado	.25
48	Greg Vaughn	.05
49	Greg Maddux	.45
50	Troy Glaus	.35

Update

Distributed as a 150-card boxed set, the main focus for this release is the inclusion of rookie cards of players called up late in the '99 season, including Rick Ankiel. Besides rookies, the set also features 10 traded players/ free agents and a 10-card Season Highlights subset.

		NM/M
Complete Set (150):		20.00
Common Player:		.10
1	Rick Ankiel **RC**	3.00
2	Peter Bergeron **RC**	.25
3	Pat Burrell **RC**	1.50
4	Eric Munson **RC**	.35
5	Alfonso Soriano **RC**	3.00
6	Tim Hudson **RC**	2.00
7	Erubiel Durazo **RC**	.25
8	Chad Hermansen	.10
9	Jeff Zimmerman	.10
10	Jesus Pena **RC**	.10
11	Ramon Hernandez	.10
12	Trent Durrington **RC**	.25
13	Tony Armas Jr.	.10
14	Mike Fyhrie **RC**	.10
15	Danny Kolb **RC**	.25
16	Mike Porzio **RC**	.10
17	Will Brunson **RC**	.10
18	Mike Duvall **RC**	.10
19	Doug Mientkiewicz **RC**	.75
20	Gabe Molina **RC**	.15
21	Luis Vizcaino **RC**	.20
22	Robinson Cancel **RC**	.10
23	Brett Laxton **RC**	.10
24	Joe McEwing **RC**	.25
25	Justin Speier **RC**	.20
26	Kip Wells **RC**	.25
27	Armando Almanza **RC**	.10
28	Joe Davenport **RC**	.10
29	Yamid Haad **RC**	.10
30	John Halama	.10
31	Adam Kennedy	.10
32	Vicente Padilla **RC**	.25
33	Travis Dawkins **RC**	.25
34	Ryan Rupe **RC**	.25
35	B.J. Ryan **RC**	.10
36	Chance Sanford **RC**	.10
37	Anthony Shumaker **RC**	.10
38	Ryan Glynn **RC**	.10
39	Matt Herges **RC**	.20
40	Ben Molina	.10
41	Scott Williamson	.10
42	Eric Gagne **RC**	1.50
43	John McDonald **RC**	.10
44	Scott Sauerbeck **RC**	.10
45	Mike Venafro **RC**	.10
46	Edwards Guzman **RC**	.10
47	Richard Barker **RC**	.10
48	Braden Looper	.10
49	Chad Meyers **RC**	.10
50	Scott Strickland **RC**	.10
51	Billy Koch	.10
52	Dave Newhan **RC**	.10
53	David Riske **RC**	.10
54	Jose Santiago	.10
55	Miguel Del Toro **RC**	.10
56	Orber Moreno **RC**	.10
57	Dave Roberts	.10
58	Tim Byrdak **RC**	.10
59	David Lee **RC**	.10
60	Guillermo Mota **RC**	.15
61	Wilton Veras **RC**	.15
62	Joe Mays **RC**	.35
63	Jose Fernandez **RC**	.10
64	Ray King **RC**	.10
65	Chris Petersen **RC**	.10
66	Vernon Wells	.15
67	Ruben Mateo	.10
68	Ben Petrick	.10
69	Chris Tremie **RC**	.10
70	Lance Berkman	.10
71	Dan Smith	.10
72	Carlos Hernandez **RC**	.10
73	Chad Harville **RC**	.25
74	Damaso Marte	.10
75	Aaron Myette **RC**	.15
76	Willis Roberts **RC**	.10
77	Erik Sabel **RC**	.10
78	Hector Almonte **RC**	.10
79	Kris Benson	.10
80	Pat Daneker **RC**	.10
81	Freddy Garcia **RC**	.50
82	Byung-Hyun Kim **RC**	.25
83	Wily Pena **RC**	1.00
84	Dan Wheeler **RC**	.15
85	Tim Harikkala **RC**	.10
86	Derrin Ebert **RC**	.10
87	Horacio Estrada **RC**	.10
88	Liu Rodriguez **RC**	.10
89	Jordan Zimmerman **RC**	.10
90	A.J. Burnett **RC**	.40
91	Doug Davis **RC**	.10
92	Robert Ramsey **RC**	.10
93	Ryan Franklin **RC**	.10
94	Charlie Greene **RC**	.10
95	Bo Porter **RC**	.10
96	Jorge Toca **RC**	.10
97	Casey Blake **RC**	.20
98	Amaury Garcia **RC**	.10
99	Jose Molina **RC**	.10
100	Melvin Mora **RC**	1.00
101	Joe Nathan **RC**	.10
102	Juan Pena **RC**	.25
103	Dave Borkowski **RC**	.10
104	Eddie Gaillard **RC**	.10
105	Rob Radlosky	.10
106	Brett Hinchliffe **RC**	.10
107	Carlos Lee	.10
108	Rob Ryan **RC**	.10
109	Jeff Weaver **RC**	.50
110	Ed Yarnall	.10
111	Nelson Cruz **RC**	.10
112	Cleatus Davidson **RC**	.10
113	Tim Kubinski **RC**	.10
114	Sean Spencer **RC**	.10
115	Joe Winkelsas **RC**	.10
116	Chris Clapinski **RC**	.10
117	Tom Davey **RC**	.10
118	Warren Morris	.10
119	Dan Murray **RC**	.10
120	Jose Nieves **RC**	.10
121	Mark Quinn **RC**	.10
122	Josh Beckett **RC**	10.00
123	Chad Allen **RC**	.10
124	Mike Figga	.10
125	Beiker Graterol **RC**	.10
126	Aaron Scheffer **RC**	.10
127	Wiki Gonzalez **RC**	.10
128	Ramon E. Martinez	.10
129	Matt Riley **RC**	.25
130	Chris Woodward **RC**	.10
131	Albert Belle	.10
132	Roger Cedeno	.10
133	Roger Clemens	.75
134	Brian Giles	.10
135	Rickey Henderson	.60
136	Randy Johnson	.60
137	Brian Jordan	.10
138	Paul Konerko	.15
139	Hideo Nomo	.50
140	Kenny Rogers	.10
141	Wade Boggs	.65
142	Jose Canseco	.45
143	Roger Clemens	.75
144	David Cone	.10
145	Tony Gwynn	.65
146	Mark McGwire	1.00
147	Cal Ripken Jr.	1.50
148	Alex Rodriguez	1.00
149	Fernando Tatis	.10
150	Robin Ventura	.10

Millennium

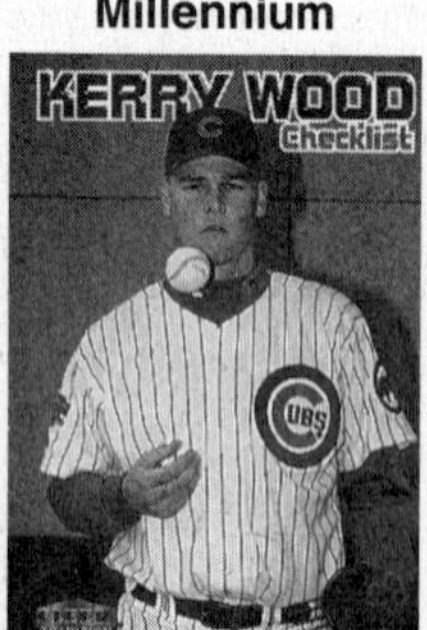

This special edition of '99 Fleer Tradition was issued only in factory sets, for sale on Shop at Home. Besides the 600 cards in the regular Tradition issue, these sets include 20 renumbered rookie and highlight cards from the Fleer Update set. Each set is sealed with gold-foil on which is a serial number from with an edition of 5,000 sets. Each card in the edition has a special gold-foil "2000" logo on front.

		NM/M
Complete Factory Set (620):		30.00
Common Player:		.50
Stars:		5X
601	Rick Ankiel	.75
602	Peter Bergeron	.50
603	Pat Burrell	2.00
604	Eric Munson	.50
605	Alfonso Soriano	2.00
606	Tim Hudson	1.25
607	Erubiel Durazo	.50
608	Chad Hermansen	.50
609	Jeff Zimmerman	.50
610	Jesus Pena	.50
611	Wade Boggs (Highlights)	.75
612	Jose Canseco (Highlights)	.50
613	Roger Clemens (Highlights)	1.00
614	David Cone (Highlights)	.50
615	Tony Gwynn (Highlights)	.75
616	Mark McGwire (Highlights)	1.50
617	Cal Ripken Jr. (Highlights)	2.00
618	Alex Rodriguez (Highlights)	1.50
619	Fernando Tatis (Highlights)	.50
620	Robin Ventura (Highlights)	.50

Brilliants Sample

To preview the introduction of its Brilliants brand of premium quality cards into baseball, Fleer issued a promo card of J.D. Drew. Like the issued cards, the sample is printed on plastic with a mirrored silver background on front. Both front and back are overprinted, "PROMOTIONAL SAMPLE."

	NM/M
J.D. Drew	3.00

Brilliants

This 175-card set features an action photo on a complete silver-foiled background swirl pattern. The featured player's name, team and postion are stamped in gold foil. Card backs have a small photo, vital information, 1998 statistics and a brief overview of the player's '98 season. Cards numbered 126-175 are part of a short-printed Rookies subset and are seeded 1:2 packs.

		NM/M
Complete Set (175):		60.00
Common Player:		.25
Common SP (126-175):		.50
Blues (1:3):		1.5X
SP Blues (1:6)		1X
Golds:		8X
SP Golds:		3X
Production 99 Sets		
24 Karat Golds:		40X
SP's:		15X
Production 24 Sets		
Pack (5):		2.00
Wax Box (24):		32.50
1	Mark McGwire	2.50
2	Derek Jeter	3.00
3	Nomar Garciaparra	1.75
4	Travis Lee	.25
5	Jeff Bagwell	.75
6	Andres Galarraga	.25
7	Pedro Martinez	.75
8	Cal Ripken Jr.	3.00
9	Vladimir Guerrero	.75
10	Chipper Jones	1.50
11	Rusty Greer	.25
12	Omar Vizquel	.25
13	Quinton McCracken	.25
14	Jaret Wright	.25
15	Mike Mussina	.50
16	Jason Giambi	.60
17	Tony Clark	.25
18	Troy O'Leary	.25
19	Troy Percival	.25
20	Kerry Wood	.50
21	Vinny Castilla	.25
22	Chris Carpenter	.25
23	Richie Sexson	.25
24	Ken Griffey Jr.	2.00
25	Barry Bonds	3.00
26	Carlos Delgado	.60
27	Frank Thomas	.75
28	Manny Ramirez	.75
29	Shawn Green	.50
30	Mike Piazza	2.00
31	Tino Martinez	.25
32	Dante Bichette	.25
33	Scott Rolen	.65
34	Gabe Alvarez	.25
35	Raul Mondesi	.25
36	Damion Easley	.25
37	Jeff Kent	.25
38	Al Leiter	.25
39	Alex Rodriguez	2.50
40	Jeff King	.25
41	Mark Grace	.25
42	Larry Walker	.25
43	Moises Alou	.25
44	Juan Gonzalez	.65
45	Rolando Arrojo	.25
46	Tom Glavine	.45
47	Johnny Damon	.45
48	Livan Hernandez	.25
49	Craig Biggio	.25
50	Dmitri Young	.25
51	Chan Ho Park	.25
52	Todd Walker	.25
53	Derrek Lee	.25
54	Todd Helton	.75
55	Ray Lankford	.25
56	Jim Thome	.65
57	Matt Lawton	.25
58	Matt Anderson	.25
59	Jose Offerman	.25
60	Eric Karros	.25
61	Orlando Hernandez	.25
62	Ben Grieve	.25
63	Bobby Abreu	.25
64	Kevin Young	.25
65	John Olerud	.25
66	Sammy Sosa	1.75
67	Andy Ashby	.25
68	Juan Encarnacion	.25
69	Shane Reynolds	.25
70	Bernie Williams	.35
71	Mike Cameron	.25
72	Troy Glaus	.75
73	Gary Sheffield	.60
74	Jeromy Burnitz	.25
75	Mike Caruso	.25
76	Chuck Knoblauch	.25
77	Kenny Rogers	.25
78	David Cone	.25
79	Tony Gwynn	1.50
80	Aramis Ramirez	.25
81	Paul O'Neill	.25
82	Charles Nagy	.25
83	Javy Lopez	.25
84	Scott Erickson	.25
85	Trevor Hoffman	.25
86	Andruw Jones	.75
87	Ray Durham	.25
88	Jorge Posada	.25
89	Edgar Martinez	.25
90	Tim Salmon	.35
91	Bobby Higginson	.25
92	Adrian Beltre	.45
93	Jason Kendall	.25
94	Henry Rodriguez	.25
95	Greg Maddux	1.50
96	David Justice	.25
97	Ivan Rodriguez	.65
98	Curt Schilling	.45
99	Matt Williams	.25
100	Darin Erstad	.50
101	Rafael Palmeiro	.65
102	David Wells	.25
103	Barry Larkin	.25
104	Robin Ventura	.25
105	Edgar Renteria	.25
106	Andy Pettitte	.50
107	Albert Belle	.25
108	Steve Finley	.25
109	Fernando Vina	.25
110	Rondell White	.25
111	Kevin Brown	.25
112	Jose Canseco	.50
113	Roger Clemens	1.75
114	Todd Hundley	.25
115	Will Clark	.35
116	Jim Edmonds	.25
117	Randy Johnson	.75
118	Denny Neagle	.25
119	Brian Jordan	.25
120	Dean Palmer	.25
121	Roberto Alomar	.45
122	Ken Caminiti	.25
123	Brian Giles	.25
124	Todd Stottlemyre	.25
125	Mo Vaughn	.25
126	J.D. Drew	1.00
127	Ryan Minor	.50
128	Gabe Kapler	.50
129	Jeremy Giambi	.50
130	Eric Chavez	1.00
131	Ben Davis	.50
132	Rob Fick	.50
133	George Lombard	.50
134	Calvin Pickering	.50
135	Preston Wilson	.50
136	Corey Koskie	.75
137	Russell Branyan	.50
138	Bruce Chen	.50
139	Matt Clement	.75
140	Pat Burrell **RC**	2.50
141	Freddy Garcia **RC**	1.00
142	Brian Simmons	.50
143	Carlos Febles	.50
144	Carlos Guillen	.50
145	Fernando Seguignol	.50
146	Carlos Beltran	1.00
147	Edgard Clemente	.50
148	Mitch Meluskey	.50
149	Ryan Bradley	.50
150	Marlon Anderson	.50
151	A.J. Burnett **RC**	1.00
152	Scott Hunter **RC**	.50
153	Mark Johnson	.50
154	Angel Pena	.50
155	Roy Halladay	.75
156	Chad Allen **RC**	.50
157	Trot Nixon	.75
158	Ricky Ledee	.50
159	Gary Bennett **RC**	.50
160	Micah Bowie **RC**	.60
161	Doug Mientkiewicz	.60
162	Danny Klassen	.50
163	Willis Otanez	.50
164	Jin Ho Cho	.50
165	Mike Lowell	.60
166	Armando Rios	.50
167	Tom Evans	.50
168	Michael Barrett	.50
169	Alex Gonzalez	.50
170	Masao Kida **RC**	.60
171	Peter Tucci **RC**	.50
172	Luis Saturria	.50
173	Kris Benson	.50
174	Mario Encarnacion **RC**	.50
175	Roosevelt Brown **RC**	.50

Brilliants Blue/Golds

The 175 Fleer Brilliants base cards are paralleled in three insert sets of differing degrees of scarcity. Brilliant Blue parallels have a mirrored blue foil background on front and a "B" suffix to the card number on back. They are seeded one per three packs (125 veterans) and one per six packs (50 rookies). Gold parallels are printed with gold foil background and a "G" suffix. Each card is serially numbered on back within an edition of 99. The 24-karat Gold parallels have gold rainbow holographic foil backgrounds, a 24-karat gold logo and are serially numbered to just 24 of each card; numbers have a TG sugffix.

	NM/M
Brilliants Blue Common:	.50
Brilliants Blue Stars:	1.5X
Brilliants Blue Rookies:	1X
Brilliants Gold Common:	3.00
Brilliants Gold Stars:	8X
Brilliants Gold Rookies:	3X
Brilliants 24K Gold Common:	10.00
Brilliants 24K Gold Stars:	40X
Brilliants 24K Gold Rookies:	15X

Brilliants Illuminators

This 15-card set highlights baseball's top young prospects on a team color-coded fully foiled front. Card backs are numbered with an "I" suffix and are inserted 1:10 packs.

		NM/M
Complete Set (15):		10.00
Common Player:		.75
Inserted 1:10		
1	Kerry Wood	2.00
2	Ben Grieve	.75
3	J.D. Drew	1.50
4	Juan Encarnacion	.75
5	Travis Lee	.75
6	Todd Helton	3.00
7	Troy Glaus	2.00
8	Ricky Ledee	.75
9	Eric Chavez	1.50
10	Ben Davis	.75
11	George Lombard	.75
12	Jeremy Giambi	.75
13	Richie Sexson	.75
14	Corey Koskie	.75
15	Russell Branyan	.75

Brilliants Shining Stars

Shining Stars is a 15-card set printed on styrene with two-sided mirrored foil. Card backs are numbered with a "S" suffix and are seeded 1:20 packs. Pulsars are a parallel set that are printed on two-sided rainbow holographic foil and styrene with an embossed star pattern in the background. Pulsars are seeded 1:400 packs.

		NM/M
Complete Set (15):		30.00
Common Player:		1.50
Inserted 1:20		
Pulsars:		4X
Inserted 1:400		
1	Ken Griffey Jr.	2.50
2	Mark McGwire	3.00
3	Sammy Sosa	2.25
4	Derek Jeter	4.00
5	Nomar Garciaparra	2.25
6	Alex Rodriguez	3.00
7	Mike Piazza	2.50
8	Juan Gonzalez	1.50
9	Chipper Jones	2.00
10	Cal Ripken Jr.	4.00
11	Frank Thomas	1.50
12	Greg Maddux	2.00
13	Roger Clemens	2.25
14	Vladimir Guerrero	1.50
15	Manny Ramirez	1.50

1999 Fleer Mystique

The "Mystique" of this issue lay partly in the fact that each four-card $4.99 pack included a card which was covered with a peel-off coating, either a short-printed star card from the #1-100 base set, one of the short-printed Rookie (#101-150) or Stars (#151-160) cards or one of the inserts. The Rookie cards are serial numbered to 2,999 apiece, while the red-foil highlighted Stars cards are in an edition of 2,500 each. Fronts have metallic foil backgrounds, backs have a player portrait photo, biographical and career notes and stats.

		NM/M
Complete Set (160):		125.00
Common Player:		.20
Common SP (1-100):		.75
Common (101-150):		1.00
Production 2,999 Sets		
Common (151-160):		2.00
Production 2,500 Sets		
Pack (4):		3.00
Wax Box (24):		60.00
1	Ken Griffey Jr./SP	2.50
2	Livan Hernandez	.20
3	Jeff Kent	.20
4	Brian Jordan	.20
5	Kevin Young	.20
6	Vinny Castilla	.20
7	Orlando Hernandez/SP	.75
8	Bobby Abreu	.20
9	Vladimir Guerrero/SP	1.50
10	Chuck Knoblauch	.20
11	Nomar Garciaparra/SP	2.25
12	Jeff Bagwell	1.00
13	Todd Walker	.20
14	Johnny Damon	.45
15	Mike Caruso	.20
16	Cliff Floyd	.20
17	Andy Pettitte	.35
18	Cal Ripken Jr./SP	4.00
19	Brian Giles	.20
20	Robin Ventura	.20
21	Alex Gonzalez	.20
22	Randy Johnson	.75
23	Raul Mondesi	.20
24	Ken Caminiti	.20
25	Tom Glavine	.40
26	Derek Jeter/SP	4.00
27	Carlos Delgado	.50
28	Adrian Beltre	.35
29	Tino Martinez	.20
30	Todd Helton	1.00
31	Juan Gonzalez/SP	1.25
32	Henry Rodriguez	.20
33	Jim Thome	.65
34	Paul O'Neill	.20
35	Scott Rolen/SP	1.25
36	Rafael Palmeiro	.65
37	Will Clark	.25
38	Todd Hundley	.20
39	Andruw Jones/SP	1.50
40	Luis Rolando Arrojo	.20
41	Barry Larkin	.20
42	Tim Salmon	.25
43	Rondell White	.20
44	Curt Schilling	.40
45	Chipper Jones/SP	2.00
46	Jeromy Burnitz	.20
47	Mo Vaughn	.20
48	Tony Clark	.20
49	Fernando Tatis	.20
50	Dmitri Young	.20
51	Wade Boggs	1.50
52	Rickey Henderson	.75
53	Manny Ramirez/SP	1.50
54	Edgar Martinez	.20
55	Jason Giambi	.65
56	Jason Kendall	.20
57	Eric Karros	.20
58	Jose Canseco/SP	1.00
59	Shawn Green	.40
60	Ellis Burks	.20
61	Derek Bell	.20
62	Shannon Stewart	.20
63	Roger Clemens/SP	2.25
64	Sean Casey/SP	.75
65	Jose Offerman	.20
66	Sammy Sosa/SP	2.25
67	Frank Thomas/SP	1.50
68	Tony Gwynn/SP	2.00
69	Roberto Alomar	.35
70	Mark McGwire/SP	3.00
71	Troy Glaus	1.00
72	Ray Durham	.20
73	Jeff Cirillo	.20
74	Alex Rodriguez/SP	3.00
75	Jose Cruz Jr.	.20
76	Juan Encarnacion	.20
77	Mark Grace	.20
78	Barry Bonds/SP	4.00
79	Ivan Rodriguez/SP	1.25
80	Greg Vaughn	.20
81	Greg Maddux/SP	2.00
82	Albert Belle	.20
83	John Olerud	.20
84	Kenny Lofton	.20
85	Bernie Williams	.30
86	Matt Williams	.20
87	Ray Lankford	.20
88	Darin Erstad	.40
89	Ben Grieve	.20
90	Craig Biggio	.20
91	Dean Palmer	.20
92	Reggie Sanders	.20
93	Dante Bichette	.20
94	Pedro Martinez/SP	1.50
95	Larry Walker	.20
96	David Wells	.20
97	Travis Lee/SP	.75
98	Mike Piazza/SP	2.50
99	Mike Mussina	.45
100	Kevin Brown	.20
101	Ruben Mateo (Rookie)	1.00
102	Roberto Ramirez (Rookie)	1.00
103	Glen Barker **RC** (Rookie)	1.00
104	Clay Bellinger **RC** (Rookie)	1.00
105	Carlos Guillen (Rookie)	1.00
106	Scott Schoeneweis (Rookie)	1.00
107	Creighton Gubanich (Rookie)	1.00
108	Scott Williamson (Rookie)	1.00
109	Edwards Guzman **RC** (Rookie)	1.00
110	A.J. Burnett **RC** (Rookie)	4.00
111	Jeremy Giambi (Rookie)	1.00
112	Trot Nixon (Rookie)	1.50
113	J.D. Drew (Rookie)	3.00
114	Roy Halladay (Rookie)	1.50
115	Jose Macias **RC** (Rookie)	2.00
116	Corey Koskie (Rookie)	2.00
117	Ryan Rupe **RC** (Rookie)	1.50
118	Scott Hunter (Rookie)	1.00
119	Rob Fick (Rookie)	1.00
120	McKay Christensen (Rookie)	1.50
121	Carlos Febles (Rookie)	2.00
122	Gabe Kapler (Rookie)	1.50
123	Jeff Liefer (Rookie)	1.00
124	Warren Morris (Rookie)	1.00
125	Chris Pritchett (Rookie)	1.00
126	Torii Hunter (Rookie)	3.00
127	Armando Rios (Rookie)	1.00
128	Ricky Ledee (Rookie)	1.00
129	Kelly Dransfeldt **RC** (Rookie)	1.00
130	Jeff Zimmerman (Rookie)	1.50
131	Eric Chavez (Rookie)	2.00
132	Freddy Garcia (Rookie)	3.00
133	Jose Jimenez (Rookie)	1.00
134	Pat Burrell **RC** (Rookie)	20.00
135	Joe McEwing **RC** (Rookie)	1.50
136	Kris Benson (Rookie)	1.00
137	Joe Mays **RC** (Rookie)	2.00
138	Rafael Roque (Rookie)	1.00
139	Cristian Guzman (Rookie)	1.50
140	Michael Barrett (Rookie)	1.50
141	Doug Mientkiewicz (Rookie)	1.50
142	Jeff Weaver **RC** (Rookie)	4.00
143	Mike Lowell (Rookie)	1.50
144	Jason Phillips **RC** (Rookie)	2.00
145	Marlon Anderson (Rookie)	1.50
146	Brett Hinchliffe **RC** (Rookie)	1.00
147	Matt Clement (Rookie)	1.50
148	Terrence Long (Rookie)	1.00
149	Carlos Beltran (Rookie)	2.50
150	Preston Wilson (Rookie)	1.50
151	Ken Griffey Jr. (Stars)	2.00
152	Mark McGwire (Stars)	3.00
153	Sammy Sosa (Stars)	1.50
154	Mike Piazza (Stars)	2.00
155	Alex Rodriguez (Stars)	3.00
156	Nomar Garciaparra (Stars)	1.50
157	Cal Ripken Jr. (Stars)	4.00
158	Greg Maddux (Stars)	1.50
159	Derek Jeter (Stars)	4.00
160	Juan Gonzalez (Stars)	1.00
	Checklist Card	.10

Gold

The first 100 cards of the base set are paralleled in this insert which features gold-foil highlights on front. Gold versions are found in one of eight packs, on average.

	NM/M
Common Player:	1.00
Stars (1-100):	1.5X
Inserted 1:8	

Masterpiece

Each of the cards in Fleer Mystique was also produced in a unique Masterpiece version. The super-rarities are labeled on front "The Only 1 of 1 / Masterpiece."

	NM/M
Common Player:	50.00

Destiny

A silver holofoil background on front and a serial number within an edition of 999 each marks this insert set. Backs have another photo along with career highlights.

		NM/M
Complete Set (10):		35.00
Common Player:		2.00
Production 999 Sets		
1	Tony Gwynn	5.00
2	Juan Gonzalez	3.00
3	Scott Rolen	4.00
4	Nomar Garciaparra	6.00
5	Orlando Hernandez	2.00
6	Andruw Jones	4.00
7	Vladimir Guerrero	4.00
8	Darin Erstad	2.00
9	Manny Ramirez	4.00
10	Roger Clemens	6.00

Established

A plastic stock, red holofoil background and silver foil highlights complement the action photo of a top star in this insert set. Backs have another photo, some career highlights and a serial number from within an edition of 100 each.

		NM/M
Complete Set (10):		300.00
Common Player:		15.00
Production 100 Sets		
1	Ken Griffey Jr.	30.00
2	Derek Jeter	60.00
3	Chipper Jones	20.00
4	Greg Maddux	20.00
5	Mark McGwire	45.00
6	Mike Piazza	30.00
7	Cal Ripken Jr.	60.00
8	Alex Rodriguez	45.00
9	Sammy Sosa	25.00
10	Frank Thomas	15.00

Feel the Game

Swatches of various game-used equipment are featured in this insert series. Each card is hand-numbered from editions which range between 345 and 450.

	NM/M
Common Player:	10.00
Adrian Beltre/Shoe/430	15.00
J.D. Drew/Jsy/450	15.00
Juan Gonzalez/Bat Glove/415	
Tony Gwynn/Jsy/435	15.00
Kevin Millwood/Jsy/435	10.00
Alex Rodriguez/Bat Glove/345	30.00
Frank Thomas/Jsy/450	15.00

Fresh Ink

These inserts, found about one per 48 packs, have a white oval at bottom front containing an autograph of the player pictured. At bottom is a white panel with a hand-printed serial number from within each card's edition, which ranged from 140 to 1,000. Backs have a Fleer seal and statement of authenticity pertinent to the autograph. The unnumbered cards are listed here in alphabetical order.

	NM/M
Complete Set (26):	300.00
Common Player:	4.00
Inserted 1:48	
Roberto Alomar/500	10.00
Michael Barrett/1,000	6.00
Kris Benson/500	8.00
Micah Bowie/1,000	4.00
A.J. Burnett/500	10.00
Pat Burrell/500	15.00
Ken Caminiti/250	10.00
Jose Canseco/250	25.00
Sean Casey/1,000	8.00
Edgard Clemente/1,000	4.00
Bartolo Colon/500	8.00
J.D. Drew/400	15.00
Juan Encarnacion/1,000	4.00
Troy Glaus/400	15.00
Juan Gonzalez/250	15.00
Shawn Green/250	15.00
Tony Gwynn/250	30.00
Chipper Jones/500	30.00
Gabe Kapler/750	6.00
Barry Larkin/250	25.00
Doug Mientkiewicz/500	6.00
Alex Rodriguez/200	80.00
Scott Rolen/140	30.00
Fernando Tatis/750	4.00
Robin Ventura/500	6.00
Todd Walker/1,000	6.00

Prophetic

Blue holofoil with silver highlights is the graphic treatment found on this insert set of young stars. Each card is numbered on front from within an edition of 1,999. Backs have a portrait photo and a few words about the player.

		NM/M
Complete Set (10):		15.00
Common Player:		1.00
Production 1,999 Sets		
1	Eric Chavez	1.50
2	J.D. Drew	2.00
3	A.J. Burnett	1.00
4	Ben Grieve	1.00
5	Gabe Kapler	1.00
6	Todd Helton	2.50
7	Troy Glaus	4.00
8	Travis Lee	1.00
9	Pat Burrell	5.00
10	Kerry Wood	1.50

Diamond Skills Commemorative Sheet

In conjunction with its sponsorship of the Diamond Skills program, Fleer distributed this eight-player sheet to 7-14 year olds participating in the event. Participants could get a sheet by redeeming Fleer wrappers at a local card store. The 10" x 9" sheet features full size Fleer Tradition cards. At top is a list of 1997 Diamond Skills winners.

	NM/M
Complete Sheet:	3.00

National Convention Commemorative Set

In conjunction with its participation at the 20th National Sports Collectors Convention in Atlanta in July 1999 Fleer distributed this cello-wrapped commemorative set to persons purchasing VIP admission packages. The set includes a specially numbered (NC1) version of the Stan Musial card from '99 Fleer Tradition, three large-format (3-1/2" x 5") cards reproducing Musial Monumental Moments inserts,

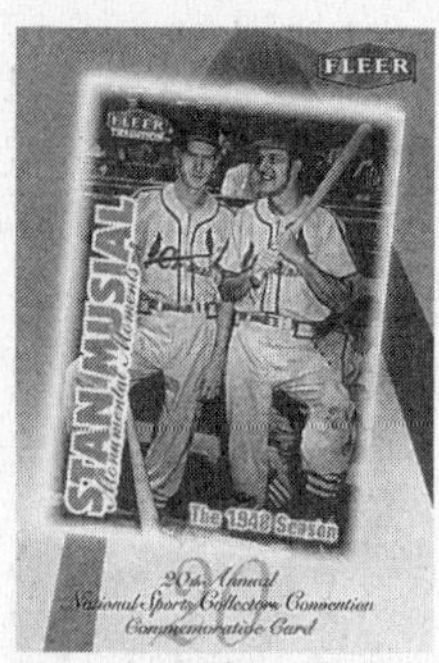

and an unnumbered header card. The Monumental Moments reproductions are printed on a red background with the famed St. Louis arch.

		NM/M
Complete Set (5):		10.00
Common Card:		2.00
NC1	Stan Musial (Fleer Tradition)	2.00
NC2	Stan Musial (Life in Donora - Monumental Moment)	2.00
NC3	Stan Musial (The 1948 Season - Monumental Moment)	2.00
NC4	Stan Musial (Hall of Fame - Monumental Season)	2.00
	Header Card	.25

2000 Fleer Focus

The 250-card base set has two versions for the Prospects subset card numbers 226-250. The portrait versions are serial numbered from 1-999, while the remaining serial numbered from 1,000 to 3,999 capture an action shot. The base set design has a white border with gold foil stamping. Card backs have complete year-by-year statistics along with a career note and small photo.

		NM/M
Complete Set (250):		100.00
Common Player:		.15
Common Prospect (226-250):		4.00
Production 2,999 Sets		
Common Portrait (226-250):		8.00
Portraits:		2X
Production 999 Sets		
Pack:		2.00
Wax Box (24):		35.00
1	Nomar Garciaparra	1.25
2	Adrian Beltre	.35
3	Miguel Tejada	.35
4	Joe Randa	.15
5	Larry Walker	.15
6	Jeff Weaver	.15
7	Jay Bell	.15
8	Ivan Rodriguez	.50
9	Edgar Martinez	.15
10	Desi Relaford	.15
11	Derek Jeter	2.50
12	Delino DeShields	.15
13	Craig Biggio	.15
14	Chuck Knoblauch	.15
15	Chuck Finley	.15
16	Brett Tomko	.15
17	Bobby Higginson	.15
18	Pedro Martinez	.75
19	Troy O"Leary	.15
20	Rickey Henderson	.75
21	Robb Nen	.15
22	Rolando Arrojo	.15
23	Rondell White	.15
24	Royce Clayton	.15
25	Rusty Greer	.15
26	Stan Spencer	.15
27	Steve Finley	.15
28	Tom Goodwin	.15
29	Troy Percival	.15
30	Wilton Guerrero	.15
31	Roberto Alomar	.30
32	Mike Hampton	.15
33	Michael Barrett	.15
34	Curt Schilling	.40
35	Bill Mueller	.15
36	Bernie Williams	.30
37	John Smoltz	.15
38	B.J. Surhoff	.15
39	Pete Harnisch	.15
40	Juan Encarnacion	.15
41	Derrek Lee	.15
42	Jeff Shaw	.15
43	David Cone	.15
44	Jason Christiansen	.15
45	Jeff Kent	.15
46	Randy Johnson	.75
47	Todd Walker	.15
48	Jose Lima	.15
49	Jason Giambi	.50
50	Ken Griffey Jr.	1.50
51	Bartolo Colon	.15
52	Mike Lieberthal	.15
53	Shane Reynolds	.15
54	Travis Lee	.15
55	Travis Fryman	.15
56	John Valentin	.15
57	Joey Hamilton	.15
58	Jay Buhner	.15
59	Brad Radke	.15
60	A.J. Burnett	.15
61	Roy Halladay	.25
62	Raul Mondesi	.15
63	Matt Mantei	.15
64	Mark Grace	.15
65	David Justice	.15
66	Billy Wagner	.15
67	Eric Milton	.15
68	Eric Chavez	.25
69	Doug Glanville	.15
70	Ray Durham	.15
71	Mike Sirotka	.15
72	Greg Vaughn	.15
73	Brian Jordan	.15
74	Alex Gonzalez	.15
75	Alex Rodriguez	2.00
76	David Nilsson	.15
77	Robin Ventura	.15
78	Kevin Young	.15
79	Wilson Alvarez	.15
80	Matt Williams	.15
81	Ismael Valdes	.15
82	Kenny Lofton	.15
83	Carlos Beltran	.45
84	Doug Mientkiewicz	.15
85	Wally Joyner	.15
86	J.D. Drew	.35
87	Carlos Delgado	.50
88	Tony Womack	.15
89	Eric Young	.15
90	Manny Ramirez	.75
91	Johnny Damon	.15
92	Torii Hunter	.25
93	Kenny Rogers	.15
94	Trevor Hoffman	.15
95	John Wetteland	.15
96	Ray Lankford	.15
97	Tom Glavine	.30
98	Carlos Lee	.15
99	Richie Sexson	.15
100	Carlos Febles	.15
101	Chad Allen	.15
102	Sterling Hitchcock	.15
103	Joe McEwing	.15
104	Justin Thompson	.15
105	Jim Edmonds	.15
106	Kerry Wood	.40
107	Jim Thome	.65
108	Jeremy Giambi	.15
109	Mike Piazza	1.50
110	Darryl Kile	.15
111	Darin Erstad	.30
112	Kyle Farnsworth	.15
113	Omar Vizquel	.15
114	Orber Moreno	.15
115	Al Leiter	.15
116	John Olerud	.15
117	Aaron Sele	.15
118	Chipper Jones	1.00
119	Paul Konerko	.25
120	Chris Singleton	.15
121	Fernando Vina	.15
122	Andy Ashby	.15
123	Eli Marrero	.15
124	Edgar Renteria	.15
125	Roberto Hernandez	.15
126	Andruw Jones	.75
127	Magglio Ordonez	.25
128	Bob Wickman	.15
129	Tony Gwynn	1.00
130	Mark McGwire	2.00
131	Albert Belle	.15
132	Pokey Reese	.15
133	Tony Clark	.15
134	Jeff Bagwell	.75
135	Mark Grudzielanek	.15
136	Dustin Hermanson	.15
137	Reggie Sanders	.15
138	Ryan Rupe	.15
139	Kevin Millwood	.15
140	Bret Saberhagen	.15
141	Juan Guzman	.15
142	Alex Gonzalez	.15
143	Gary Sheffield	.30
144	Roger Clemens	1.25
145	Ben Grieve	.15
146	Bobby Abreu	.15
147	Brian Giles	.15
148	Quinton McCracken	.15
149	Freddy Garcia	.15
150	Erubiel Durazo	.15
151	Sidney Ponson	.15
152	Scott Williamson	.15
153	Ken Caminiti	.15
154	Vladimir Guerrero	.75
155	Andy Pettitte	.25
156	Edwards Guzman	.15
157	Shannon Stewart	.15
158	Greg Maddux	1.00
159	Mike Stanley	.15
160	Sean Casey	.25
161	Cliff Floyd	.15
162	Devon White	.15
163	Scott Brosius	.15
164	Marlon Anderson	.15
165	Jason Kendall	.15
166	Ryan Klesko	.15
167	Sammy Sosa	1.25
168	Frank Thomas	.75
169	Geoff Jenkins	.15
170	Jason Schmidt	.15
171	Dan Wilson	.15
172	Jose Canseco	.40
173	Troy Glaus	.75
174	Mariano Rivera	.20
175	Scott Rolen	.65
176	J.T. Snow	.15
177	Rafael Palmeiro	.65
178	A.J. Hinch	.15
179	Jose Offerman	.15
180	Jeff Cirillo	.15
181	Dean Palmer	.15
182	Jose Rosado	.15
183	Armando Benitez	.15
184	Brady Anderson	.15
185	Cal Ripken Jr.	2.50
186	Barry Larkin	.15
187	Damion Easley	.15
188	Moises Alou	.15
189	Todd Hundley	.15
190	Tim Hudson	.25
191	Livan Hernandez	.15
192	Fred McGriff	.15
193	Orlando Hernandez	.25
194	Tim Salmon	.20
195	Mike Mussina	.40
196	Todd Helton	.75
197	Juan Gonzalez	.50
198	Kevin Brown	.15
199	Ugueth Urbina	.15
200	Matt Stairs	.15
201	Shawn Estes	.15
202	Gabe Kapler	.15
203	Javy Lopez	.15
204	Henry Rodriguez	.15
205	Dante Bichette	.15
206	Jeromy Burnitz	.15
207	Todd Zeile	.15
208	Rico Brogna	.15
209	Warren Morris	.15
210	David Segui	.15
211	Vinny Castilla	.15
212	Mo Vaughn	.15
213	Charles Johnson	.15
214	Neifi Perez	.15
215	Shawn Green	.40
216	Carl Pavano	.15
217	Tino Martinez	.15
218	Barry Bonds	2.50
219	David Wells	.15
220	Paul O'Neill	.15
221	Masato Yoshii	.15
222	Kris Benson	.15
223	Fernando Tatis	.15
224	Lee Stevens	.15
225	Jose Cruz Jr.	.15
226	Rick Ankiel (Prospect)	4.00
227	Matt Riley (Prospect)	4.00
228	Norm Hutchins (Prospect)	4.00
229	Ruben Mateo (Prospect)	4.00
230	Ben Petrick (Prospect)	4.00
231	Mario Encarnacion (Prospect)	4.00
232	Nick Johnson (Prospect)	6.00
233	Adam Piatt (Prospect)	6.00
234	Mike Darr (Prospect)	4.00
235	Chad Hermansen (Prospect)	4.00
236	Wily Pena (Prospect)	6.00
237	Octavio Dotel (Prospect)	4.00
238	Vernon Wells (Prospect)	6.00
239	Daryle Ward (Prospect)	4.00
240	Adam Kennedy (Prospect)	4.00
241	Angel Pena (Prospect)	4.00
242	Lance Berkman (Prospect)	6.00
243	Gabe Molina (Prospect)	4.00
244	Steve Lomasney (Prospect)	4.00
245	Jacob Cruz (Prospect)	4.00
246	Mark Quinn (Prospect)	4.00
247	Eric Munson (Prospect)	4.00
248	Alfonso Soriano (Prospect)	6.00
249	Kip Wells (Prospect)	4.00
250	Josh Beckett (Prospect)	6.00
	Checklist #171	.05
	Checklist #172-25, Inserts	.05
	Checklist Inserts	.05

Green

Green, rather than gold, ink is used on front for the player name, team and position to distinguish this parallel insert set. On back, each card is numbered from within an edition of 300 each.

	NM/M
Common Player:	3.00
Stars:	5-10X
Yng Stars & RC's (226-250):	1-2X
Production 300 Sets	

Masterpiece

Each of the cards in Fleer Focus was issued in a parallel edition of just one piece each. Fronts of Masterpiece 1/1s have purple metallic ink, instead of gold, for the player identification. On back, there is a notation "The Only 1 of 1 Masterpiece" along with an "M" suffix to the card number. An error version has all the attributes of the true Masterpiece, but lacks the "Only 1 . . ." notation on back (see 2000 Fleer Focus Masterpiece Errors).

	NM/M
Common Player:	100.00

Masterpiece Errors

Thousands of collectors' hopes were crushed when it was determined that an unknown number of uncompleted Masterpiece 1-of-1 cards were erroneously inserted in Focus foil packs. Like the true Masterpiece cards, the fronts of the error cards have the player name, team and position at bottom front in purple, rather than gold foil. On back, the cards even have the "M" suffix to the card number at lower-right. Unfortunately, these do not have the foil-stamped "The Only 1 of 1 Masterpiece" notation on back; greatly reducing the value.

		NM/M
Complete Set (25):		250.00
Common Player:		4.00
50M	Ken Griffey Jr.	100.00
202M	Gabe Kapler	8.00
203M	Javy Lopez	6.00
204M	Henry Rodriguez	4.00
205M	Dante Bichette	5.00
206M	Jeromy Burnitz	5.00
207M	Todd Zeile	4.00
208M	Rico Brogna	4.00
209M	Warren Morris	4.00
210M	David Segui	4.00
211M	Vinny Castilla	5.00
212M	Mo Vaughn	6.00
213M	Charles Johnson	5.00
214M	Neifi Perez	5.00
215M	Shawn Green	20.00
216M	Carl Pavano	4.00
217M	Tino Martinez	5.00
218M	Barry Bonds	30.00
219M	David Wells	8.00
220M	Paul O'Neill	6.00
221M	Masato Yoshii	5.00
222M	Kris Benson	8.00
223M	Fernando Tatis	6.00
224M	Lee Stevens	4.00
225M	Jose Cruz Jr.	6.00

Club 3000

These inserts are die-cut around the numbers 3,000 and features three players who either have 3,000 hits or strikeouts, this set spotlights Stan Musial, Steve Carlton and Paul Molitor. These are seeded 1:36 packs.

		NM/M
Complete Set (3):		4.00
Common Player:		1.50
(1)	Steve Carlton	1.50
(2)	Paul Molitor	1.50
(3)	Stan Musial	1.50

Club 3000 Memorabilia

Five tiers featuring memorabilia from game-used bats, caps etc... make up this hand numbered set. Besides a bat and cap insert others include jersey, bat and jersey combo and a bat, jersey and cap combo.

	NM/M
Steve Carlton/Bat/325	25.00
Steve Carlton/Hat/65	75.00
Steve Carlton/Jsy/750	20.00
Steve Carlton/Bat, Hat, Jsy/25	200.00
Paul Molitor/Bat/355	30.00
Paul Molitor/Hat/65	85.00
Paul Molitor/Jsy/975	20.00
Paul Molitor/Bat, Jsy/100	60.00
Stan Musial/Bat/325	50.00
Stan Musial/Hat/65	125.00
Stan Musial/Jsy/975	35.00
Stan Musial/Bat, Jsy/100	80.00

Feel the Game

This 10-card set offers pieces of player-worn jersey from some of baseball's biggest stars embedded into the card front. These were seeded 1:288 packs.

	NM/M
Common Player:	5.00
Inserted 1:288	
Adrian Beltre	7.50
Tom Glavine	10.00
Vladimir Guerrero	15.00
Randy Johnson	15.00
Javy Lopez	5.00
Alex Rodriguez	30.00
Scott Rolen	10.00
Cal Ripken Jr.	40.00
Tim Salmon	6.00
Miguel Tejada	10.00

Focal Points

This 15-card set has silver foil etching around the border and silver foil stamping. These were seeded 1:6 packs and are numbered with an "F" suffix on the card back.

		NM/M
Complete Set (15):		15.00
Common Player:		.75
Inserted 1:6		
1	Mark McGwire	2.50
2	Tony Gwynn	1.00
3	Nomar Garciaparra	2.00
4	Juan Gonzalez	.75
5	Jeff Bagwell	.75
6	Chipper Jones	1.00
7	Cal Ripken Jr.	3.00
8	Alex Rodriguez	2.50
9	Scott Rolen	.75
10	Vladimir Guerrero	.75
11	Mike Piazza	1.50
12	Frank Thomas	.75
13	Ken Griffey Jr.	1.50
14	Sammy Sosa	1.50
15	Derek Jeter	3.00

Focus Pocus

This 10-card set has a silver prismatic, holofoil background with silver foil stamping. These were seeded 1:14 packs and are numbered with an "FP" suffix.

		NM/M
Complete Set (10):		12.00
Common Player:		1.00
Inserted 1:14		
1	Cal Ripken Jr.	3.00
2	Tony Gwynn	1.50
3	Nomar Garciaparra	2.00
4	Juan Gonzalez	1.00
5	Mike Piazza	2.00
6	Mark McGwire	2.50
7	Chipper Jones	1.50
8	Ken Griffey Jr.	2.00
9	Derek Jeter	3.00
10	Alex Rodriguez	2.50

Fresh Ink

These autographed inserts are seeded 1:96 packs.

NM/M
Common Player: 5.00
Inserted 1:96
Chad Allen 5.00
Michael Barrett 5.00
Josh Beckett 30.00
Rob Bell 5.00
Adrian Beltre 15.00
Milton Bradley 8.00
Rico Brogna 5.00
Mike Cameron 8.00
Eric Chavez 15.00
Bruce Chen 5.00
Johnny Damon 20.00
Ben Davis 5.00
J.D. Drew 15.00
Erubiel Durazo 10.00
Jeremy Giambi 6.00
Jason Giambi 25.00
Doug Glanville 6.00
Troy Glaus 25.00
Shawn Green 20.00
Mike Hampton 10.00
Tim Hudson 15.00
John Jaha 5.00
Derek Jeter 150.00
D'Angelo Jimenez 5.00
Nick Johnson 8.00
Andruw Jones 20.00
Jason Kendall 10.00
Adam Kennedy 6.00
Mike Lieberthal 8.00
Edgar Martinez 15.00
Aaron McNeal 5.00
Kevin Millwood 10.00
Mike Mussina 30.00
Magglio Ordonez 15.00
Eric Owens 5.00
Rafael Palmeiro 20.00
Wily Pena 15.00
Adam Piatt 8.00
Cal Ripken Jr. 100.00
Alex Rodriguez 65.00
Scott Rolen 20.00
Tim Salmon 15.00
Chris Singleton 5.00
Mike Sweeney 10.00
Jose Vidro 8.00
Rondell White 8.00
Jaret Wright 5.00

Future Vision

This 15-card set highlights the top prospects over a holo-foiled background with red foil etching and stamping. These were seeded 1:9 packs and are numbered with an "FV" suffix.

NM/M
Complete Set (15): 8.00
Common Player: .40
Inserted 1:9
1 Rick Ankiel .40
2 Matt Riley .40
3 Ruben Mateo .40
4 Ben Petrick .40
5 Mario Encarnacion .40
6 Octavio Dotel .40
7 Vernon Wells .65
8 Adam Kennedy .40
9 Lance Berkman .40
10 Chad Hermansen .40
11 Mark Quinn .40
12 Eric Munson .40
13 Alfonso Soriano 2.00
14 Kip Wells .40
15 Josh Beckett .75

2000 Fleer Gamers

The 120-card base set has silver foil etching down the left portion of the card with vertical stripes running down the right portion of the card front. The card back has career statistical totals as well as a small photo. Two short-printed subsets also make up the 120-card set. Next Gamers (91-110) are seeded 1:3 packs and Fame Game (111-120) are seeded 1:8 packs.

NM/M
Complete Set (120): 50.00
Common Player (1-90): .15
Common (91-110): 1.00
Inserted 1:3
Common (111-120): 1.50
Inserted 1:8
Pack: 2.00
Wax Box: 35.00
1 Cal Ripken Jr. 2.00
2 Derek Jeter 2.00
3 Alex Rodriguez 1.50
4 Alex Gonzalez .15
5 Nomar Garciaparra 1.25
6 Brian Giles .15
7 Chris Singleton .15
8 Kevin Brown .15
9 J.D. Drew .25
10 Raul Mondesi .15
11 Sammy Sosa 1.25
12 Carlos Beltran .50
13 Eric Chavez .25
14 Gabe Kapler .15
15 Tim Salmon .25
16 Manny Ramirez .75
17 Orlando Hernandez .15
18 Jeff Kent .15
19 Juan Gonzalez .75
20 Moises Alou .15
21 Jason Giambi .50
22 Ivan Rodriguez .60
23 Geoff Jenkins .15
24 Ken Griffey Jr. 1.25
25 Mark McGwire 1.50
26 Jose Canseco .40
27 Roberto Alomar .40
28 Craig Biggio .15
29 Scott Rolen .65
30 Vinny Castilla .15
31 Greg Maddux 1.00
32 Pedro J. Martinez .75
33 Mike Piazza 1.25
34 Albert Belle .25
35 Frank Thomas .75
36 Bobby Abreu .15
37 Edgar Martinez .15
38 Pokey Reese .15
39 Preston Wilson .15
40 Mike Lieberthal .15
41 Andruw Jones .75
42 Damion Easley .15
43 Mike Cameron .15
44 Todd Walker .15
45 Jason Kendall .15
46 Sean Casey .25
47 Corey Koskie .15
48 Warren Morris .15
49 Andres Galarraga .15
50 Dean Palmer .15
51 Jose Vidro .15
52 Brian Jordan .15
53 Tony Clark .15
54 Vladimir Guerrero .75
55 Mo Vaughn .15
56 Richie Sexson .15
57 Tino Martinez .15
58 Eric Owens .15
59 Matt Williams .15
60 Omar Vizquel .15
61 Rickey Henderson .75
62 J.T. Snow .15
63 Mark Grace .25
64 Carlos Febles .15
65 Paul O'Neill .15
66 Randy Johnson .75
67 Kenny Lofton .15
68 Roger Cedeno .15
69 Shawn Green .35
70 Chipper Jones 1.00
71 Jeff Cirillo .15
72 Robin Ventura .15
73 Paul Konerko .15
74 Jeromy Burnitz .15
75 Ben Grieve .15
76 Troy Glaus .75
77 Jim Thome .15
78 Bernie Williams .25
79 Barry Bonds 2.00
80 Ray Durham .15
81 Adrian Beltre .15
82 Ray Lankford .15
83 Carlos Delgado .50
84 Erubiel Durazo .15
85 Larry Walker .15
86 Edgardo Alfonzo .15
87 Rafael Palmeiro .65
88 Magglio Ordonez .25
89 Jeff Bagwell .75
90 Tony Gwynn 1.00
91 Norm Hutchins (Next Gamers) 1.00
92 Derrick Turnbow **RC** (Next Gamers) 1.50
93 Matt Riley (Next Gamers) 1.00
94 David Eckstein (Next Gamers) 1.00
95 Dernell Stenson (Next Gamers) 1.00
96 Joe Crede (Next Gamers) 1.00
97 Ben Petrick (Next Gamers) 1.00
98 Eric Munson (Next Gamers) 1.00
99 Pablo Ozuna (Next Gamers) 1.00
100 Josh Beckett (Next Gamers) 3.00
101 Aaron McNeal **RC** (Next Gamers) 1.50
102 Milton Bradley (Next Gamers) 1.50
103 Alex Escobar (Next Gamers) 1.50
104 Alfonso Soriano (Next Gamers) 4.00
105 Wily Pena (Next Gamers) 1.50
106 Nick Johnson (Next Gamers) 1.50
107 Adam Piatt (Next Gamers) 1.00
108 Pat Burrell (Next Gamers) 2.00
109 Rick Ankiel (Next Gamers) 1.00
110 Vernon Wells (Next Gamers) 2.00
111 Alex Rodriguez (Fame Game) 3.00
112 Cal Ripken Jr. (Fame Game) 4.00
113 Mark McGwire (Fame Game) 3.00
114 Ken Griffey Jr. (Fame Game) 2.00
115 Mike Piazza (Fame Game) 2.00
116 Nomar Garciaparra (Fame Game) 3.00
117 Derek Jeter (Fame Game) 4.00
118 Chipper Jones (Fame Game) 1.50
119 Sammy Sosa (Fame Game) 2.00
120 Tony Gwynn (Fame Game) 1.50

Extra

A parallel to the 120-card base set, the gold foiled card front and "Extra" written down the right portion of the card can be used to differentiate these from regular cards. "Extra" is also written underneath the card number on the back as well. Extras 1-90 are seeded 1:24 packs and numbers 91-120 are seeded 1:36 packs.

Stars (1-90): 5-10X
Inserted 1:24
Next Gamers (91-110): 1-2X
Inserted 1:36
Fame Game (110-120): 1-2X
Inserted 1:36

Cal to Greatness

This 15-card tribute insert set to baseball's "Iron Man" is broken into three tiers. Cards 1-5 are seeded 1:9 packs, cards 6-10 are found 1:25 packs and cards 11-15 are inserted 1:144 packs. Card backs are numbered with a "C" suffix.

NM/M
Complete Set (15): 100.00
Common Ripken (1-5): 3.00
Inserted 1:9
Common Ripken (6-10): 6.00
Inserted 1:25
Common Ripken (11-15): 20.00
Inserted 1:144
1 Cal Ripken Jr. 3.00
2 Cal Ripken Jr. 3.00
3 Cal Ripken Jr. 3.00
4 Cal Ripken Jr. 3.00
5 Cal Ripken Jr. 3.00
6 Cal Ripken Jr. 6.00
7 Cal Ripken Jr. 6.00
8 Cal Ripken Jr. 6.00
9 Cal Ripken Jr. 6.00
10 Cal Ripken Jr. 6.00
11 Cal Ripken Jr. 20.00
12 Cal Ripken Jr. 20.00
13 Cal Ripken Jr. 20.00
14 Cal Ripken Jr. 20.00
15 Cal Ripken Jr. 20.00

Change the Game

This 15-card set has a holofoiled front with Change the Game printed behind the player image. Seeded 1:24 packs, card backs are numbered with a "CG" suffix.

NM/M
Complete Set (15): 50.00
Common Player: 1.50
Inserted 1:24
1 Alex Rodriguez 6.00
2 Cal Ripken Jr. 7.50
3 Chipper Jones 3.00
4 Derek Jeter 7.50
5 Ken Griffey Jr. 4.00
6 Mark McGwire 6.00
7 Mike Piazza 4.00
8 Nomar Garciaparra 4.00
9 Sammy Sosa 4.00
10 Tony Gwynn 3.00
11 Ivan Rodriguez 1.50
12 Pedro Martinez 2.00
13 Juan Gonzalez 2.00
14 Vladimir Guerrero 2.00
15 Manny Ramirez 2.00

Determined

This 15-card set has a holo-foiled front with two player images on the card front. The second player photo is smaller than the primary

image and is a close-up shot. Card backs are numbered with a "D" suffix and are seeded 1:12 packs.

NM/M
Complete Set (15): 25.00
Common Player: .50
Inserted 1:12
1 Nomar Garciaparra 2.50
2 Chipper Jones 2.00
3 Derek Jeter 4.00
4 Mike Piazza 2.50
5 Jeff Bagwell 1.00
6 Mark McGwire 3.00
7 Greg Maddux 2.00
8 Sammy Sosa 2.50
9 Ken Griffey Jr. 2.50
10 Alex Rodriguez 3.00
11 Tony Gwynn 2.00
12 Cal Ripken Jr. 4.00
13 Barry Bonds 4.00
14 Juan Gonzalez 1.00
15 Sean Casey .50

Lumber

Seeded 1:36 packs, these inserts have a piece of game-used bat embedded into the card front and are numbered with an "GL" suffix

NM/M
Common Player: 5.00
Inserted 1:36
1 Alex Rodriguez 30.00
2 Carlos Delgado 10.00
3 Jose Vidro 5.00
4 Carlos Febles 5.00
5 J.D. Drew 7.50
6 Mike Cameron 5.00
7 Derek Jeter 40.00
8 Eric Chavez 6.00
9 Cal Ripken Jr. 40.00
10 Gabe Kapler 5.00
11 Damion Easley 5.00
12 Frank Thomas 15.00
13 Chris Singleton 5.00
14 Norm Hutchins 5.00
15 Pokey Reese 5.00
16 Rafael Palmeiro 12.00
17 Ray Durham 5.00
18 Ray Lankford 5.00
19 Roger Cedeno 5.00
20 Shawn Green 6.00
21 Wade Boggs 20.00
22 Roberto Alomar 7.50
23 Moises Alou 5.00
24 Adrian Beltre 6.00
25 Barry Bonds 40.00
26 Jason Giambi 10.00
27 Jason Kendall 5.00
28 Paul Konerko 5.00
29 Mike Lieberthal 5.00
30 Edgar Martinez 5.00
31 Raul Mondesi 5.00
32 Scott Rolen 12.00
33 Alfonso Soriano 10.00
34 Ivan Rodriguez 10.00
35 Magglio Ordonez 7.50
36 Chipper Jones 20.00
37 Sean Casey 6.00
38 Edgardo Alfonzo 5.00
39 Robin Ventura 5.00
40 Bernie Williams 6.00
41 Vladimir Guerrero 15.00
42 Tony Clark 5.00
43 Carlos Beltran 10.00
44 Warren Morris 5.00
45 Jim Thome 5.00
46 Jeromy Burnitz 5.00
47 Matt Williams 5.00
48 Erubiel Durazo 5.00

Lumber Autograph

Twelve players also signed a limited number of their Lumber inserts. The number signed

by each player is listed after the player name. These were seeded 1:287 packs.

NM/M
Common Player: 15.00
Inserted 1:287
1 Derek Jeter 150.00
2 Eric Chavez 20.00
3 Rafael Palmeiro 40.00
4 Shawn Green 35.00
5 Roberto Alomar 45.00
6 Paul Konerko 15.00
7 Sean Casey 15.00
8 Alex Rodriguez 80.00
9 Robin Ventura 20.00
10 Erubiel Durazo 15.00
11 Tony Clark 15.00
12 Alfonso Soriano 60.00

2000 Fleer Greats of the Game

The base set consists of 107-cards of retired stars. Card fronts have a brown border with "Fleer Greats of the Game" stamped in silver foil. Backs have a small photo along with complete career statistics and a brief career highlight.

NM/M
Complete Set (108): 50.00
Common Player: .50
Pack (6): 10.00
Wax Box (24): 200.00
1 Mickey Mantle 8.00
2 Gil Hodges 1.00
3 Monte Irvin 1.00
4 Satchel Paige 2.50
5 Roy Campanella 2.00
6 Richie Ashburn 1.00
7 Roger Maris 3.00
8 Ozzie Smith 2.00
9 Reggie Jackson 2.50
10 Eddie Mathews 2.50
11 Dave Righetti .50
12 Dave Winfield 1.00
13 Lou Whitaker .50
14 Phil Garner .50
15 Ron Cey .50
16 Brooks Robinson 2.50
17 Bruce Sutter .50
18 Dave Parker .50
19 Johnny Bench 2.50
20 Fernando Valenzuela .50
21 George Brett 4.00
22 Paul Molitor 2.00
23 Hoyt Wilhelm .50
24 Luis Aparicio .50
25 Frank White .50
26 Herb Score .50
27 Kirk Gibson .50
28 Mike Schmidt 3.00
29 Don Baylor .50
30 Joe Pepitone .50
31 Hal McRae .50
32 Lee Smith .50
33 Nolan Ryan 7.00
33 Nolan Ryan/OPS 5.00
34 Bill Mazeroski .75
35 Bobby Doerr .50
36 Duke Snider 1.00
37 Dick Groat .50
38 Larry Doby .50
39 Kirby Puckett 2.00
40 Steve Carlton 1.00
41 Dennis Eckersley .50
42 Jim Bunning .50
43 Ron Guidry .50
44 Alan Trammell 1.00
45 Bob Feller 1.50
46 Dave Concepcion .50
47 Dwight Evans .50
48 Enos Slaughter .50
49 Tom Seaver 2.50

50 Tony Oliva 1.00
51 Mel Stottlemyre .50
52 Tommy John .50
53 Willie McCovey 1.00
54 Red Schoendienst .50
55 Gorman Thomas .50
56 Ralph Kiner 1.00
57 Robin Yount 2.00
58 Andre Dawson 1.00
59 Al Kaline 2.50
60 Dom DiMaggio .50
61 Juan Marichal 1.00
62 Jack Morris .50
63 Warren Spahn 1.50
64 Preacher Roe .50
65 Darrell Evans .50
66 Jim Bouton .50
67 Rocky Colavito .75
68 Bob Gibson 1.50
69 Whitey Ford 1.50
70 Moose Skowron .50
71 Boog Powell 1.00
72 Al Lopez .50
73 Lou Brock 1.00
74 Mickey Lolich .50
75 Rod Carew 2.00
76 Bob Lemon .50
77 Frank Howard .50
78 Phil Rizzuto 1.50
79 Carl Yastrzemski 2.00
80 Rico Carty .50
81 Jim Kaat .50
82 Bert Blyleven .50
83 George Kell .50
84 Jim Palmer 1.00
85 Maury Wills 1.00
86 Jim Rice .50
87 Joe Carter .50
88 Clete Boyer .50
89 Yogi Berra 2.00
90 Cecil Cooper .50
91 Davey Johnson .50
92 Lou Boudreau .50
93 Orlando Cepeda 1.00
94 Tommy Henrich .50
95 Hank Bauer .50
96 Don Larsen 1.50
97 Vida Blue 1.00
98 Ben Oglivie .50
99 Don Mattingly 5.00
100 Dale Murphy 1.00
101 Ferguson Jenkins 1.00
102 Bobby Bonds .75
103 Dick Allen .50
104 Stan Musial 3.00
105 Gaylord Perry .50
106 Willie Randolph .50
107 Willie Stargell 1.50
108 Checklist .50

Autographs

Seeded in every six packs, Autographs feature the signature on the bottom half of the card front in black Sharpie. The autographed set features 89 retired players. Some cards were issued in considerably lower quantities than others, as noted in the checklist.

NM/M
Common Player: 10.00
Inserted 1:6
Luis Aparicio 20.00
Hank Bauer 10.00
Don Baylor 20.00
Johnny Bench 180.00
Yogi Berra 150.00
Vida Blue 20.00
Bert Blyleven 10.00
Bobby Bonds 10.00
Lou Boudreau 75.00
Jim Bouton 20.00
Clete Boyer 15.00
George Brett (275 or less) 180.00
Lou Brock 20.00
Jim Bunning 30.00
Rod Carew 40.00
Steve Carlton 20.00
Joe Carter/SP 75.00
Orlando Cepeda 15.00
Ron Cey 15.00
Rocky Colavito 30.00
Dave Concepcion (Black autograph.) 15.00
Dave Concepcion (Red autograph.) 15.00
Cecil Cooper 10.00
Andre Dawson 15.00
Dom DiMaggio 75.00
Bobby Doerr 15.00
Darrell Evans 15.00
Bob Feller 20.00
Whitey Ford (300 or less) 100.00
Phil Garner 10.00
Bob Gibson 25.00
Kirk Gibson 20.00
Dick Groat 10.00
Ron Guidry 20.00
Tommy Henrich (300 or less) 100.00
Frank Howard 10.00
Reggie Jackson (250 or less) 120.00
Ferguson Jenkins 15.00
Tommy John 10.00
Davey Johnson 10.00
Jim Kaat 15.00
Al Kaline 35.00
George Kell 15.00
Ralph Kiner 20.00
Don Larsen 25.00
Mickey Lolich 10.00
Juan Marichal 40.00
Eddie Mathews 80.00
Don Mattingly (300 or less) 250.00
Bill Mazeroski 20.00
Willie McCovey 80.00
Hal McRae 10.00
Paul Molitor 40.00
Jack Morris 10.00
Dale Murphy 35.00
Stan Musial 100.00
Ben Oglivie 10.00
Tony Oliva 15.00
Jim Palmer/SP 80.00
Dave Parker 15.00
Joe Pepitone 10.00
Gaylord Perry 15.00
Boog Powell 15.00
Kirby Puckett (200 or less) 120.00
Willie Randolph 15.00
Jim Rice 15.00
Dave Righetti 10.00
Phil Rizzuto (200 or less) 140.00
Brooks Robinson 30.00
Preacher Roe 15.00
Nolan Ryan 150.00
Mike Schmidt (175 or less) 250.00
Red Schoendienst 15.00
Herb Score 25.00
Tom Seaver 75.00
Moose Skowron 15.00
Enos Slaughter 20.00
Lee Smith 10.00
Ozzie Smith/SP 150.00
Duke Snider/SP 140.00
Warren Spahn/SP 100.00
Bruce Sutter 12.50
Gorman Thomas 10.00
Alan Trammell 20.00
Frank White 10.00
Hoyt Wilhelm 15.00
Maury Wills 15.00
Dave Winfield 150.00
Carl Yastrzemski 60.00
Robin Yount/SP 125.00

Memorable Moments Autograph

NM/M
Common Player: 60.00
1 Ron Guidry/78 75.00
2 Nolan Ryan/99 300.00
3 Herb Score/55 40.00
4 Tom Seaver/69 180.00

Retrospection

The 15-card Retrospection insert set highlights some of the all-time greats with a design borrowed from 1960 Fleer. Former greats including Stan Musial and Al Kaline are featured. They were seeded 1:6 packs.

NM/M
Complete Set (15): 75.00
Common Player: 4.00
Inserted 1:6
1 Rod Carew 4.00
2 Stan Musial 8.00
3 Nolan Ryan 15.00
4 Tom Seaver 6.00
5 Brooks Robinson 5.00
6 Al Kaline 6.00
7 Mike Schmidt 10.00
8 Thurman Munson 8.00
9 Steve Carlton 4.00
10 Roger Maris 8.00
11 Duke Snider 5.00
12 Yogi Berra 6.00
13 Carl Yastrzemski 5.00
14 Reggie Jackson 6.00
15 Johnny Bench 8.00

Yankees Clippings

This 15-card memorabilia insert features an actual piece of New York Yankee uniform worn by former stars. The jersey swatch is formed in the shape of the interlocking "NY" logo and are seeded 1:48 packs.

NM/M
Common Player: 20.00
Inserted 1:48
1 Mickey Mantle 200.00
2 Ron Guidry 40.00
3 Don Larsen 40.00
4 Elston Howard 40.00
5 Mel Stottlemyre 25.00
6 Don Mattingly 100.00
7 Reggie Jackson 50.00
8 Tommy John 20.00
9 Dave Winfield 25.00
10 Willie Randolph 20.00
11 Tommy Henrich 20.00
12 Billy Martin 50.00
13 Dave Righetti 20.00
14 Joe Pepitone 20.00
15 Thurman Munson 80.00

2000 Fleer Impact

The base set consists of 200 cards with 25 of those being Prospect subset cards. The featured player's team logo appears beside the player name on the bottom portion with the Impact logo on the top left portion. Card backs have a maximum of 10 years of statistics along with a small photo and vital information. Impact was sold in 10-card packs with an SRP of $.99 per pack.

NM/M
Complete Set (200): 15.00
Common Player: .10
Pack (10): 1.00
Box (36): 20.00
1 Cal Ripken Jr. 1.50
2 Jose Canseco .25
3 Manny Ramirez .60
4 Bernie Williams .30
5 Troy Glaus .60
6 Jeff Bagwell .60
7 Corey Koskie .10
8 Barry Larkin .10
9 Mark Quinn .10
10 Russ Ortiz .10
11 Tim Salmon .15
12 Preston Wilson .10
13 Mo Vaughn .10
14 Ray Lankford .10
15 Sterling Hitchcock .10
16 Al Leiter .10
17 Jim Morris .10
18 Freddy Garcia .10
19 Adrian Beltre .20
20 Eric Chavez .20
21 Robinson Cancel .10
22 Edgar Renteria .10
23 John Jaha .10
24 Chuck Finley .10
25 Andres Galarraga .10
26 Paul Byrd .10
27 John Halama .10
28 Eric Karros .10
29 Mike Piazza 1.00
30 Ryan Rupe .10
31 Frank Thomas .60
32 Randy Velarde .10
33 Bobby Abreu .10
34 Randy Johnson .60
35 Matt Williams .10
36 Tony Gwynn .75
37 Dean Palmer .10
38 Aaron Sele .10
39 Rondell White .10
40 Erubiel Durazo .10
41 Curt Schilling .25
42 Kip Wells .10
43 Craig Biggio .10
44 Tom Glavine .25
45 Trevor Hoffman .10
46 Greg Vaughn .10
47 Edgar Martinez .10
48 Magglio Ordonez .20
49 Mark Mulder .10
50 John Rocker .10
51 Kenny Rogers .10
52 Gary Sheffield .25
53 Brian Simmons .10
54 Tony Womack .10
55 Ken Caminiti .10
56 Jeff Cirillo .10
57 Ray Durham .10
58 Mike Lieberthal .10
59 Ruben Mateo .10
60 Mike Cameron .10
61 Rusty Greer .10
62 Alex Rodriguez 1.25
63 Robin Ventura .10
64 Pokey Reese .10
65 Jose Lima .10
66 Neifi Perez .10
67 Rafael Palmeiro .50
68 Scott Rolen .50
69 Mike Hampton .10
70 Sammy Sosa 1.00
71 Mike Stanley .10
72 Dan Wilson .10
73 Kerry Wood .50
74 Mike Mussina .30
75 Masato Yoshii .10
76 Peter Bergeron .10
77 Carlos Delgado .50
78 Juan Encarnacion .10
79 Nomar Garciaparra 1.00
80 Jason Kendall .10
81 Pedro Martinez .60
82 Darin Erstad .40
83 Larry Walker .10
84 Rick Ankiel .10
85 Scott Erickson .10
86 Roger Clemens .85
87 Matt Lawton .10
88 Jon Lieber .10
89 Shane Reynolds .10
90 Ivan Rodriguez .50
91 Pat Burrell .50
92 Kent Bottenfield .10
93 David Cone .10
94 Mark Grace .15
95 Paul Konerko .10
96 Eric Milton .10
97 Lee Stevens .10
98 B.J. Surhoff .10
99 Billy Wagner .10
100 Ken Griffey Jr. 1.00
101 Randy Wolf .10
102 Henry Rodriguez .10
103 Carlos Beltran .40
104 Rich Aurilia .10
105 Chipper Jones .75
106 Homer Bush .10
107 Johnny Damon .10
108 J.D. Drew .40
109 Orlando Hernandez .10
110 Brad Radke .10
111 Wilton Veras .10
112 Dmitri Young .10
113 Jermaine Dye .10
114 Kris Benson .10
115 Derek Jeter 1.50
116 Cole Liniak .10
117 Jim Thome .10
118 Pedro Astacio .10
119 Carlos Febles .10
120 Darryl Kile .10
121 Alfonso Soriano .50
122 Michael Barrett .10
123 Ellis Burks .10
124 Chad Hermansen .10
125 Trot Nixon .10
126 Bobby Higginson .10
127 Rick Helling .10
128 Chris Carpenter .10
129 Vinny Castilla .10
130 Brian Giles .10
131 Todd Helton .60
132 Jason Varitek .10
133 Rob Ducey .10
134 Octavio Dotel .10
135 Adam Kennedy .10
136 Jeff Kent .10
137 Aaron Boone .10
138 Todd Walker .10
139 Jeromy Burnitz .10
140 Roberto Hernandez .10
141 Matt LeCroy .10
142 Ugueth Urbina .10
143 David Wells .10
144 Luis Gonzalez .25
145 Andruw Jones .50
146 Juan Gonzalez .60
147 Moises Alou .10
148 Michael Tejera .10
149 Brian Jordan .10
150 Mark McGwire 1.25
151 Shawn Green .25
152 Jay Bell .10
153 Fred McGriff .10
154 Rey Ordonez .10
155 Matt Stairs .10
156 A.J. Burnett .10
157 Omar Vizquel .10
158 Damion Easley .10
159 Dante Bichette .10
160 Javy Lopez .10
161 Fernando Seguignol .10
162 Richie Sexson .10
163 Vladimir Guerrero .60
164 Kevin Young .10
165 Josh Beckett .10
166 Albert Belle .10
167 Cliff Floyd .10
168 Gabe Kapler .10
169 Nick Johnson .15
170 Raul Mondesi .10
171 Warren Morris .10
172 Kenny Lofton .10
173 Reggie Sanders .10
174 Mike Sweeney .10
175 Robert Fick .10
176 Barry Bonds 1.50
177 Luis Castillo .10
178 Roger Cedeno .10
179 Jim Edmonds .10
180 Geoff Jenkins .10
181 Adam Piatt .10
182 Phil Nevin .10
183 Roberto Alomar .30
184 Kevin Brown .10
185 D.T. Cromer .10
186 Jason Giambi .50
187 Fernando Tatis .10
188 Brady Anderson .10
189 Tony Clark .10
190 Alex Fernandez .10
191 Matt Blank .10
192 Greg Maddux .75
193 Kevin Millwood .10
194 Jason Schmidt .10
195 Shannon Stewart .10
196 Rolando Arrojo .10
197 Darren Dreifort .10
198 Ben Grieve .10
199 Bartolo Colon .10
200 Sean Casey .10

Autographics

This autographed set has the player signature on the bottom portion of the card. These were seeded 1:216 packs.

NM/M
Common Player: 5.00
Inserted 1:216
Silvers: 1-2X
Production 250 Sets
Golds: 1-2X
Production 50 Sets
1 Bobby Abreu 15.00
2 Marlon Anderson 5.00
3 Rick Ankiel 8.00
4 Rob Bell 5.00
5 Carlos Beltran 25.00
6 Wade Boggs 30.00
7 Barry Bonds 200.00
8 Milton Bradley 8.00
9 Pat Burrell 25.00
10 Orlando Cabrera 10.00
11 Chris Carpenter 5.00
12 Sean Casey 8.00
13 Carlos Delgado 20.00
14 J.D. Drew 15.00
15 Ray Durham 8.00
16 Kelvim Escobar 6.00
17 Vladimir Guerrero 30.00
18 Tony Gwynn 35.00
19 Jerry Hairston Jr. 5.00
20 Todd Helton 25.00
21 Nick Johnson 8.00
22 Jason Kendall 8.00
23 Mark Kotsay 8.00
24 Cole Liniak 5.00
25 Jose Macias 5.00
26 Greg Maddux 60.00
27 Ruben Mateo 8.00
28 Ober Moreno 5.00
29 Eric Munson 8.00
30 Joe Nathan 5.00
31 Angel Pena 5.00
32 Adam Piatt 6.00
33 Matt Riley 5.00
34 Cal Ripken Jr. 100.00
35 Alex Rodriguez 75.00
36 Scott Rolen 25.00
37 Jimmy Rollins 15.00
38 B.J. Ryan 5.00
39 Alfonso Soriano 40.00
40 Frank Thomas 25.00
41 Wilton Veras 5.00
42 Billy Wagner 10.00
43 Jeff Weaver 8.00
44 Scott Williamson 6.00

Genuine Coverage

This memorabilia insert set has pieces of game-used batting gloves embedded into the card front. They were seeded 1:720 packs.

NM/M
Common Player: 5.00
Inserted 1:720
1 Alex Rodriguez 65.00
2 Cole Liniak 5.00
3 Barry Bonds 75.00
4 Ben Davis 5.00
5 Bobby Abreu 7.50
6 Mike Sweeney 7.50
7 Rafael Palmeiro 35.00
8 Carlos Lee 5.00
9 Glen Barker 5.00
10 Jason Giambi 30.00
11 Jacque Jones 7.50
12 Joe Nathan 5.00
13 Jason LaRue 5.00
14 Magglio Ordonez 7.50
15 Shannon Stewart 5.00
16 Matt Lawton 5.00
18 Trevor Hoffman 5.00

Mighty Fine in '99

This 40-card set honors the 1999 World Series Champion New York Yankees as well as other various award winners from the '99 season. These were seeded one per pack.

NM/M
Complete Set (40): 8.00
Common Player: .15
Inserted 1:1
1 Clay Bellinger .15
2 Scott Brosius .15
3 Roger Clemens .75
4 David Cone .15
5 Chad Curtis .15
6 Chili Davis .15
7 Joe Girardi .15
8 Jason Grimsley .15
9 Orlando Hernandez .15
10 Hideki Irabu .15
11 Derek Jeter 2.00
12 Chuck Knoblauch .15
13 Ricky Ledee .15
14 Jim Leyritz .15
15 Tino Martinez .15
16 Ramiro Mendoza .15
17 Jeff Nelson .15
18 Paul O'Neill .15
19 Andy Pettitte .25
20 Jorge Posada .25
21 Mariano Rivera .25
22 Luis Sojo .15

23 Mike Stanton .15
24 Allen Watson .15
25 Bernie Williams .30
26 Chipper Jones .60
27 Ivan Rodriguez .45
28 Randy Johnson .50
29 Pedro Martinez .50
30 Scott Williamson .15
31 Carlos Beltran .40
32 Mark McGwire 1.50
33 Ken Griffey Jr. 1.00
34 Robin Ventura .15
35 Tony Gwynn .60
36 Wade Boggs .60
37 Cal Ripken Jr. 2.00
38 Jose Canseco .40
39 Alex Rodriguez 1.50
40 Fernando Tatis .15

Point of Impact

Point of Impact honors some of the game's top sluggers on a die-cut design. Card fronts have silver foil stamping and cross hairs where the featured player finds his sweet spot. These were seeded 1:30 packs and are numbered with an "PI" suffix on the card back.

NM/M
Complete Set (10): 20.00
Common Player: 1.00
Inserted 1:30
1 Ken Griffey Jr. 2.00
2 Mark McGwire 3.00
3 Sammy Sosa 2.00
4 Jeff Bagwell 1.00
5 Derek Jeter 4.00
6 Chipper Jones 1.50
7 Nomar Garciaparra 2.00
8 Cal Ripken Jr. 4.00
9 Barry Bonds 4.00
10 Alex Rodriguez 3.00

2000 Fleer Mystique

The base set consists of 175-cards including a 50-card Prospects subset that each card is serially numbered to 2,000 and covered. The card fronts have a full bleed design with gold foil stamping. Card backs have complete year-by-year statistics and a small photo.

NM/M
Complete Set (175): 350.00
Common Player: .20
Common 126-175: 6.00
Production 2,000 Sets
Pack (5): 3.00
Box (20): 50.00
1 Derek Jeter 3.00
2 David Justice .20
3 Kevin Brown .20
4 Jason Giambi .75
5 Jose Canseco .50
6 Mark Grace .30
7 Hideo Nomo .65
8 Edgardo Alfonzo .20
9 Barry Bonds 3.00
10 Pedro Martinez 1.00
11 Juan Gonzalez 1.00
12 Vladimir Guerrero 1.00
13 Chuck Finley .20
14 Brian Jordan .20
15 Richie Sexson .20
16 Chan Ho Park .20
17 Tim Hudson .40
18 Fred McGriff .20
19 Darin Erstad .60
20 Chris Singleton .20
21 Jeff Bagwell 1.00
22 David Cone .20
23 Edgar Martinez .20
24 Greg Maddux 1.50
25 Jim Thome .20
26 Eric Karros .20
27 Bobby Abreu .20
28 Greg Vaughn .20
29 Kevin Millwood .20
30 Omar Vizquel .20
31 Marquis Grissom .20
32 Mike Lieberthal .20
33 Gabe Kapler .20
34 Brady Anderson .20
35 Jeff Cirillo .20
36 Geoff Jenkins .20
37 Scott Rolen .75
38 Rafael Palmeiro .65
39 Randy Johnson 1.00
40 Barry Larkin .20
41 Johnny Damon .40
42 Andy Pettitte .40
43 Mark McGwire 2.50
44 Albert Belle .20
45 Derrick Gibson .20
46 Corey Koskie .20
47 Curt Schilling .50
48 Ivan Rodriguez .65
49 Mike Mussina .50
50 Todd Helton 1.00
51 Matt Lawton .20
52 Jason Kendall .20
53 Kenny Rogers .20
54 Cal Ripken Jr. 3.00
55 Larry Walker .20
56 Eric Milton .20
57 Warren Morris .20
58 Carlos Delgado .50
59 Kerry Wood .65
60 Cliff Floyd .20
61 Mike Piazza 2.00
62 Jeff Kent .20
63 Sammy Sosa 2.00
64 Alex Fernandez .20
65 Mike Hampton .20
66 Livan Hernandez .20
67 Matt Williams .20
68 Roberto Alomar .45
69 Jermaine Dye .20
70 Bernie Williams .35
71 Edgar Renteria .20
72 Tom Glavine .40
73 Bartolo Colon .20
74 Jason Varitek .20
75 Eric Chavez .40
76 Fernando Tatis .20
77 Adrian Beltre .40
78 Paul Konerko .20
79 Mike Lowell .20
80 Robin Ventura .20
81 Russ Ortiz .20
82 Troy Glaus 1.00
83 Frank Thomas 1.00
84 Craig Biggio .20
85 Orlando Hernandez .20
86 John Olerud .20
87 Chipper Jones 1.50
88 Manny Ramirez 1.00
89 Shawn Green .40
90 Ben Grieve .20
91 Vinny Castilla .20
92 Tim Salmon .35
93 Dante Bichette .20
94 Ken Caminiti .20
95 Andruw Jones .75
96 Alex Rodriguez 2.50
97 Erubiel Durazo .20
98 Sean Casey .30
99 Carlos Beltran .50
100 Paul O'Neill .20
101 Ray Lankford .20
102 Troy O'Leary .20
103 Bobby Higginson .20
104 Rondell White .20
105 Tony Gwynn 1.50
106 Jim Edmonds .20
107 Magglio Ordonez .40
108 Preston Wilson .20
109 Roger Clemens 1.75
110 Ken Griffey Jr. 2.00
111 Nomar Garciaparra 2.00
112 Juan Encarnacion .20
113 Michael Barrett .20
114 Matt Clement .20
115 David Wells .20
116 Mo Vaughn .20
117 Mike Cameron .20
118 Jose Lima .20
119 Tino Martinez .20
120 J.D. Drew .40
121 Carl Everett .20
122 Tony Clark .20
123 Brad Radke .20
124 Kevin Young .20
125 Raul Mondesi .20
126 Cole Liniak (Prospects) 6.00
127 Alfonso Soriano (Prospects) 8.00
128 Lance Berkman (Prospects) 8.00
129 Danny Young (Prospects) 6.00
130 Francisco Cordero (Prospects) 6.00
131 Rob Fick (Prospects) 6.00
132 Matt LeCroy (Prospects) 6.00
133 Adam Piatt (Prospects) 6.00
134 Derrick Turnbow **RC** (Prospects) 6.00
135 Mark Quinn (Prospects) 6.00
136 Kip Wells (Prospects) 6.00
137 Rob Bell (Prospects) 6.00
138 Brad Penny (Prospects) 6.00
139 Pat Burrell (Prospects) 10.00
140 Danys Baez **RC** (Prospects) 6.00
141 Chad Hermansen (Prospects) 6.00
142 Steve Lomasney (Prospects) 6.00
143 Peter Bergeron (Prospects) 6.00
144 Jimmy Anderson (Prospects) 6.00
145 Mike Darr (Prospects) 6.00
146 Jacob Cruz (Prospects) 6.00
147 Kazuhiro Sasaki **RC** (Prospects) 10.00
148 Ben Petrick (Prospects) 6.00
149 Rick Ankiel (Prospects) 6.00
150 Aaron McNeal **RC** (Prospects) 6.00
152 Octavio Dotel (Prospects) 6.00
152 Juan Pena (Prospects) 6.00
153 Nick Johnson (Prospects) 8.00
154 Wilton Veras (Prospects) 6.00
155 Wily Pena (Prospects) 6.00
156 Mark Mulder (Prospects) 6.00
157 Daryle Ward (Prospects) 6.00
158 Chad Durbin **RC** (Prospects) 6.00
159 Angel Pena (Prospects) 6.00
160 Dewayne Wise (Prospects) 6.00
161 Tarrik Brock (Prospects) 6.00
162 Marcus Jensen (Prospects) 6.00
163 Kevin Barker (Prospects) 6.00
164 B.J. Ryan (Prospects) 6.00
165 Cesar King (Prospects) 6.00
166 Geoff Blum (Prospects) 6.00
167 Ruben Mateo (Prospects) 6.00
168 Ramon Ortiz (Prospects) 6.00
169 Eric Munson (Prospects) 6.00
170 Josh Beckett (Prospects) 8.00
171 Rafael Furcal (Prospects) 6.00
172 Matt Riley (Prospects) 6.00
173 Johan Santana **RC** (Prospects) 60.00
174 Mark Johnson (Prospects) 6.00
175 Adam Kennedy (Prospects) 6.00

Gold

These parallel inserts to the 175-card base set are identical to the base cards besides gold highlights throughout the background of the player photo. The word "Gold" also appears underneath the card number on the back. These were seeded 1:20 packs.

Stars (1-125): 4-8X
SP's (126-175): 1X
Inserted 1:20

Club 3000

This three-card set is die-cut around the 3,000 numerals with a date on the left side when the featured player reached the 3,000 milestone. The player name is stamped in silver holo-foil. Card backs are

not numbered and have a brief career note. These were seeded 1:20 packs.

NM/M
Complete Set (3): 6.00
Common Player: 1.50
Inserted 1:20
1 Cal Ripken Jr. 5.00
2 Bob Gibson 1.50
3 Dave Winfield 1.50

Club 3000 Memorabilia

Five different memorabilia versions of each player exist, using pieces of game-used bat, jersey and cap which are embedded into each card. The amount of each card produced is listed after the player name.

NM/M
Cal Ripken Jr./Jsy/825 40.00
Cal Ripken Jr./Bat/265 75.00
Cal Ripken Jr./Hat/55 120.00
Cal Ripken Jr./Bat, Jsy/100 100.00
Bob Gibson/Jsy/825 20.00
Bob Gibson/Bat/265 30.00
Bob Gibson/Bat, Jsy/100 50.00
Bob Gibson/Hat, Jsy/100 50.00
Bob Gibson/Hat/55 75.00
Dave Winfield/Jsy/825 15.00
Dave Winfield/Bat/270 25.00
Dave Winfield/Bat, Jsy/100 50.00
Dave Winfield/Hat/55 60.00

Diamond Dominators

This 10-card set spotlights baseball's most dominating performers. Card fronts have a holofoil appearance. These were seeded 1:5 packs and are numbered with an "DD" suffix.

NM/M
Complete Set (10): 15.00
Common Player: .75
Inserted 1:5
1 Manny Ramirez 1.00
2 Pedro Martinez 1.00
3 Sean Casey .75
4 Vladimir Guerrero 1.00
5 Sammy Sosa 1.50
6 Nomar Garciaparra 1.50
7 Mark McGwire 2.50
8 Ken Griffey Jr. 1.50
9 Derek Jeter 3.00
10 Alex Rodriguez 2.50

Feel the Game

This game-used memorabilia set features either game-used jerseys or bats from today's top stars. These were seeded 1:120 packs.

NM/M
Common Player: 5.00
Inserted 1:120
1 Tony Gwynn/Jsy 20.00
2 Alex Rodriguez/Jsy 25.00
3 Chipper Jones/Jsy 20.00
4 Cal Ripken Jr./Jsy 40.00
5 Derek Jeter/Pants 40.00
6 Alex Rodriguez/Bat 30.00
7 Frank Thomas/Bat 15.00
8 Barry Bonds/Bat 40.00
9 Carlos Beltran/Bat 5.00
10 Shawn Green/Bat 8.00
11 Michael Barrett/Bat 5.00
12 Rafael Palmeiro/Bat 10.00
13 Vladimir Guerrero/Bat 15.00
14 Pat Burrell/Bat 12.00

Fresh Ink

This autographed set features signatures from many of the game's top players and are seeded 1:40 packs.

NM/M
Common Player: 5.00
Inserted 1:40
1 Chad Allen 5.00
2 Glen Barker 5.00
3 Michael Barrett 5.00
4 Josh Beckett 30.00
5 Rob Bell 5.00
6 Lance Berkman 25.00
7 Kent Bottenfield 5.00
8 Milton Bradley 8.00
9 Orlando Cabrera 10.00
10 Sean Casey 10.00
11 Roger Cedeno 6.00
12 Will Clark 25.00
13 Russ Davis 5.00
14 Carlos Delgado 15.00
15 Einar Diaz 5.00
16 J.D. Drew 10.00
17 Erubiel Durazo 10.00
18 Damion Easley 5.00
19 Carlos Febles 5.00
20 Doug Glanville 6.00
21 Alex Gonzalez 5.00
22 Tony Gwynn 40.00
23 Mike Hampton 8.00
24 Bobby Howry 5.00
25 John Jaha 5.00
26 Nick Johnson 10.00
27 Andruw Jones 20.00
28 Adam Kennedy 8.00
29 Mike Lieberthal 8.00
30 Jose Macias 5.00
31 Ruben Mateo 8.00
32 Raul Mondesi 8.00
33 Heath Murray 5.00
34 Mike Mussina 30.00
35 Hideo Nomo 250.00
36 Magglio Ordonez 15.00
37 Eric Owens 5.00
38 Adam Piatt 5.00
39 Cal Ripken Jr. 100.00
40 Tim Salmon 15.00
41 Chris Singleton 5.00
42 J.T. Snow 8.00
43 Mike Sweeney 10.00
44 Wilton Veras 5.00
45 Jose Vidro 8.00
46 Rondell White 10.00
47 Jaret Wright 5.00

High Praise

This 10-card set has a holo-foiled card front with a "sky" background. These

were inserted 1:20 packs and are numbered on the card back with an "HP" suffix.

NM/M
Complete Set (10): 18.00
Common Player: .75
Inserted 1:20
1 Mark McGwire 3.00
2 Ken Griffey Jr. 2.00
3 Alex Rodriguez 3.00
4 Derek Jeter 4.00
5 Sammy Sosa 2.00
6 Mike Piazza 2.00
7 Nomar Garciaparra 2.00
8 Cal Ripken Jr. 4.00
9 Tony Gwynn 1.50
10 Shawn Green .75

Rookie I.P.O.

This 10-card set highlights the top young rookies on a holofoil design. Card backs are numbered with an "RI" suffix and are seeded 1:10 packs.

NM/M
Complete Set (10): 8.00
Common Player: .50
Inserted 1:10
1 Josh Beckett 1.00
2 Eric Munson .50
3 Pat Burrell 2.00
4 Alfonso Soriano 1.50
5 Rick Ankiel .50
6 Ruben Mateo .50
7 Mark Quinn .50
8 Kip Wells .50
9 Ben Petrick .50
10 Nick Johnson .75

Seismic Activity

This 10-card set spotlights the top power hitters in the game. The player image is in the foreground of a warp like setting with golden highlights. Card backs are numbered with an "SA" suffix and are seeded 1:40 packs. A serial numbered parallel called Richter 100 is randomly seeded and is limited to 100 serial numbered sets.

NM/M
Complete Set (10): 45.00

Common Player: 3.00
Inserted 1:40
Richter parallel: 3-5X
Production 100 Sets
1 Ken Griffey Jr. 5.00
2 Sammy Sosa 5.00
3 Derek Jeter 10.00
4 Mark McGwire 8.00
5 Manny Ramirez 3.00
6 Mike Piazza 5.00
7 Vladimir Guerrero 3.00
8 Chipper Jones 4.00
9 Alex Rodriguez 8.00
10 Jeff Bagwell 3.00

Supernaturals

This 10-card set has a warp like image of the player on the front with silver holo-foil highlights around the player image and gold foil stamping. Card backs are numbered with an "S" suffix. These were seeded 1:10 packs.

NM/M
Complete Set (10): 15.00
Common Player: 1.00
Inserted 1:10
1 Alex Rodriguez 3.00
2 Chipper Jones 1.75
3 Derek Jeter 4.00
4 Ivan Rodriguez 1.00
5 Ken Griffey Jr. 2.00
6 Mark McGwire 3.00
7 Mike Piazza 2.00
8 Nomar Garciaparra 2.00
9 Sammy Sosa 2.00
10 Vladimir Guerrero 1.50

Dave Winfield Autograph Memorabilia

This two-card set consists of 40 game-used helmet Winfield cards and 20 game-used ball cards.

NM/M
Complete Set (2):
1 Dave Winfield/Bat/20 140.00
2 Dave Winfield/Helmet/40 125.00

2000 Fleer Showcase

The base set consists of 140 cards, including 40 Prospect Showcase subset cards. Cards 101-115 are serially numbered to 1,000 and cards 116-140 are serially numbered to 2,000. The card fronts are holo-foiled, with the player name and team stamped in gold foil. Card backs have year-by-year statistics and a small close-up photo. Five-card packs carried an SRP of $4.99.

NM/M
Complete Set (140): 200.00
Common Player (1-100): .25
Common (101-115): 6.00
Production 1,000 Sets
Common (116-140): 4.00
Production 2,000 Sets
Pack (5): 2.50
Box (24): 50.00
1 Alex Rodriguez 2.50
2 Derek Jeter 3.00
3 Jeromy Burnitz .25
4 John Olerud .25
5 Paul Konerko .25
6 Johnny Damon .40
7 Curt Schilling .50
8 Barry Larkin .25
9 Adrian Beltre .40
10 Scott Rolen .75
11 Carlos Delgado .50
12 Pedro J. Martinez 1.00
13 Todd Helton 1.00
14 Jacque Jones .25
15 Jeff Kent .25
16 Darin Erstad .65
17 Juan Encarnacion .25
18 Roger Clemens 1.75
19 Tony Gwynn 1.50
20 Nomar Garciaparra 2.00
21 Roberto Alomar .40
22 Matt Lawton .25
23 Rich Aurilia .25
24 Charles Johnson .25
25 Jim Thome .25
26 Eric Milton .25
27 Barry Bonds 3.00
28 Albert Belle .25
29 Travis Fryman .25
30 Ken Griffey Jr. 2.00
31 Phil Nevin .25
32 Chipper Jones 1.50
33 Craig Biggio .25
34 Mike Hampton .25
35 Fred McGriff .25
36 Cal Ripken Jr. 3.00
37 Manny Ramirez 1.00
38 Jose Vidro .25
39 Trevor Hoffman .25
40 Tom Glavine .50
41 Frank Thomas 1.00
42 Chris Widger .25
43 J.D. Drew .50
44 Andres Galarraga .25
45 Pokey Reese .25
46 Mike Piazza 2.00
47 Kevin Young .25
48 Sean Casey .25
49 Carlos Beltran .60
50 Jason Kendall .25
51 Vladimir Guerrero 1.00
52 Jermaine Dye .25
53 Brian Giles .25
54 Andruw Jones 1.00
55 Richard Hidalgo .25
56 Robin Ventura .25
57 Ivan Rodriguez .65
58 Greg Maddux 1.50
59 Billy Wagner .25
60 Ruben Mateo .25
61 Troy Glaus 1.00
62 Dean Palmer .25
63 Eric Chavez .40
64 Edgar Martinez .25
65 Randy Johnson 1.00
66 Preston Wilson .25
67 Orlando Hernandez .25
68 Jim Edmonds .25
69 Carl Everett .25
70 Larry Walker .25
71 Ron Belliard .25
72 Sammy Sosa 2.00
73 Matt Williams .25
74 Cliff Floyd .25
75 Bernie Williams .40
76 Fernando Tatis .25
77 Steve Finley .25
78 Jeff Bagwell 1.00
79 Edgardo Alfonzo .25
80 Jose Canseco .40
81 Magglio Ordonez .40
82 Shawn Green .40
83 Bobby Abreu .25
84 Tony Batista .25
85 Mo Vaughn .25
86 Juan Gonzalez 1.00
87 Paul O'Neill .25
88 Mark McGwire 2.50
89 Mark Grace .35
90 Kevin Brown .25
91 Ben Grieve .25
92 Shannon Stewart .25
93 Erubiel Durazo .25
94 Antonio Alfonseca .25
95 Jeff Cirillo .25
96 Greg Vaughn .25
97 Kerry Wood .60
98 Geoff Jenkins .25
99 Jason Giambi .75
100 Rafael Palmeiro .65
101 Rafael Furcal 6.00
102 Pablo Ozuna 6.00
103 Brad Penny 6.00
104 Mark Mulder 8.00
105 Adam Piatt 6.00
106 Mike Lamb **RC** 6.00
107 Kazuhiro Sasaki **RC** 15.00
108 Aaron McNeal **RC** 6.00
109 Pat Burrell 8.00
110 Rick Ankiel 6.00
111 Eric Munson 6.00
112 Josh Beckett 8.00
113 Adam Kennedy 6.00
114 Alex Escobar 8.00
115 Chad Hermansen 6.00
116 Kip Wells 4.00
117 Matt LeCroy 4.00
118 Julio Ramirez 4.00
119 Ben Petrick 4.00
120 Nick Johnson 6.00
121 Gookie Dawkins 4.00
122 Julio Zuleta **RC** 4.00
123 Alfonso Soriano 8.00
124 Keith McDonald **RC** 4.00
125 Kory DeHaan 4.00
126 Vernon Wells 6.00
127 Dernell Stenson 4.00
128 David Eckstein 4.00
129 Robert Fick 4.00
130 Cole Liniak 4.00
131 Mark Quinn 4.00
132 Eric Gagne 5.00
133 Wily Pena 4.00
134 Andy Thompson **RC** 4.00
135 Steve Sisco **RC** 4.00
136 Paul Rigdon **RC** 6.00
137 Rob Bell 4.00
138 Carlos Guillen 5.00
139 Jimmy Rollins 5.00
140 Jason Conti 4.00

Legacy

A parallel to the 140-card base set these feature a matte and holo-foil design and are serially numbered to 20.

Stars (1-100): 30-50X
Prospects (101-140): 3-6X
Production 20 Sets

Masterpiece

Each card in 2000 Showcase was issued in a unique Masterpiece edition. The front is enhanced with gold ink while on back is printed the notice "The Only 1 Of 1 / Masterpiece."

Prospect Showcase First

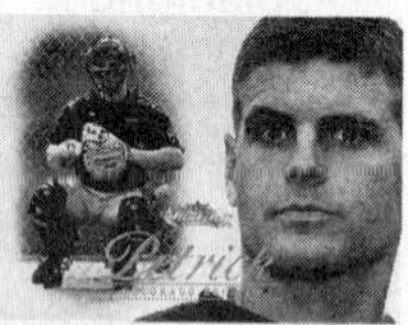

A parallel of the 40-card Prospects subset. These differ from the base cards in that they have a horizontal format and are serially numbered to 500.

Prospects (101-140): 1-2X
Production 500 Sets

Club 3000

This two-card set pays tribute to Lou Brock and Nolan Ryan. Each card is die-cut around the numerals 3,000 with a date displaying the day Brock or Ryan reached their 3,000 milestone. The player name is stamped in silver holo-foil. These were inserted 1:24 packs.

NM/M
Common Player: 3.00
Inserted 1:24
1 Lou Brock 2.00
2 Nolan Ryan 8.00

Club 3000 Memorabilia

These inserts feature actual game-used pieces of memorabilia from Nolan Ryan and Lou Brock and are serial numbered. The number produced is listed after the player name.

NM/M
Lou Brock/Jsy/680 15.00
Lou Brock/Bat/270 25.00
Lou Brock/Hat, Bat, Jsy/25 100.00
Nolan Ryan/Jsy/780 40.00
Nolan Ryan/Hat/65 120.00
Nolan Ryan/Bat/265 60.00
Nolan Ryan/Bat, Jsy/100 120.00

Consummate Prose

This 15-card set has an image of a worn scroll of paper with consummate prose written on it in the background of the player image. The Showcase logo, player name and Consummate Prose are stamped in gold foil. Card backs are numbered with an "CP" suffix and are inserted 1:6 packs.

NM/M
Complete Set (15): 20.00
Common Player: .50
Inserted 1:6
1 Jeff Bagwell 1.50
2 Alex Rodriguez 3.00
3 Chipper Jones 2.00
4 Derek Jeter 4.00
5 Manny Ramirez 1.50
6 Tony Gwynn 2.00
7 Sammy Sosa 2.50
8 Ivan Rodriguez 1.00
9 Greg Maddux 2.00
10 Ken Griffey Jr. 2.50
11 Rick Ankiel .50
12 Cal Ripken Jr. 4.00
13 Pedro Martinez 1.50
14 Mike Piazza 2.50
15 Mark McGwire 3.00

Feel the Game

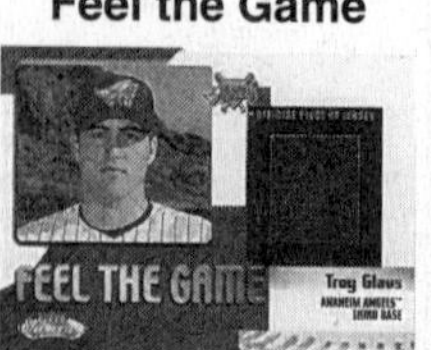

This set has swatches of game worn jersey embedded into the card front.

NM/M
Common Player: 5.00
Inserted 1:72
1 Barry Bonds 30.00
2 Gookie Dawkins 5.00
3 Darin Erstad 8.00
4 Troy Glaus 10.00
5 Scott Rolen 10.00
6 Alex Rodriguez 25.00
7 Andruw Jones 10.00
8 Robin Ventura 5.00
9 Sean Casey 5.00
10 Cal Ripken Jr. 40.00

Final Answer

These foiled inserts have a green border with the player inside a frame with question marks in the background. The card backs have trivia questions about the featured player. Card backs are numbered with a "FA" suffix. These were seeded 1:10 packs.

NM/M
Complete Set (10): 20.00
Common Player: 1.00
Inserted 1:10
1 Alex Rodriguez 3.00
2 Vladimir Guerrero 1.00
3 Cal Ripken Jr. 4.00
4 Sammy Sosa 2.00
5 Barry Bonds 4.00
6 Derek Jeter 4.00
7 Ken Griffey Jr. 2.00
8 Mike Piazza 2.00
9 Nomar Garciaparra 2.00
10 Mark McGwire 3.00

Fresh Ink

These autographed inserts are inserted 1:24 packs.

NM/M
Common Player: 5.00
Inserted 1:24
1 Rick Ankiel 8.00
2 Josh Beckett 30.00
3 Barry Bonds 200.00
4 A.J. Burnett 10.00
5 Pat Burrell 15.00
6 Ken Caminiti 8.00
7 Sean Casey 10.00
8 Jose Cruz Jr. 10.00
9 Gookie Dawkins 5.00
10 Erubiel Durazo 10.00
11 Juan Encarnacion 8.00
12 Darin Erstad 15.00
13 Rafael Furcal 15.00
14 Nomar Garciaparra 100.00
15 Jason Giambi 20.00
16 Jeremy Giambi 6.00
17 Brian Giles 15.00
18 Troy Glaus 20.00
20 Vladimir Guerrero 30.00
21 Chad Hermansen 5.00
23 Trevor Hoffman 8.00
24 Randy Johnson 60.00
25 Andruw Jones 15.00
26 Jason Kendall 8.00
27 Paul Konerko 10.00
28 Mike Lowell 10.00
29 Aaron McNeal 5.00
30 Warren Morris 5.00
31 Paul O'Neill 20.00
32 Magglio Ordonez 10.00
33 Pablo Ozuna 5.00
34 Brad Penny 8.00
35 Ben Petrick 5.00
36 Pokey Reese 5.00
37 Cal Ripken Jr. 125.00
38 Alex Rodriguez 75.00
39 Scott Rolen 30.00
40 Jose Vidro 8.00
41 Kip Wells 5.00

License to Skill

License to Skill have a rounded, die-cut top with a concentric-circles back-

ground. Silver and gold foil etching and foil stamping are used as well. Card backs are numbered with an "LS" suffix.

NM/M
Complete Set (10): 25.00
Common Player: 1.50
Inserted 1:20
1 Vladimir Guerrero 2.00
2 Pedro J. Martinez 2.00
3 Nomar Garciaparra 4.00
4 Ivan Rodriguez 1.50
5 Mark McGwire 5.00
6 Derek Jeter 6.00
7 Ken Griffey Jr. 4.00
8 Randy Johnson 2.00
9 Sammy Sosa 4.00
10 Alex Rodriguez 5.00

Long Gone

These inserts are die-cut around the card top to mimic the outfield dimensions of the featured players' stadium. Gold foil stamping is also used. Card backs are numbered with an "LG" suffix and have an insertion ratio of 1:20 packs.

NM/M
Complete Set (10): 25.00
Common Player: 2.00
Inserted 1:20
1 Sammy Sosa 4.00
2 Derek Jeter 6.00
3 Nomar Garciaparra 4.00
4 Juan Gonzalez 2.00
5 Vladimir Guerrero 2.00
6 Barry Bonds 6.00
7 Jeff Bagwell 2.00
8 Alex Rodriguez 5.00
9 Ken Griffey Jr. 4.00
10 Mark McGwire 5.00

Noise of Summer

This 10-card set has a kaleidoscope background with the insert name stamped in red foil and the logo, player name and team name stamped in gold foil. Card backs are numbered with an "NS" suffix. These were seeded 1:10 packs.

NM/M
Complete Set (10): 15.00
Common Player: 1.00
Inserted 1:10
1 Chipper Jones 1.50
2 Jeff Bagwell 1.00
3 Manny Ramirez 1.00
4 Mark McGwire 3.00
5 Ken Griffey Jr. 2.00
6 Mike Piazza 2.00
7 Pedro J. Martinez 1.00
8 Alex Rodriguez 3.00
9 Derek Jeter 4.00
10 Randy Johnson 1.00

Sweet Sigs

These autographed inserts have the featured players' autograph on an actual "sweet spot" from an authentic Major League baseball. These have an insertion ratio of 1:250 packs.

NM/M
Common Player: 10.00
Inserted 1:250
1 Nomar Garciaparra/53 150.00
2 Alex Rodriguez/67 200.00
3 Tony Gwynn 40.00
4 Roger Clemens/79 140.00
5 Scott Rolen 50.00
6 Greg Maddux 80.00
7 Jose Cruz Jr. 15.00
8 Tony Womack 10.00
9 Jay Buhner 10.00
10 Nolan Ryan 125.00

2000 Fleer Tradition

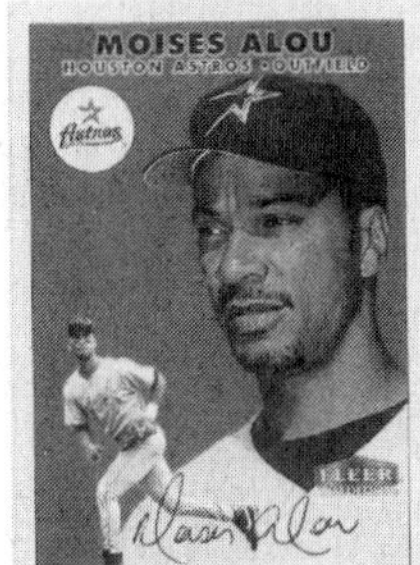

The Fleer Tradition base set consists of 450 cards including a 30-card rookies/prospects subset, 30 team cards, 10 league leaders, 6 award winners, 10 postseason recaps and 6 checklists. The card fronts have a close-up photo of the featured player as well as a small action photo surrounded by a white border. Like the fronts the card backs have a "throwback" look, which includes complete year-by-year statistics, a brief career note and vital information. 10-card packs had a SRP of $1.49.

NM/M
Complete Set (450): 50.00
Common Player: .10
Complete Glossy Factory Set (500): 450.00
Complete Glossy Factory Set (455): 75.00
Glossy (1-450): 1-2X
Common Glossy (451-500): 8.00
Five Glossy (451-500) per factory set.
1,000 produced (451-500)
Pack (10): 1.50
Wax Box: 35.00
1 AL HRs .50
2 NL HRs .50
3 AL RBIs .50
4 NL RBIs .50
5 AL Avg. .50
6 NL Avg. .15
7 AL Wins .20
8 NL Wins .40
9 AL ERA .20
10 NL ERA .25
11 Matt Mantei .10
12 John Rocker .10
13 Kyle Farnsworth .10
14 Juan Guzman .10
15 Manny Ramirez .75
16 Matt Riley-P, Calvin Pickering-1B .10
17 Tony Clark .10
18 Brian Meadows .10
19 Orber Moreno .10
20 Eric Karros .10
21 Steve Woodard .10
22 Scott Brosius .10
23 Gary Bennett .10
24 Jason Wood-3B, Dave Borkowski-P .10
25 Joe McEwing .10
26 Juan Gonzalez .75
27 Roy Halladay .25
28 Trevor Hoffman .10
29 Arizona Diamondbacks .10
30 Domingo Guzman-P **RC**, Wiki Gonzalez-C .25
31 Bret Boone .10
32 Nomar Garciaparra 2.00
33 Bo Porter .10
34 Eddie Taubensee .10
35 Pedro Astacio .10
36 Derek Bell .10
37 Jacque Jones .10
38 Ricky Ledee .10
39 Jeff Kent .10
40 Matt Williams .10
41 Alfonso Soriano-SS, D'Angelo Jimenez-3B .75
42 B.J. Surhoff .10
43 Denny Neagle .10
44 Omar Vizquel .10
45 Jeff Bagwell .75
46 Mark Grudzielanek .10
47 LaTroy Hawkins .10
48 Orlando Hernandez .10
49 Ken Griffey Jr. 2.00
50 Fernando Tatis .10
51 Quilvio Veras .10
52 Wayne Gomes .10
53 Rick Helling .10
54 Shannon Stewart .10
55 Dermal Brown-OF, Mark Quinn-OF .20
56 Randy Johnson 1.00
57 Greg Maddux 1.50
58 Mike Cameron .10
59 Matt Anderson .10
60 Milwaukee Brewers .10
61 Derrek Lee .10
62 Mike Sweeney .10
63 Fernando Vina .10
64 Orlando Cabrera .20
65 Doug Glanville .10
66 Stan Spencer .10
67 Ray Lankford .10
68 Kelly Dransfeldt .10
69 Alex Gonzalez .10
70 Russell Branyan-3B, Danny Peoples-OF .10
71 Jim Edmonds .10
72 Brady Anderson .10
73 Mike Stanley .10
74 Travis Fryman .10
75 Carlos Febles .10
76 Bobby Higginson .10
77 Carlos Perez .10
78 Steve Cox-1B, Alex Sanchez-OF .10
79 Dustin Hermanson .10
80 Kenny Rogers .10
81 Miguel Tejada .25
82 Ben Davis .10
83 Reggie Sanders .10
84 Eric Davis .10
85 J.D. Drew .45
86 Ryan Rupe .10
87 Bobby Smith .10
88 Jose Cruz Jr. .10
89 Carlos Delgado .50
90 Toronto Blue Jays .10
91 Denny Stark-P **RC**, Gil Meche-P .25
92 Randy Velarde .10
93 Aaron Boone .10
94 Javy Lopez .10
95 Johnny Damon .25
96 Jon Lieber .10
97 Montreal Expos .10
98 Mark Kotsay .10
99 Luis Gonzalez .25
100 Larry Walker .10
101 Adrian Beltre .25
102 Alex Ochoa .10
103 Michael Barrett .10
104 Tampa Bay Devil Rays .10
105 Rey Ordonez .10
106 Derek Jeter 3.00
107 Mike Lieberthal .10
108 Ellis Burks .10
109 Steve Finley .10
110 Ryan Klesko .10
111 Steve Avery .10
112 Dave Veres .10
113 Cliff Floyd .10
114 Shane Reynolds .10
115 Kevin Brown .10
116 David Nilsson .10
117 Mike Trombley .10
118 Todd Walker .10
119 John Olerud .10
120 Chuck Knoblauch .10
121 Nomar Garciaparra 2.00
122 Trot Nixon .10
123 Erubiel Durazo .10
124 Edwards Guzman .10
125 Curt Schilling .50
126 Brian Jordan .10
127 Cleveland Indians .10
128 Benito Santiago .10
129 Frank Thomas .75
130 Neifi Perez .10
131 Alex Fernandez .10
132 Jose Lima .10
133 Jorge Toca-1B, Melvin Mora-OF .10
134 Scott Karl .10
135 Brad Radke .10
136 Paul O'Neill .10
137 Kris Benson .10
138 Colorado Rockies .10
139 Jason Phillips .10
140 Robb Nen .10
141 Ken Hill .10
142 Charles Johnson .10
143 Paul Konerko .10
144 Dmitri Young .10
145 Justin Thompson .10
146 Mark Loretta .10
147 Edgardo Alfonzo .10
148 Armando Benitez .10
149 Octavio Dotel .10
150 Wade Boggs 1.50
151 Ramon Hernandez .10
152 Freddy Garcia .10
153 Edgar Martinez .10
154 Ivan Rodriguez .65
155 Kansas City Royals .10
156 Cleatus Davidson-2B, Cristian Guzman-SS .10
157 Andy Benes .10
158 Todd Dunwoody .10
159 Pedro Martinez 1.00
160 Mike Caruso .10
161 Mike Sirotka .10
162 Houston Astros .10
163 Darryl Kile .10
164 Chipper Jones 1.50
165 Carl Everett .10
166 Geoff Jenkins .10
167 Dan Perkins .10
168 Andy Pettitte .25
169 Francisco Cordova .10
170 Jay Buhner .10
171 Jay Bell .10
172 Andruw Jones .75
173 Bobby Howry .10
174 Chris Singleton .10
175 Todd Helton .75
176 A.J. Burnett .10
177 Marquis Grissom .10
178 Eric Milton .10
179 Los Angeles Dodgers .10
180 Kevin Appier .10
181 Brian Giles .10
182 Tom Davey .10
183 Mo Vaughn .10
184 Jose Hernandez .10
185 Jim Parque .10
186 Derrick Gibson .10
187 Bruce Aven .10
188 Jeff Cirillo .10
189 Doug Mientkiewicz .10
190 Eric Chavez .25
191 Al Martin .10
192 Tom Glavine .25
193 Butch Huskey .10
194 Ray Durham .10
195 Greg Vaughn .10
196 Vinny Castilla .10
197 Ken Caminiti .10
198 Joe Mays .10
199 Chicago White Sox .10
200 Mariano Rivera .20
201 Mark McGwire 2.50
202 Pat Meares .10
203 Andres Galarraga .10
204 Tom Gordon .10
205 Henry Rodriguez .10
206 Brett Tomko .10
207 Dante Bichette .10
208 Craig Biggio .10
209 Matt Lawton .10
210 Tino Martinez .10
211 Aaron Myette-P, Josh Paul-C .10
212 Warren Morris .10
213 San Diego Padres .10
214 Ramon E. Martinez .10
215 Troy Percival .10
216 Jason Johnson .10
217 Carlos Lee .10
218 Scott Williamson .10
219 Jeff Weaver .10
220 Ronnie Belliard .10
221 Jason Giambi .65
222 Ken Griffey Jr. 2.00
223 John Halama .10
224 Brett Hinchliffe .10
225 Wilson Alvarez .10
226 Rolando Arrojo .10
227 Ruben Mateo .10
228 Rafael Palmeiro .65
229 David Wells .10
230 Eric Gagne-P, Jeff Williams-P .10
231 Tim Salmon .30
232 Mike Mussina .50
233 Magglio Ordonez .25
234 Ron Villone .10
235 Antonio Alfonseca .10
236 Jeromy Burnitz .10
237 Ben Grieve .10
238 Giomar Guevara .10
239 Garret Anderson .10
240 John Smoltz .10
241 Mark Grace .15
242 Cole Liniak-3B, Jose Molina-C .10
243 Damion Easley .10
244 Jeff Montgomery .10
245 Kenny Lofton .10
246 Masato Yoshii .10
247 Philadelphia Phillies .10
248 Raul Mondesi .10
249 Marlon Anderson .10
250 Shawn Green .40
251 Sterling Hitchcock .10
252 Randy Wolf-P, Anthony Shumaker-P .10
253 Jeff Fassero .10
254 Eli Marrero .10
255 Cincinnati Reds .10
256 Rick Ankiel-P, Adam Kennedy-2B .50
257 Darin Erstad .60
258 Albert Belle .20
259 Bartolo Colon .10
260 Bret Saberhagen .10
261 Carlos Beltran .50
262 Glenallen Hill .10
263 Gregg Jefferies .10
264 Matt Clement .10
265 Miguel Del Toro .10
266 Robinson Cancel-C, Kevin Barker-1B .10
267 San Francisco Giants .10
268 Kent Bottenfield .10
269 Fred McGriff .10
270 Chris Carpenter .10
271 Atlanta Braves .10
272 Wilton Veras-3B, Tomokazu Ohka-P **RC** .50
273 Will Clark .20
274 Troy O'Leary .10
275 Sammy Sosa 2.00
276 Travis Lee .15
277 Sean Casey .25
278 Ron Gant .10
279 Roger Clemens 1.75
280 Phil Nevin .10
281 Mike Piazza 2.00
282 Mike Lowell .10
283 Kevin Millwood .10
284 Joe Randa .10
285 Jeff Shaw .10
286 Jason Varitek .10
287 Harold Baines .10
288 Gabe Kapler .10
289 Chuck Finley .10
290 Carl Pavano .10
291 Brad Ausmus .10
292 Brad Fullmer .10
293 Boston Red Sox .10
294 Bob Wickman .10
295 Billy Wagner .10
296 Shawn Estes .10
297 Gary Sheffield .40
298 Fernando Seguignol .10
299 Omar Olivares .10
300 Baltimore Orioles .10
301 Matt Stairs .10
302 Andy Ashby .10
303 Todd Greene .10
304 Jesse Garcia .10
305 Kerry Wood .50
306 Roberto Alomar .40
307 New York Mets .10
308 Dean Palmer .10
309 Mike Hampton .10
310 Devon White .10
311 Chad Hermansen-OF, Mike Garcia-P .10
312 Tim Hudson .40
313 John Franco .10
314 Jason Schmidt .10
315 J.T. Snow .10
316 Ed Sprague .10
317 Chris Widger .10
318 Ben Petrick-C, Luther Hackman-P **RC** .25
319 Jose Mesa .10
320 Jose Canseco .50
321 John Wetteland .10
322 Minnesota Twins .10
323 Jeff DaVanon-OF **RC**, Brian Cooper-P .25
324 Tony Womack .10
325 Rod Beck .10
326 Mickey Morandini .10
327 Pokey Reese .10
328 Jaret Wright .10
329 Glen Barker .10
330 Darren Dreifort .10
331 Torii Hunter .15
332 Tony Armas Jr.-P, Peter Bergeron-OF .10
333 Hideki Irabu .10
334 Desi Relaford .10
335 Barry Bonds 3.00
336 Gary DiSarcina .10
337 Gerald Williams .10
338 John Valentin .10
339 David Justice .10
340 Juan Encarnacion .10
341 Jeremy Giambi .10
342 Chan Ho Park .10
343 Vladimir Guerrero 1.00
344 Robin Ventura .10
345 Bobby Abreu .10
346 Tony Gwynn 1.50
347 Jose Jimenez .10
348 Royce Clayton .10
349 Kelvim Escobar .10
350 Chicago Cubs .10
351 Travis Dawkins-SS, Jason LaRue-C .10
352 Barry Larkin .10
353 Cal Ripken Jr. 3.00
353s Cal Ripken Jr./OPS 4.00
354 Alex Rodriguez 2.50
355 Todd Stottlemyre .10
356 Terry Adams .10
357 Pittsburgh Pirates .10
358 Jim Thome .10
359 Corey Lee-P, Doug Davis-P .10
360 Moises Alou .10
361 Todd Hollandsworth .10
362 Marty Cordova .10
363 David Cone .10
364 Joe Nathan-P, Wilson Delgado-SS .10
365 Paul Byrd .10
366 Edgar Renteria .10
367 Rusty Greer .10
368 David Segui .10
369 New York Yankees .50
370 Daryle Ward-OF/1B, Carlos Hernandez-2B .10
371 Troy Glaus .75
372 Delino DeShields .10
373 Jose Offerman .10
374 Sammy Sosa 2.00
375 Sandy Alomar Jr. .10
376 Masao Kida .10
377 Richard Hidalgo .10
378 Ismael Valdes .10
379 Ugueth Urbina .10
380 Darryl Hamilton .10
381 John Jaha .10
382 St. Louis Cardinals .10
383 Scott Sauerbeck .10
384 Russ Ortiz .10
385 Jamie Moyer .10
386 Dave Martinez .10
387 Todd Zeile .10
388 Anaheim Angels .10
389 Rob Ryan-OF, Nick Bierbrodt-P .10
390 Rickey Henderson .75
391 Alex Rodriguez 2.50
392 Texas Rangers .10
393 Roberto Hernandez .10
394 Tony Batista .10
395 Oakland Athletics .10
396 Randall Simon-1B, David Cortes-P **RC** .20
397 Gregg Olson .10
398 Sidney Ponson .10
399 Micah Bowie .10
400 Mark McGwire 2.50
401 Florida Marlins .10
402 Chad Allen .10
403 Casey Blake-3B, Vernon Wells-OF .10
404 Pete Harnisch .10
405 Preston Wilson .10
406 Richie Sexson .10
407 Rico Brogna .10
408 Todd Hundley .10
409 Wally Joyner .10
410 Tom Goodwin .10
411 Joey Hamilton .10
412 Detroit Tigers .10
413 Michael Tejera-P **RC**, Ramon Castro-C .25
414 Alex Gonzalez .10
415 Jermaine Dye .10
416 Jose Rosado .10
417 Wilton Guerrero .10
418 Rondell White .10
419 Al Leiter .10
420 Bernie Williams .25
421 A.J. Hinch .10
422 Pat Burrell .50
423 Scott Rolen .65
424 Jason Kendall .10
425 Kevin Young .10
426 Eric Owens .10
427 Derek Jeter 1.00
428 Livan Hernandez .10
429 Russ Davis .10
430 Dan Wilson .10
431 Quinton McCracken .10
432 Homer Bush .10
433 Seattle Mariners .10
434 Chad Harville-P, Luis Vizcaino-P .10
435 Carlos Beltran .45
436 Scott Williamson .10
437 Pedro Martinez .75
438 Randy Johnson .75
439 Ivan Rodriguez .60
440 Chipper Jones .75
441 AL Division (Bernie Williams) .15
442 AL Division (Pedro Martinez) .50
443 AL Champ (Derek Jeter) 1.00
444 NL Division (Brian Jordan) .10
445 NL Division (Todd Pratt) .10
446 NL Champ (Kevin Millwood) .10
447 World Series (Orlando Hernandez) .10
448 World Series (Derek Jeter) 1.00
449 World Series (Chad Curtis) .10
450 World Series (Roger Clemens) .75
451 Carlos Casimiro **RC** 8.00
452 Adam Melhuse **RC** 8.00
453 Adam Bernero **RC** 8.00
454 Dusty Allen **RC** 8.00
455 Chan Perry **RC** 8.00
456 Damian Rolls **RC** 8.00
457 Josh Phelps **RC** 10.00
458 Barry Zito **RC** 25.00
459 Hector Ortiz **RC** 8.00
460 Juan Pierre **RC** 15.00
461 Jose Ortiz **RC** 15.00
462 Chad Zerbe **RC** 8.00
463 Julio Zuleta **RC** 8.00
464 Eric Byrnes **RC** 25.00
465 Wilfredo Rodriguez **RC** 10.00
466 Wascar Serrano **RC** 8.00
467 Aaron McNeal **RC** 8.00
468 Paul Rigdon **RC** 8.00
469 John Snyder **RC** 8.00
470 J.C. Romero **RC** 8.00
471 Talmadge Nunnari **RC** 8.00
472 Mike Lamb **RC** 8.00
473 Ryan Kohlmeier **RC** 8.00
474 Rodney Lindsey **RC** 8.00
475 Elvis Pena **RC** 8.00
476 Alex Cabrera **RC** 10.00
477 Chris Richard **RC** 8.00
478 Pedro Feliz **RC** 10.00
479 Ross Gload **RC** 8.00
480 Timoniel Perez **RC** 8.00
481 Jason Woolf **RC** 8.00
482 Kenny Kelly **RC** 8.00
483 Sang-Hoon Lee **RC** 8.00
484 John Riedling **RC** 8.00
485 Chris Wakeland 8.00
486 Britt Reames **RC** 8.00
487 Greg LaRocca **RC** 8.00
488 Randy Keisler **RC** 8.00
489 Xavier Nady **RC** 20.00
490 Keith Ginter **RC** 10.00
491 Joey Nation **RC** 8.00
492 Kazuhiro Sasaki **RC** 8.00
493 Lesli Brea **RC** 8.00
494 Jace Brewer **RC** 8.00
495 Yohanny Valera **RC** 8.00
496 Adam Piatt 10.00
497 Nate Rolison 8.00
498 Aubrey Huff 10.00
499 Jason Tyner 8.00
500 Corey Patterson 10.00

Club 3000

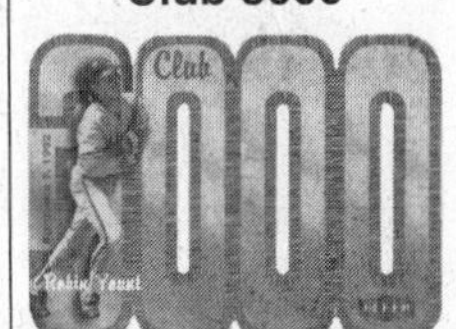

The Club 3000 inserts are die-cut around the number 3,000, commemmorating their reaching the 3,000 hit achievement. These are seeded 1:36 packs and features George Brett, Rod Carew and Robin Yount.

NM/M
Complete Set (3): 5.00
Common Player: 3.00
Inserted 1:36
(1) George Brett 4.00
(2) Rod Carew 2.00
(3) Robin Yount 2.00

Club 3000 Memorabilia

These are a parallel to the base version and has five different memorabilia based tiers. Level 2 (cap), Level 3 (bat), Level 4 (jersey), Level 5 (bat and jersey) and Level 6 (bat, jersey and cap). Each card is hand-numbered.

NM/M
George Brett/Bat/250 60.00
George Brett/Hat/100 75.00
George Brett/Jsy/445 30.00

George Brett/ Bat, Jsy/100	90.00
Rod Carew/Bat/225	30.00
Rod Carew/Hat/100	50.00
Rod Carew/Jsy/440	20.00
Rod Carew/ Bat, Jsy/100	65.00
Robin Yount/Bat/250	40.00
Robin Yount/Hat/100	60.00
Robin Yount/Jsy/440	30.00
Robin Yount/ Bat, Jsy/100	75.00

Dividends

This insert set consists of 15 cards and spotlights the top players on a horizontal format. Card fronts have silver foil stamping, a red border and are seeded 1:6 packs. They are numbered on the back with a "D" suffix.

		NM/M
Complete Set (15):		15.00
Common Player:		.50
Inserted 1:6		
1	Alex Rodriguez	2.50
2	Ben Grieve	.50
3	Cal Ripken Jr.	3.00
4	Chipper Jones	1.50
5	Derek Jeter	3.00
6	Frank Thomas	1.00
7	Jeff Bagwell	1.00
8	Sammy Sosa	2.00
9	Tony Gwynn	1.50
10	Scott Rolen	.75
11	Nomar Garciaparra	2.00
12	Mike Piazza	2.00
13	Mark McGwire	2.50
14	Ken Griffey Jr.	2.00
15	Juan Gonzalez	1.00

Fresh Ink

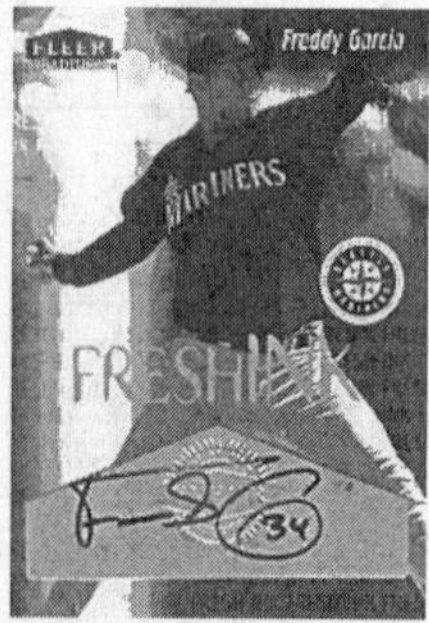

This autographed insert set consists of 38 cards on a vertical format with the autograph on the bottom third of the card below the player image. These were inserted 1:144 packs.

	NM/M
Common Player:	5.00
Inserted 1:144	
Rick Ankiel	8.00
Carlos Beltran	25.00
Pat Burrell	15.00
Miguel Cairo	5.00
Sean Casey	8.00
Will Clark	30.00
Mike Darr	5.00
J.D. Drew	10.00
Erubiel Durazo	10.00
Carlos Febles	6.00
Freddy Garcia	8.00
Greg Maddux	80.00
Jason Grilli	5.00
Vladimir Guerrero	35.00
Tony Gwynn	40.00
Jerry Hairston Jr.	8.00
Tim Hudson	15.00
John Jaha	5.00
D'Angelo Jimenez	5.00
Andruw Jones	20.00
Gabe Kapler	6.00
Cesar King	5.00
Jason LaRue	6.00
Mike Lieberthal	8.00
Pedro Martinez	50.00
Gary Matthews Jr.	5.00
Orber Moreno	5.00
Eric Munson	5.00
Rafael Palmeiro	35.00
Jim Parque	6.00
Willi Mo Pena	15.00
Cal Ripken Jr.	100.00
Alex Rodriguez	80.00
Tim Salmon	15.00
Chris Singleton	5.00
Alfonso Soriano	50.00
Ed Yarnall	5.00

Grasskickers

This 15-card set has a close-up photo of the featured player with holographic silver foil stamping. These are seeded 1:30 packs and are numbered on the back with a "GK" suffix.

		NM/M
Complete Set (15):		50.00
Common Player:		2.00
Inserted 1:30		
1	Tony Gwynn	3.00
2	Scott Rolen	2.00
3	Nomar Garciaparra	4.00
4	Mike Piazza	4.00
5	Mark McGwire	6.00
6	Frank Thomas	2.00
7	Cal Ripken Jr.	8.00
8	Chipper Jones	3.00
9	Greg Maddux	3.00
10	Ken Griffey Jr.	4.00
11	Juan Gonzalez	2.00
12	Derek Jeter	8.00
13	Sammy Sosa	4.00
14	Roger Clemens	3.50
15	Alex Rodriguez	6.00

Hall's Well

This 15-card set spotlights superstars destined for Cooperstown, featured on a transparent plastic stock with overlays of silver foil stamping. These were seeded 1:30 packs and are numbered with a "HW" suffix.

		NM/M
Complete Set (15):		50.00
Common Player:		1.50
Inserted 1:30		
1	Mark McGwire	6.00
2	Alex Rodriguez	6.00
3	Cal Ripken Jr.	8.00
4	Chipper Jones	3.00
5	Derek Jeter	8.00
6	Frank Thomas	2.00
7	Greg Maddux	3.00
8	Juan Gonzalez	2.00
9	Ken Griffey Jr.	4.00
10	Mike Piazza	4.00
11	Nomar Garciaparra	4.00
12	Sammy Sosa	4.00
13	Roger Clemens	3.50
14	Ivan Rodriguez	1.50
15	Tony Gwynn	3.00

Opening Day 2K

As part of a multi-manufacturer promotion, Fleer issued eight cards of an "Opening Day 2K" set. Packages containing some of the 32 cards in the issue were distributed by MLB teams early in the season. The cards were also available exclusively as inserts in packs sold at KMart stores early in the season. The Fleer Tradition OD2K cards have gold-foil graphic highlights on front. Backs are in the basic

format of the rest of the Tradition issue, and are numbered "XX of 32/OD."

		NM/M
Complete Set (8):		6.00
Common Player:		.50
9	Cal Ripken Jr.	2.00
10	Alex Rodriguez	2.00
11	Mike Piazza	1.00
12	Jeff Bagwell	.75
13	Randy Johnson	.75
14	Jason Kendall	.50
15	Magglio Ordonez	.50
16	Carlos Delgado	.50

Ripken Collection

This 10-card set is devoted to Cal Ripken Jr. and features 10 different Fleer retro designs. These were seeded 1:30 packs.

	NM/M
Complete Set (10):	50.00
Common Card:	6.00
Inserted 1:30	

Ten-4

This 10-card insert set focuses on baseball's home run kings on a die-cut design enhanced with silver foil stamping. These were seeded 1:18 packs and are numbered on the card back with a "TF" suffix.

		NM/M
Complete Set (10):		20.00
Common Player:		2.00
Inserted 1:18		
1	Sammy Sosa	2.00
2	Nomar Garciaparra	2.00
3	Mike Piazza	2.00
4	Mark McGwire	3.00
5	Ken Griffey Jr.	2.00
6	Juan Gonzalez	1.00
7	Derek Jeter	4.00
8	Chipper Jones	1.50
9	Cal Ripken Jr.	4.00
10	Alex Rodriguez	3.00

Who To Watch

Top prospects for the 2000 season are highlighted in this 15-card set, including Rick Ankiel. They have a die-cut design with gold foil stamping. These were inserted 1:3 packs and numbered on the back with a "WW" suffix.

		NM/M
Complete Set (15):		5.00
Common Player:		.25
Inserted 1:3		
1	Rick Ankiel	.40
2	Matt Riley	.25
3	Wilton Veras	.25
4	Ben Petrick	.25
5	Chad Hermansen	.25
6	Peter Bergeron	.25
7	Mark Quinn	.25
8	Russell Branyan	.25
9	Alfonso Soriano	1.50
10	Randy Wolf	.50
11	Ben Davis	.25
12	Jeff DaVanon	.25
13	D'Angelo Jimenez	.25
14	Vernon Wells	1.00
15	Adam Kennedy	.40

Glossy Lumberjacks

		NM/M
Common Player:		8.00
One per factory set.		
Production listed		
1	Edgardo Alfonzo/145	10.00
2	Roberto Alomar/627	10.00
3	Moises Alou/529	8.00
4	Carlos Beltran/489	8.00
5	Adrian Beltre/127	10.00
7	Barry Bonds/305	40.00
9	Pat Burrell/45	25.00
10	Sean Casey/50	15.00
11	Eric Chavez/259	10.00
12	Tony Clark/70	10.00
13	Carlos Delgado/70	20.00
14	J.D. Drew/135	10.00
15	Erubiel Durazo/70	10.00
17	Carlos Febles/120	10.00
18	Jason Giambi/220	15.00
19	Shawn Green/429	10.00
20	Vladimir Guerrero/ 809	15.00
21	Derek Jeter/180	50.00
22	Chipper Jones/725	15.00
23	Gabe Kapler/160	8.00
25	Paul Konerko/70	10.00
27	Mike Lieberthal/45	10.00
28	Edgar Martinez/211	10.00
29	Raul Mondesi/458	8.00
30	Warren Morris/35	10.00
31	Maggio Ordonez/190	10.00
32	Rafael Palmeiro/49	15.00
33	Pokey Reese/110	8.00
34	Cal Ripken/235	50.00
35	Alex Rodriguez/292	25.00
36	Ivan Rodriguez/602	10.00
37	Scott Rolen/502	10.00
38	Chris Singleton/68	8.00
39	Alfonso Soriano/285	15.00
40	Frank Thomas/489	10.00
41	Jim Thome/479	10.00
42	Robin Ventura/114	10.00
43	Jose Vidro/60	10.00
44	Bernie Williams/215	10.00
45	Matt Williams/152	8.00

2000 Fleer Tradition Update

Card #50 was supposed to be Indians prospect C.C. Sabathia but it was never issued because he was not called up during the 2000 season.

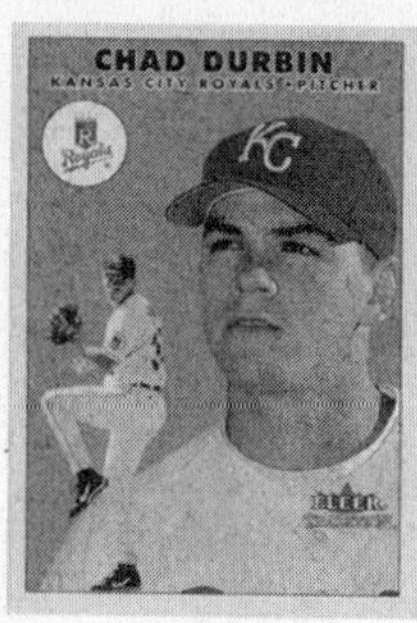

		NM/M
Complete Set (150):		20.00
Common Player:		.15
1	Ken Griffey Jr. (Season Highlights)	.50
2	Cal Ripken Jr. (Season Highlights)	1.00
3	Randy Velarde (Season Highlights)	.15
4	Fred McGriff (Season Highlights)	.15
5	Derek Jeter (Season Highlights)	1.00
6	Tom Glavine (Season Highlights)	.25
7	Brent Mayne (Season Highlights)	.15
8	Alex Ochoa (Season Highlights)	.15
9	Scott Sheldon (Season Highlights)	.15
10	Randy Johnson (Season Highlights)	.35
11	Daniel Garibay **RC**	.15
12	Brad Fullmer	.15
13	Kazuhiro Sasaki **RC**	.50
14	Andy Tracy	.15
15	Bret Boone	.15
16	Chad Durbin **RC**	.25
17	Mark Buehrle **RC**	1.50
18	Julio Zuleta **RC**	.15
19	Jeremy Giambi	.15
20	Gene Stechschulte **RC**	.15
21	Lou Pote, Bengie Molina	.15
22	Darrell Einertson	.15
23	Ken Griffey Jr.	.75
24	Jeff Sparks **RC**, Dan Wheeler	.25
25	Aaron Fultz **RC**	.15
26	Derek Bell	.15
27	Rob Bell, D.T. Cromer	.15
28	Rob Fick	.15
29	Darryl Kile	.15
30	Clayton Andrews, John Bate	.15
31	Dave Veres	.15
32	Hector Mercado **RC**	.15
33	Willie Morales	.15
34	Kelly Wunsch, Kip Wells	.15
35	Hideki Irabu	.15
36	Sean DePaula	.15
37	Dewayne Wise, Chris Woodward	.15
38	Curt Schilling	.25
39	Mark Johnson	.15
40	Mike Cameron	.15
41	Scott Sheldon, Tom Evans	.15
42	Brett Tomko	.15
43	Johan Santana **RC**	15.00
44	Andy Benes	.15
45	Matt LeCroy, Mark Redman	.15
46	Ryan Klesko	.15
47	Andy Ashby	.15
48	Octavio Dotel	.15
49	Eric Byrnes **RC**	1.00
51	Kenny Rogers	.15
52	Ben Weber	.15
53	Matt Blank, Scott Strickland	.15
54	Tom Goodwin	.15
55	Jim Edmonds	.15
56	Derrick Turnbow **RC**	.25
57	Mark Mulder	.15
58	Tarrik Brock, Ruben Quevedo	.15
59	Danny Young	.15
60	Fernando Vina	.15
61	Justin Brunette **RC**	.15
62	Jimmy Anderson	.15
63	Reggie Sanders	.15
64	Adam Kennedy	.15
65	Jesse Garcia, B.J. Ryan	.15
66	Al Martin	.15
67	Kevin Walker	.15
68	Brad Penny	.15
69	B.J. Surhoff	.15
70	Geoff Blum, Trace Coquillette	.15
71	Jose Jimenez	.15
72	Chuck Finley	.15
73	Valerio De Los Santos, Everett Stull	.15
74	Terry Adams	.15
75	Rafael Furcal	.15
76	Mike Darr, John Roskos	.15
77	Quilvio Veras	.15
78	Armando Almanza	.15
79	Greg Vaughn	.15
80	Keith McDonald **RC**	.15
81	Eric Cammack	.15
82	Horacio Estrada, Ray King	.15
83	Kory DeHaan	.15
84	Kevin Hodges	.15
85	Mike Lamb **RC**	.25
86	Shawn Green	.40
87	Dan Reichert, Jason Rakers	.15
88	Adam Piatt	.15
89	Mike Garcia	.15
90	Rodrigo Lopez **RC**	1.00
91	John Olerud	.15
92	Barry Zito, Terrence Long	1.00
93	Jimmy Rollins	.25
94	Denny Neagle	.15
95	Rickey Henderson	.50
96	Adam Eaton, Buddy Carlyle	.15
97	Brian O'Connor	.15
98	Andy Thompson	.15
99	Jason Boyd	.15
100	Carlos Guillen, Joel Piniero	.15
101	Raul Gonzalez	.15
102	Brandon Kolb **RC**	.25
103	Jason Maxwell, Mike Lincoln	.15
104	Luis Matos **RC**	.50
105	Morgan Burkhart **RC**	.25
106	Ismael Villegas, Steve Sisco	.15
107	David Justice	.15
108	Pablo Ozuna	.15
109	Jose Canseco	.40
110	Alex Cora, hawn Gilbert	.15
111	Will Clark	.25
112	Keith Luuloa, Eric Weaver	.15
113	Bruce Chen	.15
114	Adam Hyzdu	.15
115	Scott Forster, Yovanny Lara	.15
116	Allen McDill, Jose Macias	.15
117	Kevin Nicholson	.15
118	Israel Alcantara, Tim Young	.15
119	Juan Alvarez	.15
120	Julio Lugo, Mitch Meluskey	.15
121	B.J. Waszgis	.15
122	Jeff D'Amico, Brett Laxton	.15
123	Ricky Ledee	.15
124	Mark DeRosa, Jason Marquis	.15
125	Alex Cabrera **RC**	.50
126	Gary Matthews, Augie Ojeda	.15
127	Richie Sexson	.15
128	Santiago Perez, Hector Ramirez	.15
129	Rondell White	.15
130	Craig House **RC**	.15
131	Kevin Beirne, Jon Garland	.15
132	Wayne Franklin	.15
133	Henry Rodriguez	.15
134	Jay Payton, Jim Mann	.15
135	Ron Gant	.15
136	Paxton Crawford **RC**, Sang-Hoon Lee	.25
137	Kent Bottenfield	.15
138	Rocky Biddle **RC**	.15
139	Travis Lee	.15
140	Ryan Vogelsong	.15
141	Jason Conti, Geraldo Guzman	.15
142	Tim Drew, Mark Watson	.15
143	John Parrish **RC**, Chris Richard	.15
144	Javier Cardona **RC**, Brandon Villafuetre	.15
145	Tike Redman **RC**, Steve Sparks	.15
146	Brian Schneider, Matt Skrmetta	.15
147	Pasqual Coco **RC**, Leo Estrella	.15
148	Lorenzo Barcelo **RC**, Joe Crede	.15
149	Jace Brewer **RC**	.25
150	Milton Bradley, Tomas de la Rosa	.15

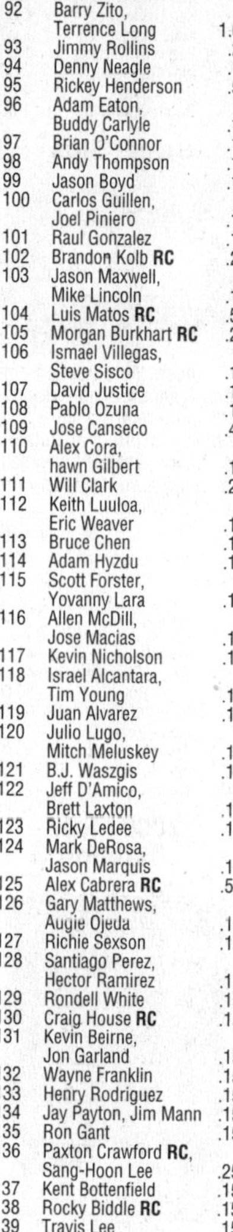

Mantle Pieces

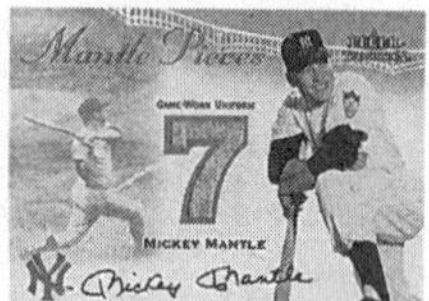

		NM/M
Inserted 1:80 Sets		
1	Mickey Mantle	150.00

Diamond Skills Commemorative Sheet

Utilizing the same format and card reproductions as the souvenir sheet issued in conjunction with the season-opener Cubs-Mets series in Japan, Fleer issued this commemorative sheet for distribution to participants in the 2000 Diamond Skills competition. The 10" x 9" sheets depict star cards from Fleer's 2000 Tradition set.

	NM/M
Derek Jeter, Chipper Jones, Pedro Martinez, Mike Piazza, Cal Ripken Jr., Ivan Rodriguez, Sammy Sosa, Mo Vaughn	10.00

Japan Commemorative Sheet

To commemorate the opening of the 2000 Major League Baseball season with a Cubs-Mets series in Japan, Fleer created this commemorative sheet for distribution at the opening game on March 29 (20,000) and at the Xebio Sporting Goods stores and Pro Pacific Hobby stores in Japan (5,000 each). The 10" x 9" sheets depict on front cards from Fleer's 2000 Tradition set.

	NM/M
Derek Jeter, Chipper Jones, Pedro Martinez, Mike Piazza, Cal Ripken Jr., Ivan Rodriguez, Sammy Sosa, Mo Vaughn	20.00

Oreo

In a nationwide promotional contest in which children stacked Oreo cookies at grocery stores, a pair of hot star cards were given away as consolation prizes. Each 2-1/2" x 3-1/2" card has blue borders with a color photo at center. Jeter's card shows him stacking cookies, while Junior's card (in his new Reds uniform) shows him holding a bag of cookies. Backs have personal information, stats, an action photo and logos of MLB, Fleer and Oreo.

		NM/M
Complete Set (2):		6.00
(1)	Ken Griffey Jr.	3.00
(2)	Derek Jeter	3.00

SportsCards Greats of the Game

The first-ever fully-licensed baseball card set to be issued in the form of a magazine insert, this set comprises the game's top players in the design of Fleer's very popular Greats of the Game issue (which depicted only former stars). The cards were issued six per month in uncut sheet form (8-1/4" x 11-1/8") in SportsCards magazine issues dated February through July 2001. The cards were only inserted in newsstand and card-shop copies. Persons who subscribed to the magazine in a special offer received the complete set in unbound format. If cut from the sheet, individual cards measure the standard 2-1/2" x 3-1/2". On front are action photos on a white background with maroon borders. Backs have player identification, licensor logos and 2000 season stats.

		NM/M
Complete Set, Sheets (6):		35.00
Complete Set, Singles (36):		25.00
Common Player:		.50
Sheet 1, February		6.00
1	Rick Ankiel	.75
2	Jeff Bagwell	1.00
3	Barry Bonds	3.00
4	Pat Burrell	.65
5	Roger Clemens	1.50
6	Carlos Delgado	.65
Sheet 2, March		4.00
7	J.D. Drew	.65
8	Jim Edmonds	.50
9	Darin Erstad	.65
10	Andres Galarraga	.50
11	Nomar Garciaparra	2.00
12	Jason Giambi	.75
Sheet 3, April		6.00
13	Troy Glaus	1.00
14	Roberto Alomar	.50
15	Ken Griffey Jr.	2.00
16	Vladimir Guerrero	1.00
17	Tony Gwynn	1.25
18	Todd Helton	1.00
Sheet 4, May		7.50
19	Derek Jeter	3.00
20	Randy Johnson	1.00
21	Chipper Jones	1.25
22	Andruw Jones	1.00
23	Greg Maddux	1.25
24	Pedro Martinez	1.00
Sheet 5, June		10.00
25	Mark McGwire	2.50
26	Magglio Ordonez	.50
27	Mike Piazza	2.00
28	Manny Ramirez	1.00
29	Cal Ripken Jr.	3.00
30	Alex Rodriguez	2.50
Sheet 6, July		4.00
31	Ivan Rodriguez	.65
32	Jeff Kent	.50
33	Gary Sheffield	.50
34	Sammy Sosa	2.00
35	Frank Thomas	1.00
36	Bernie Williams	.50

Twizzlers

A dozen of baseball's biggest stars were reproduced in a format only slightly different from 2000 Fleer Tradition for inclusion in packages of Twizzlers candy. The candy version features UV coating on both front and back, has a small Twizzlers logo at lower-right on back and is numbered "X of 12." Cards were included in large (26.5 oz.) packages of candy or a complete set could be obtained for $1.50 and 15 proofs of purchase from smaller packages.

		NM/M
Complete Set (12):		7.50
Common Player:		.25
1	Mark McGwire	1.50
2	Cal Ripken Jr.	2.00
3	Chipper Jones	.75
4	Bernie Williams	.35
5	Alex Rodriguez	1.50
6	Curt Schilling	.35
7	Ken Griffey Jr.	1.00
8	Sammy Sosa	1.00
9	Mike Piazza	1.00
10	Pedro Martinez	.50
11	Kenny Lofton	.25
12	Larry Walker	.25

2001 Fleer Authority

		NM/M
Complete Set (150):		265.00
Common Player:		.25
Common (101-150):		3.00
Production 2,001		
Pack (5):		6.00
Box (22 + 2 Graded Packs):		120.00
1	Mark Grace	.35
2	Paul Konerko	.25
3	Sean Casey	.35
4	Jim Thome	.25
5	Todd Helton	.75
6	Tony Clark	.25
7	Jeff Bagwell	.75
8	Mike Sweeney	.25
9	Eric Karros	.25
10	Richie Sexson	.25
11	Doug Mientkiewicz	.25
12	Ryan Klesko	.25
13	John Olerud	.25
14	Mark McGwire	2.00
15	Fred McGriff	.25
16	Rafael Palmeiro	.65
17	Carlos Delgado	.50
18	Roberto Alomar	.40
19	Craig Biggio	.25
20	Jose Vidro	.25
21	Edgardo Alfonzo	.25
22	Jeff Kent	.25
23	Bret Boone	.25
24	Rafael Furcal	.25
25	Nomar Garciaparra	1.50
26	Barry Larkin	.25
27	Cristian Guzman	.25
28	Derek Jeter	2.50
29	Miguel Tejada	.40
30	Jimmy Rollins	.40
31	Rich Aurilia	.25
32	Alex Rodriguez	2.00
33	Cal Ripken Jr.	2.50
34	Troy Glaus	.75
35	Matt Williams	.25
36	Chipper Jones	1.00
37	Jeff Cirillo	.25
38	Robin Ventura	.25
39	Eric Chavez	.35
40	Scott Rolen	.65
41	Phil Nevin	.25
42	Mike Piazza	1.50
43	Jorge Posada	.35
44	Jason Kendall	.25
45	Ivan Rodriguez	.65
46	Frank Thomas	.75
47	Edgar Martinez	.25
48	Darin Erstad	.25
49	Tim Salmon	.35
50	Luis Gonzalez	.35
51	Andruw Jones	.75
52	Carl Everett	.25
53	Manny Ramirez	.75
54	Sammy Sosa	1.50
55	Rondell White	.25
56	Magglio Ordonez	.40
57	Ken Griffey Jr.	1.50
58	Juan Gonzalez	.75
59	Larry Walker	.25
60	Bobby Higginson	.25
61	Cliff Floyd	.25
62	Preston Wilson	.25
63	Moises Alou	.25
64	Lance Berkman	.25
65	Richard Hidalgo	.25
66	Jermaine Dye	.25
67	Mark Quinn	.25
68	Shawn Green	.50
69	Gary Sheffield	.40
70	Jeromy Burnitz	.25
71	Geoff Jenkins	.25
72	Vladimir Guerrero	.75
73	Bernie Williams	.35
74	Johnny Damon	.40
75	Jason Giambi	.60
76	Bobby Abreu	.25
77	Pat Burrell	.50
78	Brian Giles	.25
79	Tony Gwynn	1.00
80	Barry Bonds	2.50
81	J.D. Drew	.40
82	Jim Edmonds	.25
83	Greg Vaughn	.25
84	Raul Mondesi	.25
85	Shannon Stewart	.25
86	Randy Johnson	.75
87	Curt Schilling	.50
88	Tom Glavine	.40
89	Greg Maddux	1.00
90	Pedro Martinez	.75
91	Kerry Wood	.50
92	David Wells	.25
93	Bartolo Colon	.25
94	Mike Hampton	.25
95	Kevin Brown	.25
96	Al Leiter	.25
97	Roger Clemens	1.75
98	Mike Mussina	.50
99	Tim Hudson	.35
100	Kazuhiro Sasaki	.25
101	Ichiro Suzuki **RC**	35.00
102	Albert Pujols **RC**	100.00
103	Drew Henson **RC**	5.00
104	Adam Pettyjohn	3.00
105	Adrian Hernandez **RC**	3.00
106	Andy Morales	3.00
107	Tsuyoshi Shinjo **RC**	4.00
108	Juan Uribe	3.00
109	Jack Wilson **RC**	5.00
110	Jason Smith **RC**	3.00
111	Junior Spivey **RC**	4.00
112	Wilson Betemit **RC**	4.00
113	Elpidio Guzman **RC**	3.00
114	Esix Snead **RC**	3.00
115	Winston Abreu **RC**	3.00
116	Jeremy Owens **RC**	3.00
117	Jay Gibbons **RC**	5.00
118	Luis Lopez	3.00
119	Ryan Freel **RC**	3.00
120	Rafael Soriano **RC**	4.00
121	Johnny Estrada **RC**	5.00
122	Bud Smith **RC**	3.00
123	Jackson Melian **RC**	3.00
124	Matt White **RC**	3.00
125	Travis Hafner **RC**	10.00
126	Morgan Ensberg **RC**	5.00
127	Endy Chavez **RC**	3.00
128	Bret Prinz **RC**	3.00
129	Juan Diaz **RC**	3.00
130	Erick Almonte **RC**	4.00
131	Rob Mackowiak **RC**	3.00
132	Carlos Valderrama **RC**	3.00
133	Wilkin Ruan **RC**	3.00
134	Angel Berroa **RC**	5.00
135	Henry Mateo **RC**	3.00
136	Bill Ortega	3.00
137	Billy Sylvester **RC**	3.00
138	Andres Torres **RC**	3.00
139	Nate Frese	3.00
140	Casey Fossum **RC**	4.00
141	Ricardo Rodriguez **RC**	3.00
142	Brian Roberts **RC**	8.00
143	Carlos Garcia **RC**	3.00
144	Brian Lawrence **RC**	4.00
145	Cory Aldridge **RC**	3.00
146	Mark Teixeira **RC**	25.00
147	Juan Cruz **RC**	3.00
148	Brandon Duckworth **RC**	3.00
149	Dewon Brazelton **RC**	3.00
150	Mark Prior **RC**	15.00

Graded

Mint:	1-1.5X
NrMt+:	.8-1X
NrMt:	.4-.6X

No Multipliers for Gem Mint.

Prominence

Stars (1-100):	5-10X
Production 125	
SP's (101-150):	3-5X
Production 75	

Authority Figures

		NM/M
Complete Set (20):		75.00
Common Card:		2.00
1AF	Mark McGwire, Albert Pujols	8.00
2AF	Kazuhiro Sasaki, Ichiro Suzuki	8.00
3AF	Derek Jeter, Drew Henson	10.00
4AF	Ken Griffey Jr., Jackson Melian	6.00
5AF	Wilson Betemit, Chipper Jones	4.50
6AF	Jeff Bagwell, Morgan Ensberg	4.00
7AF	Cal Ripken Jr., Jay Gibbons	10.00
8AF	Mike Piazza, Tsuyoshi Shinjo	6.00
9AF	Luis Gonzalez, Junior Spivey	2.00
10AF	Barry Bonds, Carlos Valderrama	10.00
11AF	Todd Helton, Juan Uribe	4.00
12AF	Roger Clemens, Adrian Hernandez	5.00
13AF	Alex Rodriguez, Travis Hafner	8.00
14AF	Scott Rolen, Johnny Estrada	3.00
15AF	Brian Giles, Rob Mackowiak	2.00
16AF	Randy Johnson, Bret Prinz	4.00
17AF	Carlos Delgado, Luis Lopez	3.00
18AF	Manny Ramirez, Juan Diaz	4.00
19AF	Mike Sweeney, Endy Chavez	2.00
20AF	Sammy Sosa, Jaisen Randolph	6.00

Diamond Cuts

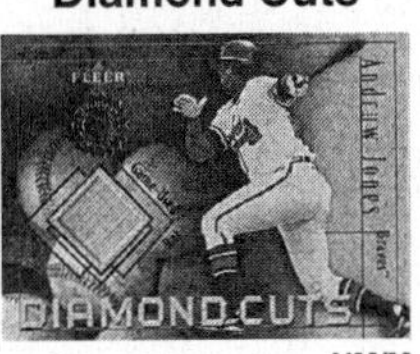

	NM/M
Common Player:	4.00
Inserted 1:10	
Rick Ankiel/Shoe	4.00
Jeff Bagwell/Jsy	8.00
Adrian Beltre/Hat	4.00
Craig Biggio/Bat	4.00
Barry Bonds/Hat	35.00
Barry Bonds/Jsy	20.00
Barry Bonds/Pants	20.00
Barry Bonds/Shoe	30.00
Barry Bonds/Wristband/100	50.00
Kevin Brown/Hat	6.00
Kevin Brown/Pants	4.00
Eric Byrnes/Bat	4.00
Sean Casey/Jsy	4.00
Eric Chavez/Hat	6.00
Chipper Jones/Jsy	10.00
Chipper Jones/Bat	10.00
Bartolo Colon/Hat	6.00
Erubiel Durazo/Bat	4.00
Ray Durham/Bat	4.00
Jim Edmonds/Hat	6.00
Jim Edmonds/Shoe	10.00
Darin Erstad/Hat	6.00
Carlos Febles/Bat	4.00
Carlos Febles/Shoe	4.00
Rafael Furcal/Hat	6.00
Juan Gonzalez/Bat Glove	10.00
Juan Gonzalez/Hat	8.00
Luis Gonzalez	6.00
Shawn Green/Bat Glove	10.00
Shawn Green/Bat	6.00
Vladimir Guerrero/Bat	8.00
Tony Gwynn/Bat	8.00
Mike Hampton/Hat	5.00
Mike Hampton/Shoe	5.00
Jerry Hairston Jr./Hat	4.00
Jason Hart/Bat	4.00
Todd Helton/Jsy	8.00
Todd Helton/Pants	8.00
Orlando Hernandez/Bat	4.00
Richard Hidalgo/Bat	4.00
Richard Hidalgo/Bat Glove	15.00
Derek Jeter/Bat	30.00
Derek Jeter/Bat Glove	60.00
Derek Jeter/Jsy	30.00
Derek Jeter/Pants	30.00
Derek Jeter/Shoe	40.00
Randy Johnson/Hat	30.00
Andruw Jones/Bat	6.00
Andruw Jones/Hat	8.00
Jason Kendall/Hat	6.00
Barry Larkin/Jsy	5.00
Matt Lawton/Hat	6.00
Mike Lieberthal/Bat Glove	6.00
Kenny Lofton/Bat	4.00
Edgar Martinez/Bat Glove	8.00
Pedro Martinez/Shoe	10.00
Raul Mondesi/Bat	4.00
Raul Mondesi/Bat Glove	6.00
Hideo Nomo/Bat	15.00
Hideo Nomo/Hat	40.00
Magglio Ordonez/Bat Glove	8.00
Magglio Ordonez/Hat	6.00
David Ortiz/Bat	4.00
Rafael Palmeiro/Bat	8.00
Rafael Palmeiro/Hat	10.00
Chan Ho Park/Hat	5.00
Mike Piazza/Bat	15.00
Mike Piazza/Jsy	15.00
Mike Piazza/Shoe	25.00
Albert Pujols/Pants	30.00
Manny Ramirez/Bat	8.00
Manny Ramirez/Bat Glove	15.00
Manny Ramirez/Hat	15.00
Cal Ripken Jr./Bat Glove	65.00
Cal Ripken Jr./Pants	25.00
Ivan Rodriguez/Bat Glove	10.00
Ivan Rodriguez/Hat	10.00
Ivan Rodriguez/Pants	8.00
Ivan Rodriguez/Shoe	10.00
Scott Rolen/Hat	10.00
Jared Sandberg/Bat	4.00
Deion Sanders/Jsy	4.00
Tsuyoshi Shinjo/Wristband	10.00
Tsuyoshi Shinjo/Bat	6.00
J.T. Snow	4.00
Alfonso Soriano/Hat	20.00
Ichiro Suzuki/Bat	50.00
Ichiro Suzuki/Hat	65.00
Mike Sweeney/Hat	6.00
Miguel Tejada/Hat	6.00
Frank Thomas/Bat	8.00
Frank Thomas/Hat	10.00
Jim Thome/Bat	8.00
Larry Walker/Bat	4.00
Larry Walker/Jsy	4.00
Bernie Williams/Bat	6.00
Brian Giles/Pants	5.00

Derek Jeter Monumental Moments

NM/M
MM4 Derek Jeter/2000 5.00
MM4AU Derek Jeter/ Auto./100 100.00

Derek Jeter Reprint Autographs

NM/M
1DJRA Derek Jeter/500 90.00

Seal of Approval

NM/M
Complete Set (15): 45.00
Common Player: 1.50
1SA Derek Jeter 6.00
2SA Alex Rodriguez 5.00
3SA Nomar Garciaparra 4.00
4SA Cal Ripken Jr. 6.00
5SA Mike Piazza 4.00
6SA Mark McGwire 5.00
7SA Tony Gwynn 3.00
8SA Barry Bonds 6.00
9SA Greg Maddux 3.00
10SA Chipper Jones 3.00
11SA Roger Clemens 3.50
12SA Ken Griffey Jr. 4.00
13SA Vladimir Guerrero 2.00
14SA Sammy Sosa 4.00
15SA Todd Helton 1.50

2001 Fleer Boston Red Sox 100th Anniversary

NM/M
Complete Set (100): 40.00
Common Player: .25
Pack (5): 6.00
Box (24): 125.00
1 Carl Yastrzemski 2.50
2 Mel Parnell .25
3 Birdie Tebbetts .25
4 Tex Hughson .25
5 Nomar Garciaparra 4.00
6 Fred Lynn .50
7 John Valentin .25
8 Rico Petrocelli .25
9 Ted Williams 5.00
10 Roger Clemens 3.00
11 Luis Aparicio .40
12 Cy Young 1.50
13 Carlton Fisk 1.00
14 Pedro Martinez 2.00
15 Joe Dobson .25
16 Babe Ruth 5.00
17 Doc Cramer .25
18 Pete Runnels .25
19 Tony Conigliaro .25
20 Bill Monbouquette .25
21 Boo Ferriss .25
22 Harry Hooper .25
23 Tony Armas .25
24 Joe Cronin 1.00
25 Rick Ferrell .25
26 Wade Boggs 2.25
27 Don Baylor .25
28 Jeff Reardon .25
29 Smokey Joe Wood .25
30 Mo Vaughn .40
31 Walt Dropo .25
32 Vern Stephens .25
33 Bernie Carbo .25
34 George Scott .25
35 Lefty Grove 1.00
36 Dom DiMaggio 1.00
37 Dennis Eckersley .75
38 Johnny Pesky .25
39 Jim Lonborg .25
40 Jimmy Piersall .25
41 Tris Speaker 1.50
42 Frank Malzone .25
43 Bobby Doerr .75
44 Jimmie Foxx 2.00
45 Tony Pena .25
46 Billy Goodman .25
47 Jim Rice .25
48 Reggie Smith .25
49 Bill Buckner .25
50 Earl Wilson .25
51 Rick Burleson .25
52 George Kell .25
53 Dick Radatz .25
54 Dwight Evans .25
55 Luis Tiant .25
56 Elijah "Pumpsie" Green .25
57 Gene Conley .25
58 Jackie Jensen .25
59 Mike Fornieles .25
60 Dutch Leonard .25
61 Jake Stahl .25
62 Don Schwall .25
63 Jimmy Collins .25
64 Herb Pennock .25
65 Red Ruffing .50
65 .25
66 Carney Lansford .25
67 Dick Stuart .25
68 Dave Morehead .25
69 Harry Agganis .25
70 Lou Boudreau .25
71 Joe Morgan .75
72 Don Zimmer .75
73 Tom Yawkey .25
74 Jean Yawkey .25
75 Origin of the Red Sox .25
76 First Season .25
77 World Series History .25
78 Carl Yastrzemski (Beantown's Best) 1.00
79 Carlton Fisk (Beantown's Best) .50
80 Dom DiMaggio (Beantown's Best) .50
81 Wade Boggs (Beantown's Best) .75
82 Nomar Garciaparra (Beantown's Best) 2.00
83 Pedro Martinez (Beantown's Best) 1.00
84 Ted Williams (Beantown's Best) 2.50
85 Jim Rice (Beantown's Best) .25
86 Fred Lynn (Beantown's Best) .25
87 Mo Vaughn (Beantown's Best) .25
88 Bobby Doerr (Beantown's Best) .40
89 Bernie Carbo (Beantown's Best) .25
90 Dennis Eckersley (Beantown's Best) .35
91 Jimmy Piersall (Beantown's Best) .25
92 Luis Tiant (Beantown's Best) .25
93 Jimmy Fund signage (Fenway Through the Years) .25
94 Green Monster w/Ads (Fenway Through the Years) .25
95 Green Monster w/All-Star logo (Fenway Through the Years) .25
96 Ladder shot on Green Monster (Fenway Through the Years) .25
97 Manual Scoreboard (Fenway Through the Years) .25
98 Panoramic of Fenway (Fenway Through the Years) .25
99 Lansdowne St. (Fenway Through the Years) .25
100 1999 All-Star Game (Fenway Through the Years) .25

Autograph Caps

Each box of Red Sox 100th Anniversary product includes one fitted, authentically autographed genuine MLB Red Sox cap. A certificate of authentication was included with each cap and each had a Fleer hologram attached.

NM/M
Complete Set (18): 825.00
Common Player: 15.00
(1) Wade Boggs 75.00
(2) Bill Buckner 20.00
(3) Bernie Carbo 15.00
(4) Roger Clemens 200.00
(5) Dom DiMaggio 30.00
(6) Bobby Doerr 25.00
(7) Dennis Eckersley 50.00
(8) Dwight Evans 40.00
(9) Carlton Fisk 125.00
(10) Nomar Garciaparra 125.00
(11) Jim Lonborg 20.00
(12) Johnny Pesky 15.00
(13) Rico Petrocelli 20.00
(14) Jimmy Piersall 30.00
(15) Jim Rice 40.00
(16) Luis Tiant 30.00
(17) Carl Yastrzemski 200.00
(18) Don Zimmer 30.00

BoSox Sigs

NM/M
Complete Set (16): 1,000
Common Autograph: 15.00
Inserted 1:96
Wade Boggs 80.00
Bill Buckner 20.00
Bernie Carbo 15.00
Roger Clemens/100 200.00
Dom DiMaggio 75.00
Bobby Doerr 40.00
Dwight Evans 35.00
Carlton Fisk 80.00
Nomar Garciaparra 100.00
Jim Lonborg 15.00
Fred Lynn 40.00
Rico Petrocelli 15.00
Jim Rice 40.00
Luis Tiant 30.00
Carl Yastrzemski/200 180.00

Field the Game

A total of 7,150 exchange cards for Field the Game memorabilia cards was inserted randomly in packs. Collectors exchanging the cards received one of four types of card.

NM/M
Complete Set (4): 75.00
(1) Piece of Green Monster outfield wall 20.00
(2) Piece of base from 100th anniver. game 20.00
(3) Piece of baseball from 100th anniv. game 20.00
(4) anniv. game 20.00

Splendid Splinters

NM/M
Complete Set (15): 20.00
Common Player: 1.00

Inserted 1:10
SS1 Babe Ruth 6.00
SS2 Dom DiMaggio 1.50
SS3 Carlton Fisk 2.00
SS4 Carl Yastrzemski 3.00
SS5 Nomar Garciaparra 5.00
SS6 Wade Boggs 2.50
SS7 Ted Williams 5.00
SS8 Jim Rice 1.00
SS9 Mo Vaughn 1.00
SS10 Tris Speaker 2.00
SS11 Dwight Evans 1.00
SS12 Jimmie Foxx 2.50
SS13 Bobby Doerr 1.50
SS14 Fred Lynn 1.00
SS15 Johnny Pesky 1.00

Splendid Splinters Game Bat

NM/M
Complete Set (8): 800.00
Common Player: 15.00
Inserted 1:96
Babe Ruth/SP/100 400.00
Carl Yastrzemski 75.00
Nomar Garciaparra 30.00
Wade Boggs 25.00
Ted Williams/SP/100 200.00
Jim Rice 15.00
Dwight Evans 15.00
Jimmie Foxx/SP/100 200.00

Threads

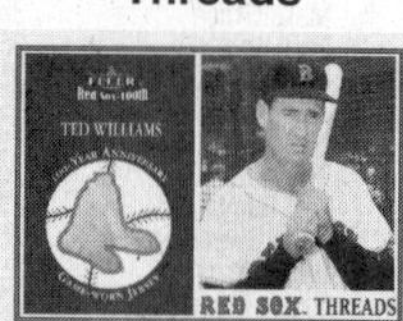

NM/M
Complete Set (9): 400.00
Common Player: 15.00
Inserted 1:96
Wade Boggs 25.00
Roger Clemens 50.00
Dwight Evans 15.00
Carlton Fisk/100 40.00
Pedro Martinez/100 40.00
Jim Rice 20.00
Ted Williams/100 180.00
Carl Yastrzemski 40.00
Don Zimmer 15.00

Yawkey's Heroes

NM/M
Complete Set (20): 15.00
Common Player: .50
Inserted 1:4
1YH Bobby Doerr .75
2YH Dom DiMaggio 1.00
3YH Jim Rice .50
4YH Wade Boggs 1.50
5YH Carlton Fisk 1.00
6YH Nomar Garciaparra 3.00
7YH Dennis Eckersley 1.00
8YH Carl Yastrzemski 2.00
9YH Ted Williams 4.00
10YH Tony Conigliaro .75
11YH Tony Armas .50
12YH Joe Cronin 1.00
13YH Mo Vaughn .50
14YH Johnny Pesky .50
15YH Jim Lonborg .50
16YH Luis Tiant .50
17YH Tony Pena .50
18YH Dwight Evans .50
19YH Fred Lynn .75
20YH Jimmy Piersall .50

2001 Fleer Cal Ripken Jr. Commemoratives

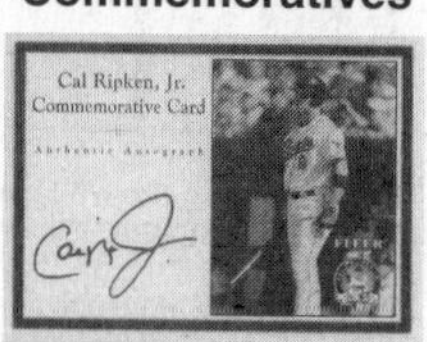

The two "commemorative cards" were produced for sale on a television home shopping program. One card is a reprint of Ripken's 1982 Fleer rookie card, with the addition of a Ripken logo at lower-right. The other is a specially designed and authentically autographed card, horizontal in format, with a game photo of Ripken at right, thre signature at left and the special logo. On back is a statement of authenticity from Fleer, along with a ghost-image portrait photo.

NM/M
Cal Ripken Jr. (1982 Reprint) 10.00
Cal Ripken Jr. (Autograph card.) 125.00

2001 E-X

NM/M
Complete Set (130): 100.00
Common Player: .25
Common SP (101-130): 4.00
Production Listed
Pack (5): 4.00
Box (24): 80.00
1 Jason Kendall .25
2 Derek Jeter 3.00
3 Greg Vaughn .25
4 Eric Chavez .40
5 Nomar Garciaparra 2.00
6 Roberto Alomar .50
7 Barry Larkin .25
8 Matt Lawton .25
9 Larry Walker .25
10 Chipper Jones 1.50
11 Scott Rolen .75
12 Carlos Lee .25
13 Adrian Beltre .40
14 Ben Grieve .25
15 Mike Sweeney .25
16 John Olerud .25
17 Gabe Kapler .25
18 Brian Giles .25
19 Luis Gonzalez .40
20 Sammy Sosa 2.00
21 Roger Clemens 1.75
22 Vladimir Guerrero 1.00
23 Ken Griffey Jr. 2.00
24 Mark McGwire 2.50
25 Orlando Hernandez .25
26 Shannon Stewart .25
27 Fred McGriff .25
28 Lance Berkman .25
29 Carlos Delgado .75
30 Mike Piazza 2.00
31 Juan Encarnacion .25
32 David Justice .25
33 Greg Maddux 1.50
34 Frank Thomas 1.00
35 Jason Giambi .75
36 Ruben Mateo .25
37 Todd Helton 1.00
38 Jim Edmonds .25
39 Steve Finley .25
40 Tom Glavine .40
41 Mo Vaughn .25
42 Phil Nevin .25
43 Richie Sexson .25
44 Craig Biggio .25
45 Kerry Wood .50
46 Pat Burrell .60
47 Edgar Martinez .25
48 Jim Thome .25
49 Jeff Bagwell 1.00
50 Bernie Williams .45
51 Andruw Jones 1.00
52 Gary Sheffield .40
53 Johnny Damon .40
54 Rondell White .25
55 J.D. Drew .50
56 Tony Batista .25
57 Paul Konerko .25
58 Rafael Palmeiro .75
59 Cal Ripken Jr. 3.00
60 Darin Erstad .60
61 Ivan Rodriguez .75
62 Barry Bonds 3.00
63 Edgardo Alfonzo .25
64 Ellis Burks .25
65 Mike Lieberthal .25
66 Robin Ventura .25
67 Richard Hidalgo .25
68 Magglio Ordonez .40
69 Kazuhiro Sasaki .25
70 Miguel Tejada .50
71 David Wells .25
72 Troy Glaus 1.00
73 Jose Vidro .25
74 Shawn Green .50
75 Barry Zito .50
76 Jermaine Dye .25
77 Geoff Jenkins .25
78 Jeff Kent .25
79 Al Leiter .25
80 Deivi Cruz .25
81 Eric Karros .25
82 Albert Belle .25
83 Pedro Martinez 1.00
84 Raul Mondesi .25
85 Preston Wilson .25
86 Rafael Furcal .25
87 Rick Ankiel .25
88 Randy Johnson 1.00
89 Kevin Brown .25
90 Sean Casey .35
91 Mike Mussina .50
92 Alex Rodriguez 2.50
93 Andres Galarraga .25
94 Juan Gonzalez 1.00
95 Manny Ramirez 1.00
96 Mark Grace .35
97 Carl Everett .25
98 Tony Gwynn 1.50
99 Mike Hampton .25
100 Ken Caminiti .25
101 Jason Hart/1,749 4.00
102 Corey Patterson/1,199 5.00
103 Timo Perez/1,999 4.00
104 Marcus Giles/1,999 4.00
105 Ichiro Suzuki/ 1,999 **RC** 50.00
106 Aubrey Huff/1,499 8.00
107 Joe Crede/1,999 5.00
108 Larry Barnes/1,499 4.00
109 Esix Snead/1,499 **RC** 4.00
110 Kenny Kelly/2,249 4.00
111 Justin Miller/2,249 4.00
112 Jack Cust/1,999 4.00
113 Xavier Nady/999 4.00
114 Eric Munson/1,499 4.00
115 Elpidio Guzman/ 1,749 **RC** 4.00
116 Juan Pierre/2,189 4.00
117 Winston Abreu/ 1,749 **RC** 4.00
118 Keith Ginter/1,999 4.00
119 Jace Brewer/2,699 4.00
120 Paxton Crawford/ 2,249 4.00
121 Jason Tyner/2,249 4.00
122 Tike Redman/1,999 4.00
123 John Riedling/2,499 4.00
124 Jose Ortiz/1,499 4.00
125 Oswaldo Mairena/ 2,499 4.00
126 Eric Byrnes/2,249 4.00
127 Brian Cole/999 4.00
128 Adam Piatt/2,249 4.00
129 Nate Rolison/2,499 4.00
130 Keith McDonald/2,249 4.00

Base Inks

NM/M
Random Inserts
Derek Jeter/AU/500 110.00

Behind the Numbers

NM/M
Common Player: 5.00

Inserted 1:33

1BN	Johnny Bench	10.00
2BN	Wade Boggs	15.00
3BN	George Brett	20.00
4BN	Lou Brock	5.00
5BN	Rollie Fingers	5.00
6BN	Carlton Fisk	10.00
7BN	Reggie Jackson	10.00
8BN	Al Kaline	10.00
10BN	Willie McCovey	5.00
11BN	Paul Molitor	10.00
12BN	Eddie Murray	10.00
13BN	Jim Palmer	5.00
14BN	Ozzie Smith	15.00
15BN	Nolan Ryan	30.00
16BN	Mike Schmidt	20.00
17BN	Tom Seaver	10.00
18BN	Dave Winfield	5.00
19BN	Ted Williams	75.00
20BN	Robin Yount	10.00
21BN	Brady Anderson	5.00
22BN	Rick Ankiel	5.00
23BN	Albert Belle	5.00
24BN	Adrian Beltre	7.50
25BN	Barry Bonds	30.00
26BN	Eric Chavez	5.00
27BN	J.D. Drew	6.00
28BN	Darin Erstad	5.00
29BN	Troy Glaus	6.00
30BN	Mark Grace	6.00
31BN	Ben Grieve	5.00
32BN	Tony Gwynn	15.00
33BN	Todd Helton	10.00
34BN	Derek Jeter	30.00
35BN	Jeff Kent	5.00
36BN	Jason Kendall	5.00
37BN	Greg Maddux	15.00
38BN	John Olerud	5.00
39BN	Cal Ripken Jr.	30.00
40BN	Chipper Jones	15.00
41BN	John Smoltz	5.00
42BN	Frank Thomas	10.00
43BN	Robin Ventura	5.00
44BN	Bernie Williams	6.00

Behind the Numbers Autograph

NM/M

Quantity produced listed

2BN	Wade Boggs/26	150.00
4BN	Lou Brock/20	100.00
5BN	Rollie Fingers/34	50.00
6BN	Carlton Fisk/27	125.00
7BN	Reggie Jackson/44	80.00
10BN	Willie McCovey/44	80.00
12BN	Eddie Murray/33	100.00
13BN	Jim Palmer/22	100.00
15BN	Nolan Ryan/34	350.00
16BN	Mike Schmidt/20	200.00
17BN	Tom Seaver/41	80.00
18BN	Dave Winfield/31	60.00
20BN	Robin Yount/19	180.00
22BN	Rick Ankiel/66	20.00
23BN	Albert Belle/88	20.00
24BN	Adrian Beltre/29	25.00
25BN	Barry Bonds/25	250.00
28BN	Darin Erstad/17	80.00
29BN	Troy Glaus/25	80.00
30BN	Mark Grace/17	100.00
32BN	Tony Gwynn/19	150.00
33BN	Todd Helton/17	125.00
35BN	Jeff Kent/21	50.00
36BN	Jason Kendall/18	40.00
37BN	Greg Maddux/31	250.00
41BN	John Smoltz/29	40.00
42BN	Frank Thomas/35	75.00
44BN	Bernie Williams/51	75.00

Derek Jeter Monumental Moments

NM/M

2DJMM	Derek Jeter (Edition of 1,996.)	5.00

2DJMM	Derek Jeter (Autographed edition of 96.)	80.00

Essential Credentials

NM/M

Stars (1-100): 3-6X
Production 299
Common (101-130): 10.00
Minor Stars (101-130): 15.00
Production 29

E-Xtra Innings

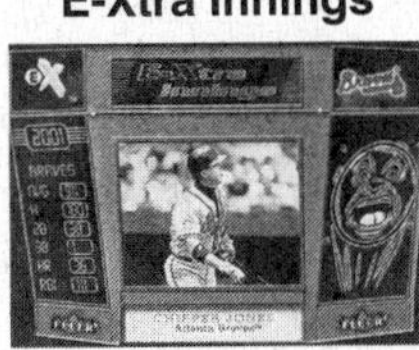

NM/M

Complete Set (10): 30.00
Common Player: 2.00
Inserted 1:20 R

1XI	Mark McGwire	5.00
2XI	Sammy Sosa	4.00
3XI	Chipper Jones	3.00
4XI	Mike Piazza	4.00
5XI	Cal Ripken Jr.	6.00
6XI	Ken Griffey Jr.	4.00
7XI	Alex Rodriguez	5.00
8XI	Vladimir Guerrero	2.00
9XI	Nomar Garciaparra	4.00
10XI	Derek Jeter	6.00

Prospects Autograph

NM/M

Common Autograph: 8.00
Prod. #'s Listed

101	Jason Hart/250	8.00
102	Corey Patterson/800	15.00
103	Timoniel Perez/1000	8.00
104	Marcus Giles/500	10.00
106	Aubrey Huff/500	15.00
107	Joe Crede/500	10.00
108	Larry Barnes/500	8.00
109	Esix Snead/500	8.00
110	Kenny Kelly/250	8.00
111	Justin Miller/250	8.00
112	Jack Cust/1000	10.00
113	Xavier Nady/1000	10.00
114	Eric Munson/1500	8.00
115	Elpidio Guzman/250	8.00
116	Juan Pierre/810	10.00
117	Winston Abreu/250	8.00
118	Keith Ginter/500	8.00
119	Jace Brewer/300	8.00
120	Paxton Crawford/250	8.00
121	Jason Tyner/250	8.00
122	Tike Redman/250	8.00
123	John Riedling/500	8.00
124	Jose Ortiz/500	8.00
125	Oswaldo Mairena/500	8.00
126	Eric Byrnes/250	8.00
127	Brian Cole/2000	8.00
128	Adam Piatt/250	8.00
129	Nate Rolison/500	8.00
130	Keith McDonald/250	8.00

Wall of Fame

NM/M

Common Player: 4.00
Inserted 1:24

1WF	Robin Yount	8.00
2WF	Paul Molitor	8.00
3WF	Geoff Jenkins	4.00
4WF	Mark McGwire	15.00
5WF	Sammy Sosa	12.00
6WF	Greg Maddux	10.00
7WF	Mike Piazza	12.00
8WF	Cal Ripken Jr.	20.00
9WF	Todd Helton	8.00
10WF	Ken Griffey Jr.	12.00
11WF	Alex Rodriguez	15.00
12WF	Vladimir Guerrero	8.00
13WF	Jeff Bagwell	8.00
14WF	Ivan Rodriguez	6.00
15WF	Juan Gonzalez	8.00
16WF	Barry Bonds	20.00
17WF	Derek Jeter	20.00
18WF	Chipper Jones	10.00
19WF	Frank Thomas	8.00
20WF	Tony Gwynn	10.00
21WF	Nomar Garciaparra	12.00
22WF	Manny Ramirez	8.00
23WF	Andruw Jones	8.00
24WF	Scott Rolen	6.00
25WF	Jason Kendall	4.00
26WF	Roger Clemens	15.00
27WF	Troy Glaus	6.00
28WF	Pedro Martinez	8.00
29WF	Jason Giambi	5.00
30WF	Pat Burrell	5.00

2001 Fleer Focus

NM/M

Complete Set (240): 100.00
Common Player: .15
Common Prospect (201-224): 3.00
Common Prospect (225-250): 3.00
Pack (10): 2.50
Box (24): 50.00

1	Derek Jeter	2.00
2	Manny Ramirez	.75
3	Ken Griffey Jr.	1.25
4	Ken Caminiti	.15
5	Joe Randa	.15
6	Jason Kendall	.15
7	Ron Coomer	.15
8	Rondell White	.15
9	Tino Martinez	.15
10	Nomar Garciaparra	1.25
11	Tony Batista	.15
12	Todd Stottlemyre	.15
13	Ryan Klesko	.15
14	Darin Erstad	.50
15	Todd Walker	.15
16	Al Leiter	.15
17	Carl Everett	.15
18	Bobby Abreu	.15
19	Raul Mondesi	.15
20	Vladimir Guerrero	.75
21	Mike Bordick	.15
22	Aaron Sele	.15
23	Ray Lankford	.15
24	Roger Clemens	1.00
25	Kevin Young	.15
26	Brad Radke	.15
27	Todd Hundley	.15
28	Ellis Burks	.15
29	Lee Stevens	.15
30	Eric Karros	.15
31	Darren Dreifort	.15
32	Ivan Rodriguez	.60
33	Pedro Martinez	.75
34	Travis Fryman	.15
35	Garret Anderson	.15
36	Rafael Palmeiro	.60
37	Jason Giambi	.50
38	Jeromy Burnitz	.15
39	Robin Ventura	.15
40	Derek Bell	.15
41	Carlos Guillen	.15
42	Albert Belle	.15
43	Henry Rodriguez	.15
44	Brian Jordan	.15
45	Mike Sweeney	.15
46	Ruben Rivera	.15
47	Greg Maddux	1.00
48	Corey Koskie	.15
49	Sandy Alomar Jr.	.15
50	Mike Mussina	.40
51	Tom Glavine	.25
52	Aaron Boone	.15
53	Frank Thomas	.75
54	Kenny Lofton	.15
55	Danny Graves	.15
56	Jose Valentin	.15
57	Travis Lee	.15
58	Jim Edmonds	.15
59	Jim Thome	.15
60	Steve Finley	.15
61	Shawn Green	.45
62	Lance Berkman	.15
63	Mark Quinn	.15
64	Randy Johnson	.75
65	Dmitri Young	.15
66	Andy Pettitte	.25
67	Paul O'Neill	.15
68	Gil Heredia	.15
69	Russell Branyan	.15
70	Alex Rodriguez	1.50
71	Geoff Jenkins	.15
72	Eric Chavez	.25
73	Cal Ripken Jr.	2.00
74	Mark Kotsay	.15
75	Jeff D'Amico	.15
76	Tony Womack	.15
77	Eric Milton	.15
78	Joe Girardi	.15
79	Peter Bergeron	.15
80	Miguel Tejada	.25
81	Luis Gonzalez	.25
82	Doug Glanville	.15
83	Gerald Williams	.15
84	Troy O'Leary	.15
85	Brian Giles	.15
86	Miguel Cairo	.15
87	Magglio Ordonez	.25
88	Rick Helling	.15
89	Bruce Chen	.15
90	Jason Varitek	.15
91	Mike Lieberthal	.15
92	Shawn Estes	.15
93	Rick Ankiel	.15
94	Tim Salmon	.25
95	Jacque Jones	.15
96	Johnny Damon	.25
97	Larry Walker	.15
98	Ruben Mateo	.15
99	Brad Fullmer	.15
100	Edgardo Alfonzo	.15
101	Mark Mulder	.15
102	Tony Gwynn	1.00
103	Mike Cameron	.15
104	Richie Sexson	.15
105	Barry Larkin	.15
106	Mike Piazza	1.25
107	Eric Young	.15
108	Edgar Renteria	.15
109	Todd Zeile	.15
110	Luis Castillo	.15
111	Sammy Sosa	1.25
112	David Justice	.15
113	Delino DeShields	.15
114	Mariano Rivera	.25
115	Edgar Martinez	.15
116	Ray Durham	.15
117	Brady Anderson	.15
118	Eric Owens	.15
119	Alex Gonzalez	.15
120	Jay Buhner	.15
121	Greg Vaughn	.15
122	Mike Lowell	.15
123	Marquis Grissom	.15
124	Matt Williams	.15
125	Dean Palmer	.15
126	Troy Glaus	.75
127	Bret Boone	.15
128	David Ortiz	.25
129	Glenallen Hill	.15
130	Chipper Jones	1.00
131	Tony Clark	.15
132	Terrence Long	.15
133	Chuck Finley	.15
134	Jeff Bagwell	.75
135	J.T. Snow	.15
136	Andruw Jones	.75
137	Carlos Delgado	.50
138	Mo Vaughn	.15
139	Derrek Lee	.15
140	Bobby Estalella	.15
141	Kerry Wood	.60
142	Jose Vidro	.15
143	Ben Grieve	.15
144	Barry Bonds	2.00
145	Javy Lopez	.15
146	Adam Kennedy	.15
147	Jeff Cirillo	.15
148	Cliff Floyd	.15
149	Carl Pavano	.25
150	Bobby Higginson	.15
151	Kevin Brown	.15
152	Fernando Tatis	.15
153	Matt Lawton	.15
154	Damion Easley	.15
155	Curt Schilling	.25
156	Mark McGwire	1.50
157	Mark Grace	.25
158	Adrian Beltre	.30
159	Jorge Posada	.25
160	Richard Hidalgo	.15
161	Vinny Castilla	.15
162	Bernie Williams	.30
163	John Olerud	.15
164	Todd Helton	.75
165	Craig Biggio	.15
166	David Wells	.15
167	Phil Nevin	.15
168	Andres Galarraga	.15
169	Moises Alou	.15
170	Denny Neagle	.15
171	Jeffrey Hammonds	.15
172	Sean Casey	.30
173	Gary Sheffield	.40
174	Carlos Lee	.15
175	Juan Encarnacion	.15
176	Roberto Alomar	.40
177	Kenny Rogers	.15
178	Charles Johnson	.15
179	Shannon Stewart	.15
180	B.J. Surhoff	.15
181	Paul Konerko	.15
182	Jermaine Dye	.15
183	Scott Rolen	.60
184	Fred McGriff	.15
185	Juan Gonzalez	.75
186	Carlos Beltran	.40
187	Jay Payton	.15
188	Chad Hermansen	.15
189	Pat Burrell	.50
190	Omar Vizquel	.15
191	Trot Nixon	.15
192	Mike Hampton	.15
193	Kris Benson	.15
194	Gabe Kapler	.15
195	Rickey Henderson	.75
196	J.D. Drew	.45
197	Pokey Reese	.15
198	Jeff Kent	.15
199	Jose Cruz Jr.	.15
200	Preston Wilson	.15
201	Eric Munson 2,499 (Prospects)	3.00
202	Alex Cabrera 2,499 (Prospects)	3.00
203	Nate Rolison 2,499 (Prospects)	3.00
204	Julio Zuleta 2,499 (Prospects)	3.00
205	Chris Richard 2,499 (Prospects)	3.00
206	Dernell Stenson 2,499 (Prospects)	3.00
207	Aaron McNeal 2,499 (Prospects)	3.00
208	Aubrey Huff 2,999 (Prospects)	5.00
209	Mike Lamb 2,999 (Prospects)	3.00
210	Xavier Nady 2,999 (Prospects)	4.00
211	Joe Crede 2,999 (Prospects)	4.00
212	Ben Petrick 3,499 (Prospects)	3.00
213	Morgan Burkhart 3,499 (Prospects)	3.00
214	Jason Tyner 1,999 (Prospects)	3.00
215	Juan Pierre 1,999 (Prospects)	5.00
216	Adam Dunn 1,999 (Prospects)	5.00
117	Adam Piatt 1,999 (Prospects)	3.00
218	Eric Byrnes 1,999 (Prospects)	4.00
219	Corey Patterson 1,999 (Prospects)	4.00
220	Kenny Kelly 1,999 (Prospects)	3.00
221	Tike Redman 1,999 (Prospects)	3.00
222	Luis Matos 1,999 (Prospects)	4.00
223	Timoniel Perez 1,999 (Prospects)	3.00
224	Vernon Wells 1,999 (Prospects)	3.00
225	Barry Zito 4,999 (Prospects)	5.00
226	Adam Bernero 4,999 (Prospects)	3.00
227	Kazuhiro Sasaki 4,999 (Prospects)	6.00
228	Oswaldo Mairena 4,999 (Prospects)	3.00
229	Mark Buehrle 4,999 (Prospects)	4.00
230	Ryan Dempster 4,999 (Prospects)	3.00
231	Tim Hudson 4,999 (Prospects)	5.00
232	Scott Downs 4,999 (Prospects)	3.00
233	A.J. Burnett 4,999 (Prospects)	4.00
234	Adam Eaton 4,999 (Prospects)	3.00
235	Paxton Crawford 4,999 (Prospects)	3.00
236	Jace Brewer 3,999 (Prospects)	3.00
237	Jose Ortiz 3,999 (Prospects)	3.00
238	Rafael Furcal 3,999 (Prospects)	4.00
239	Julio Lugo 3,999 (Prospects)	3.00
240	Tomas de la Rosa 3,999 (Prospects)	3.00

Green

NM/M

Common Player: 1.00
Random inserts in packs.
Stated print runs listed below.

1	Derek Jeter/339	10.00
2	Manny Ramirez/351	4.00
3	Ken Griffey Jr./271	8.00
4	Ken Caminiti/303	1.00
5	Joe Randa/304	1.00
6	Jason Kendall/270	1.50
7	Ron Coomer/270	1.00
8	Rondell White/258	1.50
9	Tino Martinez/258	2.00
10	Nomar Garciaparra/372	10.00
11	Tony Batista/263	1.00
12	Todd Stottlemyre/491	1.00
13	Ryan Klesko/283	1.50
14	Darin Erstad/355	1.50
15	Todd Walker/290	1.00
16	Al Leiter/320	1.00
17	Carl Everett/300	1.00
18	Bobby Abreu/316	1.50
19	Raul Mondesi/271	1.00
20	Vladimir Guerrero/345	5.00
21	Mike Bordick/285	1.00
22	Aaron Sele/451	1.00
23	Ray Lankford/253	1.00
24	Roger Clemens/370	10.00
25	Kevin Young/258	1.00
26	Brad Radke/445	1.00
27	Todd Hundley/284	1.00
28	Ellis Burks/344	1.00
29	Lee Stevens/265	1.00
30	Eric Karros/250	1.00
31	Darren Dreifort/416	1.00
32	Ivan Rodriguez/347	4.00
33	Pedro Martinez/174	5.00
34	Travis Fryman/321	1.50
35	Garret Anderson/286	2.00
36	Rafael Palmeiro/288	3.00
37	Jason Giambi/333	5.00
38	Jeromy Burnitz/232	1.00
39	Robin Ventura/232	1.50
40	Derek Bell/266	1.00
41	Carlos Guillen/257	1.00
42	Albert Belle/281	1.00
43	Henry Rodriguez/256	1.00
44	Brian Jordan/264	1.00
45	Mike Sweeney/333	1.00
46	Ruben Rivera/208	1.00
47	Greg Maddux/300	8.00
48	Corey Koskie/300	1.00
49	Sandy Alomar Jr./289	1.00
50	Mike Mussina/379	3.00
51	Tom Glavine/340	2.00
52	Aaron Boone/285	1.00
53	Frank Thomas/328	4.00
54	Kenny Lofton/278	2.00
55	Danny Graves/256	1.00
56	Jose Valentin/273	1.00
57	Travis Lee/235	1.00
58	Jim Edmonds/295	2.00
59	Jim Thome/269	4.00
60	Steve Finley/280	1.00
61	Shawn Green/269	2.00
62	Lance Berkman/297	2.00
63	Mark Quinn/294	1.00
64	Randy Johnson/264	5.00
65	Dmitri Young/303	1.00
66	Andy Pettitte/435	2.00
67	Paul O'Neill/283	2.00
68	Gil Heredia/412	1.00

69 Russell Branyan/238 1.00
70 Alex Rodriguez/316 10.00
71 Geoff Jenkins/303 1.50
72 Eric Chavez/277 2.00
73 Cal Ripken Jr./256 15.00
74 Mark Kotsay/298 1.00
75 Jeff D'Amico/266 1.00
76 Tony Womack/271 1.00
77 Eric Milton/486 1.00
78 Joe Girardi/278 1.00
79 Peter Bergeron/245 1.00
80 Miguel Tejada/275 2.00
81 Luis Gonzalez/311 2.00
82 Doug Glanville/275 1.00
83 Gerald Williams/274 1.00
84 Troy O'Leary/261 1.00
85 Brian Giles/315 2.00
86 Miguel Cairo/261 1.00
87 Magglio Ordonez/315 2.00
88 Rick Helling/448 1.00
89 Bruce Chen/329 1.00
90 Jason Varitek/248 1.00
91 Mike Lieberthal/278 1.00
92 Shawn Estes/426 1.00
93 Rick Ankiel/350 1.00
94 Tim Salmon/290 2.00
95 Jacque Jones/285 1.00
96 Johnny Damon/327 1.50
97 Larry Walker/309 2.00
98 Ruben Mateo/291 1.00
99 Brad Fullmer/295 1.00
100 Edgardo Alfonzo/324 1.00
101 Mark Mulder/544 2.00
102 Tony Gwynn/323 5.00
103 Mike Cameron/267 1.00
104 Richie Sexson/272 2.00
105 Barry Larkin/313 2.00
106 Mike Piazza/324 8.00
107 Eric Young/297 1.00
108 Edgar Renteria/278 1.00
109 Todd Zeile/268 1.00
110 Luis Castillo/334 1.00
111 Sammy Sosa/320 10.00
112 David Justice/286 1.50
113 Delino DeShields/296 1.00
114 Mariano Rivera/285 1.50
115 Edgar Martinez/324 2.00
116 Ray Durham/280 1.00
117 Brady Anderson/257 1.00
118 Eric Owens/293 1.00
119 Alex Gonzalez/252 1.00
120 Jay Buhner/253 1.00
121 Greg Vaughn/254 1.00
122 Mike Lowell/270 1.00
123 Marquis Grissom/244 1.00
124 Matt Williams/275 1.50
125 Dean Palmer/256 1.00
126 Troy Glaus/284 3.00
127 Bret Boone/251 1.50
128 David Ortiz/282 1.00
129 Glenallen Hill/293 1.00
130 Chipper Jones/311 8.00
131 Tony Clark/274 1.00
132 Terrence Long/288 1.00
133 Chuck Finley/417 1.00
134 Jeff Bagwell/310 4.00
135 J.T. Snow/284 1.00
136 Andruw Jones/303 3.00
137 Carlos Delgado/344 3.00
138 Mo Vaughn/272 1.50
139 Derek Lee/281 1.50
140 Bobby Estalella/234 1.00
141 Kerry Wood/480 3.00
142 Jose Vidro/330 1.00
143 Ben Grieve/279 1.00
144 Barry Bonds/306 12.00
145 Javy Lopez/287 2.00
146 Adam Kennedy/266 1.00
147 Jeff Cirillo/326 1.00
148 Cliff Floyd/300 1.00
149 Carl Pavano/306 1.00
150 Bobby Higginson/300 1.00
151 Kevin Brown/258 2.00
152 Fernando Tatis/253 1.00
153 Matt Lawton/305 1.00
154 Damion Easley/259 1.00
155 Curt Schilling/381 3.00
156 Mark McGwire/305 10.00
157 Mark Grace/280 2.50
158 Adrian Beltre/290 1.50
159 Jorge Posada/287 2.00
160 Richard Hidalgo/314 1.00
161 Vinny Castilla/221 1.00
162 Bernie Williams/307 3.00
163 John Olerud/285 1.50
164 Todd Helton/372 4.00
165 Craig Biggio/268 1.50
166 David Wells/411 1.00
167 Phil Nevin/303 1.00
168 Andres Galarraga/302 1.00
169 Moises Alou/355 2.00
170 Denny Neagle/452 1.00
171 Jeffrey Hammonds/335 1.00
172 Sean Casey/315 1.00
173 Gary Sheffield/325 2.00
174 Carlos Lee/301 1.00
175 Juan Encarnacion/289 1.00
176 Roberto Alomar/310 3.00
177 Kenny Rogers/455 1.00
178 Charles Johnson/315 1.00
179 Shannon Stewart/319 1.00
180 B.J. Surhoff/291 1.00
181 Paul Konerko/298 1.00
182 Jermaine Dye/321 1.00
183 Scott Rolen/298 4.00
184 Fred McGriff/277 2.00
185 Juan Gonzalez/289 4.00
186 Carlos Beltran/247 1.50
187 Jay Payton/291 1.50
188 Chad Hermansen/185 1.00
189 Pat Burrell/260 3.00
190 Omar Vizquel/287 2.00
191 Trot Nixon/276 1.00
192 Mike Hampton/314 1.00
193 Kris Benson/385 1.00
194 Gabe Kapler/302 1.00
195 Rickey Henderson/233 3.00
196 J.D. Drew/295 2.00
197 Pokey Reese/255 1.00
198 Jeff Kent/334 1.50
199 Jose Cruz Jr./242 1.00
200 Preston Wilson/264 1.00
201 Eric Munson/252 1.00
202 Alex Cabrera/263 1.00
203 Nate Rolison/77 1.00
204 Julio Zuleta/294 1.00
205 Chris Richard/265 1.00
206 Dernell Stenson/268 1.00
207 Aaron McNeal/310 1.00
208 Aubrey Huff/287 1.00
209 Mike Lamb/278 1.00
211 Joe Crede/357 2.00
212 Ben Petrick/322 1.00
213 Morgan Burkhart/288 1.00
214 Jason Tyner/226 1.00
215 Juan Pierre/310 3.00
216 Adam Dunn/281 4.00
217 Adam Piatt/299 1.00
218 Eric Byrnes/300 1.00
219 Corey Patterson/167 2.00
220 Kenny Kelly/252 1.00
221 Tike Redman/333 1.00
222 Luis Matos/225 1.00
223 Timo Perez/286 1.00
224 Vernon Wells/243 2.00
225 Barry Zito/272 3.00
226 Adam Bernero/419 1.00
227 Kazuhiro Sasaki/316 2.00
228 Oswaldo Mairena/18 5.00
229 Mark Buehrle/421 1.50
230 Ryan Dempster/366 1.00
231 Tim Hudson/414 2.00
232 Scott Downs/529 1.00
233 A.J. Burnett/479 1.00
234 Adam Eaton/413 1.00
235 Paxton Crawford/341 1.00
237 Jose Ortiz/182 1.00
238 Rafael Furcal/295 2.00
239 Julio Lugo/283 1.00
240 Tomas De La Rosa/288 1.00

Autographics

NM/M
Common Player: 5.00
Inserted 1:72
Silvers: 1-1.5X
Production 250 Sets
Golds: 1-1.5X
Production 50 Sets
Roberto Alomar 30.00
Rick Ankiel 5.00
Albert Belle 5.00
Adrian Beltre 15.00
Lance Berkman 8.00
Barry Bonds 200.00
Jeromy Burnitz 5.00
Pat Burrell 10.00
Sean Casey 8.00
Eric Chavez 10.00
Carlos Delgado 10.00
J.D. Drew 10.00
Jermaine Dye 5.00
Jim Edmonds 10.00
Troy Glaus 15.00
Ben Grieve 5.00
Tony Gwynn 30.00
Randy Johnson 40.00
Chipper Jones 40.00
Mike Lamb 5.00
Mike Lieberthal 5.00
Terrence Long 5.00
Greg Maddux 50.00
Edgar Martinez 15.00
Kevin Millwood 10.00
Mike Mussina 25.00
Corey Patterson 10.00
Jay Payton 8.00
Juan Pierre 8.00
Brad Radke 5.00
Scott Rolen 20.00
Gary Sheffield 15.00
Fernando Tatis 5.00
Robin Ventura 5.00
Kerry Wood 20.00

Bat Company

NM/M
Complete Set (10): 25.00
Common Player: 1.00
Inserted 1:24
1 Barry Bonds 5.00
2 Mark McGwire 4.00

3 Sammy Sosa 3.00
4 Ken Griffey Jr. 3.00
5 Mike Piazza 3.00
6 Derek Jeter 5.00
7 Gary Sheffield 1.00
8 Frank Thomas 1.50
9 Chipper Jones 2.00
10 Alex Rodriguez 4.00

Big Innings

NM/M
Complete Set (25): 15.00
Common Player: .50
Inserted 1:6
VIP: 5-10X
Production 50 Sets
1 Rick Ankiel .50
2 Andruw Jones 1.00
3 Brian Giles .50
4 Derek Jeter 4.00
5 Rafael Furcal .50
6 Richie Sexson .50
7 Jay Payton .50
8 Carlos Delgado .75
9 Jermaine Dye .50
10 Darin Erstad .75
11 Pat Burrell .75
12 Richard Hidalgo .50
13 Adrian Beltre .60
14 Todd Helton 1.00
15 Vladimir Guerrero 1.00
16 Nomar Garciaparra 2.00
17 Gabe Kapler .50
18 Carlos Lee .50
19 J.D. Drew .60
20 Troy Glaus 1.00
21 Scott Rolen 1.00
22 Alex Rodriguez 3.00
23 Magglio Ordonez .60
24 Miguel Tejada .60
25 Ruben Mateo .50

Diamond Vision

NM/M
Complete Set (15): 25.00
Common Player: 1.00
Inserted 1:12
1 Derek Jeter 4.00
2 Nomar Garciaparra 2.50
3 Cal Ripken Jr. 4.00
4 Jeff Bagwell 1.50
5 Mark McGwire 3.00
6 Ken Griffey Jr. 2.50
7 Pedro Martinez 1.50
8 Carlos Delgado 1.00
9 Chipper Jones 2.00
10 Barry Bonds 4.00
11 Mike Piazza 2.50
12 Sammy Sosa 2.50
13 Alex Rodriguez 3.00
14 Frank Thomas 1.50
15 Randy Johnson 1.50

Feel the Game

NM/M
Common Player: 5.00
Inserted 1:72
Moises Alou 6.00
Brady Anderson 5.00
Dante Bichette 5.00
Jermaine Dye 5.00
Brian Giles 6.00
Juan Gonzalez 10.00
Rickey Henderson 15.00
Javy Lopez 6.00
Tino Martinez 6.00
Phil Nevin 5.00
Matt Stairs 5.00
Shannon Stewart 5.00
Jose Vidro 5.00

ROY Collection

NM/M
Complete Set (25): 75.00
Common Player: 2.00
Inserted 1:24
1 Luis Aparicio 2.00
2 Johnny Bench 3.00
3 Joe Black 2.00
4 Rod Carew 2.00
5 Orlando Cepeda 2.00
6 Carlton Fisk 2.00
7 Ben Grieve 2.00
8 Frank Howard 2.00
9 Derek Jeter 10.00
10 Fred Lynn 2.00
11 Willie Mays 8.00
12 Willie McCovey 2.00
13 Mark McGwire 8.00
14 Raul Mondesi 2.00
15 Thurman Munson 4.00
16 Eddie Murray 2.00
17 Mike Piazza 6.00
18 Cal Ripken Jr. 10.00
19 Frank Robinson 2.00
20 Jackie Robinson 8.00
21 Scott Rolen 3.00
22 Tom Seaver 2.00
23 Fernando Valenzuela 2.00
24 David Justice 2.00
25 Billy Williams 2.00

ROY Collection Memorabilia

NM/M
Common Player: 8.00
Inserted 1:288
1 Luis Aparicio/Bat 8.00
2 Johnny Bench/Jsy 15.00
3 Orlando Cepeda/Bat 8.00
4 Carlton Fisk/Jsy 10.00
5 Ben Grieve/Jsy 8.00
6 Frank Howard/Bat 8.00
7 Derek Jeter/Jsy 50.00
8 Fred Lynn/Bat 8.00
9 Willie Mays/Jsy 60.00
10 Willie McCovey/Bat 10.00
11 Mark McGwire/Ball 50.00
12 Raul Mondesi/Bat 8.00
13 Thurman Munson/Bat 25.00
14 Eddie Murray/Jsy 10.00
15 Mike Piazza/Base 15.00
16 Cal Ripken/Jsy 50.00
17 Frank Robinson/Bat 10.00
18 Jackie Robinson/Jsy 75.00
19 Scott Rolen/Bat 15.00
20 Tom Seaver/Jsy 15.00
22 David Justice/Jsy 8.00

ROY Collection Signed Memorabilia

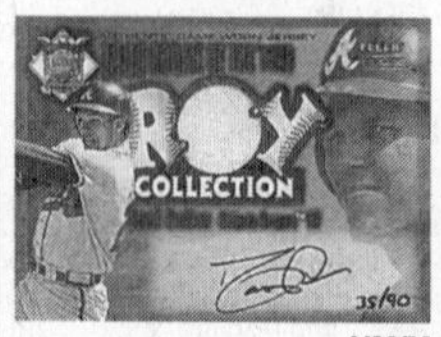

NM/M
Common Player: 25.00
1 Luis Aparicio/Jsy/56 40.00
2 Johnny Bench/68 85.00
3 Orlando Cepeda/58 25.00
4 Carlton Fisk/72 50.00
5 Ben Grieve/98 25.00
6 Frank Howard/60 25.00
7 Derek Jeter/96 200.00
8 Fred Lynn/75 25.00
9 Willie Mays/Jsy/51 200.00
10 Willie McCovey/Bat/59 40.00
11 Raul Mondesi/94 25.00
12 Eddie Murray/77 50.00
13 Cal Ripken/82 275.00
14 Frank Robinson/Bat/225 50.00
15 Scott Rolen/97 50.00
16 Tom Seaver/67 90.00
18 David Justice/90 25.00

2001 Fleer Futures

NM/M
Complete Set (220): 20.00
Common Player: .15
Pack (8): 1.50
Box (28): 30.00
1 Darin Erstad .60
2 Manny Ramirez .75
3 Darryl Kile .15
4 Troy O'Leary .15
5 Mark Quinn .15
6 Brian Giles .15
7 Randy Johnson .75
8 Todd Walker .15
9 Mike Piazza 1.50
10 Fred McGriff .15
11 Sammy Sosa 1.50
12 Chan Ho Park .15
13 John Rocker .15
14 Luis Castillo .15
15 Eric Chavez .25
16 Carlos Delgado .50
17 Sean Casey .25
18 Corey Koskie .15
19 John Olerud .15
20 Nomar Garciaparra 1.50
21 Craig Biggio .15
22 Pat Burrell .40
23 Bengie Molina .15
24 Jim Thome .15
25 Rey Ordonez .15
26 Fernando Tatis .15
27 Eric Young .15
28 Eric Karros .15
29 Adam Eaton .15
30 Brian Jordan .15
31 Jorge Posada .25
32 Gabe Kapler .15
33 Keith Foulke .15
34 Ron Coomer .15
35 Chipper Jones 1.00
36 Miguel Tejada .25
37 David Wells .15
38 Carlos Lee .15
39 Barry Bonds 2.50
40 Derrek Lee .15
41 Tim Hudson .25
42 Billy Koch .15
43 Dmitri Young .15
44 Vladimir Guerrero .75
45 Rickey Henderson .75
46 Jeff Bagwell .75
47 Robert Person .15
48 Brady Anderson .15
49 Lance Berkman .15
50 Mike Lieberthal .15
51 Adam Kennedy .15
52 Russ Branyan .15
53 Robin Ventura .15
54 Mark McGwire 2.00
55 Tony Gwynn 1.00
56 Matt Williams .15
57 Jeff Cirillo .15
58 Roger Clemens 1.25
59 Ivan Rodriguez .65
60 Brad Radke .15
61 Kazuhiro Sasaki .15
62 Cal Ripken Jr. 2.50
63 Ken Caminiti .15
64 Bobby Abreu .15
65 Troy Glaus .75
66 Sandy Alomar Jr. .15
67 Jose Vidro .15
68 Pedro Martinez .75
69 Kevin Young .15
70 Jay Bell .15
71 Larry Walker .15
72 Derek Jeter 2.50
73 Miguel Cairo .15
74 Magglio Ordonez .15
75 Jeromy Burnitz .15
76 J.T. Snow .15
77 Andres Galarraga .15
78 Ryan Dempster .15
79 Ken Griffey Jr. 1.50
80 Aaron Sele .15
81 Tom Glavine .25
82 Hideo Nomo .65
83 Orlando Hernandez .15
84 Tony Batista .15
85 Aaron Boone .15
86 Jacque Jones .15
87 Delino DeShields .15
88 Garret Anderson .15
89 Fernando Seguignol .15
90 Jim Edmonds .15
91 Frank Thomas .75
92 Adrian Beltre .30
93 Ellis Burks .15
94 Andruw Jones .75
95 Tony Clark .15
96 Danny Graves .15
97 Alex Rodriguez 2.00
98 Mike Mussina .40
99 Scott Elarton .15
100 Jason Giambi .50
101 Jay Payton .15
102 Gerald Williams .15
103 Kerry Wood .50
104 Shawn Green .35
105 Greg Maddux 1.00
106 Juan Encarnacion .15
107 Bernie Williams .30
108 Mike Lamb .15
109 Charles Johnson .15
110 Richie Sexson .15
111 Jeff Kent .15
112 Albert Belle .15
113 Cliff Floyd .15
114 Ben Grieve .15
115 Tim Salmon .25
116 Carl Pavano .15
117 Rick Ankiel .15
118 Dante Bichette .15
119 Johnny Damon .30
120 Brian Anderson .15
121 Roberto Alomar .40
122 Mike Hampton .15
123 Greg Vaughn .15
124 Carl Everett .15
125 Moises Alou .15
126 Jason Kendall .15
127 Omar Vizquel .15
128 Mark Grace .25
129 Kevin Brown .15
130 Phil Nevin .15
131 Kevin Millwood .15
132 Bobby Higginson .15
133 Ruben Mateo .15
134 Luis Gonzalez .25
135 Dean Palmer .15
136 Mariano Rivera .25
137 Rick Helling .15
138 Paul Konerko .15
139 Marquis Grissom .15
140 Robb Nen .15
141 Javy Lopez .15
142 Preston Wilson .15
143 Terrence Long .15
144 Shannon Stewart .15
145 Barry Larkin .15
146 Cristian Guzman .15
147 Jay Buhner .15
148 Jermaine Dye .15
149 Kris Benson .15
150 Curt Schilling .40
151 Todd Helton .75
152 Paul O'Neill .15
153 Rafael Palmeiro .65
154 Ray Durham .15
155 Geoff Jenkins .15
156 Livan Hernandez .15
157 Rafael Furcal .15
158 Juan Gonzalez .75
159 Tino Martinez .15
160 Raul Mondesi .15
161 Matt Lawton .15
162 Edgar Martinez .15
163 Richard Hidalgo .15
164 Scott Rolen .65
165 Chuck Finley .15
166 Edgardo Alfonzo .15
167 J.D. Drew .35
168 Trot Nixon .15
169 Carlos Beltran .50
170 Ryan Klesko .15
171 Mo Vaughn .15
172 Kenny Lofton .15
173 Al Leiter .15
174 Rondell White .15
175 Mike Sweeney .15
176 Trevor Hoffman .15
177 Steve Finley .15
178 Jeffrey Hammonds .15
179 David Justice .15
180 Gary Sheffield .40
181 Eric Munson (Bright Futures) .15
182 Luis Matos (Bright Futures) .15
183 Alex Cabrera (Bright Futures) .15
184 Randy Keisler (Bright Futures) .15
185 Nate Rolison (Bright Futures) .15
186 Jason Hart (Bright Futures) .15
187 Timo Perez (Bright Futures) .15
188 Adam Bernero (Bright Futures) .15
189 Barry Zito (Bright Futures) .50
190 Ryan Kohlmeier (Bright Futures) .15

191 Joey Nation (Bright Futures) .15
192 Oswaldo Mairena (Bright Futures) .15
193 Aubrey Huff (Bright Futures) .15
194 Mark Buehrle (Bright Futures) .15
195 Jace Brewer (Bright Futures) .15
196 Julio Zuleta (Bright Futures) .15
197 Xavier Nady (Bright Futures) .15
198 Vernon Wells (Bright Futures) .25
199 Joe Crede (Bright Futures) .15
200 Scott Downs (Bright Futures) .15
201 Ben Petrick (Bright Futures) .15
202 A.J. Burnett (Bright Futures) .15
203 Esix Snead **RC** (Bright Futures) .15
204 Dernell Stenson (Bright Futures) .15
205 Jose Ortiz (Bright Futures) .15
206 Paxton Crawford (Bright Futures) .15
207 Jason Tyner (Bright Futures) .15
208 Jimmy Rollins (Bright Futures) .25
209 Juan Pierre (Bright Futures) .25
210 Keith Ginter (Bright Futures) .15
211 Adam Dunn (Bright Futures) .40
212 Larry Barnes (Bright Futures) .15
213 Adam Piatt (Bright Futures) .15
214 Rodney Lindsey (Bright Futures) .15
215 Eric Byrnes (Bright Futures) .15
216 Julio Lugo (Bright Futures) .15
217 Corey Patterson (Bright Futures) .25
218 Reggie Taylor (Bright Futures) .15
219 Kenny Kelly (Bright Futures) .15
220 Tike Redman (Bright Futures) .15

Black Gold

Production 499 Sets: 3-6X

Bases Loaded

NM/M
Common Player: 4.00
Inserted 1:134
BL1 Ken Griffey Jr. 10.00
BL2 Mark McGwire 12.00
BL3 Carlos Delgado 4.00
BL4 Chipper Jones 7.50
BL5 Nomar Garciaparra 10.00
BL6 Cal Ripken Jr. 15.00
BL7 Sammy Sosa 10.00
BL8 Jeff Bagwell 6.00
BL9 Vladimir Guerrero 6.00
BL10 Tony Gwynn 7.50
BL11 Frank Thomas 6.00
BL12 Mike Piazza 10.00
BL13 Jason Giambi 5.00
BL14 Troy Glaus 6.00
BL15 Pat Burrell 4.00

Bats to the Future

NM/M
Complete Set (25): 60.00

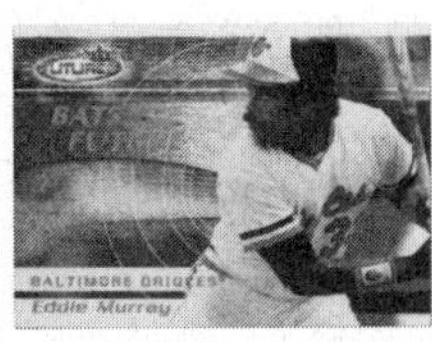

Common Player: 1.00
Inserted 1:28
1BF Mike Schmidt 6.00
2BF Carlton Fisk 3.00
3BF Paul Molitor 3.00
4BF Vladimir Guerrero 3.00
5BF Dave Parker 1.00
6BF Chipper Jones 5.00
7BF Carlos Delgado 2.00
8BF Tony Gwynn 5.00
9BF Reggie Jackson 5.00
10BF Eddie Murray 1.50
11BF Robin Yount 3.00
12BF Alan Trammell 1.00
13BF Frank Thomas 3.00
14BF Cal Ripken Jr. 8.00
15BF Don Mattingly 6.00
16BF Jim Rice 1.00
17BF Juan Gonzalez 3.00
18BF Todd Helton 3.00
19BF George Brett 6.00
20BF Barry Bonds 8.00
21BF Kirk Gibson 1.00
22BF Matt Williams 1.00
23BF Dave Winfield 1.50
24BF Ryne Sandberg 5.00
25BF Ivan Rodriguez 2.00

Bats to the Future Game Bat

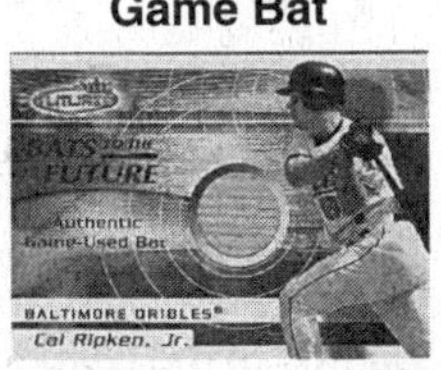

NM/M
Common Player: 5.00
Inserted 1:114
1BF Mike Schmidt 25.00
2BF Carlton Fisk 10.00
3BF Paul Molitor 15.00
4BF Vladimir Guerrero 8.00
5BF Dave Parker 5.00
6BF Chipper Jones 10.00
7BF Chris Delgado 8.00
8BF Tony Gwynn 10.00
9BF Reggie Jackson 10.00
10BF Eddie Murray 8.00
11BF Robin Yount 15.00
12BF Alan Trammell 5.00
13BF Frank Thomas 8.00
14BF Cal Ripken Jr. 30.00
15BF Don Mattingly 30.00
16BF Jim Rice 5.00
17BF Juan Gonzalez 8.00
18BF Todd Helton 8.00
19BF George Brett 25.00
20BF Barry Bonds 25.00
21BF Kirk Gibson 5.00
22BF Matt Williams 5.00
23BF Dave Winfield 8.00
24BF Ryne Sandberg 15.00
25BF Ivan Rodriguez 8.00

Bats to the Future Game Bat Autograph

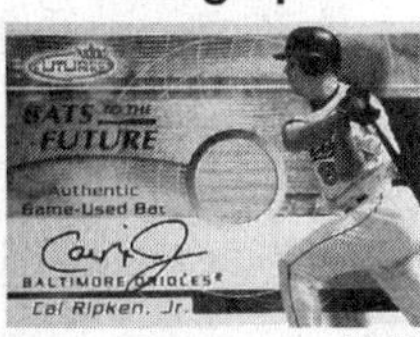

NM/M
Common Autograph: 40.00
Production 50 Sets
1BF Mike Schmidt 150.00
2BF Carlton Fisk 60.00
3BF Paul Molitor 50.00
4BF Vladimir Guerrero 80.00
5BF Dave Parker 40.00
6BF Chipper Jones 75.00
7BF Carlos Delgado 50.00
8BF Tony Gwynn 75.00
9BF Reggie Jackson 70.00
10BF Eddie Murray 70.00
11BF Robin Yount 80.00
12BF Alan Trammell 40.00
13BF Frank Thomas 60.00
14BF Cal Ripken Jr. 200.00
15BF Don Mattingly 150.00
16BF Jim Rice 40.00
17BF Juan Gonzalez 60.00
18BF Todd Helton 60.00
19BF George Brett 150.00
20BF Barry Bonds 200.00
21BF Kirk Gibson 40.00
22BF Matt Williams 40.00
23BF Dave Winfield 60.00
24BF Ryne Sandberg 125.00
25BF Ivan Rodriguez 60.00

Characteristics

NM/M
Complete Set (15): 20.00
Common Player: .75
Inserted 1:9
1C Derek Jeter 4.00
2C Mark McGwire 3.00
3C Nomar Garciaparra 2.50
4C Sammy Sosa 2.50
5C Pedro Martinez 1.50
6C Chipper Jones 2.00
7C Cal Ripken Jr. 4.00
8C Todd Helton 1.50
9C Jim Edmonds .75
10C Ken Griffey Jr. 2.50
11C Alex Rodriguez 3.00
12C Mike Piazza 2.50
13C Vladimir Guerrero 1.50
14C Frank Thomas 1.50
15C Carlos Delgado 1.00

Hot Commodities

NM/M
Complete Set (10): 20.00
Common Player: 1.00
Inserted 1:14
1HC Mark McGwire 3.00
2HC Ken Griffey Jr. 2.50
3HC Derek Jeter 4.00
4HC Cal Ripken Jr. 4.00
5HC Chipper Jones 2.00
6HC Barry Bonds 4.00
7HC Mike Piazza 2.50
8HC Sammy Sosa 2.50
9HC Alex Rodriguez 3.00
10HC Frank Thomas 1.00

September Call-Ups Memorabilia

NM/M
Common Card: 4.00
Production 200 Sets
184 Randy Keisler/Cap/Cleat 4.00
185 Nate Rolison/Bat 4.00
187 Timoniel Perez/Bat 4.00
191 Joey Nation/Glove 4.00
192 Oswaldo Mairena/Glove 4.00
195 Jace Brewer/Bat 4.00
197 Xavier Nady/Glove 6.00
199 Joe Crede/Bat 6.00
205 Jose Ortiz/Bat 4.00
208 Jimmy Rollins/Glove 6.00
210 Keith Ginter/Bat 4.00
214 Rodney Lindsey/Bat 4.00
217 Corey Patterson/Bat 8.00
218 Reggie Taylor/Bat 4.00
219 Kenny Kelly/Bat 4.00

2001 Fleer Game Time

NM/M
Complete Set (121):
Common Player: .15
Common (91-121): 3.00
Production 2,000
Pack (5): 4.00
Box (24): 80.00
1 Derek Jeter 2.00
2 Nomar Garciaparra 1.25
3 Alex Rodriguez 1.50
4 Jason Kendall .15
5 Barry Bonds 2.00
6 David Wells .15
7 Craig Biggio .15
8 Adrian Beltre .30
9 Pat Burrell .40
10 Rafael Palmeiro .60
11 Jim Thome .15
12 Mike Lowell .15
13 Trevor Hoffman .15
14 Pokey Reese .15
15 Juan Encarnacion .15
16 Shawn Green .40
17 Kerry Wood .50
18 Richard Hidalgo .15
19 Scott Rolen .60
20 Jeff Kent .15
21 Alex Gonzalez .15
22 Matt Williams .15
23 Mike Sweeney .15
24 Edgar Martinez .15
25 Sammy Sosa 1.25
26 Bobby Higginson .15
27 Kevin Brown .15
28 Mike Lieberthal .15
29 Pedro J. Martinez .75
30 Jeff Weaver .15
31 Greg Maddux 1.00
32 Mike Hampton .15
33 Vladimir Guerrero .75
34 Greg Vaughn .15
35 Manny Ramirez .75
36 Carlos Beltran .40
37 Eric Chavez .25
38 Troy Glaus .75
39 Todd Helton .75
40 Gary Sheffield .40
41 Brady Anderson .15
42 Juan Gonzalez .75
43 Tim Hudson .30
44 Kenny Lofton .15
45 Al Leiter .15
46 Eric Owens .15
47 Roberto Alomar .40
48 Preston Wilson .15
49 Tony Gwynn 1.00
50 Cal Ripken Jr. 2.00
51 Ben Petrick .15
52 Jason Giambi .50
53 Ben Grieve .15
54 Albert Belle .15
55 Jose Vidro .15
56 Barry Zito .30
57 Ivan Rodriguez .60
58 Jeff Bagwell .75
59 Geoff Jenkins .15
60 Roger Clemens 1.00
61 John Olerud .75
62 Randy Johnson .75
63 Matt Lawton .15
64 Mark McGwire 1.50
65 Brad Radke .15
66 Frank Thomas .75
67 Edgardo Alfonzo .15
68 Brian Giles .15
69 J.T. Snow .15
70 Carlos Delgado .50
71 Chipper Jones 1.00
72 Mark Quinn .15
73 Mike Mussina .40
74 Rick Ankiel .15
75 Rafael Furcal .15
76 Jim Edmonds .15
77 Vinny Castilla .15
78 Sean Casey .25
79 Derrek Lee .15
80 Mike Piazza 1.25
81 Warren Morris .15
82 Tim Salmon .25
83 Jeromy Burnitz .15
84 Freddy Garcia .15
85 Ken Griffey Jr. 1.25
86 Andruw Jones .75
87 Darryl Kile .15
88 Magglio Ordonez .15
89 Bernie Williams .30
90 Timo Perez .15
91 Ichiro Suzuki **RC** (Next Game) 35.00
92 Larry Barnes, Darin Erstad (Next Game) 3.00
93 Jaisen Randolph **RC** (Next Game) 3.00
94 Paul Phillips **RC** (Next Game) 3.00
95 Esix Snead **RC** (Next Game) 3.00
96 Matt White **RC** (Next Game) 3.00
97 Ryan Freel **RC** (Next Game) 3.00
98 Winston Abreu **RC** (Next Game) 3.00
99 Junior Spivey **RC** (Next Game) 5.00
100 Randy Keisler, Roger Clemens (Next Game) 5.00
101 Brian Cole, Mike Piazza (Next Game) 4.00
102 Aubrey Huff, Chipper Jones (Next Game) 4.00
103 Corey Patterson, Sammy Sosa (Next Game) 5.00
104 Sun-Woo Kim, Pedro Martinez (Next Game) 4.00
105 Drew Henson **RC** (Next Game) 5.00
106 Claudio Vargas **RC** (Next Game) 3.00
107 Cesar Izturis, Rafael Furcal (Next Game) 3.00
108 Paxton Crawford, Pedro Martinez (Next Game) 4.00
109 Adrian Hernandez **RC** (Next Game) 3.00
110 Jace Brewer, Derek Jeter (Next Game) 8.00
111 Andy Morales **RC** (Next Game) 3.00
112 Wilson Betemit **RC** (Next Game) 3.00
113 Juan Diaz **RC** (Next Game) 3.00
114 Erick Almonte **RC** (Next Game) 4.00
115 Nick Punto **RC** (Next Game) 3.00
116 Tsuyoshi Shinjo **RC** (Next Game) 4.00
117 Jay Gibbons **RC** (Next Game) 5.00
118 Andres Torres **RC** (Next Game) 3.00
119 Alexis Gomez **RC** (Next Game) 4.00
120 Wilken Ruan **RC** (Next Game) 3.00
121 Albert Pujols **RC** (Next Game) 80.00

Next Game Extra

Cards (91-121): 2-3X
Production 200 Sets

Famers Lumber

NM/M
Common Player: 8.00
Production 100 Sets
1FL Luis Aparicio 8.00
2FL Hank Bauer 8.00
3FL Paul Blair 8.00
4FL Bobby Bonds 8.00
5FL Orlando Cepeda 8.00
6FL Roberto Clemente 100.00
7FL Rocky Colavito 10.00
8FL Bucky Dent 8.00
9FL Bill Dickey 10.00
10FL Larry Doby 10.00
11FL Carlton Fisk 10.00
12FL Hank Greenberg 25.00
13FL Elston Howard 8.00
14FL Frank Howard 8.00
15FL Reggie Jackson 15.00
16FL Harmon Killebrew 20.00
17FL Tony Lazzeri 8.00
18FL Roger Maris 60.00
19FL Johnny Mize 10.00
20FL Thurman Munson 40.00
21FL Tony Perez 10.00
22FL Jim Rice 8.00
23FL Phil Rizzuto 10.00
24FL Bill Skowron 8.00
25FL Enos Slaughter 10.00
26FL Duke Snider 15.00
27FL Willie Stargell 15.00
28FL Bill Terry 8.00
29FL Ted Williams 100.00

Famers Lumber Autograph

NM/M
Common Player: 40.00
Production 25 Sets
1FLS Hank Bauer 40.00

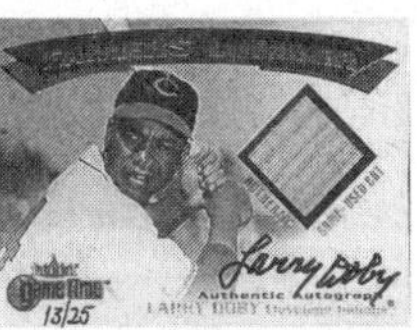

2FLS Bobby Bonds 50.00
3FLS Orlando Cepeda 50.00
4FLS Rocky Colavito 50.00
5FLS Bucky Dent 40.00
6FLS Larry Doby 50.00
7FLS Carlton Fisk 65.00
8FLS Frank Howard 40.00
9FLS Reggie Jackson 100.00
10FLS Harmon Killebrew 120.00
11FLS Tony Perez 40.00
12FLS Jim Rice 40.00
13FLS Phil Rizzuto 60.00
14FLS Bill Skowron 40.00
15FLS Enos Slaughter 40.00
16FLS Duke Snider 75.00

Derek Jeter's Monumental Moments

NM/M
Complete Set (2):
1JM Derek Jeter/1996 8.00
1JMS Derek Jeter/Auto./96 80.00

Let's Play Two!

NM/M
Complete Set (15): 30.00
Common Card: 1.50
Inserted 1:24
1LT Derek Jeter, Nomar Garciaparra 4.00
2LT Mark McGwire, Sammy Sosa 3.00
3LT Pedro J. Martinez, Randy Johnson 1.50
4LT Vladimir Guerrero, Carlos Delgado 1.50
5LT Mike Piazza, Roger Clemens 2.50
6LT Alex Rodriguez, Miguel Tejada 3.00
7LT Troy Glaus, Chipper Jones 2.00
8LT Derek Jeter, Alex Rodriguez 4.00
9LT Cal Ripken Jr., Derek Jeter 4.00
10LT Jason Giambi, Mark McGwire 3.00
11LT Jeff Bagwell, Craig Biggio 1.50
12LT Tom Glavine, Greg Maddux 2.00
13LT Ken Griffey Jr., Barry Bonds 4.00
14LT Manny Ramirez, Pedro J. Martinez 1.50
15LT Alex Rodriguez, Ivan Rodriguez 3.00

Lumber

NM/M
Common Player: 4.00
Inserted 1:40
1GL Roberto Alomar 6.00
2GL Rick Ankiel 4.00
3GL Adrian Beltre 6.00
4GL Barry Bonds 25.00
5GL Kevin Brown 4.00
7GL Ken Caminiti 4.00
8GL Eric Chavez 5.00
9GL Carlos Delgado 5.00
10GL J.D. Drew 5.00
11GL Erubiel Durazo 4.00
12GL Carl Everett 4.00
13GL Rafael Furcal 4.00
14GL Brian Giles 5.00
15GL Juan Gonzalez 6.00
16GL Todd Helton 8.00
18GL Randy Johnson 10.00
19GL Chipper Jones 10.00
20GL Pedro J. Martinez 10.00
21GL Tino Martinez 5.00
23GL Cal Ripken/SP/275 40.00

24GL Ivan Rodriguez 8.00
25GL Frank Thomas 8.00
26GL Jim Thome 8.00
27GL Bernie Williams 6.00
28GL Nomar Garciaparra 15.00

New Order

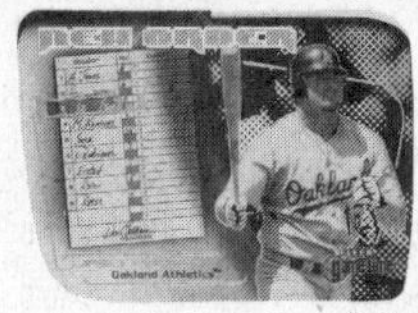

NM/M
Complete Set (15): 30.00
Common Player: 1.50
Inserted 1:12
1NO Derek Jeter 6.00
2NO Nomar Garciaparra 4.00
3NO Alex Rodriguez 5.00
4NO Mark McGwire 5.00
5NO Sammy Sosa 4.00
6NO Carlos Delgado 1.50
7NO Troy Glaus 1.50
8NO Jason Giambi 1.50
9NO Mike Piazza 4.00
10NO Todd Helton 1.50
11NO Vladimir Guerrero 2.00
12NO Manny Ramirez 1.50
13NO Frank Thomas 1.50
14NO Ken Griffey Jr. 4.00
15NO Chipper Jones 3.00

Sticktoitness

NM/M
Complete Set (20): 15.00
Common Player: .50
Inserted 1:8
1S Derek Jeter 4.00
2S Nomar Garciaparra 3.00
3S Alex Rodriguez 3.00
4S Jeff Bagwell 1.00
5S Bernie Williams .50
6S Eric Chavez .60
7S Richard Hidalgo .50
8S Ichiro Suzuki 2.00
9S Troy Glaus .75
10S Magglio Ordonez .50
11S Corey Patterson .50
12S Todd Helton 1.00
13S Jim Edmonds .50
14S Rafael Furcal .50
15S Mo Vaughn .50
16S Pat Burrell .65
17S Adrian Beltre .60
18S Andruw Jones 1.00
19S Manny Ramirez 1.00
20S Sean Casey .65

Uniformity

NM/M
Common Player: 4.00
Inserted 1:25
1GU Andres Galarraga 4.00
2GU Barry Bonds 25.00
3GU Ben Petrick 4.00
4GU Brad Radke 4.00
5GU Brian Jordan 4.00
6GU Carlos Guillen 4.00
7GU Fernando Seguignol 4.00
8GU Fred McGriff 4.00
9GU Gary Sheffield 5.00
10GU Greg Maddux 15.00
11GU Ivan Rodriguez 8.00
12GU Jay Buhner 4.00
13GU Jeromy Burnitz 4.00
14GU John Olerud 4.00
15GU Kevin Brown 4.00
16GU Larry Walker 4.00
17GU Magglio Ordonez 4.00
18GU Matt Williams 4.00
19GU Robin Ventura 4.00
20GU Rondell White 4.00
21GU Tony Gwynn 15.00
22GU Troy Glaus 8.00
23GU Vladimir Guerrero 8.00

2001 Fleer Genuine

NM/M
Complete Set (130): 150.00
Common Player: .25
Common (101-130): 3.00
Production 1,500
Pack (5): 4.00
Box (24): 80.00
1 Derek Jeter 3.00
2 Nomar Garciaparra 2.00
3 Alex Rodriguez 2.50
4 Frank Thomas 1.00
5 Travis Fryman .25
6 Gary Sheffield .40
7 Jason Giambi .75
8 Trevor Hoffman .25
9 Todd Helton 1.00
10 Ivan Rodriguez .75
11 Roberto Alomar .40
12 Barry Zito .40
13 Kevin Brown .25
14 Shawn Green .40
15 Kenny Lofton .25
16 Jeff Weaver .25
17 Geoff Jenkins .25
18 Carlos Delgado .65
19 Mark Grace .35
20 Ken Griffey Jr. 2.00
21 David Justice .25
22 Brian Giles .25
23 Scott Williamson .25
24 Richie Sexson .25
25 John Olerud .25
26 Sammy Sosa 2.00
27 Bobby Higginson .25
28 Matt Lawton .25
29 Vinny Castilla .25
30 Alex S. Gonzalez .25
31 Manny Ramirez 1.00
32 Brad Radke .25
33 Cal Ripken Jr. 3.00
34 Richard Hidalgo .25
35 Al Leiter .25
36 Freddy Garcia .25
37 Juan Encarnacion .25
38 Corey Koskie .25
39 Greg Vaughn .25
40 Rafael Palmeiro .65
41 Vladimir Guerrero 1.00
42 Troy Glaus .75
43 Mike Hampton .25
44 Jose Vidro .25
45 Ryan Rupe .25
46 Troy O'Leary .25
47 Ben Petrick .25
48 Mike Lieberthal .25
49 Mike Sweeney .25
50 Scott Rolen .75
51 Albert Belle .25
52 Mark Quinn .25
53 Mike Piazza 2.00
54 Mark McGwire 2.50
55 Brady Anderson .25
56 Carlos Beltran .45
57 Michael Barrett .25
58 Jason Kendall .25
59 Jim Edmonds .25
60 Matt Williams .25
61 Pokey Reese .25
62 Bernie Williams .25
63 Barry Bonds 3.00
64 David Wells .25
65 Chipper Jones 1.50
66 Jim Parque .25
67 Derrek Lee .25
68 Darin Erstad .60
69 Edgar Martinez .25
70 Kerry Wood .60
71 Omar Vizquel .25
72 Jeromy Burnitz .25
73 Warren Morris .25
74 Rick Ankiel .25
75 Andruw Jones 1.00
76 Paul Konerko .25
77 Mike Lowell .25
78 Roger Clemens 1.75
79 Tim Hudson .35
80 Rafael Furcal .25
81 Craig Biggio .25
82 Edgardo Alfonzo .25
83 Pat Burrell .50
84 Adrian Beltre .35
85 Tony Gwynn 1.50
86 J.T. Snow .25
87 Randy Johnson 1.00
88 Sean Casey .35
89 Preston Wilson .25
90 Mike Mussina .50
91 Eric Chavez .35
92 Tim Salmon .25
93 Pedro Martinez 1.00
94 Darryl Kile .25
95 Greg Maddux 1.50
96 Magglio Ordonez .25
97 Jeff Bagwell 1.00
98 Timo Perez .25
99 Jeff Kent .25
100 Eric Owens .25
101 Ichiro Suzuki **RC** (Genuine Upside) 35.00
102 Elpidio Guzman **RC** (Genuine Upside) 3.00
103 Tsuyoshi Shinjo **RC** (Genuine Upside) 6.00
104 Travis Hafner **RC** (Genuine Upside) 10.00
105 Larry Barnes (Genuine Upside) 3.00
106 Jaisen Randolph **RC** (Genuine Upside) 3.00
107 Paul Phillips **RC** (Genuine Upside) 3.00
108 Erick Almonte **RC** (Genuine Upside) 3.00
109 Nick Punto **RC** (Genuine Upside) 3.00
110 Jack Wilson **RC** (Genuine Upside) 3.00
111 Jeremy Owens **RC** (Genuine Upside) 3.00
112 Esix Snead **RC** (Genuine Upside) 3.00
113 Jay Gibbons **RC** (Genuine Upside) 8.00
114 Adrian Hernandez **RC** (Genuine Upside) 4.00
115 Matt White **RC** (Genuine Upside) 3.00
116 Ryan Freel **RC** (Genuine Upside) 3.00
117 Martin Vargas **RC** (Genuine Upside) 3.00
118 Winston Abreu **RC** (Genuine Upside) 3.00
119 Junior Spivey **RC** (Genuine Upside) 5.00
120 Paxton Crawford (Genuine Upside) 3.00
121 Randy Keisler (Genuine Upside) 3.00
122 Juan Diaz **RC** (Genuine Upside) 3.00
123 Aaron Rowand (Genuine Upside) 3.00
124 Toby Hall (Genuine Upside) 3.00
125 Brian Cole (Genuine Upside) 3.00
126 Aubrey Huff (Genuine Upside) 4.00
127 Corey Patterson (Genuine Upside) 4.00
128 Sun-Woo Kim (Genuine Upside) 3.00
129 Jace Brewer (Genuine Upside) 3.00
130 Cesar Izturis (Genuine Upside) 3.00

@ LG (At Large)

NM/M
Complete Set (15): 50.00
Common Player: 1.50
Inserted 1:23
1AL Derek Jeter 7.50
2AL Nomar Garciaparra 4.00
3AL Mark McGwire 6.00
4AL Pedro Martinez 3.00
5AL Tony Gwynn 3.50
6AL Roger Clemens 3.50
7AL Ivan Rodriguez 2.00
8AL Sammy Sosa 4.00
9AL Magglio Ordonez 1.50
10AL Jason Giambi 2.00
11AL Carlos Delgado 2.00
12AL Chipper Jones 3.50
13AL Mike Piazza 4.00
14AL Cal Ripken Jr. 7.50
15AL Ken Griffey Jr. 4.00

Final Cut

Final Cut cards of Ron Guidry, Don Larsen and Reggie Jackson were prepared, but not intended for release. At least a few of each have made their way into hobby channels. Because

of limited numbers extant, their values cannot be determined. Some, perhaps all, of Edgar Martinez' Final Cut cards have jersey patches rather than the described glove piece.

NM/M
Common Player: 4.00
Inserted 1:30
Miguel Tejada/SP/170 6.00
Barry Bonds/SP/330 40.00
Robin Ventura 4.00
Greg Maddux 15.00
Andruw Jones/SP/135 10.00
J.D. Drew/SP/75 10.00
Chipper Jones 10.00
Tim Salmon 4.00
Edgar Martinez/SP/130 8.00
Troy Glaus 8.00
Frank Thomas 8.00
Pokey Reese 4.00
Larry Walker 4.00
Ivan Rodriguez/SP/120 10.00
Scott Rolen 8.00
Cal Ripken Jr. 30.00
Tony Gwynn 10.00
Wade Boggs 10.00
George Brett 30.00
Sean Casey 4.00
Bob Gibson 6.00
Matt Williams 6.00
Robin Yount 8.00
Ron Guidry (Not officially released.) 150.00
Reggie Jackson (Not officially released.) 250.00
Don Larsen (Not officially released.) 140.00

Genuine Coverage PLUS

NM/M
Common Player: 6.00
Production 150 Sets
Troy Glaus 8.00
Randy Johnson 10.00
Andruw Jones 8.00
Frank Thomas 8.00
Darin Erstad 6.00
Chipper Jones 15.00
Derek Jeter 35.00
Tony Gwynn 15.00
Barry Bonds 35.00
Cal Ripken Jr. 35.00

High Interest

NM/M
Complete Set (15): 40.00
Common Player: 1.50
Inserted 1:23
1HI Derek Jeter 6.00
2HI Nomar Garciaparra 4.00
3HI Greg Maddux 3.00
4HI Todd Helton 2.00
5HI Sammy Sosa 4.00
6HI Jeff Bagwell 2.00
7HI Jason Giambi 1.50
8HI Frank Thomas 2.00
9HI Andruw Jones 2.00
10HI Jim Edmonds 1.50
11HI Bernie Williams 1.50
12HI Randy Johnson 2.00
13HI Ken Griffey Jr. 4.00
14HI Pedro Martinez 2.00
15HI Mark McGwire 5.00

Material Issue

NM/M
Common Player: 5.00
Inserted 1:30
Randy Johnson 10.00
Scott Rolen 8.00
Robin Ventura 5.00
Tony Gwynn 15.00
Troy Glaus 10.00
Kevin Millwood 5.00
Chipper Jones 15.00
Tom Glavine 5.00
Pedro Martinez/SP/60 40.00
Greg Maddux 15.00
Frank Thomas 10.00
Curt Schilling/SP/120 10.00
Edgar Martinez 5.00
Darin Erstad 5.00
J.D. Drew 5.00
Cal Ripken Jr. 30.00
Nolan Ryan 40.00
Steve Carlton 5.00

Names of the Game - Autographs

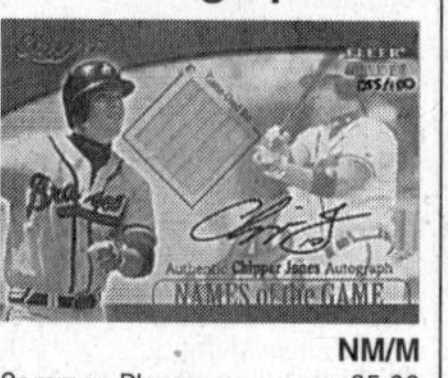

NM/M
Common Player: 25.00
Yogi Berra 60.00
Orlando Cepeda 20.00
Rocky Colavito 60.00
Andre Dawson 20.00
Bucky Dent 20.00
Rollie Fingers 20.00
Carlton Fisk 40.00
Whitey Ford 40.00
Reggie Jackson 50.00
Randy Johnson 60.00
Chipper Jones 50.00
Harmon Killebrew 60.00
Don Mattingly 90.00
Willie McCovey 25.00
Cal Ripken Jr. 150.00
Ivan Rodriguez 50.00
Preacher Roe 35.00
Nolan Ryan 100.00
Tom Seaver 50.00
Bill Skowron 25.00
Enos Slaughter 30.00
Duke Snider 40.00

Names of the Game - Game Used

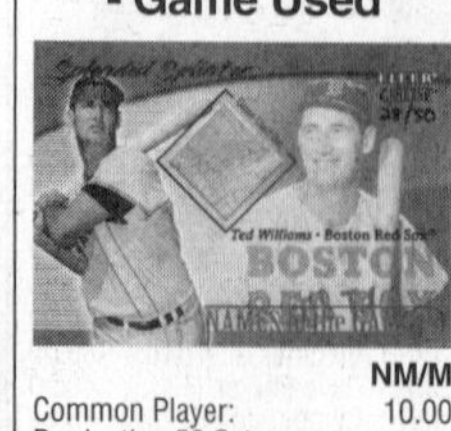

NM/M
Common Player: 10.00
Production 50 Sets
Yogi Berra/Bat 25.00
Orlando Cepeda/Bat 10.00
Rocky Colavito/Bat 20.00
Andre Dawson/Jsy 10.00
Bucky Dent/Bat 10.00
Rollie Fingers/Jsy 10.00
Carlton Fisk/Bat 15.00
Whitey Ford/Jsy 25.00
Jimmie Foxx/Bat 80.00
Hank Greenberg/Bat 50.00
"Catfish" Hunter/Jsy 10.00
Reggie Jackson/Jsy 20.00
Randy Johnson/Jsy 30.00
Chipper Jones/Bat 30.00
Harmon Killebrew/Bat 25.00
Tony Lazzeri/Bat 10.00
Don Mattingly/Bat 65.00
Willie McCovey/Bat 20.00
Johnny Mize/Bat 15.00
Pee Wee Reese/Jsy 15.00
Cal Ripken Jr./Bat 75.00
Phil Rizzuto/Bat 20.00
Ivan Rodriguez/Bat 25.00
Preacher Roe/Jsy 15.00
Babe Ruth/Bat 300.00
Nolan Ryan/Jsy 90.00
Tom Seaver/Jsy 25.00
Bill Skowron/Bat 10.00
Enos Slaughter/Bat 10.00
Duke Snider/Bat 25.00
Willie Stargell/Bat 15.00
Bill Terry/Bat 10.00
Ted Williams/Bat 200.00
Hack Wilson/Bat 75.00

Pennant Aggression

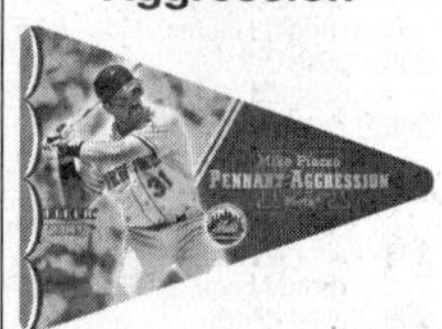

NM/M
Complete Set (10): 30.00
Inserted 1:23
1PA Derek Jeter 6.00
2PA Alex Rodriguez 5.00
3PA Nomar Garciaparra 4.00
4PA Mark McGwire 5.00
5PA Ken Griffey Jr. 4.00
6PA Mike Piazza 4.00
7PA Sammy Sosa 4.00
8PA Barry Bonds 6.00
9PA Chipper Jones 3.00
10PA Pedro Martinez 2.00

Tip of the Cap

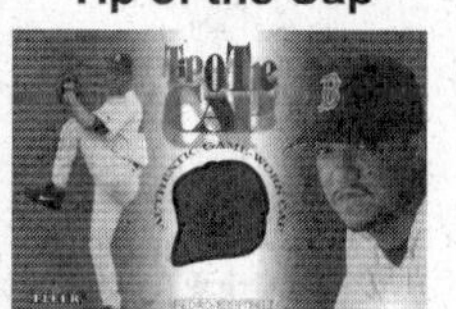

NM/M
Common Player: 8.00
Production 150 Sets
Barry Bonds 40.00
Eric Chavez 8.00
Shawn Green 8.00
Vladimir Guerrero 15.00
Randy Johnson 20.00
Andruw Jones 10.00
Javy Lopez 8.00
Rafael Palmeiro 10.00
Ivan Rodriguez 10.00
Miguel Tejada 8.00
Roberto Alomar 10.00
Pedro Martinez 15.00

2001 Fleer Greats of the Game

NM/M
Complete Set (137): 50.00
Common Player: .25
Hobby Pack (5): 10.00
Hobby Box (24): 200.00
1 Roberto Clemente 2.50
2 George "Sparky" Anderson .25
3 Babe Ruth 4.00
4 Paul Molitor 1.00
5 Don Larsen .25
6 Cy Young 1.00
7 Billy Martin .50
8 Lou Brock 1.00
9 Fred Lynn .25

10	Johnny Vander Meer	.25
11	Harmon Killebrew	1.00
12	Dave Winfield	1.00
13	Orlando Cepeda	.25
14	Johnny Mize	.75
15	Walter Johnson	1.00
16	Roy Campanella	1.00
17	Monte Irvin	.50
18	Mookie Wilson	.25
19	Elston Howard	.25
20	Walter Alston	.25
21	Rollie Fingers	.25
22	Brooks Robinson	1.00
23	Hank Greenberg	1.00
24	Maury Wills	.25
25	Rich Gossage	.25
26	Leon Day	.25
27	Jimmie Foxx	2.00
28	Alan Trammell	.50
29	Dennis Martinez	.25
30	Don Drysdale	.75
31	Bob Feller	.75
32	Jackie Robinson	3.00
33	Whitey Ford	1.00
34	Enos Slaughter	.25
35	Rod Carew	.75
36	Eddie Mathews	1.00
37	Ron Cey	.25
38	Thurman Munson	1.00
39	Henry Kimbro	.25
40	Ty Cobb	3.00
41	Rocky Colavito	.50
42	Satchel Paige	1.50
43	Andre Dawson	.50
44	Phil Rizzuto	1.00
45	Roger Maris	2.50
46	Bobby Bonds	.25
47	Joe Carter	.25
48	Christy Mathewson	.75
49	Tony Lazzeri	.25
50	Gil Hodges	.25
51	Ray Dandridge	.25
52	Gaylord Perry	.25
53	Ernie Banks	2.00
54	Lou Gehrig	3.00
55	George Kell	.25
56	Wes Parker	.25
57	Sam Jethroe	.25
58	Joe Morgan	.75
59	Steve Garvey	.50
60	Joe Torre	.75
61	Roger Craig	.25
62	Warren Spahn	1.00
63	Willie McCovey	.25
64	Cool Papa Bell	1.00
65	Frank Robinson	1.00
66	Richie Allen	.25
67	Bucky Dent	.25
68	George Foster	.25
69	Hoyt Wilhelm	.25
70	Phil Niekro	.25
71	Buck Leonard	.25
72	Preacher Roe	.25
73	Yogi Berra	1.50
74	Joe Black	.25
75	Nolan Ryan	4.00
76	Pop Lloyd	.25
77	Lester Lockett	.25
78	Paul Blair	.25
79	Ryne Sandberg	2.00
80	Bill Perkins	.25
81	Frank Howard	.25
82	Hack Wilson	1.00
83	Robin Yount	1.00
84	Harry Heilmann	.25
85	Mike Schmidt	3.00
86	Vida Blue	.25
87	George Brett	3.00
88	Juan Marichal	.50
89	Tom Seaver	1.50
90	Bill Skowron	.25
91	Don Mattingly	2.00
92	Jim Bunning	.25
93	Eddie Murray	1.00
94	Tommy Lasorda	.50
95	Pee Wee Reese	.50
96	Bill Dickey	.25
97	Ozzie Smith	1.50
98	Dale Murphy	.25
99	Artie Wilson	.25
100	Bill Terry	.25
101	Jim "Catfish" Hunter	.25
102	Don Sutton	.25
103	Luis Aparicio	.25
104	Reggie Jackson	1.50
105	Ted Radcliffe	.25
106	Carl Erskine	.25
107	Johnny Bench	2.00
108	Carl Furillo	.25
109	Stan Musial	2.00
110	Carlton Fisk	.75
111	Rube Foster	.25
112	Tony Oliva	.25
113	Hank Bauer	.25
114	Jim Rice	.25
115	Willie Mays	3.00
116	Ralph Kiner	.50
117	Al Kaline	1.00
118	Billy Williams	.25
119	Buck O'Neil	.25
120	Tony Perez	.25
121	Dave Parker	.25
122	Kirk Gibson	.25
123	Lou Piniella	.25
124	Ted Williams	4.00
125	Steve Carlton	.75
126	Dizzy Dean	.25
127	Willie Stargell	.50
128	Joe Niekro	.25
129	Lloyd Waner	.25
130	Wade Boggs	2.00
131	Wilmer Fields	.25
132	Bill Mazeroski	.50
133	Duke Snider	1.00
134	Smoky Joe Williams	.25
135	Bob Gibson	1.50
136	Jim Palmer	.75
137	Oscar Charleston	.25

Autographs

		NM/M
Common Player:		10.00
Inserted 1:8		
1	Richie Allen	10.00
2	George "Sparky" Anderson	10.00
3	Luis Aparicio	10.00
4	Ernie Banks/SP/250	80.00
5	Hank Bauer	10.00
6	Johnny Bench/SP/400	80.00
7	Yogi Berra SP/500	50.00
8	Joe Black	10.00
9	Paul Blair	10.00
9a	Paul Blair/Double Signed	10.00
10	Vida Blue	10.00
11	Wade Boggs	40.00
12	Bobby Bonds	15.00
13	George Brett/SP/247	150.00
14	Lou Brock/SP/500	40.00
15	Jim Bunning	25.00
16	Rod Carew	20.00
17	Steve Carlton	25.00
18	Joe Carter	10.00
19	Orlando Cepeda	15.00
20	Ron Cey	10.00
21	Rocky Colavito	25.00
22	Roger Craig	10.00
23	Andre Dawson	15.00
24	Bucky Dent	10.00
25	Larry Doby	35.00
26	Carl Erskine	10.00
27	Bob Feller	15.00
28	Wilmer Fields	10.00
29	Rollie Fingers	10.00
30	Carlton Fisk	40.00
31	Whitey Ford	30.00
32	George Foster	10.00
33	Steve Garvey/SP/400	40.00
34	Bob Gibson	20.00
35	Kirk Gibson	20.00
36	Rich Gossage	10.00
37	Frank Howard	10.00
38	Monte Irvin	20.00
39	Reggie Jackson/SP/400	60.00
40	Sam Jethroe	10.00
41	Al Kaline	30.00
42	George Kell	15.00
43	Harmon Killebrew	30.00
44	Ralph Kiner	20.00
45	Don Larsen	15.00
46	Tommy Lasorda/SP/400	40.00
47	Lester Lockett	10.00
48	Fred Lynn	10.00
49	Juan Marichal	20.00
50	Dennis Martinez	10.00
51	Don Mattingly	75.00
52	Willie Mays/SP/100	450.00
53	Bill Mazeroski	20.00
54	Willie McCovey	20.00
55	Paul Molitor	20.00
56	Joe Morgan	10.00
57	Dale Murphy	30.00
58	Eddie Murray/SP/140	200.00
59	Stan Musial/SP/525	75.00
60	Joe Niekro	10.00
61	Phil Niekro	10.00
62	Tony Oliva	10.00
63	Buck O'Neil	20.00
64	Jim Palmer/SP/600	20.00
65	Dave Parker	10.00
66	Tony Perez	20.00
67	Gaylord Perry	10.00
68	Lou Piniella	10.00
69	Ted Radcliffe	10.00
70	Jim Rice	10.00
71	Phil Rizzuto/SP/425	80.00
72	Brooks Robinson	25.00
73	Frank Robinson	20.00
74	Preacher Roe	20.00
75	Nolan Ryan/SP/650	100.00
76	Ryne Sandberg	50.00
77	Mike Schmidt/SP/213	175.00
78	Tom Seaver	50.00
79	Bill Skowron	10.00
80	Enos Slaughter	15.00
81	Ozzie Smith	50.00
82	Duke Snider/SP/600	50.00
83	Warren Spahn	40.00
84	Willie Stargell (Redemption card only, none signed.)	10.00
85	Don Sutton	10.00
86	Joe Torre/SP/500	40.00
87	Alan Trammell	15.00
88	Hoyt Wilhelm	10.00
89	Billy Williams	10.00
90	Maury Wills	10.00
91	Artie Wilson	10.00
92	Mookie Wilson	10.00
93	Dave Winfield/SP/370	60.00
94	Robin Yount/SP/400	80.00

Dodger Blues

		NM/M
Common Player:		10.00
Inserted 1:36		
(1)	Walter Alston/Jsy	10.00
(2)	Walt Alston/Uniform	10.00
(3)	Roy Campanella/SP/Uniform	75.00
(4)	Roger Craig/Jsy	10.00
(5)	Don Drysdale/Jsy	20.00
(6)	Carl Furillo/Jsy	10.00
(7)	Steve Garvey/Jsy	10.00
(8)	Gil Hodges/Uniform	20.00
(9)	Wes Parker/Bat	10.00
(10)	Wes Parker/Jsy	10.00
(11)	Pee Wee Reese/Jsy	15.00
(12)	Jackie Robinson/Uniform/SP	150.00
(13)	Preacher Roe/Jsy	10.00
(14)	Duke Snider/Bat/SP	75.00
(15)	Don Sutton/Jsy	10.00

Feel the Game Classics

		NM/M
Common Player:		5.00
Inserted 1:72		
1	Luis Aparicio/Bat	5.00
2	George Brett/Jsy	30.00
3	Lou Brock/Jsy	15.00
4	Orlando Cepeda/Bat	10.00
5	Whitey Ford/Jsy	15.00
6	Hank Greenberg/Bat	40.00
7	Elston Howard/Bat	5.00
8	"Catfish" Hunter/Jsy	8.00
9	Harmon Killebrew/Bat	15.00
10	Roger Maris/Bat	50.00
11	Eddie Mathews/Bat	15.00
12	W. McCovey/Bat/SP/200	15.00
13	Johnny Mize/Bat	5.00
14	Paul Molitor/Jsy	10.00
15	Jim Palmer/Jsy	10.00
16	Tony Perez/Bat	5.00
17	Brooks Robinson/Bat/144	25.00
18	Babe Ruth/Bat/250	200.00
19	Mike Schmidt/Jsy	25.00
20	Tom Seaver/Jsy	20.00
21	Enos Slaughter	10.00
22	Willie Stargell	10.00
23	Hack Wilson	10.00
24	Harry Heilmann	5.00

Retrospection Collection

		NM/M
Complete Set (10):		20.00
Common Player:		1.00
Inserted 1:6		
1	Babe Ruth	5.00
2	Stan Musial	3.00
3	Jimmie Foxx	3.00
4	Roberto Clemente	4.00
5	Ted Williams	4.00
6	Mike Schmidt	4.00
7	Cy Young	1.50

8	Satchel Paige	2.00
9	Hank Greenberg	1.50
10	Jim Bunning	1.00

2001 Fleer Legacy

		NM/M
Complete Set (105):		
Common Player:		.50
Common (91-105):		8.00
Production 799 Sets		
Pack (5):		8.00
Box (15 + Cap):		140.00
1	Pedro J. Martinez	1.50
2	Andruw Jones	1.50
3	Mike Hampton	.50
4	Gary Sheffield	.65
5	Barry Zito	.65
6	J.D. Drew	.75
7	Charles Johnson	.50
8	David Wells	.50
9	Kazuhiro Sasaki	.50
10	Vladimir Guerrero	1.50
11	Pat Burrell	.75
12	Ruben Mateo	.50
13	Greg Maddux	2.00
14	Sean Casey	.65
15	Craig Biggio	.50
16	Bernie Williams	.65
17	Jeff Kent	.50
18	Nomar Garciaparra	2.50
19	Cal Ripken Jr.	4.00
20	Larry Walker	.50
21	Adrian Beltre	.65
22	Johnny Damon	.75
23	Rick Ankiel	.50
24	Matt Williams	.50
25	Magglio Ordonez	.50
26	Richard Hidalgo	.50
27	Robin Ventura	.50
28	Jason Kendall	.50
29	Tony Batista	.50
30	Chipper Jones	2.00
31	Jim Thome	.50
32	Kevin Brown	.50
33	Mike Mussina	.65
34	Mark McGwire	3.00
35	Darin Erstad	.75
36	Manny Ramirez	1.50
37	Bobby Higginson	.50
38	Richie Sexson	.50
39	Jason Giambi	1.00
40	Alex Rodriguez	3.00
41	Mark Grace	.65
42	Ken Griffey Jr.	2.50
43	Moises Alou	.50
44	Edgardo Alfonzo	.50
45	Phil Nevin	.50
46	Rafael Palmeiro	1.25
47	Javy Lopez	.50
48	Juan Gonzalez	1.50
49	Jermaine Dye	.50
50	Roger Clemens	2.25
51	Barry Bonds	4.00
52	Carl Everett	.50
53	Ben Sheets	.50
54	Juan Encarnacion	.50
55	Jeromy Burnitz	.50
56	Miguel Tejada	.65
57	Ben Grieve	.50
58	Randy Johnson	1.50
59	Frank Thomas	1.50
60	Preston Wilson	.50
61	Mike Piazza	2.50
62	Brian Giles	.50
63	Carlos Delgado	1.00
64	Tom Glavine	.75
65	Roberto Alomar	.65
66	Mike Sweeney	.50
67	Orlando Hernandez	.50
68	Edgar Martinez	.50
69	Tim Salmon	.75
70	Kerry Wood	1.00
71	Jack Wilson **RC**	3.00
72	Matt Lawton	.50
73	Scott Rolen	1.25
74	Ivan Rodriguez	1.25
75	Steve Finley	.50
76	Barry Larkin	.50
77	Jeff Bagwell	1.50
78	Derek Jeter	4.00
79	Tony Gwynn	2.00
80	Raul Mondesi	.50
81	Rafael Furcal	.50
82	Todd Helton	1.50
83	Shawn Green	.75
84	Tim Hudson	.65
85	Jim Edmonds	.50
86	Troy Glaus	1.50
87	Sammy Sosa	2.50
88	Cliff Floyd	.50
89	Jose Vidro	.50
90	Bobby Abreu	.50
91	Drew Henson/Auto. **RC**	30.00
92	Andy Morales/Auto. **RC**	8.00
93	Wilson Betemit/Auto. **RC**	10.00
94	Elpidio Guzman **RC**	8.00
95	Esix Snead **RC**	8.00
96	Winston Abreu **RC**	8.00
97	Jeremy Owens **RC**	8.00
99	Junior Spivey **RC**	15.00
100	Jaisen Randolph **RC**	8.00
101	Ichiro Suzuki **RC**	60.00
102	Albert Pujols/499 **RC**	160.00
102	Albert Pujols/Auto./300 **RC**	750.00
103	Tsuyoshi Shinjo **RC**	10.00
104	Jay Gibbons **RC**	10.00
105	Juan Uribe **RC**	10.00

Ultimate Legacy

Stars (1-90):	3-5X
Rookies (91-100):	.3-.75X
Rookies (101-105):	.75-1X
Production 250 Sets	

Autographed MLB Fitted Cap

	NM/M
Common Player:	25.00
Inserted 1:15	
Edgardo Alfonzo	25.00
Roberto Alomar	50.00
Ernie Banks/100	100.00
Adrian Beltre	40.00
Johnny Bench/100	125.00
Lance Berkman	30.00
Yogi Berra/200	120.00
Craig Biggio	30.00
Barry Bonds	280.00
Jeromy Burnitz	25.00
Pat Burrell	30.00
Steve Carlton	40.00
Sean Casey	30.00
Orlando Cepeda	30.00
Eric Chavez	25.00
Tony Clark	25.00
Roger Clemens/100	200.00
Johnny Damon	40.00
Dom DiMaggio/200	45.00
J.D. Drew	40.00
Jermaine Dye	25.00
Darin Erstad	40.00
Carlton Fisk/150	80.00
Rafael Furcal	25.00
Nomar Garciaparra/150	150.00
Jason Giambi	50.00
Troy Glaus	35.00
Tom Glavine	50.00
Juan Gonzalez	50.00
Luis Gonzalez	30.00
Tony Gwynn	85.00
Drew Henson	30.00
Derek Jeter	250.00
Andruw Jones	40.00
David Justice	30.00
Paul Konerko	25.00
Don Mattingly	150.00
Willie McCovey	30.00
Paul Molitor	60.00
Stan Musial/200	125.00
Mike Mussina	50.00
Jim Palmer	25.00
Corey Patterson	40.00
Kirby Puckett/200	75.00
Cal Ripken/200	200.00
Brooks Robinson	60.00
Ivan Rodriguez	50.00
Scott Rolen	50.00
Nolan Ryan/150	200.00
Mike Schmidt/150	125.00
Tom Seaver/100	125.00
Ben Sheets	40.00
Ozzie Smith	85.00
Duke Snider	40.00
Miguel Tejada	50.00
Jim Thome	60.00
Matt Williams	25.00
Dave Winfield/150	75.00
Carl Yastrzemski/150	100.00
Robin Yount	100.00
Barry Zito	40.00

Hit Kings

	NM/M
Common Player:	5.00
Inserted 1:13	
Stan Musial	15.00
Barry Bonds	25.00
Corey Patterson	5.00
Shawn Green	6.00
Ralph Kiner	5.00
Troy O'Leary	5.00
Ivan Rodriguez	6.00
Jose Vidro	5.00
Carlos Beltran	8.00
Jose Canseco	6.00
Juan Encarnacion	5.00
Reggie Jackson	10.00
Ruben Mateo	5.00
Juan Pierre	5.00
Tim Salmon	5.00
Adrian Beltre	6.00
Roger Cedeno	5.00
Troy Glaus	8.00
Jason Kendall	5.00
Rick Ankiel	5.00
Andruw Jones	8.00
Jim Thome	5.00
Tony Batista	5.00
George Brett	20.00
Vladimir Guerrero	10.00
Billy Martin	5.00
Maggio Ordonez	5.00
Johnny Damon	6.00

Hit Kings Short Prints

	NM/M
Common Player:	15.00
Production 100 Sets	
Robin Yount	20.00
Scott Rolen	15.00
Johnny Bench	25.00
Steve Garvey	15.00
Joe Morgan	15.00
Frank Thomas	20.00
Eddie Mathews	20.00
Tony Gwynn	25.00
Roger Clemens	40.00
Wade Boggs	25.00

Hot Gloves

		NM/M
Common Player:		15.00
Inserted 1:180		
1HG	Andruw Jones	15.00
2HG	Mike Mussina	15.00
3HG	Roberto Alomar	15.00
4HG	Tony Gwynn	30.00
5HG	Bernie Williams	15.00
6HG	Ivan Rodriguez	15.00

7HG Ken Griffey Jr. 40.00
8HG Robin Ventura 15.00
9HG Cal Ripken Jr. 60.00
10HG Jeff Bagwell 20.00
11HG Mark McGwire 50.00
12HG Rafael Palmeiro 15.00
13HG Scott Rolen 15.00
14HG Barry Bonds 60.00
15HG Greg Maddux 30.00

MLB Game Issue - Base

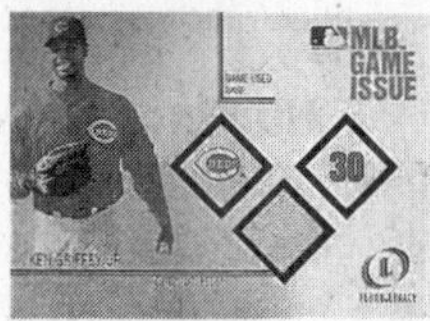

NM/M
Common Player: 4.00
Inserted 1:52
1GI Mark McGwire 15.00
2GI Ken Griffey Jr. 10.00
3GI Sammy Sosa 10.00
4GI Mike Piazza 10.00
5GI Alex Rodriguez 15.00
6GI Derek Jeter 20.00
7GI Cal Ripken Jr. 20.00
8GI Todd Helton 6.00
9GI Tony Gwynn 8.00
10GI Chipper Jones 8.00
11GI Frank Thomas 6.00
12GI Barry Bonds 20.00
13GI Troy Glaus 4.00
14GI Pat Burrell 4.00
15GI Scott Rolen 5.00

MLB Game Issue - Base/Ball

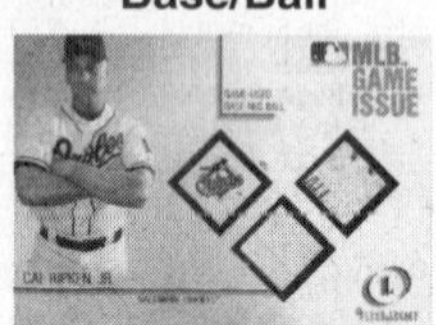

NM/M
Common Player: 10.00
Production 100 Sets
Mark McGwire 50.00
Ken Griffey Jr. 40.00
Sammy Sosa 40.00
Mike Piazza 40.00
Alex Rodriguez 50.00
Derek Jeter 60.00
Cal Ripken Jr. 60.00
Todd Helton 15.00
Tony Gwynn 25.00
Chipper Jones 25.00
Frank Thomas 15.00
Barry Bonds 60.00
Troy Glaus 10.00
Pat Burrell 10.00
Scott Rolen 12.50

MLB Game Issue - Base/Ball/Jersey

NM/M
Common Card: 25.00
Production 50 Sets
Derek Jeter 100.00
Cal Ripken Jr. 100.00
Todd Helton 30.00
Tony Gwynn 50.00
Chipper Jones 50.00
Frank Thomas 30.00
Barry Bonds 100.00
Troy Glaus 25.00
Pat Burrell 25.00
Scott Rolen 30.00

Tailor Made

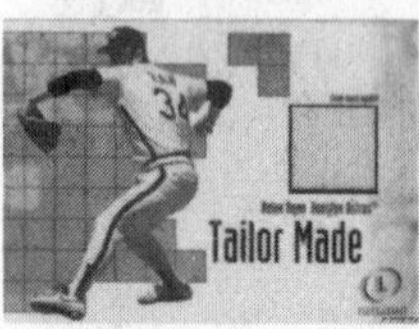

NM/M
Common Player: 4.00
Inserted 1:15
2TM Cal Ripken Jr. 40.00
3TM Orlando Cepeda 6.00
4TM Willie McCovey 6.00
5TM Dave Winfield 6.00
6TM Don Mattingly 35.00
7TM Nolan Ryan 40.00
8TM Manny Ramirez 8.00
9TM Edgardo Alfonzo 4.00
10TM Rondell White 4.00
11TM Lou Piniella 4.00
12TM Ivan Rodriguez 8.00
13TM J.D. Drew 4.00
14TM Barry Bonds 40.00
15TM Greg Maddux 15.00
16TM Rick Ankiel 4.00
17TM Carlos Delgado 8.00
18TM Kevin Brown 4.00
20TM Reggie Jackson 10.00
21TM Shawn Green 6.00
22TM Jason Kendall 4.00
23TM Rafael Palmeiro 8.00
24TM Todd Helton 8.00
25TM Curt Schilling 6.00

2001 Fleer Platinum

NM/M
Complete Set (301): 140.00
Common Player: .15
Common SP (251-300): 1.00
Inserted 1:6
Card #301 Production 1,500
Pack (10): 5.00
Box (24): 100.00
1 Bobby Abreu .15
2 Brad Radke .15
3 Bill Mueller .15
4 Adam Eaton .15
5 Antonio Alfonseca .15
6 Manny Ramirez .75
7 Adam Kennedy .15
8 Jose Valentin .15
9 Jaret Wright .15
10 Aramis Ramirez .15
11 Jeff Kent .15
12 Juan Encarnacion .15
13 Sandy Alomar Jr. .15
14 Joe Randa .15
15 Darryl Kile .15
16 Darren Dreifort .15
17 Matt Kinney .15
18 Pokey Reese .15
19 Ryan Klesko .15
20 Shawn Estes .15
21 Moises Alou .15
22 Edgar Renteria .15
23 Chuck Knoblauch .15
24 Carl Everett .15
25 Garret Anderson .15
26 Shane Reynolds .15
27 Billy Koch .15
28 Carlos Febles .15
29 Brian Anderson .15
30 Armando Rios .15
31 Ryan Kohlmeier .15
32 Steve Finley .15
33 Brady Anderson .15
34 Cal Ripken Jr. 2.50
35 Paul Konerko .15
36 Chuck Finley .15
37 Rick Ankiel .15
38 Mariano Rivera .25
39 Corey Koskie .15
40 Cliff Floyd .15
41 Kevin Appier .15
42 Henry Rodriguez .15
43 Mark Kotsay .15
44 Brook Fordyce .15
45 Brad Ausmus .15
46 Alfonso Soriano .50
47 Ray Lankford .15
48 Keith Foulke .15
49 Rich Aurilia .15
50 Alex Rodriguez 2.00
51 Eric Byrnes .15
52 Travis Fryman .15
53 Jeff Bagwell .75
54 Scott Rolen .65
55 Matt Lawton .15
56 Brad Fullmer .15
57 Tony Batista .15
58 Nate Rolison .15
59 Carlos Lee .15
60 Rafael Furcal .15
61 Jay Bell .15
62 Jimmy Rollins .25
63 Derrek Lee .15
64 Andres Galarraga .15
65 Derek Bell .15
66 Tim Salmon .25
67 Travis Lee .15
68 Kevin Millwood .15
69 Albert Belle .15
70 Kazuhiro Sasaki .15
71 Al Leiter .15
72 Britt Reames .15
73 Carlos Beltran .45
74 Curt Schilling .50
75 Curtis Leskanic .15
76 Jeremy Giambi .15
77 Adrian Beltre .35
78 David Segui .15
79 Mike Lieberthal .15
80 Brian Giles .15
81 Marvin Benard .15
82 Aaron Sele .15
83 Kenny Lofton .15
84 Doug Glanville .15
85 Kris Benson .15
86 Richie Sexson .15
87 Javy Lopez .15
88 Doug Mientkiewicz .15
89 Peter Bergeron .15
90 Gary Sheffield .40
91 Derek Lowe .15
92 Tom Glavine .40
93 Lance Berkman .15
94 Chris Singleton .15
95 Mike Lowell .25
96 Luis Gonzalez .30
97 Dante Bichette .15
98 Mike Sirotka .15
99 Julio Lugo .15
100 Juan Gonzalez .75
101 Craig Biggio .15
102 Armando Benitez .15
103 Greg Maddux 1.00
104 Mark Grace .25
105 John Smoltz .15
106 J.T. Snow .15
107 Al Martin .15
108 Danny Graves .15
109 Barry Bonds 2.50
110 Lee Stevens .15
111 Pedro Martinez .75
112 Shawn Green .40
113 Bret Boone .15
114 Matt Stairs .15
115 Tino Martinez .15
116 Rusty Greer .15
117 Mike Bordick .15
118 Garrett Stephenson .15
119 Edgar Martinez .15
120 Ben Grieve .15
121 Milton Bradley .15
122 Aaron Boone .15
123 Ruben Mateo .15
124 Ken Griffey Jr. 1.50
125 Russell Branyan .15
126 Shannon Stewart .15
127 Fred McGriff .15
128 Ben Petrick .15
129 Kevin Brown .15
130 B.J. Surhoff .15
131 Mark McGwire 2.00
132 Carlos Guillen .15
133 Adrian Brown .15
134 Mike Sweeney .15
135 Eric Milton .15
136 Cristian Guzman .15
137 Ellis Burks .15
138 Fernando Tatis .15
139 Ben Molina .15
140 Tony Gwynn 1.00
141 Jeromy Burnitz .15
142 Miguel Tejada .25
143 Raul Mondesi .15
144 Jeffrey Hammonds .15
145 Pat Burrell .40
146 Frank Thomas .75
147 Eric Munson .15
148 Mike Hampton .15
149 Mike Cameron .15
150 Jim Thome .15
151 Mike Mussina .50
152 Rick Helling .15
153 Ken Caminiti .15
154 John Vander Wal .15
155 Denny Neagle .15
156 Robb Nen .15
157 Jose Canseco .50
158 Mo Vaughn .15
159 Phil Nevin .15
160 Pat Hentgen .15
161 Sean Casey .25
162 Greg Vaughn .15
163 Trot Nixon .15
164 Roberto Hernandez .15
165 Vinny Castilla .15
166 Robin Ventura .15
167 Alex Ochoa .15
168 Orlando Hernandez .15
169 Luis Castillo .15
170 Quilvio Veras .15
171 Troy O'Leary .15
172 Livan Hernandez .15
173 Roger Cedeno .15
174 Jose Vidro .15
175 John Olerud .15
176 Richard Hidalgo .15
177 Eric Chavez .25
178 Fernando Vina .15
179 Chris Stynes .15
180 Bobby Higginson .15
181 Bruce Chen .15
182 Omar Vizquel .15
183 Rey Ordonez .15
184 Trevor Hoffman .15
185 Jeff Cirillo .15
186 Billy Wagner .15
187 David Ortiz .15
188 Tim Hudson .40
189 Tony Clark .15
190 Larry Walker .15
191 Eric Owens .15
192 Aubrey Huff .15
193 Royce Clayton .15
194 Todd Walker .15
195 Rafael Palmeiro .65
196 Todd Hundley .15
197 Roger Clemens 1.25
198 Jeff Weaver .15
199 Dean Palmer .15
200 Geoff Jenkins .15
201 Matt Clement .15
202 David Wells .15
203 Chan Ho Park .15
204 Hideo Nomo .65
205 Bartolo Colon .15
206 John Wetteland .15
207 Corey Patterson .15
208 Freddy Garcia .15
209 David Cone .15
210 Rondell White .15
211 Carl Pavano .15
212 Charles Johnson .15
213 Ron Coomer .15
214 Matt Williams .15
215 Jay Payton .15
216 Nick Johnson .15
217 Deivi Cruz .15
218 Scott Elarton .15
219 Neifi Perez .15
220 Jason Isringhausen .15
221 Jose Cruz .15
222 Gerald Williams .15
223 Timo Perez .15
224 Damion Easley .15
225 Jeff D'Amico (Photo actually Jamey Wright.) .15
226 Preston Wilson .15
227 Robert Person .15
228 Jacque Jones .15
229 Johnny Damon .25
230 Tony Womack .15
231 Adam Piatt .15
232 Brian Jordan .15
233 Ben Davis .15
234 Kerry Wood .50
235 Mike Piazza 1.50
236 David Justice .15
237 Dave Veres .15
238 Eric Young .15
239 Juan Pierre .15
240 Gabe Kapler .15
241 Ryan Dempster .15
242 Dmitri Young .15
243 Jorge Posada .35
244 Eric Karros .15
245 J.D. Drew .25
246 Todd Zeile .15
247 Mark Quinn .15
248 Kenny Kelly .15
249 Jermaine Dye .15
250 Barry Zito .30
251 Jason Hart, Larry Barnes 1.00
252 Ichiro Suzuki **RC**, Elpidio Guzman **RC** 20.00
253 Tsuyoshi Shinjo **RC**, Brian Cole 3.00
254 John Barnes, Adrian Hernandez **RC** 1.00
255 Jason Tyner, Jace Brewer 1.00
256 Brian Buchanan, Luis Rivas 1.00
257 Brent Abernathy, Jose Ortiz 1.00
258 Marcus Giles, Keith Ginter 1.00
259 Tike Redman, Jaisen Randolph **RC** 1.00
260 Dane Sardinha, David Espinosa 1.00
261 Josh Beckett, Craig House 1.00
262 Jack Cust, Hiram Bocachica 1.00
263 Alex Escobar, Esix Snead **RC** 1.00
264 Chris Richard, Vernon Wells 1.00
265 Pedro Feliz, Xavier Nady 1.00
266 Brandon Inge, Joe Crede 1.00
267 Ben Sheets, Roy Oswalt 1.00
268 Drew Henson **RC**, Andy Morales **RC** 4.00
269 C.C. Sabathia, Justin Miller 1.00
270 David Eckstein, Jason Gabrowski 1.00
271 Dee Brown, Chris Wakeland 1.00
272 Junior Spivey **RC**, Alex Cintron 3.00
273 Elvis Pena, Juan Uribe **RC** 2.00
274 Carlos Pena, Jason Romano 1.00
275 Winston Abreu **RC**, Wilson Betemit **RC** 1.50
276 Jose Mieses **RC**, Nick Neugebauer 1.00
277 Shea Hillenbrand, Dernell Stenson 1.00
278 Jared Sandberg, Toby Hall 1.00
279 Jay Gibbons **RC**, Ivanon Coffie 3.00
280 Pablo Ozuna, Santiago Perez 1.00
281 Nomar Garciaparra/AS 6.00
282 Derek Jeter/AS 6.00
283 Jason Giambi/AS 2.50
284 Magglio Ordonez/AS 1.00
285 Ivan Rodriguez/AS 2.00
286 Troy Glaus/AS 2.00
287 Carlos Delgado/AS 2.00
288 Darin Erstad/AS 1.00
289 Bernie Williams/AS 2.00
290 Roberto Alomar/AS 1.50
291 Barry Larkin/AS 1.50
292 Chipper Jones/AS 4.00
293 Vladimir Guerrero/AS 3.00
294 Sammy Sos/AS 5.00
295 Todd Helton/AS 2.00
296 Randy Johnson/AS 3.00
297 Jason Kendall/AS 1.00
298 Jim Edmonds/AS 1.50
299 Andruw Jones/AS 2.00
300 Edgardo Alfonzo/AS 1.00
301 Albert Pujols **RC**, Donaldo Mendez **RC** 80.00

Platinum Edition

Cards (1-250): 4-8X
Production 201 Sets
SP's (251-280): 8-20X
SP's (281-300): 5-10X
SP Production 21 Sets

Classic Combinations

NM/M
Common Card: 4.00
#1-10 Numbered to 250
11-20 Numbered to 500
21-30 Numbered to 1,000
31-40 Numbered to 2,000
1CC Derek Jeter, Alex Rodriguez 20.00
2CC Willie Mays, Willie McCovey 15.00
3CC Lou Gehrig, Babe Ruth 20.00
4CC Mark McGwire, Ken Griffey Jr. 15.00
5CC Johnny Bench, Roy Campanella 10.00
6CC Ted Williams, Nomar Garciaparra 20.00
7CC Yogi Berra, Mike Piazza 15.00
8CC Ernie Banks, Sammy Sosa 12.00
9CC Nolan Ryan, Randy Johnson 25.00
10CC Roberto Clemente, Vladimir Guerrero 15.00
11CC Lou Gehrig, Stan Musial 15.00
12CC Bill Mazeroski, Roberto Clemente 10.00
13CC Ernie Banks, Alex Rodriguez 10.00
14CC Phil Rizzuto, Derek Jeter 10.00
15CC Mike Piazza, Johnny Bench 8.00
16CC Mark McGwire, Sammy Sosa 10.00
17CC Ted Williams, Tony Gwynn 12.00
18CC Eddie Mathews, Mike Schmidt 10.00
19CC Barry Bonds, Willie Mays 10.00
20CC Nolan Ryan, Pedro Martinez 15.00
21CC Barry Bonds, Ken Griffey Jr. 10.00
22CC Willie McCovey, Reggie Jackson 5.00
23CC Roberto Clemente, Sammy Sosa 8.00
24CC Willie Mays, Ernie Banks 8.00
25CC Eddie Mathews, Chipper Jones 5.00
26CC Mike Schmidt, Brooks Robinson 6.00
27CC Stan Musial, Mark McGwire 8.00
28CC Ted Williams, Roger Maris 8.00
29CC Yogi Berra, Roy Campanella 5.00
30CC Johnny Bench, Tony Perez 5.00
31CC Bill Mazeroski, Joe Carter 3.00
32CC Mike Piazza, Roy Campanella 5.00
33CC Ernie Banks, Craig Biggio 4.00
34CC Frank Robinson, Brooks Robinson 4.00
35CC Mike Schmidt, Scott Rolen 5.00
36CC Roger Maris, Mark McGwire 10.00
37CC Stan Musial, Tony Gwynn 4.00
38CC Ted Williams, Bill Terry 6.00
39CC Derek Jeter, Reggie Jackson 6.00
40CC Yogi Berra, Bill Dickey 4.00

Classic Combinations Memorabilia

NM/M
Production 25 Sets
1 Yogi Berra, Bill Dickey 75.00
2 Yogi Berra, Roy Campanella 100.00
3 Roberto Clemente, Vladimir Guerrero 200.00
4 Eddie Mathews, Chipper Jones 80.00
5 Willie McCovey, Reggie Jackson 75.00
6 Phil Rizzuto, Derek Jeter 180.00
7 Brooks Robinson, Frank Robinson 85.00
8 Brooks Robinson, Mike Schmidt 180.00
9 Mike Schmidt, Scott Rolen 160.00
10 Ted Williams, Bill Terry 300.00
11 Ted Williams, Tony Gwynn 375.00

Grandstand Greats

NM/M
Complete Set (20): 25.00
Common Player: 1.00
Inserted 1:12
1GG Chipper Jones 2.00
2GG Alex Rodriguez 3.00
3GG Jeff Bagwell 1.50
4GG Troy Glaus 1.50
5GG Manny Ramirez 1.50
6GG Derek Jeter 4.00
7GG Tony Gwynn 2.00
8GG Greg Maddux 2.00
9GG Nomar Garciaparra 2.50
10GG Sammy Sosa 2.50
11GG Mike Piazza 2.50
12GG Barry Bonds 4.00
13GG Mark McGwire 3.00
14GG Vladimir Guerrero 1.50
15GG Ivan Rodriguez 1.00
16GG Ken Griffey Jr. 2.50
17GG Todd Helton 1.50
18GG Cal Ripken Jr. 4.00
19GG Pedro Martinez 1.50
20GG Frank Thomas 1.50

Nameplates

NM/M
Common Player: 15.00

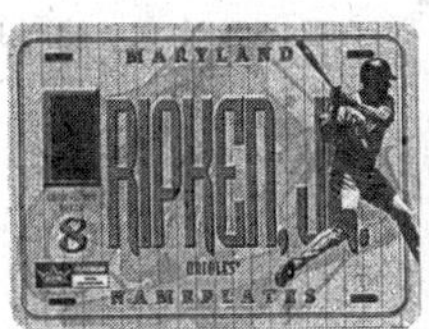

Inserted 1:12
Cal Ripken/19 200.00
Cal Ripken/21 200.00
Cal Ripken/23 200.00
Cal Ripken/110 100.00
Randy Johnson/99 40.00
Nolan Ryan/40 200.00
Javy Lopez/49 20.00
Frank Thomas/35 40.00
Frank Thomas/75 30.00
Frank Thomas/80 30.00
Jeffrey Hammonds/135 15.00
Larry Walker/79 15.00
Larry Walker/85 15.00
Dave Winfield/80 20.00
Vladimir Guerrero/80 25.00
Vladimir Guerrero/90 25.00
Kevin Millwood/130 15.00
Mike Mussina/91 25.00
Edgar Martinez/87 25.00
Edgar Martinez/120 20.00
Scott Rolen/65 30.00
Ivan Rodriguez/177 25.00
Manny Ramirez/75 25.00
Manny Ramirez/105 25.00
J.D. Drew/170 15.00
Greg Maddux/180 50.00
Chipper Jones/95 40.00
Carlos Beltran/90 15.00
Adrian Beltre 15.00
Matt Williams/175 15.00
Curt Schilling 20.00
Pedro Martinez/120 30.00
Robin Ventura/99 15.00
Tom Glavine/125 15.00
Tony Gwynn/35 75.00
Tony Gwynn/65 40.00
Tony Gwynn/70 40.00
Troy Glaus/85 20.00
Sean Casey/21 35.00
Darin Erstad/39 30.00
Stan Musial/30 150.00

National Patch Time

NM/M
Common Player: 4.00
Inserted 1:24 H
Tony Gwynn 8.00
Manny Ramirez 6.00
Freddy Garcia 4.00
Rondell White 4.00
Ivan Rodriguez 5.00
Brady Anderson 4.00
Adam Piatt 4.00
Carl Everett 4.00
Magglio Ordonez 4.00
Edgardo Alfonzo 4.00
Jason Kendall 4.00
Greg Maddux 8.00
Cal Ripken Jr. 30.00
Fred McGriff 4.00
Pedro Martinez 6.00
Roger Clemens 10.00
Wade Boggs 8.00
George Brett 15.00
Ozzie Smith 8.00
Dave Winfield 6.00
Tom Seaver 6.00
Rollie Fingers 4.00
Mike Schmidt 15.00
Eddie Murray 6.00
Nolan Ryan 30.00
Jeff Cirillo 4.00
Mike Mussina 5.00

2001 Fleer Platinum Rack Pack Autographs

NM/M
Common Player: 5.00
Hank Aaron/1997/90 100.00
Roger Clemens/1998/125 100.00
Jose Cruz Jr./1997 5.00
Bob Gibson/1998/300 25.00
Ben Grieve/100 6.00
Tony Gwynn/1998/125 50.00
Wes Helms/1997 5.00

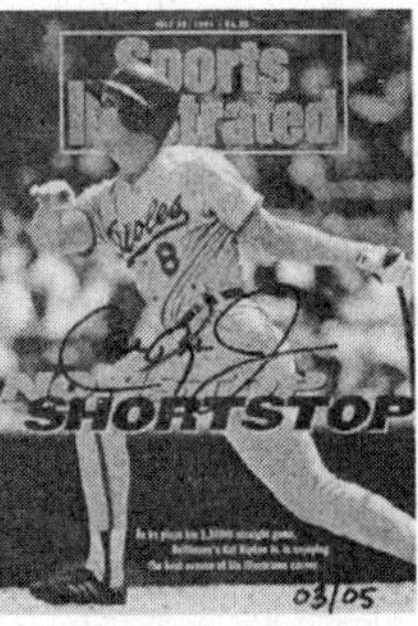

Harmon Killebrew/1998/300 30.00
Paul Konerko 135 5.00
Willie Mays/1997/115 120.00
Willie Mays/1998/120 120.00
Kirby Puckett/1997/105 50.00
Brooks Robinson/1998/40 75.00
Frank Robinson/1998/115 20.00
Scott Rolen/1998/150 25.00
Alex Rodriguez/1997/94 100.00
Alex Rodriguez/1998/150 70.00

Tickets

Complete Set (44):
Common Player:

Tickets Autographs

Complete Set (9):
Common Player:

20th Anniversary Reprints

NM/M
Complete Set (18): 25.00
Common Player: .50
Inserted 1:8
1AR Cal Ripken Jr. 4.00
2AR Wade Boggs 1.50
3AR Ryne Sandberg 1.50
4AR Tony Gwynn 1.50
5AR Don Mattingly 3.00
6AR Roger Clemens 2.00
7AR Kirby Puckett 1.50
8AR Jose Canseco .75
9AR Barry Bonds 4.00
10AR Ken Griffey Jr. 2.50
11AR Sammy Sosa 2.50
12AR Ivan Rodriguez .75
13AR Jeff Bagwell 1.00
14AR J.D. Drew .75
15AR Troy Glaus 1.00
16AR Rick Ankiel .50
17AR Xavier Nady .50
18AR Jose Ortiz .50

2001 Fleer Platinum RC

NM/M
Complete Set (300): 150.00
Common Player: .15
Common (502-601): 1.00
Inserted 1:3 Hobby
Pack (10): 7.00
Box (24): 140.00
302 Shawn Wooten .15
303 Todd Walker .15
304 Brian Buchanan .15
305 Jim Edmonds .25
306 Jarrod Washburn .15
307 Jose Rijo .15
308 Tim Raines .15
309 Matt Morris .15
310 Troy Glaus .50
311 Barry Larkin .40
312 Javier Vazquez .15
313 Placido Polanco .15
314 Darin Erstad .25
315 Marty Cordova .15
316 Vladimir Guerrero .75
317 Kerry Robinson .15
318 Byung-Hyun Kim .15
319 C.C. Sabathia .15
320 Edgardo Alfonzo .15
321 Jason Tyner .15
322 Reggie Sanders .15
323 Roberto Alomar .60
324 Matt Lawton .15
325 Brent Abernathy .15
326 Randy Johnson .75
327 Todd Helton .75
328 Andy Pettitte .40
329 Josh Beckett .40
330 Mark DeRosa .15
331 Jose Ortiz .15
332 Derek Jeter 2.00
333 Toby Hall .15
334 Wes Helms .15
335 Jose Macias .15
336 Bernie Williams .60
337 Ivan Rodriguez .75
338 Chipper Jones 1.25
339 Brandon Inge .15
340 Jason Giambi .75
341 Frank Catalanotto .15
342 Andruw Jones .50
343 Carlos Hernandez **RC** .40
344 Jermaine Dye .15
345 Mike Lamb .15
346 Ken Caminiti .15
347 A.J. Burnett .15
348 Terrence Long .15
349 Ruben Sierra .15
350 Marcus Giles .15
351 Wade Miller .15
352 Mark Mulder .25
353 Carlos Delgado .50
354 Chris Richard .15
355 Daryle Ward .15
356 Brad Penny .15
357 Vernon Wells .25
358 Jason Johnson .15
359 Tim Redding .15
360 Marlon Anderson .15
361 Carlos Pena .15
362 Nomar Garciaparra 2.00
363 Roy Oswalt .40
364 Todd Ritchie .15
365 Jose Mesa .15
366 Shea Hillenbrand .15
367 Dee Brown .15
368 Jason Kendall .25
369 Vinny Castilla .15
370 Fred McGriff .25
371 Neifi Perez .15
372 Xavier Nady .15
373 Abraham Nunez .15
374 Jon Lieber .15
375 Paul LoDuca .15
376 Bubba Trammell .15
377 Brady Clark .15
378 Joel Pineiro .15
379 Mark Grudzielanek .15
380 D'Angelo Jimenez .15
381 Junior Herndon .15
382 Magglio Ordonez .40
383 Ben Sheets .25
384 John Vander Wal .15
385 Pedro Astacio .15
386 Jose Canseco .40
387 Jose Hernandez .15
388 Eric Davis .15
389 Sammy Sosa 1.25
390 Mark Buehrle .15
391 Mark Loretta .15
392 Andres Galarraga .25
393 Scott Spiezio .15
394 Joe Crede .15
395 Luis Rivas .15
396 David Bell .15
397 Einar Diaz .15
398 Adam Dunn .75
399 A.J. Pierzynski .15
400 Jamie Moyer .15
401 Nick Johnson .15
402 Freddy Garcia 4.00
403 Hideo Nomo .50
404 Mark Mulder .25
405 Steve Sparks .15
406 Mariano Rivera .25
407 Mark Buehrle, Mike Mussina .25
408 Randy Johnson .50
409 Randy Johnson .50
410 Curt Schilling, Matt Morris .25
411 Greg Maddux .60
412 Robb Nen .15
413 Randy Johnson .50
414 Barry Bonds 1.00
415 Jason Giambi .40
416 Ichiro Suzuki 2.50
417 Ichiro Suzuki 2.50
418 Alex Rodriguez 1.00
419 Bret Boone .25
420 Ichiro Suzuki 2.50
421 Alex Rodriguez 1.00
422 Jason Giambi .40
423 Alex Rodriguez 1.00
424 Larry Walker .25
425 Rich Aurilia .15
426 Barry Bonds 1.00
427 Sammy Sosa .75
428 Jimmy Rollins, Juan Pierre .25
429 Sammy Sosa .75
430 Lance Berkman .25
431 Sammy Sosa .75
432 Carlos Delgado .25
433 Alex Rodriguez 1.00
434 Greg Vaughn .15
435 Albert Pujols 10.00
436 Ichiro Suzuki 2.50
437 Barry Bonds 1.00
438 Phil Nevin .15
439 Brian Giles .25
440 Bobby Abreu .25
441 Jason Giambi .40
442 Derek Jeter 1.00
443 Mike Piazza .75
444 Vladimir Guerrero .50
445 Corey Koskie .15
446 Richie Sexson .25
447 Shawn Green .25
448 Mike Sweeney .15
449 Jeff Bagwell .40
450 Cliff Floyd .15
451 Roger Cedeno .15
452 Todd Helton .40
453 Juan Gonzalez .30
454 Sean Casey .15
455 Magglio Ordonez .25
456 Sammy Sosa .75
457 Manny Ramirez .40
458 Jeff Conine .15
459 Chipper Jones .60
460 Luis Gonzalez .25
461 Troy Glaus .25
462 Ivan Rodriguez .40
463 Luis Gonzalez, Jack Cust .25
464 Jim Thome, C.C. Sabathia .25
465 Jason Hart, Jason Giambi .25
466 Jeff Bagwell, Roy Oswalt .30
467 Sammy Sosa, Corey Patterson .50
468 Mike Piazza, Alex Escobar .75
469 Ken Griffey Jr., Adam Dunn .75
470 Roger Clemens, Nick Johnson .75
471 Cliff Floyd, Josh Beckett .15
472 Cal Ripken Jr., Jerry Hairston Jr. .75
473 Phil Nevin, Xavier Nady .15
474 Scott Rolen, Jimmy Rollins .40
475 Barry Larkin, David Espinosa .25
476 Larry Walker, Jose Ortiz .15
477 Chipper Jones, Marcus Giles .40
478 Craig Biggio, Keith Ginter .15
479 Magglio Ordonez, Aaron Rowand .25
480 Alex Rodriguez, Carlos Pena .75
481 Derek Jeter, Alfonso Soriano .75
482 Curt Schilling (Post Season Glory) .20
483 (Post Season Glory) .25
484 (Post Season Glory) .25
485 (Post Season Glory) .25
486 (Post Season Glory) .25
487 (Post Season Glory) .25
488 (Post Season Glory) .25
489 Rudolph Giuliani (Post Season Glory) .50
490 George Bush (Post Season Glory) .50
491 (Post Season Glory) .25
492 (Post Season Glory) .25
493 (Post Season Glory) .25
494 Derek Jeter (Post Season Glory) .75
495 (Post Season Glory) .25
496 (Post Season Glory) .25
497 (Post Season Glory) .25
498 (Post Season Glory) .25
499 (Post Season Glory) .25
500 (Post Season Glory) .25
501 (Post Season Glory) .25
502 Josh Fogg **RC** 1.00
503 Elpidio Guzman 1.00
504 Corky Miller **RC** 1.00
505 Cesar Crespo **RC** 1.00
506 Carlos Garcia **RC** 1.00
507 Carlos Valderrama **RC** 1.00
508 Joe Kennedy **RC** 1.00
509 Henry Mateo **RC** 1.00
510 Brandon Duckworth **RC** 1.00
511 Ichiro Suzuki 15.00
512 Zach Day **RC** 2.00
513 Ryan Freel **RC** 1.00
514 Brian Lawrence **RC** 2.00
515 Alexis Gomez **RC** 1.00
516 Will Ohman **RC** 1.00
517 Juan Diaz **RC** 1.00
518 Juan Moreno **RC** 1.00
519 Rob Mackowiak **RC** 1.00
520 Horacio Ramirez **RC** 1.50
521 Albert Pujols 75.00
522 Tsuyoshi Shinjo 2.50
523 Ryan Drese **RC** 1.00
524 Angel Berroa **RC** 3.00
525 Josh Towers **RC** 2.50
526 Junior Spivey 1.50
527 Greg Miller **RC** 1.00
528 Esix Snead **RC** 1.00
529 Mark Prior **RC** 8.00
530 Drew Henson 3.00
531 Brian Reith **RC** 1.00
532 Andres Torres **RC** 1.00
533 Casey Fossum **RC** 2.00
534 Wilmy Caceres **RC** 1.00
535 Matt White **RC** 1.00
536 Wilkin Ruan **RC** 1.00
537 Rick Bauer **RC** 1.00
538 Morgan Ensberg **RC** 2.00
539 Geronimo Gil **RC** 1.00
540 Dewon Brazelton **RC** 1.00
541 Johnny Estrada **RC** 1.50
542 Claudio Vargas **RC** 1.00
543 Donaldo Mendez **RC** 1.00
544 Kyle Lohse **RC** 2.00
545 Nate Frese **RC** 1.00
546 Christian Parker **RC** 1.00
547 Blaine Neal **RC** 1.00
548 Travis Hafner **RC** 4.00
549 Billy Sylvester **RC** 1.00
550 Adam Pettyjohn 1.00
551 Bill Ortega 1.00
552 Jose Acevedo **RC** 1.00
553 Steve Green **RC** 1.00
554 Jay Gibbons **RC** 2.50
555 Bert Snow **RC** 1.00
556 Erick Almonte **RC** 1.50
557 Jeremy Owens **RC** 1.00
558 Sean Douglass **RC** 1.00
559 Jason Smith **RC** 1.00
560 Ricardo Rodriguez **RC** 1.00
561 Mark Teixeira **RC** 15.00
562 Tyler Walker **RC** 1.00
563 Juan Uribe **RC** 1.50
564 Bud Smith **RC** 1.00
565 Angel Santos **RC** 1.00
566 Brandon Lyon **RC** 1.00
567 Eric Hinske **RC** 2.50
568 Nick Punto **RC** 1.00
569 Winston Abreu **RC** 1.00
570 Jason Phillips **RC** 4.00
571 Rafael Soriano **RC** 1.50
572 Wilson Betemit 1.00
573 Endy Chavez **RC** 1.00
574 Juan Cruz **RC** 1.00
575 Cory Aldridge **RC** 1.00
576 Adrian Hernandez 1.00
577 Brandon Larson **RC** 1.50
578 Bret Prinz **RC** 1.00
579 Jackson Melian **RC** 1.00
580 Dave Maurer **RC** 1.00
581 Jason Michaels **RC** 1.00
582 Travis Phelps **RC** 1.00
583 Cody Ransom **RC** 1.00
584 Benito Baez **RC** 1.00
585 Brian Roberts **RC** 1.00
586 Nate Teut **RC** 1.00
587 Jack Wilson **RC** 1.00
588 Willie Harris **RC** 1.00
589 Martin Vargas **RC** 1.00
590 Steve Torrealba **RC** 1.00
591 Stubby Clapp **RC** 1.00
592 Danny Wright **RC** 1.00
593 Mike Rivera **RC** 1.00
594 Luis Pineda **RC** 1.00
595 Lance Davis **RC** 1.00
596 Ramon Vazquez **RC** 2.00
597 Dustan Mohr **RC** 1.00
598 Troy Mattes **RC** 1.00
599 Grant Balfour **RC** 1.00
600 Jared Fernandez **RC** 1.00
601 Jorge Julio **RC** 2.00

E-X
131 Albert Pujols/499 **RC** 300.00
132 Bud Smith/499 **RC** 8.00
133 Tsuyoshi Shinjo/499 **RC** 10.00
134 Wilson Betemit/499 **RC** 8.00
135 Adrian Hernandez/499 **RC** 8.00
136 Jackson Melian/499 8.00
137 Jay Gibbons/499 **RC** 10.00
138 Johnny Estrada/499 **RC** 15.00
139 Morgan Ensberg/499 **RC** 10.00
140 Drew Henson/499 **RC** 20.00

Focus
241 Tsuyoshi Shinjo/999 **RC** 5.00
242 Wilson Betemit/999 **RC** 5.00
243 Jeremy Owens/999 **RC** 5.00
244 Drew Henson/999 **RC** 8.00
245 Albert Pujols/999 **RC** 100.00
246 Travis Hafner/999 **RC** 12.00
247 Ichiro Suzuki/999 **RC** 40.00
248 Elpidio Guzman/999 **RC** 6.00
249 Matt White/999 **RC** 6.00
250 Junior Spivey/999 **RC** 8.00

Futures
221 Drew Henson/2499 **RC** 5.00
222 Johnny Estrada/2499 **RC** 5.00
223 Elpidio Guzman/2499 **RC** 3.00
224 Albert Pujols/2499 **RC** 60.00
225 Wilson Betemit/2499 **RC** 4.00
226 Mark Teixeira/2499 **RC** 15.00
227 Tsuyoshi Shinjo/2499 **RC** 5.00
228 Matt White/2499 **RC** 3.00
229 Adrian Hernandez/2499 **RC** 3.00
230 Ichiro Suzuki/2499 **RC** 30.00

Triple Crown
301 Elpidio Guzman/2999 **RC** 4.00
302 Drew Henson/2999 **RC** 5.00
303 Bud Smith/2999 **RC** 2.00
304 Carlos Valderrama/2999 **RC** 2.00
305 Tsuyoshi Shinjo/2999 **RC** 4.00
306 Ichiro Suzuki/2999 **RC** 30.00
307 Jackson Melian/2999 2.00
308 Morgan Ensberg/2999 **RC** 4.00
309 Albert Pujols/2999 **RC** 90.00
310 Johnny Estrada/2999 **RC** 5.00

Ultra
276 Junior Spivey **RC**, Juan Uribe **RC** 5.00
277 Albert Pujols **RC**, Bud Smith **RC** 80.00
278 Ichiro Suzuki **RC**, Tsuyoshi Shinjo **RC** 25.00
279 Drew Henson **RC**, Jackson Melian 5.00
280 Matt White **RC**, Adrian Hernandez **RC** 2.00

RC Platinum

Cards (302-501): 4-8X
Production 201
SP's (502-601):
Production 21 not priced.

RC Lumberjacks

NM/M
Common Player: 4.00
Inserted 1:1 Rack Pack
Barry Bonds 20.00
Derek Jeter 20.00
Luis Gonzalez 4.00
Mike Sweeney 4.00
Albert Pujols 15.00
Tony Gwynn 10.00
Adam Dunn 5.00
J.D. Drew 5.00
Brian Giles 4.00
Adrian Beltre 5.00
Bret Boone 4.00
Chipper Jones 10.00
Cliff Floyd 4.00
Darin Erstad 5.00
Gary Sheffield 4.00
Manny Ramirez 8.00
Mike Piazza 12.00
Todd Helton 8.00
Ivan Rodriguez 6.00
Lance Berkman 4.00
Vladimir Guerrero 8.00
Drew Henson 6.00
Cristian Guzman 4.00
Roberto Alomar 5.00
Moises Alou 4.00
Larry Walker 4.00

RC Lumberjacks Autographs

NM/M
Production 100 Sets
Barry Bonds 200.00
J.D. Drew 40.00
Adam Dunn 60.00

Luis Gonzalez 20.00
Derek Jeter 150.00
Albert Pujols 500.00
Cal Ripken Jr. 150.00
Mike Sweeney 20.00

RC National Patch Time

NM/M
Common Player: 4.00
Inserted 1:24 H
Edgardo Alfonzo 4.00
Brady Anderson 4.00
Adrian Beltre 4.00
Barry Bonds 20.00
Jeromy Burnitz 4.00
Eric Chavez 4.00
Roger Clemens 15.00
J.D. Drew 5.00
Darin Erstad 5.00
Carl Everett 4.00
Freddy Garcia 4.00
Jason Giambi 8.00
Juan Gonzalez 6.00
Mark Grace 6.00
Shawn Green 4.00
Ben Grieve 4.00
Vladimir Guerrero 8.00
Tony Gwynn 10.00
Randy Johnson 8.00
Chipper Jones 10.00
David Justice 4.00
Jeff Kent 4.00
Greg Maddux 10.00
Fred McGriff 4.00
John Olerud 4.00
Magglio Ordonez 4.00
Jorge Posada 5.00
Cal Ripken Jr. 20.00
Mariano Rivera 4.00
Ivan Rodriguez 6.00
Scott Rolen 6.00
Kazuhiro Sasaki 4.00
Aaron Sele 4.00
Gary Sheffield 4.00
John Smoltz 4.00
Frank Thomas 8.00
Mo Vaughn 4.00
Robin Ventura 4.00
Bernie Williams 5.00
Carlos Delgado 6.00
Chan Ho Park 4.00
Todd Helton 8.00
Craig Biggio 4.00
Jeff Bagwell 8.00
Paul LoDuca 4.00

RC Prime Numbers

NM/M
Common Player: 8.00
Inserted 1:12 Jumbo Pack
1PN Jeff Bagwell 15.00
2PN Cal Ripken Jr. 50.00
3PN Barry Bonds 50.00
4PN Todd Helton 15.00
5PN Derek Jeter 50.00
6PN Tony Gwynn 20.00
7PN Kazuhiro Sasaki 8.00
8PN Chan Ho Park 8.00
9PN Sean Casey 10.00
10PN Chipper Jones 20.00
11PN Pedro Martinez 15.00
12PN Mike Piazza 30.00
13PN Carlos Delgado 10.00
15PN Roger Clemens 25.00

RC Winning Combinations

NM/M
Common Card: 3.00
Varying quantities produced
1WC Derek Jeter, Ozzie Smith/2000 8.00
2WC Barry Bonds, Mark McGwire/500 10.00
3WC Ichiro Suzuki, Albert Pujols/250 30.00
4WC Ted Williams, Manny Ramirez/1000 10.00
5WC Tony Gwynn, Cal Ripken/250 15.00
6WC Mike Piazza, Derek Jeter/500 10.00
7WC Dave Winfield, Tony Gwynn/2000 5.00
8WC Hideo Nomo, Ichiro Suzuki/2000 10.00
9WC Cal Ripken, Ozzie Smith/1000 10.00
10WC Mark McGwire, Albert Pujols/2000 10.00
11WC Jeff Bagwell, Craig Biggio/1000 3.00
12WC Bobby Bonds, Barry Bonds/250 10.00
13WC Ted Williams, Stan Musial/250 10.00
14WC Babe Ruth, Reggie Jackson/500 15.00
15WC Kazuhiro Sasaki, Ichiro Suzuki/500 10.00
16WC Nolan Ryan, Roger Clemens/500 15.00
17WC Roger Clemens, Derek Jeter/250 15.00
18WC Ivan Rodriguez, Mike Piazza/1000 6.00
19WC Vladimir Guerrero, Sammy Sosa/2000 6.00
20WC Barry Bonds, Sammy Sosa/250 10.00
21WC Roger Clemens, Greg Maddux/1000 8.00
22WC Juan Gonzalez, Manny Ramirez/2000 3.00
23WC Todd Helton, Jason Giambi/2000 3.00
24WC Jeff Bagwell, Lance Berkman/2000 3.00
25WC Mike Sweeney, George Brett/1000 6.00
26WC Luis Gonzalez, Babe Ruth/2000 10.00
27WC Bill Skowron, Don Mattingly/250 10.00
28WC Yogi Berra, Cal Ripken/2000 10.00
29WC Pedro Martinez, Nomar Garciaparra/500 8.00
30WC Ted Kluszewski, Frank Robinson/1000 3.00
31WC Curt Schilling, Randy Johnson/1000 5.00
32WC Ken Griffey Jr., Cal Ripken/500 10.00
33WC Mike Piazza, Johnny Bench/1000 6.00
34WC Stan Musial, Albert Pujols/500 10.00
35WC Jackie Robinson, Nellie Fox/500 8.00
36WC Lefty Grove, Steve Carlton/250 5.00
37WC Ty Cobb, Tony Gwynn/250 10.00
38WC Albert Pujols, Frank Robinson/1000 10.00
39WC Ryne Sandberg, Sammy Sosa/500 10.00
40WC Cal Ripken Jr., Lou Gehrig/250 20.00

2001 Fleer Premium

NM/M
Complete Set (235):
Common Player: .15
Common SP (201-230): 4.00
Production 1,999
Cards 231-235 are redemptions.
Hobby Pack (8): 5.00
Hobby Box (24): 100.00
1 Cal Ripken Jr. 2.00
2 Derek Jeter 2.00
3 Edgardo Alfonzo .15
4 Luis Castillo .15
5 Mike Lieberthal .15
6 Kazuhiro Sasaki .15
7 Jeff Kent .15
8 Eric Karros .15
9 Tom Glavine .40
10 Jeromy Burnitz .15
11 Travis Fryman .15
12 Ron Coomer .15
13 Jeff D'Amico .15
14 Carlos Febles .15
15 Kevin Brown .15
16 Deivi Cruz .15
17 Tino Martinez .15
18 Bobby Abreu .15
19 Roger Clemens 1.00
20 Jeffrey Hammonds .15
21 Peter Bergeron .15
22 Ray Lankford .15
23 Scott Rolen .60
24 Jermaine Dye .15
25 Rusty Greer .15
26 Frank Thomas .75
27 Jeff Bagwell .75
28 Cliff Floyd .15
29 Chris Singleton .15
30 Steve Finley .15
31 Orlando Hernandez .15
32 Tom Goodwin .15
33 Larry Walker .15
34 Mike Sweeney .15
35 Tim Hudson .30
36 Kerry Wood .40
37 Mike Lowell .15
38 Andruw Jones .75
39 Alex S. Gonzalez .15
40 Juan Gonzalez .75
41 J.D. Drew .25
42 Mark McLemore .15
43 Royce Clayton .15
44 Paul O'Neill .15
45 Carlos Beltran .45
46 Phil Nevin .15
47 Rondell White .15
48 Gerald Williams .15
49 Geoff Jenkins .15
50 Marvin Benard .15
51 Alex Rodriguez 1.50
52 Moises Alou .15
53 Mike Lansing .15
54 Omar Vizquel .15
55 Eric Chavez .30
56 Mark Quinn .15
57 Mike Lamb .15
58 Rick Ankiel .15
59 Lance Berkman .15
60 Jeff Conine .15
61 B.J. Surhoff .15
62 Todd Helton .75
63 J.T. Snow .15
64 John Vander Wal .15
65 Johnny Damon .25
66 Bobby Higginson .15
67 Carlos Delgado .40
68 Shawn Green .35
69 Mike Redmond .15
70 Mike Piazza 1.25
71 Adrian Beltre .35
72 Juan Encarnacion .15
73 Chipper Jones 1.00
74 Garret Anderson .15
75 Paul Konerko .15
76 Barry Larkin .15
77 Tony Gwynn 1.00
78 Rafael Palmeiro .60
79 Randy Johnson .75
80 Mark Grace .25
81 Javy Lopez .15
82 Gabe Kapler .15
83 Henry Rodriguez .15
84 Raul Mondesi .15
85 Adam Piatt .15
86 Marquis Grissom .15
87 Charles Johnson .15
88 Sean Casey .25
89 Manny Ramirez .75
90 Curt Schilling .40
91 Fernando Tatis .15
92 Derek Bell .15
93 Tony Clark .15
94 Homer Bush .15
95 Nomar Garciaparra 1.25
96 Vinny Castilla .15
97 Ben Davis .15
98 Carl Everett .15
99 Damion Easley .15
100 Craig Biggio .15
101 Todd Hollandsworth .15
102 Jay Payton .15
103 Gary Sheffield .35
104 Sandy Alomar Jr. .15
105 Doug Glanville .15
106 Barry Bonds 2.00
107 Tim Salmon .25
108 Terrence Long .15
109 Jorge Posada .30
110 Jose Offerman .15
111 Edgar Martinez .15
112 Jeremy Giambi .15
113 Dean Palmer .15
114 Roberto Alomar .35
115 Aaron Boone .15
116 Adam Kennedy .15
117 Joe Randa .15
118 Jose Vidro .15
119 Tony Batista .15
120 Kevin Young .15
121 Preston Wilson .15
122 Jason Kendall .15
123 Mark Kotsay .15
124 Timoniel Perez .15
125 Eric Young .15
126 Greg Maddux 1.00
127 Richard Hidalgo .15
128 Brian Giles .15
129 Fred McGriff .15
130 Troy Glaus .75
131 Todd Walker .15
132 Brady Anderson .15
133 Jim Edmonds .15
134 Ben Grieve .15
135 Greg Vaughn .15
136 Robin Ventura .15
137 Sammy Sosa 1.25
138 Rich Aurilia .15
139 Jose Valentin .15
140 Trot Nixon .15
141 Troy Percival .15
142 Bernie Williams .35
143 Warren Morris .15
144 Jacque Jones .15
145 Danny Bautista .15
146 A.J. Pierzynski .15
147 Mark McGwire 1.50
148 Rafael Furcal .15
149 Ray Durham .15
150 Mike Mussina .40
151 Jay Bell .15
152 David Wells .15
153 Ken Caminiti .15
154 Jim Thome .15
155 Ivan Rodriguez .60
156 Milton Bradley .15
157 Ken Griffey Jr. 1.25
158 Al Leiter .15
159 Corey Koskie .15
160 Shannon Stewart .15
161 Mo Vaughn .15
162 Pedro Martinez .75
163 Todd Hundley .15
164 Darin Erstad .60
165 Ruben Rivera .15
166 Richie Sexson .15
167 Andres Galarraga .15
168 Darryl Kile .15
169 Jose Cruz Jr. .15
170 David Justice .15
171 Vladimir Guerrero .75
172 Jeff Cirillo .15
173 John Olerud .15
174 Devon White .15
175 Ron Belliard .15
176 Pokey Reese .15
177 Mike Hampton .15
178 David Ortiz .15
179 Magglio Ordonez .15
180 Ruben Mateo .15
181 Carlos Lee .15
182 Matt Williams .15
183 Miguel Tejada .25
184 Scott Elarton .15
185 Bret Boone .15
186 Pat Burrell .40
187 Brad Radke .15
188 Brian Jordan .15
189 Matt Lawton .15
190 Al Martin .15
191 Albert Belle .15
192 Tony Womack .15
193 Roger Cedeno .15
194 Travis Lee .15
195 Dmitri Young .15
196 Jay Buhner .15
197 Jason Giambi .50
198 Jason Tyner .15
199 Ben Petrick .15
200 Jose Canseco .40
201 Nick Johnson 4.00
202 Jace Brewer 4.00
203 Ryan Freel **RC** 4.00
204 Jaisen Randolph **RC** 4.00
205 Marcus Giles 4.00
206 Claudio Vargas **RC** 4.00
207 Brian Cole 4.00
208 Scott Hodges 4.00
209 Winston Abreu **RC** 4.00
210 Shea Hillenbrand 4.00
211 Larry Barnes 4.00
212 Paul Phillips **RC** 4.00
213 Pedro Santana **RC** 4.00
214 Ivanon Coffie 4.00
215 Junior Spivey **RC** 8.00
216 Donzell McDonald 4.00
217 Vernon Wells 5.00
218 Corey Patterson 5.00
219 Sang-Hoon Lee 4.00
220 Jack Cust 4.00
221 Jason Romano 4.00
222 Jack Wilson **RC** 8.00
223 Adam Everett 4.00
224 Esix Snead **RC** 4.00
225 Jason Hart 4.00
226 Joe Lawrence 4.00
227 Brandon Inge 4.00
228 Alex Escobar 4.00
229 Abraham Nunez 4.00
230 Jared Sandberg 4.00
231 Ichiro Suzuki **RC** 50.00
232 Tsuyoshi Shinjo **RC** 6.00
233 Albert Pujols **RC** 100.00
234 Wilson Betemit **RC** 5.00
235 Drew Henson **RC** 6.00

Star Ruby

Stars (1-200): 5-10X
SPs (201-230): .4-.8X
Production 125 Sets

A Time for Heroes

NM/M
Complete Set (20): 30.00
Common Player: 1.00
Inserted 1:20
Darin Erstad 1.00
Alex Rodriguez 4.00
Shawn Green 1.00
Jeff Bagwell 1.50
Sammy Sosa 3.00
Derek Jeter 5.00
Nomar Garciaparra 3.00
Carlos Delgado 1.00
Pat Burrell 1.00
Tony Gwynn 2.50
Chipper Jones 2.50
Jason Giambi 1.00
Magglio Ordonez 1.00
Troy Glaus 1.00
Ivan Rodriguez 1.00
Andruw Jones 1.50
Vladimir Guerrero 2.00
Ken Griffey Jr. 3.00
J.D. Drew 1.00
Todd Helton 1.50

A Time for Heroes Memorabilia

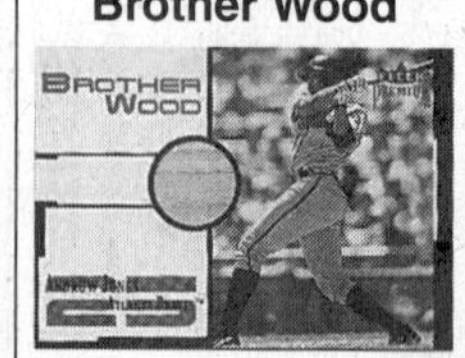

NM/M
Common Player: 4.00
Inserted 1:82
Shawn Green 5.00
Derek Jeter 25.00
Pat Burrell 5.00
Chipper Jones 10.00
Jason Giambi 8.00
Troy Glaus 6.00
Ivan Rodriguez 6.00
Andruw Jones 8.00
J.D. Drew 4.00
Todd Helton 8.00

Brother Wood

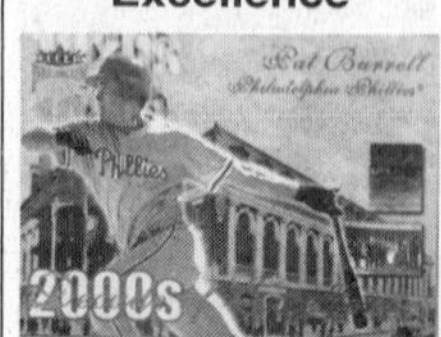

NM/M
Common Player: 5.00
Inserted 1:108
1BW Vladimir Guerrero 10.00
2BW Andruw Jones 6.00
3BW Corey Patterson 5.00
4BW Magglio Ordonez 5.00
5BW Jason Giambi 8.00
6BW Rafael Palmeiro 8.00
7BW Eric Chavez 5.00
8BW Pat Burrell 6.00
9BW Adrian Beltre 5.00

Decades of Excellence

NM/M
Complete Set (50): 140.00
Common Player: 1.00
Inserted 1:12
Card #17 does not exist.
Babe Ruth, Lou Gehrig 10.00
Lloyd Waner 1.00
Jimmie Foxx 3.00
Hank Greenberg 2.00
Ted Williams 8.00
Johnny Mize 2.00
Enos Slaughter 1.00
Jackie Robinson 6.00
Stan Musial 5.00
Duke Snider 3.00
Eddie Mathews 3.00
Roy Campanella 2.50
Yogi Berra 4.00
Pee Wee Reese 2.00
Phil Rizzuto 2.00
Al Kaline 4.00
Frank Howard 1.00
Roberto Clemente 8.00
Bob Gibson 3.00
Roger Maris 4.00
Don Drysdale 2.50
Maury Wills 1.00
Tom Seaver 2.50
Reggie Jackson 3.00
Johnny Bench 4.00
Carlton Fisk 2.50
Rod Carew 2.00
Steve Carlton 1.00
Mike Schmidt 6.00
Nolan Ryan 10.00
Rickey Henderson 3.00
Roger Clemens 5.00
Don Mattingly 6.00
George Brett 6.00
Greg Maddux 5.00
Cal Ripken Jr. 10.00
Chipper Jones 5.00
Barry Bonds 10.00
Ivan Rodriguez 2.50
Sammy Sosa, Mark McGwire 8.00
Ken Griffey Jr. 6.00
Tony Gwynn 4.00
Vladimir Guerrero 3.00
Shawn Green 1.00
Alex Rodriguez, Derek Jeter, Nomar Garciaparra 8.00
Pat Burrell 2.00
Rick Ankiel 1.00
Eric Chavez 1.00
Troy Glaus 2.00

Decades of Excellence Autograph

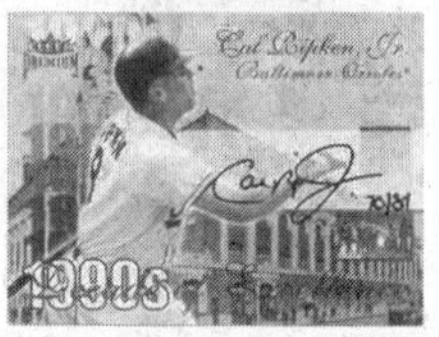

NM/M
Common Autograph: 20.00
Production #'s listed.
1 Rick Ankiel/99 10.00
2 Johnny Bench/67 65.00
3 Barry Bonds/86 200.00
4 George Brett/73 100.00
5 Rod Carew/67 30.00
6 Steve Carlton/65 30.00
7 Eric Chavez/98 20.00
8 Carlton Fisk/69 50.00
9 Bob Gibson/59 40.00
10 Tony Gwynn/82 50.00
11 Reggie Jackson/67 40.00
12 Chipper Jones/93 60.00
13 Al Kaline/53 80.00
14 Don Mattingly/82 100.00
15 Cal Ripken Jr./82 150.00
16 Nolan Ryan/66 125.00
17 Mike Schmidt/72 80.00
18 Tom Seaver/67 50.00
19 Enos Slaughter/38 40.00
20 Maury Wills/59 20.00

Decades of Excellence Memorabilia

NM/M
Common Player: 8.00
Inserted 1:217 H
1 Rick Ankiel/Jsy 8.00
2 Barry Bonds/Jsy 15.00
3 Pat Burrell/Jsy 10.00
4 Roy Campanella/Bat/50 50.00
5 Eric Chavez/Bat 8.00
6 Roberto Clemente/Bat/50 125.00
7 Carlton Fisk/Uni. 15.00
8 Jimmie Foxx/Bat/50 80.00
9 Shawn Green/Bat 8.00
10 Tony Gwynn/Jsy 15.00
11 Reggie Jackson/Jsy 15.00
12 Greg Maddux/Jsy 20.00

13 Roger Maris/Uni. 35.00
14 Pee Wee Reese/Jsy 8.00
15 Cal Ripken/Jsy/50 35.00
16 Ivan Rodriguez/Bat 8.00
17 Nolan Ryan/Jsy 25.00
18 Mike Schmidt/Jsy 20.00
19 Tom Seaver/Jsy 15.00
20 Duke Snider/Bat 15.00
21 Ted Williams/Jsy/50 250.00

Diamond Dominators

NM/M
Common Player: 4.00
Inserted 1:51
1DD Troy Glaus 6.00
2DD Darin Erstad 5.00
3DD J.D. Drew 4.00
4DD Barry Bonds 25.00
5DD Roger Clemens 20.00
6DD Vladimir Guerrero 8.00
7DD Tony Gwynn 10.00
8DD Greg Maddux 10.00
9DD Cal Ripken Jr. 25.00
10DD Ivan Rodriguez 6.00
11DD Frank Thomas 8.00
12DD Bernie Williams 4.00
13DD Jeromy Burnitz 4.00
14DD Juan Gonzalez 6.00

Diamond Dominators Patches

NM/M
Common Player: 15.00
Production 100 Sets
1DD Troy Glaus 25.00
2DD Darin Erstad 20.00
3DD J.D. Drew 15.00
4DD Barry Bonds 75.00
5DD Roger Clemens 60.00
6DD Vladimir Guerrero 25.00
7DD Tony Gwynn 50.00
8DD Greg Maddux 50.00
9DD Cal Ripken Jr. 75.00
10DD Ivan Rodriguez 20.00
11DD Frank Thomas 25.00
12DD Bernie Williams 20.00
13DD Jeromy Burnitz 15.00
14DD Juan Gonzalez 25.00

Grip It and Rip It

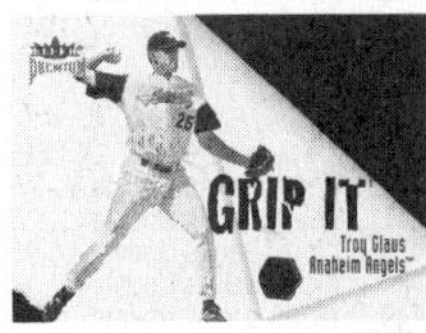

NM/M
Complete Set (15): 10.00
Common Player: .50
Inserted 1:6
1GRP Roger Clemens, Derek Jeter 2.00
2GRP Scott Rolen, Pat Burrell .50
3GRP Greg Maddux, Andruw Jones 1.00
4GRP Shannon Stewart, Carlos Delgado .50
5GRP Shawn Estes, Barry Bonds 2.00
6GRP Cal Eldred, Frank Thomas .50
7GRP Mark McGwire, Jim Edmonds 2.00
8GRP Jose Vidro, Vladimir Guerrero .75
9GRP Pedro Martinez, Nomar Garciaparra 1.50
10GRP Tom Glavine, Chipper Jones 1.00
11GRP Ken Griffey Jr., Sean Casey 1.00
12GRP Jeff Bagwell, Moises Alou .50
13GRP Troy Glaus, Darin Erstad .50
14GRP Mike Piazza, Robin Ventura 1.00
15GRP Eric Chavez, Jason Giambi .50

Grip It and Rip It Plus

NM/M
Common Card: 8.00
200 Base/Bat Produced
100 Ball/Bat Produced

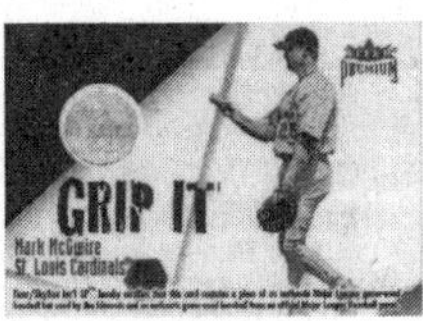

Roger Clemens, Derek Jeter/100 50.00
Scott Rolen, Pat Burrell/200 8.00
Greg Maddux, Andruw Jones/100 40.00
Shannon Stewart, Carlos Delgado/200 8.00
Shawn Estes, Barry Bonds/100 50.00
Cal Eldred, Frank Thomas/200 15.00
Mark McGwire, Jim Edmonds/100 60.00
Jose Vidro, Vladimir Guerrero/200 15.00
Pedro Martinez, Nomar Garciaparra/100 50.00
Tom Glavine, Chipper Jones/200 15.00
Ken Griffey Jr., Sean Casey/200 20.00
Jeff Bagwell, Moises Alou/200 10.00
Troy Glaus, Darin Erstad/200 10.00
Mike Piazza, Robin Ventura/100 40.00
Eric Chavez, Jason Giambi/200 10.00

Home Field Advantage

NM/M
Complete Set (15): 60.00
Common Player: 2.00
Inserted 1:72
Mike Piazza 6.00
Derek Jeter 10.00
Ken Griffey Jr. 6.00
Carlos Delgado 2.00
Chipper Jones 5.00
Alex Rodriguez 8.00
Sammy Sosa 6.00
Scott Rolen 3.00
Nomar Garciaparra 6.00
Todd Helton 3.00
Vladimir Guerrero 3.00
Jeff Bagwell 3.00
Barry Bonds 10.00
Cal Ripken Jr. 10.00
Mark McGwire 8.00

Home Field Advantage Game Wall

NM/M
Common Player: 6.00
Production 100 Sets
Mike Piazza 15.00
Derek Jeter 25.00
Ken Griffey Jr. 15.00
Carlos Delgado 6.00
Chipper Jones 10.00
Alex Rodriguez 20.00
Sammy Sosa 15.00
Scott Rolen 8.00
Nomar Garciaparra 15.00
Todd Helton 8.00
Vladimir Guerrero 8.00
Jeff Bagwell 8.00
Barry Bonds 25.00
Cal Ripken Jr. 25.00
Mark McGwire 20.00

Derek Jeter Monumental Moments

NM/M
Numbered to 1,995.
Autograph numbered to 95.
DJMM Derek Jeter 8.00

DJMM Derek Jeter/ Auto./95 80.00

Solid Performers

NM/M
Complete Set (15): 30.00
Common Player: 1.50
Inserted 1:20
1SP Mark McGwire 4.00
2SP Alex Rodriguez 4.00
3SP Nomar Garciaparra 2.50
4SP Derek Jeter 5.00
5SP Vladimir Guerrero 1.50
6SP Todd Helton 1.50
7SP Chipper Jones 2.00
8SP Mike Piazza 2.50
9SP Ivan Rodriguez 1.50
10SP Tony Gwynn 2.00
11SP Cal Ripken Jr. 5.00
12SP Barry Bonds 5.00
13SP Jeff Bagwell 1.50
14SP Ken Griffey Jr. 2.50
15SP Sammy Sosa 2.50

2001 Fleer Premium Solid Performers Game Base

NM/M
Common Player: 5.00
Production 150 Sets
1SP Mark McGwire 15.00
2SP Alex Rodriguez 15.00
3SP Nomar Garciaparra 12.00
4SP Derek Jeter 20.00
5SP Vladimir Guerrero 8.00
6SP Todd Helton 8.00
7SP Chipper Jones 10.00
8SP Mike Piazza 12.00
9SP Ivan Rodriguez 8.00
10SP Tony Gwynn 10.00
11SP Cal Ripken Jr. 20.00
12SP Barry Bonds 20.00
13SP Jeff Bagwell 8.00
14SP Ken Griffey Jr. 12.00
15SP Sammy Sosa 12.00

2001 Fleer Showcase

NM/M
Complete Set (160):
Common Player: .25
Common SP (116-125): 10.00
Production 500
Common SP (126-145): 4.00
Production 1,500
Common SP (146-160): 4.00
Production 2,000
Pack (5): 10.00
Box (24): 200.00
1 Tony Gwynn 1.50
2 Barry Larkin .25
3 Chan Ho Park .25
4 Darin Erstad .65
5 Rafael Furcal .25
6 Roger Cedeno .25
7 Timo Perez .25
8 Rick Ankiel .25
9 Pokey Reese .25
10 Jeromy Burnitz .25
11 Phil Nevin .25
12 Matt Williams .25
13 Mike Hampton .25
14 Fernando Tatis .25
15 Kazuhiro Sasaki .25
16 Jim Thome .25
17 Geoff Jenkins .25
18 Jeff Kent .25
19 Tom Glavine .40
20 Dean Palmer .25
21 Todd Zeile .25
22 Edgar Renteria .25
23 Andruw Jones 1.00
24 Juan Encarnacion .25
25 Robin Ventura .25
26 J.D. Drew .25
27 Ray Durham .25
28 Richard Hidalgo .25
29 Eric Chavez .35
30 Rafael Palmeiro .75
31 Steve Finley .25
32 Jeff Weaver .25
33 Al Leiter .25
34 Jim Edmonds .25
35 Garret Anderson .25
36 Larry Walker .25
37 Jose Vidro .25
38 Mike Cameron .25
39 Brady Anderson .25
40 Mike Lowell .25
41 Bernie Williams .35
42 Gary Sheffield .40
43 John Smoltz .25
44 Mike Mussina .40
45 Greg Vaughn .25
46 Juan Gonzalez .75
47 Matt Lawton .25
48 Robb Nen .25
49 Brad Radke .25
50 Edgar Martinez .25
51 Mike Bordick .25
52 Shawn Green .40
53 Carl Everett .25
54 Adrian Beltre .40
55 Kerry Wood .50
56 Kevin Brown .25
57 Brian Giles .25
58 Greg Maddux 1.50
59 Preston Wilson .25
60 Orlando Hernandez .25
61 Ben Grieve .25
62 Jermaine Dye .25
63 Travis Lee .25
64 Jose Cruz Jr. .25
65 Rondell White .25
66 Carlos Beltran .45
67 Scott Rolen .75
68 Brad Fullmer .25
69 David Wells .25
70 Mike Sweeney .25
71 Barry Zito .40
72 Tony Batista .25
73 Curt Schilling .40
74 Jeff Cirillo .25
75 Edgardo Alfonzo .25
76 John Olerud .25
77 Carlos Lee .25
78 Moises Alou .25
79 Tim Hudson .35
80 Andres Galarraga .25
81 Roberto Alomar .45
82 Richie Sexson .25
83 Trevor Hoffman .25
84 Omar Vizquel .25
85 Jacque Jones .25
86 J.T. Snow .25
87 Sean Casey .25
88 Craig Biggio .40
89 Mariano Rivera .35
90 Rusty Greer .25
91 Barry Bonds 3.00
92 Pedro Martinez 1.00
93 Cal Ripken Jr. 3.00
94 Pat Burrell .50
95 Chipper Jones 1.50
96 Magglio Ordonez .25
97 Jeff Bagwell 1.00
98 Randy Johnson 1.00
99 Frank Thomas 1.00
100 Jason Kendall .25
101 Nomar Garciaparra (Avant Card) 6.00
102 Mark McGwire (Avant Card) 8.00
103 Troy Glaus (Avant Card) 3.00
104 Ivan Rodriguez (Avant Card) 2.50
105 Manny Ramirez (Avant Card) 3.00
106 Derek Jeter (Avant Card) 10.00
107 Alex Rodriguez (Avant Card) 8.00
108 Ken Griffey Jr. (Avant Card) 6.00
109 Todd Helton (Avant Card) 3.00
110 Sammy Sosa (Avant Card) 6.00
111 Vladimir Guerrero (Avant Card) 3.00
112 Mike Piazza (Avant Card) 6.00
113 Roger Clemens (Avant Card) 5.00
114 Jason Giambi (Avant Card) 2.50
115 Carlos Delgado (Avant Card) 2.00
116 Ichiro Suzuki **RC** (Rookie Avant) 100.00
117 Morgan Ensberg **RC** (Rookie Avant) 20.00
118 Carlos Valderrama **RC** (Rookie Avant) 10.00
119 Erick Almonte **RC** (Rookie Avant) 10.00
120 Tsuyoshi Shinjo **RC** (Rookie Avant) 10.00
121 Albert Pujols **RC** (Rookie Avant) 240.00
122 Wilson Betemit **RC** (Rookie Avant) 10.00
123 Adrian Hernandez **RC** (Rookie Avant) 10.00
124 Jackson Melian **RC** (Rookie Avant) 10.00
125 Drew Henson **RC** (Rookie Avant) 12.00
126 Paul Phillips **RC** 4.00
127 Esix Snead **RC** 4.00
128 Ryan Freel **RC** 4.00
129 Junior Spivey **RC** 8.00
130 Elpidio Guzman **RC** 6.00
131 Juan Diaz **RC** 4.00
132 Andres Torres **RC** 4.00
133 Jay Gibbons **RC** 10.00
134 Bill Ortega 4.00
135 Alexis Gomez **RC** 4.00
136 Wilken Ruan **RC** 4.00
137 Henry Mateo **RC** 4.00
138 Juan Uribe **RC** 8.00
139 Johnny Estrada **RC** 10.00
140 Jaisen Randolph **RC** 4.00
141 Eric Hinske **RC** 8.00
142 Jack Wilson **RC** 10.00
143 Cody Ransom **RC** 4.00
144 Nate Frese **RC** 4.00
145 John Grabow **RC** 4.00
146 Christian Parker **RC** 4.00
147 Brian Lawrence **RC** 6.00
148 Brandon Duckworth **RC** 4.00
149 Winston Abreu **RC** 4.00
150 Horacio Ramirez **RC** 8.00
151 Nick Maness **RC** 4.00
152 Blaine Neal **RC** 4.00
153 Billy Sylvester **RC** 4.00
154 David Elder **RC** 4.00
155 Bert Snow **RC** 4.00
156 Claudio Vargas **RC** 4.00
157 Martin Vargas **RC** 4.00
158 Grant Balfour **RC** 4.00
159 Randy Keisler 4.00
160 Zach Day **RC** 4.00

Legacy

Stars (1-100): 10-15X
Avant (101-115): 2-4X
RC's (116-125): .75-1.5X
RC's (126-160): 1-2X
Production 50 Sets

Autographics

NM/M
Common Player: 5.00
Silvers: 1X
Production 250 Sets
Golds: 1-2X
Production 50 Sets
Roberto Alomar 30.00
Rick Ankiel 5.00
Albert Belle 8.00
Carlos Beltran 25.00
Adrian Beltre 10.00
Milton Bradley 5.00
Dee Brown 5.00
Jeromy Burnitz 5.00
Pat Burrell 10.00
Sean Casey 8.00
Joseph Crede 5.00
Jose Cruz Jr. 5.00
Ryan Dempster 5.00
J.D. Drew 10.00
Adam Dunn 15.00
Erubiel Durazo 5.00
Jermaine Dye 5.00
David Eckstein 5.00
Alex Escobar 5.00
Seth Etherton 5.00
Adam Everett 5.00
Carlos Febles 5.00
Troy Glaus 15.00
Ben Grieve 5.00
Toby Hall 5.00
Todd Helton 20.00
Shea Hillenbrand 6.00
Aubrey Huff 6.00
D'Angelo Jimenez 5.00
Paul Konerko 8.00
Mike Lamb 5.00
Matt Lawton 5.00
Derrek Lee 8.00
Mike Lieberthal 5.00
Mike Lowell 8.00
Julio Lugo 5.00
Jason Marquis 5.00
Edgar Martinez 15.00
Kevin Millwood 10.00
Eric Milton 5.00
Bengie Molina 5.00
Mike Mussina 25.00
Russ Ortiz 5.00
Corey Patterson 10.00
Jay Payton 5.00
Adam Piatt 5.00
Juan Pierre 5.00
Brad Radke 5.00
John Rocker 5.00
Alex Rodriguez 60.00
Scott Rolen 20.00
Richie Sexson 10.00
Gary Sheffield 10.00
Shannon Stewart 5.00
Miguel Tejada 25.00
Robin Ventura 5.00
Jose Vidro 5.00
Billy Wagner 8.00
Kip Wells 5.00
Rondell White 5.00
Preston Wilson 5.00
Kerry Wood 20.00
Julio Zuleta 5.00

Awards Showcase

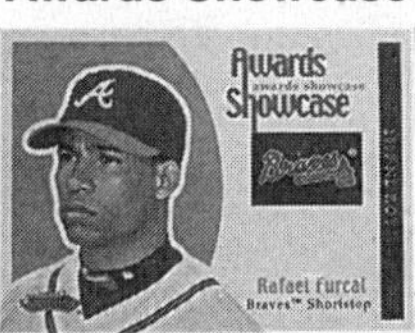

NM/M
Complete Set (20): 30.00
Common Player: 1.00
Inserted 1:20 Retail
Derek Jeter 5.00
Derek Jeter 5.00
Jason Giambi 1.50
Jeff Kent 1.00
Pedro Martinez 2.00
Randy Johnson 2.00
Kazuhiro Sasaki 1.00
Rafael Furcal 1.00
Carlos Delgado 1.50
Todd Helton 2.00
Ivan Rodriguez 1.50
Darin Erstad 1.50
Bernie Williams 1.00
Greg Maddux 3.00
Jim Edmonds 1.00
Andruw Jones 2.00
Nomar Garciaparra 4.00
Todd Helton 2.00
Troy Glaus 2.00
Sammy Sosa 4.00

Awards Showcase Autographs

NM/M
Production 25 Sets
Johnny Bench 100.00
Yogi Berra 90.00
George Brett 200.00
Steve Carlton 60.00
Roger Clemens 180.00
Andre Dawson 40.00
Whitey Ford 80.00
Tom Glavine 50.00
Juan Gonzalez 50.00
Reggie Jackson 80.00
Randy Johnson 90.00
Chipper Jones 80.00
Harmon Killebrew 75.00
Fred Lynn 25.00
Greg Maddux 150.00
Don Mattingly 175.00

Willie McCovey	40.00
Jim Palmer	40.00
Jim Rice	25.00
Brooks Robinson	75.00
Frank Robinson	50.00
Ivan Rodriguez	50.00
Mike Schmidt	125.00
Tom Seaver	100.00

Awards Showcase Memorabilia

	NM/M
Common Player:	10.00
Production 100 Sets	
Johnny Bench	20.00
Yogi Berra	15.00
George Brett	40.00
Lou Brock	10.00
Roy Campanella	25.00
Steve Carlton	10.00
Roger Clemens	40.00
Andre Dawson	10.00
Whitey Ford	15.00
Jimmie Foxx	45.00
Kirk Gibson	10.00
Tom Glavine	10.00
Juan Gonzalez	10.00
Elston Howard	10.00
Jim "Catfish" Hunter	10.00
Reggie Jackson	20.00
Randy Johnson	15.00
Chipper Jones	15.00
Harmon Killebrew	20.00
Greg Maddux	25.00
Don Mattingly	75.00
Willie McCovey	10.00
Jim Palmer	10.00
Jim Rice	10.00
Brooks Robinson	20.00
Frank Robinson	15.00
Jackie Robinson	75.00
Ivan Rodriguez	15.00
Mike Schmidt	40.00
Tom Seaver	15.00
Willie Stargell	10.00
Ted Williams	150.00
Robin Yount	25.00

Derek Jeter's Monumental Moments

	NM/M
Production 2,000:	
MM5 Derek Jeter	8.00
Derek Jeter/ Auto./100	90.00

Showcase Sticks

	NM/M
Common Player:	4.00
Inserted 1:24	
Roberto Alomar	6.00
Adrian Beltre	5.00
Pat Burrell	6.00
J.D. Drew	4.00
Juan Gonzalez	6.00
Andruw Jones	8.00
Chipper Jones	10.00
Magglio Ordonez	4.00
Ivan Rodriguez	6.00
Scott Rolen	8.00
Frank Thomas	8.00
Roger Cedeno	4.00
Shawn Green	5.00
Richard Hidalgo	4.00
Tony Clark	4.00
Preston Wilson	4.00
Barry Bonds	30.00
Rafael Furcal	4.00
Randy Johnson	8.00
Vladimir Guerrero	8.00
Al Kaline	10.00
George Kell	4.00
Jason Kendall	4.00
Carlos Delgado	5.00
Adam Piatt	4.00
Alex Gonzalez	4.00
Jorge Posada	6.00
Jose Vidro	4.00
Roger Clemens	20.00
Steve Finley	4.00
Reggie Jackson	8.00
Shannon Stewart	4.00
Rick Ankiel	4.00
Jim Thome	8.00
Tsuyoshi Shinjo	6.00
Ichiro Suzuki	25.00

Sweet Sigs

	NM/M
Common Player:	10.00
Inserted 1:24	
Prices for Lumber	
Wall:	1X
Leather:	1-1.5X
Bobby Abreu	15.00
Wilson Betemit	10.00
Russell Branyan	10.00
Pat Burrell	20.00
Eric Chavez	20.00
Rafael Furcal	15.00
Nomar Garciaparra	100.00
Juan Gonzalez	35.00
Elpidio Guzman	10.00
Drew Henson	15.00
Brandon Inge	10.00
Derek Jeter	130.00
Andruw Jones	30.00
Willie Mays	180.00
Jackson Melian	10.00
Xavier Nady	10.00
Jose Ortiz	10.00
Ben Sheets	15.00
Mike Sweeney	15.00
Miguel Tejada	35.00
Albert Pujols	450.00

2001 Fleer Tradition

		NM/M
Complete Set (450):		35.00
Common Player:		.15
Comp. Factory Set (485):		100.00
Pack (10):		2.00
Box (36):		55.00
1	Andres Galarraga	.15
2	Armando Rios	.15
3	Julio Lugo	.15
4	Darryl Hamilton	.15
5	Dave Veres	.15
6	Edgardo Alfonzo	.15
7	Brook Fordyce	.15
8	Eric Karros	.15
9	Neifi Perez	.15
10	Jim Edmonds	.15
11	Barry Larkin	.15
12	Trot Nixon	.15
13	Andy Pettitte	.35
14	Jose Guillen	.15
15	David Wells	.15
16	Magglio Ordonez	.15
17	David Segui	.15
18	Juan Encarnacion	.15
19	Robert Person	.15
20	Quilvio Veras	.15
21	Mo Vaughn	.15
22	B.J. Surhoff	.15
23	Ken Caminiti	.15
24	Frank Catalanotto	.15
25	Luis Gonzalez	.25
26	Pete Harnisch	.15
27	Alex Gonzalez	.15
28	Mark Quinn	.15
29	Luis Castillo	.15
30	Rick Helling	.15
31	Barry Bonds	2.00
32	Warren Morris	.15
33	Aaron Boone	.15
34	Ricky Gutierrez	.15
35	Preston Wilson	.15
36	Erubiel Durazo	.15
37	Jermaine Dye	.15
38	John Rocker	.15
39	Mark Grudzielanek	.15
40	Pedro Martinez	.75
41	Phil Nevin	.15
42	Luis Matos	.15
43	Orlando Hernandez	.15
44	Steve Cox	.15
45	James Baldwin	.15
46	Rafael Furcal	.15
47	Todd Zeile	.15
48	Elmer Dessens	.15
49	Russell Branyan	.15
50	Juan Gonzalez	.75
51	Mac Suzuki	.15
52	Adam Kennedy	.15
53	Randy Velarde	.15
54	David Bell	.15
55	Royce Clayton	.15
56	Greg Colbrunn	.15
57	Rey Ordonez	.15
58	Kevin Millwood	.15
59	Fernando Vina	.15
60	Eddie Taubensee	.15
61	Enrique Wilson	.15
62	Jay Bell	.15
63	Brian Moehler	.15
64	Brad Fullmer	.15
65	Ben Petrick	.15
66	Orlando Cabrera	.25
67	Shane Reynolds	.15
68	Mitch Meluskey	.15
69	Jeff Shaw	.15
70	Chipper Jones	1.00
71	Tomo Ohka	.15
72	Ruben Rivera	.15
73	Mike Sirotka	.15
74	Scott Rolen	.60
75	Glendon Rusch	.15
76	Miguel Tejada	.35
77	Brady Anderson	.15
78	Bartolo Colon	.15
79	Ron Coomer	.15
80	Gary DiSarcina	.15
81	Geoff Jenkins	.15
82	Billy Koch	.15
83	Mike Lamb	.15
84	Alex Rodriguez	1.50
85	Denny Neagle	.15
86	Michael Tucker	.15
87	Edgar Renteria	.15
88	Brian Anderson	.15
89	Glenallen Hill	.15
90	Aramis Ramirez	.15
91	Rondell White	.15
92	Tony Womack	.15
93	Jeffrey Hammonds	.15
94	Freddy Garcia	.15
95	Bill Mueller	.15
96	Mike Lieberthal	.15
97	Michael Barrett	.15
98	Derrek Lee	.15
99	Bill Spiers	.15
100	Derek Lowe	.15
101	Javy Lopez	.15
102	Adrian Beltre	.30
103	Jim Parque	.15
104	Marquis Grissom	.15
105	Eric Chavez	.25
106	Todd Jones	.15
107	Eric Owens	.15
108	Roger Clemens	1.00
109	Denny Hocking	.15
110	Roberto Hernandez	.15
111	Albert Belle	.15
112	Troy Glaus	.75
113	Ivan Rodriguez	.60
114	Carlos Guillen	.15
115	Chuck Finley	.15
116	Dmitri Young	.15
117	Paul Konerko	.15
118	Damon Buford	.15
119	Fernando Tatis	.15
120	Larry Walker	.15
121	Jason Kendall	.15
122	Matt Williams	.15
123	Henry Rodriguez	.15
124	Placido Polanco	.15
125	Bobby Estalella	.15
126	Pat Burrell	.50
127	Mark Loretta	.15
128	Moises Alou	.15
129	Tino Martinez	.15
130	Milton Bradley	.15
131	Todd Hundley	.15
132	Keith Foulke	.15
133	Robert Fick	.15
134	Cristian Guzman	.15
135	Rusty Greer	.15
136	John Olerud	.15
137	Mariano Rivera	.25
138	Jeromy Burnitz	.15
139	Dave Burba	.15
140	Ken Griffey Jr.	1.25
141	Tony Gwynn	1.00
142	Carlos Delgado	.50
143	Edgar Martinez	.15
144	Ramon Hernandez	.15
145	Pedro Astacio	.15
146	Ray Lankford	.15
147	Mike Mussina	.40
148	Ray Durham	.15
149	Lee Stevens	.15
150	Jay Canizaro	.15
151	Adrian Brown	.15
152	Mike Piazza	1.25
153	Cliff Floyd	.15
154	Jose Vidro	.15
155	Jason Giambi	.50
156	Andruw Jones	.75
157	Robin Ventura	.15
158	Gary Sheffield	.40
159	Jeff D'Amico	.15
160	Chuck Knoblauch	.15
161	Roger Cedeno	.15
162	Jim Thome	.15
163	Peter Bergeron	.15
164	Kerry Wood	.50
165	Gabe Kapler	.15
166	Corey Koskie	.15
167	Doug Glanville	.15
168	Brent Mayne	.15
169	Scott Spiezio	.15
170	Steve Karsay	.15
171	Al Martin	.15
172	Fred McGriff	.15
173	Gabe White	.15
174	Alex Gonzalez	.15
175	Mike Darr	.15
176	Bengie Molina	.15
177	Ben Grieve	.15
178	Marlon Anderson	.15
179	Brian Giles	.15
180	Jose Valentin	.15
181	Brian Jordan	.15
182	Randy Johnson	.75
183	Ricky Ledee	.15
184	Russ Ortiz	.15
185	Mike Lowell	.15
186	Curtis Leskanic	.15
187	Bobby Abreu	.15
188	Derek Jeter	2.00
189	Lance Berkman	.15
190	Roberto Alomar	.40
191	Darin Erstad	.60
192	Richie Sexson	.15
193	Alex Ochoa	.15
194	Carlos Febles	.15
195	David Ortiz	.15
196	Shawn Green	.35
197	Mike Sweeney	.15
198	Vladimir Guerrero	.75
199	Jose Jimenez	.15
200	Travis Lee	.15
201	Rickey Henderson	.75
202	Bob Wickman	.15
203	Miguel Cairo	.15
204	Steve Finley	.15
205	Tony Batista	.15
206	Jamey Wright	.15
207	Terrence Long	.15
208	Trevor Hoffman	.15
209	John Vander Wal	.15
210	Greg Maddux	1.00
211	Tim Salmon	.25
212	Herbert Perry	.15
213	Marvin Benard	.15
214	Jose Offerman	.15
215	Jay Payton	.15
216	Jon Lieber	.15
217	Mark Kotsay	.15
218	Scott Brosius	.15
219	Scott Williamson	.15
220	Omar Vizquel	.15
221	Mike Hampton	.15
222	Richard Hidalgo	.15
223	Rey Sanchez	.15
224	Matt Lawton	.15
225	Bruce Chen	.15
226	Ryan Klesko	.15
227	Garret Anderson	.15
228	Kevin Brown	.15
229	Mike Cameron	.15
230	Tony Clark	.15
231	Curt Schilling	.40
232	Vinny Castilla	.15
233	Carl Pavano	.15
234	Eric Davis	.15
235	Darrin Fletcher	.15
236	Matt Stairs	.15
237	Octavio Dotel	.15
238	Mark Grace	.25
239	John Smoltz	.15
240	Matt Clement	.15
241	Ellis Burks	.15
242	Charles Johnson	.15
243	Jeff Bagwell	.75
244	Derek Bell	.15
245	Nomar Garciaparra	1.25
246	Jorge Posada	.35
247	Ryan Dempster	.15
248	J.T. Snow	.15
249	Eric Young	.15
250	Daryle Ward	.15
251	Joe Randa	.15
252	Travis Fryman	.15
253	Mike Williams	.15
254	Jacque Jones	.15
255	Scott Elarton	.15
256	Mark McGwire	1.50
257	Jay Buhner	.15
258	Randy Wolf	.15
259	Sammy Sosa	1.25
260	Chan Ho Park	.15
261	Damion Easley	.15
262	Rick Ankiel	.15
263	Frank Thomas	.75
264	Kris Benson	.15
265	Luis Alicea	.15
266	Jeremy Giambi	.15
267	Geoff Blum	.15
268	Joe Girardi	.15
269	Livan Hernandez	.15
270	Jeff Conine	.15
271	Danny Graves	.15
272	Craig Biggio	.15
273	Jose Canseco	.35
274	Tom Glavine	.30
275	Ruben Mateo	.15
276	Jeff Kent	.15
277	Kevin Young	.15
278	A.J. Burnett	.15
279	Dante Bichette	.15
280	Sandy Alomar Jr.	.15
281	John Wetteland	.15
282	Torii Hunter	.15
283	Jarrod Washburn	.15
284	Rich Aurilia	.15
285	Jeff Cirillo	.15
286	Fernando Seguignol	.15
287	Darren Dreifort	.15
288	Deivi Cruz	.15
289	Pokey Reese	.15
290	Garrett Stephenson	.15
291	Pat Boone	.15
292	Tim Hudson	.35
293	John Flaherty	.15
294	Shannon Stewart	.15
295	Shawn Estes	.15
296	Wilton Guerrero	.15
297	Delino DeShields	.15
298	David Justice	.15
299	Harold Baines	.15
300	Al Leiter	.15
301	Wil Cordero	.15
302	Antonio Alfonseca	.15
303	Sean Casey	.25
304	Carlos Beltran	.40
305	Brad Radke	.15
306	Jason Varitek	.15
307	Shigetosi Hasegawa	.15
308	Todd Stottlemyre	.15
309	Raul Mondesi	.15
310	Mike Bordick	.15
311	Darryl Kile	.15
312	Dean Palmer	.15
313	Johnny Damon	.30
314	Todd Helton	.75
315	Chad Hermansen	.15
316	Kevin Appier	.15
317	Greg Vaughn	.15
318	Robb Nen	.15
319	Jose Cruz Jr.	.15
320	Ron Belliard	.15
321	Bernie Williams	.35
322	Melvin Mora	.15
323	Kenny Lofton	.15
324	Armando Benitez	.15
325	Carlos Lee	.15
326	Damian Jackson	.15
327	Eric Milton	.15
328	J.D. Drew	.30
329	Byung-Hyun Kim	.15
330	Chris Stynes	.15
331	Kazuhiro Sasaki	.15
332	Troy O'Leary	.15
333	Pat Hentgen	.15
334	Brad Ausmus	.15
335	Todd Walker	.15
336	Jason Isringhausen	.15
337	Gerald Williams	.15
338	Aaron Sele	.15
339	Paul O'Neill	.15
340	Cal Ripken Jr.	2.00
341	Manny Ramirez	.75
342	Will Clark	.35
343	Mark Redman	.15
344	Bubba Trammell	.15
345	Troy Percival	.15
346	Chris Singleton	.15
347	Rafael Palmeiro	.60
348	Carl Everett	.15
349	Andy Benes	.15
350	Bobby Higginson	.15
351	Alex Cabrera (Prospects)	.15
352	Barry Zito (Prospects)	.40
353	Jace Brewer (Prospects)	.15
354	Paxton Crawford (Prospects)	.15
355	Oswaldo Mairena (Prospects)	.15
356	Joe Crede (Prospects)	.15
357	A.J. Pierzynski (Prospects)	.15
358	Daniel Garibay (Prospects)	.15
359	Jason Tyner (Prospects)	.15
360	Nate Rolison (Prospects)	.15
361	Scott Downs (Prospects)	.15
362	Keith Ginter (Prospects)	.15
363	Juan Pierre (Prospects)	.15
364	Adam Bernero (Prospects)	.15
365	Chris Richard (Prospects)	.15
366	Joey Nation (Prospects)	.15
367	Aubrey Huff (Prospects)	.15
368	Adam Eaton (Prospects)	.15
369	Jose Ortiz (Prospects)	.15
370	Eric Munson (Prospects)	.15
371	Matt Kinney (Prospects)	.15
372	Eric Byrnes (Prospects)	.15
373	Keith McDonald (Prospects)	.15
374	Matt Wise (Prospects)	.15
375	Timo Perez (Prospects)	.15
376	Julio Zuleta (Prospects)	.15
377	Jimmy Rollins (Prospects)	.25
378	Xavier Nady (Prospects)	.15
379	Ryan Kohlmeier (Prospects)	.15
380	Corey Patterson (Prospects)	.15
381	Todd Helton (League Leaders)	.40
382	Moises Alou (League Leaders)	.15
383	Vladimir Guerrero (League Leaders)	.40
384	Luis Castillo (League Leaders)	.15
385	Jeffrey Hammonds (League Leaders)	.15
386	Nomar Garciaparra (League Leaders)	.75
387	Carlos Delgado (League Leaders)	.25
388	Darin Erstad (League Leaders)	.15
389	Manny Ramirez (League Leaders)	.40
390	Mike Sweeney (League Leaders)	.15
391	Sammy Sosa (League Leaders)	.75
392	Barry Bonds (League Leaders)	1.00
393	Jeff Bagwell (League Leaders)	.40
394	Richard Hidalgo (League Leaders)	.15
395	Vladimir Guerrero (League Leaders)	.40
396	Troy Glaus (League Leaders)	.30
397	Frank Thomas (League Leaders)	.40
398	Carlos Delgado (League Leaders)	.25
399	David Justice (League Leaders)	.15
400	Jason Giambi (League Leaders)	.25
401	Randy Johnson (League Leaders)	.40
402	Kevin Brown (League Leaders)	.15
403	Greg Maddux (League Leaders)	.50
404	Al Leiter (League Leaders)	.15
405	Mike Hampton (League Leaders)	.15
406	Pedro Martinez (League Leaders)	.40
407	Roger Clemens (League Leaders)	.65
408	Mike Sirotka (League Leaders)	.15
409	Mike Mussina (League Leaders)	.25
410	Bartolo Colon (League Leaders)	.15
411	World Series Update	.15
412	World Series Update	.15
413	World Series Update	.15
414	World Series Update	.15
415	World Series Update	.15
416	World Series Update	.15
417	World Series Update	.15
418	World Series Update	.15
419	World Series Update	.15
420	World Series Update	.15
421	Atlanta Braves (Team Checklists)	.15
422	New York Mets (Team Checklists)	.15
423	Florida Marlins (Team Checklists)	.15
424	Philadelphia Phillies (Team Checklists)	.15
425	Montreal Expos (Team Checklists)	.15
426	St. Louis Cardinals (Team Checklists)	.15
427	Cincinnati Reds (Team Checklists)	.15
428	Chicago Cubs (Team Checklists)	.15
429	Milwaukee Brewers (Team Checklists)	.15
430	Houston Astros (Team Checklists)	.15
431	Pittsburgh Pirates (Team Checklists)	.15
432	San Francisco Giants (Team Checklists)	.15
433	Arizona Diamondbacks (Team Checklists)	.15
434	Los Angeles Dodgers (Team Checklists)	.15
435	Colorado Rockies (Team Checklists)	.15
436	San Diego Padres (Team Checklists)	.15
437	New York Yankees (Team Checklists)	.15
438	Boston Red Sox (Team Checklists)	.15

439 Baltimore Orioles (Team Checklists) .15
440 Toronto Blue Jays (Team Checklists) .15
441 Tampa Bay Devil Rays (Team Checklists) .15
442 Chicago White Sox (Team Checklists) .15
443 Cleveland Indians (Team Checklists) .15
444 Detroit Tigers (Team Checklists) .15
445 Kansas City Royals (Team Checklists) .15
446 Minnesota Twins (Team Checklists) .15
447 Seattle Mariners (Team Checklists) .15
448 Oakland Athletics (Team Checklists) .15
449 Anaheim Angels (Team Checklists) .15
450 Texas Rangers (Team Checklists) .15
451 Albert Pujols **RC** 70.00
452 Ichiro Suzuki **RC** 15.00
453 Tsuyoshi Shinjo **RC** .75
454 Johnny Estrada **RC** .75
455 Elpidio Guzman **RC** .40
456 Adrian Hernandez **RC** .30
457 Rafael Soriano **RC** .75
458 Drew Henson **RC** 1.00
459 Juan Uribe **RC** .75
460 Matt White **RC** .40
461 Endy Chavez **RC** .30
462 Bud Smith **RC** .25
463 Morgan Ensberg **RC** .75
464 Jay Gibbons **RC** 2.00
465 Jackson Melian **RC** .30
466 Junior Spivey **RC** .75
467 Juan Cruz **RC** .50
468 Wilson Betemit **RC** .40
469 Alexis Gomez **RC** .30
470 Mark Teixeira **RC** 15.00
471 Erick Almonte **RC** .30
472 Travis Hafner **RC** 5.00
473 Carlos Valderrama **RC** .30
474 Brandon Duckworth **RC** .75
475 Ryan Freel **RC** .30
476 Wilkin Ruan **RC** .30
477 Andres Torres **RC** .30
478 Josh Towers **RC** .50
479 Kyle Lohse **RC** .75
480 Jason Michaels **RC** .30
481 Alfonso Soriano .50
482 C.C. Sabathia .15
483 Roy Oswalt .15
484 Ben Sheets .15
485 Adam Dunn .50

Diamond Tributes

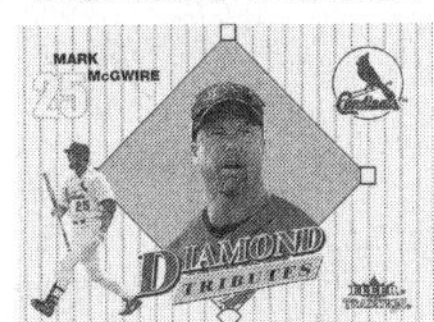

NM/M
Complete Set (30): 35.00
Common Player: .50
Inserted 1:7
1 Jackie Robinson 2.00
2 Mike Piazza 2.00
3 Alex Rodriguez 3.00
4 Barry Bonds 4.00
5 Nomar Garciaparra 2.00
6 Roger Clemens 1.75
7 Ivan Rodriguez .75
8 Cal Ripken Jr. 4.00
9 Manny Ramirez 1.00
10 Chipper Jones 1.50
11 Barry Larkin .50
12 Carlos Delgado .75
13 J.D. Drew .60
14 Carl Everett .50
15 Todd Helton 1.00
16 Greg Maddux 1.50
17 Scott Rolen .75
18 Troy Glaus 1.00
19 Brian Giles .50
20 Jeff Bagwell 1.00
21 Sammy Sosa 2.00
22 Randy Johnson 1.00
23 Andruw Jones 1.00
24 Ken Griffey Jr. 2.00
25 Mark McGwire 3.00
26 Derek Jeter 4.00
27 Vladimir Guerrero 1.00
28 Frank Thomas 1.00
29 Pedro Martinez 1.00
30 Bernie Williams .50

Grass Roots

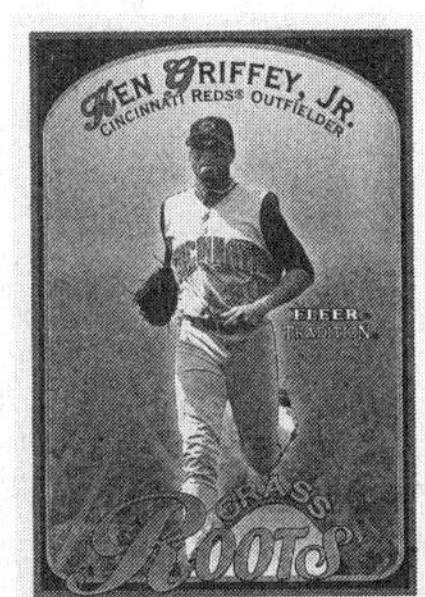

NM/M
Complete Set (15): 25.00
Common Player: 1.00
Inserted 1:18
1 Derek Jeter 4.00
2 Greg Maddux 2.00
3 Sammy Sosa 2.50
4 Alex Rodriguez 3.00
5 Vladimir Guerrero 1.50
6 Scott Rolen 1.00
7 Frank Thomas 1.50
8 Nomar Garciaparra 2.50
9 Cal Ripken Jr. 4.00
10 Mike Piazza 2.50
11 Ivan Rodriguez 1.00
12 Chipper Jones 2.00
13 Tony Gwynn 2.00
14 Ken Griffey Jr. 2.50
15 Mark McGwire 3.00

Lumber Company

NM/M
Complete Set (20): 25.00
Common Player: .50
Inserted 1:12
1 Vladimir Guerrero 1.50
2 Mo Vaughn .50
3 Ken Griffey Jr. 2.50
4 Juan Gonzalez 1.50
5 Tony Gwynn 2.00
6 Jim Edmonds .50
7 Jason Giambi 1.00
8 Alex Rodriguez 3.00
9 Derek Jeter 4.00
10 Darin Erstad 1.00
11 Andruw Jones 1.50
12 Cal Ripken Jr. 4.00
13 Magglio Ordonez .50
14 Nomar Garciaparra 2.50
15 Chipper Jones 2.00
16 Sean Casey .60
17 Shawn Green .60
18 Mike Piazza 2.50
19 Sammy Sosa 2.50
20 Barry Bonds 4.00

Season Pass

Complete Set (6):
Common Player:
Values Undetermined

Stitches in Time

NM/M
Complete Set (25): 40.00
Common Player: 1.50
Inserted 1:18
1 Henry Kimbro 1.50
2 Ernie Banks 3.00
3 James "Cool Papa" Bell 2.00
4 Joe Black 1.50
5 Roy Campanella 2.00
6 Ray Dandridge 1.50
7 Leon Day 1.50
8 Larry Doby 2.00
9 Josh Gibson 2.00
10 Elston Howard 2.00
11 Monte Irvin 2.00
12 Buck Leonard 2.00
13 Max Manning 1.50
14 Willie Mays 6.00
15 Buck O'Neil 2.00
16 Satchel Paige 3.00
17 Ted Radcliffe 2.00
18 Jackie Robinson 4.00
19 Bill Perkins 1.50
20 Andrew "Rube" Foster 2.00
21 William "Judy" Johnson 1.50
22 Oscar Charleston 1.50
23 John Henry "Pop" Lloyd 1.50
24 Artie Wilson 1.50
25 Sam Jethroe 1.50

Stitches in Time Autographs

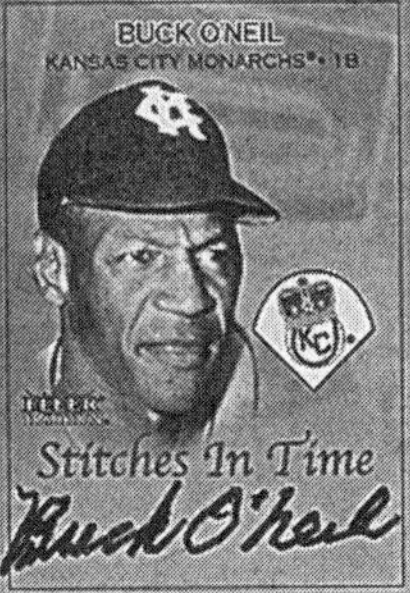

NM/M
Common Autograph: 20.00
2 Ernie Banks 50.00
4 Joe Black 20.00
11 Monte Irvin 30.00
14 Willie Mays 150.00
15 Buck O'Neil 30.00
17 Ted Radcliffe 25.00
24 Artie Wilson 20.00

Stitches in Time Game-Used

NM/M
Common Card: 25.00
5 Roy Campanella 60.00
8 Larry Doby/Bat 25.00
10 Elston Howard/Bat 25.00
14 Willie Mays/Jsy 125.00
18 Jackie Robinson/Jsy 100.00

Turn Back the Clock

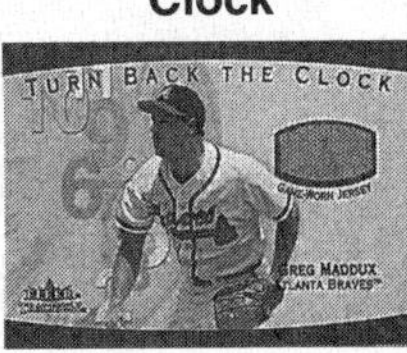

NM/M
Common Card: 8.00
Inserted 1:352
1 Tom Glavine 10.00
2 Greg Maddux 20.00
3 Sean Casey 8.00
4 Pokey Reese 8.00
5 Jason Giambi 15.00
6 Tim Hudson 8.00
7 Larry Walker 8.00
8 Jeffrey Hammonds 8.00
9 Scott Rolen 15.00
10 Pat Burrell 10.00
11 Chipper Jones 20.00
13 Troy Glaus 15.00
14 Tony Gwynn 20.00
15 Cal Ripken Jr. 50.00
16 Tom Glavine, Greg Maddux 75.00
17 Sean Casey, Pokey Reese 30.00
18 Chipper Jones, Greg Maddux 100.00
19 Larry Walker, Jeffrey Hammonds 30.00
20 Scott Rolen, Pat Burrell 40.00
21 Jason Giambi, Tim Hudson 40.00

Warning Track

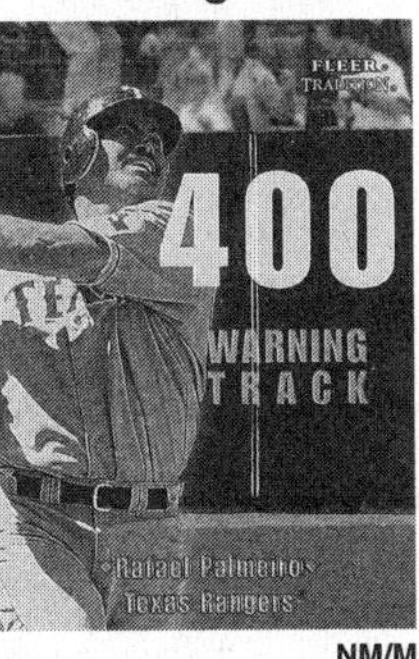

NM/M
Complete Set (25): 120.00
Common Player: 2.00
Inserted 1:72
1 Josh Gibson 5.00
2 Willie Mays 10.00
3 Mark McGwire 12.00
4 Barry Bonds 15.00
5 Jose Canseco 4.00
6 Ken Griffey Jr. 10.00
7 Cal Ripken Jr. 15.00
8 Rafael Palmeiro 5.00
9 Sammy Sosa 10.00
10 Juan Gonzalez 6.00
11 Frank Thomas 6.00
12 Jeff Bagwell 6.00
13 Gary Sheffield 2.50
14 Larry Walker 2.00
15 Mike Piazza 10.00
16 Larry Doby 4.00
17 Roy Campanella 5.00
18 Manny Ramirez 6.00
19 Chipper Jones 8.00
20 Alex Rodriguez 12.00
21 Ivan Rodriguez 5.00
22 Vladimir Guerrero 6.00
23 Nomar Garciaparra 10.00
24 Andres Galarraga 2.00
25 Jim Thome 2.00

Milwaukee Brewers

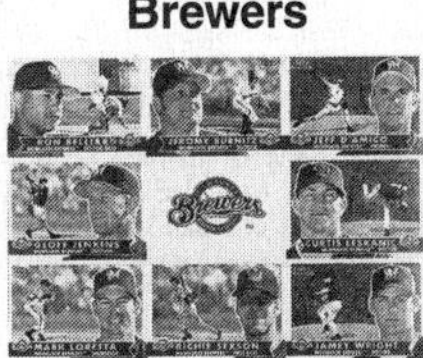

This 10-1/2" x 7-1/2" sheet was distributed to the first 10,000 fans attending the Brewers' September 2 game at Miller Park. Eight of the team's Fleer Tradition cards are reproduced on the sheet, with a team logo at center.

NM/M
Sheet: 12.00

2001 Fleer Triple Crown

NM/M
Complete Set (300): 25.00
Common Player: .15
Pack (10): 2.00
Box (24): 40.00
1 Derek Jeter 2.00
2 Vladimir Guerrero .75
3 Henry Rodriguez .15
4 Jason Giambi .50
5 Nomar Garciaparra 1.25
6 Jeff Kent .15
7 Garret Anderson .15
8 Todd Helton .75
9 Barry Bonds 2.00
10 Preston Wilson .15
11 Troy Glaus .75
12 Geoff Jenkins .15
13 Jim Edmonds .15
14 Bobby Higginson .15
15 Mark Quinn .15
16 Barry Larkin .15
17 Richie Sexson .15
18 Fernando Tatis .15
19 John Vander Wal .15
20 Darin Erstad .60
21 Shawn Green .40
22 Scott Rolen .60
23 Tony Batista .15
24 Phil Nevin .15
25 Tim Salmon .25
26 Gary Sheffield .35
27 Ben Grieve .15
28 Jermaine Dye .15
29 Andres Galarraga .15
30 Adrian Beltre .35
31 Rafael Palmeiro .60
32 J.T. Snow .15
33 Edgardo Alfonzo .15
34 Paul Konerko .15
35 Jim Thome .15
36 Andruw Jones .75
37 Mike Sweeney .15
38 Jose Cruz Jr. .15
39 David Ortiz .15
40 Pat Burrell .40
41 Chipper Jones 1.00
42 Jeff Bagwell .75
43 Raul Mondesi .15
44 Rondell White .15
45 Edgar Martinez .15
46 Cal Ripken Jr. 2.00
47 Moises Alou .15
48 Shannon Stewart .15
49 Tino Martinez .15
50 Jason Kendall .15
51 Richard Hidalgo .15
52 Albert Belle .15
53 Jay Payton .15
54 Cliff Floyd .15
55 Rusty Greer .15
56 Matt Williams .15
57 Sammy Sosa 1.25
58 Carl Everett .15
59 Carlos Delgado .50
60 Jeremy Giambi .15
61 Jose Canseco .40
62 David Segui .15
63 Jose Vidro .15
64 Matt Stairs .15
65 Travis Fryman .15
66 Ken Griffey Jr. 1.25
67 Mike Piazza 1.25
68 Mark McGwire 1.50
69 Craig Biggio .15
70 Eric Chavez .25
71 Mo Vaughn .15
72 Matt Lawton .15
73 Miguel Tejada .25
74 Brian Giles .15
75 Sean Casey .25
76 Robin Ventura .15
77 Ivan Rodriguez .60
78 Dean Palmer .15
79 Frank Thomas .75
80 Bernie Williams .30
81 Juan Encarnacion .15
82 John Olerud .15
83 Rich Aurilia .15
84 Juan Gonzalez .75
85 Ray Durham .15
86 Steve Finley .15
87 Ken Caminiti .15
88 Roberto Alomar .40
89 Jeromy Burnitz .15
90 J.D. Drew .15
91 Lance Berkman .15
92 Gabe Kapler .15
93 Larry Walker .15
94 Alex Rodriguez 1.50
95 Jeffrey Hammonds .15
96 Magglio Ordonez .15
97 David Justice .15
98 Eric Karros .15
99 Manny Ramirez .75
100 Paul O'Neill .15
101 Ron Gant .15
102 Erubiel Durazo .15
103 Jason Varitek .15
104 Chan Ho Park .15
105 Corey Koskie .15
106 Jeff Conine .15
107 Kevin Tapani .15
108 Mike Lowell .15
109 Tim Hudson .25
110 Bobby Abreu .15
111 Bret Boone .15
112 David Wells .15
113 Brian Jordan .15
114 Mitch Meluskey .15
115 Terrence Long .15
116 Matt Clement .15
117 Fernando Vina .15
118 Luis Alicea .15
119 Jay Bell .15
120 Mark Grace .25
121 Carlos Febles .15
122 Mark Redman .15
123 Kevin Jordan .15
124 Pat Meares .15
125 Mark McLemore .15
126 Chris Singleton .15
127 Trot Nixon .15
128 Carlos Beltran .40
129 Lee Stevens .15
130 Kris Benson .15
131 Jay Buhner .15
132 Greg Vaughn .15
133 Eric Young .15
134 Tony Womack .15
135 Roger Cedeno .15
136 Travis Lee .15
137 Marvin Benard .15
138 Aaron Sele .15
139 Rick Ankiel .15
140 Ruben Mateo .15
141 Randy Johnson .75
142 Jason Tyner .15
143 Mike Redmond .15
144 Ron Coomer .15
145 Scott Elarton .15
146 Javy Lopez .15
147 Carlos Lee .15
148 Tony Clark .15
149 Roger Clemens 1.00
150 Mike Lieberthal .15
151 Shawn Estes .15
152 Vinny Castilla .15
153 Alex Gonzalez .15
154 Troy Percival .15
155 Pokey Reese .15
156 Todd Hollandsworth .15
157 Marquis Grissom .15
158 Greg Maddux 1.00
159 Dante Bichette .15
160 Hideo Nomo .75
161 Jacque Jones .15
162 Kevin Young .15
163 B.J. Surhoff .15
164 Eddie Taubensee .15
165 Neifi Perez .15
166 Orlando Hernandez .15
167 Francisco Cordova .15
168 Miguel Cairo .15
169 Rafael Furcal .15
170 Sandy Alomar Jr. .15
171 Jeff Cirillo .15
172 A.J. Pierzynski .15
173 Fred McGriff .15
174 Mike Mussina .40
175 Aaron Boone .15
176 Nick Johnson .15
177 Kent Bottenfield .15
178 Felipe Crespo .15
179 Ryan Minor .15
180 Charles Johnson .15
181 Damion Easley .15
182 Michael Barrett .15
183 Doug Glanville .15
184 Ben Davis .15
185 Rickey Henderson .75
186 Edgard Clemente .15
187 Dmitri Young .15
188 Tom Goodwin .15
189 Mike Hampton .15
190 Gerald Williams .15
191 Omar Vizquel .15
192 Ben Petrick .15
193 Brad Radke .15
194 Russ Davis .15
195 Milton Bradley .15
196 John Parrish .15
197 Todd Hundley .15
198 Carl Pavano .15
199 Bruce Chen .15
200 Royce Clayton .15
201 Homer Bush .15
202 Mark Grudzielanek .15
203 Mike Lansing .15
204 Daryle Ward .15
205 Jeff D'Amico .15
206 Ray Lankford .15
207 Curt Schilling .40
208 Pedro Martinez .75
209 Johnny Damon .30
210 Al Leiter .15
211 Ruben Rivera .15
212 Kazuhiro Sasaki .15
213 Will Clark .25
214 Rick Helling .15
215 Adam Piatt .15
216 Joe Girardi .15
217 A.J. Burnett .15
218 Mike Bordick .15
219 Mike Cameron .15
220 Tony Gwynn 1.00
221 Deivi Cruz .15
222 Bubba Trammell .15
223 Scott Erickson .15
224 Kerry Wood .50
225 Derrek Lee .15
226 Peter Bergeron .15
227 Chris Gomez .15
228 Al Martin .15
229 Brady Anderson .15
230 Ramon Martinez .15
231 Darryl Kile .15
232 Devon White .15
233 Charlie Hayes .15
234 Aramis Ramirez .15
235 Mike Lamb .15
236 Tom Glavine .30
237 Troy O'Leary .15
238 Joe Randa .15
239 Dustin Hermanson .15
240 Adam Kennedy .15
241 Jose Valentin .15
242 Derek Bell .15
243 Mark Kotsay .15
244 Ron Belliard .15
245 Warren Morris .15
246 Ozzie Guillen .15
247 Andy Ashby .15
248 Jose Offerman .15

249 Kevin Brown .15
250 Jorge Posada .35
251 Alex Cabrera (Prospects) .15
252 Chan Perry (Prospects) .15
253 Augie Ojeda (Prospects) .15
254 Santiago Perez (Prospects) .15
255 Grant Roberts (Prospects) .15
256 Dusty Allen (Prospects) .15
257 Elvis Pena (Prospects) .15
258 Matt Kinney (Prospects) .15
259 Timoniel Perez (Prospects) .15
260 Adam Eaton (Prospects) .15
261 Geraldo Guzman (Prospects) .15
262 Damian Rolls (Prospects) .15
263 Alfonso Soriano (Prospects) .50
264 Corey Patterson (Prospects) .15
265 Juan Alvarez (Prospects) .15
266 Shawn Gilbert (Prospects) .15
267 Adam Bernero (Prospects) .15
268 Ben Weber (Prospects) .15
269 Tike Redman (Prospects) .15
270 Willie Morales (Prospects) .15
271 Tomas De La Rosa (Prospects) .15
272 Rodney Lindsey (Prospects) .15
273 Carlos Casimiro (Prospects) .15
274 Jim Mann (Prospects) .15
275 Pasqual Coco (Prospects) .15
276 Julio Zuleta (Prospects) .15
277 Damon Minor (Prospects) .15
278 Jose Ortiz (Prospects) .15
279 Eric Munson (Prospects) .15
280 Andy Thompson (Prospects) .15
281 Aubrey Huff (Prospects) .15
282 Chris Richard (Prospects) .15
283 Ross Gload (Prospects) .15
284 Travis Dawkins (Prospects) .15
285 Tim Drew (Prospects) .15
286 Barry Zito (Prospects) .40
287 Andy Tracy (Prospects) .15
288 Julio Lugo (Prospects) .15
289 Matt DeWitt (Prospects) .15
290 Keith McDonald (Prospects) .15
291 J.C. Romero (Prospects) .15
292 Adam Melhuse (Prospects) .15
293 Ryan Kohlmeier (Prospects) .15
294 John Bale (Prospects) .15
295 Eric Cammack (Prospects) .15
296 Morgan Burkhart (Prospects) .15
297 Kory DeHaan (Prospects) .15
298 Raul Gonzalez (Prospects) .15
299 Hector Ortiz (Prospects) .15
300 Talmadge Nunnari (Prospects) .15

Blue

NM/M
Common Player: 3.00
Produced to # of 2000 HR's
1 Derek Jeter/15 150.00
2 Vladimir Guerrero/44 25.00
3 Henry Rodriguez/20 3.00
4 Jason Giambi/43 15.00
5 Nomar Garciaparra/21 25.00
6 Jeff Kent/33 8.00
7 Garret Anderson/35 8.00
8 Todd Helton/42 15.00
9 Barry Bonds/49 40.00
10 Preston Wilson/31 3.00
11 Troy Glaus/47 10.00
12 Geoff Jenkins/34 8.00
13 Jim Edmonds/42 10.00
14 Bobby Higginson/30 3.00
15 Mark Quinn/20 5.00
16 Barry Larkin /11 15.00
17 Richie Sexson/30 10.00
18 Fernando Tatis/18 3.00
19 John Vander Wal/24 3.00
20 Darin Erstad/25 10.00
21 Shawn Green/24 10.00
22 Scott Rolen/26 15.00
23 Tony Batista/41 3.00
24 Phil Nevin/31 3.00
25 Tim Salmon/34 5.00
26 Gary Sheffield/43 8.00
27 Ben Grieve/27 5.00
28 Jermaine Dye/33 3.00
29 Andres Galarraga/28 5.00
30 Adrian Beltre/20 8.00
31 Rafael Palmeiro/39 10.00
32 J.T. Snow/19 5.00
33 Edgardo Alfonzo/25 5.00
34 Paul Konerko/21 5.00
35 Jim Thome/37 15.00
36 Andruw Jones/36 10.00
37 Mike Sweeney/29 3.00
38 Jose Cruz Jr./31 3.00
39 David Ortiz/10 8.00
40 Pat Burrell/18 15.00
41 Chipper Jones/36 15.00
42 Jeff Bagwell/47 10.00
43 Raul Mondesi/24 5.00
44 Rondell White/13 10.00
45 Edgar Martinez/37 5.00
46 Cal Ripken Jr./15 150.00
47 Moises Alou/30 5.00
48 Shannon Stewart/21 3.00
49 Tino Martinez/16 5.00
50 Jason Kendall/14 5.00
51 Richard Hidalgo/44 3.00
52 Albert Belle/23 3.00
53 Jay Payton/17 3.00
54 Cliff Floyd /22 3.00
55 Rusty Greer/8 8.00
56 Matt Williams/12 10.00
57 Sammy Sosa/50 25.00
58 Carl Everett/34 3.00
59 Carlos Delgado/41 5.00
60 Jeremy Giambi/10 5.00
61 Jose Canseco/15 10.00
62 David Segui/19 3.00
63 Jose Vidro/24 3.00
64 Matt Stairs/21 3.00
65 Travis Fryman/22 5.00
66 Ken Griffey Jr./40 15.00
67 Mike Piazza/38 15.00
68 Mark McGwire/32 20.00
69 Craig Biggio/8 10.00
70 Eric Chavez/26 10.00
71 Mo Vaughn/36 5.00
72 Matt Lawton/13 5.00
73 Miguel Tejada/30 10.00
74 Brian Giles/35 5.00
75 Sean Casey/20 5.00
76 Robin Ventura/24 5.00
77 Ivan Rodriguez/27 8.00
78 Dean Palmer/29 3.00
79 Frank Thomas/43 10.00
80 Bernie Williams/30 8.00
81 Juan Encarnacion/14 5.00
82 John Olerud/14 5.00
83 Rich Aurilia/20 3.00
84 Juan Gonzalez/22 8.00
85 Ray Durham/17 5.00
86 Steve Finley/35 3.00
87 Ken Caminiti/15 5.00
88 Roberto Alomar/19 15.00
89 Jeromy Burnitz/31 3.00
90 J.D. Drew/18 8.00
91 Lance Berkman/21 8.00
92 Gabe Kapler/14 8.00
93 Larry Walker/9 10.00
94 Alex Rodriguez/41 20.00
95 Jeffrey Hammonds/20 3.00
96 Magglio Ordonez/32 5.00
97 David Justice/41 5.00
98 Eric Karros/31 3.00
99 Manny Ramirez/38 10.00
100 Paul O'Neill/18 8.00

Green

NM/M
Common Player: 1.00
Produced to # of 2000 RBI's
1 Derek Jeter/73 20.00
2 Vladimir Guerrero/123 5.00
3 Henry Rodriguez/61 1.00
4 Jason Giambi/137 5.00
5 Nomar Garciaparra/96 10.00
6 Jeff Kent/125 3.00
7 Garret Anderson/117 3.00
8 Todd Helton/147 5.00
9 Barry Bonds/106 20.00
10 Preston Wilson/121 1.00
11 Troy Glaus/102 4.00
12 Geoff Jenkins/94 3.00
13 Jim Edmonds/108 4.00
14 Bobby Higginson/102 1.00
15 Mark Quinn/78 1.00
16 Barry Larkin/41 4.00
17 Richie Sexson/91 4.00
18 Fernando Tatis/64 1.00
19 John Vander Wal/94 1.00
20 Darin Erstad/100 3.00
21 Shawn Green/99 3.00
22 Scott Rolen/89 4.00
23 Tony Batista/114 1.00
24 Phil Nevin/107 1.00
25 Tim Salmon/97 3.00
26 Gary Sheffield/109 3.00
27 Ben Grieve/104 1.00
28 Jermaine Dye/118 1.00
29 Andres Galarraga/100 1.50
30 Adrian Beltre/85 1.00
31 Rafael Palmeiro/120 3.00
32 J.T. Snow/96 1.00
33 Edgardo Alfonzo/94 1.00
34 Paul Konerko/97 1.50
35 Jim Thome/106 4.00
36 Andruw Jones/104 4.00
37 Mike Sweeney/144 1.00
38 Jose Cruz Jr./76 1.00
39 David Ortiz/63 1.00
40 Pat Burrell/79 4.00
41 Chipper Jones/111 8.00
42 Jeff Bagwell/132 5.00
43 Raul Mondesi/67 2.00
44 Rondell White/61 1.50
45 Edgar Martinez/145 2.00
46 Cal Ripken Jr./56 25.00
47 Moises Alou/114 1.00
48 Shannon Stewart/69 1.00
49 Tino Martinez/91 2.00
50 Jason Kendall/58 1.00
51 Richard Hidalgo/122 1.00
52 Albert Belle/103 1.00
53 Jay Payton/62 1.00
54 Cliff Floyd/91 1.00
55 Rusty Greer/65 1.00
56 Matt Williams/47 2.00
57 Sammy Sosa/138 10.00
58 Carl Everett/108 1.00
59 Carlos Delgado/137 3.00
60 Jeremy Giambi/50 1.00
61 Jose Canseco/49 5.00
62 David Segui/103 1.00
63 Jose Vidro/97 1.00
64 Matt Stairs/81 1.00
65 Travis Fryman/106 2.00
66 Ken Griffey Jr./118 10.00
67 Mike Piazza/113 10.00
68 Mark McGwire/73 15.00
69 Craig Biggio/35 4.00
70 Eric Chavez/86 4.00
71 Mo Vaughn/117 3.00
72 Matt Lawton/88 1.00
73 Miguel Tejada/115 4.00
74 Brian Giles/123 3.00
75 Sean Casey/85 2.00
76 Robin Ventura/84 2.00
77 Ivan Rodriguez/83 5.00
78 Dean Palmer/102 1.00
79 Frank Thomas/143 5.00
80 Bernie Williams/121 4.00
81 Juan Encarnacion/72 1.00
82 John Olerud/103 3.00
83 Rich Aurilia/79 1.00
84 Juan Gonzalez/67 5.00
85 Ray Durham/75 1.00
86 Steve Finley/96 1.00
87 Ken Caminiti/45 1.00
88 Roberto Alomar/89 5.00
89 Jeromy Burnitz/98 1.00
90 J.D. Drew/57 3.00
91 Lance Berkman/67 2.00
92 Gabe Kapler/66 2.00
93 Larry Walker/51 3.00
94 Alex Rodriguez/132 15.00
95 Jeffrey Hammonds/106 1.00
96 Maggio Ordonez/126 3.00
97 David Justice/118 3.00
98 Eric Karros/106 1.00
99 Manny Ramirez/122 5.00
100 Paul O'Neill/100 2.00

Red

Common Player (1-100): 4-8X
Stars:
Produced to 2000 Bat Avg.

Autographics

NM/M
Common Autograph: 5.00
Inserted 1:72
Silvers: 1X
Production 250 Sets
Golds: 1-2X
Production 50 Sets
1 Roberto Alomar 30.00
2 Jimmy Anderson 5.00
3 Ryan Anderson 5.00
4 Rick Ankiel 5.00
5 Adrian Beltre 10.00
6 Peter Bergeron 5.00
7 Lance Berkman 8.00
8 Barry Bonds 200.00
9 Milton Bradley 5.00
10 Dee Brown 5.00
11 Roosevelt Brown 5.00
12 Pat Burrell 10.00
13 Sean Casey 8.00
14 Eric Chavez 10.00
15 Giuseppe Chiaramonte 5.00
16 Joe Crede 5.00
17 Jose Cruz Jr. 5.00
18 Carlos Delgado 10.00
19 Ryan Dempster 5.00
20 Adam Dunn 15.00
21 David Eckstein 5.00
22 Jim Edmonds 10.00
23 Troy Glaus 15.00
24 Chad Green 5.00
25 Tony Gwynn 30.00
26 Todd Helton 20.00
27 Chad Hermansen 5.00
28 Shea Hillenbrand 6.00
29 Aubrey Huff 6.00
30 Randy Johnson 40.00
31 Chipper Jones 40.00
32 Mike Lamb 5.00
33 Corey Lee 5.00
34 Steve Lomasney 5.00
35 Terrence Long 5.00
36 Julio Lugo 5.00
37 Jason Marquis 5.00
38 Bengie Molina 5.00
39 Mike Mussina 25.00
40 Pablo Ozuna 5.00
41 Corey Patterson 10.00
42 Jay Payton 6.00
43 Wily Pena 15.00
44 Josh Phelps 8.00
45 Adam Piatt 5.00
46 Matt Riley 5.00
47 Alex Rodriguez 75.00
48 Alex Sanchez 5.00
49 Gary Sheffield 10.00
50 Alfonso Soriano 40.00
51 Shannon Stewart 6.00
52 Fernando Tatis 5.00
53 Jose Vidro 5.00
54 Preston Wilson 8.00
55 Kerry Wood 25.00
56 Julio Zuleta 5.00

Crowning Achievements

NM/M
Complete Set (15): 15.00
Common Player: .50
Inserted 1:9
1 Troy Glaus 1.00
2 Mark McGwire 2.50
3 Barry Larkin, Craig Biggio .50
4 Ken Griffey Jr. 2.00
5 Rafael Palmeiro .75
6 Alex Rodriguez 2.50
7 Roger Clemens 1.75
8 Mike Piazza 2.00
9 Cal Ripken Jr. 3.00
10 Randy Johnson 1.00
11 Jeff Bagwell 1.00
12 Sammy Sosa 2.00
13 Greg Maddux 1.50
14 Barry Bonds 3.00
15 Fred McGriff .50

Crowns of Gold

NM/M
Common Player: 4.00
Random inserts in Hobby packs.
Rick Ankiel/Jsy 4.00
Steve Carlton/Jsy 10.00
Roger Clemens/Jsy 40.00
Carlos Delgado/Bat 8.00
Darin Erstad/Bat 6.00
Jimmie Foxx/Bat 100.00
Todd Helton/Bat 10.00
Randy Johnson/Jsy 15.00
Frank Robinson/Bat 10.00
Gary Sheffield/Jsy 8.00
Frank Thomas/Bat 10.00
Ted Williams/Bat 200.00

Crowns of Gold Autograph

NM/M
Random inserts in Hobby packs.
Steve Carlton/Jsy/72 80.00
Roger Clemens/Jsy/98 200.00
Frank Robinson/Bat/66 80.00

Feel the Game

NM/M
Common Player: 4.00
Inserted 1:72
Golds: 1.5-2X
Production 50 Sets
Adrian Beltre 6.00
Dante Bichette 4.00
Roger Cedeno 4.00
Ben Davis 4.00
Carlos Delgado 6.00
J.D. Drew 6.00
Jason Giambi 6.00
Brian Giles 4.00
Juan Gonzalez 8.00
Richard Hidalgo 4.00
Chipper Jones 10.00
Eric Karros 4.00
Javy Lopez 4.00
Tino Martinez 4.00
Raul Mondesi 4.00
Phil Nevin 4.00
Chan Ho Park 4.00
Ivan Rodriguez 6.00
Shannon Stewart 4.00
Frank Thomas 8.00
Jose Vidro 4.00
Matt Williams 4.00
Preston Wilson 4.00

Future Threats

NM/M
Complete Set (15): 15.00
Common Player: .50
Inserted 1:7
1 Derek Jeter 3.00
2 Alex Rodriguez 2.50
3 Magglio Ordonez, Shawn Green .50
4 Larry Walker .50
5 Vladimir Guerrero 1.00
6 Nomar Garciaparra 2.00
7 Ken Griffey Jr. 2.00
8 Barry Bonds 3.00
9 Chipper Jones 1.50
10 Todd Helton 1.00
11 Ivan Rodriguez .75
12 Jeff Bagwell 1.00
13 Frank Thomas 1.00
14 Carlos Delgado .65
15 Mike Piazza 2.00

Glamour Boys

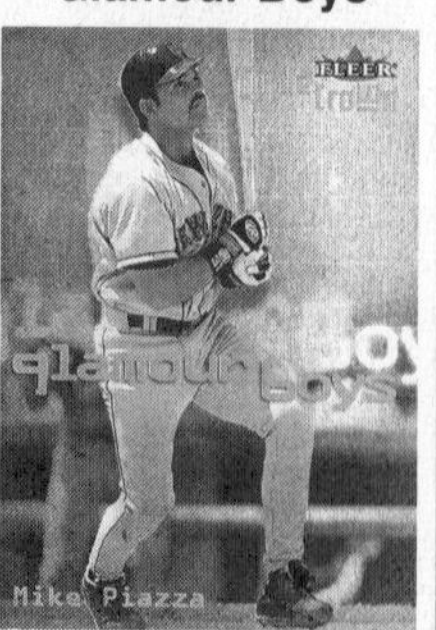

NM/M
Complete Set (15): 40.00
Common Player: 1.50
Inserted 1:24
1 Derek Jeter 6.00
2 Vladimir Guerrero 2.00
3 Scott Rolen, Jeff Bagwell 1.50
4 Sammy Sosa 4.00
5 Ken Griffey Jr. 4.00
6 Mark McGwire 5.00
7 Ivan Rodriguez 1.50
8 Mike Piazza 4.00
9 Nomar Garciaparra 4.00
10 Cal Ripken Jr. 6.00
11 Tony Gwynn 3.00
12 Barry Bonds 6.00
13 Randy Johnson 2.00
14 Alex Rodriguez 5.00
15 Pedro Martinez 2.00

Ritz-Oreo

In conjunction with its sponsorship of the 2001 All-Star Game in Seattle, Ritz-Oreo issued a pair of Jeter cards distributed in product packages. In standard 2-1/2" x 3-1/2" format, one card is bordered in red and pictures him batting; a blue bordered card has a picture of him throwing. Backs have biographical data with height measured in Oreos, and weight measured in Ritz, recent stats, a quote and logos of all parties involved. The cards were also available packaged with a pair of Upper Deck Griffey cards in a mail-in offer.

NM/M
Complete Set (2): 3.00
Common Card: 2.00
Derek Jeter/Btg 2.00
Derek Jeter/Throwing 2.00

2002 Fleer

NM/M
Complete Set (540): 75.00
Common Player: .15
Pack (10): 2.00
Box (24): 40.00
1 Darin Erstad .15
2 Randy Johnson .25
3 Chipper Jones .50
4 Jay Gibbons .15
5 Nomar Garciaparra .50
6 Sammy Sosa .50
7 Frank Thomas .50
8 Ken Griffey Jr. .75
9 Jim Thome .25
10 Todd Helton .25
11 Jeff Weaver .15
12 Cliff Floyd .15
13 Jeff Bagwell .25
14 Mike Sweeney .15
15 Adrian Beltre .25
16 Richie Sexson .25
17 Brad Radke .15
18 Vladimir Guerrero .50
19 Mike Piazza .50
20 Derek Jeter 1.00
21 Eric Chavez .15
22 Pat Burrell .15
23 Brian Giles .15
24 Trevor Hoffman .15
25 Barry Bonds 1.00
26 Ichiro Suzuki .75
27 Albert Pujols 1.00
28 Ben Grieve .15
29 Alex Rodriguez 1.00
30 Carlos Delgado .25
31 Miguel Tejada .25

32 Todd Hollandsworth .15
33 Marlon Anderson .15
34 Kerry Robinson .15
35 Chris Richard .15
36 Jamey Wright .15
37 Ray Lankford .15
38 Mike Bordick .15
39 Danny Graves .15
40 A.J. Pierzynski .15
41 Shannon Stewart .15
42 Tony Armas Jr. .15
43 Brad Ausmus .15
44 Alfonso Soriano .50
45 Junior Spivey .15
46 Brent Mayne .15
47 Jim Thome .15
48 Dan Wilson .15
49 Geoff Jenkins .15
50 Kris Benson .15
51 Rafael Furcal .15
52 Wiki Gonzalez .15
53 Jeff Kent .15
54 Curt Schilling .40
55 Ken Harvey .15
56 Roosevelt Brown .15
57 David Segui .15
58 Mario Valdez .15
59 Adam Dunn .50
60 Bob Howry .15
61 Michael Barrett .15
62 Garret Anderson .15
63 Kelvim Escobar .15
64 Ben Grieve .15
65 Randy Johnson .75
66 Jose Offerman .15
67 Jason Kendall .15
68 Joel Pineiro .15
69 Alex Escobar .15
70 Chris George .15
71 Bobby Higginson .15
72 Nomar Garciaparra 1.50
73 Pat Burrell .40
74 Lee Stevens .15
75 Felipe Lopez .15
76 Al Leiter .15
77 Jim Edmonds .15
78 Al Levine .15
79 Raul Mondesi .15
80 Jose Valentin .15
81 Matt Clement .15
82 Richard Hidalgo .15
83 Jamie Moyer .15
84 Brian Schneider .15
85 John Franco .15
86 Brian Buchanan .15
87 Roy Oswalt .25
88 Johnny Estrada .15
89 Marcus Giles .15
90 Carlos Valderrama .15
91 Mark Mulder .15
92 Mark Grace .25
93 Andy Ashby .15
94 Woody Williams .15
95 Ben Petrick .15
96 Roy Halladay .30
97 Fred McGriff .15
98 Shawn Green .40
99 Todd Hundley .15
100 Carlos Febles .15
101 Jason Marquis .15
102 Mike Redmond .15
103 Shane Halter .15
104 Trot Nixon .15
105 Jeremy Giambi .15
106 Carlos Delgado .50
107 Richie Sexson .15
108 Russ Ortiz .15
109 David Ortiz .25
110 Curtis Leskanic .15
111 Jay Payton .15
112 Travis Phelps .15
113 J.T. Snow .15
114 Edgar Renteria .15
115 Freddy Garcia .15
116 Cliff Floyd .15
117 Charles Nagy .15
118 Tony Batista .15
119 Rafael Palmeiro .65
120 Darren Dreifort .15
121 Warren Morris .15
122 Augie Ojeda .15
123 Rusty Greer .15
124 Esteban Yan .15
125 Corey Patterson .15
126 Matt Ginter .15
127 Matt Lawton .15
128 Miguel Batista .15
129 Randy Winn .15
130 Eric Milton .15
131 Jack Wilson .15
132 Sean Casey .25
133 Mike Sweeney .15
134 Jason Tyner .15
135 Carlos Hernandez .15
136 Shea Hillenbrand .15
137 Shawn Wooten .15
138 Peter Bergeron .15
139 Travis Lee .15
140 Craig Wilson .15
141 Carlos Guillen .15
142 Chipper Jones 1.00
143 Gabe Kapler .15
144 Raul Ibanez .15
145 Eric Chavez .25
146 D'Angelo Jiminez .15
147 Chad Hermansen .15
148 Joe Kennedy .15
149 Mariano Rivera .25
150 Jeff Bagwell .75
151 Joe McEwing .15
152 Ronnie Belliard .15
153 Desi Relaford .15
154 Vinny Castilla .15
155 Tim Hudson .25
156 Wilton Guerrero .15
157 Raul Casanova .15
158 Edgardo Alfonzo .15
159 Derrek Lee .15
160 Phil Nevin .15
161 Roger Clemens 1.25
162 Jason LaRue .15
163 Brian Lawrence .15
164 Adrian Beltre .30
165 Troy Glaus .75
166 Jeff Weaver .15
167 B.J. Surhoff .15
168 Eric Byrnes .15
169 Mike Sirotka .15
170 Bill Haselman .15
171 Javier Vazquez .15
172 Sidney Ponson .15
173 Adam Everett .15
174 Bubba Trammell .15
175 Robb Nen .15
176 Barry Larkin .15
177 Tony Graffanino .15
178 Rich Garces .15
179 Juan Uribe .15
180 Tom Glavine .25
181 Eric Karros .15
182 Michael Cuddyer .15
183 Wade Miller .15
184 Matt Williams .15
185 Matt Morris .15
186 Rickey Henderson .75
187 Trevor Hoffman .15
188 Wilson Betemit .15
189 Steve Karsay .15
190 Frank Catalanotto .15
191 Jason Schmidt .15
192 Roger Cedeno .15
193 Magglio Ordonez .15
194 Pat Hentgen .15
195 Mike Lieberthal .15
196 Andy Pettitte .30
197 Jay Gibbons .15
198 Rolando Arrojo .15
199 Joe Mays .15
200 Aubrey Huff .15
201 Nelson Figueroa .15
202 Paul Konerko .25
203 Ken Griffey Jr. 1.50
204 Brandon Duckworth .15
205 Sammy Sosa 1.50
206 Carl Everett .15
207 Scott Rolen .65
208 Orlando Hernandez .15
209 Todd Helton .75
210 Preston Wilson .15
211 Gil Meche .15
212 Bill Mueller .15
213 Craig Biggio .15
214 Dean Palmer .15
215 Randy Wolf .15
216 Jeff Suppan .15
217 Jimmy Rollins .25
218 Alexis Gomez .15
219 Ellis Burks .15
220 Ramon E. Martinez .15
221 Ramiro Mendoza .15
222 Einar Diaz .15
223 Brent Abernathy .15
224 Darin Erstad .25
225 Reggie Taylor .15
226 Jason Jennings .15
227 Ray Durham .15
228 John Parrish .15
229 Kevin Young .15
230 Xavier Nady .15
231 Juan Cruz .15
232 Greg Norton .15
233 Barry Bonds 2.00
234 Kip Wells .15
235 Paul LoDuca .15
236 Javy Lopez .25
237 Luis Castillo .15
238 Tom Gordon .15
239 Mike Mordecai .15
240 Damian Rolls .15
241 Julio Lugo .15
242 Ichiro Suzuki 1.00
243 Tony Womack .15
244 Matt Anderson .15
245 Carlos Lee .15
246 Alex Rodriguez 1.75
247 Bernie Williams .30
248 Scott Sullivan .15
249 Mike Hampton .15
250 Orlando Cabrera .15
251 Benito Santiago .15
252 Steve Finley .15
253 Dave Williams .15
254 Adam Kennedy .15
255 Omar Vizquel .15
256 Garrett Stephenson .15
257 Fernando Tatis .15
258 Mike Piazza 1.50
259 Scott Spiezio .15
260 Jacque Jones .15
261 Russell Branyan .15
262 Mark McLemore .15
263 Mitch Meluskey .15
264 Marlon Byrd .15
265 Kyle Farnsworth .15
266 Billy Sylvester .15
267 C.C. Sabathia .15
268 Mark Buehrle .15
269 Geoff Blum .15
270 Bret Prinz .15
271 Placido Polanco .15
272 John Olerud .15
273 Pedro J. Martinez .75
274 Doug Mientkiewicz .15
275 Jason Bere .15
276 Bud Smith .15
277 Terrence Long .15
278 Troy Percival .15
279 Derek Jeter 2.00
280 Eric Owens .15
281 Jay Bell .15
282 Mike Cameron .15
283 Joe Randa .15
284 Brian Roberts .15
285 Ryan Klesko .15
286 Ryan Dempster .15
287 Cristian Guzman .15
288 Tim Salmon .25
289 Mark Johnson .15
290 Brian Giles .15
291 Jon Lieber .15
292 Fernando Vina .15
293 Mike Mussina .40
294 Juan Pierre .15
295 Carlos Beltran .40
296 Vladimir Guerrero .75
297 Orlando Merced .15
298 Jose Hernandez .15
299 Mike Lamb .15
300 David Eckstein .15
301 Mark Loretta .15
302 Greg Vaughn .15
303 Jose Vidro .15
304 Jose Ortiz .15
305 Mark Grudzielanek .15
306 Rob Bell .15
307 Elmer Dessens .15
308 Tomas Perez .15
309 Jerry Hairston Jr. .15
310 Mike Stanton .15
311 Todd Walker .15
312 Jason Varitek .15
313 Masato Yoshii .15
314 Ben Sheets .15
315 Roberto Hernandez .15
316 Eli Marrero .15
317 Josh Beckett .50
318 Robert Fick .15
319 Aramis Ramirez .15
320 Bartolo Colon .15
321 Kenny Kelly .15
322 Luis Gonzalez .25
323 John Smoltz .15
324 Homer Bush .15
325 Kevin Millwood .15
326 Manny Ramirez .75
327 Armando Benitez .15
328 Luis Alicea .15
329 Mark Kotsay .15
330 Felix Rodriguez .15
331 Eddie Taubensee .15
332 John Burkett .15
333 Ramon Ortiz .15
334 Daryle Ward .15
335 Jarrod Washburn .15
336 Benji Gil .15
337 Mike Lowell .15
338 Larry Walker .15
339 Andruw Jones .75
340 Scott Elarton .15
341 Tony McKnight .15
342 Frank Thomas .50
343 Kevin Brown .15
344 Jermaine Dye .15
345 Luis Rivas .15
346 Jeff Conine .15
347 Bobby Kielty .15
348 Jeffrey Hammonds .15
349 Keith Foulke .15
350 Dave Martinez .15
351 Adam Eaton .15
352 Brandon Inge .15
353 Tyler Houston .15
354 Bobby Abreu .15
355 Ivan Rodriguez .65
356 Doug Glanville .15
357 Jorge Julio .15
358 Kerry Wood .50
359 Eric Munson .15
360 Joe Crede .15
361 Denny Neagle .15
362 Vance Wilson .15
363 Neifi Perez .15
364 Darryl Kile .15
365 Jose Macias .15
366 Michael Coleman .15
367 Erubiel Durazo .15
368 Darrin Fletcher .15
369 Matt White .15
370 Marvin Benard .15
371 Brad Penny .15
372 Chuck Finley .15
373 Delino DeShields .15
374 Adrian Brown .15
375 Corey Koskie .15
376 Kazuhiro Sasaki .15
377 Brent Butler .15
378 Paul Wilson .15
379 Scott Williamson .15
380 Mike Young .15
381 Toby Hall .15
382 Shane Reynolds .15
383 Tom Goodwin .15
384 Seth Etherton .15
385 Billy Wagner .15
386 Josh Phelps .15
387 Kyle Lohse .15
388 Jeremy Fikac .15
389 Jorge Posada .30
390 Bret Boone .15
391 Angel Berroa .15
392 Matt Mantei .15
393 Alex Gonzalez .15
394 Scott Strickland .15
395 Charles Johnson .15
396 Ramon Hernandez .15
397 Damian Jackson .15
398 Albert Pujols 1.50
399 Gary Bennett .15
400 Edgar Martinez .15
401 Carl Pavano .15
402 Chris Gomez .15
403 Jaret Wright .15
404 Lance Berkman .15
405 Robert Person .15
406 Brook Fordyce .15
407 Adam Pettyjohn .15
408 Chris Carpenter .15
409 Rey Ordonez .15
410 Eric Gagne .25
411 Damion Easley .15
412 A.J. Burnett .15
413 Aaron Boone .15
414 J.D. Drew .25
415 Kelly Stinnett .15
416 Mark Quinn .15
417 Brad Radke .15
418 Jose Cruz Jr. .15
419 Greg Maddux 1.00
420 Steve Cox .15
421 Torii Hunter .15
422 Sandy Alomar .15
423 Barry Zito .40
424 Bill Hall .15
425 Marquis Grissom .15
426 Rich Aurilia .15
427 Royce Clayton .15
428 Travis Fryman .15
429 Pablo Ozuna .15
430 David Dellucci .15
431 Vernon Wells .15
432 Gregg Zaun .15
433 Alex Gonzalez .15
434 Hideo Nomo .40
435 Jeromy Burnitz .15
436 Gary Sheffield .25
437 Tino Martinez .15
438 Tsuyoshi Shinjo .15
439 Chan Ho Park .15
440 Tony Clark .15
441 Brad Fullmer .15
442 Jason Giambi .50
443 Billy Koch .15
444 Mo Vaughn .15
445 Alex Ochoa .15
446 Darren Lewis .15
447 John Rocker .15
448 Scott Hatteberg .15
449 Brady Anderson .15
450 Chuck Knoblauch .15
451 Pokey Reese .15
452 Brian Jordan .15
453 Albie Lopez .15
454 David Bell .15
455 Juan Gonzalez .75
456 Terry Adams .15
457 Kenny Lofton .25
458 Shawn Estes .15
459 Josh Fogg .15
460 Dmitri Young .15
461 Johnny Damon .25
462 Chris Singleton .15
463 Ricky Ledee .15
464 Dustin Hermanson .15
465 Aaron Sele .15
466 Chris Stynes .15
467 Matt Stairs .15
468 Kevin Appier .15
469 Omar Daal .15
470 Moises Alou .15
471 Juan Encarnacion .15
472 Robin Ventura .15
473 Eric Hinske .15
474 Rondell White .15
475 Carlos Pena .15
476 Craig Paquette .15
477 Marty Cordova .15
478 Brett Tomko .15
479 Reggie Sanders .15
480 Roberto Alomar .15
481 Jeff Cirillo .15
482 Todd Zeile .15
483 John Vander Wal .15
484 Rick Helling .15
485 Jeff D'Amico .15
486 David Justice .15
487 Jason Isringhausen .15
488 Shigetoshi Hasegawa .15
489 Eric Young .15
490 David Wells .15
491 Ruben Sierra .15
492 Aaron Cook **RC** .50
493 Takahito Nomura **RC** .50
494 Austin Kearns .50
495 Kazuhisa Ishii **RC** 2.00
496 Mark Teixeira .50
497 Rene Reyes **RC** .50
498 Tim Spooneybarger .15
499 Ben Broussard .15
500 Eric Cyr **RC** .25
501 Anastacio Martinez **RC** .50
502 Morgan Ensberg .15
503 Steve Kent **RC** .25
504 Franklin Nunez **RC** .25
505 Adam Walker **RC** .25
506 Anderson Machado **RC** .50
507 Ryan Drese .15
508 Luis Ugueto **RC** .25
509 Jorge Nunez **RC** .25
510 Colby Lewis .15
511 Ron Calloway **RC** .25
512 Hansel Izquierdo **RC** .50
513 Jason Lane .15
514 Rafael Soriano .15
515 Jackson Melian .15
516 Edwin Almonte **RC** .50
517 Satoru Komiyama **RC** .50
518 Corey Thurman **RC** .25
519 Jorge De La Rosa **RC** .50
520 Victor Martinez .15
521 Dewan Brazleton .15
522 Marlon Byrd .50
523 Jae Weong Seo .15
524 Orlando Hudson .15
525 Sean Burroughs .15
526 Ryan Langerhans .15
527 David Kelton .15
528 So Taguchi **RC** .50
529 Tyler Walker .15
530 Hank Blalock .50
531 Mark Prior .75
532 Yankee Stadium .50
533 Fenway Park .50
534 Wrigley Field .50
535 Dodger Stadium .15
536 Camden Yards .15
537 PacBell Park .15
538 Jacobs Field .15
539 SAFECO Field .15
540 Miller Field .15

Mini

Mini (1-540): 8-15X
Production 50 Sets
Retail Exclusive

Tiffany

Stars (1-540): 4-8X
Production 200 Sets

Barry Bonds Career Highlights

	NM/M
Complete Set (10):	40.00
Common Bonds 1-3:	3.00
Common 4-6 inserted 1:125 H.	4.00
7-9 1:250 H	6.00
#10 1:383	6.00
1CH Barry Bonds	3.00
2CH Barry Bonds	3.00
3CH Barry Bonds	3.00
4CH Barry Bonds	4.00
5CH Barry Bonds	4.00
6CH Barry Bonds	4.00
7CH Barry Bonds	6.00
8CH Barry Bonds	6.00
9CH Barry Bonds	6.00
10CH Barry Bonds	6.00

Barry Bonds Career Highlights Autographs

No Pricing
25 Sets Produced

Barry Bonds Chasing History

This special edition of 600 was sold exclusively via a home shopping tv program. The 3-1/2" x 2-1/2" card features on front a piece of game-used Bonds bat in the form of the two 0s in "600." At right are an authentic autograph and portrait and action photos. On back is a statement of authenticity and a serial number.

	NM/M
Barry Bonds	125.00

Barry Bonds 4X MVP Super

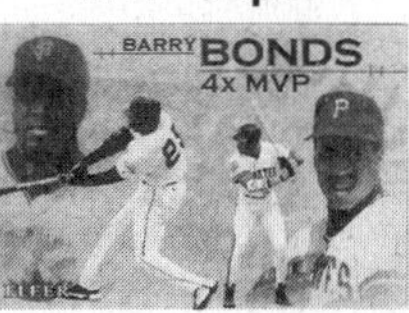

Bonds' status as the only four-time MVP winner was marked with the issue of this home shopping channel exclusive. The 5-1/2" x 3-1/2" card is serially numbered on back from within an edition of 5,000.

	NM/M
Barry Bonds	15.00

Barry Bonds 600 HR Supers

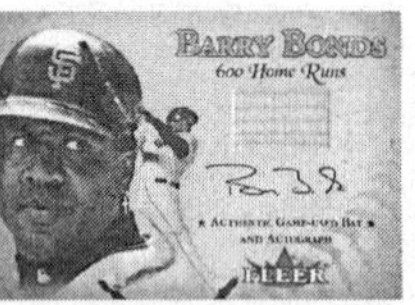

To commemorate his career 600th home run, Fleer produced a pair of jumbo-format (3-1/2" x 5") cards for sale on a TV home shopping show. One version of the card bears a facsimile autograph. A premium version, limited to 600 numbered cards, has a game-used bat chip and an authentic Bonds signature.

	NM/M
Barry Bonds (Facsimile signature.)	55.00
Barry Bonds (Autograph w/bat chip.)	250.00

Classic Cuts Autographs

		NM/M
Inserted 1:432		
LA-A	Luis Aparicio	15.00
RC-A	Ron Cey	8.00
HK-A	Harmon Killebrew	35.00
JM-A	Juan Marichal	15.00
GP-A	Gaylord Perry/SP/225	15.00
PR-A	Phil Rizzuto/SP/125	50.00
BR-A	Brooks Robinson/SP/200	40.00

Classic Cuts Game-Used

		NM/M
Common Player:		5.00
Inserted 1:24		
SA-P	Sparky Anderson/Pants	5.00
HB-B	Hank Bauer/Bat	5.00
JB-J	Johnny Bench/Jsy	15.00
PB-B	Paul Blair/Bat	5.00
WB-B	Wade Boggs/Bat/99	20.00
WB-J	Wade Boggs/Jsy	10.00
BB-B	Bobby Bonds/Bat	5.00
BB-J	Bobby Bonds/Jsy	5.00
GB-B	George Brett/Bat/250	30.00
GB-J	George Brett/Jsy/250	30.00
SC-P	Steve Carlton/Pants	6.00
OC-P	Orlando Cepeda/Pants	5.00
AD-J	Andre Dawson/Jsy	8.00
BD-B	Bill Dickey/Bat/200	20.00
LD-B	Larry Doby/Bat/250	10.00
DE-B	Dwight Evans/Bat/250	10.00
DE-J	Dwight Evans/Jsy	5.00
RF-J	Rollie Fingers/Jsy	5.00
CF-B	Carlton Fisk/Bat	10.00
CF-J	Carlton Fisk/Jsy/150	20.00
NF-B	Nellie Fox/Bat/200	20.00
SG-B	Steve Garvey/Bat	5.00
KG-B	Kirk Gibson/Bat	5.00
GH-B	Gil Hodges/Bat/200	15.00
CH-J	Jim Hunter/Jsy	10.00
BJ-J	Bo Jackson/Jsy	15.00
RJ-P	Reggie Jackson/Pants	10.00
GK-B	George Kell/Bat/150	15.00

TK-B Ted Kluszewski/Bat/200 15.00
TK-P Ted Kluszewski/Pants 10.00
RM-P Roger Maris/Pants/200 60.00
EM-B Eddie Mathews/Bat/200 20.00
DM-B Don Mattingly/Bat/200 50.00
DM-J Don Mattingly/Jsy 40.00
WM-J Willie McCovey/Jsy/300 10.00
PM-B Paul Molitor/Bat/250 25.00
JM-B Joe Morgan/Bat/250 8.00
EM-B Eddie Murray/Bat 10.00
EM-J Eddie Murray/Jsy 10.00
JP-J Jim Palmer/Jsy/273 8.00
DP-B Dave Parker/Bat 5.00
TP-B Tony Perez/Bat/250 10.00
TP-J Tony Perez/Jsy 8.00
LP-P Lou Piniella/Pants 5.00
KP-J Kirby Puckett/Jsy 15.00
JR-B Jim Rice/Bat/225 8.00
CR-BG Cal Ripken Jr./Btg Glv/100 75.00
CR-FG Cal Ripken Jr./Fld Glv/50 125.00
CR-J Cal Ripken Jr./Jsy 35.00
CR-P Cal Ripken Jr./Pants/200 40.00
BR-B Brooks Robinson/Bat/250 15.00
NR-J Nolan Ryan/Jsy 50.00
NR-P Nolan Ryan/Pants/200 60.00
RS-B Ryne Sandberg/Bat 25.00
OS-J Ozzie Smith/Jsy/250 15.00
WS-B Willie Stargell/Bat/250 15.00
JT-J Joe Torre/Jsy/125 15.00
AT-B Alan Trammell/Bat 10.00
EW-J Earl Weaver/Jsy 5.00
HW-P Hoyt Wilhelm/Pants/150 15.00
TW-B Ted Williams/Bat 85.00
TW-P Ted Williams/Pants 120.00
DW-B Dave Winfield/Bat 8.00
DW-J Dave Winfield/Jsy/231 10.00
DW-P Dave Winfield/Pants 8.00
RY-B Robin Yount/Bat 15.00

Classic Cuts Game-Used Autographs

NM/M
Varying quantities produced
LA-B Luis Aparicio/Bat/45 25.00
BR-B Brooks Robinson/Bat/45 80.00

Diamond Standouts

NM/M
Complete Set (10): 40.00
Common Player: 2.00
Production 1,200 Sets
1DS Mike Piazza 4.00
2DS Derek Jeter 8.00
3DS Ken Griffey Jr. 4.00
4DS Barry Bonds 8.00
5DS Sammy Sosa 4.00
6DS Alex Rodriguez 6.00
7DS Ichiro Suzuki 4.00
8DS Greg Maddux 3.00
9DS Jason Giambi 2.00
10DS Nomar Garciaparra 4.00

Golden Memories

NM/M
Complete Set (15): 20.00
Common Player: 1.00
Inserted 1:24
1GM Frank Thomas 1.50
2GM Derek Jeter 4.00
3GM Albert Pujols 3.00
4GM Barry Bonds 4.00
5GM Alex Rodriguez 3.00
6GM Randy Johnson 1.50
7GM Jeff Bagwell 1.50
8GM Greg Maddux 2.00
9GM Ivan Rodriguez 1.00
10GM Ichiro Suzuki 2.50
11GM Mike Piazza 2.50
12GM Pat Burrell 1.00
13GM Rickey Henderson 1.50
14GM Vladimir Guerrero 1.50
15GM Sammy Sosa 2.50

Headliners

NM/M
Complete Set (20): 10.00
Common Player: .25
Inserted 1:8
1HL Randy Johnson .75
2HL Alex Rodriguez 1.50
3HL Todd Helton .75
4HL Pedro J. Martinez .75
5HL Ichiro Suzuki 1.50
6HL Vladimir Guerrero .75
7HL Derek Jeter 2.00
8HL Adam Dunn .40
9HL Luis Gonzalez .25
10HL Kazuhiro Sasaki .25
11HL Sammy Sosa 1.25
12HL Jason Giambi .60
13HL Ken Griffey Jr. 1.25
14HL Roger Clemens 1.00
15HL Brandon Duckworth .25
16HL Nomar Garciaparra 1.25
17HL Bud Smith .25
18HL Juan Gonzalez .75
19HL Chipper Jones 1.00
20HL Barry Bonds 2.00

Rookie Flashback

NM/M
Complete Set (20): 6.00
Common Player: .25
Inserted 1:3 Retail
1RF Bret Prinz .25
2RF Albert Pujols 2.00
3RF C.C. Sabathia .25
4RF Ichiro Suzuki 1.50
5RF Juan Cruz .25
6RF Jay Gibbons .50
7RF Bud Smith .25
8RF Johnny Estrada .25
9RF Roy Oswalt .50
10RF Tsuyoshi Shinjo .25
11RF Brandon Duckworth .25
12RF Jackson Melian .25
13RF Josh Beckett 1.00
14RF Morgan Ensberg .25
15RF Brian Lawrence .25
16RF Eric Hinske .25
17RF Juan Uribe .25
18RF Matt White .25
19RF Junior Spivey .25
20RF Wilson Betemit .25

Rookie Sensations

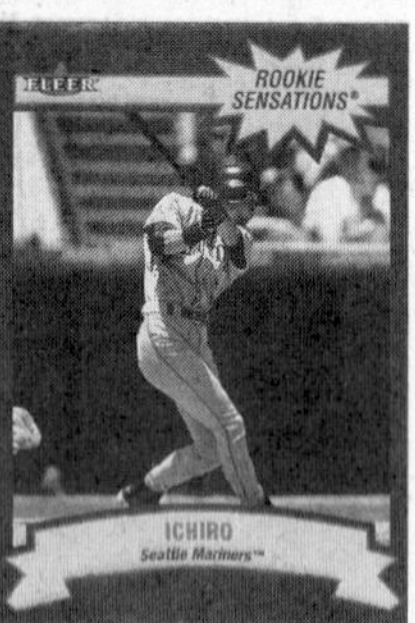

NM/M
Complete Set (20): 40.00
Common Player: 2.00
Production 1,500 Sets
1RS Bret Prinz 2.00
2RS Albert Pujols 10.00
3RS C.C. Sabathia 2.00
4RS Ichiro Suzuki 8.00
5RS Juan Cruz 2.00
6RS Jay Gibbons 3.00
7RS Bud Smith 2.00
8RS Johnny Estrada 2.00
9RS Roy Oswalt 4.00
10RS Tsuyoshi Shinjo 2.00
11RS Brandon Duckworth 2.00
12RS Jackson Melian 2.00
13RS Josh Beckett 4.00
14RS Morgan Ensberg 2.00
15RS Brian Lawrence 2.00
16RS Eric Hinske 2.00
17RS Juan Uribe 2.00
18RS Matt White 2.00
19RS Junior Spivey 2.00
20RS Wilson Betemit 2.00

Then and Now

NM/M
Common Card: 5.00
Production 275 Sets
1TN Eddie Mathews, Chipper Jones 5.00
2TN Willie McCovey, Barry Bonds 15.00
3TN Johnny Bench, Mike Piazza 5.00
4TN Ernie Banks, Alex Rodriguez 8.00
5TN Rickey Henderson, Ichiro Suzuki 10.00
6TN Tom Seaver, Roger Clemens 10.00
7TN Juan Marichal, Pedro J. Martinez 5.00
8TN Reggie Jackson, Derek Jeter 15.00
9TN Nolan Ryan, Kerry Wood 20.00
10TN Joe Morgan, Ken Griffey Jr. 10.00

2002 Fleer Authentix

NM/M
Complete Set (170): 85.00
Common Player: .25
Common SP (151-170): 3.00
Production 1,850
Pack (5): 3.00
Box (24): 60.00
1 Derek Jeter 2.00
2 Tim Hudson .35
3 Robert Fick .25
4 Javy Lopez .25
5 Alfonso Soriano .50
6 Ken Griffey Jr. 1.25
7 Rafael Palmeiro .65
8 Bernie Williams .35
9 Adam Dunn .50
10 Ivan Rodriguez .65
11 Vladimir Guerrero .75
12 Pedro J. Martinez .75
13 Bret Boone .25
14 Paul LoDuca .25
15 Tony Batista .25
16 Barry Bonds 2.00
17 Craig Biggio .25
18 Garret Anderson .25
19 Mark Mulder .25
20 Frank Thomas .75
21 Alex Rodriguez 1.50
22 Cristian Guzman .25
23 Sammy Sosa 1.25
24 Ichiro Suzuki 1.25
25 Carlos Beltran .50
26 Edgardo Alfonzo .25
27 Josh Beckett .50
28 Eric Chavez .40
29 Roberto Alomar .40
30 Raul Mondesi .25
31 Mike Piazza 1.25
32 Barry Larkin .25
33 Ruben Sierra .25
34 Tsuyoshi Shinjo .25
35 Magglio Ordonez .25
36 Ben Grieve .25
37 Richie Sexson .25
38 Manny Ramirez .75
39 Jeff Kent .25
40 Shawn Green .40
41 Andruw Jones .75
42 Aramis Ramirez .25
43 Cliff Floyd .25
44 Juan Pierre .25
45 Jose Vidro .25
46 Paul Konerko .25
47 Greg Vaughn .25
48 Geoff Jenkins .25
49 Greg Maddux 1.00
50 Ryan Klesko .25
51 Corey Koskie .25
52 Nomar Garciaparra 1.25
53 Edgar Martinez .25
54 Gary Sheffield .40
55 Randy Johnson .75
56 Bobby Abreu .25
57 Mike Sweeney .25
58 Chipper Jones 1.00
59 Brian Giles .25
60 Charles Johnson .25
61 Ben Sheets .25
62 Jason Giambi .60
63 Todd Helton .75
64 David Eckstein .25
65 Troy Glaus .75
66 Sean Casey .35
67 Gabe Kapler .25
68 Doug Mientkiewicz .25
69 Curt Schilling .40
70 Pat Burrell .40
71 Albert Pujols 1.25
72 Jermaine Dye .25
73 Miguel Tejada .40
74 Jim Thome .25
75 Carlos Delgado .40
76 Fred McGriff .25
77 Mike Cameron .25
78 Jeromy Burnitz .25
79 Jay Gibbons .25
80 Rich Aurilia .25
81 Lance Berkman .25
82 Brian Jordan .25
83 Phil Nevin .25
84 Moises Alou .25
85 Reggie Sanders .25
86 Scott Rolen .65
87 Larry Walker .25
88 Matt Williams .25
89 Roger Clemens 1.00
90 Juan Gonzalez .75
91 Jose Cruz Jr. .25
92 Tino Martinez .25
93 Kerry Wood .65
94 Freddy Garcia .25
95 Jeff Bagwell .75
96 Luis Gonzalez .35
97 Jimmy Rollins .50
98 Bobby Higginson .25
99 Rondell White .25
100 Jorge Posada .35
101 Trot Nixon .25
102 Jason Kendall .25
103 Preston Wilson .25
104 Corey Patterson .25
105 Jose Valentin .25
106 Carlos Lee .25
107 Chris Richard .25
108 Todd Walker .25
109 Ellis Burks .25
110 Brady Anderson .25
111 Kazuhiro Sasaki .25
112 Roy Oswalt .35
113 Kevin Brown .25
114 Jeff Weaver .25
115 Todd Hollandsworth .25
116 Joe Crede .25
117 Tom Glavine .40
118 Mike Lieberthal .25
119 Tim Salmon .35
120 Johnny Damon .40
121 Brad Fullmer .25
122 Mo Vaughn .25
123 Torii Hunter .25
124 Jamie Moyer .25
125 Terrence Long .25
126 Travis Lee .25
127 Jacque Jones .25
128 Lee Stevens .25
129 Russ Ortiz .25
130 Jeremy Giambi .25
131 Mike Mussina .45
132 Orlando Cabrera .25
133 Barry Zito .40
134 Robert Person .25
135 Andy Pettitte .40
136 Drew Henson .40
137 Mark Teixeira .50
138 David Espinosa .25
139 Orlando Hudson .25
140 Colby Lewis .25
141 Bill Hall .25
142 Michael Restovich .25
143 Angel Berroa .40
144 Dewon Brazelton .25
145 Joe Thurston .25
146 Mark Prior .50
147 Dane Sardinha .25
148 Marlon Byrd .25
149 Jeff Deardorff **RC** .25
150 Austin Kearns .40
151 Anderson Machado **RC** 5.00
152 Kazuhisa Ishii **RC** 8.00
153 Eric Junge **RC** 3.00
154 Mark Corey **RC** 3.00
155 So Taguchi **RC** 5.00
156 Jorge Padilla **RC** 5.00
157 Steve Kent **RC** 3.00
158 Jaime Cerda **RC** 3.00
159 Hansel Izquierdo **RC** 3.00
160 Rene Reyes **RC** 3.00
161 Jorge Nunez **RC** 3.00
162 Corey Thurman **RC** 4.00
163 Jorge Sosa **RC** 3.00
164 Franklin Nunez **RC** 3.00
165 Adam Walker **RC** 3.00
166 Ryan Baerlocher **RC** 3.00
167 Ron Calloway **RC** 3.00
168 Miguel Asencio **RC** 3.00
169 Luis Ugueto **RC** 3.00
170 Felix Escalona **RC** 3.00

Front Row

Front Row: 4-8X
Front Row SP: 1-2X
Production 150 Sets

Second Row

Second Row: 3-5X
Second Row SP: .75-1.5X
Production 250 Sets

Autographed AuthenTIX

NM/M
Common Autograph: 10.00
Inserted 1:780
Unripped No Pricing.
Numbered to 25
Derek Jeter 200.00
Mark Teixeira/25 35.00
Brooks Robinson/145 40.00
Ben Sheets/25 30.00
Mark Prior 40.00
Kazuhisa Ishii 25.00
So Taguchi 15.00
Dane Sardinha 10.00
David Espinosa 10.00

Autographed Jersey AuthenTIX

NM/M
Inserted 1:1,387
Derek Jeter 200.00
Jeff Bagwell 80.00

Ballpark Classics

NM/M
Complete Set (15): 50.00
Common Player: 1.50
Inserted 1:22
1BC Reggie Jackson 3.00
2BC Don Mattingly 6.00
3BC Duke Snider 2.00
4BC Carlton Fisk 2.00
5BC Cal Ripken Jr. 8.00
6BC Willie McCovey 1.50
7BC Robin Yount 3.00
8BC Paul Molitor 3.00
9BC George Brett 6.00
10BC Ryne Sandberg 5.00
11BC Nolan Ryan 8.00
12BC Thurman Munson 4.00
13BC Joe Morgan 1.50
14BC Jim Rice 1.50
15BC Babe Ruth 8.00

Ballpark Classics Memorabilia

NM/M
Common Player: 5.00
Inserted 1:83
Golds: 2X
Production 100
RJ Reggie Jackson 15.00
DM Don Mattingly 30.00
DS Duke Snider 15.00
CF Carlton Fisk 10.00
CR Cal Ripken Jr. 40.00
WC Willie McCovey 15.00
RY Robin Yount 25.00
PM Paul Molitor 15.00
GB George Brett 30.00
RS Ryne Sandberg/SP 75.00
NR Nolan Ryan 30.00
TM Thurman Munson/Cap/SP 50.00
JM Joe Morgan 5.00
JR Jim Rice 8.00
BR Babe Ruth/Seat 150.00

Bat AuthenTIX

NM/M
Common Player: 5.00
Inserted 1:68
Unripped: 2-3X
Production 50
Pat Burrell 8.00
Ray Durham/SP/52 5.00
Juan Gonzalez 8.00
Drew Henson 5.00
Orlando Hernandez 5.00
Hideo Nomo/SP/41 30.00
Jimmy Rollins 5.00
Manny Ramirez 8.00
Bernie Williams/SP/44 10.00
Derek Jeter/197 40.00
Andruw Jones 8.00
Chipper Jones/SP/37 20.00
Barry Bonds 20.00
Nomar Garciaparra 25.00

Jersey AuthenTIX

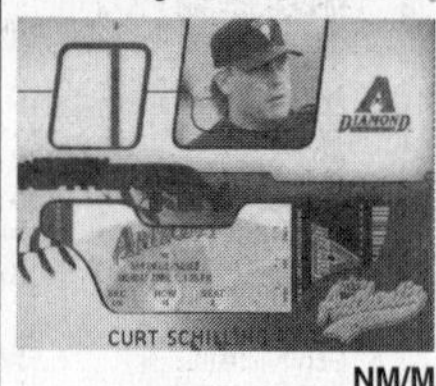

NM/M
Common Player: 5.00
Inserted 1:12
Unripped: 2-3X
Production 50
Barry Bonds 20.00
Chipper Jones 10.00
Scott Rolen/SP 12.00
Greg Maddux 10.00
Curt Schilling/SP 10.00
Mike Piazza 10.00
Nomar Garciaparra/SP 15.00
Derek Jeter 20.00
Luis Gonzalez/SP 8.00
Jeff Bagwell 8.00
Frank Thomas 8.00
Manny Ramirez/SP 10.00
Shawn Green 5.00
Todd Helton 8.00
Jim Edmonds/SP 10.00
Paul LoDuca 5.00
Alex Rodriguez 10.00
Roberto Alomar 6.00
Andruw Jones/SP 10.00
Barry Zito 8.00
J.D. Drew 5.00
Magglio Ordonez 5.00
Eric Chavez 5.00
Darin Erstad/SP 8.00
Freddy Garcia 5.00
Jim Thome/SP 12.00
Pedro J. Martinez 10.00
Ivan Rodriguez 8.00
Bernie Williams/SP 10.00
Randy Johnson 8.00

Derek Jeter 1996 Autographics

NM/M
Production 100
Derek Jeter 150.00

Power Alley

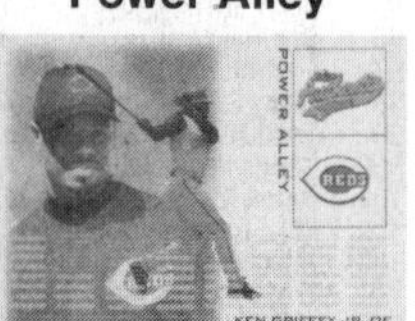

NM/M
Complete Set (15): 20.00
Common Player: .50
Inserted 1:11
1PA Sammy Sosa 2.00
2PA Ken Griffey Jr. 2.00
3PA Luis Gonzalez .50
4PA Alex Rodriguez 3.00
5PA Shawn Green .75
6PA Barry Bonds 4.00
7PA Todd Helton 1.00
8PA Jim Thome .50
9PA Troy Glaus 1.00
10PA Manny Ramirez 1.00
11PA Jeff Bagwell 1.00
12PA Jason Giambi .75
13PA Chipper Jones 1.50
14PA Mike Piazza 2.00
15PA Albert Pujols 3.00

2002 Fleer Box Score

NM/M
Complete Set (310):
Common Player: .25
Common (126-150): 3.00
Production 2,499
Complete Rising Star Set (40): 30.00
Common (151-190): 1.00
Complete Intl. Set (40): 18.00
Common (191-230): 1.00
Complete All-Star Set (40): 20.00
Common (231-270): 1.00
Comp. Cooperstown Set (40): 30.00
Common Cooperstown (271-310): 1.00
Print run for all subsets is 2,950.
Pack (7): 5.00
Box (18 Packs + Supp. Box): 80.00
1 Derek Jeter 2.00
2 Kevin Brown .25
3 Nomar Garciaparra 1.25
4 Mark Buehrle .25
5 Mike Piazza 1.25
6 David Justice .25
7 Tino Martinez .25
8 Paul Konerko .25
9 Larry Walker .25
10 Ben Sheets .25
11 Mike Cameron .25
12 David Wells .25
13 Barry Zito .35
14 Pat Burrell .45
15 Mike Mussina .50
16 Bud Smith .25
17 Brian Jordan .25
18 Chris Singleton .25
19 Daryle Ward .25
20 Russ Ortiz .25
21 Jason Kendall .25
22 Kerry Wood .65
23 Jeff Weaver .25
24 Tony Armas .25
25 Toby Hall .25
26 Brian Giles .25
27 Juan Pierre .25
28 Ken Griffey Jr. 1.25
29 Mike Sweeney .25
30 John Smoltz .25
31 Sean Casey .35
32 Jeremy Giambi .25
33 Mike Lieberthal .25
34 Rich Aurilia .25
35 Matt Lawton .25
36 Dmitri Young .25
37 Wade Miller .25
38 Jason Giambi .65
39 Jeff Cirillo .25
40 Mark Grace .35
41 Frank Thomas .75
42 Preston Wilson .25
43 Brad Radke .25
44 Greg Maddux 1.00
45 Adam Dunn .50
46 Roy Oswalt .35
47 Troy Glaus .75
48 Edgar Martinez .25
49 Billy Koch .25
50 Chipper Jones 1.00
51 Lance Berkman .25
52 Shannon Stewart .25
53 Eddie Guardado .25
54 C.C. Sabathia .25
55 Craig Biggio .25
56 Roger Clemens 1.00
57 Jimmy Rollins .25
58 Carlos Delgado .50
59 Tony Clark .25
60 Mike Hampton .25
61 Jeromy Burnitz .25
62 Jorge Posada .35
63 Todd Helton .75
64 Richie Sexson .25
65 Ryan Klesko .25
66 Cliff Floyd .25
67 Eric Milton .25
68 Scott Rolen .65
69 Steve Finley .25
70 Ray Durham .25
71 Jeff Bagwell .75
72 Geoff Jenkins .25
73 Jamie Moyer .25
74 David Eckstein .25
75 Johnny Damon .40
76 Pokey Reese .25
77 Mo Vaughn .25
78 Trevor Hoffman .25
79 Albert Pujols 1.50
80 Ben Grieve .25
81 Matt Morris .25
82 Aubrey Huff .25
83 Darin Erstad .60
84 Garret Anderson .25
85 Jacque Jones .25
86 Matt Anderson .25
87 Jose Vidro .25
88 Carlos Lee .25
89 Jeff Suppan .25
90 Al Leiter .25
91 Jeff Kent .25
92 Randy Johnson .75
93 Moises Alou .25
94 Bobby Higginson .25
95 Phil Nevin .25
96 Alex Rodriguez 1.50
97 Luis Gonzalez .40
98 A.J. Burnett .25
99 Torii Hunter .25
100 Ivan Rodriguez .60
101 Pedro J. Martinez .75
102 Brady Anderson .25
103 Paul LoDuca .25
104 Eric Chavez .35
105 Tim Salmon .35
106 Javier Vazquez .25
107 Bret Boone .25
108 Greg Vaughn .25
109 J.D. Drew .40
110 Jay Gibbons .25
111 Jim Thome .25
112 Shawn Green .40
113 Tim Hudson .35
114 John Olerud .25
115 Raul Mondesi .25
116 Curt Schilling .50
117 Corey Patterson .25
118 Robert Fick .25
119 Corey Koskie .25
120 Juan Gonzalez .75
121 Jerry Hairston Jr. .25
122 Gary Sheffield .40
123 Mark Mulder .25
124 Barry Bonds 2.00
125 Jim Edmonds .25
126 Franklyn German **RC** 3.00
127 Rodrigo Rosario **RC** 3.00
128 Ryan Ludwick 3.00
129 Jorge de la Rosa **RC** 4.00
130 Jason Lane 3.00
131 Brian Mallette **RC** 3.00
132 Chris Baker **RC** 3.00
133 Kyle Kane **RC** 3.00
134 Doug DeVore **RC** 3.00
135 Raul Chavez **RC** 3.00
136 Miguel Asencio **RC** 3.00
137 Luis Garcia 3.00
138 Nick Johnson 3.00
139 Michael Crudale **RC** 3.00
140 P.J. Bevis **RC** 3.00
141 Josh Hancock **RC** 3.00
142 Jeremy Lambert **RC** 3.00
143 Ben Broussard 3.00
144 John Ennis **RC** 3.00
145 Wilson Valdez **RC** 3.00
146 Eric Good **RC** 3.00
147 Elio Serrano **RC** 3.00
148 Jaime Cerda **RC** 3.00
149 Hank Blalock 5.00
150 Brandon Duckworth 3.00
151 Drew Henson 1.50
152 Kazuhisa Ishii **RC** 3.00
153 Earl Snyder **RC** 1.00
154 J.M. Gold 1.00
155 Satoru Komiyama **RC** 1.00
156 Marlon Byrd 1.00
157 So Taguchi **RC** 2.00
158 Eric Hinske 1.00
159 Mark Prior 3.00
160 Jorge Padilla **RC** 1.50
161 Rene Reyes **RC** 1.00
162 Jorge Nunez **RC** 1.00
163 Nelson Castro **RC** 1.00
164 Anderson Machado **RC** 2.00
165 Mark Teixeira 2.00
166 Orlando Hudson 1.00
167 Edwin Almonte **RC** 1.00
168 Luis Ugueto **RC** 1.00
169 Felix Escalona **RC** 1.00
170 Ron Calloway **RC** 1.00
171 Kevin Mench 1.00
172 Takahito Nomura **RC** 1.00
173 Sean Burroughs 1.00
174 Steve Kent **RC** 1.00
175 Jorge Sosa **RC** 1.00
176 Mike Moriarty **RC** 1.00
177 Carlos Pena 1.00
178 Anastacio Martinez **RC** 1.00
179 Reed Johnson **RC** 1.00
180 Juan Brito **RC** 1.00
181 Wilson Betemit 1.00
182 Mike Rivera 1.00
183 David Espinosa 1.00
184 Todd Donovan **RC** 1.00
185 Morgan Ensberg 1.00
186 Dewon Brazelton 1.00
187 Ben Howard **RC** 1.00
188 Austin Kearns 2.00
189 Josh Bagwell 2.00
190 Brandon Backe **RC** 1.50
191 Ichiro Suzuki 4.00
192 Tsuyoshi Shinjo 1.00
193 Hideo Nomo 2.00
194 Kazuhiro Sasaki 1.00
195 Edgardo Alfonzo 1.00
196 Chan Ho Park 1.00
197 Carlos Hernandez 1.00
198 Byung Kim 1.00
199 Omar Vizquel 1.00
200 Freddy Garcia 1.00
201 Richard Hidalgo 1.00
202 Magglio Ordonez 1.00
203 Bobby Abreu 1.00
204 Roger Cedeno 1.00
205 Andruw Jones 2.00
206 Mariano Rivera 1.50
207 Jose Macias 1.00
208 Orlando Hernandez 1.00
209 Rafael Palmeiro 2.00
210 Danys Baez 1.00
211 Bernie Williams 1.25
212 Carlos Beltran 3.00
213 Roberto Alomar 1.50
214 Jose Cruz Jr. 1.00
215 Ryan Dempster 1.00
216 Erubiel Durazo 1.00
217 Carlos Pena 1.00
218 Sammy Sosa 4.00
219 Adrian Beltre 1.50
220 Aramis Ramirez 1.00
221 Alfonso Soriano 2.00
222 Vladimir Guerrero 2.00
223 Juan Uribe 1.00
224 Cristian Guzman 1.00
225 Manny Ramirez 2.00
226 Juan Cruz 1.00
227 Ramon Ortiz 1.00
228 Juan Encarnacion 1.00
229 Bartolo Colon 1.00
230 Miguel Tejada 1.25
231 Cal Ripken Jr. 6.00
232 Derek Jeter 6.00
233 Pedro J. Martinez 2.00
234 Roberto Alomar 1.50
235 Sandy Alomar 1.00
236 Mike Piazza 4.00
237 Jeff Conine 1.00
238 Fred McGriff 1.00
239 Kirby Puckett 3.00
240 Ken Griffey Jr. 4.00
241 Roger Clemens 3.50
242 Joe Morgan 1.00
243 Willie McCovey 1.00
244 Brooks Robinson 1.00
245 Juan Marichal 1.00
246 Todd Helton 2.00
247 Alex Rodriguez 5.00
248 Barry Bonds 6.00
249 Nomar Garciaparra 4.00
250 Jeff Bagwell 2.00
251 Kenny Lofton 1.00
252 Barry Larkin 1.00
253 Tom Glavine 1.50
254 Magglio Ordonez 1.00
255 Randy Johnson 2.00
256 Chipper Jones 3.00
257 Kevin Brown 1.00
258 Rickey Henderson 2.00
259 Greg Maddux 3.00
260 Jim Thome 2.00
261 Rafael Palmeiro 1.50
262 Frank Thomas 2.00
263 Manny Ramirez 2.00
264 Travis Fryman 1.00
265 Gary Sheffield 1.25
266 Bernie Williams 1.25
267 Matt Williams 1.00
268 Ivan Rodriguez 1.50
269 Mike Mussina 1.25
270 Larry Walker 1.00
271 Jim Palmer 1.00
272 Cal Ripken Jr. 6.00
273 Brooks Robinson 1.00
274 Bobby Doerr 1.00
275 Ernie Banks 2.00
276 Fergie Jenkins 1.00
277 Luis Aparicio 1.00
278 Hoyt Wilhelm 1.00
279 Tom Seaver 1.50
280 Joe Morgan 1.00
281 Lou Boudreau 1.00
282 Larry Doby 1.00
283 Jim Bunning 1.00
284 George Kell 1.00
285 Pee Wee Reese 1.50
286 Eddie Mathews 1.00
287 Robin Yount 2.00
288 Rod Carew 1.00
289 Monte Irvin 1.00
290 Yogi Berra 2.00
291 Whitey Ford 2.00
292 Reggie Jackson 2.00
293 Rollie Fingers 1.00
294 Jim "Catfish" Hunter 1.00
295 Richie Ashburn 1.00
296 Willie Stargell 1.00
297 Ralph Kiner 1.00
298 Orlando Cepeda 1.00
299 Juan Marichal 1.00
300 Gaylord Perry 1.00
301 Willie McCovey 1.00
302 Red Schoendienst 1.00
303 Nolan Ryan 8.00
304 Bob Gibson 1.00
305 Al Kaline 1.00
306 Harmon Killebrew 1.00
307 Stan Musial 3.00
308 Phil Rizzuto 1.00
309 Mike Schmidt 4.00
310 Enos Slaughter 1.00

Classic Miniatures

NM/M
Complete Set (40): 25.00
Stars: 1.5-3X Base Card
Production 2,950 Sets
One set per classic mini box.
First Editions: 4-8X
Production 100 Sets

Classic Miniatures Game-Used

NM/M
Common Player: 6.00
One per Classic Mini box.
Derek Jeter/Bat 20.00
Mike Piazza/Jsy 10.00
Adam Dunn/Jsy 6.00
Chipper Jones/Bat 10.00
Roger Clemens/Jsy 15.00
Alex Rodriguez/Jsy 10.00
Pedro Martinez/Jsy 10.00
Jim Thome/Bat 10.00
Curt Schilling/Jsy 8.00
Barry Bonds/Bat 20.00

First Edition

Cards (1-125): 4-8X
Cards (126-150): .5-1X
Cards (151-310): 1-2X
Production 100 Sets

All-Star Lineup

NM/M
Common Card: 15.00
1:All-Stars Box
Derek Jeter, Nomar Garciaparra, Alex Rodriguez 50.00
Joe Morgan, Willie McCovey, Brooks Robinson 15.00
Alex Rodriguez, Ivan Rodriguez, Rafael Palmeiro 20.00
Derek Jeter, Mike Mussina, Bernie Williams 35.00
Barry Bonds, Cal Ripken Jr., Frank Thomas 60.00
Cal Ripken Jr., Derek Jeter, Roberto Alomar, Pedro J. Martinez 60.00
Mike Piazza, Barry Bonds, Ken Griffey Jr., Jeff Bagwell 40.00
Roger Clemens, Greg Maddux, Randy Johnson, Pedro J. Martinez 35.00
Todd Helton, Roberto Alomar, Alex Rodriguez, Chipper Jones 25.00
Ken Griffey Jr., Barry Bonds, Larry Walker, Manny Ramirez 35.00

Amazing Greats

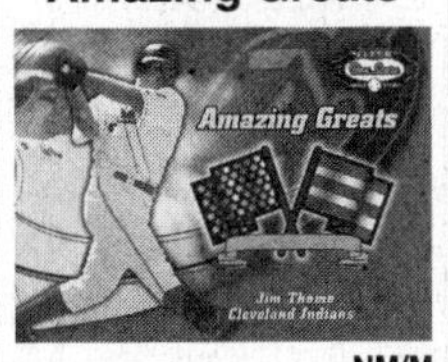

NM/M
Complete Set (20): 20.00
Common Player: .50
Inserted 1:5
1AG Derek Jeter 4.00
2AG Barry Bonds 4.00
3AG Mike Piazza 2.50
4AG Ivan Rodriguez .75
5AG Todd Helton 1.00
6AG Nomar Garciaparra 2.50
7AG Jim Thome .50
8AG Bernie Williams .50
9AG Kazuhiro Sasaki .50
10AG Torii Hunter .50
11AG Bret Boone .50
12AG Tim Hudson .50
13AG Randy Johnson 1.00
14AG Rafael Palmeiro .75
15AG Scott Rolen .75
16AG Carlos Delgado .75
17AG Chipper Jones 2.00
18AG Lance Berkman .50
19AG Frank Thomas 1.00
20AG Greg Maddux 2.00

Amazing Greats Single Swatch

NM/M
Common Player: 5.00
Inserted 1:13
Dual Swatches: 1-2X
Inserted 1:90
Derek Jeter 20.00
Barry Bonds 20.00
Mike Piazza 10.00
Ivan Rodriguez 8.00
Nomar Garciaparra 15.00
Jim Thome/bat 10.00
Bernie Williams 8.00
Kazuhiro Sasaki 5.00
Torii Hunter 6.00
Bret Boone 5.00
Rafael Palmeiro 8.00
Scott Rolen 8.00
Carlos Delgado 8.00
Lance Berkman 5.00
Frank Thomas 8.00
Greg Maddux 10.00

Amazing Greats Patch

NM/M
Common Player: 15.00
Production 150 Sets
Derek Jeter 50.00
Barry Bonds 50.00
Mike Piazza 25.00
Ivan Rodriguez 25.00
Nomar Garciaparra 40.00
Bernie Williams 25.00
Kazuhiro Sasaki 15.00
Torii Hunter 25.00
Bret Boone 15.00
Rafael Palmeiro 25.00
Scott Rolen 25.00
Carlos Delgado 20.00
Lance Berkman 15.00
Frank Thomas 25.00
Greg Maddux 30.00

Bat Rack

NM/M
Common Card: 20.00
Production 300 Sets
1BR Derek Jeter, Alfonso Soriano, Bernie Williams 60.00
2BR Mike Piazza, Roberto Alomar, Mo Vaughn 30.00
3BR Jeff Bagwell, Lance Berkman, Craig Biggio 30.00
4BR Eric Chavez, Miguel Tejada, Carlos Pena 15.00
5BR Alex Rodriguez, Ivan Rodriguez, Rafael Palmeiro 30.00
6BR Chipper Jones, Gary Sheffield, Andruw Jones 20.00
7BR Carlos Delgado, Jim Thome, Frank Thomas 20.00
8BR Derek Jeter, Nomar Garciaparra, Alex Rodriguez 60.00
9BR Barry Bonds, Adam Dunn, Chipper Jones 35.00
10BR Magglio Ordonez, Juan Gonzalez, Manny Ramirez 20.00

Bat Rack Quad

NM/M
Common Card 25.00
Production 150 Sets
Torii Hunter, Cristian Guzman, Frank Thomas, Magglio Ordonez 25.00
Alex Rodriguez, Ivan Rodriguez, Eric Chavez, Miguel Tejada 40.00
Mike Piazza, Roberto Alomar, Alfonso Soriano, Derek Jeter 80.00
Barry Bonds, Lance Berkman, Alex Rodriguez, Nomar Garciaparra 75.00
Barry Bonds, Chipper Jones, Mike Piazza, Ivan Rodriguez 75.00
Derek Jeter, Miguel Tejada, Nomar Garciaparra, Alex Rodriguez 75.00
Roberto Alomar, Mo Vaughn, Jeff Bagwell, Craig Biggio 25.00
Jim Palmer, Carlos Delgado, Jim Thome, Frank Thomas 25.00
Magglio Ordonez, Bernie Williams, Juan Gonzalez, Manny Ramirez 25.00
Chipper Jones, Adam Dunn, Jeff Bagwell, Mo Vaughn 25.00
Alex Rodriguez, Jim Palmer, Bernie Williams, Alfonso Soriano 40.00
Carlos Pena, Eric Chavez, Carlos Delgado, Juan Gonzalez 20.00
Adam Dunn, Lance Berkman, Jim Thome, Manny Ramirez 25.00

Box Score Debuts

NM/M
Complete Set (15): 40.00
Common Player: 2.50
Production 2,002 Sets
1 Hank Blalock 6.00
2 Eric Hinske 3.00
3 Kazuhisa Ishii 5.00
4 Sean Burroughs 3.00
5 Andres Torres 2.50
6 Satoru Komiyama 2.50
7 Mark Prior 10.00
8 Kevin Mench 2.50
9 Austin Kearns 3.00
10 Earl Snyder 2.50
11 Jon Rauch 2.50
12 Jason Lane 2.50
13 Ben Howard 2.50
14 Bobby Hill 2.50
15 Dennis Tankersley 2.50

Hall of Fame Material

NM/M
Common Player: 8.00
1:Cooperstown Box
Jim Palmer/Jsy 8.00
Cal Ripken Jr/Jsy 25.00
Brooks Robinson/Bat 10.00
Joe Morgan/Bat 8.00
Eddie Mathews/Bat 10.00
Robin Yount/Jsy 15.00
Reggie Jackson/Jsy 10.00
"Catfish" Hunter/Jsy 8.00
Willie McCovey/Jsy 8.00
Nolan Ryan/Jsy 30.00

Press Clippings

NM/M
Complete Set (20): 90.00
Common Player: 4.00
Inserted 1:90
1PC Mark Mulder 4.00
2PC Curt Schilling 6.00
3PC Alfonso Soriano 7.50
4PC Jeff Bagwell 7.50
5PC J.D. Drew 5.00
6PC Pedro J. Martinez 7.50
7PC Bobby Abreu 4.00
8PC Alex Rodriguez 12.00
9PC Mike Sweeney 4.00
10PC Carlos Pena 4.00
11PC Josh Beckett 6.00
12PC Roger Clemens 9.00
13PC Manny Ramirez 7.50
14PC Adam Dunn 6.00
15PC Kazuhisa Ishii 4.00
16PC Ken Griffey Jr. 10.00
17PC Sammy Sosa 10.00
18PC Ichiro Suzuki 9.00
19PC Albert Pujols 15.00
20PC Troy Glaus 7.50

Press Clippings Game-Used

NM/M
Common Player: 5.00
Inserted 1:13
Mark Mulder/Jsy 5.00
Curt Schilling/Jsy 8.00
Alfonso Soriano/Bat 10.00
Jeff Bagwell/Jsy 8.00
J.D. Drew/Jsy 5.00
Pedro Martinez/Jsy 10.00
Bobby Abreu/Jsy 5.00
Alex Rodriguez/Jsy 10.00
Mike Sweeney/Jsy 5.00
Carlos Pena/Jsy 5.00
Josh Beckett/Jsy 8.00
Manny Ramirez/Jsy 10.00
Adam Dunn/Jsy 6.00
Kazuhisa Ishii/Jsy 10.00
Ken Griffey Jr./Base 10.00
Sammy Sosa/Base 15.00
Ichiro Suzuki/Base 15.00
Albert Pujols/Base 10.00
Troy Glaus/Base 5.00

Wave of the Future

NM/M
Common Player: 4.00
1: Rising Stars Box
1WF Drew Henson/Bat 5.00
2WF Kazuhisa Ishii/Bat 5.00
3WF Marlon Byrd/Jsy 4.00
4WF So Taguchi/Bat 4.00
5WF Jorge Padilla/Pants/75 10.00
6WF Rene Reyes/Jsy 4.00
7WF Mark Teixeira/100 10.00
8WF Carlos Pena/Bat 4.00
9WF Austin Kearns/Pants 6.00
10WF Josh Beckett/Jsy/50 15.00

World Piece

NM/M
Common Player: 4.00
1:International Box
1WP Ichiro Suzuki/Base 20.00
2WP Tsuyoshi Shinjo/Bat 4.00
3WP Hideo Nomo/Jsy 20.00
4WP Kazuhiro Sasaki/Jsy 4.00
5WP Chan Ho Park/Jsy 4.00
6WP Magglio Ordonez/Jsy 6.00
7WP Andruw Jones/Jsy 8.00
8WP Rafael Palmeiro/Jsy 10.00
9WP Bernie Williams/Jsy 10.00
10WP Roberto Alomar/Bat 6.00

2002 Fleer E-X

NM/M
Complete Set (140):
Common Player: .25
Common SP (101-125): 3.00
Common (126-140): 5.00
Inserted 1:24
Pack (4): 2.50
Box (24): 40.00
1 Alex Rodriguez 1.50
2 Albert Pujols 1.50

3 Ken Griffey Jr. 1.25
4 Vladimir Guerrero .75
5 Sammy Sosa 1.25
6 Ichiro Suzuki 1.25
7 Jorge Posada .35
8 Matt Williams .25
9 Adrian Beltre .40
10 Pat Burrell .40
11 Roger Cedeno .25
12 Tony Clark .25
13 Steve Finley .25
14 Rafael Furcal .25
15 Rickey Henderson .75
16 Richard Hidalgo .25
17 Jason Kendall .25
18 Tino Martinez .25
19 Scott Rolen .65
20 Shannon Stewart .25
21 Jose Vidro .25
22 Preston Wilson .25
23 Raul Mondesi .25
24 Lance Berkman .25
25 Rick Ankiel .25
26 Kevin Brown .25
27 Jeromy Burnitz .25
28 Jeff Cirillo .25
29 Carl Everett .25
30 Eric Chavez .35
31 Freddy Garcia .25
32 Mark Grace .35
33 David Justice .25
34 Fred McGriff .25
35 Mike Mussina .50
36 John Olerud .25
37 Magglio Ordonez .25
38 Curt Schilling .50
39 Aaron Sele .25
40 Robin Ventura .25
41 Adam Dunn .50
42 Jeff Bagwell .75
43 Barry Bonds 2.00
44 Roger Clemens 1.00
45 Cliff Floyd .25
46 Jason Giambi .50
47 Juan Gonzalez .75
48 Luis Gonzalez .35
49 Cristian Guzman .25
50 Todd Helton .75
51 Derek Jeter 2.00
52 Rafael Palmeiro .65
53 Mike Sweeney .25
54 Ben Grieve .25
55 Phil Nevin .25
56 Mikes Piazza 1.25
57 Moises Alou .25
58 Ivan Rodriguez .65
59 Manny Ramirez .75
60 Brian Giles .25
61 Jim Thome .25
62 Larry Walker .25
63 Bobby Abreu .25
64 Troy Glaus .75
65 Garret Anderson .25
66 Roberto Alomar .40
67 Bret Boone .25
68 Marty Cardova .25
69 Craig Biggio .25
70 Omar Vizquel .25
71 Jermaine Dye .25
72 Darin Erstad .60
73 Carlos Delgado .50
74 Nomar Garciaparra 1.25
75 Greg Maddux 1.00
76 Tom Glavine .40
77 Frank Thomas .75
78 Shawn Green .40
79 Bobby Higginson .25
80 Jeff Kent .25
81 Chuck Knoblauch .25
82 Paul Konerko .25
83 Carlos Lee .25
84 Jon Lieber .25
85 Paul LoDuca .25
86 Mike Lowell .25
87 Edgar Martinez .25
88 Doug Mientkiewicz .25
89 Pedro J. Martinez .75
90 Randy Johnson .75
91 Aramis Ramirez .25
92 J.D. Drew .40
93 Chris Richard .25
94 Jimmy Rollins .50
95 Ryan Klesko .25
96 Gary Sheffield .40
97 Chipper Jones 1.00
98 Greg Vaughn .25
99 Mo Vaughn .25
100 Bernie Williams .35
101 John Foster/2,999 **RC** 3.00
102 Jorge De La Rosa/2,999 **RC** 4.00
103 Edwin Almonte/2,999 **RC** 3.00
104 Chris Booker/2,999 **RC** 3.00
105 Victor Alvarez/2,999 **RC** 3.00
106 Clifford Bartosh/2,999 **RC** 3.00
107 Felix Escalona/2,999 **RC** 3.00
108 Corey Thurman/2,999 **RC** 3.00
109 Kazuhisa Ishii/2,999 **RC** 6.00
110 Miguel Ascencio/2,999 **RC** 3.00
111 P.J. Bevis/2,499 **RC** 3.00
112 Gustavo Chacin/2,499 **RC** 3.00
113 Steve Kent/2,499 **RC** 3.00
114 Takahito Nomura/2,499 **RC** 3.00
115 Adam Walker/2,499 **RC** 3.00
116 So Taguchi/2,499 **RC** 5.00
117 Reed Johnson/2,499 **RC** 5.00
118 Rodrigo Rosario/2,499 **RC** 3.00
119 Luis Martinez/2,499 **RC** 4.00
120 Satoru Komiyama/2,499 **RC** 3.00
121 Sean Burroughs/1,999 3.00
122 Hank Blalock/1,999 5.00
123 Marlon Byrd/1,999 3.00
124 Nick Johnson/1,999 3.00
125 Mark Teixeira/1,999 5.00
126 David Espinosa 3.00
127 Adrian Burnside **RC** 3.00
128 Mark Corey **RC** 3.00
129 Matt Thornton 3.00
130 Dane Sardinha 3.00
131 Juan Rivera 3.00
132 Austin Kearns 5.00
134 Ben Broussard 3.00
135 Orlando Hudson 3.00
136 Carlos Pena 3.00
137 Kenny Kelly 3.00
138 Bill Hall 3.00
139 Ron Chiavacci 3.00
140 Mark Prior 6.00

Essential Credentials Future

This insert is issued in an edition inverse to the card number, paralleling the first 125 cards in two groups. Cards #1-60 include a game-used piece; card #1 is produced in an edition of 60, while card #60 is unique, etc. Cards #61-125 are inversely numbered with 125 examples of card #61 and 61 of card #125.

NM/M

Quantity produced listed
1 Alex Rodriguez/Jsy/60 30.00
2 Albert Pujols/Base/59 25.00
3 Ken Griffey Jr./Base/58 20.00
4 Vladimir Guerrero/Base/57 15.00
5 Sammy Sosa/Base/56 25.00
6 Ichiro Suzuki/Base/55 40.00
7 Jorge Posada/Bat/54 12.00
8 Matt Williams/Bat/53 8.00
9 Adrian Beltre/Bat/52 8.00
10 Pat Burrell/Bat/51 10.00
11 Roger Cedeno/Bat/50 8.00
12 Tony Clark/Bat/49 8.00
13 Steve Finley/Bat/48 8.00
14 Rafael Furcal/Bat/47 12.00
15 Rickey Henderson/Bat/46 20.00
16 Richard Hidalgo/Bat/45 10.00
17 Jason Kendall/Bat/44 10.00
18 Tino Martinez/Bat/43 15.00
19 Scott Rolen/Bat/42 20.00
20 Shannon Stewart/Bat/41 10.00
21 Jose Vidro/Bat/40 10.00
22 Preston Wilson/Bat/39 10.00
23 Raul Mondesi/Bat/38 10.00
24 Lance Berkman/Bat/37 10.00
25 Rick Ankiel/Jsy/36 8.00
26 Kevin Brown/Jsy/35 10.00
27 Jeromy Burnitz/Bat/34 8.00
28 Jeff Cirillo/Jsy/33 8.00
29 Carl Everett/Jsy/32 8.00
30 Eric Chavez/Bat/31 10.00
31 Freddy Garcia/Jsy/30 10.00
32 Mark Grace/Jsy/29 20.00
33 David Justice/Jsy/28 15.00
34 Fred McGriff/Jsy/27 15.00
37 Magglio Ordonez/Jsy/24 15.00
38 Curt Schilling/Jsy/23 30.00
61 Jim Thome/125 8.00
62 Larry Walker/124 4.00
63 Bobby Abreu/123 4.00
64 Troy Glaus/122 6.00
65 Garret Anderson/121 6.00
66 Roberto Alomar/120 6.00
67 Bret Boone/119 6.00
68 Marty Cordova/118 4.00
69 Craig Biggio/117 4.00
70 Omar Vizquel/116 4.00
71 Jermaine Dye/115 4.00
72 Darin Erstad/114 4.00
73 Carlos Delgado/113 6.00
74 Nomar Garciaparra/112 10.00
75 Greg Maddux/111 10.00
76 Tom Glavine/110 6.00
77 Frank Thomas/109 6.00
78 Shawn Green/108 5.00
79 Bobby Higginson/107 3.00
80 Jeff Kent/106 4.00
81 Chuck Knoblauch/105 3.00
82 Paul Konerko/104 3.00
83 Carlos Lee/103 3.00
84 Jon Lieber/102 3.00
85 Paul LoDuca/101 3.00
86 Mike Lowell/100 4.00
87 Edgar Martinez/99 4.00
88 Doug Mientkiewicz/98 3.00
89 Pedro J. Martinez/97 8.00
90 Randy Johnson/96 8.00
91 Aramis Ramirez/95 4.00
92 J.D. Drew/94 4.00
93 Chris Richard/93 3.00
94 Jimmy Rollins/92 4.00
95 Ryan Klesko/91 4.00
96 Gary Sheffield/90 4.00
97 Chipper Jones/89 8.00
98 Greg Vaughn/88 3.00
99 Mo Vaughn/87 3.00
100 Bernie Williams/86 5.00
101 John Foster NT/85 3.00
102 Jorge De La Rosa NT/84 3.00
103 Edwin Almonte NT/83 3.00
104 Chris Booker NT/82 3.00
105 Victor Alvarez NT/81 3.00
106 Clifford Bartosh NT/80 3.00
107 Felix Escalona NT/79 3.00
108 Corey Thurman NT/78 3.00
109 Kazuhisa Ishii NT/77 12.00
110 Miguel Asencio NT/76 3.00
111 P.J. Bevis NT/75 3.00
112 Gustavo Chacin NT/74 3.00
113 Steve Kent NT/73 3.00
114 Takahito Nomura NT/72 3.00
115 Adam Walker NT/71 3.00
116 So Taguchi NT/70 6.00
117 Reed Johnson NT/69 6.00
118 Rodrigo Rosario NT/68 4.00
119 Luis Martinez NT/67 5.00
120 Satoru Komiyama NT/66 4.00
121 Sean Burroughs NT/65 5.00
122 Hank Blalock NT/64 6.00
123 Marlon Byrd NT/63 4.00
124 Nick Johnson NT/62 4.00
125 Mark Teixeira NT/61 6.00

Essential Credentials Now

This insert parallels the first 125 cards in E-X. Each card is in an edition equal to its card number. Cards of the first 60 players include a game-used piece.

NM/M

Quantity produced listed
19 Scott Rolen/Bat/19 45.00
22 Preston Wilson/Bat/22 15.00
24 Lance Berkman/Bat/24 20.00
25 Rick Ankiel/Jsy/25 15.00
26 Kevin Brown/Jsy/26 20.00
27 Jeromy Burnitz/Bat/27 20.00
28 Jeff Cirillo/Jsy/28 15.00
29 Carl Everett/Jsy/29 15.00
30 Eric Chavez/Bat/30 20.00
31 Freddy Garcia/Jsy/31 15.00
32 Mark Grace/Jsy/32 20.00
33 David Justice/Jsy/33 15.00
34 Fred McGriff/Jsy/34 15.00
35 Mike Mussina/Jsy/35 25.00
36 John Olerud/Jsy/36 10.00
37 Magglio Ordonez/Jsy/37 15.00
38 Curt Schilling/Jsy/38 20.00
39 Aaron Sele/Jsy/39 10.00
40 Robin Ventura/Jsy/40 10.00
41 Adam Dunn/Bat/41 15.00
42 Jeff Bagwell/Jsy/42 20.00
43 Barry Bonds/Pants/43 75.00
44 Roger Clemens/Bat/44 50.00
45 Cliff Floyd/Bat/45 10.00
46 Jason Giambi/Base/46 15.00
47 Juan Gonzalez/Jsy/47 15.00
48 Luis Gonzalez/Base/48 10.00
49 Cristian Guzman/Bat/49 10.00
50 Todd Helton/Base/50 15.00
51 Derek Jeter/Bat/51 60.00
52 Rafael Palmeiro/Bat/52 20.00
53 Mike Sweeney/Bat/53 10.00
54 Ben Grieve/Jsy/54 5.00
55 Phil Nevin/Bat/55 8.00
56 Mike Piazza/Base/56 20.00
57 Moises Alou/Bat/57 10.00
58 Ivan Rodriguez/Jsy/58 15.00
59 Manny Ramirez/Base/59 10.00
60 Brian Giles/Bat/60 10.00
61 Jim Thome/61 15.00
62 Larry Walker/62 5.00
63 Bobby Abreu/63 5.00
64 Troy Glaus/64 8.00
65 Garret Anderson/65 8.00
66 Roberto Alomar/66 8.00
67 Bret Boone/67 5.00
68 Marty Cordova/68 4.00
69 Craig Biggio/69 5.00
70 Omar Vizquel/70 4.00
71 Jermaine Dye/71 4.00
72 Darin Erstad/72 5.00
73 Carlos Delgado/73 6.00
74 Nomar Garciaparra/74 15.00
75 Greg Maddux/75 15.00
76 Tom Glavine/76 5.00
77 Frank Thomas/77 8.00
78 Shawn Green/78 6.00
79 Bobby Higginson/79 4.00
80 Jeff Kent/80 5.00
81 Chuck Knoblauch/81 4.00
82 Paul Konerko/82 5.00
83 Carlos Lee/83 5.00
84 Jon Lieber/84 5.00
85 Paul LoDuca/85 5.00
86 Mike Lowell/86 6.00
87 Edgar Martinez/87 6.00
88 Doug Mientkiewicz/88 5.00
89 Pedro J. Martinez/89 10.00
90 Randy Johnson/90 10.00
91 Aramis Ramirez/91 6.00
92 J.D. Drew/92 6.00
93 Chris Richard/93 4.00
94 Jimmy Rollins/94 10.00
95 Ryan Klesko/95 6.00
96 Gary Sheffield/96 6.00
97 Chipper Jones/97 10.00
98 Greg Vaughn/98 4.00
99 Mo Vaughn/99 5.00
100 Bernie Williams/100 6.00
101 John Foster NT/101 4.00
102 Jorge De La Rosa NT/102 4.00
103 Edwin Almonte NT/103 4.00
104 Chris Booker NT/104 4.00
105 Victor Alvarez NT/105 4.00
106 Clifford Bartosh NT/106 4.00
107 Felix Escalona NT/107 4.00
108 Corey Thurman NT/108 4.00
109 Kazuhisa Ishii NT/109 10.00
110 Miguel Asencio NT/110 4.00
111 P.J. Bevis NT/111 4.00
112 Gustavo Chacin NT/112 4.00
113 Steve Kent NT/113 4.00
114 Takahito Nomura NT/114 4.00
115 Adam Walker NT/115 4.00
116 So Taguchi NT/116 6.00
117 Reed Johnson NT/117 6.00
118 Rodrigo Rosario NT/118 4.00
119 Luis Martinez NT/119 4.00
120 Satoru Komiyama NT/120 4.00
121 Sean Burroughs NT/121 5.00
122 Hank Blalock NT/122 6.00
123 Marlon Byrd NT/123 4.00
124 Nick Johnson NT/124 4.00
125 Mark Teixeira NT/125 6.00

Behind the Numbers

NM/M

Complete Set (35): 75.00
Common Player: 1.00
Inserted 1:8
1BTN Ichiro Suzuki 5.00
2BTN Jason Giambi 2.50
3BTN Mike Piazza 5.00
4BTN Brian Giles 1.00
5BTN Barry Bonds 8.00
6BTN Pedro J. Martinez 3.00
7BTN Nomar Garciaparra 5.00
8BTN Randy Johnson 3.00
9BTN Craig Biggio 1.00
10BTN Manny Ramirez 3.00
11BTN Mike Mussina 1.50
12BTN Kerry Wood 2.50
13BTN Jim Edmonds 1.00
14BTN Ivan Rodriguez 2.50
15BTN Jeff Bagwell 3.00
16BTN Roger Clemens 4.50
17BTN Chipper Jones 4.00
18BTN Shawn Green 1.25
19BTN Albert Pujols 6.00
20BTN Andruw Jones 3.00
21BTN Luis Gonzalez 1.00
22BTN Todd Helton 3.00
23BTN Jorge Posada 1.25
24BTN Scott Rolen 2.50
25BTN Ben Sheets 1.00
26BTN Alfonso Soriano 2.50
27BTN Greg Maddux 4.00
28BTN Gary Sheffield 1.25
29BTN Barry Zito 1.25
30BTN Alex Rodriguez 6.00
31BTN Larry Walker 1.00
32BTN Derek Jeter 8.00
33BTN Ken Griffey Jr. 5.00
34BTN Vladimir Guerrero 3.00
35BTN Sammy Sosa 5.00

Behind the Numbers Game Jersey

NM/M

Common Player: 5.00
Inserted 1:24
1 Jeff Bagwell 10.00
2 Craig Biggio/Pants 5.00
4 Roger Clemens 20.00
5 Jim Edmonds 5.00
6 Brian Giles 5.00
7 Luis Gonzalez 5.00
8 Shawn Green 5.00
9 Todd Helton 8.00
10 Derek Jeter/SP 30.00
11 Randy Johnson/SP 10.00
12 Andruw Jones 8.00
13 Chipper Jones 10.00
14 Greg Maddux 10.00
15 Pedro J. Martinez 10.00
16 Mike Mussina 10.00
17 Mike Piazza/Pants 10.00
18 Jorge Posada 8.00
19 Manny Ramirez 8.00
20 Alex Rodriguez 10.00
21 Ivan Rodriguez 8.00
22 Scott Rolen 8.00
23 Alfonso Soriano/SP 10.00
24 Barry Zito 6.00

Behind the Numbers Game Jersey Dual

No Pricing
Production 25 Sets

Barry Bonds 4X MVP

NM/M

Complete Set (4): 20.00

Common Bonds: 6.00
1BB4X Barry Bonds/1990 6.00
2BB4X Barry Bonds/1,992 6.00
3BB4X Barry Bonds/1,993 6.00
4BB4X Barry Bonds/2,001 6.00

Game Essentials

NM/M

Common Player: 5.00
Carlos Beltran 5.00
Kevin Brown 5.00
Jeromy Burnitz 5.00
Carlos Delgado 8.00
Jason Hart/SP 8.00
Rickey Henderson 20.00
Drew Henson/Shoe 5.00
Drew Henson/Glove 8.00
Derek Jeter/Shoe 40.00
Jason Kendall 5.00
Jeff Kent 10.00
Barry Larkin/Glove 20.00
Javy Lopez 8.00
Raul Mondesi/Btg Glove 8.00
Rafael Palmeiro 10.00
Adam Piatt 5.00
Brad Radke 5.00
Cal Ripken Jr. 30.00
Mariano Rivera 10.00
Alex Rodriguez/Btg Glove 15.00
Ivan Rodriguez/Shoe 10.00
Kazuhiro Sasaki 5.00
J.T. Snow 5.00
Mo Vaughn 5.00
Robin Ventura 8.00
Jose Vidro 5.00
Matt Williams 5.00

HardWear

NM/M

Complete Set (10): 60.00
Common Player: 4.00
Inserted 1:72Hobby
1HW Ivan Rodriguez 4.00
2HW Mike Piazza 8.00
3HW Derek Jeter 15.00
4HW Barry Bonds 15.00
5HW Todd Helton 4.00
6HW Roberto Alomar 4.00
7HW Albert Pujols 10.00
8HW Ichiro Suzuki 8.00
9HW Ken Griffey Jr. 8.00
10HW Jason Giambi 5.00

Hit and Run

NM/M

Complete Set (30): 50.00
Common Player: 1.00
Inserted 1:12
1 Adam Dunn 1.00
2 Derek Jeter 6.00
3 Frank Thomas 2.00
4 Albert Pujols 5.00
5 J.D. Drew 1.00
6 Richard Hidalgo 1.00

7 John Olerud 1.00
8 Roberto Alomar 1.00
9 Pat Burrell 1.50
10 Darin Erstad 1.50
11 Mark Grace 1.00
12 Chipper Jones 3.00
13 Jose Vidro 1.00
14 Cliff Floyd 1.00
15 Mo Vaughn 1.00
16 Nomar Garciaparra 4.00
17 Ivan Rodriguez 1.50
18 Luis Gonzalez 1.00
19 Jason Giambi 1.50
20 Bernie Williams 1.00
21 Mike Piazza 4.00
22 Barry Bonds 6.00
23 Jose Ortiz 1.00
24 Magglio Ordonez 1.00
25 Troy Glaus 2.00
26 Alex Rodriguez 5.00
27 Ichiro Suzuki 4.00
28 Sammy Sosa 4.00
29 Ken Griffey Jr. 4.00
30 Vladimir Guerrero 2.00

Hit and Run Game Base

NM/M

Inserted 1:120
1 J.D. Drew 4.00
2 Adam Dunn 6.00
3 Jason Giambi 6.00
4 Troy Glaus 6.00
5 Ken Griffey Jr. 10.00
6 Vladimir Guerrero 8.00
7 Albert Pujols 15.00
8 Sammy Sosa 10.00
9 Ichiro Suzuki 15.00
10 Bernie Williams 6.00

Hit and Run Game Bat

NM/M

Common Player: 4.00
Inserted 1:24
1 Roberto Alomar 6.00
2 J.D. Drew 4.00
3 Darin Erstad 4.00
4 Cliff Floyd 4.00
5 Nomar Garciaparra 15.00
6 Luis Gonzalez 6.00
7 Richard Hidalgo 4.00
8 Derek Jeter 25.00
9 Chipper Jones 8.00
10 John Olerud 4.00
11 Magglio Ordonez 6.00
12 Jose Ortiz 4.00
13 Mike Piazza 10.00
14 Alex Rodriguez 15.00
15 Ivan Rodriguez 8.00
16 Frank Thomas 8.00
17 Mo Vaughn 4.00
18 Jose Vidro 4.00
19 Bernie Williams 8.00

Hit and Run Game Bat and Base

NM/M

Common Player: 10.00
Inserted 1:240
1 Roberto Alomar 15.00
2 Barry Bonds/SP 50.00
3 Nomar Garciaparra 30.00
4 Derek Jeter 40.00
5 Chipper Jones 15.00
6 Mike Piazza 20.00
7 Alex Rodriguez 25.00
8 Mo Vaughn 10.00

Derek Jeter 4X Champ

NM/M

Complete Set (4): 20.00
Common Jeter: 6.00
1DJFX Derek Jeter/1,996 6.00
2DJFX Derek Jeter/1,998 6.00
3DJFX Derek Jeter/1,999 6.00
4DJFX Derek Jeter/2,000 6.00

2002 Fleer Fall Classic

NM/M

Complete Set (100): 30.00

Common Player: .25
Common SP: 3.00
Inserted 1:18 Hobby
Pack (5): 5.00
Box (24): 100.00
1 Rabbit Maranville .25
2 Tris Speaker .75
3 Harmon Killebrew 1.00
4 Lou Gehrig 2.00
5 Lou Boudreau .25
6 Al Kaline 1.00
7 Paul Molitor 1.00
7 Paul Molitor/Brewers 4.00
8 Cal Ripken Jr. 3.00
9 Yogi Berra 1.00
10 Phil Rizzuto .75
11 Luis Aparicio .25
11 Luis Aparicio/Orioles 4.00
12 Stan Musial 2.00
13 Mel Ott .75
14 Larry Doby .25
15 Ozzie Smith 1.00
16 Babe Ruth 4.00
16 Babe Ruth/Red Sox 10.00
17 Red Schoendienst .25
17 Red Schoendienst/Cards 3.00
18 Rollie Fingers .25
19 Thurman Munson 1.50
20 Lou Brock .50
21 Paul O'Neill .25
21 Paul O'Neill/Reds 3.00
22 Jim Palmer .50
23 Kirby Puckett 1.00
24 Tony Perez .25
24 Tony Perez/Phila. 3.00
25 Don Larsen .75
26 Steve Garvey .25
26 Steve Garvey/Padres 3.00
27 Jim "Catfish" Hunter .25
27 "Catfish" Hunter/Yanks 4.00
28 Juan Marichal .50
29 Pee Wee Reese .25
30 Orlando Cepeda .25
31 Rich "Goose" Gossage .25
32 Ray Knight .25
33 Eddie Murray .75
34 Nolan Ryan 3.00
35 Alan Trammell .50
36 Grover Alexander .75
37 Joe Carter .25
38 Rogers Hornsby 1.00
39 Jimmie Foxx 1.00
40 Mike Schmidt 1.50
41 Eddie Mathews 1.00
42 Jackie Robinson 1.50
43 Eddie Collins .25
43 Eddie Collins/White Sox 3.00
44 Willie McCovey .25
45 Bob Gibson 1.00
46 Keith Hernandez .50
46 Keith Hernandez/Cards 4.00
47 Brooks Robinson 1.00
48 Mordecai Brown .25
49 Gary Carter .50
50 Kirk Gibson .25
50 Kirk Gibson/Tigers 3.00
51 Johnny Mize .25
52 Johnny Podres .25
53 Darrell Porter .25
54 Willie Stargell .75
55 Lenny Dykstra .25
55 Lenny Dykstra/Phila. 3.00
56 Christy Mathewson .75
57 Walter Johnson 1.00
58 Whitey Ford .75
59 Lefty Grove .50
60 Duke Snider .75
61 Cy Young 1.00
62 Dave Winfield .75
62 Dave Winfield/Yanks 5.00
63 Robin Yount 1.00
64 Fred Lynn .25
65 Ty Cobb 2.00
66 Joe Morgan .25
67 Bill Mazeroski .25
68 Frank Baker .25
69 Chief Bender .25
70 Carlton Fisk .50
71 Jerry Coleman .25
72 Frankie Frisch .25
73 Wade Boggs 1.00
73 Wade Boggs/Yanks 4.00
74 Johnny Bench 1.00
75 Roger Maris 2.00
75 Roger Maris/Cards 8.00
76 Dom DiMaggio .25
77 George Brett 3.00
78 Dave Parker .25
78 Dave Parker/A's 3.00
79 Hank Greenberg .25
80 Pepper Martin .25
81 Graig Nettles .25
81 Graig Nettles/Padres 3.00
82 Dennis Eckersley .50
83 Donn Clendenon .25
84 Tom Seaver 1.00
85 Honus Wagner 1.50
86 Reggie Jackson .75
86 Reggie Jackson/A's 5.00
87 Goose Goslin .25
87 Goose Goslin/Tigers 3.00
88 Tony Kubek .25
89 Roy Campanella 1.00
90 Steve Carlton/Cards 4.00
91 Lou Gehrig, Mel Ott 2.00
92 Eddie Collins, Joe Morgan .25
93 George Brett, Mike Schmidt 2.00
94 Cal Ripken Jr., Ozzie Smith 3.00
95 Thurman Munson, Johnny Bench 1.50
96 Willie Stargell, Stan Musial, Pepper Martin 1.00
97 Babe Ruth, Kirby Puckett, Reggie Jackson 3.00
98 Cy Young, Bob Gibson 1.00
99 Whitey Ford, Steve Carlton 1.00
100 Paul Molitor, Lou Brock .50

Championship Gold

Golds: 5-10X
Gold SP's: 1-2X
Production 50 Sets

HOF Plaque

NM/M

Complete Set (30): 90.00
Common Player: 3.00
#'d to HOF induction year
1HOF Babe Ruth 8.00
2HOF Christy Mathewson 3.00
3HOF Honus Wagner 4.00
4HOF Ty Cobb 5.00
5HOF Walter Johnson 4.00
6HOF Cy Young 4.00
7HOF Tris Speaker 3.00
8HOF Eddie Collins 3.00
9HOF Lou Gehrig 6.00
10HOF Jimmie Foxx 4.00
11HOF Jackie Robinson 6.00
12HOF Stan Musial 5.00
13HOF Yogi Berra 4.00
14HOF Duke Snider 4.00
15HOF Juan Marichal 3.00
16HOF Luis Aparicio 3.00
17HOF Pee Wee Reese 3.00
18HOF Willie McCovey 3.00
19HOF Willie Stargell 3.00
20HOF Johnny Bench 5.00
21HOF Joe Morgan 3.00
22HOF Jim Palmer 3.00
23HOF Tom Seaver 5.00
24HOF Reggie Jackson 4.00
25HOF Steve Carlton 3.00
26HOF George Brett 6.00
27HOF Nolan Ryan 8.00
28HOF Robin Yount 4.00
29HOF Kirby Puckett 5.00
30HOF Ozzie Smith 4.00

MVP Collection Game-Used

NM/M

Common Player: 5.00
Inserted 1:100
Golds: .75-2X
Production 100 Sets
JB Johnny Bench/200 20.00
DC Donn Clendenon 5.00
RF Rollie Fingers/200 5.00
RJOK Reggie Jackson/50 20.00
RJNY Reggie Jackson 10.00
RK Ray Knight 5.00
PM Paul Molitor/250 15.00
DP Darrell Porter/250 5.00
BR Brooks Robinson/250 20.00
WS Willie Stargell/200 10.00
AT Alan Trammell 10.00

MVP Collection Patch

NM/M

Numbered to MVP year.
JB Johnny Bench/76 45.00
RF Rollie Fingers/74 20.00
RJNY Reggie Jackson/77 40.00
BR Brooks Robinson/70 40.00
AT Alan Trammell/84 30.00

October Legends

NM/M

Common Player: 5.00
Inserted 1:48
Golds: .75-1.5X
Production 100 Sets
Joe Morgan 5.00
Wade Boggs/60 20.00
Keith Hernandez/100 15.00
Robin Yount 10.00
Eddie Murray 10.00
Lenny Dykstra/200 8.00
Paul O'Neill 8.00
Red Schoendienst/210 8.00
Pepper Martin/50 15.00
Keith Hernandez/150 20.00
Willie Stargell/225 12.00
George Brett 20.00
Dave Parker/50 10.00
Tony Perez 5.00
Rollie Fingers 5.00
Gary Carter/200 10.00
Dennis Eckersley 5.00
Juan Marichal 8.00
Pee Wee Reese/200 15.00
Roger Maris 60.00
Duke Snider/200 15.00
Darrell Porter/150 5.00
Willie McCovey/150 10.00
Paul Molitor/150 15.00

October Legends Dual

NM/M

Common Card: 10.00
SP's Noted
Rollie Fingers, Dennis Eckersley 12.00
Keith Hernandez, Red Schoendienst 12.00
Joe Morgan, Tony Perez 10.00
Wade Boggs, Keith Hernandez 20.00
Lenny Dykstra, Gary Carter 12.00
Robin Yount, Paul Molitor/150 35.00
Roger Maris, Paul O'Neill/200 50.00
Duke Snider, Pee Wee Reese/200 25.00
Juan Marichal, Willie McCovey 15.00
George Brett, Darrell Porter/150 35.00
Willie Stargell, Dave Parker 15.00
Gary Carter, Keith Hernandez 10.00
Cal Ripken Jr., Eddie Murray/200 40.00
Cal Ripken Jr., Eddie Murray/100 50.00
Pepper Martin, Frankie Frisch 15.00

Pennant Chase

NM/M

Common Player: 10.00
Inserted 1:48 Hobby
Yogi Berra/Pants/150 20.00
Carlton Fisk/Bat 10.00
Reggie Jackson/Jsy 10.00
Fred Lynn/Bat 10.00
Thurman Munson/Bat 30.00
Wade Boggs/Jsy 10.00
Dave Winfield/Bat 10.00

Pennant Chase Dual

NM/M

Production 50 Sets
CFRJ Carlton Fisk/Bat, Reggie Jackson/Jsy 30.00
FLTM Fred Lynn/Bat, Thurman Munson/Bat 50.00
WBDW Wade Boggs/Jsy, Dave Winfield/Bat 30.00

Rival Factions

NM/M

Common Card: 2.00
1-24 #'d to 1,000
25-36 #'d to 500

37-43 #'d to 50
1RF Carlton Fisk, Thurman Munson 3.00
2RF Frank Baker, Babe Ruth 8.00
3RF Jimmie Foxx, Lou Gehrig 6.00
4RF Steve Carlton, Nolan Ryan 8.00
5RF Mordecai Brown, Honus Wagner 3.00
6RF Frankie Frisch, Duke Snider 3.00
7RF Ozzie Smith, Alan Trammell 3.00
8RF Larry Doby, Jackie Robinson 5.00
9RF Steve Garvey, Tony Perez 2.00
10RF Johnny Bench, Willie Stargell 4.00
11RF Ty Cobb, Eddie Collins 5.00
12RF Reggie Jackson, Brooks Robinson 4.00
13RF Yogi Berra, Roy Campanella 4.00
14RF Orlando Cepeda, Willie McCovey 2.00
15RF Al Kaline, Jim Palmer 4.00
16RF George Brett, Kirby Puckett 6.00
17RF Bob Gibson, Tom Seaver 4.00
18RF Cal Ripken Jr., Robin Yount 8.00
19RF Johnny Mize, Mel Ott 3.00
20RF Stan Musial, Pee Wee Reese 4.00
21RF Hank Greenburg, Lefty Grove 2.00
22RF Dave Parker, Mike Schmidt 4.00
23RF Bill Mazeroski, Joe Morgan 3.00
24RF Johnny Bench, Carlton Fisk 5.00
25RF George Brett, Mike Schmidt 8.00
26RF Pee Wee Reese, Phil Rizzuto 4.00
27RF Cal Ripken Jr., Alan Trammell 15.00
28RF Tom Seaver, Jim "Catfish" Hunter 4.00
29RF Ty Cobb, Honus Wagner 5.00
30RF Steve Carlton, Lefty Grove 3.00
31RF Ozzie Smith, Robin Yount 8.00
32RF Frankie Frisch, Joe Morgan 3.00
33RF Hank Greenberg, Jackie Robinson 5.00
34RF Jimmie Foxx, Pepper Martin 5.00
35RF Lou Gehrig, Cal Ripken Jr. 40.00
36RF Ozzie Smith, Honus Wagner 40.00
37RF Reggie Jackson, Dave Winfield 20.00
38RF Ty Cobb, Rogers Hornsby 35.00
39RF Babe Ruth, Roger Maris 50.00
40RF Yogi Berra, Thurman Munson 20.00
41RF Nolan Ryan, Tom Seaver 50.00
42RF Joe Morgan, Jackie Robinson 20.00
43RF Jimmie Foxx, Mel Ott 25.00

Rival Factions Game-Used Single

NM/M

Common Card: 8.00
Inserted 1:32
Carlton Fisk, Thurman Munson 25.00
Frank Baker, Babe Ruth 25.00
Jimmie Foxx, Lou Gehrig 35.00
Steve Carlton, Nolan Ryan 25.00
Frankie Frisch, Duke Snider 20.00
Ozzie Smith, Alan Trammell 15.00
Larry Doby, Jackie Robinson 15.00
Steve Garvey, Tony Perez 10.00
Johnny Bench, Willie Stargell 10.00
Reggie Jackson, Brooks Robinson 12.00
Orlando Cepeda, Willie McCovey 10.00
Al Kaline, Jim Palmer 10.00
George Brett, Kirby Puckett 25.00
Bob Gibson, Tom Seaver 20.00
Cal Ripken Jr., Robin Yount 30.00
Stan Musial, Pee Wee Reese 25.00
Hank Greenberg, Lefty Grove 20.00
Bill Mazeroski, Joe Morgan 8.00
Johnny Bench, Carlton Fisk 10.00
George Brett, Mike Schmidt 25.00
Pee Wee Reese, Phil Rizzuto 15.00
Cal Ripken Jr., Alan Trammell 35.00
Steve Carlton, Lefty Grove 15.00
Ozzie Smith, Robin Yount 15.00
Frankie Frisch, Joe Morgan 25.00
Hank Greenberg, Jackie Robinson 20.00
Jimmie Foxx, Pepper Martin 30.00
Lou Gehrig, Cal Ripken Jr. 40.00
Reggie Jackson, Dave Winfield 10.00
Babe Ruth, Roger Maris 60.00
Nolan Ryan, Tom Seaver 35.00

Rival Factions Game-Used Dual

NM/M

Common Card: 12.00
Carlton Fisk, Thurman Munson 30.00
Steve Carlton, Nolan Ryan 40.00
Frankie Frisch, Duke Snider 15.00
Ozzie Smith, Alan Trammell 25.00
Larry Doby, Jackie Robinson/75 60.00
Steve Garvey, Tony Perez 10.00
Johnny Bench, Willie Stargell 20.00
Reggie Jackson, Brooks Robinson 20.00
Orlando Cepeda, Willie McCovey/200 15.00
George Brett, Kirby Puckett 40.00
Cal Ripken Jr., Robin Yount 30.00
Johnny Bench, Carlton Fisk 20.00
Cal Ripken Jr., Alan Trammell 30.00
Jim "Catfish" Hunter, Tom Seaver 15.00
Ozzie Smith, Robin Yount 25.00
Frankie Frisch, Joe Morgan 15.00
Hank Greenberg, Jackie Robinson/50 100.00
Jimmie Foxx, Pepper Martin/200 40.00
Reggie Jackson, Dave Winfield/150 20.00
Yogi Berra, Thurman Munson 40.00
Nolan Ryan, Tom Seaver 45.00
Joe Morgan, Jackie Robinson/50 50.00

Rival Factions Dual Patch

NM/M

Production 50 Sets 12.00
Carlton Fisk, Thurman Munson 60.00
Steve Carlton, Nolan Ryan 100.00
Ozzie Smith, Alan Trammell 50.00

Steve Garvey,
Tony Perez 30.00
Johnny Bench,
Willie Stargell 50.00
Cal Ripken Jr.,
Robin Yount 125.00
Johnny Bench,
Carlton Fisk 50.00
Cal Ripken Jr.,
Alan Trammell 100.00
Ozzie Smith,
Robin Yount 60.00
Reggie Jackson,
Dave Winfield 40.00

Series of Champions

NM/M
Complete Set (19): 25.00
Common Player: 1.00
Inserted 1:6
1 Yogi Berra 2.00
2 Wade Boggs 2.00
3 Dave Parker 1.00
4 Joe Carter 1.00
5 Kirk Gibson 1.00
6 Reggie Jackson 2.00
7 Tony Kubek 1.00
8 Don Larsen 1.00
9 Bill Mazeroski 1.00
10 Eddie Murray 1.50
11 Graig Nettles 1.00
12 Tony Perez 1.00
13 Phil Rizzuto 1.50
14 Mike Schmidt 2.50
15 Red Schoendienst 1.00
16 Duke Snider 2.00
17 Ty Cobb 2.50
18 Lou Gehrig 3.00
19 Babe Ruth 4.00

Series of Champions Game-Used

NM/M
Common Player: 5.00
Inserted 1:36
Golds: .75-1.5X
Production 100 Sets
Bat Knob numbered to 10 not priced.
Yogi Berra/Bat 15.00
Wade Boggs/Jsy 10.00
Dave Parker/Bat 5.00
Joe Carter/Bat 5.00
Kirk Gibson/Bat 5.00
Reggie Jackson/Bat 10.00
Tony Kubek/Bat 10.00
Eddie Murray/Bat 10.00
Graig Nettles/Bat 5.00
Tony Perez/Bat 5.00
Red Schoendienst/Jsy 5.00
Duke Snider/Bat 10.00
Babe Ruth/Bat/25 180.00

2002 Fleer Flair

NM/M
Complete Set (138):
Common Player: .25
Common (101-138): 3.00
Production 1,750
Pack (5): 4.00
Hobby Box (20): 70.00
1 Scott Rolen .75
2 Derek Jeter 3.00
3 Sean Casey .40
4 Hideo Nomo .75
5 Craig Biggio .50
6 Randy Johnson 1.00
7 J.D. Drew .50
8 Greg Maddux 1.50
9 Paul LoDuca .25
10 John Olerud .25
11 Barry Larkin .50
12 Mark Grace .35
13 Jimmy Rollins .25
14 Todd Helton 1.00
15 Jim Edmonds .25
16 Roy Oswalt .35
17 Phil Nevin .25
18 Tim Salmon .35
19 Magglio Ordonez .25
20 Roger Clemens 1.75
21 Raul Mondesi .25
22 Edgar Martinez .25
23 Pedro J. Martinez 1.00
24 Edgardo Alfonzo .25
25 Bernie Williams .35
26 Gary Sheffield .40
27 D'Angelo Jimenez .25
28 Toby Hall .25
29 Joe Mays .25
30 Alfonso Soriano .75
31 Mike Piazza 2.00
32 Lance Berkman .25
33 Jim Thome .25
34 Ben Sheets .25
35 Brandon Inge .25
36 Luis Gonzalez .35
37 Jeff Kent .25
38 Ben Grieve .25
39 Carlos Delgado .50
40 Pat Burrell .50
41 Mark Buehrle .25
42 Cristian Guzman .25
43 Shawn Green .40
44 Nomar Garciaparra 2.00
45 Carlos Beltran .60
46 Troy Glaus .75
47 Paul Konerko .25
48 Moises Alou .25
49 Kerry Wood .75
50 Jose Vidro .25
51 Juan Encarnacion .25
52 Bobby Abreu .25
53 C.C. Sabathia .25
54 Alex Rodriguez 2.50
55 Albert Pujols 2.50
56 Bret Boone .25
57 Orlando Hernandez .25
58 Jason Kendall .25
59 Tim Hudson .40
60 Darin Erstad .60
61 Mike Mussina .40
62 Ken Griffey Jr. 2.00
63 Adrian Beltre .35
64 Jeff Bagwell 1.00
65 Vladimir Guerrero 1.00
66 Mike Sweeney .25
67 Sammy Sosa 2.00
68 Andruw Jones .75
69 Richie Sexson .25
70 Matt Morris .25
71 Ivan Rodriguez .75
72 Shannon Stewart .25
73 Barry Bonds 3.00
74 Matt Williams .25
75 Jason Giambi .60
76 Brian Giles .25
77 Cliff Floyd .25
78 Tino Martinez .25
79 Juan Gonzalez 1.00
80 Frank Thomas 1.00
81 Ichiro Suzuki 2.00
82 Barry Zito .35
83 Chipper Jones 1.50
84 Adam Dunn .75
85 Kazuhiro Sasaki .25
86 Mark Quinn .25
87 Rafael Palmeiro .60
88 Jeromy Burnitz .25
89 Curt Schilling .50
90 Chris Richards .25
91 Jon Leiber .25
92 Doug Mientkiewicz .25
93 Roberto Alomar .40
94 Rich Aurilia .25
95 Eric Chavez .35
96 Larry Walker .25
97 Manny Ramirez 1.00
98 Tony Clark .25
99 Tsuyoshi Shinjo .25
100 Josh Beckett .50
101 Dewon Brazelton 3.00
102 Jeremy Lambert **RC** 3.00
103 Andres Torres 3.00
104 Matt Childers **RC** 4.00
105 Wilson Betemit 3.00
106 Willie Harris 3.00
107 Drew Henson 4.00
108 Rafael Soriano 3.00
109 Carlos Valderrama 3.00
110 Victor Martinez 6.00
111 Juan Rivera 3.00
112 Felipe Lopez 3.00
113 Brandon Duckworth 3.00
114 Jeremy Owens 3.00
115 Aaron Cook **RC** 3.00
116 Derrick Lewis 3.00
117 Mark Teixeira 6.00
118 Ken Harvey 5.00
119 Tim Spooneybarger 3.00
120 Bill Hall 3.00
121 Adam Pettyjohn 3.00
122 Ramon Castro 3.00
123 Marlon Byrd 4.00
124 Matt White 3.00
125 Eric Cyr **RC** 3.00
126 Morgan Ensberg 3.00
127 Horacio Ramirez 4.00
128 Ron Calloway **RC** 3.00
129 Nick Punto 3.00
130 Joe Kennedy 3.00
131 So Taguchi **RC** 5.00
132 Austin Kearns 4.00
133 Mark Prior 6.00
134 Kazuhisa Ishii **RC** 8.00
135 Steve Torrealba 3.00
136 Adam Walker **RC** 3.00
137 Travis Hafner 4.00
138 Zach Day 3.00

Collection

Collection (1-100): 4-6X
Production 175
Collection (101-138): 1-2X
Production 50

Hot Numbers

NM/M
Common Player: 15.00
Production 100 Sets
Manny Ramirez 30.00
Randy Johnson 30.00
Curt Schilling 25.00
Pedro J. Martinez 30.00
Nomar Garciaparra 50.00
Barry Larkin 15.00
Todd Helton 30.00
Larry Walker 15.00
Sean Casey 20.00
Jeff Bagwell 30.00
Craig Biggio 15.00
Shawn Green 20.00
Edgardo Alfonzo 15.00
Mike Piazza 50.00
Derek Jeter 75.00
Chipper Jones 40.00
Jim Edmonds 15.00
J.D. Drew 20.00
Ivan Rodriguez 25.00
Rafael Palmeiro 25.00
Alex Rodriguez 60.00
Greg Maddux 40.00
Carlos Delgado 20.00

Jersey Heights

NM/M
Common Player: 4.00
Inserted 1:18 Hobby
1JH Edgardo Alfonzo 4.00
2JH Jeff Bagwell 8.00
3JH Craig Biggio 4.00
4JH Barry Bonds 20.00
5JH Sean Casey 4.00
6JH Roger Clemens 15.00
7JH Carlos Delgado 6.00
8JH J.D. Drew 6.00
9JH Jim Edmonds 6.00
10JH Nomar Garciaparra 15.00
11JH Shawn Green 5.00
12JH Todd Helton 8.00
13JH Derek Jeter 20.00
14JH Randy Johnson 8.00
15JH Chipper Jones 8.00
16JH Barry Larkin 6.00
17JH Greg Maddux 10.00
18JH Pedro J. Martinez 8.00
19JH Rafael Palmeiro 8.00
20JH Mike Piazza 10.00
21JH Manny Ramirez 8.00
22JH Alex Rodriguez 15.00
23JH Ivan Rodriguez 6.00
24JH Curt Schilling 6.00
25JH Larry Walker 4.00

Jersey Heights (Dual)

NM/M
Common Card: 15.00
Production 100 Sets
Randy Johnson,
Curt Schilling 30.00
Pedro J. Martinez,
Nomar Garciaparra 50.00
Edgardo Alfonzo,
Mike Piazza 30.00
Derek Jeter,
Roger Clemens 75.00
Greg Maddux,
Chipper Jones 40.00
Jim Edmonds,
Jeff Bagwell 20.00
Jeff Bagwell,
Craig Biggio 25.00
Rafael Palmeiro,
Ivan Rodriguez 25.00
Carlos Delgado,
Shawn Green 15.00
Todd Helton,
Larry Walker 20.00
Sean Casey,
Barry Larkin 25.00
Alex Rodriguez,
Manny Ramirez 40.00

Power Tools

NM/M
Common Player: 4.00
Inserted 1:19
Golds: 1-2.5X
Production 100
1PT Roberto Alomar 6.00
2PT Jeff Bagwell/150 8.00
3PT Craig Biggio 4.00
4PT Barry Bonds 15.00
5PT Bret Boone 4.00
6PT Pat Burrell/225 6.00
8PT Eric Chavez 5.00
9PT J.D. Drew/150 8.00
10PT Jim Edmonds 6.00
11PT Juan Gonzalez 6.00
12PT Luis Gonzalez 4.00
13PT Shawn Green 5.00
15PT Derek Jeter 25.00
16PT Doug Mientkiewicz 4.00
17PT Magglio Ordonez 4.00
18PT Rafael Palmeiro/100 8.00
19PT Mike Piazza 10.00
20PT Alex Rodriguez 15.00
21PT Ivan Rodriguez 8.00
22PT Scott Rolen/42 15.00
23PT Reggie Sanders/120 5.00
24PT Gary Sheffield 6.00
25PT Tsuyoshi Shinjo 5.00
26PT Miguel Tejada 6.00
27PT Frank Thomas 8.00
28PT Jim Thome/225 15.00
29PT Larry Walker 4.00
30PT Bernie Williams 6.00

Power Tools Dual

NM/M
Common Card: 10.00
Inserted 1:40
Golds: 1-2.5X
Production 50 Sets
1 Eric Chavez,
Miguel Tejada 10.00
2 Barry Bonds,
Tsuyoshi Shinjo 25.00
3 Jim Edmonds,
J.D. Drew 15.00
4 Jeff Bagwell,
Craig Biggio 15.00
5 Bernie Williams,
Derek Jeter 35.00
6 Roberto Alomar,
Mike Piazza 20.00
7 Sean Casey,
Jim Thome/40 30.00
8 Pat Burrell,
Scott Rolen 15.00
9 Gary Sheffield,
Shawn Green 10.00
10 Ivan Rodriguez,
Alex Rodriguez 15.00
11 Juan Gonzalez,
Rafael Palmeiro 15.00
12 Magglio Ordonez,
Frank Thomas 15.00
13 Larry Walker,
Todd Helton/225 10.00
14 Luis Gonzalez,
Reggie Sanders 10.00
15 Doug Mientkiewicz,
Bret Boone 10.00

Sweet Swatch Autographs

NM/M
Common Player: 15.00
Quantity produced listed
Golds: No Pricing
Production 15 Sets
Derek Jeter/375 100.00
Barry Bonds/35 200.00
Drew Henson/785 40.00
Mark Teixeira/185 40.00
Dewon Brazelton/185 15.00
Mark Prior/285 40.00
Marlon Byrd/185 15.00
Ozzie Smith/185 65.00
Ron Cey/285 20.00
Paul Molitor/85 50.00
Maury Wills/285 20.00
Dale Murphy/285 60.00
David Espinosa/485 15.00
Dane Sardinha/485 15.00
Ben Sheets/85 50.00
Tony Perez/115 20.00
Brooks Robinson/
185 50.00
So Taguchi/335 30.00
Al Kaline/285 50.00
Kazuhisa Ishii/335 30.00
Albert Pujols/50 125.00
Don Mattingly/85 150.00

Sweet Swatch Game-Used

NM/M
Common Player: 8.00
1:Hobby Box
Jeff Bagwell/490 10.00
Josh Beckett/500 10.00
Darin Erstad/525 8.00
Freddy Garcia/620 8.00
Brian Giles/445 10.00
Juan Gonzalez/505 10.00
Mark Grace/795 15.00
Derek Jeter/525 40.00
Jason Kendall/990 10.00
Paul LoDuca/440 10.00
Greg Maddux/475 15.00
Magglio Ordonez/495 10.00
Rafael Palmeiro/535 10.00
Mike Piazza/1,000 15.00
Alex Rodriguez/550 25.00
Ivan Rodriguez/475 10.00
Tim Salmon/465 8.00
Kazuhiro Sasaki/770 8.00
Alfonso Soriano/775 10.00
Larry Walker/430 8.00
Ted Williams/250 125.00

Sweet Swatch Patch

NM/M
Common Player: 25.00
Random Box Topper
Jeff Bagwell/45 75.00
Josh Beckett/60 55.00
Darin Erstad/50 40.00
Freddy Garcia/50 40.00
Juan Gonzalez/55 75.00
Mark Grace/75 60.00
Jason Kendall/120 25.00
Paul LoDuca/50 35.00
Greg Maddux/50 90.00
Magglio Ordonez/55 40.00
Rafael Palmeiro/60 40.00
Mike Piazza/95 100.00
Alex Rodriguez/50 90.00
Ivan Rodriguez/50 60.00
Tim Salmon/40 40.00
Kazuhiro Sasaki/80 50.00
Alfonso Soriano/35 65.00
Larry Walker/60 40.00

2002 Fleer Focus Jersey Edition

NM/M
Complete Set (260): 60.00
Common Player: .15
Common (226-260): 1.00
Inserted 1:4
Pack (10): 2.00
Box (24): 40.00
1 Mike Piazza 1.50
2 Jason Giambi .50
3 Jim Thome .15
4 John Olerud .15
5 J.D. Drew .30
6 Richard Hidalgo .15
7 Rusty Greer .15
8 Tony Batista .15
9 Omar Vizquel .15
10 Randy Johnson .75
11 Cristian Guzman .15
12 Mark Grace .25
13 Jeff Cirillo .15
14 Mike Cameron .15
15 Jeromy Burnitz .15
16 Pokey Reese .15
17 Richie Sexson .15
18 Joe Randa .15
19 Aramis Ramirez .15
20 Pedro J. Martinez .75
21 Todd Hollandsworth .15
22 Rondell White .15
23 Tsuyoshi Shinjo .15
24 Melvin Mora .15
25 Tim Hudson .30
26 Darrin Fletcher .15
27 Bill Mueller .15
28 Jeff Weaver .15
29 Tony Clark .15
30 Tom Glavine .40
31 Jarrod Washburn .15
32 Greg Vaughn .15
33 Lee Stevens .15
34 Charles Johnson .15
35 Lance Berkman .15
36 Bud Smith .15
37 Keith Foulke .15
38 Ben Davis .15
39 Daryle Ward .15
40 Bernie Williams .30
41 Dean Palmer .15
42 Mark Mulder .15
43 Jason LaRue .15
44 Jay Gibbons .15
45 Brandon Duckworth .15
46 Carlos Delgado .40
47 Barry Zito .25
48 Matt Morris .15
49 J.T. Snow .15
50 Albert Pujols 1.50
51 Brad Fullmer .15
52 Damion Easley .15
53 Pat Burrell .40
54 Kevin Brown .15
55 Todd Walker .15
56 Rich Garces .15
57 Carlos Pena .15
58 Paul LoDuca .15
59 Mike Lieberthal .15
60 Barry Larkin .15
61 Jon Lieber .15
62 Jose Cruz .15
63 Mo Vaughn .15
64 Ivan Rodriguez .60
65 Jorge Posada .25
66 Magglio Ordonez .15
67 Juan Encarnacion .15
68 Shawn Estes .15
69 Kevin Appier .15
70 Jeff Bagwell .75
71 Tim Wakefield .15
72 Shannon Stewart .15
73 Scott Rolen .65
74 Bobby Higginson .15
75 Jim Edmonds .15
76 Adam Dunn .50
77 Eric Chavez .30
78 Adrian Beltre .30
79 Jason Varitek .15
80 Barry Bonds 2.50
81 Edgar Renteria .15
82 Raul Mondesi .15
83 Eric Karros .15
84 Ken Griffey Jr. 1.50
85 Jermaine Dye .15
86 Carlos Beltran .40
87 Mark Quinn .15
88 Terrence Long .15
89 Shawn Green .40
90 Nomar Garciaparra 1.50
91 Sean Casey .25
92 Homer Bush .15
93 Bobby Abreu .15
94 Jamey Wright .15
95 Tony Womack .15
96 Larry Walker .15
97 Doug Mientkiewicz .15
98 Jimmy Rollins .40
99 Brady Anderson .15
100 Derek Jeter 2.50
101 Kevin Young .15
102 Juan Pierre .15
103 Edgar Martinez .15
104 Corey Koskie .15
105 Jeffrey Hammonds .15
106 Luis Gonzalez .25
107 Travis Fryman .15
108 Kerry Wood .50
109 Rafael Palmeiro .60
110 Ichiro Suzuki 1.00
111 Russ Ortiz .15
112 Jeff Kent .15
113 Scott Erickson .15
114 Bruce Chen .15
115 Craig Biggio .15
116 Robin Ventura .15
117 Alex Rodriguez 2.00
118 Roy Oswalt .25
119 Fred McGriff .15
120 Juan Gonzalez .75
121 David Justice .15

122 Pat Hentgen .15
123 Hideo Nomo .65
124 Ramon Ortiz .15
125 David Ortiz .25
126 Phil Nevin .15
127 Ryan Dempster .15
128 Toby Hall .15
129 Vladimir Guerrero .75
130 Chipper Jones 1.00
131 Russell Branyan .15
132 Jose Vidro .15
133 Bubba Trammell .15
134 Tino Martinez .15
135 Greg Maddux 1.00
136 Derrek Lee .15
137 Troy Glaus .75
138 Joe Crede .15
139 Steve Cox .15
140 Sammy Sosa 1.50
141 Corey Patterson .15
142 Vernon Wells .15
143 Matt Lawton .15
144 Gabe Kapler .15
145 Johnny Damon .25
146 Marty Cordova .15
147 Moises Alou .15
148 Fernando Tatis .15
149 Tanyon Sturtze .15
150 Roger Clemens 1.25
151 Paul Konerko .15
152 Chan Ho Park .15
153 Marcus Giles .15
154 David Eckstein .15
155 Mike Lowell .15
156 Preston Wilson .15
157 John Vander Wal .15
158 Tim Salmon .25
159 Andy Pettitte .35
160 Mike Mussina .40
161 Doug Davis .15
162 Peter Bergeron .15
163 Rich Aurilia .15
164 Eric Milton .15
165 Geoff Jenkins .15
166 Todd Helton .75
167 Bret Boone .15
168 Kris Benson .15
169 Brian Anderson .15
170 Roberto Alomar .40
171 Javier Vazquez .15
172 Scott Schoeneweis .15
173 Ryan Klesko .15
174 Jacque Jones .15
175 Andruw Jones .75
176 Aubrey Huff .15
177 Mark Buehrle .15
178 Josh Beckett .40
179 Ben Sheets .15
180 Curt Schilling .40
181 C.C. Sabathia .15
182 Denny Neagle .15
183 Jamie Moyer .15
184 Jason Kendall .15
185 Dee Brown .15
186 Frank Thomas .75
187 Damian Rolls .15
188 Carlos Lee .15
189 Kevin Jarvis .15
190 Manny Ramirez .75
191 Cliff Floyd .15
192 Freddy Garcia .15
193 Orlando Cabrera .15
194 Mike Sweeney .15
195 Gary Sheffield .35
196 Rafael Furcal .15
197 Esteban Loaiza .15
198 Mike Hampton .15
199 Brian Giles .15
200 Darin Erstad .60
201 David Wells .15
202 Kenny Lofton .15
203 Aaron Sele .15
204 Jason Schmidt .15
205 Javy Lopez .15
206 Dmitri Young .15
207 Darryl Kile .15
208 Matt Williams .15
209 Joe Kennedy .15
210 Chuck Knoblauch .15
211 Brian Jordan .15
212 Roberto Person .15
213 Alex Ochoa .15
214 Steve Finley .15
215 Ben Petrick .15
216 Al Leiter .15
217 Mark Kotsay .15
218 Miguel Tejada .35
219 David Segui .15
220 A.J. Burnett .15
221 Marlon Anderson .15
222 Wiki Gonzalez .15
223 Jeff Suppan .15
224 Dave Roberts .15
225 Jose Hernandez .15
226 Angel Berroa 1.00
227 Sean Burroughs 1.00
228 Luis Martinez **RC** 1.00
229 Adrian Burnside **RC** 1.00
230 John Ennis **RC** 1.00
231 Anastacio Martinez **RC** 1.00
232 Hank Blalock 2.00
233 Eric Hinske 1.00
234 Chris Booker **RC** 1.00
235 Colin Young **RC** 1.00
236 Mark Corey **RC** 1.00
237 Satoru Komiyama **RC** 1.00
238 So Taguchi **RC** 2.50
239 Elio Serrano **RC** 1.00
240 Reed Johnson **RC** 2.00
241 Jeremy Lambert **RC** 1.00
242 Chris Baker **RC** 1.00
243 Orlando Hudson 1.00
244 Travis Hughes **RC** 1.00
245 Kevin Frederick **RC** 1.00
246 Rodrigo Rosario **RC** 1.00
247 Jeremy Ward **RC** 1.00
248 Kazuhisa Ishii **RC** 4.00
249 Austin Kearns 1.00
250 Kyle Kane **RC** 1.00
251 Cam Esslinger **RC** 1.00
252 Jeff Austin **RC** 1.00
253 Brian Mallette **RC** 1.00
254 Mark Prior 4.00
255 Mark Teixeira 2.00
256 Carlos Valderrama 1.00
257 Jason Hart 1.00
258 Takahito Nomura **RC** 1.00
259 Matt Thornton 1.00
260 Marlon Byrd 1.00

Century

Cards (1-225): 6-10X
Cards (226-260): .75-1.5X
Production 101-199

Jersey Number Parallel

(1-225) print run 26-50: 10-25X
(1-225) p/r 51-75: 8-15X
(1-225) p/r 76-99: 5-10X
Produced to player's jsy #.

Blue Chips

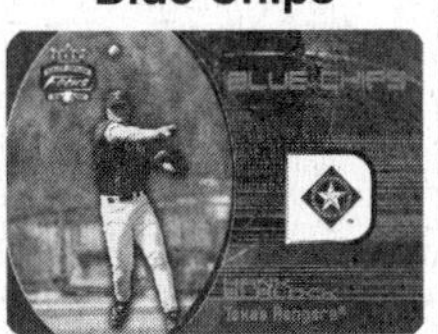

NM/M
Complete Set (15): 10.00
Common Player: .50
Inserted 1:6
1BC Albert Pujols 3.00
2BC Sean Burroughs .50
3BC Vernon Wells .50
4BC Adam Dunn 1.50
5BC Pat Burrell 1.00
6BC Juan Pierre .50
7BC Russell Branyan .50
8BC Carlos Pena .50
9BC Toby Hall .50
10BC Hank Blalock 1.00
11BC Alfonso Soriano 1.50
12BC Jimmy Rollins .75
13BC Jose Ortiz .50
14BC Eric Hinske .50
15BC Nick Johnson .50

Blue Chips Game-Used

NM/M
Inserted 1:96 Hobby
Russell Branyan/Jsy 8.00
Nick Johnson/Jsy 10.00
Nick Johnson/Patch/100 20.00

International Diamond Co.

NM/M
Complete Set (25): 25.00
Common Player: 1.00
Inserted 1:8
1 Bobby Abreu 1.00
2 Adrian Beltre 1.00
3 Jorge Posada 1.00
4 Vladimir Guerrero 3.00
5 Rafael Palmeiro 2.00
6 Sammy Sosa 4.00
7 Larry Walker 1.00
8 Manny Ramirez 3.00
9 Ichiro Suzuki 4.00
10 Jose Cruz 1.00
11 Juan Gonzalez 3.00
12 Bernie Williams 1.00
13 Ivan Rodriguez 2.00
14 Moises Alou 1.00
15 Cristian Guzman 1.00
16 Andruw Jones 3.00
17 Aramis Ramirez 1.00
18 Raul Mondesi 1.00
19 Edgar Martinez 1.00
20 Magglio Ordonez 1.00
21 Roberto Alomar 1.50
22 Chan Ho Park 1.00
23 Kazuhiro Sasaki 1.00
24 Tsuyoshi Shinjo 1.00
25 Hideo Nomo 3.00

International Diamond Co. Game-Used

NM/M
Common Player: 5.00
Inserted 1:144
Jorge Posada/Jsy 15.00
Rafael Palmeiro/Jsy 8.00
Manny Ramirez/Jsy 10.00
Ivan Rodriguez/Jsy 6.00
Andruw Jones/Jsy 6.00
Aramis Ramirez/Jsy 5.00
Raul Mondesi/Jsy 5.00
Edgar Martinez/Jsy 6.00
Chan Ho Park/Jsy 5.00
Kazuhiro Sasaki/Jsy 6.00
Hideo Nomo/Jsy 20.00

International Diamond Co. Patch

NM/M
Common Player: 15.00
Production 100
Manny Ramirez 25.00
Ivan Rodriguez 25.00
Raul Mondesi 15.00
Edgar Martinez 20.00
Chan Ho Park 20.00
Hideo Nomo 75.00

K Corps

NM/M
Complete Set (15): 20.00
Common Player: 1.00
Inserted 1:12
1KC Roger Clemens 5.00
2KC Randy Johnson 3.00
3KC Tom Glavine 1.50
4KC Josh Beckett 1.50
5KC Matt Morris 1.00
6KC Curt Schilling 1.50
7KC Greg Maddux 4.00
8KC Tim Hudson 1.00
9KC Roy Oswalt 1.00
10KC Kerry Wood 2.00
11KC Barry Zito 1.00
12KC Kevin Brown 1.00
13KC Ryan Dempster 1.00
14KC Ben Sheets 1.00
15KC Pedro J. Martinez 3.00

K Corps Game-Used

NM/M
Common Player: 5.00
Inserted 1:96
2KC Randy Johnson/Jsy 15.00
6KC Curt Schilling/Jsy 10.00
7KC Greg Maddux/Jsy 15.00
11KC Barry Zito/Jsy 8.00
12KC Kevin Brown/Jsy 5.00
15KC Pedro Martinez/Jsy 10.00

K Corps Patch

NM/M
Production 100
Curt Schilling 20.00
Kevin Brown 20.00
Pedro Martinez 30.00

Kings of Swing

NM/M
Complete Set (20): 80.00
Common Player: 2.00
Inserted 1:48
1KS Barry Bonds 10.00
2KS Mike Piazza 6.00
3KS Albert Pujols 8.00
4KS Todd Helton 3.00
5KS Ken Griffey Jr. 6.00
6KS Alex Rodriguez 8.00
7KS Sammy Sosa 6.00
8KS Troy Glaus 3.00
9KS Derek Jeter 10.00
10KS Ichiro Suzuki 6.00
11KS Manny Ramirez 3.00
12KS Roberto Alomar 2.00
13KS Juan Gonzalez 3.00
14KS Shawn Green 2.00
15KS Vladimir Guerrero 3.00
16KS Nomar Garciaparra 6.00
17KS Adam Dunn 2.00
18KS Jason Giambi 2.50
19KS Edgar Martinez 2.00
20KS Chipper Jones 4.00

Kings of Swing Game-Used

NM/M
Common Player: 5.00
Inserted 1:108
Mike Piazza 15.00
Todd Helton 8.00
Alex Rodriguez 15.00
Derek Jeter 30.00
Manny Ramirez 8.00
Shawn Green 5.00
Edgar Martinez 5.00
Chipper Jones 10.00

Kings of Swing Patch

NM/M
Production 100
Todd Helton 25.00
Manny Ramirez 25.00
Shawn Green 20.00
Edgar Martinez 25.00
Mike Piazza 40.00

Larger Than Life

NM/M
Common Player: 4.00
Inserted 1:240
1LL Jason Giambi 6.00
2LL Carlos Delgado 5.00
3LL Alex Rodriguez 20.00
4LL Preston Wilson 4.00
5LL Frank Thomas 9.00
6LL Nomar Garciaparra 15.00
7LL Jim Edmonds 4.00
8LL Jim Thome 4.00
9LL Barry Bonds 25.00
10LL Mo Vaughn 4.00
11LL Ichiro Suzuki 20.00
12LL Ivan Rodriguez 5.00
13LL Gary Sheffield 4.00
14LL Derek Jeter 25.00
15LL Jeff Bagwell 9.00
16LL Mike Piazza 15.00
17LL J.D. Drew 4.00
18LL Sammy Sosa 15.00
19LL Albert Pujols 20.00
20LL Luis Gonzalez 4.00

Larger Than Life Game-Used

NM/M
Common Player: 5.00
Inserted 1:144
Alex Rodriguez/Jsy 15.00
Preston Wilson/Jsy 5.00
Frank Thomas/Jsy 10.00
Jim Edmonds/Jsy 6.00
Mo Vaughn/Jsy 5.00
Ivan Rodriguez/Jsy 8.00
Derek Jeter/Jsy 25.00
Jeff Bagwell/Jsy/SP/20 25.00
Mike Piazza/Jsy 15.00
Luis Gonzalez/Jsy 5.00

Larger Than Life Patch

NM/M
Common Player: 15.00
Production 100
Preston Wilson 15.00
Frank Thomas 25.00
Jim Edmonds 15.00
Ivan Rodriguez 25.00
Mike Piazza 40.00
Luis Gonzalez 15.00

Lettermen

No Pricing
Production One Set

Materialistic Away

NM/M
Complete Set (15): 75.00
Common Player: 4.00
Inserted 1:24
Home: 1.5-3X
Production 50 Sets
Away Oversized: .5-1X
One per hobby box.
Home Oversized: 2-4X
Production 50 Sets
1MA Derek Jeter 12.00
2MA Alex Rodriguez 10.00
3MA Mike Piazza 8.00
4MA Ivan Rodriguez 4.00
5MA Chipper Jones 6.00
6MA Todd Helton 5.00
7MA Nomar Garciaparra 8.00
8MA Barry Bonds 12.00
9MA Ichiro Suzuki 8.00
10MA Ken Griffey Jr. 8.00
11MA Jason Giambi 4.00
12MA Sammy Sosa 8.00
13MA Albert Pujols 10.00
14MA Pedro J. Martinez 5.00
15MA Vladimir Guerrero 5.00

2002 Fleer Genuine

NM/M
Complete Set (140):
Common Player: .15
Common (101-140): 3.00
Production 2,002
Pack (5): 3.00
Box (20): 50.00
1 Alex Rodriguez 2.50
2 Manny Ramirez .75
3 Jim Thome .15
4 Eric Milton .15
5 Todd Helton .75
6 Mike Mussina .50
7 Ichiro Suzuki 1.50
8 Randy Johnson 1.00
9 Mark Mulder .15
10 Johnny Damon .25
11 Sean Casey .25
12 Albert Pujols 2.50
13 Mark Grace .25
14 Moises Alou, Mark Mulder .15
15 Raul Mondesi, Roberto Alomar .15
16 Cliff Floyd, Scott Rolen .30
17 Vladimir Guerrero, Tom Glavine .40
18 Pat Burrell, Bobby Abreu .25
19 Ryan Klesko, Nomar Garciaparra .50
20 Mike Hampton, Darin Erstad .15
21 Shawn Green, Cliff Floyd .15
22 Rich Aurilia, Tim Hudson .15
23 Matt Morris, Jim Thome .15
24 Curt Schilling, Nolan Ryan 1.00
25 Kevin Brown, Reggie Jackson .25
26 Adrian Beltre, Rafael Palmeiro .30
27 Joe Mays, Ken Griffey Jr. .75
28 Luis Gonzalez, Sammy Sosa .75
29 Barry Larkin, Vladimir Guerrero .40
30 A.J. Burnett, Ichiro Suzuki .75
31 Eric Munson .15
32 Juan Gonzalez .75
33 Lance Berkman .15
34 Fred McGriff .15
35 Paul Konerko .15
36 Pedro J. Martinez .75
37 Adam Dunn .50
38 Jeromy Burnitz .15
39 Mike Sweeney .15
40 Bret Boone .15
41 Ken Griffey Jr. 2.00
42 Eric Chavez .25
43 Mark Quinn .15
44 Roberto Alomar .35
45 Bobby Abreu .15
46 Bartolo Colon .15
47 Jimmy Rollins .25
48 Chipper Jones 1.00
49 Ben Sheets .15
50 Freddy Garcia .15
51 Sammy Sosa 2.00
52 Rafael Palmeiro .65
53 Preston Wilson .15
54 Troy Glaus .75
55 Josh Beckett .50
56 C.C. Sabathia .15
57 Magglio Ordonez .15
58 Brian Giles .15
59 Darin Erstad .60
60 Gary Sheffield .35
61 Paul LoDuca .15
62 Derek Jeter 3.00
63 Greg Maddux 1.50
64 Kerry Wood .65
65 Toby Hall .15
66 Barry Bonds 3.00
67 Jeff Bagwell .75
68 Jason Kendall .15
69 Richard Hidalgo .15
70 J.D. Drew .30
71 Tom Glavine .25
72 Javier Vazquez .15
73 Doug Mientkiewicz .15
74 Jason Giambi .50
75 Carlos Delgado .40
76 Aramis Ramirez .15
77 Torii Hunter .15
78 Ivan Rodriguez .65
79 Charles Johnson .15
80 Jeff Kent .15
81 Jacque Jones .15
82 Larry Walker .15
83 Cristian Guzman .15
84 Jermaine Dye .15
85 Roger Clemens 1.75
86 Mike Piazza 2.00
87 Craig Biggio .15
88 Phil Nevin .15
89 Jeff Cirillo .15
90 Barry Zito .25
91 Ryan Dempster .15
92 Mark Buehrle .15
93 Nomar Garciaparra 2.00
94 Frank Thomas .75
95 Jim Edmonds .15
96 Geoff Jenkins .15
97 Scott Rolen .65
98 Tim Hudson .25
99 Shannon Stewart .15
100 Richie Sexson .15

101 Orlando Hudson 3.00
102 Doug DeVore **RC** 3.00
103 Rene Reyes **RC** 3.00
104 Steve Bechler **RC** 4.00
105 Jorge Nunez **RC** 3.00
106 Mitch Wylie **RC** 3.00
107 Jaime Cerda **RC** 3.00
108 Brandon Puffer **RC** 3.00
109 Tyler Yates **RC** 6.00
110 Bill Hall 3.00
111 Peter Zamora **RC** 3.00
112 Jeff Deardorff **RC** 3.00
113 J.J. Putz **RC** 3.00
114 Scotty Layfield **RC** 3.00
115 Brandon Backe **RC** 3.00
116 Andy Pratt **RC** 3.00
117 Mark Prior 8.00
118 Franklyn German **RC** 3.00
119 Todd Donovan **RC** 3.00
120 Franklin Nunez **RC** 3.00
121 Adam Walker **RC** 3.00
122 Ron Calloway **RC** 3.00
123 Tim Kalita **RC** 3.00
124 Kazuhisa Ishii **RC** 8.00
125 Mark Teixeira 5.00
126 Nate Field **RC** 3.00
127 Nelson Castro **RC** 3.00
128 So Taguchi **RC** 8.00
129 Marlon Byrd 3.00
130 Drew Henson 3.00
131 Kenny Kelly 3.00
132 John Ennis **RC** 3.00
133 Anastacio Martinez **RC** 3.00
134 Matt Guerrier 3.00
135 Tom Wilson **RC** 3.00
136 Ben Howard **RC** 4.00
137 Chris Baker **RC** 3.00
138 Kevin Frederick **RC** 3.00
159 Wilson Valdez **RC** 3.00
140 Austin Kearns 4.00

Bat's Incredible

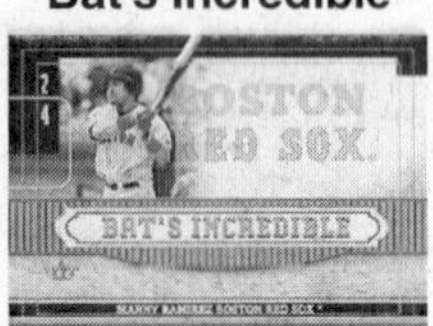

NM/M
Complete Set (25): 60.00
Common Player: 1.50
Inserted 1:10
1BI Todd Helton 2.00
2BI Chipper Jones 3.00
3BI Luis Gonzalez 1.50
4BI Barry Bonds 8.00
5BI Jason Giambi 2.00
6BI Alex Rodriguez 6.00
7BI Manny Ramirez 2.00
8BI Jeff Bagwell 2.00
9BI Shawn Green 1.50
10BI Albert Pujols 6.00
11BI Paul LoDuca 1.50
12BI Mike Piazza 5.00
13BI Derek Jeter 8.00
14BI Edgar Martinez 1.50
15BI Juan Gonzalez 2.00
16BI Magglio Ordonez 1.50
17BI Jermaine Dye 1.50
18BI Larry Walker 1.50
19BI Phil Nevin 1.50
20BI Ivan Rodriguez 1.50
21BI Ichiro Suzuki 5.00
22BI J.D. Drew 1.50
23BI Vladimir Guerrero 2.00
24BI Sammy Sosa 5.00
25BI Ken Griffey Jr. 5.00

Bat's Incredible Game-used

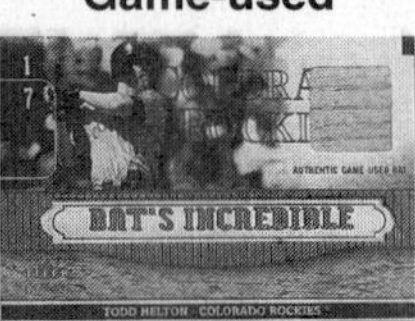

NM/M
Common Player: 5.00
Inserted 1:20
Todd Helton 10.00
Chipper Jones 10.00
J.D. Drew 8.00
Alex Rodriguez 15.00
Manny Ramirez 10.00
Shawn Green 6.00
Derek Jeter 20.00
Edgar Martinez 8.00
Juan Gonzalez 8.00
Jermaine Dye 5.00
Phil Nevin 5.00
Ivan Rodriguez 10.00

Genuine Ink

NM/M
Common Autograph 15.00
Production varies

Barry Bonds/150 150.00
Ron Cey/175 15.00
Derek Jeter/150 125.00
Al Kaline/300 60.00
Don Mattingly/50 100.00
Paul Molitor 50.00
Dale Murphy/700 40.00
Phil Rizzuto/700 30.00
Brooks Robinson/140 60.00
Maury Willis/975 15.00

Leaders

NM/M
Complete Set (15): 25.00
Common Player: 1.00
Inserted 1:6
1GL Sammy Sosa 4.00
2GL Todd Helton 2.00
3GL Alex Rodriguez 4.00
4GL Roger Clemens 3.00
5GL Barry Bonds 5.00
6GL Randy Johnson 2.00
7GL Albert Pujols 4.00
8GL Curt Schilling 1.00
9GL Bernie Williams 1.00
10GL Ken Griffey Jr. 4.00
11GL Pedro J. Martinez 2.00
12GL Juan Gonzalez 2.00
13GL Hideo Nomo 2.00
14GL Bret Boone 1.00
15GL Ichiro Suzuki 4.00

Leaders Game-Used

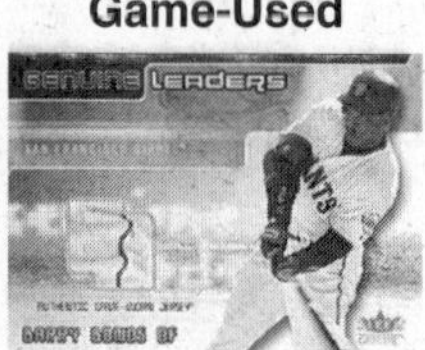

NM/M
Common Player: 8.00
Inserted 1:16
Todd Helton 10.00
Alex Rodriguez 15.00
Roger Clemens 15.00
Barry Bonds 20.00
Randy Johnson 10.00
Curt Schilling 8.00
Bernie Williams 8.00
Pedro J. Martinez 10.00
Hideo Nomo 15.00

Names of the Game

NM/M
Complete Set (30): 60.00
Common Player: 1.00
Inserted 1:10 H, 1:20 R
1 Mike Piazza 5.00
2 Chipper Jones 4.00
3 Jim Edmonds 1.00
4 Barry Larkin 1.00
5 Frank Thomas 3.00
6 Manny Ramirez 3.00
7 Carlos Delgado 1.50
8 Brian Giles 1.00
9 Kerry Wood 2.00
10 Derek Jeter 8.00
11 Adam Dunn 2.00
12 Gary Sheffield 1.50
13 Luis Gonzalez 1.00
14 Mark Mulder 1.00
15 Roberto Alomar 1.50
16 Scott Rolen 2.50
17 Tom Glavine 1.50
18 Bobby Abreu 1.00
19 Nomar Garciaparra 5.00
20 Darin Erstad 2.00
21 Cliff Floyd 1.00
22 Tim Hudson 1.00
23 Jim Thome 1.00
24 Nolan Ryan 8.00
25 Reggie Jackson 3.00
26 Rafael Palmeiro 2.00
27 Ken Griffey Jr. 5.00
28 Sammy Sosa 5.00
29 Vladimir Guerrero 3.00
30 Ichiro Suzuki 5.00

Names of the Game Memorabilia

NM/M
Common Player: 5.00
1:24 H, 1:100 R
1 Roberto Alomar 10.00
2 Carlos Delgado 8.00
3 Jim Edmonds 8.00
4 Darin Erstad 5.00
5 Cliff Floyd 5.00
6 Nomar Garciaparra/SP/90 60.00
7 Brian Giles 5.00
8 Luis Gonzalez 5.00
9 Tim Hudson 8.00
10 Derek Jeter 30.00
11 Chipper Jones 10.00
12 Barry Larkin 8.00
13 Mark Mulder 8.00
14 Rafael Palmeiro 10.00
15 Mike Piazza 15.00
16 Manny Ramirez 8.00
17 Scott Rolen 10.00
18 Nolan Ryan 40.00
19 Jim Thome 10.00

Tip of the Cap

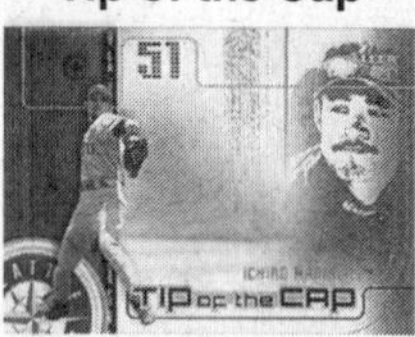

NM/M
Complete Set (25): 40.00
Common Player: .50
Inserted 1:6
1TC Alex Rodriguez 6.00
2TC Derek Jeter 8.00
3TC Kazuhiro Sasaki .50
4TC Barry Bonds 8.00
5TC J.D. Drew .75
6TC Tsuyoshi Shinjo .50
7TC Alfonso Soriano 1.50
8TC Albert Pujols 6.00
9TC Tom Seaver 1.50
10TC Drew Henson .75
11TC Dave Winfield 1.50
12TC Carlos Delgado 1.00
13TC Lou Boudreau .50
14TC Shawn Green .75
15TC Roger Clemens 3.00
16TC Randy Johnson 1.50
17TC Sammy Sosa 4.00
18TC Rafael Palmeiro 1.25
19TC Ken Griffey Jr. 5.00
20TC Ichiro Suzuki 5.00
21TC Eric Chavez .65
22TC Andruw Jones 1.50
23TC Miguel Tejada .65
24TC Pedro J. Martinez 1.50
25TC Tim Salmon .50

Tip of the Cap Game-Used

NM/M
Common Player:
Alex Rodriguez/670 20.00
Barry Bonds/32 75.00
Tom Seaver/224 25.00
Drew Henson/361 15.00
Dave Winfield/363 15.00

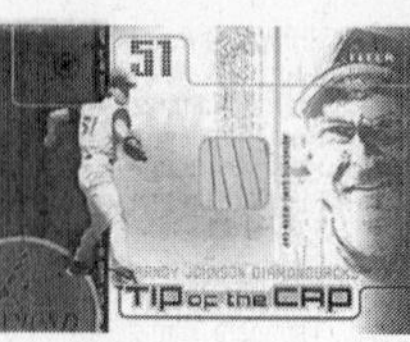

Carlos Delgado/219 15.00
Lou Boudreau/303 20.00
Randy Johnson/74 30.00
Rafael Palmeiro/300 20.00
Andruw Jones/19 40.00
Miguel Tejada/225 15.00

Touch 'Em All

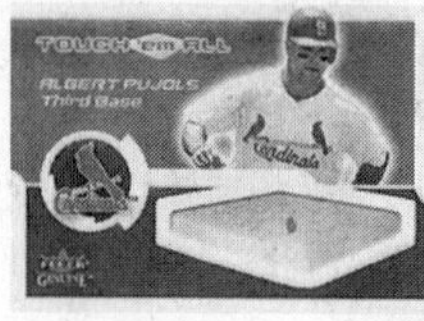

NM/M
Complete Set (25): 60.00
Common Player: 1.50
Inserted 1:10
1 Derek Jeter 8.00
2 Sammy Sosa 5.00
3 Albert Pujols 6.00
4 Vladimir Guerrero 3.00
5 Ken Griffey Jr. 5.00
6 Nomar Garciaparra 5.00
7 Luis Gonzalez 1.50
8 Barry Bonds 8.00
9 Manny Ramirez 2.50
10 Jason Giambi 2.00
11 Chipper Jones 4.00
12 Ichiro Suzuki 5.00
13 Alex Rodriguez 6.00
14 Juan Gonzalez 2.50
15 Todd Helton 2.50
16 Roberto Alomar 1.50
17 Jeff Bagwell 2.50
18 Mike Piazza 5.00
19 Gary Sheffield 1.50
20 Ivan Rodriguez 2.00
21 Frank Thomas 2.50
22 Bobby Abreu 1.50
23 J.D. Drew 1.50
24 Scott Rolen 2.00
25 Darin Erstad 1.50

Touch 'Em All Base

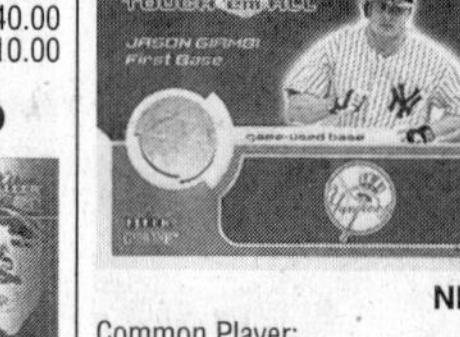

NM/M
Common Player: 4.00
Production 350 Sets
Derek Jeter 15.00
Sammy Sosa 10.00
Albert Pujols 15.00
Vladimir Guerrero 10.00
Ken Griffey Jr. 10.00
Nomar Garciaparra 10.00
Luis Gonzalez 5.00
Barry Bonds 15.00
Manny Ramirez 8.00
Jason Giambi 8.00
Chipper Jones 8.00
Ichiro Suzuki 15.00
Alex Rodriguez 10.00
Juan Gonzalez 8.00
Todd Helton 8.00
Roberto Alomar 6.00
Jeff Bagwell 8.00
Mike Piazza 10.00
Gary Sheffield 6.00
Ivan Rodriguez 8.00
Frank Thomas 8.00
Bobby Abreu 4.00
J.D. Drew 4.00
Scott Rolen 8.00
Darin Erstad 4.00

2002 Fleer Greats of the Game

NM/M
Complete Set (100): 45.00
Common Player: .40
Pack (5): 5.00
Box (24): 100.00
1 Cal Ripken Jr. 6.00
2 Paul Molitor 1.50
3 Roberto Clemente 4.00
4 Cy Young 1.50
5 Tris Speaker .75
6 Lou Brock .50
7 Fred Lynn .40
8 Harmon Killebrew 1.50
9 Ted Williams 6.00

10 Dave Winfield 1.00
11 Orlando Cepeda .40
12 Johnny Mize .40
13 Walter Johnson 1.50
14 Roy Campanella 1.50
15 George Sisler .40
16 Bo Jackson 1.00
17 Rollie Fingers .40
18 Brooks Robinson 1.50
19 Billy Williams .40
20 Maury Wills .40
21 Jimmie Foxx 1.50
22 Alan Trammell .40
23 Rogers Hornsby 1.50
24 Don Drysdale 1.00
25 Bob Feller .75
26 Jackie Robinson 5.00
27 Whitey Ford 1.50
28 Enos Slaughter .40
29 Rod Carew 1.00
30 Eddie Mathews 1.50
31 Ron Cey .40
32 Thurman Munson 2.00
33 Ty Cobb 3.00
34 Rocky Colavito .75
35 Satchel Paige 1.50
36 Andre Dawson .75
37 Phil Rizzuto .75
38 Roger Maris 3.00
39 Earl Weaver .40
40 Joe Carter .40
41 Christy Mathewson 1.50
42 Tony Lazzeri .40
43 Gil Hodges .75
44 Gaylord Perry .40
45 Steve Carlton 1.00
46 George Kell .40
47 Mickey Cochrane 1.00
48 Joe Morgan .60
49 Steve Garvey .40
50 Bob Gibson 1.50
51 Lefty Grove .40
52 Warren Spahn 1.50
53 Willie McCovey .75
54 Frank Robinson 1.50
55 Rich "Goose" Gossage .40
56 Hank Bauer .40
57 Hoyt Wilhelm .40
58 Mel Ott 1.00
59 Preacher Roe .75
60 Yogi Berra 1.50
61 Nolan Ryan 6.00
62 Dizzy Dean .75
63 Ryne Sandberg 2.00
64 Frank Howard .40
65 Hack Wilson .40
66 Robin Yount 1.50
67 Al Kaline 1.50
68 Mike Schmidt 2.00
69 Vida Blue .40
70 George Brett 3.00
71 Sparky Anderson .40
72 Tom Seaver 1.50
73 Bill "Moose" Skowron .40
74 Don Mattingly 2.50
75 Carl Yastrzemski 1.50
76 Eddie Murray 1.50
77 Jim Palmer 1.00
78 Bill Dickey .75
79 Ozzie Smith 1.50
80 Dale Murphy .75
81 Nap Lajoie 1.00
82 Jim "Catfish" Hunter 1.00
83 Duke Snider 1.00
84 Luis Aparicio .40
85 Reggie Jackson 1.50
86 Honus Wagner 1.50
87 Johnny Bench 2.00
88 Stan Musial 3.00
89 Carlton Fisk .75
90 Tony Oliva .75
91 Wade Boggs 2.00
92 Jim Rice .40
93 Bill Mazeroski .40
94 Ralph Kiner .40
95 Tony Perez .40
96 Kirby Puckett 2.00
97 Bobby Bonds .75
98 Bill Terry .40
99 Juan Marichal .75
100 Hank Greenberg 1.00

Autographs

NM/M
Common Autograph: 10.00
Inserted 1:24
SA Sparky Anderson 15.00

LA Luis Aparicio 15.00
HB Hank Bauer 10.00
JB Johnny Bench 50.00
YB Yogi Berra 40.00
PB Paul Blair 10.00
VB Vida Blue 15.00
WB Wade Boggs 20.00
BB Bobby Bonds 15.00
GB George Brett/150 125.00
LB Lou Brock/250 25.00
RC Rod Carew/250 40.00
SC Steve Carlton 25.00
JC Joe Carter 15.00
OC Orlando Cepeda 15.00
CE Ron Cey 10.00
CO Rocky Colavito 35.00
AD Andre Dawson 15.00
BF Bob Feller 15.00
RF Rollie Fingers 15.00
CF Carlton Fisk/100 65.00
WF Whitey Ford 40.00
SG Steve Garvey 15.00
BG Bob Gibson/200 30.00
RG Rich "Goose" Gossage 10.00
FH Frank Howard 15.00
RJ Reggie Jackson/150 70.00
AK Al Kaline 40.00
GK George Kell 15.00
HK Harmon Killebrew 30.00
RK Ralph Kiner/250 25.00
FL Fred Lynn 15.00
JM Juan Marichal 15.00
DM Don Mattingly/300 75.00
BM Bill Mazeroski/200 20.00
WM Willie McCovey 25.00
PM Paul Molitor 25.00
JM Joe Morgan 15.00
MU Dale Murphy 40.00
EM Eddie Murray/250 70.00
SM Stan Musial/200 75.00
TO Tony Oliva 15.00
JP Jim Palmer 20.00
DP Dave Parker 10.00
TP Tony Perez 15.00
GP Gaylord Perry/4 60.00
KP Kirby Puckett/250 60.00
JR Jim Rice 15.00
CR Cal Ripken Jr./100 180.00
PR Phil Rizzuto/300 50.00
BR Brooks Robinson 30.00
FR Frank Robinson/250 30.00
PR Preacher Roe 15.00
NR Nolan Ryan/150 100.00
RS Ryne Sandberg/200 75.00
MS Mike Schmidt/150 100.00
TS Tom Seaver/150 50.00
BS Bill "Moose" Skowron 10.00
ES Enos Slaughter 15.00
OS Ozzie Smith/300 65.00
DS Duke Snider 25.00
WS Warren Spahn 50.00
AT Alan Trammell 20.00
HW Hoyt Wilhelm 15.00
BW Billy Williams 15.00
MW Maury Wills 15.00
DW Dave Winfield/250 25.00
CY Carl Yastrzemski/200 75.00
RY Robin Yount 70.00

Dueling Duos

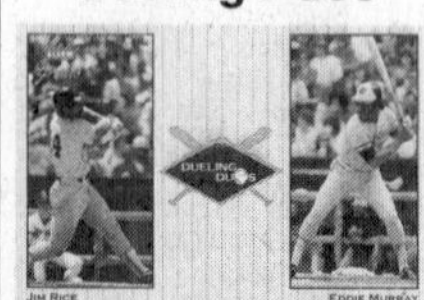

NM/M
Complete Set (29): 90.00
Common Player: 2.00
Inserted 1:6
1DD Johnny Bench, Carlton Fisk 4.00
2DD Roy Campanella, Yogi Berra 5.00
3DD Stan Musial, Ted Williams 8.00
4DD Carl Yastrzemski, Reggie Jackson 3.00
5DD Babe Ruth, Jimmie Foxx 8.00

6DD Steve Carlton, Nolan Ryan 8.00
7DD Wade Boggs, Don Mattingly 6.00
8DD Brooks Robinson, Roger Maris 5.00
9DD Paul Molitor, Don Mattingly 6.00
10DD Sparky Anderson, Earl Weaver 2.00
11DD Bob Gibson, Duke Snider 3.00
12DD Yogi Berra, Gil Hodges 4.00
13DD Joe Morgan, Ryne Sandberg 3.00
14DD Tony Perez, Carl Yastrzemski 3.00
15DD Jimmie Foxx, Bill Dickey 3.00
16DD Ralph Kiner, Duke Snider 2.00
17DD Nellie Fox, Rocky Colavito 2.00
18DD Willie McCovey, Johnny Bench 3.00
19DD Duke Snider, Eddie Mathews 4.00
20DD Reggie Jackson, Jim Rice 3.00
21DD Eddie Murray, Jim Rice 2.00
22DD Paul Molitor, Dave Winfield 3.00
23DD Robin Yount, Dave Winfield 3.00
24DD Enos Slaughter, Ted Kluszewski 2.00
25DD Wade Boggs, George Brett 4.00
26DD George Brett, Eddie Murray 4.00
27DD George Brett, Cal Ripken Jr. 8.00
28DD Kirby Puckett, Don Mattingly 6.00
29DD George Brett, Mike Schmidt 5.00

Dueling Duos Autograph

No Pricing
Production 25 Sets

Dueling Duos G-U Single

NM/M
Common Card: 15.00
Inserted 1:24
Johnny Bench, Carlton Fisk 20.00
Roy Campanella, Yogi Berra 25.00
Carl Yastrzemski, Reggie Jackson 25.00
Babe Ruth, Jimmie Foxx/75 50.00
Kirby Puckett, Don Mattingly 25.00
Steve Carlton, Nolan Ryan 80.00
Wade Boggs, Don Mattingly 25.00
Brooks Robinson, Roger Maris 25.00
Paul Molitor, Don Mattingly 25.00
Sparky Anderson, Earl Weaver 10.00
Bob Gibson, Duke Snider/200 20.00
Yogi Berra, Gil Hodges 25.00
Joe Morgan, Ryne Sandberg 25.00
Tony Perez, Carl Yastrzemski 25.00
Jimmie Foxx, Bill Dickey 20.00
Ralph Kiner, Duke Snider 20.00
Nellie Fox, Rocky Colavito 20.00
Willie McCovey, Johnny Bench 25.00
Duke Snider, Eddie Mathews 20.00
Reggie Jackson, Jim Rice 20.00
Eddie Murray, Jim Rice 15.00
Paul Molitor, Dave Winfield 15.00
Robin Yount, Dave Winfield 15.00
Enos Slaughter, Ted Kluszewski 10.00
Wade Boggs, George Brett 25.00
George Brett, Eddie Murray 20.00
George Brett, Cal Ripken Jr. 40.00

Dueling Duos Game Used Dual

No Pricing
Production 25 Sets

Through the Years Level 1

NM/M
Common Player: 10.00
Inserted 1:24
George Brett 25.00
Reggie Jackson/A's 15.00
Reggie Jackson/Angels 15.00
Ted Williams/350 100.00
Robin Yount 20.00
Willie McCovey 10.00
Paul Molitor/Brewers 15.00
Paul Molitor/Blue Jays 15.00
Jim Palmer 10.00
Brooks Robinson 15.00
Carl Yastrzemski 25.00
Don Mattingly 25.00
Carlton Fisk/Htg 15.00
Carlton Fisk/Fldg 15.00
Nolan Ryan 40.00
Eddie Murray 10.00
Wade Boggs 15.00
Tony Perez 10.00
Ted Kluszewski 10.00
Bo Jackson/Royals 15.00
Bo Jackson/White Sox 15.00
Johnny Bench 20.00
Jackie Robinson 65.00
Hoyt Wilhelm 10.00
Vida Blue 10.00
Dave Winfield 10.00
Frank Robinson 15.00
Jim Rice 10.00
Jim Rice 10.00
Cal Ripken/Htg 40.00
Cal Ripken/Fldg 40.00

Through the Years Level 2

NM/M
Common Player: 25.00
Production 100 Sets
George Brett 80.00
Reggie Jackson 30.00
Ted Williams 120.00
Robin Yount 40.00
Willie McCovey 30.00
Paul Molitor 40.00
Jim Palmer 25.00
Carl Yastrzemski 65.00
Don Mattingly 60.00
Carlton Fisk 30.00
Nolan Ryan 75.00
Eddie Murray 25.00
Wade Boggs 30.00
Ted Kluszewski 30.00
Bo Jackson/Royals 30.00
Bo Jackson/White Sox 30.00
Johnny Bench 40.00
Dave Winfield 25.00
Jim Rice 25.00
Jim Rice 25.00
Cal Ripken Jr. 60.00
Cal Ripken Jr. 60.00

Through the Years Level 3

No Pricing
Production 25 Sets

Through Years Patch Edition

NM/M
Common Player: 25.00
Production 100 Sets
George Brett 80.00
Reggie Jackson/A's 30.00
Reggie Jackson/Angels 30.00
Ted Williams 120.00
Robin Yount 50.00
Willie McCovey 30.00
Paul Molitor/Brewers 40.00
Paul Molitor/Blue Jays 40.00
Jim Palmer 25.00
Carl Yastrzemski 75.00
Don Mattingly 60.00
Carlton Fisk 30.00
Carlton Fisk 30.00
Nolan Ryan 75.00
Eddie Murray 25.00
Wade Boggs 30.00
Tony Perez 25.00
Ted Kluszewski 30.00
Bo Jackson/Royals 40.00
Bo Jackson/White Sox 40.00
Johnny Bench 40.00
Dave Winfield 30.00
Frank Robinson 30.00
Jim Rice 25.00
Jim Rice 25.00
Cal Ripken Jr. 80.00
Cal Ripken Jr. 80.00

2002 Fleer Hot Prospects

NM/M
Complete Set (125):
Common Player: .25
Common (81-105): 8.00
Production 1,000
Common (106-125): 3.00
Production 1,500
Pack (5): 4.00
Box (18): 50.00
1 Derek Jeter 3.00
2 Garret Anderson .25
3 Scott Rolen .75
4 Bret Boone .25
5 Lance Berkman .25
6 Andruw Jones 1.00
7 Ivan Rodriguez .75
8 Bernie Williams .35
9 Cristian Guzman .25
10 Mo Vaughn .25
11 Troy Glaus 1.00
12 Tim Salmon .35
13 Jason Giambi .65
14 Cliff Floyd .25
15 Tim Hudson .35
16 Curt Schilling .40
17 Sammy Sosa 2.00
18 Alex Rodriguez 2.50
19 Chuck Knoblauch .25
20 Jason Kendall .25
21 Ben Sheets .25
22 Nomar Garciaparra 2.00
23 Ryan Klesko .25
24 Greg Vaughn .25
25 Rafael Palmeiro .75
26 Miguel Tejada .35
27 Shea Hillenbrand .25
28 Jim Thome .25
29 Randy Johnson 1.00
30 Barry Larkin .25
31 Paul LoDuca .25
32 Pedro J. Martinez 1.00
33 Luis Gonzalez .35
34 Carlos Delgado .50
35 Richie Sexson .25
36 Albert Pujols 2.25
37 Bobby Abreu .25
38 Gary Sheffield .40
39 Magglio Ordonez .25
40 Eric Chavez .35
41 Jeff Bagwell 1.00
42 Doug Mientkiewicz .25
43 Moises Alou .25
44 Todd Helton 1.00
45 Ichiro Suzuki 2.00
46 Jose Cruz Jr. .25
47 Freddy Garcia .25
48 Tino Martinez .25
49 Roger Clemens 1.75
50 Greg Maddux 1.50
51 Mike Piazza 2.00
52 Roberto Alomar .50
53 Adam Dunn .50
54 Kerry Wood .75
55 Edgar Martinez .25
56 Ken Griffey Jr. 2.00
57 Juan Gonzalez 1.00
58 Pat Burrell .50
59 Corey Koskie .25
60 Jose Vidro .25
61 Ben Grieve .25
62 Barry Bonds 3.00
63 Raul Mondesi .25
64 Jimmy Rollins .50
65 Mike Sweeney .25
66 Josh Beckett .50
67 Chipper Jones 1.50
68 Jeff Kent .25
69 Tony Batista .25
70 Phil Nevin .25
71 Brian Jordan .25
72 Rich Aurilia .25
73 Brian Giles .25
74 Frank Thomas 1.00
75 Larry Walker .25
76 Shawn Green .40
77 Manny Ramirez 1.00
78 Craig Biggio .25
79 Vladimir Guerrero 1.00
80 Jeromy Burnitz .25
81 Mark Teixeira 10.00
82 Corey Thurman RC 8.00
83 Mark Prior 15.00
84 Marlon Byrd 8.00
85 Austin Kearns 10.00
86 Satoru Komiyama RC 8.00
87 So Taguchi RC 12.00
88 Jorge Padilla RC 8.00
89 Rene Reyes RC 8.00
90 Jorge Nunez RC 8.00
91 Ron Calloway RC 8.00
92 Kazuhisa Ishii RC 10.00
93 Dewon Brazelton 8.00
94 Angel Berroa 8.00
95 Felix Escalona RC 8.00
96 Sean Burroughs 8.00
97 Brandon Duckworth 8.00
98 Hank Blalock 10.00
99 Eric Hinske 8.00
100 Carlos Pena 8.00
101 Morgan Ensberg 8.00
102 Ryan Ludwick 8.00
103 Chris Snelling RC 8.00
104 Jason Lane 8.00
105 Drew Henson 10.00
106 Bobby Kielty 3.00
107 Earl Snyder RC 3.00
108 Nate Field RC 3.00
109 Juan Diaz 3.00
110 Ryan Anderson 3.00
111 Esteban German 3.00
112 Takahito Nomura RC 3.00
113 David Kelton 3.00
114 Steve Kent RC 3.00
115 Colby Lewis 3.00
116 Jason Simontacchi RC 3.00
117 Rodrigo Rosario RC 3.00
118 Ben Howard RC 3.00
119 Hansel Izquierdo RC 3.00
120 John Ennis RC 3.00
121 Anderson Machado RC 3.00
122 Luis Ugueto RC 3.00
123 Anastacio Martinez RC 3.00
124 Reed Johnson RC 6.00
125 Juan Cruz 3.00

Co-Stars

NM/M
Complete Set (15): 25.00
Common Card: 1.00
Inserted 1:6
1CS Barry Bonds, Alex Rodriguez 6.00
2CS Derek Jeter, Nomar Garciaparra 5.00
3CS Andruw Jones, Chipper Jones 3.00
4CS Juan Gonzalez, Jim Thome 2.00
5CS Pedro J. Martinez, Randy Johnson 2.00
6CS Adam Dunn, Pat Burrell 1.50
7CS Frank Thomas, Manny Ramirez 2.00
8CS Jeff Bagwell, Lance Berkman 2.00
9CS So Taguchi, Kazuhisa Ishii 4.00
10CS Jimmy Rollins, Miguel Tejada 2.00
11CS Morgan Ensberg, Carlos Pena 1.00
12CS Adam Dunn, Austin Kearns 2.00
13CS Vladimir Guerrero, Scott Rolen 3.00
14CS Drew Henson, Xavier Nady 1.00
15CS Mike Piazza, Ivan Rodriguez 4.00

Future Swatch Autograph

NM/M
Common Auto.
Production 100
83 Mark Prior 40.00
87 So Taguchi 20.00
89 Rene Reyes 10.00
105 Drew Henson 20.00

Inside Barry Bonds

NM/M
Common Bonds: 15.00
1BB Barry Bonds/Pants/1,000 20.00
2BB Barry Bonds/Pants/900 20.00
3BB Barry Bonds/Jsy/800 20.00
4BB Barry Bonds/Bat/700 20.00
5BB Barry Bonds/Base/600 15.00
6BB Barry Bonds/Cleat/500 25.00
7BB Barry Bonds/Glove/400 25.00
8BB Barry Bonds/Cap/300 30.00

Jerseygraphs

NM/M
Common Player: 10.00
Inserted 1:186
DJ Derek Jeter/108 150.00
BB Barry Bonds/65 250.00
CJ Chipper Jones/100 80.00
DH Drew Henson 30.00
ST So Taguchi/100 25.00
DE David Espinosa 10.00
DS Dane Sardinha 10.00
AB Adrian Beltre/169 35.00

MLB Hot Materials

NM/M
Common Player: 5.00
Inserted 1:9
Red Hots: 1-2X
Production 50 Sets
AD Adam Dunn 8.00
AR Alex Rodriguez 10.00
BB Bret Boone 5.00
BB2 Barry Bonds 20.00
BD Brandon Duckworth 5.00
BG Brian Giles 5.00
BW Bernie Williams 8.00
CD Carlos Delgado 6.00
CG Cristian Guzman 5.00
CP Carlos Pena 8.00
CP Corey Patterson 6.00
CS Curt Schilling 8.00
FT Frank Thomas 10.00
GK Gabe Kapler 5.00
GM Greg Maddux 15.00
GS Gary Sheffield 6.00
IR Ivan Rodriguez 10.00
JB Josh Beckett 8.00
JB2 Jeff Bagwell/108 20.00
JG Juan Gonzalez 8.00
JT Jim Thome 10.00
JU Juan Uribe 5.00
LB Lance Berkman 8.00
MM Mark Mulder 8.00
MA Moises Alou 6.00
MP Mike Piazza 15.00
MS Mike Sweeney 5.00
NJ Nick Johnson 5.00
PL Paul LoDuca 5.00
PM Pedro J. Martinez 10.00
RF Rafael Furcal 5.00
RO Roy Oswalt 5.00
RP Rafael Palmeiro 10.00
SB Sean Burroughs/350 10.00
SG Shawn Green 8.00
TA Tony Armas Jr. 5.00
TH Torii Hunter 5.00
TM Tino Martinez 8.00
VW Vernon Wells 5.00
TH Todd Helton 8.00
MO Magglio Ordonez 8.00
FG Freddy Garcia 5.00
ST So Taguchi 8.00

MLB Hot Tandems

NM/M
Common Card: 10.00
Production 100 Sets
Red Hots 10 Sets. No Pricing
Adam Dunn, Lance Berkman 15.00
Alex Rodriguez, Ivan Rodriguez 30.00
Bret Boone, Freddy Garcia 10.00
Barry Bonds, Kazuhisa Ishii 40.00
Brandon Duckworth, Roy Oswalt 10.00
Bernie Williams, Jorge Posada 15.00
Carlos Delgado, Vernon Wells 10.00
Cristian Guzman, Torii Hunter 10.00
Carlos Pena, Corey Patterson 10.00
Curt Schilling, Greg Maddux 25.00
Frank Thomas, Magglio Ordonez 15.00
Gabe Kapler, Rafael Palmeiro 12.00
Gary Sheffield, Rafael Furcal 10.00
Josh Beckett, Roy Oswalt 10.00
Brandon Duckworth, Josh Beckett 15.00
Jeff Bagwell, Lance Berkman 15.00
Juan Gonzalez, Rafael Palmeiro 15.00
Jim Thome, Shawn Green 15.00
Paul LoDuca, Shawn Green 10.00
Juan Uribe, Miguel Tejada 15.00
Mark Mulder, Miguel Tejada 15.00
Moises Alou, Magglio Ordonez 10.00
Jorge Posada, Mike Piazza 25.00
Mike Sweeney, Todd Helton 15.00
Carlos Pena, Nick Johnson 10.00
Curt Schilling, Pedro J. Martinez 25.00
Tony Armas Jr., Freddy Garcia 10.00
Tino Martinez, Todd Helton 15.00
Barry Bonds, Derek Jeter 60.00
Kazuhisa Ishii, Derek Jeter 40.00
Juan Uribe, Cristian Guzman 10.00
Kazuhisa Ishii, So Taguchi 20.00
Adam Dunn, Corey Patterson 15.00
Bernie Williams, Nick Johnson 10.00
Bret Boone, Torii Hunter 10.00
Greg Maddux, Pedro J. Martinez 20.00
Sean Burroughs, Drew Henson 10.00
Kazuhisa Ishii, Satoru Komiyama 20.00
Kazuhisa Ishii, Mark Prior 20.00
Hank Blalock, Austin Kearns 15.00
Hank Blalock, Mark Teixeira 15.00
Marlon Byrd, Jorge Padilla 10.00
Marlon Byrd, Austin Kearns 10.00
Gabe Kapler, Juan Gonzalez 15.00
Jeff Bagwell, Mike Piazza 25.00

2002 Fleer Hot Prospects We're Number One

NM/M
Complete Set (10): 35.00
Common Player: 1.50
Inserted 1:15
1WN Derek Jeter 8.00
2WN Barry Bonds 8.00
3WN Ken Griffey Jr. 5.00
4WN Roger Clemens 4.50
5WN Alex Rodriguez 6.00
6WN J.D. Drew 1.50
7WN Chipper Jones 4.00
8WN Manny Ramirez 3.00
9WN Nomar Garciaparra 5.00
10WN Todd Helton 3.00

We're Number One Autograph

NM/M
Common Player:
Barry Bonds/85 200.00

We're Number One Memorabilia

NM/M
Common Player: 5.00
Inserted 1:25
Derek Jeter/Jsy 25.00
Barry Bonds/Jsy 20.00
Ken Griffey Jr./Base 15.00
Alex Rodriguez/Jsy 15.00
J.D. Drew/Jsy 5.00
Chipper Jones/Jsy 10.00
Manny Ramirez/Jsy 10.00
Nomar Garciaparra/Jsy 20.00
Todd Helton/Jsy 10.00

2002 Fleer Maximum

NM/M
Complete Set (270):
Common Player: .15
Common (201-250): 5.00
Production 500
Common (251-270): .50
Inserted 1:Hobby Pack
Pack (15): 2.50
Box (16): 35.00
1 Barry Bonds 2.00
2 Alex Rodriguez 1.50
3 Jim Edmonds .15
4 Manny Ramirez .75
5 Jeff Bagwell .75
6 Kazuhiro Sasaki .15
7 Jason Giambi .50
8 J.D. Drew .25
9 Barry Larkin .15
10 Chipper Jones 1.00
11 Rafael Palmeiro .65
12 Roberto Alomar .35
13 Randy Johnson .75
14 Juan Gonzalez .75
15 Gary Sheffield .25
16 Larry Walker .15
17 Todd Helton .75
18 Ivan Rodriguez .65
19 Greg Maddux 1.00
20 Mike Piazza 1.25
21 Tsuyoshi Shinjo .15
22 Luis Gonzalez .25
23 Pedro Martinez .75
24 Albert Pujols 1.50
25 Jose Canseco .35
26 Edgar Martinez .15
27 Moises Alou .15
28 Vladimir Guerrero .75
29 Shawn Green .35
30 Miguel Tejada .25
31 Bernie Williams .30
32 Frank Thomas .75
33 Jim Thome .15
34 Derek Jeter 2.00
35 Julio Lugo .15
36 Mo Vaughn .15
37 Steve Cox .15
38 Brad Radke .15
39 Brian Jordan .15
40 Garret Anderson .15
41 Ichiro Suzuki 1.25
42 Mike Lieberthal .15
43 Preston Wilson .15
44 Bud Smith .15
45 Curt Schilling .40
46 Eric Chavez .25
47 Javier Vazquez .15
48 Jose Ortiz .15
49 Mike Sweeney .15
50 Travis Fryman .15
51 Brady Anderson .15
52 Chan Ho Park .15
53 C.C. Sabathia .15
54 Jack Wilson .25
55 Joe Crede .15
56 Mike Mussina .40
57 Sean Casey .30
58 Bobby Abreu .15
59 Joe Randa .15
60 Jose Vidro .15
61 Juan Uribe .15
62 Mark Grace .25
63 Matt Morris .15
64 Omar Vizquel .15
65 Darryl Kile .15
66 Dee Brown .15
67 Fernando Tatis .15
68 Jeff Cirillo .15
69 Johnny Damon .25
70 Milton Bradley .15
71 Reggie Sanders .15
72 Al Leiter .15
73 Andres Galarraga .15
74 Ellis Burks .15
75 Jermaine Dye .15
76 Juan Pierre .15
77 Junior Spivey .15
78 Mark Quinn .15
79 Ben Sheets .15
80 Brad Fullmer .15
81 Bubba Trammell .15
82 Dante Bichette .15
83 Ken Griffey Jr. 1.25
84 Paul O'Neill .15
85 Robert Fick .15
86 Bret Boone .15
87 Raul Mondesi .15
88 Josh Beckett .40
89 Geoff Jenkins .15
90 Ramon Ortiz .15
91 Robin Ventura .15
92 Tom Glavine .30
93 Jimmy Rollins .25
94 Jamie Moyer .15
95 Magglio Ordonez .15
96 Mike Lowell .15
97 Ryan Dempster .15
98 Scott Schoeneweis .15
99 Todd Zeile .15
100 A.J. Burnett .15
101 Aaron Sele .15
102 Cal Ripken Jr. 2.00
103 Carlos Beltran .45
104 David Eckstein .15
105 Jason Marquis .15
106 Matt Lawton .15
107 Ben Grieve .15
108 Brian Giles .15
109 Josh Towers .15
110 Lance Berkman .15
111 Sammy Sosa 1.25
112 Torii Hunter .15
113 Aubrey Huff .15
114 Craig Biggio .15
115 Doug Mientkiewicz .15
116 Fred McGriff .15
117 Jason Johnson .15
118 Pat Burrell .25
119 Aaron Boone .15
120 Carlos Delgado .50
121 Nomar Garciaparra 1.25
122 Richie Sexson .15
123 Russ Ortiz .15
124 Tim Hudson .25
125 Tony Clark .15
126 Jeromy Burnitz .15
127 Jose Cruz .15
128 Juan Encarnacion .15
129 Mark Mulder .15
130 Mike Hampton .15
131 Rich Aurilia .15
132 Trot Nixon .15
133 Greg Vaughn .15
134 Jacque Jones .15
135 Jason Kendall .15
136 Jay Gibbons .15
137 Mark Buehrle .15
138 Richard Hidalgo .15
139 Rondell White .15
140 Cristian Guzman .15
141 Andy Pettitte .30
142 Chris Richard .15
143 Paul LoDuca .15
144 Phil Nevin .15
145 Ray Durham .15
146 Todd Walker .15
147 Bartolo Colon .15
148 Ben Petrick .15
149 Freddy Garcia .15
150 Jon Lieber .15
151 Jose Hernandez .15
152 Matt Williams .15
153 Shannon Stewart .15
154 Adrian Beltre .30
155 Carlos Lee .15
156 Frank Catalanotto .15
157 Jorge Posada .30
158 Pokey Reese .15
159 Ryan Klesko .15
160 Ugueth Urbina .15
161 Adam Dunn .50
162 Alfonso Soriano .50
163 Ben Davis .15
164 Paul Konerko .25
165 Eric Karros .25
166 Jeff Weaver .15
167 Ruben Sierra .15
168 Bobby Higginson .15
169 Eric Milton .15
170 Kerry Wood .65
171 Roy Oswalt .30
172 Scott Rolen .65
173 Tim Salmon .25
174 Aramis Ramirez .25
175 Jason Tyner .15
176 Juan Cruz .15
177 Keith Foulke .15
178 Kevin Brown .25
179 Roger Clemens 1.00
180 Tony Batista .15
181 Andruw Jones .75
182 Cliff Floyd .15
183 Darin Erstad .25
184 Joe Mays .15
185 Mike Cameron .15
186 Robert Person .15
187 Jeff Kent .25
188 Gabe Kapler .15
189 Jason Jennings .15
190 Jason Varitek .15
191 Barry Zito .25
192 Rickey Henderson .75
193 Tino Martinez .25
194 Brandon Duckworth .15
195 Corey Koskie .15
196 Derrek Lee .25
197 Javy Lopez .25
198 John Olerud .25
199 Terrance Long .15
200 Troy Glaus .75
201 Scott MacRae 5.00
202 Scott Chiasson 5.00
203 Bart Miadich 5.00
204 Brian Bowles 5.00
205 David Williams 5.00
206 Victor Zambrano 5.00
207 Joe Beimel 5.00
208 Scott Stewart 5.00
209 Bob File 5.00
210 Ryan Jensen 5.00
211 Jason Karnuth 5.00
212 Brandon Knight 5.00
213 Andy Shibilo **RC** 5.00
214 Chad Ricketts **RC** 5.00
215 Mark Prior 8.00
216 Chad Paronto 5.00
217 Corky Miller 5.00
218 Luis Pineda 5.00
219 Ramon Vazquez 5.00
220 Tony Cogan 5.00
221 Roy Smith 5.00
222 Mark Lukasiewicz 5.00
223 Mike Rivera 5.00
224 Brad Voyles 5.00
225 Jamie Burke **RC** 5.00
226 Justin Duchscherer 5.00
227 Eric Cyr **RC** 5.00
228 Mark Lukasiewicz 5.00
229 Marlon Byrd 5.00
230 Chris Piersoll **RC** 5.00
231 Ramon Vazquez 5.00
232 Tony Cogan 5.00
233 Roy Smith 5.00
234 Franklin Nunez **RC** 5.00
235 Corky Miller 5.00
236 Jorge Nunez **RC** 5.00
237 Joe Beimel 5.00
238 Eric Knott 5.00
239 Victor Zambrano 5.00
240 Jason Karnuth 5.00
241 Jason Middlebrook 5.00
242 Scott Stewart 5.00
243 Tim Spooneybarger 5.00
244 David Williams 5.00
245 Bart Miadich 5.00
246 Mike Koplove 5.00
247 Ryan Jensen 5.00
248 Jeremy Fikac 5.00
249 Bob File 5.00
250 Craig Monroe 5.00
251 Albert Pujols 2.00
252 Ichiro Suzuki 2.00
253 Nomar Garciaparra 2.00
254 Barry Bonds 3.00
255 Jason Giambi .75
256 Derek Jeter 3.00
257 Roberto Alomar .75
258 Roger Clemens 2.00
259 Mike Piazza 1.50
260 Vladimir Guerrero 1.00
261 Todd Helton .75
262 Shawn Green .50
263 Chipper Jones 1.00
264 Pedro Martinez 1.00
265 Pat Burrell .50
266 Sammy Sosa 2.00
267 Ken Griffey Jr. 1.50
268 Cal Ripken Jr. 3.00
269 Kerry Wood 1.00
270 Alex Rodriguez 2.50

Maximum To The Max

Stars (1-200): 4-6X
Print Run 200-500
Stars (1-200): 4-8X
Print Run 121-199
Stars (1-200): 6-12X
Print Run 75-120
Stars (1-200): 10-25X
Print Run 40-75
Stars (1-200): 15-40X
Print Run 20-39
Rookies (201-250): .5-1X
Production 100
Impact (251-270): 2-4X
Production 200-400

America's Game

NM/M
Complete Set (25): 25.00
Common Player: .50
Inserted 1:10 Retail
1 Pedro Martinez 1.50
2 Miguel Tejada .75
3 Randy Johnson 1.50
4 Barry Bonds 5.00
5 Rafael Palmeiro 1.00
6 Mike Piazza 3.00
7 Greg Maddux 2.50
8 Jeff Bagwell 1.50
9 Edgar Martinez .50
10 Albert Pujols 4.00
11 Todd Helton 1.50
12 Chipper Jones 2.50
13 Luis Gonzalez .50
14 Jason Giambi 1.00
15 Kazuhiro Sasaki .50
16 Dave Winfield 1.00
17 Reggie Jackson 1.50
18 Tom Glavine .75
19 Carlos Delgado .75
20 Bobby Abreu .50
21 Larry Walker .50
22 J.D. Drew .75
23 Alex Rodriguez 4.00
24 Frank Thomas 1.50
25 C.C. Sabathia .50

Americas Game Jersey

NM/M
Common Player: 8.00
Inserted 1:24 H, 1:72 R
1 Jeff Bagwell 10.00
2 Craig Biggio 8.00
3 Barry Bonds 25.00
4 Carlos Delgado 8.00
5 J.D. Drew 5.00
6 Jason Giambi 10.00
7 Tom Glavine 10.00
8 Luis Gonzalez 5.00
9 Todd Helton 10.00
10 Reggie Jackson 10.00
11 Randy Johnson 10.00
12 Chipper Jones 10.00
13 Greg Maddux 10.00
14 Edgar Martinez 8.00
15 Pedro Martinez 10.00
16 Rafael Palmeiro 10.00
17 Chan Ho Park 5.00
18 Mike Piazza 10.00
19 Albert Pujols 20.00
20 Kazuhiro Sasaki 5.00
21 Miguel Tejada 5.00
22 Frank Thomas 10.00
23 Larry Walker 5.00
24 Dave Winfield 5.00

Americas Game Stars and Stripes

No Pricing
Production 25 Sets

Coverage

NM/M
Common Player: 15.00
Production 100 Sets
1 Roberto Alomar/Bat 25.00
2 Jeff Bagwell/Jsy 20.00
3 Barry Bonds/Bat 50.00
4 Jose Canseco/Bat 25.00
5 J.D. Drew/Bat 25.00
6 Jim Edmonds/Bat 20.00
7 Jason Giambi/Bat 25.00
8 Juan Gonzalez/Bat 25.00
9 Luis Gonzalez/Jsy 15.00
10 Todd Helton/Jsy 20.00
11 Randy Johnson/Jsy 40.00
12 Chipper Jones/Bat 25.00
13 Greg Maddux/Jsy 40.00
14 Pedro Martinez/Jsy 30.00
15 Rafael Palmeiro/Pants 25.00
16 Albert Pujols/Jsy 50.00
17 Manny Ramirez/Bat 20.00
18 Alex Rodriguez/Bat 30.00
19 Ivan Rodriguez/Bat 25.00
20 Kazuhiro Sasaki/Jsy 20.00
21 Gary Sheffield/Bat 20.00
22 Tsuyoshi Shinjo/Bat 15.00

Coverage Autographs

NM/M
Quantity produced listed
1 Barry Bonds/Pants/50 200.00
2 J.D. Drew/Bat/100 25.00
3 Jim Edmonds/Bat/100 25.00
4 Drew Henson/Bat/100 25.00
5 Chipper Jones/Bat/50 60.00
6 Albert Pujols/Jsy/100 150.00
7 Gary Sheffield/Bat/100 30.00

Derek Jeter Legacy Collection

NM/M
Inserted 1:236
DJ Derek Jeter/Bat 20.00
DJ Derek Jeter/Bat/Auto./222 150.00
DJ Derek Jeter/Jsy 20.00
DJ Derek Jeter/Jsy/Auto. 200.00

Maximum Power Bat

NM/M
Common Player: 5.00
Inserted 1:24 H
Golds: 3-4X
Production 25 Sets
Luis Gonzalez 5.00
Larry Walker 5.00
Frank Thomas 10.00
Manny Ramirez 10.00
Barry Bonds 25.00
Jim Thome 10.00
Tsuyoshi Shinjo 5.00
Bernie Williams/175 25.00
Chipper Jones 10.00
Shawn Green 5.00
Juan Gonzalez 8.00
Jim Edmonds 10.00
Moises Alou 10.00
Roberto Alomar 10.00
Jose Canseco 10.00
Ivan Rodriguez 10.00
Barry Larkin/50 40.00
Mike Piazza 15.00
Gary Sheffield 8.00
J.D. Drew/200 8.00
Alex Rodriguez 15.00
Jason Giambi 10.00
Todd Helton 8.00

Mets All-Amazin' Team

To commemorate the team's 40th anniversary, Fleer produced this set of Mets greats which was given away at Shea on August 17. The cards are printed on heavy stock and feature (mostly) color poses, game-action shots and team photos on a textured-look background. The player name, uniform number and years with the Mets appear at bottom. The anniversary logo and Fleer logo are also seen on front. Backs repeat a detail from the front photo in a circle at top. There are a few sentences about the player and stats lines for his Mets days and major league career. Appropriate logos round out the design.

NM/M
Complete Set (21): 15.00
Common Card: .50
1 Gil Hodges 1.00
2 Keith Hernandez .75
3 Edgardo Alfonzo .75
4 Howard Johnson .75
5 Bud Harrelson .50
6 Mike Piazza 3.00
7 Mookie Wilson .75
8 Darryl Strawberry .75
9 Lenny Dykstra .50
10 Tom Seaver 2.00
11 Jerry Koosman .50
12 Roger McDowell .50
13 John Franco .50
14 Ed Kranepool .50
15 Rusty Staub .75
16 Bob Murphy (Broadcaster) .50
17 Ralph Kiner (Broadcaster) .50
18 1962 Team Card 1.00
19 1969 Team Card 1.00
20 1986 Team Card 1.00
--- Checklist .10

2002 Fleer Platinum

NM/M
Complete Set (302): 125.00
Common Player: .15
Common (251-260): 2.00
Common (261-302): 1.50
Inserted 1:3 H, 1:6 Retail
Hobby Pack (10): 2.00
Hobby Box (24): 35.00
Rack Box: 70.00
1 Garrett Anderson .15
2 Randy Johnson .65
3 Chipper Jones .75
4 David Cone .15
5 Corey Patterson .15
6 Carlos Lee .15
7 Barry Larkin .15
8 Jim Thome .15
9 Larry Walker .15
10 Randall Simon .15
11 Charles Johnson .15
12 Richard Hidalgo .15
13 Mark Quinn .15
14 Paul LoDuca .15
15 Cristian Guzman .15
16 Orlando Cabrera .15
17 Al Leiter .15
18 Nick Johnson .15
19 Eric Chavez .25
20 Miguel Tejada .25
21 Mike Lieberthal .15
22 Robert Mackowiak .15
23 Ryan Klesko .15
24 Jeff Kent .15
25 Edgar Martinez .15
26 Steve Kline .15
27 Toby Hall .15
28 Rusty Greer .15
29 Jose Cruz Jr. .15
30 Darin Erstad .50
31 Reggie Sanders .15
32 Javy Lopez .15
33 Carl Everett .15
34 Sammy Sosa 1.00
35 Magglio Ordonez .15
36 Todd Walker .15
37 Omar Vizquel .15
38 Matt Anderson .15
39 Jeff Weaver .15
40 Derrek Lee .15
41 Julio Lugo .15
42 Joe Randa .15
43 Chan Ho Park .15
44 Torii Hunter .15
45 Vladimir Guerrero .65
46 Rey Ordonez .15
47 Tino Martinez .15
48 Johnny Damon .25
49 Barry Zito .25
50 Robert Person .15
51 Aramis Ramirez .15
52 Mark Kotsay .15
53 Jason Schmidt .15
54 Jamie Moyer .15
55 David Justice .15
56 Aubrey Huff .15
57 Rick Helling .15
58 Carlos Delgado .40
59 Troy Glaus .65
60 Curt Schilling .40
61 Greg Maddux .75
62 Nomar Garciaparra 1.00
63 Kerry Wood .50
64 Frank Thomas .65
65 Dmitri Young .15
66 Alex Ochoa .15
67 Jose Macias .15

68 Antonio Alfonseca .15
69 Mike Lowell .15
70 Wade Miller .15
71 Mike Sweeney .15
72 Gary Sheffield .25
73 Corey Koskie .15
74 Lee Stevens .15
75 Jay Payton .15
76 Mike Mussina .40
77 Jermaine Dye .15
78 Bobby Abreu .15
79 Scott Rolen .50
80 Todd Ritchie .15
81 D'Angelo Jimenez .15
82 Rob Nenn .15
83 John Olerud .15
84 Matt Morris .15
85 Joe Kennedy .15
86 Gabe Kapler .15
87 Chris Carpenter .15
88 David Eckstein .15
89 Matt Williams .15
90 John Smoltz .15
91 Pedro J. Martinez .65
92 Eric Young .15
93 Jose Valentin .15
94 Erubiel Durazo .15
95 Jeff Cirillo .15
96 Brandon Inge .15
97 Josh Beckett .40
98 Preston Wilson .15
99 Damian Jackson .15
100 Adrian Beltre .25
101 Jeromy Burnitz .15
102 Joe Mays .15
103 Michael Barrett .15
104 Mike Piazza 1.00
105 Brady Anderson .15
106 Jason Giambi .40
107 Marlon Anderson .15
108 Jimmy Rollins .25
109 Jack Wilson .15
110 Brian Lawrence .15
111 Russ Ortiz .15
112 Kazuhiro Sasaki .15
113 Placido Polanco .15
114 Damian Rolls .15
115 Rafael Palmeiro .50
116 Brad Fullmer .15
117 Tim Salmon .25
118 Tony Womack .15
119 Tony Batista .15
120 Trot Nixon .15
121 Mark Buehrle .15
122 Derek Jeter 1.50
123 Ellis Burks .15
124 Mike Hampton .15
125 Roger Cedeno .15
126 A.J. Burnett .15
127 Moises Alou .15
128 Billy Wagner .15
129 Kevin Brown .15
130 Jose Hernandez .15
131 Doug Mientkiewicz .15
132 Javier Vazquez .15
133 Tsuyoshi Shinjo .15
134 Andy Pettitte .30
135 Tim Hudson .25
136 Pat Burrell .40
137 Brian Giles .15
138 Kevin Young .15
139 Xavier Nady .15
140 J.T. Snow .15
141 Aaron Sele .15
142 Albert Pujols 1.25
143 Jason Tyner .15
144 Ivan Rodriguez .50
145 Raul Mondesi .15
146 Matt Lawton .15
147 Rafael Furcal .15
148 Jeff Conine .15
149 Hideo Nomo .60
150 Jose Canseco .30
151 Aaron Boone .15
152 Bartolo Colon .15
153 Todd Helton .65
154 Tony Clark .15
155 Pablo Ozuna .15
156 Jeff Bagwell .65
157 Carlos Beltran .50
158 Shawn Green .25
159 Geoff Jenkins .15
160 Eric Milton .15
161 Jose Vidro .15
162 Robin Ventura .15
163 Jorge Posada .25
164 Terrence Long .15
165 Brandon Duckworth .15
166 Chad Hermansen .15
167 Ben Davis .15
168 Phil Nevin .15
169 Bret Boone .15
170 J.D. Drew .25
171 Edgar Renteria .15
172 Randy Winn .15
173 Alex Rodriguez 1.50
174 Shannon Stewart .15
175 Steve Finley .15
176 Marcus Giles .15
177 Jay Gibbons .15
178 Manny Ramirez .65
179 Ray Durham .15
180 Sean Casey .25
181 Travis Fryman .15
182 Denny Neagle .15
183 Deivi Cruz .15
184 Luis Castillo .15
185 Lance Berkman .15
186 Dee Brown .15
187 Jeff Shaw .15
188 Mark Loretta .15
189 David Ortiz .25
190 Edgardo Alfonzo .15
191 Roger Clemens .75
192 Mariano Rivera .25
193 Jeremy Giambi .15
194 Johnny Estrada .15
195 Craig Wilson .15
196 Adam Eaton .15
197 Rich Aurilia .15
198 Mike Cameron .15
199 Jim Edmonds .15
200 Fernando Vina .15
201 Greg Vaughn .15
202 Mike Young .15
203 Vernon Wells .15
204 Luis Gonzalez .25
205 Tom Glavine .30
206 Chris Richard .15
207 Jon Lieber .15
208 Keith Foulke .15
209 Rondell White .15
210 Bernie Williams .30
211 Juan Pierre .15
212 Juan Encarnacion .15
213 Ryan Dempster .15
214 Tim Redding .15
215 Jeff Suppan .15
216 Mark Grudzielanek .15
217 Richie Sexson .15
218 Brad Radke .15
219 Armando Benitez .15
220 Orlando Hernandez .15
221 Alfonso Soriano .40
222 Mark Mulder .15
223 Travis Lee .15
224 Jason Kendall .15
225 Trevor Hoffman .15
226 Barry Bonds 1.50
227 Freddy Garcia .15
228 Darryl Kile .15
229 Ben Grieve .15
230 Frank Catalanotto .15
231 Ruben Sierra .15
232 Homer Bush .15
233 Mark Grace .25
234 Andruw Jones .60
235 Brian Roberts .15
236 Fred McGriff .15
237 Paul Konerko .15
238 Ken Griffey Jr. 1.00
239 John Burkett .15
240 Juan Uribe .15
241 Bobby Higginson .15
242 Cliff Floyd .15
243 Craig Biggio .15
244 Neifi Perez .15
245 Eric Karros .15
246 Ben Sheets .15
247 Tony Armas Jr. .15
248 Mo Vaughn .15
249 David Wells .15
250 Juan Gonzalez .60
251 Barry Bonds 5.00
252 Sammy Sosa 3.00
253 Ken Griffey Jr. 3.00
254 Roger Clemens 4.00
255 Greg Maddux 2.50
256 Chipper Jones 1.50
257 Alex Rodriguez, Derek Jeter, Nomar Garciaparra 5.00
258 Roberto Alomar 1.50
259 Jeff Bagwell 1.50
260 Mike Piazza 3.00
261 Mark Teixeira 2.00
262 Mark Prior 2.00
263 Alex Escobar 1.50
264 C.C. Sabathia 1.50
265 Drew Henson 1.50
266 Wilson Betemit 1.50
267 Roy Oswalt 1.50
268 Adam Dunn 2.00
269 Bud Smith 1.50
270 Dewon Brazelton 1.50
271 Brandon Backe **RC**, Jason Standridge 1.50
272 Wilfredo Rodriguez, Carlos Hernandez 1.50
273 Geronimo Gil, Luis Rivera 1.50
274 Carlos Pena, Jovanny Cedeno 1.50
275 Austin Kearns, Ben Broussard 1.50
276 Jorge De La Rosa **RC**, Kenny Kelly 1.50
277 Ryan Drese, Victor Martinez 1.50
278 Joel Pinero, Nate Cornejo 1.50
279 David Kelton, Carlos Zambrano 1.50
281 Donnie Bridges, Wilkin Ruan 1.50
282 Wily Mo Pena, Brandon Claussen 2.00
283 Jason Jennings, Rene Reyes **RC** 1.50
284 Steve Green, Alfredo Amezaga 1.50
285 Eric Hinske, Felipe Lopez 1.50
286 Anderson Machado **RC**, Brad Baisley 1.50
287 Carlos Garcia, Sean Douglass 1.50
288 Pat Strange, Jae Weong Seo 1.50
289 Marcus Thames, Alex Graman 1.50
290 Matt Childers **RC**, Hansel Izquierdo **RC** 1.50
291 Ron Calloway **RC**, Adam Walker **RC** 1.50
292 J.R. House, J.J. Davis 1.50
293 Ryan Anderson, Rafael Soriano 1.50
294 Mike Bynum, Dennis Tankersley 1.50
295 Kurt Ainsworth, Carlos Valderrama 1.50
296 Billy Hall, Cristian Guerrero 1.50
297 Miguel Olivo, Danny Wright 1.50
298 Marlon Byrd, Jorge Padilla **RC** 1.50
299 Juan Cruz, Ben Christensen 1.50
300 Adam Johnson, Michael Restovich 1.50
301 So Taguchi **RC** 2.00
302 Kazuhisa Ishii **RC** 3.00

Edition

Stars (1-250): 4-8X
Production 202
Cards 251-302: No Pricing
Production 22

Buy Back Autographs

Common Player:

Barry Bonds RC Autograph

NM/M
73 Cards Autographed
Barry Bonds 400.00

Clubhouse Collection - Dual

NM/M
Common Card: 10.00
Inserted 1:96
Edgardo Alfonzo 10.00
Rick Ankiel 8.00
Adrian Beltre 10.00
Barry Bonds 40.00
Sean Casey 10.00
Eric Chavez 10.00
Roger Clemens 30.00
Carlos Delgado 10.00
J.D. Drew 10.00
Darin Erstad 10.00
Jim Thome 20.00
Juan Gonzalez 15.00
Nomar Garciaparra 30.00
Derek Jeter 40.00
Randy Johnson 20.00
Andruw Jones 10.00
Johnny Damon 10.00
Paul LoDuca 10.00
Greg Maddux 20.00
Pedro J. Martinez 20.00
Magglio Ordonez 10.00
Mike Piazza 30.00
Manny Ramirez 15.00
Mariano Rivera 15.00
Ivan Rodriguez 20.00
Alex Rodriguez 25.00
Scott Rolen 20.00
Kazuhiro Sasaki 10.00
Curt Schilling 20.00
Gary Sheffield 10.00
Frank Thomas 20.00
Jim Thome 20.00
Omar Vizquel 10.00

Clubhouse Collection Memorabilia

NM/M
Common Player: 5.00
Inserted 1:32
Edgardo Alfonzo/Jsy 5.00
Rick Ankiel/Jsy 5.00
Craig Biggio/Bat 8.00
Adrian Beltre/Jsy 5.00
Sean Casey/Jsy 8.00
Barry Bonds/Jsy 25.00
Scott Rolen/Jsy 10.00
Eric Chavez/Jsy 8.00
Roger Clemens/Jsy 25.00
Carlos Delgado/Jsy 8.00
J.D. Drew/Jsy 5.00
Darin Erstad/Jsy 5.00
Jim Thome/Bat 10.00
Juan Gonzalez/Bat 8.00
Nomar Garciaparra/Jsy 15.00
Todd Helton/Jsy 8.00
Derek Jeter/Pants 25.00
Randy Johnson/Jsy 10.00
Andruw Jones/Jsy 8.00
Tim Hudson/Jsy 5.00
Jason Kendall/Jsy 5.00
Johnny Damon/Bat 5.00
Paul LoDuca/Jsy 5.00
Greg Maddux/Jsy 10.00
Pedro Martinez/Jsy 10.00
Raul Mondesi/Bat 5.00
Magglio Ordonez/Jsy 5.00
Mike Piazza/Jsy 10.00
Manny Ramirez/Jsy 8.00
Mariano Rivera/Jsy 8.00
Ivan Rodriguez/Jsy 10.00
Alex Rodriguez/Jsy 15.00
Kazuhiro Sasaki/Jsy 5.00
Frank Thomas/Jsy 10.00
Curt Schilling/Jsy 8.00
Gary Sheffield/Bat 6.00
Omar Vizquel/Jsy 5.00

Cornerstones

NM/M
Complete Set (40): 120.00
Inserted 1:12 Jumbo
1 Bill Terry, Johnny Mize 1.50
2 Cal Ripken Jr., Eddie Murray 10.00
3 Eddie Mathews, Chipper Jones 3.00
4 Albert Pujols, George Sisler 6.00
5 Sean Casey, Tony Perez 1.50
6 Jimmie Foxx, Scott Rolen 4.00
7 Wade Boggs, George Brett 8.00
8 Rod Carew, Troy Glaus 1.50
9 Jeff Bagwell, Rafael Palmeiro 2.00
10 Willie Stargell, Pie Traynor 2.00
11 Cal Ripken Jr., Brooks Robinson 10.00
12 Tony Perez, Ted Kluszewski 1.50
13 Jason Giambi, Don Mattingly 8.00
14 Hank Greenberg, Jimmie Foxx 4.00
15 Ernie Banks, Willie McCovey 3.00
16 Jim Thome, Travis Fryman 3.00
17 Ted Kluszewski, Sean Casey 1.50
18 Gil Hodges, Johnny Mize 3.00
19 Brooks Robinson, Boog Powell 3.00
20 Bill Terry, George Sisler 2.00
21 Wade Boggs, Don Mattingly 8.00
22 Jason Giambi, Carlos Delgado 2.50
23 Willie Stargell, Bill Madlock 2.00
24 Mark Grace, Matt Williams 2.00
25 Paul Molitor, George Brett 8.00
26 Carlos Delgado, Mo Vaughn 1.50
27 Bill Terry, Willie McCovey 1.50
28 Mike Sweeney, George Brett 8.00
29 Eddie Mathews, Ernie Banks 4.00
30 Eric Karros, Gil Hodges 1.50
31 Paul Molitor, Don Mattingly 8.00
32 Brooks Robinson, Rod Carew 3.00
33 Chipper Jones, Albert Pujols 8.00
34 Harry Heilmann, Hank Greenberg 1.50
35 Frank Thomas, Carlos Delgado 2.50
36 Jeff Bagwell, Todd Helton 2.00
37 Rafael Palmeiro, Fred McGriff 2.00
38 Cal Ripken Jr., Wade Boggs 10.00
39 Orlando Cepeda, Willie McCovey 2.00
40 John Olerud, Mark Grace 2.00

Cornerstones Memorabilia

No Pricing
Production 25 Sets

Cornerstones Numbered

NM/M
Complete Set (40):
#1-10: Production 250
#11-20: Production 250
#21-30: Production 1,000
#31-40: Production 2,000
1 Bill Terry, Johnny Mize 10.00
2 Cal Ripken Jr., Eddie Murray 30.00
3 Eddie Mathews, Chipper Jones 10.00
4 Albert Pujols, George Sisler 20.00
5 Sean Casey, Tony Perez 8.00
6 Jimmie Foxx, Scott Rolen 10.00
7 Wade Boggs, George Brett 20.00
8 Rod Carew, Troy Glaus 10.00
9 Jeff Bagwell, Rafael Palmeiro 10.00
10 Willie Stargell, Pie Traynor 8.00
11 Cal Ripken Jr., Brooks Robinson 20.00
12 Tony Perez, Ted Kluszewski 5.00
13 Jason Giambi, Don Mattingly 15.00
14 Hank Greenberg, Jimmie Foxx 8.00
15 Ernie Banks, Willie McCovey 8.00
16 Jim Thome, Travis Fryman 6.00
17 Ted Kluszewski, Sean Casey 5.00
18 Gil Hodges, Johnny Mize 5.00
19 Brooks Robinson, Boog Powell 8.00
20 Bill Terry, George Sisler 5.00
21 Wade Boggs, Don Mattingly 10.00
22 Jason Giambi/Yanks, Carlos Delgado 3.00
23 Willie Stargell, Bill Madlock 4.00
24 Mark Grace, Matt Williams 4.00
25 Paul Molitor, George Brett 10.00
26 Carlos Delgado, Mo Vaughn 3.00
27 Bill Terry, Willie McCovey 4.00
28 Mike Sweeney, George Brett 10.00
29 Eddie Mathews, Ernie Banks 4.00
30 Eric Karros, Gil Hodges 3.00
31 Paul Molitor, Don Mattingly 8.00
32 Brooks Robinson, Rod Carew 3.00
33 Chipper Jones, Albert Pujols 6.00
34 Harry Heilmann, Hank Greenburg 3.00
35 Frank Thomas, Carlos Delgado 3.00
36 Jeff Bagwell, Todd Helton 3.00
37 Rafael Palmeiro, Fred McGriff 3.00
38 Cal Ripken Jr., Wade Boggs 8.00
39 Orlando Cepeda, Willie McCovey 3.00
40 John Olerud, Mark Grace 3.00

Fencebusters

NM/M
Common Player: 5.00
Rack Pack Exclusive
Derek Jeter 20.00
J.D. Drew 6.00
Brian Giles 5.00
Moises Alou 5.00
Rafael Palmeiro 6.00
Jeff Bagwell 8.00
Mike Piazza 15.00
Manny Ramirez 8.00
Tino Martinez 5.00
Jim Thome 5.00
Andruw Jones 8.00
Shawn Green 6.00
Frank Thomas 8.00
Miguel Tejada 6.00
Luis Gonzalez 5.00
Alex Rodriguez 12.50
Larry Walker 5.00
Barry Bonds 20.00
Todd Helton 8.00
Chipper Jones 10.00
Roberto Alomar 6.00
Jim Edmonds 5.00

Fencebusters Autographed

NM/M
Numbered to 2001 HR Total.
Barry Bonds/73 275.00

National Patch Time

NM/M
Common Player: 20.00
Inserted 1:12 Jumbo
Barry Bonds/75 100.00
Todd Helton/110 40.00
Ivan Rodriguez/225 40.00
Kazuhiro Sasaki/310 20.00
Derek Jeter/65 100.00
Cal Ripken Jr/350 80.00
Darin Erstad/315 20.00
Jose Canseco/150 40.00
Miguel Tejada/55 35.00
Greg Maddux/775 30.00
Juan Gonzalez/50 50.00
J.D. Drew/210 25.00
Manny Ramirez/100 40.00
Pedro Martinez/45 50.00
Carlos Delgado/70 30.00
Magglio Ordonez/85 30.00
Pat Burrell/285 25.00
Adam Dunn/75 40.00
Alex Rodriguez/325 50.00

Wheelhouse

NM/M
Complete Set (20): 40.00
Common Player: 1.00
Inserted 1:12
1WH Derek Jeter 6.00
2WH Barry Bonds 6.00
3WH Luis Gonzalez 1.00
4WH Jason Giambi 1.00
5WH Ivan Rodriguez 1.50
6WH Mike Piazza 4.00
7WH Troy Glaus 1.50
8WH Nomar Garciaparra 4.00
9WH Juan Gonzalez 1.50
10WH Sammy Sosa 4.00
11WH Albert Pujols 5.00
12WH Ken Griffey Jr. 4.00
13WH Scott Rolen 1.00
14WH Jeff Bagwell 1.50
15WH Ichiro Suzuki 4.00
16WH Todd Helton 1.50
17WH Chipper Jones 3.00
18WH Alex Rodriguez 4.00
19WH Vladimir Guerrero 2.00
20WH Manny Ramirez 1.50

2002 Fleer Premium

NM/M
Complete Set (240): 50.00
Common Player: .15
Common SP (201-240): .50
Inserted 1:2
Pack (8): 2.00
Box (24): 35.00
1 Garret Anderson .20
2 Derek Jeter 2.50
3 Ken Griffey Jr. 1.50
4 Luis Castillo .15
5 Richie Sexson .20
6 Mike Mussina .40
7 Ricky Henderson .75
8 Bud Smith .15
9 David Eckstein .15

10 Nomar Garciaparra 1.50
11 Barry Larkin .20
12 Cliff Floyd .15
13 Ben Sheets .20
14 Jorge Posada .30
15 Phil Nevin .15
16 Fernando Vina .15
17 Darin Erstad .65
18 Shea Hillenbrand .15
19 Todd Walker .15
20 Charles Johnson .15
21 Cristian Guzman .15
22 Mariano Rivera .30
23 Bubba Trammell .15
24 Brent Abernathy .15
25 Troy Glaus .75
26 Pedro J. Martinez .75
27 Dmitri Young .15
28 Derrek Lee .20
29 Torii Hunter .20
30 Alfonso Soriano .65
31 Rich Aurilia .15
32 Ben Grieve .15
33 Tim Salmon .30
34 Trot Nixon .15
35 Roberto Alomar .40
36 Mike Lowell .20
37 Jacque Jones .15
38 Bernie Williams .30
39 Barry Bonds 2.50
40 Toby Hall .15
41 Mo Vaughn .20
42 Hideo Nomo .65
43 Travis Fryman .15
44 Preston Wilson .15
45 Corey Koskie .15
46 Eric Chavez .30
47 Andres Galarraga .15
48 Greg Vaughn .15
49 Shawn Wooten .15
50 Manny Ramirez .75
51 Juan Gonzalez .75
52 Moises Alou .20
53 Joe Mays .15
54 Johnny Damon .35
55 Jeff Kent .20
56 Frank Catalanotto .15
57 Steve Finley .15
58 Jason Varitek .15
59 Kenny Lofton .20
60 Jeff Bagwell .75
61 Doug Mientkiewicz .15
62 Jermaine Dye .15
63 John Vander Wal .15
64 Gabe Kapler .15
65 Luis Gonzalez .30
66 Jon Lieber .15
67 C.C. Sabathia .15
68 Lance Berkman .20
69 Eric Milton .15
70 Jason Giambi .50
71 Ichiro Suzuki 1.50
72 Rafael Palmeiro .65
73 Mark Grace .30
74 Fred McGriff .20
75 Jim Thome .20
76 Craig Biggio .20
77 A.J. Pierzynski .15
78 Ramon Hernandez .15
79 Paul Abbott .15
80 Alex Rodriguez 2.00
81 Randy Johnson .75
82 Corey Patterson .20
83 Omar Vizquel .20
84 Richard Hidalgo .15
85 Luis Rivas .15
86 Tim Hudson .30
87 Bret Boone .20
88 Ivan Rodriguez .60
89 Junior Spivey .15
90 Sammy Sosa 1.50
91 Jeff Cirillo .15
92 Roy Oswalt .30
93 Orlando Cabrera .15
94 Terrence Long .15
95 Mike Cameron .15
96 Homer Bush .15
97 Reggie Sanders .15
98 Rondell White .20
99 Mike Hampton .15
100 Carlos Beltran .50
101 Vladimir Guerrero .75
102 Miguel Tejada .30
103 Freddy Garcia .15
104 Jose Cruz Jr. .15
105 Curt Schilling .45
106 Kerry Wood .65
107 Todd Helton .75
108 Neifi Perez .15
109 Javier Vazquez .15
110 Barry Zito .30
111 Edgar Martinez .20
112 Carlos Delgado .50
113 Matt Williams .20
114 Eric Young .15
115 Alex Ochoa .15
116 Mark Quinn .15
117 Jose Vidro .15
118 Bobby Abreu .20
119 David Bell .15
120 Brad Fullmer .15
121 Rafael Furcal .15
122 Ray Durham .15
123 Jose Ortiz .15
124 Joe Randa .15
125 Edgardo Alfonzo .15
126 Marlon Anderson .15
127 Jamie Moyer .15
128 Alex Gonzalez .15
129 Marcus Giles .15
130 Keith Foulke .15
131 Juan Pierre .15
132 Mike Sweeney .15
133 Matt Lawton .15
134 Pat Burrell .40
135 John Olerud .20
136 Raul Mondesi .20
137 Tom Glavine .40
138 Paul Konerko .20
139 Larry Walker .20
140 Adrian Beltre .35
141 Al Leiter .20
142 Mike Lieberthal .15
143 Kazuhiro Sasaki .15
144 Shannon Stewart .15
145 Andruw Jones .75
146 Carlos Lee .15
147 Roger Cedeno .15
148 Kevin Brown .20
149 Jay Payton .15
150 Scott Rolen .65
151 J.D. Drew .35
152 Chipper Jones 1.00
153 Magglio Ordonez .20
154 Tony Clark .15
155 Shawn Green .35
156 Mike Piazza 1.50
157 Jimmy Rollins .25
158 Jim Edmonds .20
159 Javy Lopez .20
160 Chris Singleton .15
161 Juan Encarnacion .15
162 Eric Karros .15
163 Tsuyoshi Shinjo .15
164 Brian Giles .20
165 Darryl Kile .15
166 Greg Maddux 1.00
167 Frank Thomas .75
168 Shane Halter .15
169 Paul LoDuca .15
170 Robin Ventura .15
171 Jason Kendall .15
172 Jason Hart .15
173 Brady Anderson .15
174 Jose Valentin .15
175 Bobby Higginson .15
176 Gary Sheffield .40
177 Roger Clemens 1.25
178 Aramis Ramirez .20
179 Matt Morris .20
180 Jeff Conine .15
181 Aaron Boone .15
182 Jose Macias .15
183 Jeromy Burnitz .15
184 Carl Everett .15
185 Trevor Hoffman .15
186 Placido Polanco .15
187 Jay Gibbons .15
188 Sean Casey .35
189 Josh Beckett .40
190 Jeffrey Hammonds .15
191 Chuck Knoblauch .15
192 Ryan Klesko .15
193 Albert Pujols 1.75
194 Chris Richard .15
195 Adam Dunn .50
196 A.J. Burnett .15
197 Geoff Jenkins .25
198 Tino Martinez .15
199 Ray Lankford .15
200 Edgar Renteria .20
201 Eric Cyr **RC** 1.00
202 Travis Phelps .50
203 Rick Bauer .50
204 Mark Prior 2.00
205 Wilson Betemit .50
206 Dewon Brazelton .50
207 Cody Ransom .50
208 Donnie Bridges .50
209 Justin Duchscherer .50
210 Nate Cornejo .50
211 Jason Romano .50
212 Juan Cruz .50
213 Pedro Santana .50
214 Ryan Drese .50
215 Bert Snow .50
216 Nate Frese .50
217 Rafael Soriano .50
218 Franklin Nunez **RC** .50
219 Tim Spooneybarger .50
220 Willie Harris .50
221 Billy Sylvester .50
222 Carlos Hernandez .50
223 Mark Teixeira 3.00
224 Adrian Hernandez .50
225 Andres Torres .50
226 Marlon Byrd .50
227 Juan Rivera .50
228 Adam Johnson .50
229 Justin Kaye .50
230 Kyle Kessel .50
231 Horacio Ramirez .50
232 Brandon Larson .50
233 Luis Lopez .50
234 Robert Mackowiak .50
235 Henry Mateo .50
236 Corky Miller .50
237 Greg Miller .50
238 Dustan Mohr .50
239 Bill Ortega .50
240 Billy Hall .50

Star Ruby

Stars (1-200): 4-8X
SP's (201-240): 1-2X
Production 125 Sets

Diamond Stars

NM/M
Complete Set (20): 100.00
Common Player: 2.00
Inserted 1:72
1DS Pedro J. Martinez 4.00
2DS Derek Jeter 15.00
3DS Sammy Sosa 8.00
4DS Ken Griffey Jr. 8.00
5DS Chipper Jones 5.00
6DS Roger Clemens 10.00
7DS Ichiro Suzuki 8.00
8DS Jeff Bagwell 4.00
9DS Luis Gonzalez 2.00
10DS Manny Ramirez 4.00
11DS Alex Rodriguez 12.50
12DS Kazuhiro Sasaki 2.00
13DS Mike Piazza 8.00
14DS Vladimir Guerrero 4.00
15DS Randy Johnson 4.00
16DS Ivan Rodriguez 3.00
17DS Nomar Garciaparra 8.00
18DS Barry Bonds 15.00
19DS Todd Helton 4.00
20DS Greg Maddux 5.00

Diamond Stars Autograph

NM/M
Numbered to 100
Derek Jeter 125.00

Diamond Stars Game-Used

NM/M
Common Player: 5.00
Inserted 1:105
Barry Bonds/Jsy 20.00
Manny Ramirez/Jsy 8.00
Ivan Rodriguez/Jsy 8.00
Kazuhiro Sasaki/Jsy 5.00
Roger Clemens 20.00
Alex Rodriguez 15.00
Derek Jeter 25.00
Chipper Jones 10.00
Todd Helton 8.00
Luis Gonzalez 5.00
Mike Piazza 10.00
Nomar Garciaparra 25.00

Diamond Stars Game-Used Premium

NM/M
Production 75 Sets
Barry Bonds 60.00
Roger Clemens 60.00
Todd Helton 30.00
Chipper Jones 30.00
Manny Ramirez 25.00
Alex Rodriguez 50.00
Ivan Rodriguez 25.00
Luis Gonzalez 25.00
Mike Piazza 40.00
Kazuhiro Sasaki 20.00

Diamond Stars Dual Game-Used

NM/M
Numbered to 100.
Barry Bonds 60.00
Todd Helton 20.00
Derek Jeter 60.00
Chipper Jones 30.00
Mike Piazza 35.00
Manny Ramirez 25.00
Alex Rodriguez 40.00

Diamond Stars Dual Game-Used Premium

Production 25 Sets

International Pride

NM/M
Complete Set (15): 10.00
Common Player: .50
Inserted 1:6
1IP Larry Walker .50
2IP Albert Pujols 3.00
3IP Juan Gonzalez .75
4IP Ichiro Suzuki 2.00
5IP Rafael Palmeiro .65
6IP Carlos Delgado .50
7IP Kazuhiro Sasaki .50
8IP Vladimir Guerrero .75
9IP Bobby Abreu .50
10IP Ivan Rodriguez .60
11IP Tsuyoshi Shinjo .50
12IP Pedro J. Martinez .75
13IP Andruw Jones .75
14IP Sammy Sosa 2.00
15IP Chan Ho Park .50

International Pride Game-Used

NM/M
Common Player: 5.00
Inserted 1:90
Carlos Delgado/Jsy 8.00
Juan Gonzalez/Jsy 8.00
Andruw Jones/Jsy 8.00
Pedro Martinez/Jsy 10.00
Rafael Palmeiro/Jsy 8.00
Chan Ho Park/Jsy 5.00
Albert Pujols/Jsy 20.00
Ivan Rodriguez/Bat 10.00
Kazuhiro Sasaki/Jsy 5.00
Tsuyoshi Shinjo/Jsy 5.00

International Pride Premium

NM/M
Production 75 Sets 15.00
Carlos Delgado 25.00
Juan Gonzalez 40.00
Andruw Jones 40.00
Pedro J. Martinez 40.00
Chan Ho Park 15.00
Ivan Rodriguez 25.00
Tsuyoshi Shinjo 15.00
Rafael Palmeiro 25.00
Albert Pujols 75.00
Kazuhiro Sasaki 15.00

Legendary Dynasties

NM/M
Complete Set (36): 125.00
Common Player: 1.50
Inserted 1:18
Gold: 1X
Production 300 Sets
1LD Honus Wagner 4.00
2LD Christy Mathewson 4.00
3LD Lou Gehrig 8.00
4LD Babe Ruth 12.00
5LD Jimmie Foxx 4.00
6LD Lefty Grove 2.00
7LD Al Simmons 1.50
8LD Bill Dickey 1.50
9LD Stan Musial 5.00
10LD Enos Slaughter 1.50
11LD Johnny Mize 2.00
12LD Yogi Berra 3.00
13LD Whitey Ford 3.00
14LD Jackie Robinson 8.00
15LD Duke Snider 3.00
16LD Roger Maris 5.00
17LD Jim Palmer 2.00
18LD Don Drysdale 2.00
19LD Brooks Robinson 3.00
20LD Rollie Fingers 1.50
21LD Reggie Jackson 3.00
22LD Joe Morgan 2.00
23LD Johnny Bench 5.00
24LD Thurman Munson 4.00
25LD Jose Canseco 2.50
26LD Tom Glavine 2.00
27LD Chipper Jones 4.00
28LD Greg Maddux 5.00
29LD Roberto Alomar 3.00
30LD David Cone 1.50
31LD Jim Thome 3.00
32LD Manny Ramirez 3.00
33LD Roger Clemens 6.00
34LD Derek Jeter 8.00
35LD Bernie Williams 2.50
36LD Alfonso Soriano 3.00

Legendary Dynasties Autographs

NM/M
#'d to World Series Year
Johnny Bench/76 80.00
Yogi Berra/51 60.00
Reggie Jackson/73 60.00
Derek Jeter/96 125.00

Legendary Dynasties Game-Used

NM/M
Common Player: 8.00
Inserted 1:120
Roberto Alomar/Jsy 8.00
Johnny Bench/Jsy 15.00
Yogi Berra/Bat/SP/75 50.00
Roger Clemens/Jsy 25.00
Bill Dickey/Bat 25.00
Rollie Fingers/Jsy 8.00
Reggie Jackson/Bat 25.00
Derek Jeter/Bat 30.00
Chipper Jones/Jsy 10.00
Roger Maris/Pants/SP 50.00
Johnny Mize/Bat 15.00
Joe Morgan/Bat 8.00
Thurman Munson/Bat 35.00
Jim Palmer/Jsy 10.00
Manny Ramirez/Jsy 10.00
Brooks Robinson/Bat 30.00
Jackie Robinson/SP/150 60.00
Babe Ruth/Bat 200.00
Duke Snider/Bat 30.00
Alfonso Soriano/Bat 10.00
Bernie Williams/Jsy 8.00

Legendary Dynasties Premium

NM/M
Numbered to Highest win total.
Rollie Fingers/93 15.00
Roger Clemens/114 50.00
Roger Maris/109 70.00
Roberto Alomar/96 25.00
Reggie Jackson/93 30.00
Manny Ramirez/99 25.00
Johnny Bench/108 35.00
Jim Palmer/109 20.00
Derek Jeter/114 80.00
Alfonso Soriano/99 30.00
Chipper Jones/106 30.00
Bernie Williams/114 20.00

On Base!

NM/M
Complete Set (30): 125.00
Common Player: 2.00
#'d to 2001 OBP
1OB Frank Thomas/316 5.00
2OB Ivan Rodriguez/347 5.00
3OB Nomar Garciaparra/352 10.00
4OB Ken Griffey Jr./365 8.00
5OB Juan Gonzalez/370 4.00
6OB Shawn Green/372 3.00
7OB Vladimir Guerrero/377 5.00
8OB Derek Jeter/377 15.00
9OB Scott Rolen/378 5.00
10OB Ichiro Suzuki/381 10.00
11OB Mike Piazza/384 10.00
12OB Bernie Williams/395 3.00
13OB Moises Alou/396 3.00
14OB Jeff Bagwell/397 4.00
15OB Alex Rodriguez/399 10.00
16OB Albert Pujols/403 10.00
17OB Manny Ramirez/405 4.00
18OB Carlos Delgado/408 4.00
19OB Jim Edmonds/410 3.00
20OB Roberto Alomar/415 3.00
21OB Jim Thome/416 4.00
22OB Gary Sheffield/417 3.00
23OB Chipper Jones/427 5.00
24OB Luis Gonzalez/429 2.00
25OB Lance Berkman/430 3.00
26OB Todd Helton/432 4.00
27OB Sammy Sosa/437 10.00
28OB Larry Walker/449 2.00
29OB Jason Giambi/477 4.00
30OB Barry Bonds/515 12.00

On Base! Game-Used

NM/M
Common Player: 5.00
Production 100 Sets
Roberto Alomar 8.00
Moises Alou 5.00
Jeff Bagwell 8.00
Lance Berkman 5.00
Barry Bonds 20.00
Carlos Delgado 8.00
Jim Edmonds 6.00
Nomar Garciaparra 15.00
Jason Giambi 8.00
Juan Gonzalez 8.00
Luis Gonzalez 5.00
Shawn Green 5.00
Ken Griffey Jr. 20.00
Vladimir Guerrero 8.00
Todd Helton 8.00
Derek Jeter 25.00
Chipper Jones 10.00
Mike Piazza 15.00
Albert Pujols 20.00
Manny Ramirez 10.00
Alex Rodriguez 15.00
Ivan Rodriguez 10.00
Scott Rolen 10.00
Gary Sheffield 6.00
Sammy Sosa 20.00
Ichiro Suzuki 25.00
Frank Thomas 10.00
Jim Thome 8.00
Larry Walker 5.00
Bernie Williams 6.00

Project Liberty N.Y. Mets

"New York is Getting Stronger Every Day" was the theme of this team set distributed at a promotional game in Shea Stadium. Cards feature game-action photos and symbols of the team's efforts to respond to the 9/11/01 attack. An image of the Statue of Liberty is vignetted on front of most cards. Player cards have recent stats and highlights, other cards have information on help lines and other resources.

NM/M
Complete Set (15): 10.00
Common Card: .35
1 Mets players .35
2 Al Leiter .75
3 Mike Piazza 3.00
4 NYPD baseball cap (Al Leiter) .75
5 Mo Vaughn .75
6 Roberto Alomar 1.00
7 Edgardo Alfonzo .75
8 9-11-01 sleeve patch .35
9 Rey Ordonez .75
10 Roger Cedeno .75
11 Timo Perez .75
12 NYPD batting helmet (Mike Piazza) 1.50
13 Jeromy Burnitz .75
14 Bobby Valentine .75
15 U.S. flag at Shea .35

2002 Fleer Showcase

NM/M
Complete Set (166): 225.00
Common Player: .25
Common (126-141): 5.00
Production 500
Common (141-166) 4.00

Production 1,500
Pack (5): 3.00
Box (24): 60.00
1 Albert Pujols 2.00
2 Pedro J. Martinez .75
3 Frank Thomas .75
4 Gary Sheffield .40
5 Roberto Alomar .40
6 Luis Gonzalez .35
7 Bobby Abreu .25
8 Carlos Lee .25
9 Preston Wilson .25
10 Todd Helton .75
11 Juan Gonzalez .75
12 Chuck Knoblauch .25
13 Jason Kendall .25
14 Aaron Sele .25
15 Greg Vaughn .25
16 Fred McGriff .25
17 Doug Mientkiewicz .25
18 Richard Hidalgo .25
19 Alfonso Soriano .50
20 Matt Williams .25
21 Bobby Higginson .25
22 Mo Vaughn .25
23 Andruw Jones .75
24 Omar Vizquel .25
25 Bret Boone .25
26 Bernie Williams .35
27 Rafael Furcal .25
28 Jeff Bagwell .75
29 Marty Cardova .25
30 Lance Berkman .25
31 Vernon Wells .25
32 Garret Anderson .25
33 Larry Bigbie .25
34 Steve Finley .25
35 Barry Bonds 3.00
36 Eric Chavez .35
37 Tony Clark .25
38 Roger Clemens 1.50
39 Adam Dunn .50
40 Roger Cedeno .25
41 Carlos Delgado .50
42 Jermaine Dye .25
43 Brian Jordan .25
44 Darin Erstad .65
45 Paul LoDuca .25
46 Jim Edmonds .25
47 Tom Glavine .50
48 Cliff Floyd .25
49 Jon Lieber .25
50 Adrian Beltre .40
51 Joel Pineiro .25
52 Jim Thome .25
53 Jimmy Rollins .40
54 Pat Burrell .40
55 Jeromy Burnitz .25
56 Larry Walker .25
57 Damon Minor .25
58 John Olerud .25
59 Carlos Beltran .50
60 Vladimir Guerrero .75
61 David Justice .25
62 Phil Nevin .25
63 Tino Martinez .25
64 Curt Schilling .75
65 Corey Patterson .25
66 Aubrey Huff .25
67 Mark Grace .35
68 Rafael Palmeiro .65
69 Jorge Posada .35
70 Craig Biggio .25
71 Manny Ramirez .75
72 Mark Quinn .25
73 Raul Mondesi .25
74 Shawn Green .40
75 Brian Giles .25
76 Paul Konerko .25
77 Troy Glaus .75
78 Mike Mussina .40
79 Greg Maddux 1.00
80 Edgar Martinez .25
81 Jose Vidro .25
82 Scott Rolen .65
83 Ben Grieve .25
84 Jeff Kent .25
85 Magglio Ordonez .25
86 Freddy Garcia .25
87 Ivan Rodriguez .65
88 Pokey Reese .25
89 Shannon Stewart .25
90 Randy Johnson .75
91 Cristian Guzman .25
92 Tsuyoshi Shinjo .25
93 Steve Cox .25
94 Mike Sweeney .25
95 Robert Fick .25
96 Sean Casey .40
97 Tim Hudson .35
98 Bud Smith .25
99 Corey Koskie .25
100 Richie Sexson .25
101 Aramis Ramirez .25
102 Barry Larkin .25
103 Rich Aurilia .25
104 Charles Johnson .25
105 Ryan Klesko .25
106 Ben Sheets .25
107 J.D. Drew .40
108 Jay Gibbons .25
109 Kerry Wood .65
110 C.C. Sabathia .25
111 Eric Munson .25
112 Josh Beckett .40
113 Javier Vasquez .25
114 Barry Zito .35
115 Kazuhiro Sasaki .25
116 Bubba Trammell .25
117 Russell Branyan .25
118 Todd Walker .25
119 Mike Hampton .25
120 Jeff Weaver .25
121 Geoff Jenkins .25
122 Edgardo Alfonzo .25
123 Mike Lieberthal .25
124 Mike Lowell .25
125 Kevin Brown .25
126 Derek Jeter 8.00
127 Ichiro Suzuki 5.00
128 Nomar Garciaparra 5.00
129 Ken Griffey Jr. 5.00
130 Jason Giambi 5.00
131 Alex Rodriguez 6.00
132 Chipper Jones 5.00
133 Mike Piazza 5.00
134 Sammy Sosa 5.00
135 Hideo Nomo 5.00
136 Kazuhisa Ishii **RC** 8.00
137 Satoru Komiyama **RC** 5.00
138 So Taguchi **RC** 6.00
139 Jorge Padilla **RC** 5.00
140 Rene Reyes **RC** 5.00
141 Jorge Nunez **RC** 5.00
142 Nelson Castro **RC** 4.00
143 Anderson Machado **RC** 4.00
144 Edwin Almonte **RC** 4.00
145 Luis Ugueto **RC** 4.00
146 Felix Escalona **RC** 4.00
147 Ron Calloway **RC** 4.00
148 Hansel Izquierdo **RC** 4.00
149 Mark Teixeira 6.00
150 Orlando Hudson 4.00
151 Aaron Cook **RC** 4.00
152 Aaron Taylor **RC** 4.00
153 Takahito Nomura **RC** 4.00
154 Matt Thornton 4.00
155 Mark Prior 6.00
156 Reed Johnson **RC** 6.00
157 Doug DeVore 4.00
158 Ben Howard **RC** 4.00
159 Francis Beltran **RC** 4.00
160 Brian Mallette **RC** 4.00
161 Sean Burroughs 4.00
162 Michael Restovich 4.00
163 Austin Kearns 4.00
164 Marlon Byrd 4.00
165 Hank Blalock 6.00
166 Mike Rivera 4.00

2002 Fleer Showcase Legacy

Stars (1-125): 3-5X
Legacy (126-166): 1X
Production 175 Sets

2002 Fleer Showcase Baseball's Best

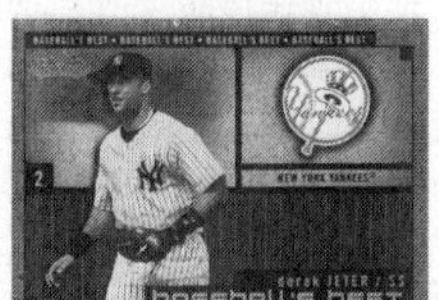

NM/M
Complete Set (20): 40.00
Common Player: 1.00
Inserted 1:8
1 Derek Jeter 5.00
2 Barry Bonds 5.00
3 Mike Piazza 3.00
4 Alex Rodriguez 4.00
5 Pat Burrell 1.00
6 Rafael Palmeiro 1.00
7 Nomar Garciaparra 3.00
8 Todd Helton 1.50
9 Roger Clemens 2.50
10 Shawn Green 1.00
11 Chipper Jones 2.00
12 Pedro J. Martinez 1.50
13 Luis Gonzalez 1.00
14 Randy Johnson 1.50
15 Ichiro Suzuki 3.00
16 Ken Griffey Jr. 3.00
17 Vladimir Guerrero 1.50
18 Sammy Sosa 3.00
19 Jason Giambi 1.00
20 Albert Pujols 4.00

Baseball's Best Memorabilia

NM/M
Common Player: 5.00
Inserted 1:24
Golds: 1-2X
Production 100 Sets
Derek Jeter/Jsy 20.00
Barry Bonds/Jsy 20.00
Mike Piazza/Jsy 10.00
Alex Rodriguez/Bat 15.00
Rafael Palmeiro/Jsy 8.00
Nomar Garciaparra/Jsy 10.00
Todd Helton/Bat 8.00
Roger Clemens/Jsy 15.00
Shawn Green/Jsy 5.00
Chipper Jones/Jsy 10.00
Pedro Martinez/Jsy 8.00
Luis Gonzalez/Jsy 5.00
Randy Johnson/Jsy 10.00
Ichiro Suzuki/Base 15.00
Ken Griffey Jr./Base 10.00
Vladimir Guerrero/Base 8.00
Sammy Sosa/Base 10.00
Jason Giambi/Base 8.00
Albert Pujols/Base 10.00

Baseball's Best Silver Autograph

NM/M
Serial numbered to 400.
Derek Jeter 125.00
Barry Bonds 200.00

Baseball's Best Gold Autograph

NM/M
Serial numbered to 100.
Derek Jeter 150.00
Barry Bonds 225.00

Derek Jeter's Legacy Collection

NM/M
Complete Set (22): 80.00
Common Jeter: 5.00
Production 1,000 Sets
1-22 Derek Jeter 5.00

Derek Jeter's Legacy Collection Memorabilia

NM/M
Quantity produced listed
Derek Jeter/Jsy/300 75.00
Derek Jeter/Combo Jsy/175 90.00
Derek Jeter/World Series Ball/50 100.00
Derek Jeter/Glove/425 60.00

Sweet Sigs Leather

NM/M
Common Player: 8.00
2 Russell Branyan/90 10.00
6 Rafael Furcal/92 15.00
8 Brandon Inge/122 8.00
10 Xavier Nady/301 8.00
11 Jose Ortiz/50 10.00
12 Ben Sheets/60 25.00
13 Mike Sweeney/103 15.00

Sweet Sigs Lumber

NM/M
Common Player: 5.00
1 Bobby Abreu/231 10.00
2 Russell Branyan/425 8.00
3 Pat Burrell/115 10.00
4 Sean Casey/64 20.00
5 Eric Chavez/256 10.00
6 Rafael Furcal/530 10.00
8 Brandon Inge/528 5.00
9 Jackson Melian/636 5.00
10 Xavier Nady/589 8.00
11 Jose Ortiz/515 8.00
12 Ben Sheets/458 15.00
13 Mike Sweeney/495 10.00

Sweet Sigs Wall

NM/M
Common Player: 8.00
1 Bobby Abreu/70 20.00
2 Russell Branyan/200 8.00
5 Eric Chavez/108 15.00
6 Rafael Furcal/207 10.00
8 Brandon Inge/187 8.00
9 Jackson Melian/146 8.00
10 Xavier Nady/286 8.00
11 Jose Ortiz/116 8.00
12 Ben Sheets/150 20.00
13 Mike Sweeney/371 10.00

2002 Fleer Tradition

NM/M
Complete Set (500): 175.00
Common Player: .15
Common SP (1-100): 1.50
Inserted 1:2
Pack (10): 2.00
Box (36): 50.00
1 Barry Bonds 10.00
2 Cal Ripken Jr. 10.00
3 Tony Gwynn 5.00
4 Brad Radke 1.50
5 Jose Ortiz 1.50
6 Mark Mulder 1.50
7 Jon Lieber 1.50
8 John Olerud 1.50
9 Phil Nevin 1.50
10 Craig Biggio 1.50
11 Pedro Martinez 4.00
12 Fred McGriff 1.50
13 Vladimir Guerrero 4.00
14 Jason Giambi 3.00
15 Mark Kotsay 1.50
16 Bud Smith 1.50
17 Kevin Brown 1.50
18 Darin Erstad 3.00
19 Julio Franco 1.50
20 C.C. Sabathia 1.50
21 Larry Walker 1.50
22 Doug Mientkiewicz 1.50
23 Luis Gonzalez 2.00
24 Albert Pujols 8.00
25 Brian Lawrence 1.50
26 Al Leiter 1.50
27 Mike Sweeney 1.50
28 Jeff Weaver 1.50
29 Matt Morris 1.50
30 Hideo Nomo 4.00
31 Tom Glavine 2.50
32 Magglio Ordonez 1.50
33 Roberto Alomar 2.50
34 Roger Cedeno 1.50
35 Greg Vaughn 1.50
36 Chan Ho Park 1.50
37 Rich Aurilia 1.50
38 Tsuyoshi Shinjo 1.50
39 Eric Young 1.50
40 Bobby Higginson 1.50
41 Marlon Anderson 1.50
42 Mark Grace 2.00
43 Steve Cox 1.50
44 Cliff Floyd 1.50
45 Brian Roberts 1.50
46 Paul Konerko 1.50
47 Brandon Duckworth 1.50
48 Josh Beckett 2.50
49 David Ortiz 2.50
50 Geoff Jenkins 1.50
51 Ruben Sierra 1.50
52 John Franco 1.50
53 Einar Diaz 1.50
54 Luis Castillo 1.50
55 Mark Quinn 1.50
56 Shea Hillenbrand 1.50
57 Rafael Palmeiro 3.00
58 Paul O'Neill 1.50
59 Andruw Jones 4.00
60 Lance Berkman 1.50
61 Jimmy Rollins 2.00
62 Jose Hernandez 1.50
63 Rusty Greer 1.50
64 Wade Miller 1.50
65 David Eckstein 1.50
66 Jose Valentin 1.50
67 Javier Vazquez 1.50
68 Roger Clemens 6.00
69 Omar Vizquel 1.50
70 Roy Oswalt 1.50
71 Shannon Stewart 1.50
72 Byung-Hyun Kim 1.50
73 Jay Gibbons 1.50
74 Barry Larkin 1.50
75 Brian Giles 1.50
76 Andres Galarraga 1.50
77 Sammy Sosa 6.00
78 Manny Ramirez 4.00
79 Carlos Delgado 2.50
80 Jorge Posada 1.50
81 Todd Ritchie 1.50
82 Russ Ortiz 1.50
83 Brent Mayne 1.50
84 Mike Mussina 3.00
85 Raul Mondesi 1.50
86 Mark Loretta 1.50
87 Tim Raines 1.50
88 Ichiro Suzuki 6.00
89 Juan Pierre 1.50
90 Adam Dunn 2.50
91 Jason Tyner 1.50
92 Miguel Tejada 1.50
93 Elpidio Guzman 1.50
94 Freddy Garcia 1.50
95 Marcus Giles 1.50
96 Junior Spivey 1.50
97 Aramis Ramirez 1.50
98 Jose Rijo 1.50
99 Paul LoDuca 1.50
100 Mike Cameron 1.50
101 Alex Hernandez .15
102 Benji Gil .15
103 Benito Santiago .15
104 Bobby Abreu .15
105 Brad Penny .15
106 Calvin Murray .15
107 Chad Durbin .15
108 Chris Singleton .15
109 Chris Carpenter .15
110 David Justice .15
111 Eric Chavez .25
112 Fernando Tatis .15
113 Frank Castillo .15
114 Jason LaRue .15
115 Jim Edmonds .15
116 Joe Kennedy .15
117 Jose Jimenez .15
118 Josh Towers .15
119 Junior Herndon .15
120 Luke Prokopec .15
121 Mac Suzuki .15
122 Mark DeRosa .15
123 Marty Cordova .15
124 Michael Tucker .15
125 Michael Young .15
126 Robin Ventura .15
127 Shane Halter .15
128 Shane Reynolds .15
129 Tony Womack .15
130 A.J. Pierzynski .15
131 Aaron Rowand .15
132 Antonio Alfonseca .15
133 Arthur Rhodes .15
134 Bob Wickman .15
135 Brady Clark .15
136 Chad Hermansen .15
137 Marlon Byrd .15
138 Dan Wilson .15
139 David Cone .15
140 Dean Palmer .15
141 Denny Neagle .15
142 Derek Jeter 2.50
143 Erubiel Durazo .15
144 Felix Rodriguez .15
145 Jason Hart .15
146 Jay Bell .15
147 Jeff Suppan .15
148 Jeff Zimmerman .15
149 Kerry Wood .65
150 Kerry Robinson .15
151 Kevin Appier .15
152 Michael Barrett .15
153 Mo Vaughn .15
154 Rafael Furcal .15
155 Sidney Ponson .15
156 Terry Adams .15
157 Tim Redding .15
158 Toby Hall .15
159 Aaron Sele .15
160 Bartolo Colon .15
161 Brad Ausmus .15
162 Carlos Pena .15
163 Jace Brewer .15
164 David Wells .15
165 David Segui .15
166 Derek Lowe .15
167 Derek Bell .15
168 Jason Grabowski .15
169 Johnny Damon .25
170 Jose Mesa .15
171 Juan Encarnacion .15
172 Ken Caminiti .15
173 Ken Griffey Jr. 1.50
174 Luis Rivas .15
175 Mariano Rivera .25
176 Mark Grudzielanek .15
177 Mark McGwire 2.00
178 Mike Bordick .15
179 Mike Hampton .15
180 Nick Bierbrodt .15
181 Paul Byrd .15
182 Robb Nen .15
183 Ryan Dempster .15
184 Ryan Klesko .15
185 Scott Spiezio .15
186 Scott Strickland .15
187 Todd Zeile .15
188 Tom Gordon .15
189 Troy Glaus .75
190 Matt Williams .15
191 Wes Helms .15
192 Jerry Hairston Jr. .15
193 Brook Fordyce .15
194 Nomar Garciaparra 1.50
195 Kevin Tapani .15
196 Mark Buehrle .15
197 Dmitri Young .15
198 John Rocker .15
199 Juan Uribe .15
200 Matt Anderson .15
201 Alex Gonzalez .15
202 Julio Lugo .15
203 Roberto Hernandez .15
204 Richie Sexson .15
205 Corey Koskie .15
206 Tony Armas Jr. .15
207 Rey Ordonez .15
208 Orlando Hernandez .15
209 Pokey Reese .15
210 Mike Lieberthal .15
211 Kris Benson .15
212 Jermaine Dye .15
213 Livan Hernandez .15
214 Bret Boone .15
215 Dustin Hermanson .15
216 Placido Polanco .15
217 Jesus Colome .15
218 Alex Gonzalez .15
219 Adam Everett .15
220 Adam Piatt .15
221 Brad Fullmer .15
222 Brian Buchanan .15
223 Chipper Jones 1.00
224 Chuck Finley .15
225 David Bell .15
226 Jack Wilson .25
227 Jason Bere .15
228 Jeff Conine .15
229 Jeff Bagwell .75
230 Joe McEwing .15
231 Kip Wells .15
232 Mike Lansing .15
233 Neifi Perez .15
234 Omar Daal .15
235 Reggie Sanders .15
236 Shawn Wooten .15
237 Shawn Chacon .15
238 Shawn Estes .15
239 Steve Sparks .15
240 Steve Kline .15
241 Tino Martinez .15
242 Tyler Houston .15
243 Xavier Nady .15
244 Bengie Molina .15
245 Ben Davis .15
246 Casey Fossum .15
247 Chris Stynes .15
248 Danny Graves .15
249 Pedro Feliz .15
250 Darren Oliver .15
251 Dave Veres .15
252 Deivi Cruz .15
253 Desi Relaford .15
254 Devon White .15
255 Edgar Martinez .15
256 Eric Munson .15
257 Eric Karros .15
258 Homer Bush .15
259 Jason Kendall .15
260 Javy Lopez .15
261 Keith Foulke .15
262 Keith Ginter .15
263 Nick Johnson .15
264 Pat Burrell .35
265 Ricky Gutierrez .15
266 Russ Johnson .15
267 Steve Finley .15
268 Terrence Long .15
269 Tony Batista .15
270 Torii Hunter .15
271 Vinny Castilla .15
272 A.J. Burnett .15
273 Adrian Beltre .35
274 Alex Rodriguez 2.00
275 Armando Benitez .15
276 Billy Koch .15
277 Brady Anderson .15
278 Brian Jordan .15
279 Carlos Febles .15
280 Daryle Ward .15
281 Eli Marrero .15
282 Garret Anderson .15
283 Jack Cust .15
284 Jacque Jones .15
285 Jamie Moyer .15
286 Jeffrey Hammonds .15
287 Jim Thome .15
288 Jon Garland .15
289 Jose Offerman .15
290 Matt Stairs .15
291 Orlando Cabrera .15
292 Ramiro Mendoza .15
293 Ray Durham .15
294 Rickey Henderson .75
295 Rob Mackowiak .15
296 Scott Rolen .65

297	Tim Hudson	.25
298	Todd Helton	.75
299	Tony Clark	.15
300	B.J. Surhoff	.15
301	Bernie Williams	.30
302	Bill Mueller	.15
303	Chris Richard	.15
304	Craig Paquette	.15
305	Curt Schilling	.40
306	Damian Jackson	.15
307	Derrek Lee	.15
308	Eric Milton	.15
309	Frank Catalanotto	.15
310	J.T. Snow	.15
311	Jared Sandberg	.15
312	Jason Varitek	.15
313	Jeff Cirillo	.15
314	Jeromy Burnitz	.15
315	Joe Crede	.15
316	Joel Pineiro	.15
317	Jose Cruz Jr.	.15
318	Kevin Young	.15
319	Marquis Grissom	.15
320	Moises Alou	.15
321	Randall Simon	.15
322	Royce Clayton	.15
323	Tim Salmon	.25
324	Travis Fryman	.15
325	Travis Lee	.15
326	Vance Wilson	.15
327	Jarrod Washburn	.15
328	Ben Petrick	.15
329	Ben Grieve	.15
330	Carl Everett	.15
331	Eric Byrnes	.15
332	Doug Glanville	.15
333	Edgardo Alfonzo	.15
334	Ellis Burks	.15
335	Gabe Kapler	.15
336	Gary Sheffield	.25
337	Greg Maddux	1.00
338	J.D. Drew	.25
339	Jamey Wright	.15
340	Jeff Kent	.15
341	Jeremy Giambi	.15
342	Joe Randa	.15
343	Joe Mays	.15
344	Jose Macias	.15
345	Kazuhiro Sasaki	.15
346	Mike Kinkade	.15
347	Mike Lowell	.15
348	Randy Johnson	.75
349	Randy Wolf	.15
350	Richard Hidalgo	.15
351	Ron Coomer	.15
352	Sandy Alomar	.15
353	Sean Casey	.25
354	Trevor Hoffman	.15
355	Adam Eaton	.15
356	Alfonso Soriano	.50
357	Barry Zito	.25
358	Billy Wagner	.15
359	Brent Abernathy	.15
360	Bret Prinz	.15
361	Carlos Beltran	.40
362	Carlos Guillen	.15
363	Charles Johnson	.15
364	Cristian Guzman	.15
365	Damion Easley	.15
366	Darryl Kile	.15
367	Delino DeShields	.15
368	Eric Davis	.15
369	Frank Thomas	.75
370	Ivan Rodriguez	.65
371	Jay Payton	.15
372	Jeff D'Amico	.15
373	John Burkett	.15
374	Melvin Mora	.15
375	Ramon Ortiz	.15
376	Robert Person	.15
377	Russell Branyan	.15
378	Shawn Green	.25
379	Todd Hollandsworth	.15
380	Tony McKnight	.15
381	Trot Nixon	.15
382	Vernon Wells	.15
383	Troy Percival	.15
384	Albie Lopez	.15
385	Alex Ochoa	.15
386	Andy Pettitte	.25
387	Brandon Inge	.15
388	Bubba Trammell	.15
389	Corey Patterson	.15
390	Damian Rolls	.15
391	Dee Brown	.15
392	Edgar Renteria	.15
393	Eric Gagne	.35
394	Jason Johnson	.15
395	Jeff Nelson	.15
396	John Vander Wal	.15
397	Johnny Estrada	.15
398	Jose Canseco	.40
399	Juan Gonzalez	.75
400	Kevin Millwood	.15
401	Lee Stevens	.15
402	Matt Lawton	.15
403	Mike Lamb	.15
404	Octavio Dotel	.15
405	Ramon Hernandez	.15
406	Ruben Quevedo	.15
407	Todd Walker	.15
408	Troy O'Leary	.15
409	Wascar Serrano	.15
410	Aaron Boone	.15
411	Aubrey Huff	.15
412	Ben Sheets	.15
413	Carlos Lee	.15
414	Chuck Knoblauch	.15
415	Steve Karsay	.15
416	Dante Bichette	.15
417	David Dellucci	.15
418	Esteban Loaiza	.15
419	Fernando Vina	.15
420	Ismael Valdes	.15
421	Jason Isringhausen	.15
422	Jeff Shaw	.15
423	John Smoltz	.15
424	Jose Vidro	.15
425	Kenny Lofton	.15
426	Mark Little	.15
427	Mark McLemore	.15
428	Marvin Benard	.15
429	Mike Piazza	1.50
430	Pat Hentgen	.15
431	Preston Wilson	.15
432	Rick Helling	.15
433	Robert Fick	.15
434	Rondell White	.15
435	Adam Kennedy	.15
436	David Espinosa	.15
437	Dewon Brazelton	.15
438	Drew Henson	.25
439	Juan Cruz	.15
440	Jason Jennings	.15
441	Carlos Garcia	.15
442	Carlos Hernandez	.15
443	Wilkin Ruan	.15
444	Wilson Betemit	.15
445	Horacio Ramirez	.15
446	Danys Baez	.15
447	Abraham Nunez	.15
448	Josh Hamilton	.25
449	Chris George	.15
450	Rick Bauer	.15
451	Donnie Bridges	.15
452	Erick Almonte	.15
453	Cory Aldridge	.15
454	Ryan Drese	.15
455	Jason Romano	.15
456	Corky Miller	.15
457	Rafael Soriano	.15
458	Mark Prior	.75
459	Mark Teixeira	.50
460	Adrian Hernandez	.15
461	Tim Spooneybarger	.15
462	Bill Ortega	.15
463	D'Angelo Jimenez	.15
464	Andres Torres	.15
465	Alexis Gomez	.15
466	Angel Berroa	.15
467	Henry Mateo	.15
468	Endy Chavez	.15
469	Billy Sylvester	.15
470	Nate Frese	.15
471	Luis Gonzalez	.25
472	Barry Bonds	2.50
473	Rich Aurilia	.15
474	Albert Pujols	2.00
475	Todd Helton	.75
476	Moises Alou	.15
477	Lance Berkman	.15
478	Brian Giles	.15
479	Cliff Floyd	.15
480	Sammy Sosa	1.50
481	Shawn Green	.30
482	Jon Lieber	.15
483	Matt Morris	.15
484	Curt Schilling	.40
485	Randy Johnson	.75
486	Manny Ramirez	.75
487	Ichiro Suzuki	1.50
488	Juan Gonzalez	.75
489	Derek Jeter	2.50
490	Alex Rodriguez	2.00
491	Bret Boone	.15
492	Roberto Alomar	.30
493	Jason Giambi	.50
494	Rafael Palmeiro	.65
495	Doug Mientkiewicz	.15
496	Jim Thome	.15
497	Freddy Garcia	.15
498	Mark Buehrle	.15
499	Mark Mulder	.15
500	Roger Clemens	1.25

Diamond Tributes

		NM/M
Complete Set (15):		15.00
Common Player:		.50
Inserted 1:6		
1DT	Cal Ripken Jr.	3.00
2DT	Tony Gwynn	1.00
3DT	Derek Jeter	3.00
4DT	Pedro Martinez	.75
5DT	Mark McGwire	2.50
6DT	Sammy Sosa	1.50
7DT	Barry Bonds	3.00
8DT	Roger Clemens	1.50
9DT	Mike Piazza	2.00
10DT	Alex Rodriguez	2.50
11DT	Randy Johnson	.75
12DT	Chipper Jones	1.00
13DT	Nomar Garciaparra	2.00
14DT	Ichiro Suzuki	2.00
15DT	Jason Giambi	.50

Grass Roots

		NM/M
Complete Set (10):		15.00
Common Player:		.75
Inserted 1:18		
1GR	Barry Bonds	5.00
2GR	Alex Rodriguez	4.00
3GR	Derek Jeter	5.00
4GR	Greg Maddux	2.50
5GR	Ivan Rodriguez	1.00
6GR	Cal Ripken Jr.	5.00
7GR	Bernie Williams	.75
8GR	Jeff Bagwell	1.50
9GR	Scott Rolen	1.00
10GR	Larry Walker	.75

Grass Roots Patch

	NM/M
Production 50 Sets	
Barry Bonds	100.00
Alex Rodriguez	75.00
Greg Maddux	50.00
Ivan Rodriguez	25.00
Cal Ripken Jr.	100.00
Bernie Williams	25.00
Jeff Bagwell	40.00
Scott Rolen	30.00
Larry Walker	20.00

Heads Up

		NM/M
Complete Set (10):		45.00
Common Player:		1.00
Inserted 1:36		
1HU	Derek Jeter	8.00
2HU	Ichiro Suzuki	5.00
3HU	Sammy Sosa	5.00
4HU	Mike Piazza	5.00
5HU	Ken Griffey Jr.	5.00
6HU	Alex Rodriguez	6.00
7HU	Barry Bonds	8.00
8HU	Nomar Garciaparra	5.00
9HU	Mark McGwire	6.00
10HU	Cal Ripken Jr.	8.00

Lumber Company

		NM/M
Complete Set (30):		40.00
Common Player:		1.00
Inserted 1:12		
1LC	Moises Alou	1.00
2LC	Luis Gonzalez	1.00
3LC	Todd Helton	2.50
4LC	Mike Piazza	4.00
5LC	J.D. Drew	1.50
6LC	Albert Pujols	5.00
7LC	Chipper Jones	3.00
8LC	Manny Ramirez	2.50
9LC	Miguel Tejada	1.00
10LC	Curt Schilling	1.50
11LC	Alex Rodriguez	5.00
12LC	Barry Larkin	1.00
13LC	Nomar Garciaparra	4.00
14LC	Cliff Floyd	1.00
15LC	Alfonso Soriano	1.50
16LC	Sean Casey	1.00
17LC	Scott Rolen	2.00
18LC	Jose Ortiz	1.00
19LC	Corey Patterson	1.00
20LC	Joe Crede	1.00
21LC	Jace Brewer	1.00
22LC	Derek Jeter	6.00
23LC	Jim Thome	1.00
24LC	Frank Thomas	2.50
25LC	Shawn Green	1.00
26LC	Drew Henson	1.00
27LC	Jimmy Rollins	1.50
28LC	Dave Justice	1.00
29LC	Roberto Alomar	1.50
30LC	Bernie Williams	1.00

Lumber Company Game-Used

	NM/M
Common Player:	5.00
Inserted 1:72	
Moises Alou	5.00
Luis Gonzalez	5.00
Todd Helton	8.00
Mike Piazza	12.00
J.D. Drew	6.00
Albert Pujols	15.00
Chipper Jones	10.00
Manny Ramirez	8.00
Miguel Tejada	6.00
Curt Schilling	6.00
Alex Rodriguez	15.00
Barry Larkin	5.00
Nomar Garciaparra	12.00
Cliff Floyd	5.00
Alfonso Soriano	8.00
Sean Casey	6.00
Scott Rolen	8.00
Jose Ortiz	5.00
Corey Patterson	5.00
Joe Crede	5.00
Jace Brewer	5.00
Derek Jeter	25.00
Jim Thome	5.00
Frank Thomas	8.00
Shawn Green	5.00
Drew Henson	5.00
Jimmy Rollins	5.00
Dave Justice	5.00
Roberto Alomar	6.00
Bernie Williams	5.00

This Day in History

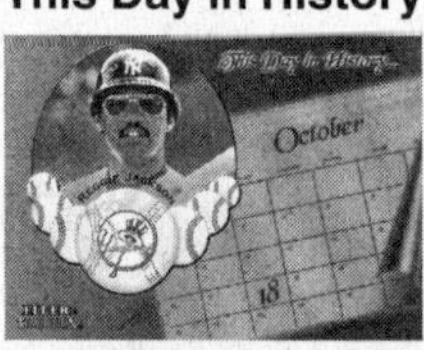

		NM/M
Complete Set (29):		120.00
Common Player:		1.50
Inserted 1:18		
1	Cal Ripken Jr.	10.00
2	Barry Bonds	10.00
3	George Brett	4.00
4	Tony Gwynn	3.00
5	Nolan Ryan	10.00
6	Reggie Jackson	3.00
7	Paul Molitor	2.00
8	Ichiro Suzuki	5.00
9	Alex Rodriguez	8.00
10	Don Mattingly	6.00
11	Sammy Sosa	5.00
12	Mark McGwire	8.00
13	Derek Jeter	10.00
14	Roger Clemens	4.00
15	Jim "Catfish" Hunter	1.50
16	Greg Maddux	3.00
17	Ken Griffey Jr.	5.00
18	Gil Hodges	1.50
19	Edgar Martinez	1.50
20	Mike Piazza	5.00
21	Jimmie Foxx	1.50
22	Albert Pujols	6.00
23	Chipper Jones	3.00
25	Jeff Bagwell	2.00
26	Nomar Garciaparra	5.00
27	Randy Johnson	2.00
28	Todd Helton	2.00
29	Ted Kluszewski	1.50
30	Ivan Rodriguez	1.75

This Day in History Autographs

		NM/M
Common Player:		
3	Derek Jeter/100	100.00
4	Randy Johnson/75	50.00
5	Don Mattingly/50	90.00
7	Albert Pujols/50	200.00
8	Cal Ripken Jr./50	125.00

This Day in History Game-Used

	NM/M
Common Player:	
Jeff Bagwell/Bat/100	15.00
Barry Bonds/Jsy/250	40.00
Roger Clemens/Jsy/150	30.00
Jimmie Foxx/Bat/250	40.00
Todd Helton/Bat/150	15.00
Jim "Catfish" Hunter/Jsy/250	15.00
Derek Jeter/Jsy/250	40.00
Greg Maddux/Jsy/100	20.00
Mike Piazza/Bat/150	20.00
Alex Rodriguez/Hat/250	30.00

Update

		NM/M
Complete Set (400):		75.00
Common Player:		.15
Common SP (1-100):		.50
Inserted 1:1		
Pack (10):		1.50
Box (36):		35.00
1	P.J. Bevis **RC**	.50
2	Michael Crudale **RC**	.50
3	Ben Howard **RC**	.75
4	Travis Driskill **RC**	.50
5	Heed Johnson **RC**	.50
6	Kyle Kane **RC**	.50
7	Deivis Santos	.50
8	Tim Kalita **RC**	.50
9	Brandon Puffer **RC**	.50
10	Chris Snelling **RC**	1.00
11	Juan Brito **RC**	.50
12	Tyler Yates **RC**	.50
13	Victor Alvarez **RC**	.50
14	Takahito Nomura **RC**	.50
15	Ron Calloway **RC**	.50
16	Satoru Komiyama **RC**	.50
17	Julius Matos **RC**	.50
18	Jorge Nunez **RC**	.50
19	Anderson Machado **RC**	.50
20	Scotty Layfield **RC**	.50
21	Aaron Cook **RC**	.50
22	Alex Pelaez **RC**	.50
23	Corey Thurman **RC**	.50
24	Nelson Castro **RC**	.50
25	Jeff Austin **RC**	.50
26	Felix Escalona **RC**	.50
27	Luis Ugueto **RC**	.50
28	Jaime Cerda **RC**	.50
29	J.J. Trujillo **RC**	.50
30	Rodrigo Rosario **RC**	.50
31	Jorge Padilla **RC**	.50
32	Shawn Sedlacek **RC**	.50
33	Nate Field **RC**	.50
34	Earl Snyder **RC**	.75
35	Miguel Asencio **RC**	.50
36	Ken Huckaby **RC**	.50
37	Valentino Pascucci	.50
38	So Taguchi **RC**	1.00
39	Brian Mallette **RC**	.50
40	Kazuhisa Ishii **RC**	2.00
41	Matt Thornton	.50
42	Mark Corey	.50
43	Kirk Saarloos	.50
44	Brandon Bracke	.50
45	Hansel Izquierdo **RC**	.50
46	Rene Reyes **RC**	.50
47	Luis Garcia	.50
48	Jason Simontacchi **RC**	.50
49	John Ennis **RC**	.75
50	Franklyn German **RC**	.50
51	Aaron Guiel **RC**	.50
52	Howie Clark **RC**	.50
53	David Ross **RC**	.50
54	Walt McKeel	.50
55	Francis Beltran **RC**	.50
56	Barry Wesson **RC**	.50
57	Runelvys Hernandez **RC**	.50
58	Oliver Perez **RC**	2.00
59	Ryan Bukvich **RC**	.50
60	Steve Kent **RC**	.50
61	Julio Mateo **RC**	.50
62	Jason Jimenez	.50
63	Jayson Durocher **RC**	.75
64	Kevin Frederick **RC**	.50
65	Kevin Gryboski **RC**	.50
66	Edwin Almonte **RC**	.50
67	John Foster **RC**	.50
68	Doug DeVore **RC**	1.00
69	Tom Shearn **RC**	.50
70	Colin Young **RC**	.50
71	Jon Adkins **RC**	.50
72	Wilbert Nieves **RC**	.50
73	Matt Duff	.50
74	Carl Sadler **RC**	.50
75	Jason Kershner	.50
76	Brandon Backe **RC**	.50
77	Wilson Valdez **RC**	.50
78	Chris Baker **RC**	.50
79	Ryan Jamison	.50
80	Steve Bechler **RC**	.75
81	Allan Simpson **RC**	.50
82	Aaron Taylor **RC**	.50
83	Kevin Cash **RC**	.50
84	Chone Figgins **RC**	1.00
85	Clay Condrey **RC**	.50
86	Shane Nance **RC**	.50
87	Freddy Sanchez **RC**	.50
88	Jim Rushford **RC**	.50
89	Jeriome Robertson **RC**	.50
90	Trey Lunsford **RC**	.50
91	Cody McKay **RC**	.50
92	Trey Hodges **RC**	.50
93	Hee Seop Choi	1.00
94	Joe Borchard	.50
95	Orlando Hudson	.50
96	Carl Crawford	.50
97	Mark Prior	2.00
98	Brett Myers	.50
99	Kenny Lofton	.50
100	Cliff Floyd	.50
101	Randy Winn	.15
102	Ryan Dempster	.15
103	Josh Phelps	.15
104	Marcus Giles	.15
105	Rickey Henderson	.75
106	Jose Leon	.15
107	Tino Martinez	.15
108	Greg Norton	.15
109	Odalis Perez	.15
110	J.C. Romero	.15
111	Gary Sheffield	.35
112	Ismael Valdes	.15
113	Juan Acevedo	.15
114	Ben Broussard	.15
115	Deivi Cruz	.15
116	Geronimo Gil	.15
117	Eric Hinske	.15
118	Ted Lilly	.15
119	Quinton McCracken	.15
120	Antonio Alfonseca	.15
121	Brent Abernathy	.15
122	Johnny Damon	.25
123	Francisco Cordova	.15
124	Sterling Hitchcock	.15
125	Vladimir Nunez	.15
126	Andres Galarraga	.15
127	Timoniel Perez	.15
128	Tsuyoshi Shinjo	.15
129	Joe Girardi	.15
130	Roberto Alomar	.35
131	Ellis Burks	.15
132	Mike DeJean	.15
133	Alex Gonzalez	.15
134	Johan Santana	.35
135	Kenny Lofton	.15
136	Juan Encarnacion	.15
137	Dewon Brazelton	.15
138	Jeromy Burnitz	.15
139	Elmer Dessens	.15
140	Juan Gonzalez	.75
141	Todd Hundley	.15
142	Tomokazu Ohka	.15
143	Robin Ventura	.15
144	Rodrigo Lopez	.15
145	Ruben Sierra	.15
146	Jason Phillips	.15
147	Ryan Rupe	.15
148	Kevin Appier	.15
149	Sean Burroughs	.15
150	Masato Yoshii	.15
151	Juan Diaz	.15
152	Tony Graffanino	.15
153	Raul Ibanez	.15
154	Kevin Mench	.15
155	Pedro Astacio	.15
156	Brent Butler	.15
157	Kirk Rueter	.15
158	Eddie Guardado	.15
159	Hideki Irabu	.15
160	Wendell Magee	.15
161	Antonio Osuna	.15
162	Jose Vizcaino	.15
163	Danny Bautista	.15
164	Vinny Castilla	.15
165	Chris Singleton	.15
166	Mark Redman	.15
167	Olmedo Saenz	.15
168	Scott Erickson	.15
169	Ty Wigginton	.15
170	Jason Isringhausen	.15
171	Lou Merloni	.15
172	Chris Magruder	.15
173	Brandon Berger	.15
174	Roger Cedeno	.15
175	Kelvim Escobar	.15
176	Jose Guillen	.15
177	Damian Jackson	.15
178	Eric Owens	.15
179	Angel Berroa	.15
180	Alex Cintron	.15
181	Jeff Weaver	.15
182	Damon Minor	.15
183	Bobby Estalella	.15
184	David Justice	.15
185	Roy Halladay	.25

186 Brian Jordan .15
187 Mike Maroth .15
188 Pokey Reese .15
189 Rey Sanchez .15
190 Hank Blalock .50
191 Jeff Cirillo .15
192 Dmitri Young .15
193 Carl Everett .15
194 Joey Hamilton .15
195 Jorge Julio .15
196 Pablo Ozuna .15
197 Jason Marquis .15
198 Dustan Mohr .15
199 Joe Borowski .15
200 Tony Clark .15
201 David Wells .15
202 Josh Fogg .15
203 Aaron Harang .15
204 John McDonald .15
205 John Stephens .15
206 Chris Reitsma .15
207 Alex Sanchez .15
208 Milton Bradley .15
209 Matt Clement .15
210 Brad Fullmer .15
211 Shigetoshi Hasegawa .15
212 Austin Kearns .50
213 Damaso Marte .15
214 Vicente Padilla .15
215 Raul Mondesi .15
216 Russell Branyan .15
217 Bartolo Colon .15
218 Moises Alou .15
219 Scott Hatteberg .15
220 Bobby Kielty .15
221 Kip Wells .15
222 Scott Stewart .15
223 Victor Martinez .40
224 Marty Cordova .15
225 Desi Relaford .15
226 Reggie Sanders .15
227 Jason Giambi .50
228 Jimmy Haynes .15
229 Billy Koch .15
230 Damian Moss .15
231 Chan Ho Park .15
232 Cliff Floyd .15
233 Todd Zeile .15
234 Jeremy Giambi .15
235 Rick Helling .15
236 Matt Lawton .15
237 Ramon Martinez .15
238 Rondell White .15
239 Scott Sullivan .15
240 Hideo Nomo .60
241 Todd Ritchie .15
242 Ramon Santiago .15
243 Jake Peavy .15
244 Brad Wilkerson .15
245 Reggie Taylor .15
246 Carlos Pena .15
247 Willis Roberts .15
248 Jason Schmidt .15
249 Mike Williams .15
250 Alan Zinter .15
251 Michael Tejera .15
252 Dave Roberts .15
253 Scott Schoeneweis .15
254 Woody Williams .15
255 John Thomson .15
256 Ricardo Rodriguez .15
257 Aaron Sele .15
258 Paul Wilson .15
259 Brett Tomko .15
260 Kenny Rogers .15
261 Mo Vaughn .15
262 John Burkett .15
263 Dennis Stark .15
264 Ray Durham .15
265 Scott Rolen .65
266 Gabe Kapler .15
267 Todd Hollandsworth .15
268 Bud Smith .15
269 Jay Payton .15
270 Tyler Houston .15
271 Brian Moehler .15
272 David Espinosa .15
273 Placido Polanco .15
274 John Patterson .15
275 Adam Hyzdu .15
276 Albert Pujols 2.00
277 Larry Walker .15
278 Magglio Ordonez .15
279 Ryan Klesko .15
280 Darin Erstad .60
281 Jeff Kent .15
282 Paul LoDuca .15
283 Jim Edmonds .15
284 Chipper Jones 1.00
285 Bernie Williams .30
286 Pat Burrell .40
287 Cliff Floyd .15
288 Troy Glaus .75
289 Brian Giles .15
290 Jim Thome .15
291 Greg Maddux 1.00
292 Roberto Alomar .30
293 Jeff Bagwell .75
294 Rafael Furcal .15
295 Josh Beckett .25
296 Carlos Delgado .35
297 Ken Griffey Jr. 1.50
298 Jason Giambi .50
299 Paul Konerko .15
300 Mike Sweeney .15
301 Alfonso Soriano .50
302 Shea Hillenbrand .15
303 Tony Batista .15
304 Robin Ventura .15
305 Alex Rodriguez 2.00
306 Nomar Garciaparra 1.50
307 Derek Jeter 2.50
308 Miguel Tejada .30
309 Omar Vizquel .15
310 Jorge Posada .25
311 A.J. Pierzynski .15
312 Ichiro Suzuki 1.50
313 Manny Ramirez .75
314 Torii Hunter .15
315 Garret Anderson .15
316 Robert Fick .15
317 Randy Winn .15
318 Mark Buehrle .15
319 Freddy Garcia .15
320 Eddie Guardado .15
321 Roy Halladay .25
322 Derek Lowe .15
323 Pedro J. Martinez .75
324 Mariano Rivera .25
325 Kazuhiro Sasaki .15
326 Barry Zito .25
327 Johnny Damon .25
328 Ugueth Urbina .15
329 Todd Helton .75
330 Richie Sexson .15
331 Jose Vidro .15
332 Luis Castillo .15
333 Junior Spivey .15
334 Scott Rolen .65
335 Mike Lowell .15
336 Jimmy Rollins .25
337 Jose Hernandez .15
338 Mike Piazza 1.50
339 Benito Santiago .15
340 Sammy Sosa 1.50
341 Barry Bonds 2.50
342 Vladimir Guerrero .75
343 Lance Berkman .15
344 Adam Dunn .40
345 Shawn Green .25
346 Luis Gonzalez .25
347 Eric Gagne .25
348 Tom Glavine .30
349 Trevor Hoffman .15
350 Randy Johnson .75
351 Byung-Hyun Kim .15
352 Matt Morris .15
353 Odalis Perez .15
354 Curt Schilling .40
355 John Smoltz .15
356 Mike Williams .15
357 Andruw Jones .75
358 Vicente Padilla .15
359 Mike Remlinger .15
360 Robb Nen .15
361 Shawn Green .25
362 Derek Jeter 2.50
363 Troy Glaus .75
364 Ken Griffey Jr. 1.50
365 Mike Piazza 1.50
366 Jason Giambi .50
367 Greg Maddux 1.00
368 Albert Pujols 2.00
369 Pedro J. Martinez .75
370 Barry Zito .25
371 Ichiro Suzuki 1.50
372 Nomar Garciaparra 1.50
373 Vladimir Guerrero .75
374 Randy Johnson .75
375 Barry Bonds 2.50
376 Sammy Sosa 1.50
377 Hideo Nomo .75
378 Jeff Bagwell .75
379 Curt Schilling .35
380 Jim Thome .15
381 Todd Helton .75
382 Roger Clemens 1.25
383 Chipper Jones 1.00
384 Alex Rodriguez 2.00
385 Manny Ramirez .40
386 Barry Bonds 2.50
387 Jim Thome .15
388 Adam Dunn .40
389 Alex Rodriguez 2.00
390 Shawn Green .25
391 Jason Giambi .50
392 Lance Berkman .15
393 Pat Burrell .40
394 Eric Chavez .25
395 Mike Piazza 1.50
396 Vladimir Guerrero .75
397 Paul Konerko .15
398 Sammy Sosa 1.50
399 Richie Sexson .15
400 Torii Hunter .15

Update Glossy

Stars (1-100): 1-2X
Cards (101-400): 4-8X
Production 200 Sets

Update Diamond Debuts

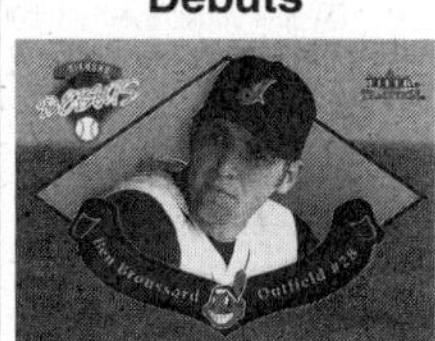

NM/M
Complete Set (15): 10.00
Common Player: .50
Inserted 1:6
1DD Mark Prior 1.50
2DD Eric Hinske .50
3DD Kazuhisa Ishii .50
4DD Ben Broussard .50
5DD Sean Burroughs .50
6DD Austin Kearns 1.00
7DD Hee Seop Choi 1.00
8DD Kirk Saarloos .50
9DD Orlando Hudson .50
10DD So Taguchi .50
11DD Kevin Mench .50
12DD Carl Crawford .50
13DD John Patterson .50
14DD Hank Blalock 1.50
15DD Brett Myers .50

Update Grass Patch

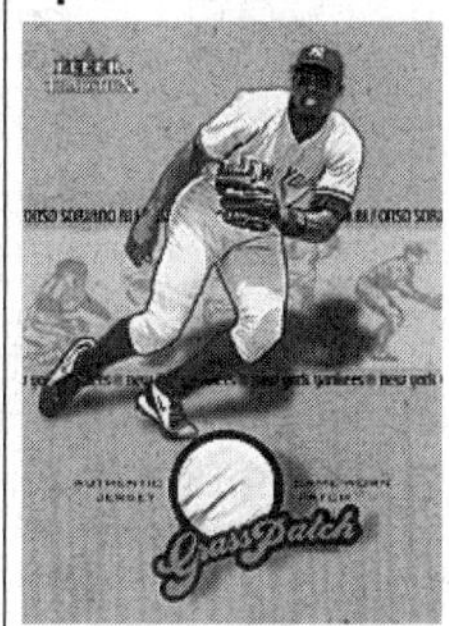

NM/M
Common Player: 20.00
Production 50 Sets
Alfonso Soriano 30.00
Torii Hunter 20.00
Andruw Jones 30.00
Jim Edmonds 20.00
Shawn Green 20.00
Nomar Garciaparra 50.00
Roberto Alomar 25.00

Update Grass Roots

NM/M
Complete Set (10): 15.00
Common Player: 1.00
Inserted 1:24
1GR Alfonso Soriano 1.50
2GR Torii Hunter 1.00
3GR Andruw Jones 1.50
4GR Jim Edmonds 1.00
5GR Shawn Green 1.00
6GR Todd Helton 1.50
7GR Nomar Garciaparra 4.00
8GR Roberto Alomar 1.00
9GR Vladimir Guerrero 1.50
10GR Ichiro Suzuki 4.00

Update Heads Up

NM/M
Complete Set (10): 25.00
Common Player: 2.00
Inserted 1:48
1HU Roger Clemens 6.00
2HU Adam Dunn 2.00
3HU Kazuhisa Ishii 1.50
4HU Barry Zito 1.50
5HU Pedro J. Martinez 4.00

6HU Alfonso Soriano 3.00
7HU Mark Prior 2.00
8HU Chipper Jones 5.00
9HU Randy Johnson 4.00
10HU Lance Berkman 1.50

Update Heads Up Game-Used

NM/M
Common Player: 5.00
Production 150 Sets
Roger Clemens 25.00
Adam Dunn 10.00
Kazuhisa Ishii 5.00
Barry Zito 5.00
Alfonso Soriano 10.00
Mark Prior 10.00
Chipper Jones 15.00
Randy Johnson 15.00
Lance Berkman 5.00
Mike Piazza 20.00
Barry Bonds 50.00

Update New York's Finest

NM/M
Complete Set (15): 60.00
Common Player: 3.00
Inserted 1:83
1 Edgardo Alfonzo 3.00
2 Roberto Alomar 4.00
3 Jeromy Burnitz 3.00
4 Satoru Komiyama 3.00
5 Rey Ordonez 3.00
6 Mike Piazza 10.00
7 Mo Vaughn 3.00
8 Roger Clemens 10.00
9 Jason Giambi 5.00
10 Derek Jeter 15.00
11 Mike Mussina 5.00
12 Jorge Posada 3.00
13 Alfonso Soriano 5.00
14 Robin Ventura 3.00
15 Bernie Williams 4.00

Update N.Y.'s Finest Single Swatch

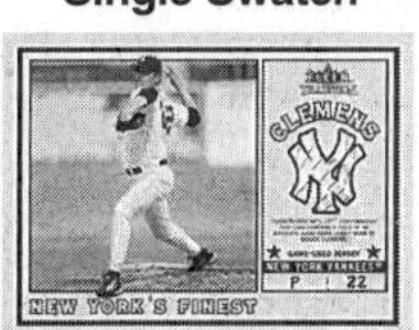

NM/M
Common Card: 5.00
Inserted 1:112
Derek Jeter/Jsy, Rey Ordonez 25.00
Alfonso Soriano/Jsy, Roberto Alomar 10.00

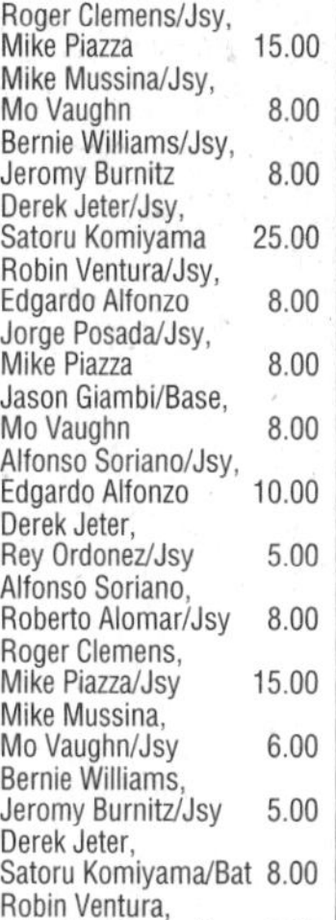

Roger Clemens/Jsy, Mike Piazza 15.00
Mike Mussina/Jsy, Mo Vaughn 8.00
Bernie Williams/Jsy, Jeromy Burnitz 8.00
Derek Jeter/Jsy, Satoru Komiyama 25.00
Robin Ventura/Jsy, Edgardo Alfonzo 8.00
Jorge Posada/Jsy, Mike Piazza 8.00
Jason Giambi/Base, Mo Vaughn 8.00
Alfonso Soriano/Jsy, Edgardo Alfonzo 10.00
Derek Jeter, Rey Ordonez/Jsy 5.00
Alfonso Soriano, Roberto Alomar/Jsy 8.00
Roger Clemens, Mike Piazza/Jsy 15.00
Mike Mussina, Mo Vaughn/Jsy 6.00
Bernie Williams, Jeromy Burnitz/Jsy 5.00
Derek Jeter, Satoru Komiyama/Bat 8.00
Robin Ventura, Edgardo Alfonzo/Jsy 5.00
Jorge Posada, Mike Piazza/Jsy 15.00
Jason Giambi, Mo Vaughn/Jsy 6.00
Alfonso Soriano, Edgardo Alfonzo/Jsy 5.00

Update N.Y.'s Finest Dual Swatch

NM/M
Common Card: 10.00
Production 100 Sets
Derek Jeter, Rey Ordonez 75.00
Alfonso Soriano, Roberto Alomar 40.00
Roger Clemens, Mike Piazza 65.00
Mike Mussina, Mo Vaughn 30.00
Bernie Williams, Jeromy Burnitz 20.00
Robin Ventura, Edgardo Alfonzo 10.00

Update Plays of the Week

NM/M
Complete Set (30): 35.00
Common Player: 1.00
Inserted 1:12
1PW Troy Glaus 1.50
2PW Andruw Jones 1.50
3PW Curt Schilling 1.25
4PW Manny Ramirez 1.50
5PW Sammy Sosa 2.50
6PW Magglio Ordonez 1.00
7PW Ken Griffey Jr. 2.50
8PW Jim Thome 1.00
9PW Larry Walker 1.00
10PW Robert Fick 1.00
11PW Josh Beckett 1.00
12PW Roy Oswalt 1.00
13PW Mike Sweeney 1.00
14PW Shawn Green 1.00
15PW Torii Hunter 1.00
16PW Vladimir Guerrero 1.50
17PW Mike Piazza 2.50
18PW Jason Giambi 1.25
19PW Eric Chavez 1.00
20PW Pat Burrell 1.25
21PW Brian Giles 1.00
22PW Ryan Klesko 1.00
23PW Barry Bonds 5.00
24PW Mike Cameron 1.00
25PW Albert Pujols 4.00
26PW Alex Rodriguez 4.00
27PW Carlos Delgado 1.00
28PW Richie Sexson 1.00
29PW Jay Gibbons 1.00
30PW Randy Winn 1.00

Update This Day in History

NM/M
Complete Set (25): 40.00
Common Player: 1.00
1 Shawn Green 1.00
2 Ozzie Smith 2.50
3 Derek Lowe 1.00
4 Ken Griffey Jr. 3.00
5 Barry Bonds 5.00
6 Juan Gonzalez 1.50
7 Wade Boggs 2.00
8 Mark Prior 1.50
9 Thurman Munson 2.00
10 Curt Schilling 1.25
11 Jason Giambi 1.25
12 Cal Ripken Jr. 5.00
13 Craig Biggio 1.00
14 Drew Henson 1.00
15 Steve Carlton 1.00
16 Greg Maddux 2.50
17 Adam Dunn 1.00
18 Vladimir Guerrero 2.00
19 Alex Rodriguez 4.00
20 Carlton Fisk 1.50
21 Ichiro Suzuki 3.00
22 Johnny Bench 2.00
23 Kazuhisa Ishii 1.00
24 Derek Jeter 5.00
25 Jim Thome 1.00

Update This Day in History Autograph

NM/M
Inserted 1:582
Barry Bonds/150 200.00
Mark Prior/64 40.00
Drew Henson 20.00
Greg Maddux/99 150.00
Derek Jeter 100.00

Update This Day in History Memorabilia

NM/M
Common Player: 5.00
Inserted 1:24
Shawn Green/Jsy 5.00
Ozzie Smith/Jsy 10.00
Barry Bonds/Bat 15.00
Barry Bonds/Jsy 15.00
Juan Gonzalez/Bat 6.00
Wade Boggs/Jsy 6.00
Wade Boggs/Pants 6.00
Curt Schilling/Jsy 6.00
Craig Biggio/Jsy 5.00
Adam Dunn/Jsy 8.00
Alex Rodriguez/Bat 10.00
Alex Rodriguez/Jsy 10.00
Carlton Fisk/Bat 8.00
Kazuhisa Ishii/Bat 5.00
Derek Jeter/Pants 20.00
Jim Thome/Jsy 8.00
Greg Maddux/Jsy 10.00

2002 Fleer Triple Crown

NM/M
Complete Set (270): 30.00
Common Player: .15
Pack (10): 1.50
Box (24): 30.00
1 Mo Vaughn .15

2 Derek Jeter 2.00
3 Ken Griffey Jr. 1.25
4 Charles Johnson .15
5 Geoff Jenkins .15
6 Chuck Knoblauch .15
7 Jason Kendall .15
8 Jim Edmonds .15
9 David Eckstein .15
10 Carl Everett .15
11 Barry Larkin .15
12 Cliff Floyd .15
13 Ben Sheets .15
14 Jeff Conine .15
15 Brian Giles .15
16 Darryl Kile .15
17 Troy Glaus .65
18 Trot Nixon .15
19 Jim Thome .15
20 Preston Wilson .15
21 Roger Clemens 1.00
22 Chad Hermansen .15
23 Matt Morris .15
24 Shawn Wooten .15
25 Manny Ramirez .65
26 Roberto Alomar .30
27 Josh Beckett .25
28 Jose Hernandez .15
29 Mike Mussina .35
30 Jack Wilson .25
31 Bud Smith .15
32 Garret Anderson .15
33 Pedro J. Martinez .65
34 Travis Fryman .15
35 Jeff Bagwell .65
36 Doug Mientkiewicz .15
37 Andy Pettitte .25
38 Ryan Klesko .15
39 Edgar Renteria .15
40 Mariano Rivera .25
41 Darin Erstad .50
42 Hideo Nomo .50
43 Ellis Burks .15
44 Craig Biggio .15
45 Corey Koskie .15
46 Jason Varitek .15
47 Xavier Nady .15
48 Aubrey Huff .15
49 Tim Salmon .25
50 Nomar Garciaparra 1.25
51 Juan Gonzalez .65
52 Moises Alou .15
53 A.J. Pierzynski .15
54 Bernie Williams .30
55 Phil Nevin .15
56 Ben Grieve .15
57 Mark Grace .25
58 Mike Lansing .15
59 Kenny Lofton .15
60 Lance Berkman .15
61 David Ortiz .25
62 Jason Giambi .40
63 Mark Kotsay .15
64 Greg Vaughn .15
65 Junior Spivey .15
66 Fred McGriff .15
67 C.C. Sabathia .15
68 Richard Hidalgo .15
69 Torii Hunter .15
70 Jason Hart .15
71 Bubba Trammell .15
72 Jace Brewer .15
73 Matt Williams .15
74 Matt Stairs .15
75 Omar Vizquel .15
76 Daryle Ward .15
77 Joe Mays .15
78 Eric Chavez .15
79 Andres Galarraga .15
80 Rafael Palmeiro .50
81 Steve Finley .15
82 Eric Young .15
83 Todd Helton .65
84 Roy Oswalt .25
85 Eric Milton .15
86 Ramon Hernandez .15
87 Jeff Kent .15
88 Ivan Rodriguez .50
89 Luis Gonzalez .25
90 Corey Patterson .15
91 Jose Ortiz .15
92 Mike Sweeney .15
93 Cristian Guzman .15
94 Johnny Damon .25
95 Barry Bonds 2.00
96 Rusty Greer .15
97 Reggie Sanders .15
98 Sammy Sosa 1.25
99 Jeff Cirillo .15
100 Carlos Febles .15
101 Jose Vidro .15
102 Jermaine Dye .15
103 Rich Aurilia .15
104 Gabe Kapler .15
105 Randy Johnson .65
106 Rondell White .15
107 Ben Petrick .15
108 Joe Randa .15
109 Fernando Tatis .15
110 Tim Hudson .25
111 John Olerud .15
112 Alex Rodriguez 1.50
113 Curt Schilling .40
114 Kerry Wood .40
115 Alex Ochoa .15
116 Carlos Beltran .40
117 Vladimir Guerrero .65
118 Mark Mulder .15
119 Bret Boone .15
120 Carlos Delgado .35
121 Marcus Giles .15
122 Paul Konerko .15
123 Juan Pierre .15
124 Mark Quinn .15
125 Edgardo Alfonzo .15
126 Barry Zito .25
127 Dan Wilson .15
128 Jose Cruz Jr. .15
129 Chipper Jones .75
130 Ray Durham .15
131 Larry Walker .15
132 Neifi Perez .15
133 Robin Ventura .15
134 Miguel Tejada .25
135 Edgar Martinez .15
136 Raul Mondesi .15
137 Javy Lopez .15
138 Jose Canseco .25
139 Mike Hampton .15
140 Eric Karros .15
141 Mike Piazza 1.25
142 Travis Lee .15
143 Ichiro Suzuki 1.25
144 Shannon Stewart .15
145 Andruw Jones .65
146 Frank Thomas .65
147 Tony Clark .15
148 Adrian Beltre .25
149 Matt Lawton .15
150 Marlon Anderson .15
151 Freddy Garcia .15
152 Brian Jordan .15
153 Carlos Lee .15
154 Eric Munson .15
155 Paul LoDuca .15
156 Jay Payton .15
157 Scott Rolen .50
158 Jamie Moyer .15
159 Tom Glavine .30
160 Magglio Ordonez .15
161 Brandon Inge .15
162 Shawn Green .25
163 Tsuyoshi Shinjo .15
164 Mike Lieberthal .15
165 Kazuhiro Sasaki .15
166 Greg Maddux .75
167 Chris Singleton .15
168 Juan Encarnacion .15
169 Gary Sheffield .25
170 Nick Johnson .15
171 Bobby Abreu .15
172 Aaron Boone .15
173 Rafael Furcal .15
174 Mark Buehrle .15
175 Bobby Higginson .15
176 Kevin Brown .15
177 Tino Martinez .15
178 Pat Burrell .30
179 Fernando Vina .15
180 Jay Gibbons .15
181 Jose Valentin .15
182 Derrek Lee .15
183 Richie Sexson .15
184 Alfonso Soriano .50
185 Jimmy Rollins .25
186 Albert Pujols 1.50
187 Brady Anderson .15
188 Sean Casey .25
189 Luis Castillo .15
190 Jeromy Burnitz .15
191 Jorge Posada .25
192 Kevin Young .15
193 Eli Marrero .15
194 Shea Hillenbrand .15
195 Adam Dunn .40
196 Mike Lowell .15
197 Jeffrey Hammonds .15
198 David Justice .15
199 Aramis Ramirez .15
200 J.D. Drew .25
201 Pedro Santana .15
202 Endy Chavez .15
203 Donnie Bridges .15
204 Travis Phelps .15
205 Drew Henson .25
206 Angel Berroa .15
207 George Perez .15
208 Billy Sylvester .15
209 Juan Cruz .15
210 Horacio Ramirez .15
211 J.J. Davis .15
212 Cody Ransom .15
213 Mark Teixeira .50
214 Nate Frese .15
215 Brian Rogers .15
216 Dewon Brazelton .15
217 Carlos Hernandez .15
218 Juan Rivera .15
219 Luis Lopez .15
220 Benito Baez .15
221 Bill Ortega .15
222 Dustan Mohr .15
223 Corky Miller .15
224 Tyler Walker .15
225 Rick Bauer .15
226 Mark Prior .50
227 Rafael Soriano .15
228 Greg Miller .15
229 Dave Williams .15
230 Bert Snow .15
231 Barry Bonds 1.50
232 Rickey Henderson .50
233 Alex Rodriguez 1.25
234 Luis Gonzalez .25
235 Derek Jeter 1.50
236 Bud Smith .15
237 Sammy Sosa .75
238 Jeff Bagwell .50
239 Jim Thome .15
240 Hideo Nomo .50
241 Greg Maddux .75
242 Ken Griffey Jr. 1.00
243 Curt Schilling .25
244 Arizona Diamondbacks .15
245 Ichiro Suzuki .75
246 Albert Pujols 1.00
247 Ichiro Suzuki .75
248 Barry Bonds 1.50
249 Roger Clemens .65
250 Randy Johnson .50
251 Todd Helton .50
252 Rafael Palmeiro .40
253 Mike Piazza 1.00
254 Alex Rodriguez 1.25
255 Manny Ramirez .50
256 Ken Griffey Jr. 1.00
257 Jason Giambi .40
258 Chipper Jones .65
259 Larry Walker .15
260 Sammy Sosa .75
261 Vladimir Guerrero .50
262 Nomar Garciaparra .75
263 Randy Johnson .50
264 Roger Clemens .65
265 Ichiro Suzuki 1.00
266 Barry Bonds 1.50
267 Paul LoDuca .15
268 Albert Pujols 1.00
269 Derek Jeter 1.50
270 Adam Dunn .40

Batting Average Parallel

Stars: 4-8X
Numbered to 2001 batting avg.

Home Run Parallel

Stars Print Run 50-75: 10-20X
Stars P/R 31-50: 15-25X
Stars P/R 21-30: 20-40X
Numbered to 2001 HR total

RBI Parallel

Stars Print Run 101-200: 4-8X
Stars P/R 76-100: 5-10X
Stars P/R 51-75: 6-12X
Stars P/R 25-50: 10-20X
Numbered to 2001 RBI total

Diamond Immortality

NM/M
Complete Set (10): 25.00
Common Player: 1.00
Inserted 1:12
1DI Derek Jeter 5.00
2DI Barry Bonds 5.00
3DI Ricky Henderson 1.00
4DI Roger Clemens 2.50
5DI Alex Rodriguez 4.00
6DI Albert Pujols 4.00
7DI Nomar Garciaparra 3.00
8DI Ichiro Suzuki 3.00
9DI Chipper Jones 2.00
10DI Ken Griffey Jr. 3.00

Diamond Immortality Game-Used

NM/M
Inserted 1:129
Barry Bonds/Jsy 25.00
Roger Clemens/Jsy 20.00
Nomar Garciaparra/Jsy/SP 40.00
Ricky Henderson/Bat 10.00
Derek Jeter/Bat 25.00
Chipper Jones/Bat 10.00
Albert Pujols/Jsy 25.00
Alex Rodriguez/Jsy 20.00

Home Run Kings

NM/M
Complete Set (25): 100.00
Common Player: 2.00
Inserted 1:24
1 Ted Williams 10.00
2 Todd Helton 4.00
3 Eddie Murray 2.00
4 Jeff Bagwell 4.00
5 Babe Ruth 15.00
6 Eddie Mathews 5.00
7 Alex Rodriguez 10.00
8 Juan Gonzalez 4.00
9 Chipper Jones 5.00
10 Luis Gonzalez 2.00
11 Johnny Bench 5.00
12 Frank Thomas 4.00
13 Ernie Banks 3.00
14 Jimmie Foxx 4.00
15 Ken Griffey Jr. 8.00
16 Rafael Palmeiro 3.00
17 Sammy Sosa 8.00
18 Reggie Jackson 4.00
19 Barry Bonds 10.00
20 Willie McCovey 2.00
21 Manny Ramirez 4.00
22 Larry Walker 2.00
23 Jason Giambi 4.00
24 Mike Piazza 8.00
25 Jose Canseco 2.00

Home Run Kings Autograph

NM/M
Common Player:
Barry Bonds/73 300.00
Alex Rodriguez/52 100.00

Home Run Kings Game-Used

NM/M
Common Player: 5.00
Inserted 1:155
Jeff Bagwell/Jsy 10.00
Johnny Bench/Bat/SP 50.00
Barry Bonds/Jsy 25.00
Jimmie Foxx/Bat 40.00
Jason Giambi/Jsy 10.00
Reggie Jackson/Bat 10.00
Eddie Mathews/Bat 15.00
Eddie Murray/Bat 10.00
Rafael Palmeiro/Bat 10.00
Mike Piazza/Jsy 15.00
Manny Ramirez/Bat/SP 50.00
Todd Helton/Bat 10.00
Alex Rodriguez/Bat 15.00
Larry Walker/Bat 5.00
Ted Williams/Jsy 100.00

RBI Kings

NM/M
Complete Set (15): 140.00
Common Player: 4.00
Inserted 1:144
1 Sammy Sosa 15.00
2 Todd Helton 8.00
3 Albert Pujols 20.00
4 Manny Ramirez 8.00
5 Luis Gonzalez 4.00
6 Shawn Green 4.00
7 Barry Bonds 20.00
8 Ken Griffey Jr. 15.00
9 Alex Rodriguez 20.00
10 Jason Giambi 8.00
11 Jeff Bagwell 8.00
12 Vladimir Guerrero 8.00
13 Juan Gonzalez 8.00
14 Chipper Jones 8.00
15 Mike Piazza 15.00

RBI Kings Game-Used

NM/M
Common Player: 5.00
Inserted 1:70
Jeff Bagwell/Jsy 10.00
Barry Bonds/Jsy 25.00
Jason Giambi/Jsy 8.00
Luis Gonzalez/Bat 5.00
Juan Gonzalez/Bat 8.00
Shawn Green/Jsy 6.00
Todd Helton/Jsy 10.00
Mike Piazza/Jsy 15.00
Albert Pujols/Bat/SP 70.00
Manny Ramirez/Bat 10.00
Alex Rodriguez/Shoe 25.00

Season Crowns

NM/M
Complete Set (10): 25.00
Common Card: 2.00
Inserted 1:12
1SC Barry Bonds, Sammy Sosa, Luis Gonzalez 4.00
2SC Larry Walker, Nomar Garciaparra, Todd Helton 4.00
3SC Sammy Sosa, Todd Helton, Manny Ramirez 4.00
4SC Pedro J. Martinez, Derek Jeter, Cal Ripken Jr. 6.00
5SC Jose Canseco, Barry Bonds, Alex Rodriguez 5.00
6SC Barry Bonds, Jeff Kent, Chipper Jones 4.00
7SC Ichiro Suzuki, Jason Giambi, Ivan Rodriguez 3.00
8SC Curt Schilling, Tom Glavine, Pedro J. Martinez 2.00
9SC Randy Johnson, Pedro J. Martinez, Greg Maddux 3.00
10SC Randy Johnson, Curt Schilling, John Smoltz 2.00

Season Crowns Autograph

NM/M
Jeter #'d to 160.
Derek Jeter/160 150.00
Barry Bonds/77 250.00

Season Crowns Game-Used

NM/M
Common Player: 5.00
Inserted 1:90
Barry Bonds/Jsy 25.00
Sammy Sosa/Base 15.00
Larry Walker/Bat 5.00
Nomar Garciaparra/Jsy 20.00
Todd Helton/Jsy 10.00
Sammy Sosa/Base 15.00
Todd Helton/Jsy 10.00
Manny Ramirez/Jsy 10.00
Pedro Martinez/Jsy 10.00
Derek Jeter/Pants 25.00
Cal Ripken Jr/Bat 60.00
Jose Canseco/Jsy 8.00
Barry Bonds/Jsy 25.00
Alex Rodriguez/Jsy 20.00
Barry Bonds/Jsy 25.00
Jeff Kent/Jsy 5.00
Ichiro Suzuki/Base 25.00
Jason Giambi/Jsy 10.00
Ivan Rodriguez/Jsy 10.00
Curt Schilling/Jsy 10.00
Tom Glavine/Jsy 10.00
Pedro Martinez/Jsy 10.00
Randy Johnson/Jsy 10.00
Pedro Martinez/Jsy 10.00
Greg Maddux/Jsy 15.00
Randy Johnson/Jsy 10.00
Curt Schilling/Jsy 10.00
John Smoltz/Jsy 5.00

Season Crowns Triple Swatch

NM/M
Production 100 Sets
Barry Bonds, Sammy Sosa, Luis Gonzalez 100.00
Larry Walker, Nomar Garciaparra, Todd Helton 40.00
Sammy Sosa, Todd Helton, Manny Ramirez 50.00
Barry Bonds, Jeff Kent, Chipper Jones 80.00
Ichiro Suzuki, Jason Giambi, Ivan Rodriguez 80.00
Curt Schilling, Tom Glavine, Pedro J. Martinez 50.00
Randy Johnson, Pedro J. Martinez, Greg Maddux 50.00
Randy Johnson, Curt Schilling, John Smoltz 50.00

Turn Two Foundation Derek Jeter

In conjunction with Jeter's charitable foundation, Fleer produced a three-card set that was given to youngsters entering an essay contest at after-school recreation centers in New York City. The 2-1/2" x 3-1/2" cards have pictures of Jeter on front and back and information about the contest and the foundation. Fleer reported production as 10,000 sets.

NM/M
Complete Set (3): 13.50
Common Card: 5.00
1 Derek Jeter (Foundation's mission) 5.00
2 Derek Jeter (W/Firefighters) 5.00
3 Derek Jeter (Stats) 5.00

Utz Yankees Starting Five

The starting rotation of the Yankees is featured on this stadium giveaway set sponsored by Utz snacks and produced by Fleer. The 3-1/2" x 2-1/2" horizontal cards have vignetted action photos. The player name is bracketed by the famed Yankee Stadium facade, with the set title in red at bottom. Backs have player biographical data, career highlights and recent stats, along with a serial number from within the edition of 25,000 sets given out to fans 14 and under on June 12. A cover card was included with the set. Autographed versions of the cards were produced for charitable purposes.

NM/M
Complete Set (6): 7.50
Common Player: 1.00
1 Roger Clemens 3.00

1 Roger Clemens/ Auto. 100.00
2 David Wells 1.00
2 David Wells/Auto. 15.00
3 Mike Mussina 2.00
3 Mike Mussina/Auto. 15.00
4 Orlando Hernandez 1.00
4 Orlando Hernandez/ Auto. 25.00
5 Andy Pettitte 1.00
5 Andy Pettitte/Auto. 15.00
-- Cover Card .25

2003 Fleer Authentix

NM/M
Complete Set (160):
Common Player: .25
Common (111-125): 3.00
Production 1,850
Common (126-160): 1.50
Exclusive to Home Team boxes.
Pack (5): 3.00
Box (24): 50.00
1 Derek Jeter 3.00
2 Tom Glavine .40
3 Jason Jennings .25
4 Craig Biggio .25
5 Miguel Tejada .40
6 Barry Bonds 3.00
7 Juan Gonzalez 1.00
8 Luis Gonzalez .40
9 Johnny Damon .40
10 Ellis Burks .25
11 Frank Thomas 1.00
12 Richie Sexson .25
13 Roger Clemens 1.50
14 Matt Morris .25
15 Troy Glaus 1.00
16 Tony Batista .25
17 Magglio Ordonez .25
18 Jose Vidro .25
19 Barry Zito .40
20 Chipper Jones 1.50
21 Moises Alou .25
22 Lance Berkman .25
23 Jacque Jones .25
24 Alfonso Soriano .75
25 Sean Burroughs .25
26 Scott Rolen 1.00
27 Mark Grace .35
28 Manny Ramirez 1.00
29 Ken Griffey Jr. 2.00
30 Josh Beckett .25
31 Kazuhisa Ishii .25
32 Pat Burrell 1.00
33 Edgar Martinez .25
34 Tim Salmon .35
35 Raul Ibanez .25
36 Vladimir Guerrero 1.00
37 Jermaine Dye .25
38 Rich Aurilia .25
39 Rafael Palmeiro .75
40 Kerry Wood .75
41 Omar Vizquel .25
42 Fred McGriff .25
43 Ben Sheets .25
44 Bernie Williams .40
45 Brian Giles .25
46 Jim Edmonds .25
47 Garret Anderson .25
48 Pedro J. Martinez 1.00
49 Adam Dunn .75
50 A.J. Burnett .25
51 Eric Gagne .25
52 Mo Vaughn .25
53 Bobby Abreu .25
54 Bret Boone .25
55 Carlos Delgado .40
56 Gary Sheffield .40
57 Sammy Sosa 2.00
58 Jim Thome .25
59 Jeff Bagwell 1.00
60 David Eckstein .25
61 Jason Kendall .25
62 Albert Pujols 2.50
63 Curt Schilling .40
64 Nomar Garciaparra 2.00
65 Sean Casey .35
66 Shawn Green .40
67 Mike Piazza 2.00
68 Ichiro Suzuki 2.00
69 Eric Hinske .25
70 Greg Maddux 1.50
71 Larry Walker .25
72 Roy Oswalt .40
73 Alex Rodriguez 2.50
74 Austin Kearns .75
75 Cliff Floyd .25
76 Kevin Brown .25
77 Jason Giambi .75
78 Jorge Julio .25
79 Carlos Lee .25
80 Mike Sweeney .25
81 Edgardo Alfonzo .25
82 Eric Chavez .40
83 Andruw Jones 1.00
84 Mark Prior .75
85 Todd Helton 1.00
86 Torii Hunter .25
87 Ryan Klesko .25
88 Aubrey Huff .25
89 Randy Johnson 1.00
90 Barry Larkin .25
91 Mike Lowell .25
92 Jimmy Rollins .40
93 Darin Erstad .65
94 Jay Gibbons .25
95 Paul Konerko .40
96 Bobby Higginson .25
97 Carlos Beltran .60
98 Bartolo Colon .25
99 Jeff Kent .25
100 Ivan Rodriguez .65
101 Joe Borchard .25
102 Mark Teixeira .50
103 Francisco Rodriguez .25
104 Chris Snelling .25
105 Hee Seop Choi .25
106 Hank Blalock .50
107 Marlon Byrd .25
108 Michael Restovich .25
109 Victor Martinez .25
110 Lyle Overbay .25
111 Brian Stokes **RC** 3.00
112 Josh Hall **RC** 4.00
113 Chris Waters **RC** 3.00
114 Lew Ford **RC** 5.00
115 Ian Ferguson **RC** 3.00
116 Josh Willingham **RC** 4.00
117 Josh Stewart **RC** 3.00
118 Pete LaForest **RC** 4.00
119 Jose Contreras **RC** 5.00
120 Terrmel Sledge **RC** 3.00
121 Guillermo Quiroz **RC** 4.00
122 Alejandro Machado **RC** 3.00
123 Nook Logan **RC** 3.00
124 Rontrez Johnson **RC** 4.00
125 Hideki Matsui **RC** 10.00
126 Phil Rizzuto 3.00
127 Robin Ventura 1.50
128 Andy Pettitte 4.00
129 Mike Mussina 3.00
130 Mariano Rivera 3.00
131 Jeff Weaver 1.50
132 David Wells 1.50
133 Tommy Lasorda 2.00
134 Pee Wee Reese 2.00
135 Hideo Nomo 4.00
136 Adrian Beltre 2.00
137 Chin-Feng Chen 4.00
138 Odalis Perez 1.50
139 Dave Roberts 1.50
140 Bobby Doerr 3.00
141 Jason Varitek 1.50
142 Trot Nixon 1.50
143 Tim Wakefield 1.50
144 John Burkett 1.50
145 Jeremy Giambi 1.50
146 Casey Fossum 1.50
147 Phil Niekro 1.50
148 Warren Spahn 4.00
149 Rafael Furcal 2.00
150 Vinny Castilla 1.50
151 Javy Lopez 1.50
152 Jason Marquis 1.50
153 Mike Hampton 1.50
154 Gaylord Perry 1.50
155 Ruben Sierra 1.50
156 Mike Cameron 1.50
157 Freddy Garcia 1.50
158 Joel Pineiro 1.50
159 Jamie Moyer 1.50
160 Carlos Guillen 1.50

Balcony

Stars (1-110): 3-6X
SP's (111-125): .5-1.5X
Production 250 Sets
Club Box (1-110): 5-10X
SP's (111-125): .75-2X
Production 100 Sets
Standing Room Only: No Pricing
Production 25 Sets

Autographed Authentix

NM/M
Quantity produced listed
DJ Derek Jeter/50 150.00
DJ Derek Jeter/150 125.00
DJ Derek Jeter/250 125.00
BB Barry Bonds/50 200.00
BB Barry Bonds/150 200.00
BB Barry Bonds/250 200.00

Autographed Jersey Authentix

NM/M
Quantity produced listed
DJ Derek Jeter/100 150.00
DJ Derek Jeter/200 150.00
DJ Derek Jeter/300 125.00
NR Nolan Ryan/100 185.00
NR Nolan Ryan/200 150.00
NR Nolan Ryan/300 125.00

Ballpark Classics

NM/M
Complete Set (10): 25.00
Common Player: 1.50
Inserted 1:12
1 Derek Jeter 6.00
2 Randy Johnson 2.00
3 Nomar Garciaparra 4.00
4 Barry Bonds 6.00
5 Alfonso Soriano 2.00
6 Alex Rodriguez 5.00
7 Jim Thome 1.50
8 Chipper Jones 3.00
9 Mike Piazza 4.00
10 Ichiro Suzuki 4.00

Bat Authentix

NM/M
Common Player: 8.00
Inserted 1:78
Unripped: 1.5-3X
Production 50 Sets
AD Adam Dunn 8.00
NG Nomar Garciaparra 15.00
JG Jason Giambi 15.00
VG Vladimir Guerrero 10.00
DJ Derek Jeter 30.00
CJ Chipper Jones 10.00
MR Manny Ramirez 10.00
SS Sammy Sosa 15.00
JT Jim Thome 15.00

Hometown Heroes Memorabilia

NM/M
Common Player: 8.00
Home Team Box Exclusive
BB Bret Boone/Jsy/200 8.00
KB Kevin Brown/Jsy/150 10.00
CC Chin-Feng Chen/ Jsy/150 35.00
RC Roger Clemens 25.00
JD Johnny Damon/ Jsy/100 8.00
FG Freddy Garcia/Jsy/200 8.00
NG Nomar Garciaparra 25.00
JG Jason Giambi/ Bat/300 20.00
SG Shawn Green/Jsy/100 8.00
KI Kazuhisa Ishii/Jsy/100 8.00
DJ Derek Jeter 40.00
AJ Andruw Jones/ Jsy/150 10.00
CJ Chipper Jones 15.00
GM Greg Maddux/Jsy 15.00
EM Edgar Martinez/ Jsy/200 10.00
PM Pedro Martinez/ Jsy/100 15.00
MR Manny Ramirez 10.00
GS Gary Sheffield/Jsy/100 8.00
AS Alfonso Soriano 15.00
I Ichiro Suzuki/ Base/100 30.00

Jersey Authentix

NM/M
Common Player: 5.00
Inserted 1:10
Unripped: 1.5-3X
Production 50 Sets
JB Jeff Bagwell 8.00
JB2 Josh Beckett 5.00
LB Lance Berkman 5.00
MB Mark Buehrle 5.00
PB Pat Burrell 10.00
SB Sean Burroughs 5.00
RC Roger Clemens 15.00
CD Carlos Delgado 5.00
AD Adam Dunn 8.00
NG Nomar Garciaparra 15.00
VG Vladimir Guerrero 8.00
EH Eric Hinske 5.00
TH Torii Hunter 6.00
DJ Derek Jeter 25.00
RJ Randy Johnson 8.00
CJ Chipper Jones 8.00
GM Greg Maddux 15.00
MP Mike Piazza 12.00
MR Manny Ramirez 8.00
AR Alex Rodriguez 12.00
AS Alfonso Soriano 10.00
SS Sammy Sosa 12.00
MT Miguel Tejada 5.00
KW Kerry Wood 8.00

Jersey Authentix Game of the Week

NM/M
Common Card: 10.00
Inserted 1:240
Unripped: 1.5-3X
Production 50 Sets
Derek Jeter, Nomar Garciaparra 45.00
Mike Piazza, Sammy Sosa 25.00
Chipper Jones, Pat Burrell 20.00
Greg Maddux, Randy Johnson 20.00
Alex Rodriguez, Miguel Tejada 20.00
Adam Dunn, Lance Berkman 10.00
Torii Hunter, Alfonso Soriano 15.00
Derek Jeter, Miguel Tejada 25.00
Eric Hinske, Torii Hunter 10.00
Alfonso Soriano, Sammy Sosa 15.00

Ticket Studs

NM/M
Complete Set (15): 25.00
Common Player: 1.00
Inserted 1:6
1TS Curt Schilling 1.00
2TS Greg Maddux 2.50
3TS Torii Hunter 1.00
4TS Mike Piazza 3.00
5TS Pedro J. Martinez 2.00
6TS Nomar Garciaparra 3.00
7TS Derek Jeter 5.00
8TS Alex Rodriguez 4.00
9TS Alfonso Soriano 2.00
10TS Pat Burrell 1.50
11TS Barry Bonds 5.00
12TS Jason Giambi 2.50
13TS Sammy Sosa 2.50
14TS Vladimir Guerrero 1.50
15TS Ichiro Suzuki 3.00

2003 Fleer Avant

NM/M
Complete Set (90): 240.00
Common Player: .50
Common Retired SP (66-75): 5.00
Production 799
Common Rk (76-90): 3.00
Production 699
Pack (4): 4.00
Box (18): 60.00
1 Adam Dunn .50
2 Barry Zito .50
3 Preston Wilson .50
4 Barry Bonds 4.00
5 Hank Blalock 1.00
6 Omar Vizquel .50
7 Brian Giles .50
8 Kerry Wood .75
9 Miguel Tejada .75
10 Magglio Ordonez .50
11 Randy Johnson 1.00
12 Jeff Bagwell 1.00
13 Pat Burrell .75
14 Jason Giambi .75
15 Mark Prior .75
16 Roger Clemens 2.00
17 Sammy Sosa 2.50
18 Jay Gibbons .50
19 Torii Hunter .75
20 Ichiro Suzuki 2.00
21 Derek Jeter 4.00
22 Tom Glavine .50
23 Alfonso Soriano 1.00
24 Manny Ramirez 1.00
25 Frank Thomas 1.00
26 Carlos Pena .50
27 Alex Rodriguez 3.00
28 Edgar Martinez .50
29 Larry Walker .50
30 Rafael Palmeiro .75
31 Mike Piazza 2.00
32 Nomar Garciaparra 2.50
33 Lance Berkman .50
34 Vladimir Guerrero 1.00
35 Troy Glaus .75
36 Ivan Rodriguez .75
37 Mark Mulder .50
38 Curt Schilling .75
39 Mike Sweeney .50
40 Albert Pujols 3.00
41 Tim Hudson .50
42 Greg Maddux 1.50
43 Shawn Green .50
44 Scott Rolen 1.00
45 Gary Sheffield .75
46 Richie Sexson .75
47 Aubrey Huff .50
48 Luis Gonzalez .50
49 Todd Helton 1.00
50 Xavier Nady .50
51 Juan Gonzalez 1.00
52 Pedro J. Martinez 1.00
53 Garret Anderson .50
54 Craig Biggio .50
55 Bret Boone .50
56 Ken Griffey Jr. 2.00
57 Kevin Millwood .50
58 Carlos Delgado .75
59 Chipper Jones 1.50
60 Hideo Nomo .50
61 Jim Edmonds .50
62 Austin Kearns .75
63 Jim Thome .50
64 Vernon Wells .50
65 Mike Lowell .50
66 Whitey Ford 5.00
67 Bob Gibson 5.00
68 Reggie Jackson 5.00
69 Willie McCovey 5.00
70 Phil Rizzuto 5.00
71 Al Kaline 6.00
72 Brooks Robinson 5.00
73 Nolan Ryan 15.00
74 Mike Schmidt 10.00
75 Tom Seaver 6.00
76 Hideki Matsui **RC** 15.00
77 Rocco Baldelli 4.00
78 Jose Contreras **RC** 6.00
79 Hee Seop Choi 3.00
80 Jeremy Bonderman 6.00
81 Bo Hart **RC** 3.00
82 Brandon Webb **RC** 10.00
83 Ron Calloway 3.00
84 Jesse Foppert 3.00
85 Kyle Snyder 3.00
86 Mark Teixeira 5.00
87 Jose Reyes 5.00
88 Dontrelle Willis 4.00
89 Reed Johnson 3.00
90 Rickie Weeks **RC** 10.00

Black/White

Stars (1-65): 4-6X
SP's (66-90): 1-2X
Production 199 Sets

Autographs

NM/M
Common Autograph: 10.00
Varying quantities produced
Parallel SP's: 1-1.5X
Production 75 or 150
DJ Derek Jeter/75 140.00
MR Manny Ramirez/100 35.00
VW Vernon Wells/250 10.00
HB Hank Blalock/150 25.00
DW Dontrelle Willis/300 30.00
AK Al Kaline/200 35.00
BR Brooks Robinson/ 300 20.00
BG Bob Gibson/250 25.00
JR Jose Reyes/300 30.00
BZ Barry Zito/150 20.00
EM Edgar Martinez/246 25.00
BH Bo Hart/300 15.00
AH Aubrey Huff/300 15.00
CP Carlos Pena/150 15.00
MT Miguel Tejada/150 20.00
ML Mike Lowell/150 10.00
CB Craig Biggio/250 15.00
BW Brandon Webb/300 25.00
RB Rocco Baldelli/250 30.00

Candid Collection

NM/M
Complete Set (15): 50.00
Common Player: 2.00
Production 500 Sets
1CC Derek Jeter 6.00
2CC Mike Piazza 4.00
3CC Albert Pujols 6.00
4CC Randy Johnson 3.00
5CC Alex Rodriguez 6.00
6CC Vladimir Guerrero 3.00
7CC Troy Glaus 2.00
8CC Ichiro Suzuki 4.00
9CC Barry Zito 2.00
10CC Jim Thome 2.00
11CC Sammy Sosa 5.00
12CC Greg Maddux 4.00
13CC Barry Bonds 8.00
14CC Jason Giambi 3.00
15CC Nomar Garciaparra 6.00

Candid Collection Memorabilia

NM/M
Common Player:
Production 150 Sets
Derek Jeter 30.00
Mike Piazza 12.00
Randy Johnson 8.00
Alex Rodriguez 15.00
Barry Zito 8.00
Jim Thome 15.00
Sammy Sosa 15.00
Greg Maddux 15.00
Jason Giambi 10.00
Nomar Garciaparra 15.00

Hall of Frame

NM/M
Complete Set (14): 80.00
Common Player: 6.00
Production 299 Sets
1 Richie Ashburn 6.00
2 Rod Carew 8.00
3 Whitey Ford 8.00
4 Bob Gibson 8.00
5 Reggie Jackson 8.00
6 Harmon Killebrew 8.00
7 Willie McCovey 6.00
8 Phil Rizzuto 8.00
9 Al Kaline 10.00
10 Brooks Robinson 8.00
11 Nolan Ryan 15.00
12 Mike Schmidt 10.00
13 Tom Seaver 8.00
14 Warren Spahn 8.00

Hall of Frame Memorabilia

NM/M
Production 99 Sets
Reggie Jackson 25.00
Willie McCovey 20.00
Al Kaline 35.00
Nolan Ryan 65.00
Mike Schmidt 40.00

Material

NM/M
Common Player:
Production 50 Sets
RB Rocco Baldelli 25.00
AR Alex Rodriguez 25.00
AS Alfonso Soriano 20.00
SS Sammy Sosa 20.00
NG Nomar Garciaparra 20.00

MT Miguel Tejada 10.00
CJ Chipper Jones 20.00
RJ Randy Johnson 15.00
JT Jim Thome 15.00
GM Greg Maddux 25.00
JG Jason Giambi 15.00
VG Vladimir Guerrero 15.00

On Display

NM/M
Complete Set (10): 50.00
Common Player: 3.00
Production 399 Sets
1OD Derek Jeter 6.00
2OD Barry Bonds 8.00
3OD Rocco Baldelli 5.00
4OD Alex Rodriguez 6.00
5OD Alfonso Soriano 4.00
6OD Sammy Sosa 6.00
7OD Nomar Garciaparra 6.00
8OD Hideki Matsui 20.00
9OD Miguel Tejada 3.00
10OD Chipper Jones 5.00

On Display Memorabilia

NM/M
Common Player: 5.00
Production 250 Sets
Derek Jeter 20.00
Barry Bonds 15.00
Rocco Baldelli 25.00
Alex Rodriguez 10.00
Alfonso Soriano 10.00
Sammy Sosa 12.00
Nomar Garciaparra 15.00
Hideki Matsui 40.00
Miguel Tejada 5.00
Chipper Jones 10.00

2003 Fleer Box Score

NM/M
Complete Set (245):
Common Player: .15
Common Box Score Debut (101-110): 4.00
Production 599
Common Rookie (111-125): 1.00
Inserted 1:6
Complete Rising Stars (30): 25.00
Common (126-155): 1.00
Complete All-Stars (30): 20.00
Common (156-185): .50
Comp. Intl. Road Trip (30): 20.00
Common (186-215): .50
Comp. Bronx Bombers (30): 30.00
Common (216-245): .50
Pack (7): 3.00
Box (18 + 1 Supplemental Box): 40.00
1 Troy Glaus .75
2 Derek Jeter 3.00
3 Alex Rodriguez 2.50
4 Barry Zito .40
5 Darin Erstad .60
6 Tim Hudson .40
7 Josh Beckett .15
8 Adam Dunn .60
9 Tim Salmon .25
10 Ivan Rodriguez .50
11 Mark Buehrle .15
12 Sammy Sosa 2.00
13 Vicente Padilla .15
14 Randy Johnson 1.00
15 Lance Berkman .15
16 Jim Thome .15
17 Luis Gonzalez .25
18 Craig Biggio .15
19 Cliff Floyd .15
20 Pat Burrell .50
21 Matt Morris .15
22 Torii Hunter .15
23 Curt Schilling .40
24 Paul Konerko .15
25 Jeff Bagwell .75
26 Mike Piazza 2.00
27 A.J. Burnett .15
28 Jimmy Rollins .25
29 Greg Maddux 1.50
30 Jeff Kent .15
31 Bobby Abreu .15
32 Chipper Jones 1.50
33 Mike Sweeney .15
34 Jason Kendall .15
35 Gary Sheffield .30
36 Carlos Beltran .50
37 Brian Giles .15
38 Jim Edmonds .15
39 Roger Clemens 1.75
40 Andruw Jones .75
41 Paul LoDuca .15
42 Ryan Klesko .15
43 Jay Gibbons .15
44 Shawn Green .40
45 Sean Burroughs .15
46 Magglio Ordonez .15
47 Tony Batista .15
48 J.D. Drew .45
49 Hideo Nomo .50
50 Edgardo Alfonzo .15
51 Nomar Garciaparra 2.00
52 Frank Thomas .75
53 Kazuhisa Ishii .15
54 Rich Aurilia .15
55 Shea Hillenbrand .15
56 Tom Glavine .40
57 Richie Sexson .15
58 Mo Vaughn .15
59 Barry Bonds 3.00
60 Carlos Delgado .50
61 Pedro J. Martinez 1.00
62 Jacque Jones .15
63 Edgar Martinez .15
64 Manny Ramirez .75
65 Bret Boone .15
66 Kerry Wood .50
67 Roy Oswalt .40
68 Cristian Guzman .15
69 Moises Alou .15
70 Bartolo Colon .15
71 Ichiro Suzuki 1.50
72 Jose Vidro .15
73 Scott Rolen .75
74 Mark Prior 1.00
75 Vladimir Guerrero .75
76 Albert Pujols 1.50
77 Aubrey Huff .15
78 Ken Griffey Jr. 2.00
79 Roberto Alomar .30
80 Ben Grieve .15
81 Miguel Tejada .40
82 Austin Kearns .50
83 Jason Giambi .75
84 John Olerud .15
85 Omar Vizquel .15
86 Juan Gonzalez .75
87 Larry Walker .15
88 Jorge Posada .25
89 Rafael Palmeiro .65
90 Todd Helton .75
91 Bernie Williams .30
92 Garret Anderson .15
93 Eric Hinske .15
94 Mike Lowell .15
95 Jason Jennings .15
96 Eric Chavez .30
97 Alfonso Soriano 1.00
98 David Eckstein .15
99 Bobby Higginson .15
100 Roy Halladay .15
101 Robby Hammock **RC** 4.00
102 Hideki Matsui **RC** 12.00
103 Chase Utley 4.00
104 Oscar Villarreal **RC** 4.00
105 Jose Contreras **RC** 8.00
106 Rocco Baldelli 4.00
107 Rontrez Johnson **RC** 4.00
108 Jeremy Bonderman 8.00
109 Shane Victorino **RC** 4.00
110 Ron Calloway 4.00
111 Brandon Webb **RC** 4.00
112 Guillermo Quiroz **RC** 2.00
113 Clint Barmes **RC** 2.00
114 Pete LaForest **RC** 1.00
115 Craig Brazell **RC** 2.00
116 Todd Wellemeyer **RC** 1.00
117 Bernie Castro **RC** 1.00
118 Alejandro Machado **RC** 1.00
119 Terrmel Sledge **RC** 1.00
120 Ian Ferguson **RC** 1.00
121 Lew Ford **RC** 3.00
122 Nook Logan **RC** 1.50
123 Mike Nicolas **RC** 1.50
124 Jeff Duncan **RC** 1.50
125 Tim Olson **RC** 1.00
126 Michael Hessman **RC** 1.00
127 Francisco Rosario **RC** 1.00
128 Felix Sanchez **RC** 1.00
129 Andrew Brown **RC** 1.50
130 Matt Bruback **RC** 2.00
131 Diegomar Markwell **RC** 2.00
132 Josh Willingham **RC** 1.00
133 Wes Obermueller 1.50
134 Phil Seibel **RC** 2.00
135 Arnie Munoz **RC** 1.00
136 Matt Kata **RC** 3.00
137 Joe Valentine **RC** 1.00
138 Ricardo Rodriguez 1.00
139 Lyle Overbay 2.00
140 Brian Stokes **RC** 1.00
141 Josh Hall **RC** 1.50
142 Kevin Hooper 1.00
143 Chien-Ming Wang **RC** 10.00
144 Prentice Redman **RC** 1.50
145 Chris Waters **RC** 1.50
146 Jon Leicester **RC** 1.00
147 Daniel Cabrera **RC** 3.00
148 Alfredo Gonzalez **RC** 1.50
149 Doug Waechter **RC** 1.50
150 Brandon Larson 1.00
151 Beau Kemp **RC** 1.50
152 Cory Stewart **RC** 1.00
153 Francisco Rodriguez 1.00
154 Hee Seop Choi 1.50
155 Mike Neu **RC** 1.00
156 Derek Jeter 3.00
157 Alex Rodriguez 2.50
158 Nomar Garciaparra 2.00
159 Barry Bonds 2.50
160 Sammy Sosa 1.50
161 Vladimir Guerrero .75
162 Roger Clemens 2.00
163 Randy Johnson 1.00
164 Greg Maddux 1.50
165 Ken Griffey Jr. 1.50
166 Mike Piazza 2.00
167 Ichiro Suzuki 1.50
168 Barry Larkin .50
169 Lance Berkman .50
170 Jim Thome .75
171 Jason Giambi 1.00
172 Gary Sheffield .50
173 Ivan Rodriguez .50
174 Miguel Tejada .50
175 Manny Ramirez .75
176 Mike Sweeney .50
177 Larry Walker .50
178 Jeff Bagwell .75
179 Chipper Jones 1.50
180 Craig Biggio .50
181 Curt Schilling .50
182 Pedro J. Martinez 1.00
183 Roberto Alomar .50
184 Bernie Williams .50
185 Magglio Ordonez .50
186 Jose Contreras 1.00
187 Rafael Palmeiro 1.00
188 Andruw Jones .75
189 Bartolo Colon .50
190 Vladimir Guerrero .75
191 Pedro Martinez 1.00
192 Albert Pujols 1.50
193 Manny Ramirez .75
194 Felix Rodriguez .50
195 Alfonso Soriano 1.00
196 Sammy Sosa 1.50
197 Miguel Tejada .50
198 Kazuhisa Ishii .50
199 Hideki Matsui 5.00
200 Hideo Nomo 1.00
201 Tomokazu Ohka .50
202 Kazuhiro Sasaki .50
203 Tsuyoshi Shinjo .50
204 Ichiro Suzuki 1.50
205 Vicente Padilla .50
206 Carlos Beltran .50
207 Jose Cruz Jr. .50
208 Carlos Delgado .50
209 Juan Gonzalez .75
210 Jorge Posada .50
211 Ivan Rodriguez .50
212 Hee Seop Choi .50
213 Bobby Abreu .50
214 Magglio Ordonez .50
215 Francisco Rodriguez .50
216 Juan Acevedo .50
217 Erick Almonte .50
218 Yogi Berra 1.50
219 Brandon Claussen 1.00
220 Roger Clemens 2.00
221 Jose Contreras 1.00
222 Whitey Ford 1.00
223 Jason Giambi 1.00
224 Chris Hammond .50
225 Michel Hernandez **RC** .50
226 Sterling Hitchcock .50
227 Jim "Catfish" Hunter .75
228 Reggie Jackson 1.00
229 Derek Jeter 3.00
230 Nick Johnson .50
231 Hideki Matsui 5.00
232 Raul Mondesi .50
233 Mike Mussina .75
234 Andy Pettitte .50
235 Jorge Posada .50
236 Mariano Rivera .50
237 Phil Rizzuto 1.00
238 Enos Slaughter .50
239 Alfonso Soriano 1.00
240 Robin Ventura .50
241 Chien-Ming Wang 2.00
242 Jeff Weaver .50
243 David Wells .50
244 Bernie Williams .75
245 Todd Zeile .50

First Edition

Stars (1-100): 4-8X
Rookies (101-125): 1.5-3X
Production 150 Sets

All-Star Lineup

NM/M
Common Card: 15.00
Inserted 1:All-Stars Set
Derek Jeter, Alex Rodriguez, Nomar Garciaparra 35.00
Barry Bonds, Sammy Sosa, Vladimir Guerrero 15.00
Roger Clemens, Randy Johnson, Greg Maddux 30.00
Jason Giambi, Alfonso Soriano, Derek Jeter 30.00
Craig Biggio, Jeff Bagwell, Lance Berkman 20.00
Chipper Jones, Gary Sheffield, Greg Maddux 30.00
Ivan Rodriguez, Mike Piazza, Randy Johnson, Roger Clemens 40.00
Roberto Alomar, Mike Piazza, Alfonso Soriano, Jason Giambi 45.00
Jim Thome, Roberto Alomar, Alex Rodriguez, Nomar Garciaparra 40.00

Bat Rack

NM/M
Common Card: 20.00
Production 250 Sets
Derek Jeter, Alfonso Soriano, Jason Giambi 35.00
Scott Rolen, Miguel Tejada, Troy Glaus 20.00
Jim Thome, Torii Hunter, Mike Piazza 25.00
Troy Glaus, Nomar Garciaparra, Alfonso Soriano 30.00
Lance Berkman, Vladimir Guerrero, Sammy Sosa 20.00
Chipper Jones, Lance Berkman, Vladimir Guerrero 20.00
Torii Hunter, Jason Giambi, Nomar Garciaparra 25.00
Derek Jeter, Miguel Tejada, Alex Rodriguez 25.00
Scott Rolen, Sammy Sosa, Alex Rodriguez 25.00

Bat Rack Quad

NM/M
Production 50 Sets
Derek Jeter, Torii Hunter, Troy Glaus, Miguel Tejada 40.00
Derek Jeter, Mike Piazza, Nomar Garciaparra, Chipper Jones 60.00
Alex Rodriguez, Jim Thome, Sammy Sosa, Barry Bonds 50.00

Bronx Bombers Jersey

NM/M
Common Player: 4.00
Inserted 1:Bronx Bombers Set
Roger Clemens 15.00
Jason Giambi 12.00
Derek Jeter 20.00
Nick Johnson 4.00
Mike Mussina 10.00
Jorge Posada 8.00
Alfonso Soriano 10.00
Robin Ventura 5.00
Bernie Williams 8.00

Classic Minatures

NM/M
Complete Set (30): 10.00
Common Player: .25
1CM Jim Thome .40
2CM Jason Giambi .50
3CM Miguel Tejada .25
4CM Alfonso Soriano 1.00
5CM Ivan Rodriguez .40
6CM Troy Glaus .40
7CM Mike Piazza 1.00
8CM Barry Bonds 1.50
9CM Sammy Sosa 1.00
10CM Lance Berkman .25
11CM Pat Burrell .25
12CM Chipper Jones .75
13CM Shawn Green .25
14CM Manny Ramirez .50
15CM Ichiro Suzuki .75
16CM Vladimir Guerrero .50
17CM Albert Pujols .75
18CM Ken Griffey Jr. 1.00
19CM Bernie Williams .40
20CM Austin Kearns .40
21CM Randy Johnson .50
22CM Greg Maddux .75
23CM Roger Clemens 1.00
24CM Hideo Nomo .25
25CM Pedro J. Martinez .50
26CM Kerry Wood .40
27CM Mark Prior .50
28CM Derek Jeter 1.50
29CM Alex Rodriguez 1.00
30CM Nomar Garciaparra 1.00

Classic Miniatures Mini Jersey

NM/M
Common Jersey: 4.00
1:Classic Miniatures Box
NG Nomar Garciaparra 10.00
JG Jason Giambi 8.00
VG Vladimir Guerrero 5.00
DJ Derek Jeter 15.00
AK Austin Kearns 8.00
GM Greg Maddux 10.00
HN Hideo Nomo 10.00
MP Mark Prior 10.00
MT Miguel Tejada 4.00
JT Jim Thome 8.00

Jersey Rack

NM/M
Common Card: 15.00
Production 350 Sets
Derek Jeter, Alfonso Soriano, Jason Giambi 40.00
Curt Schilling, Randy Johnson, Greg Maddux 25.00
Roger Clemens, Pedro J. Martinez, Barry Zito 30.00
Alex Rodriguez, Vladimir Guerrero, Sammy Sosa 25.00
Derek Jeter, Nomar Garciaparra, Alex Rodriguez 30.00
Lance Berkman, Sammy Sosa, Torii Hunter 20.00
Vladimir Guerrero, Jim Thome, Alex Rodriguez 20.00
Derek Jeter, Miguel Tejada, Nomar Garciaparra 30.00
Alfonso Soriano, Eric Chavez, Jim Thome 20.00
Miguel Tejada, Eric Chavez, Barry Zito 15.00

Jersey Rack Quad

NM/M
Common Card:
Production 150 Sets
Derek Jeter, Alex Rodriguez, Nomar Garciaparra, Miguel Tejada 60.00
Jim Thome, Jason Giambi, Sammy Sosa, Vladimir Guerrero 50.00
Randy Johnson, Greg Maddux, Roger Clemens, Pedro J. Martinez 60.00
Curt Schilling, Vladimir Guerrero, Randy Johnson, Alex Rodriguez 40.00
Alfonso Soriano, Jim Thome, Sammy Sosa, Eric Chavez 40.00
Eric Chavez, Miguel Tejada, Barry Zito, Nomar Garciaparra 20.00

Press Clippings

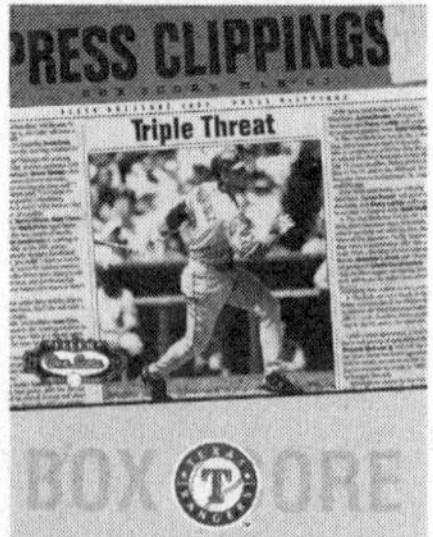

NM/M
Complete Set (20): 40.00
Common Player: 1.00
Inserted 1:18
1PC Derek Jeter 6.00
2PC Nomar Garciaparra 5.00
3PC Miguel Tejada 1.00
4PC Barry Bonds 5.00
5PC Alex Rodriguez 5.00
6PC Sammy Sosa 3.00
7PC Lance Berkman 1.00
8PC Torii Hunter 1.00
9PC Troy Glaus 1.50
10PC Eric Chavez 1.00
11PC Tim Hudson 1.00
12PC Randy Johnson 2.00
13PC Mike Piazza 4.00
14PC Roberto Alomar 1.50
15PC Jim Thome 1.50
16PC Alfonso Soriano 3.00
17PC Roger Clemens 4.00
18PC Pedro J. Martinez 2.00
19PC Mark Prior 1.50
20PC Curt Schilling 1.00

Press Clippings Game-Used

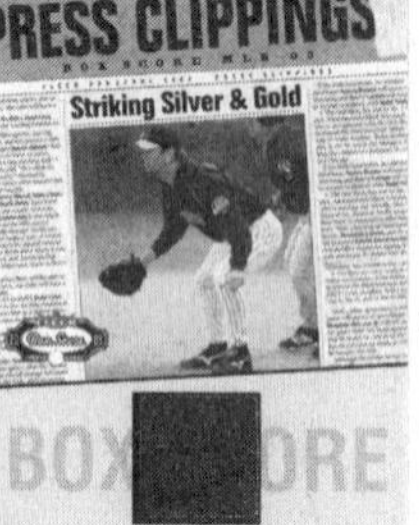

NM/M
Common Player: 4.00
Inserted 1:12
Derek Jeter 15.00
Nomar Garciaparra 15.00
Miguel Tejada 4.00
Alex Rodriguez 10.00
Sammy Sosa 12.00
Lance Berkman 4.00
Torii Hunter 6.00
Troy Glaus 5.00
Eric Chavez 4.00
Tim Hudson 4.00
Randy Johnson 8.00
Mike Piazza 12.00
Roberto Alomar 8.00
Jim Thome 10.00
Alfonso Soriano 10.00
Roger Clemens 12.00
Pedro J. Martinez 8.00
Mark Prior 6.00
Curt Schilling 4.00

Press Clippings Dual

		NM/M
Complete Set (10):		35.00
Common Player:		2.00
Production 250 Sets		
1	Derek Jeter, Nomar Garciaparra	8.00
2	Miguel Tejada, Barry Bonds	6.00
3	Alex Rodriguez, Sammy Sosa	6.00
4	Lance Berkman, Torii Hunter	2.00
5	Troy Glaus, Eric Chavez	2.00
6	Tim Hudson, Randy Johnson	3.00
7	Mike Piazza, Roberto Alomar	5.00
8	Jim Thome, Alfonso Soriano	4.00
9	Roger Clemens, Pedro J. Martinez	5.00
10	Mark Prior, Curt Schilling	2.00

Press Clippings Dual Patch

	NM/M
Common Card:	25.00
Derek Jeter, Nomar Garciaparra/100	60.00
Miguel Tejada, Troy Glaus/150	25.00
Alex Rodriguez, Sammy Sosa/150	80.00
Lance Berkman, Torii Hunter/150	30.00
Troy Glaus, Eric Chavez/150	30.00
Tim Hudson, Randy Johnson/150	30.00
Mike Piazza, Roberto Alomar/150	40.00
Jim Thome, Alfonso Soriano/100	40.00
Roger Clemens, Pedro Martinez/100	50.00
Mark Prior, Curt Schilling/150	25.00

Wave of the Future

	NM/M
Common Player:	4.00
Inserted 1:Rising Stars Set	
Jeremy Bonderman/Bat	12.00
Ron Calloway/Jsy	4.00
Hee Seop Choi/Jsy	10.00
Brandon Larson/Bat	8.00
Lyle Overbay/Bat	6.00
Francisco Rodriguez/Jsy	6.00
Chase Utley/Jsy	6.00

World Piece

	NM/M
Common Player:	4.00
Inserted 1:Intl. Road Trip Set	
Vladimir Guerrero	6.00
Pedro Martinez	10.00
Sammy Sosa	12.00
Miguel Tejada	4.00
Hideo Nomo	10.00
Jose Cruz Jr.	4.00
Ivan Rodriguez	6.00
Hee Seop Choi	10.00
Francisco Rodriguez	4.00
Kazuhiro Sasaki	4.00

2003 Fleer Double Header

		NM/M
Complete Set (300):		60.00
Common Player:		.20
Common (181-300):		.40
Pack (8):		2.00
Box (20):		35.00
1	Ramon Vazquez	.20
2	Derek Jeter	2.00
3	Orlando Hudson	.20
4	Miguel Tejada	.30
5	Steve Finley	.20
6	Brad Wilkerson	.20
7	Craig Biggio	.20
8	Marlon Anderson	.20
9	Phil Nevin	.20
10	Hideo Nomo	.50
11	Barry Larkin	.20
12	Alfonso Soriano	.75
13	Rodrigo Lopez	.20
14	Paul Konerko	.25
15	Carlos Beltran	.50
16	Garret Anderson	.20
17	Kazuhisa Ishii	.20
18	Eddie Guardado	.20
19	Juan Gonzalez	.50
20	Mark Mulder	.20
21	Sammy Sosa	1.25
22	Kazuhiro Sasaki	.20
23	Jose Cruz Jr.	.20
24	Tomokazu Ohka	.20
25	Barry Bonds	2.00
26	Carlos Delgado	.50
27	Scott Rolen	.50
28	Steve Cox	.20
29	Mike Sweeney	.20
30	Ryan Klesko	.20
31	Greg Maddux	1.00
32	Derek Lowe	.20
33	David Wells	.20
34	Kerry Wood	.40
35	Randall Simon	.20
36	Ben Howard	.20
37	Jeff Suppan	.20
38	Curt Schilling	.40
39	Eric Gagne	.20
40	Raul Mondesi	.20
41	Jeffrey Hammonds	.20
42	Mo Vaughn	.20
43	Sidney Ponson	.20
44	Adam Dunn	.50
45	Pedro J. Martinez	.75
46	Jason Simontacchi	.20
47	Tom Glavine	.40
48	Torii Hunter	.20
49	Gabe Kapler	.20
50	Andy Van Hekken	.20
51	Ichiro Suzuki	1.25
52	Andruw Jones	.50
53	Bobby Abreu	.20
54	Junior Spivey	.20
55	Ray Durham	.20
56	Mark Buehrle	.20
57	Drew Henson	.20
58	Brandon Duckworth	.20
59	Robert Mackowiak	.20
60	Josh Beckett	.20
61	Chan Ho Park	.20
62	John Smoltz	.20
63	Jimmy Rollins	.40
64	Orlando Cabrera	.20
65	Johnny Damon	.20
66	Austin Kearns	.40
67	Tsuyoshi Shinjo	.20
68	Tim Hudson	.30
69	Coco Crisp	.20
70	Darin Erstad	.60
71	Jacque Jones	.20
72	Vicente Padilla	.20
73	Hee Seop Choi	.20
74	Shea Hillenbrand	.20
75	Edgardo Alfonzo	.20
76	Pat Burrell	.50
77	Ben Sheets	.20
78	Ivan Rodriguez	.40
79	Josh Phelps	.20
80	Adam Kennedy	.20
81	Eric Chavez	.30
82	Bobby Higginson	.20
83	Nomar Garciaparra	1.50
84	J.D. Drew	.30
85	Carl Crawford	.20
86	Matt Morris	.20
87	Chipper Jones	1.00
88	Luis Gonzalez	.30
89	Richie Sexson	.20
90	Eric Milton	.20
91	Andres Galarraga	.20
92	Paul LoDuca	.20
93	Mark Grace	.30
94	Ben Grieve	.20
95	Mike Lowell	.20
96	Roberto Alomar	.35
97	Wade Miller	.20
98	Sean Casey	.20
99	Roger Clemens	1.25
100	Matt Williams	.20
101	Brian Giles	.20
102	Jim Thome	.20
103	Troy Glaus	.75
104	Joe Borchard	.20
105	Vladimir Guerrero	.75
106	Kevin Mench	.20
107	Omar Vizquel	.20
108	Magglio Ordonez	.20
109	Ken Griffey Jr.	1.50
110	Mike Piazza	1.50
111	Mark Teixeira	.40
112	Jason Jennings	.20
113	Ellis Burks	.20
114	Jason Varitek	.20
115	Larry Walker	.20
116	Frank Thomas	.75
117	Ramon Ortiz	.20
118	Mark Quinn	.20
119	Preston Wilson	.20
120	Carlos Lee	.20
121	Brian Lawrence	.20
122	Tim Salmon	.20
123	Shawn Green	.30
124	Randy Johnson	.75
125	Jeff Bagwell	.75
126	C.C. Sabathia	.20
127	Bernie Williams	.35
128	Roy Oswalt	.30
129	Albert Pujols	.75
130	Reggie Sanders	.20
131	Jeff Conine	.20
132	John Olerud	.20
133	Lance Berkman	.20
134	Geoff Jenkins	.20
135	Jim Edmonds	.20
136	Todd Helton	.65
137	Jason Kendall	.20
138	Robin Ventura	.20
139	Randy Winn	.20
140	Carl Everett	.20
141	Jose Vidro	.20
142	Pokey Reese	.20
143	Edgar Renteria	.20
144	Alex Rodriguez	1.75
145	Doug Mientkiewicz	.20
146	Aramis Ramirez	.20
147	Bobby Hill	.20
148	Jorge Posada	.35
149	Sean Burroughs	.20
150	Jeff Kent	.20
151	Tino Martinez	.20
152	Mark Prior	.50
153	Brad Radke	.20
154	Al Leiter	.20
155	Eric Karros	.20
156	Manny Ramirez	.50
157	Jason Lane	.20
158	Mike Lieberthal	.20
159	Shannon Stewart	.20
160	Robert Fick	.20
161	Derrek Lee	.20
162	Jason Giambi	.50
163	Rafael Palmeiro	.65
164	Jay Payton	.20
165	Adrian Beltre	.20
166	Marlon Byrd	.20
167	Bret Boone	.20
168	Roy Halladay	.20
169	Freddy Garcia	.20
170	Rich Aurilia	.20
171	Jared Sandberg	.20
172	Paul Byrd	.20
173	Gary Sheffield	.30
174	Edgar Martinez	.20
175	Eric Hinske	.20
176	Milton Bradley	.20
177	David Eckstein	.20
178	Jay Gibbons	.20
179	Corey Patterson	.20
180	Barry Zito	.20
181-182	Darin Erstad, Troy Glaus	.50
183-184	Curt Schilling, Randy Johnson	.75
185-186	Andruw Jones, Chipper Jones	1.00
187-188	Tony Batista, Jay Gibbons	.40
189-190	Pedro Martinez, Nomar Garciaparra	1.25
191-192	Sammy Sosa, Kerry Wood	1.00
193-194	Paul Konerko, Joe Borchard	.40
195-196	Austin Kearns, Adam Dunn	.50
197-198	Omar Vizquel, Jim Thome	.50
199-200	Larry Walker, Todd Helton	.40
201-202	Josh Beckett, Luis Castillo	.40
203-204	Craig Biggio, Jeff Bagwell	.50
205-206	Paul Byrd, Mike Sweeney	.40
207-208	Adrian Beltre, Shawn Green	.40
209-210	Jose Hernandez, Richie Sexson	.40
211-212	Jacque Jones, Torii Hunter	.40
213-214	Vladimir Guerrero, Jose Vidro	.75
215-216	Edgardo Alfonzo, Mike Piazza	1.50
217-218	Roger Clemens, Derek Jeter	2.00
219-220	Eric Chavez, Miguel Tejada	.40
221-222	Marlon Byrd, Pat Burrell	.50
223-224	Jason Kendall, Brian Giles	.40
225-226	Phil Nevin, Sean Burroughs	.40
227-228	Jeff Kent, Barry Bonds	2.00
229-230	Kazuhiro Sasaki, Ichiro Suzuki	1.25
231-232	Albert Pujols, J.D. Drew	.75
233-234	Juan Gonzalez, Ivan Rodriguez	.50
235-236	Eric Hinske, Orlando Hudson	.40
237-238	Lance Berkman, Chipper Jones	1.00
239-240	Alex Rodriguez, Derek Jeter	2.00
241-242	Ichiro Suzuki, Hideo Nomo	1.25
243-244	Manny Ramirez, Bernie Williams	.50
245-246	Tom Glavine, Roger Clemens	1.00
247-248	Ken Griffey Jr., Barry Larkin	1.25
249-250	Mark Teixeira, Mark Prior	.40
251-252	Albert Pujols, Drew Henson	.75
253-254	Jason Giambi, Todd Helton	1.00
255-256	Jose Vidro, Alfonso Soriano	.75
257-258	Shea Hillenbrand, Scott Rolen	.50
259-260	Jimmy Rollins, Alex Rodriguez	2.00
261-262	Torii Hunter, Vladimir Guerrero	.75
263-264	Ichiro Suzuki, Sammy Sosa	1.25
265-266	Barry Bonds, Manny Ramirez	2.00
267-268	Mike Piazza, Jorge Posada	1.25
269-270	Robin Yount, Ozzie Smith	1.00
271-272	Josh Hancock, Freddy Sanchez	.40
273-274	Ryan Bukvich, Shawn Sedlacek	.40
275-276	Doug DeVore, Rene Reyes	.40
277-278	Hank Blalock, Travis Hafner	.50
279-280	Eric Junge, Brett Myers	.40
281-282	Brad Lidge, Jeriome Robertson	.40
283-284	Miguel Asencio, Runelvys Hernandez	.40
285-286	Fernando Rodney, Barry Wesson	.40
287-288	Victor Alvarez, David Ross	.40
289-290	Tony Torcato, Chris Snelling	.50
291-292	Kirk Saarloos, Morgan Ensberg	.40
293-294	Josh Bard, Wilbert Nieves	.40
295-296	Jung Bong, Trey Hodges	.40
297-298	Kevin Cash, Reed Johnson	.40
299-300	Chone Figgins, John Lackey	.40

Flip Card Memorabilia

		NM/M
Common Player:		4.00
Inserted 1:20		
Golds:		.75-2X
Production 100 Sets		
1	Roberto Alomar/Bat/200	10.00
2	Jeff Bagwell/Jsy	8.00
3	Adrian Beltre/Jsy	4.00
4	Barry Bonds/Bat/200	15.00
5	Roger Clemens/Jsy/200	12.00
6	J.D. Drew/Jsy	6.00
7	Adam Dunn/Jsy/200	10.00
8	Nomar Garciaparra/Jsy/200	15.00
9	Mark Grace/Jsy	8.00
10	Todd Helton/Jsy/200	8.00
11	Derek Jeter/Jsy/200	20.00
12	Randy Johnson/Jsy/200	10.00
13	Chipper Jones/Jsy	8.00
14	Eric Karros/Jsy	4.00
15	Barry Larkin/Jsy/200	8.00
16	Greg Maddux/Jsy/200	10.00
17	Hideo Nomo/Jsy/200	10.00
18	Kazuhisa Ishii/Jsy	6.00
19	Mike Piazza/Jsy/200	10.00
20	Jorge Posada/Jsy/200	8.00
21	Mark Prior/Jsy/200	5.00
22	Alex Rodriguez/Jsy	10.00
23	Kazuhiro Sasaki/Jsy/200	6.00
24	Curt Schilling/Jsy/200	8.00
25	Alfonso Soriano/Jsy	8.00
26	Miguel Tejada/Jsy	8.00
27	Jim Thome/Jsy/200	10.00
28	Robin Ventura/Jsy	4.00
29	Bernie Williams/Jsy/200	8.00
30	Kerry Wood/Jsy/200	10.00

Keystone Combination

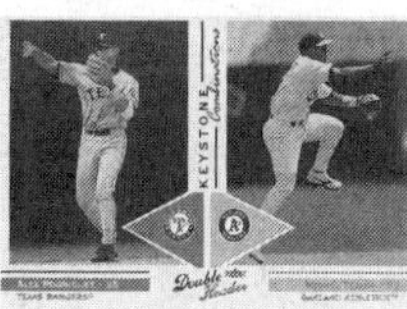

		NM/M
Complete Set (10):		25.00
Common Card:		1.00
Inserted 1:10		
1KC	Derek Jeter, Bret Boone	6.00
2KC	Miguel Tejada, Jeff Kent	1.00
3KC	Nomar Garciaparra, Ray Durham	4.00
4KC	Omar Vizquel, Roberto Alomar	1.00
5KC	Pee Wee Reese, Joe Morgan	1.00
6KC	Alex Rodriguez, Craig Biggio	5.00
7KC	Orlando Hudson, Jose Vidro	1.00
8KC	Phil Rizzuto, Alfonso Soriano	3.00
9KC	Alex Rodriguez, Miguel Tejada	5.00
10KC	Nomar Garciaparra, Derek Jeter	6.00

Keystone Combination Memorabilia

	NM/M
Common Card:	4.00
Inserted 1:40	
Derek Jeter, Bret Boone/Jsy	8.00
Miguel Tejada, Jeff Kent/Jsy	4.00
N.Garciaparra/Jsy/175, Ray Durham	12.00
Omar Vizquel, Roberto Alomar/Jsy	6.00
Alex Rodriguez, Craig Biggio/Jsy	6.00
Orlando Hudson, Jose Vidro/Jsy	4.00
Phil Rizzuto, Alfonso Soriano/Jsy/75	15.00
Alex Rodriguez/Bat, Miguel Tejada	10.00
N.Garciaparra/Jsy/175, Derek Jeter	12.00
Derek Jeter/Jsy/175, Bret Boone	20.00
Derek Jeter/Jsy/175, Nomar Garciaparra	20.00
Alex Rodriguez/Jsy/200, Craig Biggio	10.00
Miguel Tejada/Jsy, Jeff Kent	8.00
Miguel Tejada/Jsy, Alex Rodriguez	8.00

Let's Play, Too!

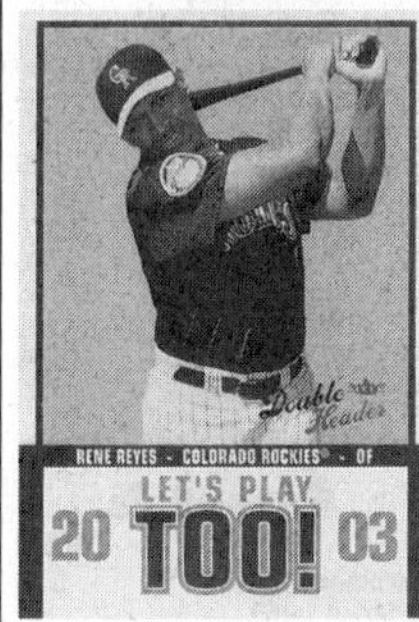

		NM/M
Complete Set (15):		8.00
Common Player:		.50
Inserted 1:5		
1LPT	Chris Snelling	1.00
2LPT	Kevin Mench	.50
3LPT	Brett Meyers	.50
4LPT	Julius Matos	.50
5LPT	Drew Henson	1.00
6LPT	Joe Borchard	.50
7LPT	Felix Escalona	.50
8LPT	Kirk Saarloos	.50
9LPT	Ben Howard	.50
10LPT	Hee Seop Choi	1.00
11LPT	Rene Reyes	.50
12LPT	Josh Bard	.50
13LPT	Marlon Byrd	.50
14LPT	Coco Crisp	.50
15LPT	Reed Johnson	.50

Matinee Idols

		NM/M
Complete Set (15):		50.00
Common Player:		2.00
Inserted 1:20		
1MI	Yogi Berra	3.00
2MI	Richie Ashburn	3.00
3MI	Whitey Ford	3.00
4MI	Eddie Mathews	3.00
5MI	Jim Palmer	2.00
6MI	Al Kaline	6.00
7MI	Brooks Robinson	3.00
8MI	Willie McCovey	3.00
9MI	Billy Williams	2.00
10MI	Willie Stargell	3.00
11MI	Nolan Ryan	15.00
12MI	Rod Carew	3.00
13MI	Reggie Jackson	3.00
14MI	Tom Seaver	4.00
15MI	Mike Schmidt	6.00

Twin Bill

		NM/M
Complete Set (20):		45.00
Common Player:		1.00
Inserted 1:10		
1a	Barry Bonds	5.00
1b	Lance Berkman	1.00
2a	Derek Jeter	6.00
2b	Alex Rodriguez	5.00
3a	Roger Clemens	3.00
3b	Pedro Martinez	2.00
4a	Roberto Alomar	1.25
4b	Chipper Jones	3.00
5a	Barry Zito	1.00
5b	Ichiro Suzuki	4.00
6a	Sammy Sosa	3.00
6b	Ken Griffey Jr.	4.00
7a	Bernie Williams	1.00
7b	Manny Ramirez	1.50
8a	Nomar Garciaparra	4.00
8b	Derek Jeter	6.00
9a	Randy Johnson	2.00
9b	Greg Maddux	3.00
10a	Albert Pujols	2.00
10b	Adam Dunn	1.50

Twin Bill Single Swatch

	NM/M
Common Player:	1.00
Barry Bonds/Cap/100	25.00
Alex Rodriguez/Cap/100	15.00
Roger Clemens/Cap/100	15.00
Pedro Martinez/Cap/100	12.00
Roberto Alomar/Cap	10.00
Barry Zito/Cap/100	15.00
Bernie Williams/Cap/100	10.00
Manny Ramirez/Cap/75	12.00

Nomar Garciaparra/ Cap/100 25.00
Derek Jeter/Cap/100 30.00
Randy Johnson/ Cap/100 15.00
Adam Dunn/Cap/100 12.00

Twin Bill Dual Swatch

NM/M
Common Card:
Production 50 Sets
Barry Bonds, Adam Dunn 40.00
Randy Johnson, Barry Zito 35.00

2003 Fleer E-X

NM/M
Complete Set (102): 125.00
Common Player: .50
Common SP (83-102): 3.00
Pack (3): 4.00
Box (20): 60.00
1 Troy Glaus .75
2 Darin Erstad .75
3 Garret Anderson .50
4 Curt Schilling .75
5 Randy Johnson 1.00
6 Luis Gonzalez .50
7 Greg Maddux 1.50
8 Chipper Jones 1.50
9 Andruw Jones 1.00
10 Melvin Mora .50
11 Jay Gibbons .50
12 Nomar Garciaparra 2.00
13 Pedro J. Martinez 1.00
14 Manny Ramirez 1.00
15 Sammy Sosa 2.00
16 Kerry Wood .75
17 Magglio Ordonez .50
18 Frank Thomas 1.00
19 Roberto Alomar .60
20 Barry Larkin .50
21 Adam Dunn 1.00
22 Austin Kearns .75
23 Omar Vizquel .50
24 Larry Walker .50
25 Todd Helton 1.00
26 Preston Wilson .50
27 Dmitri Young .50
28 Ivan Rodriguez .75
29 Mike Lowell .50
30 Jeff Kent .50
31 Jeff Bagwell 1.00
32 Roy Oswalt .75
33 Craig Biggio .50
34 Mike Sweeney .50
35 Carlos Beltran .75
36 Shawn Green .60
37 Kazuhisa Ishii .50
38 Richie Sexson .50
39 Torii Hunter .50
40 Jacque Jones .50
41 Jose Vidro .50
42 Vladimir Guerrero 1.00
43 Mike Piazza 2.00
44 Tom Glavine .60
45 Roger Clemens 1.75
46 Jason Giambi .75
47 Bernie Williams .60
48 Alfonso Soriano 1.00
49 Mike Mussina .60
50 Barry Zito .60
51 Miguel Tejada .60
52 Eric Chavez .60
53 Eric Byrnes .50
54 Jim Thome .50
55 Kevin Millwood .50
56 Brian Giles .50
57 Xavier Nady .50
58 Barry Bonds 3.00
59 Bret Boone .50
60 Edgar Martinez .50
61 Kazuhiro Sasaki .50
62 Edgar Renteria .50
63 J.D. Drew .50
64 Scott Rolen 1.00
65 Jim Edmonds .50
66 Aubrey Huff .50
67 Alex Rodriguez 2.50
68 Juan Gonzalez 1.00
69 Hank Blalock .75
70 Mark Teixeira .75
71 Carlos Delgado .75
72 Vernon Wells .50
73 Shea Hillenbrand .50
74 Gary Sheffield .60
75 Mark Prior .50
76 Ken Griffey Jr. 2.00
77 Lance Berkman .50
78 Hideo Nomo .75
79 Derek Jeter 3.00
80 Ichiro Suzuki 2.00
81 Albert Pujols 2.50
82 Rafael Palmeiro .75
83 Jose Reyes 4.00
84 Rocco Baldelli 4.00
85 Hee Seop Choi 3.00
86 Dontrelle Willis 4.00
87 Robby Hammock **RC** 3.00
88 Brandon Webb **RC** 8.00
89 Matt Kata **RC** 5.00
90 Todd Wellemeyer **RC** 3.00
91 Francisco Cruceta **RC** 3.00
92 Clint Barmes **RC** 6.00
93 Jeremy Bonderman 8.00
94 Dave Matranga **RC** 4.00
95 Ryan Wagner **RC** 5.00
96 Jeremy Griffiths 3.00
97 Hideki Matsui **RC** 15.00
98 Jose Contreras **RC** 6.00
99 Chien-Ming Wang **RC** 25.00
100 Bo Hart **RC** 4.00
101 Dan Haren 5.00
102 Rickie Weeks **RC** 10.00

Essential Credentials Now/Future

Cards serial numbered 26-50: 6-12X
Cards s/n 51-75: 4-8X
Cards s/n 76-102: 3-5X
SP's (83-102) s/n 83-102: 1-2X
Now is consectutively #'d from 1 to 102.
Future is consect. #'d from 102 to 1.

Behind the Numbers

NM/M
Complete Set (15): 50.00
Common Player: 1.50
Inserted 1:80
1 Derek Jeter 8.00
2 Alex Rodriguez 8.00
3 Randy Johnson 3.00
4 Chipper Jones 5.00
5 Jim Thome 3.00
6 Alfonso Soriano 4.00
7 Adam Dunn 2.00
8 Nomar Garciaparra 6.00
9 Roger Clemens 6.00
10 Gary Sheffield 1.50
11 Vladimir Guerrero 3.00
12 Greg Maddux 5.00
13 Sammy Sosa 6.00
14 Mike Piazza 5.00
15 Troy Glaus 2.00

2003 Fleer E-X Behind the Numbers Autograph

No pricing due to scarcity.
Numbered to jersey number.

Behind the Numbers Game-Used

NM/M
Common Player: 5.00
Inserted 1:10
Patch Version: 1.5-2.5X
DJ Derek Jeter 15.00
AR Alex Rodriguez 10.00
RJ Randy Johnson 8.00
CJ Chipper Jones 8.00
JT Jim Thome 8.00
AS Alfonso Soriano 8.00
AD Adam Dunn 6.00
NG Nomar Garciaparra 10.00
RC Roger Clemens 10.00
GS Gary Sheffield 5.00
VG Vladimir Guerrero 8.00
GM Greg Maddux 8.00
SS Sammy Sosa 10.00
MP Mike Piazza 8.00
TG Troy Glaus 5.00
HB Hank Blalock 6.00
TG Tom Glavine 5.00
BM Brett Myers 5.00
LB Lance Berkman 5.00
RB Rocco Baldelli 10.00
BZ Barry Zito 6.00
DW Dontrelle Willis 10.00
RP Rafael Palmeiro 6.00
RA Roberto Alomar 6.00
MB Marlon Byrd 5.00

Diamond Essentials

NM/M
Common Player: 5.00
Inserted 1:480
1DE Randy Johnson 15.00
2DE Ichiro Suzuki 25.00
3DE Albert Pujols 30.00
4DE Barry Bonds 40.00
5DE Hideki Matsui 30.00
6DE Derek Jeter 40.00
7DE Chipper Jones 20.00
8DE Sammy Sosa 25.00
9DE Jeff Bagwell 10.00
10DE Mike Piazza 20.00
11DE Pedro J. Martinez 15.00
12DE Mark Prior 20.00
13DE Jason Giambi 10.00
14DE Jose Reyes 5.00
15DE Alfonso Soriano 15.00

Diamond Essentials Autograph

NM/M
Common Player:
Dontrelle Willis 30.00
Ryan Wagner 20.00
Rocco Baldelli 25.00
Albert Pujols 150.00

Diamond Essentials Game-Used

NM/M
Common Player: 8.00
Same price for cards #'d 145, 245 & 345.
Patch Versions: 1.5-2.5X
Production 55
RJ Randy Johnson 8.00
DJ Derek Jeter 15.00
CJ Chipper Jones 8.00
SS Sammy Sosa 12.00
JB Jeff Bagwell 8.00
MP Mike Piazza 10.00
PM Pedro J. Martinez 8.00
MP Mark Prior 10.00
JG Jason Giambi 8.00
JR Jose Reyes 8.00

Emerald Essentials

NM/M
Complete Set (10): 60.00
Common Player: 4.00
Inserted 1:240
1 Austin Kearns 4.00
2 Alfonso Soriano 8.00
3 Miguel Tejada 4.00
4 Troy Glaus 4.00
5 Adam Dunn 4.00
6 Hideo Nomo 6.00
7 Kerry Wood 6.00
8 Nomar Garciaparra 15.00
9 Roger Clemens 15.00
10 Derek Jeter 15.00

Emerald Essentials Autograph

NM/M
Common Player:
Brandon Webb 40.00
Hank Blalock 20.00

Emerald Essentials Game-Used

NM/M
Common Player: 4.00
Same price for levels #'d 175, 250 & 375.
Patch Versions: 1.5-2.5X
Production 60
AK Austin Kearns 6.00
AS Alfonso Soriano 8.00
MT Miguel Tejada 4.00
TG Troy Glaus 6.00
AD Adam Dunn 6.00
HN Hideo Nomo 15.00
KW Kerry Wood 8.00
NG Nomar Garciaparra 12.00
RC Roger Clemens 12.00
AR Alex Rodriguez 10.00

X-tra Innings

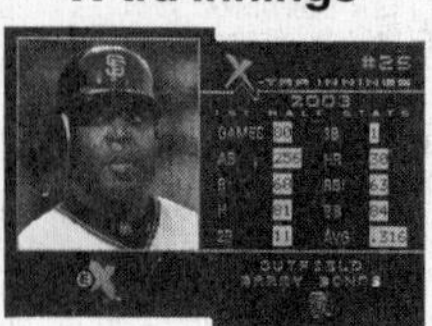

NM/M
Complete Set (10): 25.00
Common Player: 1.00
Inserted 1:32
1XI Ichiro Suzuki 3.00
2XI Albert Pujols 4.00
3XI Barry Bonds 5.00
4XI Jason Giambi 1.50
5XI Pedro J. Martinez 2.00
6XI Mark Prior 3.00
7XI Derek Jeter 5.00
8XI Curt Schilling 1.00
9XI Jeff Bagwell 1.50
10XI Alex Rodriguez 5.00

2003 Fleer Fall Classic

NM/M
Complete Set (87): 30.00
Common Player: .25
Common SP:
Hobby Pack (5): 4.00
Hobby Box (24): 75.00
1 Rod Carew .50
2 Bobby Doerr .25
3 Eddie Mathews 1.00
3 Eddie Mathews/ SP/Tigers 4.00
4 Tom Seaver 1.50
5 Lou Brock .75
6 Nolan Ryan 3.00
6 Nolan Ryan/ SP/Astros 10.00
7 Pee Wee Reese .25
8 Robin Yount 1.00
9 Bob Feller .50
10 Harmon Killebrew 1.00
11 Hal Newhouser .25
12 Al Kaline 1.00
13 Hoyt Wilhelm .25
14 Early Wynn .25
15 Yogi Berra 1.00
15 Yogi Berra/SP/Mets 4.00
16 Billy Williams .25
17 Rollie Fingers .25
18 Sparky Anderson .25
18 Sparky Anderson/ SP/Reds 3.00
19 Lou Boudreau .25
20 Warren Spahn 1.00
21 Enos Slaughter .25
22 Luis Aparicio .50
23 Phil Rizzuto .75
24 Willie McCovey .75
25 Joe Morgan .50
26 Alan Trammell .75
27 Eddie Plank .25
28 Lefty Grove .25
29 Walter Johnson 1.00
30 Roy Campanella 1.00
31 Carlton Fisk .75
32 Bill Dickey .25
33 Rogers Hornsby 1.00
33 Rogers Hornsby/ SP/Cubs 5.00
34 Wade Boggs .75
35 Chick Stahl .25
36 Don Drysdale .75
36 Don Drysdale/ SP/Dodgers 4.00
37 Jose Canseco .75
38 Roger Maris 2.00
38 Roger Maris/ SP/Yankees 8.00
39 Cal Ripken Jr. 3.00
40 Kiki Cuyler .25
40 Kiki Cuyler/SP/Cubs 3.00
41 Hank Greenberg .25
42 Don Larsen .50
43 Eddie Murray .75
43 Eddie Murray/ SP/Indians 4.00
44 Jimmy Sebring .25
45 Ozzie Smith 1.50
46 Darryl Strawberry .25
46 Darryl Strawberry/ SP/Yankees 3.00
47 Dave Parker .25
48 Gil Hodges .25
48 Gil Hodges/SP/Mets 3.00
49 Joe Carter .50
50 Leo Durocher .25
50 Leo Durocher/ SP/Giants 3.00
51 Christy Mathewson .75
52 Elston Howard .25
53 Hughie Jennings .25
54 Nellie Fox .50
55 Carl Yastrzemski 1.00
56 Frank Robinson 1.00
56 Frank Robinson/ SP/Reds 4.00
57 Dennis Eckersley .50
58 Grover Alexander .50
58 Grover Alexander/ SP/Cards 4.00
59 Carl Hubbell .25
60 Dave Winfield .75
61 Honus Wagner 1.50
62 Duke Snider 1.00
62 Duke Snider/ SP/Dodgers 5.00
63 Frankie Frisch .25
63 Frankie Frisch/ SP/Cards 3.00
64 Dizzy Dean .75
65 Bob Gibson 1.00
66 Johnny Bench 1.50
67 Ty Cobb 2.00
68 Lou Gehrig 2.50
69 Jim "Catfish" Hunter .50
70 Willie Stargell .75
71 Reggie Jackson 1.00
71 Reggie Jackson/ SP/Yankees 5.00
72 George Brett 2.50
73 Babe Ruth 3.00
73 Babe Ruth/ SP/Yankees 10.00
74 Cy Young 1.00
75 Jim Palmer .50
76 Mickey Lolich .25
77 Stan Musial 1.50
78 Steve Carlton .75
79 Roberto Clemente 2.50
80 John McGraw .25
81 Paul Molitor .75
82 Red Ruffing .25
83 Connie Mack .25
84 Mike Schmidt 2.00
85 Mickey Cochrane .50
85 Mickey Cochrane/ SP/Tigers 4.00
86 Brooks Robinson 1.00
87 Whitey Ford 1.00

Championship Gold

Cards 1-87: 3-6X
Production 50 Sets

All-American Collection

NM/M
Common Player: 8.00
OS Ozzie Smith/100 20.00
TS Tom Seaver/100 15.00
SM Stan Musial/100 30.00
CR Cal Ripken Jr/100 60.00
EM Eddie Mathews/100 10.00
NR Nolan Ryan 30.00
YB Yogi Berra 15.00
EM Eddie Murray/100 15.00
FR Frank Robinson 8.00
DS Duke Snider 8.00
RJ Reggie Jackson 8.00
LA Luis Aparicio/100 10.00
GH Gil Hodges 8.00
AK Al Kaline 10.00
BM Bill Mazeroski/100 10.00
BR Brooks Robinson/ 100 15.00
WB Wade Boggs/100 12.00
AT Alan Trammell/100 12.00

All American Collection Autograph

NM/M
Common Autograph:
Varying quantities produced
SP version #'d to 100: 1-1.5X
SP version #'d to 50: 1-2X
LA Luis Aparicio/150 10.00
VB Vida Blue/450 8.00
RB Rick Burleson/250 8.00
SC Steve Carlton/100 20.00
BF Bob Feller/300 15.00
CF Carlton Fisk/75 30.00
AL Al Kaline/325 20.00
HK Harmon Killebrew/ 150 30.00
FL Fred Lynn/275 8.00
BM Bill Mazeroski/75 20.00
JP Jim Palmer/100 15.00
BR Brooks Robinson/ 325 20.00
PR Preacher Roe/450 12.00
MS Mike Schmidt/50 60.00
BS "Moose" Skowron/ 150 10.00
OS Ozzie Smith/50 65.00
DS Duke Snider/100 25.00
WS Warren Spahn/75 40.00
AT Alan Trammell/150 15.00

All American Collection Jersey Autograph

NM/M
Production 25 Sets
GB George Brett 160.00
SC Steve Carlton 50.00

Legendary Collection

NM/M
Common Player:
Inserted 1:Legendary Star Pack
EM Eddie Mathews/SP 15.00
NR Nolan Ryan 30.00
YB Yogi Berra 15.00
EMY Eddie Murray 8.00
FR Frank Robinson 6.00
DS Duke Snider/SP 10.00
DSy Darryl Strawberry 5.00
RJ Reggie Jackson 8.00
RM Roger Maris/SP 30.00
GH Gil Hodges/SP 10.00

Pennant Aggression

NM/M
Complete Set (20): 50.00
Common Player: 3.00
Numbered to pennant year.
1PA Ty Cobb/1,908 4.00
2PA Honus Wagner/1,909 3.00
3PA Walter Johnson/1,924 3.00
4PA Jimmie Foxx/1,930 4.00
5PA Frankie Frisch/1,931 3.00
6PA Pee Wee Reese/1,947 3.00
7PA Yogi Berra/1,951 4.00
8PA Roy Campanella/ 1,953 3.00
9PA Whitey Ford/1,961 4.00
10PA Frank Robinson/1,966 3.00
11PA Carl Yastrzemski/ 1,967 3.00
12PA Brooks Robinson/ 1,970 3.00
13PA Johnny Bench/1,972 4.00
14PA Reggie Jackson/1,973 3.00
15PA Jim "Catfish" Hunter/ 1,974 3.00
16PA Joe Morgan/1,975 3.00
17PA Thurman Munson/ 1,976 4.00
18PA Willie Stargell/1,979 3.00
19PA Mike Schmidt/1,980 4.00
20PA George Brett/1,985 4.00

Pennant Aggression Game-Used

NM/M
Common Player: 8.00
Production 100
Patches: 1.5-2X
Production 50
YB Yogi Berra 15.00
FB Frank Robinson 10.00
CY Carl Yastrzemski 20.00
BR Brooks Robinson 15.00
JB Johnny Bench 15.00
RJ Reggie Jackson 12.00
CH Jim "Catfish" Hunter 8.00
JM Joe Morgan 8.00
TM Thurman Munson 15.00
WS Willie Stargell 10.00
MS Mike Schmidt 25.00
GB George Brett 35.00

Postseason Glory

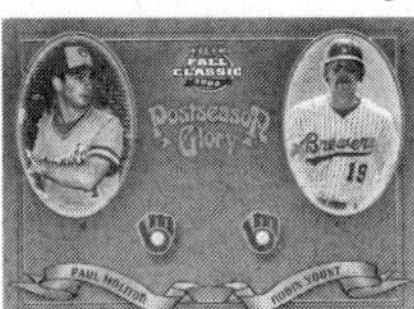

NM/M
Complete Set (30): 125.00
Common Player: 2.00
#1-15 Numbered to 1,500
16-25 Numbered to 750
26-30 Numbered to 100
1 Carlton Fisk, Carl Yastrzemski 2.00
2 Enos Slaughter, Stan Musial 4.00
3 Reggie Jackson, Thurman Munson 4.00
4 Eddie Plank, Christy Mathewson 3.00
5 Cy Young, Jimmy Sebring 3.00
6 Yogi Berra, Whitey Ford 4.00
7 Mickey Lolich, Alan Trammell 2.00
8 Eddie Mathews, Al Schoendienst 3.00
9 Roy Campanella, Pee Wee Reese 3.00
10 Joe Carter, Bill Mazeroski 2.00
11 Brooks Robinson, Frank Robinson 3.00
12 Tom Seaver, Gil Hodges 3.00
13 Robin Yount, Paul Molitor 2.50
14 Dave Parker, Willie Stargell 2.00
15 Cal Ripken Jr., Jim Palmer 6.00
16 Babe Ruth, Whitey Ford 8.00
18 Lou Brock, Bob Gibson 4.00
19 Mike Schmidt, Brooks Robinson 5.00
20 Johnny Bench, Thurman Munson 5.00
21 Nolan Ryan, Walter Johnson 10.00
22 Don Drysdale, Duke Snider 4.00
23 Joe Carter, Paul Molitor 2.00
24 Hughie Jennings, Ty Cobb 4.00
25 Cal Ripken Jr., Eddie Murray 10.00
26 Mike Schmidt, Steve Carlton 5.00
27 Roberto Clemente, Willie Stargell 15.00
28 Jim Palmer, Nolan Ryan 25.00
29 Joe Morgan, Johnny Bench 10.00
30 Lou Gehrig, Babe Ruth 25.00

Postseason Glory Dual Game-Used

NM/M
Production 100
Single Jerseys: .5X
Production 150
Carlton Fisk, Carl Yastrzemski 25.00
Reggie Jackson, Thurman Munson 25.00
Yogi Berra, Whitey Ford 30.00
Brooks Robinson, Frank Robinson 20.00
Robin Yount, Paul Molitor 25.00
Dave Parker, Willie Stargell/ Single/150 8.00
Lou Brock, Bob Gibson/ Single/150 10.00
Joe Carter, Paul Molitor/ Single/150 8.00
Don Drysdale, Duke Snider 25.00
Cal Ripken Jr., Eddie Murray 50.00
Mike Schmidt, Steve Carlton 25.00
Jim Palmer, Nolan Ryan 40.00
Joe Morgan, Johnny Bench 25.00
Babe Ruth/Single/150, Lou Gehrig 125.00

Postseason Glory Dual Patch

NM/M
Production 50
Single Patch: .5-.75X
Production 75
Carlton Fisk, Carl Yastrzemski 70.00
Robin Yount, Paul Molitor 50.00
Lou Brock, Bob Gibson 50.00
Cal Ripken Jr., Eddie Murray 120.00
Mike Schmidt, Steve Carlton 50.00
Jim Palmer, Nolan Ryan 80.00
Joe Morgan, Johnny Bench 50.00
Brooks Robinson, Frank Robinson 40.00

Series Contender

NM/M
Common Player:
Inserted 1:50 Retail
Bat Knobs: No Pricing
Production 9 or 10
SK Al Kaline 15.00
BD Bill Dickey 10.00
DS Darryl Strawberry 5.00
DM Don Mattingly 30.00
PR Phil Rizzuto/SP 10.00
WM Willie McCovey/SP 10.00
HK Harmon Killebrew 25.00
CF Carlton Fisk 6.00
JC Jose Canseco 10.00

Yankee Penstripes

NM/M
Production 100
World Series Edition: No Pricing
Production 26
RJ Reggie Jackson 40.00
BSP Bill "Moose" Skowron 15.00
WB Wade Boggs 50.00
DM Don Mattingly 75.00
DW Dave Winfield 35.00

2003 Fleer Focus Jersey Edition

NM/M
Complete Set (180): 45.00
Common Player: .15
Common Prospect (161-180): .75
Inserted 1:4
Pack (7): 1.50
Box (24): 30.00
1 Derek Jeter 2.50
2 Preston Wilson .15
3 Trevor Hoffman .15
4 Moises Alou .15
5 Roberto Alomar .35
6 Tim Salmon .25
7 Mike Lowell .15
8 Barry Bonds 2.50
9 Fred McGriff .15
10 Mo Vaughn .15
11 Junior Spivey .15
12 Roy Oswalt .25
13 Ichiro Suzuki 1.50
14 Magglio Ordonez .25
15 Adam Kennedy .15
16 Randy Johnson .75
17 Carlos Beltran .50
18 John Olerud .15
19 Joe Borchard .75
20 Alfonso Soriano .75
21 Curt Schilling .50
22 Mike Sweeney .15
23 Tino Martinez .15
24 Barry Larkin .15
25 Miguel Tejada .40
26 Chipper Jones 1.00
27 Kevin Brown .15
28 J.D. Drew .15
29 Sean Casey .15
30 Bernie Williams .35
31 Troy Percival .15
32 Jeff Bagwell .75
33 Kenny Lofton .15
34 Kerry Wood .50
35 Armando Benitez .15
36 David Eckstein .15
37 Wade Miller .15
38 Edgar Martinez .15
39 Mark Prior .75
40 Mike Piazza 1.50
41 Shea Hillenbrand .15
42 Bartolo Colon .15
43 Darin Erstad .50
44 A.J. Burnett .15
45 Jeff Kent .15
46 Corey Patterson .15
47 Derek Wigginton .15
48 Troy Glaus .75
49 Josh Beckett .15
50 Brian Lawrence .15
51 Frank Thomas .75
52 Jason Giambi .60
53 Luis Gonzalez .25
54 Raul Ibanez .15
55 Kazuhiro Sasaki .15
56 Mark Buehrle .15
57 Roger Clemens 1.25
58 Matt Williams .15
59 Joe Randa .15
60 Jamie Moyer .15
61 Paul Konerko .15
62 Mike Mussina .50
63 Javy Lopez .15
64 Brian Jordan .15
65 Scott Rolen .75
66 Aaron Boone .15
67 Eric Chavez .25
68 Mark Grace .25
69 Shawn Green .25
70 Albert Pujols 1.25
71 Sammy Sosa 1.50
72 Edgardo Alfonzo .15
73 Garret Anderson .15
74 Lance Berkman .15
75 Bret Boone .15
76 Joe Crede .15
77 Al Leiter .15
78 Jarrod Washburn .15
79 Craig Biggio .15
80 Rich Aurilia .15
81 Adam Dunn .60
82 Jermaine Dye .15
83 Tom Glavine .40
84 Eric Gagne .15
85 Jared Sandberg .15
86 Jim Thome .15
87 Barry Zito .35
88 Gary Sheffield .25
89 Paul LoDuca .15
90 Matt Morris .15
91 Juan Pierre .15
92 Randy Wolf .15
93 Jay Gibbons .15
94 Brad Radke .15
95 Carlos Delgado .35
96 Carlos Pena .15
97 Brian Giles .15
98 Rodrigo Lopez .15
99 Jacque Jones .15
100 Juan Gonzalez .75
101 Randall Simon .15
102 Mike Williams .15
103 Derek Lowe .15
104 Brad Wilkerson .15
105 Eric Hinske .15
106 Luis Castillo .15
107 Phil Nevin .15
108 Manny Ramirez .75
109 Vladimir Guerrero .75
110 Roy Halladay .15
111 Ellis Burks .15
112 Bobby Abreu .15
113 Tony Batista .15
114 Richie Sexson .15
115 Rafael Palmeiro .65
116 Todd Helton .65
117 Pat Burrell .60
118 John Smoltz .60
119 Ben Sheets .15
120 Aubrey Huff .15
121 Andruw Jones .75
122 Kazuhisa Ishii .15
123 Jim Edmonds .15
124 Austin Kearns .60
125 Mark Mulder .25
126 Greg Maddux 1.00
127 Jose Hernandez .15
128 Ben Grieve .15
129 Ken Griffey Jr. 1.50
130 Tim Hudson .35
131 Jorge Julio .15
132 Torii Hunter .15
133 Ivan Rodriguez .65
134 Jason Jennings .15
135 Jason Kendall .15
136 Nomar Garciaparra 1.50
137 Michael Cuddyer .15
138 Shannon Stewart .15
139 Larry Walker .15
140 Aramis Ramirez .15
141 Johnny Damon .15
142 Orlando Cabrera .15
143 Vernon Wells .15
144 Bobby Higginson .15
145 Sean Burroughs .15
146 Pedro J. Martinez .75
147 Jose Vidro .15
148 Orlando Hudson .15
149 Robert Fick .15
150 Ryan Klesko .15
151 Kevin Millwood .15
152 Alex Sanchez .15
153 Randy Winn .15
154 Omar Vizquel .15
155 Mike Lieberthal .15
156 Marty Cordova .15
157 Cristian Guzman .15
158 Alex Rodriguez 2.00
159 C.C. Sabathia .15
160 Jimmy Rollins .25
161 Josh Willingham **RC** 2.00
162 Lance Niekro .75
163 Nook Logan **RC** .75
164 Chase Utley .75
165 Pete LaForest **RC** .75
166 Victor Martinez .75
167 Adam LaRoche .75
168 Ian Ferguson **RC** .75
169 Mark Teixeira .75
170 Chris Waters **RC** .75
171 Hideki Matsui **RC** 5.00
172 Alejandro Machado **RC** .75
173 Francisco Rosario **RC** .75
174 Termel Sledge **RC** 1.00
175 Guillermo Quiroz **RC** .75
176 Lew Ford **RC** 3.00
177 Hank Blalock .75
178 Lyle Overbay .75
179 Matt Bruback **RC** .75
180 Jose Contreras **RC** 3.00

Century Jersey Number

Stars (1-160): 5-10X
Prospects (161-180): 2-4X
Numbered to jsy number + 100

Franchise Focus

NM/M
Complete Set (20): 15.00
Common Player: .50
Inserted 1:4
1 Troy Glaus .75
2 Randy Johnson 1.00
3 Chipper Jones 1.50
4 Nomar Garciaparra 2.00
5 Sammy Sosa 1.50
6 Ken Griffey Jr. 1.50
7 Jeff Bagwell .75
8 Mike Sweeney .50
9 Shawn Green .50
10 Torii Hunter .50
11 Vladimir Guerrero 1.00
12 Mike Piazza 2.00
13 Jason Giambi 1.00
14 Barry Zito .50
15 Pat Burrell .75
16 Barry Bonds 3.00
17 Ichiro Suzuki 1.50
18 Albert Pujols 1.00
19 Alex Rodriguez 2.50
20 Carlos Delgado .50

Home and Aways

NM/M
Common Player: 10.00
Inserted 1:288
Lance Berkman 10.00
J.D. Drew 10.00
Nomar Garciaparra 20.00
Derek Jeter 40.00
Chipper Jones 20.00
Greg Maddux 20.00
Roy Oswalt 10.00
Alex Rodriguez 30.00
Alfonso Soriano 10.00

Materialistic

NM/M
Common Player: 3.00
Inserted 1:192
Action Home: 1.5-2.5X
Production 50 Sets
Portrait Away: .75-1.5X
Inserted 1:576
Plus (Memorabilia): 1.5-2.5X
Production 250 Sets
Portrait Home: No Pricing
Production One Set
1M Greg Maddux 5.00
2M Roger Clemens 5.00
3M Nomar Garciaparra 6.00
4M Derek Jeter 10.00
5M Mike Piazza 6.00
6M Pat Burrell 3.00
7M Alfonso Soriano 5.00
8M Chipper Jones 5.00
9M Adam Dunn 3.00
10M Alex Rodriguez 8.00
11M Jason Giambi 4.00
12M Sammy Sosa 5.00
13M Albert Pujols 4.00
14M Ken Griffey Jr. 5.00
15M Ichiro Suzuki 5.00

Materialistic Flannels

Complete Set (15):
Common Player:

Materialistic Oversize

NM/M
Complete Set (16): 60.00
Common Player: 2.00
5-1/4" x 3-3/4" Box Topper
(1) Pat Burrell 2.00
(2) Roger Clemens 6.00
(3) Adam Dunn 2.00
(4) Nomar Garciaparra 4.00
(5) Jason Giambi 2.00
(6) Ken Griffey Jr. 6.00
(7) Reggie Jackson 5.00
(8) Derek Jeter 12.50
(9) Chipper Jones 5.00
(10) Greg Maddux 5.00
(11) Mike Piazza 6.00
(12) Albert Pujols 10.00
(13) Alex Rodriguez 10.00
(14) Alfonso Soriano 2.00
(15) Sammy Sosa 6.00
(16) Ichiro Suzuki 7.50

Materialistic Oversize Autographs

NM/M
Complete Set (3): 200.00
(1) Reggie Jackson/360 50.00
(2) Derek Jeter/360 100.00
(3) Chipper Jones/80 75.00

Shirtified

NM/M
Complete Set (15): 35.00

Common Player: 1.00
Inserted 1:24
1 Manny Ramirez 2.00
2 Jarrod Washburn 1.00
3 Greg Maddux 4.00
4 Austin Kearns 2.00
5 Jim Thome 2.00
6 Kazuhisa Ishii 1.00
7 Mike Piazza 5.00
8 Alfonso Soriano 3.00
9 Pat Burrell 2.00
10 Derek Jeter 8.00
11 Miguel Tejada 1.50
12 Roger Clemens 4.00
13 Alex Rodriguez 6.00
14 Barry Bonds 8.00
15 Scott Rolen 2.00

Shirtified Game-Used

NM/M
Common Player:
Inserted 1:35
Patches: 2-3X
Production 200
Manny Ramirez 8.00
Greg Maddux 12.00
Mike Piazza 10.00
Alfonso Soriano 15.00
Derek Jeter 25.00
Miguel Tejada 6.00
Roger Clemens 12.00
Alex Rodriguez 12.00

Team Colors

NM/M
Complete Set (20): 20.00
Common Player: .50
Inserted 1:12
1TC Alex Rodriguez 3.50
2TC Mark Prior 1.00
3TC Derek Jeter 4.00
4TC Curt Schilling 1.00
5TC Pat Burrell 1.00
6TC Josh Beckett .50
7TC Sean Burroughs .50
8TC Troy Glaus 1.00
9TC Torii Hunter .75
10TC Jeff Bagwell 1.00
11TC Pedro J. Martinez 1.50
12TC Mike Piazza 3.00
13TC Lance Berkman .75
14TC Nomar Garciaparra 2.50
15TC Chipper Jones 2.00
16TC Eric Chavez .75
17TC Barry Zito .75
18TC Barry Bonds 4.00
19TC Adam Dunn 1.00
20TC Randy Johnson 1.50

Team Colors Game-Used

NM/M
Common Player: 4.00
Inserted 1:28
Multi-Color: 1.5X
Production 250
Derek Jeter 25.00
Curt Schilling 5.00
Josh Beckett 4.00
Troy Glaus 8.00
Jeff Bagwell 8.00
Pedro J. Martinez 8.00
Lance Berkman 8.00
Nomar Garciaparra 15.00

Chipper Jones 10.00
Eric Chavez 6.00
Adam Dunn 8.00
Randy Johnson 8.00

2003 Fleer Genuine

NM/M
Complete Set (130): 150.00
Common Player: .25
Common Gen. Upside (101-130): 3.00
Production 799
Pack (5): 2.00
Box (24): 40.00
1 Derek Jeter 3.00
2 Mo Vaughn .25
3 Adam Dunn .75
4 Aubrey Huff .25
5 Jacque Jones .25
6 Kerry Wood .60
7 Barry Bonds 3.00
8 Kevin Brown .25
9 Sammy Sosa 2.00
10 Ray Durham .25
11 Carlos Beltran .50
12 Tony Batista .25
13 Bobby Abreu .25
14 Craig Biggio .25
15 Gary Sheffield .45
16 Jermaine Dye .25
17 Carlos Pena .25
18 Tim Salmon .35
19 Mike Piazza 2.00
20 Moises Alou .25
21 Edgardo Alfonzo .25
22 Mike Sweeney .25
23 Jay Gibbons .25
24 Kevin Millwood .25
25 A.J. Burnett .25
26 Austin Kearns .75
27 Rafael Palmeiro .75
28 Vladimir Guerrero 1.00
29 Paul Konerko .25
30 Scott Rolen .75
31 Fred McGriff .25
32 Frank Thomas 1.00
33 John Olerud .25
34 Eric Gagne .25
35 Nomar Garciaparra 2.00
36 Ryan Klesko .25
37 Lance Berkman .25
38 Andruw Jones .75
39 Pat Burrell .60
40 Juan Encarnacion .25
41 Curt Schilling .50
42 Jason Giambi .65
43 Barry Larkin .25
44 Alex Rodriguez 2.50
45 Kazuhisa Ishii .25
46 Pedro J. Martinez 1.00
47 Sean Burroughs .25
48 Roy Oswalt .40
49 Chipper Jones 1.50
50 Barry Zito .40
51 Jeff Kent .25
52 Rodrigo Lopez .25
53 Jim Thome .25
54 Ivan Rodriguez .60
55 Luis Gonzalez .40
56 Alfonso Soriano 1.00
57 Josh Beckett .25
58 Junior Spivey .25
59 Bernie Williams .40
60 Omar Vizquel .25
61 Eric Hinske .25
62 Jose Vidro .25
63 Bartolo Colon .25
64 Jim Edmonds .25
65 Ben Sheets .25
66 Mark Prior 1.00
67 Edgar Martinez .25
68 Raul Ibanez .25
69 Darin Erstad .40
70 Roger Clemens 1.75
71 C.C. Sabathia .25
72 Carlos Delgado .50
73 Tom Glavine .40
74 Magglio Ordonez .40
75 Ichiro Suzuki 1.50
76 Johnny Damon .40
77 Brian Giles .25
78 Jeff Bagwell 1.00
79 Greg Maddux 1.50
80 Eric Chavez .40
81 Larry Walker .25
82 Randy Johnson 1.00
83 Miguel Tejada .40
84 Todd Helton .75
85 Jarrod Washburn .25
86 Troy Glaus .75
87 Ken Griffey Jr. 2.00
88 Albert Pujols 2.00
89 Torii Hunter .25
90 Joe Crede .25
91 Matt Morris .25
92 Shawn Green .40
93 Manny Ramirez 1.00
94 Jason Kendall .25
95 Preston Wilson .25
96 Garret Anderson .25
97 Cliff Floyd .25
98 Sean Casey .25
99 Juan Gonzalez .75
100 Richie Sexson .25
101 Joe Borchard 3.00
102 Josh Stewart RC 3.00
103 Francisco Rodriguez 4.00
104 Jeremy Bonderman 8.00
105 Walter Young 3.00
106 Brandon Webb RC 6.00
107 Lyle Overbay 4.00
108 Jose Contreras RC 6.00
109 Victor Martinez 4.00
110 Hideki Matsui RC 10.00
111 Brian Stokes RC 3.00
112 Daniel Cabrera RC 6.00
113 Josh Willingham RC 3.00
114 Mark Teixeira 4.00
115 Pete LaForest RC 3.00
116 Chris Waters RC 3.00
117 Chien-Ming Wang RC 30.00
118 Ian Ferguson RC 3.00
119 Rocco Baldelli 4.00
120 Termel Sledge RC 4.00
121 Hank Blalock 4.00
122 Alejandro Machado RC 3.00
123 Hee Seop Choi 4.00
124 Guillermo Quiroz RC 4.00
125 Chase Utley 4.00
126 Nook Logan RC 3.00
127 Josh Hall RC 3.00
128 Ryan Church 3.00
129 Lew Ford RC 6.00
130 Francisco Rosario RC 3.00

Reflection

Cards 1-100 print run 25-50: 8-15X
Cards 101-130 p/r 101-130: .5-1.5X
Cards 1-100 p/r 51-80: 4-8X
Cards 1-100 p/r 81-130: 3-5X
Ascending consecutively #'d from 1-130.
Descending consecutively #'d from 130-1.

Article Insider

NM/M
Common Player: 4.00
Inserted 1:24
Adam Dunn 5.00
Andruw Jones 6.00
Alex Rodriguez 10.00
Alfonso Soriano 8.00
Chipper Jones 8.00
Curt Schilling 5.00
Derek Jeter 15.00
Don Mattingly 25.00
Greg Maddux 10.00
Jeff Bagwell 6.00
Jason Giambi 10.00
Lance Berkman 4.00
Magglio Ordonez 4.00
Mike Piazza 10.00
Miguel Tejada 4.00
Nomar Garciaparra 15.00
Pat Burrell 4.00
Pedro J. Martinez 8.00
Randy Johnson 6.00
Shawn Green 4.00
Sammy Sosa 10.00
Troy Glaus 5.00
Torii Hunter 5.00
Todd Helton 6.00
Vladimir Guerrero 6.00

Article Insider Autograph

NM/M
Quantity produced listed
Lance Berkman/165 25.00
Lance Berkman/100 25.00
Lance Berkman/50 40.00
Derek Jeter/100 125.00
Don Mattingly/170 85.00
Don Mattingly/100 100.00

Long Ball Threats

NM/M
Complete Set (15): 15.00
Common Card: .50
Inserted 1:8
1 Derek Jeter, Nomar Garciaparra 3.00
2 Jim Thome, Pat Burrell 1.00
3 Alex Rodriguez, Rafael Palmeiro 3.00
4 Alfonso Soriano, Hideki Matsui 3.00
5 Torii Hunter, Vladimir Guerrero 1.00
6 Mike Sweeney, Phil Nevin .50
7 Mike Piazza, Sammy Sosa 2.00
8 Shawn Green, Jason Giambi 1.00
9 Magglio Ordonez, Andruw Jones 1.00
10 Eric Chavez, Carlos Delgado .75
11 Manny Ramirez, Jeff Bagwell 1.00
12 Scott Rolen, Troy Glaus 1.00
13 Barry Bonds, Miguel Tejada 3.00
14 Albert Pujols, Lance Berkman 2.00
15 Chipper Jones, Todd Helton 1.50

Long Ball Threats Single Jersey

NM/M
Common Player: 3.00
Inserted 1:13
Derek Jeter/Jsy, Nomar Garciaparra 15.00
Derek Jeter, Nomar Garciaparra/Jsy 10.00
Jim Thome/Jsy, Pat Burrell 6.00
Jim Thome, Pat Burrell/Jsy 6.00
Alfonso Soriano/Jsy, Hideki Matsui 8.00
Torii Hunter/Jsy, Vladimir Guerrero 6.00
Torii Hunter, Vladimir Guerrero/Jsy 6.00
Mike Sweeney/Jsy, Phil Nevin 3.00
Mike Sweeney, Phil Nevin/Jsy 3.00
Mike Piazza/Jsy, Sammy Sosa 8.00
Mike Piazza, Sammy Sosa/Jsy 10.00
Shawn Green/Jsy, Jason Giambi 4.00
Magglio Ordonez/Jsy, Andruw Jones 4.00
Eric Chavez, Carlos Delgado/Jsy 5.00
Manny Ramirez/Jsy, Jeff Bagwell 8.00
Manny Ramirez, Jeff Bagwell/Jsy 8.00
Scott Rolen/Jsy, Troy Glaus 6.00
Scott Rolen, Troy Glaus/Jsy 6.00
Barry Bonds, Miguel Tejada/Jsy 5.00
Albert Pujols, Lance Berkman/Jsy 4.00
Chipper Jones/Jsy, Todd Helton 8.00
Chipper Jones, Todd Helton/Jsy 6.00

Long Ball Threats Dual Jersey

NM/M
Common Card: 5.00
Inserted 1:72
Derek Jeter, Nomar Garciaparra 30.00
Jim Thome, Pat Burrell 15.00
Alex Rodriguez, Rafael Palmeiro 15.00
Torii Hunter, Vladimir Guerrero 10.00
Mike Sweeney, Phil Nevin 5.00
Mike Piazza, Sammy Sosa 20.00
Magglio Ordonez, Andruw Jones 10.00
Scott Rolen, Troy Glaus 10.00
Chipper Jones, Todd Helton 12.00

Long Ball Threats Dual Patch

NM/M
#'d to combined 2002 HR total
Derek Jeter, Nomar Garciaparra/42 80.00
Jim Thome, Pat Burrell/89 30.00
Alex Rodriguez, Rafael Palmeiro/100 50.00
Mike Piazza, Sammy Sosa/82 75.00
Shawn Green, Jason Giambi/83 40.00
Magglio Ordonez, Andruw Jones/73 40.00
Manny Ramirez, Jeff Bagwell/64 40.00
Scott Rolen, Troy Glaus/61 50.00

Tools of the Game

NM/M
Complete Set (15): 20.00
Common Player: .75
Inserted 1:20
1 Adam Dunn 1.00
2 Chipper Jones 2.00
3 Torii Hunter .75
4 Mike Piazza 1.50
5 Hideki Matsui 8.00
6 Nomar Garciaparra 3.00
7 Derek Jeter 4.00
8 Alex Rodriguez 3.00
9 Alfonso Soriano 2.00
10 Pat Burrell .75
11 Barry Bonds 4.00
12 Jason Giambi 1.50
13 Sammy Sosa 2.00
14 Vladimir Guerrero 1.00
15 Ichiro Suzuki 2.00

Tools of the Game 1-Piece

NM/M
Common Player:
Inserted 1:42
2-Piece: 1.5-3X
Production 250
3-Piece: 3-6X
Production 100
Adam Dunn 6.00
Mike Piazza 8.00
Derek Jeter 15.00
Alex Rodriguez 10.00
Alfonso Soriano 10.00
Jason Giambi 8.00
Sammy Sosa 10.00
Vladimir Guerrero 6.00

2003 Fleer Hardball

NM/M
Complete Set (280): 85.00
Common Player: .15
Common (241-280): .75
Inserted 1:2 Hobby
Pack (7): 1.75
Box (24): 30.00

1 Barry Bonds 2.00
2 Derek Jeter 2.00
3 Jason Varitek .15
4 Magglio Ordonez .25
5 Ryan Dempster .15
6 Adam Everett .15
7 Paul LoDuca .15
8 Brad Wilkerson .15
9 Al Leiter .15
10 Jermaine Dye .15
11 Robert Mackowiak .15
12 J.T. Snow .15
13 Juan Gonzalez .60
14 Eric Hinske .15
15 Greg Maddux 1.00
16 Moises Alou .15
17 Carlos Lee .15
18 Richard Hidalgo .15
19 Jorge Posada .25
20 Mike Lieberthal .15
21 Jeff Cirillo .15
22 Corey Patterson .15
23 C.C. Sabathia .15
24 Brian Giles .15
25 Edgar Martinez .15
26 Trot Nixon .15
27 Kerry Wood .50
28 Austin Kearns .40
29 Lance Berkman .15
30 Hideo Nomo .50
31 Brad Radke .15
32 John Valentin .15
33 Tim Hudson .35
34 Aramis Ramirez .15
35 Kevin Mench .15
36 Kevin Appier .15
37 Chris Richard .15
38 Ruben Mateo .15
39 Juan Pierre .15
40 Nick Neugebauer .15
41 Mike Mussina .40
42 Rich Aurilia .15
43 Albert Pujols 1.00
44 Carlos Delgado .50
45 Junior Spivey .15
46 Marcus Giles .15
47 Johnny Damon .25
48 Mark Prior .50
49 Omar Vizquel .15
50 Craig Biggio .15
51 Chuck Knoblauch .15
52 Eric Milton .15
53 Jeromy Burnitz .15
54 Jim Thome .15
55 Steve Finley .15
56 Kevin Millwood .15
57 Alex Gonzalez .15
58 Ben Broussard .15
59 Derrek Lee .15
60 Joe Randa .15
61 Doug Mientkiewicz .15
62 Jason L. Phillips .15
63 Brett Myers .15
64 Josh Fogg .15
65 Reggie Sanders .15
66 Chipper Jones 1.00
67 Roosevelt Brown .15
68 Matt Lawton .15
69 Charles Johnson .15
70 Mark Quinn .15
71 Jacque Jones .15
72 Armando Benitez .15
73 Bobby Abreu .15
74 Jason Kendall .15
75 Jeff Kent .15
76 Mark Teixeira .50
77 Garret Anderson .15
78 Jerry Hairston Jr. .15
79 Tony Graffanino .15
80 Josh Beckett .15
81 Eric Gagne .15
82 Fernando Tatis .15
83 Brett Tomko .15
84 Fernando Vina .15
85 Rafael Palmeiro .65
86 Luis Gonzalez .35
87 Javy Lopez .15
88 Shea Hillenbrand .15
89 Hee Seop Choi .15
90 Preston Wilson .15
91 Neifi Perez .15
92 Ray Lankford .15
93 Tsuyoshi Shinjo .15
94 Ben Grieve .15
95 Jarrod Washburn .15
96 Gary Sheffield .35
97 Derek Lowe .15
98 Tony Womack .15
99 Milton Bradley .15
100 Brad Penny .15
101 Mike Sweeney .15
102 A.J. Pierzynski .15
103 Edgardo Alfonzo .15
104 Marlon Byrd .15
105 Sean Burroughs .15
106 Kazuhiro Sasaki .15
107 Damian Rolls .15
108 Troy Glaus .60
109 Rafael Furcal .15
110 Nomar Garciaparra 1.25
111 Josh Bard .15
112 Alex Gonzalez .15
113 Cristian Guzman .15
114 Roger Cedeno .15
115 Freddy Garcia .15
116 Travis Phelps .15
117 Juan Cruz .15
118 Frank Thomas .60
119 Jaret Wright .15
120 Carlos Beltran .45
121 Ronnie Belliard .15
122 Roger Clemens 1.00
123 Vicente Padilla .15
124 Joel Pineiro .15
125 Jared Sandberg .15
126 Tom Glavine .35
127 Matt Clement .15
128 Aaron Rowand .15
129 Alex Escobar .15
130 Randy Wolf .15
131 Ichiro Suzuki 1.00
132 Toby Hall .15
133 Scott Spiezio .15
134 Bobby Higginson .15
135 A.J. Burnett .15
136 Cesar Izturis .15
137 Roberto Alomar .40
138 Trevor Hoffman .15
139 Edgar Renteria .15
140 Rusty Greer .15
141 David Eckstein .15
142 Pedro J. Martinez .75
143 Joe Crede .15
144 Robert Fick .15
145 Mike Lowell .15
146 Brian Jordan .15
147 Mark Mulder .25
148 Scott Rolen .60
149 Ivan Rodriguez .60
150 Adam Kennedy .15
151 Ken Griffey Jr. 1.25
152 Larry Walker .15
153 Carlos Pena .15
154 Geoff Jenkins .15
155 Bartolo Colon .15
156 Mariano Rivera .25
157 Robb Nen .15
158 Bret Boone .15
159 Shannon Stewart .15
160 Chris Singleton .15
161 Todd Walker .15
162 Jay Payton .15
163 Zach Day .15
164 Bernie Williams .40
165 Bubba Trammell .15
166 Matt Morris .15
167 Jose Cruz Jr. .15
168 Mark Grace .40
169 Andruw Jones .75
170 Cliff Floyd .15
171 Antonio Alfonseca .15
172 Jeff Bagwell .75
173 Shawn Green .40
174 Joe Mays .15
175 Mike Piazza 1.25
176 Adam Piatt .15
177 Pokey Reese .15
178 Carl Everett .15
179 Tim Salmon .35
180 Rodrigo Lopez .15
181 Brandon Inge .15
182 Kazuhisa Ishii .15
183 Jose Vidro .15
184 Barry Zito .40
185 Phil Nevin .15
186 J.D. Drew .35
187 Vernon Wells .15
188 Darin Erstad .50
189 Barry Larkin .15
190 Jason Jennings .15
191 Luis Castillo .15
192 Adrian Beltre .35
193 Tony Armas .15
194 Terrence Long .15
195 Mark Kotsay .15
196 Tino Martinez .15
197 Jayson Werth .15
198 Eric Chavez .25
199 Matt Williams .15
200 Jon Lieber .15
201 Eddie Taubensee .15
202 Shane Reynolds .15
203 Alex Sanchez .15
204 Jason Giambi .60
205 Jimmy Rollins .25
206 Jamie Moyer .15
207 Francisco Rodriguez .15
208 Marty Cordova .15
209 Aaron Boone .15
210 Mike Hampton .15
211 Mark Redman .15
212 Richie Sexson .15
213 Andy Pettitte .40
214 Livan Hernandez .15
215 Jason Isringhausen .15
216 Curt Schilling .40
217 Manny Ramirez .75
218 Jose Valentin .15
219 Brent Butler .15
220 Billy Wagner .15
221 Ben Sheets .15

222	Jeff Weaver	.15
223	Brent Abernathy	.15
224	Jay Gibbons	.15
225	Sean Casey	.15
226	Greg Norton	.15
227	Andy Van Hekken	.15
228	Kevin Brown	.15
229	Orlando Cabrera	.15
230	Scott Hatteberg	.15
231	Ryan Klesko	.15
232	Roy Halladay	.15
233	Randy Johnson	.75
234	Mark Buehrle	.15
235	Todd Helton	.60
236	Jeffrey Hammonds	.15
237	Sidney Ponson	.15
238	Kip Wells	.15
239	John Olerud	.15
240	Aubrey Huff	.15
241	Derek Jeter	4.00
242	Barry Bonds	4.00
243	Ichiro Suzuki	2.00
244	Troy Glaus	1.00
245	Alex Rodriguez	3.00
246	Sammy Sosa	2.00
247	Lance Berkman	.75
248	Jason Giambi	2.00
249	Nomar Garciaparra	2.50
250	Miguel Tejada	.75
251	Albert Pujols	1.50
252	Mike Piazza	2.50
253	Vladimir Guerrero	1.50
254	Shawn Green	.75
255	Todd Helton	.75
256	Ken Griffey Jr.	2.00
257	Torii Hunter	.75
258	Chipper Jones	2.00
259	Alfonso Soriano	1.50
260	Luis Gonzalez	.75
261	Pedro J. Martinez	1.50
262	Tim Hudson	.75
263	Roger Clemens	2.00
264	Greg Maddux	2.00
265	Randy Johnson	1.50
266	Vinnie Chulk	.50
267	Jose Castillo	1.50
268	Craig Brazell **RC**	1.50
269	Felix Sanchez **RC**	.50
270	John Webb	.50
271	Josh Hall **RC**	.50
272	Alexis Rios	.50
273	Phil Seibel **RC**	.50
274	Prentice Redman **RC**	1.50
275	Walter Young	1.00
276	Nic Jackson	.50
277	Adam Morrissey	.50
278	Bobby Jenks	.75
279	Rodrigo Rosario	.50
280	Chin-Feng Chen	1.00

Gold

Gold (1-240):	2-3X
Gold (241-280):	1-2X
Inserted 1:4 Hobby	

Platinum

Cards (1-240):	8-15X
Cards (241-280):	3-5X
Production 50 Sets	

Discs

		NM/M
Complete Set (20):		50.00
Common Player:		1.00
Inserted 1:24		
1D	Derek Jeter	8.00
2D	Barry Bonds	8.00
3D	Ichiro Suzuki	4.00
4D	Sammy Sosa	4.00
5D	Nomar Garciaparra	5.00
6D	Lance Berkman	1.50
7D	Jason Giambi	4.00
8D	Mike Piazza	5.00
9D	Shawn Green	1.50
10D	Barry Zito	1.50
11D	Albert Pujols	3.00
12D	Alex Rodriguez	6.00
13D	Tim Salmon	1.00
14D	Eric Chavez	1.00
15D	Ken Griffey Jr.	4.00
16D	Alfonso Soriano	3.00
17D	Vladimir Guerrero	2.50
18D	Francisco Rodriguez	1.00
19D	Miguel Tejada	1.50
20D	Randy Johnson	2.50

On the Ball

		NM/M
Complete Set (15):		20.00
Common Player:		1.00
Inserted 1:12		
1	Derek Jeter	4.00

2	Barry Bonds	4.00
3	Nomar Garciaparra	2.50
4	Alfonso Soriano	1.50
5	Mike Piazza	2.50
6	Alex Rodriguez	3.00
7	Chipper Jones	2.00
8	Randy Johnson	1.50
9	Pedro J. Martinez	1.50
10	Albert Pujols	1.50
11	Vladimir Guerrero	1.50
12	Sammy Sosa	2.00
13	Ichiro Suzuki	2.00
14	Troy Glaus	1.00
15	Jason Giambi	2.00

On the Ball Memorabilia

	NM/M
Common Player:	5.00
Inserted 1:18	
Derek Jeter/Bat	15.00
Barry Bonds/Jsy	15.00
Nomar Garciaparra/Jsy	10.00
Alfonso Soriano/Jsy	10.00
Mike Piazza/Jsy	10.00
Alex Rodriguez/Jsy	10.00
Chipper Jones/Bat	8.00
Randy Johnson/Jsy	8.00
Pedro J. Martinez/Jsy	8.00
Troy Glaus/Jsy	5.00

Round Numbers

		NM/M
Complete Set (14):		50.00
Common Player:		3.00
Production 1,000 Sets		
1	Nolan Ryan	10.00
2	Al Kaline	6.00
3	Mike Schmidt	6.00
4	Yogi Berra	4.00
5	Brooks Robinson	4.00
6	Tom Seaver	4.00
7	Willie McCovey	3.00
8	Harmon Killebrew	4.00
9	Richie Ashburn	3.00
10	Lou Brock	3.00
11	Jim Palmer	3.00
12	Willie Stargell	4.00
13	Whitey Ford	4.00
14	Robin Yount	5.00

Round Numbers Memorabilia

	NM/M
Inserted 1:288	
Al Kaline/Jsy	20.00
Mike Schmidt/Jsy	15.00
Harmon Killebrew/Bat	30.00
Lou Brock/Jsy	30.00

Round Trippers

		NM/M
Complete Set (20):		15.00
Common Player:		.50
Inserted 1:8		
1	Alfonso Soriano	1.50
2	Alex Rodriguez	3.00
3	Lance Berkman	.75
4	Shawn Green	.75
5	Pat Burrell	1.00

6	Andruw Jones	.75
7	Garret Anderson	.50
8	Miguel Tejada	.75
9	Mike Piazza	2.50
10	Eric Chavez	.50
11	Rafael Palmeiro	.75
12	Chipper Jones	2.00
13	Manny Ramirez	1.00
14	Jeff Bagwell	1.00
15	Torii Hunter	.75
16	Nomar Garciaparra	2.50
17	Sammy Sosa	2.00
18	Vladimir Guerrero	1.50
19	Troy Glaus	1.00
20	Jason Giambi	2.00

Round Trippers Rounding First

	NM/M
Common Player:	5.00
Quantity produced listed	
Rounding Second:	No Pricing
Production 10 Sets	
Rounding Third:	No Pricing
Production 3 Sets	
Alfonso Soriano/Jsy/228	10.00
Alex Rodriguez/Jsy/536	12.00
Lance Berkman/Jsy/557	5.00
Shawn Green/Bat/249	5.00
Pat Burrell/Bat/502	10.00
Andruw Jones/Jsy/569	5.00
Garret Anderson/Bat/40	20.00
Miguel Tejada/Jsy/524	5.00
Mike Piazza/Bat/289	12.00
Eric Chavez/Jsy/572	5.00
Rafael Palmeiro/Jsy/515	6.00
Chipper Jones/Jsy/570	10.00
Manny Ramirez/Jsy/530	8.00
Jeff Bagwell/Bat/344	6.00
Nomar Garciaparra/Bat/529	12.00

Signatures

	NM/M
Bonds 600 HR Inscription:	1-1.5X
Barry Bonds/255	200.00
Derek Jeter	110.00

2003 Fleer Hot Prospects

		NM/M
Complete Set (120):		
Common Player:		.25
Common SP (81-120):		5.00
Production 1,250 unless noted.		
Pack (5):		4.00
Box (15):		50.00
1	Derek Jeter	3.00
2	Ryan Klesko	.25
3	Troy Glaus	.75
4	Jeff Kent	.40
5	Frank Thomas	.75
6	Gary Sheffield	.50
7	Jim Edmonds	.40

8	Pat Burrell	.50
9	Jacque Jones	.25
10	Jason Jennings	.25
11	Pedro J. Martinez	1.00
12	Rafael Palmeiro	.50
13	Jason Kendall	.25
14	Tom Glavine	.40
15	Josh Beckett	.25
16	Luis Gonzalez	.40
17	Edgar Martinez	.25
18	Miguel Tejada	.50
19	Fred McGriff	.40
20	Adam Dunn	.50
21	Lance Berkman	.50
22	Magglio Ordonez	.40
23	Darin Erstad	.40
24	Rich Aurilia	.25
25	Mike Piazza	1.50
26	Shawn Green	.50
27	Larry Walker	.40
28	Manny Ramirez	.75
29	Juan Gonzalez	.75
30	Eric Chavez	.50
31	Torii Hunter	.50
32	A.J. Burnett	.25
33	Sammy Sosa	1.50
34	Eric Hinske	.25
35	Brian Giles	.50
36	Mike Sweeney	.25
37	Sean Casey	.25
38	Chipper Jones	1.50
39	Scott Rolen	.75
40	Jason Giambi	1.00
41	Mo Vaughn	.25
42	Roy Oswalt	.25
43	Paul Konerko	.25
44	Tim Salmon	.40
45	Edgardo Alfonzo	.25
46	Jermaine Dye	.25
47	Ben Sheets	.25
48	Todd Helton	.75
49	Greg Maddux	1.50
50	Albert Pujols	2.00
51	Jim Thome	.75
52	Vladimir Guerrero	.75
53	Ivan Rodriguez	.50
54	Nomar Garciaparra	2.00
55	Alex Rodriguez	2.50
56	Alfonso Soriano	1.50
57	Kazuhisa Ishii	.25
58	Austin Kearns	.50
59	Curt Schilling	.50
60	Bret Boone	.40
61	Mark Prior	1.50
62	Garret Anderson	.40
63	Barry Bonds	2.50
64	Roger Clemens	2.00
65	Jeff Bagwell	.75
66	Omar Vizquel	.40
67	Jay Gibbons	.25
68	Aubrey Huff	.25
69	Bobby Abreu	.25
70	Richie Sexson	.50
71	Bobby Higginson	.25
72	Kerry Wood	.50
73	Carlos Delgado	.50
74	Sean Burroughs	.25
75	Jose Vidro	.25
76	Ken Griffey Jr.	1.50
77	Randy Johnson	1.00
78	Ichiro Suzuki	1.50
79	Barry Zito	.50
80	Carlos Beltran	.25
81	Joe Borchard	5.00
82	Mark Teixeira	5.00
83	Brandon Webb **RC**	8.00
84	Shane Victorino/Auto./400 **RC**	8.00
85	Hee Seop Choi	5.00
86	Hank Blalock	6.00
87	Brett Myers	6.00
88	Mike Ryan **RC**	5.00
89	Jesse Foppert	8.00
90	Lyle Overbay	6.00
91	Brian Stokes/Auto./400 **RC**	10.00
92	Josh Hall/Auto./400 **RC**	10.00
93	Chris Waters/Auto./400 **RC**	10.00
94	Lew Ford/Auto./400 **RC**	25.00
95	Ian Ferguson/Auto./500 **RC**	8.00
96	Josh Willingham **RC**	5.00
97	Josh Stewart/Auto./500 **RC**	8.00
98	Pete LaForest/Auto./500 **RC**	8.00
99	J.Contreras/Auto./Jsy/300 **RC**	40.00
100	Termel Sledge/Auto./500 **RC**	8.00
101	Guillermo Quiroz/Auto./500 **RC**	15.00
102	Alejandro Machado/Auto./500 **RC**	8.00
103	Nook Logan/Auto./Jsy./400 **RC**	10.00
104	Robby Hammock/Auto./Jsy/400 **RC**	10.00
105	Hideki Matsui/Base **RC**	15.00
106	Wilfredo Ledezma **RC**	5.00
107	Rocco Baldelli/Jsy	8.00
108	Oscar Villarreal **RC**	5.00
109	Todd Wellemeyer/Auto./400 **RC**	8.00
110	Michael Hessman/Auto./400 **RC**	8.00
111	Jeremy Bonderman/Auto./Jsy/400	35.00
112	Craig Brazell/Auto./Jsy/400 **RC**	10.00
113	Francisco Rosario/Auto./Jsy/400 **RC**	10.00
114	Jeff Duncan/Auto./Jsy/400 **RC**	10.00
115	Daniel Cabrera/Auto./Jsy/400 **RC**	25.00
116	Dontrelle Willis/Auto./Jsy/400	40.00
117	Cory Stewart/Auto./500 **RC**	10.00
118	Tim Olson/Auto./Jsy/400 **RC**	10.00
119	Chien-Ming Wang/Auto./Jsy/500 **RC**	200.00

Class Of...

	NM/M
Common Duo:	10.00
Inserted 1:15	
Barry Zito, Josh Beckett	10.00
Pat Burrell, J.D. Drew	12.00
Mark Prior, Mark Teixeira	15.00
Austin Kearns, Sean Burroughs	10.00
Troy Glaus, Lance Berkman	10.00
Darin Erstad, Todd Helton	10.00
Manny Ramirez, Shawn Green	10.00
Matt Morris, Kerry Wood	10.00
Nomar Garciaparra, Paul Konerko	15.00
Alex Rodriguez, Torii Hunter	20.00

Cream of the Crop

		NM/M
Complete Set (15):		35.00
Common Player:		1.50
Inserted 1:5		
1	Barry Bonds	5.00
2	Derek Jeter	5.00
3	Ichiro Suzuki	3.00
4	Nomar Garciaparra	3.00
5	Roger Clemens	3.00
6	Alex Rodriguez	4.00
7	Greg Maddux	2.50
8	Mike Piazza	2.50
9	Sammy Sosa	2.50
10	Jason Giambi	2.00
11	Hideki Matsui	6.00
12	Albert Pujols	4.00
13	Vladimir Guerrero	1.50
14	Jim Thome	1.50
15	Pedro J. Martinez	1.50

Hot Materials

		NM/M
Common Player:		5.00
Production 499 Sets		
Red-Hots:		1-2X
Production 50		
1HM	Derek Jeter	20.00
2HM	Torii Hunter	8.00
3HM	Mark Prior	8.00

4HM	Nomar Garciaparra	15.00
5HM	Sammy Sosa	15.00
6HM	Rafael Palmeiro	6.00
7HM	Hee Seop Choi	10.00
8HM	Mark Teixeira	5.00
9HM	Mike Piazza	10.00
10HM	Pat Burrell	8.00
11HM	Jim Thome	8.00
12HM	Lance Berkman	5.00
13HM	Vladimir Guerrero	6.00
14HM	Troy Glaus	5.00
15HM	Chipper Jones	8.00
16HM	Lyle Overbay	5.00
17HM	Jason Giambi	8.00
18HM	Alex Rodriguez	10.00
19HM	Miguel Tejada	5.00
20HM	Adam Dunn	6.00
21HM	Randy Johnson	8.00
22HM	Josh Beckett	5.00
23HM	Alfonso Soriano	10.00
24HM	Greg Maddux	10.00
25HM	Shawn Green	5.00
26HM	Carlos Delgado	5.00
27HM	Todd Helton	6.00
28HM	Mike Sweeney	5.00
29HM	Manny Ramirez	6.00
30HM	Tom Glavine	5.00

Hot Tandems

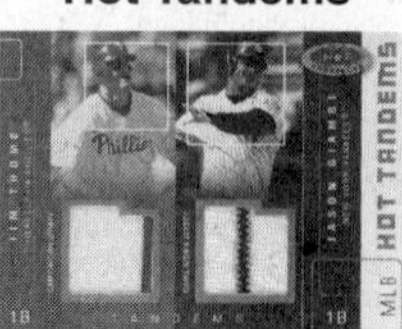

	NM/M
Common Duo:	8.00
Production 100 Sets	
Red-Hots numbered to 10.	
Derek Jeter, Chipper Jones	25.00
Derek Jeter, Mike Piazza	25.00
Derek Jeter, Miguel Tejada	25.00
Torii Hunter, Lance Berkman	10.00
Mark Prior, Sammy Sosa	25.00
Sammy Sosa, Pat Burrell	20.00
Rafael Palmeiro, Mark Teixeira	10.00
Hee Seop Choi, Lyle Overbay	15.00
Alex Rodriguez, Mark Teixeira	20.00
Mike Piazza, Chipper Jones	15.00
Pat Burrell, Jim Thome	10.00
Lance Berkman, Adam Dunn	8.00
Nomar Garciaparra, Miguel Tejada	15.00
Randy Johnson, Greg Maddux	12.00
Mark Prior, Josh Beckett	10.00
Miguel Tejada, Alex Rodriguez	15.00
Jason Giambi, Jim Thome	10.00

Hot Triple Patch

	NM/M
Production 50 Sets	
Some not priced yet.	
Derek Jeter, Nomar Garciaparra, Alex Rodriguez	125.00
Mark Prior, Josh Beckett, Greg Maddux	80.00
Mike Piazza, Pat Burrell, Jim Thome	50.00
Lance Berkman, Troy Glaus, Chipper Jones	50.00
Randy Johnson, Alfonso Soriano, Shawn Green	50.00
Derek Jeter, Torii Hunter, Mark Prior	75.00
Nomar Garciaparra, Sammy Sosa, Mike Piazza	90.00
Pat Burrell, Jim Thome, Lance Berkman	40.00
Vladimir Guerrero, Troy Glaus, Chipper Jones	60.00

Alfonso Soriano,
Greg Maddux,
Shawn Green 60.00

Playergraphs

NM/M
Common Player: 10.00
Production 400 Sets
Red-Hots: 1-1.5X
Production 100
Hank Blalock 20.00
Brett Myers 10.00
Mark Prior 35.00
Carlos Zambrano 20.00
Mark Teixeira 20.00
Francisco Rodriguez 10.00
Roy Oswalt 15.00
Xavier Nady 10.00
Jose Reyes 25.00
Aubrey Huff 10.00

MLB 3-D Stars

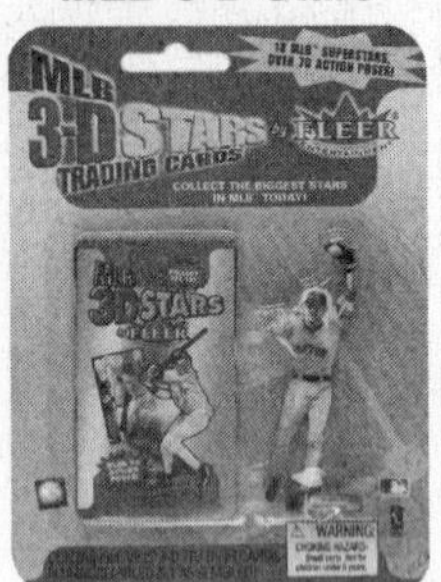

Eighteen players are included in this novelty card issue from Fleer Entertainment division. Each player is printed on a 2-1/4" x 3-1/2" card that is die-cut to allow the pieces to be punched out and assembled in a variety of action poses. Each 5-5/8" x 7-3/8" blister pack contains five 3-D cards, one assembled and four unassembled. Values shown are for unpunched cards.

NM/M
Complete Set (18): 7.50
Common Player: .25
1 Derek Jeter 1.00
2 Barry Bonds 1.00
3 Greg Maddux .40
4 Nomar Garciaparra .65
5 Curt Schilling .25
6 Jason Giambi .25
7 Pedro Martinez .25
8 Alfonso Soriano .25
9 Alex Rodriguez .75
10 Ken Griffey Jr. .60
11 Sammy Sosa .60
12 Albert Pujols .50
13 Roger Clemens .50
14 Chipper Jones .40
15 Ichiro .50
16 Miguel Tejada .25
17 Mark Prior .50
18 Mariano Rivera .25

2003 Fleer Mystique

NM/M
Complete Set (130):
Common Player: .25
Common SP (81-130): 3.00
Production 699
Pack (4): 3.00
Box (20): 40.00
1 Alex Rodriguez 2.50
2 Derek Jeter 3.00
3 Jose Vidro .25
4 Miguel Tejada .40
5 Albert Pujols 2.50
6 Rocco Baldelli .25
7 Jose Reyes .50
8 Hideo Nomo .75
9 Hank Blalock .75
10 Chipper Jones 1.50
11 Barry Larkin .25
12 Alfonso Soriano 1.00
13 Aramis Ramirez .25
14 Darin Erstad .65
15 Jim Edmonds .25
16 Garret Anderson .25
17 Todd Helton 1.00
18 Jason Kendall .25
19 Aubrey Huff .25
20 Troy Glaus .75
21 Sammy Sosa 2.00
22 Roger Clemens 1.75
23 Mark Teixeira .50
24 Barry Bonds 3.00
25 Jim Thome .25
26 Carlos Delgado .50
27 Vladimir Guerrero 1.00
28 Austin Kearns .50
29 Pat Burrell .75
30 Ken Griffey Jr. 2.00
31 Greg Maddux 1.50
32 Corey Patterson .25
33 Larry Walker .25
34 Kerry Wood .65
35 Frank Thomas 1.00
36 Dontrelle Willis .25
37 Randy Johnson 1.00
38 Curt Schilling .40
39 Jay Gibbons .25
40 Dmitri Young .25
41 Edgar Martinez .25
42 Kevin Brown .25
43 Scott Rolen 1.00
44 Adam Dunn .75
45 Pedro J. Martinez 1.00
46 Corey Koskie .25
47 Tom Glavine .40
48 Torii Hunter .25
49 Shawn Green .40
50 Nomar Garciaparra 2.00
51 Bernie Williams .40
52 Milton Bradley .25
53 Jason Giambi .75
54 Mike Lieberthal .25
55 Jeff Bagwell 1.00
56 Carlos Pena .25
57 Lance Berkman .25
58 Jose Cruz Jr. .25
59 Josh Beckett .25
60 Mark Mulder .40
61 Mike Piazza 2.00
62 Mark Prior 1.00
63 Sean Burroughs .25
64 Angel Berroa .25
65 Geoff Jenkins .25
66 Magglio Ordonez .25
67 Craig Biggio .25
68 Roberto Alomar .40
69 Hee Seop Choi .25
70 J.D. Drew .25
71 Richie Sexson .25
72 Brian Giles .25
73 Gary Sheffield .50
74 Manny Ramirez 1.00
75 Barry Zito .45
76 Andruw Jones 1.00
77 Ivan Rodriguez .65
78 Ichiro Suzuki 2.00
79 Mike Sweeney .25
80 Vernon Wells .25
81 Craig Brazell **RC** 5.00
82 Wilfredo Ledezma **RC** 3.00
83 Josh Willingham **RC** 6.00
84 Chien-Ming Wang **RC** 35.00
85 Mike Ryan **RC** 3.00
86 Mike Gallo **RC** 3.00
87 Rickie Weeks **RC** 10.00
88 Brian Stokes **RC** 3.00
89 Humberto Quintero **RC** 3.00
90 Ramon Nivar **RC** 3.00
91 Jeremy Griffiths 3.00
92 Terrmel Sledge **RC** 4.00
93 Brandon Webb **RC** 10.00
94 David DeJesus **RC** 5.00
95 Doug Waechter **RC** 3.00
96 Jeremy Bonderman 10.00
97 Felix Sanchez **RC** 3.00
98 Colin Porter **RC** 3.00
99 Francisco Cruceta **RC** 3.00
100 Hideki Matsui **RC** 15.00
101 Chris Waters **RC** 5.00
102 Dan Haren 5.00
103 Lew Ford **RC** 5.00
104 Oscar Villarreal **RC** 3.00
105 Ryan Wagner **RC** 5.00
106 Prentice Redman **RC** 3.00
107 Josh Stewart **RC** 5.00
108 Carlos Mendez **RC** 3.00
109 Michael Hessman **RC** 5.00
110 Josh Hall **RC** 5.00
111 Daniel Garcia **RC** 5.00
112 Matt Kata **RC** 5.00
113 Michel Hernandez **RC** 3.00
114 Sergio Mitre **RC** 5.00
115 Pete LaForest **RC** 5.00
116 Edwin Jackson **RC** 5.00
117 Matt Diaz **RC** 5.00
118 Greg Aquino **RC** 3.00
119 Jose Contreras **RC** 8.00
120 Jeff Duncan **RC** 6.00
121 Richard Fischer **RC** 3.00
122 Todd Wellemeyer **RC** 5.00
123 Robby Hammock **RC** 5.00
124 Delmon Young **RC** 15.00
125 Clint Barmes **RC** 5.00
126 Phil Seibel **RC** 3.00
127 Bo Hart **RC** 5.00
128 Jon Leicester **RC** 5.00
129 Chad Gaudin **RC** 6.00
130 Guillermo Quiroz **RC** 5.00

Gold

Stars (1-80): 4-8X
Production 150
SP's (81-130): 1-2X
Production 50

Awe Pairs

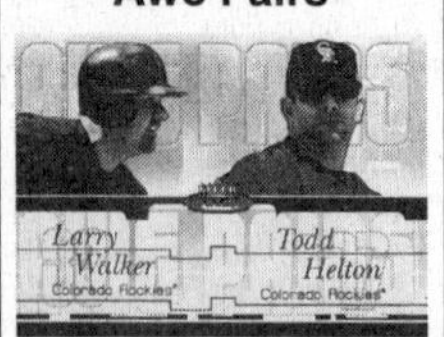

NM/M
Complete Set (20): 60.00
Common Duo: 2.00
Production 250 Sets
Golds: 1.5X
#'d to team win total for 2003
1 Nomar Garciaparra, Pedro J. Martinez 8.00
2 Derek Jeter, Alfonso Soriano 8.00
3 Rocco Baldelli, Aubrey Huff 2.00
4 Carlos Delgado, Vernon Wells 2.00
5 Troy Glaus, Garret Anderson 2.00
6 Ichiro Suzuki, Bret Boone 5.00
7 Alex Rodriguez, Hank Blalock 8.00
8 Chipper Jones, Andruw Jones 5.00
9 Dontrelle Willis, Mike Lowell 3.00
10 Vladimir Guerrero, Orlando Cabrera 4.00
11 Tom Glavine, Mike Piazza 5.00
12 Jim Thome, Mike Lieberthal 3.00
13 Sammy Sosa, Corey Patterson 6.00
14 Jeff Bagwell, Lance Berkman 3.00
15 Geoff Jenkins, Richie Sexson 2.00
16 Albert Pujols, Jim Edmonds 6.00
17 Todd Helton, Larry Walker 3.00
18 Paul LoDuca, Shawn Green 2.00
19 Ryan Klesko, Sean Burroughs 2.00
20 Barry Bonds, Rich Aurilia 8.00

Awe Pairs Game-Used

NM/M
Common Duo: 10.00
Production 100 Sets
Golds: No Pricing
Production 10 Sets
Nomar Garciaparra, Pedro J. Martinez 25.00
Derek Jeter, Alfonso Soriano 30.00
Rocco Baldelli, Aubrey Huff 15.00
Carlos Delgado, Vernon Wells 10.00
Troy Glaus, Garret Anderson 10.00
Chipper Jones, Andruw Jones 15.00
Dontrelle Willis, Mike Lowell 25.00
Vladimir Guerrero, Orlando Cabrera 10.00
Tom Glavine, Mike Piazza 20.00
Jim Thome, Mike Lieberthal 15.00
Sammy Sosa, Corey Patterson 20.00
Jeff Bagwell, Lance Berkman 15.00
Geoff Jenkins, Richie Sexson 10.00
Albert Pujols, Jim Edmonds 20.00
Todd Helton, Larry Walker 10.00
Paul LoDuca, Shawn Green 10.00
Ryan Klesko, Sean Burroughs 10.00

Diamond Dominators

NM/M
Complete Set (10): 50.00
Common Player: 3.00
Production 100 Sets
1 Mike Piazza 8.00
2 Greg Maddux 8.00
3 Alfonso Soriano 5.00
4 Barry Zito 3.00
5 Alex Rodriguez 10.00
6 Roger Clemens 10.00
7 Sammy Sosa 10.00
8 Adam Dunn 3.00
9 Randy Johnson 5.00
10 Pedro J. Martinez 5.00

Diamond Dominators Gold

NM/M
Some not priced due to scarcity.
Numbered to jersey number.
1DD Mike Piazza/31 25.00
2DD Greg Maddux/31 25.00
4DD Barry Zito/75 5.00
8DD Adam Dunn/44 6.00
9DD Randy Johnson/51 8.00
10DD Pedro Martinez/45 10.00

Diamond Dominators Game-Used

NM/M
Common Player: 6.00
Production 75 Sets
Golds: No Pricing
Production 10 Sets
RC Roger Clemens 20.00
AD Adam Dunn 6.00
RJ Randy Johnson 10.00
GM Greg Maddux 25.00
PM Pedro Martinez 12.00
MP Mike Piazza 15.00
AR Alex Rodriguez 15.00
AS Alfonso Soriano 12.00
SS Sammy Sosa 20.00
BZ Barry Zito 8.00

Ink Appeal Autographs

NM/M
Common Player: 15.00
Production 50 Sets
RB Rocco Baldelli 40.00
HB Hank Blalock 35.00
BH Bo Hart 25.00
AH Aubrey Huff 15.00
TH Torii Hunter 20.00
CP Corey Patterson 15.00
JR Jose Reyes 30.00
MR Mike Ryan 15.00
JW Josh Willingham 15.00

Ink Appeal Gold Autographs

NM/M
Numbered to jersey number.
Some not priced due to scarcity.
BH Bo Hart/31 50.00
TH Torii Hunter/48 20.00
MR Mike Ryan/54 15.00
JW Josh Willingham/70 12.00

Ink Appeal Dual Autographs

No pricing due to scarcity.
Production 20 Sets
Golds: No Pricing
Production Five Sets

Rare Finds

NM/M
Complete Set (10): 40.00
Common Trio: 3.00
Production 250 Sets

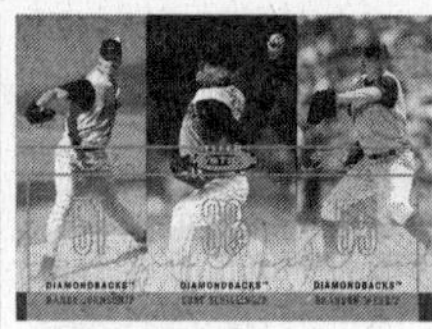

1 Jason Giambi, Roger Clemens, Derek Jeter 8.00
2 Randy Johnson, Curt Schilling, Brandon Webb 4.00
3 Nomar Garciaparra, Pedro J. Martinez, Manny Ramirez 8.00
4 Mark Prior, Kerry Wood, Sammy Sosa 5.00
5 Jeff Bagwell, Craig Biggio, Lance Berkman 3.00
6 Austin Kearns, Adam Dunn, Barry Larkin 3.00
7 Jim Edmonds, Scott Rolen, J.D. Drew 3.00
8 Chipper Jones, Andruw Jones, Greg Maddux 5.00
9 Barry Zito, Miguel Tejada, Mark Mulder 3.00
10 Alex Rodriguez, Mark Teixeira, Rafael Palmeiro 8.00

Rare Finds Autographs

No Pricing:
Production 15 Sets
Auto./Game-Used: No Pricing
Production Five Sets

Rare Finds Single Swatch

NM/M
Common Player: 6.00
Production 150 Sets
Golds: No Pricing
Production 15 Sets
JG Jason Giambi, Roger Clemens, Derek Jeter 10.00
RC Jason Giambi, Roger Clemens, Derek Jeter 15.00
DJ Jason Giambi, Roger Clemens, Derek Jeter 20.00
RJ Randy Johnson, Curt Schilling, Brandon Webb 8.00
BW Randy Johnson, Curt Schilling, Brandon Webb 10.00
NG Nomar Garciaparra, Pedro J. Martinez, Manny Ramirez 15.00
PM Nomar Garciaparra, Pedro J. Martinez, Manny Ramirez 8.00
MP Mark Prior, Kerry Wood, Sammy Sosa 10.00
SS Mark Prior, Kerry Wood, Sammy Sosa 8.00
JB Jeff Bagwell, Craig Biggio, Lance Berkman 6.00
AK Austin Kearns, Adam Dunn, Barry Larkin 6.00
BL Austin Kearns, Adam Dunn, Barry Larkin 6.00
SR Jim Edmonds, Scott Rolen, J.D. Drew 10.00
JD Jim Edmonds, Scott Rolen, J.D. Drew 6.00
CJ Chipper Jones, Andruw Jones, Greg Maddux 10.00
GM Chipper Jones, Andruw Jones, Greg Maddux 15.00
MT Barry Zito, Miguel Tejada, Mark Mulder 6.00
MM Barry Zito, Miguel Tejada, Mark Mulder 6.00
AR Alex Rodriguez, Mark Teixeira, Rafael Palmeiro 15.00
MT Alex Rodriguez, Mark Teixeira, Rafael Palmeiro 8.00

Rare Finds Dual Swatch

NM/M
Common Dual: 10.00
Production 75 Sets
Golds: No Pricing
Production 10 Sets
Jason Giambi, Roger Clemens, Derek Jeter 35.00
Jason Giambi, Roger Clemens, Derek Jeter 40.00
Randy Johnson, Curt Schilling, Brandon Webb 15.00
Randy Johnson, Curt Schilling, Brandon Webb 10.00
Nomar Garciaparra, Pedro J. Martinez, Manny Ramirez 20.00
Nomar Garciaparra, Pedro J. Martinez, Manny Ramirez 15.00
Mark Prior, Kerry Wood, Sammy Sosa 15.00
Mark Prior, Kerry Wood, Sammy Sosa 20.00
Jeff Bagwell, Craig Biggio, Lance Berkman 10.00
Austin Kearns, Adam Dunn, Barry Larkin 10.00
Jim Edmonds, Scott Rolen, J.D. Drew 15.00
Chipper Jones, Andruw Jones, Greg Maddux 20.00
Chipper Jones, Andruw Jones, Greg Maddux 20.00
Barry Zito, Miguel Tejada, Mark Mulder 10.00
Alex Rodriguez, Mark Teixeira, Rafael Palmeiro 20.00

Rare Finds Triple Swatch

NM/M
Production 50 Sets
Golds: No Pricing
Production Five Sets
Jason Giambi, Roger Clemens, Derek Jeter 50.00
Randy Johnson, Curt Schilling, Brandon Webb 25.00
Nomar Garciaparra, Pedro J. Martinez, Manny Ramirez 60.00
Mark Prior, Kerry Wood, Sammy Sosa 40.00
Jeff Bagwell, Craig Biggio, Lance Berkman 20.00
Austin Kearns, Adam Dunn, Barry Larkin 20.00
Jim Edmonds, Scott Rolen, J.D. Drew 25.00
Chipper Jones, Andruw Jones, Greg Maddux 40.00
Barry Zito, Miguel Tejada, Mark Mulder 15.00
Alex Rodriguez, Mark Teixeira, Rafael Palmeiro 40.00

Secret Weapons

NM/M
Complete Set (10): 25.00
Common Player: 2.00
Production 250 Sets
Golds: 1X
#'d to career batting average
1 Hank Blalock 3.00
2 Dontrelle Willis 3.00
3 Jose Reyes 3.00
4 Bo Hart 4.00
5 Corey Patterson 2.00
6 Hideki Matsui 8.00
7 Mark Teixeira 3.00
8 Brandon Webb 3.00
9 Rocco Baldelli 3.00
10 Mark Prior 5.00

Shining Stars

		NM/M
Complete Set (15):		50.00
Common Player:		2.00
Production 300 Sets		
1SS	Derek Jeter	8.00
2SS	Barry Bonds	8.00
3SS	Nomar Garciaparra	6.00
4SS	Austin Kearns	2.00
5SS	Vladimir Guerrero	3.00
6SS	Jim Thome	3.00
7SS	Ichiro Suzuki	5.00
8SS	Jason Giambi	3.00
9SS	Albert Pujols	6.00
10SS	Ken Griffey Jr.	5.00
11SS	Chipper Jones	5.00
12SS	Scott Rolen	3.00
13SS	Manny Ramirez	3.00
14SS	Jeff Bagwell	3.00
15SS	Torii Hunter	2.00

Shining Stars Gold

		NM/M
Numbered to career HR total.		
1SS	Derek Jeter/127	10.00
2SS	Barry Bonds/658	5.00
3SS	Nomar Garciaparra/173	10.00
4SS	Austin Kearns/28	10.00
5SS	Vladimir Guerrero/234	4.00
6SS	Jim Thome/381	3.00
7SS	Ichiro Suzuki/29	30.00
8SS	Jason Giambi/269	3.00
9SS	Albert Pujols/114	8.00
10SS	Ken Griffey Jr./481	4.00
11SS	Chipper Jones/280	5.00
12SS	Scott Rolen/192	4.00
13SS	Manny Ramirez/347	3.00
14SS	Jeff Bagwell/419	3.00
15SS	Torii Hunter/96	4.00

Shining Stars Game-Used

		NM/M
Common Player:		6.00
Production 100 Sets		
Patch:		1.5X
Production 50 Sets		
JB	Jeff Bagwell	8.00
CD	Carlos Delgado	6.00
NG	Nomar Garciaparra	15.00
JG	Jason Giambi	8.00
TH	Todd Helton	8.00
TH	Torii Hunter	8.00
DJ	Derek Jeter	20.00
AJ	Andruw Jones	6.00
CJ	Chipper Jones	10.00
AK	Austin Kearns	6.00
AP	Albert Pujols	15.00
MR	Manny Ramirez	8.00
SR	Scott Rolen	10.00
JT	Jim Thome	8.00

N.Y. Mets

While the basic format of Fleer Tradition was preserved in this stadium give-away set, different photos were used than those found in regular-issue packs. Persons attending a special Baseball Card Pack promotional game received a cello-wrapped set of seven player cards and a header card.

		NM/M
Complete Set (8):		4.00
Common Player:		.25
1	Mike Piazza	3.00
2	Tom Glavine	.50
3	Cliff Floyd	.25
4	Al Leiter	.25
5	Jae Seo	.25
6	John Franco	.25
7	Ty Wigginton	.25
---	Header Card	.10

2003 Fleer Patchworks

		NM/M
Complete Set (115):		
Common Player:		.15
Common Prospect (91-115):		3.00
Production 1,500		
Pack (5):		3.00
Box (24):		50.00
1	Luis Castillo	.15
2	Derek Jeter	2.00
3	Vladimir Guerrero	.75
4	Bobby Higginson	.15
5	Pat Burrell	.40
6	Ivan Rodriguez	.60
7	Craig Biggio	.15
8	Troy Glaus	.60
9	Barry Bonds	2.00
10	Hideo Nomo	.60
11	Barry Larkin	.15
12	Roberto Alomar	.35
13	Rodrigo Lopez	.15
14	Eric Chavez	.25
15	Shawn Green	.25
16	Joe Randa	.15
17	Mark Grace	.25
18	Jason Kendall	.15
19	Hee Seop Choi	.15
20	Luis Gonzalez	.25
21	Sammy Sosa	1.25
22	Larry Walker	.15
23	Phil Nevin	.15
24	Manny Ramirez	.75
25	Jim Thome	.15
26	Randy Johnson	.75
27	Jose Vidro	.15
28	Austin Kearns	.35
29	Mike Sweeney	.15
30	Magglio Ordonez	.15
31	Mike Piazza	1.25
32	Eric Hinske	.15
33	Alex Rodriguez	1.50
34	Kerry Wood	.60
35	Matt Morris	.15
36	Lance Berkman	.15
37	Michael Cuddyer	.15
38	Curt Schilling	.40
39	Sean Burroughs	.15
40	Ken Griffey Jr.	1.25
41	Edgardo Alfonzo	.15
42	Carlos Pena	.15
43	Adam Dunn	.50
44	Pedro J. Martinez	.75
45	Miguel Tejada	.35
46	Tom Glavine	.35
47	Torii Hunter	.15
48	Jason Giambi	.50
49	Tony Batista	.15
50	Ben Grieve	.15
51	Ichiro Suzuki	1.25
52	Bobby Abreu	.15
53	Todd Helton	.75
54	Kazuhiro Sasaki	.15
55	Nomar Garciaparra	1.25
56	Francisco Rodriguez	.15
57	Ellis Burks	.15
58	Frank Thomas	.75
59	Greg Maddux	1.00
60	Josh Beckett	.25
61	Brad Wilkerson	.15
62	Joe Borchard	.15
63	Carlos Delgado	.40
64	Alfonso Soriano	.75
65	Chipper Jones	1.00
66	J.D. Drew	.25
67	Mark Prior	.75
68	Rafael Palmeiro	.60
69	Jeff Kent	.15
70	Adrian Beltre	.25
71	Marlon Byrd	.15
72	Orlando Hudson	.15
73	Junior Spivey	.15
74	Jeff Bagwell	.75
75	Barry Zito	.35
76	Roger Clemens	1.00
77	Aubrey Huff	.15
78	Geoff Jenkins	.15
79	Andruw Jones	.75
80	Scott Rolen	.75
81	Omar Vizquel	.15
82	Darin Erstad	.50
83	Bernie Williams	.35
84	Freddy Garcia	.15
85	Richie Sexson	.15
86	Josh Phelps	.15
87	Albert Pujols	1.50
88	Aramis Ramirez	.15
89	Shea Hillenbrand	.15
90	Cristian Guzman	.15
91	Adam LaRoche	3.00
92	David Pember **RC**	3.00
93	Termel Sledge **RC**	3.00
94	Hideki Matsui **RC**	10.00
95	Nook Logan **RC**	4.00
96	Jose Contreras **RC**	4.00
97	Pete LaForest **RC**	3.00
98	Richard Fischer **RC**	3.00
99	Francisco Rosario **RC**	3.00
100	Josh Willingham **RC**	4.00
101	Alejandro Machado **RC**	3.00
102	Lew Ford **RC**	4.00
103	Joe Valentine **RC**	3.00
104	Guillermo Quiroz **RC**	4.00
105	Chien-Ming Wang **RC**	20.00
106	Jhonny Peralta	4.00
107	Shane Victorino **RC**	3.00
108	Prentice Redman **RC**	3.00
109	Matt Bruback **RC**	3.00
110	Lance Niekro	3.00
111	Travis Hughes	3.00
112	Nic Jackson	3.00
113	Hector Luna **RC**	4.00
114	Cliff Lee	3.00
115	Tim Olson **RC**	4.00

Star Ruby

Stars (1-90):	4-8X
Prospects (91-115):	1-30X
Production 100 Sets	

Diamond Ink

	NM/M
Quantity signed listed	
Derek Jeter/210	90.00
Derek Jeter/101	125.00
Derek Jeter/50	175.00
Mark Prior/88	40.00
Troy Glaus/351	25.00
Mike Schmidt/194	75.00

Licensed Apparel - Jersey

	NM/M
Common Player:	4.00
Production 500 Sets	
J.D. Drew	8.00
Magglio Ordonez	6.00
Todd Helton	8.00
Paul Konerko	4.00
Shawn Green	6.00
Carlos Beltran	4.00
Kevin Brown	4.00
Shannon Stewart	4.00
Mike Mussina	8.00
Adam Dunn	10.00
Jimmy Rollins	4.00
Darin Erstad	6.00
Chipper Jones	10.00
Mike Piazza	10.00
Derek Jeter	20.00

Licensed Apparel - Patch

	NM/M
Common Player:	10.00
Production 300 Sets	
J.D. Drew	12.00
Magglio Ordonez	15.00
Todd Helton	20.00
Paul Konerko	10.00
Shawn Green	15.00
Carlos Beltran	10.00
Kevin Brown	10.00
Shannon Stewart	10.00
Mike Mussina	15.00
Adam Dunn	20.00
Jimmy Rollins	15.00
Darin Erstad	25.00
Chipper Jones	20.00
Mike Piazza	25.00
Derek Jeter	40.00

National Pastime

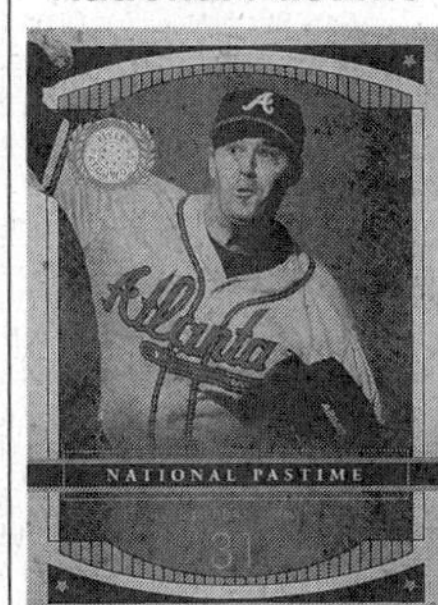

		NM/M
Complete Set (25):		40.00
Common Player:		1.00
Inserted 1:12		
1NP	Barry Bonds	6.00
2NP	Kazuhiro Sasaki	1.00
3NP	Mike Piazza	4.00
4NP	Barry Zito	1.50
5NP	Sammy Sosa	3.00
6NP	Pedro J. Martinez	2.00
7NP	Craig Biggio	1.00
8NP	Rafael Palmeiro	1.50
9NP	Greg Maddux	3.00
10NP	Manny Ramirez	2.00
11NP	Adam Dunn	1.50
12NP	Omar Vizquel	1.00
13NP	Hideo Nomo	1.00
14NP	Alex Rodriguez	5.00
15NP	Pat Burrell	1.00
16NP	Nomar Garciaparra	4.00
17NP	Randy Johnson	2.00
18NP	Juan Gonzalez	1.50
19NP	Chipper Jones	3.00
20NP	Frank Thomas	1.50
21NP	Vladimir Guerrero	2.00
22NP	Troy Glaus	2.00
23NP	Albert Pujols	3.00
24NP	Ichiro Suzuki	3.00
25NP	Ken Griffey Jr.	3.00

National Pastime - MLB logo

Production One Set:

National Patchtime - Commemorative

Production 25 Sets: No Pricing

National Patchtime - Nameplate

	NM/M
Production 50 Sets	
Vladimir Guerrero	40.00
Rafael Palmeiro	25.00
Nomar Garciaparra	40.00
Greg Maddux	30.00
Sammy Sosa	60.00
Mike Piazza	35.00
Barry Zito	40.00
Hideo Nomo	50.00
Alex Rodriguez	50.00
Pat Burrell	25.00
Randy Johnson	50.00
Chipper Jones	35.00
Frank Thomas	40.00
Troy Glaus	30.00

2003 Fleer Patchworks National Patchtime - Number

	NM/M
Common Player:	15.00
Production 75 Sets	
Vladimir Guerrero	20.00
Manny Ramirez	25.00
Craig Biggio	15.00
Rafael Palmeiro	20.00
Nomar Garciaparra	40.00
Greg Maddux	25.00
Sammy Sosa	45.00
Mike Piazza	30.00
Pedro J. Martinez	25.00
Hideo Nomo	25.00
Alex Rodriguez	30.00
Pat Burrell	20.00
Randy Johnson	45.00
Chipper Jones	35.00
Frank Thomas	30.00

National Patchtime - Team Name

	NM/M
Common Player:	15.00
Production 100 Sets	
Vladimir Guerrero	15.00
Rafael Palmeiro	20.00
Nomar Garciaparra	35.00
Sammy Sosa	40.00
Mike Piazza	30.00
Barry Zito	20.00
Hideo Nomo	30.00
Alex Rodriguez	30.00
Pat Burrell	20.00
Randy Johnson	45.00
Chipper Jones	35.00
Troy Glaus	30.00
Omar Vizquel	20.00

National Patchtime - Trim

	NM/M
Common Player:	12.00
Production 200 Sets	
Vladimir Guerrero	12.00
Manny Ramirez	15.00
Rafael Palmeiro	12.00
Nomar Garciaparra	25.00
Greg Maddux	20.00
Mike Piazza	20.00
Pedro J. Martinez	20.00
Hideo Nomo	20.00
Alex Rodriguez	25.00
Chipper Jones	20.00
Frank Thomas	20.00

Numbers Game

		NM/M
Complete Set (15):		30.00
Common Player:		1.00
Inserted 1:24		
1	Ichiro Suzuki	3.00
2	Derek Jeter	6.00
3	Alex Rodriguez	5.00
4	Miguel Tejada	1.00
5	Nomar Garciaparra	4.00
6	Jason Giambi	3.00
7	J.D. Drew	1.00
8	Barry Bonds	6.00
9	Alfonso Soriano	2.00
10	Jeff Bagwell	1.50
11	Barry Larkin	1.00
12	Roberto Alomar	1.00
13	Larry Walker	1.00
14	Roger Clemens	3.00
15	Ken Griffey Jr.	3.00

Numbers Game - Jersey

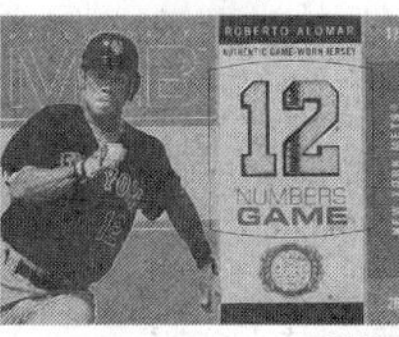

	NM/M
Common Player:	4.00
Inserted 1:25	
Barry Larkin	6.00
Roberto Alomar	4.00
Jeff Bagwell	8.00
Jason Giambi	8.00
Larry Walker	4.00
Derek Jeter	15.00
Alex Rodriguez	10.00
Alfonso Soriano	10.00
Roger Clemens	12.00
Miguel Tejada	4.00

Numbers Game - Patch

	NM/M
Common Player:	10.00
Production 300 Sets	
Barry Larkin	15.00
Roberto Alomar	15.00
Jeff Bagwell	25.00
Jason Giambi	15.00
Larry Walker	10.00
Derek Jeter	40.00
Alex Rodriguez	25.00
Alfonso Soriano	25.00
Roger Clemens	30.00
Miguel Tejada	10.00

Past, Present, Future

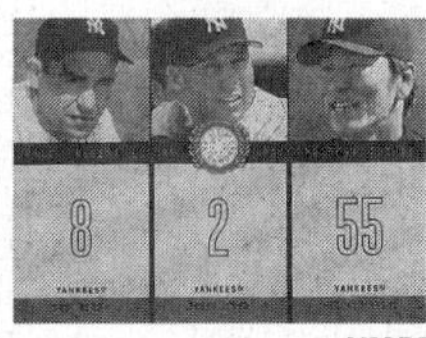

		NM/M
Complete Set (10):		40.00
Common Card:		4.00
Inserted 1:72		
1	Eddie Mathews, Rafael Palmeiro, Alex Rodriguez	5.00
2	Phil Rizzuto, Derek Jeter, Alfonso Soriano	5.00
3	Reggie Jackson, Barry Bonds, Sammy Sosa	6.00
4	Billy Williams, Sammy Sosa, Hee Seop Choi	4.00
5	Joe Morgan, Roberto Alomar, Alfonso Soriano	3.00
6	Yogi Berra, Mike Piazza, Josh Phelps	4.00
7	Nolan Ryan, Roger Clemens, Kerry Wood	6.00
8	Mike Schmidt, Scott Rolen, Eric Hinske	4.00
9	Barry Bonds, Alex Rodriguez, Alfonso Soriano	5.00
10	Yogi Berra, Derek Jeter, Hideki Matsui	6.00

Patch, Present, Future - Dual

Production 100 Sets

Patch, Present, Future - Single

	NM/M
Common Player:	10.00
Production 200 Sets	
Rafael Palmeiro	15.00
Alex Rodriguez	20.00
Derek Jeter	50.00
Alfonso Soriano	50.00
Barry Bonds	50.00
Sammy Sosa	25.00
Sammy Sosa	25.00
Roberto Alomar	25.00
Alfonso Soriano	50.00
Mike Piazza	25.00
Roger Clemens	40.00
Kerry Wood	40.00
Eric Hinske	10.00
Alex Rodriguez	20.00
Alfonso Soriano	50.00
Derek Jeter	50.00

Patchworks

		NM/M
Common Player:		8.00
Production 250 Sets		
2	Frank Thomas	12.00
8	Lance Berkman	15.00
9	Kazuhiro Sasaki	15.00
10	Roy Oswalt	15.00
11	Bernie Williams	15.00
12PW	Bob Abreu	15.00
14PW	Greg Maddux	20.00
15PW	Josh Beckett	8.00
16PW	Mark Grace	20.00
17PW	Eric Chavez	10.00
18PW	Andruw Jones	15.00
19PW	Adrian Beltre	8.00

Patchworks - Dual Color

	NM/M
Common Player:	10.00
Production 100 Sets	
Alex Rodriguez	35.00
Frank Thomas	20.00
Vladimir Guerrero	20.00
Roberto Alomar	20.00
Kerry Wood	35.00
Curt Schilling	15.00
Lance Berkman	20.00
Kazuhiro Sasaki	35.00
Roy Oswalt	20.00
Bernie Williams	25.00
Bob Abreu	10.00
Carlos Delgado	12.00
Greg Maddux	25.00
Josh Beckett	10.00
Mark Grace	15.00
Eric Chavez	15.00
Andruw Jones	15.00
Adrian Beltre	10.00

Patchworks - Multi-Color

	NM/M
Common Player:	20.00
Production 50 Sets	
Alex Rodriguez	60.00
Frank Thomas	30.00
Vladimir Guerrero	35.00
Roberto Alomar	35.00
Kerry Wood	40.00
Curt Schilling	20.00
Lance Berkman	25.00
Kazuhiro Sasaki	50.00
Roy Oswalt	40.00
Bernie Williams	35.00
Bob Abreu	25.00
Carlos Delgado	20.00
Greg Maddux	35.00
Josh Beckett	20.00
Mark Grace	30.00
Eric Chavez	30.00
Andruw Jones	30.00
Adrian Beltre	20.00

2003 Fleer Platinum

		NM/M
Complete Set (250):		40.00
Common Player:		.15
Common SP (221-250):		.50
Hobby Pack (10):		1.50
Hobby Box (14 + 4 jumbo + 1 Rack):		35.00
Jumbo Pack:		3.00
Rack Pack:		5.00
1	Barry Bonds	2.50
2	Sean Casey	.25
3	Todd Walker	.15
4	Tony Batista	.15
5	Todd Zeile	.15
6	Ruben Sierra	.15
7	Jose Cruz Jr.	.15
8	Ben Grieve	.15
9	Robert Mackowiak	.15
10	Gary Sheffield	.25
11	Armando Benitez	.15
12	Tim Hudson	.25
13	Eric Milton	.15
14	Andy Pettitte	.40
15	Jeff Bagwell	.75
16	Jeff Kent	.15
17	Joe Randa	.15
18	Benito Santiago	.15

19 Russell Branyan .15
20 Cliff Floyd .15
21 Chris Richard .15
22 Randy Winn .15
23 Freddy Garcia .15
24 Derek Lowe .15
25 Ben Sheets .15
26 Fred McGriff .15
27 Bret Boone .15
28 Jose Hernandez .15
29 Phil Nevin .15
30 Mike Piazza 1.50
31 Bobby Abreu .15
32 Darin Erstad .50
33 Andruw Jones .75
34 Brad Wilkerson .15
35 Brian Lawrence .15
36 Vladimir Nunez .15
37 Kazuhiro Sasaki .15
38 Carlos Delgado .45
39 Steve Cox .15
40 Adrian Beltre .25
41 Josh Bard .15
42 Randall Simon .15
43 Johnny Damon .25
44 Ken Griffey Jr. 1.50
45 Sammy Sosa 1.50
46 Kevin Brown .15
47 Kazuhisa Ishii .15
48 Matt Morris .15
49 Mark Prior .75
50 Kip Wells .15
51 Hee Seop Choi .15
52 Craig Biggio .15
53 Derek Jeter 2.50
54 Albert Pujols 1.25
55 Joe Borchard .15
56 Robert Fick .15
57 Jacque Jones .15
58 Juan Pierre .15
59 Bernie Williams .35
60 Elmer Dessens .15
61 Al Leiter .15
62 Curt Schilling .40
63 Carlos Pena .15
64 Tino Martinez .15
65 Fernando Vina .15
66 Aaron Boone .15
67 Michael Barrett .15
68 Frank Thomas .75
69 J.D. Drew .25
70 Vladimir Guerrero .75
71 Shannon Stewart .15
72 Mark Buehrle .15
73 Jamie Moyer .15
74 Brad Radke .15
75 Miko Williams .15
76 Ryan Klesko .15
77 Roberto Alomar .35
78 Edgardo Alfonzo .15
79 Matt Williams .15
80 Edgar Martinez .15
81 Shawn Green .25
82 Kenny Lofton .15
83 Josh Beckett .15
84 Trevor Hoffman .15
85 Kevin Millwood .15
86 Odalis Perez .15
87 Jarrod Washburn .15
88 Jason Giambi .60
89 Eric Young .15
90 Barry Larkin .15
91 Aramis Ramirez .15
92 Ivan Rodriguez .50
93 Steve Finley .15
94 Brian Jordan .15
95 Manny Ramirez .75
96 Preston Wilson .15
97 Rodrigo Lopez .15
98 Ramon Ortiz .15
99 Jim Thome .15
100 Luis Castillo .15
101 Alex Rodriguez 2.00
102 Jared Sandberg .15
103 Ellis Burks .15
104 Pat Burrell .60
105 Brian Giles .15
106 Mark Kotsay .15
107 Dave Roberts .15
108 Roy Halladay .15
109 Chan Ho Park .15
110 Erubiel Durazo .15
111 Bobby Hill .15
112 Cristian Guzman .15
113 Troy Glaus .60
114 Lance Berkman .15
115 Juan Encarnacion .15
116 Chipper Jones 1.00
117 Corey Patterson .15
118 Vernon Wells .15
119 Matt Clement .15
120 Billy Koch .15
121 Hideo Nomo .50
122 Derrek Lee .15
123 Todd Helton .75
124 Sean Burroughs .15
125 Jason Kendall .15
126 Dmitri Young .15
127 Adam Dunn .60
128 Bobby Higginson .15
129 Raul Mondesi .15
130 Bubba Trammell .15
131 A.J. Burnett .15
132 Randy Johnson .75
133 Mark Mulder .15
134 Mariano Rivera .25
135 Kerry Wood .50
136 Mo Vaughn .15
137 Jimmy Rollins .25
138 Jose Valentin .15
139 Brad Fullmer .15
140 Mike Cameron .15
141 Luis Gonzalez .25
142 Kevin Appier .15
143 Mike Hampton .15
144 Pedro J. Martinez .75
145 Javier Vazquez .15
146 Doug Mientkiewicz .15
147 Adam Kennedy .15
148 Rafael Furcal .15
149 Eric Chavez .25
150 Mike Lieberthal .15
151 Moises Alou .15
152 Jermaine Dye .15
153 Torii Hunter .15
154 Trot Nixon .15
155 Larry Walker .15
156 Jorge Julio .15
157 Mike Mussina .40
158 Kirk Rueter .15
159 Rafael Palmeiro .65
160 Pokey Reese .15
161 Miguel Tejada .35
162 Robin Ventura .15
163 Raul Ibanez .15
164 Roger Cedeno .15
165 Juan Gonzalez .65
166 Carlos Lee .15
167 Tim Salmon .25
168 Orlando Hernandez .15
169 Wade Miller .15
170 Troy Percival .15
171 Billy Wagner .15
172 Jeff Conine .15
173 Junior Spivey .15
174 Edgar Renteria .15
175 Scott Rolen .65
176 Jason Varitek .15
177 Ben Broussard .15
178 Jeremy Giambi .15
179 Gabe Kapler .15
180 Armando Rios .15
181 Ichiro Suzuki 2.00
182 Tom Glavine .35
183 Greg Maddux 1.00
184 Roy Oswalt .25
185 John Smoltz .15
186 Eric Karros .15
187 Alfonso Soriano .75
188 Nomar Garciaparra 1.50
189 Joe Crede .15
190 Javy Lopez .15
191 Carlos Beltran .50
192 Jim Edmonds .15
193 Geoff Jenkins .15
194 Magglio Ordonez .25
195 Daryle Ward .15
196 Roger Clemens 1.25
197 Byung-Hyun Kim .15
198 Robb Nen .15
199 C.C. Sabathia .15
200 Barry Zito .35
201 Mark Grace .25
202 Paul Konerko .25
203 Mike Sweeney .15
204 John Olerud .15
205 Jose Vidro .15
206 Ray Durham .15
207 Omar Vizquel .15
208 Shea Hillenbrand .15
209 Mike Lowell .15
210 Aubrey Huff .15
211 Eric Hinske .15
212 Paul LoDuca .15
213 Jay Gibbons .15
214 Austin Kearns .50
215 Richie Sexson .15
216 Garret Anderson .15
217 Eric Gagne .15
218 Jason Jennings .15
219 Damian Moss .15
220 David Eckstein .15
221 Mark Teixeira 1.00
222 Bill Hall .50
223 Bobby Jenks .75
224 Adam Morrisey .50
225 Rodrigo Rosario .50
226 Brett Myers .75
227 Tony Alvarez .50
228 Willie Bloomquist 2.00
229 Ben Howard .50
230 Nic Jackson .50
231 Carl Crawford .50
232 Omar Infante .50
233 Francisco Rodriguez 1.00
234 Andy Van Hekken .50
235 Kirk Saarloos .50
236 Dusty Wathan **RC** .75
237 Jamey Carroll 1.50
238 Jason L. Phillips 1.50
239 Jose Castillo 4.00
240 Arnaldo Munoz **RC** 2.00
241 Orlando Hudson .50
242 Drew Henson .75
243 Jason Lane .75
244 Vinnie Chulk 1.50
245 Prentice Redman **RC** 2.00
246 Marlon Byrd 1.00
247 Chin-Feng Chen 1.00
248 Craig Brazell **RC** 2.00
249 John Webb 1.50
250 Adam LaRoche 1.00

Platinum Finish

Stars (1-220): 5-10X
SP (221-250): 2-4X
Production 100 Sets

Barry Bonds Chasing History

NM/M

Production 250 Sets
Five Player card #'d to 25.
Barry Bonds, Bobby Bonds 35.00
Barry Bonds, Roger Maris 40.00
Barry Bonds, Willie McCovey 35.00
Barry Bonds, Babe Ruth 200.00
Barry Bonds 35.00
Barry Bonds, Babe Ruth, Roger Maris, Willie McCovey, Bobby Bonds 200.00

Guts and Glory

NM/M

Complete Set (20): 12.00
Common Player: .40
Inserted 1:4
1GG Jason Giambi 1.00
2GG Alfonso Soriano .75
3GG Scott Rolen .50
4GG Ivan Rodriguez .50
5GG Barry Bonds 1.50
6GG Jim Edmonds .40
7GG Darin Erstad .40
8GG Brian Giles .40
9GG Luis Gonzalez .40
10GG Adam Dunn .50
11GG Torii Hunter .40
12GG Andruw Jones .40
13GG Sammy Sosa 1.00
14GG Ichiro Suzuki 1.50
15GG Miguel Tejada .40
16GG Roger Clemens 1.00
17GG Curt Schilling .40
18GG Nomar Garciaparra 1.50
19GG Derek Jeter 2.00
20GG Alex Rodriguez 1.50

Heart of the Order

NM/M

Complete Set (20): 20.00
Common Card: .75
Inserted 1:12
1 Jason Giambi, Derek Jeter, Alfonso Soriano 3.00
2 Todd Helton, Preston Wilson, Larry Walker .75
3 Rafael Palmeiro, Alex Rodriguez, Ivan Rodriguez 3.00
4 Adam Dunn, Ken Griffey Jr., Austin Kearns 3.00
5 Jeff Bagwell, Craig Biggio, Lance Berkman 1.00
6 Eric Chavez, Miguel Tejada, Jermaine Dye .75
7 Troy Glaus, Garrett Anderson, Darin Erstad 1.00
8 Mike Piazza, Mo Vaughn, Roberto Alomar 2.50
9 Torii Hunter, Jacque Jones, Corey Koskie .75
10 Barry Bonds, Jeff Kent, Rich Aurilia 3.00
11 Pat Burrell, Bobby Abreu, Jimmy Rollins 1.50
12 Shawn Green, Adrian Beltre, Paul LoDuca .75
13 Vladimir Guerrero, Brad Wilkerson, Jose Vidro 1.50
14 Chipper Jones, Andruw Jones, Gary Sheffield 2.00
15 Ichiro Suzuki, Bret Boone, Edgar Martinez 2.50
16 Albert Pujols, Scott Rolen, J.D. Drew 1.50
17 Sammy Sosa, Fred McGriff, Moises Alou 2.00
18 Nomar Garciaparra, Shea Hillenbrand, Manny Ramirez 2.50
19 Frank Thomas, Magglio Ordonez, Paul Konerko 1.00
20 Jason Kendall, Brian Giles, Aramis Ramirez .75

Heart of the Order Memorabilia

NM/M

Common Card: 5.00
Production 400 Sets
Jason Giambi, Derek Jeter, Alfonso Soriano/Bat 15.00
Todd Helton/Jsy, Preston Wilson, Larry Walker 8.00
Rafael Palmeiro/Jsy, Alex Rodriguez, Ivan Rodriguez 6.00
Adam Dunn, Ken Griffey Jr., Austin Kearns/Pants 12.00
Troy Glaus, Garrett Anderson, Darin Erstad/Jsy 8.00
Mike Piazza/Jsy, Mo Vaughn, Roberto Alomar 10.00
Barry Bonds, Jeff Kent/Jsy, Rich Aurilia 6.00
Pat Burrell, Bobby Abreu, Jimmy Rollins/Jsy 6.00
Shawn Green, Adrian Beltre/Jsy, Paul LoDuca 5.00
Vladimir Guerrero, Brad Wilkerson, Jose Vidro/Jsy 5.00
Chipper Jones/Jsy, Andruw Jones, Gary Sheffield 10.00
Ichiro Suzuki, Bret Boone/Jsy, Edgar Martinez 5.00
Albert Pujols, Scott Rolen, J.D. Drew/Jsy 8.00
Sammy Sosa/Jsy, Fred McGriff, Moises Alou 12.00
Nomar Garciaparra, Shea Hillenbrand, Manny Ramirez/Jsy 8.00
Frank Thomas, Magglio Ordonez/Jsy, Paul Konerko 5.00
Jason Kendall, Brian Giles/Bat, Aramis Ramirez 5.00

MLB Scouting Report

NM/M

Complete Set (32): 55.00
Common Player: 1.00
Production 400 Sets
1 Jason Giambi 3.00
2 Paul Konerko 1.00
3 Jim Thome 1.50
4 Alfonso Soriano 2.00
5 Troy Glaus 1.50
6 Eric Hinske 1.00
7 Paul LoDuca 1.00
8 Mike Piazza 4.00
9 Marlon Byrd 1.00
10 Garrett Anderson 1.00
11 Barry Bonds 5.00
12 Pat Burrell 1.50
13 Joe Crede 1.00
14 J.D. Drew 1.00
15 Ken Griffey Jr. 4.00
16 Vladimir Guerrero 2.00
17 Torii Hunter 1.00
18 Chipper Jones 3.00
19 Austin Kearns 1.00
20 Albert Pujols 2.00
21 Manny Ramirez 1.50
22 Gary Sheffield 1.00
23 Sammy Sosa 3.00
24 Ichiro Suzuki 4.00
25 Bernie Williams 1.25
26 Randy Johnson 2.00
27 Greg Maddux 3.00
28 Hideo Nomo 1.00
29 Nomar Garciaparra 4.00
30 Derek Jeter 6.00
31 Alex Rodriguez 5.00
32 Miguel Tejada 1.00

MLB Scouting Report Game-Used

NM/M

Common Player: 6.00
Production 250 Sets
3 Jim Thome/Jsy 10.00
4 Alfonso Soriano/Bat 10.00
8 Mike Piazza/Jsy 15.00
11 Barry Bonds/Jsy 20.00
14 J.D. Drew/Jsy 6.00
18 Chipper Jones/Jsy 10.00
19 Austin Kearns/Pants 10.00
21 Manny Ramirez/Jsy 8.00
23 Sammy Sosa/Jsy 15.00
26 Randy Johnson/Jsy 10.00
27 Greg Maddux/Jsy 10.00
28 Hideo Nomo/Jsy 20.00
30 Derek Jeter/Jsy 20.00

Nameplates

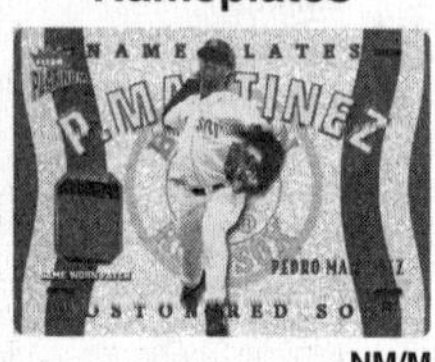

NM/M

Common Player:
Jumbo Pack Exclusive
Barry Larkin/97 30.00
Kazuhiro Sasaki/82 20.00
Greg Maddux/248 25.00
Craig Biggio/152 25.00
Pedro J. Martinez/244 35.00
Barry Zito/248 25.00
Nomar Garciaparra/258 40.00
John Olerud/180 25.00
Ivan Rodriguez/189 20.00
Jeff Bagwell/121 45.00
Chipper Jones/251 40.00
Frank Thomas/58 45.00
Roger Clemens/141 40.00
Mike Piazza/200 35.00
Mark Prior/123 25.00
Manny Ramirez/94 30.00
Kerry Wood/49 45.00
Rafael Palmeiro/245 20.00
Jimmy Rollins/74 20.00
Barry Bonds/251 50.00
Adam Dunn/117 25.00
Alex Rodriguez/248 40.00
Miguel Tejada/225 20.00
Chin-Feng Chen/110 100.00

Portraits

NM/M

Complete Set (20): 25.00
Common Player: .75
Inserted 1:20
1 Josh Beckett .75
2 Roberto Alomar 1.00
3 Alfonso Soriano 2.00
4 Mike Piazza 3.00
5 Ivan Rodriguez 1.00
6 Edgar Martinez .75
7 Barry Bonds 4.00
8 Adam Dunn 1.25
9 Juan Gonzalez 1.00
10 Chipper Jones 2.50
11 Albert Pujols 1.50
12 Magglio Ordonez .75
13 Shea Hillenbrand .75
14 Larry Walker .75
15 Pedro J. Martinez 1.50
16 Kerry Wood 1.00
17 Barry Zito 1.00
18 Nomar Garciaparra 3.00
19 Derek Jeter 5.00
20 Alex Rodriguez 4.00

Portraits Game Jersey

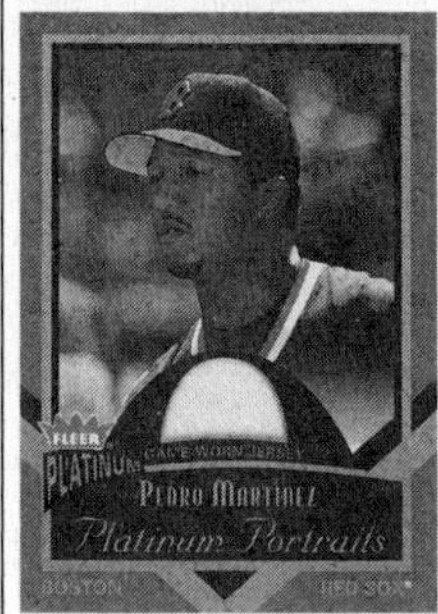

NM/M

Common Player: 5.00
Inserted 1:86
4 Mike Piazza 10.00
5 Ivan Rodriguez 6.00
7 Barry Bonds 15.00
8 Adam Dunn 8.00
10 Chipper Jones 8.00
15 Pedro J. Martinez 8.00
16 Kerry Wood 8.00
17 Barry Zito 5.00
18 Nomar Garciaparra 10.00
19 Derek Jeter/SP/150 25.00

Portraits Game Patch

NM/M

Common Player: 25.00
Production 100 Sets
4 Mike Piazza 35.00
5 Ivan Rodriguez 25.00
7 Barry Bonds 40.00
8 Adam Dunn 25.00
10 Chipper Jones 25.00
15 Pedro J. Martinez 25.00
16 Kerry Wood 25.00
17 Barry Zito 25.00
18 Nomar Garciaparra 40.00
19 Derek Jeter 45.00

2003 Fleer Rookies & Greats

NM/M

Complete Set (75): 30.00
Common Player: .25
Pack (5): 6.00
Box (20): 100.00
1 Troy Glaus .65
2 Gary Sheffield .40
3 Sammy Sosa 2.00
4 Mark Prior .75
5 Dontrelle Willis .25
6 Shawn Green .50
7 Vladimir Guerrero .75
8 Jose Reyes .50
9 Miguel Tejada .40
10 Bret Boone .25
11 Rocco Baldelli .40
12 Rafael Palmeiro .65
13 Ichiro Suzuki 1.50
14 Carlos Delgado .50
15 Garret Anderson .25
16 Richie Sexson .25
17 Roger Clemens 1.75
18 Barry Zito .40
19 Jim Thome .25
20 Alex Rodriguez 2.50
21 Randy Johnson .75
22 Chipper Jones 1.00
23 Kerry Wood .60
24 Ken Griffey Jr. 1.50
25 Ivan Rodriguez .60
26 Jeff Kent .25
27 Todd Helton .75
28 Jeff Bagwell .75
29 Hideo Nomo .60
30 Torii Hunter .25
31 Brian Giles .25
32 Albert Pujols 2.00
33 Vernon Wells .25
34 Nomar Garciaparra 2.00
35 Magglio Ordonez .25
36 C.C. Sabathia .25
37 Preston Wilson .25
38 Mike Sweeney .25
39 Jose Vidro .25
40 Jason Giambi .60
41 Derek Jeter 3.00

42 Mike Piazza 1.50
43 Rich Harden .25
44 Jason Kendall .25
45 Barry Bonds 3.00
46 Barry Larkin .25
47 Dmitri Young .25
48 Craig Biggio .25
49 Angel Berroa .25
50 Alfonso Soriano .75
51 Kevin Millwood .25
52 Edgar Martinez .25
53 Jim Edmonds .25
54 Curt Schilling .40
55 Jay Gibbons .25
56 Pedro J. Martinez .75
57 Greg Maddux 1.00
58 Manny Ramirez .75
59 Frank Thomas .75
60 Adam Dunn .60
61 Babe Ruth 3.00
62 Bob Gibson 1.00
63 Willie Stargell .75
64 Mike Schmidt 2.00
65 Nolan Ryan 3.00
66 Tom Seaver 1.00
67 Brooks Robinson 1.00
68 Willie McCovey .50
69 Harmon Killebrew 1.00
70 Al Kaline 1.00
71 Reggie Jackson 1.00
72 Eddie Mathews .75
73 Ralph Kiner .25
74 Cal Ripken Jr. 3.00
75 Phil Rizzuto .25

Ultra
Production 1,500
U-251 Chien-Ming Wang **RC** 8.00
U-252 Rickie Weeks **RC** 6.00
U-253 Brandon Webb **RC** 4.00
U-254 Hideki Matsui **RC** 8.00
U-255 Michael Hessman **RC** 2.00
U-256 Ryan Wagner **RC** 3.00
U-257 Matt Kata **RC** 3.00
U-258 Edwin Jackson **RC** 6.00
U-259 Jose Contreras **RC** 3.00
U-260 Delmon Young **RC** 8.00
U-261 Bo Hart **RC** 3.00
U-262 Jeff Duncan **RC** 3.00
U-263 Robby Hammock **RC** 2.00
U-264 Jeremy Bonderman 5.00
U-265 Clint Barmes **RC** 2.00

Authentix
Production 1,250
A-161 Chien-Ming Wang **RC** 10.00
A-162 Rickie Weeks **RC** 8.00
A-163 Brandon Webb **RC** 4.00
A-164 Craig Brazell **RC** 3.00
A-165 Michael Hessman **RC** 3.00
A-166 Ryan Wagner **RC** 5.00
A-167 Matt Kata **RC** 4.00
A-168 Edwin Jackson **RC** 8.00
A-169 Mike Ryan **RC** 3.00
A-170 Delmon Young **RC** 10.00
A-171 Bo Hart **RC** 4.00
A-172 Jeff Duncan **RC** 4.00
A-173 Robby Hammock **RC** 3.00
A-174 Jeremy Bonderman 5.00
A-175 Clint Barmes **RC** 3.00

Genuine
Production 1,000
G-131 Dan Haren 5.00
G-132 Rickie Weeks **RC** 8.00
G-133 Prentice Redman **RC** 4.00
G-134 Craig Brazell **RC** 4.00
G-135 Jon Leicester **RC** 4.00
G-136 Ryan Wagner **RC** 6.00
G-137 Matt Kata **RC** 5.00
G-138 Edwin Jackson **RC** 8.00
G-139 Mike Ryan **RC** 5.00
G-140 Delmon Young **RC** 10.00
G-141 Bo Hart **RC** 5.00
G-142 Jeff Duncan **RC** 5.00
G-143 Robby Hammock **RC** 4.00
G-144 Michael Hessman **RC** 4.00
G-145 Clint Barmes **RC** 4.00

Showcase
Production 750
S-136 Chien-Ming Wang **RC** 12.00
S-137 Rickie Weeks **RC** 10.00
S-138 Brandon Webb **RC** 5.00
S-139 Hideki Matsui **RC** 10.00
S-140 Michael Hessman **RC** 4.00
S-141 Ryan Wagner **RC** 6.00
S-142 Bo Hart **RC** 5.00
S-143 Edwin Jackson **RC** 8.00
S-144 Jose Contreras **RC** 6.00
S-145 Delmon Young **RC** 10.00

Flair
Production 500
F-126 Jeff Duncan **RC** 6.00
F-127 Rickie Weeks **RC** 12.00
F-128 Brandon Webb **RC** 10.00
F-129 Robby Hammock **RC** 5.00
F-130 Jon Leicester **RC** 5.00
F-131 Ryan Wagner **RC** 8.00
F-132 Bo Hart **RC** 6.00
F-133 Edwin Jackson **RC** 10.00
F-134 Sergio Mitre **RC** 5.00
F-135 Delmon Young **RC** 15.00

Hot Prospects
Production 250
H-120 Josh Willingham **RC** 10.00
H-121 Rickie Weeks **RC** 15.00
H-122 Prentice Redman **RC** 8.00
H-123 Mike Ryan **RC** 8.00
H-124 Oscar Villarreal **RC** 8.00
H-125 Ryan Wagner **RC** 10.00
H-126 Bo Hart **RC** 10.00
H-127 Edwin Jackson **RC** 12.00

Boyhood Idols

NM/M
Common Player: 5.00
Production 615 Sets
Carlton Fisk 8.00
Joe Carter 5.00
Cal Ripken Jr. 20.00
Mike Schmidt 15.00
Robin Yount 8.00
Joe Morgan 5.00
Jim Palmer 5.00
Harmon Killebrew 8.00
Brooks Robinson 8.00
Frank Howard 5.00
Bill "Moose" Skowron 5.00
Bucky Dent 5.00
Nolan Ryan 20.00
Don Mattingly 20.00

Boyhood Idols Autograph

NM/M
Production 50 unless noted.
Carlton Fisk 30.00
Brooks Robinson 35.00
Bucky Dent 20.00

Dynamic Debuts

NM/M
Complete Set (10): 10.00
Common Player: .50
Inserted 1:10
1DD Rickie Weeks 4.00
2DD Brandon Webb 1.00
3DD Jose Reyes 1.00
4DD Bo Hart 1.00
5DD Dontrelle Willis 1.00
6DD Rich Harden .50
7DD Ryan Wagner .50
8DD Rocco Baldelli 1.00
9DD Mark Teixeira 1.00
10DD Hideki Matsui 5.00

Dynamic Debuts Autograph

NM/M
Common Player: 10.00
Production 100
Rickie Weeks 25.00
Jose Reyes 35.00
Bo Hart 10.00
Dontrelle Willis 25.00
Ryan Wagner 10.00

Looming Large

NM/M
Complete Set (15): 30.00
Common Player: 1.50
Production 500 Sets
Uncommon: 1-2X
Production 150
Rare: No Pricing
Production 15
1LL Chien-Ming Wang 4.00
2LL Rickie Weeks 6.00
3LL Brandon Webb 3.00
4LL Hideki Matsui 6.00
5LL Michael Hessman 1.50
6LL Ryan Wagner 1.50
7LL Matt Kata 1.50
8LL Edwin Jackson 1.50
9LL Jose Contreras 1.50
10LL Delmon Young 6.00
11LL Bo Hart 3.00
12LL Jeff Duncan 1.50
13LL Robby Hammock 1.50
14LL Jeremy Bonderman 1.50
15LL Clint Barmes 1.50

The Naturals

NM/M
Complete Set (25): 45.00
Common Player: .50
Inserted 1:5
Uncommons: 2-4X
Production 75 Sets
1 Cal Ripken Jr. 5.00
2 Mike Schmidt 3.00
3 Derek Jeter 5.00
4 Joe Carter .50
5 Nomar Garciaparra 3.00
6 Frank Howard .50
7 Al Kaline 2.00
8 Albert Pujols 4.00
9 Nolan Ryan 5.00
10 Duke Snider 1.50
11 Alex Rodriguez 4.00
12 Brooks Robinson 1.50
13 Roger Clemens 4.00
14 Sammy Sosa 3.00
15 Jim Palmer 1.00
16 Alfonso Soriano 2.00
17 Don Mattingly 3.00
18 Harmon Killebrew 1.50
19 Bob Feller .50
20 Reggie Jackson 1.50
21 Ichiro Suzuki 2.50
22 Barry Bonds 5.00
23 Hideki Matsui 4.00
24 Willie Stargell .50
25 Pee Wee Reese .50

The Naturals Autograph

NM/M
Common Player:
Production 50
Joe Carter 15.00
Bob Feller 25.00
Frank Howard 25.00
Al Kaline 40.00
Harmon Killebrew 35.00
Jim Palmer 15.00
Cal Ripken Jr. 140.00
Brooks Robinson 35.00
Nolan Ryan 100.00
Duke Snider 25.00

The Naturals Jersey Autograph

NM/M
Common Player:
Production 30
Joe Carter 25.00
Frank Howard 25.00
Al Kaline 60.00
Harmon Killebrew 50.00
Jim Palmer 25.00
Cal Ripken Jr. 150.00
Brooks Robinson 50.00
Nolan Ryan 120.00
Duke Snider 40.00

The Naturals Memorabilia

NM/M
Common Player: 5.00
Production 250 unless noted.
CR Cal Ripken Jr. 30.00
MS Mike Schmidt 15.00
DJ Derek Jeter 20.00
JC Joe Carter 5.00
NG Nomar Garciaparra 15.00
FH Frank Howard/400 5.00
AK Al Kaline 15.00
AP Albert Pujols 12.00
NR Nolan Ryan/400 25.00
DS Duke Snider 10.00
AR Alex Rodriguez 10.00
BR Brooks Robinson/400 10.00
RC Roger Clemens/400 15.00
JP Jim Palmer 8.00
AS Alfonso Soriano 8.00
DM Don Mattingly 20.00
HK Harmon Killebrew/400 10.00
RJ Reggie Jackson/400 10.00

The Naturals Patch

No Pricing
Production 25
Patch Autos: No Pricing
Production 5

Through the Years

NM/M
Common Duo: 10.00
Production 360
Patches: No Pricing
Production 25
Sammy Sosa, Mark Prior 20.00
Mark Prior, Jose Reyes 10.00
Nolan Ryan, Hank Blalock 25.00
Roger Clemens, Chien-Ming Wang 35.00
Jim Thome, Mike Schmidt 25.00
Alex Rodriguez, Mark Teixeira 25.00
Randy Johnson, Brandon Webb 15.00
Phil Rizzuto, Jose Reyes 15.00
Nomar Garciaparra, Bobby Doerr 20.00
Jason Giambi, Reggie Jackson 15.00
Derek Jeter, Phil Rizzuto 45.00
Barry Larkin, Joe Morgan 10.00
Harmon Killebrew, Torii Hunter 20.00
Willie McCovey, Barry Bonds 15.00
Bo Hart, Lou Brock 15.00
Jose Contreras, Mike Mussina 10.00
Michael Hessman, Chipper Jones 12.00
Steve Carlton, Kevin Millwood 12.00
Robin Yount, Scott Podsednik 20.00
Eddie Mathews, Chipper Jones 15.00

2003 Fleer Showcase

NM/M
Complete Set (135): 50.00
Common Player: .25
Common SP (106-135): 1.00
Inserted 1:4
Pack (5): 3.00
Box (24): 60.00
1 David Eckstein .25
2 Curt Schilling .75
3 Jay Gibbons .25
4 Kerry Wood .75
5 Jeff Bagwell 1.00
6 Hideo Nomo .75
7 Tim Hudson .40
8 J.D. Drew .50
9 Josh Phelps .25
10 Bartolo Colon .25
11 Bobby Abreu .25
12 Matt Morris .25
13 Kazuhiro Sasaki .25
14 Sean Burroughs .25
15 Vicente Padilla .25
16 Jorge Posada .35
17 Torii Hunter .25
18 Richie Sexson .25
19 Lance Berkman .25
20 Todd Helton 1.00
21 Paul Konerko .25
22 Pedro J. Martinez 1.00
23 Rodrigo Lopez .25
24 Gary Sheffield .35
25 Darin Erstad .50
26 Nomar Garciaparra 2.50
27 Adam Dunn .75
28 Jason Giambi .75
29 Miguel Tejada .40
30 Chipper Jones 1.50
31 Alex Rodriguez 3.00
32 Barry Bonds 4.00
33 Roger Clemens 2.00
34 Sammy Sosa 2.50
35 Randy Johnson 1.00
36 Tim Salmon .35
37 Shea Hillenbrand .25
38 Larry Walker .25
39 A.J. Burnett .25
40 Shawn Green .50
41 Cristian Guzman .25
42 Bernie Williams .35
43 Mark Mulder .25
44 Brian Giles .25
45 Bret Boone .25
46 Juan Gonzalez .75
47 Roy Halladay .25
48 Wade Miller .25
49 Jeff Kent .25
50 Carlos Delgado .50
51 Mike Lowell .25
52 Jim Edmonds .25
53 Ivan Rodriguez .75
54 Aubrey Huff .25
55 Ryan Klesko .25
56 Paul LoDuca .25
57 Roy Oswalt .50
58 Omar Vizquel .25
59 Manny Ramirez 1.00
60 Andruw Jones 1.00
61 Troy Glaus 1.00
62 Ichiro Suzuki 2.50
63 Albert Pujols 2.50
64 Derek Jeter 4.00
65 Mark Prior 1.00
66 Ken Griffey Jr. 2.50
67 Vladimir Guerrero 1.00
68 Mike Piazza 2.50
69 Alfonso Soriano 1.00
70 Greg Maddux 1.50
71 Adam Kennedy .25
72 Junior Spivey .25
73 Tom Glavine .40
74 Derek Lowe .25
75 Magglio Ordonez .25
76 Jim Thome .25
77 Robert Fick .25
78 Josh Beckett .25
79 Mike Sweeney .25
80 Kazuhisa Ishii .25
81 Roberto Alomar .40
82 Barry Zito .40
83 Pat Burrell .65
84 Scott Rolen 1.00
85 John Olerud .25
86 Eric Hinske .25
87 Rafael Palmeiro .75
88 Edgar Martinez .25
89 Eric Chavez .40
90 Jose Vidro .25
91 Craig Biggio .25
92 Rich Aurilia .25
93 Austin Kearns .75
94 Luis Gonzalez .40
95 Garrett Anderson .25
96 Yogi Berra 1.50
97 Al Kaline 1.50
98 Robin Yount 1.00
99 Reggie Jackson 1.00
100 Harmon Killebrew 1.50
101 Eddie Mathews 1.50
102 Willie McCovey .50
103 Nolan Ryan 4.00
104 Mike Schmidt 2.50
105 Tom Seaver 1.00
106 Francisco Rodriguez 1.00
107 Carl Crawford 1.00
108 Ben Howard 1.00
109 Hank Blalock 2.00
110 Hee Seop Choi 2.00
111 Kirk Saarloos 1.00
112 Lew Ford **RC** 3.00
113 Andy Van Hekken 1.00
114 Drew Henson 1.50
115 Marlon Byrd 1.00
116 Jayson Werth 1.00
117 Willie Bloomquist 1.00
118 Joe Borchard 1.00
119 Mark Teixeira 2.00
120 Bobby Hill 1.00
121 Jason Lane 1.00
122 Omar Infante 1.00
123 Victor Martinez 1.50
124 Jorge Padilla 1.00
125 John Lackey 1.00
126 Anderson Machado 1.00
127 Rodrigo Rosario 1.00
128 Freddy Sanchez 1.00
129 Tony Alvarez 1.00
130 Matt Thornton 1.00
131 Joe Thurston 1.00
132 Brett Myers 1.00
133 Antonio Perez 1.00
134 Chris Snelling 1.00
135 Terrmel Sledge **RC** 2.00

Legacy

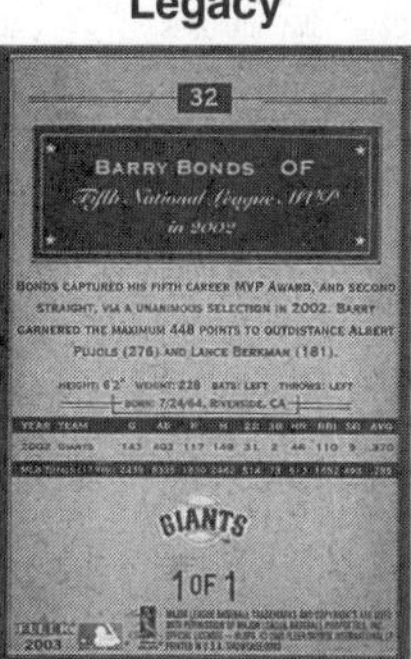

Legacy Stars (1-105): 3-6X
SP's (106-135): 1-30X
Production 150 Sets
Masterpiece 1 of 1 also exists.

Baseball's Best

NM/M
Complete Set (15): 40.00
Common Player: 1.50
Inserted 1:24
1 Curt Schilling 2.00
2 Barry Zito 2.00
3 Torii Hunter 2.00
4 Pedro J. Martinez 4.00
5 Bernie Williams 2.00
6 Magglio Ordonez 1.50
7 Alfonso Soriano 4.00
8 Hideo Nomo 2.00
9 Jason Giambi 5.00
10 Sammy Sosa 5.00
11 Vladimir Guerrero 4.00
12 Ken Griffey Jr. 5.00
13 Troy Glaus 3.00
14 Ichiro Suzuki 6.00
15 Albert Pujols 4.00

Baseball's Best Memorabilia

NM/M
Common Player: 5.00
Inserted 1:24
CS Curt Schilling 6.00
BZ Barry Zito 6.00
TH Torii Hunter 8.00
PM Pedro J. Martinez 10.00
BW Bernie Williams 8.00

MO Magglio Ordonez 5.00
AS Alfonso Soriano 15.00
HN Hideo Nomo 8.00
JG Jason Giambi 8.00
SS Sammy Sosa 15.00

Hot Gloves

NM/M
Complete Set (10): 15.00
Common Player: 1.00
Inserted 1:8
1 Greg Maddux 2.00
2 Ivan Rodriguez 1.00
3 Derek Jeter 4.00
4 Mike Piazza 2.50
5 Nomar Garciaparra 2.50
6 Andruw Jones 1.00
7 Scott Rolen 1.00
8 Barry Bonds 3.00
9 Roger Clemens 2.00
10 Alex Rodriguez 3.00

Hot Gloves Memorabilia

NM/M
Common Player: 5.00
Production 350 Sets
GM Greg Maddux 12.00
IR Ivan Rodriguez 5.00
DJ Derek Jeter 25.00
MP Mike Piazza 15.00
NG Nomar Garciaparra 15.00
AJ Andruw Jones 6.00
SR Scott Rolen 15.00
BB Barry Bonds 25.00
RC Roger Clemens 15.00
AR Alex Rodriguez 15.00

Sweet Sigs

NM/M
Quantity produced listed
DJ Derek Jeter/250 130.00
DJ Derek Jeter/50/Red 185.00
BB Barry Bonds/90 MVP/150 200.00
BB Barry Bonds/92 MVP/100 200.00
BB Barry Bonds/93 MVP/75 200.00

Sweet Stitch

NM/M
Complete Set (10): 12.00
Common Player: .75
Inserted 1:8
1SS Derek Jeter 4.00
2SS Randy Johnson 1.50
3SS Jeff Bagwell 1.00
4SS Nomar Garciaparra 2.50
5SS Roger Clemens 2.00
6SS Todd Helton .75
7SS Barry Bonds 3.00
8SS Alfonso Soriano 1.50
9SS Miguel Tejada .75
10SS Mark Prior .75

Sweet Stitch Memorabilia

NM/M
Varying quantities produced
DJ Derek Jeter 25.00
RJ Randy Johnson 8.00
JB Jeff Bagwell 8.00
NG Nomar Garciaparra 12.00
RC Roger Clemens 12.00
TH Todd Helton 5.00
BB Barry Bonds 20.00
AS Alfonso Soriano 12.00
MT Miguel Tejada 5.00
MP Mark Prior 10.00

Sweet Stitch Patch

NM/M
Common Player: 20.00
DJ Derek Jeter/50 60.00
RJ Randy Johnson/150 40.00
JB Jeff Bagwell/150 35.00
NG Nomar Garciaparra/150 45.00
RC Roger Clemens/50 45.00
TH Todd Helton/50 30.00
BB Barry Bonds/150 75.00
AS Alfonso Soriano/50 40.00
MT Miguel Tejada/150 20.00
MP Mark Prior/150 25.00

Thundersticks

NM/M
Complete Set (10): 12.00
Common Player: .75
Inserted 1:8
1TS Adam Dunn 1.00
2TS Alex Rodriguez 3.00
3TS Barry Bonds 4.00
4TS Jim Thome 1.00
5TS Chipper Jones 2.00
6TS Manny Ramirez 1.00
7TS Carlos Delgado .75
8TS Mike Piazza 2.50
9TS Shawn Green .75
10TS Pat Burrell 1.00

Thundersticks Bat

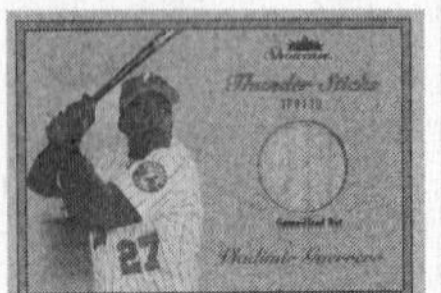

NM/M
Common Player: 5.00
Golds: 1-2.5X
Production 99 Sets
AD Adam Dunn 10.00
AR Alex Rodriguez 15.00
BB Barry Bonds 20.00
JT Jim Thome 8.00
CJS Chipper Jones 8.00
MR Manny Ramirez 8.00
SG Shawn Green 5.00
PB Pat Burrell 10.00

2003 Fleer Splendid Splinters

NM/M
Complete Set (150):
Common Player: .20
Common Wood (91-110): 6.00
Production 499
Common SP (111-140): 1.50
Inserted 1:6
Common (141-150): 3.00
Production 999
Pack (5): 3.00
Box (24): 50.00
1 David Eckstein .20
2 Barry Larkin .40
3 Edgardo Alfonzo .20
4 Darin Erstad .50
5 Ellis Burks .20
6 Omar Vizquel .40
7 Bartolo Colon .20
8 Roberto Alomar .50
9 Garret Anderson .40
10 Al Leiter .20
11 Tim Salmon .40
12 Larry Walker .40
13 Jorge Posada .50
14 Curt Schilling .50
15 Jason Jennings .20
16 Jason Giambi 1.00
17 Robert Fick .20
18 Kazuhiro Sasaki .20
19 Bernie Williams .50
20 Junior Spivey .20
21 Mike Lowell .20
22 Luis Gonzalez .40
23 Josh Beckett .20
24 John Smoltz .20
25 Mike Mussina .50
26 Gary Sheffield .40
27 Tom Glavine .40
28 Tim Hudson .40
29 Austin Kearns .75
30 Andruw Jones .50
31 Roger Clemens 1.50
32 Mark Mulder .40
33 Jay Gibbons .20
34 Jeff Kent .40
35 Barry Zito .40
36 Rodrigo Lopez .20
37 Jeff Bagwell .75
38 Eric Chavez .40
39 Pedro J. Martinez 1.00
40 Lance Berkman .50
41 Bobby Abreu .40
42 Wade Miller .20
43 Bret Boone .20
44 Vicente Padilla .20
45 Shea Hillenbrand .20
46 Roy Oswalt .40
47 Pat Burrell .75
48 Manny Ramirez .75
49 Craig Biggio .40
50 Randy Wolf .20
51 Kerry Wood .50
52 Mike Sweeney .20
53 Brian Giles .40
54 Kazuhisa Ishii .20
55 Jason Kendall .20
56 Hideo Nomo .40
57 Josh Phelps .20
58 Sean Burroughs .20
59 Paul Konerko .20
60 Shawn Green .40
61 Ryan Klesko .40
62 Magglio Ordonez .40
63 Paul LoDuca .20
64 Edgar Martinez .20
65 J.D. Drew .30
66 Phil Nevin .20
67 Jim Edmonds .40
68 Matt Morris .40
69 Aubrey Huff .20
70 Adam Dunn .75
71 John Olerud .40
72 Juan Gonzalez .50
73 Scott Rolen .50
74 Rafael Palmeiro .50
75 Roy Halladay .20
76 Kevin Brown .20
77 Ivan Rodriguez .50
78 Eric Hinske .20
79 Frank Thomas .75
80 Carlos Delgado .40
81 Bobby Higginson .20
82 Trevor Hoffman .20
83 Cliff Floyd .20
84 Derek Lowe .20
85 Richie Sexson .50
86 Rich Aurilia .20
87 Sean Casey .20
88 Cristian Guzman .20
89 Randy Winn .20
90 Jose Vidro .20
91 Mark Prior 6.00
92 Derek Jeter 15.00
93 Alex Rodriguez 12.00
94 Greg Maddux 9.00
95 Troy Glaus 7.50
96 Vladimir Guerrero 7.50
97 Todd Helton 7.50
98 Albert Pujols 10.00
99 Torii Hunter 6.00
100 Mike Piazza 10.00
101 Ichiro Suzuki 10.00
102 Sammy Sosa 10.00
103 Ken Griffey Jr. 10.00
104 Nomar Garciaparra 10.00
105 Barry Bonds 15.00
106 Chipper Jones 9.00
107 Jim Thome 6.00
108 Miguel Tejada 6.00
109 Randy Johnson 7.50
110 Alfonso Soriano 7.50
111 Guillermo Quiroz **RC** 3.00
112 Josh Willingham **RC** 3.00
113 Alejandro Machado **RC** 1.50
114 Chris Waters **RC** 2.00
115 Adam LaRoche 1.50
116 Prentice Redman **RC** 3.00
117 Jhonny Peralta 4.00
118 Francisco Rosario **RC** 1.50
119 Shane Victorino **RC** 2.00
120 Chien-Ming Wang **RC** 15.00
121 Matt Bruback **RC** 2.00
122 Rontrez Johnson **RC** 3.00
123 Josh Hall **RC** 2.00
124 Matt Kata **RC** 3.00
125 Hector Luna **RC** 2.00
126 Josh Stewart **RC** 2.00
127 Craig Brazell **RC** 2.00
128 Tim Olson **RC** 2.00
129 Michel Hernandez **RC** 1.50
130 Michael Hessman **RC** 2.00
131 Clint Barmes **RC** 5.00
132 Justin Morneau 1.50
133 Chris Snelling 1.50
134 Bobby Jenks 1.50
135 Tim Hummel **RC** 1.50
136 Adam Morrissey 1.50
137 Carl Crawford 1.50
138 Garrett Atkins 1.50
139 Jung Bong 1.50
140 Ken Harvey 1.50
141 Chin-Feng Chen 2.00
142 Hee Seop Choi 2.00
143 Lance Niekro 2.00
144 Mark Teixeira 2.00
145 Nook Logan **RC** 3.00
146 Terrmel Sledge **RC** 3.00
147 Lew Ford **RC** 6.00
148 Ian Ferguson **RC** 3.00
149 Hideki Matsui/499 **RC** 15.00
150 Jose Contreras **RC** 6.00

Bat Chips

NM/M
Common Player: 4.00
Production 425 Sets
1 Jason Giambi 8.00
2 Jeff Bagwell 8.00
3 Manny Ramirez 8.00
4 Adam Dunn 8.00
5 Derek Jeter 25.00
6 Alex Rodriguez 15.00
7 Troy Glaus 5.00
8 Mike Piazza 15.00
9 Sammy Sosa 12.00
10 Nomar Garciaparra 18.00
11 Barry Bonds 18.00
12 Jim Thome 10.00
13 Miguel Tejada 5.00
14 Alfonso Soriano 10.00
15 Ryan Klesko 4.00
16 Sean Casey 4.00
17 Bernie Williams 8.00
18 Vladimir Guerrero 8.00
19 Gary Sheffield 5.00

Family Tree

NM/M
Complete Set (10): 10.00
Common Player: .50
Inserted 1:8
1 Lance Niekro, Phil Niekro .50
2 Bob Boone, Bret Boone .50
3 Sandy Alomar Jr., Roberto Alomar .50
4 Ken Griffey Sr., Ken Griffey Jr. 2.00
5 Jason Giambi, Jeremy Giambi 1.50
6 Bobby Bonds, Barry Bonds 3.00
7 Tony Perez, Eduardo Perez .50
8 Brian Giles, Marcus Giles .75
9 Felipe Alou, Moises Alou .75
10 Pedro J. Martinez, Ramon Martinez 1.50

Home Run Club

NM/M
Complete Set (12): 50.00
Common Player: 2.00
Inserted 1:72
1 Barry Bonds 10.00
2 Jason Giambi 5.00
3 Sammy Sosa 6.00
4 Jim Thome 4.00
5 Lance Berkman 2.00
6 Alfonso Soriano 5.00
7 Vladimir Guerrero 4.00
8 Shawn Green 2.00
9 Troy Glaus 3.00
10 Pat Burrell 3.00
11 Alex Rodriguez 10.00
12 Mike Piazza 8.00

Home Run Club Autographs

NM/M
Quantity produced listed
BB1 Barry Bonds/Black Ink/150 150.00
CR1 Cal Ripken Jr./Black Ink/300 100.00
CR2 Cal Ripken Jr./Blue Ink/150 125.00
CR3 Cal Ripken Jr./Red Ink/50 200.00
DJ1 Derek Jeter/Black Ink/400 80.00
DJ2 Derek Jeter/Blue Ink/250 100.00
DJ3 Derek Jeter/Red Ink/50 125.00

Home Run Club Memorabilia

NM/M
Common Player: 5.00
Production 599 Sets
Barry Bonds/Jsy 20.00
Jason Giambi/Bat 8.00
Sammy Sosa/Jsy 12.00
Jim Thome/Bat 8.00
Lance Berkman/Bat 5.00
Alfonso Soriano/Jsy 15.00
Vladimir Guerrero/Jsy 8.00
Shawn Green/Jsy 5.00
Troy Glaus/Bat 6.00
Pat Burrell/Bat 10.00
Alex Rodriguez/Jsy 15.00
Mike Piazza/Jsy 12.00
Todd Helton/Jsy 8.00
Rafael Palmeiro/Jsy 6.00

Knot Hole Gang

NM/M
Complete Set (15): 40.00
Common Player: 1.00
Inserted 1:24
1 Derek Jeter 6.00
2 Barry Bonds 6.00
3 Sammy Sosa 3.00
4 Jason Giambi 3.00
5 Alfonso Soriano 2.00
6 Roger Clemens 3.00
7 Miguel Tejada 1.00
8 Greg Maddux 3.00
9 Randy Johnson 2.00
10 Chipper Jones 3.00
11 Nomar Garciaparra 4.00
12 Alex Rodriguez 5.00
13 Ichiro Suzuki 4.00
14 Vladimir Guerrero 2.00
15 Albert Pujols 2.00

Knot Hole Gang Game-Used

NM/M
Common Player: 4.00
Inserted 1:40
Derek Jeter 20.00
Barry Bonds 15.00
Sammy Sosa 10.00
Vladimir Guerrero 8.00
Alfonso Soriano 8.00
Roger Clemens 10.00
Miguel Tejada 5.00
Greg Maddux 10.00
Randy Johnson 8.00
Chipper Jones 8.00
Nomar Garciaparra 12.00
Alex Rodriguez 12.00
Magglio Ordonez 4.00
Lance Berkman 6.00

Knot Hole Gang Patch

NM/M
Common Player: 15.00
Production 99 Sets
Derek Jeter 45.00
Barry Bonds 45.00
Sammy Sosa 35.00
Vladimir Guerrero 25.00
Alfonso Soriano 25.00
Roger Clemens 25.00
Miguel Tejada 15.00
Greg Maddux 30.00
Randy Johnson 20.00
Chipper Jones 30.00
Nomar Garciaparra 35.00
Alex Rodriguez 35.00

Knot Hole Gang Triple

Common Player:
Production 29 Sets: No Pricing

Splendid Splinters

NM/M
Complete Set (10): 15.00
Common Player: 1.00
Inserted 1:12
1 Derek Jeter 4.00
2 Barry Bonds 4.00
3 Scott Rolen 1.00
4 Nomar Garciaparra 2.50
5 Sammy Sosa 2.00
6 Alfonso Soriano 1.50
7 Alex Rodriguez 3.00
8 Mike Piazza 2.50
9 Manny Ramirez 1.00
10 Jeff Bagwell 1.00

Splendid Splinters G-U

NM/M
Common Player: 8.00
Production 349 Sets
Derek Jeter 20.00
Barry Bonds 20.00
Nomar Garciaparra 15.00
Sammy Sosa 10.00
Alfonso Soriano 10.00
Alex Rodriguez 12.00
Mike Piazza 12.00
Manny Ramirez 8.00
Jeff Bagwell 8.00

Splendid Splinters Dual

NM/M
Production 99 Sets
Derek Jeter, Alfonso Soriano 40.00
Barry Bonds, Sammy Sosa 50.00
Alex Rodriguez, Nomar Garciaparra 40.00
Mike Piazza, Jeff Bagwell 25.00

2003 Fleer Tradition

NM/M
Complete Set (485): 150.00
Common Player: .15
Common SP (1-100): 1.00
Inserted 1:1
Hobby Pack (10): 1.50
Hobby Box (40): 40.00
1 Jarrod Washburn, Troy Glaus, Garret Anderson, Ramon Ortiz 1.50
2 Luis Gonzalez, Randy Johnson, Andruw Jones 1.50
3 Andruw Jones, Chipper Jones, Tom Glavine, Kevin Millwood 2.00
4 Tony Batista, Rodrigo Lopez 1.00
5 Manny Ramirez, Nomar Garciaparra, Derek Lowe, Pedro J. Martinez 3.00
6 Sammy Sosa, Matt Clement, Kerry Wood 3.00
7 Mark Buehrle, Magglio Ordonez, Danny Wright 1.00
8 Adam Dunn, Aaron Boone, Jimmy Haynes 1.00
9 C.C. Sabathia, Jim Thome 1.50
10 Todd Helton, Jason Jennings 1.50
11 Randall Simon, Steve Sparks, Mark Redman 1.00
12 Derrek Lee, Mike Lowell, A.J. Burnett 1.00
13 Lance Berkman, Roy Oswalt 1.50
14 Paul Byrd, Carlos Beltran 1.00
15 Shawn Green, Hideo Nomo 1.50
16 Richie Sexson, Ben Sheets 1.00
17 Torii Hunter, Kyle Lohse, Johan Santana 1.00
18 Vladimir Guerrero, Tomokazu Ohka, Javier Vazquez 2.00
19 Mike Piazza, Al Leiter 3.00
20 Jason Giambi, David Wells, Roger Clemens 4.00
21 Eric Chavez, Miguel Tejada, Barry Zito 1.50
22 Pat Burrell, Vicente Padilla, Randy Wolf 1.50
23 Brian Giles, Josh Fogg, Kip Wells 1.00
24 Ryan Klesko, Brian Lawrence 1.00
25 Barry Bonds, Russ Ortiz, Jason Schmidt 5.00
26 Mike Cameron, Bret Boone, Freddy Garcia 1.00
27 Albert Pujols, Matt Morris 3.00
28 Aubrey Huff, Randy Winn, Joe Kennedy, Tanyon Sturtze 1.00
29 Alex Rodriguez, Kenny Rogers, Chan Ho Park 5.00
30 Carlos Delgado, Roy Halladay 1.00
31 Greg Maddux 6.00
32 Nick Neugebauer 1.00
33 Larry Walker 1.50
34 Freddy Garcia 1.00
35 Rich Aurilia 1.00
36 Craig Wilson 1.00
37 Jeff Suppan 1.00
38 Joel Pineiro 1.00
39 Pedro Feliz 1.00
40 Bartolo Colon 1.50
41 Pete Walker 1.00
42 Mo Vaughn 1.50
43 Sidney Ponson 1.00
44 Jason Isringhausen 1.00
45 Hideki Irabu 1.00
46 Pedro J. Martinez 4.00
47 Tom Glavine 2.50
48 Matt Lawton 1.00
49 Kyle Lohse 1.00
50 Corey Patterson 1.00
51 Ichiro Suzuki 6.00
52 Wade Miller 1.00
53 Ben Diggins 1.00
54 Jayson Werth 1.00
55 Masato Yoshii 1.00
56 Mark Buehrle 1.00
57 Drew Henson 1.50
58 Dave Williams 1.00
59 Juan Rivera 1.00
60 Scott Schoeneweis 1.00
61 Josh Beckett 1.50
62 Vinny Castilla 1.00
63 Barry Zito 2.00
64 Jose Valentin 1.00
65 Jon Lieber 1.00
66 Jorge Padilla 1.00
67 Luis Aparicio 1.00
68 Boog Powell 1.00
69 Dick Radatz 1.00
70 Frank Malzone 1.00
71 Lou Brock 1.50
72 Billy Williams 1.00
73 Early Wynn 1.00
74 Jim Bunning 1.00
75 Al Kaline 5.00
76 Eddie Mathews 3.00
77 Harmon Killebrew 5.00
78 Gil Hodges 1.00
79 Duke Snider 3.00
80 Yogi Berra 4.00
81 Whitey Ford 3.00
82 Willie Stargell 1.50
83 Willie McCovey 1.50
84 Gaylord Perry 1.00
85 Red Schoendienst 1.00
86 Luis Castillo 1.00
87 Derek Jeter 8.00

88 Orlando Hudson 1.00
89 Bobby Higginson 1.00
90 Brent Butler 1.00
91 Brad Wilkerson 1.00
92 Craig Biggio 1.50
93 Marlon Anderson 1.00
94 Ty Wigginton 1.00
95 Hideo Nomo 3.00
96 Barry Larkin 2.00
97 Roberto Alomar 3.00
98 Omar Vizquel 1.50
99 Andres Galarraga 1.00
100 Shawn Green 1.50
101 Rafael Furcal .15
102 Bill Selby .15
103 Brent Abernathy .15
104 Nomar Garciaparra 1.50
105 Michael Barrett .15
106 Travis Hafner .15
107 Carl Crawford .15
108 Jeff Cirillo .15
109 Mike Hampton .15
110 Kip Wells .15
111 Luis Alicea .15
112 Ellis Burks .15
113 Matt Anderson .15
114 Carlos Beltran .50
115 Paul LoDuca .15
116 Lance Berkman .15
117 Moises Alou .15
118 Roger Cedeno .15
119 Brad Fullmer .15
120 Sean Burroughs .15
121 Eric Byrnes .15
122 Milton Bradley .15
123 Jason Giambi .75
124 Brook Fordyce .15
125 Kevin Appier .15
126 Steve Cox .15
127 Danny Bautista .15
128 Edgardo Alfonzo .15
129 Matt Clement .15
130 Robb Nen .15
131 Roy Halladay .15
132 Brian Jordan .15
133 A.J. Burnett .15
134 Aaron Cook .15
135 Paul Byrd .15
136 Ramon Ortiz .15
137 Adam Hyzdu .15
138 Rafael Soriano .15
139 Marty Cordova .15
140 Nelson Cruz .15
141 Jamie Moyer .15
142 Raul Mondesi .15
143 Josh Bard .15
144 Elmer Dessens .15
145 Rickey Henderson .75
146 Joe McEwing .15
147 Luis Rivas .15
148 Armando Benitez .15
149 Keith Foulke .15
150 Zach Day .15
151 Troy Lunsford .15
152 Bobby Abreu .15
153 Juan Cruz .15
154 Ramon Hernandez .15
155 Brandon Duckworth .15
156 Matt Ginter .15
157 Robert Mackowiak .15
158 Josh Pearce .15
159 Marlon Byrd .15
160 Todd Walker .15
161 Chad Hermansen .15
162 Felix Escalona .15
163 Ruben Mateo .15
164 Mark Johnson .15
165 Juan Pierre .15
166 Gary Sheffield .30
167 Edgar Martinez .15
168 Randy Winn .15
169 Pokey Reese .15
170 Kevin Mench .15
171 Albert Pujols 1.50
172 J.T. Snow .15
173 Dean Palmer .15
174 Jay Payton .15
175 Abraham Nunez .15
176 Richie Sexson .15
177 Jose Vidro .15
178 Geoff Jenkins .15
179 Dan Wilson .15
180 John Olerud .15
181 Javy Lopez .15
182 Carl Everett .15
183 Vernon Wells .15
184 Juan Gonzalez .75
185 Jorge Posada .35
186 Mike Sweeney .15
187 Cesar Izturis .15
188 Jason Schmidt .15
189 Chris Richard .15
190 Jason Phillips .15
191 Fred McGriff .15
192 Shea Hillenbrand .15
193 Ivan Rodriguez .50
194 Mike Lowell .15
195 Neifi Perez .15
196 Kenny Lofton .15
197 A.J. Pierzynski .15
198 Larry Bigbie .15
199 Juan Uribe .15
200 Jeff Bagwell .75
201 Timoniel Perez .15
202 Jeremy Giambi .15
203 Deivi Cruz .15
204 Marquis Grissom .15
205 Chipper Jones 1.00
206 Alex Gonzalez .15
207 Steve Finley .15
208 Ben Davis .15
209 Mike Bordick .15
210 Casey Fossum .15
211 Aramis Ramirez .15
212 Aaron Boone .15
213 Orlando Cabrera .15
214 Hee Seop Choi .15
215 Jeromy Burnitz .15
216 Todd Hollandsworth .15
217 Rey Sanchez .15
218 Jose Cruz Jr. .15
219 Roosevelt Brown .15
220 Odalis Perez .15
221 Carlos Delgado .40
222 Orlando Hernandez .15
223 Adam Everett .15
224 Adrian Beltre .25
225 Ken Griffey Jr. 1.50
226 Brad Penny .15
227 Carlos Lee .15
228 J.C. Romero .15
229 Ramon Martinez .15
230 Matt Morris .15
231 Ben Howard .15
232 Damon Minor .15
233 Jason Marquis .15
234 Paul Wilson .15
235 Ryan Dempster .15
236 Jeffrey Hammonds .15
237 Jaret Wright .15
238 Carlos Pena .15
239 Toby Hall .15
240 Rick Helling .15
241 Alex Escobar .15
242 Trevor Hoffman .15
243 Bernie Williams .35
244 Jorge Julio .15
245 Byung-Hyun Kim .15
246 Mike Redmond .15
247 Tony Armas .15
248 Aaron Rowand .15
249 Rusty Greer .15
250 Aaron Harang .15
251 Jeremy Fikac .15
252 Jay Gibbons .15
253 Brandon Puffer .15
254 Dewayne Wise .15
255 Chan Ho Park .15
256 David Bell .15
257 Kenny Rogers .15
258 Mark Quinn .15
259 Greg LaRocca .15
260 Reggie Taylor .15
261 Brett Tomko .15
262 Jack Wilson .15
263 Billy Wagner .15
264 Greg Norton .15
265 Tim Salmon .25
266 Joe Randa .15
267 Geronimo Gil .15
268 Johnny Damon .25
269 Robin Ventura .15
270 Frank Thomas .75
271 Terrence Long .15
272 Mark Redman .15
273 Mark Kotsay .15
274 Ben Sheets .15
275 Reggie Sanders .15
276 Mark Grace .25
277 Eddie Guardado .15
278 Julio Mateo .15
279 Bengie Molina .15
280 Bill Hall .15
281 Eric Chavez .30
282 Joe Kennedy .15
283 John Valentin .15
284 Ray Durham .15
285 Trot Nixon .15
286 Rondell White .15
287 Alex Gonzalez .15
288 Tomas Perez .15
289 Jared Sandberg .15
290 Jacque Jones .15
291 Cliff Floyd .15
292 Ryan Klesko .15
293 Morgan Ensberg .15
294 Jerry Hairston Jr. .15
295 Doug Mientkiewicz .15
296 Darin Erstad .50
297 Jeff Conine .15
298 Johnny Estrada .15
299 Mark Mulder .15
300 Jeff Kent .15
301 Roger Clemens 1.25
302 Endy Chavez .15
303 Joe Crede .15
304 J.D. Drew .30
305 David Dellucci .15
306 Eli Marrero .15
307 Josh Fogg .15
308 Mike Crudale .15
309 Bret Boone .15
310 Mariano Rivera .30
311 Mike Piazza 1.50
312 Jason Jennings .15
313 Jason Varitek .15
314 Vicente Padilla .15
315 Kevin Millwood .15
316 Nick Johnson .15
317 Shane Reynolds .15
318 Joe Thurston .15
319 Mike Lamb .15
320 Aaron Sele .15
321 Fernando Tatis .15
322 Randy Wolf .15
323 David Justice .15
324 Andy Pettitte .30
325 Freddy Sanchez .15
326 Scott Spiezio .15
327 Randy Johnson .75
328 Karim Garcia .15
329 Eric Milton .15
330 Jermaine Dye .15
331 Kevin Brown .15
332 Adam Pettyjohn .15
333 Jason Lane .15
334 Mark Prior .60
335 Mike Lieberthal .15
336 Matt White .15
337 John Patterson .15
338 Marcus Giles .15
339 Kazuhisa Ishii .15
340 Willie Harris .15
341 Travis Phelps .15
342 Randall Simon .15
343 Manny Ramirez .75
344 Kerry Wood .60
345 Shannon Stewart .15
346 Mike Mussina .40
347 Joe Borchard .15
348 Tyler Walker .15
349 Preston Wilson .15
350 Damian Moss .15
351 Eric Karros .15
352 Bobby Kielty .15
353 Jason LaRue .15
354 Phil Nevin .15
355 Tony Graffanino .15
356 Antonio Alfonseca .15
357 Eddie Taubensee .15
358 Luis Ugueto .15
359 Greg Vaughn .15
360 Corey Thurman .15
361 Omar Infante .15
362 Alex Cintron .15
363 Esteban Loaiza .15
364 Tino Martinez .15
365 David Eckstein .15
366 David Pember **RC** .15
367 Damian Rolls .15
368 Richard Hidalgo .15
369 Brad Radke .15
370 Alex Sanchez .15
371 Ben Grieve .15
372 Brandon Inge .15
373 Adam Piatt .15
374 Charles Johnson .15
375 Rafael Palmeiro .65
376 Joe Mays .15
377 Derrek Lee .15
378 Fernando Vina .15
379 Andruw Jones .75
380 Troy Glaus .75
381 Bobby Hill .15
382 C.C. Sabathia .15
383 Jose Hernandez .15
384 Al Leiter .15
385 Jarrod Washburn .15
386 Cody Ransom .15
387 Matt Stairs .15
388 Edgar Renteria .15
389 Tsuyoshi Shinjo .15
390 Matt Williams .15
391 Bubba Trammell .15
392 Jason Kendall .15
393 Scott Rolen .65
394 Chuck Knoblauch .15
395 Jimmy Rollins .25
396 Gary Bennett .15
397 David Wells .15
398 Ronnie Belliard .15
399 Austin Kearns .50
400 Tim Hudson .30
401 Andy Van Hekken .15
402 Ray Lankford .15
403 Todd Helton .75
404 Jeff Weaver .15
405 Gabe Kapler .15
406 Luis Gonzalez .40
407 Sean Casey .15
408 Kazuhiro Sasaki .15
409 Mark Teixeira .50
410 Brian Giles .15
411 Robert Fick .15
412 Wilkin Ruan .15
413 Jose Rijo .15
414 Ben Broussard .15
415 Aubrey Huff .15
416 Magglio Ordonez .25
417 Barry Bonds 2.00
418 Miguel Tejada .40
419 Randy Johnson .75
420 Barry Zito .30
421 Jason Jennings .15
422 Eric Hinske .15
423 Benito Santiago .15
424 Adam Kennedy .15
425 Troy Glaus .65
426 Brandon Phillips .15
427 Jake Peavy .15
428 Jason Romano .15
429 Jeriome Robertson .15
430 Aaron Guiel .15
431 Hank Blalock .15
432 Brad Lidge .15
433 Francisco Rodriguez .15
434 Jaime Cerda .15
435 Jung Bong .15
436 Reed Johnson .15
437 Rene Reyes .15
438 Chris Snelling .15
439 Miguel Olivo .15
440 Brian Banks .15
441 Eric Junge .15
442 Kirk Saarloos .15
443 Jamey Carroll .15
444 Josh Hancock .15
445 Michael Restovich .15
446 William Bloomquist .15
447 John Lackey .15
448 Marcus Thames .15
449 Victor Martinez .15
450 Brett Myers .15
451 Wes Obermueller .15
452 Hansel Izquierdo .15
453 Brian Tallet .15
454 Craig Monroe .15
455 Doug DeVore .15
456 John Buck .15
457 Tony Alvarez .15
458 Wily Mo Pena .15
459 John Stephens .15
460 Tony Torcato .15
461 Adam Kennedy .15
462 Alex Rodriguez .15
463 Derek Lowe .15
464 Garret Anderson .15
465 Pat Burrell .50
466 Eric Gagne .15
467 Tomokazu Ohka .15
468 Josh Phelps .15
469 Sammy Sosa 1.50
470 Jim Thome .15
471 Vladimir Guerrero .75
472 Jason Simontacchi .15
473 Adam Dunn .50
474 Jim Edmonds .15
475 Barry Bonds 2.00
476 Paul Konerko .25
477 Alfonso Soriano .75
478 Curt Schilling .40
479 John Smoltz .15
480 Torii Hunter .15
481 Rodrigo Lopez .15
482 Miguel Tejada .35
483 Eric Hinske .15
484 Roy Oswalt .25
485 Junior Spivey .15

Glossy

SP's (1-100): 1-2X
Cards (101-485): 5-10X
Production 100 Sets
Randomly inserted in Update packs.

B/W Goudey

NM/M
Complete Set (25): 80.00
Common Player: 1.50
Production 1,936 Sets
Golds: 4-8X
Production 36 Sets
1BWG Jim Thome 2.50
2BWG Derek Jeter 10.00
3BWG Alex Rodriguez 8.00
4BWG Mark Prior 1.00
5BWG Nomar Garciaparra 6.00
6BWG Curt Schilling 2.00
7BWG Pat Burrell 2.00
8BWG Frank Thomas 2.50
9BWG Roger Clemens 5.00
10BWG Chipper Jones 5.00
11BWG Barry Larkin 1.50
12BWG Hideo Nomo 2.00
13BWG Pedro J. Martinez 3.00
14BWG Jeff Bagwell 2.50
15BWG Greg Maddux 5.00
16BWG Vladimir Guerrero 3.00
17BWG Ichiro Suzuki 6.00
18BWG Mike Piazza 8.00
19BWG Drew Henson 1.50
20BWG Albert Pujols 3.00
21BWG Sammy Sosa 5.00
22BWG Jason Giambi 5.00
23BWG Randy Johnson 3.00
24BWG Ken Griffey Jr. 6.00
25BWG Barry Bonds 8.00

Checklist

NM/M
Complete Set (18): 6.00
Common Card: .50
Inserted 1:4
1CL-9CL Derek Jeter .50
10CL-18CL Barry Bonds .50

Game-Used Parallel

NM/M
Common Player: 5.00
Inserted 1:35
Golds: 1-2X

Production 100 Sets
Derek Jeter/Jsy/150 35.00
Craig Biggio/Bat 8.00
Hideo Nomo/Jsy/200 20.00
Barry Larkin/Jsy/200 10.00
Kazuhiro Sasaki/Jsy/200 10.00
Greg Maddux/Jsy 15.00
Mo Vaughn/Jsy/60 10.00
Pedro Martinez/Jsy/200 12.00
Barry Zito/Jsy 10.00
Luis Aparicio/Jsy/150 10.00
Willie Stargell/Pants/150 15.00
Nomar Garciaparra/Jsy/200 20.00
Edgardo Alfonzo/Jsy/200 8.00
John Olerud/Jsy 6.00
Juan Gonzalez/Bat/200 10.00
Jorge Posada/Bat 8.00
Shea Hillenbrand/Bat 10.00
Ivan Rodriguez/Jsy 8.00
Mike Lowell/Bat 5.00
Jeff Bagwell/Jsy/200 12.00
Chipper Jones/Jsy 15.00
Jeromy Burnitz/Jsy/200 6.00
Adrian Beltre/Jsy 6.00
Robin Ventura/Jsy 8.00
Frank Thomas/Jsy 10.00
Mark Grace/Jsy 10.00
Darin Erstad/Jsy 8.00
Roger Clemens/Jsy/150 20.00
J.D. Drew/Jsy 8.00
Mike Piazza/Jsy/150 20.00
Randy Johnson/Jsy/150 12.00
Mark Prior/Jsy/200 15.00
Kazuhisa Ishii/Jsy 10.00
Manny Ramirez/Jsy/150 10.00
Kerry Wood/Jsy/200 15.00
Mike Mussina/Jsy 10.00
Eric Karros/Jsy 5.00
Rafael Palmeiro/Jsy 8.00
Andruw Jones/Bat/150 10.00
Jason Kendall/Jsy 6.00
Jimmy Rollins/Jsy 8.00
Barry Bonds/Jsy/50 40.00
Miguel Tejada/Bat/150 8.00
Jason Jennings/Jsy 6.00

Hardball Preview

NM/M
Complete Set (10): 125.00
Common Player: 5.00
Inserted 1:400
1 Miguel Tejada 5.00
2 Derek Jeter 25.00
3 Mike Piazza 20.00
4 Barry Bonds 20.00
5 Mark Prior 4.00
6 Ichiro Suzuki 20.00
7 Alex Rodriguez 20.00
8 Nomar Garciaparra 15.00
9 Alfonso Soriano 12.00
10 Ken Griffey Jr. 15.00

Lumber Company

NM/M
Complete Set (30): 70.00
Common Player: 1.00
Inserted 1:10
1 Mike Piazza 6.00
2 Derek Jeter 8.00
3 Alex Rodriguez 6.00
4 Miguel Tejada 1.00
5 Nomar Garciaparra 5.00
6 Andruw Jones 1.50
7 Pat Burrell 1.50
8 Albert Pujols 3.00
9 Jeff Bagwell 2.00
10 Chipper Jones 4.00
11 Ichiro Suzuki 6.00
12 Alfonso Soriano 3.00
13 Eric Chavez 1.50
14 Brian Giles 1.00
15 Shawn Green 1.50
16 Jim Thome 2.00
17 Lance Berkman 1.50
18 Bernie Williams 1.50
19 Manny Ramirez 2.00
20 Vladimir Guerrero 3.00
21 Carlos Delgado 1.25
22 Scott Rolen 1.50
23 Sammy Sosa 4.00
24 Ken Griffey Jr. 5.00
25 Barry Bonds 6.00
26 Todd Helton 1.50
27 Jason Giambi 4.00
28 Austin Kearns 1.50
29 Jeff Kent 1.00
30 Magglio Ordonez 1.00

Lumber Company Bat

NM/M
Common Player: 6.00
Inserted 1:108
Jeff Bagwell/200 15.00
Lance Berkman/200 10.00
Barry Bonds/150 25.00
Pat Burrell/75 25.00
Eric Chavez/125 8.00
Carlos Delgado/200 6.00
Nomar Garciaparra/200 25.00
Brian Giles/200 8.00
Shawn Green/200 8.00
Todd Helton 8.00
Derek Jeter/96 35.00
Andruw Jones 8.00
Chipper Jones 15.00
Austin Kearns/75 18.00
Jeff Kent/200 6.00
Magglio Ordonez 6.00
Mike Piazza/200 20.00
Manny Ramirez 10.00
Alex Rodriguez 15.00
Scott Rolen/80 25.00
Alfonso Soriano/200 12.00
Miguel Tejada 10.00
Jim Thome/200 12.00
Bernie Williams 10.00

Lumber Company Bat Gold

NM/M
Numbered to 2002 HR total.
Lance Berkman/42 25.00
Barry Bonds/46 70.00
Pat Burrell/37 50.00
Eric Chavez/34 20.00
Carlos Delgado/33 35.00
Nomar Garciaparra/24 60.00
Brian Giles/38 25.00
Shawn Green/42 35.00
Todd Helton/30 35.00
Derek Jeter/18 200.00
Andruw Jones/35 25.00
Chipper Jones/26 45.00
Austin Kearns/13 35.00
Jeff Kent/37 20.00
Magglio Ordonez/38 25.00
Mike Piazza/33 65.00
Alex Rodriguez/57 40.00
Miguel Tejada/34 35.00
Jim Thome/52 30.00

Milestones

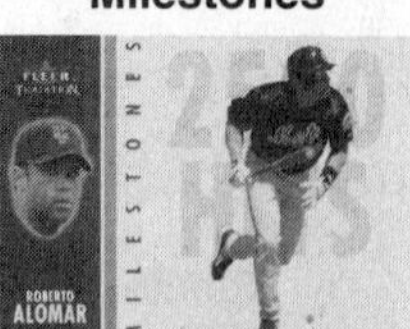

NM/M
Complete Set (25): 40.00
Common Player: 1.00
Inserted 1:5
1 Eddie Mathews 1.50
2 Rickey Henderson 1.50
3 Harmon Killebrew 1.50
4 Al Kaline 2.50
5 Willie McCovey 1.00
6 Tom Seaver 2.00
7 Reggie Jackson 2.00
8 Mike Schmidt 3.00
9 Nolan Ryan 5.00
10 Mike Piazza 4.00
11 Randy Johnson 2.00
12 Bernie Williams 1.50
13 Rafael Palmeiro 1.50
14 Juan Gonzalez 1.50
15 Ken Griffey Jr. 3.00
16 Derek Jeter 5.00
17 Roger Clemens 3.00
18 Roberto Alomar 1.50
19 Manny Ramirez 1.50
20 Luis Gonzalez 1.00
21 Barry Bonds 4.00

22 Nomar Garciaparra 3.00
23 Fred McGriff 1.00
24 Greg Maddux 2.50
25 Barry Bonds 4.00

Milestones Game-Used

NM/M
Common Player: 8.00
Inserted 1:143
Golds: 1-2X
Production 100 Sets
Roberto Alomar/Bat/200 8.00
Barry Bonds/600 HR/Bat/100 30.00
Barry Bonds/5 MVP/Jsy/200 25.00
Roger Clemens/Jsy/150 20.00
Nomar Garciaparra/Jsy/200 20.00
Juan Gonzalez/Bat/250 10.00
Derek Jeter/Jsy/150 35.00
Randy Johnson/Jsy/100 15.00
Greg Maddux 20.00
Fred McGriff 5.00
Rafael Palmeiro/Jsy/200 8.00
Mike Piazza/Jsy/100 20.00
Manny Ramirez/Jsy/150 10.00
Bernie Williams/Jsy/200 10.00

Standouts

NM/M
Complete Set (15): 60.00
Common Player: 1.50
Inserted 1:40
1SO Greg Maddux 5.00
2SO Derek Jeter 10.00
3SO Alex Rodriguez 8.00
4SO Miguel Tejada 2.00
5SO Nomar Garciaparra 6.00
6SO Barry Bonds 8.00
7SO Pat Burrell 2.00
8SO Ken Griffey Jr. 6.00
9SO Alfonso Soriano 4.00
10SO Mike Piazza 8.00
11SO Sammy Sosa 5.00
12SO Ichiro Suzuki 6.00
13SO Vladimir Guerrero 3.00
14SO Roger Clemens 5.00
15SO Adam Dunn 2.50

Update

NM/M
Complete Set (398): 175.00
Common Player: .15
Common Rookie (286-398): .50
Cards (286-299):
Inserted 1:4
Pack (10): 2.00
Box (32 + 25 count update box): 50.00
1 Aaron Boone .15
2 Carl Everett .15
3 Eduardo Perez .15
4 Jason Michaels .15
5 Karim Garcia .15
6 Rainier Olmedo .15
7 Scott Williamson .15
8 Adam Kennedy .15
9 Carl Pavano .15
10 Eli Marrero .15
11 Jason Simontacchi .15
12 Keith Foulke .15
13 Preston Wilson .15
14 Scott Hatteberg .15
15 Adam Dunn .50
16 Carlos Baerga .15
17 Elmer Dessens .15
18 Javier Vazquez .15
19 Kenny Rogers .15
20 Quinton McCracken .15
21 Shane Reynolds .15
22 Adam Eaton .15
23 Carlos Zambrano .15
24 Enrique Wilson .15
25 Jeff DaVanon .15
26 Kenny Lofton .25
27 Ramon Castro .15
28 Shannon Stewart .15
29 Al Martin .15
30 Carlos Guillen .15
31 Eric Karros .15
32 Tim Worrell .15
33 Kevin Millwood .25
34 Randall Simon .15
35 Shawn Chacon .15
36 Alex Rodriguez 1.50
37 Casey Blake .15
38 Eric Munson .15
39 Jeff Kent .25
40 Kris Benson .15
41 Randy Winn .15
42 Shea Hillenbrand .15
43 Alfonso Soriano 1.00
44 Chris George .15
45 Eric Bruntlett .15
46 Jeromy Burnitz .15
47 Kyle Farnsworth .15
48 Torii Hunter .40
49 Sidney Ponson .15
50 Andres Galarraga .25
51 Chris Singleton .15
52 Eric Gagne .25
53 Jesse Foppert .15
54 Lance Carter .15
55 Ray Durham .15
56 Tanyon Sturtze .15
57 Andy Ashby .15
58 Cliff Floyd .15
59 Eric Young .15
60 Jhonny Peralta .50
61 Livan Hernandez .15
62 Reggie Sanders .15
63 Tim Spooneybarger .15
64 Angel Berroa .15
65 Coco Crisp .15
66 Eric Hinske .15
67 Jim Edmonds .25
68 Luis Matos .15
69 Rickey Henderson .40
70 Todd Walker .15
71 Antonio Alfonseca .15
72 Corey Koskie .15
73 Erubiel Durazo .15
74 Jim Thome .50
75 Lyle Overbay .15
76 Robert Fick .15
77 Todd Hollandsworth .15
78 Aramis Ramirez .15
79 Cristian Guzman .15
80 Esteban Loaiza .15
81 Jody Gerut .15
82 Mark Grudzielanek .15
83 Roberto Alomar .40
84 Todd Hundley .15
85 Mike Hampton .15
86 Curt Schilling .40
87 Francisco Rodriguez .15
88 John Lackey .15
89 Mark Redman .15
90 Robin Ventura .25
91 Todd Zeile .15
92 B.J. Surhoff .15
93 Raul Mondesi .25
94 Frank Catalanotto .15
95 John Smoltz .25
96 Mark Ellis .15
97 Rocco Baldelli .50
98 Todd Pratt .15
99 Barry Bonds 2.00
100 Danny Graves .15
101 Fred McGriff .25
102 John Burkett .15
103 Marquis Grissom .15
104 Rocky Biddle .15
105 Tom Glavine .25
106 Bartolo Colon .25
107 Darren Bragg .15
108 Gabe Kapler .15
109 John Franco .15
110 Matt Mantei .15
111 Rod Beck .15
112 Tomokazu Ohka .15
113 Ben Petrick .15
114 Darren Dreifort .15
115 Garret Anderson .25
116 John Vander Wal .15
117 Melvin Mora .15
118 Rodrigo Lopez .15
119 Raul Ibanez .15
120 Benito Santiago .15
121 David Ortiz .15
122 Gary Bennett .15
123 Jon Garland .15
124 Michael Young .15
125 Rodrigo Rosario .15
126 Travis Lee .15
127 Bill Mueller .15
128 Derek Lowe .15
129 Gil Meche .15
130 Jose Guillen .15
131 Miguel Cabrera .40
132 Ron Calloway .15
133 Troy Percival .15
134 Billy Koch .15
135 Dmitri Young .15
136 Glendon Rusch .15
137 Jose Jimenez .15
138 Miguel Tejada .40
139 John Thomson .15
140 Troy O'Leary .15
141 Bobby Kielty .15
142 Dontrelle Willis .50
143 Greg Myers .15
144 Jose Vizcaino .15
145 Mike MacDougal .15
146 Ronnie Belliard .15
147 Tyler Houston .15
148 Brady Clark .15
149 Edgardo Alfonzo .15
150 Guillermo Mota .15
151 Jose Lima .15
152 Mike Williams .15
153 Roy Oswalt .25
154 Scott Podsednik .25
155 Brandon Lyon .15
156 Henry Mateo .15
157 Jose Macias .15
158 Mike Bordick .15
159 Royce Clayton .15
160 Vance Wilson .15
161 Brent Abernathy .15
162 Horacio Ramirez .15
163 Jose Reyes .50
164 Nick Punto .15
165 Ruben Sierra .15
166 Victor Zambrano .15
167 Brett Tomko .15
168 Ivan Rodriguez .75
169 Jose Mesa .15
170 Octavio Dotel .15
171 Russ Ortiz .15
172 Vladimir Guerrero .75
173 Brian Lawrence .15
174 Jae Weong Seo .15
175 Jose Cruz Jr. .15
176 Pat Burrell .40
177 Russell Branyan .15
178 Warren Morris .15
179 Brian Boehringer .15
180 Jason Johnson .15
181 Josh Phelps .15
182 Paul Konerko .15
183 Ryan Franklin .15
184 Wes Helms .15
185 Brooks Kieschnick .15
186 Jason Davis .15
187 Juan Pierre .15
188 Paul Wilson .15
189 Sammy Sosa 1.50
190 Wil Cordero .15
191 Byung-Hyun Kim .15
192 Juan Encarnacion .15
193 Placido Polanco .15
194 Sandy Alomar .15
195 Julio Lugo .15
196 Junior Spivey .15
197 Woody Williams .15
198 Xavier Nady .15
199 Mark Loretta .15
200 Deivi Cruz .15
201 Jorge Posada .25
202 Carlos Delgado .25
203 Alfonso Soriano .50
204 Alex Rodriguez 1.00
205 Troy Glaus .25
206 Garret Anderson .15
207 Hideki Matsui 2.00
208 Ichiro Suzuki .75
209 Esteban Loaiza .15
210 Manny Ramirez .25
211 Roger Clemens .75
212 Roy Halladay .15
213 Jason Giambi .25
214 Edgar Martinez .15
215 Bret Boone .15
216 Hank Blalock .15
217 Nomar Garciaparra .75
218 Vernon Wells .15
219 Melvin Mora .15
220 Magglio Ordonez .15
221 Mike Sweeney .15
222 Barry Zito .25
223 Carl Everett .15
224 Shigetoshi Hasegawa .15
225 Jamie Moyer .15
226 Mark Mulder .15
227 Eddie Guardado .15
228 Ramon Hernandez .15
229 Keith Foulke .15
230 Javy Lopez .15
231 Todd Helton .25
232 Marcus Giles .15
233 Edgar Renteria .15
234 Scott Rolen .25
235 Barry Bonds 1.00
236 Albert Pujols .75
237 Gary Sheffield .25
238 Jim Edmonds .25
239 Jason Schmidt .15
240 Mark Prior 1.00
241 Dontrelle Willis .25
242 Kerry Wood .25
243 Kevin Brown .15
244 Woody Williams .15
245 Paul LoDuca .15
246 Richie Sexson .15
247 Jose Vidro .15
248 Luis Castillo .15
249 Aaron Boone .15
250 Mike Lowell .15
251 Rafael Furcal .15
252 Andruw Jones .25
253 Preston Wilson .15
254 John Smoltz .15
255 Eric Gagne .15
256 Randy Wolf .15
257 Billy Wagner .15
258 Luis Gonzalez .15
259 Russ Ortiz .15
260 Jim Thome, Pedro J. Martinez .40
261 Alfonso Soriano, Jeff Bagwell .50
262 Dontrelle Willis, Rocco Baldelli .15
263 Carlos Delgado, Vladimir Guerrero .25
264 Sammy Sosa, Magglio Ordonez .50
265 Jason Giambi, Adam Dunn .25
266 Mike Sweeney, Albert Pujols .50
267 Barry Bonds, Torii Hunter .75
268 Ichiro Suzuki, Andruw Jones .50
269 Chipper Jones, Hank Blalock .50
270 Mark Prior, Vernon Wells .75
271 Nomar Garciaparra, Scott Rolen .75
272 Alex Rodriguez, Lance Berkman .75
273 Roger Clemens, Kerry Wood .75
274 Derek Jeter, Jose Reyes .75
275 Greg Maddux, Barry Zito .50
276 Carlos Delgado .25
277 J.D. Drew .15
278 Barry Bonds 1.00
279 Albert Pujols .75
280 Jim Thome .25
281 Sammy Sosa .75
282 Alfonso Soriano .50
283 Hideki Matsui 1.00
284 Mike Piazza .50
285 Vladimir Guerrero .40
286 Rich Harden .50
287 Chin-Hui Tsao .50
288 Edwin Jackson **RC** 4.00
289 Chien-Ming Wang **RC** 6.00
290 Josh Willingham **RC** 2.00
291 Matt Kata **RC** 2.00
292 Jose Contreras **RC** 2.00
293 Chris Bootcheck .50
294 Javier Lopez 1.00
295 Delmon Young **RC** 8.00
296 Pedro Liriano .50
297 Noah Lowry .50
298 Khalil Greene 3.00
299 Rob Bowen .50
300 Bo Hart **RC** 2.00
301 Beau Kemp **RC** .25
302 Gerald Laird .15
303 Miguel Ojeda **RC** .40
304 Todd Wellemeyer **RC** .75
305 Ryan Wagner **RC** 2.00
306 Jeff Duncan **RC** 1.50
307 Wilfredo Ledezma **RC** 1.50
308 Wes Obermueller .15
309 Bernie Castro **RC** .25
310 Tim Olson **RC** .25
311 Colin Porter **RC** 2.00
312 Francisco Cruceta **RC** 1.50
313 Guillermo Quiroz **RC** 1.50
314 Brian Stokes **RC** .50
315 Robby Hammock **RC** .50
316 Lew Ford **RC** 2.00
317 Todd Linden .15
318 Mike Gallo **RC** .50
319 Francisco Rosario **RC** 1.50
320 Rosman Garcia **RC** .50
321 Felix Sanchez **RC** .50
322 Chad Gaudin **RC** 1.00
323 Phil Seibel **RC** .50
324 Jason Gilfillan **RC** .50
325 Terrmel Sledge **RC** .75
326 Alfredo Gonzalez **RC** .50
327 Josh Stewart **RC** 1.00
328 Jeremy Griffiths .15
329 Cory Stewart **RC** .50
330 Josh Hall **RC** 1.00
331 Arnie Munoz **RC** .50
332 Garrett Atkins .15
333 Neal Cotts .15
334 Dan Haren 2.00
335 Shane Victorino **RC** .50
336 David Sanders **RC** .50
337 Oscar Villarreal **RC** .50
338 Michael Hessman **RC** .50
339 Andrew Brown **RC** .50
340 Kevin Hooper .15
341 Prentice Redman **RC** .50
342 Brandon Webb **RC** 3.00
343 Jimmy Gobble .15
344 Pete LaForest **RC** .50
345 Chris Waters **RC** .75
346 Hideki Matsui **RC** 8.00
347 Chris Capuano **RC** 1.00
348 Jon Leicester **RC** .50
349 Mike Nicolas **RC** .50
350 Nook Logan **RC** .50
351 Craig Brazell **RC** 1.00
352 Aaron Looper **RC** .50
353 D.J. Carrasco **RC** .50
354 Clint Barmes **RC** 1.00
355 Doug Waechter **RC** .75
356 Julio Manon **RC** .50
357 Jeremy Bonderman 3.00
358 Diegomar Markwell **RC** .50
359 Dave Matranga **RC** .75
360 Luis Ayala **RC** .50
361 Jason Stanford .15
362 Roger Deago **RC** .50
363 Geoff Geary **RC** 1.00
364 Edgar Gonzalez **RC** .50
365 Michel Hernandez **RC** .50
366 Aquilino Lopez **RC** .50
367 David Manning **RC** 1.00
368 Carlos Mendez **RC** .50
369 Matt Miller .15
370 Micheal Nakamura **RC** 1.00
371 Mike Neu **RC** .50
372 Ramon Nivar **RC** .50
373 Kevin Ohme **RC** .50
374 Alex Prieto **RC** 1.00
375 Stephen Randolph **RC** .50
376 Brian Sweeney **RC** 1.00
377 Matt Diaz **RC** .50
378 Mike Gonzalez .15
379 Daniel Cabrera **RC** 2.00
380 Fernando Cabrera **RC** .50
381 David DeJesus **RC** .50
382 Mike Ryan **RC** 1.00
383 Rick Roberts **RC** .50
384 Seung Jun Song .15
385 Rickie Weeks **RC** 6.00
386 Humberto Quintero **RC** .50
387 Alexis Rios .15
388 Aaron Miles **RC** 2.00
389 Tom Gregorio **RC** .50
390 Anthony Ferrari **RC** .75
391 Kevin Correia **RC** .75
392 Rafael Betancourt **RC** .75
393 Rett Johnson **RC** .50
394 Richard Fischer **RC** .50
395 Greg Aquino **RC** .50
396 Daniel Garcia **RC** 1.00
397 Sergio Mitre **RC** 1.00
398 Edwin Almonte .15

Update Glossy

Stars (1-285): 5-10X
Rookies (286-398): .5-1.5X
Production 100 Sets

Update Diamond Debuts

NM/M
Complete Set (25): 40.00
Common Player: 1.00
Inserted 1:10
1 Dontrelle Willis 4.00
2 Bo Hart 1.00
3 Jose Reyes 4.00
4 Chin-Hui Tsao 1.00
5 Brandon Webb 3.00
6 Rich Harden 2.00
7 Jesse Foppert 1.00
8 Rocco Baldelli 2.00
9 Hideki Matsui 5.00
10 Ron Calloway 1.00
11 Jeremy Bonderman 1.50
12 Mark Teixeira 3.00
13 Ryan Wagner 2.00
14 Jose Contreras 2.00
15 Miguel Cabrera 4.00
16 Lew Ford 1.00
17 Jeff Duncan 1.50
18 Matt Kata 1.00
19 Jeremy Griffiths 1.00
20 Todd Wellemeyer 1.00
21 Robby Hammock 1.00
22 Dave Matranga 1.00
23 Laynce Nix 1.00
24 Jhonny Peralta 1.00
25 Oscar Villarreal 1.00

Update Long GONE!

NM/M
Complete Set (20): 60.00
Common Player: 2.00
Quantity produced listed
1 Barry Bonds/475 8.00
2 Jason Giambi/440 2.00
3 Albert Pujols/452 6.00
4 Chipper Jones/420 4.00
5 Manny Ramirez/430 2.00
6 Sammy Sosa/536 5.00
7 Alfonso Soriano/440 3.00
8 Alex Rodriguez/430 6.00
9 Jim Thome/445 3.00
10 Vladimir Guerrero/502 3.00
11 Austin Kearns/430 2.00
12 Jeff Bagwell/420 2.00
13 Andruw Jones/430 2.00
14 Carlos Delgado/451 2.00
15 Nomar Garciaparra/440 6.00
16 Adam Dunn/464 2.00
17 Mike Piazza/450 4.00
18 Derek Jeter/410 6.00
19 Ken Griffey Jr./420 4.00
20 Hank Blalock/424 2.00

Update Milestones

NM/M
Complete Set (20): 25.00
Common Player: 1.00
Inserted 1:8
1 Roger Clemens 3.00
2 Rafael Palmeiro 1.00
3 Jeff Bagwell 1.00
4 Barry Bonds 4.00
5 Sammy Sosa 2.50
6 Albert Pujols 3.00
7 Ichiro Suzuki 2.00
8 Alfonso Soriano 1.50
9 Alex Rodriguez 3.00
10 Randy Johnson 1.50
11 Manny Ramirez 1.00
12 Chipper Jones 2.00
13 Todd Helton 1.00
14 Ken Griffey Jr. 2.00
15 Jim Thome 1.00
16 Frank Thomas 1.00
17 Pedro J. Martinez 1.50
18 Hideo Nomo 1.00
19 Jason Schmidt 1.00
20 Carlos Delgado 1.00

Update Milestones Memorabilia

NM/M
Common Player: 5.00
Inserted 1:20
Golds: 1-2X
Production 100 Sets
Roger Clemens 15.00
Rafael Palmeiro 5.00

Jeff Bagwell 8.00
Sammy Sosa 10.00
Alfonso Soriano 10.00
Alex Rodriguez 10.00
Randy Johnson 8.00
Manny Ramirez 5.00
Chipper Jones 8.00
Todd Helton 6.00
Jim Thome 8.00
Frank Thomas 8.00
Pedro J. Martinez 8.00
Hideo Nomo 8.00
Jason Schmidt 8.00
Carlos Delgado 5.00

Update Milestones Memorabilia Gold

Complete Set (16):
Common Player:

Update Throwback Threads

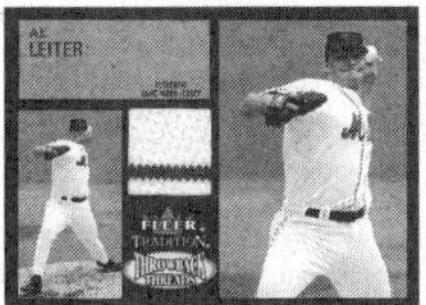

NM/M
Common Player: 4.00
Inserted 1:64
Kevin Millwood 6.00
Vladimir Guerrero 8.00
Troy Glaus 6.00
Mike Piazza 10.00
Al Leiter 4.00

Update Throwback Threads Dual

NM/M
Production 100
Vladimir Guerrero, Troy Glaus 15.00
Mike Piazza, Al Leiter 15.00

Update Throwback Threads Patch

NM/M
Common Player: 10.00
Production 100 Sets
Kevin Millwood 15.00
Vladimir Guerrero 20.00
Troy Glaus 15.00
Mike Piazza 25.00
Al Leiter 10.00

Update Turn Back the Clock

NM/M
Complete Set (10): 75.00
Common Player: 4.00
Inserted 1:160
1 Yogi Berra 8.00
2 Mike Schmidt 15.00
3 Tom Seaver 6.00
4 Reggie Jackson 5.00
5 Pee Wee Reese 4.00
6 Phil Rizzuto 4.00
7 Jim Palmer 4.00
8 Robin Yount 15.00
9 Nolan Ryan 20.00
10 Al Kaline 10.00

Cub Foods

In an unusual 2" x 2-3/4" format, these cards were distributed in 24-can cubes of soda, reportedly only at Cub Foods stores in the Upper Midwest. Fronts have player portraits over team logos on a white background. Cub Foods and Pepsi logos are at bottom. Backs have personal data, recent stats, career highlights and a team logo.

NM/M
Complete Set (10): 7.50
Common Player: .50
1 Ichiro 2.00
2 Kerry Wood .75
3 Mike Piazza 1.00
4 Randy Johnson .75
5 Magglio Ordonez .50
6 Brad Radke .50
7 Omar Vizquel .50
8 Ben Sheets .50
9 Barry Zito .50
10 Ken Griffey Jr. 2.00

Pepsi-Cola

2004 Fleer America's National Pastime

NM/M
Common Player (1-60): .25
Minor Stars (1-60): .60
Unlisted Stars (1-60): .75
Common Card (61-90): 3.00
Production 699 Sets
Pack (5): 10.00
Box (10): 100.00
1 Hideki Matsui 2.50
2 Khalil Greene 1.00
3 Pedro J. Martinez 1.00
4 Sammy Sosa 2.00
5 Mark Teixeira .40
6 Orlando Cabrera .25
7 Scott Podsednik .25
8 Miguel Tejada .60
9 Andruw Jones .75
10 Manny Ramirez .75
11 Jose Reyes .25
12 Bobby Abreu .40
13 Alex Rodriguez 2.50
14 Ivan Rodriguez .60
15 Jason Schmidt .40
16 Mike Piazza 1.50
17 Eric Chavez .40
18 Mark Prior 1.50
19 Adam Dunn .60
20 Richard Hidalgo .25
21 Todd Helton .75
22 Rocco Baldelli .60
23 Roy Oswalt .40
24 Angel Berroa .25
25 Jason Giambi 1.00
26 Jim Thome 1.00
27 Javy Lopez .40
28 Derek Jeter 3.00
29 Tom Glavine .40
30 Magglio Ordonez .40
31 Austin Kearns .60
32 Scott Rolen 1.00
33 Miguel Cabrera .75
34 Vernon Wells .40
35 Frank Thomas .75
36 Jeff Bagwell .75
37 Shannon Stewart .25
38 Richie Sexson .60
39 Hideo Nomo .40
40 Nomar Garciaparra 2.50
41 C.C. Sabathia .25
42 Albert Pujols 2.50
43 Barry Zito .60
44 Hank Blalock .60
45 Carlos Delgado .75
46 Greg Maddux 1.50
47 Randy Johnson 1.00
48 Josh Beckett .75
49 Kerry Wood .75
50 Roger Clemens 1.50
51 Garret Anderson .40
52 Ichiro Suzuki 2.00
53 Kip Wells .25
54 Vladimir Guerrero 1.00
55 Shawn Green .40
56 Chipper Jones 1.50
57 Aubrey Huff .25
58 Ken Griffey Jr. 1.50
59 Torii Hunter .60
60 Alfonso Soriano 1.00
61 Chris Shelton **RC** 8.00
62 Graham Koonce 4.00
63 Kazuo Matsui **RC** 8.00
64 Alfredo Simon **RC** 4.00
65 Mike Gosling 3.00
66 Mike Rouse 4.00
67 Mariano Gomez **RC** 3.00
68 Justin Leone **RC** 3.00
69 Jose Capellan **RC** 3.00
70 Donald Kelly **RC** 4.00
71 Merkin Valdez **RC** 4.00
72 Greg Dobbs **RC** 4.00
73 Shingo Takatsu **RC** 4.00
74 Chris Aguila **RC** 3.00
75 Jerome Gamble **RC** 4.00
76 Onil Joseph **RC** 4.00
77 Ramon Ramirez **RC** 4.00
78 Angel Chavez **RC** 3.00
79 Hector Gimenez **RC** 3.00
80 Ivan Ochoa **RC** 4.00
81 Aarom Baldiris **RC** 4.00
82 Akinori Otsuka **RC** 4.00
83 Ruddy Yan **RC** 3.00
84 Jerry Gil **RC** 3.00
85 Shawn Hill **RC** 3.00
86 John Gall **RC** 4.00
87 Jason Bartlett **RC** 4.00
88 Jorge Sequea **RC** 4.00
89 Luis Gonzalez **RC** 4.00
90 Sean Henn 3.00

Red

(1-60): 1-4X
(61-90): .75-1.25X
Production 150 Sets

White

(1-60): 2X-6X
(61-90): .75X-2X
Production 50 Sets

Blue

No Pricing
Production One Set

American Flag Box Topper

No Pricing
Numbered to indicated quantity.

American GAME

NM/M
Common Player: 1.00
Inserted 1:10 (Hobby)
Inserted 1:12 (Retail)
1 Greg Maddux 2.50
2 Randy Johnson 2.00
3 Roger Clemens 4.00
4 Mark Prior 3.00
5 Mike Piazza 2.50
6 Alex Rodriguez 4.00
7 Adam Dunn 1.00
8 Jim Thome 2.00
9 Derek Jeter 5.00
10 Scott Rolen 2.00
11 Nomar Garciaparra 4.00
12 Kerry Wood 1.50
13 Chipper Jones 2.50
14 Frank Thomas 1.50
15 Jeff Bagwell 1.50

American Game Retired - Dual

Numbered between 10 & 25.
No Pricing

American Game Retired - Single

Numbered between 6 & 31.
No Pricing

American GAME - Jersey

NM/M
Common Player: 8.00
Inserted 1:96
Patch #'d between 25 & 50: 2-6X
Patch #'d less than 25: No Pricing
Masterpiece: No Pricing
Production One Set
JB Jeff Bagwell/50 8.00
RCL Roger Clemens/47 10.00
AD Adam Dunn/30 8.00
DJ Derek Jeter/10 15.00
RJO Randy Johnson/42 8.00
CJ Chipper Jones/37 10.00
GM Greg Maddux/46 12.00
MP Mike Piazza/29 10.00
MPR Mark Prior/45 10.00
AR Alex Rodriguez/13 15.00
SR Scott Rolen/49 8.00
FT Frank Thomas/35 8.00
JT Jim Thome/47 8.00
KW Kerry Wood/43 8.00

History in the Making

NM/M
Common Player: .75
Inserted 1:5 (Hobby)
Inserted 1:4 (Retail)
1 Pedro J. Martinez 1.50
2 Alex Rodriguez 3.00
3 Sammy Sosa 2.50
4 Mike Piazza 2.00
5 Jason Giambi 1.50
6 Jim Thome 1.50
7 Derek Jeter 4.00
8 Hideo Nomo .75
9 Nomar Garciaparra 3.00
10 Albert Pujols 3.00
11 Greg Maddux 2.00
12 Randy Johnson 1.50
13 Roger Clemens 2.00
14 Ichiro Suzuki 2.50
15 Vladimir Guerrero 1.50
16 Chipper Jones 2.00
17 Ken Griffey Jr. 2.00
18 Manny Ramirez 1.00
19 Ivan Rodriguez .75
20 Mark Prior 2.00
21 Austin Kearns .75
22 Alfonso Soriano 1.50
23 Barry Zito .75
24 Josh Beckett 1.00
25 Angel Berroa .75
26 Jose Reyes .75
27 Adam Dunn .75
28 Todd Helton 1.00
29 Hank Blalock .75
30 Kazuo Matsui 6.00

History in the Making - Jersey

NM/M
Common Player: 5.00
Inserted 1:36
Patch: 2-6X
Numbered between 20 & 50.
Masterpiece: No Pricing
Production One Set
JB Josh Beckett/45 8.00
AB Angel Berroa/20 5.00
MB Hank Blalock/48 8.00
RC Roger Clemens/26 10.00
AD Adam Dunn/49 8.00
JG Jason Giambi/24 8.00
VG Vladimir Guerrero/50 8.00
TH Todd Helton/32 8.00
DJ Derek Jeter/22 15.00
RJ Randy Johnson/50 8.00
CJ Chipper Jones/48 10.00
AK Austin Kearns/41 8.00
GM Greg Maddux/47 12.00
PM Pedro J. Martinez/45 8.00
KM Kazuo Matsui/20 20.00
HN Hideo Nomo/50 5.00
MP Mike Piazza/42 10.00
MPR Mark Prior/49 10.00
AP Albert Pujols/46 15.00
MR Manny Ramirez/46 8.00
JR Jose Reyes/37 5.00
AR Alex Rodriguez/21 15.00
IR Ivan Rodriguez/43 8.00
AS Alfonso Soriano/48 8.00
SS Sammy Sosa/39 12.00
JT Jim Thome/49 8.00
BZ Barry Zito/44 8.00

History in the Making Dual Swatch

No Pricing
Production Five Sets

Nat'l Pastime National Treasures

NM/M
Common Card: 3.00
Production 500 Sets
Gold: Numbered to notable year.
#75-99: 1-30X
#25-74: 1-5X
Less than 25: No Pricing
2NT Kenesaw Landis 3.00
5NT Leo Durocher 3.00
9NT Peter Gammons 3.00
10NT Ernie Harwell 3.00
11NT Billy Martin 4.00
12NT John McGraw 3.00
13NT Red Barber 3.00
15NT Casey Stengel 3.00
16NT Sparky Anderson 3.00
17NT Harry Caray 4.00
18NT Ban Johnson 3.00
20NT Ralph Kiner 3.00

National Treasures - Red

NM/M
Peter Gammons/50 20.00
Ernie Harwell/50 20.00
Ralph Kiner/50 20.00

National Treasures - White

NM/M
Ernie Harwell/30 15.00

National Treasures - Blue

No Pricing

National Treasures - Masterpiece

No Pricing

Signature Swing - Red

NM/M
Numbered to indicated quantity.
Carlos Beltran/109 25.00
Lance Berkman/98 20.00
Hank Blalock/109 20.00
George Brett/42 120.00
Sean Casey/108 15.00
Eric Chavez/85 20.00
Bucky Dent/35 20.00
David Eckstein/76 15.00
Carlton Fisk/51 40.00
Lew Ford/109 20.00
Jay Gibbons/33 20.00
Luis Gonzalez/109 10.00
Chipper Jones/88 40.00
Al Kaline/43 50.00
Javy Lopez/65 20.00
Don Mattingly/73 50.00
Bill Mazeroski/56 30.00
Stan Musial/36 60.00
Jim Palmer/25 25.00
Dave Parker/79 15.00
Mike Piazza/31 125.00
Albert Pujols/76 150.00
Gary Sheffield/26 60.00
Bill "Moose" Skowron/59 15.00
Warren Spahn/106 40.00
Alan Trammell/89 15.00

Signature Swing - White

NM/M
Numbered to indicated quantity.
Carlos Beltran/29 25.00
Lance Berkman/42 25.00
Hank Blalock/29 30.00
George Brett/30 120.00
Joe Carter/35 20.00
Sean Casey/25 20.00
Eric Chavez/34 25.00
Jim Edmonds/42 20.00
Carlton Fisk/37 40.00
Jay Gibbons/28 20.00
Luis Gonzalez/57 20.00
Vladimir Guerrero/44 30.00
Frank Howard/48 25.00
Aubrey Huff/34 15.00
Chipper Jones/45 50.00
Al Kaline/29 50.00
Javy Lopez/43 20.00
Edgar Martinez/37 30.00
Don Mattingly/35 80.00
Stan Musial/39 60.00
Rafael Palmeiro/47 50.00
Dave Parker/34 15.00
Mike Piazza/40 125.00
Albert Pujols/43 175.00
Cal Ripken Jr./25 200.00
Ivan Rodriguez/35 50.00
Scott Rolen/28 80.00
Gary Sheffield/43 60.00
Bill "Moose" Skowron/28 20.00
Frank Thomas/43 80.00
Alan Trammell/28 20.00

Signature Swing - Blue

NM/M
Numbered to indicated quantity.
Sean Casey/37 40.00
Adam Dunn/31 20.00
David Eckstein/44 15.00
Jim Edmonds/37 20.00
Lew Ford/44 40.00
Bill Mazeroski/39 50.00
Jim Palmer/44 25.00
Dave Parker/29 15.00
Scott Podsednik/38 20.00
Warren Spahn/26 50.00

Signature Swing - Gold

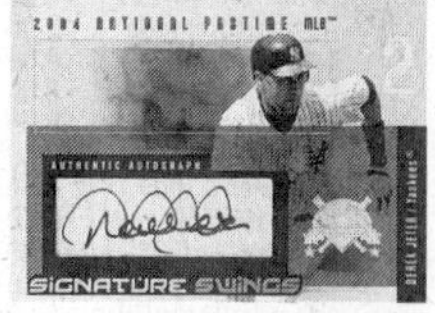

NM/M
Numbered to indicated quantity.
Carlos Beltran/176 25.00
Lance Berkman/173 15.00
Hank Blalock/265 15.00
Joe Carter/95 12.00
Sean Casey/169 12.00
Eric Chavez/138 15.00
David Eckstein/161 10.00
Carlton Fisk/36 40.00
Lew Ford/183 20.00
Luis Gonzalez/61 15.00
Frank Howard/60 20.00
Derek Jeter/35 125.00
Chipper Jones/116 40.00
Al Kaline/79 40.00
Javy Lopez/220 15.00
Edgar Martinez/85 20.00
Bill Mazeroski/61 25.00
Jim Palmer/33 25.00
Dave Parker/57 15.00
Mike Piazza/64 100.00
Albert Pujols/110 125.00
Gary Sheffield/25 60.00
Warren Spahn/182 30.00
Alan Trammell/138 10.00

Signature Swing - Masterpiece

No Pricing

Signs of the Future - Red

NM/M
Numbered to indicated quantity.
Aarom Baldiris/64 10.00
Jeremy Bonderman/120 10.00
A.J. Burnett/58 20.00
Miguel Cabrera/133 25.00
Bobby Crosby/114 20.00
Adam Everett/106 12.00
Luis Gonzalez/132 10.00
Mike Gosling/132 10.00
Khalil Greene/121 50.00
Rich Harden/133 15.00
Sean Henn/128 10.00
Koyie Hill/58 12.00
Edwin Jackson/52 15.00
Graham Koonce/55 10.00
Josh Labandeira/55 8.00
Adam LaRoche/124 8.00
Justin Leone/68 20.00

Micheal Nakamura/133 10.00
Bubba Nelson/99 10.00
Jose Reyes/93 25.00
Mike Rouse/124 8.00
Alfredo Simon/112 10.00
Ryan Wagner/98 12.00
Kerry Wood/55 30.00
Kevin Youkilis/133 20.00

Signs of the Future - White

NM/M
Numbered to indicated quantity.
Garrett Atkins/25 15.00
Miguel Cabrera/34 40.00
Bobby Crosby/52 30.00
Adam Everett/36 15.00
Luis Gonzalez/50 15.00
Mike Gosling/41 12.00
Khalil Greene/52 80.00
Rich Harden/52 20.00
Sean Henn/48 12.00
Koyie Hill/27 15.00
Tim Hudson/28 40.00
Adam LaRoche/50 12.00
Micheal Nakamura/33 15.00
Jose Reyes/52 30.00
Alexis Rios/39 15.00
Mike Rouse/40 10.00
Alfredo Simon/28 15.00
Ryan Wagner/46 15.00
Kevin Youkilis/52 25.00

Signs of the Future - Blue

NM/M
Numbered to indicated quantity.
Javier Vazquez/98 15.00
Kerry Wood/98 25.00

Signs of the Future - Gold

NM/M
Numbered to indicated quantity.
Jeremy Bonderman/300 8.00
Miguel Cabrera/300 20.00
Bobby Crosby/299 20.00
Adam Everett/285 10.00
Luis Gonzalez/264 8.00
Mike Gosling/195 8.00
Khalil Greene/300 50.00
Rich Harden/304 10.00
Sean Henn/300 8.00
Koyie Hill/340 8.00
Ryan Howard/53 60.00
Tim Hudson/72 20.00
Adam LaRoche/78 8.00
Micheal Nakamura/231 8.00
Alexis Rios/45 15.00
Alfredo Simon/258 8.00
Javier Vazquez/21 20.00
Ryan Wagner/251 10.00
Dontrelle Willis/47 40.00
Kevin Youkilis/317 15.00

1959 Fleer Ted Williams Reprint Set

May 16, 1954 — Ted Is Patched Up

NM/M
Ted Williams Card (1-81): 6.00
Production 406 Sets
Masterpiece: No Pricing
Production One Set
1-80 Ted Williams 6.00

Ted Williams Reprint Game-Used

No Pricing
Production Nine Sets

2004 Fleer Authentix

NM/M
Complete Set (130):
Common Player: .25
Common SP (101-130): 2.50
Production 999
Pack (5): 4.00
Box (24): 80.00
1 Albert Pujols 2.50
2 Derek Jeter 3.00
3 Jody Gerut .25
4 Mark Teixeira .40
5 Tom Glavine .50
6 Kerry Wood 1.00
7 Ichiro Suzuki 1.50
8 Jose Vidro .25

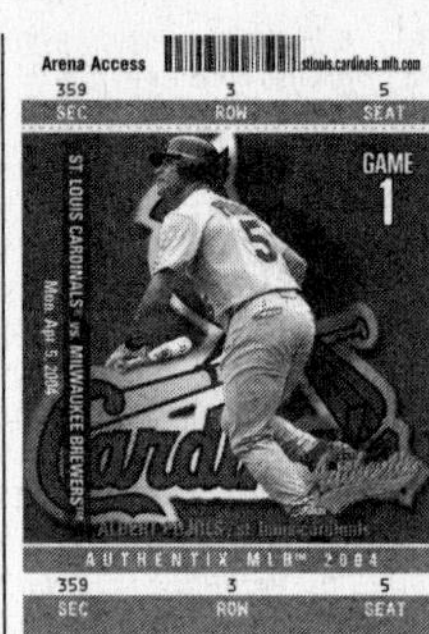

9 Mark Prior 1.50
10 Jim Edmonds .50
11 Richie Sexson .50
12 Jay Gibbons .25
13 Jason Kendall .25
14 Lance Berkman .50
15 Andruw Jones .75
16 Jim Thome 1.00
17 Josh Beckett .75
18 Troy Glaus .50
19 Jason Giambi 1.00
20 Sammy Sosa 2.00
21 Bret Boone .40
22 Eric Gagne .40
23 Nomar Garciaparra 2.00
24 Geoff Jenkins .50
25 Ivan Rodriguez .50
26 Preston Wilson .40
27 Alex Rodriguez 2.50
28 Jorge Posada .50
29 Ken Griffey Jr. 1.50
30 Rocco Baldelli .50
31 Shannon Stewart .25
32 Frank Thomas .75
33 Edgar Renteria .25
34 Torii Hunter .50
35 Corey Patterson .25
36 Edgar Martinez .40
37 Jeff Bagwell .75
38 Greg Maddux 1.50
39 Mike Lieberthal .25
40 Craig Biggio .40
41 Randy Johnson 1.00
42 Marlon Byrd .25
43 Jay Payton .25
44 Carlos Delgado .75
45 Scott Podsednik .50
46 Pedro J. Martinez 1.00
47 Carlos Beltran .40
48 Mike Sweeney .25
49 Gary Sheffield .50
50 Pat Burrell .50
51 Shawn Green .40
52 Tony Batista .25
53 Brian Giles .40
54 Roy Oswalt .40
55 Brandon Webb .40
56 Miguel Tejada .50
57 Miguel Cabrera .75
58 Luis Gonzalez .40
59 Billy Wagner .25
60 Craig Monroe .25
61 Vernon Wells .40
62 Bernie Williams .50
63 Austin Kearns .50
64 Aubrey Huff .25
65 Mike Piazza 1.50
66 Magglio Ordonez .50
67 Bo Hart .25
68 Hideo Nomo .50
69 Curt Schilling .50
70 Barry Zito .50
71 Todd Helton .75
72 Roy Halladay .50
73 Alfonso Soriano 1.00
74 Roberto Alomar .50
75 Scott Rolen 1.00
76 Manny Ramirez .75
77 Sean Burroughs .25
78 Angel Berroa .25
79 Javy Lopez .40
80 Reggie Sanders .25
81 Juan Pierre .25
82 Chipper Jones 1.50
83 Bobby Abreu .40
84 Dontrelle Willis .40
85 Tim Salmon .40
86 Eric Chavez .40
87 Adam Dunn .50
88 Rafael Palmeiro .75
89 Hideki Matsui 2.50
90 Esteban Loaiza .25
91 Darin Erstad .40
92 Vladimir Guerrero 1.00
93 David Ortiz .25
94 Jason Schmidt .40
95 Dmitri Young .25
96 Garret Anderson .50
97 Mark Mulder .25
98 Omar Vizquel .25
99 Hank Blalock .50
100 Jose Reyes .25
101 Rickie Weeks 8.00
102 Chad Gaudin 2.50
103 Ryan Wagner 3.00
104 Koyie Hill 2.50
105 Rich Harden 2.50
106 Edwin Jackson 4.00
107 Khalil Greene 3.00
108 Chien-Ming Wang 3.00
109 Matt Kata 2.50
110 Chin-Hui Tsao 2.50
111 Dan Haren 2.50
112 Delmon Young 8.00
113 Mike Hessman 2.50
114 Bobby Crosby 2.50
115 Cory Sullivan **RC** 2.50
116 Brandon Watson 2.50
117 Aaron Miles 2.50
118 Jonny Gomes 2.50
119 Graham Koonce 2.50
120 Shawn Hill **RC** 2.50
121 Garrett Atkins 2.50
122 John Gall **RC** 2.50
123 Chad Bentz **RC** 2.50
124 Alfredo Simon **RC** 2.50
125 Josh Labandeira **RC** 3.00
126 Ryan Howard 3.00
127 Jason Bartlett **RC** 2.50
128 Dallas McPherson 2.50
129 Greg Dobbs **RC** 2.50
130 Jerry Gil **RC** 2.50

Balcony

Stars (1-100): 4-8X
SP's (101-130): 1-2X
Production 100 Sets

Club Box

Stars (1-100): 10-15X
SP's (101-130): 2-4X
Production 25 Sets

Standing Room Only

No Pricing
Production Five Sets

Autographed Authentix

NM/M
Common Autograph: 15.00
Production 75
Championship: No Pricing
Production 25
Rocco Baldelli 40.00
Angel Berroa 15.00
Marlon Byrd 15.00
Miguel Cabrera 40.00
Eric Gagne 40.00
Roy Halladay 20.00
Trot Nixon 35.00
Juan Pierre 15.00
Albert Pujols 120.00
Vernon Wells 20.00

Ballpark Classics

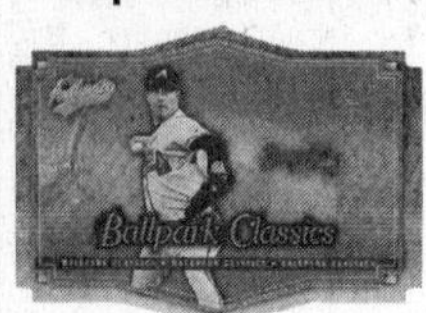

NM/M
Complete Set (10): 15.00
Common Player: 1.00
Inserted 1:12
1BC Nomar Garciaparra 3.00
2BC Alfonso Soriano 1.50
3BC Chipper Jones 1.50
4BC Albert Pujols 3.00
5BC Jason Giambi 1.00
6BC Mark Prior 2.00
7BC Sammy Sosa 2.50
8BC Derek Jeter 4.00
9BC Greg Maddux 2.00
10BC Alex Rodriguez 3.00

Ballpar Classics Game-Used

NM/M
Common Player: 8.00
Inserted 1:37
Nomar Garciaparra 10.00
Jason Giambi 8.00
Derek Jeter 15.00
Chipper Jones 8.00
Greg Maddux 10.00
Mark Prior 10.00
Albert Pujols 15.00
Alex Rodriguez 10.00
Alfonso Soriano 8.00
Sammy Sosa 12.00

Jersey Authentix Autograph

NM/M
Common Autograph: 15.00
Production 100
All-Star Autographs: 1-1.25X
Production 50
Championship Autos.: No Pricing
Production 10
Albert Pujols 125.00
Juan Pierre 15.00
Miguel Cabrera 40.00
Eric Gagne 40.00
Marlon Byrd 15.00
Rocco Baldelli 40.00
Roy Halladay 25.00
Vernon Wells 20.00
Trot Nixon 35.00

Jersey Authentix Game of the Week

NM/M
Common Duo: 10.00
Inserted 1:120
Unripped: 1-1.5X
Production 50
1 Dontrelle Willis, Kerry Wood 20.00
2 Miguel Cabrera, Mark Teixeira 15.00
3 Nomar Garciaparra, Alfonso Soriano 15.00
4 Jim Thome, Ivan Rodriguez 10.00
5 Josh Beckett, Mark Prior 15.00
6 Alex Rodriguez, Derek Jeter 35.00
7 Jeff Bagwell, Austin Kearns 15.00
8 Jason Giambi, Barry Zito 10.00
9 Jose Reyes, Juan Pierre 10.00
10 Chipper Jones, Albert Pujols 20.00

Jersey Authentix Ripped

NM/M
Common Player: 4.00
Inserted 1:16
Unripped: 2-3X
Production 50 Sets
All-Star Unripped: No Pricing
Production One Set
Jeff Bagwell 8.00
Josh Beckett 6.00
Miguel Cabrera 8.00
Hee Seop Choi 4.00
Nomar Garciaparra 10.00
Jason Giambi 8.00
Torii Hunter 5.00
Derek Jeter 15.00
Randy Johnson 8.00
Chipper Jones 8.00
Austin Kearns 6.00
Greg Maddux 8.00
Juan Pierre 4.00
Mark Prior 10.00
Albert Pujols 15.00
Jose Reyes 8.00
Alex Rodriguez 10.00
Ivan Rodriguez 6.00
Alfonso Soriano 8.00
Sammy Sosa 12.00
Mark Teixeira 6.00
Jim Thome 8.00
Dontrelle Willis 6.00
Kerry Wood 8.00
Barry Zito 6.00

Ticket for Four

NM/M
Common Quad Jersey: 20.00
Production 100 Sets
1 Dontrelle Willis, Josh Beckett, Mark Prior, Kerry Wood 20.00
2 Nomar Garciaparra, Alex Rodriguez, Derek Jeter, Jose Reyes 50.00
4 Jason Giambi, Jim Thome, Mark Teixeira, Jeff Bagwell 25.00
5 Chipper Jones, Albert Pujols, Sammy Sosa, Torii Hunter 40.00
6 Greg Maddux, Randy Johnson, Kerry Wood, Barry Zito 20.00
7 Nomar Garciaparra, Alfonso Soriano, Chipper Jones, Albert Pujols 40.00
8 Sammy Sosa, Derek Jeter, Alex Rodriguez, Jim Thome 50.00
9 Mark Prior, Greg Maddux, Austin Kearns, Ivan Rodriguez 15.00
10 Jason Giambi, Randy Johnson, Jeff Bagwell, Torii Hunter 20.00

Ticket Studs

NM/M
Complete Set (15): 20.00
Common Player: .75
Inserted 1:6
1TS Nomar Garciaparra 3.00
2TS Josh Beckett 1.00
3TS Derek Jeter 4.00

4TS Mark Prior 2.00
5TS Albert Pujols 3.00
6TS Alfonso Soriano 1.50
7TS Jim Thome 1.50
8TS Ichiro Suzuki 2.00
9TS Hideki Matsui 3.00
10TS Dontrelle Willis .75
11TS Mike Schmidt 2.00
12TS Nolan Ryan 4.00
13TS Reggie Jackson 1.00
14TS Tom Seaver 1.00
15TS Brooks Robinson 1.00

2004 Fleer Classic Clippings

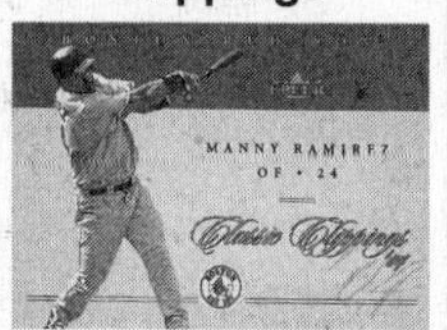

NM/M
Common Player (1-75): .25
Minor Stars (1-75): .40
Unlisted Stars (1-75): .60
Common Player (76-110): 5.00
Production 500 Sets
Pack (5): 5.00
Box (18): 90.00
1 Juan Pierre .25
2 Derek Jeter 3.00
3 Jose Reyes .40
4 Eric Chavez .40
5 Alex Rodriguez 2.50
6 Mark Prior 2.00
7 Carlos Beltran .40
8 Ichiro Suzuki 2.00
9 Shawn Green .40
10 Richie Sexson .60
11 Andruw Jones .75
12 Geoff Jenkins .40
13 Luis Gonzalez .40
14 Garret Anderson .40
15 Adam Dunn .60
16 Nomar Garciaparra 2.50
17 Albert Pujols 2.50
18 Jeff Bagwell .75
19 Rocco Baldelli .60
20 Preston Wilson .25
21 Gary Sheffield .60
22 Magglio Ordonez .40
23 Kerry Wood .75
24 Manny Ramirez .75
25 Randy Johnson 1.00
26 Ken Griffey Jr. 1.50
27 Rafael Palmeiro .40
28 Vernon Wells .25
29 Mike Piazza 1.50
30 Hank Blalock .60
31 Miguel Cabrera .75
32 Jason Giambi 1.00
33 Troy Glaus .60
34 Angel Berroa .25
35 Greg Maddux 1.50
36 Lance Berkman .40
37 Austin Kearns .60
38 Hideo Nomo .40
39 Sammy Sosa 2.00
40 Jose Vidro .25
41 Curt Schilling .60
42 Melvin Mora .25
43 Scott Podsednik .40
44 Dontrelle Willis .40
45 Roy Halladay .40
46 Hideki Matsui 2.50
47 Tom Glavine .40
48 Torii Hunter .60
49 Chipper Jones 1.50
50 Barry Zito .60
51 Vladimir Guerrero 1.00
52 Jim Thome 1.00
53 Shannon Stewart .25
54 Miguel Tejada .60
55 Roy Oswalt .40
56 Jason Kendall .40
57 Brian Giles .40
58 Jason Schmidt .40
59 Pedro J. Martinez 1.00
60 Bret Boone .40
61 Josh Beckett .75
62 Scott Rolen 1.00
63 Aubrey Huff .25
64 Pat Burrell .40
65 Mark Teixeira .40
66 Alfonso Soriano 1.00
67 Carlos Delgado .75
68 Ivan Rodriguez .60
69 Brandon Webb .25
70 Eric Gagne .40
71 Frank Thomas .75
72 Jody Gerut .25
73 Todd Helton .75
74 Andy Pettitte .60
75 Roger Clemens 1.50
76 Rickie Weeks 8.00
77 Chien-Ming Wang 8.00
78 Edwin Jackson 6.00
79 Dallas McPherson 8.00
80 John Gall **RC** 5.00
81 Ryan Wagner 6.00
82 Clint Barmes 8.00
83 Khalil Greene 6.00
84 Chin-Hui Tsao 6.00
85 Alexis Rios 6.00
86 Merkin Valdez **RC** 5.00
87 Aarom Baldiris **RC** 5.00
88 Onil Joseph **RC** 5.00
89 Ruddy Yan **RC** 5.00
90 Chad Bentz **RC** 5.00
91 Shawn Hill **RC** 5.00
92 Delmon Young 8.00
93 Hector Gimenez **RC** 5.00
94 William Bergolla **RC** 5.00
95 Ronny Cedeno **RC** 5.00
96 Angel Chavez **RC** 5.00
97 Justin Leone **RC** 5.00
98 Ivan Ochoa **RC** 5.00
99 Ian Snell **RC** 10.00
100 Rich Harden 6.00
101 Joe Mauer 10.00
102 Akinori Otsuka **RC** 10.00
103 Bobby Crosby 6.00
104 Garrett Atkins 5.00
105 Dan Haren 5.00
106 Koyie Hill 5.00
107 Kazuo Matsui **RC** 20.00
108 Adam LaRoche 5.00
109 Terrmel Sledge 5.00
110 Shingo Takatsu **RC** 5.00

First Edition

(1-75): 1-5X
(76-110): .5-1.25X
Production 150 Sets

All-Star Lineup Triple Jersey Silver

NM/M
Common Card: 15.00
Production 75 Sets
Gold Triple Patch: 2-4X
Production 25 Sets
No Gold Card For ASL-SMA
S/C/G Alfonso Soriano, Roger Clemens, Jason Giambi 25.00
R/G/R Alex Rodriguez, Nomar Garciaparra, Manny Ramirez 25.00
W/P/W Kerry Wood, Mark Prior, Dontrelle Willis 25.00
S/P/W Gary Sheffield, Albert Pujols, Preston Wilson 20.00
C/H/R Luis Castillo, Todd Helton, Scott Rolen 15.00
D/S/G Carlos Delgado, Alfonso Soriano, Troy Glaus 15.00
W/D/H Vernon Wells, Carlos Delgado, Roy Halladay 15.00
S/M/A Ichiro Suzuki, Hideki Matsui, Garret Anderson 30.00
R/R/P Edgar Renteria, Scott Rolen, Albert Pujols 50.00
S/J/L Gary Sheffield, Andruw Jones, Javy Lopez 15.00
C/Z/H Roger Clemens, Barry Zito, Roy Halladay 20.00
C/W/L Luis Castillo, Dontrelle Willis, Mike Lowell 10.00
O/B/G Magglio Ordonez, Hank Blalock, Troy Glaus 15.00
G/R/G Nomar Garciaparra, Alex Rodriguez, Jason Giambi 40.00
H/S/P Todd Helton, Richie Sexson, Albert Pujols 20.00

Bat Rack (3 Bat) - Green

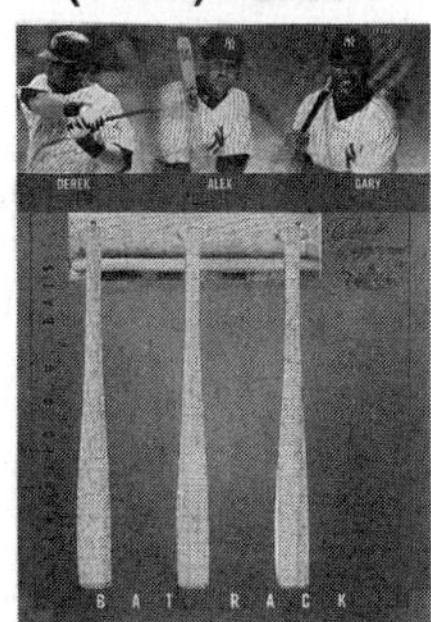

NM/M
Common Card: 10.00
Production 175 Sets
Red: .5-1.5X
Production 50 Sets
Gold: 1-2X
Production 25 Sets
Derek Jeter, Alex Rodriguez, Gary Sheffield 40.00
Sammy Sosa, Derek Lee, Mark Prior 25.00
Miguel Cabrera, Juan Pierre, Josh Beckett 15.00
Nomar Garciaparra, Manny Ramirez, Curt Schilling 20.00
Alfonso Soriano, Hank Blalock, Mark Teixeira 15.00
Mike Piazza, Jose Reyes, Kazuo Matsui 20.00
Richie Sexson, Brandon Webb, Roberto Alomar 10.00
Mark Prior, Josh Beckett, Curt Schilling 15.00
Carlos Delgado, Aubrey Huff, Jason Giambi 10.00
Albert Pujols, Scott Rolen, Jim Edmonds 30.00
Rocco Baldelli, Aubrey Huff, Carlos Delgado 10.00
Jeff Bagwell, Jim Thome, Todd Helton 15.00
Gary Sheffield, Manny Ramirez, Rocco Baldelli 10.00
Troy Glaus, Scott Rolen, Hank Blalock 15.00
Roberto Alomar, Jose Reyes, Alfonso Soriano 15.00
Alex Rodriguez, Miguel Tejada, Miguel Cabrera 15.00
Vladimir Guerrero, Juan Pierre, Chipper Jones 10.00
Jason Giambi, Jim Thome, Todd Helton 15.00
Vladimir Guerrero, Albert Pujols, Sammy Sosa 25.00
Derek Jeter, Hideki Matsui, Nomar Garciaparra 40.00

Bat Rack (4 Bat) - Green

NM/M
Common Card: 15.00
Production 75 Sets
Red: 1-2X
Production 25 Sets
Gold: No Pricing
Production 10 Sets
Derek Jeter, Alex Rodriguez, Gary Sheffield, Jason Giambi 50.00
Sammy Sosa, Mark Prior, Miguel Cabrera, Josh Beckett 30.00
Derek Jeter, Alex Rodriguez, Kazuo Matsui, Nomar Garciaparra 60.00
Juan Pierre, Gary Sheffield, Miguel Cabrera, Rocco Baldelli 15.00
Jim Thome, Jeff Bagwell, Mark Teixeira, Carlos Delgado 20.00
Albert Pujols, Mark Prior, Alex Rodriguez, Curt Schilling 40.00
Todd Helton, Jose Reyes, Kazuo Matsui, Scott Rolen 40.00
Sammy Sosa, Vladimir Guerrero, Jim Edmonds, Chipper Jones 25.00
Alfonso Soriano, Roberto Alomar, Hank Blalock, Troy Glaus 15.00
Rocco Baldelli, Chipper Jones, Juan Pierre, Manny Ramirez 20.00
Jim Thome, Jeff Bagwell, Todd Helton, Derek Lee 20.00
Curt Schilling, Nomar Garciaparra, Brandon Webb, Richie Sexson 25.00
Mike Piazza, Jose Reyes, Albert Pujols, Scott Rolen 30.00
Vladimir Guerrero, Miguel Tejada, Jason Giambi, Mike Piazza 25.00
Jeff Bagwell, Derrek Lee, Aubrey Huff, Carlos Delgado 20.00

Bat Rack Autographs-Bronze

NM/M
Common Player: 12.00
Production 75 Sets
Roberto Alomar 40.00
Josh Beckett 40.00
Hank Blalock 30.00
Miguel Cabrera 40.00
Jim Edmonds 30.00
Aubrey Huff 12.00
Edgar Martinez 20.00
Jose Reyes 25.00
Gary Sheffield 30.00
Mark Teixeira 20.00

Classic Clippings

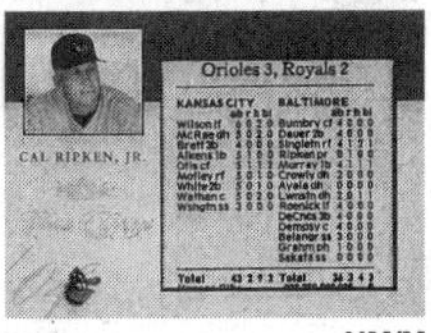

NM/M
Common Player (1-20): 4.00
Production 750 Sets
Common Player (21-25): 8.00
Production 100 Sets
1CC Nolan Ryan 15.00
2CC Mike Schmidt 6.00
3CC Cal Ripken Jr. 10.00
4CC Don Mattingly 8.00
5CC Roger Clemens 5.00
6CC Randy Johnson 4.00
7CC Mark Prior 3.00
8CC Jim Thome 5.00
9CC Sammy Sosa 5.00
10CC Pedro J. Martinez 4.00
11CC Chipper Jones 4.00
12CC Vladimir Guerrero 4.00
13CC Albert Pujols 6.00
14CC Ichiro Suzuki 6.00
15CC Derek Jeter 10.00
16CC Alex Rodriguez 8.00
17CC Greg Maddux 5.00
18CC Nomar Garciaparra 8.00
19CC Mike Piazza 6.00
20CC Ken Griffey Jr. 8.00
21CC Pie Traynor 8.00
22CC Bill Dickey 8.00
23CC George Sisler 10.00
24CC Ted Williams 20.00
25CC Enos Slaughter 8.00

C.C. Signature Edition

NM/M
Common Player: 15.00
Production 50 Sets
Masterpiece: No Pricing
Production One Set
1 Nolan Ryan 125.00
2 Mike Schmidt 75.00
3 Cal Ripken Jr. 175.00
4 Don Mattingly 75.00
5 Albert Pujols 125.00
6 Randy Johnson 60.00
7 Khalil Greene 40.00
8 Rickie Weeks 30.00
9 Edwin Jackson 15.00
10 Rich Harden 15.00
16 Vladimir Guerrero 40.00
17 Mark Prior 40.00

Jersey Rack (3 Jersey) - Blue

NM/M
Common Card: 15.00
Production 225 Sets
Bronze Jersey: .5-1.25X
Production 99 Sets
Silver Jersey: .75-1.5X
Production To Player's Jersey No.
Patch Pack Gold: No Pricing
Production 125 Sets
Derek Jeter, Alex Rodriguez, Jason Giambi 50.00
Sammy Sosa, Kerry Wood, Mark Prior 25.00
Miguel Cabrera, Dontrelle Willis, Josh Beckett 15.00
Nomar Garciaparra, Pedro J. Martinez, Curt Schilling 15.00
Alex Rodriguez, Derek Jeter, Nomar Garciaparra 40.00
Mike Piazza, Ivan Rodriguez, Javy Lopez 20.00
Roger Clemens, Mark Prior, Josh Beckett 20.00
Roger Clemens, Andy Pettitte, Roy Oswalt 40.00
Dontrelle Willis, Kerry Wood, Curt Schilling 20.00
Albert Pujols, Sammy Sosa, Manny Ramirez 20.00
Rocco Baldelli, Miguel Cabrera, Albert Pujols 20.00
Barry Zito, Tim Hudson, Mark Mulder 15.00
Randy Johnson, Richie Sexson, Brandon Webb 15.00
Dontrelle Willis, Brandon Webb, Angel Berroa 15.00
Carlos Delgado, Miguel Tejada, Alfonso Soriano 15.00

Jersey Rack Autograph - Bronze

NM/M
Common Player: 12.00
Production 149 Sets
Silver Jersey: .5-1.5X
Production 50 Sets
Patch Rack Gold: No Pricing
Production To Player's Jersey No.
Garret Anderson 15.00
Garrett Atkins 12.00
Rocco Baldelli 20.00
Josh Beckett 20.00
Angel Berroa 15.00
Marlon Byrd 12.00
Miguel Cabrera 40.00
Carlos Delgado 20.00
Jody Gerut 12.00
Roy Halladay 15.00
Dan Haren 12.00
Torii Hunter 15.00
Edwin Jackson 20.00
Barry Larkin 40.00
Mark Mulder 15.00
Mike Mussina 30.00
Andy Pettitte 40.00
Albert Pujols 120.00
Ivan Rodriguez 50.00
Scott Rolen 50.00
Ryan Wagner 12.00
Brandon Webb 15.00
Dontrelle Willis 20.00
Kerry Wood 30.00

Phenom Lineup Autograph - Red

NM/M
Common Card: 10.00
Production 150 Sets
Silver: .5-1.25X
Production 99 Sets
Gold: .5-1.5X
Production 50 Sets
Cards contain autograph of the first player listed.
Ryan Howard, Jim Thome, Todd Helton 10.00
John Gall, Albert Pujols, Scott Rolen 10.00
Jose Reyes, Kazuo Matsui, Rickie Weeks 20.00
Hank Blalock, Troy Glaus, Alex Rodriguez 20.00
Rich Harden, Roy Halladay, Barry Zito 10.00
Alexis Rios, Carlos Delgado, Vernon Wells 10.00
Laynce Nix, Alex Rodriguez, Garret Anderson 10.00
Khalil Greene, Edgar Renteria, Mike Lowell 25.00
Dontrelle Willis, Mark Prior, Kerry Wood 15.00
Rickie Weeks, Luis Castillo, Jose Reyes 20.00
Dallas McPherson, Troy Glaus, Garret Anderson 15.00
Chien-Ming Wang, Hideki Matsui, Jason Giambi 20.00
Scott Podsednik, Albert Pujols, Andruw Jones 15.00
Bobby Crosby, Nomar Garciaparra, Alex Rodriguez 18.00
Ryan Wagner, Dontrelle Willis, Mark Prior 8.00
Delmon Young, Ichiro Suzuki, Hideki Matsui 30.00
Grady Sizemore, Manny Ramirez, Garret Anderson 20.00
Adam LaRoche, Albert Pujols, Jim Thome 10.00
Edwin Jackson, Mark Prior, Kerry Wood 10.00
Miguel Cabrera, Luis Castillo, Mike Lowell 40.00
Merkin Valdez, Edwin Jackson, Dontrelle Willis 10.00
Angel Berroa, Nomar Garciaparra, Alex Rodriguez 10.00

Press Clippings

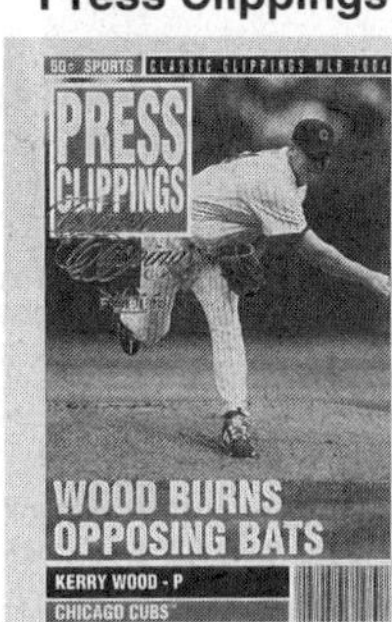

NM/M
Common Player: 1.25
Inserted 1:6
1PC Josh Beckett 1.75
2PC Albert Pujols 4.00
3PC Derek Jeter 5.00
4PC Alex Rodriguez 5.00
5PC Jim Thome 2.00
6PC Angel Berroa 1.00
7PC Dontrelle Willis 1.25
8PC Roy Halladay 1.25
9PC Kerry Wood 1.75
10PC Mark Prior 3.00
11PC Roger Clemens 3.00
12PC Hideki Matsui 4.00
13PC Ichiro Suzuki 3.50
14PC Eric Gagne 1.25
15PC Miguel Cabrera 1.75
16PC Nomar Garciaparra 4.00
17PC Hank Blalock 1.25
18PC Chipper Jones 3.00
19PC Sammy Sosa 3.50
20PC Alfonso Soriano 2.00

Press Proof Black

(1-100): No Pricing
Production One Set

Press Proof Cyan

(1-100): No Pricing
Production One Set

Press Proof Magenta

(1-100): No Pricing
Production One Set

Press Proof Yellow

(1-100): No Pricing
Production One Set

2004 Fleer EX

NM/M
Common Player (1-40): 1.50
Minor Stars (1-40): 2.00
Unlisted Stars (1-40): 2.50
Common Player (41-65): 5.00
Production 500 Sets
Die-Cuts (41-65): .75-1.25X
First 150 seq. #'d cards are die-cut.
1 Vladimir Guerrero 3.50
2 Randy Johnson 3.50
3 Chipper Jones 4.00
4 Miguel Tejada 2.50
5 Pedro J. Martinez 3.50
6 Nomar Garciaparra 6.00
7 Sammy Sosa 5.00
8 Greg Maddux 4.00
9 Frank Thomas 3.00
10 Ken Griffey Jr. 4.00
11 Omar Vizquel 2.00
12 Todd Helton 3.00
13 Ivan Rodriguez 2.50
14 Miguel Cabrera 3.00
15 Dontrelle Willis 2.00
16 Jeff Bagwell 3.00
17 Roger Clemens 4.00
18 Carlos Beltran 2.00
19 Hideo Nomo 2.00
20 Scott Podsednik 1.50
21 Torii Hunter 2.50
22 Jose Vidro 1.50
23 Mike Piazza 4.00
24 Hideki Matsui 6.00
25 Alex Rodriguez 6.00
26 Derek Jeter 8.00
27 Tim Hudson 2.00
28 Jim Thome 3.50
29 Craig Wilson 1.50
30 Brian Giles 2.00
31 Jason Schmidt 2.00
32 Ichiro Suzuki 5.00
33 Scott Rolen 3.50
34 Albert Pujols 6.00
35 Rocco Baldelli 2.50
36 Alfonso Soriano 3.50
37 Carlos Delgado 3.00
38 Curt Schilling 2.50
39 Mark Prior 4.00
40 Josh Beckett 3.00
41 Merkin Valdez **RC** 5.00
42 Akinori Otsuka **RC** 8.00
43 Ian Snell **RC** 8.00
44 Kazuo Matsui **RC** 10.00
45 Jason Bartlett **RC** 8.00
46 Dennis Sarfate **RC** 5.00
47 Sean Henn 5.00
48 David Aardsma 5.00
49 Casey Kotchman 8.00
50 John Gall **RC** 5.00
51 William Bergolla **RC** 5.00
52 Angel Chavez **RC** 5.00
53 Hector Gimenez **RC** 5.00
54 Aarom Baldiris **RC** 5.00
55 Justin Leone **RC** 8.00
56 Onil Joseph **RC** 5.00
57 Freddy Guzman **RC** 5.00
58 Andres Blanco **RC** 5.00
59 Greg Dobbs **RC** 5.00
60 Joe Mauer 5.00
61 Luis Gonzalez **RC** 8.00
62 Chris Saenz **RC** 5.00
63 Zack Greinke 5.00
64 Jose Capellan **RC** 8.00
65 Brad Halsey **RC** 10.00

Essential Credentials Future

Cards 1-25: .75-2X
Cards 26-40: 2-4X
Cards 41-65: No Pricing
Production 65 - 1 Sets

Essential Credentials Now

Cards 51-65: 1-2X
Cards 41-50: 1.25-2.25X
Cards 25-40: 3-5X
Cards 1-24: No Pricing
Production 65 - 1 Sets

Check Mates

NM/M
Production 1 or 25 Sets
1 Albert Pujols, Stan Musial/25 500.00
2 Eddie Murray, Rafael Palmeiro/25 200.00
4 Ernie Banks, Ryne Sandberg/25 300.00
9 Manny Ramirez, Pedro J. Martinez/25 300.00
10 Wade Boggs, Tony Gwynn/25 175.00
11 Reggie Jackson, Don Mattingly/25 200.00
14 Robin Yount, Kirby Puckett/25 150.00

Classic ConnEXions Doubles

No Pricing
Production 22 Sets
Emerald: No Pricing
Production One Set

Classic ConnEXions Triples

No Pricing
Production 13 Sets
Emerald: No Pricing
Production One Set

Clearly Authentics Signature Black Jersey

NM/M
Sequentially #'d to varying quantities.
Burgundy Buttons: No Pricing
Production 6 Sets
Emerald MLB Logo: No Pricing
Production One Set
Josh Beckett/50 30.00
Hank Blalock/50 50.00
Miguel Cabrera/50 30.00
Roger Clemens/50 150.00
J.D. Drew 30.00
Troy Glaus/50 25.00
Vladimir Guerrero/50 50.00
Todd Helton/50 40.00
Chipper Jones/50 60.00
Roy Oswalt/49 30.00
Rafael Palmeiro/43 60.00
Albert Pujols/50 225.00
Manny Ramirez/50 60.00
Mariano Rivera/50 80.00
Gary Sheffield/50 50.00

Frank Thomas/50 60.00
Bernie Williams/42 75.00
Dontrelle Willis/50 25.00
Kerry Wood/34 50.00

Clearly Authentics Black Patch

NM/M
Common Player: 10.00
Production 75 Sets
Jeff Bagwell 20.00
Rocco Baldelli 15.00
Josh Beckett 20.00
Lance Berkman 15.00
Hank Blalock 15.00
Pat Burrell 15.00
Miguel Cabrera 20.00
Rod Carew 30.00
Roger Clemens 30.00
Adam Dunn 15.00
Eric Gagne 15.00
Jason Giambi 25.00
Brian Giles 15.00
Troy Glaus 15.00
Shawn Green 15.00
Vladimir Guerrero 25.00
Tony Gwynn 30.00
Todd Helton 20.00
Rickey Henderson 30.00
Tim Hudson 15.00
Torii Hunter 15.00
Randy Johnson 25.00
Andruw Jones 20.00
Chipper Jones 30.00
Greg Maddux 30.00
Pedro J. Martinez 25.00
Hideki Matsui 40.00
Kazuo Matsui 40.00
Don Mattingly 40.00
Paul Molitor 30.00
Eddie Murray 50.00
Hideo Nomo 15.00
Magglio Ordonez 15.00
Rafael Palmeiro 20.00
Mike Piazza 30.00
Mark Prior 30.00
Albert Pujols 40.00
Manny Ramirez 20.00
Cal Ripken Jr. 75.00
Alex Rodriguez 40.00
Ivan Rodriguez 15.00
Scott Rolen 25.00
Curt Schilling 15.00
Ozzie Smith 25.00
Alfonso Soriano 25.00
Sammy Sosa 35.00
Mark Teixeira 15.00
Miguel Tejada 15.00
Frank Thomas 20.00
Jim Thome 25.00
Rickie Weeks 15.00
Dontrelle Willis 15.00
Kerry Wood 20.00
Barry Zito 15.00

Clearly Authentics Bronze Patch/Jersey

.75-1.5X Black Patch Version
Production 35 Sets

Clearly Authentics Burgundy Triple Patch

No Pricing
Production 13 Sets

Clearly Authentics - Double MLB Logo

No Pricing
Production One Set

Clearly Authentics Pewter

Sequentially #'d to varying quantities.

Clearly Authentics Pewter Patch/Bat

.75-1.5X Black Patch Version
Production 44 Sets

Clearly Authentics Royal Patch/ Bat/Jersey

No Pricing
Production Eight Sets

Clearly Authentics Signature Tan Patch

Sequentially #'d to varying quantities.

Clearly Authentics Tan Double Patch

No Pricing
Production 22 Sets

Clearly Authentics Tan Double Patches

No Pricing
Production 22 Sets

Clearly Authentics Turquoise Nameplate

No Pricing
Sequentially #'d to varying quantities.

ConnEXions

NM/M
Production 25 or 50 Sets
6 Casey Kotchman, Joe Mauer/50 100.00
7 Shannon Stewart, Torii Hunter/25 90.00
9 Johnny Damon, Trot Nixon/25 90.00
10 Carlos Lee, Magglio Ordonez/25 30.00
12 Scott Podsednik, Lyle Overbay/25 60.00
13 Barry Zito, Tim Hudson/25 125.00
14 Bucky Dent, Mike Torrez/50 40.00
15 Brian Giles, Marcus Giles/25 60.00
17 Dontrelle Willis, Miguel Cabrera/25 60.00
18 Michael Young, Khalil Greene/50 80.00
19 Mark Teixeira, Hank Blalock/25 100.00

Double Barrel

No Pricing
Production One Set

Signings of the Times Best Year

NM/M
Sequentially #'d to player's best year.
Emerald: No Pricing
Production One Set
Ernie Banks/Bat/58 60.00
Johnny Bench/Jsy/72 60.00
Wade Boggs/Bat/8 40.00
George Brett/Jsy/80 80.00
Jose Canseco/Jsy/88 30.00
Will Clark/Jsy/91 40.00
Tony Gwynn/Jsy/94 50.00
Rickey Henderson/ Jsy/90 75.00
Bo Jackson/Jsy/89 60.00
Don Mattingly/Jsy/85 80.00
Eddie Murray/Jsy/83 60.00
Stan Musial/Bat/48 75.00
Nolan Ryan/Jsy/73 150.00
Ryne Sandberg/ Bat/90 60.00
Mike Schmidt/Jsy/80 80.00
Tom Seaver/Jsy/69 75.00
Ozzie Smith/Jsy/87 50.00
Duke Snider/Bat/55 50.00
Carl Yastrzemski/ Bat/67 60.00

Signings of the Times Debut Year

NM/M
Sequentially #'d to player's debut year.
Ernie Banks/Bat/53 60.00
Johnny Bench/Jsy/67 60.00
Yogi Berra/Bat/46 60.00
Wade Boggs/Bat/82 40.00
Jose Canseco/Jsy/85 30.00
Will Clark/Jsy/86 40.00
Tony Gwynn/Jsy/82 50.00
Rickey Henderson/ Jsy/79 75.00
Bo Jackson/Jsy/86 60.00
Reggie Jackson/ Jsy/67 50.00
Don Mattingly/Jsy/82 80.00
Eddie Murray/Jsy/77 60.00
Stan Musial/Bat/41 75.00
Kirby Puckett/Bat/84 50.00
Nolan Ryan/Jsy/66 150.00
Ryne Sandberg/ Bat/81 60.00
Deion Sanders/ Jsy/89 40.00
Mike Schmidt/Jsy/72 80.00
Ozzie Smith/Jsy/78 50.00
Duke Snider/Bat/47 50.00
Carl Yastrzemski/ Bat/61 75.00
Robin Yount/Jsy/74 40.00

Signings of the Times HOF Year

NM/M
Sequentially #'d to player's HOF year.
Ernie Banks/Bat/77 60.00
Johnny Bench/Jsy/89 60.00
Yogi Berr/Bat/72 50.00
George Brett/Jsy/99 80.00
Reggie Jackson/ Jsy/93 50.00
Stan Musial/Bat/69 75.00
Mike Schmidt/Jsy/95 75.00
Tom Seaver/Jsy/92 50.00
Duke Snider/Bat/80 30.00
Carl Yastrzemski/ Bat/89 60.00

Signings of the Times Pewter

NM/M
Sequentially #'d to varying quantities.
Wade Boggs/Bat/32 50.00
Jose Canseco/Jsy/27 75.00
Rickey Henderson/ Jsy/32 75.00
Bo Jackson/Jsy/60 50.00
Don Mattingly/Jsy/33 80.00
Eddie Murray/Jsy/50 80.00
Stan Musial/Bat/51 80.00
Kirby Puckett/Bat/31 50.00
Ryne Sandberg/ Bat/28 60.00
Ozzie Smith/Jsy/36 80.00

2004 Fleer Flair

NM/M
Common Player (1-60): 1.00
Minor Star (1-60): 1.25
Unlisted Star (1-60): 1.75
Common Rookie (61-82): 5.00
Rookie Production 799 Sets
Collection Row (1-60): 1-30X
Collection Row (61-82): .5-2X
Row 1 Production 125 Sets
Collection Row 2: No Pricing
Production One Set
Box (1): 100.00
1 Brandon Webb 1.00
2 Todd Helton 2.00
3 Jeff Bagwell 2.00
4 Shawn Green 1.25
5 Vladimir Guerrero 3.00
6 Tom Glavine 1.25
7 Jason Giambi 3.00
8 Barry Zito 1.75
9 Jason Kendall 1.25
10 Carlos Delgado 2.00
11 Curt Schilling 1.75
12 Ken Griffey Jr. 3.50
13 Mike Piazza 3.50
14 Alfonso Soriano 3.00
15 Albert Pujols 5.00
16 Chipper Jones 3.50
17 Alex Rodriguez 5.00
18 Miguel Tejada 1.75
19 Pedro J. Martinez 3.00
20 Mark Prior 4.00
21 Magglio Ordonez 1.25
22 Scott Podsednik 1.75
23 Shannon Stewart 1.00
24 Rocco Baldelli 1.75
25 Darin Erstad 1.25
26 Omar Vizquel 1.00
27 Angel Berroa 1.00
28 Jose Vidro 1.00
29 Rich Harden 1.00
30 Andruw Jones 2.00
31 Troy Glaus 1.75
32 Sammy Sosa 4.00
33 Dontrelle Willis 1.25
34 Ivan Rodriguez 1.75
35 Nomar Garciaparra 5.00
36 Josh Beckett 2.00
37 Jose Reyes 1.00
38 Scott Rolen 3.00
39 Greg Maddux 3.50
40 Andy Pettitte 1.75
41 Jason Schmidt 1.25
42 Edgar Martinez 1.25
43 Manny Ramirez 2.00
44 Torii Hunter 1.75
45 Mark Teixeira 1.25
46 Hideo Nomo 1.00
47 Brian Giles 1.25
48 Adam Dunn 1.75
49 Fernando Vina 1.00
50 Hideki Matsui 5.00
51 Jim Thome 3.00
52 Hank Blalock 1.75
53 Miguel Cabrera 2.00
54 Randy Johnson 3.00
55 Javy Lopez 1.25
56 Frank Thomas 2.00
57 Roger Clemens 3.50
58 Marlon Byrd 1.00
59 Derek Jeter 6.00
60 Ichiro Suzuki 4.00
61 Kazuo Matsui **RC** 25.00
62 Chad Bentz **RC** 8.00
63 Greg Dobbs **RC** 5.00
64 John Gall **RC** 5.00
65 Cory Sullivan **RC** 5.00
66 Hector Gimenez **RC** 5.00
67 Graham Koonce 5.00
68 Jason Bartlett **RC** 5.00
69 Angel Chavez **RC** 5.00
70 Ronny Cedeno **RC** 5.00
71 Donald Kelly **RC** 5.00
72 Ivan Ochoa **RC** 5.00
73 Ruddy Yan **RC** 5.00
74 Mike Gosling 5.00
75 Alfredo Simon **RC** 5.00
76 Jerome Gamble **RC** 5.00
77 Chris Aguila **RC** 5.00
78 Mike Rouse 5.00
79 Justin Leone **RC** 5.00
80 Merkin Valdez **RC** 5.00
81 Aarom Baldiris **RC** 5.00
82 Chris Shelton **RC** 10.00

Autograph Collection

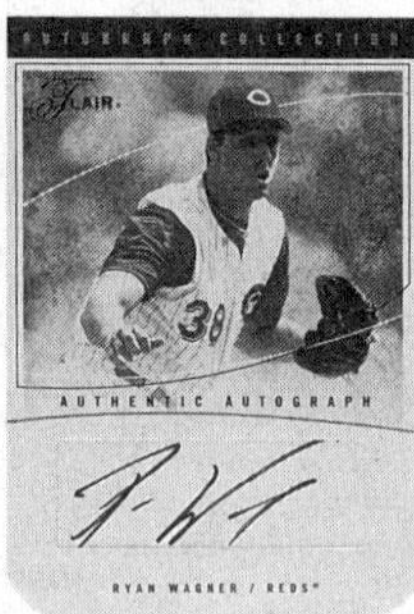

NM/M
Common Player: 10.00
Production between 65-200 Sets
Crown: .5-1X
Production 100 Sets
Parchment: 1-1.75X
Production 25 Sets
Platinum: No Pricing
Production 10 Sets
Masterpiece: No Pricing
Production One Set
Garrett Atkins/195 10.00
Rocco Baldelli/180 25.00
Aarom Baldiris/180 10.00
Jason Bartlett/95 15.00
Josh Beckett/65 40.00
Angel Berroa/178 15.00
Miguel Cabrera/172 40.00
Bobby Crosby/87 30.00
Jim Edmonds/73 25.00
John Gall/94 30.00
Khalil Greene/40 195.00
Dan Haren/195 15.00
Ryan Howard/185 75.00
Edwin Jackson/183 15.00
Andruw Jones/163 25.00
Graham Koonce/175 10.00
Josh Labandeira/166 10.00
Adam LaRoche/280 15.00
Justin Leone/180 15.00
Ryan Meaux/180 10.00
Mike Mussina/69 50.00
Micheal Nakamura/ 180 10.00
Bubba Nelson/185 10.00
Corey Patterson/172 15.00
Juan Pierre/94 15.00
Scott Podsednik/96 25.00
Mark Prior/60 60.00
Alexis Rios/185 20.00
Michael Rouse/195 10.00
Chris Shelton/170 30.00
Grady Sizemore/197 30.00
Merkin Valdez/179 10.00
Javier Vazquez/187 30.00
Ryan Wagner/175 15.00
Chien-Ming Wang/178 50.00
Brandon Webb/122 15.00
Rickie Weeks/169 30.00
Dontrelle Willis/73 30.00
Kerry Wood/73 40.00
Delmon Young/177 25.00

Cuts and Glory

NM/M
Common Player: 25.00
Production 100 Sets
Silver: .75-1.25X
Production 50 Sets
Gold: No Pricing
Production 15 Sets
Platinum: No Pricing
Production Three Sets
Masterpiece: No Pricing
Production One Set
Garret Anderson 30.00
Hank Blalock 25.00
Marlon Byrd 25.00
Carlos Delgado 30.00
Adam Dunn 40.00
Eric Gagne 40.00
Luis Gonzalez 25.00
Vladimir Guerrero 50.00
Ricky Henderson 100.00
Torii Hunter 25.00
Randy Johnson 60.00
Chipper Jones 60.00
Austin Kearns 25.00
Greg Maddux 75.00
Edgar Martinez 40.00
Magglio Ordonez 25.00
Albert Pujols 150.00
Jose Reyes 30.00
Scott Rolen 40.00
Mark Teixeira 25.00
Frank Thomas 75.00

Diamond Cuts Game-Used Blue

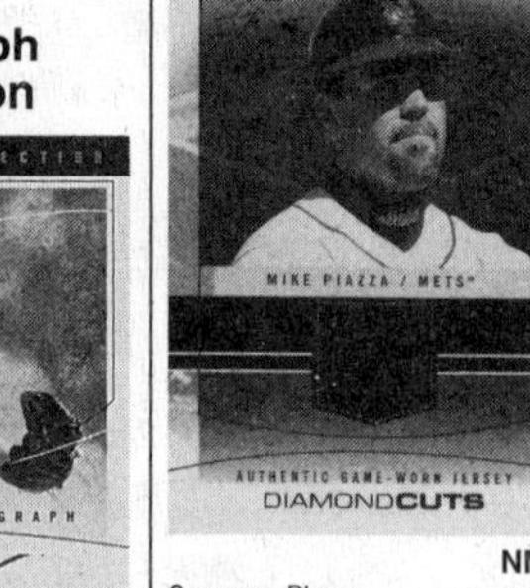

NM/M
Common Player: 5.00
Production 250 Sets
Blue Die-Cut: 1-30X
Production 25 Sets
Red: .5-1.25X
Production 175 Sets
Red Die-Cut: No Pricing
Production 18 Sets
Pewter: .5-1.5X
Production 125 Sets
Pewter Die-Cut: No Pricing
Production 13 Sets
Copper: .5-1.5X
Production 75 Sets
Die-Cut Copper: No Pricing
Production Eight Sets
Silver: .5-1.5X
Production 50 Sets
Silver Die-Cut: No Pricing
Production Five Sets
Gold: 1-5X
Numbered to player's jersey No.
Gold Die-Cut: No Pricing
Production Three Sets
Platinum: 2-5X
Numbered to 2003 HR/Win total.
Platinum Die-Cut: No Pricing
Production One Set
Purple: No Pricing
Production One Set
JB Josh Beckett 8.00
HB Hank Blalock 5.00
RC Roger Clemens 10.00
NG Nomar Garciaparra 12.00
DJ Derek Jeter 15.00
AJ Andruw Jones 8.00
CJ Chipper Jones 8.00
PM Pedro J. Martinez 8.00
HM Hideki Matsui 12.00
ANP Andy Pettitte 8.00
MIP Mike Piazza 8.00
MAP Mark Prior 8.00
ALP Albert Pujols 12.00
JR Jose Reyes 5.00
SR Scott Rolen 8.00
SS Curt Schilling 5.00
SS Sammy Sosa 10.00
IS Ichiro Suzuki 10.00
MT Mark Teixeira 5.00
DW Dontrelle Willis 5.00

Dual Patch

No Pricing
Production 10 Sets

Hot Numbers Game-Used Blue

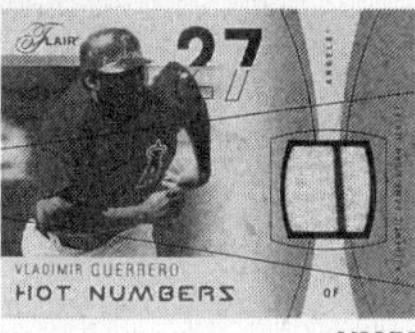

NM/M
Common Player: 5.00
Production 250 Sets
Blue Die-Cut: 1X-3X
Production 25 Sets
Red: .5X-1.25X
Production 175 Sets
Red Die-Cut: No Pricing
Production 18 Sets
Pewter: .5X-1.5X
Production 125 Sets
Pewter Die-Cut: No Pricing
Production 13 Sets
Copper: .5X-1.5X
Production 75 Sets
Die-Cut Copper: No Pricing
Production Eight Sets
Silver: .5X-1.5X
Production 50 Sets
Silver Die-Cut: No Pricing
Production Five Sets
Gold: 1X-5X
Numbered to player's jersey No.
Gold Die-Cut: No Pricing
Production Three Sets
Platinum: 2X-5X
Numbered to 2003 HR/Win total.
Platinum Die-Cut: No Pricing
Production One Set
Purple: No Pricing
Production One Set
Jeff Bagwell 8.00
Rocco Baldelli 5.00
Josh Beckett 8.00
Hank Blalock 5.00
Nomar Garciaparra 12.00
Jason Giambi 8.00
Troy Glaus 5.00
Tom Glavine 5.00
Vladimir Guerrero 8.00
Todd Helton 8.00
Derek Jeter 15.00
Randy Johnson 8.00
Chipper Jones 8.00
Barry Larkin 5.00
Greg Maddux 8.00
Pedro J. Martinez 8.00
Mike Mussina 5.00
Hideo Nomo 5.00
Mike Piazza 8.00
Mark Prior 8.00
Albert Pujols 12.00
Manny Ramirez 8.00
Alex Rodriguez 12.00
Curt Schilling 5.00
Sammy Sosa 10.00
Mark Teixeira 5.00
Frank Thomas 8.00
Jim Thome 8.00
Brandon Webb 5.00
Kerry Wood 8.00

Lettermen

No Pricing
Numbered to number of letters in player's last name.

Power Tools Game-Used Blue

NM/M
Common Player: 5.00
Production 250 Sets
Blue Die-Cut: 1X-3X
Production 25 Sets
Red: .5X-1.25X
Production 175 Sets
Red Die-Cut: No Pricing
Production 18 Sets
Pewter: .5X-1.5X
Production 125 Sets
Pewter Die-Cut: No Pricing
Production 13 Sets
Copper: .5X-1.5X
Production 75 Sets
Die-Cut Copper: No Pricing
Production Eight Sets

Silver: .5X-1.5X
Production 50 Sets
Silver Die-Cut: No Pricing
Production Five Sets
Gold: 1X-5X
Numbered to player's jersey No.
Gold Die-Cut: No Pricing
Production Three Sets
Platinum: 2X-5X
Numbered to 2003 HR total.
Platinum Die-Cut: No Pricing
Production One Set
Purple: No Pricing
Production One Set
Rocco Baldelli 5.00
Adam Dunn 5.00
Nomar Garciaparra 12.00
Jason Giambi 8.00
Vladimir Guerrero 8.00
Derek Jeter 15.00
Chipper Jones 8.00
Mike Piazza 10.00
Jorge Posada 8.00
Albert Pujols 12.00
Manny Ramirez 8.00
Alex Rodriguez 12.00
Alfonso Soriano 8.00
Sammy Sosa 10.00
Jim Thome 8.00

SIGnificant Cuts

NM/M
Serially Numbered
RA Roberto Alomar/50 60.00
JB2 Johnny Bench/25 100.00
VC Vince Carter/200 50.00
TC Ty Cobb 2,650
DE Dennis Eckersley/75 30.00
RH Roy Halladay/50 40.00
BL Barry Larkin/75 30.00
PM Paul Molitor/75 50.00
AP1 Andy Pettitte/50 40.00
JR Jose Reyes/25 40.00
MR Mariano Rivera/50 75.00
IR Ivan Rodriguez/50 50.00
NR Nolan Ryan/25 200.00
MS Mike Schmidt/25 125.00
GS Gary Sheffield/50 50.00

2004 Fleer Genuine Insider

NM/M
Common Player (1-90): .25
Minor Stars: .40
Unlisted Stars: .60
Common Rookie Insider (91-100): 4.00
Production 499 Sets
Common Upside (101-120): 4.00
Production 799 Sets
Common Mini Rookie: 4.00
Production 350 Sets
Pack (5): 4.00
Box (18): 75.00
1 Troy Glaus .60
2 Eric Chavez .40
3 Lance Berkman .40
4 Pedro J. Martinez 1.00
5 Jim Edmonds .40
6 Tom Glavine .40
7 Ken Griffey Jr. 1.50
8 Vernon Wells .40
9 Hideki Matsui 2.50
10 Jeff Bagwell .75
11 Rafael Palmeiro .40
12 Edgar Martinez .40
13 Bernie Williams .60
14 Josh Beckett .75
15 Javy Lopez .40
16 Ichiro Suzuki 2.00
17 Scott Podsednik .40
18 Sammy Sosa 2.00
19 Mark Teixeira .40
20 Jorge Posada .60
21 Miguel Cabrera .75
22 Chipper Jones 1.50
23 Sean Burroughs .25
24 Dmitri Young .25
25 Brandon Webb .25
26 Bobby Abreu .40
27 Hideo Nomo .40
28 Frank Thomas .75
29 Alex Rodriguez 2.50
30 Derek Jeter 3.00
31 Todd Helton .75
32 Andruw Jones .75
33 Jason Kendall .40
34 Eric Gagne .40
35 Omar Vizquel .40
36 Vladimir Guerrero 1.00
37 Jim Thome 1.00
38 Mike Sweeney .25
39 Manny Ramirez .75
40 Scott Rolen 1.00
41 Jose Vidro .25
42 Adam Dunn .60
43 Garret Anderson .40
44 Mike Lieberthal .25
45 Roy Oswalt .40
46 Geoff Jenkins .40
47 Magglio Ordonez .40
48 Hank Blalock .60
49 Barry Zito .60
50 Dontrelle Willis .40
51 Greg Maddux 1.50
52 Brian Giles .40
53 Shawn Green .40
54 Carlos Lee .25
55 Carlos Delgado .75
56 Alfonso Soriano 1.00
57 Angel Berroa .25
58 Kerry Wood .75
59 Rocco Baldelli .60
60 Gary Sheffield .60
61 Ivan Rodriguez .60
62 Richie Sexson .60
63 Marlon Byrd .25
64 Carlos Beltran .40
65 Mark Prior 2.00
66 Aubrey Huff .25
67 Jason Giambi 1.00
68 Curt Schilling .60
69 Reggie Sanders .25
70 Mike Piazza 1.50
71 Craig Monroe .25
72 Randy Johnson 1.00
73 Pat Burrell .40
74 Craig Biggio .40
75 Nomar Garciaparra 2.50
76 Albert Pujols 2.50
77 Jose Reyes .25
78 Preston Wilson .25
79 Miguel Tejada .60
80 Bret Boone .40
81 Shannon Stewart .25
82 Jody Gerut .25
83 Tim Salmon .25
84 Tim Hudson .40
85 Juan Pierre .25
86 Jay Gibbons .40
87 Jason Schmidt .40
88 Torii Hunter .60
89 Austin Kearns .25
90 Roy Halladay .40
91 John Gall **RC** 8.00
92 Hideki Matsui **RC** 25.00
93 Merkin Valdez **RC** 4.00
94 William Bergolla **RC** 8.00
95 Angel Chavez **RC** 4.00
96 Hector Gimenez **RC** 4.00
97 Aarom Baldiris **RC** 4.00
98 Justin Leone **RC** 6.00
99 Onil Joseph **RC** 5.00
100 Freddy Guzman **RC** 4.00
101 Rickie Weeks 6.00
102 Chad Bentz **RC** 5.00
103 Bobby Crosby 6.00
104 Dallas McPherson 5.00
105 Brandon Watson 4.00
106 Garrett Atkins 6.00
107 Graham Koonce 4.00
108 Chien-Ming Wang 4.00
109 Jonny Gomes 4.00
110 Edwin Jackson 4.00
111 Alfredo Simon **RC** 5.00
112 Delmon Young 6.00
113 Angel Guzman 4.00
114 Ryan Howard 4.00
115 Scott Hairston 10.00
116 Edwin Encarnacion 5.00
117 Byron Gettis 4.00
118 Kevin Youkilis 8.00
119 Grady Sizemore 4.00
120 Corey Hart 4.00
121 Greg Dobbs **RC** 4.00
122 Jerry Gil **RC** 4.00
123 Shawn Hill **RC** 4.00
124 John Labandeira **RC** 4.00
125 Jason Bartlett **RC** 4.00
126 Ronny Cedeno **RC** 4.00
127 Donald Kelly **RC** 8.00
128 Ivan Ochoa **RC** 5.00
129 Mariano Gomez **RC** 5.00
130 Ruddy Yan **RC** 5.00

Genuine Reflection

(1-90): .5-2X

(101-120): .5-1.25X
Production 99 Sets

Autograph Insider

NM/M
Common Player: 10.00
Production as indicated.
RA Roberto Alomar/150 30.00
MB Marlon Byrd/550 10.00
MC Miguel Cabrera/250 40.00
DE David Eckstein/350 10.00
JG Jody Gerut/550 10.00
JG2 Jay Gibbons/350 10.00
OH Orlando Hudson/550 15.00
AH Aubrey Huff/550 10.00
AK Austin Kearns/350 10.00
MO Magglio Ordonez/250 20.00
RP Rafael Palmeiro/150 50.00
SP Scott Podsednik/550 15.00
JR Jose Reyes/350 25.00
MR Mariano Rivera/150 60.00
IR Ivan Rodriguez/150 40.00
JR2 Jimmy Rollins/350 15.00
JS Jason Schmidt/300 300.00
JS2 John Smoltz/150 30.00
MT Mark Teixeira/350 20.00
BW Brandon Webb/450 10.00

Autograph Insider - Ball

No Pricing
Production 10 Sets

Autograph Insider - Bat

NM/M
Common Card: 20.00
Production 50 Sets
RA Roberto Alomar 40.00
MB Marlon Byrd 20.00
MC Miguel Cabrera 60.00
DE David Eckstein 30.00
JG Jody Gerut 25.00
JG2 Jay Gibbons 20.00
OH Orlando Hudson 20.00
AH Aubrey Huff 25.00
AK Austin Kearns 20.00
RP Rafael Palmeiro 50.00
SP Scott Podsednik 25.00
JR Jose Reyes 35.00
IR Ivan Rodriguez 50.00
JR2 Jimmy Rollins 30.00
MT Mark Teixeira 25.00

Autograph Insider-Cut Sigs

No Pricing

Autograph Insider - Jersey

NM/M
Common Player: 10.00
Production 100 Sets
RA Roberto Alomar 30.00
MB Marlon Byrd 10.00
MC Miguel Cabrera 40.00
DE David Eckstein 15.00
JG Jody Gerut 25.00
JG2 Jay Gibbons 20.00
OH Orlando Hudson 10.00
AH Aubrey Huff 20.00
AK Austin Kearns 20.00
MO Magglio Ordonez 40.00
RP Rafael Palmeiro 50.00
SP Scott Podsednik 25.00
AP Albert Pujols 100.00
JR Jose Reyes 35.00
MR Mariano Rivera 75.00
IR Ivan Rodriguez 50.00
JR2 Jimmy Rollins 20.00
JS Jason Schmidt 20.00
JS2 John Smoltz 50.00
MT Mark Teixeira 25.00
BW Brandon Webb 10.00

Classic Confrontations

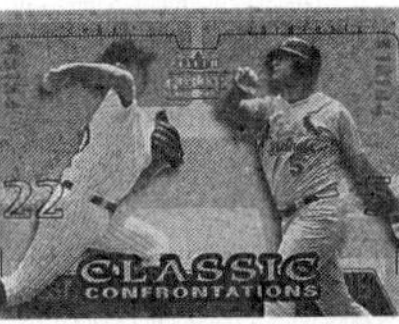

NM/M
Common Card: 3.00
Inserted 1:18
1CC Mike Piazza, Roger Clemens 4.00
2CC Pedro J. Martinez, Derek Jeter 6.00
3CC Randy Johnson, Jeff Bagwell 3.00
4CC Mark Prior, Albert Pujols 4.00
5CC Josh Beckett, Sammy Sosa 4.00
6CC Eric Gagne, Hank Blalock 3.00
7CC Mariano Rivera, Nomar Garciaparra 5.00
8CC Curt Schilling, Chipper Jones 4.00
9CC Kerry Wood, Jim Edmonds 3.00
10CC Barry Zito, Alfonso Soriano 3.00
11CC Randy Johnson, Ken Griffey Jr. 4.00
12CC Derek Jeter, John Smoltz 6.00
13CC Roy Oswalt, Ken Griffey Jr. 4.00
14CC Dontrelle Willis, Hideki Matsui 4.00
15CC Hideo Nomo, Ichiro Suzuki 4.00

2004 Fleer Genuine Insider Cl. Confrontations Jersey

NM/M
Common Card: 5.00
Production 400 Sets
JB Jeff Bagwell with Randy Johnson 6.00
JB2 Josh Beckett with Sammy Sosa 6.00
HB Hank Blalock with Eric Gagne 8.00
RC Roger Clemens with Mike Piazza 15.00
JE Jim Edmonds with Kerry Wood 5.00
EG Eric Gagne with Hank Blalock 5.00
NG Nomar Garciaparra with Mariano Rivera 8.00
DJ Derek Jeter with Pedro J. Martinez 15.00
RJ1 Randy Johnson with Jeff Bagwell 8.00
RJ2 Randy Johnson with Ken Griffey Jr. 8.00
CJ Chipper Jones with Curt Schilling 8.00
PM Pedro J. Martinez with Derek Jeter 10.00
HN Hideo Nomo with Ichiro Suzuki 12.00
RO Roy Oswalt with Ken Griffey Jr. 5.00
MP Mike Piazza with Roger Clemens 8.00
MP2 Mark Prior with Albert Pujols 8.00
AP Albert Pujols with Mark Prior 12.00
MR Mariano Rivera with Nomar Garciaparra 8.00
CS Curt Schilling with Chipper Jones 5.00
JS John Smoltz with Derek Jeter 5.00
AS Alfonso Soriano with Barry Zito 8.00
SS Sammy Sosa with Josh Beckett 8.00
DW Dontrelle Willis with Matsui 5.00
KW Kerry Wood with Jim Edmonds 8.00
BZ Barry Zito with Alfonso Soriano 5.00

Classic Confrontations Dual Jersey

NM/M
Common Card: 12.00
Production 100 Sets
Dual Patch: No Pricing
Production 10 Sets
Barry Zito, Alfonso Soriano 12.00
Curt Schilling, Chipper Jones 12.00
Eric Gagne, Hank Blalock 12.00
Josh Beckett, Sammy Sosa 12.00
Kerry Wood, Jim Edmonds 15.00
Mark Prior, Albert Pujols 15.00
Mike Piazza, Roger Clemens 15.00
Mariano Rivera, Nomar Garciaparra 20.00
Pedro J. Martinez, Derek Jeter 20.00
Randy Johnson, Jeff Bagwell 12.00

Genuine Article Insider-Jersey

NM/M
Common Player: 5.00
Production 250 Sets
Bat: .75-1.25X
Production 100 Sets
Jersey/Bat: .75-1.5X
Production 50 Sets
Jersey Tags: No Pricing
Production Five Sets
RB Rocco Baldelli 5.00
LB Lance Berkman 5.00
HB Hank Blalock 5.00
MC Miguel Cabrera 8.00
CD Carlos Delgado 6.00
AD Adam Dunn 5.00
NG Nomar Garciaparra 12.00
JG Jason Giambi 6.00
TG Troy Glaus 5.00
VG Vladimir Guerrero 8.00
TH Todd Helton 8.00
DJ Derek Jeter 18.00
CJ Chipper Jones 8.00
MO Magglio Ordonez 5.00
RP Rafael Palmeiro 5.00
MP Mike Piazza 8.00
AP Albert Pujols 12.00
MR Manny Ramirez 6.00
JR Jose Reyes 6.00
AR Alex Rodriguez 15.00
CS Gary Sheffield 6.00
AS Alfonso Soriano 8.00
SS Sammy Sosa 10.00
MT Mark Teixeira 5.00
JT Jim Thome 6.00

Tools of the Game

NM/M
Common Player: 1.00
Inserted 1:6
1TG Jason Giambi 1.50
2TG Torii Hunter 1.00
3TG Derek Jeter 4.00
4TG Nomar Garciaparra 3.00
5TG Albert Pujols 3.00
6TG Jim Thome 1.50
7TG Alex Rodriguez 4.00
8TG Chipper Jones 2.00
9TG Sammy Sosa 2.50
10TG Jose Reyes 1.00
11TG Pedro J. Martinez 1.50
12TG Greg Maddux 2.00
13TG Randy Johnson 1.50
14TG Curt Schilling 1.00
15TG Mark Prior 2.00
16TG Ichiro Suzuki 2.50
17TG Hideki Matsui 3.00
18TG Kazuo Matsui 2.50
19TG Ken Griffey Jr. 2.00
20TG Josh Beckett 1.00

Tools of Game-Game Jersey

NM/M
Common Player: 5.00
Production 250 Sets
Jersey/Bat: .75-2X
Production 125
Jersey/Bat/Cap: 1-2.5X
Production 75
NG Nomar Garciaparra 12.00
JG Jason Giambi 8.00
TH Torii Hunter 5.00
DJ Derek Jeter 15.00
RJ Randy Johnson 6.00
CJ Chipper Jones 8.00
GM Greg Maddux 6.00
PM Pedro J. Martinez 6.00
MP Mark Prior 10.00
AP Albert Pujols 12.00
JR Jose Reyes 8.00
AR Alex Rodriguez 15.00
CS Curt Schilling 5.00
SS Sammy Sosa 10.00
JT Jim Thome 6.00

2004 Fleer Greats of the Game

NM/M
Common Player: .40
Minor Stars: .75
Pack (5): 10.00
Box (15): 130.00
1 Lou Gehrig 4.00
2 Ty Cobb 3.00
3 Dizzy Dean 1.50
4 Jimmie Foxx 1.50
5 Hank Greenberg 1.00
6 Babe Ruth 6.00
7 Honus Wagner 1.50
8 Mickey Cochrane 1.50
9 Pepper Martin .40
10 Charlie Gehringer .75
11 Carl Hubbell .40
12 Bill Terry .40
13 Mel Ott .75
14 Bill Dickey 1.50
15 Ted Williams 6.00
16 Roger Maris 3.00
17 Thurman Munson 2.00
18 Phil Rizzuto 2.00
19 Stan Musial 3.00
20 Duke Snider 2.50
21 Reggie Jackson 1.50
22 Don Mattingly 1.50
23 Vida Blue .75
24 Harmon Killebrew 1.50
25 Lou Brock .75
26 Al Kaline 1.00
27 Dave Parker .40
28 Nolan Ryan 6.00
29 Jim Rice .40
30 Paul Molitor 2.00
31 Dwight Evans .40
32 Brooks Robinson 1.50
33 Jose Canseco .40
34 Alan Trammell .40
35 Johnny Bench 2.00
36 Carlton Fisk 1.00
37 Jim Palmer 1.50
38 George Brett 2.00
39 Mike Schmidt 2.00
40 Tony Perez .75
41 Paul Blair .40
42 Fred Lynn .40
43 Carl Yastrzemski 1.50
44 Steve Carlton 1.00
45 Dennis Eckersley 1.50
46 Tom Seaver 1.50
47 Juan Marichal .75
48 Tony Gwynn 2.00
49 Bill "Moose" Skowron .75
50 Bob Gibson 1.50
51 Luis Tiant .75
52 Eddie Murray 1.00
53 Frank Robinson 2.00
54 Rocky Colavito .75
55 Bobby Shantz .40
56 Ernie Banks 2.00
57 Rod Carew 1.00
58 Gorman Thomas .40
59 Bernie Carbo .40
60 Joe Rudi .40
61 Graig Nettles .75
62 Ron Guidry .75
63 Whitey Ford 1.50
64 George Kell 1.00

65 Cal Ripken Jr. 6.00
66 Willie McCovey .75
67 Bo Jackson 1.00
68 Kirby Puckett 2.00
69 Ted Kluszewski .75
70 Johnny Podres .40
71 Davey Lopes .40
72 Chris Short .40
73 Jeff Torborg .40
74 Bill Freehan .40
75 Frank Tanana .40
76 Jack Morris .75
77 Rick Dempsey .40
78 Yogi Berra 1.50
79 Tim McCarver .40
80 Rusty Staub .40
81 Tony Lazzeri .40
82 Al Rosen .40
83 Willie McGee .75
84 Preacher Roe .75
85 Dave Kingman .40
86 Luis Aparicio 1.00
87 John Kruk .40
88 Bing Miller .40
89 Joe Charboneau .40
90 Mark Fidrych .40
91 Jim "Catfish" Hunter 2.00
92 Nap Lajoie 2.00
93 Eddie Murray 2.00
94 Johnny Pesky 1.00
95 Tom Seaver 2.00
96 Frank Robinson 2.00
97 Enos Slaughter 1.00
98 Cecil Travis .40
99 Robin Yount 2.00
100 Don Zimmer .75
101 Babe Herman .40
102 Ron Santo .40
103 Willie Stargell 2.00
105 Jimmy Piersall .75
106 Johnny Sain .40
107 Joe Pepitone .75
108 Ryne Sandberg 3.00
109 Jim Thorpe 3.00
110 Steve Garvey 1.50
111 Ray Knight .75
112 Fernando Valenzuela 1.00
113 Will Clark 1.00
114 Tony Kubek .75
115 Jim Bouton .40
116 Jerry Koosman .75
117 Steve Carlton 3.00
118 Richie Ashburn .75
119 Roberto Clemente 6.00
120 Paul O'Neill .40
121 Reggie Jackson 3.00
122 Andre Dawson 1.50
123 Hoyt Wilhelm 1.00
124 Dale Murphy 1.50
125 Dwight Gooden 1.50
126 Roger Maris 1.00
127 Bill Mazeroski 1.00
128 Don Newcombe .75
129 Robin Roberts .75
130 Duke Snider 2.00
131 Eddie Mathews 3.00
132 Wade Boggs 2.00
133 Rollie Fingers 1.50
134 Frankie Frisch .40
135 Billy Williams .75
136 Rod Carew 1.50
137 Dom DiMaggio .75
138 Orel Hershiser .40
139 Gary Carter 1.00
140 Keith Hernandez .75
141 Bob Lemon .75
142 Nolan Ryan 6.00
143 Ozzie Smith 1.50
144 Rick Sutcliffe .40
145 Carlton Fisk 1.50

Blue

Cards 81-145
Cards #'d to 51-96: 3-5X
Cards #'d to 26-50: 5-10X
Cards #'d to less than 25: No Pricing

Announcing Greats

NM/M
Common Card: 6.00
Inserted 1:12 Retail
1AG Harry Kalas, Mike Schmidt 8.00
2AG Vin Scully, Steve Garvey 12.00
3AG Harry Caray, Ryne Sandberg 12.00
4AG Ned Martin, Carlton Fisk 6.00
5AG Ernie Harwell, Kirk Gibson 6.00
6AG Ken Harrelson, Carl Yastrzemski 8.00
7AG Don Mattingly, Phil Rizzuto 10.00
8AG Yogi Berra, Mel Allen 10.00
9AG Jonathan Miller, Cal Ripken Jr. 10.00
10AG Marty Brennaman, Johnny Bench 8.00

Announcing Greats Autographs

NM/M
Sequentially #'d between 1 & 50.
Ken Harrelson,
Carl Yastrzemski/50 75.00
Phil Rizzuto,
Don Mattingly/26 225.00
Johnny Bench,
Marty Brennaman/50 60.00

Battery Mates

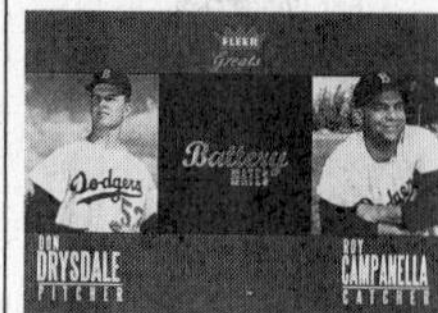

NM/M
Common Card: 5.00
Serially Numbered
1BM Steve Carlton, Tim McCarver/1972 5.00
2BM Don Drysdale, Roy Campanella/1957 5.00
3BM Tom Seaver, Johnny Bench/1979 8.00
4BM Whitey Ford, Yogi Berra/1956 8.00
5BM Ron Guidry, Thurman Munson/1978 8.00
6BM Nolan Ryan, Jeff Torborg/1973 10.00
7BM Denny McLain, Bill Freehan/1968 5.00
8BM Lefty Gomez, Bill Dickey/1934 5.00
9BM Jim Palmer, Rick Dempsey/1977 5.00
10BM Luis Tiant, Carlton Fisk 5.00

Single Panel: Battery Mates

NM/M
Common Card: 15.00
Serially Numbered
TM Steve Carlton, Tim McCarver/72 30.00
TS-JB Tom Seaver, Johnny Bench/79 60.00
WF-YB Whitey Ford, Yogi Berra/56 40.00
RG-TM Ron Guidry, Thurman Munson/78 25.00
NR-JT Nolan Ryan, Jeff Torborg/73 15.00
DM-BF Denny McLain, Bill Freehan/68 60.00
JP-RD Jim Palmer, Rick Dempsey/77 25.00

Dual Panel: Battery Mates

No Pricing
Production 10 Sets

Comparison Cuts: Dual Cut

No Pricing
Production One Set

Forever

NM/M
Common Player: 4.00
Sequentially #'d to player's rookie year.
1 Fernando Valenzuela/1980 4.00
2 Steve Garvey/1969 4.00
3 Zach Wheat/1909 4.00
4 Orel Hershiser/1983 4.00
5 Duke Snider/1947 6.00
6 Jim Rice/1974 5.00
7 Carlton Fisk/1969 6.00
8 Wade Boggs/1982 6.00
9 Ted Williams/1939 10.00
10 Carl Yastrzemski/1961 8.00
11 Dom DiMaggio/1940 5.00
12 Ron Santo/1960 4.00
13 Billy Williams/1959 5.00
14 Ryne Sandberg/1981 8.00
15 Ernie Banks/1953 8.00
16 Gabby Hartnett/1922 4.00
17 Hack Wilson/1923 6.00
18 Dwight Gooden/1984 5.00
19 Ray Knight/1974 4.00
20 Tom Seaver/1967 8.00
21 Nolan Ryan/1966 10.00
22 Keith Hernandez/1974 5.00
23 Darryl Strawberry/1983 5.00
24 Bob Gibson/1959 8.00
25 Pepper Martin/1928 4.00
26 Stan Musial/1941 8.00
27 Frankie Frisch/1919 4.00
28 Steve Carlton/1965 8.00
29 Ozzie Smith/1978 6.00

Forever Game-Used Jersey

NM/M
Common Player: 10.00
Production 149 Sets
Jersey: .75-1.5X
Production 99 Sets
Patch Number: 1-2X
Production 49 Sets
Patch Logo: No Pricing
Production 10 Sets
EB Ernie Banks 20.00
WB Wade Boggs 12.00
SC Steve Carlton 12.00
DD Dom DiMaggio 20.00
CF Carlton Fisk 15.00
SG Steve Garvey 10.00
BG Bob Gibson 15.00
DG Dwight Gooden 10.00
KH Keith Hernandez 10.00
OH Orel Hershiser 10.00
RK Ray Knight 10.00
SM Stan Musial 30.00
JR Jim Rice 12.00
NR Nolan Ryan 50.00
RS Ryne Sandberg 25.00
RST Ron Santo 10.00
TS Tom Seaver 15.00
OS Ozzie Smith 15.00
DS Darryl Strawberry 12.00
FV Fernando Valenzuela 10.00
BW Billy Williams 10.00
TW Ted Williams 75.00
CY Carl Yastrzemski 20.00

2004 Fleer Greats of the Game Gold Border Autographs

NM/M
Common Player: 10.00
Randomly Inserted
Ernie Banks 60.00
Johnny Bench 50.00
Yogi Berra 60.00
Paul Blair 10.00
Vida Blue 10.00
George Brett 125.00
Lou Brock 20.00
Jose Canseco 30.00
Bernie Carbo 10.00
Rod Carew 30.00
Steve Carlton 30.00
Rocky Colavito 100.00
Rick Dempsey 15.00
Dennis Eckersley 50.00
Dwight Evans 15.00
Carlton Fisk 40.00
Whitey Ford 40.00
Bill Freehan 10.00
Bob Gibson 25.00
Ron Guidry 20.00
Tony Gwynn 50.00
Bo Jackson 50.00
Reggie Jackson 100.00
Al Kaline 25.00
George Kell 15.00
Harmon Killebrew 30.00
Davey Lopes 10.00
Fred Lynn 10.00
Juan Marichal 20.00
Don Mattingly 80.00
Tim McCarver 15.00
Willie McCovey 40.00
Paul Molitor 40.00
Jack Morris 10.00
Eddie Murray 80.00
Stan Musial 100.00
Graig Nettles 15.00
Jim Palmer 20.00
Dave Parker 10.00
Tony Perez 30.00
Johnny Podres 10.00
Kirby Puckett 80.00
Jim Rice 20.00
Cal Ripken Jr. 150.00
Phil Rizzuto 40.00
Brooks Robinson 20.00
Frank Robinson 30.00
Joe Rudi 10.00
Nolan Ryan 150.00
Mike Schmidt 60.00
Tom Seaver 80.00
Bobby Shantz 10.00
Bill "Moose" Skowron 10.00
Duke Snider 30.00
Rusty Staub 10.00
Frank Tanana 10.00
Gorman Thomas 10.00
Luis Tiant 10.00
Jeff Torborg 10.00
Alan Trammell 10.00
Carl Yastrzemski 60.00

Gold Border Autograph Series 2

NM/M
Common Player: 15.00
Inserted 1:75
LA Luis Aparicio 20.00
WB Wade Boggs 40.00
JBO Jim Bouton 15.00
RC2 Rod Carew/Twins 40.00
SC2 Steve Carlton/Cards 30.00
GC Gary Carter 25.00
JCH Joe Charboneau 15.00
WC Will Clark 40.00
DC David Cone 40.00
AD Andre Dawson 20.00
DD Dom DiMaggio 50.00
RF Rollie Fingers 15.00
CF2 Carlton Fisk/White Sox 40.00
SG Steve Garvey 15.00
DG Dwight Gooden 20.00
KH Keith Hernandez 15.00
OH Orel Hershiser 15.00
RJ2 Reggie Jackson/Angels 60.00
DK Dave Kingman 15.00
RK Ray Knight 15.00
JK Jerry Koosman 20.00
JKR John Kruk 15.00
TK Tony Kubek 25.00
BM Bill Mazeroski 30.00
WMG Willie McGee 25.00
PM2 Paul Molitor Jays 40.00
DMU Dale Murphy 25.00
DN Don Newcombe 15.00
PO Paul O'Neill 30.00
JPP Joe Pepitone 15.00
JPS Johnny Pesky 25.00
JPI Jimmy Piersall 20.00
RR Robin Roberts 25.00
FR2 Frank Robinson O's 30.00
PRO Preacher Roe 20.00
AR Al Rosen 15.00
NR2 Nolan Ryan Angels 120.00
RS Ryne Sandberg 75.00
DS Deion Sanders 30.00
RST Ron Santo 20.00
TS2 Tom Seaver Reds 75.00
OS Ozzie Smith 40.00
DS2 Duke Snider 40.00
BW Billy Williams 20.00
RY Robin Yount 40.00
DZ Don Zimmer 25.00

Personality Cuts

No Pricing
Production One Set

Personality Cuts Series 2

No Pricing
Production One or Two Sets

Etched in Time

NM/M
No Pricing
ET-RC Roberto Clemente/1 (7/04 Auction) 6,100

Etched In Time Series 2

NM/M
Sequentially #'d to indicated quantity.
Cards #'d 25 or less: No Pricing
EA Ethan Allen/75 150.00
EAV Earl Averill/50 125.00
DC Dolph Camilli/40 250.00
BH Babe Herman/35 250.00
HK Harvey Kuenn/32 120.00
SM Sal Maglie/40 100.00
ER Edd Roush/95 100.00
PR Pete Runnels/35 200.00
CS Chris Short/30 120.00

The Glory of Their Time

NM/M
Common Player: 4.00
Serially Numbered
1GOT Harmon Killebrew/1961 4.00
2GOT Johnny Bench/1974 5.00
3GOT George Brett/1980 8.00
4GOT Tony Gwynn/1987 4.00
5GOT Paul Molitor/1987 5.00
6GOT Don Mattingly/1986 8.00
7GOT Reggie Jackson/1980 8.00
8GOT Carlton Fisk/1985 5.00
9GOT Cal Ripken Jr./1983 10.00
10GOT Brooks Robinson/1964 4.00
11GOT Eddie Murray/1980 5.00
12GOT Bill "Moose" Skowron/1960 4.00
13GOT Lou Brock/1974 5.00
14GOT Don Drysdale/1962 5.00
15GOT Tony Gwynn/1997 4.00
16GOT Mike Schmidt/1980 8.00
17GOT Carl Yastrzemski/1967 8.00
18GOT Babe Ruth/1927 10.00
19GOT Nolan Ryan/1989 10.00
20GOT Yogi Berra/1950 8.00
21GOT Al Kaline/1955 5.00
22GOT Ty Cobb/1911 5.00
23GOT Duke Snider/1955 5.00
24GOT Stan Musial/1948 8.00
25GOT Jose Canseco/1988 5.00
26GOT Rocky Colavito/1958 5.00
27GOT Dave Winfield/1979 4.00
28GOT Nolan Ryan/1982 10.00
29GOT Thurman Munson/1977 8.00
30GOT Jackie Robinson/1949 8.00
31GOT Kirby Puckett/1988 8.00
32GOT Ted Kluszewski/1954 5.00
33GOT Warren Spahn/1953 5.00
34GOT Willie McCovey/1969 4.00
35GOT Phil Rizzuto/1950 5.00

The Glory/Time: Game-Used

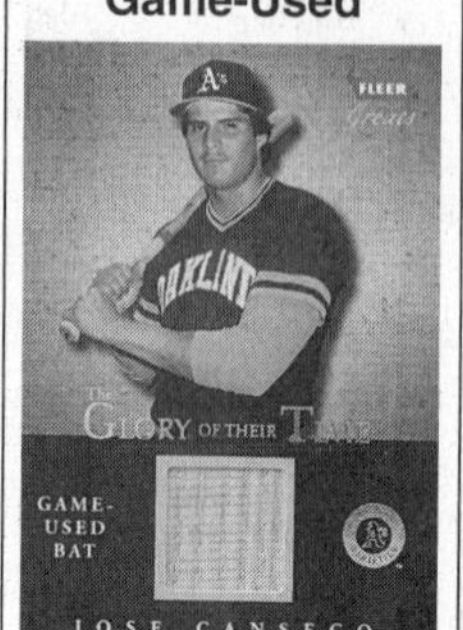

NM/M
Common Player: 10.00
Production 250 Sets
Hobby Only
Gold: 1.5-2X
Retail Only (Not Numbered)
No Rizzuto Retail Version
JB Johnny Bench/Jsy 15.00
YB Yogi Berra/Pants 15.00
GB George Brett/Jsy 15.00
LB Lou Brock/Jsy 15.00
JC1 Jose Canseco/Jsy 10.00
JC2 Jose Canseco/Bat 10.00
RC Rocky Colavito/Bat 25.00
DD Don Drysdale/Jsy 15.00
CF1 Carlton Fisk/Jsy 10.00
CF2 Carlton Fisk/Bat 10.00
TG1 Tony Gwynn/Jsy 10.00
TG2 Tony Gwynn/Jsy 10.00
RJ Reggie Jackson/Pants 20.00
AK Al Kaline/Pants 15.00
HK Harmon Killebrew/Bat 10.00
TK Ted Kluszewski/Pants 15.00
DM Don Mattingly/Pants 20.00
WM Willie McCovey/Pants 10.00
PM Paul Molitor/Jsy 15.00
TM Thurman Munson/Pants 15.00
EM Eddie Murray/Jsy 10.00
KP Kirby Puckett/Bat 20.00
CR Cal Ripken Jr./Jsy 25.00
PR Phil Rizzuto/Pants 15.00
BR Brooks Robinson/Jsy 10.00
NR1 Nolan Ryan/Jsy 20.00
NR2 Nolan Ryan/Bat 20.00
MS Mike Schmidt/Jsy 15.00
MS Bill "Moose" Skowron/Pants 10.00
WS Warren Spahn/Jsy 20.00
DW Dave Winfield/Jsy 10.00
CY Carl Yastrzemski/Jsy 20.00

The Glory/Time: G-U Patch

No Pricing
Production 25 Sets

Yankee Clippings

NM/M
Common Player: 25.00
Inserted 1:45
YB Yogi Berra 60.00
WB Wade Boggs 40.00
RJ Reggie Jackson 40.00
LG Roger Maris 400.00
DM Don Mattingly 100.00
PO Paul O'Neill 30.00
PR Phil Rizzuto 325.00
BS Bill "Moose" Skowron 25.00

Yankee Clippings Autographs

No Pricing
Sequentially #'d between 3 & 26.

2004 Fleer Hot Prospects Draft Edition

NM/M
Common Player (1-60): .25
Minor Stars (1-60): .40
Unlisted Stars (1-60): .60
Common Rookie (61-70): 3.00
Common Rookie (71-120): 15.00
Production 1,000 Sets
Cards 112 & 113 do not exist.
Production 299 Sets
Pack (5): 7.00
Box (15): 100.00
1 Miguel Tejada .50
2 Jose Vidro .25
3 Hideki Matsui 2.00
4 Roger Clemens 2.50
5 Craig Wilson .25
6 Bobby Crosby .25
7 Pat Burrell .40
8 Mike Sweeney .25
9 Craig Biggio .40
10 Scott Rolen 1.00
11 Roy Halladay .40
12 Lyle Overbay .25
13 Rocco Baldelli .50
14 Mike Piazza 1.50

15 Rafael Palmeiro .75
16 Hank Blalock .50
17 Sammy Sosa 1.50
18 Dontrelle Willis .40
19 Alfonso Soriano 1.00
20 Gary Sheffield .75
21 Jim Thome 1.00
22 Ivan Rodriguez .75
23 Adam Dunn .50
24 Kerry Wood .50
25 Khalil Greene .50
26 Richie Sexson .50
27 Nomar Garciaparra 1.00
28 Andruw Jones .75
29 Tom Glavine .40
30 Carlos Beltran .75
31 Chipper Jones 1.00
32 Jeff Bagwell .75
33 Tim Hudson .40
34 Alex Rodriguez 2.00
35 Omar Vizquel .40
36 Albert Pujols 2.50
37 Frank Thomas .75
38 Ben Sheets .40
39 Jason Schmidt .40
40 Miguel Cabrera .75
41 Carlos Delgado .75
42 Ichiro Suzuki 2.00
43 Curt Schilling .75
44 Todd Helton .75
45 Ken Griffey Jr. 1.50
46 Mark Prior .75
47 Vladimir Guerrero 1.00
48 Pedro Martinez 1.00
49 Manny Ramirez 1.00
50 Joe Mauer .50
51 Jorge Posada .75
52 Troy Glaus .50
53 Randy Johnson 1.00
54 Adrian Beltre .40
55 Eric Gagne .40
56 Josh Beckett .50
57 Jason Giambi .75
58 Barry Zito .50
59 Lance Berkman .50
60 Derek Jeter 3.00
61 Kazuo Matsui **RC** 5.00
62 Jason Bartlett **RC** 5.00
63 John Gall **RC** 3.00
64 Chris Saenz **RC** 3.00
65 Merkin Valdez **RC** 3.00
66 Akinori Otsuka **RC** 3.00
67 Joey Gathright **RC** 5.00
68 Brad Halsey **RC** 5.00
69 David Aardsma 3.00
70 Scott Kazmir 10.00
71 Matt Bush/AU **RC** 30.00
72 John Bowker/AU **RC** 25.00
73 Mike Ferris/AU **RC** 15.00
74 Brian Bixler/AU **RC** 15.00
75 Scott Elbert/AU **RC** 40.00
76 Josh Fields/AU **RC** 50.00
77 Bill Bray/AU **RC** 15.00
78 Greg Golson/AU **RC** 30.00
79 Neil Walker/AU **RC** 30.00
80 Phillip Hughes/ AU **RC** 150.00
81 Chris Nelson AU **RC** 40.00
82 Mark Rogers/AU **RC** 30.00
83 Trevor Plouffe/ AU **RC** 25.00
84 Christian Garcia/ AU **RC** 15.00
85 Thomas Diamond/ AU **RC** 30.00
86 B.J. Szymanski/ AU **RC** 25.00
87 Richie Robnett/ AU **RC** 25.00
88 Seth Smith/AU **RC** 25.00
89 Kyle Waldrop/AU **RC** 25.00
90 Curtis Thigpen/ AU **RC** 15.00
91 J.P. Howell/AU **RC** 15.00
92 Blake DeWitt/AU **RC** 30.00
93 Taylor Tankersley/ AU **RC** 15.00
94 Zach Jackson/AU **RC** 15.00
95 Justin Orenduff/ AU **RC** 15.00
96 Tyler Lumsden/ AU **RC** 15.00
97 Danny Putnam **RC** 20.00
98 Jon Poterson/AU **RC** 20.00
99 Matt Fox/AU **RC** 15.00
100 Gio Gonzalez/AU **RC** 35.00
101 Huston Street/AU **RC** 40.00
102 Jay Rainville/AU **RC** 25.00
103 Matt Durkin/AU **RC** 15.00
104 Brett Smith/AU **RC** 15.00
105 Justin Hoyman/ AU **RC** 20.00
106 Erick San Pedro/ AU **RC** 15.00
107 Jeff Marquez/AU **RC** 15.00
108 Hunter Pence/ AU **RC** 160.00
109 Dustin Pedroia/ AU **RC** 75.00
110 Kurt Suzuki/AU **RC** 25.00
111 Billy Buckner/AU **RC** 15.00
114 J.C. Holt/AU **RC** 15.00
115 Homer Bailey/AU **RC** 80.00
116 David Purcey/AU **RC** 20.00
117 Jeremy Sowers/ AU **RC** 25.00
118 Chris Lambert/AU **RC** 15.00
119 Eric Hurley/AU **RC** 40.00
120 Grant Johnson/ AU **RC** 15.00

Red Hot

Veterans (1-60): 2-4X
Rookies (61-70): 1-2X
Production 150
Rookies (71-120): No Pricing
Production 25 Sets

White Hot

Cards (1-120): No Pricing
Production One Set

Alumni Ink

No Pricing
Production 15 Sets
Red Hot: No Pricing
Production Five Sets
White Hot: No Pricing
Production One Set

Double Team Autograph Patch Red Hot

No Pricing
Production 22 Sets
White Hot: No Pricing
Production One Set

Double Team Jersey

NM/M
Common Player: 10.00
Production 100 Sets
Red Hot: No Pricing
Production 25 Sets
White Hot: No Pricing
Production One Set
Patch: .75-1.5X
Production 50 Sets
Patch Red Hot: No Pricing
Production 10 Sets
Patch White Hot: No Pricing
Production One Set
CB Carlos Beltran 15.00
RCA Rod Carew 20.00
RCL Roger Clemens 20.00
JG Jason Giambi 12.00
TG Tom Glavine 10.00
VG Vladimir Guerrero 15.00
RH Rickey Henderson 20.00
RJ Reggie Jackson 25.00
GM Greg Maddux 15.00
PM Pedro Martinez 15.00
EM Eddie Murray 20.00
HN Hideo Nomo 15.00
RP Rafael Palmeiro 12.00
MP Mike Piazza 20.00
MR Manny Ramirez 15.00
IR Ivan Rodriguez 10.00
SR Scott Rolen 15.00
NR Nolan Ryan 50.00
AS Alfonso Soriano 12.00
MT Miguel Tejada 10.00

Draft Rewind

NM/M
Common Player: 2.00
Inserted 1:5
1 Joe Mauer 2.00
2 Derek Jeter 6.00
3 Chipper Jones 3.50
4 Greg Maddux 3.50
5 Alex Rodriguez 5.00
6 Nomar Garciaparra 5.00
7 Curt Schilling 3.00
8 Kerry Wood 3.00
9 Troy Glaus 3.00
10 Pat Burrell 2.00
11 Mark Mulder 2.00
12 Josh Beckett 3.00
13 Barry Zito 3.00
14 Mark Prior 4.00
15 Rickie Weeks 2.00
16 Khalil Greene 3.00
17 Ken Griffey Jr. 3.50
18 Gary Sheffield 3.00
19 Todd Helton 3.00
20 Barry Larkin 2.00
21 Kevin Brown 2.00
22 Frank Thomas 3.00
23 Manny Ramirez 3.00
24 Roger Clemens 5.00
25 Lance Berkman 2.00
26 Randy Johnson 3.00
27 Jason Giambi 3.00
28 Ben Sheets 2.00
29 Scott Rolen 3.00
30 Tom Glavine 2.00

Draft Rewind Jersey

NM/M
Common Player: 8.00
Sequentially #'d to indicated quantity.
Red Hot: No Pricing
Production 10 Sets
White Hot: No Pricing
Production One Set
Patch
Cards #'d 41-68: .75-1.5X
Cards #'d 29 or less: No Pricing
Patch Red Hot: No Pricing
Production Five Sets
Patch White Hot: No Pricing
Production One Set
RB Rocco Baldelli/119 8.00
JB Josh Beckett/102 10.00
LB Lance Berkman/116 8.00
KB Kevin Brown/104 8.00
PB Pat Burrell/101 8.00
EC Eric Chavez/110 8.00
RC Roger Clemens/119 15.00
JG Jason Giambi/158 8.00
TG Troy Glaus/103 8.00
TG Tom Glavine/147 8.00
KG Khalil Greene/113 15.00
ZG Zack Greinke/106 8.00
TH Todd Helton/108 10.00
RJ Randy Johnson/136 10.00
CJ Chipper Jones/101 12.00
CK Casey Kotchman/113 8.00
BL Barry Larkin/104 10.00
GM Greg Maddux/131 12.00
JM Joe Mauer/101 10.00
MM Mark Mulder/102 8.00
MP Mark Prior/102 8.00
MR Manny Ramirez/113 10.00
SR Scott Rolen/146 10.00
CS Curt Schilling/139 10.00
BS Ben Sheets/110 8.00
GS Gary Sheffield/106 8.00
FT Frank Thomas/107 15.00
RW Rickie Weeks/102 8.00
KW Kerry Wood/104 10.00
BZ Barry Zito/109 8.00

Hot Tandems

NM/M
Common Card: 3.00
Inserted 1:15
1HT Mark Prior, Greg Maddux 4.00
2HT Jim Thome, Pat Burrell 3.50
3HT Ken Griffey Jr., Adam Dunn 4.00
4HT Mike Piazza, Tom Glavine 4.00
5HT Alex Rodriguez, Derek Jeter 10.00
6HT Roger Clemens, Andy Pettitte 6.00
7HT Hideki Matsui, Jason Giambi 6.00
8HT Hank Blalock, Alfonso Soriano 3.50
9HT Manny Ramirez, David Ortiz 3.50
10HT Miguel Cabrera, Dontrelle Willis 3.50
11HT Hideki Matsui, Ichiro Suzuki 6.00
12HT Albert Pujols, Scott Rolen 6.00
13HT Curt Schilling, Pedro J. Martinez 3.50
14HT Nomar Garciaparra, Sammy Sosa 5.00
15HT Kazuo Matsui, Derek Jeter 8.00

MLB Hot Materials

NM/M
Common Player: 5.00
Production 325 Sets
Red Hot: 1-2X
Production 50 Sets
White Hot Patch: No Pricing
Production One Set
JB Jeff Bagwell/Jsy 6.00
LB Lance Berkman/Jsy 5.00
HB Hank Blalock/Jsy 6.00
MC Miguel Cabrera/Jsy 8.00
RC Roger Clemens/Jsy 12.00
CD Carlos Delgado/Jsy 6.00
JD J.D. Drew/Jsy 6.00
AD Adam Dunn/Jsy 6.00
JE Jim Edmonds/Jsy 5.00
EG Eric Gagne/Jsy 6.00
VG Vladimir Guerrero/Jsy 8.00
THE Todd Helton/Jsy 6.00
THU Tim Hudson/Jsy 5.00
THN Torii Hunter/Jsy 6.00
RJ Randy Johnson/Jsy 8.00
AJ Andruw Jones/Jsy 6.00
CJ Chipper Jones/Jsy 8.00
HM Hideki Matsui/Jsy 20.00
KM Kazuo Matsui/Jsy 10.00
JM Joe Mauer/Jsy 8.00
MM Mike Mussina/Jsy 6.00
HN Hideo Nomo/Jsy 8.00
LO Lyle Overbay/Jsy 5.00
APE Andy Pettitte/Jsy 6.00
MPI Mike Piazza/Jsy 8.00
JP Jorge Posada/Jsy 6.00
MPR Mark Prior/Jsy 8.00
APU Albert Pujols/Jsy 12.00
MR Manny Ramirez/Jsy 8.00
IR Ivan Rodriguez/Jsy 6.00
CS Curt Schilling/Jsy 8.00
JS Jason Schmidt/Jsy 5.00
AS Alfonso Soriano/Jsy 8.00
SS Sammy Sosa/Jsy 10.00
MTX Mark Teixeira/Jsy 6.00
MTJ Miguel Tejada/Jsy 5.00
FT Frank Thomas/Jsy 8.00
JT Jim Thome/Jsy 8.00
DW Dontrelle Willis/Jsy 5.00
KW Kerry Wood/Jsy 8.00

Past, Present, Future Triple Autograph

NM/M
Production 33 Sets
Red Hot: No Pricing
Production Three Sets
White Hot: No Pricing
Production One Set
Matt Durkin, Mookie Wilson, Mike Piazza 150.00
Hideo Nomo, Scott Elbert, Kirk Gibson 250.00
Josh Fields, Carlton Fisk, Ryan Meaux 80.00
Greg Golson, Steve Carlton, Jim Thome 100.00
Jack Wilson, Neil Walker, Ralph Kiner 80.00
Ryne Sandberg, Mark Prior, Grant Johnson 250.00
Homer Bailey, Johnny Bench, Adam Dunn 150.00
Albert Pujols, Chris Lambert, Stan Musial 300.00
Richie Robnett, Reggie Jackson, Eric Chavez 80.00
Dustin Pedroia, Bill Buckner, Manny Ramirez 60.00

2004 Fleer InScribed

NM/M
Common Player (1-75): .25
Minor Stars (1-75): .40
Unlisted Stars (1-75): .60
Common Player (76-85): 3.00
Production 1,000 Sets
Numbered to 750 3.00
Not all 750 of each card not released.
Pack (5): 10.00
Box (12): 85.00
1 Vladimir Guerrero 1.00
2 Bartolo Colon .40
3 Troy Glaus .60
4 Richie Sexson .60
5 Randy Johnson 1.00
6 Luis Gonzalez .40
7 J.D. Drew .40
8 Chipper Jones 1.50
9 Andruw Jones .75
10 Melvin Mora .25
11 Miguel Tejada .60
12 Curt Schilling .60
13 Pedro J. Martinez 1.00
14 Nomar Garciaparra 2.50
15 Kerry Wood .75
16 Mark Prior 2.00
17 Sammy Sosa 2.00
18 Frank Thomas .75
19 Magglio Ordonez .40
20 Sean Casey .25
21 Ken Griffey Jr. 1.50
22 Adam Dunn .60
23 Jody Gerut .25
24 Omar Vizquel .25
25 Todd Helton .75
26 Vinny Castilla .25
27 Alex Sanchez .25
28 Ivan Rodriguez .60
29 Dontrelle Willis .40
30 Josh Beckett .75
31 Miguel Cabrera .75
32 Roger Clemens 1.50
33 Andy Pettitte .60
34 Jeff Bagwell .75
35 Ken Harvey .25
36 Carlos Beltran .60
37 Shawn Green .40
38 Hideo Nomo .40
39 Scott Podsednik .25
40 Ben Sheets .40
41 Torii Hunter .60
42 Jacque Jones .25
43 Jose Vidro .25
44 Mike Piazza 1.50
45 Tom Glavine .40
46 Derek Jeter 3.00
47 Alex Rodriguez 2.50
48 Jason Giambi 1.00
49 Hideki Matsui 2.50
50 Eric Chavez .40
51 Barry Zito .60
52 Tim Hudson .40
53 Mark Mulder .40
54 Jim Thome 1.00
55 Pat Burrell .40
56 Chase Utley .25
57 Jason Kendall .40
58 Jack Wilson .25
59 Khalil Greene .75
60 Brian Giles .40
61 Jason Schmidt .40
62 Marquis Grissom .25
63 Ichiro Suzuki 2.00
64 Bret Boone .40
65 Albert Pujols 2.50
66 Scott Rolen 1.00
67 Jim Edmonds .40
68 Tino Martinez .25
69 Rocco Baldelli .60
70 Alfonso Soriano 1.00
71 Michael Young .25
72 Hank Blalock .40
73 Roy Halladay .40
74 Carlos Delgado .75
75 Vernon Wells .40
76 Johnny Bench 3.00
77 Reggie Jackson 5.00
78 Al Kaline 3.00
79 Nolan Ryan 10.00
80 Tom Seaver 3.00
81 Robin Yount 6.00
82 Mike Schmidt 5.00
83 Jim Palmer 3.00
84 Harmon Killebrew 3.00
85 Joe Morgan 3.00
86 Kazuo Matsui **RC** 5.00
87 Luis Gonzalez **RC** 5.00
88 Yadier Molina **RC** 4.00
89 Jon Knott **RC** 3.00
90 Kevin Youkilis 5.00
91 Chris Saenz **RC** 3.00
92 Andres Blanco **RC** 3.00
93 David Aardsma 3.00
94 Merkin Valdez **RC** 3.00
95 Jason Bartlett **RC** 3.00
96 John Gall **RC** 3.00
97 Zack Greinke 3.00
98 Scott Hairston 3.00
99 Matt Holliday 4.00
100 Casey Kotchman 5.00

Red

No Pricing
Production Five Sets

Gold

Veterans (1-75): 2-5X
Rookies (76-100): .75-2X
Production 199 Sets

Autographs Silver

NM/M
Common Player: 10.00
Numbered to indicated quantity.
Red: No Pricing
Production 25 Sets
Purple: .5-2X
Numbered to jersey number.
RB Rocco Baldelli/34 25.00
CB Carlos Beltran/296 25.00
JB Jeremy Bonderman/ 287 10.00
EC Eric Chavez/322 15.00
EG Eric Gagne/57 40.00
BG Brian Giles/134 15.00
LG Luis Gonzalez/55 15.00
RHL Roy Halladay/139 15.00
RHR Rich Harden/235 10.00
TH Trevor Hoffman/174 15.00
BL Barry Larkin/140 20.00
JL Javy Lopez/257 15.00
WM Wade Miller/195 10.00
TN Trot Nixon/318 10.00
LO Lyle Overbay/240 10.00
SP Scott Podsednik/280 10.00
BR Brad Radke/168 15.00

Facsimile Signature Gold

Current (1-75): 3-5X
Retired (76-85): 1-2X
Rookies (86-100): .75-1.5X
Production 199 Sets

Award Winners

NM/M
Common Player:
Production 150 Sets
1 Alex Rodriguez 10.00
2 Eric Gagne 3.00
3 Miguel Tejada 4.00
4 Roy Halladay 3.00
5 Randy Johnson 5.00
6 Barry Zito 4.00
7 Chipper Jones 3.00
8 Ivan Rodriguez 4.00
9 Pedro J. Martinez 5.00
10 Barry Larkin 3.00
11 Dontrelle Willis 3.00
12 Angel Berroa 3.00
13 Kerry Wood 5.00
14 Albert Pujols 8.00
15 Hideo Nomo 3.00

Award Winners Jersey Silver

NM/M
Common Player:
Production 175 Sets
Copper: .75-1.5X
Production 99 Sets
Purple: 1-30X
Production 49 Sets
AB Angel Berroa 5.00
EG Eric Gagne 8.00
RH Roy Halladay 5.00
RJ Randy Johnson 10.00
CJ Chipper Jones 10.00
BL Barry Larkin 5.00
PM Pedro J. Martinez 10.00
HN Hideo Nomo 5.00
AP Albert Pujols 15.00
IR Ivan Rodriguez 8.00
MT Miguel Tejada 8.00
DW Dontrelle Willis 5.00
KW Kerry Wood 10.00
BZ Barry Zito 8.00

Award Winners Autographs

NM/M
Common Player: 15.00
Numbered to Award Year.
All cards not released for some cards.
AB Angel Berroa/103 15.00
RH Roy Halladay/102 20.00
BL Barry Larkin 95/50 30.00
DW Dontrelle Willis/103 25.00

Induction Ceremony

NM/M
Common Player: 6.00
Numbered to Year of Induction.
1 Carlton Fisk/100 8.00
2 Tony Perez/100 6.00
3 Nolan Ryan/99 20.00
4 Robin Yount/99 10.00
5 Orlando Cepeda/99 8.00
6 Bill Mazeroski/101 8.00
7 Larry Doby/98 6.00
8 Phil Niekro/97 6.00
9 Jim Bunning/96 6.00
10 Sparky Anderson/100 6.00
11 Phil Rizzuto/94 8.00
12 Rollie Fingers/92 6.00
13 Hal Newhouser/92 6.00
14 Rod Carew/91 8.00
15 Reggie Jackson/93 8.00
16 Tom Seaver/92 8.00
17 Bob Gibson/81 8.00
18 Jim Palmer/90 6.00

19	Joe Morgan/90	6.00
20	Al Kaline/80	10.00

Induction Ceremony Autograph Bronze

		NM/M
Common Player:		20.00
Numbered to 50		
Silver:		No Pricing
Production 15 Sets		
Gold:		No Pricing
Production Five Sets		
JB	Jim Bunning	20.00
OC	Orlando Cepeda/40	20.00
RF	Rollie Fingers	30.00
CF	Carlton Fisk	30.00
BG	Bob Gibson	40.00
AK	Al Kaline	50.00
TP	Tony Perez	30.00

Induction Ceremony Material Silver

		NM/M
Common Player:		10.00
Numbered (two-didgit) to induction year.		
Masterpiece:		No Pricing
Production One Set		
SA	Sparky Anderson/100	10.00
RC	Rod Carew/91	15.00
OC	Orlando Cepeda/99	10.00
LD	Larry Doby/98	20.00
RF	Rollie Fingers/92	10.00
CF	Carlton Fisk/100	15.00
RJ	Reggie Jackson/93	10.00
AK	Al Kaline/80	20.00
BM	Bill Mazeroski/101	10.00
JM	Joe Morgan/90	15.00
PN	Phil Niekro/97	10.00
JP	Jim Palmer/90	10.00
TP	Tony Perez/100	15.00
PR	Phil Rizzuto/94	20.00
NR	Nolan Ryan/99	25.00
TS	Tom Seaver/92	10.00
RY	Robin Yount/99	10.00

Names of the Game

		NM/M
Common Player:		2.00
Production 299 Sets		
1	Nomar Garciaparra	8.00
2	Randy Johnson	3.00
3	Hideki Matsui	8.00
4	Frank Thomas	2.00
5	Ivan Rodriguez	2.00
6	Roger Clemens	5.00
7	Chipper Jones	5.00
8	Dontrelle Willis	2.00
9	Luis Gonzalez	2.00
10	Alex Rodriguez	8.00
11	Eric Gagne	2.00
12	Juan Gonzalez	2.00
13	Hideo Nomo	2.00
14	Sean Casey	2.00
15	Greg Maddux	5.00
16	Cal Ripken Jr.	15.00
17	Carl Yastrzemski	5.00
18	Tony Perez	3.00
19	Joe Morgan	3.00
20	Carlton Fisk	3.00
21	Willie McCovey	5.00
22	Al Kaline	5.00
23	Dennis Eckersley	3.00
24	Ted Williams	10.00
25	Willie Stargell	5.00
26	Rollie Fingers	3.00
27	Yogi Berra	2.00
28	Reggie Jackson	5.00
29	Harmon Killebrew	5.00
30	Nolan Ryan	10.00

Names of the Game Autograph Silver

		NM/M
Common Player:		15.00
Stated Production 99 Sets		
All 99 not released for some cards.		
Gold:		No Pricing
Stated Production 25 Sets.		
All 25 not released for some cards.		
SC	Sean Casey	20.00
DE	Dennis Eckersley/90	25.00
RF	Rollie Fingers/90	25.00
CF	Carlton Fisk/50	30.00
LG	Luis Gonzalez/75	15.00
CJ	Chipper Jones/40	40.00
AK	Al Kaline/90	40.00
DW	Dontrelle Willis	25.00

Names of the Game Material Copper

		NM/M
Common Player:		5.00
Production 250 Sets		
Gold:		.5-1.25X
Production 150 Sets		
Red:		.75-1.5X
Production 79 Sets		
Purple:		1-2X
Production 33 Sets		
YB	Yogi Berra	10.00
SC	Sean Casey	5.00
RC	Roger Clemens	10.00
DE	Dennis Eckersley	8.00
RF	Rollie Fingers	8.00
CF	Carlton Fisk	8.00
EG	Eric Gagne	10.00
JG	Juan Gonzalez	5.00
LG	Luis Gonzalez	5.00
RJA	Reggie Jackson	10.00
RJO	Randy Johnson	8.00
CJ	Chipper Jones	8.00
AK	Al Kaline	10.00
HK	Harmon Killebrew	10.00
GM	Greg Maddux	10.00
HM	Hideki Matsui	15.00
WM	Willie McCovey	10.00
JM	Joe Morgan	8.00
HN	Hideo Nomo	5.00
TP	Tony Perez	8.00
CR	Cal Ripken Jr.	30.00
IR	Ivan Rodriguez	5.00
NR	Nolan Ryan	20.00
WS	Willie Stargell	10.00
FT	Frank Thomas	5.00
TW	Ted Williams	25.00
DW	Dontrelle Willis	5.00
CY	Carl Yastrzemski	10.00

Rookie Autographs Notation

		NM/M
Common Player:		15.00
Stated Production 750 Sets		
75 Notation Cards for each player		
87	Luis A. Gonzalez 4/6/04	15.00
89	Jon Knott 5/30/04	15.00
90	Kevin Youkilis 5/15/04	20.00
91	Chris Saenz 4/24/04	15.00
92	Andres Blanco 4/17/04	15.00
94	Merkin Valdez Go Giants	20.00
95	Jason Bartlett Go Twins	20.00
96B	John Gall Go Cards/50	20.00
98	Scott Hairston 5/17/04	15.00
100	Casey Kotchman 5/9/04	25.00

L.A. Dodgers

Persons attending April 11 (#1-7), May 30 (#8-14) and July 10 (#15-21) special Baseball Card Pack promotional games received a cello-wrapped series of seven Tradition cards and a checklist card. Fronts have game-action photos with blue borders. Backs have major/minor league stats.

		NM/M
Complete Set (22):		7.50
Common Player:		.25
1	Hideo Nomo	1.50
2	Paul LoDuca	.50
3	Alex Cora	.25
4	Paul Shuey	.25
5	Juan Encarnacion	.25
6	Steve Colyer	.25
7	Joe Thurston	.25
8	Shawn Green	.35
9	Edwin Jackson	.50
10	Dave Roberts	.25
11	Guillermo Mota	.25
12	Jolbert Cabrera	.25
13	Darren Dreifort	.25
14	David Ross	.25
15	Eric Gagne	.35
16	Adrian Beltre	.35
17	Cesar Izturis	.25
18	Robin Ventura	.25
19	Wilson Alvarez	.25
20	Bubba Trammell	.25
21	Wilkin Ruan	.25
---	Checklist	.25

2004 Fleer Legacy

		NM/M
Common Player (1-60):		1.50
Minor Stars (1-60):		2.00
Unlisted Stars (1-60):		2.50
Common Rookie (61-75):		4.00
Production 599 Sets		
Box (1 Pack, 1 Autographed Baseball):		150.00
1	Angel Berroa	1.50
2	Derek Jeter	8.00
3	Jody Gerut	1.50
4	Curt Schilling	2.50
5	Khalil Greene	3.00
6	Manny Ramirez	3.00
7	Rocco Baldelli	2.50
8	Sammy Sosa	5.00
9	Shawn Green	2.00
10	Austin Kearns	2.60
11	Frank Thomas	3.00
12	Alfonso Soriano	3.50
13	Alex Rodriguez	6.00
14	Carlos Delgado	3.00
15	Chipper Jones	4.00
16	Edgar Martinez	2.00
17	Ivan Rodriguez	2.50
18	Mark Prior	4.00
19	Mike Piazza	4.00
20	Orlando Cabrera	1.50
21	Adam Dunn	2.50
22	Andruw Jones	3.00
23	Eric Chavez	2.00
24	Mark Teixeira	2.00
25	Scott Podsednik	1.50
26	Torii Hunter	2.50
27	Miguel Cabrera	3.00
28	Hideki Matsui	6.00
29	Jose Reyes	1.50
30	Vladimir Guerrero	3.50
31	Albert Pujols	6.00
32	Greg Maddux	4.00
33	Jason Giambi	3.50
34	Randy Johnson	3.50
35	Roger Clemens	6.00
36	Casey Kotchman	2.00
37	Ken Griffey Jr.	4.00
38	Todd Helton	3.00
39	Javy Lopez	1.50
40	Jim Thome	3.50
41	Josh Beckett	3.00
42	Kerry Wood	3.00
43	Scott Rolen	3.50
44	Pat Burrell	2.00
45	Pedro J. Martinez	3.50
46	Barry Zito	2.50
47	Hank Blalock	2.00
48	Hideo Nomo	2.00
49	Jeff Bagwell	3.00
50	Magglio Ordonez	2.00
51	Ichiro Suzuki	5.00
52	Joe Mauer	2.00
53	Richie Sexson	2.50
54	Shannon Stewart	1.50
55	Craig Wilson	1.50
56	Miguel Tejada	2.50
57	Sean Casey	1.50
58	Tom Glavine	2.00
59	Jason Schmidt	2.00
60	Nomar Garciaparra	6.00
61	Kazuo Matsui **RC**	8.00
62	Justin Leone **RC**	4.00
63	Merkin Valdez **RC**	6.00
64	Shingo Takatsu **RC**	6.00
65	Andres Blanco **RC**	4.00
66	Angel Chavez **RC**	4.00
67	Hector Gimenez **RC**	4.00
68	Akinori Otsuka **RC**	4.00
69	Jason Bartlett **RC**	4.00
70	Luis Gonzalez **RC**	4.00
71	Sean Henn	4.00
72	Mike Rouse	4.00
73	Chris Aguila **RC**	4.00
74	Aarom Baldiris **RC**	4.00
75	Jerry Gil **RC**	4.00

Gold Legacy

Veterans (1-60):	2-4X
Rookies (61-75):	.75-1.5X
Production 50 Sets	

Ultimate Legacy

No Pricing
Production One Set

Franchise Legacy Patch

		NM/M
Common Player:		10.00
Production 99 Sets		
Patch 50:		.5-1.5X
Production 50 Sets		
Patch 25:		No Pricing
Production 25 Sets		
Masterpiece:		No Pricing
Production One Set		
JBA	Jeff Bagwell	15.00
JBE	Josh Beckett	15.00
RC	Roger Clemens	25.00
VG	Vladimir Guerrero	15.00
RJ	Randy Johnson	20.00
CJ	Chipper Jones	20.00
JL	Javy Lopez	10.00
GM	Greg Maddux	30.00
PM	Pedro Martinez	15.00
HM	Hideki Matsui	60.00
KM	Kazuo Matsui	20.00
DM	Don Mattingly	40.00
HN	Hideo Nomo	20.00
MP	Mike Piazza	20.00
MPR	Mark Prior	10.00
AP	Albert Pujols	50.00
CR	Cal Ripken Jr.	60.00
IR	Ivan Rodriguez	15.00
NR	Nolan Ryan	50.00
SS	Sammy Sosa	15.00
MT	Miguel Tejada	10.00
JT	Jim Thome	15.00
KW	Kerry Wood	15.00

Franchise Dual Patch

No Pricing
Sequentially #'d between 5 & 31.

Franchise Legacy Quad Patch

No Pricing
Sequentially #'d between 2 & 22.

Hit Kings Patch Silver

		NM/M
Common Player:		15.00
Production 99 Sets		
Gold:		.5-1.5X
Production 50 Sets		
Masterpiece:		No Pricing
Production One Set		
JB	Jeff Bagwell	15.00
LB	Lance Berkman	15.00
HB	Hank Blalock	20.00
MC	Miguel Cabrera	20.00
CD	Carlos Delgado	20.00
AD	Adam Dunn	30.00
JG	Jason Giambi	15.00
VG	Vladimir Guerrero	20.00
CJ	Chipper Jones	20.00
AK	Austin Kearns	15.00
HM	Hideki Matsui	50.00
MP	Mike Piazza	25.00
AP	Albert Pujols	50.00
MR	Manny Ramirez	25.00
SR	Scott Rolen	20.00
MS	Mike Schmidt	40.00
RS	Richie Sexson	15.00
GS	Gary Sheffield	20.00
SS	Sammy Sosa	20.00
MT	Mark Teixeira	15.00
FT	Frank Thomas	15.00
JT	Jim Thome	25.00

Hit Kings Dual Patch

No Pricing
Sequentially numbered between 7 & 21.

Kaz Matsui Special Edition

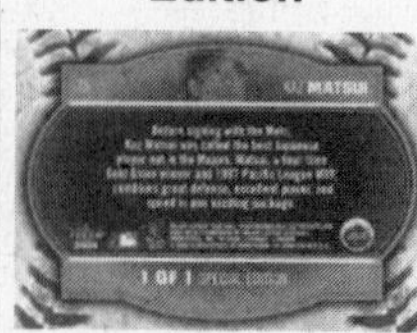

This card was produced in an edition of 25,000. It was available to customers presenting a sheet of the Fleer/N.Y. Post Mets cards at any Mets Team Store and purchasing a Fleer pack. The back is labeled "1 OF 1 SPECIAL EDITION."

		NM/M
1	Kaz Matsui	3.00

National Trading Card Day

As part of its participation in NTCD on April 3, Fleer issued a foil pack with four baseball player cards, two football and three basketball, plus a header. Only the baseball players are listed here. Fronts have game-action photos on a ghosted background; backs have recent stats and biographical data. The NTCD logo appears on both sides.

		NM/M
Unopened Pack:		3.00
Common Player:		.25
1	Derek Jeter	.50
2	Alex Rodriguez	.50
3	Nomar Garciaparra	.35
4	Jose Reyes	.25

N.Y. Mets

Persons attending a special Baseball Card Pack promotional game received a cello-wrapped set of seven player cards and a header card. Fronts have game-action photos on a blue graph background. Backs have portrait and action photos and career highlights.

		NM/M
Complete Set (8):		4.00
Common Player:		.50
1	Mike Cameron	.50
2	Cliff Floyd	.50
3	Al Leiter	.50
4	Kaz Matsui	1.00
5	Mike Piazza	1.00
6	Jose Reyes	1.00
7	Shea Stadium	.50
---	Checklist	.05

2004 Fleer Patchworks

		NM/M
Common Player (1-90):		.15
Minor Stars:		.40
Unlisted Stars:		.60
Common Rookie (91-110):		2.00
Minor Rookies:		3.00
Unlisted Rookies:		5.00
Production 799 Sets		
Pack (5):		4.00
Box (18):		70.00
1	Kerry Wood	1.00
2	Brian Giles	.40
3	Tino Martinez	.15
4	Mark Mulder	.40
5	Andy Pettitte	.60
6	Gary Sheffield	.60
7	Mark Teixeira	.40
8	Garret Anderson	.40
9	Craig Biggio	.40
10	Alfonso Soriano	1.50
11	Bret Boone	.40
12	Mike Piazza	2.00
13	Todd Helton	1.00
14	Jay Gibbons	.40
15	Eric Chavez	.40
16	Andruw Jones	1.00
17	Adam Dunn	.60
18	Corey Koskie	.15
19	Rafael Palmeiro	1.00
20	Ivan Rodriguez	.60
21	Tom Glavine	.40
22	Luis Gonzalez	.40
23	Miguel Tejada	.60
24	Jose Vidro	.15
25	Richie Sexson	.60
26	Roy Halladay	.40
27	Vladimir Guerrero	1.50
28	Randy Johnson	1.50
29	Vernon Wells	.40
30	Pat Burrell	.40
31	Jason Schmidt	.40
32	Casey Blake	.15
33	Greg Maddux	2.00
34	Mike Lowell	.15
35	Hideo Nomo	.40
36	Carlos Delgado	1.00
37	Dontrelle Willis	.40
38	Shawn Green	.40
39	Pedro Martinez	1.50
40	Josh Beckett	1.00
41	Eric Gagne	.40
42	Manny Ramirez	1.00
43	Jim Edmonds	.40
44	Curt Schilling	.60
45	Mike Sweeney	.15
46	Albert Pujols	3.00
47	Nomar Garciaparra	3.00
48	Alex Rodriguez	3.00
49	Angel Berroa	.15
50	Jim Thome	1.50
51	Edgardo Alfonzo	.15
52	Jeremy Bonderman	.15
53	Miguel Cabrera	1.00
54	Bobby Higginson	.15
55	John Smoltz	.40
56	Jason Kendall	.40
57	Torii Hunter	.60
58	Troy Glaus	.60
59	Rafael Furcal	.40
60	Austin Kearns	.60
61	Esteban Loaiza	.15
62	Darin Erstad	.40
63	Jose Reyes	.15
64	Preston Wilson	.15
65	Rocco Baldelli	.60
66	Barry Zito	.60
67	Ken Griffey Jr.	2.00
68	Frank Thomas	1.00
69	Roger Clemens	2.00
70	Brett Myers	.15
71	Billy Wagner	.15
72	Scott Podsednik	.15
73	Jody Gerut	.15
74	Bartolo Colon	.40
75	Jeff Bagwell	1.00
76	Jason Giambi	1.50
77	Edgar Martinez	.40
78	Chipper Jones	2.00
79	Jason Bay	.15
80	Doug Mientkiewicz	.15
81	Hank Blalock	.60
82	Sammy Sosa	2.00
83	Derek Jeter	4.00
84	Ichiro Suzuki	2.00
85	Ben Sheets	.40
86	Magglio Ordonez	.40
87	Carlos Beltran	.40
88	Mark Prior	2.00
89	Sean Burroughs	.15
90	Tim Hudson	.40
91	Hector Gimenez **RC**	8.00
92	Khalil Greene **RC**	5.00
93	Rickie Weeks	8.00
94	Delmon Young	10.00

95 Donald Kelly **RC** 3.00
96 Chad Bentz **RC** 5.00
97 Greg Dobbs **RC** 3.00
98 John Gall **RC** 5.00
99 Cory Sullivan **RC** 3.00
100 Kazuo Matsui **RC** 25.00
101 Graham Koonce 3.00
102 Jason Bartlett **RC** 8.00
103 Angel Chavez **RC** 2.00
104 Ronny Cedeno **RC** 3.00
105 Jerry Gil **RC** 3.00
106 Ivan Ochoa **RC** 3.00
107 Ruddy Yan **RC** 8.00
108 Mike Gosling 2.00
109 Alfredo Simon **RC** 2.00
110 Koyie Hill **RC** 2.00

Ruby

Ruby (1-90): 3-10X
Ruby (91-110): .5-2X
Production 50 Sets

Autoworks

NM/M
Common Player: 10.00
Inserted 1:54
Parallel: .5-1.25X
Production 100 Sets
Patch
Production 10 Sets
1 Garret Anderson/145 15.00
2 Josh Beckett/148 30.00
3 Angel Berroa/145 10.00
4 Eric Gagne/193 20.00
5 Jody Gerut/376 10.00
6 Roy Halladay/286 10.00
7 Mark Mulder/190 15.00
8 Andy Pettitte/148 30.00
9 Scott Podsednik/146 20.00
10 Albert Pujols/193 120.00
11 Grady Sizemore/263 25.00
12 Miguel Tejada/164 20.00

By The Numbers

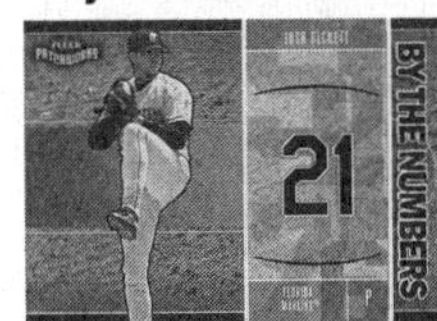

NM/M
Common Player: 3.00
Inserted 1:24
Patch: 3-8X
Production 100 Sets
1 Albert Pujols 8.00
2 Derek Jeter 10.00
3 Mike Piazza 6.00
4 Nomar Garciaparra 8.00
5 Eric Gagne 4.00
6 Sammy Sosa 6.00
7 Josh Beckett 4.00
8 Vladimir Guerrero 5.00
9 Jose Reyes 3.00
10 Bret Boone 3.00
11 Alex Rodriguez 8.00
12 Randy Johnson 6.00
13 Chipper Jones 6.00
14 Tim Hudson 4.00
15 Rocco Baldelli 4.00

Game-Used Level 1

NM/M
Common Player: 6.00
Production 200 Sets
Level 2: 1-1.5X
Production 100 Sets
Patch: 1-2X
Production 50 Sets
1 Albert Pujols 15.00
2 Andy Pettitte 6.00
3 Dontrelle Willis 6.00
4 Mike Piazza 10.00
5 Barry Zito 6.00
6 Troy Glaus 6.00
7 Carlos Delgado 8.00
8 Torii Hunter 6.00
9 Roy Halladay 6.00
10 Andruw Jones 8.00
11 Garret Anderson 6.00
12 Larry Walker 6.00
13 Shawn Green 6.00
14 Bernie Williams 6.00
15 Alfonso Soriano 10.00
16 Bret Boone 6.00
17 Hank Blalock 6.00
18 Jose Reyes 6.00
19 Mark Prior 10.00

Licensed Apparel

NM/M
Common Player: 5.00
Production 300 Sets
Team Name: 1-2X
Production 150 Sets
Number: 1-2X
Production 100 Sets
Nameplate: 1-30X
Production 50 Sets
Jersey Tags:
Production 10 Sets
MLB Logo
Production One Set
1 Albert Pujols 15.00
2 Derek Jeter 18.00
3 Alex Rodriguez 15.00
4 Jim Thome 8.00
5 Mike Piazza 10.00
6 Dontrelle Willis 5.00
7 Torii Hunter 5.00
8 Tim Hudson 5.00
9 Sammy Sosa 12.00
10 Troy Glaus 5.00
11 Andruw Jones 8.00
12 Austin Kearns 5.00
13 Jeff Bagwell 8.00
14 Mark Prior 10.00
15 Bret Boone 5.00

National Pastime

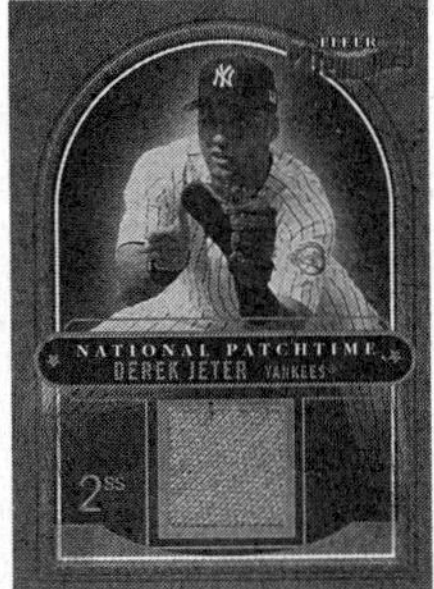

NM/M
Common Player: 5.00
Production 250 Sets
Jersey: 1-1.5X
Production 350 Sets
Gold Jersey: 1-2X
Production 200 Sets
Patch: 1-30X
Production 100 Sets
1 Albert Pujols 15.00
2 Alex Rodriguez 15.00
3 Derek Jeter 18.00
4 Nomar Garciaparra 15.00
5 Jim Thome 8.00
6 Chipper Jones 10.00
7 Mark Prior 10.00
8 Ichiro Suzuki 12.00
9 Jeff Bagwell 6.00
10 Troy Glaus 5.00
11 Randy Johnson 8.00
12 Sammy Sosa 12.00
13 Austin Kearns 5.00
14 Miguel Cabrera 6.00
15 Vladimir Guerrero 8.00

Stitches In Time

NM/M
Common Player: 2.00
Inserted 1:12
Jersey:
Production 350 Sets
Patch:
Production 150 Sets
1 Albert Pujols 5.00
2 Alex Rodriguez 5.00
3 Derek Jeter 6.00
4 Nomar Garciaparra 5.00
5 Jim Thome 3.00
6 Chipper Jones 3.00
7 Mark Prior 4.00
8 Eric Gagne 2.00
9 Jeff Bagwell 3.00
10 Troy Glaus 2.00
11 Randy Johnson 3.00
12 Sammy Sosa 4.00
13 Austin Kearns 2.00
14 Miguel Cabrera 2.00
15 Vladimir Guerrero 3.00
16 Mike Piazza 3.00
17 Jason Giambi 3.00
18 Tim Hudson 2.00
19 Carlos Delgado 3.00
20 Rocco Baldelli 2.00
21 Ichiro Suzuki 4.00
22 Barry Zito 2.00
23 Pedro Martinez 3.00
24 Torii Hunter 2.00
25 Andruw Jones 3.00

2004 Fleer Platinum

Vladimir Guerrero
MONTREAL EXPOS™ • OUTFIELD

NM/M
Complete Set (200): 35.00
Common Player: .15
Common SP (136-151): .50
Inserted 1:3
Pack (7): 2.00
Jumbo Pack (20): 5.00
Box (18 + 4 Jumbo): 55.00
1 Luis Castillo .15
2 Preston Wilson .15
3 Johan Santana .15
4 Fred McGriff .25
5 Albert Pujols 1.50
6 Reggie Sanders .15
7 Ivan Rodriguez .40
8 Roy Halladay .25
9 Brian Giles .25
10 Bernie Williams .40
11 Barry Larkin .25
12 Marlon Anderson .15
13 Ramon Ortiz .15
14 Luis Matos .15
15 Esteban Loaiza .15
16 Orlando Cabrera .15
17 Jamie Moyer .15
18 Tino Martinez .15
19 Josh Beckett .50
20 Derek Jeter 2.00
21 Derek Lowe .15
22 Jack Wilson .15
23 Bret Boone .25
24 Matt Morris .15
25 Javier Vazquez .25
26 Joe Crede .15
27 Jose Vidro .15
28 Mike Piazza 1.00
29 Curt Schilling .40
30 Alex Rodriguez 1.50
31 John Olerud .25
32 Dontrelle Willis .25
33 Larry Walker .25
34 Joe Randa .15
35 Paul LoDuca .15
36 Marlon Byrd .15
37 Bo Hart .15
38 Rafael Palmeiro .50
39 Garret Anderson .40
40 Tom Glavine .25
41 Ichiro Suzuki 1.25
42 Derek Lee .25
43 Lance Berkman .25
44 Nomar Garciaparra 1.50
45 Mike Sweeney .15
46 A.J. Burnett .15
47 Sean Casey .15
48 Eric Gagne .25
49 Joel Pineiro .15
50 Russ Ortiz .15
51 Placido Polanco .15
52 Sammy Sosa 1.25
53 Mark Teixeira .25
54 Randy Wolf .15
55 Vladimir Guerrero .75
56 Tim Hudson .25
57 Lew Ford .15
58 Carlos Delgado .50
59 Darin Erstad .25
60 Mike Lieberthal .15
61 Craig Biggio .25
62 Ryan Klesko .25
63 C.C. Sabathia .15
64 Carlos Lee .15
65 Al Leiter .15
66 Brandon Webb .15
67 Jacque Jones .15
68 Kerry Wood .50
69 Omar Vizquel .25
70 Jeremy Bonderman .15
71 Kevin Brown .25
72 Richie Sexson .40
73 Zach Day .15
74 Mike Mussina .40
75 Sidney Ponson .15
76 Andruw Jones .50
77 Woody Williams .15
78 Kazuhiro Sasaki .15
79 Matt Clement .15
80 Shea Hillenbrand .15
81 Bartolo Colon .25
82 Ken Griffey Jr. 1.00
83 Todd Helton .50
84 Dmitri Young .15
85 Richard Hidalgo .15
86 Carlos Beltran .25
87 Brad Wilkerson .15
88 Andy Pettitte .40
89 Miguel Tejada .40
90 Edgar Martinez .25
91 Vernon Wells .25
92 Magglio Ordonez .25
93 Tony Batista .15
94 Jose Reyes .15
95 Matt Stairs .15
96 Manny Ramirez .50
97 Carlos Pena .15
98 A.J. Pierzynski .15
99 Jim Thome .75
100 Aubrey Huff .15
101 Roberto Alomar .40
102 Luis Gonzalez .25
103 Chipper Jones 1.00
104 Jay Gibbons .25
105 Adam Dunn .40
106 Jay Payton .15
107 Scott Podsednik .40
108 Roy Oswalt .25
109 Milton Bradley .15
110 Shawn Green .25
111 Ryan Wagner .15
112 Eric Chavez .25
113 Pat Burrell .25
114 Frank Thomas .50
115 Jason Kendall .25
116 Jake Peavy .15
117 Mike Cameron .15
118 Jim Edmonds .25
119 Hank Blalock .40
120 Troy Glaus .40
121 Jeff Kent .25
122 Jason Schmidt .25
123 Corey Patterson .15
124 Austin Kearns .40
125 Edwin Jackson .15
126 Alfonso Soriano .75
127 Bobby Abreu .25
128 Scott Rolen .75
129 Jeff Bagwell .50
130 Shannon Stewart .15
131 Rich Aurilia .15
132 Ty Wigginton .15
133 Randy Johnson .75
134 Rocco Baldelli .40
135 Hideo Nomo .25
136 Greg Maddux 2.00
137 Johnny Damon 1.50
138 Mark Prior .75
139 Corey Koskie .50
140 Miguel Cabrera 1.50
141 Hideki Matsui 2.00
142 Jose Cruz .50
143 Barry Zito 1.00
144 Javy Lopez .50
145 Jason Varitek 1.00
146 Moises Alou 1.00
147 Torii Hunter 1.00
148 Juan Encarnacion .50
149 Jorge Posada 1.00
150 Marquis Grissom .50
151 Rich Harden 1.00
152 Gary Sheffield 4.00
153 Pedro J. Martinez 5.00
154 Brad Radke 3.00
155 Mike Lowell 3.00
156 Jason Giambi 4.00
157 Mark Mulder 4.00
158 Ben Weber .15
159 Mark DeRosa .15
160 Melvin Mora .15
161 Bill Mueller .15
162 Jon Garland .15
163 Jody Gerut .15
164 Javier Lopez .15
165 Craig Monroe .15
166 Juan Pierre .15
167 Morgan Ensberg .15
168 Angel Berroa .15
169 Geoff Jenkins .25
170 Matt LeCroy .15
171 Livan Hernandez .15
172 Jason L. Phillips .15
173 Mariano Rivera .25
174 Erubiel Durazo .15
175 Jason Michaels .15
176 Kip Wells .15
177 Ray Durham .15
178 Randy Winn .15
179 Edgar Renteria .15
180 Carl Crawford .15
181 Laynce Nix .15
182 Greg Myers .15
183 Delmon Young, Chad Gaudin 1.00
184 Humberto Quintero, Bernie Castro .50
185 Craig Brazell, Daniel Garcia .50
186 Ryan Wing, Francisco Cruceta .50
187 William Bergolla **RC**, Josh Hall .50
188 Clint Barmes, Garrett Atkins .50
189 Chris Bootcheck, Richard Fischer .50
190 Edgar Gonzalez, Matt Kata .50
191 Andrew Brown, Koyie Hill .50
192 John Gall **RC**, Dan Haren .50
193 Chad Bentz **RC**, Luis Ayala .50
194 Hector Gimenez **RC**, Eric Bruntlett .50
195 Boof Bonser, Rob Bowen .50
196 Chris Snelling, Rett Johnson .50
197 Rickie Weeks, Adam Morrissey 1.00
198 Noah Lowry, Todd Linden .50
199 Chris Waters, Brett Evert .50
200 Jorge DePaula, Chien-Ming Wang .50

Finish

Stars (1-200): 4-6X
Production 100 Sets

Big Signs

NM/M
Complete Set (15): 25.00
Common Player: .75
Inserted 1:9
1 Albert Pujols 3.00
2 Derek Jeter 4.00
3 Mike Piazza 2.00
4 Jason Giambi 1.50
5 Ichiro Suzuki 2.50
6 Nomar Garciaparra 3.00
7 Mark Prior 2.00
8 Randy Johnson 1.50
9 Greg Maddux 2.00
10 Sammy Sosa 2.50
11 Ken Griffey Jr. 2.00
12 Dontrelle Willis .75
13 Alex Rodriguez 3.00
14 Chipper Jones 2.00
15 Hank Blalock .75

Big Signs Autographs

NM/M
Production 100
Hank Blalock 25.00
Albert Pujols 150.00
Dontrelle Willis 25.00

Classic Combinations

NM/M
Complete Set (10): 50.00
Common Player: 3.00
Inserted 1:108
1 Ivan Rodriguez, Mike Piazza 6.00
2 Alex Rodriguez, Sammy Sosa 8.00
3 Dontrelle Willis, Angel Berroa 3.00
4 Nomar Garciaparra, Derek Jeter 10.00
5 Ichiro Suzuki, Hideo Nomo 6.00
6 Josh Beckett, Kerry Wood 4.00
7 Albert Pujols, Carlos Delgado 8.00
8 Alfonso Soriano, Joe Morgan 4.00
9 Jason Giambi, Reggie Jackson 4.00
10 Nolan Ryan, Tom Seaver 10.00

Clubhouse Memorabilia

NM/M
Common Player: 5.00
Inserted 1:24
Rocco Baldelli 10.00
Josh Beckett 8.00
Hank Blalock 6.00
Nomar Garciaparra 12.00
Jason Giambi 8.00
Vladimir Guerrero 8.00
Todd Helton 6.00
Torii Hunter 5.00
Derek Jeter 15.00
Chipper Jones 8.00
Austin Kearns 6.00
Greg Maddux 10.00
Hideo Nomo 8.00
Mike Piazza 8.00
Mark Prior 10.00
Albert Pujols 12.00
Alex Rodriguez 10.00
Richie Sexson 5.00
Alfonso Soriano 6.00
Sammy Sosa 12.00
Miguel Tejada 5.00
Jim Thome 8.00
Dontrelle Willis 8.00

Clubhouse Memorabilia Dual

NM/M
Common Player: 10.00
Production 50 Sets
Hank Blalock 15.00
Nomar Garciaparra 30.00
Jason Giambi 15.00
Vladimir Guerrero 20.00
Todd Helton 20.00
Torii Hunter 15.00
Derek Jeter 35.00
Chipper Jones 15.00
Austin Kearns 10.00
Greg Maddux 30.00
Hideo Nomo 25.00
Mark Prior 20.00
Albert Pujols 30.00
Alex Rodriguez 25.00
Sammy Sosa 20.00
Jim Thome 20.00

Nameplates

NM/M
Common Player: 8.00
Inserted 1:4 Jumbo
Varying quantities produced
1 Austin Kearns 10.00
2 Juan Pierre 10.00
3 Albert Pujols 30.00
4 Manny Ramirez 15.00
5 Kerry Wood 20.00
6 Alex Rodriguez 20.00
8 Barry Zito 10.00
9 Hee Seop Choi 8.00
10 Kevin Brown 10.00
11 Jose Reyes 15.00
12 Marlon Byrd 10.00
13 Nomar Garciaparra 20.00
14 Josh Beckett 15.00
16 Hideo Nomo 15.00
19 Randy Johnson 15.00
20 Hank Blalock 12.00
21 Tom Glavine/25 25.00

22 Luis Castillo 8.00
23 Mark Teixeira 12.00
24 Gary Sheffield 10.00
25 Richie Sexson 10.00
26 Miguel Cabrera 20.00
27 Sammy Sosa 25.00
28 Curt Schilling 10.00
30 Chipper Jones 20.00

Portraits

NM/M
Complete Set (10): 25.00
Common Player: 1.50
Inserted 1:18
1 Jason Giambi 1.50
2 Nomar Garciaparra 4.00
3 Vladimir Guerrero 1.50
4 Mark Prior 3.00
5 Jim Thome 1.50
6 Derek Jeter 5.00
7 Sammy Sosa 3.00
8 Alex Rodriguez 4.00
9 Greg Maddux 2.50
10 Albert Pujols 4.00

Portraits Jersey

NM/M
Common Player: 8.00
Inserted 1:48
Nomar Garciaparra 15.00
Jason Giambi 8.00
Vladimir Guerrero 8.00
Derek Jeter 15.00
Greg Maddux 8.00
Mark Prior 6.00
Albert Pujols 15.00
Alex Rodriguez 10.00
Sammy Sosa 12.00
Jim Thome 8.00

Portraits Patch

NM/M
Common Player: 10.00
Production 100 Sets
Nomar Garciaparra 20.00
Jason Giambi 10.00
Vladimir Guerrero 10.00
Derek Jeter 25.00
Mark Prior 20.00
Albert Pujols 30.00
Alex Rodriguez 15.00
Sammy Sosa 20.00
Jim Thome 12.00

Scouting Report

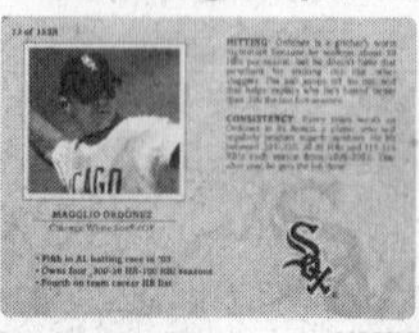

NM/M
Complete Set (15): 35.00
Common Player: 1.50
Production 400 Sets
1 Josh Beckett 2.00
2 Todd Helton 2.00
3 Rocco Baldelli 2.00
4 Pedro J. Martinez 3.00
5 Jeff Bagwell 2.00
6 Mark Prior 4.00
7 Ichiro Suzuki 4.00
8 Barry Zito 2.00
9 Manny Ramirez 2.00
10 Miguel Cabrera 2.00
11 Richie Sexson 1.50
12 Hideki Matsui 8.00
13 Magglio Ordonez 1.50
14 Brandon Webb 1.50
15 Kerry Wood 2.00

Scouting Report Memorabilia

NM/M
Common Player: 6.00
Production 250 Sets
Jeff Bagwell 8.00
Rocco Baldelli 8.00
Josh Beckett 8.00
Todd Helton 6.00
Pedro J. Martinez 8.00
Mark Prior 10.00
Manny Ramirez 6.00
Brandon Webb 6.00
Kerry Wood 8.00

2004 Fleer Showcase

NM/M
Complete Set (130):
Common Player: .25
Common SP (101-130): 1.00
Inserted 1:6
Pack (5): 4.50
Box (24): 90.00
1 Corey Patterson .25
2 Ken Griffey Jr. 1.50
3 Preston Wilson .40
4 Juan Pierre .25
5 Jose Reyes .50
6 Jason Schmidt .40
7 Rocco Baldelli .50
8 Carlos Delgado .75
9 Hideki Matsui 2.50
10 Nomar Garciaparra 2.00
11 Brian Giles .40
12 Darin Erstad .40
13 Larry Walker .40
14 Bernie Williams .50
15 Laynce Nix .25
16 Manny Ramirez .75
17 Magglio Ordonez .50
18 Khalil Greene .25
19 Jim Edmonds .40
20 Troy Glaus .50
21 Curt Schilling .50
22 Chipper Jones 1.50
23 Sammy Sosa 2.00
24 Frank Thomas .75
25 Todd Helton .75
26 Craig Biggio .40
27 Shannon Stewart .25
28 Mark Mulder .40
29 Mike Lieberthal .25
30 Reggie Sanders .25
31 Edgar Martinez .25
32 Bo Hart .25
33 Mark Teixeira .40
34 Jay Gibbons .25
35 Roberto Alomar .50
36 Kip Wells .25
37 J.D. Drew .25
38 Jason Varitek .25
39 Craig Monroe .25
40 Roy Oswalt .40
41 Edgardo Alfonzo .25
42 Roy Halladay .50
43 Gary Sheffield .50
44 Lance Berkman .50
45 Torii Hunter .50
46 Vladimir Guerrero 1.00
47 Marlon Byrd .25
48 Austin Kearns .50
49 Angel Berroa .25
50 Geoff Jenkins .50
51 Aubrey Huff .25
52 Dontrelle Willis .50
53 Tony Batista .25
54 Shawn Green .40
55 Jason Kendall .25
56 Garret Anderson .50
57 Andruw Jones .75
58 Dmitri Young .25
59 Richie Sexson .50
60 Jorge Posada .50
61 Bobby Abreu .40
62 Vernon Wells .40
63 Javy Lopez .40
64 Josh Beckett .75
65 Eric Chavez .40
66 Tim Salmon .40
67 Brandon Webb .40
68 Pedro J. Martinez 1.00
69 Kerry Wood 1.00
70 Jose Vidro .25
71 Alfonso Soriano 1.00
72 Barry Zito .50
73 Sean Burroughs .25
74 Jamie Moyer .25
75 Luis Gonzalez .40
76 Adam Dunn .50
77 Mike Piazza 1.50
78 Pat Burrell .50
79 Scott Rolen 1.00
80 Milton Bradley .25
81 Mike Sweeney .25
82 Hank Blalock .50
83 Esteban Loaiza .25
84 Hideo Nomo .50
85 Derek Jeter 3.00
86 Albert Pujols 2.50
87 Greg Maddux 1.50
88 Mark Prior 1.50
89 Mike Lowell .25
90 Jeff Bagwell .75
91 Scott Podsednik .50
92 Tom Glavine .50
93 Jason Giambi 1.00
94 Jim Thome 1.00
95 Ichiro Suzuki 2.00
96 Randy Johnson 1.00
97 Omar Vizquel .25
98 Ivan Rodriguez .50
99 Miguel Tejada .50
100 Alex Rodriguez 2.50
101 Rickie Weeks 3.00
102 Chad Gaudin 1.00
103 Rich Harden 1.00
104 Edwin Jackson 1.50
105 Chien-Ming Wang 1.00
106 Matt Kata 1.00
107 Delmon Young 3.00
108 Ryan Wagner 1.00
109 Jeff Duncan 1.00
110 Prentice Redman 1.00
111 Clint Barmes 1.00
112 Jeremy Guthrie 1.00
113 Brian Stokes 1.00
114 David DeJesus 1.00
115 Felix Sanchez 1.00
116 Josh Stewart 1.00
117 Daniel Garcia 1.00
118 Jon Leicester 1.00
119 Francisco Cruceta 1.00
120 Oscar Villarreal 1.00
121 Michael Hessman 1.00
122 Michel Hernandez 1.00
123 Richard Fischer 1.00
124 Robby Hammock 1.00
125 Guillermo Quiroz 1.00
126 Craig Brazell 1.00
127 Wilfredo Ledezma 1.00
128 Josh Willingham 1.00
129 Ramon Nivar 1.00
130 Matt Diaz 1.00

Legacy

Stars (1-100): 4-8X
SP's (101-130): 1-30X
Production 99 Sets

Masterpiece

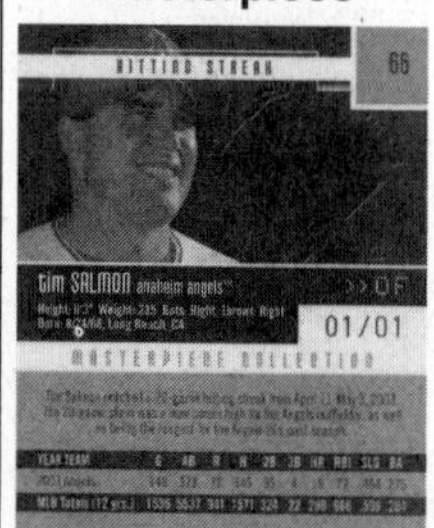

No Pricing
Production One Set

Albert Pujols Legacy Collection

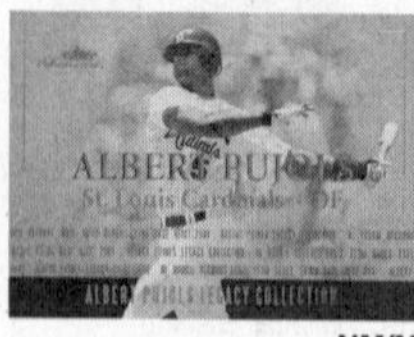

NM/M
Complete Set (10): 60.00
Common Pujols: 8.00
Production 1,000 Sets
1-10 Albert Pujols 8.00

Albert Pujols Legacy Collection Autograph

Varying quantities produced
No Pricing

Albert Pujols Legacy Collection Jersey

NM/M
Varying quantities produced
3 Albert Pujols/30 40.00
4 Albert Pujols/40 30.00
5 Albert Pujols/50 30.00
6 Albert Pujols/60 30.00
7 Albert Pujols/70 25.00
8 Albert Pujols/80 25.00
9 Albert Pujols/90 25.00
10 Albert Pujols/100 25.00

Baseball's Best

NM/M
Complete Set (15): 20.00
Common Player: .75
Inserted 1:24
1 Derek Jeter 4.00
2 Mark Prior 2.00
3 Mike Piazza 2.50
4 Jeff Bagwell 1.00
5 Kerry Wood 1.00
6 Ivan Rodriguez 1.00
7 Albert Pujols 3.00
8 Jim Thome 1.50
9 Sammy Sosa 2.50
10 Vladimir Guerrero 1.50
11 Eric Gagne .75
12 Randy Johnson 1.50
13 Todd Helton 1.00
14 Chipper Jones 2.00
15 Alex Rodriguez 4.00

Baseball's Best Memorabilia

NM/M
Common Player: 5.00
Inserted 1:72
Parallel 150: .75-1.5X
Production 150
Parallel 50: 1.5-2X
Patch Versions: 2-4X
Production 50
Derek Jeter 15.00
Mark Prior 10.00
Mike Piazza 10.00
Jeff Bagwell 8.00
Kerry Wood 8.00
Ivan Rodriguez 5.00
Albert Pujols 15.00
Jim Thome 8.00
Sammy Sosa 10.00
Vladimir Guerrero 8.00
Eric Gagne 8.00
Randy Johnson 8.00
Todd Helton 8.00
Chipper Jones 8.00
Alex Rodriguez 10.00

Grace

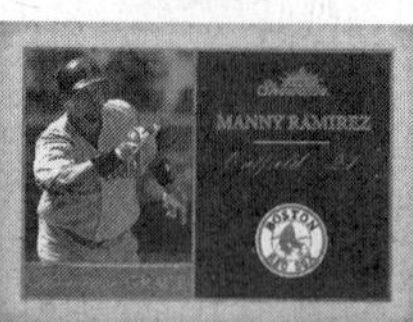

NM/M
Complete Set (20): 20.00
Common Player: .75
Inserted 1:12
1 Kerry Wood 1.50
2 Derek Jeter 4.00
3 Nomar Garciaparra 3.00
4 Mike Piazza 2.50
5 Mark Prior 2.00
6 Jose Reyes 1.00
7 Dontrelle Willis .75
8 Pedro J. Martinez 1.50
9 Tim Hudson .75
10 Troy Glaus .75
11 Hank Blalock 1.00
12 Albert Pujols 3.00
13 Juan Pierre .75
14 Angel Berroa .75
15 Rocco Baldelli 1.00
16 Carlos Delgado 1.00
17 Manny Ramirez 1.00
18 Alex Rodriguez 3.00
19 Andruw Jones 1.00
20 Luis Gonzalez .75

Grace Memorabilia

NM/M
Common Player: 5.00
Inserted 1:48
Parallel 150: 1-1.5X
Production 150
Patch: 1.5-2.5X
Production 50
Derek Jeter 15.00
Nomar Garciaparra 10.00
Mike Piazza 10.00
Mark Prior 10.00
Dontrelle Willis 5.00
Pedro J. Martinez 8.00
Albert Pujols 15.00
Rocco Baldelli 8.00
Manny Ramirez 8.00
Alex Rodriguez 10.00

Hot Gloves

NM/M
Common Player: 8.00
Inserted 1:288
1 Derek Jeter 40.00
2 Nomar Garciaparra 30.00
3 Alex Rodriguez 30.00
4 Chipper Jones 15.00
5 Torii Hunter 8.00
6 Ichiro Suzuki 35.00
7 Mark Prior 20.00
8 Vladimir Guerrero 15.00
9 Albert Pujols 30.00
10 Ivan Rodriguez 10.00
11 Hideki Matsui 30.00
12 Sammy Sosa 25.00
13 Jim Thome 15.00
14 Rocco Baldelli 10.00
15 Jeff Bagwell 10.00

Hot Gloves Memorabilia

NM/M
Common Player: 20.00
All jerseys unless noted.
Production 50 Sets
Derek Jeter 60.00
Nomar Garciaparra 50.00
Alex Rodriguez 40.00
Chipper Jones 40.00
Ichiro Suzuki/base 65.00
Mark Prior 25.00
Vladimir Guerrero 30.00
Albert Pujols 50.00
Ivan Rodriguez 20.00
Hideki Matsui/base 60.00
Sammy Sosa 40.00
Jim Thome 20.00
Rocco Baldelli 20.00
Jeff Bagwell 20.00

Sweet Sigs

NM/M
Common Player: 6.00
Inserted 1:24
Sweet Sigs Game Used: No Pricing
Production 5
Hank Blalock/824 20.00
Taylor Bucholz/ Redemp. 6.00
John Gall/Redemp. 8.00
Bo Hart/667 15.00
Torii Hunter/294 15.00
Austin Kearns/224 20.00
Wilfredo Ledezma/376 6.00
Mike Lowell/44 15.00
Corey Patterson/176 15.00
Carlos Pena/48 10.00
Albert Pujols/ Redemp. 120.00
Jose Reyes/115 40.00
Scott Rolen/200 25.00
Michael Ryan/288 12.00
Miguel Tejada/52 20.00
Ryan Wagner/ Redemp. 10.00
Brandon Webb/1,000 15.00
Rickie Weeks/416 30.00
Josh Willingham/180 6.00
Dontrelle Willis/26 60.00
Delmon Young/1,000 25.00
Barry Zito/248 25.00

2004 Fleer Sweet Sigs

NM/M
Common Player (1-75): .20
Minor Stars (1-75): .40
Unlisted Star (1-75): .60
Common Future Sig-cess (76-100): 3.00
Future Sig-cess Production 999 Sets
Pack (6): 5.00
Box (12): 80.00
1 Manny Ramirez 1.00
2 Frank Thomas 1.00
3 Josh Beckett 1.00
4 Shawn Green .40
5 Tom Glavine .40
6 Marquis Grissom .20
7 Nomar Garciaparra 3.00
8 Magglio Ordonez .40
9 Alex Rodriguez 3.00
10 Chipper Jones 2.00
11 Jody Gerut .20
12 Dontrelle Willis .40
13 Lance Berkman .40
14 Jose Vidro .20
15 Barry Zito .60
16 Jason Kendall .40
17 Scott Rolen 1.50
18 Troy Glaus .60
19 Brandon Webb .20
20 Tim Hudson .40
21 Shannon Stewart .20
22 Darin Erstad .40
23 Curt Schilling .60
24 Bret Boone .40
25 Richie Sexson .60
26 Hideki Matsui 3.00
27 Albert Pujols 3.00
28 Greg Maddux 2.00
29 Austin Kearns .60
30 Todd Helton 1.00
31 Miguel Cabrera 1.00
32 Jeff Bagwell 1.00
33 Marlon Byrd .20
34 Ichiro Suzuki 2.50
35 Rocco Baldelli .60
36 Garret Anderson .40
37 Javy Lopez .40
38 Kerry Wood 1.00
39 Adam Dunn .60
40 Geoff Jenkins .40
41 Derek Jeter 4.00
42 Rich Harden .20
43 Alfonso Soriano 1.50
44 Ken Griffey Jr. 2.00
45 Ivan Rodriguez .60
46 Pedro J. Martinez 1.50
47 Andy Pettitte .60
48 Gary Sheffield .60
49 Brian Giles .40
50 Carlos Delgado 1.00
51 Mike Piazza 2.00
52 Hank Blalock .60
53 Roger Clemens 2.00
54 Scott Podsednik .20
55 Torii Hunter .60
56 Jose Reyes .20
57 Jim Thome 1.50
58 Jason Schmidt .40
59 Jose Cruz .20
60 Mark Teixeira .40
61 Randy Johnson 1.50
62 Miguel Tejada .60
63 Sammy Sosa 2.50
64 Larry Walker .40
65 Carl Everett .20
66 Luis Castillo .20
67 Jason Giambi 1.50
68 Mike Sweeney .20
69 Andruw Jones 1.00
70 Vladimir Guerrero 1.50
71 J.D. Drew .40
72 Mark Prior 2.00
73 Angel Berroa .20
74 Hideo Nomo .40
75 Roy Halladay .40
76 John Gall **RC** 3.00
77 Angel Chavez **RC** 3.00
78 Alfredo Simon **RC** 3.00
79 Merkin Valdez **RC** 3.00
80 Chad Bentz **RC** 3.00
81 Justin Leone **RC** 6.00
82 Mike Rouse 3.00
83 Aarom Baldiris **RC** 3.00
84 Chris Shelton **RC** 8.00
85 Akinori Otsuka **RC** 6.00
86 Ruddy Yan **RC** 3.00
87 Ramon Ramirez **RC** 3.00
88 Hector Gimenez **RC** 6.00
89 Mike Gosling 3.00
90 Greg Dobbs **RC** 3.00
91 Kazuo Matsui **RC** 8.00
92 Donald Kelly **RC** 6.00
93 Shingo Takatsu **RC** 6.00
94 Ivan Ochoa **RC** 5.00
95 Chris Aguila **RC** 5.00
96 Jason Bartlett **RC** 3.00
97 Graham Koonce 5.00
98 Ronny Cedeno **RC** 3.00
99 Jerome Gamble **RC** 3.00
100 Onil Joseph **RC** 3.00

Black

(1-100): No Pricing
Production Five Sets

Gold

(1-75): 1-5X
(76-100): .5-2X
Production 99 Sets

Ballpark Heroes

NM/M
Common Player: 1.25
Inserted 1:6
1 Rocco Baldelli 1.75
2 Adam Dunn 1.75
3 Nomar Garciaparra 5.00
4 Ken Griffey Jr. 3.50
5 Vladimir Guerrero 3.00
6 Torii Hunter 1.75
7 Andruw Jones 2.00
8 Mike Piazza 3.50
9 Alfonso Soriano 3.00
10 Frank Thomas 2.00
11 Dontrelle Willis 1.25
12 Barry Zito 1.75
13 Javy Lopez 1.25
14 Miguel Cabrera 2.00
15 Kazuo Matsui 3.50
16 Josh Beckett 2.00
17 Derek Jeter 6.00
18 Greg Maddux 3.50
19 Pedro J. Martinez 3.00
20 Hideo Nomo 1.25
21 Mark Prior 4.00
22 Albert Pujols 5.00
23 Alex Rodriguez 5.00
24 Scott Rolen 3.00
25 Ichiro Suzuki 4.00

Ballpark Heroes Duals

No Pricing
Sequentially Numbered

Ballpark Heroes Quad

NM/M
Sequentially Numbered
1 Josh Beckett, Greg Maddux, Pedro J. Martinez, Mark Prior/42 150.00
2 Dontrelle Willis, Kazuo Matsui, Miguel Cabrera, Rocco Baldelli/26 75.00
4 Dontrelle Willis, Josh Beckett, Derek Jeter, Alex Rodriguez/32 150.00
5 Albert Pujols, Vladimir Guerrero, Mike Piazza, Alex Rodriguez/37 150.00

Ballpark Heroes Black Patch

NM/M
Sequentially Numbered
MP Mike Piazza/31 50.00

Ballpark Heroes Copper Jersey

NM/M
Common Player: 5.00
Production 110 Sets
Gold Patch: 1-30X
Production 50 Sets
Masterpiece Patch: No Pricing
Production One Set
RB Rocco Baldelli/110 5.00
MC Miguel Cabrera/110 6.00
AD Adam Dunn/110 5.00
VG Vladimir Guerrero/110 8.00
GM Greg Maddux/110 10.00
PM Pedro J. Martinez/110 8.00
HN Hideo Nomo/110 5.00
MP Mike Piazza/110 10.00
AP Albert Pujols/110 15.00
SR Scott Rolen/110 8.00
AS Alfonso Soriano/110 8.00
FT Frank Thomas/110 6.00
DW Dontrelle Willis/110 5.00
BZ Barry Zito/110 5.00

Ballpark Heroes Silver Jersey

NM/M
Common Player: 4.00
Sequentially Numbered
RB Rocco Baldelli/250 4.00
MC Miguel Cabrera/196 5.00
AD Adam Dunn/215 4.00
VG Vladimir Guerrero/200 6.00
GM Greg Maddux/224 8.00
PM Pedro J. Martinez/239 6.00
HN Hideo Nomo/210 4.00
MP Mike Piazza/163 8.00
AP Albert Pujols/199 12.00
SR Scott Rolen/221 6.00
AS Alfonso Soriano/235 6.00
FT Frank Thomas/242 5.00
DW Dontrelle Willis/186 4.00
BZ Barry Zito/195 4.00

Sweet Sigs Copper

NM/M
Common Player: 10.00
Sequentially Numbered
Gold: .75-1.5X
Production 30 Sets
Hideo Nomo #'d to 10.
No Roger Clemens or Ted Williams.
Gold card.
Masterpiece: No Pricing
Production One Set
GA Garret Anderson/100 20.00
RB Rocco Baldelli/75 25.00
JB Josh Beckett/75 30.00
CB Carlos Beltran/75 20.00
LB Lance Berkman/150 20.00
AB Angel Berroa/75 20.00
JB Jeremy Bonderman/150 15.00
MC Miguel Cabrera/150 30.00
MC Mike Cameron/150 20.00
RC Roger Clemens/52 400.00
CC Carl Crawford/150 15.00
JD Johnny Damon/100 30.00
JD J.D. Drew/98 40.00
DE Dennis Eckersley/75 40.00
AE Adam Everett/150 10.00
JF Julio Franco/150 30.00
LG Luis Gonzalez/150 15.00
KG Khalil Greene/150 40.00
VG Vladimir Guerrero/75 75.00
TH Torii Hunter/150 25.00
EJ Edwin Jackson/75 15.00
RJ Randy Johnson/28 150.00
CJ Chipper Jones/50 100.00
MK Matt Kata/150 10.00
BL Barry Larkin/50 50.00
CL Carlos Lee/150 15.00
AL Al Leiter/75 25.00
KL Kenny Lofton/50 50.00
JL Javy Lopez/75 25.00
GM Greg Maddux/50 75.00
PM Pedro J. Martinez/75 125.00
JM Joe Mauer/150 40.00
WM Wade Miller/150 20.00
KM Kevin Millwood/100 15.00
PM Paul Molitor/75 40.00
SM Stan Musial/25 80.00
MM Mike Mussina/50 40.00
LN Lance Niekro/150 10.00
JO John Olerud/75 30.00
MO Magglio Ordonez/150 20.00
RO Russ Ortiz/150 15.00
RO Roy Oswalt/150 20.00
AO Akinori Otsuka/150 20.00
BP Brad Penny/150 10.00
AP Andy Pettitte/50 40.00
MP Mike Piazza/50 120.00
AP Albert Pujols/73 300.00
BR Brad Radke/100 20.00
JR Jose Reyes/163 30.00
AR Alexis Rios/150 15.00
NR Nolan Ryan/50 300.00
CS C.C. Sabathia/150 20.00
TS Tim Salmon/100 40.00
DS Deion Sanders/50 50.00
JS Johan Santana/150 80.00
MS Mike Schmidt/50 60.00
SS Shannon Stewart/75 20.00
FT Frank Thomas/75 75.00
JV Jason Varitek/75 40.00
TW Tim Wakefield/150 30.00
VW Vernon Wells/150 20.00
BW Bernie Williams/50 80.00
DW Dontrelle Willis/150 20.00
KW Kerry Wood/75 60.00
CY Carl Yastrzemski/50 100.00
BZ Barry Zito/44 30.00

Sweet Sigs Jersey Number

NM/M
No. 3-25: 1-30X Copper
No. 26-57: .75-1.5X Copper
Numbered to player's jersey #.
No Hideo Nomo card.
MC Mike Cameron/44 30.00

Sweet Stitches Black Patch

NM/M
Sequentially Numbered
SS-GM Greg Maddux/32 25.00

Sweet Stitches Copper Jersey

NM/M
Common Player: 5.00
Production 125 Sets
Gold Patch: 1-30X
Production 50 Sets
Masterpiece Patch: No Pricing
Production One Set
HB Hank Blalock/125 5.00
MC Miguel Cabrera/125 8.00
RC Roger Clemens/125 8.00
JG Jason Giambi/125 8.00
VG Vladimir Guerrero/125 8.00
AJ Andruw Jones/125 10.00
GM Greg Maddux/125 8.00
MO Magglio Ordonez/125 5.00
MP Mike Piazza/125 8.00
MP; Mark Prior/125 8.00
AP Albert Pujols/125 15.00
MR Manny Ramirez/125 8.00
JR Jose Reyes/125 8.00
SR Scott Rolen/125 8.00
GS Gary Sheffield/125 8.00
AS Alfonso Soriano/125 8.00
SS Sammy Sosa/125 10.00
MT Mark Teixeira/125 5.00
MT Miguel Tejada/125 5.00
FT Frank Thomas/125 8.00
JT Jim Thome/125 8.00
KW Kerry Wood/125 8.00

Sweet Stitches Silver Jersey

NM/M
Common Player: 5.00
Sequentially Numbered
HB Hank Blalock/166 5.00
MC Miguel Cabrera/169 8.00
RC Roger Clemens/165 8.00
JG Jason Giambi/125 8.00
VG Vladimir Guerrero/172 8.00
AJ Andruw Jones/175 8.00
GM Greg Maddux/156 8.00
MO Magglio Ordonez/113 5.00
MP Mike Piazza/174 8.00
MP Mark Prior/172 8.00
AP Albert Pujols/170 12.00
MR Manny Ramirez/163 8.00
JR Jose Reyes/171 8.00
SR Scott Rolen/166 8.00
GS Gary Sheffield/88 8.00
AS Alfonso Soriano/162 8.00
SS Sammy Sosa/158 10.00
MT Mark Teixeira/158 5.00
MT Miguel Tejada/162 5.00
FT Frank Thomas/159 8.00
JT Jim Thome/8 8.00
KW Kerry Wood/134 8.00

Sweet Stitches Quad Patches

NM/M
Sequentially Numbered
No pricing for quantities less than 25.
4 Andruw Jones/31, Miguel Cabrera/31, Albert Pujols/31, Sammy Sosa/31 80.00
10 Greg Maddux/33, Sammy Sosa/33, Mark Prior/33, Kerry Wood/33 150.00

Sweet Swing

NM/M
Common Player: 2.50
Inserted 1:12
1SS Sammy Sosa 5.00
2SS Vladimir Guerrero 3.50
3SS Jason Giambi 3.50
4SS Chipper Jones 4.00
5SS Alfonso Soriano 3.50
6SS Manny Ramirez 3.00
7SS Todd Helton 3.00
8SS Alex Rodriguez 6.00

9SS Albert Pujols 6.00
10SS Jeff Bagwell 3.00
11SS Mike Piazza 4.00
12SS Hank Blalock 2.50
13SS Jim Thome 3.50
14SS Carlos Delgado 3.00
15SS Nomar Garciaparra 6.00

Sweet Swing Black Bat/Patch

Numbered to most home runs.

Sweet Swing Copper Jersey

NM/M
Common Player: 4.00
Production 200 Sets
Gold Bat/Jersey: 1.5-4X
Production 50 Sets
Masterpiece Bat/Patch
Production One Set
HB Hank Blalock/200 4.00
JG Jason Giambi/200 6.00
VG Vladimir Guerrero/200 6.00
CJ Chipper Jones/200 8.00
MP Mike Piazza/200 8.00
AP Albert Pujols/200 12.00
MR Manny Ramirez/200 5.00
AR Alex Rodriguez/200 12.00
AS Alfonso Soriano/200 6.00
SS Sammy Sosa/200 10.00
JT Jim Thome/200 6.00

Sweet Swing Silver Bat

NM/M
Common Player: 5.00
Sequentially Numbered
JG Jason Giambi/247 6.00
VG Vladimir Guerrero/250 6.00
CJ Chipper Jones/235 8.00
MP Mike Piazza/231 8.00
AP Albert Pujols/237 12.00
MR Manny Ramirez/224 5.00
AR Alex Rodriguez/213 12.00
AS Alfonso Soriano/216 6.00
SS Sammy Sosa/221 10.00
JT Jim Thome/245 6.00

Sweet Swing Quad

NM/M
Sequentially Numbered
1 Jason Giambi, Alex Rodriguez, Jeff Bagwell, Manny Ramirez/35 80.00
3 Mike Piazza, Alfonso Soriano, Todd Helton, Hank Blalock/32 125.00

2004 Fleer Tradition

NM/M
Complete Set (500): 100.00
Common Player: .15
Common SP (401-500): .25
Pack (10): 1.75
Hobby Box (36): 50.00
1 Juan Pierre .15
2 Josh Beckett .50
3 Ivan Rodriguez .50
4 Miguel Cabrera .50
5 Dontrelle Willis .25
6 Derek Jeter 2.00
7 Jason Giambi .75
8 Bernie Williams .40
9 Alfonso Soriano .75
10 Hideki Matsui 2.00
11 Garret Anderson, Ramon Ortiz, John Lackey .15
12 Luis Gonzalez, Brandon Webb, Curt Schilling .25
13 Javy Lopez, Gary Sheffield, Russ Ortiz .25
14 Tony Batista, Jay Gibbons, Sidney Ponson, Jason Johnson .15
15 Manny Ramirez, Nomar Garciaparra, Derek Lowe, Pedro J. Martinez .50
16 Sammy Sosa, Mark Prior, Kerry Wood .75
17 Frank Thomas, Carlos Lee, Esteban Loaiza .25
18 Adam Dunn, Sean Casey, Chris Reitsma, Paul Wilson .25
19 Jody Gerut, C.C. Sabathia .15
20 Preston Wilson, Darren Oliver, Jason Jennings .15
21 Dmitri Young, Mike Maroth, Jeremy Bonderman .15
22 Mike Lowell, Dontrelle Willis, Josh Beckett .25
23 Jeff Bagwell, Jeriome Robertson, Wade Miller .25
24 Carlos Beltran, Darrell May .15
25 Adrian Beltre, Shawn Green, Hideo Nomo, Kevin Brown .15
26 Richie Sexson, Ben Sheets .15
27 Torii Hunter, Brad Radke, Johan Santana .15
28 Vladimir Guerrero, Orlando Cabrera, Livan Hernandez, Javier Vazquez .25
29 Cliff Floyd, Ty Wigginton, Steve Trachsel, Al Leiter .15
30 Jason Giambi, Andy Pettitte, Mike Mussina .40
31 Eric Chavez, Miguel Tejada, Tim Hudson .25
32 Jim Thome, Randy Wolf .25
33 Reggie Sanders, Josh Fogg, Kip Wells .15
34 Ryan Klesko, Mark Loretta, Jake Peavy .15
35 Jose Cruz, Edgardo Alfonzo, Jason Schmidt .15
36 Bret Boone, Jamie Moyer, Joel Pineiro .15
37 Albert Pujols, Woody Williams .75
38 Aubrey Huff, Victor Zambrano .15
39 Alex Rodriguez, John Thomson .75
40 Carlos Delgado, Roy Halladay .25
41 Greg Maddux 1.00
42 Ben Grieve .15
43 Darin Erstad .25
44 Ruben Sierra .15
45 Byung-Hyun Kim .15
46 Freddy Garcia .15
47 Richard Hidalgo .15
48 Tike Redman .15
49 Kevin Millwood .25
50 Marquis Grissom .15
51 Jae Weong Seo .15
52 Wil Cordero .15
53 LaTroy Hawkins .15
54 Jolbert Cabrera .15
55 Kevin Appier .15
56 John Lackey .15
57 Garret Anderson .25
58 R.A. Dickey .15
59 David Segui .15
60 Erubiel Durazo .15
61 Bobby Abreu .25
62 Travis Hafner .15
63 Victor Zambrano .15
64 Randy Johnson .75
65 Bernie Williams .40
66 J.T. Snow .15
67 Sammy Sosa 1.50
68 Al Leiter .15
69 Jason Jennings .15
70 Matt Morris .15
71 Mike Hampton .15
72 Juan Encarnacion .15
73 Alex Gonzalez .15
74 Bartolo Colon .25
75 Brett Myers .15
76 Michael Young .15
77 Ichiro Suzuki 1.50
78 Jason Johnson .15
79 Brad Ausmus .15
80 Ted Lilly .15
81 Ken Griffey Jr. 1.00
82 Chone Figgins .15
83 Edgar Martinez .25
84 Adam Eaton .15
85 Ken Harvey .15
86 Francisco Rodriguez .15
87 Bill Mueller .15
88 Mike Maroth .15
89 Charles Johnson .15
90 Jhonny Peralta .15
91 Kip Wells .15
92 Cesar Izturis .15
93 Matt Clement .15
94 Lyle Overbay .15
95 Kirk Rueter .15
96 Cristian Guzman .15
97 Garrett Stephenson .15
98 Lance Berkman .25
99 Brett Tomko .15
100 Chris Stynes .15
101 Nate Cornejo .15
102 Aaron Rowand .15
103 Javier Vazquez .15
104 Jason Kendall .25
105 Mark Redman .15
106 Benito Santiago .15
107 C.C. Sabathia .15
108 David Wells .15
109 Mark Ellis .15
110 Casey Blake .15
111 Sean Burroughs .15
112 Carlos Beltran .25
113 Ramon Hernandez .15
114 Eric Hinske .15
115 Luis Gonzalez .25
116 Jarrod Washburn .15
117 Ronnie Belliard .15
118 Troy Percival .15
119 Jose Valentine .15
120 Chase Utley .15
121 Odalis Perez .15
122 Steve Finley .15
123 Bret Boone .25
124 Jeff Conine .15
125 Jason Fogg .15
126 Neifi Perez .15
127 Ben Sheets .25
128 Randy Winn .15
129 Matt Stairs .15
130 Carlos Delgado .50
131 Morgan Ensberg .15
132 Vinny Castilla .15
133 Matt Mantei .15
134 Alex Rodriguez 1.50
135 Matthew LeCroy .15
136 Woody Williams .15
137 Frank Catalanotto .15
138 Rondell White .15
139 Scott Rolen .75
140 Cliff Floyd .15
141 Chipper Jones .75
142 Robin Ventura .15
143 Mariano Rivera .25
144 Brady Clark .15
145 Ramon Ortiz .15
146 Omar Infante .15
147 Mike Matheny .15
148 Pedro J. Martinez .75
149 Carlos Baerga .15
150 Shannon Stewart .15
151 Travis Lee .15
152 Eric Byrnes .15
153 Rafael Furcal .25
154 B.J. Surhoff .15
155 Zach Day .15
156 Marlon Anderson .15
157 Mark Hendrickson .15
158 Mike Mussina .50
159 Randall Simon .15
160 Jeff DaVanon .15
161 Joel Pineiro .15
162 Vernon Wells .25
163 Adam Kennedy .15
164 Trot Nixon .15
165 Rodrigo Lopez .15
166 Curt Schilling .50
167 Horacio Ramirez .15
168 Gerald Laird .15
169 Magglio Ordonez .25
170 Scott Schoeneweis .15
171 Andruw Jones .50
172 Tino Martinez .25
173 Moises Alou .25
174 Kelvim Escobar .15
175 Xavier Nady .15
176 Ramon Martinez .15
177 Pat Hentgen .15
178 Austin Kearns .40
179 D'Angelo Jimenez .15
180 Deivi Cruz .15
181 John Smoltz .25
182 Toby Hall .15
183 Mark Buehrle .15
184 Howie Clark .15
185 David Ortiz .15
186 Raul Mondesi .15
187 Milton Bradley .15
188 Jorge Julio .15
189 Victor Martinez .15
190 Gabe Kapler .15
191 Julio Franco .15
192 Ryan Freel .15
193 Brad Fullmer .15
194 Joe Borowski .15
195 Darren Oliver .15
196 Jason Varitek .15

No.	Player	Price
197	Greg Myers	.15
198	Eric Munson	.15
199	Tim Wakefield	.15
200	Kyle Farnsworth	.15
201	John Vander Wal	.15
202	Alex Escobar	.15
203	Sean Casey	.15
204	John Thomson	.15
205	Carlos Zambrano	.15
206	Kenny Lofton	.15
207	Marcus Giles	.15
208	Wade Miller	.15
209	Geoff Blum	.15
210	Jason LaRue	.15
211	Omar Vizquel	.25
212	Carlos Pena	.15
213	Adam Dunn	.40
214	Oscar Villarreal	.15
215	Paul Konerko	.15
216	Hideo Nomo	.40
217	Mike Sweeney	.15
218	Coco Crisp	.15
219	Shawn Chacon	.15
220	Brook Fordyce	.15
221	Josh Beckett	.50
222	Paul Wilson	.15
223	Josh Towers	.15
224	Geoff Jenkins	.25
225	Shawn Green	.25
226	Derek Lee	.15
227	Karim Garcia	.15
228	Preston Wilson	.15
229	Dane Sardinha	.15
230	Aramis Ramirez	.15
231	Doug Mientkiewicz	.15
232	Jay Gibbons	.15
233	Adam Everett	.15
234	Brooks Kieschnick	.15
235	Dmitri Young	.15
236	Brad Penny	.15
237	Todd Zeile	.15
238	Eric Gagne	.25
239	Esteban Loaiza	.15
240	Billy Wagner	.15
241	Nomar Garciaparra	1.50
242	Desi Relaford	.15
243	Luis Rivas	.15
244	Andy Pettitte	.40
245	Ty Wigginton	.15
246	Edgar Gonzalez	.15
247	Brian Anderson	.15
248	Richie Sexson	.40
249	Russell Branyan	.15
250	Jose Guillen	.15
251	Chin-Hui Tsao	.15
252	Jose Hernandez	.15
253	Kevin Brown	.25
254	Pete LaForest	.15
255	Adrian Beltre	.15
256	Jacque Jones	.15
257	Jimmy Rollins	.25
258	Brandon Phillips	.15
259	Derek Jeter	2.00
260	Carl Everett	.15
261	Wes Helms	.15
262	Kyle Lohse	.15
263	Jason L. Phillips	.15
264	Jake Peavy	.15
265	Orlando Hernandez	.15
266	Keith Foulke	.15
267	Brad Wilkerson	.15
268	Corey Koskie	.15
269	Josh Hall	.15
270	Bobby Higginson	.15
271	Andres Galarraga	.15
272	Alfonso Soriano	.75
273	Carlos Rivera	.15
274	Steve Trachsel	.15
275	David Bell	.15
276	Endy Chavez	.15
277	Jay Payton	.15
278	Mark Mulder	.25
279	Terrence Long	.15
280	A.J. Burnett	.15
281	Pokey Reese	.15
282	Phil Nevin	.15
283	Jose Contreras	.25
284	Jim Thome	.75
285	Pat Burrell	.40
286	Luis Castillo	.15
287	Juan Uribe	.15
288	Raul Ibanez	.25
289	Sidney Ponson	.15
290	Shane Hatteberg	.15
291	Jack Wilson	.15
292	Reggie Sanders	.15
293	Brian Giles	.25
294	Craig Biggio	.25
295	Kazuhisa Ishii	.15
296	Jim Edmonds	.25
297	Trevor Hoffman	.15
298	Ray Durham	.15
299	Mike Lieberthal	.15
300	Todd Worrell	.15
301	Chris George	.15
302	Jamie Moyer	.15
303	Mike Cameron	.15
304	Matt Kinney	.15
305	Aubrey Huff	.15
306	Brian Lawrence	.15
307	Carlos Guillen	.15
308	J.D. Drew	.15
309	Paul LoDuca	.15
310	Tim Salmon	.25
311	Jason Schmidt	.15
312	A.J. Pierzynski	.15
313	Lance Carter	.15
314	Julio Lugo	.15
315	Johan Santana	.15
316	Laynce Nix	.15
317	John Olerud	.25
318	Robb Quinlan	.15
319	Scott Spiezio	.15
320	Tony Clark	.15
321	Jose Vidro	.15
322	Shea Hillenbrand	.15
323	Doug Glanville	.15
324	Orlando Palmeiro	.15
325	Juan Gonzalez	.40
326	Jason Giambi	.75
327	Junior Spivey	.15
328	Tom Glavine	.25
329	Reed Johnson	.15
330	David Eckstein	.15
331	Damian Jackson	.15
332	Orlando Hudson	.15
333	Barry Zito	.40
334	Robert Fick	.15
335	Aaron Boone	.15
336	Rafael Palmeiro	.50
337	Bobby Kielty	.15
338	Tony Batista	.15
339	Ryan Dempster	.15
340	Derek Lowe	.25
341	Alex Cintron	.15
342	Jermaine Dye	.15
343	John Burkett	.15
344	Javy Lopez	.25
345	Eric Karros	.15
346	Corey Patterson	.25
347	Josh Phelps	.15
348	Ryan Klesko	.25
349	Craig Wilson	.15
350	Brian Roberts	.15
351	Roberto Alomar	.40
352	Frank Thomas	.50
353	Gary Sheffield	.40
354	Alex Gonzalez	.15
355	Jose Cruz	.15
356	Jerome Williams	.15
357	Mark Kotsay	.15
358	Chris Reitsma	.15
359	Carlos Lee	.15
360	Todd Helton	.50
361	Gil Meche	.15
362	Ryan Franklin	.15
363	Josh Bard	.15
364	Juan Pierre	.15
365	Barry Larkin	.25
366	Edgar Renteria	.15
367	Alex Sanchez	.15
368	Jeff Bagwell	.50
369	Ben Broussard	.15
370	Chan Ho Park	.15
371	Darrell May	.15
372	Roy Oswalt	.25
373	Craig Monroe	.15
374	Fred McGriff	.25
375	Bengie Molina	.15
376	Aaron Guiel	.15
377	Jeriome Robertson	.15
378	Kenny Rogers	.15
379	Colby Lewis	.15
380	Jeromy Burnitz	.15
381	Orlando Cabrera	.15
382	Joe Randa	.15
383	Miguel Batista	.15
384	Brad Radke	.15
385	Jason Giambi	.75
386	Vladimir Guerrero	.75
387	Melvin Mora	.15
388	Royce Clayton	.15
389	Danny Garcia	.15
390	Manny Ramirez	.50
391	Dave McCarty	.15
392	Mark Grudzielanek	.15
393	Mike Piazza	1.00
394	Jorge Posada	.40
395	Tim Hudson	.25
396	Placido Polanco	.15
397	Mark Loretta	.15
398	Jesse Foppert	.15
399	Albert Pujols	1.50
400	Jeremi Gonzalez	.15
401	Paul Bako	.25
402	Luis Matos	.25
403	Johnny Damon	.50
404	Kerry Wood	1.00
405	Joe Crede	.25
406	Jason Davis	.25
407	Larry Walker	.50
408	Ivan Rodriguez	1.00
409	Nick Johnson	.25
410	Jose Lima	.25
411	Brian Jordan	.25
412	Eddie Guardado	.25
413	Ron Calloway	.25
414	Aaron Heilman	.25
415	Eric Chavez	.50
416	Randy Wolf	.25
417	Jason Bay	.25
418	Edgardo Alfonzo	.25
419	Kazuhiro Sasaki	.25
420	Eduardo Perez	.25
421	Carl Crawford	.25
422	Troy Glaus	1.00
423	Joaquin Benoit	.25
424	Russ Ortiz	.25
425	Larry Bigbie	.25
426	Todd Walker	.25
427	Kris Benson	.25
428	Sandy Alomar	.25
429	Jody Gerut	.25
430	Rene Reyes	.25
431	Mike Lowell	.25
432	Jeff Kent	.25
433	Mike MacDougal	.25
434	Dave Roberts	.25
435	Torii Hunter	.75
436	Tomokazu Ohka	.25
437	Jeremy Griffiths	.25
438	Miguel Tejada	.75
439	Vicente Padilla	.25
440	Bobby Hill	.25
441	Rich Aurilia	.25
442	Shigetoshi Hasegawa	.25
443	So Taguchi	.25
444	Damian Rolls	.25
445	Roy Halladay	.75
446	Rocco Baldelli	.75
447	Dontrelle Willis	.75
448	Mark Prior	2.00
449	Jason Lane	.25
450	Angel Berroa	.25
451	Jose Reyes	.75
452	Ryan Wagner	.25
453	Marlon Byrd	.25
454	Hee Seop Choi	.25
455	Brandon Webb	.50
456	Bo Hart	.75
457	Hank Blalock	1.00
458	Mark Teixeira	.75
459	Hideki Matsui	4.00
460	Scott Podsednik	.25
461	Miguel Cabrera	1.00
462	Josh Beckett	1.00
463	Mariano Rivera	.50
464	Ivan Rodriguez	1.00
465	Alex Rodriguez	3.00
466	Albert Pujols	3.00
467	Roy Halladay	.75
468	Eric Gagne	.50
469	Angel Berroa	.25
470	Dontrelle Willis	.50
471	Chris Bootcheck, Tom Gregorio, Richard Fischer	.25
472	Matt Kata, Tim Olson, Robby Hammock	.25
473	Michael Hessman, Chris Waters, Humberto Quintero	.25
474	Carlos Mendez, Daniel Cabrera, Jeremy Guthrie	.25
475	Edwin Almonte, Phil Seibel, Felix Sanchez	.25
476	Todd Wellemeyer, Jon Leicester, Sergio Mitre	.25
477	Josh Stewart, Neal Cotts, Aaron Miles	.25
478	Terrmel Sledge, Josh Hall, Brandon Claussen	.25
479	Francisco Cruceta, Jason Stanford, Rafael Betancourt	.25
480	Javier Lopez, Garrett Atkins, Clint Barmes	.25
481	Wilfredo Ledezma, Nook Logan, Jeremy Bonderman	.25
482	Josh Willingham, Kevin Hooper, Rick Roberts	.25
483	Colin Porter, Mike Gallo, Dave Matranga	.25
484	David DeJesus, Jason Gilfillan, Jimmy Gobble	.25
485	Koyie Hill, Alfredo Gonzalez, Andrew Brown	.25
486	Rickie Weeks, Pedro Liriano, Wes Obermueller	1.00
487	Alex Prieto, Mike Ryan, Lew Ford	.25
488	Julio Manon, Luis Ayala, Seung Jun Song	.25
489	Jeff Duncan, Prentice Redman, Craig Brazell	.25
490	Chien-Ming Wang, Michel Hernandez, Mike Gonzalez	.25
491	Rich Harden, Mike Neu, Geoff Geary	.25
492	Diegomar Markwell, Chad Gaudin, David Sanders	.25
493	Beau Kemp, Micheal Nakamura, D.J. Carrasco	.25
494	Khalil Greene, Miguel Ojeda, Bernie Castro	.25
495	Noah Lowry, Todd Linden, Kevin Correia	.25
496	Aaron Looper, Brian Sweeney, Rett Johnson	.25
497	Bo Hart, Dan Haren, Kevin Ohme	.50
498	Delmon Young, Doug Waechter, Matt Diaz	1.00
499	Gerald Laird, Rosman Garcia, Ramon Nivar	.25
500	Alexis Rios, Guillermo Quiroz, Francisco Rosario	.25

Career Tributes

NM/M

Complete Set (10): 30.00
Common Player: 3.00
Numbered to last season.
Die-Cuts: 2-3X
#'d to last two digits of last season

1CT	Mike Schmidt/1,989	5.00
2CT	Nolan Ryan/1,993	6.00
3CT	Tom Seaver/1,986	4.00
4CT	Reggie Jackson/1,987	3.00
5CT	Bob Gibson/1,975	4.00
6CT	Harmon Killebrew/1,975	4.00
7CT	Phil Rizzuto/1,956	3.00
8CT	Lou Brock/1,979	3.00
9CT	Eddie Mathews/1,968	3.00
10CT	Al Kaline/1,974	4.00

Diamond Tributes

NM/M

Complete Set (20): 18.00
Common Player: .50
Inserted 1:6

1DT	Derek Jeter	3.00
2DT	Chipper Jones	1.50
3DT	Vladimir Guerrero	1.00
4DT	Kerry Wood	.75
5DT	Jim Thome	1.00
6DT	Nomar Garciaparra	2.00
7DT	Alex Rodriguez	3.00
8DT	Mike Piazza	1.50
9DT	Jason Giambi	1.00
10DT	Barry Zito	.50
11DT	Dontrelle Willis	.50
12DT	Albert Pujols	2.50
13DT	Todd Helton	.75
14DT	Richie Sexson	.50
15DT	Randy Johnson	1.00
16DT	Pedro J. Martinez	1.00
17DT	Josh Beckett	.75
18DT	Manny Ramirez	.75
19DT	Roy Halladay	.50
20DT	Mark Prior	1.50

Diamond Tributes Game-Used

NM/M

Common Player: 5.00
Inserted 1:36
Patch versions: 2-3X
Production 50 Sets

Josh Beckett	8.00
Nomar Garciaparra	10.00
Jason Giambi	8.00
Vladimir Guerrero	8.00
Roy Halladay	5.00
Todd Helton	8.00
Derek Jeter	15.00
Randy Johnson	8.00
Chipper Jones	8.00
Pedro J. Martinez	10.00
Mike Piazza	8.00
Mark Prior	10.00
Albert Pujols	15.00
Manny Ramirez	8.00
Alex Rodriguez	10.00
Richie Sexson	6.00
Jim Thome	8.00
Dontrelle Willis	8.00
Kerry Wood	8.00
Barry Zito	8.00

Retrospection Collection

NM/M

Complete Set (10): 60.00
Common Player: 4.00
Inserted 1:360

1RC	Rickie Weeks	10.00
2RC	Delmon Young	12.00
3RC	Torii Hunter	5.00
4RC	Aubrey Huff	4.00
5RC	Rocco Baldelli	6.00
6RC	Mike Lowell	4.00
7RC	Dontrelle Willis	6.00
8RC	Albert Pujols	10.00
9RC	Bo Hart	8.00
10RC	Brandon Webb	4.00

Retrospection Collection Autograph

NM/M

Common Autograph: 10.00
Production 60

Hank Blalock	25.00
Bo Hart	25.00
Aubrey Huff	10.00
Torii Hunter	30.00
Austin Kearns	20.00
Corey Patterson	25.00
Albert Pujols	75.00
Jose Reyes	25.00
Scott Rolen	30.00
Mike Ryan	15.00
Ryan Wagner	15.00
Brandon Webb	20.00
Rickie Weeks	50.00
Josh Willingham	20.00
Dontrelle Willis	35.00
Delmon Young	50.00

Retrospection Collection Dual Autograph

No Pricing
Production 19 Sets

Standouts Game-Used

NM/M

Common Player: 4.00
Inserted 1:41

Rocco Baldelli	8.00
Angel Berroa	5.00
Hank Blalock	6.00
Marlon Byrd	5.00
Miguel Cabrera	8.00
Hee Seop Choi	4.00
Bo Hart	8.00
Jose Reyes	8.00
Mark Teixeira	6.00
Brandon Webb	5.00
Dontrelle Willis	6.00

Standouts Game-Used Gold

Numbered to player's age.

This Day in History

NM/M

Complete Set (15): 12.00
Common Player: .50
Inserted 1:18

1	Josh Beckett	1.00
2	Carlos Delgado	1.00
3	Javy Lopez	.50
4	Greg Maddux	2.00
5	Rafael Palmeiro	1.00
6	Sammy Sosa	2.50
7	Jeff Bagwell	1.00
8	Frank Thomas	1.00
9	Kevin Millwood	.50
10	Jose Reyes	.75
11	Rafael Furcal	.50
12	Alfonso Soriano	1.50
13	Eric Gagne	.50
14	Hideki Matsui	4.00
15	Hank Blalock	.75

This Day in History Memorabilia

NM/M

Common Player: 5.00

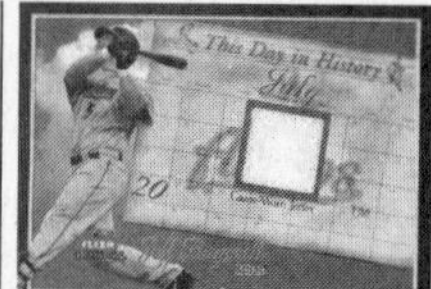

Inserted 1:288

Jeff Bagwell	8.00
Carlos Delgado	5.00
Javy Lopez	5.00
Greg Maddux	15.00
Rafael Palmeiro	8.00
Alfonso Soriano	8.00
Sammy Sosa	12.00
Frank Thomas	8.00

This Day/History Dual Memorabilia

NM/M

Production 25 Sets

Frank Thomas, Jeff Bagwell 25.00

N.Y. Daily News Yankees

Ten popular Yankees stars are featured on this promotional issue. The April 25 Sunday Daily News included a nine-card sheet produced in an edition of 1.1 million. The 7-1/2" x 12" sheet has nine standard-size player cards. Fronts have game-action photos on a dark blue background. Backs are in blue and black on white, presenting personal data and stats. A 10th card, Alex Rodriguez, in a special edition of 50,000 was available at the Yankees Clubhouse Store with the purchase of a Fleer product and a coupon found in the newspaper. Cards on the sheet are not perforated and must be hand-cut to seperate.

NM/M

Uncut Sheet: 2.00
Alex Rodriguez: 7.50

N.Y. Post Mets

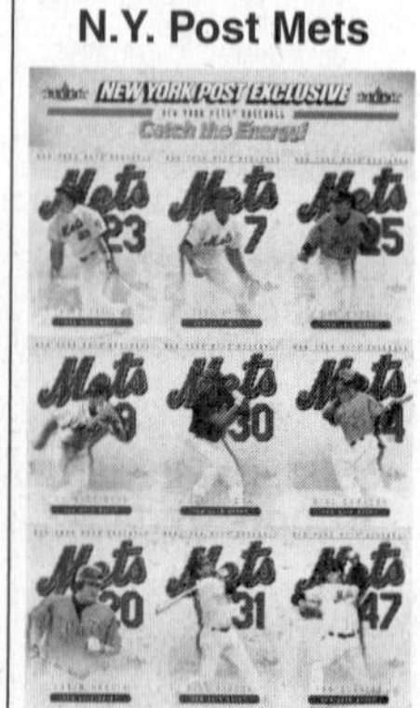

The opening day lineup of the N.Y. Mets was featured in this promotional issue. The April 19 issue of the Post included a nine-card sheet produced in an edition of 800,000. The 7-1/2" x 12" sheet has nine standard-size player cards. Fronts have game-action photos superimposed on a background resembling the team's jersey. Backs are in team colors and reproduce part of the photo while presenting personal data, stats and career highlights. A 10th card, a Kaz Matsui special edition of 25,000 was available with the purchase of a Fleer product at Mets Team Store outlets. Cards on the sheet are not perforated and must be hand-cut to seperate.

NM/M
Complete Sheet: 2.00

2005 Fleer

NM/M
Common Player (1-50): 1.00
Minor Stars (1-50): 1.25
Unlisted Stars (1-50): 1.75
Common Class '05 (51-80): 3.00
Minor Class '05 (51-80): 4.00
Production 699 Sets
Common Veteran (81-90): 3.00
Production 699 Sets
Box (1): 90.00
1 Curt Schilling 1.75
2 Jim Thome 3.00
3 Miguel Cabrera 2.00
4 Randy Johnson 3.50
5 David Ortiz 1.75
6 Vladimir Guerrero 3.00
7 Nomar Garciaparra 5.00
8 Ivan Rodriguez 1.75
9 Jason Schmidt 1.25
10 Khalil Greene 2.00
11 Jose Vidro 1.00
12 Lyle Overbay 1.00
13 Todd Helton 2.00
14 Vernon Wells 1.25
15 B.J. Upton 1.25
16 Hideki Matsui 5.00
17 Pedro Martinez 3.00
18 Victor Martinez 1.00
19 Adam Dunn 1.75
20 Andruw Jones 2.00
21 Jeff Bagwell 2.00
22 Mike Sweeney 1.00
23 Mike Piazza 3.50
24 Ben Sheets 1.25
25 Adrian Beltre 1.25
26 Chipper Jones 3.50
27 Greg Maddux 3.50
28 Manny Ramirez 2.00
29 Roger Clemens 5.00
30 Johan Santana 1.25
31 Derek Jeter 6.00
32 Jason Bay 1.00
33 Ken Griffey Jr. 3.50
34 Miguel Tejada 1.75
35 Richie Sexson 1.75
36 Scott Rolen 3.00
37 Alfonso Soriano 3.00
38 Ichiro Suzuki 4.00
39 Sammy Sosa 4.00
40 Barry Zito 1.75
41 Kazuo Matsui 3.00
42 Mark Teixeira 1.25
43 Carlos Beltran 1.75
44 Mark Prior 4.00
45 Travis Hafner 1.00
46 Alex Rodriguez 5.00
47 Lew Ford 1.00
48 Albert Pujols 5.00
49 Frank Thomas 2.00
50 Juan Pierre 1.00
51 David Aardsma 5.00
52 J.D. Durbin 3.00
53 Zack Greinke 4.00
54 Dioner Navarro 4.00
55 Edwin Encarnacion 4.00
56 Luis Hernandez **RC** 4.00
57 Jeff Baker 4.00
58 Victor Diaz 5.00
59 Joey Gathright 3.00
60 Casey Kotchman 4.00
61 David Wright 5.00
62 Jon Knott 3.00
63 Charlton Jimerson 4.00
64 Nick Swisher 5.00
65 Ryan Raburn 3.00
66 Josh Kroeger 3.00
67 Kelly Johnson 4.00
68 Justin Verlander **RC** 6.00
69 Taylor Buchholz 3.00
70 Ubaldo Jimenez **RC** 5.00
71 Russ Adams 4.00
72 Ronny Cedeno 4.00
73 Bobby Jenks 5.00
74 Dan Meyer 4.00
75 Jeff Francis 3.00
76 Scott Kazmir 5.00
77 Sean Burnett 3.00
78 Jose Lopez 4.00
79 Andres Blanco 3.00
80 Gavin Floyd 4.00
81 Tom Seaver 3.00
82 Steve Carlton 3.00
83 Al Kaline 4.00
84 Cal Ripken Jr. 10.00
85 Willie McCovey 5.00
86 Johnny Bench 5.00
87 Nolan Ryan 10.00
88 Mike Schmidt 4.00
89 Carlton Fisk 3.00
90 Don Mattingly 4.00

Row 1

Stars (1-50):
Class of '05 (51-80): .5-2X
Veterans: .5-2X
Production 100 Sets

Row 2

Cards 1-90: No Pricing
Production One Set

Cuts and Glory Jersey

NM/M
Common Card: 15.00
Production 100 Sets
Patch: 2-4X
Production 50 Sets
Jersey and Patch: No Pricing
Production 15 Sets
Masterpiece Logo: No Pricing
Production One Set
JB Johnny Bench 60.00
CC Carl Crawford 20.00
JL Javy Lopez 20.00
JP Josh Phelps 15.00
BS Ben Sheets 20.00
SS Shannon Stewart 20.00

Cuts and Glory Dual Patch

Production 35 Sets

Diamond Cuts Jersey

NM/M
Common Player: 5.00
Production 150 Sets
Die-Cut: .75-1.5X
Production 75 Sets
Patch: 1-30X
Production 50 Sets
Super Patch: No Pricing
Production 20 Sets
Die-Cut Patch: No Pricing
Production 10 Sets
MLB Logo Masterpiece: No Pricing
Production One Set
JB Jeff Bagwell 8.00
CB Carlos Beltran 6.00
HB Hank Blalock 6.00
MC Miguel Cabrera 8.00
RC Roger Clemens 12.00
AD Adam Dunn 6.00
VG Vladimir Guerrero 8.00
TH Todd Helton 8.00
RJ Randy Johnson 8.00
AJ Andruw Jones 8.00
CJ Chipper Jones 8.00
AK Austin Kearns 6.00
PM Pedro Martinez 8.00
VM Victor Martinez 5.00
HM Hideki Matsui 15.00
HN Hideo Nomo 8.00
DO David Ortiz 6.00
MP Mike Piazza 8.00
MP2 Mark Prior 8.00
AP Albert Pujols 12.00
MR Manny Ramirez 8.00
SR Scott Rolen 8.00
CS Curt Schilling 6.00
GS Gary Sheffield 6.00
AS Alfonso Soriano 8.00
SS Sammy Sosa 10.00
MT Mark Teixeira 5.00
JT Jim Thome 8.00
BU B.J. Upton 5.00
KW Kerry Wood 8.00

Diamond Cuts Dual Jersey

NM/M
Common Card: 8.00
Production 99 Sets
Die-Cut: .5-1.5X
Production 50 Sets
Patch: No Pricing
Production 15 Sets
Patch Die-Cut: No Pricing
Production Five Sets
BC Jeff Bagwell, Roger Clemens 15.00
BM Carlos Beltran, Pedro Martinez 10.00
BS Hank Blalock, Alfonso Soriano 10.00
CH Miguel Cabrera, Todd Helton 10.00
DK Adam Dunn, Austin Kearns 8.00
JJ Chipper Jones, Andruw Jones 12.00
JS Randy Johnson, Curt Schilling 10.00
MS Hideki Matsui, Gary Sheffield 20.00
MT Victor Martinez, Mark Teixeira 8.00
NU Hideo Nomo, B.J. Upton 10.00
OR David Ortiz, Manny Ramirez 10.00
PR Albert Pujols, Scott Rolen 15.00
PT Mike Piazza, Jim Thome 12.00
PW Mark Prior, Kerry Wood 10.00
SG Sammy Sosa, Vladimir Guerrero 15.00

Dynasty Cornerstones Signatures

NM/M
Sequentially Numbered
JB Jeremy Bonderman/75 20.00
DG Dwight Gooden/25 30.00
DO David Ortiz/75 40.00

Dynasty Cornerstones Dual Signatures

Sequentially Numbered

Dynasty Foundations Dual Player Jersey

NM/M
Common Card: 10.00
Production 150 Sets
Patch: 1-30X
Production 50 Sets
BO Miguel Tejada, Javy Lopez 15.00
BR Manny Ramirez, David Ortiz 10.00
CI Victor Martinez, Travis Hafner 10.00
CR1 Adam Dunn, Austin Kearns 12.00
CR2 Todd Helton, Preston Wilson 12.00
FM Miguel Cabrera, Juan Pierre 10.00
HA Jeff Bagwell, Lance Berkman 12.00
LA Vladimir Guerrero, Garret Anderson 12.00
MT Johan Santana, Torii Hunter 12.00
NM Mike Piazza, Tom Glavine 10.00
OA Barry Zito, Eric Chavez 10.00
PP Jim Thome, Bobby Abreu 10.00
SC Scott Rolen, Albert Pujols 25.00
TD B.J. Upton, Scott Kazmir 10.00
TR Mark Teixeira, Michael Young 10.00

Dynasty Foundations Three Player Jersey

NM/M
Common Card: 15.00
Production 99 Sets
Patch: No Pricing
Production 25 Sets
CR1 Adam Dunn, Austin Kearns, Joe Morgan 15.00
FM Miguel Cabrera, Josh Beckett, Juan Pierre 15.00
HA Jeff Bagwell, Lance Berkman, Roger Clemens 40.00
LA Vladimir Guerrero, Garret Anderson, Darin Erstad 20.00
MT Johan Santana, Torii Hunter, Shannon Stewart 15.00
NM Mike Piazza, Pedro Martinez, Tom Glavine 20.00
SC Scott Rolen, Albert Pujols, Jim Edmonds 40.00
TR Alfonso Soriano, Mark Teixeira, Michael Young 15.00

Dynasty Foundations Four Player Jersey

NM/M
Production 40 Sets
Patch: No Pricing
Production 15 Sets
NM Mike Piazza, Nolan Ryan, Pedro Martinez, Tom Glavine 100.00

Dynasty Foundations Five Player Jersey

No Pricing
Production 25 Sets
Patch: No Pricing
Production Nine Sets
MLB Logo Masterpiece: No Pricing
Production One Set

Head of the Class Triple Player Jersey

NM/M
Common Card: 15.00
Numbered to Debut Year.
No pricing for quantities three or less.
Patch: 1-30X
Production 33 Sets
MLB Logo Masterpiece: No Pricing
Production One Set
AGJ Bobby Abreu, Vladimir Guerrero, Andruw Jones/96 20.00
BGB Carlos Beltran, Troy Glaus, Adrian Beltre/98 15.00
BTR Jeff Bagwell, Jim Thome, Ivan Rodriguez/91 15.00
GBH Eric Gagne, A.J. Burnett, Tim Hudson/99 15.00
JDR Chipper Jones, Carlos Delgado, Manny Ramirez/93 20.00
OHS David Ortiz, Torii Hunter, Richie Sexson/97 15.00
SNP Jason Schmidt, Hideo Nomo, Andy Pettitte/95 20.00

Letterman

Sequentially numbered between 4-8.
No Pricing

Significant Signings Blue

NM/M
Common Player: 10.00
Sequentially #'d to indicated quantity.
Silver Die-Cut: 1-30X
Cards #'d 50 or less: .25-1X
Production 50 Sets
Gold Jersey: No Pricing
Production 25 Sets
Patch: No Pricing
Production 15 Sets
Masterpiece Jersey Tag: No Pricing
Production One Set
JB Jason Bay/250 15.00
AB Adrian Beltre/30 50.00
MC Miguel Cabrera/250 20.00
SC Steve Carlton/59 30.00
BC Bobby Crosby/93 15.00
GF Gavin Floyd/221 10.00
LF Lew Ford/230 10.00
ZG Zack Greinke/250 10.00
TH Travis Hafner/250 10.00
SK Scott Kazmir/250 10.00
CK Casey Kotchman/250 10.00
PM Pedro Martinez/101 40.00
VM Victor Martinez/224 10.00
DM Don Mattingly/103 40.00
JM Justin Morneau/225 25.00
JR Jeremy Reed/250 40.00
NR Nolan Ryan/92 100.00
BU B.J. Upton/250 10.00
KW Kerry Wood/200 25.00
DW David Wright/250 40.00

Significant Dual

NM/M
Common Player: 30.00
Production 40 Sets
Dual Jersey: No Pricing
Production 15 Sets
Dual Patch: No Pricing
Production Five Sets
BR Adrian Beltre, Jeremy Reed 60.00
CF Steve Carlton, Gavin Floyd 40.00
FM Lew Ford, Justin Morneau 40.00
MH Victor Martinez, Travis Hafner 30.00
SR Mike Schmidt, Cal Ripken Jr. 250.00

Dynasty Foundations

NM/M
Common Card: 6.00
Production 500 Sets
1DF Rod Carew, Nolan Ryan, Vladimir Guerrero, Garret Anderson, Darin Erstad 8.00
2DF Cal Ripken Jr., Brooks Robinson, Miguel Tejada, Javy Lopez, Jim Palmer 15.00
3DF Ted Williams, Manny Ramirez, Johnny Damon, Carl Yastrzemski, David Ortiz 15.00
4DF Ryne Sandberg, Sammy Sosa, Ernie Banks, Greg Maddux, Mark Prior 8.00
5DF Adam Dunn, Johnny Bench, Tony Perez, Austin Kearns, Joe Morgan 8.00
6DF Victor Martinez, Travis Hafner, Bob Feller, C.C. Sabathia, Larry Doby 6.00
7DF Aaron Miles, Matt Holliday, Todd Helton, Garrett Atkins, Preston Wilson 6.00
8DF Miguel Cabrera, Dontrelle Willis, Juan Pierre, Al Leiter, Josh Beckett 6.00
9DF Lance Berkman, Jeff Bagwell, Craig Biggio, Roger Clemens, Roy Oswalt 8.00
10DF Ben Sheets, Lyle Overbay, Robin Yount, Geoff Jenkins, Paul Molitor 8.00
11DF Johan Santana, Shannon Stewart, Harmon Killebrew, Torii Hunter, Lee Ford 6.00
12DF Tom Glavine, Mike Piazza, Tom Seaver, Nolan Ryan, Pedro Martinez 8.00
13DF Eric Chavez, Reggie Jackson, Bobby Crosby, Dennis Eckersley, Barry Zito 6.00
14DF Jim Thome, Bobby Abreu, Gavin Floyd, Robin Roberts, Mike Schmidt 6.00
15DF Craig Wilson, Willie Stargell, Bill Mazeroski, Jason Bay, Jack Wilson 6.00
16DF Willie McCovey, Jason Schmidt, Juan Marichal, Orlando Cepeda, Ray Durham 6.00
17DF Scott Rolen, Mark Mulder, Albert Pujols, Jim Edmonds, Stan Musial 10.00
18DF Rocco Baldelli, Scott Kazmir, Aubrey Huff, B.J. Upton, Carl Crawford 6.00
19DF Alfonso Soriano, Mark Teixeira, Hank Blalock, Nolan Ryan, Michael Young 10.00
20DF Alexis Rios, Paul Molitor, Roy Halladay, Vernon Wells, Orlando Hudson 6.00

2005 Fleer America's National Pastime

NM/M
Common Player (1-50): .25
Minor Stars (1-50): .40
Unlisted Stars (1-50): .60
Common Player (51-70): 3.00
Production 699 Sets
Common Player (71-80): 3.00
Production 699 Sets
Pack (5): 7.00
Box (10): 60.00
1 Khalil Greene .75
2 Pedro Martinez 1.00
3 Mark Teixeira .40
4 Jim Thome 1.00
5 Jack Wilson .25
6 Johan Santana .40
7 Jason Bay .25
8 Adam Dunn .60
9 Lyle Overbay .25
10 Jason Schmidt .40
11 Bobby Crosby .25
12 J.D. Drew .40
13 Ken Griffey Jr. 1.50
14 Sammy Sosa 2.00
15 Hank Blalock .60
16 Victor Martinez .25
17 Randy Johnson 1.00
18 Vernon Wells .40
19 Todd Helton .75
20 Javy Lopez .40
21 Kazuo Matsui .60
22 Ben Sheets .40
23 Brad Wilkerson .25
24 Miguel Cabrera .75
25 Mike Sweeney .25
26 Roger Clemens 2.50
27 Chipper Jones 1.50
28 Hideki Matsui 2.50
29 Manny Ramirez .75
30 Scott Rolen 1.00
31 Lance Berkman .40
32 Jim Edmonds .40
33 Derek Jeter 3.00
34 B.J. Upton .40
35 Carlos Delgado .75
36 Ichiro Suzuki 2.00
37 Nomar Garciaparra 2.50
38 Albert Pujols 2.50
39 Ivan Rodriguez .60
40 Gary Sheffield .60
41 Alfonso Soriano 1.00
42 Carlos Beltran .60
43 Magglio Ordonez .40
44 Alex Rodriguez 2.50
45 Curt Schilling .60
46 Greg Maddux 1.50
47 Vladimir Guerrero 1.00
48 Mike Piazza 1.50
49 Miguel Tejada .60
50 Adrian Beltre .40
51 Scott Kazmir 5.00
52 Gavin Floyd 4.00
53 Zack Greinke 4.00
54 David Wright 5.00
55 David Aardsma 4.00
56 Ryan Raburn 3.00
57 Joey Gathright 3.00
58 J.D. Durbin 3.00
59 Sean Burnett 3.00
60 Jose Lopez 3.00
61 Nick Swisher 4.00
62 Bobby Jenks 3.00
63 Kelly A. Johnson 3.00
65 Ronny Cedeno 4.00
66 Edwin Encarnacion 3.00
67 Jeff Baker 3.00
68 Taylor Buchholz 3.00
69 Justin Verlander **RC** 5.00
70 Luis Hernandez **RC** 5.00
71 Mike Schmidt 5.00
72 Al Kaline 3.00
73 Yogi Berra 4.00
74 Robin Yount 4.00
75 Nolan Ryan 6.00
76 Johnny Bench 5.00
77 Eddie Murray 4.00
78 Tom Seaver 4.00
79 Willie McCovey 3.00
80 Cal Ripken Jr. 6.00

Blue Foil

No Pricing
Production One Set

Red Foil

Cards 1-50: 1-30X
Cards 51-70: .75-1.5X
Cards 71-80: .75-1.5X
Production 150 Sets

White Foil

Cards 1-50 #'d to 41-57: 2-6X
Cards 1-50 #'d to 26-40: 4-8X
Cards 1-50 #'d 25 or less: No Pricing
Cards 71-80 #'d to 26-44: 1-30X
Cards 71-80 #'d 25 or less: No Pricing
Numbered to player's jersey number.

Beltway Baseball

NM/M
Common Card: 6.00
Production 202 Sets
1 Ed Delahanty 8.00
2 Benjamin Harrison 8.00
3 William Howard Taft 6.00
4 Clark Griffith 6.00
5 Bobby Burke 8.00
6 Roy Seivers 8.00
7 Tom Cheney 8.00
8 Woodrow Wilson 8.00
9 Franklin D. Roosevelt 8.00
10 John F. Kennedy 10.00
11 Frank Howard 8.00
12 Griffith Stadium 10.00
13 RFK Stadium 8.00
14 All-Star Game 6.00
15 Ted Williams 15.00
16 Harmon Killebrew 12.00
17 Jeff Burroughs 8.00
18 All-Star Game 6.00
19 Unveiling the Nationals 10.00
20 New Logo 8.00

First Name Bases Autograph Gold

NM/M
Cards #'d 25 or less: No Pricing
Sequentially #'d to indicated quantity.
AB Adrian Beltre/96 25.00
MCAM Mike Cameron/126 15.00
SH Shea Hillenbrand/99 15.00
JL Javy Lopez/73 15.00
AP Albert Pujols/73 200.00
MT Mark Teixeira/147 25.00
JV Justin Verlander/149 20.00

First Name Bases Autograph Red

NM/M
Cards #'d 25 or less: No Pricing

Sequentially #'d to indicated quantity.
MCAM Mike Cameron/90 15.00
BL Barry Larkin/27 40.00
MT Mark Teixeira/95 30.00
JV Justin Verlander/99 20.00

First Name Bases Autograph Silver

NM/M
Sequentially #'d to indicated quantity.
Blue: No Pricing
Production One Set
MCAM Mike Cameron/375 10.00
SH Shea Hillenbrand/316 10.00
JL Javy Lopez/158 15.00
MT Mark Teixeira/225 20.00
JV Justin Verlander/401 15.00

First Name Bases Autograph White

NM/M
Cards #'d 25 or less: No Pricing
Sequentially #'d to indicated quantity.
AB Adrian Beltre/48 25.00

Grand Old Gamers

NM/M
Common Player: .75
Inserted 1:5
1 Pedro Martinez 1.50
2 Jim Thome 1.50
3 Ken Griffey Jr. 2.00
4 Sammy Sosa 2.50
5 Hank Blalock 1.00
6 Randy Johnson 1.50
7 Roger Clemens 3.00
8 Chipper Jones 2.00
9 Hideki Matsui 3.00
10 Manny Ramirez 1.25
11 Derek Jeter 4.00
12 Ichiro Suzuki 2.50
13 Nomar Garciaparra 3.00
14 Albert Pujols 3.00
15 Gary Sheffield 1.00
16 Alfonso Soriano 1.50
17 Alex Rodriguez 3.00
18 Curt Schilling 1.00
19 Vladimir Guerrero 1.50
20 Mike Piazza 2.00
21 Greg Maddux 2.00
22 Frank Thomas 1.25
23 Adrian Beltre .75
24 Barry Larkin .75
25 Todd Helton 1.25
26 Kerry Wood 1.25
27 Kazuo Matsui 1.00
28 Scott Rolen 1.50
29 Ivan Rodriguez 1.00
30 Miguel Tejada 1.00
31 Mark Teixeira .75
32 Rafael Palmeiro 1.25
33 Andruw Jones 1.25
34 Carlos Beltran 1.00
35 Jeff Bagwell 1.25

Grand Old Gamers Jersey

NM/M
Common Player: 6.00
Inserted 1:36 Retail
JB Jeff Bagwell 8.00
CB Carlos Beltran 8.00
AB Adrian Beltre 6.00
HB Hank Blalock 8.00
RC Roger Clemens/SP/50 15.00
VG Vladimir Guerrero 8.00
TH Todd Helton 8.00
RJ Randy Johnson 8.00
AJ Andruw Jones 8.00
CJ Chipper Jones 8.00
BL Barry Larkin 6.00
GM Greg Maddux/SP/75 12.00
PM Pedro Martinez 8.00
HM Hideki Matsui/SP/50 15.00
KM Kazuo Matsui 8.00
RP Rafael Palmeiro 8.00
MP Mike Piazza 8.00
AP Albert Pujols 12.00
MR Manny Ramirez 8.00
IR Ivan Rodriguez 8.00
SR Scott Rolen 8.00
CS Curt Schilling 8.00
GS Gary Sheffield 8.00
AS Alfonso Soriano 8.00
SS Sammy Sosa 12.00
MT Mark Teixeira 6.00
FT Frank Thomas 8.00
JT Jim Thome 8.00
KW Kerry Wood 8.00

Grand Old Gamers Patch Blue

NM/M
Numbered to player's jersey number.
Cards numbered 25 or less: No Pricing
Masterpiece: No Pricing
Production One Set
VG Vladimir Guerrero/27 25.00
RJ Randy Johnson/51 20.00
GM Greg Maddux/31 25.00
PM Pedro Martinez/45 20.00
HM Hideki Matsui/55 50.00
MP Mike Piazza/31 25.00
SR Scott Rolen/27 25.00
CS Curt Schilling/38 15.00
FT Frank Thomas/35 15.00
KW Kerry Wood/34 20.00

Grand Old Gamers Dual Patch

NM/M
Cards #'d to 25 or less: No Pricing
Production 5-33 Sets
Ivan Rodriguez, Mike Piazza/31 75.00
Hank Blalock, Mark Teixeira/33 30.00

Historical Record

NM/M
Common Card: 2.00
Inserted 1:6
1 Ichiro Suzuki/2004 2.50
2 Greg Maddux/2004 2.00
3 Alex Rodriguez/1998 3.00
4 Mike Piazza/2004 2.00
5 Nolan Ryan/1991 5.00
6 Albert Pujols/2001 3.00
7 Mike Schmidt/1987 4.00
8 Randy Johnson/2004 2.00
9 Sammy Sosa/2003 2.50
10 Cal Ripken Jr./1996 5.00
11 Roger Clemens/2004 3.00
12 Hideki Matsui/2003 3.00
13 Hideo Nomo/1994 2.00
14 Gene Autry/1961 2.00
15 Walter O'Malley/1944 2.00

Historical Record Jersey

NM/M
Common Player: 6.00
Inserted 1:96 Retail
RC Roger Clemens 10.00
RJ Randy Johnson 8.00
GM Greg Maddux 8.00
HM Hideki Matsui 12.00
HN Hideo Nomo 6.00
MP Mike Piazza 8.00
AP Albert Pujols 10.00
CR Cal Ripken Jr. 30.00
NRO Nolan Ryan 20.00
MS Mike Schmidt 25.00
SS Sammy Sosa 10.00

Historical Record Patch Blue

No Pricing
Numbered to player's jersey number.
Masterpiece: No Pricing
Production One Set

Historical Record Dual Patch

No Pricing
Production 8-25 Sets

Signature Swings Bat Red

NM/M
Common Player: 20.00
Production 30-99 Sets
BAY Jason Bay/99 20.00
JB Johnny Bench/42 80.00
LB Lance Berkman/99 20.00
CC Carl Crawford/99 20.00
LF Lew Ford/76 20.00
CK Casey Kotchman/99 20.00
BR Brooks Robinson/64 40.00
MS Mike Schmidt/30 100.00
SS Shannon Stewart/99 20.00
DW David Wright/99 60.00

Signature Swings Jersey White

NM/M
Production 3-29 Sets
Cards #'d less than 25: No Pricing
LB Lance Berkman/29 30.00
CC Carl Crawford/29 30.00
JP Josh Phelps/27 15.00

Signature Swings Patch Blue

NM/M
Numbered to player's jersey number.
Cards #'d less than 25: No Pricing
Masterpiece: No Pricing
Production One Set
BAY Jason Bay/38 60.00
JP Josh Phelps/45 20.00

Signature Swings Silver

NM/M
Common Player: 10.00
Gold: .75-1.5X
Sequentially #'d between 50 & 199.
BAY Jason Bay 20.00
CC Carl Crawford 10.00
AE Adam Everett 10.00
CF Chone Figgins 10.00
LF Lew Ford 10.00
JG Joey Gathright 10.00
KG Khalil Greene 30.00
TH Travis Hafner 10.00
AH Aubrey Huff 10.00
CK Casey Kotchman 10.00
VAL Val Majewski 10.00
JM Joe Mauer 25.00
DM Dallas McPherson 15.00
JMO Justin Morneau 40.00
WMP Wily Mo Pena 25.00
JP Josh Phelps 10.00
RR Ryan Raburn 10.00
SS Shannon Stewart 10.00
NS Nick Swisher 15.00
BJU B.J. Upton 15.00
CU Chase Utley 12.00
DW David Wright 50.00
MY Michael Young 10.00

2005 Fleer Authentix

NM/M
Common Player (1-100): .25
Minor Stars (1-100): .40
Unlisted Stars (1-100): .60
Common Player Autograph (101-125): 10.00
Minor Stars Autograph 101-125): 15.00
Production 250 Sets
Pack (5): 3.00
Box (24): 60.00
1 Albert Pujols 2.50
2 Bernie Williams .60
3 Vinny Castilla .25
4 Rocco Baldelli .60
5 Mike Piazza 1.50
6 Sean Casey .25
7 Oliver Perez .25
8 Tony Batista .25
9 Paul Konerko .25
10 Scott Rolen 1.00
11 Justin Morneau .25
12 Nomar Garciaparra 2.50
13 Lance Berkman .40
14 Mike Sweeney .25
15 Miguel Tejada .75
16 Craig Wilson .25
17 Craig Biggio .40
18 Shea Hillenbrand .25
19 Mark Mulder .40
20 Juan Pierre .25
21 Troy Glaus .60
22 Eric Chavez .40
23 Jeromy Burnitz .25
24 Carl Crawford .25
25 Kazuo Matsui .25
26 Ivan Rodriguez .60
27 Aubrey Huff .25
28 Derek Jeter 3.00
29 Casey Blake .25
30 Mark Teixeira .40
31 Brad Wilkerson .25
32 Austin Kearns .60
33 Jim Edmonds .40
34 Johan Santana .40
35 Kerry Wood .75
36 Ichiro Suzuki 2.00
37 Lyle Overbay .25
38 Melvin Mora .25
39 Jason Bay .25
40 Jake Westbrook .25
41 Andruw Jones .75
42 Chase Utley .25
43 Carl Pavano .25
44 Luis Gonzalez .40
45 Bobby Crosby .25
46 Carlos Guillen .25
47 Carlos Delgado .75
48 Alex Rodriguez 2.50
49 Todd Helton .75
50 Michael Young .25
51 Geoff Jenkins .40
52 Pedro Martinez 1.00
53 Brian Giles .40
54 Ken Harvey .25
55 Johnny Estrada .25
56 Billy Wagner .25
57 Roger Clemens 2.50
58 Chipper Jones 1.50
59 Jim Thome 1.00
60 Miguel Cabrera .75
61 Vladimir Guerrero 1.00
62 Gary Sheffield .60
63 Travis Hafner .25
64 Alfonso Soriano 1.00
65 Richard Hidalgo .25
66 Adam Dunn .60
67 Garret Anderson .40
68 Lew Ford .25
69 Mark Prior 1.50
70 Bret Boone .40
71 Ben Sheets .40
72 David Ortiz .60
73 Mark Loretta .25
74 Eric Gagne .40
75 Curt Schilling .60
76 Jason Schmidt .40
77 Adrian Beltre .40
78 Javy Lopez .40
79 Jack Wilson .25
80 Carlos Beltran .60
81 J.D. Drew .40
82 Bobby Abreu .40
83 Jeff Bagwell .75
84 Randy Johnson 1.00
85 Tim Hudson .40
86 Carlos Pena .25
87 Vernon Wells .40
88 Tom Glavine .40
89 Victor Martinez .25
90 Hank Blalock .60
91 Jose Vidro .25
92 Magglio Ordonez .40
93 Jake Peavy .25
94 Torii Hunter .60
95 Sammy Sosa 2.00
96 Hideki Matsui 2.50
97 Shawn Green .40
98 Manny Ramirez .75
99 Khalil Greene .75
100 Jason Marquis .25
101 B.J. Upton/Auto. 20.00
102 Scott Kazmir/Auto. 20.00
103 Gavin Floyd/Auto. 20.00
104 Jeff Francis/Auto. 20.00
105 Russ Adams/Auto. Exch. 10.00
106 Zack Greinke/Auto. 15.00
107 David Wright/Auto. 60.00
108 David Aardsma/Auto. 20.00
109 Josh Kroeger/Auto. 10.00
110 Ryan Raburn/Auto. 30.00
111 Jason Kubel/Auto. 10.00
112 Casey Kotchman/Auto. 20.00
113 Joey Gathright/Auto. 15.00
114 Jon Knott/Auto. 10.00
115 J.D. Durbin/Auto. 25.00
116 Andres Blanco/Auto. 10.00
117 Charlton Jimerson/Auto. 10.00
118 Sean Burnett/Auto. 15.00
119 Joe Mauer/Auto. 30.00
120 Justin Verlander/Auto. **RC** 30.00
121 Mike Gosling/Auto. 10.00
122 Jeff Keppinger/Auto. 10.00
123 David Krynzel/Auto. 10.00
124 Jose Lopez/Auto. 15.00
125 Ruben Gotay/Auto. 15.00

General Admission

Cards 1-100: 1-2.5X
Cards 101-125: .75-1.5X
Production 100 Sets

Autographed General Admission

NM/M
Common Player: 15.00
Production 100 Sets
Mezzanine: 1-2X
Production 40 Sets
Club Box: No Pricing
Production Five Sets
Standing Room Only: No Pricing
Production One Set
JB Jason Bay 15.00
JE Johnny Estrada 15.00
CF Chone Figgins 20.00
LF Lew Ford 15.00
KG Khalil Greene 50.00
TH Travis Hafner 15.00
JM Justin Morneau 40.00
JS Johan Santana 25.00
BS Ben Sheets 20.00
CU Chase Utley 15.00
JW Jack Wilson 15.00

Mezzanine

Cards 1-100: 1-30X
Cards 101-125: .75-2X
Production 75 Sets

Club Box

Cards 1-100: 1-3.25X
Cards 101-125: 1-2X
Production 50 Sets

Standing Room Only

Cards 1-125: No Pricing
Production 10 Sets

Hot Ticket

NM/M
Common Player: 2.00
Inserted 1:12
1 Derek Jeter 6.00
2 Roger Clemens 5.00
3 Vladimir Guerrero 3.00
4 Manny Ramirez 2.00
5 Alex Rodriguez 5.00
6 Albert Pujols 5.00
7 Mike Piazza 3.50
8 Hideki Matsui 5.00
9 Sammy Sosa 4.00
10 Chipper Jones 3.50

Hot Ticket Jersey

NM/M
Common Player: 8.00
Inserted 1:87
Patch
Cards #'d to 55: 1-30X
Cards #'d to 27: 2-4X
Cards #'d to 25 or less: No Pricing
Sequentially #'d to player's jersey #.
MLB Logo: No Pricing
Production One Set
RC Roger Clemens 15.00
VG Vladimir Guerrero 8.00
CJ Chipper Jones 10.00
HM Hideki Matsui 25.00
MP Mike Piazza 10.00
AP Albert Pujols 20.00
MR Manny Ramirez 8.00
SS Sammy Sosa 12.00

Jersey Game of the Week

NM/M
Common Player: 10.00
Sequentially #'d between 10 & 200.
No pricing for cards #'d to 20 or less.
Patch: No Pricing
Production 10 Sets
BR Carlos Beltran, Scott Rolen/120 15.00
BT Tony Batista, Miguel Tejada/170 10.00
CG Eric Chavez, Troy Glaus/150 12.00
CJ Roger Clemens, Randy Johnson/70 15.00
CJ2 Miguel Cabrera, Chipper Jones/90 12.00
CP Carl Crawford, Juan Pierre/190 10.00
DT Adam Dunn, Jim Thome/110 20.00
GG Shawn Green, Vladimir Guerrero/180 12.00
GS Vladimir Guerrero, Alfonso Soriano/100 15.00
KG Scott Kazmir, Zack Greinke/80 10.00
MM Kazuo Matsui, Hideki Matsui/30 100.00
MM2 Joe Mauer, Victor Martinez/130 10.00
MR Pedro Martinez, Mariano Rivera/60 12.00
OP David Ortiz, Albert Pujols/200 15.00
OS Magglio Ordonez, Sammy Sosa/160 15.00
RH Manny Ramirez, Torii Hunter/140 10.00
SS Johan Santana, Curt Schilling/40 30.00
WO Kerry Wood, Roy Oswalt/50 30.00

Jersey General Admission

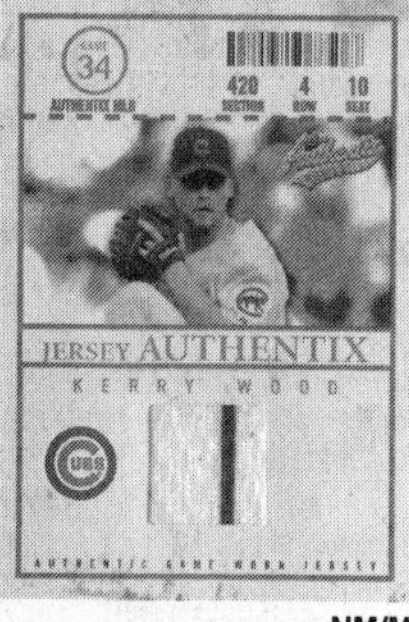

NM/M
Common Player: 5.00
Inserted 1:16
Jersey Mezzanine: 1-30X
Production 75 Sets
Jersey Club Box: No Pricing
Production 25 Sets
Jersey Standing Room Only: No Pricing
Production One Set
Patch General Admission: 2-4X
Production 75 Sets
Patch Mezzanine: No Pricing
Production 15 Sets
Patch Club Box: No Pricing
Production Five Sets
Patch Standing Room Only: No Pricing
Production One Set
CB Carlos Beltran 10.00
AB Adrian Beltre 5.00
LB Lance Berkman 5.00
HB Hank Blalock 5.00
MC Miguel Cabrera 8.00
RC Roger Clemens 12.00
AD Adam Dunn 5.00
EG Eric Gagne 5.00
KG Khalil Greene 10.00
VG Vladimir Guerrero 8.00
TH Todd Helton 5.00
RJ Randy Johnson 8.00
CJ Chipper Jones 8.00
PM Pedro Martinez 8.00
HM Hideki Matsui 20.00
KM Kazuo Matsui 10.00
JM Joe Mauer 8.00
HN Hideo Nomo 8.00
DO David Ortiz 10.00
MP Mike Piazza 8.00
AP Albert Pujols 15.00
MR Manny Ramirez 8.00
MR2 Mariano Rivera 5.00
IR Ivan Rodriguez 5.00
SR Scott Rolen 8.00
JS Johan Santana 5.00
CS Curt Schilling 5.00
GS Gary Sheffield 5.00
AS Alfonso Soriano 8.00
SS Sammy Sosa 10.00
JT Jim Thome 8.00
BU B.J. Upton 8.00
BW Bernie Williams 5.00
KW Kerry Wood 8.00
DW David Wright 15.00

Autograph Jersey General Admission

NM/M
Common Player: 20.00
Production 75 Sets
Mezzanine: No Pricing
Production 15 Sets
Club Box: No Pricing
Production Five Sets
Standing Room Only: No Pricing
Production One Set
JB Jason Bay 20.00
MC Miguel Cabrera 30.00
JE Johnny Estrada 20.00
CF Chone Figgins 25.00
LF Lew Ford 20.00
KG Khalil Greene 60.00
TH Travis Hafner 20.00
JM Justin Morneau 50.00
JS Johan Santana 30.00
MS Mike Schmidt 75.00
BS Ben Sheets 25.00
CU Chase Utley 20.00
JW Jack Wilson 20.00

Autograph Patch General Admission

NM/M
Production 40 Sets
Mezzanine: No Pricing
Production 10 Sets
Club Box: No Pricing
Production Five Sets
Standing Room Only

Production One Set
CF Chone Figgins 25.00
MP Mike Piazza 150.00
CR Cal Ripken Jr. 400.00
MS Mike Schmidt 150.00
JT Jim Thome 80.00

Showstoppers

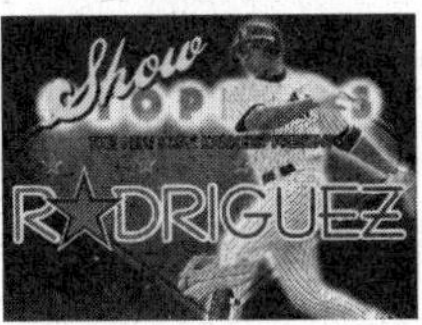

NM/M
Common Player: 2.00
Inserted 1:8
1 Nomar Garciaparra 4.00
2 Ichiro Suzuki 3.50
3 Ken Griffey Jr. 3.00
4 Alex Rodriguez 4.00
5 Albert Pujols 4.00
6 Derek Jeter 5.00
7 Roger Clemens 4.00
8 Randy Johnson 2.50
9 Hideo Nomo 2.00
10 Jim Thome 2.50
11 Mike Piazza 3.00
12 Hideki Matsui 4.00
13 Sammy Sosa 3.50
14 Kerry Wood 2.00
15 Eric Gagne 2.00

Teammate Trios

NM/M
Common Card: 12.00
Production 75 Sets
Hometown 1: 2-3X
Production 25 Sets
Hometown 2: No Pricing
Production Five Sets
BR David Ortiz, Manny Ramirez, Pedro Martinez 25.00
NY Hideki Matsui, Bernie Williams, Gary Sheffield 30.00
AB J.D. Drew, Chipper Jones, Andruw Jones 15.00
CC Sammy Sosa, Mark Prior, Nomar Garciaparra 15.00
CI Victor Martinez, Travis Hafner, Casey Blake 12.00
HA Lance Berkman, Roger Clemens, Carlos Beltran 25.00
MT Johan Santana, Torii Hunter, Corey Koskie 12.00
WN Tony Batista, Jose Vidro, Brad Wilkerson 12.00
NM Mike Piazza, David Wright, Kazuo Matsui 40.00
OA Barry Zito, Tim Hudson, Mark Mulder 12.00
PP Bobby Abreu, Jim Thome, Pat Burrell 15.00
SC Scott Rolen, Albert Pujols, Jim Edmonds 30.00
TD Scott Kazmir, Rocco Baldelli, B.J. Upton 25.00
TR Hank Blalock, Mark Teixeira, Alfonso Soriano 15.00
LD Shawn Green, Adrian Beltre, Steve Finley 12.00

2005 Fleer Classic Clippings

NM/M
Common Player (1-75): .25
Minor Stars (1-75): .40
Unlisted Stars (1-75): .60
Common Legends (76-105): 2.00
Production 999 Sets
Common Player (106-125): 3.00
Inserted 1:6
1 Frank Thomas .75
2 Vladimir Guerrero 1.00
3 Ken Griffey Jr. 1.50
4 Derek Jeter 3.00
5 Rafael Palmeiro .75
6 Adrian Beltre .40
7 Khalil Greene .75
8 Richie Sexson .60
9 Roger Clemens 2.50
10 Mike Piazza 1.50
11 Chipper Jones 1.50
12 Juan Pierre .25
13 Todd Helton .75
14 Ben Sheets .40
15 John Smoltz .40
16 Steve Finley .25
17 Jim Thome 1.00
18 Vernon Wells .40
19 Melvin Mora .25
20 Dontrelle Willis .40
21 Eric Gagne .40
22 Craig Wilson .25
23 Curt Schilling .60
24 Justin Morneau .25
25 Jason Schmidt .40
26 Kerry Wood .75
27 Ivan Rodriguez .60
28 Rocco Baldelli .60
29 Mark Prior 2.00
30 Josh Beckett .75
31 Scott Rolen 1.00
32 Nomar Garciaparra 2.50
33 Carl Crawford .25
34 Paul Konerko .40
35 Miguel Cabrera .75
36 Hank Blalock .60
37 Sammy Sosa 2.00
38 Jim Edmonds .40
39 David Ortiz .60
40 Lance Berkman .40
41 Ichiro Suzuki 2.00
42 Adam Dunn .60
43 Carlos Guillen .25
44 Alfonso Soriano 1.00
45 Victor Martinez .25
46 Torii Hunter .60
47 Kazuo Matsui .60
48 Andruw Jones .75
49 Matt Holliday .50
50 Eric Chavez .40
51 Randy Johnson 1.00
52 Lew Ford .25
53 Hideki Matsui 2.50
54 Manny Ramirez .75
55 Mark Teixeira .40
56 Jose Vidro .25
57 Mike Sweeney .25
58 Jack Wilson .25
59 Greg Maddux 1.50
60 Tony Batista .25
61 Albert Pujols 2.50
62 Miguel Tejada .60
63 Carlos Beltran .60
64 Bobby Abreu .40
65 Carlos Delgado .75
66 Travis Hafner .25
67 Scott Podsednik .25
68 Gary Sheffield .60
69 Johan Santana .40
70 Barry Zito .60
71 Pedro Martinez 1.00
72 Brian Giles .40
73 Garret Anderson .40
74 Jeff Bagwell .60
75 Alex Rodriguez 2.50
76 Johnny Bench 4.00
77 Yogi Berra 3.00
78 Lou Brock 3.00
79 Rod Carew 3.00
80 Orlando Cepeda 2.00
81 Carlton Fisk 5.00
82 Bob Gibson 3.00
83 Reggie Jackson 5.00
84 Al Kaline 4.00
85 Harmon Killebrew 3.00
86 Ralph Kiner 4.00
87 Willie McCovey 2.00
88 Eddie Murray 4.00
89 Phil Rizzuto 4.00
90 Brooks Robinson 3.00
91 Nolan Ryan 5.00
92 Mike Schmidt 4.00
93 Tom Seaver 3.00
94 Willie Stargell 2.00
95 Rollie Fingers 2.00
96 Dennis Eckersley 2.00
97 Enos Slaughter 2.00
98 Jim Palmer 2.00
99 Warren Spahn 3.00
100 Joe Morgan 2.00
101 Richie Ashburn 3.00
102 Robin Yount 3.00
103 Bob Feller 3.00
104 Pee Wee Reese 2.00
105 Eddie Mathews 3.00
106 David Wright 6.00
107 David Aardsma 3.00
108 B.J. Upton 3.00
109 Scott Kazmir 4.00
110 Gavin Floyd 3.00
111 Jeff Francis 3.00
112 Dioner Navarro 3.00
113 Zack Greinke 3.00
114 Nick Swisher 5.00
115 Josh Kroeger 3.00
116 Ryan Raburn 3.00
117 Victor Diaz 4.00
118 Casey Kotchman 4.00
119 Joey Gathright 3.00
120 Jon Knott 3.00
121 J.D. Durbin 3.00
122 Andres Blanco 3.00
123 Charlton Jimerson 3.00
124 Russ Adams 3.00
125 Justin Verlander RC 5.00

First Edition

(1-75): 2-5X
(76-105): 1-1.5X
(106-125): 1-2X
Production 150 Sets

Final Edition

No Pricing
Production One Set

Bat Rack Quad Blue

NM/M
Inserted 1:118
Silver: No Pricing
Production 10 Sets
Purple: No Pricing
Production One Set
Gary Sheffield, Vladimir Guerrero, Manny Ramirez, Sammy Sosa 20.00
Manny Ramirez, Wade Boggs, Carl Yastrzemski, Bobby Doerr 40.00
Kirby Puckett, Jacque Jones, Harmon Killebrew, Torii Hunter 40.00
Brandon Webb, Randy Johnson, Curt Schilling, Roger Clemens 40.00
Willie Stargell, Bill Madlock, Bill Mazeroski, Roberto Clemente 100.00
Al Kaline, Tony Gwynn, Frank Howard, Rocky Colavito 50.00
Jose Reyes, Gary Carter, Mike Piazza, Kazuo Matsui 25.00
Bobby Abreu, Adam Dunn, Rocco Baldelli, Hideki Matsui 30.00
Jim Thome, Albert Pujols, Jeff Bagwell, Todd Helton 40.00
Hank Blalock, Miguel Tejada, Troy Glaus, Ivan Rodriguez 25.00
Carlos Delgado, Jason Giambi, Rafael Palmeiro, Mark Teixeira 25.00

Classic Clippings

NM/M
Common Player: 3.00
Gold: 2-5X
Production 51-95 Sets
1 Nolan Ryan/1991 6.00
2 Cal Ripken Jr./1995 8.00
3 Joe Carter/1993 3.00
4 Bucky Dent/1978 3.00
5 Kirk Gibson/1988 3.00
6 Reggie Jackson/1977 5.00
7 Carlton Fisk/1975 4.00
8 Bobby Thomson/1951 3.00
9 Bill Mazeroski/1960 3.00
10 Don Larsen/1956 4.00

Cut of History Single Autograph Blue

NM/M
Common Player: 20.00
Inserted 1:161
Silver: No Pricing
Production 25 Sets
Purple: No Pricing
Production One Set
JB Johnny Bench 50.00
BB Bill Buckner 20.00
BF Bob Feller 20.00
KG Kirk Gibson 20.00
DG Dwight Gooden 30.00
DL Don Larsen 20.00
DM Don Mattingly 50.00
JP Jim Palmer 30.00
BR Brooks Robinson 40.00
DS Darryl Strawberry 25.00
MW Mookie Wilson 20.00

Cut of History Dual Autograph Blue

NM/M
Production 49 Sets
Silver: No Pricing
Production 22 Sets
Purple: No Pricing
Production One Set
GE Kirk Gibson, Dennis Eckersley 50.00
GS Dwight Gooden, Darryl Strawberry 40.00
WB Mookie Wilson, Bill Buckner 40.00

Cut of History Triple Autograph Blue

No Pricing
Production 15 Sets
Silver: No Pricing
Production Five Sets
Purple: No Pricing
Production One Set

Cut of History Single Jersey Blue

NM/M
Common Player: 6.00
Inserted 1:21
Silver Patch: No Pricing
Production 25 Sets
Purple Patch: No Pricing
Production One Set
SA Sparky Anderson 6.00
JB Johnny Bench 15.00
OC Orlando Cepeda 8.00
CF Carlton Fisk 10.00
BG Bob Gibson 8.00
DG Dwight Gooden 6.00
RJ Reggie Jackson 12.00
DM Don Mattingly 15.00
WM Willie McCovey 6.00
JM Joe Morgan/SP/82 12.00
EM Eddie Murray 10.00
CR Cal Ripken Jr. 20.00
BR Brooks Robinson 8.00
NR Nolan Ryan 20.00
MS Mike Schmidt 12.00
TS Tom Seaver 10.00
OS Ozzie Smith 15.00
WS Willie Stargell 10.00
DS Darryl Strawberry 6.00
CY Carl Yastrzemski 10.00

Cut of History Dual Jersey Blue

NM/M
Common Card: 15.00
Inserted 1:112
Silver Patch: No Pricing
Production 15 Sets
Purple Patch: No Pricing
Production One Set
BF Johnny Bench, Carlton Fisk 20.00
BS Lou Brock, Mike Schmidt 25.00
CM Orlando Cepeda, Willie McCovey 15.00
GS Dwight Gooden, Darryl Strawberry 15.00
JY Reggie Jackson, Carl Yastrzemski 20.00
RS Cal Ripken Jr., Ozzie Smith 30.00
RS Nolan Ryan, Tom Seaver 30.00
SJ Willie Stargell, Reggie Jackson 20.00

Cut of History Triple Jersey Blue

NM/M
Inserted 1:67
Silver Patch: No Pricing
Production 25 Sets
Purple Patch: No Pricing
Production One Set
ACW Hank Aaron, Roberto Clemente, Ted Williams 160.00
BSG Lou Brock, Kirk Gibson, Ozzie Smith 50.00
JKM Reggie Jackson, Harmon Killebrew, Willie McCovey 40.00
MMC Eddie Murray, Orlando Cepeda, Willie McCovey 25.00
MRS Don Mattingly, Cal Ripken Jr., Mike Schmidt 75.00
OJM Paul O'Neill, Don Mattingly, Reggie Jackson 50.00
RCJ Nolan Ryan, Roger Clemens, Randy Johnson 50.00

Diamond Signings Single Blue

NM/M
Inserted 1:29
Silver: No Pricing
Production 25 Sets
Purple: No Pricing
Production One Set
JB Jason Bay 20.00
AB Andres Blanco 15.00
CF Chone Figgins 15.00
GF Gavin Floyd 15.00
KG Khalil Greene/150 25.00
ZG Zack Greinke 15.00
TH Travis Hafner 10.00
CJ Charlton Jimerson 10.00
SK Scott Kazmir 20.00
CK Casey Kotchman 10.00
BL Brad Lidge/97 40.00
JM Justin Morneau/98 25.00
DN Dioner Navarro 10.00
JP Jake Peavy 20.00
NS Nick Swisher 15.00
BU B.J. Upton 15.00
JV Justin Verlander/150 35.00
DW David Wright/97 50.00

Diamond Signings Dual Blue

NM/M
Production 49 Sets
Silver: No Pricing
Production 22 Sets
Purple: No Pricing
Production One Set
BC Jason Bay, B. Crosby Exch 30.00
FU Gavin Floyd, Chase Utley 40.00

Diamond Signings Triple Blue

NM/M
Sequentially Numbered
Silver: No Pricing
Production Five Sets
Purple: No Pricing
Production One Set
Khalil Greene, B.J. Upton, Bobby Crosby/99 50.00
Justin Verlander, Gavin Floyd, Scott Kazmir/99 75.00
Nick Swisher, Charlton Jimerson, Chone Figgins/99 30.00
Casey Kotchman, Justin Morneau, Jason Bay/86 40.00

Jersey Rack Dual Jersey Blue

NM/M
Common Card: 10.00
Inserted 1:100
Silver Patch: No Pricing
Production 25 Sets
Purple Patch: No Pricing
Production One Set
BW Josh Beckett, Kerry Wood 10.00
CJ Miguel Cabrera, Andruw Jones 12.00
DB Adam Dunn, Lance Berkman 10.00
GS Vladimir Guerrero, Sammy Sosa 15.00
GT Khalil Greene, Miguel Tejada 10.00
HB Todd Helton, Jeff Bagwell 10.00
HE Torii Hunter, Jim Edmonds 10.00
JC Randy Johnson, Roger Clemens 20.00
JW Chipper Jones, David Wright 15.00
MM Hideki Matsui, Kazuo Matsui 25.00
OG David Ortiz, Jason Giambi 12.00
RB Scott Rolen, Adrian Beltre 12.00
RS Manny Ramirez, Gary Sheffield 12.00
SG John Smoltz, Eric Gagne 10.00
SM Jason Schmidt, Pedro Martinez 12.00
SM1 Alfonso Soriano, Kazuo Matsui 10.00
SP Curt Schilling, Mark Prior 8.00
TP Jim Thome, Mike Piazza 12.00
WS Dontrelle Willis, Johan Santana 12.00

Jersey Rack Triple Jersey Blue

NM/M
Common Card: 12.00
Inserted 1:54
Silver Patch: No Pricing
Production 25 Sets
Purple Patch: No Pricing
CJS Roger Clemens, Randy Johnson, Jason Schmidt 20.00
CSJ Roger Clemens, Curt Schilling, Randy Johnson 20.00
EHJ Jim Edmonds, Torii Hunter, Andruw Jones 12.00
GRS Vladimir Guerrero, Manny Ramirez, Gary Sheffield 15.00
GSR Eric Gagne, John Smoltz, Mariano Rivera 15.00
HSB Todd Helton, Alfonso Soriano, Adrian Beltre 12.00
MGT Kazuo Matsui, Khalil Greene, Miguel Tejada 15.00
MRG Hideki Matsui, Mariano Rivera, Jason Giambi 25.00
ORM David Ortiz, Manny Ramirez, Pedro Martinez 15.00
PRE Albert Pujols, Scott Rolen, Jim Edmonds 25.00
PTB Albert Pujols, Jim Thome, Jeff Bagwell 20.00
RBJ Scott Rolen, Adrian Beltre, Chipper Jones 15.00
SDC Sammy Sosa, Adam Dunn, Miguel Cabrera 12.00
SJJ John Smoltz, Chipper Jones, Andruw Jones 20.00
SPB Jason Schmidt, Mark Prior, Josh Beckett 10.00
STB Sammy Sosa, Miguel Tejada, Adrian Beltre 15.00
WPM David Wright, Mike Piazza, Kazuo Matsui 20.00
WSW Dontrelle Willis, Johan Santana, Kerry Wood 15.00

Press Clippings

NM/M
Common Player: 2.00
Inserted 1:6
Gold: No Pricing
Production Four Sets
1 Ichiro Suzuki 4.00
2 Manny Ramirez 2.00
3 Albert Pujols 5.00
4 David Ortiz 2.00
5 Greg Maddux 3.00
6 Ken Griffey Jr. 3.00
7 Vladimir Guerrero 3.00
8 Randy Johnson 3.00
9 Johan Santana 2.00
10 Roger Clemens 5.00
11 Bobby Crosby 2.00
12 Jason Bay 2.00

2005 Fleer Patchworks

NM/M
Complete Set (100):
Common (1-70): .40
Common (71-90): 1.50
Production 499 Sets
Common (91-100): 2.00
Production 999 Sets
Pack (5): 4.00
Box (18): 60.00
1 Bobby Abreu .50
2 Miguel Cabrera 1.00
3 J.D. Drew .40
4 Justin Morneau .40
5 David Ortiz 1.00
6 Ivan Rodriguez .75
7 Jason Schmidt .40
8 Frank Thomas .75
9 Travis Hafner .50
10 Curt Schilling 1.00
11 Jim Edmonds .75
12 Randy Johnson 1.00
13 Jose Vidro .40
14 Vernon Wells .40
15 Lance Berkman .50
16 Khalil Greene .50
17 Andruw Jones .75
18 Mark Prior .75
19 Mark Teixeira .75

20 Jack Wilson .40
21 Adrian Beltre .50
22 Lew Ford .40
23 Shawn Green .50
24 Juan Pierre .40
25 Alfonso Soriano .75
26 Mike Sweeney .40
27 Chipper Jones 1.00
28 Javy Lopez .40
29 Victor Martinez .40
30 Kazuo Matsui .40
31 Bernie Williams .50
32 Kerry Wood .50
33 Barry Zito .50
34 Austin Kearns .40
35 Todd Helton .75
36 B.J. Upton .40
37 Jeff Bagwell .75
38 Pedro Martinez 1.00
39 Lyle Overbay .40
40 Ichiro Suzuki 2.00
41 Jason Bay .50
42 Bobby Crosby .40
43 Vladimir Guerrero 1.00
44 Richie Sexson .50
45 Johan Santana 1.00
46 Magglio Ordonez .40
47 Derek Jeter 3.00
48 Eric Gagne .40
49 Albert Pujols 3.00
50 Jim Thome .75
51 Hideki Matsui 2.00
52 Torii Hunter .40
53 Greg Maddux 2.00
54 Michael Young .40
55 Carlos Beltran .75
56 Carl Crawford .40
57 Adam Dunn .75
58 Nomar Garciaparra 1.00
59 Mike Piazza 1.00
60 Alex Rodriguez 3.00
61 Scott Rolen .75
62 Ben Sheets .50
63 Sammy Sosa 1.00
64 Hank Blalock .50
65 Carlos Delgado .50
66 Ken Griffey Jr. 2.00
67 Manny Ramirez 1.00
68 Miguel Tejada .75
69 Roger Clemens 3.00
70 Gary Sheffield .75
71 Jon Knott 1.50
72 Ryan Raburn 1.50
73 Zack Greinke 1.50
74 David Aardsma 1.50
75 Justin Verlander **RC** 4.00
76 Andres Blanco 1.50
77 David Wright 4.00
78 Jeff Baker 1.50
79 Charlton Jimerson 1.50
80 Sean Burnett 1.50
81 Joey Gathright 1.50
82 Victor Diaz 1.50
83 Scott Kazmir 1.50
84 Edwin Encarnacion 1.50
85 J.D. Durbin 1.50
86 Nick Swisher 1.50
87 Casey Kotchman 1.50
88 Gavin Floyd 1.50
89 Josh Kroeger 1.50
90 Taylor Buchholz 1.50
91 Reggie Jackson 2.00
92 Nolan Ryan 6.00
93 Eddie Murray 2.00
94 Carlton Fisk 2.00
95 Mike Schmidt 4.00
96 Joe Morgan 2.00
97 Rod Carew 2.00
98 Harmon Killebrew 3.00
99 Tom Seaver 3.00
100 Brooks Robinson 3.00

Gold

Gold (1-70): 3-6X
Gold (71-100): 1-2X
Production 99 Sets

Autoworks Silver

NM/M
Production 99 Sets
RB Rocco Baldelli 12.00
JB Jason Bay 20.00
JBO Jeremy Bonderman 15.00
SB Sean Burnett 8.00
MC Miguel Cabrera 25.00
MCA Mike Cameron 12.00
CC Carl Crawford 15.00
JD J.D. Durbin 8.00
LF Lew Ford 10.00
ZG Zack Greinke 10.00
TH Travis Hafner 15.00
BL Brad Lidge 15.00
VM Victor Martinez 15.00
JM Justin Morneau 20.00
JP Josh Phelps 10.00
BS Ben Sheets 15.00
BU B.J. Upton 15.00
JV Justin Verlander 20.00
DW David Wright 60.00

Autoworks Gold

NM/M
Production 49 Sets
HA Hank Aaron 200.00
RB Rocco Baldelli 15.00
EB Ernie Banks 50.00
JB Jason Bay 20.00
LB Lance Berkman 20.00
JBO Jeremy Bonderman 20.00
SB Sean Burnett 10.00
MC Miguel Cabrera 30.00
MCA Mike Cameron 12.00
CC Carl Crawford 20.00
JD J.D. Durbin 10.00
GF Gavin Floyd 10.00
LF Lew Ford 10.00
ZG Zack Greinke 12.00
TH Travis Hafner 20.00
BL Brad Lidge 20.00
VM Victor Martinez 20.00
JM Justin Morneau 25.00
JP Josh Phelps 10.00
BS Ben Sheets 20.00
BU B.J. Upton 20.00
DW David Wright 60.00
MY Michael Young 15.00

Autoworks Copper

NM/M
Production 75-250
Masterpiece: No Pricing
Production One Set
RB Rocco Baldelli/100 12.00
JB Jason Bay/150 20.00
JBO Jeremy Bonderman/100 15.00
SB Sean Burnett/100 8.00
MC Miguel Cabrera/75 25.00
CC Carl Crawford/175 15.00
JD J.D. Durbin/100 8.00
ZG Zack Greinke/200 10.00
TH Travis Hafner/150 15.00
BL Brad Lidge/75 15.00
VM Victor Martinez/100 15.00
JM Justin Morneau/175 20.00
BU B.J. Upton/150 15.00
JV Justin Verlander/100 20.00
DW David Wright/250 50.00

Autoworks Dual

Production 25 Sets

Autoworks Quad

Production 10 Sets

By the Numbers

NM/M
Common Player: 1.00
Inserted 1:18
1 Roy Oswalt 1.00
2 Hideki Matsui 3.00
3 Curt Schilling 1.50
4 Mike Piazza 2.00
5 Alex Rodriguez 4.00
6 Vladimir Guerrero 1.50
7 Victor Martinez 1.00
8 Adrian Beltre 1.00
9 Johnny Estrada 1.00
10 Ken Griffey Jr. 3.00
11 Sammy Sosa 2.00
12 Ichiro Suzuki 3.00
13 Roger Clemens 4.00
14 David Ortiz 1.50
15 Johan Santana 1.50
16 Pedro Martinez 1.50
17 Austin Kearns 1.00
18 Randy Johnson 1.50
19 Nomar Garciaparra 1.50
20 Albert Pujols 4.00

By the Numbers Jersey

NM/M
Common Player: 4.00
AB Adrian Beltre 4.00
RC Roger Clemens/SP 10.00
JE Johnny Estrada 4.00
VG Vladimir Guerrero/SP 8.00
RJ Randy Johnson 8.00
PM Pedro Martinez 8.00
HM Hideki Matsui 20.00
RO Roy Oswalt 4.00
AP Albert Pujols 15.00
JS Johan Santana 6.00
CS Curt Schilling 8.00
SS Sammy Sosa 8.00

By the Numbers Jersey Die Cut

NM/M
Production 199 Sets
Jersey Tag: No Pricing
Production One Set
AB Adrian Beltre 4.00
RC Roger Clemens 10.00
JE Johnny Estrada 4.00
VG Vladimir Guerrero 8.00
RJ Randy Johnson 8.00
AK Austin Kearns 4.00
PM Pedro Martinez 8.00
HM Hideki Matsui 20.00
DO David Ortiz 8.00
RO Roy Oswalt 4.00
MP Mike Piazza/116 10.00
AP Albert Pujols 15.00
JS Johan Santana 6.00
CS Curt Schilling 8.00
SS Sammy Sosa 8.00

By the Numbers Patch

NM/M
Production 99 Sets
Patch Die-Cut: No Pricing
Production 25 Sets
AB Adrian Beltre 10.00
JE Johnny Estrada 8.00
VG Vladimir Guerrero 15.00
AK Austin Kearns/78 10.00
HM Hideki Matsui 30.00
DO David Ortiz/46 15.00
RO Roy Oswalt 10.00
MP Mike Piazza 20.00
AP Albert Pujols 30.00
JS Johan Santana 15.00
CS Curt Schilling 15.00
SS Sammy Sosa 20.00

By the Numbers Patch Autographs

No Pricing
Production 25 Sets

Heart of the Team

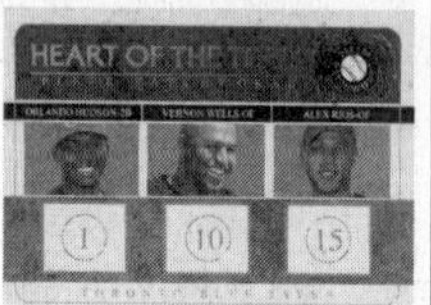

NM/M
Inserted 1:108
1 Braves/Marlins 8.00
2 Red Sox/Yankees 15.00
3 Cardinals/Astros 10.00
4 Angels/A's 8.00
5 Phillies/Mets 8.00
6 Twins/White Sox 8.00
7 Reds/Cubs 10.00
8 Mariners/Rangers 10.00
9 Orioles/Nationals 8.00
10 Blue Jays/Devil Rays 6.00

Heart of the Team Jersey

Production 199 Sets
Patch: No Pricing
Production 15 Sets

Jersey

NM/M
Common Player: 4.00
JB Josh Beckett 4.00
TH Torii Hunter 4.00
MARK Mark Prior 4.00
MR Manny Ramirez 8.00
GS Gary Sheffield 6.00
AS Alfonso Soriano 6.00
SS Shannon Stewart 4.00
BW Bernie Williams 6.00
DW Dontrelle Willis 4.00
KW Kerry Wood 4.00
DWR David Wright 15.00
MY Michael Young 4.00

Dual Jersey

NM/M
Common Duo: 6.00
Die-Cut: 1-1.5X
Production 199 Sets
Dual MLB Logo: No Pricing
Production One Set
Dual Patch: No Pricing
Production 25 Sets
Dual Patch Die-Cut: No Pricing
Production 15 Sets
DWJB Dontrelle Willis, Josh Beckett 6.00
DWMP David Wright, Mike Piazza 15.00
GSBW Gary Sheffield, Bernie Williams/SP 8.00
KWMP Kerry Wood, Mark Prior/SP 8.00
MRDO Manny Ramirez, David Ortiz 15.00
MYAS Michael Young, Alfonso Soriano 8.00
SSTH Shannon Stewart, Torii Hunter 6.00

Patch

NM/M
Production 99 Sets
Die-Cut: 1-1.5X
Production 49 Sets
JB Josh Beckett 8.00
TH Torii Hunter 10.00
DO David Ortiz/51 20.00
MIKE Mike Piazza 20.00
MARK Mark Prior 15.00
MR Manny Ramirez 20.00
AS Alfonso Soriano/73 12.00
SS Shannon Stewart 10.00
BW Bernie Williams 12.00
DW Dontrelle Willis 15.00
KW Kerry Wood 12.00
DWR David Wright 35.00
MY Michael Young 10.00

Property of

NM/M
Common Player: 1.00
Inserted 1:6
1 Vladimir Guerrero 1.50
2 Luis Gonzalez 1.00
3 Chipper Jones 1.50
4 Miguel Tejada 1.50
5 David Ortiz 1.50
6 Kerry Wood 1.00
7 Frank Thomas 1.00
8 Adam Dunn 1.00
9 Victor Martinez 1.00
10 Todd Helton 1.00
11 Ivan Rodriguez 1.50
12 Miguel Cabrera 1.50
13 Jeff Bagwell 1.50
14 Mike Sweeney 1.00
15 Eric Gagne 1.00
16 Lyle Overbay 1.00
17 Johan Santana 1.50
18 Mike Piazza 2.00
19 Derek Jeter 5.00
20 Bobby Crosby 1.00
21 Jim Thome 1.50
22 Jason Bay 1.00
23 Khalil Greene 1.00
24 Jason Schmidt 1.00
25 Ichiro Suzuki 3.00
26 Albert Pujols 5.00
27 D.J. Upton 1.00
28 Hank Blalock 1.00
29 Vernon Wells 1.00
30 Jose Vidro 1.00

Property of Jersey

NM/M
JB Jeff Bagwell 6.00
JBA Jason Bay 4.00
HB Hank Blalock 4.00
MC Miguel Cabrera 8.00
EG Eric Gagne 4.00
LG Luis Gonzalez 4.00
VG Vladimir Guerrero/SP 8.00
CJ Chipper Jones 8.00
AP Albert Pujols 15.00
IR Ivan Rodriguez 6.00
JS Johan Santana/SP 8.00
JSC Jason Schmidt 4.00
MT Miguel Tejada 6.00
FT Frank Thomas 6.00
JT Jim Thome 6.00
BU B.J. Upton 4.00
VW Vernon Wells 4.00
KW Kerry Wood 4.00

Property of Jersey Die Cut

NM/M
Production 199 Sets
MLB Logo: No Pricing
Production One Set
JB Jeff Bagwell 6.00
JBA Jason Bay 4.00
HB Hank Blalock 4.00
MC Miguel Cabrera 8.00
EG Eric Gagne 4.00
LG Luis Gonzalez 4.00
KG Khalil Greene 4.00
VG Vladimir Guerrero 8.00
CJ Chipper Jones 8.00
DO David Ortiz 8.00
LO Lyle Overbay/86 UER 4.00
MP Mike Piazza 8.00
AP Albert Pujols 15.00
IR Ivan Rodriguez 6.00
JS Johan Santana 6.00
JSC Jason Schmidt 4.00
MT Miguel Tejada 6.00
FT Frank Thomas 6.00
JT Jim Thome 6.00
BU B.J. Upton 4.00
VW Vernon Wells 4.00
KW Kerry Wood 4.00

Property of Patch

NM/M
Production 99 Sets
Die-Cut: No Pricing
Production 25 Sets
Nameplate: 1-2X
Production 49 Sets
JB Jeff Bagwell 15.00
JBA Jason Bay/84 10.00
HB Hank Blalock 12.00
MC Miguel Cabrera 15.00
AD Adam Dunn/42 10.00
EG Eric Gagne 10.00
LG Luis Gonzalez 10.00
KG Khalil Greene 10.00
VG Vladimir Guerrero 15.00
CJ Chipper Jones 15.00
DO David Ortiz/45 20.00
MP Mike Piazza 20.00
AP Albert Pujols 30.00
IR Ivan Rodriguez 15.00
JS Johan Santana 15.00
JSC Jason Schmidt 12.00
MS Mike Sweeney/77 10.00
MT Miguel Tejada 15.00
JT Jim Thome 15.00
BU B.J. Upton 10.00
VW Vernon Wells/30 10.00
KW Kerry Wood/89 15.00

2005 Fleer Platinum

NM/M
Common Players (1-100): .25
Minor Players (1-100): .40
Unlisted Stars (1-100): .50
Common Players (101-125): 3.00
Production 1,000 Sets
Pack (5): 2.00
Box (24): 40.00
1 Nomar Garciaparra 1.50
2 Matt Holliday .50
3 Rickie Weeks .25
4 Jim Thome .75
5 Roy Halladay .40
6 Paul Konerko .25
7 Lance Berkman .40
8 Ichiro Suzuki 1.25
9 Kerry Wood .60
10 Lew Ford .25
11 Omar Vizquel .40
12 Manny Ramirez .60
13 Carlos Beltran .50
14 Lyle Overbay .25
15 Billy Wagner .40
16 Jose Vidro .25
17 Vladimir Guerrero .75
18 Miguel Tejada .50
19 Alex Rodriguez 1.50
20 Rocco Baldelli .50
21 David Ortiz .50
22 Victor Martinez .25
23 Shawn Green .40
24 Jason Bay .25
25 Pedro Martinez .75
26 Travis Hafner .25
27 Eric Gagne .40
28 Jack Wilson .25
29 Ivan Rodriguez .50
30 Jody Gerut .25
31 Adrian Beltre .40
32 Craig Wilson .25
33 J.D. Drew .40
34 Craig Biggio .40
35 Mark Mulder .40
36 Mark Teixeira .50
37 Melvin Mora .25
38 Ken Griffey Jr. 1.00
39 Mike Sweeney .25
40 Khalil Greene .60
41 Rafael Palmeiro .60
42 Austin Kearns .50
43 Garret Anderson .40
44 Trevor Hoffman .25
45 Andruw Jones .60
46 Adam Dunn .50
47 Angel Berroa .25
48 Ryan Klesko .40
49 Sean Casey .25
50 Kazuo Matsui .50
51 Jim Edmonds .40
52 Magglio Ordonez .40
53 Tom Glavine .40
54 Larry Walker .40
55 Johnny Estrada .25
56 Brad Lidge .25
57 Barry Zito .50
58 Michael Young .40
59 Chipper Jones 1.00
60 Andy Pettitte .50
61 Eric Chavez .40
62 Carlos Delgado .60
63 David Eckstein .25
64 Dmitri Young .25
65 Mike Piazza 1.00
66 Albert Pujols 1.50
67 Luis Gonzalez .40
68 Hideki Matsui 1.50
69 Gary Sheffield .50
70 Carl Crawford .25
71 Curt Schilling .50
72 Todd Helton .60
73 Ben Sheets .40
74 Bobby Abreu .40
75 Jose Guillen .25
76 Richie Sexson .50
77 Miguel Cabrera .60
78 Bernie Williams .50
79 Aubrey Huff .25
80 John Smoltz .40
81 Jeff Bagwell .60
82 Tim Hudson .40
83 Alfonso Soriano .75
84 Freddy Garcia .25
85 Johan Santana .40
86 Bret Boone .40
87 Troy Glaus .50
88 Carlos Guillen .25
89 Derek Jeter 2.00
90 Scott Rolen .75
91 Sammy Sosa 1.25
92 Jacque Jones .25
93 Jason Schmidt .40
94 Randy Johnson .75
95 Dontrelle Willis .40
96 Mariano Rivera .40
97 Hank Blalock .50
98 Mark Prior 1.50
99 Torii Hunter .50
100 Roger Clemens 1.50
101 David Wright 6.00
102 Justin Morneau 4.00
103 Scott Kazmir 4.00
104 Gavin Floyd 3.00
105 Justin Verlander **RC** 8.00
106 Zack Greinke 4.00
107 David Aardsma 3.00
108 Ryan Raburn 4.00
109 Joey Gathright 3.00
110 J.D. Durbin 3.00
111 Sean Burnett 3.00
112 Jose Lopez 5.00
113 Nick Swisher 4.00
114 Bobby Jenks 3.00
115 Kelly Johnson 8.00
116 B.J. Upton 5.00
117 Ronny Cedeno 3.00
118 Edwin Encarnacion 6.00
119 Jeff Baker 3.00
120 Taylor Buchholz 3.00
121 Livan Hernandez **RC** 4.00
122 Dioner Navarro 4.00
123 Victor Diaz 4.00
124 Jon Knott 4.00
125 Russ Adams 3.00

Finish

Cards 1-100: 3-6X
Cards 101-125: .75-1.25X
Production 199 Sets

Extreme

Cards 1-125: No Pricing
Production 20 Sets

Autograph Die Cuts

NM/M
Numbered to indicated quantities.
1 Lew Ford/99 10.00
3 Jason Bay/50 15.00
4 Travis Hafner/99 15.00
6 Brad Lidge/99 30.00
7 Michael Young/99 15.00
8 David Eckstein/99 20.00
9 Carl Crawford/50 15.00
10 Miguel Cabrera/50 25.00
11 David Wright/50 50.00
13 Scott Kazmir/99 15.00
14 Gavin Floyd/99 10.00
15 Justin Verlander/99 40.00
18 Joey Gathright/50 10.00

Decade of Excellence

NM/M
Common Player: 2.00
Inserted 1:199
1 Albert Pujols 6.00
2 Derek Jeter 8.00
3 Randy Johnson 4.00
4 Ichiro Suzuki 5.00
5 Alex Rodriguez 6.00
6 Mike Piazza 4.00
7 Greg Maddux 4.00
8 Curt Schilling 3.00
9 Frank Thomas 3.00
10 Torii Hunter 3.00
11 Al Kaline 6.00
12 Travis Hafner 2.00
13 Ivan Rodriguez 3.00
14 Rafael Palmeiro 3.00
15 Mike Schmidt 8.00
16 Johnny Bench 8.00
17 Jim Edmonds 2.00
18 Pedro Martinez 4.00
19 Robin Yount 6.00
20 Sammy Sosa 5.00

Decade of Excellence Jersey Silver

NM/M

Common Player: 5.00
Inserted 1:54
Gold: .75-1.25X
Production 99 Sets
Patch Platinum: No Pricing
Production 10 Sets

JB	Johnny Bench	15.00
JE	Jim Edmonds	5.00
TF	Travis Hafner	5.00
TH	Torii Hunter	5.00
RJ	Randy Johnson	8.00
AK	Al Kaline	10.00
GM	Greg Maddux	8.00
PM	Pedro Martinez	8.00
RP	Rafael Palmeiro	8.00
MP	Mike Piazza	8.00
AP	Albert Pujols	12.00
IR	Ivan Rodriguez	5.00
CS	Curt Schilling	5.00
MS	Mike Schmidt	15.00
SS	Sammy Sosa	10.00
FT	Frank Thomas	8.00
RY	Robin Yount	10.00

Decade of Excellence Autograph Jersey Platinum

No Pricing
Production Five Sets

Diamond Dominators

NM/M

Common Player: 2.00
Inserted 1:12 Retail

1	Albert Pujols	6.00
2	Curt Schilling	3.00
3	Adrian Beltre	2.00
4	Randy Johnson	4.00
5	Ivan Rodriguez	3.00
6	Mike Piazza	4.00
7	Chipper Jones	4.00
8	Sammy Sosa	5.00
9	Tim Hudson	2.00
10	Rocco Baldelli	3.00
11	Alfonso Soriano	4.00
12	David Ortiz	3.00
13	Mariano Rivera	2.00
14	Kazuo Matsui	3.00
15	Khalil Greene	3.00
16	Eric Gagne	2.00
17	Vladimir Guerrero	4.00
18	Jason Giambi	4.00
19	Scott Rolen	4.00
20	Miguel Cabrera	3.00

Diamond Dominators Jersey Silver

NM/M

Common Player:
Inserted 1:45
Gold: .75-1.25X
Production 199 Sets (Hobby)
Red: .5-1X
Inserted 1:50 (Retail)

RB	Rocco Baldelli	5.00
AB	Adrian Beltre	5.00
MC	Miguel Cabrera	8.00
EG	Eric Gagne	5.00
JG	Jason Giambi	8.00
KG	Khalil Greene	8.00
VG	Vladimir Guerrero	8.00
TH	Tim Hudson	5.00
RJ	Randy Johnson	8.00
CJ	Chipper Jones	4.00
KM	Kazuo Matsui	5.00
DO	David Ortiz	5.00
MP	Mike Piazza	8.00
AP	Albert Pujols	12.00
IR	Ivan Rodriguez	5.00
SR	Scott Rolen	8.00
CS	Curt Schilling	5.00
AS	Alfonso Soriano	8.00
SS	Sammy Sosa	10.00

Diamond Dominators Metal

NM/M

Common Player: 2.00
Inserted 1:18 Hobby

1	Albert Pujols	6.00
2	Curt Schilling	3.00
3	Adrian Beltre	2.00
4	Randy Johnson	4.00
5	Ivan Rodriguez	3.00
6	Mike Piazza	4.00
7	Chipper Jones	4.00
8	Sammy Sosa	5.00
9	Tim Hudson	2.00
10	Rocco Baldelli	3.00
11	Alfonso Soriano	4.00
12	David Ortiz	3.00
13	Kazuo Matsui	3.00
14	Khalil Greene	3.00
15	Eric Gagne	2.00
16	Vladimir Guerrero	4.00
17	Jason Giambi	4.00
18	Scott Rolen	4.00
19	Miguel Cabrera	3.00

Diamond Dominators Metal Autograph

No Pricing
Production 10 Sets

Diamond Dominators Metal Patch

NM/M

1-2X Diamond Dominators Jersey Silver
Sequentially #'d to 30.

HA	Hank Aaron	100.00

Lumberjacks

NM/M

Common Player: .75
Inserted 1:6
Bat Silver: 2-3X
Inserted 1:9
Bat Gold: 2-4X
Production 250 Sets
Bat Patch: No Pricing
Production 20 Sets

1	Albert Pujols	2.50
2	Jim Thome	1.25
3	Andruw Jones	1.00
4	Kazuo Matsui	.75
5	Adam Dunn	.75
6	Bernie Williams	.75
7	Hank Blalock	.75
8	Bobby Abreu	.75
9	Rocco Baldelli	.75
10	Jacque Jones	.75
11	Mark Teixeira	.75
12	Ichiro Suzuki	2.00
13	Gary Sheffield	.75
14	Sean Casey	.75
15	Carl Crawford	.75

Lumberjacks Autograph Platinum

No Pricing
Production 20 Sets

Nameplates Patch Platinum

No Pricing
Production 25 Sets
Masterpiece: No Pricing
Production One Set

Nameplates Dual Patch Platinum

No Pricing
Production 25 Sets
Masterpiece: No Pricing
Production One Set

Nameplates Patch Autograph Platinum

No Pricing
Production 25 Sets

Nameplates Dual Patch Autograph Platinum

No Pricing
Production One Set

2005 Fleer Showcase

NM/M

Common Player (1-100): .25
Minor Stars (1-100): .40
Unlisted Stars (1-100): .60
Common Showcasing Talent (101-110): 2.00
Inserted 1:5
Common Showcasing History (111-135): .40
Inserted 1:20
Pack (5): 3.00
Box (20): 50.00

1	Albert Pujols	2.50
2	Rocco Baldelli	.60
3	Bernie Williams	.60
4	Shawn Green	.40
5	Garret Anderson	.40
6	Paul Konerko	.25
7	Mike Sweeney	.25
8	Jim Thome	1.00
9	Mark Teixeira	.40
10	Mark Prior	2.00
11	Angel Berroa	.25
12	Barry Zito	.60
13	Carlos Delgado	.75
14	Troy Glaus	.60
15	Travis Hafner	.25
16	Lyle Overbay	.25
17	David Ortiz	.60
18	Ivan Rodriguez	.60
19	Jack Wilson	.25
20	Jason Schmidt	.40
21	Mike Piazza	1.50
22	David Eckstein	.25
23	Ben Sheets	.40
24	Randy Johnson	1.00
25	Jacque Jones	.25
26	Jody Gerut	.25
27	Kris Benson	.25
28	Luis Gonzalez	.40
29	Victor Martinez	.25
30	Torii Hunter	.60
31	Gary Sheffield	.60
32	Miguel Tejada	.60
33	Dontrelle Willis	.60
34	Bret Boone	.40
35	Hideki Matsui	.60
36	Shea Hillenbrand	.25
37	Wily Mo Pena	.25
38	Johan Santana	.40
39	Derek Jeter	3.00
40	Chipper Jones	1.50
41	Sean Casey	.25
42	Corey Koskie	.25
43	Alex Rodriguez	2.50
44	Andruw Jones	.75
45	Austin Kearns	.60
46	Jose Vidro	.25
47	Adam Dunn	.60
48	Adrian Beltre	.40
49	Bobby Abreu	.40
50	Michael Young	.25
51	Freddy Garcia	.25
52	Eric Gagne	.40
53	Chase Utley	.25
54	Alfonso Soriano	1.00
55	Nick Johnson	.25
56	Johnny Estrada	.25
57	Jeff Bagwell	.75
58	Randy Winn	.25
59	Roy Halladay	.40
60	J.D. Drew	.40
61	Craig Biggio	.40
62	Scott Rolen	1.00
63	Nomar Garciaparra	2.50
64	Matt Holliday	.50
65	Billy Wagner	.25
66	Carl Crawford	.25
67	Pedro J. Martinez	1.00
68	Jeremy Bonderman	.25
69	Jason Bay	.25
70	A.J. Pierzynski	.25
71	Vladimir Guerrero	1.00
72	Rickie Weeks	.60
73	Mark Loretta	.25
74	Todd Helton	.75
75	Manny Ramirez	.75
76	Carlos Guillen	.25
77	Khalil Greene	.75
78	Javy Lopez	.40
79	Josh Beckett	.75
80	Ichiro Suzuki	2.00
81	Magglio Ordonez	.40
82	Ken Harvey	.25
83	Mark Mulder	.40
84	Hank Blalock	.60
85	Richard Hidalgo	.25
86	Curt Schilling	.60
87	Jeromy Burnitz	.25
88	Craig Wilson	.25
89	Aubrey Huff	.25
90	Kerry Wood	.75
91	Andy Pettitte	.60
92	Tim Hudson	.40
93	Jim Edmonds	.40
94	Melvin Mora	.25
95	Miguel Cabrera	.75
96	Trevor Hoffman	.25
97	J.T. Snow	.25
98	Sammy Sosa	2.00
99	Roger Clemens	2.50
100	Eric Chavez	4.00
101	B.J. Upton	5.00
102	Gavin Floyd	3.00
103	Casey Kotchman	3.00
104	David Wright	5.00
105	Dioner Navarro	3.00
106	Scott Kazmir	3.00
107	Andres Blanco	2.00
108	Joey Gathright	2.00
109	Jon Knott	2.00
110	Charlton Jimerson	3.00
111	Larry Doby	.75
112	Reggie Jackson	2.00
113	Enos Slaughter	.60
114	Bill "Moose" Skowron	.60
115	Duke Snider	.75
116	Harmon Killebrew	1.00
117	Willie McCovey	.75
118	Rollie Fingers	1.00
119	Preacher Roe	.40
120	Carlton Fisk	.60
121	Andre Dawson	.60
122	Orlando Cepeda	.60
123	Bucky Dent	.40
124	Cal Ripken Jr.	1.50
125	Nolan Ryan	3.00
126	Tony Perez	.60
127	Mike Schmidt	1.50
128	Johnny Bench	1.50
129	Sparky Anderson	.40
130	Ted Williams	2.50
131	Al Kaline	.75
132	Carl Yastrzemski	1.00
133	Eddie Murray	.75
134	Roberto Clemente	1.50
135	Yogi Berra	1.50

Masterpiece Legacy

Cards (1-135): No Pricing
Production One Set

Masterpiece Showpiece Patch

Cards (1-135): No Pricing
Production One Set
Autograph Patch: No Pricing
Production One Set
Patch Showdown: No Pricing
Production One Set
Patch Showtime: No Pricing
Production One Set

Autographed Legacy

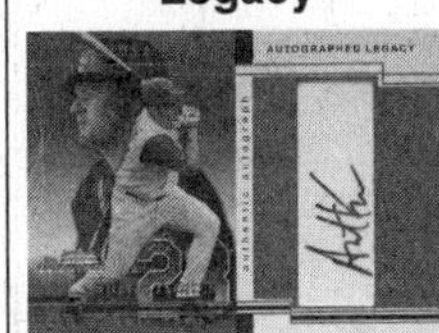

NM/M

Common Player: 15.00
Sequentially Numbered

8	Jim Thome/34	60.00
10	Mark Prior/43	30.00
12	Barry Zito/45	35.00
18	Ivan Rodriguez/217	40.00
19	Jack Wilson/298	15.00
20	Jason Schmidt/127	15.00
21	Mike Piazza/26	100.00
22	David Eckstein/40	35.00
23	Ben Sheets/427	15.00
40	Chipper Jones/41	60.00
45	Austin Kearns/460	10.00
47	Adam Dunn/52	35.00
48	Adrian Beltre/180	15.00
50	Michael Young/80	15.00
52	Eric Gagne/310	25.00
53	Chase Utley/446	25.00
59	Roy Halladay/99	15.00
68	Jeremy Bonderman/97	20.00
72	Rickie Weeks/453	15.00
75	Manny Ramirez/31	75.00
77	Khalil Greene/299	25.00
88	Craig Wilson/40	20.00
89	Aubrey Huff/453	15.00
90	Kerry Wood/28	25.00
92	Tim Hudson/183	25.00
95	Miguel Cabrera/32	35.00
99	Roger Clemens/64	100.00
100	Eric Chavez/204	15.00
103	Casey Kotchman/454	15.00
104	David Wright/298	40.00
106	Scott Kazmir/458	20.00
107	Andres Blanco/23	15.00
109	Jon Knott/402	10.00
114	Bill "Moose" Skowron/64	20.00
119	Preacher Roe/304	20.00
120	Carlton Fisk/86	30.00
123	Bucky Dent/99	15.00
135	Yogi Berra/25	75.00

Showdown

Cards (1-135): No Pricing
Production 15 Sets
Masterpiece: No Pricing
Production One Set

Showtime

Veterans (1-100): 3-6X
Showcasing Talent (101-110): 2-4X

Showcasing History (111-135): 1-30X
Production 99 Sets
Masterpiece: No Pricing
Production One Set

Measures of Greatness

NM/M

Common Player: .75
Inserted 1:5
Jersey Red: 2-4X
Production 340 Sets
Patch: No Pricing
Production 10 Sets
Masterpiece: No Pricing
Production One Set

1	Albert Pujols	4.00
2	Mike Piazza	2.50
3	Vladimir Guerrero	2.00
4	Jim Thome	2.00
5	Pedro J. Martinez	2.00
6	Rafael Palmeiro	.75
7	Adrian Beltre	.75
8	Sammy Sosa	3.00
9	Todd Helton	1.50
10	Randy Johnson	2.00
11	Jeff Bagwell	1.50
12	Jason Giambi	2.00
13	Scott Rolen	2.00
14	Greg Maddux	2.50
15	Alfonso Soriano	2.00
16	Mariano Rivera	.75
17	Curt Schilling	1.00
18	Derek Jeter	5.00
19	Chipper Jones	2.50
20	Roger Clemens	4.00

Swing Time

NM/M

Common Player: 2.50
Inserted 1:45
Jersey Red: 1-30X
Production 610 Sets
Patch: 2-5X
Production 50 Sets
Masterpiece: No Pricing
Production One Set

1	Ivan Rodriguez	2.50
2	Gary Sheffield	2.50
3	Bernie Williams	2.50
4	Vladimir Guerrero	3.50
5	Jim Edmonds	2.50
6	Manny Ramirez	3.00
7	Todd Helton	3.00
8	Hank Blalock	2.50
9	Hideki Matsui	6.00
10	David Ortiz	2.50
11	Albert Pujols	6.00
12	Miguel Tejada	2.50
13	Miguel Cabrera	3.00
14	Alex Rodriguez	6.00
15	Ichiro Suzuki	5.00

Timepiece Extreme

No Pricing
Production One Set

Timepiece Ink

No Pricing
Production 10 Sets

Timepiece Teammates

No Pricing
Production One Set

Timepiece Unique

No Pricing
Production Five Sets

Wave of the Future

NM/M

Common Player: 1.00
Inserted 1:15
Jersey Red: 1-30X
Production 610 Sets
Patch: 2-5X
Production 50 Sets
Masterpiece: No Pricing
Production One Set

1	Kazuo Matsui	5.00
2	Johan Santana	1.50
3	Khalil Greene	2.00
4	Dontrelle Willis	1.50
5	Mark Teixeira	1.50
6	Travis Hafner	1.00
7	Jason Bay	1.50
8	Angel Berroa	1.00
9	Miguel Cabrera	2.00
10	Joe Mauer	1.50
11	Adam Dunn	2.00
12	B.J. Upton	3.00
13	Victor Martinez	1.00
14	Michael Young	1.00
15	David Wright	3.00

2005 Fleer Tradition

NM/M

Common Player (1-300): .15
Minor Stars (1-300): .25
Unlisted Stars (1-300): .40
Common Card (301-330): 3.00
Unlisted Card (301-330): 4.00
Inserted 1:2
Common Player (331-350): .15
Minor Stars (331-350): .25
Unlisted Stars (331-350): .40
Cards 1-12; 331-350 Inserted 1:2
Pack (10): 1.25
Box (36): 35.00

1	Johan Santana, Curt Schilling, Jake Westbrook	.40
2	Ben Sheets, Jake Peavy, Randy Johnson	.75
3	Johan Santana, Bartolo Colon, Curt Schilling	.40
4	Carl Pavano, Roy Oswalt, Roger Clemens	1.50
5	Johan Santana, Pedro Martinez, Curt Schilling	.75

6 Jason Schmidt, Randy Johnson, Ben Sheets .75
7 Melvin Mora, Vladimir Guerrero, Ichiro Suzuki 1.25
8 Adrian Beltre, Todd Helton, Mark Loretta .50
9 Manny Ramirez, Paul Konerko, David Ortiz .50
10 Albert Pujols, Adrian Beltre, Adam Dunn 1.50
11 David Ortiz, Manny Ramirez, Miguel Tejada .50
12 Albert Pujols, Vinny Castilla, Scott Rolen 1.50
13 Jason Bay .15
14 Greg Maddux 1.00
15 Melvin Mora .15
16 Matt Stairs .15
17 Scott Podsednik .25
18 Bartolo Colon .25
19 Roger Clemens 1.50
20 Eric Hinske .15
21 Johnny Estrada .15
22 Brett Tomko .15
23 John Buck .15
24 Nomar Garciaparra 1.50
25 Milton Bradley .15
26 Craig Biggio .25
27 Kyle Denney .50
28 Brad Penny .15
29 Todd Helton .50
30 Luis Gonzalez .25
31 Bill Hall .15
32 Ruben Sierra .15
33 Zack Greinke .15
34 Sandy Alomar Jr. .15
35 Jason Giambi .75
36 Ben Sheets .25
37 Edgardo Alfonzo .15
38 Kenny Rogers .15
39 Coco Crisp .15
40 Randy Choate .50
41 Braden Looper .15
42 Adam Dunn .40
43 Adam Eaton .15
44 Luis Castillo .25
45 Casey Fossum .15
46 Mike Piazza 1.00
47 Juan Pierre .15
48 Doug Davis .15
49 Manny Ramirez .50
50 Travis Hafner .15
51 Jack Wilson .15
52 Melvin Mora .15
53 Ken Harvey .15
54 Brooks Kieschnick .15
55 Brad Fullmer .15
56 Octavio Dotel .15
57 Mike Matheny .15
58 Andruw Jones .50
59 Alfonso Soriano .75
60 Royce Clayton .15
61 Jon Garland .15
62 John Mabry .15
63 Rafael Palmeiro .25
64 Garrett Atkins .15
65 Brian Meadows .15
66 Tony Armas Jr. .15
67 Toby Hall .15
68 Carlos Baerga .15
69 Barry Larkin .25
70 Jody Gerut .15
71 Brent Mayne .15
72 Shigetoshi Hasegawa .15
73 Jose Cruz Jr. .15
74 Dan Wilson .15
75 Sidney Ponson .15
76 Jason Jennings .15
77 A.J. Burnett .15
78 Tony Batista .15
79 Kris Benson .15
80 Sean Burroughs .15
81 Eric Young .15
82 Casey Kotchman .40
83 Derrek Lee .25
84 Mariano Rivera .25
85 Julio Franco .15
86 Corey Patterson .15
87 Carlos Beltran .40
88 Trevor Hoffman .15
89 Danny Garcia .15
90 Marco Scutaro .15
91 Marquis Grissom .15
92 Aubrey Huff .15
93 Tony Womack .15
94 Placido Polanco .15
95 Bengie Molina .15
96 Roger Cedeno .15
97 Geoff Jenkins .25
98 Kip Wells .15
99 Derek Jeter 2.00
100 Omar Infante .15
101 Phil Nevin .15
102 Edgar Renteria .15
103 B.J. Surhoff .15
104 David DeJesus .15
105 Raul Ibanez .15
106 Hank Blalock .40
107 Shawn Estes .15
108 Wily Mo Pena .15
109 Shawn Green .25
110 David Wright .50
111 Kenny Lofton .15
112 Matt Clement .15
113 Cesar Izturis .15
114 John Lackey .15
115 Torii Hunter .40
116 Charles Johnson .15
117 Ray Durham .15
118 Luke Hudson .15
119 Jeremy Bonderman .15
120 Sean Casey .15
121 Johnny Damon .25
122 Eric Milton .15
123 Shea Hillenbrand .15
124 Jim Edmonds .25
125 Jim Edmonds .25
126 Javier Vazquez .15
127 Jon Adkins .15
128 Mike Lowell .15
129 Khalil Greene .50
130 Quinton McCracken .15
131 Edgar Martinez .25
132 Matt Lawton .15
133 Jeff Weaver .15
134 Marlon Byrd .15
135 John Smoltz .25
136 Grady Sizemore .25
137 Brian Roberts .15
138 Dee Brown .15
139 Joel Pineiro .15
140 David Dellucci .15
141 Bobby Higginson .15
142 Ryan Madson .15
143 Scott Hatteberg .15
144 Gregg Zaun .15
145 Brian Jordan .15
146 Jason Isringhausen .15
147 Vinnie Chulk .15
148 Al Leiter .15
149 Pedro Martinez .50
150 Carlos Guillen .15
151 Randy Wolf .15
152 Vernon Wells .25
153 Barry Zito .40
154 Pedro Feliz .15
155 Omar Vizquel .15
156 Chone Figgins .15
157 David Ortiz .40
158 Sun-Woo Kim **RC** 1.00
159 Adam Kennedy .15
160 Carlos Lee .15
161 Rick Ankiel .15
162 Roy Oswalt .25
163 Armando Benitez .15
164 Erubiel Durazo .15
165 Adam Hyzdu .15
166 Esteban Yan .15
167 Victor Santos .15
168 Kevin Millwood .15
169 Andy Pettitte .60
170 Mike Cameron .15
171 Scott Rolen .75
172 Trot Nixon .15
173 Eric Munson .15
174 Roy Halladay .25
175 Juan Encarnacion .15
176 Eric Chavez .25
177 Terrmel Sledge .15
178 Jason Schmidt .25
179 Endy Chavez .15
180 Carlos Zambrano .15
181 Carlos Delgado .50
182 Dewon Brazelton .15
183 J.D. Drew .25
184 Orlando Cabrera .15
185 Craig Wilson .15
186 Chin-Hui Tsao .15
187 Jolbert Cabrera .15
188 Rod Barajas .15
189 Craig Monroe .15
190 Dave Berg .15
191 Carlos Silva .15
192 Eric Gagne .25
193 Marcus Giles .15
194 Nick Johnson .15
195 Kelvim Escobar .15
196 Wade Miller .15
197 David Bell .15
198 Rondell White .15
199 Brian Giles .25
200 Jeromy Burnitz .15
201 Carl Pavano .15
202 Alex Rios .15
203 Ryan Freel .15
204 R.A. Dickey .15
205 Miguel Cairo .15
206 Kerry Wood .50
207 C.C. Sabathia .15
208 Jaime Cerda .15
209 Jerome Williams .15
210 Ryan Wagner .15
211 Javy Lopez .25
212 Tike Redman .15
213 Richie Sexson .40
214 Shannon Stewart .15
215 Ben Davis .15
216 Jeff Bagwell .50
217 David Wells .15
218 Justin Leone .15
219 Brad Radke .15
220 Ramon Santiago .15
221 Richard Hidalgo .15
222 Aaron Miles .15
223 Mark Loretta .15
224 Aaron Boone .15
225 Steve Trachsel .15
226 Geoff Blum .15
227 Shingo Takatsu .15
228 Kevin Youkilis .15
229 Laynce Nix .15
230 Daniel Cabrera .15
231 Kyle Lohse .15
232 Todd Pratt .15
233 Reed Johnson .15
234 Lance Berkman .25
235 Hideki Matsui 1.50
236 Randy Winn .15
237 Joe Randa .15
238 Bob Howry .15
239 Jason LaRue .15
240 Jose Valentin .15
241 Livan Hernandez .15
242 Jamie Moyer .15
243 Garret Anderson .25
244 Brad Ausmus .15
245 Russell Branyan .15
246 Paul Wilson .15
247 Tim Wakefield .15
248 Roberto Alomar .40
249 Kazuhisa Ishii .15
250 Tino Martinez .15
251 Tomokazu Ohka .15
252 Mark Redman .15
253 Paul Byrd .15
254 Greg Aquino .15
255 Adrian Beltre .25
256 Ricky Ledee .15
257 Josh Fogg .15
258 Derek Lowe .15
259 Lew Ford .15
260 Bobby Crosby .15
261 Jim Thome .75
262 Jaret Wright .15
263 Chin-Feng Chen .15
264 Troy Glaus .40
265 Jorge Sosa .15
266 Mike Lamb .15
267 Russ Ortiz .15
268 Reggie Sanders .15
269 Orlando Hudson .15
270 Rodrigo Lopez .15
271 Jose Vidro .15
272 Akinori Otsuka .15
273 Victor Martinez .15
274 Carl Crawford .15
275 Roberto Novoa .25
276 Brian Lawrence .15
277 Angel Berroa .15
278 Josh Beckett .50
279 Lyle Overbay .15
280 Dustin Hermanson .15
281 Jeff Conine .15
282 Mark Prior 1.00
283 Kevin Brown .25
284 Magglio Ordonez .25
285 Dontrelle Willis .25
286 Dallas McPherson .25
287 Rafael Furcal .25
288 Ty Wigginton .15
289 Moises Alou .25
290 A.J. Pierzynski .15
291 Todd Walker .15
292 Hideo Nomo .15
293 Larry Walker .25
294 Choo Freeman .15
295 Eduardo Perez .15
296 Miguel Tejada .40
297 Corey Koskie .15
298 Jermaine Dye .15
299 John Riedling .15
300 John Olerud .25
301 Tim Bittner, Jake Woods, Bobby Jenks 5.00
302 Josh Kroeger, Casey Daigle, Brandon Medders 5.00
303 Kelly Johnson, Charles Thomas, Dan Meyer 4.00
304 Eddy Rodriguez, Ryan Hannaman, John Maine 6.00
305 Anastacio Martinez, Jerome Gamble, Lenny Dinardo 8.00
306 Ronny Cedeno, Carlos Vasquez, Renyel Pinto 6.00
307 Arnie Munoz, Ryan Wing, Felix Diaz 6.00
308 William Bergolla, Ray Olmedo **RC**, Edwin Encarnacion 4.00
309 Mariano Gomez, Ivan Ochoa, Kazuhito Tadano 3.00
310 Toby Miller **RC**, Jeff Baker, Matt Holliday 6.00
311 Preston Larrison, Curtis Granderson, Ryan Raburn 8.00
312 Josh Wilson, Logan Kensing, Kevin Cave 5.00
313 Hector Gimenez, Willy Taveras, Taylor Buchholz 3.00
314 Ruben Gotay, Brian Bass, Andres Blanco 4.00
315 Joel Hanrahan, Willy Aybar, Yhency Brazoban 3.00
316 David Krynzel, Ben Hendrickson, Corey Hart 3.00
317 Colby Miller, Jason Kubel, J.D. Durban 5.00
318 Maicer Izturis, Chad Cordero, Brandon Watson 3.00
319 Victor Diaz, Aarom Baldiris, Wayne Lydon 8.00
320 Edwardo Sierra, Dioner Navarro, Sean Henn 3.00
321 Nick Swisher, Joe Blanton, Dan Johnson 6.00
322 Ryan Howard, Gavin Floyd, Keith Bucktrot 6.00
323 Ryan Doumit, Sean Burnett, Bobby Bradley 6.00
324 Justin Germano, Rusty Tucker, Freddy Guzman 6.00
325 David Aardsma, Justin Knoedler, Alfredo Simon 4.00
326 Jose Lopez, Rene Rivera, Cha Sueng Baek 4.00
327 Yadier Molina, Evan Rust, Adam Wainwright 4.00
328 Jorge Cantu, Scott Kazmir, B.J. Upton 5.00
329 Adrian Gonzalez, Ramon Nivar, Jason Bourgeois 6.00
330 Russ Adams, Dustin McGowan, Gustavo Chacin 8.00
331 Alfonso Soriano .75
332 Albert Pujols 1.50
333 David Ortiz .40
334 Manny Ramirez .50
335 Jason Bay .15
336 Bobby Crosby .15
337 Roger Clemens 1.50
338 Johan Santana .25
339 Jim Thome .75
340 Vladimir Guerrero .75
341 David Ortiz .40
342 Alex Rodriguez 1.50
343 Albert Pujols 1.50
344 Carlos Beltran .40
345 Johnny Damon .25
346 Scott Rolen .75
347 Larry Walker .25
348 Curt Schilling .40
349 Pedro Martinez .75
350 David Ortiz .40

Gray Backs

Cards 13-300: .75 1.5X
Cards 1-10; 301-350: .5-1.25X
Inserted 1:2

Club 3,000/500/300

NM/M
Inserted 1:360
1 Ernie Banks/500 30.00
2 Stan Musial/3,000 40.00
3 Steve Carlton/3,000 15.00
4 Greg Maddux/300 25.00
5 Dave Winfield/3,000 15.00
6 Rafael Palmeiro/500 15.00
7 Rickey Henderson/3,000 15.00
8 Roger Clemens/3,000 30.00
9 Don Sutton/300 10.00
10 George Brett/3,000 25.00
11 Reggie Jackson/500 20.00
12 Wade Boggs/3,000 20.00
13 Bob Gibson/3,000 20.00
14 Eddie Murray/3,000 20.00
15 Tom Seaver/3,000 20.00
16 Willie McCovey/500 20.00
17 Rod Carew/3,000 20.00
18 Fergie Jenkins/300 15.00
19 Phil Niekro/300 10.00
20 Frank Robinson/500 20.00

Cooperstown Tribute

NM/M
Common Player: 4.00
Sequentially #'d to HOF Induction Year.
Gold: .5-1X
Inserted 1:24
Jersey: 1-2X
Inserted 1:200
There are 20 total jersey cards for Joe Morgan & Yogi Berra.
No Pricing for Morgan & Berra jers. card
Patch: No Pricing
Production 10 Sets
1 Mike Schmidt/1995 5.00
2 Al Kaline/1980 4.00
3 Yogi Berra/1972 6.00
4 Robin Yount/1999 4.00
5 Joe Morgan/1990 4.00
6 Willie Stargell/1988 4.00
7 Harmon Killebrew/1984 5.00
8 Nolan Ryan/1999 10.00
9 Carlton Fisk/2000 5.00
10 Johnny Bench/1989 6.00

Diamond Tributes

NM/M
Common Player: 2.00

Inserted 1:6
1 Albert Pujols 5.00
2 Alex Rodriguez 5.00
3 Ken Griffey Jr. 3.50
4 Sammy Sosa 4.00
5 Chipper Jones 3.50
6 Johan Santana 2.00
7 Roger Clemens 5.00
8 Pedro Martinez 3.00
9 Jim Thome 3.00
10 Greg Maddux 3.50
11 Alfonso Soriano 3.00
12 Derek Jeter 6.00
13 Randy Johnson 3.00
14 Miguel Cabrera 2.00
15 Adrian Beltre 2.00
16 Ivan Rodriguez 2.00
17 Manny Ramirez 2.00
18 Mark Teixeira 2.00
19 Adam Dunn 2.00
20 Scott Rolen 3.00
21 Mike Piazza 3.50
22 J.D. Drew 2.00
23 Hideki Matsui 5.00
24 Nomar Garciaparra 5.00
25 Kazuo Matsui 3.00

Diamond Tribute Jersey

NM/M
Common Player: 6.00
Inserted 1:30
Patch: 1-30X
Production 50 Sets
AB Adrian Beltre/Bat 6.00
RC Roger Clemens/Jsy 12.00
JD J.D. Drew/Bat 6.00
NG Nomar Garciaparra/Bat 12.00
RJ Randy Johnson/Jsy 8.00
CJ Chipper Jones/Bat 10.00
GM Greg Maddux/Jsy 10.00
PM Pedro Martinez/Jsy 8.00
HM Hideki Matsui/Bat 15.00
KM Kazuo Matsui/Bat 8.00
MP Mike Piazza/Bat 10.00
AP Albert Pujols/Bat 15.00
MR Manny Ramirez/Bat 6.00
JS Johan Santana/Jsy 8.00
AS Alfonso Soriano/Bat 8.00
SS Sammy Sosa/Bat 10.00
MT Mark Teixeira/Bat 6.00
JT Jim Thome/Bat 8.00

Diamond Tributes Dual Patch

NM/M
Common Player: 75.00
Production 50 Sets
APSR Albert Pujols, Scott Rolen 100.00
ASMT Alfonso Soriano, Mark Teixeira 75.00
CJJD Chipper Jones, J.D. Drew 80.00
HMKM Hideki Matsui, Kazuo Matsui 125.00
JTAB Jim Thome, Adrian Beltre 75.00
MPIR Mike Piazza, Ivan Rodriguez 75.00
PMMR Pedro Martinez, Manny Ramirez 120.00
RCJS Roger Clemens, Johan Santana 100.00
RJGM Randy Johnson, Greg Maddux 75.00
SSMC Miguel Cabrera, Sammy Sosa 80.00

Standouts

NM/M
Common Player: 3.50
Inserted 1:18
1 Albert Pujols 6.00
2 Ichiro Suzuki 5.00
3 Derek Jeter 8.00
4 Randy Johnson 3.50
5 Greg Maddux 4.00
6 Hideki Matsui 6.00
7 Mike Piazza 4.00
8 Vladimir Guerrero 3.50
9 Sammy Sosa 5.00
10 Jim Thome 3.50
11 Chipper Jones 4.00
12 Alex Rodriguez 6.00
13 Roger Clemens 6.00
14 Nomar Garciaparra 6.00
15 Lance Berkman 3.50

Standouts Jersey

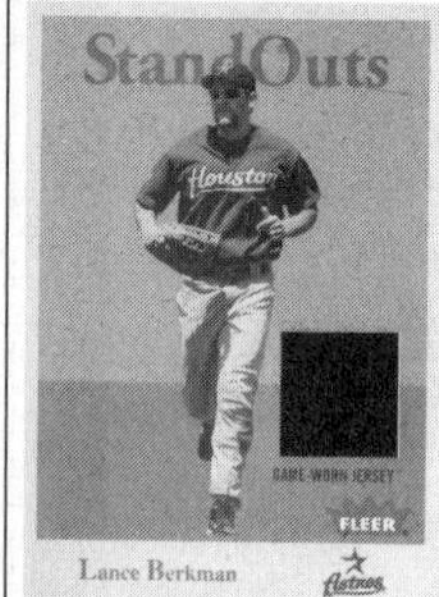

NM/M
Common Player: 10.00
Inserted 1:18
Patch: 1-30X
Production 50 Sets
LB Lance Berkman 6.00
RC Roger Clemens 18.00
VG Vladimir Guerrero 10.00
RJ Randy Johnson 10.00
CJ Chipper Jones 12.00
GM Greg Maddux 12.00
HM Hideki Matsui 20.00
MP Mike Piazza 12.00
AP Albert Pujols 18.00
SS Sammy Sosa 15.00
JT Jim Thome 10.00

2006 Fleer

NM/M
Complete Set (400): 40.00
Complete Factory Set (430): 50.00
#'s 401-430 available in Factory Set
Common Player: .15
Pack (10): 1.75
Box (36): 55.00
1 Adam Kennedy .15
2 Bartolo Colon .25
3 Bengie Molina .15
4 Chone Figgins .15
5 Dallas McPherson .15
6 Darin Erstad .15
7 Francisco Rodriguez .15
8 Garret Anderson .25
9 Jarrod Washburn .15
10 John Lackey .15
11 Orlando Cabrera .15
12 Ryan Theriot **(RC)** .50
13 Steve Finley .15
14 Vladimir Guerrero .75
15 Adam Everett .15
16 Andy Pettitte .40
17 Charlton Jimerson .15
18 Brad Lidge .15
19 Chris Burke .15
20 Craig Biggio .25
21 Jason Lane .15
22 Jeff Bagwell .40
23 Lance Berkman .50
24 Morgan Ensberg .25
25 Roger Clemens 2.00

26 Roy Oswalt .25
27 Willy Taveras .15
28 Barry Zito .25
29 Bobby Crosby .15
30 Bobby Kielty .15
31 Dan Johnson .15
32 Danny Haren .15
33 Eric Chavez .25
34 Huston Street .15
35 Jason Kendall .15
36 Jay Payton .15
37 Joe Blanton .15
38 Mark Kotsay .15
39 Nick Swisher .15
40 Rich Harden .25
41 Ron Flores **RC** .25
42 Alex Rios .15
43 John-Ford Griffin **(RC)** .15
44 David Bush .15
45 Eric Hinske .15
46 Frank Catalanotto .15
47 Gustavo Chacin .15
48 Josh Towers .15
49 Miguel Batista .15
50 Orlando Hudson .15
51 Roy Halladay .25
52 Shea Hillenbrand .15
53 Shaun Marcum **(RC)** .15
54 Vernon Wells .25
55 Adam LaRoche .15
56 Andruw Jones .50
57 Chipper Jones .75
58 Anthony Lerew **(RC)** .15
59 Jeff Francoeur .25
60 John Smoltz .40
61 Johnny Estrada .15
62 Julio Franco .15
63 Joey Devine **RC** 1.00
64 Marcus Giles .15
65 Mike Hampton .15
66 Rafael Furcal .25
67 Chuck James **(RC)** .15
68 Tim Hudson .25
69 Ben Sheets .25
70 Bill Hall .15
71 Brady Clark .15
72 Carlos Lee .25
73 Chris Capuano .15
74 Nelson Cruz **(RC)** .15
75 Derrick Turnbow .15
76 Doug Davis .15
77 Geoff Jenkins .15
78 J.J. Hardy .15
79 Lyle Overbay .15
80 Prince Fielder **(RC)** 1.00
81 Rickie Weeks .25
82 Albert Pujols 2.00
83 Chris Carpenter .25
84 David Eckstein .15
85 Jason Isringhausen .15
86 Tyler Johnson **(RC)** .15
87 Adam Wainwright **(RC)** .15
88 Jim Edmonds .25
89 Chris Duncan .15
90 Mark Grudzielanek .15
91 Mark Mulder .25
92 Matt Morris .15
93 Reggie Sanders .15
94 Scott Rolen .50
95 Yadier Molina .15
96 Aramis Ramirez .40
97 Carlos Zambrano .25
98 Corey Patterson .15
99 Derrek Lee .50
100 Glendon Rusch .15
101 Greg Maddux 1.00
102 Jeromy Burnitz .15
103 Kerry Wood .25
104 Mark Prior .50
105 Michael Barrett .15
106 Geovany Soto **(RC)** .15
107 Nomar Garciaparra .50
108 Ryan Dempster .15
109 Todd Walker .15
110 Alex Gonzalez .15
111 Aubrey Huff .15
112 Victor Diaz .15
113 Carl Crawford .25
114 Danys Baez .15
115 Joey Gathright .15
116 Jonny Gomes .25
117 Jorge Cantu .15
118 Julio Lugo .15
119 Rocco Baldelli .15
120 Scott Kazmir .15
121 Toby Hall .15
122 Tim Corcoran **RC** .40
123 Alex Cintron .15
124 Brandon Webb .15
125 Chad Tracy .15
126 Dustin Nippert **(RC)** .15
127 Claudio Vargas .15
128 Craig Counsell .15
129 Javier Vazquez .15
130 Jose Valverde .15
131 Luis Gonzalez .15
132 Royce Clayton .15
133 Russ Ortiz .15
134 Shawn Green .15
135 Tony Clark .15
136 Troy Glaus .25
137 Brad Penny .15
138 Cesar Izturis .15
139 Derek Lowe .15
140 Eric Gagne .15
141 Hee Seop Choi .15
142 J.D. Drew .15
143 Jason Phillips .15
144 Jayson Werth .15
145 Jeff Kent .25
146 Jeff Weaver .15
147 Milton Bradley .15
148 Odalis Perez .15
149 Hong-Chih Kuo .15
150 Brian Myrow **RC** .25
151 Armando Benitez .15
152 Edgardo Alfonzo .15
153 J.T. Snow .15
154 Jason Schmidt .15
155 Lance Niekro .15
156 Doug Clark .15
157 Daniel Ortmeier **(RC)** .15
158 Moises Alou .25
159 Noah Lowry .15
160 Omar Vizquel .25
161 Pedro Feliz .15
162 Randy Winn .15
163 Jeremy Accardo **RC** .15
164 Aaron Boone .15
165 Ryan Garko **(RC)** .15
166 C.C. Sabathia .15
167 Casey Blake .15
168 Cliff Lee .15
169 Coco Crisp .15
170 Grady Sizemore .40
171 Jake Westbrook .15
172 Jhonny Peralta .15
173 Kevin Millwood .15
174 Scott Elarton .15
175 Travis Hafner .50
176 Victor Martinez .25
177 Adrian Beltre .25
178 Eddie Guardado .15
179 Felix Hernandez .40
180 Gil Meche .15
181 Ichiro Suzuki 1.50
182 Jamie Moyer .15
183 Jeremy Reed .15
184 Jaime Bubela **(RC)** .15
185 Raul Ibanez .25
186 Richie Sexson .40
187 Ryan Franklin .15
188 Jeff Harris **RC** .25
189 A.J. Burnett .15
190 Josh Wilson **(RC)** .15
191 Josh Johnson **(RC)** .15
192 Carlos Delgado .40
193 Dontrelle Willis .25
194 Bernie Castro .15
195 Josh Beckett .25
196 Juan Encarnacion .15
197 Juan Pierre .15
198 Robert Andino **RC** .25
199 Miguel Cabrera .75
200 Ryan Jorgensen **RC** .25
201 Paul LoDuca .15
202 Todd Jones .15
203 Braden Looper .15
204 Carlos Beltran .50
205 Cliff Floyd .15
206 David Wright 1.00
207 Doug Mientkiewicz .15
208 Jae Weong Seo .15
209 Jose Reyes .50
210 Anderson Hernandez **(RC)** .15
211 Miguel Cairo .15
212 Mike Cameron .15
213 Mike Piazza .50
214 Pedro Martinez .75
215 Tom Glavine .25
216 Tim Hamulack .15
217 Brad Wilkerson .15
218 Darrell Rasner **(RC)** .15
219 Chad Cordero .15
220 Cristian Guzman .15
221 Jason Bergmann **RC** .50
222 John Patterson .15
223 Jose Guillen .15
224 Jose Vidro .15
225 Livan Hernandez .15
226 Nick Johnson .15
227 Preston Wilson .15
228 Ryan Zimmerman **(RC)** .25
229 Vinny Castilla .15
230 B.J. Ryan .15
231 B.J. Surhoff .15
232 Brian Roberts .25
233 Walter Young .15
234 Daniel Cabrera .15
235 Erik Bedard .15
236 Javy Lopez .15
237 Jay Gibbons .15
238 Luis Matos .15
239 Melvin Mora .25
240 Miguel Tejada .50
241 Rafael Palmeiro .25
242 Alejandro Freire **RC** .25
243 Sammy Sosa .75
244 Adam Eaton .15
245 Brian Giles .25
246 Brian Lawrence .15
247 Dave Roberts .15
248 Jake Peavy .25
249 Khalil Greene .15
250 Mark Loretta .15
251 Ramon Hernandez .15
252 Ryan Klesko .15
253 Trevor Hoffman .15
254 Woody Williams .15
255 Craig Breslow **RC** .25
256 Billy Wagner .25
257 Bobby Abreu .25
258 Brett Myers .15
259 Chase Utley .40
260 David Bell .15
261 Jim Thome .50
262 Jimmy Rollins .40
263 Jon Lieber .15
264 Danny Sandoval **RC** .25
265 Mike Lieberthal .15
266 Pat Burrell .25
267 Randy Wolf .15
268 Ryan Howard 1.00
269 J.J. Furmaniak **(RC)** .15
270 Ronny Paulino **(RC)** .15
271 Craig Wilson .15
272 Bryan Bullington .15
273 Jack Wilson .15
274 Jason Bay .25
275 Matt Capps **(RC)** .15
276 Oliver Perez .15
277 Robert Mackowiak .15
278 Tom Gorzelanny **(RC)** .15
279 Zachary Duke .15
280 Alfonso Soriano .50
281 Chris Young .15
282 David Dellucci .15
283 Francisco Cordero .15
284 Jason Botts **(RC)** .15
285 Hank Blalock .25
286 Josh Rupe .15
287 Kevin Mench .15
288 Laynce Nix .15
289 Mark Teixeira .50
290 Michael Young .25
291 Richard Hidalgo .15
292 Scott Feldman **RC** .25
293 Bill Mueller .15
294 Hanley Ramirez **(RC)** .40
295 Curt Schilling .75
296 David Ortiz .75
297 Alejandro Machado .15
298 Edgar Renteria .25
299 Jason Varitek .40
300 Johnny Damon .75
301 Keith Foulke .15
302 Manny Ramirez .75
303 Matt Clement .15
304 Craig Hansen **RC** 2.00
305 Tim Wakefield .15
306 Trot Nixon .15
307 Aaron Harang .15
308 Adam Dunn .50
309 Austin Kearns .25
310 Brandon Claussen .15
311 Chris Booker .15
312 Edwin Encarnacion .15
313 Chris Denorfia **(RC)** .15
314 Felipe Lopez .15
315 Miguel Perez **(RC)** .15
316 Ken Griffey Jr. 1.50
317 Ryan Freel .15
318 Sean Casey .15
319 Wily Mo Pena .15
320 Mike Esposito .15
321 Aaron Miles .15
322 Brad Hawpe .15
323 Brian Fuentes .15
324 Clint Barmes .15
325 Cory Sullivan .15
326 Garrett Atkins .15
327 J.D. Closser .15
328 Jeff Francis .15
329 Luis Gonzalez .15
330 Matt Holliday .25
331 Todd Helton .50
332 Angel Berroa .15
333 David DeJesus .15
334 Emil Brown .15
335 Jeremy Affeldt .15
336 Chris Demaria **RC** .50
337 Mark Teahen .15
338 Matt Stairs .15
339 Steve Stemle **RC** .25
340 Mike Sweeney .15
341 Runelvys Hernandez .15
342 Jonah Bayliss **RC** .25
343 Zack Greinke .15
344 Brandon Inge .15
345 Carlos Guillen .15
346 Carlos Pena .15
347 Chris Shelton .25
348 Craig Monroe .15
349 Dmitri Young .15
350 Ivan Rodriguez .40
351 Jeremy Bonderman .15
352 Magglio Ordonez .25
353 Mark Woodyard **(RC)** .15
354 Omar Infante .15
355 Placido Polanco .15
356 Rondell White .15
357 Brad Radke .15
358 Carlos Silva .15
359 Jacque Jones .15
360 Joe Mauer .25
361 Chris Heintz **RC** .25
362 Joe Nathan .15
363 Johan Santana .50
364 Justin Morneau .15
365 Francisco Liriano **(RC)** .50
366 Travis Bowyer .15
367 Michael Cuddyer .15
368 Scott Baker .15
369 Shannon Stewart .15
370 Torii Hunter .25
371 A.J. Pierzynski .15
372 Aaron Rowand .15
373 Carl Everett .15
374 Dustin Hermanson .15
375 Frank Thomas .40
376 Freddy Garcia .15
377 Jermaine Dye .15
378 Joe Crede .15
379 Jon Garland .15
380 Jose Contreras .15
381 Juan Uribe .15
382 Mark Buehrle .25
383 Orlando Hernandez .15
384 Paul Konerko .25
385 Scott Podsednik .15
386 Tadahito Iguchi .25
387 Alex Rodriguez 2.00
388 Bernie Williams .25
389 Chien-Ming Wang .40
390 Derek Jeter 2.00
391 Gary Sheffield .40
392 Hideki Matsui 1.00
393 Jason Giambi .40
394 Jorge Posada .25
395 Michael Vento .15
396 Mariano Rivera .25
397 Mike Mussina .25
398 Randy Johnson .75
399 Robinson Cano .25
400 Tino Martinez .25
401 Alay Soler **RC** .40
402 Boof Bonser **(RC)** .40
403 Cole Hamels **(RC)** 1.50
404 Ian Kinsler **(RC)** .40
405 Jason Kubel **(RC)** .40
406 Joel Zumaya **(RC)** 1.00
407 Jonathan Papelbon **(RC)** 2.50
408 Jered Weaver **(RC)** 2.50
409 Kendry Morales **(RC)** 1.00
410 Lastings Milledge **(RC)** 1.00
411 Matthew Kemp **(RC)** 1.00
412 Taylor Buchholz **(RC)** .40
413 Andre Ethier **(RC)** 2.50
414 Dan Uggla **(RC)** 1.00
415 Jeremy Sowers **(RC)** .40
416 Chad Billingsley **(RC)** .75
417 Josh Barfield **(RC)** .40
418 Matt Cain **(RC)** .75
419 Fausto Carmona **(RC)** .40
420 Josh Willingham **(RC)** .40
421 Jeremy Hermida **(RC)** .75
422 Conor Jackson **(RC)** .75
423 Dave Gassner **(RC)** .40
424 Brian Bannister **(RC)** .40
425 Fernando Nieve **(RC)** .40
426 Justin Verlander **(RC)** 2.50
427 Scott Olsen **(RC)** .40
428 Takashi Saito **RC** .50
429 Willie Eyre **(RC)** .40
430 Travis Ishikawa **(RC)** .40

Top 40

NM/M
Common Player: .50
Inserted 2:1 Fat Pack
1 Ken Griffey Jr. 3.00
2 Derek Jeter 4.00
3 Albert Pujols 4.00
4 Alex Rodriguez 4.00
5 Vladimir Guerrero 1.50
6 Roger Clemens 3.00
7 Derrek Lee 1.00
8 David Ortiz 1.50
9 Miguel Cabrera 1.50
10 Bobby Abreu .50
11 Mark Teixeira 1.00
12 Johan Santana 1.50
13 Hideki Matsui 2.50
14 Ichiro Suzuki 3.00
15 Andruw Jones 1.00
16 Eric Chavez .50
17 Roy Oswalt .75
18 Curt Schilling 1.00
19 Randy Johnson 1.50
20 Ivan Rodriguez 1.00
21 Chipper Jones 1.50
22 Mark Prior .50
23 Jason Bay .75
24 Pedro Martinez 1.50
25 David Wright 2.50
26 Carlos Beltran 1.00
27 Jim Edmonds .50
28 Chris Carpenter .75
29 Roy Halladay .75
30 Jake Peavy 1.00
31 Paul Konerko .75
32 Travis Hafner .75
33 Barry Zito .50
34 Miguel Tejada .75
35 Josh Beckett 1.00
36 Todd Helton 1.00
37 Dontrelle Willis .50
38 Manny Ramirez 1.50
39 Mariano Rivera 1.00
40 Jeff Kent .50

Glossy

Glossy: 2-3X
Inserted 1:12

Glossy Gold

Glossy Gold: 4-8X
Inserted 1:144

Autographics

NM/M
Inserted 1:432
AN Garrett Anderson 15.00
GA Garrett Atkins 10.00
JB Joe Blanton 15.00
EC Eric Chavez 20.00
KG Ken Griffey Jr. 85.00
TI Tadahito Iguchi 50.00
CS Chris Shelton 30.00
NS Nick Swisher 20.00
KY Kevin Youkilis 15.00

Award Winners

NM/M
Complete Set (6): 5.00
Common Player: .50
1 Albert Pujols 3.00
2 Alex Rodriguez 3.00
3 Chris Carpenter .50
4 Bartolo Colon .50
5 Ryan Howard 1.00
6 Huston Street .50

Fabrics

NM/M
Inserted 1:36
BA Bobby Abreu 6.00
CB Carlos Beltran 8.00
MC Miguel Cabrera 8.00
EC Eric Chavez 4.00
RC Roger Clemens 15.00
JD Johnny Damon 8.00
JE Jim Edmonds 6.00
EG Eric Gagne 4.00
LG Luis Gonzalez 4.00
GR Khalil Greene 4.00
KG Ken Griffey Jr. 15.00
VG Vladimir Guerrero 8.00
RH Roy Halladay 4.00
TH Todd Helton 6.00
DJ Derek Jeter 20.00
RJ Randy Johnson 8.00
AJ Andruw Jones 6.00
CJ Chipper Jones 8.00
DL Derrek Lee 8.00
GM Greg Maddux 15.00
PM Pedro Martinez 8.00
JM Joe Mauer 4.00
DO David Ortiz 8.00
JP Jake Peavy 6.00
MP Mark Prior 6.00
AP Albert Pujols 20.00
AR Aramis Ramirez 6.00
MR Manny Ramirez 8.00
IR Ivan Rodriguez 6.00
SR Scott Rolen 8.00
JS Johan Santana 8.00
CS Curt Schilling 8.00
GS Gary Sheffield/SP 10.00
SM John Smoltz 8.00
AS Alfonso Soriano 6.00
MT Mark Teixeira 8.00
TE Miguel Tejada 6.00
JT Jim Thome 6.00
RW Rickie Weeks 4.00
DW Dontrelle Willis/SP 8.00
WR David Wright 12.00
MY Michael Young 4.00

Lumber Company

NM/M
1 Adam Dunn 1.00
2 Albert Pujols 3.00
3 Alex Rodriguez 3.00
4 Alfonso Soriano .75
5 Andruw Jones .75
6 Aramis Ramirez .75
7 Bobby Abreu .75
8 Carlos Delgado .75
9 Carlos Lee .50
10 David Ortiz 1.00
11 David Wright 1.50
12 Derrek Lee 1.00
13 Eric Chavez .50
14 Gary Sheffield .75
15 Jeff Kent .50
16 Ken Griffey Jr. 2.00
17 Manny Ramirez 1.00
18 Mark Teixeira 1.00
19 Miguel Cabrera 1.00
20 Miguel Tejada .75
21 Paul Konerko .75
22 Richie Sexson .50
23 Todd Helton .75
24 Troy Glaus .50
25 Vladimir Guerrero 1.00

Smoke 'n Heat

NM/M
1 Carlos Zambrano .50
2 Chris Carpenter .50
3 Curt Schilling 1.00
4 Dontrelle Willis .50
5 Felix Hernandez 1.00
6 Jake Peavy .75
7 Johan Santana 1.00
8 John Smoltz .75
9 Mark Prior .75
10 Pedro Martinez 1.00
11 Randy Johnson 1.00
12 Roger Clemens 3.00
13 Roy Halladay .50
14 Roy Oswalt .50
15 Scott Kazmir .50

Smooth Leather

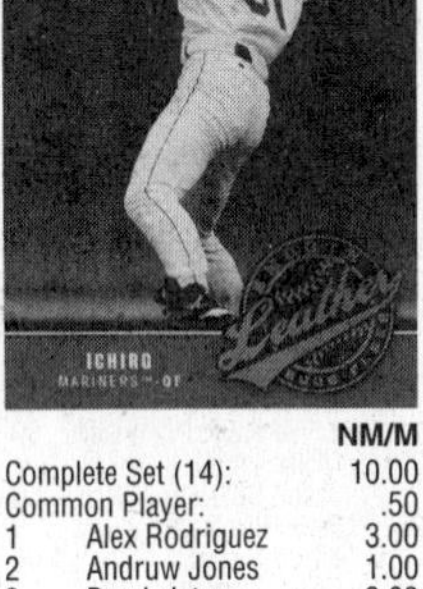
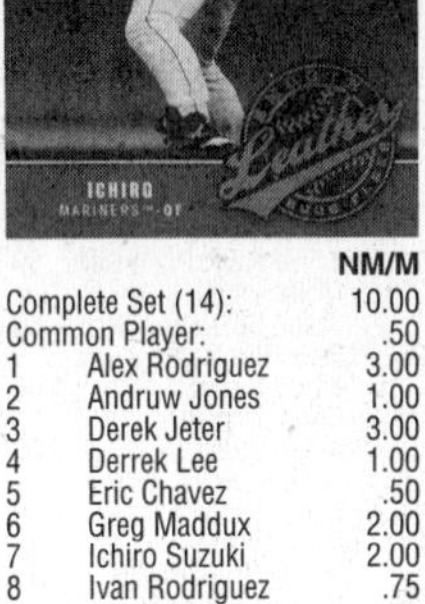

NM/M
Complete Set (14): 10.00
Common Player: .50
1 Alex Rodriguez 3.00
2 Andruw Jones 1.00
3 Derek Jeter 3.00
4 Derrek Lee 1.00
5 Eric Chavez .50
6 Greg Maddux 2.00
7 Ichiro Suzuki 2.00
8 Ivan Rodriguez .75
9 Jim Edmonds .75
10 Mike Mussina .75
11 Omar Vizquel .50
12 Scott Rolen 1.00
13 Todd Helton .75
14 Torii Hunter .50

Stars of Tomorrow

NM/M
Complete Set (10): 5.00
Common Player: .50
Inserted 1:10
1 David Wright 1.50
2 Ryan Howard 1.00
3 Felix Hernandez 1.00
4 Jeff Francoeur .50
5 Joe Mauer .50
6 Mark Prior .75
7 Mark Teixeira 1.00
8 Miguel Cabrera 1.00
9 Prince Fielder **(RC)** 1.00
10 Rickie Weeks .50

Team Fleer

NM/M
Inserted 1:Case
1 Albert Pujols 40.00
2 Alex Rodriguez 30.00
3 Alfonso Soriano 10.00
4 Andruw Jones 10.00
5 Bobby Abreu 10.00
6 David Ortiz 15.00
7 David Wright 25.00
8 Eric Gagne 8.00
9 Ichiro Suzuki 30.00
10 Jason Varitek 15.00
11 Jeff Kent 8.00
12 Johan Santana 15.00
13 Jose Reyes 10.00
14 Manny Ramirez 15.00
15 Mariano Rivera 10.00
16 Miguel Cabrera 15.00
17 Miguel Tejada 10.00
18 Mike Piazza 15.00
19 Roger Clemens 30.00
20 Torii Hunter 8.00

Team Leaders

NM/M
Complete Set (30): 15.00
Common Player: .50
1 Troy Glaus, Brandon Webb .50
2 John Smoltz, Andruw Jones .50
3 Miguel Tejada, Erik Bedard .50
4 David Ortiz, Curt Schilling .75
5 Derrek Lee, Mark Prior .75
6 Mark Buehrle, Paul Konerko .50
7 Ken Griffey Jr., Aaron Harang 1.50
8 Cliff Lee, Travis Hafner .50
9 Todd Helton, Jeff Francis .50
10 Jeremy Bonderman, Ivan Rodriguez .50
11 Miguel Cabrera, Dontrelle Willis .75
12 Lance Berkman, Roger Clemens 2.00
13 Mike Sweeney, Zack Greinke .50
14 Derek Lowe, Jeff Kent .50
15 Carlos Lee, Ben Sheets .50
16 Johan Santana, Torii Hunter .50
17 Pedro Martinez, David Wright 1.00
18 Derek Jeter, Randy Johnson 2.00
19 Barry Zito, Eric Chavez .50
20 Bobby Abreu, Brett Myers .50
21 Jason Bay, Zachary Duke .50
22 Jake Peavy, Brian Giles .50
23 Moises Alou, Jason Schmidt .50
24 Felix Hernandez, Ichiro Suzuki 1.00
25 Chris Carpenter, Albert Pujols 2.00
26 Scott Kazmir, Carl Crawford .50
27 Mark Teixeira, Kenny Rogers .50
28 Vernon Wells, Roy Halladay .50
29 Livan Hernandez, Jose Guillen .50
30 Bartolo Colon, Vladimir Guerrero .50

2006 Fleer Greats of the Game

NM/M
Complete Set (100): 35.00
Common Player: .40
Pack (5): 8.00
Box (15): 100.00
1 Al Kaline 1.50
2 Alan Trammell .50
3 Andre Dawson .75
4 Barry Larkin .75
5 Bill Buckner .40
6 Bill Freehan .40
7 Bill Madlock .40
8 Bill Mazeroski .40
9 Billy Williams .50
10 Bo Jackson 1.00
11 Bob Feller 1.00
12 Bob Gibson .50
13 Bobby Doerr .40
14 Bobby Murcer .50
15 Boog Powell .50
16 Brooks Robinson 1.50
17 Bruce Sutter .40
18 Bucky Dent .40
19 Cal Ripken Jr. 4.00
20 Rico Petrocelli .40
21 Carlton Fisk .75
22 Chris Chambliss .40
23 Dave Concepcion .40
24 Dave Parker .50
25 Dave Winfield 1.00
26 David Cone .50
27 Denny McLain .40
28 Don Mattingly 3.00
29 Don Newcombe .50
30 Don Sutton .50
31 Dusty Baker .50
32 Dwight Evans .50
33 Eric Davis .50
34 Ernie Banks 2.00
35 Fergie Jenkins .75
36 Frank Robinson 1.00
37 Fred Lynn .40
38 Fred McGriff .50
39 Andre Thornton .40
40 Garry Maddox .40
41 Gary Matthews .40
42 Gaylord Perry .40
43 George Foster .40
44 George Kell .40
45 Graig Nettles .40
46 Greg Luzinski .40
47 Harmon Killebrew 1.50
48 Jack Clark .50
49 Jack Morris .50
50 Jim Palmer .75
51 Jim Rice .75
52 Joe Morgan .75
53 John Kruk .50
54 Johnny Bench 2.00
55 Jose Canseco .75
56 Kirby Puckett 2.00
57 Kirk Gibson .50
58 Lee Mazzilli .40
59 Lou Brock .75
60 Lou Piniella .50
61 Luis Aparicio .50
62 Luis Tiant .50
63 Mark Fidrych .50
64 Mark Grace .75
65 Maury Wills .50
66 Mike Schmidt 2.00
67 Nolan Ryan 3.00
68 Ozzie Smith 1.00
69 Paul Molitor 1.00
70 Paul O'Neill .50
71 Phil Niekro .50
72 Ralph Kiner .75
73 Randy Hundley .40
74 Red Schoendienst .50
75 Reggie Jackson 1.00
76 Robin Yount 1.00
77 Rod Carew .75
78 Rollie Fingers .50
79 Ron Cey .50
80 Ron Guidry .50
81 Ron Santo .75
82 Rusty Staub .50
83 Ryne Sandberg 2.00
84 Sparky Lyle .40
85 Stan Musial 2.00
86 Steve Carlton .75
87 Steve Garvey .50
88 Steve Sax .40
89 Tommy Herr .40
90 Tim McCarver .50
91 Tim Raines .50
92 Tom Seaver 1.00
93 Tony Gwynn 1.00
94 Tony Perez .75
95 Wade Boggs .75
96 Whitey Ford 1.00
97 Will Clark .75
98 Willie Horton .40
99 Willie McCovey 1.00
100 Yogi Berra 1.50

Copper

Copper: 2-4X
Production 299 Sets

Pewter

Pewter: 2X
Inserted 1:15

AUTOGRAPHics

NM/M
Inserted 1:180
Cards are not serial numbered.
LA Luis Aparicio/25 20.00
LB Lou Brock/25 25.00
RC Rod Carew/25 30.00
SC Steve Carlton/50 25.00
WC Will Clark/25 40.00
AD Andre Dawson 25.00
BF Bob Feller/50 30.00
GF George Foster/50 20.00
SG Steve Garvey/50 25.00
BG Bob Gibson/25 40.00
KG Kirk Gibson/25 25.00
MG Mark Grace/50 30.00
RG Ron Guidry/99 50.00
BJ Bo Jackson/25 75.00
FJ Fergie Jenkins/25 30.00
AK Al Kaline/99 35.00
HK Harmon Killebrew/25 50.00
BL Barry Larkin/50 40.00
BI Bill Mazeroski/25 35.00
FM Fred McGriff/99 30.00
PM Paul Molitor/50 25.00
JM Joe Morgan/25 35.00
BM Bobby Murcer/99 30.00
DN Don Newcombe/99 15.00
PN Phil Niekro/50 20.00
JP Jim Palmer/99 20.00
DP Dave Parker/99 20.00
TP Tony Perez/99 30.00
JR Jim Rice/99 20.00
BR Brooks Robinson/50 40.00
RS Ron Santo/99 30.00
OS Ozzie Smith/25 60.00
BS Bruce Sutter/50 15.00
SU Don Sutton/50 20.00
BW Billy Williams/50 25.00
MW Maury Wills/99 20.00

Bat Barrel Autograph

No Pricing
Production 1-5

Cardinals Greats

NM/M
Complete Set (10): 8.00
LB Lou Brock 1.00
SC Steve Carlton .50
DD Dizzy Dean 1.00
BG Bob Gibson 1.00
TH Tommy Herr .25
RH Rogers Hornsby 1.00
TM Tim McCarver .50
SM Stan Musial 2.00
RS Red Schoendienst .50
OS Ozzie Smith 1.00

Cubs Greats

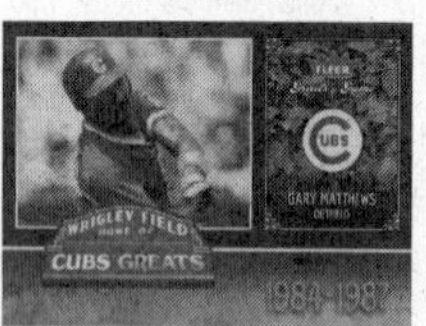

NM/M
Complete Set (10): 8.00
EB Ernie Banks 2.00
AD Andre Dawson 1.00
MG Mark Grace 1.00
RH Randy Hundley .50
FJ Fergie Jenkins .50
GM Gary Mathews .50
SA Ryne Sandberg 2.00
RS Ron Santo 1.00
BS Bruce Sutter .50
BW Billy Williams .50

Decade Greats

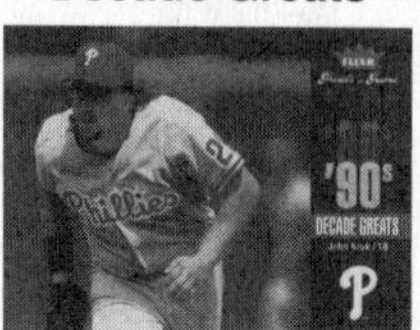

NM/M
Complete Set (30): 20.00
EA Earl Averill .50
RO Rod Carew 1.00
SC Steve Carlton .75
CC Chris Chambliss .50
JC Jack Clark .50
WC Will Clark 1.00
RC Roberto Clemente 3.00
MC Mickey Cochrane .50
BF Bob Feller 1.00
TG Tony Gwynn 1.00
BJ Bo Jackson 1.00
JK John Kruk .50
BI Bill Madlock .50
EM Eddie Mathews 1.00
BM Bill Mazeroski .50
WM Willie McCovey 1.00
JM Johnny Mize .50
PM Paul Molitor 1.00
MO Mel Ott 1.00
DP Dave Parker .50
KP Kirby Puckett 1.00
TR Tim Raines .50
CR Cal Ripken Jr. 3.00
BR Brooks Robinson 1.00
NR Nolan Ryan 2.00
TS Tom Seaver 1.00
MS Mike Schmidt 1.00
WS Willie Stargell 1.00
PT Paul Traynor .50
RY Robin Yount 1.00

Dodgers Greats

NM/M
Complete Set (10): 6.00
DB Dusty Baker .50
CA Roy Campanella 1.00
RC Ron Cey .50
DD Don Drysdale 1.00
SG Steve Garvey .50
PR Pee Wee Reese .50
JR Jackie Robinson 2.00
SS Steve Sax .50
DS Don Sutton .50
MW Maury Wills .50

Nickname Greats

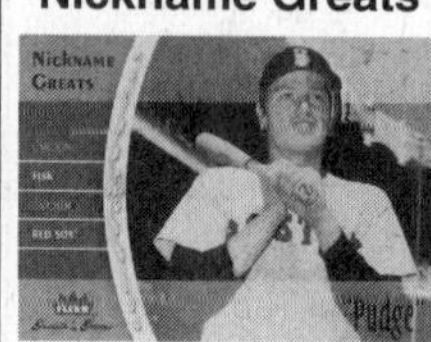

NM/M
LA Luis Aparicio .50
SB Steve Balboni .50
DB Don Baylor .50
BE Steve Bedrosian .50
JB Jim Bouton .50
TB Tom Brunansky .50
RB Rick Burleson .50
RC Ron Cey .50
CH Joe Charboneau .50
JC Jack Clark .50
WC Will Clark 1.00
DD Darren Daulton .50
DE Dwight Evans .50
BF Bob Feller 1.00
SF Sid Fernandez .50
MF Mark Fidrych .50
CF Carlton Fisk .75
DF Dan Ford .50
GF George Foster .50
AG Andres Galarraga .50
RG Ron Guidry .50
MH Mike Hargrove .50
KH Ken Harrelson .50
TH Tom Henke .50
HE Tommy Herr .50
BH Burt Hooton .50
AH Al Hrabosky .50
GH Glenn Hubbard .50
HJ Howard Johnson .50
JJ Jay Johnstone .50
ML Mike LaValliere .50
BL Bill Lee .50
SL Sparky Lyle .50
GM Garry Maddox .50
BM Bill Madlock .50
MZ Dennis Martinez .50
MA Gary Matthews .50
DM Don Mattingly 2.00
LM Lee Mazzilli .50
WM Willie McCovey 1.00
SM Sam McDowell .50
JM John Montefusco .50
DP Dave Parker .50
JP Joe Pepitone .50
LP Lou Piniella .50
RA Doug Rader .50
TR Tim Raines .50
RR Rick Reuschel .50
DR Dave Righetti .50
MR Mickey Rivers .50
FR Frank Robinson 1.00
GS George Scott .50
JS John Shelby .50
FS Fred Stanley .50
RS Rusty Staub .50
AT Andre Thornton .50
ST Steve Trout .50
EV Ellis Valentine .50
MW Mitch Williams .50
JW Jimmy Wynn .50

Red Sox Greats

NM/M
Complete Set (10): 8.00
WB Wade Boggs 1.00
BD Bobby Doerr .50
DE Dwight Evans .50
CF Carlton Fisk 1.00
JF Jimmie Foxx 2.00
FL Fred Lynn .50
RP Rico Petrocelli .50
JR Jim Rice .75
LT Luis Tiant .50
TW Ted Williams 2.00

Reds Greats

NM/M
Complete Set (10): 8.00
JB Johnny Bench 1.50
DC Dave Concepcion .50
ED Eric Davis .50
GF George Foster .50
KG Ken Griffey Sr. .50
BL Barry Larkin 1.00
JM Joe Morgan 1.00
TP Tony Perez 1.00
FR Frank Robinson 1.00
TS Tom Seaver 1.00

Tigers Greats

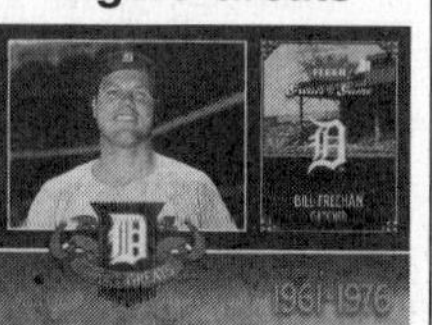

NM/M
Complete Set (10): 6.00
TC Ty Cobb 2.00
MF Mark Fidrych .50
BF Bill Freehan .50
KG Kirk Gibson 1.00
WH Willie Horton .50
AK Al Kaline 1.00
GK George Kell .50
DM Denny McLain 1.00
JM Jack Morris .50
AT Alan Trammell .50

Yankee Clippings

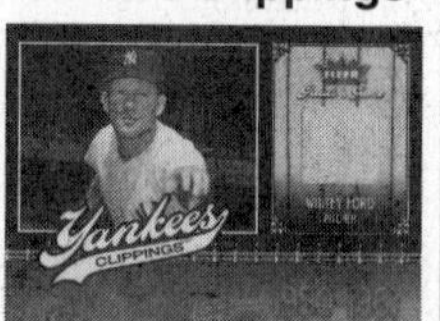

NM/M
Complete Set (10): 12.00
YB Yogi Berra 1.50
JD Joe DiMaggio 2.00
WF Whitey Ford 1.00
RG Ron Guidry .50
RJ Reggie Jackson 1.00
DM Don Mattingly 2.00
TM Thurman Munson 1.50
BM Bobby Murcer .50
GN Graig Nettles .50
BR Babe Ruth 3.00

Autographs

NM/M
Common Autograph: 10.00
1 Al Kaline 25.00
2 Alan Trammell 15.00
3 Andre Dawson 20.00
4 Barry Larkin 35.00
5 Bill Buckner 12.00
6 Bill Freehan 12.00
7 Bill Madlock 15.00
8 Bill Mazeroski 35.00
9 Billy Williams 20.00
10 Bo Jackson 60.00
11 Bob Feller 25.00
12 Bob Gibson 40.00
13 Bobby Doerr 20.00
14 Bobby Murcer 15.00
15 Boog Powell 15.00
16 Brooks Robinson 25.00
17 Bruce Sutter 15.00
18 Bucky Dent 10.00
19 Cal Ripken Jr./SP 140.00
20 Rico Petrocelli 10.00
21 Carlton Fisk 30.00
22 Chris Chambliss 15.00
23 Dave Concepcion 15.00
24 Dave Parker 20.00
25 Dave Winfield 30.00
26 David Cone 15.00
27 Denny McLain 20.00
28 Don Mattingly 60.00
29 Don Newcombe 20.00
30 Don Sutton 15.00
31 Dusty Baker 25.00
32 Dwight Evans 20.00
33 Eric Davis 20.00
34 Ernie Banks 75.00
35 Fergie Jenkins 20.00
36 Frank Robinson 30.00
37 Fred Lynn 15.00
38 Fred McGriff 30.00
39 Andre Thornton 10.00
40 Garry Maddox 20.00
41 Gary Matthews 10.00
42 Gaylord Perry 15.00
43 George Foster 15.00
44 George Kell 15.00
45 Graig Nettles 20.00
46 Greg Luzinski 15.00
47 Harmon Killebrew 35.00
48 Jack Clark/SP/50 20.00
49 Jack Morris 15.00
50 Jim Palmer 20.00
51 Jim Rice 20.00
52 Joe Morgan 25.00
53 John Kruk 20.00
54 Johnny Bench 60.00
56 Kirby Puckett 100.00
57 Kirk Gibson 20.00
58 Lee Mazzilli 15.00
59 Lou Brock 30.00
60 Lou Piniella 15.00
61 Luis Aparicio 15.00
62 Luis Tiant 15.00
63 Mark Fidrych 25.00
64 Mark Grace 25.00
65 Maury Wills 20.00
66 Mike Schmidt 50.00
67 Nolan Ryan/SP/50 100.00
68 Ozzie Smith 40.00
69 Paul Molitor 25.00
70 Paul O'Neill 25.00
71 Phil Niekro 20.00
72 Ralph Kiner 20.00
73 Randy Hundley 15.00
74 Red Schoendienst 25.00
75 Reggie Jackson 35.00
76 Robin Yount 50.00
77 Rod Carew 25.00
78 Rollie Fingers 20.00
79 Ron Cey 10.00
80 Ron Guidry/SP 50.00
81 Ron Santo 25.00
83 Ryne Sandberg/SP 50.00
84 Sparky Lyle 15.00
85 Stan Musial 65.00
86 Steve Carlton 25.00
87 Steve Garvey 25.00
88 Steve Sax 10.00
89 Tommy Herr 15.00
90 Tim McCarver 20.00
91 Tim Raines/SP 20.00
92 Tom Seaver 50.00
93 Tony Gwynn 40.00
94 Tony Perez 25.00
95 Wade Boggs 25.00
96 Whitey Ford 50.00
97 Will Clark/SP 35.00
98 Willie Horton 15.00
99 Willie McCovey 35.00
100 Yogi Berra 60.00

Cardinals Greats Memorabilia Autograph

NM/M
Production 30 Sets
LB Lou Brock 50.00
SC Steve Carlton 35.00
BG Bob Gibson 60.00
TH Tommy Herr 20.00
TM Tim McCarver 30.00
SM Stan Musial 75.00
RS Red Schoendienst 30.00
OS Ozzie Smith 50.00

Cardinals Greats Autograph

NM/M
Production 30 Sets
LB Lou Brock 40.00
SC Steve Carlton 30.00
BG Bob Gibson 50.00
TH Tommy Herr 20.00
TM Tim McCarver 30.00
SM Stan Musial 75.00
RS Red Schoendienst 25.00
OS Ozzie Smith 50.00

Cardinals Greats Memorabilia

NM/M
Common Player: 5.00
LB Lou Brock 5.00
SC Steve Carlton 5.00
DD Dizzy Dean/SP 50.00
BG Bob Gibson 15.00
TH Tommy Herr 5.00
RH Rogers Hornsby 40.00

TM	Tim McCarver	5.00
SM	Stan Musial	20.00
RS	Red Schoendienst	10.00
OS	Ozzie Smith	15.00

Cubs Greats Memorabilia Autograph

		NM/M
Production 30 Sets		
EB	Ernie Banks	60.00
AD	Andre Dawson	30.00
FJ	Fergie Jenkins	25.00
GM	Gary Matthews	25.00
SA	Ryne Sandberg	60.00
RS	Ron Santo	40.00
BS	Bruce Sutter	20.00
BW	Billy Williams	30.00

Cubs Greats Autograph

		NM/M
Production 30 Sets		
EB	Ernie Banks	60.00
AD	Andre Dawson	30.00
MG	Mark Grace	30.00
FJ	Fergie Jenkins	25.00
GM	Gary Matthews	25.00
SA	Ryne Sandberg	60.00
RS	Ron Santo	40.00
BS	Bruce Sutter	20.00
BW	Billy Williams	30.00

Cubs Greats Memorabilia

		NM/M
EB	Ernie Banks	20.00
AD	Andre Dawson	8.00
MG	Mark Grace	8.00
FJ	Fergie Jenkins	8.00
GM	Gary Matthews	15.00
SA	Ryne Sandberg	15.00
RS	Ron Santo	10.00
BS	Brian Sutter	5.00
BW	Billy Williams	8.00

Decade Greats Memorabilia Autograph

		NM/M
Production 30 Sets		
RO	Rod Carew	35.00
SC	Steve Carlton	35.00
CC	Chris Chambliss	25.00
JC	Jack Clark	25.00
WC	Will Clark	35.00
BF	Bob Feller	50.00
TG	Tony Gwynn	60.00
BJ	Bo Jackson	65.00
JK	John Kruk	25.00
BI	Bill Madlock	20.00
BM	Bill Mazeroski	35.00
WM	Willie McCovey	40.00
PM	Paul Molitor	35.00
DP	Dave Parker	20.00
KP	Kirby Puckett	100.00
TR	Tim Raines	20.00
CR	Cal Ripken Jr.	150.00
BR	Brooks Robinson	40.00
NR	Nolan Ryan	100.00
MS	Mike Schmidt	75.00
TS	Tom Seaver	50.00
RY	Robin Yount	50.00

Decade Greats Autograph

		NM/M
Production 30 Sets		
RO	Rod Carew	35.00
SC	Steve Carlton	35.00
CC	Chris Chambliss	25.00
JC	Jack Clark	25.00
WC	Will Clark	35.00
BF	Bob Feller	50.00
TG	Tony Gwynn	60.00
BJ	Bo Jackson	65.00
JK	John Kruk	25.00
BI	Bill Madlock	20.00
BM	Bill Mazeroski	35.00
WM	Willie McCovey	40.00
PM	Paul Molitor	35.00
DP	Dave Parker	20.00
KP	Kirby Puckett	100.00
TR	Tim Raines	20.00
CR	Cal Ripken Jr.	150.00
BR	Brooks Robinson	40.00
NR	Nolan Ryan	100.00
MS	Mike Schmidt	75.00
TS	Tom Seaver	50.00
RY	Robin Yount	50.00

Decade Greats Memorabilia

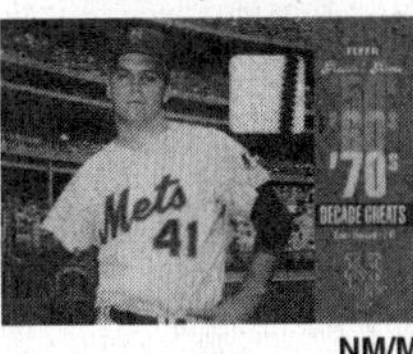

		NM/M
Common Player:		5.00
EA	Earl Averill	20.00
RO	Rod Carew	8.00
SC	Steve Carlton	5.00
CC	Chris Chambliss	5.00
JC	Jack Clark	5.00
WC	Will Clark	8.00
RC	Roberto Clemente	60.00
BF	Bob Feller	15.00
BJ	Bo Jackson	15.00
JK	John Kruk	8.00
BI	Bill Madlock	5.00
EM	Eddie Mathews	10.00
BM	Bill Mazeroski	8.00
WM	Willie McCovey	10.00
JM	Johnny Mize	15.00
PM	Paul Molitor	8.00
MO	Mel Ott/SP	50.00
DP	Dave Parker	5.00
KP	Kirby Puckett	15.00
TR	Tim Raines	5.00
CR	Cal Ripken Jr.	20.00
BR	Brooks Robinson	8.00
NR	Nolan Ryan	15.00
MS	Mike Schmidt	10.00
TS	Tom Seaver	10.00
WS	Willie Stargell	15.00
RY	Robin Yount	8.00

Dodgers Greats Memorabilia Autograph

		NM/M
Production 30 Sets		
DB	Dusty Baker	40.00
RC	Ron Cey	30.00
SG	Steve Garvey	35.00
SS	Steve Sax	20.00
DS	Don Sutton	35.00
MW	Maury Wills	35.00

Dodgers Greats Autograph

		NM/M
Production 30 Sets		
DB	Dusty Baker	40.00
RC	Ron Cey	30.00
SG	Steve Garvey	35.00
SS	Steve Sax	25.00
DS	Don Sutton	35.00
MW	Maury Wills	35.00

Dodgers Greats Memorabilia

		NM/M
Common Player:		5.00
DB	Dusty Baker	8.00
CA	Roy Campanella	35.00
RC	Ron Cey	5.00
DD	Don Drysdale	25.00
SG	Steve Garvey	8.00
PR	Pee Wee Reese	10.00
JR	Jackie Robinson	40.00
SS	Steve Sax	5.00
DS	Don Sutton	5.00
MW	Maury Wills	5.00

Nickname Greats Autograph

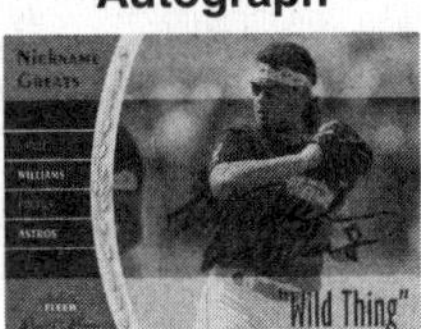

		NM/M
SB	Steve Balboni	15.00
BE	Steve Bedrosian	15.00
JB	Jim Bouton	35.00
TB	Tom Brunansky	15.00
RB	Rick Burleson	15.00
CH	Joe Charboneau	20.00
JC	Jack Clark	20.00
WC	Will Clark	30.00
DD	Darren Daulton	20.00
DE	Dwight Evans	20.00
BF	Bob Feller	50.00
SF	Sid Fernandez	15.00
MF	Mark Fidrych	35.00
CF	Carlton Fisk	50.00
DF	Dan Ford	15.00
GF	George Foster	20.00
RG	Ron Guidry	40.00
MH	Mike Hargrove	20.00
TH	Tom Henke	15.00
HE	Tommy Herr	15.00
BH	Burt Hooton	20.00
AH	Al Hrabosky	20.00
GH	Glenn Hubbard	15.00
HJ	Howard Johnson	25.00
JJ	Jay Johnstone	20.00
ML	Mike LaValliere	15.00
BL	Bill Lee	20.00
SL	Sparky Lyle	15.00
GM	Garry Maddox	20.00
BM	Bill Madlock	15.00
MZ	Dennis Martinez	20.00
MA	Gary Matthews	15.00
LM	Lee Mazzilli	15.00
WM	Willie McCovey	50.00
SM	Sam McDowell	20.00
JM	John Montefusco	20.00
DP	Dave Parker	20.00
JP	Joe Pepitone	20.00
LP	Lou Piniella	25.00
RA	Doug Rader	15.00
TR	Tim Raines	15.00
RR	Rick Reuschel	20.00
DR	Dave Righetti	20.00
MR	Mickey Rivers	20.00
FR	Frank Robinson	50.00
GS	George Scott	20.00
JS	John Shelby	15.00
FS	Fred Stanley	20.00
RS	Rusty Staub	20.00
AT	Andre Thornton	15.00
ST	Steve Trout	20.00
EV	Ellis Valentine	15.00
MW	Mitch Williams	15.00
JW	Jimmy Wynn	20.00

Red Sox Greats Memorabilia Autograph

		NM/M
Production 30 Sets		
WB	Wade Boggs	50.00
BD	Bobby Doerr	20.00
DE	Dwight Evans	25.00
CF	Carlton Fisk	35.00
FL	Fred Lynn	20.00
RP	Rico Petrocelli	20.00
JR	Jim Rice	25.00
LT	Luis Tiant	20.00

Red Sox Greats Autograph

		NM/M
Production 30 Sets		
WB	Wade Boggs	50.00
BD	Bobby Doerr	20.00
DE	Dwight Evans	25.00
CF	Carlton Fisk	35.00
FL	Fred Lynn	20.00
RP	Rico Petrocelli	20.00
JR	Jim Rice	25.00
LT	Luis Tiant	25.00

Red Sox Greats Memorabilia

		NM/M
Common Player:		
WB	Wade Boggs	10.00
BD	Bobby Doerr	8.00
DE	Dwight Evans	8.00
CF	Carlton Fisk	8.00
JF	Jimmie Foxx	50.00
FL	Fred Lynn	5.00
RP	Rico Petrocelli	5.00
JR	Jim Rice	8.00
LT	Luis Tiant	5.00
TW	Ted Williams	50.00

Reds Greats Memorabilia Autograph

		NM/M
Production 30 Sets		
JB	Johnny Bench	65.00
DC	Dave Concepcion	25.00
ED	Eric Davis	30.00
GF	George Foster	25.00
KG	Ken Griffey Sr.	30.00
BL	Barry Larkin	40.00
JM	Joe Morgan	40.00
TP	Tony Perez	40.00
FR	Frank Robinson	50.00
TS	Tom Seaver	50.00

Reds Greats Autograph

		NM/M
Production 30 Sets		
JB	Johnny Bench	65.00
DC	Dave Concepcion	25.00
ED	Eric Davis	30.00
GF	George Foster	25.00
KG	Ken Griffey Sr.	30.00
BL	Barry Larkin	40.00
JM	Joe Morgan	40.00
TP	Tony Perez	40.00
FR	Frank Robinson	50.00
TS	Tom Seaver	50.00

Reds Greats Memorabilia

		NM/M
Common Player:		5.00
JB	Johnny Bench	15.00
DC	Dave Concepcion	5.00
ED	Eric Davis	10.00
GF	George Foster	5.00
KG	Ken Griffey Sr.	5.00
BL	Barry Larkin	8.00
JM	Joe Morgan	8.00
TP	Tony Perez	8.00
FR	Frank Robinson	10.00
TS	Tom Seaver	10.00

Tigers Greats Memorabilia Autograph

		NM/M
Production 30 Sets		
MF	Mark Fidrych	35.00
BF	Bill Freehan	30.00
KG	Kirk Gibson	35.00
WH	Willie Horton	20.00
AK	Al Kaline	50.00
GK	George Kell	40.00
JM	Jack Morris	25.00
AT	Alan Trammell	35.00

Tigers Greats Autograph

		NM/M
Production 30 Sets		
MF	Mark Fidrych	35.00
BF	Bill Freehan	30.00
KG	Kirk Gibson	35.00
WH	Willie Horton	20.00
AK	Al Kaline	50.00
GK	George Kell	40.00
DM	Denny McLain	35.00
JM	Jack Morris	25.00
AT	Alan Trammell	35.00

Tigers Greats Memorabilia

		NM/M
Common Player:		5.00
TC	Ty Cobb	85.00
MF	Mark Fidrych	10.00
BF	Bill Freehan	5.00
KG	Kirk Gibson	5.00
WH	Willie Horton	5.00
AK	Al Kaline	12.00
GK	George Kell	8.00
JM	Jack Morris	5.00
AT	Alan Trammell	5.00

Yankee Clippings Memorabilia Autograph

		NM/M
Production 30 Sets		
YB	Yogi Berra	80.00
WF	Whitey Ford	60.00
RG	Ron Guidry	65.00
RJ	Reggie Jackson	50.00
DM	Don Mattingly	100.00
BM	Bobby Murcer	25.00
GN	Graig Nettles	40.00

Yankee Clippings Autograph

		NM/M
Production 30 Sets		
YB	Yogi Berra	80.00
WF	Whitey Ford	60.00
RG	Ron Guidry	65.00
RJ	Reggie Jackson	50.00
DM	Don Mattingly	100.00
BM	Bobby Murcer	25.00
GN	Graig Nettles	40.00

Yankee Clippings Memorabilia

		NM/M
Common Player:		8.00
YB	Yogi Berra	25.00
JD	Joe DiMaggio	75.00
WF	Whitey Ford	15.00
RG	Ron Guidry	15.00
RJ	Reggie Jackson	12.00
DM	Don Mattingly	15.00
TM	Thurman Munson	20.00
BM	Bobby Murcer	10.00
GN	Graig Nettles	8.00
BR	Babe Ruth	200.00

2006 Fleer Tradition

		NM/M
Complete Set (200):		35.00
Common Player:		.15
Hobby Pack (10):		2.00
Hobby Box (36):		60.00
1	Andruw Jones	.50
2	Chipper Jones	.75
3	John Smoltz	.25
4	Tim Hudson	.25
5	Joey Devine **RC**	.25
6	Chuck James **(RC)**	.25
7	Alay Soler **RC**	.50
8	Conor Jackson **(RC)**	.25
9	Luis Gonzalez	.15
10	Brandon Webb	.15
11	Chad Tracy	.15
12	Orlando Hudson	.15
13	Shawn Green	.15
14	Vladimir Guerrero	.75
15	Bartolo Colon	.15
16	Chone Figgins	.15
17	Garret Anderson	.15
18	Francisco Rodriguez	.15
19	Casey Kotchman	.15
20	Lance Berkman	.25
21	Craig Biggio	.25
22	Andy Pettitte	.25
23	Morgan Ensberg	.15
24	Brad Lidge	.15
25	Jered Weaver **(RC)**	1.00
26	Roy Oswalt	.25
27	Eric Chavez	.25
28	Rich Harden	.15
29	Cole Hamels **(RC)**	.25
30	Huston Street	.15
31	Bobby Crosby	.15
32	Nick Swisher	.25
33	Vernon Wells	.25
34	Roy Halladay	.25
35	A.J. Burnett	.15
36	Troy Glaus	.25
37	B.J. Ryan	.15
38	Bengie Molina	.15
39	Alex Rios	.15
40	Prince Fielder **(RC)**	2.00
41	Jose Capellan **(RC)**	.25
42	Rickie Weeks	.15
43	Ben Sheets	.25
44	Carlos Lee	.25
45	J.J. Hardy	.15
46	Albert Pujols	2.00
47	Skip Schumaker **(RC)**	.25
48	Adam Wainwright **(RC)**	.25
49	Jim Edmonds	.25
50	Scott Rolen	.75
51	Chris Carpenter	.25
52	David Eckstein	.15
53	Derrek Lee	.50
54	Jon Lester **(RC)**	3.00
55	Mark Prior	.40
56	Aramis Ramirez	.25
57	Juan Pierre	.15
58	Greg Maddux	1.50
59	Michael Barrett	.15
60	Carl Crawford	.15
61	Scott Kazmir	.25
62	Jorge Cantu	.15
63	Jonny Gomes	.15
64	Julio Lugo	.15
65	Aubrey Huff	.15
66	Jeff Kent	.25
67	Nomar Garciaparra	.75
68	Rafael Furcal	.15
69	Tim Hamulack **(RC)**	.25
70	Chad Billingsley **(RC)**	.25
71	Hong-Chih Kuo **(RC)**	.25
72	J.D. Drew	.15
73	Moises Alou	.25
74	Randy Winn	.15
75	Jason Schmidt	.25
76	Jeremy Accardo **RC**	.25
77	Matt Cain **(RC)**	.50
78	Joel Zumaya **(RC)**	.50
79	Travis Hafner	.50
80	Victor Martinez	.25
81	Grady Sizemore	.40
82	C.C. Sabathia	.15
83	Jhonny Peralta	.15
84	Jason Michaels	.15
85	Jeremy Sowers **(RC)**	.25
86	Ichiro Suzuki	1.50
87	Richie Sexson	.25
88	Adrian Beltre	.25
89	Felix Hernandez	.25
90	Kenji Johjima **RC**	3.00
91	Jeff Harris **RC**	.25
92	Taylor Buchholz **(RC)**	.25
93	Miguel Cabrera	.75
94	Dontrelle Willis	.25
95	Jeremy Hermida **(RC)**	.25
96	Mike Jacobs **(RC)**	.25
97	Josh Johnson **(RC)**	.25
98	Hanley Ramirez **(RC)**	.40
99	Josh Willingham **(RC)**	.25
100	Dan Uggla **(RC)**	.25
101	David Wright	1.00
102	Jose Reyes	.50
103	Pedro Martinez	.75
104	Carlos Beltran	.50
105	Carlos Delgado	.40
106	Billy Wagner	.25
107	Lastings Milledge **(RC)**	.50
108	Alfonso Soriano	.75
109	Jose Vidro	.15
110	Livan Hernandez	.15
111	Matthew Kemp **(RC)**	.25
112	Brandon Watson **(RC)**	.25
113	Ryan Zimmerman **(RC)**	2.00
114	Miguel Tejada	.50
115	Ramon Hernandez	.15
116	Brian Roberts	.15
117	Melvin Mora	.15
118	Erik Bedard	.15
119	Jay Gibbons	.15
120	Aaron Rakers **(RC)**	.25
121	Jake Peavy	.25
122	Brian Giles	.25
123	Khalil Greene	.15
124	Trevor Hoffman	.25
125	Josh Barfield **(RC)**	.25
126	Ben Johnson **(RC)**	.25
127	Ryan Howard	1.50
128	Bobby Abreu	.25
129	Chase Utley	.50
130	Pat Burrell	.25
131	Jimmy Rollins	.50
132	Brett Myers	.15
133	Mike Thompson **RC**	.25
134	Jason Bay	.40
135	Oliver Perez	.15
136	Matt Capps **(RC)**	.25
137	Paul Maholm **(RC)**	.25
138	Nate McLouth **(RC)**	.25
139	John Van Benschoten **(RC)**	.25
140	Mark Teixeira	.50
141	Michael Young	.25
142	Hank Blalock	.25
143	Kevin Millwood	.25
144	Laynce Nix	.15
145	Francisco Cordero	.15
146	Ian Kinsler **(RC)**	.25
147	David Ortiz	.75
148	Manny Ramirez	.75
149	Jason Varitek	.75
150	Curt Schilling	.75
151	Josh Beckett	.25
152	Coco Crisp	.15
153	Jonathan Papelbon **(RC)**	2.00
154	Ken Griffey Jr.	1.50
155	Adam Dunn	.50
156	Felipe Lopez	.15
157	Bronson Arroyo	.15
158	Ryan Freel	.15
159	Chris Denorfia **(RC)**	.25
160	Todd Helton	.50
161	Garrett Atkins	.15
162	Matt Holliday	.25
163	Clint Barmes	.15
164	Kendry Morales **(RC)**	.25
165	Ryan Shealy **(RC)**	.25
166	Josh Wilson **(RC)**	.25
167	Reggie Sanders	.15
168	Angel Berroa	.15
169	Mike Sweeney	.15
170	Mark Grudzielanek	.15
171	Jeremy Affeldt	.15
172	Steve Stemle **RC**	.50
173	Justin Verlander **(RC)**	2.00
174	Ivan Rodriguez	.50
175	Chris Shelton	.15
176	Jeremy Bonderman	.25
177	Magglio Ordonez	.15
178	Carlos Guillen	.15
179	Placido Polanco	.15
180	Johan Santana	.75
181	Torii Hunter	.25
182	Joe Nathan	.15
183	Joe Mauer	.50
184	David Gassner **(RC)**	.25
185	Jason Kubel **(RC)**	.25
186	Francisco Liriano **(RC)**	2.00
187	Jim Thome	.50
188	Paul Konerko	.40
189	Scott Podsednik	.25
190	Tadahito Iguchi	.25
191	A.J. Pierzynski	.15
192	Jose Contreras	.15
193	Brian Anderson **(RC)**	.25
194	Hideki Matsui	1.50
195	Wilbert Nieves **(RC)**	.25
196	Alex Rodriguez	1.00
197	Gary Sheffield	.25
198	Randy Johnson	.25
199	Johnny Damon	.40
200	Derek Jeter	1.00

Griffey Jr. 1989 Fleer Buyback Autograph

NM/M

Production 50

	Ken Griffey Jr.	250.00

Black & White

B&W (1-200): 2-3X

Printing Plates

No Pricing
Production one set per color.

Sepia Tone

Sepia (1-200): 2-3X

1934 Goudey Greats

		NM/M
Common Player:		2.00
GG-1	Andruw Jones	5.00
GG-2	Chipper Jones	8.00
GG-3	John Smoltz	4.00
GG-4	Tim Hudson	3.00
GG-5	Conor Jackson	2.00
GG-6	Luis Gonzalez	2.00
GG-7	Brandon Webb	3.00
GG-8	Vladimir Guerrero	8.00
GG-9	Bartolo Colon	2.00
GG-10	Lance Berkman	3.00
GG-11	Craig Biggio	4.00
GG-12	Andy Pettitte	3.00
GG-13	Morgan Ensberg	2.00
GG-14	Roy Oswalt	3.00
GG-15	Eric Chavez	3.00
GG-16	Rich Harden	3.00
GG-17	Huston Street	2.00
GG-18	Vernon Wells	3.00
GG-19	Roy Halladay	3.00
GG-20	Troy Glaus	3.00
GG-21	Prince Fielder	10.00
GG-22	Rickie Weeks	3.00
GG-23	Ben Sheets	3.00
GG-24	Carlos Lee	3.00
GG-25	Albert Pujols	20.00
GG-26	Jim Edmonds	4.00
GG-27	Scott Rolen	8.00
GG-28	Chris Carpenter	5.00
GG-29	Derrek Lee	5.00
GG-30	Mark Prior	5.00
GG-31	Greg Maddux	15.00
GG-32	Carl Crawford	4.00
GG-33	Scott Kazmir	3.00
GG-34	Jorge Cantu	2.00
GG-35	Jeff Kent	3.00
GG-36	Nomar Garciaparra	8.00
GG-37	J.D. Drew	2.00
GG-38	Randy Winn	2.00
GG-39	Jason Schmidt	3.00
GG-40	Travis Hafner	5.00
GG-41	Victor Martinez	3.00
GG-42	Grady Sizemore	4.00
GG-43	Jhonny Peralta	2.00
GG-44	Ichiro Suzuki	15.00
GG-45	Richie Sexson	4.00
GG-46	Felix Hernandez	4.00
GG-47	Kenji Johjima	10.00
GG-48	Miguel Cabrera	8.00
GG-49	Dontrelle Willis	4.00
GG-50	Josh Willingham	2.00
GG-51	David Wright	15.00
GG-52	Jose Reyes	5.00
GG-53	Pedro Martinez	8.00
GG-54	Carlos Beltran	5.00
GG-55	Alfonso Soriano	8.00
GG-56	Ryan Zimmerman	8.00
GG-57	Miguel Tejada	4.00
GG-58	Brian Roberts	2.00
GG-59	Jake Peavy	3.00
GG-60	Brian Giles	2.00
GG-61	Khalil Greene	2.00
GG-62	Ryan Howard	15.00
GG-63	Bobby Abreu	4.00
GG-64	Chase Utley	5.00
GG-65	Jimmy Rollins	5.00
GG-66	Jason Bay	4.00
GG-67	Mark Teixeira	5.00
GG-68	Michael Young	3.00
GG-69	Hank Blalock	3.00
GG-70	David Ortiz	8.00
GG-71	Manny Ramirez	8.00
GG-72	Curt Schilling	8.00
GG-73	Josh Beckett	3.00
GG-74	Jonathan Papelbon	10.00
GG-75	Ken Griffey Jr.	15.00
GG-76	Adam Dunn	5.00
GG-77	Todd Helton	4.00
GG-78	Garrett Atkins	2.00
GG-79	Matt Holliday	2.00
GG-80	Reggie Sanders	2.00
GG-81	Justin Verlander	10.00
GG-82	Ivan Rodriguez	5.00
GG-83	Chris Shelton	2.00
GG-84	Jeremy Bonderman	3.00
GG-85	Magglio Ordonez	2.00
GG-86	Johan Santana	6.00
GG-87	Torii Hunter	3.00
GG-88	Joe Nathan	2.00
GG-89	Joe Mauer	5.00
GG-90	Francisco Liriano	8.00
GG-91	Jim Thome	5.00
GG-92	Paul Konerko	4.00
GG-93	Scott Podsednik	3.00
GG-94	Tadahito Iguchi	4.00
GG-95	A.J. Pierzynski	2.00
GG-96	Hideki Matsui	12.00
GG-97	Alex Rodriguez	20.00
GG-98	Gary Sheffield	4.00
GG-99	Derek Jeter	25.00
GG-100	Jason Giambi	6.00

Blue Chip Prospects

		NM/M
Common Player:		.50
BC-1	Ryan Zimmerman	3.00
BC-2	Conor Jackson	.75
BC-3	Jonathan Papelbon	3.00
BC-4	Justin Verlander	3.00
BC-5	Jeremy Hermida	.75
BC-6	Josh Willingham	.50
BC-7	Hanley Ramirez	1.00
BC-8	Prince Fielder	3.00
BC-9	Francisco Liriano	2.00
BC-10	Lastings Milledge	2.00
BC-11	Jon Lester	2.00
BC-12	Matt Cain	1.50
BC-13	Adam Wainwright	.75
BC-14	Chuck James	1.00
BC-15	Kenji Johjima	3.00
BC-16	Josh Johnson	.75
BC-17	Josh Kubel	.50
BC-18	Brian Anderson	.50
BC-19	Cole Hamels	2.00
BC-20	Mike Jacobs	.50
BC-21	Jered Weaver	3.00
BC-22	Kendry Morales	.50
BC-23	Alay Soler	.50
BC-24	Chris Denorfia	.50
BC-25	Chad Billingsley	1.00

Diamond Tribute

		NM/M
Common Player:		.50
DT-1	Derek Jeter	3.00
DT-2	Ken Griffey Jr.	3.00
DT-3	Vladimir Guerrero	1.50
DT-4	Albert Pujols	3.00
DT-5	Derrek Lee	1.00
DT-6	David Ortiz	1.50
DT-7	Miguel Tejada	1.00
DT-8	Jim Thome	1.00
DT-9	Travis Hafner	1.00
DT-10	Grady Sizemore	1.00
DT-11	Chris Shelton	.50
DT-12	Dontrelle Willis	1.00
DT-13	Craig Biggio	1.00
DT-14	Roy Oswalt	1.00
DT-15	Prince Fielder	2.00
DT-16	David Wright	2.50
DT-17	Jose Reyes	1.00
DT-18	Hideki Matsui	2.00
DT-19	Rich Harden	.75
DT-20	Bobby Abreu	.75
DT-21	Jason Bay	1.00
DT-22	Jake Peavy	.75
DT-23	Felix Hernandez	.75
DT-24	Carl Crawford	.75
DT-25	Vernon Wells	.75

Grass Roots

		NM/M
Common Player:		.50
GR-1	Ken Griffey Jr.	2.50
GR-2	Albert Pujols	3.00
GR-3	Derek Jeter	3.00
GR-4	Derrek Lee	1.00
GR-5	Vladimir Guerrero	1.00
GR-6	Andruw Jones	1.00
GR-7	Manny Ramirez	1.00
GR-8	Johan Santana	1.00
GR-9	Victor Martinez	.75
GR-10	Todd Helton	1.00
GR-11	Ivan Rodriguez	1.00
GR-12	Miguel Cabrera	1.00
GR-13	Lance Berkman	.75
GR-14	Bartolo Colon	.50
GR-15	Jeff Kent	.50
GR-16	Carlos Lee	.75
GR-17	Torii Hunter	.50
GR-18	Carlos Beltran	1.00
GR-19	Alex Rodriguez	3.00
GR-20	Randy Johnson	1.00
GR-21	Eric Chavez	.50
GR-22	Ryan Howard	2.50
GR-23	Ichiro Suzuki	2.00
GR-24	Chris Carpenter	1.00
GR-25	Mark Teixeira	1.00

Signature Tradition

		NM/M
Inserted 1:1,269 Hobby		
CH	Craig Hansen	35.00
JM	Joe Mauer/SP	30.00

Traditional Threads

		NM/M
Common Player:		4.00
JB	Josh Barfield	4.00
BA	Jason Bay	8.00
EB	Erik Bedard	4.00
HB	Hank Blalock	6.00
SC	Sean Casey	4.00
JD	Johnny Damon	10.00
ZD	Zachary Duke	4.00
PF	Prince Fielder	15.00
CF	Chone Figgins	4.00
BG	Brian Giles	4.00
MG	Marcus Giles	4.00
GR	Khalil Greene	4.00
KG	Ken Griffey Jr.	15.00
VG	Vladimir Guerrero	8.00
JH	Jeremy Hermida	6.00
FH	Felix Hernandez	6.00
LH	Livan Hernandez	4.00
GJ	Geoff Jenkins	4.00
DJ	Derek Jeter	20.00
CK	Casey Kotchman/SP	4.00
CL	Carlos Lee	6.00
DL	Derrek Lee	8.00
JL	Javy Lopez	4.00
GM	Greg Maddux	10.00
MM	Melvin Mora	4.00
DO	David Ortiz	10.00
RO	Roy Oswalt	6.00
JP	Jake Peavy	6.00
AP	Albert Pujols	20.00
AR	Aramis Ramirez	6.00
AS	Alfonso Soriano	8.00
BR	Brian Roberts	6.00
BS	Ben Sheets	6.00
TE	Mark Teixeira	8.00
MT	Miguel Tejada	6.00
JV	Jose Vidro	4.00
OV	Omar Vizquel	6.00
RW	Rickie Weeks	6.00
MY	Michael Young	6.00
CZ	Carlos Zambrano	4.00
RZ	Ryan Zimmerman	15.00

Triple Crown Contenders

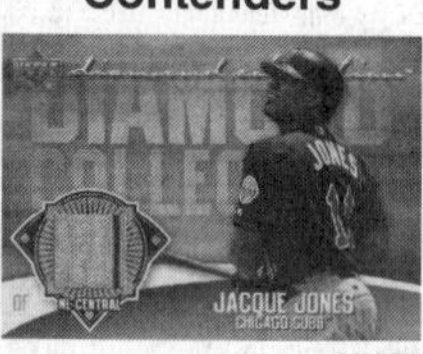

		NM/M
Common Player:		.75
TC-1	Albert Pujols	3.00
TC-2	Derrek Lee	.75
TC-3	Manny Ramirez	1.00
TC-4	David Ortiz	1.00
TC-5	Mark Teixeira	.75
TC-6	Alex Rodriguez	3.00
TC-7	Andruw Jones	.75
TC-8	Todd Helton	.75
TC-9	Vladimir Guerrero	1.00
TC-10	Miguel Cabrera	1.00
TC-11	Hideki Matsui	2.00
TC-12	Travis Hafner	.75
TC-13	David Wright	2.00
TC-14	Ken Griffey Jr.	2.50
TC-15	Jason Bay	.75

2007 Fleer

		NM/M
Complete Set (400):		75.00
Common Player:		.15
Hobby Pack (10):		1.50
Hobby Box (36):		50.00
Rack Pack (52):		4.50
Rack Box (18):		75.00
1	Chad Cordero	.15
2	Alfonso Soriano	.50
3	Nick Johnson	.15
4	Austin Kearns	.15
5	Ramon Ortiz	.15
6	Brian Schneider	.15
7	Ryan Zimmerman	.40
8	Jose Vidro	.15
9	Felipe Lopez	.15
10	Cristian Guzman	.15
11	B.J. Ryan	.15
12	Alex Rios	.25
13	Vernon Wells	.25
14	Roy Halladay	.25
15	A.J. Burnett	.15
16	Lyle Overbay	.25
17	Troy Glaus	.25
18	Bengie Molina	.15
19	Gustavo Chacin	.15
20	Aaron Hill	.15
21	Vicente Padilla	.15
22	Kevin Millwood	.15
23	Akinori Otsuka	.15
24	Adam Eaton	.15
25	Hank Blalock	.25
26	Mark Teixeira	.40
27	Michael Young	.25
28	Mark DeRosa	.15
29	Gary Matthews	.15
30	Ian Kinsler	.15
31	Carlos Lee	.25
32	James Shields	.15
33	Scott Kazmir	.25
34	Carl Crawford	.25
35	Jonny Gomes	.15
36	Tim Corcoran	.15
37	B.J. Upton	.25
38	Rocco Baldelli	.25
39	Jae Weong Seo	.15
40	Jorge Cantu	.15
41	Ty Wigginton	.15
42	Chris Carpenter	.40
43	Albert Pujols	1.50
44	Scott Rolen	.50
45	Jim Edmonds	.40
46	Jason Isringhausen	.15
47	Yadier Molina	.15
48	Adam Wainwright	.25
49	Mark Mulder	.25
50	Jason Marquis	.15
51	Juan Encarnacion	.15
52	Aaron Miles	.15
53	Ichiro Suzuki	1.00
54	Felix Hernandez	.40
55	Kenji Johjima	.25
56	Richie Sexson	.40
57	Yuniesky Betancourt	.15
58	J.J. Putz	.15
59	Jarrod Washburn	.15
60	Ben Broussard	.15
61	Adrian Beltre	.25
62	Raul Ibanez	.15
63	Jose Lopez	.15
64	Matt Cain	.25
65	Noah Lowry	.15
66	Jason Schmidt	.25
67	Pedro Feliz	.15
68	Matt Morris	.15
69	Ray Durham	.15
70	Steve Finley	.15
71	Randy Winn	.15
72	Moises Alou	.25
73	Eliezer Alfonzo	.15
74	Armando Benitez	.15
75	Omar Vizquel	.25
76	Chris Young	.25
77	Adrian Gonzalez	.25
78	Khalil Greene	.15
79	Mike Piazza	.75
80	Josh Barfield	.25
81	Brian Giles	.25
82	Jake Peavy	.25
83	Trevor Hoffman	.25
84	Mike Cameron	.15
85	Dave Roberts	.15
86	David Wells	.15
87	Zachary Duke	.15
88	Ian Snell	.15
89	Jason Bay	.40
90	Freddy Sanchez	.15
91	Jack Wilson	.15
92	Tom Gorzelanny	.15
93	Chris Duffy	.15
94	Jose Castillo	.15
95	Matt Capps	.15
96	Mike Gonzalez	.15
97	Chase Utley	.50
98	Jimmy Rollins	.50
99	Aaron Rowand	.15
100	Ryan Howard	1.00
101	Cole Hamels	.50
102	Pat Burrell	.25
103	Shane Victorino	.15
104	Jamie Moyer	.15
105	Mike Lieberthal	.15
106	Tom Gordon	.15
107	Brett Myers	.25
108	Nick Swisher	.25
109	Barry Zito	.25
110	Jason Kendall	.15
111	Milton Bradley	.25
112	Bobby Crosby	.15
113	Huston Street	.15
114	Eric Chavez	.25
115	Frank Thomas	.40
116	Danny Haren	.25
117	Jay Payton	.15
118	Randy Johnson	.50
119	Mike Mussina	.40
120	Bobby Abreu	.40
121	Jason Giambi	.40
122	Derek Jeter	1.50
123	Alex Rodriguez	1.50
124	Jorge Posada	.40
125	Robinson Cano	.40
126	Mariano Rivera	.40
127	Chien-Ming Wang	.40
128	Hideki Matsui	1.00
129	Gary Sheffield	.40
130	Lastings Milledge	.25
131	Tom Glavine	.25
132	Billy Wagner	.25
133	Pedro Martinez	.50
134	Paul LoDuca	.15
135	Carlos Delgado	.40
136	Carlos Beltran	.40
137	David Wright	.75
138	Jose Reyes	.50
139	Julio Franco	.15
140	Michael Cuddyer	.15
141	Justin Morneau	.40
142	Johan Santana	.50
143	Francisco Liriano	.25
144	Joe Mauer	.25
145	Torii Hunter	.25
146	Luis Castillo	.15
147	Joe Nathan	.15
148	Carlos Silva	.15
149	Boof Bonser	.15
150	Ben Sheets	.25
151	Prince Fielder	.50
152	Bill Hall	.25
153	Rickie Weeks	.25
154	Geoff Jenkins	.15
155	Kevin Mench	.15
156	Francisco Cordero	.15
157	Chris Capuano	.15
158	Brady Clark	.15
159	Tony Gwynn Jr.	.15
160	Chad Billingsley	.25
161	Russell Martin	.25
162	Wilson Betemit	.15
163	Nomar Garciaparra	.50
164	Kenny Lofton	.15
165	Rafael Furcal	.25
166	Julio Lugo	.15
167	Brad Penny	.15
168	Jeff Kent	.25
169	Greg Maddux	1.00
170	Derek Lowe	.15
171	Andre Ethier	.25
172	Chone Figgins	.15
173	Francisco Rodriguez	.25
174	Garret Anderson	.15
175	Orlando Cabrera	.25
176	Adam Kennedy	.15
177	John Lackey	.25
178	Vladimir Guerrero	.50
179	Bartolo Colon	.25
180	Jered Weaver	.25
181	Juan Rivera	.15
182	Howie Kendrick	.25
183	Ervin Santana	.25
184	Mark Redman	.15
185	David DeJesus	.15
186	Joey Gathright	.15
187	Mike Sweeney	.15
188	Mark Teahen	.15
189	Angel Berroa	.15
190	Ambiorix Burgos	.15
191	Luke Hudson	.15
192	Mark Grudzielanek	.15
193	Roger Clemens	1.50
194	Willy Taveras	.15
195	Craig Biggio	.25
196	Andy Pettitte	.25
197	Roy Oswalt	.40
198	Lance Berkman	.40
199	Morgan Ensberg	.25
200	Brad Lidge	.15
201	Chris Burke	.15
202	Miguel Cabrera	.50
203	Dontrelle Willis	.25
204	Josh Johnson	.15
205	Ricky Nolasco	.15
206	Dan Uggla	.15
207	Jeremy Hermida	.15
208	Scott Olsen	.25
209	Josh Willingham	.15
210	Joe Borowski	.15
211	Hanley Ramirez	.40
212	Mike Jacobs	.15
213	Kenny Rogers	.15
214	Justin Verlander	.40
215	Ivan Rodriguez	.40
216	Magglio Ordonez	.15
217	Todd Jones	.15
218	Joel Zumaya	.25
219	Jeremy Bonderman	.40
220	Nate Robertson	.15
221	Brandon Inge	.15
222	Craig Monroe	.15
223	Carlos Guillen	.15
224	Jeff Francis	.15
225	Brian Fuentes	.15
226	Todd Helton	.40
227	Matt Holliday	.25
228	Garrett Atkins	.25
229	Clint Barmes	.15
230	Jason Jennings	.15
231	Aaron Cook	.15
232	Brad Hawpe	.25
233	Cory Sullivan	.15
234	Aaron Boone	.15
235	C.C. Sabathia	.25
236	Grady Sizemore	.50
237	Travis Hafner	.40
238	Jhonny Peralta	.15
239	Jake Westbrook	.15
240	Jeremy Sowers	.15
241	Andy Marte	.15
242	Victor Martinez	.25
243	Jason Michaels	.15
244	Cliff Lee	.15
245	Bronson Arroyo	.15
246	Aaron Harang	.15
247	Ken Griffey Jr.	1.00
248	Adam Dunn	.40
249	Rich Aurilia	.15
250	Eric Milton	.15
251	David Ross	.15
252	Brandon Phillips	.15
253	Ryan Freel	.15
254	Eddie Guardado	.15
255	Jose Contreras	.15
256	Freddy Garcia	.15
257	Jon Garland	.15
258	Mark Buehrle	.25
259	Bobby Jenks	.15
260	Paul Konerko	.25
261	Jermaine Dye	.15
262	Joe Crede	.25
263	Jim Thome	.40
264	Javier Vazquez	.15
265	A.J. Pierzynski	.15
266	Tadahito Iguchi	.15
267	Carlos Zambrano	.40
268	Derrek Lee	.40
269	Aramis Ramirez	.40
270	Ryan Theriot	.15
271	Juan Pierre	.25
272	Rich Hill	.15
273	Ryan Dempster	.15
274	Jacque Jones	.15
275	Mark Prior	.25
276	Kerry Wood	.25
277	Josh Beckett	.25
278	David Ortiz	.50
279	Kevin Youkilis	.15
280	Jason Varitek	.40
281	Manny Ramirez	.50
282	Curt Schilling	.50

No.	Player	Price
283	Jon Lester	.25
284	Jonathan Papelbon	.50
285	Alex Gonzalez	.15
286	Mike Lowell	.15
287	Kyle Snyder	.15
288	Miguel Tejada	.40
289	Erik Bedard	.25
290	Ramon Hernandez	.15
291	Melvin Mora	.15
292	Nicholas Markakis	.25
293	Brian Roberts	.25
294	Corey Patterson	.15
295	Kris Benson	.15
296	Jay Gibbons	.15
297	Rodrigo Lopez	.15
298	Chris Ray	.15
299	Andruw Jones	.50
300	Brian McCann	.40
301	Jeff Francoeur	.25
302	Chuck James	.25
303	John Smoltz	.40
304	Bob Wickman	.15
305	Edgar Renteria	.25
306	Adam LaRoche	.25
307	Marcus Giles	.15
308	Tim Hudson	.25
309	Chipper Jones	.50
310	Miguel Batista	.15
311	Claudio Vargas	.15
312	Brandon Webb	.25
313	Luis Gonzalez	.15
314	Livan Hernandez	.15
315	Stephen Drew	.25
316	Johnny Estrada	.15
317	Orlando Hudson	.15
318	Conor Jackson	.15
319	Chad Tracy	.15
320	Carlos Quentin	.25
321	Alvin Colina **RC**	.50
322	Miguel Montero **(RC)**	.25
323	Jeff Fiorentino **(RC)**	.25
324	Jeff Baker **(RC)**	.25
325	Brian Burres **(RC)**	.25
326	David Murphy **(RC)**	.25
327	Francisco Cruceta **(RC)**	.25
328	Beltran Perez **(RC)**	.25
329	Scott Moore **(RC)**	.25
330	Sean Henn **(RC)**	.25
331	Ryan Sweeney **(RC)**	.25
332	Josh Fields **(RC)**	.25
333	Jerry Owens **(RC)**	.25
334	Vinny Rottino **(RC)**	.25
335	Kevin Kouzmanoff **(RC)**	.50
336	Alexi Casilla **RC**	.50
337	Justin Hampson **(RC)**	.25
338	Troy Tulowitzki **(RC)**	.50
339	Jose Garcia **RC**	.50
340	Andrew Miller **RC**	2.00
341	Glen Perkins **(RC)**	.25
342	Ubaldo Jimenez **(RC)**	.25
343	Doug Slaten **RC**	.50
344	Angel Sanchez **RC**	.50
345	Mitch Maier **RC**	.50
346	Ryan Braun **(RC)**	.50
347	Joselo Diaz **(RC)**	.25
348	Delwyn Young **(RC)**	.25
349	Kevin Hooper **(RC)**	.25
350	Dennis Sarfate **(RC)**	.25
351	Andy Cannizaro **RC**	.50
352	Devern Hansack **RC**	1.00
353	Michael Bourn **(RC)**	.50
354	Carlos Maldonado **(RC)**	.25
355	Shane Youman **RC**	.50
356	Philip Humber **(RC)**	.50
357	Hector Gimenez **(RC)**	.25
358	Fred Lewis **(RC)**	.25
359	Ryan Feierabend **(RC)**	.25
360	Juan Morillo **(RC)**	.25
361	Travis Chick **(RC)**	.25
362	Oswaldo Navarro **RC**	.50
363	Cesar Jimenez **RC**	.50
364	Brian Stokes **(RC)**	.25
365	Delmon Young **(RC)**	.50
366	Juan Salas **(RC)**	.25
367	Shawn Riggans **(RC)**	.25
368	Adam Lind **(RC)**	.50
369	Joaquin Arias **(RC)**	.25
370	Eric Stults **RC**	.50
371	Brandon Webb	.25
372	John Smoltz	.50
373	Miguel Tejada	.50
374	David Ortiz	1.00
375	Carlos Zambrano	.50
376	Jermaine Dye	.25
377	Ken Griffey Jr.	1.50
378	Victor Martinez	.25
379	Todd Helton	.50
380	Ivan Rodriguez	.50
381	Miguel Cabrera	.50
382	Lance Berkman	.50
383	Mike Sweeney	.25
384	Vladimir Guerrero	.50
385	Derek Lowe	.25
386	Bill Hall	.25
387	Johan Santana	.75
388	Carlos Beltran	.75
389	Derek Jeter	2.00
390	Nick Swisher	.50
391	Ryan Howard	1.50
392	Jason Bay	.50
393	Trevor Hoffman	.25
394	Omar Vizquel	.25
395	Ichiro Suzuki	1.00
396	Albert Pujols	2.00
397	Carl Crawford	.50
398	Mark Teixeira	.50
399	Roy Halladay	.25
400	Ryan Zimmerman	.50

Printing Plates

No Pricing
Production one set per color.

Mini Die-Cuts

Mini: 1.5-2X
Inserted 1:2
Mini Gold: No Pricing
Inserted 1:576

Autographics

Inserted 1:720

Crowning Achievement

		NM/M
Common Player:		.50
Inserted 1:5		
AP	Albert Pujols	3.00
BZ	Barry Zito	.50
CD	Carlos Delgado	.75
CS	Curt Schilling	.75
DJ	Derek Jeter	3.00
DO	David Ortiz	1.00
FT	Frank Thomas	.75
GM	Greg Maddux	2.00
IS	Ichiro Suzuki	2.00
JS	Johan Santana	.75
JT	Jim Thome	.75
KG	Ken Griffey Jr.	2.00
MC	Miguel Cabrera	1.00
MP	Mike Piazza	1.00
MR	Manny Ramirez	1.00
PM	Pedro Martinez	1.00
RC	Roger Clemens	2.50
RH	Ryan Howard	2.00
TG	Tom Glavine	.75
TH	Trevor Hoffman	.50

Fresh Ink

		NM/M
Inserted 1:720		
BB	Brandon Backe	15.00
BW	Brian Wilson	20.00
CB	Clint Barmes	20.00
CC	Craig Counsell	20.00
GQ	Guillermo Quiroz	15.00
JB	Joe Blanton	15.00
JV	John Van Benschoten	10.00
LN	Leo Nunez	10.00
MM	Matt Murton	25.00
SR	Saul Rivera	15.00

Genuine Coverage

		NM/M
Inserted 1:720		
AP	Albert Pujols	25.00
AS	Alfonso Soriano	20.00
BR	Brian Roberts	15.00
DW	Dontrelle Willis	8.00
ES	Johnny Estrada	8.00
JB	Josh Beckett	15.00
JE	Jim Edmonds	15.00
JM	Justin Morneau	15.00
JT	Jim Thome	15.00
LB	Lance Berkman	10.00
RC	Robinson Cano	20.00
SM	John Smoltz	15.00
VG	Vladimir Guerrero	15.00

In the Zone

		NM/M
Common Player:		1.00
Inserted 1:10		
AJ	Andruw Jones	1.00
AP	Albert Pujols	3.00
AR	Alex Rodriguez	2.50
DO	David Ortiz	1.50
DW	David Wright	1.50
KG	Ken Griffey Jr.	2.00
MC	Miguel Cabrera	1.00
MT	Mark Teixeira	1.00
RH	Ryan Howard	2.00
VG	Vladimir Guerrero	1.00

Perfect 10

		NM/M
Common Player:		.50
Inserted 1:5		
CC	Carl Crawford	.75
DO	David Ortiz	1.50
DJ	Derek Jeter	3.00
IR	Ivan Rodriguez	.75
JD	Jermaine Dye	.50
JS	Johan Santana	1.00
MM	Mike Mussina	.75
MY	Michael Young	.75
RH	Roy Halladay	.50
VG	Vladimir Guerrero	1.00
AP	Albert Pujols	3.00
AS	Alfonso Soriano	1.00
BH	Bill Hall	.50
CB	Carlos Beltran	1.00
CJ	Chipper Jones	1.00
CU	Chase Utley	1.00
JB	Jason Bay	.75
MC	Miguel Cabrera	1.00
RC	Roger Clemens	2.50
RH	Ryan Howard	2.00

Rookie Sensations

		NM/M
Common Player:		.50
Inserted 1:1		
BB	Boof Bonser	.50
CB	Chad Billingsley	1.00
CH	Cole Hamels	1.50
CJ	Conor Jackson	.75
DU	Dan Uggla	.50
FL	Francisco Liriano	1.00
HR	Hanley Ramirez	1.00
IK	Ian Kinsler	.75
JB	Josh Barfield	.75
JH	Jeremy Hermida	.50
JJ	Josh Johnson	.50
JL	Jon Lester	1.00
JP	Jonathan Papelbon	2.00
JS	Jeremy Sowers	.50
JV	Justin Verlander	2.00
JW	Jered Weaver	1.00
KJ	Kenji Johjima	.75
LO	James Loney	.75
MK	Matthew Kemp	.75
NM	Nicholas Markakis	1.00
PF	Prince Fielder	1.50
RG	Matt Garza	1.00
RN	Ricky Nolasco	.50
RZ	Ryan Zimmerman	2.00
SO	Scott Olsen	.75

Soaring Stars

		NM/M
Common Player:		.50
Inserted 1:2 Rack Packs		
AD	Adam Dunn	.75
AJ	Andruw Jones	1.00
AL	Alex Rodriguez	2.50
AP	Albert Pujols	3.00
AR	Alex Rios	.50
AS	Alfonso Soriano	1.00
BW	Brandon Webb	.50
BZ	Barry Zito	.50
CB	Carlos Beltran	1.00
CJ	Chipper Jones	1.00
CU	Chase Utley	1.00
DA	Johnny Damon	1.00
DJ	Derek Jeter	3.00
DL	Derrek Lee	1.00
DO	David Ortiz	1.00
DW	David Wright	1.50
HA	Roy Halladay	.50
IR	Ivan Rodriguez	.75
IS	Ichiro Suzuki	2.00
JB	Jason Bay	.75
JD	Jermaine Dye	.50
JG	Jon Garland	.50
JM	Joe Mauer	.75
JS	Johan Santana	1.00
JV	Justin Verlander	1.00
KG	Ken Griffey Jr.	2.00
LB	Lance Berkman	.75
MC	Miguel Cabrera	1.00
MP	Mike Piazza	1.50
MR	Manny Ramirez	1.00
MT	Mark Teixeira	.75
NG	Nomar Garciaparra	1.00
PF	Prince Fielder	1.00
PM	Pedro Martinez	1.00
RH	Ryan Howard	2.00
RI	Mariano Rivera	.75
RO	Roy Oswalt	.75
TE	Miguel Tejada	.75
TG	Tom Glavine	.75
TH	Travis Hafner	.75
VG	Vladimir Guerrero	1.00
WI	Dontrelle Willis	.75

Year in Review

		NM/M
Common Player:		.50
Inserted 1:5		
AP	Albert Pujols	3.00
AR	Alex Rodriguez	2.50
AS	Alfonso Soriano	1.00
BA	Bobby Abreu	1.00
CU	Chase Utley	1.00
DJ	Derek Jeter	3.00
DO	David Ortiz	1.00
FL	Francisco Liriano	.75
FS	Freddy Sanchez	.50
HO	Ryan Howard	2.00
JD	Jermaine Dye	.50
JM	Joe Mauer	.75
JR	Jose Reyes	1.00
JV	Justin Verlander	1.00
JW	Jered Weaver	1.00
KG	Ken Griffey Jr.	2.00
MD	Mark DeRosa	.50
MO	Justin Morneau	1.00
RH	Roy Halladay	.50
TH	Travis Hafner	.75

1992 Flopps Promos

Prior to the 1992 season, Pro Set announced plans to produce a set of 66 cards parodying contemporary baseball stars and teams. The name "Flopps" was used instead of Pro Set, which does not appear anywhere on the cards. While the announced checklist included players such as Craig Piggio, George Brat and Cal Ripped-One, only five promo cards were produced before the Players Union whined and the idea was dropped. Pro Set didn't want to offend the union at the time because they were attempting to get a baseball card license. Cards pictured caricatures of the players on front and funny biographies on back, all in color in the standard 2-1/2" x 3-1/2" format.

		NM/M
Complete Set (5):		6.00
Common Player:		.50
(1)	Barry Bones	4.00
(2)	Wade Bugs	2.50
(3)	Ken Groovy, Jr.	3.00
(4)	Stickey Henderson	1.50
(5)	Lance Perishable	.50

1993 Florida Agriculture Dept. Braves/Marlins

A pair of eight-card team panels of the Atlanta Braves and Florida Marlins was issued by the Florida Department of Agriculture and Consumer Services to promote the state's fruit and vegetable products. Individual cards show the player posing - sometimes comically - with one of the state's agricultural products. The photos are bordered in team colors and have a "Fresh 2 U" logo in the upper-left consisting of a fruit or vegetable superimposed on a ball diamond and crossed bats. Backs have the player's name, uniform number, and a short career summary at top. In center is a baseball with the result of an at-bat. In the bottom panel is a statistic about one of the state's crops. A card number is at top. Individual cards measure the standard 2-1/2" x 3-1/2", with the eight-card perforated sheets measuring 10" x 7". The card sheets were distributed during the Sunshine State Games in Tallahassee.

		NM/M
Complete Set (16):		18.00
Common Player:		1.00
Atlanta Braves Team Set:		10.00
1	Team Logo Card	1.00
2	Steve Avery	1.00
3	Jeff Blauser	1.00
4	Sid Bream	1.00
5	Tom Glavine	4.00
6	Mark Lemke	1.00
7	Greg Olson	1.00
8	Terry Pendleton	1.00
Florida Marlins Team Set:		9.00
1	Team Logo Card	1.00
2	Billy the Marlin (Mascot)	1.00
3	Ryan Bowen	1.00
4	Benito Santiago	1.00
5	Richie Lewis	1.00
6	Bret Barbarie	1.00
7	Rich Renteria	1.00
8	Jeff Conine	1.00

1987 Red Foley Stickers

Individual player stickers were inserted in sheets within the pages of "Red Foley's Best Baseball Book Ever." The 8-1/2" x 11", 96-page softbound book offered games, quizzes and trivia, with a space to put each sticker. Individual stickers measure about 1-3/8" x 1-3/4". Stickers have color photos on front with a number in the white border at bottom. Player identification does not appear on the sticker. Cover price of the book in 1987 was about $7.

		NM/M
Complete Book:		9.00
Complete Sticker Set (130):		7.50
Common Player:		.05
1	Julio Franco	.05
2	Willie Randolph	.05
3	Jesse Barfield	.05
4	Mike Witt	.05
5	Orel Hershiser	.05
6	Dwight Gooden	.05
7	Dan Quisenberry	.05
8	Vince Coleman	.05
9	Rich Gossage	.05
10	Kirk Gibson	.05
11	Joaquin Andujar	.05
12	Dave Concepcion	.05
13	Andre Dawson	.25
14	Tippy Martinez	.05
15	Bob James	.05
16	Ryne Sandberg	1.00
17	Bob Knepper	.05
18	Bob Stanley	.05
19	Jim Presley	.05
20	Greg Gross	.05
21	Bob Horner	.05
22	Paul Molitor	.75
23	Kirby Puckett	1.00
24	Scott Garrelts	.05
25	Tony Pena	.05
26	Charlie Hough	.05
27	Joe Carter	.05
28	Dave Winfield	.75
29	Tony Fernandez	.05
30	Bobby Grich	.05
31	Mike Marshall	.05
32	Keith Hernandez	.05
33	Dennis Leonard	.05
34	John Tudor	.05
35	Kevin McReynolds	.05
36	Lance Parrish	.05
37	Carney Lansford	.05
38	Buddy Bell	.05
39	Tim Raines	.05
40	Mike Boddicker	.05
41	Carlton Fisk	.75
42	Lee Smith	.05
43	Glenn Davis	.05
44	Jim Rice	.25
45	Mark Langston	.05
46	Mike Schmidt	1.50
47	Dale Murphy	.45
48	Cecil Cooper	.05
49	Kent Hrbek	.05
50	Will Clark	.10
51	Johnny Ray	.05
52	Darrell Porter	.05
53	Brook Jacoby	.05
54	Ron Guidry	.05
55	Lloyd Moseby	.05
56	Donnie Moore	.05
57	Fernando Valenzuela	.05
58	Darryl Strawberry	.05
59	Hal McRae	.05
60	Tommy Herr	.05
61	Steve Garvey	.35
62	Alan Trammell	.05
63	Jose Canseco	.50
64	Pete Rose	1.75
65	Jeff Reardon	.05
66	Eddie Murray	.75
67	Ozzie Guillen	.05
68	Jody Davis	.05
69	Bill Doran	.05
70	Roger Clemens	1.25
71	Alvin Davis	.05
72	Von Hayes	.05
73	Zane Smith	.05
74	Ted Higuera	.05
75	Tom Brunansky	.05
76	Chili Davis	.05
77	R.J. Reynolds	.05
78	Oddibe McDowell	.05
79	Brett Butler	.05
80	Rickey Henderson	.75
81	Dave Steib	.05
82	Wally Joyner	.05
83	Pedro Guerrero	.05
84	Jesse Orosco	.05
85	Steve Balboni	.05
86	Willie McGee	.05
87	Graig Nettles	.05
88	Lou Whitaker	.05
89	Jay Howell	.05
90	Dave Parker	.05
91	Hubie Brooks	.05
92	Rick Dempsey	.05
93	Neil Allen	.05
94	Shawon Dunston	.05
95	Jose Cruz	.05
96	Wade Boggs	1.00
97	Danny Tartabull	.05
98	Steve Bedrosian	.05
99	Ken Oberkfell	.05
100	Ben Oglivie	.05
101	Bert Blyleven	.05
102	Jeff Leonard	.05
103	Rick Rhoden	.05
104	Larry Parrish	.05
105	Tony Bernazard	.05
106	Don Mattingly	1.50
107	Willie Upshaw	.05
108	Reggie Jackson	1.00
109	Bill Madlock	.05
110	Gary Carter	.75
111	George Brett	1.50
112	Ozzie Smith	1.00
113	Tony Gwynn	1.00
114	Jack Morris	.05
115	Dave Kingman	.05
116	John Franco	.05
117	Tim Wallach	.05
118	Cal Ripken Jr.	2.00
119	Harold Baines	.05
120	Leon Durham	.05
121	Nolan Ryan	2.00
122	Dennis (Oil Can) Boyd	.05
123	Matt Young	.05
124	Shane Rawley	.05
125	Bruce Sutter	.65
126	Robin Yount	.75
127	Frank Viola	.05
128	Vida Blue	.05
129	Rick Reuschel	.05
130	Pete Incaviglia	.05

1988 Red Foley Stickers

Identical in format to the previous year's issues, the 104 player and 26 team logo stickers in this set were bound into a 96-page, 8-1/2" x 11" softbound book titled "Red Foley's Best Baseball Book Ever." Each 1-3/8" x 1-3/4" sticker could be placed in the book as an answer to trivia questions, quizzes, games, etc. Stickers have color player photos with a number in the white border at bottom. There is no player identification on the stickers. Original issue price was about $8.

		NM/M
Complete Book:		9.00
Complete Sticker Set (130):		6.00
Common Player:		.05
1	Mike Aldrete	.05
2	Andy Ashby	.05
3	Harold Baines	.05
4	Floyd Bannister	.05
5	Buddy Bell	.05
6	George Bell	.05
7	Barry Bonds	2.00
8	Scott Bradley	.05
9	Bob Brower	.05
10	Ellis Burks	.05
11	Casey Candaele	.05
12	Jack Clark	.05
13	Roger Clemens	1.25
14	Kal Daniels	.05
15	Eric Davis	.05
16	Mike Davis	.05
17	Andre Dawson	.25
18	Rob Deer	.05
19	Brian Downing	.05
20	Doug Drabek	.05
21	Dwight Evans	.05
22	Sid Fernandez	.05
23	Carlton Fisk	.75
24	Scott Fletcher	.05
25	Julio Franco	.05
26	Gary Gaetti	.05
27	Ken Gerhardt	.05
28	Ken Griffey	.05
29	Pedro Guerrero	.05
30	Billy Hatcher	.05
31	Mike Heath	.05
32	Neal Heaton	.05
33	Tom Henke	.05
34	Larry Herndon	.05
35	Brian Holton	.05
36	Glenn Hubbard	.05
37	Bruce Hurst	.05
38	Bo Jackson	.10
39	Michael Jackson	.05
40	Howard Johnson	.05
41	Wally Joyner	.05
42	Jimmy Key	.05
43	Ray Knight	.05
44	John Kruk	.05
45	Mike Krukow	.05
46	Mark Langston	.05
47	Gene Larkin	.05
48	Jeff Leonard	.05
49	Bill Long	.05
50	Fred Lynn	.05
51	Dave Magadan	.05
52	Joe Magrane	.05
53	Don Mattingly	1.50
54	Fred McGriff	.05
55	Mark McGwire	1.75
56	Kevin McReynolds	.05
57	Dave Meads	.05
58	Keith Moreland	.05
59	Dale Murphy	.30
60	Juan Nieves	.05
61	Paul Noce	.05
62	Matt Nokes	.05
63	Pete O'Brien	.05
64	Paul O'Neill	.05
65	Lance Parrish	.05
66	Larry Parrish	.05
67	Tony Pena	.05
68	Terry Pendleton	.05
69	Ken Phelps	.05
70	Dan Plesac	.05
71	Luis Polonia	.05
72	Kirby Puckett	1.00
73	Jeff Reardon	.05
74	Rick Rhoden	.05
75	Dave Righetti	.05
76	Cal Ripken Jr.	2.00
77	Bret Saberhagen	.05
78	Benito Santiago	.05
79	Mike Schmidt	1.50
80	Dick Schofield	.05
81	Mike Scott	.05
82	John Smiley	.05
83	Cory Snyder	.05
84	Franklin Stubbs	.05
85	B.J. Surhoff	.05
86	Rick Sutcliffe	.05
87	Pat Tabler	.05
88	Jose Tartabull (Danny)	.05
89	Garry Templeton	.05
90	Walt Terrell	.05
91	Andre Thornton	.05
92	Andy Van Slyke	.05
93	Ozzie Virgil	.05
94	Tim Wallach	.05
95	Gary Ward	.05
96	Mark Wasinger	.05
97	Mitch Webster	.05
98	Bob Welch	.05
99	Devon White	.05
100	Frank White	.05
101	Ed Whitson	.05
102	Bill Wilkinson	.05
103	Glenn Wilson	.05
104	Curt Young	.05
105	Braves Logo	.05
106	Phillies Logo	.05
107	Padres Logo	.05
108	Giants Logo	.05
109	Orioles Logo	.05
110	Tigers Logo	.05
111	Pirates Logo	.05
112	Royals Logo	.05
113	Astros Logo	.05
114	Indians Logo	.05
115	Brewers Logo	.05
116	Cardinals Logo	.05
117	White Sox Logo	.05
118	Blue Jays Logo	.05
119	Red Sox Logo	.05
120	Athletics Logo	.05
121	Cubs Logo	.05
122	Mariners Logo	.05
123	Rangers Logo	.05
124	Dodgers Logo	.05
125	Yankees Logo	.05
126	Mets Logo	.05
127	Twins Logo	.05
128	Expos Logo	.05
129	Angels Logo	.05
130	Reds Logo	.05

1989 Red Foley Stickers

In its third consecutive year of publication, "Red Foley's Best Baseball Book Ever" retained its 96-page softbound 8-1/2" x 11" format of trivia, quizzes and games to be illustrated by placing one of 130 player stickers in the book. Individual stickers are 1-3/8" x 1-3/4" and feature color photos with a white border. Sticker number appears in the bottom-right. There is no player identification on the sticker. Original price of the book was about $8.

		NM/M
Complete Book:		9.00
Complete Sticker Set (130):		7.50
Common Player:		.05
1	Doyle Alexander	.05
2	Luis Alicea	.05
3	Roberto Alomar	.15
4	Andy Ashby	.05
5	Floyd Bannister	.05
6	Jesse Barfield	.05
7	George Bell	.05
8	Wade Boggs	1.00
9	Barry Bonds	2.00
10	Bobby Bonilla	.05
11	Chris Bosio	.05
12	George Brett	1.50
13	Hubie Brooks	.05
14	Tom Brunansky	.05
15	Tim Burke	.05
16	Ivan Calderon	.05
17	Tom Candiotti	.05
18	Jose Canseco	.50
19	Gary Carter	.75
20	Joe Carter	.05
21	Jack Clark	.05
22	Will Clark	.10
23	Roger Clemens	1.25
24	David Cone	.05
25	Ed Correa	.05
26	Kal Daniels	.05
27	Al Davis	.05
28	Chili Davis	.05
29	Eric Davis	.05
30	Glen Davis	.05
31	Jody Davis	.05
32	Mark Davis	.05
33	Andre Dawson	.25
34	Rob Deer	.05
35	Jose DeLeon	.05
36	Bo Diaz	.05
37	Bill Doran	.05
38	Shawon Dunston	.05
39	Dennis Eckersley	.60
40	Dwight Evans	.05
41	Tony Fernandez	.05
42	Brian Fisher	.05
43	Carlton Fisk	.75
44	Mike Flanagan	.05
45	John Franco	.05
46	Gary Gaetti	.05
47	Andres Galarraga	.05
48	Scott Garrelts	.05
49	Kirk Gibson	.05
50	Dan Gladden	.05
51	Dwight Gooden	.05
52	Pedro Guerrero	.05
53	Ozzie Guillen	.05
54	Tony Gwynn	1.00
55	Mel Hall	.05
56	Von Hayes	.05
57	Keith Hernandez	.05
58	Orel Hershiser	.05
59	Ted Higuera	.05
60	Charlie Hough	.05
61	Jack Howell	.05
62	Kent Hrbek	.05
63	Pete Incaviglia	.05
64	Bo Jackson	.10
65	Brook Jacoby	.05
66	Chris James	.05
67	Lance Johnson	.05
68	Wally Joyner	.05
69	John Kruk	.05
70	Mike LaCoss	.05
71	Mark Langston	.05
72	Carney Lansford	.05
73	Barry Larkin	.05
74	Mike LaValliere	.05
75	Jose Lind	.05
76	Fred Lynn	.05
77	Greg Maddux	1.00
78	Candy Maldonado	.05
79	Don Mattingly	1.50
80	Mark McGwire	1.75
81	Paul Molitor	.75
82	Jack Morris	.05
83	Lloyd Moseby	.05
84	Dale Murphy	.30
85	Eddie Murray	.75
86	Matt Nokes	.05
87	Pete O'Brien	.05
88	Rafael Palmeiro	.65
89	Melido Perez	.05
90	Gerald Perry	.05
91	Tim Raines	.05
92	Willie Randolph	.05
93	Johnny Ray	.05
94	Jeff Reardon	.05
95	Jody Reed	.05
96	Harold Reynolds	.05
97	Dave Righetti	.05
98	Billy Ripken	.05
99	Cal Ripken Jr.	2.00
100	Nolan Ryan	2.00
101	Juan Samuel	.05
102	Benito Santiago	.05
103	Steve Sax	.05
104	Mike Schmidt	1.50
105	Rick Schu	.05
106	Mike Scott	.05
107	Kevin Seitzer	.05
108	Ruben Sierra	.05
109	Lee Smith	.05
110	Ozzie Smith	1.00
111	Zane Smith	.05
112	Dave Stewart	.05
113	Darryl Strawberry	.05
114	Bruce Sutter	.65
115	Bill Swift	.05
116	Greg Swindell	.05
117	Frank Tanana	.05
118	Danny Tartabull	.05
119	Milt Thompson	.05
120	Rob Thompson	.05
121	Alan Trammell	.05
122	John Tudor	.05
123	Fernando Valenzuela	.05
124	Dave Valle	.05
125	Frank Viola	.05
126	Ozzie Virgil	.05
127	Tim Wallach	.05
128	Dave Winfield	.75
129	Mike Witt	.05
130	Robin Yount	.75

1990 Red Foley Stickers

In its fourth consecutive year of publication, "Red Foley's Best Baseball Book Ever" retained its 96-page softbound 8-1/2" x 11" format of trivia, quizzes and games to be illustrated by placing one of 104 player or 26 team logo stickers in the book. Individual stickers are 1-3/8" x 1-3/4" and feature color photos with a white border. Sticker number appears in the bottom-right. There is no player identification on the sticker.

		NM/M
Complete Book:		9.00
Complete Sticker Set (130):		7.00
Common Player:		.05
1	Allan Anderson	.05
2	Scott Bailes	.05
3	Jeff Ballard	.05
4	Jesse Barfield	.05
5	Bert Blyleven	.05
6	Wade Boggs	1.00
7	Barry Bonds	2.00
8	Chris Bosio	.05
9	George Brett	1.50
10	Tim Burke	.05
11	Ellis Burks	.05
12	Brett Butler	.05
13	Ivan Calderon	.05
14	Jose Canseco	.50
15	Joe Carter	.05
16	Jack Clark	.05
17	Will Clark	.10
18	Roger Clemens	1.25
19	Vince Coleman	.05
20	Eric Davis	.05
21	Glenn Davis	.05
22	Mark Davis	.05
23	Andre Dawson	.25
24	Rob Deer	.05
25	Jose DeLeon	.05
26	Jim Deshaies	.05
27	Doug Drabek	.05
28	Lenny Dykstra	.05
29	Dennis Eckersley	.65
30	Steve Farr	.05
31	Tony Fernandez	.05
32	Carlton Fisk	.75
33	John Franco	.05
34	Julio Franco	.05
35	Andres Galarraga	.05
36	Tom Glavine	.25
37	Dwight Gooden	.05
38	Mark Grace	.10
39	Mike Greenwell	.05
40	Ken Griffey Jr.	1.25
41	Kelly Gruber	.05
42	Pedro Guerrero	.05
43	Tony Gwynn	1.00
44	Bryan Harvey	.05
45	Von Hayes	.05
46	Willie Hernandez	.05
47	Tommy Herr	.05
48	Orel Hershiser	.05
49	Jay Howell	.05
50	Kent Hrbek	.05
51	Bo Jackson	.10
52	Steve Jeltz	.05
53	Jimmy Key	.05
54	Ron Kittle	.05
55	Mark Langston	.05
56	Carney Lansford	.05
57	Barry Larkin	.05
58	Jeffrey Leonard	.05
59	Don Mattingly	1.50
60	Fred McGriff	.05
61	Mark McGwire	1.75
62	Kevin McReynolds	.05
63	Randy Myers	.05
64	Kevin Mitchell	.05
65	Paul Molitor	.75
66	Mike Morgan	.05
67	Dale Murphy	.30
68	Eddie Murray	.75
69	Matt Nokes	.05
70	Greg Olson	.05
71	Paul O'Neill	.05
72	Rafael Palmeiro	.65
73	Lance Parrish	.05
74	Dan Plesac	.05
75	Kirby Puckett	1.00
76	Jeff Reardon	.05
77	Rick Reuschel	.05
78	Cal Ripken Jr.	2.00
79	Dave Righetti	.05
80	Jeff Russell	.05
81	Nolan Ryan	2.00
82	Benito Santiago	.05
83	Steve Sax	.05
84	Mike Schooler	.05
85	Mike Scott	.05
86	Kevin Seitzer	.05
87	Dave Smith	.05
88	Lonnie Smith	.05
89	Ozzie Smith	1.00
90	John Smoltz	.05
91	Cory Snyder	.05
92	Darryl Strawberry	.05
93	Greg Swindell	.05
94	Mickey Tettleton	.05
95	Bobby Thigpen	.05
96	Alan Trammell	.05
97	Dave Valle	.05
98	Andy Van Slyke	.05
99	Tim Wallach	.05
100	Jerome Walton	.05
101	Lou Whitaker	.05
102	Devon White	.05
103	Mitch Williams	.05
104	Glen Wilson	.05
105	Indians Logo	.05
106	Rangers Logo	.05
107	Reds Logo	.05
108	Orioles Logo	.05
109	Red Sox Logo	.05
110	White Sox Logo	.05
111	Dodgers Logo	.05
112	Tigers Logo	.05
113	Mariners Logo	.05
114	Blue Jays Logo	.05
115	Expos Logo	.05
116	Pirates Logo	.05
117	Astros Logo	.05
118	Cardinals Logo	.05
119	Padres Logo	.05
120	Angels Logo	.05
121	Yankees Logo	.05
122	Cubs Logo	.05
123	Brewers Logo	.05
124	Twins Logo	.05
125	Giants Logo	.05
126	Royals Logo	.05
127	A's Logo	.05
128	Mets Logo	.05
129	Phillies Logo	.05
130	Braves Logo	.05

1991 Red Foley Stickers

In its fifth consecutive year of publication, "Red Foley's Best Baseball Book Ever" retained its 96-page softbound 8-1/2" x 11" format of trivia, quizzes and games to be illustrated by placing one of 112 regular player or 18 All-Star (#113-130) stickers in the book. Individual stickers are 1-3/8" x 1-3/4" and feature color photos with a white border. Sticker number appears in the bottom-right. There is no player identification on the sticker.

		NM/M
Complete Book:		10.00
Comlete Sticker Set (130):		8.00
Common Player:		.05
1	Jim Abbott	.05
2	Rick Aguilera	.05
3	Roberto Alomar	.30
4	Rob Dibble	.05
5	Wally Backman	.05
6	Harold Baines	.05
7	Steve Bedrosian	.05
8	Craig Biggio	.05
9	Wade Boggs	1.00
10	Bobby Bonilla	.05
11	George Brett	1.25
12	Greg Brock	.05
13	Hubie Brooks	.05
14	Tom Brunansky	.05
15	Tim Burke	.05
16	Tom Candiotti	.05
17	Jose Canseco	.50
18	Jack Clark	.05
19	Will Clark	.10
20	Roger Clemens	1.25
21	Vince Coleman	.05
22	Kal Daniels	.05
23	Glenn Davis	.05
24	Mark Davis	.05
25	Andre Dawson	.25
26	Rob Deer	.05
27	Delino DeShields	.05
28	Doug Drabek	.05
29	Shawon Dunston	.05
30	Lenny Dykstra	.05
31	Dennis Eckersley	.35
32	Kevin Elster	.05
33	Tony Fernandez	.05
34	Cecil Fielder	.05
35	Chuck Finley	.05
36	Carlton Fisk	.75
37	Greg Gagne	.05
38	Ron Gant	.05
39	Dan Gladden	.05
40	Dwight Gooden	.05
41	Ken Griffey Jr.	1.50
42	Kelly Gruber	.05
43	Pedro Guerrero	.05
44	Ozzie Guillen	.05
45	Pete Harnisch	.05
46	Billy Hatcher	.05
47	Von Hayes	.05
48	Rickey Henderson	.75
49	Mike Henneman	.05
50	Kent Hrbek	.05
51	Pete Incaviglia	.05
52	Howard Johnson	.05
53	Randy Johnson	.75
54	Doug Jones	.05
55	Ricky Jordan	.05
56	Wally Joyner	.05
57	Roberto Kelly	.05
58	Barry Larkin	.05
59	Craig Lefferts	.05
60	Candy Maldonado	.05
61	Don Mattingly	1.25
62	Oddibe McDowell	.05
63	Roger McDowell	.05
64	Willie McGee	.05
65	Fred McGriff	.05
66	Kevin Mitchell	.05
67	Mike Morgan	.05
68	Eddie Murray	.75
69	Gregg Olson	.05
70	Joe Orsulak	.05
71	Dan Petry	.05
72	Dan Plesac	.05
73	Jim Presley	.05
74	Kirby Puckett	1.00
75	Tim Raines	.05
76	Jeff Reardon	.05
77	Dave Righetti	.05
78	Cal Ripken Jr.	2.00
79	Nolan Ryan	2.00
80	Bret Saberhagen	.05
81	Chris Sabo	.05
82	Ryne Sandberg	1.00
83	Benito Santiago	.05
84	Steve Sax	.05
85	Mike Schooler	.05
86	Mike Scott	.05
87	Ruben Sierra	.05
88	Cory Snyder	.05
89	Dave Steib	.05
90	Dave Stewart	.05
91	Kurt Stillwell	.05
92	Bobby Thigpen	.05
93	Alan Trammell	.05
94	John Tudor	.05
95	Dave Valle	.05
96	Andy Van Slyke	.05
97	Robin Ventura	.05
98	Frank Viola	.05
99	Tim Wallach	.05
100	Matt Williams	.05
101	Mitch Williams	.05
102	Dave Winfield	.75
103	Eric Yelding	.05
104	Robin Yount	.75
105	Steve Avery	.05
106	Travis Fryman	.05
107	Juan Gonzalez	.40
108	Todd Hundley	.05
109	Ben McDonald	.05
110	Jose Offerman	.05
111	Frank Thomas	.75
112	Bernie Williams	.10
113	Sandy Alomar Jr.	.05
114	Jack Armstrong	.05
115	Wade Boggs	.40
116	Jose Canseco	.25
117	Will Clark	.10
118	Andre Dawson	.05
119	Lenny Dykstra	.05
120	Ken Griffey Jr.	.65
121	Rickey Henderson	.40
122	Mark McGwire	1.75
123	Kevin Mitchell	.05
124	Cal Ripken Jr.	1.00
125	Chris Sabo	.05
126	Ryne Sandberg	.50
127	Steve Sax	.05
128	Mike Scioscia	.05
129	Ozzie Smith	.50
130	Bob Welch	.05

1992 Red Foley Stickers

The format was unchanged when "Red Foley's Best Baseball Book Ever" was published in 1992. The 96-page, 8-1/2" x 11" softcover book features 96 pages of quizzes, trivia and games, along with 130 player stickers (#105-130 are All-Star stickers) to be placed on the proper pages. Single stickers measure 1-3/8" x 1-3/4" and have color photos with a white border. A sticker number is in the bottom-right. No player identification appears on the stickers. Issue price of the book was about $9.

		NM/M
Complete Book:		12.00
Complete Sticker Set (130):		10.00
Common Player:		.05
1	Jim Abbott	.05
2	Roberto Alomar	.15
3	Sandy Alomar Jr.	.05
4	Eric Anthony	.05
5	Kevin Appier	.05
6	Jack Armstrong	.05
7	Steve Avery	.05
8	Carlos Baerga	.05
9	Scott Bankhead	.05
10	George Bell	.05
11	Albert Belle	.05
12	Andy Benes	.05
13	Craig Biggio	.05
14	Wade Boggs	1.00
15	Barry Bonds	2.00
16	Bobby Bonilla	.05
17	Sid Bream	.05
18	George Brett	1.25
19	Hubie Brooks	.05
20	Ellis Burks	.05
21	Brett Butler	.05
22	Jose Canseco	.40
23	Joe Carter	.05
24	Jack Clark	.05
25	Will Clark	.10
26	Roger Clemens	1.25
27	Vince Coleman	.05
28	Eric Davis	.05
29	Glenn Davis	.05
30	Andre Dawson	.25
31	Rob Deer	.05
32	Delino DeShields	.05
33	Lenny Dykstra	.05
34	Scott Erickson	.05
35	Cecil Fielder	.05
36	Carlton Fisk	.75
37	Travis Fryman	.05
38	Greg Gagne	.05
39	Juan Gonzalez	.40
40	Tommy Greene	.05
41	Ken Griffey Jr.	1.50
42	Kent Hrbek	.05
43	Kelly Gruber	.05
44	Tony Gwynn	1.00
45	Dave Henderson	.05
46	Rickey Henderson	.75
47	Orel Hershiser	.05
48	Marquis Grissom	.05
49	Howard Johnson	.05
50	Felix Jose	.05
51	Wally Joyner	.05
52	David Justice	.05
53	Roberto Kelly	.05
54	Ray Lankford	.05
55	Barry Larkin	.05
56	Mark Lewis	.05
57	Kevin Maas	.05
58	Greg Maddux	1.00
59	Dennis Martinez	.05
60	Edgar Martinez	.05
61	Don Mattingly	1.50
62	Ben McDonald	.05
63	Jack McDowell	.05
64	Willie McGee	.05
65	Fred McGriff	.05
66	Brian McRae	.05
67	Mark McGwire	1.75
68	Kevin Mitchell	.05
69	Terry Mulholland	.05
70	Dale Murphy	.25
71	Eddie Murray	.75
72	John Olerud	.05
73	Rafael Palmeiro	.65
74	Terry Pendleton	.05
75	Luis Polonia	.05
76	Mark Portugal	.05
77	Kirby Puckett	1.00
78	Tim Raines	.05
79	Harold Reynolds	.05
80	Billy Ripken	.05
81	Cal Ripken Jr.	2.00
82	Nolan Ryan	2.00
83	Chris Sabo	.05
84	Ryne Sandberg	1.00
85	Benito Santiago	.05
86	Kevin Seitzer	.05
87	Gary Sheffield	.30
88	Ruben Sierra	.05
89	John Smiley	.05
90	Ozzie Smith	1.00
91	Darryl Strawberry	.05
92	B.J. Surhoff	.05
93	Frank Thomas	.75
94	Alan Trammell	.05
95	Andy Van Slyke	.05
96	Greg Vaughn	.05
97	Frank Viola	.05
98	Tim Wallach	.05
99	Matt Williams	.05
100	Dave Winfield	.75
101	Mike Witt	.05
102	Eric Yelding	.05
103	Robin Yount	.75
104	Todd Zeile	.05
105	Roberto Alomar	.10
106	Sandy Alomar Jr.	.05
107	Wade Boggs	.50
108	Bobby Bonilla	.05
109	Ivan Calderon	.05
110	Will Clark	.05
111	Andre Dawson	.05
112	Cecil Fielder	.05
113	Carlton Fisk	.30
114	Tom Glavine	.25
115	Ken Griffey Jr.	.65
116	Tony Gwynn	.50
117	Dave Henderson	.05
118	Rickey Henderson	.30
119	Felix Jose	.05
120	Jimmy Key	.05
121	Tony LaRussa	.05
122	Jack Morris	.05
123	Lou Piniella	.05
124	Cal Ripken Jr.	1.00
125	Chris Sabo	.05
126	Juan Samuel	.05
127	Ryne Sandberg	.50
128	Benito Santiago	.05
129	Ozzie Smith	.50
130	Danny Tartabull	.05

1993 Red Foley Stickers

The format was unchanged when "Red Foley's Best Baseball Book Ever" was published in 1993. The 96-page, 8-1/2" x 11" softcover book features 96 pages of quizzes, trivia and games, along with 130 player stickers (#105-130 are All-Star stickers) to be placed on the proper pages. Single stickers measure 1-3/8" x 1-3/4" and have color photos with a white border. A sticker number is in the bottom-right. No player identification appears on the stickers.

		NM/M
Complete Book:		10.00
Complete Sticker Set (130):		9.00
Common Player:		.05
1	Jim Abbott	.05
2	Roberto Alomar	.15
3	Sandy Alomar Jr.	.05
4	Steve Avery	.05
5	Jeff Bagwell	.75
6	Harold Baines	.05
7	Bret Barberie	.05
8	Derek Bell	.05
9	Jay Bell	.05
10	Albert Belle	.05
11	Andy Benes	.05
12	Craig Biggio	.05
13	Wade Boggs	1.00
14	Barry Bonds	2.00
15	Bobby Bonilla	.05
16	Jose Canseco	.40
17	Joe Carter	.05
18	Wes Chamberlain	.05
19	Will Clark	.10
20	Roger Clemens	1.25
21	Milt Cuyler	.05
22	Eric Davis	.05
23	Delino DeShields	.05
24	Rob Dibble	.05
25	Doug Drabek	.05
26	Shawon Dunston	.05
27	Lenny Dykstra	.05
28	Scott Erickson	.05
29	Cecil Fielder	.05
30	Steve Finley	.05
31	Tom Glavine	.25
32	Dwight Gooden	.05
33	Mark Grace	.10
34	Ken Griffey Jr.	1.50
35	Marquis Grissom	.05
36	Kelly Gruber	.05
37	Mark Gubicza	.05
38	Tony Gwynn	1.00
39	Mel Hall	.05
40	Pete Harnisch	.05
41	Brian Harper	.05
42	Bryan Harvey	.05
43	Rickey Henderson	.75
44	Orel Hershiser	.05
45	Gregg Jefferies	.05
46	Howard Johnson	.05
47	Felix Jose	.05
48	Wally Joyner	.05
49	David Justice	.05
50	Roberto Kelly	.05
51	Chuck Knoblauch	.05
52	John Kruk	.05
53	Barry Larkin	.05
54	Kenny Lofton	.05
55	Greg Maddux	1.00
56	Dennis Martinez	.05
57	Edgar Martinez	.05
58	Tino Martinez	.05
59	Don Mattingly	1.25
60	Jack McDowell	.05
61	Willie McGee	.05
62	Fred McGriff	.05
63	Mark McGwire	1.75
64	Brian McRae	.05
65	Randy Milligan	.05
66	Kevin Mitchell	.05
67	Paul Molitor	.75
68	Dale Murphy	.25
69	Mike Mussina	.40
70	Charles Nagy	.05
71	Gregg Olson	.05
72	Rafael Palmeiro	.65
73	Dean Palmer	.05
74	Phil Plantier	.05
75	Luis Polonia	.05
76	Kirby Puckett	1.00
77	Tim Raines	.05
78	Cal Ripken Jr.	2.00
79	Bip Roberts	.05
80	Ivan Rodriguez	.65
81	Nolan Ryan	2.00
82	Bret Saberhagen	.05
83	Ryne Sandberg	1.00
84	Deion Sanders	.10
85	Reggie Sanders	.05
86	Benito Santiago	.05
87	Mike Scoscia	.05
88	Lee Smith	.05
89	Ozzie Smith	1.00
90	Lee Stevens	.05
91	Darryl Strawberry	.05
92	B.J. Surhoff	.05
93	Danny Tartabull	.05
94	Mickey Tettleton	.05
95	Frank Thomas	.75
96	Robby Thompson	.05
97	Alan Trammell	.05
98	Greg Vaughn	.05
99	Mo Vaughn	.05
100	Andy Van Slyke	.05
101	Robin Ventura	.05
102	Matt Williams	.05
103	Robin Yount	.75
104	Todd Zeile	.05
105	Roberto Alomar	.15
106	Sandy Alomar Jr.	.05
107	Wade Boggs	.50
108	Kevin Brown	.05
109	Joe Carter	.05
110	Will Clark	.05
111	Bobby Cox	.05
112	Dennis Eckersley	.40
113	Tony Fernandez	.05
114	Tom Glavine	.05
115	Ken Griffey Jr.	.65
116	Tony Gwynn	.50
117	Tom Kelly	.05
118	John Kruk	.05
119	Fred McGriff	.05
120	Mark McGwire	.75
121	Kirby Puckett	.50
122	Cal Ripken Jr.	1.00
123	Bip Roberts	.05
124	Ivan Rodriguez	.20
125	Gary Sheffield	.25
126	Ruben Sierra	.05
127	Ozzie Smith	.50
128	Andy Van Slyke	.05
129	Robin Ventura	.05
130	Larry Walker	.05

1994 Red Foley

Beginning in 1994, major changes were seen in "Red Foley's Best Baseball Book Ever." The book remained in 8-1/2" x 11" format, but was downsized to 64 pages. The previous years' stickers were replaced with four nine-card sheets of perforated baseball cards. When separated from the sheets, cards measure the standard 2-1/2" x 3-1/2". The unnumbered cards appear in two types. "Superstar" cards feature a single player in a color action photo on front. "Team Leaders" cards have two teammates on front. Red and black printing on backs give personal data and career highlights. Original retail cost of the book was $8.95.

		NM/M
Complete Book:		15.00
Complete Set (36):		12.00
Common Card:		.25
(1)	Barry Bonds	2.00
(2)	Joe Carter	.25
(3)	Roger Clemens	1.25
(4)	Juan Gonzalez	.60
(5)	Ken Griffey Jr.	1.50
(6)	Fred McGriff	.25
(7)	Jose Rijo	.25
(8)	Ryne Sandberg	1.00
(9)	Angels (Tim Salmon, Mark Langston)	.25
(10)	Astros (Jeff Bagwell, Doug Drabek)	.50
(11)	Athletics (Mark McGwire, Dennis Eckersley)	.75
(12)	Blue Jays (Roberto Alomar, John Olerud)	.30
(13)	Braves (Greg Maddux, Tom Glavine)	.60
(14)	Brewers (Robin Yount, Cal Eldred)	.50
(15)	Cardinals (Ray Lankford, Ozzie Smith)	.60
(16)	Cubs (Mark Grace, Randy Myers)	.30
(17)	Dodgers (Mike Piazza, Orel Hershiser)	.65
(18)	Expos (Larry Walker, Marquis Grissom)	.25
(19)	Giants (Will Clark, Matt Williams)	.25
(20)	Indians (Albert Belle, Carlos Baerga)	.25
(21)	Mariners (Jay Buhner, Randy Johnson)	.40
(22)	Marlins (Gary Sheffield, Bryan Harvey)	.25
(23)	Mets (Bobby Bonilla, Dwight Gooden)	.25
(24)	Orioles (Cal Ripken Jr., Mike Mussina)	1.00
(25)	Padres (Andy Benes, Tony Gwynn)	.60
(26)	Phillies (John Kruk, Tommy Greene)	.25
(27)	Pirates (Jay Bell, Andy Van Slyke)	.25
(28)	Rangers (Jose Canseco, Kevin Brown)	.35
(29)	Reds (Barry Larkin, Reggie Sanders)	.25
(30)	Red Sox (Mo Vaughn, Frank Viola)	.25
(31)	Rockies (Charlie Hayes, Andres Galarraga)	.25
(32)	Royals (Brian McRae, David Cone)	.25
(33)	Tigers (Cecil Fielder, Mike Henneman)	.25
(34)	Twins (Kirby Puckett, Rick Aguilera)	.60
(35)	White Sox (Frank Thomas, Jack McDowell)	.50
(36)	Yankees (Don Mattingly, Jim Abbott)	.75

1995 Red Foley

The Red Foley book of children's games, quizzes, trivia and other baseball related entertainment reprised its 1994 format for 1995. The 36 perforated insert cards, 2-1/2" x 3-1/2", were again divided into single-player "Superstar" and two-player "Team Leaders" types. Designs were identical to the previous year, with color action photos on front and career highlights on back. The unnumbered cards are checklisted here in alphabetical order by type.

		NM/M
Complete Book:		15.00
Complete Set (36):		12.00
Common Card:		.25
(1)	Barry Bonds	2.00
(2)	Joe Carter	.25
(3)	Roger Clemens	1.00
(4)	Juan Gonzalez	.60
(5)	Ken Griffey Jr.	1.50
(6)	Fred McGriff	.25
(7)	Cal Ripken Jr.	2.00
(8)	Frank Thomas	.75
(9)	Angels (Tim Salmon, Steve Finley)	.35
(10)	Astros (Jeff Bagwell, Craig Biggio)	.50
(11)	Athletics (Mark McGwire, Dennis Eckersley)	.75
(12)	Blue Jays (Roberto Alomar, John Olerud)	.35
(13)	Braves (Greg Maddux, David Justice)	.60
(14)	Brewers (Cal Eldred, Dave Nillson)	.25
(15)	Cardinals (Ozzie Smith, Gregg Jefferies)	.60
(16)	Cubs (Mark Grace, Randy Myers)	.35
(17)	Dodgers (Mike Piazza, Orel Hershiser)	.65
(18)	Expos (Larry Walker, Ken Hill)	.25
(19)	Giants (Matt Williams, Rod Beck)	.25
(20)	Indians (Albert Belle, Carlos Baerga)	.25
(21)	Mariners (Jay Buhner, Randy Johnson)	.25
(22)	Marlins (Gary Sheffield, Benito Santiago)	.25
(23)	Mets (Bret Saberhagen, Bobby Bonilla)	.25
(24)	Orioles (Rafael Palmeiro, Mike Mussina)	.40
(25)	Padres (Tony Gwynn, Andy Benes)	.60
(26)	Phillies (John Kruk, Lenny Dykstra)	.25
(27)	Pirates (Andy Van Slyke, Al Martin)	.25
(28)	Rangers (Jose Canseco, Will Clark)	.35
(29)	Reds (Barry Larkin, Jose Rijo)	.25
(30)	Red Sox (Mo Vaughn, Aaron Sele)	.25
(31)	Rockies (Andres Galarraga, Dante Bichette)	.25
(32)	Royals (Brian McRae, David Cone)	.25
(33)	Tigers (Cecil Fielder, Travis Fryman)	.25
(34)	Twins (Kirby Puckett, Rick Aguilera)	.60
(35)	White Sox (Robin Ventura, Wilson Alvarez)	.25
(36)	Yankees (Don Mattingly, Jimmy Key)	.65

1996 Red Foley

The Red Foley book of children's games, quizzes, trivia and other baseball related entertainment changed little for its 1996 edition. The number of cards was decreased to 32 and the size to a 2" x 2-3/4" perforated format. Only single-player cards were produced. Designs were nearly identical to the previous year, with color action photos on front and career highlights on back. The unnumbered cards are checklisted here in alphabetical order.

		NM/M
Complete Book:		12.00
Complete Set (32):		9.00
Common Player:		.25
(1)	Roberto Alomar	.30
(2)	Moises Alou	.25
(3)	Carlos Baerga	.25
(4)	Jay Bell	.25
(5)	Craig Biggio	.25
(6)	Barry Bonds	1.50
(7)	Jeff Conine	.25
(8)	Lenny Dykstra	.25
(9)	Cecil Fielder	.25
(10)	Ken Griffey Jr.	1.00
(11a)	Tony Gwynn/Red	.75
(11b)	Tony Gwynn/Purple	.75
(12)	Rickey Henderson	.65
(13)	Wally Joyner	.25
(14)	Barry Larkin	.25
(15)	Mark McGwire	1.25
(16)	Eddie Murray	.65
(17)	Rafael Palmeiro	.50
(18)	Mike Piazza	1.00
(19)	Greg Maddux	.75
(20)	Paul O'Neill	.25
(21)	Kirby Puckett	.75
(22)	Bill Pulsipher	.25
(23)	Cal Ripken Jr.	1.50
(24)	Ivan Rodriguez	.50
(25)	Kenny Rogers	.25
(26)	Tim Salmon	.30
(27)	Kevin Seitzer	.25
(28)	Ozzie Smith	.75
(29)	Sammy Sosa	.90
(30)	Frank Thomas	.65
(31)	Mo Vaughn	.25
(32)	Larry Walker	.25

1988 Foot Locker Slam Fest

Two baseball players are among the athletes pictured in this Foot Locker set issued in conjunction with the shoe store chain's Slam Fest competition. Cards were given away at local stores. The 2-1/2" x 3-1/2" cards have color player portrait photos on a semi-gloss front. All athletes are pictured in Slam Dunk basketball jerseys. A sponsor's banner is at top; the chain's referee logo at lower-left. Backs are printed in blue with information about the televised competition and the player's career.

		NM/M
Complete Set (9):		6.00
Common Player:		.50
(1)	Carl Banks (Football)	.50
(2)	Mike Conley/SP (Track)	.50
(3)	Thomas Hearns (Boxing)	2.00
(4)	Bo Jackson	2.00
(5)	Keith Jackson (Football)	.50
(6)	Karch Kiraly (Volleyball)	.50
(7)	Ricky Sanders (Football)	.50
(8)	Dwight Stones (Track)	.50
(9)	Devon White	1.00

1989 Foot Locker Slam Fest

One baseball player is among the athletes pictured in this Foot Locker set issued in

conjunction with the shoe store chain's Slam Fest competition. Cards were given away at local stores. The 2-1/2" x 3-1/2" cards have color player portrait photos on a semi-gloss front. All athletes are pictured in Slam Dunk basketball jerseys. A sponsor's banner is at top. Backs have information about the televised competition and the player's career.

		NM/M
Complete Set (10):		3.00
Common Player:		.35
1	Mike Conley (Track)	.40
2	Keith Jackson (Football)	.75
3	Vince Coleman	1.00
4	Eric Dickerson (Football)	2.00
5	Steve Timmons (Volleyball)	.40
6	Matt Biondi (Swimming)	.50
7	Carl Lewis (Track)	.75
8	Mike Quick (Football)	.50
9	Mike Powell (Track)	.50
10	Checklist	.05

1991 Foot Locker Slam Fest

A number of baseball players were included among the various current and former athletes in this set of three 10-card series produced in conjunction with the sporting gear retailer's Slam Fest charity event. Players are pictured in color on the 2-1/2" x 3-1/2" cards wearing Nike basketball uniforms.

		NM/M
Complete Set (30):		5.00
Common Player:		.03
1-1	Ken Griffey Jr.	1.50
1-2	Delino DeShields	.10
1-3	Barry Bonds	4.00
1-4	Jack Armstrong	.10
1-5	Dave Justice	.25
1-6	Deion Sanders	.50
1-7	Michael Dean Perry (Football)	.10
1-8	Tim Brown (Football)	.10
1-9	Mike Conley (Track)	.10
1-10	Mike Powell (Track)	.10
10-1	Wilt Chamberlain (Basketball)	1.00
10-2	Carl Ramsey (Basketball)	.10
10-3	Bobby Jones (Basketball)	.10
10-4	John Havlicek (Basketball)	.10
10-5	Calvin Murphy (Basketball)	.10
10-6	Nate Thurmond (Basketball)	.10
10-7	John Havlicek (Basketball)	.10
10-8	Checklist Series 1	.05
10-9	Checklist Series 2	.05
10-10	Checklist Series 3	.05
20-1	Jerry Lucas (Basketball)	.10
20-2	Bo Jackson	.25
20-3	Elvin Hayes (Basketball)	.10
20-4	Thomas Hearns (Boxing)	.25
20-5	Matt Biondi (Swimming)	.10
20-6	Earl Monroe (Basketball)	.10
20-7	Eric Dickerson (Football)	.50
20-8	Carl Lewis (Track)	.25
20-9	Wilt and Company (Basketball)	.10
20-10	TV Schedule	.05

1981 Franchise 1966 Baltimore Orioles

One of the lesser-known producers of collectors' issues in the early 1980s was "The Franchise". Most of their card sets featured subjects of special interest to their home (Maryland) area. This set, for example, features the 1966 Baltimore Orioles World Champions. In 2-1/2" x 3-1/2" size, cards have black-and-white player photos on front surrounded by orange borders. Black-and-white backs are somewhat in the style of 1953 Bowman, with personal data, career highlights and 1966/Lifetime stats.

		NM/M
Complete Set (32):		13.50
Common Player:		.50
1	World Champs 1966	.50
2	Team photo	.50
3	Luis Aparicio	2.50
4	Steve Barber	.50
5	Hank Bauer	.50
6	Paul Blair	.50
7	Curt Blefary	.50
8	Sam Bowens	.50
9	Gene Brabender	.50
10	Harry Brecheen	.50
11	Wally Bunker	.50
12	Moe Drabowsky	.50
13	Andy Etchebarren	.50
14	Eddie Fisher	.50
15	Dick Hall	.50
16	Larry Haney	.50
17	Woody Held	.50
18	Billy Hunter	.50
19	Bob Johnson	.50
20	Dave Johnson	.50
21	Sherman Lollar	.50
22	Dave McNally	.50
23	John Miller	.50
24	Stu Miller	.50
25	Jim Palmer	2.50
26	Boog Powell	1.50
27	Brooks Robinson	3.00
28	Frank Robinson	3.00
29	Vic Roznovsky	.50
30	Russ Snyder	.50
31	Eddie Watt	.50
32	Gene Woodling	.50

1983 Franchise Brooks Robinson

This collectors' issue was produced by a Maryland company which specialized in sets of local interest. Cards detail the career of the Orioles Hall of Famer. Fronts of the 2-1/2" x 3-1/2" cards have a black-and-white photo with orange graphics. Backs are printed in

black, white and orange and provide a title and details about the front photo.

		NM/M
Complete Set (40):		35.00
Common Card:		1.00
1	Professional record	1.00
2	Youngest on team	1.00
3	All-state performer	1.00
4	Teen-ager in Texas	1.00
5	First spring training	1.00
6	Another uniform	1.00
7	First solid infield	1.00
8	Celebration time	1.00
9	Instinctive baserunner	1.00
10	Wedding day	1.00
11	First business partner	1.00
12	Second solid infield	1.00
13	Two Baltimore heroes	1.00
14	Enjoying the kids	1.00
15	Playing every game	1.00
16	Upsetting the Yankees	1.00
17	Tag out at third	1.00
18	Getting net results	1.00
19	The future MVPs	1.50
20	The original Rocky	1.00
21	Bauer's gloveman	1.00
22	World Series infield	1.00
23	Orioles' power parade	1.00
24	All-star trio	1.50
25	Lethal lumber	1.00
26	Belanger joins infield	1.00
27	Respect for Oliva	1.00
28	Out of Harm's way	1.00
29	Master trader	1.00
30	Eastern Shore visit	1.00
31	Gloves of gold	1.00
32	Ripping the Reds	1.00
33	Rappin' with Willie	2.00
34	Using the body	1.00
35	Getting the umps' attention	1.00
36	Respect from teammate	1.00
37	Touch of class	1.00
38	Bubble never burst	1.00
39	Honored by Yankees	1.00
40	Two greats at third	1.00

2002 Franz Bread Seattle Mariners

This team set was produced by Upper Deck and issued regionally with individually cello-wrapped cards inserted into loaves of bread. The cards have game-action photos which are borderless at top and sides. In a wide white strip at bottom are the team name, player name, position and uniform number and a Franz logo. In the upper corners are UD and Mariners 25th Anniversary logos. Backs have a portrait photo, a few words about the player, previous season's stats and various logos and copyright information.

		NM/M
Complete Set (16):		10.00
Common Player:		.50
1	Ichiro	5.00
2	Edgar Martinez	1.00
3	John Olerud	.75
4	Bret Boone	.75
5	Jeff Cirillo	.50
6	Carlos Guillen	.50
7	Mike Cameron	.50
8	Ruben Sierra	.50
9	Ben Davis	.50
10	Freddy Garcia	.50
11	Kazuhiro Sasaki	1.00
12	Jamie Moyer	.50
13	James Baldwin	.50
14	Jeff Nelson	.50
15	Dan Wilson	.50
16	Mark McLemore	.50

1987 French/Bray Orioles

The Baltimore Orioles and French Bray, Inc. issued a baseball card set to be handed out to fans in attendance at Memorial Stadium on July 26th. Thirty perforated, detachable cards were printed within a three-panel fold-out piece measuring 9-1/2" x 11-1/4". The card fronts feature full-color player photos surrounded by an orange border. The French/Bray logo appears on the card front. The backs are of simple design, containing only the player's name, uniform number, position and professional record.

		NM/M
Complete Set, Panel:		45.00
Complete Set, Singles (30):		40.00
Common Player:		1.00
2	Alan Wiggins	1.00
3	Bill Ripken	1.00
6	Floyd Rayford	1.00
7	Cal Ripken, Sr.	1.00
8	Cal Ripken, Jr.	25.00
9	Jim Dwyer	1.00
10	Terry Crowley	1.00
15	Terry Kennedy	1.00
16	Scott McGregor	1.00
18	Larry Sheets	1.00
19	Fred Lynn	1.00
20	Frank Robinson	4.00
24	Dave Schmidt	1.00
25	Ray Knight	1.00
27	Lee Lacy	1.00
31	Mark Wiley	1.00
32	Mark Williamson	1.00
33	Eddie Murray	12.50
38	Ken Gerhart	1.00
39	Ken Dixon	1.00
40	Jimmy Williams	1.00
42	Mike Griffin	1.00
43	Mike Young	1.00
44	Elrod Hendricks	1.00
45	Eric Bell	1.00
46	Mike Flanagan	1.00
49	Tom Niedenfuer	1.00
52	Mike Boddicker	1.00
54	John Habyan	1.00
57	Tony Arnold	1.00

1988 French/Bray Orioles

French-Bray sponsored a full-color brochure that was distributed to fans during an in-stadium promotion. A blue and orange front cover features inset photos of the Orioles in action on the upper left in a filmstrip motif. To the right is the Orioles logo and their 1988 slogan, "You Gotta Be There" above a baseball glove and ball. The 3-panel foldout measures approximately 9-1/2" x 11-1/4" and includes a team photo on the inside cover, with two perforated pages of individual cards featuring players, coaches and the team manager. Individual cards measure 2-1/4" x 3-1/8", with close-ups framed in white with an orange accent line. The player name and sponsor logo are printed beneath the photo. The black-and-white backs are numbered by player uniform and provide career stats. Additional copies of the brochure were made available from the Orioles Baseball Store following the free giveaway.

		NM/M
Complete Set, Panel:		70.00
Complete Set, Singles (31):		60.00
Common Player:		1.00
2	Don Buford	1.00
6	Joe Orsulak	1.00
7	Bill Ripken	1.00
8	Cal Ripken, Jr.	40.00
9	Jim Dwyer	1.00
10	Terry Crowley	1.00
12	Mike Morgan	1.00
14	Mickey Tettleton	1.00
15	Terry Kennedy	1.00
17	Pete Stanicek	1.00
18	Larry Sheets	1.00
19	Fred Lynn	1.00
20	Frank Robinson	5.00
23	Ozzie Peraza	1.00
24	Dave Schmidt	1.00
25	Rich Schu	1.00
28	Jim Traber	1.00
31	Herm Starrette	1.00
33	Eddie Murray	15.00
34	Jeff Ballard	1.00
38	Ken Gerhart	1.00
40	Minnie Mendoza	1.00
41	Don Aase	1.00
44	Elrod Hendricks	1.00
47	John Hart	1.00
48	Jose Bautista	1.00
49	Tom Niedenfuer	1.00
52	Mike Boddicker	1.00
53	Jay Tibbs	1.00
88	Rene Gonzales	1.00
---	Team Photo	5.00

1989 French/Bray Orioles

This 32-card team set was co-sponsored by French-Bray and the Wilcox Walter Furlong Paper Co., and was distributed as an in-stadium promotion to fans attending the May 12 game. Smaller than standard size, the cards measure 2-1/4" x 3" and feature a full-color player photo with number, name and position below. The backs, done in black-and-white, include brief player data and complete major and minor league stats.

		NM/M
Complete Set (32):		20.00
Common Player:		.50
3	Bill Ripken	.50
6	Joe Orsulak	.50
7	Cal Ripken, Sr.	.50
8	Cal Ripken, Jr.	15.00
9	Brady Anderson	1.50
10	Steve Finley	.50
11	Craig Worthington	.50
12	Mike Devereaux	.50
14	Mickey Tettleton	.50
15	Randy Milligan	.50
16	Phil Bradley	.50
18	Bob Milacki	.50
19	Larry Sheets	.50
20	Frank Robinson	4.50
21	Mark Thurmond	.50
23	Kevin Hickey	.50
24	Dave Schmidt	.50
28	Jim Traber	.50
29	Jeff Ballard	.50
30	Gregg Olson	.50
31	Al Jackson	.50
32	Mark Williamson	.50
36	Bob Melvin	.50
37	Brian Holton	.50
40	Tom McCraw	.50
42	Pete Harnisch	.50
43	Fransisco Melendez	.50
44	Elrod Hendricks	.50
46	Johnny Oates	.50
48	Jose Bautista	.50
88	Rene Gonzales	.50
---	Sponsor's Card	.50

1992 French's Mustard

In 1992 French's gave away a promotional card with the purchase of its mustard products. Each of the cards displays photographs of two players. The cards, which have team insignias air-brushed out, feature a green border, color photos and the players' statistics on the back.

		NM/M
Complete Set (18):		4.00
Common Card:		.10
1	Jeff Bagwell, Chuck Knoblauch	.50
2	Roger Clemens, Tom Glavine	.65
3	Julio Franco, Terry Pendleton	.10
4	Howard Johnson, Jose Canseco	.35
5	John Smiley, Scott Erickson	.10
6	Bryan Harvey, Lee Smith	.10
7	Kirby Puckett, Barry Bonds	1.00
8	Robin Ventura, Matt Williams	.10
9	Tony Pena, Tom Pagnozzi	.10
10	Benito Santiago, Sandy Alomar, Jr.	.10
11	Don Mattingly, Will Clark	.75
12	Ryne Sandberg, Roberto Alomar	.60
13	Cal Ripken, Jr., Ozzie Smith	1.00
14	Wade Boggs, Chris Sabo	.60
15	Ken Griffey Jr., David Justice	.75
16	Joe Carter, Tony Gwynn	.60
17	Rickey Henderson, Darryl Strawberry	.50
18	Jack Morris, Steve Avery	.10

2003 French's Mustard N.Y. Yankees

This six-card set sponsored by Yankee Stadium's long-time condiments concessionaire was distributed to fans 14 and under. Produced by Donruss, the standard-sized cards have game-action photos on front with the sponsor's ad message at bottom. Backs have player personal data, career highlights and career stats.

		NM/M
Complete Set (6):		5.00
Common Player:		.25

1 Derek Jeter 4.00
2 Alfonso Soriano 1.00
3 Jorge Posada .25
4 Jose Contreras .50
5 Jeff Weaver .25
6 Steve Karsay .25
-- Header Card .05

1983 Fritsch One-Year Winners

Larry Fritsch Cards continued its series of collector's issues under the banner of "One-Year Winners" with a 64-card color issue in 1983. Most of the player photos featured are unused Topps pictures. As in previous issues, the set features players with short major league careers, few of whom appear on any contemporary baseball card. In the style of 1966 Topps cards, the set has large player photos bordered in white with a diagonal blue strip in an upper corner containing the initials OYW. A blue strip beneath the photo has the player name in black. Backs are in red, black and white with personal data, stats and career highlights.

NM/M
Complete Set (64): 35.00
Common Player: 2.00
55 Don Prince 2.00
56 Tom Gramly 2.00
57 Roy Heiser 2.00
58 Hank Izquierdo 2.00
59 Rex Johnston 2.00
60 Jack Damaska 2.00
61 John Flavin 2.00
62 John Glenn 2.00
63 Stan Johnson 2.00
64 Don Choate 2.00
65 Bill Kern 2.00
66 Dick Luebke 2.00
67 Glen Clark 2.00
68 Lamar Jacobs 2.00
69 Rick Herrscher 2.00
70 Jim McManus 2.00
71 Len Church 2.00
72 Larry Stubing 2.00
73 Cal Emery 2.00
74 Lee Gregory 2.00
75 Mike Page 2.00
76 Benny Valenzuela 2.00
77 John Papa 2.00
78 Jim Stump 2.00
79 Brian McCall 2.00
80 Al Kenders 2.00
81 Corky Withrow 2.00
82 Verle Tiefenthaler 2.00
83 Dave Wissman 2.00
84 Tom Fletcher 2.00
85 Dale Willis 2.00
86 Larry Foster 2.00
87 Johnnie Seale 2.00
88 Jim Lehew 2.00
89 Charlie Shoemaker 2.00
90 Don Arlick 2.00
91 George Gerberman 2.00
92 John Pregenzer 2.00
93 Merlin Nippert 2.00
94 Steve Demeter 2.00
95 John Paciorek 2.00
96 Larry Loughlin 2.00
97 Alan Brice 2.00
98 Chet Boak 2.00
99 Alan Koch 2.00
100 Dan Thomas 2.00
101 Elder White 2.00
102 Jim Snyder 2.00
103 Ted Schreiber 2.00
104 Evans Killeen 2.00
105 Ray Daviault 2.00
106 Larry Foss 2.00
107 Wayne Graham 2.00
108 Santiago Rosario 2.00
109 Bob Sprout 2.00
110 Tom Hughes 2.00
111 Em Lindbeck 2.00
112 Ray Blemker 2.00
113 Shaun Fitzmaurice 2.00
114 Ron Stillwell 2.00
115 Carl Thomas 2.00
116 Mike DeGerick 2.00
117 Jay Dahl 2.00
118 Al Lary 2.00

1983 Fritsch 1953 Boston/ Milwaukee Braves

This collectors' issue commemorates the 30th anniversary of the move of the Boston Braves to Milwaukee. The black-and-white photos on the front of the cards (bordered in blue) were taken in spring training, with players still wearing Boston caps. Card backs have personal data and detailed career highlights. Cards measure about 2-5/8" x 3-3/4", which was the standard prior to 1957.

NM/M
Complete Set (33): 8.00
Common Player: .25
1 Joe Adcock .35
2 John Antonelli .25
3 Billy Bruton .25
4 Bob Buhl .25
5 Lew Burdette .35
6 Paul Burris .25
7 Dave Cole .25
8 Johnny Cooney .25
9 Walker Cooper .25
10 Del Crandall .35
11 George Crowe .25
12 Jack Dittmer .25
13 Dick Donovan .25
14 Sid Gordon .25
15 Virgil Jester .25
16 Ernie Johnson .25
17 Dave Jolly .25
18 Billy Klaus .25
19 Don Liddle .25
20 Johnny Logan .25
21 Luis Marquez .25
21s Luis Marquez (Sample overprint.) .25
22 Eddie Mathews 1.00
22s Eddie Mathews (Sample overprint.) .25
23 Andy Pafko .35
24 Jim Pendleton .25
25 Ebba St. Claire .25
26 Sibby Sisti .25
27 Warren Spahn 1.00
28 Max Surkont .25
29 Bob Thorpe .25
30 Murray Wall .25
31 Bucky Walters .25
32 Jim Wilson .25
33 1953 Braves Team .25

1986 Fritsch Negro League Baseball Stars

One of the most comprehensive collectors' issues to feature the stars of the Negro Leagues, the Fritsch set features black-and-white photos of varying quality; most of the photos are contemporary with the players' careers from the 1920s into the 1950s, with a few of the segregated leagues' earlier pioneers also included. Fronts are highlighted with red graphics. Backs are printed in blue and present a brief summary of the player's career and a list of the teams on which he played. Cards are in standard 2-1/2" x 3-1/2" format.

NM/M
Complete Set (119): 15.00
Common Player: .10
1 Buck Leonard .15
2 Ted Page .10
3 Cool Papa Bell .15
4 Oscar Charleston, Josh Gibson, Ted Page, Judy Johnson .15
5 Judy Johnson .15
6 Monte Irvin .15
7 Ray Dandridge .15
8 Oscar Charleston .15
9 Josh Gibson .15
10 Satchel Paige .25
10s Satchel Paige (SAMPLE on back.) 2.50
11 Jackie Robinson .50
12 Piper Davis .10
13 Josh Johnson .10
14 Lou Dials .15
15 Andy Porter .10
16 Pop Lloyd .15
17 Andy Watts .10
18 Rube Foster .10
19 Martin Dihigo .15
20 Lou Dials .15
21 Satchel Paige .25
22 Crush Holloway .10
23 Josh Gibson .15
24 Oscar Charleston .15
25 Jackie Robinson .50
26 Larry Brown .10
27 Hilton Smith .15
28 Moses Fleetwood Walker .25
29 Jimmie Crutchfield .10
30 Josh Gibson .15
30s Josh Gibson (SAMPLE on back.) 2.00
31 Josh Gibson .15
32 Bullet Rogan .15
33 Clint Thomas .10
34 Rats Henderson .10
35 Pat Scantlebury .10
36 Sidney Morton .10
37 Larry Kimbrough .10
38 Sam Jethroe .10
39 Normal "Tweed" Webb .10
40 Mahlon Duckett .10
41 Andy Anderson .10
42 Buster Haywood .10
43 Bob Trice .10
44 Bus Clarkson .10
45 Buck O'Neil .15
46 Jim Zapp .10
47 Piper Davis .10
48 Ed Steel .10
49 Bob Boyd .10
50 Marlin Carter .10
51 George Giles .10
52 Bill Byrd .10
53 Art Pennington .10
54 Max Manning .10
55 Ron Teasley .10
56 Ziggy Marcell .10
57 Bill Cash .10
58 Joe Scott .10
59 Joe Fillmore .10
60 Bob Thurman .10
61 Larry Kimbrough .10
62 Verdell Mathis .10
63 Josh Johnson .10
64 Double Duty Radcliffe .15
65 William Bobby Robinson .10
66 Bingo DeMoss .15
67 John Beckwith .10
68 Bill Jackman .10
69 Bill Drake .10
70 Charles Grant .15
71 Willie Wells .25
72 Jose Fernandez .10
73 Isidro Fabri .10
74 Frank Austin .10
75 Richard Lundy .10
76 Junior Gilliam .15
77 John Donaldson .10
78 Herb Dixon .10
79 Slim Jones .10
80 Sam Jones .10
81 Dave Hoskins .10
82 Jerry Benjamin .10
83 Luke Easter .10
84 Ramon Herrera .10
85 Matthew Carlisle .10
86 Smoky Joe Williams .25
87 Marv Williams .10
88 William Yancey .10
89 Monte Irvin .15
89s Monte Irvin (SAMPLE on back.) 1.00
90 Cool Papa Bell .15
91 Biz Mackey .25
92 Harry Simpson .10
93 Lazario Salazar .10
94 Bill Perkins .10
95 Johnny Davis .10
96 Jelly Jackson .10
97 Sam Bankhead .10
98 Hank Thompson .10
99 William Bell .10
100 Cliff Bell .10
101 Dave Barnhill .10
102 Dan Bankhead .10
103 Lloyd Bassett .10
104 Newt Allen .10
105 George Jefferson .10
106 Pat Paterson .10
107 Goose Tatum .15
108 Dave Malarcher .10
109 Home Run Johnson .10
110 Bill Monroe .10
111 Sammy Hughes .10
112 Dick Redding .10
113 Fats Jenkins .10
114 Jimmie Lyons .10
115 Mule Suttles .15
116 Ted Trent .10
117 George Sweatt .10
118 Frank Duncan .10
119 Checklist .05

1991 Front Row Ken Griffey Jr.

Production of this collectors' set and related promo cards was reported at 25,000 sets each. Cards trace the three-year career of Junior in photos, stats, highlights and biographic details. Fronts have various posed and color action photos, complete with team logos, and a white border. Horizontal backs are printed in black on a light blue background. Promo cards have a large "PROMO" printed on a baseball at center. Size is 2-1/2" x 3-1/2".

NM/M
Complete Set (10): 2.00
Complete Promo Set (5): 1.00
Common Card: .25
Common Promo: .25
1 Ken Griffey Jr./AS .25
1 Ken Griffey Jr./AS (Promo) .25
2 Ken Griffey Jr. (The Breakdown) .25
2 Ken Griffey Jr. (The Breakdown) (Promo) .25
3 Ken Griffey Jr. (Homers) .25
3 Ken Griffey Jr. (Homers) (Promo) .25
4 Ken Griffey Jr. (Gold Glove) .25
4 Ken Griffey Jr. (Gold Glove) (Promo)) .25
5 Ken Griffey Jr. (Drafted) .25
5 Ken Griffey Jr. (Drafted)(Promo)) .25
6 Ken Griffey Jr. (Up Close and Personal) .25
7 Ken Griffey Jr. (Background) .25
8 Ken Griffey Jr. (The Majors) .25
9 Ken Griffey Jr. (Career Highlights) .25
10 Ken Griffey Jr. (The American League) .25

1992-95 Front Row All-Time Great Series

Some of baseball's greatest living former stars were featured in this run of five-card sets. Originally intended to encompass 100 players, the issue was cut considerably short. Each single-player set contains five cards featuring black-and-white and/or color photos on front. Backs have a photo in the background, overprinted with statistical, biographical or career information. Major league uniform logos have been removed from photos for lack of licensing by MLB. Each set was issued in an edition of 25,000, with an illustrated, numbered certificate of authenticity included. Each set was also produced with the top card authentically autographed. The Perry and Spahn sets were issued some time after the first 37 players. Sets are checklisted here alphabetically; single cards are not listed because the cards are usually sold only as sets.

NM/M
Common Player Set: .25
(1) Hank Aaron (5-card set) 1.00
(1a) Hank Aaron/Auto. 40.00
(2) Ernie Banks (5-card set) .75
(2a) Ernie Banks/Auto. 15.00
(3) Al Barlick (5-card set) .25
(3a) Al Barlick/Auto. 25.00
(4) Johnny Bench (5-card set) .75
(4a) Johnny Bench/Auto. 20.00
(5) Yogi Berra (5-card set) .75
(5a) Yogi Berra/Auto. 20.00
(6) Lou Boudreau (5-card set) .25
(6a) Lou Boudreau/Auto. 16.00
(7) Lou Brock (5-card set) .25
(7a) Lou Brock/Auto. 12.50
(8) Roy Campanella (5-card set) .75
(8a) Roy Campanella/Auto. 150.00
(9) Rod Carew (5-card set) .35
(9a) Rod Carew/Auto. 20.00
(10) Ray Dandridge (5-card set) .25
(10a) Ray Dandridge/Auto. 17.50
(11) Bobby Doerr (5-card set) .25
(11a) Bobby Doerr/Auto. 12.50
(12) Rick Ferrell (5-card set) .25
(12a) Rick Ferrell/Auto. 30.00
(13) Rollie Fingers (5-card set) .25
(13a) Rollie Fingers/Auto. 12.50
(14) Whitey Ford (5-card set) .50
(14a) Whitey Ford/Auto. 22.50
(15) George Foster (5-card set) .25
(15a) George Foster/Auto. 10.00
(16) Catfish Hunter (5-card set) .25
(16a) Catfish Hunter/Auto. 15.00
(17) Monte Irvin (5-card set) .25
(17a) Monte Irvin/Auto. 5.00
(18) Al Kaline (5-card set) .50
(18a) Al Kaline/Auto. 15.00
(19) George Kell (5-card set) .25
(19a) George Kell/Auto. 12.50
(20) Ralph Kiner (5-card set) .25
(20a) Ralph Kiner/Auto. 30.00
(21) Don Larsen (5-card set) .25
(21a) Don Larsen/Auto. 15.00
(22) Bob Lemon (5-card set) .25
(22a) Bob Lemon/Auto. 25.00
(23) Buck Leonard (5-card set) .25
(23a) Buck Leonard/Auto. 22.50
(23p) Buck Leonard ("PROMO" on back.) 1.00
(24) Juan Marichal (5-card set) .35
(24a) Juan Marichal/Auto. 15.00
(25) Joe Morgan (5-card set) .25
(25a) Joe Morgan/Auto. 25.00
(26) Stan Musial (5-card set) .50
(26a) Stan Musial/Auto. 40.00
(27) Hal Newhouser (5-card set) .25
(27a) Hal Newhouser/Auto. 15.00
(28) Jim Palmer (5-card set) .35
(28a) Jim Palmer/Auto. 12.50
(29) Tony Perez (5-card set) .25
(29a) Tony Perez/Auto. 12.50
(30) Gaylord Perry (5-card set) .50
(30a) Gaylord Perry/Auto. 12.50
(31) Pee Wee Reese (5-card set) .35
(32a) Pee Wee Reese/Auto. 40.00
(32) Phil Rizzuto (5-card set) .50
(32a) Phil Rizzuto/Auto. 20.00
(33) Brooks Robinson (5-card set) .35
(33a) Brooks Robinson/ Auto. 12.50
(34) Frank Robinson (5-card set) .35
(34a) Frank Robinson/ Auto. 15.00
(35) Red Schoendienst (5-card set) .25
(35a) Red Schoendienst/ Auto. 40.00
(36) Tom Seaver (5-card set) .35
(36a) Tom Seaver/Auto. 17.50
(37) Warren Spahn (5-card set) .50
(37a) Warren Spahn/Auto. 30.00
(38) Willie Stargell (5-card set) .25
(38a) Willie Stargell/Auto. 15.00
(39) Carl Yastrzemski (5-card set) .35
(39a) Carl Yastrzemski/ Auto. 30.00

1992 Front Row Club House Series Ken Griffey, Jr.

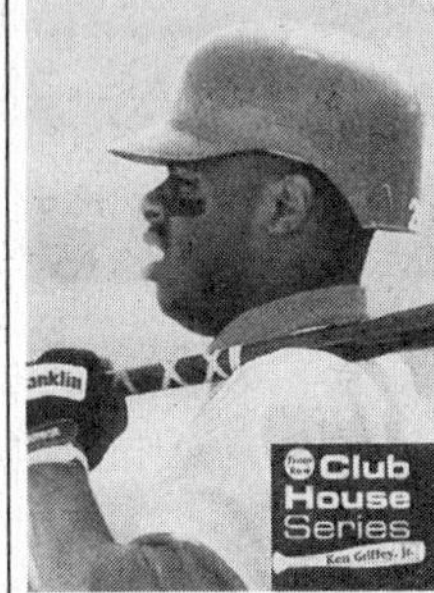

Ten cards tracing the life and career of Ken Griffey Jr. comprise this collectors' issue. Cards are standard 2-1/2" x 3-1/2" with borderless color action and posed photos. Uniform logos have been removed from the photos since the set is not licensed by MLB. A Club House Series logo is on front at bottom-right. Horizontal backs have a color photo of Griffey ghosted in the background. Printed over that are personal data, career highlights and stats.

NM/M
Complete Set (10): 1.00
Common Player: .15

1 Ken Griffey Jr. (Background) .15
2 Ken Griffey Jr. (Drafted) .15
3 Ken Griffey Jr. (The Majors) .15
4 Ken Griffey Jr. (The Breakdown) .15
5 Ken Griffey Jr. (The American League) .15
6 Ken Griffey Jr./AS .15
7 Ken Griffey Jr. (Gold Glove) .15
8 Ken Griffey Jr. (Homers) .15
9 Ken Griffey Jr. (Career Highlights) .15
10 Ken Griffey Jr. (A Closer Look) .15

Ken Griffey Jr. Holograms

This set of collectors' edition cards was produced in an issue of 50,000, with each set including a numbered certificate of authenticity. In standard 2-1/2" x 3-1/2" size, the cards have a borderless hologram picture on front. Conventionally printed backs have a color photo of the player and a few sentences about his career. Team logos have been removed from the pictures because the cards were not licensed by MLB.

		NM/M
Complete Set (3):		3.00
Common Card:		1.00
1	Ken Griffey Jr. (Making History)	1.00
2	Ken Griffey Jr. (Rewriting the Record Book)	1.00
3	Ken Griffey Jr. (Turning Up Gold)	1.00

Ken Griffey Jr. Pure Gold

This set of collectors' edition cards was produced in an issue of 20,000, with each set including a numbered certificate of authenticity. In standard 2-1/2" x 3-1/2" size, the cards have wide gold-foil borders on front. Backs have stats or a few sentences about his career. Team logos have been removed from the pictures because the cards were not licensed by MLB.

		NM/M
Complete Set (3):		3.00
Uncut Strip:		5.00
Common Card:		1.00
1	Ken Griffey Jr. (Gold Glove)	1.00
2	Ken Griffey Jr. (Background)	1.00
3	Ken Griffey Jr. (Drafted)	1.00

Holograms

The "career" seasons of three Hall of Famers are remembered in this series of cards. In standard 2-1/2" x 3-1/2" format, fronts have a borderless hologram featuring a vintage action photo. Conventionally printed backs have a color photo, a recap and stats from the named season, and a foil holographic serial number tag designating the card's place in an edition of 100,000 each.

		NM/M
Complete Set (3):		1.50
Common Player:		.50
(1)	Hank Aaron	.70
(2)	Roy Campanella	.50
(3)	Tom Seaver	.50

Pure Gold

Each of these 2-1/2" x 3-1/2" cards features 23-K gold borders on front, surrounding a color action photo on which uniform details have been air brushed away. Backs have player information.

		NM/M
Complete Set (6):		15.00
Common Player:		3.00
(1)	Hank Aaron	3.00
(2)	Roy Campanella	3.00
(3)	Tom Seaver	3.00
	Frank Thomas Strip (3):	10.00
(4)	Frank Thomas/Btg	3.00
(5)	Frank Thomas/Standing	3.00
(6)	Frank Thomas/Fldg	

Frank Thomas

Budding super slugger Frank Thomas is featured in this collectors' issue. The 2-1/2" x 3-1/2" cards have color photos on front, from which team logos have been airbrushed because the set was licensed only by the player, and not by MLB. Horizontally formatted backs have a second color photo along with a headline and a few sentences about his career to that point. The set was released in an edition of 30,000 and each was sold with a serial-numbered certificate of authenticity.

		NM/M
Complete Set (7):		3.00
Common Card:		.50
Autographed (# to 4,000):		15.00
1	Frank Thomas (A Good Start)	.50
nno	Frank Thomas (A Good Start- promo overprint on back.)	.50
2	Frank Thomas (Multi-Talented)	.50
3	Frank Thomas (Auburn Career)	.50
4	Frank Thomas (Accomplishments)	.50
5	Frank Thomas (Individual Honors)	.50
6	Frank Thomas (Minor League Stats)	.50
7	Frank Thomas (Major League Stats)	.50

1993 Front Row Gold Collection

Five borderless color photos (uniform logos removed) of Rollie Fingers are featured on the cards in this set. At bottom in a dark green stripe is the player name and, at left, the Front Row logo and the word "PREMIUM." Vertically at left is "The Gold Collection." All front printing is in gold foil. Backs have dark green borders with a ghost-image action photo and a few sentences about the player. A baseball at top carries the legend, "All Time Great / Series." Production was reported as 5,000 sets.

		NM/M
Complete Set (5):		2.00
Common Card:		.50
1-5	Rollie Fingers	.50

1999 FroZsnack's High-Screamers Lids

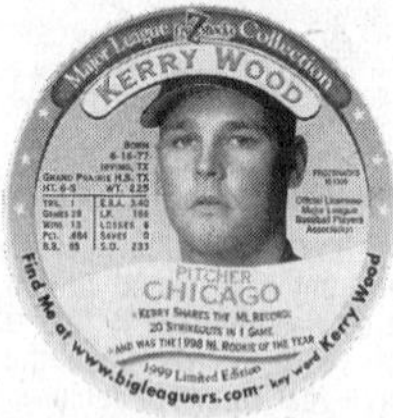

These 3-1/4" plastic lids were found on ice cream snacks sold at ballparks and possibly other outlets. A player photo with uniform logos covered is featured at center with personal data and 1998 stats on the side. The player name is in a banner at top, his team, position and career highlights are in a banner at bottom.

		NM/M
Complete Set (40):		30.00
Common Player:		.75
(1)	Roberto Alomar	.75
(2)	Jeff Bagwell	1.25
(3)	Albert Belle	.75
(4)	Dante Bichette	.75
(5)	Craig Biggio	.75
(6)	Barry Bonds	2.50
(7)	Kevin Brown	.75
(8)	Jose Canseco	1.00
(9)	Vinny Castilla	.75
(10)	Tony Clark	.75
(11)	Francisco Cordova	.75
(12)	Eric Davis	.75
(13)	Nomar Garciaparra	1.75
(14)	Tom Glavine	1.00
(15)	Ben Grieve	.75
(16)	Ken Griffey Jr.	2.00
(17)	Tony Gwynn	1.50
(18)	Rickey Henderson	1.25
(19)	Livan Hernandez	.75
(20)	Derek Jeter	2.50
(21)	Jason Kendall	.75
(22)	Randy Johnson	1.25
(23)	Barry Larkin	.75
(24)	Greg Maddux	1.50
(25)	Tino Martinez	.75
(26)	Mark McGwire	2.25
(27)	Robb Nen	.75
(28)	Mike Piazza	2.00
(29)	Manny Ramirez	1.25
(30)	Cal Ripken Jr.	2.50
(31)	Alex Rodriguez	2.25
(32)	Scott Rolen	1.00
(33)	Sammy Sosa	1.75
(34)	Frank Thomas	1.25
(35)	Greg Vaughn	.75
(36)	Fernando Vina	.75
(37)	Omar Vizquel	.75
(38)	Larry Walker	.75
(39)	Matt Williams	.75
(40)	Kerry Wood	1.00

1998 Fruit Roll-Ups All-Stars

Perforated panels of eight small (1-1/2" x 2") cards bearing the Topps logo were found on 38-count boxes of Fruit Roll-Ups snacks early in the 1998 season. The blank-back cards are printed on a 6" x 4" panel which can be removed from the box back. The front of the box pictures Rodriguez, Thomas and McGwire.

		NM/M
Complete Box:		5.00
Complete Panel:		4.00
Complete Set, Singles (8):		3.50
Common Player:		.50
(1)	Tony Gwynn	1.00
(2)	Derek Jeter	1.50
(3)	Kenny Lofton	.50
(4)	Mark McGwire	1.25
(5)	Mike Piazza	1.25
(6)	Cal Ripken Jr.	1.50
(7)	Ivan Rodriguez	.65
(8)	Frank Thomas	.75

1985 Fun Food Buttons

Fun Foods of Little Silver, N.J., issued a set of 133 full-color metal pins in 1985. The buttons, which are 1-1/4" in diameter and have a "safety pin" back, have bright borders which correspond to the player's team colors. The button backs are numbered and contain the player's 1984 batting or earned run average. The buttons were available as complete sets through hobby dealers and were also distributed in packs of three through retail stores. Cardboard 1-1/2" x 1-1/2" square proofs of the buttons' fronts are also seen in the hobby; their value is 2-3X that of the corresponding button, with production reported to be only 2,000 cardboard proofs.

		NM/M
Complete Set (133):		20.00
Common Player:		.10
Wax Pack (3):		.50
Wax Box (36):		9.00
1	Dave Winfield	1.00
2	Lance Parrish	.10
3	Gary Carter	1.00
4	Pete Rose	2.00
5	Jim Rice	.35
6	George Brett	1.75
7	Fernando Valenzuela	.10
8	Darryl Strawberry	.10
9	Steve Garvey	.45
10	Rollie Fingers	.75
11	Mike Schmidt	1.75
12	Kent Tekulve	.10
13	Ryne Sandberg	1.50
14	Bruce Sutter	.75
15	Tom Seaver	1.00
16	Reggie Jackson	1.50
17	Rickey Henderson	1.00
18	Mark Langston	.10
19	Jack Clark	.10
20	Willie Randolph	.10
21	Kirk Gibson	.10
22	Andre Dawson	.35
23	Dave Concepcion	.10
24	Tony Armas	.10
25	Dan Quisenberry	.10
26	Pedro Guerrero	.10
27	Dwight Gooden	.10
28	Tony Gwynn	1.50
29	Robin Yount	1.00
30	Steve Carlton	1.00
31	Bill Madlock	.10
32	Rick Sutcliffe	.10
33	Willie McGee	.10
34	Greg Luzinski	.10
35	Rod Carew	1.00
36	Dave Kingman	.10
37	Alvin Davis	.10
38	Chili Davis	.10
39	Don Baylor	.10
40	Alan Trammell	.10
41	Tim Raines	.10
42	Cesar Cedeno	.10
43	Wade Boggs	1.50
44	Frank White	.10
45	Steve Sax	.10
46	George Foster	.10
47	Terry Kennedy	.10
48	Cecil Cooper	.10
49	John Denny	.10
50	John Candelaria	.10
51	Jody Davis	.10
52	George Hendrick	.10
53	Ron Kittle	.10
54	Fred Lynn	.10
55	Carney Lansford	.10
56	Gorman Thomas	.10
57	Manny Trillo	.10
58	Steve Kemp	.10
59	Jack Morris	.10
60	Dan Petry	.10
61	Mario Soto	.10
62	Dwight Evans	.10
63	Hal McRae	.10
64	Mike Marshall	.10
65	Mookie Wilson	.10
66	Graig Nettles	.10
67	Ben Oglivie	.10
68	Juan Samuel	.10
69	Johnny Ray	.10
70	Gary Matthews	.10
71	Ozzie Smith	1.50
72	Carlton Fisk	1.00
73	Doug DeCinces	.10
74	Joe Morgan	1.00
75	Dave Stieb	.10
76	Buddy Bell	.10
77	Don Mattingly	1.75
78	Lou Whitaker	.10
79	Willie Hernandez	.10
80	Dave Parker	.10
81	Bob Stanley	.10
82	Willie Wilson	.10
83	Orel Hershiser	.10
84	Rusty Staub	.10
85	Goose Gossage	.10
86	Don Sutton	.75
87	Al Holland	.10
88	Tony Pena	.10
89	Ron Cey	.10
90	Joaquin Andujar	.10
91	LaMarr Hoyt	.10
92	Tommy John	.10
93	Dwayne Murphy	.10
94	Willie Upshaw	.10
95	Gary Ward	.10
96	Ron Guidry	.10
97	Chet Lemon	.10
98	Aurelio Lopez	.10
99	Tony Perez	.75
100	Bill Buckner	.10
101	Mike Hargrove	.10
102	Scott McGregor	.10
103	Dale Murphy	.50
104	Keith Hernandez	.10
105	Paul Molitor	1.00
106	Bert Blyleven	.10
107	Leon Durham	.10
108	Lee Smith	.10
109	Nolan Ryan	3.00
110	Harold Baines	.10
111	Kent Hrbek	.10
112	Ron Davis	.10
113	George Bell	.10
114	Charlie Hough	.10
115	Phil Niekro	.75
116	Dave Righetti	.10
117	Darrell Evans	.10
118	Cal Ripken, Jr.	3.00
119	Eddie Murray	1.00
120	Storm Davis	.10
121	Mike Boddicker	.10
122	Bob Horner	.10
123	Chris Chambliss	.10
124	Ted Simmons	.10
125	Andre Thornton	.10
126	Larry Bowa	.10
127	Bob Dernier	.10
128	Joe Niekro	.10
129	Jose Cruz	.10
130	Tom Brunansky	.10
131a	Garry Gaetti	50.00
131b	Gary Gaetti	.10
132	Lloyd Moseby	.10
133	Frank Tanana	.10

G

1982 Renata Galasso 20 Years of Met Baseball

The original New York Mets team of 1962 is featured on this 20-year anniversary set. The 2-1/2" x 3 1/2" cards have black-and-white photos with blue borders. The player name and position is in orange at bottom. Backs repeat the team colors with blue and orange printing on white cardboard. Card and uniform numbers appear in the top corners, there is a career summary, 1962 and career stats and a trivia question. Production was reported as 2,500 sets.

		NM/M
Complete Set (30):		10.00
Common Player:		.50
1	Marv Throneberry	.75
2	Richie Ashburn	2.00
3	Charlie Neal	.50
4	Cliff Cook	.50
5	Elio Chacon	.50
6	Chris Cannizzaro	.50
7	Jim Hickman	.50
8	Rod Kanehl	.50
9	Gene Woodling	.50
10	Gil Hodges	2.00
11	Al Jackson	.50
12	Sammy Taylor	.50
13	Felix Mantilla	.50
14	Ken MacKenzie	.50
15	Craig Anderson	.50
16	Bob Moorhead	.50
17	Joe Christopher	.50
18	Bob Miller	.50
19	Frank Thomas	.75
20	Vinegar Bend Mizell	.50
21	Bill Hunter	.50
22	Roger Craig	.50
23	Jay Hook	.50
24	Meet The Mets (Team card.)	.75
25	Choo Choo Coleman	.50
26	Casey Stengel	2.00
28	Solly Hemus	.50
29	Rogers Hornsby	2.00
31	Red Ruffing	.50
32	George Weiss	.50

1983 Renata Galasso 1933 All-Stars

The premiere All-Star Game in 1933 is commemorated in this 50th anniversary collectors' issue. In standard 2-1/2" x 3-1/2" format (though not uniformly cut to exact size), the cards feature black-and-white portrait photos on front. Many of the National League All-Stars are pictured in their special NL uniforms. In the wide white border at

bottom is the player's name, position and league. Backs are printed in red, white and blue with a large Galasso ad and a short career summary; there is little mention of the 1933 All-Star Game. Two unnumbered cards issued with the set have N.L. and A.L. team photos on front and blue-tone backs showing A-S managers Connie Mack and John McGraw "choosing up sides."

		NM/M
Complete Set (45):		15.00
Common Player:		1.00
1	Tony Cuccinello	1.00
2	Lon Warenke (Warneke)	1.00
3	Hal Schumacher	1.00
4	Wally Berger	1.00
5	Lefty O'Doul	1.00
6	Chuck Klein	1.00
7	Chick Hafey	1.00
8	Jimmie Wilson	1.00
9	John McGraw	1.00
10	Max Carey	1.00
11	Bill McKechnie	1.00
12	Dick Bartell	1.00
13	Bill Hallahan	1.00
14	Woody English	1.00
15	Paul Waner	1.00
16	Carl Hubbell	1.50
17	Frank Frisch	1.00
18	Gabby Hartnett	1.00
19	Pie Traynor	1.00
20	Bill Terry	1.00
21	Pepper Martin	1.00
22	Earl Averill	1.00
23	Jimmy Dykes	1.00
24	Charlie Gehringer	1.50
25	Rich Ferrell (Rick)	1.00
26	Joe Cronin	1.00
27	Ben Chapman	1.00
28	Eddie Rommel	1.00
29	Lefty Grove	1.50
30	Connie Mack	1.00
31	Babe Ruth	5.00
32	Sam West	1.00
33	Tony Lazzeri	1.00
34	Al Simmons	1.00
35	Wes Ferrell	1.00
36	Bill Dickey	1.00
37	General Crowder	1.00
38	Oral Hildebrand	1.00
39	Lefty Gomez	1.00
40	Jimmie Foxx	1.50
41	Art Fletcher	1.00
42	Eddie Collins	1.00
43	Lou Gehrig	3.00
(44)	1933 N.L. All-Star Team	2.00
(45)	1933 A.L. All-Star Team	2.00

1969 Seattle Pilots

The one-year American League franchise in Seattle is recalled with this collectors' issue. Full-color photos of the peripatetic Pilots are framed in team-color blue and gold on a beige background in standard 2-1/2" x 3-1/2" size. Backs are printed in red and blue on white and feature a career summary and 1969 stats. For some players, this represents their only baseball card appearance and for many more, it is their only card in a Pilots' uniform. Many of the sets were originally sold with the #1 Jim Bouton card personally autographed.

		NM/M
Complete Set (43):		12.50
Common Player:		.50
1	Jim Bouton	2.00
1(a)	Jim Bouton/Auto.	15.00
2	Joe Schultz	.50
3	Bill Edgerton	.70
4	Gary Timberlake	.70
5	Dick Baney	.50
6	Mike G. Marshall	1.00
7	Jim Gosger	.50
8	Mike Hegan	.50
9	Steve Hovley	.50
10	Don Mincher	.50
11	Miguel Fuentes	.50
12	Charlie Bates	.50
13	John O'Donoghue	.50
14	Tommy Davis	.75
15	Jerry McNertney	.50
16	Rich Rollins	.50
17	Fred Talbot	.50
18	John Gelnar	.50
19	Bob Locker	.50
20	Frank Crosetti	.75
21	Sal Maglie	.75
22	Sibby Sisti	.50
23	Ron Plaza	.50
24	Federico Velazquez	.50
25	Diego Segui	.50
26	Steve Barber	.50
27	Jack Aker	.50
28	Marty Pattin	.50
29	Ray Oyler	.50
30	Danny Walton	.75
31	Merritt Ranew	.50
32	John Donaldson	.50
33	Greg Goossen	.50
34	Gary Bell	.50
35	Jim Pagliaroni	.50
36	Mike Ferraro	.50
37	Tommy Harper	.75
38	John Morris	.50
39	Larry Haney	.50
40	Ron Clark	.50
41	Steve Whitaker	.50
42	Wayne Comer	.50
43	Gene Brabender	.50

1984 Renata Galasso Baseball Collector Series

Some of baseball's best are presented in this glossy-front black-and-white, 2-3/8" x 3-1/2", collectors' set patterned after the 1953 Bowmans. Backs are in red and black with a career summary and lifetime stats.

		NM/M
Complete Set (20):		15.00
Common Player:		.50
1	Roberto Clemente	1.50
2	Duke Snider	.75
3	Sandy Koufax	1.50
4	Carl Hubbell	.50
5	Ty Cobb	1.00
6	Willie Mays	1.50
7	Jackie Robinson	1.50
8	Joe DiMaggio	3.00
9	Stan Musial	1.00
10	Pie Traynor	.50
11	Yogi Berra	.75
12	Babe Ruth	3.00
13	Brooks Robinson	.50
14	Walter Johnson	.50
15	Ted Williams	1.50
16	Bill Dickey	.50
17	Lou Gehrig	2.00
18	Hank Aaron	1.50
19	Eddie Mathews	.50
20	Mickey Mantle	5.00

Hall of Fame Art Card Series

Painting on these 2-7/8" x 5" deckle-edge cards are by Ron Lewis and depict Hall of Famers induction between 1936-46. There are no graphics or player identification on the front. Backs are printed in red and black and have player personal data, career highlights and lifetime stats within a decorative shield.

		NM/M
Complete Set (45):		15.00
Common Player:		.50
1	Ty Cobb	3.00
2	Babe Ruth	5.00
3	Walter Johnson	1.50
4	Christy Mathewson	1.50
5	Honus Wagner	1.50
6	Napoleon Lajoie	.75
7	Tris Speaker	.75
8	Cy Young	1.50
9	Morgan Bulkeley	.50
10	Ban Johnson	.50
11	John McGraw	.50
12	Connie Mack	.50
13	George Wright	.50
14	Grover Alexander	.65
15	Alexander Cartwright	.50
16	Henry Chadwick	.50
17	Eddie Collins	.50
18	Lou Gehrig	4.00
19	Willie Keeler	.50
20	George Sisler	.50
21	Cap Anson	.50
22	Charles Comiskey	.50
23	Candy Cummings	.50
24	Buck Ewing	.50
25	Charlie Radbourne	.50
26	A.G. Spalding	.50
27	Roger (Rogers) ornsby	.75
28	Kenesaw M. Landis	.50
29	Roger Bresnahan	.50
30	Dan Brouthers	.50
31	Fred Clarke	.50
32	Jimmy Collins	.50
33	Ed Delahanty	.50
34	Hugh Duffy	.50
35	Mike "King" Kelly	.50
36	Hughie Jennings	.50
37	Jim O'Rourke	.50
38	Wilbert Robinson	.50
39	Jesse Burkett	.50
40	Frank Chance	.50
41	Jack Chesbro	.50
42	Johnny Evers	.50
43	Joe Tinker	.50
44	Eddie Plank	.50
45	Checklist	.50

Reggie Jackson

This collectors' issue chronicling the career of "Mr. October" was produced in two sizes - the standard 2-1/2" x 3-1/2" and the Topps' "mini" format of 2-1/4" x 3-1/8". Both sizes share the same design of a color or black-and-white photo on a blue border with "Reggie 44" at bottom, along with a photo of his classic swing. Backs have statistical data, career summary or part of a puzzle showing all of Jackson's Topps cards to that point. The full-size set was limited to 10,000, with 500 featuring a genuine autograph on card #1; the mini set was issued in an edition of 5,000.

	NM/M
Complete Standard-size Set (30):	7.50
Complete Set w/Autographed #1:	45.00
Complete Mini Set (30):	10.00
Common Card:	.40

Willie Mays Story

Color and black-and-white photos from the Hall of Famer's career and off-field life are featured in this collectors' set. Each photo is surrounded by a red frame and white border. Many of the photos will be familiar to collectors as having earlier appeared on Topps cards. Backs of the first 45 cards are in red, black and white, with biographical information or a description of the front photo. Backs of cards #46-90 can be assembled into a full-color puzzle of Mays' baseball cards from Topps, Bowman and others. Card #1 in each set is authentically autographed by Mays. Retail price at issue was $20.

	NM/M
Complete Set (90):	35.00
Common Card:	.50

1927 N.Y. Yankees

Paintings by Ron Lewis adorn this collectors' issue honoring what may have been been baseball's best team ever. The 2-1/2" x 3-1/2" cards have blue borders with the player's name in a banner at bottom. Backs have typical player data plus 1927 and career stats. The set was originally issued at about $5.

		NM/M
Complete Set (30):		18.00
Common Player:		.50
1	Lou Gehrig	5.00
2	Babe Ruth	7.50
3	Earle Combs	1.00
4	Ed Barrow	.50
5	Bob Shawkey	.50
6	Bob Meusel	.50
7	Urban Shocker	.50
8	Ben Paschal	.50
9	John Grabowski	.50
10	Jacob Ruppert	.50
11	Herb Pennock	1.00
12	Miller Huggins	1.00
13	Wilcy Moore	.50
14	Walter Beall	.50
15	Cedric Durst	.50
16	Tony Lazzeri	1.00
17	Mark Koenig	.50
18	Waite Hoyt	1.00
19	Myles Thomas	.50
20	Joe Dugan	.50
21	Art Fletcher	.50
22	Charlie O'Leary	.50
23	Ray Morehart	.50
24	Benny Bengough	.50
25	Pat Collins	.50
26	Dutch Reuther (Ruether)	.50
27	George Pipgras	.50
28	Mike Gazella	.50
29	Julian Wera	.50
30	Joe Giard	.50

1985 Renata Galasso Dwight Gooden

This collectors' issue was produced by Brooklyn dealer Renata Galasso as one of several to capitalize on Gooden's early fame. Card #1 features a Ron Lewis painting of Gooden, the others feature color photos from his boyhood and early career. (Card #16 pictures him shaking hands with Henry Aaron.) Photos are surrounded on front with a border of blue squares. A pink "DR. K" logo is at bottom-right. Backs are in blue and white and feature a question and answer session with the pitcher, stats, or part of a nine-piece puzzle. Five thousand sets were produced, with 500 of them featuring Gooden's autograph on Card #1. Issue price was about $11.

	NM/M
Complete Set (30):	4.00
Complete Autographed Set:	15.00
Single Card:	.15

1986 Renata Galasso Dwight Gooden

Dr. K's Cy Young Season in 1985 is recalled in this collectors' set. Numbered from 31-60, picking up where the 1985 set had left off, the series share a similar format. Fronts have black-and-white or color photos surrounded by a frame of blue dots and larger orange squares. A blue "Dr. K" appears in the lower-right corner. Backs are in blue and orange on white and narrate the 1985 season. The final nine cards in the set have pieces forming a puzzle picture of Gooden.

	NM/M
Complete Set (30):	4.00
Single Card:	.15

Don Mattingly

The life and career of the Yankees superstar is traced in this collectors' issue. The 2-1/2" x 3-1/2" cards have a mix of black-and-white and color photos on a white background with blue pinstripes. A yellow circle in a bottom corner of each card front has "THE HIT MAN" in red. Backs are printed in blue, with 21 of them featuring a question-and-answer format and nine forming a puzzle picture of Mattingly.

	NM/M
Complete Set (30):	6.00
Single Card:	.50

1961 Yankees Black-and-White

Illustrating one of the problems with collectors' issues, a person holding one of these cards might assume it is of 1961 or 1962 vintage because there is no date of actual issue, which occurred around 1986, anywhere on the cards. In a format similar to Topps' 1961 cards, this set features large black-and-white player photos on a 2-1/2" x 3-1/2" glossy stock. The player name and position are in a pair of color bars at bottom. Backs are in red and black and have personal data, season and career stats, a 1961 season summary and a trivia question. Reported production was 2,500.

		NM/M
Complete Set (30):		20.00
Common Player:		.50
1	Roger Maris	3.00
2	Bobby Richardson	.75
3	Tony Kubek	.75
4	Elston Howard	.75
5	Bill Skowron	.75
6	Clete Boyer	.50
7	Mickey Mantle	7.50
8	Yogi Berra	2.00
9	Johnny Blanchard	.50
10	Hector Lopez	.50
11	Whitey Ford	2.00
12	Ralph Terry	.50
13	Bill Stafford	.50
14	Bud Daley	.50
15	Billy Gardner	.50
16	Jim Coates	.50
17	Luis Arroyo	.50
18	Tex Clevenger	.50
19	Bob Cerv	.50
20	Art Ditmar	.50
21	Bob Turley	.50
22	Joe DeMaestri	.50
23	Rollie Sheldon	.50
24	Earl Torgeson	.50
25	Hal Reniff	.50

26	Ralph Houk	.50
27	Jim Hegan	.50
28	Johnny Sain	.60
29	Frank Crosetti	.50
30	Wally Moses	.50

1961 Yankees Color

The World Champion N.Y. Yankees of 1961 are remembered in this collectors' set. The 2-1/2" x 3-1/2" cards borrow the design of Topps' 1961 issue, with a large color photo at top and red and yellow boxes below with player name and position in contrasting color. Backs are printed in blue and red with a few biographical details, 1961 and career stats and a career summary.

		NM/M
Complete Set (37):		15.00
Common Player:		.25
1	Roger Maris	3.00
2	Yogi Berra	1.50
3	Whitey Ford	1.50
4	Hector Lopez	.25
5	Bob Turley	.25
6	Frank Crosetti	.25
7	Bob Cerv	.25
8	Jack Reed	.25
9	Luis Arroyo	.25
10	Danny McDevitt	.25
11	Duke Maas	.25
12	Jesse Gonder	.25
13	Ralph Terry	.25
14	Deron Johnson	.25
15	Johnny Blanchard	.25
16	Bill Stafford	.25
17	Earl Torgeson	.25
18	Tony Kubek	.40
19	Rollie Sheldon	.25
20	Tex Clevenger	.25
21	Art Ditmar	.25
22	Bud Daley	.25
23	Jim Coates	.25
24	Al Downing	.25
25	Johnny Sain	.25
26	Jim Hegan	.25
27	Wally Moses	.25
28	Ralph Houk	.25
29	Bill Skowron	.40
30	Bobby Richardson	.40
31	Johnny James	.25
32	Hal Reniff	.25
33	Mickey Mantle	6.00
34	Clete Boyer	.25
35	Elston Howard	.35
36	Joe DeMaestri	.25
37	Billy Gardner	.25

1983 Gardner's Brewers

Topps produced in 1983 for Gardner's Bakery of Madison, Wisconsin, a 22-card set featuring the American League champion Milwaukee Brewers. The cards, which measure 2-1/2" x 3-1/2", have colorful fronts which contain the player's name, team and position plus the Brewers and Gardner's logos. The card backs are identical to the regular Topps issue but are numbered 1-22. The cards were inserted in specially marked packages of Gardner's bread products and were susceptible to grease stains.

		NM/M
Complete Set (22):		8.00
Common Player:		.25
1	Harvey Kuenn	.25
2	Dwight Bernard	.25
3	Mark Brouhard	.25
4	Mike Caldwell	.25
5	Cecil Cooper	.25
6	Marshall Edwards	.25
7	Rollie Fingers	1.00
8	Jim Gantner	.25
9	Moose Haas	.25
10	Bob McClure	.25
11	Paul Molitor	4.00
12	Don Money	.25
13	Charlie Moore	.25
14	Ben Oglivie	.25
15	Ed Romero	.25
16	Ted Simmons	.25
17	Jim Slaton	.25
18	Don Sutton	1.00
19	Gorman Thomas	.25
20	Pete Vuckovich	.25
21	Ned Yost	.25
22	Robin Yount	4.00

1984 Gardner's Brewers

For the second straight year, Gardner's Bakery inserted baseball cards featuring the Milwaukee Brewers with its bread products. The 22-card set, entitled "1984 Series II," have multi-colored fronts that include the Brewers and Gardner's logos. The card backs are identical to the regular 1984 Topps issue except for the 1-22 numbering system. The Topps-produced cards are the standard 2-1/2" x 3-1/2" size. The cards are sometimes found with grease stains, resulting from contact with the bread.

		NM/M
Complete Set (22):		5.00
Common Player:		.25
1	Rene Lachemann	.25
2	Mark Brouhard	.25
3	Mike Caldwell	.25
4	Bobby Clark	.25
5	Cecil Cooper	.25
6	Rollie Fingers	.50
7	Jim Gantner	.25
8	Moose Haas	.25
9	Roy Howell	.25
10	Pete Ladd	.25
11	Rick Manning	.25
12	Bob McClure	.25
13	Paul Molitor	3.00
14	Charlie Moore	.25
15	Ben Oglivie	.25
16	Ed Romero	.25
17	Ted Simmons	.25
18	Jim Sundberg	.25
19	Don Sutton	.50
20	Tom Tellmann	.25
21	Pete Vuckovich	.25
22	Robin Yount	3.00

1985 Gardner's Brewers

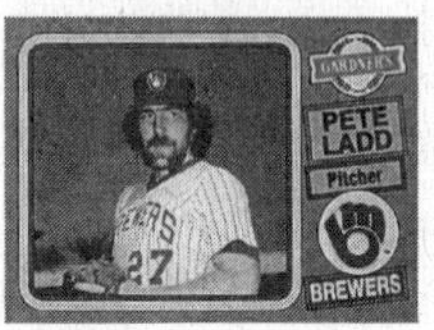

Gardner's Bakery issued a 22-card set featuring the Milwaukee Brewers for the third consecutive year in 1985. The set was produced by Topps and is designed in a horizontal format. The card fronts feature color photos inside blue, red and yellow frames. The player's name and position are placed in orange boxes to the right of the photo and are accompanied by the Brewers and Gardner's logos. The card backs are identical to the regular 1985 Topps set but are blue rather than green and are numbered 1-22. The cards, which were inserted in specially marked bread products, are often found with grease stains.

		NM/M
Complete Set (22):		5.00
Common Player:		.25
1	George Bamberger	.25
2	Mark Brouhard	.25
3	Bob Clark	.25
4	Jaime Cocanower	.25
5	Cecil Cooper	.25
6	Rollie Fingers	.50
7	Jim Gantner	.25
8	Moose Haas	.25
9	Dion James	.25
10	Pete Ladd	.25
11	Rick Manning	.25
12	Bob McClure	.25
13	Paul Molitor	3.00
14	Charlie Moore	.25
15	Ben Oglivie	.25
16	Chuck Porter	.25
17	Ed Romero	.25
18	Bill Schroeder	.25
19	Ted Simmons	.25
20	Tom Tellmann	.25
21	Pete Vuckovich	.25
22	Robin Yount	3.00

1989 Gardner's Brewers

Returning after a three-year hiatus, Gardner's Bread of Madison, Wis., issued a 15-card Milwaukee Brewers set in 1989. The blue and white-bordered cards are the standard size and feature posed portrait photos with all Brewer logos airbrushed from the players' caps. The Gardner's logo appears at the top of the card, while the player's name is below the photo. The set, which was produced in conjunction with Mike Schechter Associates, was issued with loaves of bread or packages of buns, one card per package.

		NM/M
Complete Set (15):		5.00
Common Player:		.25
1	Paul Molitor	2.50
2	Robin Yount	2.50
3	Jim Gantner	.25
4	Rob Deer	.25
5	B.J. Surhoff	.25
6	Dale Sveum	.25
7	Ted Higuera	.25
8	Dan Plesac	.25
9	Bill Wegman	.25
10	Juan Nieves	.25
11	Greg Brock	.25
12	Glenn Braggs	.25
13	Joey Meyer	.25
14	Ernest Riles	.25
15	Don August	.25

1986 Gatorade Cubs

Gatorade sponsored this set which was given away at the July 17, 1986, Cubs game.

Cards measure 2-7/8" x 4-1/4" and feature color photos inside red and white frames. The Cubs logo appears at the top of the card. Backs include statistical information and the Gatorade logo. This set marked the fifth consecutive year the Cubs had held a baseball card giveaway promotion.

		NM/M
Complete Set (28):		12.00
Common Player:		.25
4	Gene Michael	.25
6	Keith Moreland	.25
7	Jody Davis	.25
10	Leon Durham	.25
11	Ron Cey	.25
12	Shawon Dunston	.25
15	Davey Lopes	.25
16	Terry Francona	.25
18	Steve Christmas	.25
19	Manny Trillo	.25
20	Bob Dernier	.25
21	Scott Sanderson	.25
22	Jerry Mumphrey	.25
23	Ryne Sandberg	9.00
27	Thad Bosley	.25
28	Chris Speier	.25
29	Steve Lake	.25
31	Ray Fontenot	.25
34	Steve Trout	.25
36	Gary Matthews	.25
39	George Frazier	.25
40	Rick Sutcliffe	.35
43	Dennis Eckersley	1.50
46	Lee Smith	.35
48	Jay Baller	.25
49	Jamie Moyer	.25
50	Guy Hoffman	.25
---	The Coaching Staff (Ruben Amaro, Billy Connors, Johnny Oates, John Vukovich, Billy Williams)	.25

1987 Gatorade Indians

For the second year in a row, the Indians gave out a perforated set of baseball cards to fans attending the Team Photo/Baseball Card Day promotion. Sponsored by Gatorade, the individual cards measure 2-1/2" x 3-1/8". Fronts contain a color photo surrounded by a red frame inside a white border. The player's name, uniform number and the Gatorade logo are also on front. Backs are printed in black, blue and red and carry a facsimile autograph and the player's stats.

		NM/M
Complete Set, Foldout:		6.00
Complete Set, Singles (31):		6.00
Common Player:		.25
2	Brett Butler	.25
4	Tony Bernazard	.25
6	Andy Allanson	.25
7	Pat Corrales	.25
8	Carmen Castillo	.25
10	Pat Tabler	.25
11	Jamie Easterly	.25
12	Dave Clark	.25
13	Ernie Camacho	.25
14	Julio Franco	.35
17	Junior Noboa	.25
18	Ken Schrom	.25
20	Otis Nixon	.25
21	Greg Swindell	.25
22	Frank Wills	.25
23	Chris Bando	.25
24	Rick Dempsey	.25
26	Brook Jacoby	.25
27	Mel Hall	.25
28	Cory Snyder	.25
29	Andre Thornton	.35
30	Joe Carter	.75
35	Phil Niekro	.75
36	Ed Vande Berg	.25
42	Rich Yett	.25
43	Scott Bailes	.25
46	Doug Jones	.25
49	Tom Candiotti	.25
54	Tom Waddell	.25
---	Manager and Coaching Staff (Jack Aker, Bobby Bonds, Pat Corrales, Doc Edwards, Johnny Goryl)	.25
---	Team Photo	.25

1988 Gatorade Indians

This three-panel foldout was sponsored by Gatorade for distribution during an in-stadium giveaway. The cover includes four game-action photos. One panel of the 9-1/2" x 11-1/4" glossy color foldout features a team photo (with checklist), two panels consist of 30 perforated baseball cards (2-1/4" x 3") featuring team members. Posed portrait photos are framed in red on a white background. The player's name and uniform number are printed below the photo. Backs are printed in red, blue and black. A facsimile autograph appears at the top-right of the card back, opposite the player uniform number, name and position. Both major and minor league stats are listed.

		NM/M
Complete Set, Foldout:		5.00
Complete Set, Singles (31):		5.00
Common Player:		.25
2	Tom Spencer	.25
6	Andy Allanson	.25
7	Luis Issac	.25
8	Carmen Castillo	.25
9	Charlie Manuel	.25
10	Pat Tabler	.25
11	Doug Jones	.25
14	Julio Franco	.50
15	Ron Washington	.25
16	Jay Bell	.75
17	Bill Laskey	.25
20	Willie Upshaw	.25
21	Greg Swindell	.25
23	Chris Bando	.25
25	Dave Clark	.25
26	Brook Jacoby	.25
27	Mel Hall	.25
28	Cory Snyder	.25
30	Joe Carter	.75
31	Dan Schatzeder	.25
32	Doc Edwards	.25
33	Ron Kittle	.25
35	Mark Wiley	.25
42	Rich Yett	.25
43	Scott Bailes	.25
45	Johnny Goryl	.25
47	Jeff Kaiser	.25
49	Tom Candiotti	.25
50	Jeff Dedmon	.25
52	John Farrell	.25
---	Team Photo	2.00

1993 Gatorade Detroit Tigers

Color action photos are featured on these oversized (2-7/8" x 4-1/4") cards. The pictures are framed in team-color navy and orange pinstripes with a white border. Player name is in white in a navy border below the photo, with the position printed in orange at bottom. A large team logo appears in the upper-right corner. Backs are printed in orange and black and include a Gatorade logo, player identification and stats. Cards are listed here by uniform number.

		NM/M
Complete Set (28):		4.00
Common Player:		.25
1	Lou Whitaker	.75
3	Alan Trammell	1.00
4	Tony Phillips	.25
7	Scott Livingstone	.25
9	Skeeter Barnes	.25
11	Sparky Anderson	.75
15	Gary Thurman	.25
16	David Wells	.25
18	David Haas	.25
19	Chad Kreuter	.25
20	Mickey Tettleton	.25
21	Mike Moore	.25
22	Milt Cuyler	.25
23a	Kirk Gibson	.50
23b	Mark Leiter	.25
24	Travis Fryman	.50
27	Kurt Knudsen	.25
28	Rob Deer	.25
30	Bill Krueger	.25
32	Dan Gladden	.25
36	Bill Gullickson	.25
38	Bob MacDonald	.25
39	Mike Henneman	.25
42	Buddy Groom	.25
44	John Doherty	.25
45	Cecil Fielder	.50
49	Tom Bolton	.25
---	Coaches (Dick Tracewksi, Billy Muffett, Larry Herndon, Gene Roof, Dan Whitmer)	.25

1995 Gatorade Cubs

Fans attending the August 24 game at Wrigley Field received a set of oversized (2-7/8" x 4-1/4") cards of the Chicago Cubs, sponsored by Gatorade. Cards feature a color action photo at top, with the player's name, position and uniform number in a blue box at bottom. Backs have a small black-and-white portrait photo, complete minor and major league stats and the team and sponsor logos. Cards are checklisted here by player uniform number.

		NM/M
Complete Set (27):		5.00
Common Player:		.25
5	Jim Riggleman	.25
9	Scott Servais	.25
10	Scott Bullett	.25
11	Rey Sanchez	.25
12	Shawon Dunston	.25
13	Turk Wendell	.25
16	Anthony Young	.25
17	Mark Grace	.50
18	Jose Hernandez	.25
20	Howard Johnson	.25
21	Sammy Sosa	4.00
25	Luis Gonzalez	.50
27	Todd Zeile	.25
28	Randy Myers	.25
29	Jose Guzman	.25
30	Ozzie Timmons	.25
32	Kevin Foster	.25
38	Jaime Navarro	.25
46	Steve Trachsel	.25
47	Mike Perez	.25
49	Frank Castillo	.25
52	Jim Bullinger	.25
53	Chris Nabholz	.25
55	Larry Casian	.25
56	Brian McRae	.25
57	Rich Garces	.25
---	Cubs Coaches (Dave Bialas, Fergie Jenkins, Tony Muser, Max Oliveras, Dan Radison, Billy Williams)	.25

1997 Gatorade Cubs

This postcard-size set was a stadium give-away. Fronts have game-action photos on a green ivy background. Backs have player data and stats. The set is arranged here alphabetically.

		NM/M
Complete Set (26):		8.00
Common Player:		.25
(1)	Terry Adams	.25
(2)	Kent Bottenfield	.25
(3)	Brant Brown	.25
(4)	Dave Clark	.25
(5)	Shawon Dunston	.25
(6)	Kevin Foster	.25
(7)	Doug Glanville	.25
(8)	Jeremi Gonzalez	.25
(9)	Mark Grace	.50
(10)	Dave Hansen	.25
(11)	Jose Hernandez	.25
(12)	Tyler Houston	.25
(13)	Brian McRae	.25
(14)	Kevin Orie	.25
(15)	Bob Patterson	.25
(16)	Jim Riggleman	.25
(17)	Mel Rojas	.25
(18)	Rey Sanchez	.25
(19)	Ryne Sandberg	4.00
(20)	Scott Servais	.25
(21)	Sammy Sosa	4.00
(22)	Kevin Tapani	.25
(23)	Ramon Tatis	.25
(24)	Steve Traschel	.25
(25)	Turk Wendell	.25
(26)	Cubs Coaches (Rick Kranitz, Jeff Pentland, Mako Oliveras, Dan Radison, Phil Regan, Billy Williams)	.25

1985 General Mills Stickers

General Mills of Canada inserted a panel of two cellophane-wrapped baseball stickers in each box of Cheerios in 1985. The full-color sticker panels, measuring 2-3/8" x 3-3/4", are blank-backed and unnumbered and contain the player's name, team and position in both English and French. The General Mills logo appears at the top of each sticker. All team insignia on the players' uniforms and caps have been airbrushed off.

		NM/M
Complete Panel Set (15):		10.00
Complete Singles Set (26):		7.00
Common Panel:		.50
Common Player:		.25
Panel (1)		1.25
(1)	Gary Carter	.50
(2)	Tom Brunansky	.25
Panel (2)		1.25
(1)	Gary Carter	.50
(3)	Dave Steib	.25
Panel (3)		1.00
(4)	Andre Dawson	.35
(5)	Alvin Davis	.25
Panel (4)		1.00
(4)	Andre Dawson	.35
(3)	Dave Steib	.25
Panel (5)		1.00
(6)	Steve Garvey	.35
(7)	Buddy Bell	.25
Panel (6)		1.25
(6)	Steve Garvey	.35
(8)	Jim Rice	.30
Panel (7)		1.00
(9)	Jeff Leonard	.25
(10)	Eddie Murray	.50
Panel (8)		1.50
(11)	Dale Murphy	.35
(12)	Robin Yount	.50
Panel (9)		1.50
(13)	Terry Puhl	.25
(14)	Reggie Jackson	.60
Panel (10)		.50
(15)	Johnny Ray	.25
(16)	Lou Whitaker	.25
Panel (11)		1.00
(17)	Ryne Sandberg	.75
(18)	Mike Hargrove	.25
Panel (12)		2.00
(19)	Mike Schmidt	.75
(20)	George Brett	.75
Panel (13)		2.00
(21)	Ozzie Smith	.60
(22)	Dave Winfield	.50
Panel (14)		1.25
(23)	Mario Soto	.25
(24)	Carlton Fisk	.50
Panel (15)		1.00
(25)	Fernando Valenzuela	.25
(26)	Dwayne Murphy	.25

1986 General Mills Booklets

In 1986, General Mills of Canada inserted six different "Baseball Players Booklets" in specially marked boxes of Cheerios. Ten different players are featured in each booklet, with statistics for the 1985 season in both English and French. The booklet, when opened fully, measures 3-3/4" x 15". Also included in the booklet is a contest sponsored by Petro-Canada service stations to win a day with a major league player at his 1987 spring training site in Florida. Team insignias have been airbrushed off the players' uniforms and caps.

		NM/M
Complete Set (6):		12.50
Common Booklet:		1.25
1	A.L. East (Wade Boggs, Kirk Gibson, Rickey Henderson, Don Mattingly, Jack Morris, Lance Parrish, Jim Rice, Dave Righetti, Cal Ripken, Lou Whitaker)	4.00
2	A.L. West (Harold Baines, Phil Bradley, George Brett, Carlton Fisk, Ozzie Guillen, Kent Hrbek, Reggie Jackson, Dan Quisenberry, Bret Saberhagen, Frank White)	2.50
3	Toronto Blue Jays (Jesse Barfield, George Bell, Bill Caudill, Tony Fernandez, Damaso Garcia, Lloyd Moseby, Rance Mulliniks, Dave Stieb, Willie Upshaw, Ernie Whitt)	2.00
4	N.L. East (Gary Carter, Jack Clark, George Foster, Dwight Gooden, Gary Matthews, Willie McGee, Ryne Sandberg, Mike Schmidt, Lee Smith, Ozzie Smith)	2.50
5	N.L. West (Dave Concepcion, Pedro Guerrero, Terry Kennedy, Dale Murphy, Graig Nettles, Dave Parker, Tony Perez, Steve Sax, Bruce Sutter, Fernando Valenzuela)	1.25
6	Montreal Expos (Hubie Brooks, Andre Dawson, Mike Fitzgerald, Vance Law, Tim Raines, Jeff Reardon, Bryn Smith, Jason Thompson, Tim Wallach, Mitch Webster)	2.00

1987 General Mills Booklets

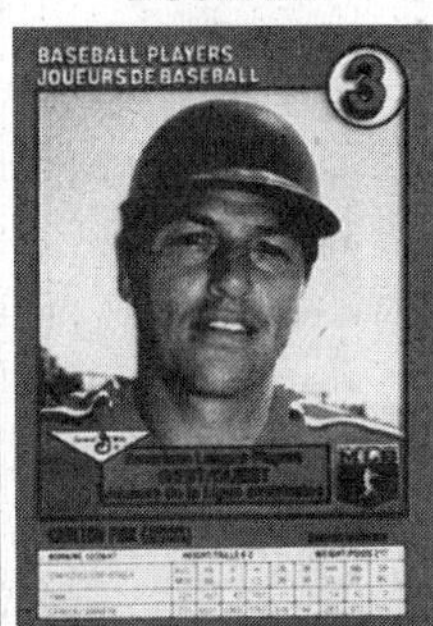

For a second straight year, General Mills of Canada inserted one of six different "Baseball Super-Stars Booklets" in specially marked boxes of Cheerios and Honey Nut Cheerios cereal. Each booklet contains ten full-color photos for a total of 60 players. The booklets, when completely unfolded, measure 15" x 3-3/4". Written in both English and French, the set was produced by Mike Schechter and Associates. All team insignias have been airbrushed off the photos.

		NM/M
Complete Set (6):		9.00
Common Booklet:		2.00
1	Toronto Blue Jays (Jesse Barfield, George Bell, Tony Fernandez, Kelly Gruber, Tom Henke, Jimmy Key, Lloyd Moseby, Dave Stieb, Willie Upshaw, Ernie Whitt)	2.00
2	A.L. East (Wade Boggs, Roger Clemens, Kirk Gibson, Rickey Henderson, Don Mattingly, Jack Morris, Eddie Murray, Pat Tabler, Dave Winfield, Robin Yount)	4.00
3	A.L. West (Phil Bradley, George Brett, Jose Canseco, Carlton Fisk, Reggie Jackson, Wally Joyner, Kirk McCaskill, Larry Parrish, Kirby Puckett, Dan Quisenberry)	2.50
4	Montreal Expos (Hubie Brooks, Mike Fitzgerald, Andres Galarraga, Vance Law, Andy McGaffigan, Bryn Smith, Jason Thompson, Tim Wallach, Mitch Webster, Floyd Youmans)	2.00
5	N.L. East (Gary Carter, Dwight Gooden, Keith Hernandez, Willie McGee, Tim Raines, R.J. Reynolds, Ryne Sandberg, Mike Schmidt, Ozzie Smith, Darryl Strawberry)	2.50
6	N.L. West (Kevin Bass, Chili Davis, Bill Doran, Pedro Guerrero, Tony Gwynn, Dale Murphy, Dave Parker, Steve Sax, Mike Scott, Fernando Valenzuela)	2.00

1990 Giant Eagle Roberto Clemente Stickers

The Giant Eagle food stores around Pittsburgh issued a collectors' poster and set of 18 stickers circa 1990. Each of the 2-1/2" x 3-1/2" stickers features one of Roberto Clemente's regular-issue Topps cards 1955-72. The stickers were originally issued in strips of three. Backs are blank. The issue was almost certainly not authorized by Topps or the Clemente estate.

	NM/M
Complete Set, Strips (6):	20.00
Common Sticker:	2.00
Poster:	16.00

1981 Granny Goose Potato Chips A's

The 1981 Granny Goose set features the Oakland A's. The 2-1/2" x 3-1/2" cards were issued in bags of potato chips and are sometimes found with grease stains. The cards have full color fronts with the graphics done in the team's green and yellow colors. The backs contain the A's logo and a short player biography. The Revering card was withdrawn from the set shortly after he was traded and is in shorter supply than the rest of the cards in the set. The cards are numbered in the checklist that follows by the player's uniform number.

		NM/M
Complete Set (15):		100.00
Common Player:		2.00
1	Billy Martin	8.00
2	Mike Heath	2.00
5	Jeff Newman	2.00
6	Mitchell Page	2.00
8	Rob Picciolo	2.00
10	Wayne Gross	2.00
13	Dave Revering	40.00
17	Mike Norris	2.00
20	Tony Armas	2.00
21	Dwayne Murphy	2.00
22	Rick Langford	2.00
27	Matt Keough	2.00
35	Rickey Henderson	35.00
39	Dave McKay	2.00
54	Steve McCatty	2.00

1982 Granny Goose Potato Chips A's

Granny Goose repeated its promotion from the previous year and issued another set featuring the Oakland A's. The 2-1/2" x 3-1/2" cards were distributed in two fashions - in bags of potato chips and at Fan Appreciation Day at Oakland-Alameda Coliseum. The cards are identical in design to the 1981 set and can be distinguished from it by the date on the copyright on the bottom of the card reverse. The cards are numbered in the checklist that follows by the player's uniform number.

		NM/M
Complete Set (15):		7.50
Common Player:		.50
1	Billy Martin	1.00
2	Mike Heath	.50
5	Jeff Newman	.50
8	Rob Picciolo	.50
10	Wayne Gross	.50
11	Fred Stanley	.50
15	Davey Lopes	.50
17	Mike Norris	.50
20	Tony Armas	.50
21	Dwayne Murphy	.50
22	Rick Langford	.50
27	Matt Keough	.50
35	Rickey Henderson	6.00
44	Cliff Johnson, Jr.	.50
54	Steve McCatty	.50

Signature Set

The cards from this very scarce 15-card set are identical to the regular Granny Goose cards, but contain a facsimile autograph on the front. The cards were initially intended as special prize-redemption inserts from Granny Goose potato chips, but were never released in any quantity.

		NM/M
Complete Set (15):		125.00
Common Player:		5.00
1	Billy Martin	30.00
2	Mike Heath	5.00
5	Jeff Newman	5.00
8	Rob Picciolo	5.00
10	Wayne Gross	5.00
11	Fred Stanley	5.00
15	Davey Lopes	7.50
17	Mike Norris	5.00
20	Tony Armas	5.00
21	Dwayne Murphy	5.00
22	Rick Langford	5.00
27	Matt Keough	5.00
35	Rickey Henderson	45.00
44	Cliff Johnson, Jr.	5.00
54	Steve McCatty	5.00

1983 Granny Goose Potato Chips A's

For the third consecutive year, Granny Goose issued a set of baseball cards featuring the Oakland A's. The cards were issued with or without a detachable coupon found at the bottom of each card. Issued in bags of potato chips were the coupon cards, which contain a scratch-off section offering prizes. The cards without the coupon section were given away to fans at Oakland-Alameda Coliseum on July 3, 1983. Cards with the detachable coupon command a 50 per cent premium over the coupon-less variety. The cards in the following checklist are numbered by the player's uniform number.

		NM/M
Complete Set (15):		8.00
Common Player:		.50
2	Mike Heath	.50
4	Carney Lansford	.50
10	Wayne Gross	.50
14	Steve Boros	.50
15	Davey Lopes	.50
16	Mike Davis	.50
17	Mike Norris	.50
21	Dwayne Murphy	.50
22	Rick Langford	.50
27	Matt Keough	.50
31	Tom Underwood	.50
33	Dave Beard	.50
35	Rickey Henderson	6.00
39	Tom Burgmeier	.50
54	Steve McCatty	.50

1999 GTE Tampa Bay Devil Rays

This team set was a stadium giveaway. Fronts have game-action color photos. On back are complete minor and major league stats along with team and sponsor logos.

		NM/M
Complete Set (30):		10.00
Common Player:		.25
1	Scott Aldred	.25
2	Wilson Alvarez	.25
3	Rolando Arrojo	.25
4	Wade Boggs	3.00
5	Miguel Cairo	.25
6	Jose Canseco	2.00

7	Coaches (Orlando Gomez, Billy Hatcher, Frank Howard, Greg Riddoch, Leon Roberts, Rick Williams)	.25
8	Mike DiFelice	.25
9	John Flaherty	.25
10	Roberto Hernandez	.25
11	David Lamb	.25
12	Aaron Ledesma	.25
13	Albie Lopez	.25
14	Dave Martinez	.25
15	Quinton McCracken	.35
16	Fred McGriff	.35
17	Herbert Perry	.25
18	Bryan Rekar	.25
19	Larry Rothschild	.25
20	Ryan Rupe	.25
21	Julio Santana	.25
22	Tony Saunders	.25
23	Paul Sorrento	.25
24	Kevin Stocker	.25
25	Rick White	.25
26	Randy Winn	.25
27	Bobby Witt	.25
28	Esteban Yan	.25
---	Literacy Champion (Quinton McCracken)	.25
---	Sponsor's Card	.25

H

1981-89 Hall of Fame Metallic Plaque-cards

Between 1981-89, the National Baseball Hall of Fame & Museum issued a set of metallic baseball cards reproducing the plaques of the baseball greats inducted. The plaques are pictured on 2-1/2" x 3-1/2" blank-backed gold anodized aluminum. Every detail of the plaque is fully and faithfully reproduced. The set was sold in series through the Hall of Fame's gift shop. The series was discontinued for economic reasons in 1989. Only 1,000 plaques of each player were produced. Values are, to some extent, based not only on player popularity, but on year of issue; later plaques tend to be more expensive because fewer were sold.

		NM/M
	Complete Set (204):	650.00
	Common Player:	3.00
(1)	Hank Aaron/1983	20.00
(2)	Grover Alexander/1982	5.00
(3)	Walter Alston/1984	4.00
(4)	Cap Anson/1981	4.00
(5)	Luis Aparicio/1984	6.50
(6)	Luke Appling/1982	3.50
(7)	Earl Averill/1983	3.00
(8)	"Home Run" Baker/1983	3.00
(9)	David Bancroft/1982	3.00
(10)	Ernie Banks/1982	8.00
(11)	Al Barlick (1989)	4.50
(12)	Ed Barrow/1982	3.00
(13)	Jacob Beckley/1982	3.00
(14)	Cool Papa Bell/1981	6.00
(15)	Johnny Bench/1989	15.00
(16)	"Chief" Bender/1982	3.50
(17)	Yogi Berra/1982	12.00
(18)	Jim Bottomley/1981	4.00
(19)	Lou Boudreau/1982	3.00
(20)	Roger Bresnahan/1982	3.00
(21)	Lou Brock/1986	12.00
(22)	Dan Brouthers/1982	3.00
(23)	Mordecai Brown/1981	4.00
(24)	Morgan Burkeley/1981	3.00
(25)	Jesse Burkett/1982	3.00
(26)	Roy Campanella/1981	12.50
(27)	Max Carey/1982	4.00
(28)	Alexander Cartwright/1981	3.00
(29)	Henry Chadwick/1982	3.00
(30)	Frank Chance/1981	4.50
(31)	Happy Chandler/1983	3.00
(32)	Oscar Charleston/1982	4.00
(33)	Jack Chesbro/1982	3.50
(34)	Fred Clarke/1983	3.00
(35)	John Clarkson/1982	3.00
(36)	Roberto Clemente/1982	30.00
(37)	Ty Cobb/1981	30.00
(38)	Mickey Cochrane/1983	5.00
(39)	Eddie Collins/1981	3.00
(40)	James Collins/1982	3.00
(41)	Earle Combs/1983	3.00
(42)	Charles Comiskey/1982	3.00
(43)	Jocko Conlan/1981	3.00
(44)	Thomas Connolly/1982	3.00
(45)	Roger Connor/1982	3.00
(46)	Stan Coveleski/1982	3.00
(47)	Sam Crawford/1983	3.50
(48)	Joe Cronin/1981	5.00
(49)	Candy Cummings/1982	3.00
(50)	Kiki Cuyler/1983	4.00
(51)	Ray Dandridge/1989	6.00
(52)	Dizzy Dean/1983	10.00
(53)	Ed Delahanty/1981	3.00
(54)	Bill Dickey/1981	5.00
(55)	Martin Dihigo/1982	6.50
(56)	Joe DiMaggio/1983	35.00
(57)	Bobby Doerr/1986	4.00
(58)	Don Drysdale/1984	10.00
(59)	Hugh Duffy/1982	3.00
(60)	Bill Evans/1983	3.00
(61)	John Evers/1982	4.50
(62)	Buck Ewing/1981	3.00
(63)	Urban Faber/1983	3.00
(64)	Bob Feller/1981	6.50
(65)	Rick Ferrell/1984	4.00
(66)	Elmer Flick/1982	3.00
(67)	Whitey Ford/1983	10.00
(68)	Rube Foster/1983	3.00
(69)	Jimmie Foxx/1982	7.50
(70)	Ford Frick/1981	3.00
(71)	Frank Frisch/1981	3.00
(72)	Pud Galvin/1982	3.00
(73)	Lou Gehrig/1982	35.00
(74)	Charles Gehringer/1983	6.50
(75)	Bob Gibson/1982	6.50
(76)	Josh Gibson/1981	6.50
(77)	Warren Giles/1983	3.00
(78)	Lefty Gomez/1981	4.00
(79)	Goose Goslin/1982	4.00
(80)	Hank Greenberg/1981	8.00
(81)	Clark Griffith/1982	3.00
(82)	Burleigh Grimes/1982	3.00
(83)	Lefty Grove/1981	4.50
(84)	Chick Hafey/1982	3.00
(85)	Pop Haines/1982	3.00
(86)	William Hamilton/1982	3.00
(87)	William Harridge/1982	3.00
(88)	Bucky Harris/1982	4.00
(89)	Gabby Hartnett/1982	3.50
(90)	Harry Heilmann/1983	3.00
(91)	Bill Herman/1982	3.00
(92)	Harry Hooper/1982	3.00
(93)	Rogers Hornsby/1981	8.00
(94)	Schoolboy Hoyt/1983	3.00
(95)	Cal Hubbard/1982	3.00
(96)	Carl Hubbell /1981	3.50
(97)	Miller Huggins/1982	3.50
(98)	Catfish Hunter/1989	6.00
(99)	Monte Irvin/1981	3.50
(100)	Travis Jackson/1983	3.00
(101)	Hugh Jennings/1983	3.00
(102)	Ban Johnson/1981	3.00
(103)	Judy Johnson/1981	3.00
(104)	Walter Johnson/1982	10.00
(105)	Addie Joss/1981	3.00
(106)	Al Kaline/1981	8.00
(107)	Timothy Keefe/1983	3.00
(108)	Willie Keeler/1982	4.00
(109)	George Kell (1984)	4.00
(110)	Joe Kelley/1983	3.00
(111)	Highpockets Kelly (?)	3.00
(112)	King Kelly/1981	4.00
(113)	Harmon Killebrew/1984	6.50
(114)	Ralph Kiner/1982	3.00
(115)	Chuck Klein/1983	4.00
(116)	Bill Klem /1981	3.00
(117)	Sandy Koufax/1982	25.00
(118)	Nap Lajoie/1982	5.00
(119)	Kenesaw Landis/1981	3.00
(120)	Buck Leonard/1982	3.50
(121)	Bob Lemon/1981	3.00
(122)	Fred Linstrom/1982	3.00
(123)	Pop Lloyd/1981	3.00
(124)	Ernie Lombardi /1986	3.00
(125)	Al Lopez/1981	3.00
(126)	Ted Lyons/1983	3.00
(127)	Connie Mack/1981	3.00
(128)	Larry MacPhail /1983	3.00
(129)	Mickey Mantle/1983	40.00
(130)	Heinie Manush/1981	3.00
(131)	Rabbit Maranville/1981	4.00
(132)	Juan Marichal /1984	5.00
(133)	Rube Marquard/1983	3.50
(134)	Eddie Mathews/1983	3.50
(135)	Christy Mathewson/1981	10.00
(136)	Willie Mays/1981	20.00
(137)	Joe McCarthy/1983	3.00
(138)	Thomas McCarthy/1983	3.00
(139)	Willie McCovey/1986	3.50
(140)	Iron Man McGinnity/1982	3.00
(141)	John McGraw/1982	3.00
(142)	Bill McKechnie/1982	3.00
(143)	Joe Medwick/1983	3.00
(144)	Johnny Mize/1982	3.00
(145)	Stan Musial /1981	15.00
(146)	Kid Nichols/1983	4.00
(147)	James O'Rourke/1982	3.00
(148)	Mel Ott/1981	4.00
(149)	Satchel Paige/1981	12.50
(150)	Herb Pennock/1983	3.00
(151)	Eddie Plank/1982	3.00
(152)	Hoss Radbourne/1983	3.00
(153)	Pee Wee Reese/1984	3.50
(154)	Sam Rice/1983	3.00
(155)	Branch Rickey/1981	3.00
(156)	Eppa Rixey/1983	3.00
(157)	Robin Roberts/1982	5.00
(158)	Brooks Robinson/1984	6.00
(159)	Frank Robinson/1983	6.50
(160)	Jackie Robinson/1981	20.00
(161)	Wilbert Robinson/1982	3.50
(162)	Edd Roush/1982	3.00
(163)	Red Ruffing/1982	4.00
(164)	Amos Rusie/1983	3.00
(165)	Babe Ruth/1981	40.00
(166)	Ray Schalk/1982	3.00
(167)	Red Schoendienst/1989	8.00
(168)	Joe Sewell/1982	3.00
(169)	Al Simmons/1982	5.00
(170)	George Sisler/1981	3.00
(171)	Enos Slaughter/1986	8.00
(172)	Duke Snider/1981	8.00
(173)	Warren Spahn/1982	8.00
(174)	Al Spalding/1982	4.00
(175)	Tris Speaker/1982	6.50
(176)	Willie Stargell/1989	3.00
(177)	Casey Stengel/1981	6.50
(178)	Bill Terry/1981	3.00
(179)	Sam Thompson/1983	3.00
(180)	Joe Tinker/1982	6.00
(181)	Pie Traynor/1982	6.00
(182)	Dazzy Vance/1983	4.00
(183)	Arky Vaughan/1986	3.00
(184)	Rube Waddell/1983	4.00
(185)	Honus Wagner/1982	15.00
(186)	Roderick Wallace/1982	3.00
(187)	Ed Walsh/1982	3.00
(188)	Lloyd Waner/1981	4.00
(189)	Paul Waner /1981	5.00
(190)	John Ward (1982)	3.00
(191)	George Weiss/1983	3.00
(192)	Mickey Welch/1983	3.00
(193)	Zack Wheat/1982	4.00
(194)	Hoyt Wilhelm/1986	6.50
(195)	Billy Williams/1989	8.00
(196)	Ted Williams/1981	27.50
(197)	Hack Wilson/1982	4.00
(198)	George Wright/1982	3.00
(199)	Harry Wright/1983	3.00
(200)	Early Wynn/1982	4.00
(201)	Carl Yastrzemski/1989	12.00
(202)	Tom Yawkey/1982	3.00
(203)	Cy Young /1981	10.00
(204)	Ross Youngs/1982	3.00

1995 Baseball's Hall of Famers Creating History

This boxed set of large-format (2-7/8" x 4-1/2") round-cornered cards was designated "Flash-Pack / Knowledge in a Nutshell." It was described as the the first in a series. Card fronts feature borderless black-and-white or color photos with no player identification or other graphics. Black-and-white backs identify the player, provide a career summary and date of selection to the Hall of Fame. The unnumbered cards are listed here alphabetically. The boxed set originally retailed for $9.95.

		NM/M
	Complete Set (36):	20.00
	Common Player:	.50
(1)	Cap Anson	.50
(2)	Ernie Banks	2.00
(3)	Edward G. Barrow	.50
(4)	Roger Bresnahan	.50
(5)	Lou Brock	1.00
(6)	Roy Campanella	2.00
(7)	Alexander Cartwright	.50
(8)	Henry Chadwick	.50
(9)	Oscar Charleston	.50
(10)	Jack Chesbro	.50
(11)	Roberto Clemente	4.00
(12)	Charles Comiskey	.50
(13)	Candy Cummings	.50
(14)	Andrew "Rube" Foster	.50
(15)	Ford Frick	.50
(16)	Josh Gibson	1.00
(17)	Burleigh Grimes	.50
(18)	Cal Hubbard	.50
(19)	Carl Hubbell	.50
(20)	Willie Keeler	.50
(21)	Bill Klem	.50
(22)	Kenesaw M. Landis	.50
(23)	Larry MacPhail	.50
(24)	Juan Marichal	1.00
(25)	Willie Mays	3.00
(26)	John McGraw	.50
(27)	Stan Musial	2.00
(28)	Charles Radbourne	.50
(29)	Branch Rickey	.50
(30)	Robin Roberts	1.00
(31)	Brooks Robinson	1.00
(32)	Warren Spahn	1.00
(33)	Albert Spalding	.50
(34)	Willie Stargell	1.00
(35)	Rube Waddell	.50
(36)	Harry Wright	.50

2001 Hall of Fame Postcards

Colorized artist's renderings of 19th Century Old Judge cabinet cards are the basis for this set of postcards produced for the Hall of Fame by R.F. Ball, who produced a similar set of lithographs in 1987. The postcards are 5" x 7" and have the central color painting bordered in black. Postcard-format backs have a few words about the player. The cards were produced in a serial-numbered edition of 2,000 each, packaged with a like-numbered checklist. Issue price at the Hall of Fame's gift shop was $12.95. A 21-1/2" x 38" uncut poster of the cards was sold for $49.95.

		NM/M
	Complete Set (10):	13.00
	Common Player:	1.50
1	Cap Anson	2.00
2	Dan Brouthers	1.50
3	John Clarkson	1.50
4	Ed Delahanty	1.50
5	Buck Ewing	1.50
6	Tim Keefe	1.50
7	Mike Kelly	2.00
8	Kid Nichols	1.50
9	Jim O'Rourke	1.50
10	Sam Thompson	1.50

2005 Hall of Fame Education Program

Each of the National Baseball Hall of Fame's educational programs is featured on a card in this special issue. Cards were issued in two 10-card cello packs.

		NM/M
	Complete Set (20):	7.50
	Common Card:	.50
(1)	Header Card	.05
(2)	American History (Joe Jackson)	1.50
(3)	Artifacts and Education (The Doubleday Ball)	.50
(4)	Civil Rights (Satchel Paige)	.75
(5)	Cultural Diversity (Jim Thorpe)	1.00
(6)	Economics (T206 Honus Wagner)	.50
(7)	Fine Art (Babe Ruth painting.)	.50
(8)	Leadership (Jackie Robinson)	.50
(9)	Popular Culture (Ichiro Suzuki bobblehead.)	.50
(10)	Women's History (Mickey Maguire)	.50
(11)	Header Card	.05
(12)	Artifacts and Education (Roberto Clemente artifacts.)	.50
(13)	Character Education (Lou Gehrig)	.75
(14)	Communication Arts (Dizzy Dean)	.50
(15)	Geography (1958 N.Y. Yankees)	.50
(16)	Industrial Technology (Roger Bresnahan)	.50
(17)	Labor History (John Montgomery Ward)	.50
(18)	Mathematics (Hank Aaron)	.75
(19)	Science (Ozzie Smith)	.50
(20)	Special Abilities (Pete Gray)	.75

1998 Hamburger Helper Home Run Heroes

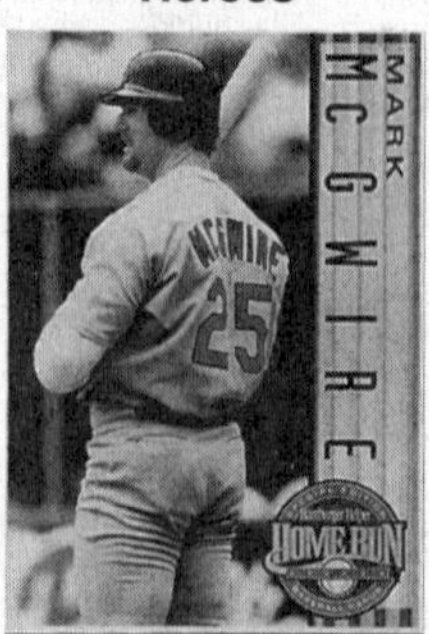

Eight top sluggers are featured in this box-back set from Hamburger Helper. The 2-1/2" x 3-1/2" cards are printed on the backs of various flavors of the skillet meal boxes. Unlike many similar issues these are fully licensed by Major League Baseball, as well as the Players Association, and the player photos have uniform logos. Also unusual is that the cards have a printed back in black-and-white offering personal data, career highlights and stats.

		NM/M
	Complete Set, Boxes (8):	15.00
	Complete Set, Singles (8):	15.00
	Common Player:	.50
1	Mark McGwire	3.00
2	Rafael Palmeiro	1.25
3	Tino Martinez	.50
4	Barry Bonds	4.00
5	Larry Walker	.50
6	Juan Gonzalez	1.25
7	Mike Piazza	2.00
8	Frank Thomas	1.50

1988 Hardee's/ Coke Conlon

Regionally issued in a promotion sponsored by Hardee's restaurants and Coca-Cola, this six-card set features the photos of Charles Martin Conlon and is closely related to the Sporting News-Wide World Conlon issues of the time. The cards feature sepia photos on front and career stats and summary on back. The unnumbered cards are checklisted here alphabetically.

		NM/M
	Complete Set (6):	3.00
	Common Player:	.40
(1)	Cool Papa Boll	.40
(2)	Ty Cobb	1.25
(3)	Lou Gehrig	1.50
(4)	Connie Mack	.40
(5)	Casey Stengel	.40
(6)	Rube Waddell	.40

1996 Hebrew National Detroit Tigers

One of the team's hot dog concessionaires sponsored a set of Tiger cards given away at the September 1 game. Originally intended to be 28 cards, only 26 were issued due to late-season trades. Cards are in a larger than normal 2-7/8" x 4-1/4" format with game-action photo on front. Down one side in team colors are the player name and position, with the stalking tiger logo at bottom. Backs have a large light blue gothic "D" in the background with player personal data and major/minor league stats and team/sponsor logos.

		NM/M
	Complete Set (26):	12.00
	Common Player:	.50
1	Kimera Bartee	.50
2	Jose Lima	.50
3	Tony Clark	.50
5	Travis Fryman	.50
7	Bobby Higginson	.50
8	Greg Keagle	.50
9	Mark Lewis	.50

10 Richie Lewis .50
11 Felipe Lira .50
12 Mike Myers .50
13 Melvin Nieves .50
14 Alan Trammell 1.00
15 Tom Urbani .50
16 Brian Williams .50
17 Eddie Williams .50
18 Curtis Pride .50
19 Mark Parent .50
20 Raul Casanova .50
21 Omar Olivares .50
22 Gregg Olson .50
23 Justin Thompson .50
24 Brad Ausmus .50
25 Andujar Cedeno .50
26 Buddy Bell .50
27 Paws (Mascot) .50
28 Detroit Tigers Coaches (Glenn Ezell, Terry Francona, Larry Herndon, Fred Kendall, John (Jon) Matlack, Ron Oester) .50

1997 Hebrew National Detroit Tigers

The hot dog concessionaire at Tiger Stadium produced a second annual team set in 1997, giving the cards away at the June 22 game. Cards feature borderless color action photos on front, with a tiny black-and-white portrait photo at bottom-right. Backs are printed in blue and yellow and have player data, complete major and minor league stats and the team and sponsor logos.

NM/M
Complete Set (28): 12.00
Common Player: .50
1 Jose Bautista .50
2 Willie Blair .50
3 Doug Brocail .50
4 Raul Casanova .50
5 Tony Clark .50
6 Deivi Cruz .50
7 John Cummings .50
8 Damion Easley .50
9 Travis Fryman .50
10 Bobby Higginson .50
11 Brian Hunter .50
12 Todd Johnson .50
13 Todd Jones .50
14 Felipe Lira .50
15 Dan Miceli .50
16 Brian Moehler .50
17 Mike Myers .50
18 Phil Nevin .50
19 Melvin Nieves .50
20 Omar Oliveras .50
21 Curtis Pride .50
22 A.J. Sager .50
23 Justin Thompson .50
24 Matt Walbeck .50
25 Jody Reed .50
26 Bob Hamelin .50
27 Buddy Bell .50
28 Tigers Coaches (Rick Adair, Larry Herndon, Perry Hill, Fred Kendall, Larry Parrish, Jerry White) .50

2005 Helmar Brewing Co.

These cards were inserted three per foil pack in packages of snack foods from a Michigan company. The product was sold only in parts of Michigan, Ohio and Pennsylvania. Fronts have color artwork. Besides major leaguers, Negro Leagues and Japanese Leagues players, the set included House of David players, wrestlers and boxers. The 1-5/8" x 2-3/4" cards are printed on thick cardboard. Backs have a scratch-off circle for prize redemptions. No checklist was ever issued for the unnumbered cards, so it is possible additions to this list may be forthcoming. Gaps have been left in the assigned numbering for that reason.

NM/M
Common Player: .50
(1) Frank "Home Run" Baker 1.00
(2) Moe Berg 2.50
(3) Mordecai Brown 1.00
(4) Slim Caldwell .50
(5) Ray Chapman 1.00
(6) Kiki Cuyler .50
(7) Bill Donovan .50
(8) Johnny "The Crab" Evers 1.00
(9) Happy Felsch 1.00
(10) Elmer Flick .50
(11) Chick Gandil 1.00
(12) Sy Gragg (Gregg) .50
(13) Miller Huggins .50
(14) Joe Jackson (Chicago) 2.50
(15) Joe Jackson (Cleveland) 2.50
(16) Hughie Jennings .50
(17) Davy Jones .50
(18) Jimmy McAleer .50
(19) John McGraw 1.00
(20) Herb Pennock .50
(21) Eppa Rixey .50
(22) Billy Rogell .50
(23) Rube Waddell .50
(24) Buck Weaver 1.50
(25) Ross Youngs .50
(30) Joe Hauser 1.00
(31) Walter Ball .50
(32) James "Cool Papa" Bell 1.00
(33) Dennis Biddle .50
(34) Sherwood Brewer .50
(35) Jim Cobbin .50
(36) Jimmie Crutchfield .50
(37) Leon (Pepper) Daniels .50
(38) Martin DiHigo 1.00
(39) Rube Foster 1.00
(40) Arthur Hamilton .50
(41) Pete Hill 1.00
(42) Dave Malarcher .50
(43) "Double Duty" Radcliffe .50
(44) Turkey Stearns (Stearnes) .50
(45) Moses Walker 1.00
(48) George Anderson .50
(49) Barnstorming Team .50
(50) Lloyd Dalager .50
(51) Eddie Deal .50
(52) Judge Dewhurst .50
(53) David Harrison .50
(54) Jesse Lee Tally .50
(55) John Tucker .50
(56) Percy Walker .50
(58) Kaoru Betto .50
(59) Sadayushi Fujimoto .50
(60) Taketoshi Goto .50
(61) Tetsuhara Kawakami 1.00
(62) Tokuji Lida .50
(63) Jiro Noguchi .50
(64) Tokyo Team (Tetsuhara Kawakami, Shigeru Chiba, Noboru Aota, Jiro Noguchi) .50

1998 Hershey's Baltimore Orioles

This team set was a stadium giveaway at a late-season game. The 2-1/2" x 3-1/2" cards have portrait or game-action photos bordered in black. An orange stripe vertically at left has the player name. Backs have a red border around complete major and minor league stats. Team and Hershey's logos are at bottom.

NM/M
Complete Set (25): 15.00
Common Player: .50
(1) Roberto Alomar .75
(2) Brady Anderson .75
(3) Harold Baines .75
(4) Rich Becker .50
(5) Armando Benitez .50
(6) Mike Bordick .50
(7) Eric Davis .60
(8) Doug Drabek .50
(9) Scott Erickson .50
(10) Chris Hoiles .50
(11) Doug Johns .50
(12) Scott Kamieniecki .50
(13) Jimmy Key .50
(14) Alan Mills .50
(15) Mike Mussina 2.00
(16) Jesse Orosco .50
(17) Rafael Palmeiro 2.00
(18) Sidney Ponson .50
(19) Jeff Reboulet .50
(20) Arthur Rhodes .50
(21) Cal Ripken 4.00
(22) Pete Smith .50
(23) B.J. Surhoff .50
(24) Lenny Webster .50
(25) Orioles Coaches (Carlos Bernhardt, Rick Down, Mike Flanagan, Elrod Hendricks, Eddie Murray, Sam Perlozzo) .50

1993 Highland Mint Mint-Cards

The Highland Mint produced replicas of several Topps rookie cards and other prominent cards in bronze and silver. Limited to 1,000 in silver and 5,000 in bronze, the company produced cards of many current stars along with a replica of Brooks Robinson's 1957 rookie card. The cards carried a suggested retail price of $235 for the silver and $50 for the bronze. Cards measure 2-1/2" x 3-1/2" and are 1/10" thick. Each Mint-Card has a serial number engraved on the edge and is sold in a heavy lucite holder, packaged with a certificate of authenticity in a plastic book-style folder.

NM/M
Common Player, Silver: 70.00
Common Player, Bronze: 12.50
(1s) Brooks Robinson (1957 Topps, silver edition of 796) 110.00
(1b) Brooks Robinson (1957 Topps, bronze edition of 2,043) 20.00
(2s) Dave Winfield (1974 Topps, silver edition of 266) 200.00
(2b) Dave Winfield (1974 Topps, bronze edition of 1,216) 20.00
(3s) George Brett (1975 Topps, silver edition of 999) 100.00
(3b) George Brett (1975 Topps, bronze edition of 3,560) 20.00
(4s) Robin Yount (1975 Topps silver edition of 349) 110.00
(4b) Robin Yount (1975 Topps, bronze edition of 1,564) 40.00
(5s) Ozzie Smith (1979 Topps, silver edition of 211) 245.00
(5b) Ozzie Smith (1979 Topps, bronze edition of 1,088) 35.00
(6s) Don Mattingly (1984 Topps, silver edition of 414) 75.00
(6b) Don Mattingly (1984 Topps, bronze edition of 1,550) 40.00
(7s) Roger Clemens (1985 Topps, silver edition of 432) 140.00
(7b) Roger Clemens (1985 Topps, bronze edition of 1,789) 25.00
(8s) Kirby Puckett (1985 Topps, silver edition of 359) 85.00
(8b) Kirby Puckett (1985 Topps, bronze edition of 1,723) 20.00
(9s) Barry Bonds (1986 Topps Traded, silver edition of 596) 125.00
(9b) Barry Bonds (1986 Topps Traded, bronze edition of 2,677) 50.00
(10s) Will Clark (1986 Topps Traded, silver edition of 150) 225.00
(10b) Will Clark (1986 Topps Traded, bronze edition of 1,0444) 20.00
(11s) Roberto Alomar (1988 Topps Traded, silver edition of 214) 90.00
(11b) Roberto Alomar(1988 Topps Traded, bronze edition of 928) 20.00
(12s) Juan Gonzalez (1990 Topps, silver edition of 365) 65.00
(12b) Juan Gonzalez (1990 Topps, bronze edition of 1,899) 15.00
(13s) Ken Griffey Jr. (1992 Topps, silver edition of 1,000) 100.00
(13b) Ken Griffey Jr. (1992 Topps, bronze edition of 5,000) 15.00
(13g) Ken Griffey Jr. (1992 Topps, gold edition of 500) 200.00
(14s) Cal Ripken, Jr. (1992 Topps, silver edition of 1,000) 100.00
(14b) Cal Ripken, Jr. (1992 Topps, bronze edition of 4,065) 15.00
(15s) Nolan Ryan (1992 Topps, silver edition of 999) 150.00
(15b) Nolan Ryan (1992 Topps, bronze edition of 5,000) 25.00
(16s) Ryne Sandberg (1992 Topps, silver edition of 430) 145.00
(16b) Ryne Sandberg (1992 Topps, bronze edition of 1,932) 15.00
(17s) Frank Thomas (1992 Topps, silver edition of 1,000) 85.00
(17b) Frank Thomas (1992 Topps, bronze edition of 5,000) 12.50
(17g) Frank Thomas (1992 Topps, gold edition of 500) 150.00

1994 Highland Mint Mint-Cards

In 1994 the Highland Mint continued its production of Mint-Cards, licensed metal replicas of Topps baseball, football and hockey cards. Maximum production of baseball players in the series was reduced to 750 in silver and halved to 2,500 in bronze. Suggested retail prices remained at $235 and $50, respectively. Once again cards were produced in the same 2-1/2" x 3-1/2" format as original Topps cards and were minted to a thickness of 1/10", with a serial number engraved on the edge. Mint-cards were sold in a heavy lucite holder, packaged with a certificate of authenticity in a plastic book-style holder. In mid-year, the company announced it was ceasing production of Topps-replica baseball cards and that henceforth all baseball Mint-Cards would reproduce the designs of Pinnacle brand cards.

NM/M
Common Player, Silver: 50.00
Common Player, Bronze: 12.00
Common Player, Gold: 200.00
(1a) Ernie Banks (1954 Topps, silver edition of 437) 65.00
(1b) Ernie Banks (1954 Topps, bronze edition of 920) 25.00
(2a) Carl Yastrzemski (1960 Topps, silver edition of 500) 75.00
(2b) Carl Yastrzemski (1960 Topps, bronze edition of 1,072) 30.00
(3a) Johnny Bench (1969 Topps, silver edition of 500) 75.00
(3b) Johnny Bench (1969 Topps, bronze edition of 1,384) 22.50
(4a) Mike Schmidt (1974 Topps, silver edition of 500) 75.00
(4b) Mike Schmidt (1974 Topps, bronze edition of 1,641) 20.00
(5a) Paul Molitor (1979 Topps, silver edition of 260) 175.00
(5b) Paul Molitor (1979 Topps, bronze edition of 639) 17.50
(6a) Deion Sanders (1989 Topps, silver edition of 187) 60.00
(6b) Deion Sanders (1989 Topps, bronze edition of 668) 12.50
(7a) Dave Justice (1990 Topps, silver edition of 265) 75.00
(7b) Dave Justice (1990 Topps, bronze edition of 1,396) 12.50
(8a) Jeff Bagwell (1992 Pinnacle, silver edition of 750) 50.00
(8b) Jeff Bagwell (1992 Pinnacle, bronze edition of 2,500) 15.00
(9a) Greg Maddux (1992 Pinnacle, silver edition of 750) 175.00
(9b) Greg Maddux (1992 Pinnacle, bronze edition of 2,500) 25.00
(10a) Mike Piazza (1992 Topps, silver edition of 750) 75.00
(10b) Mike Piazza (1992 Topps, bronze edition of 2,500) 20.00
(10c) Mike Piazza (1992 Topps, gold edition of 374) 300.00
(12a) Nolan Ryan (1992 Pinnacle Then and Now, silver edition of 1,000) 75.00
(12b) Nolan Ryan (1992 Pinnacle Then and Now, bronze edition of 5,000) 15.00
(12c) Nolan Ryan (1992 Pinnacle Then & Now, gold edition 500) 200.00
(13a) Tim Salmon (1993 Topps, silver edition of 264) 110.00
(13b) Tim Salmon (1993 Topps, bronze edition of 768) 10.00

1995 Highland Mint Mint-Cards

For 1995, the Highland Mint continued its series of precious-metal editions of cards in all major team sports. The 2-1/2" x 3-1/2" cards contain 4-1/4 oz. of bronze or silver or 24-K gold plating on silver. Each Mint-card is sold in a heavy plastic holder within a numbered album and with a certificate of authenticity. Only the firm's baseball cards are listed here.

NM/M
38b Michael Jordan (Upper Deck Rare Air, bronze, edition of 5,000.) 15.00
38s Michael Jordan (Upper Deck Rare Air, silver, edition of 1,000.) 100.00
38g Michael Jordan (Upper Deck Rare Air, gold, edition of 500.) 300.00
Mickey Mantle (1992 Pinnacle, bronze edition of 1,000) 20.00
Mickey Mantle (1992 Pinnacle, silver edition of 1,000) 75.00
Mickey Mantle (1992 Pinnacle, gold edition of 500) 300.00

1992 High 5 Decals

This issue of peelable, reusable "decals" was sold in both team sets and superstar panels. Each $2.99 panel contains five player decals and a team logo decal. The backing paper has a color 5" x 7" photo of a superstar that can be cut out and framed. Overall dimensions of the decal sheet are 7-1/2" x 7". The unnumbered decals are checklisted here in alphabetical order within team.

NM/M
Complete Set (156): 30.00
Common Player: .25
(1) Baltimore Orioles Logo .25
(2) Mike Devereaux .25
(3) Ben McDonald .25
(4) Gregg Olson .25
(5) Joe Orsulak .25
(6) Cal Ripken Jr. 3.00
(7) Boston Red Sox Logo .25
(8) Wade Boggs 2.00
(9) Roger Clemens 2.25
(10) Phil Plantier .25
(11) Jeff Reardon .25
(12) Mo Vaughn .25
(13) California Angels Logo .25
(14) Jim Abbott .25
(15) Chuck Finley .25
(16) Bryan Harvey .25
(17) Mark Langston .25
(18) Dave Winfield 1.50
(19) Chicago White Sox Logo .25
(20) Carlton Fisk 1.50
(21) Jack McDowell .25
(22) Bobby Thigpen .25
(23) Frank Thomas 1.50
(24) Robin Ventura .25

(25) Cleveland Indians Logo .25
(26) Sandy Alomar Jr. .25
(27) Carlos Baerga .25
(28) Albert Belle .25
(29) Alex Cole .25
(30) Charles Nagy .25
(31) Detroit Tigers Logo .25
(32) Cecil Fielder .25
(33) Travis Fryman .25
(34) Tony Phillips .25
(35) Alan Trammell .25
(36) Lou Whitaker .25
(37) Kansas City Royals Logo .25
(38) George Brett 2.50
(39) Jim Eisenreich .25
(40) Brian McRae .25
(41) Jeff Montgomery .25
(42) Bret Saberhagen .25
(43) Milwaukee Brewers Logo .25
(44) Chris Bosio .25
(45) Paul Molitor 1.50
(46) B.J. Surhoff .25
(47) Greg Vaughn .25
(48) Robin Yount 1.50
(49) Minnesota Twins Logo .25
(50) Rick Aguilera .25
(51) Scott Erickson .25
(52) Kent Hrbek .25
(53) Kirby Puckett 2.00
(54) Kevin Tapani .25
(55) New York Yankees Logo .25
(56) Mel Hall .25
(57) Roberto Kelly .25
(58) Kevin Maas .25
(59) Don Mattingly 2.50
(60) Steve Sax .25
(61) Oakland A's Logo .25
(62) Harold Baines .25
(63) Jose Canseco .75
(64) Dennis Eckersley 1.25
(65) Dave Henderson .25
(66) Rickey Henderson 1.50
(67) Seattle Mariners Logo .25
(68) Jay Buhner .25
(69) Ken Griffey Jr. 2.75
(70) Randy Johnson 1.50
(71) Edgar Martinez .25
(72) Harold Reynolds .25
(73) Texas Rangers Logo .25
(74) Julio Franco .25
(75) Juan Gonzalez 1.25
(76) Rafael Palmeiro 1.25
(77) Nolan Ryan 3.00
(77p) Nolan Ryan (Prototype) 6.50
(78) Ruben Sierra .25
(79) Toronto Blue Jays Logo .25
(80) Roberto Alomar .50
(81) Joe Carter .25
(82) Kelly Gruber .25
(83) John Olerud .25
(84) Devon White .25
(85) Atlanta Braves Logo .25
(86) Steve Avery .25
(87) Ron Gant .25
(88) Tom Glavine .40
(89) David Justice .25
(90) Terry Pendleton .25
(91) Chicago Cubs Logo .25
(92) George Bell .25
(93) Andre Dawson .30
(94) Mark Grace .25
(95) Greg Maddux 2.00
(96) Ryne Sandberg 2.00
(97) Cincinnati Reds Logo .25
(98) Eric Davis .25
(99) Barry Larkin .25
(100) Hal Morris .25
(101) Jose Rijo .25
(102) Chris Sabo .25
(103) Houston Astros Logo .25
(104) Jeff Bagwell 1.50
(105) Craig Biggio .25
(106) Ken Caminiti .25
(107) Luis Gonzalez .50
(108) Pete Harnisch .25
(109) Los Angeles Dodgers Logo .25
(110) Brett Butler .25
(111) Lenny Harris .25
(112) Ramon Martinez .25
(113) Eddie Murray 1.50
(114) Darryl Strawberry .25
(115) Montreal Expos Logo .25
(116) Ivan Calderon .25
(117) Delino DeShields .25
(118) Marquis Grissom .25
(119) Dennis Martinez .25
(120) Larry Walker .25
(121) New York Mets Logo .25
(122) David Cone .25
(123) Dwight Gooden .25
(124) Gregg Jefferies .25
(125) Howard Johnson .25
(126) Kevin McReynolds .25
(127) Philadelphia Phillies Logo .25
(128) Wes Chamberlain .25
(129) Lenny Dykstra .25
(130) John Kruk .25
(131) Terry Mulholland .25
(132) Mitch Williams .25
(133) Pittsburgh Pirates Logo .25
(134) Barry Bonds 3.00
(135) Doug Drabek .25
(136) John Smiley .25
(137) Zane Smith .25
(138) Andy Van Slyke .25
(139) St. Louis Cardinals Logo .25
(140) Felix Jose .25
(141) Ray Lankford .25
(142) Lee Smith .25
(143) Ozzie Smith 2.00
(144) Todd Zeile .25
(145) San Diego Padres Logo .25
(146) Tony Fernandez .25
(147) Tony Gwynn 2.00
(148) Bruce Hurst .25
(149) Fred McGriff .25
(150) Gary Sheffield .50
(151) San Francisco Giants Logo .25
(152) Will Clark .30
(152p) Will Clark (Prototype) 1.50
(153) Willie McGee .25
(154) Kevin Mitchell .25
(155) Robby Thompson .25
(156) Matt Williams .25

1989 Hills Team MVP's

This high-gloss, boxed set of superstars was produced by Topps for the Hills department store chain. The words "Hills Team MVP's" appear above the player photos, while the player's name and team are printed below. The front of the card carries a red, white and blue color scheme with yellow and gold accents. The horizontal backs include player data set against a green playing field background.

NM/M
Complete Set (33): 4.00
Common Player: .10
1 Harold Baines .10
2 Wade Boggs .75
3 George Brett 1.00
4 Tom Brunansky .10
5 Jose Canseco .35
6 Joe Carter .10
7 Will Clark .15
8 Roger Clemens .85
9 Dave Cone .10
10 Glenn Davis .10
11 Andre Dawson .25
12 Dennis Eckersley .40
13 Andres Galarraga .10
14 Kirk Gibson .10
15 Mike Greenwell .10
16 Tony Gwynn .75
17 Orel Hershiser .10
18 Danny Jackson .10
19 Mark Langston .10
20 Fred McGriff .10
21 Dale Murphy .25
22 Eddie Murray .50
23 Kirby Puckett .75
24 Johnny Ray .10
25 Juan Samuel .10
26 Ruben Sierra .10
27 Dave Stewart .10
28 Darryl Strawberry .10
29 Alan Trammell .10
30 Andy Van Slyke .10
31 Frank Viola .10
32 Dave Winfield .50
33 Robin Yount .50

1990 Hills Hit Men

The 33 slugging percentage leaders are featured in this high-gloss boxed set. The cards were produced by Topps for the Hills department store chain. Fronts feature "Hit Men" in a bat design above the photo. The player's name appears on a band below the photo. Horizontal backs feature a breakdown of the player's slugging percentage and also display career statistics.

NM/M
Complete Set (33): 5.00
Common Player: .10
1 Eric Davis .10
2 Will Clark .15
3 Don Mattingly .75
4 Darryl Strawberry .10
5 Kevin Mitchell .10
6 Pedro Guerrero .10
7 Jose Canseco .35
8 Jim Rice .15
9 Danny Tartabull .10
10 George Brett .75
11 Kent Hrbek .10
12 George Bell .10
13 Eddie Murray .50
14 Fred Lynn .10
15 Andre Dawson .25
16 Dale Murphy .15
17 Dave Winfield .50
18 Jack Clark .10
19 Wade Boggs .65
20 Ruben Sierra .10
21 Dave Parker .10
22 Glenn Davis .10
23 Dwight Evans .10
24 Jesse Barfield .10
25 Kirk Gibson .10
26 Alvin Davis .10
27 Kirby Puckett .65
28 Joe Carter .10
29 Carlton Fisk .50
30 Harold Baines .10
31 Andres Galarraga .10
32 Cal Ripken, Jr. 1.50
33 Howard Johnson .10

1993 Hills Pirates Kids Club

Stars of the Eastern Division N.L. champions are picutred on this 12-card issue. The set was issued in the form of a perforated 10" x 10-1/2" panel. Fronts have player action photos with orange frames, white borders and a team logo. Black-and-white backs have a player portrait, personal data and stats, and the Hills Pirates Kids Club logo. Cards are numbered by uniform number.

NM/M
Complete Set, Sheet: 7.00
Complete Set, Singles (12): 6.00
Common Player: .50
6 Orlando Merced .50
7 Jeff King .50
10 Jim Leyland .50
14 Tom Prince .50
23 Lloyd McClendon .50
26 Steve Cooke .50
28 Al Martin .50
32 Denny Neagle .50
36 Kevin Young .50
45 John Candelaria .50
50 Stan Belinda .50
55 Blas Minor .50

1999 Hillshire Farm Home Run Heroes

Via a special offer on packages of Hillshire Farm meats, collectors could order an autographed card of several star sluggers of the 1960s. Cards were available by sending in a package coupon and $4 for handling. The 2-1/2" x 3-1/2" cards have color player photos on which uniform logos have been removed. Borders are black and enhanced with gold foil. Black and gold backs offer lifetime stats and career highlights.

NM/M
Complete Set (4): 30.00
Common Player: 7.50
(1) Ernie Banks 10.00
(2) Harmon Killebrew 7.50
(3) Frank Robinson 7.50
(4) Willie Stargell 12.00

1988 Historic Limited Editions Brooklyn Dodgers

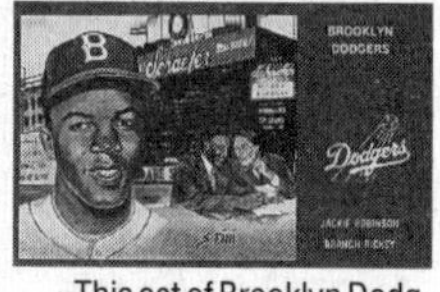

This set of Brooklyn Dodgers postcards features the artwork of Susan Rini, combining on most cards a player portrait and an action pose with Ebbets Field as the background. Fronts of the 5-1/2" x 3-1/2" cards have the artwork at left, bordered in bright blue. In the wide right border, the team name and logo, and the player name, are printed in white. Postcard-style bakcs are printed in blue. The cards were issued in three series of 12 each, but are checklisted here in alphabetical order. Two different cards each exist for Erskine and Lavagetto. Production of the series was limited to 5,000 sets; 2,000 sets were produced with a low-gloss finish to facilitate autographing, while the remaining 3,000 sets were high-gloss. Either sold for $20 at time of issue. Two hundred uncut sheets of each series were sold for $30 apiece. A special album was also made available.

NM/M
Complete Set (36): 10.00
Common Player: .50
(1) Cal Abrams .50
(2) Sandy Amoros .50
(3) Red Barber (Announcer) .50
(4) Ralph Branca .50
(5) Chuck Connors .75
(6) Roger Craig .50
(7) Roy Campanella 1.50
(8) Don Drysdale 1.00
(9) Leo Durocher .50
(10) Carl Erskine .50
(11) Carl Erskine .50
(12) Carl Furillo .50
(13) Gene Hermanski .50
(14) Gil Hodges 1.00
(15) Clyde King .50
(16) Clem Labine .50
(17) Tommy Lasorda .75
(18) Cookie Lavagetto .50
(19) Cookie Lavagetto .50
(20) Larry MacPhail (GM) .50
(21) Sal Maglie .50
(22) Eddie Miksis .50
(23) Don Newcombe .60
(24) Walter O'Malley (Owner) .50
(25) Mickey Owen .50
(26) Andy Pafko .50
(27) Johnny Podres .50
(28) Pee Wee Reese 1.00
(29) Preacher Roe .50
(30) Jackie Robinson 2.50
(31) George Shuba .50
(32) Duke Snider 1.50
(33) Red Barber, Leo Durocher .50
(34) Jackie Robinson, Branch Rickey 1.00
(35) Ebbets Field .50
(36) Dodgers Sym-Phony Band .50

1989 Historic Limited Editions Lou Gehrig Postcards

This set of postcards combines portrait and action art with a Yankee Stadium backdrop in paintings by Susan Rini. The art is set towards the top of the 3-1/2" x 5-1/2" cards which have a pinstripe background, player name beneath the art and team name and logo at bottom. Horizontal backs are postcard-style and printed in blue with appropriate credit lines, copyright notice and logos. Original issue price was $10 per set, with uncut sheets available for $15.

NM/M
Complete Set (8): 6.00
Common Card: 1.00

Don Mattingly Series 1

One of the most popular Yankees of the past 25 years is honored on this set of postcards. The 3-1/2" x 5-1/2" cards feature the artwork of Susan Rini on each card. Mattingly is shown in portrait and action art on most of the cards, though sometimes the picture of another Yankee great takes the place of the action picture. Background on the front is white with blue pinstripes. Postcard-style backs are printed in blue and announce an edition of 5,000 sets. Price at issue was about $10, with uncut sheets of the cards available for $24.

NM/M
Complete Set (12): 6.00
Common Card: .50

Negro Leagues Postcards

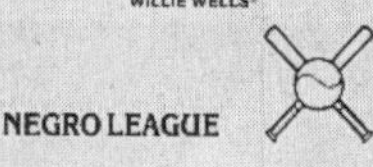

Both well-known and obscure players of the segregated Negro Leagues are included in this series of color postcards. Fronts of the 3-1/2" x 5-1/2" cards have portrait and action paintings of the players on a peach-colored background. Postcard-style backs are printed in blue and indicate a limit of 5,000 sets were produced. An edition of 200 uncut sheets was also produced.

NM/M
Complete Set (12): 7.00
Common Player: .50
Uncut Sheet: 10.00
1 Monte Irvin 1.00
2 Martin Dihigo .85
3 Clint Thomas .50
4 Buster Haywood .50
5 George Giles .50
6 Isidro Fabri .50
7 James (Cool Papa) Bell .65
8 Josh Gibson 1.50
9 Lou Dials .50
10 Willie Wells .75
11 Walter (Buck) Leonard .75
12 Jose Fernandez .50

1990 Historic Limited Editions Roberto Clemente

This set of 3-1/2" x 5-1/2" postcards details the career of the Pirates outfielder. Background of each card is beige. At top is an approximately 3" x 3-1/2" color painting of Clemente in both portrait and action poses, created by sports artist Susan Rini. Player and team name, and team logo are at bottom. Postcard-style backs are printed in blue with appropriate credit lines and copyright data. Production was reported at 5,000 sets.

NM/M
Complete Set (12): 12.50
Common Card: 1.50

Thurman Munson Postcards

The late, great Yankees catcher is memorialized in this set of color postcards from sports artist Susan Rini. Fronts of the 3-1/2" x 5-1/2" cards have a combination portrait/action painting toward the top, on a background of pinstripes. Player and team names and the Yankees logo are at bottom. Horizontal backs are in postcard style, printed in blue with appropriate licensing, copyright and credit data, and logos. Production was limited to 5,000 sets and 200 complete-set uncut sheets.

		NM/M
Complete Set (12):		10.00
Common Card:		1.25
Uncut Sheet:		55.00
1-12	Thurman Munson	1.25

Nolan Ryan Series 1

The Mets and Rangers years are graphically depicted on this set of postcards in combined portrait and action paintings by sports artist Susan Rini. The 3-1/2" x 5-1/2" cards have a light blue background on front, with the player and team name, and the team logo at bottom. Postcard-style backs are printed in blue and offer copyright and licensing information, along with a notice that the set is limited to an edition of 10,000.

	NM/M
Complete Set (12):	10.00
Common Card:	1.00

Nolan Ryan Series 2

The Astros and Angels years are graphically depicted on this set of postcards in combined portrait and action paintings by sports artist Susan Rini. The 3-1/2" x 5-1/2" cards have a beige background on front, with the player and team name, and the team logo at bottom. Post-card-style backs are printed in blue and offer copyright and

licensing information, along with a notice that the set is limited to an edition of 10,000.

	NM/M
Complete Set (12):	10.00
Common Card:	1.00

Yankees Monuments

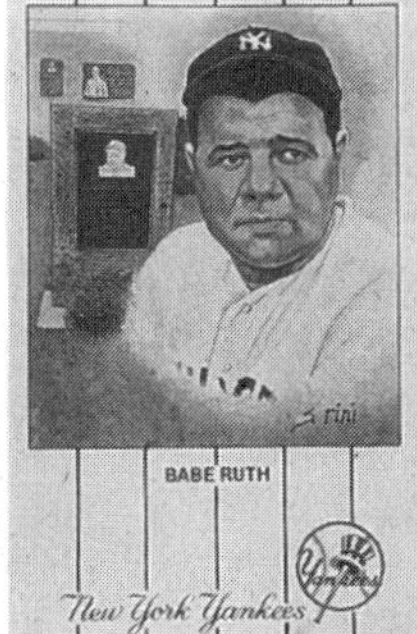

Those honored with plaques in Monument Park behind the center field wall at Yankee Stadium are presented in this series of postcards. On a pinstriped background, the fronts of the 3-1/2" x 5-1/2" cards have a portrait of the person with his plaque in the background, the work of Susan Rini. The team name and logo are at bottom. Postcard-style backs are printed in blue with various copyright and creator notices, MLB logo and an indication that the cards were produced in an edition of 5,000. At time of issue, complete sets sold for about $10; uncut sheets were available for $20.

		NM/M
Complete Set (12):		12.00
Common Player:		.70
1	Lou Gehrig	2.25
2	Babe Ruth	3.00
3	Thurman Munson	1.50
4	Elston Howard	.70
5	Phil Rizzuto	.70
6	Mickey Mantle	4.50
7	Bill Dickey	.70
8	Lefty Gomez	.70
9	Pope Paul VI	2.25
10	Jacob Ruppert	.70
11	Roger Maris	2.25
12	Joe DiMaggio	3.00

1969 Mets Postcards

This set commemorates the Amazin' Mets World Championship team of 1969. The 5-1/2" x 3-1/2" cards have bright blue front borders. At left is a portrait/action painting of the players by sports artist Susan Rini. Postcard-style backs are printed in blue with copyright and credit data, card number, logos, etc. The issue was limited to 5,000 sets and originally sold for about $20. Uncut sheets were available for $25.

		NM/M
Complete Set (36):		11.00
Common Player:		.50
1	Championship Trophy	.50
2	Shea Stadium	.50
3	Tommie Agee	.50
4	Ken Boswell	.50
5	Ed Charles	.50
6	Don Cardwell	.50
7	Donn Clendenon	.65
8	Jack DiLauro	.50
9	Duffy Dyer	.50
10	Wayne Garrett	.50
11	Jerry Grote	.50
12	Rod Gaspar	.50
13	Gary Gentry	.50
14	Bud Harrelson	.65
15	Gil Hodges	1.00
16	Cleon Jones	.65
17	Ed Kranepool	.65
18	Cal Koonce	.50
19	Jerry Koosman	.65
20	Jim McAndrew	.50
21	Tug McGraw	.75
22	J.C. Martin	.50
23	Bob Pfeil	.50
24	Nolan Ryan	4.00
25	Ron Swoboda	.50
26	Tom Seaver	1.50
27	Art Shamsky	.50
28	Ron Taylor	.50
29	Al Weis	.50
30	Joe Pignatano	.50
31	Eddie Yost	.50
32	Ralph Kiner (Announcer)	.50
33	Bob Murphy (Writer)	.50
34	Lindsey Nelson (Announcer)	.50
35	Yogi Berra	1.00
36	Rube Walker	.50

1991 Historic Limited Editions Brooklyn Dodgers

Three additional series of 12-card player postcard sets in 1991 were issued as a follow-up to the company's debut issue of 1988. Identical in format, the 5-1/2" x 3-1/2" cards have a Dodger blue background on front. At the left end is artwork by Susan Rini combining portrait and action pictures of the player against a background of Ebbets Field. Player and team identification are in white at right. Postcard backs are printed in blue with credits, copyright data, logos and series and card numbers.

		NM/M
Complete Set (36):		20.00
Common Player:		.50
SERIES 2		5.00
1	Charley Dressen	.50
2	John Roseboro	.50
3	Eddie Stanky	.50
4	Goody Rosen	.50
5	Ed Head	.50
6	Dick Williams	.50
7	Clarence (Bud) Podbielan	.50
8	Erv Palica	.50
9	Augie Galan	.50
10	Billy Loes	.50
11	Billy Cox	.50
12	Phil Phifer	.50
SERIES 3		5.00
1	Joe Black	.75
2	Jack Banta	.50
3	Whitlow Wyatt	.50
4	Gino Cimoli	.50
5	Dolph Camilli (Dolf)	.50
6	Dan Bankhead	.50
7	Henry Behrman	.50
8	Pete Reiser	.50
9	Chris Van Cuyk	.50
10	James (Junior) Gilliam	.75
11	Don Zimmer	.75
12	Ed Roebuck	.50
SERIES 4		5.00
1	Billy Herman	.50
2	Rube Walker	.50
3	Tommy Brown	.50
4	Charlie Neal	.50
5	Kirby Higbe	.50
6	Bruce Edwards	.50
7	Joe Hatten	.50
8	Rex Barney	.50
9	Al Gionfriddo	.50
10	Luis Olmo	.50
11	Dixie Walker	.50
12	Walter Alston	1.00

Don Mattingly Series 2

Two years after the release of the first series, another 12 Mattingly postcards were issued. The 3-1/2" x 5-1/2" cards feature the artwork of Susan Rini on each card. Mattingly is shown in portrait and action art on each of the cards. Background on the front is white with blue pinstripes. Postcard-style backs are printed in blue and announce an edition of 5,000 sets. Price at issue was about $10, with uncut sheets of the cards available for $24.

		NM/M
Complete Set (12):		6.00
Common Card:		.50
1-12	Don Mattingly	.50

1961 Yankees Postcards

Three series of 12 post-cards each were issued to commemorate the '61 Yanks. All cards are 5-1/2" x 3-1/2", with a pinstriped border design. At left front are combination portrait/action paintings by Susan Rini. Team name and logo are at right, along with player identification. Backs are printed in blue, in postcard style, with copyright, credits, logos, etc.

		NM/M
Complete Set (36):		16.00
Common Player:		.25
SERIES 1		3.00
1	Yogi Berra	1.00
2	Tom Tresh	.45
3	Bill Skowron	.45
4	Al Downing	.25
5	Jim Coates	.25
6	Luis Arroyo	.25
7	Johnny Blanchard	.25
8	Hector Lopez	.25
9	Tony Kubek	.50
10	Ralph Houk	.25
11	Bobby Richardson	.50
12	Clete Boyer	.35
SERIES 2		8.00
1	Roger Maris	6.00
2	Jesse Gonder	.25
3	Danny McDevitt	.25
4	Leroy Thomas	.25
5	Billy Gardner	.25
6	Ralph Terry	.25
7	Hal Reniff	.25
8	Earl Torgeson	.25
9	Art Ditmar	.25
10	Jack Reed	.25
11	Johnny James	.25
12	Elston Howard	.75
SERIES 3		6.00
1	Mickey Mantle	5.00
2	Deron Johnson	.25
3	Bob Hale	.25
4	Bill Stafford	.25
5	Duke Maas	.25
6	Bob Cerv	.25
7	Roland Sheldon	.25
8	Ryne Duren	.35
9	Bob Turley	.35
10	Whitey Ford	1.00
11	Bud Daley	.25
12	Joe DeMaestri	.25

1989 Holsum/ Schafer's Super Stars Discs

This version of the 1989 MSA bakeries disc set was issued in Canada by Ben's bakeries. The discs are nearly identical to the other regional variations except for the appearance of a red "Schafer's" logo at top.

		NM/M
Complete Set (20):		9.00
Common Player:		.25
1	Wally Joyner	.25
2	Wade Boggs	1.00
3	Ozzie Smith	1.00
4	Don Mattingly	1.25
5	Jose Canseco	.50
6	Tony Gwynn	1.00
7	Eric Davis	.25
8	Kirby Puckett	1.00
9	Kevin Seitzer	.25
10	Daryl Strawberry	.25
11	Gregg Jefferies	.25
12	Mark Grace	.25
13	Matt Nokes	.25
14	Mark McGwire	2.00
15	Don Mattingly	1.25
16	Roger Clemens	1.25
17	Frank Viola	.25
18	Orel Hershiser	.25
19	Dave Cone	.25
20	Kirk Gibson	.25

1989 Holsum Bakeries Super Stars Discs

This set of 2-3/4" diameter discs was manufactured by Mike Schechter Associates for Holsum bakeries' inclusion in various bread brands. Because the cards are licensed only by the Players Association and not MLB, the player photos have been airbrushed to remove cap and uniform logos. Cards feature white borders with red, yellow and blue decorations. Backs are printed in dark blue and include a few 1988 and career stats and some player vitals. The set was distributed in Michigan.

		NM/M
Complete Set (20):		12.00
Common Player:		.50
1	Wally Joyner	.50
2	Wade Boggs	2.00
3	Ozzie Smith	2.00
4	Don Mattingly	2.50
5	Jose Canseco	1.00
6	Tony Gwynn	2.00
7	Eric Davis	.50
8	Kirby Puckett	2.00
9	Kevin Seitzer	.50
10	Darryl Strawberry	.50
11	Gregg Jefferies	.50
12	Mark Grace	.50
13	Matt Nokes	.50
14	Mark McGwire	3.00
15	Bobby Bonilla	.50
16	Roger Clemens	2.50
17	Frank Viola	.50
18	Orel Hershiser	.50
19	Dave Cone	.50
20	Kirk Gibson	.50

1990 Holsum Bakeries Super Stars Discs

Players in this disc set are featured in round portrait photos on which uniform logos have been painted over for lack of a license from Major League Baseball (the set is licensed by the Players Union and bears their logo on back). Most of the front border on these 2-3/4" diameter discs is in red, with yellow stars and white baseballs around the portrait and the bakery's logo at top. A yellow banner beneath the photo has the "Superstars" logo. At bottom, in the white portion of the border, the player's name is presented in red, with his team and position in blue. Backs are printed in blue and include 1989 and career stats, a few biographical details, the card number and appropriate copyrights.

		NM/M
Complete Set (20):		4.00
Common Player:		.25
1	George Bell	.25
2	Tim Raines	.25
3	Tom Henke	.25
4	Andres Galarraga	.25
5	Bret Saberhagen	.25
6	Mark Davis	.25
7	Robin Yount	.75
8	Rickey Henderson	.75
9	Kevin Mitchell	.25
10	Howard Johnson	.25
11	Will Clark	.30
12	Orel Hershiser	.25
13	Fred McGriff	.25
14	Dave Stewart	.25
15	Vince Coleman	.25
16	Steve Sax	.25
17	Kirby Puckett	1.00
18	Tony Gwynn	1.00
19	Jerome Walton	.25
20	Gregg Olson	.25

1991 Holsum Bakeries Super Stars Discs

Similar to the previous year's issue, the 20 discs in the 1991 bakery set feature a color player photo (uniform logos airbrushed off) at center, with a wide white border to the edge of the 2-3/4" diameter cardboard. The player's name appears in a yellow stripe at bottom, along with his team and position. Backs are printed in dark blue and include a few stats from the previous season. The issue was distributed in Canada for Ben's Bakeries.

		NM/M
Complete Set (20):		45.00
Common Player:		.75
1	Darryl Strawberry	.75
2	Eric Davis	.75
3	Tim Wallach	.75
4	Kevin Mitchell	.75
5	Tony Gwynn	4.50
6	Ryne Sandberg	4.50

7 Doug Drabek .75
8 Randy Myers .75
9 Ken Griffey Jr. 6.50
10 Alan Trammell .75
11 Ken Griffey Sr. .75
12 Rickey Henderson 3.00
13 Roger Clemens 5.50
14 Bob Welch .75
15 Kelly Gruber .75
16 Mark McGwire 7.50
17 Cecil Fielder .75
18 Dave Steib .75
19 Nolan Ryan 9.00
20 Cal Ripken, Jr. 9.00

1983 Homeplate Sports Cards Al Kaline Story

Commemorating Al Kaline's 30th anniversary with the Detroit Tigers, this set chronicles his life and career. The 2-1/2" x 3-1/2" cards have either black-and-white front photos with orange borders or color photos with black borders. Backs reverse the color scheme and provide details about the photo on front. The first card in each set has been personally autographed by Kaline.

NM/M
Complete Set (73): 15.00
Common Card: .25
1a 30 Years a Tiger/ Auto. 12.00
1b I'd play baseball for nothing .25
2 Sandlot days in Baltimore .25
3 MVP trophy winner .25
4 Learning the ropes .25
5 Working for a living .25
6 Pleasing a young fan .25
7 Al and Louise - the newlyweds .25
8 Al and Pat Mullin .25
9 How Al does it #1 .25
10 How Al does it #2 .25
11 Silver Bat for the Champ .25
12 Al and George Stark .25
13 Al watches Gordie Howe swing a bat 2.00
14 Kaline and Mantle - Batting Champs 1.00
15 Kaline .25
16 Martin, Kaline, Kuenn, Mantle, Ford .50
17 Crossing the plate .25
18 1959 All-Star Game (W/ Bill Skowron.) .25
19 Cash, Colavito, Kaline .50
20 Kaline slides under Nellie Fox .25
21 One of many awards .25
22 Kaline, Jim Campbell, Norm Cash - 1962 .25
23 Costly catch - 1962 .25
24 Jim Bunning, Al, Norm Cash in Japan .25
25 Perfect form .25
26 Ernie Harwell, Al, George Kell .25
27 Life isn't always easy .25
28 Al, Michael and Mark Kaline .25
29 Al and Charlie Dressen - 1965 .25
30 George Kell and Al - Fielding masters .25
31 Al and Hal Newhouser .25
32 Michael, Louise, Al and Mark Kaline .25
33 Al, Charlie Gehringer, Bill Freehan .25
34 Rapping a hit in 1967 .25
35 Veteran rivals Mantle and Kaline 1.00
36 Al homers against Boston - 1968 .25
37 1968 World Series homer .25
38 Premier fielder .25
39 All-Time All-Stars (W/ Hank Greenberg, etc.) .50
40 Part of the game .25
41 Family portrait .25
42 Spring training tribute .25
43 Billy Martin and Al .25
44 First $100,000 Tiger .25
45 On deck - 1972 .25
46 A close call .25
47 On deck in Baltimore - 1974 .25
48 Hit number 3,000 - 1974 .25
49 April 17, 1955 - 3 Homers .25
50 All-Star Game record .25
51 1968 Series action - Cepeda .25
52 Celebrating 1968 .25
53 Al Kaline Day .25
54 3,000 Hit Day .25
55 Thank you - Sept. 29, 1974 .25
56 Silver salute - Sept. 29, 1974 .25
57 Al and Kell - a new career .25
58 Voices of the Tigers .25
59 Tiger record setter .25
60 1970 AL All-Star team .25
61 Pat Mullin and Al .25
62 Al and Lolich - Aug., 1980 .25
63 Hall of Fame plaque .25
64 Al and Bowie Kuhn - Aug. 4, 1980 .25
65 Al and parents - Aug., 1980 .25
66 Fame .25
67 "The Man" and the Boy (W/ Stan Musial.) .50
68 Two Kids - Ted Williams and Kaline .50
69 Master glovemen (W/ Brooks Robinson.) .45
70 Coach and Pupil - Al and Pat Underwood .25
71 Kaline career records .25
72 A Tiger Forever .25

1990 Homers Cookies Pittsburgh Pirates

This set of 4" x 6" color cards was a stadium giveaway. Fronts have borderless game-action photos. Backs are in black, white and green and have player biographical data, major and minor league stats, career highlights and a sponsor's logo.

NM/M
Complete Set (31): 20.00
Common Player: .50
(1) Wally Backman .50
(2) Doug Bair .50
(3) Jay Bell .50
(4) Rafael Belliard .50
(5) Barry Bonds 8.00
(6) Bobby Bonilla .50
(7) Sid Bream .50
(8) John Cangelosi .50
(9) Rich Donnelly .50
(10) Doug Drabek .50
(11) Billy Hatcher .50
(12) Neal Heaton .50
(13) Jeff King .50
(14) Bob Kipper .50
(15) Randy Kramer .50
(16) Gene Lamont .50
(17) Bill Landrum .50
(18) Mike LaValliere .50
(19) Jim Leyland .50
(20) Jose Lind .50
(21) Milt May .50
(22) Ray Miller .50
(23) Ted Power .50
(24) Gary Redus .50
(25) R.J. Reynolds .50
(26) Tommy Sandt .50
(27) Don Slaught .50
(28) John Smiley .50
(29) Walt Terrell .50
(30) Andy Van Slyke .50
(31) Bob Walk .50

1991 Homers Cookies

One Hall of Famer's card was inserted in each box of Homers Cookies. The cards measure 2-1/2" x 3-1/2" and feature sepia-toned photos. The card backs feature lifetime statistics and career highlights. The cards are also numbered on the back and a checklist is featured on the back of each card.

NM/M
Complete Set (9): 5.00
Common Player: .50
1 Babe Ruth 2.00
2 Satchel Paige .75
3 Lefty Gomez .50
4 Ty Cobb 1.00
5 Cy Young .50
6 Bob Feller .50
7 Roberto Clemente 2.00
8 Dizzy Dean .50
9 Lou Gehrig 1.50

1999 Homers Cookies

Former stars are featured in this set of cards inserted into specially marked boxes of cookies (suggested retail about $1). The 2-1/2" x 3-1/2" cards have color player photos (without uniform logos) with a white border. At top is player identification, at bottom is is a red stripe with "HOMERS." Horizontal backs have a cartoon, career data, biographical information and a checklist.

NM/M
Complete Set (9): 7.50
Common Player: 1.00
1 Vida Blue 1.00
2 Orlando Cepeda 1.00
3 Darrell Evans 1.00
4 Harmon Killebrew 1.00
5 Dave Kingman 1.00
6 Eddie Murray 1.50
7 Frank Robinson 1.50
8 Willie Stargell 1.00
9 Carl Yastrzemski 1.50

1985 Hostess Braves

After a five-year hiatus, Hostess returned to the production of baseball cards in 1985 with an Atlanta Braves team set. The 22 cards in the set were printed by Topps and inserted into packages of snack cake products, three cello-wrapped player cards and a header card per box. The 2-1/2" x 3-1/2" cards share a common back design with the regular-issue Topps cards of 1985.

NM/M
Complete Set (22): 4.00
Common Player: .35
1 Eddie Haas .35
2 Len Barker .35
3 Steve Bedrosian .35
4 Bruce Benedict .35
5 Rick Camp .35
6 Rick Cerone .35
7 Chris Chambliss .35
8 Terry Forster .35
9 Gene Garber .35
10 Albert Hall .35
11 Bob Horner .50
12 Glenn Hubbard .35
13 Brad Komminsk .35
14 Rick Mahler .35
15 Craig McMurtry .35
16 Dale Murphy 3.00
17 Ken Oberkfell .35
18 Pascual Perez .35
19 Gerald Perry .35
20 Rafael Ramirez .35
21 Bruce Sutter 2.50
22 Claudell Washington .35
--- Header Card .05

1987 Hostess Stickers

Hostess of Canada issued a 30-card set of stickers in specially marked bags of potato chips. One sticker, measuring 1-3/4" x 1-3/8" in size, was found in each bag. The stickers have full-color fronts with the player's name appearing in black type in a white band. The Hostess logo and the sticker number are also included on the fronts. The backs are written in both English and French and contain the player's name, position and team.

NM/M
Complete Set (30): 12.00
Common Player: .25
1 Jesse Barfield .25
2 Ernie Whitt .25
3 George Bell .25
4 Hubie Brooks .25
5 Tim Wallach .25
6 Floyd Youmans .25
7 Dale Murphy .50
8 Ryne Sandberg 2.25
9 Eric Davis .25
10 Mike Scott .25
11 Fernando Valenzuela .25
12 Gary Carter 1.50
13 Mike Schmidt 2.50
14 Tony Pena .25
15 Ozzie Smith 2.00
16 Tony Gwynn 2.00
17 Mike Krukow .25
18 Eddie Murray 1.50
19 Wade Boggs 2.00
20 Wally Joyner .25
21 Harold Baines .25
22 Brook Jacoby .25
23 Lou Whitaker .25
24 George Brett 2.50
25 Robin Yount 1.50
26 Kirby Puckett 2.00
27 Don Mattingly 2.50
28 Jose Canseco .75
29 Phil Bradley .25
30 Pete O'Brien .25

1988 Hostess Potato Chips Expos/Blue Jays

The Expos and Blue Jays are showcased in this set of 24 discs (1-1/2" diameter). Full-color portraits are framed in white, surrounded by red stars. A yellow-banner "1988 Collectors Edition" label is printed (English and French) beneath the photo, followed by the player's name in black. Numbered disc backs are bilingual, blue and white, and include player name and stats. This set was distributed inside Hostess potato chip packages sold in Canada.

NM/M
Complete Panel Set (12): 6.50
Complete Singles Set (24): 4.50
Common Panel: .50
Common Player: .35
Panel 1 .50
1 Mitch Webster .35
20 Lloyd Moseby .35
Panel 2 .50
2 Tim Burke .35
23 Tom Henke .35
Panel 3 .50
3 Tom Foley .35
13 Jim Clancy .35
Panel 4 .50
4 Herm Winningham .35
14 Rance Mulliniks .35
Panel 5 .75
5 Hubie Brooks .35
24 Jimmy Key .35
Panel 6 .75
6 Mike Fitzgerald .35
17 Dave Steib .35
Panel 7 1.50
7 Tim Wallach .35
15 Fred McGriff .50
Panel 8 1.50
8 Andres Galarraga .45
21 Tony Fernandez .35
Panel 9 .50
9 Floyd Youmans .35
18 Mark Eichhorn .35
Panel 10 .50
10 Neal Heaton .35
19 Jesse Barfield .35
Panel 11 1.00
11 Tim Raines .45
16 Ernie Whitt .35
Panel 12 .75
12 Casey Candaele .35
22 George Bell .35

1990 Hostess Blue Jays Highlight Stickers

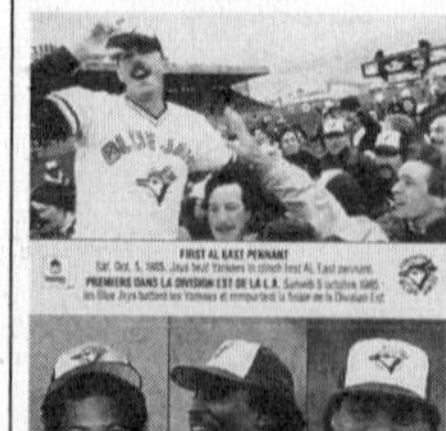

Team history highlights through the 1980 season are featured in this set of stickers. The set was produced in strips of three 2-1/4" x 3-1/4" stickers, some oriented horizontally, some vertically. Fronts have color photos with a light blue box beneath containing the highlight printed in both English and French. Black-and-white Hostess and team logos are at the left and right, respectively. Backs are blank. The set is checklisted here alphabetically based on the title of the sticker at top or left of the strip.

NM/M
Complete Set (18): 15.00
Common Sticker: .50
Panel 1 2.00
(1) First AL East Pennant (Dave Steib) .50
(2) Killer Bees Born (George Bell, Lloyd Moseby, Jesse Barfield) 1.00
(3) AL Home Run Champ (Jesse Barfield) 1.00
Panel 2 3.00
(4) First Home Run in Skydome (Fred McGriff) 1.50
(5) Club Save Leader (Tom Henke) .50
(6) Three Winning Openers in a Row (Jimmy Key) 1.00
Panel 3 2.00
(7) First 100 Wins (Jim Clancy) .50
(8) ML Home Run Record (Ernie Whitt) .50
(9) AL East Champs Again (Tom Henke) .50
Panel 4 2.00
(10) Home Run on First Pitch (Junior Felix) .50
(11) Almost Perfect (Dave Steib) .50
(12) First Game at Skydome .50
Panel 5 2.00
(13) Most Double Plays (Damaso Garcia) .50
(14) M.V.P. (George Bell) .50
(15) Hits the Cycle (Kelly Gruber) .50
Panel 6 2.00
(16) Stolen Bases (Dave Collins) .50
(17) Gold Glove Winners (Jesse Barfield, Tony Fernandez) .50
(18) Goodbye to Exhibition Stadium .50

1993 Hostess Twinkies

The Continental Baking Co., makers of Hostess Twinkies and cupcakes, returned to the baseball card market in 1993 with a 32-card set issued in two series. The promotion began around opening day with the first series; the second series was made available after the All-Star break. The cards were packaged in multi-packs with cupcakes that look like baseballs, with three cards in a box of eight cupcakes.

NM/M
Complete Set (32): 4.00
Common Player: .10
Uncut Sheet: 9.00
1 Andy Van Slyke .10
2 Ryne Sandberg .65
3 Bobby Bonilla .10
4 John Kruk .10
5 Ray Lankford .10

6 Gary Sheffield .25
7 Darryl Strawberry .10
8 Barry Larkin .10
9 Terry Pendleton .10
10 Jose Canseco .40
11 Dennis Eckersley .50
12 Brian McRae .10
13 Frank Thomas .60
14 Roberto Alomar .25
15 Cecil Fielder .10
16 Carlos Baerga .10
17 Will Clark .15
18 Andres Galarraga .10
19 Jeff Bagwell .60
20 Brett Butler .10
21 Benito Santiago .10
22 Tom Glavine .25
23 Rickey Henderson .60
24 Wally Joyner .10
25 Ken Griffey Jr. .85
26 Cal Ripken, Jr. 1.00
27 Roger Clemens .75
28 Don Mattingly .75
29 Kirby Puckett .65
30 Larry Walker .10
31 Jack McDowell .10
32 Pat Listach .10

1986 Houston Astros Police

This full-color police safety set was issued by the Houston Police Department and sponsored by Kool-Aid. The set was distributed at the Astrodome on June 14, when 15,000 sets of the first 12 cards were given away. The balance of the set was distributed throughout the summer by police. The cards feature player photos on the fronts and a safety tip on the back. The cards measure 4-1/8" x 2-5/8".

NM/M
Complete Set (26): 4.00
Common Player: .25
1 Jim Pankovits .25
2 Nolan Ryan 3.00
3 Mike Scott .25
4 Kevin Bass .25
5 Bill Doran .25
6 Hal Lanier .25
7 Denny Walling .25
8 Alan Ashby .25
9 Phil Garner .25
10 Charlie Kerfeld .25
11 Dave Smith .25
12 Jose Cruz .25
13 Craig Reynolds .25
14 Mark Bailey .25
15 Bob Knepper .25
16 Julio Solano .25
17 Dickie Thon .25
18 Mike Madden .25
19 Jeff Calhoun .25
20 Tony Walker .25
21 Terry Puhl .25
22 Glenn Davis .25
23 Billy Hatcher .25
24 Jim Deshaies .25
25 Frank DiPino .25
26 Coaching Staff (Yogi Berra, Matt Galante, Denis Menke, Les Moss, Gene Tenace) .25

1987 Houston Astros Police

The 1987 Astros safety set was produced through the combined efforts of the team, Deer Park Hospital and Sportsmedia Presentations. Cards #1-12 were handed out to youngsters 14 and under at the Astrodome on July 14. The balance of the distribution was handled by Deer Park Hospi-

tal. The cards, which measure 2-5/8" x 4-1/8", contain full-color photos. The backs offer a brief team/player history and a "Tips From The Dugout" anti-drug message.

NM/M
Complete Set (26): 5.00
Common Player: .25
1 Larry Andersen .25
2 Mark Bailey .25
3 Jose Cruz .25
4 Danny Darwin .25
5 Bill Doran .25
6 Billy Hatcher .25
7 Hal Lanier .25
8 Davey Lopes .25
9 Dave Meads .25
10 Craig Reynolds .25
11 Mike Scott .25
12 Denny Walling .25
13 Aurelio Lopez .25
14 Dickie Thon .25
15 Terry Puhl .25
16 Nolan Ryan 4.00
17 Dave Smith .25
18 Julio Solano .25
19 Jim Deshaies .25
20 Bob Knepper .25
21 Alan Ashby .25
22 Kevin Bass .25
23 Glenn Davis .25
24 Phil Garner .25
25 Jim Pankovits .25
26 Coaching Staff (Yogi Berra, Matt Galante, Denis Menke, Les Moss, Gene Tenace) .25

1988 Houston Astros Police

This set of full-color cards highlighting the Houston Astros was produced by the team, in conjunction with Deer Park Hospital and Sportsmedia Promotions for distribution to fans 14 years and younger at a ballpark giveaway. The 2-5/8" x 4-1/8" cards feature full-color player photos framed by a narrow blue border with an orange player/team name block below the photo. Blue-and-white backs have orange borders with player information, career highlights and anti-drug tips.

NM/M
Complete Set (26): 5.00
Common Player: .25
1 Juan Agosto .25
2 Larry Andersen .25
3 Joaquin Andujar .25
4 Alan Ashby .25
5 Mark Bailey .25
6 Kevin Bass .25
7 Danny Darwin .25
8 Glenn Davis .25
9 Jim Deshaies .25
10 Bill Doran .25
11 Billy Hatcher .25
12 Jeff Heathcock .25
13 Steve Henderson .25
14 Chuck Jackson .25
15 Bob Knepper .25
16 Jim Pankovits .25
17 Terry Puhl .25
18 Rafael Ramirez .25
19 Craig Reynolds .25
20 Nolan Ryan 4.00
21 Mike Scott .25
22 Dave Smith .25
23 Denny Walling .25
24 Gerald Young .25
25 Hal Lanier .25
26 Coaching Staff (Yogi Berra, Gene Clines, Matt Galante, Marc Hill, Denis Menke, Les Moss) .25

2005 Houston Astros Card Deck

This stadium giveaway was sponsored by Academy Sports+ Outdoors. Cards are 2-1/2" x 3-1/2" with rounded corners. Backs have a baseball in the background with team and sponsor's logos. Fronts have game-action photos. Many players have two cards in the deck, most with the same photo.

NM/M
Complete Set (56): 12.00
Common Player: .25
AS Roger Clemens 3.00
2S Russ Springer .25
3S Chad Harville .25
4S Brad Lidge .35
5S Jeff Bagwell 1.00
6S Jason Lane .25
7S Luke Scott .25
8S Brad Lidge .35
9S Roger Clemens 3.00
10S Jason Lane .25
JS Luke Scott .25
QS Minute Maid Park .25
KS Jeff Bagwell 1.00
AD Roy Oswalt .50
2D Brad Ausmus .25
3D Russ Springer .25
4D Raul Chavez .25
5D Morgan Ensberg .25
6D Brandon Duckworth .25
7D Orlando Palmeiro .25
8D Brandon Duckworth .25
9D Roy Oswalt .50
10D Orlando Palmeiro .25
JD Morgan Ensberg .25
QD Minute Maid Park .25
KD Brad Ausmus .25
AC Brandon Backe .25
2C Chris Burke .25
3C Dan Wheeler .25
4C Eric Bruntlett .25
5C Jose Vizcaino .25
6C Dan Wheeler .25
7C Craig Biggio .50
8C Willy Taveras .25
9C Brandon Backe .25
10C Jose Vizcaino .25
JC Willy Taveras .25
QC Minute Maid Park .25
KC Craig Biggio .50
AH Andy Pettitte .35
2H Raul Chavez .25
3H Chad Qualls .25
4H John Franco .25
5H Mike Lamb .25
6H Adam Everett .25
7H John Franco .25
8H Lance Berkman .50
9H Andy Pettitte .35
10H Mike Lamb .25
JH Adam Everett .25
QH Minute Maid Park .25
KH Lance Berkman .50
--- Phil Garner .25
--- Phil Garner .25
--- NL Wild Cardb 04 .05
--- NL Wild Card 04 .05

1989 Houston Colt .45s Fire Safety

The expansion Houston Colt .45s of 1962 are featured in this 1989 fire safety issue. The 2-1/2" x 3-1/2" cards have sepia player photos on front, with blue pistol frames and team logo, an orange name banner and brown Smokey logo. Backs are in black-and-white with a fire prevention cartoon, Forest Service logos and the player name, position and uniform number. Cards numbers are at upper-right.

NM/M
Complete Set (29): 12.50
Common Player: .50
1 Bob Bruce .50
2 Al Cicotte .50
3 Dave Giusti .50
4 Jim Golden .50
5 Ken Johnson .50
6 Tom Borland .50
7 Bobby Shantz .50
8 Dick Farrell .50
9 Jim Umbricht .50
10 Hal Woodeshick .50
11 Merritt Ranew .50
12 Hal Smith .50
13 Jim Campbell .50
14 Norm Larker .75
15 Joe Amalfitano .50
16 Bob Aspromonte .75
17 Bob Lillis .50
18 Dick Gernert .50
19 Don Buddin .50
20 Pidge Browne .50
21 Von McDaniel .50
22 Don Taussig .50
23 Al Spangler .50
24 Al Heist .50
25 Jim Pendleton .50
26 Johnny Weekly .50
27 Harry Craft .50
28 .45s Coaches (Lum Harris, Bobby Bragan, Jim Busby, Cot Deal, Jim Adair) .50
29 Team Photo .50

1993 Hoyle Legends of Baseball

Specially marked decks of Hoyle playing cards contained one of nine Hall of Famer's cards. In the 2-1/2" x 3-1/2" round-cornered poker-size format, the cards have oft-seen black-and-white photos on a glossy front. Backs have a facsimile autograph, biographical data, some stats and career highlights.

NM/M
Complete Set (9): 12.00
Common Player: 1.00
(1) Ty Cobb 2.00
(2) Dizzy Dean 1.00
(3) Lou Gehrig 2.00
(4) Walter Johnson 1.00
(5) Satchel Paige 1.00
(6) Babe Ruth 3.00
(7) Casey Stengel 1.00
(8) Honus Wagner 1.50
(9) Cy Young 1.00

1993 Humpty Dumpty

The Canadian potato chip company Humpty Dumpty issued a 50-card set of miniature cards in 1993. The UV coated cards measure 1-7/16" x 1-15/16", with a full-bleed color photo on the front along with the team logo. The backs have three-year statistics and biographical information about the player, along with appropriate product and baseball logos and a card number. Besides being packed one per bag in chips, the complete set was also available via a mail-in offer with a plastic album.

NM/M
Complete Set (50): 10.00
Complete Set, W/Album: 15.00
Common Player: .25
1 Cal Ripken, Jr. 3.00
2 Mike Mussina .50
3 Roger Clemens 2.25
4 Chuck Finley .25
5 Sandy Alomar .25
6 Frank Thomas 1.00
7 Robin Ventura .25
8 Cecil Fielder .25
9 George Brett 2.00
10 Cal Eldred .25
11 Kirby Puckett 1.50
12 Dave Winfield 1.00
13 Jim Abbott .25
14 Rickey Henderson 1.00
15 Ken Griffey Jr. 2.50
16 Nolan Ryan 3.00
17 Ivan Rodriguez .75
18 Paul Molitor 1.00
19 John Olerud .25
20 Joe Carter .25
21 Jack Morris .25
22 Roberto Alomar .40
23 Pat Borders .25
24 Devon White .25
25 Juan Guzman .25
26 Steve Avery .25
27 John Smoltz .25
28 Mark Grace .25
29 Jose Rijo .25
30 Dave Nied .25
31 Benito Santiago .25
32 Jeff Bagwell 1.00
33 Tim Wallach .25
34 Eric Karros .25
35 Delino DeShields .25
36 Wilfredo Cordero .25
37 Marquis Grissom .25
38a Ken Hill (Weight: 1915) .50
38b Ken Hill (Weight: 195) .25
39 Moises Alou .25
40 Chris Nabholz .25
41 Dennis Martinez .25
42 Larry Walker .25
43 Bobby Bonilla .25
44 Lenny Dykstra .25
45 Tim Wakefield .25
46 Andy Van Slyke .25
47 Tony Gwynn 1.50
48 Fred McGriff .25
49 Barry Bonds 3.00
50 Ozzie Smith 1.50
--- Checklist .10

1982 Hygrade Expos

This Montreal Expos team set was the object of intense collector speculation when it was first issued. Single cello-

wrapped cards were included in packages of Hygrade luncheon meat in the province of Quebec only. A mail-in offer for the complete set appeared later in the season. It remains a relatively scarce issue today. The 2" x 3" cards are printed on heavy paper, with round corners. Backs are printed in French, and contain an offer for an album to house the set.

NM/M
Complete Set (24): 15.00
Common Player: 1.00
Album: 5.00
0 Al Oliver 2.00
4 Chris Speier 1.00
5 John Milner 1.00
6 Jim Fanning 1.00
8 Gary Carter 7.50
10 Andre Dawson 5.00
11 Frank Tavaras (Taveras) 1.00
16 Terry Francona 1.00
17 Tim Blackwell 1.00
18 Jerry White 1.00
20 Bob James 1.00
21 Scott Sanderson 1.00
24 Brad Mills 1.00
29 Tim Wallach 1.00
30 Tim Raines 3.00
34 Bill Gullickson 1.00
35 Woodie Fryman 1.00
38 Bryn Smith 1.00
41 Jeff Reardon 1.00
44 Dan Norman 1.00
45 Steve Rogers 1.00
48 Ray Burris 1.00
49 Warren Cromartie 1.00
53 Charlie Lea 1.00

1987 Hygrade Baseball's All-Time Greats

(See "Baseball's All-Time Greats" for checklist and values.)

I

1994 Innovative Confections Sucker Savers

These 2-3/8" diameter discs were included in a plastic snap-top lollipop holder. A yellow strip which intersects the red border at the top contains the player name and team, while a yellow diamond graphic surrounds the player photo. Produced by Michael Schechter Assoc., the discs are licensed by the Players Union but not MLB, so team uniform logos are airbrushed off the photos. Backs are printed in blue and have 1993 and career stats. Square "proof" versions are common in the hobby and carry little or no premium.

NM/M
Complete Set (20): 25.00
Common Player: 1.00
1 Rickey Henderson 2.00
2 Ken Caminiti 1.00
3 Terry Pendleton 1.00
4 Tim Raines 1.00
5 Joe Carter 1.00
6 Benito Santiago 1.00
7 Jim Abbott 1.00
8 Ozzie Smith 2.50
9 Don Slaught 1.00
10 Tony Gwynn 2.50
11 Mark Langston 1.00
12 Darryl Strawberry 1.00
13 David Justice 1.00
14 Cecil Fielder 1.00
15 Cal Ripken Jr. 4.00
16 Jeff Bagwell 2.00
17 Mike Piazza 3.00
18 Bobby Bonilla 1.00
19 Barry Bonds 4.00
20 Roger Clemens 2.75

1994 International Playing Cards Toronto Blue Jays

Virtually identical to the team and mixed stars playing card sets issued by U.S. Playing Card Co., this Toronto team set was issued for the Canadian market. In playing card format at 2-1/2" x 3-1/2" with rounded corners, the set features Blue Jays players on front with their name and position in white in a blue stripe beneath the photo. Backs are bright blue with the team logo at top-center and sponsors' logos along the bottom. The set was sold in a colorful cardboard box.

NM/M
Complete Set (55): 4.00
Common Player: .05
AC John Olerud .15
2C Al Leiter .05
3C Dave Stewart .10
4C Pat Borders .05
5C Devon White .10
6C Joe Carter .10
7C Roberto Alomar .35
8C Woody Williams .05
9C Eddie Zosky .05
10C Willie Canate .05
JC Danny Cox .05
QC Todd Stottlemyre .10
KC Ed Sprague .05
AS Paul Molitor 1.00
2S Michael Timlin .05
3S Randy Knorr .05
4S Pat Hentgen .05
5S Darnell Coles .05
6S Juan Guzman .05
7S Roberto Alomar .35
8S Joe Carter .10
9S Scott Brow .05
10S Dick Schofield .05
JS Rob Butler .05
QS Tony Castillo .05
KS Duane Ward .05
AH Joe Carter .10
2H Woody Williams .05
3H Danny Cox .05
4H Todd Stottlemyre .10
5H Ed Sprague .05
6H John Olerud .15
7H Paul Molitor 1.00
8H Scott Brow .05
9H Pat Hentgen .05
10H Al Leiter .05
JH Dave Stewart .10
QH Pat Borders .05
KH Devon White .10
AD Roberto Alomar .35
2D Eddie Zosky .05
3D Rob Butler .05
4D Tony Castillo .05
5D Duane Ward .05
6D Paul Molitor 1.00
7D John Olerud .15
8D Carlos Delgado .75
9D Michael Timlin .05
10D Randy Knorr .05
JD Pat Hentgen .05
QD Darnell Coles .05
KD Juan Guzman .05
Joker Team Name .05
Joker A.L. Logo .05
--- Checklist .05

1995 International Playing Cards Toronto Blue Jays

For a second year the Canadian affiliate of the U.S. Playing Card Co. issued a team set of Blue Jays. Fronts have color portrait and action photos - up to three for popular players - with player identification and traditional playing card suit and value indicators in opposite corners. Backs have a large team logo. Cards are in 2-1/2" x 3-1/2" round-cornered format and were sold in a colorful flip-top box.

NM/M
Complete Set (56): 4.00
Common Player: .05
AC John Olerud .15
2C Pat Hentgen .05
3C Juan Guzman .05
4C Cecil Fielder .10
5C Roberto Alomar .35
6C Joe Carter .10
7C Mark Eichhorn .05
8C Carlos Delgado .75
9C Tom Candiotti .05
10C Dave Stewart .10
JC Tony Fernandez .05
QC Pat Borders .05
KC Dave Winfield 1.00
AS Paul Molitor 1.00
2S Todd Stottlemyre .10
3S Rickey Henderson 1.00
4S Tom Henke .05
5S Fred McGriff .10
6S Devon White .10
7S Duane Ward .05
8S David Wells .10
9S David Cone .10
10S Mike Timlin .05
JS Ed Sprague .05
QS Jack Morris .05
KS Jimmy Key .10
AH Roberto Alomar .35
2H Candy Maldonado .05
3H Mike Timlin .05
4H Ed Sprague .05
5H Pat Borders .05
6H Jimmy Key .10
7H Paul Molitor 1.00
8H Candy Maldonado .05
9H Danny Cox .05
10H Todd Stottlemyre .05
JH Rickey Henderson 1.00
QH Tom Henke .05
KH Cecil Fielder .10
AD Joe Carter .10
2D Duane Ward .05
3D Dave Stewart .10
4D Tony Fernandez .05
5D Jack Morris .05
6D Dave Winfield 1.00
7D John Olerud .15
8D Manny Lee .05
9D Pat Hentgen .05
10D Randy Knorr .05
JD Juan Guzman .05
QD Fred McGriff .10
KD Devon White .10
--- Toronto Blue Jays .05
--- Team Logo Card .05
--- A.L. Logo Card .05
--- Checklist .05

1984 Jarvis Press Rangers

For its second annual "Baseball Card Day" game promotional set, the Rangers picked up a new sponsor, Jarvis Press of Dallas. The 30 cards in the set include 27 players, the manager, trainer and a group card of the coaches. Cards measure 2-3/8" x 3-1/2".

Color game-action photos make up the card fronts. Backs, printed in black and white, include a portrait photo of the player. A source close to the promotion indicated 10,000 sets were produced.

NM/M
Complete Set (30): 4.00
Common Player: .35
1 Bill Stein .35
2 Alan Bannister .35
3 Wayne Tolleson .35
5 Billy Sample .35
6 Bobby Jones .35
7 Ned Yost .35
9 Pete O'Brien .35
11 Doug Rader .35
13 Tommy Dunbar .35
14 Jim Anderson .35
15 Larry Parrish .35
16 Mike Mason .35
17 Mickey Rivers .35
19 Curtis Wilkerson .35
20 Jeff Kunkel .35
21 Odell Jones .35
24 Dave Schmidt .35
25 Buddy Bell .35
26 George Wright .35
28 Frank Tanana .35
30 Marv Foley .35
31 Dave Stewart .50
32 Gary Ward .35
36 Dickie Noles .35
43 Donnie Scott .35
44 Danny Darwin .35
49 Charlie Hough .35
53 Joey McLaughlin .35
--- Coaching Staff (Rich Donnelly, Glenn Ezell, Merv Rettenmund, Dick Such, Wayne Terwilliger) .35
--- Trainer (Bill Zeigler) .35

1986 Jays Potato Chips

One of a handful of round baseball cards produced for inclusion in boxes of potato chips on a regional basis in 1986, the Jays set of 2-7/8" discs is believed to be the scarcest of the type. The 20 cards in the issue include the most popular Milwaukee Brewers and Chicago Cubs and White Sox players; the set having been distributed in the southern Wisconsin-northern Illinois area. Like many contemporary sets produced by Mike Schechter Associates, the '86 Jays cards feature player photos on which the team logos have been airbrushed off the caps.

NM/M
Complete Set (20): 17.50
Common Player: .50
(1) Harold Baines .50
(2) Cecil Cooper .50
(3) Jody Davis .50
(4) Bob Dernier .50
(5) Richard Dotson .50
(6) Shawon Dunston .50
(7) Carlton Fisk 3.00
(8) Jim Gantner .50
(9) Ozzie Guillen .50
(10) Teddy Higuera .50
(11) Ron Kittle .50
(12) Paul Molitor 3.00
(13) Keith Moreland .50
(14) Ernie Riles .50
(15) Ryne Sandberg 6.00
(16) Tom Seaver 3.00
(17) Lee Smith .50
(18) Rick Sutcliffe .50
(19) Greg Walker .50
(20) Robin Yount 3.00

1984 Jewel Food Chicago Cubs/ White Sox

Similar in format to previous issues by the Midwestern food company, these 16-piece sets of Chicago's National and American League teams are printed on 6" x 9" paper. Fronts feature a chest-to-cap color player photo with a black facsimile autograph. A logo and copyright notice by the Players Association is at upper-left. Backs are blank. Cards were distributed four per week with the purchase of specific sale products.

NM/M
Complete Cubs Set (16): 12.00
Complete White Sox Set (16): 12.50
Common Player: .50
(1) Larry Bowa .50
(2) Ron Cey .50
(3) Jody Davis .50
(4) Bob Dernier .50
(5) Leon Durham .50
(6) Dennis Eckersley 2.50
(7) Richie Hebner .50
(8) Gary Matthews .50
(9) Keith Moreland .50
(10) Ryne Sandberg 6.00
(11) Scott Sanderson .50
(12) Lee Smith .75
(13) Tom Stoddard .50
(14) Rick Sutcliffe .75
(15) Steve Trout .50
(16) Gary Woods .50
(1) Harold Baines .50
(2) Alan Bannister .50
(3) Julio Cruz .50
(4) Richard Dotson .50
(5) Jerry Dybzinski .50
(6) Carlton Fisk 4.00
(7) Scott Fletcher .50
(8) LaMarr Hoyt .50
(9) Ron Kittle .50
(10) Rudy Law .50
(11) Vance Law .50
(12) Greg Luzinski .50
(13) Tom Paciorek .50
(14) Tom Seaver 4.00
(15) Mike Squires .50
(16) Greg Walker .50

2003 Jewish Major Leaguers

Produced by Fleer for the American Jewish Historical Society, this set is a first-ever compilation of cards of every American Jew who played in Major League Baseball between 1871 and the All-Star break of 2003. Cards are standard 2-1/2" x 3-1/2", uv-coated on both front and back. Fronts have color or black-and-white photos, bordered in black. Backs have personal data, a career summary, an indication of what other baseball cards the player appeared on and photo/text credits. The issue was sold only as a complete boxed set with an initial price of about $100. A more limited silver-stamped version was available for $200.

NM/M
Complete Set (149): 100.00
Common Player: .75
Silver Edition: 3X
1 Sandy Koufax 15.00
2 Harry Danning .75
3 Hank Greenberg 7.50
4 Andy Cohen .75
5 Al Rosen 2.50
6 Buddy Myer .75
7 Sid Gordon .75
8 Shawn Green 3.00
9 Morrie Arnovich .75
10 "Lip" Pike 2.00
11 Nate Berkenstock .75
12 Jacob Pike (?) .75
13 Jake Goodman .75
14 Ike Samuls' 1895 St. Louis Team .75
15 Leo Fishel .75
16 Bill Cristall .75
17 Harry Kane .75
18 Barney Pelty .75
19 Moxie Manuel .75
20 Phil Cooney .75
21 Guy Zinn .75
22 Ed Mensor .75
23 Erskine Mayer .75
24 Henry Bostick .75
25 Sam Mayer .75
26 Sammy Bohne .75
27 Jake Pitler .75
28 Bob Berman .75
29 Eddie Corey .75
30 Jesse Baker .75
31 Al Schacht .75
32 Sam Fishburn .75
33 Reuben Ewing .75
34 Heinie Scheer .75
35 Lou Rosenberg .75
36 Moe Berg 7.50
37 Joe Bennett .75
38 Moe Solomon .75
39 Happy Foreman .75
40 Simon Rosenthal .75
41 Ike Danning .75
42 Jonah Goldman .75
43 Ed Wineapple .75
44 Jimmie Reese .75
45 Harry Rosenberg .75
46 Jim Levey .75
47 Alta Cohen .75
48 Max Rosenfeld .75
49 Lou Brower .75
50 Izzy Goldstein .75
51 Milt Galatzer .75
52 Phil Weintraub .75
53 Cy Malis .75
54 Syd Cohen .75
55 Fred Sington .75
56 Harry Eisenstat .75
57 Chick Starr .75
58 Goody Rosen .75
59 Harry Chozen .75
60 Eddie Feinberg .75
61 Sam Nahem .75
62 Dick Conger .75
63 Murray Franklin .75
64 Harry Feldman .75
65 Harry Shuman .75
66 Eddie Turchin .75
67 Cy Block .75
68 Hal Schacker .75
69 Mike Schemer .75
70 Herb Karpel .75
71 Bud Swartz .75
72 Mickey Rutner .75
73 Marv Rotblatt .75
74 Joe Ginsberg .75
75 Cal Abrams .75
76 Saul Rogovin .75
77 Sid Schacht .75
78 Lou Limmer .75
79 Duke Markell .75
80 Al Richter .75
81 Al Federoff .75
82 Herb Gorman .75
83 Moe Savransky .75
84 Hy Cohen .75
85 Al Silvera .75
86 Barry Latman .75
87 Ed Mayer .75
88 Larry Sherry 1.00
89 Don Taussig .75
90 Norm Sherry 1.00
91 Randy Cardinal .75
92 Alan Koch .75
93 Larry Yellen .75
94 Steve Hertz .75
95 Art Shamsky .75
96 Richie Scheinblum .75
97 Greg Goossen .75
98 Norm Miller .75
99 Ken Holtzman .75
100 Mike Epstein .75
101 Ron Blomberg .75
102 Lloyd Allen .75
103 Dave Roberts .75
104 Elliott Maddox .75
105 Steve Stone 2.00
106 Steve Yeager .75
107 Skip Jutze .75
108 Dick Sharon .75
109 Jeff Newman .75
110 Ross Baumgarten .75
111 Jeff Stember .75
112 Steve Ratzer .75
113 Bob Tufts .75
114 Larry Rothschild .75
115 Mark Gilbert .75
116 Steve Rosenberg .75
117 Roger Samuels .75
118 Steve Wapnick .75
119 Scott Radinsky .75
120 Ruben Amaro, Jr. .75
121 Wayne Rosenthal .75
122 Eddie Zosky .75
123 Jesse Levis .75
124 Brad Ausmus .75
125 Eric Helfand .75
126 Mike Lieberthal 2.00
127 Andrew Lorraine .75
128 Brian Kowitz .75
129 Brian Bark .75
130 Mike Milchin .75
131 Al Levine .75
132 Micah Franklin .75
133 Mike Saipe .75
134 Keith Glauber .75
135 Gabe Kapler 2.00
136 Scott Schoeneweis .75
137 David Newhan .75
138 Jason Marquis .75
139 Frank Charles .75
140 Tony Cogan .75
141 Justin Wayne .75
142 Matt Ford .75
--- Career Batting Leaders .10
--- Career Pitching Leaders .10
--- Alphabetical Listing A-M .10
--- Alphabetical Listing M-Z .10
--- Header Card/Credits .05
--- Credits .05
149 George Brace (Photographer) .25

2006 Jewish Major Leaguers Update Edition

Produced by the American Jewish Historical Society, this set updates the premiere edition of 2003. Cards are standard 2-1/2" x 3-1/2". Fronts have color or black-and-white photos, bordered in blue. Backs have personal data, a career summary, and photo/text credits. Ther update includes players who debuted after 2003, as well as female players, minor leaguers and many specialty cards.

NM/M
Complete Set (55): 40.00
Common Player: .50
(1) Header Card .50
(2) All-time Roster, A-F .50
(3) All-time Roster, G-Rad .50
(4) All-time Roster, Rat-Z .50
(5) Career Leaders: Batting .50
(6) Career Leaders: Pitching .50

7 Shawn Green .75
8 Brad Ausmus .75
9 Mike Lieberthal .75
10 Al Levine .75
11 Scott Schoeneweis .75
12 Jason Marquis .75
13 Gabe Kapler .75
14 John Grabow .75
15 Kevin Youkilis .75
16 Adam Stern .75
17 Craig Breslow .75
18 Adam Greenberg .75
19 Scott Feldman .75
20 Prospects (Aaron Rifkin, Scott Schneider, Tony Schrager, Jeff Pickler) .75
21 1901 Giants Team (Jacob Livingston) .50
22 Jacob Atz .75
23 Lefty Weinert .75
24 Lou Boudreau 1.50
25 Bob Davis .75
26 Jose Bautista .75
27 Sam Nahem .50
28 Thelma Eisen .50
29 Anita Foss .50
30 Blanche Schachter .50
31 Margaret Wigiser/SP (Withdrawn) .50
31A Error! (Replacement) .50
32 Cy Block .50
33 Harry Danning .50
34 Lipman Pike 1.50
35 Abe Yager .50
36 Barney Dreyfuss .50
37 Dolly Stark .50
38 Hank Greenberg 1.50
39 Allen Roth .50
40 Mel Allen .75
41 Ron Blomberg .50
42 Richie Scheinblum .50
43 Allan H. "Bud" Selig .75
44 Israel's National Baseball Team .50
45 Marvin Miller, Donald Fehr .50
46 Moe Berg, Heinie Scheer .75
47 Saul Rogovin, Lou Limmer, Joe Ginsberg .50
48 "The Cooperstown Eight" .50
49 Half a "Minyan": 1946 Giants .50
50 Clown Princes (Al Schacht, Max Patkin) .50
51 Mickey Rutner, Lou Limmer .50
52 Jake Levy, Hal Saltzman .50
53 Solomon Israel .50
54 Marty Abramowitz .50
55 Gabe Kapler, Adam Stern, Kevin Youkilis .50

1986 Jiffy Pop/ MSA Promos

This 20-card set was produced by Mike Schecter Associates in 1986 to provide attendees at a restaurant and food trade show with examples of his card promotions. The promos have the same fronts as the 1986 Jiffy Pop discs on a 2-7/8" diameter format. The backs have an advertisement for MSA's services. Like the regular issues, the uniform logos have been airbrushed from the discs due to lack of a license from Major League Baseball (the issue is licensed by the Players Union). The unnumbered promo discs are checklisted here alphabetically.

NM/M
Complete Set (20): 175.00
Common Player: 4.00
(1) Wade Boggs 10.00
(2) George Brett 15.00
(3) Gary Carter 10.00
(4) Steve Garvey 6.00
(5) Dwight Gooden 4.00
(6) Reggie Jackson 12.50
(7) Don Mattingly 15.00
(8) Willie McGee 4.00
(9) Dale Murphy 6.00
(10) Eddie Murray 10.00
(11) Lance Parrish 4.00
(12) Jim Rice 6.00
(13) Cal Ripken, Jr. 25.00
(14) Pete Rose 20.00
(15) Nolan Ryan 25.00
(16) Ryne Sandberg 12.50
(17) Mike Schmidt 15.00
(18) Fernando Valenzuela 4.00
(19) Dave Winfield 10.00
(20) Robin Yount 10.00

1986 Jiffy Pop

One of the scarcer of the 1986 regionals, the Jiffy Pop discs were inserted in packages of heat-and-eat popcorn. A production of Mike Schechter Associates, the 2-7/8" diameter discs feature 20 popular stars, many in the same pictures found in other '86 regionals. Like other MSA issues, caps have had the team logos erased, allowing Jiffy Pop to avoid paying a licensing fee to the teams. Backs have a few biographical details and stats.

NM/M
Complete Set (20): 15.00
Common Player: .50
1 Jim Rice .65
2 Wade Boggs 1.00
3 Lance Parrish .50
4 George Brett 2.00
5 Robin Yount 1.00
6 Don Mattingly 2.00
7 Dave Winfield 1.00
8 Reggie Jackson 1.50
9 Cal Ripken 3.50
10 Eddie Murray 1.00
11 Pete Rose 2.50
12 Ryne Sandberg 1.50
13 Nolan Ryan 3.50
14 Fernando Valenzuela .50
15 Willie McGee .50
16 Dale Murphy .75
17 Mike Schmidt 2.00
18 Steve Garvey .50
19 Gary Carter 1.00
20 Dwight Gooden .50

1987 Jiffy Pop

For a second year, Jiffy Pop inserted player discs in its packages of popcorn. The full-color discs measure 2-7/8" in diameter and were produced by Mike Schechter Associates. Titled "2nd Annual Collectors' Edition," the card fronts feature player photos with all team insignias airbrushed away. Information on the backs of the discs is printed in bright red on white stock. Die-cut 16-1/4" x 14" press sheets containing all 20 discs were available via a mail-in offer.

NM/M
Complete Set (20): 20.00
Uncut Sheet: 25.00
Common Player: .75
1 Ryne Sandberg 2.00
2 Dale Murphy 1.25
3 Jack Morris .75
4 Keith Hernandez .75
5 George Brett 2.50
6 Don Mattingly 2.50
7 Ozzie Smith 2.00
8 Cal Ripken, Jr. 3.50
9 Dwight Gooden .75
10 Pedro Guerrero .75
11 Lou Whitaker .75
12 Roger Clemens 2.50
13 Lance Parrish .75
14 Rickey Henderson 2.00
15 Fernando Valenzuela .75
16 Mike Schmidt 2.50
17 Darryl Strawberry .75
18 Mike Scott .75
19 Jim Rice 1.00
20 Wade Boggs 2.00

1988 Jiffy Pop

This 20-disc set is the third Jiffy Pop issue spotlighting leading players. Discs are 2-1/2" in diameter with a semi-gloss finish and feature full-color closeups on white stock. Team logos have been airbrushed off the player's caps. Fronts have a curved label "3rd Annual Collector's Edition." Disc backs are white, with dark blue lettering, and contain player information, stats and disc number. An uncut sheet (16" x 14-1/2") with all 20 discs was available in a mail-in redemption offer.

NM/M
Complete Set (20): 9.00
Uncut Sheet: 10.00
Common Player: .35
1 Buddy Bell .35
2 Wade Boggs 1.25
3 Gary Carter 1.25
4 Jack Clark .35
5 Will Clark .45
6 Roger Clemens 2.00
7 Vince Coleman .35
8 Andre Dawson .50
9 Keith Hernandez .35
10 Kent Hrbek .35
11 Wally Joyner .35
12 Paul Molitor 1.25
13 Eddie Murray 1.25
14 Tim Raines .35
15 Bret Saberhagen .35
16 Alan Trammell .35
17 Ozzie Virgil .35
18 Tim Wallach .35
19 Dave Winfield 1.25
20 Robin Yount 1.25

1998 Ronnie Joyner St. Louis Browns Heads-Up

Though there is nothing on the cards themselves to identify their origins, this set is the work of sports artist Ronnie Joyner, produced in co-operation with the St. Louis Browns Historical Society. They approximate the 1938 Goudey Heads-Up format in 2-1/2" x 2-7/8" size with sepia portraits and orange backgrounds. Backs have a vintage look with player personal data, a career summary and trivia question. Cards were sold as complete sets.

NM/M
Complete Set (20): 10.00
Common Player: .50
1 Hank Arft .50
2 Ellis Clary .50
3 Jim Delsing .50
4 Ned Garver .65
5 Don Gutteridge .50
6 Red Hayworth .50
7 Bill Jennings .50
8 Dick Kryhoski .50
9 Don Lenhardt .50
10 Bob Mahoney .50
11 Frank Mancuso .50
12 Babe Martin .50
13 Ed Mickelson .50
14 J.W. Porter .50
15 Roy Sievers .75
16 Virgil Trucks .65
17 Al Widmar .50
18 Jerry Witte .50
19 Arthur Richman (Number One Fan) .50
20 Stan Musial (Cross Town Rival) 5.00

2003 Ronnie Joyner 1953 St. Louis Browns

Though there is nothing on the cards themselves to identify their origins, or even that they do not actually date from 1953, this set is the work of sports artist Ronnie Joyner, who produced two other Brownies sets in previous years in co-operation with the St. Louis Browns Historical Society. The cards are in the modern 2-1/2" x 3-1/2" format with colorful fronts featuring Joyner portraits of the players and cartoon-style names. Backs have a vintage look with player personal data, a cartoon about the player, a career summary and 1953 and lifetime stats. Cards were sold as complete sets.

NM/M
Complete Set (40): 15.00
Common Player: .50
1 Satchel Paige 5.00
2 Les Moss .50
3 Roy Sievers .65
4 Bobby Young .50
5 Marlin Stuart .50
6 Billy Hunter .50
7 Don Lenhardt .50
8 Johnny Groth .50
9 Vic Wertz .50
10 Don Larsen 1.00
11 Clint Courtney .50
12 Dick Kryhoski .50
13 Neil Berry .50
14 Bob Cain .50
15 Willie Miranda .50
16 Hank Edwards .50
17 Dick Kokos .50
18 Jim Pisoni .50
19 Harry Brecheen .50
20 Browns 1953 Season Summary .50
21 Checklist .50
22 Lou Kretlow .50
23 Babe Martin .50
24 Ed Mickelson .50
25 Frank Kellert .50
26 Virgil Trucks .65
27 Dick Littlefield .50
28 Jim Dyck .50
29 Mike Blyzka .50
30 Bob Habenicht .75
31 Max Lanier .50
32 Bob Elliott .50
33 Duane Pillette .50
34 Johnny Lipon .50
35 Bob Turley .65
36 Vern Stephens .50
37 Hal White .50
38 Dixie Upright .75
39 Bobo Holloman .50
40 Marty Marion .65

1990 Jumbo Sunflower Seeds

The 1990 "Autograph Series" of 24 cards came in packages of sunflower seeds and

were produced by Mike Schecter Associates for Stagi & Scriven Farms Inc. The cards were found in specially-marked packages of Jumbo California Sunflower Seeds, three cards per package. Standard size with MLB logos airbrushed out, the cards are blue with a white frame. The numbered backs contain yearly statistics and biographical information along with a facsimile autograph.

NM/M
Complete Set (24): 10.00
Common Player: .25
(1) Kevin Mitchell .25
(2) Ken Griffey Jr. 1.75
(3) Howard Johnson .25
(4) Bo Jackson .35
(5) Kirby Puckett 1.25
(6) Robin Yount 1.00
(7) Dave Stieb .25
(8) Don Mattingly 1.50
(9) Barry Bonds 2.00
(10) Pedro Guerrero .25
(11) Tony Gwynn 1.25
(12) Von Hayes .25
(13) Rickey Henderson 1.00
(14) Tim Raines .25
(15) Alan Trammell .25
(16) Dave Stewart .25
(17) Will Clark .35
(18) Roger Clemens 1.50
(19) Wally Joyner .25
(20) Ryne Sandberg 1.25
(21) Eric Davis .25
(22) Mike Scott .25
(23) Cal Ripken, Jr. 2.00
(24) Eddie Murray 1.00

1991 Jumbo Sunflower Seeds

In its second year of baseball card production, Jumbo California Sunflower Seeds maintained the same basic format for its cards. Player photos, with uniform logos airbrushed away, in a white frame are surrounded by a red border with yellow pinstripe. At top left is the issuer's logo; above the photo in white is "Autograph Series II." A facsimile autograph is printed over the photo. Beneath the picture are the player's name, team and position. Backs are printed in red and include major league stats and a career summary.

NM/M
Complete Set (24): 7.50
Common Player: .25
1 Ozzie Smith 1.00
2 Wade Boggs 1.00
3 Bobby Bonilla .25
4 George Brett 1.25
5 Kal Daniels .25
6 Glenn Davis .25
7 Chuck Finley .25
8 Cecil Fielder .25
9 Len Dykstra .25
10 Dwight Gooden .25
11 Ken Griffey Jr. 1.50
12 Kelly Gruber .25
13 Kent Hrbek .25
14 Andre Dawson .35
15 Dave Justice .25
16 Barry Larkin .25
17 Ben McDonald .25
18 Mark McGwire 1.75
19 Roberto Alomar .50
20 Nolan Ryan 2.00
21 Sandy Alomar, Jr. .25
22 Bobby Thigpen .25
23 Tim Wallach .25
24 Mitch Williams .25

1992 Jumbo Sunflower Seeds

The basic format used in 1990-91 was returned for 1992 when Michael Schecter Associates produced another 24-card set for inclusion in packages of Jumbo Sunflower Seeds (the "California" identifier was dropped in 1992). Cards feature a player photo on which the uniform logos have been eliminated. Across the photo in black is a facsimile autograph. Around the photo are borders of, successively, white, blue, yellow and white. In the upper-left corner is the issuer's logo. "Autograph Series III" appears in red at upper-right. Beneath the picture, the player's name is printed in red, with his team and position in white. Backs are printed in blue, with major league stats and a career summary, along with a few personal data and the appropriate logos.

NM/M
Complete Set (24): 6.00
Common Player: .25
1 Jeff Reardon .25
2 Bill Gullickson .25
3 Todd Zeile .25
4 Terry Mulholland .25
5 Kirby Puckett 1.00
6 Howard Johnson .25
7 Terry Pendleton .25
8 Will Clark .35
9 Cal Ripken, Jr. 2.00
10 Chris Sabo .25
11 Jim Abbott .25
12 Joe Carter .25
13 Paul Molitor .75
14 Ken Griffey Jr. 1.50
15 Randy Johnson .75
16 Bobby Bonilla .25
17 John Smiley .25
18 Jose Canseco .50
19 Tom Glavine .50
20 Darryl Strawberry .25
21 Brett Butler .25
22 Devon White .25
23 Scott Erickson .25
24 Willie McGee .25

1987 Kahn's Reds

After a nearly 20-year layoff, Kahn's Wieners sponsored a baseball card set in

1987. The hot dog concessionaire sponsored a Reds team set that was distributed to fans attending the August 2 game at Riverfront Stadium. Cards are the standard 2-1/2" x 3-1/2" size. The fronts offer a full-color player photo bordered in red and white. Backs carry the Kahn's logo, a portrait photo of the player and career stats.

		NM/M
Complete Set (26):		9.00
Common Player:		.25
6	Bo Diaz	.25
10	Terry Francona	.25
11	Kurt Stillwell	.25
12	Nick Esasky	.25
13	Dave Concepcion	.25
15	Barry Larkin	3.00
16	Ron Oester	.25
21	Paul O'Neill	1.00
23	Lloyd McClendon	.25
25	Buddy Bell	.25
28	Kal Daniels	.25
29	Tracy Jones	.25
30	Guy Hoffman	.25
31	John Franco	.25
32	Tom Browning	.25
33	Ron Robinson	.25
34	Bill Gullickson	.25
35	Pat Pacillo	.25
39	Dave Parker	.25
43	Bill Landrum	.25
44	Eric Davis	.50
46	Rob Murphy	.25
47	Frank Williams	.25
48	Ted Power	.25
---	Pete Rose (Manager)	3.00
---	Reds Coaches (Scott Breeden, Billy DeMars, Tommy Helms, Bruce Kimm, Jim Lett, Tony Perez)	.25

1988 Kahn's Mets

Approximately 50,000 Mets fans received this complimentary card set during a ballpark promotion sponsored by Kahn's Wieners. Twenty-five players are featured in the set, along with manager Davey Johnson, four coaches and a team photo. Card fronts have a dark blue border with an orange rectangle framing the color player photo; Players Uniform numbers are printed in white in the upper-right corner, beside the team logo. Backs are black-and-white with red accents. In addition to player acquisition date, birthday and residence, a paragraph-style career summary is included. Cards measure 2-1/2" x 3-1/2".

		NM/M
Complete Set (31):		4.00
Common Player:		.25
1	Mookie Wilson	.25
2	Mackey Sasser	.25
3	Bud Harrelson	.25
4	Lenny Dykstra	.35
5	Davey Johnson	.25
6	Wally Backman	.25
8	Gary Carter	3.00
11	Tim Teufel	.25
12	Ron Darling	.25
13	Lee Mazzilli	.25
15	Rick Aguilera	.25
16	Dwight Gooden	.50
17	Keith Hernandez	.35
18	Darryl Strawberry	.50
19	Bob Ojeda	.25
20	Howard Johnson	.30
21	Kevin Elster	.25
22	Kevin McReynolds	.25
26	Terry Leach	.25
28	Bill Robinson	.25
29	Dave Magadan	.25
30	Mel Stottlemyre	.25
31	Gene Walter	.25
33	Barry Lyons	.25
34	Sam Perlozzo	.25
42	Roger McDowell	.25
44	David Cone	.50
48	Randy Myers	.25
50	Sid Fernandez	.25
52	Greg Pavlick	.25
---	Team Photo	.25

Reds

This 26-card team set was a giveaway during the Aug. 14, 1988 Cincinnati Reds game. The glossy cards (2-1/2" x 3-1/2") feature color action photos inside red and white borders. The Reds logo, player uniform number, name and position are printed below the photo. The backs are black and white, with small player close-ups and career stats. A promotional 25-cent coupon for Kahn's Wieners was included with each set.

		NM/M
Complete Set (26):		6.00
Common Player:		.25
6	Bo Diaz	.25
8	Terry McGriff	.25
9	Eddie Milner	.25
10	Leon Durham	.25
11	Barry Larkin	.50
12	Nick Esasky	.25
13	Dave Concepcion	.25
14	Pete Rose	3.00
15	Jeff Treadway	.25
17	Chris Sabo	.30
20	Danny Jackson	.25
21	Paul O'Neill	.30
22	Dave Collins	.25
27	Jose Rijo	.25
28	Kal Daniels	.25
29	Tracy Jones	.25
30	Lloyd McClendon	.25
31	John Franco	.25
32	Tom Browning	.25
33	Ron Robinson	.25
40	Jack Armstrong	.25
44	Eric Davis	.30
46	Rob Murphy	.25
47	Frank Williams	.25
48	Tim Birtsas	.25
---	Coaches (Danny Breeden, Tommy Helms, Bruce Kimm, Jim Lett, Lee May, Tony Perez)	.25

1989 Kahn's Cooperstown Collection

This 11-player card set was available through a mail-in offer. One dollar and three proofs of purchase from Hillshire Farms were needed to obtain the set. The card fronts feature paintings of recent Hall of Fame inductees. A coupon card was also included with each set.

		NM/M
Complete Set (11):		3.00
Common Player:		.50
(1)	Cool Papa Bell	.50
(2)	Johnny Bench	.75
(3)	Lou Brock	.60
(4)	Whitey Ford	.75
(5)	Bob Gibson	.65
(6)	Billy Herman	.50
(7)	Harmon Killebrew	.75
(8)	Eddie Mathews	.65
(9)	Brooks Robinson	.65
(10)	Willie Stargell	.65
(11)	Carl Yastrzemski	.75

1989 Kahn's Mets

This team set was sponsored by Kahn's Wieners and given to fans attending the July 6 game at Shea Stadium. Standard-size cards feature a color photo surrounded by a blue and orange border with the player's name and uniform number across the top. Backs include the Kahn's logo, along with player information and complete Major League stats. Four update cards were later added to the set.

		NM/M
Complete Set (35):		4.00
Common Player:		.20
1	Mookie Wilson	.25
2	Mackey Sasser	.20
3	Bud Harrelson	.20
5	Davey Johnson	.20
7	Juan Samuel	.20
8	Gary Carter	1.00
9	Gregg Jefferies	.50
11	Tim Teufel	.20
12	Ron Darling	.20
13	Lee Mazzilli	.20
16	Dwight Gooden	.30
17	Keith Hernandez	.20
18	Darryl Strawberry	.30
19	Bob Ojeda	.20
20	Howard Johnson	.20
21	Kevin Elster	.20
22	Kevin McReynolds	.20
28	Bill Robinson	.20
29	Dave Magadan	.20
30	Mel Stottlemyre	.20
32	Mark Carreon	.20
33	Barry Lyons	.20
34	Sam Perlozzo	.20
38	Rick Aguilera	.20
44	David Cone	.50
46	Dave West	.20
48	Randy Myers	.20
49	Don Aase	.20
50	Sid Fernandez	.20
52	Greg Pavlick	.20
---	Team Card	.20
13	Jeff Musselman	.50
25	Keith Miller	.50
28	Frank Viola	.50
40	Jeff Innis	.50

Reds

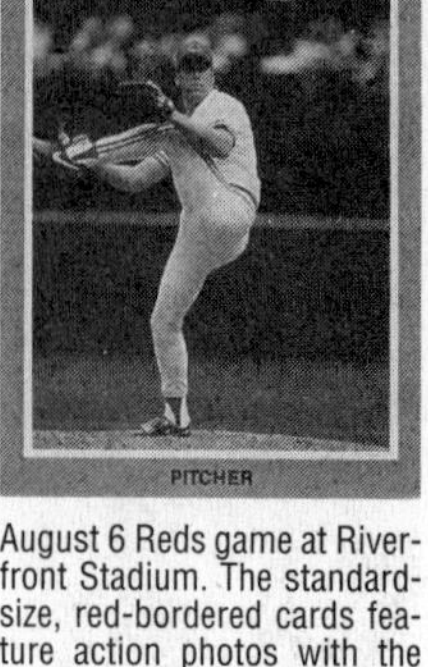

This team set, sponsored by Kahn's Wieners, was distributed to fans attending the August 6 Reds game at Riverfront Stadium. The standard-size, red-bordered cards feature action photos with the player's name in the upper-left corner, his uniform number in the upper-right and the Reds logo in the middle. Backs include a black-and-white portrait, player data and complete major and minor league stats. The Kahn's logo appears in the upper-right corner of the back.

		NM/M
Complete Set (26):		6.00
Common Player:		.20
6	Bo Diaz	.20
7	Lenny Harris	.25
11	Barry Larkin	.50
12	Joel Youngblood	.20
14	Pete Rose	3.00
16	Ron Oester	.20
17	Chris Sabo	.20
20	Danny Jackson	.20
21	Paul O'Neill	.40
25	Todd Benzinger	.20
27	Jose Rijo	.20
28	Kal Daniels	.20
29	Herm Winningham	.20
30	Ken Griffey	.25
31	John Franco	.20
32	Tom Browning	.20
33	Ron Robinson	.20
34	Jeff Reed	.20
36	Rolando Roomes	.20
37	Norm Charlton	.20
42	Rick Mahler	.20
43	Kent Tekulve	.20
44	Eric Davis	.30
48	Tim Birtsas	.20
49	Rob Dibble	.25
---	Coaches (Danny Breeden, Dave Bristol, Tommy Helms, Jim Lett, Lee May, Tony Perez)	.20

1990 Kahn's Mets

For the third consecutive year, Kahn's issued a team set of Mets baseball cards. The sets were distrubted at Shea Stadium on May 3, prior to the Mets/Reds game. Cards feature blue and orange (team colors) graphics and are numbered according to uniform number. Two coupon cards were also included with each set.

		NM/M
Complete Set (34):		3.00
Common Player:		.20
1	Lou Thornton	.20
2	Mackey Sasser	.20
3	Bud Harrelson	.20
4	Mike Cubbage	.20
5	Davey Johnson	.20
6	Mike Marshall	.20
9	Gregg Jefferies	.50
10	Dave Magadan	.20
11	Tim Teufel	.20
13	Jeff Musselman	.20
15	Ron Darling	.20
16	Dwight Gooden	.30
18	Darryl Strawberry	.30
19	Bob Ojeda	.20
20	Howard Johnson	.20
21	Kevin Elster	.20
22	Kevin McReynolds	.20
25	Keith Miller	.20
26	Alejandro Pena	.20
27	Tom O'Malley	.20
29	Frank Viola	.20
30	Mel Stottlemyre	.20
31	John Franco	.20
32	Doc Edwards	.20
33	Barry Lyons	.20
35	Orlando Mercado	.20
40	Jeff Innis	.20
44	David Cone	.35
45	Mark Carreon	.20
47	Wally Whitehurst	.20
48	Julio Machado	.20
50	Sid Fernandez	.20
52	Greg Pavlick	.20
---	Team Card	.20

Reds

This team set marks the fourth consecutive year in which Kahn's released a modern Reds issue. The cards feature color photos, red and white borders and the player's name, number, and postion on the card front. The flip sides feature biographical information, statistics, a posed photo and the Kahn's logo. The set is numbered by uniform.

		NM/M
Complete Set (27):		4.00
Common Player:		.25
7	Mariano Duncan	.25
9	Joe Oliver	.25
10	Luis Quinones	.25
11	Barry Larkin	.50
15	Glenn Braggs	.25
16	Ron Oester	.25
17	Chris Sabo	.25
20	Danny Jackson	.25
21	Paul O'Neill	.40
22	Billy Hatcher	.25
23	Hal Morris	.25
25	Todd Benzinger	.25
27	Jose Rijo	.25
28	Randy Myers	.25
29	Herm Winningham	.25
30	Ken Griffey	.25
32	Tom Browning	.25
34	Jeff Reed	.25
37	Norm Charlton	.25
40	Jack Armstrong	.25
41	Lou Pinella	.30
42	Rick Mahler	.25
43	Tim Layana	.25
44	Eric Davis	.35
48	Tim Birtsas	.25
49	Rob Dibble	.25
---	Coaches (Jackie Moore, Tony Perez, Sam Perlozzo, Larry Rothschild, Stan Williams)	.25

1991 Kahn's Mets

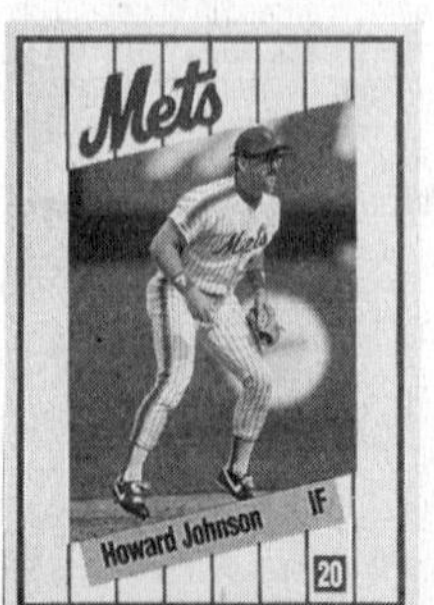

Kahn's kept its tradition in 1991 with the release of this set featuring members of the New York Mets. Cards measure 2-1/2" x 3-1/2" and the fronts feature a pinstripe design. The backs are printed horizontally and feature complete statistics. The cards are numbered according to uniform number. The complete set was distributed at a 1991 home game.

		NM/M
Complete Set (33):		4.00
Common Player:		.20
1	Vince Coleman	.20
2	Mackey Sasser	.20
3	Bud Harrelson	.20
4	Mike Cubbage	.20
5	Charlie O'Brien	.20
7	Hubie Brooks	.20
8	Daryl Boston	.20
9	Gregg Jefferies	.30
10	Dave Magadan	.20
11	Tim Teufel	.20
13	Rick Cerone	.20
15	Ron Darling	.20
16	Dwight Gooden	.30
17	David Cone	.50
20	Howard Johnson	.20
21	Kevin Elster	.20
22	Kevin McReynolds	.20
25	Keith Miller	.20
26	Alejandro Pena	.20
28	Tom Herr	.20
29	Frank Viola	.20
30	Mel Stottlemyre	.20
31	John Franco	.20
32	Doc Edwards	.20
40	Jeff Innis	.20
43	Doug Simons	.20
45	Mark Carreon	.20
47	Wally Whitehurst	.20
48	Pete Schourek	.20
50	Sid Fernandez	.20
51	Tom Spencer	.20
52	Greg Pavlick	.20
---	Team Card	.20

Reds

The World Champion Cincinnati Reds are showcased in this 28-card set. The card fronts feature small color action photos on white stock. Backs feature statistics, biographical information and the Kahn's logo. A special card of team mascot Schottzie is included in this set.

		NM/M
Complete Set (28):		4.00
Common Player:		.25
7	Mariano Duncan	.25
9	Joe Oliver	.25
10	Luis Quinones	.25
11	Barry Larkin	.50
15	Glenn Braggs	.25
17	Chris Sabo	.25
19	Bill Doran	.25
21	Paul O'Neill	.30
22	Billy Hatcher	.25
23	Hal Morris	.25
25	Todd Benzinger	.25
27	Jose Rijo	.25
28	Randy Myers	.25
29	Herm Winningham	.25
32	Tom Browning	.25
34	Jeff Reed	.25
36	Don Carman	.25
37	Norm Charlton	.25
40	Jack Armstrong	.25
41	Lou Piniella	.30
44	Eric Davis	.30
45	Chris Hammond	.25
47	Scott Scudder	.25
48	Ted Power	.25
49	Rob Dibble	.25
57	Freddie Benavides	.25
---	Schottzie (Mascot)	.25

----	Coaches (Jackie Moore, Tony Perez, Sam Perlozzo, Larry Rothschild, Stan Williams)	.25

1992 Kahn's Mets

A Mets' blue border surrounds the game-action photos in this team set. Backs are horizontally formatted and present full major league stats and the '92 Mets team slogan, "Hardball is Back." A baseball on front carries the uniform number by which the set is checklisted here. Cents-offs coupons for Kahn's hot dogs and corn dogs were packaged with the set when it was distributed at a home game, but are not considered part of the set.

		NM/M
Complete Set (33):		4.00
Common Player:		.20
1	Vince Coleman	.20
2	Mackey Sasser	.20
3	Junior Noboa	.20
4	Mike Cubbage	.20
6	Daryl Boston	.20
8	Dave Gallagher	.20
9	Todd Hundley	.35
10	Jeff Torborg	.20
11	Dick Schofield	.20
12	Willie Randolph	.20
15	Kevin Elster	.20
16	Dwight Gooden	.20
17	David Cone	.40
18	Bret Saberhagen	.35
19	Anthony Young	.20
20	Howard Johnson	.20
22	Charlie O'Brien	.20
25	Bobby Bonilla	.20
26	Barry Foote	.20
27	Tom McCraw	.20
28	Dave LaRoche	.20
29	Dave Magadan	.20
30	Mel Stottlemyre	.20
31	John Franco	.20
32	Bill Pecota	.20
33	Eddie Murray	1.00
40	Jeff Innis	.20
44	Tim Burke	.20
45	Paul Gibson	.20
47	Wally Whitehurst	.20
50	Sid Fernandez	.20
51	John Stephenson	.20
---	Mets Team	.20

Reds

This 27-card set (two coupon cards distributed with the team set are not considered part of the set) was given to fans at a promotional home date. The 2-1/2" x 3-1/2" cards have a red border with the team name at top and player name at bottom in white. The player's uniform number and position in black flank his name. A team logo appears in the lower-left corner of the photo. Backs are printed in red and black and have complete pro stats, a few biographical details and the logo of the Riverfront Stadium hot dog concessionaire. The checklist presented here is in order of uniform number.

		NM/M
Complete Set (27):		4.00
Common Player:		.25
2	Schottzie (Mascot)	.25
9	Joe Oliver	.25
10	Bip Roberts	.25
11	Barry Larkin	.45
12	Freddie Benavides	.25
15	Glenn Braggs	.25
16	Reggie Sanders	.25
17	Chris Sabo	.25
19	Bill Doran	.25
21	Paul O'Neill	.35
23	Hal Morris	.25
25	Scott Bankhead	.25
26	Darnell Coles	.25
27	Jose Rijo	.25
28	Scott Ruskin	.25
29	Greg Swindell	.25
30	Dave Martinez	.25
31	Tim Belcher	.25
32	Tom Browning	.25
34	Jeff Reed	.25
37	Norm Charlton	.25
38	Troy Afenir	.25
41	Lou Piniella	.30
45	Chris Hammond	.25
48	Dwayne Henry	.25
49	Rob Dibble	.25
---	Coaches (Jackie Moore, John McLaren, Sam Perlozzo, Tony Perez, Larry Rothschild)	.25

1993 Kahn's Mets

The Mets distributed the 1993 Kahn's team set to fans on May 23 at Shea Stadium. Cards feature color photos and a white border. The Mets logo is at the bottom center and the player's name, position and uniform number at the top. Backs include career statistics and biography inside a red border. Also included in the set is a team photo card and a title card which features the New York skyline and the stadium. Apparently not all cards, such as those of coaches, were issued in all sets.

		NM/M
Complete Set (36):		7.50
Common Player:		.25
1	Tony Fernandez	.25
4	Mike Cubbage	.50
6	Joe Orsulak	.25
7	Jeff McKnight	.25
8	Dave Gallagher	.25
9	Todd Hundley	.50
10	Jeff Torborg	.50
11	Vince Coleman	.25
12	Jeff Kent	1.00
16	Dwight Gooden	.25
18	Bret Saberhagen	.35
19	Anthony Young	.25
20	Howard Johnson	.25
21	Darren Reed	.25
22	Charlie O'Brien	.25
23	Tim Bogar	.25
25	Bobby Bonilla	.30
26	Barry Foote	.50
27	Tom McCraw	.50
28	Dave LaRoche	.50
29	Frank Tanana	.50
30	Mel Stottlemyre	.50
31	John Franco	.25
33	Eddie Murray	1.50
34	Chico Walker	.25
40	Jeff Innis	.25
44	Ryan Thompson	.25
47	Mike Draper	.25
48	Pete Schourek	.25
50	Sid Fernandez	.25
51	Mike Maddux	.25
---	John Stephenson	.50
---	Team Photo	.25
---	Header Card	.10
---	Corn Dog Coupon	.05
---	Hot Dog Coupon	.05

Reds

Kahn's produced a Reds team set which was given away to fans at Riverfront Stadium on August 1. The cards, organized by player's uniform number, show a photo of the player on the front with the player's name at the top and the Reds logo in the lower corner, surrounded by a pinstripe border. Card backs have the player's lifetime statistics and biography. Card #2 in the set portrays team owner Marge Schott and her dog Schottzie II. Coupon cards good for discounts on packages of Kahn's hot dogs and corn dogs were packaged with the set but are not considered part of the set.

		NM/M
Complete Set (28):		6.00
Common Player:		.25
2	Schottzie (Mascot) (Marge Schott)	.25
7	Kevin Mitchell	.25
8	Juan Samuel	.25
9	Joe Oliver	.25
10	Bip Roberts	.25
11	Barry Larkin	.40
15	Davey Johnson	.25
16	Reggie Sanders	.25
17	Chris Sabo	.25
19	Randy Milligan	.25
20	Jeff Branson	.25
23	Hal Morris	.25
25	Greg Cadaret	.25
27	Jose Rijo	.25
30	Bobby Kelly	.25
31	Tim Belcher	.25
32	Tom Browning	.25
40	Tim Pugh	.25
41	Jeff Reardon	.25
42	Gary Varsho	.25
43	Bill Landrum	.25
46	Jacob Brumfield	.25
49	Rob Dibble	.25
53	Kevin Wickander	.25
57	John Smiley	.25
59	Bobby Ayala	.25
---	Coaches (Jose Cardenal, Don Gullett, Ray Knight, Bobby Valentine, Dave Miley)	.25
---	Broadcasters (Marty Brennaman, Joe Nuxhall)	.25

1994 Kahn's Reds

Distributed at a promotional game and sponsored by the hot dog concessionaire at Riverfront Stadium this was the eighth consecutive Reds team set produced by Kahn's. Cards feature a player action photo with a red stripe superimposed near the left border. The stripe contains the player name and position at top and the team logo at bottom. Backs are printed in red and black and include full minor and major league stats. Cards are numbered by uniform number printed on back.

		NM/M
Complete Set (31):		4.00
Common Player:		.20
2	Schottzie (Mascot)	.20
4	Jacob Brumfield	.20
7	Kevin Mitchell	.20
9	Joe Oliver	.20
10	Eddie Taubensee	.20
11	Barry Larkin	.35
12	Deion Sanders	.50
15	Davey Johnson	.20
16	Reggie Sanders	.20
19	Jerome Walton	.20
20	Jeff Branson	.20
21	Tony Fernandez	.20
22	Thomas Howard	.20
23	Hal Morris	.20
27	Jose Rijo	.20
28	Lenny Harris	.20
29	Brett Boone	.50
31	Chuck McElroy	.20
32	Tom Browning	.20
33	Brian Dorsett	.20
39	Erik Hanson	.20
40	Tim Pugh	.20
44	John Roper	.20
45	Jeff Brantley	.20
46	Pete Schourek	.20
47	Johnny Ruffin	.20
49	Rob Dibble	.20
55	Tim Fortugno	.20
57	John Smiley	.20
58	Hector Carrasco	.20
---	Reds Coaching Staff (Bob Boone, Don Gullett, Grant Jackson, Ray Knight, Joel Youngblood)	.20

1995 Kahn's Mets

Game-action photos are featured in this edition of the annual tradition of cards sponsored by the Mets hot dog concessionaire. In standard 2-1/2" x 3-1/2" format the cards have a gray background with navy pinstripes. The player's name, uniform number and position are in team colors of blue and orange at bottom. Backs are in red, black and white with personal data, previous-year or career stats and team and sponsor logos. The cards are checklisted here by uniform number.

		NM/M
Complete Set (36):		4.00
Common Player:		.25
1	Ricky Otero	.25
4	Mike Cubbage	.25
5	Chris Jones	.25
6	Joe Orsulak	.25
7	Bobby Wine	.25
8	Steve Swisher	.25
9	Todd Hundley	.30
10	Tom McCraw	.25
11	Aaron Ledesma	.25
12	Jeff Kent	.75
13	Edgardo Alfonzo	.60
15	Jose Vizcaino	.25
17	Bret Saberhagen	.35
18	Jeff Barry	.25
19	Bill Spiers	.25
20	Ryan Thompson	.25
21	Bill Pulsipher	.25
22	Brett Butler	.25
23	Tim Bogar	.25
25	Bobby Bonilla	.25
26	Rico Brogna	.25
27	Pete Harnisch	.25
28	Bobby Jones	.25
31	John Franco	.25
33	Kelly Stinnett	.25
34	Blas Minor	.25
35	Doug Henry	.25
38	Dave Mlicki	.25
40	Eric Gunderson	.25
44	Jason Isringhausen	.25
45	Jerry DiPoto	.25
46	Dallas Green	.25
52	Greg Pavlick	.25
55	Frank Howard	.25
---	50-Cent Hot Dog Coupon	.05
---	50-Cent Corn Dog Coupon	.05

Reds

This team set continues the tradition of baseball card sponsorship by Kahn's Meats. The set was given away at the August 6 game. Team name and the year are printed in the white border above the photo; the player's name and position are in white in a red strip at bottom. A Reds logo appears in the upper-right corner of the photo, with the player's uniform number below in white. Backs have complete minor and major league stats, along with a few biographical details and the Reds and Kahn's logos. The checklist is presented here by uniform number. Two Kahn's coupons were included in each cello-wrapped set.

		NM/M
Complete Set (34):		4.50
Common Player:		.15
02	Schottzie (02)	.15
6	Ron Gant	.30
8	Damon Berryhill	.15
9	Eric Anthony	.15
10	Eddie Taubensee	.15
11	Barry Larkin	.40
12	Willie Greene	.15
15	Davey Johnson	.15
16	Reggie Sanders	.15
17	Mark Lewis	.15
18	Benito Santiago	.15
19	Jerome Walton	.15
20	Jeff Branson	.15
21	Deion Sanders	.30
22	Thomas Howard	.15
23	Hal Morris	.15
26	Johnny Ruffin	.15
27	Jose Rijo	.15
28	Lenny Harris	.15
29	Bret Boone	.40
30	Brian Hunter	.15
31	Chuck McElroy	.15
32	Kevin Jarvis	.15
37	Xavier Hernandez	.15
40	Tim Pugh	.15
41	Brad Pennington	.15
42	Mike Jackson	.15
44	John Roper	.15
45	Jeff Brantley	.15
46	Pete Schourek	.15
49	C.J. Nitkowski	.15
57	John Smiley	.15
58	Hector Carrasco	.15
---	Reds Coaches (Ray Knight, Don Gullett, Grant Jackson, Hal McRae, Joel Youngblood)	.15

1996 Kahn's Mets

This team set was handed out to attendees at the August 3 game at Shea Stadium. Sponsored by the Mets' hot dog concessionaire, the set features the players, coaches and manager in color action photos. Borders are in dark shades and include a Mets logo at lower-right. The player name and uniform number are in white. Backs are in black, red and white with personal data, 1995 stats and sponsors logos. The uniform number is repeated at lower-left. Cards are checklisted here in alphabetical order. The set was distributed cello-wrapped with two 50-cent hot dogs coupons.

		NM/M
Complete Set (32):		5.00
Common Player:		.25
(1)	Edgardo Alfonzo	.25
(2)	Tim Bogar	.25
(3)	Rico Brogna	.25
(4)	Paul Byrd	.25
(5)	Mark Clark	.25
(6)	Mike Cubbage	.25
(7)	Jerry Dipoto	.25
(8)	Carl Everett	.25
(9)	John Franco	.25
(10)	Bernard Gilkey	.25
(11)	Dallas Green	.25
(12)	Pete Harnisch	.25
(13)	Doug Henry	.25
(14)	Frank Howard	.25
(15)	Todd Hundley	.25
(16)	Butch Huskey	.25
(17)	Jason Isringhausen	.25
(18)	Lance Johnson	.25
(19)	Bobby Jones	.25
(20)	Chris Jones	.25
(21)	Brent Mayne	.25
(22)	Tom McCraw	.25
(23)	Dave Mlicki	.25
(24)	Alex Ochoa	.25
(25)	Rey Ordonez	.25
(26)	Greg Pavlick	.25
(27)	Robert Person	.25
(28)	Bill Pulsipher	.25
(29)	Steve Swisher	.25
(30)	Andy Tomberlin	.25
(31)	Paul Wilson	.25
(32)	Bobby Wine	.25

Reds

The players, manager, coaches and mascot are once again featured in a Cincinnati Reds team set sponsored by the team's hot dog concessionaire and given away to fans at the August 4 game. The 2-1/2" x 3-1/2" cards have color game-action photos on front. A red stripe at top has the team logo, player name, position and uniform number. A stripe beneath the photo has team name and year. Backs are printed in black and red on white and include personal data and complete major and minor league stats. Cards are checklisted here by uniform number.

		NM/M
Complete Set (34):		5.00
Common Player:		.25
02	Schottzie (Mascot)	.25

7 Curtis Goodwin .25
9a Eric Anthony .25
9b Joe Oliver .25
10 Eddie Taubensee .25
11 Barry Larkin .45
12 Willie Greene .25
15 Mike Kelly .25
16 Reggie Sanders .25
17 Chris Sabo .25
18 Eric Owens .25
20 Jeff Branson .25
21 Mark Portugal .25
22 Thomas Howard .25
23 Hal Morris .25
25 Ray Knight .25
26 Johnny Ruffin .25
27 Jose Rijo .25
28 Lenny Harris .25
29 Bret Boone .50
30 Eduardo Perez .25
32 Kevin Jarvis .25
34 Dave Burba .25
36 Scott Service .25
41 Jeff Shaw .25
42 Roger Salkeld .25
44 Eric Davis .30
45 Jeff Brantley .25
46 Pete Schourek .25
57 John Smiley .25
58 Hector Carrasco .25
69 Tim Belk .25
--- Coaches (Marc Bombard, Don Gullett, Tom Hume, Jim Lett, Hal McRae) .25
--- Bernie Stowe (Equipment Manager) .25

1997 Kahn's Reds

This team set was given away to fans at the August 3 game, sponsored by the Reds' hot dog concessionaire. The 2-1/2" x 3-1/2" cards have game action player photos at right and the player's name, position and uniform number in a two-toned red stripe vertically at left. Backs are printed in red and black and include complete major and minor league stats. Cards are listed here according to uniform number.

NM/M
Complete Set (34): 5.00
Common Player: .25
00 Curtis Goodwin .25
02 Schottzie (Mascot) .25
3 Pokey Reese .25
6 Brook Fordyce .25
7 Joe Oliver .25
9 Terry Pendleton .25
10 Eddie Taubensee .25
11 Barry Larkin .35
12 Willie Greene .25
15 Mike Kelly .25
16 Reggie Sanders .25
17 Aaron Boone .50
20 Jeff Branson .25
21 Deion Sanders .35
23 Hal Morris .25
25 Ray Knight .25
27 Jose Rijo .25
28 Lenny Harris .25
29 Bret Boone .50
33 Steve Gibraltar .25
34 Dave Burba .25
36 Mike Morgan .25
37 Stan Belinda .25
38 Kent Mercker .25
39 Eduardo Perez .25
40 Brett Tomko .25
41 Jeff Shaw .25
43 Mike Remlinger .25
45 Jeff Brantley .25
46 Pete Schourek .25
56 Scott Sullivan .25
57 John Smiley .25
67 Felix Rodriguez .25
--- Ken Griffey Sr., Don Gullett, Tom Hume, Denis Menke, Joel Youngblood .25

1998 Kahn's Reds

For the 12th consecutive year, the Reds hot dog concessionaire issued a team set, given away at an August 9 promotional game. The 2-1/2" x 3-1/2" cards have game-action photos at right, borderless at top, bottom and right. At left is a vertical red stripe with player name and uniform number. Horizontal backs have player data and complete major and minor league stats overprinted on a Kahn's logo. Backs are printed in red, black and white.

NM/M
Complete Set (34): 5.00
Common Player: .25
3 Pokey Reese .25
4 Damian Jackson .25
6 Brook Fordyce .25
9 Pat Watkins .25
10 Ed Taubensee .25
11 Barry Larkin .35
12 Willie Greene .25
15 Jack McKeon .25
16 Reggie Sanders .25
17 Aaron Boone .25
21 Sean Casey .75
22 Jon Nunnally .25
23 Chris Stynes .25
25 Dmitri Young .25
26 Steve Cooke .25
28 Paul Konerko .75
29 Bret Boone .50
31 Scott Sullivan .25
32 Danny Graves .25
33 John Hudek .25
34 Mike Frank .25
36 Gabe White .25
37 Stan Belinda .25
38 Pete Harnisch .25
39 Eduardo Perez .25
40 Brett Tomko .25
43 Mike Remlinger .25
44 Scott Winchester .25
46 Melvin Nieves .25
48 Rick Krivda .25
53 Todd Williams .25
58 Steve Parris .25
--- Reds Coaches (Harry Dunlop, Ken Griffey, Don Gullett, Tom Hume, Ron Oester) .25
02 Schottzie (Mascot) .25

1999 Kahn's Reds

Distribution of a Kahn's team set for the Reds attained its 13th annual celebration July 31 when the cards were handed out to fans at Cinergy Field. Cards have player action photos which are borderless at top and right. At left is a ragged-edged red strip with player identification. Team identification is in a red strip at bottom. Backs are in red and black on white with a large Kahn's logo ghosted at center. Player data and complete professional stats are provided. Cards are checklisted here by uniform number.

NM/M
Complete Set (34): 5.00
Common Player: .25
02 Schottzie (Mascot) .25
3 Pokey Reese .25
4 Jeffrey Hammonds .25
9 Hal Morris .25
10 Eddie Taubensee .25
11 Barry Larkin .35
12 Chris Stynes .25
15 Denny Neagle .25
17 Aaron Boone .25
21 Sean Casey .50
23 Greg Vaughn .25
25 Dmitri Young .25
26 Jason LaRue .25
28 Mark Lewis .25
29 Brian Johnson .25
31 Jack McKeon .25
32 Danny Graves .25
33 Steve Avery .25
34 Michael Tucker .25
36 Gabe White .25
37 Stan Belinda .25
38 Pete Harnisch .25
40 Brett Tomko .25
41 Ron Villone .25
43 Mark Wohlers .25
44 Mike Cameron .25
46 Jason Bere .25
48 Scott Williamson .25
49 Dennis Reyes .25
56 Scott Sullivan .25
58 Steve Parris .25
--- Marty Brennaman, Joe Nuxhall (Broadcasters) .25
--- Ken Griffey Sr., Ron Oester, Denis Menke, Dave Collins (Reds Coaches) .25

2000 Kahn's Reds

Some 42,500 sets of Reds cards were distributed to fans at the July 22 game at Cinergy Field. Sponsored for the 14th consecutive year by Kahn's meats, the cards do not have a Kahn's logo. Fronts have game action photos with the team logo at top-left, the player name at top-right, his position and uniform number at lower-right and "2000 Cincinnati Reds" vertically in a red stripe at left. Backs have a ghosted team logo, player data and stats. The checklist here is presented by uniform number.

NM/M
Complete Set (34): 5.00
Common Player: .25
3 Pokey Reese .25
4 Chris Stynes .25
6 Benito Santiago .25
8 Alex Ochoa .25
9 Dante Bichette .25
10 Eddie Taubensee .25
11 Barry Larkin .45
12 Juan Castro .25
15 Denny Neagle .25
17 Aaron Boone .25
21 Sean Casey .65
23 Hal Morris .25
25 Dmitri Young .25
29 Rob Bell .25
30 Ken Griffey Jr. 3.00
31 Jack McKeon .25
32 Danny Graves .25
34 Michael Tucker .25
36 Manny Aybar .25
38 Pete Harnisch .25
41 Ron Villone .25
43 Osvaldo Fernandez .25
45 Elmer Dessens .25
48 Scott Williamson .25
49 Dennis Reyes .25
56 Scott Sullivan .25
58 Steve Parris .25
--- Coaching Staff (Ken Griffey Sr., Denis Menke, Ron Oester, Dave Collins) .25
--- Coaching Staff (Don Gullett, Harry Dunlop, Tom Hume, Mark Berry) .25
--- Marty Brennaman, Joe Nuxhall (Broadcasters) .25
--- Red (Mascot) .25
--- Kahnlee (Mascot) .25
--- Coupon .05
--- Coupon .05

2001 Kahn's Reds

This team set was distributed to fans attending the August 11 game at Cinergy Field. The 2-1/2" x 3-1/2" cards have borderless game-action photos on front. Backs have brief biographical data along with minor and major league stats. The set is checklisted here by uniform number which appears on both front and back.

NM/M
Complete Set (33): 7.50
Common Player: .25
3 Pokey Reese .25
9 Bob Boone .35
11 Barry Larkin .45
12 Juan Castro .25
17 Aaron Boone .25
21 Sean Casey .50
22 Brady Clark .25
23 Jason LaRue .25
25 Dmitri Young .25
28 Ruben Rivera .25
29 Jose Acevedo .25
30 Ken Griffey Jr. 3.00
31 Kelly Stinnett .25
32 Danny Graves .25
34 Michael Tucker .25
38 Pete Harnisch .25
41 Chris Reitsma .25
43 Osvaldo Fernandez .25
44 Adam Dunn 3.00
45 Elmer Dessens .25
46 John Riedling .25
48 Scott Williamson .25
49 Dennys Reyes .25
52 Hector Mercado .25
53 Jim Brower .25
54 Bill Selby .25
56 Scott Sullivan .25
57 Chris Nichting .25
59 Lance Davis .25
--- Coaches (Don Gullett, Mark Berry, Tom Hume) .25
--- Coaches (Ken Griffey Sr., Ron Oester, Tim Foli, Bill Doran) .25
--- Broadcasters (Marty Brennaman, Joe Nuxhall) .25
--- Mr. Red (Mascot) .25

2002 Kahn's Reds

Team sets sponsored by the Reds' hot dog concessionaire were given to fans attending the August 16 game at Cinergy Field. The 2-1/2" x 3-1/2" cards have game-action photos that are borderless at top, bottom and right. At left is a vertical blue stripe with the date, team name and a 1970-2002 Riverfront Stadium logo. The player name is at bottom-right in black and red; his uniform number is in red at top-right. Horizontal backs are printed in red and black and have personal data and complete professional stats, overprinted on a large Kahn's logo.

NM/M
Complete Set (33): 10.00
Common Player: .25
(1) Aaron Boone .25
(2) Bob Boone .35
(3) Russell Branyan .25
(4) Sean Casey .50
(5) Juan Castro .25
(6) Bruce Chen .25
(7) Ryan Dempster .25
(8) Elmer Dessens .25
(9) Adam Dunn 3.00
(10) Jared Fernandez .25
(11) Danny Graves .25
(12) Ken Griffey Jr. 3.00
(13) Joey Hamilton .25
(14) Jimmy Haynes .25
(15) Austin Kearns 1.50
(16) Barry Larkin .35
(17) Jason LaRue .25
(18) Corky Miller .25
(19) Luis Pineda .25
(20) Chris Reitsma .25
(21) John Riedling .25
(22) Jose Rijo .25
(23) Jose Silva .25
(24) Kelly Stinnett .25
(25) Scott Sullivan .25
(26) Reggie Taylor .25
(27) Todd Walker .25
(28) Gabe White .25
(29) Scott Williamson .25
(30) Coaching Staff (Jim Lefebvre, Ray Knight, Tim Foli, Jose Cardenal) .25
(31) Coaching Staff (Don Gullett, Tom Hume, Mark Berry) .25
(32) Marty Brennaman, Joe Nuxhall (Broadcasters) .25
(33) Riverfront Stadium .25

2003 Kahn's Cincinnati Reds

Team sets sponsored by the Reds' hot dog concessionaire were given to fans attending the August 15 game at Cinergy Field. The 2-1/2" x 3-9/16" cards have game-action photos that are borderless at top and right. At left is a vertical black stripe with the team name. At bottom-left is a Great American Ball Park inaugural season logo. The player name and uniform number are at bottom in white on black. Horizontal backs are printed in red, yellow and black and have personal data and complete professional stats, along with a color Kahn's logo.

NM/M
Complete Set (28): 7.50
Common Player: .25
(1) Aaron Boone .50
(2) Bob Boone .50
(3) Russell Branyan .25
(4) Sean Casey .50
(5) Juan Castro .25
(6) Coaching Staff (Tom Robson, Tim Foli, Ray Knight, Jose Cardenal) .25
(7) Coaching Staff (Don Gullett, Tom Hume, Mark Berry) .25
(8) Ryan Dempster .25
(9) Adam Dunn 1.00
(10) Danny Graves .25
(11) Ken Griffey Jr. 3.00
(12) Jose Guillen .35
(13) Jimmy Haynes .25
(14) Felix Heredia .25
(15) Austin Kearns .75
(16) Barry Larkin .35
(17) Jason LaRue .25
(18) Kent Mercker .25
(19) Wily Mo Pena .25
(20) Brian Reith .25
(21) Chris Reitsma .25
(22) John Riedling .25
(23) Kelly Stinnett .25
(24) Scott Sullivan .25
(25) Reggie Taylor .25
(26) Gabe White .25
(27) Scott Williamson .25
(28) Paul Wilson .25

2004 Kahn's Cincinnati Reds

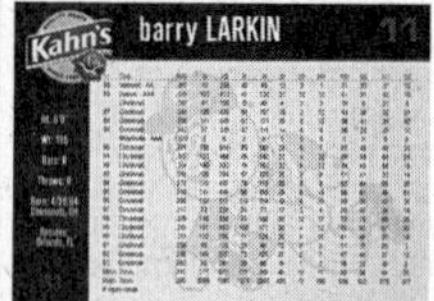

This set, sponsored by the Reds' hot dog concessionaire, was given to fans attending the Auguugst 15 game at Great American Ball Park. The 2-1/2" x 3-1/2" cards have game-action photos that are borderless at top, left and right. At left is a vertical black stripe with the team name. At bottom-left is a team logo. The player name, position and uniform number are at bottom in white on black or red. Horizontal backs are printed in red, yellow and black and have personal data and complete professional stats, along with a color Kahn's logo.

NM/M
Complete Set (29): 7.50
Common Player: .25
3 D'Angelo Jimenez .25
6 Ryan Freel .35
7 Juan Castro .25
9 Jacob Cruz .25
11 Barry Larkin .35
12 Dave Miley .25
15 Cory Lidle .25
16 Brandon Larson .25
17 Javier Valentin .25
21 Sean Casey .50
23 Jason Larue .25
25 John Vander Wal .25
26 Wily Mo Pena .25
28 Austin Kearns .50
29 Jose Acevedo .25
30 Ken Griffey Jr. 3.00
32 Danny Graves .25
34 Brandon Claussen .25
36 Gabe White .25
38 Ryan Wagner .40
39 Aaron Harang .25
40 Paul Wilson .25
44 Adam Dunn 1.50
45 Todd Van Poppel .25
46 John Riedling .25
51 Phil Norton .25
60 Tim Hummel .25
--- Mark Berry, Chris Chambliss, Don Gullett, Tom Hume .25
--- Coaching Staff (Jerry Narron, Randy Whisler, Mike Stefanski, Mark Mann) .25

2005 Kahn's Cincinnati Reds

This set, sponsored by the Reds' hot dog concessionaire, was given to fans attending the August 7 game at Great American Ball Park. The 2-1/2" x 3-1/2" cards have game-ac-

tion photos that are borderless at top, left and right. At bottom, are a team logo, player name, position and uniform number. Horizontal backs are printed in red, yellow and black and have personal data and complete professional stats, along with a color Kahn's logo.

		NM/M
	Complete Set (28):	10.00
	Common Player:	.25
2	Felipe Lopez	.25
6	Ryan Freel	.25
9	Jacob Cruz	.25
12	Edwin Encarnacion	.50
16	Joe Randa	.25
17	Javier Valentin	.25
21	Sean Casey	.60
22	Eric Milton	.25
23	Jason LaRue	.25
25	David Weathers	.25
26	Wily Mo Pena	.25
28	Austin Kearns	.50
30	Ken Griffey Jr.	3.00
31	Matt Belisle	.25
33	Rich Aurilia	.25
34	Brandon Claussen	.25
36	Ramon Ortiz	.25
38	Ryan Wagner	.25
39	Aaron Harang	.25
40	Paul Wilson	.25
41	Jerry Narron	.25
44	Adam Dunn	1.00
50	Kent Mercker	.25
54	Luke Hudson	.25
56	Todd Coffey	.25
57	Randy Keisler	.25
77	Ben Weber	.25
---	Coaching Staff (Mark Berry, Chris Chambliss, Tom Hume, John Moses, Vern Ruhle, Randy Whisler)	.25

1981 Kansas City Royals Police

Ten of the most popular Royals players are featured in this 2-1/2" x 4-1/8" set. Card fronts feature full-color photos with player name, position, facsimile autograph and team logo. Backs include player statistics, a tip from the Royals and list the four sponsoring organizations. The set was issued by the Ft. Myers, Fla., Police Department near the Royals' spring training headquarters.

		NM/M
	Complete Set (10):	20.00
	Common Player:	1.00
(1)	Willie Mays Aikens	1.00
(2)	George Brett	15.00
(3)	Rich Gale	1.00
(4)	Clint Hurdle	1.00
(5)	Dennis Leonard	1.00
(6)	Hal McRae	1.00
(7)	Amos Otis	1.00
(8)	U.L. Washington	1.00
(9)	Frank White	1.00
(10)	Willie Wilson	1.50

1983 Kansas City Royals Police

After skipping the 1982 season, the Ft. Myers, Fla., Police Department issued a Royals safety set in 1983 that is almost identical to their 1981 set. Cards are again 2-1/2" x 4-1/8" and include just 10 players. Cards are unnumbered, with vertical fronts and horizontal backs. Fronts have team logos, player name and position and facsimile autographs. Backs list the four sponsoring organizations, a "Tip from the Royals" and a "Kids and Cops Fact" about each player.

		NM/M
	Complete Set (10):	15.00
	Common Player:	.50
(1)	Willie Mays Aikens	.50
(2)	George Brett	13.50
(3)	Dennis Leonard	.50
(4)	Hal McRae	.50
(5)	Amos Otis	.50
(6)	Dan Quisenberry	.50
(7)	U.L. Washington	.50
(8)	John Wathan	.50
(9)	Frank White	.50
(10)	Willie Wilson	.75

1988 Kansas City Royals Fire Safety

This set featuring full-color player caricatures by K.K. Goodale was produced for an in-stadium promotion August 14. The 3" x 5" cards depict players, manager and coaches in action poses against a white background with a Royals logo at upper-left, opposite the Smokey Bear logo. Backs are black-and-white and contain brief player data and a Smokey cartoon.

		NM/M
	Complete Set (28):	7.50
	Common Player:	.25
1	John Wathan	.25
2	Coaches (Frank Funk, Adrian Garrett, Mike Lum, Ed Napolean, Bob Schaefer, Jim Schaefer)	.25
3	Willie Wilson	.35
4	Danny Tartabull	.25
5	Bo Jackson	1.50
6	Gary Thurman	.25
7	Jerry Don Gleaton	.25
8	Floyd Bannister	.25
9	Buddy Black	.25
10	Steve Farr	.25
11	Gene Garber	.25
12	Mark Gubicza	.25
13	Charlie Liebrandt	.25
14	Ted Power	.25
15	Dan Quisenberry	.25
16	Bret Saberhagen	.35
17	Mike Macfarlane	.25
18	Scotti Madison	.25
19	Jamie Quirk	.25
20	George Brett	5.00
21	Kevin Seitzer	.25
22	Bill Pecota	.25
23	Kurt Stillwell	.25
24	Brad Wellman	.25
25	Frank White	.25
26	Jim Eisenreich	.25
27	Smokey Bear	.10
---	Checklist	.10

1991 Kansas City Royals Police

Bo Jackson's release by the Royals in spring training caused his card to be withdrawn from distribution with the other 26 cards in this set. The 2-5/8" x 4-1/8" cards feature a color action photo on front, with the team name in royal blue and the player name and uniform number in black in the bottom border. Backs are printed in blue on white and feature a large cartoon safety message at center, career stats and bio at top, and the logos of the set's sponsors, Kansas City Life Insurance Co., and the Metro Chiefs and Sheriffs Assn., at bottom. Complete sets were distributed in a white paper envelope with team and sponsor logos.

		NM/M
	Complete Set (27) (W/Bo Jackson):	5.00
	Complete Set (26) (No Bo Jackson.):	3.00
	Common Player:	.10
1	Kurt Stillwell	.10
3	Terry Shumpert	.10
4	Danny Tartabull	.10
5	George Brett	3.00
8	Jim Eisenreich	.10
12	John Wathan	.10
14	Storm Davis	.10
15	Mike MacFarlane	.10
16	Bo Jackson	3.00
18	Bret Saberhagen	.25
21	Jeff Montgomery	.10
23	Mark Gubicza	.10
25	Gary Thurman	.10
27	Luis Aquino	.10
28	Steve Crawford	.10
30	Kirk Gibson	.15
32	Bill Pecota	.10
33	Kevin Seitzer	.10
36	Tom Gordon	.10
38	Andy McGaffigan	.10
48	Mark Davis	.10
52	Mike Boddicker	.10
55	Kevin Appier	.15
56	Brian McRae	.10
---	Royals Coaches (Pat Dobson, Adrian Garrett)	.10
---	Royals Coaches (Glenn Ezell, Lynn Jones, Bob Schaefer)	.10
---	Header Card - Royals Stadium	.10

1992 Kansas City Royals Police

Sponsored by K.C. Life Insurance and distributed by the Metropolitan Chiefs and Sheriffs Association, this 27-card set was distributed at a promotional game. Though they are checklisted, it is rumored that the cards of Kevin Seitzer (traded) and Kirk Gibson (released) were withdrawn early in the promotion, though both names appear on the checklist. The cards are numbered to match the player's uniform numbers. Cards are in the popular police-set format of 2-5/8" x 4-1/8" with white borders around color action photos. Backs have player data, stats, a fire safety message and sponsor's information.

		NM/M
	Complete Set (27):	5.00
	Common Player:	.25
2	Bob Melvin	.25
3	Terry Shumpert	.25
5	George Brett	3.00
8	Jim Eisenreich	.25
9	Gregg Jefferies	.35
11	Hal McRae	.25
12	Wally Joyner	.35
13	David Howard	.25
15	Mike McFarlane	.25
16	Keith Miller	.25
21	Jeff Montgomery	.25
22	Kevin McReynolds	.25
23	Mark Gubicza	.25
24	Brent Mayne	.25
25	Gary Thomas	.25
27	Luis Aquino	.25
29	Chris Gwynn	.25
30	Kirk Gibson	.35
33	Kevin Seitzer	.25
36	Tom Gordon	.25
37	Joel Johnson	.25
48	Mark Davis	.25
52	Mike Boddicker	.25
55	Kevin Appier	.25
56	Brian McRae	.25
57	Mike Magnante	.25
---	Coaches (Glenn Ezell, Adrian Garrett, Guy Hansen, Lynn Jones, Bruce Kison, Lee May)	.25

1993 Kansas City Royals Police

One of the longest-running police/fire safety issues continued in 1993 with a set marking the team's 25th anniversary season. The 2-5/8" x 4" cards have a light blue border, a color photo at center, an anniversary logo at lower-left and the player's name, position and uniform number at lower-right. All typography is in royal blue. Backs are printed in blue on white and feature career stats and highlights, a few biographical notes and a large safety message. Logos of the set's sponsors, Kansas City Life Insurance and the Metro Police Chiefs and Sheriffs Assn. are featured at bottom.

		NM/M
	Complete Set (27):	4.00
	Common Player:	.15
5	George Brett	3.00
7	Greg Gagne	.15
9	Craig Wilson	.15
11	Hal McRae	.15
12	Wally Joyner	.25
13	Jose Lind	.15
14	Chris Gwynn	.15
15	Mike MacFarlane	.15
16	Keith Miller	.15
17	David Cone	.25
19	Curtis Wilkerson	.15
21	Jeff Montgomery	.15
22	Kevin McReynolds	.15
23	Mark Gubicza	.15
24	Brent Mayne	.15
27	Luis Aquino	.15
28	Rusty Meacham	.15
33	Chris Haney	.15
34	Felix Jose	.15
35	Hipolito Pichardo	.15
36	Tom Gordon	.15
37	Mark Gardner	.15
40	Kevin Koslofski	.15
52	Mike Boddicker	.15
55	Kevin Appier	.15
56	Brian McRae	.15
---	Royals Coaches (Steve Boros, Glenn Ezell, Guy Hansen, Bruce Kison, Lee May)	.15

1994 Kansas City Royals Police

The team's long run of police/fire safety issues continued in 1994. The 2-5/8" x 4" cards have a pale yellow background with vertical light blue stripe, a color photo at center, team logo at top and the player's name, position and uniform number at bottom. Backs are printed in blue on white and feature career stats and highlights, a few biographical notes and a large safety message. Logos of the set's sponsors, Kansas City Life Insurance and the Metro Police Chiefs and Sheriffs Assn. are featured at bottom.

		NM/M
	Complete Set (27):	8.00
	Common Player:	.25
3	Bob Hamelin	.25
6	David Howard	.25
7	Greg Gagne	.25
8	Gary Gaetti	.25
11	Hal McRae	.25
12	Wally Joyner	.25
13	Jose Lind	.25
15	Mike MacFarlane	.25
16	Keith Miller	.25
21	Jeff Montgomery	.25
22	David Cone	.25
23	Mark Gubicza	.25
24	Brent Mayne	.25
29	Vince Coleman	.25
33	Chris Haney	.25
34	Felix Jose	.25
35	Hipolito Pichardo	.25
36	Tom Gordon	.25
40	Kevin Koslofski	.25
41	Billy Brewer	.25
42	Dave Henderson	.25
50	Stan Belinda	.25
55	Kevin Appier	.25
56	Brian McRae	.25
'94	Royals Coaches (Steve Boros, Glenn Ezell, Bruce Kison, Lee May, Jamie Quirk)	.25
---	George Brett (Royals Hall of Fame)	3.00
---	Frank White (Royals Hall of Fame)	.50

1995 Kansas City Royals Police

In 1995, the Royals safety set was sponsored by Kansas City Life Insurance Co., and distributed by law enforcement agencies in the greater Kansas City area. The cards measure about 2-5/8" x 4" and feature action photos on front. The team name is scripted at bottom with logo and the player's last name and "1995" are vertically at right. Backs have a few vital data, a career stats line, a safety message and sponsor's logo. Cards are listed here in alphabetical order.

		NM/M
	Complete Set (12):	4.00
	Common Player:	.50
(1)	Kevin Appier	.50
(2)	Bob Boone	.65
(3)	Vince Coleman	.50
(4)	Gary Gaetti	.50
(5)	Greg Gagne	.50
(6)	Tom Gordon	.50
(7)	Mark Gubicza	.50
(8)	Chris Haney	.50
(9)	Wally Joyner	.65
(10)	Brent Mayne	.50
(11)	Jeff Montgomery	.50
(12)	Hipolito Pichardo	.50

1996 Kansas City Royals Police

The 1997 Royals safety set issue is a 23-card presentation given to young fans at a promotional game. The 2-5/8" x 4" cards have game-action color photo bordered in white. Backs are in blue on white with a few personal data, career highlights and record, a cartoon safety message and the logo of sponsoring Kansas City Life Insurance, which provided the cards for distribution by the Metropolitan Chiefs and Sheriffs Assn. Cards are checklisted here alphabetically.

		NM/M
	Complete Set (27):	4.00
	Common Player:	.25
1	Bip Roberts	.25
3	Bob Hamelin	.25
4	Keith Lockhart	.25
6	David Howard	.25
8	Bob Boone	.45
15	Mike Macfarlane	.25
16	Joe Randa	.25
17	Kevin Appier	.25
18	Johnny Damon	1.50
21	Jeff Montgomery	.25
22	Jon Nunnally	.25
23	Mark Gubicza	.25
24	Terry Clark	.25
25	Les Norman	.25

28	Rusty Meacham	.25
30	Jose Offerman	.25
31	Michael Tucker	.25
33	Chris Haney	.25
35	Hipolito Pichardo	.25
37	Rick Huisman	.25
38	Jim Converse	.25
41	Tim Belcher	.25
42	Tom Goodwin	.25
44	Joe Vitiello	.25
45	Jason Jacome	.25
50	Melvin Bunch	.25
57	Mike Magnante	.25

1997 Kansas City Royals Police

In 1996 the Royals returned to safety set issue with this 27-card presentation given to fans 14 and under at the April 20 game. The 2-5/8" x 4" cards have game-action color photo bordered in white. Backs are in blue on white with a few personal data, career highlights and record, a cartoon safety message and the logo of sponsoring Kansas City Life Insurance, which provided the cards for distribution by the Metropolitan Chiefs and Sheriffs Assn. Cards are checklisted here by uniform number.

		NM/M
Complete Set (23):		4.00
Common Player:		.25
(1)	Kevin Appier	.25
(2)	Tim Belcher	.25
(3)	Jay Bell	.25
(4)	Jaime Bluma	.25
(5)	Bob Boone	.50
(6)	Johnny Damon	1.50
(7)	Chili Davis	.25
(8)	Tom Goodwin	.25
(9)	Chris Haney	.25
(10)	David Howard	.25
(11)	Rick Huisman	.25
(12)	Jason Jacome	.25
(13)	Jeff King	.25
(14)	Mike Macfarlane	.25
(15)	Jeff Montgomery	.25
(16)	Jose Offerman	.25
(17)	Craig Paquette	.25
(18)	Hipolito Pichardo	.25
(19)	Bip Roberts	.25
(20)	Jose Rosado	.25
(21)	Sluggerrr (Mascot)	.25
(22)	Mike Sweeney	.25
(23)	Joe Vitiello	.25

1998 Kansas City Royals Police

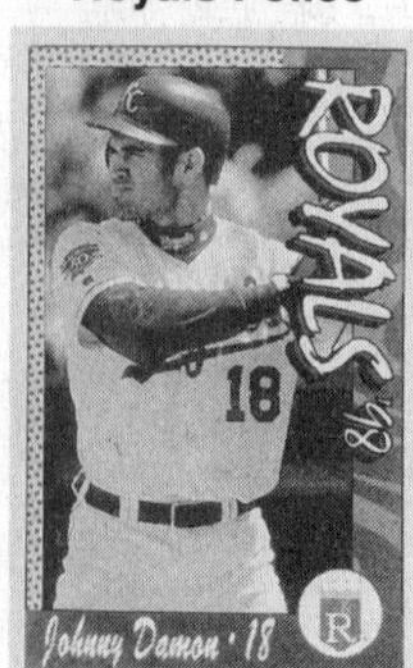

In 1998 the Royals issued this safety set to fans 14 and under at a promotional game. The 2-5/8" x 4" cards have game-action color photo bordered in white. Backs are in blue on white with a few bits of personal data, a cartoon safety message and the logo of sponsoring Kansas City Life Insurance, which provided the cards for distribution by the Metropolitan Chiefs and Sheriffs Assn. Cards are checklisted here by uniform number.

		NM/M
Complete Set (26):		4.00
Common Player:		.25
2	Jed Hansen	.25
4	Shane Halter	.25
7	Jeff King	.35
14	Felix Martinez	.25
15	Mike Macfarlane	.25
16	Dean Palmer	.25
17	Kevin Appier	.25
18	Johnny Damon	1.50
19	Jeff Conine	.50
21	Jeff Montgomery	.25
22	Larry Sutton	.25
23	Hal Morris	.25
24	Jermaine Dye	.25
27	Joe Vitiello	.25
29	Mike Sweeney	.25
30	Jose Offerman	.25
33	Chris Haney	.25
35	Hipolito Pichardo	.25
40	Tony Muser	.25
41	Tim Belcher	.25
43	Roderick Myers	.25
47	Brian Bevil	.25
50	Jose Rosado	.25
53	Glendon Rusch	.25
56	Matt Whisenant	.25
	Sluggerrr (Mascot)	.25

2000 Kansas City Royals Police

The Royals issued this safety set to the first 10,000 fans 14 and under at an April 30 promotional game. The 2-5/8" x 4" cards have game-action color photo bordered in white. Backs are in blue on white with a few bits of personal data, a cartoon safety message and the logo of sponsoring Kansas City Life Insurance, which provided the cards for distribution by the Metropolitan Chiefs and Sheriffs Assn. Cards are checklisted here by uniform number.

		NM/M
Complete Set (25):		4.00
Common Player:		.25
1	Rey Sanchez	.25
3	Carlos Febles	.50
4	Ray Holbert	.25
6	Todd Dunwoody	.25
12	Jeff Reboulet	.25
14	Mark Quinn	.25
15	Carlos Beltran	3.00
16	Joe Randa	.25
18	Johnny Damon	1.00
19	Brian Johnson	.25
24	Jermaine Dye	.25
28	Jay Witasick	.25
29	Mike Sweeney	.25
33	Chad Durbin	.25
34	Blake Stein	.25
37	Jeff Suppan	.25
38	Scott Pose	.25
40	Tony Muser	.25
41	Dan Reichert	.25
46	Jose Santiago	.25
48	Jerry Spradlin	.25
49	Chris Fussell	.25
50	Jose Rosado	.25
52	Ricky Bottalico	.25
	Sluggerrr (Mascot)	.25

2001 Kansas City Royals Police

The Royals issued this safety set to fans attending a promotional game. The 2-5/8" x 4" cards have a game-action color photo on front. The same photo is enlarged, posterized and rendered in blue as a background. A gold stripe at left and top has player identification. Backs have a few bits of personal data, a cartoon safety message and the logo of sponsoring Kansas City Life Insurance, which provided the cards for distribution by the Metropolitan Chiefs and Sheriffs Assn. Cards are checklisted here alphabetically.

		NM/M
Complete Set (27):		4.00
Common Player:		.25
(1)	Luis Alicea	.25
(2)	Carlos Beltran	2.00
(3)	Dee Brown	.25
(4)	Chad Durbin	.25
(5)	Jermaine Dye	.25
(6)	Carlos Febles	.40
(7)	Doug Henry	.25
(8)	Roberto Hernandez	.25
(9)	Dave McCarty	.25
(10)	Brian Meadows	.25
(11)	Scott Mullen	.25
(12)	Tony Muser	.25
(13)	Luis Ordaz	.25
(14)	Hector Ortiz	.25
(15)	Mark Quinn	.25
(16)	Joe Randa	.25
(17)	Dan Reichert	.25
(18)	Jose Rosado	.25
(19)	Rey Sanchez	.25
(20)	Jose Santiago	.25
(21)	Blake Stein	.25
(22)	Jeff Suppan	.25
(23)	Mac Suzuki	.25
(24)	Mike Sweeney	.25
(25)	Kris Wilson	.25
(26)	Gregg Zaun	.25
(27)	Slugger (Mascot)	.25

2002 Kansas City Royals Police

This safety set was a stadium give-away to fans attending an early-season promotional game. The 2-5/8" x 4" cards have a game-action color photo on front, with the background rendered in blue and an arc of blue at left. Backs have a few bits of personal data, a cartoon, safety message and the logo of sponsoring Kansas City Life Insurance, which provided the cards for distribution by the Metropolitan Chiefs and Sheriffs Assn. Cards are checklisted here alphabetically.

		NM/M
Complete Set (26):		4.00
Common Player:		.25
(1)	Luis Alicea	.25
(2)	Cory Bailey	.25
(3)	Carlos Beltran	2.00
(4)	Dee Brown	.25
(5)	Paul Byrd	.25
(6)	Chad Durbin	.25
(7)	Carlos Febles	.50
(8)	Jason Grimsley	.25
(9)	Roberto Hernandez	.25
(10)	A.J. Hinch	.25
(11)	Raul Ibanez	.25
(12)	Chuck Knoblauch	.25
(13)	Darrell May	.25
(14)	Brent Mayne	.25
(15)	Dave McCarty	.25
(16)	Tony Muser	.25
(17)	Neifi Perez	.25
(18)	Mark Quinn	.25
(19)	Joe Randa	.35
(20)	Dan Reichert	.25
(21)	Donnie Sadler	.25
(22)	Sluggerr (Mascot)	.25
(23)	Blake Stein	.25
(24)	Jeff Suppan	.25
(25)	Mike Sweeney	.50
(26)	Michael Tucker	.25

2003 Kansas City Royals Police

The Royals issued this safety set to fans attending an early-season promotional game. The 2-5/8" x 4" cards have a game-action color photo on front. Backs have a few bits of personal data, a cartoon, safety message and the logo of sponsoring Kansas City Life Insurance, which provided the cards for distribution by the Metropolitan Chiefs and Sheriffs Assn. Cards are checklisted here by uniform number.

		NM/M
Complete Set (27):		6.00
Common Player:		.50
2	Brent Mayne	.50
3	Carlos Febles	.50
4	Angel Berroa	1.00
6	Tony Pena	.50
12	Desi Relaford	.50
15	Carlos Beltran	2.00
16	Joe Randa	.50
18	Raul Ibanez	.50
24	Michael Tucker	.50
26	Mike DiFelice	.50
28	Ken Harvey	.50
29	Mike Sweeney	.60
30	Brandon Berger	.50
31	Albie Lopez	.50
32	Chris George	.50
33	James Baldwin	.50
34	Darrell May	.50
35	Ryan Bukvich	.50
38	Jason Grimsley	.50
40	Runelvys Hernandez	.50
45	Aaron Guiel	.50
48	Jeremy Affeldt	.50
51	Kris Wilson	.50
53	Miguel Asencio	.50
54	Mike MacDougal	.50
57	Scott Mullen	.50
---	Sluggerrr (Mascot)	.50

2004 Kansas City Royals Police

The Royals issued this safety set to fans attending an early-season promotional game. The 2-5/8" x 4" cards have a game-action color photo on front, on a dot-matrix background. Backs have a few bits of personal data, a cartoon, safety message and the logo of sponsoring Kansas City Life Insurance, which provided the cards for distribution by the Metropolitan Chiefs and Sheriffs Assn. Cards are checklisted here by uniform number.

		NM/M
Complete Set (27):		10.00
Common Player:		.50
00	Sluggerrr (Mascot)	.50
4	Angel Berroa	1.00
6	Tony Pena	.50
9	David DeJesus	.50
11	Matt Stairs	.50
12	Desi Relaford	.50
14	Tony Graffanino	.50
15	Carlos Beltran	2.00
16	Joe Randa	.50
18	Kelly Stinnett	.50
19	Brian Anderson	.50
22	Juan Gonzalez	1.00
24	Rich Thompson	.50
28	Ken Harvey	.50
29	Mike Sweeney	.65
30	Benito Santiago	.50
33	Curtis Leskanic	.50
34	Darrell May	.50
38	Jason Grimsley	.50
41	Jimmy Gobble	.50
45	Aaron Guiel	.50
47	Scott Sullivan	.50
48	Jeremy Affeldt	.50
54	Mike MacDougal	.50
55	Kevin Appier	.50
59	D.J. Carrasco	.50
61	Jaime Cerda	.50

2005 Kansas City Royals Police

The Royals issued this safety set to fans attending an early-season promotional game. The 2-5/8" x 4" cards have a game-action color photo on front, on a marbled background. Backs are printed in blue and have a few bits of personal data, a cartoon, safety message and the logo of sponsoring Kansas City Life Insurance, which provided the cards for distribution by the Metropolitan Chiefs and Sheriffs Assn. Cards are checklisted here by uniform number.

		NM/M
Complete Set (27):		8.00
Common Player:		.50
00	Sluggerrr (Mascot)	.50
2	John Buck	.50
3	Terrence Long	.50
4	Angel Berroa	.75
6	Tony Pena	.50
9	David DeJesus	.50
11	Eli Marrero	.50
12	Matt Stairs	.50
14	Tony Graffanino	.50
19	Brian Anderson	.50
23	Zack Greinke	1.50
24	Mark Teahen	.50
27	Denny Bautista	.50
28	Ken Harvey	.50
29	Mike Sweeney	.65
30	Ruben Gotay	.50
33	Jose Lima	.50
40	Runelvys Hernandez	.50
41	Jimmy Gobble	.50
45	Aaron Guiel	.50
46	Mike Wood	.50
48	Jeremy Affeldt	.50
51	Andy Sisco	.50
54	Mike MacDougal	.50
56	Jaime Cerda	.50
57	Nate Field	.50
58	Shawn Camp	.50

1993 Kansas City Star Royals All-Time Team

On the occasion of the team's 25th anniversary the Kansas City Star newspaper issued a sheet honoring the All-Time Team. The 10-3/8" x 14-3/8" sheet is perforated to allow separation of the individual 2-1/2" x 3-1/2" cards. Fronts have color photos at center with royal blue borders at the sides and gold at top and bottom. A Royals 25th anniversary logo is at lower-right. Backs are printed in black and blue on white with a career summary and the player's K.C. stats. The unnumbered cards are checklisted here alphabetically.

		NM/M
Uncut Sheet:		12.00
Complete Set (16):		10.00
Common Player:		.50
(1)	George Brett	6.00
(2)	Steve Busby	.50
(3)	Al Cowens	.50
(4)	Dick Howser	.50
(5)	Dennis Leonard	.50
(6)	John Mayberry	.50
(7)	Hal McRae	.75
(8)	Amos Otis	.50
(9)	Fred Patek	.50
(10)	Darrell Porter	.50
(11)	Dan Quisenberry	.75
(12)	Bret Saberhagen	1.00
(13)	Paul Splittorff	.50
(14)	Frank White	.75
(15)	Willie Wilson	1.00
(16)	25th Anniversary Logo	.50

1985 Kas Potato Chips Discs

One of a pair of nearly identical (see Kitty Clover) sets issued by midwestern potato chip companies, this issue features top stars of the day on 2-3/4" cardboard discs. The discs have a player portrait at center, with uniform logos airbrushed away because the producer was licensed only by the MLB Players Association and not Major League Baseball. The player's name, team and position are printed in a white diamond around the photo. The sponsor's logo is in the orange border. Backs are in black-and-white and have a few biographical data, a 1984 stats line and a Snack Time logo. The unnumbered discs are checklisted here in alphabetical order. Square versions of the discs, which have been cut from press sheets are known within the hobby and carry a small premium. KAS was based in St. Louis.

		NM/M
Complete Set (20):		75.00
Common Player:		1.50
(1)	Steve Carlton	4.50
(2)	Jack Clark	1.50
(3)	Rich Gossage	1.50
(4)	Tony Gwynn	7.50
(5)	Bob Horner	1.50
(6)	Keith Hernandez	1.50
(7)	Kent Hrbek	1.50
(8)	Willie McGee	1.50
(9)	Dan Quisenberry	1.50
(10)	Cal Ripken Jr.	20.00
(11)	Ryne Sandberg	7.50
(12)	Mike Schmidt	12.50
(13)	Tom Seaver	5.00
(14)	Ozzie Smith	7.50
(15)	Rick Sutcliffe	1.50
(16)	Bruce Sutter	4.00
(17)	Alan Trammell	1.50
(18)	Fernando Valenzuela	1.50
(19)	Willie Wilson	1.50
(20)	Dave Winfield	4.50

1986 Kas Potato Chips Cardinals

One of several of 2-7/8" round baseball card discs created by Mike Schecter Associates for inclusion in packages of potato chips, the 20-card Kas set features players of the defending National League Champion St. Louis Cardinals. Fronts feature color photos on which the team logos have been removed from the caps by airbrushing the photos' uniform logos. Card backs have minimal personal data and 1985 stats.

		NM/M
Complete Set (20):		16.00
Common Player:		.50
1	Vince Coleman	1.00
2	Ken Dayley	.50
3	Tito Landrum	.50
4	Steve Braun	.50
5	Danny Cox	.50
6	Bob Forsch	.50
7	Ozzie Smith	9.00
8	Brian Harper	.50
9	Jack Clark	.50
10	Todd Worrell	.50
11	Joaquin Andujar	.50
12	Tom Nieto	.50
13	Kurt Kepshire	.50
14	Terry Pendleton	.50
15	Tom Herr	.50
16	Darrell Porter	.50
17	John Tudor	.50
18	Jeff Lahti	.50
19	Andy Van Slyke	1.00
20	Willie McGee	1.00

1986 Kay Bee Young Superstars

One of the most-widely distributed of the specialty boxed sets of 1986, the Kay Bee toy store chain set of "Young Superstars of Baseball" was produced by Topps. The 2-1/2" x 3-1/2" cards are printed on white stock with a glossy surface finish. Backs, printed in red and black, are strongly reminiscent of the 1971 Topps cards. While the set concentrated on "young" stars of the game, few of the year's top rookies were included.

		NM/M
Complete Set (33):		2.00
Common Player:		.05
1	Rick Aguilera	.05
2	Chris Brown	.05
3	Tom Browning	.05
4	Tom Brunansky	.05
5	Vince Coleman	.05
6	Ron Darling	.05
7	Alvin Davis	.05
8	Mariano Duncan	.05
9	Shawon Dunston	.05
10	Sid Fernandez	.05
11	Tony Fernandez	.05
12	Brian Fisher	.05
13	John Franco	.05
14	Julio Franco	.05
15	Dwight Gooden	.05
16	Ozzie Guillen	.05
17	Tony Gwynn	.75
18	Jimmy Key	.05
19	Don Mattingly	1.50
20	Oddibe McDowell	.05
21	Roger McDowell	.05
22	Dan Pasqua	.05
23	Terry Pendleton	.05
24	Jim Presley	.05
25	Kirby Puckett	.75
26	Earnie Riles	.05
27	Bret Saberhagen	.05
28	Mark Salas	.05
29	Juan Samuel	.05
30	Jeff Stone	.05
31	Darryl Strawberry	.05
32	Andy Van Slyke	.05
33	Frank Viola	.05

1987 Kay Bee Superstars of Baseball

For a second year, Topps produced a boxed set for the Kay Bee toy store chain. Called "Superstars of Baseball," cards in the set measure 2-1/2" x 3-1/2". The glossy-coated fronts carry a color player photo plus the Kay Bee logo. Backs, reminiscent of those found in the 1971 Topps set, offer a black-and-white portrait of the player along with his name, postion, personal information, playing record and a brief biography.

		NM/M
Complete Set (33):		3.00
Common Player:		.05
1	Harold Baines	.05
2	Jesse Barfield	.05
3	Don Baylor	.05
4	Wade Boggs	.65
5	George Brett	.75
6	Hubie Brooks	.05
7	Jose Canseco	.30
8	Gary Carter	.50
9	Joe Carter	.05
10	Roger Clemens	.75
11	Vince Coleman	.05
12	Glenn Davis	.05
13	Dwight Gooden	.05
14	Pedro Guerrero	.05
15	Tony Gwynn	.65
16	Rickey Henderson	.50
17	Keith Hernandez	.05
18	Wally Joyner	.05
19	Don Mattingly	.75
20	Jack Morris	.05
21	Dale Murphy	.15
22	Eddie Murray	.50
23	Dave Parker	.05
24	Kirby Puckett	.65
25	Tim Raines	.05
26	Jim Rice	.05
27	Dave Righetti	.05
28	Ryne Sandberg	.65
29	Mike Schmidt	.75
30	Mike Scott	.05
31	Darryl Strawberry	.05
32	Fernando Valenzuela	.05
33	Dave Winfield	.50

1988 Kay Bee Superstars of Baseball

This boxed set was produced by Topps for exclusive distribution via Kay Bee toy stores nationwide. Card fronts are super glossy and feature color player action photos below a bright red and yellow player name banner. Photos are framed in green above a large, cartoon-style Kay Bee logo. Backs feature player closeups in a horizontal layout in blue ink on a green and white background. Backs are numbered and carry biographical information, career data and major league batting stats.

		NM/M
Complete Set (33):		3.00
Common Player:		.05
1	George Bell	.05
2	Wade Boggs	.65
3	Jose Canseco	.30
4	Joe Carter	.05
5	Jack Clark	.05
6	Alvin Davis	.05
7	Eric Davis	.05
8	Andre Dawson	.25
9	Darrell Evans	.05
10	Dwight Evans	.05
11	Gary Gaetti	.05
12	Pedro Guerrero	.05
13	Tony Gwynn	.65
14	Howard Johnson	.05
15	Wally Joyner	.05
16	Don Mattingly	.75
17	Willie McGee	.05
18	Mark McGwire	.85
19	Paul Molitor	.50
20	Dale Murphy	.25
21	Dave Parker	.05
22	Lance Parrish	.05
23	Kirby Puckett	.65
24	Tim Raines	.05
25	Cal Ripken, Jr.	1.00
26	Juan Samuel	.05
27	Mike Schmidt	.75
28	Ruben Sierra	.05
29	Darryl Strawberry	.05
30	Danny Tartabull	.05
31	Alan Trammell	.05
32	Tim Wallach	.05
33	Dave Winfield	.50

1988 Kay Bee Team Leaders

This boxed edition of 44 player and six team logo cards was produced by Fleer for distribution by Kay Bee toy stores nationwide. Color player photos are framed in black against a bright red border. "Fleer Team Leaders 1988" and Kay Bee logos appear on the front. Backs, (red, white and pink) repeat the Team Leaders logo, followed by stats, personal data, team and MLB logos. The player's name, card number and position are listed on the lower border. The set includes six team logo sticker cards that feature black-and-white stadium photos on the backs.

		NM/M
Complete Set (44):		3.00
Common Player:		.05
1	George Bell	.05
2	Wade Boggs	.65
3	Jose Canseco	.40
4	Will Clark	.10
5	Roger Clemens	.75
6	Eric Davis	.05
7	Andre Dawson	.25
8	Julio Franco	.05
9	Andres Galarraga	.05
10	Dwight Gooden	.05
11	Tony Gwynn	.65
12	Tom Henke	.05
13	Orel Hershiser	.05
14	Kent Hrbek	.05
15	Ted Higuera	.05
16	Wally Joyner	.05
17	Jimmy Key	.05
18	Mark Langston	.05
19	Don Mattingly	.75
20	Willie McGee	.05
21	Mark McGwire	.85
22	Paul Molitor	.50
23	Jack Morris	.05
24	Dale Murphy	.25
25	Larry Parrish	.05
26	Kirby Puckett	.65
27	Tim Raines	.05
28	Jeff Reardon	.05
29	Dave Righetti	.05
30	Cal Ripken, Jr.	1.00
31	Don Robinson	.05
32	Bret Saberhagen	.05
33	Juan Samuel	.05
34	Mike Schmidt	.75
35	Mike Scott	.05
36	Kevin Seitzer	.05
37	Dave Smith	.05
38	Ozzie Smith	.65
39	Zane Smith	.05
40	Darryl Strawberry	.05
41	Rick Sutcliffe	.05
42	Bobby Thigpen	.05
43	Alan Trammell	.05
44	Andy Van Slyke	.05

1989 Kay Bee Superstars of Baseball

The top stars of baseball are featured in this boxed set produced by Topps for the Kay Bee Toy store chain. The glossy, standard-size cards display the Kay Bee logo below the player photo on the front. The top of the card is headlined "Superstars of Baseball," with the player's name underneath. Backs include a small black-and-white player photo and personal data.

		NM/M
Complete Set (33):		3.00
Common Player:		.05
1	Wade Boggs	.65
2	George Brett	.75
3	Jose Canseco	.30
4	Gary Carter	.50
5	Jack Clark	.05
6	Will Clark	.10
7	Roger Clemens	.75
8	Eric Davis	.05
9	Andre Dawson	.25
10	Dwight Evans	.05
11	Carlton Fisk	.50
12	Andres Galarraga	.05
13	Kirk Gibson	.05
14	Dwight Gooden	.05
15	Mike Greenwell	.05
16	Pedro Guerrero	.05
17	Tony Gwynn	.65
18	Rickey Henderson	.50
19	Orel Hershiser	.05
20	Don Mattingly	.75
21	Mark McGwire	.85
22	Dale Murphy	.25
23	Eddie Murray	.50
24	Kirby Puckett	.65
25	Tim Raines	.05
26	Ryne Sandberg	.65
27	Mike Schmidt	.75
28	Ozzie Smith	.65
29	Darryl Strawberry	.05
30	Alan Trammell	.05
31	Frank Viola	.05
32	Dave Winfield	.50
33	Robin Yount	.50

1990 Kay Bee Kings

This boxed set was the fifth annual issue produced by Topps for the Kay Bee toy store chain. The 2-1/2" x 3-1/2" cards feature color action photos on the front and complete statistics on the flip sides. The cards are numbered alphabetically.

		NM/M
Complete Set (33):		4.00
Common Player:		.05
1	Doyle Alexander	.05
2	Bert Blyleven	.05
3	Wade Boggs	.65
4	George Brett	.75
5	John Candelaria	.05
6	Gary Carter	.50
7	Vince Coleman	.05
8	Andre Dawson	.25
9	Dennis Eckersley	.40
10	Darrell Evans	.05
11	Dwight Evans	.05
12	Carlton Fisk	.50
13	Ken Griffey	.05
14	Tony Gwynn	.65
15	Rickey Henderson	.50
16	Keith Hernandez	.05
17	Charlie Hough	.05
18	Don Mattingly	.75
19	Jack Morris	.05
20	Dale Murphy	.25
21	Eddie Murray	.50
22	Dave Parker	.05
23	Kirby Puckett	.65
24	Tim Raines	.05
25	Rick Reuschel	.05
26	Jerry Reuss	.05
27	Jim Rice	.15
28	Nolan Ryan	1.00
29	Ozzie Smith	.65
30	Frank Tanana	.05
31	Willie Wilson	.05
32	Dave Winfield	.50
33	Robin Yount	.50

1993 Keebler Texas Rangers

Over a series of eight home dates in Arlington Stadium's final season, the Keebler baking company along with a group of rotating co-sponsors produced and distributed a team set featuring "all players, manager and coaches who have ever appeared in a Rangers game." Besides the player cards there were checklists, team photo cards, team-leader cards, logo cards and other specials. The cards were made up into 8-1/2" x 11" booklets, with the cards perforated for removal. Series 2 and 3 booklets had 72 cards; the other series had 54 cards each. Single cards measure 2-1/2" x 3-1/2". Sepia-toned player portraits are featured with red frames. A blue banner at top has the team name. The player name is printed in black in the white bottom border. The Keebler logo is at the photo's lower-left, while the player's position is in a baseball diamond diagram at lower-right. Backs are printed in black, include a few biographical details and the player's Rangers' and major league career stats. The Keebler logo is repreated on the back, along with the logo of the co-sponsor of that particular series. A total of 42,000 of the first series booklets were distributed; 35,000 each of the other seven series were produced.

		NM/M
Complete Set (468):		35.00
Common Player:		.10
1	Ted Williams	5.00
2	Larry Biittner	.10
3	Rich Billings	.10
4	Dick Bosman	.10
5	Pete Broberg	.10
6	Jeff Burroughs	.10
7	Casey Cox	.10
8	Jim Drixcoll	.10
9	Jan Dukes	.10
10	Bill Fahey	.10
11	Ted Ford	.10
12	Bill Gogolewski	.10
13	Tom Grieve	.10
14	Rich Hand	.10
15	Toby Harrah	.25
16	Vic Harris	.10
17	Rich Hinton	.10
18	Frank Howard	.25
19	Gerry Janeski	.10
20	Dalton Jones	.10
21	Hal King	.10
22	Ted Kubiak	.10
23	Steve Lawson	.10
24	Paul Lindblad	.10
25	Joe Lovitto	.10
26	Elliott Maddox	.10
27	Marty Martinez	.10
28	Jim Mason	.10
29	Don Mincher	.10
30	Dave Nelson	.10
31	Jim Panther	.10
32	Mike Paul	.10
33	Horacio Pina	.10
34	Tom Ragland	.10
35	Lenny Randle	.10
36	Jim Roland	.10
37	Jim Shellenback	.10
38	Don Stanhouse	.10
39	Ken Suarez	.10
40	Joe Camacho	.10
41	Nellie Fox	2.00
42	Sid Hudson	.10
43	George Susce	.10
44	Wayne Terwilliger	.10
45	Darrel Akerfelds	.10
46	Doyle Alexander	.10
47	Gerald Alexander	.10
48	Brian Allard	.10
49	Lloyd Allen	.10
50	Sandy Alomar	.10
51	Wilson Alvarez	.10
52	Jim Anderson	.10
53	Scott Anderson	.10
54	Brad Arnsberg	.10
55	Tucker Ashford	.10
56	Doug Ault	.10
57	Bob Babcock	.10
58	Mike Bacsik	.10
59	Harold Baines	.10
60	Alan Bannister	.10
61	Floyd Bannister	.10
62	John Barfield	.10
63	Len Barker	.10
64	Steve Barr	.10
65	Randy Bass	.10
66	Lew Beasley	.10
67	Kevin Belcher	.10
68	Buddy Bell	.10
69	Juan Beniquez	.10
70	Kurt Bevacqua	.10
71	Jim Bibby	.10
72	Joe Bitker	.10

73	Larvell Blanks	.10
74	Bert Blyleven	.25
75	Terry Bogener	.10
76	Tommy Boggs	.10
77	Dan Boitano	.10
78	Bobby Bonds	.25
79	Thad Bosley	.10
80	Dennis Boyd	.10
81	Nelson Briles	.10
82	Ed Brinkman	.10
83	Bob Brower	.10
84	Jackie Brown	.10
85	Larry Brown	.10
86	Jerry Browne	.10
87	Glenn Brummer	.10
88	Kevin Buckley	.10
89	Steve Buechele	.10
90	Ray Burris	.10
91	John Butcher	.10
92	Bert Campaneris	.10
93	Mike Campbell	.10
94	John Cangelosi	.10
95	Nick Capra	.10
96	Leo Cardenas	.10
97	Don Carman	.10
98	Rico Carty	.10
99	Don Castle	.10
100	Jose Cecena	.10
101	Dave Chalk	.10
102	Scott Chiamparino	.10
103	Ken Clay	.10
104	Reggie Cleveland	.10
105	Gene Clines	.10
106	David Clyde	.10
107	Cris Colon	.10
108	Merrill Combs	.10
109	Steve Comer	.10
110	Glen Cook	.10
111	Scott Coolbaugh	.10
112	Pat Corrales	.10
113	Edwin Correa	.10
114	Larry Cox	.10
115	Keith Creel	.10
116	Victor Cruz	.10
117	Mike Cubbage	.10
118	Bobby Cuellar	.10
119	Danny Darwin	.10
120	Jack Daugherty	.10
121	Doug Davis	.10
122	Odie Davis	.10
123	Willie Davis	.10
124	Bucky Dent	.10
125	Adrian Devine	.10
126	Mario Diaz	.10
127	Rich Donnelly	.10
128	Brian Downing	.10
129	Tommy Dunbar	.10
130	Steve Dunning	.10
131	Dan Duran	.10
132	Don Durham	.10
133	Dick Egan	.10
134	Dock Ellis	.10
135	John Ellis	.10
136	Mike Epstein	.10
137	Cecil Espy	.10
138	Chuck Estrada	.10
139	Glenn Ezell	.10
140	Hector Fajardo	.10
141	Monty Fariss	.10
142	Ed Farmer	.10
143	Jim Farr	.10
144	Joe Ferguson	.10
145	Ed Figueroa	.10
146	Steve Fireovid	.10
147	Scott Fletcher	.10
148	Doug Flynn	.10
149	Marv Foley	.10
150	Tim Foli	.10
151	Tony Fossas	.10
152	Steve Foucault	.10
153	Art Fowler	.10
154	Jim Fregosi	.10
155	Pepe Frias	.10
156	Oscar Gamble	.10
157	Barbaro Garbey	.10
158	Dick Gernert	.10
159	Jim Gideon	.10
160	Jerry Don Gleaton	.10
161	Orlando Gomez	.10
162	Rich Gossage	.25
163	Gary Gray	.10
164	Gary Green	.10
165	John Grubb	.10
166	Cecilio Guante	.10
167	Jose Guzman	.10
168	Drew Hall	.10
169	Bill Hands	.10
170	Steve Hargan	.10
171	Mike Hargrove	.10
172	Toby Harrah	.10
173	Bud Harrelson	.10
174	Donald Harris	.10
175	Greg Harris	.10
176	Mike Hart	.10
177	Bill Haselman	.10
178	Ray Hayward	.10
179	Tommy Helms	.10
180	Ken Henderson	.10
181	Rick Henninger	.10
182	Dwayne Henry	.10
183	Jose Hernandez	.10
184	Whitey Herzog	.10
185	Chuck Hiller	.10
186	Joe Hoerner	.10
187	Guy Hoffman	.10
188	Gary Holle	.10
189	Rick Honeycutt	.10
190	Burt Hooton	.10
191	John Hoover	.10
192	Willie Horton	.10
193	Dave Hostetler	.10
194	Charlie Hough	.10
195	Tom House	.10
196	Art Howe	.10
197	Steve Howe	.10
198	Roy Howell	.10
199	Charles Hudson	.10
200	Billy Hunter	.10
201	Pete Incaviglia	.25
202	Mike Jeffcoat	.10
203	Ferguson Jenkins	2.00
204	Alex Johnson	.10
205	Bobby Johnson	.10
206	Cliff Johnson	.10
207	Darrell Johnson	.10
208	John Henry Johnson	.10
209	Lamar Johnson	.10
210	Bobby Jones	.10
211	Odell Jones	.10
212	Mike Jorgensen	.10
213	Don Kainer	.10
214	Mike Kekich	.10
215	Steve Kemp	.10
216	Jim Kern	.10
217	Paul Kilgus	.10
218	Ed Kirkpatrick	.10
219	Darold Knowles	.10
220	Fred Koenig	.10
221	Jim Kremmel	.10
222	Chad Kreuter	.10
223	Jeff Kunkel	.10
224	Bob Lacey	.10
225	Al Lachowicz	.10
226	Joe Lahoud	.10
227	Rick Leach	.10
228	Danny Leon	.10
229	Dennis Lewallyn	.10
230	Rick Lisi	.10
231	Davey Lopes	.10
232	John Lowenstein	.10
233	Mike Loynd	.10
234	Frank Lucceshi	.10
235	Sparky Lyle	.10
236	Pete Mackanin	.10
237	Bill Madlock	.25
238	Greg Mahlberg	.10
239	Mickey Mahler	.10
240	Bob Malloy	.10
241	Ramon Manon	.10
242	Fred Manrique	.10
243	Barry Manuel	.10
244	Mike Marshall	.10
245	Billy Martin	.50
246	Mike Mason	.10
247	Terry Mathews	.10
248	Jon Matlack	.10
249	Rob Maurer	.10
250	Dave May	.10
251	Scott May	.10
252	Lee Mazzilli	.10
253	Larry McCall	.10
254	Lance McCullers	.10
255	Oddibe McDowell	.10
256	Russ McGinnis	.10
257	Joey McLaughlin	.10
258	Craig McMurtry	.10
259	Doc Medich	.10
260	Dave Meier	.10
261	Mario Mendoza	.10
262	Orlando Mercado	.10
263	Mark Mercer	.10
264	Ron Meridith	.10
265	Jim Merritt	.10
266	Gary Mielke	.10
267	Eddie Miller	.10
268	Paul Mirabella	.10
269	Dave Moates	.10
270	Dale Mohorcic	.10
271	Willie Montanez	.10
272	Tommy Moore	.10
273	Roger Moret	.10
274	Jamie Moyer	.10
275	Dale Murray	.10
276	Al Newman	.10
277	Dickie Noles	.10
278	Eric Nolte	.10
279	Nelson Norman	.10
280	Jim Norris	.10
281	Edwin Nunez	.10
282	Pete O'Brien	.10
283	Al Oliver	.25
284	Tom O'Malley	.10
285	Tom Paciorek	.10
286	Ken Pape	.10
287	Mark Parent	.10
288	Larry Parrish	.10
289	Gaylord Perry	2.00
290	Stan Perzanowski	.10
291	Fritz Peterson	.10
292	Mark Petkovsek	.10
293	Gary Pettis	.10
294	Jim Piersall	.25
295	John Poloni	.10
296	Jim Poole	.10
297	Tom Poquette	.10
298	Darrell Porter	.10
299	Ron Pruitt	.10
300	Greg Pryor	.10
301	Luis Pujols	.10
302	Pat Putnam	.10
303	Doug Rader	.10
304	Dave Rajsich	.10
305	Kevin Reimer	.10
306	Merv Rettenmund	.10
307	Mike Richardt	.10
308	Mickey Rivers	.10
309	Dave Roberts	.10
310	Leon Roberts	.10
311	Jeff Robinson	.10
312	Tom Robson	.10
313	Wayne Rosenthal	.10
314	Dave Rozema	.10
315	Jeff Russell	.10
316	Connie Ryan	.10
317	Billy Sample	.10
318	Jim Schaffer	.10
319	Calvin Schiraldi	.10
320	Dave Schmidt	.10
321	Donnie Scott	.10
322	Tony Scruggs	.10
323	Bob Sebra	.10
324	Larry See	.10
325	Sonny Siebert	.10
326	Ruben Sierra	.10
327	Charlie Silvera	.10
328	Duke Sims	.10
329	Bill Singer	.10
330	Craig Skok	.10
331	Don Slaught	.10
332	Roy Smalley	.10
333	Dan Smith	.10
334	Keith Smith	.10
335	Mike Smithson	.10
336	Eric Soderholm	.10
337	Sammy Sosa	4.00
338	Jim Spencer	.10
339	Dick Such	.10
340	Eddie Stanky	.10
341	Mike Stanley	.10
342	Rusty Staub	.35
343	James Steels	.10
344	Bill Stein	.10
345	Rick Stelmaszek	.10
346	Ray Stephens	.10
347	Dave Stewart	.10
348	Jeff Stone	.10
349	Bill Sudakis	.10
350	Jim Sundberg	.10
351	Rich Surhoff	.10
352	Greg Tabor	.10
353	Frank Tanana	.10
354	Jeff Terpko	.10
355	Stan Thomas	.10
356	Bobby Thompson	.10
357	Danny Thompson	.10
358	Dickie Thon	.10
359	Dave Tobik	.10
360	Wayne Tolleson	.10
361	Cesar Tovar	.10
362	Jim Umbarger	.10
363	Bobby Valentine	.10
364	Ellis Valentine	.10
365	Ed Vande Berg	.10
366	Dewayne Vaughn	.10
367	Mark Wagner	.10
368	Rick Waits	.10
369	Duane Walker	.10
370	Mike Wallace	.10
371	Denny Walling	.10
372	Danny Walton	.10
373	Gary Ward	.10
374	Claudell Washington	.10
375	Larue Wasington	.10
376	Chris Welsh	.10
377	Don Werner	.10
378	Len Whitehouse	.10
379	Del Wilber	.10
380	Curtis Wilkerson	.10
381	Matt Williams	.10
382	Mitch Williams	.10
383	Bump Wills	.10
384	Paul Wilmet	.10
385	Steve Wilson	.10
386	Bobby Witt	.10
387	Clyde Wright	.10
388	George Wright	.10
389	Ricky Wright	.10
390	Ned Yost	.10
391	Don Zimmer	.10
392	Richie Zisk	.10
393	Kevin Kennedy	.10
394	Steve Balboni	.10
395	Brian Bohanon	.10
396	Jeff Bronkey	.10
397	Kevin Brown	.10
398	Todd Burns	.10
399	Jose Canseco	.75
400	Cris Carpenter	.10
401	Doug Dascenzo	.10
402	Butch Davis	.10
403	Steve Dreyer	.10
404	Rob Ducey	.10
405	Julio Franco	.10
406	Jeff Frye	.10
407	Benji Gil	.10
408	Juan Gonzalez	3.00
409	Tom Henke	.10
410	David Hulse	.10
411	Jeff Huson	.10
412	Chris James	.10
413	Manuel Lee	.10
414	Craig Lefferts	.10
415	Charlie Leibrandt	.10
416	Gene Nelson	.10
417	Robb Nen	.10
418	Darren Oliver	.10
419	Rafael Palmeiro	2.00
420	Dean Palmer	.10
421	Bob Patterson	.10
422	Roger Pavlik	.10
423	Dan Peltier	.10
424	Geno Petralli	.10
425	Gary Redus	.10
426	Rick Reed	.10
427	Bill Ripken	.10
428	Ivan Rodriguez	3.00
429	Kenny Rogers	.10
430	John Russell	.10
431	Nolan Ryan	6.00
432	Mike Schooler	.10
433	Jon Shave	.10
434	Doug Strange	.10
435	Matt Whiteside	.10
436	Mickey Hatcher	.10
437	Perry Hill	.10
438	Jackie Moore	.10
439	Dave Oliver	.10
440	Claude Osteen	.10
441	Willie Upshaw	.10
442	Checklist 1-112	.10
443	Checklist 113-224	.10
444	Checklist 225-336	.10
445	Checklist 337-446	.10
446	Arlington Stadium	.10

1999 Keebler Los Angeles Dodgers

In a promotion similar to those of Mother's Cookies in the past, Keebler sponsored a kids' trading card day August 15 distributing 28-card packs to fans 14 and under. Each pack contained 21 different cards and seven duplicates to trade in an effort to complete the set. The 2-1/2" x 3-1/2" cards have borderless player photos on front with a Dodgers logo ad team-color red and blue stripes at bottom in which the player's name appears. Color backs have a team logo, a Keebler's elf logo and a few bits of player biographical data.

		NM/M
Complete Set (28):		10.00
Common Player:		.50
1	Davey Johnson	.50
2	Eric Karros	.50
3	Gary Sheffield	.75
4	Raul Mondesi	.50
5	Kevin Brown	.60
6	Mark Grudzielanek	.50
7	Todd Hollandsworth	.50
8	Todd Hundley	.50
9	Jeff Shaw	.50
10	Pedro Borbon	.50
11	Chan Ho Park	.75
12	Jose Vizcaino	.50
13	Devon White	.50
14	Darren Dreifort	.50
15	Onan Masaoka	.50
16	Dave Hansen	.50
17	Adrian Beltre	1.50
18	Ismael Valdes	.50
19	Alan Mills	.50
20	Eric Young	.50
21	Mike Maddux	.50
22	Carlos Perez	.50
23	Tripp Cromer	.50
24	Jamie Arnold	.50
25	Angel Pena	.50
26	Trenidad Hubbard	.50
27	Doug Bochtler	.50
28	Coaches/Checklist (Rick Dempsey, Rich Down, Glenn Hoffman, Manny Mota, Claude Osteen, John Shelby, Jim Tracy)	.50

San Diego Padres

In a promotion similar to those of Mother's Cookies in the past, Keebler sponsored a kids' trading card day August 1 distributing 28-card packs to fans 14 and under. Each pack contained 21 different cards and seven duplicates to trade in an effort to complete the set. The 2-1/2" x 3-1/2"

cards have borderless player photos on front with a Padres logo and team-color orange and blue stripes at bottom in which the player's name appears. Color backs have a Padres 1969-1999 logo, a Keebler's elf logo and a few bits of player biographical data.

		NM/M
Complete Set (28):		10.00
Common Player:		.50
1	Bruce Bochy	.50
2	Tony Gwynn	4.00
3	Wally Joyner	.50
4	Sterling Hitchcock	.50
5	Jim Leyritz	.50
6	Trevor Hoffman	.75
7	Quilvio Veras	.50
8	Dave Magadan	.50
9	Andy Ashby	.50
10	Damian Jackson	.50
11	Dan Miceli	.50
12	Reggie Sanders	.50
13	Chris Gomez	.50
14	Ruben Rivera	.50
15	Greg Myers	.50
16	Ed Vosberg	.50
17	John Vandor Wal	.50
18	Donne Wall	.50
19	Eric Owens	.50
20	Brian Boehringer	.50
21	Woody Williams	.50
22	Matt Clement	.50
23	Carlos Reyes	.50
24	Stan Spencer	.50
25	George Arias	.50
26	Carlos Almanzar	.50
27	Phil Nevin	.50
28	Greg Booker, Tim Flannery, Davey Lopes, Rob Picciolo, Merv Rettenmund, Dave Smith (Padres Coaches)	.50

S.F. Giants

In a promotion similar to those of Mother's Cookies in the past, Keebler sponsored a kids' trading card day distributing 28-card packs to fans 14 and under. Each pack contained 21 different cards and seven duplicates to trade in an effort to complete the set. The 2-1/2" x 3-1/2" cards have borderless player photos on front with a farewell to Candlestick Park logo and team-color orange and black stripes at bottom in which the player's name appears. Color backs have a Keebler's elf logo and a few bits of player biographical data.

		NM/M
Complete Set (28):		12.50
Common Player:		.50
1	Dusty Baker	.50
2	Barry Bonds	7.50
3	Jeff Kent	.75
4	Robb Nen	.50
5	Bill Mueller	.50
6	Russ Ortiz	.50
7	Ellis Burks	.50
8	Marvin Benard	.50
9	Kirk Rueter	.50
10	J.T. Snow	.50
11	Stan Javier	.50
12	Chris Brock	.50
13	Charlie Hayes	.50
14	Joe Nathan	.50
15	Rich Rodriguez	.50
16	Brent Mayne	.50
17	Shawn Estes	.50
18	Rich Aurilia	.50
19	Mark Gardner	.50
20	Scott Servais	.50
21	John Johnstone	.50
22	Felix Rodriguez	.50
23	Armando Rios	.50
24	Alan Embree	.50
25	F.P. Santangelo	.50
26	Jerry Spradlin	.50
27	Lon Simmons (Broadcaster)	.50
28	Giants Coaches (Carlos Alfonso, Gene Clines, Sonny Jackson, Juan Lopez, Ron Perranoski, Ron Wotus)	.50

2000 Keebler Arizona Diamondbacks

Keebler cookies sponsored a kids' trading card day, distributing 28-card packs to fans 14 and under. Each pack contained 21 different cards and seven duplicates to trade in an effort to complete the set. Round-cornered cards have borderless portrait photos with a stripe at bottom featuring player identification and team logo. Backs have player data, uniform number, biographical information and Keebler's logo.

		NM/M
Complete Set (28):		10.00
Common Player:		.50
1	Buck Showalter	.50
2	Randy Johnson	3.00
3	Luis Gonzalez	.65
4	Todd Stottlemyre	.50
5	Matt Williams	.75
6	Curt Schilling	1.50
7	Jay Bell	.50
8	Steve Finley	.50
9	Brian Anderson	.50
10	Tony Womack	.50
11	Mike Morgan	.50
12	Damian Miller	.50
13	Greg Swindell	.50
14	Greg Colbrunn	.50
15	Dan Plesac	.50
16	Craig Counsell	.50
17	Russ Springer	.50
18	Kelly Stinnett	.50
19	Alex Cabrera	.50
20	Matt Mantei	.50
21	Danny Klassen	.50
22	Hanley Frias	.50
23	Byung-Hyun Kim	.50
24	Jason Conti	.50
25	Danny Bautista	.50
26	Erubiel Durazo	.50
27	Armando Reynoso	.50
28	Coaches/Checklist	.50

L.A. Dodgers

Keebler cookies sponsored a kids'trading card day August 20, distributing 28-card packs to fans 14 and under. Each pack contained 21 different cards and seven duplicates to trade in an effort to complete the set. Round-cornered cards have borderless portrait photos with a red stripe at bottom featuring player identification and team logo. Backs have player data, uniform number, biographical information and Keebler's logo.

NM/M
Complete Set (28): 10.00
Common Player: .50
1 Davey Johnson .50
2 Eric Karros .50
3 Gary Sheffield .75
4 Kevin Brown .60
5 Shawn Green 2.50
6 Mark Grudzielanek .50
7 Todd Hollandsworth .50
8 Todd Hundley .50
9 Jeff Shaw .50
10 Adrian Beltre 1.00
11 Chan Ho Park .60
12 Jose Vizcaino .50
13 Devon White .50
14 Darren Dreifort .50
15 Onan Masaoka .50
16 Dave Hansen .50
17 Kevin Elster .50
18 Antonio Osuna .50
19 Geronimo Berroa .50
20 Orel Hershiser .65
21 Chad Kreuter .50
22 Carlos Perez .50
23 F.P. Santangelo .50
24 Terry Adams .50
25 Alex Cora .50
26 Matt Herges .50
27 Mike Fetters .50
28 Coaches/Checklist (Rick Dempsey, Claude Osteen, Rick Down, Manny Mota, Jim Tracy, Glenn Hoffman, John Shelby) .50

San Diego Padres

Keebler cookies sponsored a kids' trading card day July 16 distributing 28-card packs to fans 14 and under. Each pack contained 21 different cards and seven duplicates to trade in an effort to complete the set. Fronts of the round-cornered 2-1/2" x 3-1/2" cards have posed photos with team-color orange and blue bars at bottom with player name and team logo. Backs have player ID, jersey number and team logo.

NM/M
Complete Set (28): 10.00
Common Player: .50
1 Bruce Bochy .50
2 Tony Gwynn 4.00
3 Ryan Klesko .50
4 Sterling Hitchcock .50
5 Al Martin .50
6 Trevor Hoffman .75
7 Bret Boone .65
8 Dave Magadan .50
9 Steve Montgomery .50
10 Damian Jackson .50
11 Woody Williams .50
12 Wiki Gonzalez .50
13 Chris Gomez .50
14 Ruben Rivera .50
15 Ed Sprague .50
16 Carlton Loewer .50
17 Kory DeHaan .50
18 Donne Wall .50
19 Eric Owens .50
20 Brian Boehringer .50
21 Phil Nevin .50
22 Matt Clement .50
23 Brian Meadows .50
24 Vincente Palacios .50
25 Carlos Hernandez .50
26 Carlos Almanzar .50
27 Kevin Walker .50
28 Coaches/Checklist (Greg Booker, Tim Flannery, Ben Oglivie, Rob Picciolo, Dave Smith, Alan Trammell) .50

S.F. Giants

Keebler cookies sponsored a trading card day August 6, distributing 25,000 28-card packs to fans. Each pack contained 21 different cards and seven duplicates to trade in an effort to complete the set.

NM/M
Complete Set (28): 10.00
Common Player: .50
1 Dusty Baker .50
2 Barry Bonds 5.00
3 Jeff Kent .75
4 Robb Nen .50
5 J.T. Snow .50
6 Russ Ortiz .50
7 Ellis Burks .50
8 Bill Mueller .50
9 Shawn Estes .50
10 Marvin Benard .50
11 Kirk Rueter .50
12 Bobby Estalella .50
13 Livan Hernandez .50
14 Rich Aurilia .50
15 Alan Embree .50
16 Armando Rios .50
17 Felix Rodriguez .50
18 Doug Mirabelli .50
19 John Johnstone .50
20 Russ Davis .50
21 Joe Nathan .50
22 Aaron Fultz .50
23 Felipe Crespo .50
24 Mark Gardner .50
25 Ramon Martinez .50
26 Calvin Murray .50
27 Carlos Alfonso .50
28 Giants Coaches (Gene Clines, Sonny Jackson, Juan Lopez, Dave Righetti, Robby Thompson, Ron Wotus) .50

Seattle Mariners

Keebler cookies sponsored a trading card day at a home game August 13, distributing 20,000 28-card packs to fans. Each pack contained 21 different cards and seven duplicates to trade in an effort to complete the set. Cards are 2-1/2" x 3-1/2" with rounded corners. Fronts have borderless posed photos with a team logo at lower-left and the player name in white in a dark blue strip. Backs have a color Keebler logo and basic player information.

NM/M
Complete Set (28): 15.00
Common Player: .50
1 Lou Piniella .50
2 Alex Rodriguez 6.00
3 Jamie Moyer .50
4 Edgar Martinez .50
5 Kazuhiro Sasaki .75
6 Jay Buhner .50
7 Rickey Henderson 2.50
8 John Olerud .50
9 Aaron Sele .50
10 Charles Gipson .50
11 Arthur Rhodes .50
12 Dan Wilson .50
13 Jose Mesa .50
14 Mike Cameron .50
15 John Halama .50
16 Mark McLemore .50
17 Brett Tomko .50
18 Tom Lampkin .50
19 Freddy Garcia .50
20 John Mabry .50
21 Paul Abbott .50
22 Stan Javier .50
23 Gil Meche .50
24 David Bell .50
25 Frankie Rodriguez .50
26 Raul Ibanez .50
27 Jose Paniagua .50
28 Coaches/Checklist .50

2001 Keebler Arizona Diamondbacks

Keebler cookies sponsored a trading card day on July 29, distributing 20,000 28-card packs to fans. Each pack contained 21 different cards and seven duplicates to

trade in an effort to complete the set. Round-cornered cards have borderless portrait photos with a stripe at bottom featuring player name and team logo. Backs have player data, uniform number, biographical information and Keebler's logo.

NM/M
Complete Set (28): 10.00
Common Player: .50
1 Bob Brenly .50
2 Randy Johnson 3.00
3 Luis Gonzalez .60
4 Curt Schilling 1.50
5 Matt Williams .65
6 Todd Stottlemyre .50
7 Jay Bell .50
8 Steve Finley .50
9 Mark Grace .60
10 Brian Anderson .50
11 Tony Womack .50
12 Damian Miller .50
13 Russ Springer .50
14 Greg Colbrunn .50
15 Craig Counsell .50
16 Greg Swindell .50
17 Reggie Sanders .50
18 Matt Mantei .50
19 Danny Bautista .50
20 Mike Morgan .50
21 Erubiel Durazo .50
22 Troy Brohawn .50
23 Byung-Hyun Kim .50
24 David Dellucci .50
25 Robert Ellis .50
26 Rod Barajas .50
27 Armando Reynoso .50
28 Coaches/Checklist (Bob Melvin, Dwayne Murphy, Eddie Rodriguez, Glenn Sherlock, Chris Speier, Bob Welch) .50

L.A. Dodgers

Keebler cookies sponsored a kids' trading card day, on August 19, distributing 28-card packs to fans 14 and under. Each pack contained 21 different cards and seven duplicates to trade in an effort to complete the set. Round-cornered cards have borderless portrait photos with a stripe at bottom featuring player name and team logo. Backs have player data, uniform number, biographical information and Keebler's logo.

NM/M
Complete Set (28): 10.00
Common Player: .50
1 Jim Tracy .50
2 Eric Karros .50
3 Shawn Green 2.00
4 Kevin Brown .60
5 Gary Sheffield .75
6 Mark Grudzielanek .50
7 Darren Dreifort .50
8 Dave Hansen .50
9 Jeff Shaw .50
10 Chad Kreuter .50
11 Chan Ho Park .60
12 Adrian Beltre 1.00
13 Marquis Grissom .50
14 Alex Cora .50
15 Tom Goodwin .50
16 Gregg Olson .50
17 Andy Ashby .50
18 Paul LoDuca .60
19 Luke Prokopec .50
20 Mike Fetters .50
21 Giovanni Carrara .50
22 Chris Donnels .50
23 Matt Herges .50
24 Jeff Reboulet .50
25 Terry Adams .50
26 Hiram Bocachica .50
27 Jesse Orosco .50
28 Dodgers coaches/checklist (Travis Barbary, Jack Clark, Jim Colborn, Glenn Hoffman, Jim Lett, Manny Mota, Jim Riggleman, John Shelby) .50

San Diego Padres

Keebler cookies sponsored a kids' trading card day July 22, distributing 15,000 28-card packs to fans 14 and under. Each pack contained 21 different cards and seven duplicates to trade in an effort to complete the set. Fronts of the round-cornered 2-1/2" x 3-1/2" cards have posed photos with a dark blue bar at bottom with player name and team logo. Backs have player data, jersey number and color team and sponsor's logos.

NM/M
Complete Set (28): 10.00
Common Player: .50
1 Bruce Bochy .50
2 Tony Gwynn 4.00
3 Trevor Hoffman .60
4 Rickey Henderson 2.00
5 Ryan Klesko .50
6 Phil Nevin .50
7 Ben Davis .50
8 Woody Williams .50
9 Chris Gomez .50
10 Dave Magadan .50
11 Wiki Gonzalez .50
12 Bobby J. Jones .50
13 Damian Jackson .50
14 Kevin Jarvis .50
15 Bubba Trammell .50
16 Kevin Walker .50
17 Mark Kotsay .50
18 Alex Arias .50
19 Jay Witasick .50
20 Mike Darr .50
21 Adam Eaton .75
22 Wascar Serrano .50
23 Jose Nunez .50
24 Brian Tollberg .50
25 Donaldo Mendez .50
26 Tom Davey .50
27 Rodney Myers .50
28 Coaches/Checklist (Greg Booker, Duane Espy, Tim Flannery, Rob Picciolo, Dave Smith, Alan Trammell) .50

San Francisco Giants

Keebler cookies sponsored a trading card day, on September 2, distributing 28-card packs to the first 25,000 fans. Each pack contained 20 different cards and eight duplicates to trade in an effort to complete the set. Round-cornered cards have borderless portrait photos with a stripe at bottom featuring player name and team logo. Backs have player data, uniform number, biographical information and Keebler's logo.

NM/M
Complete Set (28): 10.00
Common Player: .50
1 Dusty Baker .50
2 Jeff Kent .75
3 Barry Bonds 6.00
4 Robb Nen .50
5 J.T. Snow .50
6 Russ Ortiz .50
7 Rich Aurilia .50
8 Benito Santiago .50
9 Shawn Estes .50
10 Marvin Benard .50
11 Kirk Reuter .50
12 Calvin Murray .50
13 Livan Hernandez .50
14 Eric Davis .50
15 Aaron Fultz .50
16 Armando Rios .50
17 Felix Rodriguez .50
18 Shawon Dunston .50
19 Mark Gardner .50
20 Ramon Martinez .50
21 Pedro Feliz .50
22 Chad Zerbe .50
23 Felipe Crespo .50
24 Tim Worrell .50
25 Edwards Guzman .50
26 Ryan Vogelsong .50
27 Brian Boehringer .50
28 Coaches/Checklist (Carlos Alfonso, Gene Clines, Sonny Jackson, Juan Lopez, Dave Righetti, Robby Thompson, Ron Wotus) .50

Seattle Mariners

Keebler cookies sponsored a kids' trading card day at Safeco Field July 15, distributing 20,000 28-card packs to fans. Each pack contained 21 different cards and seven duplicates to trade in an effort to complete the set. Cards are 2-1/2" x 3-1/2" with rounded corners. Fronts have borderless posed photos with a team logo at lower-left and the player name in white in a dark blue strip. Backs have a color Keebler logo and basic player information.

NM/M
Complete Set (28): 10.00
Common Player: .50
1 Lou Piniella .50
2 Edgar Martinez .50
3 Mike Cameron .50
4 Jamie Moyer .50
5 Ichiro Suzuki 6.00
6 Jay Buhner .50
7 Kazuhiro Sasaki .50
8 John Olerud .50
9 Aaron Sele .50
10 Bret Boone .65
11 Arthur Rhodes .50
12 Al Martin .50
13 Jeff Nelson .50
14 Dan Wilson .50
15 John Halama .50
16 Stan Javier .50
17 Brett Tomko .50
18 Carlos Guillen .50
19 Freddy Garcia .50
20 David Bell .50
21 Paul Abbott .50
22 Mark McLemore .50
23 Tom Lampkin .50
24 Charles Gipson .50
25 Ryan Franklin .50
26 Anthony Sanders .50
27 Jose Paniagua .50
28 Coaches/Checklist (Lee Elia, John McLaren, John Moses, Dave Myers, Gerald Perry, Bryan Price, Matt Sinatro) .50

2002 Keebler Arizona Diamondbacks

Keebler cookies sponsored a kids' trading card day July 28, distributing 20,000 28-card packs to fans 14 and under. Each pack contained 20 different cards and eight duplicates to trade in an effort to complete the set. Fronts of the round-cornered 2-1/2" x 3-1/2" cards have posed photos with a purple stripe at bottom with player name and team logo. Color-printed backs have player data, jersey number and team and sponsor's logos.

NM/M
Complete Set (28): 10.00
Common Player: .50
1 Bob Brenly .50
2 Luis Gonzalez .60
3 Randy Johnson 3.00
4 Curt Schilling 1.50
5 Matt Williams .65
6 Todd Stottlemyre .50
7 Jay Bell .50
8 Steve Finley .50
9 Mark Grace .60
10 Brian Anderson .50
11 Tony Womack .50
12 Damian Miller .50
13 Erubiel Durazo .50
14 Craig Counsell .50
15 David Dellucci .50
16 Greg Swindell .50
17 Greg Colbrunn .50
18 Rick Helling .50
19 Danny Bautista .50
20 Mike Morgan .50
21 Rod Barajas .50
22 Byung-Hyun Kim .50
23 Mike Myers .50
24 Jose Guillen .50
25 Miguel Batista .50
26 Junior Spivey .50
27 Quinton McCracken .50
28 Coaches/Checklist (Chuck Kniffin, Bob Melvin, Dwayne Murphy, Eddie Rodriguez, Glenn Sherlock, Robin Yount) .50

L.A. Dodgers

Keebler cookies sponsored a kids' trading card day in August, distributing 28-card packs to fans 14 and under. Each pack contained 20 different cards and eight duplicates to trade in an effort to complete the set. Fronts of the round-cornered 2-1/2" x 3-1/2" cards have posed photos with a red stripe at bottom with player name and team logo. Color-printed backs have player data, jersey number and team and sponsor's logos.

NM/M
Complete Set (28): 10.00
Common Player: .50
1 Jim Tracy .50
2 Eric Karros .50
3 Shawn Green 1.50
4 Kevin Brown .65
5 Paul LoDuca .65
6 Mark Grudzielanek .50
7 Brian Jordan .50
8 Kazuhisa Ishii 1.00
9 Hideo Nomo 1.50
10 Dave Hansen .50
11 Chad Kreuter .50
12 Adrian Beltre 1.00
13 Marquis Grissom .50
14 Eric Gagne .65
15 Odalis Perez .50
16 Dave Roberts .50
17 Omar Daal .50
18 Alex Cora .50
19 Andy Ashby .50
20 Hiram Bocachica .50
21 Darren Dreifort .50
22 Jesse Orosco .50
23 Cesar Izturis .50
24 Terry Mulholland .50
25 Jeff Reboulet .50
26 Paul Quantrill .50
27 Giovanni Carrara .50
28 Checklist/Coaches (Robert Flippo, Jack Clark, Jim Colborn, Glenn Hoffman, Jim Lett, Manny Mota, Jim Riggleman, John Shelby) .50

San Diego Padres

Keebler cookies sponsored a kids' trading card day July 21, distributing 28-card packs to fans 14 and under. Each pack contained 21 different cards and seven duplicates to trade in an effort to complete the set. Fronts of the round-cornered 2-1/2" x 3-1/2" cards have posed photos with an orange and dark blue stripe at bottom with player name and team logo. Color-printed backs have player data, jersey number and color team and sponsor's logos.

NM/M
Complete Set (28): 7.50
Common Player: .50
1 Bruce Bochy .50
2 Trevor Hoffman .60
3 Sean Burroughs 1.50
4 Ryan Klesko .50
5 Phil Nevin .50
6 Kevin Jarvis .50
7 Ron Gant .50
8 Ramon Vazquez .50
9 Alan Embree .50
10 Wiki Gonzalez .50
11 Bobby J. Jones .50
12 Mark Kotsay .50
13 Brett Tomko .50
14 Bubba Trammell .50
15 Tom Lampkin .50
16 Steve Reed .50
17 Deivi Cruz .50
18 Brian Tollberg .50
19 Trenidad Hubbard .50
20 Jose Nunez .50
21 Ray Lankford .50
22 Kevin Walker .50
23 Dennis Tankersley .50
24 Jeremy Fikac .50
25 D'Angelo Jimenez .50
26 Brian Lawrence .50
27 Adam Eaton .50
28 Coaches/Checklist (Greg Booker, Darrel Akerfelds, Duane Espy, Tim Flannery, Rob Picciolo, Alan Trammell) .50

San Francisco Giants

Keebler cookies sponsored a kids' trading card day August 25, distributing 28-card packs to fans 14 and under. Each pack contained 21 different cards and seven duplicates to trade in an effort to complete the set. Fronts of the round-cornered 2-1/2" x 3-1/2" cards have posed photos with an orange and dark black stripe at bottom with player name and team logo. Color-printed backs have player data, jersey number and team and sponsor's logos.

NM/M
Complete Set (28): 10.00
Common Player: .50
1 Dusty Baker .50
2 Barry Bonds 6.00
3 Jeff Kent .75
4 Robb Nen .50
5 J.T. Snow .50
6 Russ Ortiz .50
7 Rich Aurilia .50
8 Marvin Benard .50
9 Kirk Reuter .50
10 Benito Santiago .50
11 Jason Schmidt .50
12 Reggie Sanders .50
13 Livan Hernandez .50
14 Tsuyoshi Shinjo .50
15 Aaron Fultz .50
16 Ramon Martinez .50
17 Felix Rodriguez .50
18 Shawon Dunston .50
19 Tim Worrell .50
20 David Bell .50
21 Pedro Feliz .50
22 Chad Zerbe .50
23 Damon Minor .50
24 Yorvit Torrealba .50
25 Jay Witasick .50
26 Ryan Jensen .50
27 Jason Christiansen .50
28 Coaches/Checklist (Carlos Alfonso, Gene Clines, Sonny Jackson, Joe Lefebvre, Juan Lopez, Dave Righetti, Ron Wotus) .50

Seattle Mariners

Keebler cookies sponsored a kids' trading card day August 4, distributing 28-card packs to fans 14 and under. Each pack contained 21 different cards and seven duplicates to trade in an effort to complete the set. Fronts of the round-cornered 2-1/2" x 3-1/2" cards have posed photos with a dark blue strip at bottom with player name and team logo. Color-printed backs have player data, jersey number and color team and sponsor's logos.

NM/M
Complete Set (28): 10.00
Common Player: .50
1 Lou Piniella .50
2 Ichiro Suzuki 5.00
3 Edgar Martinez .50
4 Jamie Moyer .50
5 Mike Cameron .50
6 Bret Boone .75
7 Kazuhiro Sasaki .65
8 Mark McLemore .50
9 John Olerud .50
10 Arthur Rhodes .50
11 Ruben Sierra .50
12 Freddy Garcia .50
13 Dan Wilson .50
14 Jeff Nelson .50
15 John Halama .50
16 Carlos Guillen .50
17 Ben Davis .50
18 James Baldwin .50
19 Jeff Cirillo .50
20 Shigetoshi Hasegawa .50
21 Paul Abbott .50
22 Desi Relaford .50
23 Ryan Franklin .50
24 Luis Ugueto .50
25 Charles Gipson .50
26 Joel Pineiro .50
27 Rafael Soriano .50
28 M's Coaches .50

2003 Keebler Arizona Diamondbacks

Keebler cookies sponsored a kids' trading card day July 27, distributing 20,000 28-card packs to fans 14 and under. Each pack contained 20 different cards and eight duplicates to trade in an effort to complete the set. Fronts of the round-cornered 2-1/2" x 3-1/2" cards have posed photos with a purple stripe at bottom with player name and team logo. Color-printed backs have player data, jersey number and team and sponsor's logos.

NM/M
Complete Set (28): 12.00
Common Player: .50
1 Bob Brenly .50
2 Luis Gonzalez .60
3 Randy Johnson 3.00
4 Curt Schilling 1.50
5 Danny Bautista .50
6 Matt Mantei .50
7 Craig Counsell .50
8 Steve Finley .50
9 Mark Grace .60
10 Alex Cintron .50
11 Tony Womack .50
12 Chad Moeller .50
13 Shea Hillenbrand .50
14 Miguel Batista .50
15 David Dellucci .50
16 Elmer Dessens .50
17 Lyle Overbay .75
18 Mike Myers .50
19 Quinton McCracken .50
20 Rod Barajas .50
21 Junior Spivey .50
22 Stephen Randolph .50
23 Carlos Baerga .50
24 Mike Koplove .50
25 Brandon Webb 1.00
26 Oscar Villarreal .50
27 Bret Prinz .50
28 Coaches/Checklist (Mark Davis, Chuck Kniffin, Dwayne Murphy, Eddie Rodriguez, Glenn Sherlock, Robin Yount) .50

L.A. Dodgers

Keebler cookies sponsored a kids' trading card night August 24, distributing 20,000 28-card packs to fans 14 and under. Each pack contained 20 different cards and eight duplicates to trade in an effort to complete the set. Fronts of the round-cornered 2-1/2" x 3-1/2" cards have posed photos with an orange stripe at bottom with player name and team logo. Color-printed backs have player data, jersey number and team and sponsor's logos.

NM/M
Complete Set (28): 7.50
Common Player: .50
1 Jim Tracy .50
2 Shawn Green 1.00
3 Paul LoDuca .60
4 Kevin Brown .60
5 Adrian Beltre 1.00
6 Eric Gagne .50
7 Brian Jordan .50
8 Kazuhisa Ishii .50
9 Fred McGriff .50
10 Dave Roberts .50
11 Hideo Nomo 1.00
12 Alex Cora .50
13 Paul Quantrill .50
14 Darren Dreifort .50
15 Odalis Perez .50
16 Cesar Izturis .50
17 Todd Hundley .50
18 Daryle Ward .50
19 Paul Shuey .50
20 Guillermo Mota .50
21 Andy Ashby .50
22 Tom Martin .50
23 Jason Romano .50
24 Jolbert Cabrera .50
25 Mike Kinkade .50
26 Ron Coomer .50
27 David Ross .50
28 Coaches .50

San Diego Padres

Keebler cookies sponsored a kids' trading card day distributing 28-card packs to fans 14 and under. Each pack contained 21 different cards and seven duplicates to trade in an effort to complete the set. Fronts of the round-cornered 2-1/2" x 3-1/2" cards have posed photos with an orange and dark blue stripe at bottom with player name and team logo. Color-printed backs have player data, jersey number and color team and sponsor's logos.

NM/M
Complete Set (28): 5.00
Common Player: .50
1 Bruce Bochy .50
2 Trevor Hoffman .50
3 Phil Nevin .50
4 Ryan Klesko .50
5 Sean Burroughs .75
6 Brian Lawrence .50
7 Rondell White .50
8 Ramon Vazquez .50
9 Mark Kotsay .50
10 Dave Hansen .50
11 Jaret Wright .50
12 Gary Bennett .50
13 Brandon Villafuerte .50
14 Lou Merloni .50
15 Jesse Orosco .50
16 Keith Lockhart .50
17 Kevin Walker .50
18 Mark Loretta .50
19 Kevin Jarvis .50
20 Xavier Nady .50
21 Jake Peavy .50
22 Mike Matthews .50
23 Brian Buchanan .50
24 Luther Hackman .50
25 Adam Eaton .50
26 Matt Herges .50
27 Jay Witasick .50
28 Coaches/Checklist (Darrel Akerfelds, Darren Balsley, Davey Lopes, Dave Magadan, Mark Merila, Tony Muser, Rob Picciolo) .50

S.F. Giants

Keebler cookies sponsored a kids' trading card day August 10, distributing 28-card packs to fans 14 and under. Each pack contained 21 different cards and seven duplicates to trade in an effort to complete the set. Fronts of the round-cornered 2-1/2" x 3-1/2" cards have posed photos with an orange stripe at bottom with player name and team logo. Color-printed backs have player data, jersey number and color team and sponsor's logos.

NM/M
Complete Set (28): 10.00
Common Player: .50
1 Felipe Alou .50
2 Barry Bonds 4.00
3 Rich Aurilia .50
4 Robb Nen .50
5 J.T. Snow .50
6 Kirk Reuter .50
7 Benito Santiago .50
8 Jose Cruz Jr. .50
9 Damian Moss .50
10 Ray Durham .50
11 Jason Schmidt .50
12 Marquis Grissom .50
13 Kurt Ainsworth .50
14 Andres Galarraga .50
15 Scott Eyre .50
16 Yorvit Torrealba .50
17 Felix Rodriguez .50
18 Edgardo Alfonzo .50
19 Tim Worrell .50
20 Pedro Feliz .50
21 Jesse Foppert .50
22 Chad Zerbe .50
23 Neifi Perez .50
24 Jason Christiansen .50
25 Marvin Benard .50
26 Jim Brower .50
27 Joe Nathan .50
28 Coaches (Carlos Alfonzo, Mark Gardner, Gene Glynn, Bill Hayes, Joe Lefebvre, Luis Pujols, Dave Righetti, Ron Wotus) .50

Seattle Mariners

Keebler cookies sponsored a kids' trading card day July 13, distributing 28-card packs to fans 14 and under. Each pack contained 21 different cards and seven duplicates to trade in an effort to complete the set. Fronts of the round-cornered 2-1/2" x 3-1/2" cards have posed photos with a dark blue stripe at bottom with player name and team logo. Color-printed backs have player data, jersey number and color team and sponsor's logos.

NM/M
Complete Set (28): 10.00
Common Player: .50
1 Bob Melvin .50
2 Ichiro Suzuki 4.00
3 Edgar Martinez .50
4 Jamie Moyer .50
5 Mike Cameron .50
6 Bret Boone .75
7 Kazuhiro Sasaki .60
8 John Olerud .50
9 Mark McLemore .50
10 Arthur Rhodes .50
11 Randy Winn .50
12 Freddy Garcia .50
13 Dan Wilson .50
14 Jeff Nelson .50
15 Carlos Guillen .50
16 Ryan Franklin .50
17 Ben Davis .50
18 Joel Pineiro .50
19 Jeff Cirillo .50
20 Shigetoshi Hasegawa .50
21 Greg Colbrunn .50
22 John Mabry .50
23 Julio Mateo .50
24 Willie Bloomquist .75
25 Gil Meche .50
26 Giovanni Carrara .50
27 Chris Snelling .50
28 M's Coaches .50

1986 Keller's Butter Phillies

It's a good thing the Keller's Butter set of six Philadelphia Phillies players is downright unattractive or their value would be sky high. One card was printed on each one pound package of butter. The 2-1/2" x 2-3/4" cards feature crude drawings of the players, the backs are blank.

NM/M
Complete Set (6): 15.00
Common Player: 1.00
(1) Steve Carlton 4.00
(2) Von Hayes 1.00
(3) Gary Redus 1.00
(4) Juan Samuel 1.00
(5) Mike Schmidt 8.00
(6) Glenn Wilson 1.00

1981 Kellogg's

"Bigger" is the word to best describe Kellogg's 1981 card set. Not only were the cards themselves larger than ever before at 2-1/2" x 3-1/2", but the size of the set was increased to 66, the largest since the 75-card issues of 1970-71. The '81 Kellogg's set was available only as complete sets by mail. It is thought that the wider format of the 1981s may help prevent the problems of curling and cracking from which other years of Kellogg's issues suffer.

		NM/M
Complete Set (66):		15.00
Common Player:		.50
1	George Foster	.50
2	Jim Palmer	1.50
3	Reggie Jackson	2.50
4	Al Oliver	.50
5	Mike Schmidt	3.00
6	Nolan Ryan	7.50
7	Bucky Dent	.50
8	George Brett	3.00
9	Jim Rice	.75
10	Steve Garvey	.75
11	Willie Stargell	1.50
12	Phil Niekro	1.00
13	Dave Parker	.50
14	Cesar Cedeno	.50
15	Don Baylor	.50
16	J.R. Richard	.50
17	Tony Perez	1.00
18	Eddie Murray	1.50
19	Chet Lemon	.50
20	Ben Oglivie	.50
21	Dave Winfield	1.50
22	Joe Morgan	1.50
23	Vida Blue	.50
24	Willie Wilson	.50
25	Steve Henderson	.50
26	Rod Carew	1.50
27	Garry Templeton	.50
28	Dave Concepcion	.50
29	Davey Lopes	.50
30	Ken Landreaux	.50
31	Keith Hernandez	.50
32	Cecil Cooper	.50
33	Rickey Henderson	3.00
34	Frank White	.50
35	George Hendrick	.50
36	Reggie Smith	.50
37	Tug McGraw	.50
38	Tom Seaver	1.50
39	Ken Singleton	.50
40	Fred Lynn	.50
41	Rich "Goose" Gossage	.50
42	Terry Puhl	.50
43	Larry Bowa	.50
44	Phil Garner	.50
45	Ron Guidry	.50
46	Lee Mazzilli	.50
47	Dave Kingman	.50
48	Carl Yastrzemski	2.00
49	Rick Burleson	.50
50	Steve Carlton	1.50
51	Alan Trammell	.75
52	Tommy John	.50
53	Paul Molitor	1.50
54	Joe Charboneau	1.00
55	Rick Langford	.50
56	Bruce Sutter	1.00
57	Robin Yount	1.50
58	Steve Stone	.50
59	Larry Gura	.50
60	Mike Flanagan	.50
61	Bob Horner	.50
62	Bruce Bochte	.50
63	Pete Rose	6.00
64	Buddy Bell	.50
65	Johnny Bench	2.00
66	Mike Hargrove	.50

1982 Kellogg's

For the second straight year in 1982, Kellogg's cards were not inserted into cereal boxes, but had to be obtained by sending cash and box tops to the company for complete sets. The '82 cards were downsized both in number of cards in the set - 64 - and in physical dimensions, 2-1/8" x 3-1/4".

		NM/M
Complete Set (64):		15.00
Common Player:		.25
1	Richie Zisk	.25
2	Bill Buckner	.25
3	George Brett	3.00
4	Rickey Henderson	1.50
5	Jack Morris	.25
6	Ozzie Smith	2.00
7	Rollie Fingers	1.00
8	Tom Seaver	2.00
9	Fernando Valenzuela	.25
10	Hubie Brooks	.25
11	Nolan Ryan	7.50
12	Dave Winfield	1.50
13	Bob Horner	.25
14	Reggie Jackson	2.50
15	Burt Hooton	.25
16	Mike Schmidt	3.00
17	Bruce Sutter	1.00
18	Pete Rose	6.00
19	Dave Kingman	.25
20	Neil Allen	.25
21	Don Sutton	1.00
22	Dave Concepcion	.25
23	Keith Hernandez	.25
24	Gary Carter	1.50
25	Carlton Fisk	1.50
26	Ron Guidry	.25
27	Steve Carlton	1.50
28	Robin Yount	1.50
29	John Castino	.25
30	Johnny Bench	2.00
31	Bob Knepper	.25
32	Rich "Goose" Gossage	.25
33	Buddy Bell	.25
34	Art Howe	.25
35	Tony Armas	.25
36	Phil Niekro	1.00
37	Len Barker	.25
38	Bobby Grich	.25
39	Steve Kemp	.25
40	Kirk Gibson	.25
41	Carney Lansford	.25
42	Jim Palmer	1.50
43	Carl Yastrzemski	2.00
44	Rick Burleson	.25
45	Dwight Evans	.25
46	Ron Cey	.25
47	Steve Garvey	.50
48	Dave Parker	.25
49	Mike Easler	.25
50	Dusty Baker	.25
51	Rod Carew	1.50
52	Chris Chambliss	.25
53	Tim Raines	.25
54	Chet Lemon	.25
55	Bill Madlock	.25
56	George Foster	.25
57	Dwayne Murphy	.25
58	Ken Singleton	.25
59	Mike Norris	.25
60	Cecil Cooper	.25
61	Al Oliver	.25
62	Willie Wilson	.25
63	Vida Blue	.25
64	Eddie Murray	1.50

1983 Kellogg's

In its 14th consecutive year of baseball card issue, Kellogg's returned to the policy of inserting single cards into cereal boxes, as well as offering complete sets by a mail-in box top redemption offer. The 3-D cards themselves returned to a narrow 1-7/8" x 3-1/4" format, while the set size was reduced to 60 cards.

		NM/M
Complete Set (60):		15.00
Common Player:		.40
1	Rod Carew	1.50
2	Rollie Fingers	1.00
3	Reggie Jackson	2.50
4	George Brett	3.00
5	Hal McRae	.40
6	Pete Rose	6.00
7	Fernando Valenzuela	.40
8	Rickey Henderson	1.50
9	Carl Yastrzemski	2.00
10	Rich "Goose" Gossage	.40
11	Eddie Murray	1.50
12	Buddy Bell	.40
13	Jim Rice	.60
14	Robin Yount	1.50
15	Dave Winfield	1.50
16	Harold Baines	.40
17	Garry Templeton	.40
18	Bill Madlock	.40
19	Pete Vuckovich	.40
20	Pedro Guerrero	.40
21	Ozzie Smith	2.00
22	George Foster	.40
23	Willie Wilson	.40
24	Johnny Ray	.40
25	George Hendrick	.40
26	Andre Thornton	.40
27	Leon Durham	.40
28	Cecil Cooper	.40
29	Don Baylor	.40
30	Lonnie Smith	.40
31	Nolan Ryan	7.50
32	Dan Quiesenberry (Quisenberry)	.40
33	Len Barker	.40
34	Neil Allen	.40
35	Jack Morris	.40
36	Dave Stieb	.40
37	Bruce Sutter	1.00
38	Jim Sundberg	.40
39	Jim Palmer	1.50
40	Lance Parrish	.40
41	Floyd Bannister	.40
42	Larry Gura	.40
43	Britt Burns	.40
44	Toby Harrah	.40
45	Steve Carlton	1.50
46	Greg Minton	.40
47	Gorman Thomas	.40
48	Jack Clark	.40
49	Keith Hernandez	.40
50	Greg Luzinski	.40
51	Fred Lynn	.40
52	Dale Murphy	.75
53	Kent Hrbek	.40
54	Bob Horner	.40
55	Gary Carter	1.50
56	Carlton Fisk	1.50
57	Dave Concepcion	.40
58	Mike Schmidt	3.00
59	Bill Buckner	.40
60	Bobby Grich	.40

1991 Kellogg's Baseball Greats

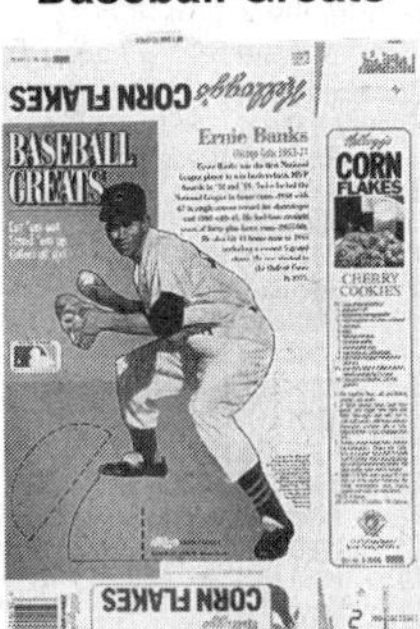

Six Hall of Famers are featured on the backs of 7- and 12-ounce Corn Flakes boxes. The photos are designed to be cut out and assembled as a stand-up figure. A career summary also appears on the box back.

		NM/M
Complete Set (6):		12.00
Common Player:		2.00
(1)	Hank Aaron	4.00
(2)	Ernie Banks	2.50
(3)	Yogi Berra	2.50
(4)	Lou Brock	2.00
(5)	Steve Carlton	2.00
(6)	Bob Gibson	2.00

1991 Kellogg's Leyendas

These bilingual (English/Spanish) cards honoring past Hispanic stars were inserted in several brands of Kellogg's cereal in selected geographic areas. Fronts have an action player photo, while backs have a black-and-white portrait photo, biographical details, career stats and highlights.

		NM/M
Complete Set (11):		9.00
Common Player:		.50
(1)	Bert Campaneris	.50
(2)	Rod Carew	1.00
(3)	Rico Carty	.50
(4)	Cesar Cedeno	.50
(5)	Orlando Cepeda	1.00
(6)	Roberto Clemente	6.00
(7)	Mike Cuellar	.50
(8)	Ed Figueroa	.50
(9)	Minnie Minoso	.75
(10)	Manny Sanguillen	.50
(11)	Header card	.25

1991 Kellogg's 3-D

In 1991, specially-marked packages of Kellogg's Corn Flakes included 3-D baseball cards, resuming a tradition that began in 1970 and continued without interruption until 1983. In the 1991 edition, there are 15 cards to collect, featuring many of the greatest living retired stars in the game. Most of the players are in the Hall of Fame. The card fronts show two pictures of the player, while the backs include career highlights and a portrait. The cards are 2-1/2" x 3-5/16", numbered and were made by Sportflics. A complete set was available via a mail-in offer for $4.95 plus proofs of purchase.

		NM/M
Complete Set (15):		4.50
Common Player:		.25
1	Gaylord Perry	.25
2	Hank Aaron	1.00
3	Willie Mays	1.00
4	Ernie Banks	.75
5	Bob Gibson	.50
6	Harmon Killebrew	.50
7	Rollie Fingers	.25
8	Steve Carlton	.50
9	Billy Williams	.25
10	Lou Brock	.25
11	Yogi Berra	.75
12	Warren Spahn	.50
13	Boog Powell	.25
14	Don Baylor	.25
15	Ralph Kiner	.25

1992 Kellogg's 3-D

Kellogg's cereal company created a 10-card 1992 All Star set of retired stars, with one card inserted in specially-marked boxes of corn flakes, and complete sets available by mail. The cards, produced by Sportflics, feature two sequential action images on each front. Red, white and blue designs comprise the border, with yellow bands above and beneath the photo. On back is a black-and-white portrait photo, plus a career summary, a few stats, and the logos of the cereal company, the Major League Baseball Players Alumni and Sportflics. As in the previous year, cards are slightly longer, at 2-1/2" x 2-5/16", than standard size. Also available by mail was a large, colorful cardboard display in which the cards could be placed.

		NM/M
Complete Set (10):		2.00
Common Player:		.25
1	Willie Stargell	.50
2	Tony Perez	.50
3	Jim Palmer	.50
4	Rod Carew	.50
5	Tom Seaver	.65
6	Phil Niekro	.50
7	Bill Madlock	.25
8	Jim Rice	.35
9	Dan Quisenberry	.25
10	Mike Schmidt	1.00

Canadian

Very similar in format to the American version, 3-D cards of 10 baseball stars of the past were found in packages of Kellogg's Frosted Flakes. Backs of the Canadian cards are printed in both English and French, which left no room for a card number, so the checklist provided here is alphabetical.

		NM/M
Complete Set (10):		8.00
Common Player:		.75
(1)	Rod Carew	1.00
(2)	Bill Madlock	.75
(3)	Phil Niekro	1.00
(4)	Jim Palmer	1.00
(5)	Tony Perez	1.00
(6)	Dan Quisenberry	.75
(7)	Jim Rice	.75
(8)	Mike Schmidt	3.00
(9)	Tom Seaver	1.50
(10)	Willie Stargell	1.00

1994 Kellogg's Clemente Collection

To commemorate the life and career of its greatest sports hero, special boxes of Kellogg's Corn Flakes sold in Puerto Rico for a time in 1994 contained one of three special cards in a cello pack. The 2-1/2" x 3-1/2" cards have color photos on front bordered in bright colors. A home plate design at top-left reads: "Kellogg's Clemente Coleccion Classico." Black-and-white backs are printed in Spanish, have personal data, career stats, highlights and a portrait photo.

		NM/M
Complete Set (3):		35.00
Common Card:		12.50
1	Roberto Clemente (Bat on shoulder.)	12.50
2	Roberto Clemente (Running, black helmet.)	12.50
3	Roberto Clemente (Running, yellow helmet.)	12.50

1987 Key Food Discs

(See 1987 Super Stars Discs for checklist and price guide.)

1988 Key Food Discs

(See 1988 Super Stars Discs for checklist and price guide.)

1988 King-B

Created by Mike Schechter Associates, this set consists of 24 numbered discs, 2-3/4" in diameter. The cards were inserted in specially marked 7/16 ounce tubs of Jerky Stuff (shredded beef jerky). Fronts feature full-color photos surrounded by a blue border. The King-B logo appears in the upper left portion of the disc. Backs are printed in blue on white stock and carry player personal and playing information. Team insignias have been airbrushed from the players' caps and jerseys.

		NM/M
Complete Set (24):		15.00
Common Player:		.50
Uncut Sheet:		20.00
1	Mike Schmidt	1.50
2	Dale Murphy	.65
3	Kirby Puckett	1.00
4	Ozzie Smith	1.00
5	Tony Gwynn	1.00
6	Mark McGwire	2.50
7	George Brett	1.50
8	Darryl Strawberry	.50
9	Wally Joyner	.50
10	Cory Snyder	.50
11	Barry Bonds	3.00
12	Darrell Evans	.50
13	Mike Scott	.50
14	Andre Dawson	.65
15	Don Mattingly	1.50
16	Candy Maldonado	.50
17	Alvin Davis	.50

18	Carlton Fisk	.75
19	Fernando Valenzuela	.50
20	Roger Clemens	1.50
21	Larry Parrish	.50
22	Eric Davis	.50
23	Paul Molitor	.75
24	Cal Ripken, Jr.	3.00

1989 King-B

The second King-B set created by Mike Schechter Associates again consists of 24 circular baseball cards measuring 2-3/4" in diameter. The cards were inserted into specially-marked tubs of "Jerky Stuff." Fronts feature full-color photos bordered in red. The King-B logo appears in the upper left portion of the disc. Like the 1988 set, the team insignias have airbrushed from uniforms and caps. The backs are printed in red and display personal information and stats.

		NM/M
Complete Set (24):		15.00
Common Player:		.50
1	Kirk Gibson	.50
2	Eddie Murray	1.50
3	Wade Boggs	2.00
4	Mark McGwire	3.00
5	Ryne Sandberg	2.00
6	Ozzie Guillen	.50
7	Chris Sabo	.50
8	Joe Carter	.50
9	Alan Trammell	.50
10	Nolan Ryan	4.00
11	Bo Jackson	.75
12	Orel Hershiser	.50
13	Robin Yount	1.50
14	Frank Viola	.50
15	Darryl Strawberry	.50
16	Dave Winfield	1.50
17	Jose Canseco	.75
18	Von Hayes	.50
19	Andy Van Slyke	.50
20	Pedro Guerrero	.50
21	Tony Gwynn	2.00
22	Will Clark	.50
23	Danny Jackson	.50
24	Pete Incaviglia	.50

1990 King-B

King-B meat products offered baseball player discs inside specially-marked packages in 1990, the third year in a row the company inserted the discs with shredded beef jerky. Each disc measures 2-3/4" across and uses full-color pictures on the front. The backs have biographical information and statistics. Team insignias have been airbrushed from caps and uniforms. As in the first two years of the promotion, there are 24 cards in the set.

		NM/M
Complete Set (24):		8.00
Common Player:		.50
1	Mike Scott	.50
2	Kevin Mitchell	.50
3	Tony Gwynn	.75
4	Ozzie Smith	.75
5	Kirk Gibson	.50
6	Tim Raines	.50
7	Von Hayes	.50
8	Bobby Bonilla	.50
9	Wade Boggs	.75
10	Chris Sabo	.50
11	Dale Murphy	.65
12	Cory Snyder	.50
13	Fred McGriff	.50
14	Don Mattingly	1.00
15	Jerome Walton	.50
16	Ken Griffey Jr.	2.50
17	Bo Jackson	.65
18	Robin Yount	.65
19	Rickey Henderson	.65
20	Jim Abbott	.50
21	Kirby Puckett	.75
22	Nolan Ryan	3.00
23	Gregg Olson	.50
24	Lou Whitaker	.50

1991 King-B

The 1991 release of baseball player discs in cans of shredded beef snack was labeled "Fourth Annual Collectors' Edition." Once again the discs are 2-3/8" in diameter and feature player photos on which uniform logos have been removed for lack of an MLB license. Front border is in green; backs are printed in blue and include 1990 and major league cumulative stats. One player from each major league team is included in the set.

		NM/M
Complete Set (24):		15.00
Common Player:		.50
1	Willie McGee	.50
2	Kevin Seitzer	.50
3	Kevin Maas	.50
4	Ben McDonald	.50
5	Rickey Henderson	1.00
6	Ken Griffey Jr.	2.00
7	John Olerud	.50
8	Dwight Gooden	.50
9	Ruben Sierra	.50
10	Luis Polonia	.50
11	Wade Boggs	1.50
12	Ramon Martinez	.50
13	Craig Biggio	.50
14	Cecil Fielder	.50
15	Will Clark	.50
16	Matt Williams	.50
17	Sandy Alomar Jr.	.50
18	David Justice	.50
19	Ryne Sandberg	1.50
20	Benito Santiago	.50
21	Barry Bonds	3.00
22	Carlton Fisk	1.00
23	Kirby Puckett	1.50
24	Jose Rijo	.50

1992 King-B

Labeled the "Fifth Annual Collectors Edition," the 1992 King-B discs were again packaged in plastic containers of shredded beef snack. The 2-3/8" diameter discs have a color player portrait at center. Uniform logos have been removed from the photos for lack of an MLB licensing agreement. The player's name and team are in white in a blue banner above his photo. Backs are printed in blue and include previous year and career stats along with a few biographical details and appropriate logos.

		NM/M
Complete Set (24):		15.00
Common Player:		.50
1	Terry Pendleton	.50
2	Chris Sabo	.50
3	Frank Thomas	1.00
4	Todd Zeile	.50
5	Bobby Bonilla	.50
6	Howard Johnson	.50
7	Nolan Ryan	3.00
8	Ken Griffey Jr.	2.00
9	Roger Clemens	1.75
10	Tony Gwynn	1.50
11	Steve Avery	.50
12	Cal Ripken Jr.	3.00
13	Danny Tartabull	.50
14	Paul Molitor	1.00
15	Willie McGee	.50
16	Wade Boggs	1.50
17	Cecil Fielder	.50
18	Jack Morris	.50
19	Ryne Sandberg	1.50
20	Kirby Puckett	1.50
21	Craig Biggio	.50
22	Harold Baines	.50
23	Scott Erickson	.50
24	Joe Carter	.50

1993 King-B

The sixth annual edition of baseball player discs inserted into packages of King-B meat snacks followed the format of previous issues. Measuring 2-3/8" in diameter, the cards have a photo (with uniform logos airbrushed away) in a yellow baseball diamond design at center. The disc is bordered in black. Backs are printed in red and contain 1992 and career stats.

		NM/M
Complete Set (24):		9.00
Common Player:		.50
1	Barry Bonds	2.00
2	Ken Griffey Jr.	1.50
3	Cal Ripken, Jr.	2.00
4	Frank Thomas	.75
5	Steve Avery	.50
6	Benito Santiago	.50
7	Luis Polonia	.50
8	Jose Rijo	.50
9	George Brett	1.25
10	Darren Daulton	.50
11	Cecil Fielder	.50
12	Ozzie Smith	1.00
13	Joe Carter	.50
14	Dwight Gooden	.50
15	Tom Henke	.50
16	Brett Butler	.50
17	Nolan Ryan	2.00
18	Sandy Alomar, Jr.	.50
19	Tom Glavine	.60
20	Rafael Palmeiro	.75
21	Roger Clemens	1.25
22	Ryne Sandberg	1.00
23	Doug Drabek	.50
24	Chuck Knoblauch	.50

1994 King-B

King-B once again created and inserted discs of 24 major league stars with its products in 1994. The entire set was also available in uncut sheet form which was found in each case. Discs measure 2-3/8" diameter and have a broad purple border with yellow and white typography surrounding the player photo at center. A black glove holds a King-B logo at bottom. Uniform logos have been airbrushed from the photos. Backs are printed in purple and include 1993 and career stats.

		NM/M
Complete Set (24):		6.00
Common Player:		.50
1	Fred McGriff	.50
2	Paul Molitor	.75
3	Jack McDowell	.50
4	Darren Daulton	.50
5	Wade Boggs	1.00
6	Ken Griffey Jr.	2.00
7	Tim Salmon	.50
8	Dennis Eckersley	.65
9	Albert Belle	.50
10	Travis Fryman	.50
11	Chris Hoiles	.50
12	Kirby Puckett	1.00
13	John Olerud	.50
14	Frank Thomas	.75
15	Lenny Dykstra	.50
16	Andres Galarraga	.50
17	Barry Larkin	.50
18	Greg Maddux	1.00
19	Mike Piazza	1.50
20	Roberto Alomar	.50
21	Robin Ventura	.50
22	Ryne Sandberg	1.00
23	Andy Van Slyke	.50
24	Barry Bonds	3.00

1995 King-B

A wood-grain background distinguishes the eighth annual baseball disc issue packaged inside shredded beef snack tins. Because they are licensed only by the Players Association, and not MLB, cards in the set have had team logos removed from the color player photos at the center of the 2-3/8" diameter discs. Backs are printed in red and have a few personal bits of data, previous season and career stats and the logos of King-B and the MLBPA.

		NM/M
Complete Set (24):		15.00
Common Player:		.35
1	Roberto Alomar	.35
2	Jeff Bagwell	.75
3	Wade Boggs	1.50
4	Barry Bonds	3.00
5	Joe Carter	.35
6	Mariano Duncan	.35
7	Lenny Dykstra	.35
8	Andres Galarraga	.35
9	Matt Williams	.35
10	Raul Mondesi	.35
11	Ken Griffey Jr.	2.00
12	Gregg Jefferies	.35
13	Fred McGriff	.35
14	Paul Molitor	.75
15	Dave Justice	.35
16	Mike Piazza	1.75
17	Kirby Puckett	1.50
18	Cal Ripken Jr.	3.00
19	Ivan Rodriguez	.65
20	Ozzie Smith	1.50
21	Gary Sheffield	.50
22	Frank Thomas	.75
23	Greg Maddux	1.50
24	Jimmy Key ("JIIMY" on back.)	.35

1996 King-B

The "9th Annual Collectors Edition" of King-B discs once again features player photos on which uniform insignia have been airbrushed away. The cards are licensed by Michael Schechter Associates only with the Players Union, not MLB, and so cannot display team logos. The 2-5/8" cardboard discs are packaged in plastic cannisters of shredded dried meat. Fronts have the 1996 date at left in a black and gold pinstriped area. The backs are in black and white with 1995 and career stats, along with a few vital data and appropriate logos and copyright information.

		NM/M
Complete Set (24):		15.00
Common Player:		.50
1	Roger Clemens	1.75
2	Mo Vaughn	.50
3	Dante Bichette	.50
4	Jeff Bagwell	1.00
5	Randy Johnson	1.00
6	Ken Griffey Jr.	2.00
7	Kirby Puckett	1.50
8	Orel Hershiser	.50
9	Albert Belle	.50
10	Tony Gwynn	1.50
11	Tom Glavine	.65
12	Jim Abbott	.50
13	Andres Galarraga	.50
14	Frank Thomas	1.00
15	Barry Larkin	.50
16	Mike Piazza	1.75
17	Matt Williams	.50
18	Greg Maddux	1.50
19	Hideo Nomo	.75
20	Roberto Alomar	.50
21	Ivan Rodriguez	.75
22	Cal Ripken Jr.	3.00
23	Barry Bonds	3.00
24	Mark McGwire	2.50

1997 King-B

The shredded beef product issued its 10th Anniversary set of player discs in 1997. The discs are packed inside the plastic canisters of the snack food and measure 2-3/8" in diameter. The '97 discs have a player action photo on front against a gold and black marbled background. Backs are in black-and-white and repeat the photo in the background, along with a few stats and personal data, logos and a disc number. One player from each team is represented in the checklist.

		NM/M
Complete Set (28):		15.00
Common Player:		.50
1	Brady Anderson	.50
2	Barry Bonds	3.00
3	Travis Fryman	.50
4	Rey Ordonez	.50
5	Kenny Lofton	.50
6	Mark McGwire	2.50
7	Jeff Bagwell	1.00
8	Roger Clemens	1.75
9	Juan Gonzalez	.75
10	Mike Piazza	1.75
11	Tim Salmon	.50
12	Jeff Montgomery	.50
13	Joe Carter	.50
14	David Cone	.50
15	Frank Thomas	1.00
16	Mickey Morandini	.50
17	Ray Lankford	.50
18	Pedro Martinez	1.00
19	Tom Glavine	.65
20	Chuck Knoblauch	.50
21	Dan Wilson	.50
22	Gary Sheffield	.65
23	Dante Bichette	.50
24	Al Martin	.50
25	Barry Larkin	.50
26	Ryne Sandberg	1.50
27	Steve Finley	.50
28	Matt Mieske	.50

1998 King-B

Except for the expansion teams, each Major League team has one player in this issue of player discs which were packed inside plastic canisters of the snack food. The cards measure 2-3/8" in diameter with a color player action photo on front (uniform logos have been removed). Backs have a few stats and personal data, logos plus a disc number.

		NM/M
Complete Set (28):		12.50
Common Player:		.50
1	Brady Anderson	.50
2	Barry Bonds	3.00
3	Tony Clark	.50
4	Rey Ordonez	.50
5	Travis Fryman	.50
6	Jason Giambi	.75
7	Jeff Bagwell	1.00
8	Tim Naehring	.50
9	Juan Gonzalez	.75
10	Mike Piazza	1.50
11	Tim Salmon	.50
12	Jeff Montgomery	.50
13	Tom Glavine	.65
14	Chuck Knoblauch	.50
15	Dan Wilson	.50
16	Gary Sheffield	.65
17	Dante Bichette	.50
18	Al Martin	.50
19	Roger Clemens	1.50
20	David Cone	.50
21	Frank Thomas	1.00
22	Mike Lieberthal	.50
23	Ray Lankford	.50
24	Rondell White	.50
25	Barry Larkin	.50
26	Matt Mieske	.50
27	Steve Finley	.50
28	Fernando Vina	.50

1999 King-B

The shredded beef product issued its 12th set of cardboard player discs in 1999. The discs are packed inside plastic canisters of the snack food and measure 2-3/8" in diameter. The cards have a color player action photo on front. Uniform logos are removed and team names are nowhere to be seen on the cards. Backs repeat the front photo in black-and-white in the background, along with a few stats and personal data, logos and a disc number. One player from each team is represented in the checklist.

		NM/M
Complete Set (30):		15.00
Common Player:		.50
1	Brady Anderson	.50
2	Barry Bonds	3.00
3	Scott Rolen	.75
4	Tony Clark	.50
5	Jeff Bagwell	1.00
6	Roberto Alomar	.50
7	Mark Kotsay	.50
8	Juan Gonzalez	.75
9	Tim Salmon	.50
10	Tom Glavine	.65
11	Frank Thomas	1.00
12	Dan Wilson	.50
13	Dante Bichette	.50
14	Mickey Morandini	.50
15	Fred McGriff	.50
16	Andy Benes	.50
17	Jeff Montgomery	.50
18	Pedro Martinez	1.00
19	Barry Larkin	.50
20	Carlos Delgado	.75
21	Mike Myers	.50
22	Ray Lankford	.50

23	Brad Radke	.50
24	Al Martin	.50
25	Raul Mondesi	.50
26	Ugueth Urbina	.50
27	Derek Jeter	3.00
28	Ben Grieve	.50
29	Mike Piazza	1.75
30	Wally Joyner	.50

2000 King-B

The shredded beef product issued its 13th annual set of cardboard player discs in 2000. The discs are packed inside plastic canisters of the snack food and measure 2-3/8" in diameter. The cards have a color player action photo on front. Uniform logos are removed and team names are nowhere to be seen on the cards. Backs have a black-and-white portrait photo, along with a few stats and personal data, logos and a disc number. One player from each team is represented in the checklist.

		NM/M
Complete Set (30):		15.00
Common Player:		.50
1	Nomar Garciaparra	1.50
2	Larry Walker	.50
3	Manny Ramirez	.75
4	Carlos Beltran	.65
5	Mark McGwire	2.00
6	Jeromy Burnitz	.50
7	Carlos Delgado	.60
8	Tom Glavine	.65
9	Shawn Green	.60
10	Mark Kotsay	.50
11	Warren Morris	.50
12	Fred McGriff	.50
13	Brady Anderson	.50
14	Jeff Bagwell	.75
15	Tony Clark	.50
16	Ben Grieve	.50
17	Vladimir Guerrero	.75
18	Tony Gwynn	1.00
19	Derek Jeter	3.00
20	Barry Larkin	.50
21	Rafael Palmeiro	.65
22	Mike Piazza	1.50
23	Brad Radke	.50
24	Scott Rolen	.65
25	Tim Salmon	.50
26	Frank Thomas	.75
27	Mark Grace	.50
28	Jeff Kent	.50
29	Dan Wilson	.50
30	Jay Bell	.50

2001 King-B

The cardboard discs for the shredded-beef snack's 14th annual issue were produced by Playoff, whose logo is among those appearing on back. The 2-3/8" diameter discs have a color action photo and black-and-white portrait on a pinstriped ball diamond background on front. Backs have another black-and-white portrait photo, along with 2000 and career stats and a few biographical bits. All photos have had team logos removed. Each disc is numbered "1 of 30" on back, so the checklist presented here is in alphabetical order.

		NM/M
Complete Set (30):		15.00
Common Player:		.50
(1)	Brady Anderson	.50
(2)	Jeff Bagwell	.75
(3)	Jay Bell	.50
(4)	Carlos Beltran	.65
(5)	Jeromy Burnitz	.50
(6)	Tony Clark	.50
(7)	Carlos Delgado	.60
(8)	Nomar Garciaparra	1.50
(9)	Tom Glavine	.65
(10)	Mark Grace	.50
(11)	Shawn Green	.60
(12)	Ben Grieve	.50
(13)	Vladimir Guerrero	.75
(14)	Tony Gwynn	1.00
(15)	Derek Jeter	2.50
(16)	Jeff Kent	.50
(17)	Mark Kotsay	.50
(18)	Barry Larkin	.50
(19)	Fred McGriff	.50
(20)	Mark McGwire	2.00
(21)	Warren Morris	.50
(22)	Rafael Palmeiro	.65
(23)	Mike Piazza	1.50
(24)	Brad Radke	.50
(25)	Manny Ramirez	.75
(26)	Scott Rolen	.65
(27)	Tim Salmon	.50
(28)	Frank Thomas	.75
(29)	Larry Walker	.50
(30)	Dan Wilson	.50

2001 King-B League Legends

For the first time in its 14 years of producing baseball player discs as a premium with its beef snacks, King B produced a set in 2001 featuring non-current players. Issued one per package of King B jerkey, the 2-3/8" diameter discs have a color portrait (with uniform logos removed) on front, against a ballpark photo background. Backs are in white and green and have a baseball design background with player data and a repeat of the "League Legends" logo.

		NM/M
Complete Set (18):		12.00
Common Player:		.50
1	Frank Robinson	1.00
2	Steve Carlton	1.00
3	Harmon Killebrew	1.00
4	Frank Torre	.50
5	Rollie Fingers	.50
6	Robin Roberts	1.00
7	Ernie Banks	1.50
8	Steve Sax	.50
9	Duke Snider	1.50
10	Gaylord Perry	.50
11	Andre Dawson	.50
12	Dave Kingman	.50
13	Reggie Jackson	2.00
14	Willie McCovey	1.00
15	Gary Carter	.50
16	Orlando Cepeda	.50
17	Willie Randolph	.50
18	Bob Gibson	1.00

2002 King-B

For the shredded-beef snack's 15th annual issue, Donruss produced the 2-3/8" diameter discs. Fronts have a large "15" over which is printed a color action photo. Backs have a portrait photo, along with 2001 and career stats and a few biographical bits. All photos have had team logos removed.

		NM/M
Complete Set (28):		12.50
Common Player:		.50
1	Randy Johnson	.75
2	Curt Schilling	.65
3	Chipper Jones	1.00
4	Greg Maddux	1.00
5	John Burkett	.50
6	Manny Ramirez	.75
7	Barry Larkin	.50
8	Roberto Alomar	.50
9	Chuck Finley	.50
10	Jim Thome	.65
11	Juan Gonzalez	.65
12	Larry Walker	.50
13	Charles Johnson	.50
14	Moises Alou	.50
15	Gary Sheffield	.65
16	Chan Ho Park	.50
17	Vladimir Guerrero	.75
18	Roger Clemens	1.25
19	Mariano Rivera	.60
20	Jason Giambi	.65
21	Rich Aurilia	.50
22	Jeff Kent	.50
23	Edgar Martinez	.50
24	Kazuhiro Sasaki	.50
25	Bret Boone	.50
26	John Olerud	.50
27	Greg Vaughn	.50
28	Ivan Rodriguez	.65

1985 Kitty Clover Potato Chips Discs

One of a pair of nearly identical (see KAS) sets issued by midwestern potato chip companies, this issue features top stars of the day on 2-3/4" cardboard discs. The discs have a player portrait at center, with uniform logos airbrushed away because the producer was licensed only by the Players Association and not Major League Baseball. The player's name, team and position are printed in a white diamond around the photo. The sponsor's logo is in the yellow border. Backs are in black-and-white and have a few biographical data, a 1984 stats line and a Snack Time logo. The unnumbered discs are checklisted here in alphabetical order. Square versions of the discs, which have been cut from press sheets are known within the hobby and carry a small premium. Kitty Clover was based in Omaha.

		NM/M
Complete Set (20):		60.00
Common Player:		1.50
(1)	Steve Carlton	6.00
(2)	Jack Clark	1.50
(3)	Rich Gossage	1.50
(4)	Tony Gwynn	7.50
(5)	Bob Horner	1.50
(6)	Keith Hernandez	1.50
(7)	Kent Hrbek	1.50
(8)	Willie McGee	1.50
(9)	Dan Quisenberry	1.50
(10)	Cal Ripken Jr.	25.00
(11)	Ryne Sandberg	7.50
(12)	Mike Schmidt	20.00
(13)	Tom Seaver	6.00
(14)	Ozzie Smith	7.50
(15)	Rick Sutcliffe	1.50
(16)	Bruce Sutter	4.00
(17)	Alan Trammell	1.50
(18)	Fernando Valenzuela	1.50
(19)	Willie Wilson	1.50
(20)	Dave Winfield	6.00

1986 Kitty Clover Potato Chips Royals

Twenty players of the 1985 World's Champion Kansas City Royals are featured in a round card set inserted into packages of potato chips in

the K.C. area. The 2-7/8" discs were similar to other contemporary snack issues produced by Mike Schechter Associates in that team logos have been airbrushed off the players' caps. The photos of some of the players can be found on other regional issues of 1986.

		NM/M
Complete Set (20):		15.00
Common Player:		.75
1	Lonnie Smith	.75
2	Buddy Biancalana	.75
3	Bret Saberhagen	1.00
4	Hal McRae	.75
5	Onix Concepcion	.75
6	Jorge Orta	.75
7	Bud Black	.75
8	Dan Quisenberry	.75
9	Dane Iorg	.75
10	Charlie Leibrandt	.75
11	Pat Sheridan	.75
12	John Wathan	.75
13	Frank White	.75
14	Darryl Motley	.75
15	Willie Wilson	1.00
16	Danny Jackson	.75
17	Steve Balboni	.75
18	Jim Sundberg	.75
19	Mark Gubicza	.75
20	George Brett	6.00

1996 Klosterman Baking Big Red Machine

Twenty years after The Big Red Machine captured the World's Championship, the 1976 Cincinnati Reds were honored on a card set issued by this Queen City bakery. One card was included with each 20-oz. loaf of bread during the run of the promotion. Cards are 2-3/8" x 3-1/2". Fronts feature color game-action photos with a large headline above and the player's name and position in white on a red strip at bottom. The Reds logo is in an upper corner of the photo, with the player's uniform number beneath. Backs have career summary and stats for the 1976 season and M.L. career, along with sponsors' logos and copyright information.

		NM/M
Complete Set (10):		10.00
Common Player:		.50
5	Johnny Bench	4.00
8	Joe Morgan	1.50
10	Sparky Anderson	1.00
13	Dave Concepcion	.50
15	George Foster	.50
20	Cesar Geronimo	.50
24	Tony Perez	1.00
30	Ken Griffey	.50
35	Don Gullett	.50
----	The Big Four (Tony Perez, Johnny Bench, Joe Morgan, Pete Rose)	3.00

2000 Klosterman Bakery Big Red Machine

The 25th anniversary of Cincinnati's 1975 World Series championship is marked with this issue by a regional bakery. The cards are printed on thin stock in a 2-3/8" x 3-1/2" format. Fronts have vintage game-action photos with red borders and a Big Red Machine 25th anniversary logo. Backs recap the player's 1975 season in words and stats. The cards were distributed singly in loaves of bread. The unnumbered cards are listed here in alphabetical order.

		NM/M
Complete Set (10):		5.00
Common Player:		.50
(1)	Sparky Anderson	.65
(2)	Johnny Bench	1.00
(3)	Jack Billingham	.50
(4)	Dave Concepcion	.50
(5)	George Foster	.50
(6)	Cesar Geronimo	.50
(7)	Ken Griffey	.50
(8)	Joe Morgan	.75
(9)	Tony Perez	.65
(10)	Pete Rose, Joe Morgan, Johnny Bench	1.00

1982 K-Mart

The first of what became dozens of boxed sets specially produced for retail chain stores by the major card producers, the 1982 K-Mart set has enjoyed little collector popularity. The theme of the set is Most Valuable Players and selected record-breaking performances of the 1962-1981 seasons. The design used miniature reproductions of Topps cards of the era, except in a few cases where designs had to be created because original cards were never issued (1962 Maury Wills, 1975 Fred Lynn). Originally sold for about $2 per boxed set of 44, large quantities were bought up by speculators who got burned when over-production and lack of demand caused the set to drop as low as 10¢. The 2-1/2" x 3-1/2" cards were printed by Topps.

		NM/M
Complete Set (44):		3.00
Common Player:		.10
1	Mickey Mantle	2.00
2	Maury Wills	.10
3	Elston Howard	.10
4	Sandy Koufax	.50
5	Brooks Robinson	.10
6	Ken Boyer	.10
7	Zoilo Versalles	.10
8	Willie Mays	.50
9	Frank Robinson	.10
10	Bob Clemente	.50
11	Carl Yastrzemski	.25
12	Orlando Cepeda	.10
13	Denny McLain	.10
14	Bob Gibson	.10
15	Harmon Killebrew	.10
16	Willie McCovey	.10
17	Boog Powell	.10
18	Johnny Bench	.10
19	Vida Blue	.10
20	Joe Torre	.10
21	Rich Allen	.10
22	Johnny Bench	.10
23	Reggie Jackson	.25
24	Pete Rose	.45
25	Jeff Burroughs	.10
26	Steve Garvey	.10
27	Fred Lynn	.10
28	Joe Morgan	.10
29	Thurman Munson	.10
30	Joe Morgan	.10
31	Rod Carew	.10
32	George Foster	.10
33	Jim Rice	.10
34	Dave Parker	.10
35	Don Baylor	.10
36	Keith Hernandez	.10
37	Willie Stargell	.10
38	George Brett	.50
39	Mike Schmidt	.50
40	Rollie Fingers	.10
41	Mike Schmidt	.50
42	Don Drysdale	.10
43	Hank Aaron	.50
44	Pete Rose	.45

1987 K-Mart

Produced by Topps for K-Mart, the 1987 K-Mart set was distributed by the department stores to celebrate their 25th anniversary. Entitled "Baseball's Stars of the Decades," the 33-card set was issued in a special cardboard box with one stick of bubblegum. Fronts feature a full-color photo set diagonally against a red background. The backs contain career highlights plus pitching or batting statistics for the decade in which the player enjoyed his greatest success. Cards are the standard 2-1/2" x 3-1/2".

		NM/M
Complete Set (33):		3.00
Common Player:		.10
1	Hank Aaron	.60
2	Roberto Clemente	.75
3	Bob Gibson	.10
4	Harmon Killebrew	.10
5	Mickey Mantle	2.00
6	Juan Marichal	.10
7	Roger Maris	.25
8	Willie Mays	.60
9	Brooks Robinson	.10
10	Frank Robinson	.10
11	Carl Yastrzemski	.25
12	Johnny Bench	.10
13	Lou Brock	.10
14	Rod Carew	.10
15	Steve Carlton	.10
16	Reggie Jackson	.25
17	Jim Palmer	.10
18	Jim Rice	.10
19	Pete Rose	.60
20	Nolan Ryan	.75
21	Tom Seaver	.10
22	Willie Stargell	.10
23	Wade Boggs	.25
24	George Brett	.50
25	Gary Carter	.10
26	Dwight Gooden	.10
27	Rickey Henderson	.10
28	Don Mattingly	.50
29	Dale Murphy	.10
30	Eddie Murray	.10
31	Mike Schmidt	.50
32	Darryl Strawberry	.10
33	Fernando Valenzuela	.10

1988 K-Mart

This 33-card boxed set, titled "Memorable Moments," was produced by Topps for distribution via K-Mart. The 1988 cards are standard-size with red, white and blue borders and a super glossy coating. Numbered card backs are printed in red and blue on white and highlight special events in the featured players' careers. The set was marketed in a bright yellow and green checklist box (gum included).

		NM/M
Complete Set (33):		2.00
Common Player:		.10
1	George Bell	.10
2	Wade Boggs	.45
3	George Brett	.50
4	Jose Canseco	.25
5	Jack Clark	.10
6	Will Clark	.10
7	Roger Clemens	.50
8	Vince Coleman	.10
9	Andre Dawson	.15
10	Dwight Gooden	.10
11	Pedro Guerrero	.10
12	Tony Gwynn	.45
13	Rickey Henderson	.35
14	Keith Hernandez	.10
15	Don Mattingly	.50
16	Mark McGwire	.75
17	Paul Molitor	.35
18	Dale Murphy	.15
19	Tim Raines	.10
20	Dave Righetti	.10
21	Cal Ripken, Jr.	1.00
22	Pete Rose	.60
23	Nolan Ryan	1.00
24	Benny Santiago	.10
25	Mike Schmidt	.50
26	Mike Scott	.10
27	Kevin Seitzer	.10
28	Ozzie Smith	.45
29	Darryl Strawberry	.10
30	Rick Sutcliffe	.10
31	Fernando Valenzuela	.10
32	Todd Worrell	.10
33	Robin Yount	.35

1989 K-Mart

This 33-card, glossy set was produced by Topps for K-Mart, where it was sold in stores nationwide. The standard-size cards feature mostly action shots on the front, and include the Topps "Dream Team" logo at the top, with the K-Mart logo in the lower right corner. The first 11 cards in the set picture the top rookies of 1988, while the next 11 picture the top A.L. rookies of the '80s, and the final 11 cards highlight the top N.L. rookies of the decade.

		NM/M
Complete Set (33):		2.00
Common Player:		.10
1	Mark Grace	.10
2	Ron Gant	.10
3	Chris Sabo	.10
4	Walt Weiss	.10
5	Jay Buhner	.10
6	Cecil Espy	.10
7	Dave Gallagher	.10
8	Damon Berryhill	.10
9	Tim Belcher	.10
10	Paul Gibson	.10
11	Gregg Jefferies	.10
12	Don Mattingly	.75
13	Harold Reynolds	.10
14	Wade Boggs	.60
15	Cal Ripken, Jr.	1.00
16	Kirby Puckett	.60
17	George Bell	.10
18	Jose Canseco	.25
19	Terry Steinbach	.10
20	Roger Clemens	.65
21	Mark Langston	.10
22	Harold Baines	.10
23	Will Clark	.10
24	Ryne Sandberg	.60
25	Tim Wallach	.10
26	Shawon Dunston	.10
27	Tim Raines	.10
28	Darryl Strawberry	.10
29	Tony Gwynn	.60
30	Tony Pena	.10
31	Doc Gooden	.10
32	Fernando Valenzuela	.10
33	Pedro Guerrero	.10

1990 K-Mart

This 33-card glossy set was produced by Topps for K-Mart, where it was available nationwide. The set is subtitled "Superstars" and features 16 A.L. players, 16 N.L. stars and a managers' card featuring both Tony LaRussa and Roger Craig. A special Superstars logo is featured on the card fronts. The 1990 issue marks the fourth consecutive year that Topps has produced a set in cooperation with K-Mart.

		NM/M
Complete Set (33):		3.00
Common Player:		.10
1	Will Clark	.10
2	Ryne Sandberg	.50
3	Howard Johnson	.10
4	Ozzie Smith	.50
5	Tony Gwynn	.50
6	Kevin Mitchell	.10
7	Jerome Walton	.10
8	Craig Biggio	.10
9	Mike Scott	.10
10	Dwight Gooden	.10
11	Sid Fernandez	.10
12	Joe Magrane	.10
13	Jay Howell	.10
14	Mark Davis	.10
15	Pedro Guerrero	.10
16	Glenn Davis	.10
17	Don Mattingly	.65
18	Julio Franco	.10
19	Wade Boggs	.50
20	Cal Ripken, Jr.	1.00
21	Jose Canseco	.25
22	Kirby Puckett	.50
23	Rickey Henderson	.35
24	Mickey Tettleton	.10
25	Nolan Ryan	1.00
26	Bret Saberhagen	.10
27	Jeff Ballard	.10
28	Chuck Finley	.10
29	Dennis Eckersley	.30
30	Dan Plesac	.10
31	Fred McGriff	.10
32	Mark McGwire	.75
33	Managers (Tony LaRussa, Roger Craig)	.10

1988 Kodak White Sox

These blank-back large format (8" x 12") cards feature borderless color action photos of team stars, overprinted with team and sponsor logos and a facsimile autograph. At top is a line of type with the card number and a "1988 Kodak Collectible Series" title.

		NM/M
Complete Set (5):		10.00
Common Player:		2.00
1	Ozzie Guillen	2.00
2	Carlton Fisk	4.00
3	Rick Horton	2.00
4	Ivan Calderon	2.00
5	Harold Baines	2.00

1989 Kodak White Sox

A series of six collectible pictures was given to fans over the course of the 1989 season. Sponsored by Kodak and Osco drug stores, the 8" x 12" sheets combine pictures of a current White Sox star with those of two former stars who played the same position. Ads for the sponsors appear on the photos' fronts, while there is a modicum of information about the former stars accompanying their portraits, including the years they played for the Sox.

		NM/M
Complete Set (6):		10.00
Common Card:		2.00
1	Greg Walker, Dick Allen, Ted Kluszewski	2.50
2	Steve Lyons, Eddie Collins, Nellie Fox	2.50
3	Carlton Fisk, Sherm Lollar, Ray Schalk	2.50
4	Harold Baines, Minnie Minoso, Jim Landis	2.00
5	Bobby Thigpen, Gerry Staley, Hoyt Wilhelm	2.00
6	Ozzie Guillen, Luke Appling, Luis Aparicio	2.00

1990 Kodak White Sox

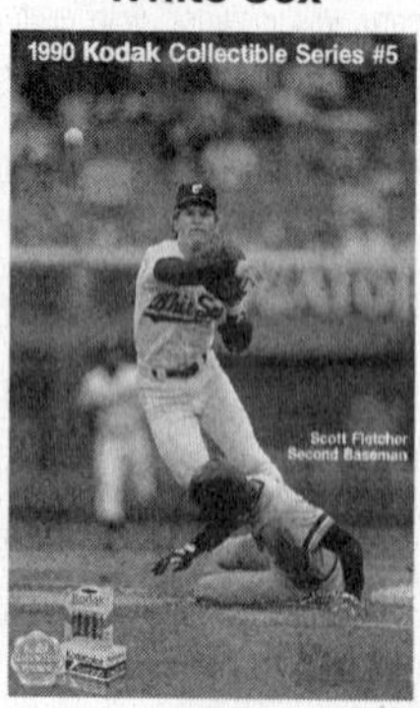

Again utilizing a large format (7" x 11") with borderless color action photos, the "1990 Kodak Collectible Series" features top stars of the South Siders. Player name and position, along with team and sponsor's logos, are superimposed over the photo, along with the title line and card number. The blank-back cards were distributed over the course of the season at various home games.

		NM/M
Complete Set (6):		10.00
Common Player:		2.00
1	Carlton Fisk	4.00
2	Melido Perez	2.00
3	Ozzie Guillen	2.00
4	Ron Kittle	2.00
5	Scott Fletcher	2.00
6	Comiskey Park	2.00

1991 Kodak White Sox

For a fourth year in a row, Kodak sponsored a White Sox team set in 1991. Fronts feature a full-bleed color action photo with the player's name and uniform number at the bottom and a commemorative logo for new Comiskey Park's inaugural season at top. Black-and-white backs have a few stats, personal details and career highlights along with the Kodak logo.

		NM/M
Complete Set (30):		24.00
Common Player:		.50
1	Lance Johnson	.50
5	Matt Merullo	.50
7	Scott Fletcher	.50
8	Bo Jackson	1.50
10	Jeff Torborg	.50
13	Ozzie Guillen	.50
14	Craig Grebeck	.50
20	Ron Karkovice	.50
21	Joey Cora	.50
22	Donn Pall	.50
23	Robin Ventura	1.00
25	Sammy Sosa	10.00
27	Greg Hibbard	.50
28	Cory Snyder	.50
29	Jack McDowell	.50
30	Tim Raines	.50
31	Scott Radinsky	.50
32	Alex Fernandez	.50
33	Melido Perez	.50
34	Ken Patterson	.50
35	Frank Thomas	5.00
37	Bobby Thigpen	.50
44	Dan Pasqua	.50
45	Wayne Edwards	.50
49	Charlie Hough	.50
50	Brian Drahman	.50
72	Carlton Fisk	3.00
---	White Sox Coaches (Terry Bevington, Sammy Ellis, Barry Foote, Walt Hriniak, Dave Laroche, Joe Nossek, John Stephenson)	.50
---	Co-captains (Ozzie Guillen, Carlton Fisk)	.50
---	No. 1 Draft Choices (Alex Fernandez, Jack McDowell, Frank Thomas, Robin Ventura)	1.00

1992 Kodak White Sox

With the theme of "Good Guys Wear Black," this set depicts the Chicago southsiders in photos featuring the team's Sunday-best black uniform jerseys. Photos on the cards are full-bleed with the GGWB logo in the upper-left corner of each card. At bottom is a black strip with the player's last name and uniform number. On back are the player's 1991 and career stats, a few biographical details, a trivia question and Kodak logo. At 2-5/8" x 3-1/2", the cards are slightly wider than current standard.

		NM/M
Complete Set (30):		10.00
Common Player:		.25
1	Lance Johnson	.25
5	Matt Merullo	.25
7	Steve Sax	.25
12	Mike Huff	.25
13	Ozzie Guillen	.25
14	Craig Grebeck	.25
20	Ron Karkovice	.25
21	George Bell	.25
22	Donn Pall	.25
23	Robin Ventura	.50
24	Warren Newson	.25
25	Kirk McCaskill	.25
27	Greg Hibbard	.25
28	Joey Cora	.25
29	Jack McDowell	.25
30	Tim Raines	.25
31	Scott Radinsky	.25
32	Alex Fernandez	.25
33	Gene Lamont	.25
34	Terry Leach	.25
35	Frank Thomas	4.00
37	Bobby Thigpen	.25
39	Roberto Hernandez	.25
40	Wilson Alvarez	.25
44	Dan Pasqua	.25
45	Shawn Abner	.25
49	Charlie Hough	.25
72	Carlton Fisk	2.50
00	Waldo (Cartoon mascot.)	.25
---	Mike Squires, Terry Bevington, Gene Lamont, Joe Nossek, Jackie Brown, Walt Hriniak, Doug Mansolino, Dave Huppert	.25

1993 Kodak White Sox

Kodak produced a White Sox set of 30 cards in 1993 that was given away prior to the July 23 game between Chicago and Milwaukee. The full color cards are slightly oversized at 2-5/8" x 3-1/2" and are printed on a very heavy card stock. The photo on the front is full bleed, with the White Sox logo appearing in the upper corner and a metallic blue stripe at the card bottom displaying the player's uniform number, name and position. The backs are white with gray borders and a Kodak logo, with year and career statistics and biographical information. The cards are unnumbered.

		NM/M
Complete Set (30):		10.00
Common Player:		.25
1	Lance Johnson	.25
7	Steve Sax	.25
8	Bo Jackson	.75
10	Mike LaValliere	.25
12	Mike Huff	.25
13	Ozzie Guillen	.25
14	Craig Grebeck	.25
20	Ron Karkovice	.25
21	George Bell	.25
22	Donn Pall	.25
23	Robin Ventura	.50
25	Kirk McCaskill	.25
26	Ellis Burks	.25
28	Joey Cora	.25
29	Jack McDowell	.25
30	Tim Raines	.25
31	Scott Radinsky	.25
32	Alex Fernandez	.25
33	Gene Lamont	.25
34	Terry Leach	.25
35	Frank Thomas	4.00
37	Bobby Thigpen	.25
39	Roberto Hernandez	.25
40	Wilson Alvarez	.25
42	Rod Bolton	.25
44	Dan Pasqua	.25
45	Chuck Cary	.25
49	Jeff Schwartz	.25
51	Jason Bere	.25
---	1993 Coaching Staff (Gene Lamont, Jackie Brown, Terry Bevington, Joe Nossek, Walt Hriniak, Doug Mansolino, Dewey Robinson, Jose Antigua)	.25

1994 Kodak White Sox

Slightly wider than standard cards, at 2-5/8" x 3-1/2" cards, this team set features borderless game-action photos on front with a silver facsimile autograph. Backs are bordered in silver and have a few stats, player personal data, career highlights and logos of the team and sponsor.

		NM/M
Complete Set (30):		12.00
Common Player:		.50
(1)	Wilson Alvarez	.50
(2)	Paul Assenmacher	.50
(3)	Jason Bere	.50
(4)	Dennis Cook	.50
(5)	Joey Cora	.50
(6)	Jose DeLeon	.50
(7)	Alex Fernandez	.50
(8)	Julio Franco	.50
(9)	Craig Grebeck	.50
(10)	Ozzie Guillen	.50
(11)	Joe Hall	.50
(12)	Roberto Hernandez	.50
(13)	Dann Howitt	.50
(14)	Darrin Jackson	.50
(15)	Dane Johnson	.50
(16)	Lance Johnson	.50
(17)	Ron Karkovice	.50
(18)	Gene Lamont	.50
(19)	Mike LaValliere	.50
(20)	Norberto Martin	.50
(21)	Kirk McCaskill	.50
(22)	Jack McDowell	.50
(23)	Warren Newson	.50
(24)	Dan Pasqua	.50
(25)	Tim Raines	.50
(26)	Scott Sanderson	.50
(27)	Frank Thomas	4.00
(28)	Robin Ventura	.75
(29)	Bob Zupcic	.50
(30)	Coaches (Terry Bevington, Jackie Brown, Roly de Armas, Walt Hriniak, Gene Lamont, Doug Mansolino, Joe Nossek, Rick Peterson)	.50

1995 Kodak Pittsburgh Pirates

This 13-1/2" x 20-1/4" perforated sheet containing 30 player and staff cards and sponsor advertising was issued to persons attending a July 23 promotional game. Individual cards measure 2-1/4" x 3-1/4". Player photos at center are flanked by the team name in gold with the player name in yellow in a red banner above. Backs are in black-and-white with just a few biographical notes and team and sponsor logos. The unnumbered cards are checklisted here alphabetically.

		NM/M
Complete Set, Sheet:		6.00
Complete Set, Singles (30):		6.00
Common Player:		.25
(1)	Rich Aude	.25
(2)	Jay Bell	.50
(3)	Jacob Brumfield	.25
(4)	Jason Christiansen	.25
(5)	Dave Clark	.25
(6)	Steve Cooke	.25
(7)	Midre Cummings	.25
(8)	Mike Dyer	.25
(9)	Angelo Encarnacion	.25
(10)	Carlos Garcia	.25
(11)	Freddy Garcia	.25
(12)	Jim Gott	.25
(13)	Mark Johnson	.25
(14)	Jeff King	.25
(15)	Jim Leyland	.25
(16)	Jon Lieber	.25
(17)	Nelson Liriano	.25
(18)	Esteban Loaiza	.25
(19)	Al Martin	.25
(20)	Jeff McCurry	.25
(21)	Orlando Merced	.25
(22)	Dan Miceli	.25
(23)	Denny Neagle	.25
(24)	Mark Parent	.25
(25)	Steve Pegues	.25
(26)	Dan Plesac	.25
(27)	Don Slaught	.25
(28)	Paul Wagner	.25
(29)	Rick White	.25
(30)	Gary Wilson	.25

1995 Kodak White Sox

Fans attending the July 21 game at Comiskey Park received a cello-wrapped 30-card team set. Fronts of the 2-5/8" x 3-1/2" cards have color player photos that are borderless at top and sides. At bottom the player's name appears in black-and-white. Backs are in black-and-white and feature the sponsor's logo and the team's 95-year anniversary logo. There are also a few biographical details, 1994 and career stats and a player trivia question. Cards are numbered by player uniform number.

		NM/M
Complete Set (30):		9.00
Common Player:		.15
1	Lance Johnson	.15
5	Ray Durham	.30
7	Norberto Martin	.15
8	Mike Devereaux	.15
10	Mike Lavalliere	.15
12	Craig Grebeck	.15
13	Ozzie Guillen	.15
14	Dave Martinez	.15
15	Kirk McCaskill	.15
18	Terry Bevington	.15
20	Ron Karkovice	.15
23	Robin Ventura	.25
24	Warren Newson	.15
25	Jim Abbott	.15
26	Brian Keyser	.15
29	John Kruk	.15
30	Tim Raines	.15
31	Scott Radinsky	.15
32	Alex Fernandez	.15
35	Frank Thomas	4.00
39	Roberto Hernandez	.15
40	Wilson Alvarez	.15
46	Jason Bere	.15
48	Jose DeLeon	.15
49	Rob Dibble	.15
51	Tim Fortugno	.15
---	Frank Thomas (1995 All-Star)	2.00
---	White Sox Coaching Staff (Terry Bevington, Don Cooper, Roly DeArmas, Walt Hriniak, Ron Jackson, Doug Mansolino, Joe Nossek, Mark Salas)	.15
---	Trainers (Herm Schneider, Mark Anderson)	.15
---	Director of Conditioning (Steve Odgers)	.15

1985 Kondritz Vince Coleman

The debut season of 1985 N.L. Rookie of the Year Vince Coleman is traced in this 20-card set issued by Illinois dealer Kondritz Trading Cards. Fronts of the 2-1/2" x 3-1/2" cards have player posed or action photos surrounded by a wide red border. Backs are in black-and-white with a few sentences about Coleman, a card number, large "Invincible" and copyright data. Sets were originally sold for about $10.

	NM/M
Complete Set (20):	5.00
Common Card:	.25

1986 Kondritz Ozzie Smith

The career of future Hall of Fame Cardinals shortstop Ozzie Smith is traced in this 20-card set issued by Illinois dealer Kondritz Trading Cards. Fronts of the 2-1/2" x 3-1/2" cards have player posed or action photos surrounded by a wide red border. Backs are in black-and-white with a few sentences about Smith, a card number, a large "THE WIZARD" and copyright data. Sets were originally sold for about $10.

		NM/M
Complete Set (20):		20.00
Common Card:		1.50
1-20	Ozzie Smith	1.50

1987 Kraft Home Plate Heroes

Kraft Foods issued a 48-card set on specially marked packages of macaroni & cheese dinners. Titled "Home Plate Heroes," 24 two-card panels measuring 3-1/2" x 7-1/8" make up the set. Individual cards measure 2-1/4" x 3-1/2". The blank-backed cards feature fronts with full-color photos, although all

team insignias have been erased. In conjunction with the card set, Kraft offered a contest to "Win A Day With A Major Leaguer." Mike Schechter Associates produced the set for Kraft. A total of 120 different panel combinations (five with each player) can be found.

		NM/M
Complete Set, Panels:		20.00
Complete Set, Singles (48):		16.00
Common Player:		.25
1	Eddie Murray	.50
2	Dale Murphy	.40
3	Cal Ripken, Jr.	1.00
4	Mike Scott	.25
5	Jim Rice	.35
6	Jody Davis	.25
7	Wade Boggs	.60
8	Ryne Sandberg	.60
9	Wally Joyner	.25
10	Eric Davis	.25
11	Ozzie Guillen	.25
12	Tony Pena	.25
13	Harold Baines	.25
14	Johnny Ray	.25
15	Joe Carter	.25
16	Ozzie Smith	.60
17	Cory Snyder	.25
18	Vince Coleman	.25
19	Kirk Gibson	.25
20	Steve Garvey	.35
21	George Brett	.75
22	John Tudor	.25
23	Robin Yount	.50
24	Von Hayes	.25
25	Kent Hrbek	.25
26	Darryl Strawberry	.25
27	Kirby Puckett	.60
28	Ron Darling	.25
29	Don Mattingly	.75
30	Mike Schmidt	.75
31	Rickey Henderson	.50
32	Fernando Valenzuela	.25
33	Dave Winfield	.50
34	Pete Rose	.85
35	Jose Canseco	.40
36	Glenn Davis	.25
37	Alvin Davis	.25
38	Steve Sax	.25
39	Pete Incaviglia	.25
40	Jeff Reardon	.25
41	Jesse Barfield	.25
42	Hubie Brooks	.25
43	George Bell	.25
44	Tony Gwynn	.60
45	Roger Clemens	.65
46	Chili Davis	.25
47	Mike Witt	.25
48	Nolan Ryan	1.00

1993 Kraft Pop-Up Action

Kraft released a set of Pop-Up Action baseball cards in 1993 that was available in specially-marked packages of Kraft Singles. The cards are similar to the 1992 Canadian Post Cereal cards with a pop-up tab. The set is made up of 15 players each from the American and National Leagues.

		NM/M
Complete Set (30):		12.00
Common Player:		.35
American League		
(1)	Jim Abbott	.35
(2)	Roberto Alomar	.35
(3)	Sandy Alomar Jr.	.35
(4)	George Brett	.75
(5)	Roger Clemens	.75
(6)	Dennis Eckersley	.50
(7)	Cecil Fielder	.35
(8)	Ken Griffey Jr.	1.00
(9)	Don Mattingly	.75
(10)	Mark McGwire	1.50
(11)	Kirby Puckett	.65
(12)	Cal Ripken, Jr.	2.00
(13)	Nolan Ryan	2.00
(14)	Robin Ventura	.35
(15)	Robin Yount	.60
National League		
(1)	Bobby Bonilla	.35
(2)	Ken Caminiti	.35
(3)	Will Clark	.35
(4)	Darren Daulton	.35
(5)	Doug Drabek	.35
(6)	Delino DeShields	.35
(7)	Tom Glavine	.45
(8)	Tony Gwynn	.65
(9)	Orel Hershiser	.35
(10)	Barry Larkin	.35
(11)	Terry Pendleton	.35
(12)	Ryne Sandberg	.65
(13)	Gary Sheffield	.50
(14)	Lee Smith	.35
(15)	Andy Van Slyke	.35

1994 Kraft Pop-Ups

Kraft offered a 30-card set in 1994 featuring major stars in a pop-up format. The cards show the players in action shots front and back, with the front picture "popping up." Kraft Singles consumers could find one 2-1/2" x 3-3/8" card in each package of cheese, with 15 players from each league. The cards were licensed by the Major League Baseball Players Association, but not by Major League Baseball, so the team logos were airbrushed from player's caps and uniforms. Through an on-pack and in-store mail-in offer, collectors could order complete sets of the cards for $1.95 per league (15 cards), plus the appropriate proofs of purchase. In a somewhat unusual move, officials of Kraft USA announced that the print run would be eight million cards, which works out to about 266,000 sets.

		NM/M
Complete Set (30):		7.50
Common Player:		.25
1	Carlos Baerga	.25
2	Dennis Eckersley	.50
3	Cecil Fielder	.25
4	Juan Gonzalez	.50
5	Ken Griffey Jr.	1.00
6	Mark Langston	.25
7	Brian McRae	.25
8	Paul Molitor	.60
9	Kirby Puckett	.75
10	Cal Ripken Jr.	1.50
11	Danny Tartabull	.25
12	Frank Thomas	.60
13	Greg Vaughn	.25
14	Mo Vaughn	.25
15	Dave Winfield	.60
16	Jeff Bagwell	.60
17	Barry Bonds	1.50
18	Bobby Bonilla	.25
19	Delino DeShields	.25
20	Lenny Dykstra	.25
21	Andres Galarraga	.25
22	Tom Glavine	.25
23	Mark Grace	.25
24	Tony Gwynn	.75
25	David Justice	.25
26	Barry Larkin	.25
27	Mike Piazza	.90
28	Gary Sheffield	.40
29	Ozzie Smith	.75
30	Andy Van Slyke	.25

1995 Kraft Singles Superstars

Once again incorporating a pop-up center action figure, these cards were available both in packages of cheese slices and via a mail-in offer. The 2-1/2" x 3-1/2" cards have a second player photo in the center which is revealed by pushing down the hinged front and back of the card, creating a stand. All photos have had uniform logos removed. A baseball design is at the bottom of each player photo. Back of the card has abbreviated stats and career highlights. The back of the pop-up figure has a paragraph about the player titled, "What Singles Him Out." Besides being packaged with cheese, the cards were available by sending in proofs of purchase and $1.95 for each 15-player A.L. or N.L. set.

		NM/M
Complete Set (30):		7.50
Common Player:		.25
1	Roberto Alomar	.25
2	Joe Carter	.25
3	Cecil Fielder	.25
4	Juan Gonzalez	.50
5	Ken Griffey Jr.	1.25
6	Jimmy Key	.25
7	Chuck Knoblauch	.25
8	Kenny Lofton	.25
9	Mike Mussina	.40
10	Paul O'Neill	.25
11	Kirby Puckett	.75
12	Cal Ripken Jr.	1.50
13	Ivan Rodriguez	.50
14	Frank Thomas	.60
15	Mo Vaughn	.25
16	Moises Alou	.25
17	Jeff Bagwell	.60
18	Barry Bonds	1.50
19	Jeff Conine	.25
20	Lenny Dykstra	.25
21	Andres Galarraga	.25
22	Tony Gwynn	.75
23	Gregg Jefferies	.25
24	Barry Larkin	.25
25	Greg Maddux	.75
26	Mike Piazza	1.00
27	Bret Saberhagen	.25
28	Ozzie Smith	.75
29	Sammy Sosa	1.00
30	Matt Williams	.25

1994 KVTU-TV San Francisco Giants

This short set was sponsored by the Giants' television broadcasting partner. Eight of the team's top names are featured on the 2-1/2" x 3-1/2" cards. Fronts have action photos framed in orange and brown with white borders. Black-and-white backs have a few career highlights and the TV station's logo.

		NM/M
Complete Set (9):		12.00
Common Player:		1.00
(1)	Dusty Baker	1.00
(2)	Rod Beck	1.00
(3)	Barry Bonds	7.50
(4)	Bobby Bonds	1.00
(5)	John Burkett	1.00
(6)	Billy Swift	1.00
(7)	Robby Thompson	1.00
(8)	Matt Williams	1.00
(9)	Header Card	.50

L

1981 L.A. Dodgers Police

Similar in format to the previous year's set, the Dodgers 1981 police set grew to 32 cards due to the acquisitions of Ken Landreaux and Dave Stewart shortly before printing of the sets. These two cards may even have been added after the initial printing run, making them slightly more difficult to obtain. The full-color cards are again 2-13/16" x 4-1/8", with a safety tip on the card back. Each card front has the line "LAPD Salutes the 1981 Dodgers."

		NM/M
Complete Set (32):		6.00
Common Player:		.25
2	Tom Lasorda	.50
3	Rudy Law	.25
6	Steve Garvey	3.00
7	Steve Yeager	.25
8	Reggie Smith	.25
10	Ron Cey	.25
12	Dusty Baker	.35
13	Joe Ferguson	.25
14	Mike Scioscia	.25
15	Davey Lopes	.25
16	Rick Monday	.25
18	Bill Russell	.25
21	Jay Johnstone	.25
26	Don Stanhouse	.25
27	Joe Beckwith	.25
28	Pete Guerrero	.25
30	Derrel Thomas	.25
34	Fernando Valenzuela	1.50
35	Bob Welch	.25
36	Pepe Frias	.25
37	Robert Castillo	.25
38	Dave Goltz	.25
41	Jerry Reuss	.25
43	Rick Sutcliffe	.25
44a	Mickey Hatcher	.25
44b	Ken Landreaux	1.25
46	Burt Hooton	.25
48	Dave Stewart	1.50

51	Terry Forster	.25
57	Steve Howe	.25
---	Coaching Staff (Monty Basgall, Mark Cresse, Tom Lasorda, Manny Mota, Danny Ozark, Ron Perranoski)	.25
---	Team Photo/Checklist	.25

1982 L.A. Dodgers Police

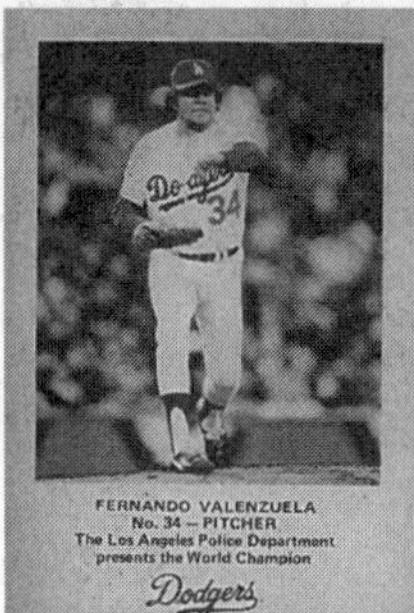

FERNANDO VALENZUELA
No. 34 -- PITCHER
The Los Angeles Police Department
presents the World Champion
Dodgers

Again issued in the same 2-13/16" x 4-1/8" size of the '80 and '81 sets, the 1982 Los Angeles set commemorates the team's 1981 World Championship. In addition to the 26 cards numbered by uniform for players and manager Tom Lasorda, there are four unnumbered cards which feature the team winning the division, league and World Series titles, plus one of the World Series trophy. The full-color card photos are once again vivid portraits on a clean white card stock. Card backs offer brief biographies and stadium information in addition to a safety tip.

		NM/M
Complete Set (30):		5.00
Common Player:		.25
2	Tom Lasorda	.50
6	Steve Garvey	2.00
7	Steve Yeager	.25
8	Mark Belanger	.25
10	Ron Cey	.25
12	Dusty Baker	.35
14	Mike Scioscia	.25
16	Rick Monday	.25
18	Bill Russell	.25
21	Jay Johnstone	.25
26	Alejandro Pena	.25
28	Pedro Guerrero	.25
30	Derrel Thomas	.25
31	Jorge Orta	.25
34	Fernando Valenzuela	.75
35	Bob Welch	.25
38	Dave Goltz	.25
40	Ron Roenicke	.25
41	Jerry Reuss	.25
44	Ken Landreaux	.25
46	Burt Hooton	.25
48	Dave Stewart	.35
49	Tom Niedenfuer	.25
51	Terry Forster	.25
52	Steve Sax	.35
57	Steve Howe	.25
---	Division Championship	.25
---	League Championship	.25
---	World Series Championship	.25
---	Trophy Card/Checklist	.25

1983 L.A. Dodgers Police

While these full-color cards remained 2-13/16" x 4-1/8" and card fronts were similar to those of previous years, the card backs are quite different. Card backs are in a horizontal design for the first time, and include a small head portrait photo of the player in the upper left corner. Fairly complete player statistics are included but there is no safety tip. The 30 cards are numbered by uniform number, with an unnumbered coaches card also included. Fronts include the year, team logo, player name and number.

		NM/M
Complete Set (30):		6.00
Common Player:		.25
2	Tom Lasorda	.50
3	Steve Sax	.25
5	Mike Marshall	.25
7	Steve Yeager	.25
12	Dusty Baker	.35
14	Mike Scioscia	.25
16	Rick Monday	.25
17	Greg Brock	.25
18	Bill Russell	.25
20	Candy Maldonado	.25
21	Ricky Wright	.25
22	Mark Bradley	.25
23	Dave Sax	.25
26	Alejandro Pena	.25
27	Joe Beckwith	.25
28	Pedro Guerrero	.25
30	Derrel Thomas	.25
34	Fernando Valenzuela	.75
35	Bob Welch	.25
38	Pat Zachry	.25
40	Ron Roenicke	.25
41	Jerry Reuss	.25
43	Jose Morales	.25
44	Ken Landreaux	.25
46	Burt Hooton	.25
47	Larry White	.25
48	Dave Stewart	.35
49	Tom Niedenfuer	.25
57	Steve Howe	.25
---	Coaches Card (Joe Amalfitano, Monty Basgall, Mark Cresse, Manny Mota, Ron Perranoski)	.25

1984 L.A. Dodgers Fire Safety

Unlike the California Angels and San Diego Padres sets issued in conjunction with the Forestry Service in 1984, the Los Angeles Dodgers set contains only three players, pictured on much larger 5" x 7" cards. Each player is pictured with Smokey in a forest scene on the full-color fronts. Backs of the unnumbered cards have brief biographical information and lifetime statistics. The cards were distributed at a Dodgers home game.

		NM/M
Complete Set (4):		7.00
Common Player:		2.50
(1)	Ken Landreaux	2.50
(2)	Tom Niedenfuer	2.50
(3)	Steve Sax	2.50
(4)	Smokey Bear	.50

1984 L.A. Dodgers Police

This was the fifth yearly effort of the Dodgers and the Los Angeles Police Department. There are 30 cards in the set, which remains 2-13/16" x 4-1/8". Card fronts are de-

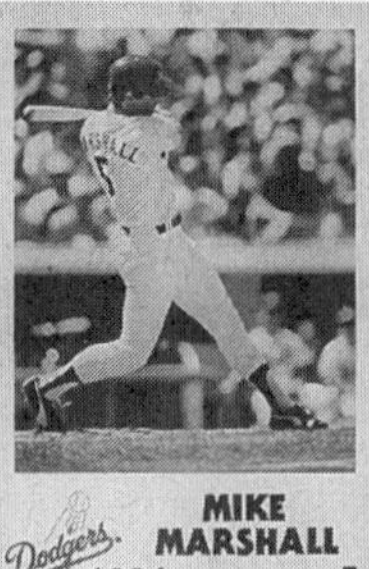

signed somewhat differently than previous years, with more posed photos, bolder player names and numbers and a different team logo. Card backs again feature a small portrait photo in the upper left corner, along with brief biographical information and an anti-drug tip. Card backs are in Dodger blue. Cards are numbered by uniform number, with an unnumbered coaches card also included.

		NM/M
Complete Set (30):		4.00
Common Player:		.25
2	Tom Lasorda	.50
3	Steve Sax	.25
5	Mike Marshall	.25
7	Steve Yeager	.25
9	Greg Brock	.25
10	Dave Anderson	.25
14	Mike Scioscia	.25
16	Rick Monday	.25
17	Rafael Landestoy	.25
18	Bill Russell	.25
20	Candy Maldonado	.25
21	Bob Bailor	.25
25	German Rivera	.25
26	Alejandro Pena	.25
27	Carlos Diaz	.25
28	Pedro Guerrero	.25
31	Jack Fimple	.25
34	Fernando Valenzuela	.75
35	Bob Welch	.25
38	Pat Zachry	.25
40	Rick Honeycutt	.25
41	Jerry Reuss	.25
43	Jose Morales	.25
44	Ken Landreaux	.25
45	Terry Whitfield	.25
46	Burt Hooton	.25
49	Tom Niedenfuer	.25
55	Orel Hershiser	3.00
56	Richard Rodas	.25
---	Coaches Card (Joe Amalfitano, Monty Basgall, Mark Cresse, Manny Mota, Ron Perranoski)	.25

1986 L.A. Dodgers Police

After skipping the 1985 season, the Los Angeles Dodgers once again issued baseball cards related to police safety. The 1986 set features 30 full-color glossy cards measuring 2-1/4" x 4-1/8", numbered according to player uniforms. The backs feature brief player data and a safety tip from the Los Angeles Police Department. The sets were given away May 18 during Baseball Card Day at Dodger Stadium.

		NM/M
Complete Set (30):		4.00
Common Player:		.20
2	Tom Lasorda	.40
3	Steve Sax	.20
5	Mike Marshall	.20
9	Greg Brock	.20
10	Dave Anderson	.20
12	Bill Madlock	.20
14	Mike Scioscia	.20
17	Len Matuszek	.20
18	Bill Russell	.20
22	Franklin Stubbs	.20
23	Enos Cabell	.20
25	Mariano Duncan	.20
26	Alejandro Pena	.20
27	Carlos Diaz	.20
28	Pedro Guerrero	.20
29	Alex Trevino	.20
31	Ed Vande Berg	.20
34	Fernando Valenzuela	.50
35	Bob Welch	.20
40	Rick Honeycutt	.20
41	Jerry Reuss	.20
43	Ken Howell	.20
44	Ken Landreaux	.20
45	Terry Whitfield	.20
48	Dennis Powell	.20
49	Tom Niedenfuer	.20
51	Reggie Williams	.20
55	Orel Hershiser	.50
---	Team Photo/Checklist	.20
---	Coaching Staff (Joe Amalfitano, Monty Basgall, Mark Cresse, Ben Hines, Don McMahon, Manny Mota, Ron Perranoski)	.20

1987 L.A. Dodgers All-Stars Fire Safety

This fire safety set features "25 Years of Dodger All-Stars." The cards, which measure 2-1/2" x 3-3/4", were given out to fans 14 and younger at the September 18 game at Dodgers Stadium. Fronts have full-color photos set in the shape of Dodger Stadium and have attractive silver borders. Backs carry the player's All-Star Game record plus a fire prevention message. Many of the photos used in the set were from team-issued picture packs sold by the Dodgers in the past.

		NM/M
Complete Set (40):		7.50
Common Player:		.25
(1)	Walt Alston	.45
(2)	Dusty Baker	.30
(3)	Jim Brewer	.25
(4)	Ron Cey	.25
(5)	Tommy Davis	.25
(6)	Willie Davis	.25
(7)	Don Drysdale	2.00
(8)	Steve Garvey	1.50
(9)	Bill Grabarkewitz	.25
(10)	Pedro Guerrero	.25
(11)	Tom Haller	.25
(12)	Orel Hershiser	.45
(13)	Burt Hooton	.25
(14)	Steve Howe	.25
(15)	Tommy John	.30
(16)	Sandy Koufax	5.00
(17)	Tom Lasorda	.45
(18)	Jim Lefebvre	.25
(19)	Davey Lopes	.25
(20)	Mike Marshall (Outfielder)	.25
(21)	Mike Marshall (Pitcher)	.25
(22)	Andy Messersmith	.25
(23)	Rick Monday	.25
(24)	Manny Mota	.25
(25)	Claude Osteen	.25
(26)	Johnny Podres	.30
(27)	Phil Regan	.25
(28)	Jerry Reuss	.25
(29)	Rick Rhoden	.25
(30)	John Roseboro	.25
(31)	Bill Russell	.25
(32)	Steve Sax	.25
(33)	Bill Singer	.25
(34)	Reggie Smith	.25
(35)	Don Sutton	1.00
(36)	Fernando Valenzuela	.50
(37)	Bob Welch	.25
(38)	Maury Wills	.45
(39)	Jim Wynn	.25
(40)	Logo Card/Checklist	.10

Police

Producing a police set for the seventh time in eight years, the 1987 edition contains 30 cards which measure 2-13/16" x 4-1/8". The set includes a special Dodger Stadium 25th Anniversary card. The card fronts contain a full-color photo plus the Dodger Stadium 25th Anniversay logo. The photos are a mix of action and posed shots. The backs contain personal player data plus a police safety tip. The cards were given out April 24th at Dodger Stadium and were distributed by the Los Angeles police department at a rate of two cards per week.

		NM/M
Complete Set (30):		4.00
Common Player:		.20
2	Tom Lasorda	.50
3	Steve Sax	.25
5	Mike Marshall	.25
10	Dave Anderson	.25
12	Bill Madlock	.25
14	Mike Scioscia	.25
15	Gilberto Reyes	.25
17	Len Matuszek	.25
21	Reggie Williams	.25
22	Franklin Stubbs	.25
23	Tim Leary	.25
25	Mariano Duncan	.25
26	Alejandro Pena	.25
28	Pedro Guerrero	.25
29	Alex Trevino	.25
33	Jeff Hamilton	.25
34	Fernando Valenzuela	.50
35	Bob Welch	.25
36	Matt Young	.25
40	Rick Honeycutt	.25
41	Jerry Reuss	.25
43	Ken Howell	.25
44	Ken Landreaux	.25
46	Ralph Bryant	.25
47	Jose Gonzalez	.25
49	Tom Niedenfuer	.25
51	Brian Holton	.25
55	Orel Hershiser	.60
---	Coaching Staff (Joe Amalfitano, Mark Cresse, Tom Lasorda, Don McMahon, Manny Mota, Ron Perranoski, Bill Russell)	.25
---	Dodger Stadium/ Checklist	.25

1988 L.A. Dodgers Fire Safety

Record-breaking Dodgers from the past three decades are featured on this perforated sheet. Individual cards measure 2-1/2" x 4" and are printed on a light blue background in a design similar to the previous year's All-Star set. Black-and-white card backs contain the player name, a summary of the player's record-breaking performance and a reproduction of one of a number of Smokey Bear fire prevention posters printed during the 1950s-1980s. The sheets were distributed to fans in Dodger Stadium.

		NM/M
Complete Set, Foldout:		9.00
Complete Set, Singles (32):		7.50
Common Player:		.25
1	Walter Alston	.30
2	John Roseboro	.25
3	Frank Howard	.30
4	Sandy Koufax	5.00
5	Manny Mota	.25
6	Record Pitchers (Sandy Koufax, Jerry Reuss, Bill Singer)	.35
7	Maury Wills	.30
8	Tommy Davis	.25
9	Phil Regan	.25
10	Wes Parker	.25
11	Don Drysdale	1.50
12	Willie Davis	.25
13	Bill Russell	.25
14	Jim Brewer	.25
15	Record Fielders (Ron Cey, Steve Garvey, Davey Lopes, Bill Russell)	.25
16	Mike Marshall (Pitcher)	.25
17	Steve Garvey	.75
18	Davey Lopes	.25
19	Burt Hooton	.25
20	Jim Wynn	.25
21	Record Hitters (Dusty Baker, Ron Cey, Steve Garvey, Reggie Smith)	.25
22	Dusty Baker	.30
23	Tom Lasorda	.40
24	Fernando Valenzuela	.50
25	Steve Sax	.25
26	Dodger Stadium	.25
27	Ron Cey	.25
28	Pedro Guerrero	.25
29	Mike Marshall (Outfielder)	.25
30	Don Sutton	.75
---	Logo Card/Checklist	.10
---	Smokey Bear	.10

Police

The Los Angeles Police Department sponsored this 30-card set (2-3/4" x 4-1/8") for use in a local crime prevention promotion. The sets include an unnumbered manager/coaches photo and three double-photo cards. The double cards feature posed closeups; the rest are action photos. The card fronts have white borders, with the team logo lower right and a bold black player name lower left. Card backs are black and white with a small closeup photo of the player, followed by personal and career info, a crime prevention tip and a LAPD badge logo. Card numbers refer to players' uniform numbers (the double-photo cards carry two numbers on both front and back).

	NM/M
Complete Set (30):	6.00

Common Player:		.15
2	Tom Lasorda	.30
3	Steve Sax	.15
5	Mike Marshall	.15
7	Alfredo Griffin	.15
9	Mickey Hatcher	.15
10	Dave Anderson	.15
12	Danny Heep	.15
14	Mike Scioscia	.15
17/21	Tito Landrum, Len Matuszek	.15
20	Don Sutton	.60
22	Franklin Stubbs	.15
23	Kirk Gibson	.40
25	Mariano Duncan	.15
26	Alejandro Pena	.15
27/52	Tim Crews, Mike Sharperson	.25
28	Pedro Guerrero	.15
29	Alex Trevino	.15
31	John Shelby	.15
33	Jeff Hamilton	.15
34	Fernando Valenzuela	.50
37	Mike Davis	.15
41	Brad Havens	.15
43	Ken Howell	.15
47	Jesse Orosco	.15
49/57	Tim Belcher, Shawn Hillegas	.15
50	Jay Howell	.15
51	Brian Holton	.15
54	Tim Leary	.15
55	Orel Hershiser	.40
---	Manager/Coaches (Joe Amalfitano, Steve Boros, Mark Cresse, Joe Ferguson, Tom Lasorda, Manny Mota, Ron Perranoski, Bill Russell)	.15

1989 L.A. Dodgers Greats Fire Safety

The largest baseball card set ever issued in conjunction with the U.S. Forest Service's Smokey the Bear fire prevention campaign was this 104-card issue featuring great players of the Brooklyn and L.A. Dodgers. Issued on perforated sheets, individual cards measure 2-1/2" x 3-1/2". White-bordered fronts have a sepia-toned photo of the player, with Dodger blue rules on the top and sides. Beneath the photo is a baseball-and-banner logo, "A Century of Dodger Greats." The player's name is beneath the ball with Smokey at left and the team logo at right. Backs are printed in blue, feature career stats and highlights and include a Smokey fire safety cartoon.

		NM/M
Complete Set (104):		20.00
Common Player:		.10
1	Tommy Lasorda, Walter Alston, Burt Shotton	.50
2	David Bancroft	.10
3	Dan Brouthers	.10
4	Roy Campanella	2.00
5	Max Carey	.10
6	Hazen "Kiki" Cuyler	.10
7	Don Drysdale	1.00
8	Burleigh Grimes	.10
9	Billy Herman	.10
10	Waite Hoyt	.10
11	Hughie Jennings	.10
12	Willie Keeler	.10
13	Joseph Kelley	.10
14	George Kelly	.10
15	Sandy Koufax	3.00
16	Heinie Manush	.10
17	Juan Marichal	.75
18	Walter Maranville	.10
19	Rube Marquard	.10
20	Thomas McCarthy	.10
21	Joseph McGinnity	.10
22	Joe Medwick	.10
23	Pee Wee Reese	2.00
24	Frank Robinson	1.00
25	Jackie Robinson	3.50
26	Babe Ruth	4.00
27	Duke Snider	2.00
28	Casey Stengel	.25
29	Dazzy Vance	.10
30	Arky Vaughan	.10
31	Mike Scioscia	.10
32	Lloyd Waner, Paul Waner	.10
33	John Monte Ward	.10
34	Zack Wheat	.10
35	Hoyt Wilhelm	.10
36	Hack Wilson	.10
37	Tony Cuccinello	.10
38	Al Lopez	.10
39	Leo Durocher	.25
40	Cookie Lavagetto	.10
41	Babe Phelps	.10
42	Dolf Camilli	.10
43	Whit Wyatt	.10
44	Mickey Owen	.10
45	Van Mungo	.10
46	Pete Coscarart	.10
47	Pete Reiser	.10
48	Augie Galan	.10
49	Dixie Walker	.10
50	Kirby Higbe	.10
51	Ralph Branca	.10
52	Bruce Edwards	.10
53	Eddie Stanky	.10
54	Gil Hodges	1.50
55	Don Newcombe	.50
56	Preacher Roe	.25
57	Willie Randolph	.10
58	Carl Furillo	.50
59	Charles Dressen	.10
60	Carl Erskine	.25
61	Clem Labine	.15
62	Gino Cimoli	.10
63	Johnny Podres	.25
64	Johnny Roseboro	.15
65	Wally Moon	.10
66	Charlie Neal	.10
67	Norm Larker	.10
68	Stan Williams	.10
69	Maury Wills	.20
70	Tommy Davis	.15
71	Jim Lefebvre	.10
72	Phil Regan	.10
73	Claude Osteen	.10
74	Tom Haller	.10
75	Bill Singer	.10
76	Bill Grabarkewitz	.10
77	Willie Davis	.15
78	Don Sutton	.50
79	Jim Brewer	.10
80	Manny Mota	.10
81	Bill Russell	.10
82	Ron Cey	.10
83	Steve Garvey	.50
84	Mike G. Marshall	.10
85	Andy Messersmith	.10
86	Jimmy Wynn	.10
87	Rick Rhoden	.10
88	Reggie Smith	.10
89	Jay Howell	.10
90	Rick Monday	.10
91	Tommy John	.15
92	Bob Welch	.10
93	Dusty Baker	.20
94	Pedro Guerrero	.10
95	Burt Hooton	.10
96	Davey Lopes	.10
97	Fernando Valenzuela	.20
98	Steve Howe	.10
99	Steve Sax	.10
100	Orel Hershiser	.40
101	Mike A. Marshall	.10
102	Wilbert Robinson	.10
103	Fred Lindstrom	.10
104	Ernie Lombardi	.10

Police

The Los Angeles Dodgers and the L.A. Police Department teamed up in 1989 to produce a 30-card police set. The cards, which measure 4-1/4" x 2-5/8", feature color action photos with the player's name and uniform number below. The Dodgers logo and "1989" appear in the upper left. The backs include player information plus a safety message.

		NM/M
Complete Set (30):		3.00
Common Player:		.15
2	Tom Lasorda	.30
3	Jeff Hamilton	.15
5	Mike Marshall	.15
7	Alfredo Griffin	.15
9	Mickey Hatcher	.15
10	Dave Anderson	.15
12	Willie Randolph	.15
14	Mike Scioscia	.15
17	Rick Dempsey	.15
20	Mike Davis	.15
21	Tracy Woodson	.15
22	Franklin Stubbs	.15
23	Kirk Gibson	.30
25	Mariano Duncan	.15
26	Alejandro Pena	.15
27	Mike Sharperson	.15
29	Ricky Horton	.15
30	John Tudor	.15
31	John Shelby	.15
33	Eddie Murray	2.00
34	Fernando Valenzuela	.35
36	Mike Morgan	.15
48	Ramon Martinez	.35
49	Tim Belcher	.15
50	Jay Howell	.15
52	Tim Crews	.15
54	Tim Leary	.15
55	Orel Hershiser	.35
57	Ray Searage	.15
---	Dodger Coaches (Joe Amalfitano, Mark Cresse, Joe Ferguson, Ben Hines, Tommy Lasorda, Manny Mota, Ron Perranoski, Bill Russell)	.15

1990 L.A. Dodgers Police

This set honors the centennial celebration of the Los Angeles Dodgers. A special 100 Anniversary logo appears on the card fronts. The cards measure 2-3/4" x 4-1/4" and feature full-color photos. The card backs are printed horizontally and contain a special safety tip or anti-drug message along with player information. The L.A.P.D. logo is featured on the bottom of the card back.

		NM/M
Complete Set (30):		3.00
Common Player:		.15
2	Tommy Lasorda	.30
3	Jeff Hamilton	.15
7	Alfredo Griffin	.15
9	Mickey Hatcher	.15
10	Juan Samuel	.15
12	Willie Randolph	.15
14	Mike Scioscia	.15
15	Chris Gwynn	.15
17	Rick Dempsey	.15
21	Hubie Brooks	.15
22	Franklin Stubbs	.15
23	Kirk Gibson	.25
27	Mike Sharperson	.15
28	Kal Daniels	.15
29	Lenny Harris	.15
31	John Shelby	.15
33	Eddie Murray	2.00
34	Fernando Valenzuela	.40
35	Jim Gott	.15
36	Mike Morgan	.15
38	Jose Gonzalez	.15
46	Mike Hartley	.15
48	Ramon Martinez	.15
49	Tim Belcher	.15
50	Jay Howell	.15
52	Tim Crews	.15
55	Orel Hershiser	.25
57	John Wetteland	.15
59	Ray Searage	.15
---	Dodgers Coaches (Joe Amalfitano, Mark Cresse, Joe Ferguson, Ben Hines, Tommy Lasorda, Manny Mota, Ron Perranoski, Bill Russell)	.15

1991 L.A. Dodgers Police

One of the longest-running police/fire safety sets continued in 1991 with this 30-card set. Players are featured in color action photos set in a tombstone shape against a white background. The date is in a banner at top with the player name, team logo and uniform number at bottom. All typography is printed in Dodger blue. Backs are printed in black-and-white and include biographical data, an anti-drug message and an LAPD badge. Cards measure 2-13/16" x 4-1/8".

		NM/M
Complete Set (30):		4.00
Common Player:		.15
3	Jeff Hamilton	.15
5	Stan Javier	.15
7	Alfredo Griffin	.15
10	Juan Samuel	.15
12	Gary Carter	1.50
14	Mike Scioscia	.15
15	Chris Gwynn	.15
17	Bob Ojeda	.15
22	Brett Butler	.15
25	Dennis Cook	.15
27	Mike Sharperson	.15
28	Kal Daniels	.15
29	Lenny Harris	.15
30	Jose Offerman	.15
31	Jim Neidlinger	.15
33	Eddie Murray	1.50
35	Jim Gott	.15
36	Mike Morgan	.15
38	Jose Gonzalez	.15
40	Barry Lyons	.15
44	Darryl Strawberry	.45
45	Kevin Gross	.15
46	Mike Hartley	.15
48	Ramon Martinez	.15
49	Tim Belcher	.15
50	Jay Howell	.15
52	Tim Crews	.15
54	John Candelaria	.15
55	Orel Hershiser	.35
---	Dodgers Coaches (Ben Hines, Ron Perranoski, Mark Cresse, Manny Mota, Tommy Lasorda, Joe Amalfitano, Joe Ferguson, Bill Russell)	.15

1992 L.A. Dodgers Police

The 1992 Dodgers Police set consists of 30 cards numbered to correspond to the player's uniform number. The set includes a card of manager Tommy Lasorda and Dodgers coaches. They were given out at promotional dates at Dodger Stadium.

		NM/M
Complete Set (30):		4.00
Common Player:		.25
2	Tommy Lasorda	.35
3	Jeff Hamilton	.25
5	Stan Javier	.25
10	Juan Samuel	.25
14	Mike Scioscia	.25
15	Dave Hansen	.25
17	Bob Ojeda	.25
20	Mitch Webster	.25
22	Brett Butler	.25
23	Eric Karros	.50
27	Mike Sharperson	.25
28	Kal Daniels	.25
29	Lenny Harris	.25
30	Jose Offerman	.25
31	Roger McDowell	.25
33	Eric Davis	.25
35	Jim Gott	.25
36	Todd Benzinger	.25
38	Steve Wilson	.25
41	Carlos Hernandez	.25
44	Darryl Strawberry	.35
46	Kevin Gross	.25
48	Ramon Martinez	.25
49	Tom Candiotti	.25
50	Jay Howell	.25
52	Tim Crews	.25
54	John Candelaria	.25
55	Orel Hershiser	.40
57	Kip Gross	.25
---	Coaches (Joe Amalfitano, Mark Cresse, Joe Ferguson, Ben Hines, Tommy Lasorda, Manny Mota, Ron Perranoski, Ron Roenicke)	.25

1993 L.A. Dodgers Police

The 1993 Los Angeles Dodgers Police Set consisted of 29 cards, including cards of manager Tommy Lasorda and his coaches. The fronts of the cards have a photo surrounded by a blue border, with the Dodgers logo and the player's name on the bottom. The set is not numbered, but the player's uniform number does appear on the front of the cards.

		NM/M
Complete Set (29):		6.00
Common Player:		.25
2	Tommy Lasorda	.35
3	Jody Reed	.25
5	Dave Hansen	.25
12	Lance Parrish	.25
17	Roger McDowell	.25
20	Mitch Webster	.25
22	Brett Butler	.25
23	Eric Karros	.25
25	Tim Wallach	.25
26	Henry Rodriguez	.25
27	Mike Sharperson	.25
28	Cory Snyder	.25
29	Lenny Harris	.25
30	Jose Offerman	.25
31	Mike Piazza	3.00
33	Eric Davis	.25
35	Jim Gott	.25
38	Todd Worrell	.25
41	Carlos Hernandez	.25
45	Pedro Martinez	2.00
46	Kevin Gross	.25
47	Tom Goodwin	.25
48	Ramon Martinez	.25
49	Tom Candiotti	.25
50	Steve Wilson	.25
55	Orel Hershiser	.45
56	Pedro Astacio	.25
57	Kip Gross	.25
---	Coaches (Joe Amalfitano, Mark Cresse, Joe Ferguson, Ben Hines, Tommy Lasorda, Manny Mota, Ron Perranoski, Ron Roenicke)	.25

1994 L.A. Dodgers Police

This 30-card set was distributed to all fans attending the Dodgers May 27 home game. Cards were produced in the form of a perforated sheet. Fronts have mostly game-action photos surrounded by a Dodger-blue border. The player's uniform number is in red in a baseball in the upper-left corner. At bottom is the team logo and the player's name in black on a yellow strip. Backs are in black on white, have a few career and biographical notes and an anti-drug message from the L.A.P.D. and the D.A.R.E. program. When removed from the sheet, cards measure the standard 2-1/2" x 3-1/2". They are checklisted here by uniform number.

		NM/M
Uncut Sheet:		6.00
Complete Set (30):		5.00
Common Player:		.25
2	Tommy Lasorda	.35
5	Dave Hansen	.25
7	Billy Ashley	.25
10	Chris Gwynn	.25
12	Jeff Treadway	.25
14	Delino DeShields	.25
15	Tom Prince	.25
17	Roger McDowell	.25
20	Mitch Webster	.25
21	Rafael Bournigal	.25
22	Brett Butler	.25
23	Eric Karros	.25
26	Carlos Hernandez	.25
28	Cory Snyder	.25
29	Tim Wallach	.25
30	Jose Offerman	.25
31	Mike Piazza	2.50
35	Jim Gott	.25
37	Darren Dreifort	.25
38	Todd Worrell	.25
40	Henry Rodriguez	.25
43	Raul Mondesi	.50
46	Kevin Gross	.25
47	Garey Wayne	.25
48	Ramon Martinez	.25
49	Tom Candiotti	.25
55	Orel Hershiser	.35
56	Pedro Astacio	.25
61	Chan Ho Park	.75
---	Coaches (Mark Cresse, Manny Mota, Bill Russell, Reggie Smith, Joe Ferguson, Ron Perranoski, Tommy Lasorda, Joe Amalfitano)	.25

1995 L.A. Dodgers Limited Edition

This special high-tech set of Brooklyn/Los Angeles Dodgers rookie of the year winners between 1947-94 was given to Dodger season ticket purchasers prior to the strike-shortened 1995 baseball season. Produced in a technique similar to Topps Finest, the cards have on front metallic backgrounds in red, green, blue or purple. A color player action photo is fea-

tured. Faux granite strips at bottom have the player's name and year of his ROY award in gold. Backs have a color portrait photo in a gold frame with career stats and highlights and a few personal details. The primary front background color is repeated on the back. A header card printed in blue on white linen-texture paper accompanies the set.

		NM/M
Complete Set (14):		50.00
Common Player:		2.00
1	Jackie Robinson	15.00
2	Don Newcombe	4.00
3	Joe Black	4.00
4	Jim Gilliam	4.00
5	Frank Howard	4.00
6	Jim Lefebvre	2.00
7	Ted Sizemore	2.00
8	Rick Sutcliffe	3.00
9	Steve Howe	2.00
10	Fernando Valenzuela	5.00
11	Steve Sax	3.00
12	Eric Karros	3.00
13	Mike Piazza	15.00
14	Raul Mondesi	3.00
---	Header Card	.10

1995 L.A. Dodgers Police

Action photos of the L.A. Dodgers are featured on this 30-card safety set which was given away to some 40,000 fans attending an early-season game. The set was produced as a perforated sheet measuring 14-13/16" x 17-1/2", with individual cards measuring 2-1/2" x 3-1/2". Fronts feature a Dodger-blue border with the player name in black in a yellow stripe at bottom. The player's uniform number is in red in a baseball in the upper-right. Backs are in black-and-white and have a few player biographical details along with an anti-drug safety message and the logos of the LAPD and D.A.R.E.

		NM/M
Uncut Sheet:		6.00
Complete Set (30):		6.00
Common Player:		.25
2	Tommy Lasorda	.35
3	Eddie Pye	.25
5	Dave Hansen	.25
7	Billy Ashley	.25
12	Jeff Treadway	.25
14	Delino DeShields	.25
16	Hideo Nomo	2.00
21	Rafael Bournigal	.25
23	Eric Karros	.25
25	Ron Coomer	.25
26	Carlos Hernandez	.25
28	Todd Hollandsworth	.25
29	Tim Wallach	.25
30	Jose Offerman	.25
31	Mike Piazza	2.00
38	Todd Worrell	.25
40	Henry Rodriguez	.25
43	Raul Mondesi	.35
45	Al Osuna	.25
48	Ramon Martinez	.25
49	Tom Candiotti	.25
50	Antonio Osuna	.25
52	Greg Hansell	.25
54	Omar Daal	.25
56	Pedro Astacio	.25
57	Rudy Seanez	.25
59	Ismael Valdes	.25
61	Chan Ho Park	.50
66	Todd Williams	.25
---	Coaches (Mark Cresse, Manny Mota, Bill Russell, Reggie Smith, Tommy Lasorda, Joe Amalfitano, Dave Wallace, Ralph Avila)	.25

1996 L.A. Dodgers Police

For the 16th time in 17 years (they skipped 1985), the Dodgers issued a safety set to fans attending the April 11 game. As in recent years, the set was issued in the form of a perforated 30-card sheet. Each card measures just under 2-1/2" wide and is 3-1/2" tall; sheet dimensions are 14-7/8" x 17-1/2". Game-action photos are bordered in Dodger blue with the uniform number in red at upper-left. Backs are in black-and-white with a few vital stats and an anti-drug abuse, anti-gang message from D.A.R.E.

		NM/M
Uncut Sheet:		6.50
Complete Set (30):		6.00
Common Player:		.10
2	Tommy Lasorda	.25
3	Chad Fonville	.10
5	Dave Hansen	.10
7	Greg Gagne	.10
12	Karim Garcia	.25
13	Antonio Osuna	.10
14	Delino DeShields	.10
16	Hideo Nomo	2.00
20	Mike Blowers	.10
21	Billy Ashley	.10
22	Brett Butler	.10
23	Eric Karros	.10
25	Mike Busch	.10
26	Carlos Hernandez	.10
27	Roger Cedeno	.10
28	Todd Hollandsworth	.10
29	Milt Thompson	.10
31	Mike Piazza	2.00
33	Garey Ingram	.10
38	Todd Worrell	.10
41	John Cummings	.10
43	Raul Mondesi	.10
44	Mark Guthrie	.10
48	Ramon Martinez	.10
49	Tom Candiotti	.10
51	Joey Eischen	.10
52	Darren Hall	.10
56	Pedro Astacio	.10
59	Ismael Valdes	.10
---	Dodgers Coaches (Joe Amalfitano, Mark Cresse, Tommy Lasorda, Manny Mota, Bill Russell, Reggie Smith, Dave Wallace)	.10

Rookies of the Year

This card was inserted into a die-cut space in the 1996 holiday greetings card sent out by the L.A. Dodgers. In 2-1/2" x 3-1/2 format it features portrait photos of the 1992-96 National League

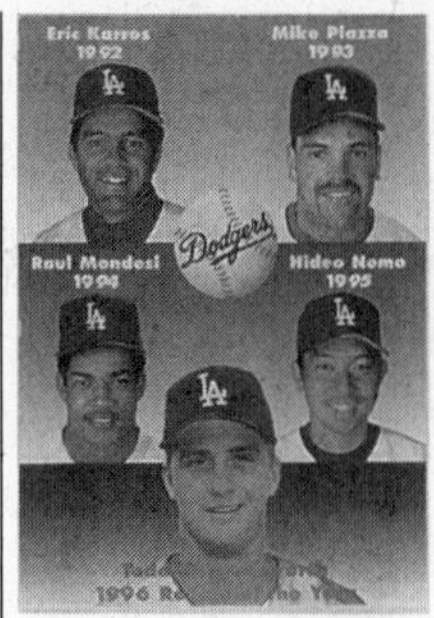

Rookies of the Year - all Dodgers. Overall background of the front is green. Back has information on previous Dodgers ROYs and the rookie season stats of the 1992-96 winners.

	NM/M
Dodger Rookies of the Year: (Eric Karros/1992, Mike Piazza/1993, Raul Mondesi/1994, Hideo Nomo/1995, Todd Hollandsworth/1996	15.00

1997 L.A. Dodgers Fan Appreciation Days

Fans attending the September 21 game were given this 11" x 8-1/2" sheet announcing a one-day sale of Dodgers souvenirs. At bottom are three differently styled cards of some of the team's most popular players. All are in color and standard 2-1/2" x 3-1/2" size, perforated for easy separation from the sheet. Card backs are in black-and-white with drawings of the players in the upper-left, biographical data and trivia. Cards are numbered by uniform number.

		NM/M
Complete Sheet:		6.00
Complete Set, Singles (3):		6.00
16	Hideo Nomo	3.00
31	Mike Piazza	4.00
61	Chan Ho Park	1.50

Police

Action photos of the 1997 Dodgers are featured on this set distributed at the April 23 game to nearly 30,500 fans. The 14-3/4" x 17-1/2" sheet has 30 cards, perforated on two, three or four sides, depending on position on the sheet. Individual cards measure 2-1/2" x 3-1/2". A central photo is surrounded with a white border. A ball with the player's uniform number in red is at top-left. At bottom is the team logo and player name. Backs are in black-and-white with biographical notes, an anti-drug message from each player and the logos of LAPD and DARE. Cards are checklisted here by uniform number.

		NM/M
Uncut Sheet:		7.00
Complete Set (30):		6.00
Common Player:		.20
3	Chad Fonville	.20
5	Chip Hale	.20
7	Greg Gagne	.20
12	Karim Garcia	.20
13	Anthony Osuna	.20
15	Tom Prince	.20
16	Hideo Nomo	1.50
18	Bill Russell	.20
21	Billy Ashley	.20
22	Brett Butler	.20
23	Eric Karros	.20
25	Juan Castro	.20
27	Todd Zeile	.20
28	Todd Hollandsworth	.20
30	Wilton Guerrero	.20
31	Mike Piazza	2.50
35	Wayne Kirby	.20
36	Scott Radinsky	.20
37	Darren Dreifort	.20
38	Todd Worrell	.20
43	Raul Mondesi	.20
44	Mark Guthrie	.20
46	Nelson Liriano	.20
48	Ramon Martinez	.20
49	Tom Candiotti	.20
52	Darren Hall	.20
56	Pedro Astacio	.20
59	Ismael Valdes	.20
61	Chan Ho Park	.20
---	Coaches (Joe Amalfitano, Mark Cresse, Manny Mota, Mike Scioscia, Reggie Smith, Dave Wallace)	.20

1998 L.A. Dodgers Fan Appreciation Days

Fans attending the Dodgers' final homestand were given this 11" x 8-1/2" sheet announcing a sale of Dodgers souvenirs. At bottom are three cards of some of the team's most popular players. All are in color and standard 2-1/2" x 3-1/2" size, perforated for easy separation from the sheet. Card backs are in black-and-white with personal data, a facsimile autograph and trivia. Cards are numbered by uniform number.

		NM/M
Complete Sheet:		6.00
Complete Set (3):		4.00
Common Player:		2.00
10	Gary Sheffield	2.50
23	Eric Karros	2.00
43	Raul Mondesi	2.00

Police

Repeating the format used in recent years, a 30-card perforated sheet, the Dodgers issued their annual D.A.R.E. drug-awareness set in April. Individual cards are the standard 2-1/2" x 3-1/2" on the 15" x 17-1/2" sheet. Fronts have action photos with blue borders. A baseball at top-left has the player's uniform number, by which the set is checklisted here.

		NM/M
Uncut Sheet:		7.00
Complete Set (30):		6.00
Common Player:		.25
7	Paul Konerko	.50
10	Jose Vizcaino	.25
12	Mike Devereaux	.25
13	Antonio Osuna	.25
15	Tom Prince	.25
16	Hideo Nomo	2.00
18	Bill Russell	.25
22	Thomas Howard	.25
23	Eric Karros	.25
25	Juan Castro	.25
26	Eric Young	.25
27	Todd Zeile	.25
28	Todd Hollandsworth	.25
30	Wilton Guerrero	.25
31	Mike Piazza	3.00
36	Scott Radinsky	.25
37	Darren Dreifort	.25
40	Matt Luke	.25
41	Tripp Cromer	.25
43	Raul Mondesi	.25
44	Mark Guthrie	.25
45	Roger Cedeno	.25
46	Jim Bruske	.25
47	Trenidad Hubbard	.25
48	Ramon Martinez	.25
49	Frank Lankford	.25
52	Darren Hall	.25
59	Ismael Valdes	.25
61	Chan Ho Park	.25
---	Joe Amalfitano, Mark Cresse, Glenn Gregson, Manny Mota, Mike Scioscia, Reggie Smith	.25

Record Breakers

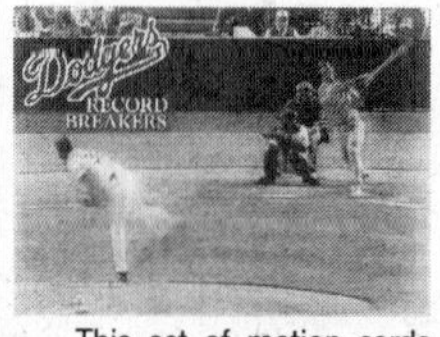

This set of motion cards was distributed one per month to members of the Dodgers Kids Clubhouse when they attended a game. The 3-1/2" x 2-1/2" cards have a borderless front with an action scene viewed by changing the angle of the card. The team logo appears in an upper corner. Backs repeat the logo and have personal data and details of the record performance. The cards are unnumbered. Distribution of the Nomo and Piazza cards was cut short when those players were traded in mid-season.

		NM/M
Complete Set (5):		17.50
Common Player:		2.00
(1)	Ramon Martinez	2.00
(2)	Raul Mondesi/Action	2.00
(3)	Raul Mondesi/Portrait (Membership card.)	2.00
(4)	Hideo Nomo	6.00
(5)	Mike Piazza	7.50

1999 L.A. Dodgers Concession Stand Cards

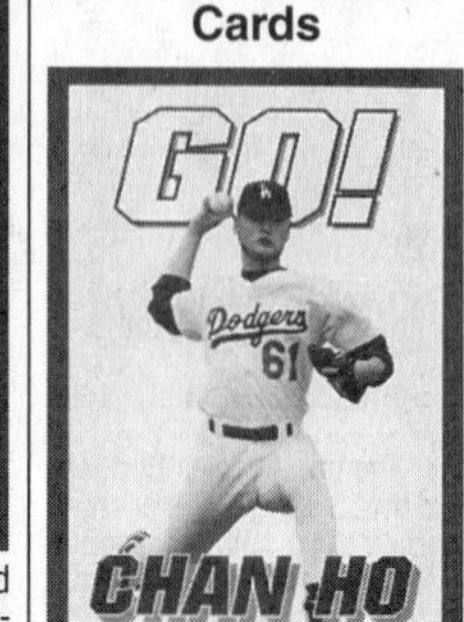

During the first five home games of the 1999 season, fans visiting the concession stands at Dodgers Stadium could receive a free player card. Fronts have color action photos on a white background with blue borders. The player's first name is printed at bottom, and a catchword at top. Backs are horizontal in black-and-white with a portrait photo career highlights and personal data, plus team and Dodger Stadium logos.

		NM/M
Complete Set (5):		4.00
Common Player:		1.00
1	Kevin Brown	1.50
2	Chan Ho Park	1.00
3	Ismael Valdes	1.00
4	Carlos Perez	1.00
5	Darren Dreifort	1.00

Fan Appreciation Days

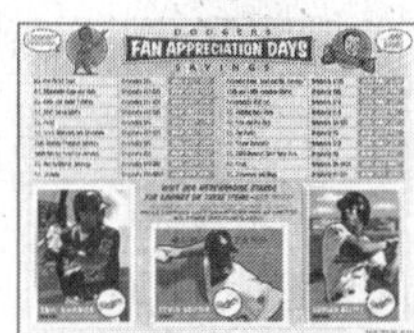

Fans attending the Dodgers' final homestand were given this 11" x 8-1/2" sheet announcing special sales of Dodgers souvenirs. At bottom are three cards of some of the team's most popular players. All are in color and standard 2-1/2" x 3-1/2" size, perforated for easy separation from the sheet. The card fronts are in the style of 1953 Topps while backs are in black-and-white 1951-Bowman format with personal data, and a career summary.

		NM/M
Complete Sheet:		5.00
Complete Set (3):		4.00
1	Adrian Beltre	2.00
2	Kevin Brown	1.00
3	Eric Karros	1.00

Library Card

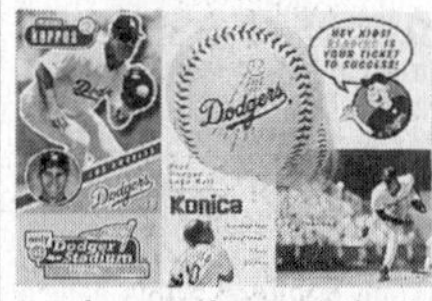

As part of a promotion to draw youngsters to the library to receive a free baseball bat, these sheets were given away at a promotional game at Dodger Stadium. The 8-1/2" x 4-3/4" sheet has a standard-size card perforated for easy removal. Front has an action photo. On back is another photo overprinted with stats.

		NM/M
(1)	Eric Karros	3.00

Police

Repeating the format used in recent years, a 30-card perforated sheet, the Dodgers issued their annual D.A.R.E.

drug-awareness set in April. Individual cards are the standard 2-1/2" x 3-1/2" on the 15" x 17-1/2" sheet. Fronts have action photos with blue borders. A baseball at top-left has the player's uniform number, by which the set is checklisted here. Backs are in black-and-white with LAPD and D.A.R.E. logos, player data and a safety message.

		NM/M
Uncut Sheet:		7.00
Complete Set (30):		6.00
Common Player:		.25
5	Jose Vizcaino	.25
7	Tripp Cromer	.25
8	Mark Grudzielanek	.25
9	Todd Hundley	.25
10	Gary Sheffield	.75
13	Antonio Osuna	.25
14	Adam Riggs	.25
15	Davey Johnson	.25
16	Paul LoDuca	.75
17	Juan Castro	.25
21	Eric Young	.25
22	Devon White	.25
23	Eric Karros	.25
25	Dave Hansen	.25
27	Kevin Brown	.45
28	Todd Hollandsworth	.25
29	Adrian Beltre	2.00
33	Carlos Perez	.25
37	Darren Dreifort	.25
41	Jeff Shaw	.25
43	Raul Mondesi	.25
46	Rick Wilkins	.25
48	Jacob Brumfield	.25
50	Pedro Borbon	.25
55	Onan Masaoka	.25
59	Ismael Valdes	.25
61	Chan Ho Park	.20
63	Angel Pena	.25
75	Alan Mills	.25
	Coaches (Rick Dempsey, Rick Down, Glenn Hoffman, Charlie Hough, Manny Mota, John Shelby, Jim Tracy)	.25

2000 L.A. Dodgers Fan Appreciation Days

Fans attending late-season Dodgers' games were given this 11" x 8-1/2" sheet announcing special sales of Dodgers souvenirs. At bottom are three cards of some of the team's most popular players. All are in color and standard 2-1/2" x 3-1/2" size, perforated for easy separation from the sheet. Card fronts have portrait and action photos while backs have 1/3 of a color team photo.

		NM/M
Complete Sheet:		5.00
Complete Set (3):		4.00
10	Gary Sheffield	1.00
15	Shawn Green	2.00
23	Eric Karros	1.00

Library Cards

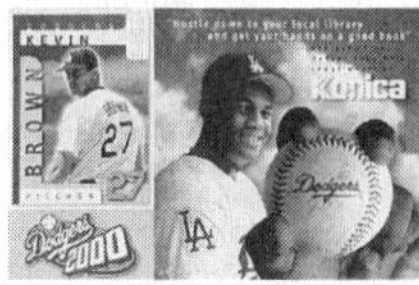

As part of a promotion to draw youngsters to the library to receive a free baseball, this sheet was given away at a promotional game at Dodger Stadium. The 8-1/2" x 4-3/4" sheet has a standard-size card perforated for easy removal. Front has both portrait and action photos. On back is another photo overprinted with stats.

		NM/M
Complete Set (2):		4.00
Common Player:		2.00
(1)	Kevin Brown	2.00
(2)	Gary Sheffield	2.00

Police

Repeating the format used in recent years, a 30-card 14-7/8" x 17-1/2" perforated sheet, the Dodgers issued their annual D.A.R.E. drug-awareness set in April. Individual cards are the standard 2-1/2" x 3-1/2". Fronts have game-action photos with blue borders. A baseball at top-left has the player's uniform number, by which the set is checklisted here. Backs are in black-and-white with LAPD and D.A.R.E. logos, player data and a safety message.

		NM/M
Uncut Sheet:		7.00
Complete Set (30):		6.00
Common Player:		.25
3	Alex Cora	.25
7	Jose Vizcaino	.25
8	Mark Grudzielanek	.25
9	Todd Hundley	.25
10	Gary Sheffield	.75
13	Antonio Osuna	.25
14	F.P. Santangelo	.25
15	Shawn Green	1.00
16	Paul LoDuca	.75
21	Chad Kreuter	.25
22	Devon White	.25
23	Eric Karros	.25
25	Dave Hansen	.25
27	Kevin Brown	.60
28	Todd Hollandsworth	.25
29	Adrian Beltre	1.00
30	Gregg Olson	.25
33	Carlos Perez	.25
36	Angel Pena	.25
37	Darren Dreifort	.25
40	Onan Masaoka	.25
41	Jeff Shaw	.25
43	Kevin Elster	.25
48	Eric Gagne	.75
51	Terry Adams	.25
55	Orel Hershiser	.50
56	Mike Fetters	.25
61	Chan Ho Park	.25
75	Alan Mills	.25
	Coaches (Rick Down, Glenn Hoffman, Davey Johnson, Manny Mota, Claude Osteen, John Shelby, Jim Tracy)	.25

2001 L.A. Dodgers Fan Appreciation Days

Fans attending late-season Dodgers' games were given this 8-1/2" x 11" tri-fold sheet announcing special sales of Dodgers souvenirs. At bottom are three cards of some of the team's most popular players. All are in color and standard 2-1/2" x 3-1/2" size, perforated for easy separation from the sheet. Card fronts action photos set on an embossed steel design background. Backs have a color portrait photo along with 2000 and 2001 highlights and stats.

		NM/M
Complete Sheet:		4.00
Complete Set (3):		3.00
1	Paul LoDuca	1.50
2	Chan Ho Park	1.00
3	Gary Sheffield	1.00

Police

All fans attending the April 29 game at Dodger Stadium received the team's annual police-sponsored drug awareness safety set. The 30-card set was produced in the format of an 14-3/4" x 17-1/2" perforated sheet. Virtually identical in design to previous years' issues, there is no 2001 identifier on the cards. Fronts have game-action photos bordered in blue with the uniform number in a baseball at top-left. Black-and-white backs have some personal data, an anti-drug message and sponsors' logos.

		NM/M
Uncut Sheet:		9.00
Complete Set (30):		6.00
Common Player:		.25
3	Alex Cora	.25
8	Mark Grudzielanek	.25
9	Marquis Grissom	.25
10	Gary Sheffield	.75
14	Jeff Reboulet	.25
15	Shawn Green	1.00
16	Paul LoDuca	.75
18	Tim Bogar	.25
21	Chad Kreuter	.25
23	Eric Karros	.25
25	Dave Hansen	.25
27	Kevin Brown	.60
28	Tom Goodwin	.25
29	Adrian Beltre	1.00
30	Gregg Olson	.25
36	Angel Pena	.25
37	Darren Dreifort	.25
38	Eric Gagne	.50
40	Onan Masaoka	.25
41	Jeff Shaw	.25
43	Andy Ashby	.25
45	Jose Antonio Nunez	.25
46	Hiram Bocachica	.25
47	Bruce Aven	.25
49	Matt Herges	.25
50	Chris Donnels	.25
51	Terry Adams	.25
56	Mike Fetters	.25
61	Chan Ho Park	.25
	Coaches (Travis Barbary, Jack Clark, Jim Colborn, Glenn Hoffman, Jim Lett, Manny Mota, Jim Riggleman, John Shelby, Jim Tracy)	.25

2002 L.A. Dodgers Police

Once again in 2002, at the April 21 game, children 14 and under received the team's annual police-sponsored drug awareness safety set, pro-

duced in the format of a 14-7/8" x 17-1/2" perforated sheet. Virtually identical in design to previous years' issues, there is no 2002 identifier on the cards. Fronts have game-action photos bordered in blue with the uniform number in a baseball at top-left. Black-and-white backs have some personal data, an anti-drug message and sponsors' logos.

		NM/M
Uncut Sheet:		10.00
Complete Set (30):		8.00
Common Player:		.25
3	Cesar Izturis	.25
7	Jeff Branson	.25
8	Mark Grudzielanek	.25
9	Marquis Grissom	.25
10	Hideo Nomo	1.50
13	Alex Cora	.25
14	Jeff Reboulet	.25
15	Shawn Green	1.00
16	Paul LoDuca	.75
17	Kazuhisa Ishii	1.50
21	Chad Kreuter	.25
23	Eric Karros	.25
25	Dave Hansen	.25
26	Hiram Bocachica	.25
27	Kevin Brown	.60
29	Adrian Beltre	1.00
30	Dave Roberts	.35
33	Brian Jordan	.25
36	Omar Daal	.25
37	Darren Dreifort	.25
38	Eric Gagne	.60
41	Odalis Perez	.25
43	Andy Ashby	.25
44	Phil Hiatt	.25
45	Terry Mulholland	.25
46	Paul Quantrill	.25
47	Jesse Orosco	.25
55	Giovanni Carrara	.25
74	Mike Kinkade	.35
---	Manager & Coaches (Jack Clark, Jim Colborn, Rob Flippo, Glenn Hoffman, Jim Lett, Manny Mota, Jim Riggleman, John Shelby, Jim Tracy)	.25

2003 L.A. Dodgers Fan Appreciation Days

Fans attending late-season Dodgers' games were given this 8-1/2" x 11" tri-fold sheet announcing special sales of Dodgers souvenirs. At bottom are three cards of some of the team's most popular players. All are in color and standard 2-1/2" x 3-1/2" size, perforated for easy separation from the sheet. Card fronts action photos and player-themed pennants. Black-and-white backs have another photo along with personal data and highlights.

		NM/M
Complete Sheet:		6.00
Complete Set (3):		5.00
10	Hideo Nomo	2.50
16	Paul Lo Duca	1.50
38	Eric Gagne	1.50

Police

At the April 20 game, children 14 and under received the team's annual police-sponsored drug awareness safety set, produced in the format of a 14-3/4" x 17-3/4" perforated sheet. Virtually identical in design to previous years' issues, there is no 2002 identifier on the cards. Fronts have game-action photos bordered in blue with the uniform number in a baseball at top-left. Black-and-white backs have some personal data, an anti-drug message and sponsors' logos.

		NM/M
Uncut Sheet:		10.00
Complete Set (30):		9.00
Common Player:		.25
3	Cesar Izturis	.25
6	Jolbert Cabrera	.25
7	Mike Kinkade	.35
8	Ron Coomer	.25
9	Todd Hundley	.25
10	Hideo Nomo	1.50
13	Alex Cora	.25
15	Shawn Green	1.00
16	Paul LoDuca	.50
17	Kazuhisa Ishii	1.00
26	Wilkin Ruan	.25
27	Kevin Brown	.45
28	Fred McGriff	.25
29	Adrian Beltre	1.00
30	Dave Roberts	.25
33	Brian Jordan	.25
36	Daryle Ward	.25
37	Darren Dreifort	.25
38	Eric Gagne	.60
40	David Ross	.25
41	Chad Hermansen	.25
43	Andy Ashby	.25
44	Paul Shuey	.25
45	Odalis Perez	.25
46	Paul Quantrill	.25
52	Chin-Feng Chen	.75
54	Troy Brohawn	.25
57	Victor Alvarez	.25
59	Guillermo Mota	.25
---	Manager & Coaches (Jack Clark, Jim Colborn, Rob Flippo, Glenn Hoffman, Jim Lett, Manny Mota, Jim Riggleman, John Shelby, Jim Tracy)	.25

2005 L.A./Brooklyn Dodgers Medallion Collection

A set of 21 commemorative medallions was sponsored by the Los Angeles Newspaper Group in this promotion. Coupons found in the newspapers between June 6-29 could be redeemed at convenience stores (along with $2.99) for that day's medallion. Larger and thicker than a quarter, the 1-3/16" diameter medals are struck in bronze (Brooklyn players) or nickel (current players) and have on their fronts an enameled portrait photo. A team logo dominates the back. A colorful, photo-filled album was available to house the pieces. The medals are listed here alphabetically.

		NM/M
Complete Set (21):		75.00
Common Player:		3.00
Album:		3.00
(1)	Wilson Alvarez	3.00
(2)	Milton Bradley	3.00
(3)	Yhency Brazoban	3.00
(4)	Roy Campanella	6.00
(5)	Hee Seop Choi	3.50
(6)	J.D. Drew	3.50
(7)	Eric Gagne	4.50
(8)	Cesar Izturis	3.00
(9)	Jeff Kent	4.50
(10)	Tommy Lasorda	3.00
(11)	Derek Lowe	3.00
(12)	Don Newcombe	3.00
(13)	Brad Penny	3.00
(14)	Odalis Perez	3.00
(15)	Jason Phillips	3.00
(16)	Jackie Robinson	10.00
(17)	Duke Snider	6.00
(18)	Jose Valentin	3.00
(19)	Jeff Weaver	3.00
(20)	Jayson Werth	3.00
(21)	50th Anniversary 1955 World Champions	3.00

1997 LaSalle Bank Ryne Sandberg

This card was part of a souvenir tribute distributed to more than 30,000 persons attending Ryne Sandberg's final game at Wrigley Field on September 20. A commemorative program and this card marked Ryno's 15 years as a Chicago Cub. The 2-1/2" x 3-1/2" card is printed on heavy, UV-coated cardboard. The front features a borderless color action photo. On the full-color back are portrait and action photos, career highlights and stats through September 14.

	NM/M
Ryne Sandberg	7.50

1985 Leaf-Donruss

In an attempt to share in the Canadian baseball card market, Donruss issued a 264-card version of its regular set to be sold in Canada.

Fronts of the 2-1/2" x 3-1/2" cards are virtually identical to the regular '85 Donruss cards of the same players, except that a green stylized leaf has been added to the logo in the upper-left. On back, player biographies have been re-written to accomodate both English and French versions, and new card numbers have been assigned. The 264 cards in this shortened set concentrate on star-caliber players, as well as those of Canada's two major league teams. A special two-card subset, "Canadian Greats," featured paintings of Dave Stieb and Tim Raines. The Leaf-Donruss cards were widely distributed in the U.S. through hobby dealers.

		NM/M
Complete Set (264):		35.00
Common Player:		.05
Wax Pack (12):		2.50
Wax Box (36):		75.00
1	Ryne Sandberg/DK	1.25
2	Doug DeCinces/DK	.05
3	Rich Dotson/DK	.05
4	Bert Blyleven/DK	.05
5	Lou Whitaker/DK	.05
6	Dan Quisenberry/DK	.05
7	Don Mattingly/DK	2.00
8	Carney Lansford/DK	.05
9	Frank Tanana/DK	.05
10	Willie Upshaw/DK	.05
11	Claudell Washington/DK	.05
12	Mike Marshall/DK	.05
13	Joaquin Andujar/DK	.05
14	Cal Ripken, Jr./DK	5.00
15	Jim Rice/DK	.25
16	Don Sutton/DK	.60
17	Frank Viola/DK	.05
18	Alvin Davis/DK	.05
19	Mario Soto/DK	.05
20	Jose Cruz/DK	.05
21	Charlie Lea/DK	.05
22	Jesse Orosco/DK	.05
23	Juan Samuel/DK	.05
24	Tony Pena/DK	.05
25	Tony Gwynn/DK	1.25
26	Bob Brenly/DK	.05
27	Steve Kiefer/RR	.05
28	Joe Morgan	.60
29	Luis Leal	.05
30	Dan Gladden	.05
31	Shane Rawley	.05
32	Mark Clear	.05
33	Terry Kennedy	.05
34	Hal McRae	.05
35	Mickey Rivers	.05
36	Tom Brunansky	.05
37	LaMarr Hoyt	.05
38	Orel Hershiser	1.00
39	Chris Bando	.05
40	Lee Lacy	.05
41	Lance Parrish	.05
42	George Foster	.05
43	Kevin McReynolds	.05
44	Robin Yount	.60
45	Craig McMurtry	.05
46	Mike Witt	.05
47	Gary Redus	.05
48	Dennis Rasmussen	.05
49	Gary Woods	.05
50	Phil Bradley	.05
51	Steve Bedrosian	.05
52	Duane Walker	.05
53	Geoff Zahn	.05
54	Dave Stieb	.05
55	Pascual Perez	.05
56	Mark Langston	.25
57	Bob Dernier	.05
58	Joe Cowley	.05
59	Dan Schatzeder	.05
60	Ozzie Smith	1.25
61	Bob Knepper	.05
62	Keith Hernandez	.05
63	Rick Rhoden	.05
64	Alejandro Pena	.05
65	Damaso Garcia	.05
66	Chili Davis	.05
67	Al Oliver	.05
68	Alan Wiggins	.05
69	Darryl Motley	.05
70	Gary Ward	.05
71	John Butcher	.05
72	Scott McGregor	.05
73	Bruce Hurst	.05
74	Dwayne Murphy	.05
75	Greg Luzinski	.05
76	Pat Tabler	.05
77	Chet Lemon	.05
78	Jim Sundberg	.05
79	Wally Backman	.05
80	Terry Puhl	.05
81	Storm Davis	.05
82	Jim Wohlford	.05
83	Willie Randolph	.05
84	Ron Cey	.05
85	Jim Beattie	.05
86	Rafael Ramirez	.05
87	Cesar Cedeno	.05
88	Bobby Grich	.05
89	Jason Thompson	.05
90	Steve Sax	.05
91	Tony Fernandez	.15
92	Jeff Leonard	.05
93	Von Hayes	.05
94	Steve Garvey	.30
95	Steve Balboni	.05
96	Larry Parrish	.05
97	Tim Teufel	.05
98	Sammy Stewart	.05
99	Roger Clemens	30.00
100	Steve Kemp	.05
101	Tom Seaver	1.00
102	Andre Thornton	.05
103	Kirk Gibson	.05
104	Ted Simmons	.05
105	David Palmer	.05
106	Roy Lee Jackson	.05
107	Kirby Puckett	4.00
108	Charlie Hough	.05
109	Mike Boddicker	.05
110	Willie Wilson	.05
111	Tim Lollar	.05
112	Tony Armas	.05
113	Steve Carlton	.60
114	Gary Lavelle	.05
115	Cliff Johnson	.05
116	Ray Burris	.05
117	Rudy Law	.05
118	Mike Scioscia	.05
119	Kent Tekulve	.05
120	George Vukovich	.05
121	Barbaro Garbey	.05
122	Mookie Wilson	.05
123	Ben Oglivie	.05
124	Jerry Mumphrey	.05
125	Willie McGee	.05
126	Jeff Reardon	.05
127	Dave Winfield	1.00
128	Lee Smith	.10
129	Ken Phelps	.05
130	Rick Camp	.05
131	Dave Concepcion	.05
132	Rod Carew	.60
133	Andre Dawson	.25
134	Doyle Alexander	.05
135	Miguel Dilone	.05
136	Jim Gott	.05
137	Eric Show	.05
138	Phil Niekro	.45
139	Rick Sutcliffe	.05
140	Two For The Title (Don Mattingly, Dave Winfield)	3.00
141	Ken Oberkfell	.05
142	Jack Morris	.05
143	Lloyd Moseby	.05
144	Pete Rose	2.00
145	Gary Gaetti	.05
146	Don Baylor	.05
147	Bobby Meacham	.05
148	Frank White	.05
149	Mark Thurmond	.05
150	Dwight Evans	.05
151	Al Holland	.05
152	Joel Youngblood	.05
153	Rance Mulliniks	.05
154	Bill Caudill	.05
155	Carlton Fisk	.60
156	Rick Honeycutt	.05
157	John Candelaria	.05
158	Alan Trammell	.05
159	Darryl Strawberry	.05
160	Aurelio Lopez	.05
161	Enos Cabell	.05
162	Dion James	.05
163	Bruce Sutter	.75
164	Razor Shines	.05
165	Butch Wynegar	.05
166	Rich Bordi	.05
167	Spike Owen	.05
168	Chris Chambliss	.05
169	Dave Parker	.05
170	Reggie Jackson	1.00
171	Bryn Smith	.05
172	Dave Collins	.05
173	Dave Engle	.05
174	Buddy Bell	.05
175	Mike Flanagan	.05
176	George Brett	1.50
177	Graig Nettles	.05
178	Jerry Koosman	.05
179	Wade Boggs	1.25
180	Jody Davis	.05
181	Ernie Whitt	.05
182	Dave Kingman	.05
183	Vance Law	.05
184	Fernando Valenzuela	.05
185	Bill Madlock	.05
186	Brett Butler	.05
187	Doug Sisk	.05
188	Dan Petry	.05
189	Joe Niekro	.05
190	Rollie Fingers	.45
191	David Green	.05
192	Steve Rogers	.05
193	Ken Griffey	.05
194	Scott Sanderson	.05
195	Barry Bonnell	.05
196	Bruce Benedict	.05
197	Keith Moreland	.05
198	Fred Lynn	.05
199	Tim Wallach	.20
200	Kent Hrbek	.05
201	Pete O'Brien	.05
202	Bud Black	.05
203	Eddie Murray	.60
204	Goose Gossage	.05
205	Mike Schmidt	1.50
206	Mike Easler	.05
207	Jack Clark	.05
208	Rickey Henderson	1.00
209	Jesse Barfield	.15
210	Ron Kittle	.05
211	Pedro Guerrero	.05
212	Johnny Ray	.05
213	Julio Franco	.05
214	Hubie Brooks	.05
215	Darrell Evans	.05
216	Nolan Ryan	5.00
217	Jim Gantner	.05
218	Tim Raines	.20
219	Dave Righetti	.05
220	Gary Matthews	.05
221	Jack Perconte	.05
222	Dale Murphy	.30
223	Brian Downing	.05
224	Mickey Hatcher	.05
225	Lonnie Smith	.05
226	Jorge Orta	.05
227	Milt Wilcox	.05
228	John Denny	.05
229	Marty Barrett	.05
230	Alfredo Griffin	.05
231	Harold Baines	.05
232	Bill Russell	.05
233	Marvell Wynne	.05
234	Dwight Gooden	.50
235	Willie Hernandez	.05
236	Bill Gullickson	.05
237	Ron Guidry	.05
238	Leon Durham	.05
239	Al Cowens	.05
240	Bob Horner	.05
241	Gary Carter	1.00
242	Glenn Hubbard	.05
243	Steve Trout	.05
244	Jay Howell	.05
245	Terry Francona	.05
246	Cecil Cooper	.05
247	Larry McWilliams	.05
248	George Bell	.15
249	Larry Herndon	.05
250	Ozzie Virgil	.05
251	Dave Stieb (Canadian Great)	.50
252	Tim Raines (Canadian Great)	2.00
253	Ricky Horton	.05
254	Bill Buckner	.05
255	Dan Driessen	.05
256	Ron Darling	.05
257	Doug Flynn	.05
258	Darrell Porter	.05
259	George Hendrick	.05
653	Lou Gehrig Puzzle Card	.05
----	Checklist 1-26 DK	.05
----	Checklist 27-102	.05
----	Checklist 103-178	.05
----	Checklist 179-259	.05

1986 Leaf

For its second Canadian card set the Donruss name was removed from the front of the company's 264-card issue, identifying the cards as "Leaf '86." Again concentrating on big-name stars and players from the Expos and Blue Jays, the 2-1/2" x 3-1/2" cards feature a design identical to the 1986 Donruss cards. Backs were altered to allow the publication of career highlights in both English and French, and card numbers were changed. The "Canadian Greats" cards in the 1986 Leaf set, painted portraits rather than photos, were Jesse Barfield and Jeff Reardon. Besides being sold in its intended market in Canada, the set was widely distributed in the U.S. through hobby vendors.

		NM/M
Complete Set (264):		12.00
Common Player:		.05
Wax Pack:		1.00
Wax Box (36):		20.00
1	Kirk Gibson/DK	.05
2	Goose Gossage/DK	.05
3	Willie McGee/DK	.05
4	George Bell/DK	.10
5	Tony Armas/DK	.05
6	Chili Davis/DK	.05
7	Cecil Cooper/DK	.05
8	Mike Boddicker/DK	.05
9	Davey Lopes/DK	.05
10	Bill Doran/DK	.05
11	Bret Saberhagen/DK	.05
12	Brett Butler/DK	.05
13	Harold Baines/DK	.05
14	Mike Davis/DK	.05
15	Tony Perez/DK	.35
16	Willie Randolph/DK	.05
17	Bob Boone/DK	.05
18	Orel Hershiser/DK	.05
19	Johnny Ray/DK	.05
20	Gary Ward/DK	.05
21	Rick Mahler/DK	.05
22	Phil Bradley/DK	.05
23	Jerry Koosman/DK	.05
24	Tom Brunansky/DK	.05
25	Andre Dawson/DK	.35
26	Dwight Gooden/DK	.05
27	Andres Galarraga/RR	2.00
28	Fred McGriff/RR	4.00
29	Dave Shipanoff/RR	.05
30	Danny Jackson	.05
31	Robin Yount	.50
32	Mike Fitzgerald	.05
33	Lou Whitaker	.05
34	Alfredo Griffin	.05
35	"Oil Can" Boyd	.05
36	Ron Guidry	.05
37	Rickey Henderson	.75
38	Jack Morris	.05
39	Brian Downing	.05
40	Mike Marshall	.05
41	Tony Gwynn	1.00
42	George Brett	1.25
43	Jim Gantner	.05
44	Hubie Brooks	.05
45	Tony Fernandez	.10
46	Oddibe McDowell	.05
47	Ozzie Smith	1.00
48	Ken Griffey	.05
49	Jose Cruz	.05
50	Mariano Duncan	.05
51	Mike Schmidt	1.25
52	Pat Tabler	.05
53	Pete Rose	1.50
54	Frank White	.05
55	Carney Lansford	.05
56	Steve Garvey	.15
57	Vance Law	.05
58	Tony Pena	.05
59	Wayne Tolleson	.05
60	Dale Murphy	.20
61	LaMarr Hoyt	.05
62	Ryne Sandberg	1.00
63	Gary Carter	1.00
64	Lee Smith	.05
65	Alvin Davis	.05
66	Edwin Nunez	.05
67	Kent Hrbek	.05
68	Dave Stieb	.05
69	Kirby Puckett	1.00
70	Paul Molitor	.75
71	Glenn Hubbard	.05
72	Lloyd Moseby	.05
73	Mike Smithson	.05
74	Jeff Leonard	.05
75	Danny Darwin	.05
76	Kevin McReynolds	.05
77	Bill Buckner	.05
78	Ron Oester	.05
79	Tommy Herr	.05
80	Mike Pagliarulo	.05
81	Ron Romanick	.05
82	Brook Jacoby	.05
83	Eddie Murray	.50
84	Gary Pettis	.05
85	Chet Lemon	.05
86	Toby Harrah	.05
87	Mike Scioscia	.05
88	Bert Blyleven	.05
89	Dave Righetti	.05
90	Bob Knepper	.05
91	Fernando Valenzuela	.05
92	Dave Dravecky	.05
93	Julio Franco	.05
94	Keith Moreland	.05
95	Darryl Motley	.05
96	Jack Clark	.05
97	Tim Wallach	.05
98	Steve Balboni	.05
99	Storm Davis	.05
100	Jay Howell	.05
101	Alan Trammell	.05
102	Willie Hernandez	.05
103	Don Mattingly	1.25
104	Lee Lacy	.05
105	Pedro Guerrero	.05
106	Willie Wilson	.05
107	Craig Reynolds	.05
108	Tim Raines	.15
109	Shane Rawley	.05
110	Larry Parrish	.05
111	Eric Show	.05
112	Mike Witt	.05
113	Dennis Eckersley	.35
114	Mike Moore	.05
115	Vince Coleman	.05
116	Damaso Garcia	.05
117	Steve Carlton	.50
118	Floyd Bannister	.05
119	Mario Soto	.05
120	Fred Lynn	.05
121	Bob Horner	.05
122	Rick Sutcliffe	.05
123	Walt Terrell	.05
124	Keith Hernandez	.05
125	Dave Winfield	.75
126	Frank Viola	.05
127	Dwight Evans	.05
128	Willie Upshaw	.05
129	Andre Thornton	.05
130	Donnie Moore	.05
131	Darryl Strawberry	.05
132	Nolan Ryan	2.00
133	Garry Templeton	.05
134	John Tudor	.05
135	Dave Parker	.05
136	Larry McWilliams	.05
137	Terry Pendleton	.05
138	Terry Puhl	.05
139	Bob Dernier	.05
140	Ozzie Guillen	.05
141	Jim Clancy	.05
142	Cal Ripken, Jr.	2.00
143	Mickey Hatcher	.05
144	Dan Petry	.05
145	Rich Gedman	.05
146	Jim Rice	.10
147	Butch Wynegar	.05
148	Donnie Hill	.05
149	Jim Sundberg	.05
150	Joe Hesketh	.05
151	Chris Codiroli	.05
152	Charlie Hough	.05
153	Herman Winningham	.05
154	Dave Rozema	.05
155	Don Slaught	.05
156	Juan Beniquez	.05
157	Ted Higuera	.05
158	Andy Hawkins	.05
159	Don Robinson	.05
160	Glenn Wilson	.05
161	Earnest Riles	.05
162	Nick Esasky	.05
163	Carlton Fisk	.50
164	Claudell Washington	.05
165	Scott McGregor	.05
166	Nate Snell	.05
167	Ted Simmons	.05
168	Wade Boggs	1.00
169	Marty Barrett	.05
170	Bud Black	.05
171	Charlie Leibrandt	.05
172	Charlie Lea	.05
173	Reggie Jackson	.50
174	Bryn Smith	.05
175	Glenn Davis	.05
176	Von Hayes	.05
177	Danny Cox	.05
178	Sam Khalifa	.05
179	Tom Browning	.05
180	Scott Garrelts	.05
181	Shawon Dunston	.05
182	Doyle Alexander	.05
183	Jim Presley	.05
184	Al Cowens	.05
185	Mark Salas	.05
186	Tom Niedenfuer	.05
187	Dave Henderson	.05
188	Lonnie Smith	.05
189	Bruce Bochte	.05
190	Leon Durham	.05
191	Terry Francona	.05
192	Bruce Sutter	.75
193	Steve Crawford	.05
194	Bob Brenly	.05
195	Dan Pasqua	.05
196	Juan Samuel	.05
197	Floyd Rayford	.05
198	Tim Burke	.05
199	Ben Oglivie	.05
200	Don Carman	.05
201	Lance Parrish	.05
202	Terry Forster	.05
203	Neal Heaton	.05
204	Ivan Calderon	.05
205	Jorge Orta	.05
206	Tom Henke	.05
207	Rick Reuschel	.05
208	Dan Quisenberry	.05
209	Ty-Breaking Hit (Pete Rose)	.25
210	Floyd Youmans	.05
211	Tom Filer	.05
212	R.J. Reynolds	.05
213	Gorman Thomas	.05
214	Canadian Great (Jeff Reardon (Canadian Great))	.45
215	Chris Brown	.05
216	Rick Aguilera	.05
217	Ernie Whitt	.05
218	Joe Orsulak	.05
219	Jimmy Key	.05
220	Atlee Hammaker	.05
221	Ron Darling	.05
222	Zane Smith	.05
223	Bob Welch	.05
224	Reid Nichols	.05
225	Fleet Feet (Vince Coleman, Willie McGee)	.10
226	Mark Gubicza	.05
227	Tim Birtsas	.05
228	Mike Hargrove	.05
229	Randy St. Claire	.05
230	Larry Herndon	.05
231	Dusty Baker	.05
232	Mookie Wilson	.05
233	Jeff Lahti	.05
234	Tom Seaver	.50
235	Mike Scott	.05
236	Don Sutton	.35
237	Roy Smalley	.05
238	Bill Madlock	.05
239	Charles Hudson	.05
240	John Franco	.05
241	Frank Tanana	.05
242	Sid Fernandez	.05
243	Knuckle Brothers (Joe Niekro, Phil Niekro)	.10
244	Dennis Lamp	.05
245	Gene Nelson	.05
246	Terry Harper	.05
247	Vida Blue	.05
248	Roger McDowell	.05
249	Tony Bernazard	.05
250	Cliff Johnson	.05
251	Hal McRae	.05
252	Garth Iorg	.05
253	Mitch Webster	.05
254	Jesse Barfield (Canadian Great)	.35
255	Dan Driessen	.05
256	Mike Brown	.05
257	Ron Kittle	.05
258	Bo Diaz	.05
259	Hank Aaron Puzzle Card	.05
260	Pete Rose (King of Kings)	1.50
----	Checklist 1-26 DK	.05
----	Checklist 27-106	.05
----	Checklist 107-186	.05
----	Checklist 187-260	.05

1987 Leaf

For the third consecutive season, Leaf-Donruss issued a Canadian baseball card set. These cards are nearly identical to the American set except for the name "Leaf" which appears on the front in place of "Donruss." The set contains 264 cards, each measuring 2-1/2" x 3-1/2", with a special emphasis being placed on players from the Montreal and Toronto teams. Backs feature career highlights in both English and French. As in the previous years, two "Canadian Greats" cards appear in the set. These painted portraits feature Mark Eichhorn and Floyd Youmans.

		NM/M
Unopened Factory Set (264):		25.00
Complete Set (264):		17.50
Common Player:		.05
Wax Pack:		1.50
Wax Box (36):		30.00
1	Wally Joyner/DK	.05
2	Roger Clemens/DK	1.00
3	Dale Murphy/DK	.15
4	Darryl Strawberry/DK	.05
5	Ozzie Smith/DK	.65
6	Jose Canseco/DK	.40
7	Charlie Hough/DK	.05
8	Brook Jacoby/DK	.05
9	Fred Lynn/DK	.05
10	Rick Rhoden/DK	.05
11	Chris Brown/DK	.05
12	Von Hayes/DK	.05
13	Jack Morris/DK	.10
14	Kevin McReynolds/DK	.05
15	George Brett/DK	.75
16	Ted Higuera/DK	.05
17	Hubie Brooks/DK	.05
18	Mike Scott/DK	.05
19	Kirby Puckett/DK	.65
20	Dave Winfield/DK	.75
21	Lloyd Moseby/DK	.10
22	Eric Davis/DK	.05
23	Jim Presley/DK	.05
24	Keith Moreland/DK	.05
25	Greg Walker/DK	.05
26	Steve Sax/DK	.05
27	Checklist 1-27	.05
28	B.J. Surhoff/RR	.05

29 Randy Myers/RR .05
30 Ken Gerhart/RR .05
31 Benito Santiago/RR .05
32 Greg Swindell/RR .05
33 Mike Birkbeck/RR .05
34 Terry Steinbach/RR .05
35 Bo Jackson/RR .25
36 Greg Maddux/RR 2.00
37 Jim Lindeman/RR .05
38 Devon White/RR .75
39 Eric Bell/RR .05
40 Will Fraser/RR .05
41 Jerry Browne/RR .05
42 Chris James/RR .05
43 Rafael Palmeiro/RR 1.00
44 Pat Dodson/RR .05
45 Duane Ward/RR .25
46 Mark McGwire/RR 4.00
47 Bruce Fields/RR (Photo actually Darnell Coles.) .05
48 Jody Davis .05
49 Roger McDowell .05
50 Jose Guzman .05
51 Oddibe McDowell .05
52 Harold Baines .05
53 Dave Righetti .05
54 Moose Haas .05
55 Mark Langston .05
56 Kirby Puckett .65
57 Dwight Evans .05
58 Willie Randolph .05
59 Wally Backman .05
60 Bryn Smith .05
61 Tim Wallach .05
62 Joe Hesketh .05
63 Garry Templeton .05
64 Rob Thompson .05
65 Canadian Greats (Floyd Youmans) .10
66 Ernest Riles .05
67 Robin Yount .50
68 Darryl Strawberry .05
69 Ernie Whitt .05
70 Dave Winfield .65
71 Paul Molitor .75
72 Dave Stieb .05
73 Tom Henke .05
74 Frank Viola .05
75 Scott Garrelts .05
76 Mike Boddicker .05
77 Keith Moreland .05
78 Lou Whitaker .05
79 Dave Parker .05
80 Lee Smith .05
81 Tom Candiotti .05
82 Greg Harris .05
83 Fred Lynn .05
84 Dwight Gooden .05
85 Ron Darling .05
86 Mike Krukow .05
87 Spike Owen .05
88 Len Dykstra .05
89 Rick Aguilera .05
90 Jim Clancy .05
91 Joe Johnson .05
92 Damaso Garcia .05
93 Sid Fernandez .05
94 Bob Ojeda .05
95 Ted Higuera .05
96 George Brett .75
97 Willie Wilson .05
98 Cal Ripken 1.50
99 Kent Hrbek .05
100 Bert Blyleven .05
101 Ron Guidry .05
102 Andy Allanson .05
103 Dave Henderson .05
104 Kirk Gibson .05
105 Lloyd Moseby .05
106 Tony Fernandez .05
107 Lance Parrish .05
108 Ozzie Smith .75
109 Gary Carter .75
110 Eddie Murray .50
111 Mike Witt .05
112 Bobby Witt .05
113 Willie McGee .05
114 Steve Garvey .10
115 Glenn Davis .05
116 Jose Cruz .05
117 Ozzie Guillen .05
118 Alvin Davis .05
119 Jose Rijo .05
120 Bill Madlock .05
121 Tommy Herr .05
122 Mike Schmidt .75
123 Mike Scioscia .05
124 Terry Pendleton .05
125 Leon Durham .05
126 Alan Trammell .05
127 Jesse Barfield .05
128 Shawon Dunston .05
129 Pete Rose 1.25
130 Von Hayes .05
131 Julio Franco .05
132 Juan Samuel .05
133 Joe Carter .10
134 Brook Jacoby .05
135 Jack Morris .05
136 Bob Horner .05
137 Calvin Schiraldi .05
138 Tom Browning .05
139 Shane Rawley .05
140 Mario Soto .05
141 Dale Murphy .15
142 Hubie Brooks .05
143 Jeff Reardon .05
144 Will Clark .15
145 Ed Correa .05
146 Glenn Wilson .05
147 Johnny Ray .05
148 Fernando Valenzuela .05
149 Tim Raines .10
150 Don Mattingly .75
151 Jose Canseco .40
152 Gary Pettis .05
153 Don Sutton .30
154 Jim Presley .05
155 Checklist 28-105 .05
156 Dale Sveum .05
157 Cory Snyder .05
158 Jeff Sellers .05
159 Denny Walling .05
160 Danny Cox .05
161 Bob Forsch .05
162 Joaquin Andujar .05
163 Roberto Clemente Puzzle Card .10
164 Paul Assenmacher .05
165 Marty Barrett .05
166 Ray Knight .05
167 Rafael Santana .05
168 Bruce Ruffin .05
169 Buddy Bell .05
170 Kevin Mitchell .05
171 Ken Oberkfell .05
172 Gene Garber .05
173 Canadian Greats (Mark Eichhorn) .15
174 Don Carman .05
175 Jesse Orosco .05
176 Mookie Wilson .05
177 Gary Ward .05
178 John Franco .05
179 Eric Davis .05
180 Walt Terrell .05
181 Phil Niekro .30
182 Pat Tabler .05
183 Brett Butler .05
184 George Bell .10
185 Pete Incaviglia .05
186 Pete O'Brien .05
187 Jimmy Key .05
188 Frank White .05
189 Mike Pagliarulo .05
190 Roger Clemens 1.00
191 Rickey Henderson .75
192 Mike Easler .05
193 Wade Boggs .75
194 Vince Coleman .05
195 Charlie Kerfeld .05
196 Dickie Thon .05
197 Bill Doran .05
198 Alfredo Griffin .05
199 Carlton Fisk .50
200 Phil Bradley .05
201 Reggie Jackson .65
202 Bob Boone .05
203 Steve Sax .05
204 Tom Niedenfuer .05
205 Tim Burke .05
206 Floyd Youmans .05
207 Jay Tibbs .05
208 Chili Davis .05
209 Larry Parrish .05
210 John Cerutti .05
211 Kevin Bass .05
212 Andre Dawson .25
213 Bob Sebra .05
214 Kevin McReynolds .05
215 Jim Morrison .05
216 Candy Maldonado .05
217 John Kruk .05
218 Todd Worrell .05
219 Barry Bonds 10.00
220 Andy McGaffigan .05
221 Andres Galarraga .10
222 Mike Fitzgerald .05
223 Kirk McCaskill .05
224 Dave Smith .05
225 Ruben Sierra .05
226 Scott Fletcher .05
227 Chet Lemon .05
228 Dan Petry .05
229 Mark Eichhorn .05
230 Cecil Cooper .05
231 Willie Upshaw .05
232 Don Baylor .05
233 Keith Hernandez .05
234 Ryne Sandberg .75
235 Tony Gwynn .65
236 Chris Brown .05
237 Pedro Guerrero .05
238 Mark Gubicza .05
239 Sid Bream .05
240 Joe Cowley .05
241 Bill Buckner .05
242 John Candelaria .05
243 Scott McGregor .05
244 Tom Brunansky .05
245 Gary Gaetti .05
246 Orel Hershiser .05
247 Jim Rice .10
248 Oil Can Boyd .05
249 Bob Knepper .05
250 Danny Tartabull .05
251 John Cangelosi .05
252 Wally Joyner .05
253 Bruce Hurst .05
254 Rich Gedman .05
255 Jim Deshaies .05
256 Tony Pena .05
257 Nolan Ryan 1.50
258 Mike Scott .05
259 Checklist 106-183 .05
260 Dennis Rasmussen .05
261 Bret Saberhagen .05
262 Steve Balboni .05
263 Tom Seaver .50
264 Checklist 184-264 .05

1987 Leaf Candy City Team

Leaf produced this set as part of its endorsement for the Special Olympics. Twelve cards feature Baseball Hall of Famers. The cards measure 2-1/2" x 3-1/2" and are numbered H1-H12. The remaining six cards in the set are numbered S1-S6 and feature unnamed Special Olympics champions. All cards feature the artwork of Dick Perez. The cards were available through a mail-in offer advertised at special store displays. Only the baseball-related subjects are listed in the checklist.

NM/M
Complete Set (12): 3.00
Common Player: .15
H1 Mickey Mantle 1.00
H2 Yogi Berra .35
H3 Roy Campanella .35
H4 Stan Musial .50
H5 Ted Williams .60
H6 Duke Snider .35
H7 Hank Aaron .60
H8 Pee Wee Reese .35
H9 Brooks Robinson .25
H10 Al Kaline .25
H11 Willie McCovey .25
H12 Cool Papa Bell .15

1988 Leaf

This 264-card set features color player photos from among the 1988 Donruss 660-card standard issue, with emphasis on players from Montreal and Toronto. A border of red, blue and black stripes duplicates the design of the Donruss set, with the exception of a "Leaf '88" logo in the upper-left corner that replaces the Donruss logo. Two special Canadian Greats cards are included in this set: Perez-Steele portraits of Tim Wallach and George Bell. The set also includes the portrait-style Diamond Kings cards (the set's first 26 cards, one for each team). The DK's carry the Donruss logo above the gold DK banner. All card backs are bilingual (French/English), numbered, and printed in black on white stock with a light blue border. This set was sold in 10-card wax packs with one triple-piece puzzle card per pack and was distributed via larger hobby and retail shops in the U.S. and Canada.

NM/M
Complete Set (264): 6.00
Common Player: .05
Wax Pack (15): .50
Wax Box (36): 9.00
1 Mark McGwire/DK 1.25
2 Tim Raines/DK .20
3 Benito Santiago/DK .05
4 Alan Trammell/DK .05
5 Danny Tartabull/DK .05
6 Ron Darling/DK .05
7 Paul Molitor/DK .75
8 Devon White/DK .20
9 Andre Dawson/DK .25
10 Julio Franco/DK .05
11 Scott Fletcher/DK .05
12 Tony Fernandez/DK .10
13 Shane Rawley/DK .05
14 Kal Daniels/DK .05
15 Jack Clark/DK .05
16 Dwight Evans/DK .05
17 Tommy John/DK .05
18 Andy Van Slyke/DK .05
19 Gary Gaetti/DK .05
20 Mark Langston/DK .05
21 Will Clark/DK .15
22 Glenn Hubbard/DK .05
23 Billy Hatcher/DK .05
24 Bob Welch/DK .05
25 Ivan Calderon/DK .05
26 Cal Ripken, Jr./DK 1.50
27 Checklist 1-27 .05
28 Mackey Sasser/RR .05
29 Jeff Treadway/RR .05
30 Mike Campbell/RR .05
31 Lance Johnson/RR .05
32 Nelson Liriano/RR .05
33 Shawn Abner/RR .05
34 Roberto Alomar/RR 2.50
35 Shawn Hillegas/RR .05
36 Joey Meyer/RR .05
37 Kevin Elster/RR .05
38 Jose Lind/RR .05
39 Kirt Manwaring/RR .05
40 Mark Grace/RR .75
41 Jody Reed/RR .05
42 John Farrell/RR .05
43 Al Leiter/RR .25
44 Gary Thurman/RR .05
45 Vincente Palacios/RR .05
46 Eddie Williams/RR .05
47 Jack McDowell/RR .20
48 Dwight Gooden .05
49 Mike Witt .05
50 Wally Joyner .05
51 Brook Jacoby .05
52 Bert Blyleven .05
53 Ted Higuera .05
54 Mike Scott .05
55 Jose Guzman .05
56 Roger Clemens 1.25
57 Dave Righetti .05
58 Benito Santiago .05
59 Ozzie Guillen .05
60 Matt Nokes .05
61 Fernando Valenzuela .05
62 Orel Hershiser .05
63 Sid Fernandez .05
64 Ozzie Virgil .05
65 Wade Boggs .50
66 Floyd Youmans .05
67 Jimmy Key .05
68 Bret Saberhagen .05
69 Jody Davis .05
70 Shawon Dunston .05
71 Julio Franco .05
72 Danny Cox .05
73 Jim Clancy .05
74 Mark Eichhorn .05
75 Scott Bradley .05
76 Charlie Liebrandt .05
77 Nolan Ryan 1.50
78 Ron Darling .05
79 John Franco .05
80 Dave Stieb .05
81 Mike Fitzgerald .05
82 Steve Bedrosian .05
83 Dale Murphy .20
84 Tim Burke .05
85 Jack Morris .05
86 Greg Walker .05
87 Kevin Mitchell .05
88 Doug Drabek .05
89 Charlie Hough .05
90 Tony Gwynn .75
91 Rick Sutcliffe .05
92 Shane Rawley .05
93 George Brett 1.00
94 Frank Viola .05
95 Tony Pena .05
96 Jim Deshaies .05
97 Mike Scioscia .05
98 Rick Rhoden .05
99 Terry Kennedy .05
100 Cal Ripken 1.50
101 Pedro Guerrero .05
102 Andy Van Slyke .05
103 Willie McGee .05
104 Mike Kingery .05
105 Kevin Seitzer .05
106 Robin Yount .50
107 Tracy Jones .05
108 Dave Magadan .05
109 Mel Hall .05
110 Billy Hatcher .05
111 Todd Benzinger .05
112 Mike LaValliere .05
113 Barry Bonds 1.50
114 Tim Raines .20
115 Ozzie Smith .75
116 Dave Winfield .75
117 Keith Hernandez .05
118 Jeffrey Leonard .05
119 Larry Parrish .05
120 Rob Thompson .05
121 Andres Galarraga .15
122 Mickey Hatcher .05
123 Mark Langston .05
124 Mike Schmidt 1.00
125 Cory Snyder .05
126 Andre Dawson .15
127 Devon White .15
128 Vince Coleman .05
129 Bryn Smith .05
130 Lance Parrish .05
131 Willie Upshaw .05
132 Pete O'Brien .05
133 Tony Fernandez .10
134 Billy Ripken .05
135 Len Dykstra .05
136 Kirk Gibson .05
137 Kevin Bass .05
138 Jose Canseco .50
139 Kent Hrbek .05
140 Lloyd Moseby .05
141 Marty Barrett .05
142 Carmelo Martinez .05
143 Tom Foley .05
144 Kirby Puckett .75
145 Rickey Henderson .75
146 Juan Samuel .05
147 Pete Incaviglia .05
148 Greg Brock .05
149 Eric Davis .05
150 Kal Daniels .05
151 Bob Boone .05
152 John Cerutti .05
153 Mike Greenwell .05
154 Oddibe McDowell .05
155 Scott Fletcher .05
156 Gary Carter .75
157 Harold Baines .05
158 Greg Swindell .05
159 Mark McLemore .05
160 Keith Moreland .05
161 Jim Gantner .05
162 Willie Randolph .05
163 Fred Lynn .05
164 B.J. Surhoff .05
165 Ken Griffey .05
166 Chet Lemon .05
167 Alan Trammell .05
168 Paul Molitor .75
169 Lou Whitaker .05
170 Will Clark .10
171 Dwight Evans .05
172 Eddie Murray .50
173 Darrell Evans .05
174 Ellis Burks .05
175 Ivan Calderon .05
176 John Kruk .05
177 Don Mattingly 1.00
178 Dick Schofield .05
179 Bruce Hurst .05
180 Ron Guidry .05
181 Jack Clark .05
182 Franklin Stubbs .05
183 Bill Doran .05
184 Joe Carter .05
185 Steve Sax .05
186 Glenn Davis .05
187 Bo Jackson .10
188 Bobby Bonilla .05
189 Willie Wilson .05
190 Danny Tartabull .05
191 Bo Diaz .05
192 Buddy Bell .05
193 Tim Wallach .05
194 Mark McGwire 1.25
195 Carney Lansford .05
196 Alvin Davis .05
197 Von Hayes .05
198 Mitch Webster .05
199 Casey Candaele .05
200 Gary Gaetti .05
201 Tommy Herr .05
202 Wally Backman .05
203 Brian Downing .05
204 Rance Mulliniks .05
205 Craig Reynolds .05
206 Ruben Sierra .05
207 Ryne Sandberg .75
208 Carlton Fisk .50
209 Checklist 28-107 .05
210 Gerald Young .05
211 MVP (Tim Raines) .25
212 John Tudor .05
213 Canadian Greats (George Bell) .60
214 MVP (George Bell) .25
215 Jim Rice .10
216 Gerald Perry .05
217 Dave Stewart .05
218 Jose Uribe .05
219 Rick Rueschel .05
220 Darryl Strawberry .05
221 Chris Brown .05
223 Lee Mazzilli .05
224 Denny Walling .05
225 Jesse Barfield .05
226 Barry Larkin .05
227 Harold Reynolds .05
228 Kevin McReynolds .05
229 Todd Worrell .05
230 Tommy John .05
231 Rick Aguilera .05
232 Bill Madlock .05
233 Roy Smalley .05
234 Jeff Musselman .05
235 Mike Dunne .05
236 Jerry Browne .05
237 Sam Horn .05
238 Howard Johnson .05
239 Candy Maldonado .05
240 Nick Esasky .05
241 Geno Petralli .05
242 Herm Winningham .05
243 Roger McDowell .05
244 Brian Fisher .05
245 John Marzano .05
246 Terry Pendleton .05
247 Rick Leach .05
248 Pascual Perez .05
249 Mookie Wilson .05
250 Ernie Whitt .05
251 Ron Kittle .05
252 Oil Can Boyd .05
253 Jim Gott .05
254 George Bell .10
255 Canadian Greats (Tim Wallach) .60
256 Luis Polonia .05
257 Hubie Brooks .05
258 Mickey Brantley .05
259 Gregg Jefferies .25
260 Johnny Ray .05
261 Checklist 108-187 .05
262 Dennis Martinez .05
263 Stan Musial Puzzle Card .05
264 Checklist 188-264 .05

1989 Leaf Blue Chip Cards

Unknown until 2001, these cards are a variation of the 1989 Donruss Grand Slammers insert set and share the back design with that issue. Instead of the GS logo in the lower-left corner of the photo, these cards have a black, white and blue logo reading "Blue Chip / CARDS / Leaf." The Blue Chip cards are printed on heavier stock and have a blue background on the back. Why they were produced and apparently not distributed is not known. It is presumed, though not confirmed, that all 12 Grand Slammers cards can also be found in the Blue Chip version.

NM/M
Complete Set (12): 1,200
Common Player: 60.00
1 Jose Canseco 125.00
2 Mike Marshall 60.00
3 Walt Weiss 60.00
4 Kevin McReynolds 60.00
5 Mike Greenwell 60.00
6 Dave Winfield 150.00
7 Mark McGwire 400.00
8 Keith Hernandez 75.00
9 Franklin Stubbs 60.00
10 Danny Tartabull 60.00
11 Jesse Barfield 60.00
12 Ellis Burks 60.00

1990 Leaf Previews

This 12-card set was produced for dealer distribution to introduce Leaf as Donruss' premium-quality brand in mid-1990. Cards have the same format as the regular-issue versions with metallic silver ink highlights on front and back. The preview cards have a white undertype on

back over the stats and career highlights. It reads "Special Preview Card."

		NM/M
Complete Set (12):		275.00
Common Player:		12.50
1	Steve Sax	12.50
2	Joe Carter	12.50
3	Dennis Eckersley	20.00
4	Ken Griffey Jr.	200.00
5	Barry Larkin	12.50
6	Mark Langston	12.50
7	Eric Anthony	12.50
8	Robin Ventura	12.50
9	Greg Vaughn	12.50
10	Bobby Bonilla	12.50
11	Gary Gaetti	12.50
12	Ozzie Smith	75.00

1990 Leaf

This 528-card set was issued in two 264-card series. The cards were printed on heavy quality stock and both the card fronts and backs have full color player photos. Cards also have an ultra-glossy finish on both the fronts and the backs. A high-tech foil Hall of Fame puzzle features former Yankee great Yogi Berra.

		NM/M
Complete Set (528):		75.00
Series 1 (264):		50.00
Series 2 (264):		25.00
Common Player:		.10
Series 1 Foil Pack (15):		4.00
Series 1 Foil Box (36):		80.00
Series 2 Foil Pack (15):		2.50
Series 2 Foil Box (36):		60.00
1	Introductory Card	.10
2	Mike Henneman	.10
3	Steve Bedrosian	.10
4	Mike Scott	.10
5	Allan Anderson	.10
6	Rick Sutcliffe	.10
7	Gregg Olson	.10
8	Kevin Elster	.10
9	Pete O'Brien	.10
10	Carlton Fisk	1.00
11	Joe Magrane	.10
12	Roger Clemens	2.50
13	Tom Glavine	.35
14	Tom Gordon	.10
15	Todd Benzinger	.10
16	Hubie Brooks	.10
17	Roberto Kelly	.10
18	Barry Larkin	.10
19	Mike Boddicker	.10
20	Roger McDowell	.10
21	Nolan Ryan	5.00
22	John Farrell	.10
23	Bruce Hurst	.10
24	Wally Joyner	.10
25	Greg Maddux	2.00
26	Chris Bosio	.10
27	John Cerutti	.10
28	Tim Burke	.10
29	Dennis Eckersley	.75
30	Glenn Davis	.10
31	Jim Abbott	.10
32	Mike LaValliere	.10
33	Andres Thomas	.10
34	Lou Whitaker	.10
35	Alvin Davis	.10
36	Melido Perez	.10
37	Craig Biggio	.10
38	Rick Aguilera	.10
39	Pete Harnisch	.10
40	David Cone	.10
41	Scott Garrelts	.10
42	Jay Howell	.10
43	Eric King	.10
44	Pedro Guerrero	.10
45	Mike Bielecki	.10
46	Bob Boone	.10
47	Kevin Brown	.10
48	Jerry Browne	.10
49	Mike Scioscia	.10
50	Chuck Cary	.10
51	Wade Boggs	2.00
52	Von Hayes	.10
53	Tony Fernandez	.10
54	Dennis Martinez	.10
55	Tom Candiotti	.10
56	Andy Benes	.10
57	Rob Dibble	.10
58	Chuck Crim	.10
59	John Smoltz	.10
60	Mike Heath	.10
61	Kevin Gross	.10
62	Mark McGwire	3.50
63	Bert Blyleven	.10
64	Bob Walk	.10
65	Mickey Tettleton	.10
66	Sid Fernandez	.10
67	Terry Kennedy	.10
68	Fernando Valenzuela	.10
69	Don Mattingly	2.50
70	Paul O'Neill	.10
71	Robin Yount	1.00
72	Bret Saberhagen	.10
73	Geno Petralli	.10
74	Brook Jacoby	.10
75	Roberto Alomar	.25
76	Devon White	.10
77	Jose Lind	.10
78	Pat Combs	.10
79	Dave Steib	.10
80	Tim Wallach	.10
81	Dave Stewart	.10
82	Eric Anthony **RC**	.10
83	Randy Bush	.10
84	Checklist	.10
85	Jaime Navarro	.10
86	Tommy Gregg	.10
87	Frank Tanana	.10
88	Omar Vizquel	.10
89	Ivan Calderon	.10
90	Vince Coleman	.10
91	Barry Bonds	5.00
92	Randy Milligan	.10
93	Frank Viola	.10
94	Matt Williams	.10
95	Alfredo Griffin	.10
96	Steve Sax	.10
97	Gary Gaetti	.10
98	Ryne Sandberg	2.00
99	Danny Tartabull	.10
100	Rafael Palmeiro	1.00
101	Jesse Orosco	.10
102	Garry Templeton	.10
103	Frank DiPino	.10
104	Tony Pena	.10
105	Dickie Thon	.10
106	Kelly Gruber	.10
107	Marquis Grissom **RC**	2.00
108	Jose Canseco	.60
109	Mike Blowers	.10
110	Tom Browning	.10
111	Greg Vaughn	.10
112	Oddibe McDowell	.10
113	Gary Ward	.10
114	Jay Buhner	.10
115	Eric Show	.10
116	Bryan Harvey	.10
117	Andy Van Slyke	.10
118	Jeff Ballard	.10
119	Barry Lyons	.10
120	Kevin Mitchell	.10
121	Mike Gallego	.10
122	Dave Smith	.10
123	Kirby Puckett	2.00
124	Jerome Walton	.10
125	Bo Jackson	.20
126	Harold Baines	.10
127	Scott Bankhead	.10
128	Ozzie Guillen	.10
129	Jose Oquendo	.10
130	John Dopson	.10
131	Charlie Hayes	.10
132	Fred McGriff	.10
133	Chet Lemon	.10
134	Gary Carter	1.00
135	Rafael Ramirez	.10
136	Shane Mack	.10
137	Mark Grace	.10
138	Phil Bradley	.10
139	Dwight Gooden	.10
140	Harold Reynolds	.10
141	Scott Fletcher	.10
142	Ozzie Smith	2.00
143	Mike Greenwell	.10
144	Pete Smith	.10
145	Mark Gubicza	.10
146	Chris Sabo	.10
147	Ramon Martinez	.10
148	Tim Leary	.10
149	Randy Myers	.10
150	Jody Reed	.10
151	Bruce Ruffin	.10
152	Jeff Russell	.10
153	Doug Jones	.10
154	Tony Gwynn	2.00
155	Mark Langston	.10
156	Mitch Williams	.10
157	Gary Sheffield	.60
158	Tom Henke	.10
159	Oil Can Boyd	.10
160	Rickey Henderson	1.00
161	Bill Doran	.10
162	Chuck Finley	.10
163	Jeff King	.10
164	Nick Esasky	.10
165	Cecil Fielder	.10
166	Dave Valle	.10
167	Robin Ventura	.10
168	Jim Deshaies	.10
169	Juan Berenguer	.10
170	Craig Worthington	.10
171	Gregg Jefferies	.10
172	Will Clark	.10
173	Kirk Gibson	.10
174	Checklist	.10
175	Bobby Thigpen	.10
176	John Tudor	.10
177	Andre Dawson	.35
178	George Brett	2.50
179	Steve Buechele	.10
180	Albert Belle	.10
181	Eddie Murray	1.00
182	Bob Geren	.10
183	Rob Murphy	.10
184	Tom Herr	.10
185	George Bell	.10
186	Spike Owen	.10
187	Cory Snyder	.10
188	Fred Lynn	.10
189	Eric Davis	.10
190	Dave Parker	.10
191	Jeff Blauser	.10
192	Matt Nokes	.10
193	Delino DeShields **RC**	.50
194	Scott Sanderson	.10
195	Lance Parrish	.10
196	Bobby Bonilla	.10
197	Cal Ripken, Jr.	5.00
198	Kevin McReynolds	.10
199	Robby Thompson	.10
200	Tim Belcher	.10
201	Jesse Barfield	.10
202	Mariano Duncan	.10
203	Bill Spiers	.10
204	Frank White	.10
205	Julio Franco	.10
206	Greg Swindell	.10
207	Benito Santiago	.10
208	Johnny Ray	.10
209	Gary Redus	.10
210	Jeff Parrett	.10
211	Jimmy Key	.10
212	Tim Raines	.10
213	Carney Lansford	.10
214	Gerald Young	.10
215	Gene Larkin	.10
216	Dan Plesac	.10
217	Lonnie Smith	.10
218	Alan Trammell	.10
219	Jeffrey Leonard	.10
220	Sammy Sosa **RC**	20.00
221	Todd Zeile	.10
222	Bill Landrum	.10
223	Mike Devereaux	.10
224	Mike Marshall	.10
225	Jose Uribe	.10
226	Juan Samuel	.10
227	Mel Hall	.10
228	Kent Hrbek	.10
229	Shawon Dunston	.10
230	Kevin Seitzer	.10
231	Pete Incaviglia	.10
232	Sandy Alomar	.10
233	Bip Roberts	.10
234	Scott Terry	.10
235	Dwight Evans	.10
236	Ricky Jordan	.10
237	John Olerud **RC**	5.00
238	Zane Smith	.10
239	Walt Weiss	.10
240	Alvaro Espinoza	.10
241	Billy Hatcher	.10
242	Paul Molitor	1.00
243	Dale Murphy	.30
244	Dave Bergman	.10
245	Ken Griffey Jr.	3.00
246	Ed Whitson	.10
247	Kirk McCaskill	.10
248	Jay Bell	.10
249	Ben McDonald **RC**	.50
250	Darryl Strawberry	.10
251	Brett Butler	.10
252	Terry Steinbach	.10
253	Ken Caminiti	.10
254	Dan Gladden	.10
255	Dwight Smith	.10
256	Kurt Stillwell	.10
257	Ruben Sierra	.10
258	Mike Schooler	.10
259	Lance Johnson	.10
260	Terry Pendleton	.10
261	Ellis Burks	.10
262	Len Dykstra	.10
263	Mookie Wilson	.10
264	Checklist (Nolan Ryan)	.10
265	Nolan Ryan (No-Hit King)	2.00
266	Brian DuBois	.10
267	Don Robinson	.10
268	Glenn Wilson	.10
269	Kevin Tapani **RC**	.25
270	Marvell Wynne	.10
271	Billy Ripken	.10
272	Howard Johnson	.10
273	Brian Holman	.10
274	Dan Pasqua	.10
275	Ken Dayley	.10
276	Jeff Reardon	.10
277	Jim Presley	.10
278	Jim Eisenreich	.10
279	Danny Jackson	.10
280	Orel Hershiser	.10
281	Andy Hawkins	.10
282	Jose Rijo	.10
283	Luis Rivera	.10
284	John Kruk	.10
285	Jeff Huson	.10
286	Joel Skinner	.10
287	Jack Clark	.10
288	Chili Davis	.10
289	Joe Girardi	.10
290	B.J. Surhoff	.10
291	Luis Sojo	.10
292	Tom Foley	.10
293	Mike Moore	.10
294	Ken Oberkfell	.10
295	Luis Polonia	.10
296	Doug Drabek	.10
297	Dave Justice **RC**	2.00
298	Paul Gibson	.10
299	Edgar Martinez	.10
300	Frank Thomas **RC**	20.00
301	Eric Yelding	.10
302	Greg Gagne	.10
303	Brad Komminsk	.10
304	Ron Darling	.10
305	Kevin Bass	.10
306	Jeff Hamilton	.10
307	Ron Karkovice	.10
308	Milt Thompson	.10
309	Mike Harkey	.10
310	Mel Stottlemyre	.10
311	Kenny Rogers	.10
312	Mitch Webster	.10
313	Kal Daniels	.10
314	Matt Nokes	.10
315	Dennis Lamp	.10
316	Ken Howell	.10
317	Glenallen Hill	.10
318	Dave Martinez	.10
319	Chris James	.10
320	Mike Pagliarulo	.10
321	Hal Morris	.10
322	Rob Deer	.10
323	Greg Olson	.10
324	Tony Phillips	.10
325	Larry Walker **RC**	8.00
326	Ron Hassey	.10
327	Jack Howell	.10
328	John Smiley	.10
329	Steve Finley	.10
330	Dave Magadan	.10
331	Greg Litton	.10
332	Mickey Hatcher	.10
333	Lee Guetterman	.10
334	Norm Charlton	.10
335	Edgar Diaz	.10
336	Willie Wilson	.10
337	Bobby Witt	.10
338	Candy Maldonado	.10
339	Craig Lefferts	.10
340	Dante Bichette	.10
341	Wally Backman	.10
342	Dennis Cook	.10
343	Pat Borders	.10
344	Wallace Johnson	.10
345	Willie Randolph	.10
346	Danny Darwin	.10
347	Al Newman	.10
348	Mark Knudson	.10
349	Joe Boever	.10
350	Larry Sheets	.10
351	Mike Jackson	.10
352	Wayne Edwards	.10
353	Bernard Gilkey **RC**	.50
354	Don Slaught	.10
355	Joe Orsulak	.10
356	John Franco	.10
357	Jeff Brantley	.10
358	Mike Morgan	.10
359	Deion Sanders	.10
360	Terry Leach	.10
361	Les Lancaster	.10
362	Storm Davis	.10
363	Scott Coolbaugh	.10
364	Checklist	.10
365	Cecilio Guante	.10
366	Joey Cora	.10
367	Willie McGee	.10
368	Jerry Reed	.10
369	Darren Daulton	.10
370	Manny Lee	.10
371	Mark Gardner	.10
372	Rick Honeycutt	.10
373	Steve Balboni	.10
374	Jack Armstrong	.10
375	Charlie O'Brien	.10
376	Ron Gant	.10
377	Lloyd Moseby	.10
378	Gene Harris	.10
379	Joe Carter	.10
380	Scott Bailes	.10
381	R.J. Reynolds	.10
382	Bob Melvin	.10
383	Tim Teufel	.10
384	John Burkett	.10
385	Felix Jose	.10
386	Larry Andersen	.10
387	David West	.10
388	Luis Salazar	.10
389	Mike Macfarlane	.10
390	Charlie Hough	.10
391	Greg Briley	.10
392	Donn Pall	.10
393	Bryn Smith	.10
394	Carlos Quintana	.10
395	Steve Lake	.10
396	Mark Whiten **RC**	.15
397	Edwin Nunez	.10
398	Rick Parker	.10
399	Mark Portugal	.10
400	Roy Smith	.10
401	Hector Villanueva	.10
402	Bob Milacki	.10
403	Alejandro Pena	.10
404	Scott Bradley	.10
405	Ron Kittle	.10
406	Bob Tewksbury	.10
407	Wes Gardner	.10
408	Ernie Whitt	.10
409	Terry Shumpert	.10
410	Tim Layana	.10
411	Chris Gwynn	.10
412	Jeff Robinson	.10
413	Scott Scudder	.10
414	Kevin Romine	.10
415	Jose DeJesus	.10
416	Mike Jeffcoat	.10
417	Rudy Seanez	.10
418	Mike Dunne	.10
419	Dick Schofield	.10
420	Steve Wilson	.10
421	Bill Krueger	.10
422	Junior Felix	.10
423	Drew Hall	.10
424	Curt Young	.10
425	Franklin Stubbs	.10
426	Dave Winfield	1.00
427	Rick Reed	.10
428	Charlie Leibrandt	.10
429	Jeff Robinson	.10
430	Erik Hanson	.10
431	Barry Jones	.10
432	Alex Trevino	.10
433	John Moses	.10
434	Dave Johnson	.10
435	Mackey Sasser	.10
436	Rick Leach	.10
437	Lenny Harris	.10
438	Carlos Martinez	.10
439	Rex Hudler	.10
440	Domingo Ramos	.10
441	Gerald Perry	.10
442	John Russell	.10
443	Carlos Baerga **RC**	.50
444	Checklist	.10
445	Stan Javier	.10
446	Kevin Maas **RC**	.10
447	Tom Brunansky	.10
448	Carmelo Martinez	.10
449	Willie Blair **RC**	.10
450	Andres Galarraga	.10
451	Bud Black	.10
452	Greg Harris	.10
453	Joe Oliver	.10
454	Greg Brock	.10
455	Jeff Treadway	.10
456	Lance McCullers	.10
457	Dave Schmidt	.10
458	Todd Burns	.10
459	Max Venable	.10
460	Neal Heaton	.10
461	Mark Williamson	.10
462	Keith Miller	.10
463	Mike LaCoss	.10
464	Jose Offerman **RC**	.25
465	Jim Leyritz **RC**	.50
466	Glenn Braggs	.10
467	Ron Robinson	.10
468	Mark Davis	.10
469	Gary Pettis	.10
470	Keith Hernandez	.10
471	Dennis Rasmussen	.10
472	Mark Eichhorn	.10
473	Ted Power	.10
474	Terry Mulholland	.10
475	Todd Stottlemyre	.10
476	Jerry Goff	.10
477	Gene Nelson	.10
478	Rich Gedman	.10
479	Brian Harper	.10
480	Mike Felder	.10
481	Steve Avery	.10
482	Jack Morris	.10
483	Randy Johnson	1.00
484	Scott Radinsky	.10
485	Jose DeLeon	.10
486	Stan Belinda **RC**	.10
487	Brian Holton	.10
488	Mark Carreon	.10
489	Trevor Wilson	.10
490	Mike Sharperson	.10
491	Alan Mills **RC**	.10
492	John Candelaria	.10
493	Paul Assenmacher	.10
494	Steve Crawford	.10
495	Brad Arnsberg	.10
496	Sergio Valdez	.10
497	Mark Parent	.10
498	Tom Pagnozzi	.10
499	Greg Harris	.10
500	Randy Ready	.10
501	Duane Ward	.10
502	Nelson Santovenia	.10
503	Joe Klink	.10
504	Eric Plunk	.10
505	Jeff Reed	.10
506	Ted Higuera	.10
507	Joe Hesketh	.10
508	Dan Petry	.10
509	Matt Young	.10
510	Jerald Clark	.10
511	John Orton **RC**	.10
512	Scott Ruskin	.10
513	Chris Hoiles **RC**	.50
514	Daryl Boston	.10
515	Francisco Oliveras	.10
516	Ozzie Canseco	.10
517	Xavier Hernandez **RC**	.10
518	Fred Manrique	.10
519	Shawn Boskie	.10
520	Jeff Montgomery	.10
521	Jack Daugherty	.10
522	Keith Comstock	.10
523	Greg Hibbard **RC**	.10
524	Lee Smith	.10
525	Dana Kiecker	.10
526	Darrel Akerfelds	.10
527	Greg Myers	.10
528	Checklist	.10

1991 Leaf Previews

Cello packs of four cards previewing the 1991 Leaf set were included in each 1991 Donruss hobby factory set. The cards are identical in format to the regular 1991 Leafs, except there is a notation, "1991 PREVIEW CARD" in white print beneath the statistics and career information on the back.

		NM/M
Complete Set (26):		20.00
Common Player:		.50
1	Dave Justice	.50
2	Ryne Sandberg	1.50
3	Barry Larkin	.50
4	Craig Biggio	.50
5	Ramon Martinez	.50
6	Tim Wallach	.50
7	Dwight Gooden	.50
8	Len Dykstra	.50
9	Barry Bonds	4.00
10	Ray Lankford	.50
11	Tony Gwynn	1.50
12	Will Clark	.60
13	Leo Gomez	.50
14	Wade Boggs	1.50
15	Chuck Finley	.50
16	Carlton Fisk	1.00
17	Sandy Alomar, Jr.	.50
18	Cecil Fielder	.50
19	Bo Jackson	.75
20	Paul Molitor	1.00
21	Kirby Puckett	1.50
22	Don Mattingly	2.00
23	Rickey Henderson	1.00
24	Tino Martinez	.50
25	Nolan Ryan	4.00
26	Dave Steib	.50

1991 Leaf

Silver borders and black insets surround the color action photos on the 1991 Leaf cards. The set was once again released in two series. Series I consists of cards 1-264. Card backs feature an additional player photo, biographical information, statistics and career highlights. The 1991 issue is not considered as scarce as the 1990 release.

		NM/M
Complete Set (528):		8.00
Common Player:		.05
Series 1 or 2 Pack (15):		.50
Series 1 or 2 Box (36):		12.50
1	The Leaf Card	.05
2	Kurt Stillwell	.05
3	Bobby Witt	.05
4	Tony Phillips	.05
5	Scott Garrelts	.05
6	Greg Swindell	.05
7	Billy Ripken	.05
8	Dave Martinez	.05
9	Kelly Gruber	.05
10	Juan Samuel	.05
11	Brian Holman	.05
12	Craig Biggio	.05
13	Lonnie Smith	.05
14	Ron Robinson	.05
15	Mike LaValliere	.05
16	Mark Davis	.05
17	Jack Daugherty	.05
18	Mike Henneman	.05
19	Mike Greenwell	.05
20	Dave Magadan	.05
21	Mark Williamson	.05
22	Marquis Grissom	.05
23	Pat Borders	.05
24	Mike Scioscia	.05
25	Shawon Dunston	.05
26	Randy Bush	.05
27	John Smoltz	.05
28	Chuck Crim	.05
29	Don Slaught	.05
30	Mike Macfarlane	.05
31	Wally Joyner	.05
32	Pat Combs	.05
33	Tony Pena	.05
34	Howard Johnson	.05
35	Leo Gomez	.05
36	Spike Owen	.05
37	Eric Davis	.05
38	Roberto Kelly	.05
39	Jerome Walton	.05
40	Shane Mack	.05
41	Kent Mercker	.05
42	B.J. Surhoff	.05
43	Jerry Browne	.05
44	Lee Smith	.05
45	Chuck Finley	.05
46	Terry Mulholland	.05
47	Tom Bolton	.05
48	Tom Herr	.05
49	Jim Deshaies	.05
50	Walt Weiss	.05
51	Hal Morris	.05
52	Lee Guetterman	.05
53	Paul Assenmacher	.05
54	Brian Harper	.05
55	Paul Gibson	.05
56	John Burkett	.05
57	Doug Jones	.05
58	Jose Oquendo	.05
59	Dick Schofield	.05
60	Dickie Thon	.05
61	Ramon Martinez	.05
62	Jay Buhner	.05
63	Mark Portugal	.05
64	Bob Welch	.05
65	Chris Sabo	.05
66	Chuck Cary	.05
67	Mark Langston	.05
68	Joe Boever	.05
69	Jody Reed	.05
70	Alejandro Pena	.05
71	Jeff King	.05
72	Tom Pagnozzi	.05
73	Joe Oliver	.05
74	Mike Witt	.05
75	Hector Villanueva	.05
76	Dan Gladden	.05
77	Dave Justice	.05
78	Mike Gallego	.05
79	Tom Candiotti	.05
80	Ozzie Smith	.60
81	Luis Polonia	.05
82	Randy Ready	.05
83	Greg Harris	.05
84	Checklist (Dave Justice)	.05
85	Kevin Mitchell	.05
86	Mark McLemore	.05
87	Terry Steinbach	.05
88	Tom Browning	.05
89	Matt Nokes	.05
90	Mike Harkey	.05
91	Omar Vizquel	.05
92	Dave Bergman	.05
93	Matt Williams	.05
94	Steve Olin	.05
95	Craig Wilson	.05
96	Dave Stieb	.05
97	Ruben Sierra	.05
98	Jay Howell	.05
99	Scott Bradley	.05
100	Eric Yelding	.05
101	Rickey Henderson	.45
102	Jeff Reed	.05
103	Jimmy Key	.05
104	Terry Shumpert	.05
105	Kenny Rogers	.05
106	Cecil Fielder	.05
107	Robby Thompson	.05
108	Alex Cole	.05
109	Randy Milligan	.05
110	Andres Galarraga	.05
111	Bill Spiers	.05
112	Kal Daniels	.05
113	Henry Cotto	.05
114	Casy Candaele	.05
115	Jeff Blauser	.05
116	Robin Yount	.45
117	Ben McDonald	.05
118	Bret Saberhagen	.05
119	Juan Gonzalez	.35
120	Lou Whitaker	.05
121	Ellis Burks	.05
122	Charlie O'Brien	.05
123	John Smiley	.05
124	Tim Burke	.05
125	John Olerud	.05
126	Eddie Murray	.45
127	Greg Maddux	.60
128	Kevin Tapani	.05
129	Ron Gant	.05
130	Jay Bell	.05
131	Chris Hoiles	.05
132	Tom Gordon	.05
133	Kevin Seitzer	.05
134	Jeff Huson	.05
135	Jerry Don Gleaton	.05
136	Jeff Brantley	.05
137	Felix Fermin	.05
138	Mike Devereaux	.05
139	Delino DeShields	.05
140	David Wells	.05
141	Tim Crews	.05
142	Erik Hanson	.05
143	Mark Davidson	.05
144	Tommy Gregg	.05
145	Jim Gantner	.05
146	Jose Lind	.05
147	Danny Tartabull	.05
148	Geno Petralli	.05
149	Travis Fryman	.05
150	Tim Naehring	.05
151	Kevin McReynolds	.05
152	Joe Orsulak	.05
153	Steve Frey	.05
154	Duane Ward	.05
155	Stan Javier	.05
156	Damon Berryhill	.05
157	Gene Larkin	.05
158	Greg Olson	.05
159	Mark Knudson	.05
160	Carmelo Martinez	.05
161	Storm Davis	.05
162	Jim Abbott	.05
163	Len Dykstra	.05
164	Tom Brunansky	.05
165	Dwight Gooden	.05
166	Jose Mesa	.05
167	Oil Can Boyd	.05
168	Barry Larkin	.05
169	Scott Sanderson	.05
170	Mark Grace	.05
171	Mark Guthrie	.05
172	Tom Glavine	.15
173	Gary Sheffield	.30
174	Checklist (Roger Clemens)	.25
175	Chris James	.05
176	Milt Thompson	.05
177	Donnie Hill	.05
178	Wes Chamberlain	.05
179	John Marzano	.05
180	Frank Viola	.05
181	Eric Anthony	.05
182	Jose Canseco	.30
183	Scott Scudder	.05
184	Dave Eiland	.05
185	Luis Salazar	.05
186	Pedro Munoz	.05
187	Steve Searcy	.05
188	Don Robinson	.05
189	Sandy Alomar	.05
190	Jose DeLeon	.05
191	John Orton	.05
192	Darren Daulton	.05
193	Mike Morgan	.05
194	Greg Briley	.05
195	Karl Rhodes	.05
196	Harold Baines	.05
197	Bill Doran	.05
198	Alvaro Espinoza	.05
199	Kirk McCaskill	.05
200	Jose DeJesus	.05
201	Jack Clark	.05
202	Daryl Boston	.05
203	Randy Tomlin	.05
204	Pedro Guerrero	.05
205	Billy Hatcher	.05
206	Tim Leary	.05
207	Ryne Sandberg	.60
208	Kirby Puckett	.60
209	Charlie Leibrandt	.05
210	Rick Honeycutt	.05
211	Joel Skinner	.05
212	Rex Hudler	.05
213	Bryan Harvey	.05
214	Charlie Hayes	.05
215	Matt Young	.05
216	Terry Kennedy	.05
217	Carl Nichols	.05
218	Mike Moore	.05
219	Paul O'Neill	.05
220	Steve Sax	.05
221	Shawn Boskie	.05
222	Rich DeLucia	.05
223	Lloyd Moseby	.05
224	Mike Kingery	.05
225	Carlos Baerga	.05
226	Bryn Smith	.05
227	Todd Stottlemyre	.05
228	Julio Franco	.05
229	Jim Gott	.05
230	Mike Schooler	.05
231	Steve Finley	.05
232	Dave Henderson	.05
233	Luis Quinones	.05
234	Mark Whiten	.05
235	Brian McRae	.05
236	Rich Gossage	.05
237	Rob Deer	.05
238	Will Clark	.10
239	Albert Belle	.05
240	Bob Melvin	.05
241	Larry Walker	.05
242	Dante Bichette	.05
243	Orel Hershiser	.05
244	Pete O'Brien	.05
245	Pete Harnisch	.05
246	Jeff Treadway	.05
247	Julio Machado	.05
248	Dave Johnson	.05
249	Kirk Gibson	.05
250	Kevin Brown	.05
251	Milt Cuyler	.05
252	Jeff Reardon	.05
253	David Cone	.05
254	Gary Redus	.05
255	Junior Noboa	.05
256	Greg Myers	.05
257	Dennis Cook	.05
258	Joe Girardi	.05
259	Allan Anderson	.05
260	Paul Marak	.05
261	Barry Bonds	2.00
262	Juan Bell	.05
263	Russ Morman	.05
264	Checklist (George Brett)	.25
265	Jerald Clark	.05
266	Dwight Evans	.05
267	Roberto Alomar	.15
268	Danny Jackson	.05
269	Brian Downing	.05
270	John Cerutti	.05
271	Robin Ventura	.05
272	Gerald Perry	.05
273	Wade Boggs	.60
274	Dennis Martinez	.05
275	Andy Benes	.05
276	Tony Fossas	.05
277	Franklin Stubbs	.05
278	John Kruk	.05
279	Kevin Gross	.05
280	Von Hayes	.05
281	Frank Thomas	.45
282	Rob Dibble	.05
283	Mel Hall	.05
284	Rick Mahler	.05
285	Dennis Eckersley	.35
286	Bernard Gilkey	.05
287	Dan Plesac	.05
288	Jason Grimsley	.05
289	Mark Lewis	.05
290	Tony Gwynn	.60
291	Jeff Russell	.05
292	Curt Schilling	.25
293	Pascual Perez	.05
294	Jack Morris	.05
295	Hubie Brooks	.05
296	Alex Fernandez	.05
297	Harold Reynolds	.05
298	Craig Worthington	.05
299	Willie Wilson	.05
300	Mike Maddux	.05
301	Dave Righetti	.05
302	Paul Molitor	.45
303	Gary Gaetti	.05
304	Terry Pendleton	.05
305	Kevin Elster	.05
306	Scott Fletcher	.05
307	Jeff Robinson	.05
308	Jesse Barfield	.05
309	Mike LaCoss	.05
310	Andy Van Slyke	.05
311	Glenallen Hill	.05
312	Bud Black	.05
313	Kent Hrbek	.05
314	Tim Teufel	.05
315	Tony Fernandez	.05
316	Beau Allred	.05
317	Curtis Wilkerson	.05
318	Bill Sampen	.05
319	Randy Johnson	.45
320	Mike Heath	.05
321	Sammy Sosa	1.00
322	Mickey Tettleton	.05
323	Jose Vizcaino	.05
324	John Candelaria	.05
325	David Howard	.05
326	Jose Rijo	.05
327	Todd Zeile	.05
328	Gene Nelson	.05
329	Dwayne Henry	.05
330	Mike Boddicker	.05
331	Ozzie Guillen	.05
332	Sam Horn	.05
333	Wally Whitehurst	.05
334	Dave Parker	.05
335	George Brett	.75
336	Bobby Thigpen	.05
337	Ed Whitson	.05
338	Ivan Calderon	.05
339	Mike Pagliarulo	.05
340	Jack McDowell	.05
341	Dana Kiecker	.05
342	Fred McGriff	.05
343	Mark Lee	.05
344	Alfredo Griffin	.05
345	Scott Bankhead	.05
346	Darrin Jackson	.05
347	Rafael Palmeiro	.35
348	Steve Farr	.05
349	Hensley Meulens	.05
350	Danny Cox	.05
351	Alan Trammell	.05
352	Edwin Nunez	.05
353	Joe Carter	.05
354	Eric Show	.05
355	Vance Law	.05
356	Jeff Gray	.05
357	Bobby Bonilla	.05
358	Ernest Riles	.05
359	Ron Hassey	.05
360	Willie McGee	.05
361	Mackey Sasser	.05
362	Glenn Braggs	.05
363	Mario Diaz	.05
364	Checklist (Barry Bonds)	.35
365	Kevin Bass	.05
366	Pete Incaviglia	.05
367	Luis Sojo	.05
368	Lance Parrish	.05
369	Mark Leonard	.05
370	Heathcliff Slocumb	.05
371	Jimmy Jones	.05
372	Ken Griffey Jr.	1.00
373	Chris Hammond	.05
374	Chili Davis	.05
375	Joey Cora	.05
376	Ken Hill	.05
377	Darryl Strawberry	.05
378	Ron Darling	.05
379	Sid Bream	.05
380	Bill Swift	.05
381	Shawn Abner	.05
382	Eric King	.05
383	Mickey Morandini	.05
384	Carlton Fisk	.45
385	Steve Lake	.05
386	Mike Jeffcoat	.05
387	Darren Holmes	.05
388	Tim Wallach	.05
389	George Bell	.05
390	Craig Lefferts	.05
391	Ernie Whitt	.05
392	Felix Jose	.05
393	Kevin Maas	.05
394	Devon White	.05
395	Otis Nixon	.05
396	Chuck Knoblauch	.05
397	Scott Coolbaugh	.05
398	Glenn Davis	.05
399	Manny Lee	.05
400	Andre Dawson	.20
401	Scott Chiamparino	.05
402	Bill Gullickson	.05
403	Lance Johnson	.05
404	Juan Agosto	.05
405	Danny Darwin	.05
406	Barry Jones	.05
407	Larry Andersen	.05
408	Luis Rivera	.05
409	Jaime Navarro	.05
410	Roger McDowell	.05
411	Brett Butler	.05
412	Dale Murphy	.15
413	Tim Raines	.05
414	Norm Charlton	.05
415	Greg Cadaret	.05
416	Chris Nabholz	.05
417	Dave Stewart	.05
418	Rich Gedman	.05
419	Willie Randolph	.05
420	Mitch Williams	.05
421	Brook Jacoby	.05
422	Greg Harris	.05
423	Nolan Ryan	2.00
424	Dave Rohde	.05
425	Don Mattingly	.75
426	Greg Gagne	.05
427	Vince Coleman	.05
428	Dan Pasqua	.05
429	Alvin Davis	.05
430	Cal Ripken, Jr.	2.00
431	Jamie Quirk	.05
432	Benito Santiago	.05
433	Jose Uribe	.05
434	Candy Maldonado	.05
435	Junior Felix	.05
436	Deion Sanders	.05
437	John Franco	.05
438	Greg Hibbard	.05
439	Floyd Bannister	.05
440	Steve Howe	.05
441	Steve Decker	.05
442	Vicente Palacios	.05
443	Pat Tabler	.05
444	Checklist (Darryl Strawberry)	.05
445	Mike Felder	.05
446	Al Newman	.05
447	Chris Donnels	.05
448	Rich Rodriguez	.05
449	Turner Ward	.05
450	Bob Walk	.05
451	Gilberto Reyes	.05
452	Mike Jackson	.05
453	Rafael Belliard	.05
454	Wayne Edwards	.05
455	Andy Allanson	.05
456	Dave Smith	.05
457	Gary Carter	.45
458	Warren Cromartie	.05
459	Jack Armstrong	.05
460	Bob Tewksbury	.05
461	Joe Klink	.05
462	Xavier Hernandez	.05
463	Scott Radinsky	.05
464	Jeff Robinson	.05
465	Gregg Jefferies	.05
466	Denny Neagle	.05
467	Carmelo Martinez	.05
468	Donn Pall	.05
469	Bruce Hurst	.05
470	Eric Bullock	.05
471	Rick Aguilera	.05
472	Charlie Hough	.05
473	Carlos Quintana	.05
474	Marty Barrett	.05
475	Kevin Brown	.05
476	Bobby Ojeda	.05
477	Edgar Martinez	.05
478	Bip Roberts	.05
479	Mike Flanagan	.05
480	John Habyan	.05
481	Larry Casian	.05
482	Wally Backman	.05
483	Doug Dascenzo	.05
484	Rick Dempsey	.05
485	Ed Sprague	.05
486	Steve Chitren	.05
487	Mark McGwire	1.50
488	Roger Clemens	.75
489	Orlando Merced	.05
490	Rene Gonzales	.05
491	Mike Stanton	.05
492	Al Osuna	.05
493	Rick Cerone	.05
494	Mariano Duncan	.05
495	Zane Smith	.05
496	John Morris	.05
497	Frank Tanana	.05
498	Junior Ortiz	.05
499	Dave Winfield	.45
500	Gary Varsho	.05
501	Chico Walker	.05
502	Ken Caminiti	.05
503	Ken Griffey Sr.	.05
504	Randy Myers	.05
505	Steve Bedrosian	.05
506	Cory Snyder	.05
507	Cris Carpenter	.05
508	Tim Belcher	.05
509	Jeff Hamilton	.05
510	Steve Avery	.05
511	Dave Valle	.05
512	Tom Lampkin	.05
513	Shawn Hillegas	.05
514	Reggie Jefferson	.05
515	Ron Karkovice	.05
516	Doug Drabek	.05
517	Tom Henke	.05
518	Chris Bosio	.05
519	Gregg Olson	.05
520	Bob Scanlan	.05
521	Alonzo Powell	.05
522	Jeff Ballard	.05
523	Ray Lankford	.05
524	Tommy Greene	.05
525	Mike Timlin	.05
526	Juan Berenguer	.05
527	Scott Erickson	.05
528	Checklist (Sandy Alomar Jr.)	.05

Gold Rookies

Special gold rookie and gold bonus cards were randomly inserted in 1991 Leaf packs. Backs have a design similar to the regular-issue cards, but have gold, rather than silver background. Fronts have gold-foil highlights. Card numbers of the issued version have a "BC" prefix, but there is a much rarer second version of the Series 1 cards, which carry card numbers between 265-276.

		NM/M
Complete Set (26):		10.00
Common Player:		.10
1	Scott Leius	.10
2	Luis Gonzalez	.40
3	Wil Cordero	.10
4	Gary Scott	.10
5	Willie Banks	.10
6	Arthur Rhodes	.10
7	Mo Vaughn	.25
8	Henry Rodriguez	.10
9	Todd Van Poppel	.10
10	Reggie Sanders	.10
11	Rico Brogna	.10
12	Mike Mussina	2.00
13	Kirk Dressendorfer	.10
14	Jeff Bagwell	6.00
15	Pete Schourek	.10
16	Wade Taylor	.10
17	Pat Kelly	.10
18	Tim Costo	.10
19	Roger Salkeld	.10
20	Andujar Cedeno	.10
21	Ryan Klesko	.10
22	Mike Huff	.10
23	Anthony Young	.10
24	Eddie Zosky	.10
25	Nolan Ryan (7th no-hitter)	.50
26	Rickey Henderson (Record Steal)	.25
	Plooey (Babe Ruth)	.01
265	Scott Leius	4.00
266	Luis Gonzalez	6.00
267	Wil Cordero	4.00
268	Gary Scott	4.00
269	Willie Banks	4.00
270	Arthur Rhodes	4.00
271	Mo Vaughn	10.00
272	Henry Rodriguez	4.00
273	Todd Van Poppel	4.00
274	Reggie Sanders	4.00
275	Rico Brogna	4.00
276	Mike Mussina	30.00

1992 Leaf Previews

In a format identical to the regular-issue 1992 Leaf cards, this 26-card preview set was issued as a bonus in packs of four cards in each 1992 Donruss hobby factory set.

		NM/M
Complete Set (26):		15.00
Common Player:		.25
1	Steve Avery	.25
2	Ryne Sandberg	1.00
3	Chris Sabo	.25
4	Jeff Bagwell	.75
5	Darryl Strawberry	.25
6	Bret Barberie	.25
7	Howard Johnson	.25
8	John Kruk	.25
9	Andy Van Slyke	.25
10	Felix Jose	.25
11	Fred McGriff	.25
12	Will Clark	.35
13	Cal Ripken, Jr.	3.00
14	Phil Plantier	.25
15	Lee Stevens	.25
16	Frank Thomas	.75
17	Mark Whiten	.25
18	Cecil Fielder	.25
19	George Brett	1.50
20	Robin Yount	.75
21	Scott Erickson	.25
22	Don Mattingly	1.50
23	Jose Canseco	.50
24	Ken Griffey Jr.	2.00
25	Nolan Ryan	3.00
26	Joe Carter	.25

1992 Leaf

Two 264-card series comprise this 528-card set. The cards feature action photos on both the front and the back. Silver borders surround the photo on the card front. Each leaf card was also produced in a gold foil version. One gold card was issued per pack and a complete Leaf Gold Edition set can be assembled. Traded players and free agents are shown in uniform with their new teams.

		NM/M
Complete Set (528):		7.50
Common Player:		.05
Series 1 or 2 Pack:		.40
Series 1 or 2 Wax Box:		7.50
1	Jim Abbott	.05
2	Cal Eldred	.05
3	Bud Black	.05
4	Dave Howard	.05
5	Luis Sojo	.05
6	Gary Scott	.05
7	Joe Oliver	.05
8	Chris Gardner	.05
9	Sandy Alomar	.05
10	Greg Harris	.05
11	Doug Drabek	.05
12	Darryl Hamilton	.05
13	Mike Mussina	.30
14	Kevin Tapani	.05
15	Ron Gant	.05
16	Mark McGwire	1.00
17	Robin Ventura	.05
18	Pedro Guerrero	.05
19	Roger Clemens	.65
20	Steve Farr	.05
21	Frank Tanana	.05
22	Joe Hesketh	.05
23	Erik Hanson	.05
24	Greg Cadaret	.05
25	Rex Hudler	.05
26	Mark Grace	.05
27	Kelly Gruber	.05
28	Jeff Bagwell	.45
29	Darryl Strawberry	.05
30	Dave Smith	.05
31	Kevin Appier	.05
32	Steve Chitren	.05
33	Kevin Gross	.05
34	Rick Aguilera	.05
35	Juan Guzman	.05
36	Joe Orsulak	.05
37	Tim Raines	.05
38	Harold Reynolds	.05
39	Charlie Hough	.05
40	Tony Phillips	.05
41	Nolan Ryan	1.50
42	Vince Coleman	.05
43	Andy Van Slyke	.05
44	Tim Burke	.05
45	Luis Polonia	.05
46	Tom Browning	.05
47	Willie McGee	.05
48	Gary DiSarcina	.05
49	Mark Lewis	.05
50	Phil Plantier	.05
51	Doug Dascenzo	.05
52	Cal Ripken, Jr.	1.50
53	Pedro Munoz	.05
54	Carlos Hernandez	.05
55	Jerald Clark	.05
56	Jeff Brantley	.05
57	Don Mattingly	.65
58	Roger McDowell	.05
59	Steve Avery	.05
60	John Olerud	.05
61	Bill Gullickson	.05
62	Juan Gonzalez	.30
63	Felix Jose	.05
64	Robin Yount	.45
65	Greg Briley	.05
66	Steve Finley	.05
67	Checklist	.05
68	Tom Gordon	.05
69	Rob Dibble	.05
70	Glenallen Hill	.05
71	Calvin Jones	.05
72	Joe Girardi	.05
73	Barry Larkin	.05
74	Andy Benes	.05
75	Milt Cuyler	.05
76	Kevin Bass	.05
77	Pete Harnisch	.05
78	Wilson Alvarez	.05
79	Mike Devereaux	.05
80	Doug Henry	.05
81	Orel Hershiser	.05
82	Shane Mack	.05
83	Mike Macfarlane	.05
84	Thomas Howard	.05
85	Alex Fernandez	.05
86	Reggie Jefferson	.05
87	Leo Gomez	.05
88	Mel Hall	.05
89	Mike Greenwell	.05
90	Jeff Russell	.05
91	Steve Buechele	.05
92	David Cone	.05
93	Kevin Reimer	.05
94	Mark Lemke	.05
95	Bob Tewksbury	.05
96	Zane Smith	.05
97	Mark Eichhorn	.05
98	Kirby Puckett	.60
99	Paul O'Neill	.05
100	Dennis Eckersley	.35
101	Duane Ward	.05
102	Matt Nokes	.05
103	Mo Vaughn	.05
104	Pat Kelly	.05
105	Ron Karkovice	.05
106	Bill Spiers	.05
107	Gary Gaetti	.05
108	Mackey Sasser	.05
109	Robby Thompson	.05
110	Marvin Freeman	.05
111	Jimmy Key	.05
112	Dwight Gooden	.05
113	Charlie Leibrandt	.05
114	Devon White	.05
115	Charles Nagy	.05
116	Rickey Henderson	.45
117	Paul Assenmacher	.05
118	Junior Felix	.05
119	Julio Franco	.05
120	Norm Charlton	.05
121	Scott Servais	.05
122	Gerald Perry	.05
123	Brian McRae	.05
124	Don Slaught	.05
125	Juan Samuel	.05
126	Harold Baines	.05
127	Scott Livingstone	.05
128	Jay Buhner	.05
129	Darrin Jackson	.05
130	Luis Mercedes	.05
131	Brian Harper	.05
132	Howard Johnson	.05
133	Checklist	.05
134	Dante Bichette	.05
135	Dave Righetti	.05
136	Jeff Montgomery	.05
137	Joe Grahe	.05
138	Delino DeShields	.05
139	Jose Rijo	.05
140	Ken Caminiti	.05
141	Steve Olin	.05
142	Kurt Stillwell	.05
143	Jay Bell	.05
144	Jaime Navarro	.05
145	Ben McDonald	.05
146	Greg Gagne	.05
147	Jeff Blauser	.05
148	Carney Lansford	.05
149	Ozzie Guillen	.05
150	Milt Thompson	.05
151	Jeff Reardon	.05
152	Scott Sanderson	.05
153	Cecil Fielder	.05
154	Greg Harris	.05
155	Rich DeLucia	.05
156	Roberto Kelly	.05
157	Bryn Smith	.05
158	Chuck McElroy	.05
159	Tom Henke	.05
160	Luis Gonzalez	.25
161	Steve Wilson	.05
162	Shawn Boskie	.05
163	Mark Davis	.05
164	Mike Moore	.05
165	Mike Scioscia	.05
166	Scott Erickson	.05
167	Todd Stottlemyre	.05
168	Alvin Davis	.05
169	Greg Hibbard	.05
170	David Valle	.05
171	Dave Winfield	.45
172	Alan Trammell	.05
173	Kenny Rogers	.05
174	John Franco	.05
175	Jose Lind	.05
176	Pete Schourek	.05
177	Von Hayes	.05
178	Chris Hammond	.05
179	John Burkett	.05
180	Dickie Thon	.05
181	Joel Skinner	.05
182	Scott Cooper	.05
183	Andre Dawson	.25
184	Billy Ripken	.05
185	Kevin Mitchell	.05
186	Brett Butler	.05
187	Tony Fernandez	.05
188	Cory Snyder	.05
189	John Habyan	.05
190	Dennis Martinez	.05
191	John Smoltz	.05
192	Greg Myers	.05
193	Rob Deer	.05
194	Ivan Rodriguez	.45
195	Ray Lankford	.05
196	Bill Wegman	.05
197	Edgar Martinez	.05
198	Darryl Kile	.05
199	Checklist	.05
200	Brent Mayne	.05
201	Larry Walker	.05
202	Carlos Baerga	.05
203	Russ Swan	.05
204	Mike Morgan	.05
205	Hal Morris	.05
206	Tony Gwynn	.60
207	Mark Leiter	.05
208	Kirt Manwaring	.05
209	Al Osuna	.05
210	Bobby Thigpen	.05
211	Chris Hoiles	.05
212	B.J. Surhoff	.05
213	Lenny Harris	.05
214	Scott Leius	.05
215	Gregg Jefferies	.05
216	Bruce Hurst	.05
217	Steve Sax	.05
218	Dave Otto	.05
219	Sam Horn	.05
220	Charlie Hayes	.05
221	Frank Viola	.05
222	Jose Guzman	.05
223	Gary Redus	.05
224	Dave Gallagher	.05
225	Dean Palmer	.05
226	Greg Olson	.05
227	Jose DeLeon	.05
228	Mike LaValliere	.05
229	Mark Langston	.05
230	Chuck Knoblauch	.05
231	Bill Doran	.05
232	Dave Henderson	.05
233	Roberto Alomar	.20
234	Scott Fletcher	.05
235	Tim Naehring	.05
236	Mike Gallego	.05
237	Lance Johnson	.05
238	Paul Molitor	.45
239	Dan Gladden	.05
240	Willie Randolph	.05
241	Will Clark	.10
242	Sid Bream	.05
243	Derek Bell	.05
244	Bill Pecota	.05
245	Terry Pendleton	.05
246	Randy Ready	.05
247	Jack Armstrong	.05
248	Todd Van Poppel	.05
249	Shawon Dunston	.05
250	Bobby Rose	.05
251	Jeff Huson	.05
252	Bip Roberts	.05
253	Doug Jones	.05
254	Lee Smith	.05
255	George Brett	.65
256	Randy Tomlin	.05
257	Todd Benzinger	.05
258	Dave Stewart	.05
259	Mark Carreon	.05
260	Pete O'Brien	.05
261	Tim Teufel	.05
262	Bob Milacki	.05
263	Mark Guthrie	.05
264	Darrin Fletcher	.05
265	Omar Vizquel	.05
266	Chris Bosio	.05
267	Jose Canseco	.30
268	Mike Boddicker	.05
269	Lance Parrish	.05
270	Jose Vizcaino	.05
271	Chris Sabo	.05
272	Royce Clayton	.05
273	Marquis Grissom	.05
274	Fred McGriff	.05
275	Barry Bonds	1.50
276	Greg Vaughn	.05
277	Gregg Olson	.05
278	Dave Hollins	.05
279	Tom Glavine	.25
280	Bryan Hickerson	.05
281	Scott Radinsky	.05
282	Omar Olivares	.05
283	Ivan Calderon	.05
284	Kevin Maas	.05
285	Mickey Tettleton	.05
286	Wade Boggs	.60
287	Stan Belinda	.05
288	Bret Barberie	.05
289	Jose Oquendo	.05
290	Frank Castillo	.05
291	Dave Stieb	.05
292	Tommy Greene	.05
293	Eric Karros	.05
294	Greg Maddux	.60
295	Jim Eisenreich	.05
296	Rafael Palmeiro	.35
297	Ramon Martinez	.05
298	Tim Wallach	.05
299	Jim Thome	.45
300	Chito Martinez	.05
301	Mitch Williams	.05
302	Randy Johnson	.45
303	Carlton Fisk	.45
304	Travis Fryman	.05
305	Bobby Witt	.05
306	Dave Magadan	.05
307	Alex Cole	.05
308	Bobby Bonilla	.05
309	Bryan Harvey	.05
310	Rafael Belliard	.05
311	Mariano Duncan	.05
312	Chuck Crim	.05
313	John Kruk	.05
314	Ellis Burks	.05
315	Craig Biggio	.05
316	Glenn Davis	.05
317	Ryne Sandberg	.60
318	Mike Sharperson	.05
319	Rich Rodriguez	.05
320	Lee Guetterman	.05
321	Benito Santiago	.05
322	Jose Offerman	.05
323	Tony Pena	.05
324	Pat Borders	.05
325	Mike Henneman	.05
326	Kevin Brown	.05
327	Chris Nabholz	.05
328	Franklin Stubbs	.05
329	Tino Martinez	.05
330	Mickey Morandini	.05
331	Checklist	.05
332	Mark Gubicza	.05
333	Bill Landrum	.05
334	Mark Whiten	.05
335	Darren Daulton	.05
336	Rick Wilkins	.05
337	Brian Jordan **RC**	.25
338	Kevin Ward	.05
339	Ruben Amaro	.05
340	Trevor Wilson	.05
341	Andujar Cedeno	.05
342	Michael Huff	.05
343	Brady Anderson	.05
344	Craig Grebeck	.05
345	Bobby Ojeda	.05
346	Mike Pagliarulo	.05
347	Terry Shumpert	.05
348	Dann Bilardello	.05
349	Frank Thomas	.45
350	Albert Belle	.05
351	Jose Mesa	.05
352	Rich Monteleone	.05
353	Bob Walk	.05
354	Monty Fariss	.05
355	Luis Rivera	.05
356	Anthony Young	.05
357	Geno Petralli	.05
358	Otis Nixon	.05
359	Tom Pagnozzi	.05
360	Reggie Sanders	.05
361	Lee Stevens	.05
362	Kent Hrbek	.05
363	Orlando Merced	.05
364	Mike Bordick	.05
365	Dion James	.05
366	Jack Clark	.05
367	Mike Stanley	.05
368	Randy Velarde	.05
369	Dan Pasqua	.05
370	Pat Listach	.05
371	Mike Fitzgerald	.05
372	Tom Foley	.05
373	Matt Williams	.05
374	Brian Hunter	.05
375	Joe Carter	.05
376	Bret Saberhagen	.05
377	Mike Stanton	.05
378	Hubie Brooks	.05
379	Eric Bell	.05
380	Walt Weiss	.05
381	Danny Jackson	.05
382	Manuel Lee	.05
383	Ruben Sierra	.05
384	Greg Swindell	.05
385	Ryan Bowen	.05
386	Kevin Ritz	.05
387	Curtis Wilkerson	.05
388	Gary Varsho	.05
389	Dave Hansen	.05
390	Bob Welch	.05
391	Lou Whitaker	.05
392	Ken Griffey Jr.	.75
393	Mike Maddux	.05
394	Arthur Rhodes	.05
395	Chili Davis	.05
396	Eddie Murray	.45
397	Checklist	.05
398	Dave Cochrane	.05
399	Kevin Seitzer	.05
400	Ozzie Smith	.60
401	Paul Sorrento	.05
402	Les Lancaster	.05
403	Junior Noboa	.05
404	Dave Justice	.05
405	Andy Ashby	.05
406	Danny Tartabull	.05
407	Bill Swift	.05
408	Craig Lefferts	.05
409	Tom Candiotti	.05
410	Lance Blankenship	.05
411	Jeff Tackett	.05
412	Sammy Sosa	.65
413	Jody Reed	.05
414	Bruce Ruffin	.05
415	Gene Larkin	.05
416	John Vanderwal	.05
417	Tim Belcher	.05
418	Steve Frey	.05
419	Dick Schofield	.05
420	Jeff King	.05
421	Kim Batiste	.05
422	Jack McDowell	.05
423	Damon Berryhill	.05
424	Gary Wayne	.05
425	Jack Morris	.05
426	Moises Alou	.05
427	Mark McLemore	.05
428	Juan Guerrero	.05
429	Scott Scudder	.05
430	Eric Davis	.05
431	Joe Slusarski	.05
432	Todd Zeile	.05
433	Dwayne Henry	.05
434	Cliff Brantley	.05
435	Butch Henry	.05
436	Todd Worrell	.05
437	Bob Scanlan	.05
438	Wally Joyner	.05
439	John Flaherty	.05
440	Brian Downing	.05
441	Darren Lewis	.05
442	Gary Carter	.45
443	Wally Ritchie	.05
444	Chris Jones	.05
445	Jeff Kent	.05
446	Gary Sheffield	.30
447	Ron Darling	.05
448	Deion Sanders	.05
449	Andres Galarraga	.05
450	Chuck Finley	.05
451	Derek Lilliquist	.05
452	Carl Willis	.05
453	Wes Chamberlain	.05
454	Roger Mason	.05
455	Spike Owen	.05
456	Thomas Howard	.05
457	Dave Martinez	.05
458	Pete Incaviglia	.05
459	Keith Miller	.05
460	Mike Fetters	.05
461	Paul Gibson	.05
462	George Bell	.05
463	Checklist	.05
464	Terry Mulholland	.05
465	Storm Davis	.05
466	Gary Pettis	.05
467	Randy Bush	.05
468	Ken Hill	.05
469	Rheal Cormier	.05
470	Andy Stankiewicz	.05
471	Dave Burba	.05
472	Henry Cotto	.05
473	Dale Sveum	.05
474	Rich Gossage	.05
475	William Suero	.05
476	Doug Strange	.05
477	Bill Krueger	.05
478	John Wetteland	.05
479	Melido Perez	.05
480	Lonnie Smith	.05
481	Mike Jackson	.05
482	Mike Gardiner	.05
483	David Wells	.05
484	Barry Jones	.05
485	Scott Bankhead	.05
486	Terry Leach	.05
487	Vince Horsman	.05
488	Dave Eiland	.05
489	Alejandro Pena	.05
490	Julio Valera	.05
491	Joe Boever	.05
492	Paul Miller	.05
493	Arci Cianfrocco **RC**	.05
494	Dave Fleming	.05
495	Kyle Abbott	.05
496	Chad Kreuter	.05
497	Chris James	.05
498	Donnie Hill	.05
499	Jacob Brumfield	.05
500	Ricky Bones	.05
501	Terry Steinbach	.05
502	Bernard Gilkey	.05
503	Dennis Cook	.05
504	Len Dykstra	.05
505	Mike Bielecki	.05
506	Bob Kipper	.05
507	Jose Melendez	.05
508	Rick Sutcliffe	.05
509	Ken Patterson	.05
510	Andy Allanson	.05
511	Al Newman	.05
512	Mark Gardner	.05
513	Jeff Schaefer	.05
514	Jim McNamara	.05
515	Peter Hoy	.05
516	Curt Schilling	.30
517	Kirk McCaskill	.05
518	Chris Gwynn	.05
519	Sid Fernandez	.05
520	Jeff Parrett	.05
521	Scott Ruskin	.05
522	Kevin McReynolds	.05
523	Rick Cerone	.05
524	Jesse Orosco	.05
525	Troy Afenir	.05
526	John Smiley	.05
527	Dale Murphy	.25
528	Leaf Set Card	.05

Gold Previews

In the same format as the chase cards which would be included in the regular 1992 Leaf packs, this preview set was produced for distribution to the Donruss dealer network. Cards feature the same black borders and gold highlights as the regular-issue Leaf Gold cards, but are numbered "X of 33" on the back.

		NM/M
Complete Set (33):		30.00
Common Player:		.50
1	Steve Avery	.50
2	Ryne Sandberg	2.00
3	Chris Sabo	.50
4	Jeff Bagwell	1.50
5	Darryl Strawberry	.50
6	Bret Barberie	.50
7	Howard Johnson	.50
8	John Kruk	.50
9	Andy Van Slyke	.50
10	Felix Jose	.50
11	Fred McGriff	.50
12	Will Clark	.60
13	Cal Ripken, Jr.	4.00
14	Phil Plantier	.50
15	Lee Stevens	.50
16	Frank Thomas	1.50
17	Mark Whiten	.50
18	Cecil Fielder	.50
19	George Brett	2.50
20	Robin Yount	1.50
21	Scott Erickson	.50
22	Don Mattingly	2.50
23	Jose Canseco	1.00
24	Ken Griffey Jr.	3.00
25	Nolan Ryan	4.00
26	Joe Carter	.50
27	Deion Sanders	.50
28	Dean Palmer	.50
29	Andy Benes	.50
30	Gary DiSarcina	.50
31	Chris Hoiles	.50
32	Mark McGwire	3.00
33	Reggie Sanders	.50

Gold Edition

This set is a parallel version of Leaf's regular 1992 set. Card fronts do not have silver borders like the regular cards do; black borders and gold foil highlights are seen instead. A Gold Edition card was inserted in each 15-card 1992 Leaf foil pack.

	NM/M
Complete Set (528):	35.00
Common Player:	.10
Stars/Rookies:	3X

Gold Rookies

Two dozen of the major leagues' most promising players are featured in this insert set. Cards 1-12 were randomly included in Series 1 foil packs, while cards 13-24 were in Series 2 packs. Cards, numbered with a BC prefix, are standard size and enhanced with gold foil.

		NM/M
Complete Set (24):		4.00
Common Player:		.25
Jumbo:		1.5X
1	Chad Curtis	.25
2	Brent Gates	.25
3	Pedro Martinez	3.00
4	Kenny Lofton	.35
5	Turk Wendell	.25
6	Mark Hutton	.25
7	Todd Hundley	.25
8	Matt Stairs	.25
9	Ed Taubensee	.25
10	David Nied	.25

11 Salomon Torres .25
12 Bret Boone .50
13 John Ruffin .25
14 Ed Martel .25
15 Rick Trlicek .25
16 Raul Mondesi .25
17 Pat Mahomes .25
18 Dan Wilson .25
19 Donovan Osborne .25
20 Dave Silvestri .25
21 Gary DiSarcina .25
22 Denny Neagle .25
23 Steve Hosey .25
24 John Doherty .25

1993 Leaf Promo

This unmarked promo of company spokesman Frank Thomas can be distinguished from the issued version of his card #195 by the presence of the Franklin logo on the batting glove he wears. The logo was airbrushed away from the issued card.

NM/M
195 Frank Thomas 10.00

1993 Leaf

Leaf issued this set in three series: two 220-card series and a 110-card update set. Card fronts have full-bleed action photos and players' names stamped in gold foil. Color-coded slate corners are used to differentiate teams. Backs have player photos against cityscapes or landmarks from the team's home city, a holographic embossed team logo and 1992 and career statistics. Players from the National League's expansion teams, the Colorado Rockies and Florida Marlins, along with the Cincinnati Reds, California Angels and Seattle Mariners were featured in Series II packs so they could be pictured in their new uniforms. The Update series included a specially numbered "DW" insert card honoring Dave Winfield's 3,000-hit landmark, plus 3,500 special Frank Thomas autographed cards.

NM/M
Complete Set (550): 12.50
Common Player: .05
Series 1 or 2 Pack (14): .65
Series 1 or 2 Box (36): 12.50
Update Pack (14): 1.50
Update Box (36): 25.00
1 Ben McDonald .05
2 Sid Fernandez .05
3 Juan Guzman .05
4 Curt Schilling .40
5 Ivan Rodriguez .65
6 Don Slaught .05
7 Terry Steinbach .05
8 Todd Zeile .05
9 Andy Stankiewicz .05
10 Tim Teufel .05
11 Marvin Freeman .05
12 Jim Austin .05
13 Bob Scanlan .05
14 Rusty Meacham .05
15 Casey Candaele .05
16 Travis Fryman .05
17 Jose Offerman .05
18 Albert Belle .05
19 John Vander Wahl (Vander Wal) .05
20 Dan Pasqua .05
21 Frank Viola .05
22 Terry Mulholland .05
23 Gregg Olson .05
24 Randy Tomlin .05
25 Todd Stottlemyre .05
26 Jose Oquendo .05
27 Julio Franco .05
28 Tony Gwynn 1.00
29 Ruben Sierra .05
30 Bobby Thigpen .05
31 Jim Bullinger .05
32 Rick Aguilera .05
33 Scott Servais .05
34 Cal Eldred .05
35 Mike Piazza 1.50
36 Brent Mayne .05
37 Wil Cordero .05
38 Milt Cuyler .05
39 Howard Johnson .05
40 Kenny Lofton .05
41 Alex Fernandez .05
42 Denny Neagle .05
43 Tony Pena .05
44 Bob Tewksbury .05
45 Glenn Davis .05
46 Fred McGriff .05
47 John Olerud .05
48 Steve Hosey .05
49 Rafael Palmeiro .65
50 Dave Justice .05
51 Pete Harnisch .05
52 Sam Militello .05
53 Orel Hershiser .05
54 Pat Mahomes .05
55 Greg Colbrunn .05
56 Greg Vaughn .05
57 Vince Coleman .05
58 Brian McRae .05
59 Len Dykstra .05
60 Dan Gladden .05
61 Ted Power .05
62 Donovan Osborne .05
63 Ron Karkovice .05
64 Frank Seminara .05
65 Bob Zupcic .05
66 Kirt Manwaring .05
67 Mike Devereaux .05
68 Mark Lemke .05
69 Devon White .05
70 Sammy Sosa 1.25
71 Pedro Astacio .05
72 Dennis Eckersley .60
73 Chris Nabholz .05
74 Melido Perez .05
75 Todd Hundley .05
76 Kent Hrbek .05
77 Mickey Morandini .05
78 Tim McIntosh .05
79 Andy Van Slyke .05
80 Kevin McReynolds .05
81 Mike Henneman .05
82 Greg Harris .05
83 Sandy Alomar Jr. .05
84 Mike Jackson .05
85 Ozzie Guillen .05
86 Jeff Blauser .05
87 John Valentin .05
88 Rey Sanchez .05
89 Rick Sutcliffe .05
90 Luis Gonzalez .25
91 Jeff Fassero .05
92 Kenny Rogers .05
93 Bret Saberhagen .05
94 Bob Welch .05
95 Darren Daulton .05
96 Mike Gallego .05
97 Orlando Merced .05
98 Chuck Knoblauch .05
99 Bernard Gilkey .05
100 Billy Ashley .05
101 Kevin Appier .05
102 Jeff Brantley .05
103 Bill Gullickson .05
104 John Smoltz .05
105 Paul Sorrento .05
106 Steve Buechele .05
107 Steve Sax .05
108 Andujar Cedeno .05
109 Billy Hatcher .05
110 Checklist .05
111 Alan Mills .05
112 John Franco .05
113 Jack Morris .05
114 Mitch Williams .05
115 Nolan Ryan 2.50
116 Jay Bell .05
117 Mike Bordick .05
118 Geronimo Pena .05
119 Danny Tartabull .05
120 Checklist .05
121 Steve Avery .05
122 Ricky Bones .05
123 Mike Morgan .05
124 Jeff Montgomery .05
125 Jeff Bagwell .75
126 Tony Phillips .05
127 Lenny Harris .05
128 Glenallen Hill .05
129 Marquis Grissom .05
130 Gerald Williams (Photo, stats actually Bernie Williams.) .20
131 Greg Harris .05
132 Tommy Greene .05
133 Chris Hoiles .05
134 Bob Walk .05
135 Duane Ward .05
136 Tom Pagnozzi .05
137 Jeff Huson .05
138 Kurt Stillwell .05
139 Dave Henderson .05
140 Darrin Jackson .05
141 Frank Castillo .05
142 Scott Erickson .05
143 Darryl Kile .05
144 Bill Wegman .05
145 Steve Wilson .05
146 George Brett 1.25
147 Moises Alou .05
148 Lou Whitaker .05
149 Chico Walker .05
150 Jerry Browne .05
151 Kirk McCaskill .05
152 Zane Smith .05
153 Matt Young .05
154 Lee Smith .05
155 Leo Gomez .05
156 Dan Walters .05
157 Pat Borders .05
158 Matt Williams .05
159 Dean Palmer .05
160 John Patterson .05
161 Doug Jones .05
162 John Habyan .05
163 Pedro Martinez .75
164 Carl Willis .05
165 Darrin Fletcher .05
166 B.J. Surhoff .05
167 Eddie Murray .75
168 Keith Miller .05
169 Ricky Jordan .05
170 Juan Gonzalez .65
171 Charles Nagy .05
172 Mark Clark .05
173 Bobby Thigpen .05
174 Tim Scott .05
175 Scott Cooper .05
176 Royce Clayton .05
177 Brady Anderson .05
178 Sid Bream .05
179 Derek Bell .05
180 Otis Nixon .05
181 Kevin Gross .05
182 Ron Darling .05
183 John Wetteland .05
184 Mike Stanley .05
185 Jeff Kent .05
186 Brian Harper .05
187 Mariano Duncan .05
188 Robin Yount .75
189 Al Martin .05
190 Eddie Zosky .05
191 Mike Munoz .05
192 Andy Benes .05
193 Dennis Cook .05
194 Bill Swift .05
195 Frank Thomas .75
196 Damon Berryhill .05
197 Mike Greenwell .05
198 Mark Grace .05
199 Darryl Hamilton .05
200 Derrick May .05
201 Ken Hill .05
202 Kevin Brown .05
203 Dwight Gooden .05
204 Bobby Witt .05
205 Juan Bell .05
206 Kevin Maas .05
207 Jeff King .05
208 Scott Leius .05
209 Rheal Cormier .05
210 Darryl Strawberry .05
211 Tom Gordon .05
212 Bud Black .05
213 Mickey Tettleton .05
214 Pete Smith .05
215 Felix Fermin .05
216 Rick Wilkins .05
217 George Bell .05
218 Eric Anthony .05
219 Pedro Munoz .05
220 Checklist .05
221 Lance Blankenship .05
222 Deion Sanders .10
223 Craig Biggio .05
224 Ryne Sandberg 1.00
225 Ron Gant .05
226 Tom Brunansky .05
227 Chad Curtis .05
228 Joe Carter .05
229 Brian Jordan .05
230 Brett Butler .05
231 Frank Bolick .05
232 Rod Beck .05
233 Carlos Baerga .05
234 Eric Karros .05
235 Jack Armstrong .05
236 Bobby Bonilla .05
237 Don Mattingly 1.25
238 Jeff Gardner .05
239 Dave Hollins .05
240 Steve Cooke .05
241 Jose Canseco .35
242 Ivan Calderon .05
243 Tim Belcher .05
244 Freddie Benavides .05
245 Roberto Alomar .25
246 Rob Deer .05
247 Will Clark .10
248 Mike Felder .05
249 Harold Baines .05
250 David Cone .05
251 Mark Guthrie .05
252 Ellis Burks .05
253 Jim Abbott .05
254 Chili Davis .05
255 Chris Bosio .05
256 Bret Barberie .05
257 Hal Morris .05
258 Dante Bichette .05
259 Storm Davis .05
260 Gary DiSarcina .05
261 Ken Caminiti .05
262 Paul Molitor .75
263 Joe Oliver .05
264 Pat Listach .05
265 Gregg Jefferies .05
266 Jose Guzman .05
267 Eric Davis .05
268 Delino DeShields .05
269 Barry Bonds 2.50
270 Mike Bielecki .05
271 Jay Buhner .05
272 Scott Pose **RC** .05
273 Tony Fernandez .05
274 Chito Martinez .05
275 Phil Plantier .05
276 Pete Incaviglia .05
277 Carlos Garcia .05
278 Tom Henke .05
279 Roger Clemens 1.25
280 Rob Dibble .05
281 Daryl Boston .05
282 Greg Gagne .05
283 Cecil Fielder .05
284 Carlton Fisk .75
285 Wade Boggs 1.00
286 Damion Easley .05
287 Norm Charlton .05
288 Jeff Conine .05
289 Roberto Kelly .05
290 Jerald Clark .05
291 Rickey Henderson .75
292 Chuck Finley .05
293 Doug Drabek .05
294 Dave Stewart .05
295 Tom Glavine .35
296 Jaime Navarro .05
297 Ray Lankford .05
298 Greg Hibbard .05
299 Jody Reed .05
300 Dennis Martinez .05
301 Dave Martinez .05
302 Reggie Jefferson .05
303 John Cummings **RC** .05
304 Orestes Destrade .05
305 Mike Maddux .05
306 David Segui .05
307 Gary Sheffield .35
308 Danny Jackson .05
309 Criag Lefferts .05
310 Andre Dawson .20
311 Barry Larkin .05
312 Alex Cole .05
313 Mark Gardner .05
314 Kirk Gibson .05
315 Shane Mack .05
316 Bo Jackson .10
317 Jimmy Key .05
318 Greg Myers .05
319 Ken Griffey Jr. 1.50
320 Monty Fariss .05
321 Kevin Mitchell .05
322 Andres Galarraga .05
323 Mark McGwire 2.00
324 Mark Langston .05
325 Steve Finley .05
326 Greg Maddux 1.00
327 Dave Nilsson .05
328 Ozzie Smith 1.00
329 Candy Maldonado .05
330 Checklist .05
331 Tim Pugh **RC** .05
332 Joe Girardi .05
333 Junior Felix .05
334 Greg Swindell .05
335 Ramon Martinez .05
336 Sean Berry .05
337 Joe Orsulak .05
338 Wes Chamberlain .05
339 Stan Belinda .05
340 Checklist .05
341 Bruce Hurst .05
342 John Burkett .05
343 Mike Mussina .40
344 Scott Fletcher .05
345 Rene Gonzales .05
346 Roberto Hernandez .05
347 Carlos Martinez .05
348 Bill Krueger .05
349 Felix Jose .05
350 John Jaha .05
351 Willie Banks .05
352 Matt Nokes .05
353 Kevin Seitzer .05
354 Erik Hanson .05
355 David Hulse **RC** .05
356 Domingo Martinez **RC** .05
357 Greg Olson .05
358 Randy Myers .05
359 Tom Browning .05
360 Charlie Hayes .05
361 Bryan Harvey .05
362 Eddie Taubensee .05
363 Tim Wallach .05
364 Mel Rojas .05
365 Frank Tanana .05
366 John Kruk .05
367 Tim Laker **RC** .05
368 Rich Rodriguez .05
369 Darren Lewis .05
370 Harold Reynolds .05
371 Jose Melendez .05
372 Joe Grahe .05
373 Lance Johnson .05
374 Jose Mesa .05
375 Scott Livingstone .05
376 Wally Joyner .05
377 Kevin Reimer .05
378 Kirby Puckett 1.00
379 Paul O'Neill .05
380 Randy Johnson .75
381 Manuel Lee .05
382 Dick Schofield .05
383 Darren Holmes .05
384 Charlie Hough .05
385 John Orton .05
386 Edgar Martinez .05
387 Terry Pendleton .05
388 Dan Plesac .05
389 Jeff Reardon .05
390 David Nied .05
391 Dave Magadan .05
392 Larry Walker .05
393 Ben Rivera .05
394 Lonnie Smith .05
395 Craig Shipley .05
396 Willie McGee .05
397 Arthur Rhodes .05
398 Mike Stanton .05
399 Luis Polonia .05
400 Jack McDowell .05
401 Mike Moore .05
402 Jose Lind .05
403 Bill Spiers .05
404 Kevin Tapani .05
405 Spike Owen .05
406 Tino Martinez .05
407 Charlie Leibrandt .05
408 Ed Sprague .05
409 Bryn Smith .05
410 Benito Santiago .05
411 Jose Rijo .05
412 Pete O'Brien .05
413 Willie Wilson .05
414 Bip Roberts .05
415 Eric Young .05
416 Walt Weiss .05
417 Milt Thompson .05
418 Chris Sabo .05
419 Scott Sanderson .05
420 Tim Raines .05
421 Alan Trammell .05
422 Mike Macfarlane .05
423 Dave Winfield .75
424 Bob Wickman .05
425 David Valle .05
426 Gary Redus .05
427 Turner Ward .05
428 Reggie Sanders .05
429 Todd Worrell .05
430 Julio Valera .05
431 Cal Ripken, Jr. 2.50
432 Mo Vaughn .05
433 John Smiley .05
434 Omar Vizquel .05
435 Billy Ripken .05
436 Cory Snyder .05
437 Carlos Quintana .05
438 Omar Olivares .05
439 Robin Ventura .05
440 Checklist .05
441 Kevin Higgins .05
442 Carlos Hernandez .05
443 Dan Peltier .05
444 Derek Lilliquist .05
445 Tim Salmon .05
446 Sherman Obando **RC** .05
447 Pat Kelly .05
448 Todd Van Poppel .05
449 Mark Whiten .05
450 Checklist .05
451 Pat Meares .05
452 Tony Tarasco **RC** .05
453 Chris Gwynn .05
454 Armando Reynoso .05
455 Danny Darwin .05
456 Willie Greene .05
457 Mike Blowers .05
458 Kevin Roberson **RC** .05
459 Graeme Lloyd **RC** .05
460 David West .05
461 Joey Cora .05
462 Alex Arias .05
463 Chad Kreuter .05
464 Mike Lansing .05
465 Mike Timlin .05
466 Paul Wagner .05
467 Mark Portugal .05
468 Jim Leyritz .05
469 Ryan Klesko .05
470 Mario Diaz .05
471 Guillermo Velasquez .05
472 Fernando Valenzuela .05
473 Raul Mondesi .05
474 Mike Pagliarulo .05
475 Chris Hammond .05
476 Torey Lovullo .05
477 Trevor Wilson .05
478 Marcos Armas **RC** .05
479 Dave Gallagher .05
480 Jeff Treadway .05
481 Jeff Branson .05
482 Dickie Thon .05
483 Eduardo Perez .05
484 David Wells .05
485 Brian Williams .05
486 Domingo Cedeno .05
487 Tom Candiotti .05
488 Steve Frey .05
489 Greg McMichael .05
490 Marc Newfield .05
491 Larry Andersen .05
492 Damon Buford .05
493 Ricky Gutierrez .05
494 Jeff Russell .05
495 Vinny Castilla .05
496 Wilson Alvarez .05
497 Scott Bullett .05
498 Larry Casian .05
499 Jose Vizcaino .05
500 J.T. Snow **RC** .75
501 Bryan Hickerson .05
502 Jeremy Hernandez .05
503 Jeromy Burnitz .05
504 Steve Farr .05
505 J. Owens .05
506 Craig Paquette .05
507 Jim Eisenreich .05
508 Matt Whiteside .05
509 Luis Aquino .05
510 Mike LaValliere .05
511 Jim Gott .05
512 Mark McLemore .05
513 Randy Milligan .05
514 Gary Gaetti .05
515 Lou Frazier .05
516 Rich Amaral .05
517 Gene Harris .05
518 Aaron Sele .05
519 Mark Wohlers .05
520 Scott Kamieniecki .05
521 Kent Mercker .05
522 Jim Deshaies .05
523 Kevin Stocker .05
524 Jason Bere .05
525 Tim Bogar .05
526 Brad Pennington .05
527 Curt Leskanic **RC** .05
528 Wayne Kirby .05
529 Tim Costo .05
530 Doug Henry .05
531 Trevor Hoffman .05
532 Kelly Gruber .05
533 Mike Harkey .05
534 John Doherty .05
535 Erik Pappas .05
536 Brent Gates .05
537 Roger McDowell .05
538 Chris Haney .05
539 Blas Minor .05
540 Pat Hentgen .05
541 Chuck Carr .05
542 Doug Strange .05
543 Xavier Hernandez .05
544 Paul Quantrill .05
545 Anthony Young .05
546 Bret Boone .05
547 Dwight Smith .05
548 Bobby Munoz .05
549 Russ Springer .05
550 Roger Pavlik .05
---- Dave Winfield (3,000 Hits) 2.00

Fasttrack

This 20-card insert set was released in two series; cards 1-10 were randomly included in Leaf Series I retail packs, while 11-20 were in Series II packs. Card fronts and backs are similar with a player photo and a diagonal white strip with "on the Fasttrack" printed in black and red. Fronts have the gold embossed Leaf logo, backs have the silver holographic team logo.

NM/M
Complete Set (20): 15.00
Common Player: .60
1 Frank Thomas 3.00
2 Tim Wakefield .60
3 Kenny Lofton .60
4 Mike Mussina 1.00
5 Juan Gonzalez 2.50
6 Chuck Knoblauch .60
7 Eric Karros .60
8 Ray Lankford .60
9 Juan Guzman .60
10 Pat Listach .60
11 Carlos Baerga .60
12 Felix Jose .60
13 Steve Avery .60
14 Robin Ventura .60
15 Ivan Rodriguez 2.50
16 Cal Eldred .60
17 Jeff Bagwell 3.00
18 Dave Justice .60
19 Travis Fryman .60
20 Marquis Grissom .60

All-Stars

Cards 1-10 in this insert set were randomly inserted one per Leaf Series I jumbo packs, while cards 11-20 were in Series II jumbo packs. Cards feature two players per card, one on each side. Only one side is numbered, but both sides have gold foil.

		NM/M
	Complete Set (20):	15.00
	Common Player:	.25
1	Ivan Rodriguez, Darren Daulton	.75
2	Don Mattingly, Fred McGriff	1.50
3	Cecil Fielder, Jeff Bagwell	.75
4	Carlos Baerga, Ryne Sandberg	1.00
5	Chuck Knoblauch, Delino DeShields	.25
6	Robin Ventura, Terry Pendleton	.25
7	Ken Griffey Jr., Andy Van Slyke	2.00
8	Joe Carter, Dave Justice	.25
9	Jose Canseco, Tony Gwynn	1.00
10	Dennis Eckersley, Rob Dibble	.60
11	Mark McGwire, Will Clark	2.50
12	Frank Thomas, Mark Grace	.75
13	Roberto Alomar, Craig Biggio	.50
14	Barry Larkin, Cal Ripken, Jr.	3.00
15	Gary Sheffield, Edgar Martinez	.50
16	Juan Gonzalez, Barry Bonds	3.00
17	Kirby Puckett, Marquis Grissom	1.00
18	Jim Abbott, Tom Glavine	.40
19	Nolan Ryan, Greg Maddux	3.00
20	Roger Clemens, Doug Drabek	1.50

Gold Rookies

These cards, numbered 1 of 20 etc., feature 1993 rookies and were randomly inserted into hobby foil packs, 10 players per series. Card fronts feature action photos, while the backs show a player photo against a landmark from his team's city. Jumbo versions in 3-1/2" x 5" format were produced as special retail box toppers, in a numbered edition of 5,000 each.

		NM/M
	Complete Set (20):	5.00
	Common Player:	.25
1	Kevin Young	.25
2	Wil Cordero	.25
3	Mark Kiefer	.25
4	Gerald Williams	.25
5	Brandon Wilson	.25
6	Greg Gohr	.25
7	Ryan Thompson	.25
8	Tim Wakefield	.25
9	Troy Neel	.25
10	Tim Salmon	.50
11	Kevin Rogers	.25
12	Rod Bolton	.25
13	Ken Ryan	.25
14	Phil Hiatt	.25
15	Rene Arocha	.25
16	Nigel Wilson	.25
17	J.T. Snow	.50
18	Benji Gil	.25
19	Chipper Jones	3.00
20	Darrell Sherman	.25

Heading for the Hall

Ten players on the way to the Baseball Hall of Fame are featured in this insert set. Series I Leaf packs had cards 1-5 randomly included; Series II packs had cards 6-10.

		NM/M
	Complete Set (10):	10.00
	Common Player:	.75
1	Nolan Ryan	2.50
2	Tony Gwynn	1.00
3	Robin Yount	1.00
4	Eddie Murray	1.00
5	Cal Ripken, Jr.	2.50
6	Roger Clemens	2.00
7	George Brett	2.00
8	Ryne Sandberg	1.00
9	Kirby Puckett	1.00
10	Ozzie Smith	1.00

Frank Thomas

Leaf signed Frank Thomas as its spokesman for 1993, and honored him with a 10-card insert set. Cards 1-5 were randomly included in Series I packs; cards 6-10 were in Series II packs. A large "Frank" logo in a holographic foil stamp is featured on each card front along with a one-word character trait. On back is a color portrait photo of Thomas superimposed on a Chicago skyline. A paragraph on back describes how the character trait on front applies to Thomas.

		NM/M
	Complete Set (10):	4.50
	Common Card:	.75
	Autographed Card:	30.00
1	Aggressive (Frank Thomas)	.75
2	Serious (Frank Thomas)	.75
3	Intense (Frank Thomas)	.75
4	Confident (Frank Thomas)	.75
5	Assertive (Frank Thomas)	.75
6	Power (Frank Thomas)	.75
7	Control (Frank Thomas)	.75
8	Strength (Frank Thomas)	.75
9	Concentration (Frank Thomas)	.75
10	Preparation (Frank Thomas)	.75

Update Gold All-Stars

These 10 cards, featuring 20 all-stars, were randomly inserted in Leaf Update packs. Each card features two players, one on each side. Cards are distinguished from the regular Gold All-Stars by indicating on the front the card is number X of 10, with a tiny white "Update" in the red stripe above the card number.

		NM/M
	Complete Set (10):	7.50
	Common Player:	.25
1	Mark Langston, Terry Mulholland	.25
2	Ivan Rodriguez, Darren Daulton	.50
3	John Olerud, John Kruk	.25
4	Roberto Alomar, Ryne Sandberg	1.00
5	Wade Boggs, Gary Sheffield	.75
6	Cal Ripken, Jr., Barry Larkin	3.00
7	Kirby Puckett, Barry Bonds	2.50
8	Marquis Grissom, Ken Griffey Jr.	2.00
9	Joe Carter, Dave Justice	.25
10	Mark Grace, Paul Molitor	.75

Update Gold Rookies

These five cards were randomly inserted in Leaf Update packs. Cards are similiar in design to the regular Gold Rookies cards, except the logo on the back indicates they are from the Update series. Jumbo 3-1/2" x 5" versions were produced as special retail box toppers in a numbered edition of 5,000 each.

		NM/M
	Complete Set (5):	3.50
	Common Player:	.25
	Jumbos:	1.5X
1	Allen Watson	.25
2	Jeffrey Hammonds	.25
3	David McCarty	.25
4	Mike Piazza	3.00
5	Roberto Meija	.25

Update Frank Thomas Autograph

This card was a random insert in '93 Leaf Update packs and features a genuine Frank Thomas autograph on front. Unlike the other cards in the set, this has a silver-gray border on front and back. Front has a gold-foil seal in upper-left. Back has a photo of Thomas in his batting follow-through. At bottom on back is a white strip bearing the card's individual serial number from an edition of 3,500.

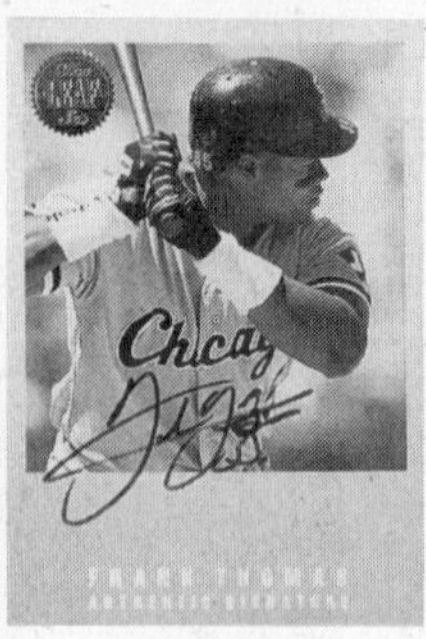

		NM/M
FT	Frank Thomas	35.00

Update Frank Thomas Super

This 10-card insert set features Leaf's 1993 spokesman, Frank Thomas. Cards, which measure 5" x 7", were included one per every Leaf Update foil box and are identical to the inserts found in Series I and II except in size. Cards are individually numbered. Thomas autographed 3,500 cards.

		NM/M
	Complete Set (10):	17.50
	Common Card:	2.00
1	Aggressive (Frank Thomas)	2.00
2	Serious (Frank Thomas)	2.00
3	Intense (Frank Thomas)	2.00
4	Confident (Frank Thomas)	2.00
5	Assertive (Frank Thomas)	2.00
6	Power (Frank Thomas)	2.00
7	Control (Frank Thomas)	2.00
8	Strength (Frank Thomas)	2.00
9	Concentration (Frank Thomas)	2.00
10	Preparation (Frank Thomas)	2.00

1994 Leaf Promos

Identical in format to the regular issue, this nine-card set was produced as a preview for the 1994 Leaf cards. The only differences on the promo cards are a large, black "Promotional Sample" notice overprinted diagonally on both the front and back of the cards. Instead of the regular card numbers, the promos are numbered "X of 9" at top to the left of the team logo hologram.

		NM/M
	Complete Set (9):	7.50
	Common Player:	.25
1	Roberto Alomar	.75
2	Darren Daulton	.25
3	Ken Griffey Jr.	2.00
4	David Justice	.25
5	Don Mattingly	1.50
6	Mike Piazza	2.00
7	Cal Ripken, Jr.	3.00
8	Ryne Sandberg	1.25
9	Frank Thomas	1.00

1994 Leaf

Donruss returned its premium-brand Leaf set in 1994 with an announced 25 percent production cut from the previous season - fewer than 20,000 20-box cases of each 220-card series. Game-action photos dominate the fronts of the cards, borderless at the top and sides. At bottom are team color-coded faux-marble borders with the player's name (last name in gold foil) and team. Backs have a background of the player's home stadium with another action photo superimposed. In a ticket-stub device at upper-left is a portrait photo and a few personal numbers. Previous season and career stats are in white stripes at bottom. The team logo is presented in holographic foil at upper-right. To feature 1994's new stadiums and uniforms, cards of the Indians, Rangers, Brewers and Astros were included only in the second series. Seven different types of insert cards were produced and distributed among the various types of Leaf packaging.

		NM/M
	Complete Set (440):	10.00
	Common Player:	.05
	Series 1 or 2 Pack (12):	.75
	Series 1 or 2 Box (36):	12.50
1	Cal Ripken, Jr.	2.50
2	Tony Tarasco	.05
3	Joe Girardi	.05
4	Bernie Williams	.20
5	Chad Kreuter	.05
6	Troy Neel	.05
7	Tom Pagnozzi	.05
8	Kirk Rueter	.05
9	Chris Bosio	.05
10	Dwight Gooden	.05
11	Mariano Duncan	.05
12	Jay Bell	.05
13	Lance Johnson	.05
14	Richie Lewis	.05
15	Dave Martinez	.05
16	Orel Hershiser	.05
17	Rob Butler	.05
18	Glenallen Hill	.05
19	Chad Curtis	.05
20	Mike Stanton	.05
21	Tim Wallach	.05
22	Milt Thompson	.05
23	Kevin Young	.05
24	John Smiley	.05
25	Jeff Montgomery	.05
26	Robin Ventura	.05
27	Scott Lydy	.05
28	Todd Stottlemyre	.05
29	Mark Whiten	.05
30	Robby Thompson	.05
31	Bobby Bonilla	.05
32	Andy Ashby	.05
33	Greg Myers	.05
34	Billy Hatcher	.05
35	Brad Holman	.05
36	Mark McLemore	.05
37	Scott Sanders	.05
38	Jim Abbott	.05
39	David Wells	.05
40	Roberto Kelly	.05
41	Jeff Conine	.05
42	Sean Berry	.05
43	Mark Grace	.05
44	Eric Young	.05
45	Rick Aguilera	.05
46	Chipper Jones	1.00
47	Mel Rojas	.05
48	Ryan Thompson	.05
49	Al Martin	.05
50	Cecil Fielder	.05
51	Pat Kelly	.05
52	Kevin Tapani	.05
53	Tim Costo	.05
54	Dave Hollins	.05
55	Kirt Manwaring	.05
56	Gregg Jefferies	.05
57	Ron Darling	.05
58	Bill Haselman	.05
59	Phil Plantier	.05
60	Frank Viola	.05
61	Todd Zeile	.05
62	Bret Barberie	.05
63	Roberto Mejia	.05
64	Chuck Knoblauch	.05
65	Jose Lind	.05
66	Brady Anderson	.05
67	Ruben Sierra	.05
68	Jose Vizcaino	.05
69	Joe Grahe	.05
70	Kevin Appier	.05
71	Wilson Alvarez	.05
72	Tom Candiotti	.05
73	John Burkett	.05
74	Anthony Young	.05
75	Scott Cooper	.05
76	Nigel Wilson	.05
77	John Valentin	.05
78	Dave McCarty	.05
79	Archi Cianfrocco	.05
80	Lou Whitaker	.05
81	Dante Bichette	.05
82	Mark Dewey	.05
83	Danny Jackson	.05
84	Harold Baines	.05
85	Todd Benzinger	.05
86	Damion Easley	.05
87	Danny Cox	.05
88	Jose Bautista	.05
89	Mike Lansing	.05
90	Phil Hiatt	.05
91	Tim Pugh	.05
92	Tino Martinez	.05
93	Raul Mondesi	.05
94	Greg Maddux	1.00
95	Al Leiter	.05
96	Benito Santiago	.05
97	Len Dykstra	.05
98	Sammy Sosa	1.25
99	Tim Bogar	.05
100	Checklist	.05
101	Deion Sanders	.10
102	Bobby Witt	.05
103	Wil Cordero	.05
104	Rich Amaral	.05
105	Mike Mussina	.50
106	Reggie Sanders	.05
107	Ozzie Guillen	.05
108	Paul O'Neill	.05
109	Tim Salmon	.05
110	Rheal Cormier	.05
111	Billy Ashley	.05
112	Jeff Kent	.05
113	Derek Bell	.05
114	Danny Darwin	.05
115	Chip Hale	.05
116	Tim Raines	.05
117	Ed Sprague	.05
118	Darrin Fletcher	.05
119	Darren Holmes	.05
120	Alan Trammell	.05
121	Don Mattingly	1.25
122	Greg Gagne	.05
123	Jose Offerman	.05
124	Joe Orsulak	.05
125	Jack McDowell	.05
126	Barry Larkin	.05
127	Ben McDonald	.05
128	Mike Bordick	.05
129	Devon White	.05
130	Mike Perez	.05
131	Jay Buhner	.05
132	Phil Leftwich	.05
133	Tommy Greene	.05
134	Charlie Hayes	.05
135	Don Slaught	.05
136	Mike Gallego	.05
137	Dave Winfield	.75
138	Steve Avery	.05
139	Derrick May	.05
140	Bryan Harvey	.05
141	Wally Joyner	.05

#	Player	Price
142	Andre Dawson	.20
143	Andy Benes	.05
144	John Franco	.05
145	Jeff King	.05
146	Joe Oliver	.05
147	Bill Gullickson	.05
148	Armando Reynoso	.05
149	Dave Fleming	.05
150	Checklist	.05
151	Todd Van Poppel	.05
152	Bernard Gilkey	.05
153	Kevin Gross	.05
154	Mike Devereaux	.05
155	Tim Wakefield	.05
156	Andres Galarraga	.05
157	Pat Meares	.05
158	Jim Leyritz	.05
159	Mike Macfarlane	.05
160	Tony Phillips	.05
161	Brent Gates	.05
162	Mark Langston	.05
163	Allen Watson	.05
164	Randy Johnson	.75
165	Doug Brocail	.05
166	Rob Dibble	.05
167	Roberto Hernandez	.05
168	Felix Jose	.05
169	Steve Cooke	.05
170	Darren Daulton	.05
171	Eric Karros	.05
172	Geronimo Pena	.05
173	Gary DiSarcina	.05
174	Marquis Grissom	.05
175	Joey Cora	.05
176	Jim Eisenreich	.05
177	Brad Pennington	.05
178	Terry Steinbach	.05
179	Pat Borders	.05
180	Steve Buechele	.05
181	Jeff Fassero	.05
182	Mike Greenwell	.05
183	Mike Henneman	.05
184	Ron Karkovice	.05
185	Pat Hentgen	.05
186	Jose Guzman	.05
187	Brett Butler	.05
188	Charlie Hough	.05
189	Terry Pendleton	.05
190	Melido Perez	.05
191	Orestes Destrade	.05
192	Mike Morgan	.05
193	Joe Carter	.05
194	Jeff Blauser	.05
195	Chris Hoiles	.05
196	Ricky Gutierrez	.05
197	Mike Moore	.05
198	Carl Willis	.05
199	Aaron Sele	.05
200	Checklist	.05
201	Tim Naehring	.05
202	Scott Livingstone	.05
203	Luis Alicea	.05
204	Torey Lovullo **RC**	.05
205	Jim Gott	.05
206	Bob Wickman	.05
207	Greg McMichael	.05
208	Scott Brosius	.05
209	Chris Gwynn	.05
210	Steve Sax	.05
211	Dick Schofield	.05
212	Robb Nen	.05
213	Ben Rivera	.05
214	Vinny Castilla	.05
215	Jamie Moyer	.05
216	Wally Whitehurst	.05
217	Frank Castillo	.05
218	Mike Blowers	.05
219	Tim Scott	.05
220	Paul Wagner	.05
221	Jeff Bagwell	.75
222	Ricky Bones	.05
223	Sandy Alomar Jr.	.05
224	Rod Beck	.05
225	Roberto Alomar	.20
226	Jack Armstrong	.05
227	Scott Erickson	.05
228	Rene Arocha	.05
229	Eric Anthony	.05
230	Jeromy Burnitz	.05
231	Kevin Brown	.05
232	Tim Belcher	.05
233	Bret Boone	.05
234	Dennis Eckersley	.60
235	Tom Glavine	.30
236	Craig Biggio	.05
237	Pedro Astacio	.05
238	Ryan Bowen	.05
239	Brad Ausmus	.05
240	Vince Coleman	.05
241	Jason Bere	.05
242	Ellis Burks	.05
243	Wes Chamberlain	.05
244	Ken Caminiti	.05
245	Willie Banks	.05
246	Sid Fernandez	.05
247	Carlos Baerga	.05
248	Carlos Garcia	.05
249	Jose Canseco	.50
250	Alex Diaz	.05
251	Albert Belle	.05
252	Moises Alou	.05
253	Bobby Ayala	.05
254	Tony Gwynn	1.00
255	Roger Clemens	1.25
256	Eric Davis	.05
257	Wade Boggs	1.00
258	Chili Davis	.05
259	Rickey Henderson	.75
260	Andujar Cedeno	.05
261	Cris Carpenter	.05
262	Juan Guzman	.05
263	Dave Justice	.05
264	Barry Bonds	2.50
265	Pete Incaviglia	.05
266	Tony Fernandez	.05
267	Cal Eldred	.05
268	Alex Fernandez	.05
269	Kent Hrbek	.05
270	Steve Farr	.05
271	Doug Drabek	.05
272	Brian Jordan	.05
273	Xavier Hernandez	.05
274	David Cone	.05
275	Brian Hunter	.05
276	Mike Harkey	.05
277	Delino DeShields	.05
278	David Hulse	.05
279	Mickey Tettleton	.05
280	Kevin McReynolds	.05
281	Darryl Hamilton	.05
282	Ken Hill	.05
283	Wayne Kirby	.05
284	Chris Hammond	.05
285	Mo Vaughn	.05
286	Ryan Klesko	.05
287	Rick Wilkins	.05
288	Bill Swift	.05
289	Rafael Palmeiro	.65
290	Brian Harper	.05
291	Chris Turner	.05
292	Luis Gonzalez	.25
293	Kenny Rogers	.05
294	Kirby Puckett	1.00
295	Mike Stanley	.05
296	Carlos Reyes	.05
297	Charles Nagy	.05
298	Reggie Jefferson	.05
299	Bip Roberts	.05
300	Darrin Jackson	.05
301	Mike Jackson	.05
302	Dave Nilsson	.05
303	Ramon Martinez	.05
304	Bobby Jones	.05
305	Johnny Ruffin	.05
306	Brian McRae	.05
307	Bo Jackson	.10
308	Dave Stewart	.05
309	John Smoltz	.05
310	Dennis Martinez	.05
311	Dean Palmer	.05
312	David Nied	.05
313	Eddie Murray	.75
314	Darryl Kile	.05
315	Rick Sutcliffe	.05
316	Shawon Dunston	.05
317	John Jaha	.05
318	Salomon Torres	.05
319	Gary Sheffield	.45
320	Curt Schilling	.30
321	Greg Vaughn	.05
322	Jay Howell	.05
323	Todd Hundley	.05
324	Chris Sabo	.05
325	Stan Javier	.05
326	Willie Greene	.05
327	Hipolito Pichardo	.05
328	Doug Strange	.05
329	Dan Wilson	.05
330	Checklist	.05
331	Omar Vizquel	.05
332	Scott Servais	.05
333	Bob Tewksbury	.05
334	Matt Williams	.05
335	Tom Foley	.05
336	Jeff Russell	.05
337	Scott Leius	.05
338	Ivan Rodriguez	.65
339	Kevin Seitzer	.05
340	Jose Rijo	.05
341	Eduardo Perez	.05
342	Kirk Gibson	.05
343	Randy Milligan	.05
344	Edgar Martinez	.05
345	Fred McGriff	.05
346	Kurt Abbott	.05
347	John Kruk	.05
348	Mike Felder	.05
349	Dave Staton	.05
350	Kenny Lofton	.05
351	Graeme Lloyd	.05
352	David Segui	.05
353	Danny Tartabull	.05
354	Bob Welch	.05
355	Duane Ward	.05
356	Tuffy Rhodes	.05
357	Lee Smith	.05
358	Chris James	.05
359	Walt Weiss	.05
360	Pedro Munoz	.05
361	Paul Sorrento	.05
362	Todd Worrell	.05
363	Bob Hamelin	.05
364	Julio Franco	.05
365	Roberto Petagine	.05
366	Willie McGee	.05
367	Pedro Martinez	.75
368	Ken Griffey Jr.	1.50
369	B.J. Surhoff	.05
370	Kevin Mitchell	.05
371	John Doherty	.05
372	Manuel Lee	.05
373	Terry Mulholland	.05
374	Zane Smith	.05
375	Otis Nixon	.05
376	Jody Reed	.05
377	Doug Jones	.05
378	John Olerud	.05
379	Greg Swindell	.05
380	Checklist	.05
381	Royce Clayton	.05
382	Jim Thome	.65
383	Steve Finley	.05
384	Ray Lankford	.05
385	Henry Rodriguez	.05
386	Dave Magadan	.05
387	Gary Redus	.05
388	Orlando Merced	.05
389	Tom Gordon	.05
390	Luis Polonia	.05
391	Mark McGwire	2.00
392	Mark Lemke	.05
393	Doug Henry	.05
394	Chuck Finley	.05
395	Paul Molitor	.75
396	Randy Myers	.05
397	Larry Walker	.05
398	Pete Harnisch	.05
399	Darren Lewis	.05
400	Frank Thomas	.75
401	Jack Morris	.05
402	Greg Hibbard	.05
403	Jeffrey Hammonds	.05
404	Will Clark	.10
405	Travis Fryman	.05
406	Scott Sanderson	.05
407	Gene Harris	.05
408	Chuck Carr	.05
409	Ozzie Smith	1.00
410	Kent Mercker	.05
411	Andy Van Slyke	.05
412	Jimmy Key	.05
413	Pat Mahomes	.05
414	John Wetteland	.05
415	Todd Jones	.05
416	Greg Harris	.05
417	Kevin Stocker	.05
418	Juan Gonzalez	.65
419	Pete Smith	.05
420	Pat Listach	.05
421	Trevor Hoffman	.05
422	Scott Fletcher	.05
423	Mark Lewis	.05
424	Mickey Morandini	.05
425	Ryne Sandberg	1.00
426	Erik Hanson	.05
427	Gary Gaetti	.05
428	Harold Reynolds	.05
429	Mark Portugal	.05
430	David Valle	.05
431	Mitch Williams	.05
432	Howard Johnson	.05
433	Hal Morris	.05
434	Tom Henke	.05
435	Shane Mack	.05
436	Mike Piazza	1.50
437	Bret Saberhagen	.05
438	Jose Mesa	.05
439	Jaime Navarro	.05
440	Checklist	.05

Clean-Up Crew

The number four spot in the line-up is featured on this 12-card insert set (six per series) found only in magazine distributor packaging. Fronts are gold-foil enhanced; backs feature an action photo set against a background of a line-up card on which the player is pencilled into the #4 spot. His 1993 stats when batting clean-up are presented.

		NM/M
Complete Set (12):		8.00
Common Player:		1.00
1	Larry Walker	1.00
2	Andres Galarraga	1.00
3	Dave Hollins	1.00
4	Bobby Bonilla	1.00
5	Cecil Fielder	1.00
6	Danny Tartabull	1.00
7	Juan Gonzalez	2.00
8	Joe Carter	1.00
9	Fred McGriff	1.00
10	Matt Williams	1.00
11	Albert Belle	1.00
12	Harold Baines	1.00

Gamers

Leaf jumbo packs are the exclusive venue for the six

cards of this insert set which were issued in each series.

		NM/M
Complete Set (12):		30.00
Common Player:		1.00
1	Ken Griffey Jr.	6.00
2	Len Dykstra	1.00
3	Juan Gonzalez	3.00
4	Don Mattingly	6.00
5	Dave Justice	1.00
6	Mark Grace	1.00
7	Frank Thomas	4.00
8	Barry Bonds	7.50
9	Kirby Puckett	4.50
10	Will Clark	1.00
11	John Kruk	1.00
12	Mike Piazza	6.00

Gold Rookies

A gold-foil rendered stadium background and huge black "94 Gold Leaf Rookie" serve as a backdrop for a player photo on these insert cards found at the rate of about one per 18 foil packs. The player's name and team are in silver at bottom. Horizontal backs have a ghosted action photo of the player in the background. A portrait photo is in the upper-right corner, above some personal data and stats. Cards are numbered "X of 20."

		NM/M
Complete Set (20):		6.00
Common Player:		.25
1	Javier Lopez	.25
2	Rondell White	.25
3	Butch Huskey	.25
4	Midre Cummings	.25
5	Scott Ruffcorn	.25
6	Manny Ramirez	3.50
7	Danny Bautista	.25
8	Russ Davis	.25
9	Steve Karsay	.25
10	Carlos Delgado	2.50
11	Bob Hamelin	.25
12	Marcus Moore	.25
13	Miguel Jimenez	.25
14	Matt Walbeck	.25
15	James Mouton	.25
16	Rich Becker	.25
17	Brian Anderson	.25
18	Cliff Floyd	.25
19	Steve Trachsel	.25
20	Hector Carrasco	.25

Gold Stars

The "Cadillac" of 1994 Leaf inserts, this 15-card series (#1-8 in Series 1; 9-15 in Series 2) is found on average of one card per 90 packs. The edition of 10,000 of each player's card is serially numbered. Fronts feature a rather small photo in a diamond-shaped frame against a green marble-look background. The border, facsimile autograph and sev-

eral other graphic elements are presented in prismatic foil. The back repeats the basic front design with a few sentences about the player and a serial number strip at bottom.

		NM/M
Complete Set (15):		60.00
Common Player:		3.00
1	Roberto Alomar	4.00
2	Barry Bonds	12.00
3	Dave Justice	3.00
4	Ken Griffey Jr.	9.00
5	Len Dykstra	3.00
6	Don Mattingly	7.50
7	Andres Galarraga	3.00
8	Greg Maddux	6.00
9	Carlos Baerga	3.00
10	Paul Molitor	5.00
11	Frank Thomas	5.00
12	John Olerud	3.00
13	Juan Gonzalez	4.00
14	Fred McGriff	3.00
15	Jack McDowell	3.00

MVP Contenders

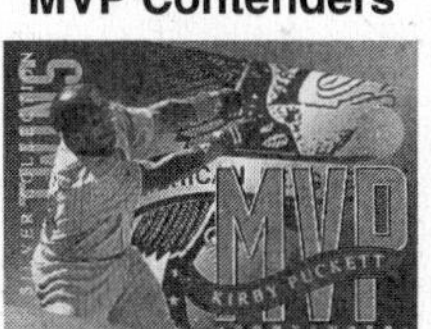

Found on an average of about once per 36-pack foil box, these inserts were produced in an edition of 10,000 each. Cards found in packs were marked "Silver Collection" on the horizontal fronts, and featured a silver-foil Leaf seal and other enhancements. Persons holding cards of the players selected as N.L. and A.L. MVPs could trade in their Contender card for an individually numbered 5" x 7" card of Leaf spokesman Frank Thomas and be entered in a drawing for one of 5,000 Gold Collection MVP Contender 28-card sets. Winning cards were punch-cancelled and returned to the winner along with his prize.

		NM/M
Complete Set, Silver (30):		20.00
Complete Set, Gold (30):		40.00
Common Player, Silver:		.25
Common Player, Gold:		.50
AMERICAN LEAGUE		2.00
1a	Albert Belle/Silver	.25
1b	Albert Belle/Gold	.50
2a	Jose Canseco/Silver	1.25
2b	Jose Canseco/Gold	2.00
3a	Joe Carter/Silver	.25
3b	Joe Carter/Gold	.50
4a	Will Clark/Silver	.35
4b	Will Clark/Gold	.60
5a	Cecil Fielder/Silver	.25
5b	Cecil Fielder/Gold	.50
6a	Juan Gonzalez/Silver	1.50
6b	Juan Gonzalez/Gold	2.50
7a	Ken Griffey Jr./Silver	4.00
7b	Ken Griffey Jr./Gold	7.50
8a	Paul Molitor/Silver	2.00
8b	Paul Molitor/Gold	4.00
9a	Rafael Palmeiro/Silver	1.50
9b	Rafael Palmeiro/Gold	2.50
10a	Kirby Puckett/Silver	2.50
10b	Kirby Puckett/Gold	5.00
11a	Cal Ripken, Jr./Silver	6.00
11b	Cal Ripken, Jr./Gold	12.50
12a	Frank Thomas/Silver	2.00
12b	Frank Thomas/Gold	4.00
13a	Mo Vaughn/Silver	.25
13b	Mo Vaughn/Gold	.50
14a	Carlos Baerga/Silver	.25
14b	Carlos Baerga/Gold	.50
15	AL Bonus Card/Silver	.25
NATIONAL LEAGUE		.60
1a	Gary Sheffield/Silver	.35
1b	Gary Sheffield/Gold	.65
2a	Jeff Bagwell/Silver	2.00
2b	Jeff Bagwell/Gold	4.00
3a	Dante Bichette/Silver	.25
3b	Dante Bichette/Gold	.50
4a	Barry Bonds/Silver	6.00
4b	Barry Bonds/Gold	12.50
5a	Darren Daulton/Silver	.25
5b	Darren Daulton/Gold	.50
6a	Andres Galarraga/Silver	.25
6b	Andres Galarraga/Gold	.50
7a	Gregg Jefferies/Silver	.25
7b	Gregg Jefferies/Gold	.50
8a	Dave Justice/Silver	.25
8b	Dave Justice/Gold	.50
9a	Ray Lankford/Silver	.25
9b	Ray Lankford/Gold	.50
10a	Fred McGriff/Silver	.25
10b	Fred McGriff/Gold	.50
11a	Barry Larkin/Silver	.25
11b	Barry Larkin/Gold	.50
12a	Mike Piazza/Silver	4.00
12b	Mike Piazza/Gold	7.50
13a	Deion Sanders/Silver	.25
13b	Deion Sanders/Gold	.50
14a	Matt Williams/Silver	.25
14b	Matt Williams/Gold	.50
15	NL Bonus Card/Silver	.25

Power Brokers

This insert set was unique to Leaf Series 2 and features top sluggers. Horizontal fronts have a player photo at left, depicting his power stroke. A fireworks display is featured in the large letters of "POWER" at top. Other gold and silver foil highlights are featured on the black background. Backs have pie charts showing home run facts along with another player photo and a few stats. Stated odds of finding a Power Brokers insert card were one per dozen packs, on average.

		NM/M
Complete Set (10):		8.00
Common Player:		.40
1	Frank Thomas	.75
2	Dave Justice	.40
3	Barry Bonds	3.00
4	Juan Gonzalez	.65
5	Ken Griffey Jr.	2.00
6	Mike Piazza	2.00
7	Cecil Fielder	.40
8	Fred McGriff	.40
9	Joe Carter	.40
10	Albert Belle	.40

Slide Show

A new level of high-tech insert card production values was reached with the creation of Leaf's "Slide Show" cards, featuring a printed acetate center sandwiched between cardboard front and back. The see-through portion of the card is bordered in white to give it the appearance of a slide. The player's name, location and date of the photo are printed on the front of the "slide," with the card number on back. The pseudo-slide is bordered in black (Series 1) or white (Series 2), with a blue "Slide Show" logo at bottom and a silver-foil Leaf logo. Backs of the Slide Show inserts have a few sentences about the featured player from Frank Thomas, Leaf's official spokesman again in 1994. The first five cards were released in Series 1; cards 6-10 in Series 2. Stated odds of finding a Slide Show insert are one per 54 packs.

		NM/M
Complete Set (10):		9.00
Common Player:		.25
1	Frank Thomas	1.00
2	Mike Piazza	2.00
3	Darren Daulton	.25
4	Ryne Sandberg	1.50
5	Roberto Alomar	.50
6	Barry Bonds	3.00
7	Juan Gonzalez	.75
8	Tim Salmon	.25
9	Ken Griffey Jr.	2.00
10	Dave Justice	.25

Statistical Standouts

Significant statistical achievements of the 1993 season are marked in this insert set found in both retail and hobby packs at a rate of about once every 12 packs. Fronts feature player action photos set against a foil background of silver at right and a team color at left. A gold embossed Leaf seal is at upper-left. Backs are bordered in the complementary team color at right, silver at left and have a vertical player photo along with the statistical achievement. Cards are numbered "X-10."

		NM/M
Complete Set (10):		10.00
Common Player:		.40
1	Frank Thomas	.75
2	Barry Bonds	2.50
3	Juan Gonzalez	.65
4	Mike Piazza	2.00
5	Greg Maddux	1.00
6	Ken Griffey Jr.	2.00
7	Joe Carter	.40
8	Dave Winfield	.75
9	Tony Gwynn	1.00
10	Cal Ripken, Jr.	2.50

Frank Thomas Super

An edition of 20,000 super-size versions of Frank Thomas' 1994 Leaf card was produced for inclusion in Series II hobby boxes as a bonus. Except for its 5" x 7" format and a white strip on back bearing a serial number, the card is identical to the normal-size issue.

		NM/M
400	Frank Thomas	5.00

5th Anniversary

The card which insured the success of the Leaf brand name when it was re-introduced in 1990, the Frank Thomas rookie card, was re-issued in a 5th anniversary commemorative form as an insert in the 1994 set. On the chase card, silver foil rays emanate from the White Sox logo at lower-left, while a silver-foil 5th anniversary logo at upper-right replaces the Leaf script on the 1990 version. The card back carries a 1994 copyright. The Thomas anniversary card is found on average of once every 36 Series I hobby packs.

		NM/M
300	Frank Thomas	2.50

1994 Leaf/Limited Promo

A single, unlabeled promo card was issued by Leaf to preview its Limited brand. The front is printed on a matte finish background as opposed to the shiny silver of the issued versions, but is otherwise identical. On back there are subtle differences in the cropping of the background photo, and a Total Bases stat is provided instead of Slugging Percentage as on the issued card. The principal difference is the use of card number 1 on the promo; the issued card is #24.

		NM/M
1	Frank Thomas	100.00

1994 Leaf/Limited

Leaf Limited is a 160-card super-premium set printed on the highest quality board stock ever used by Donruss. Production was limited to 3,000 20-box case equivalents, making this the most limited product up to that point from Donruss. Fronts feature silver holographic Spectra Tech foiling and a silhouetted player action photo over full silver foil. The team name and logo in silver and player name in black are at the bottom of the card. Leaf Limited appears in silver at the top. Backs are dull gray with a quote from a baseball personality and a player picture in the top-right corner.

		NM/M
Complete Set (160):		35.00
Common Player:		.25
Pack (5):		2.50
Wax Box (20):		40.00
1	Jeffrey Hammonds	.25
2	Ben McDonald	.25
3	Mike Mussina	.75
4	Rafael Palmeiro	1.50
5	Cal Ripken, Jr.	6.00
6	Lee Smith	.25
7	Roger Clemens	3.00
8	Scott Cooper	.25
9	Andre Dawson	.40
10	Mike Greenwell	.25
11	Aaron Sele	.25
12	Mo Vaughn	.25
13	Brian Anderson **RC**	.25
14	Chad Curtis	.25
15	Chili Davis	.25
16	Gary DiSarcina	.25
17	Mark Langston	.25
18	Tim Salmon	.25
19	Wilson Alvarez	.25
20	Jason Bere	.25
21	Julio Franco	.25
22	Jack McDowell	.25
23	Tim Raines	.25
24	Frank Thomas	2.00
25	Robin Ventura	.25
26	Carlos Baerga	.25
27	Albert Belle	.75
28	Kenny Lofton	.75
29	Eddie Murray	2.00
30	Manny Ramirez	2.00
31	Cecil Fielder	.25
32	Travis Fryman	.25
33	Mickey Tettleton	.25
34	Alan Trammell	.25
35	Lou Whitaker	.25
36	David Cone	.25
37	Gary Gaetti	.25
38	Greg Gagne	.25
39	Bob Hamelin	.25
40	Wally Joyner	.25
41	Brian McRae	.25
42	Ricky Bones	.25
43	Brian Harper	.25
44	John Jaha	.25
45	Pat Listach	.25
46	Dave Nilsson	.25
47	Greg Vaughn	.25
48	Kent Hrbek	.25
49	Chuck Knoblauch	.25
50	Shane Mack	.25
51	Kirby Puckett	2.50
52	Dave Winfield	2.00
53	Jim Abbott	.25
54	Wade Boggs	2.50
55	Jimmy Key	.25
56	Don Mattingly	3.00
57	Paul O'Neill	.25
58	Danny Tartabull	.25
59	Dennis Eckersley	1.50
60	Rickey Henderson	2.00
61	Mark McGwire	5.00
62	Troy Neel	.25
63	Ruben Sierra	.25
64	Eric Anthony	.25
65	Jay Buhner	.25
66	Ken Griffey Jr.	4.00
67	Randy Johnson	2.00
68	Edgar Martinez	.25
69	Tino Martinez	.25
70	Jose Canseco	.75
71	Will Clark	.35
72	Juan Gonzalez	1.50
73	Dean Palmer	.25
74	Ivan Rodriguez	1.50
75	Roberto Alomar	.40
76	Joe Carter	.25
77	Carlos Delgado	1.00
78	Paul Molitor	2.00
79	John Olerud	.25
80	Devon White	.25
81	Steve Avery	.25
82	Tom Glavine	.50
83	Dave Justice	.25
84	Roberto Kelly	.25
85	Ryan Klesko	.75
86	Javier Lopez	.25
87	Greg Maddux	2.50
88	Fred McGriff	.25
89	Shawon Dunston	.25
90	Mark Grace	.25
91	Derrick May	.25
92	Sammy Sosa	3.00
93	Rick Wilkins	.25
94	Bret Boone	.25
95	Barry Larkin	.25
96	Kevin Mitchell	.25
97	Hal Morris	.25
98	Deion Sanders	.25
99	Reggie Sanders	.25
100	Dante Bichette	.25
101	Ellis Burks	.25
102	Andres Galarraga	.25
103	Joe Girardi	.25
104	Charlie Hayes	.25
105	Chuck Carr	.25
106	Jeff Conine	.25
107	Bryan Harvey	.25
108	Benito Santiago	.25
109	Gary Sheffield	.60
110	Jeff Bagwell	2.00
111	Craig Biggio	.25
112	Ken Caminiti	.25
113	Andujar Cedeno	.25
114	Doug Drabek	.25
115	Luis Gonzalez	.40
116	Brett Butler	.25
117	Delino DeShields	.25
118	Eric Karros	.25
119	Raul Mondesi	.25
120	Mike Piazza	4.00
121	Henry Rodriguez	.25
122	Tim Wallach	.25
123	Moises Alou	.25
124	Cliff Floyd	.25
125	Marquis Grissom	.25
126	Ken Hill	.25
127	Larry Walker	.25
128	John Wetteland	.25
129	Bobby Bonilla	.25
130	John Franco	.25
131	Jeff Kent	.25
132	Bret Saberhagen	.25
133	Ryan Thompson	.25
134	Darren Daulton	.25
135	Mariano Duncan	.25
136	Len Dykstra	.25
137	Danny Jackson	.25
138	John Kruk	.25
139	Jay Bell	.25
140	Jeff King	.25
141	Al Martin	.25
142	Orlando Merced	.25
143	Andy Van Slyke	.25
144	Bernard Gilkey	.25
145	Gregg Jefferies	.25
146	Ray Lankford	.25
147	Ozzie Smith	2.50
148	Mark Whiten	.25
149	Todd Zeile	.25
150	Derek Bell	.25
151	Andy Benes	.25
152	Tony Gwynn	2.50
153	Phil Plantier	.25
154	Bip Roberts	.25
155	Rod Beck	.25
156	Barry Bonds	6.00
157	John Burkett	.25
158	Royce Clayton	.25
159	Bill Swift	.25
160	Matt Williams	.25

Gold

Leaf Limited Gold was an 18-card insert set randomly packed into Leaf Limited. All cards are individually numbered and feature the starting lineups at each position in both the National League and American League for the 1994 All-Star Game. There were only 10,000 cards of each player produced in this insert set.

		NM/M
Complete Set (18):		20.00
Common Player:		.25
1	Frank Thomas	1.50
2	Gregg Jefferies	.25
3	Roberto Alomar	.50
4	Mariano Duncan	.25
5	Wade Boggs	2.00
6	Matt Williams	.25
7	Cal Ripken, Jr.	4.00
8	Ozzie Smith	2.00
9	Kirby Puckett	2.00
10	Barry Bonds	4.00
11	Ken Griffey Jr.	3.00
12	Tony Gwynn	2.00
13	Joe Carter	.25
14	Dave Justice	.25
15	Ivan Rodriguez	1.25
16	Mike Piazza	3.00
17	Jimmy Key	.25
18	Greg Maddux	2.00

Rookies

Similar in format to the super-premium Leaf Limited issue, this separate issue features 80 of baseball's brightest young talents. Total production was reported as 30,000 serial numbered 20-pack foil boxes.

		NM/M
Complete Set (80):		17.50
Common Player:		.25
Pack (5):		3.00
Box (20):		60.00
1	Charles Johnson	.25
2	Rico Brogna	.25
3	Melvin Nieves	.25
4	Rich Becker	.25
5	Russ Davis	.25
6	Matt Mieske	.25
7	Paul Shuey	.25
8	Hector Carrasco	.25
9	J.R. Phillips	.25
10	Scott Ruffcorn	.25
11	Kurt Abbott	.25
12	Danny Bautista	.25
13	Rick White	.25
14	Steve Dunn	.25
15	Joe Ausanio	.25
16	Salomon Torres	.25
17	Rick Bottalico	.25
18	Johnny Ruffin	.25
19	Kevin Foster	.25
20	W. Van Landingham **RC**	.25
21	Troy O'Leary	.25
22	Mark Acre	.25
23	Norberto Martin	.25
24	Jason Jacome **RC**	.25
25	Steve Trachsel	.25
26	Denny Hocking	.25
27	Mike Lieberthal	.25
28	Gerald Williams	.25
29	John Mabry	.25
30	Greg Blosser	.25
31	Carl Everett	.25
32	Steve Karsay	.25
33	Jose Valentin	.25
34	Jon Lieber	.25
35	Chris Gomez	.25
36	Jesus Tavarez	.25
37	Tony Longmire	.25
38	Luis Lopez	.25
39	Matt Walbeck	.25
40	Rikkert Faneyte	.25
41	Shane Reynolds	.25
42	Joey Hamilton	.25
43	Ismael Valdes	.25
44	Danny Miceli	.25
45	Darren Bragg	.25
46	Alex Gonzalez	.25
47	Rick Helling	.25
48	Jose Oliva	.25
49	Jim Edmonds	4.00
50	Miguel Jimenez	.25
51	Tony Eusebio	.25
52	Shawn Green	4.00
53	Billy Ashley	.25
54	Rondell White	.25
55	Cory Bailey	.25
56	Tim Davis	.25
57	John Hudek	.25
58	Darren Hall	.25
59	Darren Dreifort	.25
60	Mike Kelly	.25
61	Marcus Moore	.25
62	Garret Anderson	.25
63	Brian Hunter	.25
64	Mark Smith	.25
65	Garey Ingram	.25
66	Rusty Greer **RC**	.25
67	Marc Newfield	.25
68	Gar Finnvold	.25
69	Paul Spoljaric	.25
70	Ray McDavid	.25
71	Orlando Miller	.25
72	Jorge Fabregas	.25
73	Ray Holbert	.25
74	Armando Benitez	.25
75	Ernie Young	.25
76	James Mouton	.25
77	Robert Perez **RC**	.25
78	Chan Ho Park **RC**	1.00
79	Roger Salkeld	.25
80	Tony Tarasco	.25

Rookies Rookie Phenoms

Similar in format to the other Leaf Limited cards for 1994, these Phenom inserts feature gold-foil background and graphics, rather than silver. Each card is numbered from within an edition of 5,000 of each player.

		NM/M
Complete Set (10):		260.00
Common Player:		1.00
Production 5,000 Sets		
1	Raul Mondesi	1.00
2	Bob Hamelin	1.00
3	Midre Cummings	1.00
4	Carlos Delgado	8.00
5	Cliff Floyd	1.00
6	Jeffrey Hammonds	1.00
7	Ryan Klesko	1.00
8	Javier Lopez	1.00
9	Manny Ramirez	10.00
10	Alex Rodriguez	250.00

1995 Leaf Promos

The lack of a "Sample" or "Promotional Card" notice makes these promos difficult to spot. They can be detected by the placement of the Registered symbol farther down and to the right compared to regular-issue cards. Also the thin line inside the gold-foil stamping enclosing the Leaf logo and inner "95" diamond is missing on the promos.

		NM/M
Complete Set (9):		35.00
Common Player:		2.00
1	Frank Thomas	4.00
10	Joe Carter	2.00
28	Matt Williams	2.00
40	Wade Boggs	6.00
60	Raul Mondesi	2.00
115	Greg Maddux	6.00
119	Jeff Bagwell	4.00
134	Cal Ripken Jr.	12.00
183	Kirby Puckett	6.00

1995 Leaf

Two series of 200 basic cards each, plus numerous insert sets, are featured in 1995 Leaf. The basic card design has a borderless action photo on front, with a small portrait photo printed at upper-left on holographic silver foil. The team name is printed in the same foil in large letters down the left side. A script rendition of the player's name is at bottom-right, with the Leaf logo under the portrait photo; both elements are in gold foil. Backs have a couple more player photos. The card number is in white in a silver-foil seal at upper-right. Previous season and career stats are at lower-left. Several of the insert sets are unique to various package configurations, while others are found in all types of packs.

		NM/M
Complete Set (400):		12.50
Common Player:		.05
Series 1 or 2 Pack (12):		.75
Series 1 or 2 Wax Box (36):		15.00
1	Frank Thomas	.75
2	Carlos Garcia	.05
3	Todd Hundley	.05
4	Damion Easley	.05
5	Roberto Mejia	.05
6	John Mabry	.05
7	Aaron Sele	.05
8	Kenny Lofton	.05
9	John Doherty	.05
10	Joe Carter	.05
11	Mike Lansing	.05
12	John Valentin	.05
13	Ismael Valdes	.05
14	Dave McCarty	.05
15	Melvin Nieves	.05
16	Bobby Jones	.05
17	Trevor Hoffman	.05
18	John Smoltz	.05
19	Leo Gomez	.05
20	Roger Pavlik	.05
21	Dean Palmer	.05
22	Rickey Henderson	.75
23	Eddie Taubensee	.05
24	Damon Buford	.05
25	Mark Wohlers	.05
26	Jim Edmonds	.05
27	Wilson Alvarez	.05
28	Matt Williams	.05
29	Jeff Montgomery	.05
30	Shawon Dunston	.05
31	Tom Pagnozzi	.05
32	Jose Lind	.05
33	Royce Clayton	.05
34	Cal Eldred	.05
35	Chris Gomez	.05
36	Henry Rodriguez	.05
37	Dave Fleming	.05
38	Jon Lieber	.05
39	Scott Servais	.05
40	Wade Boggs	1.00
41	John Olerud	.05
42	Eddie Williams	.05
43	Paul Sorrento	.05
44	Ron Karkovice	.05
45	Kevin Foster	.05
46	Miguel Jimenez	.05
47	Reggie Sanders	.05
48	Rondell White	.05
49	Scott Leius	.05
50	Jose Valentin	.05
51	William Van Landingham	.05
52	Denny Hocking	.05
53	Jeff Fassero	.05
54	Chris Hoiles	.05
55	Walt Weiss	.05
56	Geronimo Berroa	.05
57	Rich Rowland	.05
58	Dave Weathers	.05
59	Sterling Hitchcock	.05
60	Raul Mondesi	.05
61	Rusty Greer	.05
62	Dave Justice	.05
63	Cecil Fielder	.05
64	Brian Jordan	.05
65	Mike Lieberthal	.05
66	Rick Aguilera	.05
67	Chuck Finley	.05
68	Andy Ashby	.05
69	Alex Fernandez	.05
70	Ed Sprague	.05
71	Steve Buechele	.05
72	Willie Greene	.05
73	Dave Nilsson	.05
74	Bret Saberhagen	.05
75	Jimmy Key	.05
76	Darren Lewis	.05
77	Steve Cooke	.05
78	Kirk Gibson	.05
79	Ray Lankford	.05
80	Paul O'Neill	.05
81	Mike Bordick	.05
82	Wes Chamberlain	.05
83	Rico Brogna	.05
84	Kevin Appier	.05
85	Juan Guzman	.05
86	Kevin Seitzer	.05
87	Mickey Morandini	.05
88	Pedro Martinez	.75
89	Matt Mieske	.05
90	Tino Martinez	.05
91	Paul Shuey	.05
92	Bip Roberts	.05
93	Chili Davis	.05
94	Deion Sanders	.05
95	Darrell Whitmore	.05
96	Joe Orsulak	.05
97	Bret Boone	.05
98	Kent Mercker	.05
99	Scott Livingstone	.05
100	Brady Anderson	.05
101	James Mouton	.05
102	Jose Rijo	.05
103	Bobby Munoz	.05
104	Ramon Martinez	.05
105	Bernie Williams	.10
106	Troy Neel	.05
107	Ivan Rodriguez	.65
108	Salomon Torres	.05
109	Johnny Ruffin	.05
110	Darryl Kile	.05
111	Bobby Ayala	.05
112	Ron Darling	.05
113	Jose Lima	.05
114	Joey Hamilton	.05
115	Greg Maddux	1.00
116	Greg Colbrunn	.05
117	Ozzie Guillen	.05
118	Brian Anderson	.05
119	Jeff Bagwell	.75
120	Pat Listach	.05
121	Sandy Alomar	.05
122	Jose Vizcaino	.05
123	Rick Helling	.05
124	Allen Watson	.05
125	Pedro Munoz	.05
126	Craig Biggio	.05
127	Kevin Stocker	.05
128	Wil Cordero	.05
129	Rafael Palmeiro	.65
130	Gar Finnvold	.05
131	Darren Hall	.05
132	Heath Slocumb	.05
133	Darrin Fletcher	.05
134	Cal Ripken Jr.	2.50
135	Dante Bichette	.05
136	Don Slaught	.05
137	Pedro Astacio	.05
138	Ryan Thompson	.05
139	Greg Gohr	.05
140	Javier Lopez	.05
141	Lenny Dykstra	.05
142	Pat Rapp	.05
143	Mark Kiefer	.05
144	Greg Gagne	.05
145	Eduardo Perez	.05
146	Felix Fermin	.05
147	Jeff Frye	.05
148	Terry Steinbach	.05
149	Jim Eisenreich	.05
150	Brad Ausmus	.05
151	Randy Myers	.05
152	Rick White	.05
153	Mark Portugal	.05
154	Delino DeShields	.05
155	Scott Cooper	.05
156	Pat Hentgen	.05
157	Mark Gubicza	.05
158	Carlos Baerga	.05
159	Joe Girardi	.05
160	Rey Sanchez	.05
161	Todd Jones	.05
162	Luis Polonia	.05
163	Steve Trachsel	.05
164	Roberto Hernandez	.05
165	John Patterson	.05
166	Rene Arocha	.05
167	Will Clark	.10
168	Jim Leyritz	.05
169	Todd Van Poppel	.05
170	Robb Nen	.05
171	Midre Cummings	.05
172	Jay Buhner	.05
173	Kevin Tapani	.05
174	Mark Lemke	.05
175	Marcus Moore	.05
176	Wayne Kirby	.05
177	Rich Amaral	.05
178	Lou Whitaker	.05
179	Jay Bell	.05
180	Rick Wilkins	.05
181	Paul Molitor	.75
182	Gary Sheffield	.35
183	Kirby Puckett	1.00
184	Cliff Floyd	.05
185	Darren Oliver	.05
186	Tim Naehring	.05
187	John Hudek	.05
188	Eric Young	.05
189	Roger Salkeld	.05
190	Kirt Manwaring	.05
191	Kurt Abbott	.05
192	David Nied	.05
193	Todd Zeile	.05
194	Wally Joyner	.05
195	Dennis Martinez	.05
196	Billy Ashley	.05
197	Ben McDonald	.05
198	Bob Hamelin	.05
199	Chris Turner	.05
200	Lance Johnson	.05
201	Willie Banks	.05
202	Juan Gonzalez	.50
203	Scott Sanders	.05
204	Scott Brosius	.05
205	Curt Schilling	.25
206	Alex Gonzalez	.05
207	Travis Fryman	.05
208	Tim Raines	.05
209	Steve Avery	.05
210	Hal Morris	.05
211	Ken Griffey Jr.	1.50
212	Ozzie Smith	1.00
213	Chuck Carr	.05
214	Ryan Klesko	.05
215	Robin Ventura	.05
216	Luis Gonzalez	.20
217	Ken Ryan	.05
218	Mike Piazza	1.50
219	Matt Walbeck	.05
220	Jeff Kent	.05
221	Orlando Miller	.05
222	Kenny Rogers	.05
223	J.T. Snow	.05
224	Alan Trammell	.05
225	John Franco	.05
226	Gerald Williams	.05
227	Andy Benes	.05
228	Dan Wilson	.05
229	Dave Hollins	.05
230	Vinny Castilla	.05
231	Devon White	.05
232	Fred McGriff	.05
233	Quilvio Veras	.05
234	Tom Candiotti	.05
235	Jason Bere	.05
236	Mark Langston	.05
237	Mel Rojas	.05
238	Chuck Knoblauch	.05
239	Bernard Gilkey	.05
240	Mark McGwire	2.00
241	Kirk Rueter	.05
242	Pat Kelly	.05
243	Ruben Sierra	.05
244	Randy Johnson	.75
245	Shane Reynolds	.05
246	Danny Tartabull	.05
247	Darryl Hamilton	.05
248	Danny Bautista	.05
249	Tom Gordon	.05
250	Tom Glavine	.25
251	Orlando Merced	.05
252	Eric Karros	.05
253	Benji Gil	.05
254	Sean Bergman	.05
255	Roger Clemens	1.25
256	Roberto Alomar	.20
257	Benito Santiago	.05
258	Robby Thompson	.05
259	Marvin Freeman	.05
260	Jose Offerman	.05
261	Greg Vaughn	.05
262	David Segui	.05
263	Geronimo Pena	.05
264	Tim Salmon	.05
265	Eddie Murray	.75
266	Mariano Duncan	.05
267	Hideo Nomo **RC**	2.50
268	Derek Bell	.05
269	Mo Vaughn	.05
270	Jeff King	.05
271	Edgar Martinez	.05
272	Sammy Sosa	1.25
273	Scott Ruffcorn	.05
274	Darren Daulton	.05
275	John Jaha	.05
276	Andres Galarraga	.05
277	Mark Grace	.05
278	Mike Moore	.05
279	Barry Bonds	2.50
280	Manny Ramirez	.75
281	Ellis Burks	.05
282	Greg Swindell	.05
283	Barry Larkin	.05
284	Albert Belle	.05
285	Shawn Green	.35
286	John Roper	.05
287	Scott Erickson	.05
288	Moises Alou	.05
289	Mike Blowers	.05
290	Brent Gates	.05
291	Sean Berry	.05
292	Mike Stanley	.05
293	Jeff Conine	.05
294	Tim Wallach	.05
295	Bobby Bonilla	.05
296	Bruce Ruffin	.05
297	Chad Curtis	.05
298	Mike Greenwell	.05
299	Tony Gwynn	1.00
300	Russ Davis	.05
301	Danny Jackson	.05
302	Pete Harnisch	.05
303	Don Mattingly	1.25
304	Rheal Cormier	.05
305	Larry Walker	.05
306	Hector Carrasco	.05
307	Jason Jacome	.05
308	Phil Plantier	.05
309	Harold Baines	.05
310	Mitch Williams	.05
311	Charles Nagy	.05
312	Ken Caminiti	.05
313	Alex Rodriguez	2.00
314	Chris Sabo	.05
315	Gary Gaetti	.05
316	Andre Dawson	.25
317	Mark Clark	.05
318	Vince Coleman	.05
319	Brad Clontz	.05
320	Steve Finley	.05
321	Doug Drabek	.05
322	Mark McLemore	.05
323	Stan Javier	.05
324	Ron Gant	.05
325	Charlie Hayes	.05
326	Carlos Delgado	.50
327	Ricky Bottalico	.05
328	Rod Beck	.05
329	Mark Acre	.05
330	Chris Bosio	.05
331	Tony Phillips	.05
332	Garret Anderson	.05
333	Pat Meares	.05
334	Todd Worrell	.05
335	Marquis Grissom	.05
336	Brent Mayne	.05
337	Lee Tinsley	.05
338	Terry Pendleton	.05
339	David Cone	.05
340	Tony Fernandez	.05
341	Jim Bullinger	.05
342	Armando Benitez	.05
343	John Smiley	.05
344	Dan Miceli	.05
345	Charles Johnson	.05
346	Lee Smith	.05
347	Brian McRae	.05
348	Jim Thome	.65
349	Jose Oliva	.05
350	Terry Mulholland	.05
351	Tom Henke	.05
352	Dennis Eckersley	.65
353	Sid Fernandez	.05
354	Paul Wagner	.05
355	John Dettmer	.05
356	John Wetteland	.05
357	John Burkett	.05
358	Marty Cordova	.05
359	Norm Charlton	.05
360	Mike Devereaux	.05
361	Alex Cole	.05
362	Brett Butler	.05
363	Mickey Tettleton	.05
364	Al Martin	.05
365	Tony Tarasco	.05
366	Pat Mahomes	.05
367	Gary DiSarcina	.05
368	Bill Swift	.05
369	Chipper Jones	1.00
370	Orel Hershiser	.05
371	Kevin Gross	.05
372	Dave Winfield	.75
373	Andujar Cedeno	.05
374	Jim Abbott	.05
375	Glenallen Hill	.05
376	Otis Nixon	.05
377	Roberto Kelly	.05
378	Chris Hammond	.05
379	Mike Macfarlane	.05
380	J.R. Phillips	.05
381	Luis Alicea	.05
382	Bret Barberie	.05
383	Tom Goodwin	.05
384	Mark Whiten	.05
385	Jeffrey Hammonds	.05
386	Omar Vizquel	.05
387	Mike Mussina	.35
388	Rickey Bones	.05
389	Steve Ontiveros	.05
390	Jeff Blauser	.05
391	Jose Canseco	.35
392	Bob Tewksbury	.05
393	Jacob Brumfield	.05
394	Doug Jones	.05
395	Ken Hill	.05
396	Pat Borders	.05
397	Carl Everett	.05
398	Gregg Jefferies	.05
399	Jack McDowell	.05
400	Denny Neagle	.05

Checklists

Honoring the major 1994 award winners in the American (Series I) and National (Series II) Leagues, checklists for the 1995 Leaf set are not numbered among the regular issue. Horizontal cards have a player action photo at left with his name and team in gold foil at bottom. The award is printed vertically at left with the checklist beginning on the right. Backs continue the checklist on a graduated purple background with the checklist number in a silver-foil seal at top-right.

		NM/M
Complete Set (8):		1.50
Common Player:		.25
1	Checklist 1-67 (Bob Hamelin (Rookie of the Year))	.25
2	Checklist 68-134 (David Cone (Cy Young))	.25
3	Checklist 135-200 (Frank Thomas (MVP))	.45
4	Series II inserts checklist (Paul O'Neill (Batting title.))	.25
5	Checklist 201-267 (Raul Mondesi (Rookie of the Year))	.25
6	Checklist 268-334 (Greg Maddux (Cy Young))	.50
7	Checklist 335-400 (Jeff Bagwell (MVP))	.45
8	Series 2 inserts checklist (Tony Gwynn (Batting title.))	.50

Cornerstones

Cornerstones, six of the best first baseman-third baseman combos in baseball, is a six-card insert series found, on average, once every 18 packs in Series I Leaf. Card fronts are horizontally oriented and have a silver prismatic border and player names. Player defensive action photos are set against a background resembling their team logo chiseled into a stone block. Backs have player batting photos at each end with offensive and defensive stats from 1994, and a few words about the duo.

		NM/M
Complete Set (6):		3.50
Common Player:		.40
1	Frank Thomas, Robin Ventura	.75
2	Cecil Fielder, Travis Fryman	.40
3	Don Mattingly, Wade Boggs	2.00
4	Jeff Bagwell, Ken Caminiti	.75
5	Will Clark, Dean Palmer	.40
6	J.R. Phillips, Matt Williams	.40

Gold Stars

Once again the toughest pull among the Leaf inserts are the Gold Leaf Stars found in both series. Found on average of one card per 90-270 packs, depending on pack card count, each of these chase cards is numbered on back within an edition of 10,000. Cards have fronts printed on metallic foil with the player name at top, the series title at bottom and a vertical stars and stripe device at right all printed in gold foil. A die-cut star appears at bottom-left. Backs are coventionally printed with another player photo and a few sentences about the star. The serial number is in gold foil in a white strip at top.

		NM/M
Complete Set (14):		35.00
Common Player:		1.00
1	Jeff Bagwell	2.50
2	Albert Belle	1.00
3	Tony Gwynn	3.50
4	Ken Griffey Jr.	4.50
5	Barry Bonds	6.00
6	Don Mattingly	4.00
7	Raul Mondesi	1.00
8	Joe Carter	1.00
9	Greg Maddux	3.50
10	Frank Thomas	2.50
11	Mike Piazza	4.50
12	Jose Canseco	1.50
13	Kirby Puckett	3.50
14	Matt Williams	1.00

Gold Rookies

Every other pack of Series I Leaf Series I is seeded with a Gold Leaf Rookie card. Fronts have a largely white background with a large player photo at left-center and a smaller picture in a rectangle at upper-right. A team-color stripe is at left, while a smaller gray stripe is at top-right. The team name is printed in large gray letters across the center of the card, with the player name in a team color beneath that and above the gold-foil Leaf logo at lower-left. "Gold Leaf Rookies" is printed in gold foil down the right side. Backs repeat the team-color motif with a large action photo of the player in a single color and a smaller color portrait. Full career stats are at bottom.

		NM/M
Complete Set (16):		3.00
Common Player:		.10
1	Alex Rodriguez	2.50
2	Garret Anderson	.10
3	Shawn Green	.50
4	Armando Benitez	.10
5	Darren Dreifort	.10
6	Orlando Miller	.10
7	Jose Oliva	.10
8	Ricky Bottalico	.10
9	Charles Johnson	.10
10	Brian Hunter	.10
11	Ray McDavid	.10
12	Chan Ho Park	.10
13	Mike Kelly	.10
14	Cory Bailey	.10
15	Alex Gonzalez	.10
16	Andrew Lorraine	.10

Great Gloves

While the stated emphasis is on fielding prowess in this Series II chase set, players who don't also swing a big stick are ignored. Found as frequently as one per two packs, cards have a detail photo of a glove at left, with an action photo at right. The player name in the Great Gloves logo at bottom-right is in gold foil, as are the Leaf logo at top-left and the team name vertically at right.

Backs repeat the glove photo and series logo as background for another player photo and a few words and stats about the player's defense.

		NM/M
Complete Set (16):		3.00
Common Player:		.15
1	Jeff Bagwell	.35
2	Roberto Alomar	.20
3	Barry Bonds	1.00
4	Wade Boggs	.45
5	Andres Galarraga	.15
6	Ken Griffey Jr.	.60
7	Marquis Grissom	.15
8	Kenny Lofton	.15
9	Barry Larkin	.15
10	Don Mattingly	.50
11	Greg Maddux	.45
12	Kirby Puckett	.45
13	Ozzie Smith	.45
14	Cal Ripken Jr.	1.00
15	Matt Williams	.15
16	Ivan Rodriguez	.30

Heading For The Hall

Series 2 hobby packs were the home of this scarce (one per 75 packs, average) chase set. Eight players deemed to be sure shots for Cooperstown are pictured in a semblance of the famed tombstone-shaped plaque they will someday adorn at the Hall of Fame; in fact the cards are die-cut to that shape. Backs have a sepia-toned photo, career stats and a serial number placing the card within an edition of 5,000.

		NM/M
Complete Set (8):		50.00
Common Player:		4.50
1	Frank Thomas	4.50
2	Ken Griffey Jr.	9.00
3	Jeff Bagwell	4.50
4	Barry Bonds	15.00
5	Kirby Puckett	6.00
6	Cal Ripken Jr.	15.00
7	Tony Gwynn	6.00
8	Paul Molitor	4.50

Slideshow

The hold-to-light technology which Leaf debuted with its 1994 Slideshow inserts continued in 1995 with a cross-series concept. The same eight players are featured on these cards in both Series 1 and 2. Each card has three clear photos at center, between the spokes of a silver-foil wheel. When both the player's cards are placed side-by-side, the six-picture see-through photo device is complete. Slideshow inserts are found on average of just over one per box among all types of pack configurations. Cards were issued with a peelable plastic protector on the front.

		NM/M
Complete Set (16):		35.00
Complete Series 1 (1a-8a):		20.00
Complete Series 2 (1b-8b):		20.00
Same CL and prices for both series.		
Common Player:		1.50
1a	Raul Mondesi	1.50
1b	Raul Mondesi	1.50
2a	Frank Thomas	3.00
2b	Frank Thomas	3.00
3a	Fred McGriff	1.50
3b	Fred McGriff	1.50
4a	Cal Ripken Jr.	6.00
4b	Cal Ripken Jr.	6.00
5a	Jeff Bagwell	3.00
5b	Jeff Bagwell	3.00
6a	Will Clark	1.50
6b	Will Clark	1.50
7a	Matt Williams	1.50
7b	Matt Williams	1.50
8a	Ken Griffey Jr.	4.50
8b	Ken Griffey Jr.	4.50

Statistical Standouts

Embossed red stitches on the large baseball background make the Statistical Standouts chase cards stand out among the inserts in Series 1 hobby packs (one per 70, average). The leather surface of the ball is also lightly textured, as is the player action photo at center. Printed in gold foil on front are the series name at top, the player's facsimile autograph at lower-center and the Leaf logo and team name at bottom. Backs have a graduated black background with a large team logo at bottom, and a circular player portrait at center. A few words explain why the player's stats stand out among his peers. Each card is serially numbered on back to 5,000. A promo card version of each was issued without the specific serial number on back and with the upper-right corner cut off.

		NM/M
Complete Set (9):		90.00
Common Player:		3.00
Promos: 25-50 percent		
1	Joe Carter	3.00
2	Ken Griffey Jr.	25.00
3	Don Mattingly	15.00
4	Fred McGriff	3.00
5	Paul Molitor	8.00
6	Kirby Puckett	12.00
7	Cal Ripken Jr.	30.00
8	Frank Thomas	8.00
9	Matt Williams	3.00

Special Edition Jumbos

As a dealer incentive, each case of 1995 Leaf Series I cards contained one of two 3" x 5" jumbos. Similar in format to the players' regular Leaf cards, each is individually serially numbered within an edition of 5,000.

		NM/M
Complete Set (2):		7.00
1	Frank Thomas	3.00
2	Barry Bonds	5.00

Frank Thomas

The Big Hurt's six seasons in the major leagues are chronicled in this flashy insert set. Silver and gold foil squares are the background for a photo of Thomas on front. Backs repeat the motif with standard print technology and another photo, along with a few words about Thomas' season. The Frank Thomas inserts are found in all types of Series II packs, with odds varying from one in 42 packs to one in 14 packs, depending on card count per pack.

		NM/M
Complete Set (6):		7.50
Common Card:		1.50
1	The Rookie	1.50
2	Sophomore Stardom	1.50
3	Super Star	1.50
4	AL MVP	1.50
5	Back-To-Back	1.50
6	The Big Hurt	1.50

300 Club

Issued in both Series I and II Leaf, but only in the retail and magazine packs, at a rate of one per 12-30 packs, depending on pack configuration, 300 Club inserts feature the 18 active players with lifetime .300+ batting averages in a minimum of 1,000 AB. Fronts have color player photos with a large white "300" in the background and "club" in gold foil near the bottom. The player name is in gold foil in an arc above the silver Leaf logo at bottom-center. Large embossed silver triangles in each bottom corner have the team name and player position (left) and career BA (right). Backs have another player photo and highlight his place on the list of .300+ batters.

		NM/M
Complete Set (18):		12.50
Common Player:		.25
1	Frank Thomas	1.00
2	Paul Molitor	1.00
3	Mike Piazza	3.00
4	Moises Alou	.25
5	Mike Greenwell	.25
6	Will Clark	.25
7	Hal Morris	.25
8	Edgar Martinez	.25
9	Carlos Baerga	.25
10	Ken Griffey Jr.	3.00
11	Wade Boggs	1.50
12	Jeff Bagwell	1.00
13	Tony Gwynn	1.50
14	John Kruk	.25
15	Don Mattingly	2.00
16	Mark Grace	.25
17	Kirby Puckett	1.50
18	Kenny Lofton	.25

1995 Leaf/Limited

Issued in two series of 96 basic cards each, plus inserts, Leaf Limited was a hobby-only product limited to 90,000 numbered 20-pack boxes. Five-card packs had a suggested retail price of $4.99. Fronts of the basic cards have a player action photo on a background of silver holographic foil highlighted with team colors and a gold-foil Leaf Limited logo. Horizontal-format backs have two more player photos, career stats and holographic foil team logos and card numbers.

		NM/M
Complete Set (192):		20.00
Common Player:		.10
Series 1 or 2 Pack (5):		2.00
Series 1 or 2 Wax Box (20):		30.00
1	Frank Thomas	.75
2	Geronimo Berroa	.10
3	Tony Phillips	.10
4	Roberto Alomar	.25
5	Steve Avery	.10
6	Darryl Hamilton	.10
7	Scott Cooper	.10
8	Mark Grace	.10
9	Billy Ashley	.10
10	Wil Cordero	.10
11	Barry Bonds	5.00
12	Kenny Lofton	.10
13	Jay Buhner	.10
14	Alex Rodriguez	3.00
15	Bobby Bonilla	.10
16	Brady Anderson	.10
17	Ken Caminiti	.10
18	Charlie Hayes	.10
19	Jay Bell	.10
20	Will Clark	.15
21	Jose Canseco	.35
22	Bret Boone	.10
23	Dante Bichette	.10
24	Kevin Appier	.10
25	Chad Curtis	.10
26	Marty Cordova	.10
27	Jason Bere	.10
28	Jimmy Key	.10
29	Rickey Henderson	.75
30	Tim Salmon	.10
31	Joe Carter	.10
32	Tom Glavine	.35
33	Pat Listach	.10
34	Brian Jordan	.10
35	Brian McRae	.10
36	Eric Karros	.10
37	Pedro Martinez	.75
38	Royce Clayton	.10
39	Eddie Murray	.75
40	Randy Johnson	.75
41	Jeff Conine	.10
42	Brett Butler	.10
43	Jeffrey Hammonds	.10
44	Andujar Cedeno	.10
45	Dave Hollins	.10
46	Jeff King	.10
47	Benji Gil	.10
48	Roger Clemens	2.00
49	Barry Larkin	.10
50	Joe Girardi	.10
51	Bob Hamelin	.10
52	Travis Fryman	.10
53	Chuck Knoblauch	.10
54	Ray Durham	.10
55	Don Mattingly	2.00
56	Ruben Sierra	.10
57	J.T. Snow	.10
58	Derek Bell	.10
59	David Cone	.10
60	Marquis Grissom	.10
61	Kevin Seitzer	.10
62	Ozzie Smith	1.50
63	Rick Wilkins	.10
64	Hideo Nomo **RC**	3.00
65	Tony Tarasco	.10
66	Manny Ramirez	.75
67	Charles Johnson	.10
68	Craig Biggio	.10
69	Bobby Jones	.10
70	Mike Mussina	.60
71	Alex Gonzalez	.10
72	Gregg Jefferies	.10
73	Rusty Greer	.10
74	Mike Greenwell	.10
75	Hal Morris	.10
76	Paul O'Neill	.10
77	Luis Gonzalez	.25
78	Chipper Jones	1.50
79	Mike Piazza	2.50
80	Rondell White	.10
81	Glenallen Hill	.10
82	Shawn Green	.50
83	Bernie Williams	.10
84	Jim Thome	.65
85	Terry Pendleton	.10
86	Rafael Palmeiro	.65
87	Tony Gwynn	1.50
88	Mickey Tettleton	.10
89	John Valentin	.10
90	Deion Sanders	.10
91	Larry Walker	.10
92	Michael Tucker	.10
93	Alan Trammell	.10
94	Tim Raines	.10
95	Dave Justice	.10
96	Tino Martinez	.10
97	Cal Ripken Jr.	5.00
98	Deion Sanders	.10
99	Darren Daulton	.10
100	Paul Molitor	.75
101	Randy Myers	.10
102	Wally Joyner	.10
103	Carlos Perez	.10
104	Brian Hunter	.10
105	Wade Boggs	1.50
106	Bobby Higginson **RC**	.50
107	Jeff Kent	.10
108	Jose Offerman	.10
109	Dennis Eckersley	.65
110	Dave Nilsson	.10
111	Chuck Finley	.10
112	Devon White	.10
113	Bip Roberts	.10
114	Ramon Martinez	.10
115	Greg Maddux	1.50
116	Curtis Goodwin	.10
117	John Jaha	.10
118	Ken Griffey Jr.	2.50
119	Geronimo Pena	.10
120	Shawon Dunston	.10
121	Ariel Prieto	.10
122	Kirby Puckett	1.50
123	Carlos Baerga	.10
124	Todd Hundley	.10
125	Tim Naehring	.10
126	Gary Sheffield	.45
127	Dean Palmer	.10
128	Rondell White	.10
129	Greg Gagne	.10
130	Jose Rijo	.10
131	Ivan Rodriguez	.65
132	Jeff Bagwell	.75
133	Greg Vaughn	.10
134	Chili Davis	.10
135	Al Martin	.10
136	Kenny Rogers	.10
137	Aaron Sele	.10
138	Raul Mondesi	.10
139	Cecil Fielder	.10
140	Tim Wallach	.10
141	Andres Galarraga	.10
142	Lou Whitaker	.10
143	Jack McDowell	.10
144	Matt Williams	.10
145	Ryan Klesko	.10
146	Carlos Garcia	.10
147	Albert Belle	.10
148	Ryan Thompson	.10
149	Roberto Kelly	.10
150	Edgar Martinez	.10
151	Robby Thompson	.10
152	Mo Vaughn	.10
153	Todd Zeile	.10
154	Harold Baines	.10
155	Phil Plantier	.10
156	Mike Stanley	.10
157	Ed Sprague	.10
158	Moises Alou	.10
159	Quilvio Veras	.10
160	Reggie Sanders	.10
161	Delino DeShields	.10
162	Rico Brogna	.10
163	Greg Colbrunn	.10
164	Steve Finley	.10
165	Orlando Merced	.10
166	Mark McGwire	3.00
167	Garret Anderson	.10
168	Paul Sorrento	.10
169	Mark Langston	.10
170	Danny Tartabull	.10
171	Vinny Castilla	.10
172	Javier Lopez	.10
173	Bret Saberhagen	.10
174	Eddie Williams	.10
175	Scott Leius	.10
176	Juan Gonzalez	.50
177	Gary Gaetti	.10
178	Jim Edmonds	.10
179	John Olerud	.10
180	Lenny Dykstra	.10
181	Ray Lankford	.10
182	Ron Gant	.10
183	Doug Drabek	.10
184	Fred McGriff	.10
185	Andy Benes	.10
186	Kurt Abbott	.10
187	Bernard Gilkey	.10
188	Sammy Sosa	2.00
189	Lee Smith	.10
190	Dennis Martinez	.10
191	Ozzie Guillen	.10
192	Robin Ventura	.10

Bat Patrol

Yet another insert of the game's top veteran hitters was featured as chase cards in Series 2 Leaf Limited. The cards have player action photos on front with large silver-foil "BAT / PATROL" lettering at lower-left. Backs are printed on a silver background and include career stats plus another color player photo. The cards were seeded at the rate of one per pack.

		NM/M
Complete Set (24):		7.50
Common Player:		.15
1	Frank Thomas	.75
2	Tony Gwynn	1.00
3	Wade Boggs	1.00
4	Larry Walker	.25
5	Ken Griffey Jr.	1.50
6	Jeff Bagwell	.75
7	Manny Ramirez	.75
8	Mark Grace	.25
9	Kenny Lofton	.15
10	Mike Piazza	1.50
11	Will Clark	.25
12	Mo Vaughn	.25
13	Carlos Baerga	.15
14	Rafael Palmeiro	.65
15	Barry Bonds	2.50
16	Kirby Puckett	1.00
17	Roberto Alomar	.35
18	Barry Larkin	.15
19	Eddie Murray	.75
20	Tim Salmon	.25
21	Don Mattingly	1.25
22	Fred McGriff	.15
23	Albert Belle	.25
24	Dante Bichette	.15

Gold

Seeded one per pack in Series I only, this insert set follows the format of the basic Leaf Limited cards, but is distinguished by the presence of gold, rather than silver, holographic foil.

		NM/M
Complete Set (24):		10.00
Common Player:		.25
1	Frank Thomas	.60
2	Jeff Bagwell	.60
3	Raul Mondesi	.25
4	Barry Bonds	1.50
5	Albert Belle	.25

6	Ken Griffey Jr.	1.00
7	Cal Ripkin (Ripken) Jr.	1.50
8	Will Clark	.25
9	Jose Canseco	.45
10	Larry Walker	.25
11	Kirby Puckett	.75
12	Don Mattingly	1.00
13	Tim Salmon	.25
14	Roberto Alomar	.35
15	Greg Maddux	.75
16	Mike Piazza	1.00
17	Matt Williams	.25
18	Kenny Lofton	.25
19	Alex Rodriquez (Rodriguez)	1.25
20	Tony Gwynn	.75
21	Mo Vaughn	.25
22	Chipper Jones	.75
23	Manny Ramirez	.60
24	Deion Sanders	.25

Lumberjacks

Lumberjacks inserts are found in both Series 1 and 2 Leaf Limited at a rate of one per 23 packs on average (less than one per box). Fronts are printed on woodgrain veneer with a large team logo behind a batting action photo of the game's top sluggers. Backs have another photo against a background of tree trunks. A white stripe at bottom carries each card's unique serial number within an edition of 5,000.

		NM/M
Complete Set (16):		55.00
Common Player:		2.00
1	Albert Belle	2.00
2	Barry Bonds	12.00
3	Juan Gonzalez	3.50
4	Ken Griffey Jr.	7.50
5	Fred McGriff	2.00
6	Mike Piazza	7.50
7	Kirby Puckett	6.00
8	Mo Vaughn	2.00
9	Frank Thomas	4.50
10	Jeff Bagwell	4.50
11	Matt Williams	2.00
12	Jose Canseco	3.00
13	Raul Mondesi	2.00
14	Manny Ramirez	4.50
15	Cecil Fielder	2.00
16	Cal Ripken Jr.	12.00

Opening Day

Issued in celebration of the 1995's season's delayed debut, this set was only available via a mail-in offer for $2 and eight wrappers. Cards were advertised as featuring front and back photos shot on opening day. Fronts have a player photo bordered on the left with a vertical "1995 Opening Day" stripe featuring exploding fireworks at the bottom. The player's name and position appear in a silver-foil strip at bottom; a silver-foil Leaf logo is at upper-right. Backs have a player action photo set against a background of exploding fireworks and a recap of the player's 1995 Opening Day performance.

		NM/M
Complete Set (8):		6.00
Common Player:		.25
1	Frank Thomas	.50
2	Jeff Bagwell	.50
3	Barry Bonds	2.00
5	Ken Griffey Jr.	1.00
5	Mike Piazza	1.00
6	Cal Ripken Jr.	2.00
7	Jose Canseco	.35
8	Larry Walker	.25

1996 Leaf

Reverting to a single-series issue of 220 basic cards, plus numerous insert set bells and whistles, this was the final Leaf set under Donruss' ownership. Regular cards offer large action photos on front and back with a side and bottom border subdued through darkening (front) or lightening (back). Fronts feature silver prismatic-foil graphic highlights while the back includes a circular portrait photo with vital data around. Leaf was sold in both hobby and retail versions, each with some unique inserts. Basic unit was the 12-card foil pack, with suggested retail of $2.49.

		NM/M
Complete Set (220):		10.00
Common Player:		.05
Complete Gold Set (220):		100.00
Common Golds:		1.00
Gold Press Proofs:		15X
Complete Silver Set (220):		50.00
Common Silvers:		.50
Silver Press Proofs:		6X
Complete Bronze Set (220):		40.00
Common Bronze:		.25
Bronze Press Proofs:		4X
Pack (12):		1.00
Wax Box (30):		25.00
1	John Smoltz	.10
2	Dennis Eckersley	.60
3	Delino DeShields	.05
4	Cliff Floyd	.05
5	Chuck Finley	.05
6	Cecil Fielder	.05
7	Tim Naehring	.05
8	Carlos Perez	.05
9	Brad Ausmus	.05
10	Matt Lawton **RC**	.15
11	Alan Trammell	.05
12	Steve Finley	.05
13	Paul O'Neill	.05
14	Gary Sheffield	.40
15	Mark McGwire	1.50
16	Bernie Williams	.05
17	Jeff Montgomery	.05
18	Chan Ho Park	.05
19	Greg Vaughn	.05
20	Jeff Kent	.05
21	Cal Ripken Jr.	2.00
22	Charles Johnson	.05
23	Eric Karros	.05
24	Alex Rodriguez	1.50
25	Chris Snopek	.05
26	Jason Isringhausen	.05
27	Chili Davis	.05
28	Chipper Jones	.75
29	Bret Saberhagen	.05
30	Tony Clark	.05
31	Marty Cordova	.05
32	Dwayne Hosey	.05
33	Fred McGriff	.05
34	Deion Sanders	.05
35	Orlando Merced	.05
36	Brady Anderson	.05
37	Ray Lankford	.05
38	Manny Ramirez	.65
39	Alex Fernandez	.05
40	Greg Colbrunn	.05
41	Ken Griffey Jr.	1.00
42	Mickey Morandini	.05
43	Chuck Knoblauch	.05
44	Quinton McCracken	.05
45	Tim Salmon	.05
46	Jose Mesa	.05
47	Marquis Grissom	.05
48	Checklist	.05
49	Raul Mondesi	.05
50	Mark Grudzielanek	.05
51	Ray Durham	.05
52	Matt Williams	.05
53	Bob Hamelin	.05
54	Lenny Dykstra	.05
55	Jeff King	.05
56	LaTroy Hawkins	.05
57	Terry Pendleton	.05
58	Kevin Stocker	.05
59	Ozzie Timmons	.05
60	David Justice	.05
61	Ricky Bottalico	.05
62	Andy Ashby	.05
63	Larry Walker	.05
64	Jose Canseco	.40
65	Bret Boone	.05
66	Shawn Green	.35
67	Chad Curtis	.05
68	Travis Fryman	.05
69	Roger Clemens	1.00
70	David Bell	.05
71	Rusty Greer	.05
72	Bob Higginson	.05
73	Joey Hamilton	.05
74	Kevin Seitzer	.05
75	Julian Tavarez	.05
76	Troy Percival	.05
77	Kirby Puckett	.75
78	Barry Bonds	2.00
79	Michael Tucker	.05
80	Paul Molitor	.65
81	Carlos Garcia	.05
82	Johnny Damon	.35
83	Mike Hampton	.05
84	Ariel Prieto	.05
85	Tony Tarasco	.05
86	Pete Schourek	.05
87	Tom Glavine	.30
88	Rondell White	.05
89	Jim Edmonds	.05
90	Robby Thompson	.05
91	Wade Boggs	.75
92	Pedro Martinez	.65
93	Gregg Jefferies	.05
94	Albert Belle	.05
95	Benji Gil	.05
96	Denny Neagle	.05
97	Mark Langston	.05
98	Sandy Alomar	.05
99	Tony Gwynn	.75
100	Todd Hundley	.05
101	Dante Bichette	.05
102	Eddie Murray	.65
103	Lyle Mouton	.05
104	John Jaha	.05
105	Checklist	.05
106	Jon Nunnally	.05
107	Juan Gonzalez	.50
108	Kevin Appier	.05
109	Brian McRae	.05
110	Lee Smith	.05
111	Tim Wakefield	.05
112	Sammy Sosa	1.00
113	Jay Buhner	.05
114	Garret Anderson	.05
115	Edgar Martinez	.05
116	Edgardo Alfonzo	.05
117	Billy Ashley	.05
118	Joe Carter	.05
119	Javy Lopez	.05
120	Bobby Bonilla	.05
121	Ken Caminiti	.05
122	Barry Larkin	.05
123	Shannon Stewart	.05
124	Orel Hershiser	.05
125	Jeff Conine	.05
126	Mark Grace	.05
127	Kenny Lofton	.05
128	Luis Gonzalez	.25
129	Rico Brogna	.05
130	Mo Vaughn	.05
131	Brad Radke	.05
132	Jose Herrera	.05
133	Rick Aguilera	.05
134	Gary DiSarcina	.05
135	Andres Galarraga	.05
136	Carl Everett	.05
137	Steve Avery	.05
138	Vinny Castilla	.05
139	Dennis Martinez	.05
140	John Wetteland	.05
141	Alex Gonzalez	.05
142	Brian Jordan	.05
143	Todd Hollandsworth	.05
144	Terrell Wade	.05
145	Wilson Alvarez	.05
146	Reggie Sanders	.05
147	Will Clark	.10
148	Hideo Nomo	.50
149	J.T. Snow	.05
150	Frank Thomas	.65
151	Ivan Rodriguez	.60
152	Jay Bell	.05
153	Checklist	.05
154	David Cone	.05
155	Roberto Alomar	.20
156	Carlos Delgado	.40
157	Carlos Baerga	.05
158	Geronimo Berroa	.05
159	Joe Vitiello	.05
160	Terry Steinbach	.05
161	Doug Drabek	.05
162	David Segui	.05
163	Ozzie Smith	.75
164	Kurt Abbott	.05
165	Randy Johnson	.65
166	John Valentin	.05
167	Mickey Tettleton	.05
168	Ruben Sierra	.05
169	Jim Thome	.60
170	Mike Greenwell	.05
171	Quilvio Veras	.05
172	Robin Ventura	.05
173	Bill Pulsipher	.05
174	Rafael Palmeiro	.60
175	Hal Morris	.05
176	Ryan Klesko	.05
177	Eric Young	.05
178	Shane Andrews	.05
179	Brian Hunter	.05
180	Brett Butler	.05
181	John Olerud	.05
182	Moises Alou	.05
183	Glenallen Hill	.05
184	Ismael Valdes	.05
185	Andy Pettitte	.25
186	Yamil Benitez	.05
187	Jason Bere	.05
188	Dean Palmer	.05
189	Jimmy Haynes	.05
190	Trevor Hoffman	.05
191	Mike Mussina	.40
192	Greg Maddux	.75
193	Ozzie Guillen	.05
194	Pat Listach	.05
195	Derek Bell	.05
196	Darren Daulton	.05
197	John Mabry	.05
198	Ramon Martinez	.05
199	Jeff Bagwell	.65
200	Mike Piazza	1.00
201	Al Martin	.05
202	Aaron Sele	.05
203	Ed Sprague	.05
204	Rod Beck	.05
205	Checklist	.05
206	Mike Lansing	.05
207	Craig Biggio	.05
208	Jeffrey Hammonds	.05
209	Dave Nilsson	.05
210	Checklist, Inserts (Dante Bichette, Albert Belle)	.05
211	Derek Jeter	2.00
212	Alan Benes	.05
213	Jason Schmidt	.05
214	Alex Ochoa	.05
215	Ruben Rivera	.05
216	Roger Cedeno	.05
217	Jeff Suppan	.05
218	Billy Wagner	.05
219	Mark Loretta	.05
220	Karim Garcia	.10

Press Proofs

Carrying the parallel edition concept to its inevitable next level, '96 Leaf offered the Press Proof insert cards in three degrees of scarcity, each highlighted with appropriate holographic foil. At the top of the line are Gold Press Proofs in an edition of only 500 of each card. Silver and Bronze versions were produced in editions of 1,000 and 2,000, respectively. Press Proofs are inserted into both hobby and retail packs at an average rate of one card per 10 packs.

	NM/M
Complete Set, Gold (220):	200.00
Complete Set, Silver (220):	100.00
Complete Set, Bronze (220):	75.00
Common Player, Gold:	1.00
Common Player, Silver:	.50
Common Player, Bronze:	.25

All-Star MVP Contenders

A surprise insert in Leaf boxes was this interactive redemption issue. Twenty lead-

ing candidates for MVP honors at the 1996 All-Star Game in Philadelphia were presented in a silver-foil highlighted horizontal format. The player's league logo serves as a background to the color action photo on front. Backs have details of the redemption offer which expired Aug. 15, 1996. The first 5,000 persons who sent in the Mike Piazza card for redemption received a gold version of the set and had their Piazza card punch-cancelled and returned.

		NM/M
Complete Set (20):		12.50
Common Card:		.25
Golds:		1.5X
1	Frank Thomas	.75
2	Mike Piazza	1.50
2c	Mike Piazza (Redeemed and punch-cancelled.)	1.00
3	Sammy Sosa	1.50
4	Cal Ripken Jr.	2.00
5	Jeff Bagwell	.75
6	Reggie Sanders	.25
7	Mo Vaughn	.25
8	Tony Gwynn	1.00
9	Dante Bichette	.25
10	Tim Salmon	.25
11	Chipper Jones	1.00
12	Kenny Lofton	.25
13	Manny Ramirez	.75
14	Barry Bonds	2.00
15	Raul Mondesi	.25
16	Kirby Puckett	1.00
17	Albert Belle	.25
18	Ken Griffey Jr.	1.50
19	Greg Maddux	1.00
20	Bonus Card	.10

Gold Leaf Stars

A vignetted background of embossed gold metallic cardboard and a Gold Leaf Stars logo in 22-K gold foil are featured on this limited (2,500 of each) edition insert. Backs include a second color photo of the player and a serial number from within the edition. Gold Leaf Stars were included in both hobby and retail packaging, with an average insertion rate of one per 210 packs.

		NM/M
Complete Set (15):		125.00
Common Player:		3.00
1	Frank Thomas	9.00
2	Dante Bichette	3.00
3	Sammy Sosa	15.00
4	Ken Griffey Jr.	15.00
5	Mike Piazza	15.00
6	Tim Salmon	3.00
7	Hideo Nomo	6.00
8	Cal Ripken Jr.	20.00
9	Chipper Jones	12.00
10	Albert Belle	3.00
11	Tony Gwynn	12.00
12	Mo Vaughn	3.00
13	Barry Larkin	3.00
14	Manny Ramirez	9.00
15	Greg Maddux	12.00

Hats Off

The most technically innovative inserts of 1996 have to be the Hats Off series exclu-

sive to Leaf retail packs. Front player photos are on a background that is both flocked to simulate the cloth of a baseball cap, plus enhanced with a stiched team logo. The graphics are all in raised textured gold foil. Backs are conventionally printed and include a gold-foil serial number placing each card within an edition of 5,000 per player.

		NM/M
Complete Set (8):		30.00
Common Player:		3.00
1	Cal Ripken Jr.	12.00
2	Barry Larkin	3.00
3	Frank Thomas	4.50
4	Mo Vaughn	3.00
5	Ken Griffey Jr.	7.50
6	Hideo Nomo	4.00
7	Albert Belle	3.00
8	Greg Maddux	6.00

Picture Perfect

Leaf calls the glossy central area of these inserts "pearlized foil," which allows the player action photo to stand out in contrast to the actual wood veneer background. Gold-foil highlights complete the design. Backs are conventionally printed and include a gold-foil serial number from within the edition of 5,000 of each player's card. Cards #1-6 are hobby-only inserts, while #7-12 are found in retail packs. Average insertion rate is one per 140 packs. A promo version of each card was also issued.

		NM/M
Complete Set (12):		22.50
Common Player:		1.00
Promos:		2X
1	Frank Thomas	2.00
2	Cal Ripken Jr.	5.00
3	Greg Maddux	2.50
4	Manny Ramirez	2.00
5	Chipper Jones	2.50
6	Tony Gwynn	2.50
7	Ken Griffey Jr.	3.00
8	Albert Belle	1.00
9	Jeff Bagwell	2.00
10	Mike Piazza	3.00
11	Mo Vaughn	1.00
12	Barry Bonds	5.00

Statistical Standouts

The feel of leather complements the game-used baseball background on these hobby-only inserts featuring the game's top names. Backs offer statistical data and a gold-foil serial number placing the card within an edition

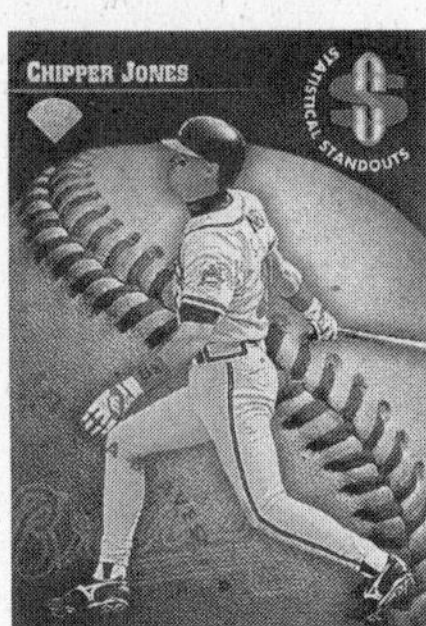

of 2,500 for each player. Average insertion rate is one per 210 packs.

		NM/M
Complete Set (8):		60.00
Common Player:		3.00
1	Cal Ripken Jr.	20.00
2	Tony Gwynn	10.00
3	Frank Thomas	7.50
4	Ken Griffey Jr.	13.50
5	Hideo Nomo	6.00
6	Greg Maddux	10.00
7	Albert Belle	3.00
8	Chipper Jones	10.00

Frank Thomas' Greatest Hits

Die-cut plastic with a background of prismatic foil to simulate a segment of a compact disc is the format for this insert issue chronicling the career-to-date of Frank Thomas. Backs include a few stats and a portrait photo, plus a gold-foil serial number from within an edition of 5,000. Cards #1-4 are found only in hobby packs; cards #5-7 are exclusive to retail packs (average insertion rate one per 210 packs) and card #8 could be had only through a wrapper redemption.

		NM/M
Complete Set (8):		12.50
Common Card:		2.00
1	1990	2.00
2	1991	2.00
3	1992	2.00
4	1993	2.00
5	1994	2.00
6	1995	2.00
7	Career	2.00
8	MVP	2.00

Total Bases

Total-base leaders from 1991-95 are featured in this hobby-only insert set. Card fronts are printed on textured canvas to simulate a base. Fronts are highlighted with gold foil. Backs have stats ranking the player in this category plus a gold-foil serial number from an edition of 5,000 of each player. Total Bases inserts are seeded at an average rate of one per 72 packs. Each player can also be found in a promo card version, marked as such on each side.

		NM/M
Complete Set (12):		25.00
Common Player:		1.00
Promos:		2X
1	Frank Thomas	2.50
2	Albert Belle	1.00
3	Rafael Palmeiro	2.00
4	Barry Bonds	6.00
5	Kirby Puckett	3.00
6	Joe Carter	1.00
7	Paul Molitor	2.50
8	Fred McGriff	1.00
9	Ken Griffey Jr.	4.00
10	Carlos Baerga	1.00
11	Juan Gonzalez	2.00
12	Cal Ripken Jr.	6.00

1996 Leaf/Limited

Leaf Limited contains 90 of the top rookies and stars. There is also a 100-card Limited Gold parallel set which includes the 90 base cards, plus 10 Limited Rookies inserts. The gold parallel cards are seeded one per 11 packs. Regular Limited Rookies inserts were seeded one per seven packs. Other insert sets were two versions of Lumberjacks and Pennant Craze.

		NM/M
Complete Set (90):		15.00
Common Player:		.10
Gold Set (90):		50.00
Gold Stars/Rookies:		3X
Pack (5):		1.50
Wax Box (14):		20.00
1	Ivan Rodriguez	.60
2	Roger Clemens	1.50
3	Gary Sheffield	.40
4	Tino Martinez	.10
5	Sammy Sosa	1.50
6	Reggie Sanders	.10
7	Ray Lankford	.10
8	Manny Ramirez	.75
9	Jeff Bagwell	.75
10	Greg Maddux	1.00
11	Ken Griffey Jr.	1.50
12	Rondell White	.10
13	Mike Piazza	1.50
14	Marc Newfield	.10
15	Cal Ripken Jr.	3.00
16	Carlos Delgado	.40
17	Tim Salmon	.10
18	Andres Galarraga	.10
19	Chuck Knoblauch	.10
20	Matt Williams	.10
21	Mark McGwire	2.00
22	Ben McDonald	.10
23	Frank Thomas	.75
24	Johnny Damon	.35
25	Gregg Jefferies	.10
26	Travis Fryman	.10
27	Chipper Jones	1.00
28	David Cone	.10
29	Kenny Lofton	.10
30	Mike Mussina	.30
31	Alex Rodriguez	2.00
32	Carlos Baerga	.10
33	Brian Hunter	.10
34	Juan Gonzalez	.60
35	Bernie Williams	.10
36	Wally Joyner	.10
37	Fred McGriff	.10
38	Randy Johnson	.75
39	Marty Cordova	.10
40	Garret Anderson	.10
41	Albert Belle	.10
42	Edgar Martinez	.10
43	Barry Larkin	.10
44	Paul O'Neill	.10
45	Cecil Fielder	.10
46	Rusty Greer	.10
47	Mo Vaughn	.10
48	Dante Bichette	.10
49	Ryan Klesko	.10
50	Roberto Alomar	.25
51	Raul Mondesi	.10
52	Robin Ventura	.10
53	Tony Gwynn	1.00
54	Mark Grace	.10
55	Jim Thome	.60
56	Jason Giambi	.50
57	Tom Glavine	.25
58	Jim Edmonds	.10
59	Pedro Martinez	.75
60	Charles Johnson	.10
61	Wade Boggs	1.00
62	Orlando Merced	.10
63	Craig Biggio	.10
64	Brady Anderson	.10
65	Hideo Nomo	.60
66	Ozzie Smith	1.00
67	Eddie Murray	.75
68	Will Clark	.15
69	Jay Buhner	.10
70	Kirby Puckett	1.00
71	Barry Bonds	3.00
72	Ray Durham	.10
73	Sterling Hitchcock	.10
74	John Smoltz	.10
75	Andre Dawson	.35
76	Joe Carter	.10
77	Ryne Sandberg	1.00
78	Rickey Henderson	.75
79	Brian Jordan	.10
80	Greg Vaughn	.10
81	Andy Pettitte	.25
82	Dean Palmer	.10
83	Paul Molitor	.75
84	Rafael Palmeiro	.60
85	Henry Rodriguez	.10
86	Larry Walker	.10
87	Ismael Valdes	.10
88	Derek Bell	.10
89	J.T. Snow	.10
90	Jack McDowell	.10

Lumberjacks

Lumberjacks inserts returned to Leaf Limited, but the 1996 versions feature an improved maple stock that puts wood grains on both sides of the card. Ten different Lumberjacks are available in two different versions. Regular versions are serial numbered to 5,000, while a special black-bordered Limited Edition version is numbered to 500. Each Lumberjacks card was also produced in a promo card version, appropriately marked on each side.

		NM/M
Complete Set (10):		40.00
Common Player:		1.50
Lumberjack Blacks (500):		2X
Promos:		2X
1	Ken Griffey Jr.	5.00
2	Sammy Sosa	5.00
3	Cal Ripken Jr.	7.50
4	Frank Thomas	3.00
5	Alex Rodriguez	6.00
6	Mo Vaughn	1.50
7	Chipper Jones	4.00
8	Mike Piazza	5.00
9	Jeff Bagwell	3.00
10	Mark McGwire	6.00

Pennant Craze

Each card in this insert set is sequentially numbered to 2,500 in silver foil on the back. The top-front of the cards have a die-cut pennant shape and is felt-textured. Appropriately marked promotional versions of each card can also be found.

		NM/M
Complete Set (10):		20.00
Common Player:		1.00
Promos:		2X
1	Juan Gonzalez	1.25
2	Cal Ripken Jr.	4.00
3	Frank Thomas	1.50
4	Ken Griffey Jr.	2.50
5	Albert Belle	1.00
6	Greg Maddux	2.00
7	Paul Molitor	1.50
8	Alex Rodriguez	3.00
9	Barry Bonds	4.00
10	Chipper Jones	2.00

Rookies

There are two versions of this 1996 Limited insert set. The cards are reprinted as part of a Limited Gold parallel set, which also includes the regular issue's 90 cards. The gold cards are seeded one per every 11 packs. The top young players are also featured on regular Limited Rookies inserts; these versions are seeded one per every seven packs.

		NM/M
Complete Set (10):		7.50
Common Player:		.50
Limited Gold:		3X
1	Alex Ochoa	.50
2	Darin Erstad	1.00
3	Ruben Rivera	.50
4	Derek Jeter	5.00
5	Jermaine Dye	.50
6	Jason Kendall	.50
7	Mike Grace	.50
8	Andruw Jones	2.50
9	Rey Ordonez	.50
10	George Arias	.50

1996 Leaf/Preferred

Leaf Preferred consists of 150 cards, a Press Proof parallel set and three insert sets, one of which has its own parallel set, too. While no individual odds are given for insert sets, the overall odds of getting an insert card are one per 10 packs. The Press Proof inserts replace the silver foil name and strip down the left side of the card with gold foil. Press Proof parallels were limited to 250 sets. Another insert set, Silver Leaf Steel, has a card seeded one per pack. This insert set is paralleled by a Gold Leaf Steel set, which appears in much more limited numbers. The two other insert sets are Steel Power and Staremaster.

		NM/M
Complete Set (150):		15.00
Common Player:		.05
Press Proofs:		12X
Pack (6):		1.00
Wax Box (24):		20.00
1	Ken Griffey Jr.	1.25
2	Rico Brogna	.05
3	Gregg Jefferies	.05
4	Reggie Sanders	.05
5	Manny Ramirez	.75
6	Shawn Green	.40
7	Tino Martinez	.05
8	Jeff Bagwell	.75
9	Marc Newfield	.05
10	Ray Lankford	.05
11	Jay Bell	.05
12	Greg Maddux	1.00
13	Frank Thomas	.75
14	Travis Fryman	.05
15	Mark McGwire	1.50
16	Chuck Knoblauch	.05
17	Sammy Sosa	1.25
18	Matt Williams	.05
19	Roger Clemens	1.25
20	Rondell White	.05
21	Ivan Rodriguez	.65
22	Cal Ripken Jr.	2.00
23	Ben McDonald	.05
24	Kenny Lofton	.05
25	Mike Piazza	1.25
26	David Cone	.05
27	Gary Sheffield	.40
28	Tim Salmon	.05
29	Andres Galarraga	.05
30	Johnny Damon	.35
31	Ozzie Smith	1.00
32	Carlos Baerga	.05
33	Raul Mondesi	.05
34	Moises Alou	.05
35	Alex Rodriguez	1.50
36	Mike Mussina	.40
37	Jason Isringhausen	.05
38	Barry Larkin	.05
39	Bernie Williams	.05
40	Chipper Jones	1.00
41	Joey Hamilton	.05
42	Charles Johnson	.05
43	Juan Gonzalez	.50
44	Greg Vaughn	.05
45	Robin Ventura	.05
46	Albert Belle	.05
47	Rafael Palmeiro	.65
48	Brian Hunter	.05
49	Mo Vaughn	.05
50	Paul O'Neill	.05
51	Mark Grace	.05
52	Randy Johnson	.75
53	Pedro Martinez	.75
54	Marty Cordova	.05
55	Garret Anderson	.05
56	Joe Carter	.05
57	Jim Thome	.60
58	Edgardo Alfonzo	.05
59	Dante Bichette	.05
60	Darryl Hamilton	.05
61	Roberto Alomar	.20
62	Fred McGriff	.05
63	Kirby Puckett	1.00
64	Hideo Nomo	.60
65	Alex Fernandez	.05
66	Ryan Klesko	.05
67	Wade Boggs	1.00
68	Eddie Murray	.75
69	Eric Karros	.05
70	Jim Edmonds	.05
71	Edgar Martinez	.05
72	Andy Pettitte	.30
73	Mark Grudzielanek	.05
74	Tom Glavine	.25
75	Ken Caminiti	.05
76	Will Clark	.10
77	Craig Biggio	.05
78	Brady Anderson	.05
79	Tony Gwynn	1.00
80	Larry Walker	.05
81	Brian Jordan	.05
82	Lenny Dykstra	.05
83	Butch Huskey	.05
84	Jack McDowell	.05
85	Cecil Fielder	.05
86	Jose Canseco	.40
87	Jason Giambi	.50
88	Rickey Henderson	.75
89	Kevin Seitzer	.05
90	Carlos Delgado	.40
91	Ryne Sandberg	1.00
92	Dwight Gooden	.05
93	Michael Tucker	.05
94	Barry Bonds	2.00
95	Eric Young	.05
96	Dean Palmer	.05
97	Henry Rodriguez	.05
98	John Mabry	.05
99	J.T. Snow	.05
100	Andre Dawson	.25
101	Ismael Valdes	.05
102	Charles Nagy	.05
103	Jay Buhner	.05
104	Derek Bell	.05
105	Paul Molitor	.75
106	Hal Morris	.05
107	Ray Durham	.05
108	Bernard Gilkey	.05
109	John Valentin	.05
110	Melvin Nieves	.05
111	John Smoltz	.05
112	Terrell Wade	.05
113	Chad Mottola	.05
114	Tony Clark	.05
115	John Wasdin	.05
116	Derek Jeter	2.00
117	Rey Ordonez	.05
118	Jason Thompson	.05
119	Robin Jennings **RC**	.05
120	Rocky Coppinger **RC**	.05
121	Billy Wagner	.05
122	Steve Gibralter	.05
123	Jermaine Dye	.05
124	Jason Kendall	.05
125	Mike Grace **RC**	.05
126	Jason Schmidt	.05
127	Paul Wilson	.05
128	Alan Benes	.05
129	Justin Thompson	.05
130	Brooks Kieschnick	.05
131	George Arias	.05
132	Osvaldo Fernandez **RC**	.20
133	Todd Hollandsworth	.05
134	Eric Owens	.05
135	Chan Ho Park	.05
136	Mark Loretta	.05
137	Ruben Rivera	.05
138	Jeff Suppan	.05
139	Ugueth Urbina	.05
140	LaTroy Hawkins	.05
141	Chris Snopek	.05
142	Edgar Renteria	.05
143	Raul Casanova	.05
144	Jose Herrera	.05
145	Matt Lawton **RC**	.05
146	Ralph Milliard **RC**	.05
147	Checklist (Frank Thomas)	.05
148	Checklist (Jeff Bagwell)	.05
149	Checklist (Ken Griffey Jr.)	.05
150	Checklist (Mike Piazza)	.05

Press Proofs

Inserted at a rate of about one per 48 packs, Press Proof parallels of the 150 cards in Leaf Preferred are identifiable only by the use of gold foil, rather than silver, on the card fronts, and gold ink on back. The cards are not otherwise marked or numbered. It is believed the issue was limited to 250-500 of each card.

	NM/M
Complete Set (150):	100.00
Common Player:	.50
Stars/Rookies:	12X

Leaf Steel Promos

Each of the 77 gold cards in the Preferred Steel set can also be found in gold, silver and bronze promo card versions. The samples differ from the issued versions only in an overprint diagonally on the back which reads "PROMOTIONAL

CARD." This parallel promo edition represents one of the largest promo card issues of the mid-1990s. Cards were reportedly distributed to dealers on the basis of one gold promo per three-case order. The silver and bronze versions were reportedly never officially released, though examples have found their way into the market in some quantity.

		NM/M
Complete Gold Set (77):		625.00
Common Gold Player:		4.00
Silver: Values Undetermined		
Bronze: Values Undetermined		
1	Frank Thomas	15.00
2	Paul Molitor	15.00
3	Kenny Lofton	4.00
4	Travis Fryman	4.00
5	Jeff Conine	4.00
6	Barry Bonds	50.00
7	Gregg Jefferies	4.00
8	Alex Rodriguez	40.00
9	Wade Boggs	20.00
10	David Justice	4.00
11	Hideo Nomo	12.50
12	Roberto Alomar	6.00
13	Todd Hollandsworth	4.00
14	Mark McGwire	40.00
15	Rafael Palmeiro	12.50
16	Will Clark	4.00
17	Cal Ripken Jr.	50.00
18	Derek Bell	4.00
19	Gary Sheffield	7.50
20	Juan Gonzalez	12.50
21	Garret Anderson	4.00
22	Mo Vaughn	4.00
23	Robin Ventura	4.00
24	Carlos Baerga	4.00
25	Tim Salmon	4.00
26	Matt Williams	4.00
27	Fred McGriff	4.00
28	Rondell White	4.00
29	Ray Lankford	4.00
30	Lenny Dykstra	4.00
31	J.T. Snow	4.00
32	Sammy Sosa	25.00
33	Chipper Jones	20.00
34	Bobby Bonilla	4.00
35	Paul Wilson	4.00
36	Darren Daulton	4.00
37	Larry Walker	4.00
38	Raul Mondesi	4.00
39	Jeff Bagwell	15.00
40	Derek Jeter	50.00
41	Kirby Puckett	20.00
42	Jason Isringhausen	4.00
43	Vinny Castilla	4.00
44	Jim Edmonds	4.00
45	Ron Gant	4.00
46	Carlos Delgado	7.50
47	Jose Canseco	7.50
48	Tony Gwynn	20.00
49	Mike Mussina	7.50
50	Charles Johnson	4.00
51	Mike Piazza	25.00
52	Ken Griffey Jr.	25.00
53	Greg Maddux	20.00
54	Mark Grace	4.00
55	Ryan Klesko	4.00
56	Dennis Eckersley	12.50
57	Rickey Henderson	15.00
58	Michael Tucker	4.00
59	Joe Carter	4.00
60	Randy Johnson	15.00
61	Brian Jordan	4.00
62	Shawn Green	7.50
63	Roger Clemens	22.50
64	Andres Galarraga	4.00
65	Johnny Damon	7.50
66	Ryne Sandberg	20.00
67	Alan Benes	4.00
68	Albert Belle	4.00
69	Barry Larkin	4.00
70	Marty Cordova	4.00
71	Dante Bichette	4.00
72	Craig Biggio	4.00
73	Reggie Sanders	4.00
74	Moises Alou	4.00
75	Chuck Knoblauch	4.00
76	Cecil Fielder	4.00
77	Manny Ramirez	15.00

Leaf Steel

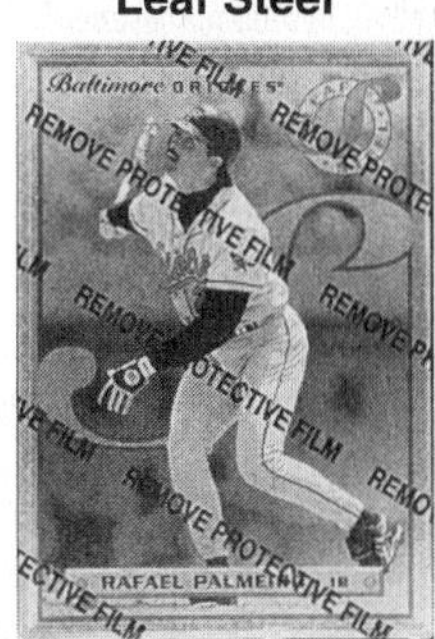

This 77-card insert set has two versions - a silver one and a much more limited gold one. A Silver Leaf Steel card is included in every pack; the parallel versions appear about one per 24 packs.

		NM/M
Complete Set (77):		25.00
Common Player:		.15
Gold:		2X
1	Frank Thomas	1.00
2	Paul Molitor	1.00
3	Kenny Lofton	.15
4	Travis Fryman	.15
5	Jeff Conine	.15
6	Barry Bonds	3.00
7	Gregg Jefferies	.15
8	Alex Rodriguez	2.50
9	Wade Boggs	1.50
10	David Justice	.15
11	Hideo Nomo	.75
12	Roberto Alomar	.30
13	Todd Hollandsworth	.15
14	Mark McGwire	2.50
15	Rafael Palmeiro	.75
16	Will Clark	.25
17	Cal Ripken Jr.	3.00
18	Derek Bell	.15
19	Gary Sheffield	.50
20	Juan Gonzalez	.65
21	Garret Anderson	.15
22	Mo Vaughn	.15
23	Robin Ventura	.15
24	Carlos Baerga	.15
25	Tim Salmon	.15
26	Matt Williams	.15
27	Fred McGriff	.15
28	Rondell White	.15
29	Ray Lankford	.15
30	Lenny Dykstra	.15
31	J.T. Snow	.15
32	Sammy Sosa	2.00
33	Chipper Jones	1.50
34	Bobby Bonilla	.15
35	Paul Wilson	.15
36	Darren Daulton	.15
37	Larry Walker	.15
38	Raul Mondesi	.15
39	Jeff Bagwell	1.00
40	Derek Jeter	3.00
41	Kirby Puckett	1.50
42	Jason Isringhausen	.15
43	Vinny Castilla	.15
44	Jim Edmonds	.15
45	Ron Gant	.15
46	Carlos Delgado	.50
47	Jose Canseco	.40
48	Tony Gwynn	1.50
49	Mike Mussina	.50
50	Charles Johnson	.15
51	Mike Piazza	2.00
52	Ken Griffey Jr.	2.00
53	Greg Maddux	1.50
54	Mark Grace	.15
55	Ryan Klesko	.15
56	Dennis Eckersley	.75
57	Rickey Henderson	1.00
58	Michael Tucker	.15
59	Joe Carter	.15
60	Randy Johnson	1.00
61	Brian Jordan	.15
62	Shawn Green	.50
63	Roger Clemens	2.00
64	Andres Galarraga	.15
65	Johnny Damon	.40
66	Ryne Sandberg	1.50
67	Alan Benes	.15
68	Albert Belle	.15
69	Barry Larkin	.15
70	Marty Cordova	.15
71	Dante Bichette	.15
72	Craig Biggio	.15
73	Reggie Sanders	.15
74	Moises Alou	.15
75	Chuck Knoblauch	.15
76	Cecil Fielder	.15
77	Manny Ramirez	1.00

Staremaster

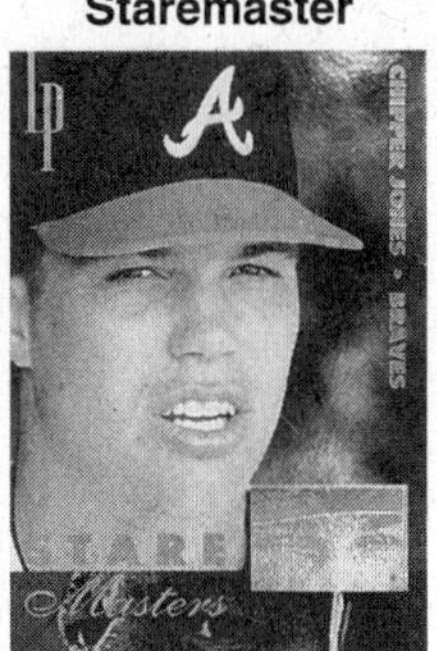

These 1996 Leaf Preferred inserts provide a photographic tribute to the stares of 12 top players. Each card is printed on silver holographic card stock and is numbered up to 2,500.

		NM/M
Complete Set (12):		50.00
Common Player:		3.00
1	Chipper Jones	5.00
2	Alex Rodriguez	7.50
3	Derek Jeter	10.00
4	Tony Gwynn	5.00
5	Frank Thomas	4.00
6	Ken Griffey Jr.	6.00
7	Cal Ripken Jr.	10.00
8	Greg Maddux	5.00
9	Albert Belle	3.00
10	Barry Bonds	10.00
11	Jeff Bagwell	4.00
12	Mike Piazza	6.00

Steel Power

This eight-card Leaf Steel insert set combines micro-etched foil with interior die-cutting to honor the game's top power hitters. Each insert card carries a serial number up to 5,000.

		NM/M
Complete Set (8):		17.50
Common Player:		1.00
1	Albert Belle	1.00
2	Mo Vaughn	1.00
3	Ken Griffey Jr.	3.50
4	Cal Ripken Jr.	5.00
5	Mike Piazza	3.50
6	Barry Bonds	5.00
7	Jeff Bagwell	2.50
8	Frank Thomas	2.50

1996 Leaf/ Signature Series

The base set which rode along with the autographed cards of more than 250 Major League players in Leaf's Signature Series (at least one authentic signature is guaranteed in every pack) features action photos with silver-foil highlights. Horizontal backs have a large photo along with a few stats and bits of personal data. One out of every 48 packs is a super pack containing nothing but autographed cards. The 150-card base set is paralleled in Gold and Platinum Press Proof insert sets. The gold version is seeded one per 12 packs in Series 1 and one per eight in the Extended Series. Platinums were issued in an edition of 150 of each of the 150 cards and are found only in the Extended Series at the rate of one per 24 packs. Four-card packs of Leaf Signature Series carried a suggested retail price at issue of $9.99.

		NM/M
Complete Set (150):		30.00
Complete 1st Series (100):		20.00
Complete Extended Series (50):		10.00
Common Player:		.05
Gold PP Stars/Rookies:		8X
Platinum PP Stars/Rookies:		20X
Pack (4):		3.50
Wax Box (12):		35.00
1	Mike Piazza	1.25
2	Juan Gonzalez	.65
3	Greg Maddux	1.00
4	Marc Newfield	.05
5	Wade Boggs	1.00
6	Ray Lankford	.05
7	Frank Thomas	.75
8	Rico Brogna	.05
9	Tim Salmon	.05
10	Ken Griffey Jr.	1.25
11	Manny Ramirez	.75
12	Cecil Fielder	.05
13	Gregg Jefferies	.05
14	Rondell White	.05
15	Cal Ripken Jr.	2.00
16	Alex Rodriguez	1.50
17	Bernie Williams	.05
18	Andres Galarraga	.05
19	Mike Mussina	.50
20	Chuck Knoblauch	.05
21	Joe Carter	.05
22	Jeff Bagwell	.75
23	Mark McGwire	1.50
24	Sammy Sosa	1.00
25	Reggie Sanders	.05
26	Chipper Jones	1.00
27	Jeff Cirillo	.05
28	Roger Clemens	1.25
29	Craig Biggio	.05
30	Gary Sheffield	.45
31	Paul O'Neill	.05
32	Johnny Damon	.35
33	Jason Isringhausen	.05
34	Jay Bell	.05
35	Henry Rodriguez	.05
36	Matt Williams	.05
37	Randy Johnson	.75
38	Fred McGriff	.05
39	Jason Giambi	.60
40	Ivan Rodriguez	.65
41	Raul Mondesi	.05
42	Barry Larkin	.05
43	Ryan Klesko	.05
44	Joey Hamilton	.05
45	Todd Hundley	.05
46	Jim Edmonds	.05
47	Dante Bichette	.05
48	Roberto Alomar	.20
49	Mark Grace	.05
50	Brady Anderson	.05
51	Hideo Nomo	.65
52	Ozzie Smith	1.00
53	Robin Ventura	.05
54	Andy Pettitte	.35
55	Kenny Lofton	.05
56	John Mabry	.05
57	Paul Molitor	.75
58	Rey Ordonez	.05
59	Albert Belle	.05
60	Charles Johnson	.05
61	Edgar Martinez	.05
62	Derek Bell	.05
63	Carlos Delgado	.50
64	Raul Casanova	.05
65	Ismael Valdes	.05
66	J.T. Snow	.05
67	Derek Jeter	2.00
68	Jason Kendall	.05
69	John Smoltz	.05
70	Chad Mottola	.05
71	Jim Thome	.60
72	Will Clark	.10
73	Mo Vaughn	.05
74	John Wasdin	.05
75	Rafael Palmeiro	.65
76	Mark Grudzielanek	.05
77	Larry Walker	.05
78	Alan Benes	.05
79	Michael Tucker	.05
80	Billy Wagner	.05
81	Paul Wilson	.05
82	Greg Vaughn	.05
83	Dean Palmer	.05
84	Ryne Sandberg	1.00
85	Eric Young	.05
86	Jay Buhner	.05
87	Tony Clark	.05
88	Jermaine Dye	.05
89	Barry Bonds	2.00
90	Ugueth Urbina	.05
91	Charles Nagy	.05
92	Ruben Rivera	.05
93	Todd Hollandsworth	.05
94	Darin Erstad **RC**	1.50
95	Brooks Kieschnick	.05
96	Edgar Renteria	.05
97	Lenny Dykstra	.05
98	Tony Gwynn	1.00
99	Kirby Puckett	1.00
100	Checklist	.05
101	Andruw Jones	.75
102	Alex Ochoa	.05
103	David Cone	.05
104	Rusty Greer	.05
105	Jose Canseco	.45
106	Ken Caminiti	.05
107	Mariano Rivera	.15
108	Ron Gant	.05
109	Darryl Strawberry	.05
110	Vladimir Guerrero	.75
111	George Arias	.05
112	Jeff Conine	.05
113	Bobby Higginson	.05
114	Eric Karros	.05
115	Brian Hunter	.05
116	Eddie Murray	.75
117	Todd Walker	.05
118	Chan Ho Park	.05
119	John Jaha	.05
120	David Justice	.05
121	Makoto Suzuki	.05
122	Scott Rolen	.65
123	Tino Martinez	.05
124	Kimera Bartee	.05
125	Garret Anderson	.05
126	Brian Jordan	.05
127	Andre Dawson	.30
128	Javier Lopez	.05
129	Bill Pulsipher	.05
130	Dwight Gooden	.05
131	Al Martin	.05
132	Terrell Wade	.05
133	Steve Gibralter	.05
134	Tom Glavine	.35
135	Kevin Appier	.05
136	Tim Raines	.05
137	Curtis Pride	.05
138	Todd Greene	.05
139	Bobby Bonilla	.05
140	Trey Beamon	.05
141	Marty Cordova	.05
142	Rickey Henderson	.75
143	Ellis Burks	.05
144	Dennis Eckersley	.65
145	Kevin Brown	.05
146	Carlos Baerga	.05
147	Brett Butler	.05
148	Marquis Grissom	.05
149	Karim Garcia	.05
150	Checklist	.05

Press Proofs

The 150-card base set of Leaf/Signature was paralleled in a pair of Press Proof versions. Identical in format to the regular issue, the Press Proofs have an embossed gold- or platinum-foil oval seal at left and "PRESS PROOF" vertically at right in the same color foil. Backs are identical to the regular version. Gold Press Proofs were inserted one per 12 packs of Series 1 and one per eight packs of Extended. Platinum Proofs are found only in Extended Series packs, at an average rate of one per 24. Total production of Platinum Press proofs was 150 of each card.

	NM/M
Common Gold:	2.00
Gold Stars:	8X
Common Platinum:	4.00
Platinum Stars:	20X

Autographs Promos

To introduce its Autograph Series, Leaf sent dealers one of two promo card versions of the Frank Thomas card. Most received a card with a pre-printed facsimile autograph, duly noted in small type beneath the signature. Others (500) received a genuine Frank Thomas autograph on their promo. All of the cards are marked "PROMOTIONAL CARD" diagonally on both front and back.

	NM/M
Frank Thomas (Facsimile signature.)	4.00
Frank Thomas (Genuine autograph.)	50.00

Autographs

Every pack of 1996 Leaf Signature Series includes at least one authentically signed card from one of over 250 players. There were 240 players who signed three versions in these quantities: 500 Gold, 1,000 Silver and 3,500 Bronze. There are also short-printed autographs for 10 players in quantities of 100 Gold, 200 Silver and 700 Bronze. The short-printed players are designated with an "SP" in the checklist. Cards are numbered alphabetically in the checklist since the autographed cards are unnumbered. Each major leaguer signed a notarized affidavit to guarantee each signature was authentic. Series 1 cards of Carlos Delgado, Brian Hunter, Phil Plantier, Jim Thome, Terrell Wade and Ernie Young were signed too late for inclusion in Series 1 packs, and were inserted with Extended. No Bronze cards of Thome were signed.

		NM/M
Common Bronze Player:		4.00
Silver:		1.5X
Gold:		2X
SPs: 100 Gold, 200 Silver, 700 Bronze		
(1)	Kurt Abbott	4.00
(2)	Juan Acevedo	4.00
(3)	Terry Adams	4.00
(4)	Manny Alexander	4.00
(5)	Roberto Alomar/SP	35.00
(6)	Moises Alou	12.00
(7)	Wilson Alvarez	4.00
(8)	Garret Anderson	10.00
(9)	Shane Andrews	4.00
(10)	Andy Ashby	4.00
(11)	Pedro Astacio	4.00
(12)	Brad Ausmus	4.00
(13)	Bobby Ayala	4.00
(14)	Carlos Baerga	4.00
(15)	Harold Baines	10.00
(16)	Jason Bates	4.00
(17)	Allen Battle	4.00
(18)	Rich Becker	4.00
(19)	David Bell	4.00
(20)	Rafael Belliard	4.00
(21)	Andy Benes	4.00
(22)	Armando Benitez	4.00
(23)	Jason Bere	4.00
(24)	Geronimo Berroa	4.00
(25)	Willie Blair	4.00
(26)	Mike Blowers	4.00
(27)	Wade Boggs/SP	50.00
(28)	Ricky Bones	4.00
(29)	Mike Bordick	4.00
(30)	Toby Borland	4.00
(31)	Ricky Bottalico	4.00
(32)	Darren Bragg	4.00
(33)	Jeff Branson	4.00
(34)	Tilson Brito	4.00
(35)	Rico Brogna	4.00
(36)	Scott Brosius	7.50
(37)	Damon Buford	4.00
(38)	Mike Busby	4.00

(39) Tom Candiotti 4.00
(40) Frank Castillo 4.00
(41) Andujar Cedeno 4.00
(42) Domingo Cedeno 4.00
(43) Roger Cedeno 4.00
(44) Norm Charlton 4.00
(45) Jeff Cirillo 4.00
(46) Will Clark 10.00
(47) Jeff Conine 4.00
(48) Steve Cooke 4.00
(49) Joey Cora 4.00
(50) Marty Cordova 4.00
(51) Rheal Cormier 4.00
(52) Felipe Crespo 4.00
(53) Chad Curtis 4.00
(54) Johnny Damon 15.00
(55) Russ Davis 4.00
(56) Andre Dawson 10.00
(57a) Carlos Delgado (Black autograph.) 15.00
(57b) Carlos Delgado (Blue autograph.) 15.00
(58) Doug Drabek 4.00
(59) Darren Dreifort 4.00
(60) Shawon Dunston 4.00
(61) Ray Durham 4.00
(62) Jim Edmonds 12.00
(63) Joey Eischen 4.00
(64) Jim Eisenreich 4.00
(65) Sal Fasano 4.00
(66) Jeff Fassero 4.00
(67) Alex Fernandez 4.00
(68) Darrin Fletcher 4.00
(69) Chad Fonville 4.00
(70) Kevin Foster 4.00
(71) John Franco 4.00
(72) Julio Franco 10.00
(73) Marvin Freeman 4.00
(74) Travis Fryman 4.00
(75) Gary Gaetti 4.00
(76) Carlos Garcia 4.00
(77) Jason Giambi 10.00
(78) Benji Gil 4.00
(79) Greg Gohr 4.00
(80) Chris Gomez 4.00
(81) Leo Gomez 4.00
(82) Tom Goodwin 4.00
(83) Mike Grace 4.00
(84) Mike Greenwell 6.00
(85) Rusty Greer 4.00
(86) Mark Grudzielanek 4.00
(87) Mark Gubicza 4.00
(88) Juan Guzman 4.00
(89) Darryl Hamilton 4.00
(90) Joey Hamilton 4.00
(91) Chris Hammond 4.00
(92) Mike Hampton 7.50
(93) Chris Haney 4.00
(94) Todd Haney 4.00
(95) Erik Hanson 4.00
(96) Pete Harnisch 4.00
(97) LaTroy Hawkins 4.00
(98) Charlie Hayes 4.00
(99) Jimmy Haynes 4.00
(100) Roberto Hernandez 4.00
(101) Bobby Higginson 4.00
(102) Glenallen Hill 4.00
(103) Ken Hill 4.00
(104) Sterling Hitchcock 4.00
(105) Trevor Hoffman 10.00
(106) Dave Hollins 4.00
(107) Dwayne Hosey 4.00
(108) Thomas Howard 4.00
(109) Steve Howe 6.00
(110) John Hudek 4.00
(111) Rex Hudler 4.00
(112) Brian Hunter 4.00
(113) Butch Huskey 4.00
(114) Mark Hutton 4.00
(115) Jason Jacome 4.00
(116) John Jaha 4.00
(117) Reggie Jefferson 4.00
(118) Derek Jeter/SP 150.00
(119) Bobby Jones 4.00
(120) Todd Jones 4.00
(121) Brian Jordan 5.00
(122) Kevin Jordan 4.00
(123) Jeff Juden 4.00
(124) Ron Karkovice 4.00
(125) Roberto Kelly 4.00
(126) Mark Kiefer 4.00
(127) Brooks Kieschnick 4.00
(128) Jeff King 4.00
(129) Mike Lansing 4.00
(130) Matt Lawton 7.50
(131) Al Leiter 6.00
(132) Mark Leiter 4.00
(133) Curtis Leskanic 4.00
(134) Darren Lewis 4.00
(135) Mark Lewis 4.00
(136) Felipe Lira 4.00
(137) Pat Listach 4.00
(138) Keith Lockhart 4.00
(139) Kenny Lofton/SP 25.00
(140) John Mabry 4.00
(141) Mike Macfarlane 4.00
(142) Kirt Manwaring 4.00
(143) Al Martin 4.00
(144) Norberto Martin 4.00
(145) Dennis Martinez 5.00
(146) Pedro Martinez 40.00
(147) Sandy Martinez 4.00
(148) Mike Matheny 4.00
(149) T.J. Mathews 4.00
(150) David McCarty 4.00
(151) Ben McDonald 4.00
(152) Pat Meares 4.00
(153) Orlando Merced 4.00
(154) Jose Mesa 4.00
(155) Matt Mieske 4.00
(156) Orlando Miller 4.00
(157) Mike Mimbs 4.00
(158) Paul Molitor/SP 40.00
(159) Raul Mondesi/SP 20.00
(160) Jeff Montgomery 4.00
(161) Mickey Morandini 4.00
(162) Lyle Mouton 4.00
(163) James Mouton 4.00
(164) Jamie Moyer 4.00
(165) Rodney Myers 4.00
(166) Denny Neagle 4.00
(167) Robb Nen 4.00
(168) Marc Newfield 4.00
(169) Dave Nilsson 4.00
(170) Jon Nunnally 4.00
(171) Chad Ogea 4.00
(172) Troy O'Leary 4.00
(173) Rey Ordonez 4.00
(174) Jayhawk Owens 4.00
(175) Tom Pagnozzi 4.00
(176) Dean Palmer 4.00
(177) Roger Pavlik 4.00
(178) Troy Percival 4.00
(179) Carlos Perez 4.00
(180) Robert Perez 4.00
(181) Andy Pettitte 30.00
(182) Phil Plantier 4.00
(183) Mike Potts 4.00
(184) Curtis Pride 4.00
(185) Ariel Prieto 4.00
(186) Bill Pulsipher 4.00
(187) Brad Radke 4.00
(188) Manny Ramirez/SP 35.00
(189) Joe Randa 4.00
(190) Pat Rapp 4.00
(191) Bryan Rekar 4.00
(192) Shane Reynolds 4.00
(193) Arthur Rhodes 4.00
(194) Mariano Rivera 45.00
(195a) Alex Rodriguez/SP (Black autograph.) 120.00
(195b) Alex Rodriguez/SP (Blue autograph.) 120.00
(196) Frank Rodriguez 4.00
(197) Mel Rojas 4.00
(198) Ken Ryan 4.00
(199) Bret Saberhagen 4.00
(200) Tim Salmon 5.00
(201) Rey Sanchez 4.00
(202) Scott Sanders 4.00
(203) Steve Scarsone 4.00
(204) Curt Schilling 25.00
(205) Jason Schmidt 20.00
(206) David Segui 4.00
(207) Kevin Seitzer 4.00
(208) Scott Servais 4.00
(209) Don Slaught 4.00
(210) Zane Smith 4.00
(211) Paul Sorrento 4.00
(212) Scott Stahoviak 4.00
(213) Mike Stanley 4.00
(214) Terry Steinbach 4.00
(215) Kevin Stocker 4.00
(216) Jeff Suppan 4.00
(217) Bill Swift 4.00
(218) Greg Swindell 4.00
(219) Kevin Tapani 4.00
(220) Danny Tartabull 4.00
(221) Julian Tavarez 4.00
(222a) Frank Thomas/SP (Blue autograph.) 40.00
(222b) Frank Thomas/SP (Black autograph.) 40.00
(223) Jim Thome/SP (Silver) 40.00
(224) Ozzie Timmons 4.00
(225a) Michael Tucker (Black autograph.) 4.00
(225b) Michael Tucker (Blue autograph.) 4.00
(226) Ismael Valdez 4.00
(227) Jose Valentin 4.00
(228) Todd Van Poppel 4.00
(229) Mo Vaughn/SP 15.00
(230) Quilvio Veras 4.00
(231) Fernando Vina 4.00
(232) Joe Vitiello 4.00
(233) Jose Vizcaino 4.00
(234) Omar Vizquel 12.00
(235) Terrell Wade 4.00
(236) Paul Wagner 4.00
(237) Matt Walbeck 4.00
(238) Jerome Walton 4.00
(239) Turner Ward 4.00
(240) Allen Watson 4.00
(241) David Weathers 4.00
(242) Walt Weiss 4.00
(243) Turk Wendell 4.00
(244) Rondell White 5.00
(245) Brian Williams 4.00
(246) George Williams 4.00
(247) Paul Wilson 4.00
(248) Bobby Witt 4.00
(249) Bob Wolcott 4.00
(250) Eric Young 4.00
(251) Ernie Young 4.00
(252) Gregg Zaun 4.00
--- Frank Thomas (Autographed jumbo edition of 1,500.) 25.00

1996 Leaf/ Signature Series Extended Autographs

Signature Series Extended Autograph cards comprise 30 short-printed stars and top prospects, and 187 other major leaguers. Most players signed 5,000 cards each, while other signees' totals are listed in parentheses. Signature cards for Alex Rodriguez, Juan Gonzalez and Andruw Jones were only available through mail-in redemption. Autographed cards were a different design from Series 1 and were seeded two per pack in Extended. The unnumbered cards are checklisted here in alphabetical order.

NM/M

Common Player: 4.00
Extended Pack: 20.00
Extended Box: 150.00
(1) Scott Aldred 4.00
(2) Mike Aldrete 4.00
(3) Rich Amaral 4.00
(4) Alex Arias 4.00
(5) Paul Assenmacher 4.00
(6) Roger Bailey 4.00
(7) Erik Bennett 4.00
(8) Sean Bergman 4.00
(9) Doug Bochtler 4.00
(10) Tim Bogar 4.00
(11) Pat Borders 4.00
(12) Pedro Borbon 4.00
(13) Shawn Boskie 4.00
(14) Rafael Bournigal 4.00
(15) Mark Brandenburg 4.00
(16) John Briscoe 4.00
(17) Jorge Brito 4.00
(18) Doug Brocail 4.00
(19) Jay Buhner/SP/1,000 17.50
(20) Scott Bullett 4.00
(21) Dave Burba 4.00
(22) Ken Caminiti/ SP/1,000 25.00
(23) John Cangelosi 4.00
(24) Cris Carpenter 4.00
(25) Chuck Carr 4.00
(26) Larry Casian 4.00
(27) Tony Castillo 4.00
(28) Jason Christiansen 4.00
(29) Archi Cianfrocco 4.00
(30) Mark Clark 4.00
(31) Terry Clark 4.00
(32) Roger Clemens/ SP/1,000 150.00
(33) Jim Converse 4.00
(34) Dennis Cook 4.00
(35) Francisco Cordova 4.00
(36) Jim Corsi 4.00
(37) Tim Crabtree 4.00
(38) Doug Creek/SP/1,950 8.00
(39) John Cummings 4.00
(40) Omar Daal 4.00
(41) Rich DeLucia 4.00
(42) Mark Dewey 4.00
(43) Alex Diaz 4.00
(44) Jermaine Dye/ SP/2,500 12.00
(45) Ken Edenfield 4.00
(46) Mark Eichhorn 4.00
(47) John Ericks 4.00
(48) Darin Erstad 10.00
(49) Alvaro Espinoza 4.00
(50) Jorge Fabregas 4.00
(51) Mike Fetters 4.00
(52) John Flaherty 4.00
(53) Bryce Florie 4.00
(54) Tony Fossas 4.00
(55) Lou Frazier 4.00
(56) Mike Gallego 4.00
(57) Karim Garcia/ SP/2,500 6.00
(58) Jason Giambi 12.00
(59) Ed Giovanola 4.00
(60) Tom Glavine/ SP/1,250 40.00
(61) Juan Gonzalez/ SP/1,000 30.00
(61) Juan Gonzalez (Redemption card.) 5.00
(62) Craig Grebeck 4.00
(63) Buddy Groom 4.00
(64) Kevin Gross 4.00
(65) Eddie Guardado 4.00
(66) Mark Guthrie 4.00
(67) Tony Gwynn/ SP/1,000 60.00
(68) Chip Hale 4.00
(69) Darren Hall 4.00
(70) Lee Hancock 4.00
(71) Dave Hansen 4.00
(72) Bryan Harvey 4.00
(73) Bill Haselman 4.00
(74) Mike Henneman 4.00
(75) Doug Henry 4.00
(76) Gil Heredia 4.00
(77) Carlos Hernandez 4.00
(78) Jose Hernandez 4.00
(79) Darren Holmes 4.00
(80) Mark Holzemer 4.00
(81) Rick Honeycutt 4.00
(82) Chris Hook 4.00
(83) Chris Howard 4.00
(84) Jack Howell 4.00
(85) David Hulse 4.00
(86) Edwin Hurtado 4.00
(87) Jeff Huson 4.00
(88) Mike James 4.00
(89) Derek Jeter/ SP/1,000 160.00
(90) Brian Johnson 4.00
(91) Randy Johnson/ SP/1,000 125.00
(92) Mark Johnson 4.00
(93) Andruw Jones/ SP/2,000 30.00
(93) Andruw Jones (Redemption card.) 5.00
(94) Chris Jones 4.00
(95) Ricky Jordan 4.00
(96) Matt Karchner 4.00
(97) Scott Karl 4.00
(98) Jason Kendall/ SP/2,500 10.00
(99) Brian Keyser 4.00
(100) Mike Kingery 4.00
(101) Wayne Kirby 4.00
(102) Ryan Klesko/ SP/1,000 17.50
(103) Chuck Knoblauch/ SP/1,000 15.00
(104) Chad Kreuter 4.00
(105) Tom Lampkin 4.00
(106) Scott Leius 4.00
(107) Jon Lieber 4.00
(108) Nelson Liriano 4.00
(109) Scott Livingstone 4.00
(110) Graeme Lloyd 4.00
(111) Kenny Lofton/ SP/1,000 10.00
(112) Luis Lopez 4.00
(113) Torey Lovullo 4.00
(114) Greg Maddux/ SP/500 250.00
(115) Mike Maddux 4.00
(116) Dave Magadan 4.00
(117) Mike Magnante 4.00
(118) Joe Magrane 4.00
(119) Pat Mahomes 4.00
(120) Matt Mantei 4.00
(121) John Marzano 4.00
(122) Terry Matthews 4.00
(123) Chuck McElroy 4.00
(124) Fred McGriff/ SP/1,000 35.00
(125) Mark McLemore 4.00
(126) Greg McMichael 4.00
(127) Blas Minor 4.00
(128) Dave Mlicki 4.00
(129) Mike Mohler 4.00
(130) Paul Molitor/ SP/1,000 25.00
(131) Steve Montgomery 4.00
(132) Mike Mordecai 4.00
(133) Mike Morgan 4.00
(134) Mike Munoz 4.00
(135) Greg Myers 4.00
(136) Jimmy Myers 4.00
(137) Mike Myers 4.00
(138) Bob Natal 4.00
(139) Dan Naulty 4.00
(140) Jeff Nelson 4.00
(141) Warren Newson 4.00
(142) Chris Nichting 4.00
(143) Melvin Nieves 4.00
(144) Charlie O'Brien 4.00
(145) Alex Ochoa 4.00
(146) Omar Olivares 4.00
(147) Joe Oliver 4.00
(148) Lance Painter 4.00
(149) Rafael Palmeiro/ SP/2,000 35.00
(150) Mark Parent 4.00
(151) Steve Parris/SP/1,800 7.50
(152) Bob Patterson 4.00
(153) Tony Pena 7.50
(154) Eddie Perez 4.00
(155) Yorkis Perez 4.00
(156) Robert Person 4.00
(157) Mark Petkovsek 4.00
(158) Andy Pettitte/ SP/1,000 60.00
(159) J.R. Phillips 4.00
(160) Hipolito Pichardo 4.00
(161) Eric Plunk 4.00
(162) Jimmy Poole 4.00
(163) Kirby Puckett/ SP/1,000 80.00
(164) Paul Quantrill 4.00
(165) Tom Quinlan 4.00
(166) Jeff Reboulet 4.00
(167) Jeff Reed 4.00
(168) Steve Reed 4.00
(169) Carlos Reyes 4.00
(170) Bill Risley 4.00
(171) Kevin Ritz 4.00
(172) Kevin Roberson 4.00
(173) Rich Robertson 4.00
(174) Alex Rodriguez/ SP/500 180.00
(174) Alex Rodriguez (Redemption card.) 15.00
(175) Ivan Rodriguez/ SP/1,250 40.00
(176) Bruce Ruffin 4.00
(177) Juan Samuel 4.00
(178) Tim Scott 4.00
(179) Kevin Sefcik 4.00
(180) Jeff Shaw 4.00
(181) Danny Sheaffer 4.00
(182) Craig Shipley 4.00
(183) Dave Silvestri 4.00
(184) Aaron Small 4.00
(185) John Smoltz/ SP/1,000 90.00
(186) Luis Sojo 4.00
(187) Sammy Sosa/ SP/1,000 160.00
(188) Steve Sparks 4.00
(189) Tim Spehr 4.00
(190) Russ Springer 4.00
(191) Matt Stairs 4.00
(192) Andy Stankiewicz 4.00
(193) Mike Stanton 4.00
(194) Kelly Stinnett 4.00
(195) Doug Strange 4.00
(196) Mark Sweeney 4.00
(197) Jeff Tabaka 4.00
(198) Jesus Tavarez 4.00
(199) Frank Thomas/ SP/1,000 45.00
(200) Larry Thomas 4.00
(201) Mark Thompson 4.00
(202) Mike Timlin 4.00
(203) Steve Trachsel 4.00
(204) Tom Urbani 4.00
(205) Julio Valera 4.00
(206) Dave Valle 4.00
(207) William Van Landingham 4.00
(208) Mo Vaughn/ SP/1,000 10.00
(209) Dave Veres 4.00
(210) Ed Vosberg 4.00
(211) Don Wengert 4.00
(212) Matt Whiteside 4.00
(213) Bob Wickman 4.00
(214) Matt Williams/ SP/1,250 12.00
(215) Mike Williams 4.00
(216) Woody Williams 4.00
(217) Craig Worthington 4.00
--- Frank Thomas (Autographed jumbo edition of 1,500.) 30.00

Extended Autographs - Century Marks

Century Marks represent the first 100 autographs by the 30 short-printed stars and prospects, plus Alex Ochoa. These are designated with a blue holographic foil "Century Marks" logo. Cards of Gonzalez, Jeter, Andruw Jones, Palmeiro and Ivan Rodriguez were available only via mail-in redemption cards.

NM/M

Common Player: 15.00
(1) Jay Buhner 30.00
(2) Ken Caminiti 30.00
(3) Roger Clemens 250.00
(4) Jermaine Dye 30.00
(5) Darin Erstad 45.00
(6) Karim Garcia 30.00
(7) Jason Giambi 75.00
(8) Tom Glavine 90.00
(9) Juan Gonzalez 90.00
(9) Juan Gonzalez (Redemption card.) 7.50
(10) Tony Gwynn 150.00
(11) Derek Jeter 350.00
(11) Derek Jeter (Redemption card.) 15.00
(12) Randy Johnson 185.00
(13) Andruw Jones 150.00
(13) Andruw Jones (Redemption card.) 7.50
(14) Jason Kendall 30.00
(15) Ryan Klesko 30.00
(16) Chuck Knoblauch 30.00
(17) Kenny Lofton 30.00
(18) Greg Maddux 200.00
(19) Fred McGriff 30.00
(20) Paul Molitor 110.00
(21) Alex Ochoa 15.00
(22) Rafael Palmeiro 110.00
(22) Rafael Palmeiro (Redemption card.) 7.50
(23) Andy Pettitte 75.00
(24) Kirby Puckett 185.00
(25) Alex Rodriguez 350.00
(25) Alex Rodriguez (Redemption card.) 15.00
(26) Ivan Rodriguez 100.00
(27) John Smoltz 100.00
(28) Sammy Sosa 350.00
(29) Frank Thomas 135.00
(30) Mo Vaughn 30.00
(31) Matt Williams 30.00

Frank Thomas The Big Heart

In one of several specialty card charitable endeavors, Frank Thomas and Leaf teamed up to issue this set as a fund raiser for "The Big Hurt's" charitable foundation. Each of the cards was available in an edition limited to 3,500 each for a $20 donation. Cards are standard 2-1/2" x 3-1/2" with posed photos on front and "THE BIG HEART," a play on his nickname. Backs have information on the foundation.

NM/M

Complete Set (4): 35.00
Common Card: 10.00
(1) Frank Thomas (Bat on shoulder.) 10.00
(2) Frank Thomas (Holding glove.) 10.00
(3) Frank Thomas (Horizontal) 10.00
(4) Frank Thomas (Seated) 10.00

1997 Leaf

Leaf produced a 400-card set in two series in 1997. The cards feature a grey border with the player photo vignetted at center. The player's name, team and a Leaf logo are displayed at bottom in silver foil. A team logo is in the upper-right corner. Besides the base cards, 10-card packs retailing for $2.99 could contain one of the following inserts: Banner Season, Dress for Success, Get-A-Grip, Knot-hole Gang, Statistical Standouts, Fractal Matrix or Fractal Matrix Die-cut.

NM/M

Complete Set (400): 25.00
Common Player: .05
Jackie Robinson 1948 Leaf Reprint: 10.00
Series 1 Pack (12): 2.00
Series 1 Wax Box (18): 30.00
Series 2 Pack (12): 1.50
Series 2 Wax Box (24): 30.00
1 Wade Boggs 1.50

2 Brian McRae .05
3 Jeff D'Amico .05
4 George Arias .05
5 Billy Wagner .05
6 Ray Lankford .05
7 Will Clark .10
8 Edgar Renteria .05
9 Alex Ochoa .05
10 Roberto Hernandez .05
11 Joe Carter .05
12 Gregg Jefferies .05
13 Mark Grace .05
14 Roberto Alomar .10
15 Joe Randa .05
16 Alex Rodriguez 2.50
17 Tony Gwynn 1.50
18 Steve Gibralter .05
19 Scott Stahoviak .05
20 Matt Williams .05
21 Quinton McCracken .05
22 Ugueth Urbina .05
23 Jermaine Allensworth .05
24 Paul Molitor .75
25 Carlos Delgado .50
26 Bob Abreu .05
27 John Jaha .05
28 Rusty Greer .05
29 Kimera Bartee .05
30 Ruben Rivera .05
31 Jason Kendall .05
32 Lance Johnson .05
33 Robin Ventura .05
34 Kevin Appier .05
35 John Mabry .05
36 Ricky Otero .05
37 Mike Lansing .05
38 Mark McGwire 2.50
39 Tim Naehring .05
40 Tom Glavine .30
41 Rey Ordonez .05
42 Tony Clark .05
43 Rafael Palmeiro .65
44 Pedro Martinez .75
45 Keith Lockhart .05
46 Dan Wilson .05
47 John Wetteland .05
48 Chan Ho Park .05
49 Gary Sheffield .40
50 Shawn Estes .05
51 Royce Clayton .05
52 Jaime Navarro .05
53 Raul Casanova .05
54 Jeff Bagwell 1.00
55 Barry Larkin .05
56 Charles Nagy .05
57 Ken Caminiti .05
58 Todd Hollandsworth .05
59 Pat Hentgen .05
60 Jose Valentin .05
61 Frank Rodriguez .05
62 Mickey Tettleton .05
63 Marty Cordova .05
64 Cecil Fielder .05
65 Barry Bonds 3.00
66 Scott Servais .05
67 Ernie Young .05
68 Wilson Alvarez .05
69 Mike Grace .05
70 Shane Reynolds .05
71 Henry Rodriguez .05
72 Eric Karros .05
73 Mark Langston .05
74 Scott Karl .05
75 Trevor Hoffman .05
76 Orel Hershiser .05
77 John Smoltz .05
78 Raul Mondesi .05
79 Jeff Brantley .05
80 Donne Wall .05
81 Joey Cora .05
82 Mel Rojas .05
83 Chad Mottola .05
84 Omar Vizquel .05
85 Greg Maddux 1.50
86 Jamey Wright .05
87 Chuck Finley .05
88 Brady Anderson .05
89 Alex Gonzalez .05
90 Andy Benes .05
91 Reggie Jefferson .05
92 Paul O'Neill .05
93 Javier Lopez .05
94 Mark Grudzielanek .05
95 Marc Newfield .05
96 Kevin Ritz .05
97 Fred McGriff .05
98 Dwight Gooden .05
99 Hideo Nomo .65
100 Steve Finley .05
101 Juan Gonzalez .65
102 Jay Buhner .05
103 Paul Wilson .05
104 Alan Benes .05
105 Manny Ramirez 1.00
106 Kevin Elster .05
107 Frank Thomas 1.00
108 Orlando Miller .05
109 Ramon Martinez .05
110 Kenny Lofton .05
111 Bernie Williams .05
112 Robby Thompson .05
113 Bernard Gilkey .05
114 Ray Durham .05
115 Jeff Cirillo .05
116 Brian Jordan .05
117 Rich Becker .05
118 Al Leiter .05
119 Mark Johnson .05
120 Ellis Burks .05
121 Sammy Sosa 2.00
122 Willie Greene .05
123 Michael Tucker .05
124 Eddie Murray .75
125 Joey Hamilton .05
126 Antonio Osuna .05
127 Bobby Higginson .05
128 Tomas Perez .05
129 Tim Salmon .05
130 Mark Wohlers .05
131 Charles Johnson .05
132 Randy Johnson .75
133 Brooks Kieschnick .05
134 Al Martin .05
135 Dante Bichette .05
136 Andy Pettitte .30
137 Jason Giambi .60
138 James Baldwin .05
139 Ben McDonald .05
140 Shawn Green .35
141 Geronimo Berroa .05
142 Jose Offerman .05
143 Curtis Pride .05
144 Terrell Wade .05
145 Ismael Valdes .05
146 Mike Mussina .40
147 Mariano Rivera .15
148 Ken Hill .05
149 Darin Erstad .25
150 Jay Bell .05
151 Mo Vaughn .05
152 Ozzie Smith 1.50
153 Jose Mesa .05
154 Osvaldo Fernandez .05
155 Vinny Castilla .05
156 Jason Isringhausen .05
157 B.J. Surhoff .05
158 Robert Perez .05
159 Ron Coomer .05
160 Darren Oliver .05
161 Mike Mohler .05
162 Russ Davis .05
163 Bret Boone .05
164 Ricky Bottalico .05
165 Derek Jeter 3.00
166 Orlando Merced .05
167 John Valentin .05
168 Andruw Jones 1.00
169 Angel Echevarria .05
170 Todd Walker .05
171 Desi Relaford .05
172 Trey Beamon .05
173 Brian Giles **RC** .75
174 Scott Rolen .60
175 Shannon Stewart .05
176 Dmitri Young .05
177 Justin Thompson .05
178 Trot Nixon .05
179 Josh Booty .05
180 Robin Jennings .05
181 Marvin Benard .05
182 Luis Castillo .05
183 Wendell Magee .05
184 Vladimir Guerrero 1.00
185 Nomar Garciaparra 2.00
186 Ryan Hancock .05
187 Mike Cameron .05
188 Cal Ripken Jr. (Legacy) 1.50
189 Chipper Jones (Legacy) .75
190 Albert Belle (Legacy) .05
191 Mike Piazza (Legacy) 1.00
192 Chuck Knoblauch (Legacy) .05
193 Ken Griffey Jr. (Legacy) 1.00
194 Ivan Rodriguez (Legacy) .30
195 Jose Canseco (Legacy) .25
196 Ryne Sandberg (Legacy) .75
197 Jim Thome (Legacy) .30
198 Andy Pettitte (Checklist) .05
199 Andruw Jones (Checklist) .50
200 Derek Jeter (Checklist) 1.50
201 Chipper Jones 1.50
202 Albert Belle .05
203 Mike Piazza 2.00
204 Ken Griffey Jr. 2.00
205 Ryne Sandberg 1.50
206 Jose Canseco .40
207 Chili Davis .05
208 Roger Clemens 2.00
209 Deion Sanders .05
210 Darryl Hamilton .05
211 Jermaine Dye .05
212 Matt Williams .05
213 Kevin Elster .05
214 John Wetteland .05
215 Garret Anderson .05
216 Kevin Brown .05
217 Matt Lawton .05
218 Cal Ripken Jr. 3.00
219 Moises Alou .05
220 Chuck Knoblauch .05
221 Ivan Rodriguez .65
222 Travis Fryman .05
223 Jim Thome .65
224 Eddie Murray .75
225 Eric Young .05
226 Ron Gant .05
227 Tony Phillips .05
228 Reggie Sanders .05
229 Johnny Damon .35
230 Bill Pulsipher .05
231 Jim Edmonds .05
232 Melvin Nieves .05
233 Ryan Klesko .05
234 David Cone .05
235 Derek Bell .05
236 Julio Franco .05
237 Juan Guzman .05
238 Larry Walker .05
239 Delino DeShields .05
240 Troy Percival .05
241 Andres Galarraga .05
242 Rondell White .05
243 John Burkett .05
244 J.T. Snow .05
245 Alex Fernandez .05
246 Edgar Martinez .05
247 Craig Biggio .05
248 Todd Hundley .05
249 Jimmy Key .05
250 Cliff Floyd .05
251 Jeff Conine .05
252 Curt Schilling .35
253 Jeff King .05
254 Tino Martinez .05
255 Carlos Baerga .05
256 Jeff Fassero .05
257 Dean Palmer .05
258 Robb Nen .05
259 Sandy Alomar Jr. .05
260 Carlos Perez .05
261 Rickey Henderson .75
262 Bobby Bonilla .05
263 Darren Daulton .05
264 Jim Leyritz .05
265 Dennis Martinez .05
266 Butch Huskey .05
267 Joe Vitiello .05
268 Steve Trachsel .05
269 Glenallen Hill .05
270 Terry Steinbach .05
271 Mark McLemore .05
272 Devon White .05
273 Jeff Kent .05
274 Tim Raines .05
275 Carlos Garcia .05
276 Hal Morris .05
277 Gary Gaetti .05
278 John Olerud .05
279 Wally Joyner .05
280 Brian Hunter .05
281 Steve Karsay .05
282 Denny Neagle .05
283 Jose Herrera .05
284 Todd Stottlemyre .05
285 Bip Roberts .05
286 Kevin Seitzer .05
287 Benji Gil .05
288 Dennis Eckersley .65
289 Brad Ausmus .05
290 Otis Nixon .05
291 Darryl Strawberry .05
292 Marquis Grissom .05
293 Darryl Kile .05
294 Quilvio Veras .05
295 Tom Goodwin .05
296 Benito Santiago .05
297 Mike Bordick .05
298 Roberto Kelly .05
299 David Justice .05
300 Carl Everett .05
301 Mark Whiten .05
302 Aaron Sele .05
303 Darren Dreifort .05
304 Bobby Jones .05
305 Fernando Vina .05
306 Ed Sprague .05
307 Andy Ashby .05
308 Tony Fernandez .05
309 Roger Pavlik .05
310 Mark Clark .05
311 Mariano Duncan .05
312 Tyler Houston .05
313 Eric Davis .05
314 Greg Vaughn .05
315 David Segui .05
316 Dave Nilsson .05
317 F.P. Santangelo .05
318 Wilton Guerrero .05
319 Jose Guillen .05
320 Kevin Orie .05
321 Derrek Lee .05
322 Bubba Trammell **RC** .50
323 Pokey Reese .05
324 Hideki Irabu **RC** .25
325 Scott Spiezio .05
326 Bartolo Colon .05
327 Damon Mashore .05
328 Ryan McGuire .05
329 Chris Carpenter .05
330 Jose Cruz Jr. **RC** .50
331 Todd Greene .05
332 Brian Moehler .05
333 Mike Sweeney .05
334 Neifi Perez .05
335 Matt Morris .05
336 Marvin Benard .05
337 Karim Garcia .05
338 Jason Dickson .05
339 Brant Brown .05
340 Jeff Suppan .05
341 Deivi Cruz **RC** .25
342 Antone Williamson .05
343 Curtis Goodwin .05
344 Brooks Kieschnick .05
345 Tony Womack **RC** .25
346 Rudy Pemberton .05
347 Todd Dunwoody .05
348 Frank Thomas (Legacy) .50
349 Andruw Jones (Legacy) .50
350 Alex Rodriguez (Legacy) 1.25
351 Greg Maddux (Legacy) .75
352 Jeff Bagwell (Legacy) .50
353 Juan Gonzalez (Legacy) .35
354 Barry Bonds (Legacy) 1.50
355 Mark McGwire (Legacy) 1.25
356 Tony Gwynn (Legacy) .75
357 Gary Sheffield (Legacy) .25
358 Derek Jeter (Legacy) 1.50
359 Manny Ramirez (Legacy) .50
360 Hideo Nomo (Legacy) .30
361 Sammy Sosa (Legacy) 1.00
362 Paul Molitor (Legacy) .40
363 Kenny Lofton (Legacy) .05
364 Eddie Murray (Legacy) .40
365 Barry Larkin (Legacy) .05
366 Roger Clemens (Legacy) 1.00
367 John Smoltz (Legacy) .05
368 Alex Rodriguez (Gamers) 1.50
369 Frank Thomas (Gamers) .40
370 Cal Ripken Jr. (Gamers) 1.50
371 Ken Griffey Jr. (Gamers) 1.50
372 Greg Maddux (Gamers) 1.00
373 Mike Piazza (Gamers) 1.25
374 Chipper Jones (Gamers) 1.00
375 Albert Belle (Gamers) .05
376 Chuck Knoblauch (Gamers) .05
377 Brady Anderson (Gamers) .05
378 David Justice (Gamers) .05
379 Randy Johnson (Gamers) .40
380 Wade Boggs (Gamers) .75
381 Kevin Brown (Gamers) .05
382 Tom Glavine (Gamers) .05
383 Raul Mondesi (Gamers) .05
384 Ivan Rodriguez (Gamers) .30
385 Larry Walker (Gamers) .05
386 Bernie Williams (Gamers) .05
387 Rusty Greer (Gamers) .05
388 Rafael Palmeiro (Gamers) .05
389 Matt Williams (Gamers) .05
390 Eric Young (Gamers) .05
391 Fred McGriff (Gamers) .05
392 Ken Caminiti (Gamers) .05
393 Roberto Alomar (Gamers) .05
394 Brian Jordan (Gamers) .05
395 Mark Grace (Gamers) .05
396 Jim Edmonds (Gamers) .05
397 Deion Sanders (Gamers) .05
398 Checklist (Vladimir Guerrero) .50
399 Checklist (Darin Erstad) .10
400 Checklist (Nomar Garciaparra) 1.00

Fractal Matrix

Leaf introduced Fractal Matrix inserts, a 400-card parallel set broken down into three colors and three unique die-cuts. One "fracture" breaks the insert set down by foil background color (80 Gold, 120 Silver and 200 Bronze). A second fracture breaks those cards down into X, Y and Z "axis" variations. There are no markings on the cards to segregate the X, Y and Z groups, though that information was printed on the box bottoms. No production numbers or insert ratios were released for either fracture. Each player is available in only one color/axis combination. The incredibly convoluted nature of the issue insured that virtually nobody understood the concept, putting a damper on collector interest.

NM/M
Common Bronze: .35
Common Silver: .50
Common Gold: 1.25
1 Wade Boggs G/Y 8.00
2 Brian McRae B/Y .35
3 Jeff D'Amico B/Y .35
4 George Arias S/Y .50
5 Billy Wagner S/Y .50
6 Ray Lankford B/Z .35
7 Will Clark S/Y .60
8 Edgar Renteria S/Y .50
9 Alex Ochoa S/Y .50
10 Roberto Hernandez B/X .35
11 Joe Carter S/Y .50
12 Gregg Jefferies B/Y .35
13 Mark Grace S/Y .75
14 Roberto Alomar G/Y 2.00
15 Joe Randa B/X .35
16 Alex Rodriguez G/Z 10.00
17 Tony Gwynn G/Z 6.00
18 Steve Gibralter B/Y .35
19 Scott Stahoviak B/X .35
20 Matt Williams S/Z .50
21 Quinton McCracken B/Y .35
22 Ugueth Urbina B/X .35
23 Jermaine Allensworth S/X .50
24 Paul Molitor G/X 5.00
25 Carlos Delgado S/Y 1.00
26 Bob Abreu S/Y .50
27 John Jaha S/Y .50
28 Rusty Greer S/Z .50
29 Kimera Bartee B/X .35
30 Ruben Rivera S/Y .50
31 Jason Kendall S/Y .50
32 Lance Johnson B/X .35
33 Robin Ventura B/Y .35
34 Kevin Appier S/X .50
35 John Mabry S/Y .50
36 Ricky Otero B/X .35
37 Mike Lansing B/X .35
38 Mark McGwire G/Z 10.00
39 Tim Naehring B/X .35
40 Tom Glavine S/Z 1.00
41 Rey Ordonez S/Y .50
42 Tony Clark S/Y .50
43 Rafael Palmeiro S/Z 2.00
44 Pedro Martinez B/X 2.00
45 Keith Lockhart B/X .35
46 Dan Wilson B/Y .35
47 John Wetteland B/Y .35
48 Chan Ho Park B/X .35
49 Gary Sheffield G/Z 3.00
50 Shawn Estes B/X .35
51 Royce Clayton B/X .35
52 Jaime Navarro B/X .35
53 Raul Casanova B/X .35
54 Jeff Bagwell G/Z 5.00
55 Barry Larkin G/X 1.25
56 Charles Nagy B/Y .35
57 Ken Caminiti G/Y 1.25
58 Todd Hollandsworth S/Z .50
59 Pat Hentgen S/X .50
60 Jose Valentin B/X .35
61 Frank Rodriguez B/X .35
62 Mickey Tettleton B/X .35
63 Marty Cordova G/X 1.25
64 Cecil Fielder S/X .50
65 Barry Bonds G/Z 13.50
66 Scott Servais B/X .35
67 Ernie Young B/X .35
68 Wilson Alvarez B/X .35
69 Mike Grace B/X .35
70 Shane Reynolds S/X .50
71 Henry Rodriguez S/Y .50
72 Eric Karros B/X .35
73 Mark Langston B/X .35
74 Scott Karl B/X .35
75 Trevor Hoffman B/X .35
76 Orel Hershiser S/X .50
77 John Smoltz G/Y 1.50
78 Raul Mondesi G/Z 1.25
79 Jeff Brantley B/X .35
80 Donne Wall B/X .35
81 Joey Cora B/X .35
82 Mel Rojas B/X .35
83 Chad Mottola B/X .35
84 Omar Vizquel B/X .35
85 Greg Maddux G/Z 6.00
86 Jamey Wright S/Y .50
87 Chuck Finley B/X .35
88 Brady Anderson G/Y 1.25
89 Alex Gonzalez S/X .50
90 Andy Benes B/X .35
91 Reggie Jefferson B/X .35
92 Paul O'Neill B/Y .35
93 Javier Lopez S/X .50
94 Mark Grudzielanek S/X .50
95 Marc Newfield B/X .35
96 Kevin Ritz B/X .35
97 Fred McGriff G/Y 1.25
98 Dwight Gooden S/X .50
99 Hideo Nomo S/Y 1.50
100 Steve Finley B/X .35
101 Juan Gonzalez G/Z 4.00
102 Jay Buhner S/Z .50
103 Paul Wilson S/Y .50
104 Alan Benes B/Y .35
105 Manny Ramirez G/Z 5.00
106 Kevin Elster B/X .35
107 Frank Thomas G/Z 5.00
108 Orlando Miller B/X .35
109 Ramon Martinez B/X .35
110 Kenny Lofton G/Z 1.25
111 Bernie Williams G/Y 1.25
112 Robby Thompson B/X .35
113 Bernard Gilkey B/Z .35
114 Ray Durham B/X .35
115 Jeff Cirillo S/Z .50
116 Brian Jordan G/Z 1.25
117 Rich Becker S/Y .50
118 Al Leiter B/X .35
119 Mark Johnson B/X .35
120 Ellis Burks B/Y .35
121 Sammy Sosa G/Z 7.50
122 Willie Greene B/X .35
123 Michael Tucker B/X .35
124 Eddie Murray G/Y 6.00
125 Joey Hamilton S/Y .50
126 Antonio Osuna B/X .35
127 Bobby Higginson S/Y .50
128 Tomas Perez B/X .35
129 Tim Salmon G/Z 1.25
130 Mark Wohlers B/X .35
131 Charles Johnson S/X .50
132 Randy Johnson S/Y 2.00
133 Brooks Kieschnick S/X .50
134 Al Martin S/Y .50
135 Dante Bichette B/X .35
136 Andy Pettitte G/Z 2.00
137 Jason Giambi G/Y 4.00
138 James Baldwin S/X .50
139 Ben McDonald B/X .35
140 Shawn Green S/X 1.00
141 Geronimo Berroa B/Y .35
142 Jose Offerman B/X .35
143 Curtis Pride B/X .35
144 Terrell Wade B/X .35
145 Ismael Valdes S/X .50
146 Mike Mussina S/Y 1.25
147 Mariano Rivera S/X .75
148 Ken Hill B/Y .35
149 Darin Erstad G/Z 4.00
150 Jay Bell B/X .35
151 Mo Vaughn G/Z 1.25
152 Ozzie Smith G/Y 8.00
153 Jose Mesa B/X .35
154 Osvaldo Fernandez B/X .35
155 Vinny Castilla B/Y .35
156 Jason Isringhausen S/Y .50
157 B.J. Surhoff B/X .35
158 Robert Perez B/X .35
159 Ron Coomer B/X .35
160 Darren Oliver B/X .35
161 Mike Mohler B/X .35
162 Russ Davis B/X .35
163 Bret Boone B/X .35
164 Ricky Bottalico B/X .35
165 Derek Jeter G/Z 13.50
166 Orlando Merced B/X .35
167 John Valentin B/X .35
168 Andruw Jones G/Z 5.00
169 Angel Echevarria B/X .35
170 Todd Walker G/Z 1.25
171 Desi Relaford B/Y .35
172 Trey Beamon S/X .50
173 Brian Giles S/Y .50
174 Scott Rolen G/Z 3.50
175 Shannon Stewart S/Z .50
176 Dmitri Young G/Z 1.25
177 Justin Thompson B/X .35
178 Trot Nixon S/Y .50
179 Josh Booty S/Y .50
180 Robin Jennings B/X .35
181 Marvin Benard B/X .35
182 Luis Castillo B/Y .35
183 Wendell Magee B/X .35
184 Vladimir Guerrero G/X 5.00
185 Nomar Garciaparra G/X 12.50
186 Ryan Hancock B/X .35
187 Mike Cameron S/X .50
188 Cal Ripken Jr. B/Z (Legacy) 5.00
189 Chipper Jones S/Z (Legacy) 4.00
190 Albert Belle S/Z (Legacy) 1.00
191 Mike Piazza B/Z (Legacy) 4.00
192 Chuck Knoblauch S/Y (Legacy) .50
193 Ken Griffey Jr. B/Z (Legacy) 3.50
194 Ivan Rodriguez G/Z (Legacy) 4.00
195 Jose Canseco S/X (Legacy) 1.25
196 Ryne Sandberg S/X (Legacy) 3.00
197 Jim Thome G/Y (Legacy) 1.50
198 Checklist (Andy Pettitte B/Y) .75
199 Checklist (Andruw Jones B/Y) 2.00
200 Checklist (Derek Jeter S/Y) 2.00
201 Chipper Jones G/X 10.00
202 Albert Belle G/Y 1.25
203 Mike Piazza G/Y 12.00
204 Ken Griffey Jr. G/X 15.00
205 Ryne Sandberg G/Z 6.00
206 Jose Canseco S/Y .75
207 Chili Davis B/X .35
208 Roger Clemens G/Z 6.50
209 Deion Sanders G/Z 1.50
210 Darryl Hamilton B/X .35
211 Jermaine Dye S/X .50

212 Matt Williams G/Y 1.25
213 Kevin Elster B/X .35
214 John Wetteland S/X .50
215 Garret Anderson G/Z 1.25
216 Kevin Brown G/Y 1.25
217 Matt Lawton S/Y .50
218 Cal Ripken Jr. G/X 16.50
219 Moises Alou G/Y 1.25
220 Chuck Knoblauch G/Z 1.25
221 Ivan Rodriguez G/Y 5.50
222 Travis Fryman B/Y .35
223 Jim Thome G/Z 2.00
224 Eddie Murray S/Z 3.00
225 Eric Young G/Z 1.25
226 Ron Gant S/X .50
227 Tony Phillips B/X .35
228 Reggie Sanders B/Y .35
229 Johnny Damon S/Z 1.00
230 Bill Pulsipher B/X .35
231 Jim Edmonds G/Z 1.25
232 Melvin Nieves B/X .35
233 Ryan Klesko G/Z 1.25
234 David Cone S/X .50
235 Derek Bell B/Y .35
236 Julio Franco S/X .50
237 Juan Guzman B/X .35
238 Larry Walker G/Z 1.25
239 Delino DeShields B/X .35
240 Troy Percival B/Y .35
241 Andres Galarraga G/Z 1.25
242 Rondell White G/Z 1.25
243 John Burkett B/X .35
244 J.T. Snow B/Y .35
245 Alex Fernandez S/Y .50
246 Edgar Martinez G/Z 1.25
247 Craig Biggio G/Z 1.25
248 Todd Hundley G/Y 1.25
249 Jimmy Key S/X .50
250 Cliff Floyd B/Y .35
251 Jeff Conine B/Y .35
252 Curt Schilling B/X .65
253 Jeff King B/X .35
254 Tino Martinez G/Z 1.25
255 Carlos Baerga S/Y .50
256 Jeff Fassero B/Y .35
257 Dean Palmer S/Y .50
258 Robb Nen B/X .35
259 Sandy Alomar Jr. S/Y .50
260 Carlos Perez B/X .35
261 Rickey Henderson S/Y 2.00
262 Bobby Bonilla S/Y .50
263 Darren Daulton B/X .35
264 Jim Leyritz B/X .35
265 Dennis Martinez B/X .35
266 Butch Huskey B/X .35
267 Joe Vitiello S/Y .50
268 Steve Trachsel B/X .35
269 Glenallen Hill B/X .35
270 Terry Steinbach B/X .35
271 Mark McLemore B/X .35
272 Devon White B/X .35
273 Jeff Kent B/X .35
274 Tim Raines B/X .35
275 Carlos Garcia B/X .35
276 Hal Morris B/X .35
277 Gary Gaetti B/X .35
278 John Olerud S/Y .50
279 Wally Joyner B/X .35
280 Brian Hunter S/X .50
281 Steve Karsay B/X .35
282 Denny Neagle S/X .50
283 Jose Herrera B/X .35
284 Todd Stottlemyre B/X .35
285 Bip Roberts S/X .50
286 Kevin Seitzer B/X .35
287 Benji Gil B/X .35
288 Dennis Eckersley S/X .50
289 Brad Ausmus B/X .35
290 Otis Nixon B/X .35
291 Darryl Strawberry B/X .35
292 Marquis Grissom S/Y .50
293 Darryl Kile B/X .35
294 Quilvio Veras B/X .35
295 Tom Goodwin B/X .35
296 Benito Santiago B/X .35
297 Mike Bordick B/X .35
298 Roberto Kelly B/X .35
299 David Justice G/Z 1.25
300 Carl Everett B/X .35
301 Mark Whiten B/X .35
302 Aaron Sele B/X .35
303 Darren Dreifort B/X .35
304 Bobby Jones B/X .35
305 Fernando Vina B/X .35
306 Ed Sprague B/X .35
307 Andy Ashby S/X .50
308 Tony Fernandez B/X .35
309 Roger Pavlik B/X .35
310 Mark Clark B/X .35
311 Mariano Duncan B/X .35
312 Tyler Houston B/X .35
313 Eric Davis S/Y .50
314 Greg Vaughn B/Y .35
315 David Segui S/Y .50
316 Dave Nilsson S/X .50
317 F.P. Santangelo S/X .50
318 Wilton Guerrero G/Z 1.25
319 Jose Guillen G/Z 1.25
320 Kevin Orie S/Y .50
321 Derrek Lee G/Z 2.50
322 Bubba Trammell S/Y .50
323 Pokey Reese G/Z 1.25
324 Hideki Irabu G/X 1.25
325 Scott Spiezio S/Z .50
326 Bartolo Colon G/Z 1.25
327 Damon Mashore S/Y .50
328 Ryan McGuire S/Y .50
329 Chris Carpenter B/X .35
330 Jose Cruz, Jr. G/X 1.25
331 Todd Greene S/Z .50
332 Brian Moehler B/X .35
333 Mike Sweeney B/Y .35
334 Neifi Perez G/Z 1.25
335 Matt Morris S/Y .50
336 Marvin Benard B/Y .35
337 Karim Garcia S/Z .75
338 Jason Dickson S/Y .50
339 Brant Brown S/Y .50
340 Jeff Suppan S/Z .50
341 Deivi Cruz B/X .35
342 Antone Williamson G/Z 1.25
343 Curtis Goodwin B/X .35
344 Brooks Kieschnick S/Y .50
345 Tony Womack B/X .35
346 Rudy Pemberton B/X .35
347 Todd Dunwoody B/X .35
348 Frank Thomas S/Y (Legacy) 2.25
349 Andruw Jones S/X (Legacy) 2.00
350 Alex Rodriguez B/Y (Legacy) 4.00
351 Greg Maddux S/Y (Legacy) 3.00
352 Jeff Bagwell B/Y (Legacy) 2.25
353 Juan Gonzalez S/Y (Legacy) 1.50
354 Barry Bonds B/Y (Legacy) 5.00
355 Mark McGwire B/Y (Legacy) 4.00
356 Tony Gwynn B/Y (Legacy) 3.00
357 Gary Sheffield B/X (Legacy) .75
358 Derek Jeter S/X (Legacy) 4.00
359 Manny Ramirez S/Y (Legacy) 2.00
360 Hideo Nomo G/Z (Legacy) 4.00
361 Sammy Sosa B/X (Legacy) 3.50
362 Paul Molitor S/Z (Legacy) 3.00
363 Kenny Lofton B/Y (Legacy) .35
364 Eddie Murray B/X (Legacy) 2.00
365 Barry Larkin S/Z (Legacy) .50
366 Roger Clemens S/Y (Legacy) 3.50
367 John Smoltz B/Z (Legacy) .35
368 Alex Rodriguez S/X (Gamers) 3.25
369 Frank Thomas B/X (Gamers) 2.25
370 Cal Ripken Jr. S/Y (Gamers) 4.00
371 Ken Griffey Jr. S/Y (Gamers) 3.25
372 Greg Maddux B/X (Gamers) 3.00
373 Mike Piazza S/X (Gamers) 3.25
374 Chipper Jones B/Y (Gamers) 3.00
375 Albert Belle B/X (Gamers) .50
376 Chuck Knoblauch B/X (Gamers) .35
377 Brady Anderson B/Z (Gamers) .35
378 David Justice S/X (Gamers) .50
379 Randy Johnson B/Z (Gamers) 2.00
380 Wade Boggs B/X (Gamers) 3.00
381 Kevin Brown B/X (Gamers) .35
382 Tom Glavine G/Y (Gamers) 3.00
383 Raul Mondesi S/X (Gamers) .50
384 Ivan Rodriguez S/X (Gamers) 1.25
385 Larry Walker B/Y (Gamers) .35
386 Bernie Williams B/Z (Gamers) .45
387 Rusty Greer G/Y (Gamers) 1.25
388 Rafael Palmeiro G/Y (Gamers) 4.50
389 Matt Williams B/X (Gamers) .35
390 Eric Young B/X (Gamers) .35
391 Fred McGriff B/X (Gamers) .35
392 Ken Caminiti B/X (Gamers) .35
393 Roberto Alomar B/Z (Gamers) .75
394 Brian Jordan B/Z (Gamers) .35
395 Mark Grace G/Z (Gamers) 1.25
396 Jim Edmonds B/Y (Gamers) .35
397 Deion Sanders S/Y (Gamers) .50
398 Checklist (Vladimir Guerrero S/Z) 1.25
399 Checklist (Darin Erstad S/Y) 1.00
400 Checklist (Nomar Garciaparra S/Z) 2.00

Fractal Matrix Die-Cut

A second parallel set to the Leaf product, the Fractal Matrix Die-Cuts offer three different die-cut designs with three colors for each. The Axis-X die-cuts comprise 200 players (150 Bronze, 40 Silver and 10 Gold), the Axis-Y die-cuts has 120 players (60 Silver, 40 Bronze, 20 Gold), and the Axis-Z die-cuts consist of 80 players (50 Gold, 20 Silver, 10 Bronze). Odds of finding any of these inserts are 1:6 packs. Each player was issued in only one color/cut combination.

NM/M
Common X- or Y-Axis: .75
Common Z-Axis: 1.25
1 Wade Boggs G/Y 6.00
2 Brian McRae B/Y .75
3 Jeff D'Amico B/Y .75
4 George Arias S/Y .75
5 Billy Wagner S/Y .75
6 Ray Lankford B/Z 1.25
7 Will Clark S/Y .75
8 Edgar Renteria S/Y .75
9 Alex Ochoa S/Y .75
11 Joe Carter S/Y .75
12 Gregg Jefferies B/Y .75
13 Mark Grace S/Y .75
14 Roberto Alomar G/Y 1.50
15 Joe Randa B/X .75
16 Alex Rodriguez G/Z 12.50
17 Tony Gwynn G/Z 7.50
18 Steve Gibralter B/Y .75
19 Scott Stahoviak B/X .75
20 Matt Williams S/Z 1.25
21 Quinton McCracken B/Y .75
22 Ugueth Urbina B/X .75
23 Jermaine Allensworth S/X .75
24 Paul Molitor G/X 5.00
25 Carlos Delgado S/Y 2.00
26 Bob Abreu S/Y .75
27 John Jaha S/Y .75
28 Rusty Greer S/Z 1.25
29 Kimera Bartee B/X .75
30 Ruben Rivera S/Y .75
31 Jason Kendall S/Y .75
32 Lance Johnson B/X .75
33 Robin Ventura B/Y .75
34 Kevin Appier S/X .75
35 John Mabry S/Y .75
36 Ricky Otero B/X .75
37 Mike Lansing B/X .75
38 Mark McGwire G/Z 12.50
39 Tim Naehring B/X .75
40 Tom Glavine S/Z 3.00
41 Rey Ordonez S/Y .75
42 Tony Clark S/Y .75
43 Rafael Palmeiro S/Z 4.00
44 Pedro Martinez B/X 5.00
45 Keith Lockhart B/X .75
46 Dan Wilson B/Y .75
47 John Wetteland B/Y .75
48 Chan Ho Park B/X .75
49 Gary Sheffield G/Z 2.50
50 Shawn Estes B/X .75
51 Royce Clayton B/X .75
52 Jaime Navarro B/X .75
53 Raul Casanova B/X .75
54 Jeff Bagwell G/Z 6.00
55 Barry Larkin G/X .75
56 Charles Nagy B/Y .75
57 Ken Caminiti G/Y .75
58 Todd Hollandsworth S/Z 1.25
59 Pat Hentgen S/X .75
60 Jose Valentin B/X .75
61 Frank Rodriguez B/X .75
62 Mickey Tettleton B/X .75
63 Marty Cordova G/X .75
64 Cecil Fielder S/X .75
65 Barry Bonds G/Z 15.00
66 Scott Servais B/X .75
67 Ernie Young B/X .75
68 Wilson Alvarez B/X .75
69 Mike Grace B/X .75
70 Shane Reynolds S/X .75
71 Henry Rodriguez S/Y .75
72 Eric Karros B/X .75
73 Mark Langston B/X .75
74 Scott Karl B/X .75
75 Trevor Hoffman B/X .75
76 Orel Hershiser S/X .75
77 John Smoltz G/Y .75
78 Raul Mondesi G/Z 1.25
79 Jeff Brantley B/X .75
80 Donne Wall B/X .75
81 Joey Cora B/X .75
82 Mel Rojas B/X .75
83 Chad Mottola B/X .75
84 Omar Vizquel B/X .75
85 Greg Maddux G/Z 7.50
86 Jamey Wright S/Y .75
87 Chuck Finley B/X .75
88 Brady Anderson G/Y .75
89 Alex Gonzalez S/X .75
90 Andy Benes B/X .75
91 Reggie Jefferson B/X .75
92 Paul O'Neill B/Y .75
93 Javier Lopez S/X .75
94 Mark Grudzielanek S/X .75
95 Marc Newfield B/X .75
96 Kevin Ritz B/X .75
97 Fred McGriff G/Y .75
98 Dwight Gooden S/X .75
99 Hideo Nomo S/Y 4.00
100 Steve Finley B/X .75
101 Juan Gonzalez G/Z 4.00
102 Jay Buhner S/Z 1.25
103 Paul Wilson S/Y .75
104 Alan Benes B/Y .75
105 Manny Ramirez G/Z 6.00
106 Kevin Elster B/X .75
107 Frank Thomas G/Z 6.00
108 Orlando Miller B/X .75
109 Ramon Martinez B/X .75
110 Kenny Lofton G/Z 1.25
111 Bernie Williams G/Y .75
112 Robby Thompson B/X .75
113 Bernard Gilkey B/Z 1.25
114 Ray Durham B/X .75
115 Jeff Cirillo S/Z 1.25
116 Brian Jordan G/Z 1.25
117 Rich Becker S/Y .75
118 Al Leiter B/X .75
119 Mark Johnson B/X .75
120 Ellis Burks B/Y .75
121 Sammy Sosa G/Z 9.00
122 Willie Greene B/X .75
123 Michael Tucker B/X .75
124 Eddie Murray G/Y 5.00
125 Joey Hamilton S/Y .75
126 Antonio Osuna B/X .75
127 Bobby Higginson S/Y .75
128 Tomas Perez B/X .75
129 Tim Salmon G/Z 1.25
130 Mark Wohlers B/X .75
131 Charles Johnson S/X .75
132 Randy Johnson S/Y 5.00
133 Brooks Kieschnick S/X .75
134 Al Martin S/Y .75
135 Dante Bichette B/X .75
136 Andy Pettitte G/Z 3.00
137 Jason Giambi G/Y 2.00
138 James Baldwin S/X .75
139 Ben McDonald B/X .75
140 Shawn Green S/X 1.25
141 Geronimo Berroa B/Y .75
142 Jose Offerman B/X .75
143 Curtis Pride B/X .75
144 Terrell Wade B/X .75
145 Ismael Valdes S/X .75
146 Mike Mussina S/Y 2.00
147 Mariano Rivera S/X 1.00
148 Ken Hill B/Y .75
149 Darin Erstad G/Z 2.50
150 Jay Bell B/X .75
151 Mo Vaughn G/Z 1.25
152 Ozzie Smith G/Y 6.00
153 Jose Mesa B/X .75
154 Osvaldo Fernandez B/X .75
155 Vinny Castilla B/Y .75
156 Jason Isringhausen S/Y .75
157 B.J. Surhoff B/X .75
158 Robert Perez B/X .75
159 Ron Coomer B/X .75
160 Darren Oliver B/X .75
161 Mike Mohler B/X .75
162 Russ Davis B/X .75
163 Bret Boone B/X .75
164 Ricky Bottalico B/X .75
165 Derek Jeter G/Z 15.00
166 Orlando Merced B/X .75
167 John Valentin B/X .75
168 Andruw Jones G/Z 6.00
169 Angel Echevarria B/X .75
170 Todd Walker G/Z 1.25
171 Desi Relaford B/Y .75
172 Trey Beamon S/X .75
173 Brian Giles S/Y .75
174 Scott Rolen G/Z 4.00
175 Shannon Stewart S/Z 1.25
176 Dmitri Young G/Z 1.25
177 Justin Thompson B/X .75
178 Trot Nixon S/Y 1.00
179 Josh Booty S/Y .75
180 Robin Jennings B/X .75
181 Marvin Benard B/X .75
182 Luis Castillo B/Y .75
183 Wendell Magee B/X .75
184 Vladimir Guerrero G/X 5.00
185 Nomar Garciaparra G/X 7.50
186 Ryan Hancock B/X .75
187 Mike Cameron S/X .75
188 Cal Ripken Jr. B/Z (Legacy) 15.00
189 Chipper Jones S/Z (Legacy) 7.50
190 Albert Belle S/Z (Legacy) 1.25
191 Mike Piazza B/Z (Legacy) 12.50
192 Chuck Knoblauch S/Y (Legacy) .75
193 Ken Griffey Jr. B/Z (Legacy) 10.00
194 Ivan Rodriguez G/Z (Legacy) 5.00
195 Jose Canseco S/X (Legacy) 1.50
196 Ryne Sandberg S/X (Legacy) 5.00
197 Jim Thome G/Y (Legacy) .75
198 Checklist (Andy Pettitte B/Y) 1.00
199 Checklist (Andruw Jones B/Y) 5.00
200 Checklist (Derek Jeter S/Y) 7.50
201 Chipper Jones G/X 6.00
202 Albert Belle G/Y .75
203 Mike Piazza G/Y 10.00
204 Ken Griffey Jr. G/X 7.50
205 Ryne Sandberg G/Z 6.00
206 Jose Canseco S/Y 1.50
207 Chili Davis B/X .75
208 Roger Clemens G/Z 9.00
209 Deion Sanders G/Z 1.50
210 Darryl Hamilton B/X .75
211 Jermaine Dye S/X .75
212 Matt Williams G/Y .75
213 Kevin Elster B/X .75
214 John Wetteland S/X .75
215 Garret Anderson G/Z 1.25
216 Kevin Brown G/Y .75
217 Matt Lawton S/Y .75
218 Cal Ripken Jr. G/X 12.50
219 Moises Alou G/Y .75
220 Chuck Knoblauch G/Z 1.25
221 Ivan Rodriguez G/Y 4.00
222 Travis Fryman B/Y .75
223 Jim Thome G/Z 2.50
224 Eddie Murray S/Z 6.00
225 Eric Young G/Z 1.25
226 Ron Gant S/X .75
227 Tony Phillips B/X .75
228 Reggie Sanders B/Y .75
229 Johnny Damon S/Z 1.25
230 Bill Pulsipher B/X .75
231 Jim Edmonds G/Z 1.25
232 Melvin Nieves B/X .75
233 Ryan Klesko G/Z 1.25
234 David Cone S/X .75
235 Derek Bell B/Y .75
236 Julio Franco S/X .75
237 Juan Guzman B/X .75
238 Larry Walker G/Z 1.25
239 Delino DeShields B/X .75
240 Troy Percival B/Y .75
241 Andres Galarraga G/Z 1.25
242 Rondell White G/Z 1.25
243 John Burkett B/X .75
244 J.T. Snow B/Y .75
245 Alex Fernandez S/Y .75
246 Edgar Martinez G/Z 1.25
247 Craig Biggio G/Z 1.25
248 Todd Hundley G/Y .75
249 Jimmy Key S/X .75
250 Cliff Floyd B/Y .75
251 Jeff Conine B/Y .75
252 Curt Schilling B/X 1.50
253 Jeff King B/X .75
254 Tino Martinez G/Z 1.25
255 Carlos Baerga S/Y .75
256 Jeff Fassero B/Y .75
257 Dean Palmer S/Y .75
258 Robb Nen B/X .75
259 Sandy Alomar Jr. S/Y .75
260 Carlos Perez B/X .75
261 Rickey Henderson S/Y 5.00
262 Bobby Bonilla S/Y .75
263 Darren Daulton B/X .75
264 Jim Leyritz B/X .75
265 Dennis Martinez B/X .75
266 Butch Huskey B/X .75
267 Joe Vitiello S/Y .75
268 Steve Trachsel B/X .75
269 Glenallen Hill B/X .75
270 Terry Steinbach B/X .75
271 Mark McLemore B/X .75
272 Devon White B/X .75
273 Jeff Kent B/X .75
274 Tim Raines B/X .75
275 Carlos Garcia B/X .75
276 Hal Morris B/X .75
277 Gary Gaetti B/X .75
278 John Olerud S/Y .75
279 Wally Joyner B/X .75
280 Brian Hunter S/X .75
281 Steve Karsay B/X .75
282 Denny Neagle S/X .75
283 Jose Herrera B/X .75
284 Todd Stottlemyre B/X .75
285 Bip Roberts S/X .75
286 Kevin Seitzer B/X .75
287 Benji Gil B/X .75
288 Dennis Eckersley S/X .75
289 Brad Ausmus B/X .75
290 Otis Nixon B/X .75
291 Darryl Strawberry B/X .75
292 Marquis Grissom S/Y .75
293 Darryl Kile B/X .75
294 Quilvio Veras B/X .75
295 Tom Goodwin B/X .75
296 Benito Santiago B/X .75
297 Mike Bordick B/X .75
298 Roberto Kelly B/X .75
299 David Justice G/Z 1.25
300 Carl Everett B/X .75
301 Mark Whiten B/X .75
302 Aaron Sele B/X .75
303 Darren Dreifort B/X .75
304 Bobby Jones B/X .75
305 Fernando Vina B/X .75
306 Ed Sprague B/X .75
307 Andy Ashby S/X .75
308 Tony Fernandez B/X .75
309 Roger Pavlik B/X .75
310 Mark Clark B/X .75
311 Mariano Duncan B/X .75
312 Tyler Houston B/X .75
313 Eric Davis S/Y .75
314 Greg Vaughn B/Y .75
315 David Segui S/Y .75
316 Dave Nilsson S/X .75
317 F.P. Santangelo S/X .75
318 Wilton Guerrero G/Z 1.25
319 Jose Guillen G/Z 1.25
320 Kevin Orie S/Y .75
321 Derrek Lee G/Z 2.50
322 Bubba Trammell S/Y .75
323 Pokey Reese G/Z 1.25
324 Hideki Irabu G/X .75
325 Scott Spiezio S/Z 1.25
326 Bartolo Colon G/Z 1.25
327 Damon Mashore S/Y .75
328 Ryan McGuire S/Y .75
329 Chris Carpenter B/X .75
330 Jose Cruz, Jr. G/X .75
331 Todd Greene S/Z 1.25
332 Brian Moehler B/X .75
333 Mike Sweeney B/Y .75
334 Neifi Perez G/Z 1.25
335 Matt Morris S/Y .75
336 Marvin Benard B/Y .75
337 Karim Garcia S/Z 1.25
338 Jason Dickson S/Y .75
339 Brant Brown S/Y .75
340 Jeff Suppan S/Z 1.25
341 Deivi Cruz B/X .75
342 Antone Williamson G/Z 1.25
343 Curtis Goodwin B/X .75
344 Brooks Kieschnick S/Y .75
345 Tony Womack B/X .75
346 Rudy Pemberton B/X .75
347 Todd Dunwoody B/X .75
348 Frank Thomas S/Y (Legacy) 5.00
349 Andruw Jones S/X (Legacy) 5.00
350 Alex Rodriguez B/Y (Legacy) 10.00
351 Greg Maddux S/Y (Legacy) 6.00
352 Jeff Bagwell B/Y (Legacy) 5.00
353 Juan Gonzalez S/Y (Legacy) 4.00
354 Barry Bonds B/Y (Legacy) 12.50
355 Mark McGwire B/Y (Legacy) 10.00
356 Tony Gwynn B/Y (Legacy) 6.00
357 Gary Sheffield B/X (Legacy) 1.50
358 Derek Jeter S/X (Legacy) 12.50
359 Manny Ramirez S/Y (Legacy) 5.00
360 Hideo Nomo G/Z (Legacy) 4.00
361 Sammy Sosa B/X (Legacy) 6.50
362 Paul Molitor S/Z (Legacy) 6.00
363 Kenny Lofton B/Y (Legacy) .75
364 Eddie Murray B/X (Legacy) 5.00
365 Barry Larkin S/Z (Legacy) 1.25
366 Roger Clemens S/Y (Legacy) 6.50
367 John Smoltz B/Z (Legacy) 1.25
368 Alex Rodriguez S/X (Gamers) 10.00
369 Frank Thomas B/X (Gamers) 5.00
370 Cal Ripken Jr. S/Y (Gamers) 12.50
371 Ken Griffey Jr. S/Y (Gamers) 7.50
372 Greg Maddux B/X (Gamers) 6.00
373 Mike Piazza S/X (Gamers) 10.00
374 Chipper Jones B/Y (Gamers) 6.00
375 Albert Belle B/X (Gamers) .75

376 Chuck Knoblauch B/X (Gamers) .75
377 Brady Anderson B/Z (Gamers) 1.25
378 David Justice S/X Gamers) .75
379 Randy Johnson B/Z (Gamers) 6.00
380 Wade Boggs B/X (Gamers) 6.00
381 Kevin Brown B/X (Gamers) .75
382 Tom Glavine G/Y (Gamers) 2.00
383 Raul Mondesi S/X (Gamers) .75
384 Ivan Rodriguez S/X (Gamers) 4.00
385 Larry Walker B/Y (Gamers) .75
386 Bernie Williams B/Z (Gamers) 1.25
387 Rusty Greer G/Y (Gamers) .75
388 Rafael Palmeiro G/Y (Gamers) 4.00
389 Matt Williams B/X (Gamers) .75
390 Eric Young B/X (Gamers) .75
391 Fred McGriff B/X (Gamers) .75
392 Ken Caminiti B/X (Gamers) .75
393 Roberto Alomar B/Z (Gamers) 2.00
394 Brian Jordan B/X (Gamers) .75
395 Mark Grace G/Z (Gamers) 1.25
396 Jim Edmonds B/Y (Gamers) .75
397 Deion Sanders S/Y (Gamers) .75
398 Checklist (Vladimir Guerrero S/Z) 3.00
399 Checklist (Darin Erstad S/Y) 1.00
400 Checklist (Nomar Garciaparra S/Z) 4.00

Banner Season

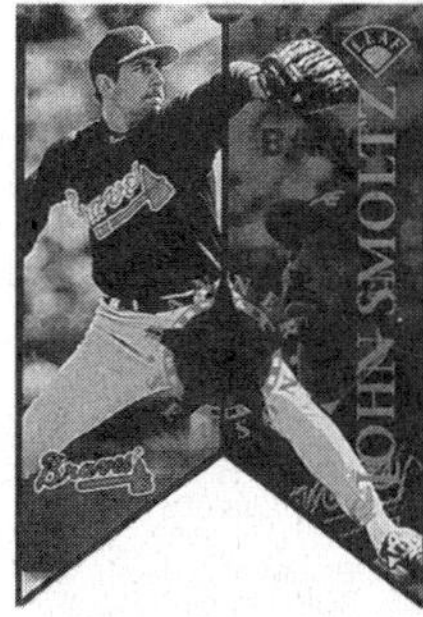

Banner Season was a 15-card insert set that was die-cut and printed on a canvas card stock. Only 2,500 individually numbered sets were produced, with cards only found in pre-priced packs.

	NM/M
Complete Set (15):	30.00
Common Player:	.50
1 Jeff Bagwell	2.50
2 Ken Griffey Jr.	5.00
3 Juan Gonzalez	1.50
4 Frank Thomas	2.50
5 Alex Rodriguez	6.00
6 Kenny Lofton	.50
7 Chuck Knoblauch	.50
8 Mo Vaughn	.50
9 Chipper Jones	4.00
10 Ken Caminiti	.50
11 Craig Biggio	.50
12 John Smoltz	.50
13 Pat Hentgen	.50
14 Derek Jeter	7.50
15 Todd Hollandsworth	.50

Dress for Success

Exclusive to retail packs was an insert called Dress for Success. It included 18 players printed on nylon and flocking card stock. Dress for Success was limited to 3,500 individually numbered sets.

	NM/M
Complete Set (18):	17.50
Common Player:	.25
1 Greg Maddux	1.50
2 Cal Ripken Jr.	3.00
3 Albert Belle	.25
4 Frank Thomas	1.00
5 Dante Bichette	.25
6 Gary Sheffield	.50
7 Jeff Bagwell	1.00
8 Mike Piazza	2.00
9 Mark McGwire	2.25
10 Ken Caminiti	.25
11 Alex Rodriguez	2.50
12 Ken Griffey Jr.	2.00
13 Juan Gonzalez	.75
14 Brian Jordan	.25
15 Mo Vaughn	.25
16 Ivan Rodriguez	.75
17 Andruw Jones	1.00
18 Chipper Jones	1.50

Get-A-Grip

Get a Grip included 16 double-sided cards, with a star hitter on one side and a star pitcher on the other. The card slated the two stars against each other and explained how the hitter would hit against the pitcher, while featuring the pitcher's top pitch. This insert was printed on silver foilboard with the right side die-cut, and limited to 3,500 numbered sets found only in hobby packs.

	NM/M
Complete Set (16):	30.00
Common Card:	1.00
1 Ken Griffey Jr., Greg Maddux	3.00
2 John Smoltz, Frank Thomas	1.50
3 Mike Piazza, Andy Pettitte	3.00
4 Randy Johnson, Chipper Jones	2.50
5 Tom Glavine, Alex Rodriguez	4.00
6 Pat Hentgen, Jeff Bagwell	1.50
7 Kevin Brown, Juan Gonzalez	1.25
8 Barry Bonds, Mike Mussina	5.00
9 Hideo Nomo, Albert Belle	1.25
10 Troy Percival, Andruw Jones	1.50
11 Roger Clemens, Brian Jordan	3.00
12 Paul Wilson, Ivan Rodriguez	1.25
13 Andy Benes, Mo Vaughn	1.00
14 Al Leiter, Derek Jeter	5.00
15 Bill Pulsipher, Cal Ripken Jr.	5.00
16 Mariano Rivera, Ken Caminiti	1.00

Knot-Hole Gang

Knot-Hole Gang pictures 12 hitters viewed through a wood picket fence. Cards are die-cut along the top of the fence and printed on a wood stock. Production was limited

to 5,000 numbered sets. A "SAMPLE" marked promo card exists for each.

	NM/M
Complete Set (12):	18.00
Common Player:	.50
Promos:	2X
1 Chuck Knoblauch	.50
2 Ken Griffey Jr.	3.50
3 Frank Thomas	1.50
4 Tony Gwynn	2.50
5 Mike Piazza	3.50
6 Jeff Bagwell	1.50
7 Rusty Greer	.50
8 Cal Ripken Jr.	5.00
9 Chipper Jones	2.50
10 Ryan Klesko	.50
11 Barry Larkin	.50
12 Paul Molitor	1.50

Leagues of the Nation

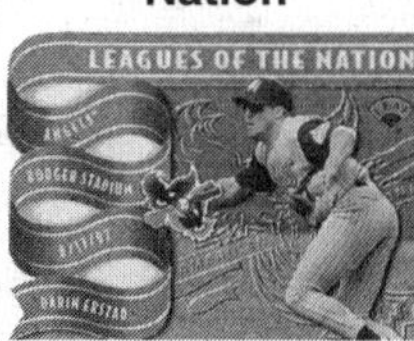

A 15-card insert set featuring a double-sided die-cut design. The players on each card represent matchups from the initial rounds of interleague play. Cards were numbered to 2,500 and feature a flocked texture.

	NM/M
Complete Set (15):	60.00
Common Card:	1.50
1 Juan Gonzalez, Barry Bonds	10.00
2 Cal Ripken Jr., Chipper Jones	10.00
3 Mark McGwire, Ken Caminiti	7.00
4 Derek Jeter, Kenny Lofton	10.00
5 Ivan Rodriguez, Mike Piazza	6.00
6 Ken Griffey Jr., Larry Walker	6.00
7 Frank Thomas, Sammy Sosa	5.00
8 Paul Molitor, Barry Larkin	3.00
9 Albert Belle, Deion Sanders	1.50
10 Matt Williams, Jeff Bagwell	3.00
11 Mo Vaughn, Gary Sheffield	1.50
12 Alex Rodriguez, Tony Gwynn	7.50
13 Tino Martinez, Scott Rolen	2.00
14 Darin Erstad, Wilton Guerrero	2.00
15 Tony Clark, Vladimir Guerrero	3.00

Statistical Standouts

Statistical Standouts were limited to only 1,000 individually numbered sets. Inserts were printed on leather and die-cut. The set included 15 top stars who excelled beyond their competition in many statistical categories.

	NM/M
Complete Set (15):	175.00
Common Player:	4.00
1 Albert Belle	4.00
2 Juan Gonzalez	9.00
3 Ken Griffey Jr.	20.00
4 Alex Rodriguez	25.00
5 Frank Thomas	12.00
6 Chipper Jones	15.00
7 Greg Maddux	15.00
8 Mike Piazza	20.00
9 Cal Ripken Jr.	30.00
10 Mark McGwire	25.00
11 Barry Bonds	30.00
12 Derek Jeter	30.00
13 Ken Caminiti	4.00
14 John Smoltz	4.00
15 Paul Molitor	12.00

Thomas Collection

This six-card insert from Series 2 features pieces of various game-used Frank Thomas items built into the texture of each card. Jerseys, bats, hats, batting gloves and sweatbands are all featured on the various cards, which are numbered to 100 each.

	NM/M
Complete Set (6):	360.00
Common Card:	60.00
1 Frank Thomas/Hat	60.00
2 Frank Thomas/Home Jersey	80.00
3 Frank Thomas/Btg Glove	60.00
4 Frank Thomas/Bat	60.00
5 Frank Thomas/Sweatband	60.00
6 Frank Thomas/Away Jersey	80.00

Warning Track

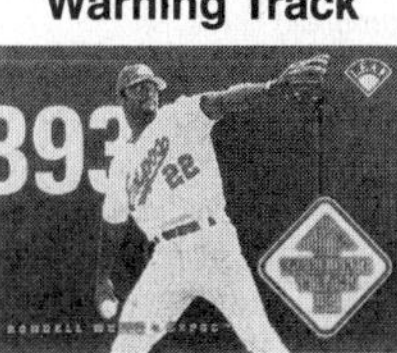

A 12-card insert printed on embossed canvas depicting players who are known for making tough catches. Cards were numbered to 3,500.

	NM/M
Complete Set (18):	40.00
Common Player:	1.00
1 Ken Griffey Jr.	6.00
2 Albert Belle	1.00
3 Barry Bonds	7.50
4 Andruw Jones	4.00
5 Kenny Lofton	1.00
6 Tony Gwynn	5.00
7 Manny Ramirez	4.00
8 Rusty Greer	1.00
9 Bernie Williams	1.00
10 Gary Sheffield	2.00
11 Juan Gonzalez	2.50
12 Raul Mondesi	1.00
13 Brady Anderson	1.00
14 Rondell White	1.00
15 Sammy Sosa	6.00
16 Deion Sanders	1.00
17 David Justice	1.00
18 Jim Edmonds	1.00

22kt Gold Stars

A 36-card insert from Series II Leaf, each card features a special 22-K. gold foil em-

bossed stamp on front which is printed on gold foil cardboard. Horizontal backs have a portrait photo on a dark background and are serially numbered to a limit of 2,500 each.

	NM/M
Complete Set (36):	115.00
Common Player:	1.00
1 Frank Thomas	4.00
2 Alex Rodriguez	8.00
3 Ken Griffey Jr.	6.50
4 Andruw Jones	4.00
5 Chipper Jones	5.50
6 Jeff Bagwell	4.00
7 Derek Jeter	10.00
8 Deion Sanders	1.00
9 Ivan Rodriguez	3.50
10 Juan Gonzalez	3.00
11 Greg Maddux	5.50
12 Andy Pettitte	2.50
13 Roger Clemens	6.00
14 Hideo Nomo	3.00
15 Tony Gwynn	5.50
16 Barry Bonds	10.00
17 Kenny Lofton	1.00
18 Paul Molitor	4.00
19 Jim Thome	3.00
20 Albert Belle	1.00
21 Cal Ripken Jr.	10.00
22 Mark McGwire	8.00
23 Barry Larkin	1.00
24 Mike Piazza	6.50
25 Darin Erstad	2.00
26 Chuck Knoblauch	1.00
27 Vladimir Guerrero	4.00
28 Tony Clark	1.00
29 Scott Rolen	3.00
30 Nomar Garciaparra	6.50
31 Eric Young	1.00
32 Ryne Sandberg	5.50
33 Roberto Alomar	2.00
34 Eddie Murray	4.00
35 Rafael Palmeiro	3.50
36 Jose Guillen	1.00

1998 Leaf

The 50th Anniversary edition of Leaf Baseball consists of a 200-card base set with three subsets, three parallels and four inserts. The base set has 148 regular cards, a 10-card Curtain Calls subset, Gold Leaf Stars subset (20 cards), Gold Leaf Rookies subset (20 cards) and three checklists. The subsets cards #148-197 are short-printed in relation to the rest of the set. Card #42 does not exist because Leaf retired the number in honor of Jackie Robinson. The base set was paralleled in Fractal Matrix, Fractal Matrix Die-Cuts and Fractal Diamond Axis. Inserts include Crusade, Heading for the Hall, State Representatives and Statistical Standouts.

	NM/M
Complete Set (200):	40.00
Common Player:	.05
Common SP (#148-197):	.40
Pack (10):	2.00
Wax Box (24):	40.00
1 Rusty Greer	.05
2 Tino Martinez	.05
3 Bobby Bonilla	.05
4 Jason Giambi	.50
5 Matt Morris	.05
6 Craig Counsell	.05
7 Reggie Jefferson	.05
8 Brian Rose	.05
9 Ruben Rivera	.05
10 Shawn Estes	.05
11 Tony Gwynn	1.00
12 Jeff Abbott	.05
13 Jose Cruz Jr.	.05
14 Francisco Cordova	.05
15 Ryan Klesko	.05
16 Tim Salmon	.05
17 Brett Tomko	.05
18 Matt Williams	.05
19 Joe Carter	.05
20 Harold Baines	.05
21 Gary Sheffield	.50
22 Charles Johnson	.05
23 Aaron Boone	.05
24 Eddie Murray	.75
25 Matt Stairs	.05
26 David Cone	.05
27 Jon Nunnally	.05
28 Chris Stynes	.05
29 Enrique Wilson	.05
30 Randy Johnson	.75
31 Garret Anderson	.05
32 Manny Ramirez	.75
33 Jeff Suppan	.05
34 Rickey Henderson	.75
35 Scott Spiezio	.05
36 Rondell White	.05
37 Todd Greene	.05
38 Delino DeShields	.05
39 Kevin Brown	.05
40 Chili Davis	.05
41 Jimmy Key	.05
43 Mike Mussina	.40
44 Joe Randa	.05
45 Chan Ho Park	.05
46 Brad Radke	.05
47 Geronimo Berroa	.05
48 Wade Boggs	1.00
49 Kevin Appier	.05
50 Moises Alou	.05
51 David Justice	.05
52 Ivan Rodriguez	.65
53 J.T. Snow	.05
54 Brian Giles	.05
55 Will Clark	.10
56 Justin Thompson	.05
57 Javier Lopez	.05
58 Hideki Irabu	.05
59 Mark Grudzielanek	.05
60 Abraham Nunez	.05
61 Todd Hollandsworth	.05
62 Jay Bell	.05
63 Nomar Garciaparra	1.25
64 Vinny Castilla	.05
65 Lou Collier	.05
66 Kevin Orie	.05
67 John Valentin	.05
68 Robin Ventura	.05
69 Denny Neagle	.05
70 Tony Womack	.05
71 Dennis Reyes	.05
72 Wally Joyner	.05
73 Kevin Brown	.05
74 Ray Durham	.05
75 Mike Cameron	.05
76 Dante Bichette	.05
77 Jose Guillen	.05
78 Carlos Delgado	.50
79 Paul Molitor	.75
80 Jason Kendall	.05
81 Mark Belhorn	.05
82 Damian Jackson	.05
83 Bill Mueller	.05
84 Kevin Young	.05
85 Curt Schilling	.25
86 Jeffrey Hammonds	.05
87 Sandy Alomar Jr.	.05
88 Bartolo Colon	.05
89 Wilton Guerrero	.05
90 Bernie Williams	.05
91 Deion Sanders	.05
92 Mike Piazza	1.25
93 Butch Huskey	.05
94 Edgardo Alfonzo	.05
95 Alan Benes	.05
96 Craig Biggio	.05
97 Mark Grace	.05
98 Shawn Green	.25
99 Derrek Lee	.60
100 Ken Griffey Jr.	1.25
101 Tim Raines	.05
102 Pokey Reese	.05
103 Lee Stevens	.05
104 Shannon Stewart	.05
105 John Smoltz	.05
106 Frank Thomas	.75
107 Jeff Fassero	.05
108 Jay Buhner	.05
109 Jose Canseco	.50
110 Omar Vizquel	.05
111 Travis Fryman	.05
112 Dave Nilsson	.05
113 John Olerud	.05
114 Larry Walker	.05
115 Jim Edmonds	.05

116 Bobby Higginson .05
117 Todd Hundley .05
118 Paul O'Neill .05
119 Bip Roberts .05
120 Ismael Valdes .05
121 Pedro Martinez .75
122 Jeff Cirillo .05
123 Andy Benes .05
124 Bobby Jones .05
125 Brian Hunter .05
126 Darryl Kile .05
127 Pat Hentgen .05
128 Marquis Grissom .05
129 Eric Davis .05
130 Chipper Jones 1.00
131 Edgar Martinez .05
132 Andy Pettitte .20
133 Cal Ripken Jr. 2.00
134 Scott Rolen .65
135 Ron Coomer .05
136 Luis Castillo .05
137 Fred McGriff .05
138 Neifi Perez .05
139 Eric Karros .05
140 Alex Fernandez .05
141 Jason Dickson .05
142 Lance Johnson .05
143 Ray Lankford .05
144 Sammy Sosa 1.25
145 Eric Young .05
146 Bubba Trammell .05
147 Todd Walker .05
148 Mo Vaughn/CC .40
149 Jeff Bagwell/CC 1.00
150 Kenny Lofton/CC .40
151 Raul Mondesi/CC .40
152 Mike Piazza/CC 2.00
153 Chipper Jones/CC 1.50
154 Larry Walker/CC .40
155 Greg Maddux/CC 1.50
156 Ken Griffey Jr./CC 2.00
157 Frank Thomas/CC 1.00
158 Darin Erstad/GLS .75
159 Roberto Alomar/GLS .60
160 Albert Belle/GLS .40
161 Jim Thome/GLS .75
162 Tony Clark/GLS .40
163 Chuck Knoblauch/GLS .40
164 Derek Jeter/GLS 3.00
165 Alex Rodriguez/GLS 2.50
166 Tony Gwynn/GLS 1.50
167 Roger Clemens/GLS 2.00
168 Barry Larkin/GLS .40
169 Andres Galarraga/GLS .40
170 Vladimir Guerrero/GLS 1.00
171 Mark McGwire/GLS 2.50
172 Barry Bonds/GLS 3.00
173 Juan Gonzalez/GLS .75
174 Andruw Jones/GLS 1.00
175 Paul Molitor/GLS 1.00
176 Hideo Nomo/GLS .75
177 Cal Ripken Jr./GLS 3.00
178 Brad Fullmer/GLR .40
179 Jaret Wright/GLR .40
180 Bobby Estalella/GLR .40
181 Ben Grieve/GLR .40
182 Paul Konerko/GLR .60
183 David Ortiz/GLR .75
184 Todd Helton/GLR 1.00
185 Juan Encarnacion/GLR .40
186 Miguel Tejada/GLR .60
187 Jacob Cruz/GLR .40
188 Mark Kotsay/GLR .40
189 Fernando Tatis/GLR .40
190 Ricky Ledee/GLR .40
191 Richard Hidalgo/GLR .40
192 Richie Sexson/GLR .40
193 Luis Ordaz/GLR .40
194 Eli Marrero/GLR .40
195 Livan Hernandez/GLR .40
196 Homer Bush/GLR .40
197 Raul Ibanez/GLR .40
198 Checklist (Nomar Garciaparra) .60
199 Checklist (Scott Rolen) .30
200 Checklist (Jose Cruz Jr.) .05
201 Al Martin .05

Crusade

Thirty cards from the cross-brand Crusade insert appear in 1998 Leaf. The cards had Green (250 sets), Purple (100 sets) and Red (25 sets) versions. Forty Crusade cards were in 1998 Donruss and 30 each in 1998 Donruss Update and Leaf Rookies & Stars.

NM/M
Complete Set (30): 400.00
Common Player: 6.00
Purples: 3X
Reds: 12X
3 Jim Edmonds 7.50
4 Darin Erstad 7.50
11 Mike Mussina 15.00
15 Albert Belle 6.00
18 Manny Ramirez 25.00
19 Jim Thome 20.00
24 Bubba Trammell 6.00
26 Bobby Higginson 6.00
28 Paul Molitor 25.00
30 Todd Walker 6.00
34 Andy Pettitte 10.00
35 Wade Boggs 30.00
40 Alex Rodriguez 60.00
41 Randy Johnson 25.00
46 Ivan Rodriguez 20.00
48 Roger Clemens 40.00
54 John Smoltz 6.00
56 Andruw Jones 25.00
58 Javier Lopez 6.00
59 Fred McGriff 6.00
64 Pokey Reese 6.00
66 Andres Galarraga 6.00
70 Eric Young 6.00
73 Moises Alou 6.00
76 Ben Grieve 6.00
79 Mike Piazza 50.00
91 Jason Kendall 6.00
95 Alan Benes 6.00
97 Tony Gwynn 30.00
98 Ken Caminiti 6.00

Heading for the Hall

This 20-card insert features players destined for the Hall of Fame. The set is sequentially numbered to 3,500. Each card is also found in a "SAMPLE" marked edition with no serial number.

NM/M
Complete Set (20): 35.00
Common Player: .75
Samples: 1X
1 Roberto Alomar 1.00
2 Jeff Bagwell 1.50
3 Albert Belle .75
4 Wade Boggs 2.00
5 Barry Bonds 5.00
6 Roger Clemens 2.50
7 Juan Gonzalez 1.50
8 Ken Griffey Jr. 3.00
9 Tony Gwynn 2.00
10 Barry Larkin .75
11 Kenny Lofton .75
12 Greg Maddux 2.00
13 Mark McGwire 4.00
14 Paul Molitor 1.50
15 Eddie Murray 1.50
16 Mike Piazza 3.00
17 Cal Ripken Jr. 5.00
18 Ivan Rodriguez 1.25
19 Ryne Sandberg 2.00
20 Frank Thomas 1.50

State Representatives/ Provincial Powers

This 30-card insert features top players. The background has a picture of the state or, in the case of Canadian teams, the province in which he plays. "State Representatives" or "Provincial Powers" is printed at the top with the player's name at the bottom. This set is sequentially numbered to 5,000.

NM/M
Complete Set (30): 40.00
Common Player: .50
1 Ken Griffey Jr. 3.00
2 Frank Thomas 2.00
3 Alex Rodriguez 4.00
4 Cal Ripken Jr. 5.00
5 Chipper Jones 2.50
6 Andruw Jones 2.00
7 Scott Rolen 1.50
8 Nomar Garciaparra 3.00
9 Tim Salmon .50
10 Manny Ramirez 2.00
11 Jose Cruz Jr. .50
12 Vladimir Guerrero 2.00
13 Tino Martinez .50
14 Larry Walker .50
15 Mo Vaughn .50
16 Jim Thome 1.50
17 Tony Clark .50
18 Derek Jeter 5.00
19 Juan Gonzalez 1.00
20 Jeff Bagwell 2.00
21 Ivan Rodriguez 1.50
22 Mark McGwire 4.00
23 David Justice .50
24 Chuck Knoblauch .50
25 Andy Pettitte .75
26 Raul Mondesi .50
27 Randy Johnson 2.00
28 Greg Maddux 2.50
29 Bernie Williams .50
30 Rusty Greer .50

Statistical Standouts

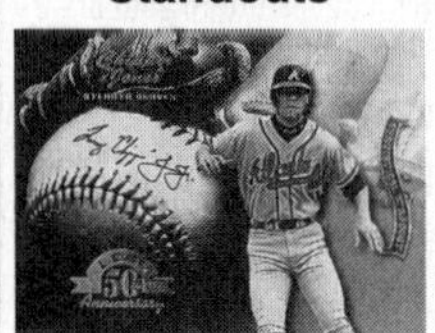

This 24-card insert features players with impressive statistics. The cards have a horizontal layout and the feel of leather. The background has a ball and glove with the player's facsimile signature on the ball. Statistical Standouts is numbered to 2,500. A parallel die-cut version of each card comprises the first 250 numbered cards.

NM/M
Complete Set (24): 55.00
Common Player: 1.00
Die-Cuts: 2X
1 Frank Thomas 2.50
2 Ken Griffey Jr. 4.00
3 Alex Rodriguez 5.00
4 Mike Piazza 4.00
5 Greg Maddux 3.00
6 Cal Ripken Jr. 6.00
7 Chipper Jones 3.00
8 Juan Gonzalez 2.00
9 Jeff Bagwell 2.50
10 Mark McGwire 5.00
11 Tony Gwynn 3.00
12 Mo Vaughn 1.00
13 Nomar Garciaparra 4.00
14 Jose Cruz Jr. 1.00
15 Vladimir Guerrero 2.50
16 Scott Rolen 2.00
17 Andy Pettitte 1.50
18 Randy Johnson 2.50
19 Larry Walker 1.00
20 Kenny Lofton 1.00
21 Tony Clark 1.00
22 David Justice 1.00
23 Derek Jeter 6.00
24 Barry Bonds 6.00

Fractal Foundation

Fractal Foundation is a stand-alone product but it parallels the 1998 Leaf set. It contains the Curtain Calls, Gold Leaf Stars and Gold Leaf Rookies subsets and is missing card #42 which Leaf retired in honor of Jackie Robinson. The set was printed on foil board and each card is

numbered to 3,999. The set is paralleled in Fractal Materials, Fractal Materials Die-Cuts and Fractal Materials Z2 Axis.

NM/M
Complete Set (200): 60.00
Common Player: .20
Semistars: .60
Unlisted Stars: 1.00
Pack (3): 2.00
Wax Box (18): 35.00
1 Rusty Greer .20
2 Tino Martinez .20
3 Bobby Bonilla .20
4 Jason Giambi .60
5 Matt Morris .20
6 Craig Counsell .20
7 Reggie Jefferson .20
8 Brian Rose .20
9 Ruben Rivera .20
10 Shawn Estes .20
11 Tony Gwynn 1.50
12 Jeff Abbott .20
13 Jose Cruz Jr. .20
14 Francisco Cordova .20
15 Ryan Klesko .20
16 Tim Salmon .20
17 Brett Tomko .20
18 Matt Williams .20
19 Joe Carter .20
20 Harold Baines .20
21 Gary Sheffield .50
22 Charles Johnson .20
23 Aaron Boone .20
24 Eddie Murray 1.00
25 Matt Stairs .20
26 David Cone .20
27 Jon Nunnally .20
28 Chris Stynes .20
29 Enrique Wilson .20
30 Randy Johnson 1.00
31 Garret Anderson .20
32 Manny Ramirez 1.00
33 Jeff Suppan .20
34 Rickey Henderson 1.00
35 Scott Spiezio .20
36 Rondell White .20
37 Todd Greene .20
38 Delino DeShields .20
39 Kevin Brown .20
40 Chili Davis .20
41 Jimmy Key .20
43 Mike Mussina .40
44 Joe Randa .20
45 Chan Ho Park .20
46 Brad Radke .20
47 Geronimo Berroa .20
48 Wade Boggs 1.50
49 Kevin Appier .20
50 Moises Alou .20
51 David Justice .20
52 Ivan Rodriguez .75
53 J.T. Snow .20
54 Brian Giles .20
55 Will Clark .20
56 Justin Thompson .20
57 Javier Lopez .20
58 Hideki Irabu .20
59 Mark Grudzielanek .20
60 Abraham Nunez .20
61 Todd Hollandsworth .20
62 Jay Bell .20
63 Nomar Garciaparra 1.75
64 Vinny Castilla .20
65 Lou Collier .20
66 Kevin Orie .20
67 John Valentin .20
68 Robin Ventura .20
69 Denny Neagle .20
70 Tony Womack .20
71 Dennis Reyes .20
72 Wally Joyner .20
73 Kevin Brown .20
74 Ray Durham .20
75 Mike Cameron .20
76 Dante Bichette .20
77 Jose Guillen .20
78 Carlos Delgado .50
79 Paul Molitor 1.00
80 Jason Kendall .20
81 Mark Belhorn .20
82 Damian Jackson .20
83 Bill Mueller .20
84 Kevin Young .20
85 Curt Schilling .40
86 Jeffrey Hammonds .20
87 Sandy Alomar Jr. .20
88 Bartolo Colon .20
89 Wilton Guerrero .20
90 Bernie Williams .20
91 Deion Sanders .20
92 Mike Piazza 2.00
93 Butch Huskey .20
94 Edgardo Alfonzo .20
95 Alan Benes .20
96 Craig Biggio .20
97 Mark Grace .20
98 Shawn Green .40
99 Derrek Lee .50
100 Ken Griffey Jr. 2.00
101 Tim Raines .20
102 Pokey Reese .20
103 Lee Stevens .20
104 Shannon Stewart .20
105 John Smoltz .20
106 Frank Thomas 1.00
107 Jeff Fassero .20
108 Jay Buhner .20
109 Jose Canseco .40
110 Omar Vizquel .20
111 Travis Fryman .20
112 Dave Nilsson .20
113 John Olerud .20
114 Larry Walker .20
115 Jim Edmonds .20
116 Bobby Higginson .20
117 Todd Hundley .20
118 Paul O'Neill .20
119 Bip Roberts .20
120 Ismael Valdes .20
121 Pedro Martinez 1.00
122 Jeff Cirillo .20
123 Andy Benes .20
124 Bobby Jones .20
125 Brian Hunter .20
126 Darryl Kile .20
127 Pat Hentgen .20
128 Marquis Grissom .20
129 Eric Davis .20
130 Chipper Jones 1.50
131 Edgar Martinez .20
132 Andy Pettitte .35
133 Cal Ripken Jr. 3.00
134 Scott Rolen .75
135 Ron Coomer .20
136 Luis Castillo .20
137 Fred McGriff .20
138 Neifi Perez .20
139 Eric Karros .20
140 Alex Fernandez .20
141 Jason Dickson .20
142 Lance Johnson .20
143 Ray Lankford .20
144 Sammy Sosa 1.75
145 Eric Young .20
146 Bubba Trammell .20
147 Todd Walker .20
148 Mo Vaughn/CC .20
149 Jeff Bagwell/CC 1.00
150 Kenny Lofton/CC .20
151 Raul Mondesi/CC .20
152 Mike Piazza/CC 2.00
153 Chipper Jones/CC 1.50
154 Larry Walker/CC .20
155 Greg Maddux/CC 1.50
156 Ken Griffey Jr./CC 2.00
157 Frank Thomas/CC 1.00
158 Darin Erstad/GLS .50
159 Roberto Alomar/GLS .40
160 Albert Belle/GLS .20
161 Jim Thome/GLS .75
162 Tony Clark/GLS .20
163 Chuck Knoblauch/GLS .20
164 Derek Jeter/GLS 3.00
165 Alex Rodriguez/GLS 2.50
166 Tony Gwynn/GLS 1.50
167 Roger Clemens/GLS 1.75
168 Barry Larkin/GLS .20
169 Andres Galarraga/GLS .20
170 Vladimir Guerrero/GLS 1.00
171 Mark McGwire/GLS 2.50
172 Barry Bonds/GLS 3.00
173 Juan Gonzalez/GLS .75
174 Andruw Jones/GLS 1.00
175 Paul Molitor/GLS 1.00
176 Hideo Nomo/GLS .75
177 Cal Ripken Jr./GLS 3.00
178 Brad Fullmer/GLR .20
179 Jaret Wright/GLR .20
180 Bobby Estalella/GLR .20
181 Ben Grieve/GLR .20
182 Paul Konerko/GLR .40
183 David Ortiz/GLR .75
184 Todd Helton/GLR 1.00
185 Juan Encarnacion/GLR .20
186 Miguel Tejada/GLR .40
187 Jacob Cruz/GLR .20
188 Mark Kotsay/GLR .20
189 Fernando Tatis/GLR .20
190 Ricky Ledee/GLR .20
191 Richard Hidalgo/GLR .20
192 Richie Sexson/GLR .20
193 Luis Ordaz/GLR .20
194 Eli Marrero/GLR .20
195 Livan Hernandez/GLR .20
196 Homer Bush/GLR .20
197 Raul Ibanez/GLR .20
198 Checklist (Nomar Garciaparra) 1.00
199 Checklist (Scott Rolen) .30
200 Checklist (Jose Cruz Jr.) .20

1998 Leaf Fractal Materials Samples

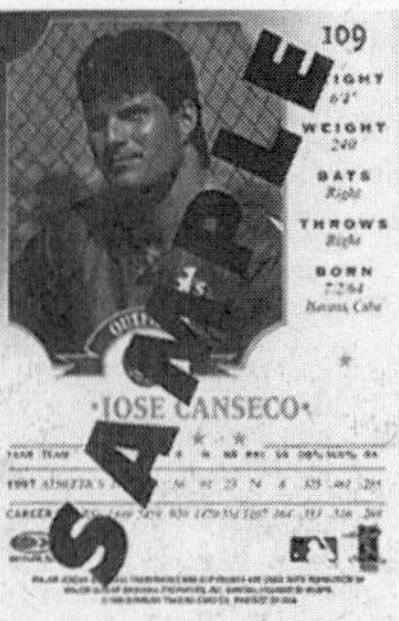

Each of the 50 Leather cards in Fractal Materials can be found in a sample version, prominently marked as such on back.

NM/M
Complete Set (50): 100.00
Common Player: 2.00
5 Matt Morris 2.00
9 Ruben Rivera 2.00
10 Shawn Estes 2.00
15 Ryan Klesko 2.00
17 Brett Tomko 2.00
22 Charles Johnson 2.00
33 Jeff Suppan 2.00
36 Rondell White 2.00
39 Kevin Brown 2.00
53 J.T. Snow 2.00
55 Will Clark 2.00
58 Hideki Irabu 2.00
66 Kevin Orie 2.00
70 Tony Womack 2.00
71 Dennis Reyes 2.00
76 Dante Bichette 2.00
78 Carlos Delgado 3.50
81 Mark Belhorn 2.00
87 Sandy Alomar Jr. 2.00
89 Wilton Guerrero 2.00
93 Butch Huskey 2.00
94 Edgardo Alfonzo 2.00
95 Alan Benes 2.00
97 Mark Grace 2.00
98 Shawn Green 3.00
99 Derrek Lee 4.00
105 John Smoltz 2.00
108 Jay Buhner 2.00
109 Jose Canseco 3.50
116 Bobby Higginson 2.00
117 Todd Hundley 2.00
136 Luis Castillo 2.00
137 Fred McGriff 2.00
138 Neifi Perez 2.00
146 Bubba Trammell 2.00
147 Todd Walker 2.00
158 Darin Erstad/GLS 3.50
160 Albert Belle/GLS 2.00
161 Jim Thome/GLS 4.00
162 Tony Clark/GLS 2.00
163 Chuck Knoblauch/GLS 2.00
167 Roger Clemens/GLS 6.50
170 Vladimir Guerrero/GLS 5.00
171 Mark McGwire/GLS 7.50
172 Barry Bonds/GLS 10.00
176 Hideo Nomo/GLS 4.00
189 Fernando Tatis/GLR 2.00
194 Eli Marrero/GLR 2.00
195 Livan Hernandez/GLR 2.00
201 Al Martin 2.00

1998 Leaf Fractal Materials

The Fractal Materials set fully parallels Fractal Foundations. Each of the inserts is sequentially numbered. The 200 card chase set was printed on four different materials: 100 plastic cards (numbered to 3,250), 50 leather (1,000), 30 nylon (500) and 20 wood (250). These parallels were inserted one per pack of Fractal Foundations. Each of the Leather cards can be found in a sample version marked as such on back.

NM/M
Complete Set (200): 375.00
Complete Plastic Set (100): 65.00
Common Plastic (3,250): .35
Complete Leather Set (50): 55.00
Common Leather (1,000): .75
Complete Nylon Set (30): 60.00
Common Nylon (500): 1.25
Complete Wood Set (20): 200.00
Common Wood (250): 5.00
Wax Box: 120.00
1 Rusty Greer/N 1.25
2 Tino Martinez/W 5.00
3 Bobby Bonilla/N 1.25
4 Jason Giambi/N 4.00
5 Matt Morris/L .75
6 Craig Counsell/P .35
7 Reggie Jefferson/P .35
8 Brian Rose/P .35
9 Ruben Rivera/L .75
10 Shawn Estes/L .75
11 Tony Gwynn/W 20.00
12 Jeff Abbott/P .35
13 Jose Cruz Jr./W 5.00
14 Francisco Cordova/P .35
15 Ryan Klesko/L .75
16 Tim Salmon/W 5.00
17 Brett Tomko/L .75
18 Matt Williams/N 1.25
19 Joe Carter/P .35
20 Harold Baines/P .35
21 Gary Sheffield/N 2.50
22 Charles Johnson/L .75
23 Aaron Boone/P .35
24 Eddie Murray/N 5.00
25 Matt Stairs/P .35
26 David Cone/P .35
27 Jon Nunnally/P .35
28 Chris Stynes/P .35
29 Enrique Wilson/P .35
30 Randy Johnson/W 15.00
31 Garret Anderson/N 1.25
32 Manny Ramirez/W 15.00
33 Jeff Suppan/L .75
34 Rickey Henderson/N 5.00
35 Scott Spiezio/P .35
36 Rondell White/L .75
37 Todd Greene/N 1.25
38 Delino DeShields/P .35
39 Kevin Brown/L .75
40 Chili Davis/P .35
41 Jimmy Key/P .35
43 Mike Mussina/N 4.00
44 Joe Randa/P .35
45 Chan Ho Park/N 1.25
46 Brad Radke/P .35
47 Geronimo Berroa/P .35
48 Wade Boggs/N 6.00
49 Kevin Appier/P .35
50 Moises Alou/N 1.25
51 David Justice/N 1.25
52 Ivan Rodriguez/W 12.50
53 J.T. Snow/L .75
54 Brian Giles/P .35
55 Will Clark/L .75
56 Justin Thompson/N 1.25
57 Javier Lopez/P .35
58 Hideki Irabu/L .75
59 Mark Grudzielanek/P .35
60 Abraham Nunez/P .35
61 Todd Hollandsworth/P .35
62 Jay Bell/P .35
63 Nomar Garciaparra/W 20.00
64 Vinny Castilla/P .35
65 Lou Collier/P .35
66 Kevin Orie/L .75
67 John Valentin/P .35
68 Robin Ventura/P .35
69 Denny Neagle/P .35
70 Tony Womack/L .75
71 Dennis Reyes/L .75
72 Wally Joyner/P .35
73 Kevin Brown/P .35
74 Ray Durham/P .35
75 Mike Cameron/N 1.25
76 Dante Bichette/L .75
77 Jose Guillen/N 1.25
78 Carlos Delgado/L 1.50
79 Paul Molitor/W 15.00
80 Jason Kendall/P .35
81 Mark Belhorn/L .75
82 Damian Jackson/P .35
83 Bill Mueller/P .35
84 Kevin Young/P .35
85 Curt Schilling/P .60
86 Jeffrey Hammonds/P .35
87 Sandy Alomar Jr./L .75
88 Bartolo Colon/P .35
89 Wilton Guerrero/L .75
90 Bernie Williams/N 1.25
91 Deion Sanders/N 1.25
92 Mike Piazza/W 25.00
93 Butch Huskey/L .75
94 Edgardo Alfonzo/L .75
95 Alan Benes/L .75
96 Craig Biggio/N 1.25
97 Mark Grace/L .75
98 Shawn Green/L 1.25
99 Derrek Lee/L 2.00
100 Ken Griffey Jr./W 25.00
101 Tim Raines/P .35
102 Pokey Reese/P .35
103 Lee Stevens/P .35
104 Shannon Stewart/N 1.25
105 John Smoltz/L .75
106 Frank Thomas/W 15.00
107 Jeff Fassero/P .35
108 Jay Buhner/L .75
109 Jose Canseco/L 1.50
110 Omar Vizquel/P .35
111 Travis Fryman/P .35
112 Dave Nilsson/P .35
113 John Olerud/P .35
114 Larry Walker/W 5.00
115 Jim Edmonds/N 1.25
116 Bobby Higginson/L .75
117 Todd Hundley/L .75
118 Paul O'Neill/P .35
119 Bip Roberts/P .35
120 Ismael Valdes/P .35
121 Pedro Martinez/N 5.00
122 Jeff Cirillo/P .35
123 Andy Benes/P .35
124 Bobby Jones/P .35
125 Brian Hunter/P .35
126 Darryl Kile/P .35
127 Pat Hentgen/P .35
128 Marquis Grissom/P .35
129 Eric Davis/P .35
130 Chipper Jones/W 20.00
131 Edgar Martinez/N 1.25
132 Andy Pettitte/W 10.00
133 Cal Ripken Jr./W 35.00
134 Scott Rolen/W 12.50
135 Ron Coomer/P .35
136 Luis Castillo/L .75
137 Fred McGriff/L .75
138 Neifi Perez/L .75
139 Eric Karros/P .35
140 Alex Fernandez/P .35
141 Jason Dickson/P .35
142 Lance Johnson/P .35
143 Ray Lankford/P .35
144 Sammy Sosa/N 7.00
145 Eric Young/P .35
146 Bubba Trammell/L .75
147 Todd Walker/L .75
148 Mo Vaughn/P/CC .35
149 Jeff Bagwell/P/CC 3.00
150 Kenny Lofton/P/CC .35
151 Raul Mondesi/P/CC .35
152 Mike Piazza/P/CC 5.00
153 Chipper Jones/P/CC 4.00
154 Larry Walker/P/CC .35
155 Greg Maddux/P/CC 4.00
156 Ken Griffey Jr./P/CC 5.00
157 Frank Thomas/P/CC 3.00
158 Darin Erstad/L/GLS 2.00
159 Roberto Alomar/P/GLS .65
160 Albert Belle/L/GLS .75
161 Jim Thome/L/GLS 2.00
162 Tony Clark/L/GLS .75
163 Chuck Knoblauch/L/GLS .75
164 Derek Jeter/P/GLS 7.50
165 Alex Rodriguez/P/GLS 6.00
166 Tony Gwynn/P/GLS 4.00
167 Roger Clemens/L/GLS 5.00
168 Barry Larkin/P/GLS .35
169 Andres Galarraga/P/GLS .35
170 Vladimir Guerrero/L/GLS 4.00
171 Mark McGwire/L/GLS 6.00
172 Barry Bonds/L/GLS 7.50
173 Juan Gonzalez/P/GLS 2.00
174 Andruw Jones/P/GLS 3.00
175 Paul Molitor/P/GLS 3.00
176 Hideo Nomo/L/GLS 2.00
177 Cal Ripken Jr./P/GLS 7.50
178 Brad Fullmer/P/GLR .35
179 Jaret Wright/N/GLR 1.25
180 Bobby Estalella/P/GLR .35
181 Ben Grieve/W/GLR 5.00
182 Paul Konerko/W/GLR 6.00
183 David Ortiz/N/GLR 2.50
184 Todd Helton/W/GLR 10.00
185 Juan Encarnacion/N/GLR 1.25
186 Miguel Tejada/N/GLR 1.50
187 Jacob Cruz/P/GLR .35
188 Mark Kotsay/N/GLR 1.25
189 Fernando Tatis/L/GLR .75
190 Ricky Ledee/P/GLR .35
191 Richard Hidalgo/P/GLR .35
192 Richie Sexson/P/GLR .35
193 Luis Ordaz/P/GLR .35
194 Eli Marrero/L/GLR .75
195 Livan Hernandez/L/GLR .75
196 Homer Bush/P/GLR .35
197 Raul Ibanez/P/GLR .35
198 Checklist (Nomar Garciaparra/P) 3.00
199 Checklist (Scott Rolen/P) .40
200 Checklist (Jose Cruz Jr./P) .35
201 Al Martin/L .75

Fractal Materials Die-Cut

This parallel set adds a die-cut to the Fractal Materials set. The first 200 of 75 plastic, 15 leather, 5 nylon and 5 wood cards have an x-axis die-cut.

The first 100 of 20 plastic, 25 leather, 10 nylon and 5 wood cards have a y-axis die-cut. The first 50 of 5 plastic, 10 leather, 15 nylon and 10 wood cards have a z-axis die-cut. The serial numbers on the backs of the die-cut cards are meaningless because they were printed prior to the die-cut fracture. This compounds the confusion engendered among collectors which has had a significant dampening effect on demand and, thus, market values.

NM/M
Common X (200 of each): 1.50
Common Y (100): 3.00
Common Z (50): 6.00
1 Rusty Greer/Z 6.00
2 Tino Martinez/Y 3.00
3 Bobby Bonilla/Y 3.00
4 Jason Giambi/Z 20.00
5 Matt Morris/Y 3.00
6 Craig Counsell/X 1.50
7 Reggie Jefferson/X 1.50
8 Brian Rose/X 1.50
9 Ruben Rivera/Y 3.00
10 Shawn Estes/Y 3.00
11 Tony Gwynn/X 12.50
12 Jeff Abbott/Y 3.00
13 Jose Cruz Jr./Z 6.00
14 Francisco Cordova/Y 3.00
15 Ryan Klesko/X 1.50
16 Tim Salmon/Y 3.00
17 Brett Tomko/Y 3.00
18 Matt Williams/Y 3.00
19 Joe Carter/X 1.50
20 Harold Baines/X 1.50
21 Gary Sheffield/Z 12.00
22 Charles Johnson/Y 3.00
23 Aaron Boone/Y 3.00
24 Eddie Murray/Y 10.00
25 Matt Stairs/X 1.50
26 David Cone/X 1.50
27 Jon Nunnally/X 1.50
28 Chris Stynes/X 1.50
29 Enrique Wilson/Y 3.00
30 Randy Johnson/Y 10.00
31 Garret Anderson/Y 3.00
32 Manny Ramirez/Y 10.00
33 Jeff Suppan/Y 3.00
34 Rickey Henderson/X 10.00
35 Scott Spiezio/Y 3.00
36 Rondell White/Y 3.00
37 Todd Greene/Z 6.00
38 Delino DeShields/Y 3.00
39 Kevin Brown/X 1.50
40 Chili Davis/X 1.50
41 Jimmy Key/X 1.50
43 Mike Mussina/Z 20.00
44 Joe Randa/X 1.50
45 Chan Ho Park/Y 3.00
46 Brad Radke/X 1.50
47 Geronimo Berroa/X 1.50
48 Wade Boggs/Y 12.50
49 Kevin Appier/X 1.50
50 Moises Alou/X 1.50
51 David Justice/Z 6.00
52 Ivan Rodriguez/X 7.50
53 J.T. Snow/X 1.50
54 Brian Giles/Y 3.00
55 Will Clark/X 1.50
56 Justin Thompson/Y 3.00
57 Javier Lopez/Y 3.00
58 Hideki Irabu/X 1.50
59 Mark Grudzielanek/X 1.50
60 Abraham Nunez/Z 6.00
61 Todd Hollandsworth/X 1.50
62 Jay Bell/X 1.50
63 Nomar Garciaparra/Z 45.00
64 Vinny Castilla/Y 3.00
65 Lou Collier/Y 3.00
66 Kevin Orie/X 1.50
67 John Valentin/X 1.50
68 Robin Ventura/X 1.50
69 Denny Neagle/X 1.50
70 Tony Womack/X 1.50
71 Dennis Reyes/Y 3.00
72 Wally Joyner/X 1.50
73 Kevin Brown/X 1.50
74 Ray Durham/X 1.50
75 Mike Cameron/Y 3.00
76 Dante Bichette/X 1.50
77 Jose Guillen/Z 6.00
78 Carlos Delgado/Y 5.00
79 Paul Molitor/X 10.00
80 Jason Kendall/X 1.50
81 Mark Belhorn/X 1.50
82 Damian Jackson/Y 3.00
83 Bill Mueller/X 1.50
84 Kevin Young/X 1.50
85 Curt Schilling/X 3.00
86 Jeffrey Hammonds/X 1.50
87 Sandy Alomar Jr./Y 3.00
88 Bartolo Colon/Y 3.00
89 Wilton Guerrero/Y 3.00
90 Bernie Williams/Z 6.00
91 Deion Sanders/Y 3.00
92 Mike Piazza/Z 55.00
93 Butch Huskey/X 1.50
94 Edgardo Alfonzo/Y 3.00
95 Alan Benes/Z 6.00
96 Craig Biggio/X 1.50
97 Mark Grace/Y 3.00
98 Shawn Green/Y 5.00
99 Derrek Lee/Y 6.00
100 Ken Griffey Jr./Z 55.00
101 Tim Raines/X 1.50
102 Pokey Reese/Y 3.00
103 Lee Stevens/X 1.50
104 Shannon Stewart/X 1.50
105 John Smoltz/Y 3.00
106 Frank Thomas/Z 30.00
107 Jeff Fassero/X 1.50
108 Jay Buhner/Y 3.00
109 Jose Canseco/X 3.00
110 Omar Vizquel/X 1.50
111 Travis Fryman/X 1.50
112 Dave Nilsson/X 1.50
113 John Olerud/X 1.50
114 Larry Walker/X 1.50
115 Jim Edmonds/Z 6.00
116 Bobby Higginson/Y 3.00
117 Todd Hundley/Z 6.00
118 Paul O'Neill/X 1.50
119 Bip Roberts/X 1.50
120 Ismael Valdes/X 1.50
121 Pedro Martinez/X 10.00
122 Jeff Cirillo/X 1.50
123 Andy Benes/X 1.50
124 Bobby Jones/X 1.50
125 Brian Hunter/X 1.50
126 Darryl Kile/X 1.50
127 Pat Hentgen/X 1.50
128 Marquis Grissom/X 1.50
129 Eric Davis/X 1.50
130 Chipper Jones/Z 45.00
131 Edgar Martinez/Z 6.00
132 Andy Pettitte/Y 6.00
133 Cal Ripken Jr./Z 75.00
134 Scott Rolen/X 7.50
135 Ron Coomer/X 1.50
136 Luis Castillo/X 1.50
137 Fred McGriff/X 1.50
138 Neifi Perez/Y 3.00
139 Eric Karros/X 1.50
140 Alex Fernandez/X 1.50
141 Jason Dickson/X 1.50
142 Lance Johnson/X 1.50
143 Ray Lankford/Y 3.00
144 Sammy Sosa/Y 17.50
145 Eric Young/Y 3.00
146 Bubba Trammell/Z 6.00
147 Todd Walker/Z 6.00
148 Mo Vaughn/X/CC 1.50
149 Jeff Bagwell/X/CC 10.00
150 Kenny Lofton/X/CC 1.50
151 Raul Mondesi/X/CC 1.50
152 Mike Piazza/X/CC 15.00
153 Chipper Jones/X/CC 12.50
154 Larry Walker/X/CC 1.50
155 Greg Maddux/X/CC 12.50
156 Ken Griffey Jr./X/CC 15.00
157 Frank Thomas/X/CC 10.00
158 Darin Erstad/Y/GLS 4.00
159 Roberto Alomar/X/GLS 2.00
160 Albert Belle/X/GLS 1.50
161 Jim Thome/X/GLS 6.00
162 Tony Clark/Z/GLS 6.00
163 Chuck Knoblauch/Z/GLS 6.00
164 Derek Jeter/X/GLS 25.00
165 Alex Rodriguez/Y/GLS 30.00
166 Tony Gwynn/X/GLS 12.50
167 Roger Clemens/Y/GLS 17.50
168 Barry Larkin/Y/GLS 3.00
169 Andres Galarraga/Y/GLS 3.00
170 Vladimir Guerrero/Y/GLS 10.00
171 Mark McGwire/Z/GLS 65.00
172 Barry Bonds/Y/GLS 35.00
173 Juan Gonzalez/Y/GLS 7.50
174 Andruw Jones/X/GLS 10.00
175 Paul Molitor/X/GLS 10.00
176 Hideo Nomo/Z/GLS 25.00
177 Cal Ripken Jr./X/GLS 25.00
178 Brad Fullmer/Z/GLR 6.00
179 Jaret Wright/Z/GLR 6.00
180 Bobby Estalella/Y/GLR 3.00
181 Ben Grieve/Z/GLR 6.00
182 Paul Konerko/Z/GLR 7.50
183 David Ortiz/Z/GLR 10.00
184 Todd Helton/Z/GLR 20.00
185 Juan Encarnacion/Z/GLR 6.00
186 Miguel Tejada/Z/GLR 12.00
187 Jacob Cruz/X/GLR 1.50
188 Mark Kotsay/Z/GLR 6.00
189 Fernando Tatis/Y/GLR 3.00
190 Ricky Ledee/X/GLR 1.50
191 Richard Hidalgo/Z/GLR 6.00
192 Richie Sexson/Z/GLR 6.00
193 Luis Ordaz/X/GLR 1.50
194 Eli Marrero/Z/GLR 6.00
195 Livan Hernandez/Z/GLR 6.00
196 Homer Bush/X/GLR 1.50
197 Raul Ibanez/X/GLR 1.50
198 Checklist (Nomar Garciaparra/X) 7.50
199 Checklist (Scott Rolen/Z) 7.50
200 Checklist (Jose Cruz Jr./X) 1.50
201 Al Martin/Y 3.00

Fractal Materials Z2 Axis

This 200-card set parallels Leaf Fractal Materials and was numbered to 20 sets.

NM/M
Common Player: 10.00
Z2 Stars: 10X
Production 20 Sets

1998 Leaf Fractal Matrix

Fractal Matrix is a parallel insert set to 1998 Leaf. Cards have a metallic finish, with 100 done in bronze, 60 in silver and 40 in gold, and each color having some cards in X, Y and Z axis. Stated print runs are: Bronze: X - 1,600; Y - 1,800; Z - 1,900. Silver: X - 600; Y - 800; Z - 900. Gold: X - 100; Y - 300; Z - 400. Each player is found only in a single color/axis combination.

NM/M
Complete Set (200): 250.00
Common Bronze: .25
Common Silver: .75
Common Gold: 2.00
1 Rusty Greer G/Z 2.00
2 Tino Martinez G/Z 2.00
3 Bobby Bonilla S/Y .75
4 Jason Giambi S/Y 1.25
5 Matt Morris S/Y .75
6 Craig Counsell B/X .25
7 Reggie Jefferson B/X .25
8 Brian Rose S/Y .75
9 Ruben Rivera B/X .25
10 Shawn Estes S/Y .75
11 Tony Gwynn G/Z 10.00
12 Jeff Abbott B/Y .25
13 Jose Cruz Jr. G/Z 2.00
14 Francisco Cordova B/X .25
15 Ryan Klesko B/X .25
16 Tim Salmon G/Y 2.00
17 Brett Tomko B/X .25
18 Matt Williams S/Y .75
19 Joe Carter B/X .25
20 Harold Baines B/X .25
21 Gary Sheffield S/Z 1.25
22 Charles Johnson S/X .75
23 Aaron Boone B/X .25
24 Eddie Murray G/Y 7.50
25 Matt Stairs B/X .25
26 David Cone B/X .25
27 Jon Nunnally B/X .25
28 Chris Stynes B/X .25
29 Enrique Wilson B/Y .25
30 Randy Johnson S/Z 2.00
31 Garret Anderson S/Y .75
32 Manny Ramirez G/Z 7.50
33 Jeff Suppan S/X .75
34 Rickey Henderson B/X 1.00
35 Scott Spiezio B/X .25
36 Rondell White S/Y .75
37 Todd Greene S/Z .75
38 Delino DeShields B/X .25
39 Kevin Brown S/X .75
40 Chili Davis B/X .25
41 Jimmy Key B/X .25
43 Mike Mussina G/Y 5.00
44 Joe Randa B/X .25
45 Chan Ho Park S/Z .75
46 Brad Radke B/X .25
47 Geronimo Berroa B/X .25
48 Wade Boggs S/Y 2.50
49 Kevin Appier B/X .25
50 Moises Alou S/Y .75
51 David Justice G/Y 2.00
52 Ivan Rodriguez G/Z 6.00
53 J.T. Snow B/X .25
54 Brian Giles B/X .25
55 Will Clark B/Y .25
56 Justin Thompson S/Y .75
57 Javier Lopez S/X .75
58 Hideki Irabu B/Z .25
59 Mark Grudzielanek B/X .25
60 Abraham Nunez S/X .75
61 Todd Hollandsworth B/X .25
62 Jay Bell B/X .25
63 Nomar Garciaparra G/Z 10.00
64 Vinny Castilla B/Y .25
65 Lou Collier B/Y .25
66 Kevin Orie S/X .75
67 John Valentin B/X .25
68 Robin Ventura B/X .25
69 Denny Neagle B/X .25
70 Tony Womack S/Y .75
71 Dennis Reyes S/Y .75
72 Wally Joyner B/X .25
73 Kevin Brown B/Y .25
74 Ray Durham B/X .25
75 Mike Cameron S/Z .75
76 Dante Bichette B/X .25
77 Jose Guillen G/Y 2.00
78 Carlos Delgado B/Y .50
79 Paul Molitor G/Z 7.50
80 Jason Kendall B/X .25
81 Mark Belhorn B/X .25
82 Damian Jackson B/X .25
83 Bill Mueller B/X .25
84 Kevin Young B/X .25
85 Curt Schilling B/X .40
86 Jeffrey Hammonds B/X .25
87 Sandy Alomar Jr. S/Y .75
88 Bartolo Colon B/Y .50
89 Wilton Guerrero B/Y .25
90 Bernie Williams G/Y 2.00
91 Deion Sanders S/Y .75
92 Mike Piazza G/X 12.50
93 Butch Huskey B/X .25
94 Edgardo Alfonzo S/X .75
95 Alan Benes S/Y .75
96 Craig Biggio S/Y .75
97 Mark Grace S/Y .75
98 Shawn Green S/Y 1.50
99 Derrek Lee S/Y 2.00
100 Ken Griffey Jr. G/Z 12.50
101 Tim Raines B/X .25
102 Pokey Reese S/X .75
103 Lee Stevens B/X .25
104 Shannon Stewart S/Y .75
105 John Smoltz S/Y .75
106 Frank Thomas G/X 7.50
107 Jeff Fassero B/X .25
108 Jay Buhner B/Y .25
109 Jose Canseco B/X .50
110 Omar Vizquel B/X .25
111 Travis Fryman B/X .25
112 Dave Nilsson B/X .25
113 John Olerud B/X .25
114 Larry Walker G/Z 2.00
115 Jim Edmonds S/Y .75
116 Bobby Higginson S/X .75
117 Todd Hundley S/X .75
118 Paul O'Neill B/X .25
119 Bip Roberts B/X .25
120 Ismael Valdes B/X .25
121 Pedro Martinez S/Y 2.00
122 Jeff Cirillo B/X .25
123 Andy Benes B/X .25
124 Bobby Jones B/X .25
125 Brian Hunter B/X .25
126 Darryl Kile B/X .25
127 Pat Hentgen B/X .25
128 Marquis Grissom B/X .25
129 Eric Davis B/X .25
130 Chipper Jones G/Z 10.00
131 Edgar Martinez S/Z .75
132 Andy Pettitte G/Z 3.00
133 Cal Ripken Jr. G/X 20.00
134 Scott Rolen G/Z 6.00
135 Ron Coomer B/X .25
136 Luis Castillo B/Y .25
137 Fred McGriff B/Y .25
138 Neifi Perez S/Y .75
139 Eric Karros B/X .25

140 Alex Fernandez B/X .25
141 Jason Dickson B/X .25
142 Lance Johnson B/X .25
143 Ray Lankford B/Y .25
144 Sammy Sosa G/Y 10.00
145 Eric Young B/Y .25
146 Bubba Trammell S/Y .75
147 Todd Walker S/Y .75
148 Mo Vaughn S/X/CC .75
149 Jeff Bagwell S/X/CC 2.00
150 Kenny Lofton S/X/CC .75
151 Raul Mondesi S/X/CC .75
152 Mike Piazza S/X/CC 4.00
153 Chipper Jones S/X/CC 3.00
154 Larry Walker S/X/CC .75
155 Greg Maddux S/X/CC 3.00
156 Ken Griffey Jr. S/X/CC 4.00
157 Frank Thomas S/X/CC 2.00
158 Darin Erstad B/Z/GLS .50
159 Roberto Alomar B/Y/GLS .35
160 Albert Belle G/Y/GLS 2.00
161 Jim Thome G/Y/GLS 4.00
162 Tony Clark G/Y/GLS 2.00
163 Chuck Knoblauch B/Y/GLS .25
164 Derek Jeter G/Z/GLS 20.00
165 Alex Rodriguez G/Z/GLS 15.00
166 Tony Gwynn B/X/GLS 1.25
167 Roger Clemens G/Z/GLS 12.00
168 Barry Larkin B/Y/GLS .25
169 Andres Galarraga B/Y/GLS .25
170 Vladimir Guerrero G/Z/GLS 7.50
171 Mark McGwire B/Z/GLS 2.00
172 Barry Bonds B/Z/GLS 3.00
173 Juan Gonzalez G/Z/GLS 4.00
174 Andruw Jones G/Z/GLS 7.50
175 Paul Molitor B/X/GLS 1.00
176 Hideo Nomo B/Z/GLS .75
177 Cal Ripken Jr. B/X/GLS 2.25
178 Brad Fullmer S/Z/GLR .75
179 Jarot Wright G/Z/GLR 2.00
180 Bobby Estalella B/Y/GLR .25
181 Ben Grieve G/X/GLR 2.00
182 Paul Konerko G/Z/GLR 3.00
183 David Ortiz G/Z/GLR 6.00
184 Todd Helton G/X/GLR 5.00
185 Juan Encarnacion G/Z/GLR 2.00
186 Miguel Tejada G/Z/GLR 4.00
187 Jacob Cruz B/Y/GLR .25
188 Mark Kotsay G/Z/GLR 2.00
189 Fernando Tatis S/Z/GLR .75
190 Ricky Ledee S/Y/GLR .75
191 Richard Hidalgo S/Y/GLR .75
192 Richie Sexson S/Y/GLR .75
193 Luis Ordaz B/X/GLR .25
194 Eli Marrero S/Z/GLR .75
195 Livan Hernandez S/Z/GLR .75
196 Homer Bush B/X/GLR .25
197 Raul Ibanez B/X/GLR .25
198 Checklist (Nomar Garciaparra B/X) .75
199 Checklist (Scott Rolen B/X) .35
200 Checklist (Jose Cruz Jr. B/X) .25
201 Al Martin B/X .25

Fractal Matrix Die-Cut

This parallel set adds a die-cut to the Fractal Matrix set. Three different die-cut versions were created: X-axis, Y-axis and Z-axis. An X-axis die-cut was added to 75 bronze, 20 silver and 5 gold cards. A Y-axis die-cut was added to 20 bronze, 30 silver and 10 gold cards. Of the 40 Z-axis cards, 5 are bronze, 10 silver and 25 gold. Stated print runs were 400 of each X-axis card; 200 Y and 100 Z.

NM/M

Complete Set (200): 950.00
Common X-Axis: 2.00
Common Y-Axis: 3.00
Common Z-Axis: 5.00
1 Rusty Greer G/Z 5.00
2 Tino Martinez G/Z 5.00
3 Bobby Bonilla S/Y 3.00
4 Jason Giambi S/Y 7.50
5 Matt Morris S/Y 3.00
6 Craig Counsell B/X 2.00
7 Reggie Jefferson B/X 2.00
8 Brian Rose S/Y 3.00
9 Ruben Rivera B/X 2.00
10 Shawn Estes S/Y 3.00
11 Tony Gwynn G/Z 35.00
12 Jeff Abbott B/Y 3.00
13 Jose Cruz Jr. G/Z 5.00
14 Francisco Cordova B/X 2.00
15 Ryan Klesko B/X 2.00
16 Tim Salmon G/Y 4.00
17 Brett Tomko B/X 2.00
18 Matt Williams S/Y 3.00
19 Joe Carter B/X 2.00
20 Harold Baines B/X 2.00
21 Gary Sheffield S/Z 15.00
22 Charles Johnson S/X 2.00
23 Aaron Boone B/X 2.00
24 Eddie Murray G/Y 10.00
25 Matt Stairs B/X 2.00
26 David Cone B/X 2.00
27 Jon Nunnally B/X 2.00
28 Chris Stynes B/X 2.00
29 Enrique Wilson B/Y 3.00
30 Randy Johnson S/Z 30.00
31 Garret Anderson S/Y 3.00
32 Manny Ramirez G/Z 30.00
33 Jeff Suppan S/X 2.00
34 Rickey Henderson B/X 6.00
35 Scott Spiezio B/X 2.00
36 Rondell White S/Y 3.00
37 Todd Greene S/Z 5.00
38 Delino DeShields B/X 2.00
39 Kevin Brown S/X 2.00
40 Chili Davis B/X 2.00
41 Jimmy Key B/X 2.00
43 Mike Mussina G/Y 7.50
44 Joe Randa B/X 2.00
45 Chan Ho Park S/Z 5.00
46 Brad Radke B/X 2.00
47 Geronimo Berroa B/X 2.00
48 Wade Boggs S/Y 12.00
49 Kevin Appier B/X 2.00
50 Moises Alou S/Y 3.00
51 David Justice G/Y 3.00
52 Ivan Rodriguez G/Z 25.00
53 J.T. Snow B/X 2.00
54 Brian Giles B/X 2.00
55 Will Clark B/Y 4.00
56 Justin Thompson S/Y 3.00
57 Javier Lopez S/X 2.00
58 Hideki Irabu B/Z 5.00
59 Mark Grudzielanek B/X 2.00
60 Abraham Nunez S/X 2.00
61 Todd Hollandsworth B/X 2.00
62 Jay Bell B/X 2.00
63 Nomar Garciaparra G/Z 40.00
64 Vinny Castilla B/Y 3.00
65 Lou Collier B/Y 3.00
66 Kevin Orie S/X 2.00
67 John Valentin B/X 2.00
68 Robin Ventura B/X 2.00
69 Denny Neagle B/X 2.00
70 Tony Womack S/Y 3.00
71 Dennis Reyes S/Y 3.00
72 Wally Joyner B/X 2.00
73 Kevin Brown B/Y 3.00
74 Ray Durham B/X 2.00
75 Mike Cameron S/Z 3.00
76 Dante Bichette B/X 2.00
77 Jose Guillen G/Y 3.00
78 Carlos Delgado B/Y 5.00
79 Paul Molitor G/Z 30.00
80 Jason Kendall B/X 2.00
81 Mark Belhorn B/X 2.00
82 Damian Jackson B/X 2.00
83 Bill Mueller B/X 2.00
84 Kevin Young B/X 2.00
85 Curt Schilling B/X 3.00
86 Jeffrey Hammonds B/X 2.00
87 Sandy Alomar Jr. S/Y 3.00
88 Bartolo Colon B/Y 3.00
89 Wilton Guerrero B/Y 3.00
90 Bernie Williams G/Y 4.00
91 Deion Sanders S/Y 3.00
92 Mike Piazza G/X 20.00
93 Butch Huskey B/X 2.00
94 Edgardo Alfonzo S/X 2.00
95 Alan Benes S/Y 3.00
96 Craig Biggio S/Y 3.00
97 Mark Grace S/Y 4.00
98 Shawn Green S/Y 5.00
99 Derrek Lee S/Y 3.00
100 Ken Griffey Jr. G/Z 40.00
101 Tim Raines B/X 2.00
102 Pokey Reese S/X 2.00
103 Lee Stevens B/X 2.00
104 Shannon Stewart S/Y 3.00
105 John Smoltz S/Y 3.00
106 Frank Thomas G/X 6.00
107 Jeff Fassero B/X 2.00
108 Jay Buhner B/Y 3.00
109 Jose Canseco B/X 4.50
110 Omar Vizquel B/X 2.00
111 Travis Fryman B/X 2.00
112 Dave Nilsson B/X 2.00
113 John Olerud B/X 2.00
114 Larry Walker G/Z 5.00
115 Jim Edmonds S/Y 3.00
116 Bobby Higginson S/X 2.00
117 Todd Hundley S/X 2.00
118 Paul O'Neill B/X 2.00
119 Bip Roberts B/X 2.00
120 Ismael Valdes B/X 2.00
121 Pedro Martinez S/Y 10.00
122 Jeff Cirillo B/X 2.00
123 Andy Benes B/X 2.00
124 Bobby Jones B/X 2.00
125 Brian Hunter B/X 2.00
126 Darryl Kile B/X 2.00
127 Pat Hentgen B/X 2.00
128 Marquis Grissom B/X 2.00
129 Eric Davis B/X 2.00
130 Chipper Jones G/Z 35.00
131 Edgar Martinez S/Z 3.00
132 Andy Pettitte G/Z 10.00
133 Cal Ripken Jr. G/X 25.00
134 Scott Rolen G/Z 25.00
135 Ron Coomer B/X 2.00
136 Luis Castillo B/Y 3.00
137 Fred McGriff B/Y 3.00
138 Neifi Perez S/Y 3.00
139 Eric Karros B/X 2.00
140 Alex Fernandez B/X 2.00
141 Jason Dickson B/X 2.00
142 Lance Johnson B/X 2.00
143 Ray Lankford B/Y 3.00
144 Sammy Sosa G/Y 20.00
145 Eric Young B/Y 3.00
146 Bubba Trammell S/Y 3.00
147 Todd Walker S/Y 3.00
148 Mo Vaughn S/X/CC 3.00
149 Jeff Bagwell S/X/CC 6.00
150 Kenny Lofton S/X/CC 2.00
151 Raul Mondesi S/X/CC 2.00
152 Mike Piazza S/X/CC 20.00
153 Chipper Jones S/X/CC 10.00
154 Larry Walker S/X/CC 2.00
155 Greg Maddux S/X/CC 10.00
156 Ken Griffey Jr. S/X/CC 15.00
157 Frank Thomas S/X/CC 6.00
158 Darin Erstad B/Z/GLS 20.00
159 Roberto Alomar B/Y/GLS 4.00
160 Albert Belle G/Y/GLS 3.50
161 Jim Thome G/Y/GLS 3.00
162 Tony Clark G/Y/GLS 3.00
163 Chuck Knoblauch B/Y/GLS 3.00
164 Derek Jeter G/Z/GLS 50.00
165 Alex Rodriguez G/Z/GLS 45.00
166 Tony Gwynn B/X/GLS10.00167
Roger Clemens G/Z/GLS 37.50
168 Barry Larkin B/Y/GLS 3.00
169 Andres Galarraga B/Y/GLS 3.00
170 Vladimir Guerrero G/Z/GLS 30.00
171 Mark McGwire B/Z/GLS 45.00
172 Barry Bonds B/Z/GLS 50.00
173 Juan Gonzalez G/Z/GLS 30.00
174 Andruw Jones G/Z/GLS 30.00
175 Paul Molitor B/X/GLS 6.00
176 Hideo Nomo B/Z/GLS 30.00
177 Cal Ripken Jr. B/X/GLS 20.00
178 Brad Fullmer S/Z/GLR 5.00
179 Jaret Wright G/Z/GLR 5.00
180 Bobby Estalella B/Y/GLR 3.00
181 Ben Grieve G/X/GLR 2.00
182 Paul Konerko G/Z/GLR 6.00
183 David Ortiz G/Z/GLR 7.50
184 Todd Helton G/X/GLR 6.00
185 Juan Encarnacion G/Z/GLR 5.00
186 Miguel Tejada G/Z/GLR 10.00
187 Jacob Cruz B/Y/GLR 3.00
188 Mark Kotsay G/Z/GLR 5.00
189 Fernando Tatis S/Z/GLR 5.00
190 Ricky Ledee S/Y/GLR 3.00
191 Richard Hidalgo S/Y/GLR 3.00
192 Richie Sexson S/Y/GLR 3.00
193 Luis Ordaz B/X/GLR 2.00
194 Eli Marrero S/Z/GLR 5.00
195 Livan Hernandez S/Z/GLR 5.00
196 Homer Bush B/X/GLR 2.00
197 Raul Ibanez B/X/GLR 2.00
198 Checklist (Nomar Garciaparra B/X) 5.00
199 Checklist (Scott Rolen B/X) 2.00
200 Checklist (Jose Cruz Jr. B/X) 2.00
201 Al Martin B/X 2.00

Fractal Matrix Diamond Axis

Production of this blue-foil finished top-shelf parallel within the 1998 Leaf set was limited to 50 serially numbered examples of each card.

NM/M

Common Player: 7.50
Stars/Rookies: 20X
SP (148-177): 12X

1998 Leaf Limited Star Factor Sample

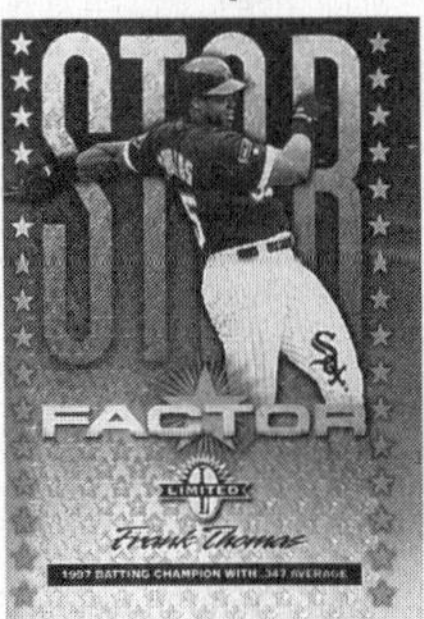

This sample card was intended to preview the 1998 Leaf Limited issue which was never released due to Pinnacle's bankruptcy. The card is printed with a refractive foil background and hundreds of embossed stars front and back. The back has a large "SAMPLE" overprint and is numbered "000."

NM/M

000 Frank Thomas 4.00

1998 Leaf Rookies & Stars

This 339-card set consists of three subsets: Power Tools, Lineup Card and Rookies. Fronts feature full-bleed photos and silver-foil graphics. Backs have complete year-by-year statistics and a small photo. The base set has short-printed base cards, numbers 131-230, 301-339, which are seeded 1:2 packs. Rookies and Stars has two parallels to the base set: True Blue and Longevity. True Blue's feature blue foil stamping and are each numbered "1 0f 500" on the card back. Longevity's are printed on a full-foiled card front with gold foil stamping and limited to 50 serially numbered sets.

NM/M

Complete Set (339): 200.00
Common Player: .10
Common SP (131-230): .20
Common SP (301-339): .50
Inserted 1:2
True Blues: 12X
SP True Blues: 2X
Production 500 Sets
Longevitys: 50X
SP Longevitys: 15X
Production 50 Sets
Pack (9): 7.50
Wax Box (24): 150.00
1 Andy Pettitte .30
2 Roberto Alomar .20
3 Randy Johnson .75
4 Manny Ramirez .75
5 Paul Molitor .75
6 Mike Mussina .50
7 Jim Thome .65
8 Tino Martinez .10
9 Gary Sheffield .50
10 Chuck Knoblauch .10
11 Bernie Williams .10
12 Tim Salmon .10
13 Sammy Sosa 1.25
14 Wade Boggs 1.00
15 Andres Galarraga .10
16 Pedro Martinez .75
17 David Justice .10
18 Chan Ho Park .10
19 Jay Buhner .10
20 Ryan Klesko .10
21 Barry Larkin .10
22 Will Clark .15
23 Raul Mondesi .10
24 Rickey Henderson .75
25 Jim Edmonds .10
26 Ken Griffey Jr. 1.25
27 Frank Thomas .75
28 Cal Ripken Jr. 2.00
29 Alex Rodriguez 1.50
30 Mike Piazza 1.25
31 Greg Maddux 1.00
32 Chipper Jones 1.00
33 Tony Gwynn 1.00
34 Derek Jeter 2.00
35 Jeff Bagwell .75
36 Juan Gonzalez .50
37 Nomar Garciaparra 1.00
38 Andruw Jones .75
39 Hideo Nomo .60
40 Roger Clemens 1.25
41 Mark McGwire 1.50
42 Scott Rolen .60
43 Vladimir Guerrero .75
44 Barry Bonds 2.00
45 Darin Erstad .25
46 Albert Belle .10
47 Kenny Lofton .10
48 Mo Vaughn .10
49 Ivan Rodriguez .60
50 Jose Cruz Jr. .10
51 Tony Clark .10
52 Larry Walker .10
53 Mark Grace .10
54 Edgar Martinez .10
55 Fred McGriff .10
56 Rafael Palmeiro .60
57 Matt Williams .10
58 Craig Biggio .10
59 Ken Caminiti .10
60 Jose Canseco .40
61 Brady Anderson .10
62 Moises Alou .10
63 Justin Thompson .10
64 John Smoltz .10
65 Carlos Delgado .50
66 J.T. Snow .10
67 Jason Giambi .50
68 Garret Anderson .10
69 Rondell White .10
70 Eric Karros .10
71 Javier Lopez .10
72 Pat Hentgen .10
73 Dante Bichette .10
74 Charles Johnson .10
75 Tom Glavine .30
76 Rusty Greer .10
77 Travis Fryman .10
78 Todd Hundley .10
79 Ray Lankford .10
80 Denny Neagle .10
81 Henry Rodriguez .10
82 Sandy Alomar Jr. .10
83 Robin Ventura .10
84 John Olerud .10
85 Omar Vizquel .10
86 Darren Dreifort .10
87 Kevin Brown .10
88 Curt Schilling .35
89 Francisco Cordova .10
90 Brad Radke .10
91 David Cone .10
92 Paul O'Neill .10
93 Vinny Castilla .10
94 Marquis Grissom .10
95 Brian Hunter .10
96 Kevin Appier .10
97 Bobby Bonilla .10
98 Eric Young .10
99 Jason Kendall .10
100 Shawn Green .40
101 Edgardo Alfonzo .10
102 Alan Benes .10
103 Bobby Higginson .10
104 Todd Greene .10
105 Jose Guillen .15
106 Neifi Perez .10
107 Edgar Renteria .10
108 Chris Stynes .10
109 Todd Walker .10
110 Brian Jordan .10
111 Joe Carter .10
112 Ellis Burks .10
113 Brett Tomko .10
114 Mike Cameron .10
115 Shannon Stewart .10
116 Kevin Orie .10
117 Brian Giles .10
118 Hideki Irabu .10
119 Delino DeShields .10
120 David Segui .10
121 Dustin Hermanson .10
122 Kevin Young .10
123 Jay Bell .10
124 Doug Glanville .10
125 John Roskos **RC** .10
126 Damon Hollins **RC** .10
127 Matt Stairs .10
128 Cliff Floyd .10
129 Derek Bell .10
130 Darryl Strawberry .10
131 Ken Griffey Jr. (Power Tools) 1.25
132 Tim Salmon (Power Tools) .20
133 Manny Ramirez (Power Tools) .75
134 Paul Konerko (Power Tools) .30
135 Frank Thomas (Power Tools) .75
136 Todd Helton (Power Tools) .75
137 Larry Walker (Power Tools) .20
138 Mo Vaughn (Power Tools) .20
139 Travis Lee (Power Tools) .20
140 Ivan Rodriguez (Power Tools) .60
141 Ben Grieve (Power Tools) .20
142 Brad Fullmer (Power Tools) .20
143 Alex Rodriguez (Power Tools) 1.50
144 Mike Piazza (Power Tools) 1.25
145 Greg Maddux (Power Tools) 1.00
146 Chipper Jones (Power Tools) 1.00
147 Kenny Lofton (Power Tools) .20
148 Albert Belle (Power Tools) .20
149 Barry Bonds (Power Tools) 2.00
150 Vladimir Guerrero (Power Tools) .75
151 Tony Gwynn (Power Tools) 1.00
152 Derek Jeter (Power Tools) 2.00
153 Jeff Bagwell (Power Tools) .75
154 Juan Gonzalez (Power Tools) .60
155 Nomar Garciaparra (Power Tools) 1.00
156 Andruw Jones (Power Tools) .75
157 Hideo Nomo (Power Tools) .60
158 Roger Clemens (Power Tools) 1.25
159 Mark McGwire (Power Tools) 1.50
160 Scott Rolen (Power Tools) .60
161 Travis Lee (Team Line-Up) .20
162 Ben Grieve (Team Line-Up) .20
163 Jose Guillen (Team Line-Up) .20
164 John Olerud (Team Line-Up) .20
165 Kevin Appier (Team Line-Up) .20
166 Marquis Grissom (Team Line-Up) .20
167 Rusty Greer (Team Line-Up) .20
168 Ken Caminiti (Team Line-Up) .20
169 Craig Biggio (Team Line-Up) .20
170 Ken Griffey Jr. (Team Line-Up) 1.25
171 Larry Walker (Team Line-Up) .20

172 Barry Larkin (Team Line-Up) .20
173 Andres Galarraga (Team Line-Up) .20
174 Wade Boggs (Team Line-Up) 1.00
175 Sammy Sosa (Team Line-Up) 1.25
176 Mike Piazza (Team Line-Up) 1.50
177 Jim Thome (Team Line-Up) .60
178 Paul Molitor (Team Line-Up) .75
179 Tony Clark (Team Line-Up) .20
180 Jose Cruz Jr. (Team Line-Up) .20
181 Darin Erstad (Team Line-Up) .25
182 Barry Bonds (Team Line-Up) 2.00
183 Vladimir Guerrero (Team Line-Up) .75
184 Scott Rolen (Team Line-Up) .60
185 Mark McGwire (Team Line-Up) 1.50
186 Nomar Garciaparra (Team Line-Up) 1.00
187 Gary Sheffield (Team Line-Up) .50
188 Cal Ripken Jr. (Team Line-Up) 2.00
189 Frank Thomas (Team Line-Up) .75
190 Andy Petitte (Team Line-Up) .30
191 Paul Konerko .35
192 Todd Helton 1.50
193 Mark Kotsay .20
194 Brad Fullmer .20
195 Kevin Millwood **RC** 8.00
196 David Ortiz 3.00
197 Kerry Wood 1.50
198 Miguel Tejada .40
199 Fernando Tatis .20
200 Jaret Wright .20
201 Ben Grieve .20
202 Travis Lee .20
203 Wes Helms .20
204 Geoff Jenkins .20
205 Russell Branyan .20
206 Esteban Yan **RC** .20
207 Ben Ford **RC** .20
208 Rich Butler **RC** .75
209 Ryan Jackson **RC** .50
210 A.J. Hinch .20
211 Magglio Ordonez **RC** 25.00
212 David Dellucci **RC** .50
213 Billy McMillon .20
214 Mike Lowell **RC** 8.00
215 Todd Erdos **RC** .20
216 Carlos Mendoza **RC** .25
217 Frank Catalanotto **RC** .75
218 Julio Ramirez **RC** .20
219 John Halama **RC** .50
220 Wilson Delgado .20
221 Mike Judd **RC** .20
222 Rolando Arrojo **RC** 1.00
223 Jason LaRue **RC** .50
224 Manny Aybar **RC** .50
225 Jorge Velandia .20
226 Mike Kinkade **RC** .75
227 Carlos Lee **RC** 20.00
228 Bobby Hughes .20
229 Ryan Christenson **RC** .50
230 Masato Yoshii **RC** 1.00
231 Richard Hidalgo .10
232 Rafael Medina .10
233 Damian Jackson .10
234 Derek Lowe .15
235 Mario Valdez .10
236 Eli Marrero .10
237 Juan Encarnacion .10
238 Livan Hernandez .10
239 Bruce Chen .10
240 Eric Milton .10
241 Jason Varitek .10
242 Scott Elarton .10
243 Manuel Barrios **RC** .10
244 Mike Caruso .10
245 Tom Evans .10
246 Pat Cline .10
247 Matt Clement .15
248 Karim Garcia .15
249 Richie Sexson .10
250 Sidney Ponson .10
251 Randall Simon .10
252 Tony Saunders .10
253 Javier Valentin .10
254 Danny Clyburn .10
255 Michael Coleman .10
256 Hanley Frias **RC** .10
257 Miguel Cairo .10
258 Rob Stanifer **RC** .10
259 Lou Collier .10
260 Abraham Nunez .10
261 Ricky Ledee .10
262 Carl Pavano .10
263 Derrek Lee .50
264 Jeff Abbott .10
265 Bob Abreu .10
266 Bartolo Colon .10
267 Mike Drumright .10
268 Daryle Ward .10
269 Gabe Alvarez .10
270 Josh Booty .10
271 Damian Moss .10
272 Brian Rose .10
273 Jarrod Washburn .10
274 Bobby Estalella .10
275 Enrique Wilson .10
276 Derrick Gibson .10
277 Ken Cloude .10
278 Kevin Witt .10
279 Donnie Sadler .10
280 Sean Casey .20
281 Jacob Cruz .10
282 Ron Wright .10
283 Jeremi Gonzalez .10
284 Desi Relaford .10
285 Bobby Smith .10
286 Javier Vazquez .10
287 Steve Woodard **RC** .20
288 Greg Norton .10
289 Cliff Politte .10
290 Felix Heredia .10
291 Braden Looper .10
292 Felix Martinez .10
293 Brian Meadows .10
294 Edwin Diaz .10
295 Pat Watkins .10
296 Marc Pisciotta **RC** .10
297 Rick Gorecki .10
298 DaRond Stovall .10
299 Andy Larkin .10
300 Felix Rodriguez .10
301 Blake Stein .50
302 John Rocker **RC** 1.00
303 Justin Baughman **RC** .50
304 Jesus Sanchez **RC** .50
305 Randy Winn .50
306 Lou Merloni .50
307 Jim Parque **RC** 1.00
308 Dennis Reyes .50
309 Orlando Hernandez **RC** 10.00
310 Jason Johnson .50
311 Torii Hunter 1.00
312 Mike Piazza 2.50
313 Mike Frank **RC** .50
314 Troy Glaus **RC** 60.00
315 Jin Cho **RC** .75
316 Ruben Mateo **RC** 1.00
317 Ryan Minor **RC** 1.00
318 Aramis Ramirez .75
319 Adrian Beltre 1.00
320 Matt Anderson **RC** 1.00
321 Gabe Kapler **RC** 2.00
322 Jeremy Giambi **RC** 1.00
323 Carlos Beltran 1.00
324 Dermal Brown .50
325 Ben Davis .50
326 Eric Chavez 1.50
327 Bob Howry **RC** 1.00
328 Roy Halladay 1.00
329 George Lombard .50
330 Michael Barrett .50
331 Fernando Seguignol **RC** 1.00
332 J.D. Drew **RC** 20.00
333 Odalis Perez **RC** 4.00
334 Alex Cora **RC** 1.00
335 Placido Polanco **RC** 8.00
336 Armando Rios **RC** .50
337 Sammy Sosa (HR Commemorative) 3.00
338 Mark McGwire (HR Commemorative) 4.00
339 Sammy Sosa, Mark McGwire (Checklist) 4.00

Longevity

Only 50 sets of this parallel edition were issued. Each card is serially numbered on back. Fronts are printed with gold foil background and have LONGEVITY printed at top. Special Longevity holographic 1 of 1 cards exist, but cannot be priced due to rarity.

	NM/M
Common Player:	3.00
Stars:	50X
SP Stars (131-230):	15X
SP Stars (301-339):	5X

True Blue

This parallel edition of the Rookies & Stars base set is labeled at top-back "1 of 500."

The parallels feature blue foil graphic highlights on front with TRUE BLUE at top.

	NM/M
Common Player:	1.00
Stars:	12X
SP Stars (131-230; 301-339):	2X

Cross Training

This 10-card insert set highlights players who excel at multiple aspects of the game. Card fronts are full-foiled and sequentially numbered on the card back to 1,000.

		NM/M
Complete Set (10):		30.00
Common Player:		1.50
Production 1,000 Sets		
1	Kenny Lofton	1.50
2	Ken Griffey Jr.	5.00
3	Alex Rodriguez	6.00
4	Greg Maddux	4.00
5	Barry Bonds	7.50
6	Ivan Rodriguez	2.50
7	Chipper Jones	4.00
8	Jeff Bagwell	3.00
9	Nomar Garciaparra	4.00
10	Derek Jeter	7.50

Crusade

This 30-card set is a continuation of this cross-brand insert. Cards are printed on a holographic green foil front and limited to 250 serial numbered sets. Two parallels are also randomly seeded: Purple and Red. Purples have purple holographic foil fronts and limited to 100 serial numbered sets. Reds are printed on red holographic foil fronts and limited to 25 serial numbered sets.

		NM/M
Complete Green Set (30):		225.00
Common Player:		7.50
Production 250 Sets		
Purples (100 Sets):		3X
Reds (25 Sets):		10X
101	Richard Hidalgo	7.50
102	Paul Konerko	15.00
103	Miguel Tejada	15.00
104	Fernando Tatis	7.50
105	Travis Lee	7.50
106	Wes Helms	7.50
107	Rich Butler	7.50
108	Mark Kotsay	7.50
109	Eli Marrero	7.50
110	David Ortiz	15.00
111	Juan Encarnacion	7.50
112	Jaret Wright	7.50
113	Livan Hernandez	7.50
114	Ron Wright	7.50
115	Ryan Christenson	7.50
116	Eric Milton	7.50
117	Brad Fullmer	7.50
118	Karim Garcia	10.00
119	Abraham Nunez	7.50
120	Ricky Ledee	7.50
121	Carl Pavano	7.50
122	Derrek Lee	15.00
123	A.J. Hinch	7.50
124	Brian Rose	7.50
125	Bobby Estalella	7.50
126	Kevin Millwood	10.00
127	Kerry Wood	30.00
128	Sean Casey	12.50
129	Russell Branyan	7.50
130	Magglio Ordonez	20.00

Extreme Measures

These inserts are printed on a full-foiled card front. Each card highlights an outstanding statistic for the featured player and is sequentially numbered to 1,000, minus the number of die-cut versions produced for each.

		NM/M
Complete Set (10):		50.00
Common Player:		3.00
1	Ken Griffey Jr./944	7.50
2	Frank Thomas/653	5.00
3	Tony Gwynn/628	6.00
4	Mark McGwire/942	9.00
5	Larry Walker/280	3.00
6	Mike Piazza/960	7.50
7	Roger Clemens/708	6.50
8	Greg Maddux/980	5.00
9	Jeff Bagwell/873	4.50
10	Nomar Garciaparra/989	6.50

Extreme Measures Die-Cuts

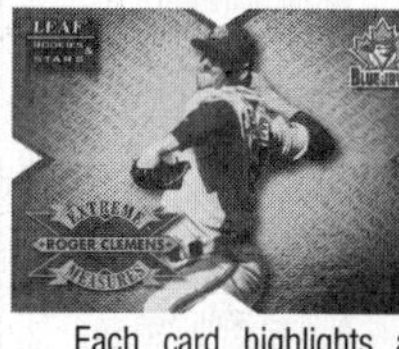

Each card highlights an outstanding statistic for each featured player, is die-cut and serially numbered to the limit of the particular statistic as shown.

		NM/M
Complete Set (10):		375.00
Common Player:		2.50
1	Ken Griffey Jr./56	65.00
2	Frank Thomas/347	11.00
3	Tony Gwynn/372	13.50
4	Mark McGwire/58	80.00
5	Larry Walker/720	2.50
6	Mike Piazza/40	75.00
7	Roger Clemens/292	16.00
8	Greg Maddux/20	100.00
9	Jeff Bagwell/127	20.00
10	Nomar Garciaparra/11	125.00

Freshman Orientation

Card fronts are printed on holographic foil with silver foil stamping and feature top prospects. Card backs highlight the date of the featured player's Major League debut, have a small photo and are serially numbered to 5,000 sets. Each card was also issued in an appropriately labeled sample version.

		NM/M
Complete Set (20):		20.00
Common Player:		.75
Production 5,000 Sets		
Samples:		1X
1	Todd Helton	4.00
2	Ben Grieve	.75
3	Travis Lee	.75
4	Paul Konerko	1.50
5	Jaret Wright	.75
6	Livan Hernandez	.75
7	Brad Fullmer	.75
8	Carl Pavano	.75
9	Richard Hidalgo	.75
10	Miguel Tejada	1.50
11	Mark Kotsay	.75
12	David Ortiz	1.50
13	Juan Encarnacion	.75
14	Fernando Tatis	.75
15	Kevin Millwood	1.50
16	Kerry Wood	2.50
17	Magglio Ordonez	1.50
18	Derrek Lee	1.50
19	Jose Cruz Jr.	.75
20	A.J. Hinch	.75

Great American Heroes

Card fronts are stamped with a holographic silver foil and done on a horizontal format. Card backs have a photo and are serially numbered to 2,500. Each card was also produced in an appropriately marked sample version.

		NM/M
Complete Set (20):		35.00
Common Player:		.75
Production 2,500 Sets		
Samples:		1X
1	Frank Thomas	1.75
2	Cal Ripken Jr.	5.00
3	Ken Griffey Jr.	3.00
4	Alex Rodriguez	4.00
5	Greg Maddux	2.25
6	Mike Piazza	3.00
7	Chipper Jones	2.25
8	Tony Gwynn	2.25
9	Jeff Bagwell	1.75
10	Juan Gonzalez	1.25
11	Hideo Nomo	1.25
12	Roger Clemens	2.50
13	Mark McGwire	4.00
14	Barry Bonds	5.00
15	Kenny Lofton	.75
16	Larry Walker	.75
17	Paul Molitor	1.75
18	Wade Boggs	2.25
19	Barry Larkin	.75
20	Andres Galarraga	.75

Greatest Hits

These inserts feature holographic silver foil stamping on the card front done on a horizontal format. Card backs have a photo and are serially numbered to 2,500.

		NM/M
Complete Set (20):		30.00
Common Player:		.50
Production 2,500 Sets		
1	Ken Griffey Jr.	2.50
2	Frank Thomas	1.50
3	Cal Ripken Jr.	4.00
4	Alex Rodriguez	3.00
5	Ben Grieve	.50
6	Mike Piazza	2.50
7	Chipper Jones	2.00
8	Tony Gwynn	2.00
9	Derek Jeter	4.00
10	Jeff Bagwell	1.50
11	Tino Martinez	.50
12	Juan Gonzalez	.75
13	Nomar Garciaparra	2.00
14	Mark McGwire	3.00
15	Scott Rolen	.75
16	David Justice	.50
17	Darin Erstad	.75
18	Mo Vaughn	.50
19	Ivan Rodriguez	1.00
20	Travis Lee	.50

Home Run Derby

This 20-card set spotlights the top home run hitters on a bronze full-foiled card front. Card backs have a portrait photo and are serially numbered to 2,500.

		NM/M
Complete Set (20):		30.00
Common Player:		.75
Production 2,500 Sets		
1	Tino Martinez	.75
2	Jim Thome	1.25
3	Larry Walker	.75
4	Tony Clark	.75
5	Jose Cruz Jr.	.75
6	Barry Bonds	5.00
7	Scott Rolen	1.00
8	Paul Konerko	1.25
9	Travis Lee	.75
10	Todd Helton	1.25
11	Mark McGwire	4.00
12	Andruw Jones	1.50
13	Nomar Garciaparra	2.50
14	Juan Gonzalez	1.00
15	Jeff Bagwell	1.50
16	Chipper Jones	2.50
17	Mike Piazza	3.00
18	Frank Thomas	1.50
19	Ken Griffey Jr.	3.00
20	Albert Belle	.75

ML Hard Drives

Card fronts are stamped with silver holographic foil. Card backs detail to which field (left, center and right) the featured player hit each of his singles, doubles, triples and home runs. Each card is serially numbered to 2,500. Each card was also produced in an appropriately marked sample version.

		NM/M
Complete Set (20):		30.00
Common Player:		.70
Production 2,500 Sets		
Samples:		1X
1	Jeff Bagwell	1.50
2	Juan Gonzalez	1.00
3	Nomar Garciaparra	2.00
4	Ken Griffey Jr.	3.00
5	Frank Thomas	1.50
6	Cal Ripken Jr.	4.50
7	Alex Rodriguez	3.50
8	Mike Piazza	3.00
9	Chipper Jones	2.00
10	Tony Gwynn	2.00
11	Derek Jeter	4.50
12	Mo Vaughn	.75
13	Ben Grieve	.75

14	Manny Ramirez	1.50
15	Vladimir Guerrero	1.50
16	Scott Rolen	1.00
17	Darin Erstad	.75
18	Kenny Lofton	.75
19	Brad Fullmer	.75
20	David Justice	.75

MVPs

This 20-card set is printed on a full silver-foil card stock and sequentially numbered to 5,000. The first 500 of each card is treated with a "Pennant Edition" logo and unique color coating.

		NM/M
Complete Set (20):		35.00
Common Player:		.50
Production 4,500 Sets		
Pennant Editions:		2X
Production 500 Sets		
1	Frank Thomas	2.00
2	Chuck Knoblauch	.50
3	Cal Ripken Jr.	5.00
4	Alex Rodriguez	4.00
5	Ivan Rodriguez	1.50
6	Albert Belle	.50
7	Ken Griffey Jr.	3.00
8	Juan Gonzalez	1.50
9	Roger Clemens	2.75
10	Mo Vaughn	.50
11	Jeff Bagwell	2.00
12	Craig Biggio	.50
13	Chipper Jones	2.50
14	Barry Larkin	.50
15	Mike Piazza	3.00
16	Barry Bonds	5.00
17	Andruw Jones	2.00
18	Tony Gwynn	2.50
19	Greg Maddux	2.50
20	Mark McGwire	4.00

Standing Ovation

Card fronts are stamped with silver holographic foil and card backs have a small photo of the featured player and are serially numbered to 5,000. Each card was also produced in an appropriately labeled sample version.

		NM/M
Complete Set (10):		12.50
Common Player:		.75
Production 5,000 Sets		
Samples:		1X
1	Barry Bonds	3.00
2	Mark McGwire	2.50
3	Ken Griffey Jr.	2.00
4	Frank Thomas	1.00
5	Tony Gwynn	1.50
6	Cal Ripken Jr.	3.00
7	Greg Maddux	1.50
8	Roger Clemens	1.75
9	Paul Molitor	1.00
10	Ivan Rodriguez	.75

Ticket Masters

Card fronts are printed on a full-foiled card stock with silver foil stamping and have a photo of one of the two players featured from the same team. Card backs have a photo of the other featured player and are serially numbered to 2,500. The first 250 of each card are die-cut.

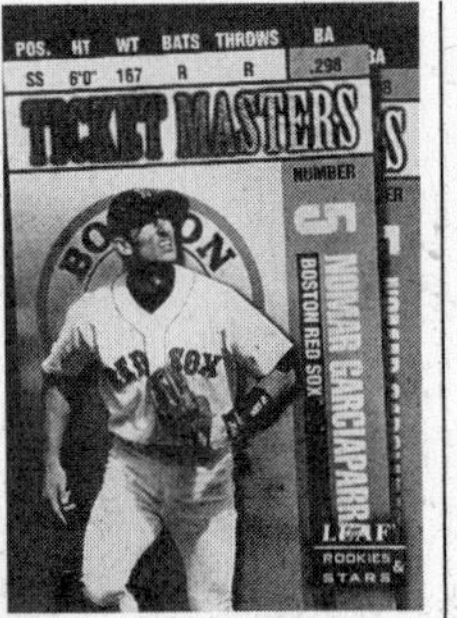

		NM/M
Complete Set (20):		32.50
Common Card:		.50
Production 2,250 Sets		
Die-Cuts:		1.5X
Production 250 Sets		
1	Ken Griffey Jr., Alex Rodriguez	4.00
2	Frank Thomas, Albert Belle	1.50
3	Cal Ripken Jr., Roberto Alomar	5.00
4	Greg Maddux, Chipper Jones	2.00
5	Tony Gwynn, Ken Caminiti	2.00
6	Derek Jeter, Andy Pettitte	5.00
7	Jeff Bagwell, Craig Biggio	1.50
8	Juan Gonzalez, Ivan Rodriguez	1.25
9	Nomar Garciaparra, Mo Vaughn	2.00
10	Vladimir Guerrero, Brad Fullmer	1.50
11	Andruw Jones, Andres Galarraga	1.50
12	Tino Martinez, Chuck Knoblauch	.50
13	Raul Mondesi, Paul Konerko	.75
14	Roger Clemens, Jose Cruz Jr.	2.25
15	Mark McGwire, Brian Jordan	4.00
16	Kenny Lofton, Manny Ramirez	1.50
17	Larry Walker, Todd Helton	1.25
18	Darin Erstad, Tim Salmon	.75
19	Travis Lee, Matt Williams	.50
20	Ben Grieve, Jason Giambi	1.00

2001 Leaf Certified Materials

		NM/M
Complete Set (160):		
Common Player:		.40
Common SP (111-160):		10.00
Production 200		
Pack (5):		15.00
Box (12):		160.00
1	Alex Rodriguez	5.00
2	Barry Bonds	6.00
3	Cal Ripken Jr.	6.00
4	Chipper Jones	3.00
5	Derek Jeter	6.00
6	Troy Glaus	2.00
7	Frank Thomas	2.00
8	Greg Maddux	3.00
9	Ivan Rodriguez	2.00
10	Jeff Bagwell	2.00
11	Eric Karros	.40
12	Todd Helton	2.00
13	Ken Griffey Jr.	4.00
14	Manny Ramirez	2.00
15	Mark McGwire	5.00
16	Mike Piazza	4.00
17	Nomar Garciaparra	4.00
18	Pedro Martinez	2.00
19	Randy Johnson	2.00
20	Rick Ankiel	.75
21	Rickey Henderson	1.50
22	Roger Clemens	3.50
23	Sammy Sosa	4.00
24	Tony Gwynn	3.00
25	Vladimir Guerrero	2.00
26	Kazuhiro Sasaki	.40
27	Roberto Alomar	.75
28	Barry Zito	.60
29	Pat Burrell	1.00
30	Harold Baines	.40
31	Carlos Delgado	1.00
32	J.D. Drew	1.00
33	Jim Edmonds	.60
34	Darin Erstad	.50
35	Jason Giambi	1.00
36	Tom Glavine	.75
37	Juan Gonzalez	2.00
38	Mark Grace	.60
39	Shawn Green	1.00
40	Tim Hudson	.60
41	Andruw Jones	1.50
42	Jeff Kent	.40
43	Barry Larkin	.40
44	Rafael Furcal	.40
45	Mike Mussina	1.00
46	Hideo Nomo	1.50
47	Rafael Palmeiro	1.25
48	Scott Rolen	1.00
49	Gary Sheffield	.60
50	Bernie Williams	.60
51	Bobby Abreu	.40
52	Edgardo Alfonzo	.40
53	Edgar Martinez	.40
54	Magglio Ordonez	.60
55	Kerry Wood	1.25
56	Adrian Beltre	.75
57	Lance Berkman	.40
58	Kevin Brown	.40
59	Sean Casey	.60
60	Eric Chavez	.60
61	Bartolo Colon	.40
62	Johnny Damon	.60
63	Jermaine Dye	.40
64	Juan Encarnacion	.40
65	Carl Everett	.40
66	Brian Giles	.40
67	Mike Hampton	.40
68	Richard Hidalgo	.40
69	Geoff Jenkins	.40
70	Jacque Jones	.40
71	Jason Kendall	.40
72	Ryan Klesko	.40
73	Chan Ho Park	.40
74	Richie Sexson	.40
75	Mike Sweeney	.40
76	Fernando Tatis	.40
77	Miguel Tejada	.60
78	Jose Vidro	.40
79	Larry Walker	.40
80	Preston Wilson	.40
81	Craig Biggio	.40
82	Fred McGriff	.40
83	Jim Thome	1.50
84	Garret Anderson	.40
85	Russell Branyan	.40
86	Tony Batista	.40
87	Terrence Long	.40
88	Deion Sanders	.40
89	Rusty Greer	.40
90	Orlando Hernandez	.40
91	Gabe Kapler	.40
92	Paul Konerko	.40
93	Carlos Lee	.40
94	Kenny Lofton	.40
95	Raul Mondesi	.40
96	Jorge Posada	.60
97	Tim Salmon	.40
98	Greg Vaughn	.40
99	Mo Vaughn	.40
100	Omar Vizquel	.40
101	Ray Durham	.40
102	Jeff Cirillo	.40
103	Dean Palmer	.40
104	Ryan Dempster	.40
105	Carlos Beltran	.40
106	Timo Perez	.40
107	Robin Ventura	.40
108	Andy Pettitte	.60
109	Aramis Ramirez	.40
110	Phil Nevin	.40
111	Alex Escobar	10.00
112	Johnny Estrada **RC**	20.00
113	Pedro Feliz	10.00
114	Nate Frese **RC**	10.00
115	Joe Kennedy **RC**	10.00
116	Brandon Larson **RC**	10.00
117	Alexis Gomez **RC**	10.00
118	Jason Hart	10.00
119	Jason Michaels **RC**	10.00
120	Marcus Giles	10.00
121	Christian Parker **RC**	10.00
122	Jackson Melian **RC**	10.00
123	Donaldo Mendez **RC**	10.00
124	Adrian Hernandez **RC**	10.00
125	Bud Smith **RC**	10.00
126	Jose Mieses **RC**	10.00
127	Roy Oswalt	10.00
128	Eric Munson	10.00
129	Xavier Nady	10.00
130	Horacio Ramirez **RC**	20.00
131	Abraham Nunez	10.00
132	Jose Ortiz	10.00
133	Jeremy Owens **RC**	10.00
134	Claudio Vargas **RC**	10.00
135	Ricardo Rodriguez **RC**	10.00
136	Aubrey Huff	10.00
137	Ben Sheets	10.00
138	Adam Dunn	10.00
139	Andres Torres **RC**	10.00
140	Elpidio Guzman **RC**	10.00
141	Jay Gibbons **RC**	20.00
142	Wilkin Ruan **RC**	10.00
143	Tsuyoshi Shinjo **RC**	10.00
144	Alfonso Soriano	15.00
145	Josh Towers **RC**	10.00
146	Ichiro Suzuki **RC**	140.00
147	Juan Uribe **RC**	15.00
148	Joe Crede	10.00
149	Carlos Valderrama **RC**	10.00
150	Matt White **RC**	10.00
151	Dee Brown	10.00
152	Juan Cruz **RC**	10.00
153	Cory Aldridge **RC**	10.00
154	Wilmy Caceres	10.00
155	Josh Beckett	10.00
156	Wilson Betemit **RC**	10.00
157	Corey Patterson	10.00
158	Albert Pujols **RC**	220.00
159	Rafael Soriano **RC**	10.00
160	Jack Wilson **RC**	20.00

Mirror Red/Gold

These randomly inserted parallels of both the base low-numbers and the short-printed Rookie Freshman Fabric high-numbers are printed on "holographic dual-sided metallized film board" with appropriate color tinting and foil highlights. Mirror red cards are individually serial numbered to 75; golds to 25. All of the mirror red SPs can be found autographed except Kennedy, Melian, Munson, Shinjo and Ichiro. Because no information was released about the number of each autographed, values cannot be attributed.

	NM/M
Common Mirror Red (1-110):	2.00
Stars (1-110):	3-5X
Common Mirror Red (111-160):	6.00
Stars (111-160):	1-2X
Production 75	
Mirror Gold:	6-8X
Production 25	

Fabric of the Game

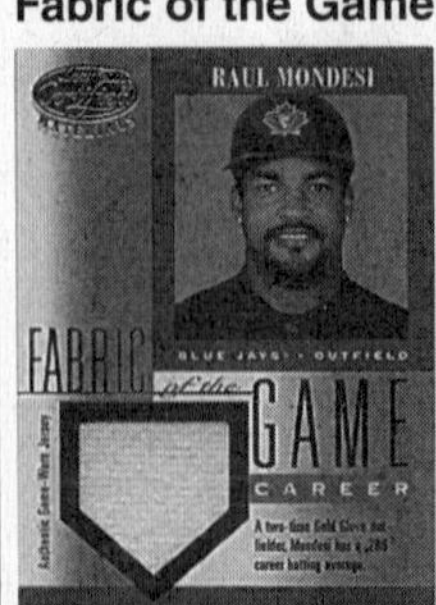

		NM/M
Common Player:		5.00
1	Lou Gehrig/184	200.00
1	Lou Gehrig/23	375.00
2	Babe Ruth/136	250.00
2	Babe Ruth/60	400.00
3	Stan Musial/177	40.00
3	Stan Musial/39	100.00
4	Nolan Ryan	40.00
4	Nolan Ryan/61	60.00
4	Nolan Ryan/34	80.00
5	Roberto Clemente/166	100.00
5	Roberto Clemente/29	250.00
6	Al Kaline/137	25.00
7	Brooks Robinson	20.00
7	Brooks Robinson/68	30.00
8	Mel Ott	30.00
8	Mel Ott/72	50.00
9	Dave Winfield/88	15.00
10	Eddie Mathews/115	25.00
10	Eddie Mathews/72	40.00
11	Ernie Banks/50	40.00
11	Ernie Banks/47	40.00
12	Frank Robinson	15.00
13	George Brett/137	40.00
14	Hank Aaron	40.00
14	Hank Aaron/98	50.00
14	Hank Aaron/47	100.00
15	Harmon Killebrew	25.00
15	Harmon Killebrew/49	50.00
16	Joe Morgan	10.00
16	Joe Morgan/96	15.00
17	Johnny Bench	20.00
17	Johnny Bench/68	30.00
18	Kirby Puckett/134	40.00
19	Mike Schmidt	40.00
19	Mike Schmidt/59	60.00
20	Phil Rizzuto/149	15.00
21	Reggie Jackson	15.00
21	Reggie Jackson/44	30.00
22	Catfish Hunter	15.00
22	Catfish Hunter/42	25.00
23	Rod Carew/92	20.00
23	Rod Carew/100	20.00
24	Bob Feller	15.00
24	Bob Feller/44	30.00
25	Lou Brock	10.00
25	Lou Brock/141	15.00
26	Tom Seaver	15.00
26	Tom Seaver/61	30.00
27	Paul Molitor	15.00
27	Paul Molitor/114	25.00
27		40.00
28	Willie McCovey/126	15.00
29	Yogi Berra	20.00
29	Yogi Berra/49	40.00
30	Don Drysdale	15.00
30	Don Drysdale/49	30.00
31	Duke Snider	20.00
31	Duke Snider/99	30.00
33	Orlando Cepeda/46	20.00
34	Casey Stengel	10.00
34	Casey Stengel/103	15.00
35	Robin Yount	20.00
35	Robin Yount/126	40.00
36	Eddie Murray	15.00
36	Eddie Murray/35	40.00
37	Jim Palmer	10.00
38	Juan Marichal	10.00
38	Juan Marichal/52	20.00
39	Willie Stargell	15.00
39	Willie Stargell/55	20.00
40	Ted Williams	150.00
40	Ted Williams/71	100.00
40	Ted Williams/43	150.00
41	Cal Ripken Jr.	30.00
41	Cal Ripken/75	50.00
41	Cal Ripken/277	40.00
42	Vladimir Guerrero/322	15.00
42	Vladimir Guerrero/44	25.00
43	Greg Maddux	15.00
43	Greg Maddux/240	20.00
44	Barry Bonds	30.00
44	Barry Bonds/49	75.00
44	Barry Bonds/289	30.00
45	Pedro Martinez	15.00
45	Pedro Martinez/268	15.00
46	Ivan Rodriguez	10.00
46	Ivan Rodriguez/304	15.00
47	Roger Maris	50.00
47	Roger Maris/275	50.00
48	Randy Johnson	15.00
48	Randy Johnson/179	20.00
49	Roger Clemens	20.00
49	Roger Clemens/260	20.00
50	Todd Helton	10.00
50	Todd Helton/334	10.00
51	Tony Gwynn	15.00
51	Tony Gwynn/119	20.00
51	Tony Gwynn/134	20.00
52	Troy Glaus	8.00
52	Troy Glaus/47	15.00
52	Troy Glaus/256	8.00
53	Phil Niekro	8.00
53	Phil Niekro/245	10.00
54	Don Sutton	8.00
54	Don Sutton/178	10.00
55	Frank Thomas	10.00
55	Frank Thomas/321	15.00
56	Jeff Bagwell	10.00
56	Jeff Bagwell/305	15.00
57	Rickey Henderson	15.00
57	Rickey Henderson/282	15.00
58	Darin Erstad/301	8.00
59	Andruw Jones	10.00
59	Andruw Jones/272	10.00
60	Roberto Alomar	10.00
60	Roberto Alomar/120	15.00
60	Roberto Alomar/170	15.00
61	Mike Piazza	20.00
61	Mike Piazza/328	20.00
62	Chipper Jones	15.00
62	Chipper Jones/189	15.00
63	Shawn Green	8.00
63	Shawn Green/143	8.00
64	Don Mattingly	50.00
64	Don Mattingly/145	50.00
64	Don Mattingly/222	40.00
65	Rafael Palmeiro	10.00
66	Wade Boggs	10.00
66	Wade Boggs/116	15.00
66	Wade Boggs/89	20.00
67	Hoyt Wilhelm	8.00
67	Hoyt Wilhelm/143	10.00
68	Andre Dawson	8.00
68	Andre Dawson/49	15.00
68	Andre Dawson/314	10.00
69	Ryne Sandberg	30.00
69	Ryne Sandberg/282	35.00
70	Nomar Garciaparra/333	25.00
71	Tom Glavine	8.00
71	Tom Glavine/208	10.00
71	Tom Glavine/247	10.00
72	Maggio Ordonez	8.00
72	Maggio Ordonez/301	8.00
72	Maggio Ordonez/126	10.00
73	Bernie Williams	10.00
73	Bernie Williams/304	15.00
74	Jim Edmonds	8.00
74	Jim Edmonds/108	10.00
74	Jim Edmonds/291	10.00
75	Hideo Nomo	20.00
75	Hideo Nomo/69	30.00
76	Barry Larkin	10.00
76	Barry Larkin/300	10.00
77	Scott Rolen	10.00
77	Scott Rolen/284	10.00
78	Miguel Tejada	8.00
78	Miguel Tejada/253	8.00
79	Freddy Garcia	5.00
79	Freddy Garcia/170	5.00
79	Freddy Garcia/249	5.00
80	Edgar Martinez	10.00
80	Edgar Martinez/320	10.00
81	Edgardo Alfonzo	5.00
81	Edgardo Alfonzo/108	5.00
81	Edgardo Alfonzo/296	5.00
82	Steve Garvey	8.00
82	Steve Garvey/272	8.00
83	Larry Walker	5.00
83	Larry Walker/311	5.00
83	Larry Walker/49	10.00
84	A.J. Burnett	5.00
84	A.J. Burnett/90	8.00
85	Richie Sexson	8.00
85	Richie Sexson/242	8.00
85	Richie Sexson/116	8.00
86	Mark Mulder	8.00
86	Mark Mulder/88	10.00
87	Kerry Wood	10.00
87	Kerry Wood/233	10.00
88	Sean Casey	5.00
88	Sean Casey/312	5.00
89	Jermaine Dye	5.00
89	Jermaine Dye/118	5.00
89	Jermaine Dye/286	5.00
90	Kevin Brown	5.00
90	Kevin Brown/170	5.00
90	Kevin Brown/257	5.00
91	Craig Biggio	5.00
91	Craig Biggio/88	8.00
91	Craig Biggio/291	5.00
92	Mike Sweeney	5.00
92	Mike Sweeney/302	5.00
92	Mike Sweeney/144	5.00
93	Jim Thome	10.00
93	Jim Thome/233	10.00
93	Jim Thome/40	20.00
94	Al Leiter	5.00
94	Al Leiter/247	5.00
94	Al Leiter/106	5.00
95	Barry Zito	8.00
95	Barry Zito/272	8.00
95	Barry Zito/78	15.00
96	Rafael Furcal	5.00
96	Rafael Furcal/295	5.00
97	J.D. Drew	5.00
97	J.D. Drew/276	5.00
98	Andres Galarraga	5.00
98	Andres Galarraga/150	5.00
98	Andres Galarraga/291	5.00
99	Kazuhiro Sasaki	5.00
99	Kazuhiro Sasaki/266	5.00
100	Chan Ho Park	5.00
100	Chan Ho Park/65	5.00
100	Chan Ho Park/217	5.00
101	Eric Milton	5.00
101	Eric Milton/163	5.00
102	Carlos Lee	5.00
102	Carlos Lee/297	5.00
103	Preston Wilson	5.00
103	Preston Wilson/266	5.00
104	Adrian Beltre	5.00
104	Adrian Beltre/85	5.00
104	Adrian Beltre/272	5.00
105	Luis Gonzalez	5.00
105	Luis Gonzalez/281	5.00
105	Luis Gonzalez/114	5.00
106	Kenny Lofton	5.00
106	Kenny Lofton/306	5.00
107	Shannon Stewart	5.00
107	Shannon Stewart/297	5.00
108	Javy Lopez	5.00
108	Javy Lopez/290	5.00
108	Javy Lopez/106	5.00
109	Raul Mondesi	5.00
109	Raul Mondesi/286	5.00
110	Mark Grace	10.00
110	Mark Grace/51	20.00
110	Mark Grace/308	15.00
111	Curt Schilling	8.00
111	Curt Schilling/235	8.00
111	Curt Schilling/110	10.00
112	Cliff Floyd	5.00

112 Cliff Floyd/275 5.00
113 Moises Alou 5.00
113 Moises Alou/124 5.00
113 Moises Alou/303 5.00
114 Aaron Sele 5.00
114 Aaron Sele/92 5.00
115 Jose Cruz Jr. 5.00
115 Jose Cruz Jr/245 5.00
116 John Olerud 5.00
116 John Olerud/186 5.00
116 John Olerud/107 5.00
117 Jose Vidro 5.00
117 Jose Vidro/296 5.00
118 John Smoltz 5.00
118 John Smoltz/334 5.00

2001 Leaf Limited

NM/M
Complete Set (375):
Common Player: .75
Common Lumberjack (151-200): 5.00
#'d to 100, 250 or 500
Common Rk (201-300): 5.00
Production 1,500
Common Auto. (301-325): 10.00
Production 1,000
Pack (3): 10.00
Box (18): 140.00
1 Curt Schilling 1.00
2 Craig Biggio .75
3 Brian Giles .75
4 Scott Brosius .75
5 Barry Larkin .75
6 Bartolo Colon .75
7 John Olerud .75
8 Cal Ripken Jr. 6.00
9 Moises Alou .75
10 Barry Zito .75
11 Ken Griffey Jr. 4.00
12 Garret Anderson .75
13 Andy Pettitte 1.00
14 Jim Edmonds 1.00
15 Tom Glavine 1.00
16 Jose Canseco 1.00
17 Fred McGriff .75
18 Robin Ventura .75
19 Tony Gwynn 3.00
20 Jeff Cirillo .75
21 Brad Radke .75
22 Ellis Burks .75
23 Scott Rolen 1.50
24 Rickey Henderson 2.00
25 Edgar Martinez .75
26 Kerry Wood 1.50
27 Al Leiter .75
28 Jose Cruz Jr. .75
29 Sean Casey .75
30 Eric Chavez .75
31 Jarrod Washburn .75
32 Gary Sheffield 1.00
33 Jermaine Dye .75
34 Bernie Williams 1.00
35 Tony Armas Jr. .75
36 Carlos Beltran 1.50
37 Geoff Jenkins .75
38 Shawn Green 1.50
39 Ryan Klesko .75
40 Richie Sexson .75
41 Pat Burrell 1.00
42 J.D. Drew 1.00
43 Larry Walker .75
44 Andres Galarraga .75
45 Tino Martinez .75
46 Rafael Furcal .75
47 Cristian Guzman .75
48 Omar Vizquel .75
49 Bret Boone .75
50 Wade Miller .75
51 Eric Milton .75
52 Gabe Kapler .75
53 Johnny Damon .75
54 Shannon Stewart .75
55 Kenny Lofton .75
56 Raul Mondesi .75
57 Jorge Posada 1.00
58 Mark Grace 1.00
59 Robert Fick .75
60 Phil Nevin .75
61 Mike Mussina 1.00
62 Joe Mays .75
63 Todd Helton 2.00
64 Tim Hudson 1.00
65 Manny Ramirez 2.00
66 Sammy Sosa 4.00
67 Darin Erstad 1.00
68 Roberto Alomar 1.00
69 Jeff Bagwell 2.00
70 Mark McGwire 5.00
71 Jason Giambi 1.50
72 Cliff Floyd .75
73 Barry Bonds 6.00
74 Juan Gonzalez 2.00
75 Jeremy Giambi .75
76 Carlos Lee .75
77 Randy Johnson 2.00
78 Frank Thomas 2.00
79 Carlos Delgado 1.00
80 Pedro Martinez 2.00
81 Rusty Greer .75
82 Brian Jordan .75
83 Vladimir Guerrero 2.00
84 Mike Sweeney .75
85 Jose Vidro .75
86 Paul LoDuca .75
87 Matt Morris .75
88 Adrian Beltre .75
89 Aramis Ramirez .75
90 Derek Jeter 6.00
91 Rich Aurilia .75
92 Freddy Garcia .75
93 Preston Wilson .75
94 Greg Maddux 3.00
95 Miguel Tejada 1.00
96 Luis Gonzalez .75
97 Torii Hunter .75
98 Nomar Garciaparra 4.00
99 Jamie Moyer .75
100 Javier Vazquez .75
101 Ben Grieve .75
102 Mike Piazza 4.00
103 Paul O'Neill .75
104 Terrence Long .75
105 Charles Johnson .75
106 Rafael Palmeiro 1.50
107 David Cone .75
108 Alex Rodriguez 5.00
109 John Burkett .75
110 Chipper Jones 3.00
111 Ryan Dempster .75
112 Bobby Abreu .75
113 Brad Fullmer .75
114 Kazuhiro Sasaki .75
115 Mariano Rivera 1.00
116 Edgardo Alfonzo .75
117 Ray Durham .75
118 Richard Hidalgo .75
119 Jeff Weaver .75
120 Paul Konerko .75
121 Jon Lieber .75
122 Mike Hampton .75
123 Mike Cameron .75
124 Kevin Brown .75
125 Doug Mientkiewicz .75
126 Jim Thome .75
127 Corey Koskie .75
128 Trot Nixon .75
129 Darryl Kile .75
130 Ivan Rodriguez 1.50
131 Carl Everett .75
132 Jeff Kent .75
133 Rondell White .75
134 Chan Ho Park .75
135 Robert Person .75
136 Troy Glaus 2.00
137 Aaron Sele .75
138 Roger Clemens 3.50
139 Tony Clark .75
140 Mark Buehrle .75
141 David Justice .75
142 Magglio Ordonez .75
143 Bobby Higginson .75
144 Hideo Nomo 2.00
145 Tim Salmon .75
146 Mark Mulder .75
147 Troy Percival .75
148 Lance Berkman .75
149 Russ Ortiz .75
150 Andruw Jones 2.00
151 Mike Piazza 25.00
152 Manny Ramirez 8.00
153 Bernie Williams 6.00
154 Nomar Garciaparra 25.00
155 Andres Galarraga 5.00
156 Kenny Lofton 5.00
157 Scott Rolen 8.00
158 Jim Thome 6.00
159 Darin Erstad 5.00
160 Garret Anderson 5.00
161 Andruw Jones 8.00
162 Juan Gonzalez 8.00
163 Rafael Palmeiro 8.00
164 Magglio Ordonez 5.00
165 Jeff Bagwell 8.00
166 Eric Chavez 5.00
167 Brian Giles 5.00
168 Adrian Beltre 5.00
169 Tony Gwynn 15.00
170 Shawn Green 5.00
171 Todd Helton 8.00
172 Troy Glaus 8.00
173 Lance Berkman 8.00
174 Ivan Rodriguez 8.00
175 Sean Casey 5.00
176 Aramis Ramirez 5.00
177 J.D. Drew 5.00
178 Barry Bonds 40.00
179 Barry Larkin 5.00
180 Cal Ripken Jr. 40.00
181 Frank Thomas 8.00
182 Craig Biggio 5.00
183 Carlos Lee 5.00
184 Chipper Jones 10.00
185 Miguel Tejada 6.00
186 Jose Vidro 5.00
187 Terrence Long 5.00
188 Moises Alou 5.00
189 Trot Nixon 5.00
190 Shannon Stewart 5.00
191 Ryan Klesko 5.00
192 Carlos Beltran 7.00
193 Vladimir Guerrero 8.00
194 Edgar Martinez 5.00
195 Luis Gonzalez 5.00
196 Richard Hidalgo 5.00
197 Roberto Alomar 6.00
198 Mike Sweeney 5.00
199 Bobby Abreu 5.00
200 Cliff Floyd 5.00
201 Jackson Melian **RC** 5.00
202 Jason Jennings 5.00
203 Toby Hall 5.00
204 Jason Karnuth **RC** 5.00
205 Jason Smith **RC** 5.00
206 Mike Maroth **RC** 5.00
207 Sean Douglass **RC** 5.00
208 Adam Johnson 5.00
209 Luke Hudson **RC** 5.00
210 Nick Maness **RC** 5.00
211 Les Walrond **RC** 5.00
212 Travis Phelps **RC** 5.00
213 Carlos Garcia **RC** 5.00
214 Bill Ortega 5.00
215 Gene Altman **RC** 5.00
216 Nate Frese 5.00
217 Bob File **RC** 5.00
218 Steve Green **RC** 5.00
219 Kris Keller **RC** 5.00
220 Matt White **RC** 5.00
221 Nate Teut **RC** 5.00
222 Nick Johnson 5.00
223 Jeremy Fikac **RC** 5.00
224 Abraham Nunez 5.00
225 Mike Penney **RC** 5.00
226 Roy Smith **RC** 5.00
227 Tim Christman **RC** 5.00
228 Carlos Pena 5.00
229 Joe Beimel **RC** 5.00
230 Mike Koplove **RC** 5.00
231 Scott MacRae **RC** 5.00
232 Kyle Lohse **RC** 10.00
233 Jerrod Riggan **RC** 5.00
234 Scott Podsednik **RC** 12.00
235 Winston Abreu **RC** 5.00
236 Ryan Freel **RC** 5.00
237 Ken Vining **RC** 5.00
238 Bret Prinz **RC** 5.00
239 Paul Phillips **RC** 5.00
240 Josh Fogg **RC** 5.00
241 Saul Rivera **RC** 5.00
242 Esix Snead **RC** 5.00
243 John Grabow **RC** 5.00
244 Tony Cogan **RC** 5.00
245 Pedro Santana **RC** 5.00
246 Jack Cust 5.00
247 Joe Crede 5.00
248 Juan Moreno **RC** 5.00
249 Kevin Joseph **RC** 5.00
250 Scott Stewart **RC** 5.00
251 Rob Mackowiak **RC** 5.00
252 Luis Pineda **RC** 5.00
253 Bert Snow **RC** 5.00
254 Dustan Mohr **RC** 5.00
255 Justin Kaye **RC** 5.00
256 Chad Paronto **RC** 5.00
257 Nick Punto **RC** 5.00
258 Brian Roberts **RC** 15.00
259 Eric Hinske **RC** 8.00
260 Victor Zambrano **RC** 5.00
261 Juan Pena 5.00
262 Rick Bauer **RC** 5.00
263 Jorge Julio **RC** 5.00
264 Craig Monroe **RC** 5.00
265 Stubby Clapp **RC** 5.00
266 Martin Vargas **RC** 5.00
267 Josue Perez **RC** 5.00
268 Cody Ransom **RC** 5.00
269 Will Ohman **RC** 5.00
270 Juan Diaz **RC** 5.00
271 Ramon Vazquez **RC** 5.00
272 Grant Balfour **RC** 5.00
273 Ryan Jensen **RC** 5.00
274 Benito Baez **RC** 5.00
275 Angel Santos **RC** 5.00
276 Brian Reith **RC** 5.00
277 Brandon Lyon **RC** 5.00
278 Erik Hiljus **RC** 5.00
279 Brandon Knight **RC** 5.00
280 Jose Acevedo **RC** 5.00
281 Cesar Crespo **RC** 5.00
282 Kevin Olsen **RC** 5.00
283 Duaner Sanchez **RC** 5.00
284 Endy Chavez **RC** 5.00
285 Blaine Neal **RC** 5.00
286 Brett Jodie **RC** 5.00
287 Brad Voyles **RC** 5.00
288 Doug Nickle **RC** 5.00
289 Junior Spivey **RC** 8.00
290 Henry Mateo **RC** 5.00
291 Xavier Nady 5.00
292 Lance Davis **RC** 5.00
293 Willie Harris **RC** 5.00
294 Mark Lukasiewicz **RC** 5.00
295 Ryan Drese **RC** 5.00
296 Morgan Ensberg **RC** 10.00
297 Jose Mieses **RC** 5.00
298 Jason Michaels **RC** 5.00
299 Kris Foster **RC** 5.00
300 Justin Duchscherer **RC** 5.00
301 Elpidio Guzman **RC** 5.00
302 Cory Aldridge **RC** 8.00
303 Angel Berroa **RC** 15.00
304 Travis Hafner **RC** 125.00
305 Horacio Ramirez **RC** 15.00
306 Juan Uribe **RC** 10.00
307 Mark Prior **RC** 80.00
308 Brandon Larson **RC** 10.00
309 Nick Neugebauer 10.00
310 Zach Day **RC** 10.00
311 Jeremy Owens **RC** 10.00
312 Dewon Brazelton **RC** 10.00
313 Brandon Duckworth **RC** 10.00
314 Adrian Hernandez **RC** 10.00
315 Mark Teixeira **RC** 160.00
316 Brian Rogers **RC** 10.00
317 David Brous **RC** 10.00
318 Geronimo Gil **RC** 10.00
319 Erick Almonte **RC** 10.00
320 Claudio Vargas **RC** 10.00
321 Wilkin Ruan **RC** 10.00
322 David Williams **RC** 10.00
323 Alexis Gomez **RC** 10.00
324 Mike Rivera **RC** 10.00
325 Brandon Berger **RC** 10.00
326 Keith Ginter 10.00
327 Brandon Inge/700 10.00
328 Brent Abernathy/700 10.00
329 Billy Sylvester/700 **RC** 10.00
330 Bart Miadich/500 **RC** 10.00
331 Tsuyoshi Shinjo/500 **RC** 15.00
332 Eric Valent 10.00
333 Dee Brown/500 10.00
334 Andres Torres/125 **RC** 10.00
335 Timo Perez/700 10.00
336 Cesar Izturis/650 10.00
337 Pedro Feliz 10.00
338 Jason Hart/200 10.00
339 Greg Miller/700 **RC** 10.00
340 Eric Munson/700 10.00
341 Aubrey Huff/450 10.00
342 Wilmy Caceres/700 **RC** 10.00
343 Alex Escobar/650 10.00
344 Brian Lawrence/700 **RC** 10.00
345 Adam Pettyjohn/650 **RC** 10.00
346 Donaldo Mendez/700 **RC** 10.00
347 Carlos Valderrama **RC** 10.00
348 Christian Parker 650 **RC** 10.00
349 Corky Miller/500 **RC** 10.00
350 Michael Cuddyer/500 10.00
351 Adam Dunn/500 20.00
352 Josh Beckett/650 10.00
353 Juan Cruz/500 **RC** 10.00
354 Ben Sheets/400 10.00
355 Roy Oswalt/100 15.00
356 Rafael Soriano/650 **RC** 10.00
357 Ricardo Rodriguez/650 **RC** 10.00
358 Jimmy Rollins/300 10.00
359 C.C. Sabathia 10.00
360 Bud Smith/500 **RC** 10.00
361 Jose Ortiz 10.00
362 Marcus Giles/400 10.00
363 Jack Wilson **RC** 20.00
364 Wilson Betemit/100 **RC** 10.00
365 Corey Patterson/650 10.00
366 Jay Gibbons/Spikes/125 **RC** 35.00
367 Albert Pujols/250 **RC** 300.00
368 Joe Kennedy **RC** 10.00
369 Alfonso Soriano/Hat/100 40.00
370 Delvin James/650 **RC** 10.00
371 Josh Towers/500 **RC** 10.00
372 Jeremy Affeldt/650 **RC** 10.00
373 Tim Redding/500 10.00
374 Ichiro Suzuki/100 **RC** 400.00
375 Johnny Estrada/100 **RC** 30.00

2001 Leaf Rookies & Stars Samples

Each January 2002 issue of Beckett Baseball Card Monthly included a sample 2002 Leaf R&S card rubber-cemented inside. The cards differ from the issued version only in the appearance on back of a (usually) silver-foil "SAMPLE" notation. Some cards were produced with the overprint in gold-foil, in much more limited quantities. The number of different players' cards involved in the promotion is unknown.

NM/M
Common Player: .10
Stars: 1.5-2X
Gold: 20X

2001 Leaf Rookies & Stars

NM/M
Complete Set (300):
Common Player: .15
Common (101-200): 1.50
Inserted 1:4
Common (201-300): 4.00
Inserted 1:24 8.00
Pack (5): 6.00
Box (24): 125.00
1 Alex Rodriguez 2.50
2 Derek Jeter 3.00
3 Aramis Ramirez .15
4 Cliff Floyd .15
5 Nomar Garciaparra 2.00
6 Craig Biggio .15
7 Ivan Rodriguez .75
8 Cal Ripken Jr. 3.00
9 Fred McGriff .15
10 Chipper Jones 1.50
11 Roberto Alomar .50
12 Moises Alou .15
13 Freddy Garcia .15
14 Bobby Abreu .15
15 Shawn Green .50
16 Jason Giambi .50
17 Todd Helton 1.00
18 Robert Fick .15
19 Tony Gwynn 1.50
20 Luis Gonzalez .35
21 Sean Casey .25
22 Roger Clemens 1.75
23 Brian Giles .15
24 Manny Ramirez 1.00
25 Barry Bonds 3.00
26 Richard Hidalgo .15
27 Vladimir Guerrero 1.00
28 Kevin Brown .15
29 Mike Sweeney .15
30 Ken Griffey Jr. 2.00
31 Mike Piazza 2.00
32 Richie Sexson .15
33 Matt Morris .15
34 Jorge Posada .25
35 Eric Chavez .25
36 Mark Buehrle .15
37 Jeff Bagwell 1.00
38 Curt Schilling .35
39 Bartolo Colon .15
40 Mark Quinn .15
41 Tony Clark .15
42 Brad Radke .15
43 Gary Sheffield .35
44 Doug Mientkiewicz .15
45 Pedro Martinez 1.00
46 Carlos Lee .15
47 Troy Glaus 1.00
48 Preston Wilson .15
49 Phil Nevin .15
50 Chan Ho Park .15
51 Randy Johnson 1.00
52 Jermaine Dye .15
53 Terrence Long .15
54 Joe Mays .15
55 Scott Rolen .75
56 Miguel Tejada .25
57 Jim Thome .15
58 Jose Vidro .15
59 Gabe Kapler .15
60 Darin Erstad .75
61 Jim Edmonds .15
62 Jarrod Washburn .15
63 Tom Glavine .40
64 Adrian Beltre .50
65 Sammy Sosa 2.00
66 Juan Gonzalez 1.00
67 Rafael Furcal .15
68 Mike Mussina .50
69 Mark McGwire 2.50
70 Ryan Klesko .15
71 Raul Mondesi .15
72 Trot Nixon .15
73 Barry Larkin .15
74 Rafael Palmeiro .75
75 Mark Mulder .25
76 Carlos Delgado .60
77 Mike Hampton .15
78 Carl Everett .15
79 Paul Konerko .15
80 Larry Walker .15
81 Kerry Wood .60
82 Frank Thomas 1.00
83 Andruw Jones 1.00
84 Eric Milton .15
85 Ben Grieve .15
86 Carlos Beltran .50
87 Tim Hudson .25
88 Hideo Nomo 1.00
89 Greg Maddux 1.50
90 Edgar Martinez .15
91 Lance Berkman .15
92 Pat Burrell .45
93 Jeff Kent .15
94 Magglio Ordonez .15
95 Cristian Guzman .15
96 Jose Canseco .30
97 J.D. Drew .60
98 Bernie Williams .40
99 Kazuhiro Sasaki .15
100 Rickey Henderson 1.00
101 Wilson Guzman **RC** 1.50
102 Nick Neugebauer 1.50
103 Lance Davis **RC** 1.50
104 Felipe Lopez 1.50
105 Toby Hall 1.50
106 Jack Cust 1.50
107 Jason Karnuth 1.50
108 Bart Miadich **RC** 1.50
109 Brian Roberts **RC** 10.00
110 Brandon Larson **RC** 2.00
111 Sean Douglass **RC** 1.50
112 Joe Crede 1.50
113 Tim Redding 1.50
114 Adam Johnson 1.50
115 Marcus Giles 1.50
116 Jose Ortiz 1.50
117 Jose Mieses **RC** 1.50
118 Nick Maness **RC** 1.50
119 Les Walrond **RC** 1.50
120 Travis Phelps **RC** 1.50
121 Troy Mattes **RC** 1.50
122 Carlos Garcia 1.50
123 Bill Ortega 1.50
124 Gene Altman **RC** 1.50
125 Nate Frese 1.50
126 Alfonso Soriano 1.00
127 Jose Nunez 1.50
128 Bob File **RC** 1.50
129 Dan Wright 1.50
130 Nick Johnson 1.50
131 Brent Abernathy 1.50
132 Steve Green **RC** 1.50
133 Billy Sylvester **RC** 1.50
134 Scott MacRae **RC** 1.50
135 Kris Keller **RC** 1.50
136 Scott Stewart **RC** 1.50
137 Henry Mateo **RC** 1.50
138 Timoniel Perez 1.50
139 Nate Teut **RC** 1.50
140 Jason Michaels **RC** 1.50
141 Junior Spivey **RC** 4.00
142 Carlos Pena 1.50
143 Wilmy Caceres **RC** 1.50
144 David Lundquist 1.50
145 Jack Wilson **RC** 6.00
146 Jeremy Fikac **RC** 1.50
147 Alex Escobar 1.50
148 Abraham Nunez 1.50
149 Xavier Nady 1.50
150 Michael Cuddyer 1.50
151 Greg Miller **RC** 1.50
152 Eric Munson 1.50
153 Aubrey Huff 1.50
154 Tim Christman **RC** 1.50
155 Erick Almonte **RC** 1.50
156 Mike Penny 1.50
157 Delvin James **RC** 1.50
158 Ben Sheets 1.50
159 Jason Hart 1.50
160 Jose Acevedo **RC** 1.50
161 Will Ohman **RC** 1.50
162 Erik Hiljus **RC** 1.50
163 Juan Moreno **RC** 1.50
164 Mike Koplove **RC** 1.50
165 Pedro Santana **RC** 1.50
166 Jimmy Rollins 1.50
167 Matt White **RC** 1.50
168 Cesar Crespo **RC** 1.50
169 Carlos Hernandez 1.50
170 Chris George 1.50
171 Brad Voyles **RC** 1.50
172 Luis Pineda **RC** 1.50
173 Carlos Zambrano 1.50
174 Nate Cornejo 1.50
175 Jason Smith **RC** 1.50
176 Craig Monroe **RC** 1.50
177 Cody Ransom **RC** 1.50
178 John Grabow **RC** 1.50
179 Pedro Feliz 1.50
180 Jeremy Owens **RC** 1.50
181 Kurt Ainsworth 1.50
182 Luis Lopez 1.50
183 Stubby Clapp **RC** 1.50
184 Ryan Freel **RC** 1.50
185 Duaner Sanchez **RC** 1.50
186 Jason Jennings 1.50
187 Kyle Lohse **RC** 3.00
188 Jerrod Riggan **RC** 1.50
189 Joe Beimel **RC** 1.50
190 Nick Punto **RC** 1.50
191 Willie Harris **RC** 1.50
192 Ryan Jensen **RC** 1.50
193 Adam Pettyjohn **RC** 1.50
194 Donaldo Mendez **RC** 1.50
195 Bret Prinz **RC** 1.50
196 Paul Phillips **RC** 1.50
197 Brian Lawrence **RC** 2.00
198 Cesar Izturis 1.50
199 Blaine Neal **RC** 1.50
200 Josh Fogg **RC** 1.50
201 Josh Towers **RC** 4.00
202 Tim Spooneybarger **RC** 4.00
203 Mike Rivera **RC** 4.00
204 Juan Cruz **RC** 4.00
205 Albert Pujols **RC** 220.00
206 Josh Beckett 4.00
207 Roy Oswalt 4.00

208	Elpidio Guzman **RC**	4.00
209	Horacio Ramirez **RC**	8.00
210	Corey Patterson	4.00
211	Geronimo Gil **RC**	4.00
212	Jay Gibbons **RC**	10.00
213	Orlando Woodwards	4.00
214	David Espinosa	4.00
215	Angel Berroa **RC**	8.00
216	Brandon Duckworth **RC**	4.00
217	Brian Reith **RC**	4.00
218	David Brous **RC**	4.00
219	Bud Smith **RC**	4.00
220	Ramon Vazquez **RC**	4.00
221	Mark Teixeira **RC**	35.00
222	Justin Atchley **RC**	4.00
223	Tony Cogan **RC**	4.00
224	Grant Balfour **RC**	4.00
225	Ricardo Rodriguez **RC**	4.00
226	Brian Rogers **RC**	4.00
227	Adam Dunn	4.00
228	Wilson Betemit **RC**	4.00
229	Juan Diaz **RC**	4.00
230	Jackson Melian **RC**	4.00
231	Claudio Vargas **RC**	4.00
232	Wilkin Ruan **RC**	4.00
233	Justin Duchscherer **RC**	4.00
234	Kevin Olsen **RC**	4.00
235	Tony Fiore	4.00
236	Jeremy Affeldt **RC**	4.00
237	Mike Maroth **RC**	4.00
238	C.C. Sabathia	4.00
239	Cory Aldridge **RC**	4.00
240	Zach Day **RC**	6.00
241	Brett Jodie **RC**	4.00
242	Winston Abreu **RC**	4.00
243	Travis Hafner **RC**	20.00
244	Joe Kennedy **RC**	4.00
245	Rick Bauer **RC**	4.00
246	Mike Young	8.00
247	Ken Vining **RC**	4.00
248	Doug Nickle **RC**	4.00
249	Pablo Ozuno	4.00
250	Dustan Mohr **RC**	4.00
251	Ichiro Suzuki **RC**	50.00
252	Ryan Drese **RC**	4.00
253	Morgan Ensberg **RC**	10.00
254	George Perez **RC**	4.00
255	Roy Smith **RC**	4.00
256	Juan Uribe **RC**	6.00
257	Dewon Brazelton **RC**	4.00
258	Endy Chavez **RC**	4.00
259	Kris Foster **RC**	4.00
260	Eric Knott **RC**	4.00
261	Corky Miller **RC**	4.00
262	Larry Bigbie	4.00
263	Andres Torres **RC**	4.00
264	Adrian Hernandez **RC**	4.00
265	Johnny Estrada **RC**	6.00
266	David Williams **RC**	4.00
267	Steve Lomasney	4.00
268	Victor Zambrano **RC**	6.00
269	Keith Ginter	4.00
270	Casey Fossum **RC**	6.00
271	Josue Perez **RC**	4.00
272	Josh Phelps	4.00
273	Mark Prior **RC**	25.00
274	Brandon Berger **RC**	4.00
275	Scott Podsednik **RC**	10.00
276	Jorge Julio **RC**	6.00
277	Esix Snead **RC**	4.00
278	Brandon Knight **RC**	4.00
279	Saul Rivera **RC**	4.00
280	Benito Baez **RC**	4.00
281	Robert Mackowiak **RC**	4.00
282	Eric Hinske **RC**	8.00
283	Juan Rivera	4.00
284	Kevin Joseph **RC**	4.00
285	Juan Pena	4.00
286	Brandon Lyon **RC**	4.00
287	Adam Everett	4.00
288	Eric Valent	4.00
289	Ken Harvey	4.00
290	Bert Snow **RC**	4.00
291	Wily Mo Pena	4.00
292	Rafael Soriano **RC**	4.00
293	Carlos Valderrama **RC**	4.00
294	Christian Parker **RC**	4.00
295	Tsuyoshi Shinjo **RC**	4.00
296	Martin Vargas **RC**	4.00
297	Luke Hudson **RC**	4.00
298	Dee Brown	4.00
299	Alexis Gomez **RC**	4.00
300	Angel Santos **RC**	4.00

Longevity

Stars (1-100): 10-20X

Production 50
#'s 101-300 Production 25

Autographs

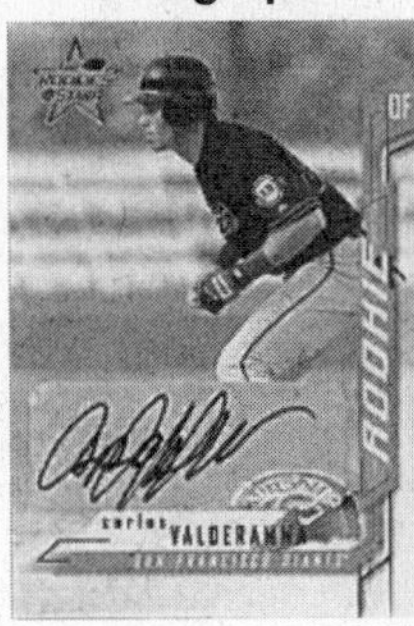

		NM/M
	Common Player:	8.00
107	Jason Karnuth	8.00
110	Brandon Larson/100	10.00
117	Jose Mieses	8.00
118	Nick Maness	8.00
119	Les Walrond	8.00
122	Carlos Garcia	8.00
123	Bill Ortega	8.00
124	Gene Altman	8.00
125	Nate Frese	8.00
130	Nick Johnson/100	15.00
133	Billy Sylvester	8.00
135	Kris Keller	8.00
139	Nate Teut	8.00
140	Jason Michaels	8.00
143	Wilmy Caceres	8.00
145	Jack Wilson/100	25.00
151	Greg Miller	8.00
155	Erick Almonte	8.00
156	Mike Penney	8.00
157	Delvin James	8.00
161	Will Ohman	8.00
167	Matt White	8.00
180	Jeremy Owens	8.00
184	Ryan Freel	10.00
185	Duaner Sanchez	8.00
193	Adam Pettyjohn/100	8.00
194	Donaldo Mendez/100	10.00
196	Paul Phillips	8.00
197	Brian Lawrence/100	15.00
199	Blaine Neal	8.00
201	Josh Towers/100	15.00
203	Michael Rivera	8.00
204	Juan Cruz/100	10.00
207	Roy Oswalt/50	50.00
208	Elpidio Guzman/100	8.00
209	Horacio Ramirez	15.00
210	Corey Patterson/SP	25.00
211	Geronimo Gil	8.00
212	Jay Gibbons/100	25.00
213	Orlando Woodards	8.00
215	Angel Berroa/100	25.00
216	Brandon Duckworth/100	10.00
218	David Brous	8.00
219	Bud Smith/50	10.00
221	Mark Teixeira/100	250.00
223	Tony Cogan	8.00
225	Ricardo Rodriguez	8.00
226	Brian Rogers	8.00
227	Adam Dunn/50	50.00
228	Wilson Betemit/100	30.00
231	Claudio Vargas	8.00
232	Wilkin Ruan	8.00
234	Kevin Olsen	8.00
236	Jeremy Affeldt	10.00
237	Mike Maroth	8.00
238	C.C. Sabathia/50	25.00
239	Cory Aldridge	8.00
240	Zach Day	10.00
243	Travis Hafner	100.00
244	Joe Kennedy/100	15.00
254	George Perez	8.00
256	Juan Uribe	10.00
257	Dewon Brazelton/100	10.00
261	Corky Miller/100	8.00
263	Andres Torres/100	8.00
265	Johnny Estrada/100	15.00
266	David Williams	10.00
270	Casey Fossum	8.00
273	Mark Prior/100	150.00
274	Brandon Berger	8.00
277	Esix Snead	8.00
282	Eric Hinske	15.00
292	Rafael Soriano	10.00
293	Carlos Valderrama	8.00
299	Alexis Gomez	8.00

Dress For Success

		NM/M
	Common Player:	8.00
	Inserted 1:96	
	Prime Cuts:	2X
	Numbered to 50 each.	
1	Cal Ripken Jr.	40.00
2	Mike Piazza	35.00
3	Barry Bonds	40.00
4	Frank Thomas	20.00
5	Nomar Garciaparra	35.00
6	Richie Sexson	8.00
7	Brian Giles	8.00
8	Todd Helton	20.00
9	Ivan Rodriguez	15.00
10	Andruw Jones	20.00
11	Juan Gonzalez	20.00
12	Vladimir Guerrero	20.00
13	Greg Maddux	25.00
14	Tony Gwynn	25.00
15	Randy Johnson	20.00
16	Jeff Bagwell	20.00
17	Kerry Wood	15.00
18	Roberto Alomar	8.00
19	Chipper Jones	25.00
20	Pedro Martinez	20.00
21	Shawn Green	10.00
22	Magglio Ordonez	10.00
23	Darin Erstad	12.00
24	Rafael Palmeiro	15.00
25	Edgar Martinez	8.00

Dress For Success Autographs

VAalues Undetermined

Freshman Orientation

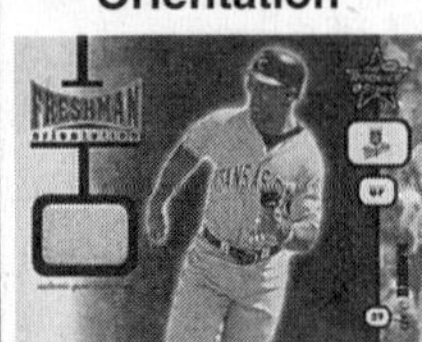

		NM/M
	Common Player:	8.00
	Inserted 1:96	
	Class Officers:	2X
	Numbered to 50 each.	
1	Adam Dunn	15.00
2	Josh Towers	8.00
3	Vernon Wells	10.00
4	Corey Patterson	10.00
6	Ben Sheets	8.00
7	Pedro Feliz	8.00
8	Keith Ginter	8.00
9	Luis Rivas	8.00
10	Andres Torres	8.00
11	Carlos Valderrama	8.00
12	Brandon Inge	8.00
13	Jay Gibbons	15.00
14	Cesar Izturis	8.00
15	Marcus Giles	8.00
16	Tsuyoshi Shinjo	12.00
17	Eric Valent	8.00
18	David Espinosa	8.00
19	Aubrey Huff	8.00
20	Wilmy Caceres	8.00
21	Bud Smith	8.00
22	Ricardo Rodriguez	8.00
23	Wes Helms	8.00
24	Jason Hart	8.00
25	Dee Brown	8.00

Freshman Orientation Autograph

Values Undetermined

Great American Treasures

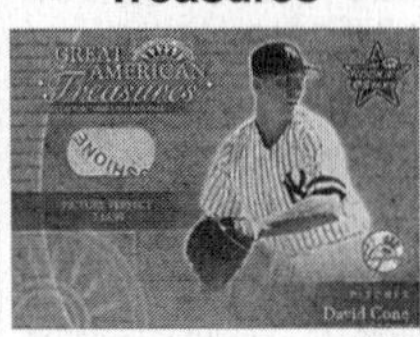

		NM/M
	Inserted 1:1,120	
1	Barry Bonds/Jsy	100.00
2	Magglio Ordonez/Bat	40.00
3	Derek Jeter/Ball	150.00
4	Nolan Ryan/Ball	600.00
5	Sammy Sosa/Ball	125.00
6	Tom Glavine/Jsy	50.00
7	Ivan Rodriguez/Bat	30.00
8	Pedro Martinez/Ball	100.00
9	Mark McGwire/Ball	250.00
10	Ted Williams/Ball	350.00
11	Ryne Sandberg/Bat	60.00
12	Barry Bonds/Ball	300.00
13	Hideo Nomo/Ball	450.00
14	Roger Maris/Ball	300.00
15	Ty Cobb/Ball	750.00
16	Harmon Killebrew/Bat	150.00
17	Magglio Ordonez/Cap	30.00
18	Wade Boggs/Bat	40.00
19	Hank Aaron/Cap	400.00
20	David Cone/Ball	100.00

Great American Treasures Autograph

		NM/M
GT-6	Tom Glavin/96 WS Jsy	125.00
GT-11	Ryne Sandberg/91 AS Bat	300.00
GT-16	Harmon Killebrew/570 HR Bat	200.00
GT-18	Wade Boggs/WS Bat	150.00

Player's Collection

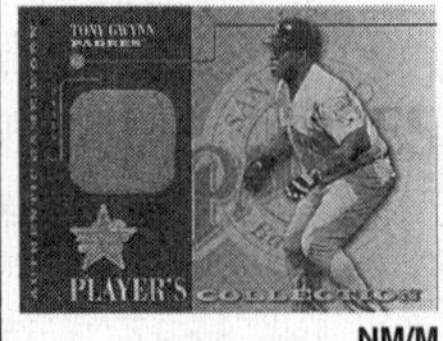

		NM/M
	Singles #'d to 100.	
1	Tony Gwynn/Bat	30.00
2	Tony Gwynn/Jsy	30.00
3	Tony Gwynn/Pants	30.00
4	Tony Gwynn/Shoe	30.00
6	Cal Ripken/Jsy	75.00
7	Cal Ripken/Bat	75.00
8	Cal Ripken/Glove	75.00
9	Cal Ripken/Jsy	75.00
11	Barry Bonds/Jsy	60.00
12	Barry Bonds/Shoe	60.00
13	Barry Bonds/Pants	60.00
14	Barry Bonds/Bat	60.00

Player's Collection Autograph

No Pricing

Slideshow

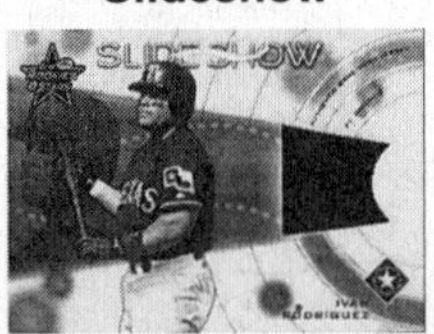

		NM/M
	Common Player:	10.00
	Production 100 Sets	
	View Masters:	1.5X
	Numbered to 25 each.	
1	Cal Ripken Jr.	40.00
2	Chipper Jones	20.00
3	Jeff Bagwell	15.00
4	Larry Walker	10.00
5	Greg Maddux	25.00
6	Ivan Rodriguez	15.00
7	Andruw Jones	15.00
8	Lance Berkman	10.00
9	Luis Gonzalez	10.00
10	Tony Gwynn	25.00
11	Troy Glaus	15.00
12	Todd Helton	20.00
13	Roberto Alomar	10.00
14	Barry Bonds	40.00
15	Vladimir Guerrero	20.00
16	Sean Casey	10.00
17	Curt Schilling	15.00
18	Frank Thomas	20.00
19	Pedro Martinez	20.00
20	Juan Gonzalez	15.00
21	Randy Johnson	20.00
22	Kerry Wood	10.00
23	Mike Sweeney	10.00
24	Maggio Ordonez	10.00
25	Kazuhiro Sasaki	10.00
26	Manny Ramirez	20.00
27	Roger Clemens	25.00
28	Albert Pujols	120.00
29	Hideo Nomo	25.00
30	Miguel Tejada	10.00

Slideshow Autographs

No Pricing

Statistical Standouts

		NM/M
	Common Player:	5.00
	Inserted 1:96	
1	Ichiro Suzuki	35.00
2	Barry Bonds	40.00
3	Ivan Rodriguez	10.00
4	Jeff Bagwell	10.00
5	Vladimir Guerrero	10.00
6	Mike Sweeney	5.00
7	Miguel Tejada	5.00
8	Mike Piazza	30.00
9	Darin Erstad	5.00
10	Alex Rodriguez	35.00
11	Jason Giambi	8.00
12	Cal Ripken Jr.	40.00
13	Albert Pujols	35.00
14	Carlos Delgado	8.00
15	Rafael Palmeiro	8.00
16	Lance Berkman	5.00
17	Luis Gonzalez	5.00
18	Sammy Sosa	30.00
19	Andruw Jones	10.00
20	Derek Jeter	40.00
21	Edgar Martinez	5.00
22	Troy Glaus	10.00
23	Maggio Ordonez	5.00
24	Mark McGwire	35.00
25	Manny Ramirez	10.00

Statistical Standouts Autograph

No Pricing

Triple Threads

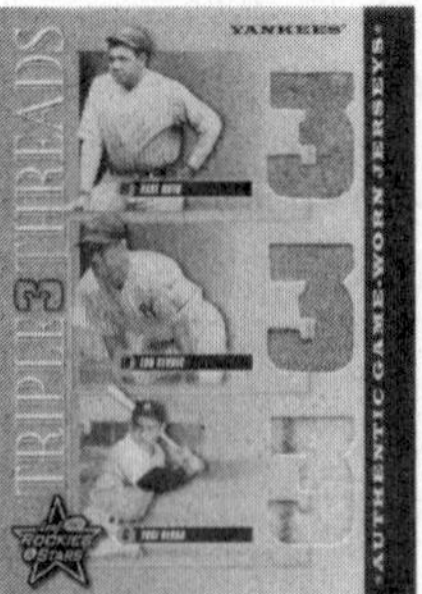

		NM/M
	Common Card:	50.00
	Numbered to 100.	
TT-1	Pedro Martinez, Manny Ramirez, Nomar Garciaparra	100.00
TT-2	Frank Robinson, Cal Ripken Jr., Brooks Robinson	200.00
TT-3	Yogi Berra, Lou Gehrig, Babe Ruth	500.00
TT-4	Andre Dawson, Ryne Sandberg, Ernie Banks	140.00
TT-5	Warren Spahn, Hank Aaron, Eddie Mathews	150.00
TT-6	Greg Maddux, Chipper Jones, Andruw Jones	75.00
TT-7	Nolan Ryan, Ivan Rodriguez, Juan Gonzalez	100.00
TT-8	Lance Berkman, Jeff Bagwell, Craig Biggio	50.00
TT-9	Rod Carew, Harmon Killebrew, Kirby Puckett	75.00
TT-10	Luis Gonzalez, Curt Schilling, Randy Johnson	60.00

2002 Leaf Samples

Each April 2002 issue of Beckett Baseball Card Monthly included a sample Leaf card rubber-cemented inside. The cards differ from the issued version only in the appearance on back of a (usually) silver-foil "SAMPLE" notation. Some cards were produced with the back overprint in gold-foil in much more limited quantities. The number of different players' cards involved in the promotion is unknown.

	NM/M
Common Player:	.10
Stars:	1.5-2X
Gold:	20X

2002 Leaf

		NM/M
	Complete Set (1-200):	80.00
	Common Player:	.15
	Common (151-200):	1.50
	Inserted 1:6	
	Pack (4):	1.50
	Box (24):	30.00
1	Tim Salmon	.25
2	Troy Glaus	.65
3	Curt Schilling	.40
4	Luis Gonzalez	.25
5	Mark Grace	.25
6	Matt Williams	.15
7	Randy Johnson	.65
8	Tom Glavine	.40
9	Brady Anderson	.15
10	Hideo Nomo	.65
11	Pedro Martinez	.65
12	Corey Patterson	.15
13	Paul Konerko	.25
14	Jon Lieber	.15
15	Carlos Lee	.15
16	Magglio Ordonez	.15
17	Adam Dunn	.40
18	Ken Griffey Jr.	1.00
19	C.C. Sabathia	.15
20	Jim Thome	.50
21	Juan Gonzalez	.65
22	Kenny Lofton	.15
23	Juan Encarnacion	.15
24	Tony Clark	.15
25	A.J. Burnett	.15
26	Josh Beckett	.25
27	Lance Berkman	.15
28	Eric Karros	.15
29	Shawn Green	.30
30	Brad Radke	.15
31	Joe Mays	.15
32	Javier Vazquez	.15
33	Alfonso Soriano	.50
34	Jorge Posada	.25
35	Eric Chavez	.25
36	Mark Mulder	.15
37	Miguel Tejada	.25
38	Tim Hudson	.25

39 Bobby Abreu .15
40 Pat Burrell .40
41 Ryan Klesko .15
43 John Olerud .15
44 Ellis Burks .15
45 Mike Cameron .15
46 Jim Edmonds .15
47 Ben Grieve .15
48 Carlos Pena .15
49 Alex Rodriguez 1.50
50 Raul Mondesi .15
51 Billy Koch .15
52 Manny Ramirez .65
53 Darin Erstad .25
54 Troy Percival .15
55 Andruw Jones .65
56 Chipper Jones .75
57 David Segui .15
58 Chris Stynes .15
59 Trot Nixon .15
60 Sammy Sosa 1.00
61 Kerry Wood .50
62 Frank Thomas .65
63 Barry Larkin .15
64 Bartolo Colon .15
65 Kazuhiro Sasaki .15
66 Roberto Alomar .35
67 Mike Hampton .15
68 Roger Cedeno .15
69 Cliff Floyd .15
70 Mike Lowell .15
71 Billy Wagner .15
72 Craig Biggio .15
73 Jeff Bagwell .65
74 Carlos Beltran .50
75 Mark Quinn .15
76 Mike Sweeney .15
77 Gary Sheffield .25
78 Kevin Brown .15
79 Paul LoDuca .15
80 Ben Sheets .15
81 Jeromy Burnitz .15
82 Richie Sexson .15
83 Corey Koskie .15
84 Eric Milton .15
85 Jose Vidro .15
86 Mike Piazza 1.00
87 Robin Ventura .15
88 Andy Pettitte .25
89 Mike Mussina .40
90 Orlando Hernandez .15
91 Roger Clemens .85
92 Barry Zito .25
93 Jermaine Dye .15
94 Jimmy Rollins .25
95 Jason Kendall .15
96 Rickey Henderson .65
97 Andres Galarraga .15
98 Bret Boone .15
99 Freddy Garcia .15
100 J.D. Drew .25
101 Jose Cruz Jr. .15
102 Greg Maddux .75
103 Javy Lopez .15
104 Nomar Garciaparra 1.00
105 Fred McGriff .15
106 Keith Foulke .15
107 Ray Durham .15
108 Sean Casey .25
109 Todd Walker .15
110 Omar Vizquel .15
111 Travis Fryman .15
112 Larry Walker .15
113 Todd Helton .65
114 Bobby Higginson .15
115 Charles Johnson .15
116 Moises Alou .15
117 Richard Hidalgo .15
118 Roy Oswalt .25
119 Neifi Perez .15
120 Adrian Beltre .30
121 Chan Ho Park .15
122 Geoff Jenkins .15
123 Doug Mientkiewicz .15
124 Torii Hunter .15
125 Vladimir Guerrero .65
126 Matt Lawton .15
127 Tsuyoshi Shinjo .15
128 Bernie Williams .40
129 Derek Jeter 2.00
130 Mariano Rivera .25
131 Tino Martinez .15
132 Jason Giambi .45
133 Scott Rolen .50
134 Brian Giles .15
135 Phil Nevin .15
136 Trevor Hoffman .15
137 Barry Bonds 2.00
138 Jeff Kent .15
139 Shannon Stewart .15
140 Shawn Estes .15
141 Edgar Martinez .15
142 Ichiro Suzuki 1.00
143 Albert Pujols 1.50
144 Bud Smith .15
145 Matt Morris .15
146 Frank Catalanotto .15
147 Gabe Kapler .15
148 Ivan Rodriguez .45
149 Rafael Palmeiro .45
150 Carlos Delgado .40
151 Marlon Byrd 2.00
152 Alex Herrera 1.50
153 Brandon Backe **RC** 2.00
154 Jorge De La Rosa **RC** 2.00
155 Corky Miller 1.50
156 Dennis Tankersley 1.50
157 Kyle Kane **RC** 2.00
158 Justin Duchscherer 1.50
159 Brian Mallette **RC** 2.00
160 Eric Hinske 1.50
161 Jason Lane 1.50
162 Hee Seop Choi 3.00
163 Juan Cruz 1.50
164 Rodrigo Rosario **RC** 2.00
165 Matt Guerrier 1.50
166 Anderson Machado **RC** 2.00
167 Geronimo Gil 1.50
168 Dewon Brazelton 1.50
169 Mark Prior 4.00
170 Bill Hall 1.50
171 Jorge Padilla **RC** 2.00
172 Josh Pearce 1.50
173 Allan Simpson **RC** 2.00
174 Doug DeVore **RC** 2.00
175 Morgan Ensberg 1.50
176 Angel Berroa 1.50
177 Steve Bechler **RC** 2.00
178 Antonio Perez 1.50
179 Mark Teixeira 3.00
180 Mark Ellis 1.50
181 Michael Cuddyer 1.50
182 Mike Rivera 1.50
183 Raul Chavez **RC** 2.00
184 Juan Pena 1.50
185 Austin Kearns 2.00
186 Ryan Ludwick 1.50
187 Ed Rogers 1.50
188 Wilson Betemit 1.50
189 Nick Neugebauer 1.50
190 Tom Shearn **RC** 2.00
191 Eric Cyr **RC** 2.00
192 Victor Martinez 1.50
193 Brandon Berger 1.50
194 Erik Bedard 1.50
195 Franklin German **RC** 2.00
196 Joe Thurston 1.50
197 John Buck 1.50
198 Jeff Deardorff **RC** 2.00
199 Ryan Jamison **RC** 2.00
200 Alfredo Amezaga 1.50
201 So Taguchi/500 **RC** 6.00
202 Kazuhisa Ishii/250 **RC** 8.00

Lineage

1999 Lineage (1-50): 2-5X
Inserted 1:12
2000 Lineage (51-100): 2-5X
Inserted 1:12
2001 Lineage (101-150): 2-5X
Inserted 1:12
Silver Holofoils: 8-15X
Production 100

Press Proof Blue

Stars (1-150): 5-10X
Inserted 1:24 Retail

Press Proof Red

Stars (1-150): 4-6X
Inserted 1:12 Retail

Autograph

Quantity produced listed

Burn n' Turn

NM/M
Complete Set (10): 50.00
Common Player: 4.00
Inserted 1:96
1 Fernando Vina, Edgar Renteria 4.00
2 Alex Rodriguez, Mike Young 10.00
3 Derek Jeter, Alfonso Soriano 15.00
4 Carlos Guillen, Bret Boone 4.00
5 Jose Vidro, Orlando Cabrera 4.00
6 Barry Larkin, Todd Walker 4.00
7 Carlos Febles, Neifi Perez 4.00
8 Jeff Kent, Rich Aurilia 4.00
9 Craig Biggio, Julio Lugo 5.00
10 Miguel Tejada, Mark Ellis 4.00

Clean Up Crew

NM/M
Complete Set (15): 90.00
Common Player: 4.00
Inserted 1:192
1 Barry Bonds 20.00
2 Sammy Sosa 12.00
3 Luis Gonzalez 4.00
4 Richie Sexson 4.00
5 Jim Thome 6.00
6 Chipper Jones 8.00
7 Alex Rodriguez 15.00
8 Troy Glaus 6.00
9 Rafael Palmeiro 5.00
10 Lance Berkman 4.00
11 Mike Piazza 12.00
12 Jason Giambi 5.00
13 Todd Helton 6.00
14 Shawn Green 5.00
15 Carlos Delgado 5.00

Clubhouse Signatures Bronze

NM/M
Common Player: 5.00
(1) Wilson Betemit/150 6.00
(2) Marlon Byrd/200 6.00
(3) Joe Crede/200 8.00
(4) Andre Dawson/100 30.00
(5) J.D. Drew/25 35.00
(6) Adam Dunn/200 25.00
(7) Jermaine Dye/125 10.00
(8) Mark Ellis/300 8.00
(9) Johnny Estrada/250 8.00
(10) Bob Feller/250 15.00
(11) Robert Fick/300 5.00
(12) Steve Garvey/200 15.00
(13) Austin Kearns/300 10.00
(14) Jason Lane/250 5.00
(15) Paul LoDuca/300 8.00
(16) Terrence Long/250 5.00
(17) Edgar Martinez/50 30.00
(18) Don Mattingly/25 100.00
(19) Joe Mays/200 6.00
(20) Mark Mulder/50 25.00
(21) Xavier Nady/200 8.00
(22) Roy Oswalt/300 10.00
(23) Aramis Ramirez/250 15.00
(24) Tim Redding/300 5.00
(25) Phil Rizzuto/25 45.00
(26) Ryne Sandberg/25 100.00
(27) Ron Santo/300 15.00
(28) Bud Smith/200 5.00
(29) Ozzie Smith/25 85.00
(30) Alfonso Soriano/75 30.00
(31) Alan Trammell/75 15.00
(32) Billy Williams/150 10.00
(33) Barry Zito/100 25.00

Clubhouse Signatures Silver

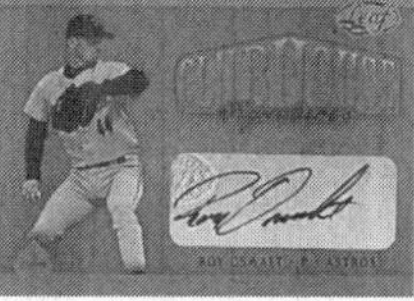

NM/M
Common Player: 10.00
(1) Rich Aurilia/100 15.00
(2) Wilson Betemit/100 15.00
(3) Marlon Byrd/100 15.00
(4) Sean Casey/50 20.00
(5) Eric Chavez/100 20.00
(6) Roger Clemens/25 150.00
(7) Joe Crede/50 20.00
(8) Andre Dawson/100 30.00
(9) Adam Dunn/75 40.00
(10) Jermaine Dye/100 15.00
(11) Mark Ellis/100 10.00
(12) Johnny Estrada/100 15.00
(13) Bob Feller/100 20.00
(14) Robert Fick/100 15.00
(15) Steve Garvey/100 20.00
(16) Vladimir Guerrero/25 60.00
(17) Todd Helton/25 50.00
(18) Austin Kearns/100 20.00
(19) Jason Lane/100 15.00
(20) Paul LoDuca/100 15.00
(21) Terrence Long/100 10.00
(22) Edgar Martinez/100 25.00
(23) Joe Mays/50 20.00
(24) Mark Mulder/100 30.00
(25) Xavier Nady/100 10.00
(26) Roy Oswalt/100 20.00
(27) Aramis Ramirez/100 20.00
(28) Tim Redding/100 10.00
(29) Cal Ripken Jr./25 225.00
(30) Phil Rizzuto/25 50.00
(31) Ron Santo/100 40.00
(32) Mike Schmidt/75 75.00
(33) Bud Smith/100 10.00
(34) Miguel Tejada/100 30.00
(35) Javier Vazquez/100 15.00
(36) Billy Williams/100 20.00
(37) Barry Zito/100 30.00

Clubhouse Signatures Gold

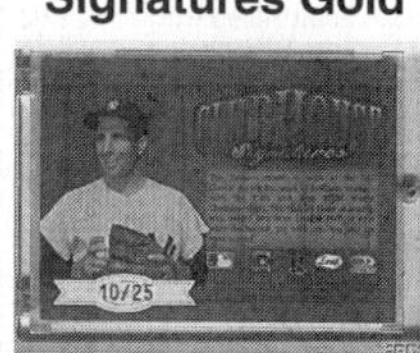

NM/M
Common Player: 15.00
Numbered to 25.
(1) Rich Aurilia 15.00
(2) Josh Beckett 60.00
(3) Wilson Betemit 15.00
(4) Marlon Byrd 15.00
(5) Sean Casey 25.00
(6) Eric Chavez 30.00
(7) Roger Clemens 150.00
(8) Joe Crede 50.00
(9) Andre Dawson 40.00
(10) J.D. Drew 40.00
(11) Adam Dunn 65.00
(12) Jermaine Dye 20.00
(13) Mark Ellis 15.00
(14) Johnny Estrada 20.00
(15) Bob Feller 45.00
(16) Robert Fick 15.00
(17) Steve Garvey 40.00
(18) Luis Gonzalez 35.00
(19) Vladimir Guerrero 75.00
(20) Todd Helton 50.00
(21) Orel Hershiser 35.00
(22) Austin Kearns 50.00
(23) Jason Lane 15.00
(24) Paul LoDuca 25.00
(25) Terrence Long 15.00
(26) Edgar Martinez 30.00
(27) Don Mattingly 125.00
(28) Joe Mays 25.00
(29) Mark Mulder 40.00
(30) Xavier Nady 20.00
(31) Roy Oswalt 30.00
(32) Chan Ho Park 15.00
(33) Kirby Puckett 125.00
(34) Aramis Ramirez 40.00
(35) Tim Redding 15.00
(36) Cal Ripken Jr. 225.00
(37) Phil Rizzuto 60.00
(38) Ryne Sandberg 125.00
(39) Ron Santo 65.00
(40) Mike Schmidt 90.00
(41) Bud Smith 20.00
(42) Ozzie Smith 100.00
(43) Alfonso Soriano 80.00
(44) Miguel Tejada 30.00
(45) Alan Trammell 25.00
(46) Javier Vazquez 20.00
(47) Billy Williams 35.00
(48) Barry Zito 50.00

Cornerstones

NM/M
Production 50 Sets
Some not priced yet
1 Andruw Jones, Chipper Jones 40.00
4 Curt Schilling, Randy Johnson 40.00
6 Larry Walker, Todd Helton 25.00
7 Carlos Delgado, Shannon Stewart 25.00
10 Bernie Williams, Roger Clemens 60.00

Future 500 Club

NM/M
Complete Set (10): 40.00
Common Player: 2.00
Inserted 1:64
1 Sammy Sosa 8.00
2 Mike Piazza 8.00
3 Alex Rodriguez 10.00
4 Chipper Jones 6.00
5 Jeff Bagwell 4.00
6 Carlos Delgado 2.00
7 Shawn Green 2.00
8 Ken Griffey Jr. 8.00
9 Rafael Palmeiro 3.00
10 Vladimir Guerrero 4.00

Game Collection

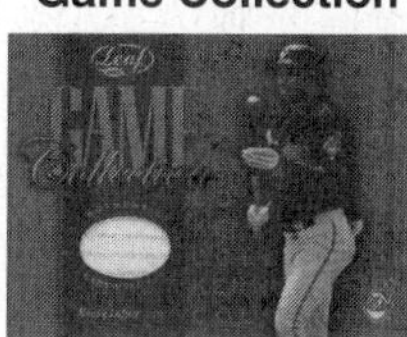

NM/M
Common Player: 5.00
Inserted 1:62 R
SP's Indicated
AB B Adrian Beltre/Bat 5.00
AD BG Adam Dunn/ Btg Glv/25 25.00
AG B Andres Galarraga/Bat 5.00
AJ B Andruw Jones/ Bat/300 8.00
BG B Brian Giles/Bat 5.00
BH B Bobby Higginson/Bat 5.00
BS H Ben Sheets/Hat/25 35.00
BW S Bernie Williams/ Shoe/25 30.00
BZ FG Barry Zito/ Fldg Glv/25 25.00
CB B Carlos Beltran/Bat 8.00
CBI B Craig Biggio/Bat 6.00
CF B Carlton Fisk/Bat 10.00
CK B Chuck Knoblauch/Bat 5.00
CP S Corey Patterson/ Shoe/25 25.00
EM B Eddie Murray/ Bat/250 15.00
GJ P Geoff Jenkins/Pants 5.00
IR BG Ivan Rodriguez/ Btg Glv/25 30.00
JB B Jeff Bagwell/Bat/100 15.00
JD H Johnny Damon/ Hat/25 25.00
JE B Juan Encarnacion/Bat 5.00
JG B Juan Gonzalez/Bat 8.00
KL B Kenny Lofton/Bat 5.00
KW S Kerry Wood/Shoe/25 40.00
LB BG Lance Berkman/ Btg Glv/25 25.00
LW B Larry Walker/Bat/50 15.00
MB BG Marlon Byrd/ Btg Glv/25 20.00
MG B Mark Grace/Bat/200 8.00
MM FG Mike Mussina/ Fldg Glv/25 55.00
MO B Magglio Ordonez/ Bat/150 6.00
MP B Mike Piazza/Bat/100 15.00
PB B Pat Burrell/Bat/100 15.00
RA B Roberto Alomar/Bat 8.00
RD B Ray Durham/Bat 5.00
RG B Rusty Greer/Bat 5.00
RJ FG Randy Johnson/ Fldg Glv 80.00
RP B Rafael Palmeiro/Bat 10.00
RP BG Rafael Palmeiro/ Btg Glv/25 30.00
RV B Robin Ventura/Bat 5.00
SC B Sean Casey/Bat 5.00
SR B Scott Rolen/Bat/250 15.00
SS H Shannon Stewart/ Hat/25 20.00
TC B Tony Clark/Bat 5.00
TG BG Tony Gwynn/ Btg Glv/25 90.00
TH B Todd Helton/Bat 10.00
TN B Trot Nixon/Bat 5.00
WB B Wade Boggs/Bat 8.00

Gold Leaf Rookies

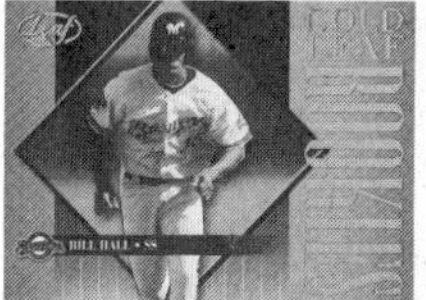

NM/M
Complete Set (10): 20.00
Common Player: 2.00
Inserted 1:24
1 Josh Beckett 4.00
2 Marlon Byrd 2.00
3 Dennis Tankersley 2.00
4 Jason Lane 2.00
5 Dewon Brazelton 2.00
6 Mark Prior 4.00
7 Bill Hall 2.00
8 Angel Berroa 2.00
9 Mark Teixeira 4.00
10 John Buck 2.00

Heading for the Hall Autographs

NM/M
Common Player: 25.00
Production 50 each.
1 Greg Maddux 125.00
2 Ozzie Smith 100.00
3 Andre Dawson 40.00
4 Dennis Eckersley 45.00
5 Roberto Alomar 25.00
6 Cal Ripken Jr. 200.00
7 Roger Clemens 150.00
8 Tony Gwynn 100.00
9 Alex Rodriguez 150.00
10 Jeff Bagwell 40.00

League of Nations

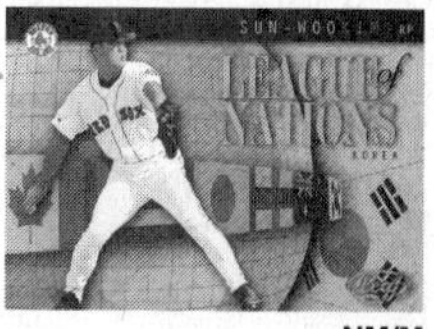

NM/M
Complete Set (10): 20.00
Common Player: 2.00
Inserted 1:60
1 Ichiro Suzuki 8.00
2 Tsuyoshi Shinjo 2.00
3 Chan Ho Park 2.00
4 Larry Walker 2.00
5 Andruw Jones 4.00
6 Hideo Nomo 4.00
7 Byung-Hyun Kim 2.00
8 Sun-Woo Kim 2.00
9 Orlando Hernandez 2.00
10 Luke Prokopec 2.00

Retired Numbers

#'d to jersey number.
No Pricing

Rookie Reprints

NM/M
Complete Set (6): 35.00
Common Player: 3.00
#'d to year of issue
1 Roger Clemens/ 1,985 10.00
2 Kirby Puckett/1,985 9.00
3 Andres Galarraga/ 1,986 3.00
4 Fred McGriff/1,986 3.00
5 Sammy Sosa/1,990 10.00
6 Frank Thomas/1,990 8.00

Shirt Off My Back

NM/M
Common Player: 5.00
Inserted 1:29
Patch Variations: 2-4X
RA Roberto Alomar 8.00
JB Jeff Bagwell/SP 20.00
MB Michael Barrett 5.00
CB Carlos Beltran 15.00
LB Lance Berkman 5.00
GB George Brett/SP 50.00
KB Kevin Brown 5.00
MB Mark Buehrle 5.00
AB A.J. Burnett 5.00
JBU Jeromy Burnitz 5.00
CD Carlos Delgado 8.00
RD Ryan Dempster 5.00
DE Darin Erstad/SP 15.00
CF Cliff Floyd 5.00
FG Freddy Garcia/SP 8.00
NG Nomar Garciaparra/ SP 40.00
TGL Troy Glaus/SP 20.00
TGL Tom Glavine 8.00
LG Luis Gonzalez 5.00
TG Tony Gwynn 25.00
MH Mike Hampton 5.00
TH Todd Helton 20.00
THU Tim Hudson 6.00
BJA Bo Jackson/SP 25.00
RJ Randy Johnson 20.00
CJ Chipper Jones/SP 30.00

AK Al Kaline/SP 20.00
EK Eric Karros 5.00
BL Barry Larkin 5.00
CL Carlos Lee 5.00
JL Javy Lopez 5.00
GM Greg Maddux/SP 30.00
EM Edgar Martinez/SP 8.00
PM Pedro Martinez/SP 20.00
DM Don Mattingly/SP 50.00
KM Kevin Millwood 5.00
HN Hideo Nomo/SP 25.00
JO John Olerud 5.00
MO Magglio Ordonez 5.00
RP Rafael Palmeiro 10.00
CHP Chan Ho Park/SP 8.00
TP Troy Percival 5.00
AP Andy Pettitte/SP 12.00
MP Mike Piazza 30.00
KP Kirby Puckett 25.00
BR Brad Radke 5.00
MR Manny Ramirez 20.00
CR Cal Ripken Jr./SP/50 100.00
AR Alex Rodriguez 35.00
SR Scott Rolen/SP 15.00
KS Kazuhiro Sasaki/SP 8.00
CS Curt Schilling/SP 15.00
RS Richie Sexson 5.00
TS Tsuyoshi Shinjo/SP 8.00
JS John Smoltz 5.00
MS Mike Sweeney 5.00
MT Miguel Tejada 6.00
LW Larry Walker/SP 8.00
MW Matt Williams 5.00
DW Dave Winfield/SP 20.00

2002 Leaf Certified Samples

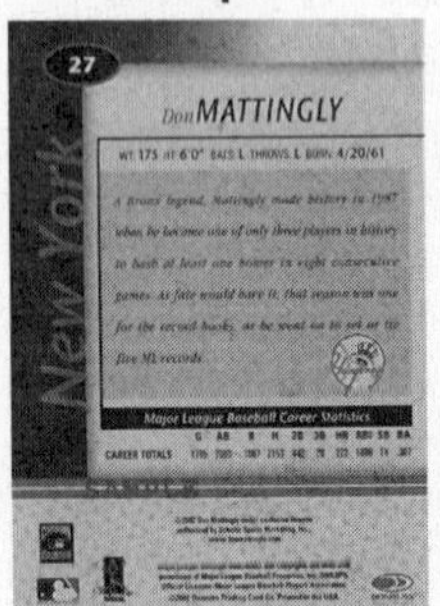

Each October 2002 issue of Beckett Baseball Card Monthly included a sample Leaf Certified card rubber-cemented inside. The cards differ from the issued version only in the appearance on back of a (usually) silver-foil "SAMPLE" notation. Some cards were produced with the back overprint in gold foil in much more limited quantities. The number of different players' cards involved in the promotion is unknown.

NM/M
Common Player: .10
Stars: 1.5X
Gold: 20X

2002 Leaf Certified

NM/M
Complete Set (200):
Common Player: .50
Common (151-200): 5.00
Production 500
Pack (5): 6.00
Box (16): 75.00
1 Alex Rodriguez 4.00
2 Luis Gonzalez .65
3 Javier Vazquez .50
4 Juan Uribe .50
5 Ben Sheets .50
6 George Brett 4.00
7 Magglio Ordonez .50
8 Randy Johnson 1.00
9 Joe Kennedy .50
10 Richie Sexson .50
11 Larry Walker .50
12 Lance Berkman .50
13 Jose Cruz Jr. .50
14 Doug Davis .50
15 Cliff Floyd .50
16 Ryan Klesko .50
17 Troy Glaus 1.00
18 Robert Person .50
19 Bartolo Colon .50
20 Adam Dunn .75
21 Kevin Brown .50
22 John Smoltz .50
23 Edgar Martinez .50
24 Eric Karros .50
25 Tony Gwynn 2.00
26 Mark Mulder .50
27 Don Mattingly 4.00
28 Brandon Duckworth .50
29 C.C. Sabathia .50
30 Nomar Garciaparra 3.00
31 Adam Johnson .50
32 Miguel Tejada .65
33 Ryne Sandberg 2.00
34 Roger Clemens 2.50
35 Edgardo Alfonzo .50
36 Jason Jennings .50
37 Todd Helton 1.00
38 Nolan Ryan 5.00
39 Paul LoDuca .50
40 Cal Ripken Jr. 5.00
41 Terrence Long .50
42 Mike Sweeney .50
43 Carlos Lee .50
44 Ben Grieve .50
45 Tony Armas Jr. .50
46 Joe Mays .50
47 Jeff Kent .50
48 Andy Pettitte .65
49 Kirby Puckett 2.00
50 Aramis Ramirez .50
51 Tim Redding .50
52 Freddy Garcia .50
53 Javy Lopez .50
54 Mike Schmidt 4.00
55 Wade Miller .50
56 Ramon Ortiz .50
57 Ray Durham .50
58 J.D. Drew .75
59 Bret Boone .50
60 Mark Buehrle .50
61 Geoff Jenkins .50
62 Greg Maddux 2.00
63 Mark Grace .65
64 Toby Hall .50
65 A.J. Burnett .50
66 Bernie Williams .65
67 Roy Oswalt .65
68 Shannon Stewart .50
69 Barry Zito .65
70 Juan Pierre .50
71 Preston Wilson .50
72 Rafael Furcal .50
73 Sean Casey .65
74 John Olerud .50
75 Paul Konerko .75
76 Vernon Wells .50
77 Juan Gonzalez 1.00
78 Ellis Burks .50
79 Jim Edmonds .75
80 Robert Fick .50
81 Michael Cuddyer .50
82 Tim Hudson .65
83 Phil Nevin .50
84 Curt Schilling .75
85 Juan Cruz .50
86 Jeff Bagwell 1.00
87 Raul Mondesi .50
88 Bud Smith .50
89 Omar Vizquel .50
90 Vladimir Guerrero 1.00
91 Garret Anderson .50
92 Mike Piazza 3.00
93 Josh Beckett .65
94 Carlos Delgado 1.00
95 Kazuhiro Sasaki .50
96 Chipper Jones 2.00
97 Jacque Jones .50
98 Pedro J. Martinez 1.00
99 Marcus Giles .50
100 Craig Biggio .50
101 Orlando Cabrera .50
102 Al Leiter .50
103 Michael Barrett .50
104 Hideo Nomo 1.00
105 Mike Mussina .75
106 Jeremy Giambi .50
107 Cristian Guzman .50
108 Frank Thomas 1.00
109 Carlos Beltran 1.00
110 Jorge Posada .65
111 Roberto Alomar .65
112 Bobby Abreu .50
113 Robin Ventura .50
114 Pat Burrell .75
115 Kenny Lofton .50
116 Adrian Beltre .75
117 Gary Sheffield .75
118 Jermaine Dye .50
119 Manny Ramirez 1.00
120 Brian Giles .50
121 Tsuyoshi Shinjo .50
122 Rafael Palmeiro .85
123 Mo Vaughn .50
124 Kerry Wood .75
125 Moises Alou .50
126 Rickey Henderson 1.00
127 Corey Patterson .50
128 Jim Thome 1.00
129 Richard Hidalgo .50
130 Darin Erstad .75
131 Johnny Damon .75
132 Juan Encarnacion .50
133 Scott Rolen 1.00
134 Tom Glavine .75
135 Ivan Rodriguez .85
136 Jay Gibbons .50
137 Trot Nixon .50
138 Nick Neugebauer .50
139 Barry Larkin .50
140 Andruw Jones 1.00
141 Shawn Green .75
142 Jose Vidro .50
143 Derek Jeter 5.00
144 Ichiro Suzuki 3.00
145 Ken Griffey Jr. 3.00
146 Barry Bonds 5.00
147 Albert Pujols 4.00
148 Sammy Sosa 3.00
149 Jason Giambi .75
150 Alfonso Soriano .75
151 Drew Henson/Bat 8.00
152 Luis Garcia/Bat 5.00
153 Geronimo Gil/Jsy 5.00
154 Corky Miller/Jsy 5.00
155 Mike Rivera/Bat 5.00
156 Mark Ellis/Jsy 5.00
157 Josh Pearce/Bat 5.00
158 Ryan Ludwick/Bat 5.00
159 So Taguchi/Bat **RC** 12.00
160 Cody Ransom/Jsy 5.00
161 Jeff Deardorff/Bat **RC** 5.00
162 Franklyn German/Bat **RC** 5.00
163 Ed Rogers/Jsy 5.00
164 Eric Cyr/Jsy **RC** 5.00
165 Victor Alvarez/Jsy **RC** 5.00
166 Victor Martinez/Jsy 15.00
167 Brandon Berger/Jsy 5.00
168 Juan Diaz/Jsy 5.00
169 Kevin Frederick/Jsy **RC** 5.00
170 Earl Snyder/Bat **RC** 5.00
171 Morgan Ensberg/Bat 8.00
172 Ryan Jamison/Jsy **RC** 5.00
173 Rodrigo Rosario/Jsy **RC** 5.00
174 Willie Harris/Bat 5.00
175 Ramon Vazquez/Bat 5.00
176 Kazuhisa Ishii/Bat **RC** 12.00
177 Hank Blalock/Jsy 10.00
178 Mark Prior/Bat 15.00
179 Dewon Brazelton/Jsy 5.00
180 Doug DeVore/Jsy **RC** 5.00
181 Jorge Padilla/Bat **RC** 5.00
182 Mark Teixeira/Jsy 10.00
183 Orlando Hudson/Bat 5.00
184 John Buck/Jsy 5.00
185 Erik Bedard/Jsy 5.00
186 Allan Simpson/Jsy **RC** 5.00
187 Travis Hafner/Jsy 10.00
188 Jason Lane/Jsy 5.00
189 Marlon Byrd/Jsy 5.00
190 Joe Thurston/Jsy 5.00
191 Brandon Backe/Jsy **RC** 5.00
192 Josh Phelps/Jsy 5.00
193 Bill Hall/Bat 5.00
194 Chris Snelling/Bat **RC** 8.00
195 Austin Kearns/Jsy 8.00
196 Antonio Perez/Bat 5.00
197 Angel Berroa/Bat 8.00
198 Anderson Machado/Jsy **RC** 5.00
199 Alfredo Amezaga/Jsy 5.00
200 Eric Hinske/Bat 8.00

Mirror Red

NM/M
Common (1-200): 5.00
Cards (151-200): .5-1X base
Production 150 Sets
Mirror Blues (1-200): .5-1.5X
Production 75 Sets
Mirror Golds not priced.
Production 25 Sets
Mirror Emerald five sets produced.
Mirror Black one set produced.
1 Alex Rodriguez/Jsy 25.00
2 Luis Gonzalez/Jsy 5.00
3 Javier Vazquez/Bat 5.00
4 Juan Uribe/Jsy 5.00
5 Ben Sheets/Jsy 8.00
6 George Brett/Jsy 40.00
7 Magglio Ordonez/Jsy 8.00
8 Randy Johnson/Jsy 15.00
9 Joe Kennedy/Jsy 5.00
10 Richie Sexson/Jsy 10.00
11 Larry Walker/Jsy 8.00
12 Lance Berkman/Jsy 8.00
13 Jose Cruz Jr./Jsy 5.00
14 Doug Davis/Jsy 5.00
15 Cliff Floyd/Jsy 5.00
16 Ryan Klesko/Bat 5.00
17 Troy Glaus/Jsy 10.00
18 Robert Person/Jsy 5.00
19 Bartolo Colon/Jsy 5.00
20 Adam Dunn/Jsy 15.00
21 Kevin Brown/Jsy 8.00
22 John Smoltz/Jsy 8.00
23 Edgar Martinez/Jsy 8.00
24 Eric Karros/Jsy 5.00
25 Tony Gwynn/Jsy 20.00
26 Mark Mulder/Jsy 8.00
27 Don Mattingly/Jsy 40.00
28 Brandon Duckworth/Jsy 5.00
29 C.C. Sabathia/Jsy 5.00
30 Nomar Garciaparra/Jsy 20.00
31 Adam Johnson/Jsy 5.00
32 Miguel Tejada/Jsy 8.00
33 Ryne Sandberg/Jsy 40.00
34 Roger Clemens/Jsy 25.00
35 Edgardo Alfonzo/Jsy 5.00
36 Jason Jennings/Jsy 5.00
37 Todd Helton/Jsy 10.00
38 Nolan Ryan/Jsy 60.00
39 Paul LoDuca/Jsy 5.00
40 Cal Ripken Jr/Jsy 55.00
41 Terrence Long/Jsy 5.00
42 Mike Sweeney/Jsy 5.00
43 Carlos Lee/Jsy 5.00
44 Ben Grieve/Jsy 5.00
45 Tony Armas Jr./Jsy 5.00
46 Joe Mays/Jsy 5.00
47 Jeff Kent/Jsy 8.00
48 Andy Pettitte/Jsy 8.00
49 Kirby Puckett/Jsy 15.00
50 Aramis Ramirez/Jsy 8.00
51 Tim Redding/Jsy 5.00
52 Freddy Garcia/Jsy 5.00
53 Javy Lopez/Jsy 6.00
54 Mike Schmidt/Jsy 35.00
55 Wade Miller/Jsy 5.00
56 Ramon Ortiz/Jsy 5.00
57 Ray Durham/Jsy 5.00
58 J.D. Drew/Jsy 5.00
59 Bret Boone/Jsy 5.00
60 Mark Buehrle/Jsy 5.00
61 Geoff Jenkins/Jsy 5.00
62 Greg Maddux/Jsy 20.00
63 Mark Grace/Jsy 10.00
64 Toby Hall/Jsy 5.00
65 A.J. Burnett/Jsy 5.00
66 Bernie Williams/Jsy 8.00
67 Roy Oswalt/Jsy 8.00
68 Shannon Stewart/Jsy 5.00
69 Barry Zito/Jsy 8.00
70 Juan Pierre/Jsy 5.00
71 Preston Wilson/Jsy 5.00
72 Rafael Furcal/Jsy 5.00
73 Sean Casey/Jsy 5.00
74 John Olerud/Jsy 5.00
75 Paul Konerko/Jsy 5.00
76 Vernon Wells/Jsy 5.00
77 Juan Gonzalez/Jsy 8.00
78 Ellis Burks/Jsy 5.00
79 Jim Edmonds/Jsy 8.00
80 Robert Fick/Jsy 5.00
81 Michael Cuddyer/Jsy 5.00
82 Tim Hudson/Jsy 5.00
83 Phil Nevin/Jsy 5.00
84 Curt Schilling/Jsy 8.00
85 Juan Cruz/Jsy 5.00
86 Jeff Bagwell/Jsy 10.00
87 Raul Mondesi/Jsy 5.00
88 Bud Smith/Jsy 5.00
89 Omar Vizquel/Jsy 5.00
90 Vladimir Guerrero/Jsy 20.00
91 Garret Anderson/Jsy 8.00
92 Mike Piazza/Jsy 15.00
93 Josh Beckett/Jsy 8.00
94 Carlos Delgado/Jsy 8.00
95 Kazuhiro Sasaki/Jsy 5.00
96 Chipper Jones/Jsy 10.00
97 Jacque Jones/Jsy 5.00
98 Pedro Martinez/Jsy 15.00
99 Marcus Giles/Jsy 5.00
100 Craig Biggio/Jsy 6.00
101 Orlando Cabrera/Jsy 5.00
102 Al Leiter/Jsy 5.00
103 Michael Barrett/Jsy 5.00
104 Hideo Nomo/Jsy 15.00
105 Mike Mussina/Jsy 12.00
106 Jeremy Giambi/Jsy 5.00
107 Cristian Guzman/Jsy 5.00
108 Frank Thomas/Jsy 10.00
109 Carlos Beltran/Bat 8.00
110 Jorge Posada/Bat 8.00
111 Roberto Alomar/Bat 12.00
112 Bobby Abreu/Bat 6.00
113 Robin Ventura/Bat 10.00
114 Pat Burrell/Bat 18.00
115 Kenny Lofton/Bat 6.00
116 Adrian Beltre/Bat 8.00
117 Gary Sheffield/Bat 6.00
118 Jermaine Dye/Bat 8.00
119 Manny Ramirez/Bat 8.00
120 Brian Giles/Bat 5.00
121 Tsuyoshi Shinjo/Bat 5.00
122 Rafael Palmeiro/Bat 10.00
123 Mo Vaughn/Bat 5.00
124 Kerry Wood/Bat 15.00
125 Moises Alou/Bat 8.00
126 Rickey Henderson/Bat 15.00
127 Corey Patterson/Bat 8.00
128 Jim Thome/Bat 15.00
129 Richard Hidalgo/Bat 5.00
130 Darin Erstad/Jsy 5.00
131 Johnny Damon/Bat 5.00
132 Juan Encarnacion/Bat 5.00
133 Scott Rolen/Bat 10.00
134 Tom Glavine/Bat 8.00
135 Ivan Rodriguez/Bat 10.00
136 Jay Gibbons/Bat 5.00
137 Trot Nixon/Bat 5.00
138 Nick Neugebauer/Bat 5.00
139 Barry Larkin/Jsy 10.00
140 Andruw Jones/Bat 8.00
141 Shawn Green/Bat 8.00
142 Jose Vidro/Jsy 5.00
143 Derek Jeter/Base 25.00
144 Ichiro Suzuki/Base 20.00
145 Ken Griffey Jr./Base 15.00
146 Barry Bonds/Base 20.00
147 Albert Pujols/Base 15.00
148 Sammy Sosa/Base 15.00
149 Jason Giambi/Base 8.00
150 Alfonso Soriano/Jsy 10.00
151 Drew Henson/Bat 5.00
152 Luis Garcia/Bat 5.00
153 Geronimo Gil/Jsy 5.00
154 Corky Miller/Jsy 5.00
155 Mike Rivera/Bat 5.00
156 Mark Ellis/Jsy 5.00
157 Josh Pearce/Bat 5.00
158 Ryan Ludwick/Bat 5.00
159 So Taguchi/Bat 12.00
160 Cody Ransom/Jsy 5.00
161 Jeff Deardorff/Bat 5.00
162 Franklyn German/Bat 5.00
163 Ed Rogers/Jsy 5.00
164 Eric Cyr/Jsy 5.00
165 Victor Alvarez/Jsy 5.00
166 Victor Martinez/Jsy 10.00
167 Brandon Berger/Jsy 5.00
168 Juan Diaz/Jsy 5.00
169 Kevin Frederick/Jsy 5.00
170 Earl Snyder/Bat 5.00
171 Morgan Ensberg/Bat 5.00
172 Ryan Jamison/Jsy 5.00
173 Rodrigo Rosario/Jsy 5.00
174 Willie Harris/Bat 5.00
175 Ramon Vazquez/Bat 5.00
176 Kazuhisa Ishii/Bat 15.00
177 Hank Blalock/Jsy 10.00
178 Mark Prior/Bat 10.00
179 Dewon Brazelton/Jsy 5.00
180 Doug DeVore/Jsy 5.00
181 Jorge Padilla/Bat 5.00
182 Mark Teixeira/Jsy 10.00
183 Orlando Hudson/Bat 5.00
184 John Buck/Jsy 5.00
185 Erik Bedard/Jsy 5.00
186 Allan Simpson/Jsy 5.00
187 Travis Hafner/Jsy 8.00
188 Jason Lane/Jsy 5.00
189 Marlon Byrd/Jsy 5.00
190 Joe Thurston/Jsy 5.00
191 Brandon Backe/Jsy 5.00
192 Josh Phelps/Jsy 5.00
193 Bill Hall/Bat 5.00
194 Chris Snelling/Bat 5.00
195 Austin Kearns/Jsy 8.00
196 Antonio Perez/Bat 5.00
197 Angel Berroa/Bat 6.00
198 Anderson Machado/Jsy 5.00
199 Alfredo Amezaga/Jsy 5.00
200 Eric Hinske/Bat 6.00

All Certified Team

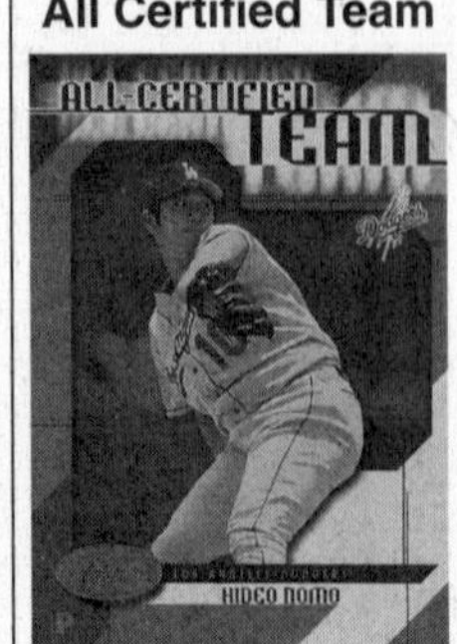

NM/M
Complete Set (25): 75.00
Common Player: 1.50
Inserted 1:17
Mirror Blues: 2-4X
Production 50 Sets
Mirror Reds: 1.5-3X
Production 75 Sets
Golds not priced 25 sets produced.
1 Ichiro Suzuki 5.00
2 Alex Rodriguez 6.00
3 Sammy Sosa 5.00
4 Jeff Bagwell 3.00
5 Greg Maddux 4.00
6 Todd Helton 3.00
7 Nomar Garciaparra 5.00
8 Ken Griffey Jr. 5.00
9 Roger Clemens 4.50
10 Adam Dunn 2.00
11 Chipper Jones 4.00
12 Hideo Nomo 3.00
13 Lance Berkman 1.50
14 Barry Bonds 8.00
15 Manny Ramirez 3.00
16 Jason Giambi 2.00
17 Rickey Henderson 3.00
18 Randy Johnson 3.00
19 Derek Jeter 8.00
20 Kazuhisa Ishii 1.50
21 Frank Thomas 3.00
22 Mike Piazza 5.00
23 Albert Pujols 6.00
24 Pedro J. Martinez 3.00
25 Vladimir Guerrero 3.00

Certified Skills

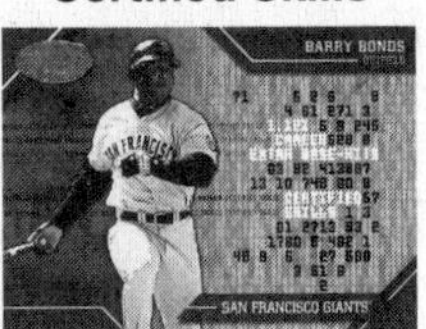

NM/M
Complete Set (20): 65.00
Common Player: 2.00
Inserted 1:17
Mirror Blues: 1.5-2.5X
Production 75 Sets
Mirror Reds: 1-2X
Production 150 Sets
Mirror Golds not priced 25 sets.
1 Barry Bonds 8.00
2 Greg Maddux 4.00
3 Rickey Henderson 2.00
4 Ichiro Suzuki 5.00
5 Pedro J. Martinez 2.00
6 Kazuhisa Ishii 1.50
7 Alex Rodriguez 6.00
8 Mike Piazza 5.00
9 Sammy Sosa 5.00
10 Derek Jeter 8.00
11 Albert Pujols 6.00
12 Roger Clemens 4.50
13 Mark Prior 1.50
14 Chipper Jones 3.00
15 Ken Griffey Jr. 5.00
16 Frank Thomas 2.00
17 Randy Johnson 2.00
18 Vladimir Guerrero 2.00
19 Nomar Garciaparra 5.00
20 Jeff Bagwell 2.00

Fabric of the Game

NM/M
Common Player:
1 Bobby Doerr/37 20.00
2 Ozzie Smith/78 40.00
3 Pee Wee Reese/40 35.00
4 Tommy Lasorda/80 8.00
4 Tommy Lasorda/54 15.00
4 Tommy Lasorda/50 15.00
5 Red Schoendienst/45 20.00
7 Harmon Killebrew/54 35.00
8 Roger Maris A's/57 75.00
10 Mel Ott/26 75.00
11 Paul Molitor/100 20.00
11 Paul Molitor/78 20.00
11 Paul Molitor/50 30.00
12 Duke Snider/47 40.00
13 Brooks Robinson/55 40.00
14 George Brett/40 75.00
14 George Brett/73 50.00
15 Johnny Bench/80 20.00
15 Johnny Bench/67 30.00
15 Johnny Bench/50 30.00
16 Lou Boudreau/38 20.00
17 Stan Musial/41 60.00
18 Al Kaline/53 30.00
19 Steve Garvey/100 8.00
19 Steve Garvey/69 15.00
19 Steve Garvey/45 15.00
20 Nomar Garciaparra/100 25.00
20 Nomar Garciaparra/96 25.00
20 Nomar Garciaparra/50 35.00
21 Joe Morgan/80 10.00
21 Joe Morgan/63 20.00
21 Joe Morgan/50 20.00
22 Willie Stargell/62 25.00
23 Andre Dawson/80 15.00
23 Andre Dawson/76 15.00
23 Andre Dawson/50 20.00
24 Gary Carter/100 10.00
24 Gary Carter/74 20.00

24 Gary Carter/50 20.00
25 Reggie Jackson/ A's/67 30.00
27 Phil Rizzuto/41 30.00
28 Luis Aparicio/56 20.00
29 Robin Yount/80 30.00
29 Robin Yount/74 30.00
29 Robin Yount/50 40.00
30 Tony Gwynn/100 20.00
30 Tony Gwynn/82 20.00
30 Tony Gwynn/50 30.00
31 Ernie Banks/53 40.00
32 Joe Torre/50 15.00
32 Joe Torre/60 15.00
33 Bo Jackson/100 20.00
33 Bo Jackson/86 20.00
33 Bo Jackson/35 50.00
34 Alfonso Soriano/80 20.00
34 Alfonso Soriano/99 20.00
34 Alfonso Soriano/50 25.00
35 Cal Ripken Jr./80 60.00
35 Cal Ripken Jr./81 60.00
35 Cal Ripken Jr./50 80.00
36 Miguel Tejada/100 10.00
36 Miguel Tejada/97 10.00
36 Miguel Tejada/50 20.00
37 Alex Rodriguez/ M's/100 20.00
37 Alex Rodriguez/ M's/94 20.00
37 Alex Rodriguez M's/50 35.00
38 Mike Schmidt/80 40.00
38 Mike Schmidt/72 40.00
38 Mike Schmidt/50 50.00
39 Lou Brock/61 25.00
40 Don Sutton/80 8.00
40 Don Sutton/66 10.00
40 Don Sutton/50 15.00
41 Roberto Clemente/ 55 125.00
42 Jim Palmer/65 20.00
43 Don Mattingly/40 75.00
43 Don Mattingly/82 50.00
44 Ryne Sandberg/40 60.00
44 Ryne Sandberg/81 40.00
45 Early Wynn/39 20.00
46 Mike Piazza/ Dodgers/100 20.00
46 Mike Piazza/ Dodgers/92 20.00
46 Mike Piazza/ Dodgers/31 40.00
46 Mike Piazza/ Dodgers/50 25.00
47 Wade Boggs/100 15.00
47 Wade Boggs/82 15.00
47 Wade Boggs/26 40.00
47 Wade Boggs/45 30.00
48 Jim "Catfish" Hunter/65 25.00
48 Jim "Catfish" Hunter/27 40.00
49 Juan Marichal/60 20.00
49 Juan Marichal/27 40.00
50 Carlton Fisk/ Red Sox/80 25.00
50 Carlton Fisk/ Red Sox/69 40.00
50 Carlton Fisk/ Red Sox/27 50.00
50 Carlton Fisk/ Red Sox/50 30.00
51 Curt Schilling/100 15.00
51 Curt Schilling/88 15.00
51 Curt Schilling/38 25.00
51 Curt Schilling/50 20.00
52 Rod Carew/ Angels/80 15.00
52 Rod Carew/ Angels/67 25.00
52 Rod Carew/ Angels/50 25.00
53 Rod Carew Twins/67 25.00
54 Joe Carter/100 8.00
54 Joe Carter/83 8.00
54 Joe Carter/29 15.00
54 Joe Carter/50 10.00
55 Nolan Ryan/ Angels/66 60.00
56 Orlando Cepeda/80 8.00
56 Orlando Cepeda/55 10.00
56 Orlando Cepeda/30 25.00
56 Orlando Cepeda/50 15.00
57 Dave Winfield/80 15.00
57 Dave Winfield/73 20.00
57 Dave Winfield/31 30.00
57 Dave Winfield/50 20.00
58 Hoyt Wilhelm/80 8.00
58 Hoyt Wilhelm/52 10.00
58 Hoyt Wilhelm/31 20.00
58 Hoyt Wilhelm/50 15.00
59 Steve Carlton/80 15.00
59 Steve Carlton/65 20.00
59 Steve Carlton/32 30.00
59 Steve Carlton/50 20.00
60 Eddie Murray/100 15.00
60 Eddie Murray/77 15.00
60 Eddie Murray/33 30.00
60 Eddie Murray/50 20.00
61 Nolan Ryan/ Rangers/40 75.00
61 Nolan Ryan/ Rangers/66 60.00
61 Nolan Ryan/ Rangers/34 75.00
62 Nolan Ryan/ Astros/40 75.00
62 Nolan Ryan/ Astros/66 60.00
62 Nolan Ryan/ Astros/34 75.00
63 Kirby Puckett/40 40.00
63 Kirby Puckett/84 20.00
63 Kirby Puckett/34 40.00
64 Yogi Berra/46 40.00
64 Yogi Berra/35 40.00
65 Phil Niekro/80 8.00
65 Phil Niekro/64 10.00
65 Phil Niekro/35 15.00
65 Phil Niekro/50 10.00
66 Gaylord Perry/80 8.00
66 Gaylord Perry/62 10.00
66 Gaylord Perry/36 15.00
66 Gaylord Perry/50 10.00
67 Pedro Martinez/ Expos/100 15.00
67 Pedro Martinez/ Expos/92 15.00
67 Pedro Martinez/ Expos/45 25.00
67 Pedro Martinez/ Expos/50 20.00
68 Alex Rodriguez/ Rgr/100 20.00
68 Alex Rodriguez/ Rgr/94 20.00
68 Alex Rodriguez/ Rgr/50 30.00
69 Dave Parker/100 8.00
69 Dave Parker/73 10.00
69 Dave Parker/39 15.00
69 Dave Parker/50 10.00
70 Darin Erstad/100 8.00
70 Darin Erstad/96 8.00
70 Darin Erstad/50 15.00
71 Eddie Matthews/52 30.00
71 Eddie Matthews/41 35.00
72 Tom Seaver Mets/67 30.00
72 Tom Seaver Mets/41 40.00
73 Tom Seaver Reds/67 30.00
73 Tom Seaver Reds/41 40.00
74 Jackie Robinson/47 100.00
74 Jackie Robinson/42 100.00
75 Randy Johnson/ M's/80 15.00
75 Randy Johnson/ M's/88 15.00
75 Randy Johnson/ M's/51 25.00
75 Randy Johnson/ M's/50 25.00
76 Reggie Jackson/ Yanks/57 30.00
76 Reggie Jackson/ Yanks/44 40.00
77 Reggie Jackson/ Angels/80 20.00
77 Reggie Jackson/ Angels/67 30.00
77 Reggie Jackson/ Angels/44 40.00
77 Reggie Jackson/ Angels/50 40.00
78 Willie McCovey/80 10.00
78 Willie McCovey/59 15.00
78 Willie McCovey/44 20.00
78 Willie McCovey/50 20.00
79 Eric Davis/100 5.00
79 Eric Davis/84 5.00
79 Eric Davis/34 10.00
79 Eric Davis/50 8.00
80 Carlos Delgado/95 6.00
80 Carlos Delgado/93 6.00
81 Dale Murphy/100 20.00
81 Dale Murphy/76 20.00
81 Dale Murphy/50 30.00
82 Brian Giles/100 5.00
82 Brian Giles/95 5.00
82 Brian Giles/50 8.00
83 Kazuhiro Sasaki/100 8.00
83 Kazuhiro Sasaki/100 8.00
83 Kazuhiro Sasaki/50 10.00
84 Phil Nevin/100 5.00
84 Phil Nevin/95 5.00
84 Phil Nevin/50 8.00
85 Frank Thomas/80 15.00
85 Frank Thomas/90 15.00
85 Frank Thomas/35 25.00
85 Frank Thomas/50 15.00
86 Raul Mondesi/100 5.00
86 Raul Mondesi/93 5.00
86 Raul Mondesi/43 8.00
86 Raul Mondesi/50 8.00
87 Don Drysdale/56 25.00
87 Don Drysdale/53 25.00
88 Gary Sheffield/100 6.00
88 Gary Sheffield/88 6.00
88 Gary Sheffield/50 10.00
89 Andy Pettitte/100 15.00
89 Andy Pettitte/95 15.00
89 Andy Pettitte/46 30.00
89 Andy Pettitte/50 20.00
90 Lance Berkman/45 20.00
90 Lance Berkman/99 10.00
91 Paul LoDuca/100 5.00
91 Paul LoDuca/98 5.00
91 Paul LoDuca/50 8.00
92 Kevin Brown/86 5.00
92 Kevin Brown/27 15.00
93 Jim Thome/100 15.00
93 Jim Thome/91 15.00
93 Jim Thome/50 25.00
94 Mike Sweeney/100 5.00
94 Mike Sweeney/95 5.00
94 Mike Sweeney/29 15.00
94 Mike Sweeney/50 10.00
95 Pedro J. Martinez/ Red Sox/100 15.00
95 Pedro J. Martinez/ Red Sox/92 15.00
95 Pedro J. Martinez/ Red Sox/45 25.00
95 Pedro J. Martinez/ Red Sox/45 25.00
96 Cliff Floyd/100 5.00
96 Cliff Floyd/93 5.00
96 Cliff Floyd/30 15.00
96 Cliff Floyd/50 10.00
97 Larry Walker/100 8.00
97 Larry Walker/89 8.00
97 Larry Walker/33 30.00
97 Larry Walker/50 10.00
98 Ivan Rodriguez/80 10.00
98 Ivan Rodriguez/91 10.00
98 Ivan Rodriguez/50 20.00
99 Aramis Ramirez/100 8.00
99 Aramis Ramirez/98 8.00
99 Aramis Ramirez/50 12.00
100 Roberto Alomar/100 10.00
100 Roberto Alomar/88 10.00
100 Roberto Alomar/50 15.00
101 Ben Sheets/100 8.00
101 Ben Sheets/101 8.00
101 Ben Sheets/50 15.00
102 Adam Dunn/101 20.00
102 Adam Dunn/39 40.00
103 Hideo Nomo/95 30.00
104 C.C. Sabathia/50 10.00
104 C.C. Sabathia/101 5.00
104 C.C. Sabathia/52 10.00
104 C.C. Sabathia/50 10.00
105 Rickey Henderson/ A's/100 20.00
105 Rickey Henderson/ A's/79 20.00
105 Rickey Henderson/ A's/30 50.00
105 Rickey Henderson/ A's/50 30.00
106 Carlton Fisk/ White Sox/80 20.00
106 Carlton Fisk/ White Sox/69 30.00
106 Carlton Fisk/ White Sox/72 30.00
106 Carlton Fisk/ White Sox/50 30.00
107 Chan Ho Park/100 5.00
107 Chan Ho Park/94 5.00
107 Chan Ho Park/61 8.00
107 Chan Ho Park/50 8.00
108 Mike Mussina/100 20.00
108 Mike Mussina/91 20.00
108 Mike Mussina/35 50.00
108 Mike Mussina/50 30.00
109 Mark Mulder/100 8.00
109 Mark Mulder/100 8.00
109 Mark Mulder/20 20.00
109 Mark Mulder/35 20.00
110 Tsuyoshi Shinjo/100 5.00
110 Tsuyoshi Shinjo/101 5.00
110 Tsuyoshi Shinjo/30 20.00
111 Pat Burrell/100 10.00
111 Pat Burrell/100 10.00
111 Pat Burrell/50 15.00
112 Edgar Martinez/100 10.00
112 Edgar Martinez/87 10.00
112 Edgar Martinez/50 15.00
113 Barry Larkin/100 10.00
113 Barry Larkin/86 10.00
113 Barry Larkin/50 15.00
114 Jeff Kent/100 6.00
114 Jeff Kent/92 6.00
114 Jeff Kent/50 8.00
115 Chipper Jones/100 15.00
115 Chipper Jones/93 15.00
115 Chipper Jones/50 30.00
116 Magglio Ordonez/100 8.00
116 Magglio Ordonez/97 8.00
116 Magglio Ordonez/30 30.00
116 Magglio Ordonez/50 15.00
117 Jim Edmonds/100 8.00
117 Jim Edmonds/93 8.00
117 Jim Edmonds/50 15.00
118 Andruw Jones/100 10.00
118 Andruw Jones/96 10.00
118 Andruw Jones/45 20.00
119 Jose Canseco/100 15.00
119 Jose Canseco/85 15.00
119 Jose Canseco/50 30.00
120 Manny Ramirez/100 10.00
120 Manny Ramirez/93 10.00
120 Manny Ramirez/50 20.00
121 Sean Casey/100 10.00
121 Sean Casey/97 10.00
121 Sean Casey/50 15.00
122 Bret Boone/100 6.00
122 Bret Boone/92 6.00
122 Bret Boone/29 15.00
122 Bret Boone/50 10.00
123 Tim Hudson/100 8.00
123 Tim Hudson/99 8.00
123 Tim Hudson/50 15.00
124 Craig Biggio/100 10.00
124 Craig Biggio/88 10.00
124 Craig Biggio/50 15.00
125 Mike Piazza/ Mets/100 20.00
125 Mike Piazza/Mets/92 20.00
125 Mike Piazza/Mets/31 40.00
125 Mike Piazza/Mets/51 25.00
126 Jack Morris/100 5.00
126 Jack Morris/77 5.00
126 Jack Morris/47 10.00
127 Roy Oswalt/100 8.00
127 Roy Oswalt/101 8.00
127 Roy Oswalt/39 15.00
127 Roy Oswalt/50 15.00
128 Shawn Green/100 8.00
128 Shawn Green/93 8.00
128 Shawn Green/50 15.00
129 Carlos Beltran/100 8.00
129 Carlos Beltran/98 8.00
129 Carlos Beltran/50 10.00
130 Todd Helton/100 10.00
130 Todd Helton/97 10.00
130 Todd Helton/50 20.00
131 Barry Zito/75 15.00
131 Barry Zito/100 10.00
131 Barry Zito/75 15.00
131 Barry Zito/30 30.00
132 J.D. Drew/100 15.00
132 J.D. Drew/98 15.00
132 J.D. Drew/50 20.00
133 Mark Grace/100 10.00
133 Mark Grace/88 10.00
133 Mark Grace/50 20.00
134 Rickey Henderson/ Mets/100 20.00
134 Rickey Henderson/ Mets/79 20.00
134 Rickey Henderson/ Mets/50 30.00
135 Greg Maddux/100 20.00
135 Greg Maddux/86 20.00
135 Greg Maddux/50 30.00
136 Garret Anderson/100 8.00
136 Garret Anderson/94 8.00
136 Garret Anderson/50 15.00
137 Rafael Palmeiro/100 15.00
137 Rafael Palmeiro/86 15.00
137 Rafael Palmeiro/50 20.00
138 Luis Gonzalez/50 10.00
138 Luis Gonzalez/90 8.00
138 Luis Gonzalez/45 15.00
139 Nick Johnson/100 5.00
139 Nick Johnson/101 5.00
139 Nick Johnson/26 20.00
139 Nick Johnson/50 10.00
140 Vladimir Guerrero/80 15.00
140 Vladimir Guerrero/96 15.00
140 Vladimir Guerrero/50 25.00
141 Mark Buehrle/100 5.00
141 Mark Buehrle/56 8.00
142 Troy Glaus/100 15.00
142 Troy Glaus/98 15.00
142 Troy Glaus/50 25.00
143 Juan Gonzalez/100 10.00
143 Juan Gonzalez/89 10.00
143 Juan Gonzalez/50 15.00
144 Kerry Wood/100 15.00
144 Kerry Wood/98 15.00
144 Kerry Wood/34 40.00
144 Kerry Wood/50 30.00
145 Roger Clemens/80 25.00
145 Roger Clemens/84 25.00
145 Roger Clemens/50 40.00
146 Bob Abreu/100 8.00
146 Bob Abreu/96 8.00
146 Bob Abreu/53 15.00
146 Bob Abreu/50 15.00
147 Bernie Williams/95 10.00
147 Bernie Williams/91 10.00
147 Bernie Williams/51 20.00
148 Tom Glavine/100 10.00
148 Tom Glavine/87 10.00
148 Tom Glavine/47 25.00
148 Tom Glavine/50 25.00
149 Jorge Posada/100 10.00
149 Jorge Posada/95 10.00
149 Jorge Posada/50 25.00
150 Randy Johnson/ D'Backs/80 15.00
150 Randy Johnson/ D'Backs/88 15.00
150 Randy Johnson/ D'Backs/51 30.00
150 Randy Johnson/ D'Backs/50 30.00

2002 Leaf Rookies & Stars Samples

Each December 2002 issue of Beckett Baseball Card Monthly included a sample Leaf R&S card rubber-cemented inside. The cards differ from the issued version only in the appearance on back of a (usually) silver-foil "SAMPLE" notation. Some cards were produced with the back overprint in gold foil in much more limited quantities. The number of different players' cards involved in the promotion is unknown.

NM/M
Common Player: .10
Stars: 1.5-2X
Gold: 20X

2002 Leaf Rookies & Stars

NM/M
Complete Set (400):
Common Player: .15
Common SP (1-300): .75
Common (301-400): .40
Inserted 1:2
Pack (6): 1.50
Box (24): 30.00

1 Darin Erstad .25
2 Garret Anderson .15
3 Troy Glaus .40
4 David Eckstein .15
5 Adam Kennedy .15
6 Kevin Appier .15
6 Kevin Appier/SP/Mets .75
6 Kevin Appier/SP/Royals .75
7 Jarrod Washburn .15
8 David Segui .15
9 Jay Gibbons .15
10 Tony Batista .15
11 Scott Erickson .15
12 Jeff Conine .15
13 Melvin Mora .15
14 Shea Hillenbrand .15
15 Manny Ramirez .65
15 Manny Ramirez/ SP/Indians 2.00
16 Pedro J. Martinez .65
16 Pedro J. Martinez/ SP/Dodgers 2.50
16 Pedro J. Martinez/ SP/Expos 2.50
17 Nomar Garciaparra 1.00
18 Rickey Henderson .65
18 Rickey Henderson/ SP/Angels 3.00
18 Rickey Henderson/ SP/A's 3.00
18 Rickey Henderson/ SP/Blue Jays 3.00
18 Rickey Henderson/ SP/M's 3.00
18 Rickey Henderson/ SP/Mets 3.00
18 Rickey Henderson/ SP/Padres 3.00
18 Rickey Henderson/ SP/Yankees 3.00
19 Johnny Damon .25
19 Johnny Damon/SP/A's 1.00
19 Johnny Damon/ SP/Royals 1.00
20 Trot Nixon .15
21 Derek Lowe .15
22 Jason Varitek .15
23 Tim Wakefield .15
24 Frank Thomas .65
25 Kenny Lofton .15
25 Kenny Lofton/ SP/Indians .75
26 Magglio Ordonez .15
27 Ray Durham .15
28 Mark Buehrle .15
29 Paul Konerko .25
29 Paul Konerko/ SP/Dodgers 1.00
29 Paul Konerko/SP/Reds 1.00
30 Jose Valentin .15
31 C.C. Sabathia .15
32 Ellis Burks .15
32 Ellis Burks/SP/Giants .75
32 Ellis Burks/SP/Red Sox .75
32 Ellis Burks/SP/Rockies .75
33 Omar Vizquel .15
33 Omar Vizquel/ SP/Mariners 1.00
34 Jim Thome .50
35 Matt Lawton .15
36 Travis Fryman .15
36 Travis Fryman/ SP/Tigers .75
37 Robert Fick .15
38 Bobby Higginson .15
39 Steve Sparks .15
40 Mike Rivera .15
41 Wendell Magee .15
42 Randall Simon .15
43 Carlos Pena .15
43 Carlos Pena/SP/A's .75
43 Carlos Pena/ SP/Rangers .75
44 Mike Sweeney .15
45 Chuck Knoblauch .15
46 Carlos Beltran .50
47 Joe Randa .15
48 Paul Byrd .15
49 Mac Suzuki .15
50 Torii Hunter .15
51 Jacque Jones .15
52 David Ortiz .35
53 Corey Koskie .15
54 Brad Radke .15
55 Doug Mientkiewicz .15
56 A.J. Pierzynski .15
57 Dustan Mohr .15
58 Derek Jeter 2.00
59 Bernie Williams .30
60 Roger Clemens .85
60 Roger Clemens/ SP/Blue Jays 4.00
60 Roger Clemens/ SP/Red Sox 4.00
61 Mike Mussina .40
61 Mike Mussina/ SP/Orioles 1.50
62 Jorge Posada .25
63 Alfonso Soriano .50
64 Jason Giambi .40
64 Jason Giambi/SP/A's 2.50
65 Robin Ventura .15
65 Robin Ventura/ SP/Mets .75
65 Robin Ventura/ SP/White Sox .75
66 Andy Pettitte .25
67 David Wells .15
67 David Wells/ SP/Blue Jays .75
67 David Wells/SP/Tigers .75
68 Nick Johnson .15
69 Jeff Weaver .15
69 Jeff Weaver/SP/Tigers .75
70 Raul Mondesi .15
70 Raul Mondesi/ SP/Blue Jays .75
70 Raul Mondesi/ SP/Dodgers .75
71 Tim Hudson .25
72 Barry Zito .25
73 Mark Mulder .25
74 Miguel Tejada .25
75 Eric Chavez .25
76 Billy Koch .15
76 Billy Koch/SP/Blue Jays .75
77 Jermaine Dye .15
77 Jermaine Dye/ SP/Royals .75
78 Scott Hatteberg .15
79 Ichiro Suzuki 1.00
80 Edgar Martinez .15
81 Mike Cameron .15
81 Mike Cameron/ SP/White Sox .75
82 John Olerud .15
82 John Olerud/ SP/Blue Jays .75
82 John Olerud/SP/Mets .75
83 Bret Boone .15
84 Dan Wilson .15
85 Freddy Garcia .15
86 Jamie Moyer .15
87 Carlos Guillen .15
88 Ruben Sierra .15
89 Kazuhiro Sasaki .15
90 Mark McLemore .15
91 Ben Grieve .15
92 Aubrey Huff .15
93 Steve Cox .15
94 Toby Hall .15
95 Randy Winn .15
96 Brent Abernathy .15
97 Chan Ho Park .15
97 Chan Ho Park/ SP/Dodgers .75
98 Alex Rodriguez 1.50
98 Alex Rodriguez/ SP/Mariners 4.00
99 Juan Gonzalez .40
99 Juan Gonzalez/ SP/Indians 1.50
99 Juan Gonzalez/ SP/Tigers 1.50
100 Rafael Palmeiro .60
100 Rafael Palmeiro/ SP/Cubs 1.00
100 Rafael Palmeiro/ SP/Orioles 1.00
101 Ivan Rodriguez .50
102 Rusty Greer .15
103 Kenny Rogers .15
103 Kenny Rogers/SP/A's .75
103 Kenny Rogers/ SP/Yankees .75
104 Hank Blalock .40
105 Mark Teixeira .25
106 Carlos Delgado .40
107 Shannon Stewart .15

108 Eric Hinske .15
109 Roy Halladay .25
110 Felipe Lopez .15
111 Vernon Wells .15
112 Curt Schilling .40
112 Curt Schilling/SP/Phillies 1.50
113 Randy Johnson .65
113 Randy Johnson/SP/Astros 3.00
113 Randy Johnson/SP/Expos 3.00
113 Randy Johnson/SP/Mariners 3.00
114 Luis Gonzalez .25
114 Luis Gonzalez/SP/Astros 1.00
114 Luis Gonzalez/SP/Cubs 1.00
115 Mark Grace .25
115 Mark Grace/SP/Cubs 1.50
116 Junior Spivey .15
117 Tony Womack .15
118 Matt Williams .15
118 Matt Williams/SP/Giants 1.00
118 Matt Williams/SP/Indians 1.00
119 Danny Bautista .15
120 Byung-Hyun Kim .15
121 Craig Counsell .15
122 Greg Maddux .75
122 Greg Maddux/SP/Cubs 4.00
123 Tom Glavine .25
124 John Smoltz .15
124 John Smoltz/SP/Tigers .75
125 Chipper Jones .75
126 Gary Sheffield .25
127 Andruw Jones .65
128 Vinny Castilla .15
129 Damian Moss .15
130 Rafael Furcal .15
131 Kerry Wood .50
132 Fred McGriff .15
132 Fred McGriff/SP/Blue Jays 1.00
132 Fred McGriff/SP/Braves 1.00
132 Fred McGriff/SP/Devil Rays 1.00
132 Fred McGriff/SP/Padres 1.00
133 Sammy Sosa 1.00
133 Sammy Sosa/SP/Rangers 4.00
133 Sammy Sosa/SP/White Sox 4.00
134 Alex Gonzalez .15
135 Corey Patterson .15
136 Moises Alou .15
137 Mark Prior .50
138 Jon Lieber .15
139 Matt Clement .15
140 Ken Griffey Jr. 1.00
140 Ken Griffey Jr./SP/Mariners 4.00
141 Barry Larkin .15
142 Adam Dunn .40
143 Sean Casey .15
143 Sean Casey/SP/Indians .75
144 Jose Rijo .15
145 Elmer Dessens .15
146 Austin Kearns .15
147 Corky Miller .15
148 Todd Walker .15
148 Todd Walker/SP/Rockies .75
148 Todd Walker/SP/Expos .75
149 Chris Reitsma .15
150 Ryan Dempster .15
151 Larry Walker .15
152 Todd Helton .65
153 Juan Uribe .15
154 Juan Pierre .15
155 Mike Hampton .15
156 Todd Zeile .15
157 Josh Beckett .25
158 Mike Lowell .15
158 Mike Lowell/SP/Yankees .75
159 Derrek Lee .15
160 A.J. Burnett .15
161 Luis Castillo .15
162 Tim Raines .15
163 Preston Wilson .15
164 Juan Encarnacion .15
165 Jeff Bagwell .65
166 Craig Biggio .15
167 Lance Berkman .15
168 Wade Miller .15
169 Roy Oswalt .25
170 Richard Hidalgo .15
171 Carlos Hernandez .15
172 Daryle Ward .15
173 Shawn Green .30
173 Shawn Green/SP/Blue Jays 1.00
174 Adrian Beltre .35
175 Paul LoDuca .15
176 Eric Karros .15
177 Kevin Brown .15
178 Hideo Nomo .65
178 Hideo Nomo/SP/Brewers 1.50
178 Hideo Nomo/SP/Mets 1.50
178 Hideo Nomo/SP/Red Sox 1.50
178 Hideo Nomo/SP/Tigers 1.50
179 Odalis Perez .15
180 Eric Gagne .35
181 Brian Jordan .15
182 Cesar Izturis .15
183 Geoff Jenkins .15
184 Richie Sexson .15
184 Richie Sexson/SP/Indians 1.00
185 Jose Hernandez .15
186 Ben Sheets .15
187 Ruben Quevedo .15
188 Jeffrey Hammonds .15
189 Alex Sanchez .15
190 Vladimir Guerrero .65
191 Jose Vidro .15
192 Orlando Cabrera .15
193 Michael Barrett .15
194 Javier Vazquez .15
195 Tony Armas Jr. .15
196 Andres Galarraga .15
197 Tomokazu Ohka .15
198 Bartolo Colon .15
198 Bartolo Colon/SP/Indians .75
199 Cliff Floyd .15
199 Cliff Floyd/SP/Marlins .75
200 Mike Piazza 1.00
200 Mike Piazza/SP/Dodgers 4.00
200 Mike Piazza/SP/Marlins 4.00
201 Jeromy Burnitz .15
202 Roberto Alomar .35
202 Roberto Alomar/SP/Blue Jays 1.50
202 Roberto Alomar/SP/Indians 1.50
202 Roberto Alomar/SP/Orioles 1.50
202 Roberto Alomar/SP/Padres 1.50
203 Mo Vaughn .15
203 Mo Vaughn/SP/Angels 1.00
203 Mo Vaughn/SP/Red Sox 1.00
204 Al Leiter .15
204 Al Leiter/SP/Blue Jays .75
205 Pedro Astacio .15
206 Edgardo Alfonzo .15
207 Armando Benitez .15
208 Scott Rolen .50
209 Pat Burrell .35
210 Bobby Abreu .15
210 Bobby Abreu/SP/Astros 1.00
211 Mike Lieberthal .15
212 Brandon Duckworth .15
213 Jimmy Rollins .40
214 Jeremy Giambi .15
215 Vicente Padilla .15
216 Travis Lee .15
217 Jason Kendall .15
218 Brian Giles .15
218 Brian Giles/SP/Indians 1.00
219 Aramis Ramirez .15
220 Pokey Reese .15
221 Kip Wells .15
222 Josh Fogg .15
222 Josh Fogg/SP/White Sox .75
223 Mike Williams .15
224 Ryan Klesko .15
224 Ryan Klesko/SP/Braves .75
225 Phil Nevin .15
225 Phil Nevin/SP/Tigers .75
226 Brian Lawrence .15
227 Mark Kotsay .15
228 Brett Tomko .15
229 Trevor Hoffman .15
229 Trevor Hoffman/SP/Marlins .75
230 Barry Bonds 2.00
230 Barry Bonds/SP/Pirates 6.00
231 Jeff Kent .15
231 Jeff Kent/SP/Blue Jays 1.00
232 Rich Aurilia .15
233 Tsuyoshi Shinjo .15
233 Tsuyoshi Shinjo/SP/Mets 1.00
234 Benito Santiago .15
234 Benito Santiago/SP/Padres .75
235 Kirk Rueter .15
236 Kurt Ainsworth .15
237 Livan Hernandez .15
238 Russ Ortiz .15
239 David Bell .15
240 Jason Schmidt .15
241 Reggie Sanders .15
242 Jim Edmonds .25
242 Jim Edmonds/SP/Angels 1.00
243 J.D. Drew .25
244 Albert Pujols 1.50
245 Fernando Vina .15
246 Tino Martinez .15
246 Tino Martinez/SP/Mariners 1.00
246 Tino Martinez/SP/Yankees 1.00
247 Edgar Renteria .15
248 Matt Morris .15
249 Woody Williams .15
250 Jason Isringhausen .15
250 Jason Isringhausen/SP/A's .75
251 Cal Ripken Jr. 2.00
252 Cal Ripken Jr. 2.00
253 Cal Ripken Jr. 2.00
254 Cal Ripken Jr. 2.00
255 Ryne Sandberg .75
256 Don Mattingly 1.00
257 Don Mattingly 1.00
258 Roger Clemens .85
259 Roger Clemens .85
260 Roger Clemens .85
261 Roger Clemens .85
262 Roger Clemens .85
263 Roger Clemens .85
264 Roger Clemens .85
265 Rickey Henderson .65
266 Rickey Henderson .65
267 Jose Canseco .40
268 Barry Bonds 2.00
269 Barry Bonds 2.00
270 Barry Bonds 2.00
271 Barry Bonds 2.00
272 Jeff Bagwell .65
273 Kirby Puckett .75
274 Kirby Puckett .75
275 Greg Maddux .75
276 Greg Maddux .75
277 Greg Maddux .75
278 Greg Maddux .75
279 Ken Griffey Jr. 1.00
280 Mike Piazza 1.00
281 Kirby Puckett .75
282 Mike Piazza 1.00
283 Frank Thomas .65
284 Hideo Nomo .65
285 Randy Johnson .65
286 Juan Gonzalez .65
287 Derek Jeter 2.00
288 Derek Jeter 2.00
289 Derek Jeter 2.00
290 Nomar Garciaparra 1.00
291 Pedro J. Martinez .65
292 Kerry Wood .50
293 Sammy Sosa 1.00
294 Chipper Jones .75
295 Ivan Rodriguez .50
296 Ivan Rodriguez .50
297 Albert Pujols 1.50
298 Ichiro Suzuki 1.00
299 Ichiro Suzuki 1.00
300 Ichiro Suzuki 1.00
301 So Taguchi **RC** 1.00
302 Kazuhisa Ishii **RC** 2.00
303 Jeremy Lambert **RC** .50
304 Sean Burroughs .40
305 P.J. Bevis **RC** .50
306 Jon Rauch .40
307 Scotty Layfield **RC** .50
308 Miguel Ascencio .40
309 Franklyn German **RC** .50
310 Luis Ugueto **RC** .50
311 Jorge Sosa **RC** .50
312 Felix Escalona **RC** .50
313 Jose Valverde **RC** .50
314 Jeremy Ward **RC** .50
315 Kevin Gryboski **RC** .50
316 Francis Beltran **RC** .50
317 Joe Thurston .40
318 Cliff Lee **RC** 1.00
319 Takahito Nomura **RC** .50
320 Bill Hall .40
321 Marlon Byrd .50
322 Andy Shibilo **RC** .50
323 Edwin Almonte **RC** .50
324 Brandon Backe **RC** .40
325 Chone Figgins **RC** 1.50
326 Brian Mallette **RC** .50
327 Rodrigo Rosario **RC** .50
328 Anderson Machado **RC** .50
329 Jorge Padilla **RC** .50
330 Allan Simpson **RC** .50
331 Doug DeVore **RC** .50
332 Drew Henson .50
333 Raul Chavez **RC** .50
334 Tom Shearn **RC** .50
335 Ben Howard **RC** .50
336 Chris Baker **RC** .50
337 Travis Hughes **RC** .50
338 Kevin Mench .40
339 Brian Tallet .40
340 Mike Moriarty **RC** .50
341 Corey Thurman **RC** .50
342 Terry Pearson **RC** .50
343 Steve Kent **RC** .50
344 Satoru Komiyama **RC** .50
345 Jason Lane .40
346 Freddy Sanchez **RC** .50
347 Brandon Puffer **RC** .50
348 Clay Condrey **RC** .50
349 Rene Reyes **RC** .50
350 Hee Seop Choi .50
351 Rodrigo Lopez .40
352 Colin Young **RC** .50
353 Jason Simontacchi **RC** .50
354 Oliver Perez **RC** 2.00
355 Kirk Saarloos .50
356 Marcus Thames .40
357 Jeff Austin **RC** .50
358 Justin Kaye .40
359 Julio Mateo **RC** .50
360 Mike Smith **RC** .50
361 Chris Snelling **RC** .75
362 Dennis Tankersley .40
363 Runelvys Hernandez **RC** .50
364 Aaron Cook **RC** .50
365 Joe Borchard .40
366 Earl Snyder **RC** .50
367 Shane Nance **RC** .50
368 Aaron Guiel **RC** .50
369 Steve Bechler **RC** .50
370 Tim Kalita **RC** .50
371 Shawn Sedlacek **RC** .50
372 Eric Good **RC** .50
373 Eric Junge **RC** .50
374 Matt Thornton .40
375 Travis Driskill **RC** .50
376 Mitch Wylie **RC** .50
377 John Ennis **RC** .50
378 Reed Johnson **RC** .75
379 Juan Brito **RC** .50
380 Ron Calloway **RC** .50
381 Adrian Burnside **RC** .50
382 Josh Bard **RC** .50
383 Matt Childers **RC** .50
384 Gustavo Chacin **RC** .50
385 Luis Martinez **RC** .50
386 Trey Hodges **RC** .50
387 Hansel Izquierdo **RC** .50
388 Jeriome Robertson **RC** .50
389 Victor Alvarez **RC** .50
390 David Ross **RC** .50
391 Ron Chiavacci .40
392 Adam Walker **RC** .50
393 Mike Gonzalez **RC** .50
394 John Foster **RC** .50
395 Kyle Kane **RC** .50
396 Cam Esslinger **RC** .50
397 Kevin Frederick **RC** .50
398 Franklin Nunez **RC** .50
399 Todd Donovan **RC** .50
400 Kevin Cash **RC** .50

Longevity

Stars (1-300): 5-10X
SP's (1-300): 1-30X
Production 100
Rookies (301-400): No Pricing
Production 25

BLC Homers

NM/M
Common Player: 20.00
Production 25 Sets
1 Luis Gonzalez 20.00
2 Luis Gonzalez 20.00
3 Luis Gonzalez 20.00
4 Todd Helton 35.00
5 Todd Helton 35.00
6 Todd Helton 35.00
7 Todd Helton 35.00
8 Todd Helton 35.00
9 Todd Helton 35.00
10 Todd Helton 35.00
11 Todd Helton 35.00
12 Jim Thome 35.00
13 Jim Thome 35.00
14 Jim Thome 35.00
15 Rafael Palmeiro 30.00
16 Rafael Palmeiro 30.00
17 Rafael Palmeiro 30.00
18 Rafael Palmeiro 30.00
19 Rafael Palmeiro 30.00
20 Troy Glaus 35.00
21 Troy Glaus 35.00
22 Troy Glaus 35.00
23 Gary Sheffield 20.00
24 Gary Sheffield 20.00
25 Gary Sheffield 20.00
26 Mike Piazza 50.00
27 Mike Piazza 50.00
28 Mike Piazza 50.00
29 Mike Piazza 50.00
30 Mike Piazza 50.00

Dress For Success

NM/M
Common Player: 8.00
Production 250 Sets
Prime Cuts: No Pricing
Production 25 Sets
1 Mike Piazza 25.00
2 Cal Ripken Jr. 40.00
3 Carlos Delgado 8.00
4 Chipper Jones 20.00
5 Bernie Williams 8.00
6 Carlos Beltran 10.00
7 Curt Schilling 10.00
8 Greg Maddux 20.00
9 Ivan Rodriguez 12.00
10 Alex Rodriguez 20.00
11 Roger Clemens 20.00
12 Todd Helton 15.00
13 Jim Edmonds 8.00
14 Manny Ramirez 15.00
15 Mark Buehrle 8.00

Freshman Orientation

NM/M
Common Player: 5.00
Inserted 1:142
Class Officer Parallel: 1.5X
Production 50 Sets
1 Andres Torres/Bat 8.00
2 Mark Ellis/Jsy 8.00
3 Erik Bedard/Bat 8.00
4 Delvin James/Jsy 5.00
5 Austin Kearns/Bat 10.00
6 Josh Pearce/Bat 5.00
7 Rafael Soriano/Jsy 8.00
8 Jason Lane/Bat 8.00
9 Mark Prior/Jsy 15.00
10 Alfredo Amezaga/Bat 5.00
11 Ryan Ludwick/Bat 5.00
12 So Taguchi/Bat 10.00
13 Duaner Sanchez/Bat 5.00
14 Kazuhisa Ishii/Jsy 15.00
15 Zach Day/Jsy 8.00
16 Eric Cyr/Bat 5.00
17 Francis Beltran/Jsy 5.00
18 Joe Borchard/Jsy 10.00
19 Jeremy Affeldt/Shoe 10.00
20 Alexis Gomez/Jsy 5.00

Great American Signings

NM/M
Common Autograph: 5.00
Inserted 1:56
Brent Abernathy/175 5.00
Brandon Backe/175 5.00
Chris Baker/175 5.00
Francis Beltran/175 5.00
Raul Chavez/175 5.00
Doug DeVore/175 5.00
Felix Escalona/100 8.00
Franklyn German/175 5.00
Jay Gibbons/150 10.00
Bill Hall/175 8.00
Drew Henson/50 35.00
Eric Hinske/175 8.00
Ben Howard/175 5.00
Aubrey Huff/175 8.00
Travis Hughes/175 5.00
Cesar Izturis/175 8.00
Nick Johnson/175 8.00
Austin Kearns/75 10.00
Satoru Komiyama/75 20.00
Jason Lane/150 8.00
Brian Lawrence/175 5.00
Anderson Machado/175 5.00
Roy Oswalt/100 15.00
Jorge Padilla/175 5.00
Oliver Perez/175 25.00
Rene Reyes/175 5.00
Mike Rivera/175 5.00
Rodrigo Rosario/175 5.00
Tom Shearn/175 5.00
Chris Snelling/175 10.00
Mac Suzuki/100 30.00
So Taguchi/50 40.00
Dennis Tankersley/175 8.00
Corey Thurman/175 5.00
Luis Ugueto/175 5.00
Kip Wells/175

Statistical Standouts

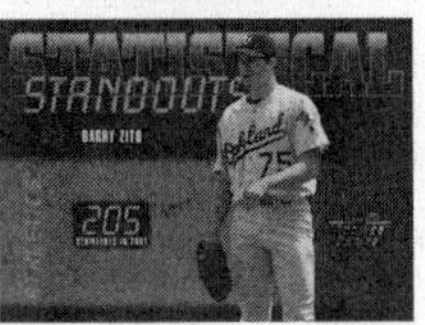

NM/M
Complete Set (50): 120.00
Common Player: 1.50
Inserted 1:12
1 Adam Dunn 2.50
2 Alex Rodriguez 8.00
3 Andruw Jones 4.00
4 Brian Giles 1.50
5 Chipper Jones 5.00
6 Cliff Floyd 1.50
7 Craig Biggio 1.50
8 Frank Thomas 4.00
9 Fred McGriff 1.50
10 Garret Anderson 1.50
11 Greg Maddux 5.00
12 Luis Gonzalez 1.50
13 Magglio Ordonez 1.50
14 Ivan Rodriguez 3.00
15 Ken Griffey Jr. 6.00
16 Ichiro Suzuki 6.00
17 Jason Giambi 2.50
18 Derek Jeter 10.00
19 Sammy Sosa 6.00
20 Albert Pujols 8.00
21 J.D. Drew 1.50
22 Jeff Bagwell 4.00
23 Jim Edmonds 1.50
24 Jose Vidro 1.50
25 Juan Encarnacion 1.50
26 Kerry Wood 3.00
27 Al Leiter 1.50
28 Curt Schilling 2.50
29 Manny Ramirez 4.00
30 Lance Berkman 1.50
31 Miguel Tejada 1.50
32 Mike Piazza 6.00
33 Nomar Garciaparra 6.00
34 Omar Vizquel 1.50
35 Pat Burrell 2.00
36 Paul Konerko 1.50
37 Rafael Palmeiro 3.00
38 Randy Johnson 4.00
39 Richie Sexson 1.50
40 Roger Clemens 5.50
41 Shawn Green 2.00
42 Todd Helton 4.00
43 Tom Glavine 1.50
44 Troy Glaus 4.00
45 Vladimir Guerrero 4.00
46 Mike Sweeney 1.50
47 Alfonso Soriano 3.00
48 Barry Zito 1.50
49 John Smoltz 1.50
50 Ellis Burks 1.50

Stat. Standouts Materials

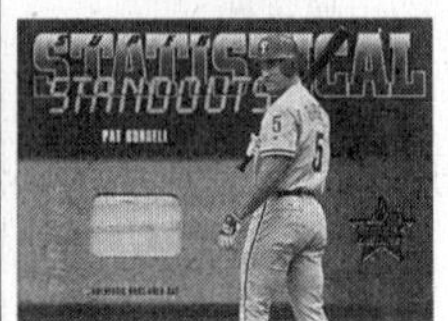

NM/M
Common Player: 5.00
Inserted 1:69
Super Materials: 2-3X
Production 25 Sets
1 Adam Dunn/Bat/200 15.00
2 Alex Rodriguez/Bat/200 15.00
3 Andruw Jones/Bat/200 10.00
4 Brian Giles/Bat 8.00
5 Chipper Jones/Bat/200 15.00
6 Cliff Floyd/Jsy 5.00
7 Craig Biggio/Jsy 8.00
8 Frank Thomas/Jsy/125 12.00
9 Fred McGriff/Bat 10.00
10 Garret Anderson/Bat 8.00
11 Greg Maddux/Jsy/200 20.00
12 Luis Gonzalez/Jsy 8.00
13 Magglio Ordonez/Bat/150 10.00
14 Ivan Rodriguez/Jsy/100 15.00
15 Ken Griffey Jr./Base/100 15.00

16 Ichiro Suzuki/Base/100 30.00
17 Jason Giambi/Base 10.00
18 Derek Jeter/Base/100 25.00
19 Sammy Sosa/Base/100 15.00
20 Albert Pujols/Base/100 15.00
21 J.D. Drew/Bat/150 10.00
22 Jeff Bagwell/Jsy/150 15.00
23 Jim Edmonds/Bat 8.00
24 Jose Vidro/Bat 5.00
25 Juan Encarnacion/Bat 5.00
26 Kerry Wood/Jsy/200 15.00
27 Al Leiter/Jsy 8.00
28 Curt Schilling/Jsy/225 12.00
29 Manny Ramirez/Bat/100 15.00
30 Lance Berkman/Bat/150 10.00
31 Miguel Tejada/Jsy 10.00
32 Mike Piazza/Bat/200 20.00
33 Nomar Garciaparra/Bat/200 20.00
34 Omar Vizquel/Jsy 8.00
35 Pat Burrell/Bat 10.00
36 Paul Konerko/Jsy 6.00
37 Rafael Palmeiro/Bat 10.00
38 Randy Johnson/Jsy/200 15.00
39 Richie Sexson/Jsy 10.00
40 Roger Clemens/Jsy/200 20.00
41 Shawn Green/Jsy 10.00
42 Todd Helton/Jsy/175 15.00
43 Tom Glavine/Jsy/125 10.00
44 Troy Glaus/Jsy 10.00
45 Vladimir Guerrero/Jsy 15.00
46 Mike Sweeney/Bat 5.00
47 Alfonso Soriano/Jsy/200 15.00
48 Barry Zito/Jsy/100 8.00
49 John Smoltz/Jsy 8.00
50 Ellis Burks/Jsy 5.00

Triple Threads

NM/M
Common Card: 25.00
Production 100 Sets
1 Reggie Jackson, Alfonso Soriano, Don Mattingly 80.00
2 Alex Rodriguez, Rafael Palmeiro, Ivan Rodriguez 30.00
3 Mike Piazza, Gary Carter, Rickey Henderson 40.00
4 Dale Murphy, Andruw Jones, Chipper Jones 40.00
5 Mike Schmidt, Steve Carlton, Scott Rolen 85.00
6 Rickey Henderson 40.00
7 Johnny Bench, Joe Morgan, Tom Seaver 50.00
8 Randy Johnson, Pedro J. Martinez, Vladimir Guerrero 35.00
9 Nolan Ryan, Rod Carew, Troy Glaus 75.00
10 Lou Brock, J.D. Drew, Stan Musial 65.00

View Masters

NM/M
Common Player: 10.00
Production 100 Sets
Slideshows: Not Priced
Production 25 Sets
1 Carlos Delgado 12.00
2 Todd Helton 20.00
3 Tony Gwynn 25.00
4 Bernie Williams 10.00
5 Luis Gonzalez 10.00
6 Larry Walker 10.00
7 Troy Glaus 20.00
8 Alfonso Soriano 15.00
9 Curt Schilling 12.00
10 Chipper Jones 25.00
11 Vladimir Guerrero 20.00
12 Adam Dunn 15.00
13 Rickey Henderson 20.00
14 Miguel Tejada 10.00
15 Kazuhisa Ishii 10.00
16 Greg Maddux 25.00
17 Pedro J. Martinez 20.00
18 Nomar Garciaparra 30.00
19 Mike Piazza 30.00
20 Lance Berkman 10.00

2003 Leaf Samples

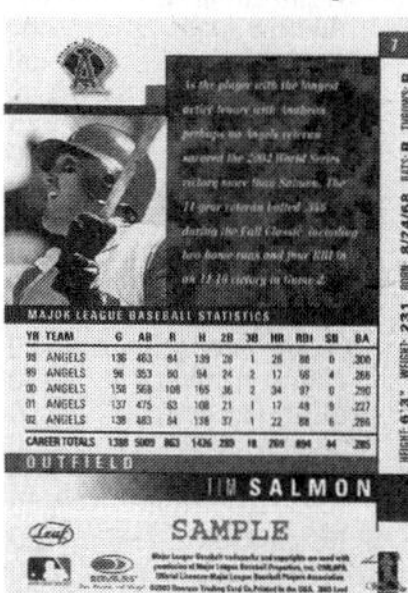

Each March 2003 issue of Beckett Baseball Card Monthly and April issue of Beckett Vintage Sports Collectibles included a sample Leaf card rubber-cemented inside. The cards differ from the issued version only in the appearance on back of a (usually) silver-foil "SAMPLE" notation. Some cards were produced with the back overprint in gold-foil in much more limited quantities. The number of different players' cards involved in the promotion is unknown.

NM/M
Common Player: .10
Stars: 1.5-2X
Gold: 20X

2003 Leaf

NM/M
Complete Set (320): 40.00
Common Player: .15
Pack (10): 1.50
Box (24): 30.00
1 Brad Fullmer .15
2 Darin Erstad .25
3 David Eckstein .15
4 Garret Anderson .15
5 Jarrod Washburn .15
6 Kevin Appier .15
7 Tim Salmon .25
8 Troy Glaus .50
9 Troy Percival .15
10 Buddy Groom .15
11 Jay Gibbons .15
12 Jeff Conine .15
13 Marty Cordova .15
14 Melvin Mora .15
15 Rodrigo Lopez .15
16 Tony Batista .15
17 Jorge Julio .15
18 Cliff Floyd .15
19 Derek Lowe .15
20 Jason Varitek .15
21 Johnny Damon .15
22 Manny Ramirez .75
23 Nomar Garciaparra 1.25
24 Pedro J. Martinez .75
25 Rickey Henderson .75
26 Shea Hillenbrand .15
27 Trot Nixon .15
28 Carlos Lee .15
29 Frank Thomas .75
30 Jose Valentin .15
31 Magglio Ordonez .15
32 Mark Buehrle .15
33 Paul Konerko .25
34 C.C. Sabathia .15
35 Danys Baez .15
36 Ellis Burks .15
37 Jim Thome .75
38 Omar Vizquel .15
39 Ricky Gutierrez .15
40 Travis Fryman .15
41 Bobby Higginson .15
42 Carlos Pena .15
43 Juan Acevedo .15
44 Mark Redman .15
45 Randall Simon .15
46 Robert Fick .15
47 Steve Sparks .15
48 Carlos Beltran .50
49 Joe Randa .15
50 Michael Tucker .15
51 Mike Sweeney .15
52 Paul Byrd .15
53 Raul Ibanez .15
54 Runelvys Hernandez .15
55 A.J. Pierzynski .15
56 Brad Radke .15
57 Corey Koskie .15
58 Cristian Guzman .15
59 David Ortiz .50
60 Doug Mientkiewicz .15
61 Dustan Mohr .15
62 Eddie Guardado .15
63 Jacque Jones .15
64 Torii Hunter .15
65 Alfonso Soriano .50
66 Andy Pettitte .35
67 Bernie Williams .30
68 David Wells .15
69 Derek Jeter 2.00
70 Jason Giambi .40
71 Jeff Weaver .15
72 Jorge Posada .25
73 Mike Mussina .30
74 Nick Johnson .15
75 Raul Mondesi .15
76 Robin Ventura .15
77 Roger Clemens 1.00
78 Barry Zito .25
79 Billy Koch .15
80 David Justice .15
81 Eric Chavez .25
82 Jermaine Dye .15
83 Mark Mulder .15
84 Miguel Tejada .30
85 Ray Durham .15
86 Scott Hatteberg .15
87 Ted Lilly .15
88 Tim Hudson .25
89 Bret Boone .15
90 Carlos Guillen .15
91 Chris Snelling .15
92 Dan Wilson .15
93 Edgar Martinez .15
94 Freddy Garcia .15
95 Ichiro Suzuki 1.25
96 Jamie Moyer .15
97 Joel Pineiro .15
98 John Olerud .15
99 Mark McLemore .15
100 Mike Cameron .15
101 Kazuhiro Sasaki .15
102 Aubrey Huff .15
103 Ben Grieve .15
104 Joe Kennedy .15
105 Paul Wilson .15
106 Randy Winn .15
107 Steve Cox .15
108 Alex Rodriguez 1.50
109 Chan Ho Park .15
110 Hank Blalock .50
111 Herbert Perry .15
112 Ivan Rodriguez .65
113 Juan Gonzalez .75
114 Kenny Rogers .15
115 Kevin Mench .15
116 Rafael Palmeiro .65
117 Carlos Delgado .40
118 Eric Hinske .15
119 Jose Cruz .15
120 Josh Phelps .15
121 Roy Halladay .25
122 Shannon Stewart .15
123 Vernon Wells .15
124 Curt Schilling .40
125 Junior Spivey .15
126 Luis Gonzalez .25
127 Mark Grace .25
128 Randy Johnson .75
129 Steve Finley .15
130 Tony Womack .15
131 Andruw Jones .75
132 Chipper Jones 1.00
133 Gary Sheffield .30
134 Greg Maddux 1.00
135 John Smoltz .25
136 Kevin Millwood .15
137 Rafael Furcal .15
138 Tom Glavine .40
139 Alex Gonzalez .15
140 Corey Patterson .15
141 Fred McGriff .15
142 Jon Lieber .15
143 Kerry Wood .65
144 Mark Prior .75
145 Matt Clement .15
146 Moises Alou .15
147 Sammy Sosa 1.25
148 Aaron Boone .15
149 Adam Dunn .50
150 Austin Kearns .15
151 Barry Larkin .15
152 Danny Graves .15
153 Elmer Dessens .15
154 Ken Griffey Jr. 1.25
155 Sean Casey .25
156 Todd Walker .15
157 Gabe Kapler .15
158 Jason Jennings .15
159 Jay Payton .15
160 Larry Walker .15
161 Mike Hampton .15
162 Todd Helton .75
163 Todd Zeile .15
164 A.J. Burnett .15
165 Derrek Lee .15
166 Josh Beckett .50
167 Juan Encarnacion .15
168 Luis Castillo .15
169 Mike Lowell .15
170 Preston Wilson .15
171 Billy Wagner .15
172 Craig Biggio .25
173 Daryle Ward .15
174 Jeff Bagwell .75
175 Lance Berkman .15
176 Octavio Dotel .15
177 Richard Hidalgo .15
178 Roy Oswalt .25
179 Adrian Beltre .40
180 Eric Gagne .40
181 Eric Karros .15
182 Hideo Nomo .65
183 Kazuhisa Ishii .15
184 Kevin Brown .15
185 Mark Grudzielanek .15
186 Odalis Perez .15
187 Paul LoDuca .15
188 Shawn Green .40
189 Alex Sanchez .15
190 Ben Sheets .15
191 Jeffrey Hammonds .15
192 Jose Hernandez .15
193 Takahito Nomura .15
194 Richie Sexson .15
195 Andres Galarraga .15
196 Bartolo Colon .15
197 Brad Wilkerson .15
198 Javier Vazquez .15
199 Jose Vidro .15
200 Michael Barrett .15
201 Tomokazu Ohka .15
202 Vladimir Guerrero .75
203 Al Leiter .15
204 Armando Benitez .15
205 Edgardo Alfonzo .15
206 Mike Piazza 1.25
207 Mo Vaughn .15
208 Pedro Astacio .15
209 Roberto Alomar .35
210 Roger Cedeno .15
211 Timoniel Perez .15
212 Bobby Abreu .15
213 Jimmy Rollins .25
214 Mike Lieberthal .15
215 Pat Burrell .25
216 Randy Wolf .15
217 Travis Lee .15
218 Vicente Padilla .15
219 Aramis Ramirez .15
220 Brian Giles .15
221 Craig Wilson .15
222 Jason Kendall .15
223 Josh Fogg .15
224 Kevin Young .15
225 Kip Wells .15
226 Mike Williams .15
227 Brett Tomko .15
228 Brian Lawrence .15
229 Mark Kotsay .15
230 Oliver Perez .15
231 Phil Nevin .15
232 Ryan Klesko .15
233 Sean Burroughs .15
234 Trevor Hoffman .15
235 Barry Bonds 2.00
236 Benito Santiago .15
237 Jeff Kent .15
238 Kirk Rueter .15
239 Livan Hernandez .15
240 Kenny Lofton .15
241 Rich Aurilia .15
242 Russ Ortiz .15
243 Albert Pujols 1.50
244 Edgar Renteria .15
245 J.D. Drew .40
246 Jason Isringhausen .15
247 Jim Edmonds .40
248 Matt Morris .15
249 Tino Martinez .15
250 Scott Rolen .75
251 Curt Schilling .25
252 Ivan Rodriguez .35
253 Mike Piazza .75
254 Sammy Sosa .75
255 Matt Williams .15
256 Frank Thomas .25
257 Barry Bonds 1.00
258 Roger Clemens .65
259 Rickey Henderson .25
260 Ken Griffey Jr. .60
261 Greg Maddux .50
262 Randy Johnson .40
263 Jeff Bagwell .25
264 Roberto Alomar .25
265 Tom Glavine .25
266 Juan Gonzalez .25
267 Mark Grace .25
268 Mike Mussina .25
269 Ryan Klesko .15
270 Fred McGriff .15
271 Joe Borchard .15
272 Chris Snelling .15
273 Brian Tallet .15
274 Cliff Lee .15
275 Freddy Sanchez .15
276 Chone Figgins .15
277 Kevin Cash .15
278 Josh Bard .15
279 Jeriome Robertson .15
280 Jeremy Hill .15
281 Shane Nance .15
282 Jeff Baker .15
283 Trey Hodges .15
284 Eric Eckenstahler .15
285 Jim Rushford .15
286 Carlos Rivera .15
287 Josh Bonifay .15
288 Garrett Atkins .15
289 Nic Jackson .15
290 Corwin Malone .15
291 Jimmy Gobble .15
292 Josh Wilson .15
293 Clint Barmes **RC** .50
294 Jon Adkins .15
295 Tim Kalita .15
296 Nelson Castro .15
297 Colin Young .15
298 Adrian Burnside .15
299 Luis Martinez .15
300 Termel Sledge **RC** .50
301 Todd Donovan .15
302 Jeremy Ward .15
303 Wilson Valdez .15
304 Jose Contreras **RC** .75
305 Marshall McDougall .15
306 Mitch Wylie .15
307 Ron Calloway .15
308 Jose Valverde .15
309 Jason Davis .15
310 Scotty Layfield .15
311 Matt Thornton .15
312 Adam Walker .15
313 Gustavo Chacin .15
314 Ron Chiavacci .15
315 Wilbert Nieves .15
316 Clifford Bartosh .15
317 Mike Gonzalez .15
318 Jeremy Guthrie .15
319 Eric Junge .15
320 Ben Kozlowski .15

Green

No Pricing
Production 25 Sets

Blue Press Proofs

Stars: 8-15X
Production 50 Sets

Red Press Proofs

Stars: 3-5X
Inserted 1:12

Clean Up Crew

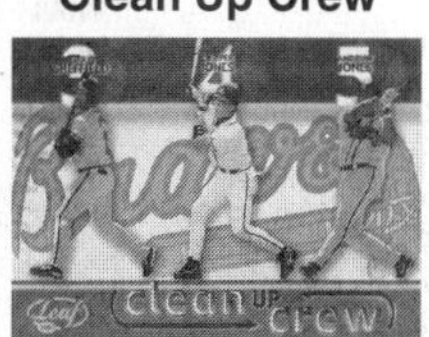

NM/M
Complete Set (10): 30.00
Common Card: 1.50
Inserted 1:49
1 Alex Rodriguez, Rafael Palmeiro, Ivan Rodriguez 6.00
2 Nomar Garciaparra, Manny Ramirez, Cliff Floyd 5.00
3 Jason Giambi, Bernie Williams, Jorge Posada 4.00
4 Rich Aurilia, Jeff Kent, Barry Bonds 6.00
5 Larry Walker, Todd Helton, Jay Payton 1.50
6 Lance Berkman, Jeff Bagwell, Daryle Ward 2.00
7 Scott Rolen, Albert Pujols, Jim Edmonds 5.00
8 Gary Sheffield, Chipper Jones, Andruw Jones 4.00
9 Miguel Tejada, Eric Chavez, Jermaine Dye 1.50
10 Sammy Sosa, Moises Alou, Fred McGriff 4.00

Clean Up Crew Memorabilia

NM/M
Production 50 Sets
1 Alex Rodriguez, Rafael Palmeiro, Ivan Rodriguez 30.00
2 Nomar Garciaparra, Manny Ramirez, Cliff Floyd 25.00
3 Jason Giambi, Bernie Williams, Jorge Posada 25.00
4 Rich Aurilia, Jeff Kent, Barry Bonds 35.00
5 Larry Walker, Todd Helton, Jay Payton 20.00
6 Lance Berkman, Jeff Bagwell, Daryle Ward 25.00
7 Scott Rolen, Albert Pujols, Jim Edmonds 40.00
8 Gary Sheffield, Chipper Jones, Andruw Jones 30.00
9 Miguel Tejada, Eric Chavez, Jermaine Dye 20.00
10 Sammy Sosa, Moises Alou, Fred McGriff 30.00

Clubhouse Signatures Bronze

NM/M
Common Bronze Auto: 8.00
Inserted 1:300
Silvers: 1-2X
Production 100 Sets
Golds: No Pricing
Production 25 Sets
Edwin Almonte 8.00
Jeff Baker 10.00
Josh Bard 10.00
Angel Berroa 8.00
Joe Crede/SP/25 15.00
Andre Dawson/SP/50 25.00
Bobby Doerr/SP/100 20.00
Dwight "Doc" Gooden 25.00
Drew Henson/SP/50 20.00
Eric Hinske 10.00
Torii Hunter/SP/75 35.00
Omar Infante 8.00
Brian Lawrence 8.00
Kevin Mench 8.00
Jack Morris/SP/100 15.00
Franklin Nunez 8.00
Magglio Ordonez/SP/50 25.00
Corey Patterson/SP/100 15.00
Jhonny Peralta 20.00
J.C. Romero 10.00
Chris Snelling/SP/100 10.00
Alfonso Soriano/SP/25 40.00
Brian Tallet/SP/100 8.00

Game Collection

NM/M
Common Player: 8.00
Production 150 Sets
1 Miguel Tejada/Cap 10.00
2 Shannon Stewart/Cap 6.00
3 Mike Schmidt/Jkt 40.00
4 Nolan Ryan/Jkt 75.00
5 Rafael Palmeiro/Glv 15.00
6 Andruw Jones/Shoe 10.00
7 Bernie Williams/Shoe 15.00
8 Ivan Rodriguez/Shoe 10.00
9 Lance Berkman/Shoe 10.00
10 Magglio Ordonez/Shoe 10.00
11 Roy Oswalt/Glv 10.00
12 Andy Pettitte/Shoe 10.00
13 Vladimir Guerrero/Glv 30.00
14 Jason Jennings/Glv 8.00
15 Mike Sweeney/Shoe 8.00
16 Joe Borchard/Shoe 10.00
17 Mark Prior/Shoe 10.00
18 Gary Carter/Jkt 10.00
19 Austin Kearns/Glv 10.00
20 Ryan Klesko/Glv 10.00

Gold Leaf Rookies

NM/M
Complete Set (10): 10.00
Common Player: 1.00
Inserted 1:24
Mirror Golds: 10-20X
Production 25 Sets
1 Joe Borchard 1.00
2 Chone Figgins 1.00
3 Alexis Gomez 1.00
4 Chris Snelling 1.00
5 Cliff Lee 1.00
6 Victor Martinez 2.00
7 Hee Seop Choi 1.50
8 Michael Restovich 1.00
9 Anderson Machado 1.00
10 Drew Henson 2.00

Hard Hats

NM/M
Complete Set (12): 15.00
Common Player: 1.00
Inserted 1:13
1 Alex Rodriguez 4.00
2 Bernie Williams 1.00
3 Ivan Rodriguez 1.25
4 Jeff Bagwell 1.50
5 Rafael Furcal 1.00
6 Rafael Palmeiro 1.50
7 Tony Gwynn 2.00
8 Vladimir Guerrero 1.50
9 Adrian Beltre 1.00
10 Shawn Green 1.00
11 Andruw Jones 1.50
12 George Brett 4.00

Hard Hats Batting Helmets

NM/M
Common Player: 15.00
Production 100 Sets
1 Alex Rodriguez 50.00
2 Bernie Williams 35.00
3 Ivan Rodriguez 30.00
4 Jeff Bagwell 40.00
5 Rafael Furcal 15.00
6 Rafael Palmeiro 35.00
7 Tony Gwynn 35.00
8 Vladimir Guerrero 35.00
9 Adrian Beltre 20.00
10 Shawn Green 20.00
11 Andruw Jones 20.00
12 George Brett 100.00

Home / Away

NM/M
Complete Set (20): 40.00
Common Player: 1.00
Home Inserted 1:34
1 Andruw Jones/Home 1.50
2 Cal Ripken Jr./Home 6.00
3 Edgar Martinez/Home 1.00
4 Jim Thome/Home 1.50
5 Larry Walker/Home 1.00
6 Nomar Garciaparra/Home 4.00
7 Mark Prior/Home 1.00
8 Mike Piazza/Home 4.00
9 Vladimir Guerrero/Home 1.50
10 Chipper Jones/Home 3.00
Away Inserted 1:34
1 Andruw Jones 1.50
2 Cal Ripken Jr. 6.00
3 Edgar Martinez 1.00
4 Jim Thome 2.00
5 Larry Walker 1.00
6 Nomar Garciaparra 4.00
7 Mark Prior 1.00
8 Mike Piazza 4.00
9 Vladimir Guerrero 2.00
10 Chipper Jones 3.00

Home / Away Memorabilia

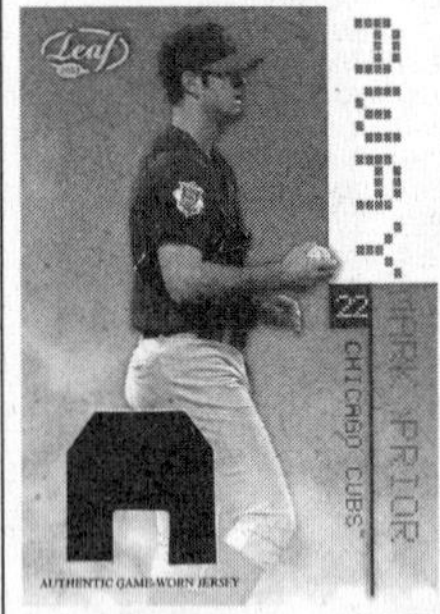

NM/M
Common Player: 6.00
Home Production 250
1 Andruw Jones/Home 8.00
2 Cal Ripken Jr./Home 45.00
3 Edgar Martinez/Home 8.00
4 Jim Thome/Home 10.00
5 Larry Walker/Home 8.00
6 Nomar Garciaparra/Home 20.00
7 Mark Prior/Home 10.00
8 Mike Piazza/Home 15.00
9 Vladimir Guerrero/Home 12.00
10 Chipper Jones/Home 15.00
Away Production 250
1 Andruw Jones 8.00
2 Cal Ripken Jr. 45.00
3 Edgar Martinez 8.00
4 Jim Thome 10.00
5 Larry Walker 6.00
6 Nomar Garciaparra 20.00
7 Mark Prior 10.00
8 Mike Piazza 15.00
9 Vladimir Guerrero 12.00
10 Chipper Jones 15.00

Maple & Ash

NM/M
Common Player: 6.00
Production 400 Sets
1 Jorge Posada 8.00
2 Mike Piazza 12.00
3 Alex Rodriguez 15.00
4 Jeff Bagwell 10.00
5 Joe Borchard 6.00
6 Miguel Tejada 6.00
7 Adam Dunn 8.00
8 Jim Thome 8.00
9 Lance Berkman 6.00
10 Torii Hunter 6.00
11 Carlos Delgado 6.00
12 Reggie Jackson 10.00
13 Juan Gonzalez 6.00
14 Vladimir Guerrero 10.00
15 Richie Sexson 6.00

Number Off My Back

NM/M
Production 50 Sets
1 Carlos Delgado 15.00
2 Don Mattingly 100.00
3 Todd Helton 30.00
4 Vernon Wells 10.00
5 Bernie Williams 20.00
6 Luis Gonzalez 20.00
7 Kerry Wood 30.00
8 Eric Chavez 10.00
9 Shawn Green 15.00
10 Roy Oswalt 15.00
11 Nomar Garciaparra 40.00
12 Robin Yount 60.00
13 Troy Glaus 20.00
14 C.C. Sabathia 10.00
15 Alex Rodriguez 50.00
16 Mark Mulder 10.00
17 Will Clark 60.00
18 Alfonso Soriano 30.00
19 Andy Pettitte 20.00
20 Curt Schilling 25.00

Shirt Off My Back

NM/M
Common Player: 5.00

Production 500 Sets
Number Off My Back: 2-4X
Production 50 Sets
1 Carlos Delgado 6.00
2 Don Mattingly 25.00
3 Todd Helton 10.00
4 Vernon Wells 5.00
5 Bernie Williams 6.00
6 Luis Gonzalez 6.00
7 Kerry Wood 8.00
8 Eric Chavez 6.00
9 Shawn Green 6.00
10 Roy Oswalt 5.00
11 Nomar Garciaparra 12.00
12 Robin Yount 15.00
13 Troy Glaus 8.00
14 C.C. Sabathia 5.00
15 Alex Rodriguez 15.00
16 Mark Mulder 5.00
17 Will Clark 10.00
18 Alfonso Soriano 10.00
19 Andy Pettitte 8.00
20 Curt Schilling 8.00

Slick Leather

NM/M
Complete Set (15): 20.00
Common Player: 1.00
Inserted 1:21
1 Omar Vizquel 1.00
2 Roberto Alomar 1.50
3 Ivan Rodriguez 2.00
4 Greg Maddux 3.00
5 Scott Rolen 2.00
6 Todd Helton 2.00
7 Andruw Jones 2.00
8 Jim Edmonds 1.50
9 Barry Bonds 6.00
10 Eric Chavez 1.00
11 Ichiro Suzuki 5.00
12 Mike Mussina 1.50
13 John Olerud 1.00
14 Torii Hunter 1.00
15 Larry Walker 1.00

60

NM/M
Complete Set (50): 80.00
Common Player: .75
Inserted 1:8
Foil Parallels: 3-5X
Production 60 Sets
1 Troy Glaus 3.00
2 Curt Schilling 2.00
3 Randy Johnson 3.00
4 Andruw Jones 3.00
5 Chipper Jones 4.00
6 Greg Maddux 4.00
7 Tom Glavine 1.00
8 Manny Ramirez 3.00
9 Nomar Garciaparra 5.00
10 Pedro J. Martinez 3.00
11 Rickey Henderson 3.00
12 Sammy Sosa 5.00
13 Frank Thomas 3.00
14 Magglio Ordonez .75
15 Mark Buehrle .75
16 Adam Dunn 1.50
17 Ken Griffey Jr. 5.00
18 Jim Thome 2.00
19 Omar Vizquel .75
20 Larry Walker .75
21 Todd Helton 3.00
22 Lance Berkman .75
23 Roy Oswalt .75
24 Mike Sweeney .75
25 Hideo Nomo 3.00
26 Kazuhisa Ishii 1.00
27 Shawn Green 1.00
28 Torii Hunter .75
29 Vladimir Guerrero 3.00
30 Mike Piazza 5.00
31 Alfonso Soriano 3.00
32 Bernie Williams 1.00
33 Derek Jeter 8.00
34 Jason Giambi 2.00
35 Roger Clemens 4.00
36 Barry Zito .75
37 Miguel Tejada .75
38 Pat Burrell 1.00
39 Ryan Klesko .75
40 Barry Bonds 8.00
41 Jeff Kent .75
42 Ichiro Suzuki 5.00
43 John Olerud .75
44 Albert Pujols 5.00
45 Jim Edmonds 1.00
46 Scott Rolen 2.50
47 Alex Rodriguez 6.00
48 Ivan Rodriguez 2.50
49 Rafael Palmeiro 2.50
50 Roy Halladay .75

2003 Leaf Certified Materials Samples

Each September 2003 issue of Beckett Baseball Card Monthly included a sample Leaf Certified Materials card rubber-cemented inside. The cards differ from the issued version only in the appearance on back of a (usually) silver-foil "SAMPLE" notation. Some cards were produced with the back overprint in gold-foil in much more limited quantities. The number of different players' cards involved in the promotion is unknown.

NM/M
Common Player: .10
Stars: 1.5X
Gold: 20X

2003 Leaf Certified Materials

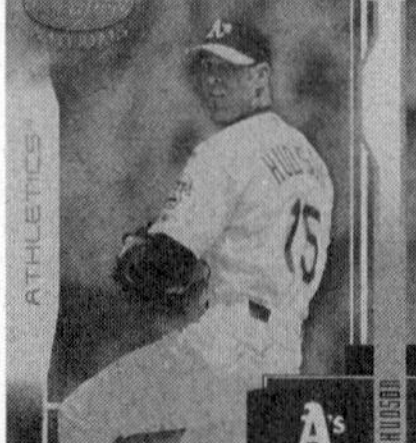

NM/M
Complete Set (250):
Common Player: .50
Common SP Auto. (206-250): 6.00
Production 400 unless noted.
Mirror Red Auto. SP's (06-250): 1-1.5X
Production 100
Mirror Blue Auto. SP's (206-250): 1-2X
Production 50
Mirror Gold Autos. (206-250): No Pricing
Production 25
Pack (5): 20.00
Box (10): 150.00
1 Troy Glaus 1.00
2 Alfredo Amezaga .50
3 Garret Anderson 1.00
4 Nolan Ryan 6.00
5 Darin Erstad .75
6 Junior Spivey .50
7 Randy Johnson 2.00
8 Curt Schilling 1.50
9 Luis Gonzalez .75
10 Steve Finley .50
11 Matt Williams .75
12 Greg Maddux 3.00
13 Chipper Jones 2.00
14 Gary Sheffield 1.00
15 Adam LaRoche .50
16 Andruw Jones 1.00
17 Robert Fick .50
18 John Smoltz 1.00
19 Javy Lopez .75
20 Jay Gibbons .50
21 Geronimo Gil .50
22 Cal Ripken Jr. 6.00
23 Nomar Garciaparra 4.00
24 Pedro J. Martinez 2.00
25 Freddy Sanchez .50
26 Rickey Henderson 1.00
27 Manny Ramirez 1.50
28 Casey Fossum .50
29 Sammy Sosa 3.00
30 Kerry Wood 2.00
31 Corey Patterson 1.00
32 Nic Jackson .50
33 Mark Prior 1.50
34 Juan Cruz .50
35 Steve Smyth .50
36 Magglio Ordonez .75
37 Joe Borchard .50
38 Frank Thomas 1.50
39 Mark Buehrle .50
40 Joe Crede .50
41 Carlos Lee .50
42 Paul Konerko .50
43 Adam Dunn 1.50
44 Corky Miller .50
45 Brandon Larson .50
46 Ken Griffey Jr. 3.00
47 Barry Larkin 1.00
48 Sean Casey .50
49 Wily Mo Pena 1.00
50 Austin Kearns .75
51 Victor Martinez 1.00
52 Brian Tallet .50
53 Cliff Lee .50
54 Jeremy Guthrie .50
55 C.C. Sabathia .50
56 Ricardo Rodriguez .50
57 Omar Vizquel 1.00
58 Travis Hafner .50
59 Todd Helton 1.50
60 Jason Jennings .50
61 Jeff Baker .50
62 Larry Walker 1.00
63 Travis Chapman .50
64 Mike Maroth .50
65 Josh Beckett 1.00
66 Ivan Rodriguez 1.50
67 Brad Penny .50
68 A.J. Burnett .50
69 Craig Biggio 1.00
70 Roy Oswalt 1.00
71 Jason Lane .50
72 Nolan Ryan 6.00
73 Wade Miller .50
74 Richard Hidalgo .50
75 Jeff Bagwell 1.50
76 Lance Berkman 1.00
77 Rodrigo Rosario .50
78 Jeff Kent 1.00
79 John Buck .50
80 Angel Berroa .50
81 Mike Sweeney .50
82 Mac Suzuki .50
83 Alexis Gomez .50
84 Carlos Beltran 1.50
85 Runelvys Hernandez .50
86 Hideo Nomo 1.00
87 Paul LoDuca .50
88 Cesar Izturis .50
89 Kazuhisa Ishii .50
90 Shawn Green 1.00
91 Joe Thurston .50
92 Adrian Beltre 1.00
93 Kevin Brown 1.00
94 Richie Sexson 1.00
95 Ben Sheets 1.00
96 Takahito Nomura .50
97 Geoff Jenkins .50
98 Bill Hall .50
99 Torii Hunter 1.00
100 A.J. Pierzynski .50
101 Michael Cuddyer .50
102 Jose Morban .50
103 Brad Radke .50
104 Jacque Jones .50
105 Eric Milton .50
106 Joe Mays .50
107 Adam Johnson .50
108 Javier Vazquez .50
109 Vladimir Guerrero 2.00
110 Jose Vidro .50
111 Michael Barrett .50
112 Orlando Cabrera .50
113 Tom Glavine 1.00
114 Roberto Alomar 1.00
115 Tsuyoshi Shinjo .50
116 Cliff Floyd .50
117 Mike Piazza 3.00
118 Al Leiter .50
119 Don Mattingly 4.00
120 Roger Clemens 4.00
121 Derek Jeter 6.00
122 Alfonso Soriano 2.00
123 Drew Henson .50
124 Brandon Claussen .50
125 Christian Parker .50
126 Jason Giambi 1.00
127 Mike Mussina 1.00
128 Bernie Williams 1.00
129 Jason Anderson .50
130 Nick Johnson .50
131 Jorge Posada 1.00
132 Andy Pettitte 1.00
133 Barry Zito 1.00
134 Miguel Tejada 1.00
135 Eric Chavez 1.00
136 Tim Hudson 1.00
137 Mark Mulder .75
138 Terrence Long .50
139 Mark Ellis .50
140 Jim Thome 1.50
141 Pat Burrell .75
142 Marlon Byrd .50
143 Bobby Abreu .75
144 Brandon Duckworth .50
145 Robert Person .50
146 Anderson Machado .50
147 Aramis Ramirez 1.00
148 Jack Wilson .50
149 Carlos Rivera .50
150 Jose Castillo .50
151 Walter Young .50
152 Brian Giles .75
153 Jason Kendall .50
154 Ryan Klesko .75
155 Mike Rivera .50
156 Sean Burroughs .50
157 Brian Lawrence .50
158 Xavier Nady .50
159 Dennis Tankersley .50
160 Phil Nevin .50
161 Barry Bonds 6.00
162 Kenny Lofton .50
163 Rich Aurilia .50
164 Ichiro Suzuki 4.00
165 Edgar Martinez .75
166 Chris Snelling .50
167 Rafael Soriano .50
168 John Olerud .75
169 Bret Boone .75
170 Freddy Garcia .50
171 Aaron Sele .50
172 Kazuhiro Sasaki .50
173 Albert Pujols 4.00
174 Scott Rolen 2.00
175 So Taguchi .50
176 Jim Edmonds 1.00
177 Edgar Renteria 1.00
178 J.D. Drew 1.00
179 Antonio Perez .50
180 Dewon Brazelton .50
181 Aubrey Huff .50
182 Toby Hall .50
183 Ben Grieve .50
184 Joe Kennedy .50
185 Alex Rodriguez 5.00
186 Rafael Palmeiro 1.50
187 Hank Blalock 1.50
188 Mark Teixeira 1.00
189 Juan Gonzalez 1.50
190 Kevin Mench .50
191 Nolan Ryan 6.00
192 Doug Davis .50
193 Eric Hinske .50
194 Vinnie Chulk .50
195 Alexis Rios .50
196 Carlos Delgado 1.00
197 Shannon Stewart .50
198 Josh Phelps .50
199 Vernon Wells .75
200 Roy Halladay .75
201 Babe Ruth 8.00
202 Lou Gehrig 6.00
203 Jackie Robinson 6.00
204 Ty Cobb 6.00
205 Thurman Munson 4.00
206 Prentice Redman **RC** 8.00
207 Craig Brazell **RC** 10.00
208 Nook Logan **RC** 15.00
209 Hong-Chih Kuo **RC** 75.00
210 Matt Kata **RC** 10.00
211 Chien-Ming Wang **RC** 225.00
212 Alejandro Machado **RC** 6.00
213 Michael Hessman **RC** 8.00
214 Francisco Rosario **RC** 8.00
215 Pedro Liriano 8.00
216 Jeremy Bonderman 35.00
217 Oscar Villarreal **RC** 10.00
218 Arnie Munoz **RC** 6.00
219 Tim Olson **RC** 10.00
220 Jose Contreras/100 **RC** 40.00
221 Francisco Cruceta **RC** 10.00
222 John Webb 10.00
223 Phil Seibel **RC** 6.00
224 Aaron Looper **RC** 10.00
225 Brian Stokes **RC** 10.00
226 Guillermo Quiroz **RC** 10.00
227 Fernando Cabrera **RC** 10.00
228 Josh Hall **RC** 10.00

229 Diegomar Markwell **RC** 8.00
230 Andrew Brown **RC** 10.00
231 Doug Waechter **RC** 10.00
232 Felix Sanchez **RC** 10.00
233 Gerardo Garcia 8.00
234 Matt Bruback **RC** 8.00
235 Michel Hernandez **RC** 8.00
236 Rett Johnson **RC** 10.00
237 Ryan Cameron **RC** 8.00
238 Rob Hammock **RC** 10.00
239 Clint Barmes **RC** 20.00
240 Brandon Webb **RC** 40.00
241 Jon Leicester **RC** 6.00
242 Shane Bazzell **RC** 10.00
243 Joe Valentine **RC** 10.00
244 Josh Stewart **RC** 10.00
245 Pete LaForest **RC** 8.00
246 Shane Victorino **RC** 8.00
247 Terrmel Sledge **RC** 10.00
248 Lew Ford **RC** 25.00
249 Todd Wellemeyer **RC** 10.00
250 Hideki Matsui/ No Auto. **RC** 15.00

Mirror Red

Stars (1-205): 2-5X
SP's (206-250): .2-.4X
Production 100 Sets
Mirror Blues (1-205): 4-10X
SP's (206-250): .3-.5X
Production 50 Sets
Mirror Golds: No Pricing
Production 25 Sets
Mirror Emeralds: No Pricing
Production Five Sets
Mirror Blacks: One Set Produced

Mirror Red Materials

NM/M
Common Player: 4.00
Production 250 unless noted.
Mirror Red SP's (206-250): .5X
Mirror Blues: 1-1.5X
Production 100
Mirror Golds: No Pricing
Production 25 Sets
Mirror Emeralds: No Pricing
Production Five Sets
Mirror Blacks: One Set Produced
1 Troy Glaus 6.00
2 Alfredo Amezaga 4.00
3 Garret Anderson 6.00
4 Nolan Ryan/35 65.00
5 Darin Erstad 5.00
6 Junior Spivey 4.00
7 Randy Johnson 8.00
8 Curt Schilling 8.00
9 Luis Gonzalez 5.00
10 Steve Finley 4.00
11 Matt Williams 5.00
12 Greg Maddux 10.00
13 Chipper Jones 10.00
14 Gary Sheffield/125 6.00
15 Adam LaRoche 4.00
16 Andruw Jones 6.00
17 Robert Fick 4.00
18 John Smoltz 6.00
19 Javy Lopez 6.00
20 Jay Gibbons 4.00
21 Geronimo Gil 4.00
22 Cal Ripken Jr/35 75.00
23 Nomar Garciaparra 15.00
24 Pedro J. Martinez 10.00
25 Freddy Sanchez 4.00
26 Rickey Henderson 10.00
27 Manny Ramirez 8.00
28 Casey Fossum 4.00
29 Sammy Sosa 15.00
30 Kerry Wood 10.00
31 Corey Patterson 6.00
32 Nic Jackson 4.00
33 Mark Prior 8.00
34 Juan Cruz 4.00
35 Steve Smyth 4.00
36 Magglio Ordonez 6.00
37 Joe Borchard 4.00
38 Frank Thomas 10.00
39 Mark Buehrle 5.00
40 Joe Crede/100 8.00
41 Carlos Lee 4.00
42 Paul Konerko 6.00
43 Adam Dunn 8.00
45 Brandon Larson/150 6.00
46 Ken Griffey Jr. 12.00
47 Barry Larkin 8.00
48 Sean Casey 6.00
49 Wily Mo Pena 6.00
50 Austin Kearns 6.00
51 Victor Martinez/100 8.00
55 C.C. Sabathia 4.00
56 Ricardo Rodriguez 4.00
57 Omar Vizquel 6.00
58 Travis Hafner 6.00
59 Todd Helton 8.00
60 Jason Jennings 4.00
62 Larry Walker 6.00
63 Travis Chapman 6.00
64 Mike Maroth 4.00
65 Josh Beckett 6.00
66 Ivan Rodriguez 8.00
67 Brad Penny 4.00
68 A.J. Burnett 4.00
69 Craig Biggio 6.00
70 Roy Oswalt 6.00
71 Jason Lane 4.00
72 Nolan Ryan/35 65.00
73 Wade Miller 5.00
74 Richard Hidalgo 4.00
75 Jeff Bagwell 10.00
76 Lance Berkman 6.00
77 Rodrigo Rosario 4.00
78 Jeff Kent 6.00
79 John Buck 4.00
80 Angel Berroa 4.00
81 Mike Sweeney 6.00
84 Carlos Beltran 8.00
86 Hideo Nomo 15.00
87 Paul LoDuca 6.00
88 Cesar Izturis 4.00
89 Kazuhisa Ishii 5.00
90 Shawn Green 6.00
91 Joe Thurston 4.00
92 Adrian Beltre 6.00
93 Kevin Brown 6.00
94 Richie Sexson 6.00
95 Ben Sheets 6.00
97 Geoff Jenkins 5.00
98 Bill Hall 4.00
99 Torii Hunter 8.00
101 Michael Cuddyer 4.00
102 Jose Morban 4.00
103 Brad Radke 6.00
104 Jacque Jones 6.00
105 Eric Milton 4.00
106 Joe Mays 5.00
107 Adam Johnson 5.00
108 Javier Vazquez 5.00
109 Vladimir Guerrero 10.00
110 Jose Vidro 4.00
111 Michael Barrett/50 6.00
112 Orlando Cabrera 5.00
113 Tom Glavine 8.00
114 Roberto Alomar 10.00
115 Tsuyoshi Shinjo 4.00
116 Cliff Floyd 5.00
117 Mike Piazza 10.00
118 Al Leiter 5.00
119 Don Mattingly/35 60.00
120 Roger Clemens 25.00
121 Derek Jeter 20.00
122 Alfonso Soriano 8.00
123 Drew Henson 6.00
124 Brandon Claussen/50 10.00
125 Christian Parker 4.00
126 Jason Giambi 6.00
127 Mike Mussina 10.00
128 Bernie Williams 8.00
130 Nick Johnson 4.00
131 Jorge Posada 8.00
132 Andy Pettitte 10.00
133 Barry Zito 6.00
134 Miguel Tejada 6.00
135 Eric Chavez 6.00
136 Tim Hudson 6.00
137 Mark Mulder 6.00
138 Terrence Long 4.00
139 Mark Ellis 4.00
140 Jim Thome 8.00
141 Pat Burrell 6.00
142 Marlon Byrd 4.00
143 Bobby Abreu 6.00
144 Brandon Duckworth 4.00
145 Robert Person 4.00
146 Anderson Machado 4.00
147 Aramis Ramirez 6.00
148 Jack Wilson 4.00
150 Jose Castillo 4.00
151 Walter Young 4.00
152 Brian Giles 6.00
153 Jason Kendall 5.00
155 Mike Rivera 4.00
157 Brian Lawrence 4.00
158 Xavier Nady/60 8.00
159 Dennis Tankersley 4.00
160 Phil Nevin 4.00
161 Barry Bonds 20.00
162 Kenny Lofton 6.00
163 Rich Aurilia 5.00
164 Ichiro Suzuki 25.00
165 Edgar Martinez/100 8.00
166 Chris Snelling 4.00
167 Rafael Soriano 4.00
168 John Olerud 4.00
169 Bret Boone 5.00
170 Freddy Garcia 4.00
171 Aaron Sele 4.00
172 Kazuhiro Sasaki 4.00
173 Albert Pujols 25.00
174 Scott Rolen 10.00
175 So Taguchi 4.00
176 Jim Edmonds 6.00
177 Edgar Renteria 8.00
178 J.D. Drew 6.00
179 Antonio Perez 4.00
180 Dewon Brazelton 4.00
181 Aubrey Huff/50 8.00
182 Toby Hall 4.00
183 Ben Grieve 4.00
184 Joe Kennedy 4.00
185 Alex Rodriguez 15.00
186 Rafael Palmeiro 8.00
187 Hank Blalock 8.00
188 Mark Teixeira 8.00
189 Juan Gonzalez 8.00
190 Kevin Mench 4.00
191 Nolan Ryan/35 65.00
192 Doug Davis 4.00
193 Eric Hinske 8.00
196 Carlos Delgado 6.00
197 Shannon Stewart 5.00
198 Josh Phelps 4.00
199 Vernon Wells 5.00
200 Roy Halladay 8.00

Mirror Red Signatures

NM/M
Common Player:
Production 100 unless noted.
Mirror Blues: 1-1.5X
Production 50
Mirror Golds: 1.5-2X
Production 25 Sets
Mirror Emeralds: No Pricing
Production Five Sets
Mirror Blacks: One Set Produced
2 Alfredo Amezaga 6.00
15 Adam LaRoche 10.00
17 Robert Fick/15 20.00
20 Jay Gibbons 15.00
21 Geronimo Gil/15 15.00
25 Freddy Sanchez 10.00
28 Casey Fossum/50 10.00
32 Nic Jackson 10.00
34 Juan Cruz/15 15.00
35 Steve Smyth/94 8.00
37 Joe Borchard/50 15.00
39 Mark Buehrle/50 20.00
40 Joe Crede/30 15.00
45 Brandon Larson 10.00
49 Wily Mo Pena 20.00
51 Victor Martinez/50 25.00
53 Cliff Lee/50 15.00
54 Jeremy Guthrie/50 15.00
56 Ricardo Rodriguez 8.00
60 Jason Jennings/50 12.00
61 Jeff Baker/50 8.00
63 Travis Chapman 10.00
64 Mike Maroth 10.00
70 Roy Oswalt/50 20.00
71 Jason Lane 10.00
73 Wade Miller/50 15.00
77 Rodrigo Rosario 10.00
80 Angel Berroa/50 15.00
85 Runelvys Hernandez 10.00
88 Cesar Izturis 6.00
91 Joe Thurston 8.00
98 Bill Hall 10.00
102 Jose Morban 10.00
107 Adam Johnson/50 10.00
117 Mike Piazza/20 150.00
124 Brandon Claussen/60 15.00
125 Christian Parker/50 10.00
129 Jason Anderson 10.00
138 Terrence Long/50 15.00
142 Marlon Byrd 10.00
144 Brandon Duckworth/ 50 10.00
145 Robert Person/50 10.00
146 Anderson Machado 8.00
149 Carlos Rivera 8.00
150 Jose Castillo 8.00
151 Walter Young 8.00
155 Mike Rivera 8.00
157 Brian Lawrence 8.00
166 Chris Snelling 10.00
167 Rafael Soriano/50 12.00
179 Antonio Perez/50 8.00
180 Dewon Brazelton/50 8.00
181 Aubrey Huff/50 15.00
182 Toby Hall/50 10.00
184 Joe Kennedy/50 12.00
187 Hank Blalock/50 40.00
188 Mark Teixeira/50 40.00
190 Kevin Mench 10.00
193 Eric Hinske 15.00
194 Vinnie Chulk 8.00
195 Alexis Rios 25.00

Fabric of the Game

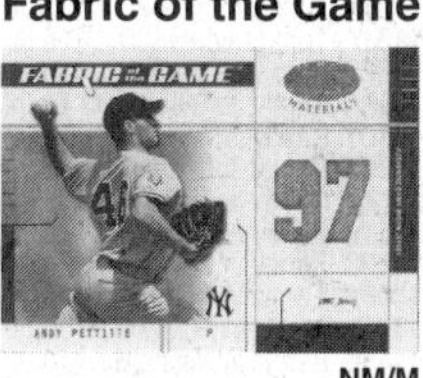

NM/M
Common Player: 4.00
Quantity produced listed
1BA Bobby Doerr/50 15.00
1JY Bobby Doerr/39 15.00
1PS Bobby Doerr/50 15.00
2BA Ozzie Smith/100 25.00
2IN Ozzie Smith/50 30.00
2JY Ozzie Smith/88 20.00
2PS Ozzie Smith/50 30.00
3DY Pee Wee Reese/32 30.00
3JY Pee Wee Reese/58 15.00
4BA Jeff Bagwell/100 10.00
4DY Jeff Bagwell/65 10.00
4IN Jeff Bagwell/50 12.00
4JY Jeff Bagwell/98 10.00
4PS Jeff Bagwell/50 12.00
5BA Tommy Lasorda/100 8.00
5DY Tommy Lasorda/58 10.00
5JY Tommy Lasorda/84 8.00
5PS Tommy Lasorda/50 10.00
6JY Red Schoendienst/55 10.00
7BA Harmon Killebrew/50 15.00
7DY Harmon Killebrew/61 15.00
7IN Harmon Killebrew/50 15.00
7JY Harmon Killebrew/71 15.00
7PS Harmon Killebrew/50 15.00
8DY Roger Maris/55 40.00
8JY Roger Maris/58 40.00
8PS Roger Maris/50 40.00
9BA Alex Rodriguez/100 15.00
9DY Alex Rodriguez/77 15.00
9IN Alex Rodriguez/50 15.00
9JY Alex Rodriguez/99 15.00
9PS Alex Rodriguez/50 15.00
10BA Alex Rodriguez/100 15.00
10DY Alex Rodriguez/72 15.00
10IN Alex Rodriguez/50 15.00
10JY Alex Rodriguez/101 15.00
10PS Alex Rodriguez/50 15.00
11BA Dale Murphy/50 15.00
11DY Dale Murphy/66 15.00
11IN Dale Murphy/50 15.00
11JY Dale Murphy/85 15.00
11PS Dale Murphy/50 15.00
12BA Alan Trammell/100 10.00
12IN Alan Trammell/50 10.00
12JY Alan Trammell/90 10.00
12PS Alan Trammell/50 10.00
13BA Babe Ruth/10 250.00
13DY Babe Ruth/13 250.00
13IN Babe Ruth/10 250.00
13JY Babe Ruth/30 200.00
13PS Babe Ruth/10 250.00
14JY Lou Gehrig/38 200.00
15JY Babe Ruth/30 250.00
16JY Mel Ott/46 30.00
17BA Paul Molitor/100 15.00
17DY Paul Molitor/70 15.00
17IN Paul Molitor/50 15.00
17JY Paul Molitor/84 15.00
17PS Paul Molitor/50 15.00
18DY Duke Snider/58 15.00
18JY Duke Snider/62 15.00
19BA Miguel Tejada/50 10.00
19DY Miguel Tejada/68 8.00
19IN Miguel Tejada/50 10.00
19JY Miguel Tejada/99 5.00
19PS Miguel Tejada/50 10.00
20JY Lou Gehrig/38 200.00
21DY Brooks Robinson/54 15.00
21JY Brooks Robinson/66 15.00
22BA George Brett/50 30.00
22DY George Brett/69 25.00
22IN George Brett/50 30.00
22JY George Brett/91 25.00
22PS George Brett/50 30.00
23BA Johnny Bench/50 15.00
23DY Johnny Bench/59 15.00
23IN Johnny Bench/50 15.00
23JY Johnny Bench/81 15.00
23PS Johnny Bench/50 15.00
24JY Lou Boudreau/48 15.00
25BA Nomar Garciaparra/ 100 20.00
25IN Nomar Garciaparra/ 50 25.00
25JY Nomar Garciaparra/ 100 20.00
25PS Nomar Garciaparra/ 50 25.00
26BA Tsuyoshi Shinjo/50 8.00
26DY Tsuyoshi Shinjo/62 8.00
26JY Tsuyoshi Shinjo/101 5.00
27BA Pat Burrell/100 8.00
27DY Pat Burrell/46 10.00
27JY Pat Burrell/101 8.00
28BA Albert Pujols/100 20.00
28IN Albert Pujols/50 25.00
28JY Albert Pujols/101 20.00
28PS Albert Pujols/50 25.00
29JY Stan Musial/43 30.00
30JY Al Kaline/64 15.00
31BA Ivan Rodriguez/100 8.00
31DY Ivan Rodriguez/72 8.00
31IN Ivan Rodriguez/50 10.00
31JY Ivan Rodriguez/101 5.00
32BA Craig Biggio/100 6.00
32DY Craig Biggio/65 8.00
32JY Craig Biggio/101 6.00
32PS Craig Biggio/50 10.00
33DY Joe Morgan/59 10.00
33JY Joe Morgan/74 8.00
34BA Willie Stargell/50 15.00
34JY Willie Stargell/68 15.00
34PS Willie Stargell/50 15.00
35BA Andre Dawson/100 8.00
35IN Andre Dawson/50 10.00
35JY Andre Dawson/87 8.00
35PS Andre Dawson/50 10.00
36BA Gary Carter/100 10.00
36DY Gary Carter/62 10.00
36IN Gary Carter/50 10.00
36JY Gary Carter/85 8.00
36PS Gary Carter/50 10.00
37BA Cal Ripken Jr./50 50.00
37DY Cal Ripken Jr./54 50.00
37IN Cal Ripken Jr./50 50.00
37JY Cal Ripken Jr./101 40.00
37PS Cal Ripken Jr./50 50.00
38JY Enos Slaughter/53 20.00
39BA Reggie Jackson/50 15.00
39DY Reggie Jackson/68 15.00
39JY Reggie Jackson/75 15.00
39PS Reggie Jackson/50 15.00
40JY Phil Rizzuto/47 15.00
41BA Chipper Jones/100 10.00
41DY Chipper Jones/66 15.00
41IN Chipper Jones/50 15.00
41JY Chipper Jones/101 10.00
41PS Chipper Jones/50 15.00
42BA Hideo Nomo/100 10.00
42DY Hideo Nomo/58 15.00
42IN Hideo Nomo/50 15.00
42JY Hideo Nomo/95 10.00
42PS Hideo Nomo/50 15.00
43JY Luis Aparicio/69 10.00
44BA Hideo Nomo/100 10.00
44IN Hideo Nomo/50 15.00
44JY Hideo Nomo/101 10.00
44PS Hideo Nomo/50 15.00
45BA Edgar Martinez/100 8.00
45DY Edgar Martinez/77 8.00
45JY Edgar Martinez/100 8.00
45PS Edgar Martinez/50 10.00
46BA Barry Larkin/100 6.00
46DY Barry Larkin/59 10.00
46JY Barry Larkin/100 6.00
46PS Barry Larkin/50 10.00
47BA Alfonso Soriano/100 10.00
47IN Alfonso Soriano/50 15.00
47JY Alfonso Soriano/102 10.00
47PS Alfonso Soriano/50 15.00
48BA Wade Boggs/100 8.00
48DY Wade Boggs/98 8.00
48IN Wade Boggs/50 10.00
48JY Wade Boggs/99 8.00
48PS Wade Boggs/50 10.00
49BA Wade Boggs/50 10.00
49IN Wade Boggs/50 10.00
49JY Wade Boggs/94 8.00
49PS Wade Boggs/50 10.00
50JY Ernie Banks/68 15.00
51BA Joe Torre/50 10.00
51DY Joe Torre/66 10.00
51IN Joe Torre/50 10.00
51JY Joe Torre/66 10.00
51PS Joe Torre/50 10.00
52BA Tim Hudson/100 4.00
52DY Tim Hudson/68 6.00
52JY Tim Hudson/101 4.00
52PS Tim Hudson/50 6.00
53BA Shawn Green/100 4.00
53DY Shawn Green/58 6.00
53JY Shawn Green/102 4.00
53PS Shawn Green/50 6.00
54BA Carlos Beltran/100 6.00
54DY Carlos Beltran/69 8.00
54JY Carlos Beltran/101 6.00
54PS Carlos Beltran/50 8.00
55BA Bo Jackson/50 15.00
55DY Bo Jackson/69 15.00
55JY Bo Jackson/90 10.00
55PS Bo Jackson/50 15.00
56BA Hal Newhouser/50 8.00
56JY Hal Newhouser/55 8.00
56PS Hal Newhouser/50 8.00
57BA Jason Giambi/100 6.00
57DY Jason Giambi/68 8.00
57IN Jason Giambi/50 8.00
57JY Jason Giambi/101 6.00
57PS Jason Giambi/50 8.00
58BA Lance Berkman/100 6.00
58DY Lance Berkman/65 8.00
58IN Lance Berkman/50 8.00
58JY Lance Berkman/102 6.00
58PS Lance Berkman/50 8.00
59BA Todd Helton/100 6.00
59DY Todd Helton/93 6.00
59JY Todd Helton/100 6.00
59PS Todd Helton/50 8.00
60BA Mark Grace/100 8.00
60JY Mark Grace/95 8.00
60PS Mark Grace/50 15.00
61BA Fred Lynn/100 6.00
61JY Fred Lynn/75 8.00
61PS Fred Lynn/50 8.00
62JY Bob Feller/52 15.00
63BA Robin Yount/100 20.00
63DY Robin Yount/70 20.00
63IN Robin Yount/50 25.00
63JY Robin Yount/88 20.00
63PS Robin Yount/50 25.00
64BA Tony Gwynn/100 15.00
64DY Tony Gwynn/69 20.00
64IN Tony Gwynn/50 20.00
64JY Tony Gwynn/99 20.00
64PS Tony Gwynn/50 20.00
65BA Tony Gwynn/100 15.00
65DY Tony Gwynn/69 15.00
65IN Tony Gwynn/50 15.00
65JY Tony Gwynn/99 15.00
65PS Tony Gwynn/50 15.00
66DY Frank Robinson/54 10.00
66JY Frank Robinson/70 10.00
67BA Mike Schmidt/50 20.00
67DY Mike Schmidt/46 20.00
67IN Mike Schmidt/50 20.00
67JY Mike Schmidt/81 20.00
67PS Mike Schmidt/50 20.00
68JY Lou Brock/66 15.00
69BA Don Sutton/50 8.00
69DY Don Sutton/58 8.00
69JY Don Sutton/72 8.00
70BA Mark Mulder/100 4.00
70DY Mark Mulder/68 6.00
70JY Mark Mulder/101 4.00
70PS Mark Mulder/50 6.00
71BA Luis Gonzalez/100 4.00
71DY Luis Gonzalez/98 4.00
71JY Luis Gonzalez/101 4.00
71PS Luis Gonzalez/50 6.00
72BA Jorge Posada/100 6.00
72JY Jorge Posada/101 6.00
72PS Jorge Posada/50 8.00
73BA Sammy Sosa/100 20.00
73IN Sammy Sosa/50 25.00
73JY Sammy Sosa/101 20.00
73PS Sammy Sosa/50 25.00
74BA Roberto Alomar/100 8.00
74DY Roberto Alomar/62 10.00
74JY Roberto Alomar/102 8.00
74PS Roberto Alomar/50 10.00
75JY Roberto Clemente/69 80.00
76BA Jeff Kent/100 4.00
76DY Jeff Kent/58 6.00
76JY Jeff Kent/101 4.00
76PS Jeff Kent/50 6.00
77DY Sean Casey/59 8.00
77JY Sean Casey/100 4.00
78BA Roger Clemens/50 25.00
78IN Roger Clemens/50 25.00
78JY Roger Clemens/95 20.00
78PS Roger Clemens/50 20.00
79DY Warren Spahn/53 15.00
79JY Warren Spahn/58 15.00
80BA Roger Clemens/100 20.00
80IN Roger Clemens/50 25.00
80JY Roger Clemens/102 25.00
80PS Roger Clemens/50 25.00
81BA Jim Palmer/50 10.00
81DY Jim Palmer/54 10.00
81JY Jim Palmer/69 10.00
81PS Jim Palmer/50 10.00
82BA Juan Gonzalez/50 10.00
82JY Juan Gonzalez/101 6.00
82PS Juan Gonzalez/50 10.00
83BA Will Clark/100 15.00
83DY Will Clark/58 15.00
83JY Will Clark/88 15.00
83PS Will Clark/50 15.00
84BA Don Mattingly/50 25.00
84IN Don Mattingly/50 25.00
84JY Don Mattingly/93 25.00
84PS Don Mattingly/50 25.00
85BA Ryne Sandberg/40 30.00
85IN Ryne Sandberg/50 30.00
85JY Ryne Sandberg/85 30.00
85PS Ryne Sandberg/50 30.00
86JY Early Wynn/55 8.00
87BA Manny Ramirez/50 8.00
87JY Manny Ramirez/102 6.00
87PS Manny Ramirez/50 8.00
88BA Rickey Henderson/100 10.00
88DY Rickey Henderson/62 15.00
88IN Rickey Henderson/50 15.00
88JY Rickey Henderson/99 10.00
88PS Rickey Henderson/50 15.00
89BA Rickey Henderson/100 10.00
89DY Rickey Henderson/69 15.00
89PS Rickey Henderson/50 15.00
90BA Jason Giambi/100 8.00
90IN Jason Giambi/50 10.00
90JY Jason Giambi/102 8.00

90PS Jason Giambi/50 10.00
91BA Carlos Delgado/100 4.00
91DY Carlos Delgado/77 4.00
91JY Carlos Delgado/100 4.00
91PS Carlos Delgado/50 6.00
92BA Jim Thome/100 8.00
92JY Jim Thome/102 10.00
92PS Jim Thome/50 10.00
93BA Andruw Jones/100 6.00
93DY Andruw Jones/66 8.00
93JY Andruw Jones/101 6.00
93PS Andruw Jones/50 8.00
94BA Rafael Palmeiro/100 8.00
94DY Rafael Palmeiro/72 8.00
94JY Rafael Palmeiro/102 8.00
94PS Rafael Palmeiro/50 8.00
95BA Troy Glaus/100 6.00
95DY Troy Glaus/97 6.00
95IN Troy Glaus/50 6.00
95JY Troy Glaus/100 6.00
95PS Troy Glaus/50 8.00
96BA Wade Boggs/100 8.00
96IN Wade Boggs/50 10.00
96JN Wade Boggs/26 25.00
96JY Wade Boggs/86 8.00
96PS Wade Boggs/50 10.00
97BA Jim "Catfish" Hunter/50 10.00
97DY Jim "Catfish" Hunter/68 10.00
97JN Jim "Catfish" Hunter/27 15.00
97JY Jim "Catfish" Hunter/68 10.00
97PS Jim "Catfish" Hunter/50 10.00
98BA Juan Marichal/50 10.00
98DY Juan Marichal/58 10.00
98JN Juan Marichal/27 20.00
98JY Juan Marichal/67 10.00
98PS Juan Marichal/50 10.00
99BA Carlton Fisk/50 15.00
99JN Carlton Fisk/27 25.00
99JY Carlton Fisk/80 10.00
99PS Carlton Fisk/50 15.00
100BA Vladimir Guerrero/100 8.00
100DY Vladimir Guerrero/69 15.00
100JN Vladimir Guerrero/27 30.00
100JY Vladimir Guerrero/101 8.00
100PS Vladimir Guerrero/50 15.00
101BA Rod Carew/100 10.00
101DY Rod Carew/65 15.00
101JN Rod Carew/29 20.00
101JY Rod Carew/85 10.00
101PS Rod Carew/50 15.00
102BA Rod Carew/50 15.00
102DY Rod Carew/61 15.00
102JN Rod Carew/29 20.00
102JY Rod Carew/71 10.00
102PS Rod Carew/50 15.00
103BA Joe Carter/50 6.00
103DY Joe Carter/77 8.00
103JN Joe Carter/29 15.00
103JY Joe Carter/94 6.00
104BA Mike Sweeney/100 4.00
104DY Mike Sweeney/69 6.00
104JN Mike Sweeney/29 15.00
104JY Mike Sweeney/101 4.00
104PS Mike Sweeney/50 6.00
105DY Nolan Ryan/65 40.00
105JN Nolan Ryan/30 50.00
105JY Nolan Ryan/70 40.00
105PS Nolan Ryan/50 40.00
106BA Orlando Cepeda/50 8.00
106DY Orlando Cepeda/58 8.00
106IN Orlando Cepeda/50 8.00
106JN Orlando Cepeda/30 15.00
106JY Orlando Cepeda/65 8.00
106PS Orlando Cepeda/50 8.00
107BA Magglio Ordonez/100 4.00
107JN Magglio Ordonez/30 15.00
107JY Magglio Ordonez/100 4.00
107PS Magglio Ordonez/50 6.00
108BA Hoyt Wilhelm/50 8.00
108JN Hoyt Wilhelm/31 15.00
108JY Hoyt Wilhelm/68 8.00
108PS Hoyt Wilhelm/50 8.00
109BA Mike Piazza/100 15.00
109DY Mike Piazza/62 20.00
109IN Mike Piazza/50 25.00
109JN Mike Piazza/31 30.00
109JY Mike Piazza/100 15.00
109PS Mike Piazza/50 20.00
110BA Greg Maddux/100 10.00
110DY Greg Maddux/66 15.00
110IN Greg Maddux/50 15.00
110JN Greg Maddux/31 30.00
110JY Greg Maddux/102 10.00
110PS Greg Maddux/50 15.00
111BA Mark Prior/100 8.00
111IN Mark Prior/50 10.00
111JY Mark Prior/102 8.00
111PS Mark Prior/50 10.00
112BA Torii Hunter/100 6.00
112DY Torii Hunter/61 8.00
112IN Torii Hunter/50 8.00
112JN Torii Hunter/48 10.00
112JY Torii Hunter/101 6.00
112PS Torii Hunter/50 8.00
113BA Steve Carlton/100 8.00
113DY Steve Carlton/46 15.00
113IN Steve Carlton/50 10.00
113JN Steve Carlton/32 15.00
113JY Steve Carlton/81 8.00
113PS Steve Carlton/50 10.00
114BA Jose Canseco/100 10.00
114DY Jose Canseco/68 10.00
114IN Jose Canseco/50 15.00
114JN Jose Canseco/33 15.00
114JY Jose Canseco/89 10.00
114PS Jose Canseco/50 15.00
115BA Nolan Ryan/50 30.00
115DY Nolan Ryan/72 30.00
115IN Nolan Ryan/50 30.00
115JN Nolan Ryan/34 40.00
115JY Nolan Ryan/90 30.00
115PS Nolan Ryan/50 30.00
116BA Nolan Ryan/50 30.00
116DY Nolan Ryan/65 30.00
116JN Nolan Ryan/34 40.00
116JY Nolan Ryan/84 30.00
116PS Nolan Ryan/50 30.00
118BA Kerry Wood/100 10.00
118JN Kerry Wood/34 25.00
118JY Kerry Wood/101 10.00
118PS Kerry Wood/50 15.00
119BA Mike Mussina/50 10.00
119JN Mike Mussina/35 25.00
119JY Mike Mussina/101 8.00
119PS Mike Mussina/50 15.00
120JN Yogi Berra/35 25.00
120JY Yogi Berra/47 25.00
121JY Thurman Munson/79 25.00
122BA Frank Thomas/100 8.00
122JN Frank Thomas/35 15.00
122JY Frank Thomas/94 6.00
122PS Frank Thomas/50 8.00
123BA Rickey Henderson/50 15.00
123DY Rickey Henderson/68 10.00
123JN Rickey Henderson/35 20.00
123JY Rickey Henderson/80 10.00
123PS Rickey Henderson/50 15.00
124BA Mike Mussina/100 6.00
124DY Mike Mussina/54 10.00
124JN Mike Mussina/35 20.00
124JY Mike Mussina/97 6.00
124PS Mike Mussina/50 10.00
125BA Gaylord Perry/100 6.00
125DY Gaylord Perry/77 6.00
125JN Gaylord Perry/36 10.00
125JY Gaylord Perry/82 6.00
125PS Gaylord Perry/50 8.00
126BA Nick Johnson/100 4.00
126JN Nick Johnson/36 6.00
126JY Nick Johnson/102 4.00
126PS Nick Johnson/50 8.00
127BA Curt Schilling/100 8.00
127DY Curt Schilling/98 8.00
127JN Curt Schilling/38 15.00
127JY Curt Schilling/102 8.00
127PS Curt Schilling/50 8.00
128BA Dave Parker/100 6.00
128JN Dave Parker/39 10.00
128JY Dave Parker/80 8.00
128PS Dave Parker/50 8.00
129DY Eddie Mathews/53 15.00
129JN Eddie Mathews/41 25.00
129JY Eddie Mathews/59 20.00
130DY Tom Seaver/62 15.00
130JN Tom Seaver/41 20.00
130JY Tom Seaver/69 15.00
131DY Tom Seaver/59 15.00
131JN Tom Seaver/41 25.00
131JY Tom Seaver/78 15.00
132JN Jackie Robinson/42 80.00
132JY Jackie Robinson/52 60.00
133BA Reggie Jackson/100 10.00
133DY Reggie Jackson/65 15.00
133IN Reggie Jackson/50 15.00
133JN Reggie Jackson/44 20.00
133JY Reggie Jackson/80 10.00
133PS Reggie Jackson/50 15.00
134BA Willie McCovey/100 8.00
134DY Willie McCovey/58 10.00
134JN Willie McCovey/44 10.00
134JY Willie McCovey/77 8.00
134PS Willie McCovey/50 10.00
135BA Eric Davis/100 6.00
135DY Eric Davis/59 8.00
135JN Eddie Davis/44 10.00
135JY Eric Davis/89 6.00
135PS Eric Davis/50 8.00
136BA Adam Dunn/100 8.00
136DY Adam Dunn/59 10.00
136JN Adam Dunn/44 15.00
136JY Adam Dunn/102 8.00
136PS Adam Dunn/50 10.00
137BA Roy Oswalt/100 4.00
137DY Roy Oswalt/65 6.00
137IN Roy Oswalt/50 6.00
137JN Roy Oswalt/44 8.00
137JY Roy Oswalt/102 4.00
137PS Roy Oswalt/50 6.00
138BA Pedro J. Martinez/50 15.00
138DY Pedro J. Martinez/69 15.00
138JN Pedro J. Martinez/45 20.00
138JY Pedro J. Martinez/95 6.00
138PS Pedro J. Martinez/50 10.00
139BA Pedro J. Martinez/100 8.00
139IN Pedro J. Martinez/50 10.00
139JN Pedro J. Martinez/45 15.00
139JY Pedro J. Martinez/102 8.00
139PS Pedro J. Martinez/50 10.00
140BA Andy Pettitte/100 6.00
140JN Andy Pettitte/46 10.00
140JY Andy Pettitte/97 6.00
140PS Andy Pettitte/50 8.00
141BA Jack Morris/100 6.00
141IN Jack Morris/50 8.00
141JN Jack Morris/47 10.00
141JY Jack Morris/85 6.00
141PS Jack Morris/50 8.00
142BA Tom Glavine/100 6.00
142DY Tom Glavine/66 10.00
142JN Tom Glavine/47 15.00
142JY Tom Glavine/100 6.00
142PS Tom Glavine/50 10.00
143BA Randy Johnson/100 10.00
143DY Randy Johnson/77 15.00
143IN Randy Johnson/50 15.00
143JN Randy Johnson/51 15.00
143JY Randy Johnson/98 10.00
143PS Randy Johnson/50 15.00
144BA Bernie Williams/100 8.00
144IN Bernie Williams/50 10.00
144JN Bernie Williams/51 10.00
144JY Bernie Williams/100 8.00
144PS Bernie Williams/50 10.00
145BA Randy Johnson/50 15.00
145DY Randy Johnson/98 10.00
145IN Randy Johnson/50 15.00
145JN Randy Johnson/51 15.00
145JY Randy Johnson/102 15.00
145PS Randy Johnson/50 15.00
146DY Don Drysdale/58 10.00
146JN Don Drysdale/53 10.00
146JY Don Drysdale/64 10.00
147BA Mark Buehrle/100 4.00
147JN Mark Buehrle/56 6.00
147JY Mark Buehrle/101 4.00
147PS Mark Buehrle/50 6.00
148BA Chan Ho Park/100 4.00
148DY Chan Ho Park/58 6.00
148JN Chan Ho Park/61 6.00
148JY Chan Ho Park/101 4.00
148PS Chan Ho Park/50 6.00
149BA Carlton Fisk/100 8.00
149IN Carlton Fisk/50 15.00
149JN Carlton Fisk/72 15.00
149JY Carlton Fisk/92 15.00
149PS Carlton Fisk/50 15.00
150BA Barry Zito/100 6.00
150DY Barry Zito/68 8.00
150JN Barry Zito/75 8.00
150JY Barry Zito/101 6.00
150PS Barry Zito/50 8.00

2003 Leaf Limited

NM/M

Complete Set (170):
Common Player (1-151): 1.50
Production 999
Common (152-170): 4.00
Production 399
Common Auto. Memor. (171-200): 15.00
Production 99
Common Auto. (171-200): 8.00
Pack (4): 75.00
Box (4): 250.00

1 Derek Jeter 6.00
2 Eric Chavez 1.50
3 Alex Rodriguez 5.00
4 Miguel Tejada 1.50
5 Nomar Garciaparra 4.00
6 Jeff Bagwell 1.50
7 Jim Thome 2.00
8 Pat Burrell 1.50
9 Albert Pujols 5.00
10 Juan Gonzalez 3.00
11 Shawn Green 1.50
12 Craig Biggio 1.50
13 Chipper Jones 3.00
14 Hideo Nomo 2.00
15 Vernon Wells 1.50
16 Gary Sheffield 2.00
17 Barry Larkin 1.50
18 Josh Beckett 1.50
19 Edgar Martinez 1.50
20 Ivan Rodriguez 2.00
21 Jeff Kent 1.50
22 Roberto Alomar 1.50
23 Alfonso Soriano 3.00
24 Jim Thome 2.00
25 Juan Gonzalez 3.00
26 Carlos Beltran 2.00
27 Shawn Green 1.50
28 Tim Hudson 1.50
29 Deion Sanders 1.50
30 Rafael Palmeiro 2.00
31 Todd Helton 3.00
32 Lance Berkman 1.50
33 Mike Mussina 2.00
34 Kazuhisa Ishii 1.50
35 Bill Burrell 1.50
36 Miguel Tejada 1.50
37 Juan Gonzalez 2.00
38 Roberto Alomar 1.50
39 Roberto Alomar 1.50
40 Luis Gonzalez 1.50
41 Jorge Posada 1.50
42 Mark Mulder 1.50
43 Sammy Sosa 4.00
44 Mark Prior 2.00
45 Roger Clemens 4.00
46 Tom Glavine 1.50
47 Mark Teixeira 1.50
48 Manny Ramirez 2.00
49 Frank Thomas 2.00
50 Troy Glaus 3.00
51 Andruw Jones 3.00
52 Jason Giambi 2.00
53 Jim Thome 2.00
54 Barry Bonds 6.00
55 Rafael Palmeiro 2.00
56 Edgar Martinez 1.50
57 Vladimir Guerrero 3.00
58 Roberto Alomar 1.50
59 Mike Sweeney 1.50
60 Magglio Ordonez 1.50
61 Ken Griffey Jr. 4.00
62 Craig Biggio 1.50
63 Greg Maddux 4.00
64 Mike Piazza 4.00
65 Tom Glavine 1.50
66 Kerry Wood 2.00
67 Frank Thomas 3.00
68 Mike Mussina 2.00
69 Nick Johnson 1.50
70 Bernie Williams 1.50
71 Scott Rolen 2.00
72 Curt Schilling 2.00
73 Adam Dunn 2.00
74 Roy Oswalt 1.50
75 Pedro J. Martinez 3.00
76 Tom Glavine 1.50
77 Torii Hunter 1.50
78 Austin Kearns 1.50
79 Randy Johnson 3.00
80 Bernie Williams 1.50
81 Ichiro Suzuki 4.00
82 Kerry Wood 2.00
83 Kazuhisa Ishii 1.50
84 Randy Johnson 3.00
85 Nick Johnson 1.50
86 Josh Beckett 1.50
87 Curt Schilling 2.00
88 Mike Mussina 2.00
89 Pedro J. Martinez 3.00
90 Barry Zito 1.50
91 Jim Edmonds 1.50
92 Rickey Henderson 3.00
93 Rickey Henderson 3.00
94 Rickey Henderson 3.00
95 Rickey Henderson 3.00
96 Rickey Henderson 3.00
97 Randy Johnson 3.00
98 Mark Grace 1.50
99 Pedro J. Martinez 3.00
100 Hee Seop Choi 1.50
101 Ivan Rodriguez 2.00
102 Jeff Kent 1.50
103 Hideo Nomo 3.00
104 Hideo Nomo 3.00
105 Mike Piazza 4.00
106 Tom Glavine 1.50
107 Roberto Alomar 1.50
108 Roger Clemens 5.00
109 Jason Giambi 2.00
110 Jim Thome 2.00
111 Alex Rodriguez 5.00
112 Juan Gonzalez 2.00
113 Torii Hunter 1.50
114 Roy Oswalt 1.50
115 Curt Schilling 2.00
116 Magglio Ordonez 1.50
117 Rafael Palmeiro 2.00
118 Andruw Jones 3.00
119 Manny Ramirez 3.00
120 Mark Teixeira 1.50
121 Mark Mulder 1.50
122 Garret Anderson 1.50
123 Tim Hudson 1.50
124 Todd Helton 3.00
125 Troy Glaus 3.00
126 Derek Jeter 6.00
127 Barry Bonds 6.00
128 Greg Maddux 4.00
129 Roger Clemens 5.00
130 Nomar Garciaparra 4.00
131 Mike Piazza 4.00
132 Alex Rodriguez 5.00
133 Ichiro Suzuki 4.00
134 Randy Johnson 3.00
135 Sammy Sosa 4.00
136 Ken Griffey Jr. 4.00
137 Alfonso Soriano 3.00
138 Jason Giambi 2.00
139 Albert Pujols 5.00
140 Chipper Jones 3.00
141 Adam Dunn 2.00
142 Pedro J. Martinez 3.00
143 Vladimir Guerrero 3.00
144 Mark Prior 2.00
145 Barry Zito 1.50
146 Jeff Bagwell 3.00
147 Lance Berkman 1.50
148 Shawn Green 1.50
149 Jason Giambi 2.00
150 Randy Johnson 3.00
151 Alex Rodriguez 5.00
152 Babe Ruth 10.00
153 Ty Cobb 6.00
154 Jackie Robinson 6.00
155 Lou Gehrig 8.00
156 Thurman Munson 6.00
157 Roberto Clemente 8.00
158 Nolan Ryan 10.00
159 Nolan Ryan 10.00
160 Nolan Ryan 10.00
161 Cal Ripken Jr. 10.00
162 Don Mattingly 8.00
163 Stan Musial 6.00
164 Tony Gwynn 3.00
165 Yogi Berra 3.00
166 Johnny Bench 5.00
167 Mike Schmidt 8.00
168 George Brett 8.00
169 Ryne Sandberg 4.00
170 Ernie Banks 5.00
171 J. Bonderman/Auto./Jsy 75.00
172 Jose Contreras/Auto. **RC** 40.00
173 Chien-Ming Wang/Auto. **RC** 350.00
174 Hideki Matsui/Base **RC** 40.00
175 Hong-Chih Kuo/Auto./Bat **RC** 120.00
176 Brandon Webb/Auto./Bat **RC** 60.00
177 Richard Fischer/Auto. 8.00
178 Robby Hammock/Auto./Bat 20.00
179 Todd Wellemeyer/Auto./49 **RC** 15.00
180 Prentice Redman/Auto./Bat **RC** 10.00
181 Nook Logan/Auto. **RC** 20.00
182 Craig Brazell/Auto. **RC** 15.00
183 Tim Olson/Auto./Bat **RC** 15.00
184 Matt Kata/Auto./Bat **RC** 20.00
185 A. Machado/Auto. 8.00
186 Michael Hessman/Auto. **RC** 10.00
187 Oscar Villarreal/Auto. **RC** 8.00
188 Guillermo Quiroz/Auto./Bat **RC** 20.00
189 Michel Hernandez/Auto. **RC** 10.00
190 Clint Barmes/Auto./Bat **RC** 40.00
191 Pete LaForest/Auto./Bat **RC** 20.00
192 Adam Loewen/Auto. **RC** 25.00
193 Terrmel Sledge/Auto./Bat **RC** 15.00
194 Lew Ford/Auto./Bat **RC** 40.00
195 Todd Wellemeyer/Auto./49 **RC** 15.00
196 Clint Barmes/Auto./Bat **RC** 40.00
197 J. Bonderman/Auto./Jsy 50.00
198 Brandon Webb/Auto./Jsy **RC** 60.00
199 Hideki Matsui/Base **RC** 30.00
200 Jose Contreras/Auto. **RC** 40.00

Silver Spotlight

Silvers (1-170): 1-2X
Production 100
Silver Auto. Memor. (171-200): 1X
Silver Memor. (171-200): 1X
Silver Auto: 1X
Production 29 to 50

Gold Spotlight

Golds (1-151): 2-4X
Golds (152-170): 1.5-3X
Production 50
Golds (171-200): No Pricing
Production 10 to 25

Jersey Numbers

NM/M

Common Player:
Production 5-100
1 Rod Carew/50 20.00
2 Nolan Ryan/50 40.00
3 Reggie Jackson/50 20.00
4 Brooks Robinson/50 25.00
5 Frank Robinson/50 15.00
6 Cal Ripken Jr./100 40.00
7 Carlton Fisk/50 15.00
8 Roger Clemens/100 15.00
10 Lou Boudreau/50 10.00
11 Bob Feller/25 30.00
13 Alan Trammell/50 10.00
14 Harmon Killebrew/50 25.00
15 Rod Carew/50 20.00
16 Kirby Puckett/50 20.00
19 Yogi Berra/50 30.00
20 Thurman Munson/50 30.00
21 Don Mattingly/100 25.00
25 Alex Rodriguez/100 10.00
26 Randy Johnson/50 10.00
27 Nolan Ryan/100 30.00
28 Dale Murphy/50 20.00
29 Warren Spahn/50 20.00
30 Eddie Mathews/50 25.00
32 Ryne Sandberg/100 30.00
33 Johnny Bench/50 30.00
34 Joe Morgan/50 10.00
35 Randy Johnson/50 10.00
36 Nolan Ryan/100 30.00
37 Pee Wee Reese/50 15.00
38 Duke Snider/50 25.00
39 Jackie Robinson/25 65.00
40 Robin Yount/50 30.00
41 Paul Molitor/50 20.00
42 Pedro Martinez/50 10.00
43 Randy Johnson/50 10.00
44 Tom Seaver/25 25.00
45 Gary Carter/50 10.00
46 Mike Schmidt/50 30.00
47 Steve Carlton/50 10.00
48 Willie Stargell/50 20.00
50 Ozzie Smith/50 35.00
51 Stan Musial/100 30.00
52 Enos Slaughter/50 10.00
53 Orlando Cepeda/50 10.00
54 Willie McCovey/50 15.00
57 Harmon Killebrew, Rod Carew/25 50.00
58 Harmon Killebrew, Kirby Puckett/25 50.00
68 Thurman Munson, Yogi Berra/25 50.00
69 Don Mattingly, Yogi Berra/25 60.00
71 Dale Murphy, Warren Spahn/25 50.00
72 Dale Murphy, Eddie Mathews/25 45.00
73 Eddie Mathews, Warren Spahn/25 60.00
74 Joe Morgan, Johnny Bench/25 40.00
75 Duke Snider, Pee Wee Reese/25 40.00
78 Paul Molitor, Robin Yount/25 75.00
81 Ozzie Smith, Stan Musial/25 60.00
82 Enos Slaughter, Stan Musial/25 60.00
83 Orlando Cepeda, Willie McCovey/25 40.00
84 Nolan Ryan, Reggie Jackson/25 60.00
90 Alex Rodriguez, Randy Johnson/25 25.00
91 Pedro J. Martinez, Randy Johnson/25 35.00
94 Reggie Jackson/25 35.00
95 Nolan Ryan/25 60.00
96 Nolan Ryan/25 60.00
97 Nolan Ryan/25 60.00
98 Nolan Ryan/25 60.00
99 Cal Ripken Jr., Rafael Palmeiro/25 90.00
100 Dale Murphy, Deion Sanders/25 50.00

Jersey Numbers Retired

NM/M

Many not priced due to scarcity.
1 Rod Carew/29 30.00
2 Nolan Ryan/30 50.00
5 Frank Robinson/20 20.00
7 Carlton Fisk/27 30.00
9 Carlton Fisk/27 15.00
16 Kirby Puckett/34 35.00
21 Don Mattingly/23 50.00
27 Nolan Ryan/34 50.00
30 Eddie Mathews/41 20.00
36 Nolan Ryan/34 50.00
39 Jackie Robinson/42 50.00
44 Tom Seaver/41 20.00
46 Mike Schmidt/20 50.00
47 Steve Carlton/32 15.00

49 Roberto Clemente/21 100.00
53 Orlando Cepeda/30 15.00
54 Willie McCovey/44 10.00

Leather

NM/M

Common Player:
Production 10-25
Golds: No Pricing
Production 5-10
Leather & Lace: No Pricing
Production 10
Leather & Lace Gold: No Pricing
Production 5
1 Alex Rodriguez/25 40.00
2 Chipper Jones/25 30.00
3 Jimmie Foxx/25 65.00
4 Kirby Puckett/25 25.00
5 Mike Schmidt/25 65.00
6 Roger Clemens/25 45.00
8 Tony Gwynn/25 40.00
10 Vladimir Guerrero/25 25.00
11 Adam Dunn/25 20.00
12 Andruw Jones/25 25.00
13 Curt Schilling/25 20.00
14 Randy Johnson/25 25.00
15 Mark Prior/25 40.00

Lineups - Bats

NM/M

Common Player:
Production 25-50
1 Paul Molitor, Robin Yount/50 35.00
2 Bernie Williams, Don Mattingly/50 40.00
4 Derek Jeter, Hideki Matsui/25 60.00
5 Andre Dawson, Ryne Sandberg/50 40.00
6 Bo Jackson, George Brett/50 40.00
7 Jose Canseco, Reggie Jackson/50 25.00
8 Mark Grace, Ryne Sandberg/50 40.00
9 Jose Canseco, Rickey Henderson/50 30.00
10 Hideo Nomo, Mike Piazza/50 30.00

Lineups - Buttons

No Pricing
Production One Set

Lineups - Jerseys

NM/M

Production 5-50
1 Paul Molitor, Robin Yount/50 35.00
2 Bernie Williams, Don Mattingly/50 40.00
3 Hee Seop Choi, Sammy Sosa/50 30.00
4 Derek Jeter, Hideki Matsui/50/Base 30.00
5 Andre Dawson, Ryne Sandberg/50 35.00
6 Bo Jackson, George Brett/50 50.00
7 Jose Canseco, Reggie Jackson/50 25.00
8 Mark Grace, Ryne Sandberg/50 35.00
9 Jose Canseco, Rickey Henderson/50 25.00
10 Hideo Nomo, Mike Piazza/50 25.00

Lineups Tag Team

No Pricing
Production 5

Lumberjacks

NM/M

Some not priced due to scarcity.
Production 1-25
Black: No Pricing
Production 1-5
Silver: No Pricing
Production 1-10
1 Babe Ruth/25 200.00
2 Lou Gehrig/25 150.00
3 Roberto Clemente/25 120.00
4 Stan Musial/25 40.00
5 Rogers Hornsby/25 50.00
6 Don Mattingly/25 50.00
7 Rickey Henderson/25 20.00
8 Cal Ripken Jr./25 75.00
9 Yogi Berra/25 30.00
10 Reggie Jackson/25 35.00
11 George Brett/25 60.00
12 Mel Ott/25 40.00
13 Roger Maris/25 60.00
14 Ryne Sandberg/25 50.00
16 Richie Ashburn/25 40.00
17 Mike Schmidt/25 40.00
18 Tony Gwynn/25 25.00
19 Ty Cobb/25 110.00
20 Thurman Munson/25 35.00
21 Jimmie Foxx/25 60.00
22 Duke Snider/25 25.00
24 Alex Rodriguez/25 30.00
25 Nomar Garciaparra/25 30.00
26 Hideki Matsui/25/Base 50.00
27 Ichiro Suzuki/25/Base 35.00
28 Barry Bonds/25/Base 35.00
29 Mike Piazza/25 30.00
30 Alfonso Soriano/25 25.00
31 Al Kaline/25 30.00
33 Dale Murphy/25 30.00
34 Orlando Cepeda/25 30.00
35 Willie McCovey/25 30.00
37 Brooks Robinson/25 30.00

Lumberjacks - Barrel

NM/M

1/1 except where indicated
No pricing due to scarcity.
21 Jimmie Foxx (7/05 Auction) 1,525

Lumberjacks - Jerseys

NM/M

Production 1-25
Black: No Pricing
Production 1-5
Silver: No Pricing
Production 1-10
4 Stan Musial/25 40.00
6 Don Mattingly/25 50.00
8 Cal Ripken Jr./25 80.00
9 Yogi Berra/25 25.00
11 George Brett/25 60.00
12 Mel Ott/25 40.00
14 Ryne Sandberg/25 50.00
15 Eddie Mathews/25 25.00
17 Mike Schmidt/25 50.00
18 Tony Gwynn/25 25.00
20 Thurman Munson/25 25.00
22 Duke Snider/25 20.00
24 Alex Rodriguez/25 30.00
25 Nomar Garciaparra/25 30.00
26 Hideki Matsui/25/Ball 50.00
27 Ichiro Suzuki/25/Ball 30.00
28 Barry Bonds/25/Ball 40.00
29 Mike Piazza/25 25.00
30 Alfonso Soriano/25 25.00
32 Harmon Killebrew/25 25.00
33 Dale Murphy/25 25.00
34 Orlando Cepeda/25 15.00
35 Willie McCovey/25 20.00
36 Willie Stargell/25 30.00
37 Brooks Robinson/25 20.00

Lumberjacks - Jerseys/Bats

NM/M

Production 1-25
Some not priced due to scarcity.
Black: No Pricing
Production 1-5
Silver: No Pricing
Production 1-10
4 Stan Musial/25 60.00
6 Don Mattingly/25 75.00
8 Cal Ripken Jr./25 140.00
9 Yogi Berra/25 30.00
11 George Brett/25 80.00
13 Roger Maris/25 100.00
14 Ryne Sandberg/25 65.00
15 Eddie Mathews/25 40.00
17 Mike Schmidt/25 65.00
18 Tony Gwynn/25 40.00
20 Thurman Munson/25 40.00
24 Alex Rodriguez/25 40.00
25 Nomar Garciaparra/25 40.00
26 Hideki Matsui/25/Base/Ball 65.00
27 Ichiro Suzuki/25/Base/Ball 60.00
28 Barry Bonds/25/Base/Ball 60.00
29 Mike Piazza/25 40.00
30 Alfonso Soriano/25 25.00
33 Dale Murphy/25 40.00
35 Willie McCovey/25 35.00
36 Willie Stargell/25 40.00
37 Brooks Robinson/25 30.00

Lumberjacks Combos

NM/M

Production 1-25
Black: No Pricing
Production 1-5
Silver: No Pricing
Production 1-10
38 Hideki Matsui, Ichiro Suzuki/25/Base 80.00
40 Don Mattingly, Lou Gehrig/25 240.00
41 Thurman Munson, Yogi Berra/25 50.00
42 Mike Schmidt, Richie Ashburn/25 60.00
43 Rogers Hornsby, Stan Musial/25 80.00
44 Don Mattingly, Roger Maris/25 100.00

Lumberjacks Combos - Jerseys

NM/M

Production 1-25
Some not priced due to scarcity.
Black: No Pricing
Production 1-5
Silver: No Pricing
Production 1-10
38 Hideki Matsui, Ichiro Suzuki/25/Ball 100.00
41 Thurman Munson, Yogi Berra/25 60.00

Lumberjacks Combos - Jerseys/Bats

NM/M

Production 1-25
Some not priced due to scarcity.
Black: No Pricing
Production 1-5
Silver: No Pricing
Production 1-10
38 Hideki Matsui, Ichiro Suzuki/25/Ball 100.00
41 Thurman Munson, Yogi Berra/25 50.00
42 Mike Schmidt, Richie Ashburn/25 60.00

Material Monikers Bats

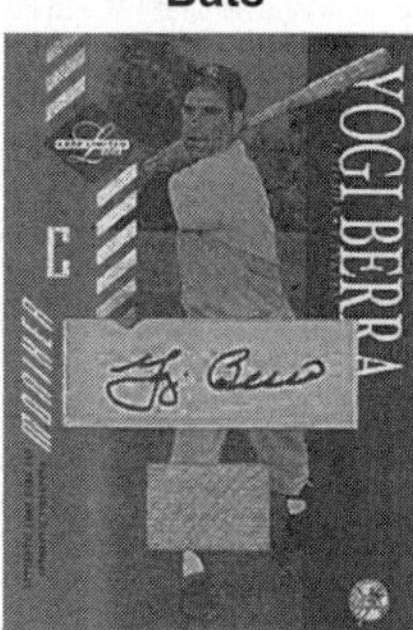

NM/M

Production 1-25
2 Eric Chavez/25 35.00
12 Craig Biggio/25 40.00
15 Vernon Wells/25 30.00
19 Edgar Martinez/25 50.00
26 Carlos Beltran/25 40.00
28 Tim Hudson/25 40.00
44 Mark Prior/25 50.00
47 Mark Teixeira/25 40.00
69 Nick Johnson/25 25.00
73 Adam Dunn/25 40.00
74 Roy Oswalt/25 30.00
77 Torii Hunter/25 30.00
85 Nick Johnson/25 25.00
113 Torii Hunter/25 30.00
114 Roy Oswalt/25 30.00
120 Mark Teixeira/25 40.00

Material Monikers Jerseys

NM/M

Common Player:
2 Eric Chavez/25 25.00
4 Miguel Tejada/25 35.00
12 Craig Biggio/25 35.00
15 Vernon Wells/25 25.00
19 Edgar Martinez/25 40.00
26 Carlos Beltran/25 50.00
28 Tim Hudson/25 25.00
44 Mark Prior/25 40.00
47 Mark Teixeira/25 30.00
69 Nick Johnson/25 20.00
73 Adam Dunn/25 40.00
74 Roy Oswalt/25 25.00
77 Torii Hunter/25 25.00
85 Nick Johnson/25 20.00
113 Torii Hunter/25 25.00
114 Roy Oswalt/25 25.00
120 Mark Teixeira/25 40.00

Material Monikers Jersey Numbers

NM/M

Production 1-25
2 Eric Chavez/25 25.00
4 Miguel Tejada/25 30.00
12 Craig Biggio/25 35.00
15 Vernon Wells/25 20.00
19 Edgar Martinez/25 30.00
26 Carlos Beltran/25 50.00
28 Tim Hudson/25 25.00
44 Mark Prior/25 40.00
47 Mark Teixeira/25 40.00
69 Nick Johnson/25 15.00
73 Adam Dunn/25 40.00
74 Roy Oswalt/25 20.00
77 Torii Hunter/25 25.00
85 Nick Johnson/25 15.00
113 Torii Hunter/25 25.00
114 Roy Oswalt/25 20.00
120 Mark Teixeira/25 40.00

Material Monikers Jersey Position

NM/M

Production 1-25
2 Eric Chavez/25 25.00
4 Miguel Tejada/25 30.00
12 Craig Biggio/25 35.00
15 Vernon Wells/25 20.00
19 Edgar Martinez/25 40.00
26 Carlos Beltran/25 50.00
28 Tim Hudson/25 25.00
29 Deion Sanders/25 50.00
44 Mark Prior/25 40.00
47 Mark Teixeira/25 40.00
69 Nick Johnson/25 20.00
73 Adam Dunn/25 40.00
74 Roy Oswalt/25 25.00
77 Torii Hunter/25 25.00
85 Nick Johnson/25 20.00
113 Torii Hunter/25 25.00
114 Roy Oswalt/25 25.00
120 Mark Teixeira/25 40.00

Player Threads

NM/M

Production 5-50
Primes: No Pricing
Production 5-10
1 Roger Clemens/50 15.00
2 Alex Rodriguez/50 15.00
3 Pedro Martinez/50 10.00
4 Randy Johnson/50 10.00
5 Curt Schilling/50 8.00
7 Nolan Ryan/50 35.00
8 Hideo Nomo/50 12.00
9 Mike Piazza/50 15.00
11 Rickey Henderson/50 15.00
12 Ivan Rodriguez/50 10.00
13 Gary Sheffield/50 8.00
14 Jeff Kent/50 8.00
15 Roberto Alomar/50 10.00
16 Rafael Palmeiro/50 10.00
17 Juan Gonzalez/50 8.00
18 Shawn Green/50 8.00
19 Jason Giambi/50 8.00
20 Jim Thome/50 10.00
21 Scott Rolen/50 12.00
22 Mike Mussina/50 10.00
23 Tom Glavine/50 8.00
24 Sammy Sosa/50 15.00

Player Threads Double

NM/M

Production 5-50
Double Primes: No Pricing
Production 5-10
1 Roger Clemens/50 25.00
2 Alex Rodriguez/50 25.00
3 Pedro Martinez/50 20.00
4 Randy Johnson/50 15.00
5 Curt Schilling/50 10.00
7 Nolan Ryan/50 50.00
8 Hideo Nomo/50 20.00
9 Mike Piazza/50 25.00
11 Rickey Henderson/50 20.00
12 Ivan Rodriguez/50 15.00
13 Gary Sheffield/50 10.00
14 Jeff Kent/50 10.00
15 Roberto Alomar/50 15.00
16 Rafael Palmeiro/50 15.00
17 Juan Gonzalez/50 15.00
18 Shawn Green/50 10.00
19 Jason Giambi/50 15.00
20 Jim Thome/50 15.00
21 Scott Rolen/50 20.00
22 Mike Mussina/50 15.00
23 Tom Glavine/50 10.00
24 Sammy Sosa/50 25.00

Player Threads Triple

NM/M

Production 50
Triple Primes: No Pricing
Production 5-10
4 Randy Johnson/50 20.00
7 Nolan Ryan/50 75.00
8 Hideo Nomo/50 60.00
11 Rickey Henderson/50 30.00
13 Gary Sheffield/50 15.00
14 Jeff Kent/50 15.00
15 Roberto Alomar/50 25.00

Limited Swatch

Complete Set (40):
Common Player:

Team Threads

NM/M

Production 10-50
Primes: No Pricing
Production 5-10
26 Alex Rodriguez, Nolan Ryan/50 50.00
27 Hideo Nomo, Mike Piazza/50 20.00
28 Cal Ripken Jr., Mike Mussina/50 50.00
29 Hideo Nomo, Kazuhisa Ishii/50 15.00
30 Nolan Ryan, Randy Johnson/50 40.00

Team Trademarks Autographs

NM/M

1 Alan Trammell/25 40.00
3 Jim Palmer/25 30.00
5 Gary Carter/25 40.00
6 Andre Dawson/25 30.00
8 Dale Murphy/25 50.00
10 Bobby Doerr/25 35.00
11 Brooks Robinson/25 50.00
12 Eric Davis/25 35.00
13 Fred Lynn/25 30.00
15 Jack Morris/25 25.00
16 Al Kaline/25 60.00
17 Deion Sanders/25 50.00
18 Luis Aparicio/25 35.00
20 Phil Rizzuto/25 40.00
24 Will Clark/25 70.00

Team Trademarks Jersey Autograph

NM/M

12 Eric Davis/44 30.00
15 Jack Morris/47 25.00
23 Rod Carew/29 50.00
25 Willie McCovey/44 25.00
27 Nolan Ryan/34 140.00
31 Rod Carew/29 50.00
32 Nolan Ryan/34 140.00
34 Nolan Ryan/30 140.00
37 Greg Maddux/31 150.00

Team Trademarks Threads Jersey Number

NM/M

Primes: 1-1.5X
Production 1-25
3 Jim Palmer/22 20.00
12 Eric Davis/44 8.00
15 Jack Morris/47 8.00
17 Deion Sanders/24 25.00
19 Orlando Cepeda/30 10.00
23 Rod Carew/29 20.00
24 Will Clark/22 50.00
25 Willie McCovey/44 10.00
27 Nolan Ryan/34 50.00
31 Rod Carew/29 20.00
32 Nolan Ryan/34 50.00
34 Nolan Ryan/30 50.00
37 Greg Maddux/31 30.00

2003 Leaf Limited Threads

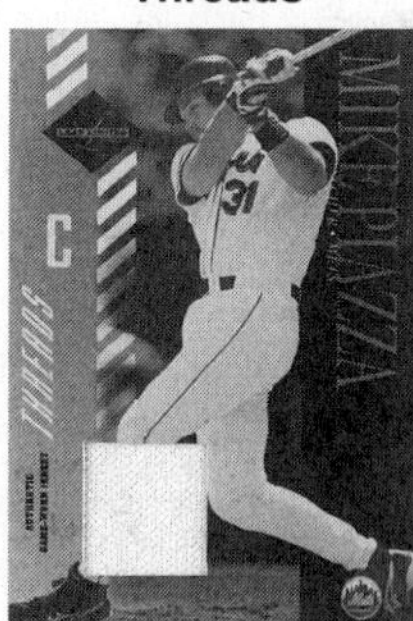

NM/M

Common Player: 8.00
Varying quantities produced
1 Derek Jeter/Base/50 20.00
2 Eric Chavez/25 10.00
3 Alex Rodriguez/100 15.00
4 Miguel Tejada/50 8.00
5 Nomar Garciaparra/100 15.00
6 Jeff Bagwell/50 10.00
7 Jim Thome/50 10.00
8 Pat Burrell/25 10.00
9 Albert Pujols/100 20.00
10 Juan Gonzalez/25 20.00
11 Shawn Green/50 10.00
12 Craig Biggio/25 10.00
13 Chipper Jones/50 20.00
14 Hideo Nomo/100 12.00
15 Vernon Wells/25 10.00
16 Gary Sheffield/25 10.00
17 Barry Larkin/25 15.00
18 Josh Beckett/25 15.00
19 Edgar Martinez/25 15.00
20 Ivan Rodriguez/25 20.00
21 Jeff Kent/25 10.00
22 Roberto Alomar/25 15.00
23 Alfonso Soriano/100 8.00
24 Jim Thome/50 10.00
25 Juan Gonzalez/25 10.00
26 Carlos Beltran/25 20.00
27 Shawn Green/50 8.00
28 Tim Hudson/25 10.00
29 Deion Sanders/25 20.00
30 Rafael Palmeiro/25 20.00
31 Todd Helton/50 10.00
32 Lance Berkman/25 10.00
33 Mike Mussina/50 10.00
34 Kazuhisa Ishii/50 8.00
35 Pat Burrell/25 10.00
36 Miguel Tejada/50 8.00
37 Juan Gonzalez/50 10.00
38 Roberto Alomar/25 15.00
39 Roberto Alomar/25 15.00
40 Luis Gonzalez/25 10.00
41 Jorge Posada/50 15.00
42 Mark Mulder/25 10.00
43 Sammy Sosa/100 15.00
44 Mark Prior/50 15.00
45 Roger Clemens/100 10.00
46 Tom Glavine/25 15.00
47 Mark Teixeira/25 10.00
48 Manny Ramirez/50 12.00
49 Frank Thomas/25 15.00
50 Troy Glaus/50 8.00
51 Andruw Jones/50 8.00
52 Jason Giambi/100 8.00
53 Jim Thome/50 10.00
54 Barry Bonds/50/Base 25.00
55 Rafael Palmeiro/25 15.00
56 Edgar Martinez/25 10.00
57 Vladimir Guerrero/50 10.00
58 Roberto Alomar/25 15.00
59 Mike Sweeney/25 10.00
60 Magglio Ordonez/25 10.00
62 Craig Biggio/25 10.00
63 Greg Maddux/100 10.00
64 Mike Piazza/100 10.00
65 Tom Glavine/25 15.00
66 Kerry Wood/25 20.00
67 Frank Thomas/25 20.00
68 Mike Mussina/25 10.00
69 Nick Johnson/25 8.00
70 Bernie Williams/50 10.00
71 Scott Rolen/25 20.00
72 Curt Schilling/25 15.00
73 Adam Dunn/50 10.00
74 Roy Oswalt/25 10.00
75 Pedro Martinez/25 20.00
76 Tom Glavine/25 15.00
77 Torii Hunter/25 10.00
78 Austin Kearns/25 10.00
79 Randy Johnson/100 8.00
80 Bernie Williams/50 10.00
81 Ichiro Suzuki/50 25.00
82 Kerry Wood/25 20.00
83 Kazuhisa Ishii/50 8.00
84 Randy Johnson/50 8.00
85 Nick Johnson/25 8.00
86 Josh Beckett/25 10.00
87 Curt Schilling/25 15.00
88 Mike Mussina/50 10.00
89 Pedro Martinez/50 15.00
90 Barry Zito/75 8.00
91 Jim Edmonds/100 6.00
92 Rickey Henderson/100 8.00
93 Rickey Henderson/50 12.00
94 Rickey Henderson/50 12.00
95 Rickey Henderson/50 12.00
96 Rickey Henderson/50 12.00
97 Randy Johnson/50 8.00
98 Mark Grace/50 10.00
99 Pedro Martinez/25 15.00
100 Hee Seop Choi/25 8.00
101 Ivan Rodriguez/25 15.00
102 Jeff Kent/25 10.00
104 Hideo Nomo/50 10.00
105 Mike Piazza/100 10.00
106 Tom Glavine/25 15.00
107 Roberto Alomar/25 15.00
108 Roger Clemens/100 10.00
109 Jason Giambi/25 10.00
110 Jim Thome/25 15.00
111 Alex Rodriguez/100 10.00
112 Juan Gonzalez/25 10.00
113 Torii Hunter/25 10.00
114 Roy Oswalt/25 10.00
115 Curt Schilling/25 15.00
116 Magglio Ordonez/25 10.00
117 Rafael Palmeiro/25 15.00
118 Andruw Jones/50 8.00
119 Manny Ramirez/50 12.00
120 Mark Teixeira/25 10.00
121 Mark Mulder/25 10.00
123 Tim Hudson/25 10.00
124 Todd Helton/50 10.00
125 Troy Glaus/50 6.00
126 Derek Jeter/Base/50 20.00
127 Barry Bonds/Base/50 25.00
128 Greg Maddux/100 10.00
129 Roger Clemens/100 10.00
130 Nomar Garciaparra/100 10.00
131 Mike Piazza/100 10.00
132 Alex Rodriguez/100 10.00
133 Ichiro Suzuki/Base/50 25.00
134 Randy Johnson/100 8.00
135 Sammy Sosa/100 15.00
137 Alfonso Soriano/100 8.00
138 Jason Giambi/100 6.00
139 Albert Pujols/100 20.00
140 Chipper Jones/25 20.00
141 Adam Dunn/50 8.00
142 Pedro Martinez/50 10.00
143 Vladimir Guerrero/50 10.00
144 Mark Prior/50 15.00
145 Barry Zito/50 8.00
146 Jeff Bagwell/50 12.00
147 Lance Berkman/Socks/25 10.00

148 Shawn Green/25 10.00
149 Jason Giambi/25 10.00
150 Randy Johnson/25 20.00
151 Alex Rodriguez/100 10.00
153 Ty Cobb/100 100.00
154 Jackie Robinson/50 50.00
156 Thurman Munson/100 15.00
158 Nolan Ryan/100 30.00
159 Nolan Ryan/100 30.00
160 Nolan Ryan/100 30.00
161 Cal Ripken Jr./100 60.00
162 Don Mattingly/100 25.00
163 Stan Musial/100 25.00
164 Tony Gwynn/100 12.00
165 Yogi Berra/100 12.00
166 Johnny Bench/100 12.00
167 Mike Schmidt/100 25.00
168 George Brett/100 30.00
169 Ryne Sandberg/100 25.00
170 Ernie Banks/50 30.00

Threads Button Up

Production 2-6
No Pricing

Threads Double

NM/M
Common Player:
Production 5 to 25.
Primes: No Pricing
Production 1 to 10
3 Alex Rodriguez/25 40.00
4 Miguel Tejada/25 25.00
10 Juan Gonzalez/25 20.00
12 Craig Biggio/25 25.00
14 Hideo Nomo/25 40.00
15 Vernon Wells/25 15.00
26 Carlos Beltran/25 25.00
28 Tim Hudson/25 20.00
31 Todd Helton/25 25.00
32 Lance Berkman/25 15.00
34 Kazuhisa Ishii/25 20.00
37 Juan Gonzalez/25 20.00
43 Sammy Sosa/25 50.00
44 Mark Prior/25 25.00
51 Andruw Jones/25 20.00
54 Barry Bonds/25 60.00
55 Rafael Palmeiro/25 30.00
60 Magglio Ordonez/25 20.00
73 Adam Dunn/25 20.00
75 Pedro Martinez/25 30.00
78 Austin Kearns/25 20.00
81 Ichiro Suzuki/25 60.00
90 Barry Zito/25 20.00
94 Rickey Henderson/25 25.00
101 Ivan Rodriguez/25 25.00
109 Jason Giambi/25 25.00
116 Magglio Ordonez/25 20.00
117 Rafael Palmeiro/25 30.00
118 Andruw Jones/25 20.00
120 Mark Teixeira/25 20.00
123 Tim Hudson/25 20.00
124 Todd Helton/25 25.00
127 Barry Bonds/25 50.00
132 Alex Rodriguez/25 40.00
133 Ichiro Suzuki/25 60.00
135 Sammy Sosa/25 50.00
141 Adam Dunn/25 30.00
142 Pedro Martinez/25 35.00
144 Mark Prior/25 40.00
145 Barry Zito/25 20.00
146 Jeff Bagwell/25 30.00
147 Lance Berkman/25 15.00
149 Jason Giambi/25 20.00
158 Nolan Ryan/25 80.00
162 Don Mattingly/25 65.00
164 Tony Gwynn/25 40.00
165 Mike Schmidt/25 65.00
168 George Brett/25 75.00
169 Ryne Sandberg/25 65.00

Number

NM/M
Common Player:
7 Jim Thome/25 20.00
18 Josh Beckett/61 10.00
24 Jim Thome/25 20.00
29 Deion Sanders/21 35.00
30 Rafael Palmeiro/25 20.00
33 Mike Mussina/35 15.00
40 Luis Gonzalez/20 15.00
41 Jorge Posada/20 25.00
42 Mark Mulder/20 15.00
43 Sammy Sosa/21 50.00
44 Mark Prior/22 25.00
45 Roger Clemens/22 50.00
46 Tom Glavine/47 8.00
47 Mark Teixeira/23 15.00
48 Manny Ramirez/24 30.00
49 Frank Thomas/35 15.00
50 Troy Glaus/25 10.00
51 Andruw Jones/25 15.00
52 Jason Giambi/52 10.00
53 Jim Thome/25 20.00
55 Rafael Palmeiro/25 20.00
57 Vladimir Guerrero/27 20.00
59 Mike Sweeney/29 10.00
60 Magglio Ordonez/30 10.00
63 Greg Maddux/31 25.00
64 Mike Piazza/31 30.00
65 Tom Glavine/47 8.00
66 Kerry Wood/52 15.00
67 Frank Thomas/35 15.00
68 Mike Mussina/35 15.00
69 Nick Johnson/36 8.00
70 Bernie Williams/51 10.00
71 Scott Rolen/27 20.00
72 Curt Schilling/38 10.00
73 Adam Dunn/44 8.00
74 Roy Oswalt/44 6.00
75 Pedro Martinez/45 10.00
76 Tom Glavine/47 8.00
77 Torii Hunter/48 8.00
78 Austin Kearns/28 10.00
79 Randy Johnson/51 10.00
80 Bernie Williams/51 10.00
82 Kerry Wood/34 20.00
84 Randy Johnson/51 10.00
85 Nick Johnson/36 8.00
86 Josh Beckett/61 8.00
87 Curt Schilling/38 10.00
88 Mike Mussina/35 15.00
89 Pedro Martinez/45 10.00
90 Barry Zito/75 8.00
93 Rickey Henderson/24 25.00
94 Rickey Henderson/35 20.00
95 Rickey Henderson/24 25.00
96 Rickey Henderson/24 25.00
97 Randy Johnson/51 10.00
99 Pedro Martinez/45 10.00
105 Mike Piazza/31 30.00
106 Tom Glavine/47 8.00
108 Roger Clemens/21 50.00
110 Jim Thome/25 15.00
112 Juan Gonzalez/22 20.00
113 Torii Hunter/48 8.00
114 Roy Oswalt/44 6.00
115 Curt Schilling/38 10.00
116 Magglio Ordonez/30 8.00
117 Rafael Palmeiro/25 20.00
118 Andruw Jones/25 10.00
119 Manny Ramirez/24 25.00
120 Mark Teixeira/23 20.00
121 Mark Mulder/20 15.00
125 Troy Glaus/25 12.00
128 Greg Maddux/31 25.00
129 Roger Clemens/22 50.00
131 Mike Piazza/31 30.00
134 Randy Johnson/51 12.00
135 Sammy Sosa/21 50.00
138 Jason Giambi/25 10.00
141 Adam Dunn/44 8.00
142 Pedro Martinez/45 10.00
143 Vladimir Guerrero/27 20.00
144 Mark Prior/22 25.00
145 Barry Zito/75 8.00
150 Randy Johnson/51 10.00
154 Jackie Robinson/42 50.00
157 Roberto Clemente/21 140.00
158 Nolan Ryan/34 50.00
159 Nolan Ryan/30 50.00
160 Nolan Ryan/34 50.00
162 Don Mattingly/23 50.00
165 Yogi Berra/42 15.00
167 Mike Schmidt/20 60.00
169 Ryne Sandberg/23 60.00

Position

NM/M
Common (2-151): 8.00
#'s 2-151
Production 25
#'s 152-170
Production 5-25
Primes: 1-1.5X
Production 25 for #'s 2-151.
2 Eric Chavez 8.00
3 Alex Rodriguez 25.00
4 Miguel Tejada 10.00
5 Nomar Garciaparra 30.00
6 Jeff Bagwell 15.00
7 Jim Thome 15.00
8 Pat Burrell 10.00
9 Albert Pujols 35.00
10 Juan Gonzalez 10.00
11 Shawn Green 10.00
12 Craig Biggio 8.00
13 Chipper Jones 25.00
14 Hideo Nomo 30.00
15 Vernon Wells 8.00
16 Gary Sheffield 10.00
17 Barry Larkin 10.00
18 Josh Beckett 15.00
19 Edgar Martinez 15.00
20 Ivan Rodriguez 15.00
21 Jeff Kent 8.00
22 Roberto Alomar 15.00
23 Alfonso Soriano 20.00
25 Juan Gonzalez 15.00
26 Carlos Beltran 8.00
27 Shawn Green 10.00
28 Tim Hudson 10.00
29 Deion Sanders 30.00
30 Rafael Palmeiro 15.00
31 Todd Helton 15.00
32 Lance Berkman 10.00
33 Mike Mussina 15.00
34 Kazuhisa Ishii 10.00
35 Pat Burrell 10.00
36 Miguel Tejada 10.00
37 Juan Gonzalez 15.00
38 Roberto Alomar 15.00
39 Roberto Alomar 15.00
40 Luis Gonzalez 10.00
41 Jorge Posada 15.00
42 Mark Mulder 10.00
43 Sammy Sosa 40.00
44 Mark Prior 25.00
45 Roger Clemens 40.00
46 Tom Glavine 15.00
47 Mark Teixeira 10.00
48 Manny Ramirez 15.00
49 Frank Thomas 15.00
50 Troy Glaus 10.00
51 Andruw Jones 15.00
52 Jason Giambi 15.00
53 Jim Thome 15.00
55 Rafael Palmeiro 15.00
56 Edgar Martinez 15.00
57 Vladimir Guerrero 15.00
58 Roberto Alomar 15.00
60 Magglio Ordonez 10.00
62 Craig Biggio 15.00
63 Greg Maddux 30.00
64 Mike Piazza 25.00
65 Tom Glavine 15.00
66 Kerry Wood 15.00
67 Frank Thomas 15.00
68 Mike Mussina 15.00
69 Nick Johnson 10.00
70 Bernie Williams 15.00
71 Scott Rolen 15.00
72 Curt Schilling 15.00
73 Adam Dunn 15.00
74 Roy Oswalt 8.00
75 Pedro J. Martinez 15.00
76 Tom Glavine 15.00
77 Torii Hunter 15.00
78 Austin Kearns 15.00
79 Randy Johnson 15.00
80 Bernie Williams 15.00
82 Kerry Wood 15.00
83 Kazuhisa Ishii 10.00
84 Randy Johnson 15.00
85 Nick Johnson 10.00
86 Josh Beckett 15.00
87 Curt Schilling 15.00
88 Mike Mussina 15.00
89 Pedro J. Martinez 15.00
90 Barry Zito 15.00
91 Jim Edmonds 15.00
93 Rickey Henderson 25.00
94 Rickey Henderson 25.00
95 Rickey Henderson 25.00
96 Rickey Henderson 25.00
97 Randy Johnson 15.00
98 Mark Grace 15.00
99 Pedro J. Martinez 15.00
100 Hee Seop Choi 10.00
101 Ivan Rodriguez 15.00
102 Jeff Kent 10.00
104 Hideo Nomo 30.00
105 Mike Piazza 25.00
106 Tom Glavine 15.00
107 Roberto Alomar 15.00
108 Roger Clemens 40.00
109 Jason Giambi 15.00
110 Jim Thome 15.00
111 Alex Rodriguez 25.00
112 Juan Gonzalez 15.00
113 Torii Hunter 15.00
114 Roy Oswalt 10.00
115 Curt Schilling 15.00
116 Magglio Ordonez 10.00
117 Rafael Palmeiro 15.00
118 Andruw Jones 15.00
119 Manny Ramirez 15.00
120 Mark Teixeira 15.00
121 Mark Mulder 10.00
123 Tim Hudson 10.00
124 Todd Helton 15.00
125 Troy Glaus 10.00
128 Greg Maddux 30.00
129 Roger Clemens 40.00
130 Nomar Garciaparra 30.00
131 Mike Piazza 25.00
132 Alex Rodriguez 25.00
134 Randy Johnson 15.00
135 Sammy Sosa 40.00
137 Alfonso Soriano 20.00
138 Jason Giambi 15.00
139 Albert Pujols 35.00
140 Chipper Jones 25.00
141 Adam Dunn 15.00
142 Pedro J. Martinez 15.00
143 Vladimir Guerrero 15.00
144 Mark Prior 25.00
145 Barry Zito 15.00
146 Jeff Bagwell 15.00
147 Lance Berkman 10.00
148 Shawn Green 10.00
149 Jason Giambi 15.00
150 Randy Johnson 15.00
151 Alex Rodriguez 25.00
153 Ty Cobb 125.00
156 Thurman Munson 30.00
158 Nolan Ryan 50.00
159 Nolan Ryan 50.00
160 Nolan Ryan 50.00
161 Cal Ripken Jr. 85.00
162 Don Mattingly 60.00
163 Stan Musial 60.00
164 Tony Gwynn 30.00
165 Yogi Berra 30.00
168 George Brett 60.00
169 Ryne Sandberg 60.00

Timber

NM/M
Common Player: 10.00
Production 25 Sets
2 Eric Chavez 10.00
3 Alex Rodriguez 25.00
4 Miguel Tejada 10.00
5 Nomar Garciaparra 30.00
6 Jeff Bagwell 15.00
7 Jim Thome 15.00
8 Pat Burrell 15.00
9 Albert Pujols 35.00
10 Juan Gonzalez 15.00
11 Shawn Green 10.00
12 Craig Biggio 10.00
13 Chipper Jones 25.00
14 Hideo Nomo 30.00
15 Vernon Wells 10.00
16 Gary Sheffield 10.00
17 Barry Larkin 15.00
18 Josh Beckett 15.00
19 Edgar Martinez 15.00
20 Ivan Rodriguez 15.00
21 Jeff Kent 10.00
22 Roberto Alomar 15.00
23 Alfonso Soriano 20.00
24 Jim Thome 15.00
25 Juan Gonzalez 15.00
26 Carlos Beltran 10.00
27 Shawn Green 10.00
28 Tim Hudson 10.00
30 Rafael Palmeiro 15.00
31 Todd Helton 15.00
32 Lance Berkman 10.00
33 Mike Mussina 15.00
34 Kazuhisa Ishii 10.00
35 Pat Burrell 15.00
36 Miguel Tejada 10.00
37 Juan Gonzalez 15.00
38 Roberto Alomar 15.00
39 Roberto Alomar 15.00
40 Luis Gonzalez 10.00
41 Jorge Posada 15.00
42 Mark Mulder 10.00
43 Sammy Sosa 40.00
44 Mark Prior 25.00
45 Roger Clemens 40.00
46 Tom Glavine 15.00
47 Mark Teixeira 15.00
48 Manny Ramirez 15.00
49 Frank Thomas 15.00
50 Troy Glaus 10.00
51 Andruw Jones 15.00
52 Jason Giambi 15.00
53 Jim Thome 15.00
55 Rafael Palmeiro 15.00
56 Edgar Martinez 15.00
57 Vladimir Guerrero 15.00
58 Roberto Alomar 15.00
59 Mike Sweeney 10.00
60 Magglio Ordonez 10.00
62 Craig Biggio 10.00
63 Greg Maddux 30.00
64 Mike Piazza 25.00
65 Tom Glavine 15.00
66 Kerry Wood 15.00
67 Frank Thomas 15.00
68 Mike Mussina 15.00
69 Nick Johnson 10.00
70 Bernie Williams 15.00
71 Scott Rolen 15.00
72 Curt Schilling 15.00
73 Adam Dunn 15.00
74 Roy Oswalt 10.00
75 Pedro J. Martinez 15.00
76 Tom Glavine 15.00
77 Torii Hunter 15.00
78 Austin Kearns 15.00
79 Randy Johnson 15.00
80 Bernie Williams 15.00
82 Kerry Wood 15.00
83 Kazuhisa Ishii 10.00
84 Randy Johnson 15.00
85 Nick Johnson 10.00
86 Josh Beckett 15.00
87 Curt Schilling 15.00
88 Mike Mussina 15.00
89 Pedro J. Martinez 15.00
90 Barry Zito 15.00
91 Jim Edmonds 10.00
92 Rickey Henderson 15.00
93 Rickey Henderson 15.00
94 Rickey Henderson 15.00
95 Rickey Henderson 15.00
96 Rickey Henderson 15.00
97 Randy Johnson 15.00
98 Mark Grace 15.00
99 Pedro J. Martinez 15.00
101 Ivan Rodriguez 15.00
102 Jeff Kent 10.00
103 Hideo Nomo 30.00
104 Hideo Nomo 30.00
105 Mike Piazza 25.00
106 Tom Glavine 15.00
107 Roberto Alomar 15.00
108 Roger Clemens 40.00
109 Jason Giambi 15.00
110 Jim Thome 15.00
111 Alex Rodriguez 25.00
112 Juan Gonzalez 15.00
113 Torii Hunter 15.00
114 Roy Oswalt 10.00
115 Curt Schilling 15.00
116 Magglio Ordonez 10.00
117 Rafael Palmeiro 15.00
118 Andruw Jones 15.00
119 Manny Ramirez 15.00
120 Mark Teixeira 15.00
121 Mark Mulder 10.00
122 Garret Anderson 10.00
123 Tim Hudson 10.00
124 Todd Helton 15.00
125 Troy Glaus 10.00
128 Greg Maddux 30.00
129 Roger Clemens 40.00
130 Nomar Garciaparra 30.00
131 Mike Piazza 25.00
132 Alex Rodriguez 25.00
134 Randy Johnson 15.00
135 Sammy Sosa 40.00
137 Alfonso Soriano 20.00
138 Jason Giambi 15.00
139 Albert Pujols 35.00
140 Chipper Jones 25.00
141 Adam Dunn 15.00
142 Pedro J. Martinez 15.00
143 Vladimir Guerrero 15.00
144 Mark Prior 25.00
145 Barry Zito 15.00
146 Jeff Bagwell 15.00
147 Lance Berkman 10.00
148 Shawn Green 10.00
149 Jason Giambi 15.00
150 Randy Johnson 15.00
151 Alex Rodriguez 25.00
152 Babe Ruth 180.00
153 Ty Cobb 125.00
155 Lou Gehrig 150.00
156 Thurman Munson 30.00
157 Roberto Clemente 140.00
158 Nolan Ryan 50.00
159 Nolan Ryan 50.00
160 Nolan Ryan 50.00
161 Cal Ripken Jr. 85.00
162 Don Mattingly 60.00
163 Stan Musial 60.00
164 Tony Gwynn 30.00
165 Yogi Berra 30.00
166 Johnny Bench 35.00
167 Mike Schmidt 60.00
168 George Brett 60.00
169 Ryne Sandberg 60.00
170 Ernie Banks/1 10.00

TNT

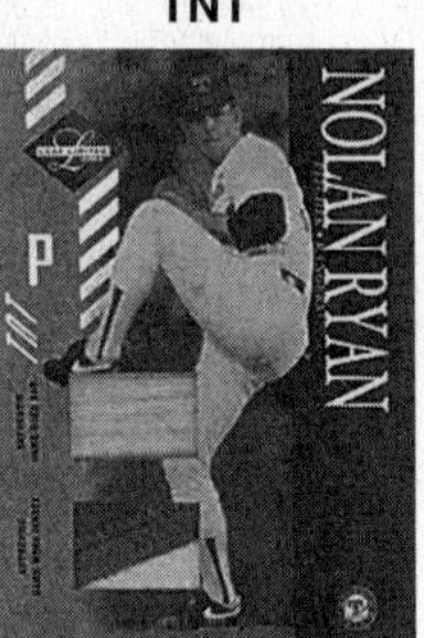

NM/M
Production 25 unless noted.
Some not priced due to scarcity.
Primes: 1X
Production 1-25
No pricing production 15 or less.
2 Eric Chavez 15.00
3 Alex Rodriguez 45.00
4 Miguel Tejada 15.00
5 Nomar Garciaparra 45.00
6 Jeff Bagwell 25.00
7 Jim Thome 30.00
8 Pat Burrell 30.00
9 Albert Pujols 60.00
10 Juan Gonzalez 25.00
11 Shawn Green 15.00
12 Craig Biggio 15.00
13 Chipper Jones 40.00
14 Hideo Nomo 50.00
15 Vernon Wells 15.00
16 Gary Sheffield 25.00
17 Barry Larkin 20.00
18 Josh Beckett 25.00
19 Edgar Martinez 25.00
20 Ivan Rodriguez 20.00
21 Jeff Kent 10.00
22 Roberto Alomar 20.00
23 Alfonso Soriano 30.00
24 Jim Thome 30.00
25 Juan Gonzalez 25.00
26 Carlos Beltran 20.00
27 Shawn Green 15.00
28 Tim Hudson 20.00
30 Rafael Palmeiro 20.00
31 Todd Helton 20.00
32 Lance Berkman 20.00
33 Mike Mussina 20.00
34 Kazuhisa Ishii 10.00
35 Pat Burrell 30.00
36 Miguel Tejada 15.00
37 Juan Gonzalez 25.00
38 Roberto Alomar 20.00
39 Roberto Alomar 20.00
40 Luis Gonzalez 15.00
41 Jorge Posada 25.00
42 Mark Mulder 20.00
43 Sammy Sosa 40.00
44 Mark Prior 25.00
45 Roger Clemens 50.00
46 Tom Glavine 20.00
47 Mark Teixeira 20.00
48 Manny Ramirez 25.00
49 Frank Thomas 35.00
50 Troy Glaus 15.00
51 Andruw Jones 20.00
52 Jason Giambi 15.00
53 Jim Thome 30.00
55 Rafael Palmeiro 25.00
56 Edgar Martinez 20.00
57 Vladimir Guerrero 30.00
58 Mike Sweeney 10.00
60 Magglio Ordonez 15.00
62 Craig Biggio 20.00
63 Greg Maddux 40.00
64 Mike Piazza 40.00
65 Tom Glavine 20.00
66 Kerry Wood 30.00
67 Frank Thomas 35.00
68 Mike Mussina 25.00
69 Nick Johnson 15.00
70 Bernie Williams 15.00
71 Scott Rolen 30.00
72 Curt Schilling 20.00
73 Adam Dunn 25.00
74 Roy Oswalt 15.00
75 Pedro J. Martinez 35.00
76 Tom Glavine 20.00
77 Torii Hunter 15.00
78 Austin Kearns 15.00
79 Randy Johnson 30.00
80 Bernie Williams 20.00
82 Kerry Wood 30.00
83 Kazuhisa Ishii 10.00
84 Randy Johnson 30.00
85 Nick Johnson 15.00
86 Josh Beckett 20.00
87 Curt Schilling 25.00
88 Mike Mussina 25.00
89 Pedro J. Martinez 35.00
90 Barry Zito 15.00
91 Jim Edmonds 20.00
92 Rickey Henderson 35.00
93 Rickey Henderson 35.00
94 Rickey Henderson 35.00
95 Rickey Henderson 35.00
96 Rickey Henderson 35.00
97 Randy Johnson 30.00
98 Mark Grace 20.00
99 Pedro J. Martinez 35.00
101 Ivan Rodriguez 20.00
102 Jeff Kent 10.00
103 Hideo Nomo 40.00
104 Hideo Nomo 40.00
105 Mike Piazza 40.00
106 Tom Glavine 20.00
107 Roberto Alomar 25.00
108 Roger Clemens 50.00
109 Jason Giambi 20.00
110 Jim Thome 30.00
111 Alex Rodriguez 45.00
112 Juan Gonzalez 25.00
113 Torii Hunter 15.00
114 Roy Oswalt 15.00
115 Curt Schilling 25.00
116 Magglio Ordonez 15.00
117 Rafael Palmeiro 25.00
118 Andruw Jones 15.00
119 Manny Ramirez 30.00
120 Mark Teixeira 25.00
121 Mark Mulder 20.00
123 Tim Hudson 20.00
124 Todd Helton 20.00
125 Troy Glaus 15.00
128 Greg Maddux 40.00
129 Roger Clemens 50.00
130 Nomar Garciaparra 40.00
131 Mike Piazza 40.00
132 Alex Rodriguez 40.00
134 Randy Johnson 30.00
135 Sammy Sosa 40.00
137 Alfonso Soriano 30.00
138 Jason Giambi 20.00
139 Albert Pujols 60.00
140 Chipper Jones 30.00
141 Adam Dunn 25.00
142 Pedro J. Martinez 35.00
143 Vladimir Guerrero 30.00
144 Mark Prior 25.00
145 Barry Zito 15.00
146 Jeff Bagwell 25.00
147 Lance Berkman 20.00
148 Shawn Green 15.00
149 Jason Giambi 20.00
150 Randy Johnson 30.00
151 Alex Rodriguez 40.00
156 Thurman Munson 50.00
158 Nolan Ryan 65.00
159 Nolan Ryan 65.00
160 Nolan Ryan 65.00
161 Cal Ripken Jr. 100.00
162 Don Mattingly 65.00
163 Stan Musial 65.00
164 Tony Gwynn 40.00
165 Yogi Berra 40.00
166 Johnny Bench 40.00
167 Mike Schmidt 65.00
168 George Brett 75.00
169 Ryne Sandberg 65.00

7th Inning Stretch

NM/M
Production 50 unless noted.
1 Alex Rodriguez 20.00
3 Sammy Sosa 25.00
4 Juan Gonzalez 10.00
5 Albert Pujols 30.00
6 Chipper Jones 15.00
7 Alfonso Soriano/40 15.00
8 Jim Thome 15.00
9 Mike Piazza 20.00
10 Rafael Palmeiro 15.00

2004 Leaf

NM/M
Complete Set (300): 50.00
Common Player: .15
Common (202-301): .25
Second Edition (1-301): 1X

Pack (8): 5.00
Box (24): 90.00
1 Darin Erstad .25
2 Garret Anderson .25
3 Jarrod Washburn .15
4 Kevin Appier .15
5 Tim Salmon .25
6 Troy Glaus .40
7 Troy Percival .15
8 Jason Johnson .15
9 Jay Gibbons .25
10 Melvin Mora .15
11 Sidney Ponson .15
12 Tony Batista .15
13 Derek Lowe .25
14 Robert Person .15
15 Manny Ramirez .50
16 Nomar Garciaparra 1.50
17 Pedro J. Martinez .75
18 Jorge de la Rosa .15
19 Bartolo Colon .25
20 Carlos Lee .15
21 Esteban Loaiza .15
22 Frank Thomas .50
23 Joe Crede .15
24 Magglio Ordonez .25
25 Ryan Ludwick .15
26 Luis Garcia .15
27 Brandon Phillips .15
28 C.C. Sabathia .15
29 Jhonny Peralta .15
30 Josh Bard .15
31 Omar Vizquel .25
32 Fernando Rodney .15
33 Mike Maroth .15
34 Bobby Higginson .15
35 Omar Infante .15
36 Dmitri Young .15
37 Eric Munson .15
38 Jeremy Bonderman .15
39 Carlos Beltran .25
40 Jeremy Affeldt .15
41 Dee Brown .15
42 .15
43 Mike Sweeney .15
44 Brent Abernathy .15
45 Runelvys Hernandez .15
46 A.J. Pierzynski .15
47 Corey Koskie .15
48 Cristian Guzman .15
49 Jacque Jones .15
50 Kenny Rogers .15
51 J.C. Romero .15
52 Torii Hunter .40
53 Alfonso Soriano .75
54 Bernie Williams .50
55 David Wells .15
56 Derek Jeter 2.00
57 Hideki Matsui 1.50
58 Jason Giambi .75
59 Jorge Posada .40
60 Jose Contreras .25
61 Mike Mussina .50
62 Nick Johnson .15
63 Roger Clemens 1.50
64 Barry Zito .40
65 Justin Duchscherer .15
66 Eric Chavez .25
67 Erubiel Durazo .15
68 Miguel Tejada .40
69 Mark Mulder .25
70 Terrence Long .15
71 Tim Hudson .25
72 Bret Boone .25
73 Dan Wilson .15
74 Edgar Martinez .25
75 Freddy Garcia .15
76 Rafael Soriano .15
77 Ichiro Suzuki 1.25
78 Jamie Moyer .15
79 John Olerud .25
80 Kazuhiro Sasaki .15
81 Aubrey Huff .15
82 Carl Crawford .15
83 Joe Kennedy .15
84 Rocco Baldelli .40
85 Toby Hall .15
86 Alex Rodriguez 1.50
87 Kevin Mench .15
88 Hank Blalock .25
89 Juan Gonzalez .50
90 Mark Teixeira .25
91 Rafael Palmeiro .50
92 Carlos Delgado .50
93 Eric Hinske .15
94 Josh Phelps .15
95 Brian Bowles .15
96 Roy Halladay .40
97 Shannon Stewart .15
98 Vernon Wells .25
99 Curt Schilling .40
100 Junior Spivey .15
101 Luis Gonzalez .25
102 Lyle Overbay .15
103 Mark Grace .25
104 Randy Johnson .75
105 Shea Hillenbrand .15
106 Andruw Jones .50
107 Chipper Jones .75
108 Gary Sheffield .40
109 Greg Maddux 1.00
110 Javy Lopez .25
111 John Smoltz .25
112 Marcus Giles .15
113 Rafael Furcal .25
114 Corey Patterson .15
115 Juan Cruz .15
116 Kerry Wood .50
117 Mark Prior 1.00
118 Moises Alou .25
119 Sammy Sosa 1.00
120 Aaron Boone .15
121 Adam Dunn .50
122 Austin Kearns .50
123 Barry Larkin .40
124 Ken Griffey Jr. 1.00
125 Brian Reith .15
126 Wily Mo Pena .15
127 Jason Jennings .15
128 Jay Payton .15
129 Larry Walker .25
130 Preston Wilson .15
131 Todd Helton .50
132 Dontrelle Willis .40
133 Ivan Rodriguez .50
134 Josh Beckett .50
135 Juan Encarnacion .15
136 Mike Lowell .15
137 Craig Biggio .25
138 Jeff Bagwell .50
139 Jeff Kent .25
140 Lance Berkman .25
141 Richard Hidalgo .15
142 Roy Oswalt .25
143 Eric Gagne .25
144 Fred McGriff .25
145 Hideo Nomo .40
146 Kazuhisa Ishii .15
147 Kevin Brown .25
148 Paul LoDuca .15
149 Shawn Green .25
150 Ben Sheets .25
151 Geoff Jenkins .25
152 Rey Sanchez .15
153 Richie Sexson .40
154 Wes Helms .15
155 Shane Nance .15
156 Fernando Tatis .15
157 Javier Vazquez .15
158 Jose Vidro .15
159 Orlando Cabrera .15
160 Henry Mateo .15
161 Vladimir Guerrero .75
162 Zach Day .15
163 Edwin Almonte .15
164 Al Leiter .15
165 Cliff Floyd .15
166 Jae Weong Seo .15
167 Mike Piazza 1.00
168 Roberto Alomar .50
169 Tom Glavine .25
170 Bobby Abreu .25
171 Brandon Duckworth .15
172 Jim Thome .75
173 Kevin Millwood .25
174 Pat Burrell .25
175 Aramis Ramirez .15
176 Jack Wilson .15
177 Brian Giles .25
178 Jason Kendall .15
179 Kenny Lofton .25
180 Kip Wells .15
181 Kris Benson .15
182 Albert Pujols 1.50
183 J.D. Drew .15
184 Jim Edmonds .25
185 Matt Morris .15
186 Scott Rolen .75
187 Woody Williams .15
188 Clifford Bartosh .15
189 Brian Lawrence .15
190 Ryan Klesko .25
191 Sean Burroughs .15
192 Xavier Nady .15
193 Dennis Tankersley .15
194 Donaldo Mendez .15
195 Barry Bonds 2.00
196 Benito Santiago .15
197 Edgardo Alfonzo .15
198 Cody Ransom .15
199 Jason Schmidt .15
200 Rich Aurilia .15
201 Ken Harvey .15
202 Adam Loewen .25
203 Alfredo Gonzalez .25
204 Arnie Munoz .25
205 Andrew Brown .25
206 Josh Hall .25
207 Josh Stewart .25
208 Clint Barmes .25
209 Brandon Webb .50
210 Chien-Ming Wang .40
211 Edgar Gonzalez .25
212 Alejandro Machado .25
213 Jeremy Griffiths .25
214 Craig Brazell .25
215 Daniel Cabrera .25
216 Fernando Cabrera .25
217 Termel Sledge .25
218 Rob Hammock .25
219 Francisco Rosario .25
220 Francisco Cruceta .25
221 Rett Johnson .25
222 Guillermo Quiroz .25
223 Hong-Chih Kuo .25
224 Ian Ferguson .25
225 Tim Olson .25
226 Todd Wellemeyer .25
227 Rich Fischer .25
228 Phil Seibel .25
229 Joe Valentine .25
230 Matt Kata .25
231 Michael Hessman .25
232 Michel Hernandez .25
233 Doug Waechter .25
234 Prentice Redman .25
235 Nook Logan .25
236 Oscar Villarreal .25
237 Pete LaForest .25
238 Matt Bruback .25
239 Josh Willingham .25
240 Greg Aquino .25
241 Lew Ford .25
242 Jeff Duncan .25
243 Chris Waters .25
244 Miguel Ojeda .25
245 Rosman Garcia .25
246 Felix Sanchez .25
247 Jon Leicester .25
248 Roger Deago .25
249 Mike Ryan .25
250 Chris Capuano .25
251 Matt White .25
252 Bernie Williams .50
253 Mark Grace .50
254 Chipper Jones 1.00
255 Greg Maddux 1.50
256 Sammy Sosa 2.00
257 Mike Mussina .75
258 Tim Salmon .50
259 Barry Larkin .50
260 Randy Johnson 1.00
261 Jeff Bagwell .75
262 Roberto Alomar .50
263 Tom Glavine .50
264 Roger Clemens 2.50
265 Barry Bonds 3.00
266 Ivan Rodriguez .75
267 Pedro J. Martinez 1.00
268 Ken Griffey Jr. 1.50
269 Jim Thome 1.00
270 Frank Thomas .75
271 Mike Piazza 1.50
272 Troy Glaus .40
273 Melvin Mora .25
274 Nomar Garciaparra 2.00
275 Magglio Ordonez .40
276 Omar Vizquel .40
277 Dmitri Young .25
278 Mike Sweeney .25
279 Torii Hunter .50
280 Derek Jeter 2.00
281 Barry Zito .50
282 Ichiro Suzuki 1.50
283 Rocco Baldelli .50
284 Alex Rodriguez 2.00
285 Carlos Delgado .50
286 Randy Johnson .75
287 Greg Maddux 1.00
288 Sammy Sosa 1.50
289 Ken Griffey Jr. 1.00
290 Todd Helton .50
291 Ivan Rodriguez .50
292 Jeff Bagwell .50
293 Hideo Nomo .50
294 Richie Sexson .50
295 Vladimir Guerrero .75
296 Mike Piazza 1.00
297 Jim Thome .75
298 Jason Kendall .40
299 Albert Pujols 1.50
300 Ryan Klesko .40
301 Barry Bonds 2.00

Black Press Proof

Stars (1-301): 5-10X
Production 50 Sets
Hot Pack Exclusive

Blue Press Proof

Stars (1-301): 4-8X
Production 100 Sets

Gold Press Proof

Cards (1-301): 12-25X
Production 25 Sets

Red Press Proof

Stars (1-301): 1-2X
Inserted 1:8

Autographs

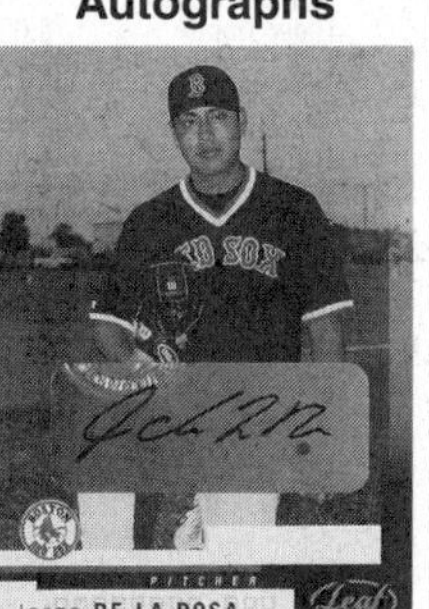

NM/M
Common Autograph 6.00
14 Robert Person 6.00
18 Jorge De La Rosa 6.00
25 Ryan Ludwick 8.00
26 Luis Garcia 6.00
29 Jhonny Peralta 6.00
30 Josh Bard 6.00
32 Fernando Rodney 6.00
33 Mike Maroth 6.00
35 Omar Infante 6.00
41 Dee Brown 6.00
44 Brent Abernathy/SP 10.00
51 J.C. Romero 6.00
65 Justin Duchscherer 10.00
70 Terrence Long/SP 15.00
76 Rafael Soriano 8.00
85 Toby Hall/SP 10.00
87 Kevin Mench 6.00
95 Brian Bowles 6.00
115 Juan Cruz 6.00
125 Brian Reith 6.00
126 Wily Mo Pena 8.00
127 Jason Jennings 6.00
155 Shane Nance 6.00
160 Henry Mateo/SP 8.00
163 Edwin Almonte 6.00
171 Brandon Duckworth 6.00
176 Jack Wilson 6.00
180 Kip Wells 6.00
188 Clifford Bartosh 6.00
189 Brian Lawrence 6.00
193 Dennis Tankersley 6.00
194 Donaldo Mendez 6.00
198 Cody Ransom/SP 8.00
247 Jon Leicester/SP 8.00

Away

NM/M
Complete Set (10): 20.00
Common Player: 1.00
Inserted 1:35
1 Greg Maddux 2.50
2 Sammy Sosa 3.00
3 Alex Rodriguez 4.00
4 Albert Pujols 4.00
5 Jason Giambi 1.50
6 Chipper Jones 2.00
7 Vladimir Guerrero 1.50
8 Mike Piazza 2.50
9 Nomar Garciaparra 3.00
10 Austin Kearns 1.00

Away Jersey

NM/M
Common Player: 5.00
Inserted 1:119
Prime: 1.5-2X
Production 50
1 Greg Maddux 8.00
2 Sammy Sosa 12.00
3 Alex Rodriguez 10.00
4 Albert Pujols 15.00
5 Jason Giambi 8.00
6 Chipper Jones 8.00
7 Vladimir Guerrero 8.00

8 Mike Piazza 10.00
9 Nomar Garciaparra 12.00
10 Austin Kearns 5.00

Clean Up Crew

NM/M
Complete Set (10): 20.00
Common Player: 1.00
Inserted 1:49
1 Sammy Sosa, Moises Alou, Hee Seop Choi 3.00
2 Jason Giambi, Alfonso Soriano, Hideki Matsui 5.00
3 Vernon Wells, Carlos Delgado, Josh Phelps 1.00
4 Alex Rodriguez, Juan Gonzalez, Hank Blalock 4.00
5 Gary Sheffield, Andruw Jones, Chipper Jones 2.50
6 Ken Griffey Jr., Austin Kearns, Aaron Boone 3.00
7 Albert Pujols, Jim Edmonds, Scott Rolen 4.00
8 Jeff Bagwell, Jeff Kent, Lance Berkman 1.50
9 Todd Helton, Preston Wilson, Larry Walker 1.50
10 Miguel Tejada, Erubiel Durazo, Eric Chavez 1.00

Clean Up Crew Materials

NM/M
Common Card: 15.00
Production 50 Sets
1 Sammy Sosa, Moises Alou, Hee Seop Choi 35.00
2 Jason Giambi, Alfonso Soriano, Hideki Matsui 60.00
3 Vernon Wells, Carlos Delgado, Josh Phelps 15.00
4 Alex Rodriguez, Juan Gonzalez, Hank Blalock 35.00
5 Gary Sheffield, Andruw Jones, Chipper Jones 20.00
6 Ken Griffey Jr., Austin Kearns, Aaron Boone 25.00
7 Albert Pujols, Jim Edmonds, Scott Rolen 40.00
8 Jeff Bagwell, Jeff Kent, Lance Berkman 25.00
9 Todd Helton, Preston Wilson, Larry Walker 20.00
10 Miguel Tejada, Erubiel Durazo, Eric Chavez 15.00

Cornerstones

NM/M
Complete Set (10): 20.00
Common Player: 1.00
Inserted 1:78
1 Alex Rodriguez, Hank Blalock 4.00
2 Kerry Wood, Mark Prior 3.00
3 Roger Clemens, Alfonso Soriano 4.00
4 Nomar Garciaparra, Manny Ramirez 4.00
5 Austin Kearns, Adam Dunn 1.00
6 Tom Glavine, Mike Piazza 2.50
7 Andruw Jones, Chipper Jones 2.50
8 Albert Pujols, Scott Rolen 4.00
9 Curt Schilling, Randy Johnson 2.00
10 Hideo Nomo, Kazuhisa Ishii 1.00

Cornerstones Materials

NM/M
Common Duo: 15.00
Production 50 Sets
1 Alex Rodriguez, Hank Blalock 25.00
2 Kerry Wood, Mark Prior 40.00
3 Roger Clemens, Alfonso Soriano 40.00
4 Nomar Garciaparra, Manny Ramirez 30.00
5 Austin Kearns, Adam Dunn 15.00
7 Andruw Jones, Chipper Jones 20.00
8 Albert Pujols, Scott Rolen 40.00
9 Curt Schilling, Randy Johnson 20.00
10 Hideo Nomo, Kazuhisa Ishii 20.00

Exhibits

NM/M
Common Player: 2.50
Production 66 Sets
Variations #'d to 63: 1X
Variations #'d to 46: 1X
Variations #'d 21 to 27: 1.5X
1 Adam Dunn 2.50
2 Albert Pujols 8.00
3 Alex Rodriguez 8.00
4 Alfonso Soriano 4.00
5 Andruw Jones 3.00
6 Barry Bonds 10.00
7 Barry Larkin 2.50
8 Barry Zito 2.50
9 Cal Ripken Jr. 10.00
10 Chipper Jones 5.00
11 Dale Murphy 2.50
12 Derek Jeter 10.00
13 Don Mattingly 8.00
14 Ernie Banks 5.00
15 Frank Thomas 4.00
16 George Brett 6.00
17 Greg Maddux 5.00
18 Hank Blalock 2.50
19 Hideo Nomo 2.50
20 Ichiro Suzuki 6.00
21 Jason Giambi 3.00
22 Jim Thome 4.00
23 Juan Gonzalez 2.50
24 Ken Griffey Jr. 5.00
25 Kirby Puckett 4.00
26 Mark Prior 5.00
27 Mike Mussina 2.50
28 Mike Piazza 5.00
29 Mike Schmidt 6.00
30 Nolan Ryan 8.00
31 Nolan Ryan 8.00
32 Nolan Ryan 8.00
33 Nomar Garciaparra 8.00
34 Ozzie Smith 2.50
35 Pedro J. Martinez 4.00
36 Randy Johnson 3.00
37 Reggie Jackson 2.50
38 Reggie Jackson 2.50
39 Rickey Henderson 2.50
40 Roberto Alomar 2.50
41 Roberto Clemente 8.00
42 Rod Carew 3.00
43 Roger Clemens 8.00
44 Sammy Sosa 6.00
45 Stan Musial 6.00
46 Tom Glavine 2.50
47 Tom Seaver 4.00
48 Tony Gwynn 4.00
49 Vladimir Guerrero 4.00
50 Yogi Berra 4.00

Gamers

NM/M
Complete Set (20): 40.00
Common Player: 1.00
Quantum: 2-4X
Production 100 Sets
1 Albert Pujols 4.00
2 Alex Rodriguez 4.00
3 Alfonso Soriano 1.50
4 Barry Bonds 5.00
5 Barry Zito 1.00
6 Chipper Jones 2.00
7 Derek Jeter 5.00

8 Greg Maddux 2.50
9 Ichiro Suzuki 3.00
10 Jason Giambi 1.50
11 Jeff Bagwell 1.50
12 Ken Griffey Jr. 2.50
13 Manny Ramirez 1.50
14 Mark Prior 3.00
15 Mike Piazza 2.50
16 Nomar Garciaparra 3.00
17 Pedro J. Martinez 2.00
18 Randy Johnson 2.00
19 Roger Clemens 3.00
20 Sammy Sosa 3.00

Gold Leaf Rookies

NM/M
Complete Set (10): 6.00
Common Player: .50
Inserted 1:23
Mirror Gold: No Pricing
Production 25 Sets
1 Adam Loewen 2.00
2 Rickie Weeks 5.00
3 Khalil Greene .50
4 Chad Tracy .50
5 Alexis Rios .50
6 Craig Brazell .50
7 Clint Barmes .50
8 Pete LaForest .50
9 Alfredo Gonzalez .50
10 Arnie Munoz .50

Home

NM/M
Complete Set (10): 20.00
Common Player: 1.00
Inserted 1:35
1 Greg Maddux 2.50
2 Sammy Sosa 3.00
3 Alex Rodriguez 4.00
4 Albert Pujols 4.00
5 Jason Giambi 1.50
6 Chipper Jones 2.00
7 Vladimir Guerrero 1.50
8 Mike Piazza 2.50
9 Nomar Garciaparra 3.00
10 Austin Kearns 1.00

Home Jersey

NM/M
Common Player: 5.00
Inserted 1:119
Primes: 1.5-2X
Production 50
1 Greg Maddux 8.00
2 Sammy Sosa 12.00
3 Alex Rodriguez 10.00
4 Albert Pujols 15.00
5 Jason Giambi 8.00
6 Chipper Jones 8.00
7 Vladimir Guerrero 8.00
8 Mike Piazza 10.00
9 Nomar Garciaparra 12.00
10 Austin Kearns 5.00

Limited Previews

NM/M
Common Player: 2.00
Production 999 Sets
Silver: 1-2X
Production 100 Sets
Gold: 2-3X
Production 50 Sets
1 Derek Jeter 8.00
2 Barry Zito 2.00
3 Ichiro Suzuki 6.00
4 Pedro J. Martinez 3.00
5 Alfonso Soriano 3.00
6 Alex Rodriguez 6.00
7 Greg Maddux 4.00
8 Mike Piazza 4.00
9 Mark Prior 2.00
10 Albert Pujols 8.00
11 Sammy Sosa 5.00
12 Ken Griffey Jr. 4.00
13 Nomar Garciaparra 4.00
14 Randy Johnson 3.00
15 Jason Giambi 2.00
16 Barry Bonds 8.00
17 Manny Ramirez 3.00
18 Chipper Jones 3.00
19 Jeff Bagwell 2.00
20 Roger Clemens 6.00

MVP Winners

NM/M
Complete Set (20): 50.00
Common Player: 1.00
Gold: 1-2X
Production 500 Sets
1 Stan Musial - 1948 NL 3.00
2 Ernie Banks - 1958 NL 2.00
3 Roberto Clemente - 1966 NL 4.00
4 George Brett - 1980 AL 4.00
5 Mike Schmidt - 1980 NL 4.00
6 Cal Ripken Jr. - 1983 AL 5.00
7 Dale Murphy - 1983 NL 1.50
8 Ryne Sandberg - 1984 NL 3.00
9 Don Mattingly - 1985 AL 3.00
10 Roger Clemens - 1986 AL 4.00
11 Rickey Henderson - 1990 AL 1.00
12 Cal Ripken Jr. - 1991 AL 5.00
13 Barry Bonds - 1992 NL 5.00
14 Barry Bonds - 1993 NL 5.00
15 Frank Thomas - 1994 AL 1.50
16 Ken Griffey Jr. - 1997 AL 2.50
17 Sammy Sosa - 1998 NL 3.00
18 Chipper Jones - 1999 NL 2.00
19 Jason Giambi - 2000 AL 1.50
20 Ichiro Suzuki - 2001 AL 3.00

Picture Perfect

NM/M
Complete Set (15): 25.00
Common Player: 1.00
Inserted 1:37
1 Albert Pujols 5.00
2 Alex Rodriguez 5.00
3 Alfonso Soriano 2.00
4 Austin Kearns 1.00
5 Carlos Delgado 1.50
6 Chipper Jones 2.50
7 Hank Blalock 1.50
8 Jason Giambi 2.00
9 Jeff Bagwell 1.50
10 Jim Thome 2.00
11 Manny Ramirez 1.50
12 Mike Piazza 3.00
13 Nomar Garciaparra 4.00
14 Sammy Sosa 4.00
15 Todd Helton 1.50

Picture Perfect Materials

NM/M
Common Player: 6.00
Inserted 1:437
1 Albert Pujols 15.00
2 Alex Rodriguez 10.00
3 Alfonso Soriano 8.00
4 Austin Kearns 6.00
5 Carlos Delgado 6.00
6 Chipper Jones 8.00
7 Hank Blalock 6.00
8 Jason Giambi 8.00
9 Jeff Bagwell 8.00
10 Jim Thome 10.00
11 Manny Ramirez 6.00
12 Mike Piazza 10.00
13 Nomar Garciaparra 10.00
14 Sammy Sosa 10.00
15 Todd Helton 8.00

Recollection Autographs

All are 1990 Leaf cards.

Shirt Off My Back

NM/M
Common Player: 4.00
Inserted 1:47
1 Shawn Green 4.00
2 Andruw Jones 6.00
3 Ivan Rodriguez 6.00
4 Hideo Nomo 6.00
5 Don Mattingly 20.00
6 Mark Prior 10.00
7 Alfonso Soriano 6.00
8 Richie Sexson 5.00
9 Vernon Wells 4.00
10 Nomar Garciaparra 8.00
11 Jason Giambi 6.00
12 Austin Kearns 5.00
13 Chipper Jones 6.00
14 Rickey Henderson 6.00
15 Alex Rodriguez 12.00
16 Garret Anderson 4.00
17 Vladimir Guerrero 4.00
18 Sammy Sosa 10.00
19 Mike Piazza 8.00
20 David Wells 4.00
21 Scott Rolen 6.00
22 Adam Dunn 5.00
23 Carlos Delgado 5.00
24 Greg Maddux 8.00
25 Hank Blalock 5.00

Shirt Off My Back Team Logo Patch

NM/M
Common Player: 10.00
Autographs: No Pricing
Production Five Sets
Jersey Number Patch: .75-1X
Production 50 Sets
Sosa #'d to 42.
Jersey Number Patch Auto.: No Pricing
Production Five Sets
1 Shawn Green/41 15.00
2 Andruw Jones/75 15.00
3 Ivan Rodriguez/75 15.00
4 Hideo Nomo/74 20.00
6 Mark Prior/46 20.00
7 Alfonso Soriano/28 25.00
8 Richie Sexson/38 15.00
9 Vernon Wells/74 10.00
10 Nomar Garciaparra/75 25.00
11 Jason Giambi/26 20.00
12 Austin Kearns/32 10.00
13 Chipper Jones/75 20.00
14 Rickey Henderson/40 20.00
15 Alex Rodriguez/75 30.00
16 Garret Anderson/71 10.00
17 Vladimir Guerrero/55 20.00
18 Sammy Sosa/39 25.00
19 Mike Piazza/75 20.00
20 David Wells/74 10.00
21 Scott Rolen/29 30.00
22 Adam Dunn/32 15.00
23 Carlos Delgado/56 15.00
24 Greg Maddux/75 20.00
25 Hank Blalock/62 15.00

Sunday Dress

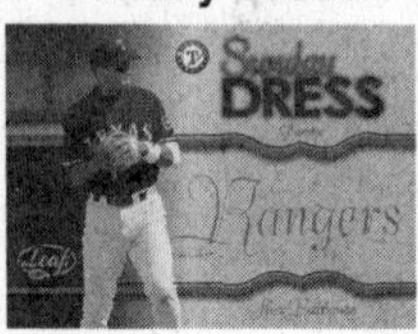

NM/M
Complete Set (10): 10.00
Common Player: .75
Inserted 1:17
1 Frank Thomas 1.00
2 Barry Zito .75
3 Mike Piazza 2.00
4 Mark Prior 2.00
5 Jeff Bagwell 1.00
6 Roy Oswalt .75
7 Todd Helton 1.00
8 Magglio Ordonez .75
9 Alex Rodriguez 3.00
10 Manny Ramirez 1.00

Sunday Dress Jersey

NM/M
Common Player: 5.00
Inserted 1:119
Prime Jersey: 1-1.5X
Production 100
1 Frank Thomas 8.00
2 Barry Zito 6.00
3 Mike Piazza 10.00
4 Mark Prior 10.00
5 Jeff Bagwell 8.00
6 Roy Oswalt 5.00
7 Todd Helton 8.00
8 Magglio Ordonez 6.00
9 Alex Rodriguez 10.00
10 Manny Ramirez 6.00

2004 Leaf Certified Cuts

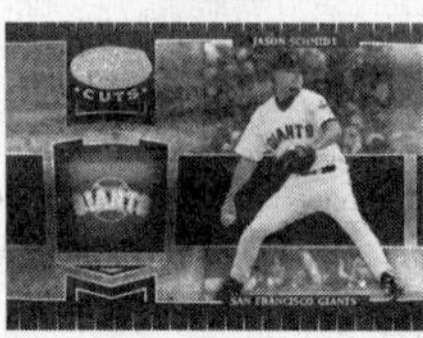

NM/M
Complete Set (300):
Common Player (1-200): .75
Common (201-250): 2.00
Production 599
Common (251-300): 5.00
Production 499
Auto. Production 99-499
Pack (5): 20.00
Box (10): 160.00
1 Vladimir Guerrero 1.50
2 Garret Anderson .75
3 John Lackey .75
4 Bartolo Colon .75
5 Troy Glaus .75
6 Tim Salmon .75
7 Shea Hillenbrand .75
8 Brandon Webb .75
9 Roberto Alomar .75
10 Randy Johnson 2.00
11 Alex Cintron .75
12 Richie Sexson .75
13 Luis Gonzalez .75
14 Adam LaRoche .75
15 Rafael Furcal .75
16 Chipper Jones 2.00
17 Marcus Giles .75
18 Andruw Jones 1.00
19 Russ Ortiz .75
20 Rafael Palmeiro 1.00
21 Melvin Mora .75
22 Luis Matos .75
23 Jay Gibbons .75
24 Adam Loewen .75
25 Larry Bigbie .75
26 Rodrigo Lopez .75
27 Javy Lopez .75
28 Miguel Tejada 1.00
29 Trot Nixon .75
30 Curt Schilling 1.00
31 Jason Varitek .75
32 Manny Ramirez 1.00
33 Keith Foulke .75
34 Derek Lowe .75
35 Pedro J. Martinez 1.50
36 Nomar Garciaparra 2.50
37 Bill Mueller .75
38 Johnny Damon .75
39 David Ortiz 1.50
40 Mark Prior 1.50
41 Kerry Wood 1.50
42 Sammy Sosa 2.50
43 Derrek Lee .75
44 Greg Maddux 2.00
45 Aramis Ramirez .75
46 Matt Clement .75
47 Carlos Zambrano .75
48 Todd Walker .75
49 Moises Alou .75
50 Corey Patterson .75
51 Frank Thomas 1.00
52 Magglio Ordonez .75
53 Carlos Lee .75
54 Mark Buehrle .75
55 Esteban Loaiza .75
56 Joe Crede .75
57 Paul Konerko .75
58 Adam Dunn 1.00
59 Austin Kearns .75
60 Barry Larkin .75
61 Ryan Wagner .75
62 Danny Graves .75
63 Sean Casey .75
64 Ken Griffey Jr. 2.00
65 Jody Gerut .75
66 Cliff Lee .75
67 Victor Martinez .75
68 C.C. Sabathia .75
69 Omar Vizquel .75
70 Travis Hafner .75
71 Todd Helton 1.00
72 Preston Wilson .75
73 Jeromy Burnitz .75
74 Larry Walker .75
75 Ivan Rodriguez 1.00
76 Rondell White .75
77 Miguel Cabrera 1.50
78 Luis Castillo .75
79 Josh Beckett .75
80 Mike Lowell .75
81 Dontrelle Willis .75
82 Brad Penny .75
83 Hee Seop Choi .75
84 Juan Pierre .75
85 Andy Pettitte .75
86 Jeff Bagwell 1.00
87 Roy Oswalt .75
88 Lance Berkman .75
89 Morgan Ensberg .75
90 Craig Biggio .75
91 Octavio Dotel .75
92 Wade Miller .75
93 Jeff Kent .75
94 Richard Hidalgo .75
95 Roger Clemens 3.00
96 Carlos Beltran 1.00
97 Angel Berroa .75
98 Jeremy Affeldt .75
99 Juan Gonzalez .75
100 Mike Sweeney .75
101 Kazuhisa Ishii .75
102 Shawn Green .75
103 Milton Bradley .75
104 Paul LoDuca .75
105 Hideo Nomo .75
106 Eric Gagne .75
107 Adrian Beltre .75
108 Scott Podsednik .75
109 Rickie Weeks .75
110 Ben Sheets .75
111 Geoff Jenkins .75
112 Jacque Jones .75
113 Johan Santana 1.00
114 Shannon Stewart .75
115 Corey Koskie .75
116 Lew Ford .75
117 Torii Hunter .75
118 Chad Cordero .75
119 Orlando Cabrera .75
120 Jose Vidro .75
121 Nick Johnson .75
122 Brad Wilkerson .75
123 Mike Piazza 2.00
124 Jae Weong Seo .75
125 Jose Reyes .75
126 Tom Glavine .75
127 Jorge Posada .75
128 Gary Sheffield 1.00
129 Bernie Williams .75
130 Mike Mussina 1.00
131 Mariano Rivera .75
132 Bubba Crosby .75
133 Kevin Brown .75
134 Javier Vazquez .75
135 Jason Giambi .75
136 Derek Jeter 4.00
137 Alex Rodriguez 4.00
138 Hideki Matsui 3.00
139 Mark Mulder .75
140 Jermaine Dye .75
141 Tim Hudson .75
142 Barry Zito .75
143 Eric Chavez .75
144 Bobby Crosby .75
145 Eric Byrnes .75
146 Marlon Byrd .75
147 Billy Wagner .75
148 Mike Lieberthal .75
149 Jimmy Rollins 1.00
150 Jim Thome 1.50
151 Bobby Abreu .75
152 Pat Burrell .75
153 Jose Castillo .75
154 Craig Wilson .75
155 Jason Bay .75
156 Jason Kendall .75
157 Raul Mondesi .75
158 Jay Payton .75
159 Trevor Hoffman .75
160 Jake Peavy .75
161 Sean Burroughs .75
162 Phil Nevin .75
163 Brian Giles .75
164 Ryan Klesko .75
165 Todd Linden .75
166 Jerome Williams .75
167 Jason Schmidt 1.00
168 Ray Durham .75
169 Marquis Grissom .75
170 Shigetoshi Hasegawa .75
171 Edgar Martinez .75
172 Freddy Garcia .75
173 Bret Boone .75
174 Raul Ibanez .75
175 Ichiro Suzuki 3.00
176 Randy Winn .75
177 Scott Rolen 1.50
178 Jim Edmonds .75
179 Albert Pujols 3.00
180 Matt Morris .75
181 Edgar Renteria .75
182 Aubrey Huff .75
183 Delmon Young .75
184 Dewon Brazelton .75
185 Rocco Baldelli .75
186 Carl Crawford .75
187 Mark Teixeira .75
188 Hank Blalock 1.00
189 Michael Young .75
190 Laynce Nix .75
191 Alfonso Soriano 1.50
192 Kevin Mench .75
193 Adrian Gonzalez .75
194 Alexis Rios .75
195 Roy Halladay .75
196 Vernon Wells .75
197 Carlos Delgado .75
198 Bill Hall .75
199 Jose Guillen .75
200 Jeremy Bonderman .75
201 Roger Clemens/SP 6.00
202 Alex Rodriguez/SP 6.00
203 Greg Maddux/SP 4.00
204 Miguel Tejada/SP 2.00
205 Alfonso Soriano/SP 3.00
206 Andy Pettitte/SP 2.00
207 Curt Schilling/SP 2.00
208 Gary Sheffield/SP 2.00
209 Ivan Rodriguez/SP 2.00
210 Jim Thome/SP 2.00
211 Mike Mussina/SP 2.00
212 Mike Piazza/SP 4.00
213 Randy Johnson/SP 3.00
214 Roger Clemens/SP 6.00
215 Sammy Sosa/SP 4.00
216 Alex Rodriguez/SP 6.00
217 Randy Johnson/SP 3.00
218 Vladimir Guerrero/SP 3.00
219 Rafael Palmeiro/SP 2.00
220 Manny Ramirez/SP 2.00
221 Mike Piazza/SP 4.00
222 Cal Ripken Jr. 10.00
223 Ted Williams 8.00
224 Duke Snider 2.00
225 Ernie Banks 4.00
226 Ryne Sandberg 8.00
227 Mark Grace 2.00
228 Andre Dawson 2.00
229 Bob Feller 2.00
230 Bob Feller 6.00
231 George Brett 8.00
232 Bo Jackson 3.00
233 Robin Yount 4.00
234 Harmon Killebrew 4.00
235 Gary Carter 2.00
236 Don Mattingly 8.00
237 Phil Rizzuto 2.00
238 Babe Ruth 8.00
239 Lou Gehrig 8.00
240 Reggie Jackson 3.00
241 Rickey Henderson 3.00
242 Mike Schmidt 8.00
243 Roberto Clemente 8.00
244 Tony Gwynn 3.00
245 Will Clark 3.00
246 Lou Brock 2.00
247 Bob Gibson 3.00
248 Stan Musial 5.00
249 Nolan Ryan 10.00
250 Dale Murphy 2.00
251 Aarom Baldiris/ Auto./499 **RC** 8.00
252 Akinori Otsuka/ Auto./99 **RC** 40.00
253 Andres Blanco/ Auto./499 **RC** 8.00
254 Angel Chavez/ Auto./499 **RC** 5.00
255 Carlos Hines/ Auto./199 **RC** 8.00
256 Carlos Vasquez/ Auto./499 **RC** 10.00
257 Casey Daigle/499 **RC** 10.00
258 Chris Oxspring/ Auto./499 **RC** 8.00
259 Colby Miller/ Auto./499 **RC** 5.00
260 David Crouthers/ Auto./199 8.00
261 Donald Kelly/ Auto./499 **RC** 5.00
262 Eddy Rodriguez/ Auto./499 **RC** 10.00
263 Edwardo Sierra/ Auto./299 **RC** 8.00
264 Edwin Moreno/ Auto./499 **RC** 10.00
265 Fernando Nieve/ Auto./499 **RC** 5.00
266 Freddy Guzman/ Auto./499 **RC** 5.00
267 Greg Dobbs/ Auto./499 **RC** 5.00
268 Brad Halsey/ Auto./499 **RC** 5.00
269 Hector Gimenez/ Auto./499 **RC** 8.00
270 Ivan Ochoa/ Auto./499 **RC** 5.00
271 Jake Woods/ Auto./499 8.00
272 Jamie Brown/ Auto./499 **RC** 5.00
273 Jason Bartlett/ Auto./499 **RC** 8.00
274 Jason Szuminski/ Auto./499 **RC** 5.00
275 John Gall/499 **RC** 5.00
276 Jorge Vasquez/ Auto./499 **RC** 5.00
277 Josh Labandeira/ Auto./499 **RC** 8.00
278 Justin Hampson/ Auto./499 **RC** 5.00
279 Kazuo Matsui/499 **RC** 15.00
280 Kevin Cave/ Auto./499 **RC** 8.00
281 Lance Cormier/ Auto./499 **RC** 5.00
282 Lincoln Holdzkom/ Auto./199 **RC** 8.00

283 Merkin Valdez/ Auto./199 **RC** 15.00
284 Mike Wuertz/ Auto./499 **RC** 8.00
285 Mike Johnston/ Auto./499 **RC** 5.00
286 Mike Rouse/Auto./329 8.00
287 Onil Joseph/ Auto./499 **RC** 5.00
288 Phil Stockman/ Auto./499 **RC** 5.00
289 Roberto Novoa/ Auto./499 **RC** 8.00
290 Ronald Belisario/ Auto./499 **RC** 5.00
291 Ronny Cedeno/ Auto./499 **RC** 5.00
292 Ryan Meaux/ Auto./499 **RC** 5.00
293 Scott Proctor/499 **RC** 5.00
294 Sean Henn/Auto./499 10.00
295 Shawn Camp/ Auto./499 **RC** 5.00
296 Shawn Hill/ Auto./499 **RC** 5.00
297 Shingo Takatsu /Auto./99 **RC** 40.00
298 Tim Bittner/ Auto./199 **RC** 8.00
299 William Bergolla/ 499 **RC** 5.00
300 Yadier Molina/ Auto./499 **RC** 15.00

Marble Black

No Pricing
Production One Set

Marble Blue

Blue 1-200: 3-5X
Blue 201-250: 2-3X
Blue 251-300: .5-1X
Production 50 Sets

Marble Emerald

No Pricing
Production Five Sets

Marble Gold

Gold 1-200: 6-8X
Gold 201-250: 2-4X
Gold 251-300: No Pricing
Production 25 Sets

Marble Red

Red 1-200: 2-3X
Red 201-250: 1-2X
Red 251-300: .4-1X
Production 100 Sets

Check Signature Blue

NM/M
Quantity produced listed
1 Al Kaline/22 60.00
2 Andre Dawson/22 25.00
22 Duke Snider/20 40.00
31 George Kell/60 35.00

Check Signature Green

No Pricing
Production 1-15

Check Signature Red

No Pricing

Check Signature Material Blue

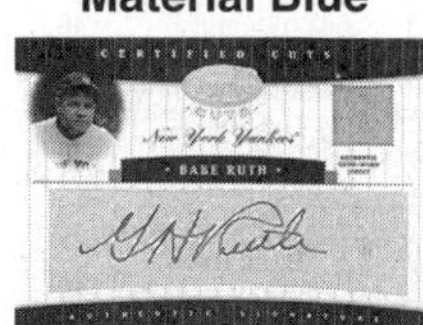

NM/M
Quantity produced listed
1 Al Kaline/Bat/50 50.00
2 Andre Dawson/ Jsy/50 20.00
4 Bob Gibson/Hat/50 30.00
5 Bobby Doerr/Jsy/50 20.00
6 Brooks Robinson/ Bat/50 50.00
7 Cal Ripken Jr. /Jsy/25 200.00
8 Cal Ripken Jr./ Jsy/25 200.00
9 Cal Ripken Jr./ Bat/25 200.00
10 Cal Ripken Jr./ Jkt/25 200.00
13 Carlton Fisk/Jkt/35 40.00
14 Carlton Fisk/Jsy/35 40.00
16 Dale Murphy/Jsy/50 30.00
17 Dale Murphy/Jsy/50 30.00
18 Don Mattingly/Jsy/25 80.00
19 Don Mattingly/ Gray Jsy/25 80.00
20 Don Mattingly/Bat/25 80.00
21 Don Mattingly/Jkt/25 80.00
22 Duke Snider/ Pants/100 40.00
23 Ozzie Smith/Jsy/40 60.00
24 Ozzie Smith/Jsy/40 60.00
25 Ozzie Smith/Bat/40 60.00
26 Frank Robinson/ Bat/50 30.00
27 George Brett/ White Jsy/30 80.00
28 George Brett/ Blue Jsy/30 80.00
29 George Brett/Bat/30 80.00
32 Hal Newhouser/ Jsy/15 30.00
33 Harmon Killebrew/ Shoe/35 60.00
34 Harmon Killebrew/ Bat/35 60.00
38 Kirby Puckett/ Fld Glv/25 60.00
39 Kirby Puckett/Bat/25 60.00
40 Lou Boudreau/ Jsy/15 100.00
41 Lou Brock/Jsy/50 30.00
43 Luis Aparicio/ Pants/50 20.00
44 Mark Grace/ Fld Glv/50 30.00
46 Mike Schmidt/ Fld Glv/25 80.00
47 Mike Schmidt/Jsy/25 80.00
48 Mike Schmidt/Jkt/25 80.00
49 Mike Schmidt/Bat/25 80.00
50 Nolan Ryan/ Astros Jkt/30 150.00
51 Nolan Ryan/ Rgr Pants/30 150.00
52 Nolan Ryan/ Angels Jkt/30 150.00
53 Paul Molitor/Bat/50 35.00
57 Red Schoendienst/ Bat/50 20.00
63 Ron Santo/Bat/25 40.00
65 Ryne Sandberg/ Jsy/50 65.00
67 Stan Musial/ White Jsy/30 80.00
68 Stan Musial/ Gray Jsy/30 80.00
69 Stan Musial/Bat/30 80.00
70 Steve Carlton/ Pants/25 40.00
71 Steve Carlton/Jsy/25 40.00
73 Tony Gwynn/ White Jsy/50 50.00
74 Tony Gwynn/ Navy Jsy/50 50.00
77 Whitey Ford/ Pants/50 30.00
78 Will Clark/Jsy/50 50.00
79 Will Clark/Bat/50 50.00

Check Signature Material Green

NM/M
Quantity produced listed
1 Al Kaline/Bat/33 65.00
2 Andre Dawson/ Jsy/33 25.00
4 Bob Gibson/Hat/15 50.00
6 Brooks Robinson/ Bat/15 80.00
22 Duke Snider/ Pants/25 50.00
26 Frank Robinson/ Bat/15 50.00
41 Lou Brock/Jsy/15 50.00
43 Luis Aparicio/ Pants/15 30.00
44 Mark Grace/ Fld Glv/15 50.00
53 Paul Molitor/Bat/15 40.00
77 Whitey Ford/ Pants/15 75.00

Check Signature Material Red

NM/M
Quantity produced listed
4 Bob Gibson/Hat/25 50.00
5 Bobby Doerr/Jsy/25 30.00
6 Brooks Robinson/ Bat/25 65.00
13 Carlton Fisk/Jkt/25 50.00
14 Carlton Fisk/Jsy/25 50.00
16 Dale Murphy/Jsy/25 40.00
17 Dale Murphy/Jsy/25 40.00
22 Duke Snider/ Pants/50 40.00
26 Frank Robinson/ Bat/25 40.00
27 George Brett/Jsy/15 100.00
28 George Brett/Jsy/15 100.00
29 George Brett/Bat/15 100.00
33 Harmon Killebrew/ Shoe/25 65.00
34 Harmon Killebrew/ Bat/25 65.00
41 Lou Brock/Jsy/25 40.00
43 Luis Aparicio/ Pants/25 25.00
44 Mark Grace/ Fld Glve/25 40.00
53 Paul Molitor/Bat/25 40.00
57 Red Schoendienst/ Bat/25 25.00
65 Ryne Sandberg/ Jsy/25 75.00
73 Tony Gwynn/Jsy/25 70.00
74 Tony Gwynn/Jsy/25 70.00
77 Whitey Ford/ Pants/25 60.00
78 Will Clark/Jsy/25 40.00
79 Will Clark/Bat/25 40.00

Hall of Fame Souvenirs

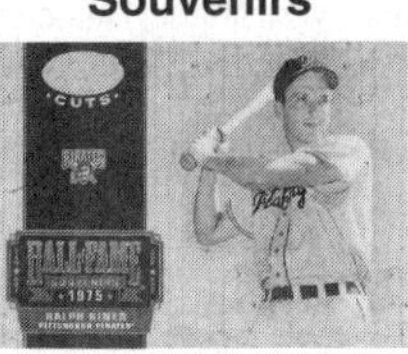

NM/M
Quantity produced listed
1 Ernie Banks/84 8.00
2 Stan Musial/93 15.00
3 Nolan Ryan/99 25.00
4 Duke Snider/87 8.00
5 Bob Feller/94 8.00
6 George Brett/98 20.00
7 Robin Yount/78 15.00
8 Harmon Killebrew/83 10.00
9 Gary Carter/78 4.00
10 Phil Rizzuto/75 8.00
11 Reggie Jackson/94 8.00
12 Mike Schmidt/97 20.00
13 Lou Brock/80 6.00
14 Bob Gibson/84 8.00
15 Bobby Doerr/75 6.00
16 Tony Perez/77 4.00
17 Whitey Ford/78 8.00
18 Juan Marichal/84 4.00
19 Monte Irvin/75 4.00
20 Fergie Jenkins/75 4.00
21 Ralph Kiner/75 8.00
22 Eddie Murray/85 10.00
23 George Kell/75 4.00
24 Hoyt Wilhelm/84 4.00
25 Carlton Fisk/80 6.00
26 Rod Carew/91 8.00
27 Frank Robinson/89 6.00
28 Gaylord Perry/77 4.00
29 Red Schoendienst/75 4.00
30 Brooks Robinson/92 8.00
31 Al Kaline/88 10.00
32 Orlando Cepeda/75 4.00
33 Steve Carlton/96 4.00
34 Luis Aparicio/85 4.00
35 Warren Spahn/83 8.00
36 Kirby Puckett/82 10.00
37 Phil Niekro/80 4.00
38 Jim Bunning/75 4.00
39 Tom Seaver/99 8.00
40 Paul Molitor/85 8.00
41 Johnny Bench/96 8.00
42 Don Sutton/82 4.00
43 Robin Roberts/87 6.00
44 Jim Palmer/93 6.00
45 Joe Morgan/82 4.00
46 Roberto Clemente/93 25.00
47 Lou Gehrig/100 10.00
48 Babe Ruth/95 20.00
49 Ty Cobb/98 10.00
50 Ted Williams/94 20.00

Hall of Fame Souvenirs Sign.

NM/M
Quantity produced listed
3 Nolan Ryan/34 150.00
4 Duke Snider/50 30.00
5 Bob Feller/50 30.00
8 Harmon Killebrew/25 50.00
9 Gary Carter/50 15.00
10 Phil Rizzuto/50 25.00
12 Mike Schmidt/20 60.00
13 Lou Brock/50 25.00
14 Bob Gibson/45 25.00
15 Bobby Doerr/50 15.00
16 Tony Perez/50 15.00
17 Whitey Ford/16 40.00
18 Juan Marichal/50 15.00
19 Monte Irvin/50 25.00
20 Fergie Jenkins/50 15.00
21 Ralph Kiner/50 25.00
22 Eddie Murray/33 60.00
23 George Kell/50 15.00
24 Hoyt Wilhelm/49 15.00
25 Carlton Fisk/27 30.00
26 Rod Carew/29 30.00
28 Gaylord Perry/50 15.00
29 Red Schoendienst/50 15.00
30 Brooks Robinson/50 40.00
31 Al Kaline/50 40.00
32 Orlando Cepeda/50 15.00
33 Steve Carlton/50 25.00
34 Luis Aparicio/50 15.00
35 Warren Spahn/21 50.00
36 Kirby Puckett/34 50.00
37 Phil Niekro/50 15.00
38 Jim Bunning/50 15.00
40 Paul Molitor/25 30.00
42 Don Sutton/50 15.00
43 Robin Roberts/50 15.00
44 Jim Palmer/22 20.00
45 Joe Morgan/25 20.00

HOF Souvenirs Material

NM/M
Production 25 Sets
1 Ernie Banks/Jsy 30.00
2 Stan Musial/Jsy 50.00
3 Nolan Ryan/Jsy 60.00
4 Duke Snider/Pants 20.00
5 Bob Feller/Jsy 20.00
6 George Brett/Jsy 50.00
7 Robin Yount/Jsy 40.00
8 Harmon Killebrew/ Jsy 25.00
9 Gary Carter/Jkt 15.00
10 Phil Rizzuto/Pants 20.00
11 Reggie Jackson/Jsy 25.00
12 Mike Schmidt/Jsy 50.00
13 Lou Brock/Jsy 20.00
14 Bob Gibson/Jsy 20.00
15 Bobby Doerr/Jsy 15.00
16 Tony Perez/Bat 10.00
17 Whitey Ford/Pants 25.00
18 Juan Marichal/Jsy 15.00
20 Fergie Jenkins/Pants 10.00
21 Ralph Kiner/Bat 25.00
22 Eddie Murray/Jsy 25.00
24 Hoyt Wilhelm/Jsy 10.00
25 Carlton Fisk/Jsy 20.00
26 Rod Carew/Jsy 20.00
27 Frank Robinson/Jsy 15.00
29 Red Schoendienst/ Jsy 15.00
30 Brooks Robinson/Bat 30.00
31 Al Kaline/Pants 30.00
32 Orlando Cepeda/Bat 10.00
33 Steve Carlton/Pants 15.00
34 Luis Aparicio/Pants 10.00
35 Warren Spahn/Pants 25.00
36 Kirby Puckett/Jsy 25.00
37 Phil Niekro/Jsy 10.00
39 Tom Seaver/Jsy 25.00
40 Paul Molitor/Bat 20.00
41 Johnny Bench/Jsy 25.00
42 Don Sutton/Jsy 10.00
43 Robin Roberts/Hat 15.00
44 Jim Palmer/Jsy 15.00
45 Joe Morgan/Jsy 15.00
46 Roberto Clemente/ Jsy 100.00
47 Lou Gehrig/Pants 150.00
48 Babe Ruth/Pants 275.00
49 Ty Cobb/Pants 150.00
50 Ted Williams/Jsy 125.00

HOF Souvenirs Sign. Material

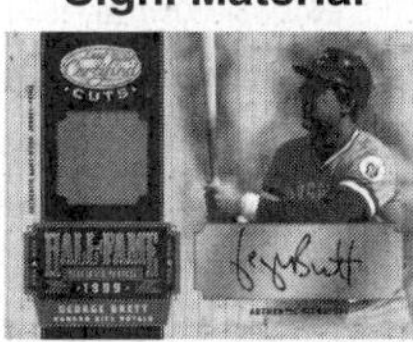

NM/M
Quantity produced listed
3 Nolan Ryan/Jsy/34 180.00
5 Bob Feller/Jsy/19 50.00
12 Mike Schmidt/Jsy/20 80.00
13 Lou Brock/Jsy/20 40.00
14 Bob Gibson/Jsy/45 30.00
16 Tony Perez/Bat/24 25.00
17 Whitey Ford/ Pants/16 50.00
18 Juan Marichal/Jsy/27 30.00
20 Fergie Jenkins/ Pants/31 30.00
22 Eddie Murray/Jsy/33 85.00
25 Carlton Fisk/Jsy/27 50.00
26 Rod Carew/Jsy/29 50.00
32 Orlando Cepeda/ Bat/30 30.00
33 Steve Carlton/ Pants/32 40.00
35 Warren Spahn/ Pants/21 75.00
36 Kirby Puckett/Jsy/34 65.00
37 Phil Niekro/Jsy/35 25.00
42 Don Sutton/Jsy/40 20.00
43 Robin Roberts/ Hat/36 25.00
44 Jim Palmer/Jsy/22 30.00
45 Joe Morgan/Jsy/16 35.00

K-Force

NM/M
Quantity produced listed
1 Nolan Ryan/500 8.00
2 Steve Carlton/500 2.00
3 Roger Clemens/500 6.00
4 Randy Johnson/500 3.00
5 Bert Blyleven/500 1.50
6 Tom Seaver/500 3.00
7 Don Sutton/500 1.50
8 Gaylord Perry/500 1.50
9 Phil Niekro/500 1.50
10 Fergie Jenkins/500 1.50
11 Bob Gibson/500 3.00
12 Nolan Ryan/383 8.00
13 Randy Johnson/308 3.00
14 Bob Feller/348 3.00
15 Curt Schilling/319 3.00
16 Pedro J. Martinez/313 3.00
17 Dwight Gooden/276 1.50
18 John Smoltz/276 2.00
19 Curt Schilling/316 3.00
20 Randy Johnson/319 3.00
21 Pedro Martinez/305 3.00
22 Roger Clemens/291 6.00
23 Roger Clemens/292 6.00
24 Tom Seaver/289 3.00
25 Hal Newhouser/275 2.00
26 Jim Bunning/201 2.00
27 Robin Roberts/198 3.00
28 Warren Spahn/191 4.00
29 Jack Morris/232 2.00
30 Nolan Ryan/270 8.00
31 Hideo Nomo/236 3.00
32 Barry Zito/205 2.00
33 Mike Mussina/214 3.00
34 Roy Oswalt/208 2.00
35 Mark Prior/245 3.00
36 Kerry Wood/266 4.00
37 Roy Halladay/204 2.00
38 Esteban Loaiza/207 1.50
39 Whitey Ford/94 6.00
40 Bob Gibson/17 12.00
41 Ben Sheets/18 8.00
42 Hoyt Wilhelm/139 3.00
43 Satchel Paige/91 10.00
44 Burleigh Grimes/136 3.00
45 Mark Prior, Kerry Wood/500 3.00
46 Nolan Ryan, Roger Clemens/500 10.00
47 Steve Carlton, Randy Johnson/500 3.00
48 Nolan Ryan, Roger Clemens/500 8.00
49 Nolan Ryan, Steve Carlton/500 8.00
50 Kerry Wood, Roger Clemens/20 30.00

K-Force Material

NM/M
Quantity produced listed
1 Nolan Ryan/Jsy/100 25.00
2 Steve Carlton/Jsy/32 12.00
3 Roger Clemens/ Jsy/25 25.00
4 Randy Johnson/ Jsy/51 15.00
5 Bert Blyleven/Jsy/28 10.00
6 Tom Seaver/Jsy/25 25.00
8 Gaylord Perry/Jsy/36 8.00
9 Phil Niekro/Jsy/35 10.00
10 Fergie Jenkins/ Pants/31 10.00
11 Bob Gibson/Jsy/45 15.00
12 Nolan Ryan/Jkt/100 25.00
13 Randy Johnson/ Jsy/51 15.00
14 Bob Feller/Jsy/25 20.00
15 Curt Schilling/Jsy/25 12.00
16 Pedro J. Martinez/ Jsy/45 15.00
17 Dwight Gooden/ Jsy/25 10.00
18 John Smoltz/Jsy/25 15.00
19 Curt Schilling/Jsy/25 12.00
20 Randy Johnson/ Jsy/51 15.00
21 Pedro Martinez/ Jsy/45 15.00
22 Roger Clemens/ Jsy/100 15.00
25 Hal Newhouser/ Jsy/25 20.00
28 Warren Spahn/Jsy/50 15.00
29 Jack Morris/Jsy/47 8.00
30 Nolan Ryan/Jkt/100 25.00
31 Hideo Nomo/Jsy/25 20.00
32 Barry Zito/Jsy/25 10.00
33 Mike Mussina/Jsy/25 20.00
34 Roy Oswalt/Jsy/44 6.00
35 Mark Prior/Jsy/50 10.00
36 Kerry Wood/Jsy/34 20.00
39 Whitey Ford/Jsy/50 15.00
40 Bob Gibson/Jsy/50 10.00
41 Ben Sheets/Jsy/25 10.00
43 Satchel Paige/ Jsy/100 60.00
44 Burleigh Grimes/ Pants/100 75.00
45 Mark Prior/Jsy, Kerry Wood/Pants/50 15.00
46 Nolan Ryan/Jsy, Roger Clemens/ Jsy/50 40.00
47 Steve Carlton/Jsy, Randy Johnson/ Jsy/50 25.00
48 Nolan Ryan/Pants, Roger Clemens/ Jsy/50 40.00
49 Nolan Ryan/Jsy, Carlton Fisk/Pants/50 35.00
50 Kerry Wood/Jsy, Roger Clemens/ Jsy/50 25.00

K-Force Signature

NM/M
Quantity produced listed
2 Steve Carlton/50 30.00
5 Bert Blyleven/50 15.00
7 Don Sutton/50 15.00
8 Gaylord Perry/50 15.00
9 Phil Niekro/50 25.00
10 Fergie Jenkins/50 15.00
14 Bob Feller/50 30.00
17 Dwight Gooden/50 20.00
26 Jim Bunning/50 25.00
27 Robin Roberts/50 20.00
29 Jack Morris/50 15.00
34 Roy Oswalt/50 15.00
38 Esteban Loaiza/50 10.00

K-Force Signature Material

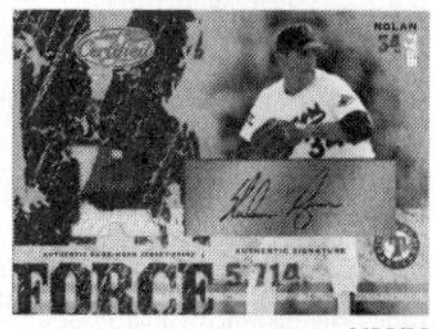

NM/M
Quantity produced listed
1 Nolan Ryan/Jsy/34 150.00
2 Steve Carlton/Jsy/32 50.00
5 Bert Blyleven/Jsy/28 25.00
8 Gaylord Perry/Jsy/36 25.00
9 Phil Niekro/Jsy/35 40.00
10 Fergie Jenkins/ Pants/31 25.00
11 Bob Gibson/Jsy/45 40.00
12 Nolan Ryan/Jkt/34 150.00
14 Bob Feller/Jsy/19 50.00
17 Dwight Gooden/ Jsy/16 30.00
28 Warren Spahn/Jsy/21 65.00
29 Jack Morris/Jsy/47 20.00
30 Nolan Ryan/Jkt/34 150.00
34 Roy Oswalt/Jsy/44 20.00
36 Kerry Wood/Jsy/34 50.00
37 Roy Halladay/Jsy/32 15.00
39 Whitey Ford/Jsy/16 50.00
40 Bob Gibson/Jsy/45 30.00

Marble Material Black

No Pricing
Production One Set

Marble Material Blue Number

NM/M
Quantity produced listed
1 Vladimir Guerrero/ Jsy/27 25.00
2 Garret Anderson/ Jsy/16 15.00
5 Troy Glaus/Jsy/25 10.00
6 Tim Salmon/Jsy/15 20.00
8 Brandon Webb/Jsy/55 5.00
10 Randy Johnson/ Jsy/51 12.00
13 Luis Gonzalez/Jsy/20 10.00
17 Marcus Giles/Jsy/22 10.00
18 Andruw Jones/Jsy/25 10.00
20 Rafael Palmeiro/ Jsy/25 15.00
22 Luis Matos/Jsy/32 10.00
23 Jay Gibbons/Jsy/31 10.00
26 Rodrigo Lopez/ Jsy/19 10.00
27 Javy Lopez/Jsy/18 15.00
30 Curt Schilling/Jsy/38 12.00
31 Jason Varitek/Jsy/33 10.00
32 Manny Ramirez/ Jsy/24 20.00
35 Pedro Martinez/ Jsy/45 15.00
39 David Ortiz/Jsy/34 20.00
40 Mark Prior/Jsy/22 15.00
41 Kerry Wood/Pants/34 20.00
42 Sammy Sosa/Jsy/21 30.00
44 Greg Maddux/Jsy/31 25.00
45 Aramis Ramirez/ Jsy/16 15.00
49 Moises Alou/Jsy/18 15.00
51 Frank Thomas/Jsy/35 20.00
52 Magglio Ordonez/ Jsy/30 10.00
53 Carlos Lee/Jsy/45 5.00
54 Mark Buehrle/Jsy/56 5.00
58 Adam Dunn/Jsy/44 12.00
59 Austin Kearns/Jsy/28 10.00
63 Sean Casey/Jsy/21 10.00
66 Cliff Lee/Jsy/34 8.00
67 Victor Martinez/Jsy/41 8.00
68 C.C. Sabathia/Jsy/52 5.00

70 Travis Hafner/Jsy/48 8.00
71 Todd Helton/Jsy/17 20.00
72 Preston Wilson/Jsy/44 5.00
73 Jeromy Burnitz/Jsy/35 5.00
74 Larry Walker/Jsy/33 10.00
77 Miguel Cabrera/Jsy/24 20.00
79 Josh Beckett/Jsy/21 12.00
81 Dontrelle Willis/Jsy/35 10.00
82 Brad Penny/Jsy/31 8.00
85 Andy Pettitte/Jsy/21 15.00
87 Roy Oswalt/Jsy/44 5.00
88 Lance Berkman/Jsy/17 10.00
95 Roger Clemens/Jsy/22 25.00
100 Mike Sweeney/Jsy/29 10.00
101 Kazuhisa Ishii/Jsy/17 15.00
107 Adrian Beltre/Jsy/29 15.00
113 Johan Santana/Jsy/57 15.00
114 Shannon Stewart/Jsy/23 10.00
117 Torii Hunter/Jsy/48 5.00
119 Orlando Cabrera/Jsy/18 20.00
123 Mike Piazza/Jsy/31 30.00
124 Jae Weong/Seo Jsy/26 10.00
126 Tom Glavine/Jsy/47 10.00
127 Jorge Posada/Jsy/20 15.00
129 Bernie Williams Jsy/51 10.00
130 Mike Mussina/Jsy/35 15.00
131 Mariano Rivera/Jsy/42 10.00
135 Jason Giambi/Jsy/25 10.00
138 Hideki Matsui/Jsy/55 40.00
139 Mark Mulder/Jsy/20 10.00
142 Barry Zito/Jsy/75 5.00
146 Marlon Byrd/Jsy/29 10.00
150 Jim Thome/Jsy/25 20.00
151 Bobby Abreu/Jsy/53 5.00
154 Craig Wilson/Jsy/36 5.00
161 Sean Burroughs/Jsy/32 10.00
163 Brian Giles/Jsy/24 8.00
164 Ryan Klesko/Jsy/30 10.00
166 Jerome Williams/Jsy/57 5.00
172 Freddy Garcia/Jsy/34 8.00
177 Scott Rolen/Jsy/27 20.00
178 Jim Edmonds/Jsy/15 15.00
180 Matt Morris/Jsy/35 10.00
181 Edgar Renteria/Jsy/15 15.00
182 Aubrey Huff/Jsy/19 10.00
184 Dewon Brazelton/Jsy/45 5.00
187 Mark Teixeira/Jsy/23 15.00
192 Kevin Mench/Jsy/28 8.00
195 Roy Halladay/Jsy/32 10.00
197 Carlos Delgado/Jsy/25 10.00
200 Jeremy Bonderman/Jsy/38 5.00
201 Roger Clemens/Jsy/22 30.00
203 Greg Maddux/Jsy/31 25.00
206 Andy Pettitte/Jsy/46 10.00
207 Curt Schilling/Jsy/38 12.00
210 Jim Thome/Jsy/25 20.00
211 Mike Mussina/Jsy/35 15.00
212 Mike Piazza/Jsy/31 30.00
213 Randy Johnson/Jsy/51 15.00
214 Roger Clemens/Jsy/21 30.00
215 Sammy Sosa/Jsy/21 30.00
217 Randy Johnson/Jsy/51 15.00
218 Vladimir Guerrero /Jsy/27 25.00
219 Rafael Palmeiro Jsy/25 15.00
221 Mike Piazza/Jsy/25 30.00
226 Ryne Sandberg/Jsy/23 40.00
227 Mark Grace/Jsy/17 25.00
229 Bob Feller/Jsy/19 20.00
232 Bo Jackson/Jsy/16 40.00
233 Robin Yount/Jsy/19 40.00
236 Don Mattingly/Jsy/23 40.00
241 Rickey Henderson/Jsy/35 25.00
242 Mike Schmidt/Jsy/20 40.00
243 Roberto Clemente/Jsy/21 100.00
245 Will Clark/Jsy/22 30.00
246 Lou Brock/Jsy/20 20.00
247 Bob Gibson/Jsy/45 15.00
249 Nolan Ryan/Jsy/34 40.00

Marble Material Emerald Prime

No Pricing
Production Five Sets

Marble Material Red Position

NM/M
Quantity produced listed
1 Vladimir Guerrero/Jsy/100 10.00
2 Garret Anderson/Jsy/100 4.00
5 Troy Glaus/Jsy/75 4.00
6 Tim Salmon/Jsy/75 6.00
10 Randy Johnson/Jsy/100 8.00
13 Luis Gonzalez/Jsy/100 4.00
15 Rafael Furcal/Jsy/100 4.00
16 Chipper Jones/Jsy/100 8.00
17 Marcus Giles/Jsy/100 4.00
18 Andruw Jones/Jsy/100 6.00
20 Rafael Palmeiro/Jsy/100 8.00
21 Melvin Mora/Jsy/50 6.00
22 Luis Matos/Jsy/50 6.00
23 Jay Gibbons/Jsy/100 4.00
25 Larry Bigbie/Jsy/50 6.00
26 Rodrigo Lopez/Jsy/50 6.00
27 Javy Lopez/Jsy/25 10.00
28 Miguel Tejada/Jsy/100 6.00
30 Curt Schilling/Jsy/50 8.00
31 Jason Varitek/Jsy/100 4.00
32 Manny Ramirez/Jsy/100 8.00
35 Pedro J. Martinez/Jsy/100 10.00
39 David Ortiz/Jsy/100 8.00
40 Mark Prior/Jsy/100 8.00
41 Kerry Wood/Pants/100 10.00
42 Sammy Sosa/Jsy/100 10.00
44 Greg Maddux/Jsy/50 15.00
45 Aramis Ramirez /Jsy/100 6.00
51 Frank Thomas/Jsy/100 8.00
52 Magglio Ordonez/Jsy/100 4.00
53 Carlos Lee/Jsy/100 4.00
54 Mark Buehrle/Jsy/100 4.00
57 Paul Konerko/Jsy/50 6.00
58 Adam Dunn/Jsy/100 8.00
59 Austin Kearns/Jsy/100 4.00
60 Barry Larkin/Jsy/100 6.00
65 Jody Gerut/Jsy/100 4.00
66 Cliff Lee/Jsy/100 4.00
67 Victor Martinez/Jsy/100 6.00
68 C.C. Sabathia/Jsy/100 4.00
69 Omar Vizquel/Jsy/100 4.00
70 Travis Hafner/Jsy/100 4.00
71 Todd Helton/Jsy/100 8.00
72 Preston Wilson/Jsy/100 4.00
75 Ivan Rodriguez/Jsy/50 10.00
77 Miguel Cabrera/Jsy/100 8.00
79 Josh Beckett/Jsy/100 6.00
81 Dontrelle Willis/Jsy/100 4.00
82 Brad Penny/Jsy/100 4.00
86 Jeff Bagwell/Jsy/100 8.00
87 Roy Oswalt/Jsy/100 4.00
88 Lance Berkman/Jsy/100 4.00
89 Morgan Ensberg/Jsy/100 4.00
90 Craig Biggio/Jsy/100 6.00
93 Jeff Kent/Jsy/100 4.00
94 Richard Hidalgo/Pants/100 4.00
95 Roger Clemens/Jsy/25 30.00
96 Carlos Beltran/Jsy/100 6.00
97 Angel Berroa/Pants/100 4.00
100 Mike Sweeney/Jsy/100 4.00
101 Kazuhisa Ishii/Jsy/100 4.00
102 Shawn Green/Jsy/100 4.00
104 Paul LoDuca/Jsy/100 4.00
105 Hideo Nomo/Jsy/100 8.00
107 Adrian Beltre/Jsy/100 8.00
110 Ben Sheets/Jsy/100 6.00
111 Geoff Jenkins/Jsy/100 4.00
112 Jacque Jones/Jsy/100 4.00
113 Johan Santana/Jsy/100 8.00
114 Shannon Stewart/Jsy/100 4.00
117 Torii Hunter/Jsy/75 4.00
123 Mike Piazza/Jsy/100 10.00
125 Jose Reyes/Jsy/75 4.00
126 Tom Glavine/Jsy/75 6.00
127 Jorge Posada/Jsy/100 8.00
129 Bernie Williams/Jsy/100 6.00
130 Mike Mussina/Jsy/25 20.00
131 Mariano Rivera/Jsy/100 8.00
138 Hideki Matsui/Jsy/100 25.00
139 Mark Mulder/Jsy/100 4.00
142 Barry Zito/Jsy/100 4.00
143 Eric Chavez/Jsy/100 4.00
146 Marlon Byrd/Jsy/100 4.00
150 Jim Thome/Jsy/100 8.00
151 Bobby Abreu/Jsy/100 4.00
152 Pat Burrell/Jsy/100 4.00
154 Craig Wilson/Jsy/100 4.00
156 Jason Kendall/Jsy/100 4.00
161 Sean Burroughs/Jsy/100 4.00
164 Ryan Klesko/Jsy/100 4.00
166 Jerome Williams/Jsy/25 10.00
171 Edgar Martinez/Jsy/100 6.00
172 Freddy Garcia/Jsy/100 4.00
177 Scott Rolen/Jsy/100 10.00
178 Jim Edmonds/Jsy/100 6.00
179 Albert Pujols/Jsy/100 20.00
180 Matt Morris/Jsy/75 4.00
181 Edgar Renteria/Jsy/25 10.00
182 Aubrey Huff/Jsy/100 4.00
185 Rocco Baldelli/Jsy/100 4.00
186 Carl Crawford/Jsy/100 4.00
187 Mark Teixeira/Jsy/25 8.00
188 Hank Blalock/Jsy/100 8.00
191 Alfonso Soriano/Jsy/100 8.00
192 Kevin Mench/Jsy/100 4.00
195 Roy Halladay/Jsy/100 4.00
196 Vernon Wells/Jsy/100 4.00
197 Carlos Delgado/Jsy/100 4.00
200 Jeremy Bonderman/Jsy/100 4.00
201 Roger Clemens/Jsy/100 10.00
202 Alex Rodriguez/Jsy/100 10.00
203 Greg Maddux/Jsy/100 10.00
204 Miguel Tejada/Jsy/100 4.00
205 Alfonso Soriano/Jsy/100 8.00
206 Andy Pettitte/Jsy/100 6.00
207 Curt Schilling/Jsy/100 8.00
208 Gary Sheffield/Jsy/50 8.00
209 Ivan Rodriguez/Jsy/100 8.00
210 Jim Thome/Jsy/25 20.00
211 Mike Mussina/Jsy/50 10.00
212 Mike Piazza/Jsy/100 10.00
213 Randy Johnson/Jsy/100 8.00
214 Roger Clemens/Jsy/100 10.00
215 Sammy Sosa/Jsy/50 15.00
216 Alex Rodriguez/Jsy/100 10.00
217 Randy Johnson/Jsy/100 8.00
218 Vladimir Guerrero Jsy/100 8.00
219 Rafael Palmeiro/Jsy/100 8.00
221 Mike Piazza/Jsy/100 10.00
222 Cal Ripken Jr./Jsy/50 50.00
223 Ted Williams/Jsy/25 100.00
225 Ernie Banks/Jsy/50 15.00
226 Ryne Sandberg/Jsy/100 15.00
227 Mark Grace/Jsy/25 20.00
228 Andre Dawson/Jsy/100 6.00
229 Bob Feller/Jsy/25 20.00
231 George Brett/Jsy/100 15.00
232 Bo Jackson/Jsy/100 10.00
233 Robin Yount/Jsy/100 12.00
234 Harmon Killebrew/Jsy/25 25.00
235 Gary Carter/Jkt/100 6.00
236 Don Mattingly/Jsy/50 25.00
237 Phil Rizzuto/Pants/25 20.00
238 Babe Ruth/Pants/50 200.00
239 Lou Gehrig/Pants/50 150.00
240 Reggie Jackson/Jsy/100 8.00
241 Rickey Henderson/Jsy/100 10.00
242 Mike Schmidt/Jsy/50 25.00
243 Roberto Clemente/Jsy/50 75.00
244 Tony Gwynn/Jsy/100 10.00
245 Will Clark/Jsy/100 10.00
246 Lou Brock/Jsy/25 20.00
247 Bob Gibson/Jsy/25 20.00
248 Stan Musial/Jsy/25 60.00
249 Nolan Ryan/Jsy/50 40.00
250 Dale Murphy/Jsy/100 10.00

Marble Signature Black

No Pricing
Production One Set

Marble Signature Blue

NM/M
Quantity produced listed
2 Garret Anderson/50 20.00
3 John Lackey/75 15.00
7 Shea Hillenbrand/75 15.00
8 Brandon Webb/75 10.00
11 Alex Cintron/75 10.00
14 Adam LaRoche/75 10.00
15 Rafael Furcal/50 20.00
17 Marcus Giles/50 15.00
19 Russ Ortiz/75 10.00
21 Melvin Mora/75 15.00
22 Luis Matos/75 10.00
23 Jay Gibbons/75 15.00
24 Adam Loewen/50 10.00
25 Larry Bigbie/75 15.00
26 Rodrigo Lopez/75 10.00
29 Trot Nixon/50 35.00
33 Keith Foulke/75 8.00
39 David Ortiz/50 40.00
40 Mark Prior/25 40.00
41 Kerry Wood/25 50.00
43 Derrek Lee/25 30.00
45 Aramis Ramirez/75 20.00
46 Matt Clement/25 15.00
47 Carlos Zambrano/75 35.00
48 Todd Walker/75 10.00
52 Magglio Ordonez/25 20.00
53 Carlos Lee/75 15.00
54 Mark Buehrle/50 15.00
55 Esteban Loaiza/25 15.00
58 Adam Dunn/25 40.00
59 Austin Kearns/25 20.00
63 Sean Casey/25 25.00
65 Jody Gerut/75 8.00
66 Cliff Lee/75 10.00
67 Victor Martinez/75 20.00
68 C.C. Sabathia/75 15.00
70 Travis Hafner/75 15.00
72 Preston Wilson/75 15.00
77 Miguel Cabrera/50 35.00
80 Mike Lowell/25 20.00
82 Brad Penny/75 10.00
87 Roy Oswalt/50 15.00
89 Morgan Ensberg/75 12.00
90 Craig Biggio/25 30.00
91 Octavio Dotel/75 15.00
92 Wade Miller/75 10.00
96 Carlos Beltran/50 50.00
97 Angel Berroa/50 10.00
98 Jeremy Affeldt/75 10.00
103 Milton Bradley/75 15.00
104 Paul LoDuca/50 15.00
108 Scott Podsednik/75 15.00
109 Rickie Weeks/25 25.00
112 Jacque Jones/75 10.00
113 Johan Santana/50 50.00
114 Shannon Stewart/50 15.00
116 Lew Ford/75 15.00
117 Torii Hunter/25 25.00
118 Chad Cordero/75 10.00
119 Orlando Cabrera/75 20.00
120 Jose Vidro/50 10.00
125 Jose Reyes/25 30.00
132 Bubba Crosby/75 10.00
139 Mark Mulder/25 25.00
140 Jermaine Dye/75 10.00
144 Bobby Crosby/75 40.00
145 Eric Byrnes/75 10.00
146 Marlon Byrd/75 10.00
148 Mike Lieberthal/75 15.00
153 Jose Castillo/75 10.00
154 Craig Wilson/75 10.00
155 Jason Bay/75 25.00
158 Jay Payton/75 10.00
161 Sean Burroughs/25 15.00
165 Todd Linden/75 8.00
170 Shigetoshi Hasegawa/50 40.00
171 Edgar Martinez/25 40.00
174 Raul Ibanez/75 10.00
177 Scott Rolen/50 35.00
182 Aubrey Huff/75 10.00
183 Delmon Young/25 25.00
184 Dewon Brazelton/75 10.00
186 Carl Crawford/75 20.00
187 Mark Teixeira/25 40.00
188 Hank Blalock/50 25.00
189 Michael Young/75 15.00
190 Laynce Nix/75 15.00
191 Alfonso Soriano/25 50.00
193 Adrian Gonzalez/75 10.00
194 Alexis Rios/75 20.00
196 Vernon Wells/50 15.00
198 Bill Hall/75 15.00
199 Jose Guillen/75 15.00
200 Jeremy Bonderman/75 10.00
222 Cal Ripken Jr./25 150.00
224 Duke Snider/35 35.00
228 Andre Dawson/50 20.00
229 Bob Feller/50 30.00
235 Gary Carter/25 20.00
237 Phil Rizzuto/25 40.00
245 Will Clark/25 50.00
246 Lou Brock/25 30.00
247 Bob Gibson/25 40.00
248 Stan Musial/25 75.00
249 Nolan Ryan/25 150.00
250 Dale Murphy/50 30.00
251 Aarom Baldiris/75 10.00
252 Akinori Otsuka/25 50.00
253 Andres Blanco/75 10.00
254 Angel Chavez/75 8.00
255 Carlos Hines/75 8.00
256 Carlos Vasquez/75 12.00
258 Chris Oxspring/75 10.00
259 Colby Miller/75 8.00
261 Donald Kelly/75 8.00
262 Eddy Rodriguez/75 8.00
263 Edwardo Sierra/65 10.00
264 Edwin Moreno/75 12.00
265 Fernando Nieve/75 8.00
266 Freddy Guzman/75 8.00
267 Greg Dobbs/75 8.00
268 Brad Halsey/75 8.00
269 Hector Gimenez/75 8.00
270 Ivan Ochoa/75 8.00
271 Jake Woods/75 10.00
272 Jamie Brown/75 8.00
273 Jason Bartlett/75 15.00
274 Jason Szuminski/75 8.00
275 John Gall/75 10.00
276 Jorge Vasquez/75 8.00
277 Josh Labandeira/75 8.00
278 Justin Hampson/75 8.00
280 Kevin Cave/75 10.00
281 Lance Cormier/75 8.00
283 Merkin Valdez/75 15.00
284 Mike Wuertz/75 10.00
285 Mike Johnston/75 8.00
287 Onil Joseph/75 8.00
288 Phil Stockman/75 8.00
289 Roberto Novoa/75 10.00
290 Ronald Belisario/75 8.00
291 Ronny Cedeno/75 8.00
292 Ryan Meaux/75 8.00
293 Scott Proctor/75 10.00
295 Shawn Camp/75 8.00
296 Shawn Hill/75 8.00
297 Shingo Takatsu/25 60.00
299 William Bergolla/75 8.00
300 Yadier Molina/75 25.00

Marble Signature Emerald

No Pricing
Production 1-5

Marble Signature Gold

No Pricing
Production 1-25

Marble Signature Material Gold Number

NM/M
Quantity produced listed
1 Vladimir Guerrero/Jsy/27 60.00
8 Brandon Webb/Jsy/55 10.00
18 Andruw Jones/Jsy/25 40.00
22 Luis Matos/Jsy/32 15.00
23 Jay Gibbons/Jsy/31 25.00
32 Manny Ramirez/Jsy/24 75.00
39 David Ortiz/Jsy/34 50.00
40 Mark Prior/Jsy/22 50.00
41 Kerry Wood/Pants/34 50.00
42 Sammy Sosa/Jsy/21 150.00
44 Greg Maddux/Jsy/31 100.00
51 Frank Thomas/Jsy/35 50.00
52 Magglio Ordonez/Jsy/30 25.00
53 Carlos Lee/Jsy/45 20.00
54 Mark Buehrle/Jsy/56 20.00
58 Adam Dunn/Jsy/44 40.00
59 Austin Kearns/Jsy/28 25.00
66 Cliff Lee/Jsy/34 15.00
67 Victor Martinez/Jsy/41 25.00
68 C.C. Sabathia/Jsy/52 20.00
70 Travis Hafner/Jsy/48 20.00
71 Todd Helton/Jsy/17 60.00
72 Preston Wilson/Jsy/44 20.00
81 Dontrelle Willis/Jsy/35 30.00
82 Brad Penny/Jsy/31 15.00
85 Andy Pettitte/Jsy/21 50.00
104 Paul LoDuca/Jsy/16 35.00
113 Johan Santana/Jsy/57 50.00
114 Shannon Stewart/Jsy/23 25.00
117 Torii Hunter/Jsy/48 20.00
119 Orlando Cabrera/Jsy/18 30.00
123 Mike Piazza/Jsy/31 100.00
124 Jae Weong/Seo Jsy/26 20.00
127 Jorge Posada/Jsy/20 40.00
130 Mike Mussina/Jsy/35 40.00
139 Mark Mulder/Jsy/20 25.00
141 Tim Hudson/Jsy/15 30.00
146 Marlon Byrd/Jsy/29 15.00
177 Scott Rolen/Jsy/27 50.00
182 Aubrey Huff/Jsy/19 30.00
184 Dewon Brazelton/Jsy/45 15.00
187 Mark Teixeira/Jsy/23 50.00
195 Roy Halladay/Jsy/32 15.00
200 Jeremy Bonderman/Jsy/38 10.00
236 Don Mattingly/Jsy/23 85.00
240 Reggie Jackson/Jsy/44 50.00
241 Rickey Henderson/Jsy/35 50.00
242 Mike Schmidt/Pants/20 100.00
244 Tony Gwynn/Jsy/19 75.00
245 Will Clark/Jsy/22 50.00
246 Lou Brock/Jsy/20 40.00
247 Bob Gibson/Jsy/45 40.00
249 Nolan Ryan/Jsy/34 150.00

Marble Signature Material Gold Position

NM/M
Quantity produced listed
2 Garret Anderson/Jsy/50 20.00
8 Brandon Webb/Jsy/50 15.00
15 Rafael Furcal/Jsy/50 20.00
17 Marcus Giles/Jsy/50 20.00
21 Melvin Mora/Jsy/50 20.00
22 Luis Matos/Jsy/50 15.00
23 Jay Gibbons/Jsy/50 15.00
25 Larry Bigbie/Jsy/50 15.00
26 Rodrigo Lopez/Jsy/50 10.00
45 Aramis Ramirez/Jsy/50 30.00
53 Carlos Lee/Jsy/50 20.00
54 Mark Buehrle/Jsy/50 20.00
59 Austin Kearns/Jsy/50 20.00
65 Jody Gerut/Jsy/50 10.00
66 Cliff Lee/Jsy/50 15.00
67 Victor Martinez/Jsy/50 25.00
68 C.C. Sabathia/Jsy/50 20.00
70 Travis Hafner/Jsy/50 20.00
72 Preston Wilson/Jsy/50 20.00
82 Brad Penny/Jsy/50 10.00
89 Morgan Ensberg/Jsy/50 10.00
96 Carlos Beltran/Jsy/50 50.00
97 Angel Berroa/Pants/50 10.00
104 Paul LoDuca/Jsy/25 25.00
112 Jacque Jones/Jsy/50 20.00
113 Johan Santana/Jsy/50 50.00
114 Shannon Stewart/Jsy/50 20.00
117 Torii Hunter/Jsy/25 25.00
119 Orlando Cabrera/Jsy/50 20.00
120 Jose Vidro/Jsy/50 10.00
139 Mark Mulder/Jsy/25 25.00
146 Marlon Byrd/Jsy/50 15.00
154 Craig Wilson/Jsy/50 15.00
161 Sean Burroughs /Jsy/50 15.00
171 Edgar Martinez/Jsy/25 50.00
182 Aubrey Huff/Jsy/50 20.00
186 Carl Crawford/Jsy/50 30.00
188 Hank Blalock/Jsy/25 50.00
200 Jeremy Bonderman/Jsy/50 10.00
228 Andre Dawson/Jsy/50 20.00
229 Bob Feller/Jsy/50 35.00
234 Harmon Killebrew/Jsy/25 65.00

Marble Signature Red

NM/M
Quantity produced listed
2 Garret Anderson/50 20.00
3 John Lackey/100 15.00
7 Shea Hillenbrand/100 15.00
8 Brandon Webb/100 10.00
11 Alex Cintron/100 10.00
14 Adam LaRoche/100 15.00
15 Rafael Furcal/50 20.00
17 Marcus Giles/50 15.00
19 Russ Ortiz/100 10.00
21 Melvin Mora/100 15.00
22 Luis Matos/100 10.00
23 Jay Gibbons/100 15.00
25 Larry Bigbie/100 15.00
26 Rodrigo Lopez/100 10.00
29 Trot Nixon/50 35.00
33 Keith Foulke/100 8.00
39 David Ortiz/50 40.00
40 Mark Prior/25 40.00
43 Derrek Lee/50 25.00
45 Aramis Ramirez/100 20.00
46 Matt Clement/25 15.00
47 Carlos Zambrano/100 35.00
48 Todd Walker/100 10.00
53 Carlos Lee/100 15.00
54 Mark Buehrle/50 15.00
55 Esteban Loaiza/100 10.00
58 Adam Dunn/25 40.00
59 Austin Kearns/25 20.00
63 Sean Casey/25 15.00
65 Jody Gerut/100 8.00
66 Cliff Lee/100 10.00
67 Victor Martinez/100 20.00
68 C.C. Sabathia/100 15.00
70 Travis Hafner/100 15.00
72 Preston Wilson/100 15.00
77 Miguel Cabrera/50 35.00
80 Mike Lowell/25 20.00
82 Brad Penny/100 10.00
89 Morgan Ensberg/100 10.00
90 Craig Biggio/25 30.00
91 Octavio Dotel/100 15.00
92 Wade Miller/100 10.00
96 Carlos Beltran/50 50.00
97 Angel Berroa/50 10.00
98 Jeremy Affeldt/100 10.00
103 Milton Bradley/100 15.00
104 Paul LoDuca/50 15.00
108 Scott Podsednik/100 15.00
109 Rickie Weeks/25 25.00
112 Jacque Jones/100 10.00
113 Johan Santana/50 50.00
114 Shannon Stewart/50 15.00
116 Lew Ford/100 15.00
117 Torii Hunter/25 25.00
118 Chad Cordero/100 10.00
119 Orlando Cabrera/100 20.00
120 Jose Vidro/50 10.00
132 Bubba Crosby/100 10.00
139 Mark Mulder/25 25.00

140 Jermaine Dye/100 10.00
144 Bobby Crosby/100 40.00
145 Eric Byrnes/100 10.00
146 Marlon Byrd/100 10.00
148 Mike Lieberthal/100 15.00
153 Jose Castillo/100 10.00
154 Craig Wilson/100 10.00
155 Jason Bay/100 25.00
158 Jay Payton/100 10.00
161 Sean Burroughs/25 15.00
165 Todd Linden/100 8.00
170 Shigetoshi Hasegawa/50 40.00
171 Edgar Martinez/25 40.00
174 Raul Ibanez/100 10.00
177 Scott Rolen/50 35.00
182 Aubrey Huff/100 10.00
183 Delmon Young/25 25.00
184 Dewon Brazelton/100 10.00
186 Carl Crawford/100 20.00
187 Mark Teixeira/25 40.00
188 Hank Blalock/50 25.00
189 Michael Young/100 15.00
190 Laynce Nix/100 15.00
191 Alfonso Soriano/25 50.00
193 Adrian Gonzalez/100 10.00
194 Alexis Rios/100 20.00
196 Vernon Wells/50 15.00
198 Bill Hall/100 10.00
199 Jose Guillen/100 15.00
200 Jeremy Bonderman/100 10.00
222 Cal Ripken Jr./25 150.00
224 Duke Snider/25 40.00
228 Andre Dawson/100 20.00
229 Bob Feller/100 25.00
235 Gary Carter/25 20.00
237 Phil Rizzuto/25 40.00
245 Will Clark/25 50.00
247 Bob Gibson/25 40.00
248 Stan Musial/25 75.00
249 Nolan Ryan/25 150.00
250 Dale Murphy/50 30.00
251 Aarom Baldiris/100 10.00
252 Akinori Otsuka/25 50.00
253 Andres Blanco/100 10.00
254 Angel Chavez/100 8.00
255 Carlos Hines/100 8.00
256 Carlos Vasquez/100 12.00
258 Chris Oxspring/100 10.00
259 Colby Miller/100 8.00
260 David Crouthers/50 8.00
261 Donald Kelly/100 8.00
262 Eddy Rodriguez/100 8.00
263 Edwardo Sierra/100 10.00
264 Edwin Moreno/100 10.00
266 Freddy Guzman/100 8.00
267 Greg Dobbs/100 8.00
268 Brad Halsey/100 8.00
269 Hector Gimenez/100 8.00
270 Ivan Ochoa/100 8.00
271 Jake Woods/100 10.00
272 Jamie Brown/100 8.00
273 Jason Bartlett/100 15.00
274 Jason Szuminski/100 8.00
275 John Gall/100 10.00
276 Jorge Vasquez/100 8.00
277 Josh Labandeira/100 8.00
280 Kevin Cave/100 10.00
281 Lance Cormier/100 8.00
283 Merkin Valdez/100 15.00
284 Mike Wuertz/100 10.00
285 Mike Johnston/100 8.00
287 Onil Joseph/100 8.00
288 Phil Stockman/100 8.00
289 Roberto Novoa/100 10.00
291 Ronny Cedeno/100 8.00
292 Ryan Meaux/100 8.00
293 Scott Proctor/100 10.00
295 Shawn Camp/100 8.00
297 Shingo Takatsu/25 60.00
299 William Bergolla/100 8.00
300 Yadier Molina/100 25.00

Stars

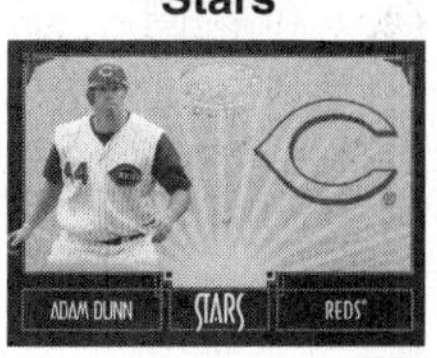

NM/M

Production 599 Sets
1 Ryne Sandberg 6.00
2 Mark Prior 2.00
3 Andre Dawson 2.00
4 Don Mattingly 6.00
5 Vladimir Guerrero 3.00
6 Garret Anderson 2.00
7 Dale Murphy 2.00
8 Cal Ripken Jr. 10.00
9 Mark Grace 3.00
10 Kerry Wood 3.00
11 Frank Thomas 3.00
12 Magglio Ordonez 2.00
13 Adam Dunn 3.00
14 Preston Wilson 2.00
15 Bo Jackson 3.00
16 Carlos Beltran 3.00
17 Tony Gwynn 4.00
18 Will Clark 3.00
19 Edgar Martinez 2.00
20 Scott Rolen 3.00
21 Alfonso Soriano 3.00
22 Randy Johnson 3.00
23 Chipper Jones 3.00
24 Andruw Jones 2.00
25 Javy Lopez 3.00
26 Curt Schilling 3.00
27 Manny Ramirez 5.00
28 Sammy Sosa 4.00
29 Greg Maddux 2.00
30 Todd Helton 3.00
31 Jeff Bagwell 3.00
32 Shawn Green 2.00
33 Mike Piazza 5.00
34 Jorge Posada 2.00
35 Gary Sheffield 3.00
36 Mike Mussina 3.00
37 Miguel Cabrera 3.00
38 Rickey Henderson 3.00
39 Albert Pujols 8.00
40 Vernon Wells 2.00
41 Fred Lynn 2.00
42 Alan Trammell 2.00
43 Lenny Dykstra 2.00
44 Dwight Gooden 2.00
45 Keith Hernandez 2.00
46 Luis Tiant 2.00
47 Orel Hershiser 2.00
48 George Foster 2.00
49 Darryl Strawberry 2.00
50 Marty Marion 2.00

Stars Signature

NM/M

Quantity produced listed
3 Andre Dawson/50 20.00
4 Don Mattingly/25 65.00
6 Garret Anderson/50 20.00
7 Dale Murphy/50 30.00
12 Magglio Ordonez/25 20.00
13 Adam Dunn/25 40.00
14 Preston Wilson/50 15.00
16 Carlos Beltran/50 40.00
18 Will Clark/25 40.00
19 Edgar Martinez/25 40.00
20 Scott Rolen/25 40.00
37 Miguel Cabrera/50 40.00
40 Vernon Wells/25 20.00
41 Fred Lynn/50 10.00
42 Alan Trammell/50 20.00
43 Lenny Dykstra/50 20.00
44 Dwight Gooden/50 20.00
45 Keith Hernandez/50 20.00
46 Luis Tiant/50 15.00
47 Orel Hershiser/50 25.00
48 George Foster/50 10.00
49 Darryl Strawberry/50 20.00

Stars Signature Jersey

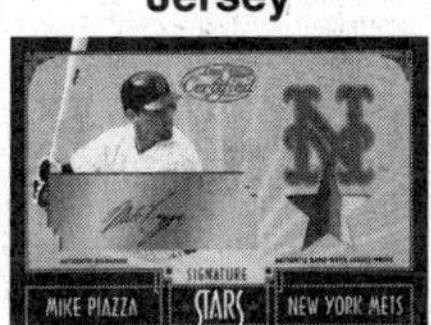

NM/M

Quantity produced listed
1 Ryne Sandberg/23 75.00
2 Mark Prior/22 40.00
4 Don Mattingly/23 75.00
5 Vladimir Guerrero/27 60.00
6 Garret Anderson/16 35.00
9 Mark Grace/17 50.00
10 Kerry Wood/34 50.00
11 Frank Thomas/35 50.00
12 Magglio Ordonez/30 25.00
13 Adam Dunn/44 50.00
14 Preston Wilson/44 20.00
15 Bo Jackson/16 125.00
16 Carlos Beltran/15 75.00
17 Tony Gwynn/19 75.00
18 Will Clark/22 65.00
20 Scott Rolen/27 60.00
24 Andruw Jones/25 40.00
28 Sammy Sosa/21 150.00
29 Greg Maddux/31 100.00
30 Todd Helton/17 50.00
34 Jorge Posada/20 50.00
37 Miguel Cabrera/24 50.00
41 Fred Lynn/19 20.00
45 Keith Hernandez/37 20.00
46 Luis Tiant/25 25.00
48 George Foster/15 25.00
49 Darryl Strawberry/18 35.00
50 Marty Marion/25 25.00

2004 Leaf Certified Materials

NM/M

Complete Set (300):
Common Player: .50
Common (201-211): 4.00
Common (212-240): 4.00
Production 500
Common Auto. (241-300): 8.00
Pack (5): 10.00
Box (10): 85.00
1 A.J. Burnett .50
2 Adam Dunn 1.00
3 Adam LaRoche .50
4 Adam Loewen .50

5 Adrian Beltre .75
6 Al Leiter .50
7 Albert Pujols 3.00
8 Alex Rodriguez 3.00
9 Alexis Rios .50
10 Alfonso Soriano 1.50
11 Andruw Jones 1.00
12 Andy Pettitte .75
13 Angel Berroa .50
14 Aramis Ramirez .75
15 Aubrey Huff .50
16 Austin Kearns .50
17 Barry Larkin .75
18 Barry Zito .75
19 Ben Sheets .75
20 Bernie Williams .75
21 Bobby Abreu .75
22 Brad Penny .50
23 Brad Wilkerson .50
24 Brandon Webb .50
25 Brendan Harris .50
26 Bret Boone .50
27 Brett Myers .50
28 Bubba Crosby .50
29 Brian Giles .50
30 Chad Cordero .50
31 Bubba Nelson .50
32 Byron Gettis .50
33 C.C. Sabathia .50
34 Carl Crawford .50
35 Carl Everett .50
36 Carlos Beltran .75
37 Carlos Delgado .75
38 Carlos Lee .50
39 Chad Gaudin .50
40 Cliff Lee .50
41 Chipper Jones 1.50
42 Cliff Floyd .50
43 Clint Barmes .50
44 Corey Patterson .75
45 Craig Biggio .75
46 Curt Schilling 1.00
47 Dan Haren .50
48 Darin Erstad .50
49 David Ortiz 1.00
50 Delmon Young .50
51 Derek Jeter 4.00
52 Dewon Brazelton .50
53 Dontrelle Willis .75
54 Edgar Martinez .75
55 Edgar Renteria .75
56 Edwin Almonte .50
57 Edwin Jackson .50
58 Eric Chavez .75
59 Eric Hinske .50
60 Eric Munson .50
61 Erubiel Durazo .50
62 Frank Thomas 1.00
63 Fred McGriff .50
64 Freddy Garcia .50
65 Garret Anderson .75
66 Garrett Atkins .50
67 Gary Sheffield .75
68 Geoff Jenkins .50
69 Greg Maddux 2.00
70 Hank Blalock 1.00
71 Hee Seop Choi .50
72 Hideki Matsui 2.50
73 Hideo Nomo .75
74 Craig Wilson .50
75 Ichiro Suzuki 2.50
76 Ivan Rodriguez 1.00
77 J.D. Drew .50
78 John Lackey .50
79 Jacque Jones .50
80 Jae Weong Seo .50
81 Jamie Moyer .50
82 Jason Giambi 1.00
83 Jason Jennings .50
84 Jason Kendall .50
85 Melvin Mora .50
86 Jason Varitek .75
87 Javier Vazquez .75
88 Javy Lopez .75
89 Jay Gibbons .50
90 Jay Payton .50
91 Jeff Bagwell 1.00
92 Jeff Baker .50
93 Jeff Kent .50
94 Jeremy Bonderman .50
95 Milton Bradley .50
96 Jerome Williams .50
97 Jim Edmonds .75
98 Jim Thome 1.50
99 Jody Gerut .50
100 Joe Borchard .50
101 Joe Crede .50
102 Johan Santana .50
103 John Olerud .50
104 John Smoltz .75
105 Johnny Damon .75
106 Jorge Posada .75
107 Jose Castillo .50
108 Jose Reyes .75
109 Jose Vidro .50
110 Josh Beckett 1.00
111 Josh Phelps .50
112 Juan Encarnacion .50
113 Juan Gonzalez 1.00
114 Junior Spivey .50
115 Kazuhisa Ishii .50
116 Kenny Lofton .50
117 Kerry Wood 1.50
118 Kevin Millwood .50
119 Kevin Youkilis .50
120 Lance Berkman .50
121 Larry Bigbie .50
122 Larry Walker .75
123 Luis Castillo .50
124 Luis Gonzalez .50
125 Luis Matos .50
126 Lyle Overbay .50
127 Magglio Ordonez .75
128 Manny Ramirez 1.00
129 Marcus Giles .50
130 Mariano Rivera .75
131 Mark Buehrle .50
132 Mark Mulder .75
133 Mark Prior 1.00
134 Mark Teixeira .75
135 Marlon Byrd .50
136 Matt Morris .50
137 Miguel Cabrera 1.00
138 Mike Lowell .50
139 Mike Mussina .75
140 Mike Piazza 2.00
141 Mike Sweeney .50
142 Morgan Ensberg .50
143 Nick Johnson .50
144 Nomar Garciaparra 2.00
145 Omar Vizquel .50
146 Orlando Cabrera .50
147 Orlando Hudson .50
148 Pat Burrell .50
149 Paul Konerko .50
150 Paul LoDuca .50
151 Pedro J. Martinez 1.50
152 Jermaine Dye .50
153 Preston Wilson .50
154 Rafael Furcal .50
155 Rafael Palmeiro 1.00
156 Randy Johnson 1.50
157 Rich Aurilia .50
158 Rich Harden .50
159 Richard Hidalgo .50
160 Richie Sexson .75
161 Rickie Weeks .75
162 Roberto Alomar .75
163 Rocco Baldelli .50
164 Roger Clemens 3.00
165 Roy Halladay .50
166 Roy Oswalt .75
167 Ryan Howard 1.50
168 Ryan Klesko .50
169 Rodrigo Lopez .50
170 Sammy Sosa 2.50
171 Scott Podsednik .50
172 Scott Rolen 1.50
173 Sean Burroughs .50
174 Sean Casey .50
175 Shannon Stewart .50
176 Shawn Green .75
177 Shea Hillenbrand .50
178 Shigetoshi Hasegawa .50
179 Steve Finley .50
180 Tim Hudson .75
181 Todd Helton 1.00
182 Tom Glavine .75
183 Torii Hunter .75
184 Trot Nixon .50
185 Troy Glaus .75
186 Vernon Wells .50
187 Victor Martinez .75
188 Vladimir Guerrero 1.50
189 Wade Miller .50
190 Brandon Larson .50
191 Travis Hafner .75
192 Tim Salmon .75
193 Tim Redding .50
194 Runelvys Hernandez .50
195 Ramon Nivar .50
196 Moises Alou .75
197 Michael Young .50
198 Laynce Nix .50
199 Tino Martinez .50
200 Randall Simon .50
201 Roger Clemens/SP 8.00
202 Greg Maddux/SP 8.00
203 Vladimir Guerrero/SP 6.00
204 Miguel Tejada/SP 4.00
205 Kevin Brown/SP 4.00
206 Jason Giambi/SP 5.00
207 Curt Schilling/SP 5.00
208 Alex Rodriguez/SP 8.00
209 Alfonso Soriano/SP 6.00
210 Ivan Rodriguez/SP 6.00
211 Rafael Palmeiro/SP 6.00
212 Gary Carter 4.00
213 Duke Snider 5.00
214 Whitey Ford 4.00
215 Bob Feller 4.00
216 Reggie Jackson 5.00
217 Ryne Sandberg 10.00
218 Dale Murphy 4.00
219 Tony Gwynn 6.00
220 Don Mattingly 10.00
221 Mike Schmidt 10.00
222 Rickey Henderson 5.00
223 Cal Ripken Jr. 20.00
224 Nolan Ryan 15.00
225 George Brett 10.00
226 Bob Gibson 5.00
227 Lou Brock 4.00
228 Andre Dawson 4.00
229 Rod Carew 4.00
230 Wade Boggs 4.00
231 Roberto Clemente 12.00
232 Roy Campanella 5.00
233 Babe Ruth 15.00
234 Lou Gehrig 10.00
235 Ty Cobb 8.00
236 Roger Maris 6.00
237 Satchel Paige 6.00
238 Ernie Banks 6.00
239 Ted Williams 10.00
240 Stan Musial 6.00
241 Hector Gimenez/Auto./500 **RC** 8.00
242 Justin Germano/Auto./500 **RC** 8.00
243 Ian Snell/Auto./500 **RC** 25.00
244 Graham Koonce/Auto./500 8.00
245 Jose Capellan/Auto./500 **RC** 25.00
246 Onil Joseph/Auto./500 **RC** 8.00
247 Shingo Takatsu/Auto./200 **RC** 40.00
248 Carlos Hines/Auto./500 **RC** 8.00
249 Lincoln Holdzkom/Auto./500 **RC** 8.00
250 Mike Gosling/Auto./500 8.00
251 Edwardo Sierra/Auto./500 **RC** 10.00
252 Renyel Pinto/Auto./500 **RC** 10.00
253 Merkin Valdez/Auto./500 **RC** 12.00
254 Angel Chavez/Auto./500 **RC** 8.00
255 Ivan Ochoa/Auto./1000 **RC** 8.00
256 Greg Dobbs/Auto./300 **RC** 8.00
257 William Bergolla/Auto./500 **RC** 8.00
258 Aarom Baldiris/Auto./500 **RC** 10.00
259 Kazuo Matsui/500 **RC** 12.00
260 Carlos Vasquez/Auto./500 **RC** 8.00
261 Freddy Guzman/Auto./500 **RC** 8.00
262 Akinori Otsuka/Auto./200 **RC** 40.00
263 Mariano Gomez/Auto./200 **RC** 8.00
264 Nick Regilio/Auto./500 **RC** 8.00
265 Jamie Brown/Auto./500 **RC** 8.00
266 Shawn Hill/Auto./500 **RC** 8.00
267 Roberto Novoa/Auto./500 **RC** 8.00
268 Sean Henn/Auto./500 10.00
269 Ramon Ramirez/Auto./500 **RC** 8.00
270 Ronny Cedeno/Auto./1000 **RC** 8.00
271 Ryan Wing/Auto./400 8.00
272 Ruddy Yan/Auto./500 **RC** 8.00
273 Fernando Nieve/Auto./500 **RC** 8.00
274 Rusty Tucker/Auto./500 **RC** 8.00
275 Jason Bartlett/Auto./500 **RC** 8.00
276 Mike Rouse/Auto./500 8.00
277 Dennis Sarfate/Auto./500 **RC** 8.00
278 Cory Sullivan/Auto./500 **RC** 8.00
279 Casey Daigle/Auto./250 **RC** 8.00
280 Chris Shelton/Auto./400 **RC** 25.00
281 Jesse Harper/Auto./400 **RC** 8.00
282 Mike Wuertz/Auto./500 **RC** 12.00
283 Tim Bausher/Auto./400 **RC** 8.00
284 Jorge Sequea/Auto./500 **RC** 8.00
285 Josh Labandeira/Auto./100 **RC** 12.00
286 Justin Leone/Auto./500 **RC** 12.00
287 Tim Bittner/Auto./500 **RC** 8.00
288 Andres Blanco/Auto./500 **RC** 8.00
289 Kevin Cave/Auto./1000 **RC** 8.00
290 Mike Johnston/Auto./1000 **RC** 8.00
291 Jason Szuminski/Auto./500 **RC** 8.00
292 Shawn Camp/500 **RC** 8.00
293 Colby Miller/Auto./500 **RC** 8.00
294 Jake Woods/Auto./500 8.00
295 Ryan Meaux/Auto./500 **RC** 8.00
296 Donald Kelly/Auto./500 **RC** 8.00
297 Edwin Moreno/Auto./500 **RC** 8.00
298 Phil Stockman/Auto./500 **RC** 8.00
299 Jorge Vasquez/500 **RC** 8.00
300 Kazuhito Tadano/Auto./500 **RC** 25.00

Fabric of the Game

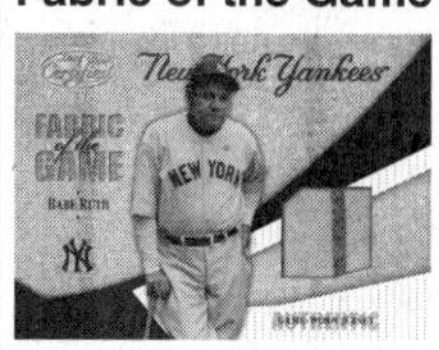

NM/M

Common Player: 6.00
Quantity produced listed
AL/NL: .75-1.5X
Production 1-100
Jersey Number: .75-2X
Production 1-72
Position: .75-2X
Production 1-100
Prime: No Pricing
Production One Set
Game Reward: .75-2X
Production 1-50
Jersey Year: .75-2X
Production 1-99
Game Stats: .75-2X
Production 1-66
No Pricing production 20 or less.
n Ozzie Smith/Jsy/100 20.00
2 Al Kaline/Pants/100 15.00
3 Alan Trammell/Jsy/100 10.00
4 Albert Pujols/Jsy/100 20.00
5 Alex Rodriguez/Jsy/100 12.00
6 Alex Rodriguez/Jsy/100 12.00
7 Andre Dawson/Jsy/100 8.00
8 Andre Dawson/Pants/100 8.00
11 Billy Williams/Jsy/100 10.00
12 Bo Jackson/Jsy/100 20.00
13 Bob Feller/Jsy/50 15.00
14 Bob Gibson/Jsy/50 15.00
15 Bobby Doerr/Jsy/100 8.00
16 Brooks Robinson/Jsy/25 25.00
17 Cal Ripken Jr./Jsy/100 30.00
18 Carl Yastrzemski/Jsy/100 20.00
19 Carlton Fisk/Jsy/100 10.00
20 Dale Murphy/Jsy/100 12.00
21 Darryl Strawberry/Pants/100 10.00
22 Darryl Strawberry/Jsy/100 10.00
23 Dave Parker/Jsy/100 10.00
24 Dave Parker/Jsy/100 10.00
25 Dave Winfield/Jsy/50 10.00
26 Dave Winfield/Jsy/100 10.00
27 Deion Sanders/Jsy/25 25.00
28 Derek Jeter/Jsy/100 20.00
29 Don Drysdale/Jsy/100 15.00
30 Don Mattingly/Jsy/100 20.00
31 Don Mattingly/Jkt/100 20.00
32 Don Sutton/Jsy/100 8.00
33 Duke Snider/Jsy/100 12.00
34 Dwight Gooden/Jsy/100 8.00
35 Early Wynn/Jsy/100 10.00
36 Eddie Mathews/Jsy/50 20.00
37 Eddie Murray/Jsy/100 15.00
38 Eddie Murray/Jsy/100 15.00
39 Enos Slaughter/Jsy/100 10.00
40 Eric Davis/Jsy/50 10.00
41 Ernie Banks/Jsy/100 15.00
42 Fergie Jenkins/Pants/100 10.00
43 Frank Robinson/Jsy/100 10.00
45 Gary Carter/Jsy/100 10.00
46 Gaylord Perry/Jsy/25 15.00

47 George Brett/White Jsy/100 20.00
48 George Foster/Jsy/100 8.00
49 Hal Newhouser/Jsy/100 8.00
50 Harmon Killebrew/Jsy/25 30.00
51 Harmon Killebrew/Pants/25 30.00
52 Harold Baines/Jsy/100 10.00
53 Hoyt Wilhelm/Jsy/50 10.00
54 Jack Morris/Jsy/100 8.00
56 Jim "Catfish" Hunter/Jsy/100 10.00
57 Jim Palmer/Jsy/100 10.00
58 Jim Rice/Jsy/100 10.00
59 Joe Carter/Jsy/100 8.00
60 Joe Morgan/Jsy/100 10.00
61 Tommy Lasorda/Jsy/100 8.00
62 Johnny Mize/Pants/100 12.00
63 Johnny Bench/Jsy/100 15.00
64 Jose Canseco/Jsy/100 10.00
65 Juan Marichal/Jsy/100 10.00
66 Kirby Puckett/Jsy/100 15.00
67 Lou Boudreau/Jsy/100 10.00
68 Lou Brock/Jsy/100 10.00
71 Luis Aparicio/Jsy/100 10.00
72 Luis Aparicio/Pants/100 10.00
73 Mariano Rivera/Jsy/100 10.00
74 Mark Grace/Jsy/100 12.00
75 Mark Prior/Jsy/100 8.00
76 Mel Ott/Jsy/25 60.00
77 Mel Ott/Pants/25 60.00
78 Mike Schmidt/Jsy/100 20.00
79 Mike Schmidt/Pants/100 20.00
80 Mike Schmidt/Jkt/100 20.00
81 Nolan Ryan/Angels Jsy/100 25.00
82 Nolan Ryan/Angels Jkt/100 25.00
83 Nolan Ryan/Astros Jsy/100 25.00
84 Nolan Ryan/Astros Jkt/100 25.00
85 Nolan Ryan/Rgr Jsy/100 25.00
86 Nolan Ryan/Rgr Pants/100 25.00
88 Ozzie Smith/Jsy/100 15.00
89 Paul Molitor/Jsy/100 12.00
90 Pee Wee Reese/Jsy/100 15.00
91 Phil Niekro/Jsy/100 8.00
92 Phil Rizzuto/Jsy/100 15.00
93 Phil Rizzuto/Pants/100 15.00
94 Red Schoendienst/Jsy/100 10.00
95 Reggie Jackson/Jkt/100 15.00
96 Reggie Jackson/Jsy/100 15.00
97 Richie Ashburn/Jsy/100 20.00
98 Rickey Henderson/Jsy/50 15.00
99 Roberto Clemente/Jsy/50 75.00
100 Robin Yount/Jsy/100 15.00
101 Rod Carew/Jsy/100 10.00
102 Rod Carew/Pants/100 10.00
103 Rod Carew/Jkt/100 10.00
104 Rod Carew/Jsy/100 10.00
105 Roger Clemens/Jsy/100 15.00
106 Roger Clemens/Jsy/100 15.00
107 Roger Maris/Jsy/100 30.00
108 Roger Maris/Pants/100 30.00
109 Roger Maris/Jsy/100 30.00
110 Roy Campanella/Pants/100 15.00
111 Ryne Sandberg/Jsy/100 25.00
112 Stan Musial/Jsy/50 30.00
113 Steve Carlton/Jsy/100 10.00
114 Ted Williams/Jsy/100 75.00
115 Ted Williams/Jkt/100 75.00
116 Thurman Munson/Jsy/100 25.00
117 Thurman Munson/Pants/100 25.00
118 Tony Gwynn/Jsy/100 15.00
119 Wade Boggs/Jsy/100 10.00
120 Wade Boggs/Jsy/100 10.00
121 Warren Spahn/Jsy/100 15.00
122 Warren Spahn/Pants/100 15.00
123 Whitey Ford/Jsy/100 15.00
124 Whitey Ford/Pants/100 15.00
125 Will Clark/Jsy/100 15.00
126 Willie McCovey/Jsy/100 10.00
127 Willie Stargell/Jsy/100 15.00
128 Yogi Berra/Jsy/25 35.00
129 Frankie Frisch/Jkt/100 15.00
130 Marty Marion/Jsy/100 10.00
131 Tommy John/Pants/100 8.00
132 Chipper Jones/Jsy/100 10.00
133 Sammy Sosa/Jsy/100 15.00
134 Rickey Henderson/Jsy/100 10.00
135 Mike Piazza/Jsy/100 12.00
136 Mike Piazza/Jsy/100 12.00
137 Nomar Garciaparra/Jsy/100 15.00
138 Hideo Nomo/Jsy/100 10.00
139 Hideo Nomo/Jsy/50 15.00
140 Randy Johnson/Jsy/100 10.00
141 Randy Johnson/Jsy/100 10.00
142 Randy Johnson/Jsy/100 10.00
143 Jason Giambi/Jsy/100 6.00
144 Jason Giambi/Jsy/100 6.00
145 Curt Schilling/Jsy/100 6.00
146 Dennis Eckersley/Jsy/100 10.00
147 Carlton Fisk/Jkt/100 10.00
148 Tom Seaver/Jsy/25 30.00
149 Joe Torre/Jsy/100 10.00
150 Pedro Martinez/Jsy/100 10.00
151 Albert Pujols/Jsy/100 20.00
152 Andre Dawson/Jsy/50 10.00
153 Bert Blyleven/Jsy/100 8.00
154 Bo Jackson/Jsy/100 15.00
155 Cal Ripken Jr./Pants/100 35.00
156 Carlton Fisk/Jsy/100 10.00
157 Curt Schilling/Jsy/100 6.00
158 Darryl Strawberry/Jsy/100 8.00
159 Dave Concepcion/Jsy/100 8.00
160 Dwight Evans/Jsy/100 8.00
161 Ernie Banks/Pants/100 15.00
163 Gary Carter/Pants/100 8.00
164 Gary Sheffield/Jsy/100 6.00
165 George Brett/Jsy/100 20.00
166 Greg Maddux/Jsy/100 10.00
167 Ivan Rodriguez/Jsy/100 10.00
168 Joe Morgan/Jsy/100 10.00
169 Jose Canseco/Jsy/100 10.00
170 Juan Gonzalez/Jsy/100 8.00
171 Juan Gonzalez/Jsy/100 8.00
172 Keith Hernandez/Jsy/100 10.00
173 Ken Boyer/Jsy/100 20.00
174 Kerry Wood/Jsy/100 10.00
175 Lee Smith/Jsy/100 8.00
176 Luis Tiant/Jsy/100 8.00
177 Manny Ramirez/Jsy/100 8.00
178 Mark Grace/Jsy/100 12.00
179 Matt Williams/Jsy/100 8.00
180 Miguel Tejada/Jsy/100 6.00
181 Mike Mussina/Jsy/100 10.00
182 Mike Piazza/Jsy/100 12.00
183 Nomar Garciaparra/Jsy/100 15.00
184 Pedro Martinez/Jsy/100 10.00
185 Rafael Palmeiro/Jsy/100 8.00
186 Reggie Jackson/Pants/100 12.00
187 Rickey Henderson/Jsy/100 10.00
188 Rickey Henderson/Pants/100 10.00
189 Rickey Henderson/Jsy/100 10.00
190 Sammy Sosa/Jsy/100 15.00
191 Satchel Paige/Jsy/100 60.00
192 Shawn Green/Jsy/100 6.00
193 Stan Musial/Jsy/50 35.00
194 Steve Carlton/Jsy/100 10.00
195 Steve Garvey/Jsy/100 8.00
196 Tom Seaver/Jsy/100 12.00
197 Tony Gwynn/Pants/100 12.00
198 Vladimir Guerrero/Jsy/100 10.00
199 Wade Boggs/Jsy/100 10.00
200 Willie Stargell/Jsy/100 10.00

Fabric of the Game

No Pricing
Production 1-10
AL/NL Auto: No Pricing
Production 1-25
Jersey Number Auto.: No Pricing
Production 1-8
Jersey Year Auto.: No Pricing
Production 1-8
Position Auto.: No Pricing
Production 1-8
Reward Auto.: No Pricing
Production 1-8
Stats Auto.: No Pricing
Production 1-8

Mirror Black

No Pricing
Production One Set

Mirror Blue

Stars (1-200): 3-5X
Mirror Blue (201-240): 1-2X
Auto. (241-300): .5X
No Auto. (241-300): 1X
Production 50 Sets

Mirror Emerald

No Pricing
Production Five Sets

Mirror Gold

Mirror Gold (1-200): 4-8X
Mirror Gold (201-240): 1.5-2X
Mirror Gold (241-300): No Pricing
Production 25 Sets

Mirror Red

Mirror Red (1-200): 2-4X
Mirror Red (201-240): .5-1X
Mirror Red (241-300): .5X
Production 100 Sets

Mirror White

Mirror White (1-200): 2-4X
Mirror White (201-240): .5-1X
Mirror White (241-300): .5X
Production 100 Sets

Mirror Autograph Black

No Pricing
Production One Set

Mirror Autograph Blue

Mirror Auto. Blue: .5-1.5X Red Auto.
Production 1-100
No pricing 25 or less.

Mirror Autograph Emerald

No Pricing
Production 1-5

Mirror Autograph Gold

No Pricing
Production 1-25

Mirror Autograph Red

NM/M
Quantity produced listed
3 Adam LaRoche/250 8.00
4 Adam Loewen/250 8.00
9 Alexis Rios/250 15.00
10 Alfonso Soriano/25 50.00
11 Andruw Jones/25 25.00
12 Andy Pettitte/25 35.00
13 Angel Berroa/100 10.00
14 Aramis Ramirez/100 25.00
15 Aubrey Huff/250 10.00
16 Austin Kearns/200 12.00
17 Barry Larkin/25 40.00
22 Brad Penny/25 15.00
24 Brandon Webb/250 8.00
25 Brendan Harris/50 10.00
27 Brett Myers/100 8.00
28 Bubba Crosby/250 8.00
30 Chad Cordero/250 8.00
31 Bubba Nelson/250 8.00
32 Byron Gettis/250 8.00
36 Carlos Beltran/100 25.00
38 Carlos Lee/250 10.00
39 Chad Gaudin/100 8.00
40 Cliff Lee/250 10.00
43 Clint Barmes/100 15.00
47 Dan Haren/250 8.00
49 David Ortiz/250 40.00
50 Delmon Young/50 30.00
52 Dewon Brazelton/250 8.00
53 Dontrelle Willis/100 20.00
56 Edwin Almonte/250 8.00
57 Edwin Jackson/250 8.00
58 Eric Chavez/25 30.00
62 Frank Thomas/50 50.00
65 Garret Anderson/250 15.00
67 Gary Sheffield/50 30.00
70 Hank Blalock/100 30.00
74 Craig Wilson/250 10.00
78 John Lackey/250 8.00
79 Jacque Jones/250 8.00
80 Jae Weong Seo/100 15.00
85 Melvin Mora/250 15.00
86 Jason Varitek/100 40.00
89 Jay Gibbons/250 8.00
90 Jay Payton/250 8.00
91 Jeff Bagwell/50 50.00
92 Jeff Baker/25 20.00
96 Jerome Williams/100 15.00
97 Jim Edmonds/25 35.00
99 Jody Gerut/250 10.00
100 Joe Borchard/250 10.00
101 Joe Crede/50 15.00
102 Johan Santana/250 25.00
106 Jorge Posada/25 50.00
107 Jose Castillo/250 8.00
109 Jose Vidro/250 10.00
110 Josh Beckett/25 50.00
113 Juan Gonzalez/25 40.00
114 Junior Spivey/25 15.00
117 Kerry Wood/50 50.00
119 Kevin Youkilis/250 10.00
120 Lance Berkman/25 30.00
121 Larry Bigbie/250 12.00
123 Luis Castillo/25 15.00
125 Luis Matos/250 8.00
127 Magglio Ordonez/250 15.00
129 Marcus Giles/250 12.00
131 Mark Buehrle/250 12.00
132 Mark Mulder/250 20.00
133 Mark Prior/100 40.00
134 Mark Teixeira/100 25.00
135 Marlon Byrd/250 8.00
137 Miguel Cabrera/250 30.00
140 Mike Piazza/25 125.00
142 Morgan Ensberg/250 8.00
146 Orlando Cabrera/25 20.00
150 Paul LoDuca/25 25.00
152 Jermaine Dye/250 10.00
153 Preston Wilson/250 10.00
154 Rafael Furcal/100 12.00
157 Rich Aurilia/25 15.00
158 Rich Harden/203 15.00
165 Roy Halladay/50 15.00
166 Roy Oswalt/50 15.00
167 Ryan Howard/100 80.00
169 Rodrigo Lopez/250 8.00
170 Sammy Sosa/50 100.00
171 Scott Podsednik/250 15.00
172 Scott Rolen/100 40.00
175 Shannon Stewart/100 8.00
176 Shawn Green/25 30.00
177 Shea Hillenbrand/250 10.00
178 Shigetoshi Hasegawa/250 40.00
179 Steve Finley/100 20.00
183 Torii Hunter/250 15.00
184 Trot Nixon/250 20.00
187 Victor Martinez/250 20.00
188 Vladimir Guerrero/50 75.00
190 Brandon Larson/200 10.00
191 Travis Hafner/250 15.00
197 Michael Young/250 15.00
212 Gary Carter/250 15.00
213 Duke Snider/250 25.00
214 Whitey Ford /50 40.00
215 Bob Feller /250 20.00
216 Reggie Jackson/50 50.00
217 Ryne Sandberg/50 60.00
218 Dale Murphy/50 30.00
219 Tony Gwynn/50 50.00
220 Don Mattingly/50 75.00
221 Mike Schmidt/50 75.00
222 Rickey Henderson/50 50.00
223 Cal Ripken Jr./50 180.00
224 Nolan Ryan/50 100.00
225 George Brett/50 75.00
226 Bob Gibson/100 25.00
227 Lou Brock/100 25.00
228 Andre Dawson/250 15.00
229 Rod Carew/50 25.00
230 Wade Boggs/50 25.00
238 Ernie Banks/50 60.00
240 Stan Musial/100 60.00
241 Hector Gimenez/200 8.00
242 Justin Germano/100 8.00
243 Ian Snell/100 25.00
244 Graham Koonce/200 8.00
245 Jose Capellan/100 40.00
246 Onil Joseph/200 8.00
247 Shingo Takatsu/50 50.00
248 Carlos Hines/200 8.00
249 Lincoln Holdzkom/100 8.00
250 Mike Gosling/100 10.00
251 Edwardo Sierra/200 10.00
252 Renyel Pinto/100 10.00
253 Merkin Valdez/200 12.00
254 Angel Chavez/200 8.00
255 Ivan Ochoa/200 8.00
257 William Bergolla/200 8.00
258 Aarom Baldiris/100 10.00
260 Carlos Vasquez/200 8.00
261 Freddy Guzman/200 8.00
262 Akinori Otsuka/50 50.00
264 Nick Regilio/200 8.00
266 Shawn Hill/200 8.00
268 Sean Henn/200 10.00
269 Ramon Ramirez/200 8.00
270 Ronny Cedeno/100 8.00
273 Fernando Nieve/200 8.00
274 Rusty Tucker/200 8.00
275 Jason Bartlett/200 8.00
276 Mike Rouse/200 8.00
277 Dennis Sarfate/200 8.00
278 Cory Sullivan/200 8.00
282 Mike Wuertz/200 8.00
284 Jorge Sequea/100 8.00
287 Tim Bittner/250 8.00
288 Andres Blanco/100 12.00
289 Kevin Cave/100 10.00
290 Mike Johnston/100 8.00
293 Colby Miller/100 8.00
294 Jake Woods/100 10.00
295 Ryan Meaux/200 8.00
296 Donald Kelly/100 8.00
297 Edwin Moreno/100 8.00
298 Phil Stockman/100 8.00

Mirror Autograph White

White Auto. (1-240):.75-1.5X Red Auto.
White Auto. (241-300): .5-1X Red Auto.
Production 1-100
No pricing 25 or less.

Mirror Bat Blue

NM/M
Blue Bat: 1-1.5X Red Price
Production 25-100
Cards listed don't have a red version.
217 Ryne Sandberg/50 40.00
219 Tony Gwynn/50 20.00
221 Mike Schmidt/50 25.00
223 Cal Ripken Jr./50 50.00
224 Nolan Ryan/50 35.00
225 George Brett/50 30.00

Mirror Bat Gold

NM/M
Gold Bat: 1.5-3X Red Price
Production 25 Sets
Cards listed don't have a red version.
69 Greg Maddux 25.00
217 Ryne Sandberg 50.00
219 Tony Gwynn 25.00
221 Mike Schmidt 40.00
223 Cal Ripken Jr. 90.00
224 Nolan Ryan 60.00
225 George Brett 40.00
231 Roberto Clemente 90.00
233 Babe Ruth 200.00
234 Lou Gehrig 150.00
235 Ty Cobb 125.00
236 Roger Maris 40.00
239 Ted Williams 80.00

Mirror Bat Red

NM/M
Common Player: 4.00
Quantity produced listed
Black: No Pricing
Production One Set
Emerald: No Pricing
Production Five Sets
2 Adam Dunn/150 6.00
3 Adam LaRoche/250 4.00
5 Adrian Beltre/150 4.00
7 Albert Pujols/150 15.00
8 Alex Rodriguez/250 10.00
9 Alexis Rios/250 4.00
10 Alfonso Soriano/150 8.00
11 Andruw Jones/150 8.00
12 Andy Pettitte/250 6.00
13 Angel Berroa/150 4.00
15 Aubrey Huff/150 4.00
16 Austin Kearns/150 4.00
17 Barry Larkin/150 6.00
20 Bernie Williams/150 6.00
21 Bobby Abreu/150 6.00
24 Brandon Webb/150 4.00
25 Brendan Harris/250 4.00
26 Bret Boone/150 4.00
29 Brian Giles/250 4.00
35 Carl Everett/250 4.00
36 Carlos Beltran/150 6.00
37 Carlos Delgado/150 6.00
38 Carlos Lee/150 4.00
41 Chipper Jones/150 8.00
42 Cliff Floyd/250 4.00
43 Clint Barmes/250 4.00
44 Corey Patterson/250 6.00
45 Craig Biggio/150 6.00
47 Dan Haren/150 4.00
48 Darin Erstad/150 4.00
49 David Ortiz/250 8.00
50 Delmon Young/250 6.00
51 Derek Jeter/150 20.00
54 Edgar Martinez/150 6.00
55 Edgar Renteria/150 6.00
59 Eric Hinske/150 4.00
60 Eric Munson/250 4.00
61 Erubiel Durazo/250 4.00
62 Frank Thomas/150 8.00
63 Fred McGriff/150 4.00
65 Garret Anderson/150 6.00
67 Gary Sheffield/250 6.00
68 Geoff Jenkins/150 4.00
70 Hank Blalock/150 8.00
71 Hee Seop Choi/250 4.00
73 Hideo Nomo/150 8.00
76 Ivan Rodriguez /250 8.00
77 J.D. Drew/250 6.00
79 Jacque Jones/150 4.00
82 Jason Giambi/150 6.00
83 Jason Jennings/150 4.00
86 Jason Varitek/150 6.00
88 Javy Lopez/250 6.00
89 Jay Gibbons/150 4.00
91 Jeff Bagwell/150 8.00
92 Jeff Baker/250 4.00
93 Jeff Kent/150 4.00
97 Jim Edmonds/150 6.00
98 Jim Thome/150 8.00
100 Joe Borchard/150 4.00
101 Joe Crede/250 4.00
103 John Olerud/150 4.00
105 Johnny Damon/250 4.00
106 Jorge Posada/150 6.00
107 Jose Castillo/250 4.00
108 Jose Reyes/150 6.00
109 Jose Vidro/150 4.00
110 Josh Beckett/150 6.00
111 Josh Phelps/150 4.00
112 Juan Encarnacion/250 4.00
113 Juan Gonzalez/250 6.00
114 Junior Spivey/250 4.00
115 Kazuhisa Ishii/150 4.00
116 Kenny Lofton/250 4.00
117 Kerry Wood/150 8.00
119 Kevin Youkilis/250 4.00
120 Lance Berkman/150 4.00
122 Larry Walker/150 4.00
123 Luis Castillo/150 4.00
124 Luis Gonzalez/150 4.00
126 Lyle Overbay/250 4.00
127 Magglio Ordonez/150 4.00
128 Manny Ramirez/150 8.00
129 Marcus Giles/250 4.00
131 Mark Buehrle/150 4.00
132 Mark Mulder/150 6.00
133 Mark Prior/150 8.00
134 Mark Teixeira/150 6.00
135 Marlon Byrd/150 4.00
137 Miguel Cabrera/250 8.00
138 Mike Lowell/150 4.00
140 Mike Piazza/150 10.00
141 Mike Sweeney/150 4.00
143 Nick Johnson/250 4.00
144 Nomar Garciaparra/150 10.00
145 Omar Vizquel/150 4.00
146 Orlando Cabrera/250 4.00
147 Orlando Hudson/150 4.00
148 Pat Burrell/150 4.00
149 Paul Konerko/150 4.00
150 Paul LoDuca/150 4.00
152 Jermaine Dye/250 4.00
153 Preston Wilson/150 4.00
154 Rafael Furcal/150 4.00
155 Rafael Palmeiro/150 8.00
157 Rich Aurilia/250 4.00
159 Richard Hidalgo/150 4.00
160 Richie Sexson/250 6.00
161 Rickie Weeks/250 6.00
162 Roberto Alomar/250 6.00
163 Rocco Baldelli/150 4.00
164 Roger Clemens/250 12.00
168 Ryan Klesko/150 4.00
170 Sammy Sosa/150 12.00
174 Sean Casey/250 4.00
175 Shannon Stewart/150 4.00
176 Shawn Green/150 4.00
181 Todd Helton/150 8.00
183 Torii Hunter/150 6.00
184 Trot Nixon/150 6.00
185 Troy Glaus/150 6.00
186 Vernon Wells/150 4.00
187 Victor Martinez/250 4.00
188 Vladimir Guerrero/250 8.00
189 Wade Miller/250 4.00
190 Brandon Larson/175 4.00
191 Travis Hafner/150 6.00
192 Tim Salmon/150 4.00
195 Ramon Nivar/150 4.00
196 Moises Alou/250 6.00
197 Michael Young/250 4.00
198 Laynce Nix/150 4.00
199 Tino Martinez/250 4.00
200 Randall Simon/250 4.00
201 Roger Clemens/150 12.00
203 Vladimir Guerrero/150 8.00
204 Miguel Tejada/150 6.00
206 Jason Giambi/150 6.00
208 Alex Rodriguez/150 10.00
209 Alfonso Soriano/150 8.00
210 Ivan Rodriguez/150 8.00
211 Rafael Palmeiro/150 8.00
212 Gary Carter/150 8.00
216 Reggie Jackson/150 10.00
220 Don Mattingly/150 20.00
222 Rickey Henderson/150 8.00
227 Lou Brock/150 6.00
228 Andre Dawson/150 6.00
229 Rod Carew /150 8.00
230 Wade Boggs/150 6.00
240 Stan Musial/100 25.00

Mirror Bat White

NM/M
White Bat: .75-1X Red Price
Production 25-200
Cards listed don't have a red version.
219 Tony Gwynn/100 15.00
221 Mike Schmidt/100 20.00
223 Cal Ripken Jr./100 40.00
224 Nolan Ryan/100 30.00
225 George Brett/100 20.00
231 Roberto Clemente/50 65.00
233 Babe Ruth/25 200.00
234 Lou Gehrig/25 150.00
235 Ty Cobb/25 125.00
236 Roger Maris/25 40.00
239 Ted Williams/25 80.00

Mirror Combo Red

NM/M
Common (2-211): 6.00
Production 250
Common (212-239): 8.00
Production 50-250
Black Prime: No Pricing
Production One Set
2 Adam Dunn/Bat-Jsy 8.00
5 Adrian Beltre/Bat-Jsy 6.00
7 Albert Pujols/Bat-Jsy 25.00
11 Andruw Jones/Bat-Jsy 8.00
13 Angel Berroa/ Bat-Pants 6.00
15 Aubrey Huff/Bat-Jsy 6.00
16 Austin Kearns/Bat-Jsy 6.00
17 Barry Larkin/Bat-Jsy 8.00
18 Barry Zito/Bat-Jsy 6.00
19 Ben Sheets/Bat-Jsy 6.00
20 Bernie Williams/ Bat-Jsy 10.00
21 Bobby Abreu/Bat-Jsy 8.00
22 Brad Penny/Bat-Jsy 6.00
24 Brandon Webb/ Bat-Jsy 6.00
26 Bret Boone/Bat-Jsy 6.00
36 Carlos Beltran/Bat-Jsy 8.00
37 Carlos Delgado/ Bat-Jsy 8.00
38 Carlos Lee/Bat-Jsy 6.00
41 Chipper Jones/ Bat-Jsy 10.00
45 Craig Biggio/Bat-Pants 6.00
47 Dan Haren/Bat-Jsy 6.00
51 Derek Jeter/Bat-Jsy 30.00
52 Dewon Brazelton/ Glv-Jsy 6.00
54 Edgar Martinez/ Bat-Jsy 8.00
55 Edgar Renteria/Bat-Jsy 8.00
58 Eric Chavez/Bat-Jsy 8.00
59 Eric Hinske/Bat-Jsy 6.00
62 Frank Thomas/ Bat-Jsy 10.00
63 Fred McGriff/Bat-Jsy 6.00
65 Garret Anderson/ Bat-Jsy 8.00
68 Geoff Jenkins/Bat-Jsy 6.00
70 Hank Blalock/Bat-Jsy 10.00
73 Hideo Nomo/Bat-Jsy 10.00
79 Jacque Jones/Bat-Jsy 6.00
82 Jason Giambi/ Bat-Jsy 10.00
83 Jason Jennings/ Bat-Jsy 6.00
86 Jason Varitek/Bat-Jsy 10.00
89 Jay Gibbons/Bat-Jsy 6.00
91 Jeff Bagwell/Bat-Jsy 10.00
93 Jeff Kent/Bat-Jsy 6.00
97 Jim Edmonds/Bat-Jsy 8.00
98 Jim Thome/Bat-Jsy 10.00
100 Joe Borchard/Bat-Jsy 6.00
103 John Olerud/Bat-Jsy 6.00
106 Jorge Posada/Bat-Jsy 8.00
108 Jose Reyes/Bat-Jsy 8.00
109 Jose Vidro/Bat-Jsy 6.00
110 Josh Beckett/Bat-Jsy 8.00
111 Josh Phelps/Bat-Jsy 6.00
115 Kazuhisa Ishii/Bat-Jsy 6.00
117 Kerry Wood/Bat-Jsy 12.00
120 Lance Berkman/ Bat-Jsy 6.00
122 Larry Walker/Bat-Jsy 6.00
123 Luis Castillo/Bat-Jsy 6.00
124 Luis Gonzalez/Bat-Jsy 6.00
127 Magglio Ordonez/ Bat-Jsy 6.00
128 Manny Ramirez/ Bat-Jsy 10.00
131 Mark Buehrle/Bat-Jsy 6.00
132 Mark Mulder/Bat-Jsy 8.00
133 Mark Prior/Bat-Jsy 8.00
134 Mark Teixeira/Bat-Jsy 8.00
135 Marlon Byrd/Bat-Jsy 6.00
138 Mike Lowell/Bat-Jsy 6.00
140 Mike Piazza/Bat-Jsy 12.00
141 Mike Sweeney/Bat-Jsy 6.00
142 Morgan Ensberg/ Bat-Jsy 6.00
144 Nomar Garciaparra/ Bat-Jsy 12.00
145 Omar Vizquel/Bat-Jsy 6.00
147 Orlando Hudson/ Bat-Jsy 6.00
148 Pat Burrell/Bat-Jsy 6.00
149 Paul Konerko/Bat-Jsy 6.00
150 Paul LoDuca/Bat-Jsy 6.00
151 Pedro J. Martinez/ Bat-Jsy 10.00
153 Preston Wilson/ Bat-Jsy 6.00
154 Rafael Furcal/Bat-Jsy 6.00
155 Rafael Palmeiro/ Bat-Jsy 10.00
156 Randy Johnson/ Bat-Jsy 12.00
159 Richard Hidalgo/ Bat-Pants 6.00
163 Rocco Baldelli/Bat-Jsy 6.00
166 Roy Oswalt/Bat-Jsy 6.00
168 Ryan Klesko/Bat-Jsy 6.00
170 Sammy Sosa/Bat-Jsy 15.00
172 Scott Rolen/Bat-Jsy 10.00
175 Shannon Stewart/ Bat-Jsy 6.00
176 Shawn Green/Bat-Jsy 6.00
180 Tim Hudson/Bat-Jsy 8.00
181 Todd Helton/Bat-Jsy 10.00
182 Tom Glavine/Bat-Jsy 8.00
183 Torii Hunter/Bat-Jsy 8.00
184 Trot Nixon/Bat-Jsy 8.00
185 Troy Glaus/Bat-Jsy 8.00
186 Vernon Wells/Bat-Jsy 6.00
191 Travis Hafner/Bat-Jsy 8.00
192 Tim Salmon/Bat-Jsy 6.00
195 Ramon Nivar/Bat-Jsy 6.00
201 Roger Clemens/ Bat-Jsy 15.00
203 Vladimir Guerrero/ Bat-Jsy 12.00
204 Miguel Tejada/Bat-Jsy 8.00
206 Jason Giambi/Bat-Jsy 8.00
207 Curt Schilling/Bat-Jsy 8.00
208 Alex Rodriguez/ Bat-Jsy 12.00
209 Alfonso Soriano/ Bat-Jsy 10.00
210 Ivan Rodriguez/ Bat-Jsy 10.00
211 Rafael Palmeiro/ Bat-Jsy 10.00
212 Gary Carter/ Bat-Pants/250 8.00
216 Reggie Jackson/ Bat-Jsy/250 12.00
217 Ryne Sandberg/ Bat-Jsy/250 25.00
218 Dale Murphy/ Bat-Jsy/250 10.00
219 Tony Gwynn/ Bat-Jsy/250 12.00
220 Don Mattingly/ Bat-Jsy/250 25.00
221 Mike Schmidt/ Bat-Pants/250 25.00
222 Rickey Henderson/ Bat-Jsy/250 10.00
223 Cal Ripken Jr./ Bat-Jsy/250 35.00
224 Nolan Ryan/ Bat-Jsy/250 35.00
225 George Brett/ Bat-Jsy/250 25.00
227 Lou Brock/ Bat-Jsy/250 8.00
228 Andre Dawson/ Bat-Jsy/250 8.00
229 Rod Carew/ Bat-Jkt/250 10.00
230 Wade Boggs/ Bat-Jsy/250 8.00
231 Roberto Clemente/ Bat-Jsy/100 100.00
232 Roy Campanella/ Bat-Pants/100 15.00
233 Babe Ruth/ Bat-Pants/50 350.00
234 Lou Gehrig/ Bat-Pants/50 200.00
235 Ty Cobb/ Bat-Pants/50 200.00
236 Roger Maris/ Bat-Pants/100 50.00
238 Ernie Banks/ Bat-Pants/100 15.00
239 Ted Williams/ Bat-Jkt/100 85.00

Mirror Fabric Blue

NM/M
Blue: 1-1.5X Red Price
Production 25-100
Cards listed don't have red version.
217 Ryne Sandberg/100 25.00
219 Tony Gwynn/100 15.00
220 Don Mattingly/100 25.00

221 Mike Schmidt/100 20.00
223 Cal Ripken Jr./100 35.00
224 Nolan Ryan/100 25.00
225 George Brett/100 15.00
231 Roberto Clemente/25 90.00
233 Babe Ruth/25 240.00
234 Lou Gehrig/25 150.00
235 Ty Cobb/25 140.00
236 Roger Maris/25 50.00
237 Satchel Paige/25 90.00
239 Ted Williams/25 100.00

Mirror Fabric Gold

NM/M
Gold: 2-3X Red Price
Production 10-25
No pricing 20 or less.
Cards listed don't have red version.
217 Ryne Sandberg/25 45.00
219 Tony Gwynn/25 30.00
220 Don Mattingly/25 60.00
221 Mike Schmidt/25 40.00
223 Cal Ripken Jr./25 90.00
224 Nolan Ryan/25 60.00
225 George Brett/25 50.00

Mirror Fabric Red

NM/M
Common Player: 4.00
Quantity produced listed
1 A.J. Burnett/Jsy/250 4.00
2 Adam Dunn/Jsy/150 6.00
5 Adrian Beltre/Jsy/150 6.00
6 Al Leiter/Jsy/250 4.00
7 Albert Pujols/Jsy/150 15.00
11 Andruw Jones/ Jsy/150 6.00
13 Angel Berroa/ Pants/150 4.00
15 Aubrey Huff/Jsy/150 4.00
16 Austin Kearns/Jsy/150 4.00
17 Barry Larkin/Jsy/150 6.00
18 Barry Zito/Jsy/150 5.00
19 Ben Sheets/Jsy/150 4.00
20 Bernie Williams/ Jsy/150 6.00
21 Bobby Abreu/Jsy/150 6.00
22 Brad Penny/Jsy/150 4.00
27 Brett Myers/Jsy/250 4.00
33 C.C. Sabathia/Jsy/250 4.00
34 Carl Crawford/Jsy/250 4.00
36 Carlos Beltran/Jsy/150 6.00
38 Carlos Lee/Jsy/150 4.00
39 Chad Gaudin/Jsy/250 4.00
41 Chipper Jones/ Jsy/150 8.00
45 Craig Biggio/ Pants/150 4.00
47 Dan Haren/Jsy/150 4.00
48 Darin Erstad/Jsy/250 4.00
51 Derek Jeter/Jsy/150 20.00
53 Dontrelle Willis/ Jsy/250 6.00
54 Edgar Martinez/ Jsy/150 6.00
55 Edgar Renteria/ Jsy/150 6.00
58 Eric Chavez/Jsy/150 4.00
59 Eric Hinske/Jsy/150 4.00
62 Frank Thomas/Jsy/150 8.00
64 Freddy Garcia/Jsy/250 4.00
66 Garrett Atkins/Jsy/250 4.00
68 Geoff Jenkins/Jsy/150 4.00
70 Hank Blalock/Jsy/150 6.00
72 Hideki Matsui/ Base/250 15.00
73 Hideo Nomo/Jsy/150 8.00
75 Ichiro Suzuki/ Base/250 15.00
79 Jacque Jones/Jsy/150 4.00
81 Jamie Moyer/Jsy/250 4.00
82 Jason Giambi/Jsy/150 6.00
83 Jason Jennings/ Jsy/150 4.00
84 Jason Kendall/Jsy/250 4.00
86 Jason Varitek/Jsy/150 6.00
89 Jay Gibbons/Jsy/150 4.00
91 Jeff Bagwell/Jsy/150 8.00
93 Jeff Kent/Jsy/150 4.00
96 Jerome Williams/ Jsy/250 4.00
97 Jim Edmonds/Jsy/150 6.00
98 Jim Thome/Jsy/150 8.00
102 Jose Santana/Jsy/250 4.00
103 John Olerud/Jsy/150 4.00
104 John Smoltz/Jsy/250 4.00
108 Jose Reyes/Jsy/150 6.00
109 Jose Vidro/Jsy/150 4.00
110 Josh Beckett/Jsy/150 6.00
111 Josh Phelps/Jsy/150 4.00
115 Kazuhisa Ishii/Jsy/150 4.00
117 Kerry Wood/Jsy/150 8.00
118 Kevin Millwood/ Jsy/250 4.00
120 Lance Berkman/ Jsy/150 4.00
121 Larry Bigbie/Jsy/250 4.00
122 Larry Walker/Jsy/150 4.00
123 Luis Castillo/Jsy/150 4.00
124 Luis Gonzalez/Jsy/150 4.00
130 Mariano Rivera/ Jsy/250 6.00
131 Mark Buehrle/Jsy/150 4.00
133 Mark Prior/Jsy/150 8.00
135 Marlon Byrd/Jsy/150 4.00
136 Matt Morris/Jsy/250 4.00
139 Mike Mussina/Jsy/250 6.00
140 Mike Piazza/Jsy/150 10.00
141 Mike Sweeney/Jsy/150 4.00
142 Morgan Ensberg/ Jsy/150 4.00
144 Nomar Garciaparra/ Jsy/150 10.00
145 Omar Vizquel/Jsy/150 4.00
147 Orlando Hudson/ Jsy/150 4.00
148 Pat Burrell/Jsy/150 4.00
151 Pedro J. Martinez/ Jsy/150 8.00
153 Preston Wilson/ Jsy/150 4.00
154 Rafael Furcal/Jsy/150 4.00
156 Randy Johnson/ Jsy/150 8.00
158 Rich Harden/Jsy/250 4.00
159 Richard Hidalgo/ Pants/150 4.00
163 Rocco Baldelli/Jsy/150 4.00
165 Roy Halladay/Jsy/250 4.00
168 Ryan Klesko/Jsy/150 4.00
170 Sammy Sosa/ Jsy/150 12.00
172 Scott Rolen/Jsy/150 8.00
173 Sean Burroughs/ Jsy/250 4.00
175 Shannon Stewart/ Jsy/150 4.00
176 Shawn Green/Jsy/150 4.00
179 Steve Finley/Jsy/250 4.00
180 Tim Hudson/Jsy/150 6.00
181 Todd Helton/Jsy/150 8.00
182 Tom Glavine/Jsy/150 6.00
185 Troy Glaus/Jsy/150 6.00
186 Vernon Wells/Jsy/150 4.00
191 Travis Hafner/Jsy/150 6.00
192 Tim Salmon/Jsy/150 6.00
193 Tim Redding/Jsy/250 4.00
194 Runelvys Hernandez/ Jsy/250 4.00
195 Ramon Nivar/Jsy/150 4.00
201 Roger Clemens/ Jsy/150 15.00
202 Greg Maddux/ Jsy/250 10.00
203 Vladimir Guerrero/ Jsy/150 8.00
204 Miguel Tejada/Jsy/150 6.00
205 Kevin Brown/Jsy/250 4.00
206 Jason Giambi/Jsy/150 6.00
207 Curt Schilling/Jsy/150 6.00
208 Alex Rodriguez/ Jsy/150 10.00
209 Alfonso Soriano/ Jsy/150 8.00
210 Ivan Rodriguez/ Jsy/150 8.00
212 Gary Carter/Pants/150 6.00
226 Bob Gibson/Jsy/250 10.00
237 Satchel Paige/ Jsy/100 50.00

Mirror Fabric White

NM/M
White: .5-1.5X Red Price
Production 25-200
Cards listed don't have red version.
217 Ryne Sandberg/25 45.00
219 Tony Gwynn/25 25.00
220 Don Mattingly/25 50.00
221 Mike Schmidt/25 40.00
223 Cal Ripken Jr./25 90.00
224 Nolan Ryan/25 60.00
225 George Brett/25 50.00
231 Roberto Clemente/25 90.00
233 Babe Ruth/25 240.00
234 Lou Gehrig/25 150.00
235 Ty Cobb/25 140.00
236 Roger Maris/25 50.00
237 Satchel Paige/25 90.00
239 Ted Williams/25 100.00

2004 Leaf Limited

NM/M
Complete Set (275):
Common Player (1-200): 1.50
Common SP (201-229): 3.00
Production 499
Common SP (251-275): 10.00
Production 99
Pack (4): 60.00
Box (4): 200.00
1 Adam Dunn 2.00
2 Adrian Beltre 2.00
3 Albert Pujols 6.00
4 Alex Rodriguez 6.00
5 Alfonso Soriano 2.50
6 Andruw Jones 1.50
7 Andy Pettitte 1.50
8 Angel Berroa 1.50
9 Aramis Ramirez 1.50
10 Aubrey Huff 1.50
11 Aubrey Huff 1.50
12 Barry Larkin 1.50
13 Barry Zito 1.50
14 Bartolo Colon 1.50
15 Ben Sheets 1.50
16 Bernie Williams 1.50
17 Bobby Abreu 1.50
18 Brandon Webb 1.50
19 Brian Giles 1.50
20 C.C. Sabathia 1.50
21 Carlos Beltran 2.00
22 Carlos Delgado 1.50
23 Chipper Jones 3.00
24 Craig Biggio 1.50
25 Curt Schilling 3.00
26 Darin Erstad 1.50
27 Delmon Young 1.50
28 Derek Jeter 6.00
29 Derek Lee 1.50
30 Dontrelle Willis 1.50
31 Edgar Renteria 1.50
32 Eric Chavez 1.50
33 Esteban Loaiza 1.50
34 Frank Thomas 2.00
35 Fred McGriff 1.50
36 Garret Anderson 1.50
37 Gary Sheffield 1.50
38 Geoff Jenkins 1.50
39 Greg Maddux 3.00
40 Hank Blalock 2.00
41 Hideki Matsui 5.00
42 Hideo Nomo 1.50
43 Ichiro Suzuki 5.00
44 Ivan Rodriguez 2.00
45 J.D. Drew 1.50
46 Jacque Jones 1.50
47 Jae Weong Seo 1.50
48 Jake Peavy 1.50
49 Jamie Moyer 1.50
50 Jason Giambi 1.50
51 Jason Kendall 1.50
52 Jason Schmidt 1.50
53 Jason Varitek 1.50
54 Javier Vazquez 1.50
55 Javy Lopez 1.50
56 Jay Gibbons 1.50
57 Jay Payton 1.50
58 Jeff Bagwell 1.50
59 Jeff Kent 1.50
60 Jeremy Bonderman 1.50
61 Jermaine Dye 1.50
62 Jeromy Burnitz 1.50
63 Jim Edmonds 2.00
64 Jim Thome 1.50
65 Jimmy Rollins 1.50
66 Jody Gerut 1.50
67 Johan Santana 2.00
68 John Olerud 1.50
69 John Smoltz 1.50
70 Johnny Damon 1.50
71 Jorge Posada 1.50
72 Jose Contreras 1.50
73 Jose Reyes 1.50
74 Jose Vidro 1.50
75 Josh Beckett 1.50
76 Juan Gonzalez 1.50
77 Juan Pierre 1.50
78 Junior Spivey 1.50
79 Kazuhisa Ishii 1.50
80 Keith Foulke 1.50
81 Ken Griffey Jr. 3.00
82 Ken Harvey 1.50
83 Kenny Rogers 1.50
84 Kerry Wood 2.50
85 Kevin Brown 1.50
86 Kevin Millwood 1.50
87 Kip Wells 1.50
88 Lance Berkman 1.50
89 Larry Bigbie 1.50
90 Larry Walker 1.50
91 Laynce Nix 1.50
92 Luis Castillo 1.50
93 Luis Gonzalez 1.50
94 Luis Matos 1.50
95 Lyle Overbay 1.50
96 Magglio Ordonez 1.50
97 Manny Ramirez 2.00
98 Marcus Giles 1.50
99 Mark Buehrle 1.50
100 Mark Mulder 1.50
101 Mark Prior 2.00
102 Mark Teixeira 1.50
103 Marlon Byrd 1.50
104 Matt Morris 1.50
105 Melvin Mora 1.50
106 Michael Young 1.50
107 Miguel Cabrera 3.00
108 Miguel Tejada 2.00
109 Mike Lowell 1.50
110 Mike Mussina 2.00
111 Mike Piazza 4.00
112 Mike Sweeney 1.50
113 Milton Bradley 1.50
114 Moises Alou 1.50
115 Morgan Ensberg 1.50
116 Nick Johnson 1.50
117 Nomar Garciaparra 4.00
118 Omar Vizquel 1.50
119 Orlando Cabrera 1.50
120 Pat Burrell 1.50
121 Paul Konerko 1.50
122 Paul LoDuca 1.50
123 Pedro J. Martinez 3.00
124 Preston Wilson 1.50
125 Rafael Furcal 1.50
126 Rafael Palmeiro 2.00
127 Randy Johnson 3.00
128 Rich Harden 1.50
129 Richard Hidalgo 1.50
130 Richie Sexson 1.50
131 Rickie Weeks 1.50
132 Roberto Alomar 1.50
133 Robin Ventura 1.50
134 Rocco Baldelli 1.50
135 Roger Clemens 6.00
136 Roy Halladay 1.50
137 Roy Oswalt 1.50
138 Russ Ortiz 1.50
139 Ryan Klesko 1.50
140 Sammy Sosa 5.00
141 Scott Podsednik 1.50
142 Scott Rolen 3.00
143 Sean Burroughs 1.50
144 Sean Casey 1.50
145 Shannon Stewart 1.50
146 Shawn Green 1.50
147 Shigetoshi Hasegawa 1.50
148 Sidney Ponson 1.50
149 Steve Finley 1.50
150 Tim Hudson 1.50
151 Tim Salmon 1.50
152 Tino Martinez 1.50
153 Todd Helton 2.00
154 Tom Glavine 2.00
155 Torii Hunter 1.50
156 Trot Nixon 1.50
157 Troy Glaus 1.50
158 Vernon Wells 1.50
159 Victor Martinez 1.50
160 Vinny Castilla 1.50
161 Vladimir Guerrero 3.00
162 Alex Rodriguez 6.00
163 Alfonso Soriano 2.50
164 Andy Pettitte 1.50
165 Curt Schilling 3.00
166 Gary Sheffield 1.50
167 Greg Maddux 3.00
168 Hideo Nomo 1.50
169 Ivan Rodriguez 2.00
170 Jason Giambi 1.50
171 Jim Thome 2.00
172 Juan Gonzalez 1.50
173 Ken Griffey Jr. 3.00
174 Kevin Brown 1.50
175 Manny Ramirez 2.00
176 Miguel Tejada 2.00
177 Mike Mussina 1.50
178 Mike Piazza 4.00
179 Pedro Martinez 3.00
180 Rafael Palmeiro 2.00
181 Randy Johnson 3.00
182 Roger Clemens 6.00
183 Scott Rolen 3.00
184 Shawn Green 1.50
185 Tom Glavine 1.50
186 Vladimir Guerrero 3.00
187 Alex Rodriguez 6.00
188 Mike Piazza 4.00
189 Randy Johnson 3.00
190 Roger Clemens 6.00
191 Albert Pujols 6.00
192 Barry Zito 1.50
193 Chipper Jones 3.00
194 Garret Anderson 1.50
195 Jeff Bagwell 2.00
196 Josh Beckett 1.50
197 Magglio Ordonez 1.50

198 Mark Prior 2.00
199 Sammy Sosa 5.00
200 Todd Helton 2.00
201 Andre Dawson 3.00
202 Babe Ruth 8.00
203 Bob Feller 4.00
204 Bob Gibson 4.00
205 Bobby Doerr 3.00
206 Cal Ripken Jr. 10.00
207 Dale Murphy 4.00
208 Don Mattingly 8.00
209 Gary Carter 3.00
210 George Brett 8.00
211 Jackie Robinson 5.00
212 Lou Brock 4.00
213 Lou Gehrig 6.00
214 Mark Grace 4.00
215 Maury Wills 3.00
216 Mike Schmidt 8.00
217 Nolan Ryan 8.00
218 Orel Hershiser 3.00
219 Paul Molitor 4.00
220 Roberto Clemente 8.00
221 Rod Carew 4.00
222 Roy Campanella 4.00
223 Ryne Sandberg 8.00
224 Stan Musial 6.00
225 Ted Williams 8.00
226 Tony Gwynn 6.00
227 Ty Cobb 5.00
228 Whitey Ford 4.00
229 Yogi Berra 4.00
230 Carlos Beltran 3.00
231 David Ortiz 3.00
232 David Ortiz 3.00
233 Carlos Zambrano 1.50
234 Carlos Lee 1.50
235 Travis Hafner 1.50
236 Brad Penny 1.50
237 Wade Miller 1.50
238 Edgar Martinez 1.50
239 Carl Crawford 1.50
240 Roy Oswalt 1.50
241 Kazuo Matsui 8.00
242 Carlos Beltran 3.00
243 Carlos Beltran 3.00
244 Miguel Cabrera 2.00
245 Scott Rolen 3.00
246 Hank Blalock 2.00
247 Vernon Wells 1.50
248 Adam Dunn 2.00
249 Preston Wilson 1.50
250 Victor Martinez 1.50
251 Aarom Baldiris **RC** 10.00
252 Akinori Otsuka **RC** 35.00
253 Andres Blanco **RC** 10.00
254 Brad Halsey **RC** 10.00
255 Joey Gathright **RC** 25.00
256 Colby Miller **RC** 10.00
257 Fernando Nieve **RC** 10.00
258 Freddy Guzman **RC** 15.00
259 Hector Gimenez **RC** 10.00
260 Jake Woods **RC** 10.00
261 Jason Bartlett **RC** 10.00
262 John Gall **RC** 15.00
263 Jose Capellan **RC** 35.00
264 Josh Labandeira **RC** 10.00
265 Justin Germano **RC** 10.00
266 Kazuhito Tadano **RC** 40.00
267 Lance Cormier **RC** 10.00
268 Merkin Valdez **RC** 20.00
269 Mike Gosling 10.00
270 Ramon Ramirez **RC** 10.00
271 Rusty Tucker **RC** 10.00
272 Shawn Hill **RC** 10.00
273 Shingo Takatsu **RC** 40.00
274 William Bergolla **RC** 10.00
275 Yadier Molina **RC** 20.00

Bronze Spotlight

Bronze: 1-2X
Production 100 Sets

Limited Silver Spotlight

Silver (1-250): 2-3X
Production 50 Sets

Gold Spotlight

Golds (1-250): 3-5X
Production 25 Sets

Platinum Spotlight

No Pricing
Production One Set

Barrels

No Pricing
Production 1-5

Cuts

NM/M
Quantity produced listed
1 Nolan Ryan/100 125.00
2 Bob Gibson/50 40.00
3 Harmon Killebrew/100 40.00
4 Duke Snider/100 30.00
5 George Brett/100 75.00
6 Stan Musial/100 80.00
7 Alan Trammell/100 20.00
8 Cal Ripken Jr./100 180.00
9 Steve Carlton/50 40.00
10 Phil Rizzuto/100 30.00
11 Mark Prior/50 40.00
12 Will Clark/100 40.00
13 Lou Brock/100 30.00
14 Ozzie Smith/100 60.00
15 Bob Feller/100 30.00
16 Gary Carter/50 25.00
17 Al Kaline/100 40.00
18 Brooks Robinson/100 40.00
19 Tony Gwynn/100 50.00
20 Mike Schmidt/100 75.00
21 Ralph Kiner/50 40.00
22 Jim Palmer/50 40.00
23 Don Mattingly/100 75.00
24 Paul Molitor/50 40.00
25 Dale Murphy/100 30.00

Cuts Gold

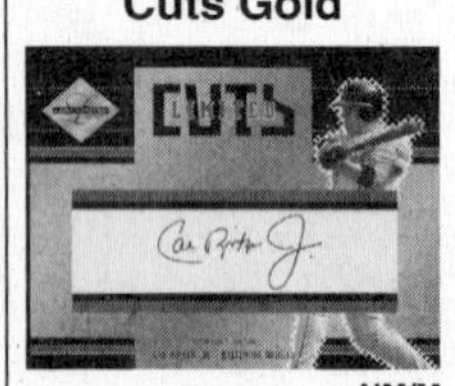

NM/M
Quantity produced listed
1 Nolan Ryan/34 200.00
2 Bob Gibson/45 40.00
9 Steve Carlton/32 50.00
11 Mark Prior/22 60.00
12 Will Clark/22 65.00
13 Lou Brock/20 50.00
15 Bob Feller/28 50.00
19 Tony Gwynn/19 100.00
20 Mike Schmidt/20 100.00
22 Jim Palmer/22 50.00
23 Don Mattingly/23 100.00

Legends Material Number

NM/M
Quantity produced listed
1 Al Kaline/Pants/50 15.00
2 Babe Ruth/Pants/50 160.00
3 Bob Feller/Jsy/50 10.00
4 Bob Gibson/Jsy/50 10.00
6 Burleigh Grimes/Pants/100 40.00
7 Carl Yastrzemski/Jsy/100 15.00
8 Harmon Killebrew/Jsy/25 25.00
9 Hoyt Wilhelm/Jsy/100 5.00
10 Johnny Mize/Pants/100 10.00
11 Ernie Banks/Pants/50 15.00
12 Lou Brock/Jsy/50 10.00
13 Luis Aparicio/Pants/100 5.00
14 Pee Wee Reese/Jsy/50 10.00
15 Reggie Jackson/Jsy/100 10.00
16 Red Schoendienst/Jsy/50 8.00
17 Roberto Clemente/Jsy/25 80.00
18 Roger Maris/Pants/100 25.00
19 Stan Musial/Jsy/100 20.00
20 Ted Williams/Jsy/50 75.00
21 Ty Cobb/Pants/50 80.00
22 Warren Spahn/Jsy/100 10.00
23 Whitey Ford/Pants/100 10.00
24 Yogi Berra/Jsy/50 15.00
25 Satchel Paige/CO Jsy/100 50.00

Legends Material Autographs Number

NM/M
Quantity produced listed
1 Al Kaline/Pants/50 50.00
3 Bob Feller/Jsy/50 30.00
4 Bob Gibson/Jsy/50 30.00
7 Carl Yastrzemski/Jsy/25 80.00
8 Harmon Killebrew/Jsy/25 65.00
9 Hoyt Wilhelm/Jsy/25 40.00
12 Lou Brock/Jsy/50 30.00
13 Luis Aparicio/Pants/50 20.00
15 Reggie Jackson/Jsy/50 50.00
16 Red Schoendienst/Jsy/50 30.00
19 Stan Musial/Jsy/50 75.00
23 Whitey Ford/Pants/25 50.00
24 Yogi Berra/Jsy/25 75.00

Legends Material Position

NM/M
Quantity produced listed
1 Al Kaline/Pants/50 15.00
2 Babe Ruth/Pants/50 160.00
3 Bob Feller/Jsy/50 10.00
4 Bob Gibson/Jsy/50 10.00
6 Burleigh Grimes/Pants/100 40.00
7 Carl Yastrzemski/Jsy/100 15.00
8 Harmon Killebrew/Jsy/25 25.00
9 Hoyt Wilhelm/Jsy/100 5.00
10 Johnny Mize/Pants/100 10.00
11 Ernie Banks/Pants/50 15.00
12 Lou Brock/Jsy/50 10.00
13 Luis Aparicio/Pants/100 5.00
14 Pee Wee Reese/Jsy/50 10.00
15 Reggie Jackson/Jsy/100 10.00
16 Red Schoendienst/Jsy/50 8.00
17 Roberto Clemente/Jsy/25 80.00
18 Roger Maris/Pants/100 25.00
19 Stan Musial/Jsy/100 20.00
20 Ted Williams/Jsy/50 75.00
21 Ty Cobb/Pants/50 80.00
22 Warren Spahn/Jsy/100 10.00
23 Whitey Ford/Pants/100 10.00
24 Yogi Berra/Jsy/50 15.00
25 Satchel Paige/CO Jsy/100 60.00

Legends Material Autographs Position

NM/M
Quantity produced listed
1 Al Kaline/Pants/50 50.00
3 Bob Feller/Jsy/50 30.00
4 Bob Gibson/Jsy/50 30.00
7 Carl Yastrzemski/Jsy/25 80.00
8 Harmon Killebrew/Jsy/25 65.00
9 Hoyt Wilhelm/Jsy/25 40.00
12 Lou Brock/Jsy/50 30.00
13 Luis Aparicio/Pants/50 20.00
15 Reggie Jackson/Jsy/50 50.00
16 Red Schoendienst/Jsy/50 30.00
19 Stan Musial/Jsy/50 75.00
23 Whitey Ford/Pants/25 50.00
24 Yogi Berra/Jsy/25 75.00

Lumberjacks

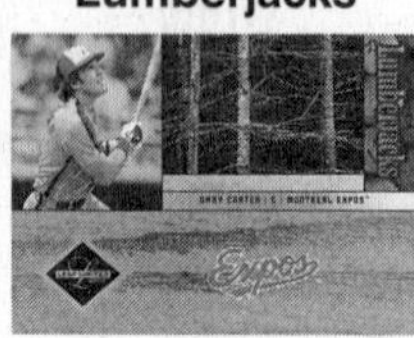

NM/M
Common Player: 2.00
Quantity produced listed
Black: 1-30X
Production 16-100
1 Al Kaline/399 4.00
2 Albert Pujols/114 15.00
3 Andre Dawson/438 2.00
4 Babe Ruth/714 8.00
5 Bo Jackson/141 5.00
6 Bobby Doerr/223 3.00
7 Brooks Robinson/268 4.00
8 Cal Ripken Jr./431 10.00
9 Carlton Fisk/376 2.00
10 Dale Murphy/398 2.00
11 Darryl Strawberry/335 2.00
12 Don Mattingly/222 6.00
13 Duke Snider/407 3.00
14 Eddie Mathews/512 3.00
15 Eddie Murray/504 3.00
16 Frank Robinson/586 3.00
17 Frank Thomas/418 3.00
18 Gary Carter/324 2.00
19 George Brett/317 6.00
20 Harmon Killebrew/573 4.00
22 Lou Gehrig/493 5.00
23 Mark Grace/173 2.00
24 Mike Piazza/358 4.00
25 Mike Schmidt/548 5.00
26 Orlando Cepeda/379 2.00
27 Rafael Palmeiro/528 2.00
28 Ralph Kiner/369 2.00
29 Reggie Jackson/563 3.00
30 Rickey Henderson/297 3.00
31 Roger Maris/275 5.00
32 Ryne Sandberg/282 4.00
33 Sammy Sosa/539 4.00
34 Scott Rolen/192 4.00
35 Stan Musial/475 4.00
36 Ted Williams/521 6.00
37 Thurman Munson/113 5.00
38 Vladimir Guerrero/234 4.00
39 Willie McCovey/521 2.00
40 Willie Stargell/475 2.00
41 Roberto Clemente, Stan Musial 6.00
42 Cal Ripken Jr., Ernie Banks 10.00
43 Babe Ruth, Lou Gehrig 8.00
44 George Brett, Mike Schmidt 8.00
45 Frank Robinson, Jackie Robinson 4.00
46 Don Mattingly, Roger Maris 8.00
47 Nomar Garciaparra, Ted Williams 8.00
48 Johnny Bench, Mike Piazza 4.00
49 Reggie Jackson, Sammy Sosa 4.00
50 Mel Ott, Willie McCovey 4.00

Lumberjacks Autographs

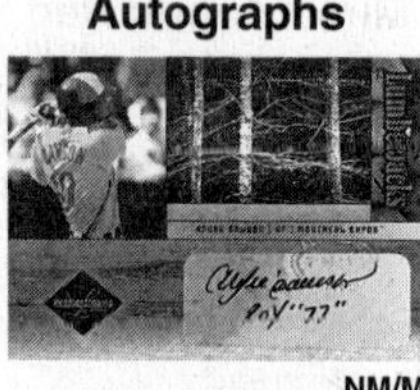

NM/M
Quantity produced listed
1 Al Kaline/100 30.00
3 Andre Dawson/100 15.00
5 Bo Jackson/25 60.00
6 Bobby Doerr/100 20.00
7 Brooks Robinson/100 50.00
8 Cal Ripken Jr./25 180.00
9 Carlton Fisk/25 30.00
10 Dale Murphy/100 20.00
11 Darryl Strawberry/100 15.00
12 Don Mattingly/25 70.00
13 Duke Snider/100 20.00
16 Frank Robinson/100 20.00
17 Frank Thomas/50 50.00
18 Gary Carter/100 15.00
19 George Brett/25 70.00
20 Harmon Killebrew/100 40.00
23 Mark Grace/25 40.00
25 Mike Schmidt/50 65.00
28 Ralph Kiner/100 20.00
29 Reggie Jackson/25 50.00
30 Rickey Henderson/25 50.00
32 Ryne Sandberg/25 90.00
34 Scott Rolen/25 40.00
35 Stan Musial/50 65.00
39 Willie McCovey/25 30.00

Lumberjacks Autographs Bat

NM/M
Quantity produced listed
1 Al Kaline/100 40.00
3 Andre Dawson/50 20.00
5 Bo Jackson/25 70.00
6 Bobby Doerr/50 25.00
7 Brooks Robinson/50 60.00
8 Cal Ripken Jr./25 200.00
9 Carlton Fisk/25 40.00
10 Dale Murphy/100 25.00
11 Darryl Strawberry/25 25.00
12 Don Mattingly/25 80.00
17 Frank Thomas/25 70.00
18 Gary Carter/50 20.00
19 George Brett/25 80.00
20 Harmon Killebrew/50 50.00
23 Mark Grace/17 50.00
25 Mike Schmidt/25 80.00
28 Ralph Kiner/100 25.00
29 Reggie Jackson/25 60.00
32 Ryne Sandberg/25 90.00
34 Scott Rolen/25 50.00
35 Stan Musial/50 75.00
39 Willie McCovey/25 40.00

Lumberjacks Autographs Jersey

NM/M
Quantity produced listed
1 Al Kaline Pants/100 40.00
3 Andre Dawson/50 20.00
5 Bo Jackson/25 70.00
6 Bobby Doerr/100 15.00
7 Brooks Robinson/25 75.00
8 Cal Ripken Jr./25 200.00
9 Carlton Fisk/50 30.00
10 Dale Murphy/100 25.00
11 Darryl Strawberry/Pants/25 25.00
12 Don Mattingly/25 80.00
15 Eddie Murray/25 70.00
16 Frank Robinson/50 30.00
17 Frank Thomas/25 70.00
18 Gary Carter/50 20.00
19 George Brett/25 80.00
20 Harmon Killebrew/25 60.00
23 Mark Grace/17 50.00
25 Mike Schmidt/25 80.00
26 Orlando Cepeda/Pants/50 20.00
29 Reggie Jackson/25 60.00
32 Ryne Sandberg/25 90.00
34 Scott Rolen/25 50.00
35 Stan Musial/50 75.00
39 Willie McCovey/25 40.00

Lumberjacks Barrel

Quantity produced listed
No Pricing
Production 1-5

Lumberjacks Bat

NM/M
Quantity produced listed
1 Al Kaline/100 15.00
2 Albert Pujols/100 15.00
3 Andre Dawson/25 15.00
4 Babe Ruth/100 125.00
5 Bo Jackson/50 15.00
6 Bobby Doerr/25 12.00
7 Brooks Robinson/100 20.00
8 Cal Ripken Jr./100 40.00
9 Carlton Fisk/100 10.00
10 Dale Murphy/50 15.00
11 Darryl Strawberry/25 15.00
12 Don Mattingly/100 20.00
14 Eddie Mathews/100 10.00
15 Eddie Murray/100 15.00
16 Frank Robinson/100 8.00
17 Frank Thomas/25 20.00
18 Gary Carter/50 10.00
19 George Brett/100 20.00
20 Harmon Killebrew/100 15.00
21 Hideki Matsui/100 25.00
22 Lou Gehrig/100 100.00
23 Mark Grace/25 15.00
24 Mike Piazza/50 15.00
25 Mike Schmidt/100 15.00
26 Orlando Cepeda/50 8.00
27 Rafael Palmeiro/50 10.00
28 Ralph Kiner/100 8.00
29 Reggie Jackson/100 10.00
30 Rickey Henderson/100 10.00
31 Roger Maris/100 25.00
32 Ryne Sandberg/100 15.00
33 Sammy Sosa/100 10.00
34 Scott Rolen/25 15.00
35 Stan Musial/100 25.00
36 Ted Williams/100 50.00
37 Thurman Munson/100 20.00
38 Vladimir Guerrero/25 15.00
39 Willie McCovey/100 10.00
40 Willie Stargell/100 10.00
41 Roberto Clemente, Stan Musial/100 85.00
42 Cal Ripken Jr., Ernie Banks/50 100.00
43 Babe Ruth, Lou Gehrig/25 250.00
44 George Brett, Mike Schmidt/50 50.00
46 Don Mattingly, Roger Maris/50 40.00
47 Nomar Garciaparra, Ted Williams/100 75.00
48 Johnny Bench, Mike Piazza/25 35.00
49 Reggie Jackson, Sammy Sosa/50 20.00
50 Mel Ott, Willie McCovey/100 40.00

Lumberjacks Jersey

NM/M
Quantity produced listed
1 Al Kaline/Pants/50 20.00
2 Albert Pujols/100 15.00
3 Andre Dawson/25 15.00
4 Babe Ruth/25 300.00
5 Bo Jackson/100 10.00
6 Bobby Doerr/100 5.00
7 Brooks Robinson/25 30.00
8 Cal Ripken Jr./100 40.00
9 Carlton Fisk/100 10.00
10 Dale Murphy/100 10.00
11 Darryl Strawberry/Pants/50 8.00
12 Don Mattingly/100 20.00
14 Eddie Mathews/100 10.00
15 Eddie Murray/50 20.00
16 Frank Robinson/50 10.00
17 Frank Thomas/100 10.00
18 Gary Carter/50 10.00
19 George Brett/100 20.00
20 Harmon Killebrew/25 30.00
21 Hideki Matsui/100 25.00
22 Lou Gehrig/25 180.00
23 Mark Grace/100 8.00
24 Mike Piazza/100 10.00
25 Mike Schmidt/100 15.00
26 Orlando Cepeda/Pants/100 5.00
27 Rafael Palmeiro/50 10.00
29 Reggie Jackson/100 10.00
30 Rickey Henderson/100 10.00
31 Roger Maris/100 25.00
32 Ryne Sandberg/100 15.00
33 Sammy Sosa/100 10.00
34 Scott Rolen/50 10.00
35 Stan Musial/50 30.00
36 Ted Williams/100 50.00
37 Thurman Munson/100 20.00
38 Vladimir Guerrero/50 10.00
39 Willie McCovey/100 10.00
40 Willie Stargell/100 8.00
41 Roberto Clemente, Stan Musial/50 120.00
42 Cal Ripken Jr., Ernie Banks/Pants/100 65.00
43 Babe Ruth, Lou Gehrig/25 400.00
44 George Brett, Mike Schmidt/Jkt/100 30.00
45 Frank Robinson, Jackie Robinson/25 30.00
46 Don Mattingly, Roger Maris/Pants/100 25.00
47 Johnny Bench, Mike Piazza/100 10.00
49 Reggie Jackson, Sammy Sosa/100 15.00
50 Mel Ott Pants, Willie McCovey/25 80.00

Lumberjacks Combos

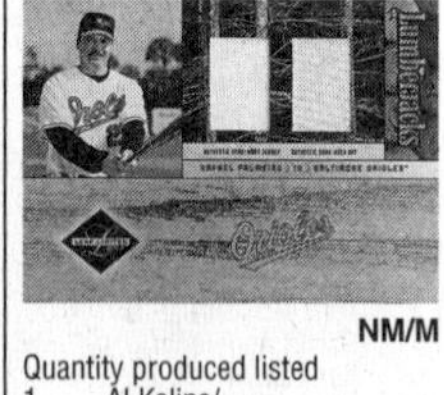

NM/M
Quantity produced listed
1 Al Kaline/Bat-Pants/100 20.00
2 Albert Pujols/Bat-Jsy/100 20.00
3 Andre Dawson/Bat-Jsy/50 15.00
4 Babe Ruth/Bat-Jsy/25 400.00
5 Bo Jackson/Bat-Jsy/50 20.00
6 Bobby Doerr/Bat-Jsy/50 12.00
7 Brooks Robinson/Bat-Jsy/25 40.00
8 Cal Ripken Jr./Bat-Jsy/100 50.00
9 Carlton Fisk/Bat-Jsy/50 15.00
10 Dale Murphy/Bat-Jsy/100 15.00
11 Darryl Strawberry/Bat-Pants/25 15.00
12 Don Mattingly/Bat-Jsy/100 25.00
14 Eddie Mathews/Bat-Jsy/50 15.00
15 Eddie Murray/Bat-Jsy/50 20.00
16 Frank Robinson/Bat-Jsy/100 15.00
17 Frank Thomas/Bat-Jsy/50 20.00

18 Gary Carter/Bat-Jsy/50 10.00
19 George Brett/Bat-Jsy/100 25.00
20 Harmon Killebrew/Bat-Jsy/50 30.00
21 Hideki Matsui/Bat-Jsy/100 30.00
22 Lou Gehrig/Bat-Jsy/25 250.00
23 Mark Grace/Bat-Jsy/17 30.00
24 Mike Piazza/Bat-Jsy/100 15.00
25 Mike Schmidt/Bat-Jsy/100 20.00
26 Orlando Cepeda/Bat-Pants/50 10.00
27 Rafael Palmeiro/Bat-Jsy/50 15.00
29 Reggie Jackson/Bat-Jsy/100 15.00
30 Rickey Henderson/Bat-Jsy/100 15.00
31 Roger Maris/Bat-Jsy/50 40.00
32 Ryne Sandberg/Bat-Jsy/50 25.00
33 Sammy Sosa/Bat-Jsy/100 15.00
34 Scott Rolen/Bat-Jsy/25 20.00
35 Stan Musial/Bat-Jsy/100 30.00
36 Ted Williams/Bat-Jsy/50 75.00
37 Thurman Munson/Bat-Jsy/100 25.00
38 Vladimir Guerrero/Bat-Jsy/50 15.00
39 Willie McCovey/Bat-Jsy/100 15.00
40 Willie Stargell/Bat-Jsy/100 12.00

Matching Numbers

NM/M
Quantity produced listed
Prime: No Pricing
Production One Set
1 Bobby Doerr/Jsy, Pee Wee Reese/Jsy/100 10.00
2 Lou Gehrig/Pants, Mel Ott/Jsy/50 160.00
3 Albert Pujols/Jsy, George Brett/Jsy/100 30.00
4 Cal Ripken Jr./Jsy, Carl Yastrzemski/Jsy/100 50.00
5 Dwight Gooden/Jsy, Whitey Ford/Pants/50 15.00
6 Mark Grace/Jsy, Todd Helton/Jsy/25 25.00
7 Robin Yount/Jsy, Tony Gwynn/Jsy/50 40.00
8 Frank Robinson/Jsy, Mike Schmidt/Jsy/100 25.00
9 Roberto Clemente/Jsy, Sammy Sosa/Jsy/100 75.00
10 Roger Clemens/Jsy, Warren Spahn/Pant/100 25.00
11 Mark Prior/Jsy, Roger Clemens/Jsy/50 15.00
12 Don Mattingly/Jkt, Ryne Sandberg/Jsy/100 30.00
13 Billy Williams/Jsy, Wade Boggs/Jsy/100 10.00
14 Jim "Catfish" Hunter/Jsy, Juan Marichal/Jsy/50 10.00
15 Fergie Jenkins/Pants, Greg Maddux/Jsy/50 20.00
16 Kerry Wood/Pants, Nolan Ryan/Jsy/100 35.00
17 Rickey Henderson/Jsy, Roger Maris/Pants/100 40.00
18 Dontrelle Willis/Jsy, Mike Mussina/Jsy/50 15.00
19 Reggie Jackson/Jsy, Willie McCovey/Jsy/100 15.00
20 Bob Gibson/Jsy, Pedro Martinez/Jsy/50 15.00
21 Duke Snider/Jsy, Paul Molitor/Jsy/100 10.00
22 Johnny Bench/Jsy, Lou Boudreau/Jsy/100 15.00
23 Andre Dawson/Jsy, Chipper Jones/Jsy/100 15.00
24 Ernie Banks/Jsy, Boyer/Jsy/100 15.00
25 Manny Ramirez/Jsy, Rickey Henderson/Jsy/100 15.00
26 Carlton Fisk/Jsy, Scott Rolen/Jsy/100 15.00
27 Nolan Ryan/Jsy, Orlando Cepeda/Pnt/100 25.00
28 Roy Halladay/Jsy, Steve Carlton/Jsy/100 8.00
29 Eddie Mathews/Jsy, Tom Seaver/Jsy/100 15.00
30 Brandon Webb/Jsy, Orel Hershiser/Jsy/100 10.00

Moniker Bat

NM/M
Quanity produced listed
1 Adam Dunn/50 30.00
5 Alfonso Soriano/25 50.00
6 Andruw Jones/25 40.00
8 Angel Berroa/25 15.00
9 Aramis Ramirez/25 25.00
10 Aubrey Huff/25 25.00
15 Ben Sheets/25 25.00
21 Carlos Beltran/50 40.00
24 Craig Biggio/25 40.00
27 Delmon Young/50 30.00
30 Dontrelle Willis/25 30.00
31 Edgar Renteria/25 25.00
34 Frank Thomas/25 70.00
35 Fred McGriff/50 30.00
36 Garret Anderson/50 20.00
37 Gary Sheffield/25 40.00
40 Hank Blalock/50 35.00
61 Jermaine Dye/25 25.00
71 Jorge Posada/25 50.00
84 Kerry Wood/25 50.00
88 Lance Berkman/25 40.00
100 Mark Mulder/50 20.00
101 Mark Prior/50 40.00
102 Mark Teixeira/25 40.00
106 Michael Young/50 15.00
107 Miguel Cabrera/40 40.00
109 Mike Lowell/25 25.00
122 Paul LoDuca/25 25.00
124 Preston Wilson/25 20.00
131 Rickie Weeks/25 25.00
137 Roy Oswalt/25 20.00
144 Sean Casey/50 20.00
145 Shannon Stewart/25 25.00
155 Torii Hunter/25 25.00
156 Trot Nixon/25 25.00
158 Vernon Wells/50 20.00
159 Victor Martinez/50 25.00
163 Alfonso Soriano/25 50.00
166 Gary Sheffield/25 35.00
194 Garret Anderson/50 20.00
198 Mark Prior/50 40.00
201 Andre Dawson/50 20.00
205 Bobby Doerr/25 25.00
207 Dale Murphy/25 25.00
208 Don Mattingly/50 75.00
209 Gary Carter/100 15.00
212 Lou Brock/50 30.00
214 Mark Grace/25 30.00
216 Mike Schmidt/50 75.00
217 Nolan Ryan/50 150.00
219 Paul Molitor/50 30.00
221 Rod Carew/50 35.00
223 Ryne Sandberg/25 80.00
224 Stan Musial/50 75.00
226 Tony Gwynn/50 50.00
230 Carlos Beltran/50 40.00
231 David Ortiz/50 60.00
232 David Ortiz/50 60.00
234 Carlos Lee/50 20.00
235 Travis Hafner/25 25.00
238 Edgar Martinez/25 40.00
240 Roy Oswalt/25 30.00
242 Carlos Beltran/50 45.00
243 Carlos Beltran/50 45.00
244 Miguel Cabrera/50 40.00
246 Hank Blalock/50 35.00
247 Vernon Wells/50 20.00
248 Adam Dunn/50 35.00
249 Preston Wilson/25 25.00
250 Victor Martinez/25 25.00

Moniker Bronze

NM/M
Quanity produced listed
Silver: .5-1.5X
Production 1-50
No pricing 15 or less.
Platinum: No Pricing
Production One Set
1 Adam Dunn/50 30.00
3 Albert Pujols/25 180.00
5 Alfonso Soriano/100 30.00
6 Andruw Jones/50 30.00
8 Angel Berroa/25 15.00
11 Austin Kearns/50 20.00
18 Brandon Webb/21 15.00
21 Carlos Beltran/50 40.00
23 Chipper Jones/25 65.00
24 Craig Biggio/5 40.00
30 Dontrelle Willis/25 30.00
31 Edgar Renteria/25 25.00
34 Frank Thomas/50 60.00
36 Garret Anderson/50 20.00
37 Gary Sheffield/50 25.00
39 Greg Maddux/25 85.00
40 Hank Blalock/50 35.00
46 Jacque Jones/25 25.00
58 Jeff Bagwell/25 75.00
71 Jorge Posada/25 50.00
76 Juan Gonzalez/25 30.00
79 Kazuhisa Ishii/25 35.00
84 Kerry Wood/25 50.00
88 Lance Berkman/50 30.00
98 Marcus Giles/25 25.00
100 Mark Mulder/100 15.00
101 Mark Prior/50 40.00
102 Mark Teixeira/50 30.00
106 Michael Young/50 15.00
107 Miguel Cabrera/50 40.00
109 Mike Lowell/25 25.00
122 Paul LoDuca/25 25.00
131 Rickie Weeks/25 25.00
137 Roy Oswalt/10 20.00
140 Sammy Sosa/25 85.00
142 Scott Rolen/25 60.00
144 Sean Casey/25 25.00
145 Shannon Stewart/25 25.00
153 Todd Helton/25 40.00
155 Torii Hunter/50 20.00
156 Trot Nixon/25 25.00
158 Vernon Wells/25 25.00
163 Alfonso Soriano/100 30.00
166 Gary Sheffield/10 30.00
167 Greg Maddux/5 80.00
172 Juan Gonzalez/25 40.00
183 Scott Rolen/25 50.00
191 Albert Pujols/5 180.00
193 Chipper Jones/5 65.00
194 Garret Anderson/10 20.00
195 Jeff Bagwell/25 75.00
198 Mark Prior/50 40.00
199 Sammy Sosa/25 80.00
200 Todd Helton/25 40.00
201 Andre Dawson/100 15.00
203 Bob Feller/100 20.00
204 Bob Gibson/100 20.00
205 Bobby Doerr/100 15.00
206 Cal Ripken Jr./25 180.00
207 Dale Murphy/100 25.00
208 Don Mattingly/100 60.00
209 Gary Carter/100 15.00
210 George Brett/25 75.00
212 Lou Brock/100 20.00
214 Mark Grace/100 20.00
215 Maury Wills/100 15.00
216 Mike Schmidt/100 60.00
217 Nolan Ryan/100 120.00
218 Orel Hershiser/25 40.00
219 Paul Molitor/100 25.00
221 Rod Carew/100 25.00
223 Ryne Sandberg/100 50.00
224 Stan Musial/100 60.00
226 Tony Gwynn/100 40.00
230 Carlos Beltran/50 45.00
231 David Ortiz/50 60.00
232 David Ortiz/50 60.00
233 Carlos Zambrano/25 30.00
234 Carlos Lee/25 20.00
238 Edgar Martinez/25 40.00
240 Roy Oswalt/50 20.00
242 Carlos Beltran/50 40.00
243 Carlos Beltran/50 40.00
244 Miguel Cabrera/50 40.00
245 Scott Rolen/25 50.00
246 Hank Blalock/50 35.00
247 Vernon Wells/25 25.00
248 Adam Dunn/50 35.00

Moniker Gold

NM/M
Quanity produced listed
5 Alfonso Soriano/25 40.00
21 Carlos Beltran/25 50.00
100 Mark Mulder/25 25.00
163 Alfonso Soriano/25 40.00
201 Andre Dawson/25 20.00
203 Bob Feller/25 35.00
204 Bob Gibson/25 40.00
205 Bobby Doerr/25 25.00
207 Dale Murphy/25 40.00
208 Don Mattingly/25 90.00
209 Gary Carter/25 25.00
212 Lou Brock/25 30.00
214 Mark Grace/25 30.00
215 Maury Wills/25 25.00
216 Mike Schmidt/25 85.00
217 Nolan Ryan/25 150.00
219 Paul Molitor/25 40.00
221 Rod Carew/25 35.00
223 Ryne Sandberg/25 75.00
224 Stan Musial/25 100.00
226 Tony Gwynn/25 50.00

Moniker Jersey

NM/M
Quanity produced listed
Prime: No Pricing
Production One Set
1 Adam Dunn/50 30.00
5 Alfonso Soriano/50 40.00
6 Andruw Jones/25 40.00
8 Angel Berroa/Pants/25 15.00
9 Aramis Ramirez/25 25.00
10 Aubrey Huff/25 25.00
11 Austin Kearns/25 25.00
15 Ben Sheets/25 25.00
18 Brandon Webb/25 15.00
20 C.C. Sabathia/25 25.00
21 Carlos Beltran/50 40.00
23 Chipper Jones/25 65.00
24 Craig Biggio/25 40.00
30 Dontrelle Willis/25 30.00
32 Eric Chavez/50 20.00
34 Frank Thomas/25 70.00
35 Fred McGriff/25 40.00
36 Garret Anderson/50 20.00
40 Hank Blalock/50 35.00
46 Jacque Jones/25 25.00
63 Jim Edmonds/25 40.00
66 Jody Gerut/25 15.00
67 Johan Santana/25 40.00
71 Jorge Posada/25 50.00
74 Jose Vidro/25 15.00
84 Kerry Wood/25 50.00
88 Lance Berkman/25 40.00
89 Larry Bigbie/25 20.00
98 Marcus Giles/25 25.00
99 Mark Buehrle/25 25.00
100 Mark Mulder/75 15.00
101 Mark Prior/50 40.00
102 Mark Teixeira/25 40.00
105 Melvin Mora/25 25.00
107 Miguel Cabrera/38 40.00
109 Mike Lowell/25 25.00
115 Morgan Ensberg/25 15.00
122 Paul LoDuca/25 25.00
124 Preston Wilson/25 25.00
137 Roy Oswalt/25 25.00
142 Scott Rolen/50 50.00
143 Sean Burroughs/25 25.00
144 Sean Casey/25 25.00
145 Shannon Stewart/25 25.00
149 Steve Finley/25 25.00
153 Todd Helton/25 40.00
154 Tom Glavine/25 40.00
155 Torii Hunter/25 25.00
156 Trot Nixon/25 25.00
158 Vernon Wells/50 20.00
159 Victor Martinez/50 20.00
163 Alfonso Soriano/50 40.00
166 Gary Sheffield/25 40.00
172 Juan Gonzalez/25 40.00
183 Scott Rolen/50 40.00
185 Tom Glavine/25 40.00
193 Chipper Jones/25 65.00
194 Garret Anderson/50 20.00
200 Todd Helton/25 40.00
201 Andre Dawson/50 20.00
204 Bob Gibson/50 30.00
205 Bobby Doerr/50 20.00
207 Dale Murphy/100 25.00
208 Don Mattingly/50 70.00
209 Gary Carter/100 15.00
216 Mike Schmidt/50 75.00
217 Nolan Ryan/100 120.00
218 Orel Hershiser/50 30.00
219 Paul Molitor/50 30.00
221 Rod Carew/50 30.00
223 Ryne Sandberg/25 100.00
224 Stan Musial/25 100.00
226 Tony Gwynn/100 40.00
228 Whitey Ford/Pants/25 40.00
229 Yogi Berra/25 75.00
230 Carlos Beltran/50 40.00
231 David Ortiz/50 60.00
232 David Ortiz/50 60.00
234 Carlos Lee/50 20.00
235 Travis Hafner/25 25.00
236 Brad Penny/25 15.00
237 Wade Miller/25 15.00
238 Edgar Martinez/50 40.00
239 Carl Crawford/25 25.00
240 Roy Oswalt/25 25.00
242 Carlos Beltran/25 45.00
243 Carlos Beltran/50 45.00
244 Miguel Cabrera/50 40.00
245 Scott Rolen/50 40.00
246 Hank Blalock/50 35.00
247 Vernon Wells/50 20.00
248 Adam Dunn/50 35.00
249 Preston Wilson/25 25.00

Moniker Jersey Number

NM/M
Quantity produced listed
Prime: No Pricing
Production One Set
1 Adam Dunn/50 30.00
5 Alfonso Soriano/50 40.00
6 Andruw Jones/25 40.00
8 Angel Berroa/Pants/25 15.00
9 Aramis Ramirez/25 25.00
10 Aubrey Huff/25 25.00
11 Austin Kearns/25 25.00
15 Ben Sheets/25 25.00
18 Brandon Webb/25 15.00
20 C.C. Sabathia/25 25.00
21 Carlos Beltran/50 40.00
23 Chipper Jones/25 65.00
24 Craig Biggio/25 40.00
30 Dontrelle Willis/25 30.00
32 Eric Chavez/50 20.00
34 Frank Thomas/25 70.00
35 Fred McGriff/25 40.00
36 Garret Anderson/50 20.00
40 Hank Blalock/50 35.00
46 Jacque Jones/25 25.00
63 Jim Edmonds/25 40.00
66 Jody Gerut/25 15.00
67 Johan Santana/25 40.00
71 Jorge Posada/25 50.00
74 Jose Vidro/25 15.00
84 Kerry Wood/25 50.00
88 Lance Berkman/25 40.00
90 Larry Walker/25 20.00
98 Marcus Giles/25 25.00
99 Mark Buehrle/25 25.00
100 Mark Mulder/75 15.00
101 Mark Prior/50 40.00
102 Mark Teixeira/25 40.00
105 Melvin Mora/25 25.00
107 Miguel Cabrera/50 30.00
109 Mike Lowell/25 25.00
115 Morgan Ensberg/25 15.00
122 Paul LoDuca/25 25.00
124 Preston Wilson/25 25.00
137 Roy Oswalt/25 25.00
140 Sammy Sosa/25 120.00
142 Scott Rolen/25 50.00
143 Sean Burroughs/25 25.00
145 Shannon Stewart/25 25.00
149 Steve Finley/25 25.00
153 Todd Helton/25 40.00
154 Tom Glavine/25 40.00
155 Torii Hunter/25 25.00
156 Trot Nixon/25 25.00
158 Vernon Wells/50 20.00
159 Victor Martinez/50 20.00
163 Alfonso Soriano/50 40.00
166 Gary Sheffield/25 40.00
172 Juan Gonzalez/25 40.00
183 Scott Rolen/50 40.00
185 Tom Glavine/25 40.00
193 Chipper Jones/25 65.00
194 Garret Anderson/50 20.00
199 Sammy Sosa/25 120.00
200 Todd Helton/25 40.00
201 Andre Dawson/50 20.00
204 Bob Gibson/25 40.00
205 Bobby Doerr/50 20.00
207 Dale Murphy/100 25.00
208 Don Mattingly/50 70.00
209 Gary Carter/100 15.00
216 Mike Schmidt/50 75.00
217 Nolan Ryan/100 120.00
218 Orel Hershiser/50 30.00
219 Paul Molitor/50 30.00
221 Rod Carew/50 30.00
223 Ryne Sandberg/25 100.00
224 Stan Musial/25 100.00
226 Tony Gwynn/100 40.00
228 Whitey Ford/Pants/25 40.00
229 Yogi Berra/25 75.00
230 Carlos Beltran/50 40.00
231 David Ortiz/50 60.00
232 David Ortiz/50 60.00
234 Carlos Lee/50 20.00
235 Travis Hafner/25 25.00
236 Brad Penny/25 15.00
237 Wade Miller/25 15.00
238 Edgar Martinez/50 40.00
239 Carl Crawford/25 25.00
240 Roy Oswalt/25 25.00
242 Carlos Beltran/50 45.00
243 Carlos Beltran/50 45.00
244 Miguel Cabrera/50 40.00
245 Scott Rolen/50 40.00
246 Hank Blalock/50 35.00
247 Vernon Wells/50 20.00
248 Adam Dunn/50 35.00
249 Preston Wilson/25 25.00
250 Victor Martinez/50 20.00

Player Threads Jersey Number

NM/M
Quantity produced listed
Prime: No Pricing
Production One Set
1 Mike Piazza/100 10.00
3 Nolan Ryan/Jkt/100 20.00
4 Reggie Jackson/100 10.00
5 Wade Boggs/50 10.00
6 Steve Carlton/Pants/100 5.00
7 Ivan Rodriguez/25 15.00
8 Pedro Martinez/50 12.00
10 Rickey Henderson/Pants/100 10.00
11 Randy Johnson/50 10.00
12 Curt Schilling/25 20.00
13 Roger Maris/50 50.00
14 Sammy Sosa/100 10.00
15 Gary Carter/Pants/50 8.00
16 Gary Sheffield/25 10.00
17 Eddie Murray/50 15.00
18 Hideo Nomo/50 10.00
19 Rafael Palmeiro/50 10.00
20 Andre Dawson/50 8.00

Player Threads Double

NM/M
Quantity produced listed
1 Mike Piazza/100 15.00
2 Roger Clemens/100 20.00
3 Nolan Ryan/100 30.00
4 Reggie Jackson/100 15.00
5 Wade Boggs/100 10.00
6 Steve Carlton/100 10.00
7 Ivan Rodriguez/100 10.00
8 Pedro Martinez/100 10.00
9 Rickey Henderson/50 25.00
10 Rickey Henderson/100 20.00
11 Randy Johnson/50 20.00
12 Curt Schilling/100 10.00
13 Roger Maris/100 40.00
14 Sammy Sosa/100 15.00
15 Gary Carter/100 8.00
16 Gary Sheffield/50 10.00
17 Eddie Murray/50 20.00
18 Hideo Nomo/50 15.00
19 Rafael Palmeiro/100 10.00
20 Andre Dawson/50 10.00

Player Threads Triple

NM/M
Quantity produced listed
1 Mike Piazza/50 30.00
2 Roger Clemens/25 50.00
3 Nolan Ryan/50 70.00
4 Reggie Jackson/25 40.00
5 Wade Boggs/25 30.00
6 Steve Carlton/25 25.00
7 Ivan Rodriguez/25 30.00
8 Pedro Martinez/25 30.00
10 Rickey Henderson/25 50.00
12 Curt Schilling/25 30.00
13 Roger Maris/25 120.00
14 Sammy Sosa/25 40.00
15 Gary Carter/25 20.00
17 Eddie Murray/25 40.00
18 Hideo Nomo/25 30.00
19 Rafael Palmeiro/50 20.00
20 Andre Dawson/25 20.00

Team Threads Jersey Number

NM/M
Common Card: 15.00
Production 100 Sets
Prime: No Pricing
Production One Set
1 Stan Musial, Albert Pujols 40.00
2 Cal Ripken Jr. Jkt, Mike Mussina 40.00
3 Carlton Fisk, Roger Clemens 25.00
4 Dale Murphy, Chipper Jones 15.00
5 Tony Gwynn, Dave Winfield 25.00
6 Don Mattingly, Hideki Matsui 50.00
7 Lou Boudreau, Early Wynn 15.00
8 Ernie Banks, Sammy Sosa 30.00
9 Nolan Ryan/Jkt, Jeff Bagwell 50.00
10 Mike Schmidt, Jim Thome 25.00

Team Trademarks

NM/M
Common Player: 5.00
Production 100 Sets
Gold: No Pricing
Production 10 Sets
1 Bob Gibson 8.00
2 Cal Ripken Jr. 30.00
3 Carl Yastrzemski 10.00
4 Dale Murphy 8.00
5 Gary Carter 5.00
6 George Brett 15.00
7 Tom Seaver 8.00
8 Kerry Wood 8.00
9 Lou Brock 8.00
10 Luis Aparicio 5.00
11 Mike Piazza 10.00
12 Nolan Ryan 15.00
13 Nolan Ryan 15.00
14 Randy Johnson 8.00
15 Reggie Jackson 8.00
16 Ricky Henderson 8.00
17 Robin Yount 10.00
18 Rod Carew 8.00
19 Ryne Sandberg 15.00
20 Steve Carlton 5.00
21 Steve Garvey 5.00
22 Johnny Bench 8.00

23 Tony Gwynn 10.00
24 Whitey Ford 8.00
25 Will Clark 8.00

Team Trademarks Autographs

NM/M
Quantity produced listed
1 Bob Gibson/100 20.00
2 Cal Ripken Jr./25 150.00
3 Carl Yastrzemski/25 60.00
4 Dale Murphy/100 20.00
5 Gary Carter/100 15.00
6 George Brett/25 65.00
7 Tom Seaver/25 50.00
8 Kerry Wood/25 40.00
9 Lou Brock/100 20.00
10 Luis Aparicio/100 15.00
12 Nolan Ryan/ Astros/25 100.00
13 Nolan Ryan Rgr/25 100.00
15 Reggie Jackson/25 50.00
17 Robin Yount/50 50.00
18 Rod Carew/50 25.00
19 Ryne Sandberg/25 65.00
20 Steve Carlton/100 20.00
21 Steve Garvey/50 15.00
22 Johnny Bench/25 50.00
23 Tony Gwynn/100 30.00
24 Whitey Ford/25 30.00
25 Will Clark/34 50.00

Team Trademarks Jersey Number

NM/M
Quantity produced listed
Prime: No Pricing
Production One Set
1 Bob Gibson/100 10.00
2 Cal Ripken Jr./ Pants/100 40.00
3 Carl Yastrzemski/100 15.00
4 Dale Murphy/100 10.00
5 Gary Carter/100 5.00
6 George Brett/100 15.00
7 Tom Seaver/100 10.00
8 Kerry Wood/Pants/50 10.00
9 Lou Brock/100 10.00
10 Luis Aparicio/ Pants/100 5.00
11 Mike Piazza/50 15.00
12 Nolan Ryan/ Astros/100 20.00
13 Nolan Ryan/Rgr/100 20.00
14 Randy Johnson/50 10.00
15 Reggie Jackson/ Pants/100 8.00
16 Ricky Henderson/100 10.00
17 Robin Yount/100 10.00
18 Rod Carew Jkt/100 8.00
19 Ryne Sandberg/100 15.00
20 Steve Carlton/50 5.00
22 Johnny Bench/100 10.00
23 Tony Gwynn/100 10.00
24 Whitey Ford/100 10.00
25 Will Clark/50 15.00

Team Trademarks Autograph Jersey Numbers

NM/M
Quantity produced listed
Prime: No Pricing
Production One Set
1 Bob Gibson/100 25.00
2 Cal Ripken Jr./ Pants/25 200.00
3 Carl Yastrzemski/25 75.00
4 Dale Murphy/100 25.00
5 Gary Carter/100 15.00
6 George Brett/25 80.00
7 Tom Seaver/25 65.00
8 Kerry Wood/Pants/25 50.00
9 Lou Brock/100 25.00
10 Luis Aparicio/ Pants/100 15.00
12 Nolan Ryan/ Astros/25 120.00
13 Nolan Ryan/Rgr/25 120.00
15 Reggie Jackson/ Pants/25 60.00
17 Robin Yount/50 75.00
18 Rod Carew/Jkt/50 30.00
19 Ryne Sandberg/50 65.00
20 Steve Carlton/25 40.00
22 Johnny Bench/50 50.00
23 Tony Gwynn/50 50.00
24 Whitey Ford/50 30.00
25 Will Clark/84 40.00

Threads Jersey

NM/M
Quanity produced listed
Prime: No Pricing
Production One Set
Button: No Pricing
Production 1-6
1 Adam Dunn/25 15.00
3 Albert Pujols/50 20.00
5 Alfonso Soriano/25 15.00
6 Andruw Jones/25 10.00
11 Austin Kearns/25 10.00
12 Barry Larkin/25 15.00
13 Barry Zito/25 8.00
16 Bernie Williams/50 8.00
21 Carlos Beltran/25 15.00
22 Carlos Delgado/25 8.00
23 Chipper Jones/50 10.00
24 Craig Biggio/25 15.00
25 Curt Schilling/25 20.00
30 Dontrelle Willis/25 8.00
31 Edgar Renteria/25 10.00
32 Eric Chavez/25 8.00
34 Frank Thomas/25 20.00
36 Garret Anderson/25 10.00
39 Greg Maddux/50 15.00
40 Hank Blalock/25 10.00
41 Hideki Matsui/50 40.00
42 Hideo Nomo/50 10.00
44 Ivan Rodriguez/25 15.00
50 Jason Giambi/50 5.00
55 Javy Lopez/25 10.00
58 Jeff Bagwell/50 10.00
59 Jeff Kent/50 5.00
63 Jim Edmonds/25 10.00
64 Jim Thome/50 10.00
69 John Smoltz/25 15.00
71 Jorge Posada/25 15.00
75 Josh Beckett/25 10.00
76 Juan Gonzalez/25 15.00
84 Kerry Wood/50 12.00
88 Lance Berkman/50 5.00
90 Larry Walker/25 15.00
93 Luis Gonzalez/25 8.00
96 Magglio Ordonez/25 8.00
97 Manny Ramirez/50 10.00
100 Mark Mulder/25 10.00
101 Mark Prior/50 8.00
107 Miguel Cabrera/25 15.00
108 Miguel Tejada/25 10.00
110 Mike Mussina/50 10.00
111 Mike Piazza/50 15.00
112 Mike Sweeney/25 10.00
123 Pedro J. Martinez/50 12.00
126 Rafael Palmeiro/25 15.00
127 Randy Johnson/25 20.00
137 Roy Oswalt/25 10.00
140 Sammy Sosa/50 15.00
142 Scott Rolen/25 20.00
146 Shawn Green/25 8.00
150 Tim Hudson/25 10.00
153 Todd Helton/50 10.00
154 Tom Glavine/25 15.00
155 Torii Hunter/25 10.00
157 Troy Glaus/25 10.00
158 Vernon Wells/25 8.00
161 Vladimir Guerrero/25 20.00
162 Alex Rodriguez/100 10.00
163 Alfonso Soriano/25 10.00
164 Andy Pettitte/25 15.00
165 Curt Schilling/25 10.00
166 Gary Sheffield/25 10.00
167 Greg Maddux/50 15.00
168 Hideo Nomo/25 20.00
169 Ivan Rodriguez/50 12.00
170 Jason Giambi/25 8.00
172 Juan Gonzalez/25 15.00
174 Kevin Brown/25 8.00
176 Miguel Tejada/25 10.00
177 Mike Mussina/50 10.00
178 Mike Piazza/25 25.00
179 Pedro Martinez/25 20.00
180 Rafael Palmeiro/25 15.00
181 Randy Johnson/50 10.00
182 Roger Clemens/100 10.00
183 Scott Rolen/25 20.00
184 Shawn Green/25 8.00
185 Tom Glavine/25 15.00
186 Vladimir Guerrero/25 20.00
187 Alex Rodriguez/100 10.00
189 Randy Johnson/50 10.00
190 Roger Clemens/100 10.00
191 Albert Pujols/50 20.00
192 Barry Zito/25 10.00
193 Chipper Jones/50 10.00
194 Garret Anderson/25 10.00
195 Jeff Bagwell/50 10.00
196 Josh Beckett/25 10.00
197 Magglio Ordonez/25 10.00
198 Mark Prior/50 8.00
199 Sammy Sosa/50 15.00
200 Todd Helton/50 10.00
201 Andre Dawson/50 5.00
202 Babe Ruth/25 350.00
203 Bob Feller/25 20.00
205 Bobby Doerr/50 8.00
206 Cal Ripken Jr./100 40.00
207 Dale Murphy/100 10.00
208 Don Mattingly/50 25.00
209 Gary Carter/50 8.00
210 George Brett/100 15.00
211 Jackie Robinson/50 40.00
212 Lou Brock/25 20.00
213 Lou Gehrig/25 140.00
214 Mark Grace/25 15.00
215 Maury Wills/50 5.00
216 Mike Schmidt/100 15.00
217 Nolan Ryan/100 20.00
218 Orel Hershiser/25 15.00
219 Paul Molitor/50 10.00
220 Roberto Clemente/25 80.00
221 Rod Carew/100 10.00
222 Roy Campanella/ Pants/50 15.00
223 Ryne Sandberg/50 25.00
224 Stan Musial/25 40.00
225 Ted Williams/50 75.00
226 Tony Gwynn/100 10.00
227 Ty Cobb Pants/100 75.00
228 Whitey Ford Pants/25 20.00
229 Yogi Berra/25 25.00
230 Carlos Beltran/25 15.00
231 David Ortiz/25 20.00
232 David Ortiz/25 20.00
238 Edgar Martinez/25 10.00
240 Roy Oswalt/25 8.00
242 Carlos Beltran/25 15.00
243 Carlos Beltran/25 15.00
244 Miguel Cabrera/25 15.00
245 Scott Rolen/25 20.00
246 Hank Blalock/25 12.00
247 Vernon Wells/25 8.00
248 Adam Dunn/25 15.00

Threads Jersey Number

NM/M
Quanity produced listed
Prime: No Pricing
Production One Set
MLB Logo: No Pricing
Production One Set
1 Adam Dunn/25 15.00
3 Albert Pujols/50 20.00
5 Alfonso Soriano/25 15.00
6 Andruw Jones/25 10.00
11 Austin Kearns/25 8.00
12 Barry Larkin/25 15.00
13 Barry Zito/25 8.00
16 Bernie Williams/50 10.00
21 Carlos Beltran/25 15.00
22 Carlos Delgado/25 8.00
23 Chipper Jones/50 10.00
24 Craig Biggio/25 10.00
25 Curt Schilling/25 20.00
30 Dontrelle Willis/25 8.00
31 Edgar Renteria/25 10.00
32 Eric Chavez/25 8.00
34 Frank Thomas/25 15.00
36 Garret Anderson/25 10.00
39 Greg Maddux/50 15.00
40 Hank Blalock/25 12.00
41 Hideki Matsui/25 40.00
42 Hideo Nomo/50 10.00
44 Ivan Rodriguez/25 20.00
50 Jason Giambi/50 5.00
55 Javy Lopez/25 8.00
58 Jeff Bagwell/50 10.00
59 Jeff Kent/25 10.00
63 Jim Edmonds/25 10.00
64 Jim Thome/50 15.00
69 John Smoltz/25 15.00
71 Jorge Posada/25 15.00
75 Josh Beckett/25 10.00
76 Juan Gonzalez/25 15.00
84 Kerry Wood/50 12.00
88 Lance Berkman/50 5.00
90 Larry Walker/25 10.00
93 Luis Gonzalez/25 8.00
96 Magglio Ordonez/25 8.00
97 Manny Ramirez/50 12.00
100 Mark Mulder/25 10.00
101 Mark Prior/50 8.00
107 Miguel Cabrera/25 15.00
108 Miguel Tejada/25 10.00
110 Mike Mussina/50 10.00
111 Mike Piazza/50 15.00
112 Mike Sweeney/25 10.00
123 Pedro J. Martinez/50 12.00
126 Rafael Palmeiro/25 15.00
127 Randy Johnson/25 20.00
137 Roy Oswalt/25 10.00
140 Sammy Sosa/50 15.00
142 Scott Rolen/25 20.00
146 Shawn Green/25 8.00
150 Tim Hudson/25 10.00
153 Todd Helton/50 10.00
154 Tom Glavine/25 15.00
155 Torii Hunter/25 10.00
157 Troy Glaus/25 8.00
158 Vernon Wells/25 8.00
161 Vladimir Guerrero/25 20.00
162 Alex Rodriguez/100 10.00
163 Alfonso Soriano/50 10.00
164 Andy Pettitte/25 15.00
165 Curt Schilling/25 10.00
166 Gary Sheffield/25 10.00
167 Greg Maddux/50 15.00
168 Hideo Nomo/25 20.00
169 Ivan Rodriguez/50 12.00
170 Jason Giambi/25 8.00
172 Juan Gonzalez/25 12.00
174 Kevin Brown/25 8.00
176 Miguel Tejada/25 10.00
177 Mike Mussina/50 10.00
178 Mike Piazza/25 25.00
179 Pedro Martinez/25 20.00
180 Rafael Palmeiro/25 15.00
181 Randy Johnson/50 10.00
182 Roger Clemens/100 10.00
183 Scott Rolen/25 20.00
184 Shawn Green/25 8.00
185 Tom Glavine/25 15.00
186 Vladimir Guerrero/25 20.00
187 Alex Rodriguez/100 10.00
189 Randy Johnson/50 10.00
190 Roger Clemens/100 10.00
191 Albert Pujols/50 20.00
192 Barry Zito/25 8.00
193 Chipper Jones/50 10.00
194 Garret Anderson/25 10.00
195 Jeff Bagwell/50 10.00
196 Josh Beckett/25 10.00
197 Magglio Ordonez/25 8.00
198 Mark Prior/50 8.00
199 Sammy Sosa/50 15.00
200 Todd Helton/50 10.00
201 Andre Dawson/50 8.00
202 Babe Ruth/25 300.00
203 Bob Feller/25 20.00
205 Bobby Doerr/50 8.00
206 Cal Ripken Jr./100 40.00
207 Dale Murphy/100 10.00
208 Don Mattingly/50 25.00
209 Gary Carter/50 8.00
210 George Brett/100 15.00
211 Jackie Robinson/100 40.00
212 Lou Brock/25 20.00
213 Lou Gehrig/25 150.00
214 Mark Grace/25 15.00
215 Maury Wills/50 8.00
216 Mike Schmidt/100 15.00
217 Nolan Ryan/100 20.00
218 Orel Hershiser/25 15.00
219 Paul Molitor/50 10.00
220 Roberto Clemente/25 80.00
221 Rod Carew/100 10.00
222 Roy Campanella/ Pants/50 15.00
223 Ryne Sandberg/50 25.00
224 Stan Musial/25 40.00
225 Ted Williams/25 75.00
226 Tony Gwynn/100 10.00
227 Ty Cobb Pants/100 60.00
228 Whitey Ford Pants/25 20.00
229 Yogi Berra/25 25.00
230 Carlos Beltran/25 15.00
231 David Ortiz/25 20.00
232 David Ortiz/25 20.00
238 Edgar Martinez/25 10.00
240 Roy Oswalt H/25 10.00
242 Carlos Beltran/25 15.00
243 Carlos Beltran/25 15.00
244 Miguel Cabrera/25 15.00
245 Scott Rolen/25 20.00
246 Hank Blalock/25 10.00
247 Vernon Wells/25 10.00
248 Adam Dunn/25 15.00

Timber

NM/M
Quanity produced listed
1 Adam Dunn/25 15.00
4 Alex Rodriguez/100 10.00
5 Alfonso Soriano/25 15.00
6 Andruw Jones/25 10.00
7 Andy Pettitte/25 15.00
11 Austin Kearns/25 8.00
12 Barry Larkin/25 15.00
13 Barry Zito/25 8.00
16 Bernie Williams/25 12.00
21 Carlos Beltran/25 15.00
22 Carlos Delgado/25 10.00
23 Chipper Jones/25 20.00
24 Craig Biggio/25 12.00
25 Curt Schilling/25 20.00
30 Dontrelle Willis/25 8.00
32 Eric Chavez/25 8.00
34 Frank Thomas/25 20.00
35 Fred McGriff/25 12.00
36 Garret Anderson/25 8.00
37 Gary Sheffield/25 10.00
39 Greg Maddux/25 25.00
40 Hank Blalock/25 10.00
41 Hideki Matsui/25 60.00
42 Hideo Nomo/25 20.00
44 Ivan Rodriguez/25 20.00
50 Jason Giambi/25 8.00
55 Javy Lopez/25 8.00
58 Jeff Bagwell/25 15.00
59 Jeff Kent/25 8.00
63 Jim Edmonds/25 10.00
64 Jim Thome/25 20.00
71 Jorge Posada/25 15.00
75 Josh Beckett/25 10.00
76 Juan Gonzalez/25 15.00
84 Kerry Wood/25 20.00
85 Kevin Brown/25 8.00
88 Lance Berkman/25 8.00
90 Larry Walker/25 10.00
93 Luis Gonzalez/25 8.00
96 Magglio Ordonez/25 8.00
97 Manny Ramirez/25 15.00
100 Mark Mulder/25 8.00
101 Mark Prior/25 15.00
102 Mark Teixeira/25 10.00
106 Michael Young/25 8.00
107 Miguel Cabrera/25 15.00
108 Miguel Tejada/25 10.00
109 Mike Lowell/25 8.00
110 Mike Mussina/25 15.00
111 Mike Piazza/25 25.00
112 Mike Sweeney/25 8.00
116 Nick Johnson/25 8.00
117 Nomar Garciaparra/ 25 20.00
122 Paul LoDuca/25 8.00
123 Pedro J. Martinez/25 20.00
126 Rafael Palmeiro/25 15.00
127 Randy Johnson/25 20.00
130 Richie Sexson/25 10.00
134 Rocco Baldelli/25 8.00
135 Roger Clemens/25 25.00
137 Roy Oswalt/25 8.00
140 Sammy Sosa/50 15.00
142 Scott Rolen/25 20.00
146 Shawn Green/25 8.00
150 Tim Hudson/25 8.00
153 Todd Helton/25 15.00
154 Tom Glavine/25 15.00
155 Torii Hunter/25 8.00
156 Trot Nixon/25 10.00
157 Troy Glaus/25 8.00
158 Vernon Wells/25 8.00
161 Vladimir Guerrero/25 20.00
162 Alex Rodriguez/100 10.00
163 Alfonso Soriano/25 15.00
164 Andy Pettitte/25 15.00
165 Curt Schilling/25 10.00
166 Gary Sheffield/25 10.00
167 Greg Maddux/25 25.00
168 Hideo Nomo/25 15.00
169 Ivan Rodriguez/25 15.00
170 Jason Giambi/25 8.00
171 Jim Thome/25 10.00
172 Juan Gonzalez/25 10.00
174 Kevin Brown/25 8.00
175 Manny Ramirez/25 15.00
176 Miguel Tejada/25 10.00
177 Mike Mussina/25 15.00
178 Mike Piazza/25 25.00
179 Pedro Martinez/25 20.00
180 Rafael Palmeiro/25 15.00
181 Randy Johnson/25 20.00
182 Roger Clemens/25 25.00
183 Scott Rolen/25 20.00
184 Shawn Green/25 8.00
185 Tom Glavine/25 15.00
186 Vladimir Guerrero/25 20.00
187 Alex Rodriguez/100 10.00
188 Mike Piazza/25 25.00
189 Randy Johnson/25 20.00
190 Roger Clemens/25 25.00
191 Albert Pujols/50 20.00
192 Barry Zito/25 8.00
193 Chipper Jones/25 20.00
194 Garret Anderson/25 8.00
195 Jeff Bagwell/25 15.00
196 Josh Beckett/25 8.00
197 Maggio Ordonez/25 8.00
198 Mark Prior/25 15.00
199 Sammy Sosa/50 15.00
200 Todd Helton/25 15.00
201 Andre Dawson/50 8.00
202 Babe Ruth/100 120.00
206 Cal Ripken Jr./100 40.00
207 Dale Murphy/50 15.00
208 Don Mattingly/50 25.00
209 Gary Carter/25 10.00
210 George Brett/50 25.00
212 Lou Brock/25 15.00
213 Lou Gehrig/100 100.00
214 Mark Grace/25 15.00
216 Mike Schmidt/50 25.00
217 Nolan Ryan/50 30.00
219 Paul Molitor/50 10.00
220 Roberto Clemente/ 100 75.00
221 Rod Carew/25 25.00
222 Roy Campanella/100 10.00
223 Ryne Sandberg/50 25.00
224 Stan Musial/100 20.00
225 Ted Williams/100 50.00
226 Tony Gwynn/50 20.00
227 Ty Cobb/100 75.00
229 Yogi Berra/100 10.00
230 Carlos Beltran/25 15.00
231 David Ortiz/25 20.00
232 David Ortiz/25 20.00
238 Edgar Martinez/25 15.00
240 Roy Oswalt/25 10.00
242 Carlos Beltran/25 15.00
243 Carlos Beltran/25 15.00
244 Miguel Cabrera/25 15.00
245 Scott Rolen/25 20.00
246 Hank Blalock/25 10.00
248 Adam Dunn/25 15.00

TNT

NM/M
Quanity produced listed
Prime: No Pricing
Production One Set
1 Adam Dunn/ Bat-Jsy/50 10.00
3 Albert Pujols/ Bat-Jsy/100 15.00
5 Alfonso Soriano/ Bat-Jsy/50 10.00
6 Andruw Jones/ Bat-Jsy/50 8.00
11 Austin Kearns/ Bat-Jsy/50 5.00
12 Barry Larkin/ Bat-Jsy/25 20.00
13 Barry Zito/Bat-Jsy/50 5.00
16 Bernie Williams/ Bat-Jsy/50 10.00
21 Carlos Beltran/ Bat-Jsy/50 10.00
22 Carlos Delgado/ Bat-Jsy/50 5.00
23 Chipper Jones/ Bat-Jsy/50 15.00
24 Craig Biggio/ Bat-Jsy/50 8.00
25 Curt Schilling/ Bat-Jsy/25 25.00
32 Eric Chavez/ Bat-Jsy/25 10.00
34 Frank Thomas/ Bat-Jsy/25 20.00
36 Garret Anderson/ Bat-Jsy/25 10.00
39 Greg Maddux/ Bat-Jsy/25 20.00
40 Hank Blalock/ Bat-Jsy/50 8.00
41 Hideki Matsui/ Bat-Jsy/50 50.00
42 Hideo Nomo/ Bat-Jsy/25 20.00
44 Ivan Rodriguez/ Bat-Jsy/25 20.00
50 Jason Giambi /Bat-Jsy/50 8.00
55 Javy Lopez/ Bat-Jsy/25 10.00
58 Jeff Bagwell/ Bat-Jsy/50 10.00
59 Jeff Kent/Bat-Jsy/25 10.00
63 Jim Edmonds/ Bat-Jsy/25 10.00
64 Jim Thome/ Bat-Jsy/50 15.00
71 Jorge Posada/ Bat-Jsy/25 20.00
75 Josh Beckett/ Bat-Jsy/25 10.00
76 Juan Gonzalez/ Bat-Jsy/25 20.00
84 Kerry Wood/ Bat-Jsy/50 15.00
88 Lance Berkman/ Bat-Jsy/50 5.00
90 Larry Walker/ Bat-Jsy/25 20.00
93 Luis Gonzalez/ Bat-Jsy/25 10.00
96 Magglio Ordonez/ Bat-Jsy/25 10.00
97 Manny Ramirez/ Bat-Jsy/50 15.00
100 Mark Mulder/ Bat-Jsy/25 10.00
101 Mark Prior/ Bat-Jsy/50 10.00
102 Mark Teixeira/ Bat-Jsy/25 10.00
107 Miguel Cabrera/ Bat-Jsy/25 20.00
108 Miguel Tejada/ Bat-Jsy/25 10.00
109 Mike Lowell/ Bat-Jsy/25 10.00
110 Mike Mussina/ Bat-Jsy/50 10.00
111 Mike Piazza/ Bat-Jsy/50 20.00
112 Mike Sweeney/ Bat-Jsy/25 10.00
123 Pedro J. Martinez/ Bat-Jsy/50 15.00
126 Rafael Palmeiro/ Bat-Jsy/25 20.00
127 Randy Johnson/ Bat-Jsy/50 15.00
137 Roy Oswalt/ Bat-Jsy/25 10.00
140 Sammy Sosa/ Bat-Jsy/50 20.00
142 Scott Rolen/ Bat-Jsy/25 25.00
146 Shawn Green/ Bat-Jsy/25 10.00
150 Tim Hudson/ Bat-Jsy/25 10.00
153 Todd Helton/ Bat-Jsy/50 10.00
154 Tom Glavine/ Bat-Jsy/25 20.00
155 Torii Hunter/ Bat-Jsy/25 10.00
157 Troy Glaus/ Bat-Jsy/25 10.00
158 Vernon Wells/ Bat-Jsy/25 10.00
161 Vladimir Guerrero/ Bat-Jsy/25 25.00
162 Alex Rodriguez/ Bat-Jsy/100 10.00
163 Alfonso Soriano/ Bat-Jsy/50 10.00
164 Andy Pettitte/ Bat-Jsy/25 20.00
165 Curt Schilling/ Bat-Jsy/25 10.00
166 Gary Sheffield/ Bat-Jsy/25 10.00
167 Greg Maddux/ Bat-Jsy/50 20.00
168 Hideo Nomo/ Bat-Jsy/25 20.00
169 Ivan Rodriguez/ Bat-Jsy/50 15.00
170 Jason Giambi/ Bat-Jsy/25 10.00

172 Juan Gonzalez/ Bat-Jsy/25 15.00
174 Kevin Brown/ Bat-Jsy/25 10.00
176 Miguel Tejada/ Bat-Jsy/25 10.00
177 Mike Mussina/ Bat-Jsy/50 10.00
178 Mike Piazza/ Bat-Jsy/50 20.00
179 Pedro Martinez/ Bat-Jsy/50 15.00
180 Rafael Palmeiro/ Bat-Jsy/50 10.00
181 Randy Johnson/ Bat-Jsy/50 15.00
182 Roger Clemens/ Bat-Jsy/100 10.00
183 Scott Rolen/ Bat-Jsy/25 25.00
184 Shawn Green/ Bat-Jsy/25 10.00
185 Tom Glavine/ Bat-Jsy/25 20.00
186 Vladimir Guerrero/ Bat-Jsy/25 25.00
187 Alex Rodriguez/ Bat-Jsy/100 10.00
189 Randy Johnson/ Bat-Jsy/50 15.00
190 Roger Clemens/ Bat-Jsy/100 10.00
191 Albert Pujols/ Bat-Jsy/50 25.00
192 Barry Zito/Bat-Jsy/25 10.00
193 Chipper Jones/ Bat-Jsy/50 15.00
194 Garret Anderson/ Bat-Jsy/25 10.00
195 Jeff Bagwell/ Bat-Jsy/50 10.00
196 Josh Beckett/ Bat-Jsy/25 10.00
197 Magglio Ordonez/ Bat-Jsy/25 10.00
198 Mark Prior/ Bat-Jsy/50 10.00
199 Sammy Sosa/ Bat-Jsy/50 20.00
200 Todd Helton/ Bat-Jsy/50 10.00
201 Andre Dawson/ Bat-Jsy/50 8.00
202 Babe Ruth/ Bat-Jsy/25 425.00
206 Cal Ripken Jr./ Bat-Jsy/100 60.00
207 Dale Murphy/ Bat-Jsy/100 10.00
208 Don Mattingly/ Bat-Jsy/100 20.00
209 Gary Carter/ Bat-Jsy/50 10.00
210 George Brett/ Bat-Jsy/100 20.00
212 Lou Brock/Bat-Jsy/25 25.00
213 Lou Gehrig/ Bat-Jsy/25 250.00
214 Mark Grace/ Bat-Jsy/25 20.00
216 Mike Schmidt/ Bat-Jsy/50 30.00
217 Nolan Ryan/ Bat-Jsy/100 25.00
219 Paul Molitor/ Bat-Jsy/25 20.00
221 Rod Carew/ Bat-Jsy/50 15.00
222 Roy Campanella/ Bat-Pants/50 20.00
223 Ryne Sandberg/ Bat-Jsy/50 30.00
224 Stan Musial/ Bat-Jsy/25 50.00
225 Ted Williams Bat-Jsy/50 100.00
226 Tony Gwynn/ Bat-Jsy/100 15.00
227 Ty Cobb/ Bat-Pants/50 120.00
230 Carlos Beltran/ Bat-Jsy/25 20.00
231 David Ortiz/ Bat-Jsy/25 25.00
232 David Ortiz/ Bat-Jsy/25 25.00
238 Edgar Martinez/ Bat-Jsy/25 15.00
240 Roy Oswalt/ Bat-Jsy/25 10.00
242 Carlos Beltran/ Bat-Jsy/25 20.00
243 Carlos Beltran/ Bat-Jsy/25 20.00
244 Miguel Cabrera/ Bat-Jsy/25 20.00
245 Scott Rolen/ Bat-Jsy/25 20.00
246 Hank Blalock/ Bat-Jsy/25 10.00
247 Vernon Wells/ Bat-Jsy/25 10.00
248 Adam Dunn/ Bat-Jsy/25 20.00

2005 Leaf

NM/M
Complete Set (300):
Common Player (1-200): .15
Common SP (201-250): 1.00
Inserted 1:3
Common SP (251-300): 1.00
#251-270 inserted 1:6
271-300 inserted 1:4
Hobby pack (8): 4.00
Hobby box (24): 80.00
1 Bartolo Colon .25
2 Casey Kotchman .15
3 Chone Figgins .15
4 Darin Erstad .25
5 Francisco Rodriguez .25
6 Garret Anderson .25
7 Jarrod Washburn .15
8 Troy Glaus .25
9 Vladimir Guerrero .50
10 Brandon Webb .15
11 Casey Fossum .15
12 Luis Gonzalez .25
13 Randy Johnson .50
14 Richie Sexson .25
15 Andruw Jones .25
16 Chipper Jones .50
17 J.D. Drew .25
18 John Smoltz .25
19 Johnny Estrada .15
20 Marcus Giles .15
21 Rafael Furcal .25
22 Russ Ortiz .15
23 Javy Lopez .25
24 Jay Gibbons .15
25 Melvin Mora .15
26 Miguel Tejada .40
27 Rafael Palmeiro .40
28 Sidney Ponson .15
29 Bill Mueller .15
30 Curt Schilling .40
31 David Ortiz .50
32 Doug Mientkiewicz .15
33 Jason Varitek .25
34 Johnny Damon .40
35 Manny Ramirez .50
36 Pedro J. Martinez .50
37 Trot Nixon .15
38 Aramis Ramirez .25
39 Corey Patterson .25
40 Derrek Lee .25
41 Greg Maddux .75
42 Kerry Wood .50
43 Mark Prior .50
44 Moises Alou .25
45 Nomar Garciaparra 1.00
46 Sammy Sosa 1.00
47 Carlos Lee .15
48 Kip Wells .15
49 Maggllo Ordonez .25
50 Mark Buehrle .15
51 Paul Konerko .25
52 Roberto Alomar .25
53 Adam Dunn .40
54 Austin Kearns .15
55 Barry Larkin .25
56 Danny Graves .15
57 Ken Griffey Jr. 1.00
58 Sean Casey .15
59 C.C. Sabathia .15
60 Cliff Lee .15
61 Jody Gerut .15
62 Omar Vizquel .25
63 Travis Hafner .15
64 Victor Martinez .25
65 Charles Johnson .15
66 Jason Jennings .15
67 Jeromy Burnitz .15
68 Preston Wilson .15
69 Todd Helton .40
70 Bobby Higginson .15
71 Dmitri Young .15
72 Eric Munson .15
73 Ivan Rodriguez .40
74 Jeremy Bonderman .15
75 Rondell White .15
76 A.J. Burnett .15
77 Carl Pavano .25
78 Dontrelle Willis .25
79 Hee Seop Choi .15
80 Josh Beckett .25
81 Juan Pierre .15
82 Miguel Cabrera .40
83 Mike Lowell .15
84 Paul LoDuca .15
85 Andy Pettitte .25
86 Carlos Beltran .40
87 Craig Biggio .25
88 Jeff Bagwell .40
89 Jeff Kent .25
90 Lance Berkman .25
91 Roger Clemens 1.50
92 Roy Oswalt .25
93 Andres Blanco .15
94 Jeremy Affeldt .15
95 Juan Gonzalez .25
96 Ken Harvey .15
97 Mike Sweeney .15
98 Zack Greinke .15
99 Adrian Beltre .25
100 Brad Penny .15
101 Eric Gagne .25
102 Kazuhisa Ishii .15
103 Milton Bradley .15
104 Shawn Green .25
105 Steve Finley .15
106 Ben Sheets .25
107 Bill Hall .15
108 Danny Kolb .15
109 Geoff Jenkins .15
110 Junior Spivey .15
111 Lyle Overbay .15
112 Scott Podsednik .15
113 A.J. Pierzynski .15
114 Brad Radke .15
115 Corey Koskie .15
116 Jacque Jones .15
117 Joe Mauer .50
118 Joe Nathan .15
119 Shannon Stewart .15
120 Torii Hunter .25
121 Brad Wilkerson .15
122 Jeff Fassero .15
123 Jose Vidro .15
124 Livan Hernandez .15
125 Nick Johnson .15
126 Al Leiter .25
127 Jose Reyes .25
128 Kazuo Matsui .25
129 Mike Cameron .15
130 Mike Piazza 1.00
131 Richard Hidalgo .15
132 Tom Glavine .25
133 Alex Rodriguez 1.50
134 Bernie Williams .25
135 Derek Jeter 1.50
136 Gary Sheffield .40
137 Jason Giambi .25
138 Javier Vazquez .25
139 Jorge Posada .25
140 Kevin Brown .15
141 Mariano Rivera .25
142 Mike Mussina .25
143 Barry Zito .25
144 Bobby Crosby .25
145 Eric Chavez .25
146 Erubiel Durazo .15
147 Jermaine Dye .15
148 Mark Mulder .25
149 Tim Hudson .25
150 Bobby Abreu .25
151 Eric Milton .15
152 Jim Thome .50
153 Kevin Millwood .15
154 Mike Lieberthal .15
155 Pat Burrell .25
156 Randy Wolf .15
157 Craig Wilson .15
158 Jack Wilson .15
159 Jason Bay .25
160 Jason Kendall .15
161 Kris Benson .15
162 Brian Giles .15
163 Jake Peavy .25
164 Jay Payton .15
165 Khalil Greene .25
166 Mark Loretta .15
167 Ryan Klesko .15
168 Sean Burroughs .15
169 David Aardsma .15
170 Edgardo Alfonzo .15
171 Jason Schmidt .25
172 Merkin Valdez .15
173 Ray Durham .15
174 Bret Boone .15
175 Dan Wilson .15
176 Ichiro Suzuki 1.25
177 Jamie Moyer .15
178 Rich Aurilia .15
179 Albert Pujols 1.50
180 Edgar Renteria .25
181 Jason Isringhausen .15
182 Jeff Suppan .15
183 Jim Edmonds .25
184 Scott Rolen .50
185 Woody Williams .15
186 Aubrey Huff .15
187 Carl Crawford .15
188 Dewon Brazelton .15
189 Jose Cruz Jr. .15
190 Rocco Baldelli .25
191 Alfonso Soriano .40
192 Hank Blalock .40
193 Kenny Rogers .15
194 Laynce Nix .15
195 Mark Teixeira .25
196 Michael Young .15
197 Alexis Rios .15
198 Carlos Delgado .25
199 Roy Halladay .15
200 Vernon Wells .15
201 Josh Kroeger 1.00
202 Angel Guzman 1.00
203 Brad Halsey 1.00
204 Bucky Jacobsen 1.00
205 Carlos Hines 1.00
206 Carlos Vasquez 1.00
207 Billy Traber 1.00
208 Bubba Crosby 1.00
209 Chris Oxspring 1.00
210 Chris Shelton 1.00
211 Colby Miller 1.00
212 David Crouthers 1.00
213 Dennis Sarfate 1.00
214 Donald Kelly 1.00
215 Edwardo Sierra 1.00
216 Edwin Moreno 1.00
217 Fernando Nieve 1.00
218 Freddy Guzman 1.00
219 Greg Dobbs 1.00
220 Hector Gimenez 1.00
221 Andy Green 1.00
222 Jason Bartlett 1.00
223 Jerry Gil 1.00
224 Jesse Crain 2.00
225 Joey Gathright 1.00
226 John Gall 1.00
227 Jorge Sequea 1.00
228 Jorge Vasquez 1.00
229 Josh Labandeira 1.00
230 Justin Leone 1.00
231 Lance Cormier 1.00
232 Lincoln Holdzkom 1.00
233 Miguel Olivo 1.00
234 Mike Rouse 1.00
235 Onil Joseph 1.00
236 Phil Stockman 1.00
237 Ramon Ramirez 1.00
238 Robb Quinlan 1.00
239 Roberto Novoa 1.00
240 Ronald Belisario 1.00
241 Ronny Cedeno 1.00
242 Ruddy Yan 1.00
243 Ryan Meaux 1.00
244 Ryan Wing 1.00
245 Scott Proctor 1.00
246 Sean Henn 1.00
247 Tim Bausher 1.00
248 Tim Bittner 1.00
249 William Bergolla 1.00
250 Yadier Molina 1.00
251 Bernie Williams 1.00
252 Craig Biggio 1.00
253 Chipper Jones 2.00
254 Greg Maddux 3.00
255 Sammy Sosa 3.00
256 Mike Mussina 1.50
257 Tim Salmon 1.00
258 Barry Larkin 1.00
259 Randy Johnson 2.00
260 Jeff Bagwell 1.50
261 Roberto Alomar 1.50
262 Tom Glavine 1.00
263 Roger Clemens 4.00
264 Alex Rodriguez 4.00
265 Ivan Rodriguez 1.50
266 Pedro J. Martinez 2.00
267 Ken Griffey Jr. 3.00
268 Jim Thome 2.00
269 Frank Thomas 1.50
270 Mike Piazza 3.00
271 Garret Anderson 1.00
272 Luis Gonzalez 1.00
273 John Smoltz 1.00
274 Rafael Palmeiro 1.50
275 Curt Schilling 1.50
276 Mark Prior 1.50
277 Magglio Ordonez 1.00
278 Adam Dunn 1.50
279 Travis Hafner 1.00
280 Jeromy Burnitz 1.00
281 Carlos Guillen 1.00
282 Dontrelle Willis 1.00
283 Carlos Beltran 1.50
284 Zack Greinke 1.00
285 Adrian Beltre 1.00
286 Ben Sheets 1.00
287 Johan Santana 1.00
288 Livan Hernandez 1.00
289 Kazuo Matsui 1.00
290 Derek Jeter 4.00
291 Tim Hudson 1.00
292 Eric Milton 1.00
293 Jason Kendall 1.00
294 Jake Peavy 1.00
295 Ray Durham 1.00
296 Ichiro Suzuki 3.00
297 Scott Rolen 2.00
298 Carl Crawford 1.00
299 Hank Blalock 1.50
300 Roy Halladay 1.00

Press Proofs Blue

Blue (1-200): 5-10X
Blue (201-250): 1-2X
Blue (251-300): 2-4X
Production 75 Sets

Press Proofs Gold

Gold (1-200): 10-20X
Gold (201-250): 2-4X
Blue (251-300): 4-8X
Production 25 Sets

Press Proofs Red

Red (1-200): 2-4X
Red (201-250): .5-1X
Red (251-300): 1-2X
Inserted 1:8

Alternate Threads

NM/M
Complete Set (25): 30.00
Common Player: 1.00
Inserted 1:18
Holo: 1-2X
Production 150 Sets
Holo Die-Cut: 2-4X
Production 50 Sets
1 Adam Dunn 1.50
2 C.C. Sabathia 1.00
3 Curt Schilling 1.50
4 Dontrelle Willis 1.00
5 Greg Maddux 3.00
6 Hank Blalock 1.50
7 Ichiro Suzuki 4.00
8 Jeff Bagwell 1.50
9 Ken Griffey Jr. 3.00
10 Ken Harvey 1.00
11 Magglio Ordonez 1.00
12 Mark Mulder 1.00
13 Mark Teixeira 1.00
14 Michael Young 1.00
15 Miguel Tejada 1.50
16 Mike Piazza 4.00
17 Pedro Martinez 2.00
18 Randy Johnson 2.00
19 Roger Clemens 6.00
20 Sammy Sosa 4.00
21 Tim Hudson 1.00
22 Todd Helton 1.50
23 Torii Hunter 1.00
24 Travis Hafner 1.00
25 Vernon Wells 1.00

Autographs

NM/M
Common Autograph: 5.00
201 Josh Kroeger 5.00
202 Angel Guzman 15.00
203 Brad Halsey 5.00
204 Bucky Jacobsen 10.00
205 Carlos Hines 5.00
207 Bill Tucker 5.00
208 Bubba Crosby 10.00
210 Chris Shelton 8.00
211 Colby Miller 5.00
212 David Crouthers 5.00
217 Fernando Nieve 10.00
220 Hector Gimenez 5.00
221 Andy Green 5.00
222 Jason Bartlett 5.00
227 Jorge Sequea/84 10.00
228 Jorge Vasquez 8.00
232 Lincoln Holdzkom 8.00
233 Miguel Olivo 8.00
234 Mike Rouse 8.00
236 Phil Stockman 8.00
237 Ramon Ramirez 8.00
242 Ruddy Yan 5.00
245 Scott Proctor 8.00
247 Tim Bausher 8.00
249 William Bergolla 10.00

Autographs Blue

No Pricing
Production 15-25
Golds: No Pricing

Autographs Red

NM/M
Common Autograph:
3 Chone Figgins/100 8.00
19 Johnny Estrada/100 15.00
24 Jay Gibbons/100 10.00
47 Carlos Lee/100 10.00
56 Danny Graves/100 8.00
60 Cliff Lee/100 10.00
63 Travis Hafner/50 15.00
74 Jeremy Bonderman/ 100 10.00
94 Jeremy Affeldt/100 8.00
96 Ken Harvey/100 8.00
103 Milton Bradley/100 10.00
111 Lyle Overbay/50 15.00
118 Joe Nathan/100 10.00
144 Bobby Crosby/100 25.00
154 Mike Lieberthal/50 15.00
157 Craig Wilson/50 15.00
158 Jack Wilson/100 12.00
163 Jake Peavy/50 25.00
172 Merkin Valdez/100 8.00
182 Jeff Suppan/100 10.00
187 Carl Crawford/50 15.00
188 Dewon Brazelton/50 10.00
194 Laynce Nix/100 10.00
201 Josh Kroeger/100 8.00
202 Angel Guzman/100 15.00
203 Brad Halsey/100 8.00
204 Bucky Jacobsen/100 10.00
205 Carlos Hines/100 8.00
207 Billy Traber/100 8.00
208 Bubba Crosby/100 10.00
210 Chris Shelton/100 8.00
211 Colby Miller/100 8.00
212 David Crouthers/100 8.00
217 Fernando Nieve/100 10.00
218 Freddy Guzman/100 10.00
220 Hector Gimenez/100 8.00
221 Andy Green/100 8.00
222 Jason Bartlett/100 8.00
224 Josh Crain/100 15.00
227 Jorge Sequea/84 10.00
228 Jorge Vasquez/100 8.00
233 Miguel Olivo/100 8.00
234 Mike Rouse/100 8.00
236 Phil Stockman/100 10.00
237 Ramon Ramirez/100 8.00
238 Robb Quinlan/100 8.00
241 Ronny Cedeno/65 10.00
242 Ruddy Yan/100 8.00
243 Ryan Meaux/93 8.00
247 Tim Bausher/100 8.00
249 William Bergolla/100 10.00
250 Yadier Molina/100 15.00

Certified Materials Preview

NM/M
Complete Set (15): 25.00
Common Player: 1.50
Inserted 1:21
Blue: 2-3X
Production 100 Sets
Gold: 4-8X
Production 25 Sets
Red: 1-2X
Production 200 Sets
1 Albert Pujols 4.00
2 Alex Rodriguez 3.00
3 Alfonso Soriano 1.50
4 Curt Schilling 1.50
5 Derek Jeter 4.00
6 Greg Maddux 2.00
7 Ichiro Suzuki 3.00
8 Jim Thome 1.50
9 Ken Griffey Jr. 2.00
10 Manny Ramirez 1.50
11 Mark Prior 1.50
12 Randy Johnson 1.50
13 Roger Clemens 4.00
14 Sammy Sosa 2.50
15 Vladimir Guerrero 1.50

Clean Up Crew

NM/M
Complete Set (15): 45.00
Common Card:
Inserted 1:49
Die-cut: 1X
Production 250 Sets
1 Albert Pujols, Jim Edmonds, Scott Rolen 6.00
2 Melvin Mora, Miguel Tejada, Rafael Palmeiro 3.00

3	Alfonso Soriano, Michael Young, Hank Blalock	3.00
4	Gary Sheffield, Alex Rodriguez, Hideki Matsui	5.00
5	Moises Alou, Sammy Sosa, Nomar Garciaparra	5.00
6	Paul LoDuca, Mike Lowell, Miguel Cabrera	3.00
7	Carlos Beltran, Lance Berkman, Jeff Bagwell	3.00
8	Paul Konerko, Magglio Ordonez, Frank Thomas	3.00
9	Sean Casey, Ken Griffey Jr., Adam Dunn	5.00
10	Vladimir Guerrero, Garret Anderson, Troy Glaus	3.00
11	Joe Morgan, Johnny Bench, Tony Perez	3.00
12	Keith Hernandez, Darryl Strawberry, Gary Carter	2.00
13	Jim Rice, Carl Yastrzemski, Dwight Evans	5.00
14	Ryne Sandberg, Andre Dawson, Mark Grace	6.00
15	Cal Ripken Jr., Eddie Murray, Rafael Palmeiro	10.00

Cornerstones

		NM/M
Complete Set (20):		50.00
Common Card:		1.50
Inserted 1:37		
1	Albert Pujols, Scott Rolen	6.00
2	Hideki Matsui, Jorge Posada	5.00
3	Nomar Garciaparra, Sammy Sosa	4.00
4	David Ortiz, Manny Ramirez	3.00
5	Miguel Cabrera, Mike Lowell	3.00
6	Hank Blalock, Mark Teixeira	2.00
7	Chipper Jones, J.D. Drew	3.00
8	Craig Biggio, Jeff Bagwell	3.00
9	Kazuo Matsui, Mike Piazza	4.00
10	Shawn Green, Adrian Beltre	1.50
11	Bobby Abreu, Jim Thome	3.00
12	Mike Schmidt, Steve Carlton	6.00
13	Cal Ripken Jr., Eddie Murray	10.00
14	Carl Yastrzemski, Dwight Evans	5.00
15	Joe Morgan, Johnny Bench	3.00
16	Dale Murphy, Phil Niekro	2.00
17	Alan Trammell, Kirk Gibson	2.00
18	Jose Canseco, Rickey Henderson	3.00
19	Paul Molitor, Robin Yount	4.00
20	Bo Jackson, George Brett	6.00

Cornerstones Bats

		NM/M
Common Dual Bat:		8.00
1	Albert Pujols, Scott Rolen	20.00
2	Hideki Matsui, Jorge Posada	35.00
3	Sammy Sosa, Nomar Garciaparra	15.00
4	Manny Ramirez, David Ortiz	20.00
5	Miguel Cabrera, Mike Lowell	10.00
6	Hank Blalock, Mark Teixeira	10.00
7	Chipper Jones, J.D. Drew	15.00
8	Craig Biggio, Jeff Bagwell	10.00
9	Mike Piazza, Kazuo Matsui	15.00
10	Shawn Green, Adrian Beltre	8.00

Cornerstones Jerseys

		NM/M
Common Dual Jersey:		8.00
1	Albert Pujols, Scott Rolen	20.00
2	Hideki Matsui, Jorge Posada	35.00
4	Manny Ramirez, David Ortiz	20.00
5	Miguel Cabrera, Mike Lowell	10.00
6	Hank Blalock, Mark Teixeira	10.00
8	Craig Biggio, Jeff Bagwell	10.00
9	Mike Piazza, Kazuo Matsui	15.00
10	Shawn Green, Adrian Beltre	8.00

Cy Young Winners

		NM/M
Complete Set (15):		30.00
Common Player:		1.50
Inserted 1:31		
Gold:		1X
Production 350 Sets		
Gold Die-Cut:		1.5-2X
Production 100 Sets		
1	Warren Spahn	3.00
2	Whitey Ford	3.00
3	Bob Gibson	3.00
4	Tom Seaver	3.00
5	Steve Carlton	2.00
6	Jim Palmer	2.00
7	Rollie Fingers	1.50
8	Dwight Gooden	1.50
9	Roger Clemens	6.00
10	Orel Hershiser	1.50
11	Greg Maddux	4.00
12	Dennis Eckersley	2.00
13	Randy Johnson	3.00
14	Pedro Martinez	3.00
15	Eric Gagne	2.00

Game Collection

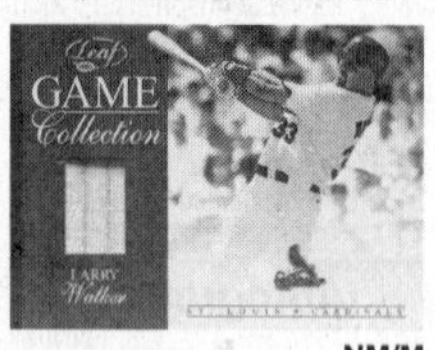

		NM/M
Inserted 1:118		
1	Cal Ripken Jr./Bat	30.00
2	Carl Crawford/Jsy	5.00
3	Dale Murphy/Bat	20.00
4	Don Mattingly/Bat	25.00
5	George Brett/Jsy	25.00
6	Victor Martinez/Bat	8.00
7	Sean Casey/Bat	5.00
8	Torii Hunter/Bat	5.00
9	Maggio Ordonez/Bat	5.00
10	Lance Berkman/Bat	5.00
11	Mike Schmidt/Bat	25.00
12	Nolan Ryan/Jkt	40.00
13	Paul LoDuca/Bat	5.00
14	Preston Wilson/Bat	5.00
15	Rod Carew/Jkt	10.00
16	Reggie Jackson/Bat	10.00
17	Ivan Rodriguez/Bat	8.00
18	Larry Walker/ Cards Bat	10.00
19	Miguel Tejada/Bat	8.00
20	Vladimir Guerrero/ Bat	10.00

Game Collection Autograph

		NM/M
Production 5-200		
2	Carl Crawford/ Jsy/200	15.00
6	Victor Martinez/ Bat/200	20.00
7	Sean Casey/Bat/200	20.00
8	Torii Hunter/Bat/50	25.00
13	Paul LoDuca/Bat/100	20.00

Gamers

		NM/M
Complete Set (15):		20.00
Common Player:		1.00
Inserted 1:13		
Quantum:		2-3X
Production 175 Sets		
Quantum Die-Cut:		3-5X
Production 50 Sets		
1	Albert Pujols	4.00
2	Alex Rodriguez	3.00
3	Alfonso Soriano	1.50
4	Chipper Jones	1.50
5	Derek Jeter	4.00
6	Greg Maddux	2.00
7	Ichiro Suzuki	3.00
8	Jim Thome	1.50
9	Ken Griffey Jr.	2.00
10	Lance Berkman	1.00
11	Miguel Tejada	1.00
12	Mike Piazza	2.50
13	Roger Clemens	4.00
14	Scott Rolen	1.50
15	Vladimir Guerrero	1.50

Gold Rookies

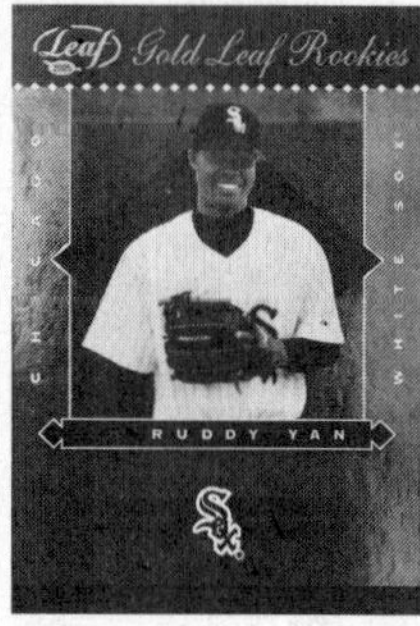

		NM/M
Complete Set (10):		15.00
Common Player:		2.00
Inserted 1:24		
Mirror:		3-5X
Production 25 Sets		
1	Dennis Sarfate	2.00
2	Donnie Kelly	2.00
3	Eddy Rodriguez	2.00
4	Edwin Moreno	2.00
5	Greg Dobbs	2.00
6	Josh Labandeira	2.00
7	Kevin Cave	2.00
8	Mariano Gomez	2.00
9	Ronald Belisario	2.00
10	Ruddy Yan	2.00

Gold Rookies Autograph

		NM/M
Common Autograph:		
Mirror:		No Pricing
Production 25 Sets		
1	Dennis Sarfate	10.00
2	Donnie Kelly	8.00
5	Greg Dobbs	8.00
7	Kevin Cave	10.00
9	Ronald Belisario	8.00
10	Ruddy Yan	8.00

Gold Stars

		NM/M
Complete Set (20):		40.00
Common Player:		.75
Inserted 1:27		
Mirror:		4-6X
Production 25 Sets		
1	Albert Pujols	4.00
2	Ichiro Suzuki	3.00
3	Derek Jeter	4.00
4	Alex Rodriguez	3.00
5	Scott Rolen	1.50
6	Randy Johnson	1.50
7	Roger Clemens	4.00
8	Greg Maddux	2.00
9	Alfonso Soriano	1.50
10	Mark Mulder	.75
11	Sammy Sosa	3.00
12	Mike Piazza	3.00
13	Rafael Palmeiro	.75
14	Ivan Rodriguez	.75
15	Miguel Cabrera	.75
16	Stan Musial	3.00
17	Nolan Ryan	6.00
18	Don Mattingly	4.00
19	George Brett	4.00
20	Cal Ripken Jr.	6.00

Home/Road

		NM/M
Common Player:		1.00
Inserted 1:22		
Home & Road price is identical.		
1H	Albert Pujols/H	4.00
1R	Albert Pujols/R	4.00
2H	Alfonso Soriano/H	1.50
2R	Alfonso Soriano/R	1.50
3H	Carlos Beltran/H	1.00
3R	Carlos Beltran/R	1.00
4H	Chipper Jones/H	1.50
4R	Chipper Jones/R	1.50
5H	Frank Thomas/H	1.50
5R	Frank Thomas/R	1.50
6H	Hank Blalock/H	1.00
6R	Hank Blalock/R	1.00
7H	Ivan Rodriguez/H	1.50
7R	Ivan Rodriguez/R	1.50
8H	Manny Ramirez/H	1.50
8R	Manny Ramirez/R	1.50
9H	Mark Prior/H	1.50
9R	Mark Prior/R	1.50
10H	Miguel Cabrera/H	1.50
10R	Miguel Cabrera/R	1.50
11H	Miguel Tejada/H	1.00
11R	Miguel Tejada/R	1.00
12H	Mike Piazza/H	2.50
12R	Mike Piazza/R	2.50
13H	Roger Clemens/H	4.00
13R	Roger Clemens/R	4.00
14H	Todd Helton/H	1.50
14R	Todd Helton/R	1.50
15H	Vladimir Guerrero/H	1.50
15R	Vladimir Guerrero/R	1.50

Home/Road Jersey

		NM/M
Common Player:		
1H	Albert Pujols/H	20.00
1R	Albert Pujols/R	20.00
2H	Alfonso Soriano/H	8.00
3H	Carlos Beltran/H	8.00
3R	Carlos Beltran/R	8.00
4R	Chipper Jones/R	8.00
5H	Frank Thomas/H	8.00
5R	Frank Thomas/R	8.00
6H	Hank Blalock/H	8.00
7H	Ivan Rodriguez/H	8.00
7R	Ivan Rodriguez/R	8.00
8R	Manny Ramirez/R	8.00
9H	Mark Prior/H	8.00
11H	Miguel Tejada/H	5.00
11R	Miguel Tejada/R	5.00
12H	Mike Piazza/H	12.00
13H	Roger Clemens/H	15.00
13R	Roger Clemens/R	15.00
14H	Todd Helton/H	8.00
14R	Todd Helton/R	8.00
15H	Vladimir Guerrero/H	8.00

Patch Off My Back

		NM/M
Common Patch:		15.00
Production 50 Sets		
1	Adam Dunn	25.00
2	Aubrey Huff	15.00
3	Austin Kearns	15.00
4	Bobby Crosby	25.00
5	C.C. Sabathia	15.00
7	David Ortiz	25.00
8	Dewon Brazelton	15.00
9	Edgar Martinez	20.00
10	Frankie Francisco	15.00
11	Garret Anderson	20.00
12	Hideki Matsui	50.00
13	Hideo Nomo	20.00
14	Jack Wilson	15.00
15	Javy Lopez	15.00
16	Jay Gibbons	15.00
17	Jim Edmonds	20.00
18	Jody Gerut	15.00
19	Joey Gathright	15.00
20	Johan Santana	20.00
21	Jose Reyes	15.00
22	Jose Vidro	15.00
23	Lance Berkman	15.00
24	Mariano Rivera	20.00
25	Mark Teixeira	20.00
26	Michael Young	15.00
27	Mike Cameron	15.00
28	Mike Sweeney	15.00
29	Omar Vizquel	15.00
30	Preston Wilson	15.00
31	Rocco Baldelli	15.00
32	Scott Rolen	25.00
33	Sean Burroughs	15.00
34	Sean Casey	15.00
35	Tim Hudson	20.00
36	Torii Hunter	20.00
37	Trevor Hoffman	20.00
38	Troy Glaus	20.00
39	Vernon Wells	15.00
40	Victor Martinez	20.00

Patch Off My Back Autograph

		NM/M
Production 10-75		
2	Aubrey Huff/50	35.00
4	Bobby Crosby/75	50.00
5	C.C. Sabathia/75	30.00
7	David Ortiz/50	100.00
8	Dewon Brazelton/75	25.00
14	Jack Wilson/75	30.00
16	Jay Gibbons/50	25.00
18	Jody Gerut/75	20.00
20	Johan Santana/50	60.00
22	Jose Vidro/75	25.00
26	Michael Young/75	35.00
33	Sean Burroughs/25	25.00
40	Victor Martinez/75	35.00

Picture Perfect

		NM/M
Complete Set (20):		30.00
Common Player:		1.00
Inserted 1:20		
Die-Cut:		2-3X
Production 100 Sets		
1	Albert Pujols	4.00
2	Alex Rodriguez	3.00
3	Alfonso Soriano	1.50
4	Derek Jeter	4.00
5	Greg Maddux	2.00
6	Hideki Matsui	3.00
7	Ichiro Suzuki	3.00
8	Ivan Rodriguez	1.00
9	Jim Thome	1.00
10	Mark Mulder	1.00
11	Mark Prior	1.50
12	Miguel Tejada	1.00
13	Mike Mussina	1.00
14	Mike Piazza	2.50
15	Nomar Garciaparra	2.50
16	Randy Johnson	1.50
17	Roger Clemens	4.00
18	Sammy Sosa	2.50
19	Scott Rolen	1.50
20	Vladimir Guerrero	1.50

Recollection Autographs

No Pricing
Production 1-29

Shirt Off My Back

		NM/M
Common Player:		5.00
Inserted 1:48		
1	Adam Dunn	15.00
4	Bobby Crosby	15.00
5	C.C. Sabathia	8.00
7	David Ortiz	15.00
8	Dewon Brazelton	5.00
9	Edgar Martinez	5.00
10	Frankie Francisco	5.00
11	Garret Anderson	5.00
12	Hideki Matsui	25.00
13	Hideo Nomo	8.00
14	Jack Wilson	5.00
15	Javy Lopez	8.00
16	Jay Gibbons	5.00
17	Jim Edmonds	15.00
18	Jody Gerut SP	5.00
19	Joey Gathright	5.00
20	Johan Santana	10.00
21	Jose Reyes	5.00
22	Jose Vidro	5.00
23	Lance Berkman	5.00
25	Mark Teixeira	5.00
26	Michael Young	5.00
27	Mike Cameron	5.00
28	Mike Sweeney	5.00
29	Omar Vizquel	8.00
30	Preston Wilson	5.00
31	Rocco Baldelli	8.00
32	Scott Rolen	10.00
33	Sean Burroughs	5.00
34	Sean Casey	5.00
35	Tim Hudson	5.00
36	Torii Hunter	5.00
37	Trevor Hoffman	5.00
38	Troy Glaus	5.00
39	Vernon Wells	5.00
40	Victor Martinez	8.00

Sportscasters 70 Green

		NM/M
Common Player:		2.00
Production 70 Sets		
Variations #'d 35-65:		1X
Variations #'d 20-30:		1.5X
No pricing 15 or less.		
1	Adam Dunn	3.00
2	Al Kaline	5.00
3	Albert Pujols	8.00
4	Alex Rodriguez	8.00
5	Alfonso Soriano	3.00
6	Bob Gibson	3.00
7	Cal Ripken Jr.	25.00
8	Carl Yastrzemski	8.00
9	Dale Murphy	3.00
10	Derek Jeter	10.00
11	Don Mattingly	10.00
12	Duke Snider	4.00
13	Eric Gagne	3.00
14	Ernie Banks	6.00
15	Frank Robinson	3.00
16	George Brett	10.00
17	Greg Maddux	6.00
18	Harmon Killebrew	5.00
19	Ichiro Suzuki	8.00
20	Ivan Rodriguez	4.00
21	Jim Edmonds	2.00
22	Jim Palmer	2.00
23	Jim Thome	4.00
24	Johnny Bench	5.00
25	Ken Griffey Jr.	6.00
26	Larry Walker	3.00
27	Mark Mulder	2.00
28	Mark Prior	4.00
29	Miguel Tejada	3.00
30	Mike Mussina	3.00
31	Mike Piazza	6.00
32	Mike Schmidt	10.00
33	Nolan Ryan	15.00
34	Nomar Garciaparra	6.00
35	Pedro Martinez	4.00
36	Rafael Palmeiro	3.00
37	Randy Johnson	4.00
38	Reggie Jackson	3.00
39	Rickey Henderson	4.00
40	Roberto Clemente	15.00
41	Rod Carew	3.00

42 Roger Clemens 8.00
43 Ryne Sandberg 8.00
44 Sammy Sosa 6.00
45 Stan Musial 8.00
46 Steve Carlton 2.00
47 Tony Gwynn 5.00
48 Vladimir Guerrero 4.00
49 Warren Spahn 4.00
50 Willie McCovey 3.00

4 Star Staffs

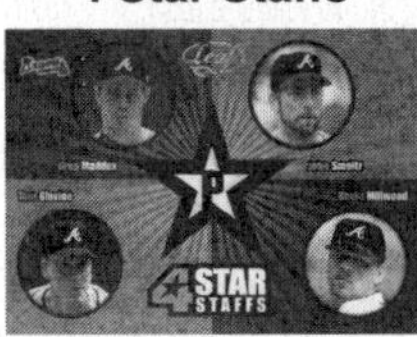

NM/M
Common Card: 2.00
Inserted 1:48
Die-Cut: 1X
Production 250 Sets
1 Kevin Millwood, Tom Glavine, Greg Maddux, John Smoltz 4.00
2 A.J. Burnett, Carl Pavano, Dontrelle Willis, Josh Beckett 2.00
3 Andy Pettitte, David Wells, Mike Mussina, Roger Clemens 6.00
4 Carlos Zambrano, Greg Maddux, Kerry Wood, Mark Prior 4.00
5 Andy Pettitte, Mariano Rivera, Mike Mussina, Roger Clemens 3.00
6 Curt Schilling, Derek Lowe, Pedro J. Martinez, Tim Wakefield 4.00
7 Barry Zito, Mark Mulder, Rich Harden, Tim Hudson 2.00
8 Brandon Webb, Byung-Hyun Kim, Curt Schilling, Randy Johnson 3.00
9 Jamie Moyer, Kenny Rogers, Kevin Brown, Nolan Ryan 8.00
10 Kelvim Escobar, Roger Clemens, Roy Halladay, Woody Williams 6.00
11 Andy Pettitte, Roger Clemens, Roy Oswalt, Wade Miller 6.00
12 Barry Zito, Billy Koch, Mark Mulder, Tim Hudson 2.00
13 Eric Gagne, Hideo Nomo, Kazuhisa Ishii, Kevin Brown 3.00
14 Greg Maddux, Jason Schmidt, John Smoltz, Tom Glavine 5.00
15 Derek Lowe, Hideo Nomo, Pedro Martinez, Tim Wakefield 4.00

Century

NM/M
Complete Set (200): 40.00
Common Player: .25
Pack (5): 12.00
Box (10): 100.00
1 Brian Roberts .25
2 Derek Jeter 2.00
3 Harmon Killebrew 1.00
4 Angel Berroa .25
5 George Brett 2.00
6 Stan Musial 1.50
7 Ivan Rodriguez .50
8 Cal Ripken Jr. 3.00
9 Hank Blalock .50
10 Miguel Tejada .50
11 Barry Larkin .40
12 Alfonso Soriano .75
13 Alex Rodriguez 2.00
14 Paul Konerko .25
15 Jim Edmonds .40
16 Garret Anderson .40
17 Todd Helton .50
18 Moises Alou .40
19 Tony Gwynn .75
20 Mike Schmidt 2.00
21 Sammy Sosa 1.25
22 Roger Clemens 2.00
23 Tony Perez .25
24 Manny Ramirez .75
25 Jim Thome .75
26 Chase Utley .40
27 Scott Rolen .75
28 Austin Kearns .25
29 John Smoltz .40
30 Ken Griffey Jr. 1.00
31 Mike Piazza 1.00
32 Steve Carlton .50
33 Larry Walker .40
34 Nolan Ryan 2.50
35 Mike Mussina .40
36 Joe Nathan .25
37 Kenny Rogers .25
38 Eric Gagne .40
39 Brett Myers .25
40 Rich Harden .25
41 Victor Martinez .40
42 Mariano Rivera .40
43 Dennis Eckersley .50
44 Roy Oswalt .25
45 Pedro Martinez .75
46 Jason Bay .40
47 Tom Glavine .40
48 Torii Hunter .25
49 Larry Bigbie .25
50 Nomar Garciaparra 1.50
51 Ichiro Suzuki 1.50
52 C.C. Sabathia .25
53 Bobby Abreu .40
54 Doug Mientkiewicz .25
55 Hideki Matsui 1.50
56 Mark Buehrle .25
57 Johan Santana .50
58 Johnny Damon .75
59 Edgar Martinez .40
60 Preston Wilson .25
61 Livan Hernandez .25
62 Eric Chavez .25
63 Lyle Overbay .25
64 Jason Schmidt .50
65 Cliff Lee .25
66 Shingo Takatsu .25
67 Jeff Bagwell .50
68 Danny Graves .25
69 Kip Wells .25
70 Steve Finley .25
71 Lew Ford .25
72 Chone Figgins .25
73 Delmon Young .40
74 Esteban Loaiza .25
75 Barry Zito .40
76 Carlos Delgado .40
77 Joe Mauer .50
78 Ryan Wagner .25
79 John Lackey .25
80 Adrian Beltre .40
81 Vernon Wells .25
82 Sean Burroughs .25
83 Francisco Cordero .25
84 Carlos Guillen .25
85 Eric Byrnes .25
86 Jose Reyes .40
87 Rocco Baldelli .25
88 Josh Beckett .40
89 Casey Kotchman .40
90 Scott Podsednik .25
91 Mike Sweeney .25
92 Khalil Greene .50
93 Trot Nixon .25
94 Chad Cordero .25
95 Derek Lowe .25
96 Jason Giambi .40
97 Jose Guillen .25
98 Craig Biggio .40
99 Pat Burrell .40
100 Kazuo Matsui .25
101 Rafael Furcal .25
102 Jack Wilson .25
103 Edgar Renteria .50
104 Carlos Beltran .75
105 Albert Pujols 2.00
106 Melvin Mora .25
107 J.D. Drew .40
108 Andre Dawson .50
109 Jody Gerut .25
110 Michael Young .25
111 Gary Sheffield .50
112 Wade Boggs .50
113 Carl Crawford .25
114 Paul LoDuca .25
115 Tim Hudson .40
116 Aramis Ramirez .40
117 Lance Berkman .40
118 Javy Lopez .40
119 Robin Yount 1.00
120 Mark Mulder .25
121 Sean Casey .25
122 Will Clark .50
123 Don Mattingly 2.00
124 Miguel Cabrera .75
125 Rafael Palmeiro .50
126 David Ortiz .75
127 Vladimir Guerrero .75
128 Ken Harvey .25
129 Rod Carew .50
130 Magglio Ordonez .25
131 Greg Maddux 1.00
132 Roy Halladay .25
133 Javier Vazquez .25
134 Kerry Wood .75
135 Frank Thomas .50
136 Tom Gordon .25
137 Jake Peavy .25
138 Curt Schilling .75
139 Dewon Brazelton .25
140 Jae Weong Seo .25
141 Danny Kolb .25
142 Jeff Kent .40
143 Juan Encarnacion .25
144 Adam Dunn .50
145 Carlos Lee .25
146 Matt Clement .25
147 Guillermo Mota .25
148 Travis Hafner .40
149 Brad Wilkerson .25
150 Eric Milton .25
151 Randy Johnson .75
152 Joe Crede .25
153 Mark Kotsay .25
154 Jason Varitek .40
155 David Wright .75
156 Brad Penny .25
157 Francisco Rodriguez .25
158 Gary Carter .50
159 Adrian Gonzalez .25
160 Derrek Lee .40
161 Mark Prior .50
162 Carlos Zambrano .40
163 Bobby Crosby .40
164 Jermaine Dye .25
165 Kris Benson .25
166 Dontrelle Willis .40
167 Dallas McPherson .40
168 Johnny Estrada .40
169 Milton Bradley .25
170 Shannon Stewart .25
171 Ben Sheets .40
172 Richard Hidalgo .25
173 Laynce Nix .25
174 B.J. Upton .50
175 Craig Wilson .25
176 Hideo Nomo .40
177 Troy Glaus .40
178 Akinori Otsuka .25
179 Rickie Weeks .40
180 Mike Lowell .40
181 Marcus Giles .25
182 Randy Wolf .25
183 A.J. Burnett .25
184 Aubrey Huff .25
185 Billy Ripken .25
186 Octavio Dotel .25
187 Kazuhisa Ishii .25
188 Mark Teixeira .50
189 Todd Walker .25
190 Dale Murphy .50
191 Alexis Rios .25
192 Reggie Sanders .25
193 Orlando Cabrera .25
194 Shawn Green .40
195 Andy Pettitte .40
196 Chipper Jones .75
197 Jose Vidro .25
198 Jacque Jones .25
199 Brian Giles .25
200 Andruw Jones .40

Post Marks Silver

Silvers: 3-6X
Production 100 Sets

Post Marks Gold

Golds: 4-8X
Production 50 Sets

Post Marks Platinum

No Pricing
Production One Set

Air Mail Bat

NM/M
Production 50-250
1 Babe Ruth/50 150.00
2 Frank Robinson/250 12.00
3 Harmon Killebrew/100 20.00
4 Sammy Sosa/100 10.00
5 Reggie Jackson/250 15.00
6 Mike Schmidt/100 20.00
7 Rafael Palmeiro/100 8.00
8 Ted Williams/50 80.00
9 Willie McCovey/250 10.00
10 Ernie Banks/100 20.00

Air Mail Bat Signature

NM/M
Production 1-25
2 Frank Robinson/25 40.00
3 Harmon Killebrew/25 60.00
9 Willie McCovey/25 35.00

Material Bat

NM/M
Common Player: 5.00
3 Harmon Killebrew/250 12.00
4 Angel Berroa/50 5.00
5 George Brett/250 15.00
6 Stan Musial/250 15.00
7 Ivan Rodriguez/100 8.00
8 Cal Ripken Jr./250 25.00
9 Hank Blalock/100 8.00
10 Miguel Tejada/100 6.00
11 Barry Larkin/100 6.00
12 Alfonso Soriano/100 8.00
14 Paul Konerko/50 5.00
15 Jim Edmonds/100 8.00
16 Garret Anderson/100 5.00
17 Todd Helton/100 8.00
18 Moises Alou/50 6.00
19 Tony Gwynn/250 10.00
20 Mike Schmidt/250 15.00
21 Sammy Sosa/100 10.00
22 Roger Clemens/100 15.00
23 Tony Perez/100 8.00
24 Manny Ramirez/100 10.00
25 Jim Thome/100 12.00
27 Scott Rolen/100 10.00
28 Austin Kearns/50 5.00
31 Mike Piazza/100 12.00
32 Steve Carlton/250 8.00
33 Larry Walker/100 8.00
34 Nolan Ryan/250 20.00
35 Mike Mussina/100 8.00
41 Victor Martinez/50 8.00
44 Roy Oswalt/100 5.00
45 Pedro Martinez/100 8.00
47 Tom Glavine/100 6.00
48 Torii Hunter/100 6.00
50 Nomar Garciaparra/100 15.00
53 Bobby Abreu/25 10.00
54 Doug Mientkiewicz/50 5.00
55 Hideki Matsui/100 25.00
56 Mark Buehrle/50 6.00
58 Johnny Damon/100 12.00
59 Edgar Martinez/100 6.00
60 Preston Wilson/50 6.00
62 Eric Chavez/100 5.00
63 Lyle Overbay/50 8.00
67 Jeff Bagwell/100 8.00
71 Lew Ford/50 5.00
73 Delmon Young/100 8.00
75 Barry Zito/100 5.00
76 Carlos Delgado/100 5.00
80 Adrian Beltre/100 8.00
81 Vernon Wells/100 5.00
86 Jose Reyes/50 8.00
87 Rocco Baldelli/100 5.00
88 Josh Beckett/100 5.00
91 Mike Sweeney/50 5.00
93 Trot Nixon/50 6.00
96 Jason Giambi/100 5.00
98 Craig Biggio/100 6.00
99 Pat Burrell/50 8.00
100 Kazuo Matsui/100 8.00
101 Rafael Furcal/50 6.00
102 Jack Wilson/50 8.00
103 Edgar Renteria/100 6.00
104 Carlos Beltran/100 8.00
105 Albert Pujols/100 15.00
106 Melvin Mora/50 5.00
107 J.D. Drew/100 5.00
108 Andre Dawson/250 6.00
109 Jody Gerut/50 6.00
110 Michael Young/250 5.00
111 Gary Sheffield/100 6.00
112 Wade Boggs/250 8.00
114 Paul LoDuca/100 10.00
115 Tim Hudson/100 5.00
116 Aramis Ramirez/50 8.00
117 Lance Berkman/250 5.00
118 Javy Lopez/100 5.00
119 Robin Yount/250 10.00
120 Mark Mulder/100 5.00
121 Sean Casey/50 5.00
122 Will Clark/250 8.00
123 Don Mattingly/250 15.00
124 Miguel Cabrera/50 12.00
125 Rafael Palmeiro/250 8.00
126 David Ortiz/250 12.00
127 Vladimir Guerrero/250 8.00
128 Ken Harvey/50 5.00
129 Rod Carew/250 8.00
130 Magglio Ordonez/250 5.00
131 Greg Maddux/100 10.00
134 Kerry Wood/100 8.00
135 Frank Thomas/100 8.00
138 Curt Schilling/100 8.00
142 Jeff Kent/250 5.00
143 Juan Encarnacion/50 5.00
144 Adam Dunn/250 8.00
145 Carlos Lee/250 5.00
148 Travis Hafner/50 6.00
149 Brad Wilkerson/50 5.00
151 Randy Johnson/100 10.00
152 Joe Crede/50 6.00
154 Jason Varitek/250 10.00
156 Brad Penny/50 5.00
158 Gary Carter/250 8.00
160 Derrek Lee/250 5.00
161 Mark Prior/100 8.00
164 Jermaine Dye/50 5.00
166 Dontrelle Willis/100 6.00
168 Johnny Estrada/50 6.00
170 Shannon Stewart/100 5.00
171 Ben Sheets/50 8.00
172 Richard Hidalgo/50 5.00
173 Laynce Nix/50 5.00
174 B.J. Upton/50 8.00
175 Craig Wilson/100 5.00
176 Hideo Nomo/100 8.00
177 Troy Glaus/250 5.00
179 Rickie Weeks/25 8.00
180 Mike Lowell/100 5.00
183 A.J. Burnett/100 5.00
184 Aubrey Huff/50 5.00
187 Kazuhisa Ishii/100 5.00
188 Mark Teixeira/250 5.00
190 Dale Murphy/250 8.00
191 Alexis Rios/50 5.00
193 Orlando Cabrera/50 6.00
194 Shawn Green/250 5.00
195 Andy Pettitte/100 6.00
196 Chipper Jones/100 8.00
197 Jose Vidro/250 5.00
198 Jacque Jones/100 5.00
199 Brian Giles/250 5.00
200 Andruw Jones/250 6.00

Material Fabric Number

NM/M
Common Player: 5.00
20 Mike Schmidt/Jsy/20 50.00
21 Sammy Sosa/Jsy/21 20.00
22 Roger Clemens/Jsy/22 40.00
23 Tony Perez/Jsy/24 15.00
24 Manny Ramirez/Jsy/24 20.00
25 Jim Thome/Jsy/25 20.00
27 Scott Rolen/Jsy/27 20.00
28 Austin Kearns/Jsy/28 15.00
29 John Smoltz/Jsy/29 20.00
31 Mike Piazza/Jsy/31 25.00
32 Steve Carlton/Pants/32 15.00
34 Nolan Ryan/Jsy/34 50.00
35 Mike Mussina/Jsy/35 15.00
39 Brett Myers/Jsy/39 8.00
41 Victor Martinez/Jsy/41 8.00
42 Mariano Rivera/Jsy/42 15.00
43 Dennis Eckersley/Jsy/43 10.00
44 Roy Oswalt/Jsy/44 8.00
45 Pedro Martinez/Jsy/45 10.00
47 Tom Glavine/Jsy/47 10.00
48 Torii Hunter/Jsy/48 8.00
52 C.C. Sabathia/Jsy/52 8.00
53 Bobby Abreu/Jsy/53 8.00
55 Hideki Matsui/Jsy/55 35.00
56 Mark Buehrle/Jsy/56 8.00
57 Johan Santana/Jsy/57 15.00
60 Preston Wilson/Jsy/44 8.00
61 Livan Hernandez/Jsy/61 5.00
65 Cliff Lee/Jsy/34 8.00
71 Lew Ford/Jsy/20 10.00
75 Barry Zito/Jsy/75 5.00
76 Carlos Delgado/Jsy/25 10.00
78 Ryan Wagner/Jsy/38 5.00
80 Adrian Beltre/Jsy/29 15.00
82 Sean Burroughs/Jsy/32 8.00
83 Francisco Cordero/Jsy/31 8.00
85 Eric Byrnes/Jsy/22 8.00
91 Mike Sweeney/Jsy/29 8.00
96 Jason Giambi/Jsy/25 10.00
100 Kazuo Matsui/Jsy/25 12.00
118 Javy Lopez/Jsy/18 15.00
119 Robin Yount/Jsy/19 30.00
120 Mark Mulder/Jsy/20 12.00
121 Sean Casey/Jsy/21 10.00
122 Will Clark/Jsy/22 20.00
123 Don Mattingly/Pants/23 40.00
124 Miguel Cabrera/Jsy/24 20.00
125 Rafael Palmeiro/Jsy/25 15.00
126 David Ortiz/Jsy/34 20.00
127 Vladimir Guerrero/Jsy/27 20.00
128 Ken Harvey/Jsy/28 10.00
129 Rod Carew/Jsy/29 20.00
130 Magglio Ordonez/Jsy/30 10.00
131 Greg Maddux/Jsy/31 25.00
132 Roy Halladay/Jsy/32 10.00
134 Kerry Wood/Jsy/34 20.00
135 Frank Thomas/Jsy/35 20.00
138 Curt Schilling/Jsy/34 15.00
139 Dewon Brazelton/Jsy/45 5.00
140 Jae Weong/Seo Jsy/40 5.00
141 Danny Kolb/Jsy/41 5.00
144 Adam Dunn/Jsy/44 15.00
145 Carlos Lee/Jsy/45 8.00
146 Matt Clement/Jsy/30 10.00
148 Travis Hafner/Jsy/48 8.00
151 Randy Johnson/Pants/51 15.00
154 Jason Varitek/Jsy/33 20.00
157 Francisco Rodriguez/Jsy/57 5.00
162 Carlos Zambrano/Jsy/38 8.00
164 Jermaine Dye/Jsy/24 10.00
166 Dontrelle Willis/Jsy/35 12.00
168 Johnny Estrada/Jsy/23 10.00
170 Shannon Stewart/Jsy/23 10.00
175 Craig Wilson/Jsy/36 5.00
177 Troy Glaus/Jsy/25 15.00
180 Mike Lowell/Jsy/19 20.00
183 A.J. Burnett/Jsy/34 10.00
188 Mark Teixeira/Jsy/23 15.00
195 Andy Pettitte/Jsy/21 20.00
200 Andruw Jones/Jsy/5 15.00

Material Fabric Position

NM/M
Common Player: 4.00
Prime: No Pricing
Production One Set
1 Brian Roberts/Jsy/250 4.00
3 Harmon Killebrew/Jsy/250 12.00
4 Angel Berroa/Jsy/250 4.00
5 George Brett/Jsy/250 15.00
6 Stan Musial/Pants/100 15.00
7 Ivan Rodriguez/Jsy/250 6.00
8 Cal Ripken Jr./Jkt/250 25.00
9 Hank Blalock/Jsy/250 8.00
10 Miguel Tejada/Jsy/250 6.00
11 Barry Larkin/Jsy/100 6.00
12 Alfonso Soriano/Jsy/250 4.00
14 Paul Konerko/Jsy/250 4.00
15 Jim Edmonds/Jsy/250 6.00
16 Garret Anderson/Jsy/250 4.00
17 Todd Helton/Jsy/250 6.00
19 Tony Gwynn/Jsy/250 10.00
20 Mike Schmidt/Jsy/250 15.00
21 Sammy Sosa/Jsy/250 10.00
22 Roger Clemens/Jsy/250 12.00
23 Tony Perez/Jsy/250 6.00
24 Manny Ramirez/Jsy/250 8.00
25 Jim Thome/Jsy/250 8.00
27 Scott Rolen/Jsy/250 8.00
28 Austin Kearns/Jsy/250 4.00
29 John Smoltz/Jsy/250 6.00
31 Mike Piazza/Jsy/250 10.00
32 Steve Carlton/Pants/250 6.00
34 Nolan Ryan/Jsy/250 20.00
35 Mike Mussina/Jsy/250 6.00
39 Brett Myers/Jsy/250 4.00
41 Victor Martinez/Jsy/250 4.00

42 Mariano Rivera /Jsy/250 6.00
43 Dennis Eckersley/ Jsy/250 6.00
44 Roy Oswalt/Jsy/250 4.00
45 Pedro Martinez/ Jsy/250 8.00
46 Jason Bay/Jsy/250 4.00
47 Tom Glavine/Jsy/250 6.00
48 Torii Hunter/Jsy/250 4.00
49 Larry Bigbie/Jsy/250 4.00
52 C.C. Sabathia/Jsy/250 4.00
53 Bobby Abreu/Jsy/250 4.00
55 Hideki Matsui/ Jsy/250 20.00
56 Mark Buehrle/Jsy/250 4.00
57 Johan Santana/ Jsy/250 8.00
59 Edgar Martinez/ Jsy/250 6.00
60 Preston Wilson/ Jsy/250 4.00
61 Livan Hernandez/ Jsy/250 4.00
62 Eric Chavez/Jsy/250 6.00
63 Lyle Overbay/Jsy/250 4.00
65 Cliff Lee/Jsy/250 4.00
67 Jeff Bagwell/Jsy/250 8.00
71 Lew Ford/Jsy/250 4.00
72 Chone Figgins/Jsy/250 4.00
75 Barry Zito/Jsy/250 4.00
76 Carlos Delgado/ Jsy/250 4.00
78 Ryan Wagner/Jsy/250 4.00
80 Adrian Beltre/Jsy/250 8.00
81 Vernon Wells/Jsy/250 4.00
82 Sean Burroughs/ Jsy/250 4.00
83 Francisco Cordero/ Jsy/250 4.00
85 Eric Byrnes/Jsy/250 10.00
86 Jose Reyes/Jsy/250 4.00
87 Rocco Baldelli/Jsy/250 4.00
88 Josh Beckett/Jsy/250 4.00
90 Scott Podsednik/ Jsy/250 4.00
91 Mike Sweeney/Jsy/250 4.00
93 Trot Nixon/Jsy/250 4.00
96 Jason Giambi/Jsy/250 4.00
98 Craig Biggio/Jsy/250 6.00
99 Pat Burrell/Jsy/250 4.00
100 Kazuo Matsui/Jsy/250 4.00
101 Rafael Furcal/Jsy/250 4.00
102 Jack Wilson/Jsy/250 4.00
103 Edgar Renteria/ Jsy/250 6.00
104 Carlos Beltran/Jsy/250 8.00
105 Albert Pujols/Jsy/250 15.00
106 Melvin Mora/Jsy/100 4.00
108 Andre Dawson/ Jsy/250 6.00
109 Jody Gerut/Jsy/250 4.00
110 Michael Young/ Jsy/250 4.00
111 Gary Sheffield/Jsy/250 6.00
112 Wade Boggs/Jsy/100 8.00
113 Carl Crawford/Jsy/250 4.00
115 Tim Hudson/Jsy/250 4.00
116 Aramis Ramirez/ Jsy/250 6.00
117 Lance Berkman/ Jsy/250 4.00
118 Javy Lopez/Jsy/250 4.00
119 Robin Yount/Jsy/250 10.00
120 Mark Mulder/Jsy/250 4.00
121 Sean Casey/Jsy/250 4.00
122 Will Clark/Jsy/250 6.00
123 Don Mattingly/ Pants/250 15.00
124 Miguel Cabrera/ Jsy/250 8.00
125 Rafael Palmeiro/ Jsy/250 8.00
126 David Ortiz/Jsy/250 8.00
127 Vladimir Guerrero/ Jsy/250 8.00
128 Ken Harvey/Jsy/250 4.00
129 Rod Carew/Jsy/250 8.00
130 Magglio Ordonez/ Jsy/250 4.00
131 Greg Maddux/ Jsy/250 10.00
132 Roy Halladay/Jsy/250 4.00
134 Kerry Wood/Jsy/250 8.00
135 Frank Thomas/Jsy/250 8.00
138 Curt Schilling/Jsy/250 8.00
139 Dewon Brazelton/ Jsy/100 4.00
140 Jae Weong/ Seo Jsy/100 4.00
141 Danny Kolb/Jsy/250 4.00
142 Jeff Kent/Jsy/100 6.00
144 Adam Dunn/Jsy/250 6.00
145 Carlos Lee/Jsy/250 4.00
146 Matt Clement/Jsy/250 4.00
148 Travis Hafner/Jsy/250 4.00
151 Randy Johnson/ Pants/250 8.00
154 Jason Varitek/ Jsy/100 15.00
157 Francisco Rodriguez/ Jsy/100 4.00
158 Gary Carter/Jsy/250 6.00
161 Mark Prior/Jsy/250 8.00
162 Carlos Zambrano/ Jsy/100 6.00
163 Bobby Crosby/Jsy/250 8.00
164 Jermaine Dye/Jsy/100 4.00
166 Dontrelle Willis/ Jsy/250 4.00
168 Johnny Estrada/ Jsy/100 4.00
170 Shannon Stewart/ Jsy/100 4.00
171 Ben Sheets/Jsy/250 6.00
173 Laynce Nix/Jsy/100 4.00
175 Craig Wilson/Jsy/100 4.00
176 Hideo Nomo/Jsy/250 8.00
177 Troy Glaus/Jsy/250 4.00
180 Mike Lowell 4.00
183 A.J. Burnett/Jsy/100 4.00
184 Aubrey Huff/Jsy/250 4.00
187 Kazuhisa Ishii/Jsy/250 4.00
188 Mark Teixeira/Jsy/250 6.00
190 Dale Murphy/Jsy/250 8.00
194 Shawn Green/Jsy/250 4.00
195 Andy Pettitte/Jsy/250 6.00
196 Chipper Jones/Jsy/250 8.00
197 Jose Vidro/Jsy/100 4.00
198 Jacque Jones/Jsy/250 4.00
200 Andruw Jones/ Jsy/250 6.00

Pennant Patches

NM/M
Production 5-25
1 Ozzie Smith/25 40.00
2 Keith Hernandez/25 20.00
3 Rickey Henderson/25 30.00
4 Paul Molitor/25 25.00
5 George Brett/25 50.00
6 Steve Garvey/25 20.00
7 Randy Johnson/25 25.00
8 Cal Ripken Jr./25 90.00
9 Darryl Strawberry/25 20.00
10 Chipper Jones/25 30.00
11 Steve Carlton/25 20.00
12 Orel Hershiser/25 20.00
13 Carlton Fisk/25 25.00
14 Dave Parker/25 20.00
15 Rollie Fingers/25 20.00
16 Dwight Gooden/25 20.00
18 Dontrelle Willis/25 15.00
19 Dave Righetti/25 15.00

Pennant Patches Signature

NM/M
Production 5-25
2 Keith Hernandez/25 40.00
6 Steve Garvey/25 35.00
9 Darryl Strawberry/25 40.00
11 Steve Carlton/25 40.00
15 Rollie Fingers/25 35.00
16 Dwight Gooden/25 40.00

Shirts

NM/M
Production 25-100
1 Rod Carew/100 10.00
2 Red Schoendienst/50 8.00
3 Harmon Killebrew/50 20.00
4 Joe Cronin/50 35.00
5 Early Wynn/50 8.00
6 Gaylord Perry/100 8.00
7 Willie McCovey/100 10.00
8 Carl Yastrzemski/100 20.00
9 Reggie Jackson/100 10.00
10 Duke Snider/50 15.00
11 Luis Aparicio/100 8.00
12 Bob Gibson/50 15.00
13 Maury Wills/50 8.00
14 Ernie Banks/50 20.00
15 Enos Slaughter/100 10.00
16 Whitey Ford/100 15.00
17 Warren Spahn/100 15.00
18 Roger Maris/100 35.00
19 Hal Newhouser/100 10.00
20 Marty Marion/25 12.00

Shirts Signature

NM/M
Production 5-50
Prime: No Pricing
Production One Set
2 Red Schoendienst/25 25.00
6 Gaylord Perry/50 20.00
7 Willie McCovey/50 30.00
11 Luis Aparicio/50 25.00
13 Maury Wills/50 20.00

Signature Post Marks Gold

NM/M
Production 1-50
36 Joe Nathan/50 20.00
39 Brett Myers/50 12.00
40 Rich Harden/50 15.00
49 Larry Bigbie/50 15.00
61 Livan Hernandez/50 15.00
63 Lyle Overbay/50 15.00
65 Cliff Lee/50 12.00
68 Danny Graves/25 20.00
71 Lew Ford/50 15.00
72 Chone Figgins/50 20.00
74 Esteban Loaiza/50 20.00
78 Ryan Wagner/50 10.00
79 John Lackey/50 15.00
83 Francisco Cordero/25 15.00
85 Eric Byrnes/25 20.00
89 Casey Kotchman/50 25.00
90 Scott Podsednik/50 15.00
94 Chad Cordero/25 15.00
97 Jose Guillen/25 20.00
102 Jack Wilson/50 15.00
106 Melvin Mora/25 20.00
109 Jody Gerut/50 10.00
128 Ken Harvey/50 10.00
136 Tom Gordon/50 15.00
137 Jake Peavy/25 25.00
139 Dewon Brazelton/50 10.00
140 Jae Weong Seo/25 20.00
141 Danny Kolb/50 20.00
145 Carlos Lee/25 20.00
147 Guillermo Mota/50 10.00
148 Travis Hafner/25 20.00
156 Brad Penny/50 10.00
159 Adrian Gonzalez/50 15.00
163 Bobby Crosby/25 30.00
164 Jermaine Dye/25 20.00
168 Johnny Estrada/25 25.00
169 Milton Bradley/25 20.00
170 Shannon Stewart/25 15.00
173 Laynce Nix/50 20.00
175 Craig Wilson/50 15.00
182 Randy Wolf/50 15.00
184 Aubrey Huff/25 20.00
185 Billy Ripken/50 10.00
186 Octavio Dotel/50 15.00
189 Todd Walker/25 20.00
191 Alexis Rios/50 15.00
198 Jacque Jones/25 15.00

Signature Post Marks Silver

NM/M
Production 1-250
Platinum: No Pricing
Production One Set
1 Brian Roberts/250 8.00
4 Angel Berroa/25 15.00
36 Joe Nathan/250 15.00
39 Brett Myers/250 8.00
40 Rich Harden/100 15.00
49 Larry Bigbie/250 10.00
52 C.C. Sabathia/25 20.00
56 Mark Buehrle/25 15.00
61 Livan Hernandez/100 10.00
63 Lyle Overbay/100 15.00
65 Cliff Lee/250 8.00
68 Danny Graves/100 10.00
71 Lew Ford/100 10.00
72 Chone Figgins/250 10.00
74 Esteban Loaiza/250 10.00
78 Ryan Wagner/250 10.00
79 John Lackey/250 10.00
82 Sean Burroughs/25 15.00
83 Francisco Cordero/ 100 8.00
85 Eric Byrnes/100 10.00
89 Casey Kotchman/250 20.00
90 Scott Podsednik/100 10.00
93 Trot Nixon/25 25.00
94 Chad Cordero/250 8.00
97 Jose Guillen/100 10.00
102 Jack Wilson/100 10.00
106 Melvin Mora/100 10.00
108 Andre Dawson/25 25.00
109 Jody Gerut/250 8.00
116 Aramis Ramirez/25 25.00
128 Ken Harvey/250 8.00
136 Tom Gordon/250 10.00
137 Jake Peavy/100 20.00
139 Dewon Brazelton/250 8.00
140 Jae Weong Seo/100 10.00
141 Danny Kolb/250 12.00
145 Carlos Lee/100 12.00
147 Guillermo Mota/250 8.00
148 Travis Hafner/100 15.00
155 David Wright/25 80.00
156 Brad Penny/250 8.00
157 Francisco Rodriguez/ 100 15.00
159 Adrian Gonzalez/250 10.00
160 Derrek Lee/25 30.00
162 Carlos Zambrano/25 25.00
163 Bobby Crosby/100 25.00
164 Jermaine Dye/250 10.00
168 Johnny Estrada/200 15.00
169 Milton Bradley/100 15.00
170 Shannon Stewart/50 15.00
173 Laynce Nix/250 10.00
175 Craig Wilson/100 15.00
181 Marcus Giles/25 20.00
182 Randy Wolf/250 12.00
184 Aubrey Huff/100 10.00
185 Billy Ripken/250 8.00
186 Octavio Dotel/250 10.00
189 Todd Walker/100 15.00
191 Alexis Rios/200 10.00
193 Orlando Cabrera/25 20.00
197 Jose Vidro/25 15.00
198 Jacque Jones/100 10.00

Stamps Centennial Autograph

NM/M
Production 1-40
2 Red Schoendienst/39 40.00
6 Bob Feller/39 40.00
11 Dwight Evans/39 30.00
15 Whitey Ford/27 50.00
22 Tony Perez/24 40.00
24 Billy Williams/39 30.00
25 Juan Marichal/39 30.00
27 Maury Wills/39 25.00
28 Fergie Jenkins/39 30.00
29 Steve Carlton/39 30.00
30 Dale Murphy/39 50.00
32 Gaylord Perry/39 25.00
33 Fred Lynn/39 30.00
35 Ron Guidry/39 40.00
38 Jack Morris/39 25.00
39 Torii Hunter/39 25.00
40 Andre Dawson/39 30.00
41 Dave Righetti/39 20.00
43 Lou Brock/20 40.00
46 Sean Casey/21 40.00
48 Ralph Kiner/39 30.00
50 Jim Rice/39 35.00
51 Duke Snider/25 50.00
52 Harold Baines/39 25.00
56 Jim Palmer/45 40.00
57 Bobby Doerr/59 30.00
59 Monte Irvin/39 35.00
61 Alan Trammell/40 30.00
62 Al Kaline/39 50.00
64 Bert Blyleven/39 25.00
65 Miguel Cabrera/39 30.00
66 Luis Tiant/39 25.00
69 Michael Young/39 25.00
70 Tony Oliva/39 35.00
71 Mark Mulder/25 40.00

Stamps Legendary Fields Autograph

NM/M
Production 1-34
11 Dwight Evans/34 30.00
22 Tony Perez/34 35.00
24 Billy Williams/34 30.00
28 Fergie Jenkins/34 30.00
29 Steve Carlton/34 30.00
33 Fred Lynn/34 30.00
35 Ron Guidry/34 50.00
38 Jack Morris/34 25.00
40 Andre Dawson/34 30.00
41 Dave Righetti/34 20.00
48 Ralph Kiner/34 30.00
50 Jim Rice/34 35.00
52 Harold Baines/34 25.00
57 Bobby Doerr/34 35.00
59 Monte Irvin/34 35.00
66 Luis Tiant/23 30.00

Stamps Masterpiece Signature Centennial

No Pricing
Production 1-2

Stamps Material Centennial

NM/M
Production 1-39
1 Pee Wee Reese/ Bat/39 20.00
3 Babe Ruth/Jsy/39 275.00
4 George Brett/Jsy/39 40.00
5 Stan Musial/Bat/39 40.00
6 Bob Feller/Pants/39 15.00
7 Cal Ripken Jr./ Pants/39 100.00
8 Ted Williams/Jsy/39 100.00
11 Dwight Evans/Jsy/39 25.00
12 Dave Concepcion/ Jsy/39 20.00
13 Ernie Banks/Jsy/39 25.00
14 Pedro J. Martinez/ Jsy/39 20.00
16 Scott Rolen/Jsy/39 25.00
17 Tony Gwynn/Jsy/39 30.00
18 Mike Schmidt/Jsy/39 60.00
19 Roberto Clemente/ Hat/21 200.00
20 Roger Clemens/ Jsy/39 35.00
21 Don Mattingly/Jsy/39 50.00
22 Tony Perez/Bat/39 15.00
23 Roger Maris/Jsy/39 75.00
24 Billy Williams/Jsy/39 15.00
25 Juan Marichal/ Pants/39 20.00
26 Hank Blalock/Jsy/39 20.00
27 Maury Wills/Jsy/39 15.00
28 Fergie Jenkins/ Pants/39 20.00
29 Steve Carlton/Jsy/39 15.00
30 Dale Murphy/Jsy/39 20.00
31 Kerry Wood/Jsy/39 20.00
32 Gaylord Perry/Jsy/39 15.00
33 Fred Lynn/Jsy/39 20.00
34 Tom Seaver/Bat/39 20.00
36 Reggie Jackson/ Pants/39 25.00
37 Bob Gibson/Jsy/39 20.00
38 Jack Morris/Jsy/39 20.00
39 Torii Hunter/Jsy/39 15.00
40 Andre Dawson/ Jsy/39 20.00
41 Dave Righetti/Jsy/39 15.00
42 Hideki Matsui/ Pants/39 65.00
43 Lou Brock/Jkt/39 25.00
44 Yogi Berra/Bat/39 30.00
45 Frankie Frisch/Jkt/39 25.00
46 Sean Casey/Jsy/39 15.00
47 Sammy Sosa/Jsy/39 30.00
48 Ralph Kiner/Bat/39 30.00
49 Hoyt Wilhelm/Jsy/39 15.00
50 Jim Rice/Jsy/39 20.00
51 Duke Snider/ Pants/39 25.00
52 Harold Baines/Jsy/39 20.00
53 Willie Stargell/Jsy/39 20.00
54 Johnny Bench/ Pants/39 25.00
55 Carlton Fisk/Jsy/39 25.00
56 Jim Palmer/Jsy/39 20.00
57 Bobby Doerr/Jsy/39 20.00
58 Mark Prior/Jsy/39 30.00
60 Lou Boudreau/Jsy/39 25.00
61 Alan Trammell/Bat/39 20.00
62 Al Kaline/Bat/39 25.00
63 Warren Spahn/ Pants/39 30.00
64 Bert Blyleven/Jsy/39 20.00
65 Miguel Cabrera/ Jsy/39 25.00
66 Luis Tiant/Jsy/39 15.00
67 Harmon Killebrew/ Jsy/39 30.00
68 Richie Ashburn/ Pants/39 25.00
69 Michael Young/ Jsy/39 15.00
70 Tony Oliva/Jsy/39 20.00
71 Mark Mulder/Jsy/39 15.00
72 Nolan Ryan/Jsy/39 75.00
73 Willie McCovey/ Jsy/39 25.00
74 Kirk Gibson/Jsy/39 20.00
75 Carl Yastrzemski/ Pants/39 40.00

Stamps Material Centennial Autograph

NM/M
Production 1-39
2 Red Schoendienst/ Jsy/39 40.00
6 Bob Feller/Pants/39 40.00
11 Dwight Evans/Jsy/39 30.00
22 Tony Perez/Bat/24 40.00
24 Billy Williams/Jsy/39 35.00
25 Juan Marichal/ Pants/39 30.00
27 Maury Wills/Jsy/39 30.00
28 Fergie Jenkins/ Pants/39 35.00
29 Steve Carlton/Jsy/39 30.00
30 Dale Murphy/Jsy/39 50.00
32 Gaylord Perry/Jsy/39 30.00
33 Fred Lynn/Jsy/39 30.00
37 Bob Gibson/Jsy/39 40.00
38 Jack Morris/Jsy/39 25.00
40 Andre Dawson/ Jsy/39 35.00
43 Lou Brock/Jkt/39 30.00
46 Sean Casey/Jsy/39 30.00
48 Ralph Kiner/Bat/39 30.00
50 Jim Rice/Jsy/39 35.00
51 Duke Snider/ Pants/39 50.00
52 Harold Baines/Jsy/39 25.00
56 Jim Palmer/Jsy/22 50.00
57 Bobby Doerr/Jsy/39 35.00
61 Alan Trammell/Bat/39 30.00
62 Al Kaline/Bat/39 50.00
64 Bert Blyleven/Jsy/39 25.00
65 Miguel Cabrera/ Jsy/39 50.00
66 Luis Tiant/Jsy/39 30.00
67 Harmon Killebrew/ Jsy/39 60.00
70 Tony Oliva/Jsy/39 35.00
71 Mark Mulder/Jsy/20 40.00
74 Kirk Gibson/Jsy/39 30.00

Stamps Material Legendary Fields

NM/M
Production 1-34
1 Pee Wee Reese/ Bat/34 30.00
11 Dwight Evans/Jsy/34 25.00
12 Dave Concepcion/ Jsy/34 20.00
13 Ernie Banks/Jsy/34 40.00
14 Pedro J. Martinez/ Jsy/34 25.00
15 Whitey Ford/Jsy/34 35.00
19 Roberto Clemente/ Hat/21 200.00
21 Don Mattingly/Jsy/34 50.00
22 Tony Perez/Bat/34 20.00
23 Roger Maris/Jsy/34 85.00
24 Billy Williams/Jsy/34 30.00
28 Fergie Jenkins/ Pants/34 20.00
29 Steve Carlton/Jsy/34 25.00
31 Kerry Wood/Jsy/34 30.00
33 Fred Lynn/Jsy/34 20.00
36 Reggie Jackson/ Pants/34 25.00
38 Jack Morris/Jsy/34 25.00
40 Andre Dawson/ Jsy/34 20.00
41 Dave Righetti/Jsy/34 20.00
42 Hideki Matsui/ Pants/34 80.00
44 Yogi Berra/Bat/34 40.00
47 Sammy Sosa/Jsy/34 40.00
48 Ralph Kiner/Bat/34 20.00
49 Hoyt Wilhelm/Jsy/34 15.00
50 Jim Rice/Jsy/34 20.00
51 Duke Snider/ Pants/34 40.00
52 Harold Baines/Jsy/34 15.00
53 Willie Stargell/Jsy/34 30.00
54 Johnny Bench/ Pants/34 40.00
55 Carlton Fisk/Jsy/34 25.00
57 Bobby Doerr/Jsy/34 25.00
58 Mark Prior/Jsy/34 40.00
61 Alan Trammell/Bat/34 30.00
62 Al Kaline/Bat/34 40.00
66 Luis Tiant/Jsy/34 25.00
74 Kirk Gibson/Jsy/34 30.00
75 Carl Yastrzemski/ Pants/34 50.00

Stamps Material Legendary Fields Auto

NM/M
Production 1-34
11 Dwight Evans/Jsy/34 30.00
22 Tony Perez/Bat/34 40.00
24 Billy Williams/Jsy/34 30.00
28 Fergie Jenkins/ Pants/34 35.00
29 Steve Carlton/Jsy/34 35.00
33 Fred Lynn/Jsy/34 30.00
38 Jack Morris/Jsy/34 30.00
40 Andre Dawson/ Jsy/34 30.00
41 Dave Righetti/Jsy/34 20.00
50 Jim Rice/Jsy/33 40.00
66 Luis Tiant/Jsy/23 35.00
74 Kirk Gibson/Jsy/23 30.00

Stamps Material Legendary Players 20

NM/M
Complete Set (2):
19 Roberto Clemente/ Hat/21 200.00

Stamps Material Legendary Players 33

NM/M
Complete Set (2):
19 Roberto Clemente/ Hat/21 200.00

Stamps Material Olympic

NM/M
Production 1-92
1 Pee Wee Reese/ Bat/92 15.00
4 George Brett/Jsy/92 30.00
5 Stan Musial/Bat/92 30.00
6 Bob Feller/Pants/92 15.00
7 Cal Ripken Jr./ Pants/92 60.00
11 Dwight Evans/Jsy/24 20.00
13 Ernie Banks/Jsy/92 25.00
14 Pedro J. Martinez /Jsy/45 20.00
16 Scott Rolen/Jsy/27 30.00
17 Tony Gwynn/Jsy/92 30.00
18 Mike Schmidt/Jsy/92 40.00
19 Roberto Clemente/ Hat/21 200.00
20 Roger Clemens/ Jsy/92 30.00
21 Don Mattingly/Jsy/23 40.00
22 Tony Perez/Bat/24 30.00
24 Billy Williams/Jsy/26 20.00
25 Juan Marichal/ Pants/92 15.00
26 Hank Blalock/Jsy/92 15.00
27 Maury Wills/Jsy/30 20.00
28 Fergie Jenkins/ Pants/92 15.00
29 Steve Carlton/Jsy/92 15.00
30 Dale Murphy/Jsy/92 20.00
31 Kerry Wood/Jsy/92 20.00
32 Gaylord Perry/Jsy/92 15.00
33 Fred Lynn/Jsy/92 15.00
34 Tom Seaver/Bat/92 20.00
36 Reggie Jackson/ Pants/44 20.00
37 Bob Gibson/Jsy/45 25.00
38 Jack Morris/Jsy/92 15.00
39 Torii Hunter/Jsy/48 15.00
41 Dave Righetti/Jsy/92 15.00
42 Hideki Matsui/ Pants/92 40.00
43 Lou Brock/Jkt/92 15.00
44 Yogi Berra/Bat/92 25.00
45 Frankie Frisch/Jkt/92 15.00
46 Sean Casey/Jsy/21 25.00
47 Sammy Sosa/Jsy/92 25.00
48 Ralph Kiner/Bat/92 15.00
49 Hoyt Wilhelm/Jsy/92 15.00
50 Jim Rice/Jsy/92 15.00
51 Duke Snider/ Pants/92 20.00
52 Harold Baines/Jsy/92 15.00
53 Willie Stargell/Jsy/92 20.00
54 Johnny Bench/ Pants/92 20.00

55 Carlton Fisk/Jsy/92 25.00
56 Jim Palmer/Jsy/92 15.00
57 Bobby Doerr/Jsy/92 15.00
58 Mark Prior/Jsy/92 20.00
60 Lou Boudreau/Jsy/92 20.00
61 Alan Trammell/Bat/92 15.00
62 Al Kaline Bat/92 20.00
63 Warren Spahn/Pants/92 25.00
65 Miguel Cabrera/Jsy/92 20.00
66 Luis Tiant/Jsy/23 20.00
67 Harmon Killebrew/Jsy/92 30.00
68 Richie Ashburn/Pants/92 20.00
70 Tony Oliva/Jsy/92 15.00
71 Mark Mulder/Jsy/20 20.00
72 Nolan Ryan/Jsy/30 100.00
73 Willie McCovey/Jsy/92 20.00
74 Kirk Gibson/Jsy/92 15.00
75 Carl Yastrzemski/Pants/92 30.00

Stamps Material Olympic Autograph

NM/M
Production 1-29
6 Bob Feller/Pants/29 45.00
11 Dwight Evans/Jsy/24 35.00
22 Tony Perez/Bat/29 40.00
24 Billy Williams/Jsy/29 35.00
25 Juan Marichal/Pants/29 35.00
27 Maury Wills/Jsy/29 30.00
28 Fergie Jenkins/Pants/29 35.00
29 Steve Carlton/Jsy/29 35.00
30 Dale Murphy/Jsy/29 50.00
32 Gaylord Perry/Jsy/29 30.00
33 Fred Lynn/Jsy/29 35.00
37 Bob Gibson/Jsy/29 40.00
38 Jack Morris/Jsy/29 30.00
40 Andre Dawson/Jsy/25 35.00
43 Lou Brock/Jkt/20 40.00
46 Sean Casey/Jsy/21 40.00
56 Jim Palmer/Jsy/22 50.00
64 Bert Blyleven/Jsy/28 30.00
65 Miguel Cabrera/Jsy/24 60.00
66 Luis Tiant/Jsy/23 30.00
71 Mark Mulder/Jsy/20 40.00
74 Kirk Gibson/Jsy/23 30.00

Stamps Material Pro Ball

NM/M
Production 1-69
1 Pee Wee Reese/Bat/69 20.00
4 George Brett/Jsy/69 40.00
5 Stan Musial/Bat/69 30.00
6 Bob Feller/Pants/69 20.00
7 Cal Ripken Jr./Pants/69 60.00
11 Dwight Evans/Jsy/24 30.00
13 Ernie Banks/Jsy/69 30.00
14 Pedro J. Martinez/Jsy/45 25.00
16 Scott Rolen/Jsy/27 40.00
17 Tony Gwynn/Jsy/69 35.00
18 Mike Schmidt/Jsy/69 60.00
19 Roberto Clemente/Hat/21 200.00
20 Roger Clemens/Jsy/69 30.00
21 Don Mattingly/Jsy/23 50.00
22 Tony Perez/Bat/24 20.00
24 Billy Williams/Jsy/69 15.00
25 Juan Marichal/Pants/69 15.00
26 Hank Blalock/Jsy/69 15.00
27 Maury Wills/Jsy/69 15.00
28 Fergie Jenkins/Pants/69 20.00
29 Steve Carlton/Jsy/69 15.00
30 Dale Murphy/Jsy/69 15.00
31 Kerry Wood/Jsy/69 20.00
32 Gaylord Perry/Jsy/69 15.00
33 Fred Lynn/Jsy/69 15.00
34 Tom Seaver/Bat/69 20.00
36 Reggie Jackson/Pants/69 15.00
37 Bob Gibson/Jsy/45 25.00
38 Jack Morris/Jsy/69 15.00
39 Torii Hunter/Jsy/48 15.00
40 Andre Dawson/Jsy/69 15.00
41 Dave Righetti/Jsy/69 15.00
42 Hideki Matsui/Pants/69 40.00
43 Lou Brock/Jkt/69 15.00
44 Yogi Berra/Bat/69 25.00
45 Frankie Frisch/Jkt/69 20.00
46 Sean Casey/Jsy/69 15.00
47 Sammy Sosa/Jsy/69 20.00
48 Ralph Kiner/Bat/69 15.00
49 Hoyt Wilhelm/Jsy/69 15.00
50 Jim Rice/Jsy/69 15.00
51 Duke Snider/Pants/69 20.00
52 Harold Baines/Jsy/69 15.00
53 Willie Stargell/Jsy/69 20.00
54 Johnny Bench/Pants/69 20.00
55 Carlton Fisk/Jsy/69 15.00
56 Jim Palmer/Jsy/69 15.00
57 Bobby Doerr/Jsy/69 15.00
58 Mark Prior/Jsy/69 20.00
60 Lou Boudreau/Jsy/69 25.00
61 Alan Trammell/Bat/69 15.00
62 Al Kaline/Bat/69 20.00
63 Warren Spahn/Pants/69 25.00
65 Miguel Cabrera/Jsy/69 15.00
66 Luis Tiant/Jsy/69 15.00
67 Harmon Killebrew/Jsy/69 35.00
68 Richie Ashburn/Pants/69 20.00
69 Michael Young/Jsy/69 15.00
70 Tony Oliva/Jsy/69 20.00
71 Mark Mulder/Jsy/20 25.00
72 Nolan Ryan/Jsy/69 60.00
73 Willie McCovey/Jsy/69 25.00
74 Kirk Gibson/Jsy/69 15.00
75 Carl Yastrzemski/Pants/69 30.00

Stamps Material Pro Ball Autograph

NM/M
Production 1-69
6 Bob Feller/Pants/69 30.00
11 Dwight Evans/Jsy/24 30.00
22 Tony Perez/Bat/24 40.00
24 Billy Williams/Jsy/26 35.00
25 Juan Marichal/Pants/27 35.00
27 Maury Wills/Jsy/69 20.00
28 Fergie Jenkins/Pants/69 25.00
29 Steve Carlton/Jsy/69 30.00
30 Dale Murphy/Jsy/69 40.00
32 Gaylord Perry/Jsy/69 20.00
33 Fred Lynn/Jsy/69 25.00
37 Bob Gibson/Jsy/45 35.00
43 Lou Brock/Jkt/20 40.00
46 Sean Casey/Jsy/21 40.00
57 Bobby Doerr/Jsy/48 30.00
65 Miguel Cabrera/Jsy/24 50.00
66 Luis Tiant/Jsy/23 30.00
71 Mark Mulder/Jsy/20 40.00
74 Kirk Gibson/Jsy/23 30.00

Stamps Material USA Flag

NM/M
Production 1-100
1 Pee Wee Reese/Bat/100 15.00
4 George Brett/Jsy/100 35.00
5 Stan Musial/Bat/100 25.00
6 Bob Feller/Pants/100 15.00
7 Cal Ripken Jr./Pants/100 65.00
11 Dwight Evans/Jsy/24 30.00
13 Ernie Banks/Jsy/100 30.00
14 Pedro J. Martinez/Jsy/45 25.00
16 Scott Rolen/Jsy/27 40.00
17 Tony Gwynn/Jsy/100 30.00
18 Mike Schmidt/Jsy/100 50.00
19 Roberto Clemente/Hat/21 200.00
20 Roger Clemens/Jsy/100 25.00
21 Don Mattingly/Jsy/100 30.00
22 Tony Perez/Bat/100 15.00
24 Billy Williams/Jsy/100 10.00
25 Juan Marichal/Pants/100 15.00
26 Hank Blalock/Jsy/100 15.00
27 Maury Wills/Jsy/100 10.00
28 Fergie Jenkins/Pants/100 15.00
29 Steve Carlton/Jsy/100 15.00
30 Dale Murphy/Jsy/100 15.00
31 Kerry Wood/Jsy/100 20.00
32 Gaylord Perry/Jsy/100 10.00
33 Fred Lynn/Jsy/100 10.00
34 Tom Seaver/Bat/100 15.00
36 Reggie Jackson/Pants/44 20.00
37 Bob Gibson/Jsy/100 20.00
38 Jack Morris/Jsy/100 10.00
39 Torii Hunter/Jsy/48 15.00
40 Andre Dawson 15.00
41 Dave Righetti/Jsy/100 10.00
42 Hideki Matsui/Pants/100 40.00
43 Lou Brock/Jkt/100 15.00
44 Yogi Berra/Bat/100 20.00
45 Frankie Frisch/Jkt/100 15.00
46 Sean Casey/Jsy/100 10.00
47 Sammy Sosa/Jsy/100 15.00
48 Ralph Kiner/Bat/100 15.00
49 Hoyt Wilhelm/Jsy/100 10.00
50 Jim Rice/Jsy/100 12.00
51 Duke Snider/Pants/100 15.00
52 Harold Baines/Jsy/100 10.00
53 Willie Stargell/Jsy/100 15.00
54 Johnny Bench/Pants/100 20.00
55 Carlton Fisk/Jsy/72 15.00
56 Jim Palmer/Jsy/100 15.00
57 Bobby Doerr/Jsy/100 15.00
58 Mark Prior/Jsy/100 15.00
62 Al Kaline/Bat/100 15.00
63 Warren Spahn/Pants/100 20.00
64 Bert Blyleven/Jsy/28 20.00
65 Miguel Cabrera/Jsy/24 25.00
66 Luis Tiant/Jsy/23 20.00
67 Harmon Killebrew/Jsy/100 30.00
68 Richie Ashburn/Pants/100 15.00
70 Tony Oliva/Jsy/100 15.00
71 Mark Mulder/Jsy/20 25.00
72 Nolan Ryan/Jsy/100 50.00
73 Willie McCovey/Jsy/44 25.00
74 Kirk Gibson/Jsy/100 10.00
75 Carl Yastrzemski/Pants/100 25.00

Stamps Material USA Flag Autograph

NM/M
Production 1-37
2 Red Schoendienst/Jsy/37 40.00
6 Bob Feller/Pants/8 40.00
11 Dwight Evans/Jsy/37 30.00
22 Tony Perez/Bat/37 35.00
24 Billy Williams/Jsy/37 30.00
25 Juan Marichal/Pants/37 30.00
27 Maury Wills/Jsy/37 25.00
28 Fergie Jenkins/Pants/37 30.00
29 Steve Carlton/Jsy/37 30.00
30 Dale Murphy/Jsy/37 50.00
32 Gaylord Perry/Jsy/37 25.00
33 Fred Lynn/Jsy/37 30.00
37 Bob Gibson/Jsy/37 40.00
38 Jack Morris/Jsy/37 25.00
41 Dave Righetti/Jsy/37 20.00
43 Lou Brock/Jkt/37 30.00
46 Sean Casey/Jsy/37 30.00
48 Ralph Kiner/Bat/37 30.00
50 Jim Rice/Jsy/37 30.00
51 Duke Snider/Pants/37 40.00
52 Harold Baines/Jsy/37 25.00
56 Jim Palmer/Jsy/37 35.00
57 Bobby Doerr/Jsy/37 40.00
61 Alan Trammell/Bat/37 30.00
62 Al Kaline/Bat/37 50.00
64 Bert Blyleven/Jsy/37 25.00
65 Miguel Cabrera/Jsy/37 50.00
66 Luis Tiant/Jsy/37 25.00
67 Harmon Killebrew/Jsy/37 60.00
70 Tony Oliva/Jsy/37 35.00
71 Mark Mulder/Jsy/37 30.00
74 Kirk Gibson/Jsy/23 30.00

Stamps Olympic Autograph

NM/M
Production 1-92
2 Red Schoendienst/92 25.00
6 Bob Feller/92 25.00
11 Dwight Evans/92 20.00
22 Tony Perez/24 40.00
24 Billy Williams/26 35.00
25 Juan Marichal/27 35.00
27 Maury Wills/92 20.00
28 Fergie Jenkins/92 25.00
29 Steve Carlton/92 20.00
30 Dale Murphy/92 30.00
32 Gaylord Perry/92 20.00
33 Fred Lynn/92 20.00
35 Ron Guidry/48 35.00
38 Jack Morris/92 20.00
39 Torii Hunter/48 25.00
40 Andre Dawson/92 25.00
43 Lou Brock/20 40.00
46 Sean Casey/21 40.00
50 Jim Rice/92 25.00
52 Harold Baines/92 20.00
56 Jim Palmer/22 50.00
57 Bobby Doerr/92 25.00
59 Monte Irvin/92 40.00
61 Alan Trammell/92 25.00
62 Al Kaline/92 40.00
64 Bert Blyleven/92 20.00
65 Miguel Cabrera/24 60.00
66 Luis Tiant/92 20.00
70 Tony Oliva/91 20.00
71 Mark Mulder/20 40.00

Stamps Pro Ball Autograph

NM/M
Production 1-69
6 Bob Feller/69 30.00
11 Dwight Evans/69 25.00
22 Tony Perez/24 40.00
24 Billy Williams/26 35.00
25 Juan Marichal/27 35.00
27 Maury Wills/69 20.00
28 Fergie Jenkins/69 25.00
29 Steve Carlton/69 30.00
30 Dale Murphy/69 40.00
32 Gaylord Perry/69 20.00
33 Fred Lynn/69 25.00
35 Ron Guidry/49 40.00
38 Jack Morris/47 20.00
39 Torii Hunter/48 25.00
43 Lou Brock/20 40.00
46 Sean Casey/21 40.00
57 Bobby Doerr/69 30.00
59 Monte Irvin/20 40.00
64 Bert Blyleven/28 25.00
65 Miguel Cabrera/24 50.00
66 Luis Tiant/23 30.00
71 Mark Mulder/20 40.00

Stamps USA Flag Autograph

NM/M
Production 1-100
2 Red Schoendienst/100 25.00
6 Bob Feller/100 25.00
11 Dwight Evans/24 35.00
22 Tony Perez/24 40.00
24 Billy Williams/26 35.00
25 Juan Marichal/27 35.00
27 Maury Wills/100 20.00
28 Fergie Jenkins/100 25.00
29 Steve Carlton/100 20.00
30 Dale Murphy/100 30.00
32 Gaylord Perry/100 20.00
33 Fred Lynn/100 20.00
35 Ron Guidry/49 35.00
38 Jack Morris/100 20.00
39 Torii Hunter/48 25.00
40 Andre Dawson/100 25.00
43 Lou Brock/20 40.00
46 Sean Casey/21 40.00
48 Ralph Kiner/100 25.00
51 Duke Snider/25 45.00
52 Harold Baines/100 20.00
56 Jim Palmer/22 50.00
57 Bobby Doerr/100 25.00
59 Monte Irvin/100 40.00
61 Alan Trammell/100 25.00
62 Al Kaline/100 40.00
64 Bert Blyleven/100 20.00
65 Miguel Cabrera/24 60.00
66 Luis Tiant/100 20.00
70 Tony Oliva/100 20.00
71 Mark Mulder/20 40.00

Timeline Threads Jersey Number

NM/M
Production 1-43
6 Orlando Cepeda/Pants/30 10.00
9 Tony Perez/Jsy/24 15.00
11 Tommy John/Jsy/25 15.00
15 Carlton Fisk/Jsy/27 20.00
17 Bert Blyleven/Jsy/28 10.00
20 Lou Brock/Jsy/20 20.00
21 Sammy Sosa/Jsy/21 20.00
22 Roger Clemens/Jsy/22 40.00
23 Don Mattingly/Jsy/23 40.00
24 Rickey Henderson/Jsy/35 15.00
26 Wade Boggs/Jsy/26 20.00
29 Jim "Catfish" Hunter/Jsy/29 15.00
30 Maury Wills/Jsy/30 10.00
31 Hoyt Wilhelm/Jsy/31 10.00
33 Eddie Murray/Pants/33 30.00
34 Nolan Ryan/Pants/34 50.00
35 Phil Niekro/Jsy/35 10.00
38 Curt Schilling/Jsy/38 15.00
40 Sandy Koufax/Jsy/32 500.00
41 Don Sutton/Jsy/20 15.00
42 Randy Johnson/Jsy/51 15.00
43 Dennis Eckersley/Jsy/43 10.00
44 Frank Thomas/Jsy/35 20.00
45 Mike Mussina/Jsy/35 15.00
46 Greg Maddux/Jsy/31 25.00
47 Jim Palmer/Pants/22 15.00
49 Mike Piazza/Jsy/31 25.00

Timeline Threads Number Autograph

Production 1-19
Position Autograph: No Pricing
Production 1-19
Prime: No Pricing
Production One Set

Timeline Threads Position

NM/M
Common Player: 4.00
1 Bobby Doerr/Jsy/39 10.00
2 Burleigh Grimes/Pants/26 50.00
3 Babe Ruth/Pants/30 200.00
4 Joe Cronin/Pants/38 20.00
5 Johnny Bench/Pants/71 15.00
6 Orlando Cepeda/Pants/62 8.00
7 Ivan Rodriguez/Jsy/103 8.00
8 Cal Ripken Jr./Jsy/78 40.00
9 Tony Perez/Jsy/78 8.00
10 Andre Dawson/Jsy/86 8.00
11 Tommy John/Jsy/86 4.00
12 Alfonso Soriano/Jsy/102 8.00
13 Ozzie Smith/Jsy/78 15.00
14 Ernie Banks/Jsy/70 15.00
15 Carlton Fisk/Jsy/80 8.00
16 Bo Jackson/Jsy/89 10.00
17 Bert Blyleven/Jsy/83 4.00
18 Darryl Strawberry/Jsy/88 6.00
19 Bob Feller/Pants/36 8.00
20 Lou Brock/Jsy/74 8.00
21 Sammy Sosa/Jsy/103 12.00
22 Roger Clemens/Jsy/101 15.00
23 Don Mattingly/Jsy/94 20.00
24 Rickey Henderson/Jsy/83 10.00
25 Albert Pujols/Jsy/103 15.00
26 Wade Boggs/Jsy/87 10.00
27 Joe Morgan/Jsy/82 8.00
28 Gary Carter/Jsy/86 8.00
29 Jim "Catfish" Hunter/Jsy/78 6.00
30 Maury Wills/Jsy/65 4.00
31 Hoyt Wilhelm/Jsy/68 4.00
32 Matt Williams/Jsy/95 4.00
33 Eddie Murray/Pants/88 8.00
34 Nolan Ryan/Pants/90 25.00
35 Phil Niekro/Jsy/80 6.00
36 Paul Molitor/Jsy/96 10.00
37 Dale Murphy/Jsy/83 8.00
38 Curt Schilling/Jsy/99 8.00
39 Fred Lynn/Jsy/75 4.00
40 Sandy Koufax/Jsy/64 260.00
41 Don Sutton/Jsy/76 4.00
42 Randy Johnson/Jsy/98 8.00
43 Dennis Eckersley/Jsy/97 6.00
44 Frank Thomas/Jsy/94 8.00
45 Mike Mussina/Jsy/100 6.00
46 Greg Maddux/Jsy/96 10.00
47 Jim Palmer/Pants/76 6.00
48 Harmon Killebrew/Jsy/62 20.00
49 Mike Piazza/Jsy/99 10.00
50 Billy Martin/Jsy/83 15.00

Certified Materials

NM/M
Complete Set (250):
Common Player: .50
Common Auto. (201-250): 6.00
Production 499 unless noted.
Hobby Pack (5): 10.00
Hobby Box (10): 90.00
1 A.J. Burnett .50
2 Adam Dunn .75
3 Adrian Beltre .75
4 Bret Boone .50
5 Albert Pujols 2.50
6 Alex Rodriguez 2.50
7 Alfonso Soriano 1.00
8 Andruw Jones 1.00
9 Andy Pettitte .75
10 Aramis Ramirez .75
11 Aubrey Huff .50
12 Austin Kearns .50
13 B.J. Upton .50
14 Brandon Webb .50
15 Barry Zito .50
16 Tim Salmon .50
17 Bobby Abreu .50
18 Bobby Crosby .50
19 Brad Penny .50
20 Preston Wilson .50
21 C.C. Sabathia .50
22 Carl Crawford .50
23 Keith Foulke .50
24 Carlos Beltran .75
25 Casey Kotchman .50
26 Chipper Jones 1.00
27 Chone Figgins .50
28 Craig Biggio .75
29 Craig Wilson .50
30 Curt Schilling 1.00
31 Danny Kolb .50
32 David Ortiz 1.00
33 Orlando Hudson .50
34 David Wright 1.50
35 Derek Jeter 2.50
36 Jake Peavy .50
37 Derrek Lee .75
38 Dontrelle Willis .75
39 Edgar Renteria .50
40 Angel Berroa .50
41 Eric Chavez .50
42 Akinori Otsuka .50
43 Francisco Rodriguez .50
44 Garret Anderson .50
45 Gary Sheffield .75
46 Greg Maddux 1.50
47 Hideki Matsui 2.00
48 Hideo Nomo .75
49 Ichiro Suzuki 2.00
50 Ivan Rodriguez .75
51 J.D. Drew .50
52 J.T. Snow .50
53 Jack Wilson .50
54 Jamie Moyer .50
55 Jason Bay .50
56 Jason Giambi .75
57 Trot Nixon .50
58 Jason Schmidt .50
59 Jason Varitek .50
60 Roy Oswalt .50
61 Javy Lopez .50
62 Eric Byrnes .50
63 Jeff Bagwell .75
64 Jeff Kent .50
65 Jeff Suppan .50
66 Jeremy Bonderman .50
67 Jermaine Dye .50
68 Kazuhito Tadano .50
69 Jim Edmonds .75
70 Jim Thome .75
71 Johan Santana 1.00
72 John Smoltz .75
73 Johnny Damon 1.00
74 Johnny Estrada .50
75 Brett Myers .50
76 Jose Guillen .50
77 Jose Vidro .50
78 Josh Beckett .50
79 Edwin Jackson .50
80 Raul Ibanez .50
81 Rich Harden .50
82 Justin Morneau .75
83 Kazuhisa Ishii .50
84 Kazuo Matsui .50
85 Ken Griffey Jr. 1.50
86 Ken Harvey .50
87 Frank Thomas .75
88 Kerry Wood .75
89 Wade Miller .50
90 Kevin Millwood .50
91 Jeremy Affeldt .50
92 Francisco Cordero .50
93 Lance Berkman .50
94 Larry Walker .50
95 Laynce Nix .50
96 Luis Gonzalez .50
97 Lyle Overbay .50
98 Carlos Zambrano .75
99 Manny Ramirez 1.00
100 Marcus Giles .50
101 Mark Buehrle .50
102 Mark Loretta .50
103 Mark Mulder .50
104 Mark Prior 1.00
105 Mark Teixeira .75
106 Marlon Byrd .50
107 Rafael Furcal .50
108 Melvin Mora .50
109 Michael Young .50
110 Miguel Cabrera 1.00
111 Miguel Tejada .75
112 Mike Lowell .50
113 Mike Mussina .75
114 Mike Piazza 1.50
115 Moises Alou .50
116 Livan Hernandez .50
117 Nomar Garciaparra 1.50
118 Omar Vizquel .50
119 Orlando Cabrera .50
120 Pat Burrell .50
121 Paul Konerko .50
122 Paul LoDuca .50
123 Pedro Martinez 1.00
124 Rafael Palmeiro .75
125 Randy Johnson 1.00
126 Richard Hidalgo .50
127 Richie Sexson .50
128 Magglio Ordonez .50
129 Roger Clemens 2.50
130 Russ Ortiz .50
131 Sammy Sosa 1.50
132 Scott Podsednik .50
133 Scott Rolen 1.00
134 Sean Burroughs .50
135 Sean Casey .50

136 Shawn Green .50
137 Jorge Posada .75
138 Roy Halladay .50
139 Steve Finley .50
140 Tim Hudson .75
141 Todd Helton .75
142 Tom Glavine .75
143 Torii Hunter .50
144 Travis Hafner .50
145 Trevor Hoffman .50
146 Troy Glaus .50
147 Vernon Wells .50
148 Victor Martinez .50
149 Vladimir Guerrero 1.00
150 Sammy Sosa 1.50
151 Hank Blalock .75
152 Danny Graves .50
153 Rocco Baldelli .50
154 Carlos Delgado .50
155 Bubba Nelson .50
156 Kevin Youkilis .50
157 Jacque Jones .50
158 Mike Lieberthal .50
159 Ben Sheets .50
160 Lew Ford .50
161 Ervin Santana .50
162 Jody Gerut .50
163 Nick Johnson .50
164 Brian Roberts .50
165 Joe Nathan .50
166 Mike Sweeney .50
167 Ryan Wagner .50
168 David Dellucci .50
169 Jae Weong Seo .50
170 Tom Gordon .50
171 Carlos Lee .50
172 Octavio Dotel .50
173 Jose Castillo .50
174 Troy Percival .50
175 Carlos Delgado .50
176 Curt Schilling 1.00
177 David Ortiz 1.00
178 Greg Maddux 1.50
179 Ivan Rodriguez .75
180 Jeff Kent .50
181 Larry Walker .50
182 Miguel Tejada .75
183 Pedro J. Martinez 1.00
184 Rafael Palmeiro .75
185 Roger Clemens 2.50
186 Shawn Green .50
187 Tim Hudson .75
188 Tom Glavine .75
189 Troy Glaus .50
190 Vladimir Guerrero 1.00
191 Cal Ripken Jr. 4.00
192 Don Mattingly 2.00
193 George Brett 2.00
194 Harmon Killebrew 1.50
195 Mike Schmidt 2.00
196 Nolan Ryan 3.00
197 Stan Musial 2.00
198 Tony Gwynn 1.00
199 Wade Boggs 1.00
200 Willie Mays 2.00
201 Ambiorix Concepcion/ Auto. **RC** 10.00
202 Agustin Montero/ Auto. **RC** 8.00
203 Carlos Ruiz/Auto. **RC** 15.00
204 Casey Rogowski/ Auto. **RC** 6.00
205 Chris Resop/Auto. **RC** 8.00
206 Chris Roberson/ Auto. **RC** 6.00
207 Colter Bean **RC** 2.00
208 Danny Rueckel/ Auto. **RC** 6.00
209 David Gassner/ Auto. **RC** 8.00
210 Devon Lowery/ Auto. **RC** 8.00
211 Norihiro Nakamura/ Auto./115 **RC** 40.00
212 Erick Threets/ Auto./299 **RC** 6.00
213 Garrett Jones/ Auto./299 **RC** 8.00
214 Geovany Soto/ Auto. **RC** 10.00
215 Jared Gothreaux/ Auto./299 **RC** 6.00
216 Jason Hammel/ Auto./299 **RC** 10.00
217 Jeff Miller/ Auto./299 **RC** 6.00
218 Jeff Niemann/ Auto./299 **RC** 20.00
219 Huston Street 2.00
220 John Hattig Jr./ Auto. **RC** 6.00
221 Justin Verlander/ Auto./299 **RC** 50.00
222 Justin Wechsler/ Auto. **RC** 6.00
223 Luke Scott/Auto. **RC** 30.00
224 Mark McLemore/ Auto. **RC** 8.00
225 Mark Woodyard/ Auto./299 **RC** 6.00
226 Matt Lindstrom/ Auto./299 **RC** 8.00
227 Miguel Negron/ Auto. **RC** 6.00
228 Mike Morse/Auto. **RC** 15.00
229 Nate McLouth/ Auto. **RC** 15.00
230 Paulino Reynoso/ Auto./299 **RC** 6.00
231 Philip Humber/ Auto./299 **RC** 15.00
232 Tony Pena/Auto. **RC** 6.00
233 Randy Messenger/ Auto. **RC** 6.00
234 Raul Tablado/Auto. **RC** 8.00
235 Russel Rohlicek/ Auto. **RC** 6.00
236 Ryan Speier/Auto. **RC** 8.00
237 Scott Munter/Auto. **RC** 8.00
238 Sean Thompson/ Auto. **RC** 6.00
239 Sean Tracey/ Auto./299 **RC** 6.00
240 Marcos Carvajal **RC** 1.50
241 Travis Bowyer/ Auto. **RC** 10.00
242 Ubaldo Jimenez/ Auto. **RC** 6.00
243 Wladimir Balentien/ Auto. **RC** 20.00
244 Eude Brito **RC** 8.00
245 Ambiorix Burgos **RC** 2.00
246 Tadahito Iguchi **RC** 5.00
247 Dae-Sung Koo **RC** 1.00
248 Chris Seddon **RC** 2.00
249 Keiichi Yabu/ Auto. **RC** 15.00
250 Yuniesky Betancourt/ Auto. **RC** 25.00

Cuts Blue

NM/M

Production 1-80
3 Willie Mays/26 150.00
7 Jim Palmer/50 25.00
12 Steve Carlton/50 25.00
15 Maury Wills/80 20.00
20 Dale Murphy/50 30.00

Cuts Green

NM/M

Production 3-50
7 Jim Palmer/50 25.00
12 Steve Carlton/50 25.00
15 Maury Wills/80 20.00
20 Dale Murphy/50 30.00

Cuts Red

NM/M

Production 1-60
7 Jim Palmer/50 25.00
12 Steve Carlton/50 25.00
15 Maury Wills/60 20.00
20 Dale Murphy/50 30.00

Materials Cuts Materials Blue

NM/M

Production 4-43
2 Hank Aaron/Bat/43 275.00
3 Willie Mays/ Pants/24 175.00
4 Sandy Koufax/ Jsy/32 400.00
6 Nolan Ryan/Jsy/34 100.00
9 Rod Carew/Jsy/29 25.00
10 Ryne Sandberg/ Jsy/23 120.00
12 Steve Carlton/ Pants/32 25.00
14 Mike Schmidt/Jsy/20 65.00
19 Don Mattingly/Jsy/23 75.00

Cuts Materials Green

NM/M

Production 4-32
3 Willie Mays/ Pants/24 175.00
9 Rod Carew/Jsy/29 25.00
10 Ryne Sandberg/ Jsy/23 120.00
12 Steve Carlton/ Pants/32 25.00
14 Mike Schmidt/Jsy/20 65.00

Cuts Materials Red

NM/M

Production 4-32
3 Willie Mays/ Pants/24 175.00
9 Rod Carew/Jsy/29 25.00
10 Ryne Sandberg/ Jsy/23 120.00
12 Steve Carlton/ Pants/32 25.00
14 Mike Schmidt/Jsy/20 65.00

Fabric of the Game

NM/M

Common Player:

Production 5-100
1 Al Oliver/Jsy/50 6.00
2 Alan Trammell/ Jsy/100 6.00
3 Andres Galarraga/ Jsy/100 4.00
4 Andres Galarraga/ Jsy/100 4.00
6 Babe Ruth/Pants/25 240.00
7 Billy Martin/ Pants/100 15.00
8 Billy Williams/Jsy/50 6.00
9 Bo Jackson/Jsy/100 10.00
10 Bo Jackson/Jsy/100 10.00
12 Bob Gibson/Jsy/25 12.00
13 Bobby Doerr/ Pants/50 10.00
14 Burleigh Grimes/ Pants/25 50.00
15 Cal Ripken Jr./Jsy/50 30.00
16 Cal Ripken Jr./Jsy/50 30.00
17 Carl Yastrzemski/ Pants/50 15.00
18 Carlton Fisk/Jkt/50 10.00
19 Jim "Catfish" Hunter/ Pants/50 8.00
20 Darryl Strawberry/ Jsy/25 8.00
21 Darryl Strawberry/ Jsy/100 4.00
22 Dave Concepcion/ Jsy/50 6.00
23 Dave Righetti/Jsy/50 8.00
24 Dave Winfield/ Pants/100 8.00
25 David Cone/Jsy/100 4.00
26 David Justice/Jsy/100 4.00
27 Deion Sanders/Jsy/50 8.00
28 Deion Sanders/Jsy/50 8.00
29 Dennis Eckersley/ Jsy/50 8.00
30 Dennis Eckersley/ Pants/50 8.00
31 Don Mattingly/ Jsy/100 15.00
32 Don Sutton/Jsy/25 8.00
33 Don Sutton/Jsy/50 6.00
37 Dwight Gooden/ Jsy/100 6.00
38 Eddie Murray/Jsy/25 15.00
39 Eddie Murray/ Pants/50 10.00
40 Edgar Martinez/ Jsy/100 4.00
41 Ernie Banks/Jsy/25 15.00
42 Fergie Jenkins/Jsy/50 8.00
43 Frankie Frisch/Jkt/50 20.00
44 Fred Lynn/Jsy/50 4.00
45 Fred McGriff/Jsy/100 6.00
46 Gary Carter/Jsy/50 6.00
47 Gary Carter/Jsy/50 6.00
48 Gaylord Perry/Jsy/50 6.00
49 Gaylord Perry/Jsy/50 6.00
50 George Brett/Jsy/25 20.00
51 Hal Newhouser/Jsy/50 8.00
54 Harmon Killebrew/ Jsy/25 15.00
55 Harmon Killebrew/ Jsy/50 12.00
56 Harold Baines/Jsy/50 8.00
57 Hoyt Wilhelm/Jsy/100 6.00
58 Jack Morris/Jsy/100 4.00
59 Jim Thorpe/Jsy/25 300.00
60 Jose Cruz/Jsy/100 4.00
61 Jim Rice/Jsy/50 8.00
62 Joe Cronin/Jsy/50 15.00
63 Joe Cronin/Pants/100 15.00
64 Joe Morgan/Jsy/50 8.00
65 Joe Torre/Jsy/50 10.00
66 John Kruk/Jsy/100 10.00
67 Johnny Bench/Jsy/50 10.00
68 Juan Marichal/ Pants/100 6.00
71 Kirk Gibson/Jsy/100 4.00
72 Lee Smith/Jsy/100 4.00
73 Lenny Dykstra/ Jsy/100 6.00
74 Lou Boudreau/Jsy/25 15.00
75 Luis Aparicio/Jsy/50 6.00
76 Luis Tiant/Pants/100 4.00
77 Mark Grace/Jsy/50 8.00
78 Hoyt Wilhelm/Jsy/100 6.00
79 Matt Williams/Jsy/100 6.00
80 Matt Williams/Jsy/50 6.00
82 Nolan Ryan/Jsy/50 20.00
84 Nolan Ryan/Jsy/25 25.00
85 Nolan Ryan/Jsy/25 25.00
86 Orlando Cepeda/ Pants/50 8.00
87 Ozzie Smith/Pants/25 15.00
88 Paul Molitor/Jsy/50 8.00
89 Paul Molitor/Jsy/50 8.00
90 Paul Molitor/Pants/50 8.00
91 Phil Niekro/Jsy/50 8.00
92 Reggie Jackson/ Pants/100 8.00
93 Reggie Jackson/ Jkt/100 8.00
94 Reggie Jackson/ Jsy/50 8.00
95 Reggie Jackson/ Jsy/50 8.00
96 Rickey Henderson/ Jkt/100 10.00
97 Rickey Henderson/ Jsy/50 10.00
98 Rickey Henderson/ Jsy/50 10.00
99 Rickey Henderson/ Jsy/50 10.00
100 Rickey Henderson/ Jsy/50 10.00
101 Rickey Henderson/ Pants/50 10.00
102 Robin Ventura/ Jsy/100 6.00
103 Robin Ventura/ Jsy/100 6.00
104 Robin Yount/Jsy/50 12.00
105 Rod Carew/Jsy/100 8.00
106 Rod Carew/Jsy/100 8.00
107 Roger Maris/ Pants/50 40.00
108 Ron Cey/Jsy/50 8.00
109 Ron Guidry/Pants/100 6.00
110 Ryne Sandberg/ Jsy/50 15.00
111 Sandy Koufax/ Jsy/25 180.00
112 Stan Musial/Jsy/25 25.00
113 Stan Musial/Pants/25 25.00
114 Steve Garvey/Jsy/100 6.00
115 Ted Williams/Jkt/50 50.00
116 Ted Williams/Jsy/25 50.00
117 Tom Seaver/Jsy/50 10.00
118 Tom Seaver/Pants/50 10.00
119 Tommy John/Jsy/100 4.00
120 Tommy John/ Pants/100 4.00
121 Tommy Lasorda/ Jsy/100 6.00
122 Tony Gwynn/Jsy/100 10.00
123 Tony Gwynn/ Pants/100 10.00
124 Tony Perez/Jsy/50 8.00
125 Wade Boggs/Jsy/100 8.00
126 Warren Spahn/Jsy/25 15.00
127 Whitey Ford/Jsy/25 15.00
128 Will Clark/Jsy/50 8.00
129 Willie Mays/Pants/50 40.00
130 Willie McCovey/ Pants/100 10.00
131 Roger Clemens/ Jsy/50 15.00
132 Roger Clemens/ Jsy/50 15.00
133 Roger Clemens/ Jsy/50 15.00
134 Randy Johnson/Jsy/50 8.00
135 Randy Johnson/Jsy/50 8.00
136 Cal Ripken Jr./Jsy/50 30.00
137 Don Mattingly/ Jsy/100 15.00
138 George Brett/Jsy/25 20.00
139 Harmon Killebrew/ Jsy/25 15.00
140 Mike Schmidt/Jsy/50 20.00
141 Nolan Ryan/Jkt/25 25.00
143 Tony Gwynn/Jsy/100 10.00
144 Wade Boggs/Jsy/50 10.00
145 Willie Mays/Jsy/25 50.00
146 Hideo Nomo/Jsy/100 10.00
147 Dale Murphy/Jsy/100 10.00
148 Dale Murphy/Jsy/100 10.00
149 Bo Jackson/Jsy/50 12.00
150 Darryl Strawberry/ Jsy/50 6.00
151 Deion Sanders/Jsy/50 8.00
152 Deion Sanders/ Pants/50 8.00
153 Dennis Eckersley/ Jsy/50 8.00
154 Dwight Gooden/ Jsy/100 6.00
155 Edgar Martinez/ Jsy/100 4.00
156 Lou Brock/Jsy/50 8.00
157 Steve Carlton/ Pants/50 6.00
158 Albert Pujols/Jsy/50 20.00
159 Tom Glavine/Jsy/100 8.00
160 Hideki Matsui/ Pants/50 20.00
161 Babe Ruth/Pants, Jim Thorpe/Jsy/25 500.00
162 Ted Williams/Jkt, Bob Gibson/Jsy/50 50.00
164 Whitey Ford/Jsy, Sandy Koufax/ Jsy/25 150.00
165 Roger Maris/Pants, Don Mattingly/Jsy/25 50.00
166 Nolan Ryan/Jsy, Tom Seaver/Jsy/50 25.00
167 Cal Ripken Jr./Jsy, George Brett/Jsy/100 40.00
168 Ryne Sandberg/Jsy, Mike Schmidt/Jsy/50 30.00
169 Tony Gwynn/Jsy, Wade Boggs/Jsy/50 15.00
170 Carlton Fisk/Jsy, Johnny Bench/ Pants/50 15.00
172 Reggie Jackson/Pants, Darryl Strawberry/ Jsy/50 10.00
173 Robin Yount/Jsy, Paul Molitor/Jsy/50 20.00
174 Warren Spahn/Pants, Juan Marichal/Jsy/50 15.00
175 Bo Jackson/Jsy, Deion Sanders/ Pants/100 15.00
176 Tony Gwynn/Jsy, Rickey Henderson/ Jsy/100 15.00
177 Hideki Matsui/Jsy, Jim Edmonds/ Jsy/100 20.00
178 Rickey Henderson/Pants, Lou Brock/Jsy/100 15.00
179 Roger Clemens/Jsy, Albert Pujols/Jsy/100 25.00
180 Hideo Nomo/Jsy, Kazuhisa Ishii/ Jsy/100 12.00

Certified Materials Fabric of the Game Autograph

No Pricing
Production One Set

Fabric of the Game Jersey Number

NM/M

Production 1-72
8 Billy Williams/Jsy/26 8.00
18 Carlton Fisk/Jkt/72 8.00
19 Jim "Catfish" Hunter/ Pants/29 10.00
20 Darryl Strawberry/ Jsy/39 6.00
21 Darryl Strawberry/ Jsy/44 6.00
24 Dave Winfield/ Pants/31 10.00
25 David Cone/Jsy/44 8.00
26 David Justice/Jsy/23 10.00
27 Deion Sanders /Jsy/21 12.00
28 Deion Sanders/ Jsy/21 12.00
29 Dennis Eckersley/ Jsy/43 8.00
30 Dennis Eckersley/ Pants/43 8.00
36 Dwight Evans/Jsy/24 10.00
38 Eddie Murray/Jsy/33 15.00
39 Eddie Murray/ Pants/33 15.00
42 Fergie Jenkins/Jsy/31 8.00
45 Fred McGriff/Jsy/29 8.00
48 Gaylord Perry/Jsy/36 8.00
49 Gaylord Perry/Jsy/36 8.00
52 Hank Aaron/Jsy/44 40.00
53 Hank Aaron/Jsy/44 40.00
57 Hoyt Wilhelm/Jsy/31 8.00
58 Jack Morris/Jsy/47 4.00
60 Jose Cruz/Jsy/25 6.00
66 John Kruk/Jsy/29 12.00
68 Juan Marichal/ Pants/27 10.00
71 Kirk Gibson/Jsy/23 10.00
72 Lee Smith/Jsy/47 10.00
76 Luis Tiant/Pants/23 10.00
78 Hoyt Wilhelm/Jsy/31 10.00
82 Nolan Ryan/Jsy/34 25.00
83 Nolan Ryan/Jsy/34 25.00
84 Nolan Ryan/Jsy/30 25.00
85 Nolan Ryan/Jsy/30 25.00
86 Orlando Cepeda/ Pants/30 10.00
91 Phil Niekro/Jsy/35 8.00
92 Reggie Jackson/ Pants/44 10.00
93 Reggie Jackson/ Jkt/44 10.00
94 Reggie Jackson/ Jsy/44 10.00
95 Reggie Jackson/ Jsy/44 10.00
96 Rickey Henderson/ Jkt/24 12.00
97 Rickey Henderson/ Jsy/25 12.00
98 Rickey Henderson/ Jsy/35 12.00
99 Rickey Henderson/ Jsy/35 12.00
100 Rickey Henderson/ Pants/24 12.00
101 Rickey Henderson/ Pants/24 12.00
105 Rod Carew/Jsy/29 15.00
106 Rod Carew/Jsy/29 15.00
109 Ron Guidry/Pants/49 8.00
110 Ryne Sandberg/ Jsy/23 35.00
111 Sandy Koufax/ Jsy/32 180.00
117 Tom Seaver/Jsy/41 10.00
118 Tom Seaver/Pants/41 10.00
119 Tommy John/Jsy/25 8.00
120 Tommy John/Pants/25 8.00
124 Tony Perez/Jsy/24 10.00
125 Wade Boggs/Jsy/26 10.00
129 Willie Mays/Pants/24 50.00
130 Willie McCovey/ Pants/44 10.00
131 Roger Clemens/ Jsy/22 20.00
132 Roger Clemens/ Jsy/22 20.00
133 Roger Clemens/ Jsy/21 20.00
134 Randy Johnson/ Jsy/51 10.00
135 Randy Johnson/ Jsy/51 10.00
137 Don Mattingly/Jsy/23 20.00
144 Wade Boggs/Jsy/26 10.00
145 Willie Mays/Jsy/24 50.00
150 Darryl Strawberry/ Jsy/44 6.00
153 Dennis Eckersley/ Jsy/43 8.00
159 Tom Glavine/Jsy/47 10.00
160 Hideki Matsui/ Pants/55 20.00
166 Nolan Ryan/Jsy, Tom Seaver/Jsy/50 25.00
167 Cal Ripken Jr./Jsy, George Brett/Jsy/25 50.00
168 Ryne Sandberg/Jsy, Mike Schmidt/Jsy/25 35.00
169 Tony Gwynn/Jsy, Wade Boggs/Jsy/50 15.00
170 Carlton Fisk/Jsy, Johnny Bench/ Pants/25 20.00
172 Reggie Jackson/Pants, Darryl Strawberry/ Jsy/50 10.00
173 Robin Yount/Jsy, Paul Molitor/Jsy/25 20.00
174 Warren Spahn/Pants, Juan Marichal/Jsy/25 20.00
175 Bo Jackson/Jsy, Deion Sanders/ Pants/50 15.00
176 Tony Gwynn/Jsy, Rickey Henderson/ Jsy/50 20.00
177 Hideki Matsui/Jsy, Jim Edmonds/Jsy/50 20.00
178 Rickey Henderson/Pants, Lou Brock/Jsy/50 20.00
179 Roger Clemens/Jsy, Albert Pujols/Jsy/50 25.00
180 Hideo Nomo/Jsy, Kazuhisa Ishii/Jsy/50 15.00

Fabric of the Game Position

NM/M

Production 3-100
1 Al Oliver/Jsy/50 6.00
2 Alan Trammell/Jsy/25 8.00
3 Andres Galarraga/ Jsy/25 8.00
4 Andres Galarraga/ Jsy/25 8.00
7 Billy Martin/Pants/50 15.00
8 Billy Williams/Jsy/25 8.00
9 Bo Jackson/Jsy/25 12.00
10 Bo Jackson/Jsy/25 12.00
13 Bobby Doerr/ Pants/25 12.00
14 Burleigh Grimes/ Pants/25 50.00
15 Cal Ripken Jr./Jsy/25 35.00
16 Cal Ripken Jr./Jsy/25 35.00
17 Carl Yastrzemski/ Pants/25 15.00
18 Carlton Fisk/Jkt/25 12.00
19 Jim "Catfish" Hunter/ Pants/100 8.00
20 Darryl Strawberry/ Jsy/25 8.00
21 Darryl Strawberry/ Jsy/25 8.00
22 Dave Concepcion/ Jsy/25 6.00
23 Dave Righetti/Jsy/50 8.00
24 Dave Winfield/ Pants/25 10.00
25 David Cone/Jsy/50 4.00
26 David Justice/Jsy/100 4.00
27 Deion Sanders/Jsy/50 8.00
28 Deion Sanders/Jsy/50 8.00
29 Dennis Eckersley/ Jsy/50 8.00
30 Dennis Eckersley/ Pants/50 8.00
32 Don Sutton/Jsy/25 8.00
37 Dwight Gooden/ Jsy/100 6.00
40 Edgar Martinez/Jsy/25 6.00
42 Fergie Jenkins/Jsy/25 10.00
43 Frankie Frisch/ Jkt/100 15.00
44 Fred Lynn/Jsy/50 4.00
45 Fred McGriff/Jsy/100 6.00
46 Gary Carter/Jsy/50 6.00
47 Gary Carter/Jsy/25 8.00
48 Gaylord Perry/Jsy/50 6.00
49 Gaylord Perry/Jsy/25 8.00
54 Harmon Killebrew/ Jsy/25 15.00
56 Harold Baines/Jsy/100 8.00
57 Hoyt Wilhelm/Jsy/100 6.00
60 Jose Cruz/Jsy/100 4.00
61 Jim Rice/Jsy/50 8.00
63 Joe Cronin/Pants/50 15.00

64 Joe Morgan/Jsy/25 10.00
66 John Kruk/Jsy/50 10.00
67 Johnny Bench/Jsy/25 12.00
68 Juan Marichal/Pants/25 10.00
71 Kirk Gibson/Jsy/50 4.00
72 Lee Smith/Jsy/50 4.00
73 Lenny Dykstra/Jsy/50 6.00
75 Luis Aparicio/Jsy/25 8.00
76 Luis Tiant/Pants/25 6.00
77 Mark Grace/Jsy/25 10.00
78 Hoyt Wilhelm/Jsy/50 8.00
79 Matt Williams/Jsy/25 8.00
82 Nolan Ryan/Jsy/25 25.00
85 Nolan Ryan/Jsy/25 25.00
86 Orlando Cepeda/Pants/50 8.00
87 Ozzie Smith/Pants/25 15.00
88 Paul Molitor/Jsy/50 8.00
89 Paul Molitor/Jsy/50 8.00
90 Paul Molitor/Pants/25 10.00
91 Phil Niekro/Jsy/25 8.00
92 Reggie Jackson/Pants/50 10.00
93 Reggie Jackson/Jkt/25 10.00
94 Reggie Jackson/Jsy/50 8.00
95 Reggie Jackson/Jsy/25 10.00
96 Rickey Henderson/Jkt/100 10.00
97 Rickey Henderson/Jsy/50 10.00
99 Rickey Henderson/Jsy/25 12.00
100 Rickey Henderson/Pants/25 12.00
101 Rickey Henderson/Pants/50 10.00
102 Robin Ventura/Jsy/50 6.00
103 Robin Ventura/Jsy/50 6.00
104 Robin Yount/Jsy/25 15.00
105 Rod Carew/Jsy/25 10.00
106 Rod Carew/Jsy/50 10.00
107 Roger Maris/Pants/25 50.00
108 Ron Cey/Jsy/50 8.00
109 Ron Guidry/Pants/50 8.00
110 Ryne Sandberg/Jsy/50 15.00
111 Sandy Koufax/Jsy/25 180.00
112 Stan Musial/Jsy/25 25.00
113 Stan Musial/Pants/25 25.00
114 Steve Garvey/Jsy/25 8.00
115 Ted Williams/Jkt/50 50.00
118 Tom Seaver/Pants/50 10.00
119 Tommy John/Jsy/50 4.00
120 Tommy John/Pants/50 4.00
121 Tommy Lasorda/Jsy/50 6.00
122 Tony Gwynn/Jsy/50 10.00
123 Tony Gwynn/Pants/50 10.00
124 Tony Perez/Jsy/50 8.00
125 Wade Boggs/Jsy/50 10.00
129 Willie Mays/Pants/25 50.00
130 Willie McCovey/Pants/50 10.00
131 Roger Clemens/Jsy/25 20.00
132 Roger Clemens/Jsy/50 15.00
133 Roger Clemens/Jsy/50 15.00
134 Randy Johnson/Jsy/50 8.00
135 Randy Johnson/Jsy/50 8.00
136 Cal Ripken Jr./Jsy/50 30.00
137 Don Mattingly/Jsy/50 15.00
138 George Brett/Jsy/25 20.00
139 Harmon Killebrew/Jsy/25 15.00
140 Mike Schmidt/Jsy/25 20.00
143 Tony Gwynn/Jsy/50 10.00
144 Wade Boggs/Jsy/50 10.00
145 Willie Mays/Jsy/25 50.00
146 Hideo Nomo/Jsy/50 10.00
147 Dale Murphy/Jsy/50 10.00
148 Dale Murphy/Jsy/50 10.00
149 Bo Jackson/Jsy/50 12.00
150 Darryl Strawberry/Jsy/50 6.00
151 Deion Sanders/Jsy/50 8.00
152 Deion Sanders/Jsy/50 8.00
153 Dennis Eckersley/Jsy/50 8.00
154 Dwight Gooden/Jsy/50 6.00
155 Edgar Martinez/Jsy/50 4.00
156 Lou Brock/Jsy/50 8.00
157 Steve Carlton/Pants/50 6.00
158 Albert Pujols/Jsy/50 20.00
159 Tom Glavine/Jsy/50 8.00
160 Hideki Matsui/Pants/50 20.00
161 Babe Ruth/Pants, Jim Thorpe/Jsy/25 500.00
162 Ted Williams/Jkt, Stan Musial/Jsy/50 50.00
164 Whitey Ford/Jsy, Sandy Koufax/Jsy/25 150.00
165 Roger Maris/Pants, Don Mattingly/Jsy/25 50.00
166 Nolan Ryan/Jsy, Tom Seaver/Jsy/100 25.00
167 Cal Ripken Jr./Jsy, George Brett/Jsy/100 40.00
168 Ryne Sandberg/Jsy, Mike Schmidt/Jsy/50 30.00
169 Tony Gwynn/Jsy, Wade Boggs/Jsy/50 15.00
170 Carlton Fisk/Jsy, Johnny Bench/Pants/25 20.00
172 Reggie Jackson/Pants, Darryl Strawberry/Jsy/50 10.00
173 Robin Yount/Jsy, Paul Molitor/Jsy/25 20.00
174 Warren Spahn/Pants, Juan Marichal/Jsy/25 20.00
175 Bo Jackson/Jsy, Deion Sanders Pants/50 15.00
176 Tony Gwynn/Jsy, Rickey Henderson/Jsy/50 20.00
177 Hideki Matsui/Jsy, Jim Edmonds/Jsy/50 20.00
178 Rickey Henderson/Pants, Lou Brock/Jsy/50 20.00
179 Roger Clemens/Jsy, Albert Pujols/Jsy/50 25.00
180 Hideo Nomo/Jsy, Kazuhisa Ishii/Jsy/50 15.00

Fabric of the Game Reward

NM/M

Production 3-50
1 Al Oliver/Jsy/50 6.00
2 Alan Trammell/Jsy/50 8.00
3 Andres Galarraga/Jsy/50 6.00
4 Andres Galarraga/Jsy/50 6.00
7 Billy Martin/Pants/50 15.00
9 Bo Jackson/Jsy/50 12.00
10 Bo Jackson/Jsy/50 12.00
13 Bobby Doerr/Pants/25 12.00
17 Carl Yastrzemski/Pants/25 15.00
19 Jim "Catfish" Hunter/Pants/50 8.00
21 Darryl Strawberry/Jsy/50 6.00
23 Dave Righetti/Jsy/25 8.00
44 Fred Lynn/Jsy/50 4.00
46 Gary Carter/Jsy/50 6.00
47 Gary Carter/Jsy/25 8.00
48 Gaylord Perry/Jsy/50 6.00
49 Gaylord Perry/Jsy/25 8.00
51 Hal Newhouser/Jsy/25 8.00
58 Jack Morris/Jsy/50 6.00
61 Jim Rice/Jsy/50 8.00
62 Joe Cronin/Jsy/25 20.00
63 Joe Cronin/Pants/25 20.00
64 Joe Morgan/Jsy/25 10.00
66 John Kruk/Jsy/50 10.00
68 Juan Marichal/Pants/25 10.00
71 Kirk Gibson/Jsy/25 8.00
72 Lee Smith/Jsy/50 4.00
75 Luis Aparicio/Jsy/25 8.00
76 Luis Tiant/Pants/25 6.00
78 Hoyt Wilhelm/Jsy/25 10.00
79 Matt Williams/Jsy/25 8.00
82 Nolan Ryan/Jsy/25 25.00
85 Nolan Ryan/Jsy/25 25.00
86 Orlando Cepeda/Pants/25 10.00
87 Ozzie Smith/Pants/25 15.00
88 Paul Molitor/Jsy/50 8.00
89 Paul Molitor/Jsy/50 8.00
90 Paul Molitor/Pants/25 10.00
91 Phil Niekro/Jsy/25 8.00
92 Reggie Jackson/Pants/50 10.00
93 Reggie Jackson/Jkt/25 10.00
95 Reggie Jackson/Jsy/25 10.00
96 Rickey Henderson/Jkt/50 10.00
97 Rickey Henderson/Jsy/50 10.00
99 Rickey Henderson/Jsy/25 12.00
102 Robin Ventura/Jsy/50 6.00
103 Robin Ventura/Jsy/50 6.00
104 Robin Yount/Jsy/50 12.00
105 Rod Carew/Jsy/25 10.00
106 Rod Carew/Jsy/50 10.00
108 Ron Cey/Jsy/50 8.00
109 Ron Guidry/Pants/50 8.00
110 Ryne Sandberg/Jsy/50 15.00
111 Sandy Koufax/Jsy/25 180.00
113 Stan Musial/Pants/25 25.00
114 Steve Garvey/Jsy/25 8.00
115 Ted Williams/Jkt/25 50.00
118 Tom Seaver/Pants/50 10.00
119 Tommy John/Jsy/50 4.00
120 Tommy John/Pants/50 4.00
121 Tommy Lasorda/Jsy/50 6.00
122 Tony Gwynn/Jsy/50 10.00
123 Tony Gwynn/Pants/50 10.00
124 Tony Perez/Jsy/50 8.00
125 Wade Boggs/Jsy/50 10.00
126 Warren Spahn/Pants/50 12.00
128 Will Clark/Jsy/50 8.00
129 Willie Mays/Pants/25 50.00
130 Willie McCovey/Pants/50 10.00
131 Roger Clemens/Jsy/25 20.00
132 Roger Clemens/Jsy/50 15.00
133 Roger Clemens/Jsy/50 15.00
134 Randy Johnson/Jsy/50 10.00
135 Randy Johnson/Jsy/50 10.00
136 Cal Ripken Jr./Jsy/50 30.00
137 Don Mattingly/Jsy/50 15.00
138 George Brett/Jsy/25 20.00
139 Harmon Killebrew/Jsy/25 15.00
140 Mike Schmidt/Jsy/25 20.00
143 Tony Gwynn/Jsy/50 10.00
144 Wade Boggs/Jsy/25 10.00
145 Willie Mays/Jsy/25 50.00
146 Hideo Nomo/Jsy/50 10.00
147 Dale Murphy/Jsy/50 10.00
148 Dale Murphy/Jsy/50 10.00
150 Darryl Strawberry/Jsy/50 6.00
151 Deion Sanders/Jsy/50 8.00
152 Deion Sanders/Pants/50 8.00
153 Dennis Eckersley/Jsy/50 8.00
154 Dwight Gooden/Jsy/50 6.00
155 Edgar Martinez/Jsy/50 4.00
156 Lou Brock/Jsy/50 8.00
157 Steve Carlton/Pants/50 6.00
158 Albert Pujols/Jsy/50 20.00
159 Tom Glavine/Jsy/50 8.00
160 Hideki Matsui/Pants/50 20.00
161 Babe Ruth/Pants, Jim Thorpe/Jsy/25 500.00
162 Ted Williams/Jkt, Stan Musial/Jsy/25 50.00
163 Willie Mays/Jsy, Bob Gibson/Jsy/25 50.00
164 Whitey Ford/Jsy, Sandy Koufax/Jsy/25 150.00
165 Roger Maris/Pants, Don Mattingly/Jsy/25 50.00
166 Nolan Ryan/Jsy, Tom Seaver/Jsy/50 25.00
167 Cal Ripken Jr./Jsy, George Brett/Jsy/50 40.00
168 Ryne Sandberg/Jsy, Mike Schmidt/Jsy/50 30.00
169 Tony Gwynn/Jsy, Wade Boggs/Jsy/50 15.00
170 Carlton Fisk/Jsy, Johnny Bench/Pants/25 20.00
172 Reggie Jackson/Pants, Darryl Strawberry/Jsy/50 10.00
173 Robin Yount/Jsy, Paul Molitor/Jsy/25 20.00
174 Warren Spahn/Pants, Juan Marichal/Jsy/25 20.00
175 Bo Jackson/Jsy, Deion Sanders/Pants/50 15.00
176 Tony Gwynn/Jsy, Rickey Henderson/Jsy/50 20.00
177 Hideki Matsui/Jsy, Jim Edmonds/Jsy/50 20.00
178 Rickey Henderson/Pants, Lou Brock/Jsy/50 20.00
179 Roger Clemens/Jsy, Albert Pujols/Jsy/50 25.00
180 Hideo Nomo/Jsy, Kazuhisa Ishii/Jsy/50 15.00

Fabric of the Game Stats

NM/M

Production 3-75
1 Al Oliver/Jsy/75 6.00
3 Andres Galarraga/Jsy/75 6.00
4 Andres Galarraga/Jsy/75 6.00
7 Billy Martin/Pants/75 15.00
8 Billy Williams/Jsy/75 6.00
9 Bo Jackson/Jsy/75 10.00
10 Bo Jackson/Jsy/75 10.00
13 Bobby Doerr/Jsy/25 12.00
14 Burleigh Grimes/Pants/25 50.00
15 Cal Ripken Jr./Jsy/75 30.00
16 Cal Ripken Jr./Jsy/75 30.00
17 Carl Yastrzemski/Pants/25 15.00
18 Carlton Fisk/Jkt/75 10.00
19 Jim "Catfish" Hunter/Pants/75 8.00
21 Darryl Strawberry/Jsy/75 6.00
22 Dave Concepcion/Jsy/75 4.00
23 Dave Righetti/Jsy/25 8.00
24 Dave Winfield/Pants/75 8.00
25 David Cone/Jsy/75 4.00
26 David Justice/Jsy/75 4.00
27 Deion Sanders/Jsy/75 8.00
28 Deion Sanders/Jsy/75 8.00
29 Dennis Eckersley/Jsy/75 8.00
30 Dennis Eckersley/Pants/75 8.00
39 Eddie Murray/Pants/75 12.00
40 Edgar Martinez/Jsy/75 4.00
43 Frankie Frisch/Jkt/75 15.00
44 Fred Lynn/Jsy/50 4.00
45 Fred McGriff/Jsy/75 6.00
46 Gary Carter/Jsy/50 6.00
47 Gary Carter/Jsy/25 8.00
48 Gaylord Perry/Jsy/50 6.00
49 Gaylord Perry/Jsy/25 8.00
51 Hal Newhouser/Jsy/25 10.00
54 Harmon Killebrew/Jsy/25 15.00
55 Harmon Killebrew/Jsy/50 12.00
56 Harold Baines/Jsy/50 8.00
57 Hoyt Wilhelm/Jsy/50 6.00
62 Joe Cronin/Jsy/25 20.00
63 Joe Cronin/Pants/25 20.00
64 Joe Morgan/Jsy/25 10.00
66 John Kruk/Jsy/75 10.00
71 Kirk Gibson/Jsy/25 8.00
72 Lee Smith/Jsy/75 4.00
73 Lenny Dykstra/Jsy/75 6.00
75 Luis Aparicio/Jsy/25 8.00
76 Luis Tiant/Pants/25 6.00
78 Hoyt Wilhelm/Jsy/25 10.00
79 Matt Williams/Jsy/25 8.00
82 Nolan Ryan/Jsy/25 25.00
85 Nolan Ryan/Jsy/25 25.00
86 Orlando Cepeda/Pants/25 10.00
87 Ozzie Smith/Pants/25 15.00
88 Paul Molitor/Jsy/50 8.00
89 Paul Molitor/Jsy/50 8.00
90 Paul Molitor/Pants/25 10.00
91 Phil Niekro/Jsy/25 8.00
92 Reggie Jackson/Pants/50 10.00
93 Reggie Jackson/Jkt/25 10.00
94 Reggie Jackson/Jsy/75 10.00
95 Reggie Jackson/Jsy/50 10.00
96 Rickey Henderson/Jkt/75 10.00
97 Rickey Henderson/Jsy/75 10.00
98 Rickey Henderson/Jsy/50 10.00
101 Rickey Henderson/Pants/75 10.00
102 Robin Ventura/Jsy/50 6.00
103 Robin Ventura/Jsy/50 6.00
104 Robin Yount/Jsy/50 12.00
105 Rod Carew/Jsy/25 10.00
106 Rod Carew/Jsy/75 8.00
107 Roger Maris/Pants/50 40.00
108 Ron Cey/Jsy/50 8.00
109 Ron Guidry/Pants/50 8.00
111 Sandy Koufax/Jsy/25 180.00
113 Stan Musial/Pants/25 25.00
114 Steve Garvey/Jsy/25 8.00
115 Ted Williams/Jkt/25 50.00
117 Tom Seaver/Jsy/75 10.00
118 Tom Seaver/Pants/50 10.00
119 Tommy John/Jsy/25 6.00
120 Tommy John/Pants/25 6.00
121 Tommy Lasorda/Jsy/75 6.00
124 Tony Perez/Jsy/75 8.00
125 Wade Boggs/Jsy/75 10.00
126 Warren Spahn/Pants/75 12.00
128 Will Clark/Jsy/50 8.00
129 Willie Mays/Pants/25 50.00
130 Willie McCovey/Pants/75 10.00
131 Roger Clemens/Jsy/25 20.00
140 Mike Schmidt/Jsy/25 20.00
144 Wade Boggs/Jsy/50 10.00
145 Willie Mays/Jsy/25 25.00
146 Hideo Nomo/Jsy/75 10.00
147 Dale Murphy/Jsy/25 10.00
148 Dale Murphy/Jsy/75 10.00
153 Dennis Eckersley/Jsy/75 8.00
154 Dwight Gooden/Jsy/75 6.00
155 Edgar Martinez/Jsy/75 4.00
156 Lou Brock/Jsy/75 8.00
157 Steve Carlton/Pants/75 6.00
159 Tom Glavine/Jsy/75 8.00
160 Hideki Matsui/Pants/75 20.00
161 Babe Ruth/Pants, Jim Thorpe/Jsy/25 500.00
162 Ted Williams/Jkt, Stan Musial/Jsy/25 50.00
163 Willie Mays/Jsy, Bob Gibson/Jsy/25 50.00
164 Whitey Ford/Jsy, Sandy Koufax/Jsy/25 150.00
165 Roger Maris/Pants, Don Mattingly/Jsy/25 50.00
166 Nolan Ryan/Jsy, Tom Seaver/Jsy/50 25.00
167 Cal Ripken Jr./Jsy, George Brett/Jsy/50 40.00
168 Ryne Sandberg/Jsy, Mike Schmidt/Jsy/50 30.00
169 Tony Gwynn/Jsy, Wade Boggs/Jsy/50 15.00
170 Carlton Fisk/Jsy, Johnny Bench/Pants/25 20.00
172 Reggie Jackson/Pants, Darryl Strawberry/Jsy/50 10.00
173 Robin Yount/Jsy, Paul Molitor/Jsy/25 20.00
174 Warren Spahn/Pants, Juan Marichal/Jsy/25 20.00
175 Bo Jackson/Jsy, Deion Sanders/Pants/50 15.00
176 Tony Gwynn/Jsy, Rickey Henderson/Jsy/50 20.00
177 Hideki Matsui/Jsy, Jim Edmonds/Jsy/50 20.00
178 Rickey Henderson/Pants, Lou Brock/Jsy/50 20.00
179 Roger Clemens/Jsy, Albert Pujols/Jsy/50 25.00
180 Hideo Nomo/Jsy, Kazuhisa Ishii/Jsy/50 15.00

Gold Team

NM/M

Complete Set (25):
Common Player: 1.00
Inserted 1:7
Mirror: 2-3X
1 Albert Pujols 4.00
2 Alex Rodriguez 3.00
3 Carlos Beltran 1.00
4 Chipper Jones 1.50
5 Curt Schilling 1.50
6 Derek Jeter 4.00
7 Greg Maddux 2.50
8 Hank Blalock 1.00
9 Ichiro Suzuki 3.00
10 Ivan Rodriguez 1.00
11 Jim Thome 1.00
12 Ken Griffey Jr. 3.00
13 Lyle Overbay 1.00
14 Manny Ramirez 1.50
15 Mark Mulder 1.00
16 Mark Prior 1.50
17 Michael Young 1.00
18 Miguel Cabrera 1.50
19 Mike Piazza 2.00
20 Pedro Martinez 1.50
21 Randy Johnson 1.50
22 Roger Clemens 4.00
23 Sammy Sosa 2.00
24 Tim Hudson 1.00
25 Todd Helton 1.50

Gold Team Autograph

No Pricing
Production 5-10

Gold Team Jersey Number

NM/M

Production 100-250
1 Albert Pujols/100 20.00
3 Carlos Beltran/200 5.00
4 Chipper Jones/100 8.00
5 Curt Schilling/250 8.00
7 Greg Maddux/100 10.00
8 Hank Blalock/250 4.00
10 Ivan Rodriguez/120 6.00
11 Jim Thome/250 6.00
13 Lyle Overbay/250 4.00
14 Manny Ramirez/250 8.00
15 Mark Mulder/250 4.00
16 Mark Prior/100 4.00
17 Michael Young/250 4.00
18 Miguel Cabrera/100 8.00
19 Mike Piazza/250 10.00
20 Pedro Martinez/100 8.00
21 Randy Johnson/250 8.00
22 Roger Clemens/250 10.00
23 Sammy Sosa/250 8.00
24 Tim Hudson/100 4.00
25 Todd Helton/100 6.00

Mirror Red

Mirror Red (1-200): 2-4X
Auto. (201-250): .4X
No Auto. (201-250): 1X
Production 100 Sets

Mirror White

Mirror White (1-200): 2-4X
Auto. (201-250): .4X
No Auto. (201-250): 1X
Production 100 Sets

Mirror Blue

Mirror Blue (1-200): 3-6X
Auto. (201-250): .5X
No Auto. (201-250): 1-2X
Production 50 Sets

Mirror Gold

Mirror Gold (1-200): 5-10X
Mirror Gol (201-250): No Pricing
Production 25 Sets

Mirror Emerald

No Pricing
Production Five Sets

Mirror Black

No Pricing
Production One Set

Mirror Autograph Red

NM/M

Production 1-250
16 Tim Salmon/25 30.00
18 Bobby Crosby/50 25.00
25 Casey Kotchman/50 12.00
33 Orlando Hudson/250 8.00
53 Jack Wilson/50 12.00
62 Eric Byrnes/50 10.00
66 Jeremy Bonderman/50 15.00
67 Jermaine Dye/50 15.00
68 Kazuhito Tadano/100 12.00
79 Edwin Jackson/250 8.00
80 Raul Ibanez/50 12.00
86 Ken Harvey/250 8.00
89 Wade Miller/250 10.00
91 Jeremy Affeldt/250 8.00
92 Francisco Cordero/25 15.00
95 Laynce Nix/100 8.00
106 Marlon Byrd/250 8.00
155 Bubba Nelson/250 6.00
156 Kevin Youkilis/50 20.00
160 Lew Ford/50 12.00
161 Ervin Santana/250 10.00
162 Jody Gerut/50 15.00
164 Brian Roberts/25 30.00
165 Joe Nathan/50 15.00
167 Ryan Wagner/50 10.00
168 David Dellucci/50 15.00
169 Jae Weong Seo/25 15.00
173 Jose Castillo/250 12.00
202 Agustin Montero/99 10.00
211 Norihiro Nakamura/99 50.00
212 Erick Threets/49 10.00
218 Jeff Niemann/49 25.00
221 Justin Verlander/49 40.00
223 Luke Scott/99 30.00
229 Nate McLouth/25 20.00
230 Paulino Reynoso/49 10.00
231 Philip Humber/49 25.00
234 Raul Tablado/99 12.00
239 Sean Tracey/49 10.00
243 Wladimir Balentien/99 15.00

Mirror Autograph White

NM/M

Production 1-50
18 Bobby Crosby/25 25.00
19 Brad Penny/25 15.00
25 Casey Kotchman/25 15.00
33 Orlando Hudson/50 8.00
53 Jack Wilson/25 15.00
62 Eric Byrnes/25 12.00
67 Jermaine Dye/25 15.00
68 Kazuhito Tadano/50 15.00
79 Edwin Jackson/25 10.00
80 Raul Ibanez/25 15.00
81 Rich Harden/50 15.00
86 Ken Harvey/50 8.00
89 Wade Miller/50 12.00
91 Jeremy Affeldt/50 10.00
95 Laynce Nix/50 10.00
106 Marlon Byrd/50 8.00
155 Bubba Nelson/50 8.00
156 Kevin Youkilis/25 25.00
160 Lew Ford/25 15.00
161 Ervin Santana/50 12.00
162 Jody Gerut/25 15.00
165 Joe Nathan/25 20.00
167 Ryan Wagner/25 10.00
168 David Dellucci/25 20.00
173 Jose Castillo/50 12.00
202 Agustin Montero/49 12.00
211 Norihiro Nakamura/49 60.00
212 Erick Threets/49 10.00
218 Jeff Niemann/49 25.00
221 Justin Verlander/49 40.00
223 Luke Scott/49 40.00
229 Nate McLouth/49 25.00
230 Paulino Reynoso/49 10.00
231 Philip Humber/49 25.00
234 Raul Tablado/49 15.00
239 Sean Tracey/49 10.00
243 Wladimir Balentien/49 20.00

Mirror Autograph Blue

NM/M
Production 1-100
Black: No Pricing
Production One Set
Emerald: No Pricing
Production 1-5
18 Bobby Crosby/25 25.00
25 Casey Kotchman/25 15.00
33 Orlando Hudson/100 10.00
53 Jack Wilson/25 15.00
62 Eric Byrnes/25 12.00
66 Jeremy Bonderman/25 20.00
67 Jermaine Dye/25 15.00
68 Kazuhito Tadano/50 15.00
79 Edwin Jackson/100 8.00
80 Raul Ibanez/25 15.00
86 Ken Harvey/100 8.00
89 Wade Miller/100 10.00
91 Jeremy Affeldt/100 8.00
95 Laynce Nix/50 10.00
106 Marlon Byrd/100 8.00
155 Bubba Nelson/100 8.00
156 Kevin Youkilis/25 25.00
160 Lew Ford/25 15.00
161 Ervin Santana/100 10.00
165 Joe Nathan/25 20.00
167 Ryan Wagner/25 10.00
168 David Dellucci/25 20.00
169 Jae Weong Seo/25 15.00
173 Jose Castillo/100 10.00
223 Luke Scott/49 30.00
229 Nate McLouth/49 20.00
234 Raul Tablado/49 10.00
243 Wladimir Balentien/49 25.00

Mirror Autograph Gold

NM/M
Production 1-25
2 Adam Dunn/25 35.00
11 Aubrey Huff/25 15.00
12 Austin Kearns/25 10.00
13 B.J. Upton/25 15.00
14 Brandon Webb/25 15.00
16 Tim Salmon/25 30.00
18 Bobby Crosby/25 25.00
19 Brad Penny/25 15.00
21 C.C. Sabathia/25 15.00
23 Keith Foulke/25 25.00
25 Casey Kotchman/25 15.00
27 Chone Figgins/25 12.00
29 Craig Wilson/25 10.00
31 Danny Kolb/25 10.00
33 Orlando Hudson/25 10.00
34 David Wright/25 70.00
36 Jake Peavy/25 35.00
37 Derrek Lee/25 40.00
39 Edgar Renteria/25 20.00
40 Angel Berroa/25 10.00
41 Eric Chavez/25 20.00
42 Akinori Otsuka/25 25.00
43 Francisco Rodriguez/25 25.00
44 Garret Anderson/25 20.00
53 Jack Wilson/25 15.00
54 Jamie Moyer/25 15.00
55 Jason Bay/25 25.00
57 Trot Nixon/25 20.00
60 Roy Oswalt/25 25.00
62 Eric Byrnes/25 12.00
63 Jeff Bagwell/25 40.00
65 Jeff Suppan/25 15.00
66 Jeremy Bonderman/25 20.00
67 Jermaine Dye/25 15.00
68 Kazuhito Tadano/25 15.00
75 Brett Myers/25 20.00
76 Jose Guillen/25 15.00
77 Jose Vidro/25 15.00
79 Edwin Jackson/25 10.00
80 Raul Ibanez/25 15.00
81 Rich Harden/25 20.00
86 Ken Harvey/25 10.00
89 Wade Miller/25 15.00
91 Jeremy Affeldt/25 12.00
92 Francisco Cordero/25 15.00
95 Laynce Nix/25 12.00
97 Lyle Overbay/25 15.00
98 Carlos Zambrano/25 30.00
101 Mark Buehrle/25 25.00
102 Mark Loretta/25 15.00
106 Marlon Byrd/25 10.00
107 Rafael Furcal/25 25.00
109 Michael Young/25 25.00
110 Miguel Cabrera/25 40.00
128 Maggio Ordonez/25 15.00
134 Sean Burroughs/25 10.00
135 Sean Casey/25 15.00
139 Steve Finley/25 15.00
143 Torii Hunter/25 20.00
144 Travis Hafner/25 20.00
147 Vernon Wells/25 15.00
152 Danny Graves/25 12.00
155 Bubba Nelson/25 10.00
156 Kevin Youkilis/25 25.00
157 Jacque Jones/25 15.00
158 Mike Lieberthal/25 15.00
160 Lew Ford/25 15.00
161 Ervin Santana/25 15.00
162 Jody Gerut/25 15.00
163 Nick Johnson/25 20.00
164 Brian Roberts/25 30.00
165 Joe Nathan/25 20.00
167 Ryan Wagner/25 10.00
168 David Dellucci/25 20.00
169 Jae Weong Seo/25 15.00
170 Tom Gordon/25 15.00
171 Carlos Lee/25 20.00
172 Octavio Dotel/25 12.00
173 Jose Castillo/25 15.00
174 Troy Percival/25 15.00
194 Harmon Killebrew/25 40.00

Mirror Bat Red

NM/M
Production 100-250
Gold: 1-2X
Production 25 Sets
2 Adam Dunn/250 6.00
5 Albert Pujols/250 15.00
8 Andruw Jones/250 6.00
11 Aubrey Huff/250 4.00
13 B.J. Upton/250 4.00
14 Brandon Webb/100 4.00
16 Tim Salmon/250 4.00
25 Casey Kotchman/250 4.00
26 Chipper Jones/250 6.00
28 Craig Biggio/50 6.00
29 Craig Wilson/250 4.00
34 David Wright/250 10.00
38 Dontrelle Willis/250 4.00
44 Garret Anderson/250 4.00
45 Gary Sheffield/250 6.00
59 Jason Varitek/250 6.00
61 Javy Lopez/250 4.00
63 Jeff Bagwell/250 6.00
77 Jose Vidro/250 4.00
93 Lance Berkman/250 4.00
99 Manny Ramirez/250 8.00
105 Mark Teixeira/250 6.00
109 Michael Young/250 4.00
110 Miguel Cabrera/250 8.00
111 Miguel Tejada/250 8.00
121 Paul Konerko/250 4.00
124 Rafael Palmeiro/250 6.00
128 Maggio Ordonez/250 4.00
136 Shawn Green/250 4.00
141 Todd Helton/250 6.00
142 Tom Glavine/250 4.00
143 Torii Hunter/200 4.00
148 Victor Martinez/250 4.00
149 Vladimir Guerrero/250 8.00
150 Sammy Sosa/250 8.00
153 Rocco Baldelli/250 4.00
160 Lew Ford/250 4.00
166 Mike Sweeney/100 4.00
184 Rafael Palmeiro/100 6.00
188 Tom Glavine/250 4.00
190 Vladimir Guerrero/250 8.00

Mirror Bat White

NM/M
Production 75-250
2 Adam Dunn/1 6.00
5 Albert Pujols/1 20.00
7 Alfonso Soriano/1 6.00
11 Aubrey Huff/10 4.00
12 Austin Kearns/5 4.00
13 B.J. Upton/5 6.00
14 Brandon Webb/50 4.00
25 Casey Kotchman/250 8.00
26 Chipper Jones/100 6.00
28 Craig Biggio/100 4.00
29 Craig Wilson/250 10.00
34 David Wright/100 6.00
37 Derrek Lee/250 6.00
38 Dontrelle Willis/100 4.00
44 Garret Anderson/100 6.00
45 Gary Sheffield/100 8.00
59 Jason Varitek/100 4.00
61 Javy Lopez/100 6.00
63 Jeff Bagwell/100 6.00
77 Jose Vidro/100 6.00
88 Kerry Wood/100 4.00
93 Lance Berkman/100 6.00
94 Larry Walker/100 8.00
99 Manny Ramirez/250 6.00
105 Mark Teixeira/250 4.00
109 Michael Young/250 8.00
110 Miguel Cabrera/250 8.00
111 Miguel Tejada/250 6.00
121 Paul Konerko/100 4.00
124 Rafael Palmeiro/75 6.00
128 Maggio Ordonez/100 4.00
136 Shawn Green/100 4.00
141 Todd Helton/100 6.00
142 Tom Glavine/100 4.00
143 Torii Hunter/100 4.00
148 Victor Martinez/100 4.00
149 Vladimir Guerrero/100 8.00
150 Sammy Sosa/100 8.00
153 Rocco Baldelli/100 4.00
160 Lew Ford/250 4.00
184 Rafael Palmeiro/250 6.00
188 Tom Glavine/100 4.00
190 Vladimir Guerrero/100 8.00

Mirror Bat Blue

NM/M
Production 75-100
Black: No Pricing
Production One Set
Emerald: No Pricing
Production Five Sets
2 Adam Dunn/100 6.00
5 Albert Pujols/100 20.00
8 Andruw Jones/100 8.00
11 Aubrey Huff/100 4.00
13 B.J. Upton/100 6.00
14 Brandon Webb/100 4.00
16 Tim Salmon/100 4.00
25 Casey Kotchman/100 4.00
26 Chipper Jones/100 8.00
32 David Ortiz/100 10.00
37 Derrek Lee/100 8.00
38 Dontrelle Willis/100 6.00
44 Garret Anderson/100 4.00
45 Gary Sheffield/100 6.00
59 Jason Varitek/100 8.00
61 Javy Lopez/100 4.00
63 Jeff Bagwell/100 6.00
77 Jose Vidro/100 4.00
93 Lance Berkman/100 4.00
99 Manny Ramirez/100 8.00
105 Mark Teixeira/100 6.00
109 Michael Young/100 4.00
110 Miguel Cabrera/5 8.00
111 Miguel Tejada/100 8.00
117 Nomar Garciaparra/100 8.00
121 Paul Konerko/100 4.00
124 Rafael Palmeiro/100 6.00
128 Magglio Ordonez/100 4.00
136 Shawn Green/100 4.00
141 Todd Helton/100 6.00
142 Tom Glavine/100 4.00
143 Torii Hunter/100 4.00
144 Travis Hafner/100 4.00
148 Victor Martinez/100 4.00
149 Vladimir Guerrero/100 8.00
150 Sammy Sosa/100 8.00
153 Rocco Baldelli/100 4.00
160 Lew Ford/100 4.00
166 Mike Sweeney/75 4.00
184 Rafael Palmeiro/100 6.00
188 Tom Glavine/100 4.00
190 Vladimir Guerrero/100 8.00

Mirror Fabric Red

NM/M
Production 100-250
Gold: 1-2X
Production 25 Sets
2 Adam Dunn/Jsy/250 6.00
5 Albert Pujols/Jsy/250 15.00
7 Alfonso Soriano/Jsy/250 6.00
8 Andruw Jones/Jsy/250 6.00
10 Aramis Ramirez/Jsy/250 4.00
11 Aubrey Huff/Jsy/250 4.00
13 B.J. Upton/Jsy/250 4.00
14 Brandon Webb/Pants/100 4.00
15 Barry Zito/Jsy/250 4.00
17 Bobby Abreu/Jsy/250 4.00
20 Preston Wilson/Jsy/250 4.00
25 Casey Kotchman/Jsy/250 4.00
26 Chipper Jones/Jsy/250 8.00
28 Craig Biggio/Jsy/250 4.00
30 Curt Schilling/Jsy/250 8.00
32 David Ortiz/Jsy/250 8.00
37 Derrek Lee/Jsy/250 8.00
38 Dontrelle Willis/Jsy/225 4.00
41 Eric Chavez/Jsy/250 4.00
43 Francisco Rodriguez/Jsy/250 4.00
44 Garret Anderson/Jsy/250 4.00
45 Gary Sheffield/Jsy/250 6.00
46 Greg Maddux/Jsy/250 10.00
47 Hideki Matsui/Jsy/250 15.00
48 Hideo Nomo/Jsy/250 6.00
50 Ivan Rodriguez/Jsy/250 4.00
57 Trot Nixon/Jsy/250 4.00
60 Roy Oswalt/Jsy/250 4.00
61 Javy Lopez/Jsy/250 4.00
63 Jeff Bagwell/Jsy/250 6.00
69 Jim Edmonds/Jsy/250 6.00
70 Jim Thome/Jsy/250 6.00
71 Johan Santana/Jsy/250 6.00
82 Justin Morneau/Jsy/250 6.00
84 Kazuo Matsui/Jsy/250 4.00
87 Frank Thomas/Jsy/250 6.00
88 Kerry Wood/Jsy/250 6.00
92 Francisco Cordero/Jsy/250 4.00
93 Lance Berkman/Jsy/250 4.00
94 Larry Walker/Jsy/250 6.00
96 Luis Gonzalez/Jsy/250 4.00
97 Lyle Overbay/Jsy/250 4.00
98 Carlos Zambrano/Jsy/250 4.00
99 Manny Ramirez/Jsy/250 8.00
104 Mark Prior/Jsy/250 8.00
109 Michael Young/Jsy/250 4.00
110 Miguel Cabrera/Jsy/250 8.00
111 Miguel Tejada/Jsy/250 6.00
114 Mike Piazza/Jsy/250 8.00
121 Paul Konerko/Jsy/250 4.00
124 Rafael Palmeiro/Jsy/100 6.00
129 Roger Clemens/Jsy/250 10.00
131 Sammy Sosa/Jsy/250 8.00
133 Scott Rolen/Jsy/250 6.00
135 Sean Casey/Jsy/250 4.00
138 Roy Halladay/Jsy/250 4.00
141 Todd Helton/Jsy/250 6.00
144 Travis Hafner/Jsy/250 4.00
147 Vernon Wells/Jsy/250 4.00
148 Victor Martinez/Jsy/250 4.00
149 Vladimir Guerrero/Jsy/250 8.00
153 Rocco Baldelli/Jsy/250 4.00
159 Ben Sheets/Jsy/250 4.00
160 Lew Ford/Jsy/250 4.00
166 Mike Sweeney/Jsy/250 4.00
178 Greg Maddux/Jsy/250 10.00
179 Ivan Rodriguez/Jsy/250 4.00
183 Pedro J. Martinez/Jsy/250 8.00
184 Rafael Palmeiro/Jsy/250 6.00
185 Roger Clemens/Jsy/250 10.00
188 Tom Glavine/Jsy/250 4.00
190 Vladimir Guerrero/Jsy/100 8.00

Mirror Fabric White

NM/M
Production 50-250
2 Adam Dunn/Jsy/250 6.00
5 Albert Pujols/Jsy/100 15.00
7 Alfonso Soriano/Jsy/100 6.00
8 Andruw Jones/Jsy/100 6.00
10 Aramis Ramirez/Jsy/100 6.00
11 Aubrey Huff/Jsy/150 4.00
13 B.J. Upton/Jsy/250 4.00
15 Barry Zito/Jsy/100 4.00
26 Chipper Jones/Jsy/250 8.00
28 Craig Biggio/Pants/250 6.00
30 Curt Schilling/Jsy/100 8.00
32 David Ortiz/Jsy/100 8.00
34 David Wright/Jsy/100 10.00
38 Dontrelle Willis/Jsy/50 4.00
41 Eric Chavez/Jsy/100 4.00
44 Garret Anderson/Jsy/100 4.00
45 Gary Sheffield/Jsy/50 6.00
46 Greg Maddux/Jsy/50 10.00
47 Hideki Matsui/Pants/100 15.00
48 Hideo Nomo/Jsy/100 6.00
57 Trot Nixon/Jsy/100 4.00
60 Roy Oswalt/Jsy/25 6.00
63 Jeff Bagwell/Jsy/100 6.00
69 Jim Edmonds/Jsy/100 6.00
70 Jim Thome/Jsy/100 6.00
71 Johan Santana/Jsy/100 6.00
78 Josh Beckett/Jsy/250 4.00
82 Justin Morneau/Jsy/100 6.00
84 Kazuo Matsui/Jsy/250 4.00
88 Kerry Wood/Jsy/50 6.00
93 Lance Berkman/Jsy/250 4.00
94 Larry Walker/Jsy/100 6.00
95 Laynce Nix/Jsy/100 4.00
96 Luis Gonzalez/Jsy/250 4.00
98 Carlos Zambrano/Jsy/100 6.00
99 Manny Ramirez/Jsy/100 8.00
104 Mark Prior/Jsy/100 8.00
109 Michael Young/Jsy/100 4.00
110 Miguel Cabrera/Jsy/150 8.00
111 Miguel Tejada/Jsy/100 8.00
113 Mike Mussina/Jsy/100 6.00
114 Mike Piazza/Jsy/100 8.00
121 Paul Konerko/Jsy/150 4.00
124 Rafael Palmeiro/Jsy/150 6.00
129 Roger Clemens/Jsy/100 10.00
131 Sammy Sosa/Jsy/150 8.00
133 Scott Rolen/Jsy/100 6.00
135 Sean Casey/Jsy/100 6.00
138 Roy Halladay/Jsy/100 4.00
141 Todd Helton/Jsy/100 6.00
144 Travis Hafner/Jsy/100 4.00
147 Vernon Wells/Jsy/250 4.00
148 Victor Martinez/Jsy/250 4.00
149 Vladimir Guerrero/Jsy/250 8.00
151 Hank Blalock/Jsy/100 4.00
159 Ben Sheets/Jsy/100 4.00
166 Mike Sweeney/Jsy/50 4.00
178 Greg Maddux/Jsy/200 10.00
179 Ivan Rodriguez/Jsy/250 4.00
184 Rafael Palmeiro/Jsy/250 6.00
185 Roger Clemens/Jsy/100 10.00
188 Tom Glavine/Jsy/250 4.00

Mirror Fabric Blue

NM/M
Production 50-100
Black: No Pricing
Production One Set
Emerald: No Pricing
Production Five Sets
2 Adam Dunn/Jsy/100 6.00
5 Albert Pujols/Jsy/100 15.00
7 Alfonso Soriano/Jsy/100 6.00
8 Andruw Jones/Jsy/100 6.00
10 Aramis Ramirez/Jsy/100 6.00
11 Aubrey Huff/Jsy/100 4.00
13 B.J. Upton/Jsy/100 4.00
14 Brandon Webb/Pants/100 4.00
15 Barry Zito/Jsy/100 4.00
17 Bobby Abreu/Jsy/100 4.00
18 Bobby Crosby/Jsy/50 6.00
25 Casey Kotchman/Jsy/100 4.00
26 Chipper Jones/Jsy/100 8.00
28 Craig Biggio/Jsy/100 4.00
30 Curt Schilling/Jsy/100 8.00
32 David Ortiz/Jsy/100 8.00
37 Derrek Lee/Jsy/100 8.00
38 Dontrelle Willis/Jsy/100 4.00
41 Eric Chavez/Jsy/100 4.00
43 Francisco Rodriguez/Jsy/100 4.00
44 Garret Anderson/Jsy/100 4.00
46 Greg Maddux/Jsy/100 10.00
47 Hideki Matsui/Pants/100 15.00
48 Hideo Nomo/Jsy/100 6.00
50 Ivan Rodriguez/Jsy/100 4.00
57 Trot Nixon/Jsy/100 4.00
60 Roy Oswalt/Jsy/50 4.00
61 Javy Lopez/Jsy/100 4.00
63 Jeff Bagwell/Jsy/100 6.00
69 Jim Edmonds/Jsy/100 6.00
70 Jim Thome/Jsy/100 6.00
71 Johan Santana/Jsy/100 6.00
73 Johnny Damon/Jsy/100 8.00
78 Josh Beckett/Jsy/100 4.00
82 Justin Morneau/Jsy/100 6.00
84 Kazuo Matsui/Jsy/100 4.00
87 Frank Thomas/Jsy/100 6.00
88 Kerry Wood/Jsy/100 6.00
92 Francisco Cordero/Jsy/100 4.00
93 Lance Berkman/Jsy/100 4.00
94 Larry Walker/Jsy/100 6.00
96 Luis Gonzalez/Jsy/100 4.00
97 Lyle Overbay/Jsy/100 4.00
98 Carlos Zambrano/Jsy/100 6.00
99 Manny Ramirez/Jsy/100 8.00
104 Mark Prior/Jsy/100 8.00
109 Michael Young/Jsy/100 4.00
110 Miguel Cabrera/Jsy/100 8.00
111 Miguel Tejada/Jsy/100 6.00
113 Mike Mussina/Jsy/50 6.00
114 Mike Piazza/Jsy/100 8.00
121 Paul Konerko/Jsy/100 4.00
124 Rafael Palmeiro/Jsy/100 6.00
129 Roger Clemens/Jsy/100 10.00
131 Sammy Sosa/Jsy/100 8.00
133 Scott Rolen/Jsy/100 6.00
135 Sean Casey/Jsy/100 4.00
138 Roy Halladay/Jsy/100 4.00
141 Todd Helton/Jsy/100 6.00
144 Travis Hafner/Jsy/100 4.00
147 Vernon Wells/Jsy/100 4.00
148 Victor Martinez/Jsy/100 4.00
149 Vladimir Guerrero/Jsy/100 8.00
151 Hank Blalock/Jsy/100 4.00
153 Rocco Baldelli/Jsy/100 4.00
159 Ben Sheets/Jsy/100 4.00
160 Lew Ford/Jsy/100 4.00
166 Mike Sweeney/Jsy/100 4.00
178 Greg Maddux/Jsy/100 10.00
179 Ivan Rodriguez/Jsy/100 4.00
183 Pedro J. Martinez/Jsy/100 8.00
184 Rafael Palmeiro/Pants/100 6.00
185 Roger Clemens/Jsy/100 10.00
188 Tom Glavine/Jsy/100 4.00
190 Vladimir Guerrero/Jsy/100 8.00

Certified Materials Skills

NM/M
Common: 1.50
Inserted 1:7
Mirror: 2X-3X
1 Andy Pettitte 1.50
2 Barry Zito 1.50
3 Bobby Crosby 2.00
4 Brandon Webb 1.50
5 Craig Biggio 2.00
6 David Ortiz 3.00
7 Dontrelle Willis 2.00
8 Francisco Rodriguez 1.50
9 Gary Sheffield 2.00
10 Jack Wilson 1.50
11 Jason Bay 1.50
12 Jeff Bagwell 2.00
13 Jim Edmonds 2.00
14 Josh Beckett 1.50
15 Kerry Wood 2.00
16 Lance Berkman 1.50
17 Mark Buehrle 1.50
18 Mark Teixeira 2.00
19 Miguel Tejada 2.00
20 Paul Konerko 1.50
21 Scott Rolen 2.00
22 Sean Burroughs 1.50
23 Vernon Wells 1.50
24 Victor Martinez 1.50
25 Vladimir Guerrero 3.00

Skills Autographs

NM/M
Production 5-25
3 Bobby Crosby/25 25.00
11 Jason Bay/25 25.00

Skills Jersey Position

NM/M
Production 100-250
Prime: No Pricing
Production 5-25
1 Andy Pettitte/250 4.00
2 Barry Zito/250 4.00
3 Bobby Crosby/100 6.00
4 Brandon Webb/Pants/100 4.00
5 Craig Biggio/250 4.00
6 David Ortiz/250 8.00
7 Dontrelle Willis/100 4.00
8 Francisco Rodriguez/250 4.00
9 Gary Sheffield/50 6.00
10 Jack Wilson/50 4.00
11 Jason Bay/100 4.00
12 Jeff Bagwell/250 6.00
13 Jim Edmonds/250 6.00
14 Josh Beckett/250 4.00
15 Kerry Wood/50 6.00
16 Lance Berkman/250 4.00
17 Mark Buehrle/150 4.00
19 Miguel Tejada/250 8.00
20 Paul Konerko/100 4.00
21 Scott Rolen/100 6.00
22 Sean Burroughs/100 4.00
23 Vernon Wells/250 4.00
24 Victor Martinez/250 4.00
25 Vladimir Guerrero/250 8.00

2005 Leaf Limited

NM/M
Complete Set (205):
Common Player (1-150): 1.00
Production 699
Common (151-175, 197): 4.00
Production 99
Commmon Auto. (176-196, 198-200): 12.00
Production 99
Pack (4): 70.00
1 Roger Clemens 5.00
2 Roger Clemens 5.00
3 Ichiro Suzuki 4.00
4 Ichiro Suzuki 4.00
5 Todd Helton 1.50
6 Todd Helton 1.50
7 Vladimir Guerrero 2.00
8 Vladimir Guerrero 2.00
9 Miguel Cabrera 2.00
10 Miguel Cabrera 2.00
11 Albert Pujols 5.00
12 Albert Pujols 5.00
13 Mark Prior 1.50
14 Mark Prior 1.50
15 Chipper Jones 2.00
16 Chipper Jones 2.00
17 Jeff Bagwell 1.50
18 Jeff Bagwell 1.50
19 Kerry Wood 1.00
20 Kerry Wood 1.00
21 Gary Sheffield 1.50
22 Carl Crawford 1.00
23 Mariano Rivera 1.50
24 Curt Schilling 2.00
25 Ben Sheets 1.00
26 Jimmy Rollins 1.00
27 Melvin Mora 1.00
28 Corey Patterson 1.00
29 Rafael Furcal 1.00
30 Jim Thome 1.50
31 Derek Jeter 5.00
32 Jake Peavy 1.50

33 Francisco Cordero 1.00
34 Aramis Ramirez 1.50
35 Javy Lopez 1.00
36 Aaron Rowand 1.00
37 Jason Bay 1.00
38 Michael Young 1.00
39 Ivan Rodriguez 1.50
40 Joe Nathan 1.00
41 Oliver Perez 1.00
42 Adam Dunn 1.50
43 Eric Chavez 1.00
44 Pedro Martinez 2.00
45 Roy Oswalt 1.00
46 Carlos Delgado 1.00
47 Jeff Kent 1.00
48 Johnny Damon 2.00
49 Edgar Renteria 1.00
50 Mark Buehrle 1.00
51 Carl Pavano 1.00
52 J.D. Drew 1.00
53 Hank Blalock 1.00
54 Moises Alou 1.00
55 Brad Radke 1.00
56 Brad Wilkerson 1.00
57 Sean Casey 1.00
58 Mike Lowell 1.00
59 Octavio Dotel 1.00
60 Francisco Rodriguez 1.00
61 Jose Guillen 1.00
62 Greg Maddux 3.00
63 A.J. Burnett 1.00
64 Chris Carpenter 1.50
65 Jose Reyes 1.50
66 Travis Hafner 1.50
67 Rich Harden 1.00
68 Bret Boone 1.00
69 Scott Podsednik 1.00
70 Andruw Jones 1.50
71 Milton Bradley 1.00
72 Zack Greinke 1.00
73 Torii Hunter 1.00
74 Paul Konerko 1.50
75 David Wells 1.00
76 Tim Hudson 1.50
77 Sammy Sosa 2.50
78 Jason Varitek 1.50
79 Lance Berkman 1.50
80 Justin Morneau 1.50
81 Troy Glaus 1.00
82 Jose Vidro 1.00
83 Joe Mauer 1.50
84 Josh Beckett 1.00
85 Craig Biggio 1.00
86 Luis Gonzalez 1.00
87 Larry Walker 1.00
88 Barry Zito 1.00
89 Jacque Jones 1.00
90 Lyle Overbay 1.00
91 Roy Halladay 1.50
92 Orlando Cabrera 1.00
93 Magglio Ordonez 1.00
94 Mike Sweeney 1.00
95 Rafael Palmeiro 1.50
96 Brandon Webb 1.00
97 Preston Wilson 1.00
98 Shannon Stewart 1.00
99 Trot Nixon 1.00
100 Mike Piazza 2.50
101 Dontrelle Willis 1.50
102 Ken Griffey Jr. 3.00
103 Andy Pettitte 1.00
104 Kazuo Matsui 1.00
105 Bobby Crosby 1.00
106 Shawn Green 1.00
107 Alfonso Soriano 2.00
108 Carlos Zambrano 1.00
109 Keith Foulke 1.00
110 Aubrey Huff 1.00
111 Adrian Beltre 1.00
112 Mark Teixeira 1.50
113 Randy Johnson 2.00
114 Miguel Tejada 1.50
115 Alex Rodriguez 4.00
116 Carlos Beltran 1.50
117 Bobby Abreu 1.50
118 Johan Santana 1.50
119 Manny Ramirez 2.00
120 Juan Pierre 1.00
121 Scott Rolen 1.50
122 Livan Hernandez 1.00
123 Carlos Lee 1.00
124 Derrek Lee 1.50
125 Brian Giles 1.00
126 Nomar Garciaparra 2.00
127 John Smoltz 1.50
128 Jim Edmonds 1.50
129 Bartolo Colon 1.00
130 Garret Anderson 1.00
131 Austin Kearns 1.00
132 Shingo Takatsu 1.00
133 Omar Vizquel 1.00
134 Tom Glavine 1.00
135 Mark Mulder 1.50
136 Bernie Williams 1.00
137 Richie Sexson 1.50
138 Mike Mussina 1.50
139 Mark Loretta 1.00
140 Vernon Wells 1.00
141 David Wright 3.00
142 Marcus Giles 1.00
143 David Ortiz 2.00
144 Victor Martinez 1.00
145 Hideki Matsui 4.00
146 C.C. Sabathia 1.00
147 Angel Berroa 1.00
148 Troy Percival 1.00
149 Paul LoDuca 1.00
150 Jorge Posada 1.50
151 Willie Mays 8.00
152 Ryne Sandberg 8.00
153 Rickey Henderson 4.00
154 Ted Williams 10.00
155 Roberto Clemente 10.00
156 George Brett 8.00
157 Whitey Ford 4.00
158 Duke Snider 4.00
159 Don Mattingly 10.00
160 Bob Gibson 4.00
161 Hank Aaron 8.00
162 Al Kaline 6.00
163 Nolan Ryan 10.00
164 Stan Musial 6.00
165 George Kell 4.00
166 Harmon Killebrew 6.00
167 Cal Ripken Jr. 15.00
168 Babe Ruth 10.00
169 Roger Clemens/SP 8.00
170 Curt Schilling/SP 4.00
171 Rafael Palmeiro/SP 4.00
172 Randy Johnson/SP 5.00
173 Mike Piazza/SP 5.00
174 Greg Maddux/SP 6.00
175 Sammy Sosa/SP 5.00
176 Hayden Penn/ Auto. **RC** 15.00
177 Ambiorix Concepcion/ Auto. **RC** 15.00
178 Casey Rogowski/ Auto. **RC** 15.00
179 Prince Fielder/Auto. 150.00
180 Geovany Soto/ Auto. **RC** 30.00
181 Wladimir Balentien/ Auto. **RC** 25.00
182 Jason Hammel/ Auto. **RC** 15.00
183 Keiichi Yabu/ Auto. **RC** 25.00
184 Brandon McCarthy/ Auto. **RC** 40.00
185 Ubaldo Jimenez/ Auto. **RC** 15.00
186 Keiichi Yabu/ Auto. **RC** 25.00
187 Miguel Negron/ Auto. **RC** 15.00
188 Mike Morse/Auto. **RC** 25.00
189 Nate McLouth/ Auto. **RC** 25.00
190 Norihiro Nakamura/ Auto. **RC** 40.00
191 Bill McCarthy/ Auto. **RC** 50.00
192 Tony Pena/ Auto. **RC** 12.00
193 Ambiorix Concepcion/ Auto. **RC** 15.00
194 Raul Tablado/ Auto. **RC** 15.00
195 Hayden Penn/ Auto. **RC** 15.00
196 Sean Thompson/ Auto. **RC** 15.00
197 Tadahito Iguchi **RC** 15.00
198 Ubaldo Jimenez/ Auto. **RC** 15.00
199 Wladimir Balentien/ Auto. **RC** 25.00
200 Prince Fielder/Auto. 150.00
201 Philip Humber/ Auto./99 **RC** 60.00
202 Jeff Niemann/ Auto./95 **RC** 40.00
203 Justin Verlander/ Auto./70 **RC** 90.00
205 Yuniesky Betancourt/ Auto./99 **RC** 50.00

Bronze Spotlight

Bronze (1-150): 1-1.5X
Bronze (151-175): 1X
Bronze (176-200): .25X
Production 99 Sets

Silver Spotlight

Silver (1-150): 1-2X
Silver (151-175): 1-1.5X
Silver (176-200): .25X
Production 50 Sets

Gold Spotlight

Gold (1-150): 2-4X
Gold (151-175): 2-3X
Production 25 Sets
Gold (176-205): No Pricing
Production 5-25

Platinum Spotlight

No Pricing
Production One Set

Cuts Silver

NM/M
Production 7-99
Platinum: No Pricing
Production One Set
1 Orlando Cepeda/30 35.00
2 Hank Aaron/44 275.00
3 Willie Mays/24 175.00
4 Sandy Koufax/32 400.00
5 Cal Ripken Jr./25 150.00
6 Nolan Ryan/34 120.00
7 Jim Palmer/22 30.00
8 Tony Gwynn/19 60.00
9 Rod Carew/29 40.00
10 Ryne Sandberg/23 70.00
11 Stan Musial/28 70.00
12 Steve Carlton/32 30.00
14 Mike Schmidt/20 60.00
15 Harmon Killebrew/25 40.00
17 Duke Snider/53 30.00
18 Don Mattingly/25 50.00
19 Dale Murphy/25 35.00
21 Juan Marichal/99 25.00
22 Greg Maddux/37 10.00
24 Paul Molitor/25 35.00
25 Wade Boggs/26 40.00
26 Mark Prior/27 40.00
28 Al Kaline/28 40.00

Cuts Gold

Production 3-30

Legends

NM/M
Common Player:
Production 50 Sets
Foil: No Pricing
Production 10 Sets
1 Billy Martin 4.00
2 Bobby Doerr 3.00
3 Carlton Fisk 4.00
4 Harmon Killebrew 5.00
5 Duke Snider 5.00
6 George Brett 6.00
7 Johnny Bench 5.00
8 Lou Boudreau 3.00
9 Brooks Robinson 4.00
10 Al Kaline 4.00
11 Stan Musial 5.00
12 Burleigh Grimes 3.00
13 Cal Ripken Jr. 10.00
14 Carl Yastrzemski 6.00
15 Willie Stargell 3.00
16 Yogi Berra 4.00
17 Enos Slaughter 3.00
18 Phil Rizzuto 3.00
19 Luis Aparicio 3.00
20 Ernie Banks 5.00
21 Hal Newhouser 3.00
22 Whitey Ford 4.00
23 Tony Gwynn 4.00
24 Bob Feller 4.00
25 Don Sutton 3.00
26 Lou Brock 3.00
27 Jim Palmer 3.00
28 Billy Williams 2.00
29 Juan Marichal 3.00
30 Rod Carew 3.00
31 Jim "Catfish" Hunter 2.00
32 Maury Wills 2.00
33 Joe Cronin 2.00
34 Fergie Jenkins 2.00
35 Sandy Koufax 5.00
36 Steve Carlton 3.00
37 Eddie Murray 3.00
38 Roger Maris 4.00
39 Gaylord Perry 2.00
40 Bob Gibson 3.00
41 Tom Seaver 3.00
42 Dennis Eckersley 2.00
43 Reggie Jackson 3.00
44 Willie McCovey 3.00
45 Willie Mays 6.00
46 Willie Mays 6.00
47 Rickey Henderson 3.00
48 Rickey Henderson 3.00
49 Nolan Ryan 6.00
50 Nolan Ryan 6.00

Legends Jersey Number

NM/M
Production 1-45
3 Carlton Fisk/50 10.00
25 Don Sutton/20 8.00
26 Lou Brock/20 10.00
27 Jim Palmer/22 8.00
28 Billy Williams/26 8.00
29 Juan Marichal/27 8.00
30 Rod Carew/29 10.00
31 Jim "Catfish" Hunter/ Pants/29 8.00
34 Fergie Jenkins/31 6.00
35 Sandy Koufax/32 250.00
36 Steve Carlton/32 8.00
37 Eddie Murray/33 12.00
39 Gaylord Perry/36 6.00
40 Bob Gibson/45 10.00
41 Tom Seaver/41 10.00
42 Dennis Eckersley/45 5.00
43 Reggie Jackson/ Pants/44 8.00
44 Willie McCovey/44 10.00
45 Willie Mays/24 40.00
46 Willie Mays/24 40.00
49 Nolan Ryan/30 25.00
50 Nolan Ryan/30 25.00

Limited Legends Signature

NM/M
Production 2-50
2 Bobby Doerr/50 15.00
4 Harmon Killebrew/50 30.00
5 Duke Snider/25 35.00
9 Brooks Robinson/50 25.00
10 Al Kaline/50 40.00
18 Phil Rizzuto/50 35.00
19 Luis Aparicio/50 20.00
24 Bob Feller/50 25.00
25 Don Sutton/50 15.00
26 Lou Brock/50 30.00
27 Jim Palmer/50 20.00
28 Billy Williams/25 20.00
29 Juan Marichal/50 25.00
30 Rod Carew/25 35.00
32 Maury Wills/50 15.00
34 Fergie Jenkins/50 15.00
36 Steve Carlton/50 25.00
39 Gaylord Perry/50 15.00
40 Bob Gibson/25 40.00
42 Dennis Eckersley/50 20.00

Legends Signature Jersey Number

NM/M
Production 5-30
2 Bobby Doerr/ Pants/25 25.00
4 Harmon Killebrew/25 40.00
11 Stan Musial/25 65.00
13 Cal Ripken Jr./25 150.00
18 Phil Rizzuto/Pants/25 40.00
19 Luis Aparicio/25 25.00
23 Tony Gwynn/25 40.00
25 Don Sutton/20 20.00
27 Jim Palmer/22 25.00
34 Fergie Jenkins/25 20.00
36 Steve Carlton/25 30.00
39 Gaylord Perry/25 20.00
40 Bob Gibson/25 40.00
42 Dennis Eckersley/25 25.00
44 Willie McCovey/25 40.00
45 Willie Mays/24 160.00
46 Willie Mays/24 160.00
49 Nolan Ryan/30 90.00
50 Nolan Ryan/30 90.00

Lettermen

NM/M
Production 4-21
DU-H Dale Murphy H/20 150.00
DU-M Dale Murphy M/20 150.00
DU-P Dale Murphy P/20 150.00
DU-R Dale Murphy R/20 150.00
DU-U Dale Murphy U/20 150.00
DU-Y Dale Murphy Y/20 150.00
NR-A Nolan Ryan A/21 200.00
NR-N Nolan Ryan N/21 200.00
NR-R Nolan Ryan R/21 200.00
NR-Y Nolan Ryan Y/21 200.00

Lumberjacks

NM/M
Common Player:
Production 50 Sets
Foil: No Pricing
1 Al Kaline 4.00
2 Albert Pujols 8.00
3 Andre Dawson 3.00
4 Babe Ruth 8.00
5 Cal Ripken Jr. 15.00
6 Chipper Jones 4.00
7 Dale Murphy 3.00
8 Dave Winfield 3.00
9 Don Mattingly 6.00
10 Duke Snider 4.00
11 Eddie Murray 3.00
12 Frank Robinson 4.00
13 Frank Thomas 4.00
14 Gary Carter 3.00
15 Hack Wilson 3.00
16 Hank Aaron 10.00
17 Harmon Killebrew 4.00
18 Joe Morgan 3.00
19 Johnny Bench 4.00
20 Kirby Puckett 4.00
21 Kirk Gibson 3.00
22 Manny Ramirez 4.00
23 Mark Grace 3.00
24 Mike Piazza 5.00
25 Mike Schmidt 6.00
26 Orlando Cepeda 3.00
27 Paul Molitor 4.00
28 Rafael Palmeiro 4.00
29 Ralph Kiner 3.00
30 Reggie Jackson 4.00
31 Richie Ashburn 3.00
32 Rickey Henderson 4.00
33 Robin Yount 5.00
34 Rod Carew 4.00
35 Ryne Sandberg 6.00
36 Stan Musial 5.00
37 Ted Williams 8.00
38 Tony Gwynn 4.00
39 Vladimir Guerrero 4.00
40 Willie Mays 8.00
41 Ernie Banks, Bernie Williams 6.00
42 Ted Williams, Joe Cronin 10.00
43 George Brett, Bo Jackson 8.00
44 John Kruk, Jim Thome 3.00
45 Willie Mays, Jim Thorpe 8.00
46 Wade Boggs, Johnny Damon 6.00
47 M. Williams, W. Clark 3.00
48 Willie Stargell, D. Parker 4.00
49 Ichiro Suzuki, Edgar Martinez 6.00
50 Carl Yastrzemski, Carlton Fisk 6.00

Lumberjacks Barrel

No Pricing
Production 1-5

Lumberjacks Bat

NM/M
Production 1-50
1 Al Kaline/50 10.00
4 Babe Ruth/25 180.00
8 Dave Winfield/50 10.00
11 Eddie Murray/25 15.00
12 Frank Robinson/50 15.00
14 Gary Carter/25 10.00
15 Hack Wilson/50 40.00
16 Hank Aaron/50 40.00
18 Joe Morgan/25 8.00
19 Johnny Bench/50 10.00
20 Kirby Puckett/50 10.00
25 Mike Schmidt/50 15.00
26 Orlando Cepeda/25 8.00
27 Paul Molitor/50 8.00
29 Ralph Kiner/25 15.00
31 Richie Ashburn/25 15.00
33 Robin Yount/25 20.00
35 Ryne Sandberg/25 20.00
36 Stan Musial/50 20.00
37 Ted Williams/50 40.00
40 Willie Mays/50 30.00
43 George Brett, Bo Jackson/50 25.00
47 M. Williams, W. Clark/50 15.00
48 Willie Stargell, D. Parker/50 15.00
50 Carl Yastrzemski, Carlton Fisk/50 20.00

Lumberjacks Combos

NM/M
Production 1-50
2 Albert Pujols/ Bat-Jsy/50 30.00
5 Cal Ripken Jr./ Bat-Jsy/50 35.00
6 Chipper Jones/ Bat-Jsy/25 15.00
7 Dale Murphy/ Bat-Jsy/50 12.00
8 Dave Winfield/ Bat-Pants/50 8.00
11 Eddie Murray/ Bat-Jsy/25 20.00
13 Frank Thomas/ Bat-Jsy/25 15.00
16 Hank Aaron/ Bat-Jsy/25 60.00
19 Johnny Bench/ Bat-Jsy/25 15.00
20 Kirby Puckett/ Bat-Jsy/25 15.00
21 Kirk Gibson/ Bat-Jsy/50 8.00
22 Manny Ramirez/ Bat-Jsy/50 12.00
23 Mark Grace/ Bat-Jsy/50 12.00
24 Mike Piazza/ Bat-Jsy/50 15.00
25 Mike Schmidt/ Bat-Jsy/25 25.00
26 Orlando Cepeda/ Bat-Pants/50 8.00
27 Paul Molitor/ Bat-Jsy/50 12.00
31 Richie Ashburn/ Bat-Jsy/25 15.00
33 Robin Yount/ Bat-Jsy/50 15.00
36 Stan Musial/ Bat-Jsy/25 35.00
40 Willie Mays/ Bat-Jsy/25 50.00

Lumberjacks Combos Prime

NM/M
Production 1-50
2 Albert Pujols/ Bat-Jsy/50 35.00
3 Andre Dawson/ Bat-Jsy/50 8.00
5 Cal Ripken Jr./ Bat-Jsy/25 50.00
6 Chipper Jones/ Bat-Jsy/50 15.00
11 Eddie Murray/ Bat-Jsy/25 25.00
12 Frank Robinson/ Bat-Jsy/50 12.00
13 Frank Thomas/ Bat-Jsy/50 15.00
14 Gary Carter/ Bat-Jsy/50 10.00
18 Joe Morgan/ Bat-Jsy/25 15.00
21 Kirk Gibson/ Bat-Jsy/50 8.00
22 Manny Ramirez/ Bat-Jsy/25 20.00
24 Mike Piazza/ Bat-Jsy/50 15.00
28 Rafael Palmeiro/ Bat-Jsy/50 12.00
32 Rickey Henderson/ Bat-Jsy/25 15.00
33 Robin Yount/ Bat-Jsy/50 25.00
34 Rod Carew/ Bat-Jsy/50 12.00
39 Vladimir Guerrero/ Bat-Jsy/50 15.00

Lumberjacks Jersey

NM/M
Production 1-50
4 Babe Ruth/25 250.00
8 Dave Winfield/ Pants/50 6.00
10 Duke Snider/ Pants/50 10.00
11 Eddie Murray/25 15.00
14 Gary Carter/50 5.00
16 Hank Aaron/25 40.00
19 Johnny Bench/25 15.00
20 Kirby Puckett/25 15.00
27 Paul Molitor/50 8.00
30 Reggie Jackson/50 10.00
31 Richie Ashburn/50 10.00
33 Robin Yount/50 12.00
35 Ryne Sandberg/50 12.00
36 Stan Musial/25 25.00
37 Ted Williams/25 50.00
40 Willie Mays/25 35.00
41 Ernie Banks, Bernie Williams/25 30.00
42 Ted Williams, Joe Cronin/25 60.00
43 George Brett, Bo Jackson/50 30.00
44 John Kruk, Jim Thome/25 20.00
45 Willie Mays, Jim Thorpe/25 200.00
46 Wade Boggs, Johnny Damon/50 20.00
47 M. Williams, W. Clark/50 20.00
48 Willie Stargell, D. Parker/25 25.00

Lumberjacks Signature

NM/M
Production 1-50
1 Al Kaline/50 40.00
3 Andre Dawson/25 20.00
5 Cal Ripken Jr./21 120.00
7 Dale Murphy/50 25.00
9 Don Mattingly/50 50.00
10 Duke Snider/50 25.00
12 Frank Robinson/50 30.00
13 Frank Thomas/25 50.00
14 Gary Carter/50 20.00
17 Harmon Killebrew/50 35.00
18 Joe Morgan/25 25.00
19 Johnny Bench/50 40.00
20 Kirby Puckett/25 40.00
23 Mark Grace/25 35.00
25 Mike Schmidt/50 40.00
27 Paul Molitor/50 30.00
29 Ralph Kiner/50 30.00
34 Rod Carew/50 25.00
35 Ryne Sandberg/50 40.00
36 Stan Musial/50 50.00
38 Tony Gwynn/50 35.00
40 Willie Mays/25 140.00

Lumberjacks Signature Bat

NM/M
Production 1-100
1 Al Kaline/50 40.00
3 Andre Dawson/100 20.00
5 Cal Ripken Jr./25 140.00
7 Dale Murphy/100 25.00
9 Don Mattingly/50 50.00
12 Frank Robinson/100 35.00
13 Frank Thomas/25 50.00
14 Gary Carter/25 25.00
18 Joe Morgan/50 25.00
19 Johnny Bench/25 50.00
21 Kirk Gibson/25 25.00
23 Mark Grace/25 40.00
26 Orlando Cepeda/100 20.00
27 Paul Molitor/25 40.00
29 Ralph Kiner/100 30.00
33 Robin Yount/25 50.00
34 Rod Carew/25 30.00
36 Stan Musial/25 65.00
38 Tony Gwynn/50 40.00

Lumberjacks Signature Jersey

NM/M
Production 1-100
3 Andre Dawson/100 20.00
5 Cal Ripken Jr./25 140.00
7 Dale Murphy/100 25.00
9 Don Mattingly/50 50.00
10 Duke Snider/ Pants/50 30.00
13 Frank Thomas/25 50.00
14 Gary Carter/50 25.00
17 Harmon Killebrew/25 40.00

19 Johnny Bench/25 50.00
23 Mark Grace/25 40.00
27 Paul Molitor/25 40.00
30 Reggie Jackson/25 40.00
33 Robin Yount/25 50.00
38 Tony Gwynn/50 40.00

Lumberjacks Signature Combos

NM/M
Production 1-100
3 Andre Dawson/ Bat-Jsy/100 20.00
5 Cal Ripken Jr./ Bat-Jsy/25 140.00
7 Dale Murphy/ Bat-Jsy/100 25.00
9 Don Mattingly/ Bat-Jsy/50 50.00
13 Frank Thomas/ Bat-Jsy/25 50.00
14 Gary Carter/ Bat-Jsy/25 25.00
23 Mark Grace/ Bat-Jsy/25 40.00
38 Tony Gwynn/ Bat-Jsy/25 45.00

Lumberjacks Signature Combos Prime

Production 1-25

Matching Numbers

NM/M
Production 5-50
Prime: No Pricing
Production 1-5
1 Ted Williams, Roger Maris/25 160.00
2 Nolan Ryan, Kerry Wood/50 35.00
3 Cal Ripken Jr., Gary Carter/50 40.00
5 Johnny Bench, Albert Pujols/50 40.00
6 Roger Clemens, W. Clark/50 35.00
7 Willie McCovey, Reggie Jackson/25 20.00
8 Ryne Sandberg, Don Mattingly/50 35.00
9 Duke Snider, Joe Cronin/25 25.00

Monikers Bronze

NM/M
Production 1-100
9 Miguel Cabrera/100 25.00
10 Miguel Cabrera/100 25.00
13 Mark Prior/50 35.00
14 Mark Prior/50 35.00
25 Ben Sheets/100 15.00
27 Melvin Mora/50 15.00
29 Rafael Furcal/25 20.00
32 Jake Peavy/50 25.00
33 Francisco Cordero/25 15.00
38 Michael Young/25 25.00
40 Joe Nathan/25 20.00
43 Eric Chavez/25 15.00
45 Roy Oswalt/50 25.00
49 Edgar Renteria/25 20.00
50 Mark Buehrle/25 30.00
57 Sean Casey/50 15.00
59 Octavio Dotel/25 12.00
60 Francisco Rodriguez/ 25 30.00
61 Jose Guillen/25 20.00
66 Travis Hafner/50 15.00
67 Rich Harden/50 15.00
71 Milton Bradley/25 15.00
73 Torii Hunter/25 25.00
74 Paul Konerko/50 30.00
76 Tim Hudson/25 25.00
80 Justin Morneau/100 25.00
82 Jose Vidro/25 15.00
84 Josh Beckett/25 30.00
85 Craig Biggio/25 30.00
89 Jacque Jones/50 15.00
91 Roy Halladay/25 15.00
93 Magglio Ordonez/100 15.00
96 Brandon Webb/50 15.00
97 Preston Wilson/50 15.00
98 Shannon Stewart/50 10.00
99 Trot Nixon/50 20.00
105 Bobby Crosby/40 15.00
107 Alfonso Soriano/25 30.00
108 Carlos Zambrano/50 25.00
109 Keith Foulke/25 30.00
110 Aubrey Huff/50 15.00
112 Mark Teixeira/100 25.00
116 Carlos Beltran/25 30.00
118 Johan Santana/100 30.00
121 Scott Rolen/25 30.00
123 Carlos Lee/50 20.00
124 Derrek Lee/50 25.00
130 Garret Anderson/100 15.00
131 Austin Kearns/100 15.00
133 Omar Vizquel/50 20.00
135 Mark Mulder/50 20.00
139 Mark Loretta/25 20.00
141 David Wright/50 60.00
144 Victor Martinez/25 15.00
151 Willie Mays/25 175.00
152 Ryne Sandberg/25 50.00
158 Duke Snider/50 25.00
159 Don Mattingly/25 50.00
160 Bob Gibson/50 50.00
162 Al Kaline/50 30.00
163 Nolan Ryan/25 80.00
164 Stan Musial/25 60.00
165 George Kell/50 15.00
166 Harmon Killebrew/50 30.00
167 Cal Ripken Jr./25 120.00
176 Hayden Penn/50 20.00
177 Ambiorix Concepcion/50 15.00
179 Prince Fielder/50 120.00
181 Wladimir Balentien/50 30.00
182 Jason Hammel/50 15.00
183 Keiichi Yabu/50 25.00
184 Brandon McCarthy/50 50.00
185 Ubaldo Jimenez/50 15.00
186 Keiichi Yabu/50 25.00
187 Miguel Negron/50 10.00
188 Mike Morse/50 30.00
189 Nate McLouth/50 25.00
190 Norihiro Nakamura/ 50 50.00
191 Brandon McCarthy/ 50 50.00
192 Tony Pena/50 10.00
193 Ambiorix Concepcion/50 15.00
194 Raul Tablado/50 15.00
195 Hayden Penn/50 20.00
196 Sean Thompson/50 12.00
198 Ubaldo Jimenez/50 15.00
199 Wladimir Balentien/ 50 30.00
200 Prince Fielder/50 120.00

Monikers Silver

NM/M
Production 1-50
9 Miguel Cabrera/50 30.00
10 Miguel Cabrera/50 30.00
13 Mark Prior/25 40.00
14 Mark Prior/25 40.00
25 Ben Sheets/50 20.00
27 Melvin Mora/25 20.00
29 Rafael Furcal/25 20.00
32 Jake Peavy/50 25.00
33 Francisco Cordero/25 15.00
38 Michael Young/25 25.00
40 Joe Nathan/25 20.00
43 Eric Chavez/25 25.00
45 Roy Oswalt/25 30.00
49 Edgar Renteria/25 20.00
50 Mark Buehrle/25 30.00
57 Sean Casey/25 20.00
59 Octavio Dotel/25 12.00
60 Francisco Rodriguez/25 30.00
61 Jose Guillen/25 20.00
66 Travis Hafner/50 15.00
67 Rich Harden/50 15.00
71 Milton Bradley/25 15.00
80 Justin Morneau/50 25.00
89 Jacque Jones/25 15.00
93 Magglio Ordonez/50 15.00
96 Brandon Webb/25 20.00
97 Preston Wilson/25 20.00
98 Shannon Stewart/25 15.00
99 Trot Nixon/25 25.00
105 Bobby Crosby/29 20.00
108 Carlos Zambrano/50 25.00
109 Keith Foulke/25 30.00
110 Aubrey Huff/25 20.00
112 Mark Teixeira/50 35.00
118 Johan Santana/50 35.00
123 Carlos Lee/50 20.00
130 Garret Anderson/50 20.00
131 Austin Kearns/50 15.00
133 Omar Vizquel/25 20.00
135 Mark Mulder/50 20.00
139 Mark Loretta/25 20.00
141 David Wright/25 70.00
144 Victor Martinez/25 15.00
151 Willie Mays/25 175.00
152 Ryne Sandberg/25 50.00
158 Duke Snider/25 30.00
159 Don Mattingly/25 50.00
162 Al Kaline/25 35.00
163 Nolan Ryan/25 80.00
164 Stan Musial/25 60.00
165 George Kell/50 15.00
166 Harmon Killebrew/25 40.00
167 Cal Ripken Jr./25 120.00

Monikers Material Bat Bronze

NM/M
Production 1-100
Platinum: No Pricing
Production One Set
9 Miguel Cabrera/50 35.00
10 Miguel Cabrera/50 35.00
13 Mark Prior/25 40.00
14 Mark Prior/25 40.00
29 Rafael Furcal/75 15.00
34 Aramis Ramirez/100 20.00
37 Jason Bay/100 20.00
38 Michael Young/100 20.00
43 Eric Chavez/50 20.00
45 Roy Oswalt/50 25.00
50 Mark Buehrle/50 25.00
57 Sean Casey/25 15.00
66 Travis Hafner/100 15.00
73 Torii Hunter/50 20.00
74 Paul Konerko/50 30.00
80 Justin Morneau/100 25.00
82 Jose Vidro/100 10.00
85 Craig Biggio/25 30.00
93 Magglio Ordonez/50 20.00
97 Preston Wilson/50 15.00
98 Shannon Stewart/50 10.00
107 Alfonso Soriano/25 30.00
110 Aubrey Huff/100 12.00
111 Adrian Beltre/25 20.00
112 Mark Teixeira/50 30.00
116 Carlos Beltran/25 30.00
121 Scott Rolen/25 30.00
123 Carlos Lee/100 15.00
124 Derrek Lee/100 20.00
130 Garret Anderson/100 15.00
131 Austin Kearns/100 15.00
140 Vernon Wells/50 15.00
141 David Wright/50 70.00
143 David Ortiz/50 50.00
144 Victor Martinez/100 15.00
147 Angel Berroa/100 10.00

Monikers Material Button Gold

No Pricing
Production 1-5
Platinum: No Pricing
Production One Set

Monikers Material Jersey Number Silver

NM/M
Production 1-75
Prime Platinum: No Pricing
Production One Set
9 Miguel Cabrera/50 35.00
10 Miguel Cabrera/50 35.00
13 Mark Prior/25 40.00
25 Ben Sheets/Pants/50 20.00
33 Francisco Cordero/25 25.00
34 Aramis Ramirez/75 20.00
38 Michael Young/50 25.00
43 Eric Chavez/75 20.00
45 Roy Oswalt/75 25.00
57 Sean Casey/75 15.00
60 Francisco Rodriguez/75 25.00
66 Travis Hafner/50 20.00
70 Andruw Jones/25 40.00
85 Craig Biggio/25 30.00
89 Jacque Jones/25 15.00
90 Lyle Overbay/75 10.00
98 Shannon Stewart/75 10.00
99 Trot Nixon/50 35.00
101 Dontrelle Willis/24 30.00
107 Alfonso Soriano/50 30.00
112 Mark Teixeira/50 30.00
117 Bobby Abreu/75 20.00
121 Scott Rolen/25 30.00
124 Derrek Lee/25 25.00
128 Jim Edmonds/25 35.00
130 Garret Anderson/50 20.00
131 Austin Kearns/75 15.00
140 Vernon Wells/50 15.00
141 David Wright/75 70.00
143 David Ortiz/75 50.00
144 Victor Martinez/75 15.00
152 Ryne Sandberg/50 40.00
158 Duke Snider/25 40.00
159 Don Mattingly/50 60.00
160 Bob Gibson/50 30.00
163 Nolan Ryan/25 100.00
164 Stan Musial/25 80.00
166 Harmon Killebrew/50 35.00
167 Cal Ripken Jr./25 140.00

Monikers Material Jersey Prime Gold

NM/M
Production 1-100
Platinum: No Pricing
Production One Set
9 Miguel Cabrera/50 40.00
10 Miguel Cabrera/50 40.00
13 Mark Prior/25 50.00
14 Mark Prior/25 50.00
25 Ben Sheets/50 25.00
34 Aramis Ramirez/100 25.00
38 Michael Young/100 25.00
43 Eric Chavez/75 25.00
45 Roy Oswalt/100 30.00
57 Sean Casey/30 20.00
60 Francisco Rodriguez/ 75 30.00
66 Travis Hafner/100 25.00
70 Andruw Jones/50 40.00
84 Josh Beckett/25 40.00
88 Barry Zito/25 30.00
89 Jacque Jones/50 15.00
98 Shannon Stewart/75 15.00
107 Alfonso Soriano/50 40.00
112 Mark Teixeira/20 50.00
117 Bobby Abreu/100 25.00
121 Scott Rolen/50 35.00
128 Jim Edmonds/25 30.00
130 Garret Anderson/25 25.00
131 Austin Kearns/75 20.00
140 Vernon Wells/50 20.00
152 Ryne Sandberg/25 75.00
159 Don Mattingly/25 85.00
160 Bob Gibson/25 50.00
163 Nolan Ryan/25 120.00
167 Cal Ripken Jr./25 175.00

Team Trademarks

NM/M
Common Player: 3.00
Production 50 Sets
Foil: No Pricing
Production 10 Sets
1 Ryne Sandberg 8.00
2 George Brett 8.00
3 Steve Carlton 3.00
4 Reggie Jackson 4.00
5 Edgar Martinez 3.00
6 Barry Larkin 4.00
7 Ozzie Smith 6.00
8 Carlton Fisk 4.00
9 Wade Boggs 5.00
10 Will Clark 4.00
11 Nolan Ryan 8.00
12 Gary Carter 3.00
13 Don Mattingly 8.00
14 Willie Stargell 4.00
15 Don Sutton 3.00
16 Kirk Gibson 3.00
17 Kirby Puckett 5.00
18 Dale Murphy 4.00
19 Rickey Henderson 4.00
20 Willie Mays 8.00
21 Cal Ripken Jr. 10.00
22 Paul Molitor 4.00
23 Tony Gwynn 5.00
24 Andre Dawson 3.00
25 Bob Feller 4.00
26 Alan Trammell 3.00
27 Dave Parker 3.00
28 Dave Righetti 3.00
29 Dwight Gooden 3.00
30 Harold Baines 3.00
31 Jack Morris 3.00
32 John Kruk 3.00
33 Lee Smith 3.00
34 Lenny Dykstra 3.00
35 Luis Tiant 3.00
36 Matt Williams 3.00
37 Ron Guidry 3.00
38 Tony Oliva 3.00

Team Trademarks Jersey Number

NM/M
Production 1-50
1 Ryne Sandberg/23 20.00
3 Steve Carlton/ Pants/32 8.00
4 Reggie Jackson/44 10.00
8 Carlton Fisk/50 8.00
9 Wade Boggs/26 10.00
11 Nolan Ryan/Pants/34 25.00
20 Willie Mays/24 40.00

Team Trademarks Jersey Number Prime

NM/M
1 Ryne Sandberg/50 25.00
2 George Brett/50 25.00
3 Steve Carlton/50 10.00
4 Reggie Jackson/50 15.00
5 Edgar Martinez/50 15.00
6 Barry Larkin/50 15.00
7 Ozzie Smith/50 20.00
8 Carlton Fisk/50 15.00
9 Wade Boggs/50 15.00
10 Will Clark/50 15.00
11 Nolan Ryan/50 25.00
12 Gary Carter/50 12.00
13 Don Mattingly/40 25.00
14 Willie Stargell/50 15.00
15 Don Sutton/25 12.00
16 Kirk Gibson/50 12.00
18 Dale Murphy/50 15.00
19 Rickey Henderson/50 15.00
21 Cal Ripken Jr./25 50.00
23 Tony Gwynn/50 20.00
24 Andre Dawson/25 15.00
26 Alan Trammell/25 12.00
27 Dave Parker/50 10.00
29 Dwight Gooden/50 15.00
30 Harold Baines/25 15.00
31 Jack Morris/47 10.00
32 John Kruk/25 15.00
33 Lee Smith/47 10.00
34 Lenny Dykstra/25 15.00
38 Tony Oliva/26 15.00

Team Trademarks Signature

NM/M
Production 5-50
1 Ryne Sandberg/25 50.00
3 Steve Carlton/25 25.00
4 Reggie Jackson/25 30.00
5 Edgar Martinez/50 20.00
6 Barry Larkin/50 25.00
7 Ozzie Smith/50 35.00
8 Carlton Fisk/50 25.00
9 Wade Boggs/25 35.00
10 Will Clark/50 25.00
11 Nolan Ryan/50 75.00
12 Gary Carter/50 15.00
13 Don Mattingly/25 50.00
15 Don Sutton/100 12.00
16 Kirk Gibson/50 20.00
17 Kirby Puckett/25 40.00
18 Dale Murphy/100 20.00
20 Willie Mays/25 160.00
21 Cal Ripken Jr./50 90.00
22 Paul Molitor/25 25.00
23 Tony Gwynn/25 40.00
24 Andre Dawson/100 15.00
25 Bob Feller/50 20.00
26 Alan Trammell/25 25.00
27 Dave Parker/50 15.00
28 Dave Righetti/25 20.00
29 Dwight Gooden/50 15.00
30 Harold Baines/50 15.00
31 Jack Morris/50 12.00
32 John Kruk/25 20.00
33 Lee Smith/50 15.00
34 Lenny Dykstra/25 20.00
35 Luis Tiant/50 15.00
36 Matt Williams/50 20.00
37 Ron Guidry/25 25.00
38 Tony Oliva/50 15.00

Team Trademarks Signature Jersey Number

NM/M
Production 1-72
4 Reggie Jackson/44 50.00
8 Carlton Fisk/72 35.00
9 Wade Boggs/26 50.00
11 Nolan Ryan/Pants/34 90.00
17 Kirby Puckett/34 60.00
27 Dave Parker/39 25.00
31 Jack Morris/47 20.00
33 Lee Smith/47 20.00
37 Ron Guidry/Pants/49 20.00

Team Trademarks Signature Jersey Number Prime

NM/M
3 Steve Carlton/25 30.00
24 Andre Dawson/25 30.00
27 Dave Parker/39 20.00
31 Jack Morris/47 20.00
33 Lee Smith/47 25.00
38 Tony Oliva/26 35.00

Threads Button

No Pricing
Production 1-7

Threads Jersey Number

NM/M
Production 1-50
Logo: No Pricing
Production One Set
152 Ryne Sandberg/50 15.00
154 Ted Williams/25 60.00
157 Whitey Ford/50 12.00
158 Duke Snider/25 15.00
164 Stan Musial/25 25.00
166 Harmon Killebrew/50 20.00

Threads Jersey Prime

NM/M
Production 5-100
1 Roger Clemens/25 25.00
5 Todd Helton/100 10.00
6 Todd Helton/100 10.00
7 Vladimir Guerrero/ 100 12.00
8 Vladimir Guerrero/ Jkt/30 20.00
9 Miguel Cabrera/100 10.00
10 Miguel Cabrera/100 10.00
12 Albert Pujols/50 30.00
13 Mark Prior/100 8.00
14 Mark Prior/25 10.00
15 Chipper Jones/100 10.00
16 Chipper Jones/100 10.00
17 Jeff Bagwell/100 8.00
18 Jeff Bagwell/100 8.00
19 Kerry Wood/100 8.00
22 Carl Crawford/100 5.00
23 Mariano Rivera/60 12.00
25 Ben Sheets/100 8.00
27 Melvin Mora/25 10.00
28 Corey Patterson/100 5.00
29 Rafael Furcal/100 5.00
30 Jim Thome/100 8.00
34 Aramis Ramirez/50 8.00
35 Javy Lopez/100 5.00
38 Michael Young/100 5.00
39 Ivan Rodriguez/100 8.00
42 Adam Dunn/100 8.00
43 Eric Chavez/100 5.00
45 Roy Oswalt/100 5.00
48 Johnny Damon/50 15.00
50 Mark Buehrle/50 8.00
53 Hank Blalock/100 5.00
55 Brad Radke/50 5.00
57 Sean Casey/50 5.00
58 Mike Lowell/100 5.00
60 Francisco Rodriguez/ 100 5.00
62 Greg Maddux/25 25.00
63 A.J. Burnett/75 5.00
66 Travis Hafner/100 5.00
68 Bret Boone/100 5.00
70 Andruw Jones/100 10.00
73 Torii Hunter/100 5.00
74 Paul Konerko/100 8.00
79 Lance Berkman/100 5.00
80 Justin Morneau/100 10.00
82 Jose Vidro/100 5.00
84 Josh Beckett/100 5.00
86 Luis Gonzalez/100 5.00
88 Barry Zito/100 5.00
91 Roy Halladay/100 5.00
94 Mike Sweeney/100 5.00
95 Rafael Palmeiro/100 8.00
97 Preston Wilson/100 5.00
98 Shannon Stewart/50 5.00
99 Trot Nixon/25 8.00
100 Mike Piazza/100 12.00
101 Dontrelle Willis/100 8.00
103 Andy Pettitte/50 10.00
104 Kazuo Matsui/100 5.00
107 Alfonso Soriano/100 8.00
110 Aubrey Huff/100 5.00
111 Adrian Beltre/50 8.00
112 Mark Teixeira/60 10.00
114 Miguel Tejada/100 8.00
117 Bobby Abreu/100 5.00
119 Manny Ramirez/60 15.00
121 Scott Rolen/100 10.00
124 Derrek Lee/50 10.00
127 John Smoltz/100 8.00
128 Jim Edmonds/100 8.00
130 Garret Anderson/60 8.00
131 Austin Kearns/100 5.00
138 Mike Mussina/50 10.00
140 Vernon Wells/100 5.00
141 David Wright/100 25.00
142 Marcus Giles/100 5.00
144 Victor Martinez/75 5.00
145 Hideki Matsui/100 40.00
146 C.C. Sabathia/100 5.00
150 Jorge Posada/75 10.00
152 Ryne Sandberg/50 25.00
153 Rickey Henderson/25 20.00
156 George Brett/50 25.00
159 Don Mattingly/50 25.00
160 Bob Gibson/25 20.00
161 Hank Aaron/25 75.00
163 Nolan Ryan/100 25.00
167 Cal Ripken Jr./100 30.00
169 Roger Clemens/50 20.00
170 Curt Schilling/100 8.00
171 Rafael Palmeiro/100 8.00
173 Mike Piazza/100 12.00
174 Greg Maddux/100 15.00
175 Sammy Sosa/100 16.00

Timber Barrel

No Pricing
Production 1-3

TNT

NM/M
Production 1-50
Prime: .50X-1.5X
Production 5-100
7 Vladimir Guerrero/ Bat-Jsy/30 15.00
10 Miguel Cabrera/ Bat-Jsy/25 12.00
11 Albert Pujols/ Bat-Jsy/50 25.00
12 Albert Pujols/ Bat-Jsy/50 25.00
13 Mark Prior/Bat-Jsy/50 8.00
14 Mark Prior/Bat-Jsy/50 8.00
15 Chipper Jones/ Bat-Jsy/50 12.00
16 Chipper Jones/ Bat-Jsy/50 12.00
39 Ivan Rodriguez/ Bat-Jsy/25 12.00
42 Adam Dunn/ Bat-Jsy/50 5.00
62 Greg Maddux/ Bat-Jsy/25 20.00
100 Mike Piazza/ Bat-Jsy/50 12.00
107 Alfonso Soriano/ Bat-Jsy/50 12.00
112 Mark Teixeira/ Bat-Jsy/50 10.00
119 Manny Ramirez/ Bat-Jsy/50 12.00
121 Scott Rolen/ Bat-Jsy/50 10.00
124 Derrek Lee/Bat-Jsy/50 8.00
143 David Ortiz/ Bat-Jsy/50 15.00
151 Willie Mays/ Bat-Jsy/25 50.00
153 Rickey Henderson/ Bat-Jsy/50 15.00
154 Ted Williams/ Bat-Jsy/25 85.00
159 Don Mattingly/ Bat-Jsy/50 20.00
161 Hank Aaron/ Bat-Jsy/25 50.00
163 Nolan Ryan/ Bat-Jsy/50 25.00
164 Stan Musial/ Bat-Jsy/25 30.00
166 Harmon Killebrew/ Bat-Jsy/25 20.00
167 Cal Ripken Jr./ Bat-Jsy/50 30.00

169	Roger Clemens/ Bat-Jsy/50	15.00
171	Rafael Palmeiro/ Bat-Jsy/50	10.00
172	Randy Johnson/ Bat-Jsy/25	15.00
174	Greg Maddux/ Bat-Jsy/50	15.00
175	Sammy Sosa/ Bat-Jsy/50	15.00

1996 Legends of the Negro Leagues Playing Cards

This set of playing cards depicting ballplayers of the pre-integration Negro Leagues was issued as a fundraiser by the International Society of Athletes in conjunction with a reunion of the players. In standard playing card finish and round-corner format, the cards have black-and-white photos at center. Backs are in black with gold printing. Size is 2-1/2" x 3-1/2". The deck's queens feature notable females of the Negro Leagues and the sponsor.

		NM/M
Complete Set (56):		10.00
Common Player:		.15
AS	Satchel Paige	1.00
2S	James "Joe" Greene	.15
3S	James "Red" Moore	.15
4S	Othello "Chico" Renfroe	.15
5S	William "Judy" Johnson	.25
6S	Willie "The Devil" Wells	.25
7S	Gene Benson	.15
8S	Willard "Sunnie" Brown	.25
9S	Martin Dihigo	.25
10S	Don Newcombe	.25
JS	Ray "Hooks" Dandridge	.25
QS	Billie Harden	.15
KS	Roy "Campy" Campanella	.75
AD	Jack "Jackie" Robinson	2.00
2D	Sam Haynes	.15
3D	Bob "The Rope" Boyd	.20
4D	William "Bonnie" Serrell	.15
5D	Orestes "Minnie" Minoso	.20
6D	Pop Lloyd	.25
7D	Art "Superman" Pennington	.15
8D	Francisco "Pancho" Coimbre	.15
9D	Sam "Jet" Jethroe	.20
10D	Joe Black	.25
JD	Monte Irvin	.25
QD	Effa "Effie" Manley	.25
KD	Henry "Hank" Aaron	1.50
AC	Joshua "Josh" Gibson	.25
2C	William "Bill" Cash	.15
3C	Francis "Fran" Matthews	.15
4C	Fred "Leap" Bankhead	.15
5C	Alex Radcliffe	.15
6C	Authur "Artie" Wilson (Arthur)	.20
7C	James "Jim" Zapp	.15
8C	Henry "Kimmie" Kimbro	.15
9C	Chester "Chet" Brewer	.15
10C	Verdell "Lefty" Mathis	.15
JC	James "Junior" Gilliam	.25
QC	Marcenia "Toni" Stone	.15
KC	Willie Mays	1.50
AH	James "Cool Papa" Bell	.25
2H	Samuel "Harriston" Hairston	.20
3H	John "Buck" O'Neil	.25
4H	Lorenzo "Piper" Davis	.15
5H	Parnell Woods	.15
6H	Thomas "Pee Wee" Butts	.15
7H	Oscar Charleston	.25
8H	Lawrence "Larry" Doby	1.00
9H	Hilton Smith	.25
10H	Leon Day	.25
JH	Walter "Buck" Leonard	.25
QH	Pamela Pryor-Fuller	.15
KH	Ernest "Ernie" Banks	.75
---	Joker (Ted "Double Duty" Radcliffe)	.25
---	Super Joker (Andrew "Rube" Foster)	.25
---	Wilmer "Red" Fields	.15
---	Clifford "Connie" Johnson	.15

2001 Legends European Tour

This two-play, four-card set was issued in conjunction with the 8th annual Baseball Legends European Tour which made a goodwill swing through 11 military bases in Germany in June. Cards feature borderless vintage color photos on front. Team logos have been airbrushed away. A Legends tour logo appears in one corner. Backs have career stats and highlights and some of the tour sponsor's logos. The cards were given away at autograph sessions, baseball clinics, softball games and other events.

		NM/M
Complete Set (4):		10.00
Common Player:		2.00
(1)	Vida Blue (Green jersey.)	3.00
(2)	Vida Blue (Yellow jersey.)	3.00
(3)	Manny Sanguillen/Btg	2.00
(4)	Manny Sanguillen/ Catching	2.00

1998 Lemon Chill Chicago White Sox

In standard 2-1/2" x 3-1/2" format, this team set was a stadium giveaway. Fronts feature game-action photos with a stylized flame-like effect at left and bottom. The team logo is at lower-left, with the player name at bottom right. Backs have player personal data, stats, career highlights and a large sponsor's logo. The cards are checklisted here in alphabetical order.

		NM/M
Complete Set (30):		12.00
Common Player:		.50
(1)	Jeff Abbott	.50
(2)	Mark Anderson (Trainer), Steve Odgers (Strength Coach), Mark Salas, Herm Schneider (Trainer)	.50
(3)	James Baldwin	.50
(4)	Albert Belle	.50
(5)	Mike Cameron	.50
(6)	Mike Caruso	.50
(7)	Carlos Castillo	.50
(8)	Nardi Contreras, Von Joshua	.50
(9)	Wil Cordero	.50
(10)	Ray Durham	.50
(11)	Scott Eyre	.50
(12)	Keith Foulke	.50
(13)	Bob Howry	.50
(14)	Wallace Johnson, Bryan Little	.50
(15)	Matt Karchner	.50
(16)	Chad Kreuter	.50
(17)	Art Kusnyer, Joe Nossek	.50
(18)	Jerry Manuel	.50
(19)	Jaime Navarro	.50
(20)	Greg Norton	.50
(21)	Charlie O'Brien	.50
(22)	Magglio Ordonez	2.00
(23)	Jim Parque	.50
(24)	Bill Simas	.50
(25)	Mike Sirotka	.50
(26)	Chris Snopek	.50
(27)	John Snyder	.50
(28)	Frank Thomas	4.00
(29)	Robin Ventura	.50
(30)	Bryan Ward	.50

1999 Lemon Chill Chicago White Sox

In standard 2-1/2" x 3-1/2" format, this team set was a stadium giveaway. Fronts feature game-action photos on a borderless ghost-photo background with the team motto, "The Kids Can Play" and logo at lower-left, with the player name at top-left in red. Backs have a red duotone photo, '98 stats, uniform and card numbers and a large sponsor's logo. A five-card 1959 World Series commemorative subset was also included.

		NM/M
Complete Set (33):		10.00
Common Player:		.25
1	Brook Fordyce	.25
2	Carlos Lee	.50
3	Greg Norton	.25
4	John Snyder	.25
5	Craig Wilson	.25
6	Chris Singleton	.25
7	Liu Rodriguez	.25
8	Magglio Ordonez	1.00
9	Mike Sirotka	.25
10	Jaime Navarro	.25
11	Mark Johnson	.25
12	Jim Parque	.25
13	Jeff Liefer	.25
14	Mike Caruso	.25
15	Ray Durham	.25
16		.25
17	Bob Howry	.25
18	James Baldwin	.25
19	Jerry Manuel	.25
20	Bill Simas	.25
21	Frank Thomas	2.00
22	Bryan Ward	.25
23	Scott Eyre	.25
24	Paul Konerko	1.00
25	Sean Lowe	.25
26	Keith Foulke	.25
---	Von Joshua, Nardi Contreras	.25
---	Joe Nossek, Art Kusnyer	.25
---	Herm Schneider (Trainer), Steve Odgers (Conditioning), Mark Salas (Bullpen), Mark Anderson (Trainer)	.25
1 of 5	1959 World Series Recap	.25
2 of 5	Billy Pierce	.25
3 of 5	Jim Landis	.25
4 of 5	Al Smith	.25
5 of 5	Al Lopez	.25

2000 Lemon Chill Chicago White Sox

The first 20,000 fans through the gates of Comiskey Park on July 16 received this team set. On front a color action photo stands out from the black-and-white background and is vignetted with black borders. The player name is in purple at bottom. A black-and-white portrait photo is featured on back along with player data, 1999 stats and the sponsor's logo.

		NM/M
Complete Set (31):		10.00
Common Player:		.35
1	James Baldwin	.35
2	Herbert Perry	.35
3	Keith Foulke	.35
4	Tony Graffanino	.35
5	Kip Wells	.35
6	Mark Johnson	.35
7	Chris Singleton	.35
8	Ray Durham	.35
9	Jose Valentin	.35
10	Kevin Beirne	.35
11	Paul Konerko	1.00
12	Greg Norton	.35
13	Bill Simas	.35
14	Jeff Abbott	.35
15	Frank Thomas	3.00
16	Mike Sirotka	.35
17	Brook Fordyce	.35
18	Cal Eldred	.35
19	Bob Howry	.35
20	Jerry Manuel	.35
21	Kelly Wunsch	.35
22	Bryan Little, Wallace Johnson	.35
23	Joe Nossek, Art Kusnyer	.35
24	Jim Parque	.35
25	Carlos Lee	.50
26	Von Joshua, Nardi Contreras	.35
27	Sean Lowe	.35
28	Magglio Ordonez	1.00
29	Jesus Pena	.35
30	Craig Wilson	.35
31	Mark Anderson, Herm Schneider, Man Soo Lee, Steve Odgers	.35

1989 Lennox/ HSE Astros

Formatted similar to a police/fire safety set, this Astros team issue is sponsored instead by a furnace company and the team's cable TV outlet. Cards measure 2-5/8" x 4-1/8" and feature portrait photos on front with orange and black team color pinstripes. Backs have biographical data, career summary and sponsors' logos.

		NM/M
Complete Set (26):		10.00
Common Player:		.25
1	Billy Hatcher	.25
2	Greg Gross	.25
3	Rick Rhoden	.25
4	Mike Scott	.25
5	Kevin Bass	.25
6	Alex Trevino	.25
7	Jim Clancy	.25
8	Bill Doran	.25
9	Dan Schatzeder	.25
10	Bob Knepper	.25
11	Jim Deshaies	.25
12	Eric Yelding	.25
13	Danny Darwin	.25
14	Coaches	.25
15	Craig Reynolds	.25
16	Rafael Ramirez	.25
17	Juan Agosto	.25
18	Larry Andersen	.25
19	Dave Smith	.25
20	Gerald Young	.25
21	Ken Caminiti	.50
22	Terry Puhl	.25
23	Bob Forsch	.25
24	Craig Biggio	6.00
25	Art Howe	.25
26	Glenn Davis	.25

1990 Lennox/ HSE Astros

Ken Oberkfell #10 - Infielder
HSE Astros LENNOX

For a second straight year Lennox, the furnace people, and HSE, the Astros cable TV outlet, sponsored a team set in an oversize (3-1/2" x 5") format on thin, semi-gloss stock. Fronts feature color player portrait photos, backs have a few biographical notes and logos for all parties. Cards are checklisted here by uniform numbers which appear on front and back.

		NM/M
Complete Set (29):		15.00
Common Player:		.50
1	Casey Candaele	.50
6	David Rohde	.50
7	Craig Biggio	5.00
9	Alex Trevino	.50
10	Ken Oberkfell	.50
11	Ken Caminiti	.50
12	Glenn Wilson	.50
13	Gerald Young	.50
15	Eric Yelding	.50
16	Rafael Ramirez	.50
18	Art Howe	.50
19	Bill Doran	.50
20	Dan Schatzeder	.50
21	Terry Puhl	.50
22	Mark Davidson	.50
23	Eric Anthony	.50
24	Franklin Stubbs	.50
27	Glenn Davis	.50
31	Xavier Hernandez	.50
33	Mike Scott	.50
36	Bill Gullickson	.50
38	Jim Clancy	.50
39	Jose Cano	.50
43	Jim Deshaies	.50
44	Danny Darwin	.50
45	Dave Smith	.50
47	Larry Andersen	.50
49	Juan Agosto	.50
51	Mark Portugal	.50

1990 Ron Lewis 1961 N.Y. Yankees

The World's Champion 1961 N.Y. Yankees are featured in this set of cards by sports artist Ron Lewis. The 42-card set contains cards of individual players, coaches and the manager, plus a team picture. The 3-1/2" x 5-1/2" cards were sold only in a complete boxed set edition of 10,000. Cards have oil painted portraits of the players set against a blue background. The card borders are pinstriped in dark blue. At bottom is a blank panel for autographing. Backs are printed in red and blue and have personal data, career summary, 1961 and career stats.

		NM/M
Complete Boxed Set (42):		10.00
Common Player:		.50
1	1961 N.Y. Yankees Team	3.00
2	Bobby Richardson	.75
3	Roger Maris	2.00
4	Elston Howard	.75
5	Bill Skowron	.60
6	Clete Boyer	.50
7	Mickey Mantle	4.00
8	Yogi Berra	1.00
9	Johnny Blanchard	.50
10	Hector Lopez	.50
11	Whitey Ford	1.00
12	Ralph Terry	.50
13	Bill Stafford	.50
14	Bud Daley	.50
15	Billy Gardner	.50
16	Jim Coates	.50
17	Luis Arroyo	.50
18	Tex Clevenger	.50
19	Bob Cerv	.50
20	Art Ditmar	.50
21	Bob Turley	.50
22	Joe DeMaestri	.50
23	Rollie Sheldon	.50
24	Earl Torgeson	.50
25	Hal Reniff	.50
26	Ralph Houk	.50
27	Johnny James	.50
28	Bob Hale	.50
29	Danny McDevitt	.50
30	Duke Maas	.50
31	Jim Hegan	.50
32	Wally Moses	.50
33	Frank Crosettl	.50
34	Lee Thomas	.50
35	Al Downing	.50
36	Jack Reed	.50
37	Ryne Duren	.50
38	Tom Tresh	.50
39	Johnny Sain	.50
40	Jesse Gonder	.50
41	Deron Johnson	.50
42	Tony Kubek	.60

1991 Ron Lewis Negro Leagues Postcards

Willie Mays

The 1991 Negro League Living Legends Postcard Set features paintings by artist Ron Lewis. Cards measure 3-1/2" x 5-1/2" and are stamped with a number within the 10,000 sets produced. Between each player's image and the player's name at the bottom of the card, is ample space for an autograph. The set, originally sold for $27, was created as a fund raiser for the Negro League Baseball Players Association. Two hundred uncut sheets were offered at $100 each.

		NM/M
Complete Set (30):		30.00
Common Player:		.75
1	George Giles	.75
2	Bill Cash	.75
3	Bob Harvey	.75
4	Lyman Bostock Sr.	.90
5	Ray Dandridge	2.50
6	Leon Day	2.00
7	Verdell "Lefty" Mathis	.75
8	Jimmie Crutchfield	.75
9	Clyde McNeal	.75
10	Bill Wright	.75
11	Mahlon Duckett	.75
12	William "Bobby" Robinson	.75
13	Max Manning	.75
14	Armando Vazquez	.75
15	Jehosie Heard	.75
16	Quincy Trouppe	.90
17	Wilmer Fields	.75
18	Lonnie Blair	.75
19	Garnett Blair	.75
20	Monte Irvin	2.50
21	Willie Mays	7.50
22	Buck Leonard	4.00
23	Frank Evans	.75
24	Josh Gibson Jr.	5.00
25	Ted "Double Duty" Radcliffe	1.50
26	Josh Johnson	.75
27	Gene Benson	.75
28	Lester Lockett	.75
29	Cowan "Bubba" Hyde	.75
30	Rufus Lewis	.75

1994 Ron Lewis Negro Leagues Postcards

A second series of postcards honoring players of the Negro Leagues was produced by artist Ron Lewis in September 1994. In this set, more emphasis was placed on multi-player cards. Many of the cards also feature detailed backgrounds of street scenes with vintage vehicles, old-time stadiums, etc. Cards measure 3-1/2" x 5-1/2" and have a wide front border with the player(s) name printed at bottom and space above for autographing. Postcard backs are printed in black and include a few career stats, a card number and the card's position among the limited edition of 10,000.

		NM/M
Complete Set (32):		25.00
Common Card:		1.00
1	Willie Mays, Ernie Banks, Hank Aaron	4.00
1p	2-1/2"	2.00
2	Bill Wright, Lester Lockett, Lyman Bostock, Sr.	1.00
3	Josh Gibson, Josh Gibson Jr., Buck Leonard	2.50
4	Max Manning, Monte Irvin, Leon Day	1.50
5	Armando Vazquez, Minnie Minoso, Martin Dihigo	1.50
6	Ted "Double Duty" Radcliffe	1.50
7	Bill Owens, Turkey Stearnes, Bobby Robinson	1.00
8	Wilmer Fields, Edsall Walker, Josh Johnson	1.00
9	Artie Wilson, Lionel Hampton	1.50
10	Earl Taborn	1.00
11	Barney "Bonnie" Serrell	1.00
12	Rodolfo "Rudy" Fernandez	1.00
13	Willie Pope	1.00
14	Ray Noble	1.00
15	Jim "Fireball" Cohen	1.00
16	Henry Kimbro	1.00
17	Charlie Biot	1.00
18	Al Wilmore	1.00
19	Sam Jethroe	1.50
20	Tommy Sampson	1.00
21	Charlie Rivera	1.00
22	Claro Duany	1.00
23	Russell Awkard	1.00
24	Art "Superman" Pennington	1.00
25	Wilmer Harris	1.00
26	Napoleon "Nap" Gulley	1.00
27	Emilio Navarro	1.00
28	Andy Porter	1.00
29	Willie Grace	1.00
30	Red Moore	1.00
31	Buck O'Neill	2.00
32	Stanley Glenn	1.00

1996 Liberty Satellite Sports

This business-to-business promotion for a cable sports network content provider features on card fronts the logo of different cable networks. Space on back is shared by player data and stats and information about a local cable network.

		NM/M
Complete Set (21):		125.00
Common Player:		2.00
1	Cal Ripken Jr.	40.00
2	Paul O'Neill	2.00
3	Mo Vaughn	2.00
4	Travis Fryman	2.00
5	Brian Jordan	2.00
6	Ken Griffey Jr.	20.00
7	Craig Biggio	2.00
8	Chili Davis	2.00
9	Greg Maddux	15.00
10	Gary Sheffield	4.00
11	Frank Thomas	10.00
12	Barry Larkin	2.00
13	John Franco	2.00
14	Albert Belle	2.00
15	Mark McGwire	20.00
16	Barry Bonds	40.00
17	Lenny Dykstra	2.00
(18)	Mickey Lopez	2.00
(19)	Tim Salmon	2.00
(20)	Matt Williams	2.00
(21)	Header Card	.35

1992 Lime Rock Griffey Baseball Holograms

This set of three hologram cards features the Griffey family of pro players. Each card carries a "GRIFFEY BASEBALL" headline at top, with a large central action photo of one of the family and his facsimile autograph. The backs have a color photo, career highlights and stats. The cards were issued in several different versions as noted below.

		NM/M
Complete Set, Silver Holograms (3):		3.00
Complete Set, Gold Holograms (3):		10.00
Complete Set, Autographed (3):		35.00
Complete Set, Blank-backed Promos (3):		6.00
Three-card strip, edition of 5,000:		6.50
1	Ken Griffey Sr. (Silver hologram, edition of 250,000.)	.50
1	Ken Griffey Sr. (Gold hologram, edition of 1,000.)	1.50
1	Ken Griffey Sr. (Autographed edition of 2,500.)	5.00
1	Ken Griffey Sr. (Blank-back promo, edition of 750.)	1.50
2	Ken Griffey Jr./Silver	2.50
2	Ken Griffey Jr./Gold	9.00
2	Ken Griffey Jr./Auto.	30.00
2	Ken Griffey Jr. (Promo)	9.00
3	Craig Griffey/Silver	.50
3	Craig GriffeyGold	1.50
3	Craig Griffey/Auto.	2.00
3	Craig Griffey (Promo)	1.50

1991 Line Drive

This set of "old-timers" includes many Hall of Famers, as well as stars who had played into the late 1980s. In standard 2-1/2" x 3-1/2", the cards have color or sepia photos framed in blue and bordered in white. Horizontal backs have biographical and career notes and stats.

		NM/M
Complete Set (50):		6.00
Common Player:		.10
1	Don Drysdale	.25
2	Joe Torre	.15
3	Bob Gibson	.25
4	Bobby Richardson	.25
5	Ron Santo	.25
6	Eric Soderholm	.10
7	Yogi Berra	.35
8	Steve Garvey	.15
9	Steve Carlton	.25
10	Toby Harrah	.10
11	Luis Tiant	.10
12	Earl Weaver	.10
13	Bill Mazeroski	.25
14	Don Baylor	.10
15	Lew Burdette	.10
16	Jim Lonborg	.10
17	Jerry Grote	.10
18	Ernie Banks	.35
19	Doug DeCinces	.10
20	Jimmy Piersall	.10
21	Ken Holtzman	.10
22	Manny Mota	.10
23	Alvin Dark	.10
24	Lou Brock	.25
25	Ralph Houk	.15
26	Graig Nettles	.15
27	Bill White	.10
28	Billy Williams	.25
29	Willie Horton	.10
30	Tommie Agee	.10
31	Rico Petrocelli	.10
32	Julio Cruz	.10
33	Robin Roberts	.25
34	Dave Johnson	.10
35	Wilbur Wood	.10
36	Cesar Cedeno	.10
37	George Foster	.10
38	Thurman Munson	.25
39	Roberto Clemente	2.00
40	Eddie Mathews	.25
41	Harmon Killebrew	.25
42	Monte Irvin	.25
43	Bob Feller	2.00
44	Jimmie Foxx	1.00
45	Walter Johnson	1.00
46	Casey Stengel	.25
47	Satchel Paige	1.00
48	Ty Cobb	2.00
49	Mickey Cochrane	.25
50	Dizzy Dean	.35

1991 Line Drive Mickey Mantle

This 20-card set was part of a collector's kit featuring the Yankees superstar. Fronts of the 2-1/2" x 3-1/2" cards have sepia or color poses or action photos. The player's name appears in white in a blue panel at bottom. Red striping seperates the graphics from the white border. The Line Drive logo appears in an upper corner. Backs are printed in red and blue and feature a facsimile autograph, a few sentences about Mantle's career, manufacturer's and licensor's logos, and a card number. The same basic cards were included in a Collectors Marketing Corp. (see CMC) in 1989, lacking the Line Drive logo on front and the Impel logo and 1991 dates on back.

		NM/M
Complete Set (20):		15.00
Common Card:		2.00
1-20	Mickey Mantle	2.00

1991 Line Drive Don Mattingly

This 20-card set was part of a collectors kit featuring the Yankees' star. Fronts of the 2-1/2" x 3-1/2" cards have color poses or action photos. The player's name appears in white in a blue panel at bottom along with the Line Drive logo in red and white. Backs are printed in red and blue and feature a facsimile autograph, a few sentences about Mattingly's career, manufacturer's and licensor's logos, and a card number.

		NM/M
Complete Set (20):		3.00
Common Card:		.15
1-20	Don Mattingly	.25

1991 Line Drive Ryne Sandberg

This 20-card set was part of a collectors kit featuring the Cubs Hall of Fame second baseman. Fronts of the 2-1/2" x 3-1/2" cards have color poses or action photos. The player's name appears in blue and red in the white border above the photo. Backs are printed in red and blue and feature a few sentences about Sandberg's career, along with manufacturer's and licensor's logos, and a card number.

		NM/M
Complete Set (20):		10.00
Common Card:		.50
1-20	Ryne Sandberg	.50

1986 Lite Beer Astros

This regional set of the Houston Astros was sponsored by Lite Beer and given away in a special stadium promotion. The 4-1/2" x 6-3/4" cards feature full-color photos surrounded by a wide, white border. Diagonal color bands of yellow, orange, red and purple extend throught the upper-right and lower-left corners of the card, which also displays the Astros' 25th Anniversary logo and the Lite Beer logo in opposite corners. The backs include player information and statistics.

		NM/M
Complete Set (22):		25.00
Common Player:		1.00
3	Phil Garner	1.00
6	Mark Bailey	1.00
10	Dickie Thon	1.00
11	Frank DiPino	1.00
12	Craig Reynolds	1.00
14	Alan Ashby	1.00
17	Kevin Bass	1.00
19	Bill Doran	1.00
20	Jim Pankovits	1.00
21	Terry Puhl	1.00
22	Hal Lanier	1.00
25	Jose Cruz	1.00
27	Glenn Davis	1.00
28	Billy Hatcher	1.00
29	Denny Walling	1.00
33	Mike Scott	1.00
34	Nolan Ryan	15.00
37	Charlie Kerfeld	1.00
39	Bob Knepper	1.00
43	Jim Deshaies	1.00
45	Dave Smith	1.00
53	Mike Madden	1.00

Rangers

This postcard-size (approximately 4" x 6") set of Texas Rangers cards was

sponsored by Lite Beer and was available by mail directly from the team. Fronts feature full-color photos surrounded by a wide, white border with the player's name, uniform number and postion appearing below. The Rangers logo is displayed in the lower-left corner, while the Lite Beer logo is in the lower-right. Backs offer personal information and stats.

		NM/M
Complete Set (28):		20.00
Common Player:		1.00
0	Oddibe McDowell	1.00
1	Scott Fletcher	1.00
2	Bobby Valentine	1.00
4	Don Slaught	1.00
5	Pete Incaviglia	2.00
9	Pete O'Brien	1.00
10	Art Howe	1.00
11	Toby Harrah	1.00
12	Geno Petralli	1.00
13	Joe Ferguson	1.00
14	Tim Foli	1.00
15	Larry Parrish	1.00
16	Mike Mason	1.00
17	Darrell Porter	1.00
18	Ed Correa	1.00
19	Curtis Wilkerson	1.00
22	Steve Buechele	1.00
23	Jose Guzman	1.00
24	Ricky Wright	1.00
27	Greg Harris	1.00
31	Tom Robson	1.00
32	Gary Ward	1.00
35	Tom House	1.00
44	Tom Paciorek	1.00
45	Dwayne Henry	1.00
48	Bobby Witt	1.00
49	Charlie Hough	1.00
---	Arlington Stadium	1.00

1994 Lite Beer Milwaukee Brewers

The 1994 baseball strike interrupted the issue of this four-series commemorative set advertised as including "Every Player in the Brewers Twenty-Five Year History." The set was produced in four booklets of 94 cards each. Individual 2-1/2" x 3-1/2" cards were perforated for easy detachment from the 13" x 7" booklets. Cards feature black-and-white player photos against a gold border. A blue, green and gold Brewers 25th anniversary logo is in the upper-left corner on front. Half of the cards (Series I, II) have a Lite beer logo at top, while half (Series III, IV) have a Miller Genuine Draft logo. Backs are in black-and-white and include a few biographical bits, a line of career stats, the years played with the Brewers and team and brewery logos. Books I and II were issued as planned to adults attending the April 24 and June 26, 1994 games. The Series IV book, containing 10 special cards honoring the Brewers 25th Anniversary Team, was given away at a June 1995 game and Book III was distributed in August of 1995. Individual cards are unnumbered and are presented here in alphabetical order within series. Cards of Bobby Clark, Tom Edens, Ken McMullen and Danny Walton, which appear in Series I or III are repeated in Series IV.

NM/M
Complete Set, Booklets (4): 30.00
Complete Set,
Singles (376): 24.00
Common Player: .10
Series I .10
Complete book: 10.00
(1) Hank Aaron 5.00
(2) Jim Adduci .10
(3) Jay Aldrich .10
(4) Andy Allanson .10
(5) Dave Baldwin .10
(6) Sal Bando .10
(7) Len Barker .10
(8) Kevin Bass .10
(9) Ken Berry .10
(10) George Canale .10
(11) Tom Candiotti .10
(12) Mike Capel .10
(13) Bobby Darwin .10
(14) Danny Darwin .10
(15) Brock Davis .10
(16) Dick Davis .10
(17) Jamie Easterley .10
(18) Tom Edens .10
(19) Marshall Edwards .10
(20) Cal Eldred .10
(21) Bob Ellis .10
(22) Ed Farmer .10
(23) Mike Felder .10
(24) John Felske .10
(25) Mike Ferraro .10
(26) Mike Fetters .10
(27) Danny Frisella .10
(28) Bob Galasso .10
(29) Jim Gantner .10
(30) Pedro Garcia .10
(31) Bob Gardner .10
(32) John Gelnar .10
(33) Moose Haas .10
(34) Darryl Hamilton .10
(35) Larry Haney .10
(36) Jim Hannan .10
(37) Bob Hansen .10
(38) Mike Ignasiak .10
(39) John Jaha .10
(40) Dion James .10
(41) Deron Johnson .10
(42) John Henry Johnson .10
(43) Tim Johnson .10
(44) Rickey Keeton .10
(45) John Kennedy .10
(46) Jim Kern .10
(47) Pete Ladd .10
(48) Joe Lahoud .10
(49) Tom Lampkin .10
(50) Dave LaPoint .10
(51) George Lauzerique .10
(52) Julio Machado .10
(53) Alex Madrid .10
(54) Candy Maldonado .10
(55) Carlos Maldonado .10
(56) Rick Manning .10
(57) Jaime Navarro .10
(58) Ray Newman .10
(59) Juan Nieves .10
(60) Dave Nilsson .10
(61) Charlie O'Brien .10
(62) Syd O'Brien .10
(63) John O'Donoghue .10
(64) Jim Paciorek .10
(65) Dave Parker .10
(66) Bill Parsons .10
(67) Marty Pattin .10
(68) Jamie Quirk .10
(69) Willie Randolph .10
(70) Paul Ratliff .10
(71) Lance Rautzhan .10
(72) Randy Ready .10
(73) Ray Sadecki .10
(74) Lenn Sakata .10
(75) Ken Sanders .10
(76) Ted Savage .10
(77) Dick Schofield .10
(78) Jim Tatum .10
(79) Chuck Taylor .10
(80) Tom Tellmann .10
(81) Frank Tepedino .10
(82) Sandy Valdespino .10
(83) Jose Valentin .10
(84) Greg Vaughn .10
(85) Carlos Velazquez .10
(86) Rick Waits .10
(87) Danny Walton .10
(88) Floyd Weaver .10
(89) Bill Wegman .10
(90) Floyd Wicker .10
(91) Al Yates .10
(92) Ned Yost .10
(93) Mike Young .10
(94) Robin Yount 3.00
Series II .10
Complete book: 8.00
(95) Hank Allen .10
(96) Felipe Alou .25
(97) Max Alvis .10
(98) Larry Anderson .10
(99) Rick Auerbach .10
(100) Don August .10
(101) Billy Bates .10
(102) Gary Beare .10
(103) Larry Bearnarth .10
(104) Andy Beene .10
(105) Jerry Bell .10
(106) Juan Bell .10
(107) Dwight Bernard .10
(108) Bernie Carbo .10
(109) Jose Cardenal .10
(110) Matias Carrillo .10
(111) Juan Castillo .10
(112) Bill Castro .10
(113) Rick Cerone .10
(114) Rob Deer .10
(115) Rick Dempsey .10
(116) Alex Diaz .10
(117) Dick Ellsworth .10
(118) Narciso Elvira .10
(119) Tom Filer .10
(120) Rollie Fingers .75
(121) Scott Fletcher .10
(122) John Flinn .10
(123) Rich Folkers .10
(124) Tony Fossas .10
(125) Chris George .10
(126) Bob L. Gibson .10
(127) Gus Gil .10
(128) Tommy Harper .10
(129) Vic Harris .10
(130) Paul Hartzell .10
(131) Tom Hausman .10
(132) Neal Heaton .10
(133) Mike Hegan .10
(134) Jack Heidemann .10
(135) Doug Jones .10
(136) Mark Kiefer .10
(137) Steve Kiefer .10
(138) Ed Kirkpatrick .10
(139) Joe Kmak .10
(140) Mark Knudson .10
(141) Kevin Kobel .10
(142) Pete Koegel .10
(143) Jack Lazorko .10
(144) Tim Leary .10
(145) Mark Lee .10
(146) Jeffrey Leonard .10
(147) Randy Lerch .10
(148) Brad Lesley .10
(149) Sixto Lezcano .10
(150) Josias Manzanillo .10
(151) Buck Martinez .10
(152) Tom Matchick .10
(153) Davey May .10
(154) Matt Maysey .10
(155) Bob McClure .10
(156) Tim McIntosh .10
(157) Tim Nordbrook .10
(158) Ben Oglivie .10
(159) Jim Olander .10
(160) Troy O'Leary .10
(161) Roberto Pena .10
(162) Jeff Peterek .10
(163) Ray Peters .10
(164) Rob Picciolo .10
(165) John Poff .10
(166) Gus Polidor .10
(167) Dan Plesac .10
(168) Kevin Reimer .10
(169) Andy Replogle .10
(170) Jerry Reuss .10
(171) Archie Reynolds .10
(172) Bob Reynolds .10
(173) Ken Reynolds .10
(174) Tommie Reynolds .10
(175) Ernest Riles .10
(176) Bill Schroeder .10
(177) George Scott .15
(178) Ray Searage .10
(179) Bob Sebra .10
(180) Kevin Seitzer .10
(181) Dick Selma .10
(182) Bill Sharp .10
(183) Ron Theobald .10
(184) Dan Thomas .10
(185) Gorman Thomas .15
(186) Randy Veres .10
(187) Bill Voss .10
(188) Jim Wohlford .10
Series III
Complete book: 8.00
(189) Jerry Augustine .10
(190) James Austin .10
(191) Rick Austin .10
(192) Kurt Bevacqua .10
(193) Tom Bianco .10
(194) Dante Bichette .10
(195) Mike Birkbeck .10
(196) Dan Boitano .10
(197) Bobby Bolin .10
(198) Mark Bomback .10
(199) Ricky Bones .10
(200) Chris Bosio .10
(201) Thad Bosley .10
(202) Steve Bowling .10
(203) Gene Brabender .10
(204) Glenn Braggs .10
(205) Mike Caldwell .10
(206) Billy Champion .10
(207) Mark Ciardi .10
(208) Bobby Clark .10
(209) Ron Clark .10
(210) Mark Clear .10
(211) Reggie Cleveland .10
(212) Bryan Clutterbuck .10
(213) Jaime Cocanower .10
(214) Jim Colborn .10
(215) Cecil Cooper .15
(216) Edgar Diaz .10
(217) Frank DiPino .10
(218) Dave Engle .10
(219) Ray Fosse .10
(220) Terry Francona .10
(221) Tito Francona .10
(222) LaVel Freeman .10
(223) Brian Giles .10
(224) Bob Heise .10
(225) Doug Henry .10
(226) Mike Hershberger .10
(227) Teddy Higuera .10
(228) Sam Hinds .10
(229) Fred Holdsworth .10
(230) Darren Holmes .10
(231) Paul Householder .10
(232) Odell Jones .10
(233) Brad Komminsk .10
(234) Andy Kosco .10
(235) Lew Krausse .10
(236) Ray Krawczyk .10
(237) Bill Krueger .10
(238) Ted Kubiak .10
(239) Jack Lind .10
(240) Frank Linzy .10
(241) Pat Listach .10
(242) Graeme Lloyd .10
(243) Bob Locker .10
(244) Skip Lockwood .10
(245) Ken McMullen .10
(246) Jerry McNertney .10
(247) Doc Medich .10
(248) Bob Meyer .10
(249) Joey Meyer .10
(250) Matt Mieske .10
(251) Roger Miller .10
(252) Paul Mirabella .10
(253) Angel Miranda .10
(254) Bobby Mitchell .10
(255) Paul Mitchell .10
(256) Paul Molitor 3.00
(257) Rafael Novoa .10
(258) Jesse Orosco .10
(259) Carlos Ponce .10
(260) Chuck Porter .10
(261) Darrell Porter .10
(262) Billy Jo Robidoux .10
(263) Ron Robinson .10
(264) Eduardo Rodriguez .10
(265) Ellie Rodriguez .10
(266) Rich Rollins .10
(267) Ed Romero .10
(268) Gary Sheffield 1.00
(269) Bob Sheldon .10
(270) Chris Short .10
(271) Bob Skube .10
(272) Jim Slaton .10
(273) Bernie Smith .10
(274) Russ Snyder .10
(275) Lary Sorenson .10
(276) Billy Spiers .10
(277) Ed Sprague .10
(278) Dickie Thon .10
(279) Bill Travers .10
(280) Pete Vuckovich .10
(281) Clyde Wright .10
(282) Jeff Yurak .10
Series IV
Complete book: 8.00
(283) Joe Azcue .10
(284) Mike Boddicker .10
(285) Ken Brett .10
(286) John Briggs .10
(287) Pete Broberg .10
(288) Greg Brock .10
(289) Jeff Bronkey .10
(290) Mark Brouhard .10
(291) Kevin Brown .10
(292) Ollie Brown .10
(293) Bruce Brubaker .10
(294) Tom Brunansky .10
(295) Steve Brye .10
(296) Bob Burda .10
(297) Ray Burris .10
(298) Jeff Cirillo .10
(299) Bobby Clark .10
(300) Bob Coluccio .10
(301) Wayne Comer .10
(302) Billy Conigliaro .10
(303) Cecil Cooper (25th Anniversary Team) .10
(304) Barry Cort .10
(305) Chuck Crim .10
(306) Lafayette Currence .10
(307) Kiki Diaz .10
(308) Bill Doran .10
(309) Al Downing .10
(310) Tom Edens .10
(311) Andy Etchebarren .10
(312) Rollie Fingers (25th) .50
(313) Jim Gantner (25th) .10
(314) Greg Goossen .10
(315) Brian Harper .10
(316) Larry Hisle .10
(317) Steve Hovley .10
(318) Wilbur Howard .10
(319) Roy Howell .10
(320) Bob Humphreys .10
(321) Jim Hunter .10
(322) Dave Huppert .10
(323) Von Joshua .10
(324) Art Kusnyer .10
(325) Doug Loman .10
(326) Jim Lonborg .10
(327) Marcelino Lopez .10
(328) Willie Lozado .10
(329) Mike Matheny .10
(330) Ken McMullen .10
(331) Jose Mercedes .10
(332) Paul Molitor (25th) 1.50
(333) Don Money .10
(334) Don Money (25th) .10
(335) Charlie Moore .10
(336) Donnie Moore .10
(337) John Morris .10
(338) Curt Motton .10
(339) Willie Mueller .10
(340) Tom Murphy .10
(341) Tony Muser .10
(342) Edwin Nunez .10
(343) Ben Oglivie (25th) .10
(344) Pat Osborn (Osburn) .10
(345) Dennis Powell .10
(346) Jody Reed .10
(347) Phil Roof .10
(348) Jimmy Rosario .10
(349) Bruce Ruffin .10
(350) Gary Ryerson .10
(351) Bob Scanlan .10
(352) Ted Simmons .10
(353) Ted Simmons (25th) .10
(354) Duane Singleton .10
(355) Steve Stanicek .10
(356) Fred Stanley .10
(357) Dave Stapleton .10
(358) Randy Stein .10
(359) Earl Stephenson .10
(360) Franklin Stubbs .10
(361) William Suero .10
(362) Jim Sundberg .10
(363) B.J. Surhoff .10
(364) Gary Sutherland .10
(365) Don Sutton .50
(366) Dale Sveum .10
(367) Gorman Thomas (25th) .10
(368) Wayne Twitchell .10
(369) Dave Valle .10
(370) Greg Vaughn (25th) .10
(371) John Vukovich .10
(372) Danny Walton .10
(373) Turner Ward .10
(374) Rick Wrona .10
(375) Jim Wynn .10
(376) Robin Yount (25th) 1.50

1990 Little Big Leaguers

This set was issued on a series of five nine-card perforated panels at the back of a book titled, "little BIG LEAGUERS / Amazing Boyhood Stories of Today's Baseball Stars." The 96 text pages of the book offer inspiring boyhood baseball tales as well as childhood and major league photos of the players. The tear-out cards measure 2-1/2" x 3-1/2" and are perforated on all four sides. Fronts have a black-and-white childhood photo of the player, nearly all in baseball uniform. The player's name is in white in a red strip at top, with the set name at bottom. Backs have the same red strips. At center in black-and-white are biographical data and career highlights. The unnumbered cards are checklisted here alphabetically.

NM/M
Complete Set, Book: 6.00
Complete Set (45): 6.00
Common Player: .25
(1) Todd Benzinger .25
(2) Bud Black .25
(3) Wade Boggs .75
(4) Chris Bosio .25
(5) George Brett 2.00
(6) Brett Butler .25
(7) Jose Canseco .65
(8) Gary Carter .75
(9) Joe Carter .25
(10) Eric Davis .25
(11) Glenn Davis .25
(12) Storm Davis .25
(13) Kevin Elster .25
(14) Tony Fernandez .25
(15) John Franco .25
(16) Gary Gaetti .25
(17) Mark Gubicza .25
(18) Tony Gwynn 1.00
(19) Bruce Hurst .25
(20) Bo Jackson .60
(21) Bob Kipper .25
(22) Ron Kittle .25
(23) Carney Lansford .25
(24) Jeffrey Leonard .25
(25) Mike A. Marshall .25
(26) Lloyd McClendon .25
(27) Andy McGaffigan .25
(28) Keith Moreland .25
(29) Lloyd Moseby .25
(30) Dale Murphy .50
(31) Pete O'Brien .25
(32) Mike Pagliarulo .25
(33) Tim Raines .25
(34) Dennis Rasmussen .25
(35) Harold Reynolds .25
(36) Billy Ripken .25
(37) Nolan Ryan 3.00
(38) Steve Sax .25
(39) Ozzie Smith 1.00
(40) Jim Sundberg .25
(41) Rick Sutcliffe .25
(42) Dave Valle .25
(43) Andy Van Slyke .25
(44) Glenn Wilson .25
(45) Todd Worrell .25

1991 Little Big Leaguers

This set was issued on a series of five nine-card perforated panels at the back of a book titled, "little BIG LEAGUERS / Amazing Boyhood Stories of Today's Baseball Stars." The 96 text pages of the book offer inspiring boyhood baseball tales as well as childhood and major league photos of the players. The tear-out cards measure 2-1/2" x 3-1/2" and are perforated on all four sides. Fronts have a black-and-white childhood photo of the player, nearly all in baseball uniform. The player's name is in white in a green strip at top, with the set name at bottom. Backs have the same green strips. At center in black-and-white are biographical data and career highlights. The unnumbered cards are checklisted here alphabetically.

NM/M
Complete Book: 6.00
Complete Set (45): 6.00
Common Player: .25
(1) Jim Abbott .25
(2) Jesse Barfield .25
(3) Kevin Bass .25
(4) Craig Biggio .25
(5) Phil Bradley .25
(6) Jeff Brantley .25
(7) Tom Brunansky .25
(8) Ken Caminiti .25
(9) Will Clark .35
(10) Vince Coleman .25
(11) David Cone .25
(12) Alvin Davis .25
(13) Andre Dawson .50
(14) Bill Doran .25
(15) Nick Esasky .25
(16) Dwight Gooden .25
(17) Tom Gordon .25
(18) Ken Griffey Jr. 2.50
(19) Kevin Gross .25
(20) Kelly Gruber .25
(21) Lee Guetterman .25
(22) Terry Kennedy .25
(23) John Kruk .25
(24) Bill Landrum .25
(25) Mark Langston .25
(26) Barry Larkin .25
(27) Dave Magadan .25
(28) Don Mattingly 2.00
(29) Mark McGwire 3.00
(30) Kevin Mitchell .25
(31) Bob Ojeda .25
(32) Gregg Olson .25
(33) Terry Pendleton .25
(34) Ted Power .25
(35) Kirby Puckett 1.50
(36) Terry Puhl .25
(37) Bret Saberhagen .25
(38) Chris Sabo .25
(39) Kevin Seitzer .25
(40) Don Slaught .25
(41) Lonnie Smith .25
(42) Darryl Strawberry .25
(43) Mickey Tettleton .25
(44) Bobby Thigpen .25
(45) Frank White .25

2005 Los Angeles Angels Card Deck

This stadium giveaway was sponsored by ValleyCrest Companies, a golf course design firm. Cards are 2-1/4" x 3-7/16" with rounded corners. Red backs have team and sponsor's logos. Each player appears four times in the deck, with an identical portrait photo on the same value card in each suit. Two wild cards complete the boxed set.

NM/M
Complete Set (54): 10.00
Common Player: .25
2 Adam Kennedy .25
3 Darin Erstad .25
4 Kelvim Escobar .25
5 Bengie Molina .25
6 Orlando Cabrera .25
7 Garret Anderson .25
8 Steve Finley .25
9 Bartolo Colon .25
10 Francisco Rodriguez .25
J Chone Figgins .25
Q Rally Money (Mascot) .25
K Mike Scioscia .25
A Vladimir Guerrero .50
WC Mascot (Brendan Donnelly) .25
WC Mascot (Brendan Donnelly) .25

1981-93 Louisville Slugger

Hillerich & Bradsby, makers of Louisville Slugger bats and gloves, produced these cards to be attached to the company's baseball gloves. A small round hole is punched in the upper-left corner of each standard-size card to enable them to be attached to the gloves. Undamaged cards are hard to find. All cards follow the same basic design - bright blue and green borders, player name and position above the full-color photo (with autograph overprint), yellow Louisville Slugger logo across the bottom border. Beneath the logo are the words "Member Louisville Slugger Bat & Glove Advisory Staff." The card backs are blue and green and include the player name, short biography and a list of personal records and information. Cards were printed with a glossy finish through 1987, when a flat finish was adopted as production moved from Taiwan to the Philippines.

		NM/M
	Common Player:	2.00
(1)	Steve Garvey/Ddgrs	5.00
(2)	Graig Nettles/Yanks	4.00
(1)	Pedro Guerrero/ Dodgers	2.00
(2)	Fred Lynn/Angels	2.00
(1)	Ray Knight/Astros	5.00
(2)	Ray Knight/Mets	2.25
(3)	Graig Nettles/Padres	3.25
(1)	Steve Garvey/Padres	3.25
(2)	Gary Matthews/Cubs	2.00
(1)	Orel Hershiser/Ddgrs	2.00
(2)	Rick Rhoden/Pirates	2.00
(1)	Eric Davis/Reds	2.00
(1)	Eric Davis/Reds	2.00
(2)	Steve Garvey/Padres	4.00
(3)	Orel Hershiser/Ddgrs	2.00
(4)	Mike Pagliarulo/Yanks	2.00
(1)	Orel Hershiser/Ddgrs	2.00
(1)	Orel Hershiser/Ddgrs	2.00
(2)	Andy Van Slyke/ Pirates	2.00
(3)	Lou Whitaker/Tigers	3.00
(1)	Wade Boggs/Red Sox	6.00
(1)	Eric Davis/Ddgrs	2.00
(2)	Jack McDowell/ White Sox	2.00

1990s Louisville Slugger TPX Advisory Staff

This series of cards issued sometime, or over a period of time, in the 1990s depicts members of Hillerich & Bradsby's Pro Advisory Staff for its TPX line-up of baseball equipment. Cards are in standard 2-1/2" x 3-1/2" format with game-action or posed color photos and a facsimile autograph on front. Backs picture a bat, glove and bat bag.

		NM/M
	Common Player:	3.00
(1)	Brett Butler/Ddgrs	3.00
(2)	Bobby Jones/Mets	3.00
(3)	Reggie Sanders/Reds	3.00
(4)	Todd Stottlemyre/ Cardinals	3.00
(5)	Robin Ventura/ White Sox	3.00

1992 Lykes Braves Team Photo Set

When Lykes Meats was awarded the Braves hot dog contract for 1992 they continued the previous years' baseball card promotions, including this early-May team photo/player card panel. Three 9-1/2" x 10-1/2" panels feature a team photo and 30 player cards. The cards have player portraits against a blue background in a tombstone shape. A blue ball at lower-left has the player's uniform number, while his name is in white in a red strip beneath the photo. Red logos of the team and hot dog vendor are at bottom. Backs are printed in red and dark blue and feature full stats, player data and a facsimile autograph. These cards are much more common than the Lykes singles distributed later in the season. The checklist here is alphabetized.

		NM/M
	Complete Foldout Set:	6.00
	Common Player:	.15
(1)	Steve Avery	.15
(2)	Rafael Belliard	.15
(3)	Juan Berenguer	.15
(4)	Damon Berryhill	.15
(5)	Mike Bielecki	.15
(6)	Jeff Blauser	.15
(7)	Sid Bream	.15
(8)	Francisco Cabrera	.15
(9)	Bobby Cox	.15
(10)	Nick Esasky	.15
(11)	Marvin Freeman	.15
(12)	Ron Gant	.15
(13)	Tom Glavine	1.00
(14)	Tommy Gregg	.15
(15)	Brian Hunter	.15
(16)	David Justice	.25
(17)	Charlie Leibrandt	.15
(18)	Mark Lemke	.15
(19)	Kent Mercker	.15
(20)	Otis Nixon	.15
(21)	Greg Olson	.15
(22)	Alejandro Pena	.15
(23)	Terry Pendleton	.15
(24)	Deion Sanders	.25
(25)	Lonnie Smith	.15
(26)	John Smoltz	1.00
(27)	Mike Stanton	.15
(28)	Jeff Treadway	.15
(29)	Jerry Willard	.15
(30)	Mark Wohlers	.15
(31)	Team Photo	.50

1992 Lykes Braves

Though Braves players no longer appeared at an autograph booth on card giveaway days in 1992, the team's hot dog vendor continued to offer small groups of cards to kids attending Tuesday home games. This distribution makes assembling complete sets very challenging. In standard 2-1/2" x 3-1/2" size, the cards have a player photo border in, successively, white, dark blue, red and white. A red-and-blue Lykes logo is at lower-right. Above is a blue ball with the year of issue, and the team and player name printed in white. Backs are in black with the player's uniform number, full minor and major league stats, and biographical vitae.

		NM/M
	Complete Set (37):	12.00
	Common Player:	.25
(1)	Steve Avery	.25
(2)	Jim Beauchamp	.25
(3)	Rafael Belliard	.25
(4)	Juan Berenguer	.25
(5)	Damon Berryhill	.25
(6)	Mike Bielecki	.25
(7)	Jeff Blauser	.25
(8)	Sid Bream	.25
(9)	Francisco Cabrera	.25
(10)	Pat Corrales	.25
(11)	Bobby Cox	.25
(12)	Marvin Freeman	.25
(13)	Ron Gant	.40
(14)	Tom Glavine	1.50
(15)	Tommy Gregg	.25
(16)	Brian Hunter	.25
(17)	Clarence Jones	.25
(18)	David Justice	.75
(19)	Charlie Leibrandt	.25
(20)	Mark Lemke	.25
(21)	Leo Mazzone	.25
(22)	Kent Mercker	.25
(23)	Otis Nixon	.25
(24)	Greg Olson	.25
(25)	Alejandro Pena	.25
(26)	Terry Pendleton	.25
(27)	Deion Sanders	.50
(28)	Lonnie Smith	.25
(29)	John Smoltz	1.50
(30)	Mike Stanton	.25
(31)	Jeff Treadway	.25
(32)	Jerry Willard	.25
(33)	Jimy Williams	.25
(34)	Mark Wohlers	.25
(35)	Ned Yost	.25
(36)	Homer the Brave (Mascot)	.25
(37)	Rally (Mascot)	.25

1993 Lykes Braves

Each Tuesday home game during the 1993 season, three player cards were distributed to youngsters, sponsored by the team's hot dog vendor. This style of distribution makes collecting a complete 38-card set very challenging. Standard 2-1/2" x 3-1/2" size cards have a player portrait photo against a blue background. The card's front border is a darker blue separated from the photo by a yellow stripe. Red-white-and-blue team and vendor logos appear at the corners and the player's name and position are in white at lower-left. Backs are printed in black with complete career stats, biographical data and sponsors' logos. The unnumbered cards are checklisted here alphabetically. The final Tuesday's handouts, Lopez, McGriff and Tarasco have slightly different back printing and are somewhat scarcer than other cards.

		NM/M
	Complete Set (38):	20.00
	Common Player:	.50
(1)	Steve Avery	.50
(2)	Jim Beauchamp	.50
(3)	Steve Bedrosian	.50
(4)	Rafael Belliard	.50
(5)	Damon Berryhill	.50
(6)	Jeff Blauser	.50
(7)	Sid Bream	.50
(8)	Francisco Cabrera	.50
(9)	Pat Corrales	.50
(10)	Bobby Cox	.50
(11)	Marvin Freeman	.50
(12)	Ron Gant	.50
(13)	Tom Glavine	1.50
(14)	Jay Howell	.50
(15)	Brian Hunter	.50
(16)	Clarence Jones	.50
(17)	David Justice	.60
(18)	Mark Lemke	.50
(19)	Javier Lopez	1.00
(20)	Greg Maddux	2.50
(21)	Leo Mazzone	.50
(22)	Fred McGriff	1.00
(23)	Greg McMichael	.50
(24)	Kent Mercker	.50
(25)	Otis Nixon	.50
(26)	Greg Olson	.50
(27)	Bill Pecota	.50
(28)	Terry Pendleton	.50
(29)	Deion Sanders	1.00
(30)	Pete Smith	.50
(31)	John Smoltz	1.50
(32)	Mike Stanton	.50
(33)	Tony Tarasco	1.00
(34)	Jimy Williams	.50
(35)	Mark Wohlers	.50
(36)	Ned Yost	.50
(37)	Homer the Brave (Mascot)	.50
(38)	Rally (Mascot)	.50

Team Photo Set

The Atlanta Braves offered a perforated, uncut sheet team set in 1992 that was handed out in an early season game. The set, sponsored by Lykes, includes 30 cards and a team photo and carries the player's name and uniform number on the front of the card along with the Braves and Lykes logos. The backs contain the player's biography, career statistics and a facsimile autograph. The first card of Fred McGriff as a Brave appears in this promotional set issued later in the season than in previous years. The 30 individual player cards also include Ryan Klesko, who was not in the single-card season-long giveaways. Three 9-1/2" x 10-1/2" panels comprise this issue, with each of the player cards perforated at the edges. Also for the first time in 1992, the same photos were used for the team sheet and single card promotions. Single cards measure 2-1/4" x 3-1/2" and are checklisted alphabetically here.

		NM/M
	Complete Foldout Set:	5.00
	Common Player:	.15
(1)	Steve Avery	.15
(2)	Steve Bedrosian	.15
(3)	Rafael Belliard	.15
(4)	Damon Berryhill	.15
(5)	Jeff Blauser	.15
(6)	Sid Bream	.15
(7)	Francisco Cabrera	.15
(8)	Bobby Cox	.15
(9)	Marvin Freeman	.15
(10)	Ron Gant	.15
(11)	Tom Glavine	1.00
(12)	Jay Howell	.15
(13)	Brian Hunter	.15
(14)	David Justice	.25
(15)	Ryan Klesko	.15
(16)	Mark Lemke	.15
(17)	Greg Maddux	2.00
(18)	Fred McGriff	.25
(19)	Greg McMichael	.15
(20)	Kent Mercker	.15
(21)	Otis Nixon	.15
(22)	Greg Olson	.15
(23)	Bill Pecota	.15
(24)	Terry Pendleton	.15
(25)	Deion Sanders	.25
(26)	Pete Smith	.15
(27)	John Smoltz	1.00
(28)	Mike Stanton	.15
(29)	Tony Tarasco	.15
(30)	Mark Wohlers	.15
(31)	Team Photo	.50

1994 Lykes Braves

While 34 cards were printed, only 27 were publicly released prior to the beginning of the 1994 baseball strike. Sponsored by the Braves' stadium hot dog concessionaire, the cards were given away at the rate of three per Tuesday home game. Because of the strike, the cards of Cox, Hill, Chipper Jones, Mike Kelly, Klesko, McGriff and Sanders were not officially released and are scarcer than the other 27. Card fronts feature a chest-to-cap player portrait photo set agaonst a blue background with an orange border and vertical blue stripe at right bearing the player's name. Backs are printed in black-and-white and have full major and minor league stats along with a few biographical details. There is no card or uniform number on the cards. They are presented here alphabetically.

		NM/M
	Complete Set (34):	40.00
	Common Player:	.25
(1)	Steve Avery	.25
(2)	Jim Beauchamp	.25
(3)	Steve Bedrosian	.25
(4)	Rafael Belliard	.25
(5)	Mike Bielecki	.25
(6)	Jeff Blauser	.25
(7)	Pat Corrales	.25
(8)	Bobby Cox	2.00
(9)	Dave Gallagher	.25
(10)	Tom Glavine	1.50
(11)	Milt Hill	2.00
(12)	Chipper Jones	10.00
(13)	Clarence Jones	.25
(14)	David Justice	.50
(15)	Mike Kelly	2.00
(16)	Ryan Klesko	6.00
(17)	Mark Lemke	.25
(18)	Javy Lopez	.25
(19)	Greg Maddux	3.00
(20)	Leo Mazzone	.25
(21)	Greg McMichael	.25
(22)	Fred McGriff	6.00
(23)	Kent Mercker	.25
(24)	Charlie O'Brien	.25
(25)	Gregg Olson	.25
(26)	Bill Pecota	.25
(27)	Terry Pendleton	.25
(28)	Deion Sanders	6.00
(29)	John Smoltz	1.50
(30)	Mike Stanton	.25
(31)	Tony Tarasco	.25
(32)	Jimy Williams	.25
(33)	Mark Wohlers	.25
(34)	Ned Yost	.25

1994 Lykes Braves Team Photo Set

Few of these team photo/player card sets have found their way into the hobby because they were intended for distribution at the August 14 Sunday home game which fell after the beginning of the 1994 baseball strike. As in past years, the set was produced as a fold-out containing a team photo and 35 player cards. Unlike previous editions, however, the player cards are identical in format to the single cards given away during the season, except that they are printed in red and blue on the back and are slightly smaller, at 2-1/8" x 3-1/8". The cards are checklisted here alphabeitcally.

		NM/M
	Complete Foldout Set:	17.50
	Common Player:	.25
(1)	Steve Avery	.25
(2)	Jim Beauchamp	.25
(3)	Steve Bedrosian	.25
(4)	Rafael Belliard	.25
(5)	Mike Bielecki	.25
(6)	Jeff Blauser	.25
(7)	Pat Corrales	.25
(8)	Bobby Cox	.25
(9)	Dave Gallagher	.25
(10)	Tom Glavine	1.50
(11)	Chipper Jones	3.50
(12)	Clarence Jones	.25
(13)	David Justice	.50
(14)	Mike Kelly	.25
(15)	Roberto Kelly	.25
(16)	Ryan Klesko	.25
(17)	Mark Lemke	.25
(18)	Javy Lopez	.25
(19)	Greg Maddux	3.50
(20)	Leo Mazzone	.25
(21)	Greg McMichael	.25
(22)	Fred McGriff	.25
(23)	Kent Mercker	.25
(24)	Mike Mordecai	.25
(25)	Charlie O'Brien	.25
(26)	Jose Oliva	.25
(27)	Gregg Olson	.25
(28)	Bill Pecota	.25
(29)	Terry Pendleton	.25
(30)	John Smoltz	1.50
(31)	Mike Stanton	.25
(32)	Tony Tarasco	.25
(33)	Jimy Williams	.25
(34)	Mark Wohlers	.25
(35)	Ned Yost	.25
(36)	Team Photo	.50

1995 Lykes Braves

For the only time since Atlanta's hot dog concessionaires began issuing cards in 1989, the team honored past, as well as current players, as part of its 30th anniversary celebration. The cards were distributed at Tuesday home games, usually three at a time, making assembly of a complete set difficult. Thus, this checklist may or may not be complete. Fronts have game-action photos with a black strip at bottom bearing the player name. A 30th anniversary logo is at top, the sponsor's logo appears over a baseball in a lower corner. Black-and-white backs have player personal data and career record.

		NM/M
	Complete Set (30):	10.00
	Common Player:	.25
(1)	Hank Aaron	2.50
(2)	Steve Avery	.25
(3)	Steve Bedrosian	.25
(4)	Jeff Blauser	.25
(5)	Sid Bream	.25
(6)	Francisco Cabrera	.25
(7)	Chris Chambliss	.25
(8)	Bobby Cox	.25
(9)	Ron Gant	.25
(10)	Tom Glavine	1.50
(11)	Marquis Grissom	.25
(12)	Bob Horner	.25
(13)	Glenn Hubbard	.25
(14)	Chipper Jones	2.00
(15)	David Justice	.25
(16)	Ryan Klesko	.25
(17)	Mark Lemke	.25
(18)	Javy Lopez	.25
(19)	Greg Maddux	2.00
(20)	Fred McGriff	.25
(21)	Kent Mercker	.25
(22)	Dale Murphy	1.50
(23)	Phil Niekro	.40
(24)	Otis Nixon	.25
(25)	Charlie O'Brien	.25
(26)	Greg Olson	.25
(27)	Pascual Perez	.25
(28)	Lonnie Smith	.25
(29)	John Smoltz	1.50
(30)	Mark Wohlers	.25

Team Photo Set

Once again this promotional giveaway by the team's hot dog concessionaire took the form of a three-panel cardboard poster. Overall 10-3/4" x 28", the foldout features a color team photo at top and 30 individual player portrait cards be-

low. Each card is 2-1/8" x 3-1/8" and perforated for separation. Backs are printed in red, white and blue with a few stats and vital data, along with team and sponsor logos. The unnumbered cards are checklisted here alphabetically.

		NM/M
Complete Foldout Set:		8.00
Common Player:		.10
(1)	Steve Avery	.10
(2)	Jim Beauchamp	.10
(3)	Rafael Belliard	.10
(4)	Jeff Blauser	.10
(5)	Pedro Borbon	.10
(6)	Brad Clontz	.10
(7)	Pat Corrales	.10
(8)	Bobby Cox	.10
(9)	Tom Glavine	.75
(10)	Marquis Grissom	.10
(11)	Chipper Jones	2.00
(12)	Clarence Jones	.10
(13)	David Justice	.25
(14)	Mike Kelly	.10
(15)	Ryan Klesko	.10
(16)	Mark Lemke	.10
(17)	Javier Lopez	.10
(18)	Greg Maddux	1.50
(19)	Leo Mazzone	.10
(20)	Fred McGriff	.10
(21)	Greg McMichael	.10
(22)	Kent Mercker	.10
(23)	Mike Mordecai	.10
(24)	Charlie O'Brien	.10
(25)	Jason Schmidt	.10
(26)	Dwight Smith	.10
(27)	John Smoltz	.75
(28)	Jimy Williams	.10
(29)	Mark Wohlers	.10
(30)	Ned Yost	.10
(31)	Team Photo	.25

1996 Lykes Braves Team Photo Set

The Braves offered a perforated, four-panel 10-3/4" x 31-1/4" uncut sheet team set in 1996 that was handed out to children 12 and under at an early season game. The set was sponsored by Lykes, the team's hot dog concessionaire. There are 35 individual player and staff portrait cards in 2-1/8" x 3-1/8" format, and a 10-3/4" x 9-1/2" team photo panel. Each card carries the player's name, position and uniform number on the front, along with the Lykes logo. Black, white and blue backs contain biographical data, 1995 and career major and minor league statistics and team and sponsor logos. The cards are checklisted alphabetically here.

		NM/M
Complete Foldout Set:		8.00
Common Player:		.10
(1)	Steve Avery	.10
(2)	Danny Bautista	.10
(3)	Jim Beauchamp	.10
(4)	Rafael Belliard	.10
(5)	Mike Bielecki	.10
(6)	Jeff Blauser	.10
(7)	Pedro Borbon	.10
(8)	Brad Clontz	.10
(9)	Pat Corrales	.10
(10)	Bobby Cox	.10
(11)	Jermaine Dye	.10
(12)	Frank Fultz	.10
(13)	Tom Glavine	1.25
(14)	Marquis Grissom	.10
(15)	Chipper Jones	3.00
(16)	Clarence Jones	.10
(17)	David Justice	.25
(18)	Ryan Klesko	.10
(19)	Mark Lemke	.10
(20)	Javy Lopez	.10
(21)	Greg Maddux	2.50
(22)	Leo Mazzone	.10
(23)	Fred McGriff	.10
(24)	Greg McMichael	.10
(25)	Mike Mordecai	.10
(26)	Eddie Perez	.10
(27)	Jason Schmidt	.10
(28)	Dwight Smith	.10
(29)	John Smoltz	1.25
(30)	Terrell Wade	.10
(31)	Jerome Walton	.10
(32)	Mark Whiten	.10
(33)	Jimy Williams	.10
(34)	Mark Wohlers	.10
(35)	Ned Yost	.10
(36)	Team Photo	.50

M

1987 M & M's

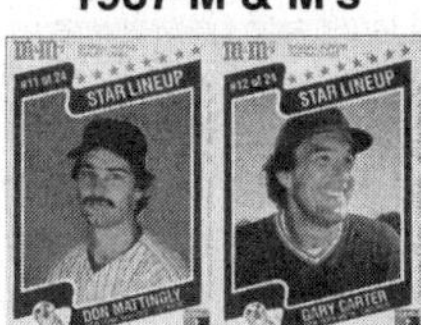

The M&M's "Star Lineup" set consists of 12 two-card panels inserted in specially marked packages of large M&M's candy. The two-card panels measure 5" x 3-1/2" with individual cards measuring 2-1/2" x 3-1/2" in size. The full-color photos are enclosed by a wavy blue frame and a white border. Card backs are printed in red ink on white stock and carry the player's career statistics and highlights. All team insignias have been airbrushed away. The set was designed and produced by Mike Schechter and Associates.

		NM/M
Complete Panel Set (12):		5.00
Complete Singles Set (24):		4.00
Common Panel:		1.00
Common Single Player:		.10
	PANEL 1	.25
1	Wally Joyner	.10
2	Tony Pena	.10
	PANEL 2	1.25
3	Mike Schmidt	.50
4	Ryne Sandberg	.40
	PANEL 3	.65
5	Wade Boggs	.40
6	Jack Morris	.10
	PANEL 4	.65
7	Roger Clemens	.45
8	Harold Baines	.10
	PANEL 5	.60
9	Dale Murphy	.25
10	Jose Canseco	.20
	PANEL 6	.75
11	Don Mattingly	.45
12	Gary Carter	.35
	PANEL 7	2.00
13	Cal Ripken Jr.	1.00
14	George Brett	.50
	PANEL 8	.65
15	Kirby Puckett	.40
16	Joe Carter	.10
	PANEL 9	.25
17	Mike Witt	.10
18	Mike Scott	.10
	PANEL 10	.45
19	Fernando Valenzuela	.15
20	Steve Garvey	.15
	PANEL 11	1.50
21	Steve Sax	.10
22	Nolan Ryan	1.00
	PANEL 12	1.25
23	Tony Gwynn	.40
24	Ozzie Smith	.40

2005 Major League Baseball Superstars Medallions

Coupons in USA Today between July 11 and August 19 allowed to collectors to purchase these medallions on a one-per-day basis for $2.99 at 7-Eleven, SuperAmerica and Speedway convenience stores.

		NM/M
Complete Set (30):		100.00
Common Player:		3.00
(1)	Roger Clemens	6.00
(2)	Ichiro Suzuki	7.50
(3)	Derek Jeter	8.00
(4)	Curt Schilling	3.00
(5)	Albert Pujols	8.00
(6)	Randy Johnson	3.00
(7)	Ivan Rodriguez	3.00
(8)	Eric Gagne	3.00
(9)	Kerry Wood	3.00
(10)	Ben Sheets	3.00
(11)	John Smoltz	3.00
(12)	Vladimir Guerrero	3.00
(13)	Torii Hunter	3.00
(14)	David Ortiz	3.00
(15)	Carlos Delgado	3.00
(16)	Scott Rolen	3.00
(17)	Jason Schmidt	3.00
(18)	Sammy Sosa	3.00
(19)	Carlos Beltran	3.00
(20)	Luis Gonzalez	3.00
(21)	Ken Griffey Jr.	4.50
(22)	Todd Helton	3.00
(23)	Alfonso Soriano	3.00
(24)	Pedro Martinez	3.00
(25)	Jim Thome	3.00
(26)	Manny Ramirez	3.00
(27)	Johan Santana	3.00
(28)	Eric Chavez	3.00
(29)	Mark Prior	3.00
(30)	Alex Rodriguez	7.50

1997-2002 Major League Dad

To promote responsible fatherhood the California Department of Child Support Services issued a series of cards picturing big league players and their children. Issued in a variety of designs, all have the phrase "Major League Dad" on front.

		NM/M
Complete Set (10):		20.00
Common Player:		2.00
(1)	Garret Anderson/2000	2.00
(2)	Marvin Benard/2000	2.00
(3)	Mike Fetters/1998	2.00
(4)	Mark Gardner/1998	2.00
(5)	Wally Joyner	2.00
(6)	Chad Kreuter	2.00
(7)	Tim Salmon	2.00
(8)	Jeff Shaw/2000	2.00
(9)	Matt Stairs/2000	2.00
(10)	Greg Vaughn/1998	2.00

1988 Mickey Mantle's Restaurant

To promote the grand opening of Mickey Mantle's restaurant in New York City, this promotional card was issued by an Oklahoma public relations firm to members of the media. In round-cornered 2-1/2" x 3-1/2" format on thin, semi-gloss cardboard, the front has a posed color photo of Mantle. The back has details of the restaurant opening and a design reminiscent of the Yankee Stadium facade, printed in white on a dark blue background.

	NM/M
Mickey Mantle	7.50

1989 Marathon Cubs

This colorful 25-card Cubs team set was sponsored by Marathon and was distributed as a stadium promotion to fans attending the Aug. 10, 1989, game at Chicago's Wrigley Field. The oversize (2-3/4" x 4-1/4") feature an action photo inside a diagonal box on the card front, with the Chicago Cubs logo at the top and the player's uniform number, name and position along the bottom. The backs include a small black-and-white photo, player data and the Cubs and Marathon logos.

		NM/M
Complete Set (25):		12.00
Common Player:		.50
2	Vance Law	.50
4	Don Zimmer	.50
7	Joe Girardi	.50
8	Andre Dawson	2.50
9	Damon Berryhill	.50
10	Lloyd McClendon	.50
12	Shawon Dunston	.50
15	Domingo Ramos	.50
17	Mark Grace	.75
18	Dwight Smith	.50
19	Curt Wilkerson	.50
20	Jerome Walton	.50
21	Scott Sanderson	.50
23	Ryne Sandberg	6.50
28	Mitch Williams	.50
31	Greg Maddux	6.00
32	Calvin Schiraldi	.50
33	Mitch Webster	.50
36	Mike Bielecki	.50
39	Paul Kilgus	.50
40	Rick Sutcliffe	.50
41	Jeff Pico	.50
44	Steve Wilson	.50
50	Les Lancaster	.50
---	Coaches (Joe Altobelli, Chuck Cottier, Larry Cox, Jose Martinez, Dick Pole)	.50

1989 Marathon Tigers

Marathon sponsored this give-away set for a 1989 Tigers home game. The oversized cards feature thin white stock and full-color player photos. The cards are numbered according to uniform number.

		NM/M
Complete Set (28):		9.00
Common Player:		.50
1	Lou Whitaker	.75
3	Alan Trammell	1.00
8	Mike Heath	.50
9	Fred Lynn	.50
10	Keith Moreland	.50
11	Sparky Anderson	.75
12	Mike Brumley	.50
14	Dave Bergman	.50
15	Pat Sheridan	.50
17	Al Pedrique	.50
18	Ramon Pena	.50
19	Doyle Alexander	.50
21	Guillermo Hernandez	.50
23	Torey Lovullo	.50
24	Gary Pettis	.50
25	Ken Williams	.50
26	Frank Tanana	.50
27	Charles Hudson	.50
32	Gary Ward	.50
33	Matt Nokes	.50
34	Chet Lemon	.50
35	Rick Schu	.50
36	Frank Williams	.50
39	Mike Henneman	.50
44	Jeff Robinson	.50
47	Jack Morris	.50
48	Paul Gibson	.50
---	Coaches (Billy Consolo, Alex Grammas, Billy Muffett, Vada Pinson, Dick Tracewksi)	.50

1990 Marathon Cubs

Marathon sponsored its second consecutive Chicago Cubs team set. The oversized cards feature thin white stock and full-color photos. The cards are numbered according to uniform number, and were distributed at a Cubs home game.

		NM/M
Complete Set (28):		6.00
Common Player:		.25
4	Don Zimmer	.35
7	Joe Girardi	.25
8	Andre Dawson	1.50
10	Lloyd McClendon	.25
11	Luis Salazar	.25
12	Shawon Dunston	.25
15	Domingo Ramos	.25
17	Mark Grace	.35
18	Dwight Smith	.25
19	Curtis Wilkerson	.25
20	Jerome Walton	.25
22	Mike Harkey	.25
23	Ryne Sandberg	4.50
25	Marvell Wynne	.25
28	Mitch Williams	.25
29	Doug Dascenzo	.25
30	Dave Clark	.25
31	Greg Maddux	4.00
32	Hector Villanueva	.25
36	Mike Bielecki	.25
37	Bill Long	.25
40	Rick Sutcliffe	.25
41	Jeff Pico	.25
44	Steve Wilson	.25
45	Paul Assenmacher	.25
47	Shawn Boskie	.25
50	Les Lancaster	.25
---	Coaches (Joe Altobelli, Chuck Cottier, Jose Martinez, Dick Pole, Phil Roof)	.25

1991 Marathon Cubs

Marathon Oil once again sponsored a set featuring the Chicago Cubs. This 28-card release features oversized cards measuring 2-7/8" x 4-1/4". The card fronts feature full-color action photos. The flip sides feature complete statistics. The cards are numbered according to uniform number. This number appears on both the front and back of the card.

		NM/M
Complete Set (28):		12.50
Common Player:		.50
7	Joe Girardi	.50
8	Andre Dawson	2.50
9	Damon Berryhill	.50
10	Luis Salazar	.50
11	George Bell	.50
12	Shawon Dunston	.50
16	Jose Vizcaino	.50
17	Mark Grace	.65
18	Dwight Smith	.50
19	Hector Villanueva	.50
20	Jerome Walton	.50
22	Mike Harkey	.50
23	Ryne Sandberg	6.50
24	Chico Walker	.50
29	Doug Dascenzo	.50
30	Bob Scanlan	.50
31	Greg Maddux	6.00
32	Danny Jackson	.50
35	Chuck McElroy	.50
36	Mike Bielecki	.50
40	Rick Sutcliffe	.50
41	Jim Essian	.50
42	Dave Smith	.50
45	Paul Assenmacher	.50
47	Shawn Boskie	.50
50	Les Lancaster	.50
51	Heathcliff Slocumb	.50
---	Coaches (Joe Altobelli, Billy Connors, Chuck Cottier, Jose Martinez, Phil Roof, Richie Zisk)	.50

1992 Marathon Cubs

The fourth consecutive year of a Cubs team set sponsored by Marathon Oil consists of 28 cards, including manager Jim Lefebvre and his coaching staff. The set was originally given away at the July 10, 1993 game at Wrigley Field. Cards are checklisted here by uniform number.

		NM/M
Complete Set (28):		9.00
Common Player:		.25
1	Doug Strange	.30
2	Frank Castillo	.30
5	Jim Lefebvre	.30
6	Rey Sanchez	.30
7	Joe Girardi	.30
8	Andre Dawson	.75
10	Luis Salazar	.30
12	Shawon Dunston	.30
16	Jose Vazcaino	.30
17	Mark Grace	.45
18	Dwight Smith	.30
19	Hector Villanueva	.30
20	Jerome Walton	.30
21	Sammy Sosa	3.50
23	Ryne Sandberg	3.50
27	Derrick May	.30
29	Doug Dascenzo	.30
30	Bob Scanlan	.30
31	Greg Maddux	3.00
32	Danny Jackson	.30
34	Ken Patterson	.30
35	Chuck McElroy	.30
36	Mike Morgan	.30
38	Jeff Robinson	.30
42	Dave Smith	.30
45	Paul Assenmacher	.30
47	Shawn Boskie	.30
---	Coaches (Tom Treblehorn, Jose Martinez, Billy Williams, Sammy Ellis, Chuck Cottier, Billy Connors)	.30

1993 Marathon Cubs

The Cubs distributed the 1993 Marathon Oil set on July 28 in a game against the Padres. The cards, measuring an oversized 4-1/4" x 2-7/8", are unnumbered, with uniform numbers appearing on the back. The cards have a vertical blue stripe down the right side with the player's last name in large, white letters. Backs carry complete major and minor league statistics. There are 27 cards in the set. The checklist is presented here by uniform number.

		NM/M
Complete Set (27):		7.50
Common Player:		.25
2	Rick Wilkins	.25
5	Jim Lefebvre	.25
6	Willie Wilson	.25
10	Steve Lake	.25
11	Rey Sanchez	.25
16	Jose Vizcaino	.25
17	Mark Grace	.35
18	Dwight Smith	.25
20	Eric Yelding	.25
21	Sammy Sosa	3.50
22	Mike Harkey	.25
23	Ryne Sandberg	3.50
24	Steve Buechele	.25
25	Candy Maldonado	.25
27	Derrick May	.25
28	Randy Myers	.25
29	Jose Guzman	.25
30	Bob Scanlan	.25
32	Dan Plesac	.25
36	Mike Morgan	.25
37	Greg Hibbard	.25
38	Jose Bautista	.25
45	Paul Assenmacher	.25
49	Frank Castillo	.25
53	Doug Jennings	.25
---	Coaches (Billy Williams, Jose Martinez, Billy Connors, Tony Muser)	.25
---	Coaches (Dan Simonds, Tom Treblehorn, Chuck Cottier)	.25

2004 Maryland Lottery Golden Ticket Baltimore Orioles

In conjunction with the 50th anniversary of the Baltimore Orioles, the Maryland Lottery issued a set of baseball cards depicting great moments and players from the past. They were issued in a four-card foil pack with the purchase of a $10 Golden Ticket scratch-off card. Cards #1-45 were reported issued in quantities of 50,000 to 100,000 each. The team highlight cards, #45-48 were issued in an edition of 25,000 each. Fifteen thousand of the Ripken Ironman card #49 were produced. Card #50, Babe Ruth (shown on a 1914 Orioles minor league baseball card), was produced in an edition of 10,000. The first 100 persons turning in a complete set won $1,000 and an Orioles prize package. Cards are in the standard 2-1/2" x 3-1/2" format, printed on thin cardboard UV-coated on both sides.

		NM/M
Complete Set (50):		40.00
Common Player:		.50
1	Luis Aparicio	.75
2	Steve Barber	.50
3	Don Baylor	.50
4	Mark Belanger	.50
5	Mike Boddicker	.50
6	Don Buford	.50
7	Al Bumbry	.50
8	Mike Cuellar	.50
9	Rich Dauer	.50
10	Storm Davis	.50
11	Doug DeCinces	.50
12	Pat Dobson	.50
13	Moe Drabowsky	.50
14	Andy Etchebarren	.50
15	Bobby Grich	.50
16	George Kell	.50
17	Tito Landrum	.50
18	Lee MacPhail	.50
19	Tippy Martinez	.50
20	Scott McGregor	.50
21	Dave McNally	.50
22	Milt Pappas	.50
23	Paul Richards	.50
24	Gary Roenicke	.50
25	Dave Schmidt	.50
26	Steve Stone	.50
27	Gus Triandos	.50
28	Gene Woodling	.50
29	Terry Crowley	.50
30	Elrod Hendricks	.50
31	Memorial Stadium	.50
32	Orioles Park	.50
33	Rex Barney	.50
34	Rick Dempsey	.50
35	Mike Flanagan	.50
36	Jim Gentile	.50
37	Reggie Jackson	2.00
38	Frank Robinson	2.00
39	Chuck Thompson	.50
40	Earl Weaver	.50
41	Opening Day 1954	.50
42	Brady Anderson	.50
43	Boog Powell	.65
44	Brooks Robinson	2.00
45	Jim Palmer	1.50
46	1966 World Series	7.50
47	1970 World Series	7.50
48	1983 World Series	7.50
49	2131 Ironman Breaks Record	7.50
50	Babe Ruth	15.00
---	Checklist/Rules	.10

1988 Master Bread Twins

This set of 12 cardboard discs (2-3/4" diameter) features full-color photos of Minnesota Twins team members. Fronts have a bright blue background with red, yellow and black printing. The player photo (with team logos airbrushed off) is centered beneath a "Master Is Good Bread" headliner and a vivid yellow player/team name banner. Backs are black-and-white with five stars printed above the player's name, team, personal data, disc number, stats and "1988 Collector's Edition" banner. The discs were printed in Canada and marketed exclusively in Minnesota in packages of Master Bread, one disc per loaf. Squares cut from sheets are known in the hobby, valued about 50 percent of the issued version.

		NM/M
Complete Set (12):		12.00
Common Player:		1.00
1	Bert Blyleven	1.00
2	Frank Viola	1.00
3	Juan Berenguer	1.00
4	Jeff Reardon	1.00
5	Tim Laudner	1.00
6	Steve Lombardozzi	1.00
7	Randy Bush	1.00
8	Kirby Puckett	5.00
9	Gary Gaetti	1.00
10	Kent Hrbek	1.00
11	Greg Gagne	1.00
12	Tom Brunansky	1.00

1989 Master Bread

For a second year Master Bread packages in the Twin Cities area contained a baseball player disc in 1989. The 2-3/4" discs are in the familiar Mike Schechter Associates format and, unlike the '88 set, featured American League players other than Twins. The issue is among the scarcer of the MSA disc issues. Fronts are trimmed in yellow banners and blue stars. Backs are in blue and have a few stats and player data, along with a disc number.

		NM/M
Complete Set (12):		20.00
Common Player:		1.00
1	Frank Viola	1.00
2	Kirby Puckett	4.00
3	Gary Gaetti	1.00
4	Alan Trammell	1.00
5	Wade Boggs	4.00
6	Don Mattingly	5.00
7	Wally Joyner	1.00
8	Paul Molitor	3.50
9	George Brett	5.00
10	Jose Canseco	2.00
11	Julio Franco	1.00
12	Cal Ripken Jr.	7.50

1989 MasterCard Masters of the Game

The reason for issue and method of distribution for this set is not known. The issue was in the form of a 7-1/2" x 10-1/2" sheet on thin cardboard, picturing eight Hall of Famers around a title card. If cut from the unperforated sheet, single cards measure the standard 2-1/2" x 3-1/2". Fronts have familiar black-and-white photos with a gold border. Backs are in black, white and red with a repeat of the Masters of the Game logo, a few biographical details, lifetime stats and an MLB licensee logo. The unnumbered cards are checklisted here in alphabetical order.

		NM/M
Uncut Sheet:		6.00
Complete Set (9):		6.00
Common Player:		1.00
(1)	Ty Cobb	1.50
(2)	Lou Gehrig	1.50
(3)	Rogers Hornsby	1.00
(4)	Christy Mathewson	1.00
(5)	Satchel Paige	1.00
(6)	Babe Ruth	2.00
(7)	Casey Stengel	1.00
(8)	Cy Young	1.00
(9)	Title Card	.05

1985 Thom McAn Discs

One of the more obscure 1985 issues, this 47-card set of "Pro Player Discs" was issued by Thom McAn as a promotion for its "Jox" tennis shoes, which are advertised on the back of the cards. The discs, which measure 2-3/4" in diameter, feature black-and-white player photos against a background of either gold, yellow, red, pink, green or blue. Although not included in the "official" checklist released by the company, cards of George Brett have also been reported. Many of the Latin players' discs are quite scarce and are believed to have been issued in more limited quantities in Hispanic communities. The discs are unnumbered and checklisted here alphabetically.

		NM/M
Complete Set (47):		50.00
Common Player:		1.00
(1)	Benny Ayala	1.25
(2)	Buddy Bell	1.00
(3)	Juan Beniquez	1.25
(4)	Tony Bernazard	1.25
(5)	Mike Boddicker	1.00
(6)	George Brett	9.00
(7)	Bill Buckner	1.00
(8)	Rod Carew	6.00
(9)	Steve Carlton	6.00
(10)	Caesar Cedeno (Cesar)	1.00
(11)	Onix Concepcion	1.00
(12)	Cecil Cooper	1.00
(13)	Al Cowens	1.00
(14)	Jose Cruz	1.25
(15)	Ivan DeJesus	1.25
(16)	Luis DeLeon	1.25
(17)	Rich Gossage	1.00
(18)	Pedro Guerrero	1.00
(19)	Ron Guidry	1.00
(20)	Tony Gwynn	7.50
(21)	Mike Hargrove	1.00
(22)	Keith Hernandez	1.25
(23)	Bob Horner	1.00
(24)	Kent Hrbek	1.00
(25)	Rick Langford	1.00
(26)	Jeff Leonard	1.00
(27)	Willie McGee	1.00
(28)	Jack Morris	1.00
(29)	Jesse Orosco	1.25
(30)	Junior Ortiz	1.25
(31)	Terry Puhl	1.00
(32)	Dan Quisenberry	1.00
(33)	Johnny Ray	1.00
(34)	Cal Ripken	12.00
(35)	Ed Romero	1.25
(36)	Ryne Sandberg	7.50
(37)	Mike Schmidt	9.00
(38)	Tom Seaver	6.00
(39)	Rick Sutcliffe	1.00
(40)	Bruce Sutter	4.50
(41)	Alan Trammell	1.00
(42)	Fernando Valenzuela	2.00
(43)	Ozzie Virgil	1.25
(44)	Greg Walker	1.00
(45)	Willie Wilson	1.00
(46)	Dave Winfield	6.00
(47)	Geoff Zahn	1.00

1990 McDonald's

This 25-card set was released exclusively at 11 McDonald's restaurants in Idaho and eastern Oregon. Four cards were given with a large fries-soda purchase. Production was reported as 4,000 each. The cards have front borders of graduated purple shades around a game-action photo. Backs are similar in format to regular 1990 Score cards and include a portrait photo. The McDonald's logo appears on front and back. Fifteen World Series trivia cards were part of the promotion.

		NM/M
Complete Set (25):		50.00
Common Player:		1.25
Trivia Card:		.60
1	Will Clark	1.25
2	Sandy Alomar, Jr.	1.25
3	Julio Franco	1.25
4	Carlton Fisk	5.00
5	Rickey Henderson	5.00
6	Matt Williams	1.25
7	John Franco	1.25
8	Ryne Sandberg	6.00
9	Kelly Gruber	1.25
10	Andre Dawson	3.00
11	Barry Bonds	12.00
12	Gary Sheffield	3.00
13	Ramon Martinez	1.25
14	Len Dykstra	1.25
15	Benito Santiago	1.25
16	Cecil Fielder	1.25
17	John Olerud	1.25
18	Roger Clemens	7.50
19	George Brett	10.00
20	George Bell	1.25
21	Ozzie Guillen	1.25
22	Steve Sax	1.25
23	Dave Stewart	1.25
24	Ozzie Smith	6.00
25	Robin Yount	5.00

1991 McDonald's Cleveland Indians

Distributed only at northern Ohio area McDonalds, this set features the players, coaches and manager of the Indians on an oversize (2-7/8" x 4-1/4") format. Color photos on front are framed in white and red with a white border all around. In the upper-left corner is a "Tribe Kids Fan Club" logo, while the McDonald's logo appears at lower-right. The player's uniform number, name and position are in black at lower-left. Backs are printed in black and have complete major and minor league statistics.

		NM/M
Complete Set (30):		5.00
Common Player:		.25
1	John McNamara	.25
2	Alex Cole	.25
4	Joel Skinner	.25
6	Jose Escobar	.25
7	Chris James	.25
8	Albert Belle	.50
9	Carlos Baerga	.25
11	Doug Jones	.25
14	Jerry Browne	.25
15	Sandy Alomar	.25
16	Felix Fermin	.25
20	Turner Ward	.25
21	Greg Swindell	.25
23	Mitch Webster	.25
26	Brook Jacoby	.25
27	Dave Otto	.25
31	Steve Olin	.25
37	Beau Allred	.25
38	Shawn Hillegas	.25
40	Eric King	.25
41	Charles Nagy	.25
44	Mike Huff	.25
45	Jeff Manto	.25
46	Bruce Egloff	.25
47	Jesse Orosco	.25
48	Mike Walker	.25
49	Tom Candiotti	.25
52	John Farrell	.25
54	Rod Nichols	.25
---	Coaches (Billy Williams, Jose Morales, Rich Dauer, Mike Hargrove, Luis Isaac, Mark Wiley)	.25

1992 McDonald's Baseball's Best

Sold in five-card cello packs with a food purchase at McDonald's stores in New York, New Jersey and Connecticut, this 44-card set was produced by Topps and carries the Topps logo, along with the Golden Arches, on front and back. Player photos on front are framed in yellow, surrounded by a black border. A red and blue "Baseball's

Best" logo appears at top-right of the photo. Above that is a gold-foil stripe announcing "Limited Edition." At lower-right is another gold-foil stripe with the McDonald's logo and the player's name embossed thereon. On cards #34-44, which were distributed one per pack, there is an additional gold embossed "Rookie" shield at upper-left. Backs have a red border with a yellow stat box at center framed in white.

		NM/M
Complete Set (44):		6.00
Common Player:		.10
1	Cecil Fielder	.10
2	Benito Santiago	.10
3	Rickey Henderson	.60
4	Roberto Alomar	.20
5	Ryne Sandberg	.75
6	George Brett	1.25
7	Terry Pendleton	.10
8	Ken Griffey Jr.	1.25
9	Bobby Bonilla	.10
10	Roger Clemens	1.00
11	Ozzie Smith	.75
12	Barry Bonds	1.50
13	Cal Ripken, Jr.	1.50
14	Ron Gant	.10
15	Carlton Fisk	.60
16	Steve Avery	.10
17	Robin Yount	.60
18	Will Clark	.10
19	Kirby Puckett	.75
20	Jim Abbott	.10
21	Barry Larkin	.10
22	Jose Canseco	.45
23	Howard Johnson	.10
24	Nolan Ryan	1.50
25	Frank Thomas	.60
26	Danny Tartabull	.10
27	Julio Franco	.10
28	David Justice	.10
29	Joe Carter	.10
30	Dale Murphy	.35
31	Andre Dawson	.25
32	Dwight Gooden	.10
33	Bo Jackson	.20
34	Jeff Bagwell	.60
35	Chuck Knoblauch	.10
36	Derek Bell	.10
37	Jim Thome	.10
38	Royce Clayton	.10
39	Ryan Klesko	.10
40	Chito Martinez	.10
41	Ivan Rodriguez	.50
42	Todd Hundley	.10
43	Eric Karros	.10
44	Todd Van Poppel	.10

Cardinals

Pacific Trading Cards and McDonald's combined in 1992 to produce this 55-card (plus checklist) team set for the benefit of Ronald McDonald Children's Charities on the occasion of the St. Louis Cardinals' 100th anniversary. Sets were sold initially for $1.49. Cards are standard 2-1/2" x 3-1/2" size and UV coated on each side. There is a sepia-toned or color photo on both front and back; generally an action photo on front and a portrait on back. Player selection is largely weighted to the last half of the 20th Century, with only a few cards of players pre-dating the Gashouse Gang era. The front design is completed with a Cardinals anniversary logo in the upper-left corner, a McDonald's logo at lower-right and gold stripes top and bottom. The player's name and position appear in red at the bottom of the photo. Besides the portrait photo, backs have a career summary stats for the player's Cardinals year and major league career and all appropriate logos.

		NM/M
Complete Set (55):		6.00
Common Player:		.10
1	Jim Bottomley	.15
2	Rip Collins	.10
3	Johnny Mize	.25
4	Rogers Hornsby	.25
5	Miller Huggins	.10
6	Marty Marion	.25
7	Frank Frisch	.25
8	Whitey Kurowski	.10
9	Joe Medwick	.10
10	Terry Moore	.10
11	Chick Hafey	.10
12	Pepper Martin	.25
13	Bob O'Farrell	.10
14	Walker Cooper	.10
15	Dizzy Dean	.50
16	Grover Cleveland Alexander	.25
17	Jesse Haines	.10
18	Bill Hallahan	.10
19	Mort Cooper	.10
20	Burleigh Grimes	.10
21	Red Schoendienst	.25
22	Stan Musial	3.00
23	Enos Slaughter	.25
24	Keith Hernandez	.25
25	Bill White	.25
26	Orlando Cepeda	.25
27	Julian Javier	.10
28	Dick Groat	.10
29	Ken Boyer	.20
30	Lou Brock	.50
31	Mike Shannon	.25
32	Curt Flood	.25
33	Joe Cunningham	.10
34	Reggie Smith	.10
35	Ted Simmons	.10
36	Tim McCarver	.25
37	Tom Herr	.10
38	Ozzie Smith	2.00
39	Joe Torre	.45
40	Terry Pendleton	.20
41	Ken Reitz	.10
42	Vince Coleman	.25
43	Willie McGee	.25
44	Bake McBride	.10
45	George Hendrick	.10
46	Bob Gibson	1.00
47	Whitey Herzog	.10
48	Harry Brecheen	.10
49	Howard Pollet	.10
50	John Tudor	.10
51	Bob Forsch	.10
52	Bruce Sutter	.50
53	Lee Smith	.15
54	Todd Worrell	.10
55	Al Hrabosky	.10
---	Checklist	.02

Ken Griffey, Jr. Pin/Cards

This set of three card-pin combinations saw limited distribution in the Northwestern U.S., with sales benefitting the Ronald McDonald Children's Charities. Cards measure 2-1/2" x 3-1/2" and have the same color photo of Ken Griffey, Jr. on the front. Fronts also have a McDonald's logo and facsimile autograph. Uniform logos have been removed from the player's photo. Backs have a description of the charity and the logo "Griffey's Golden Moments," along with a 1992 Alrak Enterprises copyright. The pins were fastened through the cardboard of the card, leaving each with a hole. Prices quoted are for card/pin combinations.

		NM/M
Complete Set (3):		7.50
Common Card/Pin:		2.50
1-3	Ken Griffey Jr.	2.50

MVP

McDonald's restaurants in Ontario released a 26-card All-Star baseball card set in 1992 featuring many of the top players in the game. The cards were sold at Canadian McDonald's in packs of four with the purchase of a meal. Additionally, the company offered a six-card Toronto Blue Jays subset. The cards were produced by Donruss.

		NM/M
Complete Set (33):		8.00
Common Player:		.25
1	Cal Ripken, Jr.	1.50
2	Frank Thomas	.65
3	George Brett	1.00
4	Roberto Kelly	.25
5	Nolan Ryan	1.50
6	Ryne Sandberg	.75
7	Darryl Strawberry	.25
8	Len Dykstra	.25
9	Fred McGriff	.25
10	Roger Clemens	.85
11	Sandy Alomar Jr.	.25
12	Robin Yount	.65
13	Jose Canseco	.45
14	Jimmy Key	.25
15	Barry Larkin	.25
16	Dennis Martinez	.25
17	Andy Van Slyke	.25
18	Will Clark	.25
19	Mark Langston	.25
20	Cecil Fielder	.25
21	Kirby Puckett	.75
22	Ken Griffey Jr.	1.00
23	David Justice	.25
24	Jeff Bagwell	.65
25	Howard Johnson	.25
26	Ozzie Smith	.75
1	Roberto Alomar	.35
2	Joe Carter	.25
3	Kelly Gruber	.25
4	Jack Morris	.25
5	Tom Henke	.25
6	Devon White	.25

WUAB Cleveland Indians

These larger-than-standard (2-7/8" x 4-1/4") cards were given to members of the Tribe Kids Fan Club, sponsored by McDonald's and television station WUAB, whose logos appear on front and back, respectively. Cards have poses or game photos with red frames, white borders and a row of vertical blue diamonds on front. Horizontally formatted backs are in black-and-white with complete career stats. Cards are listed here in order of the uniform numbers which appear on front.

		NM/M
Complete Set (30):		6.00
Common Player:		.25
0	Junior Ortiz	.25
1	Glenallen Hill	.25
2	Alex Cole	.25
4	Bob Skinner	.25
7	Kenny Lofton	.40
8	Albert Belle	.35
9	Carlos Baerga	.25
10	Mark Lewis	.25
11	Paul Sorrento	.25
15	Sandy Alomar Jr.	.25
16	Felix Fermin	.25
20	Tony Perezchica	.25
21	Mike Hargrove	.25
23	Mark Whiten	.25
25	Jim Thome	2.50
26	Brook Jacoby	.25
27	Dave Otto	.25
28	Derek Lilliquist	.25
31	Steve Olin	.25
33	Thomas Howard	.25
36	Brad Arnsberg	.25
39	Dennis Cook	.25
41	Charles Nagy	.25
44	Reggie Jefferson	.25
47	Scott Scudder	.25
48	Ted Power	.25
54	Rod Nichols	.25
63	Eric Bell	.25
77	Jack Armstrong	.25
---	The Coaches (Rick Adair, Ken Bolek, Dom Chiti, Ron Clark, Jose Morales, Dave Nelson, Jeff Newman)	.25

Cy Young

This pair of cards honoring a local hero was issued by McDonald's of Tuscarawas and Coshocton Counties in Ohio. A blue border card shows Young at bat and measures about 3-1/2" x 6". A red-bordered card has a commonly seen pitching pose and is about 3-3/4" x 5-15/16". A banner in front of crossed bats on front has his birth and death dates with a pair of McDonald's logos near the bottom. Backs are identical with biographical and statistical information.

		NM/M
Complete Set (2):		5.00
(1)	Cy Young/Btg	3.00
(2)	Cy Young/Pitching	3.00

1993 McDonald's Blue Jays

This 36-card set was produced by Donruss and distributed by McDonald's of Canada. The set features two distinct styles of cards. The first 26 are "Great Moments" cards which feature team highlights of the 1985-1992 seasons. These cards have gold-foil embossed on front with a team logo/Great Moments seal. Backs have a description of the highlight. Cards #27-35 are individual player cards. They feature full-bleed color action photos on front. Backs have a second photo and recent stats. All cards have the McDonald's and Donruss logos on front. The 36th card in the set is a header card with a checklist on back.

		NM/M
Complete Set (36):		5.00
Common Card:		.15
1	First Title - 1985 (Doyle Alexander)	.15
2	Home Run King - 1986 (Jesse Barfield)	.15
3	Major League Home Run Record - 1987 (Fred McGriff)	.15
4	Opening Bell - 1988 (George Bell)	.35
5	First Cycle - 1989 (Kelly Gruber)	.15
6	Unbelievable Comeback - 1989 (Ernie Whitt)	.15
7	Winners Again - 1989 (Tom Henke)	.15
8	First No-Hitter - 1990 (Dave Stieb)	.15
9	First 20-Gamer (Jack Morris)	.15
10	FANtastic - 1992	.15
11	Sudden Impact - 1992 (Pat Borders, Mark McGwire)	.50
12	The Turning Point - 1992 (Roberto Alomar)	.35
13	On to Atlanta - 1992 (Candy Maldonado)	.15
14	Instant Hero - 1992 (Ed Sprague)	.15
15	Old Friends - 1992 (Cito Gaston, Bobby Cox)	.15
16	The Catch - 1992 (Devon White)	.15
17	Near Triple Play - 1992 (Kelly Gruber, Deion Sanders)	.15
18	Winning Welcome - 1992 (Roberto Alomar)	.35
19	Winning Slide - 1992 (Kelly Gruber)	.15
20	Final Farewell - 1992 (Jimmy Key)	.15
21	Winning RBI - 1992 (Devon White, Candy Maldonado)	.15
22	Clincher - 1992 (Joe Carter)	.35
23	World Champions - 1992	.15
24	Trophy Presentation - 1992 (Cito Gaston, Bobby Brown)	.15
25	MVP - 1992 (Pat Borders)	.15
26	Heroes' Welcome - 1992 (Roberto Alomar)	.35
	PLAYER CARDS	.15
27	John Olerud	.35
28	Roberto Alomar	.40
29	Ed Sprague	.15
30	Dick Schofield	.15
31	Devon White	.15
32	Joe Carter	.15
33	Darrin Jackson	.15
34	Pat Borders	.15
35	Paul Molitor	1.00
36	Checklist	.05

Expos

Top players and manager's from the team's 25 years were featured in a 33-card set produced by Donruss and distributed by Canadian McDonald's outlets. Card fronts feature a full-color borderless photo with the McDonald's and Donruss logos at top. A blue strip at bottom contains the player name and uniform number. At lower-left is an embossed silver-foil 25th anniversary logo. Fronts of the 2-1/2" x 3-1/2" cards are UV coated. Backs are printed in English and French and include a career summary and the player's stats while with the Expos. Appropriate sponsor, team and licensor logos also appear. Autographed cards of Expos manager Felipe Alou were randomly packaged.

		NM/M
Complete Set (33):		12.00
Common Player:		.25
1	Moises Alou	.75
2	Andre Dawson	1.50
3	Delino DeShields	.25
4	Andres Galarraga	.50
5	Marquis Grissom	.50
6	Tim Raines	.50
7	Larry Walker	1.00
8	Tim Wallach	.25
9	Ken Hill	.25
10	Dennis Martinez	.35
11	Jeff Reardon	.25
12	Gary Carter	4.00
13	Dave Cash	.25
14	Warren Cromartie	.25
15	Mack Jones	.25
16	Al Oliver	.35
17	Larry Parrish	.25
18	Rodney Scott	.25
19	Ken Singleton	.25
20	Rusty Staub	.35
21	Ellis Valentine	.25
22	Woody Fryman	.25
23	Charlie Lea	.25
24	Bill Lee	.25
25	Mike G. Marshall	.25
26	Claude Raymond	.25
27	Steve Renko	.25
28	Steve Rogers	.25
29	Bill Stoneman	.25
30	Gene Mauch	.25
31	Felipe Alou	.45
31a	Felipe Alou/Auto.	20.00
32	Buck Rodgers	.25
33	Checklist	.05

1997 McDonald's N.Y. Yankees

Three popular Yankees stars of the 1996 World Championship team are featured in this issue which raised funds for Ronald McDonald House Charities. The 2-1/2" x 3-1/2" cards have color action photos on front with dark blue borders, a facsimile autograph and McDonald's logo. Uniform and cap logos have been removed from the photos. Backs are printed in blue with a cartoon of Ronald McDonald in baseball gear, a few biographical details about the player and some information about the charity.

		NM/M
Complete Set (3):		10.00
Common Player:		4.00
(1)	Dwight Gooden	4.00
(2)	Tino Martinez	4.00
(3)	Andy Pettitte	4.00

1998 McDonald's Arizona Diamondbacks

Marking the team's first year in the National League, this card set was given away to children 14 and under at an August 14 promotional game.

In standard 2-1/2" x 3-1/2" format, the cards feature color portrait photos. Team and sponsor logos are in the left corners, with player identification in a green stripe at bottom. Backs have a desert scene background over which is printed personal data and professional stats. At bottom is a "Diamondbacks' Fact." Cards are listed here according to uniform number appearing on front.

		NM/M
Complete Set (24):		7.50
Common Player:		.50
5	Andy Stankiewicz	.50
6	Andy Fox	.50
9	Matt Williams	.75
10	Tony Batista	.50
11	Buck Showalter	.50
12	Jorge Fabregas	.50
15	Brent Brede	.50
16	Travis Lee	1.00
19	Willie Blair	.50
20	Jeff Suppan	.50
22	Devon White	.50
24	Karim Garcia	.75
25	David Dellucci	.50
26	Damian Miller	.50
30	Gregg Olson	.50
33	Jay Bell	.50
34	Brian Anderson	.50
35	Kelly Stinnett	.50
36	Clint Sodowsky	.50
37	Omar Daal	.50
38	Joel Adamson	.50
40	Andy Benes	.50
43	Yamil Benitez	.50
47	Felix Rodriguez	.50

1999 McDonald's St. Louis Cardinals

A late-season promotion at McDonald's restaurants in the St. Louis area offered six-card packs of Upper Deck Cardinal cards at $2.49, or $1.99 with a purchase. Cards are in the basic style of UD's 1999 MVP issue, but lack the silver-foil highlights on front. Backs are also nearly identical, but include a McDonald's logo at bottom-right. Both front and back photos on the McDonald's cards differ from those used on UD MVP. Each foil pack contains four of the 15 player cards, plus two of the special Mark McGwire Milestone inserts. Checklist cards are a one-in-nine pack insert.

		NM/M
Complete Set (16):		4.00
Common Player:		.15
1	J.D. Drew	1.00
2	Jose Jiminez	.15
3	Mark McGwire	1.50
4	Fernando Tatis	.15
5	Edgar Renteria	.15
6	Ray Lankford	.15
7	Willie McGee	.15
8	Ricky Bottalico	.15
9	Eli Marrero	.15
10	Kent Bottenfield	.15
11	Eric Davis	.15
12	Darren Bragg	.15
13	Joe McEwing	.15
14	Shawon Dunston	.15
15	Darren Oliver	.15
---	Checklist	.05

1999 McDonald's Mark McGwire Milestones

A late-season promotion at McDonald's restaurants in the St. Louis area offered six-

card packs of Upper Deck Cardinal cards at $2.49, or $1.99 with a purchase. Each foil pack contains four of the 15 player cards, plus two special Mark McGwire Milestone inserts. Horizontally formatted, the Milestones inserts have an action photo of McGwire on a silver metallic-foil background with red, blue and black high-tech graphic designs. The cards mark one of McGwire important home runs of 1998. Backs have a portrait photo and recount some of his career highlights. A McDonald's logo appears in the lower-right corner.

		NM/M
Complete Set (9):		7.00
Common Card:		1.00
M1	Mark McGwire (#50)	1.00
M2	Mark McGwire (#60)	1.00
M3	Mark McGwire (#61)	1.00
M4	Mark McGwire (#62)	1.50
M5	Mark McGwire (#63)	1.00
M6	Mark McGwire (#67)	1.00
M7	Mark McGwire (#68)	1.00
M8	Mark McGwire (#69)	1.00
M9	Mark McGwire (#70)	1.50

2000 McDonald's Negro League Baseball

A set of 10 cards of former Negro Leagues ballplayers was issued by McDonald's in Milwaukee. The 2-1/2" x 3-1/2" cards have black-and-white oval photos at center, bordered in blue. A color logo reading "Yesterday's / Negro League Baseball / Players Wall of Fame" appears at top. A red starburst has the card number at upper-right. Below the photo are the McDonald's logo, the player's name and the years he was active in the Negro League. The red-on-white backs have biographical and career information and stats. Cards originally sold in one-card packs for 99 cents, or the set of 10 for about $9.

		NM/M
Complete Set (10):		20.00
Common Player:		2.00
1	William "Bobby" Robinson	2.00
2	Mamie "Peanut" Johnson	2.00
3	Carl Long	2.00
4	John "Mule" Miles	2.00
5	Sherwood Brewer	2.00
6	Ira McKnight	2.00
7	Gordon Hopkins	2.00
8	Johnny Washington	2.00
9	Jim Robinson	2.00
10	Dennis "Bose" Biddle	2.00

St. Louis Cardinals Coin/Cards

At a series of promotional games during the season, the Cardinals distributed these

coin/cards. Wrapped in cellophone was a 2-1/2" x 4" card and a 39mm (about 1-1/2") bronze medallion. The card was horizontally perforated so it could be seperated into a 2-1/2" x 2" player card and two 2-1/2" x 1" coupons. The player card has a game action photo on front. On back is the player name and career highlights. The coupons are for $1 off a McDonald's meal and for a free soft drink at Shell gas stations. Coins have the team logo on front, a player image roughly the same as pictured on the card, and the player uniform number. Back of the coin has the team and sponsor logos and the date the coin was distributed.

		NM/M
Complete Set (4):		20.00
Common Player:		4.00
1	Willie McGee (May 13)	4.00
2	Fernando Vina (June 24)	4.00
3	Jim Edmonds (July 9)	6.00
4	Mark McGwire (Sept. 3)	8.00

2003 McDonald's N.Y. Yankees

Beginning July 28, and extending until 8.75 million cards were given away, these Upper Deck-produced cards were available at 600+ McDonald's in the metro New York area with the purchase of a special Yankees-themed Happy Meal. Cards were issued in either singly in a cello pack, or in a pack with a scratch-off game card. Fronts have an action photo with a large ghost-image team logo behind. Also on front are the Yankee's 100th anniversary logo and logos of UD and McDonald's. Backs have another player photo, stats, personal data and the logos.

		NM/M
Complete Set (24):		8.00
Common Player:		.25
1	Juan Acevedo	.25
2	Roger Clemens	1.50
3	John Flaherty	.25
4	Jason Giambi	.50
5	Chris Hammond	.25
6	Sterling Hitchcock	.25
7	Derek Jeter	2.50
8	Nick Johnson	.25
9	Steve Karsay	.25
10	Hideki Matsui	1.50
11	Raul Mondesi	.25
12	Mike Mussina	.35
13	Antonio Osuna	.25
14	Andy Petitte	.35
15	Jorge Posada	.35
16	Mariano Rivera	.35
17	Alfonso Soriano	.50
18	Bubba Trammell	.25
19	Robin Ventura	.25
20	Jeff Weaver	.25
21	David Wells	.25
22	Bernie Williams	.35
23	Enrique Wilson	.25
24	Todd Zeile	.25

2004 McDonald's Philadelphia Phillies

A two-card pack was given away with each Extra Value Meal purchase at Philly area McDonald's in July. Production of 170,000 of each card was reported. Upper Deck created the cards for the promotion.

		NM/M
Complete Set (27):		6.00
Common Player:		.50
1	Jim Thome	1.00
2	Placido Polanco	.50
3	Jimmy Rollins	1.00
4	David Bell	.50
5	Bobby Abreu	.50
6	Pat Burrell	1.00
7	Marlon Byrd	.50
8	Mike Lieberthal	.75
9	Kevin Millwood	.50
10	Randy Wolf	.50
11	Vicente Padilla	.50
12	Eric Milton	.50
13	Brett Myers	.50
14	Billy Wagner	.50
15	Tim Worrell	.50
16	Rheal Cormier	.50
17	Roberto Hernandez	.50
18	Ryan Madson	.50
19	Amaury Telemaco	.50
20	Tomas Perez	.50
21	Shawn Wooten	.50
22	Doug Glanville	.50
23	Ricky Ledee	.50
24	Jason Michaels	.50
25	Todd Pratt	.50
26	Larry Bowa	.50
27	Citizens Bank Park/Checklist	.50

1992 MCI Ambassadors

Issued in conjunction with the MCI-sponsored Ambassadors of Baseball World Tour of overseas military bases, this set features retired players who participated in the tour. Cards feature color photos with a white border, a color tour logo in the lower-left and a banner across the upper-left reading, "Support MWR With MCI." The player's name and position appear in the bottom border. Horizontally oriented backs have career stats and highlights and the logos of MCI and the Major League Baseball Players Alumni in black-and-white.

		NM/M
Complete Set (16):		35.00
Common Player:		2.00
1	Earl Weaver	3.00
2	Steve Garvey	6.00
3	Doug Flynn	2.00
4	Bert Campaneris	2.00
5	Bill Madlock	2.00
6	Graig Nettles	2.00
7	Dave Kingman	3.00
8	Paul Blair	2.00
9	Jeff Burroughs	2.00
10	Rick Waits	2.00
11	Elias Sosa	2.00
12	Tug McGraw	2.00
13	Ferguson Jenkins (Photo)	4.00
14	Bob Feller	6.00
---	Ferguson Jenkins (Art)	4.00
---	Header Card	.50

1993 MCI Ambassadors

The Major League Baseball Players Alumni Association produced a set of 13 former players who were featured in 1993's MCI Ambassadors of Baseball World Tour. The card set was available free to military personnel who completed an MCI application. The tour of military bases worldwide included appearances by the players at base exchanges, clinics for dependent children and a softball game against base all-stars. The cards feature a photo of the player on the front with logos from the Ambassador tour and MCI in opposite corners.

		NM/M
Complete Set (14):		20.00
Common Player:		1.25
1	Vida Blue	1.25
2	Paul Blair	1.25
3	Mudcat Grant	1.25
4	Phil Niekro	2.00
5	Bob Feller	3.00
6	Joe Charboneau	2.00
7	Joe Rudi	1.25
8	Catfish Hunter	2.00
9	Manny Sanguillen	1.25
10	Harmon Killebrew	3.00
11	Al Oliver	1.25
12	Bob Dernier	1.25
13	Graig Nettles, Sparky Lyle	1.75
---	Header Card	.10

1994 MCI Ambassadors

Once again in 1994, the old-timers' tour of overseas military bases sponsored by MCI spawned a card set. The '94 set is similar to previous years' issues except that color player photos have had the uniform logos airbrushed away. MCI and tour logos appear in color on the front; backs are in black-and-white and contain career data and highlights along with MCI and Major League Baseball Players Alumni logos. Besides 11 numbered cards, there are four unnumbered cards in the 1994 set which include a pair honoring major leaguers who served in the military during World War II.

		NM/M
Complete Set (15):		30.00
Common Player:		2.00
1	Sparky Lyle	2.00
2	John Stearns	2.00
3	Bobby Thomson	3.00
4	Jimmy Wynn	2.00
5	Ferguson Jenkins	4.00
6	Tug McGraw	2.00
7	Paul Blair	2.00
8	Ron LeFlore	2.00
9	Manny Sanguillen	2.00
10	Doug Flynn	2.00
11	Bill North	2.00
----	Manny Sanguillen (Signing autographs.)	2.00
----	Doug Flynn (Instructing children.)	2.00
----	American Leaguers in WWII	2.00
----	National Leaguers in WWII	2.00

1995 MCI Ambassadors

For a fourth year, Major League Baseball, the Players' Union and the long distance phone provider issued a card set in conjunction with its series of softball games at military bases. Approximately 2,000 sets were issued. The 2-1/2" x 3-1/2" cards have player photos on front with MCI and the baseball tour logos in opposite corners. Backs have biographical and career information about the retired stars.

		NM/M
Complete Set (16):		30.00
Common Player:		2.00
1	Vida Blue	2.00
2	Bert Campaneris	2.00
3	Tug McGraw	2.00
4	Doug Flynn	2.00
5	Paul Blair	2.00
6	Harmon Killebrew	5.00
7	Sparky Lyle	2.00
8	Steve Garvey	4.00
9	Bert Blyleven	2.00
10	Omar Moreno	2.00
11	Bill Lee	2.00
12	Maury Wills	2.00
13	Dave Parker	2.00
14	Luis Aparicio	5.00
15	Brooks Robinson	5.00
16	George Foster	2.00

1996 MCI Ambassadors

This set of former players cards was issued in conjunction with a tour of overseas U.S. military bases by members of the Major League Baseball Players Alumni Association. Players taking part in the tour are featured on the card fronts in photos contemporary with their major league days. Backs have career summaries and stats along with sponsors logos. The cards were virtually all distributed overseas.

		NM/M
Complete Set (8):		30.00
Common Player:		5.00
(1)	Tommy Davis	6.00
(2)	Darrell Evans	6.00
(3)	Jay Howell	5.00
(4)	John Montefusco	5.00
(5)	Graig Nettles	6.00
(6)	Jim Sundberg	5.00
(7)	Header card	.50
(8)	American Airlines Sponsor Card	.50

1991 MDA All-Stars

Though the Muscular Dystrophy Association isn't mentioned on the player cards, it was the beneficiary of this set produced by SmithKline Beecham. Card fronts feature color photos of the players during their active careers. Because the set was not licensed by MLB, team uniform logos have been airbrushed off the photos. Black-and-white backs have a recent portrait photo of the player, along with biographical and career data. The set was available by mail for $3.99 plus proofs of purchase from Tums antacid.

		NM/M
Complete Set (20):		15.00
Common Player:		.50
1	Steve Carlton	1.00
2	Ted Simmons	.50
3	Willie Stargell	1.00
4	Bill Mazeroski	1.00
5	Ron Santo	.75
6	Dave Concepcion	.50
7	Bobby Bonds	.50
8	George Foster	.50
9	Billy Williams	1.00
10	Whitey Ford	2.00
11	Yogi Berra	2.00
12	Boog Powell	.60
13	Davey Johnson	.50
14	Brooks Robinson	1.00
15	Jim Fregosi	.50
16	Harmon Killebrew	1.00
17	Ted Williams	3.00
18	Al Kaline	1.00
---	MDA Fact Card (Brooks Robinson)	.50
---	Header Card	.25

1992 MVP for MDA

The Muscular Dystrophy Association was the beneficiary of this set sponsored by SmithKline Beecham. Card fronts feature color photos of the players during their active careers. Because the set was not licensed by MLB, team uniform logos have been airbrushed off the photos. Black-and-white backs have a portrait photo of the player, along with biographical and career data. A vinyl album to house the set was included in the mail-in offer.

		NM/M
Complete Set (20):		9.00
Common Player:		1.00
Album:		4.50
1	Yogi Berra	2.00
2	Dick Groat	1.00
3	Maury Wills	1.00
4	Brooks Robinson	1.50
5	Orlando Cepeda	1.50
6	Harmon Killebrew	1.50
7	Boog Powell	1.00
8	Vida Blue	1.00
9	Jeff Burroughs	1.00
10	George Foster	1.00
11	Rod Carew	1.50
12	Jim Rice	1.00
13	Don Baylor	1.00
14	Willie Stargell	1.50
15	Rollie Fingers	1.00
16	Ray Knight	1.00
17	History of the MVP	.25
18	MVP Trivia	.25
19	Harmon Killebrew (W/1992 MDA Poster Child.)	1.00
20	MLB Players Assn. Alumni Info	.25

1986 Meadow Gold Blank Backs

This was the second set to be distributed by Meadow Gold Dairy (Beatrice Foods) in 1986. It was issued on Double Play ice cream cartons, one card per package. Full-color player photos have team logos and insignias airbrushed away. This 16-card set is very similar to the Meadow Gold popsicle set, but the photos are different in some instances. The cards measure 2-3/8" x 3-1/2". The Willie McGee card is reportedly tougher to find than other cards in the set.

		NM/M
Complete Singles Set (16):		20.00
Complete Carton Set (16):		22.50
Common Player:		.75
(1)	George Brett	2.50
(2)	Wade Boggs	2.00
(3)	Carlton Fisk	1.50
(4)	Steve Garvey	1.00
(5)	Dwight Gooden	.75
(6)	Pedro Guerrero	.75
(7)	Reggie Jackson	2.50
(8)	Don Mattingly	2.50
(9)	Willie McGee	.75
(10)	Dale Murphy	1.00
(11)	Cal Ripken, Jr.	3.00
(12)	Pete Rose	3.00
(13)	Ryne Sandberg	2.00
(14)	Mike Schmidt	2.50
(15)	Fernando Valenzuela	.75
(16)	Dave Winfield	1.50

Statistic Backs

Beatrice Foods produced this set of 20 cards on specially marked boxes of Meadow Gold Double Play popsicles, fudgesicles and bubble gum coolers. They came in two-card panels and have full-color player pictures with player name, team and position printed below the photo. Card backs are printed in red ink and feature player career highlights. The cards measure 2-3/8" x 3-1/2" and were distributed in the West and Midwest. It is considered one of the toughest 1986 regional sets to complete.

		NM/M
Complete Panel Set (10):		10.00
Complete Singles Set (20):		10.00
Common Panel:		1.00
Common Single:		.30
	PANEL 1	2.00
1	George Brett	1.50
2	Fernando Valenzuela	.30
	PANEL 2	1.00
3	Dwight Gooden	.30
4	Dale Murphy	.75
	PANEL 3	3.50
5	Don Mattingly	1.50
6	Reggie Jackson	1.50
	PANEL 4	3.00
7	Dave Winfield	1.00
8	Pete Rose	2.00
	PANEL 5	1.50
9	Wade Boggs	1.25
10	Willie McGee	.30
	PANEL 6	5.00
11	Cal Ripkin (Ripken)	3.00
12	Ryne Sandberg	1.25
	PANEL 7	1.50
13	Carlton Fisk	1.00
14	Jim Rice	.50
	PANEL 8	2.50
15	Steve Garvey	.50
16	Mike Schmidt	1.50
	PANEL 9	1.00
17	Bruce Sutter	.75
18	Pedro Guerrero	.30
	PANEL 10	1.00
19	Rick Sutcliff (Sutcliffe)	.30
20	Rich Gossage	.30

Milk

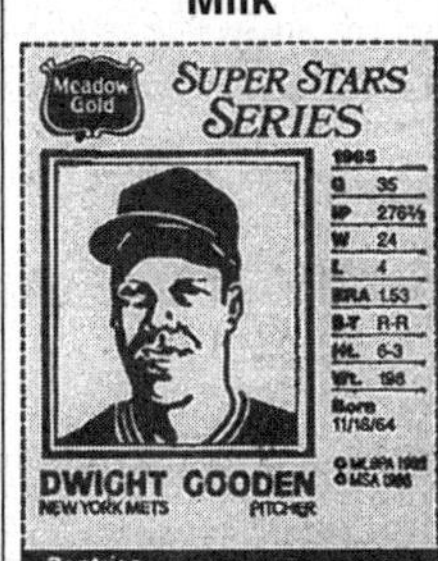

The third set from Meadow Gold from 1986 came on milk cartons; on pint, quart and half-gallon size containers. The cards measure 2-1/2" x 3-1/2" and feature drawings instead of photographs. Different dairies distributed the cards in various colors of ink. The cards can be found printed in red, brown or black ink. The crude drawings have prevented this rare set from being higher in price.

		NM/M
Complete Set (11):		75.00
Common Player:		3.50
(1)	Wade Boggs	9.00
(2)	George Brett	12.00
(3)	Steve Carlton	7.50
(4)	Dwight Gooden	3.50
(5)	Willie McGee	3.50
(6)	Dale Murphy	6.00
(7)	Cal Ripken, Jr.	17.50
(8)	Pete Rose	15.00
(9)	Ryne Sandberg	9.00
(10)	Mike Schmidt	12.00
(11)	Fernando Valenzuela	3.50

1992 Megacards Babe Ruth Prototypes

Basically identical to the regularly issued versions, these sample cards were distributed to hobby dealers to introduce Megacards Babe Ruth Collection. Most of the prototypes have different card numbers than those in the regular set, and all carry a large gray diagonal "PROTOTYPE" on back.

		NM/M
Complete Set (9):		7.50
Common Card:		1.00
14	Year in Review - 1921 (Babe Ruth)	1.00
31	World Series - 1916 (Babe Ruth)	1.00
75	Place in History - 1928 (Babe Ruth)	1.00
106	Career Highlights - 1927 (Babe Ruth)	1.00
124	Trivia - 1926 (Babe Ruth)	1.00
129	Sultan of Swat - 1925 (Babe Ruth)	1.00
134	Being Remembered - 1948 - George Bush (Babe Ruth)	1.00
138	Being Remembered - 1923 - Grantland Rice (Babe Ruth)	1.00
154	The Bambino - The Man (Babe Ruth, Lou Gehrig)	1.25

1992 Megacards Babe Ruth

This 165-card set chronicles the life and times of Babe Ruth. The set was produced by Megacards and is officially entitled "The Babe Ruth Collection." The cards feature classic black and white photos with black borders and captions below the photo. The card backs feature coordinating statistics and information.

		NM/M
Complete Set (165):		15.00
Complete Set, Tin:		20.00
Common Card:		.10
Wax Box (48):		20.00
1	Lifetime Pitching Statistics	.10
2	Lifetime Batting Statistics	.10
3	Lifetime - World Series Pitching	.10
4	Lifetime World Series Batting	.10
5	22-9 Record in the Minors	.10
6	2-1 Record First Year in the Majors	.10
7	Won 17 of his Last 21 Decisions	.10
8	Led League with 1.75 ERA and 9 Shutouts	.10
9	Defeats Walter Johnson for 6th Time	.10
10	Doubles as Pitcher and a Regular	.10
11	First Season in the Outfield	.10
12	Sold to Yankees for $100,000	.10
13	The Best Year Any Batter Ever Had	.10
14	Suspended for First 38 Games	.10
15	Wins American League MVP	.10
16	Wins Only Batting Title - .378	.10
17	The "Million Dollar Stomachache"	.10
18	Bats .372 with a .737 Slugging Average	.10
19	The Best Baseball Team in History	.20
20	Tops 50 Home Runs - 4th Time	.10
21	Clubs 500th Home Run	.10
22	Bam Bams Nine in a Week	.10
23	.700 Slugging Average for 9th Time	.10
24	Blasts Over 40 Homers for 11th Time	.10
25	Over 100 RBIs for 13th Time	.10
26	Tops 2,000 Career Walks	.10
27	Babe Retires	.10
28	Babe Coaches the Dodgers	.10
29	The Babe in Retirement	.10
30	1915 World Series - Warms Bench	.10
31	1916 World Series - Hurls 14-Inning Win	.10
32	1918 World Series - Scoreless Innings	.10
33	1921 World Series - Yankees' First	.10
34	1922 World Series - Back to the Farm	.10
35	1923 World Series - First Championship	.10
36	1926 World Series - 4 HR in Losing Cause	.15
37	1927 World Series - Destroy Bucs in Four	.15
38	1928 World Series - .625 BA and 1.375 SA	.10
39	1932 World Series - Yanks Sweep Cubs	.15
40	Lifetime - 2,056 Walks	.10
41	First to Fan 1,000 Times	.10
42	Lifetime - 2,174 Runs Scored	.15
43	Lifetime - 5,793 Total Bases	.15
44	Lifetime - 1,356 Extra-Base Hits	.10
45	Lifetime - 714 Home Runs	.10
46	Lifetime - 16 Grand Slams	.10
47	Lifetime - 8.5 Home Run Percentage	.15
48	Lifetime - Most Games, 2 or More HR	.10
49	Lifetime - 11 Seasons with 40+ HRs	.10
50	Lifetime - 2,211 RBIs	.15
51	Lifetime - .342 Batting Average	.15
52	Lifetime - .690 Slugging Average	.15
53	Season - Nine Shutouts	.10
54	Season - 170 Walks	.10
55	Season - 177 Runs Scored	.20
56	Season - .545 On-Base Percentage	.10
57	Season - 457 Total Bases	.15
58	Season - 119 Extra-Base Hits	.15
59	Season - 171 Runs Batted In	.15
60	Season - 60 Home Runs	.10
61	Season - 11.8 Home Run Percentage	.10
62	Season - .847 Slugging Average	.15
63	World Series 3-0 Record	.10
64	World Series - 0.87 ERA	.10
65	World Series - 33 Walks	.10
66	World Series - 37 Runs	.10
67	World Series - 96 Total Bases	.10
68	World Series - 15 Home Runs	.10
69	World Series - 33 RBIs	.10
70	World Series - .744 Slugging Average	.20
71	1914 - First Major League Victory	.10
72	1915 - First Major League Home Run	.10
73	1916 - Babe Derails "Big Train"	.10
74	1919 - Leads League in Fielding	.10
75	1919 First Home Run Record	.10
76	1920 - Babe Becomes a Yankee	.10
77	1923 - First Home Run in Yankee Stadium	.10
78	1923 - American League MVP	.10
79	1924 - Wins Only Batting Title	.15
80	1926 - Hits 3 Home Runs in Series Game	.10
81	1927 - Babe and Lou Smack 107 Home Runs (Lou Gehrig)	.20
82	1927 - The Babe's 60th Home Run	.20
83	1928 - Three HR in World Series Game	.10
84	1932 - Early "Called Shots" by the Bam	.10
85	1932 - The "Called Shot" - The Legend	.10
86	1932 - The "Called Shot" - The Believers	.10
87	1932 - The "Called Shot" - The Doubters	.10
88	1932 - The "Called Shot" - Babe's View	.10
89	1933 - First HR in an All-Star Game	.15
90	1933 - Last Time on the Mound	.10
91	1934 - Babe Hits 700th Home Run	.10
92	1934 - The Babe in Japan	.10
93	1935 - Last Major League Homers	.10
94	1939 - Inaugurated into Hall of Fame	.10
95	1942 - Faces Johnson Again in Exhibition	.10
96	1947 - Babe Ruth Day	.10
97	1948 - Babe's Farewell	.25
98	A Perfect Punch	.10
99	Yankees Best Base Thief	.10
100	Hub Pruett: Babe Buster	.10
101	Babe Caught Stealing, Ends 1926 Series	.10
102	Never Won a Triple Crown	.10
103	Babe Used a 54-Ounce Bat	.10
104	Babe Bats Righty	.10
105	Babe's Greatness	.10
106	The Babe's Best	.10
107	Outslugged Entire Teams	.10
108	First to Hit 30, 40, 50 and 60 Home Runs	.10
109	The Pitkin Study	.10
110	First to Put the Ball Into Orbit	.10
111	Afraid to Kill Somebody	.10
112	The Wonder Years: 1926-31	.10
113	Hit .422 With 7 Homers on Opening Days	.10
114	Babe at Bat	.10
115	"Greatest Ballplayer the Game Has Known"	.10
116	The Babe's Early Childhood	.10
117	St. Mary's Industrial School	.10
118	Babe and Brother Matthias	.10
119	The Babe's Nicknames	.10
120	Babe's First Wife, Helen	.10
121	Babe's Second Wife, Claire	.10
122	Lou Gehrig Appreciation Day	.20
123	Babe's Friendship With Herb Pennock	.10
124	The Babe and Miller Huggins	.10
125	The Babe and Ty Cobb	.15
126	Babe and Walter Johnson	.15
127	Baseball's Biggest Drawing Card	.10
128	Babe's Barnstorming	.10
129	Costly Confrontation	.10
130	He Often Played Hurt	.10
131	Babe's Big Bucks	.10
132	Want to be a Manager	.10
133	The Babe on the Links	.10
134	Babe in the Movies	.10
135	Babe Contributes to War Effort	.10
136	The Babe - Peace Negotiator	.10
137	Everyone Loved the Babe	.10
138	He Brought Children Joy	.10
139	He Always Had Time for Kids	.10
140	The Johnny Sylvester Story	.10
141	Moving with the Great	.10
142	Babe Ruth and the American Dream	.10
143	Being Remembered - Bill James	.10
144	Being Remembered - Bill James	.10
145	Being Remembered - Bill James	.10
146	Being Remembered - Mel Allen	.10
147	Being Remembered - Mel Allen	.10
148	Being Remembered - Wes Ferrell	.10
149	Being Remembered - George Bush	.50
150	Being Remembered - Ethan Allen	.20

151 Being Remembered - Daughter Dorothy .10
152 Being Remembered - Daughter Julia .10
153 Being Remembered - Daughter Julia .10
154 Being Remembered - Mark Koenig .10
155 Being Remembered - Donald Honig .10
156 Being Remembered - L. Waner, Waite Hoyt .10
157 Being Remembered - Waite Hoyt .10
158 Being Remembered - Bill Dickey .10
159 Being Remembered - Bob Meusel .10
160 Being Remembered - Jim Chapman .10
161 Being Remembered - Christy Walsh .10
162 Being Remembered - The Babe Passes Away .10
163 Being Remembered - Grantland Rice .10
164 Checklist 1-83 .10
165 Checklist 84-165 .10

1995 Megacards Ken Griffey, Jr. MegaCaps

Three different "MegaCaps" picturing Ken Griffey, Jr., were prepared for insertion into blister packs containing full sets of the Ken Griffey, Jr., Wish List Collection. Each of the 1-5/8" diameter cardboard discs has a color photo of Junior on front. Backs have trademark information. Reported print run for each of the three versions was 34,000.

NM/M
Complete Set: 1.50
Common Cap: .50
.50
1-3 Ken Griffey Jr. .50

Ken Griffey, Jr. Wish List

Sold only as a complete set in a clam-shell plastic blister pack, this set has two areas of focus. The first 14 cards details Griffey's hopes for his baseball career and his life; the second 11 cards feature projections on Junior's possible career stats based on numbers generated by baseball statstician Bill James. Each card has a different action photo of Griffey on the front. Backs have a smaller version of the front photo in the upper-right corner, and a muted background photo of Griffey at bat. Card fronts are gold-foil enhanced. Packed with each set was one of three "Mega-Caps" with Griffey's picture. With a reported print run of 100,000 sets, the issue sold for about $10 retail, with part of the purchase price going to the Make a Wish Foundation for seriously ill children.

NM/M
Complete Set (27): 7.50
Common Card: .50
1 Introduction (Ken Griffey Jr.) .50
2 Make-A-Wish Foundation (Ken Griffey Jr.) .50
3 To Make Dreams Come True (Ken Griffey Jr.) .50
4 To Play With Dad (Ken Griffey Jr. (W/Ken Griffey, Sr.)) .50
5 "The Best I Can Be" (Ken Griffey Jr.) .50
6 To Make the Majors (Ken Griffey Jr.) .50
7 To Play for a Winner (Ken Griffey Jr.) .50
8 To Assist B.A.T. (Ken Griffey Jr.) .50
9 To Enrich Inner-City Baseball (Ken Griffey Jr.) .50
10 A Lot to Live For (Ken Griffey Jr.) .50
11 To Be an All-Around Player (Ken Griffey Jr.) .50
12 To Be #1 in the Draft (Ken Griffey Jr.) .50
13 To Win the Gold (Ken Griffey Jr.) .50
14 Most Home Runs by Father/Son (Ken Griffey Jr. (W/Ken Griffey, Sr.)) .50
15 The Field of Possibilities (Ken Griffey Jr.) .50
16 The Griffey Forecast (Ken Griffey Jr.) .50
17 3,598 Career Games (Ken Griffey Jr.) .50
18 2,361 Career Runs (Ken Griffey Jr.) .50
19 3,947 Career Hits (Ken Griffey Jr.) .50
20 777 Career Doubles (Ken Griffey Jr.) .50
21 699 Career Home Runs (Ken Griffey Jr.) .50
22 2,234 Career RBIs (Ken Griffey Jr.) .50
24 1,541 Career Extra Base Hits (Ken Griffey Jr.) .50
24 40 or More Home Runs 5 Times (Ken Griffey Jr.) .50
25 28 Career Grand Slams (Ken Griffey Jr.) .50
--- Contest card .05
--- Merchandise Order Card .05

Babe Ruth 100th Anniversary

Marking the centennial of Babe Ruth's birth, Megacards issued this 25-card set chronicling the life and career of baseball's all-time greatest player. Most of the cards feature on front black-and-white photos of Ruth, although there are several colorized pictures scattered through the set. Fronts have gold-foil frames, captions and Ruth Centennial logo. Reverses have a background photo of Ruth's classic swing and a detailed vignette pertinent to the card's theme. The Babe Ruth 100th Anniversary Collection set was sold in a plastic clamshell package containing one of three Babe Ruth "Megacaps." The edition was limited to 100,000 sets.

NM/M
Complete Set (27): 5.00
Common Card: .25
1 Baseball's Greatest Ever? (Babe Ruth) .25
2 60 Home Run Club (Babe Ruth) .25
3 No Slugger Comes Close (Babe Ruth (With Jimmie Foxx, Lou Gehrig, Al Simmons.)) .25
4 History's Most Frequent Home Run Threat (Babe Ruth) .25
5 He Knew the Way Home (Babe Ruth) .25
6 He Didn't Leave Them Stranded (Babe Ruth (With Lou Gehrig.)) .25
7 50 Home Run King (Babe Ruth) .25
8 Long Ball Legend (Babe Ruth) .25
9 .342 Plus Power (Babe Ruth (With Lloyd Waner, Paul Waner, Lou Gehrig.)) .25
10 No One Hit 'Em More Often (Babe Ruth) .25
11 Greatest Pitching Prospect (Babe Ruth (Colorized, Red Sox pitcher.)) .25
12 Career Year (Babe Ruth (Colorized, fishing with Lou Gehrig.)) .25
13 Mr. Yankee (Babe Ruth (With Lou Gehrig; Don Mattingly superimposed.)) .50
14 Babe and "The Kid" (Babe Ruth (Ken Griffey, Jr., superimposed)) .50
15 Everyone Loved the Babe (Babe Ruth) .25
16 The Babe Played Hurt (Babe Ruth) .25
17 He Did It His Way (Babe Ruth) .25
18 The Rewards of Greatness (Babe Ruth) .25
19 Babe and Today's Rules (Babe Ruth) .25
20 Babe in Today's Ballparks (Babe Ruth) .25
21 Babe and Today's Best (Babe Ruth (Colorized, Ken Griffey Jr. superimposed.)) .75
22 Babe vs. Today's Pitching (Babe Ruth) .25
23 The Babe and Father Time (Babe Ruth) .25
24 How He Changed the Game (Babe Ruth (Colorized, with Dizzy Dean, Frank Frisch, Mickey Cochrane, Schoolboy Rowe.)) .25
25 Will There Be Another Babe? (Babe Ruth) .25
--- Sweepstakes Card .05
--- Babe Ruth Merchandise Order Card .05

Babe Ruth MegaCaps

One of three different 1-5/8" "MegaCaps" picturing Babe Ruth was packaged in each set of Babe Ruth 100th Anniversary Collection cards. The discs feature a photo of Ruth on front and trademark information on the back. Each cap was produced in an edition of 34,000.

NM/M
Complete Set (3): 1.50
Common Cap: .50
1-3 Babe Ruth .50

1994 Mellon Bank Phillies

This set sponsored by "The Official Bank of the Phillies" was issued in the form of a perforated fold-out, with individual cards in the standard 2-1/2" x 3-1/2" size. One panel is a 12-1/2" x 7" team photo. Fronts have game-action photos with a border of red pinstripes on white. The team name is in a box at top, the player name is in a banner at bottom. On back are personal data, stats and career highlights, along with the logos of the team, the sponsor and MLB's 125th Anniversary.

NM/M
Foldout: 12.00
Complete Set, Singles (26): 8.00
Common Player: .50
(1) Larry Anderson .50
(2) Kim Batiste .50
(3) Shawn Boskie .50
(4) Darren Daulton .75
(5) Mariano Duncan .50
(6) Lenny Dykstra .75
(7) Jim Eisenreich .50
(8) Tommy Greene .50
(9) Dave Hollins .50
(10) Pete Incaviglia .50
(11) Danny Jackson .50
(12) Doug Jones .50
(13) Ricky Jordan .50
(14) John Kruk .75
(15) Tony Longmire .50
(16) Mickey Morandini .50
(17) Bobby Munoz .50
(18) Todd Pratt .50
(19) Paul Quantrill, Billy Hatcher .50
(20) Curt Schilling 1.50
(21) Heathcliff Slocumb .50
(22) Kevin Stocker .50
(23) Milt Thompson .50
(24) David West .50
(25) Mike Williams .50
(26) Team photo 2.00

1995 Mellon Bank Phillies

This set was issued in the form of a perforated fold-out, with individual cards in the standard 2-1/2" x 3-1/2" size. Fronts have game-action photos with a border of red pinstripes on white. The team name is in a box at top, the player name is in a banner at bottom. On back are personal data and stats, along with the logos of the team, the sponsor and the Phillies "Silver Season." The unnumbered cards are checklisted here alphabetically.

NM/M
Foldout: 10.00
Complete Set, Singles (25): 8.00
Common Player: .50
(1) Kyle Abbott .50
(2) Toby Borland .50
(3) Ricky Bottalico .50
(4) Norm Charlton .50
(5) Darren Daulton .75
(6) Mariano Duncan .50
(7) Lenny Dykstra .75
(8) Jim Eisenreich .50
(9) Dave Gallagher .50
(10) Tyler Green .50
(11) Gene Harris .50
(12) Charlie Hayes .50
(13) Dave Hollins .50
(14) Gregg Jefferies .50
(15) Tony Longmire .50
(16) Michael Mimbs .50
(17) Mickey Morandini .50
(18) Paul Quantrill .50
(19) Randy Ready .50
(20) Curt Schilling 1.50
(21) Heathcliff Slocumb .50
(22) Kevin Stocker .50
(23) Gary Varsho .50
(24) Lenny Webster .50
(25) David West .50

2003 Merrick Mint Laser Line Gold Cards

These 2-1/2" x 3-1/2" cards are produced from 23-K gold foil in an intaglio printing process which gives them an engraved look and feel. Because the set is licensed only by the Player's Association, and not MLB, team logos and nicknames are not shown. Fronts have a portrait photo and facsimile autograph. Backs have information on the production process. The unnumbered cards are checklisted here alphabetically. Cards were issued in an acrylic case at an original price of about $15.

NM/M
Complete Set (17): 75.00
Common Player: 3.00
(1) Roger Clemens 5.00
(2) Nomar Garciaparra 5.00
(3) Ken Griffey Jr. 6.00
(4) Vladimir Guerrero 4.00
(5) Derek Jeter 10.00
(6) Randy Johnson 4.00
(7) Pedro Martinez 4.00
(8) Hideki Matsui 4.00
(9) Mike Piazza 6.00
(10) Mark Prior 3.00
(11) Albert Pujols 8.00
(12) Alex Rodriguez 8.00
(13) Alfonso Soriano 3.00
(14) Sammy Sosa 5.00
(15) Ichiro Suzuki 4.00
(16) Jim Thome 3.00
(17) Dontrelle Willis 3.00

2003 Merrick Mint N.Y. Yankees Stickers/Cards

To commemorate the 100th anniversary of the N.Y. Yankees, this set of stickers and cards was produced. Each player is represented on a self-adhesive 1-3/8" x 1-7/8" sticker and a 3-1/2" x 2-1/2" blank-backed card on which the sticker could be placed. Stickers were issued in sheets of nine or 16, and cards on perforated sheets of four or nine. The stickers have portrait photos, a facsimile autograph and uniform number. Cards have an action photo and facsimile autograph. Because the issued was licensed only by the Players Union and not MLB, uniform logos have been excised and the team nickname "Yankees" is nowhere to be seen. The issue was sold in sheets in either 5" x 7" or 8" x 10" format.

NM/M
Set 8x10 Sheets (2): 7.00
Set 5x7 Sheets (4): 6.00
Complete Set Stickers (17): 2.00
Common Sticker: .25
Complete Set Cards (17): 5.00
Common Card: .50
2 Derek Jeter 1.00
6 Joe Torre .25
12 Alfonso Soriano .50
18 Jeff Weaver .25
19 Robin Ventura .25
20 Jorge Posada .25
22 Jason Giambi .50
25 Roger Clemens .75
33 David Wells .25
35 Mike Mussina .35
36 Nick Johnson .25
42 Mariano Rivera .35
43 Raul Mondesi .25
46 Andy Pettitte .35
51 Bernie Williams .25
55 Hideki Matsui .50
--- 100th Anniversary Logo .25
2 Derek Jeter 2.00
6 Joe Torre .50
12 Alfonso Soriano .75
18 Jeff Weaver .50
19 Robin Ventura .50
20 Jorge Posada .50
22 Jason Giambi .75
25 Roger Clemens 1.00
33 David Wells .50
35 Mike Mussina .60
36 Nick Johnson .50
42 Mariano Rivera .60
43 Raul Mondesi .50
46 Andy Pettitte .60
51 Bernie Williams .50
55 Hideki Matsui .75
--- 100th Anniversary Logo .50

Stickers/Cards

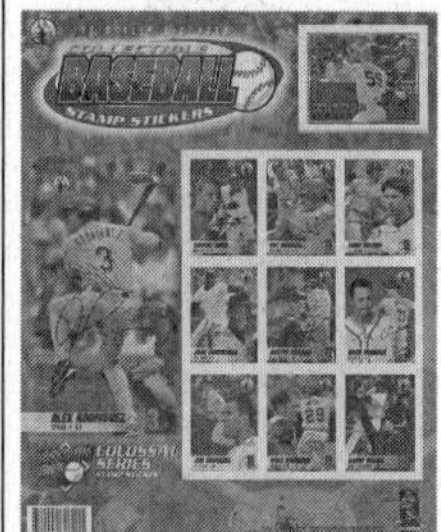

This issue comprises several types of collectibles in one cello-bagged package. Each pack consists of nine self-adhesive 1-1/2" x 2" stickers, nine 3-1/2" x 2-1/2" blank-backed cards on which the sticker could be placed, one 2-1/2" x 5" "Colossal" sticker and one of seven 2-1/2" x 1-7/8" "Rookie Star" sticker of Hideki Matsui. The stickers have color portrait and black-and-white game action photos and a facsimile autograph. Cards have a color version of the action photo. Because the issued was licensed only by the Players Union and not MLB, uniform logos have been excised and team nicknames are nowhere to be seen.

NM/M
Complete Set, Sheets (7): 20.00
Common Player Sticker + Card: .50
Package 1 5.00
(C1) Derek Jeter (Colossal) 1.00
RS1 Hideki Matsui/Btg (Rookie Star) (One hand visible.) .50
(1) Barry Bonds (Facing his right.) 1.50
(2) Roger Clemens/DP .75
(3) Ken Griffey Jr./TP .75
(4) Randy Johnson .65
(5) Pedro Martinez/DP .60
(6) Mike Piazza/DP 1.00
(7) Mark Prior .50
(8) Sammy Sosa/DP .75
(9) Ichiro/DP 1.00
Package 2 3.50
(C2) Alex Rodriguez (Colossal) .75
(RS2) Hideki Matsui/RS/Btg (No hands visible.) .50

(10) Barry Bonds/DP (Arms up.) 1.00
(11) Pat Burrell .50
(12) Jose Contreras .50
(13) Jim Edmonds .50
(14) Todd Helton .65
(15) Austin Kearns .50
(16) Greg Maddux .75
(17) Sammy Sosa/DP .75
(18) Mike Sweeney .50
Package 3 3.75
(C3) Nomar Garciaparra (Colossal) .50
(RS3) Hideki Matsui (Rookie Star)(Throwing) .50
(19) Jeff Bagwell .65
(20) Barry Bonds/DP (Arms up.) 1.00
(21) Ken Griffey Jr./TP .75
(22) Rafael Palmeiro .60
(23) Albert Pujols 1.25
(24) Alfonso Soriano .50
(25) Miguel Tedaja (Tejada) .50
(26) Larry Walker .50
(27) Dontrelle Willis .50
Package 4 3.25
(C4) Sammy Sosa (Colossal) .50
(RS4) Hideki Matsui (Rookie Star)(Thumb up.) .50
(28) Roger Clemens/DP .75
(29) Adam Dunn .50
(30) Vladimir Guerrero .65
(31) Torii Hunter .50
(32) Pedro Martinez/DP .60
(33) Magglio Ordonez .50
(34) Mike Piazza/DP 1.00
(35) Ivan Rodriguez .60
(36) John Smoltz .50
Package 5 3.50
(C5) Barry Bonds (Colossal) 1.00
(RS5) Hideki Matsui/RS (Fldg, running.) .50
(37) Lance Berkman .50
(38) Eric Chavez .50
(39) Troy Glaus .50
(40) Shawn Green .50
(41) Andruw Jones .65
(42) Manny Ramirez .65
(43) Curt Schilling .50
(44) Ichiro/DP 1.00
(45) Bernie Williams .50
Package 6 3.75
(C6) Mike Piazza (Colossal) .50
(RS6) Hideki Matsui/RS (Fldg, standing.) .50
(46) Garret Anderson .50
(47) Rocco Baldelli .50
(48) Nomar Garciaparra 1.00
(49) Juan Gonzalez .50
(50) Ken Griffey Jr./TP .75
(51) Derek Jeter 1.50
(52) Gary Sheffield .50
(53) Frank Thomas .65
(54) Jim Thome .65
Package 7 3.25
(C7) Ichiro (Colossal) .50
(RS7) Hideki Matsui/RS/Btg (Both hands visible.) .50
(55) Carlos Delgado .50
(56) Jason Giambi .60
(57) Tom Glavine .50
(58) Luis Gonzalez .50
(59) Chipper Jones .75
(60) Mike Mussina .50
(61) Alex Rodriguez 1.25
(62) Scott Rolen .60
(63) Barry Zito .50

1993 Metallic Images Cooperstown Collection

This set of retired players is produced of durable, embossed metal with rolled edges. Limited to 49,900, it came packaged in a collectors' tin with a numbered certificate of authenticity. The cards feature full-color photos on the front and back and statistics on the reverse. Half of the players in the set are members of the Hall of Fame.

		NM/M
Complete Set (20):		5.00
Common Player:		.10
1	Hank Aaron	1.50
2	Vida Blue	.10
3	Yogi Berra	.50
4	Bobby Bonds	.10
5	Lou Brock	.20
6	Lew Burdette	.10
7	Rod Carew	.20
8	Rocky Colavito	.20
9	George Foster	.10
10	Bob Gibson	.20
11	Mickey Lolich	.10
12	Willie Mays	1.50
13	Johnny Mize	.20
14	Don Newcombe	.15
15	Gaylord Perry	.20
16	Boog Powell	.20
17	Bill Skowron	.15
18	Warren Spahn	.35
19	Willie Stargell	.20
20	Luis Tiant	.10
P1	Willie Mays	1.25

1995 Metallic Images Babe Ruth

This five-card set of metal cards honors Babe Ruth in the 100th anniversary of his birth. The cards are 2-5/8" x 3-9/16" and featured gold-toned rolled edges. Fronts have familiar sepia-toned photos of the Babe with colorized backgrounds. "Cooperstown Collection" logos appear on front and back. Backs have an overall background of a ghost-image picture of Ruth at bat, along with a small sepia portrait photo, career summary and, on some cards, a few stats. The set was issued in a black embossed tin box, with cards in a cello wrapper.

		NM/M
Complete Boxed Set (5):		5.00
Common Card:		1.00
1	Babe Ruth (Batting follow-through.)	1.00
2	Babe Ruth (Seated with bat on shoulders.)	1.00
3	Babe Ruth (Batting follow-through.)	1.00
4	Babe Ruth (Standing behind 10 bats.)	1.00
5	Babe Ruth (Batting follow-through.)	1.00

Impressions Willie Mays

As part of its Cooperstown Collection series of embossed metal cards, this set traces Willie Mays' career. The set was originally marketed by Avon cosmetics and sold in a lithographed steel box with pictures of Mays on the top and sides. Each of the cards inside was sealed in a cellophane wrapper. Cards measure about 2-5/8" x 3-5/8" and feature monochrome or color photos lithographed on steel. Borders and other design details are embossed. A second photo of Mays is on back, along with a few sentences about his life and career.

		NM/M
Complete Boxed Set (5):		4.00
Common Card:		1.00
1	Willie Mays (Negro Leagues)	1.00
2	Willie Mays (Minor Leagues)	1.00
3	Willie Mays (Rookie Year)	1.00
4	Willie Mays (New York Mets)	1.00
5	Willie Mays (Willie, Mickey, and the Duke)	1.00

1996 Metallic Impressions Ken Griffey, Jr.

This set of metal cards was sold in a lithographed steel box with pictures of Griffey on the top and sides. Each of the cards inside was sealed in a cellophane wrapper. Cards measure about 2-5/8" x 3-5/8" and feature color photos lithographed on steel. Borders and other design details are embossed. Two more photos of Griffey are on back, along with a few sentences about his life and career.

		NM/M
Complete Boxed Set (5):		3.00
Common Card:		1.00
1	Ken Griffey Jr. (At bat.)	1.00
2	Ken Griffey Jr./ Throwing	1.00
3	Ken Griffey Jr./ Running	1.00
4	Ken Griffey Jr./Fldg	1.00
5	Ken Griffey Jr./ Swinging	1.00

Iron Men of Baseball

Originally sold by Avon, this set of embossed metal cards was sold in a lithographed steel box with player pictures on the top and sides. Each of the cards inside was sealed in in a cellophane wrapper. Cards measure about 2-5/8" x 3-5/8" and feature black-and-white or color photos lithographed on steel. Borders and other design details are embossed. A pair of photos is on back, along with details of each player's consecutive games streak.

		NM/M
Complete Boxed Set (5):		6.00
Common Card:		1.50
1	Lou Gehrig	1.50
2	Lou Gehrig	1.50
3	Cal Ripken Jr.	1.50
4	Cal Ripken Jr.	1.50
5	Lou Gehrig, Cal Ripken Jr.	1.50

Cal Ripken, Jr.

Two versions of this set were produced, a five-card set (#1-5) and a 10-card set (#1-10). Highlights of Cal Ripken's career are presented on these metallic baseball cards. Each 2-5/8" x 3-5/8" card has a color photo at center, surrounded by team-colored borders. Embossed at the bottom is a script version of Ripken's name with an oriole atop. In the lower-right corner is a metallic-looking home plate with "Iron Oriole." Backs repeat some of the front graphics and have identical portrait and action photos of Ripken and the magic number "2131" in lights at top. A paragraph at bottom describes a career milestone or highlight. The sets were sold in embossed lithographed metal boxes. The 10-card set is accompanied by a serial numbered certificate from an edition of 29,950.

		NM/M
Complete Boxed Set (10):		7.50
Complete Boxed Set (5):		4.00
Common Card:		1.00
1	Cal Ripken Jr. (Major League debut.)	1.00
2	Cal Ripken Jr. (1982 - Opening Day 3B)	1.00
3	Cal Ripken Jr. (Streak begins.)	1.00
4	Cal Ripken Jr. (Rookie of the Year)	1.00
5	Cal Ripken Jr. (1983)	1.00
6	Cal Ripken Jr. (Consecutive innings streak.)	1.00
7	Cal Ripken Jr. (1991 MVP)	1.00
8	Cal Ripken Jr. (Gold Glover)	1.00
9	Cal Ripken Jr. (Game 2,130.)	1.00
10	Cal Ripken Jr. (Game 2,131.)	1.00

1936 Hall of Fame Electees

As part of its Cooperstown Collection series of embossed metal cards, this set was released in the 60th anniversary year of the first Hall of Fame selections. The set was sold in a lithographed steel box with player pictures on the top and sides. Each of the cards inside was sealed in a cellophane wrapper. Cards measure about 2-5/8" x 3-5/8" and feature black-and-white photos lithographed on steel. Borders and other design details are embossed. A black-and-white photo is on back, along with "Peak Performance" stats and a career summary. Sets were originally sold through Avon.

		NM/M
Complete Boxed Set (5):		4.50
Common Player:		1.00
1	Babe Ruth	2.00
2	Ty Cobb	1.50
3	Christy Mathewson	1.00
4	Walter Johnson	1.00
5	Honus Wagner	1.00

1997 Metallic Impressions Jackie Robinson

As part of its Cooperstown Collection series of embossed metal cards, this set was released in the 50th anniversary year of Jackie Robinson's entry into the major leagues. The set was sold in a lithographed steel box with pictures of Robinson on the top and sides. Each of the cards inside was sealed in a cellophane wrapper. Cards measure about 2-5/8" x 3-5/8" and feature monochrome or color photos lithographed on steel. Borders and other design details are embossed. A black-and-white photo of Robinson is on back, along with a few sentences about his life and career.

		NM/M
Complete Boxed Set (5):		5.00
Common Card:		1.25
1	Jackie Robinson (Thigh-to-cap portrait.)	1.25
2	Jackie Robinson (Chest-to-cap portrait.)	1.25
3	Jackie Robinson/Btg (Color)	1.25
4	Jackie Robinson/Fldg	1.25
5	Jackie Robinson/Btg (B/W)	1.25

1996 Metal Universe Sample Sheet

To introduce its premiere edition of Metal Universe baseball cards, Fleer sent a nine-card sample sheet to dealers. The 8" x 11" sheet has a black border on each side of each card. The cards are identical in format to the issued version, printed on etched foil and overprinted "PROMOTIONAL SAMPLE" in gold diagonally on front and back.

	NM/M
Complete Sheet:	10.00

1996 Metal Universe

One of the most unusual baseball card issues of its era, Fleer's Metal Universe set is distinguished by its colored, textured metallic-foil backgrounds created by comic book illustrators. The effects range from gaudy to grotesque. Glossy player action photos are featured on front, with a steel-colored metallic strip at bottom carrying set and player ID. Conventionally printed backs have a heavy-metal theme with a color player portrait photo and a few stats and personal data around. The issue was sold in hobby and retail packaging with the basic eight-card pack at a suggested retail price of $2.49. Several insert sets were included, along with a platinum parallel edition of the player cards.

		NM/M
Complete Set (250):		17.50
Common Player:		.10
Platinum Set (250):		75.00
Common Platinum:		.25
Platinums:		5X
Pack (8):		1.50
Wax Box (24):		17.50
1	Roberto Alomar	.20
2	Brady Anderson	.10
3	Bobby Bonilla	.10
4	Chris Holles	.10
5	Ben McDonald	.10
6	Mike Mussina	.40
7	Randy Myers	.10
8	Rafael Palmeiro	.60
9	Cal Ripken Jr.	2.50
10	B.J. Surhoff	.10
11	Luis Alicea	.10
12	Jose Canseco	.50
13	Roger Clemens	1.25
14	Wil Cordero	.10
15	Tom Gordon	.10
16	Mike Greenwell	.10
17	Tim Naehring	.10
18	Troy O'Leary	.10
19	Mike Stanley	.10
20	John Valentin	.10
21	Mo Vaughn	.10
22	Tim Wakefield	.10
23	Garret Anderson	.10
24	Chili Davis	.10
25	Gary DiSarcina	.10
26	Jim Edmonds	.10
27	Chuck Finley	.10
28	Todd Greene	.10
29	Mark Langston	.10
30	Troy Percival	.10
31	Tony Phillips	.10
32	Tim Salmon	.10
33	Lee Smith	.10
34	J.T. Snow	.10
35	Ray Durham	.10
36	Alex Fernandez	.10
37	Ozzie Guillen	.10
38	Roberto Hernandez	.10
39	Lyle Mouton	.10
40	Frank Thomas	.75
41	Robin Ventura	.10
42	Sandy Alomar	.10
43	Carlos Baerga	.10
44	Albert Belle	.10
45	Orel Hershiser	.10
46	Kenny Lofton	.10
47	Dennis Martinez	.10
48	Jack McDowell	.10
49	Jose Mesa	.10
50	Eddie Murray	.75
51	Charles Nagy	.10
52	Manny Ramirez	.75
53	Julian Tavarez	.10
54	Jim Thome	.60
55	Omar Vizquel	.10
56	Chad Curtis	.10
57	Cecil Fielder	.10
58	John Flaherty	.10
59	Travis Fryman	.10
60	Chris Gomez	.10
61	Felipe Lira	.10
62	Kevin Appier	.10
63	Johnny Damon	.35
64	Tom Goodwin	.10
65	Mark Gubicza	.10
66	Jeff Montgomery	.10
67	Jon Nunnally	.10
68	Ricky Bones	.10
69	Jeff Cirillo	.10
70	John Jaha	.10
71	Dave Nilsson	.10
72	Joe Oliver	.10
73	Kevin Seitzer	.10
74	Greg Vaughn	.10
75	Marty Cordova	.10
76	Chuck Knoblauch	.10
77	Pat Meares	.10
78	Paul Molitor	.75
79	Pedro Munoz	.10
80	Kirby Puckett	1.00
81	Brad Radke	.10
82	Scott Stahoviak	.10
83	Matt Walbeck	.10
84	Wade Boggs	1.00
85	David Cone	.10
86	Joe Girardi	.10
87	Derek Jeter	2.50
88	Jim Leyritz	.10
89	Tino Martinez	.10
90	Don Mattingly	1.50
91	Paul O'Neill	.10
92	Andy Pettitte	.25
93	Tim Raines	.10
94	Kenny Rogers	.10
95	Ruben Sierra	.10
96	John Wetteland	.10
97	Bernie Williams	.10
98	Geronimo Berroa	.10
99	Dennis Eckersley	.65
100	Brent Gates	.10
101	Mark McGwire	2.00
102	Steve Ontiveros	.10
103	Terry Steinbach	.10
104	Jay Buhner	.10
105	Vince Coleman	.10
106	Joey Cora	.10
107	Ken Griffey Jr.	1.50
108	Randy Johnson	.75
109	Edgar Martinez	.10
110	Alex Rodriguez	2.00
111	Paul Sorrento	.10
112	Will Clark	.10

113 Juan Gonzalez .50
114 Rusty Greer .10
115 Dean Palmer .10
116 Ivan Rodriguez .65
117 Mickey Tettleton .10
118 Joe Carter .10
119 Alex Gonzalez .10
120 Shawn Green .30
121 Erik Hanson .10
122 Pat Hentgen .10
123 Sandy Martinez **RC** .10
124 Otis Nixon .10
125 John Olerud .10
126 Steve Avery .10
127 Tom Glavine .40
128 Marquis Grissom .10
129 Chipper Jones 1.00
130 David Justice .10
131 Ryan Klesko .10
132 Mark Lemke .10
133 Javier Lopez .10
134 Greg Maddux 1.00
135 Fred McGriff .10
136 John Smoltz .10
137 Mark Wohlers .10
138 Frank Castillo .10
139 Shawon Dunston .10
140 Luis Gonzalez .20
141 Mark Grace .10
142 Brian McRae .10
143 Jaime Navarro .10
144 Rey Sanchez .10
145 Ryne Sandberg 1.00
146 Sammy Sosa 1.25
147 Bret Boone .10
148 Curtis Goodwin .10
149 Barry Larkin .10
150 Hal Morris .10
151 Reggie Sanders .10
152 Pete Schourek .10
153 John Smiley .10
154 Dante Bichette .10
155 Vinny Castilla .10
156 Andres Galarraga .10
157 Bret Saberhagen .10
158 Bill Swift .10
159 Larry Walker .10
160 Walt Weiss .10
161 Kurt Abbott .10
162 John Burkett .10
163 Greg Colbrunn .10
164 Jeff Conine .10
165 Chris Hammond .10
166 Charles Johnson .10
167 Al Leiter .10
168 Pat Rapp .10
169 Gary Sheffield .40
170 Quilvio Veras .10
171 Devon White .10
172 Jeff Bagwell .75
173 Derek Bell .10
174 Sean Berry .10
175 Craig Biggio .10
176 Doug Drabek .10
177 Tony Eusebio .10
178 Brian Hunter .10
179 Orlando Miller .10
180 Shane Reynolds .10
181 Mike Blowers .10
182 Roger Cedeno .10
183 Eric Karros .10
184 Ramon Martinez .10
185 Raul Mondesi .10
186 Hideo Nomo .60
187 Mike Piazza 1.50
188 Moises Alou .10
189 Yamil Benitez .10
190 Darrin Fletcher .10
191 Cliff Floyd .10
192 Pedro Martinez .75
193 Carlos Perez .10
194 David Segui .10
195 Tony Tarasco .10
196 Rondell White .10
197 Edgardo Alfonzo .10
198 Rico Brogna .10
199 Carl Everett .10
200 Todd Hundley .10
201 Jason Isringhausen .10
202 Lance Johnson .10
203 Bobby Jones .10
204 Jeff Kent .10
205 Bill Pulsipher .10
206 Jose Vizcaino .10
207 Ricky Bottalico .10
208 Darren Daulton .10
209 Lenny Dykstra .10
210 Jim Eisenreich .10
211 Gregg Jefferies .10
212 Mickey Morandini .10
213 Heathcliff Slocumb .10
214 Jay Bell .10
215 Carlos Garcia .10
216 Jeff King .10
217 Al Martin .10
218 Orlando Merced .10
219 Dan Miceli .10
220 Denny Neagle .10
221 Andy Benes .10
222 Royce Clayton .10
223 Gary Gaetti .10
224 Ron Gant .10
225 Bernard Gilkey .10
226 Brian Jordan .10
227 Ray Lankford .10
228 John Mabry .10
229 Ozzie Smith 1.00
230 Todd Stottlemyre .10
231 Andy Ashby .10
232 Brad Ausmus .10
233 Ken Caminiti .10
234 Steve Finley .10
235 Tony Gwynn 1.00
236 Joey Hamilton .10
237 Rickey Henderson .75
238 Trevor Hoffman .10
239 Wally Joyner .10
240 Rod Beck .10
241 Barry Bonds 2.50
242 Glenallen Hill .10
243 Stan Javier .10
244 Mark Leiter .10
245 Deion Sanders .10
246 William Van Landingham .10
247 Matt Williams .10
248 Checklist .10
249 Checklist .10
250 Checklist .10

Platinum Edition

One of the eight cards in each pack of Fleer Metal baseball is a Platinum Edition parallel insert. Each of the 247 player cards (no checklists) in this special version has the textured foil background rendered only in silver. The second line of the logo/ID strip at bottom also identifies the card as part of the Platinum Edition.

NM/M
Complete Set (247): 75.00
Common Player: .25
Stars: 5X

Heavy Metal

Some of the game's biggest hitters are included in this insert set. Action photos of players at bat are set on a silver-foil background on front. Backs have a close-up photo down one side, with praise for the player's power potential down the other. The Heavy Metal inserts can be expected to turn up at an average rate of one per eight packs.

NM/M
Complete Set (10): 5.00
Common Player: .35
1 Albert Belle .35
2 Barry Bonds 1.50
3 Juan Gonzalez .50
4 Ken Griffey Jr. 1.00
5 Mark McGwire 1.25
6 Mike Piazza 1.00
7 Sammy Sosa .90
8 Frank Thomas .60
9 Mo Vaughn .35
10 Matt Williams .35

Mining for Gold

Available only in retail packs, at an average rate of one per dozen packs, the Mining for Gold insert series focuses on

1995's top rookies. Fronts have player action photos frame and backgrounded with several different gold tones in etched metal foil. Backs are conventionally printed, carrying on the same format with a portrait photo and a few words about the player.

NM/M
Complete Set (12): 12.50
Common Player: .75
1 Yamil Benitez .75
2 Marty Cordova .75
3 Shawn Green 2.00
4 Todd Greene .75
5 Brian Hunter .75
6 Derek Jeter 7.50
7 Charles Johnson .75
8 Chipper Jones 3.50
9 Hideo Nomo 2.50
10 Alex Ochoa .75
11 Andy Pettitte 1.00
12 Quilvio Veras .75

Mother Lode

Medieval designs rendered in textured silver-foil on a plain white background are the setting for the color player photos in this hobby-only insert. Backs also have a silver and white background along with another player photo and some kind words about his skills. The cards are found at an average rate of one per 12 packs.

NM/M
Complete Set (12): 15.00
Common Player: .75
1 Barry Bonds 4.50
2 Jim Edmonds .75
3 Ken Griffey Jr. 3.50
4 Kenny Lofton .75
5 Raul Mondesi .75
6 Rafael Palmeiro 1.50
7 Manny Ramirez 2.00
8 Cal Ripken Jr. 4.50
9 Tim Salmon .75
10 Ryne Sandberg 3.00
11 Frank Thomas 2.00
12 Matt Williams .75

Platinum Portraits

Close-up color photos on a plain metallic-foil background are featured in this insert set. The checklist is heavy in rookie and sophomore players, who are featured in an action photo on back, with a few career details. Platinum Portraits inserts are found in every fourth pack, on average.

NM/M
Complete Set (10): 4.00
Common Player: .40
1 Garret Anderson .40
2 Marty Cordova .40
3 Jim Edmonds .40
4 Jason Isringhausen .40
5 Chipper Jones 2.25
6 Ryan Klesko .40
7 Hideo Nomo 1.00
8 Carlos Perez .40
9 Manny Ramirez 1.50
10 Rondell White .40

1996 Metal Universe Titanium

A huge purple-highlighted silver baseball in a star-studded night sky is the background for the action photos of the game's biggest names in this insert series. Backs have a second, more up-close, photo and a few words about the player. Titanium inserts are found in Metal Universe packs at an average rate of one per 24 packs.

NM/M
Complete Set (10): 15.00
Common Player: .50
1 Albert Belle .50
2 Barry Bonds 4.00
3 Ken Griffey Jr. 2.50
4 Tony Gwynn 1.50
5 Greg Maddux 1.50
6 Mike Piazza 2.50
7 Cal Ripken Jr. 4.00
8 Frank Thomas 1.00
9 Mo Vaughn .50
10 Matt Williams .50

1997 Metal Universe

Metal Universe Baseball arrived in a 250-card set, including three checklists. Each card is printed on 100-percent etched foil with "comic book" art full-bleed backgrounds, with the player's name, team, position and the Metal Universe logo near the bottom of the card. Backs contain another player photo and key statistics. Metal Universe sold in eight-card packs and contained six different insert sets. They included: Blast Furnace, Magnetic Field, Mining for Gold, Mother Lode, Platinum Portraits and Titanium.

NM/M
Complete Set (250): 17.50
Common Player: .10
Pack (8): 1.50
Wax Box (24): 18.00
1 Roberto Alomar .20
2 Brady Anderson .10
3 Rocky Coppinger .10
4 Chris Hoiles .10
5 Eddie Murray .60
6 Mike Mussina .40
7 Rafael Palmeiro .50
8 Cal Ripken Jr. 2.00
9 B.J. Surhoff .10
10 Brant Brown .10
11 Mark Grace .10
12 Brian McRae .10
13 Jaime Navarro .10
14 Ryne Sandberg .75
15 Sammy Sosa 1.00
16 Amaury Telemaco .10
17 Steve Trachsel .10
18 Darren Bragg .10
19 Jose Canseco .40
20 Roger Clemens 1.00
21 Nomar Garciaparra 1.00
22 Tom Gordon .10
23 Tim Naehring .10
24 Mike Stanley .10
25 John Valentin .10
26 Mo Vaughn .10
27 Jermaine Dye .10
28 Tom Glavine .30
29 Marquis Grissom .10
30 Andruw Jones .60
31 Chipper Jones .75
32 Ryan Klesko .10
33 Greg Maddux .75
34 Fred McGriff .10
35 John Smoltz .10
36 Garret Anderson .10
37 George Arias .10
38 Gary DiSarcina .10
39 Jim Edmonds .10
40 Darin Erstad .25
41 Chuck Finley .10
42 Troy Percival .10
43 Tim Salmon .10
44 Bret Boone .10
45 Jeff Brantley .10
46 Eric Davis .10
47 Barry Larkin .10
48 Hal Morris .10
49 Mark Portugal .10
50 Reggie Sanders .10
51 John Smiley .10
52 Wilson Alvarez .10
53 Harold Baines .10
54 James Baldwin .10
55 Albert Belle .10
56 Mike Cameron .10
57 Ray Durham .10
58 Alex Fernandez .10
59 Roberto Hernandez .10
60 Tony Phillips .10
61 Frank Thomas .60
62 Robin Ventura .10
63 Jeff Cirillo .10
64 Jeff D'Amico .10
65 John Jaha .10
66 Scott Karl .10
67 Ben McDonald .10
68 Marc Newfield .10
69 Dave Nilsson .10
70 Jose Valentin .10
71 Dante Bichette .10
72 Ellis Burks .10
73 Vinny Castilla .10
74 Andres Galarraga .10
75 Kevin Ritz .10
76 Larry Walker .10
77 Walt Weiss .10
78 Jamey Wright .10
79 Eric Young .10
80 Julio Franco .10
81 Orel Hershiser .10
82 Kenny Lofton .10
83 Jack McDowell .10
84 Jose Mesa .10
85 Charles Nagy .10
86 Manny Ramirez .60
87 Jim Thome .50
88 Omar Vizquel .10
89 Matt Williams .10
90 Kevin Appier .10
91 Johnny Damon .35
92 Chili Davis .10
93 Tom Goodwin .10
94 Keith Lockhart .10
95 Jeff Montgomery .10
96 Craig Paquette .10
97 Jose Rosado .10
98 Michael Tucker .10
99 Wilton Guerrero .10
100 Todd Hollandsworth .10
101 Eric Karros .10
102 Ramon Martinez .10
103 Raul Mondesi .10
104 Hideo Nomo .60
105 Mike Piazza 1.25
106 Ismael Valdes .10
107 Todd Worrell .10
108 Tony Clark .10
109 Travis Fryman .10
110 Bob Higginson .10
111 Mark Lewis .10
112 Melvin Nieves .10
113 Justin Thompson .10
114 Wade Boggs .75
115 David Cone .10
116 Cecil Fielder .10
117 Dwight Gooden .10
118 Derek Jeter 2.00
119 Tino Martinez .10
120 Paul O'Neill .10
121 Andy Pettitte .20
122 Mariano Rivera .20
123 Darryl Strawberry .10
124 John Wetteland .10
125 Bernie Williams .10
126 Tony Batista .10
127 Geronimo Berroa .10
128 Scott Brosius .10
129 Jason Giambi .50
130 Jose Herrera .10
131 Mark McGwire 1.50
132 John Wasdin .10
133 Bob Abreu .10
134 Jeff Bagwell .60
135 Derek Bell .10
136 Craig Biggio .10
137 Brian Hunter .10
138 Darryl Kile .10
139 Orlando Miller .10
140 Shane Reynolds .10
141 Billy Wagner .10
142 Donne Wall .10
143 Jay Buhner .10
144 Jeff Fassero .10
145 Ken Griffey Jr. 1.25
146 Sterling Hitchcock .10
147 Randy Johnson .60
148 Edgar Martinez .10
149 Alex Rodriguez 1.50
149p Alex Rodriguez ("PROMOTIONAL SAMPLE") 1.50
150 Paul Sorrento .10
151 Dan Wilson .10
152 Moises Alou .10
153 Darrin Fletcher .10
154 Cliff Floyd .10
155 Mark Grudzielanek .10
156 Vladimir Guerrero .60
157 Mike Lansing .10
158 Pedro Martinez .60
159 Henry Rodriguez .10
160 Rondell White .10
161 Will Clark .10
162 Juan Gonzalez .50
163 Rusty Greer .10
164 Ken Hill .10
165 Mark McLemore .10
166 Dean Palmer .10
167 Roger Pavlik .10
168 Ivan Rodriguez .50
169 Mickey Tettleton .10
170 Bobby Bonilla .10
171 Kevin Brown .10
172 Greg Colbrunn .10
173 Jeff Conine .10
174 Jim Eisenreich .10
175 Charles Johnson .10
176 Al Leiter .10
177 Robb Nen .10
178 Edgar Renteria .10
179 Gary Sheffield .40
180 Devon White .10
181 Joe Carter .10
182 Carlos Delgado .40
183 Alex Gonzalez .10
184 Shawn Green .35
185 Juan Guzman .10
186 Pat Hentgen .10
187 Orlando Merced .10
188 John Olerud .10
189 Robert Perez .10
190 Ed Sprague .10
191 Mark Clark .10
192 John Franco .10
193 Bernard Gilkey .10
194 Todd Hundley .10
195 Lance Johnson .10
196 Bobby Jones .10
197 Alex Ochoa .10
198 Rey Ordonez .10
199 Paul Wilson .10
200 Ricky Bottalico .10
201 Gregg Jefferies .10
202 Wendell Magee Jr. .10
203 Mickey Morandini .10
204 Ricky Otero .10
205 Scott Rolen .50
206 Benito Santiago .10
207 Curt Schilling .25
208 Rich Becker .10
209 Marty Cordova .10
210 Chuck Knoblauch .10
211 Pat Meares .10
212 Paul Molitor .60
213 Frank Rodriguez .10
214 Terry Steinbach .10
215 Todd Walker .10
216 Andy Ashby .10
217 Ken Caminiti .10
218 Steve Finley .10
219 Tony Gwynn .75
220 Joey Hamilton .10
221 Rickey Henderson .60
222 Trevor Hoffman .10
223 Wally Joyner .10
224 Scott Sanders .10
225 Fernando Valenzuela .10
226 Greg Vaughn .10
227 Alan Benes .10
228 Andy Benes .10
229 Dennis Eckersley .50
230 Ron Gant .10
231 Brian Jordan .10
232 Ray Lankford .10

233	John Mabry	.10
234	Tom Pagnozzi	.10
235	Todd Stottlemyre	.10
236	Jermaine Allensworth	.10
237	Francisco Cordova	.10
238	Jason Kendall	.10
239	Jeff King	.10
240	Al Martin	.10
241	Rod Beck	.10
242	Barry Bonds	2.00
243	Shawn Estes	.10
244	Mark Gardner	.10
245	Glenallen Hill	.10
246	Bill Mueller	.10
247	J.T. Snow	.10
248	Checklist	.10
249	Checklist	.10
250	Checklist	.10

Blast Furnace

Blast Furnace inserts were found only in hobby packs, at a rate of one per 48 packs. The 12-card set was printed on a red-tinted plastic, with the words "Blast Furnace" near the bottom in gold foil with a fire-like border.

		NM/M
Complete Set (12):		40.00
Common Player:		1.50
1	Jeff Bagwell	4.00
2	Albert Belle	1.50
3	Barry Bonds	7.50
4	Andres Galarraga	1.50
5	Juan Gonzalez	2.50
6	Ken Griffey Jr.	5.00
7	Todd Hundley	1.50
8	Mark McGwire	6.00
9	Mike Piazza	5.00
10	Alex Rodriguez	6.00
11	Frank Thomas	4.00
12	Mo Vaughn	1.50

Emerald Autograph Redemption

Six different young stars were featured in this insert, which was found every 480 hobby packs of Metal Universe. The cards are similar to regular-issue cards, but have green foil highlights. Redemption cards are numbered AU1-AU6. The redemption period expired Jan. 15, 1998.

		NM/M
Complete Set (6):		10.00
Common Player:		1.00
1	Darin Erstad	1.50
2	Todd Hollandsworth	1.00
3	Alex Ochoa	1.00
4	Alex Rodriguez	7.50
5	Scott Rolen	1.50
6	Todd Walker	1.00

Emerald Autographs

Six different young stars were featured in this insert, which was found every 480

hobby packs of Metal Universe. The cards are similar to regular-issue cards, but have a green foil finish and autograph on the front. Redemption cards are numbered AU1-AU6, the autographed cards have a notation on back, "Certified Emerald Autograph Card."

		NM/M
Complete Set (6):		75.00
Common Autograph:		4.00
1	Darin Erstad	6.00
2	Todd Hollandsworth	4.00
3	Alex Ochoa	4.00
4	Alex Rodriguez	60.00
5	Scott Rolen	10.00
6	Todd Walker	4.00

Magnetic Field

Magnetic Field inserts are printed in a horizontal format with prismatic foil backgrounds. This 10-card insert was found every 12 packs of Metal Universe.

		NM/M
Complete Set (10):		15.00
Common Player:		.75
1	Roberto Alomar	.75
2	Jeff Bagwell	1.25
3	Barry Bonds	3.00
4	Ken Griffey Jr.	2.00
5	Derek Jeter	3.00
6	Kenny Lofton	.75
7	Edgar Renteria	.75
8	Cal Ripken Jr.	3.00
9	Alex Rodriguez	2.50
10	Matt Williams	.75

Mining for Gold

Mining for Gold was a 10-card insert that featured some of baseball's brightest stars on a die-cut "ingot" design with pearlized gold coating. This insert was found every nine packs.

		NM/M
Complete Set (10):		12.00
Common Player:		.75
1	Bob Abreu	.75
2	Kevin Brown	.75
3	Nomar Garciaparra	3.50
4	Vladimir Guerrero	3.00
5	Wilton Guerrero	.75
6	Andruw Jones	3.00
7	Curt Lyons	.75
8	Neifi Perez	.75
9	Scott Rolen	2.00
10	Todd Walker	.75

Mother Lode

Mother lode was the most difficult insert out of Metal Universe with a one per 288 pack insertion ratio. Each card in this 10-card inert was printed on etched foil with a plant-type monument in back of the player.

		NM/M
Complete Set (12):		80.00
Common Player:		2.00
1	Roberto Alomar	2.50
2	Jeff Bagwell	6.00
3	Barry Bonds	15.00
4	Ken Griffey Jr.	10.00
5	Andruw Jones	6.00
6	Chipper Jones	8.00
7	Kenny Lofton	2.00
8	Mike Piazza	10.00
9	Cal Ripken Jr.	15.00
10	Alex Rodriguez	12.50
11	Frank Thomas	6.00
12	Matt Williams	2.00

Platinum Portraits

Each card in the Platinum Portraits insert is printed on a background of platinum-colored etched foil. The 10-card set includes some of the top prospects and rising stars in baseball, and is included every 36 packs.

		NM/M
Complete Set (10):		10.00
Common Player:		.60
1	James Baldwin	.60
2	Jermaine Dye	.60
3	Todd Hollandsworth	.60
4	Derek Jeter	5.00
5	Chipper Jones	2.00
6	Jason Kendall	.60
7	Rey Ordonez	.60
8	Andy Pettitte	1.00
9	Edgar Renteria	.60
10	Alex Rodriguez	3.25

Titanium

These retail exclusive inserts include 10 cards and were found every 24 packs. Each card is die-cut on the top-left and bottom-right corner with a silver foil background. Titanium includes some of the most popular players in baseball on cards that are also embossed.

		NM/M
Complete Set (10):		24.00
Common Player:		1.50
1	Jeff Bagwell	2.00
2	Albert Belle	1.50
3	Ken Griffey Jr.	3.00
4	Chipper Jones	2.50
5	Greg Maddux	2.50
6	Mark McGwire	4.00
7	Mike Piazza	3.00
8	Cal Ripken Jr.	5.00
9	Alex Rodriguez	4.00
10	Frank Thomas	2.00

1998 Metal Universe

This 220-card single series release captured players over a foil etched, art background that related in some way to them or the city they played in. Metal Universe included a 15-card Hardball Galaxy subset and dealers and media were given an Alex Rodriguez promo card that was identical the base card except for the words "Promotional Sample" written across the back. The set arrived with a parallel called Precious Metal Gems, and included the following insert sets: All-Galactic Team, Diamond Heroes, Platinum Portraits, Titanium and Universal Language.

		NM/M
Complete Set (220):		15.00
Common Player:		.10
Pack (8):		1.50
Wax Box (24):		20.00
1	Jose Cruz Jr.	.10
2	Jeff Abbott	.10
3	Rafael Palmeiro	.65
4	Ivan Rodriguez	.65
5	Jaret Wright	.10
6	Derek Bell	.10
7	Chuck Finley	.10
8	Travis Fryman	.10
9	Randy Johnson	.75
10	Derrek Lee	.50
11	Bernie Williams	.10
12	Carlos Baerga	.10
13	Ricky Bottalico	.10
14	Ellis Burks	.10
15	Russ Davis	.10
16	Nomar Garciaparra	1.00
17	Joey Hamilton	.10
18	Jason Kendall	.10
19	Darryl Kile	.10
20	Edgardo Alfonzo	.10
21	Moises Alou	.10
22	Bobby Bonilla	.10
23	Jim Edmonds	.10
24	Jose Guillen	.10
25	Chuck Knoblauch	.10
26	Javy Lopez	.10
27	Billy Wagner	.10
28	Kevin Appier	.10
29	Joe Carter	.10
30	Todd Dunwoody	.10
31	Gary Gaetti	.10
32	Juan Gonzalez	.60
33	Jeffrey Hammonds	.10
34	Roberto Hernandez	.10
35	Dave Nilsson	.10
36	Manny Ramirez	.75
37	Robin Ventura	.10
38	Rondell White	.10
39	Vinny Castilla	.10
40	Will Clark	.10
41	Scott Hatteberg	.10
42	Russ Johnson	.10
43	Ricky Ledee	.10
44	Kenny Lofton	.10
45	Paul Molitor	.75
46	Justin Thompson	.10
47	Craig Biggio	.10
48	Damion Easley	.10
49	Brad Radke	.10
50	Ben Grieve	.10
51	Mark Bellhorn	.10
52	Henry Blanco **RC**	.10
53	Mariano Rivera	.20
54	Reggie Sanders	.10
55	Paul Sorrento	.10
56	Terry Steinbach	.10
57	Mo Vaughn	.10
58	Brady Anderson	.10
59	Tom Glavine	.40
60	Sammy Sosa	1.25
61	Larry Walker	.10
62	Rod Beck	.10
63	Jose Canseco	.45
64	Steve Finley	.10
65	Pedro Martinez	.75
66	John Olerud	.10
67	Scott Rolen	.60
68	Ismael Valdes	.10
69	Andrew Vessel	.10
70	Mark Grudzielanek	.10
71	Eric Karros	.10
72	Jeff Shaw	.10
73	Lou Collier	.10
74	Edgar Martinez	.10
75	Vladimir Guerrero	.75
76	Paul Konerko	.25
77	Kevin Orie	.10
78	Kevin Polcovich	.10
79	Brett Tomko	.10
80	Jeff Bagwell	.75
81	Barry Bonds	2.50
82	David Justice	.10
83	Hideo Nomo	.60
84	Ryne Sandberg	1.00
85	Shannon Stewart	.10
86	Derek Wallace	.10
87	Tony Womack	.10
88	Jason Giambi	.50
89	Mark Grace	.10
90	Pat Hentgen	.10
91	Raul Mondesi	.10
92	Matt Morris	.10
93	Matt Perisho	.10
94	Tim Salmon	.10
95	Jeremi Gonzalez	.10
96	Shawn Green	.25
97	Todd Greene	.10
98	Ruben Rivera	.10
99	Deion Sanders	.10
100	Alex Rodriguez	2.00
101	Will Cunnane	.10
102	Ray Lankford	.10
103	Ryan McGuire	.10
104	Charles Nagy	.10
105	Rey Ordonez	.10
106	Mike Piazza	1.50
107	Tony Saunders	.10
108	Curt Schilling	.25
109	Fernando Tatis	.10
110	Mark McGwire	2.00
111	David Dellucci **RC**	.10
112	Garret Anderson	.10
113	Shane Bowers	.10
114	David Cone	.10
115	Jeff King	.10
116	Matt Williams	.10
117	Aaron Boone	.10
118	Dennis Eckersley	.65
119	Livan Hernandez	.10
120	Richard Hidalgo	.10
121	Bobby Higginson	.10
122	Tino Martinez	.10
123	Tim Naehring	.10
124	Jose Vidro	.10
125	John Wetteland	.10
126	Jay Bell	.10
127	Albert Belle	.10
128	Marty Cordova	.10
129	Chili Davis	.10
130	Jason Dickson	.10
131	Rusty Greer	.10
132	Hideki Irabu	.10
133	Greg Maddux	1.00
134	Billy Taylor	.10
135	Jim Thome	.60
136	Gerald Williams	.10
137	Jeff Cirillo	.10
138	Delino DeShields	.10
139	Andres Galarraga	.10
140	Willie Greene	.10
141	John Jaha	.10
142	Charles Johnson	.10
143	Ryan Klesko	.10
144	Paul O'Neill	.10
145	Robinson Checo	.10
146	Roberto Alomar	.20
147	Wilson Alvarez	.10
148	Bobby Jones	.10
149	Raul Casanova	.10
150	Andruw Jones	.75
151	Mike Lansing	.10
152	Mickey Morandini	.10
153	Neifi Perez	.10
154	Pokey Reese	.10
155	Edgar Renteria	.10
156	Eric Young	.10
157	Darin Erstad	.20
158	Kelvim Escobar	.10
159	Carl Everett	.10
160	Tom Gordon	.10
161	Ken Griffey Jr.	1.50
162	Al Martin	.10
163	Bubba Trammell	.10
164	Carlos Delgado	.30
165	Kevin Brown	.10
166	Ken Caminiti	.10
167	Roger Clemens	1.25
168	Ron Gant	.10
169	Jeff Kent	.10
170	Mike Mussina	.40
171	Dean Palmer	.10
172	Henry Rodriguez	.10
173	Matt Stairs	.10
174	Jay Buhner	.10
175	Frank Thomas	.75
176	Mike Cameron	.10
177	Johnny Damon	.35
178	Tony Gwynn	1.00
179	John Smoltz	.10
180	B.J. Surhoff	.10
181	Antone Williamson	.10
182	Alan Benes	.10
183	Jeromy Burnitz	.10
184	Tony Clark	.10
185	Shawn Estes	.10
186	Todd Helton	.65
187	Todd Hundley	.10
188	Chipper Jones	1.00
189	Mark Kotsay	.10
190	Barry Larkin	.10
191	Mike Lieberthal	.10
192	Andy Pettitte	.25
193	Gary Sheffield	.35
194	Jeff Suppan	.10
195	Mark Wohlers	.10
196	Dante Bichette	.10
197	Trevor Hoffman	.10
198	J.T. Snow	.10
199	Derek Jeter	2.50
200	Cal Ripken Jr.	2.50
201	Steve Woodard **RC**	.25
202	Ray Durham	.10
203	Barry Bonds (Hardball Galaxy)	1.50
204	Tony Clark (Hardball Galaxy)	.10
205	Roger Clemens (Hardball Galaxy)	.65
206	Ken Griffey Jr. (Hardball Galaxy)	.75
207	Tony Gwynn (Hardball Galaxy)	.50
208	Derek Jeter (Hardball Galaxy)	1.50
209	Randy Johnson (Hardball Galaxy)	.40
210	Mark McGwire (Hardball Galaxy)	1.00
211	Hideo Nomo (Hardball Galaxy)	.30
212	Mike Piazza (Hardball Galaxy)	.75
213	Cal Ripken Jr. (Hardball Galaxy)	1.50
214	Alex Rodriguez (Hardball Galaxy)	1.00
215	Frank Thomas (Hardball Galaxy)	.40
216	Mo Vaughn (Hardball Galaxy)	.10
217	Larry Walker (Hardball Galaxy)	.10
218	Checklist (Ken Griffey Jr.)	.50
219	Checklist (Alex Rodriguez)	.60
220	Checklist (Frank Thomas)	.30

Precious Metal Gems

Precious Metal Gems includes 217 (no checklists) player cards from Metal Universe and are serial numbered to 50 sets. Because there were five Ultimate Metal Gems redemption cards (good for a complete set of Metal Gems) available, only serial numbers 1-45 were found in packs (46-50 were held back for the exchange program).

	NM/M
Common Player:	3.00
Stars:	25X
Production 50 Sets	

All-Galactic Team

This 18-card insert captures players over a planet holofoil background. Cards were inserted one per 192 packs.

		NM/M
Complete Set (18):		140.00
Common Player:		3.00
Inserted 1:192		
1	Ken Griffey Jr.	12.50
2	Frank Thomas	7.50
3	Chipper Jones	10.00
4	Albert Belle	3.00
5	Juan Gonzalez	5.00
6	Jeff Bagwell	7.50
7	Andruw Jones	7.50
8	Cal Ripken Jr.	20.00
9	Derek Jeter	20.00
10	Nomar Garciaparra	10.00
11	Darin Erstad	4.00
12	Greg Maddux	10.00
13	Alex Rodriguez	15.00
14	Mike Piazza	12.50
15	Vladimir Guerrero	7.50
16	Jose Cruz Jr.	3.00
17	Mark McGwire	15.00
18	Scott Rolen	5.00

Diamond Heroes

Diamond Heroes displayed six players in a comic book setting. This insert was seeded one per 18 packs and contained a foil etched image of a Marvel comic in the background.

		NM/M
Complete Set (6):		8.00
Common Player:		.50
Inserted 1:18		
1	Ken Griffey Jr.	2.00
2	Frank Thomas	1.50
3	Andruw Jones	1.50
4	Alex Rodriguez	2.50
5	Jose Cruz Jr.	.50
6	Cal Ripken Jr.	3.00

Platinum Portraits

This 12-card insert set featured color portraits of top players highlighted with a platinum-colored etched foil frame over it. Platinum Portraits are seeded one per 360 packs of Metal Universe.

		NM/M
Complete Set (12):		90.00
Common Player:		4.00
Inserted 1:360		
1	Ken Griffey Jr.	12.00
2	Frank Thomas	7.50
3	Chipper Jones	9.00
4	Jose Cruz Jr.	4.00
5	Andruw Jones	7.50
6	Cal Ripken Jr.	17.50
7	Derek Jeter	17.50
8	Darin Erstad	4.00
9	Greg Maddux	9.00
10	Alex Rodriguez	15.00
11	Mike Piazza	12.00
12	Vladimir Guerrero	7.50

Titanium

This die-cut 15-card insert contained color photos printed on embossed, sculpted cards on etched foil. Titanium inserts were seeded one per 96 packs.

		NM/M
Complete Set (15):		50.00
Common Player:		2.00
Inserted 1:96		
1	Ken Griffey Jr.	5.00
2	Frank Thomas	3.00
3	Chipper Jones	4.00
4	Jose Cruz Jr.	2.00
5	Juan Gonzalez	2.50
6	Scott Rolen	2.50
7	Andruw Jones	3.00
8	Cal Ripken Jr.	7.50
9	Derek Jeter	7.50
10	Nomar Garciaparra	4.00
11	Darin Erstad	2.50
12	Greg Maddux	4.00
13	Alex Rodriguez	6.00
14	Mike Piazza	5.00
15	Vladimir Guerrero	3.00

Universal Language

This 20-card insert features illustration and copy done in the player's native language. Cards were die-cut and inserted one per six packs.

		NM/M
Complete Set (20):		16.00
Common Player:		.40
Inserted 1:6		
1	Ken Griffey Jr.	1.25
2	Frank Thomas	.75
3	Chipper Jones	1.00
4	Albert Belle	.40
5	Juan Gonzalez	.60
6	Jeff Bagwell	.75
7	Andruw Jones	.75
8	Cal Ripken Jr.	2.00
9	Derek Jeter	2.00
10	Nomar Garciaparra	1.00
11	Darin Erstad	.50
12	Greg Maddux	1.00
13	Alex Rodriguez	1.50
14	Mike Piazza	1.25
15	Vladimir Guerrero	.75
16	Jose Cruz Jr.	.40
17	Hideo Nomo	.60
18	Kenny Lofton	.40
19	Tony Gwynn	1.00
20	Scott Rolen	.60

1999 Metal Universe Sample Sheet

To introduce its annual issue of embossed cards this six-card sheet of Metal Universe samples was issued. The 5" x 10-1/2" sheet has five regular cards and an example of the Building Blocks insert set. Cards on the sheet are virtually identical to the issued versions except they have the word "SAMPLE" on back in place of card numbers. At the February Hawaii trade show, 325 sheets with a special gold seal, serial numbered and autographed by J.D. Drew were distributed to attendees.

	NM/M
Complete Sheet:	7.50
Complete Autographed Sheet:	60.00

1999 Metal Universe

The 300-card base set offers 232 player cards and three subsets: Building Blocks, M.L.P.D. and Caught on the Fly. Base cards feature an action photo framed in an etched-foil and metallic, embossed name plate. Packs consist of eight cards with an S.R.P. of $2.69. There are two parallels, Precious Metal Gems and Gem Masters. Metal Gems are numbered to 50 with gold-foil etching. Gem Masters are limited to only one set, with silver foil etching and serial numbered "one of one."

		NM/M
Complete Set (300):		15.00
Common Player:		.10
Pack (8):		1.00
Wax Box (24):		20.00
1	Mark McGwire	1.50
2	Jim Edmonds	.10
3	Travis Fryman	.10
4	Tom Gordon	.10
5	Jeff Bagwell	.65
6	Rico Brogna	.10
7	Tom Evans	.10
8	John Franco	.10
9	Juan Gonzalez	.50
10	Paul Molitor	.65
11	Roberto Alomar	.20
12	Mike Hampton	.10
13	Orel Hershiser	.10
14	Todd Stottlemyre	.10
15	Robin Ventura	.10
16	Todd Walker	.10
17	Bernie Williams	.10
18	Shawn Estes	.10
19	Richie Sexson	.10
20	Kevin Millwood	.10
21	David Ortiz	.50
22	Mariano Rivera	.15
23	Ivan Rodriguez	.60
24	Mike Sirotka	.10
25	David Justice	.10
26	Carl Pavano	.10
27	Albert Belle	.10
28	Will Clark	.10
29	Jose Cruz Jr.	.10
30	Trevor Hoffman	.10
31	Dean Palmer	.10
32	Edgar Renteria	.10
33	David Segui	.10
34	B.J. Surhoff	.10
35	Miguel Tejada	.15
36	Bob Wickman	.10
37	Charles Johnson	.10
38	Andruw Jones	.65
39	Mike Lieberthal	.10
40	Eli Marrero	.10
41	Neifi Perez	.10
42	Jim Thome	.50
43	Barry Bonds	2.00
44	Carlos Delgado	.30
45	Chuck Finley	.10
46	Brian Meadows	.10
47	Tony Gwynn	.75
48	Jose Offerman	.10
49	Cal Ripken Jr.	2.00
50	Alex Rodriguez	1.50
51	Esteban Yan	.10
52	Matt Stairs	.10
53	Fernando Vina	.10
54	Rondell White	.10
55	Kerry Wood	.30
56	Dmitri Young	.10
57	Ken Caminiti	.10
58	Alex Gonzalez	.10
59	Matt Mantei	.10
60	Tino Martinez	.10
61	Hal Morris	.10
62	Rafael Palmeiro	.60
63	Troy Percival	.10
64	Bobby Smith	.10
65	Ed Sprague	.10
66	Brett Tomko	.10
67	Steve Trachsel	.10
68	Ugueth Urbina	.10
69	Jose Valentin	.10
70	Kevin Brown	.10
71	Shawn Green	.30
72	Dustin Hermanson	.10
73	Livan Hernandez	.10
74	Geoff Jenkins	.10
75	Jeff King	.10
76	Chuck Knoblauch	.10
77	Edgar Martinez	.10
78	Fred McGriff	.10
79	Mike Mussina	.40
80	Dave Nilsson	.10
81	Kenny Rogers	.10
82	Tim Salmon	.10
83	Reggie Sanders	.10
84	Wilson Alvarez	.10
85	Rod Beck	.10
86	Jose Guillen	.10
87	Bob Higginson	.10
88	Gregg Olson	.10
89	Jeff Shaw	.10
90	Masato Yoshii	.10
91	Todd Helton	.50
92	David Dellucci	.10
93	Johnny Damon	.35
94	Cliff Floyd	.10
95	Ken Griffey Jr.	1.00
96	Juan Guzman	.10
97	Derek Jeter	2.00
98	Barry Larkin	.10
99	Quinton McCracken	.10
100	Sammy Sosa	.85
101	Kevin Young	.10
102	Jay Bell	.10
103	Jay Buhner	.10
104	Jeff Conine	.10
105	Ryan Jackson	.10
106	Sidney Ponson	.10
107	Jeromy Burnitz	.10
108	Roberto Hernandez	.10
109	A.J. Hinch	.10
110	Hideki Irabu	.10
111	Paul Konerko	.20
112	Henry Rodriguez	.10
113	Shannon Stewart	.10
114	Tony Womack	.10
115	Wilton Guerrero	.10
116	Andy Benes	.10
117	Jeff Cirillo	.10
118	Chili Davis	.10
119	Eric Davis	.10
120	Vladimir Guerrero	.65
121	Dennis Reyes	.10
122	Rickey Henderson	.65
123	Mickey Morandini	.10
124	Jason Schmidt	.10
125	J.T. Snow	.10
126	Justin Thompson	.10
127	Billy Wagner	.10
128	Armando Benitez	.10
129	Sean Casey	.15
130	Brad Fullmer	.10
131	Ben Grieve	.10
132	Robb Nen	.10
133	Shane Reynolds	.10
134	Todd Zeile	.10
135	Brady Anderson	.10
136	Aaron Boone	.10
137	Orlando Cabrera	.10
138	Jason Giambi	.50
139	Randy Johnson	.65
140	Jeff Kent	.10
141	John Wetteland	.10
142	Rolando Arrojo	.10
143	Scott Brosius	.10
144	Mark Grace	.10
145	Jason Kendall	.10
146	Travis Lee	.10
147	Gary Sheffield	.40
148	David Cone	.10
149	Jose Hernandez	.10
150	Todd Jones	.10
151	Al Martin	.10
152	Ismael Valdes	.10
153	Wade Boggs	.75
154	Garret Anderson	.10
155	Bobby Bonilla	.10
156	Darryl Kile	.10
157	Ryan Klesko	.10
158	Tim Wakefield	.10
159	Kenny Lofton	.10
160	Jose Canseco	.40
161	Doug Glanville	.10
162	Todd Hundley	.10
163	Brian Jordan	.10
164	Steve Finley	.10
165	Tom Glavine	.25
166	Al Leiter	.10
167	Raul Mondesi	.10
168	Desi Relaford	.10
169	Bret Saberhagen	.10
170	Omar Vizquel	.10
171	Larry Walker	.10
172	Bobby Abreu	.10
173	Moises Alou	.10
174	Mike Caruso	.10
175	Royce Clayton	.10
176	Bartolo Colon	.10
177	Marty Cordova	.10
178	Darin Erstad	.30
179	Nomar Garciaparra	.75
180	Andy Ashby	.10
181	Dan Wilson	.10
182	Larry Sutton	.10
183	Tony Clark	.10
184	Andres Galarraga	.10
185	Ray Durham	.10
186	Hideo Nomo	.60
187	Steve Woodard	.10
188	Scott Rolen	.35
189	Mike Stanley	.10
190	Jaret Wright	.10
191	Vinny Castilla	.10
192	Jason Christiansen	.10
193	Paul Bako	.10
194	Carlos Perez	.10
195	Mike Piazza	1.00
196	Fernando Tatis	.10
197	Mo Vaughn	.10
198	Devon White	.10
199	Ricky Gutierrez	.10
200	Charlie Hayes	.10
201	Brad Radke	.10
202	Rick Helling	.10
203	John Smoltz	.10
204	Frank Thomas	.65
205	David Wells	.10
206	Roger Clemens	.85
207	Mark Grudzielanek	.10
208	Chipper Jones	.75
209	Ray Lankford	.10
210	Pedro Martinez	.65
211	Manny Ramirez	.65
212	Greg Vaughn	.10
213	Craig Biggio	.10
214	Rusty Greer	.10
215	Greg Maddux	.75
216	Rick Aguilera	.10
217	Andy Pettitte	.20
218	Dante Bichette	.10
219	Damion Easley	.10
220	Matt Morris	.10
221	John Olerud	.10
222	Chan Ho Park	.10
223	Curt Schilling	.25
224	John Valentin	.10
225	Matt Williams	.10
226	Ellis Burks	.10
227	Tom Goodwin	.10
228	Javy Lopez	.10
229	Eric Milton	.10
230	Paul O'Neill	.10
231	Magglio Ordonez	.15
232	Derrek Lee	.45
233	Ken Griffey Jr. (Caught on the Fly)	.60
234	Randy Johnson (Caught on the Fly)	.30
235	Alex Rodriguez (Caught on the Fly)	.75
236	Darin Erstad (Caught on the Fly)	.15
237	Juan Gonzalez (Caught on the Fly)	.20
238	Derek Jeter (Caught on the Fly)	1.00
239	Tony Gwynn (Caught on the Fly)	.40
240	Kerry Wood (Caught on the Fly)	.20
241	Cal Ripken Jr. (Caught on the Fly)	1.00
242	Sammy Sosa (Caught on the Fly)	.50
243	Greg Maddux (Caught on the Fly)	.40
244	Mark McGwire (Caught on the Fly)	.75
245	Chipper Jones (Caught on the Fly)	.40
246	Barry Bonds (Caught on the Fly)	1.00
247	Ben Grieve (Caught on the Fly)	.10
248	Ben Davis (Building Blocks)	.10
249	Robert Fick (Building Blocks)	.10
250	Carlos Guillen (Building Blocks)	.10
251	Mike Frank (Building Blocks)	.10
252	Ryan Minor (Building Blocks)	.10
253	Troy Glaus (Building Blocks)	.65
254	Matt Anderson (Building Blocks)	.10
255	Josh Booty (Building Blocks)	.10
256	Gabe Alvarez (Building Blocks)	.10
257	Gabe Kapler (Building Blocks)	.10
258	Enrique Wilson (Building Blocks)	.10
259	Alex Gonzalez (Building Blocks)	.10
260	Preston Wilson (Building Blocks)	.10
261	Eric Chavez (Building Blocks)	.20
262	Adrian Beltre (Building Blocks)	.30
263	Corey Koskie (Building Blocks)	.10
264	Robert Machado **RC** (Building Blocks)	.10
265	Orlando Hernandez (Building Blocks)	.10
266	Matt Clement (Building Blocks)	.10
267	Luis Ordaz (Building Blocks)	.10
268	Jeremy Giambi (Building Blocks)	.10
269	J.D. Drew (Building Blocks)	.50
269a	J.D. Drew (Building Blocks "Sample" autographed edition of 35.)	30.00
270	Cliff Politte (Building Blocks)	.10
271	Carlton Loewer (Building Blocks)	.10
272	Aramis Ramirez (Building Blocks)	.10
273	Ken Griffey Jr. (M.L.P.D.)	.60
274	Randy Johnson (M.L.P.D.)	.30
275	Alex Rodriguez (M.L.P.D.)	.75
276	Darin Erstad (M.L.P.D.)	.20
277	Scott Rolen (M.L.P.D.)	.25
278	Juan Gonzalez (M.L.P.D.)	.20
279	Jeff Bagwell (M.L.P.D.)	.30
280	Mike Piazza (M.L.P.D.)	.65
281	Derek Jeter (M.L.P.D.)	1.00
282	Travis Lee (M.L.P.D.)	.10
283	Tony Gwynn (M.L.P.D.)	.40
284	Kerry Wood (M.L.P.D.)	.20
285	Albert Belle (M.L.P.D.)	.10
286	Sammy Sosa (M.L.P.D.)	.50
287	Mo Vaughn (M.L.P.D.)	.10
288	Nomar Garciaparra (M.L.P.D.)	.45
289	Frank Thomas (M.L.P.D.)	.30
290	Cal Ripken Jr. (M.L.P.D.)	1.00
291	Greg Maddux (M.L.P.D.)	.40
292	Chipper Jones (M.L.P.D.)	.40
293	Ben Grieve (M.L.P.D.)	.10
294	Andruw Jones (M.L.P.D.)	.30
295	Mark McGwire (M.L.P.D.)	.75
296	Roger Clemens (M.L.P.D.)	.50
297	Barry Bonds (M.L.P.D.)	1.00
298	Ken Griffey Jr.-Checklist (M.L.P.D.)	.60

#	Player	Price
299	Kerry Wood-Checklist (M.L.P.D.)	.20
300	Alex Rodriguez-Checklist (M.L.P.D.)	.75

Precious Metal Gems

A 300-card parallel of the base set, these cards feature gold-foil etching and are inserted exclusively in hobby packs. Each card is serially numbered to 50. A Gem Master 1 of 1 parallel was also issued, but is too rare to value.

	NM/M
Common Player:	3.00
Stars:	25X
Gem Master 1 of 1:	(Value Undetermined)

Boyz With The Wood

The top hitters in the game are featured on these folded cards with four sides. These are inserted 1:18.

		NM/M
Complete Set (15):		17.50
Common Player:		.60
Inserted 1:18		
1	Ken Griffey Jr.	2.00
2	Frank Thomas	1.00
3	Jeff Bagwell	1.00
4	Juan Gonzalez	.75
5	Mark McGwire	2.50
6	Scott Rolen	.60
7	Travis Lee	.60
8	Tony Gwynn	2.00
9	Mike Piazza	2.00
10	Chipper Jones	2.00
11	Nomar Garciaparra	2.00
12	Derek Jeter	3.00
13	Cal Ripken Jr.	3.00
14	Andruw Jones	1.00
15	Alex Rodriguez	2.50

Diamond Soul

Utilizing lenticular technology these inserts showcase a soulful "galactic" design. The set consists of 15 cards which are seeded at 1:72 packs.

		NM/M
Complete Set (15):		60.00
Common Player:		1.50
Inserted 1:72		
1	Cal Ripken Jr.	12.00
2	Alex Rodriguez	9.00
3	Chipper Jones	6.00
4	Derek Jeter	12.00
5	Frank Thomas	4.00
6	Greg Maddux	6.00
7	Juan Gonzalez	3.00
8	Ken Griffey Jr.	7.50
9	Kerry Wood	3.00
10	Mark McGwire	9.00
11	Mike Piazza	7.50
12	Nomar Garciaparra	6.00
13	Scott Rolen	2.50
14	Tony Gwynn	6.00
15	Travis Lee	1.50

Linchpins

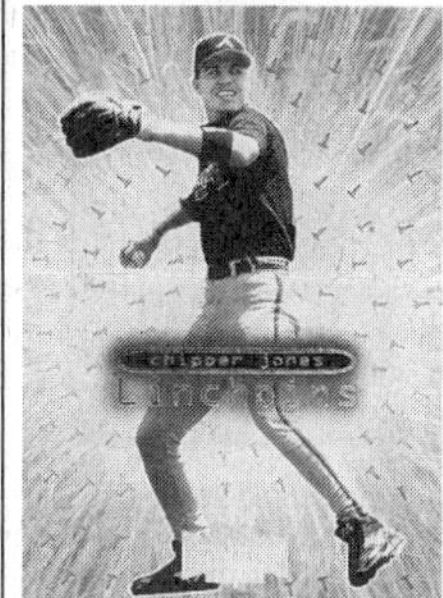

This 10-card set features a laser die-cut background and highlights key players who hold their teams together on the field and in the clubhouse. These are seeded 1:360 packs.

		NM/M
Complete Set (10):		75.00
Common Player:		5.00
Inserted 1:360		
1	Mike Piazza	10.00
2	Mark McGwire	12.50
3	Kerry Wood	5.00
4	Ken Griffey Jr.	10.00
5	Greg Maddux	7.50
6	Frank Thomas	6.00
7	Derek Jeter	15.00
8	Chipper Jones	7.50
9	Cal Ripken Jr.	15.00
10	Alex Rodriguez	12.50

Neophytes

This 15-card insert set showcases young stars like J.D. Drew and Troy Glaus. The cards feature silver foil stamping on a horizontal format, found on an average of 1:6 packs.

		NM/M
Complete Set (15):		7.50
Common Player:		.35
Inserted 1:6		
1	Troy Glaus	3.00
2	Travis Lee	.75
3	Scott Elarton	.35
4	Ricky Ledee	.35
5	Richard Hidalgo	.35
6	J.D. Drew	1.50
7	Paul Konerko	.75
8	Orlando Hernandez	.75
9	Mike Caruso	.35
10	Mike Frank	.35
11	Miguel Tejada	.50
12	Matt Anderson	.35
13	Kerry Wood	1.00
14	Gabe Alvarez	.35
15	Adrian Beltre	.50

Planet Metal

These die-cut cards feature a metallic view of the planet behind pop-out action photography. The 15-card set features the top players in the game and are seeded 1:36 packs.

		NM/M
Complete Set (15):		45.00
Common Player:		1.50
Inserted 1:36		
1	Alex Rodriguez	9.00
2	Andruw Jones	3.50
3	Cal Ripken Jr.	12.00
4	Chipper Jones	5.00
5	Darin Erstad	2.00
6	Derek Jeter	12.00
7	Frank Thomas	3.50
8	Travis Lee	1.50
9	Scott Rolen	2.50
10	Nomar Garciaparra	5.00
11	Mike Piazza	6.50
12	Mark McGwire	9.00
13	Ken Griffey Jr.	6.50
14	Juan Gonzalez	2.50
15	Jeff Bagwell	3.50

2000 Metal

		NM/M
Complete Set (250):		20.00
Common Player:		.10
Common Prospect (201-250):		.50
Inserted 1:2		
Pack (10):		1.50
Wax Box (28):		25.00
1	Tony Gwynn	1.00
2	Derek Jeter	2.50
3	Johnny Damon	.35
4	Javy Lopez	.10
5	Preston Wilson	.10
6	Derek Bell	.10
7	Richie Sexson	.10
8	Vinny Castilla	.10
9	Billy Wagner	.10
10	Carlos Beltran	.50
11	Chris Singleton	.10
12	Nomar Garciaparra	1.00
13	Carlos Febles	.10
14	Jason Varitek	.10
15	Luis Gonzalez	.20
16	Jon Lieber	.10
17	Mo Vaughn	.10
18	Dave Burba	.10
19	Brady Anderson	.10
20	Carlos Lee	.20
21	Chuck Finley	.10
22	Alex Gonzalez	.10
23	Matt Williams	.10
24	Chipper Jones	1.00
25	Pokey Reese	.10
26	Todd Helton	.65
27	Mike Mussina	.40
28	Butch Huskey	.10
29	Jeff Bagwell	.75
30	Juan Encarnacion	.10
31	A.J. Burnett	.10
32	Micah Bowie	.10
33	Brian Jordan	.10
34	Scott Erickson	.10
35	Sean Casey	.25
36	John Smoltz	.10
37	Edgard Clemente	.10
38	Mike Hampton	.10
39	Tom Glavine	.35
40	Albert Belle	.10
41	Jim Thome	.60
42	Jermaine Dye	.10
43	Sammy Sosa	1.25
44	Pedro Martinez	.75
45	Paul Konerko	.20
46	Damion Easley	.10
47	Cal Ripken Jr.	2.50
48	Jose Lima	.10
49	Mike Lowell	.10
50	Randy Johnson	.75
51	Dean Palmer	.10
52	Tim Salmon	.10
53	Kevin Millwood	.10
54	Mark Grace	.10
55	Aaron Boone	.10
56	Omar Vizquel	.10
57	Moises Alou	.10
58	Travis Fryman	.10
59	Erubiel Durazo	.10
60	Carl Everett	.10
61	Charles Johnson	.10
62	Trot Nixon	.10
63	Andres Galarraga	.10
64	Magglio Ordonez	.10
65	Pedro Astacio	.10
66	Roberto Alomar	.20
67	Pete Harnisch	.10
68	Scott Williamson	.10
69	Alex Fernandez	.10
70	Robin Ventura	.10
71	Chad Allen	.10
72	Darin Erstad	.20
73	Ron Coomer	.10
74	Ellis Burks	.10
75	Kent Bottenfield	.10
76	Ken Griffey Jr.	1.50
77	Mike Piazza	1.50
78	Jorge Posada	.20
79	Dante Bichette	.10
80	Adrian Beltre	.25
81	Andruw Jones	.75
82	Wilson Alvarez	.10
83	Edgardo Alfonzo	.10
84	Brian Giles	.10
85	Gary Sheffield	.25
86	Matt Stairs	.10
87	Bret Boone	.10
88	Kenny Rogers	.10
89	Barry Bonds	2.50
90	Scott Rolen	.60
91	Edgar Renteria	.10
92	Larry Walker	.10
93	Roger Cedeno	.10
94	Kevin Brown	.10
95	Lee Stevens	.10
96	Brad Radke	.10
97	Andy Pettitte	.25
98	Bobby Higginson	.10
99	Eric Chavez	.25
100	Alex Rodriguez	2.00
100s	Alex Rodriguez/OPS	2.00
101	Shannon Stewart	.10
102	Ryan Rupe	.10
103	Freddy Garcia	.10
104	John Jaha	.10
105	Greg Maddux	1.00
106	Hideki Irabu	.10
107	Rey Ordonez	.10
108	Troy O'Leary	.10
109	Frank Thomas	.75
110	Corey Koskie	.10
111	Bernie Williams	.10
112	Barry Larkin	.10
113	Kevin Appier	.10
114	Curt Schilling	.35
115	Bartolo Colon	.10
116	Edgar Martinez	.10
117	Ray Lankford	.10
118	Todd Walker	.10
119	John Wetteland	.10
120	David Nilsson	.10
121	Tino Martinez	.10
122	Phil Nevin	.10
123	Ben Grieve	.10
124	Ron Gant	.10
125	Jeff Kent	.10
126	Rick Helling	.10
127	Russ Ortiz	.10
128	Troy Glaus	.65
129	Chan Ho Park	.10
130	Jeromy Burnitz	.10
131	Aaron Sele	.10
132	Mike Sirotka	.10
133	Brad Ausmus	.10
134	Jose Rosado	.10
135	Mariano Rivera	.25
136	Jason Giambi	.50
137	Mike Lieberthal	.10
138	Chris Carpenter	.10
139	Henry Rodriguez	.10
140	Mike Sweeney	.10
141	Vladimir Guerrero	.75
142	Charles Nagy	.10
143	Jason Kendall	.10
144	Matt Lawton	.10
145	Michael Barrett	.10
146	David Cone	.10
147	Bobby Abreu	.10
148	Fernando Tatis	.10
149	Jose Canseco	.40
150	Craig Biggio	.10
151	Matt Mantei	.10
152	Jacque Jones	.10
153	John Halama	.10
154	Trevor Hoffman	.10
155	Rondell White	.10
156	Reggie Sanders	.10
157	Steve Finley	.10
158	Roberto Hernandez	.10
159	Geoff Jenkins	.10
160	Chris Widger	.10
161	Orel Hershiser	.10
162	Tim Hudson	.20
163	Kris Benson	.10
164	Kevin Young	.10
165	Rafael Palmeiro	.60
166	David Wells	.10
167	Ben Davis	.10
168	Jamie Moyer	.10
169	Randy Wolf	.10
170	Jeff Cirillo	.10
171	Warren Morris	.10
172	Billy Koch	.10
173	Marquis Grissom	.10
174	Geoff Blum	.10
175	Octavio Dotel	.10
176	Orlando Hernandez	.20
177	J.D. Drew	.25
178	Carlos Delgado	.40
179	Sterling Hitchcock	.10
180	Shawn Green	.25
181	Tony Clark	.10
182	Joe McEwing	.10
183	Fred McGriff	.10
184	Tony Batista	.10
185	Al Leiter	.10
186	Roger Clemens	1.25
187	Al Martin	.10
188	Eric Milton	.10
189	Bobby Smith	.10
190	Rusty Greer	.10
191	Shawn Estes	.10
192	Ken Caminiti	.10
193	Eric Karros	.10
194	Manny Ramirez	.75
195	Jim Edmonds	.10
196	Paul O'Neill	.10
197	Rico Brogna	.10
198	Ivan Rodriguez	.60
199	Doug Glanville	.10
200	Mark McGwire	2.00
201	Mark Quinn (Prospect)	.50
202	Norm Hutchins (Prospect)	.50
203	Ramon Ortiz (Prospect)	.50
204	Brett Laxton (Prospect)	.50
205	Jimmy Anderson (Prospect)	.50
206	Calvin Murray (Prospect)	.50
207	Wilton Veras (Prospect)	.50
208	Chad Hermansen (Prospect)	.50
209	Nick Johnson (Prospect)	.50
210	Kevin Barker (Prospect)	.50
211	Casey Blake (Prospect)	.50
212	Chad Meyers (Prospect)	.50
213	Kip Wells (Prospect)	.50
214	Eric Munson (Prospect)	.50
215	Lance Berkman (Prospect)	.50
216	Wily Pena (Prospect)	.50
217	Gary Matthews Jr. (Prospect)	.50
218	Travis Dawkins (Prospect)	.50
219	Josh Beckett (Prospect)	.75
220	Tony Armas Jr. (Prospect)	.50
221	Alfonso Soriano (Prospect)	1.00
222	Pat Burrell (Prospect)	1.00
223	Danys Baez **RC** (Prospect)	.50
224	Adam Kennedy (Prospect)	.50
225	Ruben Mateo (Prospect)	.50
226	Vernon Wells (Prospect)	.75
227	Brian Cooper (Prospect)	.50
228	Jeff DaVanon **RC** (Prospect)	.50
229	Glen Barker (Prospect)	.50
230	Robinson Cancel (Prospect)	.50
231	D'Angelo Jimenez (Prospect)	.50
232	Adam Piatt (Prospect)	.50
233	Buddy Carlyle (Prospect)	.50
234	Chad Hutchinson (Prospect)	.50
235	Matt Riley (Prospect)	.50
236	Cole Liniak (Prospect)	.50
237	Ben Petrick (Prospect)	.50
238	Peter Bergeron (Prospect)	.50
239	Cesar King (Prospect)	.50
240	Aaron Myette (Prospect)	.50
241	Eric Gagne (Prospect)	.60
242	Joe Nathan (Prospect)	.50
243	Bruce Chen (Prospect)	.50
244	Rob Bell (Prospect)	.50
245	Juan Sosa **RC** (Prospect)	.60
246	Julio Ramirez (Prospect)	.50
247	Wade Miller (Prospect)	.50
248	Trace Coquillette **RC** (Prospect)	.50
249	Robert Ramsay (Prospect)	.50
250	Rick Ankiel (Prospect)	.60

Emerald

A green tone at the top 1/4 of the card fronts, and a small circled "E" at top-right on back differentiate these parallels from the regular-issue cards. The first 200 cards in the set

are found in this version about one every four packs. The odds double for the Prospects cards (#201-250) that were short-printed in the regular version as well.

	NM/M
Complete Set (250):	100.00
Common Player:	.25
Stars:	2.5X
Inserted 1:4	
Prospects (201-250):	2.5X
Inserted 1:8	

Fusion

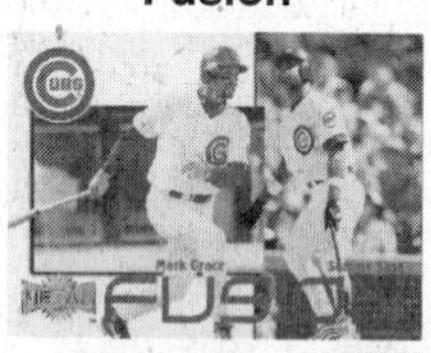

		NM/M
Complete Set (15):		12.50
Common Player:		.50
Inserted 1:4		
1	Ken Griffey Jr., Alex Rodriguez	2.00
2	Mark McGwire, Rick Ankiel	2.00
3	Scott Rolen, Curt Schilling	.50
4	Pedro Martinez, Nomar Garciaparra	1.25
5	Carlos Beltran, Carlos Febles	.60
6	Sammy Sosa, Mark Grace	1.50
7	Vladimir Guerrero, Ugueth Urbina	1.00
8	Roger Clemens, Derek Jeter	3.00
9	Jeff Bagwell, Craig Biggio	1.00
10	Chipper Jones, Andruw Jones	1.50
11	Cal Ripken Jr., Mike Mussina	2.50
12	Manny Ramirez, Roberto Alomar	1.00
13	Sean Casey, Barry Larkin	.50
14	Ivan Rodriguez, Rafael Palmeiro	.75
15	Mike Piazza, Robin Ventura	1.50

Autographics

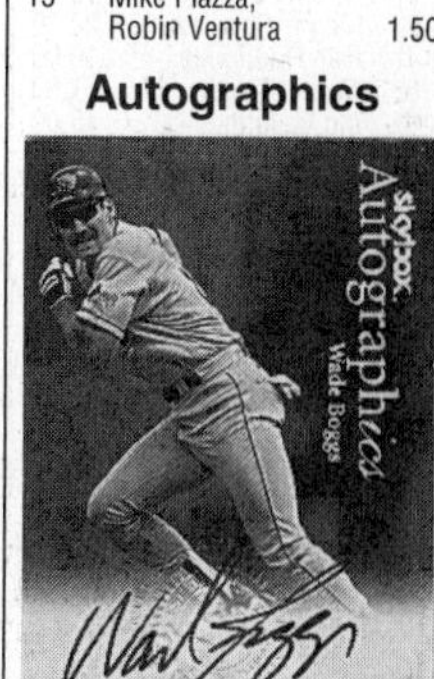

	NM/M
Common Player:	4.00
Bobby Abreu	8.00
Chad Allen	4.00
Marlon Anderson	4.00
Rick Ankiel	6.00
Glen Barker	4.00
Rob Bell	4.00
Mark Bellhorn	5.00
Peter Bergeron	4.00
Lance Berkman	8.00
Wade Boggs	25.00
Barry Bonds	150.00
Kent Bottenfield	4.00

Pat Burrell	10.00
Miguel Cairo	4.00
Mike Cameron	6.00
Chris Carpenter	6.00
Roger Cedeno	4.00
Mike Darr	6.00
Einar Diaz	4.00
J.D. Drew	15.00
Erubiel Durazo	6.00
Ray Durham	6.00
Damion Easley	4.00
Scott Elarton	4.00
Jeremy Giambi	4.00
Doug Glanville	4.00
Shawn Green	10.00
Jerry Hairston Jr.	4.00
Bob Howry	4.00
Norm Hutchins	4.00
Randy Johnson	40.00
Jacque Jones	4.00
Gabe Kapler	6.00
Cesar King	4.00
Mark Kotsay	4.00
Cole Liniak	4.00
Greg Maddux	50.00
Pedro Martinez	30.00
Ruben Mateo	4.00
Warren Morris	4.00
Heath Murray	4.00
Joe Nathan	4.00
Jim Parque	4.00
Angel Pena	4.00
Cal Ripken Jr.	100.00
Alex Rodriguez	60.00
Ryan Rupe	4.00
Randall Simon	4.00
Chris Singleton	4.00
Mike Sweeney	6.00
Wilton Veras	4.00
Scott Williamson	4.00
Randy Wolf	6.00
Tony Womack	6.00

Base Shredders

	NM/M
Complete Set (18):	160.00
Common Player:	5.00
Inserted 1:288	
(1) Roberto Alomar	7.50
(2) Michael Barrett	5.00
(3) Tony Clark	5.00
(4) Ben Davis	5.00
(5) Erubiel Durazo	5.00
(6) Troy Glaus	12.50
(7) Ben Grieve	5.00
(8) Vladimir Guerrero	15.00
(9) Tony Gwynn	25.00
(10) Todd Helton	12.50
(11) Eric Munson	5.00
(12) Rafael Palmeiro	10.00
(13) Manny Ramirez	20.00
(14) Ivan Rodriguez	10.00
(15) Miguel Tejada	7.50
(16) Mo Vaughn	5.00
(17) Larry Walker	5.00
(18) Matt Williams	5.00

Heavy Metal

	NM/M
Complete Set (10):	15.00
Common Player:	1.50
Inserted 1:20	
1 Sammy Sosa	2.25
2 Mark McGwire	3.00
3 Ken Griffey Jr.	2.50
4 Mike Piazza	2.50
5 Nomar Garciaparra	2.00
6 Alex Rodriguez	3.00
7 Manny Ramirez	1.50
8 Jeff Bagwell	1.50
9 Chipper Jones	2.00
10 Vladimir Guerrero	1.50

Hit Machines

	NM/M
Complete Set (10):	20.00
Common Player:	1.00
Inserted 1:20	
1 Ken Griffey Jr.	3.00
2 Mark McGwire	4.00
3 Frank Thomas	1.50
4 Tony Gwynn	2.00
5 Rafael Palmeiro	1.25
6 Bernie Williams	1.00
7 Derek Jeter	6.00
8 Sammy Sosa	2.50
9 Mike Piazza	3.00
10 Chipper Jones	2.00

Platinum Portraits

	NM/M
Complete Set (10):	6.00
Common Player:	.25
Inserted 1:8	
1 Carlos Beltran	.50
2 Vladimir Guerrero	.75
3 Manny Ramirez	.75
4 Ivan Rodriguez	.65
5 Sean Casey	.40
6 Alex Rodriguez	1.50
7 Derek Jeter	2.00
8 Nomar Garciaparra	1.00
9 Vernon Wells	.25
10 Shawn Green	.50

Talent Show

	NM/M
Complete Set (15):	6.00
Common Player:	.30
Inserted 1:4	
1 Rick Ankiel	.45
2 Matt Riley	.30
3 Chad Hermansen	.30
4 Ruben Mateo	.30
5 Eric Munson	.30
6 Alfonso Soriano	1.50
7 Wilton Veras	.30
8 Vernon Wells	.75
9 Erubiel Durazo	.30
10 Pat Burrell	1.50
11 Ben Davis	.30
12 A.J. Burnett	.30
13 Peter Bergeron	.30
14 Mark Quinn	.30
15 Ben Petrick	.30

1993 Metz Bakeries

Metz Baking Co. of Sioux City, Iowa, produced this set utilizing drawings of players rather than photos. The company also made available uncut sheets of the sets via a mail-in offer. Cards have either a yellow background with blue pinstripes or a blue background with yellow pinstripes. Players are shown in a red, white and black porthole at center. Backs are printed in black-and-white with complete major and minor league stats. Because the cards are licensed only by the Players Union and not Major League Baseball, the player paintings omit uniform logos. The unnumbered cards are checklisted here in alphabetical order. A special collectors tin to house the set was also available.

	NM/M
Complete Set (40):	35.00
Common Player:	.75
(1) Dante Bichette	.75
(2) Wade Boggs	2.00
(3) Barry Bonds	4.00
(4) Bobby Bonilla	.75
(5) Jose Canseco	1.00
(6) Joe Carter	.75
(7) Will Clark	.75
(8) Roger Clemens	2.25
(9) Doug Drabek	.75
(10) Shawon Dunston	.75
(11) Dennis Eckersley	1.25
(12) Cecil Fielder	.75
(13) Carlton Fisk	1.50
(14) Andres Galarraga	.75
(15) Kirk Gibson	.75
(16) Dwight Gooden	.75
(17) Mark Grace	.75
(18) Ken Griffey Jr.	2.50
(19) Tony Gwynn	2.00
(20) Rickey Henderson	1.50
(21) Kent Hrbek	.75
(22) Howard Johnson	.75
(23) Wally Joyner	.75
(24) Dave Justice	.75
(25) Barry Larkin	.75
(26) Don Mattingly	2.50
(27) Jack McDowell	.75
(28) Paul Molitor	1.50
(29) Terry Pendleton	.75
(30) Kirby Puckett	2.00
(31) Cal Ripken, Jr.	4.00
(32) Nolan Ryan	4.00
(33) Ryne Sandberg	2.00
(34) Ozzie Smith	2.00
(35) Darryl Strawberry	.75
(36) Danny Tartabull	.75
(37) Mickey Tettleton	.75
(38) Alan Trammell	.75
(39) Andy Van Slyke	.75
(40) Dave Winfield	1.50

1993 Milk Bone Super Stars

1993 Limited Edition
Mark McGwire 1B
Ellis & Sam

Milk Bone Flavor Snacks and Dog Treats issued a 20-card Super Stars set in 1993 in a format comprable to the NFL Pro Line cards. The cards show the player at home with his dog, with the player shown in an action photo in the lower left corner of the card. The card backs have the player's stats and biography, along with information about the pet and a quote from the player about his dog. The cards were available, two at a time, in specially-marked packages of the company's products. The set also could be obtained through the mail by following instructions on the boxes.

	NM/M
Complete Set (20):	12.50
Common Player:	.50
(1) Paul Molitor	1.00
(2) Tom Glavine	.65
(3) Barry Larkin	.50
(4) Mark McGwire	2.50
(5) Bill Swift	.50
(6) Ken Caminiti	.50
(7) Will Clark	.50
(8) Rafael Palmeiro	.75
(9) Matt Young	.50
(10) Todd Zeile	.50
(11) Wally Joyner	.50
(12) Cal Ripken Jr.	3.50
(13) Tom Foley	.50
(14) Ben McDonald	.50
(15) Larry Walker	.50
(16) Rob Dibble	.50
(17) Brett Butler	.50
(18) Joe Girardi	.50
(19) Brady Anderson	.50
(20) Craig Biggio	.50

1989 Milk Duds Pittsburgh Pirates

This set of Pirates photocards carries on its backs advertising for various brands of Leaf candies, principally Milk Duds. The 3-3/8" x 5-1/2" cards have color portrait photo on front with the player's name near the bottom and a team logo at bottom center. Backs have a few vital statistics, candy advertising and/or free ticket or contest offers. The cards are numbered by uniform number, but are listed here in alphabetical order.

	NM/M
Complete Set (38):	20.00
Common Player:	.75
(1) Pirate Parrot (Mascot)	.75
(2) Rafael Belliard	.75
(3) Dann Bilardello	.75
(4) Barry Bonds	9.00
(5) Sid Bream	.75
(6) Bobby Bonilla	1.00
(7) John Cangelosi	.75
(8) Benny Distefano	.75
(9) Rich Donnelly	.75
(10) Doug Drabek	.75
(11) Brian Fisher	.75
(12) Miguel Garcia	.75
(13) Jim Gott	.75
(14) Neal Heaton	.75
(15) Bruce Kimm	.75
(16) Jeff King	1.00
(17) Bob Kipper	.75
(18) Randy Kramer	.75
(19) Gene Lamont	.75
(20) Bill Landrum	.75
(21) Mike LaValliere	.75
(22) Jim Leyland	.75
(23) Jose Lind	.75
(24) Morris Madden	.75
(25) Milt May	.75
(26) Ray Miller	.75
(27) Junior Ortiz	.75
(28) Tom Prince	.75
(29) Rey Quinones	.75
(30) Gary Redus	.75
(31) R.J. Reynolds	.75
(32) Jeff Robinson	.75
(33) Tommy Sandt	.75
(34) John Smiley	.75
(35) Dorn Taylor	.75
(36) Andy Van Slyke	1.00
(37) Bob Walk	.75
(38) Glenn Wilson	.75

1997 Milk Mustache Trading Cards

Sponsored by the National Fluid Milk Processor Promotion Board (really), this nine-card panel was an advertising insert in the October 1997, issue of Sports Illustrated for Kids. The perforated panel measures about 7-1/2" x 10-1/2", with each card measuring the standard 2-1/2" x 3-1/2" and perforated on two, three or four sides, depending on its placement on the sheet. Player portrait photos are set on a silver-look background. Cap and uniform logos have been eliminated and a milk moustache added. "MILK" appears in white in a purple stripe at the top of each player's card. Backs have a baseball tip and a milk tip ascribed to each player.

	NM/M
Complete Sheet:	5.00
Complete Set (9):	5.00
Common Player:	.25
1 Alex Rodriguez	2.50
2 Nomar Garciaparra	1.00
3 Andy Pettitte	.35
4 Darin Erstad	.45
5 Jason Kendall	.25
6 Vladimir Guerrero	1.00
7 Scott Rolen	.60
8 Tony Clark	.25
-- Header Card	.05

1990 Miller Beer Milwaukee Brewers

This 32-card set was given away with an album to adults attending an August Brewers game. Cards are standard 2-1/2" x 3-1/2" and feature borderless color photos above gold and black bottom stripes. The beer company's logo is featured in the upper-right corner, with the team logo at lower-left. Black-and-white backs feature player stats. The set has been checklisted below in alphabetical order. Cards are not numbered.

	NM/M
Complete Set w/Album (32):	10.00
Common Player:	.25
(1) Chris Bosio	.25
(2) Greg Brock	.25
(3) Chuck Crim	.25
(4) Rob Deer	.25
(5) Edgar Diaz	.25
(6) Tom Edens	.25
(7) Mike Felder	.25
(8) Tom Filer	.25
(9) Jim Gantner	.25
(10) Darryl Hamilton	.25
(11) Teddy Higuera	.25
(12) Mark Knudson	.25
(13) Bill Krueger	.25
(14) Paul Mirabella	.25
(15) Paul Molitor	4.00
(16) Jaime Navarro	.25
(17) Charlie O'Brien	.25
(18) Dave Parker	.25
(19) Dan Plesac	.25
(20) Dennis Powell	.25
(21) Ron Robinson	.25
(22) Bob Sebra	.25
(23) Gary Sheffield	2.00
(24) Bill Spiers	.25
(25) B.J. Surhoff	.25
(26) Dale Sveum	.25
(27) Tom Trebelhorn	.25
(28) Greg Vaughn	.25
(29) Randy Veres	.25
(30) Bill Wegman	.25
(31) Robin Yount	4.00
(32) Coaches (Don Baylor, Ray Burris, Duffy Dyer, Andy Etchebarren, Larry Haney)	.25

1991 Miller Beer Milwaukee Brewers

The Miller High Life Brewing Co., in conjunction with the Milwaukee Brewers, sponsored a 32-card limited edition baseball card set in 1991. The set, which features 30 cards of Brewer players plus additional cards of manager Tom Trebelhorn and his coaching staff, employs a home plate window for the front photo, with the player's name and words "Miller High Life" along the bottom of the card. Complete major and minor league stats are printed on the black-and-white backs, which also include sponsors' logos.

	NM/M
Complete Set w/Album (32):	10.00
Common Player:	.25
(1) Don August	.25
(2) James Austin	.25
(3) Dante Bichette	.35
(4) Chris Bosio	.25
(5) Kevin Brown	.25
(6) Chuck Crim	.25
(7) Rick Dempsey	.25
(8) Jim Gantner	.25
(9) Darryl Hamilton	.25
(10) Teddy Higuera	.25
(11) Darren Holmes	.25
(12) Jim Hunter	.25
(13) Mark Knudson	.25
(14) Mark Lee	.25
(15) Julio Machado	.25
(16) Candy Maldonado	.25
(17) Paul Molitor	4.00
(18) Jaime Navarro	.25
(19) Edwin Nunez	.25
(20) Dan Plesac	.25
(21) Willie Randolph	.25
(22) Ron Robinson	.25
(23) Gary Sheffield	1.00
(24) Bill Spiers	.25
(25) Franklin Stubbs	.25
(26) B.J. Surhoff	.25

(27)	Dale Sveum	.25
(28)	Tom Treblehorn	.25
(29)	Greg Vaughn	.25
(30)	Bill Wegman	.25
(31)	Robin Yount	4.00

1994 Miller Genuine Draft Milwaukee Brewers

No Pricing

1984 Milton Bradley

In 1984 Milton Bradley printed their baseball game cards in full-color and adopted the standard baseball card size of 2-1/2" x 3-1/2". A total of 30 cards were in the set. The card fronts show the player photos with the team insignias and logos airbrushed away. The game is called Championship Baseball. Card backs varied in style; some had player statistics plus game information, and others only game information.

		NM/M
Complete Boxed Set:		12.00
Complete Card Set (30):		7.50
Common Player:		.25
(1)	Wade Boggs	.75
(2)	George Brett	1.50
(3)	Rod Carew	.50
(4)	Steve Carlton	.50
(5)	Gary Carter	.50
(6)	Dave Concepcion	.25
(7)	Cecil Cooper	.25
(8)	Andre Dawson	.40
(9)	Carlton Fisk	.50
(10)	Steve Garvey	.40
(11)	Pedro Guerrero	.25
(12)	Ron Guidry	.25
(13)	Rickey Henderson	.50
(14)	Reggie Jackson	1.50
(15)	Ron Kittle	.25
(16)	Bill Madlock	.25
(17)	Dale Murphy	.40
(18)	Al Oliver	.25
(19)	Darrell Porter	.25
(20)	Cal Ripken, Jr.	2.50
(21)	Pete Rose	1.50
(22)	Steve Sax	.25
(23)	Mike Schmidt	1.50
(24)	Ted Simmons	.25
(25)	Ozzie Smith	.75
(26)	Dave Stieb	.25
(27)	Fernando Valenzuela	.25
(28)	Lou Whitaker	.25
(29)	Dave Winfield	.50
(30)	Robin Yount	.50

1982 Milwaukee Brewers Police

ROBIN YOUNT
No. 19 — Shortstop
New Berlin Police Department
Salutes The 1982
Milwaukee Brewers

The inaugural Milwaukee Brewers police set contains 30 cards in a 2-13/16" x 4-1/8" format. There are 26 players included in the set, which is numbered by player uniform number. Unnumbered cards were also issued for general manager Harry Dalton, manager Buck Rodgers, the coaches and a team card with checklist. The full-color photos are especially attractive, printed on the cards' crisp white stock. A number of Wisconsin law enforcement agencies distributed the cards and credit lines on the card fronts were changed accordingly.

		NM/M
Complete Set (30):		12.00
Common Player:		.25
4	Paul Molitor	4.00
5	Ned Yost	.25
7	Don Money	.25
9	Larry Hisle	.25
10	Bob McClure	.25
11	Ed Romero	.25
13	Roy Howell	.25
15	Cecil Cooper	.25
17	Jim Gantner	.25
19	Robin Yount	4.00
20	Gorman Thomas	.25
22	Charlie Moore	.25
23	Ted Simmons	.25
24	Ben Oglivie	.25
26	Kevin Bass	.25
28	Jamie Easterly	.25
29	Mark Brouhard	.25
30	Moose Haas	.25
34	Rollie Fingers	2.00
35	Randy Lerch	.25
37	Buck Rodgers	.25
41	Jim Slaton	.25
45	Doug Jones	.25
46	Jerry Augustine	.25
47	Dwight Bernard	.25
48	Mike Caldwell	.25
50	Pete Vuckovich	.25
---	Team Photo/Checklist	.25
---	Harry Dalton (General Mgr.)	.25
---	Coaches Card (Pat Dobson, Larry Haney, Ron Hansen, Cal McLish, Buck Rogers, Harry Warner)	.25

1983 Milwaukee Brewers Police

Similar to 1982, a number of issuer variations exist for the 1983 Brewers police set, as law enforcement agencies throughout the state distributed the set with their own credit lines on the cards. At least 28 variations are known to exist, with those issued by smaller agencies being scarcest. Prices quoted below are for the most common variations, generally the Milwaukee Police Department and a few small-town departments whose entire supply of police cards seem to have fallen into dealers' hands. Some specialists are willing to pay a premium for the scarcer departments' issues. The 30, 2-13/16" x 4-1/8" cards include 29 players and coaches, along with a team card (with a checklist back). The team card and group coaches' card are unnumbered, while the others are numbered by uniform number.

		NM/M
Complete Set (30):		6.00
Common Player:		.25
4	Paul Molitor	3.00
5	Ned Yost	.25
7	Don Money	.25
8	Rob Picciolo	.25
10	Bob McClure	.25
11	Ed Romero	.25
13	Roy Howell	.25
15	Cecil Cooper	.25
16	Marshall Edwards	.25
17	Jim Gantner	.25
19	Robin Yount	3.00
20	Gorman Thomas	.25
21	Don Sutton	1.00
22	Charlie Moore	.25
23	Ted Simmons	.25
24	Ben Oglivie	.25
26	Bob Skube	.25
27	Pete Ladd	.25
28	Jamie Easterly	.25
30	Moose Haas	.25
32	Harvey Kuenn	.25
34	Rollie Fingers	1.00
40	Bob L. Gibson	.25
41	Jim Slaton	.25
42	Tom Tellmann	.25
46	Jerry Augustine	.25
48	Mike Caldwell	.25
50	Pete Vuckovich	.25
---	Team Photo/Checklist	.25
---	Coaches Card (Pat Dobson, Dave Garcia, Larry Haney, Ron Hansen)	.25

1984 Milwaukee Brewers Police

The king of the variations again in 1984, the Milwaukee Brewers set has been found with 57 different police agencies' credit lines on the front of the cards. Once again, law enforcement agencies statewide participated in distributing the sets. Some departments also include a badge of the participating agency on the card backs. The full-color cards measure 2-13/16" x 4-1/8". There are 28 numbered player and manager cards, along with an unnumbered coaches card and a team card. Player names, uniform numbers and positions are listed on each card front. Prices listed are for the most common variety (Milwaukee Police Department); sets issued by smaller departments may be worth a premium to specialists. Reported print runs varied from 120,000 sets for the Milwaukee P.D., to just 500 sets for the community of Verona.

		NM/M
Complete Set (30):		6.00
Common Player:		.15
2	Randy Ready	.15
4	Paul Molitor	2.50
8	Jim Sundberg	.15
9	Rene Lachemann	.15
10	Bob McClure	.15
11	Ed Romero	.15
13	Roy Howell	.15
14	Dion James	.15
15	Cecil Cooper	.15
17	Jim Gantner	.15
19	Robin Yount	2.50
20	Don Sutton	1.00
21	Bill Schroeder	.15
22	Charlie Moore	.15
23	Ted Simmons	.15
24	Ben Oglivie	.15
25	Bobby Clark	.15
27	Pete Ladd	.15
28	Rick Manning	.15
29	Mark Brouhard	.15
30	Moose Haas	.15
34	Rollie Fingers	1.00
42	Tom Tellmann	.15
43	Chuck Porter	.15
46	Jerry Augustine	.15
47	Jaime Cocanower	.15
48	Mike Caldwell	.15
50	Pete Vuckovich	.15
---	Team Photo/Checklist	.15
---	Coaches Card (Pat Dobson, Dave Garcia, Larry Haney, Tom Trebelhorn)	.15

1985 Milwaukee Brewers Police

49 Ted Higuera P
The Milwaukee Police Department
and The Milwaukee Journal
present the 1985
Milwaukee Brewers

The Brewers changed the size of their annual police set in 1985, but almost imperceptibly. The full-color cards are 2-3/4" x 4-1/8", a slight 1/16" narrower than the four previous efforts. Player and team name on the card fronts are much bolder than in previous years. Once again, numerous area police groups distributed the sets, leading to nearly 60 variations, as each agency put their own credit line on the cards. Card backs include the Brewers logo, a safety tip and, in some cases, a badge of the participating law enforcement group. There are 27 numbered player cards (by uniform number) and three unnumbered cards - team roster, coaches and a newspaper carrier card. Prices are for the most common departments.

		NM/M
Complete Set (30):		6.00
Common Player:		.15
2	Randy Ready	.15
4	Paul Molitor	2.50
5	Doug Loman	.15
7	Paul Householder	.15
10	Bob McClure	.15
11	Ed Romero	.15
14	Dion James	.15
15	Cecil Cooper	.15
17	Jim Gantner	.15
18	Danny Darwin	.15
19	Robin Yount	2.50
21	Bill Schroeder	.15
22	Charlie Moore	.15
23	Ted Simmons	.15
24	Ben Oglivie	.15
26	Brian Giles	.15
27	Pete Ladd	.15
28	Rick Manning	.15
29	Mark Brouhard	.15
30	Moose Haas	.15
31	George Bamberger	.15
34	Rollie Fingers	1.00
40	Bob L. Gibson	.15
41	Ray Searage	.15
47	Jaime Cocanower	.15
48	Ray Burris	.15
49	Ted Higuera	.15
50	Pete Vuckovich	.15
---	Coaches Card (Andy Etchebarren, Larry Haney, Frank Howard, Tony Muser, Herm Starrette)	.15
---	Team Photo	.15

1986 Milwaukee Brewers Police

The Milwaukee Brewers, in conjunction with the Milwaukee Police Department, WTMJ Radio and Kinney Shoes, produced this attractive police safety set of 30 cards. The cards measure 2-13/16" x 4-1/2". A thin black border encloses a full-color player photo on the front. The card backs give a safety tip and promos for the sponsor. The cards were distributed throughout the state of Wisconsin by numerous police

departments; those of the smaller departments generally being scarcer than those issued in the big cities. Prices quoted below are for the most common departments' issues.

		NM/M
Complete Set (30):		4.00
Common Player:		.15
1	Ernest Riles	.15
2	Randy Ready	.15
3	Juan Castillo	.15
4	Paul Molitor	2.00
7	Paul Householder	.15
10	Bob McClure	.15
11	Rick Cerone	.15
13	Billy Jo Robidoux	.15
15	Cecil Cooper	.15
16	Mike Felder	.15
17	Jim Gantner	.15
18	Danny Darwin	.15
19	Robin Yount	2.00
20	Juan Nieves	.15
21	Bill Schroeder	.15
22	Charlie Moore	.15
24	Ben Oglivie	.15
25	Mark Clear	.15
28	Rick Manning	.15
31	George Bamberger	.15
37	Dan Plesac	.15
39	Tim Leary	.15
41	Ray Searage	.15
43	Chuck Porter	.15
45	Rob Deer	.15
46	Bill Wegman	.15
47	Jamie Cocanower	.15
49	Ted Higuera	.15
---	Coaches Card (Andy Etchebarren, Larry Haney, Frank Howard, Tony Muser, Herm Starrette)	.15
---	Team Photo/Roster	.15

1987 Milwaukee Brewers Police

The Milwaukee Brewers issued a safety set in 1987 for the sixth consecutive year. As in the past, many local police departments throughout Wisconsin participated in the give-away program. The Milwaukee version was sponsored by Kinney Shoe Stores and WTMJ Radio and was handed out to youngsters attending the Baseball Card Day at County Stadium on May 9th. The cards, which measure 2-1/4" x 4-1/8", feature full-color photos plus a safety tip on the backs. Chris Bosio can be found with a uniform number of 26 or 29. The card was corrected to #29 in later printings.

		NM/M
Complete Set (30):		5.00
Common Player:		.15
1	Ernest Riles	.15
2	Edgar Diaz	.15
3	Juan Castillo	.15
4	Paul Molitor	2.00
5	B.J. Surhoff	.15
7	Dale Sveum	.15
9	Greg Brock	.15
13	Billy Jo Robidoux	.15
14	Jim Paciorek	.15
15	Cecil Cooper	.15
16	Mike Felder	.15
17	Jim Gantner	.15
19	Robin Yount	2.00
20	Juan Nieves	.15
21	Bill Schroeder	.15
25	Mark Clear	.15
26a	Glenn Braggs	.15
26b	Chris Bosio	.30
28	Rick Manning	.15
29	Chris Bosio	.30
32	Chuck Crim	.15
34	Mark Ciardi	.15
37	Dan Plesac	.15
38	John Henry Johnson	.15
40	Mike Birbeck	.15
42	Tom Trebelhorn	.15
45	Rob Deer	.15
46	Bill Wegman	.15
49	Ted Higuera	.15
---	Coaches Card (Andy Etchebarren, Larry Haney, Chuck Hartenstein, Dave Hilton, Tony Muser)	.15
---	Team Photo/Roster	.15

1988 Milwaukee Brewers Police

3 Juan Castillo IF
The Marathon County Sheriff's Dept. and
Brickner Chrysler Center Inc.
2525 Grand Avenue, Wausau, WI 54401
present the 1988
Milwaukee Brewers

This 30-card set is the 7th annual issue sponsored by the Milwaukee Police Department for local distribution during a crime prevention promotion. The full-color card fronts (2-3/4" x 4-1/8") feature the same design as the 1987 set with white borders and a black frame outlining the player photo and name. Sponsor credits and the team name are listed below the photo. The vertical card backs are blue on white with messages from the player and sponsors. Two group photos - one of the team's five coaches and one of the team (with a checklist back) - are unnumbered and printed horizontally. Card numbers refer to the players' uniform numbers.

		NM/M
Complete Set (30):		4.00
Common Player:		.15
1	Ernest Riles	.15
3	Juan Castillo	.15
4	Paul Molitor	2.00
5	B.J. Surhoff	.15
7	Dale Sveum	.15
9	Greg Brock	.15
11	Charlie O'Brien	.15
14	Jim Adduci	.15
16	Mike Felder	.15
17	Jim Gantner	.15
19	Robin Yount	2.00
20	Juan Nieves	.15
21	Bill Schroeder	.15
23	Joey Meyer	.15
25	Mark Clear	.15
26	Glenn Braggs	.15
28	Odell Jones	.15
29	Chris Bosio	.15
30	Steve Kiefer	.15
32	Chuck Crim	.15
33	Jay Aldrich	.15
37	Dan Plesac	.15
40	Mike Birkbeck	.15
42	Tom Trebelhorn	.15
43	Dave Stapleton	.15
45	Rob Deer	.15

46	Bill Wegman	.15
49	Ted Higuera	.15
---	Coaches Card (Andy Etchebarren, Larry Haney, Chuck Hartenstein, Dave Hilton, Tony Muser)	.15
---	Team Photo	.15

1989 Milwaukee Brewers Police

30 Terry Francona OF
Iola, Manawa & Marion Police Depts. and Wisconsin Power and Light present the 1989
Milwaukee Brewers

The Milwaukee Brewers, in conjunction with various corporate and civic sponsors, issued a 30-card police set in 1989, the eighth consecutive police set issued by the club. Some 95 law enforcement agencies in Wisconsin participated in the program, each releasing their own version of the same set. The cards measure 2-13/16" x 4-1/8" and feature full-color action photos with the player's name, uniform number and position below, along with the sponsoring agencies. The backs include the traditional safety messages. The cards were distributed in complete sets at a stadium promotion and also handed out individually over the course of the summer by uniformed police officers in various Wisconsin cities and counties.

		NM/M
Complete Set (30):		5.00
Common Player:		.15
1	Gary Sheffield	2.00
4	Paul Molitor	1.50
5	B.J. Surhoff	.15
6	Bill Spiers	.15
7	Dale Sveum	.15
9	Greg Brock	.15
14	Gus Polidor	.15
16	Mike Felder	.15
17	Jim Gantner	.15
19	Robin Yount	1.50
20	Juan Nieves	.15
22	Charlie O'Brien	.15
23	Joey Meyer	.15
25	Dave Engle	.15
26	Glenn Braggs	.15
27	Paul Mirabella	.15
29	Chris Bosio	.15
30	Terry Francona	.15
32	Chuck Crim	.15
37	Dan Plesac	.15
40	Mike Birkbeck	.15
41	Mark Knudson	.15
42	Tom Trebelhorn	.15
45	Rob Deer	.15
46	Bill Wegman	.15
48	Bryan Clutterbuck	.15
49	Teddy Higuera	.15
---	Team Photo	.15
---	Coaching Staff	.15

Yearbook Cards

Included in the team's special 20th anniversary edition yearbook was a set of 18 player cards stapled into the center of the book. Printed on a 16-1/2" x 11" cardboard sheet, there are nine cards per page, perforated on two, three or four sides, depending on sheet position. Cards have a pale yellow background. A blue and bright yellow 20th Anniversary team logo appears in the lower-right corner with the player's uniform number, name and position stacked at left in black. All but one of the photos are game-action shots. Backs are printed in black and include complete major and minor league stats. Cards are checklisted here by uniform number.

		NM/M
Complete Set, Singles (18):		8.00
Complete Yearbook:		10.00
Common Player:		.25
1	Gary Sheffield	2.00
4	Paul Molitor	4.00
5	B.J. Surhoff	.25
7	Dale Sveum	.25
9	Greg Brock	.25
17	Jim Gantner	.25
19	Robin Yount	4.00
20	Juan Nieves	.25
26	Glenn Braggs	.25
29	Chris Bosio	.25
32	Chuck Crim	.25
37	Dan Plesac	.25
38	Don August	.25
40	Mike Birkbeck	.25
42	Tom Trebelhorn	.25
45	Rob Deer	.25
46	Bill Wegman	.25
49	Teddy Higuera	.25

1990 Milwaukee Brewers Police

Brewers
4 Paul Molitor IF
The Chilton Police Department
Chilton Food Mart & Valley Bank-Chilton
present the 1990
Milwaukee Brewers

Blue borders are featured on the front of the 1990 Brewer Police/Fire Safety set. The cards are numbered according to uniform number and public service messages appear on the card backs. The 2-13/16" x 4-1/8" cards were distributed by various Wisconsin police departments.

		NM/M
Complete Set (30):		4.00
Common Player:		.15
2	Eddie Diaz	.15
4	Paul Molitor	1.50
5	B. J. Surhoff	.15
6	Bill Spiers	.15
7	Dale Sveum	.15
9	Greg Brock	.15
11	Gary Sheffield	.75
14	Gus Polidor	.15
16	Mike Felder	.15
17	Jim Gantner	.15
19	Robin Yount	1.50
22	Charlie O'Brien	.15
23	Greg Vaughn	.15
26	Glenn Braggs	.15
27	Paul Mirabella	.15
28	Tom Filer	.15
29	Chris Bosio	.15
31	Jaime Navarro	.15
32	Chuck Crim	.15
34	Billy Bates	.15
36	Tony Fossas	.15
37	Dan Plesac	.15
38	Don August	.15
39	Dave Parker	.15
41	Mark Knudson	.15
42	Tom Trebelhorn	.15
45	Rob Deer	.15
49	Ted Higuera	.15
---	Coaches (Don Baylor, Ray Burris, Duffy Dyer, Larry Haney, Andy Etchebarren)	.15
---	Team photo/roster card	.15

Yearbook Cards

Printed on cardboard stock and stapled into the center of the team's 1990 yearbook was a set of 18 cards. The sheet is 16-1/2" x 11" overall. Each page has nine 2-5/8" x 3-1/2" cards perforated on two, three or four sides, depending on sheet position. Above-left and below-right of the color player poses are yellow triangles with blue pinstripes. The team's scrip logo is in the same team colors in the lower-left of the photo. The player's name, position abbreviation and uniform number are in yellow in the upper-right corner. Backs are printed in blue and include complete major and minor league stats. The checklist is presented here by uniform number.

		NM/M
Complete Set, Singles (18):		8.00
Complete Yearbook:		10.00
Common Player:		.25
4	Paul Molitor	4.00
5	B.J. Surhoff	.25
6	Bill Spiers	.25
7	Dale Sveum	.25
9	Greg Brock	.25
17	Jim Gantner	.25
19	Robin Yount	4.00
26	Glenn Braggs	.25
28	Tom Filer	.25
29	Chris Bosio	.25
31	Jaime Navarro	.25
32	Chuck Crim	.25
37	Dan Plesac	.25
38	Don August	.25
39	Dave Parker	.25
42	Tom Trebelhorn	.25
45	Rob Deer	.25
49	Ted Higuera	.25

1991 Milwaukee Brewers Police

The Milwaukee Brewers are featured on a 1991 team set sponsored by several Milwaukee area police departments and Delicious Brand Cookies and Crackers. The 30-card set is in full color with light gray border on the front and the backs are unnumbered and contain safety tips from the players.

		NM/M
Complete Set (30):		4.00
Common Player:		.25
(1)	Robin Yount	1.50
(2)	Rick Dempsey	.25
(3)	Jamie Navarro	.25
(4)	Darryl Hamilton	.25
(5)	Bill Spiers	.25
(6)	Dante Bichette	.25
(7)	Dan Plesac	.25
(8)	Don August	.25
(9)	Willie Randolph	.25
(10)	Franklin Stubbs	.25
(11)	Julio Machado	.25
(12)	Greg Vaughn	.25
(13)	Chris Bosio	.25
(14)	Mark Knudson	.25
(15)	Paul Molitor	1.50
(16)	Kevin Brown	.25
(17)	Ron Robinson	.25
(18)	Bill Wegman	.25
(19)	Teddy Higuera	.25
(20)	Mark Lee	.25
(21)	B.J. Surhoff	.25
(22)	Candy Maldonado	.25
(23)	Chuck Crim	.25
(24)	Dale Sveum	.25
(25)	Jim Gantner	.25
(26)	Greg Brock	.25
(27)	Gary Sheffield	.75
(28)	Edwin Nunez	.25
(29)	Tom Trebelhorn	.25
(30)	Coaches (Don Baylor, Ray Burris, Duffy Dyer, Andy Etchebarren, Larry Haney, Fred Stanley)	.25

1992 Milwaukee Brewers Police

BREWERS '92
DANTE BICHETTE • OF
Presented by
The Waukesha Police Department
& Waukesha Sports Cards

The 1992 Milwaukee Brewers Police set consists of 30-cards in the standard, 2-1/2" x 3-1/2" format. The yellow-bordered cards were produced by Delicious Brand Cookies and Crackers and distributed by local Wisconsin police departments in co-operation with the Brewers.

		NM/M
Complete Set (30):		4.00
Common Player:		.15
(1)	Andy Allanson	.15
(2)	James Austin	.15
(3)	Dante Bichette	.15
(4)	Ricky Bones	.15
(5)	Chris Bosio	.15
(6)	Mike Fetters	.15
(7)	Scott Fletcher	.15
(8)	Jim Gantner	.15
(9)	Phil Garner	.15
(10)	Darryl Hamilton	.15
(11)	Doug Henry	.15
(12)	Teddy Higuera	.15
(13)	Pat Listach	.15
(14)	Jamie Navarro	.15
(15)	Edwin Nunez	.15
(16)	Tim McIntosh	.15
(17)	Paul Molitor	1.50
(18)	Jesse Orosco	.15
(19)	Dan Plesac	.15
(20)	Ron Robinson	.15
(21)	Bruce Ruffin	.15
(22)	Kevin Seitzer	.15
(23)	Bill Spiers	.15
(24)	Franklin Stubbs	.15
(25)	William Suero	.15
(26)	B.J. Surhoff	.15
(27)	Greg Vaughn	.15
(28)	Bill Wegman	.15
(29)	Robin Yount	1.50
(30)	Coaches (Bill Castro, Duffy Dyer, Mike Easler, Tim Foli, Don Rowe)	.15

1993 Milwaukee Brewers Police

The 1993 Milwaukee Brewers Police set included 30 cards with a graduated blue border. The left side has a '93 Brewers flag along the border in yellow, with the player's name in the upper right corner in white. The backs, which are white with black print, feature quotes from the player pictured. The cards are not numbered and the set also includes a card commemorating Robin Yount's 3,000th hit.

		NM/M
Complete Set (30):		3.00
Common Player:		.15
(1)	Bernie Brewer (Mascot)	.15
(2)	Phil Garner	.15
(3)	Yount's 3,000th Hit (Robin Yount)	1.00
(4)	Mark Kiefer	.15
(5)	Bill Spiers	.15
(6)	John Jaha	.15
(7)	Bill Wegman	.15
(8)	Ted Higuera	.15
(9)	Greg Vaughn	.15
(10)	Kevin Reimer	.15
(11)	Doug Henry	.15
(12)	William Suero	.15
(13)	Dave Nilsson	.15
(14)	James Austin	.15
(15)	Mike Fetters	.15
(16)	Ricky Bones	.15
(17)	Jaime Navarro	.15
(18)	Jesse Orosco	.15
(19)	Darryl Hamilton	.15
(20)	Cal Eldred	.15
(21)	Tim McIntosh	.15
(22)	Dickie Thon	.15
(23)	Graeme Lloyd	.15
(24)	Pat Listach	.15
(25)	Joe Kmak	.15
(26)	Alex Diaz	.15
(27)	Robin Yount	1.50
(28)	Tom Brunansky	.15
(29)	B.J. Surhoff	.15
(30)	Bill Doran	.15

1994 Milwaukee Brewers Police

TURNER WARD 27
'94 BREWERS
Pick'n Save
SNICKERS
Presented by
The Milwaukee Police Department

All youngsters attending the April 23 Brewers game received this 30-card set sponsored by Pick'n Save supermarkets and Snickers candy bar, whose logos appear on both front and back. Cards featured posed player photos in their new 25th anniversary uniforms, against a lime green fabric backdrop or game action photos. Two green borders surround the photos. Navy blue bars above and below the photo have the player's name, team and uniform number. A 25th anniversary logo is at lower-right. The name of one of the many Wisconsin police agencies which distributed the cards is printed in black at bottom. Backs are printed in black-on-white and feature full major and minor league stats. The traditional safety message or anti-drug warning is not included on this issue. Cards are checklisted here by uniform number. Cards are in the 2-1/2" x 3-1/2" format.

		NM/M
Complete Set (30):		3.00
Common Player:		.25
2	Jose Valentin	.25
3	Phil Garner	.25
5	B.J. Surhoff	.25
8	Jody Reed	.25
9	Bill Spiers	.25
11	Dave Nilsson	.25
12	Brian Harper	.25
16	Pat Listach	.25
18	Tom Brunansky	.25
20	Kevin Seitzer	.25
21	Cal Eldred	.25
23	Greg Vaughn	.25
24	Darryl Hamilton	.25
25	Ricky Bones	.25
27	Turner Ward	.25
28	Doug Henry	.25
29	Jeff Bronkey	.25
30	Matt Mieske	.25
31	Jaime Navarro	.25
32	John Jaha	.25
36	Mike Fetters	.25
37	Graeme Lloyd	.25
39	Bob Scanlan	.25
40	Mike Ignasiak	.25
43	Mark Kiefer	.25
46	Bill Wegman	.25
47	Jesse Orosco	.25
49	Teddy Higuera	.25
63	Jeff D'Amico, Kelly Wunsch	.25
---	Bernie Brewer (Mascot)	.25

1995 Milwaukee Brewers Police

Some of the finest portrait photos seen on modern baseball cards are combined with game-action shots in the annual Brewers police set, sponsored by Old Fashioned Foods (makers of Squeeze Cheese). The 2-1/2" x 3-1/2" cards feature forest green borders with the player and team name, and uniform number in white on a deep blue band beneath. A tan panel at bottom has the name of the Milwaukee P.D. Many of the cards are presented in horizontal format. Backs are in black-and-white and include career stats and a safety tip. Cards are checklisted here according to uniform number.

		NM/M
Complete Set (33):		3.00
Common Player:		.25
1	Fernando Vina	.25
2	Jose Valentin	.25
3	Phil Garner	.25
5	B.J. Surhoff	.25
9	Joe Oliver	.25
10	Brewers Coaches (Bill Castro, Duffy Dyer, Tim Foli, Lamar Johnson, Don Rowe)	.25
11	Dave Nilsson	.25
12	Derrick May	.25
15	Dave Hulse	.25
16	Pat Listach	.25
20	Kevin Seitzer	.25
21	Cal Eldred	.25
22	Mike Matheny, Jeff Cirillo	.25
23	Greg Vaughn	.25
24	Darryl Hamilton	.25
25	Ricky Bones	.25
27	Turner Ward	.25
29	Jeff Bronkey	.25
30	Matt Mieske	.25
32	John Jaha	.25
36	Mike Fetters	.25
37	Graeme Lloyd	.25
38	Angel Miranda	.25
39	Bob Scanlan	.25
40	Michael Ignasiak	.25
41	Jose Mercedes, Mark Kiefer	.25
42	Scott Karl, Al Reyes, Steve Sparks	.25
46	Bill Wegman	.25
---	Bob Uecker (Announcer)	1.50
---	Charlie the Mouse (Sponsor)	.05

---	Iris the Cow (Sponsor)	.05
---	Squeezasaurus (Sponsor)	.05
---	Squeeze Cheese (Coupon)	.05

1996 Milwaukee Brewers Police

Metallic gold borders are featured on the Brewers' 14th annual safety set issued June 16 as a stadium giveaway. Cards are a mix of horizontal and vertical design with a large color photo at left. In a gold strip at right is the team logo-type, player name, position and uniform number. Backs are in black-and-white with a safety message from the pictured player and the team logo. No sponsoring company or police agency is mentioned on the card. A special card in the set illustrates the proposed new Brewers stadium. Cards are listed here by uniform number.

		NM/M
Complete Set (30):		3.00
Common Player:		.15
1	Fernando Vina	.15
2	Jose Valentin	.15
3	Phil Garner	.15
4	Pat Listach	.15
8	Mark Loretta	.15
14	Dave Nilsson	.15
15	David Hulse	.15
16	Jesse Levis	.15
20	Kevin Seitzer	.15
21	Cal Eldred	.15
22	Mike Matheny	.15
23	Greg Vaughn	.15
24	Chuckie Carr	.15
25	Ricky Bones	.15
26	Jeff Cirillo	.15
27	Turner Ward	.15
30	Matt Mieske	.15
32	John Jaha	.15
36	Mike Fetters	.15
37	Graeme Lloyd	.15
38	Angel Miranda	.15
40	Ben McDonald	.15
42	Scott Karl	.15
48	Marshall Boze	.15
49	Mike Potts	.15
50	Steve Sparks	.15
51	Ramon Garcia	.15
52	Kevin Wickander	.15
---	Brewers Coaches	.15
---	Miller Park	.15

1997 Milwaukee Brewers Police

One of the more attractive safety sets of recent years, the 1997 Brewers team issue features action photos of each player in the standard 2-1/2" x 3-1/2" format. Down one side of the photo is the player's name in outline type. A team logo is at bottom-right. Backs are in black-and-white with a few bits of personal data and a cartoon figure presenting a safety tip for youngsters. The set was distributed to children attending the May 30 game at County Stadium. The checklist here is arranged by uniform number.

		NM/M
Complete Set (30):		3.00
Common Player:		.25
1	Fernando Vina	.25
2	Jose Valentin	.25
3	Phil Garner	.25
8	Mark Loretta	.25
9	Tim Unroe	.25
10	Marc Newfield	.25
13	Jeff D'Amico	.25
14	Dave Nillson	.25
15	Jeff Huson	.25
16	Jesse Levis	.25
20	Jeromy Burnitz	.50
21	Cal Eldred	.25
22	Mike Matheny	.25
24	Chuckie Carr	.25
25	Angel Miranda	.25
26	Jeff Cirillo	.25
27	Bob Wickman	.25
29	Gerald Williams	.25
30	Matt Mieske	.25
32	John Jaha	.25
36	Mike Fetters	.25
39	Bryce Florie	.25
40	Ben McDonald	.25
41	Jose Mercedes	.25
42a	Scott Karl	.25
42b	Jackie Robinson (Tribute)	2.00
43	Doug Jones	.25
49	Ron Villone	.25
51	Eddy Diaz	.25
---	Coaches (Chris Bando, Bill Castro, Jim Gantner, Lamar Johnson, Don Rowe)	.25

1998 Milwaukee Brewers Diamond Celebration

Persons attending a January 30 banquet in Milwaukee received a set of these cards highlighting the team's award winners for 1997. The set was sponsored by the Milwaukee Metropolitan Association of Commerce; their logo appears on the back. Fronts have color photos centered on a white background. The players are pictured in action, the staff in portraits. "Diamond Celebration" and the name are in script. The banquet date and specific honor also appear on front. Backs are in black-and-white with season highlights. The unnumbered cards are checklisted here alphabetically.

		NM/M
Complete Set (10):		15.00
Common Card:		.50
(1)	Hank Aaron	6.00
(2)	Jeromy Burnitz	2.00
(3)	Jeff Cirillo	2.00
(4)	Dick Hackett (Staff)	.50
(5)	Bill Haig (Staff)	.50
(6)	John Jaha	1.00
(7)	Doug Jones (MV Pitcher)	1.00
(8)	Doug Jones (MVP)	1.00
(9)	Bob Uecker (MC)	3.00
(10)	Bob Wickman	1.00

Police

For 1998, the Brewers cable television outlet sponsored the team's annual safety

Presented by: Midwest Sports Channel and The Milwaukee Brewers

set, given away to kids at the June 21 game. Card fronts have player action photos vignetted on a close-up baseball background. Team and sponsor logos appear in opposite corners. Backs have a few bits of player data, a safety tip, sponsor's logo and uniform number.

		NM/M
Complete Set (30):		3.00
Common Player:		.25
1	Fernando Vina	.25
2	Jose Valentin	.25
3	Phil Garner	.25
5	Geoff Jenkins	.60
7	Dave Nillson	.25
8	Mark Loretta	.25
9	Marquis Grissom	.25
10	Marc Newfield	.25
13	Jeff D'Amico	.25
14	Jeff Juden	.25
16	Jesse Levis	.25
20	Jeromy Burnitz	.50
21	Cal Eldred	.25
22	Mike Matheny	.25
24	Darrin Jackson	.25
26	Jeff Cirillo	.25
27	Bob Wickman	.25
28	Mike Myers	.25
30	Bob Hamelin	.25
32	John Jaha	.25
33/39	Bobby Hughes, Eric Owens	.25
37	Steve Woodard	.25
40	Chad Fox	.25
41	Jose Mercedes	.25
42	Scott Karl	.25
43	Doug Jones	.25
46	Paul Wagner	.25
47	Al Reyes	.25
48/30	Brad Woodall, Bronswell Patrick	.25
---	Coaches (Chris Bando, Bill Castro, Lamar Johnson, Doug Mansolino, Don Rowe, Joel Youngblood)	.25

1999 Milwaukee Brewers Diamond Celebration

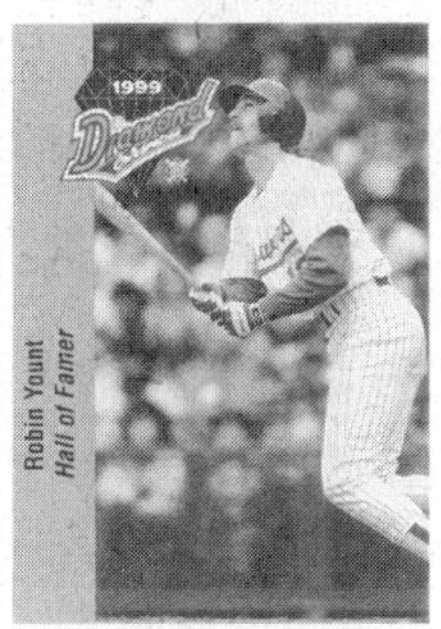

Persons attending a January 22 banquet in Milwaukee received a set of these cards highlighting the team's award winners for 1997. The set was sponsored by the Milwaukee Metropolitan Association of Commerce, whose logo appears on the back. Fronts have color photos. The players are pictured in action, the staff in portraits. "Diamond Celebration" and team logo are at left. The specific honor also appears on front. Backs are in black-and-white with season highlights. The unnumbered cards are checklisted here alphabetically.

		NM/M
Complete Set (11):		15.00
Common Player:		.50
(1)	Bob Betts (P.A. Announcer)	.50
(2)	Jeromy Burnitz (HR Champ)	2.00
(3)	Jeromy Burnitz (MVP)	2.00
(4)	Jeff Cirillo	1.00
(5)	Peter Gammons (Writer)	.50
(6)	Mark Loretta (Manager's award.)	1.00
(7)	Mark Loretta (Community service.)	1.00
(8)	Bud Selig (Owner)	.50
(9)	Bob Wickman	1.00
(10)	Steve Woodard	1.00
(11)	Robin Yount	6.00

Police

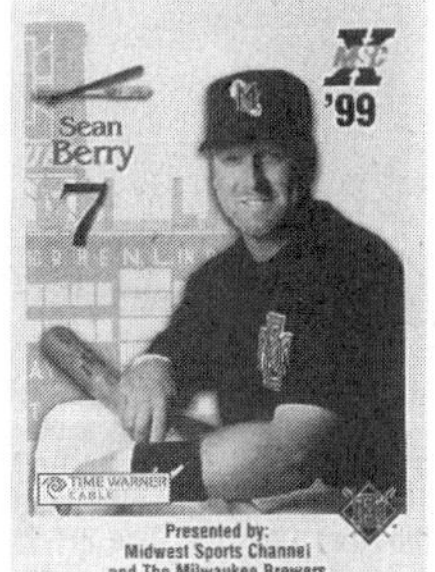

Presented by: Midwest Sports Channel and The Milwaukee Brewers

The regional cable station which carries Brewers games was the principal sponsor of the team's safety set given to fans on May 29. Cards feature color player poses against a sepia background showing Milwaukee County Stadium throughout the course of its 46-year history. Sponsor and team logos are in various corners on front along with the player's name and uniform number. Backs have a few bits of personal data, a safety message and an ad from the sponsor. Cards are checklisted here in order of uniform number.

		NM/M
Complete Set (30):		3.00
Common Player:		.25
1	Fernando Vina	.25
2	Jose Valentin	.25
3	Phil Garner	.25
5	Geoff Jenkins	.60
7	Sean Berry	.25
8	Mark Loretta	.25
9	Marquis Grissom	.25
14	David Nilsson	.25
16	Lou Collier	.25
20	Jeromy Burnitz	.50
21	Cal Eldred	.25
22/48	Rich Becker, Steve Falteisek	.25
23	Brian Banks	.25
24	Alex Ochoa	.25
25	Jim Abbott	.35
26	Jeff Cirillo	.25
27	Bob Wickman	.25
28	Mike Myers	.25
31	Bobby Hughes	.25
37	Steve Woodard	.25
38	Eric Plunk	.25
40	Chad Fox	.25
42	Scott Karl	.25
46	Bill Pulsipher	.25
47	Al Reyes	.25
49	David Weathers	.25
52	Rafael Roque	.25
58	Valerio de los Santos	.25
---	Coaches (Bill Campbell, Bill Castro, Ron Jackson, Jim Lefebvre, Doug Mansolino, Bob Melvin)	.25
---	Milwaukee County Stadium	.25

2000 Milwaukee Brewers Diamond Celebration

Winners of various annual awards by the Milwaukee Brewers are featured in this standard-size card set which was issued at the team's Diamond Celebration dinner on January 21. A large portrait photo is featured along the left or right edge on front. Down

the other side is player identification and the name of the award won. Backs have season highlights. The unnumbered cards are checklisted here alphabetically.

		NM/M
Complete Set (10):		15.00
Common Player:		.50
(1)	Kevin Barker	1.50
(2)	Ron Belliard	1.50
(3)	Jeromy Burnitz (HR Champ)	2.50
(4)	Jeromy Burnitz (MVP)	2.50
(5)	Jeff Cirillo	1.50
(6)	Marquis Grissom	1.50
(7)	Geoff Jenkins	3.00
(8)	Tim Kurkjian	.50
(9)	Dean Taylor, Davey Lopes	.50
(10)	Bob Wickman	1.00

Police

Presented by: Midwest Sports Channel and The Milwaukee Brewers

In its third season of sponsoring the team's safety set, the Brewers' cable franchisee offered the cards to the first 10,000 youngsters at a May promotional game. Other sets were distributed by police agencies. Card fronts have the players posed in their dark blue jerseys against a black background lit by a colorful Milwaukee Brewers neon sign. In a lower corner are the sponsor's logo, player name and uniform number. A Time-Warner Cable logo is in the white border at bottom. Backs have player identification and a safety message. Cards are checklisted here by uniform number.

		NM/M
Complete Set (30):		3.00
Common Player:		.25
00	Curtis Leskanic	.25
1	Luis Lopez	.25
2	Tyler Houston	.25
5	Geoff Jenkins	.50
7	Sean Berry	.25
8	Mark Loretta	.25
9	Marquis Grissom	.25
10	Ron Belliard	.25
12	Henry Blanco	.25
14	Charlie Hayes	.25
18	Jose Hernandez	.25
20	Jeromy Burnitz	.45
22	Kevin Barker	.25
24	James Mouton	.25
27	Bob Wickman	.25
28	Valerio de los Santos	.25
30	Davey Lopes	.25
31	Everett Stull	.25
33	Lyle Mouton	.25
37	Steve Woodard	.25
38	Jaime Navarro	.25
41	Matt Williams	.25
47	Jason Bere	.25
49	David Weathers	.25
51	Jimmy Haynes	.25
53	Juan Acevedo	.25
59	John Snyder	.25
88	Jim Bruske	.25
---	Coaches (Jerry Royster, Rod Carew, Bill Castro, Bob Apodaca, Chris Speier, Gary Allenson)	.25
---	Matt Vasgersian, Bill Schroeder (Broadcasters)	.25

2001 Milwaukee Brewers Diamond Celebration

Winners of various annual awards by the Milwaukee Brewers are featured in this standard-size card set which was issued at the team's Diamond Celebration dinner on January 19. Fronts have a large portrait photo along the left or right edge side. Down the other side is player identification and the name of the award won. Backs have season highlights and the Miller Park logo. The unnumbered cards are checklisted here alphabetically.

		NM/M
Complete Set (9):		20.00
Common Player:		2.00
(1)	Rod Carew (Community Service Award)	3.00
(2)	Jeff D'Amico (Most Valuable Pitcher)	2.00
(3)	Geoff Jenkins (Harvey Kuenn Award)	2.50
(4)	Geoff Jenkins (Home Run Leader)	2.50
(5)	Geoff Jenkins (MVP)	2.50
(6)	Tommy Lasorda (Bud Selig Award)(SP)	5.00
(7)	Curtis Leskanic (Newcomer of the Year)	2.00
(8)	Richie Sexson (Manager's Award)	2.00
(9)	Ben Sheets (Minor League Player/Year)	4.00

Police

Presented by: Fox Sports Net and The Milwaukee Brewers

This team set was given to youngsters attending a special promotional game. The 2-1/2" x 3-1/2" cards have close-up player portraits over a large logo in one of several colors. Also appearing in the photo area are Miller Park and Fox Sports Net logos and the player's name, position and uniform number. There is a white border, at the bottom of which is sponsor credits. Backs have a safety or character-building message from the player. Sets were also distributed locally by more than six dozen Wisconsin police agencies.

	NM/M
Complete Set (30):	4.00

Common Player: .25
1 Luis Lopez .25
2 Tyler Houston .25
5 Geoff Jenkins .50
7 Tony Fernandez .25
8 Mark Loretta .25
10 Ronnie Belliard .25
11 Richie Sexson .50
12 Henry Blanco .25
13 Jeff D'Amico .25
15 Ben Sheets .50
18 Jose Hernandez .25
20 Jeromy Burnitz .50
21 Jamey Wright .25
22 Devon White .35
23 Mark Leiter .25
24 James Mouton .25
25 Raul Casanova .25
30 Davey Lopes .25
31 Paul Rigdon .25
33 Will Cunnane .25
39 Angel Echevarria .25
40 Chad Fox .25
41 Jeffrey Hammonds .25
46 Ray King .25
48 Mike DeJean .25
49 David Weathers .25
51 Jimmy Haynes .25
00 Curtis Leskanic .25
--- Brewers Coaches (Bob Apodaca, Gary Allenson, Rod Carew, Bill Castro, Jerry Royster, Luis Salazar) .25
--- Bill Schroeder, Matt Vasgersian .25

2002 Milwaukee Brewers Diamond Celebration

Winners of various annual awards by the Milwaukee Brewers are featured in this 2-1/2" x 3-1/2" card set which was issued at the team's Diamond Celebration dinner on January 25. Fronts have a photo set against a solid colored background on which the last name is ghosted vertically. An identification strip is vertically at right, including the name of the award won. Backs have season highlights in black-and-white. The unnumbered cards are checklisted here alphabetically.

NM/M
Complete Set (10): 18.00
Common Player: 2.00
(1) Bill Castro (Unsung Hero) 2.00
(2) Cecil Cooper (Walk of Fame) 2.00
(3) Chad Fox (Most Valuable Pitcher) 2.50
(4) Ray King (Manager's Award) 2.00
(5) Ray King (Community Service Award) 2.00
(6) Mark Loretta (Harvey Kuenn Award) 2.50
(7) Allan H. (Bud) Selig (Walk of Fame) 2.50
(8) Richie Sexson (Home Run Champion) 3.00
(9) Richie Sexson (MVP) 3.00
(10) Ben Sheets (Newcomer of the Year) 3.00

Police

Fans at the May 30 Brewers game received this team set of 2-1/2" x 3-1/2" safety cards. Fronts have action photos with a black-and-white photo of an architectural detail of Miller Park in the top-left corner. Backs repeat the Miller Park photo and have a safety message from the player. Cards are checklisted here by uniform number.

LOPEZ
INFIELDER
Presented by: The Milwaukee Brewers Baseball Club

NM/M
Complete Set (30): 3.00
Common Player: .25
00 Curtis Leskanic .25
1 Luis Lopez .25
2 Tyler Houston .25
5 Geoff Jenkins .50
7 Eric Young .25
8 Mark Loretta .25
9 Paul Bako .25
10 Ron Belliard .25
11 Richie Sexson .50
12 Matt Stairs .25
15 Ben Sheets .35
16 Lenny Harris .25
18 Jose Hernandez .25
21 Jamey Wright .25
22 Alex Sanchez .25
23 Alex Ochoa .25
25 Raul Casanova .25
31 Paul Rigdon .25
32 Nick Neugebauer .25
37 Ruben Quevedo .25
29 Glendon Rusch .25
40 Chad Fox .25
41 Jeffrey Hammonds .25
46 Ray King .25
47 Mike Buddie .25
48 Mike DeJean .25
49 Jose Cabrera .25
51 Luis Vizcaino .25
52 Nelson Figueroa .25
95 Takahito Nomura .25

2003 Milwaukee Brewers Diamond Celebration

Winners of various annual awards by the Milwaukee Brewers are featured in this 3" x 5" card set which was issued at the team's Diamond Celebration dinner, January 31, one cello-wrapped set per place setting. Fronts have a black-and-sepia photo with a black frameline. A dinner logo is at bottom with the honoree's name, award and uniform number (for players) in white. Backs have season highlights in black and red. Production was reported as 1,000 sets. The unnumbered cards are checklisted here alphabetically.

NM/M
Complete Set (10): 15.00
Common Card: 1.00
(1) Harry Dalton (Walk of Fame) 1.00
(2) Mike DeJean (Most Valuable Pitcher) 1.50
(3) Jeffrey Hammonds (Community Service Award) 2.00
(4) Ernie Harwell (Bud Selig Award) 1.50
(5) Alex Sanchez (Harvey Kuenn Award) 1.50
(6) Richie Sexson (Home Run Champion) 5.00
(7) Bob Uecker (Walk of Fame) 3.00
(8) Luis Vizcaino (Newcomer of the Year) 2.00
(9) Eric Young (Unsung Hero Award) 2.00
(10) Doug Melvin, Ned Yost, Ulice Payne, Jr. (Dawning of a New Era) 1.00

Safety

This team set was a stadium giveaway to the first 10,000 youngsters attending the April 19 game. The 2-1/2" x 3-1/2" cards have neck-to-cap color portraits on front, with player name, position and uniform number. Backs are in gold with a health or safety tip.

NM/M
Complete Set (29): 3.00
Common Player: .25
3 Ned Yost .25
5 Geoff Jenkins .50
6 Keith Ginter .25
7 Eric Young .25
9 Enrique Cruz .25
10 Royce Clayton .25
11 Richie Sexson .50
12 Eddie Perez .25
15 Ben Sheets .35
18 Wes Helms .25
20 Scott Podsednik .50
21 Keith Osik .25
22 Alex Sanchez .25
24 John Vander Wal .25
26 Wayne Franklin .25
27 Brady Clark .25
28 Valerio de los Santos .25
29 Jason Conti .25
33 Curtis Leskanic .25
39 Glendon Rusch .25
40 John Foster .25
41 Jeffrey Hammonds .25
46 Todd Ritchie .25
47 Shane Nance .25
48 Mike DeJean .25
50 Matt Kinney .25
51 Luis Vizcaino .25
52 Matt Ford .25
56 Jayson Durocher .25
--- Brewers Coaches .25

2004 Milwaukee Brewers Safety

OUTFIELDER
#5 GEOFF JENKINS
PRESENTED BY THE MILWAUKEE BREWERS BASEBALL CLUB

This team set was a stadium giveaway to youngsters attending the May 1 game. The 2-1/2" x 3-1/2" cards have color portraits on front, with player name, position and uniform number. Backs have a health or safety tip.

NM/M
Complete Set (30): 5.00
Common Player: .25
1 Bernie Brewer (Mascot) .25
2 Bill Hall .25
3 Ned Yost .25
4 Paul Molitor 2.00
5 Geoff Jenkins .45
6 Keith Ginter .25
11 Lyle Overbay .50
12 Ben Grieve .25
15 Ben Sheets .50
18 Wes Helms .25
20 Scott Podsednik .50
21 Chad Moeller .25
22 Trent Durrington .25
27 Brady Clark .25
29 Gary Bennett .25
30 Craig Counsell .25
31 Adrian Hernandez .25
33 Wes Obermueller .25
37 Junior Spivey .25
39 Chris Capuano .25
41 Dan Kolb .25
43 Dave Burba .25
48 Ben Ford .25
49 Doug Davis .25
50 Matt Kinney .25
51 Luis Vizcaino .25
55 Brooks Kieschnick .25
57 Jeff Bennett .25
--- Brewers Coaches .25
--- Klements Sausages .25

2005 Milwaukee Brewers Safety

This team set was a stadium giveaway to the first 10,000 youngsters attending the May 1 game. The 2-1/2" x 3-1/2" cards have color portraits on front, with player name, position and uniform number. Backs have a health or safety tip.

NM/M
Complete Set (30): 6.00
Common Player: .25
2 Bill Hall .25
3 Ned Yost .25
5 Geoff Jenkins .50
6 Jeff Cirillo .25
7 J.J. Hardy .35
10 David Krynzel .35
11 Lyle Overbay .50
15 Ben Sheets .50
18 Wes Helms .25
21 Chad Moeller .25
24 Chris Magruder .25
26 Damian Miller .25
27 Brady Clark .25
31 Russell Branyan .25
33 Wes Obermueller .25
37 Junior Spivey .25
38 Matt Wise .25
39 Chris Capuano .25
40 Ben Hendrickson .25
41 Tommy Phelps .25
45 Carlos Lee .50
46 Mike Adams .25
47 Jorge de la Rosa .25
49 Doug Davis .25
52 Ricky Bottalico .25
53 Victor Santos .25
57 Jeff Bennett .25
58 Gary Glover .25
59 Derrick Turnbow .25
--- Coaches (Ned Yost, Butch Wynegar, Bill Castro, Marcus Hanel, Dave Nelson, Rich Dauer, Mike Maddux, Rich Donnelly) .25

2000 Milwaukee Journal Sentinel 1970s Brewers

As selected by fan balloting, an All-Decade team of 1970s Milwaukee Brewers is honored on this set of cards given to fans at a promotional game in July. The standard 2-1/2" x 3-1/2" cards have borderless game-action photos on front with a gold-foil diamond naming the player, his position and uniform number. The newspaper sponsor's logo is at bottom. Backs have a team logo, player personal data, stats and career highlights. The unnumbered cards are checklisted here in alphabetical order.

NM/M
Complete Set (13): 12.00
Common Player: .50
(1) Hank Aaron 6.00
(2) George Bamberger .50
(3) Mike Caldwell .50
(4) Cecil Cooper .75
(5) Tommy Harper .50
(6) Larry Hisle .50
(7) Sixto Lezcano .50
(8) Don Money .50
(9) Charlie Moore .50
(10) Ken Sanders .50
(11) Jim Slaton .50
(12) Gorman Thomas .50
(13) Robin Yount 4.00

1980s Brewers

As selected by fan balloting, an All-Decade team of 1980s Milwaukee Brewers is honored on this set of cards given to fans at a promotional game August 11. The standard 2-1/2" x 3-1/2" cards have game-action photos on front with a gold-foil diamond naming the player, his position and uniform number. The newspaper sponsor's logo is at bottom. Backs have a team logo, player personal data, stats and career highlights. The unnumbered cards are checklisted here in alphabetical order.

NM/M
Complete Set (13): 12.00
Common Player: .50
(1) Mike Caldwell .50
(2) Cecil Cooper .50
(3) Rollie Fingers .75
(4) Jim Gantner .50
(5) Harvey Kuenn .50
(6) Paul Molitor (DH) 3.00
(7) Paul Molitor (3B) 3.00
(8) Ben Oglivie .50
(9) Ted Simmons .50
(10) Gorman Thomas .50
(11) Pete Vuckovich .50
(12) Robin Yount (OF) 3.00
(13) Robin Yount (SS) 3.00

1990s Brewers

As selected by fan balloting, an All-Decade team of 1990s Milwaukee Brewers is honored on this set of cards given to fans at a promotional game September 8. The standard 2-1/2" x 3-1/2" cards have game-action photos on front with a gold-foil diamond naming the player, his position and uniform number. The newspaper sponsor's logo is at bottom. Backs have a team logo, player personal data, stats and career highlights. The unnumbered cards are checklisted here in alphabetical order.

NM/M
Complete Set (13): 9.00
Common Player: .50
(1) Chris Bosio .50
(2) Jeromy Burnitz 1.00
(3) Jeff Cirillo .50
(4) Phil Garner .50
(5) John Jaha .50
(6) Geoff Jenkins 2.00
(7) David Nilsson .50
(8) B.J. Surhoff .50
(9) Jose Valentin .50
(10) Fernando Vina .50
(11) Bill Wegman .50
(12) Bob Wickman .50
(13) Robin Yount 3.00

1983 Minnesota Twins team issue

The Minnesota Twins produced a 36-card set in 1983 to be sold at concession stands and through the mail. The full-color borderless cards measure 2-1/2" x 3-1/2" and displayed the player's uniform number on a white Twins jersey at the bottom of the card. The backs contain full career statistics.

NM/M
Complete Set (36): 7.00
Common Player: .25
1 John Castino .25
2 Jim Eisenreich .50
3 Ray Smith .25
4 Scott Ullger .25
5 Gary Gaetti .75
6 Mickey Hatcher .25
7 Bobby Mitchell .25
8 Len Faedo .25
9 Kent Hrbek 2.00
10 Tim Laudner .25
11 Frank Viola 1.00
12 Bryan Oelkers .25
13 Rick Lysander .25
14 Dave Engle .25
15 Len Whitehouse .25
16 Pete Filson .25
17 Tom Brunansky .25
18 Randy Bush .25
19 Brad Havens .25
20 Al Williams .25
21 Gary Ward .25
22 Jack O'Connor .25
23 Bobby Castillo .25
24 Ron Washington .25
25 Ron Davis .25
26 Tom Kelly .25
27 Billy Gardner .25
28 Rick Stelmaszek .25
29 Jim Lemon .25
30 Johnny Podres .25
31 Minnesota's Native Sons (Jim Eisenreich, Kent Hrbek, Tim Laudner) .75
32 Twins' Catchers (Dave Engle, Tim Laudner) .25
33 The Lumber Company (Tom Brunansky, Gary Gaetti, Kent Hrbek, Gary Ward) .75
34 Twins' Coaches (Billy Gardner, Tom Kelly, Jim Lemon, Johnny Podres, Rick Stelmaszek) .25
35 Team Photo .40
36 Metrodome/Checklist .25

1984 Minnesota Twins Team Issue

This team-issued set from the Minnesota Twins consists of 36 full-color, bor-

derless cards, each measuring 2-1/2" x 3-1/2". As in the previous year, the player's uniform number appears on a white Twins jersey at the bottom of the card. The backs are printed in red and blue on white stock and include career stats. The set features several special cards, including one of Harmon Killebrew.

	NM/M
Complete Set (36):	7.50
Common Player:	.25
1 John Castino	.25
2 Jim Eisenreich	.35
3 Al Jimenez	.25
4 Dave Meier	.25
5 Gary Gaetti	.50
6 Mickey Hatcher	.25
7 Jeff Reed	.25
8 Tim Teufel	.25
9 Len Faedo	.25
10 Kent Hrbek	1.00
11 Tim Laudner	.25
12 Frank Viola	.50
13 Ken Schrom	.25
14 Larry Pashnick	.25
15 Dave Engle	.25
16 Keith Comstock	.25
17 Pete Filson	.25
18 Tom Brunansky	.25
19 Randy Bush	.25
20 Darrell Brown	.25
21 Al Williams	.25
22 Mike Walters	.25
23 John Butcher	.25
24 Bobby Castillo	.25
25 Ron Washington	.25
26 Ron Davis	.25
27 Tom Kelly	.25
28 Billy Gardner	.25
29 Rick Stelmaszek	.25
30 Jim Lemon	.25
31 Johnny Podres	.25
32 Mike Smithson	.25
33 Harmon Killebrew	4.00
34 Team Photo	.50
35 Logo Card	.25
36 Metrodome/Checklist	.25

1985 Minnesota Twins Team Issue

Similar in format to the previous two years, this 36-card team-issued set features full-color, borderless cards. The player's uniform number is again displayed on a white Twins jersey in the lower right corner, and the 1985 All-Star Game logo is shown in the lower left. The All-Star Game logo also appears on a special card in the set that lists on the back all Twins who have been selected for previous All-Star Games. The set was sold at ballpark concession stands and through the mail.

	NM/M
Complete Set (36):	15.00
Common Player:	.20
1 Alvaro Espinoza	.25
2 Roy Smalley	.25
3 Pedro Oliva	.75
4 Dave Meier	.25
5 Gary Gaetti	.50
6 Mickey Hatcher	.25
7 Jeff Reed	.25
8 Tim Teufel	.25
9 Mark Salas	.25
10 Kent Hrbek	1.00
11 Tim Laudner	.25
12 Frank Viola	.50
13 Ken Schrom	.25
14 Rick Lysander	.25
15 Dave Engle	.25
16 Andre David	.25
17 Len Whitehouse	.25
18 Pete Filson	.25
19 Tom Brunansky	.25
20 Randy Bush	.25
21 Greg Gagne	.75
22 John Butcher	.25
23 Mike Stenhouse	.25
24 Kirby Puckett	10.00
25 Tom Klawitter	.25
26 Curt Wardle	.25
27 Rich Yett	.25
28 Ron Washington	.25
29 Ron Davis	.25
30 Tom Kelly	.25
31 Billy Gardner	.25
32 Rick Stelmaszek	.25
33 Johnny Podres	.40
34 Mike Smithson	.25
35 1985 All-Star Game Logo Card	.25
36 Twins Logo/Checklist	.25

1986 Minnesota Twins team issue

This team-issued set contains 36 2-9/16" x 3-1/2" full-color cards. Fronts feature the Twins 25th anniversary logo and a jersey at the bottom of each card with the player's uniform number. All cards, except an action shot of Bert Blyleven, are posed photos, with a facsimile autograph on each. The set also includes a checklist and a team photo.

	NM/M
Complete Set (36):	6.00
Common Player:	.15
1 Chris Pittaro	.15
2 Steve Lombardozzi	.15
3 Roy Smalley	.15
4 Pedro Oliva	.50
5 Gary Gaetti	.30
6 Mickey Hatcher	.15
7 Jeff Reed	.15
8 Mark Salas	.15
9 Kent Hrbek	.50
10 Tim Laudner	.15
11 Frank Viola	.30
12 Dennis Burtt	.15
13 Alex Sanchez	.15
14 Roy Smith	.15
15 Billy Beane	.15
16 Pete Filson	.15
17 Tom Brunansky	.15
18 Randy Bush	.15
19 Frank Eufemia	.15
20 Mark Davidson	.15
21 Bert Blyleven	.40
22 Greg Gagne	.25
23 John Butcher	.15
24 Kirby Puckett	5.00
25 Bill Latham	.15
26 Ron Washington	.15
27 Ron Davis	.15
28 Tom Kelly	.15
29 Dick Such	.15
30 Rick Stelmaszek	.15
31 Ray Miller	.15
32 Wayne Terwilliger	.15
33 Mike Smithson	.15
34 Alvis Woods	.15
35 Team Photo	.25
36 Twins Logo/Checklist	.15

1987 Minnesota Twins Team Issue

The Minnesota Twins produced a 32-card set of 2-1/2" x 3-1/2" full-color baseball cards to be sold at the ballpark and through their souvenir catalog. The card fronts are borderless, containing only the player photo. The backs are printed in blue and red on white card stock and carry the player's personal data and career record. The Twins also produced a post card set that was similar in design to the standard-size card set, but utilized different photos.

	NM/M
Complete Set (33):	12.50
Common Player:	.25
1 Steve Lombardozzi	.25
2 Roy Smalley	.25
3 Pedro Oliva	.50
4 Greg Gagne	.25
5 Gary Gaetti	.30
6 Tom Kelly	.25
7 Tom Nieto	.25
8 Mark Salas	.25
9 Kent Hrbek	.50
10 Tim Laudner	.25
11 Frank Viola	.35
12 Les Straker	.25
13 George Frazier	.25
14 Keith Atherton	.25
15 Tom Brunansky	.25
16 Randy Bush	.25
17 Al Newman	.25
18 Mark Davidson	.25
19 Bert Blyleven	.35
20 Dan Gladden	.25
21 Kirby Puckett	7.50
22 Mark Portugal	.25
23 Juan Berenguer	.25
24 Jeff Reardon	.25
25 Dick Such	.25
26 Rick Stelmaszek	.25
27 Rick Renick	.25
28 Wayne Terwilliger	.25
29 Joe Klink	.25
30 Mike Smithson	.25
31 Team Photo	.25
32 Twins Champions Logo	.25
33 Twins Logo/Checklist	.25

1988 Minnesota Twins Fire Safety

This 8-1/4" x 3-3/4" booklet contains a dozen postcards called Color-Grams featuring caricatures (suitable for coloring) of star players. Postcards are attached along a perforated edge to a baseball card-size stub with a black-and-white photo of the featured player. Backs include the player name and personal information. The card stubs include the same information, along with a fire prevention tip. Twins Color-Grams were produced as a public service by the U.S. Forest Service and Dept. of Agriculture and were distributed to fans at the Metrodome.

	NM/M
Complete Booklet:	10.00
Complete Set, Singles (12):	7.50
Common Player:	.50
(1) Bert Blyleven	.75
(2) Randy Bush	.50
(3) Gary Gaetti	.60
(4) Greg Gagne	.50
(5) Dan Gladden	.50
(6) Kent Hrbek	1.00
(7) Gene Larkin	.50
(8) Tim Laudner	.50
(9) Al Newman	.50
(10) Kirby Puckett	4.00
(11) Jeff Reardon	.50
(12) Frank Viola	.50

1988 Minnesota Twins team issue

The Twins issued this set to commemorate the team's 1987 World Series victory. The slightly oversized cards (2-5/8" x 3-7/16") feature color player photos printed on heavy stock with a gold-embossed "1987 World Champions" logo in the lower-left corner. Numbered card backs are red, white and blue and contain player name, personal info and stats. A limited edition of 5000 sets were printed but only a few hundred were sold before the cards were taken off the market due to Major League Baseball licensing restrictions on the use of the World Series logo.

	NM/M
Complete Set (33):	60.00
Common Player:	1.50
1 Steve Lombardozzi	1.50
2 Roy Smalley	1.50
3 Pedro Oliva	4.00
4 Greg Gagne	3.00
5 Gary Gaetti	4.00
6 Gene Larkin	2.00
7 Tom Kelly	2.00
8 Kent Hrbek	6.00
9 Tim Laudner	2.00
10 Frank Viola	4.00
11 Les Straker	1.50
12 Don Baylor	4.00
13 George Frazier	1.50
14 Keith Atherton	1.50
15 Tom Brunansky	1.50
16 Randy Bush	1.50
17 Al Newman	1.50
18 Mark Davidson	1.50
19 Bert Blyleven	4.00
20 Dan Schatzeder	1.50
21 Dan Gladden	2.00
22 Sal Butera	1.50
23 Kirby Puckett	25.00
24 Joe Niekro	2.00
25 Juan Berenguer	1.50
26 Jeff Reardon	3.00
27 Dick Such	1.50
28 Rick Stelmaszek	1.50
29 Rick Renick	1.50
30 Wayne Terwilliger	1.50
31 Team Photo	1.50
32 World Champions Team Logo Card	1.50
33 Team Logo Card/Checklist	1.50

1997 Minnesota Twins 10th Anniversary

The 10th anniversary of the team's 1987 World Series victory is recalled with this set given to fans on August 8 during the reunion weekend at the Metrodome. The 2-1/2" x 3-1/2" cards have 10-year-old color action photos on front with the anniversary logo and player identification. On back are a black-and-white portrait photo, uniform number, biographical details, the player's 1987 season and post-season performance and the sponsor's logo. The cards are checklisted here in alphabetical order.

	NM/M
Complete Set (25):	10.00
Common Player:	.25
(1) Keith Atherton	.25
(2) Don Baylor	.40
(3) Juan Berenguer	.25
(4) Bert Blyleven	.35
(5) Tom Brunansky	.25
(6) Randy Bush	.25
(7) Sal Butera	.25
(8) Mark Davidson	.25
(9) George Frazier	.25
(10) Gary Gaetti	.50
(11) Greg Gagne	.50
(12) Dan Gladden	.25
(13) Kent Hrbek	1.00
(14) Tom Kelly	.25
(15) Gene Larkin	.25
(16) Tim Laudner	.25
(17) Steve Lombardozzi	.25
(18) Al Newman	.25
(19) Joe Niekro	.40
(20) Kirby Puckett	5.00
(21) Jeff Reardon	.25
(22) Dan Schatzeder	.25
(23) Roy Smalley	.25
(24) Les Straker	.25
(25) Frank Viola	.40

2002 Minnesota Twins Police

More than 300 agencies comprising the Minnesota Crime Prevention Association distributed this multi-sport set. Eight players each from the Twins, Vikings and Wild were included, along with McGruff the Crime Dog. Distribution of the baseball players cards was between August 6-19. The baseball cards have game-action photos which are borderless at top and sides. Two team logos are in the top corners and a blue strip at bottom has player name, uniform number and position. Backs have a black-and-white portrait photo, a safety tip and sponsors logos. Only the baseball players from the issue are listed here.

	NM/M
Complete (Baseball) Set (8):	5.00
Common Player:	.50
1 Eddie Guardado	.50
2 Cristian Guzman	1.00
3 Jacque Jones	1.00
4 Corey Koskie	1.00
5 Doug Mientkiewicz	.50
6 A.J. Pierzynski	.50
7 Luis Rivas	.50
8 Torii Hunter	1.50

2003 Minnesota Twins Police

Sponsored by the Minnesota Crime Prevention Association, this set features eight popular players and McGruff the Crime Dog. Standard 2-1/2" x 3-1/2" cards have game-action photos on front, borderless at top and sides. A blue stripe at bottom has uniform number, player name and position. The team's 2002 A.L. Central Division Champions logo and "Gotta See 'Em" 2003 season logo are in the top corners. A facsimile autograph appears on front. Backs are in black, white and blue with a portrait photo, player data and a safety tip, along with the sponsor's and printer's logos.

	NM/M
Complete Set (9):	5.00
Common Player:	.50
1 Torii Hunter	1.00
2 Doug Mientkiewicz	.75
3 Corey Koskie	.75
4 A.J. Pierzynski	.75
5 Brad Radke	.50
6 Jacque Jones	.75
7 Eddie Guardado	.50
8 Eric Milton	.50
9 McGruff the Crime Dog	.50

2004 Minnesota Twins Police

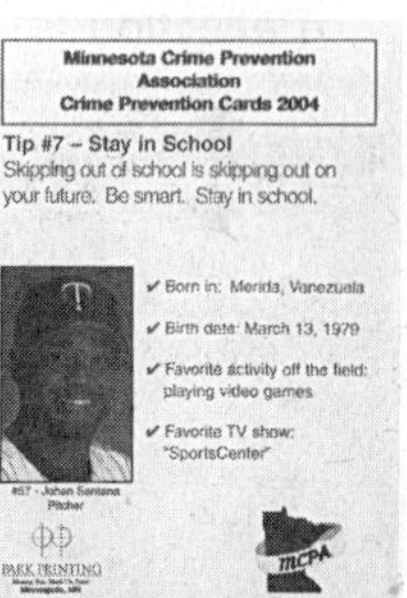

Sponsored by the Minnesota Crime Prevention Association, this set features eight popular players. Standard 2-1/2" x 3-1/2" cards have game-action photos on front, borderless at top and sides. A blue stripe at bottom has uniform number, player name and position. The team's 2003 A.L. Central Division Champions logo is in the top-right corner. A facsimile autograph appears on front. Backs are in black and white with a portrait photo, player data and a safety tip, along with the sponsor's and printer's logos.

	NM/M
Complete Set (8):	5.00
Common Player:	.50
1 Torii Hunter	.75
2 Doug Mientkiewicz	.50
3 Corey Koskie	.50
4 Shannon Stewart	.50
5 Brad Radke	.50
6 Cristian Guzman	.50
7 Johan Santana	2.00
8 Kyle Lohse	.50

2004 Minnesota Twins Team Issue

To build support in its drive to retain Major League Baseball in the Twin Cities and build a new outdoor stadium, the team issued this card set at its winter TwinsFest. Cards are 2-1/2" x 3-1/2" printed on thin semi-gloss stock. There are five player cards and seven depicting artists' views of the proposed ballpark.

		NM/M
Complete Set (12):		6.00
Common Player:		.50
16	Doug Mientkiewicz	.50
22	Brad Radke	.50
23	Shannon Stewart	.75
47	Corey Koskie	.75
48	Torii Hunter	1.00
---	A Ballpark for Minnesota ("As the new home . . .")	.50
---	A Ballpark for Minnesota ("Got off the bench . . .")	.50
---	A Ballpark for Minnesota ("Minnesota's new ballpark will honor. . .")	.50
---	A Ballpark for Minnesota ("Minnesota's new ballpark will mark. . .")	.50
---	A Ballpark for Minnesota ("Much like those . . .")	.50
---	A Ballpark for Minnesota ("The exterior . . .")	.50
---	A Ballpark for Minnesota ("With total seating . . .")	.50

2005 Star Tribune Minnesota Twins Medallion Collection

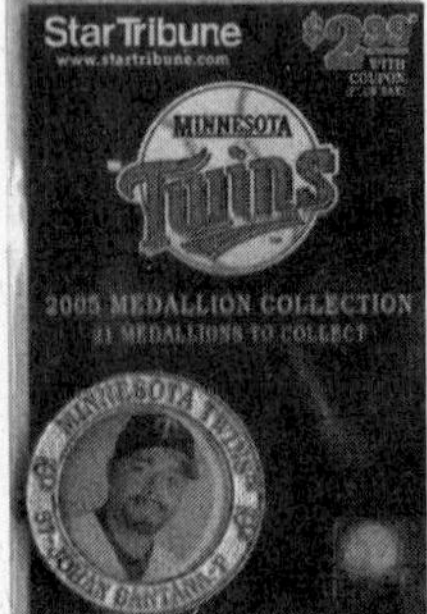

A set of 21 commemorative medallions was sponsored by the Star Tribune in this promotion. Coupons found in the newspaper between May 2-25 could be redeemed at newsstands (along with $2.99) for that day's medallion. Larger and thicker than a quarter, the 1-3/16" diameter medals are struck in nickel and have on their fronts an enameled portrait photo. A team logo dominates the back. A colorful, photo-filled 7-3/4" x 13" album was available to house the pieces. The medals are listed here in alphabetical order.

		NM/M
Complete Set (21):		90.00
Common Player:		3.00
Album:		3.00
(1)	Grant Balfour	3.00
(2)	Juan Castro	3.00
(3)	Michael Cuddyer	3.00
(4)	Lew Ford	3.00
(5)	Ron Gardenhire	3.00
(6)	Torii Hunter	4.50
(7)	Jacque Jones	4.50
(8)	Matthew LeCroy	3.00
(9)	Kyle Lohse	3.00
(10)	Joe Mauer	10.00
(11)	Joe Mays	3.00
(12)	Justin Morneau	10.00
(13)	Joe Nathan	3.00
(14)	Brad Radke	4.50
(15)	Juan Rincon	3.00
(16)	Luis Rivas	3.00
(17)	J.C. Romero	3.00
(18)	Johan Santana	12.50
(19)	Carlos Silva	3.00
(20)	Shannon Stewart	3.00
(21)	Twins Back To Back To Back Championships	3.00

2005 Minnesota Twins Police

Sponsored by the Minnesota Crime Prevention Association, this set features seven popular players and McGruff the Crime Dog. Standard 2-1/2" x 3-1/2" cards have game-action photos on front, bordered in dark blue. A strip at bottom has uniform number, player name and position. Team logos are in each upper corner. Backs are in black-and-white with a small portrait photo, player information, safety tip, along with the sponsor's and printer's logos. The set was distributed by area police agencies and at a Twins game in May.

		NM/M
Complete Set (8):		8.00
Common Player:		1.00
7	Joe Mauer	2.00
22	Brad Radke	1.00
23	Shannon Stewart	1.00
36	Joe Nathan	1.50
48	Torii Hunter	1.50
49	Kyle Lohse	1.00
57	Johan Santana	1.50
---	McGruff The Crime Dog	1.00

1992 MJB Holoprisms

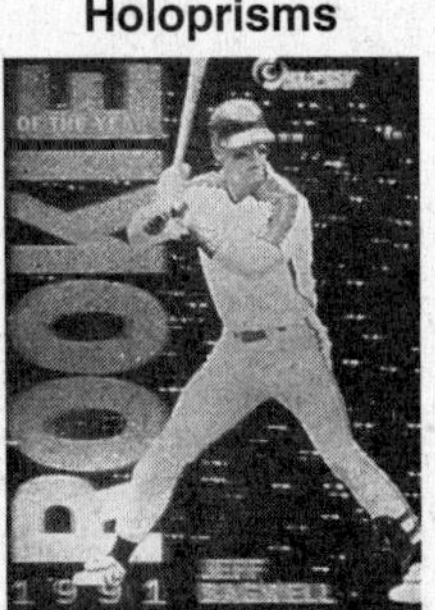

The Holoprism set consists of two 4-card hologram sets of Rookies of the Year Jeff Bagwell and Chuck Knoblauch. Each player set was packaged in a special plastic case. The production was limited to 250,000 of each set, numbered and with a letter of authenticity. Each player autographed 500 cards, which were randomly inserted.

		NM/M
Complete Bagwell Set (4):		6.00
Common Bagwell Card:		1.50
Complete Knoblauch Set (4):		6.00
Common Knoblauch Card:		1.00
Autographed Bagwell Card:		75.00
Autographed Knoblauch Card:		40.00
R1	Jeff Bagwell/Btg	2.00
R1a	Jeff Bagwell (Overprinted "PROTOTYPE" on back.)	2.00
R2	Jeff Bagwell/Fldg	2.00
R3	Jeff Bagwell/Btg	2.00
R4	Jeff Bagwell/Btg	2.00
R1	Chuck Knoblauch/Btg	1.00
R1a	Chuck Knoblauch (Overprinted "PROTOTYPE" on back.)	1.00
R2	Chuck Knoblauch/Fldg	1.00
R3	Chuck Knoblauch/Btg	1.00
R4	Chuck Knoblauch/Btg	1.00

2000 MLB Showdown Promos

To introduce its baseball card game, Wizards of the Coast produced a series of promo cards that were locally distributed to hobby stores to encourage people to join gaming leagues. The promos differ from the issued cards in the use of silver-foil highlights and the presence of large "FUTURE STAR" or "DIAMOND STAR" in the background, instead of a team logo, or "HOME RUN HITTER" at top. Because of the manner of distribution, some promos are more difficult to find in the hobby market.

		NM/M
Complete Set (43):		10.00
Common Player:		.40
(1)	Sandy Alomar Jr.	.40
(2)	Craig Biggio	.40
(3)	Carlos Delgado	.60
(4)	Damion Easley	.40
(5)	Mark Grace	.40
(6)	Rusty Greer	.40
(7)	Tony Gwynn	1.00
(8a)	Andruw Jones (8 OB)	.60
(8b)	Andruw Jones (10 OB)	1.00
(9)	Chipper Jones	1.00
(10)	Jeff Kent	.40
(11)	Edgar Martinez	.40
(12)	Gary Sheffield	.60
(13)	B.J. Surhoff	.40
(14)	Jason Varitek	.40
(15)	Robin Ventura	.40
(16)	Bernie Williams	.40
(1)	Bob Abreu	.40
(2)	Ron Belliard	.40
(3)	Sean Casey	.40
(4)	Luis Castillo	.40
(5)	J.D. Drew	.60
(6)	Erubiel Durazo	.40
(7)	Carlos Febles	.40
(8)	Troy Glaus	.65
(9)	Ben Grieve	.40
(10)	Todd Helton	.65
(11)	Corey Koskie	.40
(12)	Warren Morris	.40
1	Barry Bonds	2.00
2	Jose Canseco	.60
3	Nomar Garciaparra	1.00
4	Jason Giambi	.60
5	Shawn Green	.50
6	Ken Griffey Jr.	1.25
7	Andruw Jones	.75
8	Chipper Jones	1.00
9	Mark McGwire	1.50
10	Rafael Palmeiro	.65
11	Mike Piazza	1.25
12	Manny Ramirez	.75
13	Alex Rodriguez	1.50
14	Sammy Sosa	1.25

2000 MLB Showdown 1st Edition

Yet another attempt to bridge the gap between baseball cards as player-related collectibles and as interactive game, MLB Showdown from veteran gamers Wizards of the Coast enjoyed significant initial interest. Issued as a starter deck and in nine-card booster packs, the debut set has 462 player cards, including 63 premium holofoil star cards and 75 strategy cards. The holo premium foils were inserted in booster packs at a rate of 1:3. Promo cards were locally distributed. While collectors compete with gamers for these cards in the market, relative values placed on the cards by each group of buyers may differ. Cards without the silver-foil "1st Edition" logo were released in booster packs and are worth about half the values shown here.

		NM/M
Complete Set (517):		200.00
Common Player:		.15
Starter Box:		6.00
Starter Deck:		2.00
Booster Box (36):		25.00
Booster Pack (9):		1.00
1	Garret Anderson	.15
2	Tim Belcher	.15
3	Gary DiSarcina (Photo is Tim Salmon.)	.15
4	Darin Erstad	.30
5	Chuck Finley (Foil)	2.00
6	Troy Glaus	.65
7	Todd Greene	.15
8	Jeff Huson	.15
9	Orlando Palmeiro	.15
10	Troy Percival	.15
11	Mark Petkovsek	.15
12	Tim Salmon	.15
13	Steve Sparks	.15
14	Mo Vaughn	.15
15	Matt Walbeck	.15
16	Jay Bell (Foil)	2.00
17	Andy Benes	.15
18	Omar Daal	.15
19	Steve Finley	.15
20	Andy Fox	.15
21	Hanley Frias	.15
22	Bernard Gilkey	.15
23	Luis Gonzalez (Foil)	2.00
24	Randy Johnson (Foil)	3.00
25	Travis Lee	.15
26	Matt Mantei	.15
27	Dan Plesac	.15
28	Kelly Stinnett	.15
29	Greg Swindell	.15
30	Matt Williams (Foil)	2.00
31	Tony Womack	.15
32	Bret Boone	.15
33	Tom Glavine	.40
34	Jose Hernandez	.15
35	Brian Hunter	.15
36	Andruw Jones	.75
37	Chipper Jones (Foil)	4.00
38	Brian Jordan	.15
39	Ryan Klesko	.15
40	Keith Lockhart	.15
41	Greg Maddux (Foil)	4.00
42	Kevin Millwood (Foil)	2.00
43	Eddie Perez	.15
44	Mike Remlinger	.15
45	John Rocker	.15
46	John Smoltz	.15
47	Walt Weiss	.15
48	Gerald Williams	.15
49	Rich Amaral	.15
50	Brady Anderson	.15
51	Albert Belle	.15
52	Mike Bordick	.15
53	Jeff Conine	.15
54	Delino DeShields	.15
55	Scott Erickson	.15
56	Charles Johnson	.15
57	Mike Mussina	.35
58	Jesse Orosco	.15
59	Sidney Ponson	.15
60	Jeff Reboulet	.15
61	Cal Ripken Jr. (Foil)	7.00
62	B.J. Surhoff	.15
63	Mike Timlin	.15
64	Rod Beck	.15
65	Damon Buford	.15
66	Rheal Cormier	.15
67	Nomar Garciaparra (Foil)	4.00
68	Butch Huskey	.15
69	Darren Lewis	.15
70	Derek Lowe	.15
71	Pedro Martinez (Foil)	3.00
72	Trot Nixon	.15
73	Jose Offerman	.15
74	Troy O'Leary	.15
75	Mark Portugal	.15
76	Pat Rapp	.15
77	Mike Stanley	.15
78	John Valentin	.15
79	Jason Varitek	.25
80	Tim Wakefield	.15
81	Rick Aguilera	.15
82	Jeff Blauser	.15
83	Kyle Farnsworth	.15
84	Gary Gaetti	.15
85	Mark Grace	.15
86	Lance Johnson	.15
87	Jon Lieber	.15
88	Mickey Morandini	.15
89	Jose Nieves	.15
90	Jeff Reed	.15
91	Henry Rodriguez	.15
92	Scott Sanders	.15
93	Benito Santiago	.15
94	Sammy Sosa	4.50
95	Steve Trachsel	.15
96	James Baldwin	.15
97	Mike Caruso	.15
98	Ray Durham	.15
99	Brook Fordyce	.15
100	Bob Howry	.15
101	Paul Konerko	.25
102	Carlos Lee	.35
103	Greg Norton	.15
104	Magglio Ordonez	.15
105	Jim Parque	.15
106	Bill Simas	.15
107	Chris Singleton	.15
108	Mike Sirotka	.15
109	Frank Thomas (Foil)	3.00
110	Craig Wilson	.15
111	Aaron Boone	.15
112	Mike Cameron	.15
113	Sean Casey (Foil)	2.00
114	Danny Graves	.15
115	Pete Harnisch	.15
116	Barry Larkin (Foil)	2.00
117	Pokey Reese	.15
118	Scott Sullivan	.15
119	Eddie Taubensee	.15
120	Brett Tomko	.15
121	Michael Tucker	.15
122	Greg Vaughn	.15
123	Ron Villone	.15
124	Scott Williamson (Foil)	2.00
125	Dmitri Young	.15
126	Roberto Alomar (Foil)	2.00
127	Harold Baines	.15
128	Dave Burba	.15
129	Bartolo Colon	.15
130	Einar Diaz	.15
131	Travis Fryman	.15
132	Mike Jackson	.15
133	David Justice	.15
134	Kenny Lofton (Foil)	2.00
135	Charles Nagy	.15
136	Manny Ramirez (Foil)	3.00
137	Richie Sexson	.15
138	Paul Shuey	.15
139	Jim Thome (Foil)	2.50
140	Omar Vizquel	.15
141	Enrique Wilson	.15
142	Kurt Abbott	.15
143	Pedro Astacio	.15
144	Jeff Barry	.15
145	Dante Bichette	.15
146	Henry Blanco	.15
147	Brian Bohanon	.15
148	Vinny Castilla	.15
149	Jerry Dipoto	.15
150	Todd Helton	.65
151	Darryl Kile	.15
152	Curtis Leskanic	.15
153	Neifi Perez	.15
154	Terry Shumpert	.15
155	Dave Veres	.15
156	Larry Walker (Foil)	2.00
157	Brad Ausmus	.15
158	Frank Catalanotto	.15
159	Tony Clark	.15
160	Deivi Cruz	.15
161	Damion Easley	.15
162	Juan Encarnacion	.15
163	Karim Garcia	.15
164	Bobby Higginson	.15
165	Todd Jones	.15
166	Gabe Kapler	.15
167	Dave Mlicki	.15
168	Brian Moehler	.15
169	C.J. Nitkowski	.15
170	Dean Palmer (Foil)	2.00
171	Jeff Weaver	.15
172	Antonio Alfonseca	.15
173	Bruce Aven	.15
174	Dave Berg	.15
175	Luis Castillo (Foil)	2.00
176	Ryan Dempster	.15
177	Brian Edmondson	.15
178	Alex Gonzalez	.15
179	Mark Kotsay	.15
180	Derrek Lee	.50
181	Braden Looper	.15
182	Mike Lowell	.15
183	Brian Meadows	.15
184	Mike Redmond	.15
185	Dennis Springer	.15
186	Preston Wilson	.15
187	Jeff Bagwell (Foil)	3.00
188	Derek Bell	.15
189	Craig Biggio	.15
190	Tim Bogar	.15
191	Ken Caminiti	.15
192	Scott Elarton	.15
193	Tony Eusebio	.15
194	Carl Everett (Foil)	2.00
195	Mike Hampton (Foil)	2.00
196	Richard Hidalgo	.15
197	Stan Javier	.15
198	Jose Lima	.15
199	Jay Powell	.15
200	Shane Reynolds	.15
201	Bill Spiers	.15
202	Billy Wagner (Foil)	2.00
203	Carlos Beltran (Foil)	2.50
204	Johnny Damon	.35
205	Jermaine Dye	.15
206	Carlos Febles	.15
207	Jeremy Giambi	.15
208	Chad Kreuter	.15
209	Jeff Montgomery	.15
210	Joe Randa	.15
211	Jose Rosado	.15
212	Rey Sanchez	.15
213	Scott Service	.15
214	Tim Spehr	.15
215	Jeff Suppan	.15
216	Mike Sweeney	.15
217	Jay Witasick	.15
218	Adrian Beltre	.50
219	Pedro Borbon	.15
220	Kevin Brown (Foil)	2.00
221	Mark Grudzielanek	.15
222	Dave Hansen	.15
223	Todd Hundley	.15
224	Eric Karros	.15
225	Raul Mondesi	.15
226	Chan Ho Park	.15
227	Jeff Shaw	.15
228	Gary Sheffield (Foil)	2.50
229	Ismael Valdes	.15
230	Jose Vizcaino	.15
231	Devon White	.15
232	Eric Young	.15
233	Ron Belliard	.15
234	Sean Berry	.15
235	Jeromy Burnitz (Foil)	2.00
236	Jeff Cirillo	.15
237	Marquis Grissom	.15
238	Geoff Jenkins	.15
239	Scott Karl	.15
240	Mark Loretta	.15
241	Mike Myers	.15
242	David Nilsson (Foil)	2.00
243	Hideo Nomo	.50
244	Alex Ochoa	.15
245	Jose Valentin	.15
246	Bob Wickman	.15
247	Steve Woodard	.15
248	Chad Allen	.15
249	Ron Coomer	.15
250	Cristian Guzman	.15
251	Denny Hocking	.15
252	Torii Hunter	.15
253	Corey Koskie	.15
254	Matt Lawton	.15
255	Joe Mays	.15
256	Doug Mientkiewicz	.15
257	Eric Milton	.15
258	Brad Radke (Foil)	2.00
259	Terry Steinbach	.15
260	Mike Trombley	.15
261	Todd Walker	.15
262	Bob Wells	.15
263	Shane Andrews	.15
264	Michael Barrett	.15
265	Orlando Cabrera	.15
266	Brad Fullmer	.15
267	Vladimir Guerrero (Foil)	3.00
268	Wilton Guerrero	.15
269	Dustin Hermanson	.15
270	Steve Kline	.15
271	Manny Martinez	.15
272	Mike Thurman	.15
273	Ugueth Urbina	.15
274	Javier Vazquez	.15
275	Jose Vidro	.15
276	Rondell White	.15
277	Chris Widger	.15
278	Edgardo Alfonzo (Foil)	2.00
279	Armando Benitez	.15
280	Roger Cedeno	.15
281	Dennis Cook	.15
282	Shawon Dunston	.15
283	Matt Franco	.15
284	Darryl Hamilton	.15
285	Rickey Henderson (Foil)	3.00
286	Orel Hershiser	.15
287	Al Leiter	.15
288	John Olerud	.15
289	Rey Ordonez	.15
290	Mike Piazza (Foil)	5.00
291	Kenny Rogers	.15
292	Robin Ventura	.15
293	Turk Wendell	.15
294	Masato Yoshii	.15
295	Scott Brosius	.15
296	Roger Clemens (Foil)	4.50
297	David Cone (Foil)	2.00
298	Chad Curtis	.15
299	Chili Davis	.15
300	Orlando Hernandez	.15
301	Derek Jeter (Foil)	7.00
302	Chuck Knoblauch	.15
303	Ricky Ledee	.15
304	Tino Martinez	.15
305	Ramiro Mendoza	.15
306	Paul O'Neill	.15
307	Andy Pettitte	.35
308	Jorge Posada	.15
309	Mariano Rivera (Foil)	2.00
310	Mike Stanton	.15
311	Bernie Williams (Foil)	2.00
312	Kevin Appier	.15
313	Eric Chavez	.25
314	Ryan Christensen	.15
315	Jason Giambi (Foil)	2.50
316	Ben Grieve	.15
317	Buddy Groom	.15
318	Gil Heredia	.15
319	A.J. Hinch	.15
320	John Jaha	.15
321	Doug Jones	.15

322 Omar Olivares .15
323 Tony Phillips .15
324 Matt Stairs .15
325 Miguel Tejada .25
326 Randy Velarde (Foil) 2.00
327 Bobby Abreu (Foil) 2.00
328 Marlon Anderson .15
329 Alex Arias .15
330 Rico Brogna .15
331 Paul Byrd .15
332 Ron Gant .15
333 Doug Glanville .15
334 Wayne Gomes .15
335 Kevin Jordan .15
336 Mike Lieberthal .15
337 Steve Montgomery .15
338 Chad Ogea .15
339 Scott Rolen .60
340 Curt Schilling (Foil) 2.50
341 Kevin Sefcik .15
342 Mike Benjamin .15
343 Kris Benson .15
344 Adrian Brown .15
345 Brant Brown .15
346 Brad Clontz .15
347 Brian Giles (Foil) 2.00
348 Jason Kendall (Foil) 2.00
349 Al Martin .15
350 Warren Morris .15
351 Todd Ritchie .15
352 Scott Sauerbeck .15
353 Jason Schmidt .15
354 Ed Sprague .15
355 Mike Williams .15
356 Kevin Young .15
357 Andy Ashby .15
358 Ben Davis .15
359 Tony Gwynn (Foil) 4.00
360 Sterling Hitchcock .15
361 Trevor Hoffman (Foil) 2.00
362 Damian Jackson .15
363 Wally Joyner .15
364 Phil Nevin .15
365 Eric Owens .15
366 Ruben Rivera .15
367 Reggie Sanders .15
368 John Vander Wal .15
369 Quilvio Veras .15
370 Matt Whisenant .15
371 Woody Williams .15
372 Rich Aurilia .15
373 Marvin Benard .15
374 Barry Bonds (Foil) 7.00
375 Ellis Burks .15
376 Alan Embree .15
377 Shawn Estes .15
378 John Johnstone .15
379 Jeff Kent .15
380 Brent Mayne .15
381 Bill Mueller .15
382 Robb Nen .15
383 Russ Ortiz .15
384 Kirk Rueter .15
385 F.P. Santangelo .15
386 J.T. Snow .15
387 David Bell .15
388 Jay Buhner .15
389 Russ Davis .15
390 Freddy Garcia .15
391 Ken Griffey Jr. (Foil) 5.00
392 John Halama .15
393 Brian L. Hunter .15
394 Raul Ibanez .15
395 Tom Lampkin .15
396 Edgar Martinez (Foil) 2.00
397 Jose Mesa .15
398 Jamie Moyer .15
399 Jose Paniagua .15
400 Alex Rodriguez (Foil) 6.00
401 Dan Wilson .15
402 Manny Aybar .15
403 Ricky Bottalico .15
404 Kent Bottenfield .15
405 Darren Bragg .15
406 Alberto Castillo .15
407 J.D. Drew .60
408 Jose Jiminez .15
409 Ray Lankford .15
410 Joe McEwing .15
411 Willie McGee .15
412 Mark McGwire (Foil) 6.00
413 Darren Oliver .15
414 Lance Painter .15
415 Edgar Renteria .15
416 Fernando Tatis (Foil) 2.00
417 Wilson Alvarez .15
418 Rolando Arrojo .15
419 Wade Boggs 1.00
420 Miguel Cairo .15
421 Jose Canseco (Foil) 2.50
422 John Flaherty .15
423 Roberto Hernandez .15
424 Dave Martinez .15
425 Fred McGriff .15
426 Paul Sorrento .15
427 Kevin Stocker .15
428 Bubba Trammell .15
429 Rick White .15
430 Randy Winn .15
431 Bobby Witt .15
432 Royce Clayton .15
433 Tim Crabtree .15
434 Juan Gonzalez .45
435 Tom Goodwin .15
436 Rusty Greer .15
437 Rick Helling .15
438 Mark McLemore .15
439 Mike Morgan .15
440 Rafael Palmeiro (Foil) 3.00
441 Ivan Rodriguez (Foil) 3.00
442 Aaron Sele .15
443 Lee Stevens .15
444 Mike Venafro .15
445 John Wetteland .15
446 Todd Zeile .15
447 Jeff Zimmerman (Foil) 2.00
448 Tony Batista .15
449 Homer Bush .15
450 Jose Cruz Jr. .15
451 Carlos Delgado .40
452 Kelvim Escobar .15
453 Tony Fernandez (Foil) 2.00
454 Darrin Fletcher .15
455 Shawn Green (Foil) 2.00
456 Pat Hentgen .15
457 Billy Koch .15
458 Graeme Lloyd .15
459 Brian McRae .15
460 David Segui .15
461 Shannon Stewart .15
462 David Wells .15
S1 Bad Call/Umpire .10
S2 Big Inning (Mike Stanley) .10
S3 Bobbled in the Outfield (Tony Phillips) .10
S4 Clutch Hitting (Manny Ramirez) .10
S5 Do or Die (Chuck Knoblauch) .10
S6 Down the Middle (?) .10
S7 Ducks on the Pond (Carl Everett) .10
S8 Favorable Matchup (Barry Bonds) .30
S9 Free Steal (Juan Encarnacion) .10
S10 Get Under It (Jose Offerman) .10
S11 Great Lead (Rickey Henderson) .20
S12 Hard Slide (Damian Jackson) .10
S13 High Fives (Derek Jeter) .10
S14 Last Chance (Paul O'Neill) .10
S15 Long Single (Derek Jeter) .30
S16 Out of Gas (Jeff Zimmerman) .10
S17 Out of Position (Rickey Henderson, Ryan Klesko) .15
S18 Play the Percentages (Chipper Jones) .10
S19 Rally Cap (Omar Vizquel) .10
S20 Rattled (Mike Henneman) .10
S21 Runner Not Held (Miguel Tejada) .10
S22 Slow Roller (Brian Bohanon) .10
S23 Stick a Fork in Him (Kevin Millwood) .10
S24 Swing for the Fences (Sammy Sosa) .15
S25 To the Warning Track (Ricky Ledee) .10
S26 Whiplash (Mark McGwire) .25
S27 Wide Throw (Roberto Alomar) .10
S28 Wild Pitch (Eddie Taubensee) .10
S29 By the Book (Walt Weiss) .10
S30 Dominating (Billy Wagner) .10
S31 Full Windup (Orlando Hernandez) .10
S32 Good Fielding (Rey Ordonez, Ryan Klesko) .10
S33 Gun 'Em Down! (Jason Kendall) .10
S34 He's Got a Gun (Sammy Sosa) .10
S35 In the Groove (David Cone) .10
S36 In the Zone (Pedro Martinez) .10
S37 Infield In (S.F. Giants) .10
S38 Intimidation (Randy Johnson) .15
S39 Just Over the Wall (Ken Griffey, Jr.) .25
S40 Knock the Ball Down (?) .10
S41 Lefty Specialist (Jesse Orosco) .10
S42 Nerves of Steel (Mariano Rivera) .10
S43 Nothing but Heat (Randy Johnson) .10
S44 Pitch Out (Bobby Hughes) .10
S45 Pumped Up (John Rocker) .10
S46 Quick Pitch (Greg Maddux) .10
S47 Rally Killer (Carlos Baerga) .10
S48 Short Fly (Chuck Knoblauch, Bernie Williams) .10
S49 Three Up, Three Down (Pedro Martinez) .10
S50 Trick Pitch (Derek Jeter) .30
S51 Belt-High (Sammy Sosa) .15
S52 Change In Strategy (Joe Torre) .10
S53 Grounder to Second (Pokey Reese) .10
S54 Stealing Signals (Mark Grace) .10
S55 Swing at Anything (Cal Ripken, Jr.) .30

2000 MLB Showdown Pennant Run Promos

To promote its forthcoming Pennant Run edition, Wizards of the Coast issued eight specially marked sample cards. The promos have silver-foil player names and a large "W." The promos were issued one per copy of Top-Deck magazine (a gamer's publication) which carried a $5.99 cover price.

NM/M
Complete Set (8): 3.00
Common Player: .50
1 Peter Bergeron .50
2 Matt Clement .50
3 Ramon Hernandez .50
4 Gabe Kapler .50
5 Adam Kennedy .50
6 Sean Lowe .50
7 Joe Nathan .50
8 Daryle Ward .50

2000 MLB Showdown Pennant Run

Issued just after the 2000 season opened, this is essentially an update to the interactive game MLB Showdown from veteran gamers Wizards of the Coast. Players in the set are generally those who changed teams during the off-season, or promising rookies. The Pennant Run edition was issued in a Booster box of 36 nine-card (seven player, two strategy) packs. The set has 130 "regular" player cards, 20 premium holofoil star cards and 25 strategy cards. The holo premium cards were inserted in packs at a rate of 1:3. While collectors compete with gamers for these cards in the market, relative values placed on the cards by each group of buyers may differ.

NM/M
Complete Set (175): 30.00
Common Player: .15
Booster Pack (9): 1.00
Booster Box (36): 20.00
1 Kent Bottenfield .15
2 Ken Hill .15
3 Adam Kennedy .15
4 Ben Molina .15
5 Scott Spiezio .15
6 Brian Anderson .15
7 Erubiel Durazo (Foil) 1.00
8 Armando Reynoso .15
9 Russ Springer .15
10 Todd Stottlemyre .15
11 Tony Womack .15
12 Andres Galarraga (Foil) 1.00
13 Javy Lopez (Foil) 1.00
14 Kevin McGlinchy .15
15 Terry Mulholland .15
16 Reggie Sanders .15
17 Harold Baines .15
18 Will Clark .15
19 Mike Trombley .15
20 Manny Alexander .15
21 Carl Everett (Foil) 1.00
22 Ramon Martinez (Foil) 1.00
23 Bret Saberhagen .15
24 John Wasdin .15
25 Joe Girardi .15
26 Ricky Gutierrez .15
27 Glenallen Hill .15
28 Kevin Tapani .15
29 Kerry Wood (Foil) 2.00
30 Eric Young .15
31 Keith Foulke (Foil) 1.00
32 Mark Johnson .15
33 Sean Lowe .15
34 Jose Valentin .15
35 Dante Bichette .15
36 Ken Griffey Jr. (Foil) 6.00
37 Denny Neagle .15
38 Steve Parris .15
39 Dennis Reyes .15
40 Sandy Alomar Jr. .15
41 Chuck Finley (Foil) 1.00
42 Steve Karsay .15
43 Steve Reed .15
44 Jaret Wright .15
45 Jeff Cirillo .15
46 Tom Goodwin .15
47 Jeffrey Hammonds .15
48 Mike Lansing .15
49 Aaron Ledesma .15
50 Brent Mayne .15
51 Doug Brocail .15
52 Robert Fick .15
53 Juan Gonzalez .60
54 Hideo Nomo .60
55 Luis Polonia .15
56 Brant Brown .15
57 Alex Fernandez .15
58 Cliff Floyd .15
59 Dan Miceli .15
60 Vladimir Nunez .15
61 Moises Alou (Foil) 1.00
62 Roger Cedeno (Foil) 1.00
63 Octavio Dotel .15
64 Mitch Meluskey .15
65 Daryle Ward .15
66 Mark Quinn (Foil) 1.00
67 Brad Rigby .15
68 Blake Stein .15
69 Mac Suzuki .15
70 Terry Adams .15
71 Darren Dreifort .15
72 Kevin Elster .15
73 Shawn Green (Foil) 1.50
74 Todd Hollandsworth .15
75 Gregg Olson .15
76 Kevin Barker .15
77 Jose Hernandez .15
78 Dave Weathers .15
79 Hector Carrasco .15
80 Eddie Guardado .15
81 Jacque Jones .25
82 David Ortiz .50
83 Peter Bergeron .15
84 Hideki Irabu .15
85 Lee Stevens .15
86 Anthony Telford .15
87 Derek Bell .15
88 John Franco .15
89 Mike Hampton (Foil) 1.00
90 Bobby J. Jones .15
91 Todd Pratt .15
92 Todd Zeile .15
93 Jason Grimsley .15
94 Roberto Kelly .15
95 Jim Leyritz .15
96 Ramiro Mendoza .15
97 Rich Becker .15
98 Ramon Hernandez .15
99 Tim Hudson (Foil) 2.00
100 Jason Isringhausen .15
101 Mike Magnante .15
102 Olmedo Saenz .15
103 Mickey Morandini .15
104 Robert Person .15
105 Desi Relaford .15
106 Jason Christiansen .15
107 Wil Cordero .15
108 Francisco Cordova .15
109 Chad Hermansen .15
110 Pat Meares .15
111 Aramis Ramirez .15
112 Bret Boone .15
113 Matt Clement .15
114 Carlos Hernandez .15
115 Ryan Klesko .15
116 Dave Magadan .15
117 Al Martin .15
118 Bobby Estalella .15
119 Livan Hernandez .15
120 Doug Mirabelli .15
121 Joe Nathan .15
122 Mike Cameron .15
123 Mark McLemore .15
124 Gil Meche .15
125 John Olerud .15
126 Arthur Rhodes .15
127 Aaron Sele (Foil) 1.00
128 Jim Edmonds (Foil) 1.00
129 Pat Hentgen .15
130 Darryl Kile .15
131 Eli Marrero .15
132 Dave Veres .15
133 Fernando Vina .15
134 Vinny Castilla .15
135 Juan Guzman .15
136 Ryan Rupe .15
137 Greg Vaughn (Foil) 1.00
138 Gerald Williams .15
139 Esteban Yan .15
140 Tom Evans .15
141 Gabe Kapler .15
142 Ruben Mateo (Foil) 1.00
143 Kenny Rogers .15
144 David Segui .15
145 Tony Batista .15
146 Chris Carpenter .15
147 Brad Fullmer .15
148 Alex Gonzalez .15
149 Roy Halladay .15
150 Raul Mondesi (Foil) 1.00
S1 Afterburners (Aaron Boone) .10
S2 Change Sides (Chipper Jones) .15
S3 Patience is a Virtue (Bob Abreu) .10
S4 Payoff Pitch (Fernando Tatis) .10
S5 Pointers (Rod Carew) .15
S6 Professional Baserunner (J.D. Drew) .10
S7 Professional Hitter (John VanderWal) .10
S8 Protect the Runner (Pokey Reese) .10
S9 Rough Outing (Greg Maddux) .15
S10 Shelled (Cincinnati Reds) .10
S11 Take What is Given (Larry Walker) .10
S12 Tricky Hop (Alex Rodriguez) .40
S13 Aggressive Coaching (Alex Rodriguez) .40
S14 Cut Off in the Gap (N.Y. Mets) .10
S15 Great Start (Kevin Brown) .10
S16 Insult to Injury (Paul O'Neill) .10
S17 Job Well Done (Scott Williamson) .10
S18 Low and Away (Jamie Moyer) .10
S19 Outfield In (Bernie Williams) .10
S20 Put Out the Fire (John Franco) .10
S21 Rotation Play (Pittsburgh Pirates) .10
S22 Swiss Army Closer (John Rocker) .10
S23 Whoops (Mike Lansing) .10
S24 Pep Talk (Roger Clemens, Joe Torre) .15
S25 Revenue Sharing (Derek Jeter) .50

2001 MLB Showdown Promos

To introduce its 2001 card game, Wizards of the Coast produced a series of promo cards which were locally distributed to hobby stores to encourage people to join gaming leagues. The promos differ from the issued cards in the use of a designation at top of "ACE PITCHER," "FUTURE STAR" or "DIAMOND STAR" and the absence of the large team logo in the background. Because of the manner of distribution, some promos are more difficult to find in the hobby market.

NM/M
Complete Set (64): 35.00
Common Player: .50
(1) Kris Benson .50
(2) Kevin Brown .50
(3) Roger Clemens 1.75
(4) Bartolo Colon .50
(5) Jeff D'Amico .50
(6) Ryan Dempster .50
(7) Adam Eaton .50
(8) Scott Elarton .50
(9) Livan Hernandez .50
(10) Tim Hudson .65
(11) Randy Johnson 1.00
(12) Darryl Kile .50
(13) Al Leiter .50
(14) Jon Lieber .50
(15) Greg Maddux 1.50
(16) Pedro Martinez 1.00
(17) Brad Radke .50
(18) Javier Vazquez .50
(19) Jeff Weaver .50
(20) David Wells .50
(1) Roberto Alomar .50
(2) Carlos Delgado .65
(3) Jason Giambi .75
(4) Troy Glaus .75
(5) Bobby Higginson .50
(6) David Justice .50
(7) Jeff Kent .50
(8) Ivan Rodriguez .65
(9) Gary Sheffield .75
(10) Frank Thomas 1.00
(11) Greg Vaughn .50
(12) Robin Ventura .50
(13) Rondell White .50
(1) Peter Bergeron .50
(2) Pat Burrell .75
(3) Sean Casey .50
(4) J.D. Drew .75
(5) Richard Hidalgo .50
(6) Melvin Mora .50
(7) Eric Owens .50
(8) Aramis Ramirez .50
(9) Preston Wilson .50
(1) Joe Crede .50
(2) Corey Patterson .50
(3) Albert Pujols 15.00
(4) Ben Sheets .50
(5) Alfonso Soriano .75

2001 MLB Showdown 1st Edition

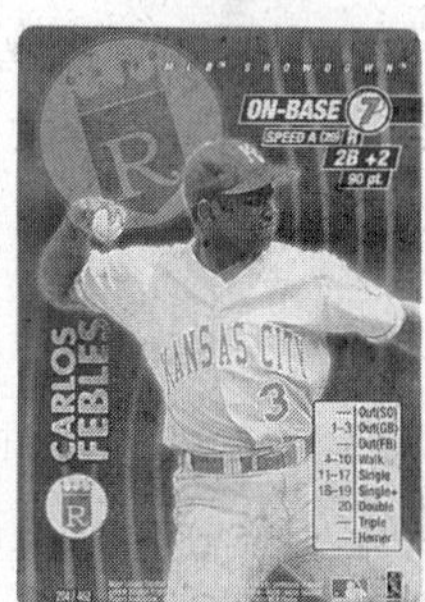

MLB Showdown returned for a second season in 2001. Issued as a 50-card starter set, a 60-card "Draft Pack" and in nine-card booster packs, the set has 416 "regular" player cards, 46 premium holofoil star cards and 75 strategy cards. The holo premium cards were inserted in booster packs at a rate of 1:3. Promo cards were locally distributed. While collectors compete with gamers for these cards in the market, relative values placed on the cards by each group of buyers may differ. Cards without the silver-foil "1st Edition" logo were released in booster packs and are worth about half the prices shown here.

NM/M
Complete Set (537): 195.00
Common Player: .15
Starter Box: 12.00
Booster Pack (9): 1.50
Booster Box (36): 25.00
1 Garret Anderson .15
2 Darin Erstad (Foil) 2.00
3 Ron Gant .15
4 Troy Glaus (Foil) 3.00
5 Shigetosi Hasegawa .15
6 Adam Kennedy .15
7 Al Levine .15
8 Ben Molina .15
9 Troy Percival .15
10 Mark Petkovsek .15
11 Tim Salmon .15
12 Scott Schoeneweis .15
13 Scott Spezio .15
14 Mo Vaughn .15
15 Jarrod Washburn .15
16 Brian Anderson .15
17 Danny Bautista .15
18 Jay Bell .15
19 Greg Colbrunn .15
20 Steve Finley .15

21 Luis Gonzalez (Foil) 2.00
22 Randy Johnson (Foil) 3.50
23 Byung-Hyun Kim .15
24 Matt Mantei .15
25 Mike Morgan .15
26 Curt Schilling .30
27 Kelly Stinnett .15
28 Greg Swindell .15
29 Matt Williams .15
30 Tony Womack .15
31 Andy Ashby .15
32 Bobby Bonilla .15
33 Rafael Furcal (Foil) 2.00
34 Andres Galarraga .15
35 Tom Glavine (Foil) 2.50
36 Andruw Jones .50
37 Chipper Jones (Foil) 4.00
38 Brian Jordan .15
39 Wally Joyner .15
40 Keith Lockhart .15
41 Javy Lopez .15
42 Greg Maddux (Foil) 4.00
43 Kevin Millwood .15
44 Mike Remlinger .15
45 John Rocker .15
46 B.J. Surhoff .15
47 Quilvio Veras .15
48 Brady Anderson .15
49 Albert Belle .15
50 Jeff Conine .15
51 Delino DeShields .15
52 Buddy Groom .15
53 Trenidad Hubbard .15
54 Luis Matos .15
55 Jose Mercedes .15
56 Melvin Mora .15
57 Mike Mussina (Foil) 2.50
58 Sidney Ponson .15
59 Pat Rapp .15
60 Chris Richard .15
61 Cal Ripken Jr. (Foil) 7.00
62 Mike Trombley .15
63 Rolando Arrojo .15
64 Dante Bichette .15
65 Rheal Cormier .15
66 Carl Everett .15
67 Rich Garces .15
68 Nomar Garciaparra (Foil) 4.00
69 Mike Lansing .15
70 Darren Lewis .15
71 Derek Lowe .15
72 Pedro Martinez (Foil) 3.50
73 Ramon Martinez .15
74 Trot Nixon .15
75 Jose Offerman .15
76 Troy O'Leary .15
77 Jason Varitek .15
78 Rick Aguilera .15
79 Damon Buford .15
80 Joe Girardi .15
81 Mark Grace .15
82 Willie Greene .15
83 Ricky Gutierrez .15
84 Felix Heredia .15
85 Jon Lieber .15
86 Jeff Reed .15
87 Sammy Sosa (Foil) 4.50
88 Kevin Tapani .15
89 Todd Van Poppel .15
90 Rondell White .15
91 Kerry Wood .35
92 Eric Young .15
93 James Baldwin .15
94 Ray Durham .15
95 Keith Foulke (Foil) 2.00
96 Bob Howry .15
97 Charles Johnson (Foil) 2.00
98 Mark L. Johnson .15
99 Paul Konerko .25
100 Carlos Lee .25
101 Magglio Ordonez .15
102 Jim Parque .15
103 Herbert Perry .15
104 Bill Simas .15
105 Chris Singleton .15
106 Mike Sirotka .15
107 Frank Thomas (Foil) 3.50
108 Jose Valentin .15
109 Kelly Wunsch .15
110 Aaron Boone .15
111 Sean Casey .15
112 Danny Graves .15
113 Ken Griffey Jr. (Foil) 5.00
114 Pete Harnisch .15
115 Barry Larkin (Foil) 2.00
116 Alex Ochoa .15
117 Steve Parris .15
118 Pokey Reese .15
119 Chris Stynes .15
120 Scott Sullivan .15
121 Eddie Taubensee .15
122 Michael Tucker .15
123 Ron Villone .15
124 Dmitri Young .15
125 Roberto Alomar (Foil) 2.00
126 Sandy Alomar Jr. .15
127 Jason Bere .15
128 Dave Burba .15
129 Bartolo Colon .15
130 Wil Cordero .15
131 Chuck Finley .15
132 Travis Fryman .15
133 Steve Karsay .15
134 Kenny Lofton .15
135 Manny Ramirez (Foil) 3.50
136 David Segui .15
137 Jim Thome .45
138 Omar Vizquel .15
139 Bob Wickman .15
140 Pedro Astacio .15
141 Brian Bohannon .15
142 Jeff Cirillo .15
143 Jeff Frye .15
144 Jeffrey Hammonds .15
145 Todd Helton (Foil) 3.00
146 Todd Hollandsworth .15
147 Butch Huskey .15
148 Jose Jimenez .15
149 Brent Mayne .15
150 Neifi Perez .15
151 Terry Shumpert .15
152 Larry Walker .15
153 Gabe White (Foil) 2.00
154 Masato Yoshii .15
155 Matt Anderson .15
156 Brad Ausmus .15
157 Rich Becker .15
158 Tony Clark .15
159 Deivi Cruz .15
160 Damion Easley .15
161 Juan Encarnacion .15
162 Juan Gonzalez .30
163 Shane Halter .15
164 Bobby Higginson .15
165 Todd Jones (Foil) 2.00
166 Brian Moehler .15
167 Hideo Nomo .35
168 Dean Palmer .15
169 Jeff Weaver .15
170 Antonio Alfonseca .15
171 Luis Castillo (Foil) 2.00
172 Ryan Dempster (Foil) 2.00
173 Cliff Floyd .15
174 Alex Gonzalez .15
175 Mark Kotsay .15
176 Derrek Lee .35
177 Braden Looper .15
178 Mike Lowell .15
179 Brad Penny .15
180 Mike Redmond .15
181 Henry Rodriguez .15
182 Jesus Sanchez .15
183 Mark Smith .15
184 Preston Wilson .15
185 Moises Alou .15
186 Jeff Bagwell (Foil) 3.50
187 Lance Berkman .15
188 Craig Biggio .15
189 Tim Bogar .15
190 Jose Cabrera .15
191 Octavio Dotel .15
192 Scott Elarton (Foil) 2.00
193 Richard Hidalgo .15
194 Chris Holt .15
195 Jose Lima .15
196 Julio Lugo .15
197 Mitch Meluskey .15
198 Bill Spiers .15
199 Daryle Ward .15
200 Carlos Beltran .40
201 Ricky Bottalico .15
202 Johnny Damon (Foil) 2.50
203 Jermaine Dye .15
204 Carlos Febles .15
205 Dave McCarty .15
206 Mark Quinn .15
207 Joe Randa .15
208 Dan Reichert .15
209 Rey Sanchez .15
210 Jose Santiago .15
211 Jeff Suppan .15
212 Mac Suzuki .15
213 Mike Sweeney .15
214 Gregg Zaun .15
215 Terry Adams .15
216 Adrian Beltre .15
217 Kevin Brown (Foil) 2.00
218 Alex Cora .15
219 Darren Dreifort .15
220 Tom Goodwin .15
221 Shawn Green .25
222 Mark Grudzielanek .15
223 Dave Hansen .15
224 Todd Hundley .15
225 Eric Karros .15
226 Chad Kreuter .15
227 Chan Ho Park .15
228 Jeff Shaw .15
229 Gary Sheffield (Foil) 2.50
230 Juan Acevedo .15
231 Ron Belliard .15
232 Henry Blanco .15
233 Jeromy Burnitz .15
234 Jeff D'Amico (Foil) 2.00
235 Valerio de los Santos .15
236 Marquis Grissom .15
237 Charlie Hayes .15
238 Jimmy Haynes .15
239 Jose Hernandez .15
240 Geoff Jenkins .15
241 Curtis Leskanic .15
242 Mark Loretta .15
243 Richie Sexson .15
244 Dave Weathers .15
245 Jay Canizaro .15
246 Ron Coomer .15
247 Cristian Guzman .15
248 LaTroy Hawkins .15
249 Denny Hocking .15
250 Torii Hunter .15
251 Jacque Jones .15
252 Corey Koskie .15
253 Matt Lawton .15
254 Matt LeCroy .15
255 Eric Milton .15
256 David Ortiz .40
257 Brad Radke (Foil) 2.00
258 Mark Redman .15
259 Bob Wells .15
260 Michael Barrett .15
261 Peter Bergeron .15
262 Milton Bradley .15
263 Orlando Cabrera .15
264 Vladimir Guerrero (Foil) 3.50
265 Wilton Guerrero .15
266 Dustin Hermanson .15
267 Terry Jones .15
268 Steve Kline .15
269 Felipe Lira .15
270 Mike Mordecai .15
271 Lee Stevens .15
272 Anthony Telford .15
273 Javier Vazquez .15
274 Jose Vidro (Foil) 2.00
275 Edgardo Alfonzo (Foil) 2.00
276 Derek Bell .15
277 Armando Benitez .15
278 Mike Bordick .15
279 Mike Hampton (Foil) 2.00
280 Lenny Harris .15
281 Al Leiter .15
282 Jay Payton .15
283 Mike Piazza (Foil) 5.00
284 Todd Pratt .15
285 Glendon Rusch .15
286 Bubba Trammell .15
287 Robin Ventura .15
288 Turk Wendell .15
289 Rick White .15
290 Todd Zeile .15
291 Scott Brosius .15
292 Roger Clemens (Foil) 4.50
293 Jason Grimsley .15
294 Orlando Hernandez .15
295 Derek Jeter (Foil) 7.00
296 Dave Justice .15
297 Chuck Knoblauch .15
298 Tino Martinez .15
299 Denny Neagle .15
300 Jeff Nelson .15
301 Paul O'Neill .15
302 Andy Pettitte .25
303 Jorge Posada .15
304 Mariano Rivera (Foil) 2.00
305 Jose Vizcaino .15
306 Bernie Williams (Foil) 2.00
307 Kevin Appier .15
308 Eric Chavez .15
309 Ryan Christenson .15
310 Jason Giambi (Foil) 3.00
311 Jeremy Giambi .15
312 Ben Grieve .15
313 Gil Heredia .15
314 Ramon Hernandez .15
315 Tim Hudson (Foil) 2.50
316 Jason Isringhausen .15
317 Terrence Long (Foil) 2.00
318 Jim Mecir .15
319 Mark Mulder .15
320 Matt Stairs .15
321 Miguel Tejada .25
322 Randy Velarde .15
323 Bobby Abreu .15
324 Jeff Brantley .15
325 Pat Burrell .45
326 Omar Daal .15
327 Rob Ducey .15
328 Doug Glanville .15
329 Wayne Gomes .15
330 Kevin Jordan .15
331 Travis Lee .15
332 Mike Lieberthal .15
333 Vicente Padilla .15
334 Robert Person .15
335 Scott Rolen (Foil) 2.50
336 Kevin Sefcik .15
337 Randy Wolf .15
338 Jimmy Anderson .15
339 Mike Benjamin .15
340 Kris Benson .15
341 Adrian Brown .15
342 Brian Giles (Foil) 2.00
343 Jason Kendall (Foil) 2.00
344 Pat Meares .15
345 Wayne Morris .15
346 Aramis Ramirez .15
347 Todd Ritchie .15
348 Scott Sauerbeck .15
349 Jose Silva .15
350 John Vander Wal .15
351 Mike Williams .15
352 Kevin Young .15
353 Carlos Almanzar .15
354 Bret Boone .15
355 Matt Clement .15
356 Adam Eaton .15
357 Wiki Gonzalez .15
358 Trevor Hoffman (Foil) 2.00
359 Damian Jackson .15
360 Ryan Klesko .15
361 Phil Nevin (Foil) 2.00
362 Eric Owens .15
363 Desi Relaford .15
364 Ruben Rivera .15
365 Kevin Walker .15
366 Woody Williams .15
367 Jay Witasick .15
368 Rich Aurilia .15
369 Marvin Benard .15
370 Barry Bonds (Foil) 7.00
371 Ellis Burks .15
372 Bobby Estella .15
373 Doug Henry .15
374 Livan Hernandez .15
375 Jeff Kent (Foil) 2.00
376 Doug Mirabelli .15
377 Bill Mueller .15
378 Calvin Murray .15
379 Robb Nen (Foil) 2.00
380 Russ Ortiz .15
381 Armando Rios .15
382 Felix Rodriguez .15
383 Kirk Rueter .15
384 J.T. Snow .15
385 Paul Abbott .15
386 David Bell .15
387 Jay Buhner .15
388 Mike Cameron .15
389 John Halama .15
390 Rickey Henderson .50
391 Al Martin .15
392 Edgar Martinez (Foil) 2.00
393 Mark McLemore .15
394 John Olerud .15
395 Jose Paniagua .15
396 Arthur Rhodes .15
397 Alex Rodriguez (Foil) 6.00
398 Kazuhiro Sasaki (Foil) 2.00
399 Aaron Sele .15
400 Dan Wilson .15
401 Rick Ankiel (Foil) 2.00
402 Will Clark .15
403 J.D. Drew .45
404 Jim Edmonds (Foil) 2.00
405 Pat Hentgen .15
406 Darryl Kile .15
407 Ray Lankford .15
408 Mike Matheny .15
409 Mark McGwire (Foil) 6.00
410 Craig Paquette .15
411 Placido Polanco .15
412 Edgar Renteria .15
413 Garrett Stephenson .15
414 Fernando Tatis .15
415 Mike Timlin .15
416 Dave Veres .15
417 Fernando Vina .15
418 Miguel Cairo .15
419 Vinny Castilla .15
420 Steve Cox .15
421 Doug Creek .15
422 John Flaherty .15
423 Jose Guillen .15
424 Roberto Hernandez (Foil) 2.00
425 Russ Johnson .15
426 Albie Lopez .15
427 Felix Martinez .15
428 Fred McGriff .15
429 Bryan Rekar .15
430 Greg Vaughn .15
431 Gerald Williams .15
432 Esteban Yan .15
433 Luis Alicea .15
434 Frank Catalanotto .15
435 Royce Clayton .15
436 Tim Crabtree .15
437 Chad Curtis .15
438 Rusty Greer .15
439 Rick Helling .15
440 Gabe Kapler .15
441 Mike Lamb .15
442 Ricky Ledee .15
443 Rafael Palmeiro .45
444 Ivan Rodriguez (Foil) 3.00
445 Kenny Rogers .15
446 Mike Venafro .15
447 John Wetteland .15
448 Tony Batista (Foil) 2.00
449 Jose Cruz, Jr. .15
450 Carlos Delgado (Foil) 2.50
451 Kelvim Escobar .15
452 Darrin Fletcher .15
453 Brad Fullmer .15
454 Alex S. Gonzalez .15
455 Mark Guthrie .15
456 Billy Koch .15
457 Esteban Loaiza .15
458 Raul Mondesi .15
459 Mickey Morandini .15
460 Paul Quantrill .15
461 Shannon Stewart .15
462 David Wells (Foil) 2.00
S1 Change Sides (Jorge Posada) .05
S2 Clutch Hitter (Nomar Garciaparra) .15
S3 Clutch Hitting (Manny Ramirez) .10
S4 Contact Hitter (Bernie Williams) .05
S5 Deep in the Gap (Sammy Sosa) .15
S6 Dog Meat (Brian Buchanon) .05
S7 Double Steal (Jay Canizaro) .05
S8 Down the Middle (Michael Tucker) .05
S9 Drag Bunt (Unidentified) .05
S10 Drained (Luis Castillo) .05
S11 Ducks on the Pond (Carl Everett) .05
S12 Favorable Matchup (Carlos Delgado) .10
S13 Fight It Off (Unidentified) .05
S14 Free Swinger (Benji Molina) .05
S15 Fuel on the Fire (Eric Young) .05
S16 Hiding an Injury (Unidentified) .05
S17 In Motion (Nomar Garciaparra) .15
S18 Last Chance (Alex Ochoa) .05
S19 Lean Into It (Unidentified) .05
S20 Nuisance (Rickey Henderson) .10
S21 Off-Balance (Alex Gonzalez) .05
S22 Out of Gas (Hideo Nomo) .10
S23 Overthrow (Sean Casey) .05
S24 Play the Percentages (Unidentified) .05
S25 Power Hitter (Unidentified) .05
S26 Protect the Runner (Chuck Knoblauch) .05
S27 Pull the Ball (Todd Helton) .10
S28 Rally Cap (Tim Salmon) .05
S29 Rough Outing (Randy Johnson) .10
S30 Runner Not Held (Johnny Damon) .05
S31 Running on Fumes (Unidentified) .05
S32 Ruptured Duck (Alex Rodriguez) .25
S33 Sail Into Center (Pokey Reese) .05
S34 Say the Magic Word (Mark McGwire) .25
S35 Shell Shocked (Unidentified) .05
S36 Singles Hitter (Homer Bush) .05
S37 Smash up the Middle (Unidentified) .05
S38 Stick a Fork in Him (Unidentified) .05
S39 Take What's Given (Unidentified) .05
S40 To the Warning Track (Brian Giles) .05
S41 Turn On It (Shawon Dunston) .05
S42 Anointed Closer (Cutis Leskanic) .05
S43 By the Book (Unidentified) .05
S44 Cannon (Bobby Higginson) .05
S45 Choke (Unidentified) .05
S46 Fast Worker (Greg Maddux) .15
S47 Flamethrower (unidentified) .05
S48 Full Windup (Kevin Brown) .05
S49 Goose Egg (Omar Vizquel) .05
S50 Great Start (Tom Glavine) .10
S51 Great Throw (Neifi Perez) .05
S52 Gutsy Play (Mike Lamb) .05
S53 Highlight Reel (Pokey Reese) .05
S54 Insult to Injury (Unidentified) .05
S55 In the Groove (Randy Johnson) .10
S56 Job Well Done (Unidentified) .05
S57 Just Foul (Unidentified) .05
S58 Just Over the Wall (Bernie Williams) .05
S59 Leaping Catch (Barry Bonds) .35
S60 Lefty Specialist (Jason Christensen) .05
S61 Low and Away (Eddie Taubensee) .05
S62 Mound Conference (Unidentified) .05
S63 Nerves of Steel (Todd Jones) .05
S64 Pitchout (Unidentified) .05
S65 Scuff the Ball (Brian Moehler) .05
S66 Sloppy Bunt (Livan Hernandez) .05
S67 Soft Hands (Omar Vizquel) .05
S68 Submarine Pitch (Byung-Hyun Kim) .05
S69 Visibly Upset (Unidentified) .05
S70 What Were You Thinking??? (Benito Santiago) .05
S71 Air It Out (Kevin Brown) .05
S72 Bear Down (Pedro Martinez) .10
S73 Brainstorm (Bobby Cox) .05
S74 Game of Inches (Dmitri Young) .05
S75 Second Look (Moises Alou) .05

2001 MLB Showdown Pennant Run Promos

To promote its Pennant Run update edition, Wizards of the Coast issued eight specially marked sample cards to persons attending All-Star FanFest, the National Sports Collectors Convention and the Origins Gaming Convention (Gen Con) in the summer of 2001. The promos are virtually identical to the issued versions of the same players' cards except for the presence on front of a large logo indicating the show at which the cards were distributed.

		NM/M
Complete Set (6):		7.50
Common Player:		1.00
008	C.C. Sabathia	1.00
017	Juan Pierre	1.00
084	Wes Helms	1.00
087	Ben Sheets	1.00
127	Luis Rivas	1.00
169	Ichiro (Suzuki)	3.50

2001 MLB Showdown Pennant Run

Issued after the 2002 season opened, this is essentially an update to the interactive MLB Showdown game. Players in the set are generally those who changed teams during the off-season, or promising rookies. The Pennant Run edition was issued in a Booster box of 36 nine-card (seven player, two strategy) packs. The set has 100 "regular" player cards, 25 SP (1:3) holofoil star cards and 25 strategy cards. Cards #91-125 are a Super Season player subset. While collectors compete with gamers for these cards in the market, relative values placed on the cards by each group of buyers may differ.

		NM/M
Complete Set (200):		75.00
Common Player:		.15
Booster Pack (9):		1.50
Booster Box (36):		25.00
001	Randy Velarde	.15
002	Dustin Hermanson	.15
003	Jamie Moyer	.15
004	Aaron Fultz	.15
005	Barry Zito (Foil)	2.50
006	Adam Piatt	.15
007	Ben Grieve	.15
008	C.C. Sabathia (Foil)	2.00

009 Eddie Guardado .15
010 Matt Kinney .15
011 Blake Stein .15
012 Billy Wagner (Foil) 2.00
013 Chris Holt .15
014 Homer Bush .15
015 Vladimir Nunez .15
016 C.J. Nitkowski .15
017 Juan Pierre .25
018 Jose Valentin .15
019 Juan Gonzalez .30
020 Derek Bell .15
021 Wade Miller .15
022 Shawn Estes .15
023 Enrique Wilson .15
024 Dave Magadan .15
025 Jason Christiansen .15
026 Paul Shuey .15
027 Mark Wohlers .15
028 John Riedling .15
029 Francisco Cordova .15
030 Craig House .15
031 Scott Strickland .15
032 Octavio Dotel .15
033 Jimmy Rollins (Foil) 2.00
034 Carl Pavano .15
035 Sandy Alomar Jr. .15
036 Hideki Irabu .15
037 Tom Gordon .15
038 Roosevelt Brown .15
039 Alex Rodriguez (Foil) 4.00
040 Andres Galarraga .15
041 Rob Bell .15
042 Jason Schmidt .15
043 Rod Beck .15
044 Paul Rigdon .15
045 Dan Miceli .15
046 Ricky Bones .15
047 Mike Hampton (Foil) 2.00
048 Cliff Politte .15
049 Chris Stynes .15
050 Ramiro Mendoza .15
051 Todd Walker .15
052 Fernando Seguignol .15
053 Mark Guthrie .15
054 Tony Armas Jr. .15
055 Billy McMillon .15
056 Gary Bennett .15
057 Corey Patterson (Foil) 2.00
058 Juan Guzman .15
059 Joe Crede .25
060 A.J. Pierzynski .15
061 Ben Davis .15
062 Alan Embree .15
063 Jon Garland (Foil) 2.00
064 Ryan Kohlmeier .15
065 Andy Benes .15
066 Ron Gant .15
067 Jerry Hairston Jr. .15
068 Odalis Perez .15
069 Lance Painter .15
070 David Segui .15
071 Russ Davis .15
072 Jeff Zimmerman .15
073 Dennys Reyes .15
074 Jamey Wright .15
075 Rico Brogna .15
076 Geraldo Guzman .15
077 Eric Gagne .15
078 Bruce Chen .15
079 Justin Speier .15
080 Randy Keisler .15
081 Ellis Burks (Foil) 2.00
082 Alfonso Soriano .50
083 Jeff Nelson .15
084 Wes Helms .15
085 Freddy Garcia (Foil) 2.00
086 Erubiel Durazo .15
087 Ben Sheets (Foil) 2.00
088 Jose Ortiz (Foil) 2.00
089 Paul Wilson .15
090 Onan Masaoka .15
091 Jose Rosado .15
092 A.J. Burnett .15
093 Bubba Trammell .15
094 Mike Fetters .15
095 Jacob Cruz .15
096 John Franco .15
097 Armando Reynoso .15
098 Lou Pote .15
099 D'Angelo Jiminez (Foil) 2.00
100 Julio Zuleta .15
101 Charles Johnson (Foil) 2.00
102 Tsuyoshi Shinjo .15
103 Brett Tomko .15
104 Marcus Giles .15
105 Craig Counsell .15
106 Ruben Mateo .15
107 Andy Ashby .15
108 Marlon Anderson .15
109 Mark Grace .15
110 Russ Branyan .15
111 Julian Tavarez .15
112 Joey Hamilton .15
113 Jason LaRue .15
114 Benji Gil .15
115 Bill Mueller .15
116 Mike Stanton .15
117 Ray King .15
118 Timoniel Perez .15
119 Johnny Damon (Foil) 2.50
120 Matt Morris .15
121 Kevin Appier .15
122 Frank Castillo .15
123 Mike Darr .15
124 Felipe Crespo .15
125 John Smoltz (Foil) 2.00
126 Ben Weber .15
127 Luis Rivas .15
128 Travis Harper .15
129 Aubrey Huff .15
130 Paul LoDuca .15
131 Eric Davis .15
132 Fernando Tatis .15
133 Ugueth Urbina .15
134 Steve Kline .15
135 Tanyon Sturtze .15
136 Scott Hatteberg .15
137 Tomokazu Ohka (Foil) 2.00
138 Melvin Mora .15
139 Kip Wells .15
140 Ken Caminiti .15
141 Dave Martinez .15
142 Robert Fick .15
143 Mike Bordick .15
144 Doug Mientkiewicz .15
145 Darryl Hamilton .15
146 Shane Reynolds .15
147 Vernon Wells (Foil) 2.00
148 Rey Ordonez .15
149 Brad Ausmus .15
150 Jay Powell .15
151 Todd Hundley .15
152 Travis Miller .15
153 Tyler Houston .15
154 Nelson Cruz .15
155 Manny Ramirez (Foil) 3.00
156 Luis Lopez .15
157 Luis Sojo .15
158 Tony Gwynn (Foil) 3.50
159 Roger Cedeno .15
160 Royce Clayton .15
161 Olmedo Saenz .15
162 Brook Fordyce .15
163 Dee Brown .15
164 David Wells (Foil) 2.00
165 Jack Wilson .15
166 Pedro Feliz .15
167 Hideo Nomo .40
168 Albert Pujols (Foil) 20.00
169 Ichiro (Suzuki) (Foil) 6.00
170 Ramon Ortiz .15
171 Mike Holtz .15
172 Chris Woodward .15
173 Mike Mussina (Foil) 2.50
174 Carlos Guillen .15
175 Ben Petrick .15
S1 Advance on Throw (Johnny Damon, Shane Halter) .05
S2 Ball in the Dirt (Roberto Alomar, Ruben Mateo) .05
S3 Constant Pressure (Sammy Sosa, Mark McGwire) .35
S4 Emergency Bunt (Jeff Leifer) .05
S5 First-Pitch Swinging (Cal Ripken, Jr.) .50
S6 Go Up Hacking (Mike Piazza) .35
S7 Speedster (Derek Jeter) .50
S8 Sprint to Second (Jose Valentin) .05
S9 Wild Thing (Benito Santiago) .05
S10 Wipeout (J.D. Drew) .10
S11 Caught Napping (Tony Gwynn) .20
S12 Comebacker (Greg Maddux) .20
S13 Confusion (Julio Zuleta, Dmitri Young) .05
S14 Double-Play Whiz (Ray Durham) .05
S15 Fired Up (Abraham Nunez) .05
S16 Focused (Rey Ordonez) .05
S17 Going the Distance (Roger Clemens) .25
S18 Great Pickoff Move (Rick Ankiel) .05
S19 Groundball Pitcher (Greg Maddux) .20
S20 Hung It (Danny Graves) .05
S21 Pitch Around (Mark McGwire) .40
S22 Pour It On (Al Leiter) .05
S23 Clutch Performance (Barry Bonds) .50
S24 Dot Racing (Mascots) .05
S25 It's Crunch Time (Dennys Reyes) .05
Checklist 1 (001-066) .05
Checklist 2 (067-132) .05
Checklist 3 (133-S25) .05
Pitcher Usage Card .05

2002 MLB Showdown Promos

		NM/M
Complete Set (10):		20.00
Common Player:		2.00
(1)	Shawn Green	2.00
(2)	Ichiro	4.00
(3)	Derek Jeter	5.00
(4)	Andruw Jones	2.50
(5)	Trot Nixon	2.00
(6)	Andy Pettitte	2.00
(7)	Alex Rodriguez	4.00
(8)	Sammy Sosa	3.00
(9)	Kerry Wood	2.00
(10)	Jeff Zimmerman	2.00

2002 MLB Showdown

MLB Showdown's third season issue in 2002 has 300 "regular" player cards, 56 premium holofoil star cards and 50 strategy cards, including short-prints. The holo premium cards were inserted in booster packs at a rate of 1:3. While collectors compete with gamers for these cards in the market, relative values placed on the cards by each group of buyers may differ.

NM/M
Complete Set (406): 175.00
Common Player: .15
Starter Set: 6.00
Booster Pack: 1.50
Booster Box (36): 20.00
1 Garret Anderson .15
2 David Eckstein .15
3 Darin Erstad .30
4 Troy Glaus (Foil) 2.50
5 Adam Kennedy .15
6 Ben Molina .15
7 Ramon Ortiz .15
8 Troy Percival .15
9 Tim Salmon .15
10 Scott Schoeneweis .15
11 Scott Spiezio .15
12 Jarrod Washburn .15
13 Miguel Batista .15
14 Jay Bell .15
15 Craig Counsell .15
16 David Dellucci .15
17 Erubiel Durazo .15
18 Steve Finley .15
19 Luis Gonzalez (Foil) 2.00
20 Mark Grace .15
21 Randy Johnson (Foil) 3.00
22 Byun-Hun Kim .15
23 Albie Lopez .15
24 Curt Schilling (Foil) 2.50
25 Matt Williams .15
26 Tony Womack .15
27 Marcus Giles (Foil) 2.00
28 Tom Glavine .25
29 Andruw Jones .45
30 Chipper Jones (Foil) 4.00
31 Brian Jordan .15
32 Steve Karsay .15
33 Javy Lopez .15
34 Greg Maddux (Foil) 4.00
35 Jason Marquis .15
36 Mike Remlinger .15
37 Rey Sanchez .15
38 B.J. Surhoff .15
39 Brady Anderson .15
40 Tony Batista (Foil) 2.00
41 Mike Bordick .15
42 Jeff Conine .15
43 Buddy Groom .15
44 Jerry Hairston Jr. .15
45 Jason Johnson .15
46 Melvin Mora .15
47 Chris Richard .15
48 B.J. Ryan .15
49 Josh Towers .15
50 Rolando Arrojo .15
51 Rod Beck .15
52 Dante Bichette .15
53 David Cone .15
54 Carl Everett .15
55 Rich Garces .15
56 Derek Lowe .15
57 Trot Nixon .15
58 Hideo Nomo .35
59 Jose Offerman .15
60 Troy O'Leary .15
61 Manny Ramirez (Foil) 3.00
62 Delino DeShields .15
63 Kyle Farnsworth .15
64 Jeff Fassero .15
65 Ricky Gutierrez .15
66 Todd Hundley .15
67 Jon Lieber .15
68 Fred McGriff .15
69 Bill Mueller .15
70 Corey Patterson .15
71 Sammy Sosa (Foil) 5.00
72 Julian Tavares .15
73 Kerry Wood .30
74 Eric Young .15
75 Mark Buehrle (Foil) 2.00
76 Royce Clayton .15
77 Joe Crede .15
78 Ray Durham .15
79 Keith Foulke .15
80 Bob Howry .15
81 Mark L. Johnson .15
82 Paul Konerko .25
83 Carlos Lee .25
84 Sean Lowe .15
85 Magglio Ordonez .15
86 Jose Valentin .15
87 Aaron Boone .15
88 Jim Brower .15
89 Sean Casey .15
90 Brady Clark .15
91 Adam Dunn (Foil) 2.00
92 Danny Graves .15
93 Ken Griffey Jr. (Foil) 6.00
94 Pokey Reese .15
95 Chris Reitsma .15
96 Kelly Stinnett .15
97 Dmitri Young .15
98 Roberto Alomar (Foil) 2.00
99 Danys Baez .15
100 Russell Branyan .15
101 Ellis Burks .15
102 Bartolo Colon .15
103 Marty Cordova .15
104 Einar Diaz .15
105 Juan Gonzalez .30
106 Ricardo Rincon .15
107 C.C. Sabathia (Foil) 2.00
108 Paul Shuey .15
109 Jim Thome (Foil) 2.50
110 Omar Vizquel .15
111 Bob Wickman .15
112 Shawn Chacon .15
113 Jeff Cirillo .15
114 Mike Hampton .15
115 Todd Helton (Foil) 2.50
116 Greg Norton .15
117 Ben Petrick .15
118 Juan Pierre .15
119 Terry Shumpert .15
120 Larry Walker (Foil) 2.00
121 Matt Anderson .15
122 Roger Cedeno .15
123 Tony Clark .15
124 Deivi Cruz .15
125 Damion Easley .15
126 Shane Halter .15
127 Bobby Higginson (Foil) 2.00
128 Jose Macias .15
129 Steve Sparks .15
130 Jeff Weaver .15
131 Antonio Alfonseca .15
132 Josh Beckett (Foil) 2.50
133 A.J. Burnett .15
134 Luis Castillo .15
135 Ryan Dempster .15
136 Cliff Floyd .15
137 Alex Gonzalez .15
138 Braden Looper .15
139 Mike Lowell .15
140 Eric Owens .15
141 Brad Penny .15
142 Preston Wilson .15
143 Moises Alou .15
144 Brad Ausmus .15
145 Jeff Bagwell (Foil) 3.00
146 Lance Berkman (Foil) 2.00
147 Craig Biggio .15
148 Octavio Dotel .15
149 Richard Hidalgo .15
150 Julio Lugo .15
151 Wade Miller .15
152 Roy Oswalt (Foil) 2.00
153 Shane Reynolds .15
154 Jose Vizcaino .15
155 Daryle Ward .15
156 Carlos Beltran (Foil) 2.50
157 Dee Brown .15
158 Roberto Hernandez .15
159 Mark Quinn .15
160 Joe Randa .15
161 Dan Reichert .15
162 Jeff Suppan .15
163 Mike Sweeney .15
164 Kris Wilson .15
165 Terry Adams .15
166 Adrian Beltre .15
167 Alex Cora .15
168 Tom Goodwin .15
169 Shawn Green .25
170 Marquis Grissom .15
171 Mark Grudzielanek .15
172 Eric Karros .15
173 Paul LoDuca (Foil) 2.00
174 Chan Ho Park .15
175 Luke Prokopec .15
176 Gary Sheffield .30
177 Ronnie Belliard .15
178 Henry Blanco .15
179 Jeromy Burnitz .15
180 Mike DeJean .15
181 Chad Fox .15
182 Jose Hernandez .15
183 Geoff Jenkins .15
184 Mark Loretta .15
185 Nick Neugebauer .15
186 Richie Sexson .15
187 Ben Sheets (Foil) 2.00
188 Devon White .15
189 Cristian Guzman (Foil) 2.00
190 Torii Hunter .15
191 Jacque Jones .15
192 Corey Koskie .15
193 Joe Mays .15
194 Doug Mientkiewicz .15
195 Eric Milton .15
196 David Ortiz .40
197 A.J. Pierzynski .15
198 Brad Radke .15
199 Luis Rivas .15
200 Tony Armas Jr. .15
201 Michael Barrett .15
202 Peter Bergeron .15
203 Orlando Cabrera .15
204 Vladimir Guerrero (Foil) 3.00
205 Graeme Lloyd .15
206 Scott Strickland .15
207 Fernando Tatis .15
208 Mike Thurman .15
209 Javier Vazquez .15
210 Jose Vidro .15
211 Brad Wilkerson .15
212 Edgardo Alfonzo .15
213 Kevin Appier .15
214 Armando Benitez .15
215 Alex Escobar .15
216 John Franco .15
217 Al Leiter .15
218 Rey Ordonez .15
219 Mike Piazza (Foil) 6.00
220 Glendon Rusch .15
221 Tsuyoshi Shinjo .15
222 Steve Trachsel .15
223 Todd Zeile .15
224 Roger Clemens (Foil) 5.00
225 Derek Jeter (Foil) 9.00
226 Nick Johnson .15
227 David Justice .15
228 Tino Martinez .15
229 Ramiro Mendoza .15
230 Mike Mussina (Foil) 2.50
231 Andy Pettitte .25
232 Jorge Posada .15
233 Mariano Rivera (Foil) 2.00
234 Alfonso Soriano .40
235 Mike Stanton .15
236 Bernie Williams (Foil) 2.00
237 Eric Chavez .15
238 Johnny Damon .30
239 Jermaine Dye .15
240 Jason Giambi (Foil) 2.50
241 Jeremy Giambi .15
242 Ramon Hernandez .15
243 Tim Hudson (Foil) 2.00
244 Jason Isringhausen .15
245 Terrence Long .15
246 Mark Mulder (Foil) 2.00
247 Olmedo Saenz .15
248 Miguel Tejada .25
249 Barry Zito .25
250 Bobby Abreu .15
251 Marlon Anderson .15
252 Ricky Bottalico .15
253 Pat Burrell .35
254 Omar Daal .15
255 Johnny Estrada .15
256 Nelson Figueroa .15
257 Travis Lee .15
258 Robert Person .15
259 Scott Rolen (Foil) 2.50
260 Jimmy Rollins (Foil) 2.00
261 Randy Wolf .15
262 Brian Giles (Foil) 2.00
263 Jason Kendall .15
264 Josias Manzanillo .15
265 Warren Morris .15
266 Aramis Ramirez .15
267 Todd Ritchie .15
268 Craig Wilson .15
269 Jack Wilson .15
270 Kevin Young .15
271 Ben Davis .15
272 Wiki Gonzalez .15
273 Rickey Henderson .45
274 Junior Herndon .15
275 Trevor Hoffman .15
276 Damian Jackson .15
277 D'Angelo Jiminez .15
278 Mark Kotsay .15
279 Phil Nevin (Foil) 2.00
280 Bubba Trammell .15
281 Rich Aurilia (Foil) 2.00
282 Marvin Benard .15
283 Barry Bonds (Foil) 9.00
284 Shawn Estes .15
285 Pedro Feliz .15
286 Jeff Kent (Foil) 2.00
287 Robb Nen .15
288 Russ Ortiz .15
289 Felix Rodriguez .15
290 Kirk Rueter .15
291 Benito Santiago .15
292 J.T. Snow .15
293 John Vander Wal .15
294 Bret Boone (Foil) 2.00
295 Mike Cameron .15
296 Freddy Garcia (Foil) 2.00
297 Carlos Guillen .15
298 Edgar Martinez (Foil) 2.00
299 Mark McLemore .15
300 Jamie Moyer .15
301 Jeff Nelson .15
302 John Olerud .15
303 Arthur Rhodes .15
304 Kazuhiro Sasaki (Foil) 2.00
305 Aaron Sele .15
306 Ichiro (Foil) 9.00
307 Dan Wilson .15
308 J.D. Drew (Foil) 2.50
309 Jim Edmonds (Foil) 2.00
310 Dustin Hermanson .15
311 Darryl Kile .15
312 Steve Kline .15
313 Mike Matheny .15
314 Matt Morris .15
315 Craig Paquette .15
316 Placido Polanco .15
317 Albert Pujols (Foil) 8.00
318 Edgar Renteria .15
319 Bud Smith .15
320 Dave Veres .15
321 Fernando Vina .15
322 Brent Abernathy .15
323 Steve Cox .15
324 Ben Grieve .15
325 Aubrey Huff .15
326 Joe Kennedy (Foil) 2.00
327 Tanyon Sturtze .15
328 Jason Tyner .15
329 Greg Vaughn .15
330 Paul Wilson .15
331 Esteban Yan .15
332 Frank Catalanotto .15
333 Chad Curtis .15
334 Doug Davis .15
335 Gabe Kapler .15
336 Mike Lamb .15
337 Darren Oliver .15
338 Rafael Palmeiro .40
339 Alex Rodriguez (Foil) 8.00
340 Ivan Rodriguez (Foil) 2.50
341 Mike Venafro .15
342 Michael Young .15
343 Jeff Zimmerman .15
344 Chris Carpenter .15
345 Jose Cruz .15
346 Carlos Delgado (Foil) 2.50
347 Kelvim Escobar .15
348 Darrin Fletcher .15
349 Brad Fullmer .15
350 Alex S. Gonzalez .15
351 Billy Koch .15
352 Esteban Loaiza .15
353 Raul Mondesi .15
354 Paul Quantrill .15
355 Shannon Stewart .15
356 Vernon Wells .15
S01 Bad Call (Bernie Williams) .05
S02 Clutch Hitting (Mike Piazza) .25
S03 Crowd the Plate (Troy Glaus) .10
S04 Down the Middle/SP (Unidentified) .50
S05 Drag Bunt/SP (Corey Patterson) .50
S06 Ducks on the Pond (Unidentified) .05
S07 Fuel on the Fire/SP (Barry Bonds) 1.50
S08 Last Chance (Craig Biggio) .05
S09 Nuisance/SP (Unidentified) .50
S10 Out of Gas (Unidentified) .05
S11 Payoff Pitch/SP (Manny Ramirez) .75
S12 Professional Baserunner/SP (Unidentified) .50
S13 Protect the Runner/SP (Unidentified) .50
S14 Pull the Ball (Rafael Palmeiro) .10
S15 Rally Cap (Tom Goodwin) .05
S16 Rough Outing (Unidentified) .05
S17 Runner Not Held (Unidentified) .05
S18 Running on Fumes/SP (Unidentified) .50
S19 Ruptured Duck/SP (Unidentified) .50
S20 Sit on the Fastball (Jose Cruz) .05
S21 Stick a Fork in Him (Kevin Appier) .05
S22 Sweet Swing (Barry Bonds) .75
S23 Take What's Given/SP (Johnny Damon) .60
S24 To the Warning Track (Unidentified) .05
S25 Turn On It (Lance Berkman) .05
S26 By the Book (Brad Radke) .05
S27 Cut Off in the Gap/SP (Unidentified) .50
S28 Full Windup (Andy Pettitte) .05
S29 Great Start (Barry Zito) .05
S30 Great Throw (Ichiro) .30
S31 Highlight Reel/SP (Brent Abernathy) .50
S32 Insult to Injury (Curt Schilling) .05
S33 In the Groove (Mark Mulder) .05
S34 Intimidation (Mariano Rivera) .05
S35 Job Well Done/SP (Arthur Rhodes) .50

S36	Just Over the Wall (Unidentified)(SP)	.50
S37	Knock the Ball Down (Abraham Nunez)	.05
S38	Lefty Specialist (Billy Wagner)	.05
S39	Low and Away (Randy Johnson)	.10
S40	Nerves of Steel (Trevor Hoffman)	.05
S41	Pitchout/SP (Unidentified)	.50
S42	Pumped Up (Unidentified)	.05
S43	Put Out the Fire (Kazuhrio Sasaki)	.05
S44	Rally Killer/SP (Unidentified)	.50
S45	Sloppy Bunt/SP (Unidentified)	.50
S46	Submarine Pitch/SP (Byung-Hyun Kim)	.50
S47	Change in Strategy (Unidentified)	.05
S48	Grounder to Second/SP (Unidentified)	.50
S49	It's Crunch Time/SP (Unidentified)	.50
S50	Second Look (Sean Casey)	.05

All-Star Edition

This specially marked edition of the MLB Showdown interactive game cards was produced for distribution at the All-Star FanFest. Cards have an All-Star Game logo on front and most picture the players in All-Star uniforms.

		NM/M
Complete Game Set (50):		20.00
Common Player:		.50
1	Garret Anderson	.50
2	Tony Batista	.50
3	Mark Buehrle	.50
4	Johnny Damon	.65
5	Robert Fick	.50
6	Freddy Garcia	.50
7	Nomar Garciaparra	1.00
8	Jason Giambi	.65
9	Roy Halladay	.50
10	Shea Hillenbrand	.50
11	Torii Hunter	.50
12	Ichiro	1.50
13	Derek Jeter	2.00
14	Paul Konerko	.60
15	Derek Lowe	.50
16	Jorge Posada	.50
17	Manny Ramirez	.75
18	Mariano Rivera	.50
19	Alex Rodriguez	1.50
20	Kazuhiro Sasaki	.50
21	Alfonso Soriano	.60
22	Mike Sweeney	.50
23	Robin Ventura	.50
24	Omar Vizquel	.50
25	Barry Zito	.50
26	Lance Berkman	.50
27	Barry Bonds	2.00
28	Luis Castillo	.50
29	Adam Dunn	.50
30	Eric Gagne	.50
31	Luis Gonzalez	.50
32	Shawn Green	.50
33	Vladimir Guerrero	.75
34	Todd Helton	.60
35	Jose Hernandez	.50
36	Andruw Jones	.75
37	Mike Lowell	.50
38	Robb Nen	.50
39	Vicente Padilla	.50
40	Odalis Perez	.50
41	Mike Piazza	1.25
42	Scott Rolen	.60
43	Jimmy Rollins	.60
44	Benito Santiago	.50
45	Curt Schilling	.60
46	John Smoltz	.50
47	Sammy Sosa	1.25
48	Junior Spivey	.50
49	Jose Vidro	.50
50	Mike Williams	.50

League Prize Cards

		NM/M
Complete Set (15):		15.00
Common Card:		.25
(1)	Bobby Abreu	2.00
(2)	Miguel Batista	2.00
(3)	Armando Benitez	2.00
(4)	Mike Cameron	2.00
(5)	Magglio Ordonez	2.00
(6)	Rafael Palmeiro	3.00
(7)	Brad Penny	2.00
(8)	Aramis Ramirez	2.00
(9)	Miguel Tejada	2.00
(10)	Bad Call	.25
(11)	By the Book	.25
(12)	Change in Strategy	.25
(13)	Ducks on the Pond	.25
(14)	Lefty Specialist	.25
(15)	Rally Cap	.25

Pennant Run

Issued after the 2001 season opened, this is essentially an update to the interactive game MLB Showdown from veteran gamers Wizards of the Coast. Many players in the set changed teams during the off-season, or were promising rookies. The Pennant Run edition was issued in a Booster box of 36 nine-card (seven player, two strategy) packs. The set has 130 "regular" player cards, 25 premium holofoil star cards and 25 strategy cards. The holo premium cards were inserted in packs at a rate of 1:3. While collectors compete with gamers for these cards in the market, relative values placed on the cards by each group of buyers may differ.

		NM/M
Complete Set (150):		60.00
Common Player:		.15
Booster Pack (9):		1.50
Booster Box (36):		20.00
1	J.C. Romero	.15
2	Robb Nen	.15
3	Raul Mondesi	.15
4	Mike Piazza	.65
5	Scott Rolen	.30
6	Shigetoshi Hasegawa	.15
7	Shannon Stewart	.15
8	David Eckstein (Foil)	2.00
9	Melvin Mora	.15
10	Jose Rijo	.15
11	Einar Diaz	.15
12	A.J. Burnett	.15
13	Mike Sweeney	.15
14	Jorge Posada (Foil)	2.00
15	Mark Kotsay	.15
16	Doug Davis	.15
17	Steve Woodard	.15
18	Sun voo Kim	.15
19	Sean Casey	.15
20	Juan Acevedo	.15
21	Dustan Mohr	.15
22	Mariano Rivera	.15
23	Kip Wells	.15
24	Kenny Lofton (Foil)	2.00
25	Steve Cox	.15
26	Josh Fogg (Foil)	2.00
27	Ruben Sierra	.15
28	Sandy Alomar Jr.	.15
29	Vicente Padilla (Foil)	2.00
30	Carlos Beltran	.30
31	Mike Lowell	.15
32	Omar Vizquel	.15
33	Ricky Stone	.15
34	Geoff Jenkins	.15
35	Eric Karros	.15
36	Ryan Drese	.15
37	Adam Dunn	.25
38	Hank Blalock	.40
39	Marcus Giles	.15
40	Joe Randa	.15
41	Bob Wickman	.15
42	Roy Halladay	.15
43	Craig Counsell	.15
44	Derek Lowe	.15
45	Ray Durham	.15
46	Paul Shuey	.15
47	Cliff Floyd	.15
48	Shawn Green	.25
49	Torii Hunter (Foil)	2.00
50	Edgardo Alfonzo	.15
51	Carlos Pena	.15
52	Sean Burroughs	.15
53	Placido Polanco	.15
54	Rafael Palmeiro	.45
55	Nate Cornejo	.15
56	Tim Salmon	.15
57	Craig Biggio	.15
58	Eric Hinske (Foil)	2.00
59	Rickey Henderson	.45
60	Nick Johnson	.15
61	Rey Ordonez	.15
62	Jose Hernandez	.15
63	Antonio Alfonseca	.15
64	Alfonso Soriano (Foil)	2.50
65	Eric Chavez	.25
66	B.J. Surhoff (Foil)	2.00
67	Austin Kearns (Foil)	2.00
68	Jacob Cruz	.15
69	Armando Benitez	.15
70	Derek Jeter	1.00
71	Ryan Jensen	.15
72	Kevin Mench	.15
73	Mike Remlinger	.15
74	Luis Castillo	.15
75	Kazuhisa Ishii (Foil)	2.00
76	Bobby Abreu	.15
77	Dave Veres	.15
78	Tony Batista	.15
79	Rey Sanchez	.15
80	Jason Grimsley	.15
81	Al Leiter (Foil)	2.00
82	Kerry Wood (Foil)	2.00
83	Ellis Burks	.15
84	Corey Patterson	.15
85	Adrian Beltre	.15
86	Barry Zito	.25
87	Doug Mientkiewicz	.15
88	Jeffrey Hammonds	.15
89	Jeremy Giambi	.15
90	Tsuyoshi Shinjo	.15
91	Roger Clemens (Foil)	3.50
92	John Franco	.15
93	Alex Rodriguez (Foil)	5.00
94	Barry Bonds (Foil)	15.00
95	Fred McGriff	.15
96	Chuck Finley	.15
97	Jose Rijo	.15
98	Jeff Bagwell (Foil)	2.50
99	Ron Gant	.15
100	Tom Glavine	.25
101	Mike Mussina	.25
102	Gary Sheffield	.30
103	Barry Larkin	.15
104	Jim Thome	.45
105	Chipper Jones (Foil)	3.00
106	Rickey Henderson	.50
107	Randy Johnson (Foil)	2.50
108	Mike Piazza (Foil)	4.00
109	John Smoltz	.15
110	Edgar Martinez	.15
111	Larry Walker	.15
112	Pedro Martinez (Foil)	2.50
113	Sammy Sosa (Foil)	3.50
114	Roberto Alomar (Foil)	2.00
115	Curt Schilling (Foil)	2.00
116	Chuck Knoblauch	.15
117	Frank Thomas	6.00
118	Jeff Kent	.15
119	Kenny Lofton	.15
120	Ken Griffey Jr.	7.50
121	Trevor Hoffman (Foil)	2.00
122	Mo Vaughn	.15
123	Robin Ventura	.15
124	Ellis Burks	.15
125	Tim Raines	.15
S1	Bad Call (Bernie Williams)	.05
S2	Clutch Hitting (Mike Piazza)	.10
S3	Crowd the Plate (Troy Glaus)	.05
S4	Down the Middle (Unidentified)	.05
S5	Ducks on the Pond (Unidentified)	.05
S6	Free Steal (Alex Rodriguez)	.10
S7	Overthrow (Unidentified)	.05
S8	Payoff Pitch (Unidentified)	.05
S9	Rally Cap (Tom Goodwin)	.05
S10	Rattled (Nate Cornejo)	.05
S11	Shell Shocked (Rick Ankiel)	.05
S12	Shelled (Scott Sullivan)	.05
S13	Comebacker (Dave Williams)	.05
S14	Fast Worker (Unidentified)	.05
S15	Full Windup (Andy Pettitte)	.05
S16	Great Thrower (Ichiro Suzuki)	.15
S17	Hung It (Unidentified)	.05
S18	In the Groove (Mark Mulder)	.05
S19	In the Zone (Curt Schilling)	.05
S20	Insult to Injury (Trevor Hoffman)	.05
S21	Nerves of Steel (Unidentified)	.05
S22	Pitchout (Unidentified)	.05
S23	Scuff the Ball (Brian Moehler)	.05
S24	Bear Down (Brian Giles)	.05
S25	Change in Strategy (Unidentified)	.05

2002 MLB Showdown Stars Promos

These four cards were made available at MLB Showdown Spring Training events. They are similar in format to other cards in the series.

		NM/M
Complete Set (4):		6.00
Common Player:		2.00
1	Eric Chavez	2.00
2	Nick Johnson	2.00
3	Jason Marquis	2.00
4	Bud Smith	2.00

Trading Deadline

Issued after the 2002 season opened, this is an update to the interactive game MLB Showdown from Wizards of the Coast. Players in the set are generally those who changed teams during the off-season, or promising rookies. The Trading Deadline edition was issued in a Booster box of 36 nine-card (seven player, two strategy) packs. The set has 125 "regular" player cards, 25 premium holofoil star cards and 25 strategy cards. The holo premium cards were inserted in packs at a rate of 1:3. While collectors compete with gamers for these cards in the market, relative values placed on the cards by each group of buyers may differ.

		NM/M
Complete Set (175):		55.00
Common Player:		.15
Booster Pack (7+2):		1.50
Booster Box (36):		20.00
1	Jason Giambi (Foil)	2.50
2	Chris Singleton	.15
3	Ben Davis	.15
4	Tsuyoshi Shinjo	.15
5	Brian Jordan	.15
6	Tony Clark	.15
7	Moises Alou (Foil)	2.00
8	Todd Walker	.15
9	Ricky Gutierrez	.15
10	Brad Fullmer	.15
11	Jeromy Burnitz	.15
12	Gary Sheffield (Foil)	2.50
13	Marty Cordova (Foil)	2.00
14	Todd Zeile	.15
15	Alex Gonzalez	.15
16	Kenny Lofton	.15
17	Vinny Castilla	.15
18	Craig Paquette	.15
19	Michael Tucker	.15
20	Cesar Izturis	.15
21	Eric Young	.15
22	Chuck Knoblauch	.15
23	Roberto Alomar (Foil)	2.00
24	David Bell	.15
25	Johnny Damon	.35
26	Roger Cedeno	.15
27	Robin Ventura	.15
28	David Justice (Foil)	2.00
29	Brady Anderson	.15
30	Pokey Reese	.15
31	Reggie Sanders (Foil)	2.00
32	Jeff Cirillo (Foil)	2.00
33	Juan Encarnacion	.15
34	Tino Martinez (Foil)	2.00
35	Carl Everett (Foil)	2.00
36	Danny Bautista	.15
37	Rafael Furcal	.15
38	Dmitri Young	.15
39	Jay Gibbons	.15
40	Brian Buchanan	.15
41	David Segui	.15
42	Barry Larkin (Foil)	2.00
43	John Vander Wal	.15
44	Brent Mayne	.15
45	Neifi Perez	.15
46	Lenny Harris	.15
47	Jason LaRue	.15
48	Travis Fryman	.15
49	Juan Uribe	.15
50	Shea Hillenbrand	.15
51	Aaron Rowand	.15
52	Jose Ortiz	.15
53	Robert Fick	.15
54	Doug Glanville	.15
55	Charles Johnson (Foil)	2.00
56	Derrek Lee	.45
57	Carlos Febles	.15
58	Luis Rivas	.15
59	Lee Stevens	.15
60	Mike Lieberthal	.15
61	Ryan Klesko (Foil)	2.00
62	Chris Gomez	.15
63	Randy Winn	.15
64	Rusty Greer	.15
65	Felipe Lopez	.15
66	Carlos Pena	.15
67	Toby Hall	.15
68	Milton Bradley	.15
69	Matt Lawton	.15
70	Gregg Zaun	.15
71	Eric Hinske	.15
72	Alex Ochoa	.15
73	Rondell White	.15
74	Armando Rios	.15
75	Desi Relaford	.15
76	Nomar Garciaparra (Foil)	4.00
77	Frank Thomas (Foil)	3.00
78	Mitch Meluskey	.15
79	Morgan Ensberg	.15
80	Mo Vaughn (Foil)	2.00
81	Adrian Brown	.15
82	Juan Gonzalez (Foil)	2.50
83	Tom Wilson	.15
84	Matt Stairs	.15
85	Andres Galarraga	.15
86	Sidney Ponson	.15
87	Jesus Colome	.15
88	Juan Cruz	.15
89	Eddie Guardado	.15
90	Jon Garland	.15
91	Denny Neagle	.15
92	Chad Durbin	.15
93	Kevin Brown (Foil)	2.00
94	Elmer Dessens	.15
95	Eric Gagne	.15
96	Jamey Wright	.15
97	Pedro Martinez (Foil)	3.00
98	Jason Bere	.15
99	Ugueth Urbina	.15
100	Carl Pavano	.15
101	Kip Wells	.15
102	Paul Abbott	.15
103	Billy Wagner (Foil)	2.00
104	Erik Hiljus	.15
105	Brandon Duckworth	.15
106	Ruben Quevedo	.15
107	Jimmy Anderson	.15
108	Bobby Jones	.15
109	Livan Hernandez	.15
110	Curtis Leskanic	.15
111	Tom Gordon	.15
112	Jeff Austin	.15
113	Joel Pineiro	.15
114	Chad Bradford	.15
115	Woody Williams	.15
116	Victor Zambrano (Foil)	2.00
117	Jose Mesa	.15
118	Roy Halladay	.15
119	Steve Karsay	.15
120	Hideo Nomo	.50
121	Jeff Farnsworth	.15
122	Dave Weathers	.15
123	Sean Lowe	.15
124	Mike Myers	.15
125	Jason Schmidt	.15
126	Mike Williams	.15
127	Terry Adams	.15
128	Chan Ho Park (Foil)	2.00
129	Jeff D'Amico	.15
130	Kevin Appier (Foil)	2.00
131	Glendon Rusch	.15
132	Jason Isringhausen	.15
133	Todd Ritchie	.15
134	Shawn Estes	.15
135	Kevin Millwood	.15
136	Aaron Sele	.15
137	Rick Helling	.15
138	Billy Koch	.15
139	Paul Quantrill	.15
140	Tim Spooneybarger	.15
141	Jorge Julio	.15
142	Carlos Hernandez	.15
143	Rick Ankiel	.15
144	Scott Erickson	.15
145	Denny Hocking	.15
146	Kazuhisa Ishii	.15
147	Pedro Astacio	.15
148	Satoru Komiyama	.15
149	Kurt Ainsworth	.15
150	John Smoltz (Foil)	2.00
S1	Big Inning (Luis Gonzalez)	.05
S2	Do or Die (Jeff Cirillo)	.05
S3	Free Steal (Alex Rodriguez)	.15
S4	Lean into It (Tsuyoshi Shinjo)	.05
S5	Overthrow (Cubs, Mets)	.05
S6	Pointers (Corey Patterson)	.05
S7	Professional Hitter (David Justice)	.05
S8	Rattled (Nate Cornejo)	.05
S9	Shelled (Scott Sullivan)	.05
S10	Shell Shocked (Rick Ankiel)	.05
S11	Swing for the Fences (Unidentified)	.05
S12	Tricky Hop (Marlon Anderson)	.05
S13	Whiplash (Unidentified)	.05
S14	Choke (Aaron Boone)	.05
S15	Comebacker (Dave Williams)	.05
S16	Fast Worker (Takahito Nomura)	.05
S17	Focused (Paul Abbott)	.05
S18	Hung It (Unidentified)	.05
S19	In the Zone (Rick Helling)	.05
S20	Scuff the Ball (Brian Moehler)	.05
S21	Swiss Army Closer (Joel Piniero)	.05
S22	What Were You Thinking??? (Unidentified)	.05
S23	Whoops! (Alex Gonzalez)	.05
S24	Bear Down (Brian Giles)	.05
S25	Game of Inches (Rich Aurilia)	.05

2003 MLB Showdown Promos

		NM/M
Complete Set (50):		35.00
Common Player:		1.00
P01	Aaron Guiel	1.00
P02	Abraham Nunez	1.00
P03	Al Levine	1.00
P04	Armando Rios	1.00
P05	Aubrey Huff	1.00
P06	Brandon Berger	1.00
P07	Carlos Baerga	1.00
P08	Chris Richard	1.00
P09	Corky Miller	1.00
P10	Damaso Marte	1.00
P11	Darren Holmes	1.00
P12	Denny Hocking	1.00
P13	Erubiel Durazo	1.00
P14	Giovanni Carrara	1.00
P15	Joe McEwing	1.00
P16	Kerry Robinson	1.00
P17	Lenny Harris	1.00
P18	Mark Derosa	1.00
P19	Mark Ellis	1.00
P20	Michael Tejera	1.00
P21	Olmedo Saenz	1.00
P22	Pedro Feliz	1.00
P23	Tomas Perez	1.00
P24	Wendell Magee	1.00
P25	Willis Roberts	1.00
P26	Benito Santiago	1.00
P27	Mike Sweeney	1.00
P28	Fernando Vina	1.00
P29	Troy Glaus	1.50
P30	Barry Larkin	1.00
P31	Manny Ramirez	1.50
P32	Steve Finley	1.00
P33	Shannon Stewart	1.00
P34	Frank Thomas	1.50
P35	Jamie Moyer	1.00
P36	Jon Lieber	1.00
P37	Mark Mulder	1.00
P38	Roger Clemens	2.50
P39	Jorge Posada	1.00
P40	Corey Koskie	1.00
P41	Shawn Green	1.00
P42	Phil Nevin	1.00
P43	Gary Sheffield	1.00
P44	Craig Biggio	1.00
P45	Alan Embree	1.00
P46	Jesse Orosco	1.00
P47	Mike Stanton	1.00
P48	Brandon Duckworth	1.00
P49	Troy Percival	1.00
P50	Robb Nen	1.00

2003 MLB Showdown

MLB Showdown's 2003 edition has has 300 "regular" player cards, 56 premium holofoil star cards and 50 strategy cards. The foil premium cards were inserted in booster packs at a rate of 1:3. While collectors compete with gamers for these cards in the market, relative values placed on the cards by each group of buyers may differ.

NM/M
Complete Set (354): 150.00
Common Player: .15
Two-Player Starter Set: 9.00
Draft Pack: 7.50
Booster Pack (7+2): 2.00
Booster Box (36): 40.00
1 Garret Anderson (Foil) 2.00
2 David Eckstein (Foil) 2.00
3 Darin Erstad .30
4 Brad Fullmer .15
5 Troy Glaus .35
6 Adam Kennedy .15
7 Bengie Molina .15
8 Ramon Ortiz .15
9 Orlando Palmeiro .15
10 Troy Percival .15
11 Tim Salmon .15
12 Jarrod Washburn (Foil) 2.00
13 Miguel Batista .15
14 Danny Bautista .15
15 Craig Counsell .15
16 Steve Finley .15
17 Luis Gonzalez (Foil) 2.00
18 Mark Grace .15
19 Randy Johnson (Foil) 7.50
20 Byung-Hyun Kim .15
21 Quinton McCracken .15
22 Curt Schilling (Foil) 4.50
23 Junior Spivey (Foil) 2.00
24 Tony Womack .15
25 Vinny Castilla .15
26 Julio Franco .15
27 Rafael Furcal (Foil) 2.00
28 Marcus Giles .15
29 Tom Glavine (Foil) 3.50
30 Andruw Jones (Foil) 7.50
31 Keith Lockhart .15
32 Javy Lopez .15
33 Greg Maddux (Foil) 8.00
34 Kevin Millwood .15
35 Gary Sheffield .30
36 John Smoltz (Foil) 2.00
37 Tony Batista .15
38 Mike Bordick .15
39 Jeff Conine .15
40 Marty Cordova .15
41 Jay Gibbons .15
42 Geronimo Gil .15
43 Jerry Hairston .15
44 Jorge Julio .15
45 Rodrigo Lopez .15
46 Gary Matthews Jr. .15
47 Melvin Mora .15
48 Sidney Ponson .15
49 Chris Singleton .15
50 John Burkett .15
51 Tony Clark .15
52 Johnny Damon .35
53 Alan Embree .15
54 Nomar Garciaparra (Foil) 8.00
55 Shea Hillenbrand .15
56 Derek Lowe (Foil) 2.00
57 Pedro Martinez (Foil) 7.50
58 Trot Nixon .15
59 Manny Ramirez .35
60 Rey Sanchez .15
61 Ugueth Urbina .15
62 Jason Varitek .15
63 Moises Alou .15
64 Mark Bellhorn .15
65 Roosevelt Brown .15
66 Matt Clement .15
67 Joe Girardi .15
68 Alex Gonzalez .15
69 Todd Hundley .15
70 Jon Lieber .15
71 Fred McGriff .15
72 Bill Mueller .15
73 Corey Patterson .15
74 Mark Prior (Foil) 6.00
75 Sammy Sosa (Foil) 9.00
76 Mark Buehrle (Foil) 2.00
77 Jon Garland .15
78 Tony Graffanino .15
79 Paul Konerko (Foil) 3.50
80 Carlos Lee .25
81 Magglio Ordonez (Foil) 2.00
82 Frank Thomas .35
83 Dan Wright .15
84 Aaron Boone .15
85 Sean Casey .15
86 Elmer Dessens .15
87 Adam Dunn .15
88 Danny Graves .15
89 Joey Hamilton .15
90 Jimmy Haynes .15
91 Austin Kearns (Foil) 2.00
92 Barry Larkin .15
93 Jason LaRue .15
94 Reggie Taylor .15
95 Todd Walker .15
96 Danys Baez .15
97 Milton Bradley .15
98 Ellis Burks .15
99 Einar Diaz .15
100 Ricky Gutierrez .15
101 Matt Lawton .15
102 Chris Magruder .15
103 C.C. Sabathia .15
104 Lee Stevens .15
105 Jim Thome (Foil) 3.50
106 Omar Vizquel .15
107 Bob Wickman .15
108 Gary Bennett .15
109 Mike Hampton .15
110 Todd Helton .35
111 Jose Jimenez .15
112 Denny Neagle .15
113 Jose Ortiz .15
114 Juan Pierre .15
115 Juan Uribe .15
116 Larry Walker (Foil) 2.00
117 Todd Zeile .15
118 Juan Acevedo .15
119 Robert Fick .15
120 Bobby Higginson .15
121 Damian Jackson .15
122 Craig Paquette .15
123 Carlos Pena .15
124 Mark Redman .15
125 Randall Simon .15
126 Steve Sparks .15
127 Dmitri Young .15
128 A.J. Burnett .15
129 Luis Castillo .15
130 Juan Encarnacion .15
131 Alex Gonzalez .15
132 Charles Johnson .15
133 Derrek Lee .40
134 Mike Lowell .15
135 Vladimir Nunez .15
136 Eric Owens .15
137 Preston Wilson .15
138 Brad Ausmus .15
139 Lance Berkman (Foil) 2.00
140 Craig Biggio .15
141 Geoff Blum .15
142 Richard Hidalgo .15
143 Julio Lugo .15
144 Orlando Merced .15
145 Billy Wagner .15
146 Carlos Beltran .40
147 Paul Byrd .15
148 Raul Ibanez .15
149 Chuck Knoblauch .15
150 Brent Mayne .15
151 Neifi Perez .15
152 Joe Randa .15
153 Mike Sweeney .15
154 Adrian Beltre .25
155 Eric Gagne (Foil) 2.00
156 Shawn Green .25
157 Marquis Grissom .15
158 Mark Grudzielanek .15
159 Kazuhisa Ishii (Foil) 2.00
160 Cesar Izturis .15
161 Brian Jordan .15
162 Eric Karros .15
163 Paul LoDuca (Foil) 2.00
164 Hideo Nomo .30
165 Jesse Orosco .15
166 Odalis Perez .15
167 Mike DeJean .15
168 Jose Hernandez .15
169 Geoff Jenkins .15
170 Alex Sanchez .15
171 Richie Sexson .15
172 Ben Sheets .15
173 Eric Young .15
174 Eddie Guardado .15
175 Cristian Guzman .15
176 Torii Hunter (Foil) 2.00
177 Jacque Jones .15
178 Corey Koskie .15
179 Doug Mientkiewicz .15
180 Eric Milton .15
181 A.J. Pierzynski .15
182 Michael Barrett .15
183 Orlando Cabrera .15
184 Cliff Floyd .15
185 Vladimir Guerrero (Foil) 7.50
186 Tomo Ohka .15
187 Fernando Tatis .15
188 Javier Vazquez .15
189 Jose Vidro (Foil) 2.00
190 Brad Wilkerson .15
191 Edgardo Alfonzo .15
192 Roberto Alomar .30
193 Pedro Astacio .15
194 Armando Benitez .15
195 Jeromy Burnitz .15
196 Al Leiter .15
197 Rey Ordonez .15
198 Timo Perez .15
199 Mike Piazza (Foil) 10.00
200 Steve Trachsel .15
201 Mo Vaughn .15
202 Roger Clemens .50
203 Jason Giambi (Foil) 4.50
204 Derek Jeter 1.00
205 Nick Johnson .15
206 Steve Karsay .15
207 Mike Mussina (Foil) 2.50
208 Jorge Posada .15
209 Mariano Rivera (Foil) 2.00
210 Alfonso Soriano (Foil) 4.50
211 Mike Stanton .15
212 Robin Ventura .15
213 Jeff Weaver .15
214 Rondell White .15
215 Bernie Williams (Foil) 2.00
216 Eric Chavez .15
217 Jermaine Dye .15
218 Scott Hatteberg .15
219 Tim Hudson .15
220 Billy Koch .15
221 Terrence Long .15
222 Mark Mulder .15
223 Miguel Tejada (Foil) 2.00
224 Barry Zito (Foil) 2.50
225 Bobby Abreu .15
226 Marlon Anderson .15
227 Pat Burrell .35
228 Brandon Duckworth .15
229 Jeremy Giambi .15
230 Doug Glanville .15
231 Mike Lieberthal .15
232 Jose Mesa .15
233 Vicente Padilla .15
234 Jimmy Rollins .25
235 Adrian Brown .15
236 Josh Fogg .15
237 Brian Giles .15
238 Jason Kendall .15
239 Pokey Reese .15
240 Kip Wells .15
241 Mike Williams (Foil) 2.00
242 Craig Wilson .15
243 Jack Wilson .15
244 Kevin Young .15
245 Trevor Hoffman (Foil) 2.00
246 Mark Kotsay .15
247 Ray Lankford .15
248 Brian Lawrence .15
249 Phil Nevin .15
250 Kurt Ainsworth .15
251 David Bell .15
252 Barry Bonds (Foil) 65.00
253 Ryan Jensen .15
254 Jeff Kent (Foil) 2.00
255 Robb Nen .15
256 Reggie Sanders .15
257 Benito Santiago .15
258 Tsuyoshi Shinjo .15
259 J.T. Snow .15
260 Bret Boone .15
261 Mike Cameron .15
262 Jeff Cirillo .15
263 Freddy Garcia .15
264 Carlos Guillen .15
265 Mark McLemore .15
266 Jamie Moyer .15
267 John Olerud .15
268 Joel Pineiro (Foil) 2.00
269 Kazuhiro Sasaki (Foil) 2.00
270 Ruben Sierra .15
271 Dan Wilson .15
272 Ichiro (Foil) 12.50
273 J.D. Drew .30
274 Jim Edmonds (Foil) 2.00
275 Jason Isringhausen .15
276 Matt Morris (Foil) 2.00
277 Albert Pujols (Foil) 12.50
278 Edgar Renteria .15
279 Scott Rolen (Foil) 2.50
280 Jason Simontacchi .15
281 Fernando Vina .15
282 Brent Abernathy .15
283 Steve Cox .15
284 Chris Gomez .15
285 Ben Grieve .15
286 Joe Kennedy .15
287 Tanyon Sturtze .15
288 Paul Wilson .15
289 Randy Winn (Foil) 2.00
290 Juan Gonzalez .30
291 Hideki Irabu .15
292 Rafael Palmeiro (Foil) 6.00
293 Herbert Perry .15
294 Alex Rodriguez (Foil) 10.00
295 Ivan Rodriguez .40
296 Kenny Rogers .15
297 Ismael Valdes .15
298 Mike Young .15
299 Dave Berg .15
300 Carlos Delgado .30
301 Kelvim Escobar .15
302 Roy Halladay (Foil) 2.50
303 Eric Hinske (Foil) 2.00
304 Shannon Stewart .15
S1 Bad Call (Sean Casey) .10
S2 Clutch Hitting (Ellis Burks) .10
S3 Down the Middle (Danny Graves) .10
S4 Drag Bunt (Mark Mulder) .10
S5 Ducks on the Pond (Unidentified) .10
S6 Furl on the Fire (Benito Santiago) .10
S7 Goodbye Baseball! (Ichiro Suzuki) .40
S8 Great Addition (Ichiro Suzuki) .40
S9 Last Chance (Ichiro Suzuki) .40
S10 Nuisance (Barry Larkin) .10
S11 Protect the Runner (Jacque Jones) .10
S12 Pull the Ball (Jim Thome) .10
S13 Rally Cap (Tino Martinez) .10
S14 Rookie's Big Chance (Eric Hinske) .10
S15 Runner Not Held (Unidentified) .10
S16 See It Clearly (Vladimir Guerrero) .20
S17 Serious Wheels (Deivi Cruz) .10
S18 Sit on the Fastball (Carlos Guillen) .10
S19 Take What's Given (David Eckstein) .10
S20 Turn On It (Derek Jeter) .50
S21 Valuable Asset (Barry Bonds) .50
S22 Aces Up (Mark Mulder) .10
S23 By the Book (Dan Reichert) .10
S24 Change It Up (Denny Neagle) .10
S25 Cut Off in the Gap (Juan Encarnacion) .10
S26 Full Windup (Chris Reitsma) .10
S27 Good Leather (Juan Encarnacion) .10
S28 Great Start (Mark Mulder) .10
S29 Great Throw (Danny Bautista) .10
S30 Highlight Reel (Jose Hernandez) .10
S31 In the Groove (Unidentified) .10
S32 Insult to Injury (David Eckstein) .10
S33 Job Well Done (Unidentified) .10
S34 Just Over the Wall (David Justice) .10
S35 Knock the Ball Down (Luis Gonzalez) .10
S36 Lefty Specialist (Ricardo Rincon) .10
S37 Nerves of Steel (Eric Gagne) .10
S38 Paint the Corner (Carlos Febles) .10
S39 Pumped Up (Raul Ibanez) .10
S40 Put Out the Fire (Mark Wohlers) .10
S41 Rally Killer (Abraham Nunez) .10
S42 Submarine Pitch (Byung-Hyun Kim) .10
S43 Throwing Heat (Dave Roberts) .10
S44 What a Relief! (Unidentified) .10
S45 Change in Strategy (Unidentified) .10
S46 Feast of Famine (Giovanni Carrara) .10
S47 Grounder to Second (Barry Larkin) .10
S48 It's Crunch Time (Unidentified) .10
S49 Just Over the Rail (Shane Halter) .10
S50 Outmanaged (Art Howe, Ray Knight) .10

Trading Deadline

NM/M
Complete Set (170): 75.00
Common Player: .15
Booster Pack (9): 1.50
Booster Box (36): 40.00
1 So Taguchi .15
2 Ryan Drese .15
3 Mike Hampton .15
4 Sandy Alomar Jr. .15
5 Steve Sparks .15
6 Chan Ho Park .15
7 Roger Cedeno .15
8 Antonio Osuna .15
9 Ryan Dempster .15
10 Jesse Orosco .15
11 Angel Berroa .15
12 Sean Burroughs .15
13 Matt Mantei .15
14 Einar Diaz .15
15 Ken Griffey Jr. 1.00
16 Rey Sanchez .15
17 Antonio Alfonseca .15
18 Carl Crawford .15
19 Rey Ordonez .15
20 Brandon Inge .15
21 Hank Blalock .40
22 Albie Lopez .15
23 Aaron Sele .15
24 Willie Bloomquist .15
25 Shigetoshi Hasegawa .15
26 Steve Kline .15
27 Ramiro Mendoza .15
28 Mike Stanton .15
29 Carlos Zambrano .15
30 Dean Palmer .15
31 Mark Grudzielanek .15
32 Matt Williams .15
33 Michael Cuddyer .15
34 Glendon Rusch .15
35 Hee Seop Choi .15
36 Mike Bordick .15
37 Ray King .15
38 Bill Mueller .15
39 John McDonald .15
40 Brent Butler .15
41 Josh Bard .15
42 Xavier Nady .15
43 J.C. Romero .15
44 Paul Shuey .15
45 Eric Karros .15
46 Runelvys Hernandez .15
47 Braden Looper .15
48 Dave Roberts .15
49 Deivi Cruz .15
50 Todd Hollandsworth .15
51 Billy Koch .15
52 Brandon Villafuerte .15
53 Ricardo Rincon .15
54 Joe Crede .15
55 Juan Pierre .15
56 Tsuyoshi Shinjo .15
57 Ugueth Urbina .15
58 Luis Vizcaino (Foil) 2.00
59 Ben Weber .15
60 Kerry Wood .30
61 Tim Worrell .15
62 Royce Clayton .15
63 Chone Figgins .15
64 Ken Huckaby .15
65 Brian Anderson .15
66 Aramis Ramirez .15
67 Edgar Martinez .15
68 Keith Foulke .15
69 LaTroy Hawkins .15
70 Mike Remlinger .15
71 Lyle Overbay .15
72 Buddy Groom .15
73 Orlando Hudson .15
74 Francisco Rodriguez (Foil) 2.00
75 Craig Biggio .15
76 Todd Zeile .15
77 Vernon Wells .15
78 Casey Fossum .15
79 Wes Helms .15
80 Robert Fick .15
81 Scott Spiezio .15
82 Ty Wigginton .15
83 Elmer Dessens .15
84 Arthur Rhodes .15
85 Matt Stairs .15
86 Miguel Olivo .15
87 Tino Martinez .15
88 Travis Hafner .15
89 Octavio Dotel .15
90 Jimmy Rollins .30
91 Placido Polanco .15
92 Kevin Brown .15
93 John Patterson .15
94 Andy Pettitte .15
95 Bobby Kielty .15
96 Jeremy Giambi .15
97 Brandon Phillips .15
98 Fred McGriff .15
99 Damian Moss .15
100 Russ Ortiz .15
101 Mark Teixeira .35
102 Tom Glavine (Foil) 2.50
103 Chris Woodward .15
104 Brad Radke .15
105 Edgardo Alfonzo .15
106 Jose Contreras (Foil) 2.00
107 Josh Beckett .30
108 Johan Santana .30
109 Brandon Larson .15
110 Randall Simon .15
111 Randy Winn (Foil) 2.00
112 Ray Durham .15
113 Omar Daal (Foil) 2.00
114 David Wells (Foil) 2.00
115 Wade Miller .15
116 Bartolo Colon (Foil) 2.00
117 Ryan Klesko (Foil) 2.00
118 Jeff Bagwell .50
119 Roy Oswalt (Foil) 2.00
120 Orlando Hernandez (Foil) 2.00
121 Ivan Rodriguez (Foil) 4.00
122 Tim Wakefield .15
123 Josh Phelps .15
124 Woody Williams .15
125 Chipper Jones (Foil) 5.00
126 Randy Wolf .15
127 Kevin Millwood (Foil) 2.00
128 Rocco Baldelli (Foil) 4.00
129 Jeff Kent (Foil) 2.00
130 Hideki Matsui (Foil) 7.00
131 Jim Thome (Foil) 3.00
132 Kazuhiro Sasaki .15
133 Jason Jennings (Foil) 2.00
134 Rafael Furcal .15
135 Derek Jeter (Foil) 7.50
136 Benito Santiago .15
137 Jeff Bagwell .50
138 Carlos Beltran .25
139 Scott Rolen (Foil) 2.50
140 Kerry Wood (Foil) 2.50
141 Tim Salmon .15
142 Ichiro (Foil) 12.00
143 Mike Piazza (Foil) 6.00
144 Albert Pujols 6.00
145 Nomar Garciaparra (Foil) 5.00
S1 Clutch Hitting .10
S2 Clutch Rookie .10
S3 Great Addition .10
S4 Headed Home .10
S5 High Fives .10
S6 Long Gone? .10
S7 On the Move .10
S8 Take What's Given .10
S9 Who is This Guy? .10
S10 Addition by Subtraction .10
S11 De-nied! .10
S12 Digging Deep .10
S13 Lock it Down .10
S14 New Arrival .10
S15 Not So Fast .10
S16 Pitch Around .10
S17 Rookie Fireballer .10
S18 Split-Finger Fastball .10
S19 Still Learning .10
S20 Three Up, Three Down .10
S21 Triple Dip .10
S22 Brainstorm .10
S23 Outmanaged .10
S24 Stealing Signals .10
S25 Swing at Anything .10

Pennant Run

Ten-player Super Season and Hall of Fame Heroes subsets were added to the 105 regular player cards and 25 strategy cards in this late-season card gaming issue. As with all MLB Showdown issues, baseball card collectors compete with game players for examples in the market, with each group often placing different values on specific cards.

NM/M
Complete Set (150): 100.00
Common Player: .15
Booster Pack (7+2): 2.00
Booster Box (36): 40.00
1 Josh Beckett .40
2 Jeremy Bonderman .15
3 Carlos Febles .15
4 Tom Goodwin .15
5 Luis Rivas .15
6 Scott Sullivan .15
7 John Thomson .15
8 Lance Carter .15
9 Terry Mulholland .15
10 Jake Westbrook .15
11 Chris George .15
12 Jake Peavy .15
13 Felix Rodriguez .15
14 Marlon Byrd .15
15 Toby Hall .15
16 Rocky Biddle .15
17 Brandon Lyon .15
18 Roberto Hernandez .15
19 Carlos Silva .15
20 Chris Hammond .15
21 Eric Munson .15
22 David Dellucci .15
23 R.A. Dickey .15
24 Cliff Politte .15
25 Russ Springer .15
26 Kirk Reuter .15
27 Vance Wilson .15
28 Scott Williamson .15
29 Ryan Franklin .15
30 Juan Castro .15
31 Craig Monroe .15
32 Joe Beimel .15
33 Scott Schoeneweis .15
34 John Halama .15
35 Eli Marrero .15
36 Felipe Lopez .15
37 Casey Blake .15
38 Mike MacDougal .15
39 Kris Benson .15
40 Francisco Cordero .15
41 Tom Gordon .15
42 Neifi Perez .15
43 Chad Bradford .15
44 Miguel Cairo .15
45 Mike Matheny .15
46 Mike Timlin .15
47 D.J. Carrasco .15
48 Eddie Perez .15
49 Gregg Zaun .15
50 Ronnie Belliard .15
51 Ricardo Rodriguez .15
52 B.J. Ryan .15
53 Michael Tucker .15
54 Rheal Cormier .15
55 Felix Heredia .15

56 Alex Cora .15
57 Travis Lee .15
58 Ted Lilly .15
59 Tom Wilson .15
60 Jeff D'Amico .15
61 Adam Eaton .15
62 Travis Harper .15
63 Mark Loretta .15
64 Ricky Stone .15
65 Wil Cordero .15
66 Cliff Floyd .15
67 Livan Hernandez .15
68 Paul Quantrill .15
69 Ben Davis .15
70 Shawn Estes .15
71 Chris Stynes .15
72 Jay Payton .15
73 Ramon Hernandez .15
74 Jason Johnson .15
75 John Vander Wal .15
76 Shawn Chacon (Foil) 2.00
77 D'Angelo Jiminez .15
78 Desi Relaford .15
79 Rich Aurilia .15
80 Rod Barajas .15
81 Jose Cruz (Foil) 2.00
82 Kyle Lohse .15
83 Rondell White .15
84 Gil Meche (Foil) 2.00
85 Jose Guillen .15
86 Kenny Lofton .15
87 Zach Day (Foil) 2.00
88 Mark Redman .15
89 Melvin Mora (Foil) 2.00
90 Todd Walker .15
91 Torii Hunter .15
92 Frank Catalanotto .15
93 Andres Galarraga .15
94 Jason Schmidt .15
95 Eric Byrnes .15
96 Hank Blalock (Foil) 4.00
97 Jacque Jones (Foil) 2.00
98 Michael Young .15
99 Carl Everett .15
100 Preston Wilson .15
101 Esteban Loaiza .15
102 Raul Mondesi (Foil) 2.00
103 Carlos Delgado (Foil) 2.50
104 Gary Sheffield (Foil) 2.50
105 Kevin Appier .15
106 Jesse Orosco .15
107 Pat Hentgen .15
108 Matt Williams .15
109 David Cone (Foil) 2.00
110 Mark Grace (Foil) 2.00
111 Carlos Baerga (Foil) 2.00
112 Greg Maddux (Foil) 5.00
113 Kevin Brown (Foil) 2.00
114 Ivan Rodriguez (Foil) 3.00
115 John Olerud (Foil) 2.00
116 Larry Doby .75
117 Yogi Berra (Foil) 7.50
118 Hoyt Wilhelm (Foil) 6.00
119 Pee Wee Reese .75
120 Brooks Robinson (Foil) 7.50
121 Robin Yount (Foil) 7.50
122 Reggie Jackson (Foil) 7.50
123 Harmon Killebrew (Foil) 7.50
124 Rod Carew (Foil) 6.00
125 Nolan Ryan (Foil) 12.00
S1 Change Sides .10
S2 Emergency Bunt .10
S3 Get Under It .10
S4 In Motion .10
S5 Out of Position .10
S6 Passed Ball .10
S7 Say the Magic Word .10
S8 Suicide Squeeze .10
S9 To the Warning Track .10
S10 Block the Plate .10
S11 Comebacker .10
S12 Good Matchup .10
S13 Ground Rule Double .10
S14 In the Zone .10
S15 Infield In .10
S16 Pickoff Attempt .10
S17 Play the Odds .10
S18 Playing Shallow .10
S19 Quick Pitch .10
S20 Sinker .10
S21 Up and In .10
S22 Good Scouting .10
S23 Looking Ahead .10
S24 Old Tricks .10
S25 Think Twice .10

2004 MLB Showdown Promo

This promo card was inserted into each issue of the September 2004, Beckett Baseball Monthly.

NM/M
P71 Alex Rodriguez .50

2004 MLB Showdown

MLB Showdown's 2004 edition has 298 "regular" player cards, 50 premium holofoil star cards and 50 strategy cards. The foil premium cards were inserted in booster packs at a rate of 1:3. While collectors compete with gamers for these cards in the market, relative values placed on the cards by each group of buyers may differ.

NM/M
Complete Set (398): 200.00
Common Player: .15
Two-Player Starter Set: 17.50
Draft Pack (60): 10.00
Booster Pack (8+3): 2.00
Booster Box: 75.00
1 Garret Anderson (Foil) 2.00
2 David Eckstein .15
3 Darin Erstad .25
4 Troy Glaus .25
5 Bengie Molina .15
6 Ramon Ortiz .15
7 Eric Owens .15
8 Tim Salmon .15
9 Scot Shields .15
10 Scott Spezio .15
11 Jarrod Washburn .15
12 Rod Barajas .15
13 Alex Cintron .15
14 Elmer Dessens .15
15 Steve Finley .15
16 Luis Gonzalez (Foil) 2.00
17 Mark Grace .15
18 Shea Hillenbrand .15
19 Matt Kata .15
20 Quinton McCracken .15
21 Curt Schilling (Foil) 2.50
22 Vinny Castilla .15
23 Robert Fick .15
24 Rafael Furcal .15
25 Marcus Giles .15
26 Andruw Jones .35
27 Chipper Jones (Foil) 7.50
28 Ray King .15
29 Javy Lopez (Foil) 2.00
30 Greg Maddux .50
31 Russ Ortiz .15
32 Gary Sheffield (Foil) 2.50
33 Tony Batista .15
34 Deivi Cruz .15
35 Travis Driskill .15
36 Brook Fordyce .15
37 Jay Gibbons .15
38 Pat Hentgen .15
39 Jorge Julio .15
40 Rodrigo Lopez .15
41 Luis Matos (Foil) 2.00
42 Melvin Mora .15
43 Brian Roberts .15
44 B.J. Surhoff .15
45 Johnny Damon .30
46 Alan Embree .15
47 Nomar Garciaparra (Foil) 7.50
48 Byung-Hyun Kim .15
49 Derek Lowe .15
50 Pedro Martinez (Foil) 6.00
51 Bill Mueller (Foil) 2.00
52 Trot Nixon .15
53 David Ortiz .35
54 Manny Ramirez .15
55 Jason Varitek .15
56 Tim Wakefield .15
57 Todd Walker .15
58 Antonio Alfonseca .15
59 Moises Alou .15
60 Paul Bako .15
61 Alex Gonzalez .15
62 Tom Goodwin .15
63 Mark Grudzielanek .15
64 Eric Karros .15
65 Kenny Lofton .15
66 Ramon Martinez .15
67 Corey Patterson .15
68 Mark Prior (Foil) 7.50
69 Aramis Ramirez .15
70 Mike Remlinger .15
71 Sammy Sosa (Foil) 9.00
72 Kerry Wood (Foil) 4.50
73 Carlos Zambrano .15
74 Mark Buehrle .15
75 Bartolo Colon .15
76 Joe Crede .15
77 Tom Gordon .15
78 Paul Konerko .25
79 Carlos Lee .25
80 Damaso Marte .15
81 Miguel Olivo .15
82 Magglio Ordonez (Foil) 2.00
83 Frank Thomas .35
84 Jose Valentin .15
85 Sean Casey .15
86 Juan Castro .15
87 Adam Dunn .15
88 Denny Graves .15
89 Ken Griffey Jr. 1.00
90 D'Angelo Jimenez .15
91 Austin Kearns .15
92 Barry Larkin .15
93 Jason LaRue .15
94 Chris Reitsma .15
95 Reggie Taylor .15
96 Paul Wilson .15
97 Danys Baez .15
98 Josh Bard .15
99 Casey Blake .15
100 Jason Boyd .15
101 Milton Bradley (Foil) 2.00
102 Ellis Burks .15
103 Coco Crisp .15
104 Jody Gerut .15
105 Travis Hafner .15
106 Matt Lawton .15
107 John McDonald .15
108 Terry Mulholland .15
109 C.C. Sabathia .15
110 Omar Vizquel .15
111 Ronnie Belliard .15
112 Shawn Chacon .15
113 Todd Helton (Foil) 3.00
114 Charles Johnson .15
115 Darren Oliver .15
116 Jay Payton .15
117 Justin Speier .15
118 Chris Stynes .15
119 Larry Walker .15
120 Preston Wilson .15
121 Jeremy Bonderman .15
122 Shane Halter .15
123 Bobby Higginson .15
124 Brandon Inge .15
125 Wilfredo Ledezma .15
126 Chris Mears .15
127 Warren Morris .15
128 Carlos Pena .15
129 Ramon Santiago .15
130 Andres Torres .15
131 Dmitri Young .15
132 Josh Beckett .25
133 Miguel Cabrera .15
134 Luis Castillo .15
135 Juan Encarnacion .15
136 Alex Gonzalez .15
137 Derrek Lee .35
138 Braden Looper .15
139 Mike Lowell .15
140 Juan Pierre .15
141 Mark Redman .15
142 Ivan Rodriguez (Foil) 4.50
143 Tim Spooneybarger .15
144 Dontrelle Willis (Foil) 2.00
145 Brad Ausmus .15
146 Jeff Bagwell .35
147 Lance Berkman .15
148 Craig Biggio .15
149 Geoff Blum .15
150 Octavio Dotel (Foil) 2.00
151 Morgan Ensberg .15
152 Adam Everett .15
153 Richard Hidalgo (Foil) 2.00
154 Jeff Kent .15
155 Brad Lidge .15
156 Roy Oswalt .15
157 Jeriome Robertson .15
158 Billy Wagner (Foil) 2.00
159 Carlos Beltran (Foil) 2.50
160 Angel Berroa .15
161 Jason Grimsley .15
162 Aaron Guiel .15
163 Runelvys Hernandez .15
164 Raul Ibanez .15
165 Curtis Leskanic .15
166 Jose Lima .15
167 Mike MacDougal .15
168 Brent Mayne .15
169 Joe Randa .15
170 Desi Relaford .15
171 Mike Sweeney .15
172 Michael Tucker .15
173 Adrian Beltre .25
174 Kevin Brown (Foil) 2.00
175 Ron Coomer .15
176 Alex Cora .15
177 Eric Gagne (Foil) 2.00
178 Shawn Green .15
179 Cesar Izturis .15
180 Brian Jordan .15
181 Paul LoDuca .15
182 Fred McGriff .15
183 Hideo Nomo .25
184 Paul Quantrill .15
185 Dave Roberts .15
186 Royce Clayton .15
187 Keith Ginter .15
188 Wes Helms .15
189 Geoff Jenkins .15
190 Brooks Kieschnick .15
191 Eddie Perez .15
192 Scott Podsednik (Foil) 2.00
193 Richie Sexson (Foil) 2.00
194 Ben Sheets .15
195 John Vander Wal .15
196 Chris Gomez .15
197 Cristian Guzman .15
198 LaTroy Hawkins .15
199 Torii Hunter .15
200 Jacque Jones .15
201 Corey Koskie .15
202 Doug Mientkiewicz .15
203 A.J. Pierzynski .15
204 Brad Radke .15
205 Shannon Stewart (Foil) 2.00
206 Michael Barrett .15
207 Orlando Cabrera (Foil) 2.00
208 Endy Chavez .15
209 Zach Day .15
210 Vladimir Guerrero (Foil) 6.00
211 Fernando Tatis .15
212 Javier Vazquez .15
213 Jose Vidro .15
214 Brad Wilkerson .15
215 Tony Clark .15
216 Cliff Floyd .15
217 John Franco .15
218 Joe McEwing .15
219 Timo Perez .15
220 Jason Phillips .15
221 Mike Piazza .65
222 Jose Reyes (Foil) 3.00
223 Steve Traschel .15
224 Dave Weathers .15
225 Ty Wigginton .15
226 Roger Clemens (Foil) 9.00
227 Chris Hammond .15
228 Derek Jeter (Foil) 12.00
229 Nick Johnson .15
230 Hideki Matsui .35
231 Mike Mussina (Foil) 4.50
232 Andy Pettitte .15
233 Jorge Posada .15
234 Mariano Rivera .15
235 Alfonso Soriano .25
236 Jeff Weaver .15
237 Bernie Williams .15
238 Enrique Wilson .15
239 Chad Bradford .15
240 Eric Byrnes .15
241 Mark Ellis .15
242 Keith Foulke (Foil) 2.00
243 Scott Hatteberg .15
244 Ramon Hernandez .15
245 Tim Hudson (Foil) 3.00
246 Terrence Long .15
247 Mark Mulder (Foil) 2.00
248 Ricardo Rincon .15
249 Chris Singleton .15
250 Miguel Tejada .15
251 Barry Zito .15
252 Bobby Abreu .15
253 David Bell .15
254 Pat Burrell .30
255 Marlon Byrd .15
256 Rheal Cormier .15
257 Vicente Padilla .15
258 Tomas Perez .15
259 Placido Polanco .15
260 Jimmy Rollins .15
261 Carlos Silva .15
262 Jim Thome (Foil) 3.00
263 Randy Wolf (Foil) 2.00
264 Kris Benson .15
265 Jeff D'Amico .15
266 Adam Hyzdu .15
267 Jason Kendall (Foil) 2.00
268 Brian Meadows .15
269 Abraham Nunez .15
270 Reggie Sanders .15
271 Matt Stairs .15
272 Jack Wilson .15
273 Gary Bennett .15
274 Sean Burroughs .15
275 Adam Eaton .15
276 Luther Hackman .15
277 Ryan Klesko .15
278 Brian Lawrence .15
279 Mark Loretta .15
280 Phil Nevin .15
281 Ramon Vazquez .15
282 Edgardo Alfonzo .15
283 Rich Aurilia .15
284 Jim Brower .15
285 Jose Cruz .15
286 Ray Durham .15
287 Andres Galarraga .15
288 Marquis Grissom .15
289 Neifi Perez .15
290 Felix Rodriguez .15
291 Benito Santiago .15
292 Jason Schmidt (Foil) 2.00
293 J.T. Snow .15
294 Tim Worrell .15
295 Bret Boone (Foil) 2.00
296 Mike Cameron .15
297 Ryan Franklin .15
298 Carlos Guillen .15
299 Shigetoshi Hasegawa .15
300 Edgar Martinez .15
301 Mark McLemore .15
302 Jamie Moyer (Foil) 2.00
303 John Olerud .15
304 Ichiro (Foil) 10.00
305 Dan Wilson .15
306 Randy Winn .15
307 J.D. Drew .30
308 Jeff Fassero .15
309 Bo Hart .15
310 Jason Isringhausen .15
311 Tino Martinez .15
312 Mike Matheny .15
313 Orlando Palmeiro .15
314 Albert Pujols (Foil) 10.00
315 Edgar Renteria (Foil) 2.00
316 Garrett Stephenson .15
317 Woody Williams (Foil) 2.00
318 Rocco Baldelli .35
319 Lance Carter .15
320 Carl Crawford .15
321 Toby Hall .15
322 Travis Harper .15
323 Aubrey Huff (Foil) 2.00
324 Travis Lee .15
325 Julio Lugo .15
326 Damian Rolls .15
327 Jorge Sosa .15
328 Hank Blalock .35
329 Francisco Cordero .15
330 Aaron Fultz .15
331 Juan Gonzalez .25
332 Rafael Palmeiro .35
333 Alex Rodriguez (Foil) 12.00
334 Mark Teixeira .35
335 John Thompson .15
336 Ismael Valdes .15
337 Michael Young .15
338 Frank Catalanotto .15
339 Carlos Delgado .15
340 Kelvim Escobar .15
341 Roy Halliday (Foil) 2.00
342 Eric Hinske .15
343 Orlando Hudson .15
344 Greg Myers .15
345 Josh Phelps .15
346 Cliff Politte .15
347 Vernon Wells (Foil) 2.00
348 Chris Woodward .15
S1 Bad Call .10
S2 Burned .10
S3 Check Swing .10
S4 Deep in the Gap .10
S5 Drained .10
S6 Ducks on the Pond .10
S7 Great Addition .10
S8 Hard Slide .10
S9 Inside the Park Home Run .10
S10 Options .10
S11 Out of the Frying Pan .10
S12 Play the Percentages .10
S13 Pointers .10
S14 Poor Positioning .10
S15 Pull the Ball .10
S16 Rough Outing .10
S17 Slow Roller .10
S18 Stick a Fork in Him .10
S19 Sweet Swing .10
S20 Take What's Given .10
S21 Think Again .10
S22 Turn on It .10
S23 Aces Up .10
S24 Caught Him Leaning .10
S25 Caught the Corner .10
S26 Choke .10
S27 Cover Second .10
S28 Dominating .10
S29 Foul Ball .10
S30 Good Leather .10
S31 Hooking Foul .10
S32 In the Zone .10
S33 Infield In .10
S34 Lined out of Play .10
S35 Locate .10
S36 Locked In .10
S37 Nerves of Steel .10
S38 Paint the Corner .10
S39 Power Pitching .10
S40 Short Fly .10
S41 Sloppy Bunt .10
S42 Split-Finger Fastball .10
S43 Top-Level Strategy .10
S44 Tough As Nails .10
S45 Change in Strategy .10
S46 Close Call .10
S47 New Strategies .10
S48 Second Look .10
S49 Swing at Anything .10
S50 Think Twice .10

NM/M
Complete Set (50): 125.00
Common Player: 3.00
P01 Barry Larkin 3.00
P02 Barry Zito 3.00
P03 C.C. Sabathia 3.00
P04 Carlos Delgado 3.00
P05 Derek Lowe 3.00
P06 Fernando Tatis 3.00
P07 Frank Thomas 4.00
P08 Greg Maddux 6.00
P09 Hideki Matsui 6.00
P10 Jason Isringhausen 3.00
P11 Jeff Kent 3.00
P12 Jimmy Rollins 3.00
P13 Mike Piazza 4.50
P14 Josh Beckett 3.00
P15 Juan Pierre 3.00
P16 Ken Griffey Jr. 5.00
P17 Luis Castillo 3.00
P18 Mike Remlinger 3.00
P19 Moises Alou 3.00
P20 Paul LoDuca 3.00
P21 Preston Wilson 3.00
P22 Rafael Furcal 3.00
P23 Reggie Sanders 3.00
P24 Shigetoshi Hasegawa 3.00
P25 Tony Batista 3.00
P26 Brady Clark 3.00
P27 Carlos Febles 3.00
P28 Damian Jackson 3.00
P29 Darren Bragg 3.00
P30 David Segui 3.00
P31 Jesse Foppert 3.00
P32 Greg Norton 3.00
P33 Hee Seop Choi 3.00
P34 Henry Mateo 3.00
P35 Jake Peavy 3.00
P36 Jeff Reboulet 3.00
P37 Kevin Witt 3.00
P38 Livan Hernandez 3.00
P39 Mike Kinkade 3.00
P40 Paul Shuey 3.00
P41 Ricky Ledee 3.00
P42 Ricky Stone 3.00
P43 Roger Cedeno 3.00
P44 Ron Calloway 3.00
P45 Ryan Wagner 3.00
P46 Shawn Estes 3.00
P47 Todd Pratt 3.00
P48 Tom Wilson 3.00
P49 Tony Graffanino 3.00
P50 Troy O'Leary 3.00

Pennant Run

NM/M
Complete Set (125): 250.00
Common Player: .15
Booster Box (36): 75.00
Booster Pack (9+2): 2.00
001 Shawn Chacon .15
002 Bobby Crosby .15
003 Russ Ortiz .15
004 Jason Simontacchi .15
005 Oscar Villarreal .15
006 Rocky Biddle .15
007 Joe Borowski .15
008 Shawn Estes .15
009 Adam LaRoche .15
010 Carl Everett .15
011 Willie Harris .15
012 Carlos Silva .15
013 Aaron Rowand .15
014 Francisco Cordero .15
015 Ryan Freel .15
016 Trevor Hoffman .15
017 Edgar Renteria .15
018 Mike Maroth .15
019 Carlos Pena .15
020 John Smoltz .15
021 Carlos Guillen .15
022 Buddy Groom .15
023 Aaron Miles .15
024 Jason Schmidt (Foil) 2.00
025 Danny Kolb .15
026 Marco Scutaro .15
027 Gary Sheffield .35
028 Eric Gagne (Foil) 4.50
029 Kazuhisa Ishii .15
030 B.J. Ryan .15
031 Mark Mulder (Foil) 2.00
032 Gerald Laird .15
033 Joe Mauer .40
034 Nate Robertson .15
035 Hideki Matsui 1.50
036 Ray Lankford .15
037 Jacob Peavy .15
038 Esteban Loaiza .15
039 Mike Stanton .15
040 Kevin Gregg .15
041 Steve Traschel .15
042 Albert Pujols (Foil) 12.00
043 Shingo Takatsu .15
044 Ichiro (Foil) 10.00
045 Milton Bradley .15
046 Eric Chavez .25
047 Paul LoDuca (Foil) 2.00
048 Kip Wells .15
049 Miguel Cabrera (Foil) 3.00
050 Johnny Estrada .15
051 Pedro Martinez (Foil) 6.00
052 Jason Giambi .40
053 Kenny Rogers .15
054 Alex Rodriguez (Foil) 12.00
055 Chone Figgins .15
056 Ken Harvey .15
057 Todd Helton .35
058 Javy Lopez .15
059 R.A. Dickey .15
060 J.D. Drew .15
061 Melvin Mora .15
062 Denny Bautista .15
063 Kerry Wood .30
064 Randy Johnson .40
065 Scott Rolen (Foil) 4.50
066 Roger Clemens (Foil) 7.50
067 Brad Penny .15
068 Matt Clement .15
069 Ron Belliard (Foil) 2.00
070 Alfonso Soriano (Foil) 4.00
071 Lew Ford .15
072 Sean Casey (Foil) 2.00
073 Troy Glaus .30
074 Mike Lowell .15

075 Juan Uribe .15
076 Adrian Beltre .25
077 Jack Wilson .15
078 Craig Wilson .15
079 Lyle Overbay (Foil) 2.00
080 Jose Contreras .15
081 Jason Jennings .15
082 Matt Mantei .15
083 Luis Vizcaino .15
084 Luis Ayala .15
085 Danny Patterson .15
086 C.J. Nitkowski .15
087 Larry Bigbie .15
088 Mike Lieberthal .15
089 Mike Timlin .15
090 Robert Mackowiak .15
091 Kevin Cash .15
092 Danys Baez .15
093 J.C. Romero .15
094 Dan Miceli .15
095 Armando Benitez .15
096 Hank Blalock .40
097 Vinny Castilla .15
098 Danny Graves .15
099 Derek Jeter 2.50
100 Jim Thome (Foil) 4.50
101 Mark Loretta .15
102 Victor Martinez .30
103 Ken Griffey Jr. 2.00
104 Miguel Tejada .25
105 Mike Piazza 1.50
106 Ivan Rodriguez .35
107 Tom Glavine .15
108 Carl Crawford (Foil) 2.00
109 Jeff Kent .15
110 Ben Sheets .15
111 Sammy Sosa 1.25
112 Vladimir Guerrero .40
113 Curt Schilling .30
114 Carl Pavano .15
115 Manny Ramirez (Foil) 6.00
116 Billy Williams (Cooperstown) 6.00
117 Ralph Kiner (Cooperstown) 6.00
118 Whitey Ford (Foil)(Cooperstown) 8.00
119 Jim Palmer (Foil)(Cooperstown) 8.00
120 Willie McCovey (Foil)(Cooperstown) 8.00
121 Phil Rizzuto (Cooperstown) 6.00
122 Orlando Cepeda (Cooperstown) 6.00
123 Eddie Mathews (Foil)(Cooperstown) 8.00
124 Tom Seaver (Foil)(Cooperstown) 8.00
125 Bob Feller (Foil)(Cooperstown) 10.00
S1 Down the Middle .10
S2 Grooved .10
S3 Lost in the Sun .10
S4 Protect the Runner .10
S5 Running on Fumes .10
S6 Serious Wheels .10
S7 Smash Up the Middle .10
S8 Superior Talent .10
S9 Swat! .10
S10 Timing .10
S11 Calculated Risk .10
S12 Chin Music .10
S13 Great Start .10
S14 High and Tight .10
S15 Intimidation .10
S16 On Your Toes .10
S17 Rally Killer .10
S18 Setup Man .10
S19 Whiff! .10
S20 Dugout General .10
S21 Old Tricks .10
S22 Out of Sync .10
S23 Revelation .10
S24 Stealing Signals .10
S25 Superstar .10

Trading Deadline

NM/M

Complete Set (150): 200.00
Common Player: .25
Booster Box (36): 75.00
Booster Pack (9+2): 2.00
1 Jose Mesa .15
2 Pokey Reese .15
3 Rey Sanchez .15
4 Jeff Weaver .15
5 Todd Zeile .15
6 Carlos Rivera .15
7 Orlando Palmeiro .15
8 Roberto Alomar .15
9 Doug Glanville .15
10 Khalil Greene .30
11 Victor Martinez .25
12 Jeffrey Hammonds .15
13 Bobby Kielty .15
14 Brian Schneider .15
15 Arthur Rhodes .15
16 David Dellucci .15
17 Eric Young Jr. .15
18 Grant Balfour .15
19 Javy Lopez .15
20 Jeff Nelson .15
21 Kelvim Escobar .15
22 Braden Looper .15
23 Tino Martinez .15
24 Laynce Nix .15
25 Horacio Ramirez .15
26 Hideki Matsui .50
27 Kevin Mench .15
28 Scott Sullivan .15
29 Michael Barrett .15
30 Jose Cruz .15
31 Robert Fick .15
32 Brad Fullmer .15
33 Eric Karros .15
34 Mark Kotsay .15
35 Fernando Vina .15
36 Tim Worrell .15
37 Mike Cameron .15
38 Howie Clark .15
39 Tom Gordon .15
40 Adam Kennedy .15
41 Rafael Palmeiro .35
42 Reed Johnson .15
43 Aquilino Lopez .15
44 Julian Tavarez .15
45 Ben Broussard .15
46 Miguel Cabrera .25
47 Raul Ibanez .15
48 Randall Simon .15
49 Ronnie Belliard .15
50 Scott Spiezio .15
51 Ellis Burks .15
52 LaTroy Hawkins .15
53 Pat Hentgen .15
54 Eddie Guardado .15
55 Todd Walker .15
56 Ivan Rodriguez .35
57 Raul Mondesi .15
58 Jeromy Burnitz .15
59 Rich Aurilia .15
60 Keith Foulke .15
61 Ramon Hernandez .15
62 Kenny Lofton .15
63 Rafael Soriano (Foil) 2.00
64 Jody Gerut .15
65 Randy Johnson .40
66 John Burkett .15
67 Brian Giles (Foil) 2.00
68 Matt Morris .15
69 Derrek Lee .35
70 Miguel Tejada .25
71 Ted Lilly .15
72 David Wells .15
73 Carl Everett .15
74 A.J. Pierzynski .15
75 Gary Sheffield .25
76 Juan Gonzalez .20
77 Brandon Webb .15
78 Joel Pineiro .15
79 Scott Rolen (Foil) 3.00
80 Jim Edmonds (Foil) 4.00
81 Curt Schilling (Foil) 4.00
82 Kevin Brown (Foil) 2.00
83 Chad Cordero .15
84 Rich Harden .15
85 Lyle Overbay .15
86 Paul Quantrill .15
87 Rondell White .15
88 Joe Nathan .15
89 Jose Valverde .15
90 Francisco Rodriguez .15
91 Billy Wagner .15
92 Jason Giambi .25
93 Jason Lane .15
94 Frank Thomas .45
95 Greg Maddux .50
96 Andy Pettitte .20
97 Jay Payton .15
98 Roger Clemens .50
99 Bartolo Colon (Foil) 2.00
100 Vladimir Guerrero .45
101 Kazuo Matsui (Foil) 4.00
102 Javier Vazquez .15
103 Esteban Loaiza (Foil) 2.00
104 Alex Rodriguez (Foil) 20.00
105 Javy Lopez (Super Season)(Foil) 3.00
106 Tino Martinez (Super Season) 2.00
107 Vladimir Guerrero (Super Season)(Foil) 7.50
108 Derek Jeter (Super Season)(Foil) 12.00
109 Craig Biggio (Super Season) 3.00
110 Tom Glavine (Super Season) 2.00
111 Nomar Garciaparra (Super Season)(Foil) 7.50
112 Mike Mussina (Super Season)(Foil) 4.50
113 Todd Helton (Super Season)(Foil) 4.50
114 Greg Maddux (Super Season)(Foil) 6.00
115 Roger Clemens (Super Season)(Foil) 7.50
116 Rollie Fingers (Cooperstown)(Foil) 9.00
117 Luis Aparicio (Cooperstown) 9.00
118 Lou Brock (Cooperstown) 9.00
119 Joe Morgan (Cooperstown)(Foil) 9.00
120 Richie Ashburn (Cooperstown)(Foil) 9.00
121 Al Kaline (Cooperstown)(Foil) 9.00
122 Bob Gibson (Cooperstown)(Foil) 9.00
123 Willie Stargell (Cooperstown) 9.00
124 Warren Spahn (Cooperstown)(Foil) 9.00
125 Mike Schmidt (Cooperstown)(Foil) 75.00
S1 Dialed In .10
S2 En Fuego! .10
S3 Last Chance .10
S4 On the Move .10
S5 Opposite-Field Power .10
S6 Out of Gas .10
S7 Quick Thinking .10
S8 Swing for the Fences .10
S9 Wheelhouse .10
S10 Beaned .10
S11 Broken Bat .10
S12 Caught Napping .10
S13 Chopper .10
S14 Dying Quail .10
S15 Great Reactions .10
S16 Insult to Injury .10
S17 Lefty Shift .10
S18 Pumped Up .10
S19 Punched Out .10
S20 Robbed! .10
S21 Feast or Famine .10
S22 Home-Field Advantage .10
S23 Just Over the Rail .10
S24 Late Call .10
S25 Outmanaged .10

2005 MLB Showdown League Promos

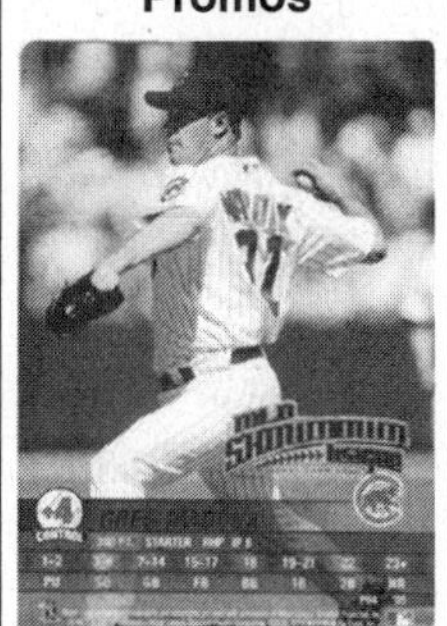

NM/M

Complete Set (25): 30.00
Common Player: 3.00
P01 Scot Shields 3.00
P02 Mark Derosa 3.00
P03 Larry Bigbie 3.00
P04 Greg Maddux 6.00
P05 Aaron Rowand 3.50
P06 C.C. Sabathia 3.00
P07 Jason Johnson 3.50
P08 Tim Spooneybarger 3.00
P09 Jeff Kent 4.50
P10 Nate Field 3.00
P11 Jimmy Gobble 3.00
P12 Edwin Jackson 3.50
P13 Jose Lima 3.00
P14 Justin Morneau 3.00
P15 Juan Rincon 3.00
P16 Luis Rivas 3.00
P17 Joe McEwing 3.00
P18 Eric Valent 3.00
P19 Billy Wagner 5.00
P20 Jack Wilson 3.00
P21 Pedro Feliz 4.50
P22 Willie Bloomquist 4.00
P23 Geoff Blum 4.00
P24 Mark Teixeira 3.50
P25 Michael Young 4.50

2005 MLB Showdown

MLB Showdown's 2004 edition has 298 "regular" player cards, 50 premium holofoil star cards and 50 strategy cards. The foil premium cards were inserted in booster packs at a rate of 1:3. While collectors compete with gamers for these cards in the market, rel-

ative values placed on the cards by each group of buyers may differ.

NM/M

Complete Set (398): 300.00
Common Player: .15
Two-Player Starter: 12.50
Booster Box (36): 65.00
Booster Pack (8+3): 2.50
1 Garret Anderson .15
2 David Eckstein .15
3 Darin Erstad .15
4 Chone Figgins .15
5 Troy Glaus .15
6 Kevin Gregg .15
7 Vladimir Guerrero (Foil) 5.00
8 Jose Guillen .15
9 Adam Kennedy .15
10 Troy Percival .15
11 Francisco Rodriguez .15
12 Tim Salmon .15
13 Danny Bautista .15
14 Alex Cintron .15
15 Luis Gonzalez .15
16 Scott Hairston .15
17 Shea Hillenbrand .15
18 Randy Johnson (Foil) 7.50
19 Mike Koplove .15
20 Chad Tracy .15
21 Brandon Webb .15
22 Antonio Alfonseca .15
23 J.D. Drew (Foil) 3.00
24 Johnny Estrada (Foil) 3.00
25 Julio Franco .15
26 Rafael Furcal .15
27 Marcus Giles .15
28 Andruw Jones .35
29 Chipper Jones .35
30 Eli Marrero .15
31 John Smoltz .15
32 John Thomson .15
33 Jaret Wright .15
34 Buddy Groom .15
35 Jerry Hairston .15
36 Jorge Julio .15
37 Rodrigo Lopez .15
38 Melvin Mora .15
39 Rafael Palmeiro .30
40 Brian Roberts .25
41 B.J. Ryan .15
42 B.J. Surhoff .15
43 Miguel Tejada (Foil) 3.00
44 Mark Bellhorn .15
45 Johnny Damon .30
46 Alan Embree .15
47 Keith Foulke .15
48 Gabe Kapler .15
49 Pedro Martinez .35
50 Bill Mueller .15
51 David Ortiz (Foil) 5.00
52 Manny Ramirez (Foil) 5.00
53 Pokey Reese .15
54 Curt Schilling .30
55 Mike Timlin .15
56 Jason Varitek .15
57 Moises Alou .15
58 Michael Barrett .15
59 Matt Clement .15
60 Kyle Farnsworth .15
61 Nomar Garciaparra .35
62 LaTroy Hawkins .15
63 Todd Hollandsworth .15
64 Derrek Lee .30
65 Greg Maddux .35
66 Kent Mercker .15
67 Corey Patterson .15
68 Aramis Ramirez .15
69 Kerry Wood .25
70 Mark Buehrle .15
71 Joe Crede .15
72 Freddy Garcia .15
73 Paul Konerko (Foil) 3.00
74 Carlos Lee .25
75 Damaso Marte .15
76 Aaron Rowand .15
77 Shingo Takatsu .15
78 Juan Uribe .15
79 Jose Valentin .15
80 Sean Casey .15
81 Juan Castro .15
82 Adam Dunn (Foil) 3.00
83 Ryan Freel .15
84 Aaron Harang .15
85 D'Angelo Jimenez .15
86 Barry Larkin .15
87 Jason LaRue .15
88 Wily Mo Pena .15
89 Phil Norton .15
90 John Riedling .15
91 Paul Wilson .15
92 Ronnie Belliard .15
93 Casey Blake .15
94 Ben Broussard .15
95 Coco Crisp .30
96 Travis Hafner (Foil) 3.00
97 Matt Lawton .15
98 Cliff Lee .15
99 Victor Martinez .15
100 David Riske .15
101 C.C. Sabathia .15
102 Omar Vizquel .15
103 Jake Westbrook .15
104 Jeromy Burnitz .15
105 Vinny Castilla .15
106 Shawn Chacon .15
107 Royce Clayton .15
108 Todd Helton (Foil) 3.00
109 Jason Jennings .15
110 Charles Johnson .15
111 Aaron Miles .15
112 Steve Reed .15
113 Mark Sweeney .15
114 Carlos Guillen .15
115 Omar Infante .15
116 Mike Maroth .15
117 Craig Monroe .15
118 Carlos Pena .15
119 Nate Robertson .15
120 Ivan Rodriguez (Foil) 3.00
121 Alex Sanchez .15
122 Ugueth Urbina .15
123 Rondell White .15
124 Esteban Yan .15
125 Dmitri Young .15
126 Josh Beckett .25
127 Armando Benitez .15
128 Miguel Cabrera (Foil) 4.00
129 Luis Castillo .15
130 Jeff Conine .15
131 Alex Gonzalez .15
132 Mike Lowell .15
133 Carl Pavano .15
134 Matt Perisho .15
135 Juan Pierre .15
136 Tim Spooneybarger .15
137 Dontrelle Willis .15
138 Brad Ausmus .15
139 Jeff Bagwell .30
140 Carlos Beltran (Foil) 5.00
141 Lance Berkman (Foil) 2.00
142 Craig Biggio .15
143 Roger Clemens .40
144 Morgan Ensberg .15
145 Adam Everett .15
146 Mike Gallo .15
147 Jeff Kent .15
148 Mike Lamb .15
149 Brad Lidge .15
150 Dan Miceli .15
151 Wade Miller .15
152 Roy Oswalt .15
153 Angel Berroa .15
154 Shawn Camp .15
155 Tony Graffanino .15
156 Ken Harvey .15
157 Darrell May .15
158 Joe Randa .15
159 Desi Relaford .15
160 Matt Stairs .15
161 Scott Sullivan .15
162 Mike Sweeney .15
163 Wilson Alvarez .15
164 Adrian Beltre (Foil) 4.00
165 Milton Bradley .15
166 Hee Seop Choi .15
167 Eric Gagne .15
168 Shawn Green .15
169 Kazuhisa Ishii .15
170 Cesar Izturis .15
171 Jose Lima .15
172 Jeff Weaver .15
173 Jeff Bennett .15
174 Javy Lopez .15
175 Brady Clark .15
176 Craig Counsell .15
177 Doug Davis .15
178 Bill Hall .15
179 Geoff Jenkins .15
180 Brooks Kieschnick .15
181 Dan Kolb .15
182 Chad Moeller .15
183 Lyle Overbay .15
184 Scott Podsednik .15
185 Victor Santos .15
186 Henry Blanco .15
187 Michael Cuddyer .15
188 Lew Ford .15
189 Cristian Guzman .15
190 Torii Hunter .15
191 Jacque Jones .15
192 Corey Koskie .15
193 Scott Linebrink .15
194 Brad Radke .15
195 Johan Santana 20.00
196 Ben Sheets .15
197 Wes Helms .15
198 Ken Griffey Jr. .45
199 Danny Graves .15
200 Runelvys Hernandez .15
201 Chris Woodward .15
202 Paul LoDuca .15
203 Scot Shields .15
204 Todd Walker .15
205 Gregg Zaun .15
206 Ricky Bottalico .15
207 Mike Cameron .15
208 Cliff Floyd .15
209 Tom Glavine .15
210 Richard Hidalgo .15
211 Al Leiter .15
212 Braden Looper .15
213 Kazuo Matsui .15
214 Jason Phillips .15
215 Mike Piazza (Foil) 5.00
216 Jose Reyes .25
217 David Wright .50
218 Kevin Brown .15
219 Miguel Cairo .15
220 Tom Gordon .15
221 Derek Jeter .50
222 Kenny Lofton .15
223 Jorge Posada (Foil) 2.00
224 Paul Quantrill .15
225 Mariano Rivera .15
226 Alex Rodriguez (Foil) 15.00
227 Gary Sheffield (Foil) 3.00
228 Javier Vazquez .15
229 Enrique Wilson .15
230 Eric Byrnes .15
231 Eric Chavez (Foil) 3.00
232 Bobby Crosby .15
233 Erubiel Durazo (Foil) 2.00
234 Jermaine Dye .15
235 Scott Hatteberg .15
236 Bobby Kielty .15
237 Mark Kotsay .15
238 Mark Mulder .15
239 Ricardo Rincon .15
240 Marco Scutaro .15
241 Barry Zito .15
242 Bobby Abreu (Foil) 2.00
243 David Bell .15
244 Pat Burrell .30
245 Rheal Cormier .15
246 Mike Lieberthal .15
247 Jason Michaels .15
248 Eric Milton .15
249 Vicente Padilla .15
250 Placido Polanco .15
251 Lance Carter .15
252 Jimmy Rollins .15
253 Jim Thome (Foil) 4.00
254 Chase Utley .15
255 Billy Wagner .15
256 Randy Wolf .15
257 Jason Bay .15
258 Jose Castillo .15
259 Jason Kendall (Foil) 2.00
260 Robert Mackowiak .15
261 Jose Mesa .15
262 Oliver Perez .15
263 Tike Redman .15
264 Salomon Torres .15
265 Daryle Ward .15
266 Kip Wells .15
267 Eric Munson .15
268 Craig Wilson .15
269 Jack Wilson .15
270 Sean Burroughs .15
271 Brian Giles .15
272 Khalil Greene .25
273 Ramon Hernandez .15
274 Trevor Hoffman .15
275 Ryan Klesko .15
276 Mark Loretta (Foil) 2.00
277 Phil Nevin .15
278 Akinori Otsuka .15
279 Jay Payton .15
280 Jake Peavey .15
281 David Wells .15
282 Edgardo Alfonzo .15
283 Jim Brower .15
284 Deivi Cruz .15
285 Ray Durham .15
286 Scott Eyre .15
287 Marquis Grissom .15
288 Dustan Mohr .15
289 A.J. Pierzynski .15
290 Jason Schmidt .15
291 J.T. Snow (Foil) 2.00
292 Brett Tomko .15
293 Michael Tucker .15
294 Bret Boone .15
295 Ryan Franklin .15
296 Eddie Guardado .15
297 Shigetoshi Hasegawa .15
298 Raul Ibanez .15
299 Edgar Martinez .15
300 Joel Pineiro .15
301 Scott Spezio .15
302 Ichiro Suzuki (Foil) 10.00
303 Dan Wilson .15
304 Randy Winn .15
305 Chris Carpenter .15
306 Jim Edmonds (Foil) 2.00
307 Jason Isringhausen .15
308 Ray King .15
309 Mike Matheny .15
310 Matt Morris .15
311 Albert Pujols (Foil) 12.50
312 Edgar Renteria .15
313 Scott Rolen (Foil) 4.00
314 Reggie Sanders .15
315 Julian Tavarez .15
316 Larry Walker .15
317 Woody Williams .15
318 Tony Womack .15
319 Danys Baez .15
320 Rocco Baldelli .25
321 Dewan Brazleton .15
322 Carl Crawford .15
323 Jose Cruz .15

324 Toby Hall .15
325 Travis Harper .15
326 Aubrey Huff .15
327 Julio Lugo .15
328 Tino Martinez .15
329 Rod Barajas .15
330 Hank Blalock (Foil) 4.00
331 Francisco Cordero .15
332 Chan Ho Park .15
333 Kevin Mench .15
334 Laynce Nix .15
335 Kenny Rogers .15
336 Brian Shouse .15
337 Alfonso Soriano (Foil) 4.00
338 Mark Teixeira .25
339 Michael Young .25
340 Miguel Batista .15
341 Frank Catalanotto .15
342 Carlos Delgado .15
343 Roy Halliday .15
344 Eric Hinske .15
345 Orlando Hudson .15
346 Reed Johnson .15
347 Justin Speier .15
348 Vernon Wells .15
S01 Goodbye Baseball .10
S02 Great Addition .10
S03 Hacker .10
S04 Helping Himself .10
S05 High Pitch Count .10
S06 Hit the Foul Pole .10
S07 Make Contact .10
S08 Pull the Ball .10
S09 Rattled .10
S10 Role Player .10
S11 Scuffing .10
S12 See it Clearly .10
S13 Serious Wheels .10
S14 Sprint to Second .10
S15 Steal the Sign .10
S16 Turn on It .10
S17 Upper-Deck Shot .10
S18 Valuable Asset .10
S19 Weakest Link .10
S20 Work the Count .10
S21 6-4-3 .10
S22 Aces Up .10
S23 Can of Corn .10
S24 De-nied! .10
S25 Fireballer .10
S26 Full Windup .10
S27 Good Leather .10
S28 Hooking Foul .10
S29 Knuckleball .10
S30 Lined out of Play .10
S31 Masterpiece .10
S32 Out Pitch .10
S33 Paint the Corner .10
S34 Playing Shallow .10
S35 Robbed! .10
S36 Shut the Door .10
S37 Up and In .10
S38 Working the Edge .10
S39 25th Man .10
S40 Change in Strategy .10
S41 Close Call .10
S42 Fake to Third .10
S43 Fan Interference .10
S44 Field General .10
S45 Intensity .10
S46 Mind Games .10
S47 New Strategies .10
S48 Scouting Report .10
S49 Second Look .10
S50 Swing at Anything .10

Trading Deadline

NM/M
Complete Set (200): 90.00
Common Player: .25
Booster Pack (8+3): 3.00
Booster Box (36): 65.00
1 Steve Finley .25
2 Josh Phelps .25
3 Magglio Ordonez .25
4 Nick Johnson .25
5 Carlos Lee (Foil) 3.00
6 Quinton McCracken .25
7 Shawn Estes .25
8 J.J. Putz .25
9 Mike DeJean .25
10 Juan Gonzalez .25
11 Eric Young .25
12 Matt Mantei .25
13 Neal Cotts .25
14 Mike Sweeney .25
15 Glendon Rusch .25
16 Terrmel Sledge .25
17 Ron Villone .25
18 Troy Glaus .25
19 Wilson Valdez .25
20 B.J. Surhoff .25
21 Kazuhisa Ishii .25
22 Dustin Hermanson .25
23 Al Leiter .25
24 Octavio Dotel .25
25 Henry Blanco .25
26 J.D. Drew (Foil) 5.00
27 Kevin Millwood .25
28 Sandy Alomar Jr. .25
29 John Riedling .25
30 Rich Harden (Foil) 3.00
31 Aaron Sele .25
32 Carlos Beltran (Foil) 4.00
33 Jose Lima .25
34 Richard Hidalgo .25
35 Placido Polanco .25
36 Neifi Perez .25
37 Wilson Alvarez .25
38 So Taguchi .25
39 Matt Perisho .25
40 Roberto Hernandez .25
41 Todd Walker .25
42 Jason Kendall .25
43 Brett Myers .25
44 Carlos Silva .25
45 Randy Johnson (Foil) 8.00
46 Jeremy Bonderman .25
47 Orlando Cabrera .25
48 Carlos Delgado (Foil) 4.00
49 A.J. Pierzynski .25
50 Omar Vizquel .25
51 Lenny Harris .25
52 Chris Carpenter .25
53 Miguel Cairo .25
54 Sammy Sosa (Foil) 8.00
55 Royce Clayton .25
56 Cal Eldred .25
57 Rich Aurilia .25
58 Orlando Palmeiro .25
59 Bengie Molina .25
60 Ismael Valdez .25
61 Nate Bump .25
62 David Wells .25
63 Jermaine Dye .25
64 Carlos Zambrano .25
65 David Newhan .25
66 Russ Springer .25
67 Elmer Dessens .25
68 Kris Benson .25
69 Al Reyes .25
70 Tino Martinez .25
71 Ruben Sierra .25
72 Antonio Osuna .25
73 Moises Alou .25
74 Brad Wilkerson (Foil) 3.00
75 Jason Christiansen .25
76 Geoff Blum .25
77 Dennys Reyes .25
78 Craig Counsell .25
79 Rey Sanchez .25
80 Mark Hendrickson .25
81 Doug Mirabelli .25
82 Jeromy Burnitz .25
83 Carl Pavano .25
84 Richie Sexson .25
85 Eric Milton .25
86 Mark DeRosa .25
87 Bob Wickman .25
88 Hideo Nomo .25
89 Tony Armas Jr. .25
90 Desi Relaford .25
91 Russ Ortiz .25
92 Jose Vidro .25
93 Jeff Kent (Foil) 7.00
94 Esteban Yan .25
95 Tim Hudson (Foil) 3.00
96 Jay Payton .25
97 Tony Womack .25
98 Gregg Zaun .25
99 David Weathers .25
100 Scott Podsednik (Foil) 3.00
101 Mark Mulder (Foil) 3.00
102 Jose Guillen .25
103 Grady Sizemore .25
104 Paul Bako .25
105 Jeff DaVanon .25
106 Jeff Nelson .25
107 Troy Percival .25
108 Brian Lawrence .25
109 Mike Redmond .25
110 Odalis Perez .25
111 John Franco .25
112 Doug Brocail .25
113 Einar Diaz .25
114 Mark Grudzielanek .25
115 Jason Marquis .25
116 Jayson Werth .25
117 John Mabry .25
118 Alexis Rios .25
119 Livan Hernandez .25
120 Zack Greinke .25
121 Chris Hammond .25
122 Kent Mercker .25
123 Ryan Drese .25
124 Pedro Martinez (Foil) 8.00
125 Alex Cora .25
126 Kenny Lofton .25
127 Adrian Beltre (Foil) 3.00
128 David Eckstein .25
129 Derek Lowe .25
130 Joe Randa .25
131 Jose Valentin .25
132 David Bush .25
133 Brian Schneider .25
134 Matt Clement .25
135 Paul Byrd .25
136 Jose Vizcaino .25
137 Todd Pratt .25
138 Jose Offerman .25
139 Dan Wilson .25
140 Frank Francisco .25
141 Woody Williams .25
142 Juan Castro .25
143 Jerry Hairston Jr. .25
144 Jeff Suppan .25
145 Steve Reed .25
146 Jon Lieber .25
147 Cristian Guzman .25
148 Shawn Green (Foil) 5.00
149 Damion Easley .25
150 Bronson Arroyo .25
151 Raul Mondesi .25
152 Roger Cedeno .25
153 Carlos Baerga .25
154 Jose Hernandez .25
155 Antonio Alfonseca .25
156 Ricky Ledee .25
157 Armando Benitez .25
158 Esteban Loaiza .25
159 Steve Kline .25
160 Corey Koskie .25
161 Vinny Castilla (Foil) 3.00
162 Tony Clark .25
163 Edgar Renteria (Foil) 3.00
164 Brian Jordan .25
165 David Dellucci .25
166 Hoyt Wilhelm (Foil) 5.00
167 Pee Wee Reese .25
168 Larry Doby .25
169 Yogi Berra (Foil) 8.00
170 Robin Yount (Foil) 5.00
171 Brooks Robinson (Foil) 5.00
172 Reggie Jackson (Foil) 8.00
173 Rod Carew (Foil) 5.00
174 Harmon Killebrew (Foil) 4.00
175 Nolan Ryan (Foil) 15.00
S1 Free Steal .25
S2 Get Under It .25
S3 Go Yard! .25
S4 Just Called Up .25
S5 Leadoff Man .25
S6 Lofted .25
S7 Missed the Cutoff .25
S8 Momentum Swing .25
S9 Shaken .25
S10 Shelled .25
S11 Texas Leaguer .25
S12 Caught Looking .25
S13 Great Range .25
S14 High Heat .25
S15 Just Over the Wall .25
S16 Slider .25
S17 Stranded .25
S18 Superior Athlete .25
S19 Taking a Risk .25
S20 Team Defense .25
S21 Brainstorm .25
S22 Change the Scorecard .25
S23 Good Coaching .25
S24 Preparation .25
S25 Shell Game .25

1992 Modell's Team Mets

Team Mets, the junior fan club, included in its 1992 membership benefits a nine-card perforated sheet sponsored by Modell's Sporting Goods. Cards feature color action photos highlighted by team-color stripes of blue and orange, with a white outer border. The 7-1/2" x 10-1/2" sheet can be separated into standard-size 2-1/2" x 3-1/2" cards. Team Mets and Modell's logos are featured on back, along with 1991 stats and highlights, career numbers and personal data. Cards are checklisted here according to the uniform numbers found on the front.

NM/M
Complete Set (9): 5.00
Common Player: .50
1 Vince Coleman .50
9 Todd Hundley .50
12 Willie Randolph .50
16 Dwight Gooden .50
17 David Cone .50
18 Bret Saberhagen .50
20 Howard Johnson .50
25 Bobby Bonilla .50
33 Eddie Murray 2.00

1991 MooTown Snackers

Produced by the Sargento Cheese Co., cards were available in Mootown Snacker packages or by sending in a special set redemption cou-

pon from a package to obtain the entire set for $5.95 and three UPCs. Fronts feature action photos with uniform logos airbrushed off. Photos are bordered at top and bottom in red. Backs are in red, black and white and feature statistics and a facsimile autograph. Each player card is attached to a perforated panel on its right which has the checklist and a coupon to order the complete set. Cards without the offer coupon still attached are worth 50percent of the values quoted here.

NM/M
Complete Set (24): 10.00
Common Player: .25
1 Jose Canseco .50
2 Kirby Puckett 1.00
3 Barry Bonds 2.00
4 Ken Griffey Jr. 1.50
5 Ryne Sandberg 1.00
6 Tony Gwynn 1.00
7 Kal Daniels .25
8 Ozzie Smith 1.00
9 Dave Justice .25
10 Sandy Alomar, Jr. .25
11 Wade Boggs 1.00
12 Ozzie Guillen .25
13 Dave Magadan .25
14 Cal Ripken, Jr. 2.00
15 Don Mattingly 1.25
16 Ruben Sierra .25
17 Robin Yount .75
18 Len Dykstra .25
19 George Brett 1.25
20 Lance Parrish .25
21 Chris Sabo .25
22 Craig Biggio .25
23 Kevin Mitchell .25
24 Cecil Fielder .25

1992 MooTown Snackers

The unusual venue of cheese snack packs was the source for these cards. Produced as two-piece panels, there is a player card attached by perforations to a card offering a complete set for $7 and proofs of purchase. The player cards have cheese-yellow borders at top and bottom with an action photo at center. Produced by Michael Schecter Assoc., the cards have had uniform and cap logos removed because they are licensed only by the Players Association and not by MLB. Backs are printed in black and yellow on white and include a facsimile autograph. Cards with the complete set offer no longer attached are worth 50% of the values shown here.

NM/M
Complete Set (24): 7.50
Common Player: .25
1 Albert Belle .25
2 Jeff Bagwell .75
3 Jose Rijo .25
4 Roger Clemens 1.25
5 Kevin Maas .25
6 Kirby Puckett 1.00
7 Ken Griffey Jr. 1.50
8 Will Clark .25
9 Felix Jose .25
10 Cecil Fielder .25
11 Darryl Strawberry .25
12 John Smiley .25
13 Roberto Alomar .35
14 Paul Molitor .75
15 Andre Dawson .25
16 Terry Mulholland .25
17 Fred McGriff .25
18 Dwight Gooden .25
19 Rickey Henderson .75
20 Nolan Ryan 2.00
21 George Brett 1.25
22 Tom Glavine .40
23 Cal Ripken Jr. 2.00
24 Frank Thomas .75

1983 Mother's Cookies Giants

After putting out Pacific Coast League sets in 1952-53, Mother's Cookies distributed this full-color set of 20 San Francisco Giants cards three decades later. The 2-1/2" x 3-1/2" cards were produced by hobbyist Barry Colla and include the Giants logo and player's name on the card fronts. Backs are numbered and contain biographical information, sponsor's logo and a space for the player's autograph. Fifteen cards were given to every fan at the Aug. 7, 1983, Giants game, with each fan also receiving a coupon good for five additional cards.

NM/M
Complete Set (20): 6.00
Common Player: .35
1 Frank Robinson 2.00
2 Jack Clark .50
3 Chili Davis .45
4 Johnnie LeMaster .35
5 Greg Minton .35
6 Bob Brenly .35
7 Fred Breining .35
8 Jeff Leonard .35
9 Darrell Evans .50
10 Tom O'Malley .35
11 Duane Kuiper .35
12 Mike Krukow .35
13 Atlee Hammaker .35
14 Gary Lavelle .35
15 Bill Laskey .35
16 Max Venable .35
17 Joel Youngblood .35
18 Dave Bergman .35
19 Mike Vail .35
20 Andy McGaffigan .35

1984 Mother's Cookies A's

Following the success of their one set in 1983, Mother's Cookies issued five more team sets of cards in 1984. Cards measure 2-1/2" x 3-1/2" with rounded corners. Fronts feature unbordered color photos. Horizontal backs have biographical data, card number, Mother's Cookies logo and space for player autograph. There are 28 cards in the A's set, with 20 of the cards distributed during a stadium promotion. Fans also received a

coupon redeemable for eight additional cards. Since those cards did not necessarily complete collectors' sets, Mother's Cookies cards become very popular among card traders. The A's set includes cards for the manager, coaches and a checklist.

NM/M
Complete Set (28): 9.00
Common Player: .25
1 Steve Boros .25
2 Rickey Henderson 5.00
3 Joe Morgan 2.00
4 Dwayne Murphy .25
5 Mike Davis .25
6 Bruce Bochte .25
7 Carney Lansford .25
8 Steve McCatty .25
9 Mike Heath .25
10 Chris Codiroli .25
11 Bill Almon .25
12 Bill Caudill .25
13 Donnie Hill .25
14 Lary Sorenson .25
15 Dave Kingman .50
16 Garry Hancock .25
17 Jeff Burroughs .25
18 Tom Burgmeier .25
19 Jim Essian .25
20 Mike Warren .25
21 Davey Lopes .25
22 Ray Burris .25
23 Tony Phillips .25
24 Tim Conroy .25
25 Jeff Bettendorf .25
26 Keith Atherton .25
27 A's Coaches (Clete Boyer, Bob Didier, Jackie Moore, Ron Schueler, Billy Williams) .25
28 Oakland Coliseum/Checklist .25

Astros

Mother's Cookies issued a full-color team set for the Astros in 1984. Cards measure 2-1/2" x 3-1/2" with rounded corners. Card fronts feature unbordered color photos. Horizontal backs have biographical data, card number, Mother's Cookies logo and space for player autograph. There are 28 cards in the Astros set, with 20 of the cards distributed during a stadium promotion. Fans also received a coupon redeemable for eight additional cards. Since those cards did not necessarily complete collectors' sets, Mother's Cookies cards became very popular among traders. The Astros set includes one card for the coaches and a checklist.

NM/M
Complete Set (28): 7.00

	Common Player:	.25
1	Nolan Ryan	6.00
2	Joe Niekro	.25
3	Alan Ashby	.25
4	Bill Doran	.25
5	Phil Garner	.25
6	Ray Knight	.25
7	Dickie Thon	.25
8	Jose Cruz	.25
9	Jerry Mumphrey	.25
10	Terry Puhl	.25
11	Enos Cabell	.25
12	Harry Spilman	.25
13	Dave Smith	.25
14	Mike Scott	.25
15	Bob Lillis	.25
16	Bob Knepper	.25
17	Frank DiPino	.25
18	Tom Wieghaus	.25
19	Denny Walling	.25
20	Tony Scott	.25
21	Alan Bannister	.25
22	Bill Dawley	.25
23	Vern Ruhle	.25
24	Mike LaCoss	.25
25	Mike Madden	.25
26	Craig Reynolds	.25
27	Astros Coaches (Cot Deal, Don Leppert, Denis Menke, Les Moss, Jerry Walker)	.25
28	Astros Logo/Checklist	.25

Giants

Mother's Cookies issued a second annual full-color card set for the S.F. Giants in 1984. Cards measure 2-1/2" x 3-1/2" with rounded corners. Fronts feature drawings of former Giant All-Star team selections. Horizontal backs have brief biographical information, card number and Mother's Cookies logo and autograph space. There are 28 cards in the Giants set, with 20 of the cards distributed during a stadium promotion. Fans also received a coupon redeemable for eight additional cards. Since those cards did not necessarily complete collectors' sets, Mother's Cookies cards became very popular among card traders.

		NM/M
	Complete Set (28):	7.50
	Common Player:	.15
1	Willie Mays	4.50
2	Willie McCovey	1.00
3	Juan Marichal	.50
4	Gaylord Perry	.50
5	Tom Haller	.15
6	Jim Davenport	.15
7	Jack Clark	.25
8	Greg Minton	.15
9	Atlee Hammaker	.15
10	Gary Lavelle	.15
11	Orlando Cepeda	.50
12	Bobby Bonds	.25
13	John Antonelli	.15
14	Bob Schmidt (Photo actually Wes Westrum.)	.15
15	Sam Jones	.15
16	Mike McCormick	.15
17	Ed Bailey	.15
18	Stu Miller	.15
19	Felipe Alou	.25
20	Jim Hart	.15
21	Dick Dietz	.15
22	Chris Speier	.15
23	Bobby Murcer	.25
24	John Montefusco	.15
25	Vida Blue	.15
26	Ed Whitson	.15
27	Darrell Evans	.25
28	All-Star Game Logo/Checklist	.15

Mariners

Mother's Cookies issued a full-color set for the Mariners in 1984. Cards measure

2-1/2" x 3-1/2" with rounded corners. Fronts feature unbordered color photos. Horizontal backs have brief biographical data, card number, Mother's Cookies logo and space for player autograph. There are 28 cards in the set with 20 of the cards distributed during a stadium promotion. Fans also received a coupon redeemable for eight additional cards. Since those cards did not necessarily complete collectors' sets, Mother's Cookies cards became very popular among traders. The set includes one card each for the manager, coaches and a checklist.

		NM/M
	Complete Set (28):	6.00
	Common Player:	.25
1	Del Crandall	.25
2	Barry Bonnell	.25
3	Dave Henderson	.25
4	Bob Kearney	.25
5	Mike Moore	.25
6	Spike Owen	.25
7	Gorman Thomas	.25
8	Ed Vande Berg	.25
9	Matt Young	.25
10	Larry Milbourne	.25
11	Dave Beard	.25
12	Jim Beattie	.25
13	Mark Langston	.25
14	Orlando Mercado	.25
15	Jack Perconte	.25
16	Pat Putnam	.25
17	Paul Mirabella	.25
18	Domingo Ramos	.25
19	Al Cowens	.25
20	Mike Stanton	.25
21	Steve Henderson	.25
22	Bob Stoddard	.25
23	Alvin Davis	.25
24	Phil Bradley	.25
25	Roy Thomas	.25
26	Darnell Coles	.25
27	Mariners Coaches (Chuck Cottier, Frank Funk, Ben Hines, Phil Roof, Rick Sweet)	.25
28	Seattle Kingdome/Checklist	.25

Padres

Mother's Cookies issued a full-color set for the Padres in 1984. Cards measure 2-1/2" x 3-1/2", with rounded corners. Fronts feature unbordered color photos. Horizontal backs have brief biographical data, card number, sponsor's logo and space for player autograph. There are 28 cards in the set, with 20 of the cards distributed during a stadium promotion. Fans also received a coupon redeemable for eight additional cards. Since those cards did not necessarily complete collectors' sets, Mother's Cookies cards became very popular among traders. The Padres set includes one card each for the manager, coaches and a checklist.

		NM/M
	Complete Set (28):	9.00
	Common Player:	.25
1	Dick Williams	.25
2	Rich Gossage	.50
3	Tim Lollar	.25
4	Eric Show	.25
5	Terry Kennedy	.25
6	Kurt Bevacqua	.25
7	Steve Garvey	1.50
8	Garry Templeton	.25
9	Tony Gwynn	5.00
10	Alan Wiggins	.25
11	Dave Dravecky	.25
12	Tim Flannery	.25
13	Kevin McReynolds	.25
14	Bobby Brown	.25
15	Ed Whitson	.25
16	Doug Gwosdz	.25
17	Luis DeLeon	.25
18	Andy Hawkins	.25
19	Craig Lefferts	.25
20	Carmelo Martinez	.25
21	Sid Monge	.25
22	Graig Nettles	.25
23	Mario Ramirez	.25
24	Luis Salazar	.25
25	Champ Summers	.25
26	Mark Thurmond	.25
27	Padres Coaches (Harry Dunlop, Deacon Jones, Jack Krol, Norm Sherry, Ozzie Virgil)	.25
28	Jack Murphy Stadium/Checklist	.25

1985 Mother's Cookies A's

Mother's Cookies again issued five full-color sets for Major League teams in 1985. Cards measure 2-1/2" x 3-1/2" with rounded corners. Fronts feature unbordered color photos. Horizontal backs have brief biographical data, card number, Mother's Cookies logo and space for player autograph. The set was distributed in its entirety during a stadium promotion.

		NM/M
	Complete Set (28):	7.00
	Common Player:	.25
1	Jackie Moore	.25
2	Dave Kingman	.40
3	Don Sutton	1.25
4	Mike Heath	.25
5	Alfredo Griffin	.25
6	Dwayne Murphy	.25
7	Mike Davis	.25
8	Carney Lansford	.25
9	Chris Codiroli	.25
10	Bruce Bochte	.25
11	Mickey Tettleton	.25
12	Donnie Hill	.25
13	Rob Picciolo	.25
14	Dave Collins	.25
15	Dusty Baker	.50
16	Tim Conroy	.25
17	Keith Atherton	.25
18	Jay Howell	.25
19	Mike Warren	.25
20	Steve McCatty	.25
21	Bill Krueger	.25
22	Curt Young	.25
23	Dan Meyer	.25
24	Mike Gallego	.25
25	Jeff Kaiser	.25
26	Steve Henderson	.25
27	A's Coaches (Clete Boyer, Bob Didier, Dave McKay, Wes Stock, Billy Williams)	.25
28	Oakland Coliseum/Checklist	.25

Astros

Mother's Cookies issued a second annual full-color set for the Astros in 1985. Cards measure 2-1/2" x 3-1/2" with rounded corners. Fronts feature unbordered color photos. Horizontal backs have biographical information, card number, Mother's Cookies logo and space for player autograph. The set was distributed in its entirety during a stadium promotion.

		NM/M
	Complete Set (28):	8.00
	Common Player:	.25
1	Bob Lillis	.25
2	Nolan Ryan	7.50
3	Phil Garner	.25
4	Jose Cruz	.25
5	Denny Walling	.25
6	Joe Niekro	.30
7	Terry Puhl	.25
8	Bill Doran	.25
9	Dickie Thon	.25
10	Enos Cabell	.25
11	Frank Dipino (DiPino)	.25
12	Julio Solano	.25
13	Alan Ashby	.25
14	Craig Reynolds	.25
15	Jerry Mumphrey	.25
16	Bill Dawley	.25
17	Mark Bailey	.25
18	Mike Scott	.25
19	Harry Spilman	.25
20	Bob Knepper	.25
21	Dave Smith	.25
22	Kevin Bass	.25
23	Tim Tolman	.25
24	Jeff Calhoun	.25
25	Jim Pankovits	.25
26	Ron Mathis	.25
27	Astros Coaches (Cot Deal, Matt Galante, Don Leppert, Denis Menke, Jerry Walker)	.25
28	Astros Logo/Checklist	.25

Giants

Mother's Cookies issued a third annual full-color set for the Giants in 1985. Cards measure 2-1/2" x 3-1/2" with rounded corners. Fronts feature unbordered color photos. Horizontal backs have brief biographical information, card number, Mother's Cookies logo and space for player autograph. The set was distributed in its entirety during a stadium promotion.

		NM/M
	Complete Set (28):	6.00
	Common Player:	.25
1	Jim Davenport	.25
2	Chili Davis	.25
3	Dan Gladden	.25
4	Jeff Leonard	.25
5	Manny Trillo	.25
6	Atlee Hammaker	.25
7	Bob Brenly	.25
8	Greg Minton	.25
9	Bill Laskey	.25
10	Vida Blue	.30
11	Mike Krukow	.25
12	Frank Williams	.25
13	Jose Uribe	.25
14	Johnnie LeMaster	.25
15	Scot Thompson	.25
16	Dave LaPoint	.25
17	David Green	.25
18	Chris Brown	.25
19	Joel Youngblood	.25
20	Mark Davis	.25
21	Jim Gott	.25
22	Doug Gwosdz	.25
23	Scott Garrelts	.25
24	Gary Rajsich	.25
25	Rob Deer	.25
26	Brad Wellman	.25
27	Coaches (Rocky Bridges, Chuck Hiller, Tom McCraw, Bob Miller, Jack Mull)	.25
28	Candlestick Park/Checklist	.25

Mariners

Mother's Cookies issued a second annual full-color set for the Mariners in 1985. Cards measure 2-1/2" x 3-1/2" with rounded corners. Fronts feature unbordered color photos. Horizontal backs have biographical information, card number, Mother's Cookies logo and space for player autograph. The set was distributed in its entirety during a stadium promotion.

		NM/M
	Complete Set (28):	6.00
	Common Player:	.25
1	Chuck Cottier	.25
2	Alvin Davis	.25
3	Mark Langston	.25
4	Dave Henderson	.25
5	Ed Vande Berg	.25
6	Al Cowens	.25
7	Spike Owen	.25
8	Mike Moore	.25
9	Gorman Thomas	.25
10	Barry Bonnell	.25
11	Jack Perconte	.25
12	Domingo Ramos	.25
13	Bob Kearney	.25
14	Matt Young	.25
15	Jim Beattie	.25
16	Mike Stanton	.25
17	David Valle	.25
18	Ken Phelps	.25
19	Salome Barojas	.25
20	Jim Presley	.25
21	Phil Bradley	.25
22	Dave Geisel	.25
23	Harold Reynolds	.50
24	Edwin Nunez	.25
25	Mike Morgan	.25
26	Ivan Calderon	.25
27	Mariners Coaches (Deron Johnson, Jim Mahoney, Marty Martinez, Phil Regan, Phil Roof)	.25
28	Seattle Kingdome/Checklist	.25

Padres

Mother's Cookies issued a second annual full-color Padres team set in 1985. Cards have rounded corners and measure 2-1/2" x 3-1/2". Glossy fronts feature unbordered color photos. Horizontal backs have biographical data, card number, Mother's Cookies logo and space for player autograph. The set was distributed in its entirety during a stadium promotion.

		NM/M
	Complete Set (28):	6.00
	Common Player:	.25
1	Dick Williams	.25
2	Tony Gwynn	4.50
3	Kevin McReynolds	.25
4	Graig Nettles	.25
5	Rich Gossage	.40
6	Steve Garvey	1.50
7	Garry Templeton	.25
8	Dave Dravecky	.25
9	Eric Show	.25
10	Terry Kennedy	.25
11	Luis DeLeon	.25
12	Bruce Bochy	.25
13	Andy Hawkins	.25
14	Kurt Bevacqua	.25
15	Craig Lefferts	.25
16	Mario Ramirez	.25
17	LaMarr Hoyt	.25
18	Jerry Royster	.25
19	Tim Stoddard	.25
20	Tim Flannery	.25
21	Mark Thurmond	.25
22	Greg Booker	.25
23	Bobby Brown	.25
24	Carmelo Martinez	.25
25	Al Bumbry	.25
26	Jerry Davis	.25
27	Padres Coaches (Galen Cisco, Harry Dunlop, Deacon Jones, Jack Krol, Ozzie Virgil)	.25
28	Jack Murphy Stadium/Checklist	.25

1986 Mother's Cookies A's

Mother's Cookies produced four full-color team sets in 1986, with only the San Diego Padres not repeating from the 1985 group. The third annual set for the Oakland A's measures 2-1/2" x 3-1/2" with rounded corners. Glossy fronts feature unbordered color photos. Horizontal backs have brief biographical information, card number and Mother's Cookies logo. There are 28 cards in the A's set, with 20 of the cards distributed during a stadium promotion. Each fan also received a coupon redeemable for eight additional cards which could be traded to complete a set.

		NM/M
	Complete Set (28):	10.00
	Common Player:	.25
1	Jackie Moore	.25
2	Dave Kingman	.40
3	Dusty Baker	.40
4	Joaquin Andujar	.25
5	Alfredo Griffin	.25
6	Dwayne Murphy	.25
7	Mike Davis	.25
8	Carney Lansford	.25
9	Jose Canseco	6.00
10	Bruce Bochte	.25
11	Mickey Tettleton	.25
12	Donnie Hill	.25
13	Jose Rijo	.25
14	Rick Langford	.25
15	Chris Codiroli	.25
16	Moose Haas	.25
17	Keith Atherton	.25
18	Jay Howell	.25

19 Tony Phillips .25
20 Steve Henderson .25
21 Bill Krueger .25
22 Steve Ontiveros .25
23 Bill Bathe .25
24 Rickey Peters .25
25 Tim Birtsas .25
26 Trainers (Frank Ciensczyk, Larry Davis, Steve Vucinich, Barry Weinberg) .25
27 Coaches (Bob Didier, Dave McKay, Jeff Newman, Ron Plaza, Wes Stock, Bob Watson) .25
28 Oakland Coliseum/Checklist .25

Astros

Mother's Cookies produced a third annual Astros team set in 1985. The round-cornered, glossy front 2-1/2" x 3-1/2" cards feature unbordered color paintings of Houston's past All-Star Game performers. Backs have biographical information, card number and Mother's Cookies logo. There are 28 cards in the set, with 20 of the cards distributed during a stadium promotion. Each fan also received a coupon redeemable for eight additional cards that could be traded to complete a set.

NM/M
Complete Set (28): 9.00
Common Player: .25
1 Dick Farrell .25
2 Hal Woodeschick (Woodeshick) .25
3 Joe Morgan 1.00
4 Claude Raymond .25
5 Mike Cuellar .25
6 Rusty Staub .25
7 Jimmy Wynn .25
8 Larry Dierker .25
9 Denis Menke .25
10 Don Wilson .25
11 Cesar Cedeno .25
12 Lee May .25
13 Bob Watson .25
14 Ken Forsch .25
15 Joaquin Andujar .25
16 Terry Puhl .25
17 Joe Niekro .30
18 Craig Reynolds .25
19 Joe Sambito .25
20 Jose Cruz .25
21 J.R. Richard .30
22 Bob Knepper .25
23 Nolan Ryan 7.50
24 Ray Knight .25
25 Bill Dawley .25
26 Dickie Thon .25
27 Jerry Mumphrey .25
28 Astros Logo/Checklist .25

Giants

Mother's Cookies produced a fourth annual set for the Giants in 1985. Round-cornered, glossy front cards measure 2-1/2" x 3-1/2" and feature unbordered color photos. Horizontal backs have biographical data, card number, and Mother's Cookies logo. There are 28 cards in the set, with 20 of the cards distributed during a stadium promotion. Each fan also received a coupon redeemable for eight additional cards which could be traded to complete the set.

NM/M
Complete Set (28): 6.00
Common Player: .25
1 Roger Craig .25
2 Chili Davis .25
3 Dan Gladden .25
4 Jeff Leonard .25
5 Bob Brenly .25
6 Atlee Hammaker .25
7 Will Clark 5.00
8 Greg Minton .25
9 Candy Maldonado .25
10 Vida Blue .25
11 Mike Krukow .25
12 Bob Melvin .25
13 Jose Uribe .25
14 Dan Driessen .25
15 Jeff Robinson .25
16 Rob Thompson .25
17 Mike LaCoss .25
18 Chris Brown .25
19 Scott Garrelts .25
20 Mark Davis .25
21 Jim Gott .25
22 Brad Wellman .25
23 Roger Mason .25
24 Bill Laskey .25
25 Brad Gulden .25
26 Joel Youngblood .25
27 Juan Berenguer .25
28 Coaches/Checklist (Bill Fahey, Bob Lillis, Gordy MacKenzie, Jose Morales, Norm Sherry) .25

Mariners

Mother's Cookies produced a third annual set for the M's in 1985. Round-cornered, glossy front cards measure 2-1/2" x 3-1/2" and feature unbordered color photos. Horizontal backs have brief biographical information, card number and sponsor's logo. There are 28 cards in the set, with 20 distributed during a stadium promotion. Each fan also received a coupon redeemable for eight additional cards which could be traded to complete the set.

NM/M
Complete Set (28): 6.00
Common Player: .25
1 Dick Williams .25
2 Alvin Davis .25
3 Mark Langston .25
4 Dave Henderson .25
5 Steve Yeager .25
6 Al Cowens .25
7 Jim Presley .25
8 Phil Bradley .25
9 Gorman Thomas .25
10 Barry Bonnell .25
11 Milt Wilcox .25
12 Domingo Ramos .25
13 Paul Mirabella .25
14 Matt Young .25
15 Ivan Calderon .25
16 Bill Swift .25
17 Pete Ladd .25
18 Ken Phelps .25
19 Karl Best .25
20 Spike Owen .25
21 Mike Moore .25
22 Danny Tartabull .25
23 Bob Kearney .25
24 Edwin Nunez .25
25 Mike Morgan .25
26 Roy Thomas .25
27 Jim Beattie .25
28 Coaches/Checklist (Deron Johnson, Marty Martinez, Phil Regan, Phil Roof, Ozzie Virgil) .25

1987 Mother's Cookies A's

Continuing with a tradition of producing beautiful baseball cards, Mother's Cookies of Oakland, Calif. issued a 28-card set featuring every Oakland A's player to have been elected to the All-Star Game since 1968. The full-color photos came from the private collection of nationally known photographer Doug McWilliams. Twenty of the 28 cards were given out to fans attending the A's game on July 5. An additional eight cards were available by redeeming a mail-in certificate. The cards measure 2-1/2" x 3-1/2" and feature rounded corners. Backs carry the player's All-Star Game statistics.

NM/M
Complete Set (28): 12.00
Common Player: .25
1 Bert Campaneris .25
2 Rick Monday .25
3 John Odom .25
4 Sal Bando .25
5 Reggie Jackson 2.50
6 Catfish Hunter 1.00
7 Vida Blue .25
8 Dave Duncan .25
9 Joe Rudi .25
10 Rollie Fingers .75
11 Ken Holtzman .25
12 Dick Williams .25
13 Alvin Dark .25
14 Gene Tenace .25
15 Claudell Washington .25
16 Phil Garner .25
17 Wayne Gross .25
18 Matt Keough .25
19 Jeff Newman .25
20 Rickey Henderson 1.50
21 Tony Armas .25
22 Mike Norris .25
23 Billy Martin .40
24 Bill Caudill .25
25 Jay Howell .25
26 Jose Canseco 2.00
27 Jose and Reggie (Jose Canseco, Reggie Jackson) 2.50
28 A's Logo/Checklist .25

Astros

Twenty of 28 cards featuring Astros players were given out to the first 25,000 fans attending the July 17 game at the Astrodome. An additional eight cards (though not necessarily the exact eight needed to complete a set) were available from the sponsor by redeeming a mail-in certificate. The cards have rounded corners, glossy fronts and measure 2-1/2" x 3-1/2". Backs are printed in purple and orange and contain personal data, the Mother's Cookies logo, card number and a spot for the player's autograph.

NM/M
Complete Set (28): 10.00
Common Player: .25
1 Hal Lanier .25
2 Mike Scott .25
3 Jose Cruz .25
4 Bill Doran .25
5 Bob Knepper .25
6 Phil Garner .25
7 Terry Puhl .25
8 Nolan Ryan 7.50
9 Kevin Bass .25
10 Glenn Davis .25
11 Alan Ashby .25
12 Charlie Kerfeld .25
13 Denny Walling .25
14 Danny Darwin .25
15 Mark Bailey .25
16 Davey Lopes .25
17 Dave Meads .25
18 Aurelio Lopez .25
19 Craig Reynolds .25
20 Dave Smith .25
21 Larry Anderson (Andersen) .25
22 Jim Pankovits .25
23 Jim Deshaies .25
24 Bert Pena .25
25 Dickie Thon .25
26 Billy Hatcher .25
27 Coaches (Yogi Berra, Matt Galante, Denis Menke, Les Moss, Gene Tenace) .25
28 Houston Astrodome/Checklist .25

Dodgers

Mother's Cookies produced for the first time in 1987 a team set featuring the L.A. Dodgers. Twenty of the 28 cards were given to youngsters 14 and under at Dodger Stadium on August 9. An additional eight cards were available from Mother's Cookies via a mail-in coupon. The borderless, full-color cards measure 2-1/2" x 3-1/2" and have rounded corners. A special album designed to house the set was available for $3.95 through a mail-in offer.

NM/M
Complete Set (28): 10.00
Common Player: .25
1 Tom Lasorda .40
2 Pedro Guerrero .25
3 Steve Sax .25
4 Fernando Valenzuela .25
5 Mike Marshall .25
6 Orel Hershiser .75
7 Mariano Duncan .25
8 Bill Madlock .25
9 Bob Welch .25
10 Mike Scioscia .25
11 Mike Ramsey .25
12 Matt Young .25
13 Franklin Stubbs .25
14 Tom Niedenfuer .25
15 Reggie Williams .25
16 Rick Honeycutt .25
17 Dave Anderson .25
18 Alejandro Pena .25
19 Ken Howell .25
20 Len Matuszek .25
21 Tim Leary .25
22 Tracy Woodson .25
23 Alex Trevino .25
24 Ken Landreaux .25
25 Mickey Hatcher .25
26 Brian Holton .25
27 Coaches (Joey Amalfitano, Mark Cresse, Don McMahon, Manny Mota, Ron Perranoski, Bill Russell) .25
28 Dodger Stadium/Checklist .25

Giants

Distribution of the 1987 Mother's Cookies Giants cards took place at Candlestick Park on June 27. Twenty of the 28 cards in the set were given to the first 25,000 fans entering the park. The starter packet of 20 cards contained a mail-in coupon card which was good for an additional eight cards. The glossy-front cards measure 2-1/2" x 3-1/2" with rounded corners. Backs are printed in red and purple and contain personal and statistical information along with the Mother's Cookies logo.

NM/M
Complete Set (28): 9.00
Common Player: .25
1 Roger Craig .25
2 Will Clark 1.00
3 Chili Davis .25
4 Bob Brenly .25
5 Chris Brown .25
6 Mike Krukow .25
7 Candy Maldonado .25
8 Jeffrey Leonard .25
9 Greg Minton .25
10 Robby Thompson .25
11 Scott Garrelts .25
12 Bob Melvin .25
13 Jose Uribe .25
14 Mark Davis .25
15 Eddie Milner .25
16 Harry Spilman .25
17 Kelly Downs .25
18 Chris Speier .25
19 Jim Gott .25
20 Joel Youngblood .25
21 Mike LaCoss .25
22 Matt Williams 3.00
23 Roger Mason .25
24 Mike Aldrete .25
25 Jeff Robinson .25
26 Mark Grant .25
27 Coaches (Bill Fahey, Bob Lillis, Gordon MacKenzie, Jose Morales, Norm Sherry, Don Zimmer) .25
28 Candlestick Park/Checklist .25

Mariners

For the fourth consecutive year, Mother's Cookies issued a team set featuring the Mariners. Twenty of the 28 cards were distributed to the first 20,000 fans entering the Kingdome on August 9. An additional eight cards (though not necessarily the eight cards needed to complete the set) were available by redeeming a mail-in certificate. Collectors were encouraged to trade to complete a set. The 2-1/2" x 3-1/2" full-color cards feature glossy fronts and rounded corners. A specially designed album to house the set was available.

NM/M
Complete Set (28): 6.00
Common Player: .25
1 Dick Williams .25
2 Alvin Davis .25
3 Mike Moore .25
4 Jim Presley .25
5 Mark Langston .25
6 Phil Bradley .25
7 Ken Phelps .25
8 Mike Morgan .25
9 David Valle .25
10 Harold Reynolds .40
11 Edwin Nunez .25
12 Bob Kearney .25
13 Scott Bankhead .25
14 Scott Bradley .25
15 Mickey Brantley .25
16 Mark Huismann .25
17 Mike Kingery .25
18 John Moses .25
19 Donell Nixon .25
20 Rey Quinones .25
21 Domingo Ramos .25
22 Jerry Reed .25
23 Rich Renteria .25
24 Rich Monteleone .25
25 Mike Trujillo .25
26 Bill Wilkinson .25
27 John Christensen .25
28 Coaches/Checklist (Billy Connors, Frank Howard, Phil Roof, Bobby Tolan, Ozzie Virgil) .25

Rangers

While Mother's Cookies of Oakland had produced high-quality baseball card sets of various teams since 1983, the Rangers participated in the promotion for the first time in 1987. Twenty cards from the 28-card set were handed out to the first 25,000 fans entering Arlington Stadium on July 17. An additional eight cards (though not necessarily the eight needed to complete a set) were available by redeeming a mail-in certificate. The cards measure 2-1/2" x 3-1/2" with rounded corners and glossy finish, like all Mother's Cookies issued in 1987.

NM/M
Complete Set (28): 9.00
Common Player: .25
1 Bobby Valentine .25
2 Pete Incaviglia .50
3 Charlie Hough .25
4 Oddibe McDowell .25
5 Larry Parrish .25
6 Scott Fletcher .25
7 Steve Buechele .25
8 Tom Paciorek .25
9 Pete O'Brien .25
10 Darrell Porter .25
11 Greg Harris .25
12 Don Slaught .25

13	Ruben Sierra	.50
14	Curtis Wilkerson	.25
15	Dale Mohorcic	.25
16	Ron Meredith	.25
17	Mitch Williams	.25
18	Bob Brower	.25
19	Edwin Correa	.25
20	Geno Petralli	.25
21	Mike Loynd	.25
22	Jerry Browne	.25
23	Jose Guzman	.25
24	Jeff Kunkel	.25
25	Bobby Witt	.25
26	Jeff Russell	.25
27	Trainers (Danny Wheat, Bill Zeigler)	.25
28	Coaches/Checklist (Joe Ferguson, Tim Foli, Tom House, Art Howe, Dave Oliver, Tom Robson)	.25

Mark McGwire

A four-card set featuring outstanding rookie Mark McGwire of the Oakland A's was produced by Mother's Cookies in 1987. Cards are 2-1/2" x 3-1/2" and have rounded corners and glossy finish like other Mother's issues. The set was obtainable by sending in eight proof-of-purchase seals or could be secured at the National Sports Collectors Convention held July 9-12 in San Francisco. Convention goers received one card as a bonus for each Mother's Cookies baseball card album purchased.

		NM/M
Complete Set (4):		10.00
Uncut Strip:		10.00
Common Card:		3.00
1	Mark McGwire/Portrait	3.00
2	Mark McGwire (Leaning on bat rack.)	3.00
3	Mark McGwire (Beginning batting swing.)	3.00
4	Mark McGwire (Batting follow-through.)	3.00

1988 Mother's Cookies A's

Complete at 28 cards, the 1988 Mother's Cookies A's set features full-color, borderless cards with rounded corners in the standard 2-1/2" x 3-1/2" format. Backs are printed in red and purple and include biographical information, the Mother's Cookies logo and card number. Starter sets of 20 cards were distributed at the stadium along with a promotional card redeemable for another eights cards (not necessarily those needed to complete the set). An album to house the cards was also available.

		NM/M
Complete Set (28):		16.00
Common Player:		.35
1	Tony LaRussa	.50
2	Mark McGwire	6.00
3	Dave Stewart	.35
4	Mickey Tettleton	.35
5	Dave Parker	.35
6	Carney Lansford	.35
7	Jose Canseco	.75
8	Don Baylor	.50
9	Bob Welch	.35
10	Dennis Eckersley	1.25
11	Walt Weiss	.50
12	Tony Phillips	.35
13	Steve Ontiveros	.35
14	Dave Henderson	.35
15	Stan Javier	.35
16	Ron Hassey	.35
17	Curt Young	.35
18	Glenn Hubbard	.35
19	Storm Davis	.35
20	Eric Plunk	.35
21	Matt Young	.35
22	Mike Gallego	.35
23	Rick Honeycutt	.35
24	Doug Jennings	.35
25	Gene Nelson	.35
26	Greg Cadaret	.35
27	Coaches (Dave Duncan, Rene Lachemann, Jim Lefebvre, Dave McKay, Mike Paul, Bob Watson)	.35
28	Jose Canseco, Mark McGwire	2.50

Astros

One of six team sets issued by Mother's Cookies in 1988, the 28-card Astros set is similar in design to other Mother's Cookies sets. Glossy-front cards are 2-1/2" x 3-1/2" size with rounded corners and feature full-color, borderless photos on the fronts. Backs feature red and purple printing and include brief biographical information, the Mother's logo and card number. Twenty of the cards were distributed in a stadium promotion, along with a redemption card that could be exchanged for an additional eight cards (but not necessarily the eight needed to complete the set). An album was also available to house the set.

		NM/M
Complete Set (28):		12.00
Common Player:		.35
1	Hal Lanier	.35
2	Mike Scott	.35
3	Gerald Young	.35
4	Bill Doran	.35
5	Bob Knepper	.35
6	Billy Hatcher	.35
7	Terry Puhl	.35
8	Nolan Ryan	10.00
9	Kevin Bass	.35
10	Glenn Davis	.35
11	Alan Ashby	.35
12	Steve Henderson	.35
13	Denny Walling	.35
14	Danny Darwin	.35
15	Mark Bailey	.35
16	Ernie Camacho	.35
17	Rafael Ramirez	.35
18	Jeff Heathcock	.35
19	Craig Reynolds	.35
20	Dave Smith	.35
21	Larry Andersen	.35
22	Jim Pankovits	.35
23	Jim Deshaies	.35
24	Juan Agosto	.35
25	Chuck Jackson	.35
26	Joaquin Andujar	.35
27	Coaches (Yogi Berra, Gene Clines, Matt Galante, Marc Hill, Denis Menke, Les Moss)	.35
28	Trainers/Checklist (Doc Ewell, Dave Labossiere, Dennis Liborio)	.35

Dodgers

Similar in design to other Mother's Cookies sets, the 1988 Dodgers issue features full-color, borderless photos with backs printed in red and purple. The 28 cards in the set measure 2-1/2" x 3-1/2" with rounded corners. Starter packs of 20 cards were distributed at a ballpark promotion along with a coupon card that could be exchanged for an additional eight cards at a local card show or through the mail. Backs include brief player information, the Mother's Cookies logo and card number. The promotion also included a special album to house the set.

		NM/M
Complete Set (28):		8.00
Common Player:		.35
1	Tom Lasorda	.45
2	Pedro Guerrero	.35
3	Steve Sax	.35
4	Fernando Valenzuela	.35
5	Mike Marshall	.35
6	Orel Hershiser	.50
7	Alfredo Griffin	.35
8	Kirk Gibson	.35
9	Don Sutton	1.25
10	Mike Scioscia	.35
11	Franklin Stubbs	.35
12	Mike Davis	.35
13	Jesse Orosco	.35
14	John Shelby	.35
15	Rick Dempsey	.35
16	Jay Howell	.35
17	Dave Anderson	.35
18	Alejandro Pena	.35
19	Jeff Hamilton	.35
20	Danny Heep	.35
21	Tim Leary	.35
22	Brad Havens	.35
23	Tim Belcher	.35
24	Ken Howell	.35
25	Mickey Hatcher	.35
26	Brian Holton	.35
27	Mike Devereaux	.35
28	Coaches/Checklist (Joe Amalfitano, Mark Cresse, Joe Ferguson, Ben Hines, Manny Mota, Ron Perranoski, Bill Russell)	.35

Giants

One of six team sets issued in 1988 by Mother's Cookies, this 28-card Giants set featured full-color borderless photos on a standard-size card with rounded corners. Backs, printed in red and purple, include brief player data, the Mother's Cookies logo and card number. Twenty different cards were distributed as a starter set at a stadium promotion along with a coupon card that could be redeemed for an additional eight cards (not necessarily those needed to complete the set). The redemption cards could be exchanged through the mail or redeemed at a local card show.

		NM/M
Complete Set (28):		10.00
Common Player:		.35
1	Roger Craig	.35
2	Will Clark	.75
3	Kevin Mitchell	.35
4	Bob Brenly	.35
5	Mike Aldrete	.35
6	Mike Krukow	.35
7	Candy Maldonado	.35
8	Jeffrey Leonard	.35
9	Dave Dravecky	.35
10	Robby Thompson	.35
11	Scott Garrelts	.35
12	Bob Melvin	.35
13	Jose Uribe	.35
14	Brett Butler	.35
15	Rick Reuschel	.35
16	Harry Spilman	.35
17	Kelly Downs	.35
18	Chris Speier	.35
19	Atlee Hammaker	.35
20	Joel Youngblood	.35
21	Mike LaCoss	.35
22	Don Robinson	.35
23	Mark Wasinger	.35
24	Craig Lefferts	.35
25	Phil Garner	.35
26	Joe Price	.35
27	Coaches (Dusty Baker, Bill Fahey, Bob Lillis, Gordie MacKenzie, Jose Morales, Norm Sherry)	.35
28	Logo Card/Checklist	.35

Mariners

Similar in design to other Mother's Cookies sets, the 28-card Mariners issue features full-color, borderless photos on a 2-1/2" x 3-1/2" card with rounded corners. Backs, printed in red and purple, include brief biographical information, the Mother's Cookies logo and card number. Twenty-card starter packs were distributed at a stadium promotion, where fans also received a coupon card that could be exchanged for an additional eight cards (not necessarily those needed to complete the set). The coupon card could be redeemed through the mail or exchanged at a local baseball card show. As with the rest of the 1988 Mother's Cookies sets, an album was also available to house the cards.

		NM/M
Complete Set (28):		6.00
Common Player:		.35
1	Dick Williams	.35
2	Alvin Davis	.35
3	Mike Moore	.35
4	Jim Presley	.35
5	Mark Langston	.35
6	Henry Cotto	.35
7	Ken Phelps	.35
8	Steve Trout	.35
9	David Valle	.35
10	Harold Reynolds	.50
11	Edwin Nunez	.35
12	Glenn Wilson	.35
13	Scott Bankhead	.35
14	Scott Bradley	.35
15	Mickey Brantley	.35
16	Bruce Fields	.35
17	Mike Kingery	.35
18	Mike Campbell	.35
19	Mike Jackson	.35
20	Rey Quinones	.35
21	Mario Diaz	.35
22	Jerry Reed	.35
23	Rich Renteria	.35
24	Julio Solano	.35
25	Bill Swift	.35
26	Bill Wilkinson	.35
27	Coaches (Billy Connors, Frank Howard, Phil Roof, Jim Snyder, Ozzie Virgil)	.35
28	Trainers/Checklist (Henry Genzale, Rick Griffin)	.35

Rangers

This 28-card issue was one of six team sets issued in 1988 by Mother's Cookies. The Rangers issue features full-color, borderless cards printed in standard 2-1/2" x 3-1/2" format with rounded corners. Backs are printed in red and purple and include player information, Mother's Cookies logo and card number. Twenty-card starter packs were distributed as a stadium promotion that included a redemption card good for another eight cards (not necessarily those needed to complete the set) either through the mail or at a local card show.

		NM/M
Complete Set (28):		7.00
Common Player:		.35
1	Bobby Valentine	.35
2	Pete Incaviglia	.35
3	Charlie Hough	.35
4	Oddibe McDowell	.35
5	Larry Parrish	.35
6	Scott Fletcher	.35
7	Steve Buechele	.35
8	Steve Kemp	.35
9	Pete O'Brien	.35
10	Ruben Sierra	.35
11	Mike Stanley	.35
12	Jose Cecena	.35
13	Cecil Espy	.35
14	Curtis Wilkerson	.35
15	Dale Mohorcic	.35
16	Ray Hayward	.35
17	Mitch Williams	.35
18	Bob Brower	.35
19	Paul Kilgus	.35
20	Geno Petralli	.35
21	James Steels	.35
22	Jerry Browne	.35
23	Jose Guzman	.35
24	DeWayne Vaughn	.35
25	Bobby Witt	.35
26	Jeff Russell	.35
27	Coaches (Richard Egan, Tom House, Art Howe, Davey Lopes, David Oliver, Tom Robson)	.35
28	Trainers/Checklist (Danny Wheat, Bill Zeigler)	.35

Will Clark

In a baseball spring training-related promotion, Mother's Cookies of Oakland, Calif. produced a full-color four-card set featuring San Francisco Giants first baseman Will Clark. The cards, which have glossy finishes and rounded corners, came cellophane-wrapped in specially marked 18-ounce packages of Mother's Cookies products. The cards are identical in style to the other Mother's Cookies issues.

		NM/M
Complete Set (4):		4.00
4-Card Uncut Panel:		4.00
Common Card:		1.00
1	Will Clark (Bat on shoulder.)	1.00
2	Will Clark/Kneeling	1.00
3	Will Clark (Batting follow-through.)	1.00
4	Will Clark (Heading for first base.)	1.00

Mark McGwire

For the second consecutive year, Mother's Cookies devoted a four-card set to Oakland A's slugger Mark McGwire. The full-color cards have rounded corners and measure 2-1/2" x 3-1/2". The cards were issued in specially marked 18-ounce packages of Mother's Cookies products in the northern California area. The cards are identical in design to the team issues produced by Mother's.

		NM/M
Complete Set (4):		7.00
4-Card Uncut Panel:		9.00
Common Card:		2.00
1	Mark McGwire (Holding oversized bat.)	2.00
2	Mark McGwire/Fldg	2.00
3	Mark McGwire/ Kneeling	2.00
4	Mark McGwire (Bat in air.)	2.00

1989 Mother's Cookies A's

The 1989 Mother's Cookies A's set consists of 28 cards designed in the traditional style: a glossy 2-1/2" x 3-1/2" card with a borderless photo and rounded corners. A starter set of the cards was used as a stadium promotion and distributed to fans attending the July 30 Oakland game.

		NM/M
Complete Set (28):		13.50
Common Player:		.35
1	Tony LaRussa	.35
2	Mark McGwire	5.00
3	Terry Steinbach	.35
4	Dave Parker	.35
5	Carney Lansford	.35
6	Dave Stewart	.35
7	Jose Canseco	1.00
8	Walt Weiss	.35
9	Bob Welch	.35
10	Dennis Eckersley	1.25
11	Tony Phillips	.35
12	Mike Moore	.35
13	Dave Henderson	.35
14	Curt Young	.35
15	Ron Hassey	.35
16	Eric Plunk	.35
17	Luis Polonia	.35
18	Storm Davis	.35
19	Glenn Hubbard	.35
20	Greg Cadaret	.35

21 Stan Javier .35
22 Felix Jose .35
23 Mike Gallego .35
24 Todd Burns .35
25 Rick Honeycutt .35
26 Gene Nelson .35
27 A's Coaches (Dave Duncan, Rene Lacheman, Art Kusnyer, Tommie Reynolds, Merv Rettenmund) .35
28 Walt Weiss, Mark McGwire, Jose Canseco 2.50

Astros

The 1989 Astros team set issued by Mother's Cookies consists of 28 cards in 2-1/2" x 3-1/2" format in the traditional style of glossy borderless photos and rounded corners. Partial sets were distributed to fans attending the July 22 game at the Astrodome. The cards feature the photography of Barry Colla and display the Mother's Cookies logo on the back.

NM/M
Complete Set (28): 11.00
Common Player: .35
1 Art Howe .35
2 Mike Scott .35
3 Gerald Young .35
4 Bill Doran .35
5 Billy Hatcher .35
6 Terry Puhl .35
7 Bob Knepper .35
8 Kevin Bass .35
9 Glenn Davis .35
10 Alan Ashby .35
11 Bob Forsch .35
12 Greg Gross .35
13 Danny Darwin .35
14 Craig Biggio 3.00
15 Jim Clancy .35
16 Rafael Ramirez .35
17 Alex Trevino .35
18 Craig Reynolds .35
19 Dave Smith .35
20 Larry Andersen .35
21 Eric Yelding .35
22 Jim Deshaies .35
23 Juan Agosto .35
24 Rick Rhoden .35
25 Ken Caminiti 1.00
26 Dave Meads .35
27 Astros Coaches (Yogi Berra, Matt Galante, Phil Garner, Les Moss, Ed Napoleon, Ed Ott) .35
28 Trainers/Checklist (Dave Labossiere, Doc Ewell, Dennis Liborio) .35

Dodgers

This 28-card set features the players and coaches of the L.A. Dodgers. The cards follow the traditional Mother's Cookies style featuring rounded corners, borderless color photos, horizontal backs and 2-1/2" x 3-1/2" size. Initially 20 cards were given away as starter sets at Dodger Stadium.

NM/M
Complete Set (28): 9.00
Common Player: .35
1 Tom Lasorda .40
2 Eddie Murray 2.00
3 Mike Scioscia .35
4 Fernando Valenzuela .35
5 Mike Marshall .35
6 Orel Hershiser .50
7 Alfredo Griffin .35
8 Kirk Gibson .35
9 John Tudor .35
10 Willie Randolph .35
11 Franklin Stubbs .35
12 Mike Davis .35
13 Mike Morgan .35
14 John Shelby .35
15 Rick Dempsey .35
16 Jay Howell .35
17 Dave Anderson .35
18 Alejandro Pena .35
19 Jeff Hamilton .35
20 Ricky Horton .35
21 Tim Leary .35
22 Ray Searage .35
23 Tim Belcher .35
24 Tim Crews .35
25 Mickey Hatcher .35
26 Mariano Duncan .35
27 Coaches (Joe Amalfitano, Mark Cresse, Joe Ferguson, Ben Hines, Manny Mota, Ron Perranoski, Bill Russell) .35
28 Checklist .35

Giants

The 1989 Mother's Cookies Giants set consists of 28 cards, all featuring borderless, color photos with rounded corners. Starter sets of the cards were distributed as a stadium promotion to fans attending the August 6 game at Candlestick Park.

NM/M
Complete Set (28): 9.00
Common Player: .35
1 Roger Craig .35
2 Will Clark 1.00
3 Kevin Mitchell .35
4 Kelly Downs .35
5 Brett Butler .35
6 Mike Krukow .35
7 Candy Maldonado .35
8 Terry Kennedy .35
9 Dave Dravecky .35
10 Robby Thompson .35
11 Scott Garrelts .35
12 Matt Williams 1.00
13 Jose Uribe .35
14 Tracy Jones .35
15 Rick Reuschel .35
16 Ernest Riles .35
17 Jeff Brantley .35
18 Chris Speier .35
19 Atlee Hammaker .35
20 Ed Jurak .35
21 Mike LaCoss .35
22 Don Robinson .35
23 Kirt Manwaring .35
24 Craig Lefferts .35
25 Donnell Nixon .35
26 Joe Price .35
27 Rich Gossage .75
28 Coaches/Checklist (Bill Fahey, Dusty Baker, Bob Lillis, Wendell Kim, Norm Sherry) .35

Mariners

For the sixth straight season, Mother's Cookies released a Mariners team set. The 1989 issue features 28 cards. Starter sets of 20 cards were distributed at a Mariners home game. The cards are 2-1/2" x 3-1/2" and feature borderless, glossy full color photos. Card backs are horizontal. Rookie sensation Ken Griffey Jr. was included in the 1989 issue.

NM/M
Complete Set (28): 12.50
Common Player: .35
1 Jim Lefebvre .35
2 Alvin Davis .35
3 Ken Griffey Jr. 9.00
4 Jim Presley .35
5 Mark Langston .35
6 Henry Cotto .35
7 Mickey Brantley .35
8 Jeffrey Leonard .35
9 Dave Valle .35
10 Harold Reynolds .50
11 Edgar Martinez 3.00
12 Tom Niedenfuer .35
13 Scott Bankhead .35
14 Scott Bradley .35
15 Omar Vizquel .35
16 Erik Hanson .35
17 Bill Swift .35
18 Mike Campbell .35
19 Mike Jackson .35
20 Rich Renteria .35
21 Mario Diaz .35
22 Jerry Reed .35
23 Darnell Coles .35
24 Steve Trout .35
25 Mike Schooler .35
26 Julio Solano .35
27 Coaches (Gene Clines, Bob Didier, Rusty Kuntz, Mike Paul, Bill Plummer) .35
28 Checklist/Trainers (Henry Genzale, Rick Griffin) .35

Rangers

The 1989 Mother's Cookies Rangers team set features the traditional glossy borderless photos and rounded corners. The 2-1/2" x 3-1/2" set of 28 cards features the photography of Barry Colla. Partial sets were distributed to fans attending the July 30 game at Arlington Stadium.

NM/M
Complete Set (28): 8.00
Common Player: .35
1 Bobby Valentine .35
2 Nolan Ryan 6.00
3 Julio Franco .35
4 Charlie Hough .35
5 Rafael Palmeiro 4.00
6 Jeff Russell .35
7 Ruben Sierra .35
8 Steve Buechele .35
9 Buddy Bell .35
10 Pete Incaviglia .35
11 Geno Petralli .35
12 Cecil Espy .35
13 Scott Fletcher .35
14 Bobby Witt .35
15 Brad Arnsberg .35
16 Rick Leach .35
17 Jamie Moyer .35
18 Kevin Brown .35
19 Jeff Kunkel .35
20 Craig McMurtry .35
21 Kenny Rogers .35
22 Mike Stanley .35
23 Cecilio Guante .35
24 Jim Sundberg .35
25 Jose Guzman .35
26 Jeff Stone .35
27 Coaches (Dick Egan, Tom Robson, Toby Harrah, Dave Oliver, Tom House, Davey Lopes) .35
28 Trainers/Checklist (Bill Ziegler, Danny Wheat) .35

Jose Canseco

This special insert glossy set features Canseco in two posed (one standing, one kneeling) and two action (one batting, one running) shots. Full-color card fronts have rounded corners. Flip sides are numbered, printed in red and purple, and carry 1988 stats and career notes. Cards are individually cello-wrapped and inserted in Mother's Fudge 'N Chips, Oatmeal Raisin and Cocadas cookie bags.

NM/M
Complete Set (4): 5.00
Four Card Uncut Panel: 6.00
Common Card: 1.50
1 Jose Canseco (Ball in hand.) 1.50
2 Jose Canseco (On one knee grasping bat.) 1.50
3 Jose Canseco (Swinging-in action.) 1.50
4 Jose Canseco (Baserunning) 1.50

Will Clark

Will Clark is featured on a special-edition glossy set inserted in Mother's big bag chocolate chip cookies. The standard-size (2-1/2" x 3-1/2") cards feature Clark in two posed (batting and catching) and two action (batting and running) shots. Purple and red backs list 1986-88 stats.

NM/M
Complete Set (4): 4.00
Four Card Uncut Panel: 4.00
Common Card: 1.00
1 Will Clark (Displaying ball in glove.) 1.00
2 Will Clark (Batting stance.) 1.00
3 Will Clark (In action-after swing.) 1.00
4 Will Clark (Heading towards first.) 1.00

Ken Griffey, Jr.

This set featuring Ken Griffey, Jr. was issued by Mother's Cookies and was available only in cookie packages in Washington and Oregon. The cards were also available at a Seattle Mariners Kingdome baseball card show on August 20, where the set was introduced. The cards were then packed inside specially marked bags of cookies, one card per bag.

NM/M
Complete Set (4): 15.00
Four Card Uncut Panel: 20.00
Common Card: 5.00
1 Ken Griffey Jr. (Arms folded.) 5.00
2 Ken Griffey Jr. (Ball in hand.) 5.00
3 Ken Griffey Jr. (Bat over left shoulder.) 5.00
4 Ken Griffey Jr. (Back of jersey showing.) 5.00

Mark McGwire

This special edition features full-color glossy player photos by Barry Colla on standard-size (2-1/2" x 3-1/2") cards with rounded corners. Photos feature four different batting poses. Numbered flip sides, printed in purple and red, carry 1987-88 statistics. Cards are individually cello-wrapped and were inserted in Mother's Cookie Parade variety cookie bags.

NM/M
Complete Set (4): 6.00
Common Player: 1.50
1 Mark McGwire (Bat on shoulder.) 1.50
2 Mark McGwire (Batting stance.) 1.50
3 Mark McGwire (Bat in front.) 1.50
4 Mark McGwire (Batting follow through.) 1.50

Rookies of the Year

This four-card set features the American League Rookies of the Year for 1986, 1987 and 1988, all members of the Oakland A's. The 2-1/2" x 3-1/2" cards feature full color photos in the traditional Mother's Cookies format. One card was devoted to each player along with a special card showcasing all three players. The cards were distributed one per box in Mother's Cookies.

NM/M
Complete Set (4): 15.00
Four Card Uncut Panel: 15.00
Common Card: .75
1 Jose Canseco 2.25
2 Mark McGwire 7.50
3 Walt Weiss .75
4 Walt Weiss, Mark McGwire, Jose Canseco 5.50

1990 Mother's Cookies A's

This 28-card set features cards distributed at an A's home game. Cards measure 2-1/2" x 3-1/2" and feature rounded corners. Backs include biographical information and autograph space.

NM/M
Complete Set (28): 15.00
Common Player: .35
1 Tony LaRussa .35
2 Mark McGwire 4.00
3 Terry Steinbach .35
4 Rickey Henderson 2.00
5 Dave Stewart .35
6 Jose Canseco .75
7 Dennis Eckersley 1.00
8 Carney Lansford .35
9 Mike Moore .35
10 Walt Weiss .35
11 Scott Sanderson .35
12 Ron Hassey .35
13 Rick Honeycutt .35
14 Ken Phelps .35
15 Jamie Quirk .35
16 Bob Welch .35
17 Felix Jose .35
18 Dave Henderson .35
19 Mike Norris .35
20 Todd Burns .35
21 Lance Blankenship .35
22 Gene Nelson .35
23 Stan Javier .35
24 Curt Young .35
25 Mike Gallego .35
26 Joe Klink .35
27 Coaches (Dave Duncan, Art Kuysner, Rene Lacheman, Dave McKay, Merv Rettenmund, Tommie Reynolds) .35
28 Checklist/Trainers (Frank Ciensczyk, Larry Davis, Steve Vucinich, Barry Weinberg) .35

Astros

This 28-card set features cards styled like past Mother's Cookies releases. The cards were distributed in 20-card packs at an Astros home game. The cards were never distributed in complete set form.

NM/M
Complete Set (28): 10.00
Common Player: .35
1 Art Howe .35
2 Glenn Davis .35
3 Eric Anthony .35
4 Mike Scott .35
5 Craig Biggio 2.00
6 Ken Caminiti .50
7 Bill Doran .35
8 Gerald Young .35
9 Terry Puhl .35
10 Mark Portugal .35
11 Mark Davidson .35
12 Jim Deshaies .35
13 Bill Gullickson .35
14 Franklin Stubbs .35
15 Danny Darwin .35
16 Ken Oberkfell .35
17 Dave Smith .35
18 Dan Schatzeder .35
19 Rafael Ramirez .35
20 Larry Andersen .35
21 Alex Trevino .35
22 Glenn Wilson .35
23 Jim Clancy .35
24 Eric Yelding .35
25 Casey Candaele .35
26 Juan Agosto .35
27 Coaches (Bill Bowman, Bob Cluck, Phil Garner, Matt Galante, Rudy Jaramillo, Ed Napoleon) .35
28 Checklist/Trainers (Doc Ewell, Dave Labossiere, Dennis Liborio) .35

Dodgers

Distributed as a promotional item, these cards are styled like past Mother's Cookies releases. Fans 14 and under received a 20-card pack at a Dodgers home game. Cards were also available at a Labor Day card show in Anaheim. The cards were not distributed in complete set form.

NM/M
Complete Set (28): 10.00
Common Player: .35
1 Tom Lasorda .45
2 Fernando Valenzuela .35
3 Kal Daniels .35
4 Mike Scioscia .35
5 Eddie Murray 3.00
6 Mickey Hatcher .35
7 Juan Samuel .35
8 Alfredo Griffin .35
9 Tim Belcher .35
10 Hubie Brooks .35
11 Jose Gonzalez .35
12 Orel Hershiser .45
13 Kirk Gibson .35
14 Chris Gwynn .35
15 Jay Howell .35
16 Rick Dempsey .35
17 Ramon Martinez .50
18 Lenny Harris .35
19 John Wetteland .35
20 Mike Sharperson .35
21 Mike Morgan .35
22 Ray Searage .35
23 Jeff Hamilton .35
24 Jim Gott .35
25 John Shelby .35
26 Tim Crews .35
27 Don Aase .35

28	Coaches (Joe Amalfitano, Mark Cresse, Joe Ferguson, Ben Hines, Manny Mota, Ron Perranoski, Bill Russell)	.35

Giants

Like the other Mother's Cookies issues of 1990, Giants cards were distributed as a promotional item. Fans 14 and under were given a 20-card starter set at a Giants game. Cards could also be obtained at the Labor Day card show in San Francisco. The cards were not released in complete set form.

		NM/M
Complete Set (28):		10.00
Common Player:		.35
1	Roger Craig	.35
2	Will Clark	1.00
3	Gary Carter	3.00
4	Kelly Downs	.35
5	Kevin Mitchell	.35
6	Steve Bedrosian	.35
7	Brett Butler	.35
8	Rick Reuschel	.35
9	Matt Williams	1.00
10	Robby Thompson	.35
11	Mike LaCoss	.35
12	Terry Kennedy	.35
13	Atlee Hammaker	.35
14	Rick Leach	.35
15	Ernest Riles	.35
16	Scott Garrelts	.35
17	Jose Uribe	.35
18	Greg Litton	.35
19	Dave Anderson	.35
20	Don Robinson	.35
21	Coaches (Dusty Baker, Bill Fahey, Wendell Kim, Bob Lillis, Norm Sherry)	.35
22	Bill Bathe	.35
23	Randy O'Neal	.35
24	Kevin Bass	.35
25	Jeff Brantley	.35
26	John Burkett	.35
27	Ernie Camacho	.35
28	Checklist	.35

Mariners

This 28-card set features the traditional Mother's Cookies style with borderless full-color photos with rounded corners. Backs feature biographical information and autograph space. The cards were released as a promotion at a Mariners home game and at a Kingdome card show.

		NM/M
Complete Set (28):		17.50
Common Player:		.35
1	Jim Lefebvre	.35
2	Alvin Davis	.35
3	Ken Griffey Jr.	7.00
4	Jeffrey Leonard	.35
5	David Valle	.35
6	Harold Reynolds	.35
7	Jay Buhner	.75
8	Erik Hanson	.35
9	Henry Cotto	.35
10	Edgar Martinez	.35
11	Bill Swift	.35
12	Omar Vizquel	.75
13	Randy Johnson	5.00
14	Greg Briley	.35
15	Gene Harris	.35
16	Matt Young	.35
17	Pete O'Brien	.35
18	Brent Knackert	.35
19	Mike Jackson	.35
20	Brian Holman	.35
21	Mike Schooler	.35
22	Darnell Coles	.35
23	Keith Comstock	.35
24	Scott Bankhead	.35
25	Scott Bradley	.35
26	Mike Brumley	.35
27	Coaches (Gene Clines, Bob Didier, Rusty Kuntz, Mike Paul, Bill Plummer)	.35
28	Checklist/Trainers (Henry Genzale, Rick Griffin, Tom Newberg)	.35

Rangers

Putting together a complete set of these cards was not an easy task. The cards were distributed in 20-card packs at a Rangers home game and also could be obtained at a Dallas card convention. The cards were not released in complete set form. The cards feature the traditional Mother's Cookies style of glossy photos and rounded corners.

		NM/M
Complete Set (28):		12.50
Common Player:		.35
1	Bobby Valentine	.35
2	Nolan Ryan	6.00
3	Ruben Sierra	.35
4	Pete Incaviglia	.35
5	Charlie Hough	.35
6	Harold Baines	.35
7	Gino Petralli	.35
8	Jeff Russell	.35
9	Rafael Palmeiro	2.00
10	Julio Franco	.35
11	Jack Daugherty	.35
12	Gary Pettis	.35
13	Brian Bohanon	.35
14	Steve Buechele	.35
15	Bobby Witt	.35
16	Thad Bosley	.35
17	Gary Mielke	.35
18	Jeff Kunkel	.35
19	Mike Jeffcoat	.35
20	Mike Stanley	.35
21	Kevin Brown	.35
22	Kenny Rogers	.35
23	Jeff Huson	.35
24	Jamie Moyer	.35
25	Cecil Espy	.35
26	John Russell	.35
27	Coaches (Toby Harrah, Tom House, Davey Lopes, Dave Oliver, Tom Robson)	.35
28	Checklist/Trainers (Joe Macko, Marty Stajduhar, Danny Wheat, Bill Zeigler)	.35

Jose Canseco

This special insert glossy set features Canseco in four posed shots. Full-color card fronts have rounded corners. Flip sides are numbered, printed in red and purple and feature the Mother's Cookies logo. The cards are individually cello-wrapped and inserted one per Mother's Cookies bag.

		NM/M
Complete Set (4):		4.00
Four Card Uncut Panel:		5.00
Common Card:		1.50
1	Jose Canseco/Sitting (Bat on shoulder.)	1.50
2	Jose Canseco (Bat behind neck.)	1.50
3	Jose Canseco (Batting stance.)	1.50
4	Jose Canseco (On dugout step.)	1.50

Will Clark

1990 marks the third consecutive year that Mother's Cookies devoted a set to Giants slugger Will Clark. The set features four posed full-color shots. The cards follow the same design as all recent Mother's Cookies cards.

		NM/M
Complete Set (4):		4.00
Four Card Uncut Panel:		4.00
Common Card:		1.00
1	Will Clark (Bat on shoulder.)	1.00
2	Will Clark (Closeup in stance.)	1.00
3	Will Clark (Open in stance.)	1.00
4	Will Clark (Bat behind neck.)	1.00

Mark McGwire

1990 marks the fourth year that A's slugger Mark McGwire was featured on a special four-card Mother's Cookies set. The photos for the cards were once again by Barry Colla. Four different posed shots of McGwire are showcased.

		NM/M
Complete Set (4):		6.00
4-Card Uncut Panel:		7.50
Common Card:		2.00
1	Mark McGwire (Bat on shoulder.)	2.00
2	Mark McGwire (Leaning against bat rack.)	2.00
3	Mark McGwire (Glove in hand.)	2.00
4	Mark McGwire (On dugout step.)	2.00

Nolan Ryan

Unlike other special Mother's Cookies player sets, the Nolan Ryan cards feature "5000 K's" along with his name and team on the card fronts. The set honors the strikout king's monumental feat. The cards follow the classic Mother's Cookies style.

		NM/M
Complete Set (4):		4.00
Four Card Uncut Panel:		5.00
Common Card:		2.00
1	Nolan Ryan (Facing with ball in hand.)	2.00
2	Nolan Ryan (Standing in dugout.)	2.00
3	Nolan Ryan (Gripping ball behind back.)	2.00
4	Nolan Ryan (Sitting on dugout step.)	2.00

Matt Williams

Matt Williams made his Mother's Cookies single-player card set debut in 1990. Four posed shots of the Giants third baseman are showcased. Williams is featured twice in batting poses and twice as a fielder on the glossy, round-cornered 2-1/2" x 3-1/2" cards.

		NM/M
Complete Set (4):		2.50
Four Card Uncut Panel:		2.50
Common Card:		.75
1	Matt Williams (Bat on shoulder.)	.75
2	Matt Williams (In batting stance.)	.75
3	Matt Williams (Glove in hand.)	.75
4	Matt Williams/Fldg	.75

1991 Mother's Cookies A's

The incomparable photography of Barry Colla captures the Oakland A's in their home-field environs for the 28 cards in this set. Glossy fronts feature borderless posed photos. The player's name and team appear in white in an upper corner. Backs have minimal biographical data, player position, uniform and card numbers and appropriate logos.

		NM/M
Complete Set (28):		12.00
Common Player:		.25
1	Tony LaRussa	.25
2	Mark McGwire	3.50
3	Terry Steinbach	.25
4	Rickey Henderson	1.50
5	Dave Stewart	.25
6	Jose Canseco	.75
7	Dennis Eckersley	1.00
8	Carney Lansford	.25
9	Bob Welch	.25
10	Walt Weiss	.25
11	Mike Moore	.25
12	Vance Law	.25
13	Rick Honeycutt	.25
14	Harold Baines	.25
15	Jamie Quirk	.25
16	Ernest Riles	.25
17	Willie Wilson	.25
18	Dave Henderson	.25
19	Kirk Dressendorfer	.25
20	Todd Burns	.25
21	Lance Blankenship	.25
22	Gene Nelson	.25
23	Eric Show	.25
24	Curt Young	.25
25	Mike Gallego	.25
26	Joe Klink	.25
27	Steve Chitren	.25
28	Coaches/Checklist (Rene Lacheman, Dave Duncan, Dave McKay, Tommie Reynolds, Art Kuysner, Reggie Jackson, Rick Burleson)	.25

Astros

This 28-card set was produced in the now-familiar Mother's Cookies card format. Glossy fronts feature rounded corners and full-bleed posed color photos (apparently taken at San Francisco's Candlestick Park, home base of photographer Barry Colla) with the player's name and team in white in an upper corner. Backs are printed in red and purple and include a few biographical details, along with cookie company and MLB logos, uniform and card numbers and a line for autographing.

		NM/M
Complete Set (28):		10.00
Common Player:		.25
1	Art Howe	.25
2	Steve Finley	.25
3	Pete Harnisch	.25
4	Mike Scott	.25
5	Craig Biggio	.50
6	Ken Caminiti	.25
7	Eric Yelding	.25
8	Jeff Bagwell	6.00
9	Jim Deshaies	.25
10	Mark Portugal	.25
11	Mark Davidson	.25
12	Jimmy Jones	.25
13	Luis Gonzalez	2.00
14	Karl Rhodes	.25
15	Curt Schilling	.25
16	Ken Oberkfell	.25
17	Mark McLemore	.25
18	David Rohde	.25
19	Rafael Ramirez	.25
20	Al Osuna	.25
21	Jim Corsi	.25
22	Carl Nichols	.25
23	Jim Clancy	.25
24	Dwayne Henry	.25
25	Casey Candaele	.25
26	Xavier Hernandez	.25
27	Darryl Kile	.25
28	Coaches/Checklist (CluckGalante, Rudy Jaramillo, Phil Garner, Bob Cluck, Ed Ott)	.25

Dodgers

Dodger Stadium is the background for Barry Colla's portraits of the Los Angeles manager, coaches and players appearing in this 28-card set. Standard-size cards with rounded corners feature borderless UV-coated fronts on which the only printing is the player's name and team in white in an upper corner. Backs are in red and purple and include a few biographical details, position, uniform and card numbers, a space for an autograph and the logos of the cookie company and MLB.

		NM/M
Complete Set (28):		7.50
Common Player:		.25
1	Tom Lasorda	.40
2	Darryl Strawberry	.25
3	Kal Daniels	.25
4	Mike Scioscia	.25
5	Eddie Murray	2.00
6	Brett Butler	.25
7	Juan Samuel	.25
8	Alfredo Griffin	.25
9	Tim Belcher	.25
10	Ramon Martinez	.25
11	Jose Gonzalez	.25
12	Orel Hershiser	.40
13	Bob Ojeda	.25
14	Chris Gwynn	.25
15	Jay Howell	.25
16	Gary Carter	2.00
17	Kevin Gross	.25
18	Lenny Harris	.25
19	Mike Hartley	.25
20	Mike Sharperson	.25
21	Mike Morgan	.25
22	John Candelaria	.25
23	Jeff Hamilton	.25
24	Jim Gott	.25
25	Barry Lyons	.25
26	Tim Crews	.25
27	Stan Javier	.25
28	Coaches/Checklist (Ron Perranoski, Bill Russell, Manny Mota, Joe Ferguson, Ben Hines, Joe Amalfitano, Mark Cresse)	.25

Giants

For the ninth consecutive year Mother's Cookies sponsored a promotional card set for the Giants. As in the beginning, the cards highlight the work of photographer Barry Colla with posed portraits of the personnel in Candlestick Park. Fronts of the round-cornered borderless cards are UV-coated and have the player's name and team printed in white in an upper corner. Backs are in red and purple and include cookie company and Major League Baseball logos along with a few biographical details and both uniform and card numbers.

		NM/M
Complete Set (28):		7.00
Common Player:		.25
1	Roger Craig	.25
2	Will Clark	.50
3	Steve Decker	.25
4	Kelly Downs	.25
5	Kevin Mitchell	.25
6	Willie McGee	.25
7	Buddy Black	.25
8	Dave Righetti	.25
9	Matt Williams	.50
10	Robby Thompson	.25
11	Mike LaCoss	.25
12	Terry Kennedy	.25
13	Mark Leonard	.25
14	Rick Reuschel	.25
15	Mike Felder	.25
16	Scott Garrelts	.25
17	Jose Uribe	.25
18	Greg Litton	.25
19	Dave Anderson	.25
20	Don Robinson	.25
21	Mike Kingery	.25
22	Trevor Wilson	.25
23	Kirt Manwaring	.25
24	Kevin Bass	.25
25	Jeff Brantley	.25
26	John Burkett	.25
27	Coaches (Norm Sherry, Wendell Kim, Bob Lillis, Dusty Baker, Bill Fahey)	.25
28	Trainers/Checklist (Mark Letendre, Greg Lynn)	.25

Rangers

The unusual venue of the players' locker room provides the backdrop for photos for this 28-card set sponsored by Mother's Cookies. Besides a look at the player's wardrobe, the full-bleed glossy front photos feature the player's name and position vertically along the left side. Backs have uniform and card numbers, some biographical data and logos of the cookie company and Major League Baseball.

		NM/M
Complete Set (28):		12.50
Common Player:		.25
1	Bobby Valentine	.25
2	Nolan Ryan	6.00
3	Ruben Sierra	.25
4	Juan Gonzalez	3.00
5	Steve Buechele	.25
6	Bobby Witt	.25
7	Geno Petralli	.25
8	Jeff Russell	.25
9	Rafael Palmeiro	2.00
10	Julio Franco	.25
11	Jack Daugherty	.25
12	Gary Pettis	.25
13	John Barfield	.25
14	Scott Chiamparino	.25
15	Kevin Reimer	.25
16	Rich Gossage	.25
17	Brian Downing	.25
18	Denny Walling	.25
19	Mike Jeffcoat	.25
20	Mike Stanley	.25
21	Kevin Brown	.25
22	Kenny Rogers	.25
23	Jeff Huson	.25
24	Mario Diaz	.25
25	Brad Arnsberg	.25
26	John Russell	.25
27	Gerald Alexander	.25

28 Coaches/Checklist (Orlando Gomez, Toby Harrah, Tom House, Davey Lopes, Dave Oliver, Tom Robson) .25

Griffeys

This four-card set was packaged with Mother's Cookies sold in the Pacific Northwest. Each card features a borderless glossy posed photo on front. The traditional rounded corners of Mother's cards are found on the issue. Backs have a few stats and career notes.

		NM/M
Complete Set, Singles (4):		5.00
Complete Set, Uncut Strip:		5.00
Common Card:		1.00
1	Ken Griffey Jr.	3.00
2	Ken Griffey, Sr.	1.00
3	Ken Griffey Jr., Ken Griffey Sr. (Holding gloves.)	1.00
4	Ken Griffey Jr., Ken Griffey Sr. (Holding bats.)	1.50

Nolan Ryan 300 Wins

Mother's Cookies in 1991 created a four-card Nolan Ryan set honoring baseball's most recent 300-game winner. One card was included in specially marked packages of cookies. Card fronts have the traditional Mother's Cookies look: Barry Colla photography on full-bleed cards with rounded corners. Backs have a few statistics and career notes.

		NM/M
Complete Set (4):		2.00
Four Card Uncut Panel:		2.00
Common Card:		.75
1	Nolan Ryan/Standing (Front view.)	.75
2	Nolan Ryan/Kneeling	.75
3	Nolan Ryan/Standing (Side view.)	.75
4	Nolan Ryan (Gripping "300" ball.)	.75

1992 Mother's Cookies A's

The commemorative patch marking the Oakland A's 25th season on the West Coast is visible on several of Barry Colla's photos in this 28-card issue. The traditional Mother's Cookies card format of 2-1/2" x 3-1/2", round-cornered cards with UV-coated borderless front photos is followed in this set. The player's name and team are in white in an upper

corner. Backs have cookie company and Major League Baseball logos, along with the player's position, uniform and card numbers, space for an autograph and minimal biographical data. Back printing is in red and purple on white.

		NM/M
Complete Set (28):		7.50
Common Player:		.25
1	Tony LaRussa	.25
2	Mark McGwire	3.50
3	Terry Steinbach	.25
4	Rickey Henderson	1.50
5	Dave Stewart	.25
6	Jose Canseco	.75
7	Dennis Eckersley	1.00
8	Carney Lansford	.25
9	Bob Welch	.25
10	Walt Weiss	.25
11	Mike Moore	.25
12	Goose Gossage	.25
13	Rick Honeycutt	.25
14	Harold Baines	.25
15	Jamie Quirk	.25
16	Jeff Parrett	.25
17	Willie Wilson	.25
18	Dave Henderson	.25
19	Joe Slusarski	.25
20	Mike Bordick	.25
21	Lance Blankenship	.25
22	Gene Nelson	.25
23	Vince Horsman	.25
24	Ron Darling	.25
25	Randy Ready	.25
26	Scott Hemond	.25
27	Scott Brosius	.25
28	Coaches/Checklist (Tommie Reynolds, Dave Duncan, Doug Rader, Rene Lacheman, Art Kusnyer, Dave McKay)	.25

Astros

The Astrodome provides the backdrop for Barry Colla's photos of Astros personnel seen on this 28-card set sponsored by Mother's Cookies. Cards are in standard 2-1/2" x 3-1/2" and feature rounded corners. Glossy fronts are borderless and have no graphics except the player's name and team in an upper corner. Backs are printed in red and purple and have a few biographical details along with uniform and card numbers, the player's position, an autograph line and the logos of the cookie company and MLB.

		NM/M
Complete Set (28):		7.50
Common Player:		.25
1	Art Howe	.25
2	Steve Finley	.25
3	Pete Harnisch	.25
4	Pete Incaviglia	.25
5	Craig Biggio	.50
6	Ken Caminiti	.25
7	Eric Anthony	.25
8	Jeff Bagwell	4.00
9	Andujar Cedeno	.25
10	Mark Portugal	.25
11	Eddie Taubensee	.25
12	Jimmy Jones	.25
13	Joe Boever	.25
14	Benny Distefano	.25
15	Juan Guerrero	.25
16	Doug Jones	.25
17	Scott Servais	.25
18	Butch Henry	.25
19	Rafael Ramirez	.25
20	Al Osuna	.25
21	Rob Murphy	.25
22	Chris Jones	.25
23	Rob Mallicoat	.25
24	Darryl Kile	.25
25	Casey Candaele	.25
26	Xavier Hernandez	.25
27	Coaches (Bob Cluck, Matt Galante, Rudy Jaramillo, Ed Ott, Tom Spencer)	.25
28	Trainers / Checklist (Doc Ewell, Dennis Liborio, Dave Labossiere)	.25

Dodgers

A commemorative patch marking Dodger Stadium's 30th anniversary is featured on some of the Barry Colla photos seen on this 28-card set. Cards have the now-traditional round-corner, glossy-front borderless format with player name and team in white in an upper corner. Printed in red and purple, the backs have a few biographical details along with uniform and card numbers and appropriate logos.

		NM/M
Complete Set (28):		6.00
Common Player:		.25
1	Tom Lasorda	.35
2	Brett Butler	.25
3	Tom Candiotti	.25
4	Eric Davis	.25
5	Lenny Harris	.25
6	Orel Hershiser	.35
7	Ramon Martinez	.25
8	Jose Offerman	.25
9	Mike Scioscia	.25
10	Darryl Strawberry	.25
11	Todd Benzinger	.25
12	John Candelaria	.25
13	Tim Crews	.25
14	Kal Daniels	.25
15	Jim Gott	.25
16	Kevin Gross	.25
17	Dave Hansen	.25
18	Carlos Hernandez	.25
19	Jay Howell	.25
20	Stan Javier	.25
21	Eric Karros	.50
22	Roger McDowell	.25
23	Bob Ojeda	.25
24	Juan Samuel	.25
25	Mike Sharperson	.25
26	Mitch Webster	.25
27	Steve Wilson	.25
28	Coaches/Checklist (Joe Amalfitano, Mark Cresse, Joe Ferguson, Ben Hines, Manny Mota, Ron Perranoski, Ron Roenicke)	.25

Giants

In 1983 Mother's Cookies re-entered the baseball card world with a set of S.F. Giants cards. In 1992, the company sponsored its 10th consecutive Giants team issue. As in the '83 set, the cards feature the photography of Barry Colla. In 2-1/2" x 3-1/2" size with

rounded corners and UV-coating on the borderless fronts, the cards continue the format used since 1984. Backs are also in the familiar style, with a bit of biographical data and appropriate logos.

		NM/M
Complete Set (28):		7.50
Common Player:		.25
1	Roger Craig	.25
2	Will Clark	.50
3	Bill Swift	.25
4	Royce Clayton	.25
5	John Burkett	.25
6	Willie McGee	.25
7	Buddy Black	.25
8	Dave Righetti	.25
9	Matt Williams	.50
10	Robby Thompson	.25
11	Darren Lewis	.25
12	Mike Jackson	.25
13	Mark Leonard	.25
14	Rod Beck	.25
15	Mike Felder	.25
16	Bryan Hickerson	.25
17	Jose Uribe	.25
18	Greg Litton	.25
19	Cory Snyder	.25
20	Jim McNamara	.25
21	Kelly Downs	.25
22	Trevor Wilson	.25
23	Kirt Manwaring	.25
24	Kevin Bass	.25
25	Jeff Brantley	.25
26	Dave Burba	.25
27	Chris James	.25
28	Coaches/Checklist (Carlos Alfonso, Dusty Baker, Bob Brenly, Wendell Kim, Bob Lillis)	.25

Mariners

After a one-year absence from the Mother's Cookies lineup, the M's returned in 1992 with a set. Standard-size cards have rounded corners and UV-coated fronts. The only graphics appearing on the borderless photos are the player and team name in white in an upper corner. Backs are printed in red and purple and have basic biographical data, uniform and card numbers, space for an autograph and appropriate sponsor and licensor logos.

		NM/M
Complete Set (28):		12.50
Common Player:		.25
1	Bill Plummer	.25
2	Ken Griffey Jr.	4.00
3	Harold Reynolds	.25
4	Kevin Mitchell	.25
5	David Valle	.25
6	Jay Buhner	.40
7	Erik Hanson	.25
8	Pete O'Brien	.25
9	Henry Cotto	.25
10	Mike Schooler	.25
11	Tino Martinez	1.00
12	Dennis Powell	.25
13	Randy Johnson	2.00
14	Dave Cochrane	.25
15	Greg Briley	.25
16	Omar Vizquel	.40
17	Dave Fleming	.25
18	Matt Sinatro	.25
19	Jeff Nelson	.25
20	Edgar Martinez	.25
21	Calvin Jones	.25
22	Russ Swan	.25
23	Jim Acker	.25
24	Jeff Schaffer	.25
25	Clay Parker	.25
26	Brian Holman	.25
27	Coaches (Marty Martinez, Gene Clines, Roger Hansen, Dan Warthen, Russ Nixon, Rusty Kuntz)	.25
28	Mascot/Checklist	.25

Padres

The Padres ended a six-year hiatus when they re-appeared in the Mother's Cookies lineup for 1992. The 28-card set follows the traditional Mother's format: 2-1/2" x 3-1/2" cards with rounded corners, glossy borderless front photos and the player and team name in white in an upper corner. Backs have appropriate logos, uniform and card numbers, player data and room for an autograph, all printed in red and purple.

		NM/M
Complete Set (28):		10.00
Common Player:		.25
1	Greg Riddoch	.25
2	Greg Harris	.25
3	Gary Sheffield	1.00
4	Fred McGriff	.40
5	Kurt Stillwell	.25
6	Benito Santiago	.25
7	Tony Gwynn	4.00
8	Tony Fernandez	.25
9	Jerald Clark	.25
10	Dave Eiland	.25
11	Randy Myers	.25
12	Oscar Azocar	.25
13	Dann Bilardello	.25
14	Jose Melendez	.25
15	Darrin Jackson	.25
16	Andy Benes	.25
17	Tim Teufel	.25
18	Jeremy Hernandez	.25
19	Kevin Ward	.25
20	Bruce Hurst	.25
21	Larry Andersen	.25
22	Rich Rodriguez	.25
23	Pat Clements	.25
24	Craig Lefferts	.25
25	Craig Shipley	.25
26	Mike Maddux	.25
27	Coaches (Bruce Kimm, Rob Picciolo, Merv Rettenmund, Mike Roarke, Jim Snyder)	.25
28	Team Logo/Checklist	.25

Rangers

The clubhouse wall provides the universal backdrop for the posed photos in this 28-card set. Standard-size cards have a high-gloss borderless front photo with rounded corners and the player and team name in white in an upper corner. Backs are in red and purple and have a few player biographical details along with uniform and card numbers, space for an autograph and the logos of the sponsor and licensor.

		NM/M
Complete Set (28):		15.00
Common Player:		.25
1	Bobby Valentine	.25
2	Nolan Ryan	5.00
3	Ruben Sierra	.25
4	Juan Gonzalez	2.00
5	Ivan Rodriguez	4.00
6	Bobby Witt	.25
7	Geno Petralli	.25
8	Jeff Russell	.25
9	Rafael Palmeiro	1.50
10	Julio Franco	.25
11	Jack Daugherty	.25
12	Dickie Thon	.25
13	Floyd Bannister	.25
14	Scott Chiamparino	.25
15	Kevin Reimer	.25
16	Jeff Robinson	.25
17	Brian Downing	.25
18	Brian Bohanon	.25
19	Jose Guzman	.25
20	Terry Mathews	.25
21	Kevin Brown	.25
22	Kenny Rogers	.25
23	Jeff Huson	.25
24	Monty Fariss	.25
25	Al Newman	.25
26	Dean Palmer	.25
27	John Cangelosi	.25
20	Coaches/Checklist (Ray Burris, Orlando Gomez, Toby Harrah, Tom House, Dave Oliver, Tom Robson)	.25

Jeff Bagwell

The set consists of four standard-size cards with a full-bleed color photo on the fronts of the cards and rounded corners. Bagwell's name appears horizontally in white on the front of the card and the backs are printed in purple and red. Along with the Major League merchandise logo on the bottom of the card there is an area for the player's autograph.

		NM/M
Complete Set (4):		9.00
4-Card Uncut Panel:		10.00
Common Card:		2.50
1	Jeff Bagwell (Head and shoulders.)	2.50
2	Jeff Bagwell (Bat on shoulder.)	2.50
3	Jeff Bagwell (Waist-up.)	2.50
4	Jeff Bagwell (Ball in glove.)	2.50

Chuck Knoblauch

American League 1991 Rookie of the Year Chuck Knoblauch is featured in this four-card set. Similar in format to other Mother's cards, the glossy fronts have rounded corners and feature full-bleed color photos. The red and pur-

ple backs have statistical and biographical data along with appropriate logos.

		NM/M
Complete Set (4):		4.00
Common Card:		1.00
1	Chuck Knoblauch (Bat on shoulder.)	1.00
2	Chuck Knoblauch (Head and shoulders.)	1.00
3	Chuck Knoblauch (Waist-up.)	1.00
4	Chuck Knoblauch/Fldg	1.00

Nolan Ryan 7 No-Hitters

Mother's Cookie Co. produced an eight-card set in 1992 commemorating Nolan Ryan's seven no-hitters. Cards were found in specially marked packages of Mother's Cookies. The company also made available uncut sheets of the eight cards through the mail. Fronts feature photos contemporary with Ryan's no-hitters in a borderless, round-cornered format with glossy surface. "Nolan Ryan/7 No-Hitters" appears in white vertically in the upper-left corner. Backs are printed in red and purple and include a bit of biographical data along with details of each no-hitter. The eighth card in the set offers room to write in information about a future no-hitter which never materialized prior to Ryan's retirement following the 1993 season.

		NM/M
Complete Set (8):		6.00
8-Card Uncut Panel:		6.00
Common Card:		1.00
1	Nolan Ryan/ Potrait/Angels	1.00
2	Nolan Ryan/ Pitching/Angels	1.00
3	Nolan Ryan/ Waving/Angels	1.00
4	Nolan Ryan/Angels (Holding four "0" balls.)	1.00
5	Nolan Ryan/Astros	1.00
6	Nolan Ryan/ Pitching/Rangers	1.00
7	Nolan Ryan/ Pointing/Rangers	1.00
8	Nolan Ryan/Rangers (Palms up.)	1.00

1993 Mother's Cookies Angels

In its 11th year of renewed baseball card production, Mother's Cookies sponsored trading card promotions with

seven major league teams including, for the first time, the California Angels. At special promotional games, youngsters entering the ballpark were given packs of 28 cards. Each of the paper envelopes contained 20 different player cards and eight cards of another player. Instructions on the envelope encouraged trading to complete a set of 28. All of the team sets were identical in format. Cards measure the standard 2-1/2" x 3-1/2" with rounded corners. Fronts feature borderless posed photos, the work of photographer Barry Colla. The only graphic elements on the front are the player's name and team in white, generally in an upper corner. In 1993 the Mother's cards featured a somewhat less glossy front finish than in previous years. Backs are printed in red and purple. Data includes the player's position, uniform and card numbers, a few biographical bits, a "How Obtained" statement and a space for an autograph, along with the logos of the cookie company and Major League Baseball.

		NM/M
Complete Set (28):		9.00
Common Player:		.25
1	Buck Rodgers	.25
2	Gary DiSarcina	.25
3	Chuck Finley	.25
4	J.T. Snow	.50
5	Gary Gaetti	.25
6	Chili Davis	.25
7	Tim Salmon	2.50
8	Mark Langston	.25
9	Scott Sanderson	.25
10	John Orton	.25
11	Julio Valera	.25
12	Chad Curtis	.25
13	Kelly Gruber	.25
14	Rene Gonzalez	.25
15	Luis Polonia	.25
16	Greg Myers	.25
17	Gene Nelson	.25
18	Torey Lovullo	.25
19	Scott Lewis	.25
20	Chuck Crim	.25
21	John Farrell	.25
22	Steve Frey	.25
23	Stan Javier	.25
24	Ken Patterson	.25
25	Ron Tingley	.25
26	Damion Easley	.25
27	Joe Grahe	.25
28	Coaches/Checklist (Jimmie Reese, Rod Carew, Bobby Knoop, Chuck Hernandez, Ken Macha, John Wathan, Rick Turner)	.25

A's

		NM/M
Complete Set (28):		6.00
Common Player:		.25
1	Tony LaRussa	.25
2	Mark McGwire	2.00
3	Terry Steinbach	.25
4	Dennis Eckersley	.75
5	Ruben Sierra	.25
6	Rickey Henderson	1.00
7	Mike Bordick	.25
8	Rick Honeycutt	.25
9	Dave Henderson	.25
10	Bob Welch	.25
11	Dale Sveum	.25
12	Ron Darling	.25
13	Jerry Browne	.25
14	Bobby Witt	.25
15	Troy Neel	.25
16	Goose Gossage	.25
17	Brent Gates	.25
18	Storm Davis	.25
19	Scott Hemond	.25
20	Kelly Downs	.25
21	Kevin Seitzer	.25
22	Lance Blankenship	.25
23	Mike Mohler	.25
24	Edwin Nunez	.25
25	Joe Boever	.25
26	Shawn Hillegas	.25
27	Coaches (Dave Duncan, Art Kusnyer, Greg Luzinski, Dave McKay, Tommie Reynolds)	.25
28	Checklist (Frank Ciensczyk (equipment manager))	.25

Astros

		NM/M
Complete Set (28):		9.00
Common Player:		.25
1	Art Howe	.25
2	Steve Finley	.25
3	Pete Harnisch	.25
4	Craig Biggio	.50
5	Doug Drabek	.25
6	Scott Servais	.25
7	Jeff Bagwell	2.50
8	Eric Anthony	.25
9	Ken Caminiti	.25
10	Andujar Cedeno	.25
11	Mark Portugal	.25
12	Jose Uribe	.25
13	Rick Parker	.25
14	Doug Jones	.25
15	Luis Gonzalez	.50
16	Kevin Bass	.25
17	Greg Swindell	.25
18	Eddie Taubensee	.25
19	Darryl Kile	.25
20	Brian Williams	.25
21	Chris James	.25
22	Chris Donnels	.25
23	Xavier Hernandez	.25
24	Casey Candaele	.25
25	Eric Bell	.25
26	Mark Grant	.25
27	Tom Edens	.25
28	Coaches/Checklist (Bill Bowman, Bob Cluck, Matt Galante, Rudy Jaramillo, Ed Ott, Tom Spencer)	.25

Dodgers

		NM/M
Complete Set (28):		20.00
Common Player:		.25
1	Tommy Lasorda	.35
2	Eric Karros	.25
3	Brett Butler	.25
4	Mike Piazza	9.00
5	Jose Offerman	.25
6	Tim Wallach	.25
7	Eric Davis	.25
8	Darryl Strawberry	.25
9	Jody Reed	.25
10	Orel Hershiser	.35
11	Tom Candiotti	.25
12	Ramon Martinez	.25
13	Lenny Harris	.25
14	Mike Sharperson	.25
15	Omar Daal	.25
16	Pedro Martinez	6.00
17	Jim Gott	.25
18	Carlos Hernandez	.25
19	Kevin Gross	.25
20	Cory Snyder	.25
21	Todd Worrell	.25
22	Mitch Webster	.25
23	Steve Wilson	.25
24	Dave Hansen	.25
25	Roger McDowell	.25
26	Pedro Astacio	.25
27	Rick Trlicek	.25
28	Coaches/Checklist (Joe Amalfitano, Mark Cresse, Joe Ferguson, Ben Hines, Manny Mota, Ron Perranoski, Ron Roenicke)	.25

Giants

		NM/M
Complete Set (28):		8.00
Common Player:		.25
1	Dusty Baker	.40
2	Will Clark	.50
3	Matt Williams	.50
4	Barry Bonds	7.50
5	Bill Swift	.25
6	Royce Clayton	.25
7	John Burkett	.25
8	Willie McGee	.25
9	Kirt Manwaring	.25
10	Dave Righetti	.25
11	Todd Benzinger	.25
12	Rod Beck	.25
13	Darren Lewis	.25
14	Robby Thompson	.25
15	Mark Carreon	.25
16	Dave Martinez	.25
17	Jeff Brantley	.25
18	Dave Burba	.25
19	Mike Benjamin	.25
20	Mike Jackson	.25
21	Craig Colbert	.25
22	Bud Black	.25
23	Trevor Wilson	.25
24	Kevin Rogers	.25
25	Jeff Reed	.25
26	Bryan Hickerson	.25
27	Gino Minutelli	.25
28	Coaches / Checklist (Bobby Bonds, Bob Brenly, Wendell Kim, Bob Lillis, Dick Pole, Denny Sommers)	.25

Mariners

		NM/M
Complete Set (28):		10.00
Common Player:		.25
1	Lou Piniella	.25
2	Dave Fleming	.25
3	Pete O'Brien	.25
4	Ken Griffey Jr.	6.00
5	Henry Cotto	.25
6	Jay Buhner	.25
7	David Valle	.25
8	Dwayne Henry	.25
9	Mike Felder	.25
10	Norm Charlton	.25
11	Edgar Martinez	.25
12	Erik Hanson	.25
13	Mike Blowers	.25
14	Omar Vizquel	.25
15	Randy Johnson	2.00
16	Russ Swan	.25
17	Tino Martinez	.25
18	Rich DeLucia	.25
19	Jeff Nelson	.25
20	Chris Bosio	.25
21	Tim Leary	.25
22	Mackey Sasser	.25
23	Dennis Powell	.25
24	Mike Hampton	.25
25	Fernando Vina	.25
26	John Cummings	.25
27	Rich Amaral	.25
28	Coaches/Checklist (Sammy Ellis, John McLaren, Ken Griffey Sr., Sam Perlozzo, Sam Mejias, Lee Elia)	.25

Padres

		NM/M
Complete Set (28):		10.00
Common Player:		.25
1	Jim Riggleman	.25
2	Gary Sheffield	1.00
3	Tony Gwynn	6.00
4	Fred McGriff	.25
5	Greg Harris	.25
6	Tim Teufel	.25
7	Dave Eiland	.25
8	Phil Plantier	.25
9	Bruce Hurst	.25
10	Ricky Gutierrez	.25
11	Rich Rodriguez	.25
12	Derek Bell	.25
13	Bob Geren	.25
14	Andy Benes	.25
15	Darrell Sherman	.25
16	Frank Seminara	.25
17	Guillermo Velasquez	.25
18	Gene Harris	.25
19	Dan Walters	.25
20	Craig Shipley	.25
21	Phil Clark	.25
22	Jeff Gardner	.25
23	Mike Scioscia	.25
24	Wally Whitehurst	.25
25	Roger Mason	.25
26	Kerry Taylor	.25
27	Tim Scott	.25
28	Coaches/Checklist (Dave Bialas, Bruce Bochy, Rob Picciolo, Dan Radison, Merv Rettenmund, Mike Roarke)	.25

Nolan Ryan Farewell

Nolan Ryan's final 10 major league seasons with the Astros and Rangers are captured in this set. Cards are in standard Mother's Cookies format: 2-1/2" x 3-1/2" with rounded corners, borderless front photos and UV-coated. Each card has a "Nolan Ryan Farewell Set" diamond logo in an upper corner. Backs are printed in red and purple and have a few biographical details along with the year the picture on front was created. Each card has stats for one year from 1984-1992 or cumulative All-Star stats along with Major League totals. Cards were available either cello-wrapped singly in cookie packages or as a complete set via a mail-in offer.

		NM/M
Complete Set (10):		6.00
Uncut Sheet (10):		6.00
Common Card:		.75
1	Nolan Ryan (1984 Astros)	.75
2	Nolan Ryan (1985 Astros)	.75
3	Nolan Ryan (1986 Astros)	.75
4	Nolan Ryan (1987 Astros)	.75
5	Nolan Ryan (1988 Astros)	.75
6	Nolan Ryan (1989 Rangers)	.75
7	Nolan Ryan (1990 Rangers)	.75
8	Nolan Ryan (1991 Rangers)	.75
9	Nolan Ryan (1992 Rangers)	.75
10	Nolan Ryan (All-Star Stats)	.75

1994 Mother's Cookies Angels

Originally scheduled to be given away at a promotional date during the 1994 season, these cards were caught in the strike and not distributed until the March 30-April 1 home-and-home series between the replacement players of the Angels and those of the Oakland A's. The cards were distributed in a paper envelope containing 20 different cards and eight cards of a 21st player. The idea was to trade to complete a set. The 2-1/2" x 3-1/2" cards have rounded corners and feature borderless color photos on front with the player's name and team in one of the corners. Backs are printed in red and purple and include some biographical data, uniform and card numbers, logos of Mother's Cookies and Major League Baseball and a line for an autograph.

		NM/M
Complete Set (28):		12.50
Common Player:		.25
1	Marcel Lacheman	.25
2	Mark Langston	.25
3	J.T. Snow	.25
4	Chad Curtis	.25
5	Tim Salmon	1.00
6	Gary DiSarcina	.25
7	Bo Jackson	2.50
8	Dwight Smith	.25
9	Chuck Finley	.25
10	Rod Correia	.25
11	Spike Owen	.25
12	Harold Reynolds	.25
13	Chris Turner	.25
14	Chili Davis	.25
15	Bob Patterson	.25
16	Jim Edmonds	4.00
17	Joe Magrane	.25
18	Craig Lefferts	.25
19	Scott Lewis	.25
20	Rex Hudler	.25
21	Mike Butcher	.25
22	Brian Anderson	.25
23	Greg Myers	.25
24	Mark Leiter	.25
25	Joe Grahe	.25
26	Jorge Fabregas	.25
27	John Dopson	.25
28	Angels Coaches/Checklist (Chuck Hernandez, Ken Macha, Bobby Knoop, Joe Maddon, Rod Carew, Max Oliveras)	.25

A's

Departing little from previous years, this 28-card set of the players, manager and coaches of the Oakland A's features the inimitable photography of Barry Colla. Cards are 2-1/2" x 3-1/2" with rounded corners and borderless photos. The player's name and team are in white in one of the corners. Backs are printed in red and purple and feature a few biographical bits, a uniform number and card number, a line for an autograph and the logos of Mother's Cookies and Major League Baseball. Originally intended to be given away at a game during the strike-shortened 1994 season, the cards were instead given out at the March 30-April 1 home-and-home exhibition series between the A's and the California Angels. To promote old-fashioned card trading, each package of cards contained 20 different cards, plus eight cards of a 21st player. Considerable trading was thus required to complete a set.

		NM/M
Complete Set (28):		12.00
Common Player:		.25
1	Tony LaRussa	.25
2	Mark McGwire	5.00
3	Terry Steinbach	.25
4	Dennis Eckersley	1.50
5	Mike Bordick	.25
6	Rickey Henderson	2.00
7	Ruben Sierra	.25
8	Stan Javier	.25
9	Todd Van Poppel	.25
10	Bob Welch	.25
11	Miguel Jiminez	.25
12	Steve Karsay	.25
13	Geronimo Berroa	.25
14	Bobby Witt	.25
15	Troy Neel	.25
16	Ron Darling	.25
17	Scott Hemond	.25
18	Steve Ontiveros	.25
19	Mike Aldrete	.25
20	Carlos Reyes	.25
21	Brent Gates	.25
22	Mark Acre	.25
23	Eric Helfand	.25
24	Vince Horsman	.25
25	Bill Taylor	.25
26	Scott Brosius	.25
27	John Briscoe	.25
28	Athletics' Coaches/Checklist (Dave Duncan, Jim Lefebvre, Carney Lansford, Tommie Reynolds, Art Kusnyer, Dave McKay)	.25

Astros

Distributed at an early 1995 game because the 1994 strike wiped out the planned promotional date, these cards were handed out in packages that contained 20 different cards and eight cards of a 21st player. The idea was to trade the duplicates to form a team set. The round-cornered 2-1/2" x 3-1/2" cards have a borderless color photo on front. Backs are printed in red and purple and include a few biographical notes, uniform and card numbers, a line for an autograph and logos of Mother's Cookies and Major League Baseball.

		NM/M
Complete Set (28):		10.00
Common Player:		.25
1	Terry Collins	.25
2	Mitch Williams	.25
3	Jeff Bagwell	2.50
4	Luis Gonzalez	.50
5	Craig Biggio	.50
6	Darryl Kile	.25
7	Ken Caminiti	.25
8	Steve Finley	.25
9	Pete Harnisch	.25
10	Sid Bream	.25
11	Mike Felder	.25
12	Tom Edens	.25
13	James Mouton	.25
14	Doug Drabek	.25
15	Greg Swindell	.25
16	Chris Donnels	.25
17	John Hudek	.25
18	Andujar Cedeno	.25
19	Scott Servais	.25
20	Todd Jones	.25
21	Kevin Bass	.25
22	Shane Reynolds	.25
23	Brian Williams	.25
24	Tony Eusebio	.25
25	Mike Hampton	.25
26	Andy Stankiewicz	.25
27	Astros Coaches (Ben Hines, Julio Linares, Matt Galante, Steve Henderson, Mel Stottlemyre, Sr.)	.25
28	Astros Trainers/Checklist (Dave Labossiere, Dennis Liborio, Rex Jones)	.25

Dodgers

Plans to distribute this set were postponed when the players' strike wiped out the latter part of the 1994 season. Instead, the cards were distributed at an early 1995 promotional contest. Each package of 28 cards contained 20 different cards and eight cards of a 21st player. This required extensive trading to complete a team set. Cards feature borderless color photos on a 2-1/2" x 3-1/2" round-cornered format. Backs are printed in red and purple and include uniform and card numbers, biographical data, an autograph line and the logos of Mother's Cookies and Major League Baseball.

		NM/M
Complete Set (28):		9.00
Common Player:		.25
1	Tommy Lasorda	.25
2	Mike Piazza	5.00
3	Delino DeShields	.25
4	Eric Karros	.25
5	Jose Offerman	.25
6	Brett Butler	.25
7	Orel Hershiser	.35
8	Henry Rodriguez	.25
9	Raul Mondesi	.25
10	Tim Wallach	.25
11	Ramon Martinez	.25
12	Mitch Webster	.25
13	Todd Worrell	.25
14	Jeff Treadway	.25
15	Tom Candiotti	.25
16	Pedro Astacio	.25
17	Chris Gwynn	.25
18	Jim Gott	.25
19	Omar Daal	.25
20	Cory Snyder	.25
21	Kevin Gross	.25
22	Dave Hansen	.25
23	Al Osuna	.25
24	Darren Dreifort	.25
25	Roger McDowell	.25
26	Carlos Hernandez	.25
27	Gary Wayne	.25
28	Dodgers Coaches/Checklist (Ron Perranoski, Joe Amalfitano, Reggie Smith, Joe Ferguson, Bill Russell, Mark Cresse)	.25

Giants

Unable to distribute these cards in 1994 because the strike wiped out a promotional date, the Giants gave away the cards at an early 1995 game. Cards were distributed in packages containing 20 different players and eight cards of a 21st player; requiring extensive trading to complete a team set. The 2-1/2" x 3-1/2" round-cornered cards feature borderless color photos on front. Backs have red and purple printing and include a few biographical notes, card and uniform numbers, Mother's Cookies and Major League Baseball logos and a line for an autograph.

		NM/M
Complete Set (28):		15.00
Common Player:		.25
1	Dusty Baker	.40
2	Robby Thompson	.25
3	Barry Bonds	7.50
4	Royce Clayton	.25
5	John Burkett	.25
6	Bill Swift	.25
7	Matt Williams	.50
8	Rod Beck	.25
9	Steve Scarsone	.25
10	Mark Portugal	.25
11	John Patterson	.25
12	Darren Lewis	.25
13	Kirt Manwaring	.25
14	Salomon Torres	.25
15	Willie McGee	.25
16	Dave Martinez	.25
17	Darryl Strawberry	.25
18	Steve Frey	.25
19	Rich Monteleone	.25
20	Todd Benzinger	.25
21	Jeff Reed	.25
22	Mike Benjamin	.25
23	Mike Jackson	.25
24	Pat Gomez	.25
25	Dave Burba	.25
26	Bryan Hickerson	.25
27	Mark Carreon	.25
28	Giants Coaches/Checklist (Bobby Bonds, Bob Lillis, Wendell Kim, Bob Brenly, Dick Pole, Denny Sommers)	.25

Mariners

When the players struck on Aug. 12, 1994, it killed the Mariners' plans to distribute these cards at a promotional date. Instead, packages of the cards were given away during the winter as players and management toured the Northwest drumming up fan interest. Cards were issued in a group containing 20 different players and eight cards of a 21st player. It was necessary to trade the duplicates to finish a team set. Cards are 2-1/2" x 3-1/2" with round corners and feature borderless color photos on front. Backs are in red and purple and include biographical bits, uniform and card numbers and the logos of Mother's Cookies and Major League Baseball.

		NM/M
Complete Set (28):		10.00
Common Player:		.25
1	Lou Piniella	.25
2	Randy Johnson	2.00
3	Eric Anthony	.25
4	Ken Griffey Jr.	5.00
5	Felix Fermin	.25
6	Jay Buhner	.25
7	Chris Bosio	.25
8	Reggie Jefferson	.25
9	Greg Hibbard	.25
10	Dave Fleming	.25
11	Rich Amaral	.25
12	Rich Gossage	.25
13	Edgar Martinez	.25
14	Bobby Ayala	.25
15	Darren Bragg	.25
16	Tino Martinez	.25
17	Mike Blowers	.25
18	John Cummings	.25
19	Keith Mitchell	.25
20	Bill Haselman	.25
21	Greg Pirkl	.25
22	Mackey Sasser	.25
23	Tim Davis	.25
24	Dan Wilson	.25
25	Jeff Nelson	.25
26	Kevin King	.25
27	Torey Lovullo	.25
28	Mariners Coaches/Checklist (Sam Perlozzo, Lee Elia, Sammy Ellis, John McLaren, Sam Mejias)	.25

Padres

The cancellation of the latter part of the 1994 season by the players' strike wiped out a planned promotional date on which these cards were to have been given out. Instead, the cards were distributed at an early 1995 game. Packages were given out consisting of 20 different cards plus eight cards of a 21st player, which could be traded to complete a team set. Cards are 2-1/2" x 3-1/2" with rounded corners and a borderless color photo on front. Backs are printed in red and purple and have a few biographical notes, card and uniform numbers, an autograph line and logos of Mother's Cookies and Major League Baseball.

		NM/M
Complete Set (28):		9.00
Common Player:		.25
1	Jim Riggleman	.25
2	Tony Gwynn	5.00
3	Andy Benes	.25
4	Bip Roberts	.25
5	Phil Clark	.25
6	Wally Whitehurst	.25
7	Archi Cianfrocco	.25
8	Derek Bell	.25
9	Ricky Gutierrez	.25
10	Mark Davis	.25
11	Phil Plantier	.25
12	Brian Johnson	.25
13	Billy Bean	.25
14	Craig Shipley	.25
15	Tim Hyers	.25
16	Gene Harris	.25
17	Scott Sanders	.25
18	A.J. Sager	.25
19	Keith Lockhart	.25
20	Tim Mauser	.25
21	Andy Ashby	.25
22	Brad Ausmus	.25
23	Trevor Hoffman	.25
24	Luis Lopez	.25
25	Doug Brocail	.25
26	Dave Staton	.25
27	Pedro A. Martinez	.25
28	Padres Coaches/Checklist (Sonny Siebert, Rob Picciolo, Dave Bialas, Dan Radison, Merv Rettenmund, Bruce Bochy)	.25

Rookies of the Year

In 1994 Mother's Cookies issued three different four-card sets of the 1993 Rookies of the Year. Cards of Mike Piazza of the Dodgers and Tim Salmon of California were available, one per package, in each of six varieties of Mother's Big Cookies. There was also a four-card set featuring both players on each of the four cards. These cards were packaged one per bag of Mother's Major League Double Headers. The specially marked packages with the trading cards inside also carried details about Mother's Commemorative Uncut Strips of each of the three different sets in a mail-in offer. In addition, the company created two chase cards designed to put the real cookie fans to the test. The "One in a Thousand - Rookies of the Year" - foil trading cards were inserted one in every 1,000 packages, with either blue or red foil, and fewer than 10,000 of the foil cards produced.

		NM/M
Complete Set (12):		8.00
Four-Card Uncut Piazza Panel:		6.00
Four-Card Uncut Salmon Panel:		2.00
Four-Card Uncut Piazza-Salmon Panel:		4.00
Common Card:		.50
1	Tim Salmon (Bat on shoulder.)	.50
2	Tim Salmon (Batting stance.)	.50
3	Tim Salmon (Dugout pose.)	.50
4	Tim Salmon/Fldg	.50
5	Mike Piazza (Bat on shoulder.)	1.50
6	Mike Piazza (Batting stance.)	1.50
7	Mike Piazza (Dugout pose.)	1.50
8	Mike Piazza/Catching	1.50
9	Tim Salmon, Mike Piazza (Bats on shoulders.)	.50
10	Tim Salmon, Mike Piazza (Arm around shoulder.)	.50
11	Tim Salmon, Mike Piazza (Shaking hands.)	.50
12	Tim Salmon, Mike Piazza (Back to back.)	.50
BF	Tim Salmon, Mike Piazza (Shaking hands; 1 in 1,000 blue foil.)	9.00
RF	Tim Salmon, Mike Piazza (Kneeling; 1 in 1,000 red foil.)	9.00

Nolan Ryan Final Farewell

A virtual reprint of the 1993 Farewell Set, the 1994 version uses the same photos and, except for card #10, presents the same information on the card backs. Card #10 in the 1994 set offers 1993 season and final Major League stats instead of the All-Star stats on the 1993 version. Some minor differences in photo cropping between the two sets will be noticed, as well as the fact that many of the back elements which had been printed in red on the 1993 cards are in purple on the 1994 cards, and vice versa. Cards can be distinguished by the presence of a 1993 or 1994 copyright line on the back.

		NM/M
Complete Set (10):		6.00
10-Card Uncut Panel:		10.00
Common Card:		1.00
1	Nolan Ryan (1984 Astros)	1.00
2	Nolan Ryan (1985 Astros)	1.00
3	Nolan Ryan (1986 Astros)	1.00
4	Nolan Ryan (1987 Astros)	1.00
5	Nolan Ryan (1988 Astros)	1.00
6	Nolan Ryan (1989 Rangers)	1.00
7	Nolan Ryan (1990 Rangers)	1.00
8	Nolan Ryan (1991 Rangers)	1.00
9	Nolan Ryan (1992 Rangers)	1.00
10	Nolan Ryan (1993 Rangers)	1.00

1995 Mother's Cookies Angels

Seven teams in the Western U.S. participated in Mother's Cookies 13th season of sponsoring team sets. Virtually identical in format to previous years, the 2-1/2" x 3-1/2" round-cornered cards were given away at promotional dates. To promote old-fashioned card trading, the cards were distributed in a paper envelope containing 20 different cards, plus eight cards of a 21st player. Considerable trading was thus required to complete a team set. As in previous years, Barry Colla's superb photos capture the players, manager and coaches of each team in a 28-card set. Backs are again printed in red and purple with a few bits of biographical data, uniform and card numbers and space for an autograph, along with the sponsor's logo.

		NM/M
Complete Set (28):		9.00
Common Player:		.25
1	Marcel Lachemann	.25
2	Mark Langston	.25
3	J.T. Snow	.25
4	Tim Salmon	1.50
5	Chili Davis	.25
6	Gary DiSarcina	.25
7	Tony Phillips	.25
8	Jim Edmonds	2.50
9	Chuck Finley	.25
10	Mark Dalesandro	.25
11	Greg Myers	.25
12	Spike Owen	.25
13	Lee Smith	.25
14	Eduardo Perez	.25
15	Bob Patterson	.25
16	Mitch Williams	.25
17	Garret Anderson	.50
18	Mike Bielecki	.25
19	Shawn Boskie	.25
20	Damion Easley	.25
21	Mike Butcher	.25
22	Brian Anderson	.25
23	Andy Allanson	.25
24	Scott Sanderson	.25
25	Troy Percival	.25
26	Rex Hudler	.25
27	Mike James	.25
28	Coaches/checklist (Mick Billmeyer, Rick Burleson, Rod Carew, Chuck Hernandez, Bobby Knoop, Bill Lachemann, Joe Maddon)	.25

A's

		NM/M
Complete Set (29):		7.50
Common Player:		.25
1	Tony LaRussa	.25
2	Mark McGwire	2.50
3	Terry Steinbach	.25
4	Dennis Eckersley	.75
5	Rickey Henderson	1.00
6	Ron Darling	.25
7	Ruben Sierra	.25
8	Mike Aldrete	.25
9	Stan Javier	.25
10	Mike Bordick	.25
11	Dave Stewart	.25
12	Geronimo Berroa	.25
13	Todd Van Poppel	.25
14	Todd Stottlemyre	.25
15	Eric Helfand	.25
16	Dave Leiper	.25
17	Rick Honeycutt	.25
18	Steve Ontiveros	.25
19	Mike Gallego	.25
20	Carlos Reyes	.25
21	Brent Gates	.25
22	Craig Paquette	.25
23	Mike Harkey	.25
24	Andy Tomberlin	.25
25	Jim Corsi	.25
26	Mark Acre	.25
27	Scott Brosius	.25
28	Coaches/Checklist (Dave Duncan, Art Kusnyer, Carney Lansford, Jim Lefebvre, Dave McKay, Tommie Reynolds)	.25
29	Ariel Prieto (Late-season update.)	2.50
---	Mother's Coupon (Spanish)	.05

Astros

		NM/M
Complete Set (28):		9.00
Common Player:		.25
1	Terry Collins	.25
2	Jeff Bagwell	2.50
3	Luis Gonzalez	.50
4	Darryl Kile	.25
5	Derek Bell	.25
6	Scott Servais	.25
7	Craig Biggio	.50
8	Dave Magadan	.25
9	Milt Thompson	.25
10	Derrick May	.25
11	Doug Drabek	.25
12	Tony Eusebio	.25
13	Phil Nevin	.25
14	James Mouton	.25
15	Phil Plantier	.25
16	Pedro Martinez	.25
17	Orlando Miller	.25
18	John Hudek	.25
19	Doug Brocail	.25
20	Craig Shipley	.25
21	Shane Reynolds	.25
22	Mike Hampton	.25
23	Todd Jones	.25
24	Greg Swindell	.25
25	Jim Dougherty	.25
26	Brian Hunter	.25
27	Dave Veres	.25
28	Coaches/Checklist (Jesse Barfield, Matt Galante, Steve Henderson, Julio Linares, Mel Stottlemyre)	.25

Dodgers

		NM/M
Complete Set (28):		12.00
Common Player:		.25
1	Tommy Lasorda	.25
2	Mike Piazza	4.00
3	Raul Mondesi	.25
4	Ramon Martinez	.25
5	Eric Karros	.25
6	Roberto Kelly	.25
7	Tim Wallach	.25
8	Jose Offerman	.25
9	Delino DeShields	.25
10	Dave Hansen	.25
11	Pedro Astacio	.25
12	Mitch Webster	.25
13	Hideo Nomo	6.00
14	Billy Ashley	.25
15	Chris Gwynn	.25
16	Todd Hollandsworth	.25
17	Omar Daal	.25
18	Todd Worrell	.25
19	Todd Williams	.25
20	Carlos Hernandez	.25
21	Tom Candiotti	.25
22	Antonio Osuna	.25
23	Ismael Valdes	.25
24	Rudy Seanez	.25
25	Joey Eischen	.25
26	Greg Hansell	.25
27	Rick Parker	.25
28	Coaches/Checklist (Joe Amalfitano, Mark Cresse, Manny Mota, Bill Russell, Reggie Smith, Dave Wallace)	.25

Giants

		NM/M
Complete Set (28):		12.00
Common Player:		.25
1	Dusty Baker	.40
2	Robby Thompson	.25
3	Barry Bonds	6.00
4	Royce Clayton	.25
5	Glenallen Hill	.25
6	Terry Mulholland	.25
7	Matt Williams	.50
8	Mark Portugal	.25
9	John Patterson	.25
10	Rod Beck	.25
11	Mark Leiter	.25
12	Kirt Manwaring	.25
13	Steve Scarsone	.25
14	Darren Lewis	.25
15	Tom Lampkin	.25
16	William Van Landingham	.25
17	Joe Rosselli	.25
18	Chris Hook	.25
19	Mark Dewey	.25
20	J.R. Phillips	.25
21	Jeff Reed	.25
22	Pat Gomez	.25
23	Mike Benjamin	.25
24	Trevor Wilson	.25
25	Dave Burba	.25
26	Jose Bautista	.25
27	Mark Carreon	.25
28	Coaches/Checklist (Bobby Bonds, Bob Brenly, Wendell Kim, Bob Lillis, Dick Pole)	.25

Mariners

		NM/M
Complete Set (28):		12.00
Common Player:		.25
1	Lou Piniella	.25
2	Randy Johnson	2.00
3	Dave Fleming	.25
4	Ken Griffey Jr.	4.00
5	Edgar Martinez	.25
6	Jay Buhner	.25
7	Alex Rodriguez	7.50
8	Joey Cora	.25
9	Tim Davis	.25
10	Mike Blowers	.25
11	Chris Bosio	.25
12	Dan Wilson	.25
13	Rich Amaral	.25
14	Bobby Ayala	.25
15	Darren Bragg	.25
16	Bob Wells	.25
17	Doug Strange	.25
18	Chad Kreuter	.25
19	Rafael Carmona	.25
20	Luis Sojo	.25
21	Tim Belcher	.25
22	Steve Frey	.25
23	Tino Martinez	.25
24	Felix Fermin	.25
25	Jeff Nelson	.25
26	Alex Diaz	.25
27	Bill Risley	.25
28	Coaches/Checklist (Bobby Cuellar, Lee Elia, John McLaren, Sam Mejias, Sam Perlozzo, Matt Sinatro)	.25

Padres

		NM/M
Complete Set (28):		9.00
Common Player:		.25
1	Bruce Bochy	.25
2	Tony Gwynn	4.00
3	Ken Caminiti	.25
4	Bip Roberts	.25
5	Andujar Cedeno	.25
6	Andy Benes	.25
7	Phil Clark	.25
8	Fernando Valenzuela	.25
9	Roberto Petagine	.25
10	Brian Johnson	.25
11	Scott Livingstone	.25
12	Brian Williams	.25
13	Jody Reed	.25
14	Steve Finley	.25
15	Jeff Tabaka	.25
16	Ray Holbert	.25
17	Tim Worrell	.25
18	Eddie Williams	.25
19	Brad Ausmus	.25
20	Willie Blair	.25
21	Trevor Hoffman	.25
22	Scott Sanders	.25
23	Andy Ashby	.25
24	Joey Hamilton	.25
25	Andres Berumen	.25
26	Melvin Nieves	.25
27	Bryce Florie	.25
28	Coaches/Checklist (Davey Lopes, Graig Nettles, Rob Picciolo, Merv Rettenmund, Sonny Siebert)	.25

1996 Mother's Cookies Angels

After a four-year absence, the California Angels returned to participate in Mother's Cookies 14th season of sponsoring team sets. Virtually identical in format to previous years, the 2-1/2" x 3-1/2" round-cornered cards were given away at promotional dates. To promote old-fashioned card trading, the cards were distributed in a paper envelope containing 20 different cards, plus eight cards of a 21st player. Considerable trading was thus required to complete a team set. As in previous years, superb photos capture the players, manager and coaches of each team in a 28-card set. Backs are again printed in red and purple with a few bits of biographical data, uniform and card numbers and space for an autograph, along with the sponsor's logo.

		NM/M
Complete Set (28):		7.50
Common Player:		.25
1	Marcel Lachemann	.25
2	Chili Davis	.25
3	Mark Langston	.25
4	Tim Salmon	.75
5	Jim Abbott	.25
6	Jim Edmonds	1.00
7	Gary DiSarcina	.25
8	J.T. Snow	.25
9	Chuck Finley	.25
10	Tim Wallach	.25
11	Lee Smith	.25
12	George Arias	.25
13	Troy Percival	.25
14	Randy Velarde	.25
15	Garret Anderson	.35
16	Jorge Fabregas	.25
17	Shawn Boskie	.25
18	Mark Eichhorn	.25
19	Jack Howell	.25
20	Jason Grimsley	.25
21	Rex Hudler	.25
22	Mike Aldrete	.25
23	Mike James	.25
24	Scott Sanderson	.25
25	Don Slaught	.25
26	Mark Holzemer	.25
27	Dick Schofield	.25
28	Coaches/Checklist (Mick Billmeyer, Rick Burleson, Rod Carew, Chuck Hernandez, Bobby Knoop, Bill Lachemann, Joe Maddon)	.25

A's

		NM/M
Complete Set (28):		7.50
Common Player:		.25
1	Art Howe	.25
2	Mark McGwire	2.00
3	Jason Giambi	2.50
4	Terry Steinbach	.25
5	Mike Bordick	.25
6	Brent Gates	.25
7	Scott Brosius	.25
8	Doug Johns	.25
9	Jose Herrera	.25
10	John Wasdin	.25
11	Ernie Young	.25
12	Pedro Munoz	.25
13	Steve Wojciechowski	.25
14	Geronimo Berroa	.25
15	Phil Plantier	.25
16	Bobby Chouinard	.25
17	George Williams	.25
18	Jim Corsi	.25
19	Mike Mohler	.25
20	Torey Lovullo	.25
21	Carlos Reyes	.25
22	Buddy Groom	.25
23	Don Wengert	.25
24	Bill Taylor	.25
25	Todd Van Poppel	.25
26	Rafael Bournigal	.25
27	Damon Mashore	.25
28	Coaches/Checklist (Bob Alejo, Bob Cluck, Duffy Dyer, Brad Fischer, Denny Walling, Ron Washington)	.25

Astros

		NM/M
Complete Set (28):		7.50
Common Player:		.25
1	Terry Collins	.25
2	Jeff Bagwell	2.50
3	Craig Biggio	.50
4	Derek Bell	.25
5	Darryl Kile	.25
6	Sean Berry	.25
7	Doug Drabek	.25
8	Derrick May	.25
9	Orlando Miller	.25
10	Mike Hampton	.25
11	Rick Wilkins	.25
12	Brian Hunter	.25
13	Shane Reynolds	.25
14	James Mouton	.25
15	Greg Swindell	.25
16	Bill Spiers	.25
17	Alvin Morman	.25
18	Tony Eusebio	.25
19	John Hudek	.25
20	Doug Brocail	.25
21	Anthony Young	.25
22	John Cangelosi	.25
23	Jeff Tabaka	.25
24	Mike Simms	.25
25	Todd Jones	.25
26	Ricky Gutierrez	.25
27	Mark Small	.25
28	Coaches/Checklist (Matt Galante, Steve Henderson, Julio Linares, Brent Strom, Rick Sweet)	.25

Dodgers

		NM/M
Complete Set (28):		10.00
Common Player:		.25
1	Tommy Lasorda	.25
2	Mike Piazza	4.00
3	Hideo Nomo	2.50
4	Raul Mondesi	.25
5	Eric Karros	.25
6	Delino DeShields	.25
7	Greg Gagne	.25
8	Brett Butler	.25
9	Todd Hollandsworth	.25
10	Mike Blowers	.25
11	Ismael Valdes	.25
12	Pedro Astacio	.25
13	Billy Ashley	.25
14	Tom Candiotti	.25
15	Dave Hansen	.25
16	Joey Eischen	.25
17	Milt Thompson	.25
18	Chan Ho Park	1.50
19	Antonio Osuna	.25
20	Carlos Hernandez	.25
21	Ramon Martinez	.25
22	Scott Radinsky	.25
23	Chad Fonville	.25
24	Darren Hall	.25
25	Todd Worrell	.25
26	Mark Guthrie	.25
27	Roger Cedeno	.25
28	Coaches/Checklist (Joe Amalfitano, Mark Cresse, Manny Mota, Bill Russell, Reggie Smith, Dave Wallace)	.25

Giants

		NM/M
Complete Set (28):		9.00
Common Player:		.25
1	Dusty Baker	.40
2	Barry Bonds	5.00
3	Rod Beck	.25
4	Matt Williams	.50
5	Robby Thompson	.25
6	Glenallen Hill	.25
7	Kirt Manwaring	.25
8	Mark Carreon	.25
9	Osvaldo Fernandez	.25
10	J.R. Phillips	.25
11	Shawon Dunston	.25
12	Mark Leiter	.25
13	William Van Landingham	.25
14	Stan Javier	.25
15	Allen Watson	.25
16	Mel Hall	.25
17	Doug Creek	.25
18	Steve Scarsone	.25
19	Mark Dewey	.25
20	Mark Gardner	.25
21	David McCarty	.25
22	Tom Lampkin	.25
23	Jeff Juden	.25
24	Steve Decker	.25
25	Rich DeLucia	.25
26	Kim Batiste	.25
27	Steve Bourgeois	.25
28	Checklist/Coaches (Carlos Alfonso, Bobby Bonds, Jim Davenport, Wendell Kim, Bob Lillis, Juan Lopez, Dick Pole, Mike Sadek)	.25

Mariners

		NM/M
Complete Set (28):		15.00
Common Player:		.25
1	Lou Piniella	.25
2	Randy Johnson	1.00
3	Jay Buhner	.25
4	Ken Griffey Jr.	3.00
5	Ricky Jordan	.25
6	Rich Amaral	.25
7	Edgar Martinez	.25
8	Joey Cora	.25
9	Alex Rodriguez	6.00
10	Sterling Hitchcock	.25
11	Chris Bosio	.25
12	John Marzano	.25
13	Bob Wells	.25
14	Rafäel Carmona	.25
15	Dan Wilson	.25
16	Norm Charlton	.25
17	Paul Sorrento	.25
18	Mike Jackson	.25
19	Luis Sojo	.25
20	Bobby Ayala	.25
21	Alex Diaz	.25
22	Doug Strange	.25
23	Bob Wolcott	.25
24	Darren Bragg	.25
25	Paul Menhart	.25
26	Edwin Hurtado	.25
27	Russ Davis	.25
28	Cocahes/Checklist (Bobby Cuellar, Lee Elia, John McLaren, Sam Mejias, Matt Sinatro, Steve Smith)	.25

Padres

		NM/M
Complete Set (28):		9.00
Common Player:		.25
1	Bruce Bochy	.25
2	Tony Gwynn	3.50
3	Wally Joyner	.25
4	Rickey Henderson	1.50
5	Ken Caminiti	.25
6	Scott Sanders	.25
7	Steve Finley	.25
8	Fernando Valenzuela	.25
9	Brian Johnson	.25
10	Jody Reed	.25
11	Bob Tewksbury	.25
12	Andujar Cedeno	.25
13	Sean Bergman	.25
14	Marc Newfield	.25
15	Craig Shipley	.25
16	Scott Livingstone	.25
17	Trevor Hoffman	.25
18	Doug Bochtler	.25
19	Archi Cianfrocco	.25
20	Joey Hamilton	.25
21	Andy Ashby	.25
22	Chris Gwynn	.25
23	Luis Lopez	.25
24	Tim Worrell	.25
25	Brad Ausmus	.25
26	Willie Blair	.25
27	Bryce Florie	.25
28	Coaches/Checklist (Tim Flannery, Grady Little, Davey Lopes, Rob Picciolo, Merv Rettenmund, Dan Warthen)	.25

Rangers

		NM/M
Complete Set (28):		9.00
Common Player:		.25
1	Johnny Oates	.25
2	Will Clark	.50
3	Juan Gonzalez	2.50
4	Ivan Rodriguez	3.50
5	Darryl Hamilton	.25
6	Dean Palmer	.25
7	Mickey Tettleton	.25
8	Craig Worthington	.25
9	Rusty Greer	.25
10	Kevin Gross	.25
11	Rick Helling	.25
12	Kevin Elster	.25
13	Bobby Witt	.25
14	Mark McLemore	.25
15	Warren Newson	.25
16	Mike Henneman	.25
17	Ken Hill	.25
18	Gil Heredia	.25
19	Roger Pavlik	.25
20	Dave Valle	.25
21	Mark Brandenburg	.25
22	Kurt Stillwell	.25
23	Ed Vosberg	.25
24	Dennis Cook	.25
25	Damon Buford	.25
26	Benji Gil	.25
27	Darren Oliver	.25
28	Cocahes/Checklist (Dick Bosman, Bucky Dent, Larry Hardy, Rudy Jaramillo, Ed Napoleon, Jerry Narron)	.25

1997 Mother's Cookies Angels

Fans attending the August 3 game at Anaheim Stadium received a starter set of 21 of the 28 cards in this team set, plus seven duplicates. They were encouraged to trade to fill their sets. The 2-1/2" x 3-1/2" round-corner cards have player portrait photos on front. To the left and bottom are red and blue stripes. The player name is at bottom in white, and the team logo is at bottom-right. Backs have minimal player data, a sponsor's logo and space for an autograph.

		NM/M
Complete Set (28):		7.50
Common Player:		.25
1	Terry Collins	.25
2	Tim Salmon	.50
3	Eddie Murray	2.50
4	Mark Langston	.25
5	Jim Edmonds	.75
6	Tony Phillips	.25
7	Gary DiSarcina	.25
8	Garret Anderson	.25
9	Chuck Finley	.25
10	Darin Erstad	2.00
11	Jim Leyritz	.25
12	Shigetosi Hasegawa	.25
13	Luis Alicea	.25
14	Troy Percival	.25
15	Allen Watson	.25
16	Craig Grebeck	.25
17	Mike Holtz	.25
18	Chad Kreuter	.25
19	Dennis Springer	.25
20	Jason Dickson	.25
21	Mike James	.25
22	Orlando Palmeiro	.25
23	Dave Hollins	.25
24	Mark Gubicza	.25
25	Pep Harris	.25
26	Jack Howell	.25
27	Rich DeLucia	.25
28	Angels Coaches/Checklist (Larry Bowa, Rod Carew, Joe Coleman, Marcel Lachemann, Joe Maddon, Dave Parker)	.25

A's

Fans attending the August 10 game at the Coliseum received a starter set of 21 of the 28 cards in this team set, plus seven duplicates. They were encouraged to trade to fill their sets. The 2-1/2" x 3-1/2" round-corner cards have player portrait photos on front. To the left and bottom are green and gold stripes. The player name is at bottom in white, and the team logo is at bottom-right. Backs have minimal player data, a sponsor's logo and space for an autograph.

		NM/M
Complete Set (28):		9.00
Common Player:		.25
1	Art Howe	.25
2	Mark McGwire	2.50
3	Jose Canseco	1.00
4	Jason Giambi	1.50
5	Geronimo Berroa	.25
6	Ernie Young	.25
7	Scott Brosius	.25
8	Dave Magadan	.25
9	Mike Mohler	.25
10	George Williams	.25
11	Tony Batista	.25
12	Steve Karsay	.25
13	Rafael Bournigal	.25
14	Ariel Prieto	.25
15	Buddy Groom	.25
16	Matt Stairs	.25
17	Brent Mayne	.25
18	Bill Taylor	.25
19	Scott Spiezio	.25
20	Richie Lewis	.25
21	Mark Acre	.25
22	Dave Telgheder	.25
23	Willie Adams	.25
24	Izzy Molina	.25
25	Don Wengert	.25
26	Damon Mashore	.25
27	Aaron Small	.25
28	A's Coaches/Checklist (Bob Alejo, Bob Cluck, Duffy Dyer, Brad Fischer, Denny Walling, Ron Washington)	.25

Astros

Children attending a promotional game at the Astrodome received a starter set of 21 of the 28 cards in this team set, plus seven duplicates. They were encouraged to trade to fill their sets. The 2-1/2" x 3-1/2" round-corner cards have portrait photos on front. To the left and bottom are navy and gold stripes. The player name is at bottom in white, and the team logo is at bottom-right. Backs have minimal player data, a sponsor's logo and space for an autograph.

		NM/M
Complete Set (28):		9.00
Common Player:		.25
1	Larry Dierker	.25
2	Jeff Bagwell	2.50
3	Craig Biggio	.50
4	Darryl Kile	.25
5	Luis Gonzalez	.50
6	Shane Reynolds	.25
7	James Mouton	.25
8	Sean Berry	.25
9	Billy Wagner	.75
10	Ricky Gutierrez	.25
11	Mike Hampton	.25
12	Tony Eusebio	.25
13	Derek Bell	.25
14	Ray Montgomery	.25
15	Bill Spiers	.25
16	Sid Fernandez	.25
17	Brad Ausmus	.25
18	John Hudek	.25
19	Bob Abreu	.25
20	Russ Springer	.25
21	Chris Holt	.25
22	Tom Martin	.25
23	Donne Wall	.25
24	Thomas Howard	.25
25	Jose Lima	.25
26	Pat Listach	.25
27	Ramon Garcia	.25
28	Astros Coaches/Checklist (Alan Ashby, Jose Cruz, Mike Cubbage, Tom McCraw, Vern Ruhle, Bill Virdon)	.25

Dodgers

Children attending the July 13 game at Dodger Stadium received a starter set of 21 of the 28 cards in this team set, plus seven duplicates. They were encouraged to trade to fill their sets. The 2-1/2" x 3-1/2" round-corner cards have player portrait photos on front. To the left and bottom are red and blue stripes. The player name is at bottom in white, and the team logo is at bottom-right. Backs have minimal player data, a sponsor's logo and space for an autograph.

		NM/M
Complete Set (28):		12.00
Common Player:		.25
1	Bill Russell	.25
2	Eric Karros	.25
3	Mike Piazza	4.00
4	Raul Mondesi	.25
5	Hideo Nomo	2.00
6	Todd Hollandsworth	.25
7	Greg Gagne	.25
8	Brett Butler	.25
9	Ramon Martinez	.25
10	Todd Zeile	.25
11	Ismael Valdes	.25
12	Chip Hale	.25
13	Tom Candiotti	.25
14	Billy Ashley	.25
15	Chan Ho Park	.50
16	Wayne Kirby	.25
17	Mark Guthrie	.25
18	Juan Castro	.25
19	Todd Worrell	.25
20	Tom Prince	.25
21	Scott Radinsky	.25
22	Pedro Astacio	.25
23	Wilton Guerrero	.25
24	Darren Hall	.25
25	Darren Dreifort	.25
26	Nelson Liriano	.25
27	Dodgers Coaches (Joe Amalfitano, Mark Cresse, Manny Mota, Mike Scioscia, Reggie Smith, Dave Wallace)	.25
28	Robinson 50th Anniversary Logo/Checklist	.25

Giants

Twenty thousand fans attending the July 27 game at 3Com Park received a starter set of 21 of the 28 cards in this team set, plus seven duplicates. They were encouraged to trade to fill their sets. The 2-1/2" x 3-1/2" round-corner cards have player portrait photos on front. To the left and bottom are black and orange stripes. The player name is at bottom in white, and the team logo is at bottom-right. Backs have minimal player data, a sponsor's logo and space for an autograph.

		NM/M
Complete Set (28)		10.00
Common Player:		.25
1	Dusty Baker	.25
2	Barry Bonds	5.00
3	J.T. Snow	.25
4	Rod Beck	.25
5	Glenallen Hill	.25
6	Rick Wilkins	.25
7	Jeff Kent	.50
8	Shawn Estes	.25
9	Darryl Hamilton	.25
10	Jose Vizcaino	.25
11	Julian Tavares	.25
12	Mark Gardner	.25
13	Stan Javier	.25
14	Osvaldo Fernandez	.25
15	Jim Poole	.25
16	Marvin Benard	.25
17	William Van Landingham	.25
18	Bill Mueller	.25
19	Mark Lewis	.25
20	Damon Berryhill	.25
21	Doug Henry	.25
22	Rich Rodriguez	.25
23	Kirk Rueter	.25
24	Rich Aurilia	.25
25	Joe Roa	.25
26	Marcus Jensen	.25
27	Miguel Murphy (Equipment Manager)	.25
28	Giants Coaches/Checklist (Carlos Alfonso, Gene Clines, Sonny Jackson, Juan Lopez, Ron Perranoski, Dick Pole)	.25

Padres

Partial sets of Mother's Cookies Padres were given to children 14 and under attending the June 22 game at Jack Murphy Stadium. Team colors of royal blue and orange form border strips to the left and bottom of the posed photo. A team logo appears at lower-right.

		NM/M
Complete Set (28):		9.00
Common Player:		.25
1	Bruce Bochy	.25
2	Tony Gwynn	3.00
3	Ken Caminiti	.25
4	Wally Joyner	.25
5	Rickey Henderson	1.50
6	Greg Vaughn	.25
7	Steve Finley	.25
8	Fernando Valenzuela	.25
9	John Flaherty	.25
10	Sterling Hitchcock	.25
11	Quilvio Veras	.25
12	Don Slaught	.25
13	Sean Bergman	.25
14	Chris Gomez	.25
15	Craig Shipley	.25
16	Joey Hamilton	.25
17	Scott Livingstone	.25
18	Trevor Hoffman	.25
19	Doug Bochtler	.25
20	Chris Jones	.25
21	Andy Ashby	.25
22	Archi Cianfrocco	.25
23	Tim Worrell	.25
24	Will Cunnane	.25
25	Carlos Hernandez	.25
26	Tim Scott	.25
27	Dario Veras	.25
28	Coaches/Checklist (Greg Booker, Tim Flannery, Davey Lopes, Rob Picciolo, Merv Rettenmund, Dan Warthen)	.25

Rangers

Fans attending a promotional game at the Ballpark in Arlington received a starter set of 21 of the 28 cards in this team set, plus seven duplicates. They were encouraged to trade to fill their sets. The 2-1/2" x 3-1/2" round-corner cards have player portrait photos on front. To the left and bottom are red and blue stripes. The player name is at bottom in white, and the team logo is at bottom-right. Backs have minimal player data, a sponsor's logo and space for an autograph.

		NM/M
Complete Set (28):		8.00
Common Player:		.25
1	Johnny Oates	.25
2	Will Clark	.50
3	Juan Gonzalez	2.50
4	Ivan Rodriguez	3.50
5	John Wetteland	.25
6	Mickey Tettleton	.25
7	Dean Palmer	.25
8	Rusty Greer	.25
9	Ed Vosberg	.25
10	Lee Stevens	.25
11	Benji Gil	.25
12	Mike Devereaux	.25
13	Bobby Witt	.25
14	Mark McLemore	.25
15	Warren Newson	.25
16	Eric Gunderson	.25
17	Ken Hill	.25
18	Damon Buford	.25
19	Roger Pavlik	.25
20	Billy Ripken	.25
21	John Burkett	.25
22	Darren Oliver	.25
23	Mike Simms	.25
24	Julio Santana	.25
25	Henry Mercedes	.25
26	Xavier Hernandez	.25
27	Danny Patterson	.25
28	Rangers Coaches/Checklist (Dick Bosman, Bucky Dent, Larry Hardy, Rudy Jaramillo, Ed Napoleon, Jerry Narron)	.25

1998 Mother's Cookies A's

The first 25,000 fans at the August 2 game in Oakland received a starter set of 21 of the 28 cards in this team set, plus seven duplicates. They were encouraged to trade to fill their sets. The 2-1/2" x 3-1/2" round-corner cards have player portrait photos on front. To the left and bottom are green and gold stripes. The player name is at the bottom in white, and the team logo is at bottom-left. Backs have minimal player data, a sponsor's logo and space for an autograph, all printed in red and purple on a purple background.

		NM/M
Complete Set (28):		8.00
Common Player:		.25
1	Art Howe	.25
2	Rickey Henderson	1.00
3	Jason Giambi	2.00
4	Tom Candiotti	.25
5	Matt Stairs	.25
6	Kenny Rogers	.25
7	Scott Spiezio	.25
8	Ben Grieve	.50
9	Kevin Mitchell	.25
10	A.J. Hinch	.25
11	Bill Taylor	.25
12	Rafael Bournigal	.25
13	Miguel Tejada	3.00
14	Kurt Abbott	.25
15	Buddy Groom	.25
16	Dave Magadan	.25
17	Mike Oquist	.25
18	Mike Macfarlane	.25
19	Mike Fetters	.25
20	Ryan Christenson	.25
21	T.J. Mathews	.25
22	Mike Mohler	.25
23	Jason McDonald	.25
24	Blake Stein	.25
25	Mike Blowers	.25
26	Jimmy Haynes	.25
27	Aaron Small	.25
28	Cocahes/Checklist (Duffy Dyer, Brad Fischer, Gary Jones, Rick Peterson, Denny Walling, Ron Washington)	.25

Astros

The first 25,000 fans at the September 13 game at the Astrodome received a starter set of 21 of the 28 cards in this team set, plus seven duplicates. They were encouraged to trade to fill their sets. The 2-1/2" x 3-1/2" round-corner cards have player portrait photos on front. To the left and bottom are team-color blue and gold stripes. The player name is at the bottom in white, and the team logo is at bottom-left. Backs have minimal player data, a sponsor's logo and space for an autograph, all printed in red and purple on a purple background.

		NM/M
Complete Set (28):		9.00
Common Player:		.25
1	Larry Dierker	.25
2	Jeff Bagwell	3.00
3	Craig Biggio	.50
4	Derek Bell	.25
5	Shane Reynolds	.25
6	Sean Berry	.25
7	Moises Alou	.25
8	Carl Everett	.25
9	Billy Wagner	.25
10	Tony Eusebio	.25
11	Mike Hampton	.25
12	Ricky Gutierrez	.25
13	Jose Lima	.25
14	Brad Ausmus	.25
15	Bill Spiers	.25
16	C.J. Nitkowski	.25
17	Randy Johnson	4.00
18	Mike Magnante	.25
19	Dave Clark	.25
20	Sean Bergman	.25
21	Richard Hidalgo	.25
22	Pete Shourek	.25
23	Jay Powell	.25
24	Trever Miller	.25
25	Tim Bogar	.25
26	Doug Henry	.25
27	Scott Elarton	.25
28	Coaches (Jose Cruz, Mike Cubbage, Dave Engle, Matt Galante, Tom McCraw, Vern Ruhle)	.25

Dodgers

The first 25,000 kids at the August 16 game in Los Angeles received a starter set of 21 of the 28 cards in this team set, plus seven duplicates. They were encouraged to trade to fill their sets. The 2-1/2" x 3-1/2" round-corner cards have player portrait photos on front. To the left and bottom are red and blue stripes. The player name is at the bottom in white, and the team logo is at bottom-left. Backs have minimal player data, a sponsor's logo and space for an autograph, all printed in red and purple on a purple background.

		NM/M
Complete Set (28):		7.50
Common Player:		.25
1	Glenn Hoffman	.25
2	Eric Karros	.25
3	Bobby Bonilla	.25
4	Raul Mondesi	.25
5	Gary Sheffield	1.00
6	Ramon Martinez	.25
7	Charles Johnson	.25
8	Jose Vizcaino	.25
9	Scott Radinsky	.25
10	Jim Eisenreich	.25
11	Ismael Valdes	.25
12	Eric Young	.25
13	Chan Ho Park	.25
14	Roger Cedeno	.25
15	Antonio Osuna	.25
16	Dave Mlicki	.25
17	Mark Guthrie	.25
18	Juan Castro	.25
19	Darren Dreifort	.25
20	Tom Prince	.25
21	Jeff Shaw	.25
22	Alex Cora	.25
23	Matt Luke	.25
24	Darren Hall	.25
25	Trenidad Hubbard	.25
26	Jim Bruske	.25
27	Tripp Cromer	.25
28	Dodgers Coaches (Joe Amalfitano, Mickey Hatcher, Charlie Hough, Manny Mota, Mike Scioscia, John Shelby)	.25

Giants

The first 25,000 fans at the July 26 game at 3Com Park received a starter set of 21 of the 28 cards in this team set, plus seven duplicates. They were encouraged to trade to fill their sets. The 2-1/2" x 3-1/2" round-corner cards have player portrait photos on front. To the left and bottom are black and orange stripes. The player name is at the bottom in white, and the team logo is at bottom-left. Backs have minimal player data, a sponsor's logo and space for an autograph, all printed in red and purple on a purple background.

		NM/M
Complete Set (28):		9.00
Common Player:		.25
1	Dusty Baker	.25
2	Barry Bonds	5.00
3	Shawn Estes	.25
4	Jeff Kent	.50
5	Orel Hershiser	.25
6	Brian Johnson	.25
7	J.T. Snow	.25
8	Bill Mueller	.25
9	Kirk Rueter	.25
10	Darryl Hamilton	.25
11	Rich Aurilia	.25
12	Mark Gardner	.25
13	Stan Javier	.25
14	Robb Nen	.25
15	Rich Rodriguez	.25
16	Brent Mayne	.25
17	Julian Tavares	.25
18	Rey Sanchez	.25
19	Chris Jones	.25
20	Charlie Hayes	.25
21	Danny Darwin	.25
22	Jim Poole	.25
23	Marvin Benard	.25
24	Steve Reed	.25
25	Alex Diaz	.25
26	John Johnstone	.25
27	Rene De La Rosa, Mike Krukow, Duane Kuiper, Jon Miller, Amaury Pi-Gonzalez, Ted Robinson (Broadcasters)	.25
28	Giants Coaches/Checklist (Carlos Alfonso, Gene Clines, Sonny Jackson, Juan Lopez, Ron Perranoski, Ron Wotus)	.25

Padres

Fans at a designated Pads' home game received a starter set of 21 of the 28 cards in this team set, plus seven duplicates. They were encouraged to trade to fill their sets. The 2-1/2" x 3-1/2" round-corner cards have player portrait photos on front. To the left and bottom are blue and orange stripes. The player name is at the bottom in white, and the team logo is at bottom-left. Backs have minimal player data, a sponsor's logo and space for an autograph, all printed in red and purple on a purple background.

		NM/M
Complete Set (28):		9.00
Common Player:		.25
1	Bruce Bochy	.25
2	Tony Gwynn	4.00
3	Ken Caminiti	.25
4	Kevin Brown	.40
5	Wally Joyner	.25
6	Sterling Hitchcock	.25
7	Greg Vaughn	.25
8	Steve Finley	.25
9	Joey Hamilton	.25
10	Carlos Hernandez	.25
11	Quilvio Veras	.25
12	Trevor Hoffman	.25
13	Chris Gomez	.25
14	Andy Ashby	.25
15	Greg Myers	.25
16	Mark Langston	.25
17	Andy Sheets	.25
18	Dan Miceli	.25
19	James Mouton	.25
20	Brian Boehringer	.25
21	Archi Cianfrocco	.25
22	Mark Sweeney	.25
23	Pete Smith	.25
24	Eddie Williams	.25
25	Ed Giovanola	.25
26	Carlos Reyes	.25
27	Donne Wall	.25
28	Padres Coaches (Greg Booker, Tim Flannery, Davey Lopes, Rob Picciolo, Merv Rettenmund, Dave Stewart)	.25

1998 Mr. Sub Roger Clemens

The date attributed is speculative, since the cards carry no copyright. This set appears to have been issued by a Canadian sub sandwich chain to honor Roger Clemens first four Cy Young Awards. Borderless fronts of the 2-1/2" x 3-1/2" cards have color portrait and action artwork of Clemens in a Blue Jays uniform, with a sepia multi-exposure image of Cy Young in the background, all four cards in the set share the front design, with the only difference being the card number at top-left. Backs are dominated by a large coin-like design with black-and-white artwork of Clemens. The first three cards have back pictures in a Red Sox uniform, the last card shows him with Toronto. The date of his CY Award is shown on each "coin." Beneath the central design on the graduated blue background are MLB and Mr. Sub logos and "www.RocketRoger.com."

		NM/M
Complete Set (4):		6.00
Common Card:		1.50
1	Roger Clemens/1986	1.50
2	Roger Clemens/1987	1.50
3	Roger Clemens/1991	1.50
4	Roger Clemens/1997	1.50

1992 Mr. Turkey

Mr. Turkey, a division of Sara Lee, offered a set of Major League Superstar cards during the 1992 season. A total of 26 cards, one player representing each team, were included in various Mr. Turkey meat packages. The cardboard packaging allows for the printing directly on the carton instead of inserting the cards inside the package. Collectors were able to collect the cards individually or as an uncut sheet, available by sending to the company.

		NM/M
Complete Set (26):		10.00
Uncut Sheet:		15.00
Common Player:		.35
1	Jim Abbott	.40
2	Roberto Alomar	.50
3	Sandy Alomar, Jr.	.40
4	Craig Biggio	.40
5	George Brett	2.00
6	Will Clark	.40
7	Roger Clemens	2.00
8	Cecil Fielder	.40
9	Carlton Fisk	1.00
10	Andres Galarraga	.40
11	Dwight Gooden	.40
12	Ken Griffey Jr.	3.00
13	Tony Gwynn	1.50
14	Rickey Henderson	1.00
15	Dave Justice	.40
16	Don Mattingly	2.00
17	Dale Murphy	.75
18	Kirby Puckett	1.50
19	Cal Ripken, Jr.	3.50
20	Nolan Ryan	3.50
21	Chris Sabo	.40
22	Ryne Sandberg	1.50
23	Ozzie Smith	1.50
24	Darryl Strawberry	.40
25	Andy Van Slyke	.40
26	Robin Yount	1.00

1995 Mr. Turkey

Five retired players are featured in this issue. The 2-1/2" x 3-1/2" cards have a sepia or color photo on front, along with a Baseball Greats logo. Uniform logos have been removed from the photos. Backs have personal and career data, and logos of the sponsor and the players' licensing agent. The cards are unnumbered.

		NM/M
Complete Set (5):		10.00
Common Player:		2.00
(1)	Bob Feller	2.00
(2)	Al Kaline	2.00
(3)	Tug McGraw	2.00
(4)	Boog Powell	2.00
(5)	Warren Spahn	2.00

1983 Mr. Z's Pizza Milwaukee Brewers

These 5" x 7" color cards were given away (bagged in cellophane) with the purchase of frozen pizzas.

		NM/M
Complete Set (3):		7.50
Common Player:		1.00
(1)	Cecil Cooper	1.00
(2)	Paul Molitor	4.00
(3)	Robin Yount	4.00

1984 Mr. Z's Pizza Milwaukee Brewers

These 5x7" color cards were given away with the purchase of frozen pizza and other Brewer-logo food products.

		NM/M
Complete Set (3):		4.00
Common Player:		1.00
(1)	George Bamberger	1.00
(2)	Rollie Fingers	2.00
(3)	Jim Gantner	1.00

1985 Mr. Z's Pizza Pete Rose

These 5" x 7" cards were issued in Mr. Z's pizzas, each one picturing Pete Rose. Fronts have borderless action photos with a headline in black or white and a facsimile autograph. Backs have a red border with photos of Reds team merchandise which could be obtained by saving pizza labels.

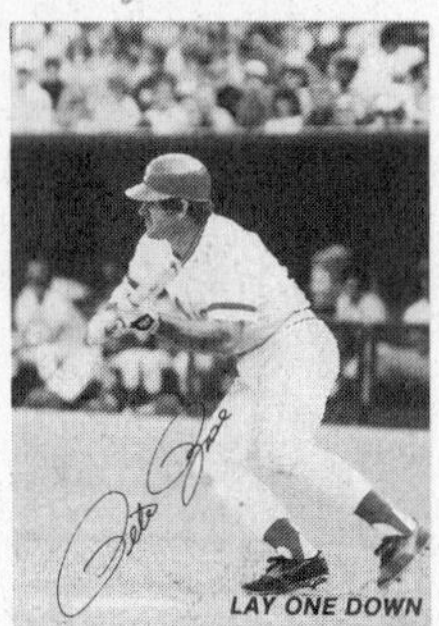

		NM/M
Complete Set (11):		35.00
Common Card:		4.00
(1)	Another Hit! (Pete Rose)	4.00
(2)	Classic Rose (Pete Rose)	4.00
(3)	Lay One Down (Pete Rose)	4.00
(4)	Line Up Time (Pete Rose)	4.00
(5)	On Deck (Pete Rose)	4.00
(6)	One Hit Closer! (Pete Rose (No facsimile autograph.))	4.00
(7)	Pete's Back (Pete Rose)	4.00
(8)	Play Ball! (Pete Rose)	4.00
(9)	Player-Manager (Pete Rose)	4.00
(10)	Rounding Third Heading for Home (Pete Rose)	4.00
(11)	Send in the Lefty (Pete Rose)	4.00

2001 Mrs. Baird's Breadwinners Texas Rangers

Every third loaf of Mrs. Baird's bread and buns included one of 10 Texas Rangers cards; other packages had ticket discount coupons, autographed memorabilia or cards, or one of 500 foil parallel sets. The cards feature game-action photos on a red and white background. The player's name is vertically in white on a blue strip at left. A Mrs. Baird's logo and "BREAD WINNERS" appear in the black band at top. A team logo is at lower-left. Horizontal backs have another photo with the Rangers stadium at top, personal data at left and 2000 season notes at right. Series 1 (#1-5) cards were available from April through June, Series 2 (#6-10) cards were in packages during July-August. Headquartered in the Dallas area, the bakery's products were distributed throughout Texas and Oklahoma and in parts of Louisiana and New Mexico.

		NM/M
Complete Set (11):		7.50
Common Player:		.50
Foil Parallel:		3X
1	Pudge Rodriguez	1.50
2	Gabe Kapler	.50
3	Rusty Greer	.50
4	Rafael Palmeiro	1.50
5	Kenny Rogers	.50
6	Alex Rodriguez	2.50
7	Ruben Mateo	.50
8	Rick Helling	.50
9	Ken Caminiti	.50
10	Andres Galarraga	.50
---	Header/Checklist	.05

1981 MSA Discs

Unlike the contemporary Peter Pan/Sunbeam blank-back discs, this set of 2-3/4" diameter discs carry on their backs the advertising of Michael Schechter Associates, their producer.

		NM/M
Complete Set (32):		135.00
Common Player:		4.00
(1)	Buddy Bell	4.00
(2)	Johnny Bench	8.00
(3)	Bruce Bochte	4.00
(4)	George Brett	12.50
(5)	Bill Buckner	4.00
(6)	Rod Carew	8.00
(7)	Steve Carlton	8.00
(8)	Cesar Cedeno	4.00
(9)	Jack Clark	4.00
(10)	Cecil Cooper	4.00
(11)	Bucky Dent	4.00
(12)	Carlton Fisk	8.00
(13)	Steve Garvey	6.50
(14)	Goose Gossage	4.00
(15)	Mike Hargrove	4.00
(16)	Keith Hernandez	4.00
(17)	Bob Horner	4.00
(18)	Reggie Jackson	12.50
(19)	Steve Kemp	4.00
(20)	Ron LeFlore	4.00
(21)	Fred Lynn	4.00
(22)	Lee Mazzilli	4.00
(23)	Eddie Murray	8.00
(24)	Mike Norris	4.00
(25)	Dave Parker	4.00
(26)	J.R. Richard	4.00
(27)	Pete Rose	15.00
(28)	Mike Schmidt	12.50
(29)	Tom Seaver	9.00
(30)	Roy Smalley	4.00
(31)	Willie Stargell	8.00
(32)	Garry Templeton	4.00

1981 MSA/Peter Pan-Sunbeam Bakery Discs

Only the MSA copyright is found on these 2-3/4" diameter player discs, the names of Peter Pan or Sunbeam Bakery, the sponsors that packed the discs in loaves of bread, are nowhere to be seen. Like other MSA disc issues, the black-and-white player picture appears on a baseball design with side panels in various colors. Player information appears at each side and in the center panel, along with the Players Association logo. Because the discs are not licensed by the leagues, uniform logos have been removed from the photos. Backs are blank. The unnumbered discs are checklisted here in alphabetical order. A 16-3/4" x 22-5/8" red, white and blue display poster with slots for inserting the discs is known bearing the Peter Pan advertising.

		NM/M
Complete Set (32):		75.00
Common Player:		2.00
Pete Pan Poster:		25.00
(1)	Buddy Bell	2.00
(2)	Johnny Bench	4.50
(3)	Bruce Bochte	2.00
(4)	George Brett	7.50
(5)	Bill Buckner	2.00
(6)	Rod Carew	4.50
(7)	Steve Carlton	4.50
(8)	Cesar Cedeno	2.00
(9)	Jack Clark	2.00
(10)	Cecil Cooper	2.00
(11)	Bucky Dent	2.00
(12)	Carlton Fisk	4.50
(13)	Steve Garvey	3.50
(14)	Goose Gossage	2.00
(15)	Mike Hargrove	2.00
(16)	Keith Hernandez	2.00
(17)	Bob Horner	2.00
(18)	Reggie Jackson	7.50
(19)	Steve Kemp	2.00
(20)	Ron LeFlore	2.00
(21)	Fred Lynn	2.00
(22)	Lee Mazzilli	2.00
(23)	Eddie Murray	4.50
(24)	Mike Norris	2.00
(25)	Dave Parker	2.00
(26)	J.R. Richard	2.00
(27)	Pete Rose	9.00
(28)	Mike Schmidt	7.50
(29)	Tom Seaver	5.00
(30)	Roy Smalley	2.00
(31)	Willie Stargell	4.50
(32)	Garry Templeton	2.00

1985 MSA/Subway Sandwiches Discs

Identical in form and format to other Schechter discs of the era, the Subway giveaways are nowhere marked as such, only the MSA copyright appears. The 2-3/4" diameter discs have black-and-white player portraits in the white center panel of a baseball design. The variously colored end panels contain player information and a 1985 date. The Players Association logo appears beneath the photo. Because the discs are not licensed by Major League Baseball, team logos have been airbrushed off uniforms. The unnumbered, blank-backed discs are checklisted here in alphabetical order.

		NM/M
Complete Set (36):		95.00
Common Player:		3.00
(1)	Buddy Bell	3.00
(2)	Mike Boddicker	3.00
(3)	George Brett	10.00
(4)	Bill Buckner	3.00
(5)	Rod Carew	6.50
(6)	Steve Carlton	6.50
(7)	Cesar Cedeno	3.00
(8)	Dave Concepcion	3.00
(9)	Cecil Cooper	3.00
(10)	Al Cowens	3.00
(11)	Goose Gossage	3.00
(12)	Pedro Guerrero	3.00
(13)	Ron Guidry	3.00
(14)	Tony Gwynn	9.00
(15)	Mike Hargrove	3.00
(16)	Bob Horner	3.00
(17)	Kent Hrbek	3.00
(18)	Rick Langford	3.00
(19)	Dennis Leonard	3.00
(20)	Willie McGee	3.00
(21)	Jack Morris	3.00
(22)	Terry Puhl	3.00
(23)	Dan Quisenberry	3.00
(24)	Johnny Ray	3.00
(25)	Cal Ripken Jr.	15.00
(26)	Ryne Sandberg	9.00
(27)	Mike Schmidt	10.00
(28)	Tom Seaver	6.50
(29)	Rick Sutcliffe	3.00
(30)	Bruce Sutter	4.50
(31)	Alan Trammell	3.00
(32)	Fernando Valenzuela	3.00
(33)	Greg Walker	3.00
(34)	Willie Wilson	3.00
(35)	Dave Winfield	6.50
(36)	Geoff Zahn	3.00

1992 MTV Rock n' Jock

The third annual softball charity game featuring music and sports personalities was the occasion for issue of this three-card set. Fronts have a

multi-colored starred border with the player action photo (presumably taken at the previous year's game). Backs are in black-and-white with the MTV and event logos, the date and place of the game and the notation that the card is from a "Limited Edition of 20,000."

		NM/M
Complete Set (3):		6.00
Common Player:		.50
1	M.C. Hammer	.50
2	Frank Thomas	2.00
3	Ken Griffey Jr.	4.00

1989 Nabisco Don Mattingly

Issued as a mail-in premium for Ritz cracker proofs of purchase, this sheet measures 10-5/8" x 13-15/16" and includes eight 2-1/2" x 3-1/2" cards and a 5" x 7" card. The individual cards are not perforated and are seldom seen cut from the sheet. For lack of licensing by Major League Baseball, the photos on front have generally had the team logos airbrushed away. Cards are numbered on front and back with a year identifying the photo. Backs are printed in red, white and blue and contain biographical data and career highlights on the small cards, while the large card offers complete major and minor league stats and major awards won. The sheet was produced for Nabisco by Topps.

		NM/M
Complete Sheet:		7.50
Common Card:		1.00
72	Don Mattingly (Boyhood photo.)	1.00
81	Don Mattingly (Minor league photo.)	1.00
84	Don Mattingly/Fldg	1.00
85	Don Mattingly/Btg	1.00
86	Don Mattingly/Btg	1.00
87	Don Mattingly/Btg	1.00
88	Don Mattinglyv	1.00
89	Don Mattingly/Btg	1.00
----	Don Mattingly (5" x 7" pose)	1.00

1992 Nabisco Canadian Tradition

Nabisco released a 36-card set of former Toronto Blue Jays and Montreal Expos

inside several of its products in 1992. Three cards were included per box. A colorful 9" x 12" album with plastic sheets was available via a mail-in offer. The cards are artist renderings of the players, similar in style to the famous sports drawings that appeared on the pages of the Sporting News over the years. Text on the drawings is in both English and French. Backs are printed in red, white and blue and include the team and Nabisco logos along with English and French descriptions of the Famous Moment.

		NM/M
Complete Set (36):		25.00
Common Player:		.75
Album:		7.50
1	Bill Lee	.75
2	Cliff Johnson	.75
3	Ken Singleton	.75
4	Al Woods	.75
5	Ron Hunt	.75
6	Barry Bonnell	.75
7	Tony Perez	4.00
8	Willie Upshaw	.75
9	Coco Laboy	.75
10	Famous Moments (Blue Jays Win A.L. East - 1985)	.75
11	Bob Bailey	.75
12	Dave McKay	.75
13	Rodney Scott	.75
14	Jerry Garvin	.75
15	Famous Moments (Expos Win N.L. East - 1981)	.75
16	Rick Bosetti	.75
17	Larry Parrish	.75
18	Bill Singer	.75
19	Ron Fairly	.75
20	Damaso Garcia	.75
21	Al Oliver	1.50
22	Famous Moments (Blue Jays Win Eastern Division - 1989)	.75
23	Claude Raymond	.75
24	Buck Martinez	.75
25	Rusty Staub	1.50
26	Otto Velez	.75
27	Mack Jones	.75
28	Garth Iorg	.75
29	Bill Stoneman	.75
30	Doug Ault	.75
31	Famous Moments (Expos Host All-Star Game 1982)	.75
32	Jesse Jefferson	.75
33	Steve Rogers	.75
34	Ernie Whitt	.75
35	John Boccabella	.75
36	Bob Bailor	.75

1993 Nabisco All-Star Autographs

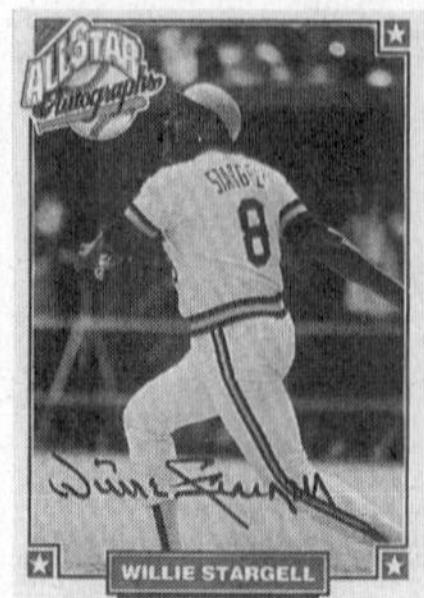

In a promotion with the Major League Baseball Players Alumni, Nabisco produced this six-card set of former stars. For $5 and proofs of purchase, collectors could receive an authentically autographed card. The 2-1/2" x 3-1/2" cards featured color photos on front on which the team logos have been airbrushed away, since Major League Baseball did not license the issue. Backs gave biographical and career information along with a black-and-white childhood photo of the player. The unnumbered cards are checklisted here in alphabetical order. Don Drysdale's death on July 3, in the midst of the promotion, curtailed availability of cards with his autograph. Each card came cased with a certificate of authenticity. Unautographed cards and 12-card uncut sheets are known.

		NM/M
Complete Set (6):		90.00
Common Player:		6.00
(1)	Ernie Banks	13.50
(2)	Don Drysdale	45.00
(3)	Catfish Hunter	20.00
(4)	Phil Niekro	6.00
(5)	Brooks Robinson	7.50
(6)	Willie Stargell	25.00

1994 Nabisco All-Star Legends Autographs

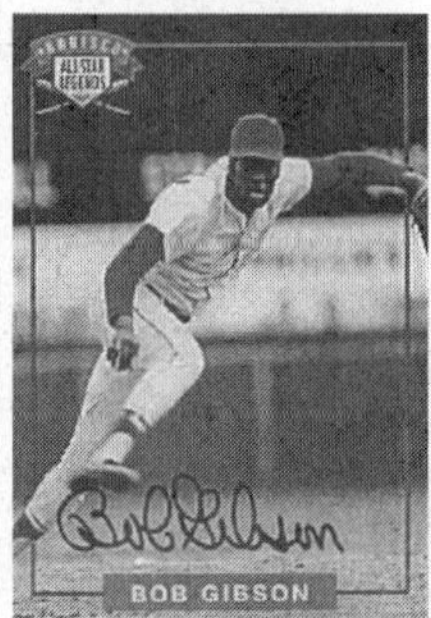

For a second year in 1994, Nabisco continued its program of offering autographed cards of former stars for $5 and proofs of purchase from its snack products. Cards retained the same basic format of using airbrushed color photos on front and black-and-white childhood photos on back. Fronts have a "Nabisco All-Star Legends" logo in the upper-left. Backs have career and biographical data and the logos of the sponsor and the Major League Baseball Players Alumni. The unnumbered cards are checklisted here alphabetically. Each card came with a certificate of authenticity. The Sparky Lyle card was not part of the mail-in promotion but was distributed in person during the Legends' tour. Unautographed cards and 12-card uncut sheets are also known.

		NM/M
Complete Set (5):		30.00
Common Player:		6.00
(1)	Bob Gibson	9.00
(2)	Sparky Lyle	12.00
(3)	Jim Palmer	6.00
(4)	Frank Robinson	8.00
(5)	Duke Snider	10.00

2000 Team Nabisco All Stars

This series was issued in Nabisco snack and cookie packages. Fronts have color photos on which team logos have been removed. The player figure is set against a background that has a large purple-blue baseball at bottom and red and white rays at top. The sponsor logo is at top-right. Backs have a small-

er version of the photo, career stats and highlights. The unnumbered cards are checklisted here alphabetically.

		NM/M
Complete Set (11):		9.00
Common Player:		.50
(1)	Lawrence "Yogi" Berra	1.50
(2)	Gary Carter	1.00
(3)	Orlando Cepeda	1.00
(4)	George Foster	.50
(5)	Steve Garvey	.75
(6)	John Kruk	.50
(7)	Joe Morgan	1.00
(8)	Dot Richardson	.50
(9)	Brooks Robinson	1.00
(10)	Mike Schmidt	2.00
(11)	Ozzie Smith	2.00

2001 Nabisco Latino Legends of Baseball

A trio of popular Latino former stars are featured in this in-store giveaway from Nabisco. Fronts have portrait and action photos of the player in an 8" x 10" format. Because the cards are not licensed by MLB, uniform logos have been removed from the photos. Backs have personal information and career data printed in Spanish.

		NM/M
Complete Set (3):		20.00
Common Player:		4.00
(1)	Roberto Clemente	15.00
(2)	Minnie Minoso	4.00
(3)	Tony Perez	6.00

2002 Nabisco Philadelphia Phillies

At the July 7 game at Veterans Stadium, youngsters 14 and under received this set. On thin card stock, the 2-1/2" x 3-1/2" cards have red, white and blue borders around game-action photos. Nabisco and Acme logos are in the upper corners. At bottom is the team logo and player name. Horizontal backs are also in red, white and blue with a large batter silhouette, biographical data and a line each of minor and major league stats. The checklist is arranged by uniform numbers which appear on back.

		NM/M
Complete Set (35):		9.00
Common Player:		.25
3	Todd Pratt	.25
5	Pat Burrell	1.00
6	Doug Glanville	.25
7	Jeremy Giambi	.25
8	Marlon Anderson	.35
9	Tomas Perez	.25
10	Larry Bowa	.25
11	Jimmy Rollins	.75
13	Turk Wendell	.25
15	Dave Hollins	.25
16	Travis Lee	.35
17	Scott Rolen	.75
18	John Vukovich	.25
19	Dan Plesac	.25
21	Greg Gross	.25
22	Jason Michaels	.25
24	Mike Lieberthal	.35
25	Gary Varsho	.25
27	Ricky Bottalico	.25
30	Tony Scott	.25
31	Robert Person	.25
33	Ricky Ledee	.25
37	Rheal Cormier	.25
40	Jose Santiago	.25
43	Randy Wolf	.25
44	Vicente Padilla	.25
46	Vern Ruhle	.25
48	David Coggin	.25
49	Jose Mesa	.25
50	Doug Nickle	.25
51	Terry Adams	.25
52	Carlos Silva	.25
53	Bobby Abreu	.35
56	Brandon Duckworth	.25
59	Ramon Henderson	.25

1983 Nalley Potato Chips Mariners

These large (8-11/16" x 10-11/16") photo cards were issued only in the area of Washington state by Nalley Potato Chips. The six Seattle Mariners are pictured in full color on the entire back panel of each box. On the side panels, detailed player stats and biographies are listed on one side, with a Mariners schedule and ticket discount offer on the other side.

		NM/M
Complete Set (6):		45.00
Common Player:		7.50
8	Rick Sweet	7.50
16	Al Cowens	7.50
21	Todd Cruz	7.50
22	Richie Zisk	7.50
36	Gaylord Perry	20.00
37	Bill Caudill	7.50

1995 National Packtime

An unusual joint venture by the six major baseball card licensees resulted in this 18-card set which was available only via a mail-in offer. The set was obtained by sending in $2 and 28 wrappers from any of the companies' 1995 baseball cards prior to June 30, 1995. Most of the card designs were similar to the respective company's regular issues of the same brand. Each card is gold-foil enhanced and each carries the crossed-bats National Packtime logo on front. Cards are numbered on back from 1-18. A reported 130,000 of the sets were exchanged for wrappers.

		NM/M
Complete Set (18):		3.00
Common Player:		.15
1	Frank Thomas (Donruss)	.40
2	Matt Williams (Fleer Ultra)	.15
3	Juan Gonzalez (Pacific Crown)	.35
4	Bob Hamelin (Pinnacle)	.15
5	Mike Piazza (Topps)	.50
6	Ken Griffey Jr. (Upper Deck)	.50
7	Barry Bonds (Donruss)	.75
8	Tim Salmon (Fleer Ultra)	.15
9	Jose Canseco (Pacific Crown)	.25
10	Cal Ripken Jr. (Pinnacle)	.75
11	Raul Mondesi (Topps)	.15
12	Alex Rodriguez (Upper Deck)	.60
13	Will Clark (Donruss)	.20
14	Fred McGriff (Fleer Ultra)	.15
15	Tony Gwynn (Pacific Crown)	.45
16	Kenny Lofton (Pinnacle)	.15
17	Deion Sanders (Topps)	.20
18	Jeff Bagwell (Upper Deck)	.40

Welcome to the Show

This special set was another joint venture by the major card manufacturers, Major League Baseball and the Players Association. Sets of six cards were given to attendees at the National Sports Collectors Convention. In designs similar to the companies' regular-issue cards of 1995, these handouts carry a National Packtime logo on front and a red, white and black "WELCOME TO THE SHOW" logo on back. Cards are variously numbered "of" 5, 6 or 8, though only six were issued. A paper accompanying the six-card packs assured collectors they were receiving the entire set.

		NM/M
Complete Set (6):		3.00
Common Player:		.50
1 of 6	Greg Maddux (Leaf)	1.00
1/8	Albert Belle (Upper Deck)	.60
2 of 6	Darren Daulton (Ultra)	.50
2 of 6	Don Mattingly (Topps)	1.50
3 of 5	Hideo Nomo (Pinnacle)	.75
3 of 6	Randy Johnson (Pacific)	.75

1986 National Photo Royals

These 2-7/8" x 4-1/4" cards were a team issue produced in conjunction with National Photo. The 24-card set includes 21 players, manager Dick Howser, a Royals' 1985 World Championship commemorative card and a discount offer card from National Photo. Card fronts feature full-color action photos with a blue

"Kansas City Royals" at the top of each card. Each player's name, number and position are also included. Card backs list complete professional career statistics, along with the National Photo logo.

		NM/M
Complete Set (24):		3.50
Common Player:		.15
1	Buddy Biancalana	.15
3	Jorge Orta	.15
4	Greg Pryor	.15
5	George Brett	3.00
6	Willie Wilson	.25
8	Jim Sundberg	.15
10	Dick Howser	.15
11	Hal McRae	.15
20	Frank White	.15
21	Lonnie Smith	.15
22	Dennis Leonard	.15
23	Mark Gubicza	.15
24	Darryl Motley	.15
25	Danny Jackson	.15
26	Steve Farr	.15
29	Dan Quisenberry	.25
31	Bret Saberhagen	.25
35	Lynn Jones	.15
37	Charlie Leibrandt	.15
38	Mark Huismann	.15
40	Buddy Black	.15
45	Steve Balboni	.15
----	Header Card	.15
----	Discount Card	.15

1988 Negro League Stars

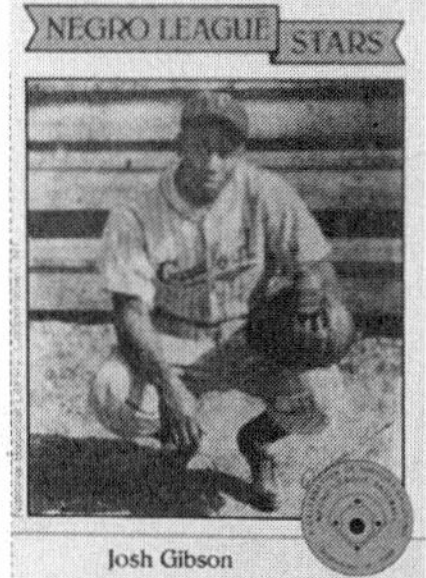

Josh Gibson

Players associated with the segregated Negro Leagues around Pittsburgh are featured on this set sponsored by the Duquesne Light Co. and the Pittsburgh Pirates and handed out at the September 10 Pirates game. The 2-1/2" x 3-1/2" cards were issued on a perforated sheet. Fronts have sepia photos. A yellow banner at top reads "NEGRO LEAGUE STARS," a commemorative circle logo appears at lower-right. Backs are in black-and-white with a career summary, biographical data, and the Pirates logo.

		NM/M
Complete Set (20):		12.00
Uncut Sheet:		12.50
Common Player:		.40
1	Rube Foster	.60
2	1913 Homestead Grays	.40
3	Cum Posey	.75
4	1926 Pittsburgh Crawford	.40
5	Gus Greenlee	.40
6	Pop Lloyd	.60
7	Oscar Charleston	.60
8	Smoky Joe Williams	.60
9	Judy Johnson	.60
10	Martin Dihigo	.60
11	Satchel Paige	1.50
12	Josh Gibson	1.50
13	Sam Streeter	.40
14	Cool Papa Bell	.60
15	Ted Page	.40
16	Buck Leonard	1.00
17	Ray Dandridge	.60
18	Lefty Melix, Willis Moody	.40
19	Harold Tinker	.40
20	Monte Irvin	.80

1984 Nestle

The 792 cards in the 1984 Nestle set are identical to the Topps regular issue except that the candy company's logo replaces the Topps logo in the upper-right corner of the front. The set was offered as a premium in uncut 132-card sheet form (24" x 48"). A few enterprising individuals bought up the majority of the reported 4,000 set production and had the sheets cut into single cards. Due to the ease in handling individual cards, as opposed to large press sheets, sets of single cards sell for more than sheet sets.

	NM/M
Complete Set, Sheets (6)	100.00
Complete Set, Singles (792)	130.00
Common Player:	.25
Sheet A:	60.00
Sheet B:	10.00
Sheet C:	10.00
Sheet D:	10.00
Sheet E:	10.00
Sheet F:	10.00

Don Mattingly "Proof/Test"

This fantasy card has been frequently encountered in the market since the days of Mattingly's dominance in the baseball card world in the late 1980s. The card is seen in several variations, always in black-and-white with a blank-back. Some versions of this unauthorized collectors issues carry notations of proof- or test-card status on front and/or back.

Dream Team

This set was issued by the Nestle candy company in conjunction with Topps. Cards are in standard 2-1/2" x 3-1/2" size and feature the top 22 players of 1984, 11 from each league. This full-color "Dream Team" includes one player at each position, plus right- and left-handed starting pitchers and one reliever. Card fronts and

backs each have a Nestle logo An unnumbered checklist was included with the set.

		NM/M
Complete Set (23):		9.00
Common Player:		.35
Uncut Sheet:		10.00
1	Eddie Murray	.75
2	Lou Whitaker	.35
3	George Brett	2.00
4	Cal Ripken	3.50
5	Jim Rice	.50
6	Dave Winfield	.75
7	Lloyd Moseby	.35
8	Lance Parrish	.35
9	LaMarr Hoyt	.35
10	Ron Guidry	.35
11	Dan Quisenberry	.35
12	Steve Garvey	.50
13	Johnny Ray	.35
14	Mike Schmidt	2.00
15	Ozzie Smith	1.50
16	Andre Dawson	.50
17	Tim Raines	.35
18	Dale Murphy	.50
19	Tony Pena	.35
20	John Denny	.35
21	Steve Carlton	.75
22	Al Holland	.35
----	Checklist	.05

1987 Nestle

Nestle, in conjunction with Topps, issued a 33-card set in 1987. Cards #1-11 feature black-and-white photos of players from the "Golden Era." Cards #12-33 feature full-color photos of American (12-22) and National League (23-33) players from the "Modern Era" of baseball. The cards measure 2-1/2" x 3-1/2" and have all team emblems airbrushed away. Three cards were inserted in specially marked six-packs of various Nestle candy bars. Two complete sets were available through a mail-in offer for $1.50 and three proofs of purchase.

		NM/M
Complete Set (33):		10.00
Common Player:		.30
1	Lou Gehrig	.75
2	Rogers Hornsby	.30
3	Pie Traynor	.30
4	Honus Wagner	.50
5	Babe Ruth	2.00
6	Tris Speaker	.30
7	Ty Cobb	.65
8	Mickey Cochrane	.30
9	Walter Johnson	.30
10	Carl Hubbell	.30
11	Jimmie Foxx	.30
12	Rod Carew	.30
13	Nellie Fox	.30
14	Brooks Robinson	.30
15	Luis Aparicio	.30
16	Frank Robinson	.30
17	Mickey Mantle	3.00
18	Ted Williams	.75
19	Yogi Berra	.30

20	Bob Feller	.30
21	Whitey Ford	.30
22	Harmon Killebrew	.30
23	Stan Musial	.60
24	Jackie Robinson	.75
25	Eddie Mathews	.30
26	Ernie Banks	.30
27	Roberto Clemente	1.50
28	Willie Mays	.75
29	Hank Aaron	.75
30	Johnny Bench	.30
31	Bob Gibson	.30
32	Warren Spahn	.30
33	Duke Snider	.30

1988 Nestle

This 44-card set was produced by Mike Schechter Associates for Nestle. "Dream Team" packets of three player cards and one checklist card were inserted in six-packs of Nestle's candy bars. The issue features current players divided into four Dream Teams (East and West teams for each league). The "1988 Nestle" header appears at the top of the red and yellow-bordered cards. Below the player close up (in an airbrushed cap) is a blue oval player name banner. Card backs are red, white and blue with personal stats, career highlights and major league totals. The bright red, blue and yellow checklist card outlines two special offers; one for an uncut sheet of all 44 player cards and one for a 1988 replica autographed baseball.

		NM/M
Complete Set, Singles (44):		10.00
Complete Set, Uncut Sheet:		10.00
Common Player:		.25
1	Roger Clemens	2.25
2	Dale Murphy	.50
3	Eric Davis	.25
4	Gary Gaetti	.25
5	Ozzie Smith	2.00
6	Mike Schmidt	2.25
7	Ozzie Guillen	.25
8	John Franco	.25
9	Andre Dawson	.50
10	Mark McGwire	2.50
11	Bret Saberhagen	.25
12	Benny Santiago	.25
13	Jose Uribe	.25
14	Will Clark	.25
15	Don Mattingly	2.25
16	Juan Samuel	.25
17	Jack Clark	.25
18	Darryl Strawberry	.25
19	Bill Doran	.25
20	Pete Incaviglia	.25
21	Dwight Gooden	.25
22	Willie Randolph	.25
23	Tim Wallach	.25
24	Pedro Guerrero	.25
25	Steve Bedrosian	.25
26	Gary Carter	1.00
27	Jeff Reardon	.25
28	Dave Righetti	.25
29	Frank White	.25
30	Buddy Bell	.25
31	Tim Raines	.25
32	Wade Boggs	2.00
33	Dave Winfield	1.00
34	George Bell	.25
35	Alan Trammell	.25
36	Joe Carter	.25
37	Jose Canseco	.75
38	Carlton Fisk	1.00
39	Kirby Puckett	2.00
40	Tony Gwynn	2.00
41	Matt Nokes	.25
42	Keith Hernandez	.25
43	Nolan Ryan	3.00
44	Wally Joyner	.25

2002 Nestle

Specially marked boxes of Nestle's ice cream novelties contained one of six Topps-

produced cards sealed to the cardboard in a protective plastic pouch. The 2-1/2" x 3-1/2" cards have a color action photo and black-and-white portrait photo on front. Both pictures have had uniform logos removed because the cards are licensed only by the players, and not by MLB. Topps and Nestle's logos appear at top. Backs have another color photo, biographical data, recent stats, career highlights and sponsor/copyright information. Authentically autographed A-Rod and Chipper cards were random inserts.

		NM/M
Complete Set (6):		12.00
Common Player:		2.00
1	Barry Bonds	3.50
2	Chipper Jones	2.00
2	Chipper Jones/Auto.	35.00
3	Mike Piazza	2.50
4	Alex Rodriguez	2.50
4	Alex Rodriguez/Auto.	60.00
5	Sammy Sosa	2.00
6	Ichiro	3.00

1991-1992 NewSport

This set of glossy player cards was issued in France as four-card panels stapled into issues of a monthly magazine devoted to American sports; hence all of the text is in French. The approximately 4" x 6" cards have a month of issue in tiny type on the back. Fronts have large color game-action photos or poses bordered in white. At top is the player's last name and initial, and his position. The NewSport and MLB logos are at bottom. Backs are in black-and-white with biographical details, major league stats and career summary. The unnumbered cards are checklisted here in alphabetical order. In 2001 a hoard of more than 14,000 of the cards, comprising 175 sets and thousands of four-card panels, was offered in a major hobby auction but did not meet a $5,000 minimum bid.

		NM/M
Complete Set (32):		55.00
Common Player:		1.00
(1)	Roberto Alomar	1.50
(2)	Wade Boggs	4.00
(3)	George Brett	4.50
(4)	Will Clark	1.00
(5)	Eric Davis	1.00
(6)	Rob Dibble	1.00
(7)	Doug Drabek	1.00
(8)	Cecil Fielder	1.00
(9)	Julio Franco	1.00
(10)	Ken Griffey Jr.	5.00
(11)	Rickey Henderson	3.00
(12)	Kent Hrbek	1.00
(13)	Bo Jackson	1.50
(14)	Howard Johnson	1.00
(15)	Barry Larkin	1.00
(16)	Don Mattingly	4.50
(17)	Fred McGriff	1.00
(18)	Mark McGwire	6.00
(19)	Jack Morris	1.00
(20)	Lloyd Moseby	1.00
(21)	Terry Pendleton	1.00
(22)	Kirby Puckett	4.00
(23)	Cal Ripken Jr.	7.50
(24)	Nolan Ryan	7.50
(25)	Bret Saberhagen	1.00
(26)	Ryne Sandberg	4.00
(27)	Benito Santiago	1.00
(28)	Mike Scioscia	1.00
(29)	Ozzie Smith	4.00
(30)	Darryl Strawberry	1.00
(31)	Andy Van Slyke	1.00
(32)	Frank Viola	1.00

1989 J.J. Nissen Super Stars

Distributed with bakery products, these standard-size cards feature central color photos on which uniform logos have been airbrushed away due to lack of a Major League Baseball license by Michael Schechter Associates, the cards' manufacturer. Front graphics are in shades of red, orange and yellow. Backs are printed in black-and-white. The complete set price does not include the Mark Grace card with Vance Law's photo.

		NM/M
Complete Set (20):		7.00
Common Player:		.25
1	Wally Joyner	.25
2	Wade Boggs	1.00
3	Ellis Burks	.25
4	Don Mattingly	1.25
5	Jose Canseco	.75
6	Mike Greenwell	.25
7	Eric Davis	.25
8	Kirby Puckett	1.00
9	Kevin Seitzer	.25
10	Darryl Strawberry	.25
11	Gregg Jefferies	.25
12a	Mark Grace (Photo actually Vance Law.)	3.00
12b	Mark Grace (Correct photo.)	.35
13	Matt Nokes	.25
14	Mark McGwire	1.50
15	Bobby Bonilla	.25
16	Roger Clemens	1.25
17	Frank Viola	.25
18	Orel Hershiser	.25
19	David Cone	.25
20	Ted Williams	2.00

2001 Norstan Milwaukee Brewers Walk of Fame

To commemorate the Walk of Fame in their newly opened ballpark, the Brewers gave this set of inaugural inductees' cards to the first 30,000 fans at the July 12 game. Sponsored by Norstan, whose logo appears in red on front, the 2-1/2" x 3-1/2" cards have sepia toned game-action photos on front with facsimile autograph; at left is a vertical

bar with player name and uniform number. Black-and-white backs have another action photo.

		NM/M
Complete Set (4):		8.00
Common Player:		1.00
(1)	Hank Aaron	4.00
(2)	Rollie Fingers	1.00
(3)	Paul Molitor	2.00
(4)	Robin Yount	2.00

1984 N.Y. Mets M.V.P. Club

This nine-card, uncut panel was issued - along with other souvenir items - as a promotion by the New York Mets M.V.P. (Most Valuable Person) Club. Available from the club by mail, the perforated panel features eight full-color player cards, plus a special promotional card in the center. The full panel measures 7-1/2" x 10-1/2", with individual cards measuring the standard 2-1/2" x 3-1/2". Card backs are numbered in the upper right corner and include player stats and career highlights.

		NM/M
Complete Singles Set (9):		3.00
Common Player:		.25
Panel:		4.50
1	Dave Johnson	.25
2	Ron Darling	.25
3	George Foster	.25
4	Keith Hernandez	.50
5	Jesse Orosco	.25
6	Rusty Staub	.40
7	Darryl Strawberry	1.50
8	Mookie Wilson	.35
----	Membership Card	.05

1985 N.Y. Mets Super Fan Club

This nine-card panel was issued as part of a souvenir package by the New York Mets Super Fan Club. The full-color, perforated panel measures 7-1/2" x 10-1/2" and features eight standard-size player cards, plus a special promotional card in the center. The uncut sheet was available by mail directly from the club. The backs are numbered in the upper right corner and include player statistics and career highlights.

		NM/M
Complete Singles Set (9):		3.50
Common Player:		.25
Panel:		4.50
1	Wally Backman	.25
2	Bruce Berenyi	.25
3	Gary Carter	2.00
4	George Foster	.25
5	Dwight Gooden	1.00
6	Keith Hernandez	.50
7	Doug Sisk	.25
8	Darryl Strawberry	.35
----	Membership Card	.05

1985 N.Y. Mets Police

This collectors' issue came out of Florida, where the Mets conducted spring training. The cards were not authorized by the team, the Kiwanis Club or any police agency; they were manufactured strictly for sale to unsuspecting collectors. In format they resemble contemporary safety issues, measuring 2-5/8" x 4-1/4" with color player photos on front and an anti-drug message on back (ironic, considering the percentage of players in the set who had well-publicized substance abuse problems). Because of their unlicensed nature no collectible value is quoted.

1986 N.Y. Mets Super Fan Club

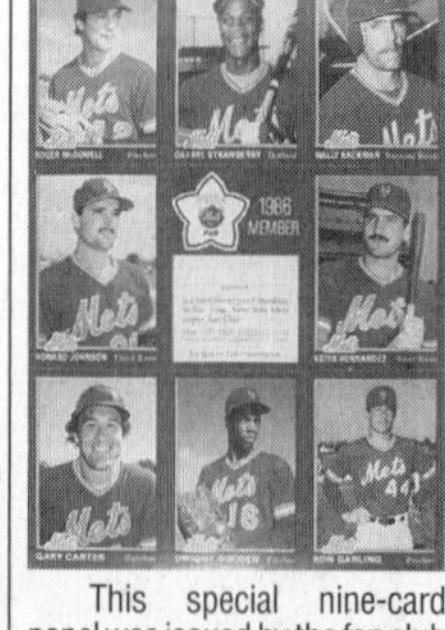

This special nine-card panel was issued by the fan club of the 1986 World Champion New York Mets, along with other souvenir items gained with membership in the club. Included in the full-color set are eight top Mets players, with a promotional card in the center of the panel. Individual cards measure 2-1/2" x 3-1/2", and are perforated at the edges to facilitate separation. The full panel measures 70-1/2" x 10-1/2". Card fronts feature posed photos of each player, along with name, position and team logo. Backs feature career and personal data, and are printed in the team's blue and orange colors.

		NM/M
Complete Singles Set (9):		2.00
Common Player:		.15
Panel:		2.00
1	Wally Backman	.25
2	Gary Carter	1.00
3	Ron Darling	.25
4	Dwight Gooden	.35
5	Keith Hernandez	.45
6	Howard Johnson	.25
7	Roger McDowell	.25
8	Darryl Strawberry	.35
----	Membership Card	.05

1992 N.Y. Mets Spring Training Superstars

A series of large-format (13-3/4" x 22-3/4") color pictures of Mets players was issued during spring training 1992 by The Port St. Lucie News and The Stuart News in Florida. The pictures are printed on heavy newspaper stock and feature color action photos with a light blue frame and white border. A box at bottom has the player's major league career stats. Various advertisements appear on back. The unnumbered pictures are listed here alphabetically and it is possible this list is not complete.

		NM/M
Complete Set (9):		35.00
Common Player:		4.00
(1)	Bobby Bonilla	4.00
(2)	Kevin Elster	4.00
(3)	John Franco	4.00
(4)	Todd Hundley	4.00
(5)	Howard Johnson	4.00
(6)	Dave Magadan	4.00
(7)	Eddie Murray	8.00
(8)	Willie Randolph	4.00
(9)	Bret Saberhagen	6.00

1997 N.Y. Mets Motion Cards

This issue was handed out to fans as a stadium promotion. The 3-1/2" x 2-1/2" cards have a borderless action scene on front, in which the players move when the card is tilted. Backs are conventionally printed with another player action photo, 1996 stats and biographical details.

		NM/M
Complete Set (4):		9.00
Common Player:		2.00
0	Rey Ordonez	3.00
1	Lance Johnson	2.00
9	Todd Hundley	2.50
31	John Franco	2.00

2003 N.Y. Mets Spring Training

Several media outlets at the team's spring training headquarters in Port St. Luice, Fla., sponsored this set of cards as a stadium giveaway on March 12. Several of the cards are the first to show the team's newest stars in their Mets uniforms. Distributed in a paper envelope, the cards are a mix of portrait and action photos in a blank-back 3-1/8" x 4-7/8" format.

		NM/M
Complete Set (7):		15.00
Common Player:		.50
(1)	Roberto Alomar	1.50
(2)	Armando Benitez	.50
(3)	Cliff Floyd	.50
(4)	Tom Glavine	2.50
(5)	Al Leiter	.50
(6)	Mike Piazza	10.00
(7)	Mo Vaughn	1.50

2004 N.Y. Post Yankees Medallion Collection

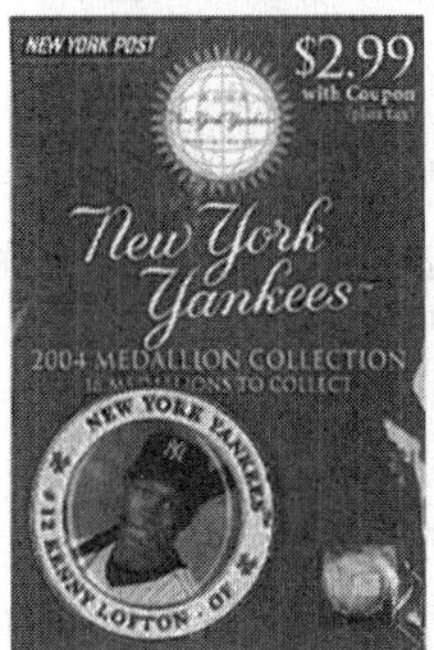

A set of 16 commemorative medallions was issued by the N.Y. Post in this early-season promotion. Coupons found in the newspaper between April 27 and May 16 could be redeemed at newsstands (along with $2.99) for that day's medallion. Larger and thicker than a quarter, the 1-3/16" diameter medals are struck in nickel and have on their fronts an enameled portrait photo. Backs have the team logo. A bronze "Next Century" medallion was available with the complete set and a colorful, photo-filled 9-1/2" x 9" album was available to house the pieces. The medals are listed here by uniform number.

		NM/M
Complete Set (16):		60.00
Common Player:		3.00
Album:		3.00
2	Derek Jeter	7.50
11	Gary Sheffield	4.50
12	Kenny Lofton	3.00
13	Alex Rodriguez	6.00
14	Enrique Wilson	3.00
20	Jorge Posada	3.00
22	Jon Lieber	3.00
25	Jason Giambi	4.50
27	Kevin Brown	3.00
33	Javier Vazquez	3.00
35	Mike Mussina	4.50
42	Mariano Rivera	3.00
51	Bernie Williams	3.00
52	Jose Contreras	3.00
55	Hideki Matsui	7.50
---	Next Century	3.00

2005 N.Y. Post Yankees Immortals Medallion Collection

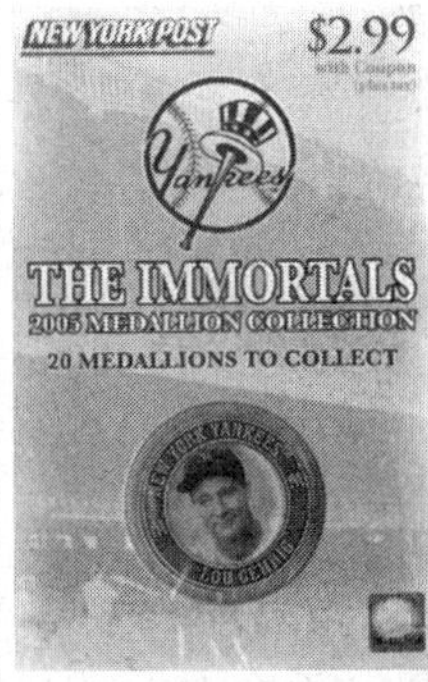

A set of 20 commemorative medallions was issued by the N.Y. Post in this promotion. Coupons found in the newspaper between April 18 and May 13 could be redeemed at newsstands (along with $2.99) for that day's medallion. Larger and thicker than a quarter, the 1-3/16" diameter medals are struck in nickel and have on their fronts an enameled portrait photo. Backs have a pinstriped jersey with the player's number. A triple-fold, colorful, photo-filled 14" x 22" album was available to house the pieces. The medals are listed here in the order of their issue.

		NM/M
Complete Set (20):		75.00
Common Player:		3.00
Album:		3.00
(1)	Lou Gehrig	7.50
(2)	Mickey Mantle	10.00
(3)	Graig Nettles	3.00
(4)	Jim "Catfish" Hunter	3.00
(5)	Reggie Jackson	5.00
(6)	Yogi Berra	5.00
(7)	Ron Guidry	3.00
(8)	Lefty Gomez	3.00
(9)	Tony Lazzeri	3.00
(10)	Phil Rizzuto	3.00
(11)	Roger Maris	4.50
(12)	Don Mattingly	4.50
(13)	Don Larsen	3.00
(14)	Elston Howard	3.00
(15)	Thurman Munson	4.50
(16)	Joe DiMaggio	7.50
(17)	Whitey Ford	4.50
(18)	Billy Martin	3.00
(19)	Casey Stengel	3.00
(20)	Babe Ruth	9.00

1982 N.Y. Yankees Yearbook

American League stars of the 1940s-1960s are featured in a two-page cardboard panel stapled into the Yankees yearbook in 1982. The cards were the work of TCMA and done in the style of early-1950s Bowman cards, although the size is the standard 2-1/2" x 3-1/2". Like the '51 Bowmans, the yearbook cards have a color painting of the player on front with his name in a black strip near the bottom. Backs have a career summary and a bit of personal data along with the TCMA copyright notice. The yearbook originally sold for $3.

		NM/M
Complete Yearbook:		18.00
Complete Set, Singles (18):		16.00
Common Player:		1.00
1	Joe DiMaggio	6.00
2	Billy Pierce	1.00
3	Phil Rizzuto	2.00
4	Ted Williams	5.00
5	Billy Martin	1.50
6	Mel Parnell	1.00
7	Harmon Killebrew	1.50
8	Yogi Berra	2.00
9	Roy Sievers	1.00
10	Bill Dickey	1.50
11	Hank Greenberg	2.00
12	Allie Reynolds	1.00
13	Joe Sewell	1.00
14	Virgil Trucks	1.00
15	Mickey Mantle	8.00
16	Boog Powell	1.00
17	Whitey Ford	1.50
18	Lou Boudreau	1.00

1985 N.Y. Yankees Police

This collectors' issue came out of Florida, where the Yankees conducted spring training. The cards were not authorized by the team, the Kiwanis Club of any police agency; they were manufactured strictly for sale to unsuspecting collectors. In format they resemble contemporary safety issues, measuring 2-5/8" x 4-1/4" with color player photos on front and an anti-drug message on back. Because they were unlicensed, no collector value is attributed.

2004 N.Y. Yankees Collector's Series

Each spring training program sold at 2004 Yankees games at Legends Field in Tampa included one 8" x 10" color card of a current or former Yankees player. Each card was issued only on a single day, making assembly of complete sets difficult. Fronts have a large color game-action photo with the famous Yankee Stadium facade at top. Backs have biographical data, a few stats or, in the case of retired players, a career summary.

		NM/M
Complete Set (13):		75.00
Common Player:		5.00
1	Jorge Posada	6.00
2	Ron Guidry	5.00
3	Mike Mussina	5.00
4	Gary Sheffield	5.00
5	Mariano Rivera	5.00
6	Hideki Matsui	7.50
7	Don Mattingly	10.00
8	Jason Giambi	6.00
9	Reggie Jackson	6.00
10	Yogi Berra	6.00
11	Bucky Dent	5.00
12	Derek Jeter	10.00
13	Alex Rodriguez	10.00

O

1981 O-Pee-Chee

The Canadian version of the 1981 Topps set consists of 374 cards. This O-Pee-Chee set features many cards which note a player team change on front. These notations could be accomplished as the OPC cards were printed after the Topps. The cards measure 2-1/2" x 3-1/2" and have texts that are written in both English and French. The cards were printed on both white and gray stock. Cards with gray stock are valued 2-3X those with white stock.

		NM/M
Complete Set (374):		40.00
Common Player:		.10
Wax Pack (8):		2.50
Wax Box (36):		60.00
1	Frank Pastore	.10
2	Phil Huffman	.10
3	Len Barker	.10
4	Robin Yount	2.00
5	Dave Stieb	.15
6	Gary Carter	4.00
7	Butch Hobson	.10
8	Lance Parrish	.10
9	Bruce Sutter	1.50
10	Mike Flanagan	.10
11	Paul Mirabella	.10
12	Craig Reynolds	.10
13	Joe Charboneau	.50
14	Dan Driessen	.10
15	Larry Parrish	.10
16	Ron Davis	.10
17	Cliff Johnson	.10
18	Bruce Bochte	.10
19	Jim Clancy	.10
20	Bill Russell	.10
21	Ron Oester	.10
22	Danny Darwin	.10
23	Willie Aikens	.10
24	Don Stanhouse	.10
25	Sixto Lezcano	.10
26	U.L. Washington	.10
27	Champ Summers	.10
28	Enrique Romo	.10
29	Gene Tenace	.10
30	Jack Clark	.10
31	Checklist 1-125	.10
32	Ken Oberkfell	.10
33	Rick Honeycutt	.10
34	Al Bumbry	.10
35	John Tamargo	.10
36	Ed Farmer	.10
37	Gary Roenicke	.10
38	Tim Foli	.10
39	Eddie Murray	2.00
40	Roy Howell	.10
41	Bill Gullickson	.15
42	Jerry White	.10
43	Tim Blackwell	.10
44	Steve Henderson	.10
45	Enos Cabell	.10
46	Rick Bossetti	.10
47	Bill North	.10
48	Rich Gossage	.15
49	Bob Shirley	.10
50	Dave Lopes	.10
51	Shane Rawley	.10
52	Lloyd Moseby	.75
53	Burt Hooton	.10
54	Ivan DeJesus	.10
55	Mike Norris	.10
56	Del Unser	.10
57	Dave Revering	.10
58	Joel Youngblood	.10
59	Steve McCatty	.10
60	Willie Randolph	.10
61	Butch Wynegar	.10
62	Gary Lavelle	.10
63	Willie Montanez	.10
64	Terry Puhl	.10
65	Scott McGregor	.10
66	Buddy Bell	.10
67	Toby Harrah	.10
68	Jim Rice	.45
69	Darrell Evans	.10
70	Al Oliver	.10
71	Hal Dues	.10
72	Barry Evans	.10
73	Doug Bair	.10
74	Mike Hargrove	.10
75	Reggie Smith	.10
76	Mario Mendoza	.10
77	Mike Barlow	.10
78	Garth Iorg	.10
79	Jeff Reardon	1.00
80	Roger Erickson	.10
81	Dave Stapleton	.10
82	Barry Bonnell	.10
83	Dave Concepcion	.10
84	Johnnie LeMaster	.10
85	Mike Caldwell	.10
86	Wayne Gross	.10
87	Rick Camp	.10
88	Joe Lefebvre	.10
89	Darrell Jackson	.10
90	Bake McBride	.10
91	Tim Stoddard	.10
92	Mike Easler	.10
93	Jim Bibby	.10
94	Kent Tekulve	.10
95	Jim Sundberg	.10
96	Tommy John	.15
97	Chris Speier	.10
98	Clint Hurdle	.10
99	Phil Garner	.10
100	Rod Carew	2.00
101	Steve Stone	.10
102	Joe Niekro	.10
103	Jerry Martin	.10
104	Ron LeFlore	.10
105	Jose Cruz	.10
106	Don Money	.10
107	Bobby Brown	.10
108	Larry Herndon	.10
109	Dennis Eckersley	1.50
110	Carl Yastrzemski	2.50
111	Greg Minton	.10
112	Dan Schatzeder	.10
113	George Brett	4.00
114	Tom Underwood	.10
115	Roy Smalley	.10
116	Carlton Fisk	2.00
117	Pete Falcone	.10
118	Dale Murphy	1.00
119	Tippy Martinez	.10
120	Larry Bowa	.10
121	Julio Cruz	.10
122	Jim Gantner	.10
123	Al Cowens	.10
124	Jerry Garvin	.10
125	Andre Dawson	3.00
126	Charlie Leibrandt	.10
127	Willie Stargell	2.00
128	Andre Thornton	.10
129	Art Howe	.10
130	Larry Gura	.10
131	Jerry Remy	.10
132	Rick Dempsey	.10
133	Alan Trammell	.15
134	Mike LaCoss	.10
135	Gorman Thomas	.10
136	Expos Future Stars (Bobby Pate, Tim Raines, Roberto Ramos)	3.00
137	Bill Madlock	.10
138	Rich Dotson	.10
139	Oscar Gamble	.10
140	Bob Forsch	.10
141	Miguel Dilone	.10
142	Jackson Todd	.10
143	Dan Meyer	.10
144	Garry Templeton	.10
145	Mickey Rivers	.10
146	Alan Ashby	.10
147	Dale Berra	.10
148	Randy Jones	.10
149	Joe Nolan	.10
150	Mark Fidrych	.25
151	Tony Armas	.10
152	Steve Kemp	.10
153	Jerry Reuss	.10
154	Rick Langford	.10
155	Chris Chambliss	.10
156	Bob McClure	.10
157	John Wathan	.10
158	John Curtis	.10
159	Steve Howe	.10
160	Garry Maddox	.10
161	Dan Graham	.10
162	Doug Corbett	.10
163	Rob Dressler	.10
164	Bucky Dent	.10
165	Alvis Woods	.10
166	Floyd Bannister	.10
167	Lee Mazzilli	.10
168	Don Robinson	.10
169	John Mayberry	.10
170	Woodie Fryman	.10
171	Gene Richards	.10
172	Rick Burleson	.10
173	Bump Wills	.10
174	Glenn Abbott	.10
175	Dave Collins	.10
176	Mike Krukow	.10
177	Rick Monday	.10
178	Dave Parker	.10
179	Rudy May	.10
180	Pete Rose	6.00
181	Elias Sosa	.10
182	Bob Grich	.10
183	Fred Norman	.10
184	Jim Dwyer	.10
185	Dennis Leonard	.10
186	Gary Matthews	.10
187	Ron Hassey	.10
188	Doug DeCinces	.10
189	Craig Swan	.10
190	Cesar Cedeno	.10
191	Rick Sutcliffe	.10
192	Kiko Garcia	.10
193	Pete Vuckovich	.10
194	Tony Bernazard	.10
195	Keith Hernandez	.10
196	Jerry Mumphrey	.10
197	Jim Kern	.10
198	Jerry Dybzinski	.10
199	John Lowenstein	.10
200	George Foster	.10
201	Phil Niekro	1.50
202	Bill Buckner	.10
203	Steve Carlton	2.00
204	John D'Acquisto	.10
205	Rick Reuschel	.10
206	Dan Quisenberry	.10
207	Mike Schmidt	4.00
208	Bob Watson	.10
209	Jim Spencer	.10
210	Jim Palmer	1.50
211	Derrel Thomas	.10
212	Steve Nicosia	.10
213	Omar Moreno	.10
214	Richie Zisk	.10
215	Larry Hisle	.10
216	Mike Torrez	.10
217	Rich Hebner	.10
218	Britt Burns	.10
219	Ken Landreaux	.10
220	Tom Seaver	2.00
221	Bob Davis	.10
222	Jorge Orta	.10
223	Bobby Bonds	.10
224	Pat Zachry	.10
225	Ruppert Jones	.10
226	Duane Kuiper	.10
227	Rodney Scott	.10
228	Tom Paciorek	.10
229	Rollie Fingers	1.50
230	George Hendrick	.10
231	Tony Perez	2.50
232	Grant Jackson	.10
233	Damaso Garcia	.10
234	Lou Whitaker	.10
235	Scott Sanderson	.10
236	Mike Ivie	.10
237	Charlie Moore	.10
238	Blue Jays Future Stars (Luis Leal, Brian Milner, Ken Schrom)	.45
239	Rick Miller	.10
240	Nolan Ryan	9.00
241	Checklist 126-250	.10
242	Chet Lemon	.10
243	Dave Palmer	.10
244	Ellis Valentine	.10
245	Carney Lansford	.10
246	Ed Ott	.10
247	Glenn Hubbard	.10
248	Joey McLaughlin	.10
249	Jerry Narron	.10
250	Ron Guidry	.10
251	Steve Garvey	.75
252	Victor Cruz	.10
253	Bobby Murcer	.10
254	Ozzie Smith	3.00
255	John Stearns	.10
256	Bill Campbell	.10
257	Rennie Stennett	.10
258	Rick Waits	.10
259	Gary Lucas	.10
260	Ron Cey	.10
261	Rickey Henderson	8.00
262	Sammy Stewart	.10
263	Brian Downing	.10
264	Mark Bomback	.10
265	John Candelaria	.10
266	Renie Martin	.10
267	Stan Bahnsen	.10
268	Expos Team	.50
269	Ken Forsch	.10
270	Greg Luzinski	.10
271	Ron Jackson	.10
272	Wayne Garland	.10
273	Milt May	.10
274	Rick Wise	.10
275	Dwight Evans	.10
276	Sal Bando	.10
277	Alfredo Griffin	.10
278	Rick Sofield	.10
279	Bob Knepper	.10
280	Ken Griffey	.10
281	Ken Singleton	.10
282	Ernie Whitt	.10
283	Billy Sample	.10
284	Jack Morris	.10
285	Dick Ruthven	.10
286	Johnny Bench	2.00
287	Dave Smith	.10
288	Amos Otis	.10
289	Dave Goltz	.10
290	Bob Boone	.10
291	Aurelio Lopez	.10
292	Tom Hume	.10
293	Charlie Lea	.10
294	Bert Blyleven	.10
295	Hal McRae	.10
296	Bob Stanley	.10

297 Bob Bailor .10
298 Jerry Koosman .10
299 Eliott Maddox .10
300 Paul Molitor 2.50
301 Matt Keough .10
302 Pat Putnam .10
303 Dan Ford .10
304 John Castino .10
305 Barry Foote .10
306 Lou Piniella .15
307 Gene Garber .10
308 Rick Manning .10
309 Don Baylor .10
310 Vida Blue .10
311 Doug Flynn .10
312 Rick Rhoden .10
313 Fred Lynn .10
314 Rich Dauer .10
315 Kirk Gibson 2.50
316 Ken Reitz .10
317 Lonnie Smith .10
318 Steve Yeager .10
319 Rowland Office .10
320 Tom Burgmeier .10
321 Leon Durham .10
322 Neil Allen .10
323 Ray Burris .10
324 Mike Willis .10
325 Ray Knight .10
326 Rafael Landestoy .10
327 Moose Haas .10
328 Ross Baumgarten .10
329 Joaquin Andujar .10
330 Frank White .10
331 Blue Jays Team .50
332 Dick Drago .10
333 Sid Monge .10
334 Joe Sambito .10
335 Rick Cerone .10
336 Eddie Whitson .10
337 Sparky Lyle .10
338 Checklist 251-374 .10
339 Jon Matlack .10
340 Ben Oglivie .10
341 Dwayne Murphy .10
342 Terry Crowley .10
343 Frank Taveras .10
344 Steve Rogers .10
345 Warren Cromartie .10
346 Bill Caudill .10
347 Harold Baines 1.50
348 Frank LaCorte .10
349 Glenn Hoffman .10
350 J.R. Richard .10
351 Otto Velez .10
352 Ted Simmons .10
353 Terry Kennedy .10
354 Al Hrabosky .10
355 Bob Horner .10
356 Cecil Cooper .10
357 Bob Welch .10
358 Paul Moskau .10
359 Dave Rader .10
360 Willie Wilson .10
361 Dave Kingman .10
362 Joe Rudi .10
363 Rich Gale .10
364 Steve Trout .10
365 Graig Nettles .10
366 Lamar Johnson .10
367 Denny Martinez .10
368 Manny Trillo .10
369 Frank Tanana .10
370 Reggie Jackson 2.50
371 Bill Lee .10
372 Jay Johnstone .10
373 Jason Thompson .10
374 Tom Hutton .10

Posters

Inserted inside the regular 1981 O-Pee-Chee wax packs, these full-color posters measure approximately 4-7/8" x 6-7/8". The set is complete at 24 posters and includes 12 players each from the Blue Jays and Expos. The blank-backed posters are numbered in the border below the photo where the caption is written in both French and English. The photos are surrounded by a blue border for Blue Jays players or a red border for Expos. Because they were inserted in wax packs, the posters are usually found quarter-folded; such folds are not considered in grading.

NM/M
Complete Set (24): 10.00
Common Player: .50
1 Willie Montanez .50
2 Rodney Scott .50
3 Chris Speier .50
4 Larry Parrish .50
5 Warren Cromartie .50
6 Andre Dawson 2.00
7 Ellis Valentine .50
8 Gary Carter 5.00
9 Steve Rogers .50
10 Woodie Fryman .50
11 Jerry White .50
12 Scott Sanderson .50
13 John Mayberry .50
14 Damasa Garcia (Damaso) .50
15 Alfredo Griffin .50
16 Garth Iorg .50
17 Alvis Woods .50
18 Rick Bosetti .50
19 Barry Bonnell .50
20 Ernie Whitt .50
21 Jim Clancy .50
22 Dave Stieb 1.50
23 Otto Velez .50
24 Lloyd Moseby .50

1982 O-Pee-Chee

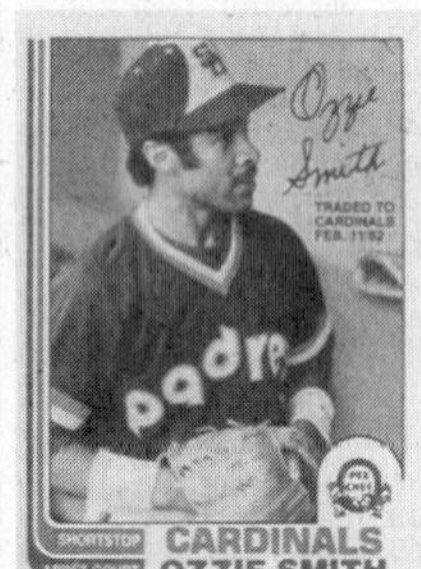

The 1982 O-Pee-Chee set, complete at 396 cards, is nearly identical in design to the 1982 Topps set, except the Canadian-issued cards display the O-Pee-Chee logo on the front of the card and list the player's position in both French and English. The backs of the cards, which measure the standard 2-1/2" x 3-1/2", are also bilingual. Some of the cards carry an extra line on the front indicating an off-season team change.

NM/M
Complete Set (396): 35.00
Common Player: .10
Wax Pack: 1.50
Wax Box (36): 40.00
1 Dan Spillner .10
2 Ken Singleton/AS .10
3 John Candelaria .10
4 Frank Tanana .10
5 Reggie Smith .10
6 Rick Monday .10
7 Scott Sanderson .10
8 Rich Dauer .10
9 Ron Guidry .15
10 Ron Guidry/IA .10
11 Tom Brookens .10
12 Moose Haas .10
13 Chet Lemon .10
14 Steve Howe .10
15 Ellis Valentine .10
16 Toby Harrah .10
17 Darrell Evans .10
18 Johnny Bench 2.00
19 Ernie Whitt .10
20 Garry Maddox .10
21 Graig Nettles/IA .10
22 Al Oliver/IA .10
23 Bob Boone .10
24 Pete Rose/IA 2.00
25 Jerry Remy .10
26 Jorge Orta .10
27 Bobby Bonds .10
28 Jim Clancy .10
29 Dwayne Murphy .10
30 Tom Seaver 2.00
31 Tom Seaver/IA 1.00
32 Claudell Washington .10
33 Bob Shirley .10
34 Bob Forsch .10
35 Willie Aikens .10
36 Rod Carew/AS .60
37 Willie Randolph .10
38 Charlie Lea .10
39 Lou Whitaker .10
40 Dave Parker .10
41 Dave Parker/IA .10
42 Mark Belanger .10
43 Rick Langford .10
44 Rollie Fingers/IA .10
45 Rick Cerone .10
46 Johnny Wockenfuss .10
47 Jack Morris/AS .10
48 Cesar Cedeno .10
49 Alvis Woods .10
50 Buddy Bell .10
51 Mickey River/IA .10
52 Steve Rogers .10
53 Blue Jays Team .50
54 Ron Hassey .10
55 Rick Burleson .10
56 Harold Baines .10
57 Craig Reynolds .10
58 Carlton Fisk/AS .60
59 Jim Kern .10
60 Tony Armas .10
61 Warren Cromartie .10
62 Graig Nettles .10
63 Jerry Koosman .10
64 Pat Zachry .10
65 Terry Kennedy .10
66 Richie Zisk .10
67 Rich Gale .10
68 Steve Carlton 2.00
69 Greg Luzinski/IA .10
70 Tim Raines 2.00
71 Roy Lee Jackson .10
72 Carl Yastrzemski 2.00
73 John Castino .10
74 Joe Niekro .10
75 Tommy John .15
76 Dave Winfield/AS .75
77 Miguel Dilone .10
78 Gary Gray .10
79 Tom Hume .10
80 Jim Palmer 1.50
81 Jim Palmer/IA .75
82 Vida Blue/IA .10
83 Garth Iorg .10
84 Rennie Stennett .10
85 Davey Lopes/IA .10
86 Dave Concepcion .10
87 Matt Keough .10
88 Jim Spencer .10
89 Steve Henderson .10
90 Nolan Ryan 7.50
91 Carney Lansford .10
92 Bake McBride .10
93 Dave Stapleton .10
94 Expos Team .50
95 Ozzie Smith 4.00
96 Rich Hebner .10
97 Tim Foli .10
98 Darrell Porter .10
99 Barry Bonnell .10
100 Mike Schmidt 3.00
101 Mike Schmidt/IA 1.50
102 Dan Briggs .10
103 Al Cowens .10
104 Grant Jackson .10
105 Kirk Gibson .10
106 Dan Schatzeder .10
107 Juan Berenguer .10
108 Jack Morris .15
109 Dave Revering .10
110 Carlton Fisk 2.00
111 Carlton Fisk/IA 1.00
112 Billy Sample .10
113 Steve McCatty .10
114 Ken Landreaux .10
115 Gaylord Perry 1.00
116 Elias Sosa .10
117 Rich Gossage/IA .10
118 Expos Future Stars (Terry Francona, Brad Mills, Bryn Smith) .25
119 Billy Almon .10
120 Gary Lucas .10
121 Ken Oberkfell .10
122 Steve Carlton/IA 1.00
123 Jeff Reardon .50
124 Bill Buckner .10
125 Danny Ainge 2.50
126 Paul Splittorff .10
127 Lonnie Smith .10
128 Rudy May .10
129 Checklist 1-132 .10
130 Julio Cruz .10
131 Stan Bahnsen .10
132 Pete Vuckovich .10
133 Luis Salazar .10
134 Dan Ford .10
135 Denny Martinez .10
136 Lary Sorensen .10
137 Fergie Jenkins 1.50
138 Rick Camp .10
139 Wayne Nordhagen .10
140 Ron LeFlore .10
141 Rick Sutcliffe .10
142 Rick Waits .10
143 Mookie Wilson .10
144 Greg Minton .10
145 Bob Horner .10
146 Joe Morgan/IA 1.00
147 Larry Gura .10
148 Alfredo Griffin .10
149 Pat Putnam .10
150 Ted Simmons .10
151 Gary Matthews .10
152 Greg Luzinski .10
153 Mike Flanagan .10
154 Jim Morrison .10
155 Otto Velez .10
156 Frank White .10
157 Doug Corbett .10
158 Brian Downing .10
159 Willie Randolph/IA .10
160 Luis Tiant .10
161 Andre Thornton .10
162 Amos Otis .10
163 Paul Mirabella .10
164 Bert Blyleven .10
165 Rowland Office .10
166 Gene Tenace .10
167 Cecil Cooper .10
168 Bruce Benedict .10
169 Mark Clear .10
170 Jim Bibby .10
171 Ken Griffey Sr./IA .10
172 Bill Gullickson .10
173 Mike Scioscia .10
174 Doug DeCinces .10
175 Jerry Mumphrey .10
176 Rollie Fingers 1.00
177 George Foster/IA .10
178 Mitchell Page .10
179 Steve Garvey .50
180 Steve Garvey/IA .25
181 Woodie Fryman .10
182 Larry Herndon .10
183 Frank White/IA .10
184 Alan Ashby .10
185 Phil Niekro 1.00
186 Leon Roberts .10
187 Rod Carew 2.00
188 Willie Stargell/IA 1.00
189 Joel Youngblood .10
190 J.R. Richard .10
191 Tim Wallach .50
192 Broderick Perkins .10
193 Johnny Grubb .10
194 Larry Bowa .10
195 Paul Molitor 3.00
196 Willie Upshaw .10
197 Roy Smalley .10
198 Chris Speier .10
199 Don Aase .10
200 George Brett 3.00
201 George Brett/IA 1.50
202 Rick Manning .10
203 Blue Jays Future Stars (Jesse Barfield, Brian Milner, Boomer Wells) 2.00
204 Rick Reuschel .10
205 Neil Allen .10
206 Leon Durham .10
207 Jim Gantner .10
208 Joe Morgan 2.00
209 Gary Lavelle .10
210 Keith Hernandez .10
211 Joe Charboneau .10
212 Mario Mendoza .10
213 Willie Randolph/AS .10
214 Lance Parrish .10
215 Mike Krukow .10
216 Ron Cey .10
217 Ruppert Jones .10
218 Dave Lopes .10
219 Steve Yeager .10
220 Manny Trillo .10
221 Dave Concepcio/IA .10
222 Butch Wynegar .10
223 Lloyd Moseby .20
224 Bruce Bochte .10
225 Ed Ott .10
226 Checklist 133-264 .10
227 Ray Burris .10
228 Reggie Smith/IA .10
229 Oscar Gamble .10
230 Willie Wilson .10
231 Brian Kingman .10
232 John Stearns .10
233 Duane Kuiper .10
234 Don Baylor .10
235 Mike Easler .10
236 Lou Piniella .10
237 Robin Yount 2.00
238 Kevin Saucier .10
239 Jon Matlack .10
240 Bucky Dent .10
241 Bucky Dent/IA .10
242 Milt May .10
243 Lee Mazzilli .10
244 Gary Carter 3.00
245 Ken Reitz .10
246 Scott McGregor/AS .10
247 Pedro Guerrero .10
248 Art Howe .10
249 Dick Tidrow .10
250 Tug McGraw .10
251 Fred Lynn .10
252 Fred Lynn/IA .10
253 Gene Richards .10
254 Jorge Bell 4.00
255 Tony Perez 2.50
256 Tony Perez/IA .10
257 Rich Dotson .10
258 Bo Diaz .10
259 Rodney Scott .10
260 Bruce Sutter 1.50
261 George Brett/AS 1.00
262 Rick Dempsey .10
263 Mike Phillips .10
264 Jerry Garvin .10
265 Al Bumbry .10
266 Hubie Brooks .10
267 Vida Blue .10
268 Rickey Henderson 3.00
269 Rick Peters .10
270 Rusty Staub .20
271 Sixto Lezcano .10
272 Bump Wills .10
273 Gary Allenson .10
274 Randy Jones .10
275 Bob Watson .10
276 Dave Kingman .10
277 Terry Puhl .10
278 Jerry Reuss .10
279 Sammy Stewart .10
280 Ben Oglivie .10
281 Kent Tekulve .10
282 Ken Macha .10
283 Ron Davis .10
284 Bob Grich .10
285 Sparky Lyle .10
286 Rich Gossage/AS .10
287 Dennis Eckersley 1.00
288 Garry Templeton .10
289 Bob Stanley .10
290 Ken Singleton .10
291 Mickey Hatcher .10
292 Dave Palmer .10
293 Damaso Garcia .10
294 Don Money .10
295 George Hendrick .10
296 Steve Kemp .10
297 Dave Smith .10
298 Bucky Dent/AS .10
299 Steve Trout .10
300 Reggie Jackson 2.50
301 Reggie Jackson/IA 1.00
302 Doug Flynn .10
303 Wayne Gross .10
304 Johnny Bench/IA 1.00
305 Don Sutton 1.00
306 Don Sutton (IA) .40
307 Mark Bomback .10
308 Charlie Moore .10
309 Jeff Burroughs .10
310 Mike Hargrove .10
311 Enos Cabell .10
312 Lenny Randle .10
313 Ivan DeJesus .10
314 Buck Martinez .10
315 Burt Hooton .10
316 Scott McGregor .10
317 Dick Ruthven .10
318 Mike Heath .10
319 Ray Knight .10
320 Chris Chambliss .10
321 Chris Chamblissv .10
322 Ross Baumgarten .10
323 Bill Lee .10
324 Gorman Thomas .10
325 Jose Cruz .10
326 Al Oliver .10
327 Jackson Todd .10
328 Ed Farmer .10
329 U.L. Washington .10
330 Ken Griffey .10
331 John Milner .10
332 Don Robinson .10
333 Cliff Johnson .10
334 Fernando Valenzuela .15
335 Jim Sundberg .10
336 George Foster .10
337 Pete Rose/AS 1.50
338 Davey Lopes/AS .10
339 Mike Schmidt/AS 1.00
340 Dave Concepcionv .10
341 Andre Dawson/AS .25
342 George Foster/AS .10
343 Dave Parker/AS .10
344 Gary Carter/AS 1.00
345 Fernando Valenzuela/AS .10
346 Tom Seaver/AS .60
347 Bruce Sutter/AS .75
348 Darrell Porter/IA .10
349 Dave Collins .10
350 Amos Otis/IA .10
351 Frank Taveras .10
352 Dave Winfield 3.00
353 Larry Parrish .10
354 Roberto Ramos .10
355 Dwight Evans .10
356 Mickey Rivers .10
357 Butch Hobson .10
358 Carl Yastrzemski/IA 1.00
359 Ron Jackson .10
360 Len Barker .10
361 Pete Rose 4.00
362 Kevin Hickey .10
363 Rod Carew/IA 1.00
364 Hector Cruz .10
365 Bill Madlock .10
366 Jim Rice .40
367 Ron Cey/IA .10
368 Luis Leal .10
369 Dennis Leonard .10
370 Mike Norris .10
371 Tom Paciorek .10
372 Willie Stargell 2.00
373 Dan Driessen .10
374 Larry Bowa/IA .10
375 Dusty Baker .10
376 Joey McLaughlin .10
377 Reggie Jackson/AS .60
378 Mike Caldwell .10
379 Andre Dawson 1.00
380 Dave Stieb .20
381 Alan Trammell .10
382 John Mayberry .10
383 John Wathan .10
384 Hal McRae .10
385 Ken Forsch .10
386 Jerry White .10
387 Tom Veryzer .10
388 Joe Rudi .10
389 Bob Knepper .10
390 Eddie Murray 2.00
391 Dale Murphy .50
392 Bob Boone/IA .10
393 Al Hrabosky .10
394 Checklist 265-396 .10
395 Omar Moreno .10
396 Rich Gossage .15

Posters

The 24 posters in this Canadian set, which features 12 players from the Expos and 12 from the Blue Jays, were inserted in regular 1982 O-Pee-Chee wax packs. The posters measure approximately 4-7/8" x 6-7/8" and are usually found quarter-folded for pack insertion. Such fold lines are not considered in grading. The blank-backed posters are numbered in the bottom border where the captions appear in both French and English. Red borders surround the photos of Blue Jays players, while blue borders are used for the Expos.

NM/M
Complete Set (24): 12.00
Common Player: .50
1 John Mayberry .50
2 Damaso Garcia .50
3 Ernie Whitt .50
4 Lloyd Moseby .50
5 Alvis Woods .50
6 Dave Stieb .75
7 Roy Lee Jackson .50
8 Joey McLaughlin .50
9 Luis Leal .50
10 Aurelio Rodriguez .50
11 Otto Velez .50
12 Juan Berenger (Berenguer) .50
13 Warren Cromartie .50
14 Rodney Scott .50
15 Larry Parrish .50
16 Gary Carter 5.00
17 Tim Raines 2.00
18 Andre Dawson 2.00
19 Terry Francona .50
20 Steve Rogers .50
21 Bill Gullickson .50
22 Scott Sanderson .50
23 Jeff Reardon .50
24 Jerry White .50

Stickers

The Canadian OPC stickers are identical to the Topps version except for the bi-lingual printing on backs.

1983 O-Pee-Chee

Again complete at 396 cards, the 1983 O-Pee-Chee set borrows its design from the 1983 Topps set, except the Canadian-issued cards display the O-Pee-Chee logo on the front of the card and show the player's position in both French and English. The backs of the cards are also printed in both languages. The cards measure the standard 2-1/2" x 3-1/2". Some cards carry the extra line on the front indicating an off-season trade.

		NM/M
Complete Set (396):		30.00
Common Player:		.05
Wax Pack:		3.00
Wax Box (36):		60.00
1	Rusty Staub	.15
2	Larry Parrish	.05
3	George Brett	1.75
4	Carl Yastrzemski	1.50
5	Al Oliver (Super Veteran)	.05
6	Bill Virdon	.05
7	Gene Richards	.05
8	Steve Balboni	.05
9	Joey McLaughlin	.05
10	Gorman Thomas	.05
11	Chris Chambliss	.05
12	Ray Burris	.05
13	Larry Herndon	.05
14	Ozzie Smith	1.50
15	Ron Cey	.05
16	Willie Wilson	.05
17	Kent Tekulve	.05
18	Kent Tekulve (Super Veteran)	.05
19	Oscar Gamble	.05
20	Carlton Fisk	1.25
21	Dale Murphy/AS	.05
22	Randy Lerch	.05
23	Dale Murphy	.45
24	Steve Mura	.05
25	Hal McRae	.05
26	Dennis Lamp	.05
27	Ron Washington	.05
28	Bruce Bochte	.05
29	Randy Jones	.05
30	Jim Rice	.15
31	Bill Gullickson	.05
32	Dave Concepcion/AS	.05
33	Ted Simmons (Super Veteran)	.05
34	Bobby Cox	.05
35	Rollie Fingers	.60
36	Rollie Fingers (Super Veteran)	.10
37	Mike Hargrove	.05
38	Roy Smalley	.05
39	Terry Puhl	.05
40	Fernando Valenzuela	.05
41	Garry Maddox	.05
42	Dale Murray	.05
43	Bob Dernier	.05
44	Don Robinson	.05
45	John Mayberry	.05
46	Richard Dotson	.05
47	Wayne Nordhagen	.05
48	Lary Sorenson	.05
49	Willie McGee	.15
50	Bob Horner	.05
51	Rusty Staub (Super Veteran)	.05
52	Tom Seaver	1.25
53	Chet Lemon	.05
54	Scott Sanderson	.05
55	Mookie Wilson	.05
56	Reggie Jackson	1.50
57	Tim Blackwell	.05
58	Keith Moreland	.05
59	Alvis Woods	.05
60	Johnny Bench	1.25
61	Johnny Bench (Super Veteran)	.30
62	Jim Gott	.05
63	Rick Monday	.05
64	Gary Matthews	.05
65	Jack Morris	.15
66	Lou Whitaker	.05
67	U.L. Washington	.05
68	Eric Show	.05
69	Lee Lacy	.05
70	Steve Carlton	1.25
71	Steve Carlton (Super Veteran)	.10
72	Tom Paciorek	.05
73	Manny Trillo	.05
74	Tony Perez (Super Veteran)	.05
75	Amos Otis	.05
76	Rick Mahler	.05
77	Hosken Powell	.05
78	Bill Caudill	.05
79	Dan Petry	.05
80	George Foster	.05
81	Joe Morgan	.05
82	Burt Hooton	.05
83	Ryne Sandberg	8.00
84	Alan Ashby	.05
85	Ken Singleton	.05
86	Tom Hume	.05
87	Dennis Leonard	.05
88	Jim Gantner	.05
89	Leon Roberts	.05
90	Jerry Reuss	.05
91	Ben Oglivie	.05
92	Sparky Lyle (Super Veteran)	.05
93	John Castino	.05
94	Phil Niekro	.60
95	Alan Trammell	.10
96	Gaylord Perry	.05
97	Tom Herr	.05
98	Vance Law	.05
99	Dickie Noles	.05
100	Pete Rose	2.00
101	Pete Rose (Super Veteran)	.50
102	Dave Concepcion	.05
103	Darrell Porter	.05
104	Ron Guidry	.05
105	Don Baylor	.05
106	Steve Rogers (AS)	.05
107	Greg Minton	.05
108	Glenn Hoffman	.05
109	Luis Leal	.05
110	Ken Griffey	.05
111	Expos Team	.05
112	Luis Pujols	.05
113	Julio Cruz	.05
114	Jim Slaton	.05
115	Chili Davis	.05
116	Pedro Guerrero	.05
117	Mike Ivie	.05
118	Chris Welsh	.05
119	Frank Pastore	.05
120	Len Barker	.05
121	Chris Speier	.05
122	Bobby Murcer	.05
123	Bill Russell	.05
124	Lloyd Moseby	.05
125	Leon Durham	.05
126	Carl Yastrzemski (Super Veteran)	.05
127	John Candelaria	.05
128	Phil Garner	.05
129	Checklist 1-132	.05
130	Dave Stieb	.10
131	Geoff Zahn	.05
132	Todd Cruz	.05
133	Tony Pena	.05
134	Hubie Brooks	.05
135	Dwight Evans	.05
136	Willie Aikens	.05
137	Woodie Fryman	.05
138	Rick Dempsey	.05
139	Bruce Berenyi	.05
140	Willie Randolph	.05
141	Eddie Murray	1.25
142	Mike Caldwell	.05
143	Tony Gwynn	8.00
144	Tommy John (Super Veteran)	.05
145	Don Sutton	.60
146	Don Sutton (Super Veteran)	.10
147	Rick Manning	.05
148	George Hendrick	.05
149	Johnny Ray	.05
150	Bruce Sutter	1.00
151	Bruce Sutter (Super Veteran)	.25
152	Jay Johnstone	.05
153	Jerry Koosman	.05
154	Johnnie LeMaster	.05
155	Dan Quisenberry	.05
156	Luis Salazar	.05
157	Steve Bedrosian	.05
158	Jim Sundberg	.05
159	Gaylord Perry (Super Veteran)	.10
160	Dave Kingman	.05
161	Dave Kingman (Super Veteran)	.05
162	Mark Clear	.05
163	Cal Ripken	8.00
164	Dave Palmer	.05
165	Dan Driessen	.05
166	Tug McGraw	.05
167	Denny Martinez	.10
168	Juan Eichelberger	.05
169	Doug Flynn	.05
170	Steve Howe	.05
171	Frank White	.05
172	Mike Flanagan	.05
173	Andre Dawson/AS	.15
174	Manny Trillo/AS	.05
175	Bo Diaz	.05
176	Dave Righetti	.05
177	Harold Baines	.05
178	Vida Blue	.05
179	Luis Tiant (Super Veteran)	.05
180	Rickey Henderson	1.50
181	Rick Rhoden	.05
182	Fred Lynn	.05
183	Ed Vande Berg	.05
184	Dwayne Murphy	.05
185	Tim Lollar	.05
186	Dave Tobik	.05
187	Tug McGraw (Super Veteran)	.05
188	Rick Miller	.05
189	Dan Schatzeder	.05
190	Cecil Cooper	.05
191	Jim Beattie	.05
192	Rich Dauer	.05
193	Al Cowens	.05
194	Roy Lee Jackson	.05
195	Mike Gates	.05
196	Tommy John	.10
197	Bob Forsch	.05
198	Steve Garvey	.15
199	Brad Mills	.05
200	Rod Carew	1.25
201	Rod Carew (Super Veteran)	.05
202	Blue Jays Team	.05
203	Floyd Bannister	.05
204	Bruce Benedict	.05
205	Dave Parker	.05
206	Ken Oberkfell	.05
207	Graig Nettles (Super Veteran)	.05
208	Sparky Lyle	.05
209	Jason Thompson	.05
210	Jack Clark	.05
211	Jim Kaat	.05
212	John Stearns	.05
213	Tom Burgmeier	.05
214	Jerry White	.05
215	Mario Soto	.05
216	Scott McGregor	.05
217	Tim Stoddard	.05
218	Bill Laskey	.05
219	Reggie Jackson (Super Veteran)	.05
220	Dusty Baker	.05
221	Joe Niekro	.05
222	Damaso Garcia	.05
223	John Montefusco	.05
224	Mickey Rivers	.05
225	Enos Cabell	.05
226	LaMarr Hoyt	.05
227	Tim Raines	.20
228	Joaquin Andujar	.05
229	Tim Wallach	.15
230	Fergie Jenkins	.05
231	Fergie Jenkins (Super Veteran)	.05
232	Tom Brunansky	.05
233	Ivan DeJesus	.05
234	Bryn Smith	.05
235	Claudell Washington	.05
236	Steve Renko	.05
237	Dan Norman	.05
238	Cesar Cedeno	.05
239	Dave Stapleton	.05
240	Rich Gossage	.10
241	Rich Gossage (Super Veteran)	.05
242	Bob Stanley	.05
243	Rich Gale	.05
244	Sixto Lezcano	.05
245	Steve Sax	.05
246	Jerry Mumphrey	.05
247	Dave Smith	.05
248	Bake McBride	.05
249	Checklist 133-264	.05
250	Bill Buckner	.05
251	Kent Hrbek	.05
252	Gene Tenace	.05
253	Charlie Lea	.05
254	Rick Cerone	.05
255	Gene Garber	.05
256	Gene Garber (Super Veteran)	.05
257	Jesse Barfield	.30
258	Dave Winfield	1.50
259	Don Money	.05
260	Steve Kemp	.05
261	Steve Yeager	.05
262	Keith Hernandez	.05
263	Tippy Martinez	.05
264	Joe Morgan (Super Veteran)	.05
265	Joel Youngblood	.05
266	Bruce Sutter/AS	.25
267	Terry Francona	.05
268	Neil Allen	.05
269	Ron Oester	.05
270	Dennis Eckersley	.60
271	Dale Berra	.05
272	Al Bumbry	.05
273	Lonnie Smith	.05
274	Terry Kennedy	.05
275	Ray Knight	.05
276	Mike Norris	.05
277	Rance Mulliniks	.05
278	Dan Spillner	.05
279	Bucky Dent	.05
280	Bert Blyleven	.05
281	Barry Bonnell	.05
282	Reggie Smith	.05
283	Reggie Smith (Super Veteran)	.05
284	Ted Simmons	.05
285	Lance Parrish	.05
286	Larry Christenson	.05
287	Ruppert Jones	.05
288	Bob Welch	.05
289	John Wathan	.05
290	Jeff Reardon	.05
291	Dave Revering	.05
292	Craig Swan	.05
293	Graig Nettles	.05
294	Alfredo Griffin	.05
295	Jerry Remy	.05
296	Joe Sambito	.05
297	Ron LeFlore	.05
298	Brian Downing	.05
299	Jim Palmer	1.00
300	Mike Schmidt	1.75
301	Mike Schmidt (Super Veteran)	.35
302	Ernie Whitt	.05
303	Andre Dawson	.75
304	Bobby Murcer (Super Veteran)	.05
305	Larry Bowa	.05
306	Lee Mazzilli	.05
307	Lou Piniella	.05
308	Buck Martinez	.05
309	Jerry Martin	.05
310	Greg Luzinski	.05
311	Al Oliver	.05
312	Mike Torrez	.05
313	Dick Ruthven	.05
314	Gary Carter/AS	.05
315	Rick Burleson	.05
316	Phil Niekro (Super Veteran)	.10
317	Moose Haas	.05
318	Carney Lansford	.05
319	Tim Foli	.05
320	Steve Rogers	.05
321	Kirk Gibson	.05
322	Glenn Hubbard	.05
323	Luis DeLeon	.05
324	Mike Marshall	.05
325	Von Hayes	.05
326	Garth Iorg	.05
327	Jose Cruz	.05
328	Jim Palmer (Super Veteran)	.10
329	Darrell Evans	.05
330	Buddy Bell	.05
331	Mike Krukow	.05
332	Omar Moreno	.05
333	Dave LaRoche	.05
334	Dave LaRoche (Super Veteran)	.05
335	Bill Madlock	.05
336	Garry Templeton	.05
337	John Lowenstein	.05
338	Willie Upshaw	.05
339	Dave Hostetler	.05
340	Larry Gura	.05
341	Doug DeCinces	.05
342	Mike Schmidt (AS)	.25
343	Charlie Hough	.05
344	Andre Thornton	.05
345	Jim Clancy	.05
346	Ken Forsch	.05
347	Sammy Stewart	.05
348	Alan Bannister	.05
349	Checklist 265-396	.05
350	Robin Yount	1.25
351	Warren Cromartie	.05
352	Tim Raines/AS	.05
353	Tony Armas	.05
354	Tom Seaver (Super Veteran)	.30
355	Tony Perez	1.00
356	Toby Harrah	.05
357	Dan Ford	.05
358	Charlie Puleo	.05
359	Dave Collins	.05
360	Nolan Ryan	6.00
361	Nolan Ryan (Super Veteran)	2.50
362	Bill Almon	.05
363	Eddie Milner	.05
364	Gary Lucas	.05
365	Dave Lopes	.05
366	Bob Boone	.05
367	Biff Pocoroba	.05
368	Richie Zisk	.05
369	Tony Bernazard	.05
370	Gary Carter	1.50
371	Paul Molitor	1.50
372	Art Howe	.05
373	Pete Rose/AS	.50
374	Glenn Adams	.05
375	Pete Vukovich	.05
376	Gary Lavelle	.05
377	Lee May	.05
378	Lee May (Super Veteran)	.05
379	Butch Wynegar	.05
380	Ron Davis	.05
381	Bob Grich	.05
382	Gary Roenicke	.05
383	Jim Kaat	.10
384	Steve Carlton/AS	.05
385	Mike Easler	.05
386	Rod Carew/AS	.05
387	Bobby Grich/AS	.05
388	George Brett/AS	.25
389	Robin Yount/AS	.05
390	Reggie Jackson/AS	.05
391	Rickey Henderson/AS	.25
392	Fred Lynn/AS	.05
393	Carlton Fisk/AS	.05
394	Pete Vuckovich/AS	.05
395	Larry Gura/AS	.05
396	Dan Quisenberry/AS	.05

1984 O-Pee-Chee

Almost identical in design to the 1984 Topps set, the 1984 O-Pee-Chee set contains 396 cards. The O-Pee-Chee cards display the Canadian company's logo in the upper right corner and the backs of the cards are printed in both English and French. The cards measure 2-1/2" x 3-1/2", and some include the extra line on the front of the card to indicate a trade.

		NM/M
Complete Set (396):		22.50
Common Player:		.05
Wax Pack:		1.00
Wax Box (36):		25.00
1	Pascual Perez	.10
2	Cal Ripken	6.00
3	Lloyd Moseby	.15
4	Mel Hall	.05
5	Willie Wilson	.05
6	Mike Morgan	.05
7	Gary Lucas	.05
8	Don Mattingly	8.00
9	Jim Gott	.05
10	Robin Yount	1.50
11	Joey McLaughlin	.05
12	Billy Sample	.05
13	Oscar Gamble	.05
14	Bill Russell	.05
15	Burt Hooton	.05
16	Omar Moreno	.05
17	Dave Lopes	.05
18	Dale Berra	.05
19	Rance Mulliniks	.05
20	Greg Luzinski	.05
21	Doug Sisk	.05
22	Don Robinson	.05
23	Keith Moreland	.05
24	Richard Dotson	.05
25	Glenn Hubbard	.05
26	Rod Carew	1.50
27	Alan Wiggins	.05
28	Frank Viola	.05
29	Phil Niekro	1.00
30	Wade Boggs	2.50
31	Dave Parker	.05
32	Bobby Ramos	.05
33	Tom Burgmeier	.05
34	Eddie Milner	.05
35	Don Sutton	1.00
36	Glenn Wilson	.05
37	Mike Krukow	.05
38	Dave Collins	.05
39	Garth Iorg	.05
40	Dusty Baker	.05
41	Tony Bernazard	.05
42	Claudell Washington	.05
43	Cecil Cooper	.05
44	Dan Driessen	.05
45	Jerry Mumphrey	.05
46	Rick Rhoden	.05
47	Rudy Law	.05
48	Julio Franco	.05
49	Mike Norris	.05
50	Chris Chambliss	.05
51	Pete Falcone	.05
52	Mike Marshall	.05
53	Amos Otis	.05
54	Jesse Orosco	.05
55	Dave Concepcion	.05
56	Gary Allenson	.05
57	Dan Schatzeder	.05
58	Jerry Remy	.05
59	Carney Lansford	.05
60	Paul Molitor	2.50
61	Chris Codiroli	.05
62	Dave Hostetler	.05
63	Ed Vande Berg	.05
64	Ryne Sandberg	2.50
65	Kirk Gibson	.05
66	Nolan Ryan	6.00
67	Gary Ward	.05
68	Luis Salazar	.05
69	Dan Quisenberry	.05
70	Gary Matthews	.05
71	Pete O'Brien	.05
72	John Wathan	.05
73	Jody Davis	.05
74	Kent Tekulve	.05
75	Bob Forsch	.05
76	Alfredo Griffin	.05
77	Bryn Smith	.05
78	Mike Torrez	.05
79	Mike Hargrove	.05
80	Steve Rogers	.05
81	Bake McBride	.05
82	Doug DeCinces	.05
83	Richie Zisk	.05
84	Randy Bush	.05
85	Atlee Hammaker	.05
86	Chet Lemon	.05
87	Frank Pastore	.05
88	Alan Trammell	.05
89	Terry Francona	.05
90	Pedro Guerrero	.05
91	Dan Spillner	.05
92	Lloyd Moseby	.05
93	Bob Knepper	.05
94	Ted Simmons	.05
95	Aurelio Lopez	.05
96	Bill Buckner	.05
97	LaMarr Hoyt	.05
98	Tom Brunansky	.05
99	Ron Oester	.05
100	Reggie Jackson	1.50
101	Ron Davis	.05
102	Ken Oberkfell	.05
103	Dwayne Murphy	.05
104	Jim Slaton	.05
105	Tony Armas	.05
106	Ernie Whitt	.05
107	Johnnie LeMaster	.05
108	Randy Moffitt	.05
109	Terry Forster	.05
110	Ron Guidry	.05
111	Bill Virdon	.05
112	Doyle Alexander	.05
113	Lonnie Smith	.05
114	Checklist	.05
115	Andre Thornton	.05
116	Jeff Reardon	.15
117	Tom Herr	.05
118	Charlie Hough	.05
119	Phil Garner	.05
120	Keith Hernandez	.05
121	Rich Gossage	.10
122	Ted Simmons	.05
123	Butch Wynegar	.05
124	Damaso Garcia	.05
125	Britt Burns	.05
126	Bert Blyleven	.05
127	Carlton Fisk	1.50
128	Rick Manning	.05
129	Bill Laskey	.05
130	Ozzie Smith	2.50
131	Bo Diaz	.05
132	Tom Paciorek	.05
133	Dave Rozema	.05
134	Dave Stieb	.15
135	Brian Downing	.05
136	Rick Camp	.05
137	Willie Aikens	.05
138	Charlie Moore	.05
139	George Frazier	.05
140	Storm Davis	.05
141	Glenn Hoffman	.05
142	Charlie Lea	.05
143	Mike Vail	.05
144	Steve Sax	.05
145	Gary Lavelle	.05
146	Gorman Thomas	.05
147	Dan Petry	.05
148	Mark Clear	.05
149	Dave Beard	.05
150	Dale Murphy	.75
151	Steve Trout	.05
152	Tony Pena	.05
153	Geoff Zahn	.05
154	Dave Henderson	.05
155	Frank White	.05
156	Dick Ruthven	.05
157	Gary Gaetti	.05
158	Lance Parrish	.05
159	Joe Price	.05
160	Mario Soto	.05
161	Tug McGraw	.05
162	Bob Ojeda	.05
163	George Hendrick	.05
164	Scott Sanderson	.05
165	Ken Singleton	.05
166	Terry Kennedy	.05
167	Gene Garber	.05
168	Juan Bonilla	.05
169	Larry Parrish	.05
170	Jerry Reuss	.05
171	John Tudor	.05
172	Dave Kingman	.05
173	Garry Templeton	.05
174	Bob Boone	.05
175	Graig Nettles	.05
176	Lee Smith	.05
177	LaMarr Hoyt	.05
178	Bill Krueger	.05
179	Buck Martinez	.05
180	Manny Trillo	.05
181	Lou Whitaker	.05
182	Darryl Strawberry	1.00
183	Neil Allen	.05
184	Jim Rice	.25
185	Sixto Lezcano	.05
186	Tom Hume	.05
187	Garry Maddox	.05
188	Bryan Little	.05
189	Jose Cruz	.05
190	Ben Oglivie	.05
191	Cesar Cedeno	.05
192	Nick Esasky	.05
193	Ken Forsch	.05
194	Jim Palmer	1.25
195	Jack Morris	.15
196	Steve Howe	.05
197	Harold Baines	.05
198	Bill Doran	.05
199	Willie Hernandez	.05
200	Andre Dawson	1.25
201	Bruce Kison	.05
202	Bobby Cox	.05
203	Matt Keough	.05
204	Ron Guidry	.05
205	Greg Minton	.05
206	Al Holland	.05
207	Luis Leal	.05
208	Jose Oquendo	.05
209	Leon Durham	.05
210	Joe Morgan	1.50
211	Lou Whitaker/AS	.05
212	George Brett/AS	.75
213	Bruce Hurst	.05
214	Steve Carlton	1.50
215	Tippy Martinez	.05

216 Ken Landreaux .05
217 Alan Ashby .05
218 Dennis Eckersley 1.00
219 Craig McMurtry .05
220 Fernando Valenzuela .05
221 Cliff Johnson .05
222 Rick Honeycutt .05
223 George Brett 3.00
224 Rusty Staub .20
225 Lee Mazzilli .05
226 Pat Putnam .05
227 Bob Welch .05
228 Rick Cerone .05
229 Lee Lacy .05
230 Rickey Henderson 2.50
231 Gary Redus .05
232 Tim Wallach .25
233 Checklist .05
234 Rafael Ramirez .05
235 Matt Young .05
236 Ellis Valentine .05
237 John Castino .05
238 Eric Show .05
239 Bob Horner .05
240 Eddie Murray 1.50
241 Billy Almon .05
242 Greg Brock .05
243 Bruce Sutter 1.00
244 Dwight Evans .05
245 Rick Sutcliffe .05
246 Terry Crowley .05
247 Fred Lynn .05
248 Bill Dawley .05
249 Dave Stapleton .05
250 Bill Madlock .05
251 Jim Sundberg .05
252 Steve Yeager .05
253 Jim Wohlford .05
254 Shane Rawley .05
255 Bruce Benedict .05
256 Dave Geisel .05
257 Julio Cruz .05
258 Luis Sanchez .05
259 Von Hayes .05
260 Scott McGregor .05
261 Tom Seaver 1.50
262 Doug Flynn .05
263 Wayne Gross .05
264 Larry Gura .05
265 John Montefusco .05
266 Dave Winfield/AS 1.00
267 Tim Lollar .05
268 Ron Washington .05
269 Mickey Rivers .05
270 Mookie Wilson .05
271 Moose Haas .05
272 Rick Dempsey .05
273 Dan Quisenberry .05
274 Steve Henderson .05
275 Len Matuszek .05
276 Frank Tanana .05
277 Dave Righetti .05
278 Jorge Bell .35
279 Ivan DeJesus .05
280 Floyd Bannister .05
281 Dale Murray .05
282 Andre Robertson .05
283 Rollie Fingers 1.00
284 Tommy John .10
285 Darrell Porter .05
286 Lary Sorensen .05
287 Warren Cromartie .05
288 Jim Beattie .05
289 Blue Jays Team .25
290 Dave Dravecky .05
291 Eddie Murray/AS .50
292 Greg Bargar .05
293 Tom Underwood .05
294 U.L. Washington .05
295 Mike Flanagan .05
296 Rich Gedman .05
297 Bruce Berenyi .05
298 Jim Gantner .05
299 Bill Caudill .05
300 Pete Rose 4.00
301 Steve Kemp .05
302 Barry Bonnell .05
303 Joel Youngblood .05
304 Rick Langford .05
305 Roy Smalley .05
306 Ken Griffey .05
307 Al Oliver .05
308 Ron Hassey .05
309 Len Barker .05
310 Willie McGee .05
311 Jerry Koosman .05
312 Jorge Orta .05
313 Pete Vuckovich .05
314 George Wright .05
315 Bob Grich .05
316 Jesse Barfield .25
317 Willie Upshaw .05
318 Bill Gullickson .10
319 Ray Burris .05
320 Bob Stanley .05
321 Ray Knight .05
322 Ken Schrom .05
323 Johnny Ray .05
324 Brian Giles .05
325 Darrell Evans .05
326 Mike Caldwell .05
327 Ruppert Jones .05
328 Chris Speier .05
329 Bobby Castillo .05
330 John Candelaria .05
331 Bucky Dent .05
332 Expos Team .25
333 Larry Herndon .05
334 Chuck Rainey .05
335 Don Baylor .05
336 Bob James .05
337 Jim Clancy .05
338 Duane Kuiper .05
339 Roy Lee Jackson .05
340 Hal McRae .05
341 Larry McWilliams .05
342 Tim Foli .05
343 Fergie Jenkins 2.00
344 Dickie Thon .05
345 Kent Hrbek .05
346 Larry Bowa .05
347 Buddy Bell .05
348 Toby Harrah .05
349 Dan Ford .05
350 George Foster .05
351 Lou Piniella .05
352 Dave Stewart .25
353 Mike Easler .05
354 Jeff Burroughs .05
355 Jason Thompson .05
356 Glenn Abbott .05
357 Ron Cey .05
358 Bob Dernier .05
359 Jim Acker .05
360 Willie Randolph .05
361 Mike Schmidt 3.00
362 David Green .05
363 Cal Ripken Jr./AS 2.00
364 Jim Rice/AS .05
365 Steve Bedrosian .05
366 Gary Carter 2.50
367 Chili Davis .05
368 Hubie Brooks .05
369 Steve McCatty .05
370 Tim Raines .35
371 Joaquin Andujar .05
372 Gary Roenicke .05
373 Ron Kittle .05
374 Rich Dauer .05
375 Dennis Leonard .05
376 Rick Burleson .05
377 Eric Rasmussen .05
378 Dave Winfield 2.50
379 Checklist .05
380 Steve Garvey .50
381 Jack Clark .05
382 Odell Jones .05
383 Terry Puhl .05
384 Joe Niekro .05
385 Tony Perez 2.00
386 George Hendrick/AS .05
387 Johnny Ray/AS .05
388 Mike Schmidtv .75
389 Ozzie Smith/AS .75
390 Tim Raines/AS .25
391 Dale Murphy/AS .25
392 Andre Dawson/AS .35
393 Gary Carter/AS 1.00
394 Steve Rogers/AS .15
395 Steve Carlton/AS .50
396 Jesse Orosco/AS .05

Stickers

83 RICK MONDAY
357 PETE O'BRIEN

Bi-lingual backs are the only difference between the OPC 1984 sticker set and the Topps issue. The sets share a checklist and, generally, values, although some Blue Jays and Expos stars may command a small premium in the Canadian version.

1985 O-Pee-Chee

This 396-card set is almost identical in design to the 1985 Topps set. Measuring 2-1/2" x 3-1/2", the fronts of the Canadian-issued cards display the O-Pee-Chee logo in the upper left corner, and the backs of the cards are printed in both French and English. A "traded" line appears on the front of some of the cards to indicate a change in teams.

NM/M
Complete Set (396): 15.00
Common Player: .05
Wax Pack (15): 1.50
Wax Box (36): 40.00
1 Tom Seaver 1.50
2 Gary Lavelle .05
3 Tim Wallach .15
4 Jim Wohlford .05
5 Jeff Robinson .05
6 Willie Wilson .05
7 Cliff Johnson .05
8 Willie Randolph .05
9 Larry Herndon .05
10 Kirby Puckett 4.00
11 Mookie Wilson .05
12 Dave Lopes .05
13 Tim Lollar .05
14 Chris Bando .05
15 Jerry Koosman .05
16 Bobby Meacham .05
17 Mike Scott .05
18 Rich Gedman .05
19 George Frazier .05
20 Chet Lemon .05
21 Dave Concepcion .05
22 Jason Thompson .05
23 Bret Saberhagen .05
24 Jesse Barfield .15
25 Steve Bedrosian .05
26 Roy Smalley .05
27 Bruce Berenyi .05
28 Butch Wynegar .05
29 Alan Ashby .05
30 Cal Ripken 4.00
31 Luis Leal .05
32 Dave Dravecky .05
33 Tito Landrum .05
34 Pedro Guerrero .05
35 Graig Nettles .05
36 Fred Breining .05
37 Roy Lee Jackson .05
38 Steve Henderson .05
39 Gary Pettis .05
40 Phil Niekro .75
41 Dwight Gooden .10
42 Luis Sanchez .05
43 Lee Smith .05
44 Dickie Thon .05
45 Greg Minton .05
46 Mike Flanagan .05
47 Bud Black .05
48 Tony Fernandez .50
49 Carlton Fisk 1.50
50 John Candelaria .05
51 Bob Watson .05
52 Rick Leach .05
53 Rick Rhoden .05
54 Cesar Cedeno .05
55 Frank Tanana .05
56 Larry Bowa .05
57 Willie McGee .05
58 Rich Dauer .05
59 Jorge Bell .35
60 George Hendrick .05
61 Donnie Moore .05
62 Mike Ramsey .05
63 Nolan Ryan 4.00
64 Mark Bailey .05
65 Bill Buckner .05
66 Jerry Reuss .05
67 Mike Schmidt 2.50
68 Von Hayes .05
69 Phil Bradley .05
70 Don Baylor .05
71 Julio Cruz .05
72 Rick Sutcliffe .05
73 Storm Davis .05
74 Mike Krukow .05
75 Willie Upshaw .05
76 Craig Lefferts .05
77 Lloyd Moseby .05
78 Ron Davis .05
79 Rick Mahler .05
80 Keith Hernandez .05
81 Vance Law .05
82 Joe Price .05
83 Dennis Lamp .05
84 Gary Ward .05
85 Mike Marshall .05
86 Marvell Wynne .05
87 David Green .05
88 Bryn Smith .05
89 Sixto Lezcano .05
90 Rich Gossage .10
91 Jeff Burroughs .05
92 Bobby Brown .05
93 Oscar Gamble .05
94 Rick Dempsey .05
95 Jose Cruz .05
96 Johnny Ray .05
97 Joel Youngblood .05
98 Eddie Whitson .05
99 Milt Wilcox .05
100 George Brett 2.50
101 Jim Acker .05
102 Jim Sundberg .05
103 Ozzie Virgil .05
104 Mike Fitzgerald .05
105 Ron Kittle .05
106 Pascual Perez .05
107 Barry Bonnell .05
108 Lou Whitaker .05
109 Gary Roenicke .05
110 Alejandro Pena .05
111 Doug DeCinces .05
112 Doug Flynn .05
113 Tom Herr .05
114 Bob James .05
115 Rickey Henderson 2.00
116 Pete Rose 3.00
117 Greg Gross .05
118 Eric Show .05
119 Buck Martinez .05
120 Steve Kemp .05
121 Checklist 1-132 .05
122 Tom Brunansky .05
123 Dave Kingman .05
124 Garry Templeton .05
125 Kent Tekulve .05
126 Darryl Strawberry .05
127 Mark Gubicza .05
128 Ernie Whitt .05
129 Don Robinson .05
130 Al Oliver .05
131 Mario Soto .05
132 Jeff Leonard .05
133 Andre Dawson .35
134 Bruce Hurst .05
135 Bobby Cox .05
136 Matt Young .05
137 Bob Forsch .05
138 Ron Darling .05
139 Steve Trout .05
140 Geoff Zahn .05
141 Ken Forsch .05
142 Jerry Willard .05
143 Bill Gullickson .05
144 Mike Mason .05
145 Alvin Davis .05
146 Gary Redus .05
147 Willie Aikens .05
148 Steve Yeager .05
149 Dickie Noles .05
150 Jim Rice .25
151 Moose Haas .05
152 Steve Balboni .05
153 Frank LaCorte .05
154 Argenis Salazar .05
155 Bob Grich .05
156 Craig Reynolds .05
157 Bill Madlock .05
158 Pat Tabler .05
159 Don Slaught .05
160 Lance Parrish .05
161 Ken Schrom .05
162 Wally Backman .05
163 Dennis Eckersley .75
164 Dave Collins .05
165 Dusty Baker .05
166 Claudell Washington .05
167 Rick Camp .05
168 Garth Iorg .05
169 Shane Rawley .05
170 George Foster .05
171 Tony Bernazard .05
172 Don Sutton .75
173 Jerry Remy .05
174 Rick Honeycutt .05
175 Dave Parker .05
176 Buddy Bell .05
177 Steve Garvey .20
178 Miguel Dilone .05
179 Tommy John .10
180 Dave Winfield 2.00
181 Alan Trammell .05
182 Rollie Fingers .75
183 Larry McWilliams .05
184 Carmen Castillo .05
185 Al Holland .05
186 Jerry Mumphrey .05
187 Chris Chambliss .05
188 Jim Clancy .05
189 Glenn Wilson .05
190 Rusty Staub .05
191 Ozzie Smith 2.00
192 Howard Johnson .05
193 Jimmy Key 1.00
194 Terry Kennedy .05
195 Glenn Hubbard .05
196 Pete O'Brien .05
197 Keith Moreland .05
198 Eddie Milner .05
199 Dave Engle .05
200 Reggie Jackson 1.50
201 Burt Hooton .05
202 Gorman Thomas .05
203 Larry Parrish .05
204 Bob Stanley .05
205 Steve Rogers .05
206 Phil Garner .05
207 Ed Vande Berg .05
208 Jack Clark .05
209 Bill Campbell .05
210 Gary Matthews .05
211 Dave Palmer .05
212 Tony Perez 1.50
213 Sammy Stewart .05
214 John Tudor .05
215 Bob Brenly .05
216 Jim Gantner .05
217 Bryan Clark .05
218 Doyle Alexander .05
219 Bo Diaz .05
220 Fred Lynn .05
221 Eddie Murray 1.50
222 Hubie Brooks .05
223 Tom Hume .05
224 Al Cowens .05
225 Mike Boddicker .05
226 Len Matuszek .05
227 Danny Darwin .05
228 Scott McGregor .05
229 Dave LaPoint .05
230 Gary Carter 2.00
231 Joaquin Andujar .05
232 Rafael Ramirez .05
233 Wayne Gross .05
234 Neil Allen .05
235 Gary Maddox .05
236 Mark Thurmond .05
237 Julio Franco .05
238 Ray Burris .05
239 Tim Teufel .05
240 Dave Stieb .15
241 Brett Butler .05
242 Greg Brock .05
243 Barbaro Garbey .05
244 Greg Walker .05
245 Chili Davis .05
246 Darrell Porter .05
247 Tippy Martinez .05
248 Terry Forster .05
249 Harold Baines .05
250 Jesse Orosco .05
251 Brad Gulden .05
252 Mike Hargrove .05
253 Nick Esasky .05
254 Frank Williams .05
255 Lonnie Smith .05
256 Daryl Sconiers .05
257 Bryan Little .05
258 Terry Francona .05
259 Mark Langston .15
260 Dave Righetti .05
261 Checklist 133-264 .05
262 Bob Horner .05
263 Mel Hall .05
264 John Shelby .05
265 Juan Samuel .05
266 Frank Viola .05
267 Jim Fanning .05
268 Dick Ruthven .05
269 Bobby Ramos .05
270 Dan Quisenberry .05
271 Dwight Evans .05
272 Andre Thornton .05
273 Orel Hershiser .50
274 Ray Knight .05
275 Bill Caudill .05
276 Charlie Hough .05
277 Tim Raines .25
278 Mike Squires .05
279 Alex Trevino .05
280 Ron Romanick .05
281 Tom Niedenfuer .05
282 Mike Stenhouse .05
283 Terry Puhl .05
284 Hal McRae .05
285 Dan Driessen .05
286 Rudy Law .05
287 Walt Terrell .05
288 Jeff Kunkel .05
289 Bob Knepper .05
290 Cecil Cooper .05
291 Bob Welch .05
292 Frank Pastore .05
293 Dan Schatzeder .05
294 Tom Nieto .05
295 Joe Niekro .05
296 Ryne Sandberg 2.00
297 Gary Lucas .05
298 John Castino .05
299 Bill Doran .05
300 Rod Carew 1.50
301 John Montefusco .05
302 Johnnie LeMaster .05
303 Jim Beattie .05
304 Gary Gaetti .05
305 Dale Berra .05
306 Rick Reuschel .05
307 Ken Oberkfell .05
308 Kent Hrbek .05
309 Mike Witt .05
310 Manny Trillo .05
311 Jim Gott .05
312 LaMarr Hoyt .05
313 Dave Schmidt .05
314 Ron Oester .05
315 Doug Sisk .05
316 John Lowenstein .05
317 Derrel Thomas .05
318 Ted Simmons .05
319 Darrell Evans .05
320 Dale Murphy .50
321 Ricky Horton .05
322 Ken Phelps .05
323 Lee Mazzilli .05
324 Don Mattingly 2.50
325 John Denny .05
326 Ken Singleton .05
327 Brook Jacoby .05
328 Greg Luzinski .05
329 Bob Ojeda .05
330 Leon Durham .05
331 Bill Laskey .05
332 Ben Oglivie .05
333 Willie Hernandez .05
334 Bob Dernier .05
335 Bruce Benedict .05
336 Rance Mulliniks .05
337 Rick Cerone .05
338 Britt Burns .05
339 Danny Heep .05
340 Robin Yount 1.50
341 Andy Van Slyke .05
342 Curt Wilkerson .05
343 Bill Russell .05
344 Dave Henderson .05
345 Charlie Lea .05
346 Terry Pendleton .05
347 Carney Lansford .05
348 Bob Boone .05
349 Mike Easler .05
350 Wade Boggs 2.00
351 Atlee Hammaker .05
352 Joe Morgan 1.50
353 Damaso Garcia .05
354 Floyd Bannister .05
355 Bert Blyleven .05
356 John Butcher .05
357 Fernando Valenzuela .05
358 Tony Pena .05
359 Mike Smithson .05
360 Steve Carlton 1.50
361 Alfredo Griffin .05
362 Craig McMurtry .05
363 Bill Dawley .05
364 Richard Dotson .05
365 Carmelo Martinez .05
366 Ron Cey .05
367 Tony Scott .05
368 Dave Bergman .05
369 Steve Sax .05
370 Bruce Sutter 1.00
371 Mickey Rivers .05
372 Kirk Gibson .05
373 Scott Sanderson .05
374 Brian Downing .05
375 Jeff Reardon .15
376 Frank DiPino .05
377 Checklist 265-396 .05
378 Alan Wiggins .05
379 Charles Hudson .05
380 Ken Griffey .05
381 Tom Paciorek .05
382 Jack Morris .15
383 Tony Gwynn 2.00
384 Jody Davis .05
385 Jose DeLeon .05
386 Bob Kearney .05
387 George Wright .05
388 Ron Guidry .05
389 Rick Manning .05
390 Sid Fernandez .05
391 Bruce Bochte .05
392 Dan Petry .05
303 Tim Stoddard .05
394 Tony Armas .05
395 Paul Molitor 2.00
396 Mike Heath .05

Posters

The 1985 O-Pee-Chee poster set consists of 12 players each from the Expos and Blue Jays. The blank-backed posters measure approximately 4-7/8" x 6-7/8" and generally have fold marks because they were inserted in the OPC wax packs. The card number, written in both French and English, appears in the bottom border. The full-color player photos are surrounded by a red border for Expos and a blue border for Blue Jays.

NM/M
Complete Set (24): 9.00
Common Player: .50
1 Mike Fitzgerald .50
2 Dan Driessen .50
3 Dave Palmer .50
4 U.L. Washington .50
5 Hubie Brooks .50
6 Tim Wallach .75
7 Tim Raines 2.50
8 Herm Winningham .50
9 Andre Dawson 2.50
10 Charlie Lea .50
11 Steve Rogers .50
12 Jeff Reardon .60
13 Buck Martinez .50
14 Willie Upshaw .50
15 Damaso Garcia .50
16 Tony Fernandez 1.00
17 Rance Mulliniks .50
18 George Bell 1.00
19 Lloyd Moseby .50
20 Jesse Barfield .60

21	Doyle Alexander	.50
22	Dave Stieb	.85
23	Bill Caudill	.50
24	Gary Lavelle	.50

Stickers

Bi-lingual backs are the only difference between the OPC 1985 sticker set and the Topps issue. The sets share a checklist and, generally, values, although some Blue Jays and Expos stars may command a small premium in the Canadian version.

1986 O-Pee-Chee

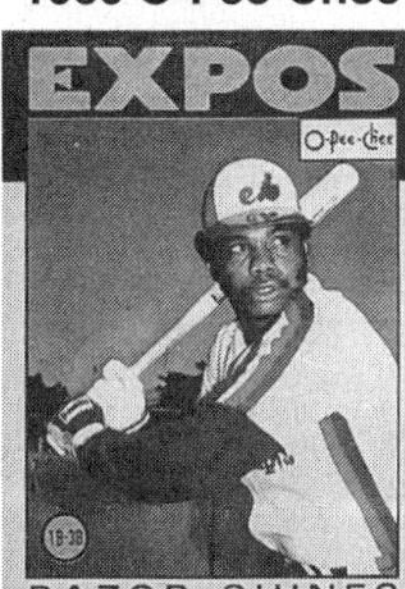

As usual, the 1986 O-Pee-Chee set was issued in close simulation of the Topps cards for the same year. The 396 cards in the set are 2-1/2" x 3-1/2" and use almost all of the same pictures as the Topps set. The O-Pee-Chee cards, being a Canadian issue, list player information in both English and French. There is an abundance of players from the two Canadian teams - Toronto and Montreal. As the O-Pee-Chee set was issued later in the year than the Topps regular issue, players who changed teams after the printing date are noted with a traded line at the bottom of the player photo. O-Pee-Chee's logo appears in the upper right of each card front.

		NM/M
Complete Set (396):		12.00
Common Player:		.05
Wax Box (36):		16.00
1	Pete Rose	1.50
2	Ken Landreaux	.05
3	Rob Picciolo	.05
4	Steve Garvey	.10
5	Andy Hawkins	.05
6	Rudy Law	.05
7	Lonnie Smith	.05
8	Dwayne Murphy	.05
9	Moose Haas	.05
10	Tony Gwynn	1.00
11	Bob Ojeda	.05
12	Jose Uribe	.05
13	Bob Kearney	.05
14	Julio Cruz	.05
15	Eddie Whitson	.05
16	Rick Schu	.05
17	Mike Stenhouse	.05
18	Lou Thornton	.05
19	Ryne Sandberg	1.00
20	Lou Whitaker	.05
21	Mark Brouhard	.05
22	Gary Lavelle	.05
23	Manny Lee	.05
24	Don Slaught	.05
25	Willie Wilson	.05
26	Mike Marshall	.05
27	Ray Knight	.05
28	Mario Soto	.05
29	Dave Anderson	.05
30	Eddie Murray	.75
31	Dusty Baker	.05
32	Steve Yeager	.05
33	Andy Van Slyke	.05
34	Dave Righetti	.05
35	Jeff Reardon	.05
36	Burt Hooton	.05
37	Johnny Ray	.05
38	Glenn Hoffman	.05
39	Rick Mahler	.05
40	Ken Griffey	.05
41	Brad Wellman	.05
42	Joe Hesketh	.05
43	Mark Salas	.05
44	Jorge Orta	.05
45	Damaso Garcia	.05
46	Jim Acker	.05
47	Bill Madlock	.05
48	Bill Almon	.05
49	Rick Manning	.05
50	Dan Quisenberry	.05
51	Jim Gantner	.05
52	Kevin Bass	.05
53	Len Dykstra	.05
54	John Franco	.05
55	Fred Lynn	.05
56	Jim Morrison	.05
57	Bill Doran	.05
58	Leon Durham	.05
59	Andre Thornton	.05
60	Dwight Evans	.05
61	Larry Herndon	.05
62	Bob Boone	.05
63	Kent Hrbek	.05
64	Floyd Bannister	.05
65	Harold Baines	.05
66	Pat Tabler	.05
67	Carmelo Martinez	.05
68	Ed Lynch	.05
69	George Foster	.05
70	Dave Winfield	1.00
71	Ken Schrom	.05
72	Toby Harrah	.05
73	Jackie Gutierrez	.05
74	Rance Mulliniks	.05
75	Jose DeLeon	.05
76	Ron Romanick	.05
77	Charlie Leibrandt	.05
78	Bruce Benedict	.05
79	Dave Schmidt	.05
80	Darryl Strawberry	.05
81	Wayne Krenchicki	.05
82	Tippy Martinez	.05
83	Phil Garner	.05
84	Darrell Porter	.05
85	Tony Perez	1.00
86	Tom Waddell	.05
87	Tim Hulett	.05
88	Barbaro Garbey	.05
89	Randy St. Claire	.05
90	Garry Templeton	.05
91	Tim Teufel	.05
92	Al Cowens	.05
93	Scot Thompson	.05
94	Tom Herr	.05
95	Ozzie Virgil	.05
96	Jose Cruz	.05
97	Gary Gaetti	.05
98	Roger Clemens	2.00
99	Vance Law	.05
100	Nolan Ryan	2.50
101	Mike Smithson	.05
102	Rafael Santana	.05
103	Darrell Evans	.05
104	Rich Gossage	.05
105	Gary Ward	.05
106	Jim Gott	.05
107	Rafael Ramirez	.05
108	Ted Power	.05
109	Ron Guidry	.05
110	Scott McGregor	.05
111	Mike Scioscia	.05
112	Glenn Hubbard	.05
113	U.L. Washington	.05
114	Al Oliver	.05
115	Jay Howell	.05
116	Brook Jacoby	.05
117	Willie McGee	.05
118	Jerry Royster	.05
119	Barry Bonnell	.05
120	Steve Carlton	.75
121	Alfredo Griffin	.05
122	David Green	.05
123	Greg Walker	.05
124	Frank Tanana	.05
125	Dave Lopes	.05
126	Mike Krukow	.05
127	Jack Howell	.05
128	Greg Harris	.05
129	Herm Winningham	.05
130	Alan Trammell	.05
131	Checklist 1-132	.05
132	Razor Shines	.05
133	Bruce Sutter	.65
134	Carney Lansford	.05
135	Joe Niekro	.05
136	Ernie Whitt	.05
137	Charlie Moore	.05
138	Mel Hall	.05
139	Roger McDowell	.05
140	John Candelaria	.05
141	Bob Rodgers	.05
142	Manny Trillo	.05
143	Dave Palmer	.05
144	Robin Yount	.75
145	Pedro Guerrero	.05
146	Von Hayes	.05
147	Lance Parrish	.05
148	Mike Heath	.05
149	Brett Butler	.05
150	Joaquin Andujar	.05
151	Graig Nettles	.05
152	Pete Vuckovich	.05
153	Jason Thompson	.05
154	Bert Roberge	.05
155	Bob Grich	.05
156	Roy Smalley	.05
157	Ron Hassey	.05
158	Bob Stanley	.05
159	Orel Hershiser	.05
160	Chet Lemon	.05
161	Terry Puhl	.05
162	Dave LaPoint	.05
163	Onix Concepcion	.05
164	Steve Balboni	.05
165	Mike Davis	.05
166	Dickie Thon	.05
167	Zane Smith	.05
168	Jeff Burroughs	.05
169	Alex Trevino	.05
170	Gary Carter	1.00
171	Tito Landrum	.05
172	Sammy Stewart	.05
173	Wayne Gross	.05
174	Britt Burns	.05
175	Steve Sax	.05
176	Jody Davis	.05
177	Joel Youngblood	.05
178	Fernando Valenzuela	.05
179	Storm Davis	.05
180	Don Mattingly	1.25
181	Steve Bedrosian	.05
182	Jesse Orosco	.05
183	Gary Roenicke	.05
184	Don Baylor	.05
185	Rollie Fingers	.50
186	Ruppert Jones	.05
187	Scott Fletcher	.05
188	Bob Dernier	.05
189	Mike Mason	.05
190	George Hendrick	.05
191	Wally Backman	.05
192	Oddibe McDowell	.05
193	Bruce Hurst	.05
194	Ron Cey	.05
195	Dave Concepcion	.05
196	Doyle Alexander	.05
197	Dale Murray	.05
198	Mark Langston	.05
199	Dennis Eckersley	.50
200	Mike Schmidt	1.50
201	Nick Esasky	.05
202	Ken Dayley	.05
203	Rick Cerone	.05
204	Larry McWilliams	.05
205	Brian Downing	.05
206	Danny Darwin	.05
207	Bill Caudill	.05
208	Dave Rozema	.05
209	Eric Show	.05
210	Brad Komminsk	.05
211	Chris Bando	.05
212	Chris Speier	.05
213	Jim Clancy	.05
214	Randy Bush	.05
215	Frank White	.05
216	Dan Petry	.05
217	Tim Wallach	.05
218	Mitch Webster	.05
219	Dennis Lamp	.05
220	Bob Horner	.05
221	Dave Henderson	.05
222	Dave Smith	.05
223	Willie Upshaw	.05
224	Cesar Cedeno	.05
225	Ron Darling	.05
226	Lee Lacy	.05
227	John Tudor	.05
228	Jim Presley	.05
229	Bill Gullickson	.05
230	Terry Kennedy	.05
231	Bob Knepper	.05
232	Rick Rhoden	.05
233	Richard Dotson	.05
234	Jesse Barfield	.10
235	Butch Wynegar	.05
236	Jerry Reuss	.05
237	Juan Samuel	.05
238	Larry Parrish	.05
239	Bill Buckner	.05
240	Pat Sheridan	.05
241	Tony Fernandez	.05
242	Rich Thompson	.05
243	Rickey Henderson	1.00
244	Craig Lefferts	.05
245	Jim Sundberg	.05
246	Phil Niekro	.50
247	Terry Harper	.05
248	Spike Owen	.05
249	Bret Saberhagen	.05
250	Dwight Gooden	.05
251	Rich Dauer	.05
252	Keith Hernandez	.05
253	Bo Diaz	.05
254	Ozzie Guillen	.05
255	Tony Armas	.05
256	Andre Dawson	.25
257	Doug DeCinces	.05
258	Tim Burke	.05
259	Dennis Boyd	.05
260	Tony Pena	.05
261	Sal Butera	.05
262	Wade Boggs	1.00
263	Checklist 133-254	.05
264	Ron Oester	.05
265	Ron Davis	.05
266	Keith Moreland	.05
267	Paul Molitor	1.00
268	John Denny	.05
269	Frank Viola	.05
270	Jack Morris	.10
271	Dave Collins	.05
272	Bert Blyleven	.05
273	Jerry Willard	.05
274	Matt Young	.05
275	Charlie Hough	.05
276	Dave Dravecky	.05
277	Garth Iorg	.05
278	Hal McRae	.05
279	Curt Wilkerson	.05
280	Tim Raines	.20
281	Bill Laskey	.05
282	Jerry Mumphrey	.05
283	Pat Clements	.05
284	Bob James	.05
285	Buddy Bell	.05
286	Tom Brookens	.05
287	Dave Parker	.05
288	Ron Kittle	.05
289	Johnnie LeMaster	.05
290	Carlton Fisk	.75
291	Jimmy Key	.05
292	Gary Matthews	.05
293	Marvell Wynne	.05
294	Danny Cox	.05
295	Kirk Gibson	.05
296	Mariano Duncan	.05
297	Ozzie Smith	1.00
298	Craig Reynolds	.05
299	Bryn Smith	.05
300	George Brett	1.50
301	Walt Terrell	.05
302	Greg Gross	.05
303	Claudell Washington	.05
304	Howard Johnson	.05
305	Phil Bradley	.05
306	R.J. Reynolds	.05
307	Bob Brenly	.05
308	Hubie Brooks	.05
309	Alvin Davis	.05
310	Donnie Hill	.05
311	Dick Schofield	.05
312	Tom Filer	.05
313	Mike Fitzgerald	.05
314	Marty Barrett	.05
315	Mookie Wilson	.05
316	Alan Knicely	.05
317	Ed Romero	.05
318	Glenn Wilson	.05
319	Bud Black	.05
320	Jim Rice	.20
321	Terry Pendleton	.05
322	Dave Kingman	.05
323	Gary Pettis	.05
324	Dan Schatzeder	.05
325	Juan Beniquez	.05
326	Kent Tekulve	.05
327	Mike Pagliarulo	.05
328	Pete O'Brien	.05
329	Kirby Puckett	1.00
330	Rick Sutcliffe	.05
331	Alan Ashby	.05
332	Willie Randolph	.05
333	Tom Henke	.05
334	Ken Oberkfell	.05
335	Don Sutton	.50
336	Dan Gladden	.05
337	George Vuckovich	.05
338	Jorge Bell	.10
339	Jim Dwyer	.05
340	Cal Ripken	2.50
341	Willie Hernandez	.05
342	Gary Redus	.05
343	Jerry Koosman	.05
344	Jim Wohlford	.05
345	Donnie Moore	.05
346	Floyd Youmans	.05
347	Gorman Thomas	.05
348	Cliff Johnson	.05
349	Ken Howell	.05
350	Jack Clark	.05
351	Gary Lucas	.05
352	Bob Clark	.05
353	Dave Stieb	.05
354	Tony Bernazard	.05
355	Lee Smith	.05
356	Mickey Hatcher	.05
357	Ed Vande Berg	.05
358	Rick Dempsey	.05
359	Bobby Cox	.05
360	Lloyd Moseby	.05
361	Shane Rawley	.05
362	Garry Maddox	.05
363	Buck Martinez	.05
364	Ed Nunez	.05
365	Luis Leal	.05
366	Dale Berra	.05
367	Mike Boddicker	.05
368	Greg Brock	.05
369	Al Holland	.05
370	Vince Coleman	.05
371	Rod Carew	.75
372	Ben Oglivie	.05
373	Lee Mazzilli	.05
374	Terry Francona	.05
375	Rich Gedman	.05
376	Charlie Lea	.05
377	Joe Carter	.50
378	Bruce Bochte	.05
379	Bobby Meacham	.05
380	LaMarr Hoyt	.05
381	Jeff Leonard	.05
382	Ivan Calderon	.05
383	Chris Brown	.05
384	Steve Trout	.05
385	Cecil Cooper	.05
386	Cecil Fielder	1.50
387	Tim Flannery	.05
388	Chris Codiroli	.05
389	Glenn Davis	.05
390	Tom Seaver	.75
391	Julio Franco	.05
392	Tom Brunansky	.05
393	Rob Wilfong	.05
394	Reggie Jackson	.75
395	Scott Garrelts	.05
396	Checklist 255-396	.05

Box Panels

The Canadian card company licensed by Topps to distribute cards in Canada is O-Pee-Chee. In 1986, O-Pee-Chee is-

sued wax pack boxes with baseball cards printed on the box bottoms. Four cards appear on four different boxes making a complete set of 16. The cards are identical to the 1986 Topps wax box issue with the exception of the OPC logo replacing Topps' and the addition of French on the card backs. These bilingual cards were issued in Canada but are readily available in the USA. The cards are the standard 2-1/2" x 3-1/2" size, printed in full-color with black and red backs. The panel cards are not numbered but instead are lettered from A through P.

		NM/M
Complete Panel Set (4):		12.00
Complete Singles Set (16):		11.00
Common Panel:		3.50
Common Single Player:		.15
Panel		4.50
A	Jorge Bell	.50
B	Wade Boggs	1.00
C	George Brett	1.50
D	Vince Coleman	.20
Panel		3.50
E	Carlton Fisk	1.00
F	Dwight Gooden	.20
G	Pedro Guerrero	.20
H	Ron Guidry	.20
Panel		4.00
I	Reggie Jackson	1.50
J	Don Mattingly	2.00
K	Oddibe McDowell	.15
L	Willie McGee	.15
Panel		3.00
M	Dale Murphy	.65
N	Pete Rose	2.50
O	Bret Saberhagen	.15
P	Fernando Valenzuela	.15

Stickers

Bi-lingual backs are the only difference between the OPC 1986 sticker set and the Topps issue. The sets share a checklist and, generally, values, although some Blue Jays and Expos stars may command a small premium in the Canadian version.

	NM/M
Complete Set:	15.00
Common Player:	.05
Album:	2.00

Tattoos

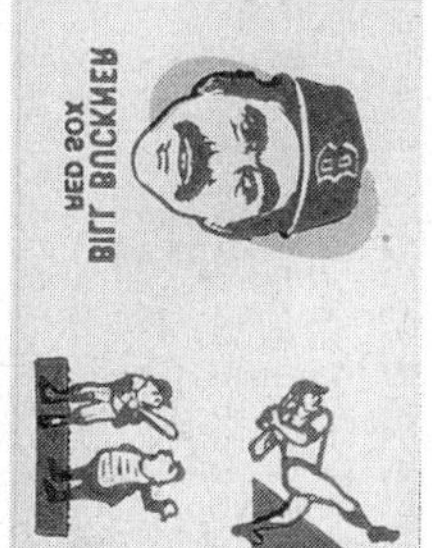

Topps and its Canadian shadow O-Pee-Chee returned to tattoos in 1986, marketing a set of 24 different tattoo sheets. Each sheet of tattoos measures 3-7/16" x 14" and includes both player portrait and smaller generic action tattoos. The player tattoos measure about 1-1/2" x 2-1/2". With 24 sheets, eight players per sheet, there are 192 players represented in the set. The sheets are numbered. The OPC version is distinguished from Topps by copyright notice.

1987 O-Pee-Chee

O-Pee-Chee of London, Ont., under license from the Topps Chewing Gum Co., continued a practice started in 1965 by issuing a baseball card set for 1987. The 396-card set is identical in design to the regular Topps set, save the name "O-Pee-Chee" replacing "Topps" in the lower right corner. Because the set is issued after its American counterpart, several cards appear with trade notations and corrected logos on the fronts. The cards, which are printed on white stock and are the standard 2-1/2" x 3-1/2", feature backs written in both English and French.

		NM/M
Complete Set (396):		15.00
Common Player:		.05
Wax Pack:		1.00
Wax Box (36):		17.50
1	Ken Oberkfell	.05
2	Jack Howell	.05
3	Hubie Brooks	.05
4	Bob Grich	.05
5	Rick Leach	.05
6	Phil Niekro	.50
7	Rickey Henderson	1.00
8	Terry Pendleton	.05
9	Jay Tibbs	.05
10	Cecil Cooper	.05
11	Mario Soto	.05
12	George Bell	.15
13	Nick Esasky	.05
14	Larry McWilliams	.05
15	Dan Quisenberry	.05
16	Ed Lynch	.05
17	Pete O'Brien	.05
18	Luis Aguayo	.05
19	Matt Young	.05
20	Gary Carter	1.00
21	Tom Paciorek	.05
22	Doug DeCinces	.05
23	Lee Smith	.05
24	Jesse Barfield	.05
25	Bert Blyleven	.05
26	Greg Brock	.05
27	Dan Petry	.05
28	Rick Dempsey	.05
29	Jimmy Key	.05
30	Tim Raines	.15
31	Bruce Hurst	.05
32	Manny Trillo	.05
33	Andy Van Slyke	.05
34	Ed Vande Berg	.05
35	Sid Bream	.05
36	Dave Winfield	1.00
37	Scott Garrelts	.05
38	Dennis Leonard	.05
39	Marty Barrett	.05
40	Dave Righetti	.05
41	Bo Diaz	.05
42	Gary Redus	.05
43	Tom Niedenfuer	.05
44	Greg Harris	.05
45	Jim Presley	.05
46	Danny Gladden	.05
47	Roy Smalley	.05
48	Wally Backman	.05
49	Tom Seaver	.75
50	Dave Smith	.05
51	Mel Hall	.05
52	Tim Flannery	.05
53	Julio Cruz	.05
54	Dick Schofield	.05
55	Tim Wallach	.05
56	Glenn Davis	.05
57	Darren Daulton	.05
58	Chico Walker	.05

59 Garth Iorg .05
60 Tony Pena .05
61 Ron Hassey .05
62 Dave Dravecky .05
63 Jorge Orta .05
64 Al Nipper .05
65 Tom Browning .05
66 Marc Sullivan .05
67 Todd Worrell .05
68 Glenn Hubbard .05
69 Carney Lansford .05
70 Charlie Hough .05
71 Lance McCullers .05
72 Walt Terrell .05
73 Bob Kearney .05
74 Dan Pasqua .05
75 Ron Darling .05
76 Robin Yount .75
77 Pat Tabler .05
78 Tom Foley .05
79 Juan Nieves .05
80 Wally Joyner .05
81 Wayne Krenchicki .05
82 Kirby Puckett 1.00
83 Bob Ojeda .05
84 Mookie Wilson .05
85 Kevin Bass .05
86 Kent Tekulve .05
87 Mark Salas .05
88 Brian Downing .05
89 Ozzie Guillen .05
90 Dave Stieb .05
91 Rance Mulliniks .05
92 Mike Witt .05
93 Charlie Moore .05
94 Jose Uribe .05
95 Oddibe McDowell .05
96 Ray Soff .05
97 Glenn Wilson .05
98 Brook Jacoby .05
99 Darryl Motley .05
100 Steve Garvey .10
101 Frank White .05
102 Mike Moore .05
103 Rick Aguilera .05
104 Buddy Bell .05
105 Floyd Youmans .05
106 Lou Whitaker .05
107 Ozzie Smith 1.00
108 Jim Gantner .05
109 R.J. Reynolds .05
110 John Tudor .05
111 Alfredo Griffin .05
112 Mike Flanagan .05
113 Neil Allen .05
114 Ken Griffey .05
115 Donnie Moore .05
116 Bob Horner .05
117 Ron Shepherd .05
118 Cliff Johnson .05
119 Vince Coleman .05
120 Eddie Murray .75
121 Dwayne Murphy .05
122 Jim Clancy .05
123 Ken Landreaux .05
124 Tom Nieto .05
125 Bob Brenly .05
126 George Brett 1.25
127 Vance Law .05
128 Checklist 1-132 .05
129 Bob Knepper .05
130 Dwight Gooden .05
131 Juan Bonilla .05
132 Tim Burke .05
133 Bob McClure .05
134 Scott Bailes .05
135 Mike Easler .05
136 Ron Romanick .05
137 Rich Gedman .05
138 Bob Dernier .05
139 John Denny .05
140 Bret Saberhagen .05
141 Herm Winningham .05
142 Rick Sutcliffe .05
143 Ryne Sandberg 1.00
144 Mike Scioscia .05
145 Charlie Kerfeld .05
146 Jim Rice .15
147 Steve Trout .05
148 Jesse Orosco .05
149 Mike Boddicker .05
150 Wade Boggs 1.00
151 Dane Iorg .05
152 Rick Burleson .05
153 Duane Ward .05
154 Rick Reuschel .05
155 Nolan Ryan 2.00
156 Bill Caudill .05
157 Danny Darwin .05
158 Ed Romero .05
159 Bill Almon .05
160 Julio Franco .05
161 Kent Hrbek .05
162 Chili Davis .05
163 Kevin Gross .05
164 Carlton Fisk .75
165 Jeff Reardon .05
166 Bob Boone .05
167 Rick Honeycutt .05
168 Dan Schatzeder .05
169 Jim Wohlford .05
170 Phil Bradley .05
171 Ken Schrom .05
172 Ron Oester .05
173 Juan Beniquez .05
174 Tony Armas .05
175 Bob Stanley .05
176 Steve Buechele .05
177 Keith Moreland .05
178 Cecil Fielder .50
179 Gary Gaetti .05
180 Chris Brown .05
181 Tom Herr .05
182 Lee Lacy .05
183 Ozzie Virgil .05
184 Paul Molitor 1.00
185 Roger McDowell .05
186 Mike Marshall .05
187 Ken Howell .05
188 Rob Deer .05
189 Joe Hesketh .05
190 Jim Sundberg .05
191 Kelly Gruber .10
192 Cory Snyder .05
193 Dave Concepcion .05
194 Kirk McCaskill .05
195 Mike Pagliarulo .05
196 Rick Manning .05
197 Brett Butler .05
198 Tony Gwynn 1.00
199 Mariano Duncan .05
200 Pete Rose 1.25
201 John Cangelosi .05
202 Danny Cox .05
203 Butch Wynegar .05
204 Chris Chambliss .05
205 Graig Nettles .05
206 Chet Lemon .05
207 Don Aase .05
208 Mike Mason .05
209 Alan Trammell .05
210 Lloyd Moseby .05
211 Richard Dotson .05
212 Mike Fitzgerald .05
213 Darrell Porter .05
214 Checklist 133-264 .05
215 Mark Langston .05
216 Steve Farr .05
217 Dann Bilardello .05
218 Gary Ward .05
219 Cecilio Guante .05
220 Joe Carter .15
221 Ernie Whitt .05
222 Denny Walling .05
223 Charlie Leibrandt .05
224 Wayne Tolleson .05
225 Mike Smithson .05
226 Zane Smith .05
227 Terry Puhl .05
228 Eric Davis .05
229 Don Mattingly 1.25
230 Don Baylor .05
231 Frank Tanana .05
232 Tom Brookens .05
233 Steve Bedrosian .05
234 Wallace Johnson .05
235 Alvin Davis .05
236 Tommy John .05
237 Jim Morrison .05
238 Ricky Horton .05
239 Shane Rawley .05
240 Steve Balboni .05
241 Mike Krukow .05
242 Rick Mahler .05
243 Bill Doran .05
244 Mark Clear .05
245 Willie Upshaw .05
246 Hal McRae .05
247 Jose Canseco .45
248 George Hendrick .05
249 Doyle Alexander .05
250 Teddy Higuera .05
251 Tom Hume .05
252 Denny Martinez .05
253 Eddie Milner .05
254 Steve Sax .05
255 Juan Samuel .05
256 Dave Bergman .05
257 Bob Forsch .05
258 Steve Yeager .05
259 Don Sutton .50
260 Vida Blue .05
261 Tom Brunansky .05
262 Joe Sambito .05
263 Mitch Webster .05
264 Checklist 265-396 .05
265 Darrell Evans .05
266 Dave Kingman .05
267 Howard Johnson .05
268 Greg Pryor .05
269 Tippy Martinez .05
270 Jody Davis .05
271 Steve Carlton .75
272 Andres Galarraga .15
273 Fernando Valenzuela .05
274 Jeff Hearron .05
275 Ray Knight .05
276 Bill Madlock .05
277 Tom Henke .05
278 Gary Pettis .05
279 Jimy Williams .05
280 Jeffrey Leonard .05
281 Bryn Smith .05
282 John Cerutti .05
283 Gary Roenicke .05
284 Joaquin Andujar .05
285 Dennis Boyd .05
286 Tim Hulett .05
287 Craig Lefferts .05
288 Tito Landrum .05
289 Manny Lee .05
290 Leon Durham .05
291 Johnny Ray .05
292 Franklin Stubbs .05
293 Bob Rodgers .05
294 Terry Francona .05
295 Len Dykstra .05
296 Tom Candiotti .05
297 Frank DiPino .05
298 Craig Reynolds .05
299 Jerry Hairston Sr. .05
300 Reggie Jackson 1.00
301 Luis Aquino .05
302 Greg Walker .05
303 Terry Kennedy .05
304 Phil Garner .05
305 John Franco .05
306 Bill Buckner .05
307 Kevin Mitchell .05
308 Don Slaught .05
309 Harold Baines .05
310 Frank Viola .05
311 Dave Lopes .05
312 Cal Ripken 2.00
313 John Candelaria .05
314 Bob Sebra .05
315 Bud Black .05
316 Brian Fisher .05
317 Clint Hurdle .05
318 Ernie Riles .05
319 Dave LaPoint .05
320 Barry Bonds 6.00
321 Tim Stoddard .05
322 Ron Cey .05
323 Al Newman .05
324 Jerry Royster .05
325 Garry Templeton .05
326 Mark Gubicza .05
327 Andre Thornton .05
328 Bob Welch .05
329 Tony Fernandez .05
330 Mike Scott .05
331 Jack Clark .05
332 Danny Tartabull .05
333 Greg Minton .05
334 Ed Correa .05
335 Candy Maldonado .05
336 Dennis Lamp .05
337 Sid Fernandez .05
338 Greg Gross .05
339 Willie Hernandez .05
340 Roger Clemens 1.50
341 Mickey Hatcher .05
342 Bob James .05
343 Jose Cruz .05
344 Bruce Sutter .65
345 Andre Dawson .25
346 Shawon Dunston .05
347 Scott McGregor .05
348 Carmelo Martinez .05
349 Storm Davis .05
350 Keith Hernandez .05
351 Andy McGaffigan .05
352 Dave Parker .05
353 Ernie Camacho .05
354 Eric Show .05
355 Don Carman .05
356 Floyd Bannister .05
357 Willie McGee .05
358 Atlee Hammaker .05
359 Dale Murphy .30
360 Pedro Guerrero .05
361 Will Clark .10
362 Bill Campbell .05
363 Alejandro Pena .05
364 Dennis Rasmussen .05
365 Rick Rhoden .05
366 Randy St. Claire .05
367 Willie Wilson .05
368 Dwight Evans .05
369 Moose Haas .05
370 Fred Lynn .05
371 Mark Eichhorn .05
372 Dave Schmidt .05
373 Jerry Reuss .05
374 Lance Parrish .05
375 Ron Guidry .05
376 Jack Morris .05
377 Willie Randolph .05
378 Joel Youngblood .05
379 Darryl Strawberry .05
380 Rich Gossage .05
381 Dennis Eckersley .50
382 Gary Lucas .05
383 Ron Davis .05
384 Pete Incaviglia .05
385 Orel Hershiser .10
386 Kirk Gibson .05
387 Don Robinson .05
388 Darnell Coles .05
389 Von Hayes .05
390 Gary Matthews .05
391 Jay Howell .05
392 Tim Laudner .05
393 Rod Scurry .05
394 Tony Bernazard .05
395 Damaso Garcia .05
396 Mike Schmidt 1.25

Box Panels

For the second consecutive year, O-Pee-Chee placed baseball cards on the bottoms of its wax pack boxes. The 2-1/8" x 3" cards were issued in panels of four and are slightly smaller in size than the regular issue OPC cards. The card fronts are identical in design to the regular issue, while the backs contain a newspaper-

type commentary in both French and English. Collectors may note the 1987 Topps wax box cards were issued on side panels as opposed to box bottoms. Because the OPC wax boxes are smaller in size than their U.S. counterparts, printing cards on side panels was not possible.

		NM/M
Complete Panel Set (2):		5.00
Complete Singles Set (8):		5.00
Common Single Player:		.15
Panel		2.00
A	Don Baylor	.15
B	Steve Carlton	.50
C	Ron Cey	.15
D	Cecil Cooper	.15
Panel		4.00
E	Rickey Henderson	1.00
F	Jim Rice	.35
G	Don Sutton	.50
H	Dave Winfield	1.00

Stickers

Bi-lingual backs are the only difference between the OPC 1987 sticker set and the Topps issue. The sets share a checklist and, generally, values, although some Blue Jays and Expos stars may command a small premium in the Canadian version.

1988 O-Pee-Chee

Under license from Topps, O-Pee-Chee uses the same player photos as the Topps issue, but the Canadian edition includes only 396 cards (one-half the number in the Topps set). The OPC set was printed after the U.S. press run, so several cards carry overprints on the fronts, indicating changes in players' teams. New teams are named in the overprints; card headers bear the former team names. This set follows the same basic design as the 1988 Topps cards. The OPC logo appears in place of the Topps logo, both front and back. A four-card subset consists of #1 and #2 draft choices for the Expos (Nathan Minchey and Delino DeShields) and Blue Jays (Alex Sanchez and Derek Bell). These cards are distinguished by a yellow or orange triangle in the lower-right corner bearing the player's name above the words "Choisi au repecharge." Card backs are bilingual (English-French) and printed in black on orange. This series was marketed primarily in Canada in four separate display boxes, with four cards printed one each box bottom. Individual card packs contain seven cards and one stick of gum.

	NM/M
Unopened Fact. Set (396):	9.00
Complete Set (396):	7.50
Common Player:	.05
Wax Pack (7):	.25
Wax Box (48):	7.50

1 Chris James .05
2 Steve Buechele .05
3 Mike Henneman .05
4 Eddie Murray .60
5 Bret Saberhagen .05
6 Nathan Minchey/DP .05
7 Harold Reynolds .05
8 Bo Jackson .10
9 Mike Easler .05
10 Ryne Sandberg .75
11 Mike Young .05
12 Tony Phillips .05
13 Andres Thomas .05
14 Tim Burke .05
15 Chili Davis .05
16 Jim Lindeman .05
17 Ron Oester .05
18 Craig Reynolds .05
19 Juan Samuel .05
20 Kevin Gross .05
21 Cecil Fielder .25
22 Greg Swindell .05
23 Jose DeLeon .05
24 Jim Deshaies .05
25 Andres Galarraga .10
26 Mitch Williams .05
27 R.J. Reynolds .05
28 Jose Nunez .05
29 Angel Salazar .05
30 Sid Fernandez .05
31 Keith Moreland .05
32 John Kruk .05
33 Rob Deer .05
34 Ricky Horton .05
35 Harold Baines .05
36 Jamie Moyer .05
37 Kevin McReynolds .05
38 Ozzie Smith .75
39 Ron Darling .05
40 Orel Hershiser .05
41 Bob Melvin .05
42 Alfredo Griffin .05
43 Dick Schofield .05
44 Terry Steinbach .05
45 Kent Hrbek .05
46 Darnell Coles .05
47 Jimmy Key .05
48 Alan Ashby .05
49 Julio Franco .05
50 Hubie Brooks .05
51 Chris Bando .05
52 Fernando Valenzuela .05
53 Kal Daniels .05
54 Jim Clancy .05
55 Phil Bradley .05
56 Andy McGaffigan .05
57 Mike LaVaillere .05
58 Dave Magadan .05
59 Danny Cox .05
60 Rickey Henderson .75
61 Jim Rice .20
62 Calvin Schiraldi .05
63 Jerry Mumphrey .05
64 Ken Caminiti .05
65 Leon Durham .05
66 Shane Rawley .05
67 Ken Oberkfell .05
68 Keith Hernandez .05
69 Bob Brenly .05
70 Roger Clemens .90
71 Gary Pettis .05
72 Dennis Eckersley .50
73 Dave Smith .05
74 Cal Ripken 1.00
75 Joe Carter .15
76 Denny Martinez .05
77 Juan Beniquez .05
78 Tim Laudner .05
79 Ernie Whitt .05
80 Mark Langston .05
81 Dale Sveum .05
82 Dion James .05
83 Dave Valle .05
84 Bill Wegman .05
85 Howard Johnson .05
86 Benito Santiago .05
87 Casey Candaele .05
88 Delino DeShields/DP 3.00
89 Dave Winfield .75
90 Dale Murphy .20
91 Jay Howell .05
92 Ken Williams .05
93 Bob Sebra .05
94 Tim Wallach .10
95 Lance Parrish .05
96 Todd Benzinger .05
97 Scott Garrelts .05
98 Jose Guzman .05
99 Jeff Reardon .05
100 Jack Clark .05
101 Tracy Jones .05
102 Barry Larkin .05
103 Curt Young .05
104 Juan Nieves .05
105 Terry Pendleton .05
106 Rob Ducey .05
107 Scott Bailes .05
108 Eric King .05
109 Mike Pagliarulo .05
110 Teddy Higuera .05
111 Pedro Guerrero .05
112 Chris Brown .05
113 Kelly Gruber .05
114 Jack Howell .05
115 Johnny Ray .05
116 Mark Eichhorn .05
117 Tony Pena .05
118 Bob Welch .05
119 Mike Kingery .05
120 Kirby Puckett .75
121 Charlie Hough .05
122 Tony Bernazard .05
123 Tom Candiotti .05
124 Ray Knight .05
125 Bruce Hurst .05
126 Steve Jeltz .05
127 Ron Guidry .05
128 Duane Ward .05
129 Greg Minton .05
130 Buddy Bell .05
131 Denny Walling .05
132 Donnie Hill .05
133 Wayne Tolleson .05
134 Bob Rodgers .05
135 Todd Worrell .05
136 Brian Dayett .05
137 Chris Bosio .05
138 Mitch Webster .05
139 Jerry Browne .05
140 Jesse Barfield .05
141 Doug DeCinces .05
142 Andy Van Slyke .05
143 Doug Drabek .05
144 Jeff Parrett .05
145 Bill Madlock .05
146 Larry Herndon .05
147 Bill Buckner .05
148 Carmelo Martinez .05
149 Ken Howell .05
150 Eric Davis .05
151 Randy Ready .05
152 Jeffrey Leonard .05
153 Dave Steib .05
154 Jeff Stone .05
155 Dave Righetti .05
156 Gary Matthews .05
157 Gary Carter .75
158 Bob Boone .05
159 Glenn Davis .05
160 Willie McGee .05
161 Bryn Smith .05
162 Mark McLemore .05
163 Dale Mohorcic .05
164 Mike Flanagan .05
165 Robin Yount .60
166 Bill Doran .05
167 Rance Mulliniks .05
168 Wally Joyner .05
169 Cory Snyder .05
170 Rich Gossage .05
171 Rick Mahler .05
172 Henry Cotto .05
173 George Bell .15
174 B.J. Surhoff .05
175 Kevin Bass .05
176 Jeff Reed .05
177 Frank Tanana .05
178 Darryl Strawberry .05
179 Lou Whitaker .05
180 Terry Kennedy .05
181 Mariano Duncan .05
182 Ken Phelps .05
183 Bob Dernier .05
184 Ivan Calderon .05
185 Rick Rhoden .05
186 Rafael Palmeiro .50
187 Kelly Downs .05
188 Spike Owen .05
189 Bobby Bonilla .05
190 Candy Maldonado .05
191 John Cerutti .05
192 Devon White .25
193 Brian Fisher .05
194 Alex Sanchez/DP .20
195 Dan Quisenberry .05
196 Dave Engle .05
197 Lance McCullers .05
198 Franklin Stubbs .05
199 Scott Bradley .05
200 Wade Boggs .75
201 Kirk Gibson .05
202 Brett Butler .05
203 Dave Anderson .05
204 Donnie Moore .05
205 Nelson Liriano .05
206 Danny Gladden .05
207 Dan Pasqua .05
208 Robbie Thompson .05
209 Richard Dotson .05
210 Willie Randolph .05
211 Danny Tartabull .05
212 Greg Brock .05
213 Albert Hall .05
214 Dave Schmidt .05
215 Von Hayes .05
216 Herm Winningham .05
217 Mike Davis .05
218 Charlie Leibrandt .05
219 Mike Stanley .05
220 Tom Henke .05

221 Dwight Evans .05
222 Willie Wilson .05
223 Stan Jefferson .05
224 Mike Dunne .05
225 Mike Scioscia .05
226 Larry Parrish .05
227 Mike Scott .05
228 Wallace Johnson .05
229 Jeff Musselman .05
230 Pat Tabler .05
231 Paul Molitor .75
232 Bob James .05
233 Joe Niekro .05
234 Oddibe McDowell .05
235 Gary Ward .05
236 Ted Power .05
237 Pascual Perez .05
238 Luis Polonia .05
239 Mike Diaz .05
240 Lee Smith .05
241 Willie Upshaw .05
242 Tom Neidenfuer .05
243 Tim Raines .20
244 Jeff Robinson .05
245 Rich Gedman .05
246 Scott Bankhead .05
247 Andre Dawson .25
248 Brook Jacoby .05
249 Mike Marshall .05
250 Nolan Ryan 1.00
251 Tom Foley .05
252 Bob Brower .05
253 Checklist 1-132 .05
254 Scott McGregor .05
255 Ken Griffey .05
256 Ken Schrom .05
257 Gary Gaetti .05
258 Ed Nunez .05
259 Frank Viola .05
260 Vince Coleman .05
261 Reid Nichols .05
262 Tim Flannery .05
263 Glenn Braggs .05
264 Garry Templeton .05
265 Bo Diaz .05
266 Matt Nokes .05
267 Barry Bonds 1.00
268 Bruce Ruffin .05
269 Ellis Burks .05
270 Mike Witt .05
271 Ken Gerhart .05
272 Lloyd Moseby .05
273 Garth Iorg .05
274 Mike Greenwell .05
275 Kevin Seitzer .05
276 Luis Salazar .05
277 Shawon Dunston .05
278 Rick Reuschel .05
279 Randy St. Claire .05
280 Pete Incaviglia .05
281 Mike Boddicker .05
282 Jay Tibbs .05
283 Shane Mack .05
284 Walt Terrell .05
285 Jim Presley .05
286 Greg Walker .05
287 Dwight Gooden .05
288 Jim Morrison .05
289 Gene Garber .05
290 Tony Fernandez .05
291 Ozzie Virgil .05
292 Carney Lansford .05
293 Jim Acker .05
294 Tommy Hinzo .05
295 Bert Blyleven .05
296 Ozzie Guillen .05
297 Zane Smith .05
298 Milt Thompson .05
299 Len Dykstra .05
300 Don Mattingly .85
301 Bud Black .05
302 Jose Uribe .05
303 Manny Lee .05
304 Sid Bream .05
305 Steve Sax .05
306 Billy Hatcher .05
307 John Shelby .05
308 Lee Mazzilli .05
309 Bill Long .05
310 Tom Herr .05
311 Derek Bell/DP 3.00
312 George Brett .85
313 Bob McClure .05
314 Jimy Williams .05
315 Dave Parker .05
316 Doyle Alexander .05
317 Dan Plesac .05
318 Mel Hall .05
319 Ruben Sierra .05
320 Alan Trammell .05
321 Mike Schmidt .85
322 Wally Ritchie .05
323 Rick Leach .05
324 Danny Jackson .05
325 Glenn Hubbard .05
326 Frank White .05
327 Larry Sheets .05
328 John Cangelosi .05
329 Bill Gullickson .05
330 Eddie Whitson .05
331 Brian Downing .05
332 Gary Redus .05
333 Wally Backman .05
334 Dwayne Murphy .05
335 Claudell Washington .05
336 Dave Concepcion .05
337 Jim Gantner .05
338 Marty Barrett .05
339 Mickey Hatcher .05
340 Jack Morris .05
341 John Franco .05
342 Ron Robinson .05
343 Greg Gagne .05
344 Steve Bedrosian .05
345 Scott Fletcher .05
346 Vance Law .05
347 Joe Johnson .05
348 Jim Eisenreich .05
349 Alvin Davis .05
350 Will Clark .10
351 Mike Aldrete .05
352 Billy Ripken .05
353 Dave Stewart .05
354 Neal Heaton .05
355 Roger McDowell .05
356 John Tudor .05
357 Floyd Bannister .05
358 Rey Quinones .05
359 Glenn Wilson .05
360 Tony Gwynn .75
361 Greg Maddux .75
362 Juan Castillo .05
363 Willie Fraser .05
364 Nick Esasky .05
365 Floyd Youmans .05
366 Chet Lemon .05
367 Matt Young .05
368 Gerald Young .05
369 Bob Stanley .05
370 Jose Canseco .45
371 Joe Hesketh .05
372 Rick Sutcliffe .05
373 Checklist 133-264 .05
374 Checklist 265-396 .05
375 Tom Brunansky .05
376 Jody Davis .05
377 Sam Horn .05
378 Mark Gubicza .05
379 Rafael Ramirez .05
380 Joe Magrane .05
381 Pete O'Brien .05
382 Lee Guetterman .05
383 Eric Bell .05
384 Gene Larkin .05
385 Carlton Fisk .60
386 Mike Fitzgerald .05
387 Kevin Mitchell .05
388 Jim Winn .05
389 Mike Smithson .05
390 Darrell Evans .05
391 Terry Leach .05
392 Charlie Kerfeld .05
393 Mike Krukow .05
394 Mark McGwire .90
395 Fred McGriff .10
396 DeWayne Buice .05

Box Panels

A Topps licensee, O-Pee-Chee of Canada issued this 16-card set on wax display box bottoms. Cards feature popular current players and are identified by alphabet (A-P) rather than numbers. Player photos are the same ones used on the Topps U.S. issue and cards follow the same design as Topps' regular issue set. The OPC logo replaces the Topps logo on both front and back. Orange and black card backs are bilingual (French/English) and include complete major and minor league career stats.

NM/M
Complete Panel Set (4): 8.00
Complete Singles Set (16): 8.00
Common Single Player: .10
Panel 1.00
A Don Baylor .10
B Steve Bedrosian .10
C Juan Beniquez .10
D Bob Boone .15
Panel 2.00
E Darrell Evans .10
F Tony Gwynn 1.00
G John Kruk .10
H Marvell Wynne .10
Panel 1.00
I Joe Carter .25
J Eric Davis .10
K Howard Johnson .10
L Darryl Strawberry .10
Panel 5.00
M Rickey Henderson 1.00
N Nolan Ryan 3.00
O Mike Schmidt 1.50
P Kent Tekulve .10

Stickers/ Stickercards

This is the Canadian version of Topps' sticker issue for 1988, virtually identical except for the substitution of the OPC logo and copyright notice on the front of the stickercard. The Canadian version shares the Topps' checklists and, essentially, the price structure, although Canadian star players command a small premium in the OPC version.

1989 O-Pee-Chee

At 396 cards, the 1989 O-Pee-Chee issue is half the size of the corresponding Topps set. As in previous years, the design of the OPC cards is virtually identical to the Topps version, though the Topps logo on front has been replaced with an O-Pee-Chee logo in one of the upper corners and the backs are printed in both English and French for the Canadian market. Cards of players who changed teams often contain an overprint indicating the player's new team and date of the transaction.

NM/M
Complete Set (396): 10.00
Common Player: .05
Wax Box (48): 12.00
1 Brook Jacoby .05
2 Atlee Hammaker .05
3 Jack Clark .05
4 Dave Steib .10
5 Bud Black .05
6 Damon Berryhill .05
7 Mike Scioscia .05
8 Jose Uribe .05
9 Mike Aldrete .05
10 Andre Dawson .25
11 Bruce Sutter .45
12 Dale Sveum .05
13 Dan Quisenberry .05
14 Tom Niedenfeur .05
15 Robby Thompson .05
16 Ron Robinson .05
17 Brian Downing .05
18 Rick Rhoden .05
19 Greg Gagne .05
20 Allan Anderson .05
21 Eddie Whitson .05
22 Billy Ripken .05
23 Mike Fitzgerald .05
24 Shane Rawley .05
25 Frank White .05
26 Don Mattingly .75
27 Fred Lynn .05
28 Mike Moore .05
29 Kelly Gruber .05
30 Dwight Gooden .05
31 Dan Pasqua .05
32 Dennis Rasmussen .05
33 B.J. Surhoff .05
34 Sid Fernandez .05
35 John Tudor .05
36 Mitch Webster .05
37 Doug Drabek .05
38 Bobby Witt .05
39 Mike Maddux .05
40 Steve Sax .05
41 Orel Hershiser .05
42 Pete Incaviglia .05
43 Guillermo Hernandez .05
44 Kevin Coffman .05
45 Kal Daniels .05
46 Carlton Fisk .50
47 Carney Lansford .05
48 Tim Burke .05
49 Alan Trammell .05
50 George Bell .15
51 Tony Gwynn .60
52 Bob Brenly .05
53 Ruben Sierra .05
54 Otis Nixon .05
55 Julio Franco .05
56 Pat Tabler .05
57 Alvin Davis .05
58 Kevin Seitzer .05
59 Mark Davis .05
60 Tom Brunansky .05
61 Jeff Treadway .05
62 Alfredo Griffin .05
63 Keith Hernandez .05
64 Alex Trevino .05
65 Rick Reuschel .05
66 Bob Walk .05
67 Dave Palmer .05
68 Pedro Guerrero .05
69 Jose Oquendo .05
70 Mark McGwire .85
71 Mike Boddicker .05
72 Wally Backman .05
73 Pascual Perez .05
74 Joe Hesketh .05
75 Tom Henke .05
76 Nelson Liriano .05
77 Doyle Alexander .05
78 Tim Wallach .10
79 Scott Bankhead .05
80 Cory Snyder .05
81 Dave Magadan .05
82 Randy Ready .05
83 Steve Buechele .05
84 Bo Jackson .10
85 Kevin McReynolds .05
86 Jeff Reardon .05
87 Tim Raines .25
88 Melido Perez .05
89 Dave LaPoint .05
90 Vince Coleman .05
91 Floyd Youmans .05
92 Buddy Bell .05
93 Andres Galarraga .15
94 Tony Pena .05
95 Gerald Young .05
96 Rick Cerone .05
97 Ken Oberkfell .05
98 Larry Sheets .05
99 Chuck Crim .05
100 Mike Schmidt .75
101 Ivan Calderon .05
102 Kevin Bass .05
103 Chili Davis .05
104 Randy Myers .05
105 Ron Darling .05
106 Willie Upshaw .05
107 Jose DeLeon .05
108 Fred Manrique .05
109 Johnny Ray .05
110 Paul Molitor .60
111 Rance Mulliniks .05
112 Jim Presley .05
113 Lloyd Moseby .05
114 Lance Parrish .05
115 Jody Davis .05
116 Matt Nokes .05
117 Dave Anderson .05
118 Checklist .05
119 Rafael Belliard .05
120 Frank Viola .05
121 Roger Clemens .85
122 Luis Salazar .05
123 Mike Stanley .05
124 Jim Traber .05
125 Mike Krukow .05
126 Sid Bream .05
127 Joel Skinner .05
128 Milt Thompson .05
129 Terry Clark .05
130 Gerald Perry .05
131 Bryn Smith .05
132 Kirby Puckett .60
133 Bill Long .05
134 Jim Gantner .05
135 Jose Rijo .05
136 Joey Meyer .05
137 Geno Petralli .05
138 Wallace Johnson .05
139 Mike Flanagan .05
140 Shawon Dunston .05
141 Eric Plunk .05
142 Bobby Bonilla .05
143 Jack McDowell .05
144 Mookie Wilson .05
145 Dave Stewart .10
146 Gary Pettis .05
147 Eric Show .05
148 Eddie Murray .50
149 Lee Smith .05
150 Fernando Valenzuela .05
151 Bob Walk .05
152 Harold Baines .05
153 Albert Hall .05
154 Don Carman .05
155 Marty Barrett .05
156 Chris Sabo .05
157 Bret Saberhagen .05
158 Danny Cox .05
159 Tom Foley .05
160 Jeffrey Leonard .05
161 Brady Anderson .05
162 Rich Gossage .05
163 Greg Brock .05
164 Joe Carter .10
165 Mike Dunne .05
166 Jeff Russell .05
167 Dan Plesac .05
168 Willie Wilson .05
169 Mike Jackson .05
170 Tony Fernandez .05
171 Jamie Moyer .05
172 Jim Gott .05
173 Mel Hall .05
174 Mark McGwire .85
175 John Shelby .05
176 Jeff Parrett .05
177 Tim Belcher .05
178 Rich Gedman .05
179 Ozzie Virgil .05
180 Mike Scott .05
181 Dickie Thon .05
182 Rob Murphy .05
183 Oddibe McDowell .05
184 Wade Boggs .60
185 Claudell Washington .05
186 Randy Johnson 2.00
187 Paul O'Neill .05
188 Todd Benzinger .05
189 Kevin Mitchell .05
190 Mike Witt .05
191 Sil Campusano .05
192 Ken Gerhart .05
193 Bob Rodgers .05
194 Floyd Bannister .05
195 Ozzie Guillen .05
196 Ron Gant .05
197 Neal Heaton .05
198 Bill Swift .05
199 Dave Parker .05
200 George Brett .75
201 Bo Diaz .05
202 Brad Moore .05
203 Rob Ducey .05
204 Bert Blyleven .05
205 Dwight Evans .05
206 Roberto Alomar .60
207 Henry Cotto .05
208 Harold Reynolds .05
209 Jose Guzman .05
210 Dale Murphy .15
211 Mike Pagliarulo .05
212 Jay Howell .05
213 Rene Gonzalez .05
214 Scott Garrelts .05
215 Kevin Gross .05
216 Jack Howell .05
217 Kurt Stillwell .05
218 Mike LaValliere .05
219 Jim Clancy .05
220 Gary Gaetti .05
221 Hubie Brooks .05
222 Bruce Ruffin .05
223 Jay Buhner .05
224 Cecil Fielder .15
225 Willie McGee .05
226 Bill Doran .05
227 John Farrell .05
228 Nelson Santovenia .05
229 Jimmy Key .05
230 Ozzie Smith .60
231 Dave Schmidt .05
232 Jody Reed .05
233 Gregg Jefferies .05
234 Tom Browning .05
235 John Kruk .05
236 Charles Hudson .05
237 Todd Stottlemyre .10
238 Don Slaught .05
239 Tim Laudner .05
240 Greg Maddux .60
241 Brett Butler .05
242 Checklist .05
243 Bob Boone .05
244 Willie Randolph .05
245 Jim Rice .15
246 Rey Quinonez .05
247 Checklist .05
248 Stan Javier .05
249 Tim Leary .05
250 Cal Ripken, Jr. 1.00
251 John Dopson .05
252 Billy Hatcher .05
253 Robin Yount .50
254 Mickey Hatcher .05
255 Bob Horner .05
256 Benito Santiago .05
257 Luis Rivera .05
258 Fred McGriff .10
259 Dave Wells .10
260 Dave Winfield .60
261 Rafael Ramirez .05
262 Nick Esasky .05
263 Barry Bonds 1.00
264 Joe Magrane .05
265 Kent Hrbek .05
266 Jack Morris .10
267 Jeff Robinson .05
268 Ron Kittle .05
269 Candy Maldonado .05
270 Wally Joyner .05
271 Glenn Braggs .05
272 Ron Hassey .05
273 Jose Lind .05
274 Mark Eichhorn .05
275 Danny Tartabull .05
276 Paul Kilgus .05
277 Mike Davis .05
278 Andy McGaffigan .05
279 Scott Bradley .05
280 Bob Knepper .05
281 Gary Redus .05
282 Rickey Henderson .60
283 Andy Allenson .05
284 Rick Leach .05
285 John Candelaria .05
286 Dick Schofield .05
287 Bryan Harvey .05
288 Randy Bush .05
289 Ernie Whitt .05
290 John Franco .05
291 Todd Worrell .05
292 Teddy Higuera .05
293 Keith Moreland .05
294 Juan Berenguer .05
295 Scott Fletcher .05
296 Roger McDowell .05
297 Mark Grace .10
298 Chris James .05
299 Frank Tanana .05
300 Darryl Strawberry .05
301 Charlie Leibrandt .05
302 Gary Ward .05
303 Brian Fisher .05
304 Terry Steinbach .05
305 Dave Smith .05
306 Greg Minton .05
307 Lance McCullers .05
308 Phil Bradley .05
309 Terry Kennedy .05
310 Rafael Palmeiro .45
311 Ellis Burks .05
312 Doug Jones .05
313 Dennis Martinez .10
314 Pete O'Brien .05
315 Greg Swindell .05
316 Walt Weiss .05
317 Pete Stanicek .05
318 Gene Nelson .05
319 Danny Jackson .05
320 Lou Whitaker .05
321 Will Clark .10
322 John Smiley .05
323 Mike Marshall .05
324 Gary Carter .60
325 Jesse Barfield .05
326 Dennis Boyd .05
327 Dave Henderson .05
328 Chet Lemon .05
329 Bob Melvin .05
330 Eric Davis .05
331 Ted Power .05
332 Carmelo Martinez .05
333 Bob Ojeda .05
334 Steve Lyons .05
335 Dave Righetti .05
336 Steve Balboni .05
337 Calvin Schiraldi .05
338 Vance Law .05
339 Zane Smith .05
340 Kirk Gibson .05
341 Jim Deshaies .05
342 Tom Brookens .05
343 Pat Borders .10
344 Devon White .10
345 Charlie Hough .05
346 Rex Hudler .05
347 John Cerutti .05
348 Kirk McCaskill .05
349 Len Dykstra .05
350 Andy Van Slyke .05
351 Jeff Robinson .05
352 Rick Schu .05
353 Bruce Benedict .05
354 Bill Wegman .05
355 Mark Langston .05
356 Steve Farr .05
357 Richard Dotson .05
358 Andres Thomas .05
359 Alan Ashby .05
360 Ryne Sandberg .60
361 Kelly Downs .05
362 Jeff Musselman .05
363 Barry Larkin .05
364 Rob Deer .05
365 Mike Henneman .05
366 Nolan Ryan 1.00
367 Johnny Paredes .05
368 Bobby Thigpen .05
369 Mickey Brantley .05
370 Dennis Eckersley .45
371 Manny Lee .05
372 Juan Samuel .05
373 Tracy Jones .05
374 Mike Greenwell .05
375 Terry Pendleton .05
376 Steve Lombardozzi .05
377 Mitch Williams .05
378 Glenn Davis .05
379 Mark Gubicza .05
380 Orel Hershiser .05
381 Jimy Williams .05
382 Kirk Gibson .05
383 Howard Johnson .05
384 Dave Cone .05
385 Von Hayes .05
386 Luis Polonia .05
387 Dan Gladden .05
388 Pete Smith .05
389 Jose Canseco .35
390 Mickey Hatcher .05

391	Wil Tejada	.05
392	Duane Ward	.05
393	Rick Mahler	.05
394	Rick Sutcliffe	.05
395	Dave Martinez	.05
396	Ken Dayley	.05

Box Panels

Continuing its practice of printing baseball cards on the bottom panels of its wax pack boxes, OPC in 1989 issued a special 16-card set, printing four cards on each of four different box-bottom panels. The cards are identical in design to the regular 1989 OPC cards. They are designated by letter (from A through P) rather than by number.

		NM/M
Complete Panel Set (4):		10.00
Complete Singles Set (16):		10.00
Common Panel:		1.50
Common Single Player:		.10
	Panel	2.50
A	George Brett	1.50
B	Bill Buckner	.10
C	Darrell Evans	.10
D	Rich Gossage	.10
	Panel	1.50
E	Greg Gross	.10
F	Rickey Henderson	1.00
G	Keith Hernandez	.10
H	Tom Lasorda	.25
	Panel	7.50
I	Jim Rice	.50
J	Cal Ripken, Jr.	3.00
K	Nolan Ryan	3.00
L	Mike Schmidt	1.50
	Panel	1.50
M	Bruce Sutter	.75
N	Don Sutton	.50
O	Kent Tekulve	.10
P	Dave Winfield	1.00

Stickers/ Stickercards

Once again sharing a checklist with the 1989 Topps sticker issue, the OPC version differs only in the substitution of the O-Pee-Chee logo and copyright notice on the front of the stickercard. Values are also essentially the same, although Expos and Blue Jays stars carry a small premium in the OPC version.

1990 O-Pee-Chee

Virtually identical to the contemporary 1990 Topps set, the OPC issue features the same 792 cards. On most cards the fronts are indistinguishable, even to the use of a Topps logo on the Canadian product. A number of the OPC cards differ from their Topps

counterparts in that there is a notice of team change printed in black on the front. Backs of the OPC cards feature a few lines of French in areas such as the stat headings, the career summary and monthly scoreboard. The OPC cards omit the Topps copyright line and feature an OPC copyright line on back.

	NM/M
Unopened Fact. Set (792):	15.00
Complete Set (792):	12.00
Common Player:	.05
Wax Pack:	.75
Wax Box (36):	20.00

Stickers

Once again sharing a checklist with the 1990 Topps sticker issue, the OPC version differs only in the substitution of the O-Pee-Chee logo and copyright notice on the stickercard. Values are also essentially the same, although Expos and Blue Jays stars carry a small premium in the OPC version.

1991 O-Pee-Chee Sample Sheet

This 7-1/2" x 10-1/2" sample sheet debuts the 1991 OPC set. Fronts reproduce the basic design while the back, printed in blue on white, contains an ad for OPC.

	NM/M
Complete Sheet:	5.00

1991 O-Pee-Chee

Once again for 1991, OPC utilized the contemporary Topps set of 792 cards as the basis for its own issue. The OPC cards are again printed on a lighter, whiter stock and differ from the Topps cards in the addition of French to the card backs, along with the OPC copyright. Many card fronts in OPC carry a small black typographical notice concerning team changes by the players.

	NM/M
Complete Set (792):	10.00
Common Player:	.05
Wax Box (36):	9.00

Premier

The O-Pee-Chee Co. of London, Ontario, Canada produced this 132-card set. The card fronts feature action photos, while the flip sides display a posed photo and career statistics. The cards were packaged seven cards per pack in a tamper-proof foil wrap. Several Expo and Blue Jay players are featured. Two special cards are included in this set. Card #62 honors Rickey Henderson's stolen base record, while card #102 commemorates Nolan Ryan's seventh no-hitter. Traded players and free agents are featured with their new teams.

		NM/M
Unopened Fact. Set (132):		4.00
Complete Set (132):		3.00
Common Player:		.05
Wax Pack (7):		.75
Wax Box (36):		9.00
1	Roberto Alomar	.40
2	Sandy Alomar	.05
3	Moises Alou	.20
4	Brian Barnes	.05
5	Steve Bedrosian	.05
6	George Bell	.10
7	Juan Bell	.05
8	Albert Belle	.05
9	Bud Black	.05
10	Mike Boddicker	.05
11	Wade Boggs	.75
12	Barry Bonds	1.00
13	Denis Boucher	.10
14	George Brett	.85
15	Hubie Brooks	.05
16	Brett Butler	.05
17	Ivan Calderon	.05
18	Jose Canseco	.25
19	Gary Carter	.75
20	Joe Carter	.10
21	Jack Clark	.05
22	Will Clark	.05
23	Roger Clemens	.90
24	Alex Cole	.05
25	Vince Coleman	.05
26	Jeff Conine	.05
27	Milt Cuyler	.05
28	Danny Darwin	.05
29	Eric Davis	.05
30	Glenn Davis	.05
31	Andre Dawson	.25
32	Ken Dayley	.05
33	Steve Decker	.05
34	Delino DeShields	.10
35	Lance Dickson	.05
36	Kirk Dressendorfer	.05
37	Shawon Dunston	.05
38	Dennis Eckersley	.50
39	Dwight Evans	.05
40	Howard Farmer	.05
41	Junior Felix	.05
42	Alex Fernandez	.10
43	Tony Fernandez	.05
44	Cecil Fielder	.15
45	Carlton Fisk	.60
46	Willie Fraser	.05
47	Gary Gaetti	.05
48	Andres Galarraga	.10
49	Ron Gant	.05
50	Kirk Gibson	.05
51	Bernard Gilkey	.05
52	Leo Gomez	.05
53	Rene Gonzalez	.05
54	Juan Gonzalez	.45
55	Doc Gooden	.05
56	Ken Griffey Jr.	.90
57	Kelly Gruber	.05
58	Pedro Guerrero	.05
59	Tony Gwynn	.75
60	Chris Hammond	.05
61	Ron Hassey	.05
62	Rickey Henderson	.75
63	Tom Henke	.05
64	Orel Hershiser	.05
65	Chris Hoiles	.05
66	Todd Hundley	.05
67	Pete Incaviglia	.05
68	Danny Jackson	.05
69	Barry Jones	.05
70	David Justice	.05
71	Jimmy Key	.05
72	Ray Lankford	.05
73	Darren Lewis	.05
74	Kevin Maas	.05
75	Denny Martinez	.10
76	Tino Martinez	.05
77	Don Mattingly	.85
78	Willie McGee	.05
79	Fred McGriff	.15
80	Hensley Meulens	.05
81	Kevin Mitchell	.05
82	Paul Molitor	.75
83	Mickey Morandini	.05
84	Jack Morris	.05
85	Dale Murphy	.15
86	Eddie Murray	.60
87	Chris Nabholz	.05
88	Tim Naehring	.05
89	Otis Nixon	.05
90	Jose Offerman	.05
91	Bob Ojeda	.05
92	John Olerud	.15
93	Gregg Olson	.05
94	Dave Parker	.05
95	Terry Pendleton	.05
96	Kirby Puckett	.75
97	Rock Raines	.10
98	Jeff Reardon	.05
99	Dave Righetti	.05
100	Cal Ripken	1.00
101	Mel Rojas	.10
102	Nolan Ryan	1.00
103	Ryne Sandberg	.75
104	Scott Sanderson	.05
105	Benito Santiago	.05
106	Pete Schourek	.05
107	Gary Scott	.05
108	Terry Shumpert	.05
109	Ruben Sierra	.05
110	Doug Simons	.05
111	Dave Smith	.05
112	Ozzie Smith	.75
113	Cory Snyder	.05
114	Luis Sojo	.05
115	Dave Stewart	.10
116	Dave Stieb	.05
117	Darryl Strawberry	.05
118	Pat Tabler	.05
119	Wade Taylor	.05
120	Bobby Thigpen	.05
121	Frank Thomas	.60
122	Mike Timlin	.05
123	Alan Trammell	.05
124	Mo Vaughn	.05
125	Tim Wallach	.05
126	Devon White	.10
127	Mark Whiten	.05
128	Bernie Williams	.10
129	Willie Wilson	.05
130	Dave Winfield	.75
131	Robin Yount	.60
132	Checklist	.05

1992 O-Pee-Chee

Once again closely following the format of the 1992 Topps set, and for the most part corresponding to its 792-card checklist, the 1992 OPCs differ on the front only in the substitution of an O-Pee-Chee logo for the Topps logo, and in the inclusion of team-change information for many of the players who moved after the Topps cards were printed. On backs, the light blue "Topps" logo printed behind the stats and beneath the card number changed from "Topps" to "O-Pee-Chee." The addition of a few lines of French above the stats and in the career summary can be seen on the OPC cards, as well as the substitution of an OPC copyright line for that of Topps. Where the 1992 Topps set features All-Star cards in the number range 386-407, the OPC set has a group of player cards who are not represented in the Topps set, including four "Tribute" cards honoring Gary Carter. Card #45 in the OPC set is also a Carter Trbitue card, whereas in the Topps set it is a regular card.

		NM/M
Unopened Fact. Set (792):		15.00
Complete Set (792):		10.00
Common Player:		.05
Wax Box (36):		12.00
45	Gary Carter - Tribute	1.00
386	Lance Blankenship	.10
387	Gary Carter - Tribute	1.00
388	Ron Tingley	.10
389	Gary Carter - Tribute	1.00
390	Gene Harris	.10
391	Jeff Schaefer	.10
392	Mark Grant	.10
393	Carl Willis	.10
394	Al Leiter	.25
395	Ron Robinson	.10
396	Tim Hullett	.10
397	Craig Worthington	.10
398	John Orton	.10
399	Gary Carter - Tribute	1.00
400	John Dopson	.10
401	Moises Alou	.60
402	Gary Carter - Tribute	1.00
403	Matt Young	.10
404	Wayne Edwards	.10
405	Nick Esasky	.10
406	Dave Eiland	.10
407	Mike Brumley	.10

Premier

O-Pee-Chee increased the number of cards in its premier set to 198 for 1992. The cards feature white borders surrounding full-color player photos. The O-Pee-Chee banner appears at the top of the card and the player's name and position appear at the bottom. The backs feature an additional player photo, statistics and player information. Traded players and free agents are featured with their new teams.

		NM/M
Factory Set (198):		5.00
Complete Set (198):		4.00
Common Player:		.10
Wax Box (36):		9.00
1	Wade Boggs	.75
2	John Smiley	.10
3	Checklist	.10
4	Ron Gant	.10
5	Mike Bordick	.10
6	Charlie Hayes	.10
7	Kevin Morton	.10
8	Checklist	.10
9	Chris Gwynn	.10
10	Melido Perez	.10
11	Danny Gladden	.10
12	Brian McRae	.10
13	Denny Martinez	.15
14	Bob Scanlan	.10
15	Julio Franco	.10
16	Ruben Amaro	.10
17	Mo Sanford	.10
18	Scott Bankhead	.10
19	Dickie Thon	.10
20	Chris James	.10
21	Mike Huff	.10
22	Orlando Merced	.10
23	Chris Sabo	.10
24	Jose Canseco	.40
25	Reggie Sanders	.10
26	Chris Nabholz	.10
27	Kevin Seitzer	.10
28	Ryan Bowen	.10
29	Gary Carter	.75
30	Wayne Rosenthal	.10
31	Alan Trammell	.10
32	Doug Drabek	.10
33	Craig Shipley	.10
34	Ryne Sandberg	.75
35	Chuck Knoblauch	.10
36	Bret Barberie	.10
37	Tim Naehring	.10
38	Omar Olivares	.10
39	Royce Clayton	.10
40	Brent Mayne	.10
41	Darrin Fletcher	.10
42	Howard Johnson	.10
43	Steve Sax	.10
44	Greg Swindell	.10
45	Andre Dawson	.25
46	Kent Hrbek	.10
47	Doc Gooden	.10
48	Mark Leiter	.10
49	Tom Glavine	.25
50	Mo Vaughn	.10
51	Doug Jones	.10
52	Brian Barnes	.10
53	Rob Dibble	.10
54	Kevin McReynolds	.10
55	Ivan Rodriguez	.50
56	Scott Livingstone	.10
57	Mike Magnante	.10
58	Pete Schourek	.10
59	Frank Thomas	.60
60	Kirk McCaskill	.10
61	Wally Joyner	.10
62	Rick Aguilera	.10
63	Eric Karros	.10
64	Tino Martinez	.10
65	Bryan Hickerson	.10
66	Ruben Sierra	.10
67	Willie Randolph	.10
68	Bill Landrum	.10
69	Bip Roberts	.10
70	Cecil Fielder	.15
71	Pat Kelly	.10
72	Kenny Lofton	.10
73	John Franco	.10
74	Phil Plantier	.10
75	Dave Martinez	.10
76	Warren Newson	.10
77	Chito Martinez	.10
78	Brian Hunter	.10
79	Jack Morris	.10
80	Eric King	.10
81	Nolan Ryan	1.50
82	Bret Saberhagen	.10
83	Roberto Kelly	.10
84	Ozzie Smith	.75
85	Chuck McElroy	.10
86	Carlton Fisk	.60
87	Mike Mussina	.50
88	Mark Carreon	.10
89	Ken Hill	.10
90	Rick Cerone	.10
91	Deion Sanders	.15
92	Don Mattingly	.85
93	Danny Tartabull	.10
94	Keith Miller	.10
95	Gregg Jefferies	.10
96	Barry Larkin	.10
97	Kevin Mitchell	.10
98	Rick Sutcliffe	.10
99	Mark McGwire	1.25
100	Albert Belle	.10
101	Gregg Olson	.10
102	Kirby Puckett	.75
103	Luis Gonzalez	.10
104	Randy Myers	.10
105	Roger Clemens	.90
106	Tony Gwynn	.75
107	Jeff Bagwell	.60
108	John Wetteland	.10
109	Bernie Williams	.10
110	Scott Kamieniecki	.10
111	Robin Yount	.60
112	Dean Palmer	.10
113	Tim Belcher	.10
114	George Brett	.85
115	Frank Viola	.10
116	Kelly Gruber	.10
117	David Justice	.10
118	Scott Leuis	.10
119	Jeff Fassero	.10
120	Sammy Sosa	.90
121	Al Osuna	.10
122	Wilson Alvarez	.10
123	Jose Offerman	.10
124	Mel Rojas	.10
125	Shawon Dunston	.10
126	Pete Incaviglia	.10
127	Von Hayes	.10
128	Dave Gallagher	.10
129	Eric Davis	.10
130	Roberto Alomar	.35
131	Mike Gallego	.10
132	Robin Ventura	.10
133	Bill Swift	.10
134	John Kruk	.10
135	Craig Biggio	.10
136	Eddie Taubensee	.10
137	Cal Ripken, Jr.	1.50
138	Charles Nagy	.10
139	Jose Melendez	.10

140 Jim Abbott .10
141 Paul Molitor .75
142 Tom Candiotti .10
143 Bobby Bonilla .10
144 Matt Williams .10
145 Brett Butler .10
146 Will Clark .10
147 Rickey Henderson .75
148 Ray Lankford .10
149 Bill Pecota .10
150 Dave Winfield .75
151 Darren Lewis .10
152 Bob MacDonald .10
153 David Segui .10
154 Benny Santiago .10
155 Chuck Finley .10
156 Andujar Cedeno .10
157 Barry Bonds 1.50
158 Joe Grahe .10
159 Frank Castillo .10
160 Dave Burba .10
161 Leo Gomez .10
162 Orel Hershiser .10
163 Delino DeShields .15
164 Sandy Alomar .10
165 Denny Neagle .10
166 Fred McGriff .15
167 Ken Griffey Jr. 1.00
168 Juan Guzman .10
169 Bobby Rose .10
170 Steve Avery .10
171 Rich DeLucia .10
172 Mike Timlin .10
173 Randy Johnson .65
174 Paul Gibson .10
175 David Cone .10
176 Marquis Grissom .15
177 Kurt Stillwell .10
178 Mark Whiten .10
179 Darryl Strawberry .10
180 Mike Morgan .10
181 Scott Scudder .10
182 George Bell .15
183 Alvin Davis .10
184 Len Dykstra .10
185 Kyle Abbott .10
186 Chris Haney .10
187 Junior Noboa .10
188 Dennis Eckersley .50
189 Derek Bell .20
190 Lee Smith .10
191 Andres Galarraga .15
192 Jack Armstrong .10
193 Eddie Murray .60
194 Joe Carter .15
195 Terry Pendleton .10
196 Darryl Kile .10
197 Rod Beck .10
198 Hubie Brooks .10

1993 O-Pee-Chee

For the first time in history, the 1993 O-Pee-Chee set differed significantly from the Topps set; photographs and designs are entirely different. Team names are scripted across the top, but a yellow triangle with a new team name appears on the front for players who have been traded. Two insert sets honoring the 1992 World Champion Toronto Blue Jays were also produced.

NM/M
Complete Set (396): 15.00
Common Player: .10
Wax Pack (8): .75
Wax Box: 15.00
1 Jim Abbott .10
2 Eric Anthony .10
3 Harold Baines .10
4 Roberto Alomar .45
5 Steve Avery .10
6 James Austin .10
7 Mark Wohlers .10
8 Steve Buechele .10
9 Pedro Astacio .10
10 Moises Alou .20
11 Rod Beck .10
12 Sandy Alomar .10
13 Brett Boone .10
14 Bryan Harvey .10
15 Bobby Bonilla .10
16 Brady Anderson .10
17 Andy Benes .10
18 Ruben Amaro .10
19 Jay Bell .10
20 Kevin Brown .10
21 Scott Bankhead .10
22 Denis Boucher .10
23 Kevin Appier .10
24 Pat Kelly .10
25 Rick Aguilera .10
26 George Bell .10
27 Steve Farr .10
28 Chad Curtis .10
29 Jeff Bagwell .60
30 Lance Blankenship .10
31 Derek Bell .10
32 Damon Berryhill .10
33 Ricky Bones .10
34 Rheal Cormier .10
35 Andre Dawson .30
36 Brett Butler .10
37 Sean Berry .10
38 Bud Black .10
39 Carlos Baerga .10
40 Jay Buhner .10
41 Charlie Hough .10
42 Sid Fernandez .10
43 Luis Mercedes .10
44 Jerald Clark .10
45 Wes Chamberlain .10
46 Barry Bonds 1.50
47 Jose Canseco .30
48 Tim Belcher .10
49 David Nied .10
50 George Brett .85
51 Cecil Fielder .30
52 Chili Davis .10
53 Alex Fernandez .15
54 Charlie Hayes .10
55 Rob Ducey .10
56 Craig Biggio .10
57 Mike Bordick .10
58 Pat Borders .10
59 Jeff Blauser .10
60 Chris Bosio .10
61 Bernard Gilkey .10
62 Shawon Dunston .10
63 Tom Candiotti .10
64 Darrin Fletcher .10
65 Jeff Brantley .10
66 Albert Belle .10
67 Dave Fleming .10
68 John Franco .10
69 Glenn Davis .10
70 Tony Fernandez .10
71 Darren Daulton .10
72 Doug Drabek .10
73 Julio Franco .10
74 Tom Browning .10
75 Tom Gordon .10
76 Travis Fryman .10
77 Scott Erickson .10
78 Carlton Fisk .60
79 Roberto Kelly .10
80 Gary DiSarcina .10
81 Ken Caminiti .10
82 Ron Darling .10
83 Joe Carter .15
84 Sid Bream .10
85 Cal Eldred .10
86 Mark Grace .10
87 Eric Davis .10
88 Ivan Calderon .10
89 John Burkett .10
90 Felix Fermin .10
91 Ken Griffey Jr. 1.00
92 Doc Gooden .10
93 Mike Devereaux .10
94 Tony Gwynn .75
95 Mariano Duncan .10
96 Jeff King .10
97 Juan Gonzalez .50
98 Norm Charlton .10
99 Mark Gubicza .10
100 Danny Gladden .10
101 Greg Gagne .10
102 Ozzie Guillen .10
103 Don Mattingly .85
104 Damion Easley .10
105 Casey Candaele .10
106 Dennis Eckersley .50
107 David Cone .10
108 Ron Gant .10
109 Mike Fetters .10
110 Mike Harkey .10
111 Kevin Gross .10
112 Archi Cianfrocco .10
113 Will Clark .10
114 Glenallen Hill .10
115 Erik Hanson .10
116 Todd Hundley .10
117 Leo Gomez .10
118 Bruce Hurst .10
119 Len Dykstra .10
120 Jose Lind .10
121 Jose Guzman .10
122 Rob Dibble .10
123 Gregg Jefferies .10
124 Bill Gulickson .10
125 Brian Harper .10
126 Roberto Hernandez .10
127 Sam Millitello .10
128 Junior Felix .10
129 Andujar Cedeno .10
130 Rickey Henderson .75
131 Bob MacDonald .10
132 Tom Glavine .25
133 Scott Fletcher .10
134 Brian Jordan .10
135 Greg Maddux .75
136 Orel Hershiser .10
137 Greg Colbrunn .10
138 Royce Clayton .10
139 Thomas Howard .10
140 Randy Johnson .75
141 Jeff Innis .10
142 Chris Hoiles .10
143 Darrin Jackson .10
144 Tommy Greene .10
145 Mike LaValliere .10
146 David Hulse .10
147 Barry Larkin .10
148 Wally Joyner .10
149 Mike Henneman .10
150 Kent Hrbek .10
151 Bo Jackson .15
152 Rich Monteleone .10
153 Chuck Finley .10
154 Steve Finley .10
155 Dave Henderson .10
156 Kelly Gruber .10
157 Brian Hunter .10
158 Darryl Hamilton .10
159 Derrick May .10
160 Jay Howell .10
161 Wil Cordero .10
162 Bryan Hickerson .10
163 Reggie Jefferson .10
164 Edgar Martinez .10
165 Nigel Wilson .10
166 Howard Johnson .10
167 Tim Hulett .10
168 Mike Maddux .10
169 Dave Hollins .10
170 Zane Smith .10
171 Rafael Palmeiro .45
172 Dave Martinez .10
173 Rusty Meacham .10
174 Mark Leiter .10
175 Chuck Knoblauch .10
176 Lance Johnson .10
177 Matt Nokes .10
178 Luis Gonzalez .10
179 Jack Morris .10
180 David Justice .10
181 Doug Henry .10
182 Felix Jose .10
183 Delino DeShields .15
184 Rene Gonzales .10
185 Pete Harnisch .10
186 Mike Moore .10
187 Juan Guzman .10
188 John Olerud .20
189 Ryan Klesko .10
190 John Jaha .10
191 Ray Lankford .10
192 Jeff Fassero .10
193 Darren Lewis .10
194 Mark Lewis .10
195 Alan Mills .10
196 Wade Boggs .75
197 Hal Morris .10
198 Ron Karkovice .10
199 John Grahe .10
200 Butch Henry .10
201 Mark McGwire 1.25
202 Tom Henke .10
203 Ed Sprague .10
204 Charlie Leibrandt .10
205 Pat Listach .10
206 Omar Olivares .10
207 Mike Morgan .10
208 Eric Karros .10
209 Marquis Grissom .15
210 Willie McGee .10
211 Derek Lilliquist .10
212 Tino Martinez .10
213 Jeff Kent .10
214 Mike Mussina .35
215 Randy Myers .10
216 John Kruk .10
217 Tom Brunansky .10
218 Paul O'Neill .10
219 Scott Livingstone .10
220 John Valentin .10
221 Eddie Zosky .10
222 Pete Smith .10
223 Bill Wegman .10
224 Todd Zeile .10
225 Tim Wallach .10
226 Mitch Williams .10
227 Tim Wakefield .10
228 Frank Viola .10
229 Nolan Ryan 1.50
230 Kirk McCaskill .10
231 Melido Perez .10
232 Mark Langston .10
233 Xavier Hernandez .10
234 Jerry Browne .10
235 Dave Stieb .15
236 Mark Lemke .10
237 Paul Molitor .75
238 Geronimo Pena .10
239 Ken Hill .10
240 Jack Clark .10
241 Greg Myers .10
242 Pete Incaviglia .10
243 Ruben Sierra .10
244 Todd Stottlemyre .10
245 Pat Hentgen .10
246 Melvin Nieves .10
247 Jaime Navarro .10
248 Donovan Osborne .10
249 Brian Barnes .10
250 Cory Snyder .10
251 Kenny Lofton .10
252 Kevin Mitchell .10
253 Dave Magadan .10
254 Ben McDonald .10
255 Fred McGriff .20
256 Mickey Morandini .10
257 Randy Tomlin .10
258 Dean Palmer .10
259 Roger Clemens 1.00
260 Joe Oliver .10
261 Jeff Montgomery .10
262 Tony Phillips .10
263 Shane Mack .10
264 Jack McDowell .10
265 Mike Macfarlane .10
266 Luis Polonia .10
267 Doug Jones .10
268 Terry Steinbach .10
269 Jimmy Key .10
270 Pat Tabler .10
271 Otis Nixon .10
272 Dave Nilsson .10
273 Tom Pagnozzi .10
274 Ryne Sandberg .75
275 Ramon Martinez .10
276 Tim Laker .10
277 Bill Swift .10
278 Charles Nagy .10
279 Harold Reynolds .10
280 Eddie Murray .60
281 Gregg Olson .10
282 Frank Seminara .10
283 Terry Mulholland .10
284 Kevin Palmer .10
285 Mike Greenwell .10
286 Jose Rijo .10
287 Brian McRae .10
288 Frank Tanana .10
289 Pedro Munoz .10
290 Tim Raines .15
291 Andy Stankiewicz .10
292 Tim Salmon .10
293 Jimmy Jones .10
294 Dave Stewart .15
295 Mike Timlin .10
296 Greg Olson .10
297 Dan Plesac .10
298 Mike Perez .10
299 Jose Offerman .10
300 Denny Martinez .15
301 Robby Thompson .10
302 Bret Saberhagen .10
303 Joe Orsulak .10
304 Tim Naehring .10
305 Bip Roberts .10
306 Kirby Puckett .75
307 Steve Sax .10
308 Danny Tartabull .10
309 Jeff Juden .10
310 Duane Ward .10
311 Alejandro Pena .10
312 Kevin Seitzer .10
313 Ozzie Smith .75
314 Mike Piazza 1.00
315 Chris Nabholz .10
316 Tony Pena .10
317 Gary Sheffield .25
318 Mark Portugal .10
319 Walt Weiss .10
320 Manuel Lee .10
321 David Wells .15
322 Terry Pendleton .10
323 Billy Spiers .10
324 Lee Smith .10
325 Bob Scanlan .10
326 Mike Scioscia .10
327 Spike Owen .10
328 Mackey Sasser .10
329 Arthur Rhodes .10
330 Ben Rivera .10
331 Ivan Rodriguez .50
332 Phil Plantier .10
333 Chris Sabo .10
334 Mickey Tettleton .10
335 John Smiley .10
336 Bobby Thigpen .10
337 Randy Velarde .10
338 Luis Sojo .10
339 Scott Servais .10
340 Bob Welch .10
341 Devon White .15
342 Jeff Reardon .10
343 B.J. Surhoff .10
344 Bob Tewksbury .10
345 Jose Vizcaino .10
346 Mike Sharperson .10
347 Mel Rojas .10
348 Matt Williams .10
349 Steve Olin .10
350 Mike Schooler .10
351 Ryan Thompson .10
352 Cal Ripken 1.50
353 Benny Santiago .10
354 Curt Schilling .25
355 Andy Van Slyke .10
356 Kenny Rogers .10
357 Jody Reed .10
358 Reggie Sanders .10
359 Kevin McReynolds .10
360 Alan Trammell .10
361 Kevin Tapani .10
362 Frank Thomas .60
363 Bernie Williams .10
364 John Smoltz .10
365 Robin Yount .60
366 John Wetteland .10
367 Bob Zupcic .10
368 Julio Valera .10
369 Brian Williams .10
370 Willie Wilson .10
371 Dave Winfield .75
372 Deion Sanders .10
373 Greg Vaughn .10
374 Todd Worrell .10
375 Darryl Strawberry .10
376 John Vander Wal .10
377 Mike Benjamin .10
378 Mark Whiten .10
379 Omar Vizquel .10
380 Anthony Young .10
381 Rick Sutcliffe .10
382 Candy Maldonado .10
383 Francisco Cabrera .10
384 Larry Walker .20
385 Scott Cooper .10
386 Gerald Williams .10
387 Robin Ventura .10
388 Carl Willis .10
389 Lou Whitaker .10
390 Hipolito Pichardo .10
391 Rudy Seanez .10
392 Greg Swindell .10
393 Mo Vaughn .10
394 Checklist 1 of 3 .10
395 Checklist 2 of 3 .10
396 Checklist 3 of 3 .10

World Champs

This 18-card insert set commemorates the Toronto Blue Jays' 1992 World Series victory; 17 players and Manager Cito Gaston are featured. Cards were randomly inserted, one World Champs or World Series Heroes card per every 69-cent, eight-card pack. Fronts and backs each feature the World's Championship logo. Backs include stats from the 1992 ALCS and World Series.

NM/M
Complete Set (18): 4.00
Common Player: .25
1 Roberto Alomar 1.00
2 Pat Borders .25
3 Joe Carter .65
4 David Cone .35
5 Kelly Gruber .25
6 Juan Guzman .25
7 Tom Henke .25
8 Jimmy Key .35
9 Manuel Lee .25
10 Candy Maldonado .25
11 Jack Morris .35
12 John Olerud .50
13 Ed Sprague .25
14 Todd Stottlemyre .25
15 Duane Ward .25
16 Devon White .35
17 Dave Winfield 1.50
18 Cito Gaston .25

World Series Heroes

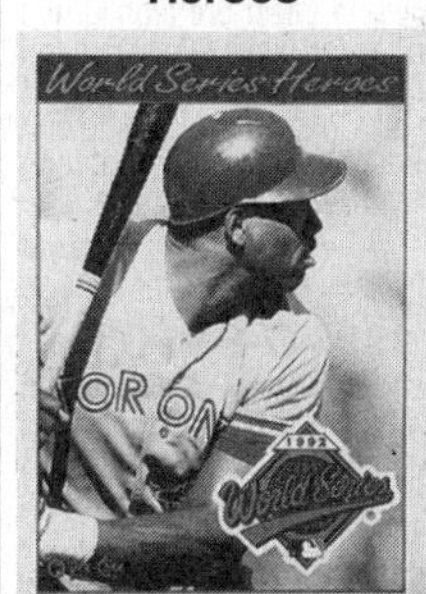

This insert set honors four of the Toronto Blue Jays' World Series stars. Cards were randomly inserted in every 69-cent, eight-card pack, one World Champs or World Series Heroes card per pack.

NM/M
Complete Set (4): 1.50
Common Player: .25
1 Pat Borders .25
2 Jimmy Key .25
3 Ed Sprague .25
4 Dave Winfield 1.50

Premier

For the third consecutive year, O-Pee-Chee produced a set under its Premier brand name. The regular set, issued in three series, has 132 cards and 48 insert cards. The insert sets are titled Star Performers (gold borders), Foil Star Performers (full-bleed photos and gold stamping), and Top Draft Picks (two each featuring the Toronto Blue Jays and Montreal Expos top picks). O-Pee-Chee announced it produced only 4,000 cases for this set.

NM/M
Complete Set (132): 4.00
Common Player: .05
Wax Box: 8.00
1 Barry Bonds 1.50
2 Chad Curtis .05
3 Chris Bosio .05
4 Cal Eldred .05
5 Dan Walter .05
6 Rene Arocha .05
7 Delino DeShields .05
8 Spike Owen .05
9 Jeff Russell .05
10 Phil Plantier .05
11 Mike Christopher .05
12 Darren Daulton .05
13 Scott Cooper .05
14 Paul O'Neill .05
15 Jimmy Key .05
16 Dickie Thon .05
17 Greg Gohr .05
18 Andre Dawson .25
19 Steve Cooke .05
20 Tony Fernandez .05
21 Mark Gardner .05
22 Dave Martinez .05
23 Jose Guzman .05
24 Chili Davis .05
25 Randy Knorr .05
26 Mike Piazza 1.00
27 Benji Gil .05
28 Dave Winfield .45
29 Wil Cordero .05
30 Butch Henry .05
31 Eric Young .05
32 Orestes Destrade .05
33 Randy Myers .05
34 Tom Brunansky .05
35 Dan Wilson .05
36 Juan Guzman .05
37 Tim Salmon .05
38 Bill Krueger .05
39 Larry Walker .25
40 David Hulse .05
41 Ken Ryan .05
42 Jose Lind .05
43 Benny Santiago .05
44 Ray Lankford .05
45 Dave Stewart .05
46 Don Mattingly .60
47 Fernando Valenzuela .05
48 Scott Fletcher .05
49 Wade Boggs .50
50 Norm Charlton .05
51 Carlos Baerga .05
52 John Olerud .15
53 Willie Wilson .05
54 Dennis Moeller .05
55 Joe Orsulak .05
56 John Smiley .05
57 Al Martin .05
58 Andres Galarraga .15
59 Billy Ripken .05
60 Dave Stieb .05
61 Dave Magadan .05
62 Todd Worrell .05
63 Sherman Obando .05
64 Kent Bottenfield .05
65 Vinny Castilla .05
66 Charlie Hayes .05

#	Player	Price
67	Mike Hartley	.05
68	Harold Baines	.05
69	John Cummings	.05
70	J.T. Snow	.05
71	Graeme Lloyd	.05
72	Frank Bolick	.05
73	Doug Drabek	.05
74	Milt Thompson	.05
75	Tim Pugh	.05
76	John Kruk	.05
77	Tom Henke	.05
78	Kevin Young	.05
79	Ryan Thompson	.05
80	Mike Hampton	.05
81	Jose Canseco	.30
82	Mike Lansing	.15
83	Candy Maldonado	.05
84	Alex Arias	.05
85	Troy Neel	.05
86	Greg Swindell	.05
87	Tim Wallach	.05
88	Andy Van Slyke	.05
89	Harold Baines	.05
90	Bryan Harvey	.05
91	Jerald Clark	.05
92	David Cone	.05
93	Ellis Burks	.05
94	Scott Bankhead	.05
95	Pete Incaviglia	.05
96	Cecil Fielder	.10
97	Sean Berry	.05
98	Gregg Jefferies	.05
99	Billy Brewer	.05
100	Scott Sanderson	.05
101	Walt Weiss	.05
102	Travis Fryman	.05
103	Barry Larkin	.05
104	Darren Holmes	.05
105	Ivan Calderon	.05
106	Terry Jorgensen	.05
107	David Nied	.05
108	Tim Bogar	.05
109	Roberto Kelly	.05
110	Mike Moore	.05
111	Carlos Garcia	.05
112	Mike Bielecki	.05
113	Trevor Hoffman	.05
114	Rich Amaral	.05
115	Jody Reed	.05
116	Charlie Leibrandt	.05
117	Greg Gagne	.05
118	Darrell Sherman	.05
119	Jeff Conine	.05
120	Tim Laker	.05
121	Kevin Seitzer	.05
122	Jeff Mutis	.05
123	Rico Rossy	.05
124	Paul Molitor	.45
125	Cal Ripken	1.50
126	Greg Maddux	.60
127	Greg McMichael	.05
128	Felix Jose	.05
129	Dick Schofield	.05
130	Jim Abbott	.05
131	Kevin Reimer	.05
132	Checklist	.05

Premier Star Performers

O-Pee-Chee released a 22-card insert set in two forms: Star Performers (featuring a gold border design) and Foil Star Performers (featuring full-bleed photos and gold stamping). The players are identical in both sets, but foil cards are generally worth more. There are 34 Star Performers per 36-card wax box and one Foil Star Performer card per box.

#		NM/M
	Complete Set (22):	4.50
	Common Player:	.10
	Foil:	6X
1	Frank Thomas	.50
2	Fred McGriff	.15
3	Roberto Alomar	.40
4	Ryne Sandberg	.65
6	Gary Sheffield	.25
7	Juan Gonzalez	.40
8	Eric Karros	.10
9	Ken Griffey Jr.	.75
10	Deion Sanders	.10
11	Kirby Puckett	.65
12	Will Clark	.10
13	Joe Carter	.15
14	Barry Bonds	1.50
15	Pat Listach	.10
16	Mark McGwire	1.00
17	Kenny Lofton	.10
18	Roger Clemens	.75
19	Greg Maddux	.65
20	Nolan Ryan	1.50
21	Tom Glavine	.20
22	Dennis Eckersley	.40

Premier Top Draft Picks

These randomly inserted cards feature four prospects; two each for Montreal and Toronto. Card fronts are foil-stamped and have a vertical banner with the player's name. The OPC Premier logo is in the corner. On back is another player photo, a team logo and a bi-lingual rationale for the player's draft status.

#		NM/M
	Complete Set (4):	2.50
	Common Player:	.50
1	B.J. Wallace	.50
2	Shannon Stewart	2.00
3	Rod Henderson	.50
4	Todd Steverson	.50

1994 O-Pee-Chee Sample Sheet

The basic '94 OPC card set and all of its chase card sets were previewed on this sample sheet sent to dealers. Measuring 8" x 11", the sheet's cards vary slightly from issued cards in terms of foil highlights. Card fronts on the sample sheet are highlighted in red foil while there is no foil on the backs. Each of the card backs (except the jumbo All-Star) includes the notation "Pre-Production Sample."

	NM/M
Complete Sheet:	6.00

1994 O-Pee-Chee

Limited to 2,500 cases (about 112,000 of each card in the regular 270-card set) the '94 OPC issue features color photos on front and back along with complete major league stats (and some minor league stats) on back. Team names are in a color-coded strip at left. Career summaries and some other data are printed in both English and French.

#		NM/M
	Complete Set (270):	15.00
	Common Player:	.05
	Wax Pack (15):	.75
	Wax Box (36):	15.00
1	Paul Molitor	.75
2	Kirt Manwaring	.05
3	Brady Anderson	.05
4	Scott Cooper	.05
5	Kevin Stocker	.05
6	Alex Fernandez	.05
7	Jeff Montgomery	.05
8	Danny Tartabull	.05
9	Damion Easley	.05
10	Andujar Cedeno	.05
11	Steve Karsay	.05
12	Dave Stewart	.05
13	Fred McGriff	.05
14	Jaime Navarro	.05
15	Allen Watson	.05
16	Ryne Sandberg	.75
17	Arthur Rhodes	.05
18	Marquis Grissom	.05
19	John Burkett	.05
20	Robby Thompson	.05
21	Denny Martinez	.05
22	Ken Griffey Jr.	1.00
23	Orestes Destrade	.05
24	Dwight Gooden	.05
25	Rafael Palmeiro	.40
26	Pedro Martinez	.05
27	Wes Chamberlain	.05
28	Juan Gonzalez	.50
29	Kevin Mitchell	.05
30	Dante Bichette	.05
31	Howard Johnson	.05
32	Mickey Tettleton	.05
33	Robin Ventura	.05
34	Terry Mulholland	.05
35	Bernie Williams	.05
36	Eduardo Perez	.05
37	Rickey Henderson	.65
38	Terry Pendleton	.05
39	John Smoltz	.05
40	Derrick May	.05
41	Pedro Martinez	.60
42	Mark Portugal	.05
43	Albert Belle	.05
44	Edgar Martinez	.05
45	Gary Sheffield	.35
46	Bret Saberhagen	.05
47	Ricky Gutierrez	.05
48	Orlando Merced	.05
49	Mike Greenwell	.05
50	Jose Rijo	.05
51	Jeff Granger	.05
52	Mike Henneman	.05
53	Dave Winfield	.65
54	Don Mattingly	.85
55	J.T. Snow	.05
56	Todd Van Poppel	.05
57	Chipper Jones	.75
58	Darryl Hamilton	.05
59	Delino DeShields	.05
60	Rondell White	.05
61	Eric Anthony	.05
62	Charlie Hough	.05
63	Sid Fernandez	.05
64	Derek Bell	.05
65	Phil Plantier	.05
66	Curt Schilling	.20
67	Roger Clemens	1.00
68	Jose Lind	.05
69	Andres Galarraga	.05
70	Tim Belcher	.05
71	Ron Karkovice	.05
72	Alan Trammell	.05
73	Pete Harnisch	.05
74	Mark McGwire	1.50
75	Ryan Klesko	.05
76	Ramon Martinez	.05
77	Gregg Jefferies	.05
78	Steve Buechele	.05
79	Bill Swift	.05
80	Matt Williams	.05
81	Randy Johnson	.60
82	Mike Mussina	.50
83	Andy Benes	.05
84	Dave Staton	.05
85	Steve Cooke	.05
86	Andy Van Slyke	.05
87	Ivan Rodriguez	.50
88	Frank Viola	.05
89	Aaron Sele	.05
90	Ellis Burks	.05
91	Wally Joyner	.05
92	Rick Aguilera	.05
93	Kirby Puckett	.75
94	Roberto Hernandez	.05
95	Mike Stanley	.05
96	Roberto Alomar	.25
97	James Mouton	.05
98	Chad Curtis	.05
99	Mitch Williams	.05
100	Carlos Delgado	.40
101	Greg Maddux	.75
102	Brian Harper	.05
103	Tom Pagnozzi	.05
104	Jose Offerman	.05
105	John Wetteland	.05
106	Carlos Baerga	.05
107	Dave Magadan	.05
108	Bobby Jones	.05
109	Tony Gwynn	.75
110	Jeromy Burnitz	.05
111	Bip Roberts	.05
112	Carlos Garcia	.05
113	Jeff Russell	.05
114	Armando Reynoso	.05
115	Ozzie Guillen	.05
116	Bo Jackson	.10
117	Terry Steinbach	.05
118	Deion Sanders	.05
119	Randy Myers	.05
120	Mark Whiten	.05
121	Manny Ramirez	.60
122	Ben McDonald	.05
123	Darren Daulton	.05
124	Kevin Young	.05
125	Barry Larkin	.05
126	Cecil Fielder	.05
127	Frank Thomas	.60
128	Luis Polonia	.05
129	Steve Finley	.05
130	John Olerud	.05
131	John Jaha	.05
132	Darren Lewis	.05
133	Orel Hershiser	.05
134	Chris Bosio	.05
135	Ryan Thompson	.05
136	Chris Sabo	.05
137	Tommy Greene	.05
138	Andre Dawson	.25
139	Bobby Kelly	.05
140	Ken Hill	.05
141	Greg Gagne	.05
142	Julio Franco	.05
143	Chili Davis	.05
144	Dennis Eckersley	.50
145	Joe Carter	.05
146	Mark Grace	.05
147	Mike Piazza	.90
148	J.R. Phillips	.05
149	Rich Amaral	.05
150	Benny Santiago	.05
151	Jeff King	.05
152	Dean Palmer	.05
153	Hal Morris	.05
154	Mike MacFarlane	.05
155	Chuck Knoblauch	.05
156	Pat Kelly	.05
157	Greg Swindell	.05
158	Chuck Finley	.05
159	Devon White	.05
160	Duane Ward	.05
161	Sammy Sosa	.85
162	Javier Lopez	.05
163	Eric Karros	.05
164	Royce Clayton	.05
165	Salomon Torres	.05
166	Jeff Kent	.05
167	Chris Hoiles	.05
168	Len Dykstra	.05
169	Jose Canseco	.35
170	Bret Boone	.05
171	Charlie Hayes	.05
172	Lou Whitaker	.05
173	Jack McDowell	.05
174	Jimmy Key	.05
175	Mark Langston	.05
176	Darryl Kile	.05
177	Juan Guzman	.05
178	Pat Borders	.05
179	Cal Eldred	.05
180	Jose Guzman	.05
181	Ozzie Smith	.75
182	Rod Beck	.05
183	Dave Fleming	.05
184	Eddie Murray	.60
185	Cal Ripken	2.00
186	Dave Hollins	.05
187	Will Clark	.05
188	Otis Nixon	.05
189	Joe Oliver	.05
190	Roberto Mejia	.05
191	Felix Jose	.05
192	Tony Phillips	.05
193	Wade Boggs	.75
194	Tim Salmon	.05
195	Ruben Sierra	.05
196	Steve Avery	.05
197	B.J. Surhoff	.05
198	Todd Zeile	.05
(199)	Raul Mondesi (No card number on back.)	.25
200	Barry Bonds	2.00
201	Sandy Alomar	.05
202	Bobby Bonilla	.05
203	Mike Devereaux	.05
204	Rickey Bottalico	.05
205	Kevin Brown	.05
206	Jason Bere	.05
207	Reggie Sanders	.05
208	David Nied	.05
209	Travis Fryman	.05
210	James Baldwin	.05
211	Jim Abbott	.05
212	Jeff Bagwell	.60
213	Bob Welch	.05
214	Jeff Blauser	.05
215	Brett Butler	.05
216	Pat Listach	.05
217	Bob Tewksbury	.05
218	Mike Lansing	.05
219	Wayne Kirby	.05
220	Chuck Carr	.05
221	Harold Baines	.05
222	Jay Bell	.05
223	Cliff Floyd	.05
224	Rob Dibble	.05
225	Kevin Appier	.05
226	Eric Davis	.05
227	Matt Walbeck	.05
228	Tim Raines	.05
229	Paul O'Neill	.05
230	Craig Biggio	.05
231	Brent Gates	.05
232	Rob Butler	.05
233	Dave Justice	.05
234	Rene Arocha	.05
235	Mike Morgan	.05
236	Denis Boucher	.05
237	Kenny Lofton	.05
238	Jeff Conine	.05
239	Bryan Harvey	.05
240	Danny Jackson	.05
241	Al Martin	.05
242	Tom Henke	.05
243	Erik Hanson	.05
244	Walt Weiss	.05
245	Brian McRae	.05
246	Kevin Tapani	.05
247	David McCarty	.05
248	Doug Drabek	.05
249	Troy Neel	.05
250	Tom Glavine	.20
251	Ray Lankford	.05
252	Wil Cordero	.05
253	Larry Walker	.05
254	Charles Nagy	.05
255	Kirk Rueter	.05
256	John Franco	.05
257	John Kruk	.05
258	Alex Gonzalez	.05
259	Mo Vaughn	.05
260	David Cone	.05
261	Kent Hrbek	.05
262	Lance Johnson	.05
263	Luis Gonzalez	.10
264	Mike Bordick	.05
265	Ed Sprague	.05
266	Moises Alou	.05
267	Omar Vizquel	.05
268	Jay Buhner	.05
269	Checklist	.05
270	Checklist	.05

All-Star Redemption Cards

A series of 25 All-Star redemption cards was one of the several inserts which were found at the rate of one per pack in '94 OPC foil. Fronts feature a color photo floating over a white background. The player's name is displayed in gold script at top and the card number is repeated along the top and left or right of the photo. Backs have information on how to redeem the cards for a super-size version of the set. Approximately 78,000 of each of the 25 cards in the insert set were produced.

#		NM/M
	Complete Set (25):	9.00
	Common Player:	.50
1	Frank Thomas	.65
2	Paul Molitor	1.00
3	Barry Bonds	2.50
4	Juan Gonzalez	.60
5	Jeff Bagwell	.75
6	Carlos Baerga	.50
7	Ryne Sandberg	1.00
8	Ken Griffey Jr.	2.00
9	Mike Piazza	1.50
10	Tim Salmon	.50
11	Marquis Grissom	.50
12	Albert Belle	.50
13	Fred McGriff	.50
14	Jack McDowell	.50
14p	Jack McDowell ("Pre-Production Sample")	.50
15	Cal Ripken, Jr.	2.50
16	John Olerud	.50
17	Kirby Puckett	1.00
18	Roger Clemens	1.50
19	Larry Walker	.60
20	Cecil Fielder	.50
21	Roberto Alomar	.60
22	Greg Maddux	1.00
23	Joe Carter	.50
24	Dave Justice	.50
25	Kenny Lofton	.50

Jumbo All-Stars

Each of the 60,000 foil-pack boxes of '94 OPC contained one jumbo (5" x 7") All-Star card from a set of 25. Fronts are identical to the All-Star redemption card inserts found in foil packs, with a UV coating. Backs are blank. Each of the jumbo All-Stars was produced in a quantity of 2,100. A factory-set version of the jumbo All-Stars was also available by redeeming five of the AS inserts and $20. The factory-set AS jumbos differ from the box-toppers in that they have gold-foil enhancements and are numbered to 5,000 each.

#		NM/M
	Complete Set (25):	75.00
	Common Player:	2.00
	Complete Factory Set:	35.00
	Factory Set Singles:	.75X
1	Frank Thomas	4.00
2	Paul Molitor	5.00
3	Barry Bonds	9.00
4	Juan Gonzalez	3.00
5	Jeff Bagwell	4.00
6	Carlos Baerga	2.00
7	Ryne Sandberg	5.00
8	Ken Griffey Jr.	7.50
9	Mike Piazza	6.00
10	Tim Salmon	2.00
11	Marquis Grissom	2.50
12	Albert Belle	2.00
13	Fred McGriff	2.50
14	Jack McDowell	2.00
15	Cal Ripken	9.00
16	John Olerud	2.50
17	Kirby Puckett	5.00
18	Roger Clemens	6.00
19	Larry Walker	2.50
20	Cecil Fielder	2.50
21	Roberto Alomar	3.00
22	Greg Maddux	5.00
23	Joe Carter	2.50
24	Dave Justice	2.00
25	Kenny Lofton	2.00

Diamond Dynamos

"Baseball's brightest new stars" was the stated criteria for inclusion in this chase card set. Fronts feature a full-bleed action photo with the player's name and "Diamond Dynamos" logo at bottom in red foil. Backs have a second player photo, personal data, a bilingual career summary and gold-foil presentation of the player's name and "Twenty-first Century Stars." An average of 1-2 of the cards was inserted per foil box, creating a production run of 5,000 of each card.

		NM/M
Complete Set (18):		5.00
Common Player:		.25
1	Mike Piazza	4.00
2	Roberto Mejia	.25
3	Wayne Kirby	.25
4	Kevin Stocker	.25
5	Chris Gomez	.25
6	Bobby Jones	.25
7	David McCarty	.25
8	Kirk Rueter	.25
9	J.T. Snow	.25
10	Wil Cordero	.25
11	Tim Salmon	.25
12	Jeff Conine	.25
13	Jason Bere	.25
14	Greg McMichael	.25
15	Brent Gates	.25
16	Allen Watson	.25
17	Aaron Sele	.25
18	Carlos Garcia	.25

Hot Prospects

Nine of 1994's hottest rookies are featured in this insert set. Fronts feature full-bleed photos with the player's name in gold foil at bottom. An "O-Pee-Chee Hot Prospects" logo appears in an upper corner. Backs are in shades of red, yellow and orange and include another player photo, biographical data, a career summary and complete minor league stats.

		NM/M
Complete Set (9):		7.50
Common Player:		.50
1	Cliff Floyd	.50
2	James Mouton	.50
3	Salomon Torres	.50
4	Raul Mondesi	.50
5	Carlos Delgado	3.00
6	Manny Ramirez	3.00
7	Javier Lopez	.50
8	Alex Gonzalez	.50
9	Ryan Klesko	.50

Toronto Blue Jays

The Blue Jays' starting line-up for the final game of the 1993 World Series is honored on this insert set. Fronts have a blue typographic background of "World Series Champions '92 & '93." There is a color player photo with his name in red foil at bottom. Backs repeat the typographic background in black and include 1992 and 1993 World Series stats along with the player's Series highlights in both English and French. A gold-foil seal marking the back-to-back championships is at top center. Stated odds of finding a Blue Jays insert card are one per foil box, indicating a production of about 6,666 of each card.

		NM/M
Complete Set (9):		6.00
Common Player:		.50
1	Rickey Henderson	2.00
2	Devon White	.75
3	Paul Molitor	2.00
4	Joe Carter	.75
5	John Olerud	1.00
6	Roberto Alomar	1.50
7	Ed Sprague	.50
8	Pat Borders	.50
9	Tony Fernandez	.50

1987 Oakland Athletics Fire Safety

The 1987 Smokey Bear A's set is not comparable to earlier Forestry Service issues. The cards are bound together in a book titled "Smokey Bear's Fire Prevention Color-Grams." Each Color-Gram features two cards in one. A near-standard size (2-1/2" x 3-3/4") black-and-white card is attached to a large perforated (3-3/4" x 6") card, also black-and-white. The large card, which has a postcard back, features a caricature of the player and is intended to be colored and mailed. Backs contain personal and statistical information and carry a Snokey the Bear cartoon fire sfaety message. The books were distributed at an A's game during the 1987 season.

		NM/M
Complete Book:		4.50
Complete Singles Set (12):		3.00
Common Player:		.25
(1)	Joaquin Andujar	.25
(2)	Jose Canseco	1.50
(3)	Mike Davis	.25
(4)	Alfredo Griffin	.25
(5)	Moose Haas	.25
(6)	Jay Howell	.25
(7)	Reggie Jackson	1.50
(8)	Carney Lansford	.25
(9)	Dwayne Murphy	.25
(10)	Tony Phillips	.25
(11)	Dave Stewart	.25
(12)	Curt Young	.25

1992 Oakland A's Dream Team

Following fan balloting in 1991, the Oakland A's named an all-time Dream Team for their 25th anniversary season in 1992 and issued a card set of those players. Cards were distributed in two versions. Perforated sheets of eight cards each were included in the second and third editions of the team's magazine. Imperforate four-card strips were also handed out to the first 10,000 fans attending each of four selected home games in 1992. Cards measure 2-9/16" x 3-3/4". Fronts have gray borders. At upper-left is a green and yellow Dream Team pennant; a 25th anniversary logo at lower-right is in team colors. A red box beneath the color player photo has the name and position in red and white. Black-and-white backs have uniform and card numbers, career stats and highlights and a few biographical bits.

		NM/M
Complete Set (16):		20.00
Common Player:		1.00
1	Mark McGwire	5.00
2	Mike Gallego	1.00
3	Bert Campaneris	1.00
4	Carney Lansford	1.00
5	Reggie Jackson	4.00
6	Rickey Henderson	3.00
7	Jose Canseco	3.00
8	Dave Parker	1.00
9	Terry Steinbach	1.00
10	Dave Stewart	1.00
11	Jim "Catfish" Hunter	2.00
12	Vida Blue	1.00
13	Bob Welch	1.00
14	Dennis Eckersley	2.00
15	Rollie Fingers	2.00
16	Tony LaRussa	1.00

1995 Oakland A's CHP

This safety set was sponsored by the California Highway Patrol, Fronts of the 2-1/2" x 3-1/2" cards have borderless game-action photos with a pair of team logos in the upper corner, a CHIPs badge at bottom-left and the player's name at lower-right. Black-and-white backs have player data and a driving safety tip.

		NM/M
Complete Set (8):		15.00
Common Player:		.50
1	Brent Gates	.50
2	Mark McGwire	10.00
3	Geronimo Berroa	.50
4	Jason Giambi	7.00
5	Terry Steinbach	.50
6	Mike Bordick	.50
7	Todd Van Poppel	.50
8	Ariel Prieto	.50

1999 Plumbers Local 342 Oakland A's

Borrowing from the concept used for many years by Mother's Cookies, this team set was designed to encourage trading when it was distributed to 15,000 fans on May 2. Cards were given away in shrink-wrapped packs of 28, containing 20 single cards and eight of one of the others. Sponsored by a trade union, the Plumbers Steamfitters Refrigeration Local 342, the set has color photos on front, surrounded by borders which morph from yellow to dark green. A "Generation '99 A's" logo is at lower-left. Backs have minimal player data.

		NM/M
Complete Set (28):		12.50
Common Player:		.25
1	Art Howe	.25
2	Ben Grieve	.50
3	Jason Giambi	3.00
4	Kenny Rogers	.25
5	Matt Stairs	.25
6	Tom Candiotti	.25
7	Tony Phillips	.25
8	Eric Chavez	1.50
9	Tim Raines	.50
10	A.J. Hinch	.50
11	Bill Taylor	.25
12	Miguel Tejada	1.50
13	Tim Worrell	.25
14	Scott Spezio	.25
15	Buddy Groom	.25
16	Olmedo Saenz	.25
17	T.J. Mathews	.25
18	Mike Macfarlane	.25
19	Brad Rigby	.25
20	Ryan Christenson	.25
21	Doug Jones	.25
22	Terry Clark	.25
23	Jorge Velandia	.25
24	Gil Heredia	.25
25	John Jaha	.25
26	Jimmy Haynes	.25
27	Jason McDonald	.25
28	A's Coaches/Checklist (Thad Bosley, Brad Fischer, Dave Hudgens, Ken Macha, Rick Peterson, Ron Washington)	.25

2000 Plumbers Local 342 Oakland A's

This team set was designed to encourage trading when it was distributed to fans at a promotional game. Cards were given away in packs of 28, containing 20 single cards and eight of one of the others. Sponsored by a trade union, the Plumbers Steamfitters Refrigeration Local 342, the set has color photos on front, surrounded by green borders. Backs have minimal player data.

		NM/M
Complete Set (28):		15.00
Common Player:		.50
1	Art Howe	.50
2	Jason Giambi	4.00
3	Tim Hudson	2.00
4	Matt Stairs	.50
5	Kevin Appier	.50
6	Ben Grieve	.50
7	Randy Velarde	.50
8	Eric Chavez	1.50
9	Mark Mulder	.75
10	Sal Fasano	.50
11	Doug Jones	.50
12	Miguel Tejada	1.50
13	Omar Oliveres	.50
14	Jeremy Giambi	.50
15	Gil Heredia	.50
16	Olmedo Saenz	.50
17	T.J. Mathews	.50
18	Ramon Hernandez	.50
19	Jeff Tam	.50
20	Ryan Christenson	.50
21	John Jaha	.50
22	Rich Sauveur	.50
23	Terrence Long	.50
24	Mike Magnante	.50
25	Scott Service	.50
26	Frank Menechino	.50
27	Jason Isringhausen	.50
28	Coaches/Checklist	.50

2001 Oakland A's Cal Ripken Farewell

To mark his final trip to Oakland as a player, the A's issued these cards to the first 20,000 fans at the September 3-5 games. The cards commemorate career highlights. Fronts have action photos from earlier seasons and a smaller second photo of more current vintage. Red-and-black backs have a ghost-image photo details of the highlight and specifics of the giveaway.

		NM/M
Complete Set (3):		9.00
Common Card:		3.00
1	Cal Ripken Jr. (Rookie Season 1982)	3.00
2	Cal Ripken Jr. (All-Star Game 1987)	3.00
3	Cal Ripken Jr. (2,131 - Record Breaker)	3.00

2002 Plumbers Local 342 Oakland A's

This team set was designed to encourage trading when it was distributed to 15,000 fans on August 18. Cards were given away in shrink-wrapped packs of 28, containing 20 single cards and eight of one of the others. Sponsored by a trade union, the Plumbers Steamfitters Refrigeration Local 342, the set has borderless color photos on front. A team-colors green and gold strip at bottom has the the player name and "BASEBALL A's STYLE." Backs are in black, green and gold with player data and a large union logo.

		NM/M
Complete Set (28):		15.00
Common Player:		.50
1	Art Howe	.50
2	Tim Hudson	2.00
3	David Justice	.50
4	Mark Mulder	.75
5	Jermaine Dye	.50
6	Barry Zito	2.00
7	Miguel Tejada	1.50
8	Eric Chavez	1.50
9	Terrence Long	.50
10	John Mabry	.50
11	Billy Koch	.50
12	Adam Piatt	.50
13	Ramon Hernandez	.50
14	Randy Velarde	.50
15	Scott Hatteberg	.50
16	Mike Magnante	.50
17	Greg Myers	.50
18	Cory Lidle	.50
19	Olmedo Saenz	.50
20	Jim Mecir	.50
21	Eric Byrnes	.50
22	Mark Ellis	.50
23	Mike Venafro	.50
24	Carlos Pena	.50
25	Mike Fyhrie	.50
26	Aaron Harang	.50
27	Chad Bradford	.50
28	A's Coaches (Thad Bosley, Brad Fischer, Ken Macha, Rick Peterson, Mike Quade, Ron Washington)	.50

2003 Plumbers Local 342 Oakland A's

This team set was designed to encourage trading when it was distributed to fans at a promotional game. Twenty-eight cards were given away in paper envelopes, containing 20 single cards and eight of one of the others. Sponsored by the Plumbers Steamfitters Refrigeration Local 342, the set has borderless color photos on front. A team-colors green and gold strip at bottom has the player name, position and team logo. Backs are in white, green and gold with player data and a large union logo.

		NM/M
Complete Set (28):		15.00
Common Player:		.50
1	Ken Macha	.50
2	Tim Hudson	2.00
3	Miguel Tejada	1.50
4	Mark Mulder	.75
5	Ramon Hernandez	.50
6	Barry Zito	2.00
7	Jose Guillen	.50
8	Eric Chavez	1.50
9	Terrence Long	.50
10	Ricardo Rincon	.50
11	Erubiel Durazo	.50
12	Mark Ellis	.50
13	Keith Foulke	.50
14	Eric Byrnes	.50
15	Ted Lilly	.50
16	Scott Hatteberg	.50
17	Rich Harden	1.00
18	Chris Singleton	.50
19	Chad Bradford	.50
20	Jermaine Dye	.50
21	Chad Harville	.50
22	Adam Melhuse	.50
23	Jim Mecir	.50
24	John Halama	.50
25	Mike Neu	.50
26	Billy McMillon	.50
27	Frank Menechino	.50
28	A's Coaches (Brad Fischer, Terry Francona, Bob Geren, Dave Hudgens, Rick Peterson, Ron Washington)	.50

1983 O'Connell & Son Ink Baseball Greats

This set of 4-1/2" x 6-1/2" blank-back cards features the artwork of T.S. O'Connell done in the style of 1959 Topps cards. Player portraits are in black-and-white, while backgrounds and team logos are in color. Production was limited to 2,000 sets.

NM/M
Complete Set (20): 65.00
Common Player: 2.50
(1) Hank Aaron 6.50
(2) Johnny Bench 2.50
(3) Yogi Berra 3.50
(4) George Brett 4.50
(5) Roy Campanella 3.50
(6) Rod Carew 2.50
(7) Roberto Clemente 10.00
(8) Bob Gibson 2.50
(9) Al Kaline 3.00
(10) Mickey Mantle 12.50
(11) Joe Morgan 2.50
(12) Stan Musial 3.50
(13) Jim Rice 2.50
(14) Frank Robinson 2.50
(15) Pete Rose 6.50
(16) Tom Seaver 2.50
(17) Duke Snider 3.50
(18) Honus Wagner 4.50
(19) Carl Yastrzemski 2.50
(20) Robin Yount 2.50

1984-91 O'Connell & Son Ink Mini Prints

This series of 2-1/2" x 3-1/2" blank-backed cards was issued over the period of 1984-91. Cards #1-180 were sold in annual series of 36 each from 1984-88; the 21-card Sixth Series was issued in 1990. The final 43 cards, plus unnumbered checklists for the first six series were distributed in issues of the company's newsletter, "The Infield Dirt." All cards feature black-and-white pen-and-ink player portraits by T.S. O'Connell and have only the player name and card number on front. Several styles of background, some in color, are found among the various series. Production was limited to 2,000 of each card.

NM/M
Complete Set (250): 450.00
Common Player: 1.50
First Series 45.00
1 Ted Williams 7.50
2 Minnie Minoso 1.50
3 Sandy Koufax 9.00
4 Al Kaline 4.50
5 Whitey Ford 3.00
6 Wade Boggs 3.00
7 Nolan Ryan 12.00
8 Greg Luzinski 1.50
9 Cal Ripken 12.00
10 Carl Yastrzemski 4.50
11 Dale Murphy 2.00
12 Rocky Colavito 7.50
13 George Brett 7.50
14 Willie McCovey 3.00
15 Rod Carew 2.50
16 Bob Gibson 2.50
17 Robin Yount 3.00
18 Steve Carlton 2.50
19 Harmon Killebrew 2.50
20 Willie Mays 7.50
21 Reggie Jackson 5.00
22 Eddie Mathews 2.50
23 Eddie Murray 2.50
24 Johnny Bench 2.50
25 Mickey Mantle 18.00
26 Willie Stargell 2.50
27 Rickey Henderson 2.50
28 Roger Maris 6.00
29 Darryl Strawberry 1.50
30 Pete Rose 9.00
31 Jim Rice 1.50
32 Thurman Munson 3.00
33 Brooks Robinson 2.50
34 Fernando Valenzuela 1.50
35 Tony Oliva 1.50
36 Hank Aaron 7.50
Second Series 45.00
37 Joe Morgan 2.50
38 Kent Hrbek 1.50
39 Yogi Berra 3.00
40 Stan Musial 7.50
41 Gary Matthews 1.50
42 Larry Doby 1.50
43 Steve Garvey 2.50
44 Bob Horner 1.50
45 Ron Guidry 1.50
46 Ernie Banks 3.00
47 Carlton Fisk 2.50
48 "Pee Wee" Reese 2.50
49 Bobby Shantz 1.50
50 Joe DiMaggio 12.00
51 Enos Slaughter 1.50
52 Gary Carter 2.50
53 Bob Feller 1.50
54 Phil Rizzuto 2.50
55 Dave Concepcion 1.50
56 Ron Kittle 1.50
57 Dwight Evans 1.50
58 Johnny Mize 1.50
59 Richie Ashburn 2.50
60 Roberto Clemente 12.00
61 Fred Lynn 1.50
62 Billy Williams 1.50
63 Dave Winfield 2.50
64 Robin Roberts 2.50
65 Billy Martin 1.50
66 Duke Snider 3.00
67 Luis Aparicio 2.50
68 Mickey Vernon 1.50
69 Mike Schmidt 6.00
70 Frank Robinson 2.50
71 Bill Madlock 1.50
72 Rollie Fingers 1.50
Third Series 45.00
73 Rod Carew 2.50
74 Carl Erskine 1.50
75 Lou Brock 2.50
76 Brooks Robinson 2.50
77 Roberto Clemente 12.00
78 Nellie Fox 2.50
79 Bud Harrelson 1.50
80 Ted Williams 7.50
81 Walter Johnson 2.50
82 Cal Ripken 12.00
83 Lefty Grove 2.00
84 Lou Whitaker 1.50
85 Johnny Bench 2.50
86 Ty Cobb 6.00
87 Mike Schmidt 6.00
88 George Brett 7.50
89 Jim Bunning 1.50
90 Babe Ruth 12.00
91 Satchel Paige 5.00
92 Warren Spahn 1.50
93 Dale Murphy 2.50
94 Early Wynn 1.50
95 Reggie Jackson 2.50
96 Charlie Gehringer 1.50
97 Jackie Robinson 9.00
98 Lou Gehrig 10.00
99 Hank Aaron 7.50
100 Mickey Mantle 18.00
101 Sandy Koufax 9.00
102 Ryne Sandberg 4.00
103 Don Mattingly 6.00
104 Darryl Strawberry 1.50
105 Tom Seaver 2.50
106 Bill Klem 1.50
107 Dwight Gooden 1.50
108 Pete Rose 9.00
Fourth Series 45.00
109 Elston Howard 2.50
110 Honus Wagner 3.00
111 Waite Hoyt 1.50
112 Bill Bruton 1.50
113 Gil Hodges 2.50
114 Vic Power 1.50
115 Al Kaline 4.50
116 Al Lopez 1.50
117 Rocky Bridges 1.50
118 Jim Gilliam 1.50
119 Christy Mathewson 2.50
120 Hank Greenberg 3.00
121 Eddie Mathews 1.50
122 Van Mungo 1.50
123 Harry Simpson 1.50
124 Carl Yastrzemski 2.50
125 Pete Rose 9.00
126 Dizzy Dean 3.00
127 Chi Chi Olivo 1.50
128 Johnny Vander Meer 1.50
129 Roberto Clemente 12.00
130 Carl Hubbell 1.50
131 Willie Mays 7.50
132 Willie Stargell 2.50
133 Sam Jethroe 1.50
134 Pete Rose 9.00
135 Jackie Robinson 9.00
136 Yogi Berra 3.00
137 Grover Alexander 2.00
138 Joe Morgan 2.50
139 Rube Foster 1.50
140 Mickey Mantle 18.00
141 Ted Williams 7.50
142 Jimmie Foxx 2.50
143 Pepper Martin 1.50
144 Hank Aaron 7.50
Fifth Series 45.00
145 Vida Blue 1.50
146 Carl Furillo 2.00
147 Lloyd Waner 1.50
148 Eddie Dyer 1.50
149 Casey Stengel 2.50
150 Mickey Mantle 18.00
151 Gil Hodges 2.50
152 Don Mossi 1.50
153 Ron Swoboda 1.50
154 Hoyt Wilhelm 1.50
155 Ed Roush (Edd) 1.50
156 Mickey Lolich 2.00
157 Jim Palmer 2.50
158 Thurman Munson 3.00
159 Don Zimmer 1.50
160 Hank Aaron 7.50
161 Johnny Bench 2.50
162 Orlando Cepeda 1.50
163 Honus Wagner 3.00
164 Tom Seaver 2.50
165 Willie Mays 7.50
166 Elmer Riddle 1.50
167 Tony Oliva 1.50
168 Elmer Flick 1.50
169 Curt Flood 1.50
170 Carl Yastrzemski 2.50
171 Charlie Keller 1.50
172 Christy Mathewson 2.50
173 Eddie Plank 1.50
174 Lou Gehrig 10.00
175 John McGraw 1.50
176 Mule Haas 1.50
177 Paul Waner 1.50
178 Steve Blass 1.50
179 Honus Wagner 3.00
180 Jack Barry 1.50
Sixth Series 45.00
181 Rocky Colavito 4.50
182 Danny Murtaugh 1.50
183 John Edwards 1.50
184 Pete Rose 9.00
185 Roy Campanella 3.00
186 Jerry Grote 1.50
187 Leo Durocher 1.50
188 Rollie Fingers 2.50
189 Wes Parker 1.50
190 Joe Rudi 1.50
191 Bill Veeck 2.50
192 Mark Fidrych 2.50
193 George Foster 1.50
194 Early Wynn 1.50
195 Frank Howard 1.50
196 Graig Nettles 2.50
197 Juan Pizzaro 1.50
198 Jose Cruz 1.50
199 Joe Jackson 12.00
200 Stan Musial 7.50
201 Chuck Klein 1.50
Seventh Series 45.00
202 Ryne Sandberg 6.00
203 Richie Allen 2.50
204 Bo Jackson 2.50
205 Kevin Mitchell 1.50
206 Al Smith, Early Wynn, Larry Doby 1.50
207 Mickey Mantle 18.00
208 Will Clark 2.50
209 Cecil Fielder 1.50
210 Bobby Richardson 2.50
211 Nolan Ryan 12.00
212 Casey Stengel 2.50
213 Ted Kluszewski 3.00
214 Gaylord Perry 2.50
215 Johnny Vander Meer 1.50
216 Willie Mays 7.50
217 Goose Goslin 1.50
218 Bobby Shantz 1.50
219 Terry Pendleton 1.50
220 Richie Ashburn 2.50
221 Robin Yount 3.00
222 Cal Ripken 12.00
223 Danny Ainge 1.50
224 Bob Friend 1.50
225 Orel Hershiser 2.50
226 Wade Boggs 3.00
227 Bill Mazeroski (1960 World Series home run) 3.00
228 Stan Musial 7.50
229 Chris Short 1.50
230 Johnny Bench 2.50
231 Nellie Fox 2.50
232 Ron Santo 2.50
233 Tony Gwynn 6.00
234 Phil Niekro 2.50
235 Frank Thomas 4.50
236 Greg Gross 1.50
237 Ken Griffey Jr. 9.00
238 Benito Santiago 1.50
239 Dwight Gooden 1.50
240 Darryl Strawberry 1.50
241 Roy Campanella 3.00
242 Roger Clemens 6.00
243 Kirby Puckett 7.50
244 Nolan Ryan 12.00
--- First Series Checklist .25
--- Second Series Checklist .25
--- Third Series Checklist .25
--- Fourth Series Checklist .25
--- Fifth Series Checklist .25
--- Sixth Series Checklist .25

1986 Oh Henry! Cleveland Indians

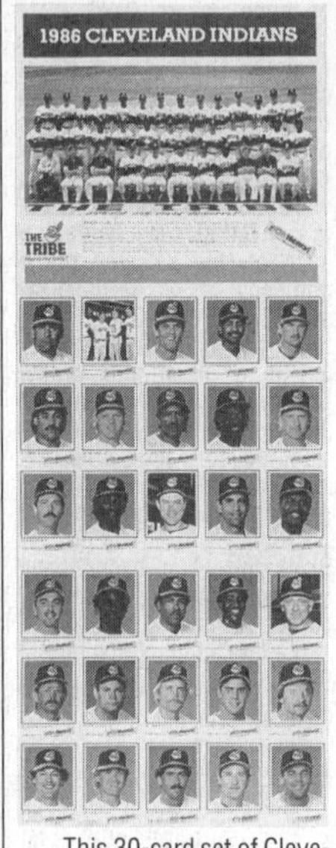

This 30-card set of Cleveland Indians players was distributed by the team at a special Photo/Baseball Card Day at Municipal Stadium. The cards were printed on an 11" x 29" three-panel, perforated foldout piece which featured four action shots of the Indians on the cover. Unfolded, there are two panels containing the baseball cards and a third which contains a team photo. Cards measure 2-1/4" x 3-1/8". The players' studio portraits are framed in blue with a white border and list player name, number and position. Card fronts also include a picture of the sponsoring candy bar. Card backs include facsimile autograph and professional records. Each card is perforated for separation.

NM/M
Complete Set, Foldout: 9.00
Common Player: .40
2 Brett Butler .40
4 Tony Bernazard .40
6 Andy Allanson .40
7 Pat Corrales .40
8 Carmen Castillo .40
10 Pat Tabler .40
13 Ernie Camacho .40
14 Julio Franco .50
15 Dan Rohn .40
18 Ken Schrom .40
20 Otis Nixon .40
22 Fran Mullins .40
23 Chris Bando .40
24 Ed Williams .40
26 Brook Jacoby .40
27 Mel Hall .40
29 Andre Thornton .50
30 Joe Carter .75
35 Phil Niekro 2.00
36 Jamie Easterly .40
37 Don Schulze .40
42 Rich Yett .40
43 Scott Bailes .40
44 Neal Heaton .40
46 Jim Kern .40
48 Dickie Noles .40
49 Tom Candiotti .40
53 Reggie Ritter .40
54 Tom Waddell .40
--- Coaching Staff (Jack Aker, Bobby Bonds, Doc Edwards, John Goryl) .40
--- Team Photo 2.00

1995 Oh Henry! Toronto Blue Jays

The candy bar company, Oh Henry!, sponsored this card set giveaway. The 2-1/2" x 3-1/2" cards have an action photo on a green background with the team name repeated in white diagonally. A large colorful "LET'S PLAY BALL" team logo is at top-left. The player name and uniform number are overprinted at bottom. Backs are printed in black-and-white with personal data, career highlights, stats, and sponsor's logo. Cards are listed here alphabetically.

NM/M
Complete Set (36): 12.00
Common Player: .25
(1) Roberto Alomar .75
(2) Bob Bailor .25
(3) Howard Battle .25
(4) Joe Carter .45
(5) Tony Castillo .25
(6) Domingo Cedeno .25
(7) Galen Cisco .25
(8) David Cone .35
(9) Brad Cornett .25
(10) Danny Cox .25
(11) Tim Crabtree .25
(12) Carlos Delgado 1.00
(13) Cito Gaston .25
(14) Alex Gonzalez .50
(15) Shawn Green 2.00
(16) Juan Guzman .25
(17) Darren Hall .25
(18) Pat Hentgen .25
(19) Larry Hisle .25
(20) Dennis Holmberg .25
(21) Michael Huff .25
(22) Randy Knorr .25
(23) Al Leiter .25
(24) Nick Leyva .25
(25) Angel Martinez .25
(26) Paul Molitor 2.50
(27) John Olerud .50
(28) Tomas Perez .25
(29) Aaron Small .25
(30) Paul Spoljaric .25
(31) Ed Sprague .25
(32) Gene Tenace .25
(33) Mike Timlin .25
(34) Duane Ward .25
(35) Devon White .40
(36) Woody Williams .25

1996 Oh Henry! Toronto Blue Jays

In celebration of the team's 20th anniversary, Oh Henry! sponsored a card set giveaway at SkyDome on June 11. The first 25,000 fans received a boxed set of current and former players. The 2-1/2" x 3-1/2" cards have a borderless photo on front. The central portion of the picture is in color, the edges are in black-and-white. The player name and uniform number are overprinted at bottom. The team's anniversary logo is in the upper-left corner. On former players' cards there is a gold "ALUMNI" banner under the logo ball. Backs are printed in blue and white with career summary and stats, a few bits of personal data and logos of the team and sponsor. Cards are listed here alphabetically.

NM/M
Complete Set (36): 8.00
Common Player: .25
(1) George Bell .35
(2) Brian Bohanon .25
(3) Joe Carter .40
(4) Tony Castillo .25
(5) Domingo Cedeno .25
(6) Tim Crabtree .25
(7) Felipe Crespo .25
(8) Carlos Delgado 1.50
(9) Cito Gaston .25
(10) Alex Gonzalez .50
(11) Shawn Green 1.00
(12) Alfredo Griffin .25
(13) Kelly Gruber .25
(14) Juan Guzman .25
(15) Erik Hanson .25
(16) Pat Hentgen .25
(17) Marty Janzen .25
(18) Nick Leyva .25
(19) Sandy Martinez .25
(20) Lloyd Moseby .35
(21) Otis Nixon .25
(22) Charlie O'Brien .25
(23) John Olerud .75
(24) Robert Perez .25
(25) Paul Quantrill .25
(26) Mel Queen .25
(27) Bill Risley .25
(28) Juan Samuel .25
(29) Ed Sprague .25
(30) Dave Steib .35
(31) Gene Tenace .25
(32) Mike Timlin .25
(33) Willie Upshaw .25
(34) Jeffrey Ware .25
(35) Ernie Whitt .25
(36) Woody Williams .25

1997 Oh Henry! Toronto Blue Jays

The first 25,000 fans entering SkyDome for the Blue Jays' May 6 game received a team card set sponsored by the candy bar company. In 2-1/2" x 3-1/2" size, fronts feature color action photos with a splash of "infield dirt" vertically at left. The player's name and uniform number appear at top-left. "Oh!" and the team logo are printed in bottom corners. Backs are printed in blue and white with a few personal data, stats and career highlights.

NM/M
Complete Set (36): 7.50
Common Player: .25
2 Otis Nixon .25
3 Felipe Crespo .25
4 Alfredo Griffin .25
5 Jacob Brumfield .25
6 Orlando Merced .25
7 Shannon Stewart .50
8 Alex Gonzalez .40
10 Jim Lett .25
11 Juan Samuel .25
12 Tilson Brito .25
13 Carlos Garcia .25
15 Shawn Green 1.00

16	Nick Leyva	.25
17	Robert Perez	.25
18	Benito Santiago	.25
19	Dan Plesac	.25
21	Roger Clemens	2.50
22	Charlie O'Brien	.25
24	Paul Spoljaric	.25
25	Carlos Delgado	1.50
26	Willie Upshaw	.25
29	Joe Carter	.30
31	Robert Person	.25
33	Ed Sprague	.25
34	Mel Queen	.25
37	Tim Crabtree	.25
39	Erik Hanson	.25
40	Mike Timlin	.25
41	Pat Hentgen	.25
43	Cito Gaston	.25
44	Gene Tenace	.25
48	Paul Quantrill	.25
49	Luis Andujar	.25
54	Woody Williams	.25
55	Bill Risley	.25
57	Juan Guzman	.25

1998 Oh Henry! Toronto Blue Jays

This stadium giveaway card set was issued in a flip-top cardboard box decorated with the team logo and checklist. The 2-1/2" x 3-1/2" cards have (mostly) game action photos on their borderless fronts. Sponsor logo at player name and uniform number are at top, team logo and motto "BRING IT ON." are at bottom. Backs are blue-and-white with player data, stats and career highlights. The checklist is arranged by uniform number.

		NM/M
Complete Set (36):		7.50
Common Player:		.25
1	Tony Fernandez	.25
3	Felipe Crespo	.25
4	Craig Grebeck	.25
5	Mark Dalesandro	.25
7	Eddie Rodriguez	.25
8	Alex Gonzalez	.45
9	Darren Fletcher	.25
10	Jim Lett	.25
11	Juan Samuel	.25
14	Kevin Brown	.25
15	Shawn Green	1.00
16	Jack Hubbard	.25
17	Tim Johnson	.25
18	Benito Santiago	.25
19	Dan Plesac	.25
20	Mike Stanley	.25
21	Roger Clemens	3.00
22	Sal Butera	.25
23	Jose Cruz Jr.	.35
24	Shannon Stewart	.35
25	Carlos Delgado	1.50
26	Chris Carpenter	.25
28	Randy Myers	.25
30	Woody Williams	.25
31	Robert Person	.25
33	Ed Sprague	.25
34	Mel Queen	.25
36	Gary Matthews	.25
39	Erik Hanson	.25
40	Carlos Almanzar	.25
41	Pat Hentgen	.25
44	Jose Canseco	1.00
45	Kelvim Escobar	.25
48	Paul Quantrill	.25
55	Bill Risley	.25
57	Juan Guzman	.25

1999 Oh Henry! Toronto Blue Jays

This boxed set was a stadium give-away. Fronts of the 2-1/2" x 3-1/2" cards have game-action photos on a wood-look background. Backs have personal data, career

highlights and stats printed in blue. The checklist is arranged by uniform number.

		NM/M
Complete Set (36):		7.50
Common Player:		.25
1	Tony Fernandez	.25
3	Norberto Martin	.25
4	Craig Grebeck	.25
5	Mark Dalesandro	.25
7	Pat Kelly	.25
8	Alex Gonzalez	.25
9	Darrin Fletcher	.25
10	Jim Lett	.25
11	Jim Fregosi	.25
12	Willie Greene	.25
13	Pete Munro	.25
15	Shawn Green	.75
16	Lloyd Moseby	.25
17	Dave Hollins	.25
18	Homer Bush	.25
19	Dan Plesac	.25
22	Mike Matheny	.25
23	Jose Cruz	.25
24a	Paul Spoljaric	.25
24b	Shannon Stewart	.35
25	Carlos Delgado	1.50
26	Chris Carpenter	.25
29	Geronimo Berroa	.25
30	Marty Pevey	.25
32	Roy Halladay	.75
33	David Wells	.25
34	Mel Queen	.25
35	Terry Bevington	.25
36	Gary Matthews	.25
37	Graeme Lloyd	.25
41	Pat Hentgen	.25
43	Tom Davey	.25
47	Kelvim Escobar	.25
48	Paul Quantrill	.25
50	Joey Hamilton	.25
77	Bill Risley	.25

2000 Oh Henry! Toronto Blue Jays

This boxed set was a stadium give-away. Fronts of the 2-1/2" x 3-1/2" cards have game-action photos on a dark blue background. Backs have personal data, career highlights and stats printed in blue.

		NM/M
Complete Set (36):		10.00
Common Player:		.25
3	Lee Elia	.25
4	Craig Grebeck	.25
7	Tony Batista	.25
8	Alex Gonzalez	.25
9	Darrin Fletcher	.25
10	Vernon Wells	.50
11	Jim Fregosi	.25
13	Peter Munro	.25
15	Marty Cordova	.25
18	Homer Bush	.25
20	Brad Fullmer	.25
22	Rick Langford	.25
23	Jose Cruz	.25
24	Shannon Stewart	.50
25	Carlos Delgado	1.50
26	Chris Carpenter	.25
28	Lance Painter	.25
29	Bobby Knoop	.25
30	Alberto Castillo	.25
32	Roy Halladay	.75
33	David Wells	.50
34	Clayton Andrews	.25
35	Terry Bevington	.25
37	Frank Castillo	.25
41	Cito Gaston	.25
43	Raul Mondesi	.25
44	Billy Koch	.25
47	Kelvim Escobar	.25
48	Paul Quantrill	.25
49	John Bale	.25
50	Joey Hamilton	.25
51	Pedro Borbon	.25
52	John Frascatore	.25
55	DeWayne Wise	.25
56	Roly de Armas	.25
77/00	Diamond / Ace (Mascots)	.25

2001 Oh Henry! Toronto Blue Jays

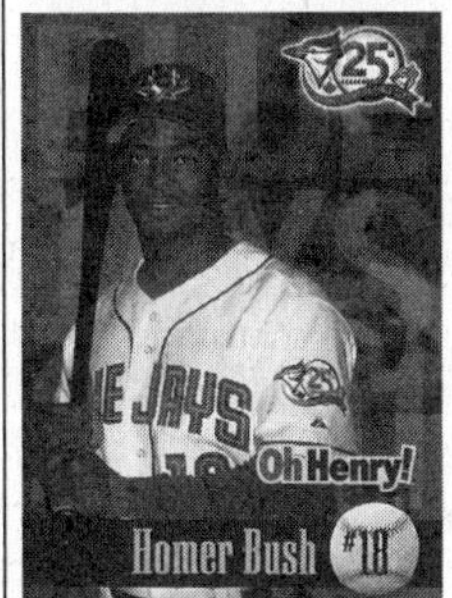

The team's 25th season is commemorated with this stadium give-away boxed set. Fronts have action photos on a blue background with team and sponsor logos. Backs have a large 25th anniversary logo, complete stats, personal data and career highlights.

		NM/M
Complete Set (36):		8.00
Common Player:		.25
1	Cookie Rojas	.25
2	Jeff Frye	.25
5	Chris Woodward	.25
7	Tony Batista	.25
8	Alex Gonzalez	.35
9	Darrin Fletcher	.25
13	Buck Martinez	.25
14	Ryan Freel	.25
16	Garth Iorg	.25
17	Chris Michalak	.25
18	Homer Bush	.25
19	Dan Plesac	.25
20	Brad Fullmer	.25
21	Esteban Loaiza	.25
22	Brian Simmons	.25
23	Jose Cruz Jr.	.25
24	Shannon Stewart	.50
25	Carlos Delgado	1.00
26	Chris Carpenter	.25
28	Lance Painter	.25
30	Alberto Castillo	.25
33	Mike Sirotka	.25
35	Terry Bevington	.25
39	Steve Parris	.25
41	Cito Gaston	.25
43	Raul Mondesi	.25
44	Billy Koch	.25
45	Kelvim Escobar	.25
47	Gil Patterson	.25
48	Paul Quantrill	.25
50	Joey Hamilton	.25
51	Pedro Borbon	.25
52	John Frascatore	.25
53	Mark Connor	.25
---	First Pitch (Bill Singer)	.25
---	Home Run Record (Raul Mondesi, Tony Batista, Jose Cruz Jr., Carlos Delgado)	.25

1982-1988 Ohio Baseball Hall of Fame

Ohio natives and players who made their mark playing in the Buckeye State are featured in this collectors' issue, along with executives and a few other figures. Fronts of the 3-3/8" x 5-5/8" cards have black-and-white player photos surrounded by red borders. The player's name and year of induction are at bottom. Black-and-white backs have lengthy career summaries. Original production was 2,500 sets which were sold into the hobby at $7 apiece. Later inductees were added to the set through at least 1988, but the checklist after #65 is incomplete and may represent skip-numbering.

		NM/M
Complete Set (93):		100.00
Common Player:		2.00
1	Ohio Baseball Hall of Fame	2.00
2	Checklist	.50
3	Nick Cullop	2.00
4	Dean Chance	2.00
5	Bob Feller	3.00
6	Jesse Haines	2.00
7	Waite Hoyt	2.00
8	Ernie Lombardi	2.00
9	Mike Powers	2.00
10	Edd Roush	2.00
11	Red Ruffing	2.00
12	Luke Sewell	2.00
13	Tris Speaker	2.00
14	Cy Young	3.00
15	Walter Alston	2.00
16	Lou Boudreau	2.00
17	Warren Giles	2.00
18	Ted Kluszewski	3.00
19	William McKinley	2.00
20	Roger Peckinpaugh	2.00
21	Johnny Vander Meer	2.00
22	Early Wynn	2.00
23	Earl Averill	2.00
24	Stan Coveleski	2.00
25	Lefty Grove	2.00
26	Nap Lajoie	2.00
27	Al Lopez	2.00
28	Eddie Onslow	2.00
29	Branch Rickey	2.00
30	Frank Robinson	3.00
31	George Sisler	2.00
32	Bob Lemon	2.00
33	Satchel Paige	3.00
34	Bucky Walters	2.00
35	Gus Bell	2.00
36	Rocky Colavito	3.00
37	Mel Harder	2.00
38	Tommy Henrich	2.00
39	Miller Huggins	2.00
40	Fred Hutchinson	2.00
41	Eppa Rixey	2.00
42	Joe Sewell	2.00
43	George Uhle	2.00
44	Bill Veeck	2.00
45	Estel Crabtree	2.00
46	Harvey Haddix	2.00
47	Noodles Hahn	2.00
48	Joe Jackson	4.00
49	Kenesaw Landis	2.00
50	Thurman Munson	3.00
51	Gabe Paul	2.00
52	Vada Pinson	2.00
53	Wally Post	2.00
54	Vic Wertz	2.00
55	Paul Derringer	2.00
56	John Galbreath	2.00
57	Richard Marquard	2.00
58	Bill McKechnie	2.00
59	Rocky Nelson	2.00
60	Al Rosen	2.00
61	Lew Fonseca	2.00
62	Larry MacPhail	2.00
63	Joe Nuxhall	2.00
64	Birdie Tebbetts	2.00
65	Gene Woodling	2.00
66	Ethan Allen	2.00
67	Mike Garcia	2.00
68	Bob Howsam	2.00
69	Addie Joss	2.00
70	Ken Keltner	2.00
71	"Tot" Pressnell	2.00
72	Roger Bresnahan	2.00
73	Bill Mazeroski	3.00
75a	Frank McCormick	2.00
75b	George H. Sisler	2.00
76	Bill Wambsganss	2.00
79	Woody English	2.00
80	Roy McMillan	3.00
81	Frank Baumholtz	2.00
83	Sam McDowell	2.50
84	James Campbell	2.00
86	Ned Garver	2.00
87	Bob Purkey	2.00
90	Harold Cooper	2.00
91	Dennis Galehouse	2.00
92	Brooks Lawrence	2.50
93	Tony Lucadello	2.00

1992 Old Style Chicago Cubs

More than two dozens Cubs stars are featured in this set of 2-1/2" x 3-1/2" cards. Front have sepia player photos with their years at Chicago indicated on top. Backs are printed in black, red and blue on white with a few stats and career highlights, sponsor and team logos and a picture of the Cubs uniform in the player's debut year. The unnumbered cards are checklisted here in alphabetical order.

		NM/M
Complete Set (28):		15.00
Common Player:		.50
(1)	Grover Alexander	.50
(2)	Cap Anson	.50
(3)	Ernie Banks	3.00
(4)	Mordecai Brown	.50
(5)	Phil Cavarretta	.50
(6)	Frank Chance	.50
(7)	Kiki Cuyler	.50
(8)	Johnny Evers	.50
(9)	Charlie Grimm	.50
(10)	Stan Hack	.50
(11)	Gabby Hartnett	.50
(12)	Billy Herman	.50
(13)	Rogers Hornsby	.50
(14)	Ken Hubbs	1.00
(15)	Randy Hundley	.50
(16)	Fergie Jenkins	.75
(17)	Bill Lee	.50
(18)	Andy Pafko	.50
(19)	Rick Reuschel	.50
(20)	Charlie Root	.50
(21)	Ron Santo	.75
(22)	Hank Sauer	.50
(23)	Riggs Stephenson	.50
(24)	Bruce Sutter	.75
(25)	Joe Tinker	.50
(26)	Hippo Vaughn	.50
(27)	Billy Williams	1.00
(28)	Hack Wilson	.50

1993 Old Style Billy Williams

The career of long-time Cubs star, batting coach and Hall of Famer Billy Williams is traced in this four-card set given to fans attending the August 17, 1993, game at Wrigley Field between the Cubs and Expos. Fronts of the first three cards have black-and-white photos, the last card is in color. Backs have biographical and career information along with the sponsor's logo.

		NM/M
Complete Set (4):		8.00
Common Card:		2.00
(1)	Billy Williams/Btg (Personal)	2.00
(2)	Billy Williams/Fldg (Playing Career)	2.00
(3)	Billy Williams/Btg (Playing Career)	2.00
(4)	Billy Williams/Portrait (Coaching Career)	2.00

1999 Old Style Chicago Cubs All-Century Team

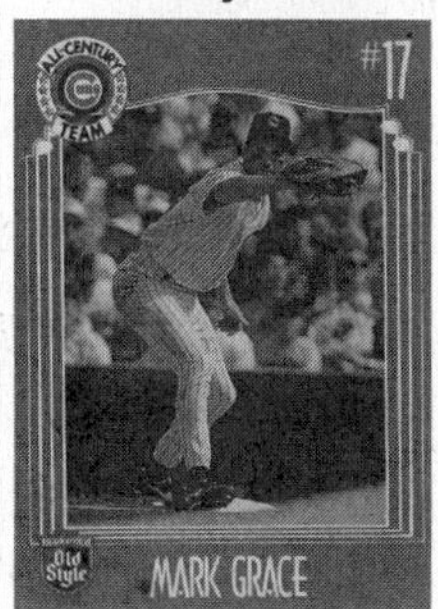

Cubs greats of the 20th Century are featured in this stadium give-away card set. The set was distributed over the course of three games at Wrigley Field in seven-card cello-wrapped packs. With the exception of all-time manager Frank Chance, the cards were packaged alphabetically; Chance was included in the third "series" pack. Fronts of the 2-1/2" x 3-1/2" cards have black-and-white or color photos in a fancy white frame on a tan background. Color team and sponsor logos appear in the left-hand corners. Black-and-white backs have player data, career highlights and lifetime Cubs stats. The player's uniform number, if any, appears on both front and back. Cards have a glossy surface on both front and back.

		NM/M
Complete Set (21):		20.00
Common Player:		.50
(1)	Grover Alexander	.50
(2)	Ernie Banks	2.50
(3)	Mordecai Brown	.50
(4)	Phil Cavarretta	.50
(5)	Frank Chance	.50
(6)	Andre Dawson	1.00
(7)	Mark Grace	2.00
(8)	Charlie Grimm	.50
(9)	Stan Hack	.50
(10)	Gabby Hartnett	.50
(11)	Billy Herman	.50
(12)	Fergie Jenkins	.75
(13)	Andy Pafko	.50
(14)	Ryne Sandberg	2.50
(15)	Ron Santo	1.50
(16)	Lee Smith	.50
(17)	Sammy Sosa	3.00
(18)	Bruce Sutter	.75
(19)	Joe Tinker	.50
(20)	Billy Williams	.75
(21)	Hack Wilson	.50

1982 On Deck Cookies Discs

These 2-3/4" discs were packaged with a large cookie and sold for 25-29 cents in areas including Florida and New Jersey. The fronts have a 1981 copyright date, but the backs indicate "1982 Collectors Series." Fronts have black-and-white player portraits in the center panel of a baseball design. The end panels can be any one of several pastel colors. Backs are in red and black and repeat the baseball motif and include a copyright for "All sports baking Co., Inc." Each side carries the Players Union logo through which the discs were licensed by Michael Schechter Associates. Because they are not licensed through Major League Baseball, player pictures have no uniform logos.

		NM/M
Complete Set (32):		60.00
Common Player:		1.50
(1)	Buddy Bell	1.50
(2)	Johnny Bench	4.00
(3)	Bruce Bochte	1.50
(4)	George Brett	7.50
(5)	Bill Buckner	1.50
(6)	Rod Carew	4.00
(7)	Steve Carlton	4.00
(8)	Cesar Cedeno	1.50
(9)	Jack Clark	1.50
(10)	Cecil Cooper	1.50
(11)	Bucky Dent	1.50
(12)	Carlton Fisk	4.00
(13)	Steve Garvey	2.50
(14)	Goose Gossage	1.50
(15)	Mike Hargrove	1.50
(16)	Keith Hernandez	1.50
(17)	Bob Horner	1.50
(18)	Reggie Jackson	7.50
(19)	Steve Kemp	1.50
(20)	Ron LeFlore	1.50
(21)	Fred Lynn	1.50
(22)	Lee Mazilli	1.50
(23)	Eddie Murray	4.00
(24)	Mike Norris	1.50
(25)	Dave Parker	1.50
(26)	J.R. Richard	1.50
(27)	Pete Rose	9.00
(28)	Mike Schmidt	7.50
(29)	Tom Seaver	4.00
(30)	Willie Stargell	4.00
(31)	Roy Smalley	1.50
(32)	Garry Templeton	1.50

1994 Oscar Mayer Superstar Pop-Ups

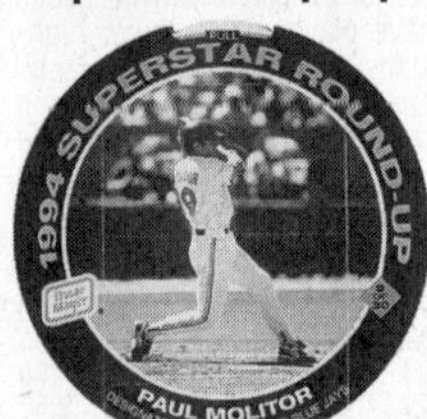

Oscar Mayer Bologna packages in 1994 included one pop-up card in each, but unlike the similar Kraft cards, in this case it was 30 round cards (2-1/2 inches in diameter), with the Oscar Mayer logo on the front and trivia questions on the backs. The promotion ran from April through May, or as long as the supplies lasted. The cards were licensed by the Major League Baseball Players Association, but not by Major League Baseball, so the team logos were airbrushed from player's caps and uniforms. Through an on-pack and in-store mail-in offer, collectors could order complete sets of cards for $1.95 per league (15 cards), plus the appropriate proofs of purchase. Officials of Kraft USA, parent company of Oscar Mayer, announced that they printed 266,000 sets.

		NM/M
Complete Set (30):		10.00
Common Player:		.50
1	Jim Abbott	.50
2	Kevin Appier	.50
3	Roger Clemens	1.25
4	Cecil Fielder	.50
5	Juan Gonzalez	.60
6	Ken Griffey Jr.	1.50
7	Kenny Lofton	.50
8	Jack McDowell	.50
9	Paul Molitor	.75
10	Kirby Puckett	1.00
11	Cal Ripken Jr.	2.00
12	Tim Salmon	.50
13	Ruben Sierra	.50
14	Frank Thomas	.75
15	Greg Vaughn	.50
16	Jeff Bagwell	.75
17	Barry Bonds	2.00
18	Bobby Bonilla	.50
19	Jeff Conine	.50
20	Lenny Dykstra	.50
21	Andres Galarraga	.50
22	Marquis Grissom	.50
23	Tony Gwynn	1.00
24	Gregg Jefferies	.50
25	John Kruk	.50
26	Greg Maddux	1.00
27	Mike Piazza	1.25
28	Jose Rijo	.50
29	Ryne Sandberg	1.00
30	Andy Van Slyke	.50

1987-89 Our Own Tea Discs

Our Own Tea was one of the regional brands which appears on the series of player disc folders which were packaged with various iced tea mixes and other products between 1987-89.

P

1988 Pacific Baseball Legends

Pacific Trading Cards rounded up 110 photos of the greatest baseball players from the past 40 years for its 1988 "Baseball Legends" set. All players featured in the set are (or were) members of the Major League Baseball Alumni Association. Card fronts feature silver outer borders and large, clear full-color player photos outlined in black against colorful banner-style inner borders of red, blue, green, orange or gold. The player's name and position are printed in white letters on the lower portion of the banner. Card backs are numbered and carry the Baseball Legends logo, player biography, major league career stats, and personal information. The cards were sold in boxed sets via candy wholesalers, with emphasis on Midwest and New England states. Complete collector sets in clear plastic boxes were made available via dealers or directly from Pacific Trading Cards. Four cards were issued in both error and corrected versions.

		NM/M
Complete Set (110) (No checklist.):		15.00
Common Player:		.10
Wax Pack (10):		.75
Wax Box (36):		15.00
1	Hank Aaron	2.00
2	Red Shoendienst (Schoendienst)	.30
3	Brooks Robinson	.50
4	Luke Appling	.30
5	Gene Woodling	.10
6	Stan Musial	1.00
7	Mickey Mantle	6.00
8	Richie Ashburn	.50
9	Ralph Kiner	.40
10	Phil Rizzuto	.50
11	Harvey Haddix	.10
12	Ken Boyer	.20
13	Clete Boyer	.10
14	Ken Harrelson	.10
15	Robin Roberts	.40
16	Catfish Hunter	.40
17	Frank Howard	.20
18	Jim Perry	.10
19a	Elston Howard (Reversed photo.)	.20
19b	Elston Howard (Correct photo.)	.20
20	Jim Bouton	.20
21	Pee Wee Reese	.50
22a	Mel Stottlemyer	.20
22b	Mel Stottlemyre	.20
23	Hank Sauer	.10
24	Willie Mays	1.00
25	Tom Tresh	.20
26	Roy Sievers	.10
27	Leo Durocher	.30
28	Al Dark	.20
29	Tony Kubek	.30
30	Johnny Vander Meer	.20
31	Joe Adcock	.20
32	Bob Lemon	.40
33	Don Newcombe	.40
34	Thurman Munson	.50
35	Earl Battey	.10
36	Ernie Banks	.60
37	Matty Alou	.10
38	Dave McNally	.10
39	Mickey Lolich	.20
40	Jackie Robinson	1.00
41	Allie Reynolds	.30
42a	Don Larson	.20
42b	Don Larsen	.20
43	Fergie Jenkins	.30
44	Jim Gilliam	.20
45	Bobby Thomson	.20
46	Sparky Anderson	.20
47	Roy Campanella	.60
48	Marv Throneberry	.20
49	Bill Virdon	.10
50	Ted Williams	1.00
51	Minnie Minoso	.20
52	Bob Turley	.20
53	Yogi Berra	.60
54	Juan Marichal	.40
55	Duke Snider	.60
56	Harvey Kuenn	.20
57	Nellie Fox	.40
58	Felipe Alou	.10
59	Tony Oliva	.20
60	Bill Mazeroski	.40
61	Bobby Shantz	.20
62	Mark Fidrych	.20
63	Johnny Mize	.30
64	Ralph Terry	.10
65	Gus Bell	.10
66	Jerry Koosman	.20
67	Mike McCormick	.10
68	Lou Burdette	.20
69	George Kell	.30
70	Vic Raschi	.20
71	Chuck Connors	.40
72	Ted Kluszewski	.50
73	Bobby Doerr	.30
74	Bobby Richardson	.30
75	Carl Erskine	.30
76	Hoyt Wilhelm	.40
77	Bob Purkey	.10
78	Bob Friend	.10
79	Monte Irvin	.30
80a	Jim Longborg	.20
80b	Jim Lonborg	.20
81	Wally Moon	.10
82	Moose Skowron	.20
83	Tommy Davis	.20
84	Enos Slaughter	.40
85	Sal Maglie	.20
86	Harmon Killebrew	.50
87	Gil Hodges	.50
88	Jim Kaat	.20
89	Roger Maris	.60
90	Billy Williams	.40
91	Luis Aparicio	.40
92	Jim Bunning	.40
93	Bill Freehan	.10
94	Orlando Cepeda	.30
95	Early Wynn	.40
96	Tug McGraw	.20
97	Ron Santo	.30
98	Del Crandall	.10
99	Sal Bando	.10
100	Joe DiMaggio	2.00
101	Bob Feller	.50
102	Larry Doby	.40
103	Rollie Fingers	.30
104	Al Kaline	.60
105	Johnny Podres	.20
106	Lou Boudreau	.30
107	Zoilo Versalles	.10
108	Dick Groat	.10
109	Warren Spahn	.50
110	Johnny Bench	.60
----	Checklist	2.00

1989 Pacific Legends II

Pacific Trading Cards issued its Baseball Legends II set as a carry over of its initial set. The photos are printed on silver background and have colorful inner borders of red, blue, orange or gold. Players' names and positions are printed in white letters below the photos. The card backs once again present the "Baseball Legends" logo, player biography, major league career statistics, and personal information. The Baseball Legends II are numbered 110-220 and were available in wax packs at a limited number of retail chains. The complete set was also made available via dealers or could be ordered directly from Pacific Trading Cards.

		NM/M
Complete Set (110) (no checklist):		12.50
Common Player:		.10
Wax Pack (10):		.75
Wax Box (36):		15.00
111	Reggie Jackson	.50
112	Rich Reese	.10
113	Frankie Frisch	.10
114	Ed Kranepool	.10
115	Al Hrabosky	.10
116	Eddie Mathews	.20
117	Ty Cobb	1.00
118	Jim Davenport	.10
119	Buddy Lewis	.10
120	Virgil Trucks	.10
121	Del Ennis	.10
122	Dick Radatz	.10
123	Andy Pafko	.10
124	Wilbur Wood	.10
125	Joe Sewell	.10
126	Herb Score	.10
127	Paul Waner	.10
128	Lloyd Waner	.10
129	Brooks Robinson	.20
130	Bo Belinsky	.10
131	Phil Cavaretta	.10
132	Claude Osteen	.10
133	Tito Francona	.10
134	Billy Pierce	.10
135	Roberto Clemente	3.00
136	Spud Chandler	.10
137	Enos Slaughter	.10
138	Ken Holtzman	.10
139	John Hopp	.10
140	Tony LaRussa	.20
141	Ryne Duren	.10
142	Glenn Beckert	.10
143	Ken Keltner	.10
144	Hank Bauer	.10
145	Roger Craig	.10
146	Frank Baker	.10
147	Jim O'Toole	.10
148	Rogers Hornsby	.20
149	Jose Cardenal	.10
150	Bobby Doerr	.10
151	Mickey Cochrane	.10
152	Gaylord Perry	.10
153	Frank Thomas	.10
154	Ted Williams	1.00
155	Sam McDowell	.10
156	Bob Feller	.20
157	Bert Campaneris	.10
158	Thornton Lee	.10
159	Gary Peters	.10
160	Joe Medwick	.10
161	Joe Nuxhall	.10
162	Joe Schultz	.10
163	Harmon Killebrew	.20
164	Bucky Walters	.10
165	Bobby Allison	.10
166	Lou Boudreau	.10
167	Joe Cronin	.10
168	Mike Torrez	.10
169	Rich Rollins	.10
170	Tony Cuccinello	.10
171	Hoyt Wilhelm	.10
172	Ernie Harwell	.10
173	George Foster	.10
174	Lou Gehrig	1.50
175	Dave Kingman	.10
176	Babe Ruth	2.00
177	Joe Black	.10
178	Roy Face	.10
179	Earl Weaver	.10
180	Johnny Mize	.10
181	Roger Cramer	.10
182	Jim Piersall	.10
183	Ned Garver	.10
184	Billy Williams	.10
185	Lefty Grove	.10
186	Jim Grant	.10
187	Elmer Valo	.10
188	Ewell Blackwell	.10
189	Mel Ott	.10
190	Harry Walker	.10
191	Bill Campbell	.10
192	Walter Johnson	.40
193	Jim "Catfish" Hunter	.10
194	Charlie Keller	.10
195	Hank Greenberg	.40
196	Bobby Murcer	.10
197	Al Lopez	.10
198	Vida Blue	.10
199	Shag Crawford	.10
200	Arky Vaughan	.10
201	Smoky Burgess	.10
202	Rip Sewell	.10
203	Earl Averill	.10
204	Milt Pappas	.10
205	Mel Harder	.10
206	Sam Jethroe	.10
207	Randy Hundley	.10
208	Jessie Haines	.10
209	Jack Brickhouse	.10
210	Whitey Ford	.20
211	Honus Wagner	1.25
212	Phil Niekro	.10
213	Gary Bell	.10
214	Jon Matlack	.10
215	Moe Drabowsky	.10
216	Edd Roush	.10
217	Joel Horlen	.10
218	Casey Stengel	.20
219	Burt Hooton	.10
220	Joe Jackson	3.00
----	Checklist	2.00

1990 Pacific Legends

The cards in this 110-card set feature the same style as the previous Pacific Legends releases. The cards were available in wax packs as well as in complete set form. Several players found in the first two legends releases are also found in this issue along with new players.

		NM/M
Complete Set (110):		10.00
Common Player:		.10
Wax Pack (10):		.50
Wax Box (36):		12.50
1	Hank Aaron	2.00
2	Tommie Agee	.10
3	Luke Appling	.20
4	Sal Bando	.10
5	Ernie Banks	1.00
6	Don Baylor	.20
7	Yogi Berra	.75
8	Vida Blue	.10
9	Lou Boudreau	.10
10	Clete Boyer	.10
11	George Bamberger	.10
12	Lou Brock	.30
13	Ralph Branca	.10
14	Carl Erskine	.10
15	Bert Campaneris	.10
16	Steve Carlton	.50
17	Rod Carew	.50
18	Rocky Colovito	.40
19	Frank Crosetti	.10
20	Larry Doby	.20
21	Bobby Doerr	.10
22	Walt Dropo	.10
23	Rick Ferrell	.10
24	Joe Garagiola	.50
25	Ralph Garr	.10
26	Dick Groat	.10
27	Steve Garvey	.40
28	Bob Gibson	.50
29	Don Drysdale	.40
30	Billy Herman	.10
31	Bobby Grich	.10
32	Monte Irvin	.20
33	Dave Johnson	.10
34	Don Kessinger	.10
35	Harmon Killebrew	.50
36	Ralph Kiner	.20
37	Vern Law	.20
38	Ed Lopat	.10
39	Bill Mazeroski	.40
40	Rick Monday	.10
41	Manny Mota	.10
42	Don Newcombe	.20
43	Gaylord Perry	.20
44	Jim Piersall	.20
45	Johnny Podres	.20
46	Boog Powell	.20
47	Robin Roberts	.20
48	Ron Santo	.30
49	Herb Score	.20
50	Enos Slaughter	.20
51	Warren Spahn	.50
52	Rusty Staub	.20
53	Frank Torre	.10
54	Bob Horner	.10
55	Lee May	.10
56	Bill White	.20
57	Hoyt Wilhelm	.10
58	Billy Williams	.20
59	Ted Williams	1.50
60	Tom Seaver	.50
61	Carl Yaztrzemski	.75
62	Marv Throneberry	.10
63	Steve Stone	.10
64	Rico Petrocelli	.10
65	Orlando Cepeda	.30
66	Eddie Mathews	.50
67	Joe Sewell	.10
68	Jim "Catfish" Hunter	.20
69	Alvin Dark	.10
70	Richie Ashburn	.30
71	Dusty Baker	.10
72	George Foster	.10
73	Eddie Yost	.10
74	Buddy Bell	.10
75	Manny Sanguillen	.10
76	Jim Bunning	.20
77	Smoky Burgess	.10
78	Al Rosen	.20
79	Gene Conley	.10
80	Dave Dravecky	.10
81	Charlie Gehringer	.20
82	Billy Pierce	.10
83	Willie Horton	.10
84	Ron Hunt	.10
85	Bob Feller	.40
86	George Kell	.20
87	Dave Kingman	.20
88	Jerry Koosman	.10
89	Clem Labine	.10
90	Tony LaRussa	.20
91	Dennis Leonard	.10
92	Dale Long	.10
93	Sparky Lyle	.10
94	Gil McDougald	.10
95	Don Mossi	.10
96	Phil Niekro	.10
97	Tom Paciorek	.10
98	Mel Parnell	.10
99	Lou Pinella	.20
100	Bobby Richardson	.20
101	Phil Rizzuto	.60
102	Brooks Robinson	.40
103	Pete Runnels	.10
104	Diego Segui	.10
105	Bobby Shantz	.10
106	Bobby Thomson	.20
107	Joe Torre	.30
108	Earl Weaver	.30
109	Willie Wilson	.10
110	Jesse Barfield	.10

Senior League

An early supporter of the short-lived "old-timers" league, Pacific issued a card set depicting the players of the Senior Professional Baseball Association. Sold in wax packs as well as complete boxed sets, the cards have silver borders on front with yellow stars above and to the right of the player photo. Color team logos are at bottom-left. Red, white and blue backs have appropriate logos, card number, a few biographical details and a short career summary in a horizontal format. The cards were issued with a set of 15 team logo stickers with a puzzle back. Shades of the 1989 Fleer Billy Ripken card, the card of Jim Nettles contains a photo which shows a vulgarity written on the knob of his bat. A cleaned-up version was issued later, and is much scarcer. Many other errors from the regular-edition set were corrected in a glossy edition of 20,000 complete sets, while several new errors were created.

NM/M
Complete Set (220): 4.00
Common Player: .05
Glossy: 2X
1 Bobby Tolan .05
2 Sergio Ferrer .05
3 David Rajsich .05
4 Ron LeFlore .10
5 Steve Henderson .05
6 Jerry Martin .05
7 Gary Rajsich .05
8 Elias Sosa .05
9 Jon Matlack .05
10 Steve Kemp .05
11 Lenny Randle .05
12 Roy Howell .05
13 Milt Wilcox .05
14 Alan Bannister .05
15 Dock Ellis .05
16 Mike Williams .05
17 Luis Gomez .05
18 Joe Sambito .05
19 Bake McBride .05
20a Pat Zachry (Photo actually Dick Bosman.) .05
20b Dick Bosman .10
21 Dwight Lowry .05
22 Ozzie Virgil Sr. .05
23 Randy Lerch .05
24 Butch Benton .05
25 Tom Zimmer .05
26a Al Holland (Photo actually Nardi Contreras.) .05
26b Nardi Contreras .10
27 Sammy Stewart .05
28 Bill Lee .05
29 Ferguson Jenkins .50
30 Leon Roberts .05
31 Rick Wise .05
32 Butch Hobson .05
33 Pete LaCock .05
34 Bill Campbell .05
35 Doug Simunic .05
36 Mario Guerrero .05
37 Jim Willoughby .05
38 Joe Pittman .05
39 Mark Bomback .05
40 Tommy McMillian .05
41 Gary Allanson .05
42 Cecil Cooper .10
43 John LaRosa .05
44 Darrell Brandon .05
45 Bernie Carbo .05
46 Mike Cuellar .10
47 Al Bumbry .05
48a Gene Richards (Photo actually Tony Scott.) .05
49b Tony Scott .10
49 Pedro Borbon .05
50 Julio Solo .05
51a Ed Nottle (Back reads Sun Sox.) .05
51b Ed Nottle (Back reads Super Sox.) .10
52 Jim Bibby .05
53 Doug Griffin .05
54 Ed Clements .05
55 Dalton Jones .05
56 Earl Weaver .25
57 Jesus DeLaRosa .05
58 Paul Casanova .05
59 Frank Riccelli .05
60 Rafael Landestoy .05
61 George Hendrick .05
62 Cesar Cedeno .10
63 Bert Campaneris .10
64 Derrel Thomas .05
65 Bobby Ramos .05
66 Grant Jackson .05
67 Steve Whitaker .05
68 Pedro Ramos .05
69 Joe Hicks .05
70 Taylor Duncan .05
71 Tom Shopay .05
72 Ken Clay .05
73 Mike Kekich .05
74 Ed Halicki .05
75 Ed Figueroa .05
76 Paul Blair .05
77 Luis Tiant .10
78 Stan Bahnsen .05
79 Rennie Stennett .05
80 Bobby Molinaro .05
81 Jim Gideon .05
82 Orlando Gonzalez .05
83 Amos Otis .05
84 Dennis Leonard .05
85 Pat Putman .05
86 Rick Manning .05
87 Pat Dobson .05
88 Marty Castillo .05
89 Steve McCatty .05
90 Doug Bird .05
91 Rick Waits .05
92 Ron Jackson .05
93 Tim Hosley .05
94 Steve Luebber .05
95 Rich Gale .05
96 Champ Summers .05
97 Dave LaRoche .05
98 Bobby Jones .05
99 Kim Allen .05
100 Wayne Garland .05
101 Tom Spencer .05
102 Dan Driessen .05
103 Ron Pruitt .05
104 Tim Ireland .05
105 Dan Driessen .05
106 Pepe Frias .05
107 Eric Rasmussen .05
108 Don Hood .05
109a Joe Coleman (Photo actually Tony Torchia.) .05
109b Tony Torchia .10
110 Jim Slaton .05
111 Clint Hurdle .05
112 Larry Milbourne .05
113 Al Holland .05
114 George Foster .10
115 Graig Nettles .10
116 Oscar Gamble .05
117 Ross Grimsley .05
118 Bill Travers .05
119 Jose Beniquez .05
120a Jerry Grote/IA .05
120b Jerry Grote (Catcher) .10
121 John D'Acquisto .05
122 Tom Murphy .05
123 Walt Williams .05
124 Roy Thomas .05
125a Jerry Grote (Photo actually Fred Stanley.) .05
125b Fred Stanley (Jerry Grote back.) .10
126a Jim Nettles (Vulgarity on bat knob.) .50
126b Jim Nettles (No vulgarity.) 3.00
127 Randy Niemann .05
128a Bobby Bonds .10
128b Bobby Bonds (No name/position on front.) .50
129 Ed Glynn .05
130 Ed Hicks .05
131 Ivan Murrell .05
132 Graig Nettles .10
133 Hal McRae .20
134 Pat Kelly .05
135 Sammy Stewart .05
136 Bruce Kison .05
137 Jim Morrison .05
138 Omar Moreno .05
139 Tom Brown .05
140 Steve Dillard .05
141 Gary Alexander .05
142 Al Oliver .10
143 Rick Lysander .05
144 Tippy Martinez .05
145 Al Cowens .05
146 Gene Clines .05
147 Willie Aikens .05
148 Tommy Moore .05
149 Clete Boyer .05
150 Stan Cliburn .05
151 Ken Kravec .05
152 Garth Iorg .05
153 Rick Peterson .05
154 Wayne Nordhagen .05
155 Danny Meyer .05
156 Wayne Garrett .05
157 Wayne Krenchicki .05
158 Graig Nettles .10
159 Earl Stephenson .05
160 Carl Taylor .05
161 Rollie Fingers .50
162 Toby Harrah .10
163 Mickey Rivers .05
164 Dave Kingman .10
165 Paul Mirabella .05
166 Dick Williams .05
167 Luis Pujols .05
168 Tito Landrum .05
169 Tom Underwood .05
170 Mark Wagner .05
171 Odell Jones .05
172 Doug Capilla .05
173 Alfie Rondon .05
174 Lowell Palmer .05
175 Juan Eichelberger .05
176 Wes Clements .05
177 Rodney Scott .05
178 Ron Washington .05
179 Al Hrabosky .05
180 Sid Monge .05
181 Randy Johnson .05
182 Tim Stoddard .05
183 Dick Williams .05
184 Lee Lacy .05
185 Jerry White .05
186 Dave Kingman .10
187 Checklistt 1-110 .05
188 Jose Cruz .10
189 Jamie Easterly .05
190 Ike Blessit .05
191 Johnny Grubb .05
192 Dave Cash .05
193 Doug Corbett .05
194 Bruce Bochy .05
195 Mark Corey .05
196 Gil Rondon .05
197 Jerry Martin .05
198 Gerry Pirtle .05
199 Gates Brown .05
200 Bob Galasso .05
201 Bake McBride .05
202 Wayne Granger .05
203 Larry Milbourne .05
204 Tom Paciorek .05
205 U.L. Washington .05
206 Larvell Blanks .05
207 Bob Shirley .05
208 Pete Falcone .05
209 Sal Butera .05
210 Roy Branch .05
211 Dyar Miller .05
212 Paul Siebert .05
213 Ken Reitz .05
214 Bill Madlock .10
215 Vida Blue .15
216 Dave Hilton .05
217 Pedro Ramos, Charlie Bree .05
218 Checklist 111-220 .05
219 Pat Dobson, Earl Weaver .25
220 Curt Flood .15

1991 Pacific Senior League

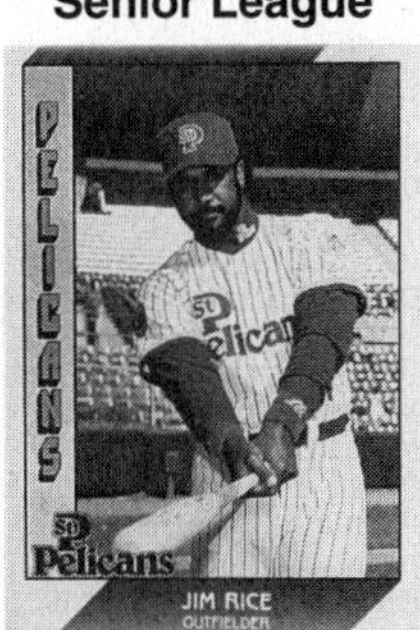

In 1991 Pacific Trading Cards produced its second set of cards of Senior Professional Baseball Association players. The cards feature color photos on the front, with the player's name and position along the bottom and team nickname and logo on a banner vertically on the left side. There are 160 cards in the glossy set, with some multi-player and in-action cards included. For reasons unknown, some of the cards (including those of Rice, Fingers, Blue, Dave Cash, Dan Norman, Ron LeFlore, Cesar Cedeno, Rafael Landestoy and Dan Driessen) were apparently printed in two versions.

NM/M
Complete Set (160): 3.00
Common Player: .05
1 Dan Driessen .05
2 Marty Castillo .05
3 Jerry White .05
4 Bud Anderson .05
5 Ron Jackson .05
6 Fred Stanley .05
7 Steve Luebber .05
8 Jery Terrell .05
9 Pat Dobson .05
10 Ken Kravec .05
11 Gil Rondon .05
12 Dyar Miller .05
13 Bobby Molinaro .05
14 Jerry Martin .05
15 Rick Waits .05
16 Steve McCatty .05
17 Roger Slagle .05
18 Mike Ramsey .05
19 Rich Gale .05
20 Larry Harlow .05
21 Dan Rohn .05
22 Don Cooper .05
23 Marv Foley .05
24 Rafael Landestoy .05
25 Eddie Milner .05
26a Amos Otis (Green jersey pose.) .05
26b Amos Otis (White jersey action.) .05
27 Odell Jones .05
28 Tippy Martinez .05
29 Stu Cliburn .05
30 Stan Cliburn .05
31 Tony Cloninger .05
32 Jeff Jones .05
33 Ken Reitz .05
34 Dave Sax .05
35 Orlando Gonzalez .05
36 Jose Cruz .10
37 Mickey Mahler .05
38 Derek Botelho .05
39 Rick Lysander .05
40 Cesar Cedeno .10
41 Garth Iorg .05
42 Wayne Krenchicki .05
43 Clete Boyer .05
44 Dan Boone .05
45 George Vukovich .05
46 Omar Moreno .05
47 Ron Washington .05
48 Ron Washington (MVP) .05
49 Rick Peterson .05
50 Tack Wilson .05
51 Stan Cliburn, Stu Cliburn .05
52 Rick Lysander (POY) .05
53 Cesar Cedeno, Pete LaCock .05
54 Jim Marshall, Clete Boyer .05
55 Doug Simunic .05
56 Pat Kelly .05
57 Roy Branch .05
58 Dave Cash .05
59 Bobby Jones .05
60 Hector Cruz .05
61 Reggie Cleveland .05
62 Gary Lance .05
63 Ron LeFlore .05
64 Dan Norman .05
65 Renie Martin .05
66 Pete Mackanin .05
67 Frank Riccelli .05
68 Alfie Rondon .05
69 Rodney Scott .05
70 Jim Tracy .05
71 Ed Dennis .05
72 Rick Lindell .05
73 Stu Pepper .05
74 Jeff Youngbauer .05
75 Russ Foster .05
76 Jeff Capriati .05
77 Art DeFreites .05
78 Alfie Rondon/Action .05
79 Reggie Cleveland/Action .05
80 Dave Cash/Action .05
81 Vida Blue .15
82 Ed Glynn .05
83 Bob Owchinko .05
84 Bill Fleming .05
85 Ron Roenicke, Gary Roenicke .05
86 Tom Thompson .05
87 Derrell Thomas .05
88 Jim Willoughby .05
89 Jim Pankovits .05
90 Jack Cooley .05
91 Lenn Sakata .05
92 Mike Brocki .05
93 Chuck Fick .05
94 Tom Benedict .05
95 Anthony Davis .05
96 Cardell Camper .05
97 Leon Roberts .05
98 Roger Erickson .05
99 Kim Allen .05
100 Dave Skaggs .05
101 Joe Decker .05
102 U.L. Washington .05
103 Don Fletcher .05
104 Gary Roenicke .05
105 Rich Dauer .05
106 Ron Roenicke .05
107 Mike Norris .05
108 Ferguson Jenkins .50
109 Ronn Reynolds .05
110 Pete Falcone .05
111 Gary Allenson .05
112 Mark Wagner .05
113 Jack Lazorko .05
114 Bob Galasso .05
115 Ron Davis .05
116 Lenny Randle .05
117 Ricky Peters .05
118 Jim Dwyer .05
119 Juan Eichelberger .05
120 Pete LaCock .05
121 Tony Scott .05
122 Rick Lancellotti .05
123 Barry Bonnell .05
124 Dave Hilton .05
125 Bill Campbell .05
126 Rollie Fingers .50
127 Jim Marshall .05
128 Razor Shines .05
129 Guy Sularz .05
130 Roy Thomas .05
131 Joel Youngblood .05
132 Ernie Camacho .05
133 Dave Hilton, Jim Marshall, Fred Stanley .05
134 Ken Landreaux .05
135 Dave Rozema .05
136 Tom Zimmer .05
137 Elias Sosa .05
138 Ozzie Virgil Sr. .05
139 Al Holland .05
140 Milt Wilcox .05
141 Jerry Reed .05
142 Chris Welch .05
143 Luis Gomez .05
144 Steve Henderson .05
145 Butch Benton .05
146 Bill Lee .05
147 Todd Cruz .05
148 Jim Rice .45
149 Tito Landrum .05
150 Ozzie Virgil Jr. .05
151 Joe Pittman .05
152 Bobby Tolan .05
153 Len Barker .05
154 Dave Rajsich .05
155 Glenn Gulliver .05
156 Gary Rajsich .05
157 Joe Sambito .05
158 Frank Vito .05
159 Ozzie Virgil Sr., Ozzie Virgil Jr. .05
160 Dave Rajsich, Gary Rajsich .05

Nolan Ryan

The career and family life of Nolan Ryan (to 1991) were the subject matter of this 110-card set by Pacific Trading Card Co. Sold in both foil packs and factory sets, the cards have a UV-coated front featuring a photo flanked on the left by "Nolan Ryan" printed vertically in a color accent stripe. At lower left is a flaming baseball "Texas Express" logo. A photo caption appears beneath the photo. On back the blazing ball motif is repeated, with a photo or career highlights in its center.

NM/M
Factory Set (110): 8.00
Complete Set (110): 5.00
Common Card: .10
Wax Pack (12): .50
Wax Box (36): 12.00
1 Future Hall of Famer .10
2 From Little League to the Major Leagues .10
3 A Dream Come True .10
4 Signed by the Mets .10
5 Fireball Pitcher .10
6 Mets Rookie Pitcher .10
7 First Major League Win .10
8 Early in 1969 .10
9 Tensions of a Pennant Race .10
10 Mets Clinch NL East .10
11 Keep the Ball Down .10
12 Playoff Victory .10
13 World Series Victory .10
14 The Amazin' Mets .10
15 Met Strikeout Record .10
16 One of the Worst Trades in Baseball .10
17 Slow Start with Mets .10
18 Pitcher New York Mets .10
19 Traded to the Angels .10
20 Meeting New Friends .10
21 Throwing Fast Balls .10
22 Move the Ball Around .10
23 Nolan Heat .10
24 No-Hitter Number 1 .10
25 Looking Back on Number 1 .10
26 No-Hitter Number 2 .10
27 Single Season Strikeout Record .10
28 21 Wins in 1973 .10
29 Fastest Pitch Ever Thrown at 100.9 MPH .10
30 No-Hitter Number 3 .10
31 No-Hitter Number 4 .10
32 Ryan and Tanana .10
33 Learning Change-Up .10
34 Pitcher California Angels .10
35 Nolan Joins Astros .10
36 Starting Pitcher Nolan Ryan .10
37 Taking Batting Practice .10
38 The Game's Greatest Power Pitcher .10
39 3000 Career Strikeouts .10
40 A Ryan Home Run .10
41 The Fast Ball Grip .10
42 Record 5th No-Hitter .10
43 No-Hitter Number 5 .10
44 A Dream Fulfilled .10
45 Nolan Passes Walter Johnson .10
46 Strikeout 4000 .10
47 Astros Win Western Division Title .10
48 Pitcher Houston Astros .10
49 Milestone Strikeouts .10
50 Post Season Participant .10
51 Hurling for Houston .10
52 135 N.L. Wins .10
53 Through with Chew .10
54 Signed by Rangers 1989 .10
55 Pleasant Change for Nolan .10
56 Real Special Moment .10
57 1989 All-Star Game .10
58 Pitching in 1989 All-Star Game .10
59 5000 Strikeouts; A Standing Ovation .10
60 Great Moments in 1989 .10
61 Nolan with Dan Smith, Rangers First Pic .10
62 Ranger Club Record 16 Strikeouts .10
63 Last Pitch No-Hitter Number 6 .10
64 Sweet Number 6 .10
65 Oldest to Throw No-Hitter .10
66 Another Ryan Win .10
67 20th Pitcher to Win 300 .10
68 300 Win Battery .10
69 300 Game Winner .10
70 Perfect Mechanics .10
71 22 Seasons with 100 or more Strikeouts .10
72 11th Strikeout Title .10
73 232 Strikeouts, 1990 .10
74 The 1990 Season .10
75 Pitcher Texas Rangers .10
76 1991, Nolan's 25th Season .10
77 Throwing Spirals .10
78 Running the Steps .10
79 Hard Work and Conditioning .10
80 The Rigid Workout .10
81 Ryan's Routine .10
82 Ryan's Routine Between Starts .10
83 Running in Outfield .10
84 B.P. in Texas .10
85 18 Career Low-Hitters .10
86 My Job is to Give My Team/Chance to Win .10
87 The Spring Workout .10
88 Power versus Power .10
89 Awesome Power .10
90 Blazing Speed .10
91 The Pick Off .10
92 Real Gamer .10
93 Ranger Battery Mates .10
94 The Glare .10
95 The High Leg Kick .10
96 Day Off .10
97 A New Ball .10
98 Going to Rosin Bag .10
99 Time for Relief .10
100 Lone Star Legend .10
101 Fans' Favorite .10
102 Watching Nolan Pitch .10
103 Our Family of Five .10
104 Texas Beefmaster .10
105 Gentleman Rancher .10
106 Texas Cowboy Life .10
107 The Ryan Family .10
108 Participating in Cutting Horse Contest .10
109 Nolan Interviews .10
110 Lynn Nolan Ryan .10

Nolan Ryan Milestones

Issued as inserts in the 1991 Nolan Ryan foil packs was this set of eight career highlight cards. The format is basically the same as the regular-issue cards, except that the inserts are bordered in either silver (edition of 10,000) or gold (edition of 1,000). The unnumbered cards are checklisted here in chronolgical order. The inserts were found only in foil and wax packs.

		NM/M
Complete Set, Silver (8):		50.00
Complete Set, Gold (8):		65.00
Common Card, Silver:		7.50
Common Card, Gold:		12.00
(1a)	Rookie Pitcher/Silver	7.50
(1b)	Rookie Pitcher/Gold	12.00
(2a)	No-Hitter 1/Silver	7.50
(2b)	No-Hitter 1/Gold	12.00
(3a)	No-Hitter 2/Silver	7.50
(3b)	No-Hitter 2/Gold	12.00
(4a)	No-Hitter 3/Silver	7.50
(4b)	No-Hitter 3/Gold	12.00
(5a)	No-Hitter 4/Silver	7.50
(5b)	No-Hitter 4/Gold	12.00
(6a)	No-Hitter 5/Silver	7.50
(6b)	No-Hitter 5/Gold	12.00
(7a)	Sweet 6/Silver	7.50
(7b)	Sweet 6/Gold	12.00
(8a)	25th Season/Silver	7.50
(8b)	25th Season/Gold	12.00

Nolan Ryan 7th No-Hitter

On May 1, 1991, before the home crowd at Arlington, Nolan Ryan posted his seventh career no-hitter, blanking the Blue Jays. In commemoration of the event, Pacific produced a seven-card insert set for random inclusion in its Nolan Ryan "Texas Express" foil packs. Each card was produced in an edition of 10,000 silver-foil bordered cards and 1,000 with gold-foil borders. The design follows the basic format of the regular Ryan issue, with the flaming baseball series logo at lower-left on the front, the card's title in a colored stripe beneath the photo, and Ryan's name printed vertically in a colored stripe at left. Backs repeat the flaming ball design at center, containing information about the no-hitter.

		NM/M
Complete Set, Silver (7):		50.00
Complete Set, Gold (7):		125.00
Common Card, Silver:		12.00
Common Card, Gold:		25.00
1a	Last Pitch/Silver	12.00
1b	Last Pitch/Gold	25.00
2a	No-Hitter #7/Silver	12.00
2b	No-Hitter #7/Gold	25.00
3a	The Best/Silver	12.00
3b	The Best/Gold	25.00
4a	Time to Celebrate/ Silver	12.00
4b	Time to Celebrate/ Gold	25.00
5a	Congratulations from Rangers Fans/Silver	12.00
5b	Congratulations from Rangers Fans/Gold	25.00
6a	Catcher Mike Stanley/ Silver	12.00
6b	Catcher Mike Stanley/ Gold	25.00
7a	All in a Day's Work/ Silver	12.00
7b	All in a Day's Work/ Gold	25.00

Nolan Ryan 7th No-Hitter Hologram

Even more elusive and exclusive than the gold- and silver-foil bordered "7th No-Hit-

ter" inserts found in wax and foil packs was this edition produced with gold and silver holographic borders (1,000 each in gold and silver. The hologram 7th No-Hitter inserts were found only in 99-cent cello packs.

		NM/M
Complete Set, Silver (7):		300.00
Complete Set, Gold (7):		300.00
Common Card, Silver:		50.00
Common Card, Gold:		50.00
1a	Last Pitch/Silver	50.00
1b	Last Pitch/Gold	50.00
2a	No-Hitter #7/Silver	50.00
2b	No-Hitter #7/Gold	50.00
3a	The Best/Silver	50.00
3b	The Best/Gold	50.00
4a	Time to Celebrate/ Silver	50.00
4b	Time to Celebrate/ Gold	50.00
5a	Congratulations from Rangers Fans/Silver	50.00
5b	Congratulations from Rangers Fans/Gold	50.00
6a	Catcher Mike Stanley/ Silver	50.00
6b	Catcher Mike Stanley/ Gold	50.00
7a	All in a Day's Work/ Silver	50.00
7b	All in a Day's Work/ Gold	50.00

1992 Pacific Nolan Ryan

The 1992 Nolan Ryan "Texas Express" Series 2 is numbered 111 to 220, featuring the same design as the original 110-card issue of 1991. The set includes photos of Ryan from boyhood to his seventh no-hitter, and two bonus subsets were also randomly inserted in the foil packs.

		NM/M
Complete Set (110):		6.00
Common Player:		.10
111	The Golden Arm	.10
112	Little League All-Star	.10
113	All-State Pitcher	.10
114	Nolan Ryan Field	.10
115	Nolan at Age 20	.10
116	Nolan Ryan Jacksonville Suns	.10
117	Surrounded By Friends	.10
118	Nolan the Cowboy	.10
119	The Simple Life	.10
120	Nolan Loves Animals	.10
121	Growing Up in New York	.10
122	New York Strikeout Record	.10
123	Traded	.10
124	Hall of Fame Victims	.10
125	Number 500	.10
126	California Victory	.10
127	20 Win Season	.10
128	Throwing Heat	.10
129	Strikeout Record	.10
130	Number One	.10
131	1,000th Strikeout	.10
132	Number Two	.10
133	2,000th Strikeout	.10
134	Number Three	.10
135	Pure Speed	.10
136	Independence Day Fireworks	.10
137	Fast Ball Pitcher	.10
138	Number Four	.10
139	Free Agent	.10
140	Houston Bound	.10
141	Big Dollars	.10
142	Strong Houston Staff	.10
143	Number Five	.10
144	Astro MVp	.10
145	Western Divison Game	.10
146	National League All-Star	.10
147	Major League Record	.10
148	Nolan Breaks Johnson's Record	.10
149	Reese and Nolan	.10
150	100th National League Win	.10
151	4,000th Strikeout	.10
152	League Leader	.10
153	250th Career Win	.10
154	The Seldom of Swat	.10
155	4,500th Strikeout	.10
156	Like Father Like Son	.10
157	Spoiled in the Ninth	.10
158	Leaving Houston	.10
159	Houston Star	.10
160	Ryan Test Free Agency	.10
161	Awesome Heat	.10
162	Brotherly Love	.10
163	Astros Return	.10
164	Texas Size Decision	.10
165	Texas Legend	.10
166	Drawing a Crowd	.10
167	Great Start	.10
168	5,000th Strikeout	.10
169	Texas All-Star	.10
170	Number Six	.10
171	300th Win	.10
172	1990 League Leader	.10
173	Man of the Year	.10
174	Spring Training 1991	.10
175	Fast Ball Grip	.10
176	Strong Arm	.10
177	Stanley's Delight	.10
178	After Nolan's 7th No-Hitter	.10
179	Stretching Before the Game	.10
180	The Rangers Sign Nolan for 1992 and 199	.10
181	Heading to the Bullpen	.10
182	Nolan Ryan - Banker	.10
183	Time with Fans	.10
184	Solid 1992 Season	.10
185	Ranger Team Leader	.10
186	More Records	.10
187	Number Seven	.10
188	Nolan Passes Niekro	.10
189	Ryan Trails Sutton	.10
190	Ranger Strikeout Mark	.10
191	Consecutive K's	.10
192	5,500th Strikeout	.10
193	Twenty-Five First Timers	.10
194	No-Hitters Ended in the Ninth	.10
195	Constant Work-Outs	.10
196	Nolan in Motion	.10
197	Pitching in Fenway Park	.10
198	Goose and Nolan	.10
199	Talking Over Strategy	.10
200	Don't Mess With Texas	.10
201	314-278 Thru 1991	.10
202	All-Time Leader	.10
203	High Praise	.10
204	Manager's Delight	.10
205	733 Major League Starts	.10
206	Ryan the Quarterback	.10
207	Hard Work Pays Off	.10
208	Passing Along Wisdom	.10
209	Still Dominant	.10
210	Nolan's Fast Ball	.10
211	Seven No-Hitters	.10
212	Training for Perfection	.10
213	Nolan's Edge - Speed	.10
214	This One was for Them	.10
215	Another Day's Work	.10
216	Pick Off at Third	.10
217	Ready to Pitch	.10
218	Spring Training 1992	.10
219	Nolan Receives The Victor Award	.10
220	Nolan's 26th Season	.10

Nolan Ryan Gold Inserts

Pacific produced this insert set for the 1992 Nolan Ryan "Texas Express" sequel. There are eight different gold-foil bordered cards, one for each of Ryan's no-hitters, plus an additional card combining all seven. Design is similar to the 1991-92 Ryan cards from Pacific. Backs feature box scores of the no-hitters. The cards are unnumbered. According to the manufacturer, 10,000 of each insert were produced.

		NM/M
Complete Set (8):		65.00
Common Ryan:		10.00
(1)	Number One	10.00
(2)	Number Two	10.00
(3)	Number Three	10.00
(4)	Number Four	10.00
(5)	Number Five	10.00
(6)	Number Six	10.00
(7)	Number Seven	10.00
(8)	Seven No-Hitters	10.00

Nolan Ryan Limited

One of two insert sets included in both regular and jumbo foil packs of 1992 Pacific Nolan Ryan cards was this six-card presentation. Cards have the basic format of the regular issue except the "Texas Express" logo on front has been replaced by a Rangers team logo. Vertically formatted backs have a color photo at left and a few paragraphs of career summary at center. Each card was printed in an edition of 3,000, and Ryan personally autographed 1,000 of card #1. A second version of these cards, without the words "Limited Edition" on back beneath the Rangers and MLB logos, was produced for inclusion in the July, 1992, issue of "Trading Cards" magazine. The magazine versions of these cards are worth about 10 percent of the inserts.

		NM/M
Complete Set (6):		30.00
Common Card:		7.50
1	Nolan Ryan	7.50
1a	Nolan Ryan/Auto.	90.00
2	Nolan Ryan	7.50
3	The Texas Express	7.50
4	Seventh No-Hitter	7.50
5	Texas Legacy	7.50
6	Quarter Century	7.50

1992 Pacific Tom Seaver

In a style similar to its popular Nolan Ryan sets, Pacific produced a Tom Seaver set of 110 cards in 1992. The company also produced two limited edition subsets as part of the "Tom Terrific" card series. Cards were sold in both foil packs and factory sets. UV-coated fronts have white borders with silver, violet or magenta highlight stripes. A baseball symbol at lower-left has "Tom" above and "Terrific" beneath. This image is duplicated on back, with the ball containing either a photo or career highlights.

		NM/M
Complete Set (110):		4.00
Common Player:		.05
1	Stand-out High School Basketball Player	.05
2	Pro Ball Player	.05
3	Destined to be a Met	.05
4	Brave or Met	.05
5	Mets Luck of the Draw	.05
6	Sent to Jacksonville	.05
7	First Major League Win	.05
8	1967 Rookie of the Year	.05
9	Humble Beginnings	.05
10	Predicting the Future	.05
11	Rookie All-Star	.05
12	16 Wins in 1968	.05
13	1968 N.L. All-Star	.05
14	The Amazing Mets	.05
15	1969 Cy Young Winner	.05
16	Pitcher of the Year	.05
17	Strikeout Leader	.05
18	Ties Major League Record	.05
19	Mr. Consistency	.05
20	Finishing in Style	.05
21	Twenty-Game Winner	.05
22	Second Cy Young Award	.05
23	Batting Star	.05
24	At Bat in the World Series	.05
25	Championship Series Record	.05
26	Injury Plagued Season	.05
27	Comeback	.05
28	Super September	.05
29	Sporting News All-Star	.05
30	Strikeout Record	.05
31	USC Alumni Star	.05
32	Winning Smile	.05
33	One-Hitter	.05
34	Traded to the Reds	.05
35	New York Mets Pitcher	.05
36	Winning with the Reds	.05
37	No-Hitter	.05
38	N.L. Leader	.05
39	Smooth Swing	.05
40	No Decision in the Championship Series	.05
41	Injury Shortened Season	.05
42	Bouncing Back	.05
43	Eighth All-Star Appearance	.05
44	Spring Training 1982	.05
45	Back to New York	.05
46	Cincinnati Reds Pitcher	.05
47	Back in the Big Apple	.05
48	Opening Day Star	.05
49	Not Much Run Support	.05
50	Pair of Shutouts	.05
51	4,000 Inning Mark	.05
52	One Season in New York	.05
53	Chicago Bound	.05
54	Chicago White Sox Pitcher	.05
55	Win 300	.05
56	16 Wins in 1985	.05
57	Blast From the Past	.05
58	Moving Up in the Record Book	.05
59	Cy Young Winners	.05
60	Two Legends of the Game	.05
61	Singing Praise	.05
62	300th Win Tribute	.05
63	The Seaver Family	.05
64	20th Major League Season	.05
65	Traded to the Red Sox	.05
66	Chicago White Sox Career Record	.05
67	Red Sox Man	.05
68	Boston Red Sox Pitcher	.05
69	One Last Try	.05
70	Major League Records	.05
71	Lowest N.L. Career ERA	.05
72	Pitching in Comsikey Park	.05
73	273 N.L. Wins	.05
74	300 Win Honors	.05
75	311 Major League Wins	.05
76	41 Retired	.05
77	Championship Series 2.84 ERA	.05
78	June 1976 Age 32	.05
79	8-Time N.L. All-Star	.05
80	Broadcasting Career	.05
81	300th Win Celebration	.05
82	Tom and Nolan	.05
83	4th Best ERA All-Time	.05
84	15th All-Time in Victories	.05
85	300 Win Club	.05
86	Hall of Fame	.05
87	Pitching in Wrigley Field	.05
88	Power Pitching	.05
89	Spring Training 1980	.05
90	Pitching in Riverfront Stadium 1980	.05
91	Tom Terrific	.05
92	Super Seaver	.05
93	Top 10 All-Time	.05
94	16 Opening Day Starts	.05
95	3,272 Strikeouts	.05
96	Six Opening Day Wins	.05
97	239 Innings Pitched in 1985	.05
98	A Day Off	.05
99	Concentration (You Can't Let Up)	.05
100	Velocity, Movement, and Location	.05
101	Strikeout King	.05
102	The Most Important Pitch	.05
103	Cincinnati Reds Number 41	.05
104	George Thomas Seaver	.05
105	Dazzling Dean of the Reds' Staff	.05
106	Tom Receives the Judge Emil Fuchs Award	.05
107	Boston Mound Ace	.05
108	Fly Ball to Center	.05
109	August 4, 1985 Yankee Stadium	.05
110	Breaking Walter Johnson's Record	.05

Tom Seaver Milestones

Inserted into foil packs of its 1992 Seaver set, Pacific produced a gold-foil bordered set limited to 10,000 each of six different cards featuring career milestones. A white-bordered version of 3,000 cards each was also produced. One thousand of the "Rookie Phenomenon" cards were personally autographed by Seaver among the inserts. On each card, an action photo of Seaver is flanked at left with his name vertically printed in a fading color stripe. The "Tom Terrific" baseball logo carried is carried over from the regular set at lower-left. Backs have a second photo at left, and a summary of the career highlight.

		NM/M
Complete Set (6):		12.50
Complete Set, Gold (6):		15.00
Common Card:		2.50
Common Card, Gold:		3.50
1a	Rookie Phenomenon	2.50
1b	Rookie Phenomenon/ Gold	3.50
1c	Rookie Phenomenon (auto. edition of 1,000)	25.00
2a	Miracle Mets	2.50
2b	Miracle Mets/Gold	3.50
3a	Strikeout Record	2.50
3b	Strikeout Record/Gold	3.50
4a	No-Hitter	2.50
4b	No-Hitter/Gold	3.50
5a	300th Win	2.50
5b	300th Win/Gold	3.50
6a	Hall of Fame	2.50
6b	Hall of Fame/Gold	3.50

1993 Pacific Nolan Ryan 27th Season

Pacific marked the record-breaking 27th season of Nolan Ryan's career by re-issuing all 220 cards in its popular Nolan Ryan set with a special logo. The first series of the set (110 cards) had been issued in 1991 and the second series was issued in 1992 and numbered 111-220. In 1993 the company released a 30-card update for

the pitcher's final season, complete with the special logo. Later the company decided to reissue cards 1-220 with the same logo because of the demand for the cards. Refer to 1991 and 1992 sets for card 1-220 checklists.

		NM/M
Complete Set (250):		10.00
Common Player:		.10
221	Rangers' Opening Night	.10
222	Slow Start in 1992	.10
223	Still Productive	.10
224	Getting Hot	.10
225	Closing Strong	.10
226	No Decision	.10
227	No Run Support	.10
228	Two Complete Games	.10
229	8-2/3 Inning Shutout	.10
230	Multiple Stikeout Games	.10
231	Ejectedl	.10
232	319 and Counting	.10
233	Strikeout	.10
234	24 of 26 Seasons	.10
235	Smile, Nolanl	.10
236	Texas Ranger Marks	.10
237	Ranger Ace	.10
238	Another Record	.10
239	6th Place All-Time Innings Pitched	.10
240	27 Games Started in 1992	.10
241	Seaver & Ryan	.10
242	Angels' Number 30 Retired	.10
243	Angels' Nolan Ryan Night	.10
244	Angels' Hall of Fame	.10
245	Great Friends	.10
246	Cowboys	.10
247	Spring Training	.10
248	Smokin' Fastball	.10
249	The Texas Express	.10
250	Pacific Pride	.10

Limited

Continuing with its "Limited Edition" insert set from the 1992 Nolan Ryan issue, this insert set picks up with numbers 7-12, featuring 1992 highlights in Ryan's career.

		NM/M
Complete Set (6):		20.00
Common Player:		5.00
7-12	Nolan Ryan	5.00

Limited Gold

A gold-foil bordered version of the six 1993 Nolan Ryan "Limited Edition" insert cards was created as a card show give-away and random pack insert. Gold versions of cards #7-9 were given out at a Bellevue, Wash., show, while gold cards of #10-12

were found in foil packs. Just 3,000 of each foil-pack insert was produced.

		NM/M
Complete Set (6):		35.00
Common Player:		7.50
7	Nolan Ryan	7.50
8	Nolan Ryan	7.50
9	Nolan Ryan	7.50
10	Nolan Ryan	7.50
11	Nolan Ryan	7.50
12	Nolan Ryan	7.50

Prism

An insert set unique to the 1993 Pacific Nolan Ryan 27th Season set was this issue of 20 prism cards. Fronts feature an action photo of Ryan against a prismatic background. Backs have another photo and a few brief biographical notes on a marbled background. Each prism card was produced in a silver edition of 10,000, a gold edition of 1,500 and a gold-edition uncut sheet of 20 cards serially numbered to 1,000. The prism cards were inserted into 25-cent foil packs of Pacific's 1993 Nolan Ryan issue.

		NM/M
Complete Set (Silver)(20):		55.00
Common Card (Silver):		3.50
1	Nolan Ryan/Silver	3.50
1a	Nolan Ryan/Gold	6.00
2	Nolan Ryan/Silver	3.50
2a	Nolan Ryan/Gold	6.00
3	Nolan Ryan/Silver	3.50
3a	Nolan Ryan/Gold	6.00
4	Nolan Ryan/Silver	3.50
4a	Nolan Ryan/Gold	6.00
5	Nolan Ryan/Silver	3.50
5a	Nolan Ryan/Gold	6.00
6	Nolan Ryan/Silver	3.50
6a	Nolan Ryan/Gold	6.00
7	Nolan Ryan/Silver	3.50
7a	Nolan Ryanv	6.00
8	Nolan Ryan/Silver	3.50
8a	Nolan Ryan/Gold	6.00
9	Nolan Ryan/Silver	3.50
9a	Nolan Ryan/Gold	6.00
10	Nolan Ryan/Silver	3.50
10a	Nolan Ryan/Gold	6.00
11	Nolan Ryan/Silver	3.50
11a	Nolan Ryan/Gold	6.00
12	Nolan Ryan/Silver	3.50
12a	Nolan Ryan/Gold	6.00
13	Nolan Ryan/Silver	3.50
13a	Nolan Ryan/Gold	6.00
14	Nolan Ryan/Silver	3.50
14a	Nolan Ryan/Gold	6.00
15	Nolan Ryan/Silver	3.50
15a	Nolan Ryan/Gold	6.00
16	Nolan Ryan/Silver	3.50
16a	Nolan Ryan/Gold	6.00
17	Nolan Ryan/Silver	3.50
17a	Nolan Ryan/Gold	6.00
18	Nolan Ryan/Silver	3.50
18a	Nolan Ryan/Gold	6.00
19	Nolan Ryan/Silver	3.50
19a	Nolan Ryan/Gold	6.00
20	Nolan Ryanv	3.50
20a	Nolan Ryan/Gold	6.00
Complete Set (Gold) (20):		85.00
Common Card (Gold):		6.00
Uncut Sheeet (Gold):		110.00

1993 Pacific/ McCormick Nolan Ryan Milestones

Great moments in Nolan Ryan's career are featured in this set produced by Pacific for McCormick & Co., a food products company. Fronts are similar to several of Pacific's other Ryan issues and include a "Farewell to a Legend" logo in the lower-left corner. The career highlight represented by the photo is named in a red strip at bottom. Backs share an action photo of Ryan over which are printed stats, information about the highlight or other data. Sponsors' logos are in the corners. Cards are UV coated on both sides.

		NM/M
Complete Set (21):		7.50
Common Player:		.50
1	No-Hitter #1 (Nolan Ryan)	.50
2	No-Hitter #2 (Nolan Ryan)	.50
3	No-Hitter #3 (Nolan Ryan)	.50
4	No-Hitter #4 (Nolan Ryan)	.50
5	No-Hitter #5 (Nolan Ryan)	.50
6	Last Pitch No-Hitter #6 (Nolan Ryan)	.50
7	No-Hitter #7 (Nolan Ryan)	.50
8	1st Strikeout (Nolan Ryan)	.50
9	1,000 Strikeout (Nolan Ryan)	.50
10	2,000 Strikeout (Nolan Ryan)	.50
11	3,000 Strikeout (Nolan Ryan)	.50
12	Nolan Breaks Johnson's Record (Nolan Ryan)	.50
13	4,000 Strikeout (Nolan Ryan)	.50
14	5,000 Strikeout (Nolan Ryan)	.50
15	5,500th Strikeout (Nolan Ryan)	.50
16	First Major League Win (Nolan Ryan)	.50
17	250th Career Win (Nolan Ryan)	.50
18	300th Win (Nolan Ryan)	.50
19	100.9 MPH Pitch (Nolan Ryan)	.50
20	Lone Star Legend (Nolan Ryan)	.50
---	Header card	.10

1993 Pacific

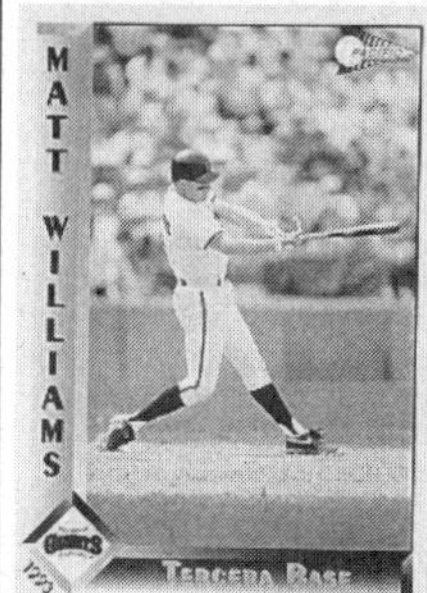

This set marks the first time a major league set was designed entirely for the Spanish-speaking market. Distribution areas included retail markets in the United States, Mexico, South America and the Caribbean. The cards are glossy and feature Spanish text on both sides. Cards are numbered in alphabetical order by team, beginning with Atlanta. Insert sets are: Prism (20 cards featuring Spanish players and their accomplishments), Beisbol De Estralla (Stars of Baseball), Hot Players and Amigos (a 30-card set which features two or more players per card).

		NM/M
Complete Set (660):		20.00
Common Player:		.05
1	Rafael Belliard	.05
2	Sid Bream	.05
3	Francisco Cabrera	.05
4	Marvin Freeman	.05
5	Ron Gant	.05
6	Tom Glavine	.25
7	Brian Hunter	.05
8	Dave Justice	.05
9	Ryan Klesko	.05
10	Melvin Nieves	.05
11	Deion Sanders	.05
12	John Smoltz	.05
13	Mark Wohlers	.05
14	Brady Anderson	.05
15	Glenn Davis	.05
16	Mike Devereaux	.05
17	Leo Gomez	.05
18	Chris Hoiles	.05
19	Chito Martinez	.05
20	Ben McDonald	.05
21	Mike Mussina	.40
22	Gregg Olson	.05
23	Joe Orsulak	.05
24	Cal Ripken, Jr.	1.50
25	David Segui	.05
26	Rick Sutcliffe	.05
27	Wade Boggs	.65
28	Tom Brunansky	.05
29	Ellis Burks	.05
30	Roger Clemens	.75
31	John Dopson	.05
32	John Flaherty	.05
33	Mike Greenwell	.05
34	Tony Pena	.05
35	Carlos Quintana	.05
36	Luis Rivera	.05
37	Mo Vaughn	.05
38	Frank Viola	.05
39	Matt Young	.05
40	Scott Bailes	.05
41	Bert Blyleven	.05
42	Chad Curtis	.05
43	Gary DiSarcina	.05
44	Chuck Finley	.05
45	Mike Fitzgerald	.05
46	Gary Gaetti	.05
47	Rene Gonzales	.05
48	Mark Langston	.05
49	Scott Lewis	.05
50	Luis Polonia	.05
51	Tim Salmon	.05
52	Lee Stevens	.05
53	Steve Buechele	.05
54	Frank Castillo	.05
55	Doug Dascenzo	.05
56	Andre Dawson	.25
57	Shawon Dunston	.05
58	Mark Grace	.05
59	Mike Morgan	.05
60	Luis Salazar	.05
61	Rey Sanchez	.05
62	Ryne Sandberg	.65
63	Dwight Smith	.05
64	Jerome Walton	.05
65	Rick Wilkins	.05
66	Wilson Alvarez	.05
67	George Bell	.05
68	Joey Cora	.05
69	Alex Fernandez	.05
70	Carlton Fisk	.50
71	Craig Grebeck	.05
72	Ozzie Guillen	.05
73	Jack McDowell	.05
74	Scott Radinsky	.05
75	Tim Raines	.05
76	Bobby Thigpen	.05
77	Frank Thomas	.50
78	Robin Ventura	.05
79	Tom Browning	.05
80	Jacob Brumfield	.05
81	Rob Dibble	.05
82	Bill Doran	.05
83	Billy Hatcher	.05
84	Barry Larkin	.05
85	Hal Morris	.05
86	Joe Oliver	.05
87	Jeff Reed	.05
88	Jose Rijo	.05
89	Bip Roberts	.05
90	Chris Sabo	.05
91	Sandy Alomar, Jr.	.05
92	Brad Arnsberg	.05
93	Carlos Baerga	.05
94	Albert Belle	.05
95	Felix Fermin	.05
96	Mark Lewis	.05
97	Kenny Lofton	.05
98	Carlos Martinez	.05
99	Rod Nicholos	.05
100	Dave Rohde	.05
101	Scott Scudder	.05
102	Paul Sorrento	.05
103	Mark Whiten	.05
104	Mark Carreon	.05
105	Milt Cuyler	.05
106	Rob Deer	.05
107	Cecil Fielder	.05
108	Travis Fryman	.05
109	Dan Gladden	.05
110	Bill Gullickson	.05
111	Les Lancaster	.05
112	Mark Leiter	.05
113	Tony Phillips	.05
114	Mickey Tettleton	.05
115	Alan Trammell	.05
116	Lou Whitaker	.05
117	Jeff Bagwell	.50
118	Craig Biggio	.05
119	Joe Boever	.05
120	Casey Candaele	.05
121	Andujar Cedeno	.05
122	Steve Finley	.05
123	Luis Gonzalez	.05
124	Pete Harnisch	.05
125	Jimmy Jones	.05
126	Mark Portugal	.05
127	Rafael Ramirez	.05
128	Mike Simms	.05
129	Eric Yelding	.05
130	Luis Aquino	.05
131	Kevin Appier	.05
132	Mike Boddicker	.05
133	George Brett	.75
134	Tom Gordon	.05
135	Mark Gubicza	.05
136	David Howard	.05
137	Gregg Jefferies	.05
138	Wally Joyner	.05
139	Brian McRae	.05
140	Jeff Montgomery	.05
141	Terry Shumpert	.05
142	Curtis Wilkerson	.05
143	Brett Butler	.05
144	Eric Davis	.05
145	Kevin Gross	.05
146	Dave Hansen	.05
147	Lenny Harris	.05
148	Carlos Hernandez	.05
149	Orel Hershiser	.05
150	Jay Howell	.05
151	Eric Karros	.05
152	Ramon Martinez	.05
153	Jose Offerman	.05
154	Mike Sharperson	.05
155	Darryl Strawberry	.05
156	Jim Gantner	.05
157	Darryl Hamilton	.05
158	Doug Henry	.05
159	John Jaha	.05
160	Pat Listach	.05
161	Jaime Navarro	.05
162	Dave Nilsson	.05
163	Jesse Orosco	.05
164	Kevin Seitzer	.05
165	B.J. Surhoff	.05
166	Greg Vaughn	.05
167	Robin Yount	.50
168	Rick Aguilera	.05
169	Scott Erickson	.05
170	Mark Guthrie	.05
171	Kent Hrbek	.05
172	Chuck Knoblauch	.05
173	Gene Larkin	.05
174	Shane Mack	.05
175	Pedro Munoz	.05
176	Mike Pagliarulo	.05
177	Kirby Puckett	.65
178	Kevin Tapani	.05
179	Gary Wayne	.05
180	Moises Alou	.05
181	Brian Barnes	.05
182	Archie Cianfrocco	.05
183	Delino DeShields	.05
184	Darrin Fletcher	.05
185	Marquis Grissom	.05
186	Ken Hill	.05
187	Dennis Martinez	.05
188	Bill Sampen	.05
189	John VanderWal	.05
190	Larry Walker	.05
191	Tim Wallach	.05
192	Bobby Bonilla	.05
193	Daryl Boston	.05
194	Vince Coleman	.05
195	Kevin Elster	.05
196	Sid Fernandez	.05
197	John Franco	.05
198	Dwight Gooden	.05
199	Howard Johnson	.05
200	Willie Randolph	.05
201	Bret Saberhagen	.05
202	Dick Schofield	.05
203	Pete Schourek	.05
204	Greg Cadaret	.05
205	John Habyan	.05
206	Pat Kelly	.05
207	Kevin Maas	.05
208	Don Mattingly	.75
209	Matt Nokes	.05
210	Melido Perez	.05
211	Scott Sanderson	.05
212	Andy Stankiewicz	.05
213	Danny Tartabull	.05
214	Randy Velarde	.05
215	Bernie Williams	.05
216	Harold Baines	.05
217	Mike Bordick	.05
218	Scott Brosius	.05
219	Jerry Browne	.05
220	Ron Darling	.05
221	Dennis Eckersley	.40
222	Rickey Henderson	.50
223	Rick Honeycutt	.05
224	Mark McGwire	1.25
225	Ruben Sierra	.05
226	Terry Steinbach	.05
227	Bob Welch	.05
228	Willie Wilson	.05
229	Ruben Amaro	.05
230	Kim Batiste	.05
231	Juan Bell	.05
232	Wes Chamberlain	.05
233	Darren Daulton	.05
234	Mariano Duncan	.05
235	Len Dykstra	.05
236	Dave Hollins	.05
237	Stan Javier	.05
238	John Kruk	.05
239	Mickey Morandini	.05
240	Terry Mulholland	.05
241	Mitch Williams	.05
242	Stan Belinda	.05
243	Jay Bell	.05
244	Carlos Garcia	.05
245	Jeff King	.05
246	Mike LaValliere	.05
247	Lloyd McClendon	.05
248	Orlando Merced	.05
249	Paul Miller	.05
250	Gary Redus	.05
251	Don Slaught	.05
252	Zane Smith	.05
253	Andy Van Slyke	.05
254	Tim Wakefield	.05
255	Andy Benes	.05
256	Dann Bilardello	.05
257	Tony Gwynn	.65
258	Greg Harris	.05
259	Darrin Jackson	.05
260	Mike Maddux	.05
261	Fred McGriff	.05
262	Rich Rodriguez	.05
263	Benito Santiago	.05
264	Gary Sheffield	.35
265	Kurt Stillwell	.05
266	Tim Teufel	.05
267	Bud Black	.05
268	John Burkett	.05
269	Will Clark	.05
270	Royce Calyton	.05
271	Bryan Hickerson	.05
272	Chris James	.05
273	Darren Lewis	.05
274	Willie McGee	.05
275	Jim McNamara	.05
276	Francisco Oliveras	.05
277	Robby Thompson	.05
278	Matt Williams	.05
279	Trevor Wilson	.05
280	Bret Boone	.05
281	Greg Briley	.05
282	Jay Buhner	.05
283	Henry Cotto	.05
284	Rich DeLucia	.05
285	Dave Fleming	.05
286	Ken Griffey Jr.	1.00
287	Erik Hanson	.05
288	Randy Johnson	.50
289	Tino Martinez	.05
290	Edgar Martinez	.05
291	Dave Valle	.05
292	Omar Vizquel	.05
293	Luis Alicea	.05
294	Bernard Gilkey	.05
295	Felix Jose	.05
296	Ray Lankford	.05
297	Omar Olivares	.05
298	Jose Oquendo	.05
299	Tom Pagnozzi	.05
300	Geronimo Pena	.05
301	Gerald Perry	.05
302	Ozzie Smith	.65
303	Lee Smith	.05
304	Bob Tewksbury	.05
305	Todd Zeile	.05
306	Kevin Brown	.05
307	Todd Burns	.05
308	Jose Canseco	.35
309	Hector Fajardo	.05
310	Julio Franco	.05
311	Juan Gonzalez	.25
312	Jeff Huson	.05
313	Rob Maurer	.05
314	Rafael Palmeiro	.45
315	Dean Palmer	.05
316	Ivan Rodriguez	.45
317	Nolan Ryan	1.50
318	Dickie Thon	.05
319	Roberto Alomar	.20
320	Derek Bell	.05
321	Pat Borders	.05
322	Joe Carter	.05
323	Kelly Gruber	.05
324	Juan Guzman	.05
325	Manny Lee	.05
326	Jack Morris	.05
327	John Olerud	.05

No.	Player	Value
328	Ed Sprague	.05
329	Todd Stottlemyre	.05
330	Duane Ward	.05
331	Steve Avery	.05
332	Damon Berryhill	.05
333	Jeff Blauser	.05
334	Mark Lemke	.05
335	Greg Maddux	.65
336	Kent Mercker	.05
337	Otis Nixon	.05
338	Greg Olson	.05
339	Bill Pecota	.05
340	Terry Pendleton	.05
341	Mike Stanton	.05
342	Todd Frohwirth	.05
343	Tim Hulett	.05
344	Mark McLemore	.05
345	Luis Mercedes	.05
346	Alan Mills	.05
347	Sherman Obando	.05
348	Jim Poole	.05
349	Harold Reynolds	.05
350	Arthur Rhodes	.05
351	Jeff Tackett	.05
352	Fernando Valenzuela	.05
353	Scott Bankhead	.05
354	Ivan Calderon	.05
355	Scott Cooper	.05
356	Danny Darwin	.05
357	Scott Fletcher	.05
358	Tony Fossas	.05
359	Greg Harris	.05
360	Joe Hesketh	.05
361	Jose Melendez	.05
362	Paul Quantrill	.05
363	John Valentin	.05
364	Mike Butcher	.05
365	Chuck Crim	.05
366	Chili Davis	.05
367	Damion Easley	.05
368	Steve Frey	.05
369	Joe Grahe	.05
370	Greg Myers	.05
371	John Orton	.05
372	J.T. Snow	.05
373	Ron Tingley	.05
374	Julio Valera	.05
375	Paul Assenmacher	.05
376	Jose Bautista	.05
377	Jose Guzman	.05
378	Greg Hibbard	.05
379	Candy Maldonado	.05
380	Derrick May	.05
381	Dan Plesac	.05
382	Tommy Shields	.05
383	Sammy Sosa	.75
384	Jose Vizcaino	.05
385	Greg Walbeck	.05
386	Ellis Burks	.05
387	Roberto Hernandez	.05
388	Mike Huff	.05
389	Bo Jackson	.10
390	Lance Johnson	.05
391	Ron Karkovice	.05
392	Kirk McCaskill	.05
393	Donn Pall	.05
394	Dan Pasqua	.05
395	Steve Sax	.05
396	Dave Stieb	.05
397	Bobby Ayala	.05
398	Tim Belcher	.05
399	Jeff Branson	.05
400	Cesar Hernandez	.05
401	Roberto Kelly	.05
402	Randy Milligan	.05
403	Kevin Mitchell	.05
404	Juan Samuel	.05
405	Reggie Sanders	.05
406	John Smiley	.05
407	Dan Wilson	.05
408	Mike Christopher	.05
409	Dennis Cook	.05
410	Alvaro Espinoza	.05
411	Glenallen Hill	.05
412	Reggie Jefferson	.05
413	Derek Lilliquist	.05
414	Jose Mesa	.05
415	Charles Nagy	.05
416	Junior Ortiz	.05
417	Eric Plunk	.05
418	Ted Power	.05
419	Scott Aldred	.05
420	Andy Ashby	.05
421	Freddie Benavides	.05
422	Dante Bichette	.05
423	Willie Blair	.05
424	Vinny Castilla	.05
425	Jerald Clark	.05
426	Alex Cole	.05
427	Andres Galarraga	.05
428	Joe Girardi	.05
429	Charlie Hayes	.05
430	Butch Henry	.05
431	Darren Holmes	.05
432	Dale Murphy	.20
433	David Nied	.05
434	Jeff Parrett	.05
435	Steve Reed **RC**	.05
436	Armando Reynoso	.05
437	Bruce Ruffin	.05
438	Bryn Smith	.05
439	Jim Tatum	.05
440	Eric Young	.05
441	Skeeter Barnes	.05
442	Tom Bolton	.05
443	Kirk Gibson	.05
444	Chad Krueter	.05
445	Bill Krueger	.05
446	Scott Livingstone	.05
447	Bob McDonald	.05
448	Mike Moore	.05
449	Mike Munoz	.05
450	Gary Thurman	.05
451	David Wells	.05
452	Alex Arias	.05
453	Jack Armstrong	.05
454	Bret Barberie	.05
455	Ryan Bowen	.05
456	Cris Carpenter	.05
457	Chuck Carr	.05
458	Jeff Conine	.05
459	Steve Decker	.05
460	Orestes Destrade	.05
461	Monty Fariss	.05
462	Junior Felix	.05
463	Bryan Harvey	.05
464	Trevor Hoffman	.05
465	Charlie Hough	.05
466	Dave Magadan	.05
467	Bob McClure	.05
468	Rob Natal	.05
469	Scott Pose	.05
470	Rich Renteria	.05
471	Benito Santiago	.05
472	Matt Turner	.05
473	Walt Weiss	.05
474	Eric Anthony	.05
475	Chris Donnels	.05
476	Doug Drabek	.05
477	Xavier Hernandez	.05
478	Doug Jones	.05
479	Darryl Kile	.05
480	Scott Servais	.05
481	Greg Swindell	.05
482	Eddie Taubensee	.05
483	Jose Uribe	.05
484	Brian Williams	.05
485	Billy Brewer	.05
486	David Cone	.05
487	Greg Gagne	.05
488	Phil Hiatt	.05
489	Jose Lind	.05
490	Brent Mayne	.05
491	Kevin McReynolds	.05
492	Keith Miller	.05
493	Hipolito Pichardo	.05
494	Harvey Pulliam	.05
495	Rico Rossy	.05
496	Pedro Astacio	.05
497	Tom Candiotti	.05
498	Tom Goodwin	.05
499	Jim Gott	.05
500	Pedro Martinez	.50
501	Roger McDowell	.05
502	Mike Piazza	.75
503	Jody Reed	.05
504	Rick Trlicek	.05
505	Mitch Weber	.05
506	Steve Wilson	.05
507	James Austin	.05
508	Ricky Bones	.05
509	Alex Diaz	.05
510	Mike Fetters	.05
511	Teddy Higuera	.05
512	Graeme Lloyd	.05
513	Carlos Maldonado	.05
514	Josias Manzanillo	.05
515	Kevin Reimer	.05
516	Bill Spiers	.05
517	Bill Wegman	.05
518	Willie Banks	.05
519	J.T. Bruett	.05
520	Brian Harper	.05
521	Terry Jorgensen	.05
522	Scott Leius	.05
523	Pat Mahomes	.05
524	Dave McCarty	.05
525	Jeff Reboulet	.05
526	Mike Trombley	.05
527	Carl Willis	.05
528	Dave Winfield	.50
529	Sean Berry	.05
530	Frank Bolick	.05
531	Kent Bottenfield	.05
532	Wil Cordero	.05
533	Jeff Fassero	.05
534	Tim Laker	.05
535	Mike Lansing	.05
536	Chris Nabholz	.05
537	Mel Rojas	.05
538	John Wetteland	.05
539	Ted Wood (Front photo actually Frank Bollick.)	.05
540	Mike Draper	.05
541	Tony Fernandez	.05
542	Todd Hundley	.05
543	Jeff Innis	.05
544	Jeff McKnight	.05
545	Eddie Murray	.50
546	Charlie O'Brien	.05
547	Frank Tanana	.05
548	Ryan Thompson	.05
549	Chico Walker	.05
550	Anthony Young	.05
551	Jim Abbott	.05
552	Wade Boggs	.75
553	Steve Farr	.05
554	Neal Heaton	.05
555	Steve Howe	.05
556	Dion James	.05
557	Scott Kamieniecki	.05
558	Jimmy Key	.05
559	Jim Leyritz	.05
560	Paul O'Neill	.05
561	Spike Owen	.05
562	Lance Blankenship	.05
563	Joe Boever	.05
564	Storm Davis	.05
565	Kelly Downs	.05
566	Eric Fox	.05
567	Rich Gossage	.05
568	Dave Henderson	.05
569	Shawn Hillegas	.05
570	Mike Mohler **RC**	.05
571	Troy Neel	.05
572	Dale Sveum	.05
573	Larry Anderson	.05
574	Bob Ayrault	.05
575	Jose DeLeon	.05
576	Jim Eisenreich	.05
577	Pete Incaviglia	.05
578	Danny Jackson	.05
579	Ricky Jordan	.05
580	Ben Rivera	.05
581	Curt Schilling	.25
582	Milt Thompson	.05
583	David West	.05
584	John Candelaria	.05
585	Steve Cooke	.05
586	Tom Foley	.05
587	Al Martin	.05
588	Blas Minor	.05
589	Dennis Moeller	.05
590	Denny Neagle	.05
591	Tom Prince	.05
592	Randy Tomlin	.05
593	Bob Walk	.05
594	Kevin Young	.05
595	Pat Gomez	.05
596	Ricky Gutierrez	.05
597	Gene Harris	.05
598	Jeremy Hernandez	.05
599	Phil Plantier	.05
600	Tim Scott	.05
601	Frank Seminara	.05
602	Darrell Sherman	.05
603	Craig Shipley	.05
604	Guillermo Velasquez	.05
605	Dan Walters	.05
606	Mike Benjamin	.05
607	Barry Bonds	1.50
608	Jeff Brantley	.05
609	Dave Burba	.05
610	Craig Colbert	.05
611	Mike Jackson	.05
612	Kirt Manwaring	.05
613	Dave Martinez	.05
614	Dave Righetti	.05
615	Kevin Rogers	.05
616	Bill Swift	.05
617	Rich Amaral	.05
618	Mike Blowers	.05
619	Chris Bosio	.05
620	Norm Charlton	.05
621	John Cummings	.05
622	Mike Felder	.05
623	Bill Haselman	.05
624	Tim Leary	.05
625	Pete O'Brien	.05
626	Russ Swan	.05
627	Fernando Vina	.05
628	Rene Arocha	.05
629	Rod Brewer	.05
630	Ozzie Canseco	.05
631	Rheal Cormier	.05
632	Brian Jordan	.05
633	Joe Magrane	.05
634	Donovan Osborne	.05
635	Mike Perez	.05
636	Stan Royer	.05
637	Hector Villanueva	.05
638	Tracy Woodson	.05
639	Benji Gil	.05
640	Tom Henke	.05
641	David Hulse	.05
642	Charlie Leibrandt	.05
643	Robb Nen	.05
644	Dan Peltier	.05
645	Billy Ripken	.05
646	Kenny Rogers	.05
647	John Russell	.05
648	Dan Smith	.05
649	Matt Whiteside	.05
650	William Canate	.05
651	Darnell Coles	.05
652	Al Leiter	.05
653	Dominigo Martinez	.05
654	Paul Molitor	.50
655	Luis Sojo	.05
656	Dave Stewart	.05
657	Mike Timlin	.05
658	Turner Ward	.05
659	Devon White	.05
660	Eddie Zosky	.05

Beisbol Amigos

In groups of two, three or more, and generally from the same team, Latin players are paired in this second series insert set. The cards feature player photos (sometimes posed, sometimes superimposed) on a background of red, white and black baseballs. The players' last names and a card title are printed in Spanish on front and repeated on back. Also on back a few career highlights and stats are printed in red on a marbled background - again all in Spanish.

		NM/M
Complete Set (30):		7.50
Common Player:		.50
1	Edgar Martinez	.50
2	Luis Polonia, Stan Javier	.50
3	George Bell, Julio Franco	.50
4	Ozzie Guillen, Ivan Rodriguez	.60
5	Carlos Baerga, Sandy Alomar Jr.	.50
6	Sandy Alomar Jr., Alvaro Espinoza, Paul Sorrento, Carlos Baerga, Felix Fermin, Junior Ortiz, Jose Mesa, Carlos Martinez	.50
7	Sandy Alomar Jr., Roberto Alomar	1.00
8	Jose Lind, Felix Jose	.50
9	Ricky Bones, Jaime Navarro	.50
10	Jaime Navarro, Jesse Orosco	.50
11	Tino Martinez, Edgar Martinez	.50
12	Juan Gonzalez, Ivan Rodriguez	.75
13	Juan Gonzalez, Julio Franco	.60
14	Julio Franco, Jose Canseco, Rafael Palmeiro	.60
15	Juan Gonzalez, Jose Canseco	.65
16	Ivan Rodriguez, Benji Gil	.60
17	Jose Guzman, Frank Castillo	.50
18	Rey Sanchez, Jose Vizcaino	.50
19	Derrick May, Sammy Sosa	2.00
20	Sammy Sosa, Candy Maldonado	2.00
21	Jose Rijo, Juan Samuel	.50
22	Freddie Benavides, Andres Galarraga	.50
23	Guillermo Velasquez, Benito Santiago	.50
24	Luis Gonzalez, Andujar Cedeno	.50
25	Wil Cordero, Dennis Martinez	.50
26	Moises Alou, Wil Cordero	.50
27	Ozzie Canseco, Jose Canseco	.75
28	Jose Oquendo, Luis Alicea	.50
29	Luis Alicea, Rene Arocha	.50
30	Geronimo Pena, Luis Alicea	.50

Estrellas de Beisbol

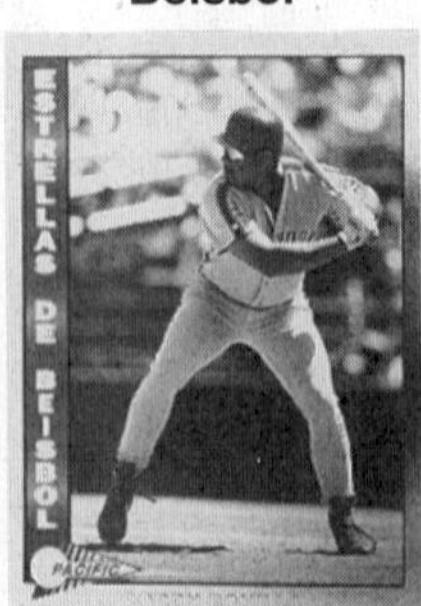

Pacific produced a gold-foil "Stars of Baseball" set of 20 that was randomly inserted as part of the company's first series Spanish language major league set in 1993. Each card features a color action photo on the front surrounded by a gold-foil border. Production was limited to 10,000 of each card.

		NM/M
Complete Set (20):		6.00
Common Player:		.50
1	Moises Alou	.50
2	Bobby Bonilla	.50
3	Tony Fernandez	.50
4	Felix Jose	.50
5	Dennis Martinez	.50
6	Orlando Merced	.50
7	Jose Oquendo	.50
8	Geronimo Pena	.50
9	Jose Rijo	.50
10	Benito Santiago	.50
11	Sandy Alomar Jr.	.50
12	Carlos Baerga	.50
13	Jose Canseco	1.50
14	Juan "Igor" Gonzalez	2.00
15	Juan Guzman	.50
16	Edgar Martinez	.50
17	Rafael Palmeiro	2.00
18	Ruben Sierra	.50
19	Danny Tartabull	.50
20	Omar Vizquel	.50

Jugadores Calientes

Three dozen "hot players" with a decidedly Hispanic predominance are featured in this glittery Series 2 insert set. Player action photos appear in front of a silver prismatic foil background. Names appear at bottom in boldly styled, but hard to read, letters in bright colors. Horizontal backs have a pair of player photos and a large team logo, along with a few stats, all printed in Spanish.

		NM/M
Complete Set (36):		20.00
Common Player:		.50
1	Rich Amaral	.50
2	George Brett	1.75
3	Jay Buhner	.50
4	Roger Clemens	2.00
5	Kirk Gibson	.50
6	Juan Gonzalez	1.00
7	Ken Griffey Jr.	2.00
8	Bo Jackson	.75
9	Kenny Lofton	.50
10	Mark McGwire	2.25
11	Sherman Obando	.50
12	John Olerud	.50
13	Carlos Quintana	.50
14	Ivan Rodriguez	1.00
15	Nolan Ryan	2.50
16	J.T. Snow	.50
17	Fernando Valenzuela	.50
18	Dave Winfield	1.25
19	Moises Alou	.50
20	Jeff Bagwell	1.25
21	Barry Bonds	2.50
22	Bobby Bonilla	.50
23	Vinny Castilla	.50
24	Andujar Cedeno	.50
25	Orestes Destrade	.50
26	Andres Galarraga	.50
27	Mark Grace	.50
28	Tony Gwynn	1.50
29	Roberto Kelly	.50
30	John Kruk	.50
31	Dave Magadan	.50
32	Derrick May	.50
33	Orlando Merced	.50
34	Mike Piazza	2.00
35	Armadno Reynoso	.50
36	Jose Vizcaino	.50

Prism Insert

Pacific produced a prism card that was randomly inserted in its Series 1 Spanish-language set in 1993. Each of the 20 cards has a color photo of a star Latino player on the front superimposed over a prismatic silver-foil background. Card backs contain an action photo and a brief player biography on a marbled background. Production was limited to 10,000 of each card.

		NM/M
Complete Set (20):		60.00
Common Player:		3.00
1	Francisco Cabrera	3.00
2	Jose Lind	3.00
3	Dennis Martinez	3.00
4	Ramon Martinez	3.00
5	Jose Rijo	3.00
6	Benito Santiago	3.00
7	Roberto Alomar	9.00
8	Sandy Alomar Jr.	3.00
9	Carlos Baerga	3.00
10	George Bell	3.00
11	Jose Canseco	6.00
12	Alex Fernandez	3.00
13	Julio Franco	3.00
14	Igor (Juan) Gonzalez	12.00
15	Ozzie Guillen	3.00
16	Teddy Higuera	3.00
17	Edgar Martinez	3.00
18	Hipolito Pichardo	3.00
19	Luis Polonia	3.00
20	Ivan Rodriguez	7.50

1994 Pacific Crown Promos

Virtually identical in format to the regular 1994 Pacific Crown issue, the eight cards in the promo set have a "P-" prefix to the card number. Each side has a large "For Promotional Use Only" printed diagonally in black. The cards were sent to dealers as a preview to Pacific's 1994 bilingual issue.

		NM/M
Complete Set (8):		6.00
Common Player:		.75
1	Carlos Baerga	.75
2	Joe Carter	.75
3	Juan Gonzalez	.75
4	Ken Griffey Jr.	2.00
5	Greg Maddux	1.50
6	Mike Piazza	1.75
7	Tim Salmon	.75
8	Frank Thomas	1.25

1994 Pacific Crown

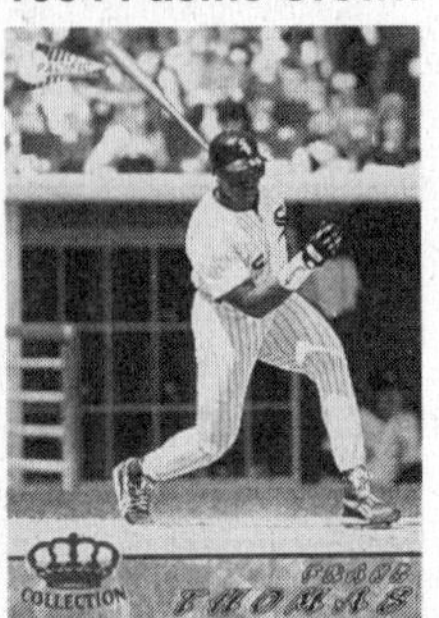

Following its 1993 Spanish-language set, Pacific's 1994 "Crown Collection" offering is bilingual, featuring both English and Spanish for most of the back printing. Fronts have an action photo which is borderless at the top and sides. A gold-foil line separates the bottom of the photo from a marbled strip that is color-coded by team. The player's name appears in two lines at the left of the strip, a gold-foil crown logo is at left. A Pacific logo appears in one of the upper corners of the photo. Backs have a photo, again borderless at top and sides, with a Pacific logo in one upper corner and the card number and MLB logos in the lower corners. At bottom is a gray marble strip with a few biographical details, 1993 and career stats and a ghost-image color team logo. The 660 cards in the set were issued in a single series.

		NM/M
Complete Set (660):		20.00
Common Player:		.05
Pack (12):		1.00
Wax Box (36):		20.00
1	Steve Avery	.05
2	Steve Bedrosian	.05
3	Damon Berryhill	.05
4	Jeff Blauser	.05
5	Sid Bream	.05
6	Francisco Cabrera	.05
7	Ramon Caraballo	.05
8	Ron Gant	.05
9	Tom Glavine	.25
10	Chipper Jones	.75
11	Dave Justice	.05
12	Ryan Klesko	.05
13	Mark Lemke	.05
14	Javier Lopez	.05
15	Greg Maddux	.75
16	Fred McGriff	.05
17	Greg McMichael	.05
18	Kent Mercker	.05
19	Otis Nixon	.05
20	Terry Pendleton	.05
21	Deion Sanders	.05
22	John Smoltz	.05
23	Tony Tarasco	.05
24	Manny Alexander	.05
25	Brady Anderson	.05
26	Harold Baines	.05
27	Damion Buford (Damon)	.05
28	Paul Carey	.05
29	Mike Devereaux	.05
30	Todd Frohwirth	.05
31	Leo Gomez	.05
32	Jeffrey Hammonds	.05
33	Chris Hoiles	.05
34	Tim Hulett	.05
35	Ben McDonald	.05
36	Mark McLemore	.05
37	Alan Mills	.05
38	Mike Mussina	.35
39	Sherman Obando	.05
40	Gregg Olson	.05
41	Mike Pagliarulo	.05
42	Jim Poole	.05
43	Harold Reynolds	.05
44	Cal Ripken, Jr.	2.00
45	David Segui	.05
46	Fernando Valenzuela	.05
47	Jack Voight	.05
48	Scott Bankhead	.05
49	Roger Clemens	1.00
50	Scott Cooper	.05
51	Danny Darwin	.05
52	Andre Dawson	.20
53	John Dopson	.05
54	Scott Fletcher	.05
55	Tony Fossas	.05
56	Mike Greenwell	.05
57	Billy Hatcher	.05
58	Jeff McNeely	.05
59	Jose Melendez	.05
60	Tim Naehring	.05
61	Tony Pena	.05
62	Carlos Quintana	.05
63	Paul Quantrill	.05
64	Luis Rivera	.05
65	Jeff Russell	.05
66	Aaron Sele	.05
67	John Valentin	.05
68	Mo Vaughn	.05
69	Frank Viola	.05
70	Bob Zupcic	.05
71	Mike Butcher	.05
72	Ron Correia	.05
73	Chad Curtis	.05
74	Chili Davis	.05
75	Gary DiSarcina	.05
76	Damion Easley	.05
77	John Farrell	.05
78	Chuck Finley	.05
79	Joe Grahe	.05
80	Stan Javier	.05
81	Mark Langston	.05
82	Phil Leftwich	.05
83	Torey Lovullo	.05
84	Joe Magrane	.05
85	Greg Myers	.05
86	Eduardo Perez	.05
87	Luis Polonia	.05
88	Tim Salmon	.05
89	J.T. Snow	.05
90	Kurt Stillwell	.05
91	Ron Tingley	.05
92	Chris Turner	.05
93	Julio Valera	.05
94	Jose Bautista	.05
95	Shawn Boskie	.05
96	Steve Buechele	.05
97	Frank Castillo	.05
98	Mark Grace	.05
99	Jose Guzman	.05
100	Mike Harkey	.05
101	Greg Hibbard	.05
102	Doug Jennings	.05
103	Derrick May	.05
104	Mike Morgan	.05
105	Randy Myers	.05
106	Karl Rhodes	.05
107	Kevin Robinson	.05
108	Rey Sanchez	.05
109	Ryne Sandberg	.75
110	Tommy Shields	.05
111	Dwight Smith	.05
112	Sammy Sosa	.75
113	Jose Vizcaino	.05
114	Turk Wendell	.05
115	Rick Wilkins	.05
116	Willie Wilson	.05
117	Eddie Zambrano	.05
118	Wilson Alvarez	.05
119	Tim Belcher	.05
120	Jason Bere	.05
121	Rodney Bolton	.05
122	Ellis Burks	.05
123	Joey Cora	.05
124	Alex Fernandez	.05
125	Ozzie Guillen	.05
126	Craig Grebeck	.05
127	Roberto Hernandez	.05
128	Bo Jackson	.10
129	Lance Johnson	.05
130	Ron Karkovice	.05
131	Mike Lavalliere	.05
132	Norberto Martin	.05
133	Kirk McCaskill	.05
134	Jack McDowell	.05
135	Scott Radinsky	.05
136	Tim Raines	.05
137	Steve Sax	.05
138	Frank Thomas	.60
139	Dan Pasqua	.05
140	Robin Ventura	.05
141	Jeff Branson	.05
142	Tom Browning	.05
143	Jacob Brumfield	.05
144	Tim Costo	.05
145	Rob Dibble	.05
146	Brian Dorsett	.05
147	Steve Foster	.05
148	Cesar Hernandez	.05
149	Roberto Kelly	.05
150	Barry Larkin	.05
151	Larry Luebbers	.05
152	Kevin Mitchell	.05
153	Joe Oliver	.05
154	Tim Pugh	.05
155	Jeff Reardon	.05
156	Jose Rijo	.05
157	Bip Roberts	.05
158	Chris Sabo	.05
159	Juan Samuel	.05
160	Reggie Sanders	.05
161	John Smiley	.05
162	Jerry Spradlin	.05
163	Gary Varsho	.05
164	Sandy Alomar Jr.	.05
165	Carlos Baerga	.05
166	Albert Belle	.05
167	Mark Clark	.05
168	Alvaro Espinoza	.05
169	Felix Fermin	.05
170	Reggie Jefferson	.05
171	Wayne Kirby	.05
172	Tom Kramer	.05
173	Jesse Levis	.05
174	Kenny Lofton	.05
175	Candy Maldonado	.05
176	Carlos Martinez	.05
177	Jose Mesa	.05
178	Jeff Mutis	.05
179	Charles Nagy	.05
180	Bob Ojeda	.05
181	Junior Ortiz	.05
182	Eric Plunk	.05
183	Manny Ramirez	.60
184	Paul Sorrento	.05
185	Jeff Treadway	.05
186	Bill Wertz	.05
187	Freddie Benavides	.05
188	Dante Bichette	.05
189	Willie Blair	.05
190	Daryl Boston	.05
191	Pedro Castellano	.05
192	Vinny Castilla	.05
193	Jerald Clark	.05
194	Alex Cole	.05
195	Andres Galarraga	.05
196	Joe Girardi	.05
197	Charlie Hayes	.05
198	Darren Holmes	.05
199	Chris Jones	.05
200	Curt Leskanic	.05
201	Roberto Mejia	.05
202	David Nied	.05
203	J. Owens	.05
204	Steve Reed	.05
205	Armando Reynoso	.05
206	Bruce Ruffin	.05
207	Keith Shepherd	.05
208	Jim Tatum	.05
209	Eric Young	.05
210	Skeeter Barnes	.05
211	Danny Bautista	.05
212	Tom Bolton	.05
213	Eric Davis	.05
214	Storm Davis	.05
215	Cecil Fielder	.05
216	Travis Fryman	.05
217	Kirk Gibson	.05
218	Dan Gladden	.05
219	John Doherty	.05
220	Chris Gomez	.05
221	David Haas	.05
222	Bill Krueger	.05
223	Chad Kreuter	.05
224	Mark Leiter	.05
225	Bob MacDonald	.05
226	Mike Moore	.05
227	Tony Phillips	.05
228	Rich Rowland	.05
229	Mickey Tettleton	.05
230	Alan Trammell	.05
231	David Wells	.05
232	Lou Whitaker	.05
233	Luis Aquino	.05
234	Alex Arias	.05
235	Jack Armstrong	.05
236	Ryan Bowen	.05
237	Chuck Carr	.05
238	Matias Carrillo	.05
239	Jeff Conine	.05
240	Henry Cotto	.05
241	Orestes Destrade	.05
242	Chris Hammond	.05
243	Bryan Harvey	.05
244	Charlie Hough	.05
245	Richie Lewis	.05
246	Mitch Lyden	.05
247	Dave Magadan	.05
248	Bob Natal	.05
249	Benito Santiago	.05
250	Gary Sheffield	.30
251	Matt Turner	.05
252	David Weathers	.05
253	Walt Weiss	.05
254	Darrell Whitmore	.05
255	Nigel Wilson	.05
256	Eric Anthony	.05
257	Jeff Bagwell	.60
258	Kevin Bass	.05
259	Craig Biggio	.05
260	Ken Caminiti	.05
261	Andujar Cedeno	.05
262	Chris Donnels	.05
263	Doug Drabek	.05
264	Tom Edens	.05
265	Steve Finley	.05
266	Luis Gonzalez	.05
267	Pete Harnisch	.05
268	Xavier Hernandez	.05
269	Todd Jones	.05
270	Darryl Kile	.05
271	Al Osuna	.05
272	Rick Parker	.05
273	Mark Portugal	.05
274	Scott Servais	.05
275	Greg Swindell	.05
276	Eddie Taubensee	.05
277	Jose Uribe	.05
278	Brian Williams	.05
279	Kevin Appier	.05
280	Billy Brewer	.05
281	David Cone	.05
282	Greg Gagne	.05
283	Tom Gordon	.05
284	Chris Gwynn	.05
285	John Habyan	.05
286	Chris Haney	.05
287	Phil Hiatt	.05
288	David Howard	.05
289	Felix Jose	.05
290	Wally Joyner	.05
291	Kevin Koslofski	.05
292	Jose Lind	.05
293	Brent Mayne	.05
294	Mike Mcfarlane	.05
295	Brian McRae	.05
296	Kevin McReynolds	.05
297	Keith Miller	.05
298	Jeff Montgomery	.05
299	Hipolito Pichardo	.05
300	Rico Rossy	.05
301	Curtis Wilkerson	.05
302	Pedro Astacio	.05
303	Rafael Bournigal	.05
304	Brett Butler	.05
305	Tom Candiotti	.05
306	Omar Daal	.05
307	Jim Gott	.05
308	Kevin Gross	.05
309	Dave Hansen	.05
310	Carlos Hernandez	.05
311	Orel Hershiser	.05
312	Eric Karros	.05
313	Pedro Martinez	.60
314	Ramon Martinez	.05
315	Roger McDowell	.05
316	Raul Mondesi	.05
317	Jose Offerman	.05
318	Mike Piazza	1.00
319	Jody Reed	.05
320	Henry Rodriguez	.05
321	Cory Snyder	.05
322	Darryl Strawberry	.05
323	Tim Wallach	.05
324	Steve Wilson	.05
325	Juan Bell	.05
326	Ricky Bones	.05
327	Alex Diaz	.05
328	Cal Eldred	.05
329	Darryl Hamilton	.05
330	Doug Henry	.05
331	John Jaha	.05
332	Pat Listach	.05
333	Graeme Lloyd	.05
334	Carlos Maldonado	.05
335	Angel Miranda	.05
336	Jaime Navarro	.05
337	Dave Nilsson	.05
338	Rafael Novoa	.05
339	Troy O'Leary	.05
340	Jesse Orosco	.05
341	Kevin Seitzer	.05
342	Bill Spiers	.05
343	William Suero	.05
344	B.J. Surhoff	.05
345	Dickie Thon	.05
346	Jose Valentin	.05
347	Greg Vaughn	.05
348	Robin Yount	.60
349	Willie Banks	.05
350	Bernardo Brito	.05
351	Scott Erickson	.05
352	Mark Guthrie	.05
353	Chip Hale	.05
354	Brian Harper	.05
355	Kent Hrbek	.05
356	Terry Jorgenson	.05
357	Chuck Knoblauch	.05
358	Gene Larkin	.05
359	Scott Leius	.05
360	Shane Mack	.05
361	David McCarty	.05
362	Pat Meares	.05
363	Pedro Munoz	.05
364	Derek Parks	.05
365	Kirby Puckett	.75
366	Jeff Reboulet	.05
367	Kevin Tapani	.05
368	Mike Trombley	.05
369	George Tsamis	.05
370	Carl Willis	.05
371	Dave Winfield	.60
372	Moises Alou	.05
373	Brian Barnes	.05
374	Sean Berry	.05
375	Frank Bolick	.05
376	Wil Cordero	.05
377	Delino DeShields	.05
378	Jeff Fassero	.05
379	Darren Fletcher	.05
380	Cliff Floyd	.05
381	Lou Frazier	.05
382	Marquis Grissom	.05
383	Gil Heredia	.05
384	Mike Lansing	.05
385	Oreste Marrero	.05
386	Dennis Martinez	.05
387	Curtis Pride	.05
388	Mel Rojas	.05
389	Kirk Rueter	.05
390	Joe Siddall	.05
391	John Vander Wal	.05
392	Larry Walker	.05
393	John Wetteland	.05
394	Rondell White	.05
395	Tom Bogar	.05
396	Bobby Bonilla	.05
397	Jeromy Burnitz	.05
398	Mike Draper	.05
399	Sid Fernandez	.05
400	John Franco	.05
401	Dave Gallagher	.05
402	Dwight Gooden	.05
403	Eric Hillman	.05
404	Todd Hundley	.05
405	Butch Huskey	.05
406	Jeff Innis	.05
407	Howard Johnson	.05
408	Jeff Kent	.05
409	Ced Landrum	.05
410	Mike Maddux	.05
411	Josias Manzanillo	.05
412	Jeff McKnight	.05
413	Eddie Murray	.60
414	Tito Navarro	.05
415	Joe Orsulak	.05
416	Bret Saberhagen	.05
417	Dave Telgheder	.05
418	Ryan Thompson	.05
419	Chico Walker	.05
420	Jim Abbott	.05
421	Wade Boggs	.75
422	Mike Gallego	.05
423	Mark Hutton	.05
424	Dion James	.05
425	Domingo Jean	.05
426	Pat Kelly	.05
427	Jimmy Key	.05
428	Jim Leyritz	.05
429	Kevin Maas	.05
430	Don Mattingly	1.00
431	Bobby Munoz	.05
432	Matt Nokes	.05
433	Paul O'Neill	.05
434	Spike Owen	.05
435	Melido Perez	.05
436	Lee Smith	.05
437	Andy Stankiewicz	.05
438	Mike Stanley	.05
439	Danny Tartabull	.05
440	Randy Velarde	.05
441	Bernie Williams	.05
442	Gerald Williams	.05
443	Mike Witt	.05
444	Marcos Armas	.05
445	Lance Blankenship	.05
446	Mike Bordick	.05
447	Ron Darling	.05
448	Dennis Eckersley	.45
449	Brent Gates	.05
450	Goose Gossage	.05
451	Scott Hemond	.05
452	Dave Henderson	.05
453	Shawn Hillegas	.05
454	Rick Honeycutt	.05
455	Scott Lydy	.05
456	Mark McGwire	1.50
457	Henry Mercedes	.05
458	Mike Mohler	.05
459	Troy Neel	.05
460	Edwin Nunez	.05
461	Craig Paquette	.05
462	Ruben Sierra	.05
463	Terry Steinbach	.05
464	Todd Van Poppel	.05
465	Bob Welch	.05
466	Bobby Witt	.05
467	Ruben Amaro	.05
468	Larry Anderson	.05
469	Kim Batiste	.05
470	Wes Chamberlain	.05
471	Darren Daulton	.05
472	Mariano Duncan	.05
473	Len Dykstra	.05
474	Jim Eisenreich	.05
475	Tommy Greene	.05
476	Dave Hollins	.05
477	Pete Incaviglia	.05
478	Danny Jackson	.05
479	John Kruk	.05
480	Tony Longmire	.05
481	Jeff Manto	.05
482	Mike Morandini	.05
483	Terry Mulholland	.05
484	Todd Pratt	.05
485	Ben Rivera	.05
486	Curt Schilling	.25
487	Kevin Stocker	.05
488	Milt Thompson	.05
489	David West	.05
490	Mitch Williams	.05
491	Jeff Ballard	.05
492	Jay Bell	.05
493	Scott Bullett	.05
494	Dave Clark	.05
495	Steve Cooke	.05
496	Midre Cummings	.05
497	Mark Dewey	.05
498	Carlos Garcia	.05
499	Jeff King	.05
500	Al Martin	.05
501	Lloyd McClendon	.05
502	Orlando Merced	.05
503	Blas Minor	.05
504	Denny Neagle	.05
505	Tom Prince	.05
506	Don Slaught	.05
507	Zane Smith	.05
508	Randy Tomlin	.05
509	Andy Van Slyke	.05
510	Paul Wagner	.05
511	Tim Wakefield	.05
512	Bob Walk	.05
513	John Wehner	.05
514	Kevin Young	.05
515	Billy Bean	.05
516	Andy Benes	.05
517	Derek Bell	.05
518	Doug Brocail	.05
519	Jarvis Brown	.05
520	Phil Clark	.05
521	Mark Davis	.05
522	Jeff Gardner	.05
523	Pat Gomez	.05
524	Ricky Gutierrez	.05
525	Tony Gwynn	.75
526	Gene Harris	.05
527	Kevin Higgins	.05
528	Trevor Hoffman	.05
529	Luis Lopez	.05
530	Pedro A. Martinez	.05
531	Melvin Nieves	.05
532	Phil Plantier	.05
533	Frank Seminara	.05
534	Craig Shipley	.05
535	Tim Tuefel	.05
536	Guillermo Velasquez	.05
537	Wally Whitehurst	.05
538	Rod Beck	.05
539	Todd Benzinger	.05
540	Barry Bonds	2.00
541	Jeff Brantley	.05
542	Dave Burba	.05
543	John Burkett	.05
544	Will Clark	.05
545	Royce Clayton	.05
546	Brian Hickerson (Bryan)	.05
547	Mike Jackson	.05
548	Darren Lewis	.05
549	Kirt Manwaring	.05
550	Dave Martinez	.05
551	Willie McGee	.05
552	Jeff Reed	.05
553	Dave Righetti	.05
554	Kevin Rogers	.05
555	Steve Scarsone	.05
556	Bill Swift	.05
557	Robby Thompson	.05
558	Salomon Torres	.05
559	Matt Williams	.05
560	Trevor Wilson	.05
561	Rich Amaral	.05
562	Mike Blowers	.05
563	Chris Bosio	.05
564	Jay Buhner	.05
565	Norm Charlton	.05
566	Jim Converse	.05
567	Rich DeLucia	.05
568	Mike Felder	.05
569	Dave Fleming	.05
570	Ken Griffey Jr.	1.00
571	Bill Haselman	.05
572	Dwayne Henry	.05
573	Brad Holman	.05
574	Randy Johnson	.60
575	Greg Litton	.05
576	Edgar Martinez	.05
577	Tino Martinez	.05
578	Jeff Nelson	.05
579	Mark Newfield	.05
580	Roger Salkeld	.05
581	Mackey Sasser	.05
582	Brian Turang	.05
583	Omar Vizquel	.05
584	Dave Valle	.05
585	Luis Alicea	.05
586	Rene Arocha	.05
587	Rheal Cormier	.05
588	Tripp Cromer	.05
589	Bernard Gilkey	.05
590	Lee Guetterman	.05
591	Gregg Jefferies	.05
592	Tim Jones	.05
593	Paul Kilgus	.05
594	Les Lancaster	.05
595	Omar Olivares	.05
596	Jose Oquendo	.05
597	Donovan Osborne	.05
598	Tom Pagnozzi	.05
599	Erik Pappas	.05
600	Geronimo Pena	.05
601	Mike Perez	.05
602	Gerald Perry	.05
603	Stan Royer	.05
604	Ozzie Smith	.75
605	Bob Tewksbury	.05
606	Allen Watson	.05
607	Mark Whiten	.05
608	Todd Zeile	.05
609	Jeff Bronkey	.05
610	Kevin Brown	.05
611	Jose Canseco	.35
612	Doug Dascenzo	.05
613	Butch Davis	.05
614	Mario Diaz	.05
615	Julio Franco	.05
616	Benji Gil	.05
617	Juan Gonzalez	.30
618	Tom Henke	.05
619	Jeff Huson	.05
620	David Hulse	.05
621	Craig Lefferts	.05
622	Rafael Palmeiro	.50
623	Dean Palmer	.05
624	Bob Patterson	.05
625	Roger Pavlik	.05
626	Gary Redus	.05
627	Ivan Rodriguez	.50
628	Kenny Rogers	.05
629	Jon Shave	.05
630	Doug Strange	.05
631	Matt Whiteside	.05
632	Roberto Alomar	.15
633	Pat Borders	.05
634	Scott Brow	.05
635	Rob Butler	.05
636	Joe Carter	.05
637	Tony Castillo	.05
638	Mark Eichhorn	.05
639	Tony Fernandez	.05
640	Huck Flener **RC**	.05
641	Alfredo Griffin	.05
642	Juan Guzman	.05
643	Rickey Henderson	.60
644	Pat Hentgen	.05
645	Randy Knorr	.05
646	Al Leiter	.05
647	Dominigo Martinez	.05
648	Paul Molitor	.60
649	Jack Morris	.05
650	John Olerud	.05
651	Ed Sprague	.05
652	Dave Stewart	.05
653	Devon White	.05
654	Woody Williams	.05
655	Barry Bonds (MVP)	1.00
656	Greg Maddux (CY)	.40
657	Jack McDowell (CY)	.05
658	Mike Piazza (ROY)	.65
659	Tim Salmon (ROY)	.05
660	Frank Thomas (MVP)	.25

All Latino All-Star Team

Latino All-Stars is the theme of the third insert set found randomly packed in Pacific Spanish for 1994. Cards feature a player action photo on front, with a gold foil pinstripe around the sides and top. The player's name appears in gold script at bottom and there is a baseball logo in the corner. On backs a portrait photo of the player is set against a background of his native flag. Season highlights of 1993 are presented in English and Spanish. Eight thousand sets were produced.

		NM/M
Complete Set (20):		4.00
Common Player:		.25
1	Benito Santiago	.25
2	Dave Magadan	.25
3	Andres Galarraga	.25
4	Luis Gonzalez	.25
5	Jose Offerman	.25
6	Bobby Bonilla	.25
7	Dennis Martinez	.25
8	Mariano Duncan	.25
9	Orlando Merced	.25
10	Jose Rijo	.25
11	Danny Tartabull	.25
12	Ruben Sierra	.25
13	Ivan Rodriguez	1.00
14	Juan Gonzalez	1.00
15	Jose Canseco	.50
16	Rafael Palmeiro	1.00
17	Roberto Alomar	.50
18	Eduardo Perez	.25
19	Alex Fernandez	.25
20	Omar Vizquel	.25

Homerun Leaders

A gold prismatic background behind a color action player photo is the featured design on this Pacific insert set. Backs have another player photo against a ballfield backdrop. A huge baseball is overprinted with the player's name and number of 1993 homers. A league designation is among the logos featured on back. A total of 8,000 of these inserts sets was the announced production.

		NM/M
Complete Set (20):		25.00
Common Player:		1.00
1	Juan Gonzalez	1.50
2	Ken Griffey Jr.	3.00
3	Frank Thomas	2.50
4	Albert Belle	1.00
5	Rafael Palmeiro	1.50
6	Joe Carter	1.00
7	Dean Palmer	1.00
8	Mickey Tettleton	1.00
9	Tim Salmon	1.00
10	Danny Tartabull	1.00
11	Barry Bonds	5.00
12	Dave Justice	1.00
13	Matt Williams	1.00
14	Fred McGriff	1.00
15	Ron Gant	1.00
16	Mike Piazza	3.00
17	Bobby Bonilla	1.00
18	Phil Plantier	1.00
19	Sammy Sosa	3.00
20	Rick Wilkins	1.00

Jewels of the Crown

One of three inserts into 1994 Pacific Spanish foil packs. The design features a player action photo set against a silver prismatic background. On back is another color player photo against a background of colored silk and a large jewel. Season highlight stats and awards won are presented in both English and Spanish. The announced production run of these inserts was 8,000 sets.

		NM/M
Complete Set (36):		40.00
Common Player:		1.00
1	Robin Yount	2.50
2	Juan Gonzalez	1.25
3	Rafael Palmeiro	2.00
4	Paul Molitor	2.50
5	Roberto Alomar	1.25
6	John Olerud	1.00
7	Randy Johnson	2.50
8	Ken Griffey Jr.	4.00
9	Wade Boggs	3.00
10	Don Mattingly	3.50
11	Kirby Puckett	3.00
12	Tim Salmon	1.00
13	Frank Thomas	2.50
14	Fernando Valenzuela (Comeback Player)	1.00
15	Cal Ripken, Jr.	6.00
16	Carlos Baerga	1.00
17	Kenny Lofton	1.00
18	Cecil Fielder	1.00
19	John Burkett	1.00
20	Andres Galarraga (Comeback Player)	1.00
21	Charlie Hayes	1.00
22	Orestes Destrade	1.00
23	Jeff Conine	1.00
24	Jeff Bagwell	2.50
25	Mark Grace	1.00
26	Ryne Sandberg	3.00
27	Gregg Jefferies	1.00
28	Barry Bonds	6.00
29	Mike Piazza	3.50
30	Greg Maddux	3.00
31	Darren Daulton	1.00
32	John Kruk	1.00
33	Len Dykstra	1.00
34	Orlando Merced	1.00
35	Tony Gwynn	3.00
36	Robby Thompson	1.00

Jewels of the Crown - Retail

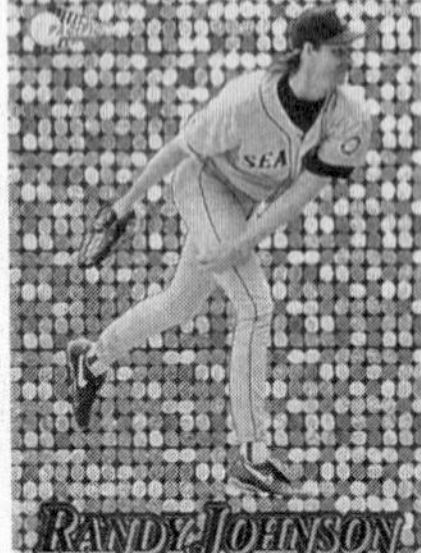

Using the same design, photos, graphics and card numbers, the retail version of the Jewels of the Crown insert set varies only in the silver prismatic foil background on front. While the scarcer hobby version has a diamond-shaped pattern to the foil, the retail version has numerous circles as a background pattern. The retail cards were inserted one per pack of retail product and are thus much more common than the hobby version.

		NM/M
Complete Set (36):		40.00
Common Player:		.75
1	Robin Yount	2.50
2	Juan Gonzalez	1.25
3	Rafael Palmeiro	1.25
4	Paul Molitor	2.50
5	Roberto Alomar	1.00
6	John Olerud	.75
7	Randy Johnson	2.50
8	Ken Griffey Jr.	4.00
9	Wade Boggs	3.00
10	Don Mattingly	3.50
11	Kirby Puckett	3.00
12	Tim Salmon	.75
13	Frank Thomas	2.50
14	Fernando Valenzuela (Comeback Player)	.75
15	Cal Ripken, Jr.	5.00
16	Carlos Baerga	.75
17	Kenny Lofton	.75
18	Cecil Fielder	.75
19	John Burkett	.75
20	Andres Galarraga (Comeback Player)	.75
21	Charlie Hayes	.75
22	Orestes Destrade	.75
23	Jeff Conine	.75
24	Jeff Bagwell	2.50
25	Mark Grace	.75
26	Ryne Sandberg	3.00
27	Gregg Jefferies	.75
28	Barry Bonds	5.00
29	Mike Piazza	3.50
30	Greg Maddux	3.00
31	Darren Daulton	.75
32	John Kruk	.75
33	Len Dykstra	.75
34	Orlando Merced	.75
35	Tony Gwynn	3.00
36	Robby Thompson	.75

1995 Pacific

The base cards in Pacific's Crown Collection baseball issue for 1995 feature borderless color action photos on front, graphically highlighted by the player name at bottom in gold foil and a color team logo in a baseball at lower-left. Backs have a playing field design in the background with a portrait photo at left. At right are 1994 stats, career highlights and a ghosted image of the team logo. Most back printing is in both English and Spanish. The 450 cards in the series are arranged alphabetically within team, with the teams arranged in city-alpha order. Several chase cards series are found in the 12-card foil packs.

		NM/M
Complete Set (450):		20.00
Common Player:		.05
Pack (12):		1.00
Wax Box (36):		20.00
1	Steve Avery	.05
2	Rafael Belliard	.05
3	Jeff Blauser	.05
4	Tom Glavine	.25
5	Dave Justice	.05
6	Mike Kelly	.05
7	Roberto Kelly	.05
8	Ryan Klesko	.05
9	Mark Lemke	.05
10	Javier Lopez	.05
11	Greg Maddux	.75
12	Fred McGriff	.05
13	Greg McMichael	.05
14	Jose Oliva	.05
15	John Smoltz	.05
16	Tony Tarasco	.05
17	Brady Anderson	.05
18	Harold Baines	.05
19	Armando Benitez	.05
20	Mike Devereaux	.05
21	Leo Gomez	.05
22	Jeffrey Hammonds	.05
23	Chris Hoiles	.05
24	Ben McDonald	.05
25	Mark McLemore	.05
26	Jamie Moyer	.05
27	Mike Mussina	.40
28	Rafael Palmeiro	.50
29	Jim Poole	.05
30	Cal Ripken Jr.	2.00
31	Lee Smith	.05
32	Mark Smith	.05
33	Jose Canseco	.35
34	Roger Clemens	1.00
35	Scott Cooper	.05
36	Andre Dawson	.25
37	Tony Fossas	.05
38	Mike Greenwell	.05
39	Chris Howard	.05
40	Jose Melendez	.05
41	Nate Minchey	.05
42	Tim Naehring	.05
43	Otis Nixon	.05
44	Carlos Rodriguez	.05
45	Aaron Sele	.05
46	Lee Tinsley	.05
47	Sergio Valdez	.05
48	John Valentin	.05
49	Mo Vaughn	.05
50	Brian Anderson	.05
51	Garret Anderson	.05
52	Rod Correia	.05
53	Chad Curtis	.05
54	Mark Dalesandro	.05
55	Chili Davis	.05
56	Gary DiSarcina	.05
57	Damion Easley	.05
58	Jim Edmonds	.05
59	Jorge Fabregas	.05
60	Chuck Finley	.05
61	Bo Jackson	.10
62	Mark Langston	.05
63	Eduardo Perez	.05
64	Tim Salmon	.05
65	J.T. Snow	.05
66	Willie Banks	.05
67	Jose Bautista	.05
68	Shawon Dunston	.05
69	Kevin Foster	.05
70	Mark Grace	.05
71	Jose Guzman	.05
72	Jose Hernandez	.05
73	Blaise Ilsley	.05
74	Derrick May	.05
75	Randy Myers	.05
76	Karl Rhodes	.05
77	Kevin Roberson	.05
78	Rey Sanchez	.05
79	Sammy Sosa	.75
80	Steve Trachsel	.05
81	Eddie Zambrano	.05
82	Wilson Alvarez	.05
83	Jason Bere	.05
84	Joey Cora	.05
85	Jose DeLeon	.05
86	Alex Fernandez	.05
87	Julio Franco	.05
88	Ozzie Guillen	.05
89	Joe Hall	.05
90	Roberto Hernandez	.05
91	Darrin Jackson	.05
92	Lance Johnson	.05
93	Norberto Martin	.05
94	Jack McDowell	.05
95	Tim Raines	.05
96	Olmedo Saenz	.05
97	Frank Thomas	.60
98	Robin Ventura	.05
99	Bret Boone	.05
100	Jeff Brantley	.05
101	Jacob Brumfield	.05
102	Hector Carrasco	.05
103	Brian Dorsett	.05
104	Tony Fernandez	.05
105	Willie Greene	.05
106	Erik Hanson	.05
107	Kevin Jarvis	.05
108	Barry Larkin	.05
109	Kevin Mitchell	.05
110	Hal Morris	.05
111	Jose Rijo	.05
112	Johnny Ruffin	.05
113	Deion Sanders	.05
114	Reggie Sanders	.05
115	Sandy Alomar Jr.	.05
116	Ruben Amaro	.05
117	Carlos Baerga	.05
118	Albert Belle	.05
119	Alvaro Espinoza	.05
120	Rene Gonzales	.05
121	Wayne Kirby	.05
122	Kenny Lofton	.05
123	Candy Maldonado	.05
124	Dennis Martinez	.05
125	Eddie Murray	.60
126	Charles Nagy	.05
127	Tony Pena	.05
128	Manny Ramirez	.60
129	Paul Sorrento	.05
130	Jim Thome	.40
131	Omar Vizquel	.05
132	Dante Bichette	.05
133	Ellis Burks	.05
134	Vinny Castilla	.05
135	Marvin Freeman	.05
136	Andres Galarraga	.05
137	Joe Girardi	.05
138	Charlie Hayes	.05
139	Mike Kingery	.05
140	Nelson Liriano	.05
141	Roberto Mejia	.05
142	David Nied	.05
143	Steve Reed	.05
144	Armando Reynoso	.05
145	Bruce Ruffin	.05
146	John Vander Wal	.05
147	Walt Weiss	.05
148	Skeeter Barnes	.05
149	Tim Belcher	.05
150	Junior Felix	.05
151	Cecil Fielder	.05
152	Travis Fryman	.05
153	Kirk Gibson	.05
154	Chris Gomez	.05
155	Buddy Groom	.05
156	Chad Kreuter	.05
157	Mike Moore	.05
158	Tony Phillips	.05
159	Juan Samuel	.05
160	Mickey Tettleton	.05
161	Alan Trammell	.05
162	David Wells	.05
163	Lou Whitaker	.05
164	Kurt Abbott	.05
165	Luis Aquino	.05
166	Alex Arias	.05
167	Bret Barberie	.05
168	Jerry Browne	.05
169	Chuck Carr	.05
170	Matias Carrillo	.05
171	Greg Colbrunn	.05
172	Jeff Conine	.05
173	Carl Everett	.05
174	Robb Nen	.05
175	Yorkis Perez	.05
176	Pat Rapp	.05
177	Benito Santiago	.05
178	Gary Sheffield	.35
179	Darrell Whitmore	.05
180	Jeff Bagwell	.60
181	Kevin Bass	.05
182	Craig Biggio	.05
183	Andujar Cedeno	.05
184	Doug Drabek	.05
185	Tony Eusebio	.05
186	Steve Finley	.05
187	Luis Gonzalez	.05
188	Pete Harnisch	.05
189	John Hudek	.05
190	Orlando Miller	.05
191	James Mouton	.05
192	Roberto Petagine	.05
193	Shane Reynolds	.05
194	Greg Swindell	.05
195	Dave Veres	.05
196	Kevin Appier	.05
197	Stan Belinda	.05
198	Vince Coleman	.05
199	David Cone	.05
200	Gary Gaetti	.05
201	Greg Gagne	.05
202	Mark Gubicza	.05
203	Bob Hamelin	.05
204	Dave Henderson	.05
205	Felix Jose	.05
206	Wally Joyner	.05
207	Jose Lind	.05
208	Mike Macfarlane	.05
209	Brian McRae	.05
210	Jeff Montgomery	.05
211	Hipolito Pichardo	.05
212	Pedro Astacio	.05
213	Brett Butler	.05
214	Omar Daal	.05
215	Delino DeShields	.05
216	Darren Dreifort	.05
217	Carlos Hernandez	.05
218	Orel Hershiser	.05
219	Garey Ingram	.05
220	Eric Karros	.05
221	Ramon Martinez	.05
222	Raul Mondesi	.05
223	Jose Offerman	.05
224	Mike Piazza	1.00
225	Henry Rodriguez	.05
226	Ismael Valdes	.05
227	Tim Wallach	.05
228	Jeff Cirillo	.05
229	Alex Diaz	.05
230	Cal Eldred	.05
231	Mike Fetters	.05
232	Brian Harper	.05
233	Ted Higuera	.05
234	John Jaha	.05
235	Graeme Lloyd	.05
236	Jose Mercedes	.05
237	Jaime Navarro	.05
238	Dave Nilsson	.05
239	Jesse Orosco	.05
240	Jody Reed	.05
241	Jose Valentin	.05
242	Greg Vaughn	.05
243	Turner Ward	.05
244	Rick Aguilera	.05
245	Rich Becker	.05
246	Jim Deshaies	.05
247	Steve Dunn	.05
248	Scott Erickson	.05
249	Kent Hrbek	.05
250	Chuck Knoblauch	.05
251	Scott Leius	.05
252	David McCarty	.05
253	Pat Meares	.05
254	Pedro Munoz	.05
255	Kirby Puckett	.75
256	Carlos Pulido	.05
257	Kevin Tapani	.05
258	Matt Walbeck	.05
259	Dave Winfield	.60
260	Moises Alou	.05
261	Juan Bell	.05
262	Freddie Benavides	.05
263	Sean Berry	.05
264	Wil Cordero	.05
265	Jeff Fassero	.05
266	Darrin Fletcher	.05
267	Cliff Floyd	.05
268	Marquis Grissom	.05
269	Gil Heredia	.05
270	Ken Hill	.05
271	Pedro Martinez	.60
272	Mel Rojas	.05
273	Larry Walker	.05
274	John Wetteland	.05
275	Rondell White	.05
276	Tim Bogar	.05
277	Bobby Bonilla	.05
278	Rico Brogna	.05
279	Jeromy Burnitz	.05
280	John Franco	.05
281	Eric Hillman	.05
282	Todd Hundley	.05
283	Jeff Kent	.05
284	Mike Maddux	.05
285	Joe Orsulak	.05
286	Luis Rivera	.05
287	Bret Saberhagen	.05
288	David Segui	.05
289	Ryan Thompson	.05
290	Fernando Vina	.05
291	Jose Vizcaino	.05
292	Jim Abbott	.05
293	Wade Boggs	.75
294	Russ Davis	.05
295	Mike Gallego	.05
296	Xavier Hernandez	.05
297	Steve Howe	.05
298	Jimmy Key	.05
299	Don Mattingly	1.00
300	Terry Mulholland	.05
301	Paul O'Neill	.05
302	Luis Polonia	.05
303	Mike Stanley	.05
304	Danny Tartabull	.05
305	Randy Velarde	.05
306	Bob Wickman	.05
307	Bernie Williams	.05
308	Mark Acre	.05
309	Geronimo Berroa	.05
310	Mike Bordick	.05
311	Dennis Eckersley	.50
312	Rickey Henderson	.60
313	Stan Javier	.05
314	Miguel Jimenez	.05
315	Francisco Matos	.05
316	Mark McGwire	1.50
317	Troy Neel	.05
318	Steve Ontiveros	.05
319	Carlos Reyes	.05
320	Ruben Sierra	.05
321	Terry Steinbach	.05
322	Bob Welch	.05
323	Bobby Witt	.05
324	Larry Andersen	.05
325	Kim Batiste	.05
326	Darren Daulton	.05
327	Mariano Duncan	.05
328	Lenny Dykstra	.05
329	Jim Eisenreich	.05
330	Danny Jackson	.05
331	John Kruk	.05
332	Tony Longmire	.05
333	Tom Marsh	.05
334	Mickey Morandini	.05
335	Bobby Munoz	.05
336	Todd Pratt	.05
337	Tom Quinlan	.05
338	Kevin Stocker	.05
339	Fernando Valenzuela	.05
340	Jay Bell	.05
341	Dave Clark	.05
342	Steve Cooke	.05
343	Carlos Garcia	.05
344	Jeff King	.05
345	Jon Lieber	.05
346	Ravelo Manzanillo	.05
347	Al Martin	.05
348	Orlando Merced	.05
349	Denny Neagle	.05
350	Alejandro Pena	.05
351	Don Slaught	.05
352	Zane Smith	.05
353	Andy Van Slyke	.05
354	Rick White	.05
355	Kevin Young	.05
356	Andy Ashby	.05
357	Derek Bell	.05
358	Andy Benes	.05
359	Phil Clark	.05
360	Donnie Elliott	.05
361	Ricky Gutierrez	.05
362	Tony Gwynn	.75
363	Trevor Hoffman	.05
364	Tim Hyers	.05
365	Luis Lopez	.05
366	Jose Martinez	.05
367	Pedro A. Martinez	.05
368	Phil Plantier	.05
369	Bip Roberts	.05
370	A.J. Sager	.05
371	Jeff Tabaka	.05
372	Todd Benzinger	.05
373	Barry Bonds	2.00

374	John Burkett	.05
375	Mark Carreon	.05
376	Royce Clayton	.05
377	Pat Gomez	.05
378	Erik Johnson	.05
379	Darren Lewis	.05
380	Kirt Manwaring	.05
381	Dave Martinez	.05
382	John Patterson	.05
383	Mark Portugal	.05
384	Darryl Strawberry	.05
385	Salomon Torres	.05
386	Bill Van Landingham	.05
387	Matt Williams	.05
388	Rich Amaral	.05
389	Bobby Ayala	.05
390	Mike Blowers	.05
391	Chris Bosio	.05
392	Jay Buhner	.05
393	Jim Converse	.05
394	Tim Davis	.05
395	Felix Fermin	.05
396	Dave Fleming	.05
397	Goose Gossage	.05
398	Ken Griffey Jr.	1.00
399	Randy Johnson	.60
400	Edgar Martinez	.05
401	Tino Martinez	.05
402	Alex Rodriguez	1.50
403	Dan Wilson	.05
404	Luis Alicea	.05
405	Rene Arocha	.05
406	Bernard Gilkey	.05
407	Gregg Jefferies	.05
408	Ray Lankford	.05
409	Terry McGriff	.05
410	Omar Olivares	.05
411	Jose Oquendo	.05
412	Vicente Palacios	.05
413	Geronimo Pena	.05
414	Mike Perez	.05
415	Gerald Perry	.05
416	Ozzie Smith	.75
417	Bob Tewksbury	.05
418	Mark Whiten	.05
419	Todd Zeile	.05
420	Esteban Beltre	.05
421	Kevin Brown	.05
422	Cris Carpenter	.05
423	Will Clark	.05
424	Hector Fajardo	.05
425	Jeff Frye	.05
426	Juan Gonzalez	.30
427	Rusty Greer	.05
428	Rick Honeycutt	.05
429	David Hulse	.05
430	Manny Lee	.05
431	Junior Ortiz	.05
432	Dean Palmer	.05
433	Ivan Rodriguez	.50
434	Dan Smith	.05
435	Roberto Alomar	.15
436	Pat Borders	.05
437	Scott Brow	.05
438	Rob Butler	.05
439	Joe Carter	.05
440	Tony Castillo	.05
441	Domingo Cedeno	.05
442	Brad Cornett	.05
443	Carlos Delgado	.35
444	Alex Gonzalez	.05
445	Juan Guzman	.05
446	Darren Hall	.05
447	Paul Molitor	.60
448	John Olerud	.05
449	Robert Perez	.05
450	Devon White	.05

Gold Crown Die-Cut

A die-cut gold holographic foil crown in the background is featured in this chase set. The player's name at bottom is rendered in the same foil. Backs have a dark blue background, a portrait photo and a 1994 season recap.

		NM/M
Complete Set (20):		30.00
Common Player:		.45
1	Greg Maddux	2.50
2	Fred McGriff	.45
3	Rafael Palmeiro	1.50
4	Cal Ripken Jr.	4.50
5	Jose Canseco	1.00
6	Frank Thomas	2.00
7	Albert Belle	.45
8	Manny Ramirez	2.00
9	Andres Galarraga	.45
10	Jeff Bagwell	2.00
11	Chan Ho Park	.45
12	Raul Mondesi	.45
13	Mike Piazza	3.00
14	Kirby Puckett	2.50
15	Barry Bonds	4.50
16	Ken Griffey Jr.	3.00
17	Alex Rodriguez	3.50
18	Juan Gonzalez	1.00
19	Roberto Alomar	1.00
20	Carlos Delgado	1.25

Hot Hispanics

Acknowledging its bilingual card license and market niche, this insert set of Latinos Destacados (Hot Hispanics) features top Latin players in the majors. The series logo and a gold-foil holographic player name rise from a row of flames at bottom-front. On the reverse is another player photo, on an inferno background, along with 1994 season highlights and a large team logo.

		NM/M
Complete Set (36):		20.00
Common Player:		.25
1	Roberto Alomar	1.25
2	Moises Alou	.25
3	Wilson Alvarez	.25
4	Carlos Baerga	.25
5	Geronimo Berroa	.25
6	Jose Canseco	1.00
7	Hector Carrasco	.25
8	Wil Cordero	.25
9	Carlos Delgado	1.50
10	Damion Easley	.25
11	Tony Eusebio	.25
12	Hector Fajardo	.25
13	Andres Galarraga	.25
14	Carlos Garcia	.25
15	Chris Gomez	.25
16	Alex Gonzalez	.25
17	Juan Gonzalez	1.25
18	Luis Gonzalez	.25
19	Felix Jose	.25
20	Javier Lopez	.25
21	Luis Lopez	.25
22	Dennis Martinez	.25
23	Orlando Miller	.25
24	Raul Mondesi	.25
25	Jose Oliva	.25
26	Rafael Palmeiro	2.00
27	Yorkis Perez	.25
28	Manny Ramirez	2.50
29	Jose Rijo	.25
30	Alex Rodriguez	4.00
31	Ivan Rodriguez	2.00
32	Carlos Rodriguez	.25
33	Sammy Sosa	3.00
34	Tony Tarasco	.25
35	Ismael Valdes	.25
36	Bernie Williams	.25

Marquee Prism

Etched gold holographic foil is the background to the action photos in this insert set. Player names at bottom-front are shadowed in team colors. Backs repeat the front photo in miniature version in a box at one side that offers career stats and a highlight. On the other end is a portrait photo on a background of baseballs.

		NM/M
Complete Set (36):		22.50
Common Player:		.35
1	Jose Canseco	.65
2	Gregg Jefferies	.35
3	Fred McGriff	.35
4	Joe Carter	.35
5	Tim Salmon	.35
6	Wade Boggs	1.25
7	Dave Winfield	1.00
8	Bob Hamelin	.35
9	Cal Ripken Jr.	3.00
10	Don Mattingly	1.50
11	Juan Gonzalez	.50
12	Carlos Delgado	.65
13	Barry Bonds	3.00
14	Albert Belle	.35
15	Raul Mondesi	.35
16	Jeff Bagwell	1.00
17	Mike Piazza	1.50
18	Rafael Palmeiro	.75
19	Frank Thomas	1.00
20	Matt Williams	.35
21	Ken Griffey Jr.	2.00
22	Will Clark	.35
23	Bobby Bonilla	.35
24	Kenny Lofton	.35
25	Paul Molitor	1.00
26	Kirby Puckett	1.25
27	Dave Justice	.35
28	Jeff Conine	.35
29	Bret Boone	.35
30	Larry Walker	.35
31	Cecil Fielder	.35
32	Manny Ramirez	1.00
33	Javier Lopez	.35
34	Jimmy Key	.35
35	Andres Galarraga	.35
36	Tony Gwynn	1.25

1995 Pacific Prism

The rainbow prismatic foil background on the card fronts provides the visual punch to Pacific's premium brand cards. In a throwback to the 1950s, the cards were sold in single-card packs for $1.75. Production was limited to 2,999 cases of 36-pack boxes. Backs have a large portrait photo on a conventionally printed rainbow background. In keeping with the company's license, the 1994 season summary printed at bottom on back is in both English and Spanish. One checklist, team or Pacific logo was inserted into each pack to protect the Prism card.

		NM/M
Complete Set (144):		65.00
Common Player:		.25
Pack (2):		.60
Wax Box (36):		12.50
1	Dave Justice	.25
2	Ryan Klesko	.25
3	Javier Lopez	.25
4	Greg Maddux	2.00
5	Fred McGriff	.25
6	Tony Tarasco	.25
7	Jeffrey Hammonds	.25
8	Mike Mussina	.75
9	Rafael Palmeiro	1.25
10	Cal Ripken Jr.	5.00
11	Lee Smith	.25
12	Roger Clemens	2.50
13	Scott Cooper	.25
14	Mike Greenwell	.25
15	Carlos Rodriguez	.25
16	Mo Vaughn	.25
17	Chili Davis	.25
18	Jim Edmonds	.25
19	Jorge Fabregas	.25
20	Bo Jackson	.35
21	Tim Salmon	.25
22	Mark Grace	.25
23	Jose Guzman	.25
24	Randy Myers	.25
25	Rey Sanchez	.25
26	Sammy Sosa	2.50
27	Wilson Alvarez	.25
28	Julio Franco	.25
29	Ozzie Guillen	.25
30	Jack McDowell	.25
31	Frank Thomas	1.50
32	Bret Boone	.25
33	Barry Larkin	.25
34	Hal Morris	.25
35	Jose Rijo	.25
36	Deion Sanders	.25
37	Carlos Baerga	.25
38	Albert Belle	.25
39	Kenny Lofton	.25
40	Dennis Martinez	.25
41	Manny Ramirez	1.50
42	Omar Vizquel	.25
43	Dante Bichette	.25
44	Marvin Freeman	.25
45	Andres Galarraga	.25
46	Mike Kingery	.25
47	Danny Bautista	.25
48	Cecil Fielder	.25
49	Travis Fryman	.25
50	Tony Phillips	.25
51	Alan Trammell	.25
52	Lou Whitaker	.25
53	Alex Arias	.25
54	Bret Barberie	.25
55	Jeff Conine	.25
56	Charles Johnson	.25
57	Gary Sheffield	.65
58	Jeff Bagwell	1.50
59	Craig Biggio	.25
60	Doug Drabek	.25
61	Tony Eusebio	.25
62	Luis Gonzalez	.25
63	David Cone	.25
64	Bob Hamelin	.25
65	Felix Jose	.25
66	Wally Joyner	.25
67	Brian McRae	.25
68	Brett Butler	.25
69	Garey Ingram	.25
70	Ramon Martinez	.25
71	Raul Mondesi	.25
72	Mike Piazza	2.50
73	Henry Rodriguez	.25
74	Ricky Bones	.25
75	Pat Listach	.25
76	Dave Nilsson	.25
77	Jose Valentin	.25
78	Rick Aguilera	.25
79	Denny Hocking	.25
80	Shane Mack	.25
81	Pedro Munoz	.25
82	Kirby Puckett	2.00
83	Dave Winfield	1.50
84	Moises Alou	.25
85	Wil Cordero	.25
86	Cliff Floyd	.25
87	Marquis Grissom	.25
88	Pedro Martinez	1.50
89	Larry Walker	.25
90	Bobby Bonilla	.25
91	Jeromy Burnitz	.25
92	John Franco	.25
93	Jeff Kent	.25
94	Jose Vizcaino	.25
95	Wade Boggs	2.00
96	Jimmy Key	.25
97	Don Mattingly	2.50
98	Paul O'Neill	.25
99	Luis Polonia	.25
100	Danny Tartabull	.25
101	Geronimo Berroa	.25
102	Rickey Henderson	1.50
103	Ruben Sierra	.25
104	Terry Steinbach	.25
105	Darren Daulton	.25
106	Mariano Duncan	.25
107	Lenny Dykstra	.25
108	Mike Lieberthal	.25
109	Tony Longmire	.25
110	Tom Marsh	.25
111	Jay Bell	.25
112	Carlos Garcia	.25
113	Orlando Merced	.25
114	Andy Van Slyke	.25
115	Derek Bell	.25
116	Tony Gwynn	2.00
117	Luis Lopez	.25
118	Bip Roberts	.25
119	Rod Beck	.25
120	Barry Bonds	5.00
121	Darryl Strawberry	.25
122	Bill Van Landingham	.25
123	Matt Williams	.25
124	Jay Buhner	.25
125	Felix Fermin	.25
126	Ken Griffey Jr.	3.00
127	Randy Johnson	1.50
128	Edgar Martinez	.25
129	Alex Rodriguez	4.00
130	Rene Arocha	.25
131	Gregg Jefferies	.25
132	Mike Perez	.25
133	Ozzie Smith	2.00
134	Jose Canseco	.65
135	Will Clark	.25
136	Juan Gonzalez	1.00
137	Ivan Rodriguez	1.25
138	Roberto Alomar	.50
139	Joe Carter	.25
140	Carlos Delgado	.75
141	Alex Gonzalez	.25
142	Juan Guzman	.25
143	Paul Molitor	1.50
144	John Olerud	.25

Team Logos

Inserted one card per pack to provide some protection to the Prism card was a checklist, team or Pacific logo card. The large color logos are on a background of a playing field. Backs have a short English/Spanish history of the team.

		NM/M
Complete Set (31):		2.00
Common Player:		.10
1	Baltimore Orioles	.10
2	Boston Red Sox	.10
3	California Angels	.10
4	Chicago White Sox	.10
5	Cleveland Indians	.10
6	Detroit Tigers	.10
7	Kansas City Royals	.10
8	Milwaukee Brewers	.10
9	Minnesota Twins	.10
10	New York Yankees	.10
11	Oakland Athletics	.10
12	Seattle Mariners	.10
13	Texas Rangers	.10
14	Toronto Blue Jays	.10
15	Atlanta Braves	.10
16	Chicago Cubs	.10
17	Cincinnati Reds	.10
18	Colorado Rockies	.10
19	Florida Marlins	.10
20	Houston Astros	.10
21	Los Angeles Dodgers	.10
22	Montreal Expos	.10
23	New York Mets	.10
24	Philadelphia Phillies	.10
25	Pittsburgh Pirates	.10
26	St. Louis Cardinals	.10
27	San Diego Padres	.10
28	San Francisco Giants	.10
1	Checklist 1-72	.05
2	Checklist 73-144	.05
---	Pacific Logo Card	.05

Mariners Memories

To commemorate the M's magical 1995 season leading up to the A.L. Western Division pennant and the American League championship series, Pacific issued this boxed set. The first 17 cards in the set depict post-season action, with backs done in newspaper style. The rest of the set features the individual players in borderless action photos on front and smaller color portraits on back. All cards feature silver-foil highlights on front. The set was sold in a team-colors cardboard box. The set was released in late December and includes full 1995 stats for the players.

		NM/M
Complete Set (50):		10.00
Common Player:		.10
1	Griffey slams M's to brink (Ken Griffey Jr.)	.50
2	Mariners clinch tie in Texas (Vince Coleman)	.10
3	Mariners win the West (Luis Sojo)	.10
4	At last, something to celebrate (Randy Johnson)	.25
5	Johnson stands tall (Randy Johnson)	.25
6	Griffey has big debut (Ken Griffey Jr.)	.50
7	Tino ignites Mariners (Edgar Martinez, Tino Martinez)	.10
8	Mariners tie Yankee series (Edgar Martinez)	.10
9	Griffey scores winning run (Ken Griffey Jr.)	.50
10	Thunder in the Kingdome	.10
11	Series win ends years of futility	.10
12	Bob who? beats Cleveland (Bob Wolcott)	.10
13	Buhner rocks Cleveland (Jay Buhner)	.10
14	Johnson salutes Kingdome crowd (Randy Johnson)	.25
15	Fans give their all (Lou Piniella)	.10
16	Cora eludes tag (Joey Cora)	.10
17	Voice of M's calls winner (Dave Niehaus)	.10
18	Rich Amaral	.10
19	Bobby Ayala	.10
20	Tim Belcher	.10
21	Andy Benes	.10
22	Mike Blowers	.10
23	Chris Bosio	.10
24	Darren Bragg	.10
25	Jay Buhner	.25
26	Rafael Carmona	.10
27	Norm Charlton	.10
28	Vince Coleman	.10
29	Joey Cora	.10
30	Alex Diaz	.10
31	Felix Fermin	.10
32	Ken Griffey Jr.	3.00
33	Lee Guetterman	.10
34	Randy Johnson	3.00
35	Edgar Martinez	.25
36	Tino Martinez	.25
37	Jeff Nelson	.10
38	Warren Newson	.10
39	Greg Pirkl	.10
40	Arquimedez Pozo	.10
41	Bill Risley	.10
42	Alex Rodriguez (Rodriguez)	5.00
43	Luis Sojo	.10
44	Doug Strange	.10
45	Salomon Torres	.10
46	Bob Wells	.10
47	Chris Widger	.10
48	Dan Wilson	.10
49	Bob Wolcott	.10
50	Lou Piniella	.25

1996 Pacific Crown

Pacific's base set for 1996 features 450 gold-foil enhanced cards. Fronts have borderless game-action photos with the issuer's logo in an upper corner and the player's name at bottom center in gold. Horizontal backs have a portrait photo at right, career highlights in both English and Spanish at left, and 1995 stats at top. Cards were sold in 12-card foil packs which could include one of six types of insert cards.

	NM/M
Complete Set (450):	17.50
Common Player:	.05
Pack (12):	1.00
Wax Box (36):	25.00

#	Player	Price
1	Steve Avery	.05
2	Ryan Klesko	.05
3	Pedro Borbon	.05
4	Chipper Jones	1.00
5	Kent Mercker	.05
6	Greg Maddux	1.00
7	Greg McMichael	.05
8	Mark Wohlers	.05
9	Fred McGriff	.05
10	John Smoltz	.05
11	Rafael Belliard	.05
12	Mark Lemke	.05
13	Tom Glavine	.30
14	Javier Lopez	.05
15	Jeff Blauser	.05
16	Dave Justice	.05
17	Marquis Grissom	.05
18	Greg Maddux (NL Cy Young)	.50
19	Randy Myers	.05
20	Scott Servais	.05
21	Sammy Sosa	1.00
22	Kevin Foster	.05
23	Jose Hernandez	.05
24	Jim Bullinger	.05
25	Mike Perez	.05
26	Shawon Dunston	.05
27	Rey Sanchez	.05
28	Frank Castillo	.05
29	Jaime Navarro	.05
30	Brian McRae	.05
31	Mark Grace	.05
32	Roberto Rivera	.05
33	Luis Gonzalez	.05
34	Hector Carrasco	.05
35	Bret Boone	.05
36	Thomas Howard	.05
37	Hal Morris	.05
38	John Smiley	.05
39	Jeff Brantley	.05
40	Barry Larkin	.05
41	Mariano Duncan	.05
42	Xavier Hernandez	.05
43	Pete Schourek	.05
44	Reggie Sanders	.05
45	Dave Burba	.05
46	Jeff Branson	.05
47	Mark Portugal	.05
48	Ron Gant	.05
49	Benito Santiago	.05
50	Barry Larkin (NL MVP)	.05
51	Steve Reed	.05
52	Kevin Ritz	.05
53	Dante Bichette	.05
54	Darren Holmes	.05
55	Ellis Burks	.05
56	Walt Weiss	.05
57	Armando Reynoso	.05
58	Vinny Castilla	.05
59	Jason Bates	.05
60	Mike Kingery	.05
61	Bryan Rekar	.05
62	Curtis Leskanic	.05
63	Bret Saberhagen	.05
64	Andres Galarraga	.05
65	Larry Walker	.05
66	Joe Girardi	.05
67	Quilvio Veras	.05
68	Robb Nen	.05
69	Mario Diaz	.05
70	Chuck Carr	.05
71	Alex Arias	.05
72	Pat Rapp	.05
73	Rich Garces	.05
74	Kurt Abbott	.05
75	Andre Dawson	.25
76	Greg Colbrunn	.05
77	John Burkett	.05
78	Terry Pendleton	.05
79	Jesus Tavarez	.05
80	Charles Johnson	.05
81	Yorkis Perez	.05
82	Jeff Conine	.05
83	Gary Sheffield	.45
84	Brian Hunter	.05
85	Derrick May	.05
86	Greg Swindell	.05
87	Derek Bell	.05
88	Dave Veres	.05
89	Jeff Bagwell	.75
90	Todd Jones	.05
91	Orlando Miller	.05
92	Pedro A. Martinez	.05
93	Tony Eusebio	.05
94	Craig Biggio	.05
95	Shane Reynolds	.05
96	James Mouton	.05
97	Doug Drabek	.05
98	Dave Magadan	.05
99	Ricky Gutierrez	.05
100	Hideo Nomo	.50
101	Delino DeShields	.05
102	Tom Candiotti	.05
103	Mike Piazza	1.50
104	Ramon Martinez	.05
105	Pedro Astacio	.05
106	Chad Fonville	.05
107	Raul Mondesi	.05
108	Ismael Valdes	.05
109	Jose Offerman	.05
110	Todd Worrell	.05
111	Eric Karros	.05
112	Brett Butler	.05
113	Juan Castro	.05
114	Roberto Kelly	.05
115	Omar Daal	.05
116	Antonio Osuna	.05
117	Hideo Nomo (NL Rookie of Year)	.50
118	Mike Lansing	.05
119	Mel Rojas	.05
120	Sean Berry	.05
121	David Segui	.05
122	Tavo Alvarez	.05
123	Pedro Martinez	.75
124	F.P. Santangelo **RC**	.05
125	Rondell White	.05
126	Cliff Floyd	.05
127	Henry Rodriguez	.05
128	Tony Tarasco	.05
129	Yamil Benitez	.05
130	Carlos Perez	.05
131	Wil Cordero	.05
132	Jeff Fassero	.05
133	Moises Alou	.05
134	John Franco	.05
135	Rico Brogna	.05
136	Dave Mlicki	.05
137	Bill Pulsipher	.05
138	Jose Vizcaino	.05
139	Carl Everett	.05
140	Edgardo Alfonzo	.05
141	Bobby Jones	.05
142	Alberto Castillo	.05
143	Joe Orsulak	.05
144	Jeff Kent	.05
145	Ryan Thompson	.05
146	Jason Isringhausen	.05
147	Todd Hundley	.05
148	Alex Ochoa	.05
149	Charlie Hayes	.05
150	Michael Mimbs	.05
151	Darren Daulton	.05
152	Toby Borland	.05
153	Andy Van Slyke	.05
154	Mickey Morandini	.05
155	Sid Fernandez	.05
156	Tom Marsh	.05
157	Kevin Stocker	.05
158	Paul Quantrill	.05
159	Gregg Jefferies	.05
160	Ricky Bottalico	.05
161	Lenny Dykstra	.05
162	Mark Whiten	.05
163	Tyler Green	.05
164	Jim Eisenreich	.05
165	Heathcliff Slocumb	.05
166	Esteban Loaiza	.05
167	Rich Aude	.05
168	Jason Christiansen	.05
169	Ramon Morel	.05
170	Orlando Merced	.05
171	Paul Wagner	.05
172	Jeff King	.05
173	Jay Bell	.05
174	Jacob Brumfield	.05
175	Nelson Liriano	.05
176	Dan Miceli	.05
177	Carlos Garcia	.05
178	Denny Neagle	.05
179	Angelo Encarnacion	.05
180	Al Martin	.05
181	Midre Cummings	.05
182	Eddie Williams	.05
183	Roberto Petagine	.05
184	Tony Gwynn	1.00
185	Andy Ashby	.05
186	Melvin Nieves	.05
187	Phil Clark	.05
188	Brad Ausmus	.05
189	Bip Roberts	.05
190	Fernando Valenzuela	.05
191	Marc Newfield	.05
192	Steve Finley	.05
193	Trevor Hoffman	.05
194	Andujar Cedeno	.05
195	Jody Reed	.05
196	Ken Caminiti	.05
197	Joey Hamilton	.05
198	Tony Gwynn (NL Batting Champ)	.50
199	Shawn Barton	.05
200	Deion Sanders	.05
201	Rikkert Faneyte	.05
202	Barry Bonds	2.50
203	Matt Williams	.05
204	Jose Bautista	.05
205	Mark Leiter	.05
206	Mark Carreon	.05
207	Robby Thompson	.05
208	Terry Mulholland	.05
209	Rod Beck	.05
210	Royce Clayton	.05
211	J.R. Phillips	.05
212	Kirt Manwaring	.05
213	Glenallen Hill	.05
214	William Van Landingham	.05
215	Scott Cooper	.05
216	Bernard Gilkey	.05
217	Allen Watson	.05
218	Donovan Osborne	.05
219	Ray Lankford	.05
220	Tony Fossas	.05
221	Tom Pagnozzi	.05
222	John Mabry	.05
223	Tripp Cromer	.05
224	Mark Petkovsek	.05
225	Mike Morgan	.05
226	Ozzie Smith	1.00
227	Tom Henke	.05
228	Jose Oquendo	.05
229	Brian Jordan	.05
230	Cal Ripken Jr.	2.50
231	Scott Erickson	.05
232	Harold Baines	.05
233	Jeff Manto	.05
234	Jesse Orosco	.05
235	Jeffrey Hammonds	.05
236	Brady Anderson	.05
237	Manny Alexander	.05
238	Chris Hoiles	.05
239	Rafael Palmeiro	.60
240	Ben McDonald	.05
241	Curtis Goodwin	.05
242	Bobby Bonilla	.05
243	Mike Mussina	.60
244	Kevin Brown	.05
245	Armando Benitez	.05
246	Jose Canseco	.50
247	Erik Hanson	.05
248	Mo Vaughn	.05
249	Tim Naehring	.05
250	Vaughn Eshelman	.05
251	Mike Greenwell	.05
252	Troy O'Leary	.05
253	Tim Wakefield	.05
254	Dwayne Hosey	.05
255	John Valentin	.05
256	Rick Aguilera	.05
257	Mike MacFarlane	.05
258	Roger Clemens	1.50
259	Luis Alicea	.05
260	Mo Vaughn (AL MVP)	.05
261	Mark Langston	.05
262	Jim Edmonds	.05
263	Rod Correia	.05
264	Tim Salmon	.05
265	J.T. Snow	.05
266	Orlando Palmeiro	.05
267	Jorge Fabregas	.05
268	Jim Abbott	.05
269	Eduardo Perez	.05
270	Lee Smith	.05
271	Gary DiSarcina	.05
272	Damion Easley	.05
273	Tony Phillips	.05
274	Garret Anderson	.05
275	Chuck Finley	.05
276	Chili Davis	.05
277	Lance Johnson	.05
278	Alex Fernandez	.05
279	Robin Ventura	.05
280	Chris Snopek	.05
281	Brian Keyser	.05
282	Lyle Mouton	.05
283	Luis Andujar **RC**	.05
284	Tim Raines	.05
285	Larry Thomas	.05
286	Ozzie Guillen	.05
287	Frank Thomas	.75
288	Roberto Hernandez	.05
289	Dave Martinez	.05
290	Ray Durham	.05
291	Ron Karkovice	.05
292	Wilson Alvarez	.05
293	Omar Vizquel	.05
294	Eddie Murray	.75
295	Sandy Alomar	.05
296	Orel Hershiser	.05
297	Jose Mesa	.05
298	Julian Tavarez	.05
299	Dennis Martinez	.05
300	Carlos Baerga	.05
301	Manny Ramirez	.75
302	Jim Thome	.60
303	Kenny Lofton	.05
304	Tony Pena	.05
305	Alvaro Espinoza	.05
306	Paul Sorrento	.05
307	Albert Belle	.05
308	Danny Bautista	.05
309	Chris Gomez	.05
310	Jose Lima	.05
311	Phil Nevin	.05
312	Alan Trammell	.05
313	Chad Curtis	.05
314	John Flaherty	.05
315	Travis Fryman	.05
316	Todd Steverson	.05
317	Brian Bohanon	.05
318	Lou Whitaker	.05
319	Bobby Higginson	.05
320	Steve Rodriguez	.05
321	Cecil Fielder	.05
322	Felipe Lira	.05
323	Juan Samuel	.05
324	Bob Hamelin	.05
325	Tom Goodwin	.05
326	Johnny Damon	.25
327	Hipolito Pichardo	.05
328	Dilson Torres	.05
329	Kevin Appier	.05
330	Mark Gubicza	.05
331	Jon Nunnally	.05
332	Gary Gaetti	.05
333	Brent Mayne	.05
334	Brent Cookson	.05
335	Tom Gordon	.05
336	Wally Joyner	.05
337	Greg Gagne	.05
338	Fernando Vina	.05
339	Joe Oliver	.05
340	John Jaha	.05
341	Jeff Cirillo	.05
342	Pat Listach	.05
343	Dave Nilsson	.05
344	Steve Sparks	.05
345	Ricky Bones	.05
346	David Hulse	.05
347	Scott Karl	.05
348	Darryl Hamilton	.05
349	B.J. Surhoff	.05
350	Angel Miranda	.05
351	Sid Roberson	.05
352	Matt Mieske	.05
353	Jose Valentin **RC**	.05
354	Matt Lawton **RC**	.25
355	Eddie Guardado	.05
356	Brad Radke	.05
357	Pedro Munoz	.05
358	Scott Stahoviak	.05
359	Erik Schullstrom	.05
360	Pat Meares	.05
361	Marty Cordova	.05
362	Scott Leius	.05
363	Matt Walbeck	.05
364	Rich Becker	.05
365	Kirby Puckett	1.00
366	Oscar Munoz	.05
367	Chuck Knoblauch	.05
368	Marty Cordova (AL Rookie of Year)	.05
369	Bernie Williams	.05
370	Mike Stanley	.05
371	Andy Pettitte	.25
372	Jack McDowell	.05
373	Sterling Hitchcock	.05
374	David Cone	.05
375	Randy Velarde	.05
376	Don Mattingly	1.50
377	Melido Perez	.05
378	Wade Boggs	1.00
379	Ruben Sierra	.05
380	Tony Fernandez	.05
381	John Wetteland	.05
382	Mariano Rivera	.15
383	Derek Jeter	2.50
384	Paul O'Neill	.05
385	Mark McGwire	2.00
386	Scott Brosius	.05
387	Don Wengert	.05
388	Terry Steinbach	.05
389	Brent Gates	.05
390	Craig Paquette	.05
391	Mike Bordick	.05
392	Ariel Prieto	.05
393	Dennis Eckersley	.65
394	Carlos Reyes	.05
395	Todd Stottlemyre	.05
396	Rickey Henderson	.75
397	Geronimo Berroa	.05
398	Steve Ontiveros	.05
399	Mike Gallego	.05
400	Stan Javier	.05
401	Randy Johnson	.75
402	Norm Charlton	.05
403	Mike Blowers	.05
404	Tino Martinez	.05
405	Dan Wilson	.05
406	Andy Benes	.05
407	Alex Diaz	.05
408	Edgar Martinez	.05
409	Chris Bosio	.05
410	Ken Griffey Jr.	1.50
411	Luis Sojo	.05
412	Bob Wolcott	.05
413	Vince Coleman	.05
414	Rich Amaral	.05
415	Jay Buhner	.05
416	Alex Rodriguez	2.00
417	Joey Cora	.05
418	Randy Johnson (AL Cy Young)	.25
419	Edgar Martinez (AL Batting Champ)	.05
420	Ivan Rodriguez	.65
421	Mark McLemore	.05
422	Mickey Tettleton	.05
423	Juan Gonzalez	.40
424	Will Clark	.05
425	Kevin Gross	.05
426	Dean Palmer	.05
427	Kenny Rogers	.05
428	Bob Tewksbury	.05
429	Benji Gil	.05
430	Jeff Russell	.05
431	Rusty Greer	.05
432	Roger Pavlik	.05
433	Esteban Beltre	.05
434	Otis Nixon	.05
435	Paul Molitor	.75
436	Carlos Delgado	.50
437	Ed Sprague	.05
438	Juan Guzman	.05
439	Domingo Cedeno	.05
440	Pat Hentgen	.05
441	Tomas Perez	.05
442	John Olerud	.05
443	Shawn Green	.25
444	Al Leiter	.05
445	Joe Carter	.05
446	Robert Perez	.05
447	Devon White	.05
448	Tony Castillo	.05
449	Alex Gonzalez	.05
450	Roberto Alomar	.20
450p	Roberto Alomar (Unmarked promo card, "Games: 128" on back.)	1.50

Cramer's Choice

One of the most unusually shaped baseball cards of all time is the Cramer's Choice insert set from the 1996 Pacific Crown Collection. The set features the 10 best players as

chosen by Pacific founder and president, Mike Cramer. Cards are in a die-cut pyramidal design 3-1/2" tall and 2-1/2" at the base. They player picture on front is set against a silver-foil background, while the player name and other information is in gold foil on a faux marble base at bottom; the effect is a simulation of a trophy. Backs repeat the marbled background and have a bilingual justification from Cramer concerning his choice of the player as one of the 10 best. Average insertion rate is one card per case (720 packs). Cards are numbered with a "CC" prefix.

		NM/M
Complete Set (10):		150.00
Common Player:		6.00
1	Roberto Alomar	7.50
2	Wade Boggs	15.00
3	Cal Ripken Jr.	30.00
4	Greg Maddux	15.00
5	Frank Thomas	12.50
6	Tony Gwynn	15.00
7	Mike Piazza	20.00
8	Ken Griffey Jr.	25.00
9	Manny Ramirez	12.50
10	Edgar Martinez	6.00

Estrellas Latinas

Three dozen of the best contemporary Latino ballplayers are honored in this chase set. Cards feature action photos silhouetted on a black background shot through with gold-foil streaks and stars. The player name, set and insert set logos are in gold at left. Backs have a portrait photo and English/Spanish career summary. The Latino Stars insert cards are inserted at an average rate of one per nine packs; about four per foil box. Cards are numbered with an "EL" prefix.

		NM/M
Complete Set (36):		16.00
Common Player:		.25
1	Roberto Alomar	.50
2	Moises Alou	.25
3	Carlos Baerga	.25
4	Geronimo Berroa	.25
5	Ricky Bones	.25
6	Bobby Bonilla	.25
7	Jose Canseco	.65
8	Vinny Castilla	.25
9	Pedro Martinez	1.50
10	John Valentin	.25
11	Andres Galarraga	.25
12	Juan Gonzalez	.75
13	Ozzie Guillen	.25
14	Esteban Loaiza	.25
15	Javier Lopez	.25
16	Dennis Martinez	.25
17	Edgar Martinez	.25
18	Tino Martinez	.25
19	Orlando Merced	.25
20	Jose Mesa	.25
21	Raul Mondesi	.25
22	Jaime Navarro	.25
23	Rafael Palmeiro	.75
24	Carlos Perez	.25
25	Manny Ramirez	1.50
26	Alex Rodriguez	3.50
27	Ivan Rodriguez	1.25
28	David Segui	.25
29	Ruben Sierra	.25
30	Sammy Sosa	2.00
31	Julian Tavarez	.25
32	Ismael Valdes	.25
33	Fernando Valenzuela	.25
34	Quilvio Veras	.25
35	Omar Vizquel	.25
36	Bernie Williams	.25

Gold Crown Die-Cuts

One of Pacific's most popular inserts of the previous year returns in 1996. The Gold Crown die-cuts have the top of the card cut away to form a gold-foil crown design with an action photo below. The player's name is also in gold foil. Backs repeat the gold crown design at top, have a portrait photo at lower-right and a few words about the player, in both English and Spanish. Insertion rate was advertised as one per 37 packs, on average. Cards are numbered with a "DC" prefix.

		NM/M
Complete Set (36):		45.00
Common Player:		.75
1	Roberto Alomar	1.00
2	Will Clark	.75
3	Johnny Damon	1.00
4	Don Mattingly	2.50
5	Edgar Martinez	.75
6	Manny Ramirez	1.50
7	Mike Piazza	2.50
8	Quilvio Veras	.75
9	Rickey Henderson	1.50
10	Jeff Bagwell	1.50
11	Andres Galarraga	.75
12	Tim Salmon	.75
13	Ken Griffey Jr.	2.50
14	Sammy Sosa	2.00
15	Cal Ripken Jr.	4.50
16	Raul Mondesi	.75
17	Jose Canseco	1.00
18	Frank Thomas	1.50
19	Hideo Nomo	1.00
20	Wade Boggs	2.00
21	Reggie Sanders	.75
22	Carlos Baerga	.75
23	Mo Vaughn	.75
24	Ivan Rodriguez	1.25
25	Kirby Puckett	2.00
26	Albert Belle	.75
27	Vinny Castilla	.75
28	Greg Maddux	2.00
29	Dante Bichette	.75
30	Deion Sanders	.75
31	Chipper Jones	2.00
32	Cecil Fielder	.75
33	Randy Johnson	1.50
34	Mark McGwire	3.50
35	Tony Gwynn	2.00
36	Barry Bonds	4.50

Hometown of the Players

The hometown roots of 20 top players are examined in this chase set. Fronts have action photos with large areas of the background replaced with textured gold foil, including solid and outline versions of the player's name. Backs have a portrait photo, a representation of the player's native flag and a few

words about his hometown. Card numbers have an "HP" prefix and are inserted at an average rate of one per 18 packs; about two per box.

		NM/M
Complete Set (20):		15.00
Common Player:		.50
1	Mike Piazza	1.50
2	Greg Maddux	1.00
3	Tony Gwynn	1.00
4	Carlos Baerga	.50
5	Don Mattingly	1.50
6	Cal Ripken Jr.	2.50
7	Chipper Jones	1.00
8	Andres Galarraga	.50
9	Manny Ramirez	.75
10	Roberto Alomar	.60
11	Ken Griffey Jr.	1.50
12	Jose Canseco	.60
13	Frank Thomas	.75
14	Vinny Castilla	.50
15	Roberto Kelly	.50
16	Dennis Martinez	.50
17	Kirby Puckett	1.00
18	Raul Mondesi	.50
19	Hideo Nomo	.60
20	Edgar Martinez	.50

Milestones

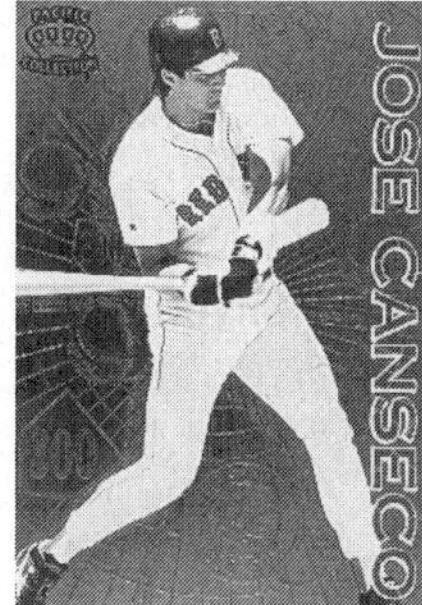

A textured metallic blue-foil background is featured on this insert set. Behind the player action photo is a spider's web design with flying baseballs, team logo and a number representing the milestone. The player's name is in purple foil, outlined in white, vertically at right. Backs have a portrait photo and bilingual description of the milestone. Average insertion rate for this insert series is one per 37 packs. Cards are numbered with a "M" prefix.

		NM/M
Complete Set (10):		12.50
Common Player:		.50
1	Albert Belle	.50
2	Don Mattingly	2.25
3	Tony Gwynn	2.00
4	Jose Canseco	1.00
5	Marty Cordova	.50
6	Wade Boggs	2.00
7	Greg Maddux	2.00
8	Eddie Murray	1.50
9	Ken Griffey Jr.	2.50
10	Cal Ripken Jr.	3.00

October Moments

Post-season baseball has never been better represented on a card than in Pacific's "October Moments" chase set. Action photos are set against a background of a stadium decked in the traditional Fall Classic bunting, all rendered in metallic copper foil. At bot-

tom is a textured silver strip with the player name in copper and a swirl of fallen leaves. Backs have a repeat of the leaves and bunting themes with a player portrait at center and English/Spanish description of his October heroics. These cards are found at an average rate of once per 37 packs. Cards are numbered with an "OM" prefix.

		NM/M
Complete Set (20):		30.00
Common Player:		.60
1	Carlos Baerga	.60
2	Albert Belle	.75
3	Dante Bichette	.60
4	Jose Canseco	1.25
5	Tom Glavine	1.00
6	Ken Griffey Jr.	5.00
7	Randy Johnson	2.50
8	Chipper Jones	3.50
9	Dave Justice	.60
10	Ryan Klesko	.60
11	Kenny Lofton	.60
12	Javier Lopez	.60
13	Greg Maddux	3.50
14	Edgar Martinez	.60
15	Don Mattingly	4.00
16	Hideo Nomo	1.25
17	Mike Piazza	4.00
18	Manny Ramirez	2.50
19	Reggie Sanders	.60
20	Jim Thome	1.50

1996 Pacific Prism

Only the best in baseball make the cut for the Prism checklist. Sold in one-card foil packs the cards feature action photos set against an etched silver-foil background highlighted by slashes approximating team colors. Backs are conventionally printed in a horizontal format with a player portrait photo at left center on a purple background. A short 1995 season recap is feature in both English and Spanish. Card numbers are prefixed with a "P."

		NM/M
Complete Set (144):		50.00
Common Player:		.35
Golds:		1.5X
Pack (2):		.65
Wax Box (36):		20.00
1	Tom Glavine	.75
2	Chipper Jones	2.00
3	David Justice	.35
4	Ryan Klesko	.35
5	Javier Lopez	.35
6	Greg Maddux	2.00
7	Fred McGriff	.35
8	Frank Castillo	.35
9	Luis Gonzalez	.35
10	Mark Grace	.35
11	Brian McRae	.35
12	Jaime Navarro	.35
13	Sammy Sosa	2.00
14	Bret Boone	.35
15	Ron Gant	.35
16	Barry Larkin	.35
17	Reggie Sanders	.35
18	Benito Santiago	.35
19	Dante Bichette	.35
20	Vinny Castilla	.35
21	Andres Galarraga	.35
22	Bryan Rekar	.35
23	Roberto Alomar	1.00
23p	Roberto Alomar ("Azulejos" rather than "Los Azulajos" on back, unmarked promo card.)	1.00
24	Jeff Conine	.35
25	Andre Dawson	.50
26	Charles Johnson	.35
27	Gary Sheffield	1.00
28	Quilvio Veras	.35
29	Jeff Bagwell	1.50
30	Derek Bell	.35
31	Craig Biggio	.35
32	Tony Eusebio	.35
33	Karim Garcia	.35
34	Eric Karros	.35
35	Ramon Martinez	.35
36	Raul Mondesi	.35
37	Hideo Nomo	1.00
38	Mike Piazza	3.00
39	Ismael Valdes	.35
40	Moises Alou	.35
41	Wil Cordero	.35
42	Pedro Martinez	1.50
43	Mel Rojas	.35
44	David Segui	.35
45	Edgardo Alfonzo	.35
46	Rico Brogna	.35
47	John Franco	.35
48	Jason Isringhausen	.35
49	Jose Vizcaino	.35
50	Ricky Bottalico	.35
51	Darren Daulton	.35
52	Lenny Dykstra	.35
53	Tyler Green	.35
54	Gregg Jefferies	.35
55	Jay Bell	.35
56	Jason Christiansen	.35
57	Carlos Garcia	.35
58	Esteban Loaiza	.35
59	Orlando Merced	.35
60	Andujar Cedeno	.35
61	Tony Gwynn	2.00
62	Melvin Nieves	.35
63	Phil Plantier	.35
64	Fernando Valenzuela	.35
65	Barry Bonds	4.50
66	J.R. Phillips	.35
67	Deion Sanders	.35
68	Matt Williams	.35
69	Bernard Gilkey	.35
70	Tom Henke	.35
71	Brian Jordan	.35
72	Ozzie Smith	2.00
73	Manny Alexander	.35
74	Bobby Bonilla	.35
75	Mike Mussina	1.00
76	Rafael Palmeiro	1.00
77	Cal Ripken Jr.	4.50
78	Jose Canseco	1.00
79	Roger Clemens	2.50
80	John Valentin	.35
81	Mo Vaughn	.35
82	Tim Wakefield	.35
83	Garret Anderson	.35
84	Damion Easley	.35
85	Jim Edmonds	.35
86	Tim Salmon	.35
87	Wilson Alvarez	.35
88	Alex Fernandez	.35
89	Ozzie Guillen	.35
90	Roberto Hernandez	.35
91	Frank Thomas	1.50
92	Robin Ventura	.35
93	Carlos Baerga	.35
94	Albert Belle	.35
95	Kenny Lofton	.35
96	Dennis Martinez	.35
97	Eddie Murray	1.50
98	Manny Ramirez	1.50
99	Omar Vizquel	.35
100	Chad Curtis	.35
101	Cecil Fielder	.35
102	Felipe Lira	.35
103	Alan Trammell	.35
104	Kevin Appier	.35
105	Johnny Damon	.35
106	Gary Gaetti	.35
107	Wally Joyner	.35
108	Ricky Bones	.35
109	John Jaha	.35
110	B.J. Surhoff	.35
111	Jose Valentin	.35
112	Fernando Vina	.35
113	Marty Cordova	.35
114	Chuck Knoblauch	.35
115	Scott Leius	.35
116	Pedro Munoz	.35
117	Kirby Puckett	2.00
118	Wade Boggs	2.00
119	Don Mattingly	2.50
120	Jack McDowell	.35
121	Paul O'Neill	.35
122	Ruben Rivera	.35
123	Bernie Williams	.35
124	Geronimo Berroa	.35
125	Rickey Henderson	1.50
126	Mark McGwire	3.50
127	Terry Steinbach	.35
128	Danny Tartabull	.35
129	Jay Buhner	.35
130	Joey Cora	.35
131	Ken Griffey Jr.	3.00
132	Randy Johnson	1.50
133	Edgar Martinez	.35
134	Tino Martinez	.35
135	Will Clark	.35
136	Juan Gonzalez	.75
137	Dean Palmer	.35
138	Ivan Rodriguez	1.25
139	Mickey Tettleton	.35
140	Larry Walker	.35
141	Joe Carter	.35
142	Carlos Delgado	1.00
143	Alex Gonzalez	.35
144	Paul Molitor	1.50

Gold

Exactly paralleling the cards in the regular Prism set, this chase card insert replaces the silver foil on front with gold foil. All else remains the same. Stated odds of picking a Gold Prism parallel card are about one per 18 packs, on average (two per box).

	NM/M
Complete Set (144):	100.00
Common Player:	.50
Stars:	1.5X

Fence Busters

Home run heroes are featured in this insert set. The player's big swing is photographed in the foreground while a baseball flies out of the etched metallic foil stadium background. The player's name is in blue foil. Backs have another player photo and details of his 1995 season home run output, in both English and Spanish. Cards are numbered with an FB prefix. Stated odds of finding a Fence Busters insert are one per 37 packs, on average.

		NM/M
Complete Set (19):		50.00
Common Player:		1.50
1	Albert Belle	1.50
2	Dante Bichette	1.50
3	Barry Bonds	7.50
4	Jay Buhner	1.50
5	Jose Canseco	2.25
6	Ken Griffey Jr.	5.00
7	Chipper Jones	4.00
8	David Justice	1.50
9	Eric Karros	1.50
10	Edgar Martinez	1.50
11	Mark McGwire	6.00
12	Eddie Murray	3.00
13	Mike Piazza	5.00
14	Kirby Puckett	4.00
15	Cal Ripken Jr.	7.50
16	Tim Salmon	1.50
17	Sammy Sosa	4.00
18	Frank Thomas	3.00
19	Mo Vaughn	1.50

Flame Throwers

Burning baseballs are the background for the game's best pitchers in this die-cut insert set. The gold-foil high-

lighted flames have their tails die-cut at the card's left end. The featured pitcher is shown in action in the foreground. The name at bottom and company logo are in gold foil. Backs are conventionally printed with another action photo and 1995 highlight printed in both English and Spanish. Card numbers carry an FT prefix. Stated odds of finding a Flame Throwers card are one in 73 packs, about every two boxes.

		NM/M
Complete Set (10):		25.00
Common Player:		1.50
1	Roger Clemens	6.50
2	David Cone	1.50
3	Tom Glavine	2.50
4	Randy Johnson	4.50
5	Greg Maddux	6.00
6	Ramon Martinez	1.50
7	Jose Mesa	1.50
8	Mike Mussina	2.50
9	Hideo Nomo	3.00
10	Jose Rijo	1.50

Red Hot Stars

Bright red metallic foil provides the background for these inserts. Color action photos are in the foreground, while player name and multiple team logos are worked into the background. Backs are conventionally printed with another player photo and a few words - in both English and Spanish - about the player's 1995 season. Card numbers have an RH prefix. Stated odds of finding a Red Hot Stars insert are one per 37 packs.

		NM/M
Complete Set (20):		25.00
Common Player:		.50
1	Roberto Alomar	.75
2	Jeff Bagwell	1.50
3	Albert Belle	.50
4	Wade Boggs	2.00
5	Barry Bonds	4.00
6	Jose Canseco	1.00
7	Ken Griffey Jr.	2.50
8	Tony Gwynn	2.00
9	Randy Johnson	1.50
10	Chipper Jones	2.00
11	Greg Maddux	2.00
12	Edgar Martinez	.50
13	Don Mattingly	2.50
14	Mike Piazza	2.50
15	Kirby Puckett	2.00
16	Manny Ramirez	1.50
17	Cal Ripken Jr.	4.00
18	Tim Salmon	.50
19	Frank Thomas	1.50
20	Mo Vaughn	.50

Carlos Baerga Celebrities Softball

This set was produced for distribution to fans attending the second annual Carlos Baerga Celebrities Softball Game in Puerto Rico. Packs were handed out containing two of the

cards from this set, a regular Pacific Crown Collection card, a Pacific logo card and an information card about card shops on the island. The softball celebrities cards have a blue and red marbled border with player names at bottom in gold foil. Players are shown in action during the '95 game. Backs feature a portrait photo of the player and English/Spanish description of his participation in the event.

		NM/M
Complete Set (8):		12.00
Common Player:		1.00
1	Carlos Baerga	1.00
2	Mike Piazza	4.00
3	Bernie Williams	1.00
4	Frank Thomas	2.50
5	Roberto Alomar	1.25
6	Edgar Martinez	1.00
7	Kenny Lofton	1.00
8	Sammy Sosa	4.00

Nolan Ryan Career Highlights

Highlights of Ryan's career with the Texas Rangers are featured in this 11-card set given to fans attending the September 13 game at Arlington during Nolan Ryan Appreciation Week, when the team retired his jersey. Ten cards feature action photos on front with gold-foil graphics. Backs share a background photo of Ryan's classic windup and describe the action pictured on front. Sponsors' and licensors' logos are at top and bottom. An 11th unnumbered card is a checklist.

		NM/M
Complete Set (11):		9.00
Common Player:		1.00
---	Header card/checklist	.25
1	King of K's (Nolan Ryan)	1.00
2	324 Career Wins (Nolan Ryan)	1.00
3	Miracle Man (Nolan Ryan)	1.00
4	Low-Hit Nolan (Nolan Ryan)	1.00
5	Milestone K's (Nolan Ryan)	1.00
6	Pure Heat (Nolan Ryan)	1.00
7	No-Hit Nolan (Nolan Ryan)	1.00
8	Ryan's Farewell (Nolan Ryan)	1.00
9	Legendary Career (Nolan Ryan)	1.00
10	Retiring #34 (Nolan Ryan)	1.00

Advil Nolan Ryan

Nolan Ryan, who starred in TV commericals for Advil pain reliever at the end of his career continued his association with the product via a baseball card set in 1996. A pair of cards marking the all-time strikeout leader's first and last Ks were available in-store with the purchase of a bottle of Advil. A 27-card set of career highlight cards was available by mail for $5.50 and proof of purchase. All of the Ryan cards have full-bleed front photos with gold-foil highlights and the Advil and Pacific logos. Backs have a background photo of Ryan pitching, with a description of the highlight. Cards are UV coated on each side. The mail-in set was issued in a collectors' box.

		NM/M
Complete Set (29):		6.00
Common Card:		.25
IN-STORE CARDS		
1a	First Strikeout (Nolan Ryan)	.50
2a	Last strikeout (Nolan Ryan)	.50
MAIL-IN SET		
1	New York Mets Rookie Pitcher (Nolan Ryan)	.25
2	California Angels (Nolan Ryan)	.25
3	Houston Astros (Nolan Ryan)	.25
4	Texas Rangers (Nolan Ryan)	.25
5	No-Hitter #1 (Nolan Ryan)	.25
6	No-Hitter #2 (Nolan Ryan)	.25
7	No-Hitter #3 (Nolan Ryan)	.25
8	No-Hitter #4 (Nolan Ryan)	.25
9	No-Hitter #5 (Nolan Ryan)	.25
10	No-Hitter #6 (Nolan Ryan)	.25
11	No-Hitter #7 (Nolan Ryan)	.25
12	First Major League Win (Nolan Ryan)	.25
13	250th Win (Nolan Ryan)	.25
14	300th Win (Nolan Ryan)	.25
15	324th Win (Nolan Ryan)	.25
16	1,000th Strikeout (Nolan Ryan)	.25
17	2,000th Strikeout (Nolan Ryan)	.25
18	3,000th Strikeout (Nolan Ryan)	.25
19	Nolan Breaks Johnson Record (Nolan Ryan)	.25
20	4,000th Strikeout (Nolan Ryan)	.25
21	5,000th Strikeout (Nolan Ryan)	.25
22	World Series Victory (Nolan Ryan)	.25
23	Fastest Pitch Ever Thrown (Nolan Ryan)	.25
24	Ryan Home Run (Nolan Ryan)	.25
25	The Greatest Power Pitcher (Nolan Ryan)	.25
26	1989 All-Star Game (Nolan Ryan)	.25
27	Last Appearance (Nolan Ryan)	.25

1997 Pacific Crown

The 450-card, regular-sized set was available in 12-card packs. The card fronts feature the player's name in gold foil along the left border with

the team logo in the bottom right corner. The card backs feature a head shot of the player in the lower left quadrant with a short highlight in both Spanish and English. Inserted in packs were: Card-Supials, Cramer's Choice, Latinos Of The Major Leagues, Fireworks Die-Cuts, Gold Crown Die-Cuts and Triple Crown Die-Cuts. A parallel silver version (67 sets) was available.

		NM/M
Complete Set (450):		30.00
Common Player:		.05
Silver Stars/RC's:		15X
Light Blue:		1X
Pack (12):		1.25
Wax Box (36):		32.50
1	Garret Anderson	.05
2	George Arias	.05
3	Chili Davis	.05
4	Gary DiSarcina	.05
5	Jim Edmonds	.05
6	Darin Erstad	.15
7	Jorge Fabregas	.05
8	Chuck Finley	.05
9	Rex Hudler	.05
10	Mark Langston	.05
11	Orlando Palmeiro	.05
12	Troy Percival	.05
13	Tim Salmon	.05
14	J.T. Snow	.05
15	Randy Velarde	.05
16	Manny Alexander	.05
17	Roberto Alomar	.25
18	Brady Anderson	.05
19	Armando Benitez	.05
20	Bobby Bonilla	.05
21	Rocky Coppinger	.05
22	Scott Erickson	.05
23	Jeffrey Hammonds	.05
24	Chris Hoiles	.05
25	Eddie Murray	.75
26	Mike Mussina	.60
27	Randy Myers	.05
28	Rafael Palmeiro	.65
29	Cal Ripken Jr.	2.50
30	B.J. Surhoff	.05
31	Tony Tarasco	.05
32	Esteban Beltre	.05
33	Darren Bragg	.05
34	Jose Canseco	.60
35	Roger Clemens	1.50
36	Wil Cordero	.05
37	Alex Delgado	.05
38	Jeff Frye	.05
39	Nomar Garciaparra	1.00
40	Tom Gordon	.05
41	Mike Greenwell	.05
42	Reggie Jefferson	.05
43	Tim Naehring	.05
44	Troy O'Leary	.05
45	Heathcliff Slocumb	.05
46	Lee Tinsley	.05
47	John Valentin	.05
48	Mo Vaughn	.05
49	Wilson Alvarez	.05
50	Harold Baines	.05
51	Ray Durham	.05
52	Alex Fernandez	.05
53	Ozzie Guillen	.05
54	Roberto Hernandez	.05
55	Ron Karkovice	.05
56	Darren Lewis	.05
57	Norberto Martin	.05
58	Dave Martinez	.05
59	Lyle Mouton	.05
60	Jose Munoz	.05
61	Tony Phillips	.05
62	Rich Sauveur	.05
63	Danny Tartabull	.05
64	Frank Thomas	.75
65	Robin Ventura	.05
66	Sandy Alomar Jr.	.05
67	Albert Belle	.05
68	Julio Franco	.05
69	Brian Giles **RC**	.50
70	Danny Graves	.05
71	Orel Hershiser	.05
72	Jeff Kent	.05
73	Kenny Lofton	.05
74	Dennis Martinez	.05
75	Jack McDowell	.05
76	Jose Mesa	.05
77	Charles Nagy	.05
78	Manny Ramirez	.75
79	Julian Tavarez	.05
80	Jim Thome	.60
81	Jose Vizcaino	.05
82	Omar Vizquel	.05
83	Brad Ausmus	.05
84	Kimera Bartee	.05
85	Raul Casanova	.05
86	Tony Clark	.05
87	Travis Fryman	.05
88	Bobby Higginson	.05
89	Mark Lewis	.05
90	Jose Lima	.05
91	Felipe Lira	.05
92	Phil Nevin	.05
93	Melvin Nieves	.05
94	Curtis Pride	.05
95	Ruben Sierra	.05
96	Alan Trammell	.05
97	Kevin Appier	.05
98	Tim Belcher	.05
99	Johnny Damon	.35
100	Tom Goodwin	.05
101	Bob Hamelin	.05
102	David Howard	.05
103	Jason Jacome	.05
104	Keith Lockhart	.05
105	Mike Macfarlane	.05
106	Jeff Montgomery	.05
107	Jose Offerman	.05
108	Hipolito Pichardo	.05
109	Joe Randa	.05
110	Bip Roberts	.05
111	Chris Stynes	.05
112	Mike Sweeney	.05
113	Joe Vitiello	.05
114	Jeromy Burnitz	.05
115	Chuck Carr	.05
116	Jeff Cirillo	.05
117	Mike Fetters	.05
118	David Hulse	.05
119	John Jaha	.05
120	Scott Karl	.05
121	Jesse Levis	.05
122	Mark Loretta	.05
123	Mike Matheny	.05
124	Ben McDonald	.05
125	Matt Mieske	.05
126	Angel Miranda	.05
127	Dave Nilsson	.05
128	Jose Valentin	.05
129	Fernando Vina	.05
130	Ron Villone	.05
131	Gerald Williams	.05
132	Rick Aguilera	.05
133	Rich Becker	.05
134	Ron Coomer	.05
135	Marty Cordova	.05
136	Eddie Guardado	.05
137	Denny Hocking	.05
138	Roberto Kelly	.05
139	Chuck Knoblauch	.05
140	Matt Lawton	.05
141	Pat Meares	.05
142	Paul Molitor	.75
143	Greg Myers	.05
144	Jeff Reboulet	.05
145	Scott Stahoviak	.05
146	Todd Walker	.05
147	Wade Boggs	1.00
148	David Cone	.05
149	Mariano Duncan	.05
150	Cecil Fielder	.05
151	Dwight Gooden	.05
152	Derek Jeter	2.50
153	Jim Leyritz	.05
154	Tino Martinez	.05
155	Paul O'Neill	.05
156	Andy Pettitte	.25
157	Tim Raines	.05
158	Mariano Rivera	.15
159	Ruben Rivera	.05
160	Kenny Rogers	.05
161	Darryl Strawberry	.05
162	John Wetteland	.05
163	Bernie Williams	.05
164	Tony Batista	.05
165	Geronimo Berroa	.05
166	Mike Bordick	.05
167	Scott Brosius	.05
168	Brent Gates	.05
169	Jason Giambi	.65
170	Jose Herrera	.05
171	Brian Lesher	.05
172	Damon Mashore **RC**	.05
173	Mark McGwire	2.00
174	Ariel Prieto	.05
175	Carlos Reyes	.05
176	Matt Stairs	.05
177	Terry Steinbach	.05
178	John Wasdin	.05
179	Ernie Young	.05
180	Rich Amaral	.05
181	Bobby Ayala	.05
182	Jay Buhner	.05
183	Rafael Carmona	.05
184	Norm Charlton	.05
185	Joey Cora	.05
186	Ken Griffey Jr.	1.50
187	Sterling Hitchcock	.05
188	Dave Hollins	.05
189	Randy Johnson	.75
190	Edgar Martinez	.05
191	Jamie Moyer	.05
192	Alex Rodriguez	2.00
193	Paul Sorrento	.05
194	Salomon Torres	.05
195	Bob Wells	.05
196	Dan Wilson	.05
197	Will Clark	.05
198	Kevin Elster	.05
199	Rene Gonzales	.05
200	Juan Gonzalez	.40
201	Rusty Greer	.05
202	Darryl Hamilton	.05
203	Mike Henneman	.05
204	Ken Hill	.05
205	Mark McLemore	.05
206	Darren Oliver	.05
207	Dean Palmer	.05
208	Roger Pavlik	.05
209	Ivan Rodriguez	.65
210	Kurt Stillwell	.05
211	Mickey Tettleton	.05
212	Bobby Witt	.05
213	Tilson Brito	.05
214	Jacob Brumfield	.05
215	Miguel Cairo	.05
216	Joe Carter	.05
217	Felipe Crespo	.05
218	Carlos Delgado	.60
219	Alex Gonzalez	.05
220	Shawn Green	.15
221	Juan Guzman	.05
222	Pat Hentgen	.05
223	Charlie O'Brien	.05
224	John Olerud	.05
225	Robert Perez	.05
226	Tomas Perez	.05
227	Juan Samuel	.05
228	Ed Sprague	.05
229	Mike Timlin	.05
230	Rafael Belliard	.05
231	Jermaine Dye	.05
232	Tom Glavine	.25
233	Marquis Grissom	.05
234	Andruw Jones	.75
235	Chipper Jones	1.00
236	David Justice	.05
237	Ryan Klesko	.05
238	Mark Lemke	.05
239	Javier Lopez	.05
240	Greg Maddux	1.00
241	Fred McGriff	.05
242	Denny Neagle	.05
243	Eddie Perez	.05
244	John Smoltz	.05
245	Mark Wohlers	.05
246	Brant Brown	.05
247	Scott Bullett	.05
248	Leo Gomez	.05
249	Luis Gonzalez	.05
250	Mark Grace	.05
251	Jose Hernandez	.05
252	Brooks Kieschnick	.05
253	Brian McRae	.05
254	Jaime Navarro	.05
255	Mike Perez	.05
256	Rey Sanchez	.05
257	Ryne Sandberg	1.00
258	Scott Servais	.05
259	Sammy Sosa	1.00
260	Pedro Valdes **RC**	.05
261	Turk Wendell	.05
262	Bret Boone	.05
263	Jeff Branson	.05
264	Jeff Brantley	.05
265	Dave Burba	.05
266	Hector Carrasco	.05
267	Eric Davis	.05
268	Willie Greene	.05
269	Lenny Harris	.05
270	Thomas Howard	.05
271	Barry Larkin	.05
272	Hal Morris	.05
273	Joe Oliver	.05
274	Eric Owens	.05
275	Jose Rijo	.05
276	Reggie Sanders	.05
277	Eddie Taubensee	.05
278	Jason Bates	.05
279	Dante Bichette	.05
280	Ellis Burks	.05
281	Vinny Castilla	.05
282	Andres Galarraga	.05
283	Quinton McCracken	.05
284	Jayhawk Owens	.05
285	Jeff Reed	.05
286	Bryan Rekar	.05
287	Armando Reynoso	.05
288	Kevin Ritz	.05
289	Bruce Ruffin	.05
290	John Vander Wal	.05
291	Larry Walker	.05
292	Walt Weiss	.05
293	Eric Young	.05
294	Kurt Abbott	.05
295	Alex Arias	.05
296	Miguel Batista	.05
297	Kevin Brown	.05
298	Luis Castillo	.05
299	Greg Colbrunn	.05
300	Jeff Conine	.05
301	Charles Johnson	.05
302	Al Leiter	.05
303	Robb Nen	.05
304	Joe Orsulak	.05
305	Yorkis Perez	.05
306	Edgar Renteria	.05
307	Gary Sheffield	.30
308	Jesus Tavarez	.05
309	Quilvio Veras	.05
310	Devon White	.05
311	Jeff Bagwell	.75
312	Derek Bell	.05
313	Sean Berry	.05
314	Craig Biggio	.05
315	Doug Drabek	.05
316	Tony Eusebio	.05
317	Ricky Gutierrez	.05
318	Xavier Hernandez	.05
319	Brian L. Hunter	.05
320	Darryl Kile	.05
321	Derrick May	.05
322	Orlando Miller	.05
323	James Mouton	.05
324	Bill Spiers	.05
325	Pedro Astacio	.05
326	Brett Butler	.05
327	Juan Castro	.05
328	Roger Cedeno	.05
329	Delino DeShields	.05
330	Karim Garcia	.10
331	Todd Hollandsworth	.05
332	Eric Karros	.05
333	Oreste Marrero	.05
334	Ramon Martinez	.05
335	Raul Mondesi	.05
336	Hideo Nomo	.50
337	Antonio Osuna	.05
338	Chan Ho Park	.05
339	Mike Piazza	1.50
340	Ismael Valdes	.05
341	Moises Alou	.05
342	Omar Daal	.05
343	Jeff Fassero	.05
344	Cliff Floyd	.05
345	Mark Grudzielanek	.05
346	Mike Lansing	.05
347	Pedro Martinez	.75
348	Sherman Obando	.05
349	Jose Paniagua	.05
350	Henry Rodriguez	.05
351	Mel Rojas	.05
352	F.P. Santangelo	.05
353	Dave Segui	.05
354	Dave Silvestri	.05
355	Ugueth Urbina	.05
356	Rondell White	.05
357	Edgardo Alfonzo	.05
358	Carlos Baerga	.05
359	Tim Bogar	.05
360	Rico Brogna	.05
361	Alvaro Espinoza	.05
362	Carl Everett	.05
363	John Franco	.05
364	Bernard Gilkey	.05
365	Todd Hundley	.05
366	Butch Huskey	.05
367	Jason Isringhausen	.05
368	Bobby Jones	.05
369	Lance Johnson	.05
370	Brent Mayne	.05
371	Alex Ochoa	.05
372	Rey Ordonez	.05
373	Ron Blazier	.05
374	Ricky Bottalico	.05
375	David Doster	.05
376	Lenny Dykstra	.05
377	Jim Eisenreich	.05
378	Bobby Estalella	.05
379	Gregg Jefferies	.05
380	Kevin Jordan	.05
381	Ricardo Jordan	.05
382	Mickey Morandini	.05
383	Ricky Otero	.05
384	Benito Santiago	.05
385	Gene Schall	.05
386	Curt Schilling	.25
387	Kevin Sefcik	.05
388	Kevin Stocker	.05
389	Jermaine Allensworth	.05
390	Jay Bell	.05
391	Jason Christiansen	.05
392	Francisco Cordova	.05
393	Mark Johnson	.05
394	Jason Kendall	.05
395	Jeff King	.05
396	Jon Lieber	.05
397	Nelson Liriano	.05
398	Esteban Loaiza	.05
399	Al Martin	.05
400	Orlando Merced	.05
401	Ramon Morel	.05
402	Luis Alicea	.05
403	Alan Benes	.05
404	Andy Benes	.05
405	Terry Bradshaw	.05
406	Royce Clayton	.05
407	Dennis Eckersley	.65
408	Gary Gaetti	.05
409	Mike Gallego	.05
410	Ron Gant	.05
411	Brian Jordan	.05
412	Ray Lankford	.05
413	John Mabry	.05
414	Willie McGee	.05
415	Tom Pagnozzi	.05
416	Ozzie Smith	1.00
417	Todd Stottlemyre	.05
418	Mark Sweeney	.05
419	Andy Ashby	.05
420	Ken Caminiti	.05
421	Archi Cianfrocco	.05
422	Steve Finley	.05
423	Chris Gomez	.05
424	Tony Gwynn	1.00
425	Joey Hamilton	.05
426	Rickey Henderson	.75
427	Trevor Hoffman	.05
428	Brian Johnson	.05
429	Wally Joyner	.05
430	Scott Livingstone	.05
431	Jody Reed	.05
432	Craig Shipley	.05
433	Fernando Valenzuela	.05
434	Greg Vaughn	.05
435	Rich Aurilia	.05
436	Kim Batiste	.05
437	Jose Bautista	.05
438	Rod Beck	.05
439	Marvin Benard	.05
440	Barry Bonds	2.50
441	Shawon Dunston	.05
442	Shawn Estes	.05
443	Osvaldo Fernandez	.05
444	Stan Javier	.05
445	David McCarty	.05
446	Bill Mueller **RC**	.15
447	Steve Scarsone	.05
448	Robby Thompson	.05
449	Rick Wilkins	.05
450	Matt Williams	.05

Light Blue

This parallel insert was produced exclusively for insertion in Wal-Mart/Sam's jumbo packs at the rate of one per pack. Following the format of the regular-issue, they use light blue foil, rather than the standard gold. Light blue inserts should not be confused with the much scarcer silver inserts which are visually similar.

	NM/M
Complete Set (450):	60.00
Common Player:	.25
Stars:	1X

Silver

This parallel insert was produced in an edition of only 67 cards per player. Following the format of the regular-issue, they use silver foil, rather than the standard gold. Silver parallels were inserted at an advertised rate of one per 73 packs. Silver inserts should not be confused with the much more common light blue inserts which are visually similar.

	NM/M
Common Player:	1.00
Stars/Rookies:	12X

Card-Supials

The 36-card, regular-sized set was inserted every 37 packs of 1997 Pacific Crown baseball. The card fronts feature a gold-foil spiral with the player's name printed along a curve on the bottom edge. The team logo appears in the lower right corner. The card backs feature an action shot and are numbered "x of 36." The cards come with a mini (1-1/4" x 1-3/4") card that slides into a pocket on the back. The mini cards depict the same action shot as the larger card backs.

		NM/M
Complete Set (72):		80.00
Complete Large Set (36):		60.00
Complete Small Set (36):		45.00
Common Large:		.75
Small Cards: 75 Percent		
1	Roberto Alomar	1.00
2	Brady Anderson	.75
3	Eddie Murray	2.00
4	Cal Ripken Jr.	5.00
5	Jose Canseco	1.00
6	Mo Vaughn	.75
7	Frank Thomas	2.00
8	Albert Belle	.75
9	Omar Vizquel	.75
10	Chuck Knoblauch	.75
11	Paul Molitor	2.00
12	Wade Boggs	2.50
13	Derek Jeter	5.00
14	Andy Pettitte	1.00
15	Mark McGwire	3.50
16	Jay Buhner	.75
17	Ken Griffey Jr.	3.00
18	Alex Rodriguez	3.50
19	Juan Gonzalez	1.00
20	Ivan Rodriguez	1.50
21	Andruw Jones	2.00
22	Chipper Jones	2.50
23	Ryan Klesko	.75
24	Greg Maddux	2.50
25	Ryne Sandberg	2.50
26	Andres Galarraga	.75
27	Gary Sheffield	1.00
28	Jeff Bagwell	2.00
29	Todd Hollandsworth	.75
30	Hideo Nomo	1.00
31	Mike Piazza	3.00
32	Todd Hundley	.75
33	Dennis Eckersley	1.50
34	Ken Caminiti	.75
35	Tony Gwynn	2.50
36	Barry Bonds	5.00

Cramer's Choice Awards

The 10-card, regular-sized set was inserted every 721 packs and features a die-cut pyramid design. A color player photo is imaged over silver foil with the player's name and position in gold foil over a green marble background along the bottom. The card backs feature a headshot with a brief career highlight in both Spanish and English. The cards are numbered with a "CC" prefix.

		NM/M
Complete Set (10):		75.00
Common Player:		4.50
1	Roberto Alomar	5.00
2	Frank Thomas	9.00
3	Albert Belle	4.50
4	Andy Pettitte	4.50
5	Ken Griffey Jr.	17.50
6	Alex Rodriguez	25.00
7	Chipper Jones	12.00
8	John Smoltz	4.50
9	Mike Piazza	15.00
10	Tony Gwynn	12.00

Fireworks Die-Cuts

The 20-card, regular-sized, die-cut set was inserted every 73 packs of 1997 Crown.

The card fronts feature a color action shot with generic fireworks over a stadium on the upper half. The horizontal card backs contain close-up shots with highlights in Spanish and English. The cards are numbered with the "FW" prefix.

		NM/M
Complete Set (20):		40.00
Common Player:		.75
1	Roberto Alomar	1.00
2	Brady Anderson	.75
3	Eddie Murray	2.50
4	Cal Ripken Jr.	7.50
5	Frank Thomas	2.50
6	Albert Belle	.75
7	Derek Jeter	7.50
8	Andy Pettitte	1.00
9	Bernie Williams	.75
10	Mark McGwire	6.50
11	Ken Griffey Jr.	5.00
12	Alex Rodriguez	6.50
13	Juan Gonzalez	1.25
14	Andruw Jones	2.50
15	Chipper Jones	3.50
16	Hideo Nomo	1.25
17	Mike Piazza	5.00
18	Henry Rodriguez	.75
19	Tony Gwynn	3.50
20	Barry Bonds	7.50

Gold Crown Die-Cuts

The 36-card, regular-sized, die-cut set was inserted every 37 packs. The card fronts feature a die-cut, gold-foil crown on the top border and the player's name appears in gold along the bottom edge. The card backs contain a headshot and a Spanish/English highlight and are numbered with the "GC" prefix.

		NM/M
Complete Set (36):		65.00
Common Player:		1.00
1	Roberto Alomar	1.25
2	Brady Anderson	1.00
3	Mike Mussina	1.50
4	Eddie Murray	2.75
5	Cal Ripken Jr.	8.50
6	Jose Canseco	2.00
7	Frank Thomas	2.75
8	Albert Belle	1.00
9	Omar Vizquel	1.00
10	Wade Boggs	3.50
11	Derek Jeter	8.50
12	Andy Pettitte	1.25
13	Mariano Rivera	1.25
14	Bernie Williams	1.00
15	Mark McGwire	6.50
16	Ken Griffey Jr.	5.00
17	Edgar Martinez	1.00
18	Alex Rodriguez	6.50
19	Juan Gonzalez	1.50
20	Ivan Rodriguez	2.50
21	Andruw Jones	2.75
22	Chipper Jones	3.50
23	Ryan Klesko	1.00
24	John Smoltz	1.00
25	Ryne Sandberg	3.50
26	Andres Galarraga	1.00
27	Edgar Renteria	1.00
28	Jeff Bagwell	2.75
29	Todd Hollandsworth	1.00
30	Hideo Nomo	1.50
31	Mike Piazza	5.00
32	Todd Hundley	1.00
33	Brian Jordan	1.00
34	Ken Caminiti	1.00
35	Tony Gwynn	3.50
36	Barry Bonds	8.50

Latinos of the Major Leagues

The 36-card, regular-sized set was inserted twice every 37 packs. The card fronts feature a color action shot over the player's name in gold foil. The card backs have another action shot and a Spanish/English highlight.

		NM/M
Complete Set (36):		45.00
Common Player:		1.00
1	George Arias	1.00
2	Roberto Alomar	1.50
3	Rafael Palmeiro	2.50
4	Bobby Bonilla	1.00
5	Jose Canseco	2.00
6	Wilson Alvarez	1.00
7	Dave Martinez	1.00
8	Julio Franco	1.00
9	Manny Ramirez	3.00
10	Omar Vizquel	1.00
11	Marty Cordova	1.00
12	Roberto Kelly	1.00
13	Tino Martinez	1.00
14	Mariano Rivera	1.50
15	Ruben Rivera	1.00
16	Bernie Williams	1.00
17	Geronimo Berroa	1.00
18	Joey Cora	1.00
19	Edgar Martinez	1.00
20	Alex Rodriguez	6.00
21	Juan Gonzalez	2.00
22	Ivan Rodriguez	2.50
23	Andruw Jones	3.00
24	Javier Lopez	1.00
25	Sammy Sosa	4.50
26	Vinny Castilla	1.00
27	Andres Galarraga	1.00
28	Ramon Martinez	1.00
29	Raul Mondesi	1.00
30	Ismael Valdes	1.00
31	Pedro Martinez	3.00
32	Henry Rodriguez	1.00
33	Carlos Baerga	1.00
34	Rey Ordonez	1.00
35	Fernando Valenzuela	1.00
36	Osvaldo Fernandez	1.00

Triple Crown Die-Cuts

The 20-card, regular-sized, die-cut set was inserted every 145 packs of Crown baseball. The horizontal card fronts feature the same gold-foil, die-cut crown as on the Gold Crown Die-Cut inserts. The card backs feature a headshot, Spanish/English text and are numbered with the "TC" prefix.

		NM/M
Complete Set (20):		75.00
Common Player:		2.00
1	Brady Anderson	2.00
2	Rafael Palmeiro	4.00
3	Mo Vaughn	2.00
4	Frank Thomas	5.00
5	Albert Belle	2.00
6	Jim Thome	4.00
7	Cecil Fielder	2.00
8	Mark McGwire	10.00
9	Ken Griffey Jr.	7.50
10	Alex Rodriguez	10.00
11	Juan Gonzalez	3.00
12	Andruw Jones	5.00
13	Chipper Jones	6.00
14	Dante Bichette	2.00
15	Ellis Burks	2.00
16	Andres Galarraga	2.00
17	Jeff Bagwell	5.00
18	Mike Piazza	7.50
19	Ken Caminiti	2.00
20	Barry Bonds	12.50

1997 Pacific Invincible

The 1997 Pacific Invincible 150-card set was sold in three-card packs. The card fronts feature gold foil parallel lines with a color action shot. The bottom right quadrant contains a transparent cel headshot. The card backs have Spanish/English text and another color action shot. The reverse cel has the player's hat team logo air-brushed off to prevent reverse print. Insert sets are: Sluggers & Hurlers, Sizzling Lumber, Gate Attractions, Gems of the Diamond (2:1), and Light Blue (retail only) and Platinum (hobby) parallel sets of the 150 base cards.

		NM/M
Complete Set (150):		30.00
Common Player:		.25
Light Blues:		1X
Platinums:		2X
Pack (3):		1.00
Wax Box (36):		25.00
1	Chili Davis	.25
2	Jim Edmonds	.25
3	Darin Erstad	.50
4	Orlando Palmeiro	.25
5	Tim Salmon	.25
6	J.T. Snow	.25
7	Roberto Alomar	.50
8	Brady Anderson	.25
9	Eddie Murray	1.50
10	Mike Mussina	1.00
11	Rafael Palmeiro	1.25
12	Cal Ripken Jr.	4.00
13	Jose Canseco	1.00
14	Roger Clemens	2.50
15	Nomar Garciaparra	2.00
16	Reggie Jefferson	.25
17	Mo Vaughn	.25
18	Wilson Alvarez	.25
19	Harold Baines	.25
20	Alex Fernandez	.25
21	Danny Tartabull	.25
22	Frank Thomas	1.50
23	Robin Ventura	.25
24	Sandy Alomar Jr.	.25
25	Albert Belle	.25
26	Kenny Lofton	.25
27	Jim Thome	.75
28	Omar Vizquel	.25
29	Raul Casanova	.25
30	Tony Clark	.25
31	Travis Fryman	.25
32	Bobby Higginson	.25
33	Melvin Nieves	.25
34	Justin Thompson	.25
35	Johnny Damon	.50
36	Tom Goodwin	.25
37	Jeff Montgomery	.25
38	Jose Offerman	.25
39	John Jaha	.25
40	Jeff Cirillo	.25
41	Dave Nilsson	.25
42	Jose Valentin	.25
43	Fernando Vina	.25
44	Marty Cordova	.25
45	Roberto Kelly	.25
46	Chuck Knoblauch	.25
47	Paul Molitor	1.50
48	Todd Walker	.25
49	Wade Boggs	2.00
50	Cecil Fielder	.25
51	Derek Jeter	4.00
52	Tino Martinez	.25
53	Andy Pettitte	.40
54	Mariano Rivera	.40
55	Bernie Williams	.25
56	Tony Batista	.25
57	Geronimo Berroa	.25
58	Jason Giambi	.75
59	Mark McGwire	3.00
60	Terry Steinbach	.25
61	Jay Buhner	.25
62	Joey Cora	.25
63	Ken Griffey Jr.	2.50
64	Edgar Martinez	.25
65	Alex Rodriguez	3.00
66	Paul Sorrento	.25
67	Will Clark	.25
68	Juan Gonzalez	.75
69	Rusty Greer	.25
70	Dean Palmer	.25
71	Ivan Rodriguez	1.25
72	Joe Carter	.25
73	Carlos Delgado	.75
74	Juan Guzman	.25
75	Pat Hentgen	.25
76	Ed Sprague	.25
77	Jermaine Dye	.25
78	Andruw Jones	1.50
79	Chipper Jones	2.00
80	Ryan Klesko	.25
81	Javier Lopez	.25
82	Greg Maddux	2.00
83	John Smoltz	.25
84	Mark Grace	.25
85	Luis Gonzalez	.25
86	Brooks Kieschnick	.25
87	Jaime Navarro	.25
88	Ryne Sandberg	2.00
89	Sammy Sosa	2.00
90	Bret Boone	.25
91	Jeff Brantley	.25
92	Eric Davis	.25
93	Barry Larkin	.25
94	Reggie Sanders	.25
95	Ellis Burks	.25
96	Dante Bichette	.25
97	Vinny Castilla	.25
98	Andres Galarraga	.25
99	Eric Young	.25
100	Kevin Brown	.25
101	Jeff Conine	.25
102	Charles Johnson	.25
103	Edgar Renteria	.25
104	Gary Sheffield	.75
105	Jeff Bagwell	1.50
106	Derek Bell	.25
107	Sean Berry	.25
108	Craig Biggio	.25
109	Shane Reynolds	.25
110	Karim Garcia	.25
111	Todd Hollandsworth	.25
112	Ramon Martinez	.25
113	Raul Mondesi	.25
114	Hideo Nomo	.75
115	Mike Piazza	2.50
116	Ismael Valdes	.25
117	Moises Alou	.25
118	Mark Grudzielanek	.25
119	Pedro Martinez	1.50
120	Henry Rodriguez	.25
121	F.P. Santangelo	.25
122	Carlos Baerga	.25
123	Bernard Gilkey	.25
124	Todd Hundley	.25
125	Lance Johnson	.25
126	Alex Ochoa	.25
127	Rey Ordonez	.25
128	Lenny Dykstra	.25
129	Gregg Jefferies	.25
130	Ricky Otero	.25
131	Benito Santiago	.25
132	Jermaine Allensworth	.25
133	Francisco Cordova	.25
134	Carlos Garcia	.25
135	Jason Kendall	.25
136	Al Martin	.25
137	Dennis Eckersley	1.25
138	Ron Gant	.25
139	Brian Jordan	.25
140	John Mabry	.25
141	Ozzie Smith	2.00
142	Ken Caminiti	.25
143	Steve Finley	.25
144	Tony Gwynn	2.00
145	Wally Joyner	.25
146	Fernando Valenzuela	.25
147	Barry Bonds	4.00
148	Jacob Cruz	.25
149	Osvaldo Fernandez	.25
150	Matt Williams	.25

Gate Attractions

The 32-card, regular-sized set was inserted every 73 packs of Pacific Invincible baseball. The card fronts feature a generic baseball glove background with the player's name and position in a gold-foil circle. The center of the card is a cel action shot within a common baseball image. The player's team logo appears in the upper right corner. The card backs contain a headshot in the upper left corner with highlights in Spanish and English. The player's image in the cel is etched in gray in reverse. The cards are numbered with the "GA" prefix.

		NM/M
Complete Set (32):		80.00
Common Player:		1.00
1	Roberto Alomar	1.00
2	Brady Anderson	1.00
3	Cal Ripken Jr.	8.00
4	Frank Thomas	2.50
5	Kenny Lofton	1.00
6	Omar Vizquel	1.00
7	Paul Molitor	2.50
8	Wade Boggs	3.00
9	Derek Jeter	8.00
10	Andy Pettitte	1.50
11	Bernie Williams	1.00
12	Geronimo Berroa	1.00
13	Mark McGwire	6.00
14	Ken Griffey Jr.	4.50
15	Alex Rodriguez	6.00
16	Juan Gonzalez	1.50
17	Andruw Jones	2.50
18	Chipper Jones	3.00
19	Greg Maddux	3.00
20	Ryne Sandberg	3.00
21	Sammy Sosa	3.00
22	Andres Galarraga	1.00
23	Jeff Bagwell	2.50
24	Todd Hollandsworth	1.00
25	Hideo Nomo	1.50
26	Mike Piazza	4.50
27	Todd Hundley	1.00
28	Lance Johnson	1.00
29	Ozzie Smith	3.00
30	Ken Caminiti	1.00
31	Tony Gwynn	3.00
32	Barry Bonds	8.00

Gems of the Diamond

Essentially the base set for 1997 Pacific Prism Invincible, these cards are found two per three-card pack. Fronts of the 2-1/2" x 3-1/2" cards have action photos with earth-tone borders and a color team logo at bottom. Backs have a large player portrait photos in a diamond at right-center and are numbered with a "GD-" prefix.

		NM/M
Complete Set (220):		20.00
Common Player:		.10
1	Jim Abbott	.10
2	Shawn Boskie	.10
3	Gary DiSarcina	.10
4	Jim Edmonds	.10
5	Todd Greene	.10
6	Jack Howell	.10
7	Jeff Schmidt	.10
8	Shad Williams	.10
9	Roberto Alomar	.35
10	Cesar Devarez	.10
11	Alan Mills	.10
12	Eddie Murray	.75
13	Jesse Orosco	.10

14 Arthur Rhodes .10
15 Bill Ripken .10
16 Cal Ripken Jr. 2.50
17 Mark Smith .10
18 Roger Clemens 1.50
19 Vaughn Eshelman .10
20 Rich Garces .10
21 Bill Haselman .10
22 Dwayne Hosey .10
23 Mike Maddux .10
24 Jose Malave .10
25 Aaron Sele .10
26 James Baldwin .10
27 Pat Borders .10
28 Mike Cameron .10
29 Tony Castillo .10
30 Domingo Cedeno .10
31 Greg Norton .10
32 Frank Thomas .75
33 Albert Belle .10
34 Einar Diaz .10
35 Alan Embree .10
36 Albie Lopez .10
37 Chad Ogea .10
38 Tony Pena .10
39 Joe Roa .10
40 Fausto Cruz .10
41 Joey Eischen .10
42 Travis Fryman .10
43 Mike Myers .10
44 A.J. Sager .10
45 Duane Singleton .10
46 Justin Thompson .10
47 Jeff Granger .10
48 Les Norman .10
49 Jon Nunnally .10
50 Craig Paquette .10
51 Michael Tucker .10
52 Julio Valera .10
53 Kevin Young .10
54 Cal Eldred .10
55 Ramon Garcia .10
56 Marc Newfield .10
57 Al Reyes .10
58 Tim Unroe .10
59 Tim Vanegmond .10
60 Turner Ward .10
61 Bob Wickman .10
62 Chuck Knoblauch .10
63 Paul Molitor .75
64 Kirby Puckett 1.00
65 Tom Quinlan .10
66 Rich Robertson .10
67 Dave Stevens .10
68 Matt Walbeck .10
69 Wade Boggs 1.00
70 Tony Fernandez .10
71 Andy Fox .10
72 Joe Girardi .10
73 Charlie Hayes .10
74 Pat Kelly .10
75 Jeff Nelson .10
76 Melido Perez .10
77 Mark Acre .10
78 Allen Battle .10
79 Rafael Bournigal .10
80 Mark McGwire 2.00
81 Pedro Munoz .10
82 Scott Spiezio .10
83 Don Wengert .10
84 Steve Wojciechowski .10
85 Alex Diaz .10
86 Ken Griffey Jr. 1.50
87 Raul Ibanez .10
88 Mike Jackson .10
89 John Marzano .10
90 Greg McCarthy .10
91 Alex Rodriguez 2.00
92 Andy Sheets .10
93 Makoto Suzuki .10
94 Benji Gil .10
95 Juan Gonzalez .40
96 Kevin Gross .10
97 Gil Heredia .10
98 Luis Ortiz .10
99 Jeff Russell .10
100 Dave Valle .10
101 Marty Janzen .10
102 Sandy Martinez .10
103 Julio Mosquera .10
104 Otis Nixon .10
105 Paul Spoljaric .10
106 Shannon Stewart .10
107 Woody Williams .10
108 Steve Avery .10
109 Mike Bielecki .10
110 Pedro Borbon .10
111 Ed Giovanola .10
112 Chipper Jones 1.00
113 Greg Maddux 1.00
114 Mike Mordecai .10
115 Terrell Wade .10
116 Terry Adams .10
117 Brian Dorsett .10
118 Doug Glanville .10
119 Tyler Houston .10
120 Robin Jennings .10
121 Ryne Sandberg 1.00
122 Terry Shumpert .10
123 Amaury Telemaco .10
124 Steve Trachsel .10
125 Curtis Goodwin .10
126 Mike Kelly .10
127 Chad Mottola .10
128 Mark Portugal .10
129 Roger Salkeld .10
130 John Smiley .10
131 Lee Smith .10
132 Roger Bailey .10
133 Andres Galarraga .10
134 Darren Holmes .10
135 Curtis Leskanic .10
136 Mike Munoz .10
137 Jeff Reed .10
138 Mark Thompson .10
139 Jamey Wright .10
140 Andre Dawson .25
141 Craig Grebeck .10
142 Matt Mantei .10
143 Billy McMillon .10
144 Kurt Miller .10
145 Ralph Milliard .10
146 Bob Natal .10
147 Joe Siddall .10
148 Bob Abreu .25
149 Doug Brocail .10
150 Danny Darwin .10
151 Mike Hampton .10
152 Todd Jones .10
153 Kirt Manwaring .10
154 Alvin Morman .10
155 Billy Ashley .10
156 Tom Candiotti .10
157 Darren Dreifort .10
158 Greg Gagne .10
159 Wilton Guerrero .10
160 Hideo Nomo .40
161 Mike Piazza 1.50
162 Tom Prince .10
163 Todd Worrell .10
164 Moises Alou .10
165 Shane Andrews .10
166 Derek Aucoin .10
167 Raul Chavez .10
168 Darrin Fletcher .10
169 Mark Leiter .10
170 Henry Rodriguez .10
171 Dave Veres .10
172 Paul Byrd .10
173 Alberto Castillo .10
174 Mark Clark .10
175 Rey Ordonez .10
176 Roberto Petagine .10
177 Andy Tomberlin .10
178 Derek Wallace .10
179 Paul Wilson .10
180 Ruben Amaro Jr. .10
181 Toby Borland .10
182 Rich Hunter .10
183 Tony Longmire .10
184 Wendell Magee Jr. .10
185 Bobby Munoz .10
186 Scott Rolen .60
187 Mike Williams .10
188 Trey Beamon .10
189 Jason Christiansen .10
190 Elmer Dessens .10
191 Angelo Encarnacion .10
192 Carlos Garcia .10
193 Mike Kingery .10
194 Chris Peters .10
195 Tony Womack .10
196 Brian Barber .10
197 David Bell .10
198 Tony Fossas .10
199 Rick Honeycutt .10
200 T.J. Mathews .10
201 Miguel Mejia .10
202 Donovan Osborne .10
203 Ozzie Smith 1.00
204 Andres Berumen .10
205 Ken Caminiti .10
206 Chris Gwynn .10
207 Tony Gwynn 1.00
208 Rickey Henderson .75
209 Scott Sanders .10
210 Jason Thompson .10
211 Fernando Valenzuela .10
212 Tim Worrell .10
213 Barry Bonds 2.50
214 Jay Canizaro .10
215 Doug Creek .10
216 Jacob Cruz .10
217 Glenallen Hill .10
218 Tom Lampkin .10
219 Jim Poole .10
220 Desi Wilson .10

Sizzling Lumber

The 36-card, regular-sized, die-cut set was inserted every 37 packs of Invincible. The cards have die-cut flames along the right border with a bat running parallel. The player's name appears in gold foil along the top border with his position in English and Spanish in gold foil along the bottom. The card backs feature a headshot in the upper half and contain Spanish and English text. The cards are numbered with the "SL" prefix.

NM/M
Complete Set (36): 50.00
Common Player: .50
1A Cal Ripken Jr. 6.50
1B Rafael Palmeiro 2.50
1C Roberto Alomar 1.00
2A Frank Thomas 3.00
2B Robin Ventura .50
2C Harold Baines .50
3A Albert Belle .50
3B Manny Ramirez 3.00
3C Kenny Lofton .50
4A Derek Jeter 6.50
4B Bernie Williams .50
4C Wade Boggs 3.50
5A Mark McGwire 5.00
5B Jason Giambi 2.00
5C Geronimo Berroa .50
6A Ken Griffey Jr. 4.00
6B Alex Rodriguez 5.00
6C Jay Buhner .50
7A Juan Gonzalez 1.50
7B Dean Palmer .50
7C Ivan Rodriguez 2.50
8A Ryan Klesko .50
8B Chipper Jones 3.50
8C Andruw Jones 3.00
9A Dante Bichette .50
9B Andres Galarraga .50
9C Vinny Castilla .50
10A Jeff Bagwell 3.00
10B Craig Biggio .50
10C Derek Bell .50
11A Mike Piazza 4.00
11B Raul Mondesi .50
11C Karim Garcia .50
12A Tony Gwynn 3.50
12B Ken Caminiti .50
12C Grog Vaughn .50

Sluggers & Hurlers

The 24-card, regular-sized set was inserted every 145 packs of Pacific Invincible baseball. The cards are numbered with an "SH-xA" or "SH-xaB." Each "A" card is the left half of a two-card set with the two players from the same team having their logo in the fit-together center. Each card has the player's name printed in gold foil along the bottom border with gold-foil swirls around the team logo. The card backs have a circular headshot with text in English and Spanish.

NM/M
Complete Set (24): 80.00
Common Player: 2.00
SH-1a Cal Ripken Jr. 10.00
SH-1b Mike Mussina 2.50
SH-2a Jose Canseco 2.50
SH-2b Roger Clemens 6.00
SH-3a Frank Thomas 3.50
SH-3b Wilson Alvarez 2.00
SH-4a Kenny Lofton 2.00
SH-4b Orel Hershiser 2.00
SH-5a Derek Jeter 10.00
SH-5b Andy Pettitte 2.00
SH-6a Ken Griffey Jr. 6.00
SH-6b Randy Johnson 3.50
SH-7a Alex Rodriguez 7.50
SH-7b Jamie Moyer 2.00
SH-8a Andruw Jones 3.50
SH-8b Greg Maddux 4.50
SH-9a Chipper Jones 4.50
SH-9b John Smoltz 2.00
SH-10a Jeff Bagwell 3.50
SH-10b Shane Reynolds 2.00
SH-11a Mike Piazza 6.00
SH-11b Hideo Nomo 2.50
SH-12a Tony Gwynn 4.50
SH-12b Fernando Valenzuela 2.00

Carlos Baerga Celebrities Softball

This set was produced for distribution to fans attending the third annual Carlos Baerga Celebrities Softball Game in Puerto Rico on December 14. Packs were handed out containing two cards from this set, a 1997 Pacific Crown Collection card, a '97 Pacific Invincible card, a Pacific logo card and an information card about card shops on the island. The softball celebrities cards have gold-foil highlighted borderless action photos from the 1996 game. Pacific and the charity game's logos are in upper-right and lower left. Horizontal backs have a player portrait photo at left and English/Spanish description of his participation in the event.

NM/M
Complete Set (10): 16.00
Common Player: 1.00
1 Carlos Baerga 1.00
2 Bernie Williams 1.00
3 Ivan Rodriguez 5.00
4 Sandy Alomar Jr. 1.00
5 Joey Cora 1.00
6 Roberto Alomar 1.50
7 Moises Alou 1.00
8 Rey Ordonez 1.00
9 Derek Jeter 10.00
10 David Justice 1.00

NationsBank Florida Marlins

Certainly one of the nicest team card sets ever given away at a promotional game was this Marlins set produced by Pacific and sponsored by NationsBank. The cello-wrapped set was given out to the first 16,000 children attending the June 27 Marlins game. The 2-1/2" x 3-1/2" cards are UV-coated on both sides with a gold-foil "wave" containing the player names on front. The producer, sponsor and team logos also appear on front. Backs have a swirling teal background with a player color portrait in the upper-right. Personal data, 1996 and career stats and a short career summary - in both English and Spanish - are also found on back.

NM/M
Complete Set (33): 6.00
Common Player: .25
1 Kurt Abbott .25
2 Moises Alou .25
3 Alex Arias .25
4 Bobby Bonilla .25
5 Kevin Brown .25
6 John Cangelosi .25
7 Luis Castillo .25
8 Jeff Conine .25
9 Jim Eisenreich .25
10 Alex Fernandez .25
11 Cliff Floyd .25
12 Rick Helling .25
13 Felix Heredia .25
14 Mark Hutton .25
15 Charles Johnson .25
16 Al Leiter .25
17 Robb Nen .25
18 Jay Powell .25
19 Pat Rapp .25
20 Edgar Renteria .25
21 Tony Saunders .25
22 Gary Sheffield .75
23 Devon White .25
24 Gregg Zaun .25
25 Jim Leyland .25
26 Rich Donnelly .25
27 Bruce Kimm .25
28 Jerry Manuel .25
29 Milt May .25
30 Larry Rothschild .25
31 Tommy Sandt .25
32 Billy the Marlin (Mascot) .25
(33) Header Card/Checklist .10

1998 Pacific

Pacific Baseball for 1998 is a 450-card, bilingual set. The base set features full-bleed photos with the Pacific Crown Collection logo in the upper-left and the player's name, position and team at the bottom. Inserts include Cramer's Choice Awards, In The Cage Laser-Cuts, Home Run Hitters, Team Checklist Laser-Cuts, Gold Crown Die-Cuts and Latinos of the Major Leagues. Three foil-color parallels were issued: Reds were found one per Wal-Mart exclusive retail pack; Silvers were found one per Hobby pack. Platinum Blues, numbered to 67 each, were found one per 73 packs.

NM/M
Complete Set (450): 40.00
Common Player: .05
Silvers: 3X
Inserted 1:1 H
Reds: 6X
Inserted 1:1 R
Platinum Blues: 15X
Inserted 1:73
Pack (12): 1.00
Wax Box (36): 20.00
1 Luis Alicea .05
2 Garret Anderson .05
3 Jason Dickson .05
4 Gary DiSarcina .05
5 Jim Edmonds .05
6 Darin Erstad .15
7 Chuck Finley .05
8 Shigetosi Hasegawa .05
9 Rickey Henderson .75
10 Dave Hollins .05
11 Mark Langston .05
12 Orlando Palmeiro .05
13 Tony Percival .05
14 Tony Phillips .05
15 Tim Salmon .05
16 Allen Watson .05
17 Roberto Alomar .25
18 Brady Anderson .05
19 Harold Baines .05
20 Armando Benitez .05
21 Geronimo Berroa .05
22 Mike Bordick .05
23 Eric Davis .05
24 Scott Erickson .05
25 Chris Hoiles .05
26 Jimmy Key .05
27 Aaron Ledesma .05
28 Mike Mussina .50
29 Randy Myers .05
30 Jesse Orosco .05
31 Rafael Palmeiro .65
32 Jeff Reboulet .05
33 Cal Ripken Jr. 2.00
34 B.J. Surhoff .05
35 Steve Avery .05
36 Darren Bragg .05
37 Wil Cordero .05
38 Jeff Frye .05
39 Nomar Garciaparra 1.00
40 Tom Gordon .05
41 Bill Haselman .05
42 Scott Hatteberg .05
43 Butch Henry .05
44 Reggie Jefferson .05
45 Tim Naehring .05
46 Troy O'Leary .05
47 Jeff Suppan .05
48 John Valentin .05
49 Mo Vaughn .05
50 Tim Wakefield .05
51 James Baldwin .05
52 Albert Belle .05
53 Tony Castillo .05
54 Doug Drabek .05
55 Ray Durham .05
56 Jorge Fabregas .05
57 Ozzie Guillen .05
58 Matt Karchner .05
59 Norberto Martin .05
60 Dave Martinez .05
61 Lyle Mouton .05
62 Jaime Navarro .05
63 Frank Thomas .75
64 Mario Valdez .05
65 Robin Ventura .05
66 Sandy Alomar Jr. .05
67 Paul Assenmacher .05
68 Tony Fernandez .05
69 Brian Giles .05
70 Marquis Grissom .05
71 Orel Hershiser .05
72 Mike Jackson .05
73 David Justice .05
74 Albie Lopez .05
75 Jose Mesa .05
76 Charles Nagy .05
77 Chad Ogea .05
78 Manny Ramirez .75
79 Jim Thome .60
80 Omar Vizquel .05
81 Matt Williams .05
82 Jaret Wright .05
83 Willie Blair .05
84 Raul Casanova .05
85 Tony Clark .05
86 Deivi Cruz .05
87 Damion Easley .05
88 Travis Fryman .05
89 Bobby Higginson .05
90 Brian Hunter .05
91 Todd Jones .05
92 Dan Miceli .05
93 Brian Moehler .05
94 Melvin Nieves .05
95 Jody Reed .05
96 Justin Thompson .05
97 Bubba Trammell .05
98 Kevin Appier .05
99 Jay Bell .05
100 Yamil Benitez .05
101 Johnny Damon .35
102 Chili Davis .05
103 Jermaine Dye .05
104 Jed Hansen .05
105 Jeff King .05
106 Mike Macfarlane .05
107 Felix Martinez .05
108 Jeff Montgomery .05
109 Jose Offerman .05
110 Dean Palmer .05
111 Hipolito Pichardo .05
112 Jose Rosado .05
113 Jeromy Burnitz .05
114 Jeff Cirillo .05
115 Cal Eldred .05
116 John Jaha .05
117 Doug Jones .05
118 Scott Karl .05
119 Jesse Levis .05
120 Mark Loretta .05
121 Ben McDonald .05
122 Jose Mercedes .05
123 Matt Mieske .05
124 Dave Nilsson .05
125 Jose Valentin .05
126 Fernando Vina .05
127 Gerald Williams .05
128 Rick Aguilera .05
129 Rich Becker .05
130 Ron Coomer .05
131 Marty Cordova .05
132 Eddie Guardado .05
133 LaTroy Hawkins .05
134 Denny Hocking .05
135 Chuck Knoblauch .05
136 Matt Lawton .05
137 Pat Meares .05
138 Paul Molitor .75
139 David Ortiz .50
140 Brad Radke .05

141 Terry Steinbach .05
142 Bob Tewksbury .05
143 Javier Valentin .05
144 Wade Boggs 1.00
145 David Cone .05
146 Chad Curtis .05
147 Cecil Fielder .05
148 Joe Girardi .05
149 Dwight Gooden .05
150 Hideki Irabu .05
151 Derek Jeter 2.00
152 Tino Martinez .05
153 Ramiro Mendoza .05
154 Paul O'Neill .05
155 Andy Pettitte .20
156 Jorge Posada .05
157 Mariano Rivera .15
158 Rey Sanchez .05
159 Luis Sojo .05
160 David Wells .05
161 Bernie Williams .05
162 Rafael Bournigal .05
163 Scott Brosius .05
164 Jose Canseco .50
165 Jason Giambi .60
166 Ben Grieve .05
167 Dave Magadan .05
168 Brent Mayne .05
169 Jason McDonald .05
170 Izzy Molina .05
171 Ariel Prieto .05
172 Carlos Reyes .05
173 Scott Spiezio .05
174 Matt Stairs .05
175 Bill Taylor .05
176 Dave Telgheder .05
177 Steve Wojciechowski .05
178 Rich Amaral .05
179 Bobby Ayala .05
180 Jay Buhner .05
181 Rafael Carmona .05
182 Ken Cloude .05
183 Joey Cora .05
184 Russ Davis .05
185 Jeff Fassero .05
186 Ken Griffey Jr. 1.25
187 Raul Ibanez .05
188 Randy Johnson .75
189 Roberto Kelly .05
190 Edgar Martinez .05
191 Jamie Moyer .05
192 Omar Olivares .05
193 Alex Rodriguez 1.50
194 Heathcliff Slocumb .05
195 Paul Sorrento .05
196 Dan Wilson .05
197 Scott Bailes .05
198 John Burkett .05
199 Domingo Cedeno .05
200 Will Clark .05
201 Hanley Frias **RC** .05
202 Juan Gonzalez .40
203 Tom Goodwin .05
204 Rusty Greer .05
205 Wilson Heredia .05
206 Darren Oliver .05
207 Billy Ripken .05
208 Ivan Rodriguez .65
209 Lee Stevens .05
210 Fernando Tatis .05
211 John Wetteland .05
212 Bobby Witt .05
213 Jacob Brumfield .05
214 Joe Carter .05
215 Roger Clemens 1.25
216 Felipe Crespo .05
217 Jose Cruz Jr. .05
218 Carlos Delgado .50
219 Mariano Duncan .05
220 Carlos Garcia .05
221 Alex Gonzalez .05
222 Juan Guzman .05
223 Pat Hentgen .05
224 Orlando Merced .05
225 Tomas Perez .05
226 Paul Quantrill .05
227 Benito Santiago .05
228 Woody Williams .05
229 Rafael Belliard .05
230 Jeff Blauser .05
231 Pedro Borbon .05
232 Tom Glavine .25
233 Tony Graffanino .05
234 Andruw Jones .75
235 Chipper Jones 1.00
236 Ryan Klesko .05
237 Mark Lemke .05
238 Kenny Lofton .05
239 Javier Lopez .05
240 Fred McGriff .05
241 Greg Maddux 1.00
242 Denny Neagle .05
243 John Smoltz .05
244 Michael Tucker .05
245 Mark Wohlers .05
246 Manny Alexander .05
247 Miguel Batista .05
248 Mark Clark .05
249 Doug Glanville .05
250 Jeremi Gonzalez .05
251 Mark Grace .05
252 Jose Hernandez .05
253 Lance Johnson .05
254 Brooks Kieschnick .05
255 Kevin Orie .05
256 Ryne Sandberg 1.00
257 Scott Servais .05
258 Sammy Sosa 1.00
259 Kevin Tapani .05
260 Ramon Tatis .05
261 Bret Boone .05
262 Dave Burba .05
263 Brook Fordyce .05
264 Willie Greene .05
265 Barry Larkin .05
266 Pedro A. Martinez .05
267 Hal Morris .05
268 Joe Oliver .05
269 Eduardo Perez .05
270 Pokey Reese .05
271 Felix Rodriguez .05
272 Deion Sanders .05
273 Reggie Sanders .05
274 Jeff Shaw .05
275 Scott Sullivan .05
276 Brett Tomko .05
277 Roger Bailey .05
278 Dante Bichette .05
279 Ellis Burks .05
280 Vinny Castilla .05
281 Frank Castillo .05
282 Mike DeJean **RC** .05
283 Andres Galarraga .05
284 Darren Holmes .05
285 Kirt Manwaring .05
286 Quinton McCracken .05
287 Neifi Perez .05
288 Steve Reed .05
289 John Thomson .05
290 Larry Walker .05
291 Walt Weiss .05
292 Kurt Abbott .05
293 Antonio Alfonseca .05
294 Moises Alou .05
295 Alex Arias .05
296 Bobby Bonilla .05
297 Kevin Brown .05
298 Craig Counsell .05
299 Darren Daulton .05
300 Jim Eisenreich .05
301 Alex Fernandez .05
302 Felix Heredia .05
303 Livan Hernandez .05
304 Charles Johnson .05
305 Al Leiter .05
306 Robb Nen .05
307 Edgar Renteria .05
308 Gary Sheffield .45
309 Devon White .05
310 Bob Abreu .10
311 Brad Ausmus .05
312 Jeff Bagwell .75
313 Derek Bell .05
314 Sean Berry .05
315 Craig Biggio .05
316 Ramon Garcia .05
317 Luis Gonzalez .05
318 Ricky Gutierrez .05
319 Mike Hampton .05
320 Richard Hidalgo .05
321 Thomas Howard .05
322 Darryl Kile .05
323 Jose Lima .05
324 Shane Reynolds .05
325 Bill Spiers .05
326 Tom Candiotti .05
327 Roger Cedeno .05
328 Greg Gagne .05
329 Karim Garcia .05
330 Wilton Guerrero .05
331 Todd Hollandsworth .05
332 Eric Karros .05
333 Ramon Martinez .05
334 Raul Mondesi .05
335 Otis Nixon .05
336 Hideo Nomo .40
337 Antonio Osuna .05
338 Chan Ho Park .05
339 Mike Piazza 1.25
340 Dennis Reyes .05
341 Ismael Valdes .05
342 Todd Worrell .05
343 Todd Zeile .05
344 Darrin Fletcher .05
345 Mark Grudzielanek .05
346 Vladimir Guerrero .75
347 Dustin Hermanson .05
348 Mike Lansing .05
349 Pedro Martinez .75
350 Ryan McGuire .05
351 Jose Paniagua .05
352 Carlos Perez .05
353 Henry Rodriguez .05
354 F.P. Santangelo .05
355 David Segui .05
356 Ugueth Urbina .05
357 Marc Valdes .05
358 Jose Vidro .05
359 Rondell White .05
360 Juan Acevedo .05
361 Edgardo Alfonzo .05
362 Carlos Baerga .05
363 Carl Everett .05
364 John Franco .05
365 Bernard Gilkey .05
366 Todd Hundley .05
367 Butch Huskey .05
368 Bobby Jones .05
369 Takashi Kashiwada .05
370 Greg McMichael .05
371 Brian McRae .05
372 Alex Ochoa .05
373 John Olerud .05
374 Rey Ordonez .05
375 Turk Wendell .05
376 Ricky Bottalico .05
377 Rico Brogna .05
378 Lenny Dykstra .05
379 Bobby Estalella .05
380 Wayne Gomes .05
381 Tyler Green .05
382 Gregg Jefferies .05
383 Mark Leiter .05
384 Mike Lieberthal .05
385 Mickey Morandini .05
386 Scott Rolen .60
387 Curt Schilling .25
388 Kevin Stocker .05
389 Danny Tartabull .05
390 Jermaine Allensworth .05
391 Adrian Brown .05
392 Jason Christiansen .05
393 Steve Cooke .05
394 Francisco Cordova .05
395 Jose Guillen .05
396 Jason Kendall .05
397 Jon Lieber .05
398 Esteban Loaiza .05
399 Al Martin .05
400 Kevin Polcovich **RC** .05
401 Joe Randa .05
402 Ricardo Rincon .05
403 Tony Womack .05
404 Kevin Young .05
405 Andy Benes .05
406 Royce Clayton .05
407 Delino DeShields .05
408 Mike Difelice .05
409 Dennis Eckersley .60
410 John Frascatore .05
411 Gary Gaetti .05
412 Ron Gant .05
413 Brian Jordan .05
414 Ray Lankford .05
415 Willie McGee .05
416 Mark McGwire 1.50
417 Matt Morris .05
418 Luis Ordaz .05
419 Todd Stottlemyre .05
420 Andy Ashby .05
421 Jim Bruske .05
422 Ken Caminiti .05
423 Will Cunnane .05
424 Steve Finley .05
425 John Flaherty .05
426 Chris Gomez .05
427 Tony Gwynn 1.00
428 Joey Hamilton .05
429 Carlos Hernandez .05
430 Sterling Hitchcock .05
431 Trevor Hoffman .05
432 Wally Joyner .05
433 Greg Vaughn .05
434 Quilvio Veras .05
435 Wilson Alvarez .05
436 Rod Beck .05
437 Barry Bonds 2.00
438 Jacob Cruz .05
439 Shawn Estes .05
440 Darryl Hamilton .05
441 Roberto Hernandez .05
442 Glenallen Hill .05
443 Stan Javier .05
444 Brian Johnson .05
445 Jeff Kent .05
446 Bill Mueller .05
447 Kirk Rueter .05
448 J.T. Snow .05
449 Julian Tavarez .05
450 Jose Vizcaino .05

Red/Silver/Blue

Red, Silver and Platinum Blue parallels were printed for all 450 cards in Pacific, with the gold foil found on base cards being replaced by one of those foils. Red foil versions were inserted one per Wal-Mart pack (retail). Silver versions were inserted one per hobby pack. Platinum Blues, limited to 67 sets, were a one per 73 pack insert.

NM/M

Common Red: 1.50
Red Stars: 6X
Common Silver: .75
Silver Stars: 3X
Common Platinum Blue: 3.00
Platinum Blue Stars: 15X

Cramer's Choice

Cramer's Choice Awards is a 10-card die-cut insert. The cards feature the top player at each position as selected by Pacific CEO Mike Cramer. Each card is shaped like a trophy.

NM/M

Complete Set (10): 150.00
Common Player: 7.50
Inserted 1:721
1 Greg Maddux 15.00
2 Roberto Alomar 7.50
3 Cal Ripken Jr. 30.00
4 Nomar Garciaparra 15.00
5 Larry Walker 7.50
6 Mike Piazza 17.50

7 Mark McGwire 25.00
8 Tony Gwynn 15.00
9 Ken Griffey Jr. 20.00
10 Roger Clemens 17.50

Gold Crown Die-Cuts

Gold Crown Die-Cuts is a 36-card insert seeded one per 37 packs. Each card has a holographic silver foil background and gold etching. The cards are die-cut around a crown design at the top.

NM/M

Complete Set (36): 85.00
Common Player: 1.50
1 Chipper Jones 4.00
2 Greg Maddux 4.00
3 Denny Neagle 1.50
4 Roberto Alomar 2.00
5 Rafael Palmeiro 2.50
6 Cal Ripken Jr. 8.00
7 Nomar Garciaparra 4.00
8 Mo Vaughn 1.50
9 Frank Thomas 3.00
10 Sandy Alomar Jr. 1.50
11 David Justice 1.50
12 Manny Ramirez 3.00
13 Andres Galarraga 1.50
14 Larry Walker 1.50
15 Moises Alou 1.50
16 Livan Hernandez 1.50
17 Gary Sheffield 2.00
18 Jeff Bagwell 3.00
19 Raul Mondesi 1.50
20 Hideo Nomo 2.00
21 Mike Piazza 4.50
22 Derek Jeter 8.00
23 Tino Martinez 1.50
24 Bernie Williams 1.50
25 Ben Grieve 1.50
26 Mark McGwire 6.50
27 Tony Gwynn 4.00
28 Barry Bonds 8.00
29 Ken Griffey Jr. 5.00
30 Randy Johnson 3.00
31 Edgar Martinez 1.50
32 Alex Rodriguez 6.50
33 Juan Gonzalez 2.00
34 Ivan Rodriguez 2.50
35 Roger Clemens 4.50
36 Jose Cruz Jr. 1.50

Home Run Hitters

This 20-card set was inserted one per 73 packs. The full-foil cards feature a color player photo with their home run total from 1997 embossed in the background.

NM/M

Complete Set (20): 50.00
Common Player: 1.00
1 Rafael Palmeiro 3.00
2 Mo Vaughn 1.00
3 Sammy Sosa 4.00
4 Albert Belle 1.00
5 Frank Thomas 3.50
6 David Justice 1.00
7 Jim Thome 3.00
8 Matt Williams 1.00
9 Vinny Castilla 1.00
10 Andres Galarraga 1.00
11 Larry Walker 1.00
12 Jeff Bagwell 3.50
13 Mike Piazza 4.50
14 Tino Martinez 1.00
15 Mark McGwire 6.00
16 Barry Bonds 7.50
17 Jay Buhner 1.00
18 Ken Griffey Jr. 5.00
19 Alex Rodriguez 6.00
20 Juan Gonzalez 2.00

In the Cage

This insert set features top players in a die-cut batting cage. The netting on the cage is laser-cut. In The Cage laser-cuts were inserted one per 145 packs.

NM/M

Complete Set (20): 175.00
Common Player: 4.00
1 Chipper Jones 12.00
2 Roberto Alomar 4.00
3 Cal Ripken Jr. 25.00
4 Nomar Garciaparra 12.00
5 Frank Thomas 10.00
6 Sandy Alomar Jr. 4.00
7 David Justice 4.00
8 Larry Walker 4.00
9 Bobby Bonilla 4.00
10 Mike Piazza 16.00
11 Tino Martinez 4.00
12 Bernie Williams 4.00
13 Mark McGwire 20.00
14 Tony Gwynn 12.00
15 Barry Bonds 25.00
16 Ken Griffey Jr. 16.00
17 Edgar Martinez 4.00
18 Alex Rodriguez 20.00
19 Juan Gonzalez 6.00
20 Ivan Rodriguez 7.50

Latinos of the Major Leagues

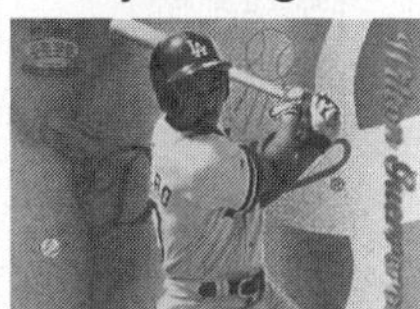

This 36-card set features Major League players of Hispanic descent. The background has a world map on the left, the player's team logo in the center and an American flag on the right.

NM/M

Complete Set (36): 30.00
Common Player: .50
Inserted 2:37
1 Andruw Jones 2.50
2 Javier Lopez .50
3 Roberto Alomar 1.25
4 Geronimo Berroa .50
5 Rafael Palmeiro 2.00
6 Nomar Garciaparra 3.00
7 Sammy Sosa 3.00
8 Ozzie Guillen .50
9 Sandy Alomar Jr. .50
10 Manny Ramirez 2.50
11 Omar Vizquel .50
12 Vinny Castilla .50
13 Andres Galarraga .50
14 Moises Alou .50
15 Bobby Bonilla .50
16 Livan Hernandez .50
17 Edgar Renteria .50
18 Wilton Guerrero .50
19 Raul Mondesi .50
20 Ismael Valdes .50
21 Fernando Vina .50
22 Pedro Martinez 2.50
23 Edgardo Alfonzo .50
24 Carlos Baerga .50
25 Rey Ordonez .50
26 Tino Martinez .50
27 Mariano Rivera 1.00
28 Bernie Williams .50
29 Jose Canseco 1.50
30 Joey Cora .50
31 Roberto Kelly .50
32 Edgar Martinez .50
33 Alex Rodriguez 3.50
34 Juan Gonzalez 1.50
35 Ivan Rodriguez 2.00
36 Jose Cruz Jr. .50

Team Checklists

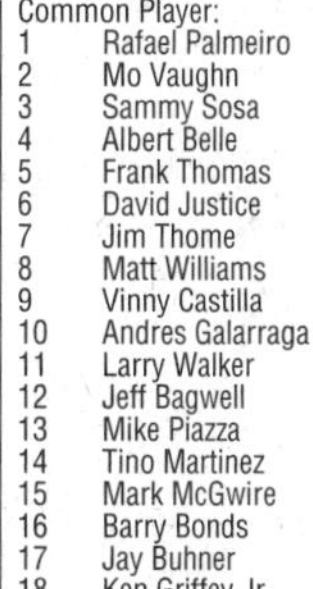

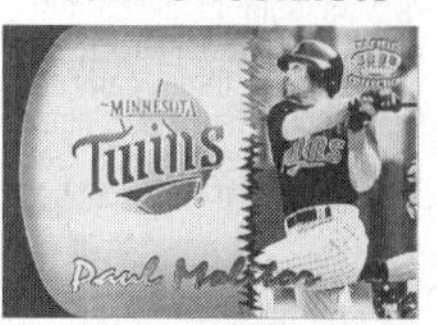

Team Checklists is a 30-card insert in the bilingual Pacific Baseball set. One card was created for each team. A player photo is featured on the right with the team logo laser-cut into a bat barrel design on the left.

NM/M

Complete Set (30): 60.00
Common Player: .50
1 Tim Salmon, Jim Edmonds .50
2 Cal Ripken Jr., Roberto Alomar 6.00
3 Nomar Garciaparra, Mo Vaughn 3.50
4 Frank Thomas, Albert Belle 2.50
5 Sandy Alomar Jr., Manny Ramirez 2.50
6 Justin Thompson, Tony Clark .50
7 Johnny Damon, Jermaine Dye .75
8 Dave Nilsson, Jeff Cirillo .50
9 Paul Molitor, Chuck Knoblauch 2.50
10 Tino Martinez, Derek Jeter 6.00
11 Ben Grieve, Jose Canseco 1.00
12 Ken Griffey Jr., Alex Rodriguez 5.00
13 Juan Gonzalez, Ivan Rodriguez 2.00
14 Jose Cruz Jr., Roger Clemens 4.00
15 Greg Maddux, Chipper Jones 3.50
16 Sammy Sosa, Mark Grace 3.50
17 Barry Larkin, Deion Sanders .50
18 Larry Walker, Andres Galarraga .50
19 Moises Alou, Bobby Bonilla .50
20 Jeff Bagwell, Craig Biggio 2.50
21 Mike Piazza, Hideo Nomo 4.00
22 Pedro Martinez, Henry Rodriguez 2.50
23 Rey Ordonez, Carlos Baerga .50
24 Curt Schilling, Scott Rolen 1.50
25 Al Martin, Tony Womack .50
26 Mark McGwire, Dennis Eckersley 5.00
27 Tony Gwynn, Wally Joyner 3.50
28 Barry Bonds, J.T. Snow 6.00
29 Matt Williams, Jay Bell .50
30 Fred McGriff, Roberto Hernandez .50

1998 Pacific Aurora

The Aurora base set consists of 200 cards printed on 24-point board. The cards have a color photo bordered on two sides by a thick green (National League) or red (A.L.) border. A portrait photo appears in the upper-right corner. Back has another portrait photo, 1997 and career stats, career highlights and personal data. Aurora was sold in six-card foil packs. Inserts include Pennant Fever (with three parallels), Hardball Cel-Fusions, Kings of the Major Leagues, On Deck Laser-Cuts and Pacific Cubes.

		NM/M
Complete Set (200):		20.00
Common Player:		.05
Pack (6):		1.00
Wax Box (36):		20.00
1	Garret Anderson	.05
2	Jim Edmonds	.05
3	Darin Erstad	.15
4	Cecil Fielder	.05
5	Chuck Finley	.05
6	Todd Greene	.05
7	Ken Hill	.05
8	Tim Salmon	.05
9	Roberto Alomar	.20
10	Brady Anderson	.05
11	Joe Carter	.05
12	Mike Mussina	.35
13	Rafael Palmeiro	.65
14	Cal Ripken Jr.	2.50
15	B.J. Surhoff	.05
16	Steve Avery	.05
17	Nomar Garciaparra	1.00
18	Pedro Martinez	.75
19	John Valentin	.05
20	Jason Varitek	.05
21	Mo Vaughn	.05
22	Albert Belle	.05
23	Ray Durham	.05
24	Magglio Ordonez **RC**	1.50
25	Frank Thomas	.75
26	Robin Ventura	.05
27	Sandy Alomar Jr.	.05
28	Travis Fryman	.05
29	Dwight Gooden	.05
30	David Justice	.05
31	Kenny Lofton	.05
32	Manny Ramirez	.75
33	Jim Thome	.60
34	Omar Vizquel	.05
35	Enrique Wilson	.05
36	Jaret Wright	.05
37	Tony Clark	.05
38	Bobby Higginson	.05
39	Brian Hunter	.05
40	Bip Roberts	.05
41	Justin Thompson	.05
42	Jeff Conine	.05
43	Johnny Damon	.35
44	Jermaine Dye	.05
45	Jeff King	.05
46	Jeff Montgomery	.05
47	Hal Morris	.05
48	Dean Palmer	.05
49	Terry Pendleton	.05
50	Rick Aguilera	.05
51	Marty Cordova	.05
52	Paul Molitor	.75
53	Otis Nixon	.05
54	Brad Radke	.05
55	Terry Steinbach	.05
56	Todd Walker	.05
57	Chili Davis	.05
58	Derek Jeter	2.50
59	Chuck Knoblauch	.05
60	Tino Martinez	.05
61	Paul O'Neill	.05
62	Andy Pettitte	.20
63	Mariano Rivera	.15
64	Bernie Williams	.05
65	Jason Giambi	.50
66	Ben Grieve	.05
67	Rickey Henderson	.75
68	A.J. Hinch	.05
69	Kenny Rogers	.05
70	Jay Buhner	.05
71	Joey Cora	.05
72	Ken Griffey Jr.	1.50
73	Randy Johnson	.75
74	Edgar Martinez	.05
75	Jamie Moyer	.05
76	Alex Rodriguez	2.00
77	David Segui	.05
78	Rolando Arrojo **RC**	.35
79	Wade Boggs	1.00
80	Roberto Hernandez	.05
81	Dave Martinez	.05
82	Fred McGriff	.05
83	Paul Sorrento	.05
84	Kevin Stocker	.05
85	Will Clark	.05
86	Juan Gonzalez	.40
87	Tom Goodwin	.05
88	Rusty Greer	.05
89	Ivan Rodriguez	.65
90	John Wetteland	.05
91	Jose Canseco	.40
92	Roger Clemens	1.25
93	Jose Cruz Jr.	.05
94	Carlos Delgado	.50
95	Pat Hentgen	.05
96	Jay Bell	.05
97	Andy Benes	.05
98	Karim Garcia	.05
99	Travis Lee	.05
100	Devon White	.05
101	Matt Williams	.05
102	Andres Galarraga	.05
103	Tom Glavine	.30
104	Andruw Jones	.75
105	Chipper Jones	1.00
106	Ryan Klesko	.05
107	Javy Lopez	.05
108	Greg Maddux	1.00
109	Walt Weiss	.05
110	Rod Beck	.05
111	Jeff Blauser	.05
112	Mark Grace	.05
113	Lance Johnson	.05
114	Mickey Morandini	.05
115	Henry Rodriguez	.05
116	Sammy Sosa	1.00
117	Kerry Wood	.35
118	Lenny Harris	.05
119	Damian Jackson	.05
120	Barry Larkin	.05
121	Reggie Sanders	.05
122	Brett Tomko	.05
123	Dante Bichette	.05
124	Ellis Burks	.05
125	Vinny Castilla	.05
126	Todd Helton	.75
127	Darryl Kile	.05
128	Larry Walker	.05
129	Bobby Bonilla	.05
130	Livan Hernandez	.05
131	Charles Johnson	.05
132	Derrek Lee	.50
133	Edgar Renteria	.05
134	Gary Sheffield	.35
135	Moises Alou	.05
136	Jeff Bagwell	.75
137	Derek Bell	.05
138	Craig Biggio	.05
139	John Halama **RC**	.15
140	Mike Hampton	.05
141	Richard Hidalgo	.05
142	Wilton Guerrero	.05
143	Todd Hollandsworth	.05
144	Eric Karros	.05
145	Paul Konerko	.05
146	Raul Mondesi	.05
147	Hideo Nomo	.40
148	Chan Ho Park	.05
149	Mike Piazza	1.25
150	Jeromy Burnitz	.05
151	Todd Dunn	.05
152	Marquis Grissom	.05
153	John Jaha	.05
154	Dave Nilsson	.05
155	Fernando Vina	.05
156	Mark Grudzielanek	.05
157	Vladimir Guerrero	.75
158	F.P. Santangelo	.05
159	Jose Vidro	.05
160	Rondell White	.05
161	Edgardo Alfonzo	.05
162	Carlos Baerga	.05
163	John Franco	.05
164	Todd Hundley	.05
165	Brian McRae	.05
166	John Olerud	.05
167	Rey Ordonez	.05
168	Masato Yoshii **RC**	.25
169	Ricky Bottalico	.05
170	Doug Glanville	.05
171	Gregg Jefferies	.05
172	Desi Relaford	.05
173	Scott Rolen	.60
174	Curt Schilling	.30
175	Jose Guillen	.05
176	Jason Kendall	.05
177	Al Martin	.05
178	Abraham Nunez	.05
179	Kevin Young	.05
180	Royce Clayton	.05
181	Delino DeShields	.05
182	Gary Gaetti	.05
183	Ron Gant	.05
184	Brian Jordan	.05
185	Ray Lankford	.05
186	Willie McGee	.05
187	Mark McGwire	2.00
188	Kevin Brown	.05
189	Ken Caminiti	.05
190	Steve Finley	.05
191	Tony Gwynn	1.00
192	Wally Joyner	.05
193	Ruben Rivera	.05
194	Quilvio Veras	.05
195	Barry Bonds	2.50
196	Shawn Estes	.05
197	Orel Hershiser	.05
198	Jeff Kent	.05
199	Robb Nen	.05
200	J.T. Snow	.05

Cubes

A cardboard cube presenting player photos on top and three sides, plus a side of stats was created as a hobby-only insert for Pacific Aurora. The assembled, shrink-wrapped cubes were packed one per box.

		NM/M
Complete Set (20):		75.00
Common Player:		1.50
Inserted 1:Box		
1	Travis Lee	1.50
2	Chipper Jones	4.00
3	Greg Maddux	4.00
4	Cal Ripken Jr.	10.00
5	Nomar Garciaparra	4.00
6	Frank Thomas	3.00
7	Manny Ramirez	3.00
8	Larry Walker	1.50
9	Hideo Nomo	2.00
10	Mike Piazza	5.00
11	Derek Jeter	10.00
12	Ben Grieve	1.50
13	Mark McGwire	7.50
14	Tony Gwynn	4.00
15	Barry Bonds	10.00
16	Ken Griffey Jr.	6.00
17	Alex Rodriguez	7.50
18	Wade Boggs	4.00
19	Juan Gonzalez	2.00
20	Jose Cruz Jr.	1.50

Hardball Cel-Fusion

Hardball Cel-Fusion features a die-cut celluloid baseball fused to a foiled and etched card.

		NM/M
Complete Set (20):		60.00
Common Player:		2.00
Inserted 1:73		
1	Travis Lee	2.00
2	Chipper Jones	6.00
3	Greg Maddux	6.00
4	Cal Ripken Jr.	15.00
5	Nomar Garciaparra	6.00
6	Frank Thomas	4.50
7	David Justice	2.00
8	Jeff Bagwell	4.50
9	Hideo Nomo	3.00
10	Mike Piazza	7.50
11	Derek Jeter	15.00
12	Ben Grieve	2.00
13	Scott Rolen	3.00
14	Mark McGwire	12.00
15	Tony Gwynn	6.00
16	Ken Griffey Jr.	9.00
17	Alex Rodriguez	12.00
18	Ivan Rodriguez	3.50
19	Roger Clemens	7.50
20	Jose Cruz Jr.	2.00

Kings of the Major Leagues

This 10-card insert features star players on fully-foiled cards. A marble-look semi-circular panel at bottom has the player identification. The action photo at center is set against a bronze orb and concentric circles of gold-foil repeat the "Kings of the Major Leagues" title. Backs have a color portrait on a red and black background along with a few sentences about the player.

		NM/M
Complete Set (10):		75.00
Common Player:		7.50
Inserted 1:361		
1	Chipper Jones	9.00
2	Greg Maddux	9.00
3	Cal Ripken Jr.	20.00
4	Nomar Garciaparra	9.00
5	Frank Thomas	7.50
6	Mike Piazza	10.00
7	Mark McGwire	15.00
8	Tony Gwynn	9.00
9	Ken Griffey Jr.	12.00
10	Alex Rodriguez	15.00

On Deck Laser-Cut

On Deck Laser-Cut is a 20-card insert in packs of 1998 Pacific Aurora. Fronts have an action photo at top, with an intricately die-cut pattern in gold foil below. Backs feature a portrait photo.

		NM/M
Complete Set (20):		30.00
Common Player:		.60
Inserted 1:9		
1	Travis Lee	.60
2	Chipper Jones	2.25
3	Greg Maddux	2.25
4	Cal Ripken Jr.	6.00
5	Nomar Garciaparra	2.25
6	Frank Thomas	1.50
7	Manny Ramirez	1.50
8	Larry Walker	.60
9	Hideo Nomo	1.00
10	Mike Piazza	2.50
11	Derek Jeter	6.00
12	Ben Grieve	.60
13	Mark McGwire	4.50
14	Tony Gwynn	2.25
15	Barry Bonds	6.00
16	Ken Griffey Jr.	3.00
17	Alex Rodriguez	4.50
18	Wade Boggs	2.25
19	Juan Gonzalez	1.00
20	Jose Cruz Jr.	.60

Pennant Fever

Pennant Fever is a 50-card insert seeded one per pack. Each card is fully foiled and etched. The color player image is duplicated in the upper-left corner with an image stamped in gold foil. Pennant Fever has four parallels. Red cards are a 1:4 retail insert. The Silver retail parallel is numbered to 250, Platinum Blue is numbered to 100 and the Copper hobby parallel is numbered to 20. Tony Gwynn signed his card serially numbered one in each insert.

		NM/M
Complete Set (50):		25.00
Common Player:		.20
Inserted 1:1		
Reds (1:4 Retail):		2X
Silvers (250 Sets):		4X
Platinum Blues (100 Sets):		12X
Coppers (20 Sets):		40X
1	Tony Gwynn	1.00
2	Derek Jeter	2.00
3	Alex Rodriguez	1.50
4	Paul Molitor	.75
5	Nomar Garciaparra	1.00
6	Jeff Bagwell	.75
7	Ivan Rodriguez	.65
8	Cal Ripken Jr.	2.00
9	Matt Williams	.20
10	Chipper Jones	1.00
11	Edgar Martinez	.20
12	Wade Boggs	1.00
13	Paul Konerko	.30
14	Ben Grieve	.20
15	Sandy Alomar Jr.	.20
16	Travis Lee	.20
17	Scott Rolen	.65
18	Ryan Klesko	.20
19	Juan Gonzalez	.40
20	Albert Belle	.20
21	Roger Clemens	1.25
22	Javy Lopez	.20
23	Jose Cruz Jr.	.20
24	Ken Griffey Jr.	1.25
25	Mark McGwire	1.50
26	Brady Anderson	.20
27	Jaret Wright	.20
28	Roberto Alomar	.30
29	Joe Carter	.20
30	Hideo Nomo	40
31	Mike Piazza	1.25
32	Andres Galarraga	.20
33	Larry Walker	.20
34	Tim Salmon	.20
35	Frank Thomas	.75
36	Moises Alou	.20
37	David Justice	.20
38	Manny Ramirez	.75
39	Jim Edmonds	.20
40	Barry Bonds	2.00
41	Jim Thome	.65
42	Mo Vaughn	.20
43	Rafael Palmeiro	.65
44	Darin Erstad	.30
45	Pedro Martinez	.75
46	Greg Maddux	1.00
47	Jose Canseco	.45
48	Vladimir Guerrero	.75
49	Bernie Williams	.20
50	Randy Johnson	.75

1998 Pacific Crown Royale

The Crown Royale base set consists of 144 die-cut cards. The cards have a horizontal layout and are die-cut around a crown design at the top. The cards are double-foiled and etched. Inserts include Diamond Knights, Pillars of the Game, Race to the Record, All-Star Die-Cuts, Firestone on Baseball and Cramer's Choice Awards.

		NM/M
Complete Set (144):		60.00
Common Player:		.20
Pack (6):		1.00
Wax Box (24):		20.00
1	Garret Anderson	.20
2	Jim Edmonds	.20
3	Darin Erstad	.50
4	Tim Salmon	.20
5	Jarrod Washburn	.20
6	David Dellucci	.20
7	Travis Lee	.20
8	Devon White	.20
9	Matt Williams	.20
10	Andres Galarraga	.20
11	Tom Glavine	.35
12	Andruw Jones	2.00
13	Chipper Jones	3.00
14	Ryan Klesko	.20
15	Javy Lopez	.20
16	Greg Maddux	3.00
17	Walt Weiss	.20
18	Roberto Alomar	.75
19	Harold Baines	.20
20	Eric Davis	.20
21	Mike Mussina	1.00
22	Rafael Palmeiro	1.50
23	Cal Ripken Jr.	5.00
24	Nomar Garciaparra	3.00
25	Pedro Martinez	2.00
26	Troy O'Leary	.20
27	Mo Vaughn	.20
28	Tim Wakefield	.20
29	Mark Grace	.20
30	Mickey Morandini	.20
31	Sammy Sosa	3.00
32	Kerry Wood	.50
33	Albert Belle	.20
34	Mike Caruso	.20
35	Ray Durham	.20
36	Frank Thomas	2.00
37	Robin Ventura	.20
38	Bret Boone	.20
39	Sean Casey	.25
40	Barry Larkin	.20
41	Reggie Sanders	.20
42	Sandy Alomar Jr.	.20
43	David Justice	.20
44	Kenny Lofton	.20
45	Manny Ramirez	2.00
46	Jim Thome	1.00
47	Omar Vizquel	.20
48	Jaret Wright	.20
49	Dante Bichette	.20
50	Ellis Burks	.20
51	Vinny Castilla	.20
52	Todd Helton	2.00
53	Larry Walker	.20
54	Tony Clark	.20
55	Damion Easley	.20
56	Bobby Higginson	.20
57	Cliff Floyd	.20
58	Livan Hernandez	.20
59	Derrek Lee	.75
60	Edgar Renteria	.20
61	Moises Alou	.20
62	Jeff Bagwell	2.00
63	Derek Bell	.20
64	Craig Biggio	.20
65	Johnny Damon	.35
66	Jeff King	.20
67	Hal Morris	.20
68	Dean Palmer	.20
69	Bobby Bonilla	.20
70	Eric Karros	.20
71	Raul Mondesi	.20
72	Gary Sheffield	.75
73	Jeromy Burnitz	.20
74	Jeff Cirillo	.20
75	Marquis Grissom	.20
76	Fernando Vina	.20
77	Marty Cordova	.20
78	Pat Meares	.20
79	Paul Molitor	2.00
80	Terry Steinbach	.20
81	Todd Walker	.20
82	Brad Fullmer	.20
83	Vladimir Guerrero	2.00
84	Carl Pavano	.20
85	Rondell White	.20
86	Carlos Baerga	.20
87	Hideo Nomo	1.00
88	John Olerud	.20
89	Rey Ordonez	.20
90	Mike Piazza	3.00
91	Masato Yoshii **RC**	.75
92	Orlando Hernandez **RC**	.75
93	Hideki Irabu	.20
94	Derek Jeter	5.00
95	Chuck Knoblauch	.20
96	Ricky Ledee	.20
97	Tino Martinez	.20
98	Paul O'Neill	.20
99	Bernie Williams	.20
100	Jason Giambi	1.25
101	Ben Grieve	.20
102	Rickey Henderson	2.00
103	Matt Stairs	.20
104	Bob Abreu	.25
105	Doug Glanville	.20
106	Scott Rolen	1.50
107	Curt Schilling	.35
108	Jose Guillen	.20
109	Jason Kendall	.20
110	Jason Schmidt	.20
111	Kevin Young	.20
112	Delino DeShields	.20
113	Brian Jordan	.20
114	Ray Lankford	.20
115	Mark McGwire	4.00
116	Tony Gwynn	3.00
117	Wally Joyner	.20
118	Ruben Rivera	.20
119	Greg Vaughn	.20
120	Rich Aurilia	.20
121	Barry Bonds	5.00
122	Bill Mueller	.20
123	Robb Nen	.20
124	Jay Buhner	.20
125	Ken Griffey Jr.	3.50
126	Edgar Martinez	.20
127	Shane Monahan	.20
128	Alex Rodriguez	4.00
129	David Segui	.20
130	Rolando Arrojo **RC**	.75
131	Wade Boggs	3.00

132	Quinton McCracken	.20
133	Fred McGriff	.20
134	Bobby Smith	.20
135	Will Clark	.20
136	Juan Gonzalez	1.00
137	Rusty Greer	.20
138	Ivan Rodriguez	1.50
139	Aaron Sele	.20
140	John Wetteland	.20
141	Jose Canseco	1.00
142	Roger Clemens	3.50
143	Carlos Delgado	1.25
144	Shawn Green	.50

All-Stars

This 20-card insert was seeded one per 25 packs. The featured players all participated in the 1998 All-Star Game. The background features the sun rising over a mountain with a die-cut at the top of the card.

		NM/M
Complete Set (20):		110.00
Common Player:		1.50
Inserted 1:25		
1	Roberto Alomar	2.00
2	Cal Ripken Jr.	15.00
3	Kenny Lofton	1.50
4	Jim Thome	5.00
5	Derek Jeter	15.00
6	David Wells	1.50
7	Ken Griffey Jr.	10.00
8	Alex Rodriguez	12.00
9	Juan Gonzalez	4.00
10	Ivan Rodriguez	5.00
11	Gary Sheffield	2.50
12	Chipper Jones	7.50
13	Greg Maddux	7.50
14	Walt Weiss	1.50
15	Larry Walker	1.50
16	Craig Biggio	1.50
17	Mike Piazza	10.00
18	Mark McGwire	12.00
19	Tony Gwynn	7.50
20	Barry Bonds	15.00

Cramer's Choice Awards

Premium-sized Cramer's Choice Awards were inserted one per box. The ten players in the set are featured on a die-cut card designed to resemble a trophy. Pacific CEO Mike Cramer signed and hand-numbered 10 sets of Cramer's Choice Awards.

		NM/M
Complete Set (10):		65.00
Common Player:		4.00
Inserted 1:box		
1	Cal Ripken Jr.	15.00
2	Ken Griffey Jr.	9.00
3	Alex Rodriguez	12.00
4	Juan Gonzalez	5.00
5	Travis Lee	4.00
6	Chipper Jones	7.50
7	Greg Maddux	7.50
8	Kerry Wood	5.00
9	Mark McGwire	12.00
10	Tony Gwynn	7.50

Diamond Knights

Diamond Knights is a 25-card, one per pack insert. Each card features a color action photo and the player's name, team and position listed on a Medieval-type border at the bottom.

		NM/M
Complete Set (25):		20.00
Common Player:		.35
Inserted 1:1		
1	Andres Galarraga	.35
2	Chipper Jones	1.00
3	Greg Maddux	1.00
4	Cal Ripken Jr.	2.50
5	Nomar Garciaparra	1.50
6	Mo Vaughn	.35
7	Kerry Wood	.45
8	Frank Thomas	.75
9	Vinny Castilla	.35
10	Jeff Bagwell	.75
11	Craig Biggio	.35
12	Paul Molitor	.75
13	Mike Piazza	1.50
14	Orlando Hernandez	.35
15	Derek Jeter	2.50
16	Ricky Ledee	.35
17	Mark McGwire	2.00
18	Tony Gwynn	1.00
19	Barry Bonds	2.50
20	Ken Griffey Jr.	1.75
21	Alex Rodriguez	2.00
22	Wade Boggs	1.00
23	Juan Gonzalez	.45
24	Ivan Rodriguez	.65
25	Jose Canseco	.50

Firestone on Baseball

This 26-card insert features star players with commentary by sports personality Roy Firestone. The fronts have a color photo of the player and a portrait of Firestone in the lower-right corner. The card backs have text by Firestone on what makes the featured player great. Firestone signed a total of 300 cards in this insert.

		NM/M
Complete Set (26):		50.00
Common Player:		.35
Firestone Auto. Card:		18.00
Inserted 1:12		
1	Travis Lee	.35
2	Chipper Jones	3.00
3	Greg Maddux	3.00
4	Cal Ripken Jr.	6.00
5	Nomar Garciaparra	3.00
6	Mo Vaughn	.35
7	Kerry Wood	1.00
8	Frank Thomas	2.25
9	Manny Ramirez	2.25
10	Larry Walker	.35
11	Gary Sheffield	1.00
12	Paul Molitor	2.25
13	Hideo Nomo	1.50
14	Mike Piazza	3.50
15	Ben Grieve	.35
16	Mark McGwire	5.00
17	Tony Gwynn	3.00
18	Barry Bonds	6.00
19	Ken Griffey Jr.	4.00
20	Randy Johnson	2.25
21	Alex Rodriguez	5.00
22	Wade Boggs	3.00
23	Juan Gonzalez	1.50
24	Ivan Rodriguez	1.75
25	Roger Clemens	3.50
26	Roy Firestone	.35

Home Run Fever

Home Run Fever features players who had a shot at breaking Roger Maris' home run record in 1998. Fronts have a player photo on the left and a blackboard with numbers from 1 to 60 on the right. Ten circles featuring disappearing ink contained numbers 61 through 70. Collectors could rub the circles to reveal the player's potential record home run total.

		NM/M
Complete Set (10):		30.00
Common Player:		1.50
Inserted 1:73		
1	Andres Galarraga	1.50
2	Sammy Sosa	4.50
3	Albert Belle	1.50
4	Jim Thome	3.00
5	Mark McGwire	7.50
6	Greg Vaughn	1.50
7	Ken Griffey Jr.	6.00
8	Alex Rodriguez	7.50
9	Juan Gonzalez	2.50
10	Jose Canseco	2.50

Pillars of the Game

This 25-card insert was seeded one per pack. Each card features a star player with a background of holographic silver foil.

		NM/M
Complete Set (25):		20.00
Common Player:		.35
Inserted 1:1		
1	Jim Edmonds	.35
2	Travis Lee	.35
3	Chipper Jones	1.00
4	Tom Glavine, John Smoltz, Greg Maddux	1.00
5	Cal Ripken Jr.	2.50
6	Nomar Garciaparra	1.00
7	Mo Vaughn	.35
8	Sammy Sosa	1.00
9	Kerry Wood	.40
10	Frank Thomas	.75
11	Jim Thome	.65
12	Larry Walker	.35
13	Moises Alou	.35
14	Raul Mondesi	.35
15	Mike Piazza	1.25
16	Hideki Irabu	.35
17	Bernie Williams	.35
18	Ben Grieve	.35
19	Scott Rolen	.65
20	Mark McGwire	2.00
21	Tony Gwynn	1.00
22	Ken Griffey Jr.	1.50
23	Alex Rodriguez	2.00
24	Juan Gonzalez	.40
25	Roger Clemens	1.25

1998 Pacific Invincible

Invincible consists of a 150-card base set with a horizontal format featuring a player photo on the left and a portrait in a cel window on the right. The regular cards were inserted one per five-card pack. Silver (2:37) and Platinum Blue (1:73) parallels were also created. Inserts include Moments in Time, Team Checklists, Photoengravings, Interleague Players, Gems of the Diamond and Cramer's Choice Awards.

		NM/M
Complete Set (150):		60.00
Common Player:		.20
Silvers:		4X
Inserted 2:37		
Platinum Blues:		6X
Inserted 1:73		
Pack (5):		1.25
Wax Box (36):		32.50
1	Garret Anderson	.20
2	Jim Edmonds	.20
3	Darin Erstad	.35
4	Chuck Finley	.20
5	Tim Salmon	.20
6	Roberto Alomar	.35
7	Brady Anderson	.20
8	Geronimo Berroa	.20
9	Eric Davis	.20
10	Mike Mussina	.50
11	Rafael Palmeiro	1.00
12	Cal Ripken Jr.	6.00
13	Steve Avery	.20
14	Nomar Garciaparra	2.50
15	John Valentin	.20
16	Mo Vaughn	.20
17	Albert Belle	.20
18	Ozzie Guillen	.20
19	Norberto Martin	.20
20	Frank Thomas	1.50
21	Robin Ventura	.20
22	Sandy Alomar Jr.	.20
23	David Justice	.20
24	Kenny Lofton	.20
25	Manny Ramirez	1.50
26	Jim Thome	1.00
27	Omar Vizquel	.20
28	Matt Williams	.20
29	Jaret Wright	.20
30	Raul Casanova	.20
31	Tony Clark	.20
32	Deivi Cruz	.20
33	Bobby Higginson	.20
34	Justin Thompson	.20
35	Yamil Benitez	.20
36	Johnny Damon	.35
37	Jermaine Dye	.20
38	Jed Hansen	.20
39	Larry Sutton	.20
40	Jeromy Burnitz	.20
41	Jeff Cirillo	.20
42	Dave Nilsson	.20
43	Jose Valentin	.20
44	Fernando Vina	.20
45	Marty Cordova	.20
46	Chuck Knoblauch	.20
47	Paul Molitor	1.50
48	Brad Radke	.20
49	Terry Steinbach	.20
50	Wade Boggs	2.50
51	Hideki Irabu	.20
52	Derek Jeter	6.00
53	Tino Martinez	.20
54	Andy Pettitte	.30
55	Mariano Rivera	.30
56	Bernie Williams	.20
57	Jose Canseco	.75
58	Jason Giambi	.75
59	Ben Grieve	.20
60	Aaron Small	.20
61	Jay Buhner	.20
62	Ken Cloude	.20
63	Joey Cora	.20
64	Ken Griffey Jr.	3.50
65	Randy Johnson	1.50
66	Edgar Martinez	.20
67	Alex Rodriguez	5.00
68	Will Clark	.20
69	Juan Gonzalez	.75
70	Rusty Greer	.20
71	Ivan Rodriguez	1.00
72	Joe Carter	.20
73	Roger Clemens	3.00
74	Jose Cruz Jr.	.20
75	Carlos Delgado	.75
76	Andruw Jones	1.50
77	Chipper Jones	2.50
78	Ryan Klesko	.20
79	Javier Lopez	.20
80	Greg Maddux	2.50
81	Miguel Batista	.20
82	Jeremi Gonzalez	.20
83	Mark Grace	.20
84	Kevin Orie	.20
85	Sammy Sosa	2.50
86	Barry Larkin	.20
87	Deion Sanders	.20
88	Reggie Sanders	.20
89	Chris Stynes	.20
90	Dante Bichette	.20
91	Vinny Castilla	.20
92	Andres Galarraga	.20
93	Neifi Perez	.20
94	Larry Walker	.20
95	Moises Alou	.20
96	Bobby Bonilla	.20
97	Kevin Brown	.20
98	Craig Counsell	.20
99	Livan Hernandez	.20
100	Edgar Renteria	.20
101	Gary Sheffield	.60
102	Jeff Bagwell	1.50
103	Craig Biggio	.20
104	Luis Gonzalez	.20
105	Darryl Kile	.20
106	Wilton Guerrero	.20
107	Eric Karros	.20
108	Ramon Martinez	.20
109	Raul Mondesi	.20
110	Hideo Nomo	.75
111	Chan Ho Park	.20
112	Mike Piazza	3.00
113	Mark Grudzielanek	.20
114	Vladimir Guerrero	1.50
115	Pedro Martinez	1.50
116	Henry Rodriguez	.20
117	David Segui	.20
118	Edgardo Alfonzo	.20
119	Carlos Baerga	.20
120	John Franco	.20
121	John Olerud	.20
122	Rey Ordonez	.20
123	Ricky Bottalico	.20
124	Gregg Jefferies	.20
125	Mickey Morandini	.20
126	Scott Rolen	1.00
127	Curt Schilling	.45
128	Jose Guillen	.20
129	Esteban Loaiza	.20
130	Al Martin	.20
131	Tony Womack	.20
132	Dennis Eckersley	1.00
133	Gary Gaetti	.20
134	Curtis King	.20
135	Ray Lankford	.20
136	Mark McGwire	5.00
137	Ken Caminiti	.20
138	Steve Finley	.20
139	Tony Gwynn	2.50
140	Carlos Hernandez	.20
141	Wally Joyner	.20
142	Barry Bonds	6.00
143	Jacob Cruz	.20
144	Shawn Estes	.20
145	Stan Javier	.20
146	J.T. Snow	.20
147	Nomar Garciaparra (ROY)	1.00
148	Scott Rolen (ROY)	.60
149	Ken Griffey Jr. (MVP)	1.75
150	Larry Walker (MVP)	.20

Cramer's Choice

The 10-card Cramer's Choice Awards insert features top players on cards with a die-cut trophy design. This set has six different foil variations, each with a different production number. Green (99 hand-numbered sets), Dark Blue (80), Light Blue (50), Red (25), Gold (15) and Purple (10) versions were included in Invincible.

		NM/M
Complete Green Set (10):		200.00
Common Green (99 Sets):		10.00
Dark Blues (80 Sets):		1X
Light Blues (50 Sets):		1.5X
Reds (25 Sets):		2X
Golds (15 Sets):		3X
Purples (10 Sets):		5X
1	Greg Maddux	20.00
2	Roberto Alomar	10.00
3	Cal Ripken Jr.	40.00
4	Nomar Garciaparra	20.00
5	Larry Walker	10.00
6	Mike Piazza	22.50
7	Mark McGwire	30.00
8	Tony Gwynn	20.00
9	Ken Griffey Jr.	25.00
10	Roger Clemens	22.50

Gems of the Diamond

Gems of the Diamond is a 220-card insert seeded four per pack. The cards feature a color photo inside a white border.

		NM/M
Complete Set (220):		20.00
Common Player:		.10
1	Jim Edmonds	.10
2	Todd Greene	.10
3	Ken Hill	.10
4	Mike Holtz	.10
5	Mike James	.10
6	Chad Kreuter	.10
7	Tim Salmon	.10
8	Roberto Alomar	.20
9	Brady Anderson	.10
10	David Dellucci	.10
11	Jeffrey Hammonds	.10
12	Mike Mussina	.40
13	Rafael Palmeiro	.65
14	Arthur Rhodes	.10
15	Cal Ripken Jr.	2.50
16	Nerio Rodriguez	.10
17	Tony Tarasco	.10
18	Lenny Webster	.10
19	Mike Benjamin	.10
20	Rich Garces	.10
21	Nomar Garciaparra	1.00
22	Shane Mack	.10
23	Jose Malave	.10
24	Jesus Tavarez	.10
25	Mo Vaughn	.10
26	John Wasdin	.10
27	Jeff Abbott	.10
28	Albert Belle	.10
29	Mike Cameron	.10
30	Al Levine	.10
31	Robert Machado	.10
32	Greg Norton	.10
33	Magglio Ordonez	.20
34	Mike Sirotka	.10
35	Frank Thomas	.75
36	Mario Valdez	.10
37	Sandy Alomar Jr.	.10
38	David Justice	.10
39	Jack McDowell	.10
40	Eric Plunk	.10
41	Manny Ramirez	.75
42	Kevin Seitzer	.10
43	Paul Shuey	.10
44	Omar Vizquel	.10
45	Kimera Bartee	.10
46	Glenn Dishman	.10
47	Orlando Miller	.10
48	Mike Myers	.10
49	Phil Nevin	.10
50	A.J. Sager	.10
51	Ricky Bones	.10
52	Scott Cooper	.10
53	Shane Halter	.10
54	David Howard	.10
55	Glendon Rusch	.10
56	Joe Vitiello	.10
57	Jeff D'Amico	.10
58	Mike Fetters	.10
59	Mike Matheny	.10
60	Jose Mercedes	.10
61	Ron Villone	.10
62	Jack Voigt	.10
63	Brent Brede	.10
64	Chuck Knoblauch	.10
65	Paul Molitor	.75
66	Todd Ritchie	.10
67	Frankie Rodriguez	.10
68	Scott Stahoviak	.10
69	Greg Swindell	.10
70	Todd Walker	.10
71	Wade Boggs	1.00
72	Hideki Irabu	.10
73	Derek Jeter	2.50
74	Pat Kelly	.10
75	Graeme Lloyd	.10
76	Tino Martinez	.10
77	Jeff Nelson	.10
78	Scott Pose	.10
79	Mike Stanton	.10
80	Darryl Strawberry	.10
81	Bernie Williams	.10
82	Tony Batista	.10
83	Mark Bellhorn	.10
84	Ben Grieve	.10
85	Pat Lennon	.10
86	Brian Lesher	.10

87 Miguel Tejada .20
88 George Williams .10
89 Joey Cora .10
90 Rob Ducey .10
91 Ken Griffey Jr. 1.50
92 Randy Johnson .75
93 Edgar Martinez .10
94 John Marzano .10
95 Greg McCarthy .10
96 Alex Rodriguez 2.00
97 Andy Sheets .10
98 Mike Timlin .10
99 Lee Tinsley .10
100 Damon Buford .10
101 Alex Diaz .10
102 Benji Gil .10
103 Juan Gonzalez .40
104 Eric Gunderson .10
105 Danny Patterson .10
106 Ivan Rodriguez .65
107 Mike Simms .10
108 Luis Andujar .10
109 Joe Carter .10
110 Roger Clemens 1.25
111 Jose Cruz Jr. .10
112 Shawn Green .30
113 Robert Perez .10
114 Juan Samuel .10
115 Ed Sprague .10
116 Shannon Stewart .10
117 Danny Bautista .10
118 Chipper Jones 1.00
119 Ryan Klesko .10
120 Keith Lockhart .10
121 Javier Lopez .10
122 Greg Maddux 1.00
123 Kevin Millwood .10
124 Mike Mordecai .10
125 Eddie Perez .10
126 Randall Simon .10
127 Miguel Cairo .10
128 Dave Clark .10
129 Kevin Foster .10
130 Mark Grace .10
131 Tyler Houston .10
132 Mike Hubbard .10
133 Kevin Orie .10
134 Ryne Sandberg 1.00
135 Sammy Sosa 1.00
136 Lenny Harris .10
137 Kent Mercker .10
138 Mike Morgan .10
139 Deion Sanders .10
140 Chris Stynes .10
141 Gabe White .10
142 Jason Bates .10
143 Vinny Castilla .10
144 Andres Galarraga .10
145 Curtis Leskanic .10
146 Jeff McCurry .10
147 Mike Munoz .10
148 Larry Walker .10
149 Jamey Wright .10
150 Moises Alou .10
151 Bobby Bonilla .10
152 Kevin Brown .10
153 John Cangelosi .10
154 Jeff Conine .10
155 Cliff Floyd .10
156 Jay Powell .10
157 Edgar Renteria .10
158 Tony Saunders .10
159 Gary Sheffield .40
160 Jeff Bagwell .75
161 Tim Bogar .10
162 Tony Eusebio .10
163 Chris Holt .10
164 Ray Montgomery .10
165 Luis Rivera .10
166 Eric Anthony .10
167 Brett Butler .10
168 Juan Castro .10
169 Tripp Cromer .10
170 Raul Mondesi .10
171 Hideo Nomo .40
172 Mike Piazza 1.25
173 Tom Prince .10
174 Adam Riggs .10
175 Shane Andrews .10
176 Shayne Bennett .10
177 Raul Chavez .10
178 Pedro Martinez .75
179 Sherman Obando .10
180 Andy Stankiewicz .10
181 Alberto Castillo .10
182 Shawn Gilbert .10
183 Luis Lopez .10
184 Roberto Petagine .10
185 Armando Reynoso .10
186 Midre Cummings .10
187 Kevin Jordan .10
188 Desi Relaford .10
189 Scott Rolen .65
190 Ken Ryan .10
191 Kevin Sefcik .10
192 Emil Brown .10
193 Lou Collier .10
194 Francisco Cordova .10
195 Kevin Elster .10
196 Mark Smith .10
197 Marc Wilkins .10
198 Manny Aybar .10
199 Jose Bautista .10
200 David Bell .10
201 Rigo Beltran .10
202 Delino DeShields .10
203 Dennis Eckersley .65
204 John Mabry .10
205 Eli Marrero .10
206 Willie McGee .10
207 Mark McGwire 2.00
208 Ken Caminiti .10
209 Tony Gwynn 1.00
210 Chris Jones .10
211 Craig Shipley .10
212 Pete Smith .10
213 Jorge Velandia .10
214 Dario Veras .10
215 Rich Aurilia .10
216 Damon Berryhill .10
217 Barry Bonds 2.50
218 Osvaldo Fernandez .10
219 Dante Powell .10
220 Rich Rodriguez .10

Interleague Players

Interleague Players is a 30-card insert featuring 15 sets of players - one National League and one American League player. The dark blue backgrounds have red lightning bolts and the white borders are made of a leather-like material. When a set of players is placed next to each other, they form the MLB Interleague logo in the center. Interleague Players cards were inserted one per 73 packs.

NM/M
Complete Set (30): 120.00
Common Player: 1.50
Inserted 1:73
1A Roberto Alomar 2.50
1N Craig Biggio 1.50
2A Cal Ripken Jr. 12.00
2N Chipper Jones 6.00
3A Nomar Garciaparra 6.00
3N Scott Rolen 3.50
4A Mo Vaughn 1.50
4N Andres Galarraga 1.50
5A Frank Thomas 4.50
5N Tony Gwynn 6.00
6A Albert Belle 1.50
6N Barry Bonds 12.00
7A Hideki Irabu 1.50
7N Hideo Nomo 2.50
8A Derek Jeter 12.00
8N Rey Ordonez 1.50
9A Tino Martinez 1.50
9N Mark McGwire 10.00
10A Alex Rodriguez 10.00
10N Edgar Renteria 1.50
11A Ken Griffey Jr. 7.50
11N Larry Walker 1.50
12A Randy Johnson 4.50
12N Greg Maddux 6.00
13A Ivan Rodriguez 3.50
13N Mike Piazza 6.50
14A Roger Clemens 6.50
14N Pedro Martinez 4.50
15A Jose Cruz Jr. 1.50
15N Wilton Guerrero 1.50

Moments in Time

Moments in Time (20 cards, 1:145) is designed as a baseball scoreboard. The cards have a horizontal layout with the date of an important game in the player's career at the top. The player's stats from the game are featured and a picture is located on the scoreboard screen.

NM/M
Complete Set (20): 100.00
Common Player: 3.00
Inserted 1:145
1 Chipper Jones 10.00
2 Cal Ripken Jr. 17.50
3 Frank Thomas 7.50
4 David Justice 3.00
5 Andres Galarraga 3.00
6 Larry Walker 3.00
7 Livan Hernandez 3.00
8 Wilton Guerrero 3.00
9 Hideo Nomo 4.50
10 Mike Piazza 12.00
11 Pedro Martinez 7.50
12 Bernie Williams 3.00
13 Ben Grieve 3.00
14 Scott Rolen 6.00
15 Mark McGwire 15.00
16 Tony Gwynn 10.00
17 Ken Griffey Jr. 13.50
18 Alex Rodriguez 15.00
19 Juan Gonzalez 4.50
20 Jose Cruz Jr. 3.00

Photoengravings

Photoengravings is an 18-card insert seeded one per 37 packs. Each card has a unique "old-style" design with a player photo in a frame in the center.

NM/M
Complete Set (18): 50.00
Common Player: 1.00
Inserted 1:37
1 Greg Maddux 3.50
2 Cal Ripken Jr. 7.50
3 Nomar Garciaparra 3.50
4 Frank Thomas 2.50
5 Larry Walker 1.00
6 Mike Piazza 4.00
7 Hideo Nomo 2.00
8 Pedro Martinez 2.50
9 Derek Jeter 7.50
10 Tino Martinez 1.00
11 Mark McGwire 6.00
12 Tony Gwynn 3.50
13 Barry Bonds 7.50
14 Ken Griffey Jr. 5.00
15 Alex Rodriguez 6.00
16 Ivan Rodriguez 2.25
17 Roger Clemens 4.00
18 Jose Cruz Jr. 1.00

Team Checklists

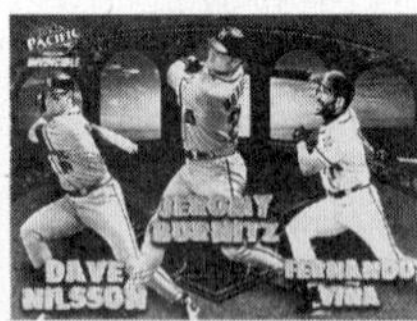

Team Checklists is a 30-card insert seeded 2:37. The fronts feature a player collage with the team logo in the background. The back has a complete checklist for that team in Invincible and more player photos.

NM/M
Complete Set (30): 60.00
Common Player: 1.00
Inserted 2:37
1 Anaheim Angels (Jim Edmonds, Tim Salmon, Darin Erstad, Garret Anderson, Rickey Henderson) 2.50
2 Atlanta Braves (Greg Maddux, Chipper Jones, Javy Lopez, Ryan Klesko, Andruw Jones) 3.00
3 Baltimore Orioles (Cal Ripken Jr., Roberto Alomar, Brady Anderson, Mike Mussina, Rafael Palmeiro) 6.00
4 Boston Red Sox (Nomar Garciaparra, Mo Vaughn, Steve Avery, John Valentin) 3.00
5 Chicago Cubs (Sammy Sosa, Mark Grace, Ryne Sandberg, Jeremi Gonzalez) 3.00
6 Chicago White Sox (Frank Thomas, Albert Belle, Robin Ventura, Ozzie Guillen) 2.50
7 Cincinnati Reds (Barry Larkin, Deion Sanders, Reggie Sanders, Brett Tomko) 1.00
8 Cleveland Indians (Sandy Alomar Jr., Manny Ramirez, David Justice, Jim Thome, Omar Vizquel) 2.50
9 Colorado Rockies (Andres Galarraga, Larry Walker, Vinny Castilla, Dante Bichette, Ellis Burks) 1.00
10 Detroit Tigers (Jason Thompson, Tony Clark, Deivi Cruz, Bobby Higginson) 1.00
11 Florida Marlins (Gary Sheffield, Edgar Renteria, Livan Hernandez, Charles Johnson, Bobby Bonilla) 1.00
12 Houston Astros (Jeff Bagwell, Craig Biggio, Richard Hidalgo, Darryl Kile) 2.50
13 Kansas City Royals (Johnny Damon, Jermaine Dye, Chili Davis, Jose Rosado) 1.00
14 Los Angeles Dodgers (Mike Piazza, Wilton Guerrero, Raul Mondesi, Hideo Nomo, Ramon Martinez) 4.00
15 Milwaukee Brewers (David Nilsson, Fernando Vina, Jeromy Burnitz, Julio Franco, Jeff Cirillo) 1.00
16 Minnesota Twins (Paul Molitor, Chuck Knoblauch, Brad Radke, Terry Steinbach, Marty Cordova) 2.50
17 Montreal Expos (Henry Rodriguez, Vladimir Guerrero, Pedro Martinez, David Segui, Mark Grudzielanek) 2.50
18 New York Mets (Carlos Baerga, Todd Hundley, Rey Ordonez, John Olerud, Edgardo Alfonzo) 1.00
19 New York Yankees (Derek Jeter, Tino Martinez, Bernie Williams, Andy Pettitte, Mariano Rivera) 6.00
20 Oakland Athletics (Jose Canseco, Ben Grieve, Jason Giambi, Matt Stairs) 1.75
21 Philadelphia Phillies (Curt Schilling, Scott Rolen, Gregg Jefferies, Lenny Dykstra, Ricky Bottalico) 1.75
22 Pittsburgh Pirates (Al Martin, Tony Womack, Jose Guillen, Esteban Loiaza) 1.00
23 St. Louis Cardinals (Mark McGwire, Dennis Eckersley, Delino DeShields, Willie McGee, Ray Lankford) 4.50
24 San Diego Padres (Tony Gwynn, Ken Caminiti, Wally Joyner, Steve Finley) 3.00
25 San Francisco Giants (Barry Bonds, J.T. Snow, Stan Javier, Rod Beck, Jose Vizcaino) 6.00
26 Seattle Mariners (Ken Griffey Jr., Alex Rodriguez, Edgar Martinez, Randy Johnson, Jay Buhner) 4.50
27 Texas Rangers (Juan Gonzalez, Ivan Rodriguez, Will Clark, John Wetteland, Rusty Greer) 2.00
28 Toronto Blue Jays (Jose Cruz Jr., Roger Clemens, Pat Hentgen, Joe Carter) 4.00
29 Arizona Diamondbacks (Yamil Benitez, Devon White, Matt Williams, Jay Bell) 1.00
30 Tampa Bay Devil Rays (Wade Boggs, Paul Sorrento, Fred McGriff, Roberto Hernandez) 3.00

1998 Pacific Omega

The Omega base set consists of 250 three-image cards. The horizontal cards feature a color player photo in the center with the image duplicated in foil on the right. Another color photo is on the left. The photos are divided by a baseball seam design. Red-foil parallels were a 1:4 pack insert in Wal-Mart exclusive packaging.

NM/M
Complete Set (250): 25.00
Common Player: .10
Reds: 4X
Pack (6): 1.00
Wax Box (36): 15.00
1 Garret Anderson .10
2 Gary DiSarcina .10
3 Jim Edmonds .10
4 Darin Erstad .20
5 Cecil Fielder .10
6 Chuck Finley .10
7 Shigetosi Hasegawa .10
8 Tim Salmon .10
9 Brian Anderson .10
10 Jay Bell .10
11 Andy Benes .10
12 Yamil Benitez .10
13 Jorge Fabregas .10
14 Travis Lee .10
15 Devon White .10
16 Matt Williams .10
17 Andres Galarraga .10
18 Tom Glavine .35
19 Andruw Jones .75
20 Chipper Jones 1.00
21 Ryan Klesko .10
22 Javy Lopez .10
23 Greg Maddux 1.00
24 Kevin Millwood **RC** .50
25 Denny Neagle .10
26 John Smoltz .10
27 Roberto Alomar .20
28 Brady Anderson .10
29 Joe Carter .10
30 Eric Davis .10
31 Jimmy Key .10
32 Mike Mussina .40
33 Rafael Palmeiro .65
34 Cal Ripken Jr. 2.50
35 B.J. Surhoff .10
36 Dennis Eckersley .65
37 Nomar Garciaparra 1.00
38 Reggie Jefferson .10
39 Derek Lowe .10
40 Pedro Martinez .75
41 Brian Rose .10
42 John Valentin .10
43 Jason Varitek .10
44 Mo Vaughn .10
45 Jeff Blauser .10
46 Jeremi Gonzalez .10
47 Mark Grace .10
48 Lance Johnson .10
49 Kevin Orie .10
50 Henry Rodriguez .10
51 Sammy Sosa 1.00
52 Kerry Wood .35
53 Albert Belle .10
54 Mike Cameron .10
55 Mike Caruso .10
56 Ray Durham .10
57 Jaime Navarro .10
58 Greg Norton .10
59 Magglio Ordonez **RC** 1.50
60 Frank Thomas .75
61 Robin Ventura .10
62 Bret Boone .10
63 Willie Greene .10
64 Barry Larkin .10
65 Jon Nunnally .10
66 Eduardo Perez .10
67 Reggie Sanders .10
68 Brett Tomko .10
69 Sandy Alomar Jr. .10
70 Travis Fryman .10
71 David Justice .10
72 Kenny Lofton .10
73 Charles Nagy .10
74 Manny Ramirez .75
75 Jim Thome .65
76 Omar Vizquel .10
77 Enrique Wilson .10
78 Jaret Wright .10
79 Dante Bichette .10
80 Ellis Burks .10
81 Vinny Castilla .10
82 Todd Helton .75
83 Darryl Kile .10
84 Mike Lansing .10
85 Neifi Perez .10
86 Larry Walker .10
87 Raul Casanova .10
88 Tony Clark .10
89 Luis Gonzalez .10
90 Bobby Higginson .10
91 Brian Hunter .10
92 Bip Roberts .10
93 Justin Thompson .10
94 Josh Booty .10
95 Craig Counsell .10
96 Livan Hernandez .10
97 Ryan Jackson **RC** .10
98 Mark Kotsay .10
99 Derrek Lee .50
100 Mike Piazza 1.25
101 Edgar Renteria .10
102 Cliff Floyd .10
103 Moises Alou .10
104 Jeff Bagwell .75
105 Derrick Bell .10
106 Sean Berry .10
107 Craig Biggio .10
108 John Halama **RC** .15
109 Richard Hidalgo .10
110 Shane Reynolds .10
111 Tim Belcher .10
112 Brian Bevil .10
113 Jeff Conine .10
114 Johnny Damon .25
115 Jeff King .10
116 Jeff Montgomery .10
117 Dean Palmer .10
118 Terry Pendleton .10
119 Bobby Bonilla .10
120 Wilton Guerrero .10
121 Todd Hollandsworth .10
122 Charles Johnson .10
123 Eric Karros .10
124 Paul Konerko .20
125 Ramon Martinez .10
126 Raul Mondesi .10
127 Hideo Nomo .40
128 Gary Sheffield .45
129 Ismael Valdes .10
130 Jeromy Burnitz .10
131 Jeff Cirillo .10
132 Todd Dunn .10
133 Marquis Grissom .10
134 John Jaha .10
135 Scott Karl .10
136 Dave Nilsson .10
137 Jose Valentin .10
138 Fernando Vina .10
139 Rick Aguilera .10
140 Marty Cordova .10
141 Pat Meares .10
142 Paul Molitor .75
143 David Ortiz .50
144 Brad Radke .10
145 Terry Steinbach .10
146 Todd Walker .10
147 Shane Andrews .10
148 Brad Fullmer .10
149 Mark Grudzielanek .10
150 Vladimir Guerrero .75
151 F.P. Santangelo .10
152 Jose Vidro .10
153 Rondell White .10
154 Carlos Baerga .10
155 Bernard Gilkey .10
156 Todd Hundley .10
157 Butch Huskey .10
158 Bobby Jones .10
159 Brian McRae .10
160 John Olerud .10
161 Rey Ordonez .10
162 Masato Yoshii **RC** .25
163 David Cone .10
164 Hideki Irabu .10
165 Derek Jeter 2.50
166 Chuck Knoblauch .10
167 Tino Martinez .10
168 Paul O'Neill .10
169 Andy Pettitte .30
170 Mariano Rivera .15
171 Darryl Strawberry .10
172 David Wells .10
173 Bernie Williams .10
174 Ryan Christenson **RC** .15
175 Jason Giambi .60
176 Ben Grieve .10
177 Rickey Henderson .75
178 A.J. Hinch .10
179 Kenny Rogers .10
180 Ricky Bottalico .10
181 Rico Brogna .10
182 Doug Glanville .10
183 Gregg Jefferies .10

184 Mike Lieberthal .10
185 Scott Rolen .65
186 Curt Schilling .35
187 Jermaine Allensworth .10
188 Lou Collier .10
189 Jose Guillen .10
190 Jason Kendall .10
191 Al Martin .10
192 Tony Womack .10
193 Kevin Young .10
194 Royce Clayton .10
195 Delino DeShields .10
196 Gary Gaetti .10
197 Ron Gant .10
198 Brian Jordan .10
199 Ray Lankford .10
200 Mark McGwire 2.00
201 Todd Stottlemyre .10
202 Kevin Brown .10
203 Ken Caminiti .10
204 Steve Finley .10
205 Tony Gwynn 1.00
206 Carlos Hernandez .10
207 Wally Joyner .10
208 Greg Vaughn .10
209 Barry Bonds 2.50
210 Shawn Estes .10
211 Orel Hershiser .10
212 Stan Javier .10
213 Jeff Kent .10
214 Bill Mueller .10
215 Robb Nen .10
216 J.T. Snow .10
217 Jay Buhner .10
218 Ken Cloude .10
219 Joey Cora .10
220 Ken Griffey Jr. 1.50
221 Glenallen Hill .10
222 Randy Johnson .75
223 Edgar Martinez .10
224 Jamie Moyer .10
225 Alex Rodriguez 2.00
226 David Segui .10
227 Dan Wilson .10
228 Rolando Arrojo **RC** .25
229 Wade Boggs 1.00
230 Miguel Cairo .10
231 Roberto Hernandez .10
232 Quinton McCracken .10
233 Fred McGriff .10
234 Paul Sorrento .10
235 Kevin Stocker .10
236 Will Clark .10
237 Juan Gonzalez .40
238 Rusty Greer .10
239 Rick Helling .10
240 Roberto Kelly .10
241 Ivan Rodriguez .65
242 Aaron Sele .10
243 John Wetteland .10
244 Jose Canseco .50
245 Roger Clemens 1.25
246 Jose Cruz Jr. .10
247 Carlos Delgado .50
248 Alex Gonzalez .10
249 Ed Sprague .10
250 Shannon Stewart .10

EO Portraits

EO Portraits is a 20-card insert seeded 1:73. Each card has a color action photo with a player portrait laser-cut into the card. A "1-of-1" parallel features a laser-cut number on the card as well. The "EO" stands for "Electro Optical" technology.

NM/M
Complete Set (20): 70.00
Common Player: 1.25
Inserted 1:73
1 Cal Ripken Jr. 10.00
2 Nomar Garciaparra 5.00
3 Mo Vaughn 1.25
4 Frank Thomas 4.00
5 Manny Ramirez 4.00
6 Ben Grieve 1.25
7 Ken Griffey Jr. 6.50
8 Alex Rodriguez 7.50
9 Juan Gonzalez 2.00
10 Ivan Rodriguez 3.50
11 Travis Lee 1.25
12 Greg Maddux 5.00
13 Chipper Jones 5.00
14 Kerry Wood 2.00
15 Larry Walker 1.25
16 Jeff Bagwell 4.00
17 Mike Piazza 6.00
18 Mark McGwire 7.50
19 Tony Gwynn 5.00
20 Barry Bonds 10.00

Face to Face

Face to Face features two star players on each card. It is a 10-card insert seeded one per 145 packs.

NM/M
Complete Set (10): 50.00
Common Player: 2.00
Inserted 1:145
1 Alex Rodriguez, Nomar Garciaparra 9.00
2 Mark McGwire, Ken Griffey Jr. 9.00
3 Mike Piazza, Sandy Alomar Jr. 6.00
4 Kerry Wood, Roger Clemens 6.00
5 Cal Ripken Jr., Paul Molitor 10.00
6 Tony Gwynn, Wade Boggs 5.00
7 Frank Thomas, Chipper Jones 5.00
8 Travis Lee, Ben Grieve 2.00
9 Hideo Nomo, Hideki Irabu 3.50
10 Juan Gonzalez, Manny Ramirez 3.50

Online

Online is a 36-card insert seeded about one per nine packs. The foiled and etched cards feature a color player photo in front of a hi-tech designed background. The card fronts also include the internet address for the player's web site on bigleaguers.com.

NM/M
Complete Set (36): 35.00
Common Player: .45
Inserted 1:9
1 Cal Ripken Jr. 5.00
2 Nomar Garciaparra 2.00
3 Pedro Martinez 1.50
4 Mo Vaughn .45
5 Frank Thomas 1.50
6 Sandy Alomar Jr. .45
7 Manny Ramirez 1.50
8 Jaret Wright .45
9 Paul Molitor 1.50
10 Derek Jeter 5.00
11 Bernie Williams .45
12 Ben Grieve .45
13 Ken Griffey Jr. 3.00
14 Edgar Martinez .45
15 Alex Rodriguez 4.00
16 Wade Boggs 2.00
17 Juan Gonzalez .75
18 Ivan Rodriguez 1.00
19 Roger Clemens 2.50
20 Travis Lee .45
21 Matt Williams .45
22 Andres Galarraga .45
23 Chipper Jones 2.00
24 Greg Maddux 2.00
25 Sammy Sosa 2.00
26 Kerry Wood .75
27 Barry Larkin .45
28 Larry Walker .45
29 Derrek Lee 1.00
30 Jeff Bagwell 1.50
31 Hideo Nomo .75
32 Mike Piazza 2.50
33 Scott Rolen 1.00
34 Mark McGwire 4.00
35 Tony Gwynn 2.00
36 Barry Bonds 5.00

Prism

This 20-card insert was seeded one per 37 packs. Horizontal card fronts feature prismatic foil technology.

NM/M
Complete Set (20): 30.00
Common Player: .75
Inserted 1:37
1 Cal Ripken Jr. 4.50
2 Nomar Garciaparra 2.50
3 Pedro Martinez 1.50
4 Frank Thomas 1.50
5 Manny Ramirez 1.50
6 Brian Giles .75
7 Derek Jeter 4.50
8 Ben Grieve .75
9 Ken Griffey Jr. 3.00
10 Alex Rodriguez 3.50
11 Juan Gonzalez 1.00
12 Travis Lee .75
13 Chipper Jones 2.50
14 Greg Maddux 2.50
15 Kerry Wood 1.00
16 Larry Walker .75
17 Hideo Nomo 1.00
18 Mike Piazza 3.00
19 Mark McGwire 3.50
20 Tony Gwynn 2.50

Rising Stars

Rising Stars is a multi-tiered hobby-only insert. The 20 base cards are found about 1:9 packs. Each card has two or three prospects from the same team. Five tiers of partial parallels of the insert are sequentially numbered.

NM/M
Complete Set (30): 15.00
Common Player: .50
Inserted 1:9
Tier 1 (# to 100): 3X
Tier 2 (# to 75): 4X
Tier 3 (# to 50): 5X
Tier 4 (# to 25): 10X
Tier 5 (1 of 1): Value Undetermined
1 Nerio Rodriguez, Sidney Ponson .50
2 Frank Catalanotto, Roberto Duran, Sean Runyan .50
3 Kevin L. Brown, Carlos Almanzar .50
4 Aaron Boone, Pat Watkins, Scott Winchester .50
5 Brian Meadows, Andy Larkin, Antonio Alfonseca .50
6 DaRond Stovall, Trey Moore, Shayne Bennett .50
7 Felix Martinez, Larry Sutton, Brian Bevil .50
8 Homer Bush, Mike Buddie .50
9 Rich Butler, Esteban Yan .50
10 Damon Hollins, Brian Edmondson .50
11 Lou Collier, Jose Silva, Javier Martinez .50
12 Steve Sinclair, Mark Dalesandro .50
13 Jason Varitek, Brian Rose, Brian Shouse .50
14 Mike Caruso, Jeff Abbott, Tom Fordham .50
15 Jason Johnson, Bobby Smith .50
16 Dave Berg, Mark Kotsay, Jesus Sanchez .50
17 Richard Hidalgo, John Halama, Trever Miller .50
18 Geoff Jenkins, Bobby Hughes, Steve Woodard .50
19 Eli Marrero, Cliff Politte, Mike Busby .50
20 Desi Relaford, Darrin Winston .50
21 Todd Helton, Bobby Jones 1.50
22 Rolando Arrojo, Miguel Cairo, Dan Carlson .50
23 David Ortiz, Javier Valentin, Eric Milton 1.25
24 Magglio Ordonez, Greg Norton 1.00
25 Brad Fullmer, Javier Vazquez, Rick DeHart .50
26 Paul Konerko, Matt Luke 1.00
27 Derrek Lee, Ryan Jackson, John Roskos 1.25
28 Ben Grieve, A.J. Hinch, Ryan Christenson .50
29 Travis Lee, Karim Garcia, David Dellucci .65
30 Kerry Wood, Marc Pisciotta 1.00

1998 Pacific Online

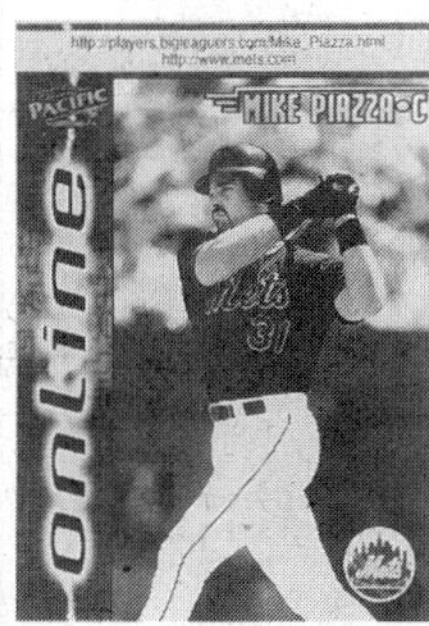

Online consists of an 800-card base set featuring 750 players on cards that list the internet address of the player's home page on the bigleaguers.com Web site. Twenty players have two cards, each with different front and back photos but sharing a card number. Each of the 30 teams has a checklist that lists the team's web site. The Web Cards set parallels the 750 player cards. It has a serial number that can be entered at the bigleaguers.com web site to determine if a prize has been won. Red-foil versions of each card were produced for retail-only jumbo packs; they may carry a modest premium.

NM/M
Complete Set (800): 60.00
Common Player: .05
Web Stars/RC's: 2X
Inserted 1:1
Pack (9): .75
Wax Box (36): 20.00
1 Garret Anderson .05
2 Rich DeLucia **RC** .05
3 Jason Dickson .05
4 Gary DiSarcina .05
5 Jim Edmonds .05
6 Darin Erstad .15
7 Cecil Fielder .05
8 Chuck Finley .05
9 Carlos Garcia .05
10 Shigetosi Hasegawa .05
11 Ken Hill .05
12 Dave Hollins .05
13 Mike Holtz .05
14 Mike James .05
15 Norberto Martin .05
16 Damon Mashore .05
17 Jack McDowell .05
18 Phil Nevin .05
19 Omar Olivares .05
20 Troy Percival .05
21 Rich Robertson .05
22 Tim Salmon .05
23 Craig Shipley .05
24 Matt Walbeck .05
25 Allen Watson .05
26 Jim Edmonds (Angels Checklist) .05
27 Brian Anderson .05
28 Tony Batista .05
29 Jay Bell .05
30 Andy Benes .05
31 Yamil Benitez .05
32 Willie Blair .05
33 Brent Brede .05
34 Scott Brow .05
35 Omar Daal .05
36 David Dellucci .05
37 Edwin Diaz .05
38 Jorge Fabregas .05
39 Andy Fox .05
40 Karim Garcia .05
41a Travis Lee/Btg .05
41b Travis Lee/Fldg .05
42 Barry Manuel .05
43 Gregg Olson .05
44 Felix Rodriguez .05
45 Clint Sodowsky .05
46 Russ Springer .05
47 Andy Stankiewicz .05
48 Kelly Stinnett .05
49 Jeff Suppan .05
50 Devon White .05
51 Matt Williams .05
52 Travis Lee (Diamondbacks Checklist) .05
53 Danny Bautista .05
54 Rafael Belliard .05
55 Adam Butler **RC** .10
56 Mike Cather .05
57 Brian Edmondson .05
58 Alan Embree .05
59 Andres Galarraga .05
60 Tom Glavine .35
61 Tony Graffanino .05
62 Andruw Jones .65
63a Chipper Jones/Btg .75
63b Chipper Jones/Fldg .75
64 Ryan Klesko .05
65 Keith Lockhart .05
66 Javy Lopez .05
67a Greg Maddux/Btg .75
67b Greg Maddux/Pitching .75
68 Dennis Martinez .05
69 Kevin Millwood **RC** .50
70 Denny Neagle .05
71 Eddie Perez .05
72 Curtis Pride .05
73 John Smoltz .05
74 Michael Tucker .05
75 Walt Weiss .05
76 Gerald Williams .05
77 Mark Wohlers .05
78 Chipper Jones (Braves Checklist) .40
79 Roberto Alomar .15
80 Brady Anderson .05
81 Harold Baines .05
82 Armando Benitez .05
83 Mike Bordick .05
84 Joe Carter .05
85 Norm Charlton .05
86 Eric Davis .05
87 Doug Drabek .05
88 Scott Erickson .05
89 Jeffrey Hammonds .05
90 Chris Hoiles .05
91 Scott Kamieniecki .05
92 Jimmy Key .05
93 Terry Mathews .05
94 Alan Mills .05
95 Mike Mussina .25
96 Jesse Orosco .05
97 Rafael Palmeiro .60
98 Sidney Ponson .05
99 Jeff Reboulet .05
100 Arthur Rhodes .05
101a Cal Ripken Jr./Btg 2.00
101b Cal Ripken Jr./Btg (Close-up.) 2.00
102 Nerio Rodriguez .05
103 B.J. Surhoff .05
104 Lenny Webster .05
105 Cal Ripken Jr. (Orioles Checklist) 1.00
106 Steve Avery .05
107 Mike Benjamin .05
108 Darren Bragg .05
109 Damon Buford .05
110 Jim Corsi .05
111 Dennis Eckersley .60
112 Rich Garces .05
113a Nomar Garciaparra/Btg .75
113b Nomar Garciaparra/Fldg .75
114 Tom Gordon .05
115 Scott Hatteberg .05
116 Butch Henry .05
117 Reggie Jefferson .05
118 Mark Lemke .05
119 Darren Lewis .05
120 Jim Leyritz .05
121 Derek Lowe .05
122 Pedro Martinez .65
123 Troy O'Leary .05
124 Brian Rose .05
125 Bret Saberhagen .05
126 Donnie Sadler .05
127 Brian Shouse .05
128 John Valentin .05
129 Jason Varitek .05
130 Mo Vaughn .05
131 Tim Wakefield .05
132 John Wasdin .05
133 Nomar Garciaparra (Red Sox Checklist) .45
134 Terry Adams .05
135 Manny Alexander .05
136 Rod Beck .05
137 Jeff Blauser .05
138 Brant Brown .05
139 Mark Clark .05
140 Jeremi Gonzalez .05
141 Mark Grace .05
142 Jose Hernandez .05
143 Tyler Houston .05
144 Lance Johnson .05
145 Sandy Martinez .05
146 Matt Mieske .05
147 Mickey Morandini .05
148 Terry Mulholland .05
149 Kevin Orie .05
150 Bob Patterson .05
151 Marc Pisciotta .05
152 Henry Rodriguez .05
153 Scott Servais .05
154 Sammy Sosa .75
155 Kevin Tapani .05
156 Steve Trachsel .05
157a Kerry Wood/Pitching .30
157b Kerry Wood/Pitching (Close-up.) .30
158 Kerry Wood (Cubs Checklist) .20
159 Jeff Abbott .05
160 James Baldwin .05
161 Albert Belle .05
162 Jason Bere .05
163 Mike Cameron .05
164 Mike Caruso .05
165 Carlos Castillo .05
166 Tony Castillo .05
167 Ray Durham .05
168 Scott Eyre .05
169 Tom Fordham .05
170 Keith Foulke .05
171 Lou Frazier .05
172 Matt Karchner .05
173 Chad Kreuter .05
174 Jaime Navarro .05
175 Greg Norton .05
176 Charlie O'Brien .05
177 Magglio Ordonez .15
178 Ruben Sierra .05
179 Bill Simas .05
180 Mike Sirotka .05
181 Chris Snopek .05
182a Frank Thomas (In batter's box.) .65
182b Frank Thomas/ Swinging .65
183 Robin Ventura .05
184 Frank Thomas (White Sox Checklist) .40
185 Stan Belinda .05
186 Aaron Boone .05
187 Bret Boone .05
188 Brook Fordyce .05
189 Willie Greene .05
190 Pete Harnisch .05
191 Lenny Harris .05
192 Mark Hutton .05
193 Damian Jackson .05
194 Ricardo Jordan .05
195 Barry Larkin .05
196 Eduardo Perez .05
197 Pokey Reese .05
198 Mike Remlinger .05
199 Reggie Sanders .05
200 Jeff Shaw .05
201 Chris Stynes .05
202 Scott Sullivan .05
203 Eddie Taubensee .05
204 Brett Tomko .05
205 Pat Watkins .05
206 David Weathers .05
207 Gabe White .05
208 Scott Winchester .05
209 Barry Larkin (Reds Checklist) .05
210 Sandy Alomar Jr. .05
211 Paul Assenmacher .05
212 Geronimo Berroa .05
213 Pat Borders .05
214 Jeff Branson .05
215 Dave Burba .05
216 Bartolo Colon .05
217 Shawon Dunston .05
218 Travis Fryman .05
219 Brian Giles .05
220 Dwight Gooden .05
221 Mike Jackson .05
222 David Justice .05
223 Kenny Lofton .05
224 Jose Mesa .05
225 Alvin Morman .05
226 Charles Nagy .05
227 Chad Ogea .05
228 Eric Plunk .05
229 Manny Ramirez .65
230 Paul Shuey .05
231 Jim Thome .65
232 Ron Villone .05
233 Omar Vizquel .05
234 Enrique Wilson .05
235 Jaret Wright .05
236 Manny Ramirez (Indians Checklist) .40
237 Pedro Astacio .05
238 Jason Bates .05
239 Dante Bichette .05
240 Ellis Burks .05
241 Vinny Castilla .05
242 Greg Colbrunn .05
243 Mike DeJean .05
244 Jerry Dipoto .05
245 Curtis Goodwin .05
246 Todd Helton .65
247 Bobby Jones .05
248 Darryl Kile .05

249 Mike Lansing .05
250 Curtis Leskanic .05
251 Nelson Liriano .05
252 Kirt Manwaring .05
253 Chuck McElroy .05
254 Mike Munoz .05
255 Neifi Perez .05
256 Jeff Reed .05
257 Mark Thompson .05
258 John Vander Wal .05
259 Dave Veres .05
260a Larry Walker/Btg .05
260b Larry Walker/Btg (Close-up.) .05
261 Jamey Wright .05
262 Larry Walker (Rockies Checklist) .05
263 Kimera Bartee .05
264 Doug Brocail .05
265 Raul Casanova .05
266 Frank Castillo .05
267 Frank Catalanotto .05
268 Tony Clark .05
269 Deivi Cruz .05
270 Roberto Duran .05
271 Damion Easley .05
272 Bryce Florie .05
273 Luis Gonzalez .05
274 Bob Higginson .05
275 Brian Hunter .05
276 Todd Jones .05
277 Greg Keagle .05
278 Jeff Manto .05
279 Brian Moehler .05
280 Joe Oliver .05
281 Joe Randa .05
282 Billy Ripken .05
283 Bip Roberts .05
284 Sean Runyan .05
285 A.J. Sager .05
286 Justin Thompson .05
287 Tony Clark (Tigers Checklist) .05
288 Antonio Alfonseca .05
289 Dave Berg .05
290 Josh Booty .05
291 John Cangelosi .05
292 Craig Counsell .05
293 Vic Darensbourg .05
294 Cliff Floyd .05
295 Oscar Henriquez .05
296 Felix Heredia .05
297 Ryan Jackson **RC** .05
298 Mark Kotsay .05
299 Andy Larkin .05
300 Derrek Lee .60
301 Brian Meadows .05
302 Rafael Medina .05
303 Jay Powell .05
304 Edgar Renteria .05
305 Jesus Sanchez **RC** .05
306 Rob Stanifer .05
307 Gregg Zaun .05
308 Derrek Lee (Marlins Checklist) .30
309 Moises Alou .05
310 Brad Ausmus .05
311a Jeff Bagwell/Btg .65
311b Jeff Bagwell/Fldg .65
312 Derek Bell .05
313 Sean Bergman .05
314 Sean Berry .05
315 Craig Biggio .05
316 Tim Bogar .05
317 Jose Cabrera .05
318 Dave Clark .05
319 Tony Eusebio .05
320 Carl Everett .05
321 Ricky Gutierrez .05
322 John Halama .05
323 Mike Hampton .05
324 Doug Henry .05
325 Richard Hidalgo .05
326 Jack Howell .05
327 Jose Lima .05
328 Mike Magnante .05
329 Trever Miller .05
330 C.J. Nitkowski .05
331 Shane Reynolds .05
332 Bill Spiers .05
333 Billy Wagner .05
334 Jeff Bagwell (Astros Checklist) .40
335 Tim Belcher .05
336 Brian Bevil .05
337 Johnny Damon .35
338 Jermaine Dye .05
339 Sal Fasano .05
340 Shane Halter .05
341 Chris Haney .05
342 Jed Hansen .05
343 Jeff King .05
344 Jeff Montgomery .05
345 Hal Morris .05
346 Jose Offerman .05
347 Dean Palmer .05
348 Terry Pendleton .05
349 Hipolito Pichardo .05
350 Jim Pittsley .05
351 Pat Rapp .05
352 Jose Rosado .05
353 Glendon Rusch .05
354 Scott Service .05
355 Larry Sutton .05
356 Mike Sweeney .05
357 Joe Vitiello .05
358 Matt Whisenant .05
359 Ernie Young .05
360 Jeff King (Royals Checklist) .05
361 Bobby Bonilla .05
362 Jim Bruske .05
363 Juan Castro .05
364 Roger Cedeno .05
365 Mike Devereaux .05
366 Darren Dreifort .05
367 Jim Eisenreich .05
368 Wilton Guerrero .05
369 Mark Guthrie .05
370 Darren Hall .05
371 Todd Hollandsworth .05
372 Thomas Howard .05
373 Trenidad Hubbard .05
374 Charles Johnson .05
375 Eric Karros .05
376 Paul Konerko .20
377 Matt Luke .05
378 Ramon Martinez .05
379 Raul Mondesi .05
380 Hideo Nomo .35
381 Antonio Osuna .05
382 Chan Ho Park .05
383 Tom Prince .05
384 Scott Radinsky .05
385 Gary Sheffield .40
386 Ismael Valdes .05
387 Jose Vizcaino .05
388 Eric Young .05
389 Gary Sheffield (Dodgers Checklist) .10
390 Jeromy Burnitz .05
391 Jeff Cirillo .05
392 Cal Eldred .05
393 Chad Fox .05
394 Marquis Grissom .05
395 Bob Hamelin .05
396 Bobby Hughes .05
397 Darrin Jackson .05
398 John Jaha .05
399 Geoff Jenkins .05
400 Doug Jones .05
401 Jeff Juden .05
402 Scott Karl .05
403 Jesse Levis .05
404 Mark Loretta .05
405 Mike Matheny .05
406 Jose Mercedes .05
407 Mike Myers .05
408 Marc Newfield .05
409 Dave Nilsson .05
410 Al Reyes .05
411 Jose Valentin .05
412 Fernando Vina .05
413 Paul Wagner .05
414 Bob Wickman .05
415 Steve Woodard .05
416 Marquis Grissom (Brewers Checklist) .05
417 Rick Aguilera .05
418 Ron Coomer .05
419 Marty Cordova .05
420 Brent Gates .05
421 Eddie Guardado .05
422 Denny Hocking .05
423 Matt Lawton .05
424 Pat Meares .05
425 Orlando Merced .05
426 Eric Milton .05
427 Paul Molitor .65
428 Mike Morgan .05
429 Dan Naulty .05
430 Otis Nixon .05
431 Alex Ochoa .05
432 David Ortiz .40
433 Brad Radke .05
434 Todd Ritchie .05
435 Frank Rodriguez .05
436 Terry Steinbach .05
437 Greg Swindell .05
438 Bob Tewksbury .05
439 Mike Trombley .05
440 Javier Valentin .05
441 Todd Walker .05
442 Paul Molitor (Twins Checklist) .40
443 Shane Andrews .05
444 Miguel Batista .05
445 Shayne Bennett .05
446 Rick DeHart .05
447 Brad Fullmer .05
448 Mark Grudzielanek .05
449 Vladimir Guerrero .65
450 Dustin Hermanson .05
451 Steve Kline .05
452 Scott Livingstone .05
453 Mike Maddux .05
454 Derrick May .05
455 Ryan McGuire .05
456 Trey Moore .05
457 Mike Mordecai .05
458 Carl Pavano .05
459 Carlos Perez .05
460 F.P. Santangelo .05
461 DaRond Stovall .05
462 Anthony Telford .05
463 Ugueth Urbina .05
464 Marc Valdes .05
465 Jose Vidro .05
466 Rondell White .05
467 Chris Widger .05
468 Vladimir Guerrero (Expos Checklist) .40
469 Edgardo Alfonzo .05
470 Carlos Baerga .05
471 Rich Becker .05
472 Brian Bohanon .05
473 Alberto Castillo .05
474 Dennis Cook .05
475 John Franco .05
476 Matt Franco .05
477 Bernard Gilkey .05
478 John Hudek .05
479 Butch Huskey .05
480 Bobby Jones .05
481 Al Leiter .05
482 Luis Lopez .05
483 Brian McRae .05
484 Dave Mlicki .05
485 John Olerud .05
486 Rey Ordonez .05
487 Craig Paquette .05
488a Mike Piazza/Btg 1.00
488b Mike Piazza/Btg (Close-up.) 1.00
489 Todd Pratt .05
490 Mel Rojas .05
491 Tim Spehr .05
492 Turk Wendell .05
493 Masato Yoshii **RC** .25
494 Mike Piazza (Mets Checklist) .45
495 Willie Banks .05
496 Scott Brosius .05
497 Mike Buddie .05
498 Homer Bush .05
499 David Cone .05
500 Chad Curtis .05
501 Chili Davis .05
502 Joe Girardi .05
503 Darren Holmes .05
504 Hideki Irabu .05
505a Derek Jeter/Btg 2.00
505b Derek Jeter/Fldg 2.00
506 Chuck Knoblauch .05
507 Graeme Lloyd .05
508 Tino Martinez .05
509 Ramiro Mendoza .05
510 Jeff Nelson .05
511 Paul O'Neill .05
512 Andy Pettitte .20
513 Jorge Posada .05
514 Tim Raines .05
515 Mariano Rivera .15
516 Luis Sojo .05
517 Mike Stanton .05
518 Darryl Strawberry .05
519 Dale Sveum .05
520 David Wells .05
521 Bernie Williams .05
522 Bernie Williams (Yankees Checklist) .05
523 Kurt Abbott .05
524 Mike Blowers .05
525 Rafael Bournigal .05
526 Tom Candiotti .05
527 Ryan Christenson .05
528 Mike Fetters .05
529 Jason Giambi .50
530a Ben Grieve/Btg .05
530b Ben Grieve/Running .05
531 Buddy Groom .05
532 Jimmy Haynes .05
533 Rickey Henderson .65
534 A.J. Hinch .05
535 Mike Macfarlane .05
536 Dave Magadan .05
537 T.J. Mathews .05
538 Jason McDonald .05
539 Kevin Mitchell .05
540 Mike Mohler .05
541 Mike Oquist .05
542 Ariel Prieto .05
543 Kenny Rogers .05
544 Aaron Small .05
545 Scott Spiezio .05
546 Matt Stairs .05
547 Bill Taylor .05
548 Dave Telgheder .05
549 Jack Voigt .05
550 Ben Grieve (A's Checklist) .05
551 Bob Abreu .10
552 Ruben Amaro .05
553 Alex Arias .05
554 Matt Beech .05
555 Ricky Bottalico .05
556 Billy Brewer .05
557 Rico Brogna .05
558 Doug Glanville .05
559 Wayne Gomes .05
560 Mike Grace .05
561 Tyler Green .05
562 Rex Hudler .05
563 Gregg Jefferies .05
564 Kevin Jordan .05
565 Mark Leiter .05
566 Mark Lewis .05
567 Mike Lieberthal .05
568 Mark Parent .05
569 Yorkis Perez .05
570 Desi Relaford .05
571 Scott Rolen .50
572 Curt Schilling .35
573 Kevin Sefcik .05
574 Jerry Spradlin .05
575 Garrett Stephenson .05
576 Darrin Winston .05
577 Scott Rolen (Phillies Checklist) .20
578 Jermaine Allensworth .05
579 Jason Christiansen .05
580 Lou Collier .05
581 Francisco Cordova .05
582 Elmer Dessens .05
583 Freddy Garcia .05
584 Jose Guillen .05
585 Jason Kendall .05
586 Jon Lieber .05
587 Esteban Loaiza .05
588 Al Martin .05
589 Javier Martinez .05
590 Chris Peters **RC** .05
591 Kevin Polcovich .05
592 Ricardo Rincon .05
593 Jason Schmidt .05
594 Jose Silva .05
595 Mark Smith .05
596 Doug Strange .05
597 Turner Ward .05
598 Marc Wilkins .05
599 Mike Williams .05
600 Tony Womack .05
601 Kevin Young .05
602 Tony Womack (Pirates Checklist) .05
603 Manny Aybar .05
604 Kent Bottenfield .05
605 Jeff Brantley .05
606 Mike Busby .05
607 Royce Clayton .05
608 Delino DeShields .05
609 John Frascatore .05
610 Gary Gaetti .05
611 Ron Gant .05
612 David Howard .05
613 Brian Hunter .05
614 Brian Jordan .05
615 Tom Lampkin .05
616 Ray Lankford .05
617 Braden Looper .05
618 John Mabry .05
619 Eli Marrero .05
620 Willie McGee .05
621a Mark McGwire/Btg 1.50
621b Mark McGwire/Fldg 1.50
622 Kent Mercker .05
623 Matt Morris .05
624 Donovan Osborne .05
625 Tom Pagnozzi .05
626 Lance Painter .05
627 Mark Petkovsek .05
628 Todd Stottlemyre .05
629 Mark McGwire (Cardinals Checklist) .75
630 Andy Ashby .05
631 Brian Boehringer .05
632 Kevin Brown .05
633 Ken Caminiti .05
634 Steve Finley .05
635 Ed Giovanola .05
636 Chris Gomez .05
637a Tony Gwynn (Blue jersey.) .75
637b Tony Gwynn (White jersey.) .75
SAMPLETony Gwynn (SAMPLE overprint on back.) 1.00
638 Joey Hamilton .05
639 Carlos Hernandez .05
640 Sterling Hitchcock .05
641 Trevor Hoffman .05
642 Wally Joyner .05
643 Dan Miceli .05
644 James Mouton .05
645 Greg Myers .05
646 Carlos Reyes .05
647 Andy Sheets .05
648 Pete Smith .05
649 Mark Sweeney .05
650 Greg Vaughn .05
651 Quilvio Veras .05
652 Tony Gwynn (Padres Checklist) .40
653 Rich Aurilia .05
654 Marvin Benard .05
655a Barry Bonds/Btg 2.00
655b Barry Bonds/Btg (Close-up.) 2.00
656 Danny Darwin .05
657 Shawn Estes .05
658 Mark Gardner .05
659 Darryl Hamilton .05
660 Charlie Hayes .05
661 Orel Hershiser .05
662 Stan Javier .05
663 Brian Johnson .05
664 John Johnstone .05
665 Jeff Kent .05
666 Brent Mayne .05
667 Bill Mueller .05
668 Robb Nen .05
669 Jim Poole .05
670 Steve Reed .05
671 Rich Rodriguez .05
672 Kirk Rueter .05
673 Rey Sanchez .05
674 J.T. Snow .05
675 Julian Tavarez .05
676 Barry Bonds (Giants Checklist) 1.00
677 Rich Amaral .05
678 Bobby Ayala .05
679 Jay Buhner .05
680 Ken Cloude .05
681 Joey Cora .05
682 Russ Davis .05
683 Rob Ducey .05
684 Jeff Fassero .05
685 Tony Fossas .05
686a Ken Griffey Jr./Btg 1.25
686b Ken Griffey Jr./Fldg 1.25
687 Glenallen Hill .05
688 Jeff Huson .05
689 Randy Johnson .65
690 Edgar Martinez .05
691 John Marzano .05
692 Jamie Moyer .05
693a Alex Rodriguez/Btg 1.50
693b Alex Rodriguez/Fldg 1.50
694 David Segui .05
695 Heathcliff Slocumb .05
696 Paul Spoljaric .05
697 Bill Swift .05
698 Mike Timlin .05
699 Bob Wells .05
700 Dan Wilson .05
701 Ken Griffey Jr. (Mariners Checklist) .50
702 Wilson Alvarez .05
703 Rolando Arrojo **RC** .30
704a Wade Boggs/Btg .75
704b Wade Boggs/Fldg .75
705 Rich Butler .05
706 Miguel Cairo .05
707 Mike Difelice .05
708 John Flaherty .05
709 Roberto Hernandez .05
710 Mike Kelly .05
711 Aaron Ledesma .05
712 Albie Lopez .05
713 Dave Martinez .05
714 Quinton McCracken .05
715 Fred McGriff .05
716 Jim Mecir .05
717 Tony Saunders .05
718 Bobby Smith .05
719 Paul Sorrento .05
720 Dennis Springer .05
721 Kevin Stocker .05
722 Ramon Tatis .05
723 Bubba Trammell .05
724 Esteban Yan .05
725 Wade Boggs (Devil Rays Checklist) .40
726 Luis Alicea .05
727 Scott Bailes .05
728 John Burkett .05
729 Domingo Cedeno .05
730 Will Clark .05
731 Kevin Elster .05
732a Juan Gonzalez/Bat .35
732b Juan Gonzalez (No bat.) .35
733 Tom Goodwin .05
734 Rusty Greer .05
735 Eric Gunderson .05
736 Bill Haselman .05
737 Rick Helling .05
738 Roberto Kelly .05
739 Mark McLemore .05
740 Darren Oliver .05
741 Danny Patterson .05
742 Roger Pavlik .05
743a Ivan Rodriguez/Btg .60
743b Ivan Rodriguez/Fldg .60
744 Aaron Sele .05
745 Mike Simms .05
746 Lee Stevens .05
747 Fernando Tatis .05
748 John Wetteland .05
749 Bobby Witt .05
750 Juan Gonzalez (Rangers Checklist) .20
751 Carlos Almanzar .05
752 Kevin Brown .05
753 Jose Canseco .40
754 Chris Carpenter .05
755 Roger Clemens 1.00
756 Felipe Crespo .05
757 Jose Cruz Jr. .05
758 Mark Dalesandro .05
759 Carlos Delgado .50
760 Kelvim Escobar .05
761 Tony Fernandez .05
762 Darrin Fletcher .05
763 Alex Gonzalez .05
764 Craig Grebeck .05
765 Shawn Green .35
766 Juan Guzman .05
767 Erik Hanson .05
768 Pat Hentgen .05
769 Randy Myers .05
770 Robert Person .05
771 Dan Plesac .05
772 Paul Quantrill .05
773 Bill Risley .05
774 Juan Samuel .05
775 Steve Sinclair .05
776 Ed Sprague .05
777 Mike Stanley .05
778 Shannon Stewart .05
779 Woody Williams .05
780 Roger Clemens (Blue Jays Checklist) .45

Web Cards

This 800-card parallel set allowed collectors to use Pacific's web site to find out the prize they had won. The cards used gold foil on the front instead of the silver foil used on base cards, and contained an eight-digit code on the back that was the claim number.

Web Stars/RC's: 2X
Inserted 1:1

1998 Pacific Paramount

Paramount was Pacific's first fully-licensed baseball card product. The 250 base cards feature full-bleed photos with the player's name and team listed at the bottom. The base set is paralleled three times. Gold retail (1:1), Copper hobby (1:1) and Platinum Blue (1:73) versions were included. Inserts in the product are Special Delivery Die-Cuts, Team Checklist Die-Cuts, Cooperstown Bound, Fielder's Choice Laser-Cuts and Inaugural Issue.

	NM/M
Complete Set (250):	20.00
Common Player:	.10
Gold (1:1R):	1X
Copper (1:1H):	1X
Red (1:1 ANCO):	2X
Platinum Blue (1:73):	4X
Holographic Silver:	20X
Production 99 Sets	
Pack (6):	1.00
Wax Box (36):	15.00

1 Garret Anderson .10
2 Gary DiSarcina .10
3 Jim Edmonds .10
4 Darin Erstad .20
5 Cecil Fielder .10
6 Chuck Finley .10
7 Todd Greene .10
8 Shigetosi Hasegawa .10
9 Tim Salmon .10
10 Roberto Alomar .20
11 Brady Anderson .10
12 Joe Carter .10
13 Eric Davis .10
14 Ozzie Guillen .10
15 Mike Mussina .40
16 Rafael Palmeiro .65
17 Cal Ripken Jr. 2.50
18 B.J. Surhoff .10
19 Steve Avery .10
20 Nomar Garciaparra 1.00
21 Reggie Jefferson .10
22 Pedro Martinez .75
23 Tim Naehring .10
24 John Valentin .10
25 Mo Vaughn .10
26 James Baldwin .10
27 Albert Belle .10
28 Ray Durham .10
29 Benji Gil .10
30 Jaime Navarro .10
31 Maggio Ordonez **RC** 1.50
32 Frank Thomas .75
33 Robin Ventura .10
34 Sandy Alomar Jr. .10
35 Geronimo Berroa .10
36 Travis Fryman .10
37 David Justice .10
38 Kenny Lofton .10
39 Charles Nagy .10
40 Manny Ramirez .75
41 Jim Thome .65
42 Omar Vizquel .10
43 Jaret Wright .10

44 Raul Casanova .10
45 Frank Catalanotto **RC** .20
46 Tony Clark .10
47 Bobby Higginson .10
48 Brian Hunter .10
49 Todd Jones .10
50 Bip Roberts .10
51 Justin Thompson .10
52 Kevin Appier .10
53 Johnny Damon .35
54 Jermaine Dye .10
55 Jeff King .10
56 Jeff Montgomery .10
57 Dean Palmer .10
58 Jose Rosado .10
59 Larry Sutton .10
60 Rick Aguilera .10
61 Marty Cordova .10
62 Pat Meares .10
63 Paul Molitor .75
64 Otis Nixon .10
65 Brad Radke .10
66 Terry Steinbach .10
67 Todd Walker .10
68 Hideki Irabu .10
69 Derek Jeter 2.50
70 Chuck Knoblauch .10
71 Tino Martinez .10
72 Paul O'Neill .10
73 Andy Pettitte .20
74 Mariano Rivera .15
75 Bernie Williams .10
76 Mark Bellhorn .10
77 Tom Candiotti .10
78 Jason Giambi .50
79 Ben Grieve .10
80 Rickey Henderson .75
81 Jason McDonald .10
82 Aaron Small .10
83 Miguel Tejada .20
84 Jay Buhner .10
85 Joey Cora .10
86 Jeff Fassero .10
87 Ken Griffey Jr. 1.50
88 Randy Johnson .75
89 Edgar Martinez .10
90 Alex Rodriguez 2.00
91 David Segui .10
92 Dan Wilson .10
93 Wilson Alvarez .10
94 Wade Boggs 1.00
95 Miguel Cairo .10
96 John Flaherty .10
97 Dave Martinez .10
98 Quinton McCracken .10
99 Fred McGriff .10
100 Paul Sorrento .10
101 Kevin Stocker .10
102 John Burkett .10
103 Will Clark .10
104 Juan Gonzalez .40
105 Rusty Greer .10
106 Roberto Kelly .10
107 Ivan Rodriguez .65
108 Fernando Tatis .10
109 John Wetteland .10
110 Jose Canseco .40
111 Roger Clemens 1.25
112 Jose Cruz Jr. .10
113 Carlos Delgado .50
114 Alex Gonzalez .10
115 Pat Hentgen .10
116 Ed Sprague .10
117 Shannon Stewart .10
118 Brian Anderson .10
119 Jay Bell .10
120 Andy Benes .10
121 Yamil Benitez .10
122 Jorge Fabregas .10
123 Travis Lee .10
124 Devon White .10
125 Matt Williams .10
126 Bob Wolcott .10
127 Andres Galarraga .10
128 Tom Glavine .35
129 Andruw Jones .75
130 Chipper Jones 1.00
131 Ryan Klesko .10
132 Javy Lopez .10
133 Greg Maddux 1.00
134 Denny Neagle .10
135 John Smoltz .10
136 Rod Beck .10
137 Jeff Blauser .10
138 Mark Grace .10
139 Lance Johnson .10
140 Mickey Morandini .10
141 Kevin Orie .10
142 Sammy Sosa 1.00
143 Aaron Boone .10
144 Bret Boone .10
145 Dave Burba .10
146 Lenny Harris .10
147 Barry Larkin .10
148 Reggie Sanders .10
149 Brett Tomko .10
150 Pedro Astacio .10
151 Dante Bichette .10
152 Ellis Burks .10
153 Vinny Castilla .10
154 Todd Helton .75
155 Darryl Kile .10
156 Jeff Reed .10
157 Larry Walker .10
158 Bobby Bonilla .10
159 Todd Dunwoody .10
160 Livan Hernandez .10
161 Charles Johnson .10
162 Mark Kotsay .10
163 Derrek Lee .60
164 Edgar Renteria .10
165 Gary Sheffield .50
166 Moises Alou .10
167 Jeff Bagwell .75
168 Derek Bell .10
169 Craig Biggio .10
170 Mike Hampton .10
171 Richard Hidalgo .10
172 Chris Holt .10
173 Shane Reynolds .10
174 Wilton Guerrero .10
175 Eric Karros .10
176 Paul Konerko .20
177 Ramon Martinez .10
178 Raul Mondesi .10
179 Hideo Nomo .40
180 Chan Ho Park .10
181 Mike Piazza 1.25
182 Ismael Valdes .10
183 Jeromy Burnitz .10
184 Jeff Cirillo .10
185 Todd Dunn .10
186 Marquis Grissom .10
187 John Jaha .10
188 Doug Jones .10
189 Dave Nilsson .10
190 Jose Valentin .10
191 Fernando Vina .10
192 Orlando Cabrera .10
193 Steve Falteisek .10
194 Mark Grudzielanek .10
195 Vladimir Guerrero .75
196 Carlos Perez .10
197 F.P. Santangelo .10
198 Jose Vidro .10
199 Rondell White .10
200 Edgardo Alfonzo .10
201 Carlos Baerga .10
202 John Franco .10
203 Bernard Gilkey .10
204 Todd Hundley .10
205 Butch Huskey .10
206 Bobby Jones .10
207 Brian McRae .10
208 John Olerud .10
209 Rey Ordonez .10
210 Ricky Bottalico .10
211 Bobby Estalella .10
212 Doug Glanville .10
213 Gregg Jefferies .10
214 Mike Lieberthal .10
215 Desi Relaford .10
216 Scott Rolen .65
217 Curt Schilling .35
218 Adrian Brown .10
219 Emil Brown .10
220 Francisco Cordova .10
221 Jose Guillen .10
222 Al Martin .10
223 Abraham Nunez .10
224 Tony Womack .10
225 Kevin Young .10
226 Alan Benes .10
227 Royce Clayton .10
228 Gary Gaetti .10
229 Ron Gant .10
230 Brian Jordan .10
231 Ray Lankford .10
232 Mark McGwire 2.00
233 Todd Stottlemyre .10
234 Kevin Brown .10
235 Ken Caminiti .10
236 Steve Finley .10
237 Tony Gwynn 1.00
238 Wally Joyner .10
239 Ruben Rivera .10
240 Greg Vaughn .10
241 Quilvio Veras .10
242 Barry Bonds 2.50
243 Jacob Cruz .10
244 Shawn Estes .10
245 Orel Hershiser .10
246 Stan Javier .10
247 Brian Johnson .10
248 Jeff Kent .10
249 Robb Nen .10
250 J.T. Snow .10

Gold/Copper/Red

Gold, Copper and Red foil versions of all 250 cards in Paramount were inserted at a rate of one per pack. Gold versions were retail exclusive, Copper versions were hobby exclusive and Red versions were ANCO pack exclusive. The only difference is these parallels use a different color foil than the base cards.

NM/M
Common Gold/Copper Player: .25
Gold/Copper Stars: 1X
Inserted 1:1
Common Red Player: .30
Red Stars: 2X

Holographic Silver

Holographics Silver parallel cards were issued for all 250 cards in the Paramount set. These were inserted into hobby packs, with only 99 sets produced.

NM/M
Common Player: 1.00
Holographic Silver Stars: 20X
Production 99 Sets

Platinum Blue

This paralled set reprinted all 250 cards in Paramount using blue foil stamping on the card front. These were inserted one per 73 packs.

NM/M
Common Platinum Blue Player: 1.00
Platinum Blue Stars: 4X
Inserted 1:73

Cooperstown Bound

Cooperstown Bound is a 10-card insert seeded one per 361 packs. Each card features a color player photo with a silver foil column on the left. The cards are fully foiled and etched.

NM/M
Complete Set (10): 60.00
Common Player: 8.00
Inserted 1:361
Pacific Proofs: 6X
Production 20 Sets
1 Greg Maddux 10.00
2 Cal Ripken Jr. 15.00
3 Frank Thomas 8.00
4 Mike Piazza 8.00
5 Paul Molitor 8.00
6 Mark McGwire 12.00
7 Tony Gwynn 8.00
8 Barry Bonds 15.00
9 Ken Griffey Jr. 10.00
10 Wade Boggs 8.00

Fielder's Choice

Fielder's Choice Laser-Cuts is a 20-card insert seeded one per 73 packs. Each card is die-cut around a baseball

glove that appears in the background. The webbing of the glove is laser-cut.

NM/M
Complete Set (20): 45.00
Common Player: .75
Inserted 1:73
1 Chipper Jones 3.00
2 Greg Maddux 3.00
3 Cal Ripken Jr. 6.00
4 Nomar Garciaparra 3.00
5 Frank Thomas 2.50
6 David Justice .75
7 Larry Walker .75
8 Jeff Bagwell 2.50
9 Hideo Nomo 1.25
10 Mike Piazza 3.50
11 Derek Jeter 6.00
12 Ben Grieve .75
13 Mark McGwire 4.50
14 Tony Gwynn 3.00
15 Barry Bonds 6.00
16 Ken Griffey Jr. 4.00
17 Alex Rodriguez 4.50
18 Wade Boggs 3.00
19 Ivan Rodriguez 2.00
20 Jose Cruz Jr. .75

Special Delivery

Special Delivery cards are die-cut to resemble a postage stamp. Each card front is foiled and etched and features three photos of the player. Special Delivery is a 20-card insert seeded one per 37 packs.

NM/M
Complete Set (20): 30.00
Common Player: .50
Inserted 1:37
1 Chipper Jones 2.50
2 Greg Maddux 2.50
3 Cal Ripken Jr. 5.00
4 Nomar Garciaparra 2.50
5 Pedro Martinez 2.00
6 Frank Thomas 2.00
7 David Justice .50
8 Larry Walker .50
9 Jeff Bagwell 2.00
10 Hideo Nomo 1.00
11 Mike Piazza 3.00
12 Vladimir Guerrero 2.00
13 Derek Jeter 5.00
14 Ben Grieve .50
15 Mark McGwire 4.00
16 Tony Gwynn 2.50
17 Barry Bonds 5.00
18 Ken Griffey Jr. 3.50
19 Alex Rodriguez 4.00
20 Jose Cruz Jr. .50

Team Checklists

Team Checklists (30 cards, 2:37) feature a player photo surrounded by two bats. The card is die-cut around the photo and the bats at the top. The bottom has the player's name, position and team.

NM/M
Complete Set (30): 25.00
Common Player: .25
Inserted 1:18
1 Tim Salmon .25
2 Cal Ripken Jr. 4.00
3 Nomar Garciaparra 1.50
4 Frank Thomas 1.00
5 Manny Ramirez 1.00
6 Tony Clark .25
7 Dean Palmer .25
8 Paul Molitor 1.00
9 Derek Jeter 4.00
10 Ben Grieve .25
11 Ken Griffey Jr. 2.50
12 Wade Boggs 1.50
13 Ivan Rodriguez .75
14 Roger Clemens 2.00
15 Matt Williams .25
16 Chipper Jones 1.50
17 Sammy Sosa 1.50
18 Barry Larkin .25
19 Larry Walker .25
20 Livan Hernandez .25
21 Jeff Bagwell 1.00
22 Mike Piazza 2.00
23 John Jaha .25
24 Vladimir Guerrero 1.00
25 Todd Hundley .25
26 Scott Rolen .75
27 Kevin Young .25
28 Mark McGwire 3.00
29 Tony Gwynn 1.50
30 Barry Bonds 4.00

1998 Pacific Revolution

Pacific Revolution consists of a 150-card base set. The base cards are dual-foiled, etched and embossed. Inserts include Showstoppers, Prime Time Performers Laser-Cuts, Foul Pole Laser-Cuts, Major League Icons and Shadow Series.

NM/M
Complete Set (150): 65.00
Common Player: .25
Pack (3): 1.00
Wax Box (24): 20.00
1 Garret Anderson .25
2 Jim Edmonds .25
3 Darin Erstad .40
4 Chuck Finley .25
5 Tim Salmon .25
6 Jay Bell .25
7 Travis Lee .25
8 Devon White .25
9 Matt Williams .25
10 Andres Galarraga .25
11 Tom Glavine .45
12 Andruw Jones 2.50
13 Chipper Jones 3.50
14 Ryan Klesko .25
15 Javy Lopez .25
16 Greg Maddux 3.50
17 Walt Weiss .25
18 Roberto Alomar .40
19 Joe Carter .25
20 Mike Mussina 1.25
21 Rafael Palmeiro 2.00
22 Cal Ripken Jr. 6.00
23 B.J. Surhoff .25
24 Nomar Garciaparra 3.00
25 Reggie Jefferson .25
26 Pedro Martinez 2.50
27 Troy O'Leary .25
28 Mo Vaughn .25
29 Mark Grace .25
30 Mickey Morandini .25
31 Henry Rodriguez .25
32 Sammy Sosa 3.00
33 Kerry Wood 1.25
34 Albert Belle .25
35 Ray Durham .25
36 Magglio Ordonez **RC** 2.00
37 Frank Thomas 2.50
38 Robin Ventura .25
39 Bret Boone .25
40 Barry Larkin .25
41 Reggie Sanders .25
42 Brett Tomko .25
43 Sandy Alomar .25
44 David Justice .25
45 Kenny Lofton .25
46 Manny Ramirez 2.50
47 Jim Thome 2.00
48 Omar Vizquel .25
49 Jaret Wright .25
50 Dante Bichette .25
51 Ellis Burks .25
52 Vinny Castilla .25
53 Todd Helton 2.50
54 Larry Walker .25
55 Tony Clark .25
56 Deivi Cruz .25
57 Damion Easley .25
58 Bobby Higginson .25
59 Brian Hunter .25
60 Cliff Floyd .25
61 Livan Hernandez .25
62 Derrek Lee 1.50
63 Edgar Renteria .25
64 Moises Alou .25
65 Jeff Bagwell 2.50
66 Derek Bell .25
67 Craig Biggio .25
68 Richard Hidalgo .25
69 Johnny Damon .40
70 Jeff King .25
71 Hal Morris .25
72 Dean Palmer .25
73 Bobby Bonilla .25
74 Charles Johnson .25
75 Paul Konerko .35
76 Raul Mondesi .25
77 Gary Sheffield .75
78 Jeromy Burnitz .25
79 Marquis Grissom .25
80 Dave Nilsson .25
81 Fernando Vina .25
82 Marty Cordova .25
83 Pat Meares .25
84 Paul Molitor 2.50
85 Brad Radke .25
86 Terry Steinbach .25
87 Todd Walker .25
88 Brad Fullmer .25
89 Vladimir Guerrero 2.50
90 Carl Pavano .25
91 Rondell White .25
92 Bernard Gilkey .25
93 Hideo Nomo 1.25
94 John Olerud .25
95 Rey Ordonez .25
96 Mike Piazza 4.00
97 Masato Yoshii **RC** .65
98 Hideki Irabu .25
99 Derek Jeter 6.00
100 Chuck Knoblauch .25
101 Tino Martinez .25
102 Paul O'Neill .25
103 Darryl Strawberry .25
104 Bernie Williams .25
105 Jason Giambi 1.50
106 Ben Grieve .25
107 Rickey Henderson 2.50
108 Matt Stairs .25
109 Doug Glanville .25
110 Desi Relaford .25
111 Scott Rolen 1.50
112 Curt Schilling .45
113 Jason Kendall .25
114 Al Martin .25
115 Jason Schmidt .25
116 Kevin Young .25
117 Delino DeShields .25
118 Gary Gaetti .25
119 Brian Jordan .25
120 Ray Lankford .25
121 Mark McGwire 5.00
122 Kevin Brown .25
123 Steve Finley .25
124 Tony Gwynn 3.50
125 Wally Joyner .25
126 Greg Vaughn .25
127 Barry Bonds 6.00
128 Orel Hershiser .25
129 Jeff Kent .25
130 Bill Mueller .25
131 Jay Buhner .25
132 Ken Griffey Jr. 4.50
133 Randy Johnson 2.50
134 Edgar Martinez .25
135 Alex Rodriguez 5.00
136 David Segui .25
137 Rolando Arrojo **RC** .75
138 Wade Boggs 3.50
139 Quinton McCracken .25
140 Fred McGriff .25
141 Will Clark .25
142 Juan Gonzalez 1.25
143 Tom Goodwin .25
144 Ivan Rodriguez 2.00
145 Aaron Sele .25
146 John Wetteland .25
147 Jose Canseco .50
148 Roger Clemens 4.00
149 Jose Cruz Jr. .25
150 Carlos Delgado .65

Shadows

Shadows is a full parallel of the Revolution base set. Limited to 99 sequentially numbered sets, each card is embossed with a special "Shadow Series" stamp.

	NM/M
Common Player:	2.00
Stars/Rookies:	6X

Foul Pole

Foul Pole Laser-Cuts is a 20-card insert seeded one per 49 packs. Each card features a color player photo on the left and a foul pole on the right. The foul pole design includes netting that is laser cut.

		NM/M
Complete Set (20):		100.00
Common Player:		2.00
Inserted 1:49		
1	Cal Ripken Jr.	15.00
2	Nomar Garciaparra	7.50
3	Mo Vaughn	2.00
4	Frank Thomas	6.00
5	Manny Ramirez	6.00
6	Bernie Williams	2.00
7	Ben Grieve	2.00
8	Ken Griffey Jr.	10.00
9	Alex Rodriguez	12.00
10	Juan Gonzalez	3.00
11	Ivan Rodriguez	5.00
12	Travis Lee	2.00
13	Chipper Jones	7.50
14	Sammy Sosa	7.50
15	Vinny Castilla	2.00
16	Moises Alou	2.00
17	Gary Sheffield	3.00
18	Mike Piazza	9.00
19	Mark McGwire	12.00
20	Barry Bonds	15.00

Major League Icons

Major League Icons is a 10-card insert seeded one per 121 packs. Each card features a player photo on a die-cut shield, with the shield on a flaming stand.

		NM/M
Complete Set (10):		50.00
Common Player:		4.50
Inserted 1:121		
1	Cal Ripken Jr.	15.00
2	Nomar Garciaparra	7.50
3	Frank Thomas	6.00
4	Ken Griffey Jr.	10.00
5	Alex Rodriguez	12.50
6	Chipper Jones	7.50
7	Kerry Wood	4.50
8	Mike Piazza	9.00
9	Mark McGwire	12.50
10	Tony Gwynn	7.50

Prime Time Performers

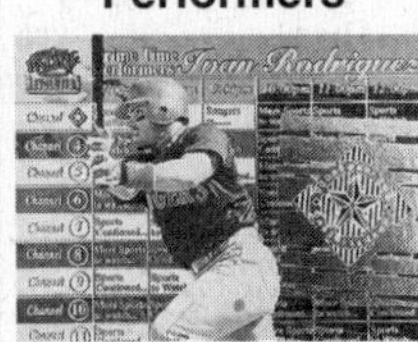

Prime Time Performers is a 20-card insert seeded one per 25 packs. The cards are designed like a TV program guide with the team logo laser-cut on the TV screen. The color player photo is located on the left.

		NM/M
Complete Set (20):		25.00
Common Player:		.50
Inserted 1:25		
1	Cal Ripken Jr.	4.50
2	Nomar Garciaparra	2.00
3	Frank Thomas	1.50
4	Jim Thome	1.25
5	Hideki Irabu	.50
6	Derek Jeter	4.50
7	Ben Grieve	.50
8	Ken Griffey Jr.	3.00
9	Alex Rodriguez	3.50
10	Juan Gonzalez	.75
11	Ivan Rodriguez	1.25
12	Travis Lee	.50
13	Chipper Jones	2.00
14	Greg Maddux	2.00
15	Kerry Wood	.75
16	Larry Walker	.50
17	Jeff Bagwell	1.50
18	Mike Piazza	2.50
19	Mark McGwire	3.50
20	Tony Gwynn	2.00

Rookies and Hardball Heroes

This hobby-only insert combines 20 hot prospects with 10 veteran stars. Horizontal cards have action photos on a flashy metallic-foil background. A portrait photo is on back. The first 20 cards in the set, the youngsters, are paralleled in a gold edition which was limited to just 50 cards of each.

		NM/M
Complete Set (30):		20.00
Common Player:		.25
Inserted 1:6		
Gold (1-20):		10X
Production 50 Sets		
1	Justin Baughman	.25
2	Jarrod Washburn	.25
3	Travis Lee	.25
4	Kerry Wood	.50
5	Maggio Ordonez	.50
6	Todd Helton	1.00
7	Derrek Lee	.25
8	Richard Hidalgo	.25
9	Mike Caruso	.25
10	David Ortiz	.75
11	Brad Fullmer	.25
12	Masato Yoshii	.25
13	Orlando Hernandez	.25
14	Ricky Ledee	.25
15	Ben Grieve	.25
16	Carlton Loewer	.25
17	Desi Relaford	.25
18	Ruben Rivera	.25
19	Rolando Arrojo	.25
20	Matt Perisho	.25
21	Chipper Jones	2.00
22	Greg Maddux	2.00
23	Cal Ripken Jr.	5.00
24	Nomar Garciaparra	2.00
25	Frank Thomas	1.00
26	Mark McGwire	4.00
27	Tony Gwynn	2.00
28	Ken Griffey Jr.	3.00
29	Alex Rodriguez	4.00
30	Juan Gonzalez	.50

Showstoppers

This 36-card insert was seeded two per 25 packs. The cards feature holographic foil. The color photo is centered above the team logo and the Showstoppers logo.

		NM/M
Complete Set (36):		30.00
Common Player:		.45
Inserted 1:12		
1	Cal Ripken Jr.	5.00
2	Nomar Garciaparra	2.50
3	Pedro Martinez	2.00
4	Mo Vaughn	.45
5	Frank Thomas	2.00
6	Manny Ramirez	2.00
7	Jim Thome	1.75
8	Jaret Wright	.45
9	Paul Molitor	2.00
10	Orlando Hernandez	.60
11	Derek Jeter	5.00
12	Bernie Williams	.45
13	Ben Grieve	.45
14	Ken Griffey Jr.	3.50
15	Alex Rodriguez	4.00
16	Wade Boggs	2.50
17	Juan Gonzalez	1.00
18	Ivan Rodriguez	1.75
19	Jose Canseco	.75
20	Roger Clemens	3.00
21	Travis Lee	.45
22	Andres Galarraga	.45
23	Chipper Jones	2.50
24	Greg Maddux	2.50
25	Sammy Sosa	2.50
26	Kerry Wood	.75
27	Vinny Castilla	.45
28	Larry Walker	.45
29	Moises Alou	.45
30	Raul Mondesi	.45
31	Gary Sheffield	.75
32	Hideo Nomo	1.00
33	Mike Piazza	3.00
34	Mark McGwire	4.00
35	Tony Gwynn	2.50
36	Barry Bonds	5.00

Nestle's Latinos

Produced by Pacific this set of Latino ballplayers' cards was issued in three-card packs with the purchase of certain Nestle's food products in Los Angeles, Miami, Houston and San Antonio. Cards are found in two styles. Five of the cards have gold-foil graphic highlights on both top and bottom on front. On back the card number is in a white circle. The second style has foil only at bottom front and on back the card number is in a black circle. Both types have Pacific and Nestle logos on front and back.

		NM/M
Complete Set (20):		8.00
Common Player:		.25
1	Ismael Valdes	.25
2	Juan Gonzalez	.50
3	Ivan Rodriguez	.65
4	Joey Cora	.25
5	Livan Hernandez	.25
1	Bernie Williams	.25
2	Tino Martinez	.25
3	Alex Rodriguez	1.50
4	Edgar Martinez	.25
5	Andres Galarraga	.25
6	Manny Ramirez	.75
7	Carlos Baerga	.25
8	Pedro Martinez	.75
9	Vinny Castilla	.25
10	Sammy Sosa	1.00
11	Nomar Garciaparra	1.00
12	Javy Lopez	.25
13	Sandy Alomar	.25
14	Roberto Alomar	.40
15	Jose Canseco	.50

Home Run Heroes

This retail exclusive product was sold as a complete set sealed in a tin lithographed can. The 2-1/2" x 3-1/2" cards have color action photos on front of the players in the follow-through of their home run swing. The figures are set on an artificial background which includes a sign giving the date and distance of their final home run of the 1998 season. Their team logo is in the "turf" at their feet. Fronts are highlighted with gold foil. On back are a portrait photo, a season summary and 1998 stats, along with appropriate licensor and manufacturer logos.

		NM/M
Complete Set (6):		2.50
Common Player:		.25
1	Mark McGwire	1.00
2	Sammy Sosa	.65
3	Ken Griffey Jr.	.75
4	Greg Vaughn	.25
5	Albert Belle	.25
6	Jose Canseco	.50

Home Run History

This boxed set commemorating the great home run chase of 1998 was an exclusive to one of the television home-shopping shows. Each player is featured on 35 cards, with several depicting both players. Fronts have portraits or action shots which are borderless at the top and sides. At bottom is a gold-foil highlighted panel with the player's name, card title and date. Backs have another photo and details of the highlight. A pair of die-cut bonus cards were included in the boxed set.

		NM/M
Complete Set (70+2):		10.00
Common Card:		.50
1	Mark McGwire (Portrait of a Hero)	.50
2	Sammy Sosa (Portrait of a Hero)	.50
3	Mark McGwire (Fan Favorite)	.50
4	Sammy Sosa (Fan Favorite)	.50
5	Mark McGwire (Well-Rounded Superstar)	.50
6	Sammy Sosa (Well-Rounded Superstar)	.50
7	Mark McGwire (Cardinals Slugger)	.50
8	Sammy Sosa (Cubs Slugger)	.50
9	Mark McGwire (Home Run #48)	.50
10	Sammy Sosa (20 HRs in June)	.50
11	Mark McGwire (Home Run #50)	.50
12	Sammy Sosa (Home Run #50)	.50
13	Mark McGwire (Home Run #57)	.50
14	Sammy Sosa (Home Run #51)	.50
15	Mark McGwire (Home Run #58)	.50
16	Sammy Sosa (Home Run #56)	.50
17	Mark McGwire (Home Run #59)	.50
18	Sammy Sosa (Home Run #59)	.50
19	Mark McGwire (Home Run #60)	.50
20	Sammy Sosa (Home Run #60)	.50
21	Mark McGwire (Home Run #61)	.50
22	Sammy Sosa (Home Run #61)	.50
23	Mark McGwire (Home Run #62)	.50
24	Sammy Sosa (Home Run #62)	.50
25	Mark McGwire (The Record Falls)	.50
26	Sammy Sosa (Tied at 62!)	.50
27	Mark McGwire (The Home Run Ball)	.50
28	Sammy Sosa (Sammy Sosa Day)	.50
29	Mark McGwire (Achievement Award)	.50
30	Sammy Sosa (Achievement Award)	.50
31	Mark McGwire (What a Ride!)	.50
32	Sammy Sosa (A Season of Accolades)	.50
33	Mark McGwire (Home Run #63)	.50
34	Sammy Sosa (Sammy, You're the Man)	.50
35	Mark McGwire (Home Run #64)	.50
36	Sammy Sosa (Home Run #63)	.50
37	Mark McGwire (Home Run #65)	.50
38	Sammy Sosa (Home Run #64)	.50
39	Mark McGwire (Home Run #67)	.50
40	Sammy Sosa (Home Run #65)	.50
41	Mark McGwire (Home Run #68)	.50
42	Sammy Sosa (Home Run #66)	.50
43	Mark McGwire (70!!!)	.50
44	Sammy Sosa (Cubs Win Wild Card)	.50
45	Mark McGwire (Last Swing of the Bat)	.50
46	Sammy Sosa (18 Stolen Bases)	.50
47	Mark McGwire (Power at the Plate)	.50
48	Sammy Sosa (Grand Sam)	.50
49	Mark McGwire (130 Runs Scored)	.50
50	Sammy Sosa (134 Runs Scored)	.50
51	Mark McGwire (32 HRs on the Road)	.50
52	Sammy Sosa (31 HRs on the Road)	.50
53	Mark McGwire (38 HRs at Home)	.50
54	Sammy Sosa (35 HRs at Home)	.50
55	Mark McGwire (11 First-Inning Home Runs)	.50
56	Sammy Sosa (12 First-Inning Home Runs)	.50
57	Mark McGwire (10 Multiple-HR Games)	.50
58	Sammy Sosa (11 Multiple-HR Games)	.50
59	Mark McGwire (545-Foot Blast)	.50
60	Sammy Sosa (500-Foot Blast)	.50
61	Mark McGwire (St. Louis' Favorite Son)	.50
62	Sammy Sosa (Chicago's Favorite Son)	.50
63	Mark McGwire (A Season of Celebration)	.50
64	Sammy Sosa (A Season of Celebration)	.50
65	Mark McGwire/CC	.50
66	Sammy Sosa/CC	.50
67	Mark McGwire, Sammy Sosa (Awesome Power)	.50
68	Mark McGwire, Sammy Sosa (Ambassadors of the Game)	.50
69	Mark McGwire, Sammy Sosa (Transcending Sports)	.50
70	Mark McGwire, Sammy Sosa (Friends to the End/Checklist)	.50

Home Run History Bonus Cards

Though they are not identified as such, this pair of Gold Crown-style die-cut cards were bonus inserts in the Home Run History boxed set. Fronts have gold-foil highlights with the pivotal number in blue-sky tones. Backs have portrait photos and a few words about the remarkable record.

		NM/M
1	Mark McGwire (Home Run Champ)	1.50
1	Cal Ripken Jr. (Consecutive Games)	2.00

National Convention Redemption

This card of Pacific spokesman Tony Gwynn was given away at the card company's booth in a redemption program during the 1998 National Sports Collectors Convention in August 1998. The card front has a color photo of Gwynn on red and yellow rayed background. At lower-right is a gold-foil convention logo. Back has an action photo, copyright information and logos.

		NM/M
1998	Tony Gwynn	3.00

1999 Pacific Sample

This card of Pacific spokesman Tony Gwynn introduces the 1999 series. The

sample card follows the format of the issued version but is overprinted "SAMPLE" on back and lacks Gwynn's 1998 season and career stats.

NM/M
Tony Gwynn 2.00

1999 Pacific

The 450-card base set features full bleed fronts enhanced with silver foil stamping. Card backs have year-by-year statistics, a small photo and a brief career highlight caption. There are two parallels, Platinum Blues and Reds. Platinum Blues have blue foil stamping and are seeded 1:73 packs. Reds are retail exclusive with red foil stamping and are seeded one per retail pack.

NM/M
Complete Set (500): 30.00
Common Player: .10
Platinum Blues (1:73): 15X
Reds (1:1R): 2.5X
Pack (10): 1.00
Wax Box (36): 35.00
1 Garret Anderson .10
2 Jason Dickson .10
3 Gary DiSarcina .10
4 Jim Edmonds .10
5 Darin Erstad .25
6 Chuck Finley .10
7 Shigetosi Hasegawa .10
8 Ken Hill .10
9 Dave Hollins .10
10 Phil Nevin .10
11 Troy Percival .10
12a Tim Salmon/Action .10
12b Tim Salmon/Portrait .10
13 Brian Anderson .10
14 Tony Batista .10
15 Jay Bell .10
16 Andy Benes .10
17 Yamil Benitez .10
18 Omar Daal .10
19 David Dellucci .10
20 Karim Garcia .10
21 Bernard Gilkey .10
22a Travis Lee/Action .10
22b Travis Lee/Portrait .10
23 Aaron Small .10
24 Kelly Stinnett .10
25 Devon White .10
26 Matt Williams .10
27a Bruce Chen/Action .10
27b Bruce Chen/Portrait .10
28a Andres Galarraga/Action .10
28b Andres Galarraga/Portrait .10
29 Tom Glavine .35
30 Ozzie Guillen .10
31 Andruw Jones 1.00
32a Chipper Jones/Action 1.50
32b Chipper Jones/Portrait 1.50
33 Ryan Klesko .10
34 George Lombard .10
35 Javy Lopez .10
36a Greg Maddux/Action 1.50
36b Greg Maddux/Portrait 1.50
37a Marty Malloy/Action .10
37b Marty Malloy/Portrait .10
38 Dennis Martinez .10
39 Kevin Millwood .10
40a Alex Rodriguez/Action 2.50
40b Alex Rodriguez /Portrait 2.50
41 Denny Neagle .10
42 John Smoltz .10
43 Michael Tucker .10
44 Walt Weiss .10
45a Roberto Alomar/Action .25
45b Roberto Alomar/Portrait .25
46 Brady Anderson .10
47 Harold Baines .10
48 Mike Bordick .10
49a Danny Clyburn/Action .10
49b Danny Clyburn/Portrait .10
50 Eric Davis .10
51 Scott Erickson .10
52 Chris Hoiles .10
53 Jimmy Key .10
54a Ryan Minor/Action .10
54b Ryan Minor/Portrait .10
55 Mike Mussina .40
56 Jesse Orosco .10
57a Rafael Palmeiro/Action .75
57b Rafael Palmeiro/Portrait .75
58 Sidney Ponson .10
59 Arthur Rhodes .10
60a Cal Ripken Jr/Action 3.00
60b Cal Ripken Jr./Portrait 3.00
61 B.J. Surhoff .10
62 Steve Avery .10
63 Darren Bragg .10
64 Dennis Eckersley .75
65a Nomar Garciaparra/Action 1.50
65b Nomar Garciaparra/Portrait 1.50
66a Sammy Sosa/Action 1.50
66b Sammy Sosa/Portrait 1.50
67 Tom Gordon .10
68 Reggie Jefferson .10
69 Darren Lewis .10
70a Mark McGwire/Action 2.50
70b Mark McGwire/Portrait 2.50
71 Pedro Martinez 1.00
72 Troy O'Leary .10
73 Bret Saberhagen .10
74 Mike Stanley .10
75 John Valentin .10
76 Jason Varitek .10
77 Mo Vaughn .10
78 Tim Wakefield .10
79 Manny Alexander .10
80 Rod Beck .10
81 Brant Brown .10
82 Mark Clark .10
83 Gary Gaetti .10
84 Mark Grace .10
85 Jose Hernandez .10
86 Lance Johnson .10
87a Jason Maxwell/Action .10
87b Jason Maxwell/Portrait .10
88 Mickey Morandini .10
89 Terry Mulholland .10
90 Henry Rodriguez .10
91 Scott Servais .10
92 Kevin Tapani .10
93 Pedro Valdes .10
94 Kerry Wood .40
95 Jeff Abbott .10
96 James Baldwin .10
97 Albert Belle .10
98 Mike Cameron .10
99 Mike Caruso .10
100 Wil Cordero .10
101 Ray Durham .10
102 Jaime Navarro .10
103 Greg Norton .10
104 Magglio Ordonez .25
105 Mike Sirotka .10
106a Frank Thomas/Action 1.00
106b Frank Thomas/Portrait 1.00
107 Robin Ventura .10
108 Craig Wilson .10
109 Aaron Boone .10
110 Bret Boone .10
111 Sean Casey .15
112 Pete Harnisch .10
113 John Hudek .10
114 Barry Larkin .10
115 Eduardo Perez .10
116 Mike Remlinger .10
117 Reggie Sanders .10
118 Chris Stynes .10
119 Eddie Taubensee .10
120 Brett Tomko .10
121 Pat Watkins .10
122 Dmitri Young .10
123 Sandy Alomar Jr. .10
124 Dave Burba .10
125 Bartolo Colon .10
126 Joey Cora .10
127 Brian Giles .10
128 Dwight Gooden .10
129 Mike Jackson .10
130 David Justice .10
131 Kenny Lofton .10
132 Charles Nagy .10
133 Chad Ogea .10
134a Manny Ramirez/Action 1.00
134b Manny Ramirez/Portrait 1.00
135 Richie Sexson .10
136a Jim Thome/Action .75
136b Jim Thome/Portrait .75
137 Omar Vizquel .10
138 Jaret Wright .10
139 Pedro Astacio .10
140 Jason Bates .10
141a Dante Bichette/Action .10
141b Dante Bichette/Portrait .10
142a Vinny Castilla/Action .10
142b Vinny Castilla/Portrait .10
143a Edgar Clemente/Action .10
143b Edgar Clemente/Portrait .10
144a Derrick Gibson/Action .10
144b Derrick Gibson/Portrait .10
145 Curtis Goodwin .10
146a Todd Helton/Action 1.00
146b Todd Helton/Portrait 1.00
147 Bobby Jones .10
148 Darryl Kile .10
149 Mike Lansing .10
150 Chuck McElroy .10
151 Neifi Perez .10
152 Jeff Reed .10
153 John Thomson .10
154a Larry Walker/Action .10
154b Larry Walker/Portrait .10
155 Jamey Wright .10
156 Kimera Bartee .10
157 Geronimo Berroa .10
158 Raul Casanova .10
159 Frank Catalanotto .10
160 Tony Clark .10
161 Deivi Cruz .10
162 Damion Easley .10
163 Juan Encarnacion .10
164 Luis Gonzalez .10
165 Seth Greisinger .10
166 Bob Higginson .10
167 Brian Hunter .10
168 Todd Jones .10
169 Justin Thompson .10
170 Antonio Alfonseca .10
171 Dave Berg .10
172 John Cangelosi .10
173 Craig Counsell .10
174 Todd Dunwoody .10
175 Cliff Floyd .10
176 Alex Gonzalez .10
177 Livan Hernandez .10
178 Ryan Jackson .10
179 Mark Kotsay .10
180 Derrek Lee .65
181 Matt Mantei .10
182 Brian Meadows .10
183 Edgar Renteria .10
184a Moises Alou/Action .10
184b Moises Alou/Portrait .10
185 Brad Ausmus .10
186a Jeff Bagwell/Action 1.00
186b Jeff Bagwell/Portrait 1.00
187 Derek Bell .10
188 Sean Berry .10
189 Craig Biggio .10
190 Carl Everett .10
191 Ricky Gutierrez .10
192 Mike Hampton .10
193 Doug Henry .10
194 Richard Hidalgo .10
195 Randy Johnson 1.00
196a Russ Johnson/Action .10
196b Russ Johnson/Portrait .10
197 Shane Reynolds .10
198 Bill Spiers .10
199 Kevin Appier .10
200 Tim Belcher .10
201 Jeff Conine .10
202 Johnny Damon .35
203 Jermaine Dye .10
204a Jeremy Giambi (Batting stance.) .10
204b Jeremy Giambi (Follow-through.) .10
205 Jeff King .10
206 Shane Mack .10
207 Jeff Montgomery .10
208 Hal Morris .10
209 Jose Offerman .10
210 Dean Palmer .10
211 Jose Rosado .10
212 Glendon Rusch .10
213 Larry Sutton .10
214 Mike Sweeney .10
215 Bobby Bonilla .10
216 Alex Cora .10
217 Darren Dreifort .10
218 Mark Grudzielanek .10
219 Todd Hollandsworth .10
220 Trenidad Hubbard .10
221 Charles Johnson .10
222 Eric Karros .10
223 Matt Luke .10
224 Ramon Martinez .10
225 Raul Mondesi .10
226 Chan Ho Park .10
227 Jeff Shaw .10
228 Gary Sheffield .40
229 Eric Young .10
230 Jeromy Burnitz .10
231 Jeff Cirillo .10
232 Marquis Grissom .10
233 Bobby Hughes .10
234 John Jaha .10
235 Geoff Jenkins .10
236 Scott Karl .10
237 Mark Loretta .10
238 Mike Matheny .10
239 Mike Myers .10
240 Dave Nilsson .10
241 Bob Wickman .10
242 Jose Valentin .10
243 Fernando Vina .10
244 Rick Aguilera .10
245 Ron Coomer .10
246 Marty Cordova .10
247 Denny Hocking .10
248 Matt Lawton .10
249 Pat Meares .10
250a Paul Molitor/Action 1.00
250b Paul Molitor/Portrait 1.00
251 Otis Nixon .10
252 Alex Ochoa .10
253 David Ortiz .65
254 A.J. Pierzynski .10
255 Brad Radke .10
256 Terry Steinbach .10
257 Bob Tewksbury .10
258 Todd Walker .10
259 Shane Andrews .10
260 Shayne Bennett .10
261 Orlando Cabrera .10
262 Brad Fullmer .10
263 Vladimir Guerrero 1.00
264 Wilton Guerrero .10
265 Dustin Hermanson .10
266 Terry Jones .10
267 Steve Kline .10
268 Carl Pavano .10
269 F.P. Santangelo .10
270a Fernando Seguignol/Action .10
270b Fernando Seguignol/Portrait .10
271 Ugueth Urbina .10
272 Jose Vidro .10
273 Chris Widger .10
274 Edgardo Alfonzo .10
275 Carlos Baerga .10
276 John Franco .10
277 Todd Hundley .10
278 Butch Huskey .10
279 Bobby Jones .10
280 Al Leiter .10
281 Greg McMichael .10
282 Brian McRae .10
283 Hideo Nomo .50
284 John Olerud .10
285 Rey Ordonez .10
286a Mike Piazza/Action 1.75
286b Mike Piazza/Portrait 1.75
287 Turk Wendell .10
288 Masato Yoshii .10
289 David Cone .10
290 Chad Curtis .10
291 Joe Girardi .10
292 Orlando Hernandez .10
293a Hideki Irabu/Action .10
293b Hideki Irabu/Portrait .10
294a Derek Jeter/Action 3.00
294b Derek Jeter/Portrait 3.00
295 Chuck Knoblauch .10
296a Mike Lowell/Action .10
296b Mike Lowell/Portrait .10
297 Tino Martinez .10
298 Ramiro Mendoza .10
299 Paul O'Neill .10
300 Andy Pettitte .25
301 Jorge Posada .10
302 Tim Raines .10
303 Mariano Rivera .15
304 David Wells .10
305a Bernie Williams/Action .10
305b Bernie Williams/Portrait .10
306 Mike Blowers .10
307 Tom Candiotti .10
308a Eric Chavez/Action .15
308b Eric Chavez/Portrait .15
309 Ryan Christenson .10
310 Jason Giambi .65
311a Ben Grieve/Action .10
311b Ben Grieve/Portrait .10
312 Rickey Henderson 1.00
313 A.J. Hinch .10
314 Jason McDonald .10
315 Bip Roberts .10
316 Kenny Rogers .10
317 Scott Spiezio .10
318 Matt Stairs .10
319 Miguel Tejada .20
320 Bob Abreu .20
321 Alex Arias .10
322a Gary Bennett/Action **RC** .10
322b Gary Bennett/Portrait **RC** .10
323 Ricky Bottalico .10
324 Rico Brogna .10
325 Bobby Estalella .10
326 Doug Glanville .10
327 Kevin Jordan .10
328 Mark Leiter .10
329 Wendell Magee .10
330 Mark Portugal .10
331 Desi Relaford .10
332 Scott Rolen .65
333 Curt Schilling .35
334 Kevin Sefcik .10
335 Adrian Brown .10
336 Emil Brown .10
337 Lou Collier .10
338 Francisco Cordova .10
339 Freddy Garcia .10
340 Jose Guillen .10
341 Jason Kendall .10
342 Al Martin .10
343 Abraham Nunez .10
344 Aramis Ramirez .10
345 Ricardo Rincon .10
346 Jason Schmidt .10
347 Turner Ward .10
348 Tony Womack .10
349 Kevin Young .10
350 Juan Acevedo .10
351 Delino DeShields .10
352a J.D. Drew/Action .40
352b J.D. Drew/Portrait .40
353 Ron Gant .10
354 Brian Jordan .10
355 Ray Lankford .10
356 Eli Marrero .10
357 Kent Mercker .10
358 Matt Morris .10
359 Luis Ordaz .10
360 Donovan Osborne .10
361 Placido Polanco .10
362 Fernando Tatis .10
363 Andy Ashby .10
364 Kevin Brown .10
365 Ken Caminiti .10
366 Steve Finley .10
367 Chris Gomez .10
368a Tony Gwynn/Action 1.50
368b Tony Gwynn/Portrait 1.50
369 Joey Hamilton .10
370 Carlos Hernandez .10
371 Trevor Hoffman .10
372 Wally Joyner .10
373 Jim Leyritz .10
374 Ruben Rivera .10
375 Greg Vaughn .10
376 Quilvio Veras .10
377 Rich Aurilia .10
378a Barry Bonds/Action 3.00
378b Barry Bonds/Portrait 3.00
379 Ellis Burks .10
380 Joe Carter .10
381 Stan Javier .10
382 Brian Johnson .10
383 Jeff Kent .10
384 Jose Mesa .10
385 Bill Mueller .10
386 Robb Nen .10
387a Armando Rios/Action .10
387b Armando Rios/Portrait .10
388 Kirk Rueter .10
389 Rey Sanchez .10
390 J.T. Snow .10
391 David Bell .10
392 Jay Buhner .10
393 Ken Cloude .10
394 Russ Davis .10
395 Jeff Fassero .10
396a Ken Griffey Jr./Action 2.00
396b Ken Griffey Jr./Portrait 2.00
397 Giomar Guevara **RC** .10
398 Carlos Guillen .10
399 Edgar Martinez .10
400 Shane Monahan .10
401 Jamie Moyer .10
402 David Segui .10
403 Makoto Suzuki .10
404 Mike Timlin .10
405 Dan Wilson .10
406 Wilson Alvarez .10
407 Rolando Arrojo .10
408 Wade Boggs 1.50
409 Miguel Cairo .10
410 Roberto Hernandez .10
411 Mike Kelly .10
412 Aaron Ledesma .10
413 Albie Lopez .10
414 Dave Martinez .10
415 Quinton McCracken .10
416 Fred McGriff .10
417 Bryan Rekar .10
418 Paul Sorrento .10
419 Randy Winn .10
420 John Burkett .10
421 Will Clark .10
422 Royce Clayton .10
423a Juan Gonzalez/Action .50
423b Juan Gonzalez/Portrait .50
424 Tom Goodwin .10
425 Rusty Greer .10
426 Rick Helling .10
427 Roberto Kelly .10
428 Mark McLemore .10
429a Ivan Rodriguez/Action .75
429b Ivan Rodriguez/Portrait .75
430 Aaron Sele .10
431 Lee Stevens .10
432 Todd Stottlemyre .10
433 John Wetteland .10
434 Todd Zeile .10
435 Jose Canseco .50
436a Roger Clemens/Action 1.75
436b Roger Clemens/Portrait 1.75
437 Felipe Crespo .10
438a Jose Cruz Jr./Action .10
438b Jose Cruz Jr./Portrait .10
439 Carlos Delgado .50
440a Tom Evans/Action .10
440b Tom Evans/Portrait .10
441 Tony Fernandez .10
442 Darrin Fletcher .10
443 Alex Gonzalez .10
444 Shawn Green .30
445 Roy Halladay .10
446 Pat Hentgen .10
447 Juan Samuel .10
448 Benito Santiago .10
449 Shannon Stewart .10
450 Woody Williams .10

Cramer's Choice

Pacific CEO Michael Cramer personally chose this 10-card set. Die-cut in a trophy

shape, the cards are enhanced with silver holographic etching and gold foil stamping across the card bottom. Cards are serially numbered to 299.

NM/M
Complete Set (10): 65.00
Common Player: 7.50
Inserted 1:721
1 Cal Ripken Jr. 20.00
2 Nomar Garciaparra 12.50
3 Frank Thomas 10.00
4 Ken Griffey Jr. 15.00
5 Alex Rodriguez 17.50
6 Greg Maddux 12.50
7 Sammy Sosa 12.50
8 Kerry Wood 7.50
9 Mark McGwire 17.50
10 Tony Gwynn 12.50

Dynagon Diamond

Dynagon Diamond captures 20 of baseball's biggest stars in action against a mirror-patterned full-foil background. These are seeded about 1:9. A Titanium parallel with each card numbered to 99 was exclusive to hobby packs.

NM/M
Complete Set (20): 20.00
Common Player: .40
Inserted 1:9
Titanium (99 Sets): 8X
1 Cal Ripken Jr. 2.50
2 Nomar Garciaparra 1.00
3 Frank Thomas .75
4 Derek Jeter 2.50
5 Ben Grieve .40
6 Ken Griffey Jr. 1.50
7 Alex Rodriguez 2.00
8 Juan Gonzalez .50
9 Travis Lee .40
10 Chipper Jones 1.00
11 Greg Maddux 1.00
12 Sammy Sosa 1.00
13 Kerry Wood .50
14 Jeff Bagwell .75
15 Hideo Nomo .50
16 Mike Piazza 12.50
17 J.D. Drew .50
18 Mark McGwire 2.00
19 Tony Gwynn 1.00
20 Barry Bonds 2.50

Gold Crown Die-Cuts

This 36-card die-cut set is shaped like a crown at the top and features dual foiling, 24-pt. stock and gold foil stamping. These are seeded 1:37 packs.

NM/M
Complete Set (36): 75.00
Common Player: .75
Inserted 1:37
1 Darin Erstad 1.00
2 Cal Ripken Jr. 7.50
3 Nomar Garciaparra 4.00
4 Pedro Martinez 3.00
5 Mo Vaughn .75

6	Frank Thomas	3.00
7	Kenny Lofton	.75
8	Manny Ramirez	3.00
9	Paul Molitor	3.00
10	Derek Jeter	7.50
11	Bernie Williams	.75
12	Ben Grieve	.75
13	Ken Griffey Jr.	5.00
14	Alex Rodriguez	6.00
15	Wade Boggs	4.00
16	Juan Gonzalez	1.50
17	Ivan Rodriguez	2.50
18	Jose Canseco	1.50
19	Roger Clemens	4.50
20	Travis Lee	.75
21	Chipper Jones	4.00
22	Greg Maddux	4.00
23	Sammy Sosa	4.00
24	Kerry Wood	1.50
25	Todd Helton	3.00
26	Larry Walker	.75
27	Jeff Bagwell	3.00
28	Craig Biggio	.75
29	Raul Mondesi	.75
30	Vladimir Guerrero	3.00
31	Mike Piazza	4.50
32	Scott Rolen	2.00
33	J.D. Drew	1.50
34	Mark McGwire	6.00
35	Tony Gwynn	4.00
36	Barry Bonds	7.50

Hot Cards

This dealer-only 10-card set was awarded to any dealer that had sold any packs/boxes that produced a card for the Pacific Hot Cards Registry Program. Fronts have a metallic foil background. Backs have a portrait photo and are serial numbered within an edition of 500 each.

		NM/M
Complete Set (10):		75.00
Common Player:		3.00
1	Alex Rodriguez	12.50
2	Tony Gwynn	7.50
3	Ken Griffey Jr.	10.00
4	Sammy Sosa	7.50
5	Ivan Rodriguez	6.00
6	Derek Jeter	15.00
7	Cal Ripken Jr.	15.00
8	Mark McGwire	12.50
9	J.D. Drew	4.50
10	Bernie Williams	3.00

Team Checklists

This 30-card horizontal insert set features a star player from each team on the card front, with each team's complete checklist on the card back. Fronts feature a holographic silver-foiled and embossed logo of the player's respective team. These are seeded 2:37 packs.

		NM/M
Complete Set (30):		30.00
Common Player:		.30
Inserted 1:18		
1	Darin Erstad	.50
2	Cal Ripken Jr.	3.00
3	Nomar Garciaparra	1.50
4	Frank Thomas	1.00
5	Manny Ramirez	1.00
6	Damion Easley	.30
7	Jeff King	.30
8	Paul Molitor	1.00
9	Derek Jeter	3.00
10	Ben Grieve	.30
11	Ken Griffey Jr.	2.00
12	Wade Boggs	1.50
13	Juan Gonzalez	.60
14	Roger Clemens	1.75
15	Travis Lee	.30
16	Chipper Jones	1.50
17	Sammy Sosa	1.50
18	Barry Larkin	.30
19	Todd Helton	1.00
20	Mark Kotsay	.30
21	Jeff Bagwell	1.00
22	Raul Mondesi	.30
23	Jeff Cirillo	.30
24	Vladimir Guerrero	1.00
25	Mike Piazza	1.75
26	Scott Rolen	.75
27	Jason Kendall	.30
28	Mark McGwire	2.50
29	Tony Gwynn	1.50
30	Barry Bonds	3.00

Timelines

Timelines features 20 superstars, giving a chronological history of each player complete with photos from early in their careers. Three photos of the player are on the card front. Inserted exclusively in hobby packs these are limited to 199 serially numbered sets.

		NM/M
Complete Set (20):		200.00
Common Player:		6.00
Inserted 1:181 H		
1	Cal Ripken Jr.	30.00
2	Frank Thomas	12.00
3	Jim Thome	10.00
4	Paul Molitor	12.00
5	Bernie Williams	6.00
6	Derek Jeter	30.00
7	Ken Griffey Jr.	20.00
8	Alex Rodriguez	25.00
9	Wade Boggs	15.00
10	Jose Canseco	9.00
11	Roger Clemens	17.50
12	Andres Galarraga	6.00
13	Chipper Jones	15.00
14	Greg Maddux	15.00
15	Sammy Sosa	15.00
16	Larry Walker	6.00
17	Randy Johnson	12.00
18	Mike Piazza	17.50
19	Mark McGwire	25.00
20	Tony Gwynn	15.00

1999 Pacific Aurora

The 200-card set features two photos on the card front and one on the back. Card backs also have '98 and career stats along with personal information. The player's name and Aurora logo are stamped with gold foil. A parallel "Opening Day" issued is stamped with a gold foil seal and numbered within an edition of 31 each.

		NM/M
Complete Set (200):		20.00
Common Player:		.10
Opening Days:		20X
Production 31 Sets		
Reds:		2X
Retail Only (1:6)		
Pack (6):		1.50
Wax Box (36):		22.50
1	Garret Anderson	.10
2	Jim Edmonds	.10
3	Darin Erstad	.30
4	Matt Luke	.10
5	Tim Salmon	.10
6	Mo Vaughn	.10
7	Jay Bell	.10
8	David Dellucci	.10
9	Steve Finley	.10
10	Bernard Gilkey	.10
11	Randy Johnson	1.00
12	Travis Lee	.10
13	Matt Williams	.10
14	Andres Galarraga	.10
15	Tom Glavine	.35
16	Andruw Jones	1.00
17	Chipper Jones	1.50
18	Brian Jordan	.10
19	Javy Lopez	.10
20	Greg Maddux	1.50
21	Albert Belle	.10
22	Will Clark	.10
23	Scott Erickson	.10
24	Mike Mussina	.40
25	Cal Ripken Jr.	3.00
26	B.J. Surhoff	.10
27	Nomar Garciaparra	1.50
28	Reggie Jefferson	.10
29	Darren Lewis	.10
30	Pedro Martinez	1.00
31	John Valentin	.10
32	Rod Beck	.10
33	Mark Grace	.10
34	Lance Johnson	.10
35	Mickey Morandini	.10
36	Sammy Sosa	1.50
37	Kerry Wood	.40
38	James Baldwin	.10
39	Mike Caruso	.10
40	Ray Durham	.10
41	Magglio Ordonez	.25
42	Frank Thomas	1.00
43	Aaron Boone	.10
44	Sean Casey	.20
45	Barry Larkin	.10
46	Hal Morris	.10
47	Denny Neagle	.10
48	Greg Vaughn	.10
49	Pat Watkins	.10
50	Roberto Alomar	.25
51	Sandy Alomar Jr.	.10
52	David Justice	.10
53	Kenny Lofton	.10
54	Manny Ramirez	1.00
55	Richie Sexson	.10
56	Jim Thome	.75
57	Omar Vizquel	.10
58	Dante Bichette	.10
59	Vinny Castilla	.10
60	Edgard Clemente **RC**	.10
61	Derrick Gibson	.10
62	Todd Helton	1.00
63	Darryl Kile	.10
64	Larry Walker	.10
65	Tony Clark	.10
66	Damion Easley	.10
67	Bob Higginson	.10
68	Brian Hunter	.10
69	Dean Palmer	.10
70	Justin Thompson	.10
71	Craig Counsell	.10
72	Todd Dunwoody	.10
73	Cliff Floyd	.10
74	Alex Gonzalez	.10
75	Livan Hernandez	.10
76	Mark Kotsay	.10
77	Derrek Lee	.65
78	Moises Alou	.10
79	Jeff Bagwell	1.00
80	Derek Bell	.10
81	Craig Biggio	.10
82	Ken Caminiti	.10
83	Richard Hidalgo	.10
84	Shane Reynolds	.10
85	Jeff Conine	.10
86	Johnny Damon	.35
87	Jermaine Dye	.10
88	Jeff King	.10
89	Jeff Montgomery	.10
90	Mike Sweeney	.10
91	Kevin Brown	.10
92	Mark Grudzielanek	.10
93	Eric Karros	.10
94	Raul Mondesi	.10
95	Chan Ho Park	.10
96	Gary Sheffield	.40
97	Jeromy Burnitz	.10
98	Jeff Cirillo	.10
99	Marquis Grissom	.10
100	Geoff Jenkins	.10
101	Dave Nilsson	.10
102	Jose Valentin	.10
103	Fernando Vina	.10
104	Marty Cordova	.10
105	Matt Lawton	.10
106	David Ortiz	.60
107	Brad Radke	.10
108	Todd Walker	.10
109	Shane Andrews	.10
110	Orlando Cabrera	.10
111	Brad Fullmer	.10
112	Vladimir Guerrero	1.00
113	Wilton Guerrero	.10
114	Carl Pavano	.10
115	Fernando Seguignol	.10
116	Ugueth Urbina	.10
117	Edgardo Alfonzo	.10
118	Bobby Bonilla	.10
119	Rickey Henderson	1.00
120	Hideo Nomo	.60
121	John Olerud	.10
122	Rey Ordonez	.10
123	Mike Piazza	2.00
124	Masato Yoshii	.10
125	Scott Brosius	.10
126	Orlando Hernandez	.10
127	Hideki Irabu	.10
128	Derek Jeter	3.00
129	Chuck Knoblauch	.10
130	Tino Martinez	.10
131	Jorge Posada	.10
132	Bernie Williams	.10
133	Eric Chavez	.20
134	Ryan Christenson	.10
135	Jason Giambi	.65
136	Ben Grieve	.10
137	A.J. Hinch	.10
138	Matt Stairs	.10
139	Miguel Tejada	.20
140	Bob Abreu	.20
141	Gary Bennett **RC**	.10
142	Desi Relaford	.10
143	Scott Rolen	.75
144	Curt Schilling	.35
145	Kevin Sefcik	.10
146	Brian Giles	.10
147	Jose Guillen	.10
148	Jason Kendall	.10
149	Aramis Ramirez	.10
150	Tony Womack	.10
151	Kevin Young	.10
152	Eric Davis	.10
153	J.D. Drew	.50
154	Ray Lankford	.10
155	Eli Marrero	.10
156	Mark McGwire	2.50
157	Luis Ordaz	.10
158	Edgar Renteria	.10
159	Andy Ashby	.10
160	Tony Gwynn	1.50
161	Trevor Hoffman	.10
162	Wally Joyner	.10
163	Jim Leyritz	.10
164	Ruben Rivera	.10
165	Reggie Sanders	.10
166	Quilvio Veras	.10
167	Rich Aurilia	.10
168	Marvin Benard	.10
169	Barry Bonds	3.00
170	Ellis Burks	.10
171	Jeff Kent	.10
172	Bill Mueller	.10
173	J.T. Snow	.10
174	Jay Buhner	.10
175	Jeff Fassero	.10
176	Ken Griffey Jr.	2.25
177	Carlos Guillen	.10
178	Edgar Martinez	.10
179	Alex Rodriguez	2.50
180	David Segui	.10
181	Dan Wilson	.10
182	Rolando Arrojo	.10
183	Wade Boggs	1.50
184	Jose Canseco	.40
185	Aaron Ledesma	.10
186	Dave Martinez	.10
187	Quinton McCracken	.10
188	Fred McGriff	.10
189	Juan Gonzalez	.60
190	Tom Goodwin	.10
191	Rusty Greer	.10
192	Roberto Kelly	.10
193	Rafael Palmeiro	.75
194	Ivan Rodriguez	.75
195	Roger Clemens	2.00
196	Jose Cruz Jr.	.10
197	Carlos Delgado	.60
198	Alex Gonzalez	.10
199	Roy Halladay	.10
200	Pat Hentgen	.10

Complete Players

The 10 players featured in this serial numbered 20-card set each have two cards, designed to fit together. Card fronts feature a red border on the top and bottom with the rest of the card done in gold foil etching. Each card is serially numbered to 299.

		NM/M
Complete Set (10):		40.00
Common Player:		3.00
Production 299 Sets		
1	Cal Ripken Jr.	9.00
2	Nomar Garciaparra	4.50
3	Sammy Sosa	4.50
4	Kerry Wood	3.00
5	Frank Thomas	4.00
6	Mike Piazza	5.00
7	Mark McGwire	7.50
8	Tony Gwynn	4.50
9	Ken Griffey Jr.	6.00
10	Alex Rodriguez	7.50

Kings of the Major Leagues

The full foiled card fronts also utilize gold foil stamping. Pacific's crown as well as the featured player's team are shadow boxed in the background with the player's image in the foreground. These are seeded 1:361.

		NM/M
Complete Set (10):		80.00
Common Player:		5.00
Inserted 1:361		
1	Cal Ripken Jr.	17.50
2	Nomar Garciaparra	9.00
3	Sammy Sosa	9.00
4	Kerry Wood	5.00
5	Frank Thomas	7.50
6	Mike Piazza	10.00
7	Mark McGwire	15.00
8	Tony Gwynn	9.00
9	Ken Griffey Jr.	12.50
10	Alex Rodriguez	15.00

On Deck

Twenty of the game's hottest players are featured in this laser-cut and silver foil stamped set. The player's team logo is laser cut into the bottom half of the card beneath the player photo.

		NM/M
Complete Set (20):		17.50
Common Player:		.50
Inserted 1:9		
1	Chipper Jones	1.00
2	Cal Ripken Jr.	3.00
3	Nomar Garciaparra	1.00
4	Sammy Sosa	1.00
5	Frank Thomas	.75
6	Manny Ramirez	.75
7	Todd Helton	.75
8	Larry Walker	.50
9	Jeff Bagwell	.75
10	Vladimir Guerrero	.75
11	Mike Piazza	1.50
12	Derek Jeter	3.00
13	Bernie Williams	.50
14	J.D. Drew	.50
15	Mark McGwire	2.50
16	Tony Gwynn	1.00
17	Ken Griffey Jr.	2.00
18	Alex Rodriguez	2.50
19	Juan Gonzalez	.50
20	Ivan Rodriguez	.65

Pennant Fever

Regular Pennant Fever inserts feature gold foil stamping of 20 of the hottest players in the hobby. These are seeded 4:37 packs. There are also three parallel versions: Platinum Blue, Silver and Copper. Platinum Blues are limited to 100 serial numbered sets, Silvers are retail exclusive and limited to 250 numbered sets and Coppers are hobby exclusive and limited to 20 numbered sets. Pacific spokesman Tony Gwynn autographed 97 regular Pennent Fever cards and one each of the Silver, Blue and Copper.

		NM/M
Complete Set (20):		30.00
Common Player:		.75
Silver (250 Sets):		2X
Platinum Blue (100):		6X
Copper (20):		20X
Tony Gwynn Autograph:		25.00
1	Chipper Jones	2.00
2	Greg Maddux	2.00
3	Cal Ripken Jr.	5.00
4	Nomar Garciaparra	2.00
5	Sammy Sosa	2.00
6	Kerry Wood	.75
7	Frank Thomas	1.50
8	Manny Ramirez	1.50
9	Todd Helton	1.50
10	Jeff Bagwell	1.50
11	Mike Piazza	2.50
12	Derek Jeter	5.00
13	Bernie Williams	.75
14	J.D. Drew	.75
15	Mark McGwire	4.00
16	Tony Gwynn	2.00
17	Ken Griffey Jr.	3.00
18	Alex Rodriguez	4.00
19	Juan Gonzalez	.75
20	Ivan Rodriguez	1.25

Styrotechs

This 20-card set features styrene stock, making the cards more resilient. Fronts have a black border highlighted with gold foil. Backs have a photo and brief career highlights. These are seeded 1:37 packs.

		NM/M
Complete Set (20):		35.00
Common Player:		1.00
Inserted 1:37		
1	Chipper Jones	3.00
2	Greg Maddux	3.00
3	Cal Ripken Jr.	6.00
4	Nomar Garciaparra	3.00
5	Sammy Sosa	3.00
6	Kerry Wood	1.25
7	Frank Thomas	2.00
8	Manny Ramirez	2.00
9	Larry Walker	1.00

10 Jeff Bagwell 2.00
11 Mike Piazza 4.00
12 Derek Jeter 6.00
13 Bernie Williams 1.00
14 J.D. Drew 1.25
15 Mark McGwire 5.00
16 Tony Gwynn 3.00
17 Ken Griffey Jr. 4.50
18 Alex Rodriguez 5.00
19 Juan Gonzalez 1.25
20 Ivan Rodriguez 1.50

1999 Pacific Crown Collection Sample

This card of Pacific spokesman Tony Gwynn introduces the 1999 Crown series. The sample card follows the format of the issued version but is overprinted "SAMPLE" on back.

NM/M
Tony Gwynn 2.00

1999 Pacific Crown Collection

Released in one series the 300-card set has white borders and gold-foil highlights on front. Backs have a small photo along with English and Spanish narrative. A Platinum Blue parallel to the base set utilizes platinum blue holographic foil and is seeded 1:73 packs. A WalMart-exclusive red-foiled parallel is seeded 1:9 packs. Twelve-card packs had an S.R.P. of $2.49.

NM/M
Complete Set (300): 20.00
Common Player: .10
Red Stars: 6X
Inserted 1:9
Platinum Blue Stars: 30X
Inserted 1:73
Pack (12): 1.00
Wax Box (36): 22.50
1 Garret Anderson .10
2 Gary DiSarcina .10
3 Jim Edmonds .10
4 Darin Erstad .25
5 Shigetosi Hasegawa .10
6 Norberto Martin .10
7 Omar Olivares .10
8 Orlando Palmeiro .10
9 Tim Salmon .10
10 Randy Velarde .10
11 Tony Batista .10
12 Jay Bell .10
13 Yamil Benitez .10
14 Omar Daal .10
15 David Dellucci .10
16 Karim Garcia .10
17 Travis Lee .10
18 Felix Rodriguez .10
19 Devon White .10
20 Matt Williams .10
21 Andres Galarraga .10
22 Tom Glavine .35
23 Ozzie Guillen .10
24 Andruw Jones 1.00
25 Chipper Jones 1.50
26 Ryan Klesko .10
27 Javy Lopez .10
28 Greg Maddux 1.50
29 Dennis Martinez .10
30 Odaliz Perez .10
31 Rudy Seanez .10
32 John Smoltz .10
33 Roberto Alomar .25
34 Armando Benitez .10
35 Scott Erickson .10
36 Juan Guzman .10
37 Mike Mussina .35
38 Jesse Orosco .10
39 Rafael Palmeiro .75
40 Sidney Ponson .10
41 Cal Ripken Jr. 3.00
42 B.J. Surhoff .10
43 Lenny Webster .10
44 Dennis Eckersley .75
45 Nomar Garciaparra 1.50
46 Darren Lewis .10
47 Pedro Martinez 1.00
48 Troy O'Leary .10
49 Bret Saberhagen .10
50 John Valentin .10
51 Mo Vaughn .10
52 Tim Wakefield .10
53 Manny Alexander .10
54 Rod Beck .10
55 Gary Gaetti .10
56 Mark Grace .10
57 Felix Heredia .10
58 Jose Hernandez .10
59 Henry Rodriguez .10
60 Sammy Sosa 1.50
61 Kevin Tapani .10
62 Kerry Wood .45
63 James Baldwin .10
64 Albert Belle .10
65 Mike Caruso .10
66 Carlos Castillo .10
67 Wil Cordero .10
68 Jaime Navarro .10
69 Magglio Ordonez .25
70 Frank Thomas 1.00
71 Robin Ventura .10
72 Bret Boone .10
73 Sean Casey .20
74 Guillermo Garcia **RC** .10
75 Barry Larkin .10
76 Melvin Nieves .10
77 Eduardo Perez .10
78 Roberto Petagine .10
79 Reggie Sanders .10
80 Eddie Taubensee .10
81 Brett Tomko .10
82 Sandy Alomar Jr. .10
83 Bartolo Colon .10
84 Joey Cora .10
85 Einar Diaz .10
86 David Justice .10
87 Kenny Lofton .10
88 Manny Ramirez 1.00
89 Jim Thome .75
90 Omar Vizquel .10
91 Enrique Wilson .10
92 Pedro Astacio .10
93 Dante Bichette .10
94 Vinny Castilla .10
95 Edgard Clemente **RC** .10
96 Todd Helton 1.00
97 Darryl Kile .10
98 Mike Munoz .10
99 Neifi Perez .10
100 Jeff Reed .10
101 Larry Walker .10
102 Gabe Alvarez .10
103 Kimera Bartee .10
104 Frank Castillo .10
105 Tony Clark .10
106 Deivi Cruz .10
107 Damion Easley .10
108 Luis Gonzalez .10
109 Marino Santana .10
110 Justin Thompson .10
111 Antonio Alfonseca .10
112 Alex Fernandez .10
113 Cliff Floyd .10
114 Alex Gonzalez .10
115 Livan Hernandez .10
116 Mark Kotsay .10
117 Derrek Lee .65
118 Edgar Renteria .10
119 Jesus Sanchez .10
120 Moises Alou .10
121 Jeff Bagwell 1.00
122 Derek Bell .10
123 Craig Biggio .10
124 Tony Eusebio .10
125 Ricky Gutierrez .10
126 Richard Hidalgo .10
127 Randy Johnson 1.00
128 Jose Lima .10
129 Shane Reynolds .10
130 Johnny Damon .40
131 Carlos Febles .10
132 Jeff King .10
133 Mendy Lopez .10
134 Hal Morris .10
135 Jose Offerman .10
136 Jose Rosado .10
137 Jose Santiago .10
138 Bobby Bonilla .10
139 Roger Cedeno .10
140 Alex Cora .10
141 Eric Karros .10
142 Raul Mondesi .10
143 Antonio Osuna .10
144 Chan Ho Park .10
145 Gary Sheffield .30
146 Ismael Valdes .10
147 Jeromy Burnitz .10
148 Jeff Cirillo .10
149 Valerio de los Santos .10
150 Marquis Grissom .10
151 Scott Karl .10
152 Dave Nilsson .10
153 Al Reyes .10
154 Rafael Roque .10
155 Jose Valentin .10
156 Fernando Vina .10
157 Rick Aguilera .10
158 Hector Carrasco .10
159 Marty Cordova .10
160 Eddie Guardado .10
161 Paul Molitor 1.00
162 Otis Nixon .10
163 Alex Ochoa .10
164 David Ortiz .45
165 Frank Rodriguez .10
166 Todd Walker .10
167 Miguel Batista .10
168 Orlando Cabrera .10
169 Vladimir Guerrero 1.00
170 Wilton Guerrero .10
171 Carl Pavano .10
172 Robert Perez .10
173 F.P. Santangelo .10
174 Fernando Seguignol .10
175 Ugueth Urbina .10
176 Javier Vazquez .10
177 Edgardo Alfonzo .10
178 Carlos Baerga .10
179 John Franco .10
180 Luis Lopez .10
181 Hideo Nomo .50
182 John Olerud .10
183 Rey Ordonez .10
184 Mike Piazza 1.75
185 Armando Reynoso .10
186 Masato Yoshii .10
187 David Cone .10
188 Orlando Hernandez .10
189 Hideki Irabu .10
190 Derek Jeter 3.00
191 Ricky Ledee .10
192 Tino Martinez .10
193 Ramiro Mendoza .10
194 Paul O'Neill .10
195 Jorge Posada .10
196 Mariano Rivera .15
197 Luis Sojo .10
198 Bernie Williams .10
199 Rafael Bournigal .10
200 Eric Chavez .20
201 Ryan Christenson .10
202 Jason Giambi .60
203 Ben Grieve .10
204 Rickey Henderson 1.00
205 A.J. Hinch .10
206 Kenny Rogers .10
207 Miguel Tejada .20
208 Jorge Velandia .10
209 Bobby Abreu .20
210 Marlon Anderson .10
211 Alex Arias .10
212 Bobby Estalella .10
213 Doug Glanville .10
214 Scott Rolen .65
215 Curt Schilling .35
216 Kevin Sefcik .10
217 Adrian Brown .10
218 Francisco Cordova .10
219 Freddy Garcia .10
220 Jose Guillen .10
221 Jason Kendall .10
222 Al Martin .10
223 Abraham Nunez .10
224 Aramis Ramirez .10
225 Ricardo Rincon .10
226 Kevin Young .10
227 J.D. Drew .40
228 Ron Gant .10
229 Jose Jimenez .10
230 Brian Jordan .10
231 Ray Lankford .10
232 Eli Marrero .10
233 Mark McGwire 2.50
234 Luis Ordaz .10
235 Placido Polanco .10
236 Fernando Tatis .10
237 Andy Ashby .10
238 Kevin Brown .10
239 Ken Caminiti .10
240 Steve Finley .10
241 Chris Gomez .10
242 Tony Gwynn 1.50
243 Carlos Hernandez .10
244 Trevor Hoffman .10
245 Wally Joyner .10
246 Ruben Rivera .10
247 Greg Vaughn .10
248 Quilvio Veras .10
249 Rich Aurilia .10
250 Barry Bonds 3.00
251 Stan Javier .10
252 Jeff Kent .10
253 Ramon Martinez .10
254 Jose Mesa .10
255 Armando Rios .10
256 Rich Rodriguez .10
257 Rey Sanchez .10
258 J.T. Snow .10
259 Julian Tavarez .10
260 Jeff Fassero .10
261 Ken Griffey Jr. 2.00
262 Giomar Guevara **RC** .10
263 Carlos Guillen .10
264 Raul Ibanez .10
265 Edgar Martinez .10
266 Jamie Moyer .10
267 Alex Rodriguez 2.50
268 David Segui .10
269 Makoto Suzuki .10
270 Wilson Alvarez .10
271 Rolando Arrojo .10
272 Wade Boggs 1.50
273 Miguel Cairo .10
274 Roberto Hernandez .10
275 Aaron Ledesma .10
276 Albie Lopez .10
277 Quinton McCracken .10
278 Fred McGriff .10
279 Esteban Yan .10
280 Luis Alicea .10
281 Will Clark .10
282 Juan Gonzalez .50
283 Rusty Greer .10
284 Rick Helling .10
285 Xavier Hernandez .10
286 Roberto Kelly .10
287 Esteban Loaiza .10
288 Ivan Rodriguez .75
289 Aaron Sele .10
290 John Wetteland .10
291 Jose Canseco .40
292 Roger Clemens 1.75
293 Felipe Crespo .10
294 Jose Cruz Jr. .10
295 Carlos Delgado .60
296 Kelvim Escobar .10
297 Tony Fernandez .10
298 Alex Gonzalez .10
299 Tomas Perez .10
300 Juan Samuel .10

In The Cage

These die-cut inserts have a netting like background with laser cutting, giving the look that the player is hitting in a batting cage. These are seeded 1:145 packs.

NM/M
Complete Set (20): 80.00
Common Player: 2.00
Inserted 1:145
1 Chipper Jones 7.50
2 Cal Ripken Jr. 15.00
3 Nomar Garciaparra 7.50
4 Sammy Sosa 7.50
5 Frank Thomas 5.00
6 Manny Ramirez 5.00
7 Todd Helton 5.00
8 Moises Alou 2.00
9 Vladimir Guerrero 5.00
10 Mike Piazza 9.00
11 Derek Jeter 15.00
12 Ben Grieve 2.00
13 J.D. Drew 3.00
14 Mark McGwire 12.00
15 Tony Gwynn 7.50
16 Ken Griffey Jr. 10.00
17 Edgar Martinez 2.00
18 Alex Rodriguez 12.00
19 Juan Gonzalez 2.50
20 Ivan Rodriguez 4.00

Latinos/Major Leagues

This 36-card set salutes the many Latino players in the major leagues.

NM/M
Complete Set (36): 25.00
Common Player: .30
Inserted 1:18
1 Roberto Alomar .60
2 Rafael Palmeiro 2.00
3 Nomar Garciaparra 3.50
4 Pedro Martinez 2.50
5 Magglio Ordonez 1.50
6 Sandy Alomar Jr. .30
7 Bartolo Colon .30
8 Manny Ramirez 2.50
9 Omar Vizquel .30
10 Enrique Wilson .30
11 David Ortiz 1.50
12 Orlando Hernandez .30
13 Tino Martinez .30
14 Mariano Rivera .45
15 Bernie Williams .30
16 Edgar Martinez .30
17 Alex Rodriguez 5.00
18 David Segui .30
19 Rolando Arrojo .30
20 Juan Gonzalez 1.25
21 Ivan Rodriguez 2.00
22 Jose Canseco 1.00
23 Jose Cruz Jr. .30
24 Andres Galarraga .30
25 Andruw Jones 2.50
26 Javy Lopez .30
27 Sammy Sosa 3.50
28 Vinny Castilla .30
29 Alex Gonzalez .30
30 Moises Alou .30
31 Bobby Bonilla .30
32 Raul Mondesi .30
33 Fernando Vina .30
34 Vladimir Guerrero 2.50
35 Carlos Baerga .30
36 Rey Ordonez .30

Pacific Cup

These die-cut inserts are shaped like a trophy with the featured player's photo in the foreground. These are seeded 1:721 packs.

NM/M
Complete Set (10): 80.00
Common Player: 5.00
Inserted 1:721
1 Cal Ripken Jr. 20.00
2 Nomar Garciaparra 8.00
3 Frank Thomas 6.00
4 Ken Griffey Jr. 12.00
5 Alex Rodriguez 16.00
6 Greg Maddux 8.00
7 Sammy Sosa 8.00
8 Kerry Wood 5.00
9 Mark McGwire 16.00
10 Tony Gwynn 8.00

Players Choice

In conjunction with the annual Players Choice Awards ceremonies, Pacific produced a special edition of the cards of some of the players involved. Cards have a "Players Choice" foil stamp on front. Quantities produced were in the range of 25-40 of each.

NM/M
Complete Set (6): 55.00
Common Player: 5.00
10 Randy Velarde 5.00
41 Cal Ripken Jr. 30.00
47 Pedro Martinez 12.00
88 Manny Ramirez 12.00
112 Alex Fernandez 5.00
128 Jose Lima 5.00

Tape Measure

This 20-card insert set is fully foiled in platinum blue with rainbow highlights in the background of the player photo.

NM/M
Complete Set (20): 20.00
Common Player: .60
Inserted 1:73
1 Andres Galarraga .60
2 Chipper Jones 2.50
3 Nomar Garciaparra 2.50
4 Sammy Sosa 2.50
5 Frank Thomas 1.50
6 Manny Ramirez 1.50
7 Vinny Castilla .60
8 Moises Alou .60
9 Jeff Bagwell 1.50
10 Raul Mondesi .60
11 Vladimir Guerrero 1.50
12 Mike Piazza 2.75
13 J.D. Drew 1.00
14 Mark McGwire 3.50
15 Greg Vaughn .60
16 Ken Griffey Jr. 3.00
17 Alex Rodriguez 3.50
18 Juan Gonzalez 1.00
19 Ivan Rodriguez 1.25
20 Jose Canseco 1.00

Team Checklists

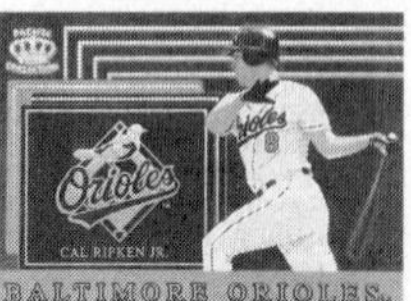

This features holographic silver-foil stamping and a horizontal format. The backs have a complete team checklist for the featured player's team.

NM/M
Complete Set (30): 25.00
Common Player: .50
Inserted 1:37
1 Darin Erstad .60
2 Travis Lee .50
3 Chipper Jones 1.75
4 Cal Ripken Jr. 4.00
5 Nomar Garciaparra 1.75
6 Sammy Sosa 1.75
7 Frank Thomas 1.25
8 Barry Larkin .50
9 Manny Ramirez 1.25
10 Larry Walker .50
11 Bob Higginson .50
12 Livan Hernandez .50
13 Moises Alou .50
14 Jeff King .50
15 Raul Mondesi .50
16 Marquis Grissom .50
17 David Ortiz 1.00
18 Vladimir Guerrero 1.25
19 Mike Piazza 2.00
20 Derek Jeter 4.00
21 Ben Grieve .50
22 Scott Rolen .75
23 Jason Kendall .50
24 Mark McGwire 3.00
25 Tony Gwynn 1.75
26 Barry Bonds 4.00
27 Ken Griffey Jr. 2.50
28 Wade Boggs 1.75
29 Juan Gonzalez .75
30 Jose Canseco .60

1999 Pacific Crown Royale

The Crown Royale 144-card base set has a horizontal format die-cut around a crown design at the top. The cards are double foiled and etched. There are 18 short-printed rookies and prospects cards, which were inserted at a rate of about one per eight packs. There are two parallels: Limited Series and Opening Day. Limited Series is produced on 24-point stock with silver foil and limited to 99 numbered sets. Opening Day is limited to 72 numbered sets.

		NM/M
Complete Set (144):		75.00
Common Player:		.25
Common SP:		.50
Limited Series (99 Sets):		6X
SP's:		2X
Opening Day (72 Sets):		12X
SP's:		2X
Pack (6):		2.00
Wax Box (24):		35.00
1	Jim Edmonds	.25
2	Darin Erstad	.50
3	Troy Glaus	2.00
4	Tim Salmon	.25
5	Mo Vaughn	.25
6	Jay Bell	.25
7	Steve Finley	.25
8	Randy Johnson	2.00
9	Travis Lee	.25
10	Matt Williams	.25
11	Andruw Jones	2.00
12	Chipper Jones	3.00
13	Brian Jordan	.25
14	Ryan Klesko	.25
15	Javy Lopez	.25
16	Greg Maddux	3.00
17	Randall Simon/SP	.50
18	Albert Belle	.25
19	Will Clark	.25
20	Delino DeShields	.25
21	Mike Mussina	.50
22	Cal Ripken Jr.	6.00
23	Nomar Garciaparra	3.00
24	Pedro Martinez	2.00
25	Jose Offerman	.25
26	John Valentin	.25
27	Mark Grace	.25
28	Lance Johnson	.25
29	Henry Rodriguez	.25
30	Sammy Sosa	3.00
31	Kerry Wood	1.00
32	Mike Caruso	.25
33	Ray Durham	.25
34	Magglio Ordonez	.40
35	Brian Simmons/SP	.50
36	Frank Thomas	2.00
37	Mike Cameron	.25
38	Barry Larkin	.25
39	Greg Vaughn	.25
40	Dmitri Young	.25
41	Roberto Alomar	.40
42	Sandy Alomar Jr.	.25
43	David Justice	.25
44	Kenny Lofton	.25
45	Manny Ramirez	2.00
46	Jim Thome	1.50
47	Dante Bichette	.25
48	Vinny Castilla	.25
49	Todd Helton	2.00
50	Larry Walker	.25
51	Tony Clark	.25
52	Damion Easley	.25
53	Bob Higginson	.25
54	Brian Hunter	.25
55	Gabe Kapler/SP	.50
56	Jeff Weaver/SP **RC**	2.50
57	Cliff Floyd	.25
58	Alex Gonzalez/SP	.50
59	Mark Kotsay	.25
60	Derrek Lee	1.00
61	Preston Wilson/SP	.75
62	Moises Alou	.25
63	Jeff Bagwell	2.00
64	Derek Bell	.25
65	Craig Biggio	.25
66	Ken Caminiti	.25
67	Carlos Beltran/SP	2.00
68	Johnny Damon	.45
69	Carlos Febles/SP	.65
70	Jeff King	.25
71	Kevin Brown	.25
72	Todd Hundley	.25
73	Eric Karros	.25
74	Raul Mondesi	.25
75	Gary Sheffield	.75
76	Jeromy Burnitz	.25
77	Jeff Cirillo	.25
78	Marquis Grissom	.25
79	Fernando Vina	.25
80	Chad Allen/SP **RC**	.50
81	Matt Lawton	.25
82	Doug Mientkiewicz/SP	.75
83	Brad Radke	.25
84	Todd Walker	.25
85	Michael Barrett/SP	.50
86	Brad Fullmer	.25
87	Vladimir Guerrero	2.00
88	Wilton Guerrero	.25
89	Ugueth Urbina	.25
90	Bobby Bonilla	.25
91	Rickey Henderson	2.00
92	Rey Ordonez	.25
93	Mike Piazza	3.50
94	Robin Ventura	.25
95	Roger Clemens	3.50
96	Orlando Hernandez	.25
97	Derek Jeter	6.00
98	Chuck Knoblauch	.25
99	Tino Martinez	.25
100	Bernie Williams	.25
101	Eric Chavez/SP	1.50
102	Jason Giambi	1.00
103	Ben Grieve	.25
104	Tim Raines	.25
105	Marlon Anderson/SP	.65
106	Doug Glanville	.25
107	Scott Rolen	1.25
108	Curt Schilling	.40
109	Brian Giles	.25
110	Jose Guillen	.25
111	Jason Kendall	.25
112	Kevin Young	.25
113	J.D. Drew/SP	2.00
114	Jose Jimenez/SP	.50
115	Ray Lankford	.25
116	Mark McGwire	5.00
117	Fernando Tatis	.25
118	Matt Clement/SP	.75
119	Tony Gwynn	3.00
120	Trevor Hoffman	.25
121	Wally Joyner	.25
122	Reggie Sanders	.25
123	Barry Bonds	6.00
124	Ellis Burks	.25
125	Jeff Kent	.25
126	J.T. Snow	.25
127	Freddy Garcia/SP **RC**	1.00
128	Ken Griffey Jr.	4.00
129	Edgar Martinez	.25
130	Alex Rodriguez	5.00
131	David Segui	.25
132	Rolando Arrojo	.25
133	Wade Boggs	3.00
134	Jose Canseco	.65
135	Quinton McCracken	.25
136	Fred McGriff	.25
137	Juan Gonzalez	1.00
138	Rusty Greer	.25
139	Rafael Palmeiro	1.50
140	Ivan Rodriguez	1.50
141	Jose Cruz Jr.	.25
142	Carlos Delgado	.75
143	Shawn Green	.75
144	Roy Halladay/SP	1.00

Century 21

This 10-card set features some of baseball's most dominating players, on a full silver foil front. These are seeded 1:25 packs.

		NM/M
Complete Set (10):		30.00
Common Player:		2.00
Inserted 1:25		
1	Cal Ripken Jr.	7.50
2	Nomar Garciaparra	4.00
3	Sammy Sosa	4.00
4	Frank Thomas	3.00
5	Mike Piazza	4.50
6	J.D. Drew	2.00
7	Mark McGwire	6.00
8	Tony Gwynn	4.00
9	Ken Griffey Jr.	5.00
10	Alex Rodriguez	6.00

Cramer's Choice Premiums

This enlarged (about 5" x 7") 10-card set is die-cut into a trophy shape. Cards are enhanced with silver holographic fronts with silver holographic etching and gold-foil stamping across the bottom. They are found one per box. Six serially numbered parallels were randomly seeded: Dark Blue (35 each), Green (30), Red (25), Light Blue (20), Gold (10) and Purple (1).

		NM/M
Complete Set (10):		20.00
Common Player:		2.00
Inserted 1:Box		
Dark Blue (35 Sets):		5X
Green (30):		6X
Red (25):		8X
Light Blue (20):		10X
Gold (10):		15X
Purple (1): Value Undetermined		
1	Cal Ripken Jr.	6.50
2	Nomar Garciaparra	3.00
3	Sammy Sosa	3.00
4	Frank Thomas	2.50
5	Mike Piazza	3.50
6	Derek Jeter	6.50
7	J.D. Drew	2.00
8	Mark McGwire	5.00
9	Tony Gwynn	3.00
10	Ken Griffey Jr.	4.00

Gold Crown Die-Cut Premiums

This enlarged six-card set was an unannounced premium box-topper. They were limited to 1,036 numbered sets, found less than once every other box.

		NM/M
Complete Set (6):		15.00
Common Player:		2.50
Inserted 6:10 boxes.		
1	Cal Ripken Jr.	7.00
2	Mike Piazza	4.50
3	Ken Griffey Jr.	5.00
4	Tony Gwynn	3.00
5	Mark McGwire	6.00
6	J.D. Drew	2.50

Living Legends

This 10-card set spotlights baseball's top stars on a fully foiled card front. These are serial numbered to 375 sets.

		NM/M
Complete Set (10):		100.00
Common Player:		7.50
Production 375 Sets		
1	Greg Maddux	10.00
2	Cal Ripken Jr.	20.00
3	Nomar Garciaparra	10.00
4	Sammy Sosa	10.00
5	Frank Thomas	7.50
6	Mike Piazza	12.00
7	Mark McGwire	15.00
8	Tony Gwynn	10.00
9	Ken Griffey Jr.	13.50
10	Alex Rodriguez	15.00

Master Performers

This 20-card set features a full foiled front with the player photo in a frame like border. Master Performers are seeded 2:25 packs.

		NM/M
Complete Set (20):		40.00
Common Player:		1.00
Inserted 2:25		
1	Chipper Jones	2.50
2	Greg Maddux	2.50
3	Cal Ripken Jr.	5.00
4	Nomar Garciaparra	2.50
5	Sammy Sosa	2.50
6	Frank Thomas	2.00
7	Raul Mondesi	1.00
8	Vladimir Guerrero	2.00
9	Mike Piazza	3.00
10	Roger Clemens	3.00
11	Derek Jeter	5.00
12	Scott Rolen	1.75
13	J.D. Drew	1.50
14	Mark McGwire	4.00
15	Tony Gwynn	2.50
16	Barry Bonds	5.00
17	Ken Griffey Jr.	3.50
18	Alex Rodriguez	4.00
19	Juan Gonzalez	1.50
20	Ivan Rodriguez	1.75

Pillars of the Game

This 25-card set features holographic silver foil fronts on a horizontal format.

		NM/M
Complete Set (25):		30.00
Common Player:		.50
Inserted 1:1		
1	Mo Vaughn	.50
2	Chipper Jones	2.00
3	Greg Maddux	2.00
4	Albert Belle	.50
5	Cal Ripken Jr.	4.00
6	Nomar Garciaparra	2.00
7	Sammy Sosa	2.00
8	Frank Thomas	1.50
9	Manny Ramirez	1.50
10	Jeff Bagwell	1.50
11	Raul Mondesi	.50
12	Vladimir Guerrero	1.50
13	Mike Piazza	2.25
14	Roger Clemens	2.25
15	Derek Jeter	4.00
16	Bernie Williams	.50
17	Ben Grieve	.50
18	J.D. Drew	1.00
19	Mark McGwire	3.00
20	Tony Gwynn	2.00
21	Barry Bonds	4.00
22	Ken Griffey Jr.	2.50
23	Alex Rodriguez	3.00
24	Juan Gonzalez	1.00
25	Ivan Rodriguez	1.25

Pivotal Players

This 25-card set features holographic silver foil fronts with a flame in the background of the player photo.

		NM/M
Complete Set (25):		20.00
Common Player:		.50
Inserted 1:1		
1	Mo Vaughn	.50
2	Chipper Jones	2.00
3	Greg Maddux	2.00
4	Albert Belle	.50
5	Cal Ripken Jr.	4.00
6	Nomar Garciaparra	2.00
7	Sammy Sosa	2.00
8	Frank Thomas	1.50

9	Manny Ramirez	1.50
10	Craig Biggio	.50
11	Raul Mondesi	.50
12	Vladimir Guerrero	1.50
13	Mike Piazza	2.25
14	Roger Clemens	2.50
15	Derek Jeter	4.00
16	Bernie Williams	.50
17	Ben Grieve	.50
18	Scott Rolen	.60
19	J.D. Drew	.75
20	Mark McGwire	3.00
21	Tony Gwynn	2.00
22	Ken Griffey Jr.	2.50
23	Alex Rodriguez	3.00
24	Juan Gonzalez	.75
25	Ivan Rodriguez	1.00

Home Run Heroes

These cards were part of an unannounced multi-manufacturer (Fleer, Upper Deck, Topps, Pacific) insert program which was exclusive to Wal-Mart. Each company produced cards of Mark McGwire and Sammy Sosa, along with two other premier sluggers. Each company's cards share a "Power Elite" logo at top and "Home Run Heroes" logo vertically at right.

		NM/M
Complete Set (4):		3.50
Common Player:		.50
13	Mark McGwire	1.50
14	Sammy Sosa	1.25
15	Juan Gonzalez	.50
16	Manny Ramirez	.50

1999 Pacific Invincible

The base set consists of 150 cards. Each features an action photo with a portrait in a cel window at bottom. There are two parallels to the base set: Opening Day and Platinum Blue. Both parallels are limited to 67 serial numbered sets.

		NM/M
Complete Set (150):		60.00
Common Player:		.25
Opening Day (69 Sets):		6X
Platinum Blues (67):		6X
Pack (3):		1.50
Wax Box (24):		35.00
1	Jim Edmonds	.25
2	Darin Erstad	.50
3	Troy Glaus	2.50
4	Tim Salmon	.25
5	Mo Vaughn	.25
6	Steve Finley	.25
7	Randy Johnson	2.50
8	Travis Lee	.25
9	Dante Powell	.25
10	Matt Williams	.25
11	Bret Boone	.25
12	Andruw Jones	2.50
13	Chipper Jones	3.00
14	Brian Jordan	.25
15	Ryan Klesko	.25
16	Javy Lopez	.25
17	Greg Maddux	3.00
18	Brady Anderson	.25
19	Albert Belle	.25
20	Will Clark	.25
21	Mike Mussina	.75
22	Cal Ripken Jr.	6.00
23	Nomar Garciaparra	3.00
24	Pedro Martinez	2.50
25	Trot Nixon	.25
26	Jose Offerman	.25
27	Donnie Sadler	.25
28	John Valentin	.25
29	Mark Grace	.25
30	Lance Johnson	.25
31	Henry Rodriguez	.25
32	Sammy Sosa	3.00
33	Kerry Wood	1.25
34	McKay Christensen	.25
35	Ray Durham	.25
36	Jeff Liefer	.25
37	Frank Thomas	2.50
38	Mike Cameron	.25
39	Barry Larkin	.25
40	Greg Vaughn	.25
41	Dmitri Young	.25
42	Roberto Alomar	.50
43	Sandy Alomar Jr.	.25
44	David Justice	.25
45	Kenny Lofton	.25
46	Manny Ramirez	2.50
47	Jim Thome	2.25
48	Dante Bichette	.25
49	Vinny Castilla	.25
50	Darryl Hamilton	.25
51	Todd Helton	2.50
52	Neifi Perez	.25
53	Larry Walker	.25
54	Tony Clark	.25
55	Damion Easley	.25
56	Bob Higginson	.25
57	Brian Hunter	.25
58	Gabe Kapler	.25
59	Cliff Floyd	.25
60	Alex Gonzalez	.25
61	Mark Kotsay	.25
62	Derrek Lee	2.00
63	Braden Looper	.25
64	Moises Alou	.25
65	Jeff Bagwell	2.50
66	Craig Biggio	.25
67	Ken Caminiti	.25
68	Scott Elarton	.25
69	Mitch Meluskey	.25
70	Carlos Beltran	.65
71	Johnny Damon	.50
72	Carlos Febles	.25
73	Jeremy Giambi	.25
74	Kevin Brown	.25
75	Todd Hundley	.25
76	Paul LoDuca	.25
77	Raul Mondesi	.25
78	Gary Sheffield	1.00
79	Geoff Jenkins	.25
80	Jeromy Burnitz	.25
81	Marquis Grissom	.25
82	Jose Valentin	.25
83	Fernando Vina	.25
84	Corey Koskie	.25
85	Matt Lawton	.25
86	Christian Guzman	.25
87	Torii Hunter	.25
88	Doug Mientkiewicz	.25
89	Michael Barrett	.25
90	Brad Fullmer	.25
91	Vladimir Guerrero	2.50
92	Fernando Seguignol	.25
93	Ugueth Urbina	.25
94	Bobby Bonilla	.25
95	Rickey Henderson	2.50
96	Rey Ordonez	.25
97	Mike Piazza	3.50
98	Robin Ventura	.25
99	Roger Clemens	3.50
100	Derek Jeter	6.00
101	Chuck Knoblauch	.25
102	Tino Martinez	.25
103	Paul O'Neill	.25
104	Bernie Williams	.25
105	Eric Chavez	.50
106	Ryan Christenson	.25
107	Jason Giambi	1.25
108	Ben Grieve	.25
109	Miguel Tejada	.50
110	Marlon Anderson	.25
111	Doug Glanville	.25
112	Scott Rolen	2.25
113	Curt Schilling	.50

114	Brian Giles	.25
115	Warren Morris	.25
116	Jason Kendall	.25
117	Kris Benson	.25
118	J.D. Drew	1.25
119	Ray Lankford	.25
120	Mark McGwire	5.00
121	Matt Clement	.25
122	Tony Gwynn	3.00
123	Trevor Hoffman	.25
124	Wally Joyner	.25
125	Reggie Sanders	.25
126	Barry Bonds	6.00
127	Ellis Burks	.25
128	Jeff Kent	.25
129	Stan Javier	.25
130	J.T. Snow	.25
131	Jay Buhner	.25
132	Freddy Garcia **RC**	2.00
133	Ken Griffey Jr.	4.00
134	Russ Davis	.25
135	Edgar Martinez	.25
136	Alex Rodriguez	5.00
137	David Segui	.25
138	Rolando Arrojo	.25
139	Wade Boggs	3.00
140	Jose Canseco	1.00
141	Quinton McCracken	.25
142	Fred McGriff	.25
143	Juan Gonzalez	1.25
144	Tom Goodwin	.25
145	Rusty Greer	.25
146	Ivan Rodriguez	2.25
147	Jose Cruz Jr.	.25
148	Carlos Delgado	1.00
149	Shawn Green	.75
150	Roy Halladay	.25

Diamond Magic

This 10-card set features a horizontal format with silver foil stamping on the front. Diamond Magic's are seeded 1:49 packs.

		NM/M
	Complete Set (10):	35.00
	Common Player:	3.00
	Inserted 1:49	
1	Cal Ripken Jr.	7.50
2	Nomar Garciaparra	4.00
3	Sammy Sosa	4.00
4	Frank Thomas	3.50
5	Mike Piazza	4.50
6	J.D. Drew	3.00
7	Mark McGwire	6.00
8	Tony Gwynn	4.00
9	Ken Griffey Jr.	5.00
10	Alex Rodriguez	6.00

Flash Point

This 20-card set features gold etching and gold foil stamping on the card front. These were seeded 1:25 packs.

		NM/M
	Complete Set (20):	50.00
	Common Player:	1.25
	Inserted 1:25	
1	Mo Vaughn	1.25
2	Chipper Jones	3.50
3	Greg Maddux	3.50
4	Cal Ripken Jr.	9.00
5	Nomar Garciaparra	3.50
6	Sammy Sosa	3.50
7	Frank Thomas	2.50
8	Manny Ramirez	2.50
9	Vladimir Guerrero	2.50
10	Mike Piazza	4.00
11	Roger Clemens	4.00
12	Derek Jeter	9.00
13	Ben Grieve	1.25
14	Scott Rolen	2.00
15	J.D. Drew	1.50
16	Mark McGwire	7.50
17	Tony Gwynn	3.50
18	Ken Griffey Jr.	5.00
19	Alex Rodriguez	7.50
20	Juan Gonzalez	1.50

Giants of the Game

This jumbo mail-in redemption set of baseball's top stars is limited to 10 serially numbered specimens of each card.

		NM/M
	Complete Set (10):	300.00
	Common Player:	25.00
	Production 10 Sets	
1	Cal Ripken Jr.	75.00
2	Nomar Garciaparra	35.00
3	Sammy Sosa	35.00
4	Frank Thomas	30.00
5	Mike Piazza	40.00
6	J.D. Drew	25.00
7	Mark McGwire	60.00
8	Tony Gwynn	35.00
9	Ken Griffey Jr.	50.00
10	Alex Rodriguez	60.00

Sandlot Heroes

Sandlot Heroes salutes baseball's top players on a horizontal format with holographic silver foil stamping on front. These were inserted one per pack. Each player can be found in two versions. A special edition, serially numbered to 10 of each and overprinted with a SportsFest logo, was created for use as a redemption prize at Pacific's booth at the show.

		NM/M
	Complete Set (20):	15.00
	Common Player:	.50
	Inserted 1:1	
	SportsFest (10 Sets):	25X
1	Mo Vaughn	.50
2	Chipper Jones	1.00
3	Greg Maddux	1.00
4	Cal Ripken Jr.	3.00
5	Nomar Garciaparra	1.00
6	Sammy Sosa	1.00
7	Frank Thomas	.75
8	Manny Ramirez	.75
9	Vladimir Guerrero	.75
10	Mike Piazza	1.25
11	Roger Clemens	1.25
12	Derek Jeter	3.00
13	Eric Chavez	.50
14	Ben Grieve	.50
15	J.D. Drew	.60
16	Mark McGwire	2.00
17	Tony Gwynn	1.00
18	Ken Griffey Jr.	1.50
19	Alex Rodriguez	2.00
20	Juan Gonzalez	.60

Seismic Force

This 20-card set has a dot pattern behind the featured player with the left side and bottom of the card in a gold border. These were seeded one per pack. A specially marked SportsFest version was created for use as a redemption prize at Pacific's booth at the show. These are serially numbered to just 20 apiece.

		NM/M
	Complete Set (20):	15.00
	Common Player:	.50
	Inserted 1:1	
	SportsFest (20 Sets):	15X
1	Mo Vaughn	.50
2	Chipper Jones	1.00
3	Greg Maddux	1.00
4	Cal Ripken Jr.	3.00
5	Nomar Garciaparra	1.00
6	Sammy Sosa	1.00
7	Frank Thomas	.75
8	Manny Ramirez	.75
9	Vladimir Guerrero	.75
10	Mike Piazza	1.25
11	Bernie Williams	.50
12	Derek Jeter	3.00
13	Ben Grieve	.50
14	J.D. Drew	.60
15	Mark McGwire	2.00
16	Tony Gwynn	1.00
17	Ken Griffey Jr.	1.50
18	Alex Rodriguez	2.00
19	Juan Gonzalez	.50
20	Ivan Rodriguez	.65

Thunder Alley

Thunder Alley focuses on baseball's top power hitters. These were inserted 1:121 packs.

		NM/M
	Complete Set (20):	75.00
	Common Player:	2.50
	Inserted 1:121	
1	Mo Vaughn	2.50
2	Chipper Jones	6.00
3	Cal Ripken Jr.	12.00
4	Nomar Garciaparra	6.00
5	Sammy Sosa	6.00
6	Frank Thomas	5.00
7	Manny Ramirez	5.00
8	Todd Helton	5.00
9	Vladimir Guerrero	5.00
10	Mike Piazza	7.50
11	Derek Jeter	12.00
12	Ben Grieve	2.50
13	Scott Rolen	4.50
14	J.D. Drew	3.00
15	Mark McGwire	10.00
16	Tony Gwynn	6.00
17	Ken Griffey Jr.	9.00
18	Alex Rodriguez	10.00
19	Juan Gonzalez	3.00
20	Ivan Rodriguez	4.50

1999 Pacific Omega Sample

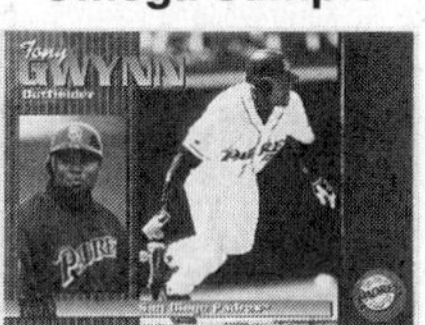

The Omega brand for '99 was launched with this sample card of spokesman Tony Gwynn. The card is in the same format as the regular-issue cards, except for the "SAMPLE" overprint on back and in the card-number circle at bottom-right.

	NM/M
SAMPLE Tony Gwynn	2.00

1999 Pacific Omega

This single-series product features both portrait and action photos on front in a horizontal format. Four parallel versions distinguished by the color of foil highlights were random inserts in the six-card packs. Gold parallels are serially numbered to 299 each; Copper to 99; Platinum Blue to 75 and Premiere Date to 50.

		NM/M
	Complete Set (250):	20.00
	Common Player:	.10
	Gold (299 Sets):	4X
	Copper (99):	10X
	Platinum Blue (75):	15X
	Premiere Date (50):	20X
	Wax Pack (6):	1.50
	Wax Box (36):	35.00
1	Garret Anderson	.10
2	Jim Edmonds	.10
3	Darin Erstad	.20
4	Chuck Finley	.10
5	Troy Glaus	.75
6	Troy Percival	.10
7	Chris Pritchett	.10
8	Tim Salmon	.10
9	Mo Vaughn	.10
10	Jay Bell	.10
11	Steve Finley	.10
12	Luis Gonzalez	.10
13	Randy Johnson	.75
14	Byung-Hyun Kim **RC**	.75
15	Travis Lee	.10
16	Matt Williams	.10
17	Tony Womack	.10
18	Bret Boone	.10
19	Mark DeRosa	.10
20	Tom Glavine	.35
21	Andruw Jones	.75
22	Chipper Jones	1.00
23	Brian Jordan	.10
24	Ryan Klesko	.10
25	Javy Lopez	.10
26	Greg Maddux	1.00
27	John Smoltz	.10
28	Bruce Chen, Odalis Perez	.10
29	Brady Anderson	.10
30	Harold Baines	.10
31	Albert Belle	.10
32	Will Clark	.10
33	Delino DeShields	.10
34	Jerry Hairston Jr.	.10
35	Charles Johnson	.10
36	Mike Mussina	.40
37	Cal Ripken Jr.	2.50
38	B.J. Surhoff	.10
39	Jin Ho Cho	.10
40	Nomar Garciaparra	1.00
41	Pedro Martinez	.75
42	Jose Offerman	.10
43	Troy O'Leary	.10
44	John Valentin	.10
45	Jason Varitek	.10
46	Juan Pena **RC**, Brian Rose	.10
47	Mark Grace	.10
48	Glenallen Hill	.10
49	Tyler Houston	.10
50	Mickey Morandini	.10
51	Henry Rodriguez	.10
52	Sammy Sosa	1.00
53	Kevin Tapani	.10
54	Mike Caruso	.10
55	Ray Durham	.10
56	Paul Konerko	.20
57	Carlos Lee	.10
58	Magglio Ordonez	.20
59	Mike Sirotka	.10
60	Frank Thomas	.75
61	Mark L. Johnson, Chris Singleton	.10
62	Mike Cameron	.10
63	Sean Casey	.20
64	Pete Harnisch	.10
65	Barry Larkin	.10
66	Pokey Reese	.10
67	Greg Vaughn	.10
68	Scott Williamson	.10
69	Dmitri Young	.10
70	Roberto Alomar	.25
71	Sandy Alomar Jr.	.10
72	Travis Fryman	.10
73	David Justice	.10
74	Kenny Lofton	.10
75	Manny Ramirez	.75
76	Richie Sexson	.10
77	Jim Thome	.65
78	Omar Vizquel	.10
79	Jaret Wright	.10
80	Dante Bichette	.10
81	Vinny Castilla	.10
82	Todd Helton	.75
83	Darryl Hamilton	.10
84	Darryl Kile	.10
85	Neifi Perez	.10
86	Larry Walker	.10
87	Tony Clark	.10
88	Damion Easley	.10
89	Juan Encarnacion	.10
90	Bobby Higginson	.10
91	Gabe Kapler	.10
92	Dean Palmer	.10
93	Justin Thompson	.10
94	Masao Kida **RC**, Jeff Weaver **RC**	1.00
95	Bruce Aven	.10
96	Luis Castillo	.10
97	Alex Fernandez	.10
98	Cliff Floyd	.10
99	Alex Gonzalez	.10
100	Mark Kotsay	.10
101	Preston Wilson	.10
102	Moises Alou	.10
103	Jeff Bagwell	.75
104	Derek Bell	.10
105	Craig Biggio	.10
106	Mike Hampton	.10
107	Richard Hidalgo	.10
108	Jose Lima	.10
109	Billy Wagner	.10
110	Russ Johnson, Daryle Ward	.10
111	Carlos Beltran	.50
112	Johnny Damon	.35
113	Jermaine Dye	.10
114	Carlos Febles	.10
115	Jeremy Giambi	.10
116	Joe Randa	.10
117	Mike Sweeney	.10
118	Orber Moreno **RC**, Jose Santiago	.10
119	Kevin Brown	.10
120	Todd Hundley	.10
121	Eric Karros	.10
122	Raul Mondesi	.10
123	Chan Ho Park	.10
124	Angel Pena	.10
125	Gary Sheffield	.45
126	Devon White	.10
127	Eric Young	.10
128	Ron Belliard	.10
129	Jeromy Burnitz	.10
130	Jeff Cirillo	.10
131	Marquis Grissom	.10
132	Geoff Jenkins	.10
133	David Nilsson	.10
134	Hideo Nomo	.40
135	Fernando Vina	.10
136	Ron Coomer	.10
137	Marty Cordova	.10
138	Corey Koskie	.10
139	Brad Radke	.10
140	Todd Walker	.10
141	Chad Allen **RC**, Torii Hunter	.10
142	Cristian Guzman, Jacque Jones	.10
143	Michael Barrett	.10
144	Orlando Cabrera	.10
145	Vladimir Guerrero	.75
146	Wilton Guerrero	.10
147	Ugueth Urbina	.10
148	Rondell White	.10
149	Chris Widger	.10
150	Edgardo Alfonzo	.10
151	Roger Cedeno	.10
152	Octavio Dotel	.10
153	Rickey Henderson	.75
154	John Olerud	.10
155	Rey Ordonez	.10
156	Mike Piazza	1.25
157	Robin Ventura	.10
158	Scott Brosius	.10
159	Roger Clemens	1.25
160	David Cone	.10
161	Chili Davis	.10
162	Orlando Hernandez	.10
163	Derek Jeter	2.50
164	Chuck Knoblauch	.10
165	Tino Martinez	.10
166	Paul O'Neill	.10
167	Bernie Williams	.10
168	Jason Giambi	.60
169	Ben Grieve	.10
170	Chad Harville **RC**	.10
171	Tim Hudson **RC**	2.00
172	Tony Phillips	.10
173	Kenny Rogers	.10
174	Matt Stairs	.10
175	Miguel Tejada	.25
176	Eric Chavez	.25
177	Bobby Abreu	.20
178	Ron Gant	.10
179	Doug Glanville	.10
180	Mike Lieberthal	.10
181	Desi Relaford	.10
182	Scott Rolen	.65
183	Curt Schilling	.35
184	Marlon Anderson, Randy Wolf	.10
185	Brant Brown	.10
186	Brian Giles	.10
187	Jason Kendall	.10
188	Al Martin	.10
189	Ed Sprague	.10
190	Kevin Young	.10
191	Kris Benson, Warren Morris	.10
192	Kent Bottenfield	.10
193	Eric Davis	.10
194	J.D. Drew	.45
195	Ray Lankford	.10
196	Joe McEwing **RC**	.25
197	Mark McGwire	2.00
198	Edgar Renteria	.10
199	Fernando Tatis	.10
200	Andy Ashby	.10
201	Ben Davis	.10
202	Tony Gwynn	1.00
203	Trevor Hoffman	.10
204	Wally Joyner	.10
205	Gary Matthews Jr.	.10
206	Ruben Rivera	.10
207	Reggie Sanders	.10
208	Rich Aurilia	.10
209	Marvin Benard	.10
210	Barry Bonds	2.50
211	Ellis Burks	.10
212	Stan Javier	.10
213	Jeff Kent	.10
214	Robb Nen	.10
215	J.T. Snow	.10
216	David Bell	.10
217	Jay Buhner	.10
218	Freddy Garcia **RC**	.50
219	Ken Griffey Jr.	1.50
220	Brian Hunter	.10
221	Butch Huskey	.10
222	Edgar Martinez	.10
223	Jamie Moyer	.10
224	Alex Rodriguez	2.00
225	David Segui	.10
226	Rolando Arrojo	.10
227	Wade Boggs	1.00
228	Miguel Cairo	.10
229	Jose Canseco	.60
230	Dave Martinez	.10
231	Fred McGriff	.10
232	Kevin Stocker	.10
233	Mike Duvall **RC**, David Lamb	.10
234	Royce Clayton	.10
235	Juan Gonzalez	.40
236	Rusty Greer	.10
237	Ruben Mateo	.10
238	Rafael Palmeiro	.65
239	Ivan Rodriguez	.65
240	John Wetteland	.10
241	Todd Zeile	.10
242	Jeff Zimmerman	.10
243	Homer Bush	.10
244	Jose Cruz Jr.	.10
245	Carlos Delgado	.60
246	Tony Fernandez	.10
247	Shawn Green	.35
248	Shannon Stewart	.10
249	David Wells	.10
250	Roy Halladay, Billy Koch	.10

Debut Duos

The careers of two players who made their major league debuts the same season are compared in this scarce (1:145) insert series. Fronts feature action photos of the pair, backs have portraits.

		NM/M
	Complete Set (10):	45.00
	Common Player:	2.50
	Inserted 1:145	
1	Nomar Garciaparra, Vladimir Guerrero	6.00
2	Derek Jeter, Andy Pettitte	12.00
3	Garret Anderson, Alex Rodriguez	9.00
4	Chipper Jones, Raul Mondesi	6.00
5	Pedro Martinez, Mike Piazza	6.50
6	Mo Vaughn, Bernie Williams	2.50
7	Juan Gonzalez, Ken Griffey Jr.	7.50
8	Sammy Sosa, Larry Walker	6.00
9	Barry Bonds, Mark McGwire	12.00
10	Wade Boggs, Tony Gwynn	6.00

Diamond Masters

		NM/M
	Complete Set (36):	27.50
	Common Player:	.25
	Inserted 1:9	
1	Darin Erstad	.35
2	Mo Vaughn	.25
3	Matt Williams	.25
4	Andruw Jones	.75
5	Chipper Jones	1.00
6	Greg Maddux	1.00
7	Cal Ripken Jr.	3.00
8	Nomar Garciaparra	1.00
9	Pedro Martinez	.75
10	Sammy Sosa	1.00
11	Frank Thomas	.75

12	Kenny Lofton	.25
13	Manny Ramirez	.75
14	Larry Walker	.25
15	Gabe Kapler	.25
16	Jeff Bagwell	.75
17	Craig Biggio	.25
18	Raul Mondesi	.25
19	Vladimir Guerrero	.75
20	Mike Piazza	1.25
21	Roger Clemens	1.25
22	Derek Jeter	3.00
23	Bernie Williams	.25
24	Scott Rolen	.65
25	J.D. Drew	.60
26	Mark McGwire	2.00
27	Fernando Tatis	.25
28	Tony Gwynn	1.00
29	Barry Bonds	3.00
30	Ken Griffey Jr.	1.50
31	Alex Rodriguez	2.00
32	Jose Canseco	.60
33	Juan Gonzalez	.40
34	Ruben Mateo	.25
35	Ivan Rodriguez	.65
36	Rusty Greer	.25

EO Portraits

		NM/M
Complete Set (20):		60.00
Common Player:		1.00
Inserted 1:73		
1-of-1 Numbered Parallels Exist		
1	Mo Vaughn	1.00
2	Chipper Jones	5.00
3	Greg Maddux	5.00
4	Cal Ripken Jr.	10.00
5	Nomar Garciaparra	5.00
6	Sammy Sosa	5.00
7	Frank Thomas	4.00
8	Manny Ramirez	4.00
9	Jeff Bagwell	4.00
10	Mike Piazza	5.50
11	Roger Clemens	5.50
12	Derek Jeter	10.00
13	Scott Rolen	3.00
14	Mark McGwire	8.00
15	Tony Gwynn	5.00
16	Barry Bonds	10.00
17	Ken Griffey Jr.	6.00
18	Alex Rodriguez	8.00
19	Jose Canseco	2.50
20	Juan Gonzalez	2.00

Hit Machine 3000

Within days of Tony Gwynn's 3,000 hit on August 6, Pacific had rushed into production a special insert set honoring the achievement of its long-time spokesman. A total of 3,000 serially numbered sets of 20 cards were issued as random pack inserts in Omega. Fronts feature various game-action and studio photos of Gwynn, and are highlighted in silver foil. Backs have two more color photos of Gwynn and a few sentences about the player. A serial number in printed on front.

		NM/M
Complete Set (20):		24.00
Common Card:		1.50
1	The Hitting Machine	1.50
2	The Eyes Have It	1.50
3	The Art of Hitting	1.50
4	Solid as a Rock	1.50
5	Seeing Doubles	1.50
6	Pithcer's Worst Nightmare	1.50
7	Portrait of an All-Star	1.50
8	An American Hero	1.50
9	Fan Favorite	1.50
10	Mr. Batting Title	1.50
11	4-for-5!	1.50
12	Mission Accomplished	1.50
13	One Hit Away	1.50
14	A Tip of the Hat	1.50
15	It's a Base Hit!	1.50
16	2997th - Grand Slam!	1.50
17	2998th Hit	1.50
18	2999th Hit - 2-Run Double	1.50
19	3000th Hit!	1.50
20	3000 Hits, 8874 At-Bats, 18 Years	1.50

HR '99

		NM/M
Complete Set (20):		20.00
Common Player:		.25
Inserted 1:37		
1	Mo Vaughn	.25
2	Matt Williams	.25
3	Chipper Jones	2.00
4	Albert Belle	.25
5	Nomar Garciaparra	2.00
6	Sammy Sosa	2.00
7	Frank Thomas	1.25
8	Manny Ramirez	1.25
9	Jeff Bagwell	1.25
10	Raul Mondesi	.25
11	Vladimir Guerrero	1.25
12	Mike Piazza	2.25
13	Derek Jeter	4.00
14	Mark McGwire	3.00
15	Fernando Tatis	.25
16	Barry Bonds	4.00
17	Ken Griffey Jr.	2.50
18	Alex Rodriguez	3.00
19	Jose Canseco	.75
20	Juan Gonzalez	.65

5-Tool Talents

		NM/M
Complete Set (30):		40.00
Common Player:		.40
Inserted 4:37		
1	Randy Johnson	1.50
2	Greg Maddux	2.00
3	Pedro Martinez	1.50
4	Kevin Brown	.40
5	Roger Clemens	2.50
6	Carlos Lee	.40
7	Gabe Kapler	.40
8	Carlos Beltran	.75
9	J.D. Drew	.75
10	Ruben Mateo	.40
11	Chipper Jones	2.00
12	Sammy Sosa	2.00
13	Manny Ramirez	1.50
14	Vladimir Guerrero	1.50
15	Mark McGwire	4.00
16	Ken Griffey Jr.	3.00
17	Jose Canseco	.75
18	Nomar Garciaparra	2.00
19	Frank Thomas	1.50
20	Larry Walker	.40
21	Jeff Bagwell	1.50
22	Mike Piazza	2.50
23	Tony Gwynn	2.00
24	Juan Gonzalez	.75
25	Cal Ripken Jr.	5.00
26	Derek Jeter	5.00
27	Scott Rolen	1.25
28	Barry Bonds	5.00
29	Alex Rodriguez	4.00
30	Ivan Rodriguez	1.25

5-Tool Talents Tiered

A parallel of the 5-Tool Talents inserts is fractured into five tiers of increasing scarcity, differentiated by the color of foil highlights and the serially numbered limited edition. The breakdown is: Tier 1, blue, 100 sets; Tier 2, red, 75 sets; Tier 3, green, 50 sets; Tier 4, purple, 25 sets; Tier 5, gold, one set. The unique gold cards are not priced due to their rarity.

		NM/M
1	Randy Johnson	4.00
6	Carlos Lee	2.00
11	Chipper Jones	5.00
18	Nomar Garciaparra	5.00
21	Jeff Bagwell	4.00
28	Barry Bonds	7.50
2	Greg Maddux	7.50
7	Gabe Kapler	2.00
13	Manny Ramirez	6.00
16	Ken Griffey Jr.	10.00
19	Frank Thomas	6.00
30	Ivan Rodriguez	5.00
3	Pedro Martinez	12.50
8	Carlos Beltran	6.00
15	Mark McGwire	20.00
20	Larry Walker	2.00
25	Cal Ripken Jr.	30.00
26	Derek Jeter	30.00
4	Kevin Brown	7.50
9	J.D. Drew	15.00
12	Sammy Sosa	25.00
17	Jose Canseco	20.00
23	Tony Gwynn	25.00
29	Alex Rodriguez	35.00

1999 Pacific Paramount Sample

Pacific spokesman Tony Gwynn is featured on the sample card issued to introduce the brand for 1999. The card carries a large "SAMPLE" overprint diagonally on back.

	NM/M
Tony Gwynn	2.00

1999 Pacific Paramount

The 250-card base set is highlighted by silver foil stamping and a white border. Card backs have a small photo along with 1998 statistics and career totals and a brief career note. There are six parallels to the base set: Copper, Platinum Blue, Holographic Silver, Opening Day Issue, Gold and Holographic Gold. Each parallel is enhanced with the appropriate foil color. Coppers are found exclusively in hobby packs at a rate of one per pack. Platinum Blues are seeded one per 73 packs. Holographic Silvers are hobby only and limited to 99 serial numbered sets. Opening Day Issue is limited to 74 numbered sets. Golds are found one per retail pack. Holographic Golds are limited to 199 numbered sets.

		NM/M
Complete Set (250):		25.00
Common Player:		.10
Copper (1:1H):		2X
Red (1:1R):		2X
Gold (1:1R):		2X
Platinum Blue (1:73):		4X
Holographic Gold (199):		10X
Holographic Silver (99 Sets):		15X
Opening Day (74):		15X
Pack (6):		1.00
Wax Box (36):		25.00
1	Garret Anderson	.10
2	Gary DiSarcina	.10
3	Jim Edmonds	.10
4	Darin Erstad	.25
5	Chuck Finley	.10
6	Troy Glaus	.75
7	Troy Percival	.10
8	Tim Salmon	.10
9	Mo Vaughn	.10
10	Tony Batista	.10
11	Jay Bell	.10
12	Andy Benes	.10
13	Steve Finley	.10
14	Luis Gonzalez	.10
15	Randy Johnson	.75
16	Travis Lee	.10
17	Todd Stottlemyre	.10
18	Matt Williams	.10
19	David Dellucci	.10
20	Bret Boone	.10
21	Andres Galarraga	.10
22	Tom Glavine	.35
23	Andruw Jones	.75
24	Chipper Jones	1.50
25	Brian Jordan	.10
26	Ryan Klesko	.10
27	Javy Lopez	.10
28	Greg Maddux	1.50
29	John Smoltz	.10
30	Brady Anderson	.10
31	Albert Belle	.10
32	Will Clark	.10
33	Delino DeShields	.10
34	Charles Johnson	.10
35	Mike Mussina	.40
36	Cal Ripken Jr.	3.00
37	B.J. Surhoff	.10
38	Nomar Garciaparra	1.50
39	Reggie Jefferson	.10
40	Darren Lewis	.10
41	Pedro Martinez	.75
42	Troy O'Leary	.10
43	Jose Offerman	.10
44	Donnie Sadler	.10
45	John Valentin	.10
46	Rod Beck	.10
47	Gary Gaetti	.10
48	Mark Grace	.10
49	Lance Johnson	.10
50	Mickey Morandini	.10
51	Henry Rodriguez	.10
52	Sammy Sosa	1.50
53	Kerry Wood	.40
54	Mike Caruso	.10
55	Ray Durham	.10
56	Paul Konerko	.20
57	Jaime Navarro	.10
58	Greg Norton	.10
59	Magglio Ordonez	.30
60	Frank Thomas	.75
61	Aaron Boone	.10
62	Mike Cameron	.10
63	Barry Larkin	.10
64	Hal Morris	.10
65	Pokey Reese	.10
66	Brett Tomko	.10
67	Greg Vaughn	.10
68	Dmitri Young	.10
69	Roberto Alomar	.25
70	Sandy Alomar Jr.	.10
71	Bartolo Colon	.10
72	Travis Fryman	.10
73	David Justice	.10
74	Kenny Lofton	.10
75	Manny Ramirez	.75
76	Richie Sexson	.10
77	Jim Thome	.65
78	Omar Vizquel	.10
79	Dante Bichette	.10
80	Vinny Castilla	.10
81	Darryl Hamilton	.10
82	Todd Helton	.75
83	Darryl Kile	.10
84	Mike Lansing	.10
85	Neifi Perez	.10
86	Larry Walker	.10
87	Tony Clark	.10
88	Damion Easley	.10
89	Bob Higginson	.10
90	Brian Hunter	.10
91	Dean Palmer	.10
92	Justin Thompson	.10
93	Todd Dunwoody	.10
94	Cliff Floyd	.10
95	Alex Gonzalez	.10
96	Livan Hernandez	.10
97	Mark Kotsay	.10
98	Derrek Lee	.60
99	Kevin Orie	.10
100	Moises Alou	.10
101	Jeff Bagwell	.75
102	Derek Bell	.10
103	Craig Biggio	.10
104	Ken Caminiti	.10
105	Ricky Gutierrez	.10
106	Richard Hidalgo	.10
107	Billy Wagner	.10
108	Jeff Conine	.10
109	Johnny Damon	.35
110	Carlos Febles	.10
111	Jeremy Giambi	.10
112	Jeff King	.10
113	Jeff Montgomery	.10
114	Joe Randa	.10
115	Kevin Brown	.10
116	Mark Grudzielanek	.10
117	Todd Hundley	.10
118	Eric Karros	.10
119	Raul Mondesi	.10
120	Chan Ho Park	.10
121	Gary Sheffield	.40
122	Devon White	.10
123	Eric Young	.10
124	Jeromy Burnitz	.10
125	Jeff Cirillo	.10
126	Marquis Grissom	.10
127	Geoff Jenkins	.10
128	Dave Nilsson	.10
129	Jose Valentin	.10
130	Fernando Vina	.10
131	Rick Aguilera	.10
132	Ron Coomer	.10
133	Marty Cordova	.10
134	Matt Lawton	.10
135	David Ortiz	.50
136	Brad Radke	.10
137	Terry Steinbach	.10
138	Javier Valentin	.10
139	Todd Walker	.10
140	Orlando Cabrera	.10
141	Brad Fullmer	.10
142	Vladimir Guerrero	.75
143	Wilton Guerrero	.10
144	Carl Pavano	.10
145	Ugueth Urbina	.10
146	Rondell White	.10
147	Chris Widger	.10
148	Edgardo Alfonzo	.10
149	Bobby Bonilla	.10
150	Rickey Henderson	.75
151	Brian McRae	.10
152	Hideo Nomo	.40
153	John Olerud	.10
154	Rey Ordonez	.10
155	Mike Piazza	1.75
156	Robin Ventura	.10
157	Masato Yoshii	.10
158	Roger Clemens	1.75
159	David Cone	.10
160	Orlando Hernandez	.10
161	Hideki Irabu	.10
162	Derek Jeter	3.00
163	Chuck Knoblauch	.10
164	Tino Martinez	.10
165	Paul O'Neill	.10
166	Darryl Strawberry	.10
167	Bernie Williams	.10
168	Eric Chavez	.20
169	Ryan Christenson	.10
170	Jason Giambi	.50
171	Ben Grieve	.10
172	Tony Phillips	.10
173	Tim Raines	.10
174	Scott Spiezio	.10
175	Miguel Tejada	.20
176	Bobby Abreu	.20
177	Rico Brogna	.10
178	Ron Gant	.10
179	Doug Glanville	.10
180	Desi Relaford	.10
181	Scott Rolen	.65
182	Curt Schilling	.35
183	Brant Brown	.10
184	Brian Giles	.10
185	Jose Guillen	.10
186	Jason Kendall	.10
187	Al Martin	.10
188	Ed Sprague	.10
189	Kevin Young	.10
190	Eric Davis	.10
191	J.D. Drew	.40
192	Ray Lankford	.10
193	Eli Marrero	.10
194	Mark McGwire	2.50
195	Edgar Renteria	.10
196	Fernando Tatis	.10
197	Andy Ashby	.10
198	Tony Gwynn	1.50
199	Carlos Hernandez	.10
200	Trevor Hoffman	.10
201	Wally Joyner	.10
202	Jim Leyritz	.10
203	Ruben Rivera	.10
204	Matt Clement	.10
205	Quilvio Veras	.10
206	Rich Aurilia	.10
207	Marvin Benard	.10
208	Barry Bonds	3.00
209	Ellis Burks	.10
210	Jeff Kent	.10
211	Bill Mueller	.10
212	Robb Nen	.10
213	J.T. Snow	.10
214	Jay Buhner	.10
215	Jeff Fassero	.10
216	Ken Griffey Jr.	2.00
217	Carlos Guillen	.10
218	Butch Huskey	.10
219	Edgar Martinez	.10
220	Alex Rodriguez	2.50
221	David Segui	.10
222	Dan Wilson	.10
223	Rolando Arrojo	.10
224	Wade Boggs	1.50
225	Jose Canseco	.50
226	Roberto Hernandez	.10
227	Dave Martinez	.10
228	Quinton McCracken	.10
229	Fred McGriff	.10
230	Kevin Stocker	.10
231	Randy Winn	.10
232	Royce Clayton	.10
233	Juan Gonzalez	.40
234	Tom Goodwin	.10
235	Rusty Greer	.10
236	Rick Helling	.10
237	Rafael Palmeiro	.65
238	Ivan Rodriguez	.65
239	Aaron Sele	.10
240	John Wetteland	.10
241	Todd Zeile	.10
242	Jose Cruz Jr.	.10
243	Carlos Delgado	.50
244	Tony Fernandez	.10
245	Cecil Fielder	.10
246	Alex Gonzalez	.10
247	Shawn Green	.35
248	Roy Halladay	.10
249	Shannon Stewart	.10
250	David Wells	.10

Cooperstown Bound

This 10-card set focuses on players who seem destined for the Hall of Fame. These inserts feature silver foil stamping and are seeded 1:361 packs.

		NM/M
Complete Set (10):		35.00
Common Player:		3.00
Inserted 1:361		
1	Greg Maddux	4.00
2	Cal Ripken Jr.	10.00
3	Nomar Garciaparra	4.00
4	Sammy Sosa	4.00
5	Frank Thomas	3.00
6	Mike Piazza	5.00
7	Mark McGwire	10.00
8	Tony Gwynn	4.00
9	Ken Griffey Jr.	6.00
10	Alex Rodriguez	8.00

Fielder's Choice

This 20-card set is die-cut into a glove shape and enhanced with gold foil stamping. These are seeded 1:73 packs.

		NM/M
Complete Set (20):		60.00
Common Player:		2.50
Inserted 1:73		
1	Chipper Jones	5.00
2	Greg Maddux	5.00
3	Cal Ripken Jr.	10.00
4	Nomar Garciaparra	5.00
5	Sammy Sosa	5.00
6	Kerry Wood	3.00
7	Frank Thomas	4.00
8	Manny Ramirez	4.00
9	Todd Helton	4.00
10	Jeff Bagwell	4.00
11	Mike Piazza	5.50
12	Derek Jeter	10.00

13	Bernie Williams	2.50
14	J.D. Drew	3.00
15	Mark McGwire	7.50
16	Tony Gwynn	5.00
17	Ken Griffey Jr.	6.00
18	Alex Rodriguez	7.50
19	Juan Gonzalez	2.50
20	Ivan Rodriguez	3.50

Personal Bests

This 36-card set features holographic silver foil stamping on the card front. Card backs include a close-up photo of the featured playcr and a career note. These are seeded 1:37 packs.

		NM/M
Complete Set (36):		45.00
Common Player:		.50
Inserted 1:37		
1	Darin Erstad	.65
2	Mo Vaughn	.50
3	Travis Lee	.50
4	Chipper Jones	3.00
5	Greg Maddux	3.00
6	Albert Belle	.50
7	Cal Ripken Jr.	6.00
8	Nomar Garciaparra	3.00
9	Sammy Sosa	3.00
10	Kerry Wood	1.00
11	Frank Thomas	2.00
12	Greg Vaughn	.50
13	Manny Ramirez	2.00
14	Todd Helton	2.00
15	Larry Walker	.50
16	Jeff Bagwell	2.00
17	Craig Biggio	.50
18	Raul Mondesi	.50
19	Vladimir Guerrero	2.00
20	Hideo Nomo	1.00
21	Mike Piazza	3.50
22	Roger Clemens	3.50
23	Derek Jeter	6.00
24	Bernie Williams	.50
25	Eric Chavez	.75
26	Ben Grieve	.50
27	Scott Rolen	1.50
28	J.D. Drew	1.25
29	Mark McGwire	4.50
30	Tony Gwynn	3.00
31	Barry Bonds	6.00
32	Ken Griffey Jr.	4.00
33	Alex Rodriguez	4.50
34	Jose Canseco	1.25
35	Juan Gonzalez	1.00
36	Ivan Rodriguez	1.50

Team Checklists

This 30-card set features gold foil etching and stamping on the card front. Card backs show the featured player's team checklist for the base set. These were seeded 2:37 packs.

		NM/M
Complete Set (30):		40.00
Common Player:		.50
Inserted 2:37		
1	Mo Vaughn	.50
2	Travis Lee	.50
3	Chipper Jones	3.00
4	Cal Ripken Jr.	6.00
5	Nomar Garciaparra	3.00
6	Sammy Sosa	3.00
7	Frank Thomas	2.50
8	Greg Vaughn	.50
9	Manny Ramirez	2.50
10	Larry Walker	.50
11	Damion Easley	.50
12	Mark Kotsay	.50
13	Jeff Bagwell	2.50
14	Jeremy Giambi	.50
15	Raul Mondesi	.50
16	Marquis Grissom	.50
17	Brad Radke	.50
18	Vladimir Guerrero	2.50
19	Mike Piazza	3.50
20	Roger Clemens	3.50
21	Ben Grieve	.50
22	Scott Rolen	2.00
23	Brian Giles	.50
24	Mark McGwire	5.00
25	Tony Gwynn	3.00
26	Barry Bonds	6.00
27	Ken Griffey Jr.	4.00
28	Jose Canseco	1.25
29	Juan Gonzalez	1.25
30	Jose Cruz Jr.	.50

1999 Pacific Prism Sample

This card of Pacific spokesman Tony Gwynn introduces the 1999 Prism series. The sample card follows the format of the issued version but is overprinted "SAMPLE" on back.

	NM/M
Tony Gwynn	2.00

1999 Pacific Prism

This 150-card base set has a full, holographic silver card front. Card backs feature two more player photos along with 1998 and career statistics. Hobby packs consist of five cards. There are also five parallels including Holographic Gold, Holographic Mirror, Holographic Blue, Holographic Purple and Red. Golds are limited to 480 serial numbered sets, Mirrors 160 sets, Blues 80 numbered sets, and, Purples 320 sets. Red parallels are a retail-only insert and are seeded at a rate of one per 12.5 packs.

		NM/M
Complete Set (150):		50.00
Common Player:		.15
Red (2:25R):		3X
HoloGold (480 Sets):		3X
HoloPurple (320):		4X
HoloMirror (160):		8X
HoloBlue (80):		15X
Retail Pack (3):		1.00
Hobby Pack (5):		1.50
1	Garret Anderson	.15
2	Jim Edmonds	.15
3	Darin Erstad	.30
4	Chuck Finley	.15
5	Tim Salmon	.15
6	Jay Bell	.15
7	David Dellucci	.15
8	Travis Lee	.15
9	Matt Williams	.15
10	Andres Galarraga	.15
11	Tom Glavine	.40
12	Andruw Jones	1.50
13	Chipper Jones	2.00
14	Ryan Klesko	.15
15	Javy Lopez	.15
16	Greg Maddux	2.00
17	Roberto Alomar	.50
18	Ryan Minor	.15
19	Mike Mussina	.40
20	Rafael Palmeiro	1.25
21	Cal Ripken Jr.	4.00
22	Nomar Garciaparra	2.00
23	Pedro Martinez	1.50
24	John Valentin	.15
25	Mo Vaughn	.15
26	Tim Wakefield	.15
27	Rod Beck	.15
28	Mark Grace	.15
29	Lance Johnson	.15
30	Sammy Sosa	2.00
31	Kerry Wood	.50
32	Albert Belle	.15
33	Mike Caruso	.15
34	Magglio Ordonez	.30
35	Frank Thomas	1.50
36	Robin Ventura	.15
37	Aaron Boone	.15
38	Barry Larkin	.15
39	Reggie Sanders	.15
40	Brett Tomko	.15
41	Sandy Alomar Jr	.15
42	Bartolo Colon	.15
43	David Justice	.15
44	Kenny Lofton	.15
45	Manny Ramirez	1.50
46	Richie Sexson	.15
47	Jim Thome	1.00
48	Omar Vizquel	.15
49	Dante Bichette	.15
50	Vinny Castilla	.15
51	Edgard Clemente **RC**	.15
52	Todd Helton	1.50
53	Quinton McCracken	.15
54	Larry Walker	.15
55	Tony Clark	.15
56	Damion Easley	.15
57	Luis Gonzalez	.15
58	Bob Higginson	.15
59	Brian Hunter	.15
60	Cliff Floyd	.15
61	Alex Gonzalez	.15
62	Livan Hernandez	.15
63	Derrek Lee	.65
64	Edgar Renteria	.15
65	Moises Alou	.15
66	Jeff Bagwell	1.50
67	Derek Bell	.15
68	Craig Biggio	.15
69	Randy Johnson	1.50
70	Johnny Damon	.35
71	Jeff King	.15
72	Hal Morris	.15
73	Dean Palmer	.15
74	Eric Karros	.15
75	Raul Mondesi	.15
76	Chan Ho Park	.15
77	Gary Sheffield	.50
78	Jeromy Burnitz	.15
79	Jeff Cirillo	.15
80	Marquis Grissom	.15
81	Jose Valentin	.15
82	Fernando Vina	.15
83	Paul Molitor	1.50
84	Otis Nixon	.15
85	David Ortiz	.65
86	Todd Walker	.15
87	Vladimir Guerrero	1.50
88	Carl Pavano	.15
89	Fernando Seguignol	.15
90	Ugueth Urbina	.15
91	Carlos Baerga	.15
92	Bobby Bonilla	.15
93	Hideo Nomo	.75
94	John Olerud	.15
95	Rey Ordonez	.15
96	Mike Piazza	2.25
97	David Cone	.15
98	Orlando Hernandez	.15
99	Hideki Irabu	.15
100	Derek Jeter	4.00
101	Tino Martinez	.15
102	Bernie Williams	.15
103	Eric Chavez	.25
104	Jason Giambi	1.00
105	Ben Grieve	.15
106	Rickey Henderson	1.50
107	Bob Abreu	.25
108	Doug Glanville	.15
109	Scott Rolen	1.00
110	Curt Schilling	.40
111	Emil Brown	.15
112	Jose Guillen	.15
113	Jason Kendall	.15
114	Al Martin	.15
115	Aramis Ramirez	.15
116	Kevin Young	.15
117	J.D. Drew	.75
118	Ron Gant	.15
119	Brian Jordan	.15
120	Eli Marrero	.15
121	Mark McGwire	3.00
122	Kevin Brown	.15
123	Tony Gwynn	2.00
124	Trevor Hoffman	.15
125	Wally Joyner	.15
126	Greg Vaughn	.15
127	Barry Bonds	4.00
128	Ellis Burks	.15
129	Jeff Kent	.15
130	Robb Nen	.15
131	J.T. Snow	.15
132	Jay Buhner	.15
133	Ken Griffey Jr.	2.50
134	Edgar Martinez	.15
135	Alex Rodriguez	3.00
136	David Segui	.15
137	Rolando Arrojo	.15
138	Wade Boggs	2.00
139	Aaron Ledesma	.15
140	Fred McGriff	.15
141	Will Clark	.15
142	Juan Gonzalez	.75
143	Rusty Greer	.15
144	Ivan Rodriguez	1.25
145	Aaron Sele	.15
146	Jose Canseco	.40
147	Roger Clemens	2.25
148	Jose Cruz Jr.	.15
149	Carlos Delgado	.50
150	Alex Gonzalez	.15

Ahead of the Game

Each card features full gold foil and etching with a close-up photo of baseball's top 20 stars. These are seeded 1:49 packs.

		NM/M
Complete Set (20):		40.00
Common Player:		1.00
Inserted 1:49		
1	Darin Erstad	1.25
2	Travis Lee	1.00
3	Chipper Jones	3.00
4	Cal Ripken Jr.	6.00
5	Nomar Garciaparra	3.00
6	Sammy Sosa	3.00
7	Kerry Wood	1.25
8	Frank Thomas	2.00
9	Manny Ramirez	2.00
10	Todd Helton	2.00
11	Jeff Bagwell	2.00
12	Mike Piazza	3.50
13	Derek Jeter	6.00
14	Bernie Williams	1.00
15	J.D. Drew	1.25
16	Mark McGwire	5.00
17	Tony Gwynn	3.00
18	Ken Griffey Jr.	4.00
19	Alex Rodriguez	5.00
20	Ivan Rodriguez	1.50

Ballpark Legends

This 10 card set salutes baseball's biggest stars. These inserts feature silver foil stamping and etching with an image of a ballpark in the background of the player photo. These are seeded 1:193 packs.

		NM/M
Complete Set (10):		40.00
Common Player:		2.50
Inserted 1:193		
1	Cal Ripken Jr.	10.00
2	Nomar Garciaparra	5.00
3	Frank Thomas	4.00
4	Ken Griffey Jr.	6.00
5	Alex Rodriguez	7.50
6	Greg Maddux	5.00
7	Sammy Sosa	5.00
8	Kerry Wood	2.50
9	Mark McGwire	7.50
10	Tony Gwynn	5.00

Diamond Glory

Card fronts feature full copper foil stamping with a star in the background of the player's photo. The 20-card set features 20 of baseball's most exciting players including several top 1999 rookies. These are seeded 2:25 packs.

		NM/M
Complete Set (20):		25.00
Common Player:		.60
Inserted 2:25		
1	Darin Erstad	.60
2	Travis Lee	.60
3	Chipper Jones	2.00
4	Greg Maddux	2.00
5	Cal Ripken Jr.	3.50
6	Nomar Garciaparra	2.00
7	Sammy Sosa	2.00
8	Kerry Wood	.75
9	Frank Thomas	1.50
10	Todd Helton	1.50
11	Jeff Bagwell	1.50
12	Mike Piazza	2.25
13	Derek Jeter	3.50
14	Bernie Williams	.60
15	J.D. Drew	.75
16	Mark McGwire	3.00
17	Tony Gwynn	2.00
18	Ken Griffey Jr.	2.50
19	Alex Rodriguez	3.00
20	Juan Gonzalez	.75

Epic Performers

This hobby-only set features top hobby favorites and is seeded at 1:97 packs.

		NM/M
Complete Set (10):		60.00
Common Player:		4.00
Inserted 1:97 H		
1	Cal Ripken Jr.	15.00
2	Nomar Garciaparra	7.50
3	Frank Thomas	6.00
4	Ken Griffey Jr.	10.00
5	Alex Rodriguez	12.50
6	Greg Maddux	7.50
7	Sammy Sosa	7.50
8	Kerry Wood	4.00
9	Mark McGwire	12.50
10	Tony Gwynn	7.50

1999 Pacific Private Stock

The premiere issue of Private Stock base cards features holographic silver foil on 30-pt. cardboard. Card backs have selected box scores from the '98 season, with a brief commentary on the player. Packs consist of six cards.

		NM/M
Complete Set (150):		25.00
Common Player:		.10
Pack (6):		1.50
Wax Box (24):		20.00
Wax Box (36):		25.00
1	Jeff Bagwell	1.00
2	Roger Clemens	1.75
3	J.D. Drew	.60
4	Nomar Garciaparra	1.50
5	Juan Gonzalez	.50
6	Ken Griffey Jr.	2.00
7	Tony Gwynn	1.50
8	Derek Jeter	3.00
9	Chipper Jones	1.50
10	Travis Lee	.10
11	Greg Maddux	1.50
12	Mark McGwire	2.50
13	Mike Piazza	1.75
14	Manny Ramirez	1.00
15	Cal Ripken Jr.	3.00
16	Alex Rodriguez	2.50
17	Ivan Rodriguez	.75
18	Sammy Sosa	1.50
19	Frank Thomas	1.00
20	Kerry Wood	.40
21	Roberto Alomar	.25
22	Moises Alou	.10
23	Albert Belle	.10
24	Craig Biggio	.10
25	Wade Boggs	1.50
26	Barry Bonds	3.00
27	Jose Canseco	.50
28	Jim Edmonds	.10
29	Darin Erstad	.25
30	Andres Galarraga	.10
31	Tom Glavine	.35
32	Ben Grieve	.10
33	Vladimir Guerrero	1.00
34	Wilton Guerrero	.10
35	Todd Helton	1.00
36	Andruw Jones	1.00
37	Ryan Klesko	.10
38	Kenny Lofton	.10
39	Javy Lopez	.10
40	Pedro Martinez	1.00
41	Paul Molitor	1.00
42	Raul Mondesi	.10
43	Rafael Palmeiro	.75
44	Tim Salmon	.10
45	Jim Thome	.75
46	Mo Vaughn	.10
47	Larry Walker	.10
48	David Wells	.10
49	Bernie Williams	.10
50	Jaret Wright	.10
51	Bobby Abreu	.15
52	Garret Anderson	.10
53	Rolando Arrojo	.10
54	Tony Batista	.10
55	Rod Beck	.10
56	Derek Bell	.10
57	Marvin Benard	.10
58	Dave Berg	.10
59	Dante Bichette	.10
60	Aaron Boone	.10
61	Bret Boone	.10
62	Scott Brosius	.10
63	Brant Brown	.10
64	Kevin Brown	.10
65	Jeromy Burnitz	.10
66	Ken Caminiti	.10
67	Mike Caruso	.10
68	Sean Casey	.20
69	Vinny Castilla	.10
70	Eric Chavez	.20
71	Ryan Christenson	.10
72	Jeff Cirillo	.10
73	Tony Clark	.10
74	Will Clark	.10
75	Edgard Clemente **RC**	.10
76	David Cone	.10
77	Marty Cordova	.10
78	Jose Cruz Jr.	.10
79	Eric Davis	.10
80	Carlos Delgado	.50
81	David Dellucci	.10
82	Delino DeShields	.10
83	Gary DiSarcina	.10
84	Damion Easley	.10
85	Dennis Eckersley	.65
86	Cliff Floyd	.10
87	Jason Giambi	.65
88	Doug Glanville	.10
89	Alex Gonzalez	.10
90	Mark Grace	.10
91	Rusty Greer	.10
92	Jose Guillen	.10
93	Carlos Guillen	.10
94	Jeffrey Hammonds	.10
95	Rick Helling	.10
96	Bob Henley	.10
97	Livan Hernandez	.10
98	Orlando Hernandez	.10
99	Bob Higginson	.10
100	Trevor Hoffman	.10

101	Randy Johnson	1.00
102	Brian Jordan	.10
103	Wally Joyner	.10
104	Eric Karros	.10
105	Jason Kendall	.10
106	Jeff Kent	.10
107	Jeff King	.10
108	Mark Kotsay	.10
109	Ray Lankford	.10
110	Barry Larkin	.10
111	Mark Loretta	.10
112	Edgar Martinez	.10
113	Tino Martinez	.10
114	Quinton McCracken	.10
115	Fred McGriff	.10
116	Ryan Minor	.10
117	Hal Morris	.10
118	Bill Mueller	.10
119	Mike Mussina	.40
120	Dave Nilsson	.10
121	Otis Nixon	.10
122	Hideo Nomo	.50
123	Paul O'Neill	.10
124	Jose Offerman	.10
125	John Olerud	.10
126	Rey Ordonez	.10
127	David Ortiz	.50
128	Dean Palmer	.10
129	Chan Ho Park	.10
130	Aramis Ramirez	.10
131	Edgar Renteria	.10
132	Armando Rios	.10
133	Henry Rodriguez	.10
134	Scott Rolen	.75
135	Curt Schilling	.35
136	David Segui	.10
137	Richie Sexson	.10
138	Gary Sheffield	.45
139	John Smoltz	.10
140	Matt Stairs	.10
141	Justin Thompson	.10
142	Greg Vaughn	.10
143	Omar Vizquel	.10
144	Tim Wakefield	.10
145	Todd Walker	.10
146	Devon White	.10
147	Rondell White	.10
148	Matt Williams	.10
149	Enrique Wilson **RC**	.25
150	Kevin Young	.10

Exclusive Series

This 20-card set is a partial parallel to the base set. Taking the first 20 cards from the set and serially numbering them to 299 sets. These are inserted exclusively in hobby packs.

		NM/M
Complete Set (20):		50.00
Common Player:		1.00
Production: 299 Sets H		
1	Jeff Bagwell	2.00
2	Roger Clemens	3.50
3	J.D. Drew	1.25
4	Nomar Garciaparra	3.00
5	Juan Gonzalez	1.25
6	Ken Griffey Jr.	4.00
7	Tony Gwynn	3.00
8	Derek Jeter	6.00
9	Chipper Jones	3.00
10	Travis Lee	1.00
11	Greg Maddux	3.00
12	Mark McGwire	5.00
13	Mike Piazza	3.50
14	Manny Ramirez	2.00
15	Cal Ripken Jr.	6.00
16	Alex Rodriguez	5.00
17	Ivan Rodriguez	1.50
18	Sammy Sosa	3.00
19	Frank Thomas	2.00
20	Kerry Wood	1.25

Platinum Series

Another partial parallel of the first 50 cards in the base set. Cards have a platinum holographic sheen to them with a Platinum stamp on the front. These are limited to 199 numbered sets.

		NM/M
Complete Set (50):		160.00
Common Player:		.75
Production 199 Sets		
1	Jeff Bagwell	5.00
2	Roger Clemens	6.50
3	J.D. Drew	3.00
4	Nomar Garciaparra	6.00
5	Juan Gonzalez	2.50
6	Ken Griffey Jr.	8.00
7	Tony Gwynn	6.00
8	Derek Jeter	12.00
9	Chipper Jones	6.00
10	Travis Lee	.75
11	Greg Maddux	6.00
12	Mark McGwire	10.00
13	Mike Piazza	6.50
14	Manny Ramirez	5.00
15	Cal Ripken Jr.	12.00
16	Alex Rodriguez	10.00
17	Ivan Rodriguez	4.00
18	Sammy Sosa	6.00
19	Frank Thomas	5.00
20	Kerry Wood	2.00
21	Roberto Alomar	1.50
22	Moises Alou	.75
23	Albert Belle	.75
24	Craig Biggio	.75
25	Wade Boggs	6.00
26	Barry Bonds	12.00
27	Jose Canseco	3.00
28	Jim Edmonds	.75
29	Darin Erstad	1.50
30	Andres Galarraga	.75
31	Tom Glavine	2.00
32	Ben Grieve	.75
33	Vladimir Guerrero	5.00
34	Wilton Guerrero	.75
35	Todd Helton	5.00
36	Andruw Jones	5.00
37	Ryan Klesko	.75
38	Kenny Lofton	.75
39	Javy Lopez	.75
40	Pedro Martinez	5.00
41	Paul Molitor	5.00
42	Raul Mondesi	.75
43	Rafael Palmeiro	4.00
44	Tim Salmon	.75
45	Jim Thome	3.50
46	Mo Vaughn	.75
47	Larry Walker	.75
48	David Wells	.75
49	Bernie Williams	.75
50	Jaret Wright	.75

Preferred Series

Another partial parallel of the first 20 base cards. Each card is stamped with a holographic Preferred logo and are numbered to 399 sets.

		NM/M
Complete Set (20):		37.50
Common Player:		.60
Production: 399 Sets		
1	Jeff Bagwell	1.50
2	Roger Clemens	2.25
3	J.D. Drew	.75
4	Nomar Garciaparra	2.00
5	Juan Gonzalez	.75
6	Ken Griffey Jr.	2.50
7	Tony Gwynn	2.00
8	Derek Jeter	5.00
9	Chipper Jones	2.00
10	Travis Lee	.60
11	Greg Maddux	2.00
12	Mark McGwire	3.50
13	Mike Piazza	2.25
14	Manny Ramirez	1.50
15	Cal Ripken Jr.	5.00
16	Alex Rodriguez	3.50
17	Ivan Rodriguez	1.25
18	Sammy Sosa	2.00
19	Frank Thomas	1.50
20	Kerry Wood	.75

Vintage Series

This insert set is a partial parallel of the first 50 cards in the base set and has a Vintage holograpic stamp on the card fronts. These are limited to 99 numbered sets.

		NM/M
Complete Set (50):		375.00
Common Player:		2.50
Production: 99 Sets		
1	Jeff Bagwell	12.50
2	Roger Clemens	17.50
3	J.D. Drew	7.50
4	Nomar Garciaparra	15.00
5	Juan Gonzalez	6.00
6	Ken Griffey Jr.	20.00
7	Tony Gwynn	15.00
8	Derek Jeter	30.00
9	Chipper Jones	15.00
10	Travis Lee	2.50
11	Greg Maddux	15.00
12	Mark McGwire	25.00
13	Mike Piazza	17.50
14	Manny Ramirez	12.50
15	Cal Ripken Jr.	30.00
16	Alex Rodriguez	25.00
17	Ivan Rodriguez	10.00
18	Sammy Sosa	15.00
19	Frank Thomas	12.50
20	Kerry Wood	6.00
21	Roberto Alomar	3.50
22	Moises Alou	2.50
23	Albert Belle	2.50
24	Craig Biggio	2.50
25	Wade Boggs	15.00
26	Barry Bonds	30.00
27	Jose Canseco	5.00
28	Jim Edmonds	2.50
29	Darin Erstad	3.50
30	Andres Galarraga	2.50
31	Tom Glavine	5.00
32	Ben Grieve	2.50
33	Vladimir Guerrero	12.50
34	Wilton Guerrero	2.50
35	Todd Helton	12.50
36	Andruw Jones	12.50
37	Ryan Klesko	2.60
38	Kenny Lofton	2.50
39	Javy Lopez	2.50
40	Pedro Martinez	12.50
41	Paul Molitor	12.50
42	Raul Mondesi	2.50
43	Rafael Palmeiro	10.00
44	Tim Salmon	2.50
45	Jim Thome	10.00
46	Mo Vaughn	2.50
47	Larry Walker	2.50
48	David Wells	2.50
49	Bernie Williams	2.50
50	Jaret Wright	2.50

PS-206

This 150-card set takes reverent reach back into collecting history with its smaller format (1.5" x 2.5"). Card fronts have a white border with silver foil stamping and a blue back, these are found one per pack. A parallel also exists with a red back, which are seeded 1:25 packs.

		NM/M
Complete Set (150):		20.00
Common Player:		.15
Inserted 1:1		
Red Parallels:		4X
Inserted 1:25		
1	Jeff Bagwell	.75
2	Roger Clemens	1.25
3	J.D. Drew	.50
4	Nomar Garciaparra	1.00
5	Juan Gonzalez	.40
6	Ken Griffey Jr.	1.50
7	Tony Gwynn	1.00
8	Derek Jeter	3.00
9	Chipper Jones	1.00
10	Travis Lee	.15
11	Greg Maddux	1.00
12	Mark McGwire	2.00
13	Mike Piazza	1.25
14	Manny Ramirez	.75
15	Cal Ripken Jr.	3.00
16	Alex Rodriguez	2.00
17	Ivan Rodriguez	.65
18	Sammy Sosa	1.00
19	Frank Thomas	.75
20	Kerry Wood	.40
21	Roberto Alomar	.30
22	Moises Alou	.15
23	Albert Belle	.15
24	Craig Biggio	.15
25	Wade Boggs	1.00
26	Barry Bonds	3.00
27	Jose Canseco	.50
28	Jim Edmonds	.15
29	Darin Erstad	.30
30	Andres Galarraga	.15
31	Tom Glavine	.35
32	Ben Grieve	.15
33	Vladimir Guerrero	.75
34	Wilton Guerrero	.15
35	Todd Helton	.75
36	Andruw Jones	.75
37	Ryan Klesko	.15
38	Kenny Lofton	.15
39	Javy Lopez	.15
40	Pedro Martinez	.75
41	Paul Molitor	.75
42	Raul Mondesi	.15
43	Rafael Palmeiro	.65
44	Tim Salmon	.15
45	Jim Thome	.65
46	Mo Vaughn	.15
47	Larry Walker	.15
48	David Wells	.15
49	Bernie Williams	.15
50	Jaret Wright	.15
51	Bobby Abreu	.15
52	Garret Anderson	.15
53	Rolando Arrojo	.15
54	Tony Batista	.15
55	Rod Beck	.15
56	Derek Bell	.15
57	Marvin Benard	.15
58	Dave Berg	.15
59	Dante Bichette	.15
60	Aaron Boone	.15
61	Bret Boone	.15
62	Scott Brosius	.15
63	Brant Brown	.15
64	Kevin Brown	.15
65	Jeromy Burnitz	.15
66	Ken Caminiti	.15
67	Mike Caruso	.15
68	Sean Casey	.25
69	Vinny Castilla	.15
70	Eric Chavez	.25
71	Ryan Christenson	.15
72	Jeff Cirillo	.15
73	Tony Clark	.15
74	Will Clark	.15
75	Edgard Clemente	.15
76	David Cone	.15
77	Marty Cordova	.15
78	Jose Cruz Jr.	.15
79	Eric Davis	.15
80	Carlos Delgado	.60
81	David Dellucci	.15
82	Delino DeShields	.15
83	Gary DiSarcina	.15
84	Damion Easley	.15
85	Dennis Eckersley	.65
86	Cliff Floyd	.15
87	Jason Giambi	.60
88	Doug Glanville	.15
89	Alex Gonzalez	.15
90	Mark Grace	.15
91	Rusty Greer	.15
92	Jose Guillen	.15
93	Carlos Guillen	.15
94	Jeffrey Hammonds	.15
95	Rick Helling	.15
96	Bob Henley	.15
97	Livan Hernandez	.15
98	Orlando Hernandez	.15
99	Bob Higginson	.15
100	Trevor Hoffman	.15
101	Randy Johnson	.75
102	Brian Jordan	.15
103	Wally Joyner	.15
104	Eric Karros	.15
105	Jason Kendall	.15
106	Jeff Kent	.15
107	Jeff King	.15
108	Mark Kotsay	.15
109	Ray Lankford	.15
110	Barry Larkin	.15
111	Mark Loretta	.15
112	Edgar Martinez	.15
113	Tino Martinez	.15
114	Quinton McCracken	.15
115	Fred McGriff	.15
116	Ryan Minor	.15
117	Hal Morris	.15
118	Bill Mueller	.15
119	Mike Mussina	.40
120	Dave Nilsson	.15
121	Otis Nixon	.15
122	Hideo Nomo	.40
123	Paul O'Neill	.15
124	Jose Offerman	.15
125	John Olerud	.15
126	Rey Ordonez	.15
127	David Ortiz	.50
128	Dean Palmer	.15
129	Chan Ho Park	.15
130	Aramis Ramirez	.15
131	Edgar Renteria	.15
132	Armando Rios	.15
133	Henry Rodriguez	.15
134	Scott Rolen	.60
135	Curt Schilling	.35
136	David Segui	.15
137	Richie Sexson	.15
138	Gary Sheffield	.50
139	John Smoltz	.15
140	Matt Stairs	.15
141	Justin Thompson	.15
142	Greg Vaughn	.15
143	Omar Vizquel	.15
144	Tim Wakefield	.15
145	Todd Walker	.15
146	Devon White	.15
147	Rondell White	.15
148	Matt Williams	.15
149	Enrique Wilson	.15
150	Kevin Young	.15

Homerun History

This holographic silver foiled commemorative set honors Mark McGwire and Sammy Sosa's historic '98 seasons. Two cards were added to the end of the set, which are Silver Crown Die-Cuts honoring Ripken Jr.'s consecutive games streak and McGwire's 70 home runs. These are inserted 2:25 packs.

		NM/M
Complete Set (22):		25.00
Common McGwire:		1.50
Common Sosa:		1.00
Inserted 1:12		
1	Home Run #61 (Mark McGwire)	3.00
2	Home Run #59 (Sammy Sosa)	1.00
3	Home Run #62 (Mark McGwire)	1.50
4	Home Run #60 (Sammy Sosa)	1.00
5	Home Run #63 (Mark McGwire)	1.50
6	Home Run #61 (Sammy Sosa)	3.00
7	Home Run #64 (Mark McGwire)	1.50
8	Home Run #62 (Sammy Sosa)	1.00
9	Home Run #65 (Mark McGwire)	1.50
10	Home Run #63 (Sammy Sosa)	1.00
11	Home Run #67 (Mark McGwire)	1.50
12	Home Run #64 (Sammy Sosa)	1.00
13	Home Run #68 (Mark McGwire)	1.50
14	Home Run #65 (Sammy Sosa)	1.00
15	Home Run #70 (Mark McGwire)	5.00
16	Home Run #66 (Sammy Sosa)	3.00
17	A Season of Celebration (Mark McGwire)	1.50
18	A Season of Celebration (Sammy Sosa)	1.00
19	Awesome Power (Sammy Sosa, Mark McGwire)	1.50
20	Transcending Sports (Mark McGwire, Sammy Sosa)	1.50
21	Crown Die-Cut (Mark McGwire)	1.50
22	Crown Die-Cut (Cal Ripken Jr.)	1.00

1999 Pacific Revolution

The 150-card set features dual foiled etching and embossing enhanced by gold-foil stamping. Card backs have year-by- year statistics along with a close-up photo. There are 25 short-printed rookie and prospect cards, which were inserted at a rate of about one per four packs. There are three parallels to the base set: Premiere Date, Red and Shadow. Reds are retail exclusive and are limited to 299 numbered sets. Shadows have light blue foil stamping and are limited to 99 numbered sets. Premiere Date are seeded exclusively in hobby packs at a rate of 1:25 packs.

		NM/M
Complete Set (150):		60.00
Common Player:		.15
Shadow (99 Sets H):		6X
SP:		3X
Red (299 R):		2X
SP:		1.5X
Premiere Date (49 H):		12X
SP:		6X
Wax Pack (3):		2.00
Wax Box (24):		35.00
1	Jim Edmonds	.15
2	Darin Erstad	.30
3	Troy Glaus	1.00
4	Tim Salmon	.15
5	Mo Vaughn	.15
6	Steve Finley	.15
7	Luis Gonzalez	.15
8	Randy Johnson	1.00
9	Travis Lee	.15
10	Matt Williams	.15
11	Andruw Jones	1.00
12	Chipper Jones	1.50
13	Brian Jordan	.15
14	Javy Lopez	.15
15	Greg Maddux	1.50
16	Kevin McGlinchy/SP **RC**	1.00
17	John Smoltz	.15
18	Brady Anderson	.15
19	Albert Belle	.15
20	Will Clark	.15
21	Willis Otanez/SP **RC**	.25
22	Calvin Pickering/SP **RC**	.25
23	Cal Ripken Jr.	4.00
24	Nomar Garciaparra	1.50
25	Pedro Martinez	1.00
26	Troy O'Leary	.15
27	Jose Offerman	.15
28	Mark Grace	.15
29	Mickey Morandini	.15
30	Henry Rodriguez	.15
31	Sammy Sosa	1.50
32	Ray Durham	.15
33	Carlos Lee/SP	.50
34	Jeff Liefer/SP **RC**	.35
35	Magglio Ordonez	.30
36	Frank Thomas	1.00
37	Mike Cameron	.15
38	Sean Casey	.35
39	Barry Larkin	.15
40	Greg Vaughn	.15
41	Roberto Alomar	.35
42	Sandy Alomar Jr.	.15
43	David Justice	.15
44	Kenny Lofton	.15
45	Manny Ramirez	1.00
46	Richie Sexson	.15
47	Jim Thome	.65
48	Dante Bichette	.15
49	Vinny Castilla	.15
50	Darryl Hamilton	.15
51	Todd Helton	1.00
52	Larry Walker	.15
53	Tony Clark	.15
54	Damion Easley	.15
55	Bob Higginson	.15
56	Gabe Kapler/SP	.25
57	Alex Gonzalez/SP **RC**	.35
58	Mark Kotsay	.15
59	Kevin Orie	.15

60 Preston Wilson/SP 1.00
61 Jeff Bagwell 1.00
62 Derek Bell .15
63 Craig Biggio .15
64 Ken Caminiti .15
65 Carlos Beltran/SP .65
66 Johnny Damon .35
67 Jermaine Dye .15
68 Carlos Febles/SP .35
69 Kevin Brown .15
70 Todd Hundley .15
71 Eric Karros .15
72 Raul Mondesi .15
73 Gary Sheffield .45
74 Jeromy Burnitz .15
75 Jeff Cirillo .15
76 Marquis Grissom .15
77 Fernando Vina .15
78 Chad Allen/SP **RC** .25
79 Corey Koskie/SP **RC** 1.50
80 Doug Mientkiewicz/ SP **RC** 1.00
81 Brad Radke .15
82 Todd Walker .15
83 Michael Barrett/SP **RC** .35
84 Vladimir Guerrero 1.00
85 Wilton Guerrero .15
86 Guillermo Mota/SP **RC** .35
87 Rondell White .15
88 Edgardo Alfonzo .15
89 Rickey Henderson 1.00
90 John Olerud .15
91 Mike Piazza 2.00
92 Robin Ventura .15
93 Roger Clemens 2.00
94 Chili Davis .15
95 Derek Jeter 4.00
96 Chuck Knoblauch .15
97 Tino Martinez .15
98 Paul O'Neill .15
99 Bernie Williams .15
100 Eric Chavez/SP .35
101 Jason Giambi .65
102 Ben Grieve .15
103 John Jaha .15
104 Olmedo Saenz/SP **RC** .25
105 Bobby Abreu .25
106 Doug Glanville .15
107 Desi Relaford .15
108 Scott Rolen .75
109 Curt Schilling .35
110 Brian Giles .15
111 Jason Kendall .15
112 Pat Meares .15
113 Kevin Young .15
114 J.D. Drew/SP 1.00
115 Ray Lankford .15
116 Eli Marrero .15
117 Joe McEwing/SP **RC** .35
118 Mark McGwire 3.00
119 Fernando Tatis .15
120 Tony Gwynn 1.50
121 Trevor Hoffman .15
122 Wally Joyner .15
123 Reggie Sanders .15
124 Barry Bonds 4.00
125 Ellis Burks .15
126 Jeff Kent .15
127 Ramon Martinez/SP **RC** .25
128 Joe Nathan/SP **RC** .25
129 Freddy Garcia/SP **RC** 1.00
130 Ken Griffey Jr. 2.50
131 Brian Hunter .15
132 Edgar Martinez .15
133 Alex Rodriguez 3.00
134 David Segui .15
135 Wade Boggs 1.50
136 Jose Canseco .45
137 Quinton McCracken .15
138 Fred McGriff .15
139 Kelly Dransfeldt/SP **RC** .25
140 Juan Gonzalez .50
141 Rusty Greer .15
142 Rafael Palmeiro .75
143 Ivan Rodriguez .75
144 Lee Stevens .15
145 Jose Cruz Jr. .15
146 Carlos Delgado .60
147 Shawn Green .50
148 Roy Halladay/SP **RC** 1.50
149 Shannon Stewart .15
150 Kevin Witt/SP **RC** .35

Shadow

This hobby-only parallel insert features blue metallic-foil background and graphics on front. Backs are identical to the base version except they include a dot-matrix applied serial number at left within an edition of 99.

NM/M
Common Player: 4.00
Stars: 6X
SP's: 3X

Diamond Legacy

This 36-card set features a holographic patterned foil card front. Card backs have a small close-up photo along with a career note. These were seeded 2:25 packs.

NM/M
Complete Set (36): 60.00
Common Player: .50
Inserted 2:25
1 Troy Glaus 2.00
2 Mo Vaughn .50
3 Matt Williams .50
4 Chipper Jones 3.00
5 Andruw Jones 2.00
6 Greg Maddux 3.00
7 Albert Belle .50
8 Cal Ripken Jr. 6.00
9 Nomar Garciaparra 3.00
10 Sammy Sosa 3.00
11 Frank Thomas 2.00
12 Manny Ramirez 2.00
13 Todd Helton 2.00
14 Larry Walker .50
15 Gabe Kapler .50
16 Jeff Bagwell 2.00
17 Craig Biggio .50
18 Raul Mondesi .50
19 Vladimir Guerrero 2.00
20 Mike Piazza 3.50
21 Roger Clemens 3.50
22 Derek Jeter 6.00
23 Bernie Williams .50
24 Ben Grieve .50
25 Scott Rolen 1.75
26 J.D. Drew 1.50
27 Mark McGwire 5.00
28 Fernando Tatis .50
29 Tony Gwynn 3.00
30 Barry Bonds 6.00
31 Ken Griffey Jr. 4.00
32 Alex Rodriguez 5.00
33 Jose Canseco 1.25
34 Juan Gonzalez 1.00
35 Ivan Rodriguez 1.75
36 Shawn Green 1.50

Foul Pole

This 20-card set features netting down the right side of each card, with the player photo on the left side. The player name, position and logo are stamped with gold foil. These were seeded 1:49 packs.

NM/M
Complete Set (20): 100.00
Common Player: 1.50
Inserted 1:49
1 Chipper Jones 8.00
2 Andruw Jones 6.00
3 Cal Ripken Jr. 16.00
4 Nomar Garciaparra 8.00
5 Sammy Sosa 8.00
6 Frank Thomas 6.00
7 Manny Ramirez 6.00
8 Jeff Bagwell 6.00
9 Raul Mondesi 1.50
10 Vladimir Guerrero 6.00
11 Mike Piazza 9.00
12 Derek Jeter 16.00
13 Bernie Williams 1.50
14 Scott Rolen 5.00
15 J.D. Drew 3.00
16 Mark McGwire 12.00
17 Tony Gwynn 8.00
18 Ken Griffey Jr. 10.00
19 Alex Rodriguez 12.00
20 Juan Gonzalez 3.00

Icons

This 10-card set spotlights the top players, each card is die-cut in the shape of a shield with silver foil etching and stamping. These were seeded 1:121 packs.

NM/M
Complete Set (10): 50.00
Common Player: 4.00
Inserted 1:121
1 Cal Ripken Jr. 10.00
2 Nomar Garciaparra 5.00
3 Sammy Sosa 5.00
4 Frank Thomas 4.00
5 Mike Piazza 6.50
6 Derek Jeter 10.00
7 Mark McGwire 8.00
8 Tony Gwynn 5.00
9 Ken Griffey Jr. 7.50
10 Alex Rodriguez 8.00

Thorn in the Side

This 20-card set features full holographic silver foil and is die-cut in the upper right portion. Card backs analyzes the featured player's success against a certain opponent over the years. These were seeded 1:25 packs.

NM/M
Complete Set (20): 35.00
Common Player: 1.00
Inserted 1:25
1 Mo Vaughn 1.00
2 Chipper Jones 3.00
3 Greg Maddux 3.00
4 Cal Ripken Jr. 6.00
5 Nomar Garciaparra 3.00
6 Sammy Sosa 3.00
7 Frank Thomas 2.25
8 Manny Ramirez 2.25
9 Jeff Bagwell 2.25
10 Mike Piazza 3.50
11 Derek Jeter 6.00
12 Bernie Williams 1.00
13 J.D. Drew 1.50
14 Mark McGwire 4.50
15 Tony Gwynn 3.00
16 Barry Bonds 6.00
17 Ken Griffey Jr. 4.00
18 Alex Rodriguez 4.50
19 Juan Gonzalez 1.50
20 Ivan Rodriguez 2.00

Tripleheader

This 30-card set features spotted gold foil blotching around the player image with the name, postion, team and logo stamped in gold foil. These were seeded 4:25 hobby packs. The set is also broken down into three separate tiers of 10 cards. Tier 1 (cards 1-10) are limited to 99 numbered sets. Tier 2 (11-20) 199 numbered sets and Tier 3 (21-30) 299 numbered sets.

NM/M
Complete Set (30): 30.00
Common Player: .25
Inserted 4:25 H
Tier 1 (1-10)
Production 99 Sets H
Tier 2 (11-20)
Production 199 Sets H
Tier 3 (21-30)
Production 299 Sets H
1 Greg Maddux 1.50
2 Cal Ripken Jr. 3.00
3 Nomar Garciaparra 1.50
4 Sammy Sosa 1.50
5 Frank Thomas 1.00
6 Mike Piazza 1.75
7 Mark McGwire 2.50
8 Tony Gwynn 1.50
9 Ken Griffey Jr. 2.00
10 Alex Rodriguez 2.50
11 Mo Vaughn .25
12 Chipper Jones 1.50
13 Manny Ramirez 1.00
14 Larry Walker .25
15 Jeff Bagwell 1.00
16 Vladimir Guerrero 1.00
17 Derek Jeter 3.00
18 J.D. Drew .60
19 Barry Bonds 3.00
20 Juan Gonzalez .50
21 Troy Glaus 1.00
22 Andruw Jones 1.00
23 Matt Williams .25
24 Craig Biggio .25
25 Raul Mondesi .25
26 Roger Clemens 1.75
27 Bernie Williams .25
28 Scott Rolen .75
29 Jose Canseco .50
30 Ivan Rodriguez .75

2000 Pacific Sample

Tony Gwynn was once again the spokesman for Pacific's 2000 line-up of baseball cards products. To showcase its base brand for the year, Pacific produced this sample card, so overprinted and "numbered" on back, but otherwise virtually identical to the issued version.

NM/M
SAMPLE Tony Gwynn 3.00

2000 Pacific

The base set consists of 500-cards with the Pacific logo and player name stamped in silver foil on the card front. Card backs have a small photo along with complete career statistics and a brief career highlight. 50 players in the base set also have another version and are priced equally.

NM/M
Complete Set (500): 60.00
Common Player: .10
Pack (12): 1.50
Wax Box (24): 25.00
1 Garret Anderson .15
2 Tim Belcher .10
3 Gary DiSarcina .10
4 Trent Durrington .10
5 Jim Edmonds .15
6a Darin Erstad/Action .35
6b Darin Erstad/Portrait .35
7 Chuck Finley .10
8 Troy Glaus .75
9 Todd Greene .10
10 Bret Hemphill .10
11 Ken Hill .10
12 Ramon Ortiz .10
13 Troy Percival .10
14 Mark Petkovsek .10
15 Tim Salmon .20
16a Mo Vaughn .15
16b Mo Vaughn/Portrait .15
17 Jay Bell .10
18 Omar Daal .10
19 Erubiel Durazo .10
20 Steve Finley .10
21 Bernard Gilkey .10
22 Luis Gonzalez .20
23 Randy Johnson .75
24 Byung-Hyun Kim .10
25 Travis Lee .10
26 Matt Mantei .10
27 Armando Reynoso .10
28 Rob Ryan .10
29 Kelly Stinnett .10
30 Todd Stottlemyre .10
31a Matt Williams/Action .15
31b Matt Williams/Portrait .15
32 Tony Womack .10
33 Bret Boone .10
34 Andres Galarraga .15
35 Tom Glavine .35
36 Ozzie Guillen .10
37a Andruw Jones/Action .75
37b Andruw Jones/Portrait .75
38a Chipper Jones/Action 1.00
38b Chipper Jones/Portrait 1.00
39 Brian Jordan .10
40 Ryan Klesko .10
41 Javy Lopez .15
42a Greg Maddux/Action 1.00
42b Greg Maddux/Portrait 1.00
43 Kevin Millwood .15
44 John Rocker .10
45 Randall Simon .10
46 John Smoltz .15
47 Gerald Williams .10
48 Brady Anderson .15
49a Albert Belle/Action .15
49b Albert Belle/Portrait .15
50 Mike Bordick .10
51 Will Clark .25
52 Jeff Conine .10
53 Delino DeShields .10
54 Jerry Hairston Jr. .10
55 Charles Johnson .10
56 Eugene Kingsale .10
57 Ryan Minor .10
58 Mike Mussina .35
59 Sidney Ponson .10
60a Cal Ripken Jr./Action 2.50
60b Cal Ripken Jr./Portrait 2.50
61 B.J. Surhoff .10
62 Mike Timlin .10
63 Rod Beck .10
64a Nomar Garciaparra/ Action 1.50
64b Nomar Garciaparra/ Portrait 1.50
65 Tom Gordon .10
66 Butch Huskey .10
67 Derek Lowe .10
68a Pedro Martinez/Action .75
68b Pedro Martinez/Portrait .75
69 Trot Nixon .10
70 Jose Offerman .10
71 Troy O'Leary .10
72 Pat Rapp .10
73 Donnie Sadler .10
74 Mike Stanley .10
75 John Valentin .10
76 Jason Varitek .10
77 Wilton Veras .15
78 Tim Wakefield .10
79 Rick Aguilera .10
80 Manny Alexander .10
81 Roosevelt Brown .10
82 Mark Grace .20
83 Glenallen Hill .10
84 Lance Johnson .10
85 Jon Lieber .10
86 Cole Liniak .10
87 Chad Meyers .10
88 Mickey Morandini .10
89 Jose Nieves .10
90 Henry Rodriguez .10
91a Sammy Sosa/Action 1.50
91b Sammy Sosa/Portrait 1.50
92 Kevin Tapani .10
93 Kerry Wood .50
94 Mike Caruso .10
95 Ray Durham .10
96 Brook Fordyce .10
97 Bobby Howry .10
98 Paul Konerko .25
99 Carlos Lee .10
100 Aaron Myette .10
101 Greg Norton .10
102 Magglio Ordonez .25
103 Jim Parque .10
104 Liu Rodriguez .10
105 Chris Singleton .10
106 Mike Sirotka .10
107a Frank Thomas/Action .75
107b Frank Thomas/Portrait .75
108 Kip Wells .10
109 Aaron Boone .10
110 Mike Cameron .10
111a Sean Casey/Action .20
111b Sean Casey/Portrait .20
112 Jeffrey Hammonds .10
113 Pete Harnisch .10
114a Barry Larkin/Portrait .15
114b Barry Larkin/Portrait .15
115 Jason LaRue .10
116 Denny Neagle .10
117 Pokey Reese .10
118 Scott Sullivan .10
119 Eddie Taubensee .10
120 Greg Vaughn .10
121 Scott Williamson .10
122 Dmitri Young .10
123a Roberto Alomar/Action .35
123b Roberto Alomar/Portrait .35
124 Sandy Alomar Jr. .10
125 Harold Baines .10
126 Russell Branyan .10
127 Dave Burba .10
128 Bartolo Colon .10
129 Travis Fryman .15
130 Mike Jackson .10
131 David Justice .15
132a Kenny Lofton/Action .15
132b Kenny Lofton/Portrait .15
133 Charles Nagy .10
134a Manny Ramirez/Action .75
134b Manny Ramirez/Portrait .75
135 Dave Roberts .10
136 Richie Sexson .15
137 Jim Thome .60
138 Omar Vizquel .15
139 Jaret Wright .10
140 Pedro Astacio .10
141 Dante Bichette .10
142 Brian Bohanon .10
143a Vinny Castilla/Action .10
143b Vinny Castilla/Portrait .10
144 Edgard Clemente .10
145 Derrick Gibson .10
146 Todd Helton .75
147 Darryl Kile .10
148 Mike Lansing .10
149 Kirt Manwaring .10
150 Neifi Perez .10
151 Ben Petrick .10
152 Juan Sosa **RC** .20
153 Dave Veres .10
154a Larry Walker/Action .15
154b Larry Walker/Portrait .15
155 Brad Ausmus .10
156 Dave Borkowski .10
157 Tony Clark .10
158 Francisco Cordero .10
159 Deivi Cruz .10
160 Damion Easley .10
161 Juan Encarnacion .10
162 Robert Fick .10
163 Bobby Higginson .10
164 Gabe Kapler .15
165 Brian Moehler .10
166 Dean Palmer .10
167 Luis Polonia .10
168 Justin Thompson .10
169 Jeff Weaver .10
170 Antonio Alfonseca .10
171 Bruce Aven .10
172 A.J. Burnett .15
173 Luis Castillo .10
174 Ramon Castro .10
175 Ryan Dempster .10
176 Alex Fernandez .10
177 Cliff Floyd .10
178 Amaury Garcia .10
179 Alex Gonzalez .10
180 Mark Kotsay .10
181 Mike Lowell .15
182 Brian Meadows .10
183 Kevin Orie .10
184 Julio Ramirez .10
185 Preston Wilson .15
186 Moises Alou .15
187a Jeff Bagwell/Action .75
187b Jeff Bagwell/Portrait .75
188 Glen Barker .10
189 Derek Bell .10
190a Craig Biggio/Action .15
190b Craig Biggio/Portrait .15
191 Ken Caminiti .10
192 Scott Elarton .10
193 Carl Everett .10
194 Mike Hampton .10
195 Carlos Hernandez .10

196 Richard Hidalgo .10
197 Jose Lima .10
198 Shane Reynolds .15
199 Bill Spiers .10
200 Billy Wagner .15
201a Carlos Beltran/Action .50
201b Carlos Beltran/Portrait .50
202 Dermal Brown .10
203 Johnny Damon .25
204 Jermaine Dye .10
205 Carlos Febles .10
206 Jeremy Giambi .10
207 Mark Quinn .10
208 Joe Randa .10
209 Dan Reichert .10
210 Jose Rosado .10
211 Rey Sanchez .10
212 Jeff Suppan .10
213 Mike Sweeney .10
214a Kevin Brown/Action .15
214b Kevin Brown/Portrait .15
215 Darren Dreifort .10
216 Eric Gagne .10
217 Mark Grudzielanek .10
218 Todd Hollandsworth .10
219 Todd Hundley .10
220 Eric Karros .15
221 Raul Mondesi .15
222 Chan Ho Park .10
223 Jeff Shaw .10
224a Gary Sheffield/Action .30
224b Gary Sheffield/Portrait .30
225 Ismael Valdes .10
226 Devon White .10
227 Eric Young .10
228 Kevin Barker .10
229 Ron Belliard .10
230a Jeromy Burnitz/Action .10
230b Jeromy Burnitz/Portrait .10
231 Jeff Cirillo .10
232 Marquis Grissom .10
233 Geoff Jenkins .10
234 Mark Loretta .10
235 David Nilsson .10
236 Hideo Nomo .75
237 Alex Ochoa .10
238 Kyle Peterson .10
239 Fernando Vina .10
240 Bob Wickman .10
241 Steve Woodard .10
242 Chad Allen .10
243 Ron Coomer .10
244 Marty Cordova .10
245 Cristian Guzman .10
246 Denny Hocking .10
247 Jacque Jones .10
248 Corey Koskie .10
249 Matt Lawton .10
250 Joe Mays .10
251 Eric Milton .10
252 Brad Radke .10
253 Mark Redman .10
254 Terry Steinbach .10
255 Todd Walker .10
256 Tony Armas Jr. .10
257 Michael Barrett .10
258 Peter Bergeron .10
259 Geoff Blum .10
260 Orlando Cabrera .10
261 Trace Coquillette **RC** .15
262 Brad Fullmer .10
263a Vladimir Guerrero/ Action .75
263b Vladimir Guerrero/ Portrait .75
264 Wilton Guerrero .10
265 Dustin Hermanson .10
266 Manny Martinez .10
267 Ryan McGuire .10
268 Ugueth Urbina .10
269 Jose Vidro .10
270 Rondell White .15
271 Chris Widger .10
272 Edgardo Alfonzo .15
273 Armando Benitez .10
274 Roger Cedeno .10
275 Dennis Cook .10
276 Octavio Dotel .10
277 John Franco .10
278 Darryl Hamilton .10
279 Rickey Henderson .75
280 Orel Hershiser .10
281 Al Leiter .15
282a John Olerud/Action .15
282b John Olerud/Portrait .15
283 Rey Ordonez .10
284a Mike Piazza/Action 1.50
284b Mike Piazza/Portrait 1.50
285 Kenny Rogers .10
286 Jorge Toca .10
287 Robin Ventura .15
288 Scott Brosius .10
289a Roger Clemens/Action 1.25
289b Roger Clemens/ Portrait 1.25
290 David Cone .15
291 Chili Davis .10
292 Orlando Hernandez .15
293 Hideki Irabu .10
294a Derek Jeter/Action 2.50
294b Derek Jeter/Portrait 2.50
295 Chuck Knoblauch .10
296 Ricky Ledee .10
297 Jim Leyritz .10
298 Tino Martinez .15
299 Paul O'Neill .15
300 Andy Pettitte .25
301 Jorge Posada .15
302 Mariano Rivera .25
303 Alfonso Soriano .75
304a Bernie Williams/Action .20
304b Bernie Williams/Portrait .20
305 Ed Yarnall .10
306 Kevin Appier .10
307 Rich Becker .10
308 Eric Chavez .25
309 Jason Giambi .60
310 Ben Grieve .10
311 Ramon Hernandez .10
312 Tim Hudson .25
313 John Jaha .10
314 Doug Jones .10
315 Omar Olivares .10
316 Mike Oquist .10
317 Matt Stairs .10
318 Miguel Tejada .25
319 Randy Velarde .10
320 Bobby Abreu .15
321 Marlon Anderson .10
322 Alex Arias .10
323 Rico Brogna .10
324 Paul Byrd .10
325 Ron Gant .10
326 Doug Glanville .10
327 Wayne Gomes .10
328 Mike Lieberthal .10
329 Robert Person .10
330 Desi Relaford .10
331a Scott Rolen/Action .60
331b Scott Rolen/Portrait .60
332a Curt Schilling/Action .35
332b Curt Schilling/Portrait .35
333 Kris Benson .10
334 Adrian Brown .10
335 Brant Brown .10
336 Brian Giles .15
337 Chad Hermansen .10
338 Jason Kendall .15
339 Al Martin .10
340 Pat Meares .10
341a Warren Morris/Action .10
341b Warren Morris/Portrait .10
342 Todd Ritchie .10
343 Jason Schmidt .10
344 Ed Sprague .10
345 Mike Williams .10
346 Kevin Young .10
347 Rick Ankiel .15
348 Ricky Bottalico .10
349 Kent Bottenfield .10
350 Darren Bragg .10
351 Eric Davis .15
352a J.D. Drew/Action .35
352b J.D. Drew/Portrait .35
353 Adam Kennedy .10
354 Ray Lankford .10
355 Joe McEwing .10
356a Mark McGwire/Action 2.00
356b Mark McGwire/Portrait 2.00
357 Matt Morris .10
358 Darren Oliver .10
359 Edgar Renteria .10
360 Fernando Tatis .10
361 Andy Ashby .10
362 Ben Davis .10
363a Tony Gwynn/Action 1.00
363b Tony Gwynn/Portrait 1.00
364 Sterling Hitchcock .10
365 Trevor Hoffman .10
366 Damian Jackson .10
367 Wally Joyner .10
368 Dave Magadan .10
369 Gary Matthews Jr. .10
370 Phil Nevin .10
371 Eric Owens .10
372 Ruben Rivera .10
373a Reggie Sanders/Action .10
373b Reggie Sanders/Portrait .10
374 Quilvio Veras .10
375 Rich Aurilia .10
376 Marvin Benard .10
377a Barry Bonds/Action 2.50
377b Barry Bonds/Portrait 2.50
378 Ellis Burks .10
379 Shawn Estes .10
380 Livan Hernandez .10
381a Jeff Kent/Action .15
381b Jeff Kent/Portrait .15
382 Brent Mayne .10
383 Bill Mueller .10
384 Calvin Murray .10
385 Robb Nen .10
386 Russ Ortiz .10
387 Kirk Rueter .10
388 J.T. Snow .10
389 David Bell .10
390 Jay Buhner .15
391 Russ Davis .10
392a Freddy Garcia/Action .10
392b Freddy Garcia/Portrait .10
393a Ken Griffey Jr./Action 1.50
393b Ken Griffey Jr./Portrait 1.50
394 Carlos Guillen .10
395 John Halama .10
396 Brian Hunter .10
397 Ryan Jackson .10
398 Edgar Martinez .10
399 Gil Meche .10
400 Jose Mesa .10
401 Jamie Moyer .10
402a Alex Rodriguez/Action 2.00
402b Alex Rodriguez/ Portrait 2.00
403 Dan Wilson .10
404 Wilson Alvarez .10
405 Rolando Arrojo .10
406a Wade Boggs/Action 1.00
406b Wade Boggs/Portrait 1.00
407 Miguel Cairo .10
408a Jose Canseco/Action .40
408b Jose Canseco/Portrait .40
409 John Flaherty .10
410 Jose Guillen .10
411 Roberto Hernandez .10
412 Terrell Lowery .10
413 Dave Martinez .10
414 Quinton McCracken .10
415a Fred McGriff/Action .15
415b Fred McGriff/Portrait .15
416 Ryan Rupe .10
417 Kevin Stocker .10
418 Bubba Trammell .10
419 Royce Clayton .10
420a Juan Gonzalez/Action .75
420b Juan Gonzalez/Portrait .75
421 Tom Goodwin .10
422 Rusty Greer .10
423 Rick Helling .10
424 Roberto Kelly .10
425 Ruben Mateo .10
426 Mark McLemore .10
427 Mike Morgan .10
428 Rafael Palmeiro .65
429a Ivan Rodriguez/Action .65
429b Ivan Rodriguez/Portrait .65
430 Aaron Sele .10
431 Lee Stevens .10
432 John Wetteland .10
433 Todd Zeile .10
434 Jeff Zimmerman .10
435 Tony Batista .10
436 Casey Blake .10
437 Homer Bush .10
438 Chris Carpenter .10
439 Jose Cruz Jr. .10
440a Carlos Delgado/Action .50
440b Carlos Delgado/Portrait .50
441 Tony Fernandez .10
442 Darrin Fletcher .10
443 Alex Gonzalez .10
444a Shawn Green/Action .35
444b Shawn Green/Portrait .35
445 Roy Halladay .20
446 Billy Koch .10
447 David Segui .10
448 Shannon Stewart .10
449 David Wells .10
450 Vernon Wells .15

Copper

Coppers are a parallel set to the 500-card base set and are identical to the base cards besides the copper foil stamping. Inserted exclusively in hobby packs Coppers are limited to 99 serial numbered sets.

NM/M
Common Copper: 5.00
Stars: 4-8X
Production 99 Sets

Platinum Blue

A parallel to the 500-card base set these have identical photos as the regular cards besides platinum blue foil stamping. A total of 75 serial numbered sets were produced.

NM/M
Common Player: 8.00
Stars: 6-10X
Production 75 Sets

Premiere Date

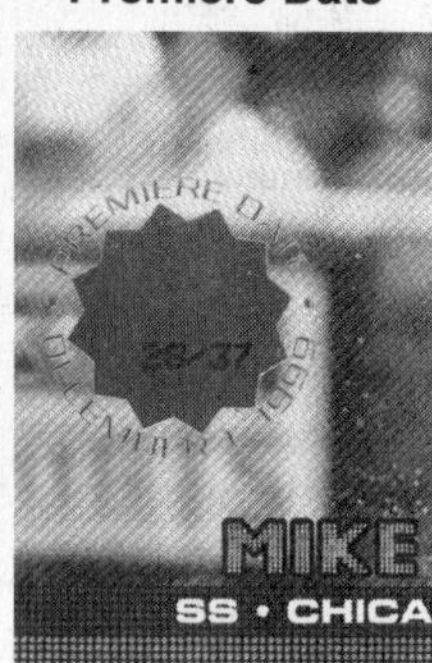

A parallel to the 500-card base set these are sequentially numbered to 37 sets.

NM/M
Common Player: 15.00
Stars: 8X to15X
Production 37 Sets

Ruby Red (Seven-11)

This parallel to the base set of 2000 Pacific was available only in 10-card retail "Jewel Collection" packs at Seven-11 convenience stores. Other than the use of red metallic foil for the player name and Pacific logo, the cards are identical to the regular-issue version.

NM/M
Complete Set (500): 65.00
Common Player: .15
Stars/Rookies 1.5X

Command Performers

NM/M
Complete Set (20): 45.00
Common Player: 1.00
Inserted 1:24 Retail
1 Chipper Jones 3.00
2 Greg Maddux 3.00
3 Cal Ripken Jr. 6.00
4 Nomar Garciaparra 4.00
5 Sammy Sosa 4.00
6 Sean Casey 1.00
7 Manny Ramirez 2.00
8 Larry Walker 1.00
9 Jeff Bagwell 2.00
10 Vladimir Guerrero 2.00
11 Mike Piazza 4.00
12 Roger Clemens 3.50
13 Derek Jeter 6.00
14 Mark McGwire 5.00
15 Tony Gwynn 3.00
16 Barry Bonds 6.00
17 Ken Griffey Jr. 4.00
18 Alex Rodriguez 5.00
19 Ivan Rodriguez 1.50
20 Shawn Green 1.25

Cramer's Choice Awards

This die-cut set is shaped in a trophy-like design on a holographic silver foil design.

Cramer's Choice are seeded 1:721 packs.

NM/M
Complete Set (10): 300.00
Common Player: 25.00
Inserted 1:721
1 Chipper Jones 25.00
2 Cal Ripken Jr. 50.00
3 Nomar Garciaparra 30.00
4 Sammy Sosa 30.00
5 Mike Piazza 30.00
6 Derek Jeter 50.00
7 Mark McGwire 40.00
8 Tony Gwynn 25.00
9 Ken Griffey Jr. 30.00
10 Alex Rodriguez 40.00

Diamond Leaders

Designed on a horizontal format each card features three statistical leaders from the 1999 season for each respective team. Card fronts have gold holofoil stamping while card backs give statistical leaders for eight categories for the featured team. These were seeded 2:25 packs.

NM/M
Complete Set (30): 25.00
Common Card: .50
Inserted 2:25
1 Anaheim Angels (Garret Anderson, Chuck Finley, Troy Percival, Mo Vaughn) .50
2 Baltimore Orioles (Albert Belle, Mike Mussina, B.J. Surhoff) .50
3 Boston Red Sox (Nomar Garciaparra, Pedro J. Martinez, Troy O'Leary) 3.00
4 Chicago White Sox (Ray Durham, Magglio Ordonez, Frank Thomas) 1.50
5 Cleveland Indians (Bartolo Colon, Manny Ramirez, Omar Vizquel) 1.50
6 Detroit Tigers (Deivi Cruz, Dave Mlicki, David Palmer) .50
7 Kansas City Royals (Johnny Damon, Jermaine Dye, Jose Rosado, Mike Sweeney) .50
8 Minnesota Twins (Corey Koskie, Eric Milton, Brad Radke) .50
9 New York Yankees (Orlando Hernandez, Derek Jeter, Mariano Rivera, Bernie Williams) 4.00
10 Oakland Athletics (Jeremy Giambi, Tim Hudson, Matt Stairs) 1.00
11 Seattle Mariners (Freddy Garcia, Ken Griffey Jr., Edgar Martinez) 3.00
12 Tampa Bay Devil Rays (Jose Canseco, Roberto Hernandez, Fred McGriff) .75
13 Texas Rangers (Rafael Palmeiro, Ivan Rodriguez, John Wetteland) 1.00

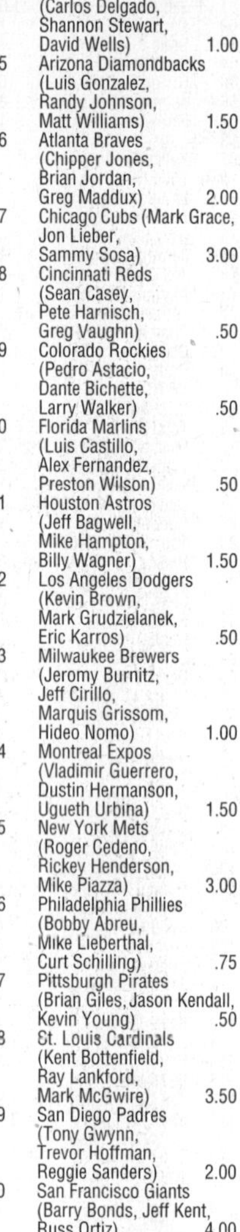

14 Toronto Blue Jays (Carlos Delgado, Shannon Stewart, David Wells) 1.00
15 Arizona Diamondbacks (Luis Gonzalez, Randy Johnson, Matt Williams) 1.50
16 Atlanta Braves (Chipper Jones, Brian Jordan, Greg Maddux) 2.00
17 Chicago Cubs (Mark Grace, Jon Lieber, Sammy Sosa) 3.00
18 Cincinnati Reds (Sean Casey, Pete Harnisch, Greg Vaughn) .50
19 Colorado Rockies (Pedro Astacio, Dante Bichette, Larry Walker) .50
20 Florida Marlins (Luis Castillo, Alex Fernandez, Preston Wilson) .50
21 Houston Astros (Jeff Bagwell, Mike Hampton, Billy Wagner) 1.50
22 Los Angeles Dodgers (Kevin Brown, Mark Grudzielanek, Eric Karros) .50
23 Milwaukee Brewers (Jeromy Burnitz, Jeff Cirillo, Marquis Grissom, Hideo Nomo) 1.00
24 Montreal Expos (Vladimir Guerrero, Dustin Hermanson, Ugueth Urbina) 1.50
25 New York Mets (Roger Cedeno, Rickey Henderson, Mike Piazza) 3.00
26 Philadelphia Phillies (Bobby Abreu, Mike Lieberthal, Curt Schilling) .75
27 Pittsburgh Pirates (Brian Giles, Jason Kendall, Kevin Young) .50
28 St. Louis Cardinals (Kent Bottenfield, Ray Lankford, Mark McGwire) 3.50
29 San Diego Padres (Tony Gwynn, Trevor Hoffman, Reggie Sanders) 2.00
30 San Francisco Giants (Barry Bonds, Jeff Kent, Russ Ortiz) 4.00

Gold Crown Die-Cuts

Printed on a 24-point stock this set features Pacific's classic crown shaped design on a dual foiled holographic gold and silver stock. These were seeded 1:25 packs.

NM/M
Complete Set (36): 150.00
Common Player: 1.50
Inserted 1:25
1 Mo Vaughn 1.50
2 Matt Williams 1.50
3 Andruw Jones 6.00
4 Chipper Jones 8.00
5 Greg Maddux 8.00
6 Cal Ripken Jr. 15.00
7 Nomar Garciaparra 10.00
8 Pedro Martinez 6.00
9 Sammy Sosa 10.00
10 Magglio Ordonez 2.50
11 Frank Thomas 6.00
12 Sean Casey 1.50
13 Roberto Alomar 2.50
14 Manny Ramirez 6.00
15 Larry Walker 1.50
16 Jeff Bagwell 6.00
17 Craig Biggio 1.50

18 Carlos Beltran 4.00
19 Vladimir Guerrero 6.00
20 Mike Piazza 10.00
21 Roger Clemens 9.00
22 Derek Jeter 15.00
23 Bernie Williams 2.00
24 Scott Rolen 5.00
25 Warren Morris 1.50
26 J.D. Drew 2.00
27 Mark McGwire 12.00
28 Tony Gwynn 8.00
29 Barry Bonds 15.00
30 Ken Griffey Jr. 10.00
31 Alex Rodriguez 12.00
32 Jose Canseco 2.00
33 Juan Gonzalez 6.00
34 Rafael Palmeiro 5.00
35 Ivan Rodriguez 5.00
36 Shawn Green 3.00

Reflections

This 20-card die-cut set features a unique sunglasses-on-cap design utilizing cel technology for added effect on the sunglasses portion of the insert. The backs have a small photo of the featured player. These were seeded 1:97 packs.

NM/M
Common Player: 3.00
Inserted 1:97
1 Andruw Jones 6.00
2 Chipper Jones 8.00
3 Cal Ripken Jr. 20.00
4 Nomar Garciaparra 12.00
5 Sammy Sosa 12.00
6 Frank Thomas 6.00
7 Manny Ramirez 6.00
8 Jeff Bagwell 6.00
9 Vladimir Guerrero 6.00
10 Mike Piazza 12.00
11 Derek Jeter 20.00
12 Bernie Williams 3.00
13 Scott Rolen 5.00
14 J.D. Drew 3.00
15 Mark McGwire 15.00
16 Tony Gwynn 8.00
17 Ken Griffey Jr. 12.00
18 Alex Rodriguez 15.00
19 Juan Gonzalez 6.00
20 Ivan Rodriguez 5.00

Past & Present

Inserted exclusively in hobby packs at a rate of 1:49, these inserts have a silver prism front and a cardboard textured back. The fronts have a current photo of the player while the backs have a photo taken years before.

NM/M
Complete Set (20): 80.00
Common Player: 1.50
Inserted 1:49 H
1 Chipper Jones 5.00
2 Greg Maddux 5.00
3 Cal Ripken Jr. 10.00
4 Nomar Garciaparra 6.00
5 Pedro Martinez 4.00
6 Sammy Sosa 6.00
7 Frank Thomas 4.00
8 Manny Ramirez 4.00
9 Larry Walker 1.50
10 Jeff Bagwell 4.00
11 Mike Piazza 6.00
12 Roger Clemens 5.50
13 Derek Jeter 10.00
14 Mark McGwire 8.00
15 Tony Gwynn 5.00
16 Barry Bonds 10.00
17 Ken Griffey Jr. 6.00
18 Alex Rodriguez 8.00
19 Wade Boggs 5.00
20 Ivan Rodriguez 3.00

Ornaments

This 20-card set features a number of different Christmas patterned die-cut shapes, including ornaments, wreaths and Christmas trees. Each card comes with a string intended to hang from a tree on a holographic foil design. These were seeded 2:25 packs.

NM/M
Complete Set (20): 40.00
Common Player: 1.00
Inserted 2:25
1 Mo Vaughn 1.00
2 Chipper Jones 3.00
3 Greg Maddux 3.00
4 Cal Ripken Jr. 6.00
5 Nomar Garciaparra 4.00
6 Sammy Sosa 4.00
7 Frank Thomas 2.00
8 Manny Ramirez 2.00
9 Larry Walker 1.00
10 Jeff Bagwell 2.00
11 Mike Piazza 4.00
12 Roger Clemens 3.50
13 Derek Jeter 6.00
14 Scott Rolen 1.50
15 J.D. Drew 1.25
16 Mark McGwire 5.00
17 Tony Gwynn 3.00
18 Ken Griffey Jr. 4.00
19 Alex Rodriguez 5.00
20 Ivan Rodriguez 1.50

2000 Pacific Aurora Sample

Nearly identical to the issued version of spokesman Tony Gwynn's card, this features a large white diagonal "SAMPLE" overprint on back and in the space where a card number usually appears.

NM/M
Tony Gwynn 3.00

2000 Pacific Aurora

NM/M
Complete Set (151): 25.00
Common Player: .15
Pack (10): 2.00
Wax Box (24): 30.00
1 Darin Erstad .25
2 Troy Glaus .75
3 Tim Salmon .25
4 Mo Vaughn .15
5 Jay Bell .15
6 Erubiel Durazo .15
7 Luis Gonzalez .25
8 Randy Johnson .75
9 Matt Williams .15
10 Tom Glavine .35
11 Andruw Jones .75
12 Chipper Jones 1.00
13 Brian Jordan .15
14 Greg Maddux 1.00
15 Kevin Millwood .15
16 Albert Belle .15
17 Will Clark .25
18 Mike Mussina .35
19 Cal Ripken Jr. 2.50
20 B.J. Surhoff .15
21 Nomar Garciaparra 1.50
22 Pedro Martinez .75
23 Troy O'Leary .15
24 Wilton Veras .15
25 Mark Grace .25
26 Henry Rodriguez .15
27 Sammy Sosa 1.50
28 Kerry Wood .50
29 Ray Durham .15
30 Paul Konerko .25
31 Carlos Lee .15
32 Magglio Ordonez .25
33 Chris Singleton .15
34 Frank Thomas .75
35 Mike Cameron .15
36 Sean Casey .25
37 Barry Larkin .15
38 Pokey Reese .15
39 Eddie Taubensee .15
40 Roberto Alomar .40
41 David Justice .15
42 Kenny Lofton .15
43 Manny Ramirez .75
44 Richie Sexson .15
45 Jim Thome .60
46 Omar Vizquel .15
47 Todd Helton .75
48 Mike Lansing .15
49 Neifi Perez .15
50 Ben Petrick .15
51 Larry Walker .15
52 Tony Clark .15
53 Damion Easley .15
54 Juan Encarnacion .15
55 Juan Gonzalez .75
56 Dean Palmer .15
57 Luis Castillo .15
58 Cliff Floyd .15
59 Alex Gonzalez .15
60 Mike Lowell .15
61 Preston Wilson .15
62 Jeff Bagwell .75
63 Craig Biggio .15
64 Ken Caminiti .15
65 Jose Lima .15
66 Billy Wagner .15
67 Carlos Beltran .50
68 Johnny Damon .25
69 Jermaine Dye .15
70 Mark Quinn .15
71 Mike Sweeney .15
72 Kevin Brown .15
73 Shawn Green .35
74 Eric Karros .15
75 Chan Ho Park .15
76 Gary Sheffield .40
77 Ron Belliard .15
78 Jeromy Burnitz .15
79 Marquis Grissom .15
80 Geoff Jenkins .15
81 David Nilsson .15
82 Ron Coomer .15
83 Jacque Jones .15
84 Brad Radke .15
85 Todd Walker .15
86 Michael Barrett .15
87 Peter Bergeron .15
88 Vladimir Guerrero .75
89 Jose Vidro .15
90 Rondell White .15
91 Edgardo Alfonzo .15
92 Darryl Hamilton .15
93 Rey Ordonez .15
94 Mike Piazza 1.50
95 Robin Ventura .15
96 Roger Clemens 1.25
97 Orlando Hernandez .15
98 Derek Jeter 2.50
99 Tino Martinez .15
100 Mariano Rivera .25
101 Bernie Williams .25
102 Eric Chavez .25
103 Jason Giambi .60
104 Ben Grieve .15
105 Tim Hudson .25
106 John Jaha .15
107 Matt Stairs .15
108 Bobby Abreu .15
109 Doug Glanville .15
110 Mike Lieberthal .15
111 Scott Rolen .60
112 Curt Schilling .40
113 Brian Giles .15
114 Chad Hermansen .15
115 Jason Kendall .15
116 Warren Morris .15
117 Kevin Young .15
118 Rick Ankiel .25
119 J.D. Drew .25
120 Ray Lankford .15
121 Mark McGwire 2.00
122 Edgar Renteria .15
123 Fernando Tatis .15
124 Ben Davis .15
125 Tony Gwynn 1.00
126 Trevor Hoffman .15
127 Phil Nevin .15
128 Barry Bonds 2.50
129 Ellis Burks .15
130 Jeff Kent .15
131 J.T. Snow .15
132 Freddy Garcia .15
133 Ken Griffey Jr. 1.50
133a Ken Griffey Jr. Reds 2.00
134 Edgar Martinez .15
135 Alex Rodriguez 2.00
136 Dan Wilson .15
137 Jose Canseco .40
138 Roberto Hernandez .15
139 Dave Martinez .15
140 Fred McGriff .15
141 Rusty Greer .15
142 Ruben Mateo .15
143 Rafael Palmeiro .65
144 Ivan Rodriguez .65
145 Jeff Zimmerman .15
146 Homer Bush .15
147 Carlos Delgado .50
148 Raul Mondesi .15
149 Shannon Stewart .15
150 Vernon Wells .15

Copper

Stars: 2-4X
Production 399 Sets

Platinum Blue

Stars: 5-10X
Production 67 Sets

Silver

Stars: 3-6X
Production 199 Sets

At-Bat Styrotechs

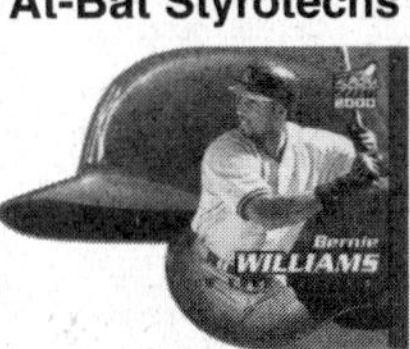

NM/M
Complete Set (20): 125.00
Common Player: 2.00
Production 299 Sets
1 Chipper Jones 7.50
2 Cal Ripken Jr. 15.00
3 Nomar Garciaparra 10.00
4 Sammy Sosa 10.00
5 Frank Thomas 6.00
6 Manny Ramirez 6.00
7 Larry Walker 2.00
8 Jeff Bagwell 6.00
9 Carlos Beltran 2.00
10 Vladimir Guerrero 6.00
11 Mike Piazza 10.00
12 Derek Jeter 15.00
13 Bernie Williams 2.00
14 Mark McGwire 12.00
15 Tony Gwynn 7.50
16 Barry Bonds 15.00
17 Ken Griffey Jr. 10.00
18 Alex Rodriguez 12.00
19 Jose Canseco 3.00
20 Ivan Rodriguez 5.00

Dugout View Net-Fusions

NM/M
Complete Set (20): 110.00
Common Player: 2.50
Inserted 1:37
1 Mo Vaughn 2.50
2 Chipper Jones 8.00
3 Cal Ripken Jr. 15.00
4 Nomar Garciaparra 10.00
5 Sammy Sosa 10.00
6 Manny Ramirez 6.00
7 Larry Walker 2.50
8 Juan Gonzalez 6.00
9 Jeff Bagwell 6.00
10 Craig Biggio 2.50
11 Shawn Green 3.00
12 Vladimir Guerrero 6.00
13 Mike Piazza 10.00
14 Derek Jeter 15.00
15 Scott Rolen 5.00
16 Mark McGwire 12.00
17 Tony Gwynn 8.00
18 Ken Griffey Jr. 10.00
19 Alex Rodriguez 12.00
20 Rafael Palmeiro 4.00

Pennant Fever

NM/M
Complete Set (20): 25.00
Common Player: 1.00
T. Gwynn Auto./147 75.00
Inserted 4:37
1 Andruw Jones 1.50
2 Chipper Jones 2.00
3 Greg Maddux 2.00
4 Cal Ripken Jr. 4.00
5 Nomar Garciaparra 2.50
6 Pedro Martinez 1.50
7 Sammy Sosa 2.50
8 Manny Ramirez 1.50
9 Jim Thome 1.50
10 Jeff Bagwell 1.50
11 Mike Piazza 2.50
12 Roger Clemens 2.25
13 Derek Jeter 4.00
14 Bernie Williams 1.00
15 Mark McGwire 3.00
16 Tony Gwynn 2.00
17 Ken Griffey Jr. 2.50
18 Alex Rodriguez 3.00
19 Rafael Palmeiro 1.00
20 Ivan Rodriguez 1.00

Pinstripes

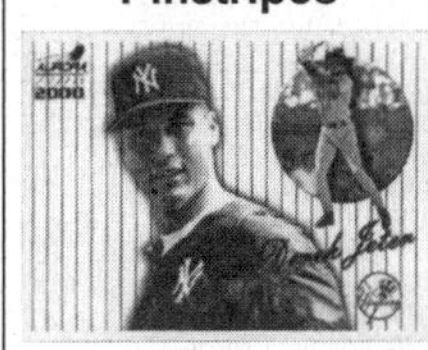

NM/M
Complete Set (50): 30.00
Common Player: .25
Premiere Date: 3-6X
Production 51 Sets
4 Mo Vaughn .25
8 Randy Johnson 1.50
9 Matt Williams .25
11 Andruw Jones 1.50
12 Chipper Jones 2.00
14 Greg Maddux 2.00
19 Cal Ripken Jr. 4.00
21 Nomar Garciaparra 2.50
22 Pedro Martinez 1.50
27 Sammy Sosa 2.50
32 Magglio Ordonez .35
34 Frank Thomas 1.50
36 Sean Casey .35
37 Barry Larkin .25
42 Kenny Lofton .25
43 Manny Ramirez 1.50
45 Jim Thome 1.50
47 Todd Helton 1.50
51 Larry Walker .25
55 Juan Gonzalez 1.50
62 Jeff Bagwell 1.50
63 Craig Biggio .25
67 Carlos Beltran .50
73 Shawn Green .40
76 Gary Sheffield .40
78 Jeromy Burnitz .25
88 Vladimir Guerrero 1.50
91 Edgardo Alfonzo .25
94 Mike Piazza 2.50
96 Roger Clemens 2.25
97 Orlando Hernandez .25
98 Derek Jeter 4.00
101 Bernie Williams .35
102 Eric Chavez .35
105 Tim Hudson .35
111 Scott Rolen 1.25
112 Curt Schilling .50
113 Brian Giles .25
114 Rick Ankiel .25
121 Mark McGwire 3.00
125 Tony Gwynn 2.00
128 Barry Bonds 4.00
130 Jeff Kent .25
133 Ken Griffey Jr. 2.50
135 Alex Rodriguez 3.00
137 Jose Canseco .50
140 Fred McGriff .25
143 Rafael Palmeiro .75
144 Ivan Rodriguez .75
147 Carlos Delgado 1.00

Star Factor

NM/M
Complete Set (10): 200.00
Common Player: 20.00
Inserted 1:361
1 Chipper Jones 20.00
2 Cal Ripken Jr. 40.00
3 Nomar Garciaparra 25.00
4 Sammy Sosa 25.00
5 Mike Piazza 25.00
6 Derek Jeter 40.00
7 Mark McGwire 30.00
8 Tony Gwynn 20.00
9 Ken Griffey Jr. 25.00
10 Alex Rodriguez 30.00

2000 Pacific Crown Collection Sample

Nearly identical to the issued version of spokesman Tony Gwynn's card, this features a large white diagonal "SAMPLE" overprint on back and in the space where a card number usually appears.

NM/M
Tony Gwynn 3.00

2000 Pacific Crown Collection

This 300-card base set has a white bordered design with the logo, player name and team stamped in gold foil. Card backs have a small close-up photo, a brief career highlight and 1999 statistics along with career totals.

NM/M
Complete Set (300): 25.00
Common Player: .10
Pack (10): 1.50
Wax Box (36): 30.00
1 Garret Anderson .10

2	Darin Erstad	.25
3	Ben Molina	.10
4	Ramon Ortiz	.10
5	Orlando Palmeiro	.10
6	Troy Percival	.10
7	Tim Salmon	.15
8	Mo Vaughn	.10
9	Checklist (Mo Vaughn)	.10
10	Jay Bell	.10
11	Omar Daal	.10
12	Erubiel Durazo	.10
13	Steve Finley	.10
14	Hanley Frias	.10
15	Luis Gonzalez	.25
16	Randy Johnson	.75
17	Matt Williams	.10
18	Checklist (Matt Williams)	.10
19	Andres Galarraga	.10
20	Tom Glavine	.35
21	Andruw Jones	.75
22	Chipper Jones	1.00
23	Brian Jordan	.10
24	Javy Lopez	.10
25	Greg Maddux	1.00
26	Kevin Millwood	.10
27	Eddie Perez	.10
28	John Smoltz	.10
29	Checklist (Chipper Jones)	.50
30	Albert Belle	.15
31	Jesse Garcia	.10
32	Jerry Hairston Jr.	.10
33	Charles Johnson	.10
34	Mike Mussina	.30
35	Sidney Ponson	.10
36	Cal Ripken Jr.	2.50
37	B.J. Surhoff	.10
38	Checklist (Cal Ripken Jr.)	1.00
39	Nomar Garciaparra	1.50
40	Pedro Martinez	.75
41	Ramon Martinez	.10
42	Trot Nixon	.10
43	Jose Offerman	.10
44	Troy O'Leary	.10
45	John Valentin	.10
46	Wilton Veras	.10
47	Checklist (Nomar Garciaparra)	.75
48	Mark Grace	.15
49	Felix Heredia	.10
50	Jose Molina	.10
51	Jose Nieves	.10
52	Henry Rodriguez	.10
53	Sammy Sosa	1.50
54	Kerry Wood	.65
55	Checklist (Sammy Sosa)	.60
56	Mike Caruso	.10
57	Carlos Castillo	.10
58	Jason Dellaero	.10
59	Carlos Lee	.10
60	Magglio Ordonez	.25
61	Jesus Pena	.10
62	Liu Rodriguez	.10
63	Frank Thomas	.75
64	Checklist (Magglio Ordonez)	.15
65	Aaron Boone	.10
66	Mike Cameron	.10
67	Sean Casey	.20
68	Juan Guzman	.10
69	Barry Larkin	.10
70	Pokey Reese	.10
71	Eddie Taubensee	.10
72	Greg Vaughn	.10
73	Checklist (Sean Casey)	.15
74	Roberto Alomar	.25
75	Sandy Alomar Jr.	.10
76	Bartolo Colon	.10
77	Jacob Cruz	.10
78	Einar Diaz	.10
79	David Justice	.10
80	Kenny Lofton	.10
81	Manny Ramirez	.75
82	Richie Sexson	.10
83	Jim Thome	.75
84	Omar Vizquel	.10
85	Enrique Wilson	.10
86	Checklist (Manny Ramirez)	.40
87	Pedro Astacio	.10
88	Henry Blanco	.10
89	Vinny Castilla	.10
90	Edgard Clemente	.10
91	Todd Helton	.75
92	Neifi Perez	.10
93	Terry Shumpert	.10
94	Juan Sosa **RC**	.20
95	Larry Walker	.10
96	Checklist (Vinny Castilla)	.10
97	Tony Clark	.10
98	Deivi Cruz	.10
99	Damion Easley	.10
100	Juan Encarnacion	.10
101	Karim Garcia	.10
102	Luis Garcia	.10
103	Juan Gonzalez	.75
104	Jose Macias	.10
105	Dean Palmer	.10
106	Checklist (Juan Encarnacion)	.10
107	Antonio Alfonseca	.10
108	Armando Almanza	.10
109	Bruce Aven	.10
110	Luis Castillo	.10
111	Ramon Castro	.10
112	Alex Fernandez	.10
113	Cliff Floyd	.10
114	Alex Gonzalez	.10
115	Michael Tejera **RC**	.10
116	Preston Wilson	.10
117	Checklist (Luis Castillo)	.10
118	Jeff Bagwell	.75
119	Craig Biggio	.10
120	Jose Cabrera	.10
121	Tony Eusebio	.10
122	Carl Everett	.10
123	Ricky Gutierrez	.10
124	Mike Hampton	.10
125	Richard Hidalgo	.10
126	Jose Lima	.10
127	Billy Wagner	.10
128	Checklist (Jeff Bagwell)	.40
129	Carlos Beltran	.50
130	Johnny Damon	.25
131	Jermaine Dye	.10
132	Carlos Febles	.10
133	Jeremy Giambi	.10
134	Jose Rosado	.10
135	Rey Sanchez	.10
136	Jose Santiago	.10
137	Checklist (Carlos Beltran)	.10
138	Kevin Brown	.10
139	Craig Counsell	.10
140	Shawn Green	.40
141	Eric Karros	.10
142	Angel Pena	.10
143	Gary Sheffield	.25
144	Ismael Valdes	.10
145	Jose Vizcaino	.10
146	Devon White	.10
147	Checklist (Eric Karros)	.10
148	Ron Belliard	.10
149	Jeromy Burnitz	.10
150	Jeff Cirillo	.10
151	Marquis Grissom	.10
152	Geoff Jenkins	.10
153	Dave Nilsson	.10
154	Rafael Roque	.10
155	Jose Valentin	.10
156	Fernando Vina	.10
157	Jeromy Burnitz	.10
158	Chad Allen	.10
159	Ron Coomer	.10
160	Eddie Guardado	.10
161	Cristian Guzman	.10
162	Jacque Jones	.10
163	Javier Valentin	.10
164	Todd Walker	.10
165	Checklist (Ron Coomer)	.10
166	Michael Barrett	.10
167	Miguel Batista	.10
168	Vladimir Guerrero	.75
169	Wilton Guerrero	.10
170	Fernando Seguignol	.10
171	Ugueth Urbina	.10
172	Javier Vazquez	.10
173	Jose Vidro	.10
174	Rondell White	.10
175	Checklist (Vladimir Guerrero)	.25
176	Edgardo Alfonzo	.10
177	Armando Benitez	.10
178	Roger Cedeno	.10
179	Octavio Dotel	.10
180	Melvin Mora	.10
181	Rey Ordonez	.10
182	Mike Piazza	1.50
183	Jorge Toca	.10
184	Robin Ventura	.10
185	Checklist (Edgardo Alfonzo)	.10
186	Roger Clemens	1.25
187	David Cone	.10
188	Orlando Hernandez	.10
189	Derek Jeter	2.50
190	Ricky Ledee	.10
191	Tino Martinez	.10
192	Ramiro Mendoza	.10
193	Jorge Posada	.10
194	Mariano Rivera	.15
195	Alfonso Soriano	.75
196	Bernie Williams	.30
197	Checklist (Derek Jeter)	1.00
198	Eric Chavez	.15
199	Jason Giambi	.60
200	Ben Grieve	.10
201	Ramon Hernandez	.10
202	Tim Hudson	.25
203	John Jaha	.10
204	Omar Olivares	.10
205	Olmedo Saenz	.10
206	Matt Stairs	.10
207	Miguel Tejada	.20
208	Checklist (Tim Hudson)	.20
209	Rico Brogna	.10
210	Bobby Abreu	.10
211	Marlon Anderson	.10
212	Alex Arias	.10
213	Doug Glanville	.10
214	Robert Person	.10
215	Scott Rolen	.60
216	Curt Schilling	.35
217	Checklist (Scott Rolen)	.25
218	Francisco Cordova	.10
219	Brian Giles	.10
220	Jason Kendall	.10
221	Warren Morris	.10
222	Abraham Nunez	.10
223	Aramis Ramirez	.10
224	Jose Silva	.10
225	Kevin Young	.10
226	Checklist (Brian Giles)	.10
227	Rick Ankiel	.15
228	Ricky Bottalico	.10
229	J.D. Drew	.25
230	Ray Lankford	.10
231	Mark McGwire	2.00
232	Eduardo Perez	.10
233	Placido Polanco	.10
234	Edgar Renteria	.10
235	Fernando Tatis	.10
236	Checklist (Mark McGwire)	.85
237	Carlos Almanzar	.10
238	Wiki Gonzalez	.10
239	Tony Gwynn	1.00
240	Trevor Hoffman	.10
241	Damian Jackson	.10
242	Wally Joyner	.10
243	Ruben Rivera	.10
244	Reggie Sanders	.10
245	Quilvio Veras	.10
246	Checklist (Tony Gwynn)	.50
247	Rich Aurilia	.10
248	Marvin Benard	.10
249	Barry Bonds	2.50
250	Ellis Burks	.10
251	Miguel Del Toro	.10
252	Edwards Guzman	.10
253	Livan Hernandez	.10
254	Jeff Kent	.10
255	Russ Ortiz	.10
256	Armando Rios	.10
257	Checklist (Barry Bonds)	1.00
258	Rafael Bournigal	.10
259	Freddy Garcia	.10
260	Ken Griffey Jr.	15.00
261	Carlos Guillen	.10
262	Raul Ibanez	.10
263	Edgar Martinez	.10
264	Jose Mesa	.10
265	Jamie Moyer	.10
266	John Olerud	.10
267	Jose Paniagua	.10
268	Alex Rodriguez	2.00
269	Checklist (Alex Rodriguez)	1.00
270	Wilson Alvarez	.10
271	Rolando Arrojo	.10
272	Wade Boggs	1.00
273	Miguel Cairo	.10
274	Jose Canseco	.40
275	Jose Guillen	.10
276	Roberto Hernandez	.10
277	Albie Lopez	.10
278	Fred McGriff	.10
279	Esteban Yan	.10
280	Checklist (Jose Canseco)	.20
281	Rusty Greer	.10
282	Roberto Kelly	.10
283	Esteban Loaiza	.10
284	Ruben Mateo	.10
285	Rafael Palmeiro	.65
286	Ivan Rodriguez	.65
287	Aaron Sele	.10
288	John Wetteland	.10
289	Checklist (Ivan Rodriguez)	.25
290	Tony Batista	.10
291	Jose Cruz Jr.	.10
292	Carlos Delgado	.50
293	Kelvim Escobar	.10
294	Tony Fernandez	.10
295	Billy Koch	.10
296	Raul Mondesi	.10
297	Willis Otanez	.10
298	David Segui	.10
299	David Wells	.10
300	Checklist (Carlos Delgado)	.20

Holographic Purple

A parallel to the 300-card base set, holographic purple stamping replaces the gold foil to differentiate these from the base cards. These are limited to 199 numbered sets.

Stars:	4-8X
Production 199 Sets	

Platinum Blue

A parallel to the 300-card base set, these have blue foil stamping in place of gold foil and are limited to 67 serial numbered sets.

Stars:	8-15X
Production 67 Sets	

In The Cage

These inserts have a die-cut design around an image of a batting cage, with net-fusion technology used to mimic the netting in a batting cage. These were inserted 1:145 packs.

		NM/M
Complete Set (20):		250.00
Common Player:		5.00
Inserted 1:145		
1	Mo Vaughn	5.00
2	Chipper Jones	15.00
3	Cal Ripken Jr.	30.00
4	Nomar Garciaparra	20.00
5	Sammy Sosa	20.00
6	Frank Thomas	10.00
7	Roberto Alomar	6.00
8	Manny Ramirez	10.00
9	Larry Walker	5.00
10	Jeff Bagwell	10.00
11	Vladimir Guerrero	10.00
12	Mike Piazza	20.00
13	Derek Jeter	30.00
14	Bernie Williams	5.00
15	Mark McGwire	25.00
16	Tony Gwynn	15.00
17	Ken Griffey Jr.	20.00
18	Alex Rodriguez	25.00
19	Rafael Palmeiro	8.00
20	Ivan Rodriguez	8.00

Latinos of the Major Leagues

This set salutes major league's who have a latino heritage. These were seeded 2:37 packs and have a horizontal format with two images of the featured player on the card front.

		NM/M
Complete Set (36):		20.00
Common Player:		.25
Inserted 2:37		
Parallel:		2-4X
Production 99 Sets		
1	Erubiel Durazo	.25
2	Luis Gonzalez	.25
3	Andruw Jones	1.00
4	Nomar Garciaparra	2.00
5	Pedro Martinez	1.00
6	Sammy Sosa	2.00
7	Carlos Lee	.25
8	Magglio Ordonez	.25
9	Roberto Alomar	.65
10	Manny Ramirez	1.00
11	Omar Vizquel	.25
12	Vinny Castilla	.25
13	Juan Gonzalez	1.00
14	Luis Castillo	.25
15	Jose Lima	.25
16	Carlos Beltran	.75
17	Vladimir Guerrero	1.00
18	Edgardo Alfonzo	.25
19	Roger Cedeno	.25
20	Rey Ordonez	.25
21	Orlando Hernandez	.25
22	Tino Martinez	.25
23	Mariano Rivera	.35
24	Bernie Williams	.50
25	Miguel Tejada	.50
26	Bobby Abreu	.25
27	Fernando Tatis	.25
28	Freddy Garcia	.25
29	Edgar Martinez	.25
30	Alex Rodriguez	3.00
31	Jose Canseco	.65
32	Ruben Mateo	.25
33	Rafael Palmeiro	.75
34	Ivan Rodriguez	.75
35	Carlos Delgado	.65
36	Raul Mondesi	.25

Moment of Truth

These inserts feature gold foil stamping and a shadow image of the player in the background of the player photo. These were inserted 1:37 packs.

		NM/M
Complete Set (30):		50.00
Common Player:		.50
Inserted 1:37		
1	Mo Vaughn	.50
2	Chipper Jones	3.00
3	Greg Maddux	3.00
4	Albert Belle	.50
5	Cal Ripken Jr.	6.00
6	Nomar Garciaparra	4.00
7	Pedro Martinez	2.00
8	Sammy Sosa	4.00
9	Frank Thomas	2.00
10	Barry Larkin	.50
11	Kenny Lofton	.50
12	Manny Ramirez	2.00
13	Larry Walker	.50
14	Juan Gonzalez	2.00
15	Jeff Bagwell	2.00
16	Craig Biggio	.50
17	Carlos Beltran	1.00
18	Vladimir Guerrero	2.00
19	Mike Piazza	4.00
20	Roger Clemens	3.50
21	Derek Jeter	6.00
22	Bernie Williams	.75
23	Mark McGwire	5.00
24	Tony Gwynn	3.00
25	Barry Bonds	6.00
26	Ken Griffey Jr.	4.00
27	Alex Rodriguez	5.00
28	Rafael Palmeiro	1.50
29	Ivan Rodriguez	1.50
30	Carlos Delgado	1.00

Pacific Cup

Pacific Cup's have a horizontal format with gold foil stamping and an image of a trophy cup beside the player photo. These were inserted 1:721 packs.

		NM/M
Complete Set (10):		220.00
Inserted 1:721		
1	Cal Ripken Jr.	40.00
2	Nomar Garciaparra	25.00
3	Pedro Martinez	15.00
4	Sammy Sosa	25.00
5	Vladimir Guerrero	15.00
6	Derek Jeter	40.00
7	Mark McGwire	35.00
8	Tony Gwynn	20.00
9	Ken Griffey Jr.	25.00
10	Alex Rodriguez	35.00

Timber 2000

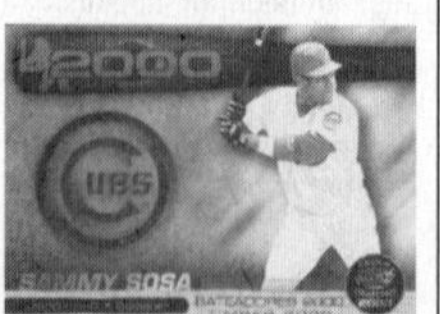

These 1:73 pack inserts have a horizontal format highlighted by gold foil stamping. A black bat is in the background of the player image with 2000 written in the bat head.

		NM/M
Complete Set (20):		100.00
Common Player:		2.00
Inserted 1:73		
1	Chipper Jones	8.00
2	Nomar Garciaparra	10.00
3	Sammy Sosa	10.00
4	Magglio Ordonez	2.00
5	Manny Ramirez	6.00
6	Vinny Castilla	2.00
7	Juan Gonzalez	6.00
8	Jeff Bagwell	6.00
9	Shawn Green	3.00
10	Vladimir Guerrero	6.00
11	Mike Piazza	10.00
12	Derek Jeter	15.00
13	Bernie Williams	2.00
14	Mark McGwire	12.00
15	Ken Griffey Jr.	10.00
16	Alex Rodriguez	12.00
17	Jose Canseco	3.00
18	Rafael Palmeiro	5.00
19	Ivan Rodriguez	5.00
20	Carlos Delgado	4.00

2000 Pacific Crown Royale

The Crown Royale 144-card base set has a horizontal format die-cut around a crown design at the top. The cards are double foiled with gold and silver foil etching.

		NM/M
Complete Set (144):		40.00
Common Player:		.25
Common SP:		1.00
Pack (6):		2.50
Box (24):		45.00
1	Darin Erstad	.40
2	Troy Glaus	1.00
3	Adam Kennedy/SP	1.00
4	Derrick Turnbow/SP **RC**	1.00
5	Mo Vaughn	.25
6	Erubiel Durazo	.25
7	Steve Finley	.25
8	Randy Johnson	1.00
9	Travis Lee	.25
10	Matt Williams	.25
11	Rafael Furcal/SP	1.00
12	Andres Galarraga	.25
13	Andruw Jones	1.00
14	Chipper Jones	1.50
15	Javy Lopez	.25
16	Greg Maddux	1.50
17	Albert Belle	.25
18	Will Clark	.35
19	Mike Mussina	.40
20	Cal Ripken Jr.	3.00
21	Carl Everett	.25
22	Nomar Garciaparra	2.00
23	Pedro Martinez	1.00
24	Jason Varitek	.25
25	Scott Downs/SP **RC**	1.00
26	Mark Grace	.35
27	Sammy Sosa	2.00
28	Kerry Wood	.65
29	Ray Durham	.25
30	Paul Konerko	.25
31	Carlos Lee	.25
32	Magglio Ordonez	.40
33	Frank Thomas	1.00
34	Rob Bell/SP	1.00
35	Sean Casey	.25
36	Ken Griffey Jr.	2.00
37	Barry Larkin	.25
38	Pokey Reese	.25
39	Roberto Alomar	.40
40	David Justice	.25
41	Kenny Lofton	.25
42	Manny Ramirez	1.00
43	Richie Sexson	.25
44	Jim Thome	.75
45	Rolando Arrojo	.25
46	Jeff Cirillo	.25
47	Tom Goodwin	.25
48	Todd Helton	1.00
49	Larry Walker	.25
50	Tony Clark	.25
51	Juan Encarnacion	.25
52	Juan Gonzalez	1.00
53	Hideo Nomo	1.00
54	Dean Palmer	.25
55	Cliff Floyd	.25
56	Alex Gonzalez	.25
57	Mike Lowell	.25
58	Brad Penny/SP	1.00
59	Preston Wilson	.25
60	Moises Alou	.25
61	Jeff Bagwell	1.00
62	Craig Biggio	.25
63	Roger Cedeno	.25
64	Julio Lugo SP	1.00
65	Carlos Beltran	.60
66	Johnny Damon	.40
67	Jermaine Dye	.25
68	Carlos Febles	.25
69	Mark Quinn/SP	1.00
70	Kevin Brown	.25
71	Shawn Green	.50
72	Eric Karros	.25
73	Gary Sheffield	.50
74	Kevin Barker/SP	1.00
75	Ron Belliard	.25
76	Jeromy Burnitz	.25
77	Geoff Jenkins	.25
78	Jacque Jones	.25
79	Corey Koskie	.25

80 Matt LeCroy/SP 1.00
81 Brad Radke .25
82 Peter Bergeron/SP 1.00
83 Matt Blank/SP 1.00
84 Vladimir Guerrero 1.00
85 Hideki Irabu .25
86 Rondell White .25
87 Edgardo Alfonzo .25
88 Mike Hampton .25
89 Rickey Henderson 1.00
90 Rey Ordonez .25
91 Jay Payton/SP 1.00
92 Mike Piazza 2.00
93 Roger Clemens 1.75
94 Orlando Hernandez .25
95 Derek Jeter 3.00
96 Tino Martinez .25
97 Alfonso Soriano/SP 2.50
98 Bernie Williams .40
99 Eric Chavez .40
100 Jason Giambi .75
101 Ben Grieve .25
102 Tim Hudson .50
103 Terrence Long/SP 1.00
104 Mark Mulder/SP 1.00
105 Adam Piatt/SP 1.00
106 Bobby Abreu .25
107 Doug Glanville .25
108 Mike Lieberthal .25
109 Scott Rolen .75
110 Brian Giles .25
111 Chad Hermansen/SP 1.00
112 Jason Kendall .25
113 Warren Morris .25
114 Rick Ankiel SP 1.00
115 Justin Brunette/SP **RC** 1.00
116 J.D. Drew .40
117 Mark McGwire 2.50
118 Fernando Tatis .25
119 Wiki Gonzalez/SP 1.00
120 Tony Gwynn 1.50
121 Trevor Hoffman .25
122 Ryan Klesko .25
123 Barry Bonds 3.00
124 Ellis Burks .25
125 Jeff Kent .25
126 Calvin Murray/SP 1.00
127 J.T. Snow .25
128 Freddy Garcia .25
129 John Olerud .25
130 Alex Rodriguez 2.50
131 Kazuhiro Sasaki/SP **RC** 3.00
132 Jose Canseco .50
133 Vinny Castilla .25
134 Fred McGriff .25
135 Greg Vaughn .25
136 Gabe Kapler .25
137 Mike Lamb/SP **RC** 1.00
138 Ruben Mateo/SP 1.00
139 Rafael Palmeiro .75
140 Ivan Rodriguez .75
141 Tony Batista .25
142 Carlos Delgado .75
143 Raul Mondesi .25
144 Shannon Stewart .25

Limited Series

A parallel to the 144-card base set, silver foil replaces gold foil to differentiate these from regular cards. They are also limited to 144 serial numbered sets.

Stars: 2-4X
Production 144 Sets

Red

Identical in design to the base set, these have red foil instead of gold and are the base cards in retail packaging.

All singles: 1X
Base cards in retail packs.

Platinum Blue

A parallel to the 144-card base set these have blue foil in place of gold foil to differentiate them from regular cards. They are limited to 75 serial numbered sets.

Stars: 3-6X
Production 75 Sets

Premiere Date

A parallel to the 144-card base set these are found exclusively in hobby packs and are limited to 121 serial numbered sets.

Stars: 2-4X
Production 121 Sets

Card-Supials

These inserts feature a superstar's regular sized card paired with a top prospect teammate's smaller card. The standard sized card has a hor-

izontal format with gold foil stamping, the small prospect card has gold foil stamping on a vertical format. These were seeded 2:25 packs.

NM/M
Complete Set (20): 40.00
Common Card: 1.00
Inserted 2:25
1 Randy Johnson, Erubiel Durazo 2.00
2 Chipper Jones, Andruw Jones 3.00
3 Cal Ripken Jr., Matt Riley 6.00
4 Nomar Garciaparra, Jason Varitek 4.00
5 Sammy Sosa, Kerry Wood 4.00
6 Frank Thomas, Magglio Ordonez 2.00
7 Ken Griffey Jr., Sean Casey 4.00
8 Manny Ramirez, Richie Sexson 2.00
9 Larry Walker, Ben Petrick 1.00
10 Juan Gonzalez, Juan Encarnacion 2.00
11 Jeff Bagwell, Lance Berkman 2.00
12 Shawn Green, Eric Gagne 1.00
13 Vladimir Guerrero, Peter Bergeron 2.00
14 Mike Piazza, Edgardo Alfonzo 4.00
15 Derek Jeter, Alfonso Soriano 5.00
16 Scott Rolen, Bobby Abreu 1.50
17 Mark McGwire, Rick Ankiel 5.00
18 Tony Gwynn, Ben Davis 3.00
19 Alex Rodriguez, Freddy Garcia 5.00
20 Ivan Rodriguez, Ruben Mateo 1.50

Cramer's Choice Jumbo

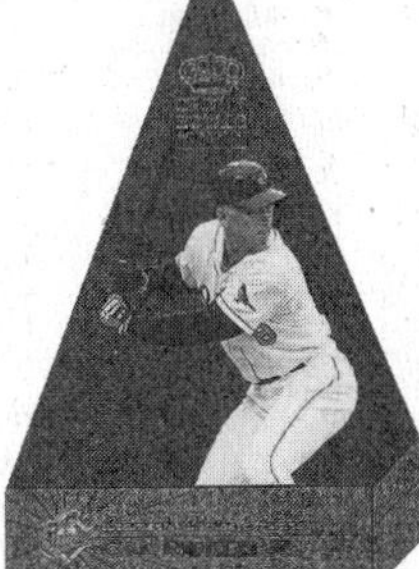

This enlarged 10-card set is die-cut into a trophy shape. The jumbo cards are enhanced with a silver holo-foiled front with gold foil stamping and etching across the bottom portion. These were found one per box exclusively in hobby boxes. Six parallels also were randomly inserted with each individual color replacing the gold foil stamping. Aqua's are limited to 20 numbered sets, Blue's 35 sets, Gold's 10 sets, Green's 30 sets, Purple's one set and Red's 25 sets.

NM/M
Complete Set (10): 35.00
Common Player: 1.00
Inserted 1:Box H
Aqua: 5-10X
Production 20 Sets
Blue: 2-5X
Production 35 Sets
Gold: 10-20X
Production 10 Sets
Green: 3-6X
Production 30 Sets
Red: 4-8X
Production 25 Sets
1 Cal Ripken Jr. 6.00
2 Nomar Garciaparra 4.00
3 Ken Griffey Jr. 4.00
4 Sammy Sosa 4.00
5 Mike Piazza 4.00
6 Derek Jeter 6.00
7 Rick Ankiel 1.00
8 Mark McGwire 5.00
9 Tony Gwynn 2.00
10 Alex Rodriguez 5.00

Feature Attractions

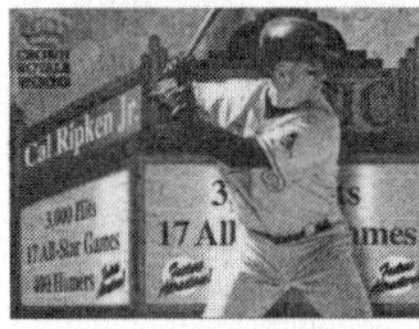

This 25-card set has a horizontal format with the featured player's achievements on a billboard in the background. These were seeded one per hobby pack and one per two retail packs. An Exclusive Showing parallel is also randomly inserted and is limited to 20 serial numbered sets.

NM/M
Complete Set (25): 10.00
Common Player: .25
Inserted 1:1
Exclusive Showing: 30-50X
Production 20 Sets
1 Erubiel Durazo .25
2 Chipper Jones 1.00
3 Greg Maddux 1.00
4 Cal Ripken Jr. 2.50
5 Nomar Garciaparra 1.50
6 Pedro Martinez .75
7 Sammy Sosa 1.50
8 Frank Thomas .75
9 Ken Griffey Jr. 1.50
10 Manny Ramirez .75
11 Larry Walker .25
12 Juan Gonzalez .75
13 Jeff Bagwell .75
14 Carlos Beltran .50
15 Shawn Green .50
16 Vladimir Guerrero .75
17 Mike Piazza 1.50
18 Roger Clemens 1.25
19 Derek Jeter 2.50
20 Ben Grieve .25
21 Rick Ankiel .35
22 Mark McGwire 2.00
23 Tony Gwynn 1.00
24 Alex Rodriguez 2.00
25 Ivan Rodriguez .65

Final Numbers

These inserts are found one per hobby pack and one per two retail packs. The logo, player name and team are stamped in silver foil and has "Final Numbers" written down the right hand portion of the front. A holographic parallel limited to 10 serial numbered sets is also randomly inserted.

NM/M
Complete Set (25): 10.00
Common Player: .25
Inserted 1:1
1 Randy Johnson .75
2 Andruw Jones .75
3 Chipper Jones 1.00
4 Cal Ripken Jr. 2.50
5 Nomar Garciaparra 1.50
6 Pedro Martinez .75
7 Sammy Sosa 1.50
8 Ken Griffey Jr. 1.50
9 Sean Casey .35
10 Manny Ramirez .75
11 Larry Walker .25
12 Jeff Bagwell .75
13 Craig Biggio .25
14 Shawn Green .50
15 Vladimir Guerrero .75
16 Mike Piazza 1.50
17 Derek Jeter 2.50
18 Bernie Williams .35
19 Scott Rolen .65
20 Mark McGwire 2.00
21 Tony Gwynn 1.00
22 Barry Bonds 2.50
23 Alex Rodriguez 2.00
24 Jose Canseco .40
25 Ivan Rodriguez .65

Jumbo

These jumbo cards are identical in design to the base cards besides their enlarged size. These were found exclusively in hobby boxes and were found as a box topper in 6:10 boxes.

NM/M
Complete Set (6): 25.00
Inserted 6:10 boxes H
1 Cal Ripken Jr. 6.00
2 Nomar Garciaparra 4.00
3 Ken Griffey Jr. 4.00
4 Derek Jeter 6.00
5 Mark McGwire 5.00
6 Alex Rodriguez 5.00

Proofs

Proofs are the actual printer's proofs used to produce this set. The inserts are transparent and have a coal black tint. These were inserted 1:25 packs. A parallel is also randomly inserted and is limited to 50 serial numbered sets.

NM/M
Complete Set (36): 90.00
Common Player: 1.00
Inserted 1:25
Proofs: 2-3X
1 Erubiel Durazo 1.50
2 Randy Johnson 3.00
3 Chipper Jones 5.00
4 Greg Maddux 5.00
5 Cal Ripken Jr. 10.00
6 Nomar Garciaparra 8.00
7 Pedro Martinez 3.00
8 Sammy Sosa 5.00
9 Frank Thomas 2.50
10 Sean Casey 1.50
11 Ken Griffey Jr. 5.00
12 Manny Ramirez 2.50
13 Jim Thome 2.50
14 Larry Walker 1.50
15 Juan Gonzalez 2.50
16 Jeff Bagwell 2.50
17 Craig Biggio 1.50
18 Carlos Beltran 2.00
19 Shawn Green 2.00
20 Vladimir Guerrero 2.50
21 Edgardo Alfonzo 1.00
22 Mike Piazza 5.00
23 Roger Clemens 6.00
24 Derek Jeter 10.00
25 Alfonso Soriano 4.00
26 Bernie Williams 2.00
27 Ben Grieve 1.00
28 Rick Ankiel 1.00
29 Mark McGwire 8.00
30 Tony Gwynn 3.00
31 Barry Bonds 8.00
32 Alex Rodriguez 8.00
33 Jose Canseco 2.00
34 Vinny Castilla 1.00
35 Ivan Rodriguez 2.00
36 Rafael Palmeiro 2.00

Sweet Spot Signatures

These die-cut autographed cards are done on a horizontal format with an image of a baseball beside the player photo. The signature is on the "sweet spot" of the baseball image. Red foil stamping is used on the seams of the baseball and the player name. No insertion ratio was announced.

NM/M
Common Player: 5.00
1 Adam Kennedy 5.00
2 Trot Nixon 8.00
3 Magglio Ordonez 10.00
4 Sean Casey 8.00
5 Travis Dawkins 5.00
6 Todd Helton 25.00
7 Ben Petrick 5.00
8 Jeff Weaver 6.00
9 Preston Wilson 5.00
10 Lance Berkman 10.00
11 Roger Cedeno 5.00
12 Eric Gagne 10.00
13 Kevin Barker 5.00
14 Kyle Peterson 5.00
15 Tony Armas Jr. 5.00
16 Peter Bergeron 5.00
17 Alfonso Soriano 40.00
18 Ben Grieve 5.00
19 Ramon Hernandez 5.00
20 Brian Giles 8.00
21 Chad Hermansen 5.00
22 Warren Morris 5.00
23 Ben Davis 5.00
24 Rick Ankiel 5.00
25 Chad Hutchinson 5.00
26 Freddy Garcia 10.00
27 Gabe Kapler 5.00
28 Ruben Mateo 5.00
29 Billy Koch 5.00
30 Vernon Wells 5.00

2000 Pacific Invincible

The base set consists of 150 cards. The player image is on an acetate stock with a blue sky background. The rest of the card is on standard UV coated stock and has the player name stamped in gold foil.

NM/M
Complete Set (150): 75.00
Common Player: .25
Pack (3): 2.00
Box (36): 50.00
1 Darin Erstad .50
2 Troy Glaus 1.50
3 Ramon Ortiz .25
4 Tim Salmon .35
5 Mo Vaughn .25
6 Erubiel Durazo .25
7 Luis Gonzalez .35
8 Randy Johnson 1.50
9 Matt Williams .25
10 Rafael Furcal .25
11 Andres Galarraga .25
12 Tom Glavine .40
13 Andruw Jones 1.50
14 Chipper Jones 2.00
15 Greg Maddux 2.00
16 Kevin Millwood .25
17 Albert Belle .25
18 Will Clark .35
19 Mike Mussina .40
20 Matt Riley .25
21 Cal Ripken Jr. 4.00
22 Carl Everett .25
23 Nomar Garciaparra 2.50
24 Steve Lomasney .25
25 Pedro Martinez 1.50
26 Tomo Ohka **RC** .75
27 Wilton Veras .25
28 Mark Grace .35
29 Sammy Sosa 2.50
30 Kerry Wood .75
31 Eric Young .25
32 Julio Zuleta **RC** .25
33 Paul Konerko .35
34 Carlos Lee .25
35 Magglio Ordonez .35
36 Josh Paul .25
37 Frank Thomas 1.50
38 Rob Bell .25
39 Dante Bichette .25
40 Sean Casey .35
41 Ken Griffey Jr. 2.50
42 Barry Larkin .25
43 Pokey Reese .25
44 Roberto Alomar .40
45 Manny Ramirez 1.50
46 Richie Sexson .25
47 Jim Thome 1.50
48 Omar Vizquel .25
49 Jeff Cirillo .25
50 Todd Helton 1.50
51 Neifi Perez .25
52 Larry Walker .25
53 Tony Clark .25
54 Juan Encarnacion .25
55 Juan Gonzalez 1.50
56 Hideo Nomo 1.00
57 Luis Castillo .25
58 Alex Gonzalez .25
59 Brad Penny .25
60 Preston Wilson .25
61 Moises Alou .25
62 Jeff Bagwell 1.50
63 Lance Berkman .25
64 Craig Biggio .25
65 Roger Cedeno .25
66 Jose Lima .25
67 Carlos Beltran .50
68 Johnny Damon .35
69 Chad Durbin **RC** .50
70 Jermaine Dye .25
71 Carlos Febles .25
72 Mark Quinn .25
73 Kevin Brown .25
74 Eric Gagne .25
75 Shawn Green .50
76 Eric Karros .25
77 Gary Sheffield .40
78 Kevin Barker .25
79 Ron Belliard .25
80 Jeromy Burnitz .25
81 Geoff Jenkins .25
82 Jacque Jones .25
83 Corey Koskie .25
84 Matt LeCroy .25
85 David Ortiz .35
86 Johan Santana **RC** 20.00
87 Todd Walker .25
88 Peter Bergeron .25
89 Vladimir Guerrero 1.50
90 Jose Vidro .25
91 Rondell White .25
92 Edgardo Alfonzo .25
93 Derek Bell .25
94 Mike Hampton .25
95 Rey Ordonez .25
96 Mike Piazza 2.50
97 Robin Ventura .25
98 Roger Clemens 2.25
99 Orlando Hernandez .25
100 Derek Jeter 4.00
101 Alfonso Soriano .75
102 Bernie Williams .35
103 Eric Chavez .40
104 Jason Giambi .75
105 Ben Grieve .25
106 Tim Hudson .40
107 Miguel Tejada .40
108 Bobby Abreu .25
109 Doug Glanville .25
110 Mike Lieberthal .25
111 Scott Rolen .75
112 Brian Giles .25
113 Chad Hermansen .25
114 Jason Kendall .25
115 Warren Morris .25
116 Aramis Ramirez .25
117 Rick Ankiel .25
118 J.D. Drew .40
119 Mark McGwire 3.00
120 Fernando Tatis .25
121 Fernando Vina .25
122 Bret Boone .25
123 Ben Davis .25
124 Tony Gwynn 2.00
125 Trevor Hoffman .25
126 Ryan Klesko .25
127 Rich Aurilia .25
128 Barry Bonds 4.00
129 Ellis Burks .25
130 Jeff Kent .25
131 Freddy Garcia .25
132 Carlos Guillen .25
133 Edgar Martinez .25
134 John Olerud .25
135 Robert Ramsay .25
136 Alex Rodriguez 3.00
137 Kazuhiro Sasaki **RC** 3.00
138 Jose Canseco .50
139 Vinny Castilla .25
140 Fred McGriff .25
141 Greg Vaughn (Front photo is Mo Vaughn.) .25
142 Dan Wheeler .25
143 Gabe Kapler .25
144 Ruben Mateo .25
145 Rafael Palmeiro .75
146 Ivan Rodriguez .75
147 Tony Batista .25
148 Carlos Delgado .65
149 Raul Mondesi .25
150 Vernon Wells .25

Holographic Purple

A parallel to the 150-card set, holographic purple stamping replaces the gold foil from the base cards. These are limited to 299 serial numbered sets.

Stars: 2-3X
Production 299 Sets

Platinum Blue

A parallel to the 150-card base set these differ only from the regular cards in that blue foil stamping replaces gold. Each card is also serially numbered on the card front in an edition of 67 sets.

Stars: 4-8X
Production 67 Sets

Diamond Aces

This insert set highlights the top pitchers in the game. Silver-foil stamping is used on the card fronts, which are designed to duplicate the look of an Ace in a deck of of playing cards. These were seeded 1 per pack. A parallel limited to 399 serial numbered sets is also randomly seeded.

NM/M
Complete Set (20): 5.00
Common Player: .25
Inserted 1:1
Edition of 399 Parallel: 2-3X
1 Randy Johnson .75
2 Greg Maddux 1.00
3 Tom Glavine .40
4 John Smoltz .25
5 Mike Mussina .50
6 Pedro Martinez .75
7 Kerry Wood .60
8 Bartolo Colon .25
9 Brad Penny .25
10 Billy Wagner .25
11 Kevin Brown .25
12 Mike Hampton .25
13 Roger Clemens 1.50
14 David Cone .25
15 Orlando Hernandez .25
16 Mariano Rivera .40
17 Tim Hudson .40
18 Trevor Hoffman .25
19 Rick Ankiel .25
20 Freddy Garcia .25

Eyes of the World

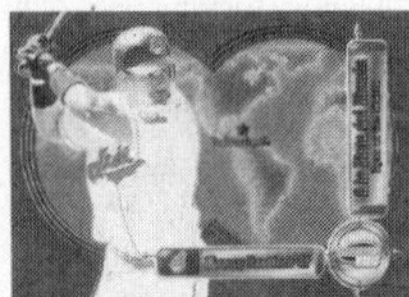

This 20-card set has a horizontal format with gold foil stamping. The background of the player photo has a partial globe with a star and the country the featured player is from stamped in gold foil. These were inserted 1:25 packs.

NM/M
Complete Set (20): 30.00
Common Player: .75
Inserted 1:25
1 Erubiel Durazo .75
2 Andruw Jones 2.00
3 Cal Ripken Jr. 6.00
4 Nomar Garciaparra 4.00
5 Pedro Martinez 2.00
6 Sammy Sosa 4.00
7 Ken Griffey Jr. 4.00
8 Manny Ramirez 2.00
9 Larry Walker .75
10 Juan Gonzalez 2.00
11 Carlos Beltran 1.25
12 Vladimir Guerrero 2.00
13 Orlando Hernandez .75
14 Derek Jeter 6.00
15 Mark McGwire 5.00
16 Tony Gwynn 3.00
17 Freddy Garcia .75
18 Alex Rodriguez 5.00
19 Jose Canseco 1.25
20 Ivan Rodriguez 1.50

Game Gear

NM/M
Common Card: 4.00
1 Jeff Bagwell/Jsy/1,000 8.00
2 Tom Glavine/Jsy/1,000 6.00
3 Mark Grace/Jsy/1,000 8.00
4 Eric Karros/Jsy/1,000 4.00
5 Edgar Martinez/Jsy/800 6.00
6 Manny Ramirez/Jsy/975 8.00
7 Cal Ripken Jr./Jsy/1,000 25.00
8 Alex Rodriguez/Jsy/900 15.00
9 Ivan Rodriguez/Jsy/675 6.00
10 Mo Vaughn Jsy/1000 4.00
11 Edgar Martinez/Dat-Jsy/200 8.00
12 Manny Ramirez/Jsy/145 15.00
13 Alex Rodriguez/Bat-Jsy/200 25.00
14 Ivan Rodriguez/Bat-Jsy/200 10.00
15 Edgar Martinez/Bat/200 10.00
16 Manny Ramirez/Bat/200 15.00
17 Ivan Rodriguez/Bat/200 8.00
18 Alex Rodriguez/Bat/200 20.00
19 Jeff Bagwell/Patch/125 30.00
20 Tom Glavine/Patch/110 25.00
21 Mark Grace/Patch/125 25.00
22 Tony Gwynn/Patch/65 40.00
23 Chipper Jones/Patch/80 40.00
24 Eric Karros/Patch/125 15.00
25 Greg Maddux/Patch/80 50.00
26 Edgar Martinez/Patch/125 20.00
27 Manny Ramirez/Patch/125 30.00
28 Cal Ripken Jr./Patch/125 65.00
29 Alex Rodriguez/Patch/125 50.00
30 Ivan Rodriguez/Patch/125 25.00
31 Frank Thomas/Patch/125 25.00
32 Mo Vaughn/Patch/125 15.00

Kings of the Diamond

Twenty of the top hitters in the game are featured on a design intended to duplicate the look of a King card in a playing deck of cards. These were seeded one per pack. A parallel version limited to 299 serial numbered sets is also randomly seeded.

NM/M
Complete Set (30): 10.00
Common Player: .20
Inserted 1:1
1 Mo Vaughn .20
2 Erubiel Durazo .20

3 Andruw Jones .65
4 Chipper Jones .75
5 Cal Ripken Jr. 1.50
6 Nomar Garciaparra 1.00
7 Sammy Sosa 1.00
8 Frank Thomas .65
9 Sean Casey .25
10 Ken Griffey Jr. 1.00
11 Manny Ramirez .65
12 Larry Walker .20
13 Juan Gonzalez .65
14 Jeff Bagwell .65
15 Craig Biggio .20
16 Carlos Beltran .50
17 Shawn Green .35
18 Vladimir Guerrero .65
19 Mike Piazza 1.00
20 Derek Jeter 1.50
21 Bernie Williams .40
22 Ben Grieve .20
23 Scott Rolen .40
24 Mark McGwire 1.25
25 Tony Gwynn .75
26 Barry Bonds 1.50
27 Alex Rodriguez 1.25
28 Jose Canseco .25
29 Rafael Palmeiro .50
30 Ivan Rodriguez .50

Lighting The Fire

These full-foiled inserts are die-cut in the shape of a flame, with an image of a baseball at the core of the fiery image. These were inserted 1:49 packs.

NM/M
Complete Set (20): 120.00
Common Player: 3.00
Inserted 1:49
1 Chipper Jones 8.00
2 Greg Maddux 8.00
3 Cal Ripken Jr. 15.00
4 Nomar Garciaparra 10.00
5 Pedro Martinez 6.00
6 Ken Griffey Jr. 10.00
7 Sammy Sosa 10.00
8 Manny Ramirez 6.00
9 Juan Gonzalez 6.00
10 Jeff Bagwell 6.00
11 Shawn Green 3.00
12 Vladimir Guerrero 6.00
13 Mike Piazza 10.00
14 Roger Clemens 9.00
15 Derek Jeter 15.00
16 Mark McGwire 12.00
17 Tony Gwynn 8.00
18 Alex Rodriguez 12.00
19 Jose Canseco 3.00
20 Ivan Rodriguez 5.00

Ticket To Stardom

These unique cards have a design intended to replicate a ticket stub. Two images of the featured player are on the front, the bigger primary photo is vertical, while the smaller photo is horizontal. Silver foil stamping is used throughout. These are found 1:121 packs.

NM/M
Complete Set (20): 250.00
Common Player: 5.00
Inserted 1:121
1 Andruw Jones 10.00
2 Chipper Jones 15.00

3 Cal Ripken Jr. 30.00
4 Nomar Garciaparra 20.00
5 Pedro Martinez 10.00
6 Ken Griffey Jr. 20.00
7 Sammy Sosa 20.00
8 Manny Ramirez 10.00
9 Jeff Bagwell 10.00
10 Shawn Green 5.00
11 Vladimir Guerrero 10.00
12 Mike Piazza 20.00
13 Derek Jeter 30.00
14 Alfonso Soriano 8.00
15 Scott Rolen 6.00
16 Rick Ankiel 5.00
17 Mark McGwire 25.00
18 Tony Gwynn 15.00
19 Alex Rodriguez 25.00
20 Ivan Rodriguez 8.00

Wild Vinyl

This scarce 10-card insert set is serial numbered on the card front, limited to only 10 sets.

Complete Set (10):
Common Player:
Production 10 Sets

2000 Pacific Omega

NM/M
Complete Set (255): 300.00
Common Player: .10
Common (151-255): 4.00
Production 999 Sets
1 Garret Anderson .10
2 Darin Erstad .25
3 Troy Glaus .75
4 Tim Salmon .20
5 Mo Vaughn .10
6 Jay Bell .10
7 Steve Finley .10
8 Luis Gonzalez .20
9 Randy Johnson .75
10 Matt Williams .10
11 Andres Galarraga .10
12 Andruw Jones .75
13 Chipper Jones 1.00
14 Brian Jordan .10
15 Greg Maddux 1.00
16 B.J. Surhoff .10
17 Brady Anderson .10
18 Albert Belle .10
19 Mike Mussina .40
20 Cal Ripken Jr. 2.50
21 Carl Everett .10
22 Nomar Garciaparra 1.50
23 Pedro Martinez .75
24 Jason Varitek .10
25 Mark Grace .20
26 Sammy Sosa 1.50
27 Rondell White .10
28 Kerry Wood .35
29 Eric Young .10
30 Ray Durham .10
31 Carlos Lee .10
32 Magglio Ordonez .25
33 Frank Thomas .75
34 Sean Casey .20
35 Ken Griffey Jr. 1.50
36 Barry Larkin .10
37 Pokey Reese .10
38 Roberto Alomar .40
39 Kenny Lofton .10
40 Manny Ramirez .75
41 David Segui .10
42 Jim Thome .60
43 Omar Vizquel .10
44 Jeff Cirillo .10
45 Jeffrey Hammonds .10
46 Todd Helton .75
47 Todd Hollandsworth .10
48 Larry Walker .10
49 Tony Clark .10
50 Juan Encarnacion .10
51 Juan Gonzalez .75
52 Bobby Higginson .10
53 Hideo Nomo .75
54 Dean Palmer .10
55 Luis Castillo .10
56 Cliff Floyd .10
57 Derrek Lee .10
58 Mike Lowell .10
59 Henry Rodriguez .10
60 Preston Wilson .10
61 Moises Alou .10
62 Jeff Bagwell .75
63 Craig Biggio .10
64 Ken Caminiti .10
65 Richard Hidalgo .10
66 Carlos Beltran .40
67 Johnny Damon .25
68 Jermaine Dye .10
69 Joe Randa .10
70 Mike Sweeney .10
71 Adrian Beltre .20
72 Kevin Brown .10
73 Shawn Green .35
74 Eric Karros .10
75 Chan Ho Park .10
76 Gary Sheffield .30
77 Ron Belliard .10
78 Jeromy Burnitz .10
79 Geoff Jenkins .10
80 Richie Sexson .10
81 Ron Coomer .10
82 Jacque Jones .10
83 Corey Koskie .10
84 Matt Lawton .10
85 Vladimir Guerrero .75
86 Lee Stevens .10
87 Jose Vidro .10
88 Edgardo Alfonzo .10
89 Derek Bell .10
90 Mike Bordick .10
91 Mike Piazza 1.50
92 Robin Ventura .10
93 Jose Canseco .40
94 Roger Clemens 1.25
95 Orlando Hernandez .10
96 Derek Jeter 2.50
97 David Justice .10
98 Tino Martinez .10
99 Jorge Posada .10
100 Bernie Williams .40
101 Eric Chavez .20
102 Jason Giambi .50
103 Ben Grieve .10
104 Miguel Tejada .25
105 Bobby Abreu .10
106 Doug Glanville .10
107 Travis Lee .10
108 Mike Lieberthal .10
109 Scott Rolen .65
110 Brian S. Giles .10
111 Jason Kendall .10
112 Warren Morris .10
113 Kevin Young .10
114 Will Clark .20
115 J.D. Drew .20
116 Jim Edmonds .10
117 Mark McGwire 2.00
118 Edgar Renteria .10
119 Fernando Tatis .10
120 Fernando Vina .10
121 Bret Boone .10
122 Tony Gwynn 1.00
123 Trevor Hoffman .10
124 Phil Nevin .10
125 Eric Owens .10
126 Barry Bonds 2.50
127 Ellis Burks .10
128 Jeff Kent .10
129 J.T. Snow .10
130 Jay Buhner .10
131 Mike Cameron .10
132 Rickey Henderson .75
133 Edgar Martinez .10
134 John Olerud .10
135 Alex Rodriguez 2.00
136 Kazuhiro Sasaki **RC** 1.00
137 Fred McGriff .10
138 Greg Vaughn .10
139 Gerald Williams .10
140 Rusty Greer .10
141 Gabe Kapler .10
142 Ricky Ledee .10
143 Rafael Palmeiro .65
144 Ivan Rodriguez .65
145 Tony Batista .10
146 Jose Cruz Jr. .10
147 Carlos Delgado .50
148 Brad Fullmer .10
149 Shannon Stewart .10
150 David Wells .10
151 Juan Alvarez, Jeff DaVanon 6.00
152 Seth Etherton, Adam Kennedy 4.00
153 Ramon Ortiz, Lou Pote 4.00
154 Derrick Turnbow **RC**, Eric Weaver 4.00
155 Rod Barajas, Jason Conti 4.00
156 Byung-Hyun Kim, Rob Ryan 4.00
157 David Cortes, George Lombard 4.00
158 Ivanon Coffie, Melvin Mora 4.00
159 Ryan Kohlmeier **RC**, Luis Matos **RC** 6.00
160 Willie Morales, John Parrish **RC** 4.00
161 Chris Richard **RC**, Jay Spurgeon **RC** 5.00
162 Israel Alcantara, Tomokazu Ohka **RC** 5.00
163 Paxton Crawford **RC**, Sang-Hoon Lee **RC** 4.00
164 Mike Mahoney **RC**, Wilton Veras 4.00
165 Daniel Garibay **RC**, Ross Gload **RC** 4.00
166 Gary Matthews Jr., Phil Norton 4.00
167 Roosevelt Brown, Ruben Quevedo 4.00
168 Lorenzo Barcelo **RC**, Rocky Biddle **RC** 4.00
169 Mark Buehrle **RC**, John Garland 8.00
170 Aaron Myette, Josh Paul 4.00
171 Kip Wells, Kelly Wunsch 4.00
172 Rob Bell, Travis Dawkins 4.00
173 Hector Mercado **RC**, John Riedling **RC** 4.00
174 Russell Branyan, Sean DePaula 4.00
175 Tim Drew, Mark Watson 4.00
176 Craig House **RC**, Ben Petrick 5.00
177 Robert Fick, Jose Macias 4.00
178 Javier Cardona **RC**, Brandon Villafuerte 4.00
179 Armando Almanza, A.J. Burnett 4.00
180 Ramon Castro, Pablo Ozuna 4.00
181 Lance Berkman, Jason Green 4.00
182 Julio Lugo, Tony McKnight 4.00
183 Mitch Meluskey, Wade Miller 4.00
184 Chad Durbin **RC**, Hector Ortiz **RC** 5.00
185 Dermal Brown, Mark Quinn 4.00
186 Eric Gagne, Mike Judd 4.00
187 Kane Davis **RC**, Valerio de los Santos 4.00
188 Santiago Perez, Paul Rigdon **RC** 4.00
189 Matt Kinney, Matt LeCroy 4.00
190 Jason Maxwell, A.J. Pierzynski 4.00
191 J.C. Romero **RC**, Johan Santana **RC** 50.00
192 Tony Armas Jr., Peter Bergeron 4.00
193 Matt Blank, Milton Bradley 4.00
194 Tomas De La Rossa, Scott Forster 4.00
195 Yovanny Lara **RC**, Talmadge Nunnari **RC** 4.00
196 Brian Schneider, Andy Tracy 4.00
197 Scott Strickland, T.J. Tucker 4.00
198 Eric Cammack, Jim Mann **RC** 4.00
199 Grant Roberts, Jorge Toca 4.00
200 Alfonso Soriano, Jay Tessmer 8.00
201 Terrence Long, Mark Mulder 4.00
202 Pat Burrell, Cliff Politte 4.00
203 Jimmy Anderson, Bronson Arroyo 4.00
204 Mike Darr, Kory DeHaan 4.00
205 Adam Eaton, Wiki Gonzalez 4.00
206 Brandon Kolb **RC**, Kevin Walker 4.00
207 Damon Minor, Calvin Murray 4.00
208 Kevin Hodges, Joel Pineiro **RC** 40.00
209 Rob Ramsay **RC**, Kazuhiro Sasaki **RC** 8.00

#	Player	NM/M
210	Rick Ankiel, Mike Matthews	4.00
211	Steve Cox, Travis Harper	4.00
212	Kenny Kelly **RC**, Damian Rolls **RC**	4.00
213	Doug Davis, Scott Sheldon	4.00
214	Brian Sikorski, Pedro Valdes	4.00
215	Francisco Cordero, B.J. Waszgis	4.00
216	Matt DeWitt, Josh Phelps **RC**	8.00
217	Vernon Wells, Dewayne Wise	4.00
218	Geraldo Guzman **RC**, Jason Marquis	4.00
219	Rafael Furcal, Steve Sisco **RC**	4.00
220	B.J. Ryan, Kevin Beirne	4.00
221	Matt Ginter **RC**, Brad Penny	4.00
222	Julio Zuleta **RC**, Eric Munson	5.00
223	Dan Reichert, Jeff Williams	4.00
224	Jason LaRue, Danny Ardoin	4.00
225	Ray King, Mark Redman	4.00
226	Joe Crede, Mike Bell	4.00
227	Juan Pierre **RC**, Jay Payton	6.00
228	Wayne Franklin, Randy Choate **RC**	4.00
229	Chris Truby, Adam Piatt	4.00
230	Kevin Nicholson, Chris Woodward	4.00
231	Barry Zito **RC**, Jason Boyd	15.00
232	Brian O'Connor **RC**, Miguel Del Toro	4.00
233	Carlos Guillen, Aubrey Huff	4.00
234	Chad Hermansen, Jason Tyner	4.00
235	Aaron Fultz, Ryan Vogelsong	4.00
236	Shawn Wooten, Vance Wilson	4.00
237	Danny Klassen, Mike Lamb **RC**	4.00
238	Chad Bradford, Gene Stechschulte **RC**	4.00
239	Ismael Villegas, Hector Ramirez, Matt T. Williams, Luis Vizcaino	4.00
240	Mike Garcia, Domingo Guzman, Justin Brunette **RC**, Pasqual Coco **RC**	4.00
241	Frank Charles, Keith McDonald **RC**	4.00
242	Carlos Casimiro **RC**, Morgan Burkhart **RC**	4.00
243	Raul Gonzalez **RC**, Shawn Gilbert	4.00
244	Darrell Einertson, Jeff Sparks **RC**	4.00
245	Augie Ojeda **RC**, Brady Clark, Todd Belitz, Eric Byrnes **RC**	6.00
246	Leo Estrella **RC**, Charlie Greene	4.00
247	Trace Coquillette, Pedro Feliz **RC**	6.00
248	Tike Redman **RC**, David Newhan	4.00
249	Rodrigo Lopez **RC**, John Bales	6.00
250	Corey Patterson, Jose Ortiz **RC**	6.00
251	Britt Reames **RC**, Oswaldo Mairena **RC**	4.00
252	Xavier Nady **RC**, Timoniel Perez **RC**	6.00
253	Tom Jacquez, Vicente Padilla	4.00
254	Elvis Pena **RC**, Adam Melhuse **RC**	4.00
255	Ben Weber, Alex Cabrera **RC**	6.00

Copper

Stars (1-150): 8-15X
Production 45 Sets

Gold

Stars (1-150): 4-8X
Production 120 Sets

Platinum Blue

Stars (1-150): 6-10X
Production 55 Sets

Premiere Date

Stars (1-150): 4-8X
Production 77 Sets

AL Contenders

		NM/M
Complete Set (18):		20.00
Common Player:		.50
Inserted 2:37		
1	Darin Erstad	.75
2	Troy Glaus	1.50
3	Mo Vaughn	.50
4	Albert Belle	.50
5	Cal Ripken Jr.	4.00
6	Nomar Garciaparra	3.00
7	Pedro Martinez	1.50
8	Frank Thomas	1.50
9	Manny Ramirez	1.50
10	Jim Thome	1.25
11	Juan Gonzalez	1.50
12	Roger Clemens	2.50
13	Derek Jeter	4.00
14	Bernie Williams	.75
15	Jason Giambi	1.00
16	Alex Rodriguez	3.50
17	Edgar Martinez	.50
18	Carlos Delgado	1.00

EO Portraits

		NM/M
Complete Set (20):		125.00
Common Player:		3.00
Inserted 1:73		
1-of-1 Die-Cut Parallels Exist		
1	Chipper Jones	8.00
2	Greg Maddux	8.00
3	Cal Ripken Jr.	15.00
4	Pedro Martinez	6.00
5	Nomar Garciaparra	10.00
6	Sammy Sosa	10.00
7	Frank Thomas	6.00
8	Ken Griffey Jr.	10.00
9	Gary Sheffield	4.00
10	Vladimir Guerrero	6.00
11	Mike Piazza	10.00
12	Roger Clemens	9.00
13	Derek Jeter	15.00
14	Pat Burrell	4.00
15	Tony Gwynn	8.00
16	Barry Bonds	15.00
17	Alex Rodriguez	12.00
18	Rick Ankiel	3.00
19	Mark McGwire	12.00
20	Ivan Rodriguez	5.00

Full Count

		NM/M
Complete Set (36):		30.00
Common Player:		.50
Inserted 4:37 H		
1	Magglio Ordonez	.50
2	Manny Ramirez	1.50
3	Todd Helton	1.50
4	David Justice	.50
5	Bernie Williams	.50
6	Jason Giambi	1.00
7	Scott Rolen	1.00
8	Jeff Kent	.50
9	Edgar Martinez	.50
10	Randy Johnson	1.50
11	Greg Maddux	2.00
12	Mike Mussina	.60
13	Pedro Martinez	1.50
14	Chuck Finley	.50
15	Kevin Brown	.50
16	Roger Clemens	2.25
17	Tim Hudson	.50
18	Rick Ankiel	.50
19	Troy Glaus	1.50
20	Chipper Jones	2.00
21	Nomar Garciaparra	2.50
22	Jeff Bagwell	1.50
23	Shawn Green	.60
24	Vladimir Guerrero	1.50
25	Mike Piazza	2.50
26	Jim Edmonds	.50
27	Rafael Palmeiro	.75
28	Cal Ripken Jr.	4.00
29	Sammy Sosa	2.50
30	Frank Thomas	1.50
31	Ken Griffey Jr.	2.50
32	Gary Sheffield	.50
33	Barry Bonds	4.00
34	Alex Rodriguez	3.00
35	Mark McGwire	3.00
36	Carlos Delgado	1.00

MLB Generations

		NM/M
Complete Set (20):		100.00
Common Card:		3.00
Inserted 1:145		
1	Mark McGwire, Pat Burrell	12.00
2	Cal Ripken Jr., Alex Rodriguez	15.00
3	Randy Johnson, Rick Ankiel	6.00
4	Tony Gwynn, Darin Erstad	8.00
5	Barry Bonds, Magglio Ordonez	15.00
6	Frank Thomas, Jason Giambi	6.00
7	Roger Clemens, Kerry Wood	10.00
8	Mike Piazza, Mitch Meluskey	10.00
9	Ken Griffey Jr., Andruw Jones	10.00
10	Bernie Williams, J.D. Drew	4.00
11	Chipper Jones, Troy Glaus	8.00
12	Andres Galarraga, Todd Helton	6.00
13	Juan Gonzalez, Vladimir Guerrero	6.00
14	Craig Biggio, Rafael Furcal	3.00
15	Sammy Sosa, Jermaine Dye	10.00
16	Larry Walker, Richard Hidalgo	3.00
17	Greg Maddux, Adam Eaton	8.00
18	Barry Larkin, Derek Jeter	15.00
19	Roberto Alomar, Jose Vidro	4.00
20	Jeff Kent, Edgardo Alfonzo	3.00

NL Contenders

		NM/M
Complete Set (18):		20.00
Common Player:		.50
Inserted 2:37		
1	Randy Johnson	1.50
2	Chipper Jones	2.00
3	Greg Maddux	2.00
4	Sammy Sosa	2.50
5	Sean Casey	.50
6	Ken Griffey Jr.	2.50
7	Todd Helton	1.50
8	Jeff Bagwell	1.50
9	Shawn Green	.50
10	Gary Sheffield	.75
11	Vladimir Guerrero	1.50
12	Mike Piazza	2.50
13	Scott Rolen	1.00
14	Barry Bonds	4.00
15	Rick Ankiel	.50
16	J.D. Drew	.50
17	Jim Edmonds	.50
18	Mark McGwire	3.00

Signatures

		NM/M
Common Player:		5.00
1	Darin Erstad	10.00
2	Nomar Garciaparra	125.00
3	Cal Eldred	5.00
4	Magglio Ordonez	10.00
5	Frank Thomas	30.00
6	Brady Clark	5.00
7	Richard Hidalgo	5.00
8	Gary Sheffield	10.00
9	Pat Burrell	15.00
10	Jim Edmonds	10.00

Stellar Performers

		NM/M
Complete Set (20):		50.00
Common Player:		1.00
Inserted 1:37		
1	Darin Erstad	1.00
2	Chipper Jones	3.00
3	Greg Maddux	3.00
4	Cal Ripken Jr.	6.00
5	Pedro Martinez	2.00
6	Nomar Garciaparra	4.00
7	Sammy Sosa	4.00
8	Frank Thomas	2.00
9	Ken Griffey Jr.	4.00
10	Todd Helton	2.00
11	Jeff Bagwell	2.00
12	Vladimir Guerrero	2.00
13	Mike Piazza	4.00
14	Derek Jeter	6.00
15	Roger Clemens	3.50
16	Tony Gwynn	3.00
17	Barry Bonds	6.00
18	Alex Rodriguez	5.00
19	Mark McGwire	5.00
20	Ivan Rodriguez	1.50

Opening Day 2K

As part of a multi-manufacturer promotion, Pacific issued eight cards of an "Opening Day 2K" set. Packages containing some of the 32 cards in the issue were distributed by MLB teams early in the season. The cards were also available exclusively as inserts in Pacific Crown Collection and Pacific Aurora packs sold at K-Mart stores early in the season. The Pacific OD2K cards have gold-foil graphic highlights on front. Backs have a portrait photo and are numbered with an "OD" prefix.

		NM/M
Complete Set (8):		4.00
Common Player:		.50
25	Mo Vaughn	.50
26	Chipper Jones	1.00
27	Nomar Garciaparra	1.00
28	Larry Walker	.65
29	Corey Koskie	.50
30	Scott Rolen	.75
31	Tony Gwynn	1.00
32	Jose Canseco	.65

2000 Pacific Paramount Sample

Nearly identical to the issued version of spokesman Tony Gwynn's card, this features a large white diagonal "SAMPLE" overprint on back and in the space where a card number usually appears.

	NM/M
Tony Gwynn	3.00

2000 Pacific Paramount

		NM/M
Complete Set (250):		25.00
Common Player:		.10
Pack (6):		1.50
Wax Box (36):		40.00
1	Garret Anderson	.10
2	Jim Edmonds	.10
3	Darin Erstad	.25
4	Chuck Finley	.10
5	Troy Glaus	.75
6	Troy Percival	.10
7	Tim Salmon	.20
8	Mo Vaughn	.10
9	Jay Bell	.10
10	Erubiel Durazo	.10
11	Steve Finley	.10
12	Luis Gonzalez	.20
13	Randy Johnson	.75
14	Travis Lee	.10
15	Matt Mantei	.10
16	Matt Williams	.10
17	Tony Womack	.10
18	Bret Boone	.10
19	Tom Glavine	.35
20	Andruw Jones	.75
21	Chipper Jones	1.00
22	Brian Jordan	.10
23	Javy Lopez	.10
24	Greg Maddux	1.00
25	Kevin Millwood	.10
26	John Rocker	.10
27	John Smoltz	.10
28	Brady Anderson	.10
29	Albert Belle	.10
30	Will Clark	.20
31	Charles Johnson	.10
32	Mike Mussina	.35
33	Cal Ripken Jr.	2.00
34	B.J. Surhoff	.10
35	Nomar Garciaparra	1.25
36	Derek Lowe	.10
37	Pedro Martinez	.75
38	Trot Nixon	.10
39	Troy O'Leary	.10
40	Jose Offerman	.10
41	John Valentin	.10
42	Jason Varitek	.10
43	Mark Grace	.20
44	Glenallen Hill	.10
45	Jon Lieber	.10
46	Cole Liniak	.10
47	Jose Nieves	.10
48	Henry Rodriguez	.10
49	Sammy Sosa	1.25
50	Kerry Wood	.65
51	Jason Dellaero	.10
52	Ray Durham	.10
53	Paul Konerko	.10
54	Carlos Lee	.10
55	Greg Norton	.10
56	Magglio Ordonez	.10
57	Chris Singleton	.10
58	Frank Thomas	.75
59	Aaron Boone	.10
60	Mike Cameron	.10
61	Sean Casey	.20
62	Pete Harnisch	.10
63	Barry Larkin	.10
64	Pokey Reese	.10
65	Greg Vaughn	.10
66	Scott Williamson	.10
67	Roberto Alomar	.35
68	Sean DePaula **RC**	.20
69	Travis Fryman	.10
70	David Justice	.10
71	Kenny Lofton	.10
72	Manny Ramirez	.75
73	Richie Sexson	.10
74	Jim Thome	.65
75	Omar Vizquel	.10
76	Pedro Astacio	.10
77	Vinny Castilla	.10
78	Derrick Gibson	.10
79	Todd Helton	.75
80	Neifi Perez	.10
81	Ben Petrick	.10
82	Larry Walker	.10
83	Brad Ausmus	.10
84	Tony Clark	.10
85	Deivi Cruz	.10
86	Damion Easley	.10
87	Juan Encarnacion	.10
88	Juan Gonzalez	.75
89	Bobby Higginson	.10
90	Dave Mlicki	.10
91	Dean Palmer	.10
92	Bruce Aven	.10
93	Luis Castillo	.10
94	Ramon Castro	.10
95	Cliff Floyd	.10
96	Alex Gonzalez	.10
97	Mike Lowell	.10
98	Preston Wilson	.10
99	Jeff Bagwell	.75
100	Derek Bell	.10
101	Craig Biggio	.10
102	Ken Caminiti	.10
103	Carl Everett	.10
104	Mike Hampton	.10
105	Jose Lima	.10
106	Billy Wagner	.10
107	Daryle Ward	.10
108	Carlos Beltran	.40
109	Johnny Damon	.25
110	Jermaine Dye	.10
111	Carlos Febles	.10
112	Mark Quinn	.10
113	Joe Randa	.10
114	Jose Rosado	.10
115	Mike Sweeney	.10
116	Kevin Brown	.10
117	Shawn Green	.35
118	Mark Grudzielanek	.10
119	Todd Hollandsworth	.10
120	Eric Karros	.10
121	Chan Ho Park	.10
122	Gary Sheffield	.35
123	Devon White	.10
124	Eric Young	.10
125	Kevin Barker	.10
126	Ron Belliard	.10
127	Jeromy Burnitz	.10
128	Jeff Cirillo	.10
129	Marquis Grissom	.10
130	Geoff Jenkins	.10
131	David Nilsson	.10
132	Chad Allen	.10
133	Ron Coomer	.10
134	Jacque Jones	.10
135	Corey Koskie	.10
136	Matt Lawton	.10
137	Brad Radke	.10
138	Todd Walker	.10
139	Michael Barrett	.10
140	Peter Bergeron	.10
141	Brad Fullmer	.10
142	Vladimir Guerrero	.75
143	Ugueth Urbina	.10
144	Jose Vidro	.10
145	Rondell White	.10

146 Edgardo Alfonzo .10
147 Armando Benitez .10
148 Roger Cedeno .10
149 Rickey Henderson .75
150 Melvin Mora .10
151 John Olerud .10
152 Rey Ordonez .10
153 Mike Piazza 1.25
154 Jorge Toca .10
155 Robin Ventura .10
156 Roger Clemens 1.00
157 David Cone .10
158 Orlando Hernandez .10
159 Derek Jeter 2.00
160 Chuck Knoblauch .10
161 Ricky Ledee .10
162 Tino Martinez .10
163 Paul O'Neill .10
164 Mariano Rivera .20
165 Alfonso Soriano .75
166 Bernie Williams .25
167 Eric Chavez .25
168 Jason Giambi .50
169 Ben Grieve .10
170 Tim Hudson .25
171 John Jaha .10
172 Matt Stairs .10
173 Miguel Tejada .25
174 Randy Velarde .10
175 Bobby Abreu .10
176 Marlon Anderson .10
177 Rico Brogna .10
178 Ron Gant .10
179 Doug Glanville .10
180 Mike Lieberthal .10
181 Scott Rolen .65
182 Curt Schilling .35
183 Brian Giles .10
184 Chad Hermansen .10
185 Jason Kendall .10
186 Al Martin .10
187 Pat Meares .10
188 Warren Morris .10
189 Ed Sprague .10
190 Kevin Young .10
191 Rick Ankiel .20
192 Kent Bottenfield .10
193 Eric Davis .10
194 J.D. Drew .25
195 Adam Kennedy .10
196 Ray Lankford .10
197 Joe McEwing .10
198 Mark McGwire 1.50
199 Edgar Renteria .10
200 Fernando Tatis .10
201 Mike Darr .10
202 Ben Davis .10
203 Tony Gwynn 1.00
204 Trevor Hoffman .10
205 Damian Jackson .10
206 Phil Nevin .10
207 Reggie Sanders .10
208 Quilvio Veras .10
209 Rich Aurilia .10
210 Marvin Benard .10
211 Barry Bonds 2.00
212 Ellis Burks .10
213 Livan Hernandez .10
214 Jeff Kent .10
215 Russ Ortiz .10
216 J.T. Snow .10
217 Paul Abbott .10
218 David Bell .10
219 Freddy Garcia .10
220 Ken Griffey Jr. 1.50
221 Carlos Guillen .10
222 Brian Hunter .10
223 Edgar Martinez .10
224 Jamie Moyer .10
225 Alex Rodriguez 1.50
226 Wade Boggs 1.00
227 Miguel Cairo .10
228 Jose Canseco .40
229 Roberto Hernandez .10
230 Dave Martinez .10
231 Quinton McCracken .10
232 Fred McGriff .10
233 Kevin Stocker .10
234 Royce Clayton .10
235 Rusty Greer .10
236 Ruben Mateo .10
237 Rafael Palmeiro .65
238 Ivan Rodriguez .65
239 Aaron Sele .10
240 John Wetteland .10
241 Todd Zeile .10
242 Tony Batista .10
243 Homer Bush .10
244 Carlos Delgado .50
245 Tony Fernandez .10
246 Billy Koch .10
247 Raul Mondesi .10
248 Shannon Stewart .10
249 David Wells .10
250 Vernon Wells .10

Copper

Stars: 2X
Inserted 1:1 H

Emerald

Stars: 1-2X
Yng Stars & RC's: 1X
Inserted 1:1 7-11 pack.

Gold

Inserted 1:1 R
Stars: 1-2X
Yng Stars & Rc's: 1X

Holographic Gold

Stars: 3-6X
Production 199 Sets

Holographic Green

Stars: 6-10X
Production 99 Sets, 7-11 insert.

Holographic Silver

Stars: 5-10X
Production 99 Sets

Platinum Blue

Stars: 6-12X
Production 67 Sets

Premiere Date

Stars: 8-15X
Production 50 Sets

Ruby Red

Stars: 1-2X
RC's: 1X
Inserted 9 per 7-11 pack.

Cooperstown Bound

NM/M
Complete Set (10): 220.00
Common Player: 20.00
Inserted 1:361
Proofs: 2X
Production 20 Sets, hobby only.
Canvas Proofs: Values Undetermined
Production One Set
1 Greg Maddux 20.00
2 Cal Ripken Jr. 40.00
3 Nomar Garciaparra 25.00
4 Sammy Sosa 25.00
5 Roger Clemens 30.00
6 Derek Jeter 40.00
7 Mark McGwire 30.00
8 Tony Gwynn 20.00
9 Ken Griffey Jr. 25.00
10 Alex Rodriguez 30.00

Double Vision

NM/M
Complete Set (36): 220.00
Common Player: 3.00
Inserted 1:37
1 Chipper Jones 8.00
2 Cal Ripken Jr. 15.00
3 Nomar Garciaparra 10.00
4 Pedro Martinez 6.00
5 Sammy Sosa 10.00
6 Manny Ramirez 6.00
7 Jeff Bagwell 6.00
8 Craig Biggio 3.00
9 Vladimir Guerrero 6.00
10 Mike Piazza 10.00
11 Roger Clemens 9.00
12 Derek Jeter 15.00
13 Mark McGwire 12.00
14 Tony Gwynn 8.00
15 Ken Griffey Jr. 10.00
16 Alex Rodriguez 12.00
17 Rafael Palmeiro 5.00
18 Ivan Rodriguez 5.00
19 Chipper Jones 8.00
20 Cal Ripken Jr. 15.00
21 Nomar Garciaparra 10.00
22 Pedro Martinez 6.00
23 Sammy Sosa 10.00
24 Manny Ramirez 6.00
25 Jeff Bagwell 6.00
26 Craig Biggio 3.00
27 Vladimir Guerrero 6.00
28 Mike Piazza 10.00
29 Roger Clemens 9.00
30 Derek Jeter 15.00
31 Mark McGwire 12.00
32 Tony Gwynn 8.00
33 Ken Griffey Jr. 10.00
34 Alex Rodriguez 12.00
35 Rafael Palmeiro 5.00
36 Ivan Rodriguez 5.00

Fielder's Choice

NM/M
Complete Set (20): 150.00
Common Player: 3.00
Inserted 1:73
Gold Parallel (10 Sets issued): 6-8X
1 Andruw Jones 5.00
2 Chipper Jones 8.00
3 Greg Maddux 8.00
4 Cal Ripken Jr. 20.00
5 Nomar Garciaparra 10.00
6 Sammy Sosa 10.00
7 Sean Casey 3.00
8 Manny Ramirez 5.00
9 Larry Walker 3.00
10 Jeff Bagwell 5.00
11 Mike Piazza 10.00
12 Derek Jeter 20.00
13 Bernie Williams 3.00
14 Scott Rolen 4.00
15 Mark McGwire 15.00
16 Tony Gwynn 8.00
17 Barry Bonds 20.00
18 Ken Griffey Jr. 10.00
19 Alex Rodriguez 15.00
20 Ivan Rodriguez 4.00

Maximum Impact

NM/M
Complete Set (20): 25.00
Common Player: .50
Inserted 2:25 7-11 packs.
1 Chipper Jones 2.00
2 Cal Ripken Jr. 4.00
3 Nomar Garciaparra 2.50
4 Pedro Martinez 1.50
5 Sammy Sosa 2.50
6 Manny Ramirez 1.50
7 Larry Walker .50
8 Jeff Bagwell 1.50
9 Carlos Beltran .75
10 Vladimir Guerrero 1.50
11 Mike Piazza 2.50
12 Derek Jeter 4.00
13 Roger Clemens 2.25
14 Mark McGwire 3.00
15 Tony Gwynn 2.00
16 Barry Bonds 4.00
17 Ken Griffey Jr. 2.50
18 Alex Rodriguez 3.00
19 Ivan Rodriguez 1.00
20 Carlos Delgado .75

Season in Review

NM/M
Complete Set (30): 25.00
Common Player: .50
Inserted 2:37
1 Randy Johnson 1.50
2 Matt Williams .50
3 Chipper Jones 2.00
4 Greg Maddux 2.00
5 Cal Ripken Jr. 4.00
6 Nomar Garciaparra 2.50
7 Pedro Martinez 1.50
8 Sammy Sosa 2.50
9 Manny Ramirez 1.50
10 Larry Walker .50
11 Jeff Bagwell 1.50
12 Craig Biggio .50
13 Carlos Beltran .75
14 Mark Quinn .50
15 Vladimir Guerrero 1.50
16 Mike Piazza 2.50
17 Robin Ventura .50
18 Roger Clemens 2.25
19 David Cone .50
20 Derek Jeter 4.00
21 Mark McGwire 3.00
22 Fernando Tatis .50
23 Tony Gwynn 2.00
24 Barry Bonds 4.00
25 Ken Griffey Jr. 2.50
26 Alex Rodriguez 3.00
27 Wade Boggs 2.00
28 Jose Canseco .65
29 Rafael Palmeiro 1.00
30 Ivan Rodriguez 1.00

Update

NM/M
Complete Set (100): 10.00
Common Player: .10
Production 12,500 Sets; retail exclusive
1-U Adam Kennedy .10
2-U Bengie Molina .10
3-U Derrick Turnbow .10
4-U Randy Johnson .75
5-U Danny Klassen .10
6-U Vicente Padilla .10
7-U Rafael Furcal .10
8-U Andres Galarraga .10
9-U Chipper Jones 1.00
10-U Fernando Lunar .10
11-U Willie Morales .10
12-U Cal Ripken Jr. 2.00
13-U B.J. Ryan .10
14-U Carl Everett .10
15-U Nomar Garciaparra 1.25
16-U Pedro Martinez .75
17-U Wilton Veras .10
18-U Scott Downs .10
19-U Daniel Garibay .10
20-U Sammy Sosa 1.25
21-U Julio Zuleta .10
22-U Josh Paul .10
23-U Frank Thomas .75
24-U Rob Bell .10
25-U Dante Bichette .10
26-U Travis Dawkins .10
27-U Ken Griffey Jr. 1.25
28-U Chuck Finley .10
29-U Manny Ramirez .75
30-U Paul Rigdon .10
31-U Jeff Cirillo .10
32-U Larry Walker .10
33-U Masato Yoshii .10
34-U Robert Fick .10
35-U Jose Macias .10
36-U Juan Gonzalez .75
37-U Hideo Nomo .75
38-U Jason Grilli .10
39-U Pablo Ozuna .10
40-U Brad Penny .10
41-U Jeff Bagwell .75
42-U Lance Berkman .10
43-U Roger Cedeno .10
44-U Octavio Dotel .10
45-U Chad Durbin .10
46-U Eric Gagne .10
47-U Shawn Green .35
48-U Jose Hernandez .10
49-U Matt LeCroy .10
50-U Johan Santana .10
51-U Vladimir Guerrero .75
52-U Hideki Irabu .10
53-U Andrew Tracy .10
54-U Derek Bell .10
55-U Eric Cammack .10
56-U Mike Hampton .10
57-U Jay Payton .10
58-U Mike Piazza 1.25
59-U Todd Zeile .10
60-U Roger Clemens 1.00
61-U Darrell Einertson .10
62-U Derek Jeter 2.00
63-U Jason Giambi .60
64-U Terrence Long .10
65-U Mark Mulder .10
66-U Adam Piatt .10
67-U Luis Vizcaino .10
68-U Pat Burrell .35
69-U Scott Rolen .65
70-U Chad Hermansen .10
71-U Rick Ankiel .15
72-U Jim Edmonds .10
73-U Mark McGwire 1.50
74-U Gene Stechschulte .10
75-U Fernando Vina .10
76-U Bret Boone .10
77-U Tony Gwynn 1.00
78-U Ryan Klesko .10
79-U David Newhan .10
80-U Kevin Walker .10
81-U Barry Bonds 2.00
82-U Aaron Fultz .10
83-U Ben Weber .10
84-U Rickey Henderson .75
85-U Kevin Hodges .10
86-U John Olerud .10
87-U Robert Ramsay .10
88-U Alex Rodriguez 1.50
89-U Kazuhiro Sasaki .15
90-U Vinny Castilla .10
91-U Jeff Sparks .10
92-U Greg Vaughn .10
93-U Francisco Cordero .10
94-U Gabe Kapler .10
95-U Mike Lamb .10
96-U Ivan Rodriguez .65
97-U Clayton Andrews .10
98-U Brad Fullmer .10
99-U Raul Mondesi .10
100-U Dewayne Wise .10

2000 Pacific Prism

NM/M
Complete Set (150): 10.00
Common Player: .10
Pack (5): 1.50
Wax Box (24): 15.00
1 Jeff DaVanon **RC** .50
2 Troy Glaus .50
3 Tim Salmon .15
4 Mo Vaughn .10
5 Jay Bell .10
6 Erubiel Durazo .10
7 Luis Gonzalez .20
8 Randy Johnson .50
9 Matt Williams .10
10 Andres Galarraga .10
11 Andruw Jones .50
12 Chipper Jones .65
13 Brian Jordan .10
14 Greg Maddux .65
15 Kevin Millwood .10
16 John Smoltz .10
17 Albert Belle .15
18 Mike Mussina .25
19 Calvin Pickering .10
20 Cal Ripken Jr. 1.50
21 B.J. Surhoff .10
22 Nomar Garciaparra 1.00
23 Pedro Martinez .50
24 Troy O'Leary .10
25 John Valentin .10
26 Jason Varitek .10
27 Mark Grace .15
28 Henry Rodriguez .10
29 Sammy Sosa 1.00
30 Kerry Wood .25
31 Ray Durham .10
32 Carlos Lee .10
33 Magglio Ordonez .10
34 Chris Singleton .10
35 Frank Thomas .50
36 Sean Casey .15
37 Travis Dawkins .10
38 Barry Larkin .10
39 Pokey Reese .10
40 Scott Williamson .10
41 Roberto Alomar .20
42 Bartolo Colon .10
43 David Justice .10
44 Manny Ramirez .50
45 Richie Sexson .10
46 Jim Thome .50
47 Omar Vizquel .10
48 Pedro Astacio .10
49 Todd Helton .50
50 Neifi Perez .10
51 Ben Petrick .10
52 Larry Walker .10
53 Tony Clark .10
54 Damion Easley .10
55 Juan Gonzalez .50
56 Dean Palmer .10
57 A.J. Burnett .10
58 Luis Castillo .10
59 Cliff Floyd .10
60 Alex Gonzalez .10
61 Preston Wilson .10
62 Jeff Bagwell .50
63 Craig Biggio .10
64 Ken Caminiti .10
65 Jose Lima .10
66 Billy Wagner .10
67 Carlos Beltran .30
68 Johnny Damon .25
69 Jermaine Dye .10
70 Carlos Febles .10
71 Mike Sweeney .10
72 Kevin Brown .10
73 Shawn Green .25
74 Eric Karros .10
75 Chan Ho Park .10
76 Gary Sheffield .30
77 Ron Belliard .10
78 Jeromy Burnitz .10
79 Marquis Grissom .10
80 Geoff Jenkins .10
81 Mark Loretta .10
82 Ron Coomer .10
83 Jacque Jones .10
84 Corey Koskie .10
85 Brad Radke .10
86 Todd Walker .10
87 Michael Barrett .10
88 Peter Bergeron .10
89 Vladimir Guerrero .50
90 Jose Vidro .10
91 Rondell White .10
92 Edgardo Alfonzo .10
93 Rickey Henderson .50
94 Rey Ordonez .10
95 Mike Piazza 1.00
96 Robin Ventura .10
97 Roger Clemens .75
98 Orlando Hernandez .10
99 Derek Jeter 1.50
100 Tino Martinez .10
101 Mariano Rivera .15
102 Alfonso Soriano .50
103 Bernie Williams .20
104 Eric Chavez .15
105 Jason Giambi .30
106 Ben Grieve .10
107 Tim Hudson .20
108 John Jaha .10
109 Bobby Abreu .10
110 Doug Glanville .10
111 Mike Lieberthal .10
112 Scott Rolen .40
113 Curt Schilling .25
114 Brian Giles .10
115 Jason Kendall .10
116 Warren Morris .10
117 Kevin Young .10
118 Rick Ankiel .10
119 J.D. Drew .15
120 Chad Hutchinson .10
121 Ray Lankford .10
122 Mark McGwire 1.25
123 Fernando Tatis .10
124 Bret Boone .10
125 Ben Davis .10
126 Tony Gwynn .65
127 Trevor Hoffman .10
128 Barry Bonds 1.50
129 Ellis Burks .10
130 Jeff Kent .10

#	Player	Price
131	J.T. Snow	.10
132	Freddy Garcia	.10
133	Ken Griffey Jr.	1.00
134	Edgar Martinez	.10
135	John Olerud	.10
136	Alex Rodriguez	1.25
137	Jose Canseco	.20
138	Vinny Castilla	.10
139	Roberto Hernandez	.10
140	Fred McGriff	.10
141	Rusty Greer	.10
142	Ruben Mateo	.10
143	Rafael Palmeiro	.40
144	Ivan Rodriguez	.40
145	Lee Stevens	.10
146	Tony Batista	.10
147	Carlos Delgado	.35
148	Shannon Stewart	.10
149	David Wells	.10
150	Vernon Wells	.10

Drops Silver

One of eight silver-foil parallels to Prism, this version features a raindrop-like patterned background. Inserted into both hobby and retail packaging, production was reported as 799 of 100 of the cards, and 916 of the other 50 cards (indicated with a (*) in the checklist. The cards are not serially numbered.

		NM/M
	Common Player:	.50
	Stars:	2-4X
1	Jeff DaVanon **RC**	.50
2	Troy Glaus	1.00
3	Tim Salmon	.60
4	Mo Vaughn (*)	.50
5	Jay Bell	.50
6	Erubiel Durazo	.50
7	Luis Gonzalez	.60
8	Randy Johnson (*)	1.00
9	Matt Williams (*)	.50
10	Andres Galarraga	.50
11	Andruw Jones (*)	1.00
12	Chipper Jones (*)	1.50
13	Brian Jordan	.50
14	Greg Maddux (*)	1.50
15	Kevin Millwood	.50
16	John Smoltz	.50
17	Albert Belle	.50
18	Mike Mussina (*)	.60
19	Calvin Pickering	.50
20	Cal Ripken Jr. (*)	3.00
21	B.J. Surhoff	.50
22	Nomar Garciaparra (*)	2.00
23	Pedro Martinez (*)	1.00
24	Troy O'Leary	.50
25	John Valentin	.50
26	Jason Varitek	.50
27	Mark Grace	.60
28	Henry Rodriguez	.50
29	Sammy Sosa (*)	2.00
30	Kerry Wood (*)	.65
31	Ray Durham	.50
32	Carlos Lee	.50
33	Magglio Ordonez (*)	.50
34	Chris Singleton	.50
35	Frank Thomas (*)	1.00
36	Sean Casey (*)	.50
37	Travis Dawkins	.50
38	Barry Larkin	.50
39	Pokey Reese	.50
40	Scott Williamson	.50
41	Roberto Alomar (*)	.60
42	Bartolo Colon	.50
43	David Justice	.50
44	Manny Ramirez (*)	1.00
45	Richie Sexson	.50
46	Jim Thome (*)	1.00
47	Omar Vizquel	.50
48	Pedro Astacio	.50
49	Todd Helton (*)	1.00
50	Neifi Perez	.50
51	Ben Petrick	.50
52	Larry Walker (*)	.50
53	Tony Clark	.50
54	Damion Easley	.50
55	Juan Gonzalez (*)	1.00
56	Dean Palmer	.50
57	A.J. Burnett	.50
58	Luis Castillo	.50
59	Cliff Floyd	.50
60	Alex Gonzalez	.50
61	Preston Wilson (*)	.50
62	Jeff Bagwell (*)	1.00
63	Craig Biggio (*)	.50
64	Ken Caminiti	.50
65	Jose Lima	.50
66	Billy Wagner	.50
67	Carlos Beltran (*)	.65
68	Johnny Damon	.65
69	Jermaine Dye	.50
70	Carlos Febles	.50
71	Mike Sweeney	.50
72	Kevin Brown (*)	.50
73	Shawn Green (*)	.75
74	Eric Karros	.50
75	Chan Ho Park	.50
76	Gary Sheffield (*)	.60
77	Ron Belliard	.50
78	Jeromy Burnitz (*)	.50
79	Marquis Grissom	.50
80	Geoff Jenkins	.50
81	Mark Loretta	.50
82	Ron Coomer	.50
83	Jacque Jones	.50
84	Corey Koskie	.50
85	Brad Radke	.50
86	Todd Walker	.50
87	Michael Barrett	.50
88	Peter Bergeron	.50
89	Vladimir Guerrero (*)	1.00
90	Jose Vidro	.50
91	Rondell White	.50
92	Edgardo Alfonzo (*)	.50
93	Rickey Henderson	1.00
94	Rey Ordonez	.50
95	Mike Piazza (*)	2.00
96	Robin Ventura	.50
97	Roger Clemens (*)	1.75
98	Orlando Hernandez	.50
99	Derek Jeter (*)	3.00
100	Tino Martinez	.50
101	Mariano Rivera	.50
102	Alfonso Soriano	.75
103	Bernie Williams (*)	.60
104	Eric Chavez	.50
105	Jason Giambi	.75
106	Ben Grieve	.50
107	Tim Hudson	.75
108	John Jaha	.50
109	Bobby Abreu	.50
110	Doug Glanville	.50
111	Mike Lieberthal	.50
112	Scott Rolen (*)	.75
113	Curt Schilling	.60
114	Brian Giles (*)	.50
115	Jason Kendall	.50
116	Warren Morris	.50
117	Kevin Young	.50
118	Rick Ankiel (*)	.50
119	J.D. Drew (*)	.60
120	Chad Hutchinson	.50
121	Ray Lankford	.50
122	Mark McGwire (*)	2.50
123	Fernando Tatis	.50
124	Bret Boone	.60
125	Ben Davis	.50
126	Tony Gwynn (*)	1.50
127	Trevor Hoffman	.50
128	Barry Bonds (*)	3.00
129	Ellis Burks	.50
130	Jeff Kent	.50
131	J.T. Snow	.50
132	Freddy Garcia (*)	.50
133	Ken Griffey Jr. (*)	2.00
134	Edgar Martinez	.50
135	John Olerud	.50
136	Alex Rodriguez (*)	2.50
137	Jose Canseco (*)	.60
138	Vinny Castilla	.50
139	Roberto Hernandez	.50
140	Fred McGriff	.50
141	Rusty Greer	.50
142	Ruben Mateo (*)	.50
143	Rafael Palmeiro (*)	.75
144	Ivan Rodriguez (*)	.75
145	Lee Stevens	.50
146	Tony Batista	.50
147	Carlos Delgado (*)	.60
148	Shannon Stewart	.50
149	David Wells	.50
150	Vernon Wells	.50

Holographic Blue

	NM/M
Common Player:	1.00
Stars:	4-6X
Production 80 Sets	

Holographic Gold

	NM/M
Common Player:	.50
Stars:	2-4X
Production 480 Sets	

Holographic Mirror

	NM/M
Common Player:	1.50
Stars:	4-6X
Production 160 Sets	

Holographic Purple

	NM/M
Common Player:	1.00
Stars:	6-8X
Production 99 Sets	

Pebbly Dots

One of eight silver-foil versions of Prism, there is virtually no way to describe the silver metallic foil background of this parallel set dubbed "Pebbly Dots" by the maker to allow its differentiation from the set labeled "Texture Silver," other than perhaps the vaguely vertical orientation of the texture. Production of 100 of the cards was 691 apiece, with the other 50 cards produced in an edition of 448 each indicated with an (*) in the checklist. They were inserted into both hobby and retail packaging. The cards are not serially numbered.

		NM/M
	Complete Set (150):	50.00
	Common Player:	.50
1	Jeff DaVanon **RC**	.50
2	Troy Glaus	.75
3	Tim Salmon	.60
4	Mo Vaughn (*)	.50
5	Jay Bell	.50
6	Erubiel Durazo	.50
7	Luis Gonzalez	.60
8	Randy Johnson (*)	.75
9	Matt Williams (*)	.50
10	Andres Galarraga	.50
11	Andruw Jones (*)	.75
12	Chipper Jones (*)	1.00
13	Brian Jordan	.50
14	Greg Maddux (*)	1.00
15	Kevin Millwood	.50
16	John Smoltz	.50
17	Albert Belle	.50
18	Mike Mussina (*)	.60
19	Calvin Pickering	.50
20	Cal Ripken Jr. (*)	3.00
21	B.J. Surhoff	.50
22	Nomar Garciaparra (*)	2.00
23	Pedro Martinez (*)	.75
24	Troy O'Leary	.50
25	John Valentin	.50
26	Jason Varitek	.50
27	Mark Grace	.60
28	Henry Rodriguez	.50
29	Sammy Sosa (*)	2.00
30	Kerry Wood (*)	.65
31	Ray Durham	.50
32	Carlos Lee	.50
33	Magglio Ordonez (*)	.50
34	Chris Singleton	.50
35	Frank Thomas (*)	.75
36	Sean Casey (*)	.60
37	Travis Dawkins	.50
38	Barry Larkin	.50
39	Pokey Reese	.50
40	Scott Williamson	.50
41	Roberto Alomar (*)	.60
42	Bartolo Colon	.50
43	David Justice	.50
44	Manny Ramirez (*)	.75
45	Richie Sexson	.50
46	Jim Thome (*)	.75
47	Omar Vizquel	.50
48	Pedro Astacio	.50
49	Todd Helton (*)	.75
50	Neifi Perez	.50
51	Ben Petrick	.50
52	Larry Walker (*)	.50
53	Tony Clark	.50
54	Damion Easley	.50
55	Juan Gonzalez (*)	.75
56	Dean Palmer	.50
57	A.J. Burnett	.50
58	Luis Castillo	.50
59	Cliff Floyd	.50
60	Alex Gonzalez	.50
61	Preston Wilson (*)	.50
62	Jeff Bagwell (*)	.75
63	Craig Biggio (*)	.50
64	Ken Caminiti	.50
65	Jose Lima	.50
66	Billy Wagner	.50
67	Carlos Beltran (*)	.65
68	Johnny Damon	.60
69	Jermaine Dye	.50
70	Carlos Febles	.50
71	Mike Sweeney	.50
72	Kevin Brown (*)	.50
73	Shawn Green (*)	.65
74	Eric Karros	.50
75	Chan Ho Park	.50
76	Gary Sheffield (*)	.60
77	Ron Belliard	.50
78	Jeromy Burnitz (*)	.50
79	Marquis Grissom	.50
80	Geoff Jenkins	.50
81	Mark Loretta	.50
82	Ron Coomer	.50
83	Jacque Jones	.50
84	Corey Koskie	.50
85	Brad Radke	.50
86	Todd Walker	.50
87	Michael Barrett	.50
88	Peter Bergeron	.50
89	Vladimir Guerrero (*)	.75
90	Jose Vidro	.50
91	Rondell White	.50
92	Edgardo Alfonzo (*)	.50
93	Rickey Henderson	.75
94	Rey Ordonez	.50
95	Mike Piazza (*)	2.00
96	Robin Ventura	.50
97	Roger Clemens (*)	1.50
98	Orlando Hernandez	.50
99	Derek Jeter (*)	3.00
100	Tino Martinez	.50
101	Mariano Rivera	.50
102	Alfonso Soriano	.65
103	Bernie Williams (*)	.60
104	Eric Chavez	.50
105	Jason Giambi	.60
106	Ben Grieve	.50
107	Tim Hudson	.60
108	John Jaha	.50
109	Bobby Abreu	.50
110	Doug Glanville	.50
111	Mike Lieberthal	.50
112	Scott Rolen (*)	.60
113	Curt Schilling	.60
114	Brian Giles (*)	.50
115	Jason Kendall	.50
116	Warren Morris	.50
117	Kevin Young	.50
118	Rick Ankiel (*)	.50
119	J.D. Drew (*)	.60
120	Chad Hutchinson	.50
121	Ray Lankford	.50
122	Mark McGwire (*)	2.50
123	Fernando Tatis	.50
124	Bret Boone	.50
125	Ben Davis	.50
126	Tony Gwynn (*)	1.00
127	Trevor Hoffman	.50
128	Barry Bonds (*)	3.00
129	Ellis Burks	.50
130	Jeff Kent	.50
131	J.T. Snow	.50
132	Freddy Garcia (*)	.50
133	Ken Griffey Jr. (*)	2.00
134	Edgar Martinez	.50
135	John Olerud	.50
136	Alex Rodriguez (*)	2.50
137	Jose Canseco (*)	.60
138	Vinny Castilla	.50
139	Roberto Hernandez	.50
140	Fred McGriff	.50
141	Rusty Greer	.50
142	Ruben Mateo (*)	.50
143	Rafael Palmeiro (*)	.65
144	Ivan Rodriguez (*)	.65
145	Lee Stevens	.50
146	Tony Batista	.50
147	Carlos Delgado (*)	.60
148	Shannon Stewart	.50
149	David Wells	.50
150	Vernon Wells	.50

Premiere Date

Sixty-one of each card in '00 Prism were embossed with a round seal at center: "PREMIERE DATE / PRISM / 2000 / APR. 12, 2000" and have a dot-matrix serial number at bottom-right on front.

	NM/M
Common Player:	1.50

Stars:	8-10X
Production 61 Sets	

Rapture Gold

This complete-set parallel to Prism, features a diagonally striped metallic gold-foil background. A retail-only insert, 565 sets were produced. The cards are not serially numbered.

	NM/M
Complete Set (150):	50.00
Common Player:	.50
Stars:	2-3X

Rapture Silver

One of eight silver-foil parallels to Prism, this version features a diagonally striped background. A hobby-only insert, 916 sets were produced. The cards are not serially numbered.

	NM/M
Complete Set (150):	50.00
Common Player:	.50
Stars:	2-3X

Sheen Silver

One of eight silver-foil versions of Prism, there is virtually no way to describe the silver metallic foil background of this partial-parallel set dubbed "Sheen Silver" by the maker, other than perhaps the diagonal orientation of the jagged-edged forms. Production was reported as 565 each for cards in the numberical range of #1-40 and #80-110, and 448 each for cards skip-numbered between #42-79 and #111-150. They were inserted into both hobby and retail packaging. The cards are not serially numbered. The 100-card partial-parallel does not include most of the top stars.

		NM/M
	Complete Set (100):	40.00
	Common Player:	.50
1	Jeff DaVanon **RC**	.50
2	Troy Glaus	1.50
3	Tim Salmon	.50
5	Jay Bell	.50
6	Erubiel Durazo	.50
7	Luis Gonzalez	.50
10	Andres Galarraga	.50
13	Brian Jordan	.50
15	Kevin Millwood	.50
16	John Smoltz	.50
17	Albert Belle	.50
19	Calvin Pickering	.50
21	B.J. Surhoff	.50
24	Troy O'Leary	.50
25	John Valentin	.50
26	Jason Varitek	.50
27	Mark Grace	.50
28	Henry Rodriguez	.50
31	Ray Durham	.50
32	Carlos Lee	.50
34	Chris Singleton	.50
37	Travis Dawkins	.50
38	Barry Larkin	.50
39	Pokey Reese	.50
40	Scott Williamson	.50
42	Bartolo Colon	.50
43	David Justice	.50
45	Richie Sexson	.50
47	Omar Vizquel	.50
48	Pedro Astacio	.50
50	Neifi Perez	.50
51	Ben Petrick	.50
53	Tony Clark	.50
54	Damion Easley	.50
56	Dean Palmer	.50
57	A.J. Burnett	.50
58	Luis Castillo	.50
59	Cliff Floyd	.50
60	Alex Gonzalez	.50
64	Ken Caminiti	.50
65	Jose Lima	.50
66	Billy Wagner	.50
68	Johnny Damon	.50
69	Jermaine Dye	.50
70	Carlos Febles	.50
71	Mike Sweeney	.50
74	Eric Karros	.50
75	Chan Ho Park	.50
77	Ron Belliard	.50
79	Marquis Grissom	.50
80	Geoff Jenkins	.50
81	Mark Loretta	.50
82	Ron Coomer	.50
83	Jacque Jones	.50
84	Corey Koskie	.50
85	Brad Radke	.50
86	Todd Walker	.50
87	Michael Barrett	.50
88	Peter Bergeron	.50
90	Jose Vidro	.50
91	Rondell White	.50
93	Rickey Henderson	1.50
94	Rey Ordonez	.50
96	Robin Ventura	.50
98	Orlando Hernandez	.50
100	Tino Martinez	.50
101	Mariano Rivera	.50
102	Alfonso Soriano	1.00
104	Eric Chavez	.50
105	Jason Giambi	1.00
106	Ben Grieve	.50
107	Tim Hudson	.50
108	John Jaha	.50
109	Bobby Abreu	.50
110	Doug Glanville	.50
111	Mike Lieberthal	.50
113	Curt Schilling	.50
115	Jason Kendall	.50
116	Warren Morris	.50
117	Kevin Young	.50
120	Chad Hutchinson	.50
121	Ray Lankford	.50
123	Fernando Tatis	.50
124	Bret Boone	.50
125	Ben Davis	.50
127	Trevor Hoffman	.50
129	Ellis Burks	.50
130	Jeff Kent	.50
131	J.T. Snow	.50
134	Edgar Martinez	.50
135	John Olerud	.50
138	Vinny Castilla	.50
139	Roberto Hernandez	.50
140	Fred McGriff	.50
141	Rusty Greer	.50
145	Lee Stevens	.50

146 Tony Batista .50
148 Shannon Stewart .50
149 David Wells .50
150 Vernon Wells .50

Slider Silver

One of eight silver-foil versions of Prism, there is virtually no way to describe the silver metallic foil background of this parallel set dubbed "Slider Silver" by the maker, other than perhaps noting the horizontally oriented arrowhead-shaped forms in the background. Production was reported as either 334 each, 448, or 565, depending on press sheet. The number of each card produced is noted parenthetically in this checklist. They were inserted into both hobby and retail packaging. The cards are not serially numbered.

		NM/M
Complete Set (150):		50.00
Common Player:		.50
1	Jeff DaVanon/334 RC	.50
2	Troy Glaus/334	.75
3	Tim Salmon/334	.60
4	Mo Vaughn/565	.50
5	Jay Bell/334	.50
6	Erubiel Durazo/334	.50
7	Luis Gonzalez/334	.60
8	Randy Johnson/565	.75
9	Matt Williams/565	.50
10	Andres Galarraga/334	.50
11	Andruw Jones/565	.75
12	Chipper Jones/565	1.00
13	Brian Jordan/334	.50
14	Greg Maddux/565	1.00
15	Kevin Millwood/334	.50
16	John Smoltz/334	.50
17	Albert Belle/334	.50
18	Mike Mussina/565	.45
19	Calvin Pickering/334	.50
20	Cal Ripken Jr./565	3.00
21	B.J. Surhoff/334	.50
22	Nomar Garciaparra/565	2.00
23	Pedro Martinez/565	.75
24	Troy O'Leary/334	.50
25	John Valentin/334	.50
26	Jason Varitek/334	.50
27	Mark Grace/334	.50
28	Henry Rodriguez/334	.50
29	Sammy Sosa/565	2.00
30	Kerry Wood/565	.60
31	Ray Durham/334	.50
32	Carlos Lee/334	.50
33	Magglio Ordonez/565	.60
34	Chris Singleton/334	.50
35	Frank Thomas/565	.75
36	Sean Casey/565	.60
37	Travis Dawkins/334	.50
38	Barry Larkin/334	.50
39	Pokey Reese/334	.50
40	Scott Williamson/334	.50
41	Roberto Alomar/565	.60
42	Bartolo Colon/448	.50
43	David Justice/448	.50
44	Manny Ramirez/565	.75
45	Richie Sexson/448	.50
46	Jim Thome/565	.65
47	Omar Vizquel/448	.50
48	Pedro Astacio/448	.50
49	Todd Helton/565	.75
50	Neifi Perez/448	.50
51	Ben Petrick/448	.50
52	Larry Walker/565	.50
53	Tony Clark/448	.50
54	Damion Easley/448	.50
55	Juan Gonzalez/565	.75
56	Dean Palmer/448	.50
57	A.J. Burnett/448	.50
58	Luis Castillo/448	.50
59	Cliff Floyd/448	.50
60	Alex Gonzalez/448	.50
61	Preston Wilson/565	.50
62	Jeff Bagwell/565	.75
63	Craig Biggio/565	.50
64	Ken Caminiti/448	.50
65	Jose Lima/448	.50
66	Billy Wagner/448	.50
67	Carlos Beltran/565	.65
68	Johnny Damon/448	.50
69	Jermaine Dye/448	.50
70	Carlos Febles/448	.50
71	Mike Sweeney/448	.50
72	Kevin Brown/565	.50
73	Shawn Green/565	.60
74	Eric Karros/448	.50
75	Chan Ho Park/448	.50
76	Gary Sheffield/565	.60
77	Ron Belliard/448	.50
78	Jeromy Burnitz/565	.50
79	Marquis Grissom/448	.50
80	Geoff Jenkins/334	.50
81	Mark Loretta/334	.50
82	Ron Coomer/334	.50
83	Jacque Jones/334	.50
84	Corey Koskie/334	.50
85	Brad Radke/334	.50
86	Todd Walker/334	.50
87	Michael Barrett/334	.50
88	Peter Bergeron/334	.50
89	Vladimir Guerrero/565	.75
90	Jose Vidro/334	.50
91	Rondell White/334	.50
92	Edgardo Alfonzo/565	.50
93	Rickey Henderson/334	.75
94	Rey Ordonez/334	.50
95	Mike Piazza/565	2.00
96	Robin Ventura/334	.50
97	Roger Clemens/565	1.50
98	Orlando Hernandez/334	.50
99	Derek Jeter/565	3.00
100	Tino Martinez/334	.50
101	Mariano Rivera/334	.50
102	Alfonso Soriano/334	2.00
103	Bernie Williams/334	.60
104	Eric Chavez/334	.50
105	Jason Giambi/334	.75
106	Ben Grieve/334	.50
107	Tim Hudson/334	.60
108	John Jaha/334	.50
109	Bobby Abreu/334	.50
110	Doug Glanville/334	.50
111	Mike Lieberthal/448	.50
112	Scott Rolen/565	.65
113	Curt Schilling/448	.60
114	Brian Giles/565	.50
115	Jason Kendall/448	.50
116	Warren Morris/448	.50
117	Kevin Young/448	.50
118	Rick Ankiel/565	.50
119	J.D. Drew/565	.60
120	Chad Hutchinson/448	.50
121	Ray Lankford/448	.50
122	Mark McGwire/565	2.50
123	Fernando Tatis/448	.50
124	Bret Boone/448	.50
125	Ben Davis/448	.50
126	Tony Gwynn/565	1.00
127	Trevor Hoffman/448	.50
128	Barry Bonds/565	3.00
129	Ellis Burks/448	.50
130	Jeff Kent/448	.50
131	J.T. Snow/448	.50
132	Freddy Garcia/565	.50
133	Ken Griffey Jr./565	2.00
134	Edgar Martinez/448	.50
135	John Olerud/448	.50
136	Alex Rodriguez/565	2.50
137	Jose Canseco/565	.60
138	Vinny Castilla/448	.50
139	Roberto Hernandez/448	.50
140	Fred McGriff/448	.50
141	Rusty Greer/448	.50
142	Ruben Mateo/565	.50
143	Rafael Palmeiro/565	.65
144	Ivan Rodriguez/565	.65
145	Lee Stevens/448	.50
146	Tony Batista/448	.50
147	Carlos Delgado/565	.60
148	Shannon Stewart/448	.50
149	David Wells/448	.50
150	Vernon Wells/448	.50

Texture Silver

One of eight silver-foil versions of Prism, there is virtually no way to describe the silver metallic foil background of this parallel set dubbed "Texture Silver" by the maker to allow its differentiation from the set labeled "Silver Pebbly Drops," other than perhaps the vaguely diagonal orientation of the texture. Production was reported as 448 sets inserted only into retail packaging. The cards are not serially numbered.

	NM/M
Complete Set (150):	50.00
Common Player:	.50
Stars:	2-3X

Tinsel Silver

One of eight silver-foil parallels to Prism, this version features a horizontally striped background that the makers labeled "Tinsel Silver." Inserted only into hobby packaging, production was reported as 331 sets. The cards are not serially numbered.

	NM/M
Complete Set (150):	50.00
Common Player:	.50
Stars:	2-3X

Woodgrain Silver

One of eight silver-foil parallels to Prism, this version features a mottled patterned background which the makers insist resembles woodgrain. Inserted only into retail packaging, production was reported as 331 sets. The cards are not serially numbered.

	NM/M
Complete Set (150):	50.00
Common Player:	.50
Stars:	2-3X

A.L. Legends

		NM/M
Complete Set (10):		15.00
Common Player:		.50
Inserted 1:25		
1	Mo Vaughn	.50
2	Cal Ripken Jr.	4.00
3	Nomar Garciaparra	2.50
4	Manny Ramirez	1.50
5	Roger Clemens	2.00
6	Derek Jeter	4.00
7	Ken Griffey Jr.	2.50
8	Alex Rodriguez	3.00
9	Jose Canseco	.75
10	Rafael Palmeiro	1.00

Center Stage

		NM/M
Complete Set (20):		40.00
Common Player:		1.00

Inserted 1:25		
1	Chipper Jones	3.00
2	Cal Ripken Jr.	6.00
3	Nomar Garciaparra	4.00
4	Pedro Martinez	2.00
5	Sammy Sosa	4.00
6	Sean Casey	1.00
7	Manny Ramirez	2.00
8	Jim Thome	1.50
9	Jeff Bagwell	2.00
10	Carlos Beltran	1.50
11	Vladimir Guerrero	2.00
12	Mike Piazza	4.00
13	Derek Jeter	6.00
14	Bernie Williams	1.00
15	Scott Rolen	1.50
16	Mark McGwire	5.00
17	Tony Gwynn	3.00
18	Ken Griffey Jr.	4.00
19	Alex Rodriguez	5.00
20	Ivan Rodriguez	1.50

Diamond Dial-A-Stats

		NM/M
Complete Set (10):		90.00
Common Player:		8.00
Inserted 1:193		
1	Chipper Jones	8.00
2	Greg Maddux	8.00
3	Cal Ripken Jr.	20.00
4	Sammy Sosa	10.00
5	Mike Piazza	10.00
6	Roger Clemens	9.00
7	Mark McGwire	15.00
8	Tony Gwynn	8.00
9	Ken Griffey Jr.	10.00
10	Alex Rodriguez	15.00

N.L. Legends

		NM/M
Complete Set (10):		15.00
Common Player:		.50
Inserted 1:25		
1	Chipper Jones	2.00
2	Greg Maddux	2.00
3	Sammy Sosa	2.50
4	Larry Walker	.50
5	Jeff Bagwell	1.00
6	Vladimir Guerrero	1.00
7	Mike Piazza	2.50
8	Mark McGwire	3.00
9	Tony Gwynn	2.00
10	Barry Bonds	4.00

Prospects

		NM/M
Complete Set (10):		12.00
Common Player:		1.00
Inserted 1:97		
1	Erubiel Durazo	1.00
2	Wilton Veras	1.00
3	Ben Petrick	1.00
4	Mark Quinn	1.00
5	Peter Bergeron	1.00
6	Alfonso Soriano	5.00
7	Tim Hudson	2.00
8	Chad Hermansen	1.00
9	Rick Ankiel	1.50
10	Ruben Mateo	1.00

2000 Pacific Private Stock

This base set consists of 150-cards, each card image uses an artist's computer generated brush strokes. Short-printed prospects are seeded 1:4 packs. The logo, player name and team are stamped in gold foil.

		NM/M
Complete Set (150):		50.00
Common Player:		.15
Common SP Prospect:		1.00
Inserted 1:4		
Pack (7):		2.00
Wax Box (24):		35.00
1	Darin Erstad	.25
2	Troy Glaus	.75
3	Tim Salmon	.25
4	Mo Vaughn	.15
5	Jay Bell	.15
6	Luis Gonzalez	.25
7	Randy Johnson	.75
8	Matt Williams	.15
9	Andruw Jones	.75
10	Chipper Jones	1.00
11	Brian Jordan	.15
12	Greg Maddux	1.00
13	Kevin Millwood	.15
14	Albert Belle	.20
15	Mike Mussina	.35
16	Cal Ripken Jr.	2.00
17	B.J. Surhoff	.15
18	Nomar Garciaparra	1.25
19	Butch Huskey	.15
20	Pedro Martinez	.75
21	Troy O'Leary	.15
22	Mark Grace	.25
23	Bo Porter/SP	1.00
24	Henry Rodriguez	.15
25	Sammy Sosa	1.25
26	Kerry Wood	.40
27	Jason Dellaero/SP	1.00
28	Ray Durham	.15
29	Paul Konerko	.20
30	Carlos Lee	.15
31	Magglio Ordonez	.25
32	Frank Thomas	.75
33	Mike Cameron	.15
34	Sean Casey	.25
35	Barry Larkin	.15
36	Greg Vaughn	.15
37	Roberto Alomar	.40
38	Russell Branyan/SP	1.00
39	Kenny Lofton	.15
40	Manny Ramirez	.75
41	Richie Sexson	.15
42	Jim Thome	.75
43	Omar Vizquel	.15
44	Dante Bichette	.15
45	Vinny Castilla	.15
46	Todd Helton	.75
47	Ben Petrick/SP	1.00
48	Juan Sosa/SP	1.00
49	Larry Walker	.15
50	Tony Clark	.15
51	Damion Easley	.15
52	Juan Encarnacion	.15
53	Robert Fick/SP	1.00
54	Dean Palmer	.15
55	A.J. Burnett/SP	1.00
56	Luis Castillo	.15
57	Alex Gonzalez	.15
58	Julio Ramirez/SP	1.00
59	Preston Wilson	.15
60	Jeff Bagwell	.75
61	Craig Biggio	.15
62	Ken Caminiti	.15
63	Carl Everett	.15
64	Mike Hampton	.15
65	Billy Wagner	.15
66	Carlos Beltran	.50
67	Dermal Brown/SP	1.00
68	Jermaine Dye	.15
69	Carlos Febles	.15
70	Mark Quinn/SP	1.00
71	Mike Sweeney	.15
72	Kevin Brown	.15
73	Eric Gagne/SP	1.50
74	Eric Karros	.15
75	Raul Mondesi	.15
76	Gary Sheffield	.40
77	Jeromy Burnitz	.15
78	Jeff Cirillo	.15
79	Geoff Jenkins	.15
80	David Nilsson	.15
81	Ron Coomer	.15
82	Jacque Jones	.15
83	Corey Koskie	.15
84	Brad Radke	.15
85	Tony Armas Jr./SP	1.50
86	Peter Bergeron/SP	1.00
87	Vladimir Guerrero	.75
88	Jose Vidro	.15
89	Rondell White	.15
90	Edgardo Alfonzo	.15
91	Roger Cedeno	.15
92	Rickey Henderson	.75
93	Jay Payton/SP	1.00
94	Mike Piazza	1.25
95	Jorge Toca/SP	1.00
96	Robin Ventura	.15
97	Roger Clemens	1.00
98	David Cone	.15
99	Derek Jeter	2.00
100	D'Angelo Jimenez/SP	1.00
101	Tino Martinez	.15
102	Alfonso Soriano/SP	3.00
103	Bernie Williams	.25
104	Jason Giambi	.50
105	Ben Grieve	.15
106	Tim Hudson	.25
107	Matt Stairs	.15
108	Bobby Abreu	.15
109	Doug Glanville	.15
110	Scott Rolen	.65
111	Curt Schilling	.40
112	Brian Giles	.15
113	Chad Hermansen (SP)	1.00
114	Jason Kendall	.15
115	Warren Morris	.15
116	Rick Ankiel (SP)	1.00
117	J.D. Drew	.25
118	Adam Kennedy (SP)	1.00
119	Ray Lankford	.15
120	Mark McGwire	1.50
121	Fernando Tatis	.15
122	Mike Darr (SP)	1.00
123	Ben Davis	.15
124	Tony Gwynn	1.00
125	Trevor Hoffman	.15
126	Reggie Sanders	.15
127	Barry Bonds	2.00
128	Ellis Burks	.15
129	Jeff Kent	.15
130	J.T. Snow	.15
131	Freddy Garcia	.15
132	Ken Griffey Jr.	1.25
133	Carlos Guillen/SP	1.00
134	Edgar Martinez	.15
135	Alex Rodriguez	1.50
136	Miguel Cairo	.15
137	Jose Canseco	.40
138	Steve Cox/SP	1.00
139	Roberto Hernandez	.15
140	Fred McGriff	.15
141	Juan Gonzalez	.75
142	Rusty Greer	.15
143	Ruben Mateo/SP	1.00
144	Rafael Palmeiro	.65
145	Ivan Rodriguez	.65
146	Carlos Delgado	.50
147	Tony Fernandez	.15
148	Shawn Green	.35
149	Shannon Stewart	.15
150	Vernon Wells/SP	1.00

Gold Portraits

A parallel to the 150-card base set these have a gold foiled border. These are found exclusively in hobby packs and are limited to 99 serial numbered sets.

Stars:	5-10X

Prospects: 1-2X
Production 99 Sets

Silver Portraits

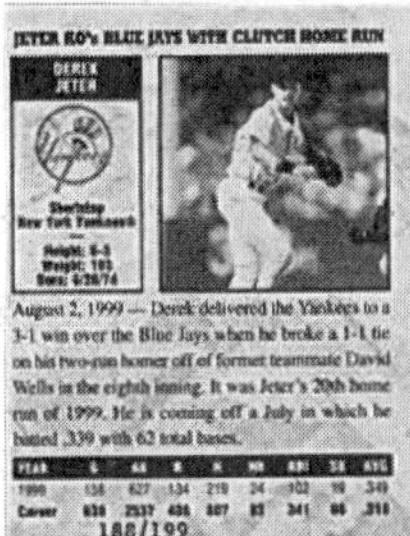

A parallel to the 150-card base set. These have a silver foiled border. Found exclusively in retail packs, these are limited to 199 serial numbered sets.

Stars: 3-6X
Prospects: 1-2X
Production 199 Sets

Premiere Date

A parallel to the 150-card base set these are limited to 34 serial numbered sets.

Stars: 5-10X
Prospects: 1-2X
Inserted 1:24

Canvas

This 20-card set is printed on real artist's canvas and has the look of a miniature piece of art.

		NM/M
Complete Set (20):		120.00
Common Player:		2.00
Inserted 1:49		
1	Chipper Jones	8.00
2	Greg Maddux	8.00
3	Cal Ripken Jr.	15.00
4	Nomar Garciaparra	10.00
5	Sammy Sosa	10.00
6	Frank Thomas	6.00
7	Manny Ramirez	6.00
8	Larry Walker	2.00
9	Jeff Bagwell	6.00
10	Vladimir Guerrero	6.00
11	Mike Piazza	10.00
12	Roger Clemens	9.00
13	Derek Jeter	15.00
14	Mark McGwire	12.00
15	Tony Gwynn	8.00
16	Barry Bonds	15.00
17	Ken Griffey Jr.	10.00
18	Alex Rodriguez	12.00
19	Juan Gonzalez	6.00
20	Ivan Rodriguez	5.00

Extreme Action

The focus of this 20-card set is the action photography, hence the name Extreme Action. They are seeded 2:25 packs.

		NM/M
Complete Set (20):		25.00
Common Player:		.50
Inserted 2:25		
1	Andruw Jones	1.50
2	Chipper Jones	2.00
3	Cal Ripken Jr.	4.00
4	Nomar Garciaparra	2.50
5	Sammy Sosa	2.50
6	Frank Thomas	1.50
7	Roberto Alomar	.60
8	Manny Ramirez	1.50
9	Larry Walker	.50
10	Jeff Bagwell	1.50
11	Vladimir Guerrero	1.50
12	Mike Piazza	2.50
13	Derek Jeter	4.00
14	Bernie Williams	.50
15	Scott Rolen	1.00
16	Mark McGwire	3.00
17	Tony Gwynn	2.00
18	Ken Griffey Jr.	2.50
19	Alex Rodriguez	3.00
20	Ivan Rodriguez	1.00

Reserve

Found exclusively in hobby packs these have a paper thin stock, enhanced with gold foil stamping. These are seeded 1:25 packs.

		NM/M
Complete Set (20):		50.00
Common Player:		1.00
Inserted 1:25		
1	Chipper Jones	3.00
2	Greg Maddux	3.00
3	Cal Ripken Jr.	6.00
4	Nomar Garciaparra	4.00
5	Sammy Sosa	4.00
6	Frank Thomas	2.00
7	Manny Ramirez	2.00
8	Larry Walker	1.00
9	Jeff Bagwell	2.00
10	Vladimir Guerrero	2.00
11	Mike Piazza	4.00
12	Roger Clemens	3.50
13	Derek Jeter	6.00
14	Mark McGwire	5.00
15	Tony Gwynn	3.00
16	Barry Bonds	6.00
17	Ken Griffey Jr.	4.00
18	Alex Rodriguez	5.00
19	Ivan Rodriguez	1.50
20	Shawn Green	1.25

PS-2000

This miniature 60-card set has a white border with gold foil stamping and are seeded two per pack.

		NM/M
Complete Set (60):		15.00
Common Player:		.15
Inserted 2:Pack		
1	Mo Vaughn	.15
2	Greg Maddux	1.00
3	Andruw Jones	.75
4	Chipper Jones	1.00
5	Cal Ripken Jr.	2.50
6	Nomar Garciaparra	1.50
7	Pedro Martinez	.75
8	Sammy Sosa	1.50
9	Jason Dellaero	.15
10	Magglio Ordonez	.15
11	Frank Thomas	.75
12	Sean Casey	.25
13	Russell Branyan	.15
14	Manny Ramirez	.75
15	Richie Sexson	.15
16	Ben Petrick	.15
17	Juan Sosa	.15
18	Larry Walker	.15
19	Robert Fick	.15
20	Craig Biggio	.15
21	Jeff Bagwell	.75
22	Carlos Beltran	.50
23	Dermal Brown	.15
24	Mark Quinn	.15
25	Eric Gagne	.15
26	Jeromy Burnitz	.15
27	Tony Armas Jr.	.15
28	Peter Bergeron	.15
29	Vladimir Guerrero	.75
30	Edgardo Alfonzo	.15
31	Mike Piazza	1.50
32	Jorge Toca	.15
33	Roger Clemens	1.25
34	Alfonso Soriano	.65
35	Bernie Williams	.25
36	Derek Jeter	2.50
37	Tim Hudson	.25
38	Bobby Abreu	.15
39	Scott Rolen	.65
40	Brian Giles	.15
41	Chad Hermansen	.15
42	Warren Morris	.15
43	Rick Ankiel	.15
44	J.D. Drew	.25
45	Adam Kennedy	.15
46	Mark McGwire	2.00
47	Mike Darr	.15
48	Tony Gwynn	1.00
49	Barry Bonds	2.50
50	Ken Griffey Jr.	1.50
51	Carlos Guillen	.15
52	Alex Rodriguez	1.50
53	Juan Gonzalez	.75
54	Ruben Mateo	.15
55	Ivan Rodriguez	.65
56	Rafael Palmeiro	.65
57	Jose Canseco	.40
58	Steve Cox	.15
59	Shawn Green	.30
60	Vernon Wells	.15

PS-2000 New Wave

This miniature 20-card set has copper foil stamping and is limited to 199 serial numbered sets.

		NM/M
Complete Set (20):		40.00
Common Player:		1.00
Production 199 Sets		
1	Andruw Jones	3.50
2	Chipper Jones	5.00
3	Nomar Garciaparra	6.00
4	Magglio Ordonez	1.00
5	Sean Casey	1.00
6	Manny Ramirez	3.50
7	Richie Sexson	1.00
8	Carlos Beltran	2.00
9	Jeromy Burnitz	1.00
10	Vladimir Guerrero	3.50
11	Edgardo Alfonzo	1.00
12	Derek Jeter	10.00
13	Tim Hudson	1.00
14	Bobby Abreu	1.00
15	Scott Rolen	2.50
16	Brian Giles	1.00
17	Warren Morris	1.00
18	J.D. Drew	1.25
19	Alex Rodriguez	8.00
20	Shawn Green	1.25

PS-2000 Rookies

This miniature 20-card set has holographic silver foil stamping and is limited to 99 serial numbered sets.

		NM/M
Complete Set (20):		20.00
Common Player:		1.00
Inserted 99 Sets		
1	Jason Dellaero	1.00
2	Russell Branyan	1.00
3	Ben Petrick	1.00
4	Juan Sosa	1.00
5	Robert Fick	1.00
6	Dermal Brown	1.00
7	Mark Quinn	1.00
8	Eric Gagne	1.50
9	Tony Armas Jr.	1.00
10	Peter Bergeron	1.00
11	Jorge Toca	1.00
12	Alfonso Soriano	6.00
13	Chad Hermansen	1.00
14	Rick Ankiel	1.00
15	Adam Kennedy	1.50
16	Mike Darr	1.00
17	Carlos Guillen	1.00
18	Steve Cox	1.00
19	Ruben Mateo	1.00
20	Vernon Wells	1.50

PS-2000 Stars

This miniature 20-card set is limited to 299 serial numbered sets.

		NM/M
Complete Set (20):		40.00
Common Player:		1.00
Production 299 Sets		
1	Mo Vaughn	1.00
2	Greg Maddux	4.00
3	Cal Ripken Jr.	8.00
4	Pedro Martinez	3.00
5	Sammy Sosa	5.00
6	Frank Thomas	3.00
7	Larry Walker	1.00
8	Craig Biggio	1.00
9	Jeff Bagwell	3.00
10	Mike Piazza	5.00
11	Roger Clemens	4.50
12	Bernie Williams	1.00
13	Mark McGwire	6.00
14	Tony Gwynn	4.00
15	Barry Bonds	8.00
16	Ken Griffey Jr.	5.00
17	Juan Gonzalez	3.00
18	Ivan Rodriguez	2.00
19	Rafael Palmeiro	2.00
20	Jose Canseco	1.50

2000 Pacific Revolution

The base set consists of 150 cards with silver holofoil throughout the card front. "Revolution" is embossed on the left portion and the logo is stamped in gold foil. Twenty-five short-printed prospects are seeded 1:4 packs.

		NM/M
Complete Set (150):		60.00
Common Player:		.25
Common SP:		1.00
Pack (3):		2.00
Box:		35.00
1	Darin Erstad	.50
2	Troy Glaus	1.00
3	Adam Kennedy/SP	1.50
4	Mo Vaughn	.25
5	Erubiel Durazo	.25
6	Steve Finley	.25
7	Luis Gonzalez	.35
8	Randy Johnson	1.00
9	Travis Lee	.25
10	Vicente Padilla/SP	1.00
11	Matt Williams	.25
12	Rafael Furcal/SP	1.00
13	Andres Galarraga	.25
14	Andruw Jones	1.00
15	Chipper Jones	1.50
16	Greg Maddux	1.50
17	Luis Rivera/SP	1.00
18	Albert Belle	.25
19	Mike Bordick	.25
20	Will Clark	.35
21	Mike Mussina	.40
22	Cal Ripken Jr.	3.00
23	B.J. Surhoff	.25
24	Carl Everett	.25
25	Nomar Garciaparra	2.00
26	Pedro Martinez	1.00
27	Jason Varitek	.25
28	Wilton Veras/SP	1.00
29	Shane Andrews	.25
30	Scott Downs/SP **RC**	1.00
31	Mark Grace	.35
32	Sammy Sosa	2.00
33	Kerry Wood	.50
34	Ray Durham	.25
35	Paul Konerko	.35
36	Carlos Lee	.25
37	Magglio Ordonez	.25
38	Frank Thomas	1.00
39	Rob Bell/SP	1.00
40	Sean Casey	.40
41	Ken Griffey Jr.	2.00
42	Barry Larkin	.25
43	Pokey Reese	.25
44	Roberto Alomar	.40
45	David Justice	.25
46	Kenny Lofton	.25
47	Manny Ramirez	1.00
48	Richie Sexson	.25
49	Jim Thome	1.00
50	Jeff Cirillo	.25
51	Jeffrey Hammonds	.25
52	Todd Helton	1.00
53	Larry Walker	.25
54	Tony Clark	.25
55	Juan Gonzalez	1.00
56	Hideo Nomo	1.00
57	Dean Palmer	.25
58	Alex Gonzalez	.25
59	Mike Lowell	.25
60	Pablo Ozuna/SP	1.00
61	Brad Penny/SP	1.00
62	Preston Wilson	.25
63	Moises Alou	.25
64	Jeff Bagwell	1.00
65	Craig Biggio	.25
66	Ken Caminiti	.25
67	Julio Lugo/SP	1.00
68	Carlos Beltran	.60
69	Johnny Damon	.40
70	Jermaine Dye	.25
71	Carlos Febles	.25
72	Mark Quinn/SP	1.00
73	Kevin Brown	.25
74	Shawn Green	.65
75	Chan Ho Park	.25
76	Gary Sheffield	.50
77	Kevin Barker/SP	1.00
78	Ron Belliard	.25
79	Jeromy Burnitz	.25
80	Geoff Jenkins	.25
81	Cristian Guzman	.25
82	Jacque Jones	.25
83	Corey Koskie	.25
84	Matt Lawton	.25
85	Peter Bergeron/SP	1.00
86	Vladimir Guerrero	1.00
87	Andy Tracy/SP	1.00
88	Jose Vidro	.25
89	Rondell White	.25
90	Edgardo Alfonzo	.25
91	Derek Bell	.25
92	Eric Cammack/SP	1.00
93	Mike Piazza	2.00
94	Robin Ventura	.25
95	Roger Clemens	1.75
96	Orlando Hernandez	.25
97	Derek Jeter	3.00
98	Tino Martinez	.25
99	Alfonso Soriano/SP	3.00
100	Bernie Williams	.35
101	Eric Chavez	.35
102	Jason Giambi	.75
103	Ben Grieve	.25
104	Terrence Long/SP	1.00
105	Mark Mulder/SP	1.00
106	Adam Piatt /SP	1.00
107	Bobby Abreu	.25
108	Rico Brogna	.25
109	Doug Glanville	.25
110	Mike Lieberthal	.25
111	Scott Rolen	.75
112	Brian Giles	.25
113	Chad Hermansen/SP	1.00
114	Jason Kendall	.25
115	Warren Morris	.25
116	Rick Ankiel/SP	1.00
117	J.D. Drew	.40
118	Jim Edmonds	.25
119	Mark McGwire	2.50
120	Fernando Tatis	.25
121	Fernando Vina	.25
122	Tony Gwynn	1.50
123	Trevor Hoffman	.25
124	Ryan Klesko	.25
125	Eric Owens	.25
126	Barry Bonds	3.00
127	Ellis Burks	.25
128	Bobby Estalella	.25
129	Jeff Kent	.25
130	Scott Linebrink/SP **RC**	1.00
131	Jay Buhner	.25
132	Stan Javier	.25
133	Edgar Martinez	.25
134	John Olerud	.25
135	Alex Rodriguez	2.50
136	Kazuhiro Sasaki/SP **RC**	2.00
137	Jose Canseco	.40
138	Vinny Castilla	.25
139	Fred McGriff	.25
140	Greg Vaughn	.25
141	Gabe Kapler	.25
142	Mike Lamb/SP **RC**	1.00
143	Ruben Mateo	.25
144	Rafael Palmeiro	.75
145	Ivan Rodriguez	.75
146	Tony Batista	.25
147	Jose Cruz Jr.	.25
148	Carlos Delgado	.75
149	Brad Fullmer	.25
150	Raul Mondesi	.25

Red

A parallel to the 150-card base set these insert have red foil in place of the gold from the base version. These are also serial numbered on the card front, limited to 299 sets.

Stars: 1-2X
SP's: 1X
Production 299 Sets

Shadow

This parallel to the 150-card base set replaces the gold foil highlights with blue foil on front and has an embossed box at center which reads "SHADOW SERIES." Backs have a serial number ink-jetted from within an edition of 99 each.

Stars: 3-6X
SP's: 1-2X
Production 99 Sets

Foul Pole Net-Fusions

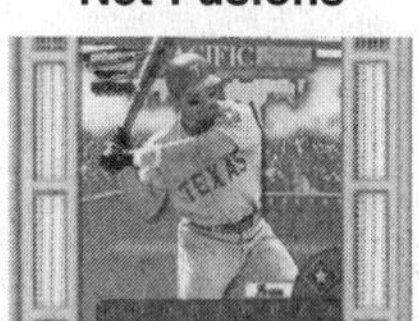

These inserts utilize net-fusion technology, with netting infused in the left and right portion. The player name and logo are stamped in gold foil. These are found on the average of 1:49 packs.

		NM/M
Complete Set (20):		110.00
Common Player:		2.00
Inserted 1:49		
1	Chipper Jones	8.00
2	Cal Ripken Jr.	15.00
3	Nomar Garciaparra	10.00
4	Pedro Martinez	6.00
5	Sammy Sosa	10.00
6	Frank Thomas	6.00
7	Ken Griffey Jr.	10.00
8	Manny Ramirez	6.00
9	Jeff Bagwell	6.00
10	Shawn Green	3.00
11	Vladimir Guerrero	6.00
12	Mike Piazza	10.00
13	Derek Jeter	15.00
14	Bernie Williams	2.00
15	Rick Ankiel	2.00
16	Mark McGwire	12.00
17	Tony Gwynn	8.00
18	Barry Bonds	15.00
19	Alex Rodriguez	12.00
20	Ivan Rodriguez	5.00

Game-Ball Signatures

This 25-card autographed set has a piece of baseball leather embedded into the front on which the player penned his signature.

		NM/M
Common Player:		5.00
1	Randy Johnson	40.00
2	Greg Maddux	90.00
3	Rafael Furcal	7.50
4	Shane Andrews	5.00
5	Sean Casey	10.00
6	Travis Dawkins	5.00
7	Alex Gonzalez	5.00
8	Shane Reynolds	5.00
9	Eric Gagne	10.00
10	Kevin Barker	5.00
11	Eric Milton	5.00
12	Mark Quinn	5.00
13	Alfonso Soriano	40.00
14	Brian Giles	6.00
15	Mark Mulder	10.00
16	Adam Piatt	5.00
17	Warren Morris	5.00
18	Rick Ankiel	6.00
19	Adam Kennedy	6.00
20	Fernando Tatis	5.00
21	Barry Bonds	100.00
22	Alex Rodriguez	75.00
23	Ruben Mateo	5.00
24	Billy Koch	5.00
25	Brad Penny	5.00

Icons

These die-cut cards feature silver foil stamping and the player's team logo in the background. These are found on the average of 1:121 packs.

		NM/M
Complete Set (20):		250.00
Common Player:		8.00
Inserted 1:121		
1	Randy Johnson	10.00
2	Chipper Jones	15.00
3	Greg Maddux	15.00
4	Cal Ripken Jr.	30.00
5	Nomar Garciaparra	20.00
6	Pedro Martinez	10.00
7	Sammy Sosa	20.00
8	Frank Thomas	10.00
9	Ken Griffey Jr.	20.00
10	Juan Gonzalez	10.00
11	Jeff Bagwell	10.00
12	Vladimir Guerrero	10.00
13	Mike Piazza	20.00
14	Roger Clemens	17.50
15	Derek Jeter	30.00
16	Mark McGwire	25.00
17	Tony Gwynn	15.00
18	Barry Bonds	30.00
19	Alex Rodriguez	25.00
20	Ivan Rodriguez	8.00

On Deck

These inserts have a die-cut rounded bottom and feature the player in a simulated on-deck circle enhanced by green foil stamping. These are seeded 1:25 packs.

		NM/M
Complete Set (20):		40.00
Common Player:		1.00
Inserted 1:25		
1	Chipper Jones	3.00
2	Cal Ripken Jr.	6.00
3	Nomar Garciaparra	4.00
4	Sammy Sosa	4.00
5	Frank Thomas	2.00
6	Ken Griffey Jr.	4.00
7	Manny Ramirez	2.00
8	Larry Walker	1.00
9	Juan Gonzalez	2.00
10	Jeff Bagwell	2.00
11	Shawn Green	1.50
12	Vladimir Guerrero	2.00
13	Mike Piazza	4.00
14	Derek Jeter	6.00
15	Scott Rolen	1.50
16	Mark McGwire	5.00
17	Tony Gwynn	3.00
18	Alex Rodriguez	5.00
19	Jose Canseco	1.50
20	Ivan Rodriguez	1.75

Season Opener

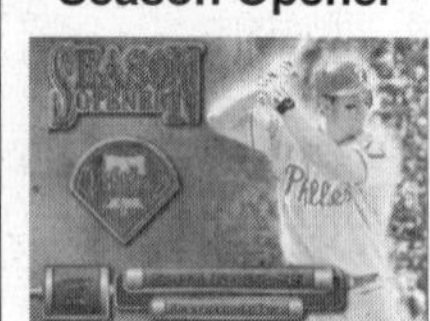

This 36-card set has a horizontal format with the set name, team logo, player name and Revolution logo stamped in gold foil. These are seeded 2:25 packs.

		NM/M
Complete Set (36):		35.00
Common Player:		.50
Inserted 2:25		
1	Erubiel Durazo	.50
2	Randy Johnson	1.50
3	Andruw Jones	1.50
4	Chipper Jones	2.00
5	Greg Maddux	2.00
6	Cal Ripken Jr.	4.00
7	Nomar Garciaparra	3.00
8	Pedro Martinez	1.50
9	Sammy Sosa	2.50
10	Frank Thomas	1.50
11	Magglio Ordonez	.50
12	Ken Griffey Jr.	2.50
13	Barry Larkin	.50
14	Kenny Lofton	.50
15	Manny Ramirez	1.50
16	Jim Thome	1.50
17	Larry Walker	.50
18	Juan Gonzalez	1.50
19	Jeff Bagwell	1.50
20	Craig Biggio	.50
21	Carlos Beltran	.75
22	Shawn Green	.75
23	Vladimir Guerrero	1.50
24	Mike Piazza	2.50
25	Orlando Hernandez	.50
26	Derek Jeter	4.00
27	Bernie Williams	.50
28	Eric Chavez	.50
29	Scott Rolen	1.00
30	Jim Edmonds	.50
31	Tony Gwynn	2.00
32	Barry Bonds	4.00
33	Alex Rodriguez	3.00
34	Jose Canseco	.65
35	Ivan Rodriguez	1.00
36	Rafael Palmeiro	1.00

Triple Header

This 30-card set is broken down into three tiers with cards 1-10 spotlighting batting average leaders, 11-20 home run leaders and 21-30 strikeout leaders. The base versions are seeded 4:25 packs. A parallel version for each of the three groups is also inserted. Cards 1-20 are limited to 99 serial numbered sets while cards 21-30 are limited to 599 serial numbered sets.

		NM/M
Complete Set (30):		25.00
Common Player:		.25
Inserted 4:25		
Parallel (1-10):		3-6X
99 Sets Produced		
Parallel (11-20):		3-6X
99 Sets Produced		
Parallel (21-30):		1-2X
599 Sets Produced		
1	Chipper Jones	1.50
2	Cal Ripken Jr.	3.00
3	Nomar Garciaparra	2.00
4	Frank Thomas	1.00
5	Larry Walker	.25
6	Vladimir Guerrero	1.00
7	Mike Piazza	2.00
8	Derek Jeter	3.00
9	Tony Gwynn	1.50
10	Ivan Rodriguez	.75
11	Sammy Sosa	2.00
12	Ken Griffey Jr.	2.00
13	Manny Ramirez	1.00
14	Jeff Bagwell	1.00
15	Shawn Green	.40
16	Mark McGwire	2.50
17	Barry Bonds	3.00
18	Alex Rodriguez	2.50
19	Jose Canseco	.50
20	Rafael Palmeiro	.75
21	Randy Johnson	1.00
22	Tom Glavine	.40
23	Greg Maddux	1.50
24	Mike Mussina	.40
25	Pedro Martinez	1.00
26	Kerry Wood	.60
27	Chuck Finley	.25
28	Kevin Brown	.25
29	Roger Clemens	1.75
30	Rick Ankiel	.25

2000 Pacific Vanguard Sample

To introduce the hobby to its new Vanguard brand, Pacific issued this card of principal spokesman Tony Gwynn. Using the same "Vision-Glow" technology as the regular-issue cards, the sample has a large white diagonal overprint on back and "SAMPLE" instead of a card number.

	NM/M
Tony Gwynn	3.00

2000 Pacific Vanguard

		NM/M
Complete Set (100):		30.00
Common Player:		.15
Pack (4):		2.00
Wax Box (24):		35.00
1	Troy Glaus	1.00
2	Tim Salmon	.25
3	Mo Vaughn	.15
4	Albert Belle	.15
5	Mike Mussina	.35
6	Cal Ripken Jr.	3.00
7	Nomar Garciaparra	2.00
8	Pedro Martinez	1.00
9	Troy O'Leary	.15
10	Wilton Veras	.15
11	Magglio Ordonez	.15
12	Chris Singleton	.15
13	Frank Thomas	1.00
14	Roberto Alomar	.40
15	Russell Branyan	.15
16	Manny Ramirez	1.00
17	Jim Thome	.75
18	Omar Vizquel	.15
19	Tony Clark	.15
20	Juan Gonzalez	1.00
21	Dean Palmer	.15
22	Carlos Beltran	.50
23	Johnny Damon	.30
24	Jermaine Dye	.15
25	Mark Quinn	.15
26	Jacque Jones	.15
27	Corey Koskie	.15
28	Brad Radke	.15
29	Roger Clemens	1.75
30	Derek Jeter	3.00
31	Alfonso Soriano	.75
32	Bernie Williams	.30
33	Eric Chavez	.30
34	Jason Giambi	.75
35	Ben Grieve	.15
36	Tim Hudson	.30
37	Mike Cameron	.15
38	Freddy Garcia	.15
39	Edgar Martinez	.15
40	Alex Rodriguez	2.50
41	Jose Canseco	.50
42	Vinny Castilla	.15
43	Fred McGriff	.15
44	Rusty Greer	.15
45	Ruben Mateo	.15
46	Rafael Palmeiro	.75
47	Ivan Rodriguez	.65
48	Carlos Delgado	.75
49	Shannon Stewart	.15
50	Vernon Wells	.15
51	Erubiel Durazo	.15
52	Randy Johnson	1.00
53	Matt Williams	.15
54	Andruw Jones	1.00
55	Chipper Jones	1.50
56	Greg Maddux	1.50
57	Mark Grace	.25
58	Sammy Sosa	2.00
59	Kerry Wood	.50
60	Sean Casey	.25
61	Ken Griffey Jr.	2.00
62	Barry Larkin	.15
63	Todd Helton	1.00
64	Ben Petrick	.15
65	Larry Walker	.15
66	Luis Castillo	.15
67	Alex Gonzalez	.15
68	Preston Wilson	.15
69	Jeff Bagwell	1.00
70	Craig Biggio	.15
71	Billy Wagner	.15
72	Kevin Brown	.15
73	Shawn Green	.40
74	Gary Sheffield	.40
75	Kevin Barker	.15
76	Ron Belliard	.15
77	Jeromy Burnitz	.15
78	Michael Barrett	.15
79	Peter Bergeron	.15
80	Vladimir Guerrero	1.00
81	Edgardo Alfonzo	.15
82	Rey Ordonez	.15
83	Mike Piazza	2.00
84	Robin Ventura	.15
85	Bobby Abreu	.15
86	Mike Lieberthal	.15
87	Scott Rolen	.75
88	Brian Giles	.15
89	Chad Hermansen	.15
90	Jason Kendall	.15
91	Rick Ankiel	.15
92	J.D. Drew	.25
93	Mark McGwire	2.50
94	Fernando Tatis	.15
95	Ben Davis	.15
96	Tony Gwynn	1.50
97	Trevor Hoffman	.15
98	Barry Bonds	3.00
99	Ellis Burks	.15
100	Jeff Kent	.15

Gold

A.L. (1-50):	2-4X
Production 199 Sets R	
N.L. (51-100):	3-6X
Production 99 Sets R	

Green

A.L. (1-50):	3-6X
Production 99 Sets	
N.L. (51-100):	2-4X
Production 199 Sets	

Purple

Production 10 Sets
(Values Undetermined)

Premiere Date

Stars:	3-5X
Production 135 Sets H	

A.L. Vanguard Press

		NM/M
Complete Set (10):		10.00
Common Player:		.65
Inserted 2:25		
1	Cal Ripken Jr.	3.00
2	Nomar Garciaparra	2.00
3	Pedro Martinez	1.00
4	Manny Ramirez	1.00
5	Carlos Beltran	.65
6	Roger Clemens	1.50
7	Derek Jeter	3.00
8	Alex Rodriguez	2.50
9	Rafael Palmeiro	.75
10	Ivan Rodriguez	.75

Cosmic Force

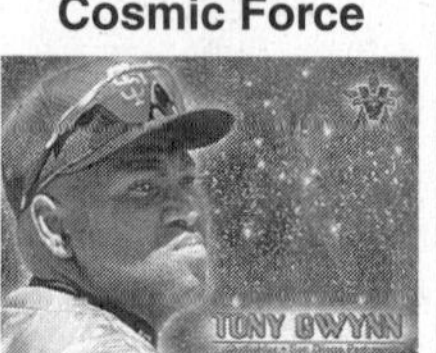

		NM/M
Complete Set (10):		30.00
Common Player:		3.00
Inserted 1:73		
1	Chipper Jones	3.00
2	Cal Ripken Jr.	6.00
3	Nomar Garciaparra	4.00
4	Sammy Sosa	4.00
5	Ken Griffey Jr.	4.00
6	Mike Piazza	4.00
7	Derek Jeter	6.00
8	Mark McGwire	5.00
9	Tony Gwynn	3.00
10	Alex Rodriguez	5.00

Diamond Architects

		NM/M
Complete Set (20):		25.00
Common Player:		.50
Inserted 1:25		
1	Chipper Jones	2.00
2	Greg Maddux	2.00
3	Cal Ripken Jr.	4.00
4	Nomar Garciaparra	2.50
5	Sammy Sosa	2.50
6	Ken Griffey Jr.	2.50
7	Manny Ramirez	1.50
8	Larry Walker	.50
9	Jeff Bagwell	1.50
10	Vladimir Guerrero	1.50
11	Mike Piazza	2.50
12	Roger Clemens	2.25
13	Derek Jeter	4.00
14	Bernie Williams	.50
15	Scott Rolen	1.00
16	Mark McGwire	3.00
17	Tony Gwynn	2.00
18	Alex Rodriguez	3.00
19	Rafael Palmeiro	1.00
20	Ivan Rodriguez	.75

Game Worn Jersey

		NM/M
Inserted 1:120		
1	Greg Maddux	10.00
2	Tony Gwynn	10.00
3	Alex Rodriguez	20.00
4	Frank Thomas	8.00
5	Chipper Jones	10.00

High Voltage

		NM/M
Complete Set (36):		10.00
Common Player:		.15
Inserted 1:1		
1	Mo Vaughn	.15
2	Erubiel Durazo	.15
3	Randy Johnson	.60
4	Andruw Jones	.60
5	Chipper Jones	.75
6	Greg Maddux	.75
7	Cal Ripken Jr.	2.00
8	Nomar Garciaparra	1.25
9	Pedro Martinez	.60
10	Sammy Sosa	1.25
11	Frank Thomas	.60
12	Sean Casey	.25
13	Ken Griffey Jr.	1.25
14	Barry Larkin	.15
15	Manny Ramirez	.60
16	Jim Thome	.50
17	Larry Walker	.15
18	Jeff Bagwell	.60
19	Craig Biggio	.15
20	Carlos Beltran	.40
21	Shawn Green	.25
22	Vladimir Guerrero	.60
23	Edgardo Alfonzo	.15
24	Mike Piazza	1.50
25	Roger Clemens	1.00
26	Derek Jeter	2.00
27	Bernie Williams	.25
28	Scott Rolen	.60
29	Brian Giles	.15
30	Rick Ankiel	.15
31	Mark McGwire	1.50
32	Tony Gwynn	.75
33	Barry Bonds	2.00
34	Alex Rodriguez	1.50
35	Rafael Palmeiro	.60
36	Ivan Rodriguez	.60

N.L. Vanguard Press

		NM/M
Complete Set (10):		10.00
Common Player:		.50
Inserted 2:37		
1	Chipper Jones	1.50
2	Greg Maddux	1.50
3	Sammy Sosa	2.00
4	Ken Griffey Jr.	2.00
5	Larry Walker	.50
6	Jeff Bagwell	1.00
7	Vladimir Guerrero	1.00
8	Mike Piazza	2.00
9	Mark McGwire	2.50
10	Tony Gwynn	1.50

2001 Pacific

	NM/M
Complete Set (500):	40.00

Common Player:		.10
Pack (12):		1.00
Box (36):		25.00
1	Garret Anderson	.10
2	Gary DiSarcina	.10
3	Darin Erstad	.25
4	Seth Etherton	.10
5	Ron Gant	.10
6	Troy Glaus	.75
7	Shigetosi Hasegawa	.10
8	Adam Kennedy	.10
9	Ben Molina	.10
10	Ramon Ortiz	.10
11	Troy Percival	.10
12	Tim Salmon	.20
13	Scott Schoeneweis	.10
14	Mo Vaughn	.10
15	Jarrod Washburn	.10
16	Brian Anderson	.10
17	Danny Bautista	.10
18	Jay Bell	.10
19	Greg Colbrunn	.10
20	Erubiel Durazo	.10
21	Steve Finley	.10
22	Luis Gonzalez	.20
23	Randy Johnson	.75
24	Byung-Hyun Kim	.10
25	Matt Mantei	.10
26	Armando Reynoso	.10
27	Todd Stottlemyre	.10
28	Matt Williams	.10
29	Tony Womack	.10
30	Andy Ashby	.10
31	Bobby Bonilla	.10
32	Rafael Furcal	.10
33	Andres Galarraga	.10
34	Tom Glavine	.35
35	Andruw Jones	.75
36	Chipper Jones	1.00
37	Brian Jordan	.10
38	Wally Joyner	.10
39	Keith Lockhart	.10
40	Javy Lopez	.10
41	Greg Maddux	1.00
42	Kevin Millwood	.10
43	John Rocker	.10
44	Reggie Sanders	.10
45	John Smoltz	.10
46	B.J. Surhoff	.10
47	Quilvio Veras	.10
48	Walt Weiss	.10
49	Brady Anderson	.10
50	Albert Belle	.15
51	Jeff Conine	.10
52	Delino DeShields	.10
53	Brook Fordyce	.10
54	Jerry Hairston Jr.	.10
55	Mark Lewis	.10
56	Luis Matos	.10
57	Melvin Mora	.10
58	Mike Mussina	.35
59	Chris Richard	.10
60	Cal Ripken Jr.	2.00
61	Manny Alexander	.10
62	Rolando Arrojo	.10
63	Midre Cummings	.10
64	Carl Everett	.10
65	Nomar Garciaparra	1.25
66	Mike Lansing	.10
67	Darren Lewis	.10
68	Derek Lowe	.10
69	Pedro Martinez	.75
70	Ramon Martinez	.10
71	Trot Nixon	.10
72	Troy O'Leary	.10
73	Jose Offerman	.10
74	Tomo Ohka	.10
75	Jason Varitek	.10
76	Rick Aguilera	.10
77	Shane Andrews	.10
78	Brant Brown	.10
79	Damon Buford	.10
80	Joe Girardi	.10
81	Mark Grace	.20
82	Willie Greene	.10
83	Ricky Gutierrez	.10
84	Jon Lieber	.10
85	Sammy Sosa	1.25
86	Kevin Tapani	.10
87	Rondell White	.10
88	Kerry Wood	.50
89	Eric Young	.10
90	Harold Baines	.10
91	James Baldwin	.10
92	Ray Durham	.10
93	Cal Eldred	.10
94	Keith Foulke	.10
95	Charles Johnson	.10
96	Paul Konerko	.20
97	Carlos Lee	.10
98	Magglio Ordonez	.10
99	Jim Parque	.10
100	Herbert Perry	.10
101	Chris Singleton	.10
102	Mike Sirotka	.10
103	Frank Thomas	.75
104	Jose Valentin	.10
105	Rob Bell	.10
106	Aaron Boone	.10
107	Sean Casey	.20
108	Danny Graves	.10
109	Ken Griffey Jr.	1.25
110	Pete Harnisch	.10
111	Brian L. Hunter	.10
112	Barry Larkin	.10
113	Pokey Reese	.10
114	Benito Santiago	.10
115	Chris Stynes	.10
116	Michael Tucker	.10
117	Ron Villone	.10
118	Scott Williamson	.10
119	Dmitri Young	.10
120	Roberto Alomar	.35
121	Sandy Alomar Jr.	.10
122	Russell Branyan	.10
123	Dave Burba	.10
124	Bartolo Colon	.10
125	Wil Cordero	.10
126	Einar Diaz	.10
127	Chuck Finley	.10
128	Travis Fryman	.10
129	Kenny Lofton	.10
130	Charles Nagy	.10
131	Manny Ramirez	.75
132	David Segui	.10
133	Jim Thome	.65
134	Omar Vizquel	.10
135	Brian Bohanon	.10
136	Jeff Cirillo	.10
137	Jeff Frye	.10
138	Jeffrey Hammonds	.10
139	Todd Helton	.75
140	Todd Hollandsworth	.10
141	Jose Jimenez	.10
142	Brent Mayne	.10
143	Neifi Perez	.10
144	Ben Petrick	.10
145	Juan Pierre	.10
146	Larry Walker	.10
147	Todd Walker	.10
148	Masato Yoshii	.10
149	Brad Ausmus	.10
150	Rich Becker	.10
151	Tony Clark	.10
152	Deivi Cruz	.10
153	Damion Easley	.10
154	Juan Encarnacion	.10
155	Robert Fick	.10
156	Juan Gonzalez	.75
157	Bobby Higginson	.10
158	Todd Jones	.10
159	Wendell Magee Jr.	.10
160	Brian Moehler	.10
161	Hideo Nomo	.75
162	Dean Palmer	.10
163	Jeff Weaver	.10
164	Antonio Alfonseca	.10
165	David Berg	.10
166	A.J. Burnett	.10
167	Luis Castillo	.10
168	Ryan Dempster	.10
169	Cliff Floyd	.10
170	Alex Gonzalez	.10
171	Mark Kotsay	.10
172	Derrek Lee	.10
173	Mike Lowell	.10
174	Mike Redmond	.10
175	Henry Rodriguez	.10
176	Jesus Sanchez	.10
177	Preston Wilson	.10
178	Moises Alou	.10
179	Jeff Bagwell	.75
180	Glen Barker	.10
181	Lance Berkman	.10
182	Craig Biggio	.10
183	Tim Bogar	.10
184	Ken Caminiti	.10
185	Roger Cedeno	.10
186	Scott Elarton	.10
187	Tony Eusebio	.10
188	Richard Hidalgo	.10
189	Jose Lima	.10
190	Mitch Meluskey	.10
191	Shane Reynolds	.10
192	Bill Spiers	.10
193	Billy Wagner	.10
194	Daryle Ward	.10
195	Carlos Beltran	.40
196	Ricky Bottalico	.10
197	Johnny Damon	.25
198	Jermaine Dye	.10
199	Jorge Fabregas	.10
200	David McCarty	.10
201	Mark Quinn	.10
202	Joe Randa	.10
203	Jeff Reboulet	.10
204	Rey Sanchez	.10
205	Blake Stein	.10
206	Jeff Suppan	.10
207	Mac Suzuki	.10
208	Mike Sweeney	.10
209	Gregg Zaun	.10
210	Adrian Beltre	.25
211	Kevin Brown	.10
212	Alex Cora	.10
213	Darren Dreifort	.10
214	Tom Goodwin	.10
215	Shawn Green	.30
216	Mark Grudzielanek	.10
217	Todd Hundley	.10
218	Eric Karros	.10
219	Chad Kreuter	.10
220	Jim Leyritz	.10
221	Chan Ho Park	.10
222	Jeff Shaw	.10
223	Gary Sheffield	.25
224	Devon White	.10
225	Ron Belliard	.10
226	Henry Blanco	.10
227	Jeromy Burnitz	.10
228	Jeff D'Amico	.10
229	Marquis Grissom	.10
230	Charlie Hayes	.10
231	Jimmy Haynes	.10
232	Tyler Houston	.10
233	Geoff Jenkins	.10
234	Mark Loretta	.10
235	James Mouton	.10
236	Richie Sexson	.10
237	Jamey Wright	.10
238	Jay Canizaro	.10
239	Ron Coomer	.10
240	Cristian Guzman	.10
241	Denny Hocking	.10
242	Torii Hunter	.10
243	Jacque Jones	.10
244	Corey Koskie	.10
245	Matt Lawton	.10
246	Matt LeCroy	.10
247	Eric Milton	.10
248	David Ortiz	.25
249	Brad Radke	.10
250	Mark Redman	.10
251	Michael Barrett	.10
252	Peter Bergeron	.10
253	Milton Bradley	.10
254	Orlando Cabrera	.10
255	Vladimir Guerrero	.75
256	Wilton Guerrero	.10
257	Dustin Hermanson	.10
258	Hideki Irabu	.10
259	Fernando Seguignol	.10
260	Lee Stevens	.10
261	Andy Tracy	.10
262	Javier Vazquez	.10
263	Jose Vidro	.10
264	Edgardo Alfonzo	.10
265	Derek Bell	.10
266	Armando Benitez	.10
267	Mike Bordick	.10
268	John Franco	.10
269	Darryl Hamilton	.10
270	Mike Hampton	.10
271	Lenny Harris	.10
272	Al Leiter	.10
273	Joe McEwing	.10
274	Rey Ordonez	.10
275	Jay Payton	.10
276	Mike Piazza	1.25
277	Glendon Rusch	.10
278	Bubba Trammell	.10
279	Robin Ventura	.10
280	Todd Zeile	.10
281	Scott Brosius	.10
282	Jose Canseco	.25
283	Roger Clemens	1.00
284	David Cone	.10
285	Dwight Gooden	.10
286	Orlando Hernandez	.10
287	Glenallen Hill	.10
288	Derek Jeter	2.00
289	David Justice	.10
290	Chuck Knoblauch	.10
291	Tino Martinez	.10
292	Denny Neagle	.10
293	Paul O'Neill	.10
294	Andy Pettitte	.20
295	Jorge Posada	.10
296	Mariano Rivera	.20
297	Luis Sojo	.10
298	Jose Vizcaino	.10
299	Bernie Williams	.25
300	Kevin Appier	.10
301	Eric Chavez	.20
302	Ryan Christenson	.10
303	Jason Giambi	.50
304	Jeremy Giambi	.10
305	Ben Grieve	.10
306	Gil Heredia	.10
307	Ramon Hernandez	.10
308	Tim Hudson	.20
309	Jason Isringhausen	.10
310	Terrence Long	.10
311	Mark Mulder	.10
312	Adam Piatt	.10
313	Matt Stairs	.10
314	Miguel Tejada	.25
315	Randy Velarde	.10
316	Alex Arias	.10
317	Pat Burrell	.25
318	Omar Daal	.10
319	Travis Lee	.10
320	Mike Lieberthal	.10
321	Randy Wolf	.10
322	Bobby Abreu	.10
323	Jeff Brantley	.10
324	Bruce Chen	.10
325	Doug Glanville	.10
326	Kevin Jordan	.10
327	Robert Person	.10
328	Scott Rolen	.65
329	Jimmy Anderson	.10
330	Mike Benjamin	.10
331	Kris Benson	.10
332	Adam Brown	.10
333	Brian Giles	.10
334	Jason Kendall	.10
335	Pat Meares	.10
336	Warren Morris	.10
337	Aramis Ramirez	.10
338	Todd Ritchie	.10
339	Jason Schmidt	.10
340	John Vander Wal	.10
341	Mike Williams	.10
342	Enrique Wilson	.10
343	Kevin Young	.10
344	Rick Ankiel	.10
345	Andy Benes	.10
346	Will Clark	.15
347	Eric Davis	.10
348	J.D. Drew	.20
349	Shawon Dunston	.10
350	Jim Edmonds	.10
351	Pat Hentgen	.10
352	Darryl Kile	.10
353	Ray Lankford	.10
354	Mike Matheny	.10
355	Mark McGwire	1.50
356	Craig Paquette	.10
357	Edgar Renteria	.10
358	Garrett Stephenson	.10
359	Fernando Tatis	.10
360	Dave Veres	.10
361	Fernando Vina	.10
362	Bret Boone	.10
363	Matt Clement	.10
364	Ben Davis	.10
365	Adam Eaton	.10
366	Wiki Gonzalez	.10
367	Tony Gwynn	1.00
368	Damian Jackson	.10
369	Ryan Klesko	.10
370	John Mabry	.10
371	Dave Magadan	.10
372	Phil Nevin	.10
373	Eric Owens	.10
374	Desi Relaford	.10
375	Ruben Rivera	.10
376	Woody Williams	.10
377	Rich Aurilia	.10
378	Marvin Bernard	.10
379	Barry Bonds	2.00
380	Ellis Burks	.10
381	Bobby Estalella	.10
382	Shawn Estes	.10
383	Mark Gardner	.10
384	Livan Hernandez	.10
385	Jeff Kent	.10
386	Bill Mueller	.10
387	Robb Nen	.10
388	Russ Ortiz	.10
389	Armando Rios	.10
390	Kirk Rueter	.10
391	J.T. Snow	.10
392	David Bell	.10
393	Jay Buhner	.10
394	Mike Cameron	.10
395	Freddy Garcia	.10
396	Carlos Guillen	.10
397	John Halama	.10
398	Rickey Henderson	.75
399	Al Martin	.10
400	Edgar Martinez	.10
401	Mark McLemore	.10
402	Jamie Moyer	.10
403	John Olerud	.10
404	Joe Oliver	.10
405	Alex Rodriguez	1.50
406	Kazuhiro Sasaki	.15
407	Aaron Sele	.10
408	Dan Wilson	.10
409	Miguel Cairo	.10
410	Vinny Castilla	.10
411	Steve Cox	.10
412	John Flaherty	.10
413	Jose Guillen	.10
414	Roberto Hernandez	.10
415	Russ Johnson	.10
416	Felix Martinez	.10
417	Fred McGriff	.10
418	Greg Vaughn	.10
419	Gerald Williams	.10
420	Luis Alicea	.10
421	Frank Catalanotto	.10
422	Royce Clayton	.10
423	Chad Curtis	.10
424	Rusty Greer	.10
425	Bill Haselman	.10
426	Rick Helling	.10
427	Gabe Kapler	.10
428	Mike Lamb	.10
429	Ricky Ledee	.10
430	Ruben Mateo	.10
431	Rafael Palmeiro	.65
432	Ivan Rodriguez	.65
433	Kenny Rogers	.10
434	John Wetteland	.10
435	Jeff Zimmerman	.10
436	Tony Batista	.10
437	Homer Bush	.10
438	Chris Carpenter	.10
439	Marty Cordova	.10
440	Jose Cruz Jr.	.10
441	Carlos Delgado	.40
442	Darrin Fletcher	.10
443	Brad Fullmer	.10
444	Alex S. Gonzalez	.10
445	Billy Koch	.10
446	Raul Mondesi	.10
447	Mickey Morandini	.10
448	Shannon Stewart	.10
449	Steve Trachsel	.10
450	David Wells	.10
451	Juan Alvarez	.10
452	Shawn Wooten	.10
453	Ismael Villegas	.10
454	Carlos Casimiro	.10
455	Morgan Burkhart	.10
456	Paxton Crawford	.10
457	Dernell Stenson	.10
458	Ross Gload	.10
459	Raul Gonzalez	.10
460	Corey Patterson	.10
461	Julio Zuleta	.10
462	Rocky Biddle	.10
463	Joe Crede	.10
464	Matt Ginter	.10
465	Aaron Myette	.10
466	Mike Bell	.10
467	Travis Dawkins	.10
468	Mark Watson	.10
469	Elvis Pena	.10
470	Eric Munson	.10
471	Pablo Ozuna	.10
472	Frank Charles	.10
473	Mike Judd	.10
474	Hector Ramirez	.10
475	Jack Cressend	.10
476	Talmadge Nunnari	.10
477	Jorge Toca	.10
478	Alfonso Soriano	.65
479	Jay Tessmer	.10
480	Jake Westbrook	.10
481	Todd Belitz	.10
482	Eric Byrnes	.10
483	Jose Ortiz	.10
484	Tike Redman	.10
485	Domingo Guzman	.10
486	Rodrigo Lopez	.10
487	Pedro Feliz	.10
488	Damon Minor	.10
489	Ryan Vogelsong	.10
490	Joel Pineiro	.10
491	Justin Brunette	.10
492	Keith McDonald	.10
493	Aubrey Huff	.10
494	Kenny Kelly	.10
495	Damian Rolls	.10
496	John Bale	.10
497	Pasqual Coco	.10
498	Matt DeWitt	.10
499	Leo Estrella	.10
500	Josh Phelps	.10

Hobby Limited

Stars: 8-15X
Production 70 Sets

Retail Limited

Stars: 4-8X
Production 85 Sets

Premiere Date

Stars: 20-30X
Production 35 Sets

Extreme

Stars: 15-25X
Production 45 Sets

AL Decade's Best

		NM/M
Complete Set (18):		20.00
Common Player:		.50
Inserted 2:37		
1	Rickey Henderson	1.50
2	Rafael Palmeiro	1.00
3	Cal Ripken Jr.	4.00
4	Jose Canseco	.75
5	Juan Gonzalez	1.50
6	Frank Thomas	1.50
7	Albert Belle	.50
8	Edgar Martinez	.50
9	Mo Vaughn	.50
10	Derek Jeter	4.00
11	Mark McGwire	3.00
12	Alex Rodriguez	3.00
13	Ken Griffey Jr.	2.50
14	Nomar Garciaparra	2.50
15	Roger Clemens	2.00
16	Bernie Williams	.50
17	Ivan Rodriguez	1.00
18	Pedro Martinez	1.50

Cramer's Choice Awards

		NM/M
Complete Set (10):		275.00
Common Player:		15.00
Inserted 1:721		
Styrene & Canvas pricing unavailable.		
1	Cal Ripken Jr.	50.00
2	Nomar Garciaparra	30.00
3	Sammy Sosa	30.00
4	Frank Thomas	15.00
5	Ken Griffey Jr.	30.00
6	Mike Piazza	30.00
7	Derek Jeter	50.00
8	Mark McGwire	40.00
9	Barry Bonds	50.00
10	Alex Rodriguez	40.00

Gold Crown Die-Cuts

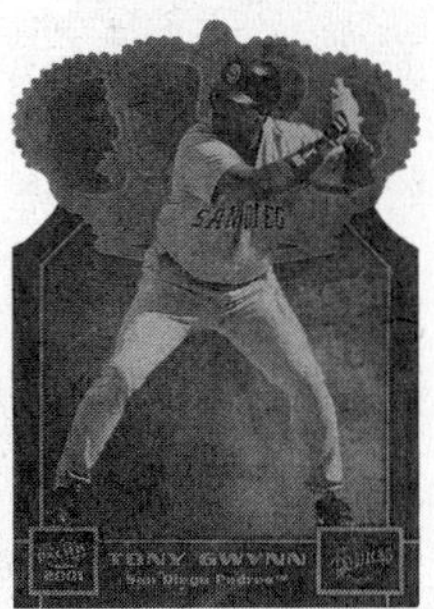

		NM/M
Complete Set (36):		100.00
Common Player:		1.50
Inserted 1:73		
1	Darin Erstad	1.50
2	Troy Glaus	4.00
3	Randy Johnson	4.00
4	Rafael Furcal	1.50
5	Andruw Jones	4.00
6	Chipper Jones	5.00
7	Greg Maddux	5.00
8	Cal Ripken Jr.	10.00
9	Nomar Garciaparra	8.00
10	Pedro Martinez	4.00
11	Sammy Sosa	8.00
12	Kerry Wood	2.50
13	Frank Thomas	4.00
14	Ken Griffey Jr.	8.00
15	Manny Ramirez	4.00

16 Todd Helton 4.00
17 Jeff Bagwell 4.00
18 Shawn Green 1.50
19 Gary Sheffield 1.50
20 Vladimir Guerrero 4.00
21 Mike Piazza 8.00
22 Jose Canseco 2.00
23 Roger Clemens 6.00
24 Derek Jeter 10.00
25 Jason Giambi 2.50
26 Pat Burrell 2.00
26 Rick Ankiel (Should be #27.) 1.50
28 Jim Edmonds 1.50
29 Mark McGwire 9.00
30 Tony Gwynn 5.00
31 Barry Bonds 10.00
32 Rickey Henderson 4.00
33 Edgar Martinez 1.50
34 Alex Rodriguez 9.00
35 Ivan Rodriguez 3.00
36 Carlos Delgado 2.00

NL Decade's Best

NM/M
Complete Set (18): 15.00
Common Player: .50
Inserted 2:37
1 Barry Bonds 4.00
2 Jeff Bagwell 1.00
3 Tom Glavine .65
4 Gary Sheffield .65
5 Fred McGriff .50
6 Greg Maddux 1.50
7 Mike Piazza 2.00
8 Tony Gwynn 1.50
9 Hideo Nomo 1.00
10 Andres Galarraga .50
11 Larry Walker .50
12 Scott Rolen .75
13 Pedro Martinez 1.00
14 Sammy Sosa 2.00
15 Mark McGwire 3.00
16 Kerry Wood .75
17 Chipper Jones 1.50
18 Mark Grace .75

On The Horizon

NM/M
Complete Set (10): 20.00
Common Player: 2.00
Inserted 1:145
1 Rafael Furcal 2.00
2 Corey Patterson 2.50
3 Russell Branyan 2.00
4 Juan Pierre 2.50
5 Mark Quinn 2.00
6 Alfonso Soriano 6.00
7 Adam Piatt 2.00
8 Pat Burrell 4.50
9 Kazuhiro Sasaki 2.50
10 Aubrey Huff 2.00

Ornaments

NM/M
Complete Set (24): 25.00
Common Player: .50
Inserted 2:37
1 Rafael Furcal .50
2 Chipper Jones 2.00
3 Greg Maddux 2.00
4 Cal Ripken Jr. 4.00
5 Nomar Garciaparra 2.50
6 Pedro Martinez 1.50
7 Sammy Sosa 2.50
8 Frank Thomas 1.50
9 Ken Griffey Jr. 2.50
10 Manny Ramirez 1.50
11 Todd Helton 1.50
12 Vladimir Guerrero 1.50
13 Mike Piazza 2.50
14 Roger Clemens 2.25
15 Derek Jeter 4.00
16 Pat Burrell 1.00
17 Rick Ankiel .50
18 Mark McGwire 3.00
19 Barry Bonds 4.00
20 Alex Rodriguez 3.00
21 Troy Glaus 1.50
22 Tom Glavine .50
23 Jim Edmonds .50
24 Ivan Rodriguez 1.00

Paramount Samples

While the Paramount brand was never produced due to Pacific's loss of its licensing

early in 2001, a trio of base-set sample cards were created and distributed to media and dealers. Fronts have vignetted photos and silver-foil highlights. Backs have portrait photos and the usual data and stats. Cards have "SAMPLE" in place of the card number on back.

NM/M
Complete Set (3): 7.50
Common Player: 3.00
(1) Barry Bonds 3.00
(2) Vladimir Guerrero 3.00
(3) Greg Maddux 3.00

2001 Pacific Private Stock

NM/M
Complete Set (150): 50.00
Common Player: .25
Common (126-150): 1.00
Inserted 1:4
Hobby Pack (7): 10.00
Hobby Box (10): 75.00
1 Darin Erstad .50
2 Troy Glaus 1.00
3 Tim Salmon .35
4 Mo Vaughn .25
5 Steve Finley .25
6 Luis Gonzalez .35
7 Randy Johnson 1.00
8 Matt Williams .25
9 Rafael Furcal .25
10 Andres Galarraga .25
11 Tom Glavine .45
12 Andruw Jones 1.00
13 Chipper Jones 1.50
14 Greg Maddux 1.50
15 B.J. Surhoff .25
16 Brady Anderson .25
17 Albert Belle .25
18 Mike Mussina .45
19 Cal Ripken Jr. 3.00
20 Carl Everett .25
21 Nomar Garciaparra 2.00
22 Pedro Martinez 1.00
23 Mark Grace .35
24 Sammy Sosa 2.00
25 Kerry Wood .50
26 Carlos Lee .25
27 Magglio Ordonez .25
28 Frank Thomas 1.00
29 Sean Casey .35
30 Ken Griffey Jr. 2.00
31 Barry Larkin .25
32 Pokey Reese .25
33 Roberto Alomar .40
34 Kenny Lofton .25
35 Manny Ramirez 1.00
36 Jim Thome .75
37 Omar Vizquel .25
38 Jeff Cirillo .25
39 Jeffrey Hammonds .25
40 Todd Helton 1.00
41 Larry Walker .25
42 Tony Clark .25
43 Juan Encarnacion .25
44 Juan Gonzalez 1.00
45 Hideo Nomo 1.00
46 Cliff Floyd .25
47 Derrek Lee .25
48 Henry Rodriguez .25
49 Preston Wilson .25
50 Jeff Bagwell 1.00
51 Craig Biggio .25
52 Richard Hidalgo .25
53 Moises Alou .25
54 Carlos Beltran .50
55 Johnny Damon .40
56 Jermaine Dye .25
57 Mac Suzuki .25
58 Mike Sweeney .25
59 Adrian Beltre .40
60 Kevin Brown .25
61 Shawn Green .50
62 Eric Karros .25
63 Chan Ho Park .25
64 Gary Sheffield .40
65 Jeromy Burnitz .25
66 Geoff Jenkins .25
67 Richie Sexson .25
68 Jacque Jones .25
69 Matt Lawton .25
70 Eric Milton .25
71 Vladimir Guerrero 1.00
72 Jose Vidro .25
73 Edgardo Alfonzo .25
74 Mike Hampton .25
75 Mike Piazza 2.00
76 Robin Ventura .25
77 Jose Canseco .50
78 Roger Clemens 1.75
79 Derek Jeter 3.00
80 David Justice .25
81 Jorge Posada .25
82 Bernie Williams .35
83 Jason Giambi .65
84 Ben Grieve .25
85 Tim Hudson .35
86 Terrence Long .25
87 Miguel Tejada .35
88 Bobby Abreu .25
89 Pat Burrell .50
90 Mike Lieberthal .25
91 Scott Rolen .75
92 Kris Benson .25
93 Brian Giles .25
94 Jason Kendall .25
95 Aramis Ramirez .25
96 Rick Ankiel .25
97 Will Clark .35
98 J.D. Drew .25
99 Jim Edmonds .25
100 Mark McGwire 2.50
101 Fernando Tatis .25
102 Adam Eaton .25
103 Tony Gwynn 1.50
104 Phil Nevin .25
105 Eric Owens .25
106 Barry Bonds 3.00
107 Jeff Kent .25
108 J.T. Snow .25
109 Rickey Henderson 1.00
110 Edgar Martinez .25
111 John Olerud .25
112 Alex Rodriguez 2.50
113 Kazuhiro Sasaki .25
114 Vinny Castilla .25
115 Fred McGriff .25
116 Greg Vaughn .25
117 Gabe Kapler .25
118 Ruben Mateo .25
119 Rafael Palmeiro .75
120 Ivan Rodriguez .75
121 Tony Batista .25
122 Jose Cruz Jr. .25
123 Carlos Delgado .75
124 Shannon Stewart .25
125 David Wells .25
126 Shawn Wooten 1.00
127 George Lombard 1.00
128 Morgan Burkhart 1.00
129 Ross Gload 1.00
130 Corey Patterson 1.00
131 Julio Zuleta 1.00
132 Joe Crede 1.00
133 Matt Ginter 1.00
134 Travis Dawkins 1.00
135 Eric Munson 1.00
136 Dee Brown 1.00
137 Luke Prokopec 1.00
138 Timoniel Perez 1.00
139 Alfonso Soriano 2.00
140 Jake Westbrook 1.00
141 Eric Byrnes 1.00
142 Adam Hyzdu 1.00
143 Jimmy Rollins 1.50
144 Xavier Nady 1.00
145 Ryan Vogelsong 1.00
146 Joel Pineiro 2.00
147 Aubrey Huff 1.00
148 Kenny Kelly 1.00
149 Josh Phelps 1.00
150 Vernon Wells 1.00

Silver

Stars: .5-1.5X
SP's: .5-1X
Base cards in retail.

Gold Portraits

Stars: 6-10X
SP's (126-150): 1-2X
Production 75 Sets H

Silver Portraits

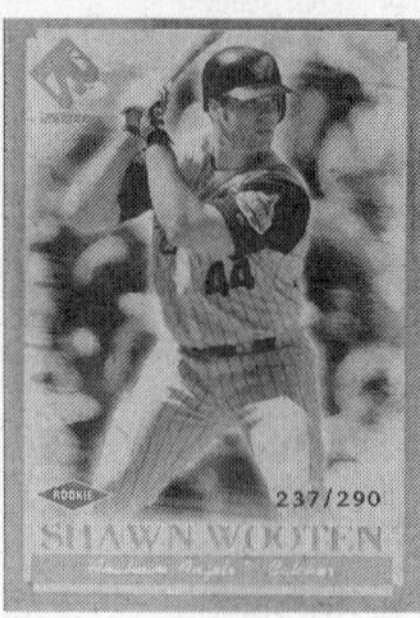

Stars: 2-5X
SP's: 1X
Production 290 Sets R

Premiere Date

Stars: 4-8X
SP's: 1-2X
Production 90 Sets

Artist's Canvas

NM/M
Complete Set (20): 50.00
Common Player: 1.00
Inserted 1:21
1 Randy Johnson 2.50
2 Chipper Jones 4.00
3 Greg Maddux 4.00
4 Cal Ripken Jr. 8.00
5 Nomar Garciaparra 5.00
6 Pedro Martinez 2.50
7 Sammy Sosa 5.00
8 Frank Thomas 2.50
9 Ken Griffey Jr. 5.00
10 Manny Ramirez 2.50
11 Vladimir Guerrero 2.50
12 Mike Piazza 5.00
13 Roger Clemens 4.50
14 Derek Jeter 6.00
15 Jason Giambi 2.50
16 Rick Ankiel 1.00
17 Mark McGwire 6.00
18 Barry Bonds 8.00
19 Alex Rodriguez 6.00
20 Ivan Rodriguez 2.00

Extreme Action

NM/M
Complete Set (20): 20.00
Common Player: .50
Inserted 1:11
1 Troy Glaus 1.00
2 Rafael Furcal .50
3 Chipper Jones 1.50
4 Cal Ripken Jr. 3.00
5 Nomar Garciaparra 2.00
6 Sammy Sosa 2.00
7 Ken Griffey Jr. 2.00
8 Manny Ramirez 1.00
9 Todd Helton 1.00
10 Jeff Bagwell 1.00
11 Vladimir Guerrero 1.00
12 Derek Jeter 3.00
13 Mike Piazza 2.00
14 Pat Burrell .75
15 Jim Edmonds .50
16 Mark McGwire 2.50
17 Barry Bonds 3.00
18 Alex Rodriguez 2.50
19 Ivan Rodriguez .75
20 Carlos Delgado .75

Game Gear

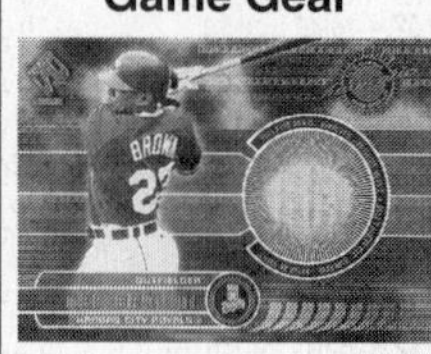

NM/M
Common Player: 4.00
Inserted 1:1 H
1 Garret Anderson/Bat 6.00
2 Darin Erstad/Jsy 5.00
3 Ron Gant/Bat 4.00
4 Troy Glaus/Jsy 8.00
5 Tim Salmon/Bat 5.00
6 Mo Vaughn/Jsy/Gray 4.00
7 Mo Vaughn/Jsy/White 4.00
8 Mo Vaughn/Bat 4.00
9 Jay Bell/Jsy 4.00
10 Jay Bell/Bat 4.00
11 Erubiel Durazo/Jsy/Black 4.00
12 Erubiel Durazo/Jsy/White 4.00
13 Erubiel Durazo/Bat 4.00
14 Steve Finley/Bat 4.00
15 Randy Johnson/Jsy 10.00
16 Byung-Hyun Kim/Jsy/White 4.00
17 Byung-Hyun Kim/Jsy/Gray 4.00
18 Matt Williams/Jsy/Gray 4.00
19 Matt Williams/Jsy/White 4.00
20 Matt Williams/Jsy/Purple 4.00
21 Bobby Bonilla/Jsy 4.00
22 Rafael Furcal/Bat 5.00
23 Andruw Jones/Bat 8.00
24 Chipper Jones/Jsy 10.00
25 Chipper Jones/Bat 10.00
26 Brian Jordan/Jsy 4.00
27 Javier Lopez/Bat 4.00
28 Greg Maddux/Jsy 15.00
29 Greg Maddux/Bat 15.00
30 Brady Anderson/Bat 4.00
31 Albert Belle/Bat 4.00
32 Nomar Garciaparra/Bat 15.00
33 Pedro Martinez/Bat 10.00
34 Jose Offerman/Bat 4.00
35 Damon Buford/Jsy 4.00
36 Jose Nieves/Bat 4.00
38 Kerry Wood/Bat 8.00
39 James Baldwin/Jsy 4.00
40 Ray Durham/Jsy 4.00
41 Ray Durham/Bat 4.00
42 Carlos Lee/Bat 4.00
43 Magglio Ordonez/Jsy 6.00
44 Magglio Ordonez/Bat 6.00
45 Chris Singleton/Jsy 4.00
46 Aaron Boone/Bat 4.00
47 Sean Casey/Bat 4.00
48 Barry Larkin/Jsy 6.00
49 Pokey Reese/Jsy 4.00
50 Pokey Reese/Bat 4.00
51 Dmitri Young/Bat 4.00
52 Roberto Alomar/Bat 8.00
53 Einar Diaz/Bat 4.00
54 Kenny Lofton/Jsy 4.00
55 David Segui/Bat 4.00
56 Omar Vizquel/Jsy 5.00
57 Luis Castillo/Jsy 4.00
58 Jeff Cirillo/Jsy 4.00
59 Jeff Frye/Bat 4.00
60 Todd Helton/Jsy 8.00
61 Todd Helton/Bat 8.00
62 Neifi Perez/Bat 4.00
63 Larry Walker/Jsy 4.00
64 Larry Walker/Bat 4.00
65 Masato Yoshii/Jsy 4.00
66 Brad Ausmus/Jsy 4.00
67 Rich Becker/Bat 4.00
68 Tony Clark/Bat 4.00
69 Deivi Cruz/Bat 4.00
70 Juan Gonzalez/Bat 6.00
71 Dean Palmer/Bat 4.00
72 Cliff Floyd/Jsy/White 4.00
73 Cliff Floyd/Jsy/Teal 4.00
74 Cliff Floyd/Bat 4.00
75 Alex Gonzalez/Jsy 4.00
76 Alex Gonzalez/Marlins Bat 4.00
77 Mark Kotsay/Bat 4.00
78 Derrek Lee/Bat 4.00
79 Pablo Ozuna/Jsy 4.00
80 Craig Biggio/Bat 4.00
81 Ken Caminiti/Bat 4.00
82 Roger Cedeno/Bat 4.00
83 Ricky Bottalico/Bat 4.00
84 Dee Brown/Bat 4.00
85 Jermaine Dye/Bat 4.00
86 David McCarty/Bat 4.00
87 Hector Ortiz/Bat 4.00
88 Joe Randa/Bat 4.00
89 Adrian Beltre/Jsy 4.00
90 Kevin Brown/Jsy 6.00
91 Alex Cora/Bat 4.00
92 Darren Dreifort/Bat 4.00
93 Shawn Green/Jsy/White 6.00
94 Shawn Green/Jsy/Gray 6.00
95 Shawn Green/Bat 6.00
96 Todd Hundley/Jsy 4.00
97 Eric Karros/Bat 4.00
98 Chan Ho Park/Jsy 4.00
99 Chan Ho Park/Bat 4.00
101 Gary Sheffield/Bat 6.00
102 Ismael Valdes/Bat 4.00
103 Jeromy Burnitz/Bat 4.00
104 Marquis Grissom/Bat 4.00
105 Matt Lawton/Bat 4.00
106 Fernando Seguignol/Bat 4.00
107 Edgardo Alfonzo/White Swing 4.00
108 Edgardo Alfonzo/Jsy/White Drop 4.00
109 Edgardo Alfonzo/Jsy/Black 4.00
110 Derek Bell/Jsy/White 4.00
111 Derek Bell/Jsy/Black 4.00
112 Armando Benitez/Bat 4.00
113 Al Leiter/Bat 4.00
114 Rey Ordonez/Jsy/Gray Field 4.00
115 Rey Ordonez/Jsy/White 4.00
116 Rey Ordonez/Jsy/Gray Bunt 4.00
117 Rey Ordonez/Bat 4.00
118 Jay Payton/Bat 4.00
119 Mike Piazza/Jsy 10.00
120 Robin Ventura/Jsy/Black Hit 4.00
121 Robin Ventura/Jsy/Black Field 4.00
122 Robin Ventura/Jsy/White 4.00
123 Luis Polonia/Bat 4.00
124 Bernie Williams/Bat 6.00
125 Eric Chavez/Jsy 4.00
126 Jason Giambi/Jsy 8.00
127 Jason Giambi/Bat 8.00
128 Ben Grieve/Jsy 4.00
129 Ben Grieve/Bat 4.00
130 Ramon Hernandez/Bat 4.00
131 Tim Hudson/Jsy 6.00
132 Terrence Long/Bat 4.00
133 Mark Mulder/Jsy 6.00
134 Adam Piatt/Jsy 4.00
135 Olmedo Saenz/Bat 4.00
136 Matt Stairs/Bat 4.00
137 Mike Stanley/Bat 4.00
138 Miguel Tejada/Bat 6.00
139 Travis Lee/Bat 4.00
140 Brian Giles/Bat 5.00
141 Jason Kendall/Jsy 4.00
142 Will Clark/Bat 6.00
143 J.D. Drew/Bat 4.00
144 Jim Edmonds/Bat 6.00
145 Mark McGwire/Bat 50.00
146 Edgar Renteria/Bat 4.00
147 Garrett Stephenson/Jsy 4.00
148 Tony Gwynn/Jsy 10.00
149 Ruben Rivera/Bat 4.00
150 Barry Bonds/Jsy 40.00
151 Barry Bonds/Bat 40.00
152 Ellis Burks/Jsy 4.00
153 J.T. Snow/Bat 4.00
154 Jay Buhner/Jsy 4.00
155 Jay Buhner/Bat 4.00
156 Carlos Guillen/Jsy 4.00
157 Carlos Guillen/Bat 4.00
158 Rickey Henderson/Bat 15.00
159 Edgar Martinez/Bat 6.00
160 Gil Meche/Jsy 4.00
161 John Olerud/Bat 5.00
162 Joe Oliver/Bat 4.00
163 Alex Rodriguez/Jsy 30.00
164 Kazuhiro Sasaki/Jsy 4.00
165 Dan Wilson/Jsy 4.00
166 Dan Wilson/Bat 4.00
167 Vinny Castilla/Bat 4.00
168 Jose Guillen/Bat 4.00
169 Fred McGriff/Jsy 5.00
170 Rusty Greer/Bat 4.00
171 Mike Lamb/Bat 4.00
172 Ruben Mateo/Jsy 4.00
173 Ruben Mateo/Bat 4.00
174 Rafael Palmeiro/Jsy 8.00
175 Rafael Palmeiro/Bat 8.00
178 Tony Batista/Bat 4.00
179 Marty Cordova/Bat 4.00
180 Jose Cruz Jr./Bat 4.00
181 Alex Gonzalez/Blue Jays Bat 4.00
182 Raul Mondesi/Bat 4.00

Game Jersey Patch

		NM/M
	Common Player:	8.00
2	Darin Erstad	8.00
4	Troy Glaus	15.00
6	Mo Vaughn/Gray	8.00
7	Mo Vaughn/White	8.00
9	Jay Bell	8.00
11	Erubiel Durazo/Black	8.00
12	Erubiel Durazo/White	8.00
15	Randy Johnson	40.00
16	Byung-Hyun Kim/White	8.00
17	Byung-Hyun Kim/Gray	8.00
18	Matt Williams/Gray	8.00
19	Matt Williams/White	8.00
20	Matt Williams/Purple	8.00
21	Bobby Bonilla	8.00
24	Chipper Jones	25.00
26	Brian Jordan	8.00
28	Greg Maddux	80.00
35	Damon Buford	8.00
39	James Baldwin	8.00
40	Ray Durham	8.00
43	Magglio Ordonez	20.00
45	Chris Singleton	8.00
48	Barry Larkin	15.00
49	Pokey Reese	8.00
54	Kenny Lofton	10.00
56	Omar Vizquel	10.00
57	Luis Castillo	8.00
58	Jeff Cirillo	8.00
60	Todd Helton	20.00
63	Larry Walker	10.00
65	Masato Yoshii	8.00
66	Brad Ausmus	8.00
72	Cliff Floyd/White	8.00
73	Cliff Floyd Teal	8.00
75	Alex Gonzalez	8.00
79	Pablo Ozuna	8.00
89	Adrian Beltre	8.00
90	Kevin Brown	15.00
93	Shawn Green/White	15.00
94	Shawn Green/Gray	15.00
96	Todd Hundley	8.00
98	Chan Ho Park	8.00
107	Edgardo Alfonzo/White Swing	8.00
108	Edgardo Alfonzo/White Drop	8.00
109	Edgardo Alfonzo/Black	8.00
110	Derek Bell/White	8.00
111	Derek Bell/Black	8.00
114	Rey Ordonez/Gray Field	8.00
115	Rey Ordonez/White	8.00
116	Rey Ordonez/Gray Bunt	8.00
119	Mike Piazza	75.00
120	Robin Ventura/Black Hit	10.00
121	Robin Ventura/Black Field	10.00
122	Robin Ventura/White	10.00
125	Eric Chavez	15.00
126	Jason Giambi	15.00
128	Ben Grieve	8.00
131	Tim Hudson	15.00
133	Mark Mulder	15.00
134	Adam Piatt	8.00
141	Jason Kendall	10.00
147	Garrett Stephenson	8.00
148	Tony Gwynn	40.00
150	Barry Bonds	90.00
152	Ellis Burks	8.00
154	Jay Buhner	8.00
156	Carlos Guillen	8.00
160	Gil Meche	8.00
164	Kazuhiro Sasaki	15.00
165	Dan Wilson	8.00
169	Fred McGriff	10.00
172	Ruben Mateo	8.00
174	Rafael Palmeiro	25.00

Reserve

		NM/M
	Complete Set (20):	25.00
	Common Player:	.50
	Inserted 1:21 H	
1	Randy Johnson	1.50
2	Chipper Jones	2.00
3	Greg Maddux	2.00
4	Cal Ripken Jr.	4.00
5	Nomar Garciaparra	2.50
6	Pedro Martinez	1.50
7	Sammy Sosa	2.50
8	Frank Thomas	1.50
9	Ken Griffey Jr.	2.50
10	Todd Helton	1.50
11	Vladimir Guerrero	1.50
12	Mike Piazza	2.50
13	Roger Clemens	2.25
14	Derek Jeter	4.00
15	Rick Ankiel	.50
16	Mark McGwire	3.00
17	Tony Gwynn	2.00
18	Barry Bonds	4.00
19	Alex Rodriguez	3.00
20	Ivan Rodriguez	1.00

PS-206 Action

		NM/M
	Complete Set (60):	20.00
	Common Player:	.15
	Inserted 2:Pack	
1	Darin Erstad	.25
2	Troy Glaus	.65
3	Randy Johnson	.65
4	Rafael Furcal	.15
5	Tom Glavine	.40
6	Andruw Jones	.65
7	Chipper Jones	.75
8	Greg Maddux	.75
9	Albert Belle	.15
10	Mike Mussina	.40
11	Cal Ripken Jr.	1.50
12	Nomar Garciaparra	1.00
13	Pedro Martinez	.65
14	Mark Grace	.25
15	Sammy Sosa	1.00
16	Kerry Wood	.35
17	Magglio Ordonez	.15
18	Frank Thomas	.65
19	Ken Griffey Jr.	1.00
20	Barry Larkin	.15
21	Roberto Alomar	.35
22	Manny Ramirez	.65
23	Jim Thome	.60
24	Jeff Cirillo	.15
25	Todd Helton	.65
26	Larry Walker	.15
27	Juan Gonzalez	.65
28	Hideo Nomo	.65
29	Preston Wilson	.15
30	Jeff Bagwell	.65
31	Craig Biggio	.15
32	Johnny Damon	.25
33	Jermaine Dye	.15
34	Shawn Green	.30
35	Gary Sheffield	.25
36	Vladimir Guerrero	.65
37	Mike Piazza	1.00
38	Jose Canseco	.40
39	Roger Clemens	.85
40	Derek Jeter	1.50
41	Bernie Williams	.30
42	Jason Giambi	.50
43	Ben Grieve	.15
44	Pat Burrell	.40
45	Scott Rolen	.50
46	Rick Ankiel	.15
47	J.D. Drew	.25
48	Jim Edmonds	.15
49	Mark McGwire	1.25
50	Tony Gwynn	.75
51	Barry Bonds	1.50
52	Jeff Kent	.15
53	Edgar Martinez	.15
54	Alex Rodriguez	1.25
55	Kazuhiro Sasaki	.15
56	Fred McGriff	.15
57	Rafael Palmeiro	.50
58	Ivan Rodriguez	.50
59	Tony Batista	.15
60	Carlos Delgado	.45

PS-206 New Wave

		NM/M
	Complete Set (20):	30.00
	Common Player:	1.00
	Inserted 2:Hobby Case	
1	Darin Erstad	1.50
2	Troy Glaus	5.00
3	Rafael Furcal	1.00
4	Andruw Jones	5.00
5	Magglio Ordonez	1.00
6	Carlos Lee	1.00
7	Todd Helton	5.00
8	Johnny Damon	1.50
9	Jermaine Dye	1.00
10	Vladimir Guerrero	5.00
11	Jason Giambi	4.00
12	Ben Grieve	1.00
13	Pat Burrell	3.00
14	Rick Ankiel	1.00
15	J.D. Drew	1.50
16	Adam Eaton	1.00
17	Kazuhiro Sasaki	1.00
18	Ruben Mateo	1.00
19	Tony Batista	1.00
20	Carlos Delgado	3.00

PS-206 Rookies

		NM/M
	Complete Set (20):	50.00
	Common Player:	3.00
	Inserted 1:Case	
1	George Lombard	3.00
2	Morgan Burkhart	3.00
3	Corey Patterson	5.00
4	Julio Zuleta	3.00
5	Joe Crede	3.00
6	Matt Ginter	3.00
7	Aaron Myette	3.00
8	Travis Dawkins	3.00
9	Eric Munson	3.00
10	Dee Brown	3.00
11	Luke Prokopec	3.00
12	Jorge Toca	3.00
13	Alfonso Soriano	7.50
14	Eric Byrnes	3.00
15	Adam Hyzdu	3.00
16	Jimmy Rollins	4.00
17	Joel Pineiro	5.00
18	Aubrey Huff	4.00
19	Kenny Kelly	3.00
20	Vernon Wells	3.00

PS-206 Stars

		NM/M
	Complete Set (20):	50.00
	Common Player:	1.00
	Inserted 3:Hobby Case	
1	Chipper Jones	3.00
2	Greg Maddux	3.00
3	Cal Ripken Jr.	6.00
4	Nomar Garciaparra	4.00
5	Pedro Martinez	2.00
6	Sammy Sosa	4.00
7	Frank Thomas	2.00
8	Ken Griffey Jr.	4.00
9	Manny Ramirez	2.00
10	Jeff Bagwell	2.00
11	Gary Sheffield	1.00
12	Mike Piazza	4.00
13	Roger Clemens	3.50
14	Derek Jeter	6.00
15	Rick Ankiel	1.00
16	Mark McGwire	5.00
17	Tony Gwynn	3.00
18	Barry Bonds	6.00
19	Alex Rodriguez	5.00
20	Ivan Rodriguez	1.50

1991 Pacific Gas & Electric S.F. Giants

Perforated panels of six 2-3/4" x 3-3/4" Giants cards were included in each of five editions of Giants Magazine, the team's official program, for 1991. The set was sponsored by PG&E. Cards have color action photos on front with a graduated gray frame and white borders. At bottom is a team typographical logo, crossed bats and a red ribbon with player identification. A pentagon at top has the date "91." Backs are in black-and-white with a large sponsor's ad, the player's career stats, a few biographical details and uniform and card numbers.

		NM/M
	Complete Set (30):	15.00
	Common Player:	.50
1	Kevin Mitchell	.50
2	Robby Thompson	.50
3	John Burkett	.50
4	Kelly Downs	.50
5	Terry Kennedy	.50
6	Roger Craig	.50
7	Jeff Brantley	.50
8	Greg Litton	.50
9	Trevor Wilson	.50
10	Kevin Bass	.50
11	Matt Williams	1.00
12	Jose Uribe	.50
13	Steve Decker	.50
14	Will Clark	1.00
15	Dave Righetti	.50
16	Mike Kingery	.50
17	Mike LaCoss	.50
18	Dave Anderson	.50
19	Bud Black	.50
20	Mike Benjamin	.50
21	Don Robinson	.50
22	Mark Leonard	.50
23	Willie McGee	.50
24	Francisco Oliveras	.50
25	Kirt Manwaring	.50
26	Rick Parker	.50
27	Mike Remlinger	.50
28	Mike Felder	.50
29	Scott Garrelts	.50
30	Tony Perezchica	.50

1992 Pacific Gas & Electric S.F. Giants

Perforated panels of six 2-3/4" x 3-3/4" Giants cards were included in each of six editions of Giants Magazine, the team's official program, for 1992. The set was sponsored by PG&E. Cards have color action photos on front with a wood-look frame and white borders. At top is a gold ribbon with player name and position. At bottom is the team logo, crossed bats, uniform number and the year of issue. Horizontal backs are in black-and-white with a large sponsor's ad, the player's career stats, a few biographical details, uniform number and energy conservation tip. Cards are unnumbered and are listed here by panel.

		NM/M
	Complete Set, Panels (6):	25.00
	Complete Set, Singles (36):	20.00
	Common Player:	.50
	PANEL 1	5.00
(1)	Rod Beck	.50
(2)	Wendell Kim	.50
(3)	Gil Heredia	.50
(4)	Mike Benjamin	.50
(5)	Matt Williams	1.00
(6)	Robby Thompson	.50
	PANEL 2	5.00
(7)	Will Clark/AS	1.00
(8)	Bob Brenly	.50
(9)	Bryan Hickerson	.50
(10)	Bob Lillis	.50
(11)	Royce Clayton	.50
(12)	Mark Leonard (Dropping bat.)	.50
	PANEL 3	5.00
(13)	Roger Craig	.50
(14)	Jeff Brantley	.50
(15)	Darren Lewis	.50
(16)	Mark Leonard/Btg	.50
(17)	John Burkett	.50
(18)	Mike Felder	.50
	PANEL 4	5.00
(19)	Kelly Downs	.50
(20)	Jose Uribe	.50
(21)	Bud Black	.50
(22)	Kirt Manwaring	.50
(23)	Trevor Wilson	.50
(24)	Kevin Bass	.50
	PANEL 5	5.00
(25)	Mike Jackson	.50
(26)	Will Clark	1.00
(27)	Jim McNamara	.50
(28)	Dusty Baker	.50
(29)	Scott Garrelts	.50
(30)	Chris James	.50
	PANEL 6	5.00
(31)	Dave Righetti	.50
(32)	Cory Snyder	.50
(33)	Dave Burba	.50
(34)	Carlos Alfonso	.50
(35)	Bill Swift	.50
(36)	Willie McGee	.50

2000 Palm Beach Post Montreal Expos

At each of the spring training games between March 3-April 1 each copy of the newspaper sold at the ballpark contained a random insert of two Expos and two Cardinals cards. The 3-1/8" x 4-3/4" blank-back cards have action color photos on front.

		NM/M
	Complete Set (20):	15.00
	Common Player:	.50
(1)	Felipe Alou	.65
(2)	Michael Barrett	.50
(3)	Geoff Blum	.50
(4)	Orlando Cabrera	.75
(5)	Brad Fullmer	.65
(6)	Vladimir Guerrero	5.00
(7)	Dustin Hermanson	.75
(8)	Hideki Irabu	.50
(9)	Steve Kline	.50
(10)	Graeme Lloyd	.50
(11)	Trey Moore	.50
(12)	Mickey Morandini	.50
(13)	Mike Mordecai	.50
(14)	Carl Pavano	.75
(15)	Anthony Telford	.50
(16)	Ugueth Urbina	.50
(17)	Jose Vidro	.75
(18)	Rondell White/Btg	1.00
(19)	Rondell White/Standing	1.00
(20)	Chris Widger	.50

2000 Palm Beach Post St. Louis Cardinals

During spring training each copy of the newspaper sold at the ballpark contained a random insert of two Expos and two Cardinals cards. The 3-1/8" x 4-3/4" blank-back cards have action color photos on front.

		NM/M
	Complete Set (20):	20.00
	Common Player:	.50
(1)	Rick Ankiel	.50
(2)	Andy Benes	.50
(3)	Kent Bottenfield	.50
(4)	Eric Davis	.50
(5)	J.D. Drew	2.00
(6)	Pat Hentgen	.50
(7)	Chad Hutchinson	.50
(8)	Darryl Kile	.50
(9)	Ray Lankford	.50
(10)	Tony LaRussa	.50
(11)	Eli Marrero	.50
(12)	Joe McEwing	.50
(13)	Mark McGwire/Btg	5.00
(14)	Mark McGwire/Standing	5.00
(15)	Matt Morris	.50
(16)	Edgar Renteria	.50
(17)	Heathcliff Slocumb	.50
(18)	Fernando Tatis	.50
(19)	Dave Veres	.50
(20)	Fernando Vina	.50

2001 Palm Beach Post N.Y. Mets

During spring training the local newspaper distributed (in unknown manner) this set of 2-1/2" x 3-1/2" cards printed on thin stock. Fronts have purplish-gray gray borders and game-action photos. Backs are in black-and-white with a portrait photo, career notes, stats and player personal data. The set is checklisted here by uniform number, as printed on front and back.

		NM/M
	Complete Set (10):	10.00
	Common Player:	.50
4	Robin Ventura	.50
9	Todd Zeile	.50
10	Rey Ordonez	.50
13	Edgardo Alfonzo	.50
22	Al Leiter	.50
31	Mike Piazza	6.00
35	Rick Reed	.50
45	John Franco	.50
49	Armando Benitez	.50
50	Benny Agbayani	.50

2002 Palm Beach Post N.Y. Mets

During spring training the local newspaper distributed (in unknown manner) this set of 2-1/2" x 3-1/2" cards printed on thin stock. Fronts have purple borders and posed or game-action photos. Backs are in black-and-white and have a large team logo and minimal player personal data. The set is checklisted here by uniform number, as printed on front and back.

		NM/M
	Complete Set (10):	8.00
	Common Player:	.50
2	Bobby Valentine	.50
6	Timo Perez	.50
10	Rey Ordonez	.50
13	Edgardo Alfonzo	.50
22	Al Leiter	.50
31	Mike Piazza	5.00
44	Jay Payton	.50
45	John Franco	.50
47	Joe McEwing	.50
49	Armando Benitez	.50

1988 Panini Stickers

This set of 480 stickers features 312 major league players, both rookies and superstar veterans. The full-color stickers measure 2-11/16" x 1-7/8" (team emblem and uniform stickers are slightly larger). Individual players, duos and group action shots are included in the set which also contains 14 stickers that depict 1987 season highlights. Panini also produced a 64-page album with Don Mattingly on the cover and two pages devoted to each team with a space marked for each sticker in the set. Individual sticker packets contained a total of six stickers; four players, one team logo and one uniform sticker. Panini offered a collectors' sticker exchange service in which up to 30 stickers could be traded or specific stickers purchased for 10 cents each. The 26 team logo/pennant stickers (numbered A-1 through Z-1) are listed as #455-480 in the following checklist.

		NM/M
	Complete Set (480):	15.00
	Common Player:	.05
	Sticker Album:	1.00
	Wax Pack (6):	.25
	Wax Box (100):	7.50
1	World Series Trophy	.05
2	Orioles Logo	.05
3	Orioles Uniform	.05
4	Eric Bell	.05
5	Mike Boddicker	.05
6	Dave Schmidt	.05
7	Terry Kennedy	.05
8	Eddie Murray	.45
9	Bill Ripken	.05
10	Orioles Action (Tony Armas, Cal Ripken Jr.)	.25
11	Orioles Action (Tony Armas, Cal Ripken Jr.)	.25
12	Ray Knight	.05
13	Cal Ripken, Jr.	1.00
14	Ken Gerhart	.05
15	Fred Lynn	.05
16	Larry Sheets	.05
17	Mike Young	.05
18	Red Sox Logo	.05
19	Red Sox Uniform	.05
20	Oil Can Boyd	.05
21	Roger Clemens	.65
22	Bruce Hurst	.05
23	Bob Stanley	.05
24	Rich Gedman	.05
25	Dwight Evans	.05
26	Red Sox Action (Marty Barrett, Tim Laudner)	.05
27	Red Sox Action (Marty Barrett, Tim Laudner)	.05
28	Marty Barrett	.05
29	Wade Boggs	.50
30	Spike Owen	.05
31	Ellis Burks	.05
32	Mike Greenwell	.05
33	Jim Rice	.10
34	Angels Logo	.05
35	Angels Uniform	.05
36	Kirk McCaskill	.05
37	Don Sutton	.40
38	Mike Witt	.05

39 Bob Boone .05
40 Wally Joyner .05
41 Mark McLemore .05
42 Angels Action (Juan Bonilla, Devon White) .05
43 Angels Action (Juan Bonilla, Devon White) .05
44 Jack Howell .05
45 Dick Schofield .05
46 Brian Downing .05
47 Ruppert Jones .05
48 Gary Pettis .05
49 Devon White .05
50 White Sox Logo .05
51 White Sox Uniform .05
52 Floyd Bannister .05
53 Richard Dotson .05
54 Bob James .05
55 Carlton Fisk .45
56 Greg Walker .05
57 Fred Manrique .05
58 White Sox Action (Ozzie Guillen, Donnie Hill, Pat Sheridan) .05
59 White Sox Action (Ozzie Guillen, Donnie Hill, Pat Sheridan) .05
60 Steve Lyons .05
61 Ozzie Guillen .05
62 Harold Baines .05
63 Ivan Calderon .05
64 Gary Redus .05
65 Ken Williams .05
66 Indians Logo .05
67 Indians Uniform .05
68 Scott Bailes .05
69 Tom Candiotti .05
70 Greg Swindell .05
71 Chris Bando .05
72 Joe Carter .05
73 Tommy Hinzo .05
74 Indians Action (Juan Bonilla, Joe Carter) .05
75 Indians Action (Juan Bonilla, Joe Carter) .05
76 Brook Jacoby .05
77 Julio Franco .05
78 Brett Butler .05
79 Mel Hall .05
80 Cory Snyder .05
81 Pat Tabler .05
82 Tigers Logo .05
83 Tigers Uniform .05
84 Willie Hernandez .05
85 Jack Morris .05
86 Frank Tanana .05
87 Walt Terrell .05
88 Matt Nokes .05
89 Darrell Evans .05
90 Tigers Action (Darrell Evans, Carlton Fisk) .05
91 Tigers Action (Darrell Evans, Carlton Fisk) .05
92 Lou Whitaker .05
93 Tom Brookens .05
94 Alan Trammell .05
95 Kirk Gibson .05
96 Chet Lemon .05
97 Pat Sheridan .05
98 Royals Logo .05
99 Royals Uniform .05
100 Charlie Leibrandt .05
101 Dan Quisenberry .05
102 Bret Saberhagen .05
103 Jamie Quirk .05
104 George Brett .60
105 Frank White .05
106 Royals Action (Bret Saberhagen) .05
107 Royals Action (Bret Saberhagen) .05
108 Kevin Seitzer .05
109 Angel Salazar .05
110 Bo Jackson .10
111 Lonnie Smith .05
112 Danny Tartabull .05
113 Willie Wilson .05
114 Brewers Logo .05
115 Brewers Uniform .05
116 Ted Higuera .05
117 Juan Nieves .05
118 Dan Plesac .05
119 Bill Wegman .05
120 B.J. Surhoff .05
121 Greg Brock .05
122 Brewers Action (Jim Gantner, Lou Whitaker) .05
123 Brewers Action (Jim Gantner, Lou Whitaker) .05
124 Jim Gantner .05
125 Paul Molitor .45
126 Dale Sveum .05
127 Glenn Braggs .05
128 Rob Deer .05
129 Robin Yount .45
130 Twins Logo .05
131 Twins Uniform .05
132 Bert Blyleven .05
133 Jeff Reardon .05
134 Frank Viola .05
135 Tim Laudner .05
136 Kent Hrbek .05
137 Steve Lombardozzi .05
138 Twins Action (Steve Lombardozzi, Frank White) .05
139 Twins Action (Steve Lombardozzi, Frank White) .05
140 Gary Gaetti .05
141 Greg Gagne .05
142 Tom Brunansky .05
143 Dan Gladden .05
144 Kirby Puckett .50
145 Gene Larkin .05
146 Yankees Logo .05
147 Yankees Uniform .05
148 Tommy John .05
149 Rick Rhoden .05
150 Dave Righetti .05
151 Rick Cerone .05
152 Don Mattingly .60
153 Willie Randolph .05
154 Yankees Action (Scott Fletcher, Don Mattingly) .25
155 Yankees Action (Scott Fletcher, Don Mattingly) .20
156 Mike Pagliarulo .05
157 Wayne Tolleson .05
158 Rickey Henderson .45
159 Dan Pasqua .05
160 Gary Ward .05
161 Dave Winfield .45
162 Athletics Logo .05
163 Athletics Uniform .05
164 Dave Stewart .05
165 Curt Young .05
166 Terry Steinbach .05
167 Mark McGwire .75
168 Tony Phillips .05
169 Carney Lansford .05
170 Athletics Action (Mike Gallego, Tony Phillips) .05
171 Athletics Action (Mike Gallego, Tony Phillips) .05
172 Alfredo Griffin .05
173 Jose Canseco .30
174 Mike Davis .05
175 Reggie Jackson .60
176 Dwayne Murphy .05
177 Luis Polonia .05
178 Mariners Logo .05
179 Mariners Uniform .05
180 Scott Bankhead .05
181 Mark Langston .05
182 Edwin Nunez .05
183 Scott Bradley .05
184 Dave Valle .05
185 Alvin Davis .05
186 Mariners Action (Jack Howell, Rey Quinones) .05
187 Mariners Action (Jack Howell, Rey Quinones) .05
188 Harold Reynolds .05
189 Jim Presley .05
190 Rey Quinones .05
191 Phil Bradley .05
192 Mickey Brantley .05
193 Mike Kingery .05
194 Rangers Logo .05
195 Rangers Uniform .05
196 Edwin Correa .05
197 Charlie Hough .05
198 Bobby Witt .05
199 Mike Stanley .05
200 Pete O'Brien .05
201 Jerry Browne .05
202 Rangers Action (Steve Buechele, Eddie Murray) .05
203 Rangers Action (Steve Buechele, Eddie Murray) .05
204 Steve Buechele .05
205 Larry Parrish .05
206 Scott Fletcher .05
207 Pete Incaviglia .05
208 Oddibe McDowell .05
209 Ruben Sierra .05
210 Blue Jays Logo .05
211 Blue Jays Uniform .05
212 Mark Eichhorn .05
213 Tom Henke .05
214 Jimmy Key .05
215 Dave Stieb .05
216 Ernie Whitt .05
217 Willie Upshaw .05
218 Blue Jays Action (Harold Reynolds, Willie Upshaw) .05
219 Blue Jays Action (Harold Reynolds, Willie Upshaw) .05
220 Garth Iorg .05
221 Kelly Gruber .05
222 Tony Fernandez .05
223 Jesse Barfield .05
224 George Bell .05
225 Lloyd Moseby .05
226 National League Logo .05
227 Terry Kennedy, Don Mattingly .20
228 Wade Boggs, Willie Randolph .05
229 Bret Saberhagen .05
230 George Bell, Cal Ripken Jr. .45
231 Rickey Henderson, Dave Winfield .10
232 Gary Carter, Jack Clark .05
233 Mike Scott .05
234 Ryne Sandberg, Mike Schmidt .25
235 Ozzie Smith, Eric Davis .10
236 Andre Dawson, Darryl Strawberry .05
237 Braves Logo .05
238 Braves Uniform .05
239 Rick Mahler .05
240 Zane Smith .05
241 Ozzie Virgil .05
242 Gerald Perry .05
243 Glenn Hubbard .05
244 Ken Oberkfell .05
245 Braves Action (Glenn Hubbard, Jeffrey Leonard) .05
246 Braves Action (Glenn Hubbard, Jeffrey Leonard) .05
247 Rafael Ramirez .05
248 Ken Griffey .05
249 Albert Hall .05
250 Dion James .05
251 Dale Murphy .20
252 Gary Roenicke .05
253 Cubs Logo .05
254 Cubs Uniform .05
255 Jamie Moyer .05
256 Lee Smith .05
257 Rick Sutcliffe .05
258 Jody Davis .05
259 Leon Durham .05
260 Ryne Sandberg .50
261 Cubs Action (Jody Davis) .05
262 Cubs Action (Jody Davis) .05
263 Keith Moreland .05
264 Shawon Dunston .05
265 Andre Dawson .25
266 Dave Martinez .05
267 Jerry Mumphrey .05
268 Rafael Palmeiro .45
269 Reds Logo .05
270 Reds Uniform .05
271 John Franco .05
272 Ted Power .05
273 Bo Diaz .05
274 Nick Esasky .05
275 Dave Concepcion .05
276 Kurt Stillwell .05
277 Reds Action (Bob Melvin, Dave Parker) .05
278 Reds Action (Bob Melvin, Dave Parker) .05
279 Buddy Bell .05
280 Barry Larkin .05
281 Kal Daniels .05
282 Eric Davis .05
283 Tracy Jones .05
284 Dave Parker .05
285 Astros Logo .05
286 Astros Uniform .05
287 Jim Deshaies .05
288 Nolan Ryan 1.00
289 Mike Scott .05
290 Dave Smith .05
291 Alan Ashby .05
292 Glenn Davis .05
293 Astros Action (Alan Ashby, Gary Carter) .05
294 Astros Action (Alan Ashby, Gary Carter) .05
295 Bill Doran .05
296 Denny Walling .05
297 Craig Reynolds .05
298 Kevin Bass .05
299 Jose Cruz .05
300 Billy Hatcher .05
301 Dodgers Logo .05
302 Dodgers Uniform .05
303 Orel Hershiser .05
304 Fernando Valenzuela .05
305 Bob Welch .05
306 Matt Young .05
307 Mike Scioscia .05
308 Franklin Stubbs .05
309 Dodgers Action (Mariano Duncan, Junior Ortiz) .05
310 Dodgers Action (Mariano Duncan, Junior Ortiz) .05
311 Steve Sax .05
312 Jeff Hamilton .05
313 Dave Anderson .05
314 Pedro Guerrero .05
315 Mike Marshall .05
316 John Shelby .05
317 Expos Logo .05
318 Expos Uniform .05
319 Neal Heaton .05
320 Bryn Smith .05
321 Floyd Youmans .05
322 Mike Fitzgerald .05
323 Andres Galarraga .05
324 Vance Law .05
325 Expos Action (John Kruk, Tim Raines) .05
326 Expos Action (John Kruk, Tim Raines) .05
327 Tim Wallach .05
328 Hubie Brooks .05
329 Casey Candaele .05
330 Tim Raines .05
331 Mitch Webster .05
332 Herm Winningham .05
333 Mets Logo .05
334 Mets Uniform .05
335 Ron Darling .05
336 Sid Fernandez .05
337 Dwight Gooden .05
338 Gary Carter .45
339 Keith Hernandez .05
340 Wally Backman .05
341 Mets Action (Mike Diaz, Darryl Strawberry, Tim Teufel, Mookie Wilson) .05
342 Mets Action (Mike Diaz, Darryl Strawberry, Tim Teufel, Mookie Wilson) .05
343 Howard Johnson .05
344 Rafael Santana .05
345 Lenny Dykstra .05
346 Kevin McReynolds .05
347 Darryl Strawberry .05
348 Mookie Wilson .05
349 Phillies Logo .05
350 Phillies Uniform .05
351 Steve Bedrosian .05
352 Shane Rawley .05
353 Bruce Ruffin .05
354 Kent Tekulve .05
355 Lance Parrish .05
356 Von Hayes .05
357 Phillies Action (Tony Pena, Glenn Wilson) .05
358 Phillies Action (Tony Pena, Glenn Wilson) .05
359 Juan Samuel .05
360 Mike Schmidt .60
361 Steve Jeltz .05
362 Chris James .05
363 Milt Thompson .05
364 Glenn Wilson .05
365 Pirates Logo .05
366 Pirates Uniform .05
367 Mike Dunne .05
368 Brian Fisher .05
369 Mike LaValliere .05
370 Sid Bream .05
371 Jose Lind .05
372 Bobby Bonilla .05
373 Pirates Action (Bobby Bonilla) .05
374 Pirates Action (Bobby Bonilla) .05
375 Al Pedrique .05
376 Barry Bonds 1.00
377 John Cangelosi .05
378 Mike Diaz .05
379 R.J. Reynolds .05
380 Andy Van Slyke .05
381 Cardinals Logo .05
382 Cardinals Uniform .05
383 Danny Cox .05
384 Bob Forsch .05
385 Joe Magrane .05
386 Todd Worrell .05
387 Tony Pena .05
388 Jack Clark .05
389 Cardinals Action (Jody Davis, Tom Herr) .05
390 Cardinals Action (Jody Davis, Tom Herr) .05
391 Tom Herr .05
392 Terry Pendleton .05
393 Ozzie Smith .50
394 Vince Coleman .05
395 Curt Ford .05
396 Willie McGee .05
397 Padres Logo .05
398 Padres Uniform .05
399 Lance McCullers .05
400 Eric Show .05
401 Ed Whitson .05
402 Benito Santiago .05
403 John Kruk .05
404 Tim Flannery .05
405 Padres Action (Randy Ready, Benito Santiago) .05
406 Padres Action (Randy Ready, Benito Santiago) .05
407 Randy Ready .05
408 Chris Brown .05
409 Garry Templeton .05
410 Tony Gwynn .50
411 Stan Jefferson .05
412 Carmelo Martinez .05
413 Giants Logo .05
414 Giants Uniform .05
415 Kelly Downs .05
416 Scott Garrelts .05
417 Mike Krukow .05
418 Mike LaCoss .05
419 Bob Brenly .05
420 Will Clark .05
421 Giants Action (Will Clark, Mike Fitzgerald) .05
422 Giants Action (Will Clark, Mike Fitzgerald) .05
423 Robby Thompson .05
424 Kevin Mitchell .05
425 Jose Uribe .05
426 Mike Aldrete .05
427 Jeffrey Leonard .05
428 Candy Maldonado .05
429 Mike Schmidt .40
430 Don Mattingly .40
431 Juan Nieves .05
432 Paul Molitor .25
433 Benito Santiago .05
434 Rickey Henderson .25
435 Nolan Ryan .65
436 Kevin Seitzer .05
437 Tony Gwynn .35
438 Mark McGwire .55
439 Howard Johnson .05
440 Steve Bedrosian .05
441 Darrell Evans .05
442 Eddie Murray .25
443 1987 A.L. Championship Series (Kirby Puckett, Alan Trammell, Lou Whitaker) .05
444 1987 A.L. Championship Series (Kirby Puckett, Alan Trammell, Lou Whitaker) .05
445 American League Championship Series MVP (Gary Gaetti) .05
446 National League Championship Series MVP (Jeffrey Leonard) .05
447 1987 N.L. Championship Series (Kevin Mitchell, Tony Pena) .05
448 1987 N.L. Championship Series (Kevin Mitchell, Tony Pena) .05
449 1987 World Series (Tom Brunansky, Tony Pena) .05
450 1987 World Series (Tom Brunansky, Tony Pena) .05
451 World Series Celebration .05
452 World Series Celebration .05
453 World Series Celebration .05
454 World Series Celebration .05
(455) Orioles Logo/Pennant .05
(456) Red Sox Logo/Pennant .05
(457) Angels Logo/Pennant .05
(458) White Sox Logo/Pennant .05
(459) Indians Logo/Pennant .05
(460) Tigers Logo/Pennant .05
(461) Royals Logo/Pennant .05
(462) Brewers Logo/Pennant .05
(463) Twins Logo/Pennant .05
(464) Yankees Logo/Pennant .05
(465) Athletics Logo/Pennant .05
(466) Mariners Logo/Pennant .05
(467) Rangers Logo/Pennant .05
(468) Blue Jays Logo/Pennant .05
(469) Braves Logo/Pennant .05
(470) Cubs Logo/Pennant .05
(471) Reds Logo/Pennant .05
(472) Astros Logo/Pennant .05
(473) Dodgers Logo/Pennant .05
(474) Expos Logo/Pennant .05
(475) Mets Logo/Pennant .05
(476) Phillies Logo/Pennant .05
(477) Pirates Logo/Pennant .05
(478) Cardinals Logo/Pennant .05
(479) Padres Logo/Pennant .05
(480) Giants Logo/Pennant .05

1989 Panini Stickers

For a second straight year, the Italian sticker manufacturer produced a 480-piece set for the American market. The 1-7/8" x 2-11/16" stickers were sold in packs of six for 30 cents. Packs contain five player stickers and a foil depicting team logos, lettering or ballparks. A 64-page album depicting Jose Canseco on the cover was offered for 69 cents. The 1989 Panini stickers used more action photos than the previous year. Color photos had banners at the bottom with team and player name. Backs had appropriate logos, sticker number and ads for Panini's sticker book.

NM/M
Complete Set (480): 12.50
Common Player: .05
Sticker Album: 1.00
Wax Pack (6): .25
Wax Box (100): 7.50

1 World Series Trophy .05
2 World Series Trophy .05
3 Mike Schmidt .40
4 Tom Browning .05
5 Doug Jones .05
6 Wrigley Field .05
7 Wade Boggs .30
8 Jose Canseco .20
9 Orel Hershiser .05
10 Oakland A's Win ALCS .05
11 Oakland A's Win ALCS .05
12 Dennis Eckersley (ALCS MVP) .20
13 Orel Hershiser (NLCS MVP) .05
14 Dodgers Win NLCS .05
15 Dodgers Win NLCS .05
16 Kirk Gibson .05
17 Kirk Gibson .05
18 Orel Hershiser .05
19 Orel Hershiser .05
20 Mark McGwire .50
21 Tim Belcher .05
22 Jay Howell .05
23 Mickey Hatcher .05
24 Mike Davis .05
25 Orel Hershiser (World Series MVP) .05
26 Dodgers Win World Series .05
27 Dodgers Win World Series .05
28 Dodgers Win World Series .05
29 Dodgers Win World Series .05
30 Braves Logo .05
31 Jose Alvarez .05
32 Tommy Gregg .05
33 Paul Assenmacher .05
34 Tom Glavine .25
35 Rick Mahler .05
36 Pete Smith .05
37 Atlanta Stadium .05
38 Braves Script .05
39 Bruce Sutter .20
40 Gerald Perry .05
41 Jeff Blauser .05
42 Ron Gant .05
43 Andres Thomas .05
44 Dion James .05
45 Dale Murphy .20
46 Cubs Logo .05
47 Doug Dascenzo .05
48 Mike Harkey .05
49 Greg Maddux .50
50 Jeff Pico .05
51 Rick Sutcliffe .05
52 Damon Berryhill .05
53 Wrigley Field .05
54 Cubs Script .05
55 Mark Grace .15
56 Ryne Sandberg .50
57 Vance Law .05
58 Shawon Dunston .05
59 Andre Dawson .25
60 Rafael Palmeiro .40
61 Mitch Webster .05
62 Reds Logo .05
63 Jack Armstrong .05
64 Chris Sabo .05
65 Tom Browning .05
66 John Franco .05
67 Danny Jackson .05
68 Jose Rijo .05
69 Riverfront Stadium .05
70 Reds Script .05
71 Bo Diaz .05
72 Nick Esasky .05
73 Jeff Treadway .05
74 Barry Larkin .05
75 Kal Daniels .05
76 Eric Davis .05
77 Paul O'Neill .05
78 Astros Logo .05
79 Craig Biggio .05
80 John Fishel .05
81 Juan Agosto .05
82 Bob Knepper .05
83 Nolan Ryan 1.00
84 Mike Scott .05
85 The Astrodome .05
86 Astros Script .05
87 Dave Smith .05
88 Glenn Davis .05
89 Bill Doran .05
90 Rafael Ramirez .05
91 Kevin Bass .05
92 Billy Hatcher .05
93 Gerald Young .05
94 Dodgers Logo .05
95 Tim Belcher .05
96 Tim Crews .05

97 Orel Hershiser .05
98 Jay Howell .05
99 Tim Leary .05
100 John Tudor .05
101 Dodgers Stadium .05
102 Dodgers Script .05
103 Fernando Valenzuela .05
104 Mike Scioscia .05
105 Mickey Hatcher .05
106 Steve Sax .05
107 Kirk Gibson .05
108 Mike Marshall .05
109 John Shelby .05
110 Expos Logo .05
111 Randy Johnson .40
112 Nelson Santovenia .05
113 Tim Burke .05
114 Dennis Martinez .05
115 Pascual Perez .05
116 Bryn Smith .05
117 Olympic Stadium .05
118 Expos Script .05
119 Andres Galarraga .05
120 Wallace Johnson .05
121 Tom Foley .05
122 Tim Wallach .05
123 Hubie Brooks .05
124 Tracy Jones .05
125 Tim Raines .05
126 Mets Logo .05
127 Kevin Elster .05
128 Gregg Jefferies .05
129 David Cone .05
130 Ron Darling .05
131 Dwight Gooden .05
132 Roger McDowell .05
133 Shea Stadium .05
134 Mets Script .05
135 Randy Myers .05
136 Gary Carter .40
137 Keith Hernandez .05
138 Lenny Dykstra .05
139 Kevin McReynolds .05
140 Darryl Strawberry .05
141 Mookie Wilson .05
142 Phillies Logo .05
143 Ron Jones .05
144 Ricky Jordan .05
145 Steve Bedrosian .05
146 Don Carman .05
147 Kevin Gross .05
148 Bruce Ruffin .05
149 Veterans Stadium .05
150 Phillies Script .05
151 Von Hayes .05
152 Juan Samuel .05
153 Mike Schmidt .55
154 Phil Bradley .05
155 Bob Dernier .05
156 Chris James .05
157 Milt Thompson .05
158 Pirates Logo .05
159 Randy Kramer .05
160 Scott Medvin .05
161 Doug Drabek .05
162 Mike Dunne .05
163 Jim Gott .05
164 Jeff Robinson .05
165 Three Rivers Stadium .05
166 Pirates Script .05
167 John Smiley .05
168 Mike LaValliere .05
169 Sid Bream .05
170 Jose Lind .05
171 Bobby Bonilla .05
172 Barry Bonds 1.00
173 Andy Van Slyke .05
174 Cardinals Logo .05
175 Luis Alicea .05
176 John Costello .05
177 Jose DeLeon .05
178 Joe Magrane .05
179 Todd Worrell .05
180 Tony Pena .05
181 Busch Stadium .05
182 Cardinals Script .05
183 Pedro Guerrero .05
184 Jose Oquendo .05
185 Terry Pendleton .05
186 Ozzie Smith .50
187 Tom Brunansky .05
188 Vince Coleman .05
189 Willie McGee .05
190 Padres Logo .05
191 Roberto Alomar .15
192 Sandy Alomar, Jr. .05
193 Mark Davis .05
194 Andy Hawkins .05
195 Dennis Rasmussen .05
196 Eric Show .05
197 Jack Murphy Stadium .05
198 Padres Script .05
199 Benito Santiago .05
200 John Kruk .05
201 Randy Ready .05
202 Garry Templeton .05
203 Tony Gwynn .50
204 Carmelo Martinez .05
205 Marvell Wynne .05
206 Giants Logo .05
207 Dennis Cook .05
208 Kirt Manwaring .05
209 Kelly Downs .05
210 Rick Reuschel .05
211 Don Robinson .05
212 Will Clark .05
213 Candlestick Park .05
214 Giants Script .05
215 Robby Thompson .05
216 Kevin Mitchell .05
217 Jose Uribe .05
218 Matt Williams .05
219 Mike Aldrete .05
220 Brett Butler .05
221 Candy Maldonado .05
222 Tony Gwynn .30
223 Darryl Strawberry .05
224 Andres Galarraga .05
225 Orel Hershiser, Danny Jackson .05
226 Nolan Ryan .50
227 Dwight Gooden/AS .05
228 Gary Carter/AS .05
229 Vince Coleman/AS .05
230 Andre Dawson/AS .05
231 Darryl Strawberry/AS .05
232 Will Clark/AS .05
233 Ryne Sandberg/AS .25
234 Bobby Bonilla/AS .05
235 Ozzie Smith/AS .30
236 Terry Steinbach/AS .05
237 Frank Viola/AS .05
238 Jose Canseco/AS .10
239 Rickey Henderson/AS .20
240 Dave Winfield/AS .20
241 Cal Ripken, Jr./AS .50
242 Wade Boggs/AS .25
243 Paul Molitor/AS .20
244 Mark McGwire/AS .40
245 Wade Boggs .30
246 Jose Canseco .10
247 Kirby Puckett .30
248 Frank Viola .05
249 Roger Clemens .35
250 Orioles Logo .05
251 Bob Milacki .05
252 Craig Worthington .05
253 Jeff Ballard .05
254 Tom Niedenfeur .05
255 Dave Schmidt .05
256 Terry Kennedy .05
257 Memorial Stadium .05
258 Orioles Script .05
259 Mickey Tettleton .05
260 Eddie Murray .40
261 Billy Ripken .05
262 Cal Ripken, Jr. 1.00
263 Joe Orsulak .05
264 Larry Sheets .05
265 Pete Stanicek .05
266 Red Sox Logo .05
267 Steve Curry .05
268 Jody Reed .05
269 "Oil Can" Boyd .05
270 Roger Clemens .55
271 Bruce Hurst .05
272 Lee Smith .05
273 Fenway Park .05
274 Red Sox Script .05
275 Todd Benzinger .05
276 Marty Barrett .05
277 Wade Boggs .50
278 Ellis Burks .05
279 Dwight Evans .05
280 Mike Greenwell .05
281 Jim Rice .10
282 Angels Logo .05
283 Dante Bichette .05
284 Bryan Harvey .05
285 Kirk McCaskill .05
286 Mike Witt .05
287 Bob Boone .05
288 Brian Downing .05
289 Anaheim Stadium .05
290 Angels Script .05
291 Wally Joyner .05
292 Johnny Ray .05
293 Jack Howell .05
294 Dick Schofield .05
295 Tony Armas .05
296 Chili Davis .05
297 Devon White .05
298 White Sox Logo .05
299 Dave Gallagher .05
300 Melido Perez .05
301 Shawn Hillegas .05
302 Jack McDowell .05
303 Bobby Thigpen .05
304 Carlton Fisk .40
305 Comiskey Park .05
306 White Sox Script .05
307 Greg Walker .05
308 Steve Lyons .05
309 Ozzie Guillen .05
310 Harold Baines .05
311 Daryl Boston .05
312 Lance Johnson .05
313 Dan Pasqua .05
314 Indians Logo .05
315 Luis Medina .05
316 Ron Tingley .05
317 Tom Candiotti .05
318 John Farrell .05
319 Doug Jones .05
320 Greg Swindell .05
321 Cleveland Stadium .05
322 Indians Script .05
323 Andy Allanson .05
324 Willie Upshaw .05
325 Julio Franco .05
326 Brook Jacoby .05
327 Joe Carter .05
328 Mel Hall .05
329 Cory Snyder .05
330 Tigers Logo .05
331 Paul Gibson .05
332 Torey Luvello .05
333 Mike Henneman .05
334 Jack Morris .05
335 Jeff Robinson .05
336 Frank Tanana .05
337 Tiger Stadium .05
338 Tigers Script .05
339 Matt Nokes .05
340 Tom Brookens .05
341 Lou Whitaker .05
342 Luis Salazar .05
343 Alan Trammell .05
344 Chet Lemon .05
345 Gary Pettis .05
346 Royals Logo .05
347 Luis de los Santos .05
348 Gary Thurman .05
349 Steve Farr .05
350 Mark Gubicza .05
351 Charlie Leibrandt .05
352 Bret Saberhagen .05
353 Royals Stadium .05
354 Royals Script .05
355 George Brett .55
356 Frank White .05
357 Kevin Seitzer .05
358 Bo Jackson .10
359 Pat Tabler .05
360 Danny Tartabull .05
361 Willie Wilson .05
362 Brewers Logo .05
363 Joey Meyer .05
364 Gary Sheffield .25
365 Don August .05
366 Ted Higuera .05
367 Dan Plesac .05
368 B.J. Surhoff .05
369 County Stadium .05
370 Brewers Script .05
371 Greg Brock .05
372 Jim Gantner .05
373 Paul Molitor .40
374 Dale Sveum .05
375 Glenn Braggs .05
376 Rob Deer .05
377 Robin Yount .40
378 Twins Logo .05
379 German Gonzalez .05
380 Kelvin Torve .05
381 Allan Anderson .05
382 Jeff Reardon .05
383 Frank Viola .05
384 Tim Laudner .05
385 HHH Metrodome .05
386 Twins Script .05
387 Kent Hrbek .05
388 Gene Larkin .05
389 Gary Gaetti .05
390 Greg Gagne .05
391 Randy Bush .05
392 Dan Gladden .05
393 Kirby Puckett .50
394 Yankees Logo .05
395 Roberto Kelly .05
396 Al Leiter .05
397 John Candelaria .05
398 Rich Dotson .05
399 Rick Rhoden .05
400 Dave Righetti .05
401 Yankee Stadium .05
402 Yankees Script .05
403 Don Slaught .05
404 Don Mattingly .55
405 Willie Randolph .05
406 Mike Pagliarulo .05
407 Rafael Santana .05
408 Rickey Henderson .40
409 Dave Winfield .40
410 A's Logo .05
411 Todd Burns .05
412 Walt Weiss .05
413 Storm Davis .05
414 Dennis Eckersley .35
415 Dave Stewart .05
416 Bob Welch .05
417 Oakland Coliseum .05
418 A's Script .05
419 Terry Steinbach .05
420 Mark McGwire .75
421 Carney Lansford .05
422 Jose Canseco .35
423 Dave Henderson .05
424 Dave Parker .05
425 Luis Polonia .05
426 Mariners Logo .05
427 Mario Diaz .05
428 Edgar Martinez .05
429 Scott Bankhead .05
430 Mark Langston .05
431 Mike Moore .05
432 Scott Bradley .05
433 The Kingdome .05
434 Mariners Script .05
435 Alvin Davis .05
436 Harold Reynolds .05
437 Jim Presley .05
438 Rey Quinonez .05
439 Mickey Brantley .05
440 Jay Buhner .05
441 Henry Cotto .05
442 Rangers Logo .05
443 Cecil Espy .05
444 Chad Kreuter .05
445 Jose Guzman .05
446 Charlie Hough .05
447 Jeff Russell .05
448 Bobby Witt .05
449 Arlington Stadium .05
450 Rangers Script .05
451 Geno Petralli .05
452 Pete O'Brien .05
453 Steve Buechele .05
454 Scott Fletcher .05
455 Pete Incaviglia .05
456 Oddibe McDowell .05
457 Ruben Sierra .05
458 Blue Jays Logo .05
459 Rob Ducey .05
460 Todd Stottlemyre .05
461 Tom Henke .05
462 Jimmy Key .05
463 Dave Steib .05
464 Pat Borders .05
465 Exhibition Stadium .05
466 Blue Jays Script .05
467 Fred McGriff .05
468 Manny Lee .05
469 Kelly Gruber .05
470 Tony Fernandez .05
471 Jesse Barfield .05
472 George Bell .05
473 Lloyd Moseby .05
474 Orel Hershiser .05
475 Frank Viola .05
476 Chris Sabo .05
477 Jose Canseco .10
478 Walt Weiss .05
479 Kirk Gibson .05
480 Jose Canseco .10

1990 Panini Stickers

Nearly 400 individual player and specialty stickers comprise the 1990 issue from this Italian company. Sold in packs of five regular and one foil sticker, the set includes 388 2-1/8" x 3" stickers. Fronts feature color action photos. Backs are printed in black-and-white and include a sticker number and appropriate logos. A 68-page album with Nolan Ryan on the cover was sold as an adjunct to the stickers. Among the foil stickers in the set are those featuring the team logo and batting helmet of each team.

	NM/M
Complete Set (388):	9.00
Common Player:	.05
English Album:	1.00
French Album:	3.00
Wax Pack (5+1):	.25
Wax Box (100):	7.50

1 Randy Milligan .05
2 Gregg Olson .05
3 Bill Ripken .05
4 Phil Bradley .05
5 Joe Orsulak .05
6 Bob Milacki .05
7 Cal Ripken, Jr. 1.00
8 Mickey Tettleton .05
9 Orioles Logo (Foil) .05
10 Orioles Helmet (Foil) .05
11 Craig Worthington .05
12 Mike Devereaux .05
13 Jeff Ballard .05
14 Lee Smith .05
15 Marty Barrett .05
16 Mike Greenwell .05
17 Dwight Evans .05
18 John Dopson .05
19 Wade Boggs .50
20 Mike Boddicker .05
21 Ellis Burks .05
22 Red Sox Logo (Foil) .05
23 Red Sox Helmet (Foil) .05
24 Roger Clemens .55
25 Jody Reed .05
26 Nick Esasky .05
27 Brian Downing .05
28 Bert Blyleven .05
29 Devon White .05
30 Claudell Washington .05
31 Wally Joyner .05
32 Chuck Finley .05
33 Johnny Ray .05
34 Jim Abbott .05
35 Angels Logo (Foil) .05
36 Angels Helmet (Foil) .05
37 Kirk McCaskill .05
38 Lance Parrish .05
39 Chili Davis .05
40 Steve Lyons .05
41 Ozzie Guillen .05
42 Melido Perez .05
43 Scott Fletcher .05
44 Carlton Fisk .40
45 Greg Walker .05
46 Dave Gallagher .05
47 Ivan Calderon .05
48 White Sox Logo (Foil) .05
49 White Sox Helmet (Foil) .05
50 Bobby Thigpen .05
51 Ron Kittle .05
52 Daryl Boston .05
53 John Farrell .05
54 Jerry Browne .05
55 Pete O'Brien .05
56 Cory Snyder .05
57 Tom Candiotti .05
58 Brook Jacoby .05
59 Greg Swindell .05
60 Felix Fermin .05
61 Indians Logo (Foil) .05
62 Indians Helmet (Foil) .05
63 Doug Jones .05
64 Dion James .05
65 Joe Carter .05
66 Mike Heath .05
67 Dave Bergman .05
68 Gary Ward .05
69 Mike Henneman .05
70 Alan Trammell .05
71 Lou Whitaker .05
72 Frank Tanana .05
73 Fred Lynn .05
74 Tigers Logo (Foil) .05
75 Tigers Helmet (Foil) .05
76 Jack Morris .05
77 Chet Lemon .05
78 Gary Pettis .05
79 Kurt Stillwell .05
80 Jim Eisenreich .05
81 Bret Saberhagen .05
82 Mark Gubicza .05
83 Frank White .05
84 Bo Jackson .10
85 Jeff Montgomery .05
86 Kevin Seitzer .05
87 Royals Logo (Foil) .05
88 Royals Helmet (Foil) .05
89 Tom Gordon .05
90 Danny Tartabull .05
91 George Brett .55
92 Robin Yount .40
93 B.J. Surhoff .05
94 Jim Gantner .05
95 Dan Plesac .05
96 Ted Higuera .05
97 Glenn Braggs .05
98 Paul Molitor .40
99 Chris Bosio .05
100 Brewers Logo (Foil) .05
101 Brewers Helmet (Foil) .05
102 Rob Deer .05
103 Chuck Crim .05
104 Greg Brock .05
105 Kirby Puckett .50
106 Gary Gaetti .05
107 Roy Smith .05
108 Jeff Reardon .05
109 Randy Bush .05
110 Al Newman .05
111 Dan Gladden .05
112 Kent Hrbek .05
113 Twins Logo (Foil) .05
114 Twins Helmet (Foil) .05
115 Greg Gagne .05
116 Brian Harper .05
117 Allan Anderson .05
118 Lee Guetterman .05
119 Roberto Kelly .05
120 Jesse Barfield .05
121 Alvaro Espinoza .05
122 Mel Hall .05
123 Chuck Cary .05
124 Dave Righetti .05
125 Don Mattingly .55
126 Yankees Logo (Foil) .05
127 Yankees Helmet (Foil) .05
128 Bob Geren .05
129 Steve Sax .05
130 Andy Hawkins .05
131 Bob Welch .05
132 Mark McGwire .75
133 Dave Henderson .05
134 Carney Lansford .05
135 Walt Weiss .05
136 Mike Moore .05
137 Dennis Eckersley .35
138 Rickey Henderson .40
139 A's Logo (Foil) .05
140 A's Helmet (Foil) .05
141 Dave Stewart .05
142 Jose Canseco .30
143 Terry Steinbach .05
144 Harold Reynolds .05
145 Darnell Coles .05
146 Brian Holman .05
147 Scott Bankhead .05
148 Greg Briley .05
149 Alvin Davis .05
150 Jeffrey Leonard .05
151 Mike Schooler .05
152 Mariners Logo (Foil) .05
153 Mariners Helmet (Foil) .05
154 Randy Johnson .40
155 Ken Griffey Jr. .65
156 Dave Valle .05
157 Pete Incaviglia .05
158 Fred Manrique .05
159 Jeff Russell .05
160 Nolan Ryan 1.00
161 Geno Petralli .05
162 Ruben Sierra .05
163 Julio Franco .05
164 Rafael Palmeiro .35
165 Rangers Logo (Foil) .05
166 Rangers Helmet (Foil) .05
167 Harold Baines .05
168 Kevin Brown .05
169 Steve Buechele .05
170 Fred McGriff .05
171 Kelly Gruber .05
172 Todd Stottlemyre .05
173 Dave Steib .05
174 Mookie Wilson .05
175 Pat Borders .05
176 Tony Fernandez .05
177 John Cerutti .05
178 Blue Jays Logo (Foil) .05
179 Blue Jays Helmet (Foil) .05
180 George Bell .05
181 Jimmy Key .05
182 Nelson Liriano .05
183 Kirby Puckett (BA leader) .30
184 Carney Lansford (Stats leader.) .05
185 Nolan Ryan (K Leader) .50
186 American League Logo (Foil) .05
187 National League Logo (Foil) .05
188 World's Championship Trophy (Foil) .05
189 1988 L.A. Dodgers World Series Ring (Foil) .05
190 1987 Minnesota Twins World Series Ring (Foil) .05
191 1986 N.Y. Mets World Series Ring (Foil) .05
192 1985 K.C. Royals World Series Ring (Foil) .05
193 1984 Detroit Tigers World Series Ring (Foil) .05
194 1983 Baltimore Orioles World Series Ring (Foil) .05
195 1982 Cardinals World Series Ring (Foil) .05
196 1981 L.A. Dodgers World Series Ring (Foil) .05
197 1980 Phillies World Series Ring (Foil) .05
198 Dave Stewart, Bo Jackson/AS .05
199 Wade Boggs, Kirby Puckett/AS .15
200 Harold Baines/AS .05
201 Julio Franco/AS .05
202 Cal Ripken, Jr./AS .50
203 Ruben Sierra/AS .05
204 Mark McGwire/AS .40
205 Terry Steinbach/AS .05
206 Rick Reuschel, Ozzie Smith/AS .05
207 Tony Gwynn, Will Clark/AS .05
208 Kevin Mitchell/AS .05
209 Eric Davis/AS .05
210 Howard Johnson/AS .05
211 Pedro Guerrero/AS .05
212 Ryne Sandberg/AS .25
213 Benito Santiago/AS .05
214 Kevin Mitchell (HR Leaders) .05
215 Mark Davis (Saves leader.) .05
216 Vince Coleman (SB Leader) .05
217 Jeff Blauser .05
218 Jeff Treadway .05
219 Tom Glavine .20
220 Joe Boever .05
221 Oddibe McDowell .05
222 Dale Murphy .20
223 Derek Lilliquist .05
224 Tommy Gregg .05
225 Braves Logo (Foil) .05
226 Braves Helmet (Foil) .05
227 Lonnie Smith .05
228 John Smoltz .05
229 Andres Thomas .05
230 Jerome Walton .05
231 Ryne Sandberg .50
232 Mitch Williams .05
233 Rick Sutcliffe .05
234 Damon Berryhill .05
235 Dwight Smith .05
236 Shawon Dunston .05
237 Greg Maddux .50
238 Cubs Logo (Foil) .05
239 Cubs Helmet (Foil) .05
240 Andre Dawson .25
241 Mark Grace .05
242 Mike Bielecki .05
243 Jose Rijo .05
244 John Franco .05
245 Paul O'Neill .05
246 Eric Davis .05
247 Tom Browning .05
248 Chris Sabo .05
249 Rob Dibble .05

250 Todd Benzinger .05
251 Reds Logo (Foil) .05
252 Reds Helmet (Foil) .05
253 Barry Larkin .05
254 Rolando Roomes .05
255 Danny Jackson .05
256 Terry Puhl .05
257 Dave Smith .05
258 Glenn Davis .05
259 Craig Biggio .05
260 Ken Caminiti .05
261 Kevin Bass .05
262 Mike Scott .05
263 Gerald Young .05
264 Astros Logo (Foil) .05
265 Astros Helmet (Foil) .05
266 Rafael Ramirez .05
267 Jim Deshaies .05
268 Bill Doran .05
269 Fernando Valenzuela .05
270 Alfredo Griffin .05
271 Kirk Gibson .05
272 Mike Marshall .05
273 Eddie Murray .40
274 Jay Howell .05
275 Orel Hershiser .05
276 Mike Scioscia .05
277 Dodgers Logo (Foil) .05
278 Dodgers Helmet (Foil) .05
279 Willie Randolph .05
280 Kal Daniels .05
281 Tim Belcher .05
282 Pascual Perez .05
283 Tim Raines .05
284 Andres Galarraga .05
285 Spike Owen .05
286 Tim Wallach .05
287 Mark Langston .05
288 Dennis Martinez .05
289 Nelson Santovenia .05
290 Expos Logo (Foil) .05
291 Expos Helmet (Foil) .05
292 Tom Foley .05
293 Dave Martinez .05
294 Tim Burke .05
295 Ron Darling .05
296 Kevin Elster .05
297 Dwight Gooden .05
298 Gregg Jefferies .05
299 Sid Fernandez .05
300 Dave Magadan .05
301 David Cone .05
302 Darryl Strawberry .05
303 Mets Logo (Foil) .05
304 Mets Helmet (Foil) .05
305 Kevin McReynolds .05
306 Howard Johnson .05
307 Randy Myers .05
308 Roger McDowell .05
309 Tom Herr .05
310 John Kruk .05
311 Randy Ready .05
312 Jeff Parrett .05
313 Lenny Dykstra .05
314 Ken Howell .05
315 Ricky Jordan .05
316 Phillies Logo (Foil) .05
317 Phillies Helmet (Foil) .05
318 Dickie Thon .05
319 Von Hayes .05
320 Dennis Cook .05
321 Jay Bell .05
322 Barry Bonds 1.00
323 John Smiley .05
324 Andy Van Slyke .05
325 Bobby Bonilla .05
326 Bill Landrum .05
327 Randy Kramer .05
328 Jose Lind .05
329 Pirates Logo (Foil) .05
330 Pirates Helmet (Foil) .05
331 Gary Redus .05
332 Doug Drabek .05
333 Mike LaValliere .05
334 Jose DeLeon .05
335 Pedro Guerrero .05
336 Vince Coleman .05
337 Terry Pendleton .05
338 Ozzie Smith .50
339 Willie McGee .05
340 Todd Worrell .05
341 Jose Oquendo .05
342 Cardinals Logo (Foil) .05
343 Cardinals Helmet (Foil) .05
344 Tom Brunansky .05
345 Milt Thompson .05
346 Joe Magrane .05
347 Ed Whitson .05
348 Jack Clark .05
349 Roberto Alomar .10
350 Chris James .05
351 Tony Gwynn .50
352 Mark Davis .05
353 Greg W. Harris .05
354 Garry Templeton .05
355 Padres Logo (Foil) .05
356 Padres Helmet (Foil) .05
357 Bruce Hurst .05
358 Benito Santiago .05
359 Bip Roberts .05
360 Dave Dravecky .05
361 Kevin Mitchell .05
362 Craig Lefferts .05
363 Will Clark .05
364 Steve Bedrosian .05
365 Brett Butler .05
366 Matt Williams .05
367 Scott Garrelts .05
368 Giants Logo (Foil) .05
369 Giants Helmet (Foil) .05
370 Rick Reuschel .05
371 Robby Thompson .05
372 Jose Uribe .05
373 Ben McDonald (Headliner) .05
374 Carlos Martinez (Headliner) .05
375 Steve Olin (Headliner) .05
376 Bill Spiers (Headliner) .05
377 Junior Felix (Headliner) .05
378 Joe Oliver (Headliner) .05
379 Eric Anthony (Headliner) .05
380 Ramon Martinez (Headliner) .05
381 Todd Zeile (Headliner) .05
382 Andy Benes (Headliner) .05
383 Vince Coleman (Highlight) .05
384 Bo Jackson (Highlight) .05
385 Howard Johnson (Highlight) .05
386 Dave Dravecky (Highlight) .05
387 Nolan Ryan (Highlight) .50
388 Cal Ripken, Jr. (Highlight) .50

1991 Panini Stickers

For 1991 the Panini stickers were considerably downsized in both the number of pieces in the set (271) and in the size of each sticker (1-1/2" x 2-9/16"). Player stickers have a color action photo at center with a few stats at bottom. There are foil pennant and team logo stickers for each team as well as 1990 season highlights kicking off the set. Backs are printed in black-and-white and have MLB and Players Association logos, along with Panini advertising. A colorful album was available to house the stickers, featuring on its cover Ken Griffey, Jr., Ryne Sandberg and Rickey Henderson.

NM/M
Complete Set (271): 12.50
Common Player: .05
Album: 1.00
Wax Pack (5+1): .25
Wax Box (100): 9.00
1 Mark Langston, Mike Witt (No-hitter.) .05
2 Randy Johnson (No-hitter.) .20
3 Nolan Ryan (No-hitter.) .50
4 Dave Stewart (No-hitter.) .05
5 Fernando Valenzuela (No-hitter.) .05
6 Andy Hawkins (No-hitter.) .05
7 Melido Perez (No-hitter.) .05
8 Terry Mullholland (No-hitter.) .05
9 Dave Steib (No-hitter.) .05
10 Craig Biggio .05
11 Jim Deshaies .05
12 Dave Smith .05
13 Eric Yelding .05
14 Astros Pennant .05
15 Astros Logo .05
16 Mike Scott .05
17 Ken Caminiti .05
18 Danny Darwin .05
19 Glenn Davis .05
20 Braves Pennant .05
21 Braves Logo .05
22 Lonnie Smith .05
23 Charlie Leibrandt .05
24 Jim Presley .05
25 Greg Olson .05
26 John Smoltz .05
27 Ron Gant .05
28 Jeff Treadway .05
29 Dave Justice .05
30 Jose Oquendo .05
31 Joe Magrane .05
32 Cardinals Pennant .05
33 Cardinals Logo .05
34 Todd Zeile .05
35 Vince Coleman .05
36 Bob Tewksbury .05
37 Pedro Guerrero .05
38 Lee Smith .05
39 Ozzie Smith .50
40 Ryne Sandberg .50
41 Andre Dawson .25
42 Cubs Pennant .05
43 Greg Maddux .50
44 Jerome Walton .05
45 Cubs Logo .05
46 Mike Harkey .05
47 Shawon Dunston .05
48 Mark Grace .05
49 Joe Girardi .05
50 Ramon Martinez .05
51 Lenny Harris .05
52 Mike Morgan .05
53 Eddie Murray .40
54 Dodgers Pennant .05
55 Dodgers Logo .05
56 Hubie Brooks .05
57 Mike Scioscia .05
58 Kal Daniels .05
59 Fernando Valenzuela .05
60 Expos Pennant .05
61 Expos Logo .05
62 Spike Owen .05
63 Tim Raines .05
64 Tim Wallach .05
65 Larry Walker .05
66 Dave Martinez .05
67 Mark Gardner .05
68 Dennis Martinez .05
69 Delino DeShields .05
70 Jeff Brantley .05
71 Kevin Mitchell .05
72 Giants Pennant .05
73 Giants Logo .05
74 Don Robinson .05
75 Brett Butler .05
76 Matt Williams .05
77 Robby Thompson .05
78 John Burkett .05
79 Will Clark .05
80 David Cone .05
81 Dave Magadan .05
82 Mets Pennant .05
83 Gregg Jefferies .05
84 Frank Viola .05
85 Mets Logo .05
86 Howard Johnson .05
87 John Franco .05
88 Darryl Strawberry .05
89 Dwight Gooden .05
90 Joe Carter .05
91 Ed Whitson .05
92 Andy Benes .05
93 Benito Santiago .05
94 Padres Pennant .05
95 Padres Logo .05
96 Roberto Alomar .10
97 Bip Roberts .05
98 Jack Clark .05
99 Tony Gwynn .50
100 Phillies Pennant .05
101 Phillies Logo .05
102 Charlie Hayes .05
103 Lenny Dykstra .05
104 Dale Murphy .20
105 Von Hayes .05
106 Dickie Thon .05
107 John Kruk .05
108 Ken Howell .05
109 Darren Daulton .05
110 Jay Bell .05
111 Bobby Bonilla .05
112 Pirates Pennant .05
113 Pirates Logo .05
114 Barry Bonds 1.00
115 Neal Heaton .05
116 Doug Drabek .05
117 Jose Lind .05
118 Andy Van Slyke .05
119 Sid Bream .05
120 Paul O'Neill .05
121 Randy Myers .05
122 Reds Pennant .05
123 Mariano Duncan .05
124 Eric Davis .05
125 Red Logo .05
126 Jack Armstrong .05
127 Chris Sabo .05
128 Rob Dibble .05
129 Barry Larkin .05
130 National League Logo .05
131 American League Logo .05
132 Dave Winfield .40
133 Lance Parrish .05
134 Chili Davis .05
135 Chuck Finley .05
136 Angels Pennant .05
137 Angels Logo .05
138 Johnny Ray .05
139 Dante Bichette .05
140 Jim Abbott .05
141 Wally Joyner .05
142 A's Pennant .05
143 A's Logo .05
144 Dave Stewart .05
145 Mark McGwire .75
146 Rickey Henderson .40
147 Walt Weiss .05
148 Dennis Eckersley .35
149 Jose Canseco .30
150 Dave Henderson .05
151 Bob Welch .05
152 Tony Fernandez .05
153 David Wells .05
154 Blue Jays Pennant .05
155 Blue Jays Logo .05
156 Pat Borders .05
157 Fred McGriff .05
158 George Bell .05
159 John Olerud .05
160 Dave Steib .05
161 Kelly Gruber .05
162 Billy Spiers .05
163 Dan Plesac .05
164 Brewers Pennant .05
165 Mark Knudson .05
166 Robin Yount .40
167 Brewers Logo .05
168 Paul Molitor .40
169 B.J. Surhoff .05
170 Gary Sheffield .30
171 Dave Parker .05
172 Sandy Alomar .05
173 Doug Jones .05
174 Tom Candiotti .05
175 Mitch Webster .05
176 Indians Pennant .05
177 Indians Logo .05
178 Brook Jacoby .05
179 Candy Maldonado .05
180 Carlos Baerga .05
181 Chris James .05
182 Mariners Pennant .05
183 Mariners Logo .05
184 Mike Schooler .05
185 Alvin Davis .05
186 Erik Hanson .05
187 Edgar Martinez .05
188 Randy Johnson .40
189 Ken Griffey Jr. .60
190 Jay Buhner .05
191 Harold Reynolds .05
192 Cal Ripken Jr. 1.00
193 Gregg Olson .05
194 Orioles Pennant .05
195 Orioles Logo .05
196 Mike Devereaux .05
197 Ben McDonald .05
198 Craig Worthington .05
199 Dave Johnson .05
200 Joe Orsulak .05
201 Randy Milligan .05
202 Ruben Sierra .05
203 Bobby Witt .05
204 Rangers Pennant .05
205 Nolan Ryan 1.00
206 Jeff Huson .05
207 Rangers Logo .05
208 Kevin Brown .05
209 Steve Buechele .05
210 Julio Franco .05
211 Rafael Palmeiro .05
212 Ellis Burks .05
213 Dwight Evans .05
214 Wade Boggs .50
215 Roger Clemens .55
216 Red Sox Pennant .05
217 Red Sox Logo .05
218 Jeff Reardon .05
219 Tony Pena .05
220 Jody Reed .05
221 Carlos Quintana .05
222 Royals Pennant .05
223 Royals Logo .05
224 George Brett .55
225 Bret Saberhagen .05
226 Bo Jackson .10
227 Kevin Seitzer .05
228 Mark Gubicza .05
229 Jim Eisenreich .05
230 Gerald Perry .05
231 Tom Gordon .05
232 Cecil Fielder .05
233 Lou Whitaker .05
234 Tigers Pennant .05
235 Tigers Logo .05
236 Mike Henneman .05
237 Mike Heath .05
238 Alan Trammell .05
239 Lloyd Moseby .05
240 Dan Petry .05
241 Dave Bergman .05
242 Brian Harper .05
243 Rick Aguilera .05
244 Twins Pennant .05
245 Greg Gagne .05
246 Gene Larkin .05
247 Twins Logo .05
248 Kirby Puckett .50
249 Kevin Tapani .05
250 Gary Gaetti .05
251 Kent Hrbek .05
252 Bobby Thigpen .05
253 Lance Johnson .05
254 Greg Hibbard .05
255 Carlton Fisk .40
256 White Sox Pennant .05
257 White Sox Logo .05
258 Ivan Calderon .05
259 Barry Jones .05
260 Robin Ventura .05
261 Ozzie Guillen .05
262 Yankees Pennant .05
263 Yankees Logo .05
264 Kevin Maas .05
265 Bob Geren .05
266 Dave Righetti .05
267 Don Mattingly .55
268 Roberto Kelly .05
269 Alvaro Espinosa .05
270 Oscar Azocar .05
271 Steve Sax .05

Canadian

While the U.S. sticker set from Panini was downsized both in physical format and number of stickers in the set, a special issue for the Canadian market was produced in the 2-1/8" x 3" size to a total of 360 pieces. The relatively simple design has a color game-action photo with a wide white border. The black player name and team at bottom are highlighted by a red (American League) or blue (National League) splash of color at lower-left. Black-and-white backs have a sticker number and a few words about the collection in English and French. Besides player stickers there are foil specialty stickers for the teams and a subset of All-Star stickers.

NM/M
Complete Set (360): 20.00
Common Player: .05
Album: 3.00
1 Major League Baseball Logo (foil) .05
2 MLB Players Association Logo (foil) .05
3 Panini Logo (foil) .05
4 Houston Astros Pennant (Foil) .05
5 Houston Astros Logo (Foil) .05
6 Craig Biggio .05
7 Glenn Davis .05
8 Casey Candaele .05
9 Ken Caminiti .05
10 Rafael Ramirez .05
11 Glenn Wilson .05
12 Eric Yelding .05
13 Franklin Stubbs .05
14 Mike Scott .05
15 Danny Darwin .05
16 Atlanta Braves Pennant (Foil) .05
17 Atlanta Braves Logo (Foil) .05
18 Greg Olson .05
19 Tommy Gregg .05
20 Jeff Treadway .05
21 Jim Presley .05
22 Jeff Blauser .05
23 Ron Gant .05
24 Lonnie Smith .05
25 Dave Justice .05
26 John Smoltz .05
27 Charlie Leibrandt .05
28 St. Louis Cardinals Pennant (Foil) .05
29 St. Louis Cardinals Logo (Foil) .05
30 Tom Pagnozzi .05
31 Pedro Guerrero .05
32 Jose Oquendo .05
33 Todd Zeile .05
34 Ozzie Smith .50
35 Vince Coleman .05
36 Milt Thompson .05
37 Rex Hudler .05
38 Joe Magrane .05
39 Lee Smith .05
40 Chicago Cubs Pennant (Foil) .05
41 Chicago Cubs Logo (Foil) .05
42 Joe Girardi .05
43 Mark Grace .05
44 Ryne Sandberg .50
45 Luis Salazar .05
46 Shawon Dunston .05
47 Dwight Smith .05
48 Jerome Walton .05
49 Andre Dawson .25
50 Greg Maddux .50
51 Mike Harkey .05
52 Los Angeles Dodgers Pennant (Foil) .05
53 Los Angeles Dodgers Logo (Foil) .05
54 Mike Scioscia .05
55 Eddie Murray .40
56 Juan Samuel .05
57 Lenny Harris .05
58 Alfredo Griffin .05
59 Hubie Brooks .05
60 Kal Daniels .05
61 Stan Javier .05
62 Ramon Martinez .05
63 Mike Morgan .05
64 San Francisco Giants Pennant (Foil) .05
65 San Francisco Giants Logo (Foil) .05
66 Terry Kennedy .05
67 Will Clark .05
68 Robby Thompson .05
69 Matt Williams .05
70 Jose Uribe .05
71 Kevin Mitchell .05
72 Brett Butler .05
73 Don Robinson .05
74 John Burkett .05
75 Jeff Brantley .05
76 New York Mets Pennant (Foil) .05
77 New York Mets Logo (Foil) .05
78 Mackey Sasser .05
79 Dave Magadan .05
80 Gregg Jefferies .05
81 Howard Johnson .05
82 Kevin Elster .05
83 Kevin McReynolds .05
84 Daryl Boston .05
85 Darryl Strawberry .05
86 Dwight Gooden .05
87 Frank Viola .05
88 San Diego Padres Pennant (Foil) .05
89 San Diego Padres Logo (Foil) .05
90 Benito Santiago .05
91 Jack Clark .05
92 Roberto Alomar .10
93 Mike Pagliarulo .05
94 Garry Templeton .05
95 Joe Carter .05
96 Bip Roberts .05
97 Tony Gwynn .50
98 Ed Whitson .05
99 Andy Benes .05
100 Philadelphia Phillies Pennant (Foil) .05
101 Philadelphia Phillies Logo (Foil) .05
102 Darren Daulton .05
103 Ricky Jordan .05
104 Randy Ready .05
105 Charlie Hayes .05
106 Dickie Thon .05
107 Von Hayes .05
108 Lenny Dykstra .05
109 Dale Murphy .20
110 Ken Howell .05
111 Roger McDowell .05
112 Pittsburgh Pirates Pennant (Foil) .05
113 Pittsburgh Pirates Logo (Foil) .05
114 Mike LaValliere .05
115 Sid Bream .05
116 Jose Lind .05
117 Jeff King .05
118 Jay Bell .05
119 Barry Bonds 1.00
120 Bobby Bonilla .05
121 Andy Van Slyke .05
121 Doug Drabek .05
123 Neal Heaton .05
124 Cincinnati Reds Pennant (Foil) .05
125 Cincinnati Reds Logo (Foil) .05
126 Joe Oliver .05
127 Todd Benzinger .05
128 Mariano Duncan .05
129 Chris Sabo .05
130 Barry Larkin .05
131 Eric Davis .05
132 Billy Hatcher .05
133 Paul O'Neill .05
134 Jose Rijo .05
135 Randy Myers .05
136 Montreal Expos Pennant (Foil) .05
137 Montreal Expos Logo (Foil) .05
138 Mike Fitzgerald .05
139 Andres Galarraga .05
140 Delino DeShields .05
141 Tim Wallach .05
142 Spike Owen .05
143 Tim Raines .05
144 Dave Martinez .05
145 Larry Walker .05

146 Expos batting Helmet (Foil) .05
147 Dennis Boyd .05
148 Tim Burke .05
149 Bill Sampen .05
150 Dennis Martinez .05
151 Marquis Grissom .05
152 Otis Nixon .05
153 Jerry Goff .05
154 Steve Frey .05
155 National League Logo (Foil) .05
156 American League Logo (Foil) .05
157 Benito Santiago/AS .05
158 Will Clark/AS .05
159 Ryne Sandberg/AS .25
160 Chris Sabo/AS .05
161 Ozzie Smith/AS .25
162 Kevin Mitchell/AS .05
163 Lenny Dykstra/AS .05
164 Darryl Strawberry/AS .05
165 Jack Armstrong/AS .05
166 Sandy Alomar, Jr./AS .05
167 Mark McGwire/AS .45
168 Steve Sax/AS .05
169 Wade Boggs/AS .25
170 Cal Ripken, Jr./AS .50
171 Rickey Henderson/AS .20
172 Ken Griffey Jr./AS .40
173 Jose Canseco/AS .15
174 Bob Welch/AS .05
175 All-Star Game - Wrigley Field .05
176 World's Championship Trophy (Foil) .05
177 California Angels pennant (Foil) .05
178 California Angels Logo (Foil) .05
179 Lance Parrish .05
180 Wally Joyner .05
181 Johnny Ray .05
182 Jack Howell .05
183 Dick Schofield .05
184 Dave Winfield .40
185 Devon White .05
186 Dante Bichette .05
187 Chuck Finley .05
188 Jim Abbott .05
189 Oakland A's Pennant (Foil) .05
190 Oakland A's Logo (Foil) .05
191 Terry Steinbach .05
192 Mark McGwire .85
193 Willie Randolph .05
194 Carney Lansford .05
195 Walt Weiss .05
196 Rickey Henderson .40
197 Dave Henderson .05
198 Jose Canseco .30
199 Dave Stewart .05
200 Dennis Eckersley .35
201 Milwaukee Brewers Pennant (Foil) .05
202 Milwaukee Brewers Logo (Foil) .05
203 B.J. Surhoff .05
204 Greg Brock .05
205 Paul Molitor .40
206 Gary Sheffield .20
207 Billy Spiers .05
208 Robin Yount .40
209 Rob Deer .05
210 Dave Parker .05
211 Mark Knudson .05
212 Dan Plesac .05
213 Cleveland Indians Pennant (Foil) .05
214 Cleveland Indians Logo (Foil) .05
215 Sandy Alomar, Jr. .05
216 Brook Jacoby .05
217 Jerry Browne .05
218 Carlos Baerga .05
219 Felix Fermin .05
220 Candy Maldonado .05
221 Cory Snyder .05
222 Alex Cole, Jr. .05
223 Tom Candiotti .05
224 Doug Jones .05
225 Seattle Mariners Pennant (Foil) .05
226 Seattle Mariners Logo (Foil) .05
227 Dave Valle .05
228 Pete O'Brien .05
229 Harold Reynolds .05
230 Edgar Martinez .05
231 Omar Vizquel .05
232 Henry Cotto .05
233 Ken Griffey Jr. .75
234 Jay Buhner .05
235 Eric Hanson (Erik) .05
236 Mike Schooler .05
237 Baltimore Orioles Pennant (Foil) .05
238 Baltimore Orioles Logo (Foil) .05
239 Mickey Tettleton .05
240 Randy Milligan .05
241 Billy Ripken .05
242 Craig Worthington .05
243 Cal Ripken, Jr. 1.00
244 Steve Finley .05
245 Mike Devereaux .05
246 Joe Orsulak .05
247 Ben McDonald .05
248 Gregg Olson .05
249 Texas Rangers Pennant (Foil) .05
250 Texas Rangers Logo (Foil) .05
251 Geno Petralli .05
252 Rafael Palmeiro .40
253 Julio Franco .05
254 Steve Buechele .05
255 Jeff Huson .05
256 Gary Pettis .05
257 Ruben Sierra .05
258 Pete Incaviglia .05
259 Nolan Ryan 1.00
260 Bobby Witt .05
261 Boston Red Sox Pennant (Foil) .05
262 Boston Red Sox Logo (Foil) .05
263 Tony Pena .05
264 Carlos Quintana .05
265 Jody Reed .05
266 Wade Boggs .50
267 Luis Rivera .05
268 Mike Greenwell .05
269 Ellis Burks .05
270 Tom Brunansky .05
271 Roger Clemens .60
272 Jeff Reardon .05
273 Kansas City Royals Pennant (Foil) .05
274 Kansas City Royals Logo (Foil) .05
275 Mike Macfarlane .05
276 George Brett .60
277 Bill Pecota .05
278 Kevin Seitzer .05
279 Kurt Stillwell .05
280 Jim Eisenreich .05
281 Bo Jackson .10
282 Danny Tartabull .05
283 Bret Saberhagen .05
284 Tom Gordon .05
285 Detroit Tigers Pennant (Foil) .05
286 Detroit Tigers Logo (Foil) .05
287 Mike Heath .05
288 Cecil Fielder .05
289 Lou Whitaker .05
290 Tony Phillips .05
291 Alan Trammell .05
292 Chet Lemon .05
293 Lloyd Moseby .05
294 Gary Ward .05
295 Dan Petry .05
296 Jack Morris .05
297 Minnesota Twins Pennant (Foil) .05
298 Minnesota Twins Logo (Foil) .05
299 Brian Harper .05
300 Kent Hrbek .05
301 Al Newman .05
302 Gary Gaetti .05
303 Greg Gagne .05
304 Dan Gladden .05
305 Kirby Puckett .50
306 Gene Larkin .05
307 Kevin Tapani .05
308 Rick Aguilera .05
309 Chicago White Sox Pennant (Foil) .05
310 Chicago White Sox Logo (Foil) .05
311 Carlton Fisk .40
312 Carlos Martinez .05
313 Scott Fletcher .05
314 Robin Ventura .05
315 Ozzie Guillen .05
316 Sammy Sosa .65
317 Lance Johnson .05
318 Ivan Calderon .05
319 Greg Hibbard .05
320 Bobby Thigpen .05
321 New York Yankees Pennant (Foil) .05
322 New York Yankees Logo (Foil) .05
323 Bob Geren .05
324 Don Mattingly .60
325 Steve Sax .05
326 Jim Leyritz .05
327 Alvaro Espinoza .05
328 Roberto Kelly .05
329 Oscar Azocar .05
330 Jesse Barfield .05
331 Chuck Cary .05
332 Dave Righetti .05
333 Toronto Blue Jays Pennant (Foil) .05
334 Toronto Blue Jays Logo (Foil) .05
335 Pat Borders .05
336 Fred McGriff .05
337 Manny Lee .05
338 Kelly Gruber .05
339 Tony Fernandez .05
340 George Bell .05
341 Mookie Wilson .05
342 Junior Felix .05
343 Blue Jays Batting Helmet (Foil) .05
344 Dave Steib .05
345 Tom Henke .05
346 Greg Myers .05
347 Glenallen Hill .05
348 John Olerud .05
349 Todd Stottlemyre .05
350 David Wells .05
351 Jimmy Key .05
352 Mark Langston (No-hitter.) .05
353 Randy Johnson (No-hitter.) .20
354 Nolan Ryan (No-hitter.) .50
355 Dave Stewart (No-hitter.) .05
356 Fernando Valenzuela (No-hitter.) .05
357 Andy Hawkins (No-hitter.) .05
358 Melido Perez (No-hitter.) .05
359 Terry Mulholland (No-hitter.) .05
360 Dave Stieb (No-hitter.) .05

Top 15 Stickers (Canadian)

The four leaders from each league in major statistical categories from the 1990 season are featured in this set of stickers marketed in Canada. The 2-1/2" x 3-1/2" stickers feature a large color photo at top. In the white border at bottom is the player's name and team, the stat in which he excelled (printed in both English and French), the number achieved, and, at lower-left, his rank among the top four. A series of team logo metallic stickers honors the teams which led in various stats. Backs are printed in black with appropriate logos and sticker number. A colorful album could be purchased to the house the sticker collection.

NM/M
Complete Set (136): 10.00
Common Player: .10
1 Willie McGee .10
2 Eddie Murray .30
3 Dave Magadan .10
4 Lenny Dykstra .10
5 George Brett .45
6 Rickey Henderson .30
7 Rafael Palmeiro .30
8 Alan Trammell .10
9 Ryne Sandberg .40
10 Darryl Strawberry .10
11 Kevin Mitchell .10
12 Barry Bonds .75
13 Cecil Fielder .10
14 Mark McGwire .65
15 Jose Canseco .15
16 Fred McGriff .10
17 Matt Williams .10
18 Bobby Bonilla .10
19 Joe Carter .10
20 Barry Bonds .75
21 Cecil Fielder .10
22 Kelly Gruber .10
23 Mark McGwire .65
24 Jose Canseco .15
25 Brett Butler .10
26 Lenny Dykstra .10
27 Ryne Sandberg .40
28 Barry Larkin .10
29 Rafael Palmeiro .30
30 Wade Boggs .40
31 Roberto Kelly .10
32 Mike Greenwell .10
33 Barry Bonds .75
34 Ryne Sandberg .40
35 Kevin Mitchell .10
36 Ron Gant .10
37 Cecil Fielder .10
38 Rickey Henderson .30
39 Jose Canseco .15
40 Fred McGriff .10
41 Vince Coleman .10
42 Eric Yelding .10
43 Barry Bonds .75
44 Brett Butler .10
45 Rickey Henderson .30
46 Steve Sax .10
47 Roberto Kelly .10
48 Alex Cole, Jr. .10
49 Ryne Sandberg .40
50 Bobby Bonilla .10
51 Brett Butler .10
52 Ron Gant .10
53 Rickey Henderson .30
54 Cecil Fielder .10
55 Harold Reynolds .10
56 Robin Yount .30
57 Doug Drabek .10
58 Ramon Martinez .10
59 Frank Viola .10
60 Dwight Gooden .10
61 Bob Welch .10
62 Dave Stewart .10
63 Roger Clemens .45
64 Dave Stieb .10
65 Danny Darwin .10
66 Zane Smith .10
67 Ed Whitson .10
68 Frank Viola .10
69 Roger Clemens .45
70 Chuck Finley .10
71 Dave Stewart .10
72 Kevin Appier .10
73 David Cone .10
74 Dwight Gooden .10
75 Ramon Martinez .10
76 Frank Viola .10
77 Nolan Ryan .75
78 Bobby Witt .10
79 Erik Hanson .10
80 Roger Clemens .45
81 John Franco .10
82 Randy Myers .10
83 Lee Smith .10
84 Craig Lefferts .10
85 Bobby Thigpen .10
86 Dennis Eckersley .25
87 Doug Jones .10
88 Gregg Olson .10
89 Mike Morgan .10
90 Bruce Hurst .10
91 Mark Gardner .10
92 Doug Drabek .10
93 Dave Stewart .10
94 Roger Clemens .45
95 Kevin Appier .10
96 Melido Perez .10
97 National League Logo .10
98 Greg Maddux .40
99 Benito Santiago .10
100 Andres Galarraga .10
101 Ryne Sandberg .40
102 Tim Wallach .10
103 Ozzie Smith .40
104 Tony Gwynn .40
105 Barry Bonds .75
106 Andy Van Slyke .10
107 American League Logo .10
108 Mike Boddicker .10
109 Sandy Alomar Jr. .10
110 Mark McGwire .65
111 Harold Reynolds .10
112 Kelly Gruber .10
113 Ozzie Guillen .10
114 Ellis Burks .10
115 Gary Pettis .10
116 Ken Griffey Jr. .50
117 Cincinnati Reds Logo .10
118 New York Mets Logo .10
119 New York Mets Script .10
120 Chicago Cubs Logo .10
121 Montreal Expos Logo .10
122 Boston Red Sox Logo .10
123 Detroit Tigers Logo .10
124 Toronto Blue Jays Logo .10
125 Boston Red Sox Script .10
126 Milwaukee Brewers Logo .10
127 Philadelphia Phillies Logo .10
128 Cincinnati Reds Logo .10
129 Montreal Expos Logo .10
130 New York Mets Logo .10
131 Cincinnati Reds Logo .10
132 California Angels Logo .10
133 Toronto Blue Jays Logo .10
134 Oakland A's Logo .10
135 Oakland A's Script .10
136 Chicago White Sox Logo .10

1992 Panini Stickers

A 288-piece set comprised Panini's annual baseball issue in 1992. Stickers were sold in packs of six for 39 cents. A colorful album for housing the stickers was also available, picturing members of the World Champion Twins. Individual stickers measured 2-1/8" x 3". Player stickers feature a color action photo at center, with a shark's tooth border at right. A colored diamond is overprinted on the first letters of the name, while a rule of the same color is printed around the photo. On American League stickers the color highlights are in magenta; teal for N.L. Stickers are numbered by position within team, and each team set includes a foil-glitter team logo stickers. Similar special stickers honor the 1991 All-Star Game starters and a few other special themes. Backs of the foils are printed in blue and promote sticker collecting. Backs of the player stickers are special themes. Backs of the foils are printed in blue and in full color and include trivia questions, "Play Ball" game situations and score cards for the game.

NM/M
Complete Set (288): 10.00
Common Player: .05
Album: 1.00
Wax Pack (5+1): .25
Wax Box (50): 5.00
1 Panini Logo (Foil) .05
2 Major League Baseball Logo (Foil) .05
3 Players Association Logo (Foil) .05
4 Lance Parrish .05
5 Wally Joyner .05
6 Luis Sojo .05
7 Gary Gaetti .05
8 Dick Schofield .05
9 Junior Felix .05
10 Luis Polonia .05
11 Mark Langston .05
12 Jim Abbott .05
13 California Angels Logo (Foil) .05
14 Terry Steinbach .05
15 Mark McGwire .75
16 Mike Gallego .05
17 Carney Lansford .05
18 Walt Weiss .05
19 Jose Canseco .30
20 Dave Henderson .05
21 Rickey Henderson .40
22 Dennis Eckersley .35
23 Oakland A's Logo (Foil) .05
24 Pat Borders .05
25 John Olerud .05
26 Roberto Alomar .20
27 Kelly Gruber .05
28 Manuel Lee .05
29 Joe Carter .05
30 Devon White .05
31 Candy Maldonado .05
32 Jimmy Key .05
33 Toronto Blue Jays Logo (Foil) .05
34 B.J. Surhoff .05
35 Franklin Stubbs .05
36 Willie Randolph .05
37 Jim Gantner .05
38 Bill Spiers .05
39 Dante Bichette .05
40 Robin Yount .40
41 Greg Vaughn .05
42 Jaime Navarro .05
43 Milwaukee Brewers Logo (Foil) .05
44 Sandy Alomar Jr. .05
45 Mike Aldrete .05
46 Mark Lewis .05
47 Carlos Baerga .05
48 Felix Fermin .05
49 Mark Whiten .05
50 Alex Cole .05
51 Albert Belle .10
52 Greg Swindell .05
53 Cleveland Indians Logo (Foil) .05
54 Dave Valle .05
55 Pete O'Brien .05
56 Harold Reynolds .05
57 Edgar Martinez .05
58 Omar Vizquel .05
59 Jay Buhner .05
60 Ken Griffey Jr. .60
61 Greg Briley .05
62 Randy Johnson .40
63 Seattle Mariners Logo (Foil) .05
64 Chris Hoiles .05
65 Randy Milligan .05
66 Billy Ripken .05
67 Leo Gomez .05
68 Cal Ripken Jr. 1.00
69 Dwight Evans .05
70 Mike Devereaux .05
71 Joe Orsulak .05
72 Gregg Olson .05
73 Baltimore Orioles Logo (Foil) .05
74 Ivan Rodriguez .40
75 Rafael Palmeiro .40
76 Julio Franco .05
77 Dean Palmer .05
78 Jeff Huson .05
79 Ruben Sierra .05
80 Gary Pettis .05
81 Juan Gonzalez .40
82 Nolan Ryan 1.00
83 Texas Rangers Logo (Foil) .05
84 Tony Pena .05
85 Carlos Quintana .05
86 Jody Reed .05
87 Wade Boggs .50
88 Luis Rivera .05
89 Tom Brunansky .05
90 Ellis Burks .05
91 Mike Greenwell .05
92 Roger Clemens .55
93 Boston Red Sox Logo (Foil) .05
94 Todd Benzinger .05
95 Terry Shumpert .05
96 Bill Pecota .05
97 Kurt Stillwell .05
98 Danny Tartabull .05
99 Brian McRae .05
100 Kirk Gibson .05
101 Bret Saberhagen .05
102 George Brett .55
103 Kansas City Royals Logo (Foil) .05
104 Mickey Tettleton .05
105 Cecil Fielder .05
106 Lou Whitaker .05
107 Travis Fryman .05
108 Alan Trammell .05
109 Rob Deer .05
110 Milt Cuyler .05
111 Lloyd Moseby .05
112 Bill Gullickson .05
113 Detroit Tigers Logo (Foil) .05
114 Brian Harper .05
115 Kent Hrbek .05
116 Chuck Knoblauch .05
117 Mike Pagliarulo .05
118 Greg Gagne .05
119 Shane Mack .05
120 Kirby Puckett .50
121 Dan Gladden .05
122 Jack Morris .05
123 Minnesota Twins Logo (Foil) .05
124 Carlton Fisk .40
125 Frank Thomas .40
126 Joey Cora .05
127 Robin Ventura .05
128 Ozzie Guillen .05
129 Sammy Sosa .60
130 Lance Johnson .05
131 Tim Raines .05
132 Bobby Thigpen .05
133 Chicago White Sox Logo (Foil) .05
134 Matt Nokes .05
135 Don Mattingly .55
136 Steve Sax .05
137 Pat Kelly .05
138 Alvaro Espinoza .05
139 Jesse Barfield .05
140 Roberto Kelly .05
141 Mel Hall .05
142 Scott Sanderson .05
143 New York Yankees Logo (Foil) .05
144 A.L. HR Leaders (Cecil Fielder, Jose Canseco) .05
145 A.L. BA Leader (Julio Franco) .05
146 A.L. ERA Leader (Roger Clemens) .25
147 N.L. HR Leader (Howard Johnson) .05
148 N.L. BA Leader (Terry Pendleton) .05
149 N.L. ERA Leader (Dennis Martinez) .05
150 Houston Astros Logo (foil) .05
151 Craig Biggio .05
152 Jeff Bagwell .40
153 Casey Candaele .05
154 Ken Caminiti .05
155 Andujar Cedeno .05
156 Mike Simms .05
157 Steve Finley .05
158 Luis Gonzalez .05
159 Pete Harnisch .05
160 Atlanta Braves Logo (Foil) .05
161 Greg Olson .05
162 Sid Bream .05
163 Mark Lemke .05
164 Terry Pendleton .05

165 Rafael Belliard .05
166 Dave Justice .05
167 Ron Gant .05
168 Lonnie Smith .05
169 Steve Avery .05
170 St. Louis Cardinals Logo (Foil) .05
171 Tom Pagnozzi .05
172 Pedro Guerrero .05
173 Jose Oquendo .05
174 Todd Zeile .05
175 Ozzie Smith .50
176 Felix Jose .05
177 Ray Lankford .05
178 Jose DeLeon .05
179 Lee Smith .05
180 Chicago Cubs Logo (Foil) .05
181 Hector Villanueva .05
182 Mark Grace .10
183 Ryne Sandberg .50
184 Luis Salazar .05
185 Shawon Dunston .05
186 Andre Dawson .20
187 Jerome Walton .05
188 George Bell .05
189 Greg Maddux .50
190 Los Angeles Dodgers Logo (Foil) .05
191 Mike Scioscia .05
192 Eddie Murray .40
193 Juan Samuel .05
194 Lenny Harris .05
195 Alfredo Griffin .05
196 Darryl Strawberry .05
197 Brett Butler .05
198 Kal Daniels .05
199 Orel Hershiser .05
200 Montreal Expos Logo (Foil) .05
201 Gilberto Reyes .05
202 Andres Galarraga .05
203 Delino DeShields .05
204 Tim Wallach .05
205 Spike Owen .05
206 Larry Walker .05
207 Marquis Grissom .05
208 Ivan Calderon .05
209 Dennis Martinez .05
210 San Francisco Giants Logo (Foil) .05
211 Steve Decker .05
212 Will Clark .10
213 Robby Thompson .05
214 Matt Williams .05
215 Jose Uribe .05
216 Kevin Bass .05
217 Willie McGee .05
218 Kevin Mitchell .05
219 Dave Righetti .05
220 New York Mets Logo (Foil) .05
221 Rick Cerone .05
222 Dave Magadan .05
223 Gregg Jefferies .05
224 Howard Johnson .05
225 Kevin Elster .05
226 Hubie Brooks .05
227 Vince Coleman .05
228 Kevin McReynolds .05
229 Frank Viola .05
230 San Diego Padres Logo (Foil) .05
231 Benito Santiago .05
232 Fred McGriff .05
233 Bip Roberts .05
234 Jack Howell .05
235 Tony Fernandez .05
236 Tony Gwynn .50
237 Darrin Jackson .05
238 Bruce Hurst .05
239 Craig Lefferts .05
240 Philadelphia Phillies Logo (Foil) .05
241 Darren Daulton .05
242 John Kruk .05
243 Mickey Morandini .05
244 Charlie Hayes .05
245 Dickie Thon .05
246 Dale Murphy .25
247 Lenny Dykstra .05
248 Von Hayes .05
249 Terry Mulholland .05
250 Pittsburgh Pirates Logo (Foil) .05
251 Mike LaValliere .05
252 Orlando Merced .05
253 Jose Lind .05
254 Steve Buechele .05
255 Jay Bell .05
256 Bobby Bonilla .05
257 Andy Van Slyke .05
258 Barry Bonds 1.00
259 Doug Drabek .05
260 Cincinnati Reds Logo (Foil) .05
261 Joe Oliver .05
262 Hal Morris .05
263 Bill Doran .05
264 Chris Sabo .05
265 Barry Larkin .05
266 Paul O'Neill .05
267 Eric Davis .05
268 Glenn Braggs .05
269 Jose Rijo .05
270 Toronto Sky Dome (Foil) .05
271 Sandy Alomar Jr. (All-Star Foil) .05
272 Cecil Fielder (All-Star Foil) .05
273 Roberto Alomar (All-Star Foil) .10
274 Wade Boggs (All-Star Foil) .25
275 Cal Ripken Jr. (All-Star Foil) .50
276 Dave Henderson (All-Star Foil) .05
277 Ken Griffey Jr. (All-Star Foil) .40
278 Rickey Henderson (All-Star Foil) .20
279 Jack Morris (All-Star Foil) .05
280 Benito Santiago (All-Star Foil) .05
281 Will Clark (All-Star Foil) .05
282 Ryne Sandberg (All-Star Foil) .25
283 Chris Sabo (All-Star Foil) .05
284 Ozzie Smith (All-Star Foil) .25
285 Andre Dawson (All-Star Foil) .05
286 Tony Gwynn (All-Star Foil) .25
287 Ivan Calderon (All-Star Foil) .05
288 Tom Glavine (All-Star Foil) .05

Canadian

The Canadian version of the 1992 Panini stickers mirrors the U.S. set's checklist (and price guide). In the same size (2-1/8" x 3") and format, the Canadian stickers differ from the U.S. version in the addition of French position on front and bilingual back.

	NM/M
Complete Set (288):	10.00
Common Player:	.05
Album:	1.00

1993 Panini Stickers

The 1993 issue is complete at 300 stickers. Besides 10 player stickers for each major league team, there are stickers for league leaders and major 1992-season award winners. There is a gold-foil team logo sticker for each team and one of the player stickers on each team is produced in a glitter technology. Stickers measure 2-3/8" x 3-3/8". Fronts have an action photo at center with team logo in the lower-left corner. Backs are printed in green and include the sticker number and appropriate Panini and baseball logos. A 58-page album was available to house the stickers.

	NM/M
Complete Set (300):	10.00
Common Player:	.05
Sticker Album:	1.00

1 California Angels Logo .05
2 Mark Langston .05
3 Ron Tingley .05
4 Gary Gaetti .05
5 Kelly Gruber .05
6 Gary Disarcina .05
7 Damion Easley (Glitter) .05
8 Luis Polonia .05
9 Lee Stevens .05
10 Chad Curtis .05
11 Rene Gonzales .05
12 Oakland A's Logo .05
13 Dennis Eckersley .35
14 Terry Steinbach .05
15 Mark McGwire .75
16 Mike Bordick (Glitter) .05
17 Carney Lansford .05
18 Jerry Browne .05
19 Rickey Henderson .40
20 Dave Henderson .05
21 Ruben Sierra .05
22 Ron Darling .05
23 Toronto Blue Jays Logo .05
24 Jack Morris .05
25 Pat Borders .05
26 John Olerud .05
27 Roberto Alomar .10
28 Luis Sojo .05
29 Dave Stewart .05
30 Devon White .05
31 Joe Carter .05
32 Derek Bell .05
33 Juan Guzman (Glitter) .05
34 Milwaukee Brewers Logo .05
35 Jaime Navarro .05
36 B.J. Surhoff .05
37 Franklin Stubbs .05
38 Billy Spiers .05
39 Pat Listach (Glitter) .05
40 Kevin Seitzer .05
41 Darryl Hamilton .05
42 Robin Yount .40
43 Kevin Reimer .05
44 Greg Vaughn .05
45 Cleveland Indians Logo .05
46 Charles Nagy .05
47 Sandy Alomar Jr. .05
48 Reggie Jefferson .05
49 Mark Lewis .05
50 Felix Fermin .05
51 Carlos Baerga .05
52 Albert Belle .05
53 Kenny Lofton (Glitter) .05
54 Mark Whiten .05
55 Paul Sorrento .05
56 Seattle Mariners Logo .05
57 Dave Fleming .05
58 Dave Valle .05
59 Pete O'Brien .05
60 Randy Johnson .40
61 Omar Vizquel .05
62 Edgar Martinez .05
63 Ken Griffey Jr. (Glitter) .75
64 Henry Cotto .05
65 Jay Buhner .05
66 Tino Martinez .05
67 Baltimore Orioles Logo .05
68 Ben McDonald .05
69 Mike Mussina (Glitter) .35
70 Chris Hoiles .05
71 Randy Milligan .05
72 Billy Ripken .05
73 Cal Ripken Jr. 1.00
74 Leo Gomez .05
75 Mike Devereaux .05
76 Brady Anderson .05
77 Joe Orsulak .05
78 Texas Rangers Logo .05
79 Kevin Brown .05
80 Ivan Rodriguez (Glitter) .40
81 Rafael Palmeiro .40
82 Julio Franco .05
83 Jeff Huson .05
84 Dean Palmer .05
85 Jose Canseco .30
86 Juan Gonzalez .40
87 Nolan Ryan 1.00
88 Brian Downing .05
89 Boston Red Sox Logo .05
90 Roger Clemens .55
91 Tony Pena .05
92 Mo Vaughn .05
93 Scott Cooper .05
94 Luis Rivera .05
95 Ellis Burks .05
96 Mike Greenwell .05
97 Andre Dawson .20
98 Ivan Calderon .05
99 Phil Plantier (Glitter) .05
100 Kansas City Royals Logo .05
101 Kevin Appier .05
102 Mike MacFarlane .05
103 Wally Joyner .05
104 Jim Eisenreich .05
105 Greg Gagne .05
106 Gregg Jefferies .05
107 Kevin McReynolds .05
108 Brian McRae (Glitter) .05
109 Keith Miller .05
110 George Brett .55
111 Detroit Tigers Logo .05
112 Bill Gullickson .05
113 Mickey Tettleton .05
114 Cecil Fielder .05
115 Tony Phillips .05
116 Scott Livingstone .05
117 Travis Fryman (Glitter) .05
118 Dan Gladden .05
119 Rob Deer .05
120 Frank Tanana .05
121 Skeeter Barnes .05
122 Minnesota Twins Logo .05
123 Scott Erickson .05
124 Brian Harper .05
125 Kent Hrbek .05
126 Chuck Knoblauch (Glitter) .05
127 Willie Banks .05
128 Scott Leius .05
129 Shane Mack .05
130 Kirby Puckett .50
131 Chili Davis .05
132 Pedro Munoz .05
133 Chicago White Sox Logo .05
134 Jack McDowell .05
135 Carlton Fisk .40
136 Frank Thomas (Glitter) .45
137 Steve Sax .05
138 Ozzie Guillen .05
139 Robin Ventura .05
140 Tim Raines .05
141 Lance Johnson .05
142 Ron Karkovice .05
143 George Bell .05
144 New York Yankees Logo .05
145 Scott Sanderson .05
146 Matt Nokes .05
147 Kevin Maas (Glitter) .05
148 Randy Velarde .05
149 Andy Stankiewicz .05
150 Pat Kelly .05
151 Paul O'Neill .05
152 Wade Boggs .50
153 Danny Tartabull .05
154 Don Mattingly .55
155 Edgar Martinez (B.A. Leader) .05
156 Kevin Brown (W-L Record) .05
157 Dennis Eckersley (Saves leader.) .15
158 Gary Sheffield (B.A. leader.) .05
159 Tom Glavine, Greg Maddux (W-L Leaders) .05
160 Lee Smith (Saves leader.) .05
161 Dennis Eckersley (Cy Young) .15
162 Dennis Eckersley (MVP) .15
163 Pat Listach (Rookie/Year) .05
164 Greg Maddux (Cy Young) .50
165 Barry Bonds (MVP) .50
166 Eric Karros (Rookie/Year) .05
167 Houston Astros Logo .05
168 Pete Harnisch .05
169 Eddie Taubensee .05
170 Jeff Bagwell (Glitter) .45
171 Craig Biggio .05
172 Andujar Cedeno .05
173 Ken Caminiti .05
174 Steve Finley .05
175 Luis Gonzalez .05
176 Eric Anthony .05
177 Casey Candaele .05
178 Atlanta Braves Logo .05
179 Tom Glavine .25
180 Greg Olson .05
181 Sid Bream .05
182 Mark Lemke .05
183 Jeff Blauser .05
184 Terry Pendleton .05
185 Ron Gant .05
186 Otis Nixon .05
187 Dave Justice .05
188 Deion Sanders (Glitter) .20
189 St. Louis Cardinals Logo .05
190 Bob Tewksbury .05
191 Tom Pagnozzi .05
192 Lee Smith .05
193 Geronimo Pena .05
194 Ozzie Smith .50
195 Todd Zeile .05
196 Ray Lankford .05
197 Bernard Gilkey .05
198 Felix Jose .05
199 Donovan Osborne (Glitter) .05
200 Chicago Cubs Logo .05
201 Mike Morgan .05
202 Rick Wilkins .05
203 Mark Grace (Glitter) .05
204 Ryne Sandberg .50
205 Shawon Dunston .05
206 Steve Buechele .05
207 Kal Daniels .05
208 Sammy Sosa .50
209 Derrick May .05
210 Doug Dascenzo .05
211 Los Angeles Dodgers Logo .05
212 Ramon Martinez .05
213 Mike Scioscia .05
214 Eric Karros (Glitter) .05
215 Tim Wallach .05
216 Jose Offerman .05
217 Mike Sharperson .05
218 Brett Butler .05
219 Darryl Strawberry .05
220 Lenny Harris .05
221 Eric Davis .05
222 Montreal Expos Logo .05
223 Ken Hill .05
224 Darrin Fletcher .05
225 Greg Colbrunn (Glitter) .05
226 Delino DeShields .05
227 Wil Cordero .05
228 Dennis Martinez .05
229 John Vander Wal .05
230 Marquis Grissom .05
231 Larry Walker .05
232 Moises Alou .05
233 San Francisco Giants Logo .05
234 Billy Swift .05
235 Kirt Manwaring .05
236 Will Clark .05
237 Robby Thompson .05
238 Royce Clayton (Glitter) .05
239 Matt Williams .05
240 Willie McGee .05
241 Mark Leonard .05
242 Cory Snyder .05
243 Barry Bonds 1.00
244 New York Mets Logo .05
245 Dwight Gooden .05
246 Todd Hundley (Glitter) .05
247 Eddie Murray .40
248 Sid Fernandez .05
249 Tony Fernandez .05
250 Dave Magadan .05
251 Howard Johnson .05
252 Vince Coleman .05
253 Bobby Bonilla .05
254 Daryl Boston .05
255 San Diego Padres Logo .05
256 Bruce Hurst .05
257 Dan Walters .05
258 Fred McGriff .05
259 Kurt Stillwell .05
260 Craig Shipley .05
261 Gary Sheffield (Glitter) .35
262 Tony Gwynn .50
263 Oscar Azocar .05
264 Darrin Jackson .05
265 Andy Benes .05
266 Philadelphia Phillies Logo .05
267 Terry Mulholland .05
268 Curt Schilling .25
269 Darren Daulton .05
270 John Kruk .05
271 Mickey Morandini (Glitter) .05
272 Mariano Duncan .05
273 Dave Hollins .05
274 Lenny Dykstra .05
275 Wes Chamberlain .05
276 Stan Javier .05
277 Pittsburgh Pirates Logo .05
278 Zane Smith .05
279 Tim Wakefield (Glitter) .05
280 Mike LaValliere .05
281 Orlando Merced .05
282 Stan Belinda .05
283 Jay Bell .05
284 Jeff King .05
285 Andy Van Slyke .05
286 Bob Walk .05
287 Gary Varsho .05
288 Cincinnati Reds Logo .05
289 Jose Rijo .05
290 Joe Oliver .05
291 Hal Morris .05
292 Bip Roberts .05
293 Barry Larkin .05
294 Chris Sabo .05
295 Roberto Kelly .05
296 Kevin Mitchell .05
297 Rob Dibble .05
298 Reggie Sanders (Glitter) .05
299 Florida Marlins Logo .05
300 Colorado Rockies Logo .05

1994 Panini Stickers

With set size at the reduced count of 268, Panini retained the larger format 2-3/8" x 3-3/8" sticker size. Stickers featured green borders surrounding a color action photo on front. Below the player photo is a pennant with the team logo and player name. Backs have a sticker number at center, with appropriate licensor logos and Panini advertising in black-and-white. The set includes 16 foil stickers honoring major 1993 season award winners in the A.L. and N.L. and four World Series action stickers. The set is arranged alphabetically within team and league. Stickers were sold in packs of six for 49 cents. A colorful album to house the stickers was also available.

	NM/M
Complete Set (268):	5.00
Common Player:	.05

1 World Series Action (Foil) .05
2 World Series Action (Foil) .05
3 World Series Action (Foil) .05
4 World Series Action (Foil) .05
5 BA Leader (John Olerud (Foil)) .05
6 HR Leader (Juan Gonzalez (Foil)) .20
7 RBI Leader (Albert Belle (Foil)) .05
8 Wins Leader (Jack McDowell (Foil)) .05
9 K Leader (Randy Johnson (Foil)) .20
10 Saves Leader (Jeff Montgomery (Foil)) .05
11 BA Leader (Andres Galarraga (Foil)) .05
12 HR Leader (Barry Bonds (Foil)) .50
13 RBI Leade r (Barry Bonds (Foil)) .50
14 Wins Leaders (Tom Glavine, John Burkett (Foil)) .05
15 K Leader (Jose Rijo (Foil)) .05
16 Saves Leader (Randy Myers (Foil)) .05
17 Brady Anderson .05
18 Harold Baines .05
19 Mike Devereaux .05
20 Chris Hoiles .05
21 Mike Mussina .30
22 Harold Reynolds .05
23 Cal Ripken Jr. 1.00
24 David Segui .05
25 Fernando Valenzuela .05
26 Roger Clemens .60
27 Scott Cooper .05
28 Andre Dawson .20
29 Scott Fletcher .05
30 Mike Greenwell .05
31 Billy Hatcher .05
32 Tony Pena .05
33 John Valentin .05
34 Mo Vaughn .05
35 Chad Curtis .05
36 Gary DiSarcina .05
37 Damion Easley .05
38 Mark Langston .05
39 Torey Lovullo .05
40 Greg Myers .05
41 Luis Polonia .05
42 Tim Salmon .05
43 J.T. Snow .05
44 George Bell .05
45 Ellis Burks .05
46 Joey Cora .05
47 Ozzie Guillen .05
48 Roberto Hernandez .05
49 Bo Jackson .10
50 Jack McDowell .05
51 Frank Thomas .40
52 Robin Ventura .05
53 Sandy Alomar Jr. .05
54 Carlos Baerga .05
55 Albert Belle .05
56 Felix Fermin .05
57 Wayne Kirby .05
58 Kenny Lofton .05
59 Charles Nagy .05
60 Paul Sorrento .05
61 Jeff Treadway .05
62 Eric Davis .05
63 Cecil Fielder .05
64 Travis Fryman .05
65 Bill Gullickson .05
66 Mike Moore .05
67 Tony Phillips .05
68 Mickey Tettleton .05

69	Alan Trammell	.05
70	Lou Whitaker	.05
71	Kevin Appier	.05
72	Greg Gagne	.05
73	Tom Gordon	.05
74	Felix Jose	.05
75	Wally Joyner	.05
76	Jose Lind	.05
77	Mike Macfarlane	.05
78	Brian McRae	.05
79	Kevin McReynolds	.05
80	Darryl Hamilton	.05
81	Teddy Higuera	.05
82	John Jaha	.05
83	Pat Listach	.05
84	Dave Nilsson	.05
85	Kevin Reimer	.05
86	Kevin Seitzer	.05
87	B. J. Surhoff	.05
88	Greg Vaughn	.05
89	Willie Banks	.05
90	Brian Harper	.05
91	Kent Hrbek	.05
92	Chuck Knoblauch	.05
93	Shane Mack	.05
94	Pat Meares	.05
95	Pedro Munoz	.05
.5	Kirby Puckett	.50
97	Dave Winfield	.40
98	Jim Abbott	.05
99	Wade Boggs	.50
100	Mike Gallego	.05
101	Pat Kelly	.05
102	Don Mattingly	.60
103	Paul O'Neill	.05
104	Mike Stanley	.05
105	Danny Tartabull	.05
106	Bernie Williams	.05
107	Mike Bordick	.05
108	Dennis Eckersley	.35
109	Dave Henderson	.05
110	Mark McGwire	.75
111	Troy Neel	.05
112	Ruben Sierra	.05
113	Terry Steinbach	.05
114	Todd Van Poppel	.05
115	Bob Welch	.05
116	Bret Boone	.05
117	Jay Buhner	.05
118	Ken Griffey Jr.	.65
119	Randy Johnson	.40
120	Rich Amaral	.05
121	Edgar Martinez	.05
122	Tino Martinez	.05
123	Dave Valle	.05
124	Omar Vizquel	.05
125	Jose Canseco	.25
126	Julio Franco	.05
127	Juan Gonzalez	.20
128	Tom Henke	.05
129	Manuel Lee	.05
130	Rafael Palmeiro	.35
131	Dean Palmer	.05
132	Ivan Rodriguez	.35
133	Doug Strange	.05
134	Roberto Alomar	.10
135	Pat Borders	.05
136	Joe Carter	.05
137	Tony Fernandez	.05
138	Juan Guzman	.05
139	Rickey Henderson	.40
140	Paul Molitor	.40
141	John Olerud	.05
142	Devon White	.05
143	Jeff Blauser	.05
144	Ron Gant	.05
145	Tom Glavine	.20
146	Dave Justice	.05
147	Greg Maddux	.50
148	Fred McGriff	.05
149	Terry Pendleton	.05
150	Deion Sanders	.05
151	John Smoltz	.05
152	Shawon Dunston	.05
153	Mark Grace	.05
154	Derrick May	.05
155	Randy Myers	.05
156	Ryne Sandberg	.50
157	Dwight Smith	.05
158	Sammy Sosa	.50
159	Jose Vizcaino	.05
160	Rick Wilkins	.05
161	Tom Browning	.05
162	Roberto Kelly	.05
163	Barry Larkin	.05
164	Kevin Mitchell	.05
165	Hal Morris	.05
166	Joe Oliver	.05
167	Jose Rijo	.05
168	Chris Sabo	.05
169	Reggie Sanders	.05
170	Freddie Benavides	.05
171	Dante Bichette	.05
172	Vinny Castilla	.05
173	Jerald Clark	.05
174	Andres Galarraga	.05
175	Charlie Hayes	.05
176	Chris Jones	.05
177	Roberto Mejia	.05
178	Eric Young	.05
179	Bret Barberie	.05
180	Chuck Carr	.05
181	Jeff Conine	.05
182	Orestes Destrade	.05
183	Bryan Harvey	.05
184	Rich Renteria	.05
185	Benito Santiago	.05
186	Gary Sheffield	.20
187	Walt Weiss	.05
188	Eric Anthony	.05
189	Jeff Bagwell	.40
190	Craig Biggio	.05
191	Ken Caminiti	.05
192	Andujar Cedeno	.05
193	Doug Drabek	.05
194	Steve Finley	.05
195	Doug Jones	.05
196	Darryl Kile	.05
197	Brett Butler	.05
198	Tom Candiotti	.05
199	Dave Hansen	.05
200	Orel Hershiser	.05
201	Eric Karros	.05
202	Jose Offerman	.05
203	Mike Piazza	.60
204	Cory Snyder	.05
205	Darryl Strawberry	.05
206	Moises Alou	.05
207	Sean Berry	.05
208	Wil Cordero	.05
209	Delino DeShields	.05
210	Marquis Grissom	.05
211	Ken Hill	.05
212	Mike Lansing	.05
213	Larry Walker	.05
214	John Wetteland	.05
215	Bobby Bonilla	.05
216	Jeromy Burnitz	.05
217	Dwight Gooden	.05
218	Todd Hundley	.05
219	Howard Johnson	.05
220	Jeff Kent	.05
221	Eddie Murray	.40
222	Bret Saberhagen	.05
223	Ryan Thompson	.05
224	Darren Daulton	.05
225	Mariano Duncan	.05
226	Lenny Dykstra	.05
227	Jim Eisenreich	.05
228	Dave Hollins	.05
229	John Kruk	.05
230	Curt Schilling	.20
231	Kevin Stocker	.05
232	Mitch Williams	.05
233	Jay Bell	.05
234	Steve Cooke	.05
235	Carlos Garcia	.05
236	Jeff King	.05
237	Orlando Merced	.05
238	Don Slaught	.05
239	Zane Smith	.05
240	Andy Van Slyke	.05
241	Kevin Young	.05
242	Bernard Gilkey	.05
243	Gregg Jefferies	.05
244	Brian Jordan	.05
245	Ray Lankford	.05
246	Tom Pagnozzi	.05
247	Geronimo Pena	.05
248	Ozzie Smith	.50
249	Bob Tewksbury	.05
250	Mark Whiten	.05
251	Brad Ausmus	.05
252	Derek Bell	.05
253	Andy Benes	.05
254	Phil Clark	.05
255	Jeff Gardner	.05
256	Tony Gwynn	.50
257	Trevor Hoffman	.05
258	Phil Plantier	.05
259	Craig Shipley	.05
260	Rod Beck	.05
261	Barry Bonds	1.00
262	John Burkett	.05
263	Will Clark	.05
264	Royce Clayton	.05
265	Willie McGee	.05
266	Bill Swift	.05
267	Robby Thompson	.05
268	Matt Williams	.05
Album:		1.00
Wax Pack (5+1):		.25
Wax Box (50):		5.00

2005 Parody Productions Boston Baseball Heroes

This deck of poker-format (2-1/2" x 3-1/2", round-cornered, linen finish) playing cards features color caricatures of past and contemporary Red Sox stars. Player name, sometimes a nickname, and his dates of service with the team are included. Backs have a baseball on a red background with white borders. The issue is apparently not licensed by MLB or the players.

		NM/M
Complete Set (55):		10.00
Common Player:		.25
AS	Curt Schilling	.35
2S	Jason Varitek	.25
3S	Mo Vaughn	.25
4S	Bill Mueller	.25
5S	Wade Boggs	1.00
6S	Nomar Garciaparra	1.00
7S	Manny Ramirez	1.00
8S	Johnny Damon	.40
9S	Trot Nixon	.25
10S	Tim Wakefield	.25
JS	Pedro Martinez	.35
QS	Roger Clemens	1.50
KS	David Ortiz	.50
AD	Mel Parnell	.25
2D	Sammy White	.25
3D	Billy Goodman	.25
4D	Bobby Doerr	.25
5D	Frank Malzone	.25
6D	Johnny Pesky	.25
7D	Jimmy Piersall	.35
8D	Dominic DiMaggio	.35
9D	Jackie Jensen	.35
10D	Vern Stephens	.25
JD	Dave Ferriss	.25
QD	Tex Hughson	.25
KD	Ted Williams	2.00
AC	Cy Young	.50
2C	Wally Schang	.25
3C	Jimmy Foxx	.50
4C	Jack Berry (Barry)	.25
5C	Jimmy Collins	.25
6C	Joe Cronin	.25
7C	Duffy Lewis	.25
8C	Doc Cramer	.25
9C	Harry Hooper	.25
10C	Bill Carrigan	.25
JC	Lefty Grove	.35
QC	Joe Wood	.25
KC	Tris Speaker	.40
AH	Luis Tiant	.35
2H	Carlton Fisk	.40
3H	George Scott	.25
4H	Tony Conigliaro	.35
5H	Rico Petrocelli	.25
6H	Rick Burleson	.25
7H	Reggie Smith	.25
8H	Fred Lynn	.35
9H	Dwight Evans	.35
10H	Jim Rice	.35
JH	Dick Radatz	.25
QH	Bill Lee	.25
KH	Carl Yastrzemski	1.50
---	Ken Coleman (Broadcaster)	.25
---	Ned Martin (Broadcaster)	.25
---	Tom Yawkey (Owner)	.25

Chicago (Cubs) Baseball Heroes

This deck of poker-format (2-1/2" x 3-1/2", round-cornered, linen finish) playing cards features color caricatures of past and contemporary Cubs stars. Player name, sometimes a nickname, and his dates of service with the team are included. Backs have a baseball on a blue background with white borders. The issue is apparently not licensed by MLB or the players.

		NM/M
Complete Set (55):		10.00
Common Player:		.25
AS	Mark Prior	1.00
2S	Joe Girardi	.25
3S	Mark Grace	.35
4S	Ryne Sandberg	2.00
5S	Aramis Ramirez	.25
6S	Shawon Dunston	.25
7S	Moises Alou	.25
8S	Corey Patterson	.25
9S	Andre Dawson	.50
10S	Carlos Zambrano	.35
JS	Kerry Wood	.35
QS	Lee Smith	.35
KS	Sammy Sosa	1.50
AD	Fergie Jenkins	.50
2D	Randy Hundley	.25
3D	Phil Cavarretta	.25
4D	Glenn Beckert	.35
5D	Ron Santo	.50
6D	Don Kessinger	.25
7D	Billy Williams	.75
8D	Hank Sauer	.25
9D	Jose Cardenal	.25
10D	Billy Herman	.35
JD	Bill Hands	.25
QD	Ken Holtzman	.25
KD	Ernie Banks	2.00
AC	Mordecai Brown	.25
2C	Gabby Hartnett	.25
3C	Frank Chance	.35
4C	Johnny Evers	.35
5C	Stan Hack	.35
6C	Joe Tinker	.35
7C	Bill Nicholson	.25
8C	Andy Pafko	.35
9C	Lewis Wilson	.35
10C	Kiki Cuyler	.25
JC	Charley Root	.25
QC	Grover Cleveland Alexander	.35
KC	Cap Anson	.35
AH	Greg Maddux	1.50
2H	Jody Davis	.25
3H	Bill Buckner	.25
4H	Manny Trillo	.25
5H	Bill Madlock	.25
6H	Ivan DeJesus	.25
7H	Gary Matthews	.25
8H	Leon Durham	.25
9H	Keith Moreland	.25
10H	Rick Reuschel	.25
JH	Rick Sutcliffe	.25
QH	Bruce Sutter	.50
KH	Dave Kingman	.25
---	Jack Brickhouse (Broadcaster)	.25
---	Harry Carey (Caray) (Broadcaster)	.50
---	Charlie Grimm	.25

Cincinnati Baseball Heroes

This deck of poker-format (2-1/2" x 3-1/2", round-cornered, linen finish) playing cards features color caricatures of past and contemporary Reds stars. Player name, sometimes a nickname, and his dates of service with the team are included. Backs have a baseball on a red background with white borders. The issue is apparently not licensed by MLB or the players.

		NM/M
Complete Set (55):		10.00
Common Player:		.25
AS	Don Gullett	.25
2S	Johnny Bench	1.50
3S	Tony Perez	1.50
4S	Joe Morgan	1.50
5S	Pete Rose	2.00
6S	Dave Concepcion	.50
7S	George Foster	.50
8S	Cesar Geronimo	.25
9S	Ken Griffey	.50
10S	Sparky Anderson	1.00
JS	Rawly Eastwick	.25
QS	Pedro Borbon	.25
KS	Fred Norman	.25
AD	Johnny Vander Meer	.25
2D	Ernie Lombardi	.25
3D	Ted Kluszewski	1.00
4D	Johnny Temple	.25
5D	Ray Knight	.25
6D	Roy McMillan	.25
7D	Gus Bell	.25
8D	Eric Davis	.25
9D	Vada Pinson	.50
10D	Fred Hutchinson	.25
JD	Joe Nuxhall	.35
QD	Bucky Walters	.25
KD	Frank Robinson	1.50
AC	Eppa Rixey	.25
2C	Bubbles Hargrave	.25
3C	Frank McCormick	.25
4C	Hughie Critz	.25
5C	Heinie Groh	.25
6C	Billy Myers	.25
7C	Wally Post	.25
8C	Edd Roush	.25
9C	Red Lucas	.25
10C	Bill McKechnie	.25
JC	Dolf Luque	.25
QC	Paul Derringer	.25
KC	Noodles Hahn	.25
AH	Jose Rijo	.25
2H	Jason LaRue	.35
3H	Sean Casey	.50
4H	Tommy Helms	.25
5H	Chris Sabo	.25
6H	Barry Larkin	.25
7H	Adam Dunn	.50
8H	Ken Griffey Jr.	2.00
9H	Paul O'Neill	.25
10H	Lou Piniella	.25
JH	Mario Soto	.25
QH	Rob Dibble	.25
KH	Tom Browning	.25
---	Marty Brennaman (Announcer)	.25
---	Powel Crosley (Owner)	.25
---	Marge Schott (Owner)	.25

L.A. & Brooklyn Baseball Heroes

This deck of poker-format (2-1/2" x 3-1/2", round-cornered, linen finish) playing cards features color caricatures of past and contemporary Dodgers stars. Player name, sometimes a nickname, and his dates of service with the team are included. Backs have a baseball on a blue background with white borders. The issue is apparently not licensed by MLB or the players.

		NM/M
Complete Set (55):		10.00
Common Player:		.25
AS	Eric Gagne	.25
2S	Mike Scioscia	.25
3S	Eric Karros	.25
4S	Steve Sax	.25
5S	Adrian Beltre	.25
6S	Cesar Izturis	.25
7S	Gary Sheffield	.25
8S	Milton Bradley	.25
9S	Shawn Green	.35
10S	Ramon Martinez	.25
JS	Hideo Nomo	.50
QS	Kevin Brown	.25
KS	Mike Piazza	1.00
AD	Sandy Koufax	2.00
2D	John Roseboro	.25
3D	Wes Parker	.25
4D	Jim Gilliam	.25
5D	Bill Buckner	.25
6D	Maury Wills	.35
7D	Tommy Davis	.25
8D	Willie Davis	.25
9D	Ron Fairly	.25
10D	Ron Perranoski	.25
JD	Johnny Podres	.25
QD	Don Drysdale	.50
KD	Frank Howard	.40
AC	Don Newcombe	.25
2C	Roy Campanella	.50
3C	Gil Hodges	.50
4C	Jackie Robinson	1.50
5C	Billy Cox	.25
6C	Pee Wee Reese	.50
7C	Zach Wheat	.25
8C	Duke Snider	.50
9C	Carl Furillo	.25
10C	Dazzy Vance	.25
JC	Clem Labine	.25
QC	Carl Erskine	.25
KC	Jake Daubert	.25
AH	Orel Hershiser	.25
2H	Steve Yeager	.25
3H	Steve Garvey	.35
4H	Davey Lopes	.25
5H	Ron Cey	.25
6H	Bill Russell	.25
7H	Dusty Baker	.25
8H	Claude Osteen	.25
9H	Reggie Smith	.25
10H	Burt Hooten (Hooton)	.25
JH	Fernando Valenzuela	.35
QH	Don Sutton	.25
KH	Kirk Gibson	.25
---	Walter Alston	.25
---	Tommy Lasorda	.25
---	Vin Scully (Announcer)	.25

N.Y. (Yankees) Baseball Heroes

This deck of poker-format (2-1/2" x 3-1/2", round-cornered, linen finish) playing cards features color caricatures of past and contemporary Yankees stars. Player name, sometimes a nickname, and his dates of service with the team are included. Backs have a baseball on a white pinstriped background. The issue is apparently not licensed by MLB or the players.

		NM/M
Complete Set (55):		10.00
Common Player:		.25
AS	Roger Clemens	1.50
2S	Jorge Posada	.25
3S	Tino Martinez	.25
4S	Alfonso Soriano	.25
5S	Alex Rodriguez	1.50
6S	Derek Jeter	1.50
7S	Hideki Matsui	.50
8S	Bernie Williams	.25
9S	Paul O'Neill	.25
10S	Mike Mussina	.25
JS	Andy Petitte	.25
QS	Mariano Rivera	.25
KS	Don Mattingly	1.00
AD	Whitey Ford	.50
2D	Yogi Berra	.50
3D	Joe Pepitone	.35
4D	Bobby Richardson	.35
5D	Clete Boyer	.25
6D	Phil Rizzuto	.35
7D	Roy White	.25
8D	Roger Maris	.50
9D	Hank Bauer	.25
10D	Allie Reynolds	.25
JD	Ed Lopat	.25
QD	Mel Stottlemyre	.25
KD	Mickey Mantle	2.00
AC	Charles Ruffing	.25
2C	Bill Dickey	.25
3C	Lou Gehrig	2.00
4C	Tony Lazzeri	.25
5C	Red Rolfe	.25
6C	Frank Crosetti	.25
7C	Earle Combs	.25
8C	Joe DiMaggio	2.00
9C	Charlie Keller	.25
10C	Waite Hoyt	.25
JC	Herb Pennock	.25
QC	Lefty Gomez	.25
KC	George Herman Ruth	2.00
AH	Ron Guidry	.25
2H	Thurman Munson	.50
3H	Chris Chambliss	.25
4H	Willie Randolph	.25
5H	Graig Nettles	.25
6H	Bucky Dent	.25
7H	Dave Winfield	.50
8H	Mickey Rivers	.25
9H	Bobby Murcer	.25
10H	Jim Hunter	.35
JH	Dave Righetti	.25
QH	Rich Gossage	.25
KH	Reggie Jackson	.50
---	Billy Martin	.40
---	Casey Stengel	.40
---	Joe Torre	.40

1988 Pepsi-Cola/ Kroger Tigers

Approximately 38,000 sets of cards were given to fans at Tiger Stadium on July 30th, 1988. The set, sponsored by

Pepsi-Cola and Kroger, includes 25 oversized (2-7/8" x 4-1/4") cards printed on glossy white stock with blue and orange borders. The card backs include small black and white close-up photos, the players' professional records and sponsor logos. The numbers in the following checklist refer to the players' uniform.

		NM/M
	Complete Set (25):	4.00
	Common Player:	.25
1	Lou Whitaker	.50
2	Alan Trammell	1.00
8	Mike Heath	.25
11	Sparky Anderson	.50
12	Luis Salazar	.25
14	Dave Bergman	.25
15	Pat Sheridan	.25
16	Tom Brookens	.25
19	Doyle Alexander	.25
21	Guillermo Hernandez	.25
22	Ray Knight	.25
24	Gary Pettis	.25
25	Eric King	.25
26	Frank Tanana	.25
31	Larry Herndon	.25
32	Jim Walewander	.25
33	Matt Nokes	.25
34	Chet Lemon	.25
35	Walt Terrell	.25
39	Mike Henneman	.25
41	Darrell Evans	.50
44	Jeff Robinson	.25
47	Jack Morris	.25
48	Paul Gibson	.25
---	Coaches (Billy Consolo, Alex Grammas, Billy Muffett, Vada Pinson, Dick Tracewski)	.25

1989 Pepsi-Cola Mark McGwire

During the summer of 1989, selected Pepsi products in the Northern California area carried these special McGwire cards. Photos were posed with McGwire wearing a generic white uniform trimmed in A's colors and bearing his number 25 and a Pepsi logo patch. Backs have the same biographical details, recent stats and career highlights. A card number is printed at lower-right.

		NM/M
	Complete Set (12):	10.00
	Common Card:	1.50
1	Mark McGwire/Btg (Left foot raised.)	1.50
2	Mark McGwire/Fldg	1.50
3	Mark McGwire (Reaching for ball with glove.)	1.50
4	Mark McGwire/Btg (Foot down.)	1.50
5	Mark McGwire (Kneeling with bat.)	1.50
6	Mark McGwire (Stretching for throw at first.)	1.50
7	Mark McGwire (Bat on shoulder.)	1.50
8	Mark McGwire (Holding bat.)	1.50
9	Mark McGwire (Bat on shoulder.)	1.50
10	Mark McGwire (Holding bat.)	1.50
11	Mark McGwire (Holding bat.)	1.50
12	Mark McGwire (Batting follow-through.)	1.50

1990 Pepsi-Cola Boston Red Sox

Pepsi combined with Score to produce this special 20-card Boston Red Sox team set. Cards were inserted regionally in 12-packs of Pepsi and Diet Pepsi. The card fronts feature full-color action photos with the team name across the top border and the player's name along the bottom border. The Pepsi and Diet Pepsi logos also appear on the bottom border. The card backs represent standard Score card backs, but are not numbered and also once again feature the Pepsi and Diet Pepsi logos.

		NM/M
	Complete Set (20):	5.00
	Common Player:	.25
(1)	Marty Barrett	.25
(2)	Mike Boddicker	.25
(3)	Wade Boggs	1.50
(4)	Bill Buckner	.35
(5)	Ellis Burks	.25
(6)	Roger Clemens	3.00
(7)	John Dopson	.25
(8)	Dwight Evans	.35
(9)	Wes Gardner	.25
(10)	Rich Gedman	.25
(11)	Mike Greenwell	.25
(12)	Dennis Lamp	.25
(13)	Rob Murphy	.25
(14)	Tony Pena	.25
(15)	Carlos Quintana	.25
(16)	Jeff Reardon	.25
(17)	Jody Reed	.25
(18)	Luis Rivera	.25
(19)	Kevin Romine	.25
(20)	Lee Smith	.25

Jose Canseco

Single cards from this issue were distributed in packs of Pepsi products in the San Francisco Bay area. Each card has a photo of Canseco in a generic red, white and blue uniform. Fronts have a blue border with a Pepsi logo. Backs have biographical data, recent stats and career highlights. The cards are numbered in the lower-right corner.

		NM/M
	Complete Set (10):	5.00
	Common Card:	.75
1	Jose Canseco (Batting follow-through.)	.75
2	Jose Canseco (Batting follow-through.)	.75
3	Jose Canseco/Fldg	.75
4	Jose Canseco/Btg	.75
5	Jose Canseco (Holding glove.)	.75
6	Jose Canseco (Batting follow-through.)	.75
7	Jose Canseco (On dugout steps.)	.75
8	Jose Canseco/Btg	.75
9	Jose Canseco/Portrait	.75
10	Jose Canseco/Portrait	.75

1991 Pepsi-Cola Superstars

This Florida regional issue was distributed by gluing cards inside of specially marked Pepsi products. Both front and back feature a "Flavor of Baseball" headline and logo of a glove catching a flying Pepsi can. Fronts have an action photo with colored strips at top and bottom. Player photos have uniform logos deleted. Backs have career stats, a few biographical details and a card number. The cards are slightly larger than current standards, measuring 2-5/8" x 3-1/2".

		NM/M
	Complete Set (17):	18.50
	Common Player:	.35
1	Dwight Gooden	.35
2	Andre Dawson	.65
3	Ryne Sandberg	2.00
4	Dave Steib	.35
5	Jose Rijo	.35
6	Roger Clemens	2.50
7	Barry Bonds	4.00
8	Cal Ripken, Jr.	4.00
9	Dave Justice	.35
10	Cecil Fielder	.35
11	Don Mattingly	2.50
12	Ozzie Smith	2.00
13	Kirby Puckett	2.00
14	Rafael Palmeiro	1.50
15	Bobby Bonilla	.35
16	Len Dykstra	.35
17	Jose Canseco	1.00

Cincinnati Reds

This team set was produced for inclusion in packages of Pepsi products in the Ohio area by Michael Schecheter Assoc. Like most MSA issues, the cards have had cap and uniform logos airbrushed away because they are licensed only by the Players Union, and not MLB. Fronts have red borders with Pepsi, Diet Pepsi and MLBPA logos. Backs are in red, white and blue with the soda logos at top a few biographical notes, complete major and minor league stats and a facsimile autograph. The unnumbered cards are checklisted here alphabetically.

		NM/M
	Complete Set (20):	8.00
	Common Player:	.50
(1)	Jack Armstrong	.50
(2)	Todd Benzinger	.50
(3)	Glenn Braggs	.50
(4)	Tom Browning	.50
(5)	Norm Charlton	.50
(6)	Eric Davis	.75
(7)	Rob Dibble	.50
(8)	Bill Doran	.50
(9)	Mariano Duncan	.50
(10)	Billy Hatcher	.50
(11)	Barry Larkin	.75
(12)	Hal Morris	.50
(13)	Randy Myers	.50
(14)	Joe Oliver	.50
(15)	Paul O'Neill	.75
(16)	Lou Piniella	.50
(17)	Jeff Reed	.50
(18)	Jose Rijo	.50
(19)	Chris Sabo	.50
(20)	Herm Winningham	.50

Red Sox

For the second consecutive year, Pepsi/Diet Pepsi sponsored Boston Red Sox trading cards. The cards were inserted in specially marked packs of Pepsi and Diet Pepsi and were made available from July 1 through August 10. A consumer sweepstakes was also included with this promotion. Player jersey numbers are featured on the backs of the cards. Danny Darwin's jersey is incorrectly listed as #46. He actually wears #44 for the BoSox. Wade Boggs is not featured on a 1991 Pepsi-Cola Red Sox card.

		NM/M
	Complete Set (20):	6.00
	Common Player:	.25
2	Luis Rivera	.25
3	Jody Reed	.25
6	Tony Pena	.25
11	Tim Naehring	.25
12	Ellis Burks	.25
15	Dennis Lamp	.25
18	Carlos Quintana	.25
19	Dana Kiecker	.25
20	John Marzano	.25
21	Roger Clemens	5.00
23	Tom Brunansky	.25
25	Jack Clark	.25
27	Greg Harris	.25
29	Phil Plantier	.25
30	Matt Young	.25
38	Jeff Gray	.25
39	Mike Greenwell	.25
41	Jeff Reardon	.25
46	Danny Darwin	.25
50	Tom Bolton	.25

Griffeys

This regionally released set features Ken Griffey, Sr. and Jr. and was distributed in Pepsi products. In the photos the players are shown in generic white uniforms with Pepsi logo patches. Backs are printed in black-and-white and include biographical data, recent stats and career highlights. Card numbers are in the lower-right.

		NM/M
	Complete Set (8):	7.50
	Common Card:	.25
1	Ken Griffey Jr. (Swinging bat.)	2.00
2	Ken Griffey Jr./Throwing	2.00
3	Ken Griffey Jr./Catching	2.00
4	Ken Griffey Jr. (Bat on shoulder.)	2.00
5	Ken Griffey Jr. (Leaning on father.)	.75
6	Ken Griffey Jr. (Standing with father.)	.75
7	Ken Griffey Sr./Btg	.25
8	Ken Griffey Sr./Fldg	.25

Rickey Henderson

A third annual issue distributed with Pepsi products in the San Francisco Bay area this set features photos of the all-time base stealing king in airbrushed uniforms. Borders are red, white and blue pinstripes. A line-art figure of a base runner appears in the lower-right. Backs have a few bits of biographical data, career stats and a career highlight. Card numbers are printed in the lower-right.

		NM/M
	Complete Set (10):	9.00
	Common Card:	1.00
	Uncut Prize Sheet:	25.00
1	Rickey Henderson (Batting follow-through.)	1.00
2	Rickey Henderson (Base running.)	1.00
3	Rickey Henderson (Warm-up stretches.)	1.00
4	Rickey Henderson (Taking lead-off.)	1.00
5	Rickey Henderson (Bat on shoulder.)	1.00
6	Rickey Henderson (Batting follow-through.)	1.00
7	Rickey Henderson (Squatting with bat.)	1.00
8	Rickey Henderson (Throwing follow-through.)	1.00
9	Rickey Henderson (Leading off.)	1.00
10	Rickey Henderson (Warm-up swings.)	1.00

Rickey Henderson Discs

Intended as a giveaway with Pepsi fountain drinks, this four-piece set of "3-D" discs pictures Rickey Henderson in a generic Pepsi-logo uniform. Each 2-1/4" diameter disc has two pictures of Henderson which change when the disc is moved. There is a purple border around the color photos, with "Pepsi," decorative stars and Henderson's name in white. Backs are printed in red and blue on white and are identical and unnumbered. The date and Pepsi logo are at top with 1990 season and career stats beneath.

		NM/M
	Complete Set (4):	2.50
	Common Disc:	1.00
(1)	Rickey Henderson (Bat on shoulder/follow-through.)	1.00
(2)	Rickey Henderson (Warm-up swing/batting follow-through.)	1.00
(3)	Rickey Henderson (Lead-off/running for 2nd.)	1.00
(4)	Rickey Henderson (Lead-off/headfirst slide.)	1.00

1996 Pepsi-Cola Cubs Convention

In conjunction with the Chicago Cubs 11th annual winter fan convention, Pepsi issued this boxed set featuring past and current Cubs with an emphasis on those appearing as convention guests. Individual cards are 4" x 5-1/2" and feature black-and-white or color photos inside a black border with white piping. The team and convention logos are printed in red, white and blue. Backs are printed in black on white and feature stats and biographical data plus the team and sponsor logos. The unnumbered cards are checklisted here in alphabetical order.

		NM/M
	Complete Set (24):	8.00
	Common Player:	.25
(1)	Ernie Banks	3.00
(2)	Glenn Beckert	.25
(3)	Larry Bowa	.25
(4)	Harry Caray	.25
(5)	Frank Castillo	.25
(6)	Jody Davis	.25
(7)	Dynamic Duo (Scott Bullett, Ozzie Timmons)	.25
(8)	Flashback Favorites (Milt Pappas, Tim Stoddard)	.25
(9)	Golden Voices (Jack Brickhouse, Vince Lloyd)	.25
(10)	Randy Hundley	.25
(11)	Fergie Jenkins	.50
(12)	Don Kessinger	.35
(13)	Gary Matthews	.25
(14)	Brian McRae	.25
(15)	Jim Riggleman	.25
(16)	Ron Santo	.50
(17)	Sensational 70's (Jose Cardenal, Rick Monday)	.25
(18)	Scott Servais	.25
(19)	Rick Sutcliffe	.25
(20)	Steve Trachsel	.25
(21)	Billy Williams	.75
(22)	Wrigleyville Sluggers (Keith Moreland, Richie Hebner)	.25

(23)	Young Guns (Turk Wendell, Terry Adams)	.25
(24)	Vine Line subscription offer (Ernie Banks)	.25

1998 Pepsi-Cola Arizona Diamondbacks

Pepsi-Cola and Circle K stores ran a baseball-season promotion to distribute 15 cards of Arizona Diamondback players on a regional basis. By use of a punchcard to record the purchase of five 20-oz. or one-liter Pepsi products a customer could receive a series of three players cards each month. Produced by Pinnacle, the D'back cards have action photos on front against a stylized semi-circular background. Team, Pinnacle and Pepsi logos are in three of the corners with the player name at lower-right. Backs have a red, white and blue Pepsi-style whirlpool background, another player photo, major league stats, a career highlight and licensor logos. Final production of the cards differs considerably from the player checklist provided on the punchcard and ads.

		NM/M
Complete Set (15):		6.00
Common Player:		.50
1	Andy Benes	.50
2	Willie Blair	.50
3	Jorge Fabregas	.50
4	Jay Bell	.50
5	Travis Lee	1.00
6	Matt Williams	.50
7	Devon White	.50
8	Karim Garcia	.65
9	Yamil Benitez	.50
10	Brian Anderson	.50
11	Scott Brow	.50
12	Felix Rodriguez	.50
13	Jeff Suppan	.50
14	Andy Fox	.50
15	Andy Stankiewicz	.50

Cubs Convention

In conjunction with the Chicago Cubs 13th annual winter fan convention, Pepsi issued this boxed set featuring past and current Cubs with an emphasis on those appearing as convention guests. Individual cards are 3-1/2" x 4" and feature black-and-white or color photos bordered in blue and sand. The team and convention logos are printed in red, white and blue. Backs are printed in black on white and feature stats and biographical data plus the team and sponsor logos. The unnumbered cards are checklisted here in alphabetical order.

		NM/M
Complete Set (30):		7.00
Common Card:		.25
(1)	Terry Adams	.25
(2)	Alumni Club (Carmen Fanzone, Paul Reuschel)	.25
(3)	Alumni Club (Oscar Gamble, Larry Bowa)	.25
(4)	Ernie Banks	2.00
(5)	Behind the Plate (Randy Hundley, Jody Davis)	.25
(6)	Booth Banter (Pat Hughes, Josh Lewin)	.25
(7)	Jack Brickhouse	.25
(8)	Harry Caray	.25
(9)	Catching Corps (Mike Hubbard, Tyler Houston)	.25
(10)	Andre Dawson	.50
(11)	Flame-Throwers (Kevin Foster, Marc Pisciotta)	.25
(12)	Future Stars (Kerry Wood, Pat Cline)	.50
(13)	Mark Grace	.50
(14)	Hot Prospects (Robin Jennings, Rodney Myers)	.25
(15)	Mound Mates (Mark Clark, Jeremi Gonzalez)	.25
(16)	New Cubs (Jeff Blauser, Mickey Morandini)	.25
(17)	No-Hit Hurlers (Milt Pappas, Don Cardwell)	.25
(18)	Kevin Orie	.25
(19)	Outfield Greats (Andy Pafko, Gary Matthews)	.35
(20)	Jim Riggleman	.25
(21)	Ron Santo	1.00
(22)	Scott Servais	.25
(23)	Sammy Sosa	2.00
(24)	Rick Sutcliffe	.25
(25)	Steve Trachsel	.25
(26)	Veteran Hurlers (Bob Patterson, Kevin Tapani)	.25
(27)	Billy Williams	1.00
(28)	1969 Cubs (Dick Selma, Willie Smith)	.25
(29)	1969 Infield (Glenn Beckert, Don Kessinger)	.50
(30)	89er's (Mike Bielecki, Vance Law)	.25

1999 Pepsi-Cola Arizona Diamondbacks

Sponsored by Pepsi and produced by Fleer, this team-set promotion features action photos on front on a metallic-foil background which approximates the colors and design of the soft drink logo, which also appears at lower-left. The player's uniform is at top-left. On back is a portrait photo on a repeat of the red, white and blue background. Full Major League stats are provided, along with career highlights and biographical data. At bottom is a row of licensor and sponsor logos.

		NM/M
Complete Set (15):		9.00
Common Player:		.50
1	Jay Bell	.50
2	Andy Benes	.50
3	Randy Johnson	3.00
4	Matt Williams	.50
5	Steve Finley	.50
6	Todd Stottlemyre	.50
7	Omar Daal	.50
8	Travis Lee	.50
9	Armando Reynoso	.50
10	Gregg Olson	.50
11	Tony Batista	.50
12	Greg Swindell	.50
13	Greg Colbrunn	.50
14	Damian Miller	.50
15	Kelly Stinnett	.50
---	Checklist 1	.10
---	Checklist 2	.10
---	Checklist 3	.10
---	Checklist 4	.10

2000 Pepsi-Cola Arizona Diamondbacks

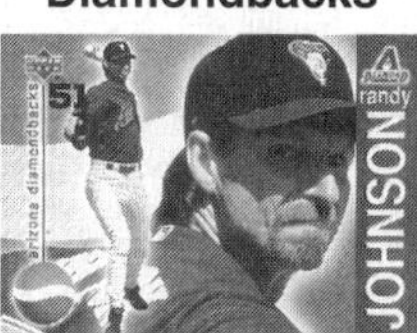

Pepsi-Cola and Circle K stores ran a baseball-season promotion to distribute 15 cards of Arizona Diamondback players on a regional basis. Produced by Upper Deck, the D'back cards have large portrait and smaller action photos in a horizontal format on a red, white and blue wave background. Team, UD and Pepsi logos appear in the corners with the player name at right. Backs have the same background, another player photo, major league stats, a career highlight and licensor logos. Cards were distributed in three five-card series, with a checklist card in each pack.

		NM/M
Complete Set (18):		9.00
Common Player:		.50
1	Jay Bell	.50
2	Matt Mantei	.50
3	Greg Swindell	.50
4	Matt Williams	.50
5	Erubiel Durazo	.50
6	Todd Stottlemyre	.50
7	Randy Johnson	3.00
8	Tony Womack	.50
9	Greg Colbrunn	.50
10	Brian Anderson	.50
11	Omar Daal	.50
12	Travis Lee	.50
13	Steve Finley	.50
14	Luis Gonzalez	.50
15	Kelly Stinnett	.50
	Checklist 1	.10
	Checklist 2	.10
	Checklist 3	.10

Detroit Tigers

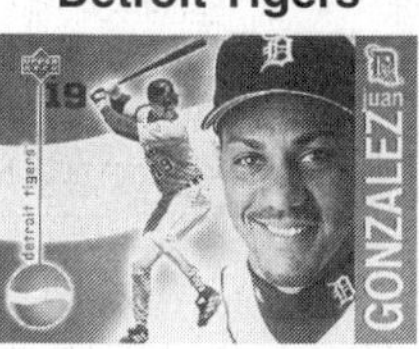

Pepsi-Cola ran a late-season promotion to distribute 15 cards of Detroit Tigers players on a regional basis. Produced by Upper Deck, the cards have large portrait and smaller action photos in a horizontal format on a red, white and blue wave background. Team, UD and Pepsi logos appear in the corners with the player name at right. Backs have the same background, another action photo, major league stats, a careeer highlight and licensor logos. Cards were distributed in one per 12-pack of Pepsi products.

		NM/M
Complete Set (15):		5.00
Common Player:		.50
1	Damion Easley	.50
2	Dave Mlicki	.50
3	Jeff Weaver	.50
4	Deivi Cruz	.50
5	Juan Encarnacion	.50
6	Brian Moehler	.50
7	Robert Fick	.50
8	Juan Gonzalez	1.50
9	Phil Garner	.50
10	Brad Ausmus	.50
11	Todd Jones	.50
12	Bobby Higginson	.50
13	Tony Clark	.50
14	Dean Palmer	.50
15	Doug Brocail	.50

2001 Pepsi-Cola Arizona Diamondbacks

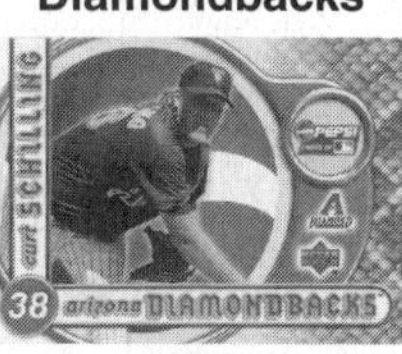

Pepsi-Cola ran a baseball-season promotion to distribute 15 cards of Arizona Diamondback players on a regional basis. Produced by Upper Deck, the D'back cards have a circular action photo in a horizontal format on a red, white and blue wave background at left. At right is a rattlesnake skin design. Team, UD and Pepsi logos appear at right, with the player name at left. Backs have the same background, another player photo, recent major league stats, a career highlight and licensor logos. Cards were distributed in five three-card series. They are checklisted here by uniform number which appears on front.

		NM/M
Complete Set (15):		10.00
Common Player:		.25
5	Tony Womack	.25
9	Matt Williams	.25
12	Steve Finley	.25
16	Reggie Sanders	.25
17	Mark Grace	.50
20	Luis Gonzalez	.25
22	Greg Swindell	.25
27	Armando Reynoso	.25
28	Greg Colbrunn	.25
30	Todd Stottlemyre	.25
31	Matt Mantei	.25
33	Jay Bell	.25
34	Brian Anderson	.25
38	Curt Schilling	2.00
51	Randy Johnson	3.00

2002 Pepsi-Cola Seattle Mariners

Pepsi-Cola and the Mariners teamed up for this 25th Anniversary promotion distributing eight cards on a regional basis. Produced by Upper Deck, the M's cards have a game-action photo at left. At right is the team name along with Pepsi and anniversary logos. Backs have player stats and career highlights, a few sentences of team history and licensor logos. Cards were distributed in two-card cello packs.

		NM/M
Complete Set (8):		10.00
Common Player:		.50
1	John Olerud	.50
2	Mike Cameron	.50
3	Edgar Martinez	.75
4	Ichiro	6.00
5	Bret Boone	.75
6	Jeff Nelson	.50
7	Freddy Garcia	.50
8	Jamie Moyer	.50

2003 Pepsi-Cola

Unusual for modern promotional cards, Pepsi chose a smaller, 2" x 2-3/4" format for its Fleer-produced issue. Specially marked 24-can "Value Cubes" of Pepsi products included one of the cards. A total of 9.75 million (about 325,000 sets) were reportedly produced. Fronts have action photos in a format similar to the soda logo, with red border at top and blue at bottom. Fleer, Pepsi and MLB logos appear. Backs have a team logo, player data, recent stats and career highlights, along with appropriate logos and copyright information. There is one player from each team in the issue.

		NM/M
Complete Set (30):		6.00
Common Player:		.15
1	Troy Glaus	.30
2	Chipper Jones	.35
3	Randy Johnson	.30
4	Tony Batista	.15
5	Magglio Ordonez	.15
6	Ken Griffey Jr.	.40
7	Omar Vizquel	.15
8	Todd Helton	.30
9	Bobby Higginson	.15
10	Luis Castillo	.15
11	Jeff Bagwell	.30
12	Mike Sweeney	.15
13	Shawn Green	.25
14	Richie Sexson	.15
15	Torii Hunter	.15
16	Vladimir Guerrero	.30
17	Mike Piazza	.35
18	Jason Giambi	.25
19	Barry Zito	.15
20	Pat Burrell	.25
21	Brian Giles	.15
22	Trevor Hoffman	.15
23	Barry Bonds	.75
24	Ichiro	.50
25	Albert Pujols	.60
26	Ben Grieve	.15
27	Alex Rodriguez	.60
28	Carlos Delgado	.25
29	Kerry Wood	.20
30	Pedro Martinez	.30

2004 Pepsi-Cola Arizona Diamondbacks

Pepsi-Cola offered this team set of Arizona Diamondback players as a stadium giveaway. Produced by Upper Deck, the cards have a game-action photo on a blue background. Backs have the same background, two more player photos, recent major league stats, a career highlight and licensor logos.

		NM/M
Complete Set (15):		7.00
Common Player:		.25
1	Randy Johnson	5.00
2	Richie Sexson	.35
3	Roberto Alomar	.35
4	Shea Hillenbrand	.35
5	Alex Cintron	.25
6	Matt Kata	.25
7	Robby Hammock	.25
8	Luis Gonzalez	.25
9	Steve Finley	.25
10	Danny Bautista	.25
11	Matt Mantei	.25
12	Brandon Webb	.35
13	Elmer Dessens	.25
14	Oscar Villarreal	.25
15	Jose Valverde	.25

1980-2001 Perez-Steele Hall of Fame Postcards

In 1980, Perez-Steele Galleries of Ft. Washington, Pa., produced the first in an ongoing series of limited-edition (10,000 each) postcards devoted to members of the Hall of Fame. The company updated its series regularly through 2001 to add new inductees. The 3-1/2" x 5-1/2" cards feature color portrait and smaller sepia action watercolor paintings by Dick Perez. Decorative postcard backs have a few words about the player, card and series number and individual set number from within the edition of 10,000. Cards were sold by series only, in a color-coded box which includes a checklist. To a great degree, value of unsigned Perez-Steele cards depends on whether the player is still alive to autograph them.

		NM/M
Complete Set (270):		750.00
Common Player:		2.00
	First Series, 1980	75.00
1	Ty Cobb	20.00
2	Walter Johnson	6.00
3	Christy Mathewson	7.50
4	Babe Ruth	25.00
5	Honus Wagner	7.50
6	Morgan Bulkeley	2.00
7	Ban Johnson	2.00
8	Nap Lajoie	4.00
9	Connie Mack	4.00
10	John McGraw	2.00
11	Tris Speaker	4.00
12	George Wright	2.00
13	Cy Young	7.50
14	Grover Alexander	4.00
15	Alexander Cartwright	2.00
16	Henry Chadwick	2.00
17	Cap Anson	2.00
18	Eddie Collins	2.00
19	Candy Cummings	2.00
20	Charles Comiskey	2.00
21	Buck Ewing	2.00
22	Lou Gehrig	20.00
23	Willie Keeler	2.00
24	Hoss Radbourne	2.00
25	George Sisler	2.00
26	A.G. Spalding	2.00
27	Rogers Hornsby	4.00
28	Kenesaw Landis	2.00
29	Roger Breshnahan	2.00
30	Dan Brouthers	2.00
---	**First Series Checklist**	1.00
	Second Series, 1980	50.00
31	Fred Clarke	2.00

32	Jimmy Collins	2.00
33	Ed Delahanty	2.00
34	Hugh Duffy	2.00
35	Hughie Jennings	2.00
36	King Kelly	2.00
37	Jim O'Rourke	2.00
38	Wilbert Robinson	2.00
39	Jesse Burkett	2.00
40	Frank Chance	2.00
41	Jack Chesbro	2.00
42	Johnny Evers	2.00
43	Clark Griffith	2.00
44	Thomas McCarthy	2.00
45	Joe McGinnity	2.00
46	Eddie Plank	2.00
47	Joe Tinker	2.00
48	Rube Waddell	2.00
49	Ed Walsh	2.00
50	Mickey Cochrane	2.00
51	Frankie Frisch	2.00
52	Lefty Grove	2.00
53	Carl Hubbell	2.00
54	Herb Pennock	2.00
55	Pie Traynor	2.00
56	Mordecai Brown	2.00
57	Charlie Gehringer	2.00
58	Kid Nichols	2.00
59	Jimmie Foxx	4.00
60	Mel Ott	2.00
---	**Second Series Checklist**	1.00
	Third Series, 1980	75.00
61	Harry Heilmann	2.00
62	Paul Waner	2.00
63	Ed Barrow	2.00
64	Chief Bender	2.00
65	Tom Connolly	2.00
66	Dizzy Dean	7.50
67	Bill Klem	2.00
68	Al Simmons	2.00
69	Bobby Wallace	2.00
70	Harry Wright	2.00
71	Bill Dickey	2.00
72	Rabbit Maranville	2.00
73	Bill Terry	2.00
74	Frank Baker	2.00
75	Joe DiMaggio	20.00
76	Gabby Hartnett	2.00
77	Ted Lyons	2.00
78	Ray Schalk	2.00
79	Dazzy Vance	2.00
80	Joe Cronin	2.00
81	Hank Greenberg	7.50
82	Sam Crawford	2.00
83	Joe McCarthy	2.00
84	Zack Wheat	2.00
85	Max Carey	2.00
86	Billy Hamilton	2.00
87	Bob Feller	6.00
88	Bill McKechnie	2.00
89	Jackie Robinson	10.00
90	Edd Roush	2.00
---	**Third Series Checklist**	1.00
	Fourth Series, 1981	65.00
91	John Clarkson	2.00
92	Elmer Flick	2.00
93	Sam Rice	2.00
94	Eppa Rixey	2.00
95	Luke Appling	2.00
96	Red Faber	2.00
97	Burleigh Grimes	2.00
98	Miller Huggins	2.00
99	Tim Keefe	2.00
100	Heinie Manush	2.00
101	John Ward	2.00
102	Pud Galvin	2.00
103	Casey Stengel	3.00
104	Ted Williams	20.00
105	Branch Rickey	2.00
106	Red Ruffing	2.00
107	Lloyd Waner	2.00
108	Kiki Cuyler	2.00
109	Goose Goslin	2.00
110	Joe Medwick	2.00
111	Roy Campanella	7.50
112	Stan Coveleski	2.00
113	Waite Hoyt	2.00
114	Stan Musial	10.00
115	Lou Boudreau	2.00
116	Earle Combs	2.00
117	Ford Frick	2.00
118	Jesse Haines	2.00
119	David Bancroft	2.00
120	Jake Beckley	2.00
---	**Fourth Series Checklist**	1.00
	Fifth Series, 1981	85.00
121	Chick Hafey	2.00
122	Harry Hooper	2.00
123	Joe Kelley	2.00
124	Rube Marquard	2.00
125	Satchel Paige	10.00
126	George Weiss	2.00
127	Yogi Berra	6.00
128	Josh Gibson	4.00
129	Lefty Gomez	2.00
130	William Harridge	2.00
131	Sandy Koufax	15.00
132	Buck Leonard	2.00
133	Early Wynn	2.00
134	Ross Youngs	2.00
135	Roberto Clemente	20.00
136	Billy Evans	2.00
137	Monte Irvin	4.00
138	George Kelly	2.00
139	Warren Spahn	2.00
140	Mickey Welch	2.00
141	Cool Papa Bell	2.00
142	Jim Bottomley	2.00
143	Jocko Conlan	2.00
144	Whitey Ford	5.00
145	Mickey Mantle	25.00
146	Sam Thompson	2.00
147	Earl Averill	2.00
148	Bucky Harris	2.00
149	Billy Herman	2.00
150	Judy Johnson	2.00
---	**Fifth Series Checklist**	1.00
	Sixth Series, 1981	85.00
151	Ralph Kiner	2.00
152	Oscar Charleston	2.00
153	Roger Connor	2.00
154	Cal Hubbard	2.00
155	Bob Lemon	2.00
156	Freddie Lindstrom	2.00
157	Robin Roberts	4.00
158	Ernie Banks	6.00
159	Martin DiHigo	2.00
160	John Lloyd	2.00
161	Al Lopez	2.00
162	Amos Rusie	2.00
163	Joe Sewell	2.00
164	Addie Joss	2.00
165	Larry MacPhail	2.00
166	Eddie Mathews	2.00
167	Warren Giles	2.00
168	Willie Mays	15.00
169	Hack Wilson	2.00
170	Al Kaline	5.00
171	Chuck Klein	2.00
172	Duke Snider	5.00
173	Tom Yawkey	2.00
174	Rube Foster	2.00
175	Bob Gibson	4.00
176	Johnny Mize	2.00
A	Abner Doubleday	2.00
B	Stephen Clark	2.00
C	Paul Kerr	2.00
D	Edward W. Stack	2.00
---	**Sixth Series Checklist**	1.00
	Seventh Series, 1983	55.00
177	Hank Aaron	20.00
178	Happy Chandler	3.00
179	Travis Jackson	3.00
180	Frank Robinson	10.00
181	Walter Alston	3.00
182	George Kell	6.00
183	Juan Marichal	7.50
184	Brooks Robinson	10.00
	Eighth Series, 1985	55.00
185	Luis Aparicio	7.50
186	Don Drysdale	3.00
187	Rick Ferrell	3.00
188	Harmon Killebrew	6.00
189	Pee Wee Reese	3.00
190	Lou Brock	6.00
191	Enos Slaughter	3.00
192	Arky Vaughn	3.00
193	Hoyt Wilhelm	3.00
	Ninth Series, 1987.	15.00
194	Bobby Doerr	2.00
195	Ernie Lombardi	2.00
196	Willie McCovey	2.00
197	Ray Dandridge	2.00
198	Catfish Hunter	2.00
199	Billy Williams	4.00
E	Frank Steele, Peggy Steele, Dick Perez	2.00
	Tenth Series, 1989	20.00
200	Willie Stargell	2.00
201	Al Barlick	2.00
202	Johnny Bench	4.00
203	Red Schoendienst	4.00
204	Carl Yastrzemski	4.00
F	George Bush, Edward Stack	4.00
	Eleventh Series, 1991	30.00
205	Joe Morgan	4.00
206	Jim Palmer	4.00
207	Rod Carew	4.00
208	Ferguson Jenkins	4.00
209	Tony Lazzeri	2.00
210	Gaylord Perry	4.00
211	Bill Veeck	2.00
	Twelfth Series, 1993	35.00
212	Rollie Fingers	4.00
213	Bill McGowan	3.00
214	Hal Newhouser	3.00
215	Tom Seaver	6.00
216	Reggie Jackson	7.50
217	Steve Carlton	6.00
218	Leo Durocher	3.00
219	Phil Rizzuto	6.00
	Thirteenth Series, 1995	40.00
220	Richie Ashburn	4.00
221	Leon Day	3.00
222	William Hulbert	3.00
223	Mike Schmidt	10.00
224	Vic Willis	3.00
225	Jim Bunning	6.00
226	Andrew "Rube" Foster	3.00
227	Ned Hanlon	3.00
228	Earl Weaver	6.00
	Fourteenth Series, 1997	85.00
229	Nellie Fox	6.00
230	Tommy Lasorda	6.00
231	Phil Niekro	4.00
232	Willie Wells	3.00
233	George Davis	3.00
234	Larry Doby	4.00
235	Lee MacPhail	4.00
236	Joe Rogan	3.00
237	Don Sutton	4.00
238	George Brett	15.00
239	Orlando Cepeda	6.00
240	Nestor Chylak	3.00
241	Nolan Ryan	20.00
242	Frank Selee	3.00
243	Joe Williams	3.00
244	Robin Yount	7.50
	Fifteenth Series, 2001	50.00
245	Sparky Anderson	6.00
246	Carlton Fisk	7.50
247	Bid McPhee	3.00
248	Tony Perez	6.00
249	Turkey Stearnes	3.00
250	Bill Mazeroski	7.50
251	Kirby Puckett	7.50
252	Hilton Smith	3.00
253	Dave Winfield	7.50
G	Franklin A. Steele	5.00

Autographed

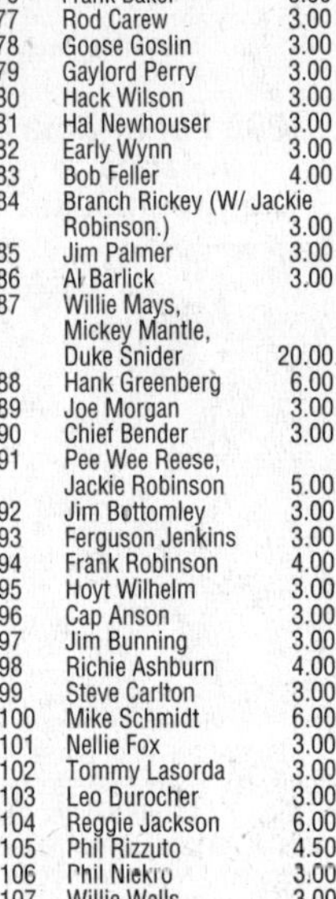

Because the cards are so popular with autograph collectors, a listing of Perez-Steele Hall of Fame postcards which are possible to acquire in authentically autographed form is provided here, along with current retail values. Only those players who were alive at the time of their cards' issue are included in this listings; no cards from Series 1 and very few from Series 2 are available in autographed form.

		NM/M
	Common Player:	15.00
53	Carl Hubbell	80.00
57	Charlie Gehringer	80.00
71	Bill Dickey	65.00
73	Bill Terry	90.00
75	Joe DiMaggio	325.00
77	Ted Lyons	235.00
80	Joe Cronin	750.00
81	Hank Greenberg	300.00
87	Bob Feller	25.00
90	Edd Roush	75.00
95	Luke Appling	50.00
97	Burleigh Grimes	190.00
104	Ted Williams	300.00
106	Red Ruffing	450.00
107	Lloyd Waner	2,250
111	Roy Campanella	300.00
112	Stan Coveleski	300.00
113	Waite Hoyt	495.00
114	Stan Musial	75.00
115	Lou Boudreau	25.00
125	Satchel Paige	2,500
127	Yogi Berra	40.00
129	Lefty Gomez	60.00
131	Sandy Koufax	90.00
132a	Buck Leonard (Pre-stroke.)	45.00
132b	Buck Leonard (Post-stroke.)	25.00
133	Early Wynn	40.00
137	Monte Irvin	20.00
138	George Kelly	350.00
139	Warren Spahn	30.00
141	Cool Papa Bell	75.00
143	Jocko Conlan	60.00
144	Whitey Ford	40.00
145	Mickey Mantle	300.00
147	Earl Averill	450.00
149	Billy Herman	35.00
150	Judy Johnson	60.00
151	Ralph Kiner	30.00
155	Bob Lemon	30.00
157	Robin Roberts	25.00
158	Ernie Banks	30.00
161	Al Lopez	75.00
163	Joe Sewell	45.00
166	Eddie Mathews	40.00
168	Willie Mays	75.00
170	Al Kaline	25.00
172	Duke Snider	30.00
175	Bob Gibson	25.00
176	Johnny Mize	35.00
D	Edward W. Stack	15.00
177	Hank Aaron	45.00
178	Happy Chandler	50.00
179	Travis Jackson	80.00
180	Frank Robinson	35.00
181	Walter Alston	675.00
182	George Kell	20.00
183	Juan Marichal	20.00
184	Brooks Robinson	22.50
185	Luis Aparicio	22.50
186	Don Drysdale	40.00
187	Rick Ferrell	25.00
188	Harmon Killebrew	30.00
189	Pee Wee Reese	55.00
190	Lou Brock	25.00
191	Enos Slaughter	20.00
193	Hoyt Wilhelm	20.00
194	Bobby Doerr	17.50
196	Willie McCovey	35.00
197	Ray Dandridge	30.00
198	Catfish Hunter	40.00
199	Billy Williams	22.50
E	Frank Steele, Peggy Steele, Dick Perez	15.00
200	Willie Stargell	35.00
201	Al Barlick	20.00
202	Johnny Bench	45.00
203	Red Schoendienst	25.00
204	Carl Yastrzemski	65.00
F	George Bush, Edward Stack	60.00
205	Joe Morgan	35.00
206	Jim Palmer	25.00
207	Rod Carew	45.00
208	Ferguson Jenkins	30.00
210	Gaylord Perry	17.50
212	Rollie Fingers	35.00
214	Hal Newhouser	60.00
215	Tom Seaver	60.00
216	Reggie Jackson	75.00
217	Steve Carlton	45.00
219	Phil Rizzuto	40.00
220	Richie Ashburn	30.00
223	Mike Schmidt	75.00
225	Jim Bunning	35.00
228	Earl Weaver	35.00
230	Tommy Lasorda	35.00
231	Phil Niekro	35.00
234	Larry Doby	90.00
235	Lee MacPhail	35.00
237	Don Sutton	35.00
238	George Brett	100.00
239	Orlando Cepeda	40.00
241	Nolan Ryan	100.00
244	Robin Yount	100.00
245	Sparky Anderson	45.00
246	Carlton Fisk	60.00
248	Tony Perez	45.00
250	Bill Mazeroski	45.00
251	Kirby Puckett	85.00
253	Dave Winfield	85.00

1981 Perez-Steele Yankee Greats Promotional Postcard

To advertise the availability of a "Yankee Greats" lithograph by Dick Perez, the Perez-Steele Galleries issued this promotional postcard. The 3-1/2" x 5-1/2" card is printed on thin cardboard with a reproduction of the lithograph on front. Printed in blue, the postcard-style back has information on the lithograph, which was issued in a size of 19" x 24-1/2" in an edition of 1,000 signed pieces.

	NM/M
Yankee Greats (Babe Ruth, Lou Gehrig, Earle Combs)	4.00

1985-95 Perez-Steele Great Moments Postcards

Yet another collectors issue devoted solely to Hall of Fame players, the Great Moments series borrows the format of the 1911 Turkey Red cabinet cards. The 5-3/4" x 8" cards are printed on textured cardboard (which was noticeably downgraded beginning with the 1993 series). Fronts have Dick Perez paintings surrounded by a greenish-brown border; backs are in black-and-white. Each card carries a series checklist on back and an individual set serial number from within an edition of 5,000. Cards were issued in series of 12.

		NM/M
	Complete Set (108):	400.00
	Common Player:	3.00
1	Babe Ruth	20.00
2	Al Kaline	6.00
3	Jackie Robinson	10.00
4	Lou Gehrig	15.00
5	Whitey Ford	6.00
6	Christy Mathewson	5.00
7	Roy Campanella	7.50
8	Walter Johnson	6.00
9	Hank Aaron	12.50
10	Cy Young	5.00
11	Stan Musial	12.50
12	Ty Cobb	15.00
13	Ted Williams	15.00
14	Warren Spahn	3.00
15	Lloyd Waner, Paul Waner	3.00
16	Sandy Koufax	12.50
17	Robin Roberts	3.00
18	Dizzy Dean	4.00
19	Mickey Mantle	25.00
20	Satchel Paige	10.00
21	Ernie Banks	6.00
22	Willie McCovey	3.00
23	Johnny Mize	3.00
24	Honus Wagner	7.50
25	Willie Keeler	3.00
26	Pee Wee Reese	3.00
27	Monte Irvin	3.00
28	Eddie Mathews	3.00
29	Enos Slaughter	3.00
30	Rube Marquard	3.00
31	Charlie Gehringer	3.00
32	Roberto Clemente	15.00
33	Duke Snider	4.50
34	Ray Dandridge	3.00
35	Carl Hubbell	3.00
36	Bobby Doerr	3.00
37	Bill Dickey	3.00
38	Willie Stargell	3.00
39	Brooks Robinson	3.00
40	Joe Tinker, Johnny Evers, Frank Chance	5.00
41	Billy Herman	3.00
42	Grover Alexander	4.00
43	Luis Aparicio	3.00
44	Lefty Gomez	3.00
45	Eddie Collins	3.00
46	Judy Johnson	3.00
47	Harry Heilmann	3.00
48	Harmon Killebrew	3.00
49	Johnny Bench	4.50
50	Max Carey	3.00
51	Cool Papa Bell	3.00
52	Rube Waddell	3.00
53	Yogi Berra	6.00
54	Herb Pennock	3.00
55	Red Schoendienst	3.00
56	Juan Marichal	3.00
57	Frankie Frisch	3.00
58	Buck Leonard	3.00
59	George Kell	3.00
60	Chuck Klein	3.00
61	King Kelly	3.00
62	Jim Hunter	3.00
63	Lou Boudreau	3.00
64	Al Lopez	3.00
65	Willie Mays	12.50
66	Lou Brock	3.00
67	Bob Lemon	3.00
68	Joe Sewell	3.00
69	Billy Williams	3.00
70	Rick Ferrell	3.00
71	Arky Vaughn	3.00
72	Carl Yastrzemski	4.50
73	Tom Seaver	6.00
74	Rollie Fingers	3.00
75	Ralph Kiner	3.00
76	Frank Baker	3.00
77	Rod Carew	3.00
78	Goose Goslin	3.00
79	Gaylord Perry	3.00
80	Hack Wilson	3.00
81	Hal Newhouser	3.00
82	Early Wynn	3.00
83	Bob Feller	4.00
84	Branch Rickey (W/ Jackie Robinson.)	3.00
85	Jim Palmer	3.00
86	Al Barlick	3.00
87	Willie Mays, Mickey Mantle, Duke Snider	20.00
88	Hank Greenberg	6.00
89	Joe Morgan	3.00
90	Chief Bender	3.00
91	Pee Wee Reese, Jackie Robinson	5.00
92	Jim Bottomley	3.00
93	Ferguson Jenkins	3.00
94	Frank Robinson	4.00
95	Hoyt Wilhelm	3.00
96	Cap Anson	3.00
97	Jim Bunning	3.00
98	Richie Ashburn	4.00
99	Steve Carlton	3.00
100	Mike Schmidt	6.00
101	Nellie Fox	3.00
102	Tommy Lasorda	3.00
103	Leo Durocher	3.00
104	Reggie Jackson	6.00
105	Phil Rizzuto	4.50
106	Phil Niekro	3.00
107	Willie Wells	3.00
108	Earl Weaver	3.00

Autographed

Because the Perez-Steele postcards are so popular with autograph collectors, separate listings for authentically autographed examples of the cards are provided here. Those cards not listed cannot possibly have been signed because the player was deceased prior to issue.

		NM/M
	Complete Set (70):	1,800
	Common Player:	17.50
2	Al Kaline	30.00
5	Whitey Ford	35.00
7	Roy Campanella	400.00
9	Hank Aaron	60.00
11	Stan Musial	60.00
13	Ted Williams	300.00
14	Warren Spahn	30.00
16	Sandy Koufax	95.00
17	Robin Roberts	25.00
19	Mickey Mantle	300.00
21	Ernie Banks	55.00
22	Willie McCovey	40.00
23	Johnny Mize	40.00
26	Pee Wee Reese	60.00
27	Monte Irvin	20.00
28	Eddie Mathews	50.00
29	Enos Slaughter	27.50
31	Charlie Gehringer	65.00
33	Duke Snider	40.00
34	Ray Dandridge	45.00
35	Carl Hubbell	65.00
36	Bobby Doerr	17.50
37	Bill Dickey	65.00
38	Willie Stargell	35.00
39	Brooks Robinson	30.00
41	Billy Herman	40.00
43	Luis Aparicio	25.00
44	Lefty Gomez	55.00
48	Harmon Killebrew	35.00
49	Johnny Bench	40.00
51	Cool Papa Bell	90.00
53	Yogi Berra	35.00
55	Red Schoendienst	25.00
56	Juan Marichal	25.00
58	Buck Leonard	40.00
59	George Kell	20.00
62	Jim Hunter	55.00
63	Lou Boudreau	30.00
64	Al Lopez	60.00
65	Willie Mays	80.00
66	Lou Brock	30.00
67	Bob Lemon	35.00
68	Joe Sewell	50.00

69	Billy Williams	25.00
70	Rick Ferrell	35.00
72	Carl Yastrzemski	60.00
73	Tom Seaver	50.00
74	Rollie Fingers	32.50
75	Ralph Kiner	27.50
77	Rod Carew	35.00
79	Gaylord Perry	25.00
81	Hal Newhouser	30.00
82	Early Wynn	40.00
83	Bob Feller	30.00
85	Jim Palmer	32.50
86	Al Barlick	25.00
87	Willie Mays, Mickey Mantle, Duke Snider	325.00
89	Joe Morgan	30.00
93	Ferguson Jenkins	20.00
94	Frank Robinson	40.00
95	Hoyt Wilhelm	30.00
97	Jim Bunning	30.00
98	Richie Ashburn	25.00
99	Steve Carlton	45.00
100	Mike Schmidt	75.00
102	Tommy Lasorda	50.00
104	Reggie Jackson	50.00
105	Phil Rizzuto	35.00
106	Phil Niekro	30.00
108	Earl Weaver	30.00

1989 Perez-Steele Celebration Postcards

The Celebrations postcard issue from Perez-Steele was an attempt to offer collectors an original medium on which to obtain auotgraphs of Hall of Famers. All 44 of the players included in the issue were alive when the set was conceived and most were still around when it was actually issued. The 3-1/2" x 5-1/2" cards have color portrait and action paintings by Dick Perez on front, which features a linen texture. Backs have postcard indicia, Perez-Steele and Hall of Fame logos, card number and individual serial number from within the edition limit of 10,000. Cards were originally sold only as complete sets.

		NM/M
Complete Set (45):		100.00
Common Player:		2.50
1	Hank Aaron	10.00
2	Luis Aparicio	2.50
3	Ernie Banks	6.00
4	Cool Papa Bell	2.50
5	Johnny Bench	2.50
6	Yogi Berra	6.00
7	Lou Boudreau	2.50
8	Roy Campanella	7.50
9	Happy Chandler	2.50
10	Jocko Conlan	2.50
11	Ray Dandridge	2.50
12	Bill Dickey	3.00
13	Bobby Doerr	2.50
14	Rick Ferrell	2.50
15	Charlie Gehringer	3.00
16	Lefty Gomez	3.00
17	Billy Herman	2.50
18	Catfish Hunter	2.50
19	Monte Irvin	2.50
20	Judy Johnson	2.50
21	Al Kaline	6.00
22	George Kell	2.50
23	Harmon Killebrew	2.50
24	Ralph Kiner	2.50
25	Bob Lemon	2.50
26	Buck Leonard	2.50
27	Al Lopez	2.50
28	Mickey Mantle	20.00
29	Juan Marichal	2.50
30	Eddie Mathews	2.50
31	Willie McCovey	2.50
32	Johnny Mize	2.50
33	Stan Musial	7.50
34	Pee Wee Reese	2.50
35	Brooks Robinson	2.50
36	Joe Sewell	2.50
37	Enos Slaughter	2.50
38	Duke Snider	6.00
39	Warren Spahn	2.50
40	Willie Stargell	2.50
41	Bill Terry	2.50
42	Billy Williams	2.50
43	Ted Williams	15.00
44	Carl Yastrzemski	2.50
---	Checklist	1.00

Autographed

Because of their popularity as an autograph vehicle, values for authentically signed examples of the Perez-Steele Celebrations postcards are presented here. Cards of Lefty Gomez (#16), Judy Johnson (#20) and Bill Terry (#41) cannot exist with genuine autographs because those players were deceased by the time the cards were issued.

		NM/M
Common Player:		15.00
1	Hank Aaron	40.00
2	Luis Aparicio	15.00
3	Ernie Banks	30.00
4	Cool Papa Bell	60.00
5	Johnny Bench	35.00
6	Yogi Berra	35.00
7	Lou Boudreau	20.00
8	Roy Campanella	400.00
9	Happy Chandler	35.00
10	Jocko Conlan	450.00
11	Ray Dandridge	30.00
12	Bill Dickey	65.00
13	Bobby Doerr	15.00
14	Rick Ferrell	20.00
15	Charlie Gehringer	45.00
17	Billy Herman	30.00
18	Catfish Hunter	40.00
19	Monte Irvin	22.50
21	Al Kaline	25.00
22	George Kell	20.00
23	Harmon Killebrew	30.00
24	Ralph Kiner	25.00
25	Bob Lemon	30.00
26	Buck Leonard	30.00
27	Al Lopez	75.00
28	Mickey Mantle	300.00
29	Juan Marichal	30.00
30	Eddie Mathews	40.00
31	Willie McCovey	30.00
32	Johnny Mize	30.00
33	Stan Musial	50.00
34	Pee Wee Reese	55.00
35	Brooks Robinson	25.00
36	Joe Sewell	40.00
37	Enos Slaughter	25.00
38	Duke Snider	30.00
39	Warren Spahn	25.00
40	Willie Stargell	30.00
42	Billy Williams	20.00
43	Ted Williams	250.00
44	Carl Yastrzemski	60.00

1990-92 Perez-Steele Master Works Postcards

A blending of the designs of classic early baseball cards with the artwork of one of today's most recognized baseball artists produced the Perez-Steele Master Works postcard series. Each of the players in the collection (living players selected for inclusion on the basis of autograph possibilities) is shown on five different cards, one of original design and four adapting the formats of the 1909 Ramly (T204), 1911 "Gold Borders" (T205) and 1908 Rose Co. postcards (PC760) and 1888 Goodwin Champions (N162). The Ramly and Rose takeoffs feature gold-foil embossing. Postcard backs are printed in brown (#1-25) or dark green (#26-50). Information on back includes a description of the card set on which the design is based, card and series number and the individual set serial number from within the edition of 10,000. Series 1 (#1-25) was issued in 1990; Series 2 (#26-50) in 1992. Each was available only as a complete boxed set.

		NM/M
Complete Set (52):		150.00
Common Player:		3.00
1	Charlie Gehringer (Ramly)	3.00
2	Charlie Gehringer (Goodwin)	3.00
3	Charlie Gehringer (Rose)	3.00
4	Charlie Gehringer (Gold Border)	3.00
5	Charlie Gehringer (Perez-Steele)	3.00
6	Mickey Mantle (Ramly)	15.00
7	Mickey Mantle (Goodwin)	15.00
8	Mickey Mantle (Rose)	15.00
9	Mickey Mantle (Gold Border)	15.00
10	Mickey Mantle (Perez-Steele)	15.00
11	Willie Mays (Ramly)	9.00
12	Willie Mays (Goodwin)	9.00
13	Willie Mays (Rose)	9.00
14	Willie Mays (Gold Border)	9.00
15	Willie Mays (Perez-Steele)	9.00
16	Duke Snider (Ramly)	6.00
17	Duke Snider (Goodwin)	6.00
18	Duke Snider (Rose)	6.00
19	Duke Snider (Gold Border)	6.00
20	Duke Snider (Perez-Steele)	6.00
21	Warren Spahn (Ramly)	3.00
22	Warren Spahn (Goodwin)	3.00
23	Warren Spahn (Rose)	3.00
24	Warren Spahn (Gold Border)	3.00
25	Warren Spahn (Perez-Steele)	3.00
---	Checklist 1-25	1.00
26	Yogi Berra (Ramly)	5.00
27	Yogi Berra (Goodwin)	5.00
28	Yogi Berra (Rose)	5.00
29	Yogi Berra (Gold Border)	5.00
30	Yogi Berra (Perez-Steele)	5.00
31	Johnny Mize (Ramly)	3.00
32	Johnny Mize (Goodwin)	3.00
33	Johnny Mize (Rose)	3.00
34	Johnny Mize (Gold Border)	3.00
35	Johnny Mize (Perez-Steele)	3.00
36	Willie Stargell (Ramly)	3.00
37	Willie Stargell (Goodwin)	3.00
38	Willie Stargell (Rose)	3.00
39	Willie Stargell (Gold Border)	3.00
40	Willie Stargell (Perez-Steele)	3.00
41	Ted Williams (Ramly)	12.00
42	Ted Williams (Goodwin)	12.00
43	Ted Williams (Rose)	12.00
44	Ted Williams (Gold Border)	12.00
45	Ted Williams (Perez-Steele)	12.00
46	Carl Yastrzemski (Ramly)	4.00
47	Carl Yastrzemski (Goodwin)	4.00
48	Carl Yastrzemski (Rose)	4.00
49	Carl Yastrzemski (Gold Border)	4.00
50	Carl Yastrzemski (Perez-Steele)	4.00
---	Checklist 26-50	1.00

1985 Performance Printing Texas Rangers

A local printing company sponsored this 28-card set of the Texas Rangers. The 2-3/8" x 3-1/2" cards are in full color and are numbered on the back by uniform number. Card fronts feature full-color, game-action photos. The 25 players on the Rangers' active roster at press time are included, along with manager Bobby Valentine and unnumbered coaches and trainer cards. The black and white card backs have a smaller portrait photo of each player, as well as biographical information and career statistics.

		NM/M
Complete Set (28):		9.00
Common Player:		.50
0	Oddibe McDowell	.50
1	Bill Stein	.50
2	Bobby Valentine	.50
3	Wayne Tolleson	.50
4	Don Slaught	.50
5	Alan Bannister	.50
6	Bobby Jones	.50
7	Glenn Brummer	.50
8	Luis Pujols	.50
9	Pete O'Brien	.50
11	Toby Harrah	.50
13	Tommy Dunbar	.50
15	Larry Parrish	.50
16	Mike Mason	.50
19	Curtis Wilkerson	.50
24	Dave Schmidt	.50
25	Buddy Bell	.50
27	Greg Harris	.50
30	Dave Rozema	.50
32	Gary Ward	.50
36	Dickie Noles	.50
41	Chris Welsh	.50
44	Cliff Johnson	.50
46	Burt Hooton	.50
48	Dave Stewart	.50
49	Charlie Hough	.50
----	Trainers (Danny Wheat, Bill Ziegler)	.50
----	Rangers Coaches (Rich Donnelly, Glenn Ezell, Tom House, Art Howe, Wayne Terwilliger)	.50

1986 Performance Printing Texas Rangers

For the second time, the Texas Rangers issued a full-color card set in conjunction with this local printing company. Fronts of the 28-card set include player name, position and team logo beneath the color photo. Backs of the 2-3/8" x 3-1/2" cards are in black and white, with a small portrait photo of each player along with personal and professional statistics. Cards were distributed at the August 23 Rangers home game, and the set includes all of the Rangers' fine rookies such as Bobby Witt, Pete Incaviglia, Edwin Correa and Ruben Sierra.

		NM/M
Complete Set (28):		5.00
Common Player:		.25
0	Oddibe McDowell	.25
1	Scott Fletcher	.25
2	Bobby Valentine	.25
3	Ruben Sierra	.35
4	Don Slaught	.25
9	Pete O'Brien	.25
11	Toby Harrah	.25
12	Geno Petralli	.25
15	Larry Parrish	.25
16	Mike Mason	.25
17	Darrell Porter	.25
18	Edwin Correa	.25
19	Curtis Wilkerson	.25
22	Steve Buechele	.25
23	Jose Guzman	.25
24	Ricky Wright	.25
27	Greg Harris	.25
28	Mitch Williams	.25
29	Pete Incaviglia	.50
32	Gary Ward	.25
34	Dale Mohorcic	.25
40	Jeff Russell	.25
44	Tom Paciorek	.25
46	Mike Loynd	.25
48	Bobby Witt	.25
49	Charlie Hough	.25
----	Coaching Staff (Joe Ferguson, Tim Foli, Tom House, Art Howe, Tom Robson)	.25
----	Trainers (Danny Wheat, Bill Zeigler)	.25

1981 Perma-Graphics All-Star Credit Cards

Using the same "credit card" style of its previous 1981 issue, Perma-Graphics issued an 18-card set in the fall of 1981 featuring the starting players from the 1981 All-Star Game. The front of the card contains a full-color photo, plus the player's name, position and team. The back includes personal data, career records, highlights and an "autograph panel."

		NM/M
Complete Set (18):		15.00
Common Player:		1.00
1	Gary Carter	1.50
2	Dave Concepcion	1.00
3	Andre Dawson	1.25
4	George Foster	1.00
5	Davey Lopes	1.00
6	Dave Parker	1.00
7	Pete Rose	5.00
8	Mike Schmidt	4.00
9	Fernando Valenzuela	1.00
10	George Brett	4.00
11a	Rod Carew (Outfield)	2.50
11b	Rod Carew (First base.)	2.50
11c	Rod Carew (First base, #20 on back.)	2.50
11d	Rod Carew (First base, #29 on back.)	2.50
12	Bucky Dent	1.00
13	Carlton Fisk	1.50
14	Reggie Jackson	3.00
15	Jack Morris	1.00
16	Willie Randolph	1.00
17	Ken Singleton	1.00
18	Dave Winfield	1.50

Super Star Credit Cards

Issued in 1981 by Perma-Graphics of Maryland Heights, Mo., this innovative 32-card set was printed on high-impact, permanently laminated vinyl to give the appearance of a real credit card. The front of the wallet-sized cards includes career statistics and highlights, along with an "autograph panel" for obtaining the player's signature.

		NM/M
Complete Set (32):		25.00
Common Player:		1.00
1	Johnny Bench	2.00
2	Mike Schmidt	4.00
3	George Brett	4.00
4	Carl Yastrzemski	2.00
5	Pete Rose	5.00
6	Bob Horner	1.00
7	Reggie Jackson	3.00
8	Keith Hernandez	1.00
9	George Foster	1.00
10	Garry Templeton	1.00
11	Tom Seaver	2.00
12	Steve Garvey	1.25
13	Dave Parker	1.00
14	Willie Stargell	1.50
15	Cecil Cooper	1.00
16	Steve Carlton	1.50
17	Ted Simmons	1.00
18	Dave Kingman	1.00
19	Rickey Henderson	1.50
20	Fred Lynn	1.00
21	Dave Winfield	1.50
22a	Rod Carew (Uniform #20 on back.)	2.00
22b	Rod Carew (Uniform #29 on back.)	2.00
23	Jim Rice	1.25
24	Bruce Sutter	1.50
25	Cesar Cedeno	1.00
26	Nolan Ryan	6.00
27	Dusty Baker	1.00
28	Jim Palmer	1.50
29	Gorman Thomas	1.00
30	Ben Oglivie	1.00
31	Willie Wilson	1.00
32	Gary Carter	1.50

1982 Perma-Graphics All-Star Credit Cards

Perma-Graphics issued its second "All-Star Credit Card" set in the fall of 1982. Consisting of 18 cards, the set pictured the starters from both leagues in the 1982 All-Star Game. The set was also available in a more limited "gold" version.

		NM/M
Complete Set (18):		15.00
Common Player:		1.00
Gold:		3X
1	Dennis Eckersley	1.50
2	Cecil Cooper	1.00
3	Carlton Fisk	2.00
4	Robin Yount	2.00
5	Bobby Grich	1.00
6	Rickey Henderson	2.00
7	Reggie Jackson	3.00
8	Fred Lynn	1.00
9	George Brett	4.00
10	Gary Carter	2.00

11	Dave Concepcion	1.00
12	Andre Dawson	1.25
13	Tim Raines	1.00
14	Dale Murphy	1.25
15	Steve Rogers	1.00
16	Pete Rose	5.00
17	Mike Schmidt	4.00
18	Manny Trillo	1.00

Super Star Credit Cards

Perma-Graphics reduced its "Superstar Credit Card Set" to 24 players in 1982, maintaining the same basic credit card appearance. The player photos on the front of the cards are surrounded by a woodtone border and the backs include the usual personal data, career statistics, highlights and autograph panel. The set was also issued in a limited-edition "gold" version.

		NM/M
Complete Set (24):		25.00
Common Player:		1.00
Gold:		3X
1	Johnny Bench	2.00
2	Tom Seaver	2.00
3	Mike Schmidt	4.00
4	Gary Carter	1.50
5	Willie Stargell	1.50
6	Tim Raines	1.00
7	Bill Madlock	1.00
8	Keith Hernandez	1.00
9	Pete Rose	5.00
10	Steve Carlton	1.50
11	Steve Garvey	1.25
12	Fernando Valenzuela	1.00
13	Carl Yastrzemski	2.00
14	Dave Winfield	1.50
15	Carney Lansford	1.00
16	Rollie Fingers	1.00
17	Tony Armas	1.00
18	Cecil Cooper	1.00
19	George Brett	4.00
20	Reggie Jackson	3.00
21	Rod Carew	1.50
22	Eddie Murray	1.50
23	Rickey Henderson	1.50
24	Kirk Gibson	1.00

1983 Perma-Graphics All-Star Credit Cards

The final issue from Perma-Graphics, this 18-card set was produced in the fall of 1983 and features the 18 starting players from the 1983 All-Star Game. Similar to other Perma-Graphics sets, the cards were printed on wallet-size vinyl to give the appearance of a real credit card. The set was also available in a limited-edition "gold" version.

		NM/M
Complete Set (18):		17.50
Common Player:		1.00
Gold:		3X
1	George Brett	4.00
2	Rod Carew	2.00
3	Fred Lynn	1.00
4	Jim Rice	1.50
5	Ted Simmons	1.00
6	Dave Stieb	1.00
7	Manny Trillo	1.00
8	Dave Winfield	2.00
9	Robin Yount	2.00
10	Gary Carter	2.00
11	Andre Dawson	1.50
12	Dale Murphy	1.50
13	Al Oliver	1.00
14	Tim Raines	1.00
15	Steve Sax	1.00
16	Mike Schmidt	4.00
17	Ozzie Smith	3.00
18	Mario Soto	1.00

Super Star Credit Cards

Similar in design to its previous sets, Perma-Graphics increased the number of cards in its 1983 "Superstar" set to 36, including 18 players from each league. The front of the vinyl card has a full-color photo with the player's name, team, league and position below. The backs contain career records, highlights and autograph panel. The cards were also issued in a special "gold" version, more limited than the regular edition.

		NM/M
Complete Set (36):		25.00
Common Player:		1.00
Gold:		3X
1	Bill Buckner	1.00
2	Steve Carlton	2.00
3	Gary Carter	2.00
4	Andre Dawson	1.25
5	Pedro Guerrero	1.00
6	George Hendrick	1.00
7	Keith Hernandez	1.00
8	Bill Madlock	1.00
9	Dale Murphy	1.25
10	Al Oliver	1.00
11	Dave Parker	1.00
12	Darrell Porter	1.00
13	Pete Rose	5.00
14	Mike Schmidt	4.00
15	Lonnie Smith	1.00
16	Ozzie Smith	2.50
17	Bruce Sutter	1.50
18	Fernando Valenzuela	1.00
19	George Brett	4.00
20	Rod Carew	2.00
21	Cecil Cooper	1.00
22	Doug DeCinces	1.00
23	Rollie Fingers	1.50
24	Damaso Garcia	1.00
25	Toby Harrah	1.00
26	Rickey Henderson	2.00
27	Reggie Jackson	3.00
28	Hal McRae	1.00
29	Eddie Murray	2.00
30	Lance Parrish	1.00
31	Jim Rice	1.25
32	Gorman Thomas	1.00
33	Willie Wilson	1.00
34	Dave Winfield	2.00
35	Carl Yastrzemski	2.50
36	Robin Yount	2.00

1983 Gaylord Perry Career Highlights

Although their name does not appear anywhere on the six cards in this set, Topps was the manufacturer of this career highlights issue which was distributed by Perry's own memorabilia company. In standard 2-1/2" x 3-1/2" format, card fronts feature a color photo with various colored borders and name plates. The year of the career highlight printed on back is presented in the lower-right. Backs have a card number in a peanut and a write-up of the career accomplishment, printed in brown and orange.

		NM/M
Complete Set (6):		8.00
Common Card:		1.50
1	Gaylord Perry (First win.)	1.50
2	Gaylord Perry (No-hitter.)	1.50
3	Gaylord Perry (Cy Young Award)	1.50
4	Gaylord Perry (2,500th K)	1.50
5	Gaylord Perry (Cy Young/3,000th K)	1.50
6	Gaylord Perry (300th win)	1.50

1981 Peter Pan Bakery Discs

(See 1981 MSA/Peter Pan - Sunbeam Bakery Discs.)

1991 Petro Canada All-Star FanFest Standups

Petro-Canada Standups are vaguely reminiscent of the 1964 Topps Standups. The set was distributed at Fanfest in Toronto in conjunction with the All-Star Game. The folded card as issued measures 2-7/8" x 3-9/16". The card can be unfolded to reveal a die-cut action figure of the player superimposed in front of a photo of stadium surroundings. The base which the player stands on has major league and All-Star Game statistics, with career highlights on the back and a player quiz.

		NM/M
Complete Set (26):		12.50
Common Player:		.25
1	Cal Ripken, Jr.	3.00
2	Greg Olson	.25
3	Roger Clemens	2.00
4	Ryne Sandberg	1.50
5	Dave Winfield	1.00
6	Eric Davis	.25
7	Carlton Fisk	1.00
8	Mike Scott	.25
9	Sandy Alomar, Jr.	.25
10	Tim Wallach	.25
11	Cecil Fielder	.25
12	Dwight Gooden	.25
13	George Brett	2.00
14	Dale Murphy	.50
15	Paul Molitor	1.00
16	Barry Bonds	3.00
17	Kirby Puckett	1.50
18	Ozzie Smith	1.50
19	Don Mattingly	2.00
20	Will Clark	.25
21	Rickey Henderson	1.00
22	Orel Hershiser	.25
23	Ken Griffey Jr.	2.50
24	Tony Gwynn	1.50
25	Nolan Ryan	3.00
26	Kelly Gruber	.25

1998-99 Philadelphia A's Historical Society

A major undertaking by the Philadelphia A's Historical Society was the creation of this collectors card set in conjunction with the group's fourth reunion in 1998. Card designs are strongly reminiscent of the classic Topps and Bowman cards of the early 1950s. Fronts have a painting of each player by Ron Joyner, noted sports artist. Backs have a cartoon, career stats with the A's and lifetime, biographical data and career highlights. Backs are printed in blue and black on white. A card of 1908-09 A's Joe Jackson has been printed in a limited edition of 500 numbered cards and is available only in those sets sold directly through the Society at its original $18.50 price. Seventy-five sets of the cards, which included a sample Joe Jackson card and a pair of large-format cards of Jimmie Foxx and Roger Cramer, were sold as uncut sheets.

		NM/M
Complete Set, W/Jackson (42):		24.00
Complete Set, No/Jackson (41):		18.50
Complete Set, uncut sheet:		60.00
Common Player:		.50
1	Connie Mack	.75
2	Sam Chapman	.50
3	Bobby Shantz	.60
4	Al Brancato	.50
5	Bob Dillinger	.50
6	Irv Hall	.50
7	Joe Hauser	.50
8	Taffy Wright	.50
9	Gus Zernial	.60
10	Ray Murray	.50
11	Skeeter Kell	.50
12	Morrie Martin	.50
13	Pete Suder	.50
14	Pinky Higgins	.50
15	Allie Clark	.50
16	Hank Wyse	.50
17	George Kell	.75
18	Hank Majeski	.50
19	Jimmie Foxx	1.00
20	Crash Davis	.50
21	Elmer Valo	.50
22	Ray Coleman	.50
23	Carl Scheib	.50
24	Billy Hitchcock	.50
25	Earle Brucker Jr.	.50
26	Dave Philley	.50
27	Joe DeMaestri	.50
28	Eddie Collins Jr.	.50
29	Eddie Joost	.50
30	Spook Jacobs	.50
31	Ferris Fain	.60
32	Eddie Robinson	.50
33	Vic Power	.60
34	Lou Brissie	.50
35	Bill Renna	.50
36	Nellie Fox	1.00
37	Lou Limmer	.50
38	Eddie Collins Sr.	1.00
39	Roger Cramer	.50
40	Joe Astroth	.50
---	Joe Jackson (# of 500)	8.00
---	Joe Jackson (Sample overprint.)	4.00
---	Roger Cramer (3-1/2" x 6")	2.00
---	Jimmie Foxx (3-1/2" x 8-1/2")	4.00
41	Bill Werber (Issued 1999)	.50

2001 Philadelphia A's Historical Society Update

Selected by the Society's members as "Fan Favorites" of each decade from the 1900s through the 1930s, this collectors' issue updates the group's original 1998-99 card issue. Cards are in 2-5/8" x 3-3/4" format with painted portraits on front. Black, blue and white backs have a cartoon highlight, personal data, career summary and lifetime A's and major league stats. The cards were also pictured on a 10-3/4" x 12-3/4" "Decades of Greatness" uncut sheet.

		NM/M
Complete Set (4):		6.00
Common Player:		2.00
Uncut Sheet:		10.00
42	Rube Oldring	2.00
43	Stuffy McInnis	2.00
44	Bing Miller	2.00
45	Bob Johnson	2.00

1985 Philadelphia Phillies Police

This is a brilliantly colored 2-5/8" x 4-1/8" set, co-sponsored by the Phillies and Cigna Corp. Card fronts include the player name, number, position and team logo. The 16 cards are numbered on the back and include biographical information and a safety tip. The cards were distributed by several Philadelphia area police departments.

		NM/M
Complete Set (16):		4.00
Common Player:		.15
1	Juan Samuel	.15
2	Von Hayes	.15
3	Ozzie Virgil	.15
4	Mike Schmidt	3.50
5	Greg Gross	.15
6	Tim Corcoran	.15
7	Jerry Koosman	.15
8	Jeff Stone	.15
9	Glenn Wilson	.15
10	Steve Jeltz	.15
11	Garry Maddox	.15
12	Steve Carlton	1.50
13	John Denny	.15
14	Kevin Gross	.15
15	Shane Rawley	.15
16	Charlie Hudson	.15

1986 Philadelphia Phillies Fire Safety

For the second straight year, the Philadelphia Phillies issued a 16-card safety set. However, in 1986 the set was issued in conjunction with the Philadelphia Fire Department rather than the police. Cigna Corp., remained a sponsor. The cards, which measure 2-5/8" x 4-1/8" in size, feature full color photos. Along with other pertinent information, the card backs contain a short player biography and a "Tips From The Dugout" fire safety hint.

		NM/M
Complete Set (16):		3.00
Common Player:		.15
1	Juan Samuel	.15
2	Don Carman	.15
3	Von Hayes	.15
4	Kent Tekulve	.15
5	Greg Gross	.15
6	Shane Rawley	.15
7	Darren Daulton	.25
8	Kevin Gross	.15
9	Steve Jeltz	.15
10	Mike Schmidt	3.00
11	Steve Bedrosian	.15
12	Gary Redus	.15
13	Charles Hudson	.15
14	John Russell	.15
15	Fred Toliver	.15
16	Glenn Wilson	.15

2005 Philadelphia Phillies Medallion Collection

A set of 21 commemorative medallions was sponsored by the Philadelphia Daily News and The Inquirer in this early-season promotion. Coupons found in the newspapers between April 18 and May 18 could be redeemed at newsstands (along with $2.99) for that day's medallion. Larger and thicker than a quarter, the

1-3/16" diameter medals are struck in nickel and have on their fronts an enameled portrait photo. A team logo dominates the back. A colorful, photo-filled 7-3/4" x 13" album was available to house the pieces. The medals are listed here in order of their issue.

		NM/M
Complete Set (21):		65.00
Common Player:		3.00
Album:		3.00
(1)	Jim Thome	5.00
(2)	Placido Polanco	3.00
(3)	Randy Wolf	3.00
(4)	Mike Lieberthal	3.00
(5)	Jon Lieber	3.00
(6)	Jimmy Rollins	4.50
(7)	Kenny Lofton	3.00
(8)	Brett Myers	3.00
(9)	Tomas Perez	3.00
(10)	Rheal Cormier	3.00
(11)	Vicente Padilla	3.00
(12)	David Bell	3.00
(13)	Bobby Abreu	4.50
(14)	Tim Worrell	3.00
(15)	Ryan Madson	3.00
(16)	Chase Utley	4.50
(17)	Charlie Manuel	3.00
(18)	Jason Michaels	3.00
(19)	Pat Burrell	5.00
(20)	Billy Wagner	3.00
(21)	Phillie Phanatic (Mascot)	3.00

1989 Phoenix Holsum Super Stars Discs

(See 1989 Holsum for checklist and price guide. Distributed in Arizona.)

1992 Pinnacle

Score entered the high-end card market with the release of this 620-card set. The cards feature black borders surrounding a white frame with a full-color action photo inside. The player extends beyond the natural background. The backs are horizontal and feature a closeup photo, statistics, team logo, biographical information and career notes. Several subsets can be found within the set including "Idols, Sidelines, Grips, Shades" and "Technicians." The set was released in two 310-card series.

		NM/M
Complete Set (620):		15.00
Common Player:		.05
Foil Pack (16):		.75
Foil Box (36):		17.50
Jumbo Pack (24+3):		1.50
Jumbo Box (12):		22.50
1	Frank Thomas	.75
2	Benito Santiago	.05
3	Carlos Baerga	.05
4	Cecil Fielder	.05
5	Barry Larkin	.05
6	Ozzie Smith	1.00
7	Willie McGee	.05
8	Paul Molitor	.75
9	Andy Van Slyke	.05
10	Ryne Sandberg	1.00
11	Kevin Seitzer	.05
12	Len Dykstra	.05
13	Edgar Martinez	.05
14	Ruben Sierra	.05
15	Howard Johnson	.05
16	Dave Henderson	.05
17	Devon White	.05
18	Terry Pendleton	.05
19	Steve Finley	.05
20	Kirby Puckett	1.00
21	Orel Hershiser	.05
22	Hal Morris	.05
23	Don Mattingly	1.25
24	Delino DeShields	.05
25	Dennis Eckersley	.60
26	Ellis Burks	.05
27	Jay Buhner	.05
28	Matt Williams	.05
29	Lou Whitaker	.05
30	Alex Fernandez	.05
31	Albert Belle	.05
32	Todd Zeile	.05
33	Tony Pena	.05
34	Jay Bell	.05
35	Rafael Palmeiro	.65
36	Wes Chamberlain	.05
37	George Bell	.05
38	Robin Yount	.75
39	Vince Coleman	.05
40	Bruce Hurst	.05
41	Harold Baines	.05
42	Chuck Finley	.05
43	Ken Caminiti	.05
44	Ben McDonald	.05
45	Roberto Alomar	.15
46	Chili Davis	.05
47	Bill Doran	.05
48	Jerald Clark	.05
49	Jose Lind	.05
50	Nolan Ryan	2.00
51	Phil Plantier	.05
52	Gary DiSarcina	.05
53	Kevin Bass	.05
54	Pat Kelly	.05
55	Mark Wohlers	.05
56	Walt Weiss	.05
57	Lenny Harris	.05
58	Ivan Calderon	.05
59	Harold Reynolds	.05
60	George Brett	1.25
61	Gregg Olson	.05
62	Orlando Merced	.05
63	Steve Decker	.05
64	John Franco	.05
65	Greg Maddux	1.00
66	Alex Cole	.05
67	Dave Hollins	.05
68	Kent Hrbek	.05
69	Tom Pagnozzi	.05
70	Jeff Bagwell	.75
71	Jim Gantner	.05
72	Matt Nokes	.05
73	Brian Harper	.05
74	Andy Benes	.05
75	Tom Glavine	.35
76	Terry Steinbach	.05
77	Dennis Martinez	.05
78	John Olerud	.05
79	Ozzie Guillen	.05
80	Darryl Strawberry	.05
81	Gary Gaetti	.05
82	Dave Righetti	.05
83	Chris Hoiles	.05
84	Andujar Cedeno	.05
85	Jack Clark	.05
86	David Howard	.05
87	Bill Gullickson	.05
88	Bernard Gilkey	.05
89	Kevin Elster	.05
90	Kevin Maas	.05
91	Mark Lewis	.05
92	Greg Vaughn	.05
93	Bret Barberie	.05
94	Dave Smith	.05
95	Roger Clemens	1.25
96	Doug Drabek	.05
97	Omar Vizquel	.05
98	Jose Guzman	.05
99	Juan Samuel	.05
100	Dave Justice	.05
101	Tom Browning	.05
102	Mark Gubicza	.05
103	Mickey Morandini	.05
104	Ed Whitson	.05
105	Lance Parrish	.05
106	Scott Erickson	.05
107	Jack McDowell	.05
108	Dave Stieb	.05
109	Mike Moore	.05
110	Travis Fryman	.05
111	Dwight Gooden	.05
112	Fred McGriff	.05
113	Alan Trammell	.05
114	Roberto Kelly	.05
115	Andre Dawson	.25
116	Bill Landrum	.05
117	Brian McRae	.05
118	B.J. Surhoff	.05
119	Chuck Knoblauch	.05
120	Steve Olin	.05
121	Robin Ventura	.05
122	Will Clark	.05
123	Tino Martinez	.05
124	Dale Murphy	.25
125	Pete O'Brien	.05
126	Ray Lankford	.05
127	Juan Gonzalez	.40
128	Ron Gant	.05
129	Marquis Grissom	.05
130	Jose Canseco	.50
131	Mike Greenwell	.05
132	Mark Langston	.05
133	Brett Butler	.05
134	Kelly Gruber	.05
135	Chris Sabo	.05
136	Mark Grace	.05
137	Tony Fernandez	.05
138	Glenn Davis	.05
139	Pedro Munoz	.05
140	Craig Biggio	.05
141	Pete Schourek	.05
142	Mike Boddicker	.05
143	Robby Thompson	.05
144	Mel Hall	.05
145	Bryan Harvey	.05
146	Mike LaValliere	.05
147	John Kruk	.05
148	Joe Carter	.05
149	Greg Olson	.05
150	Julio Franco	.05
151	Darryl Hamilton	.05
152	Felix Fermin	.05
153	Jose Offerman	.05
154	Paul O'Neill	.05
155	Tommy Greene	.05
156	Ivan Rodriguez	.65
157	Dave Stewart	.05
158	Jeff Reardon	.05
159	Felix Jose	.05
160	Doug Dascenzo	.05
161	Tim Wallach	.05
162	Dan Plesac	.05
163	Luis Gonzalez	.05
164	Mike Henneman	.05
165	Mike Devereaux	.05
166	Luis Polonia	.05
167	Mike Sharperson	.05
168	Chris Donnels	.05
169	Greg Harris	.05
170	Deion Sanders	.05
171	Mike Schooler	.05
172	Jose DeJesus	.05
173	Jeff Montgomery	.05
174	Milt Cuyler	.05
175	Wade Boggs	1.00
176	Kevin Tapani	.05
177	Bill Spiers	.05
178	Tim Raines	.05
179	Randy Milligan	.05
180	Rob Dibble	.05
181	Kirt Manwaring	.05
182	Pascual Perez	.05
183	Juan Guzman	.05
184	John Smiley	.05
185	David Segui	.05
186	Omar Olivares	.05
187	Joe Slusarski	.05
188	Erik Hanson	.05
189	Mark Portugal	.05
190	Walt Terrell	.05
191	John Smoltz	.05
192	Wilson Alvarez	.05
193	Jimmy Key	.05
194	Larry Walker	.05
195	Lee Smith	.05
196	Pete Harnisch	.05
197	Mike Harkey	.05
198	Frank Tanana	.05
199	Terry Mulholland	.05
200	Cal Ripken, Jr.	2.00
201	Dave Magadan	.05
202	Bud Black	.05
203	Terry Shumpert	.05
204	Mike Mussina	.40
205	Mo Vaughn	.05
206	Steve Farr	.05
207	Darrin Jackson	.05
208	Jerry Browne	.05
209	Jeff Russell	.05
210	Mike Scioscia	.05
211	Rick Aguilera	.05
212	Jaime Navarro	.05
213	Randy Tomlin	.05
214	Bobby Thigpen	.05
215	Mark Gardner	.05
216	Norm Charlton	.05
217	Mark McGwire	1.75
218	Skeeter Barnes	.05
219	Bob Tewksbury	.05
220	Junior Felix	.05
221	Sam Horn	.05
222	Jody Reed	.05
223	Luis Sojo	.05
224	Jerome Walton	.05
225	Darryl Kile	.05
226	Mickey Tettleton	.05
227	Dan Pasqua	.05
228	Jim Gott	.05
229	Bernie Williams	.05
230	Shane Mack	.05
231	Steve Avery	.05
232	Dave Valle	.05
233	Mark Leonard	.05
234	Spike Owen	.05
235	Gary Sheffield	.20
236	Steve Chitren	.05
237	Zane Smith	.05
238	Tom Gordon	.05
239	Jose Oquendo	.05
240	Todd Stottlemyre	.05
241	Darren Daulton	.05
242	Tim Naehring	.05
243	Tony Phillips	.05
244	Shawon Dunston	.05
245	Manuel Lee	.05
246	Mike Pagliarulo	.05
247	Jim Thome (Rookie Prospect)	.65
248	Luis Mercedes (Rookie Prospect)	.05
249	Cal Eldred (Rookie Prospect)	.05
250	Derek Bell (Rookie Prospect)	.05
251	Arthur Rhodes (Rookie Prospect)	.05
252	Scott Cooper (Rookie Prospect)	.05
253	Roberto Hernandez (Rookie Prospect)	.05
254	Mo Sanford (Rookie Prospect)	.05
255	Scott Servais (Rookie Prospect)	.05
256	Eric Karros (Rookie Prospect)	.05
257	Andy Mota	.05
258	Keith Mitchell	.05
259	Joel Johnston (Rookie Prospect)	.05
260	John Wehner (Rookie Prospect)	.05
261	Gino Minutelli (Rookie Prospect)	.05
262	Greg Gagne	.05
263	Stan Royer (Rookie Prospect)	.05
264	Carlos Garcia (Rookie Prospect)	.05
265	Andy Ashby (Rookie Prospect)	.05
266	Kim Batiste (Rookie Prospect)	.05
267	Julio Valera (Rookie Prospect)	.05
268	Royce Clayton (Rookie Prospect)	.05
269	Gary Scott (Rookie Prospect)	.05
270	Kirk Dressendorfer (Rookie Prospect)	.05
271	Sean Berry (Rookie Prospect)	.05
272	Lance Dickson (Rookie Prospect)	.05
273	Rob Maurer (Rookie Prospect)	.05
274	Scott Brosius (Rookie Prospect)	.05
275	Dave Fleming (Rookie Prospect)	.05
276	Lenny Webster (Rookie Prospect)	.05
277	Mike Humphreys	.05
278	Freddie Benavides (Rookie Prospect)	.05
279	Harvey Pulliam (Rookie Prospect)	.05
280	Jeff Carter (Rookie Prospect)	.05
281	Jim Abbott, Nolan Ryan (Idols)	.25
282	Wade Boggs, George Brett (Idols)	.25
283	Ken Griffey Jr., Rickey Henderson (Idols)	.50
284	Dale Murphy, Wally Joyner (Idols)	.10
285	Chuck Knoblauch, Ozzie Smith (Idols)	.20
286	Robin Ventura, Lou Gehrig (Idols)	.20
287	Robin Yount (Sidelines - Motocross)	.30
288	Bob Tewksbury (Sidelines - Cartoonist)	.05
289	Kirby Puckett (Sidelines - Pool Player)	.50
290	Kenny Lofton (Sidelines - Basketball Player)	.05
291	Jack McDowell (Sidelines - Guitarist)	.05
292	John Burkett (Sidelines - Bowler)	.05
293	Dwight Smith (Sidelines - Singer)	.05
294	Nolan Ryan (Sidelines - Cattle Rancher)	1.00
295	Manny Ramirez **RC** (1st Round Draft Pick)	2.50
296	Cliff Floyd **RC** (1st Round Draft Pick)	.50
297	Al Shirley **RC** (1st Round Draft Pick)	.05
298	Brian Barber **RC** (1st Round Draft Pick)	.05
299	Jon Farrell **RC** (1st Round Draft Pick)	.05
300	Scott Ruffcorn **RC** (1st Round Draft Pick)	.05
301	Tyrone Hill **RC** (1st Round Draft Pick)	.05
302	Benji Gil **RC** (1st Round Draft Pick)	.05
303	Tyler Green **RC** (1st Round Draft Pick)	.05
304	Allen Watson (Shades)	.05
305	Jay Buhner (Shades)	.05
306	Roberto Alomar (Shades)	.05
307	Chuck Knoblauch (Shades)	.05
308	Darryl Strawberry (Shades)	.05
309	Danny Tartabull (Shades)	.05
310	Bobby Bonilla (Shades)	.05
311	Mike Felder	.05
312	Storm Davis	.05
313	Tim Teufel	.05
314	Tom Brunansky	.05
315	Rex Hudler	.05
316	Dave Otto	.05
317	Jeff King	.05
318	Dan Gladden	.05
319	Bill Pecota	.05
320	Franklin Stubbs	.05
321	Gary Carter	.75
322	Melido Perez	.05
323	Eric Davis	.05
324	Greg Myers	.05
325	Pete Incaviglia	.05
326	Von Hayes	.05
327	Greg Swindell	.05
328	Steve Sax	.05
329	Chuck McElroy	.05
330	Gregg Jefferies	.05
331	Joe Oliver	.05
332	Paul Faries	.05
333	David West	.05
334	Craig Grebeck	.05
335	Chris Hammond	.05
336	Billy Ripken	.05
337	Scott Sanderson	.05
338	Dick Schofield	.05
339	Bob Milacki	.05
340	Kevin Reimer	.05
341	Jose DeLeon	.05
342	Henry Cotto	.05
343	Daryl Boston	.05
344	Kevin Gross	.05
345	Milt Thompson	.05
346	Luis Rivera	.05
347	Al Osuna	.05
348	Rob Deer	.05
349	Tim Leary	.05
350	Mike Stanton	.05
351	Dean Palmer	.05
352	Trevor Wilson	.05
353	Mark Eichhorn	.05
354	Scott Aldred	.05
355	Mark Whiten	.05
356	Leo Gomez	.05
357	Rafael Belliard	.05
358	Carlos Quintana	.05
359	Mark Davis	.05
360	Chris Nabholz	.05
361	Carlton Fisk	.75
362	Joe Orsulak	.05
363	Eric Anthony	.05
364	Greg Hibbard	.05
365	Scott Leius	.05
366	Hensley Meulens	.05
367	Chris Bosio	.05
368	Brian Downing	.05
369	Sammy Sosa	1.00
370	Stan Belinda	.05
371	Joe Grahe	.05
372	Luis Salazar	.05
373	Lance Johnson	.05
374	Kal Daniels	.05
375	Dave Winfield	.75
376	Brook Jacoby	.05
377	Mariano Duncan	.05
378	Ron Darling	.05
379	Randy Johnson	.75
380	Chito Martinez	.05
381	Andres Galarraga	.05
382	Willie Randolph	.05
383	Charles Nagy	.05
384	Tim Belcher	.05
385	Duane Ward	.05
386	Vicente Palacios	.05
387	Mike Gallego	.05
388	Rich DeLucia	.05
389	Scott Radinsky	.05
390	Damon Berryhill	.05
391	Kirk McCaskill	.05
392	Pedro Guerrero	.05
393	Kevin Mitchell	.05
394	Dickie Thon	.05
395	Bobby Bonilla	.05
396	Bill Wegman	.05
397	Dave Martinez	.05
398	Rick Sutcliffe	.05
399	Larry Andersen	.05
400	Tony Gwynn	1.00
401	Rickey Henderson	.75
402	Greg Cadaret	.05
403	Keith Miller	.05
404	Bip Roberts	.05
405	Kevin Brown	.05
406	Mitch Williams	.05
407	Frank Viola	.05
408	Darren Lewis	.05
409	Bob Walk	.05
410	Bob Walk	.05
411	Todd Frohwirth	.05
412	Brian Hunter	.05
413	Ron Karkovice	.05
414	Mike Morgan	.05
415	Joe Hesketh	.05
416	Don Slaught	.05
417	Tom Henke	.05
418	Kurt Stillwell	.05
419	Hector Villanueva	.05
420	Glenallen Hill	.05
421	Pat Borders	.05
422	Charlie Hough	.05
423	Charlie Leibrandt	.05
424	Eddie Murray	.75
425	Jesse Barfield	.05
426	Mark Lemke	.05
427	Kevin McReynolds	.05
428	Gilberto Reyes	.05
429	Ramon Martinez	.05
430	Steve Buechele	.05
431	David Wells	.05
432	Kyle Abbott (Rookie Prospect)	.05
433	John Habyan	.05
434	Kevin Appier	.05
435	Gene Larkin	.05
436	Sandy Alomar, Jr.	.05
437	Mike Jackson	.05
438	Todd Benzinger	.05
439	Teddy Higuera	.05
440	Reggie Sanders (Rookie Prospect)	.05
441	Mark Carreon	.05
442	Bret Saberhagen	.05
443	Gene Nelson	.05
444	Jay Howell	.05
445	Roger McDowell	.05
446	Sid Bream	.05
447	Mackey Sasser	.05
448	Bill Swift	.05
449	Hubie Brooks	.05
450	David Cone	.05
451	Bobby Witt	.05
452	Brady Anderson	.05
453	Lee Stevens	.05
454	Luis Aquino	.05
455	Carney Lansford	.05
456	Carlos Hernandez (Rookie Prospect)	.05
457	Danny Jackson	.05
458	Gerald Young	.05
459	Tom Candiotti	.05
460	Billy Hatcher	.05
461	John Wetteland	.05
462	Mike Bordick	.05
463	Don Robinson	.05
464	Jeff Johnson	.05
465	Lonnie Smith	.05
466	Paul Assenmacher	.05
467	Alvin Davis	.05
468	Jim Eisenreich	.05
469	Brent Mayne	.05
470	Jeff Brantley	.05
471	Tim Burke	.05
472	Pat Mahomes **RC** (Rookie Prospect)	.05
473	Ryan Bowen	.05
474	Bryn Smith	.05
475	Mike Flanagan	.05
476	Reggie Jefferson (Rookie Prospect)	.05
477	Jeff Blauser	.05
478	Craig Lefferts	.05
479	Todd Worrell	.05
480	Scott Scudder	.05
481	Kirk Gibson	.05
482	Kenny Rogers	.05
483	Jack Morris	.05
484	Russ Swan	.05
485	Mike Huff	.05
486	Ken Hill	.05
487	Geronimo Pena	.05
488	Charlie O'Brien	.05
489	Mike Maddux	.05
490	Scott Livingstone (Rookie Prospect)	.05
491	Carl Willis	.05
492	Kelly Downs	.05
493	Dennis Cook	.05
494	Joe Magrane	.05
495	Bob Kipper	.05
496	Jose Mesa	.05
497	Charlie Hayes	.05
498	Joe Girardi	.05
499	Doug Jones	.05
500	Barry Bonds	2.00
501	Bill Krueger	.05
502	Glenn Braggs	.05
503	Eric King	.05
504	Frank Castillo	.05
505	Mike Gardiner	.05
506	Cory Snyder	.05
507	Steve Howe	.05
508	Jose Rijo	.05
509	Sid Fernandez	.05
510	Archi Cianfrocco **RC** (Rookie Prospect)	.05
511	Mark Guthrie	.05
512	Bob Ojeda	.05
513	John Doherty (Rookie Prospect)	.05
514	Dante Bichette	.05
515	Juan Berenguer	.05
516	Jeff Robinson	.05
517	Mike MacFarlane	.05
518	Matt Young	.05
519	Otis Nixon	.05
520	Brian Holman	.05
521	Chris Haney	.05
522	Jeff Kent **RC** (Rookie Prospect)	.75
523	Chad Curtis **RC** (Rookie Prospect)	.25
524	Vince Horsman	.05
525	Rod Nichols	.05
526	Peter Hoy **RC** (Rookie Prospect)	.05
527	Shawn Boskie	.05
528	Alejandro Pena	.05
529	Dave Burba (Rookie Prospect)	.05
530	Ricky Jordan	.05
531	David Silvestri (Rookie Prospect)	.05
532	John Patterson (Rookie Prospect)	.05
533	Jeff Branson (Rookie Prospect)	.05
534	Derrick May (Rookie Prospect)	.05
535	Esteban Beltre (Rookie Prospect)	.05
536	Jose Melendez	.05
537	Wally Joyner	.05

538	Eddie Taubensee (Rookie Prospect)	.05
539	Jim Abbott	.05
540	Brian Williams **RC** (Rookie Prospect)	.05
541	Donovan Osborne (Rookie Prospect)	.05
542	Patrick Lennon (Rookie Prospect)	.05
543	Mike Groppuso **RC** (Rookie Prospect)	.05
544	Jarvis Brown **RC** (Rookie Prospect)	.05
545	Shawn Livesy **RC** (1st Round Draft Pick)	.05
546	Jeff Ware (1st Round Draft Pick)	.05
547	Danny Tartabull	.05
548	Bobby Jones **RC** (1st Round Draft Pick)	.05
549	Ken Griffey Jr.	1.50
550	Rey Sanchez **RC** (Rookie Prospect)	.05
551	Pedro Astacio **RC** (Rookie Prospect)	.10
552	Juan Guerrero **RC** (Rookie Prospect)	.05
553	Jacob Brumfield **RC** (Rookie Prospect)	.05
554	Ben Rivera **RC** (Rookie Prospect)	.05
555	Brian Jordan **RC** (Rookie Prospect)	.40
556	Denny Neagle (Rookie Prospect)	.05
557	Cliff Brantley (Rookie Prospect)	.05
558	Anthony Young (Rookie Prospect)	.05
559	John VanderWal **RC** (Rookie Prospect)	.05
560	Monty Fariss **RC** (Rookie Prospect)	.05
561	Russ Springer **RC** (Rookie Prospect)	.05
562	Pat Listach **RC** (Rookie Prospect)	.05
563	Pat Hentgen (Rookie Prospect)	.05
564	Andy Stankiewicz (Rookie Prospect)	.05
565	Mike Perez (Rookie Prospect)	.05
566	Mike Bielecki	.05
567	Butch Henry (Rookie Prospect)	.05
568	Dave Nilsson **RC** (Rookie Prospect)	.05
569	Scott Hatteberg **RC** (Rookie Prospect)	.05
570	Ruben Amaro Jr. (Rookie Prospect)	.05
571	Todd Hundley (Rookie Prospect)	.05
572	Moises Alou (Rookie Prospect)	.05
573	Hector Fajardo (Rookie Prospect)	.05
574	Todd Van Poppel (Rookie Prospect)	.05
575	Willie Banks (Rookie Prospect)	.05
576	Bob Zupcic (Rookie Prospect)	.05
577	J.J. Johnson **RC** (1st Round Draft Pick)	.05
578	John Burkett	.05
579	Trever Miller (1st Round Draft Pick)	.05
580	Scott Bankhead	.05
581	Rich Amaral (Rookie Prospect)	.05
582	Kenny Lofton (Rookie Prospect)	.05
583	Matt Stairs (Rookie Prospect)	.05
584	Don Mattingly, Rod Carew (Idols)	.25
585	Jack Morris, Steve Avery (Idols)	.05
586	Roberto Alomar, Sandy Alomar (Idols)	.10
587	Scott Sanderson, Catfish Hunter (Idols)	.05
588	Dave Justice, Willie Stargell (Idols)	.05
589	Rex Hudler, Roger Staubach (Idols)	.05
590	David Cone, Jackie Gleason (Idols)	.05
591	Willie Davis, Tony Gwynn (Idols)	.15
592	Orel Hershiser (Sidelines)	.05
593	John Wetteland (Sidelines)	.05
594	Tom Glavine (Sidelines)	.05
595	Randy Johnson (Sidelines)	.25
596	Jim Gott (Sidelines)	.05
597	Donald Harris	.05
598	Shawn Hare **RC**	.05
599	Chris Gardner	.05
600	Rusty Meacham	.05
601	Benito Santiago (Shades)	.05
602	Eric Davis (Shades)	.05
603	Jose Lind (Shades)	.05
604	Dave Justice (Shades)	.05
605	Tim Raines (Shades)	.05
606	Randy Tomlin (Grips)	.05
607	Jack McDowell (Grips)	.05
608	Greg Maddux (Grips)	.30
609	Charles Nagy (Grips)	.05
610	Tom Candiotti (Grips)	.05
611	David Cone (Grips)	.05
612	Steve Avery (Grips)	.05
613	Rod Beck **RC**	.10
614	Rickey Henderson (Technician)	.25
615	Benito Santiago (Technician)	.05
616	Ruben Sierra (Technician)	.05
617	Ryne Sandberg (Technician)	.50
618	Nolan Ryan (Technician)	1.00
619	Brett Butler (Technician)	.05
620	Dave Justice (Technician)	.05

Rookie Idols

Carrying on with the Idols subset theme in the regular issue, these Series 2 foil-pack inserts feature 18 young prospects sharing cards with their baseball heroes. Both front and back are horizontal in format and include photos of both the rookie and his idol.

		NM/M
Complete Set (18):		20.00
Common Player:		.50
1	Reggie Sanders, Eric Davis	.50
2	Hector Fajardo, Jim Abbott	.50
3	Gary Cooper, George Brett	3.50
4	Mark Wohlers, Roger Clemens	3.50
5	Luis Mercedes, Julio Franco	.50
6	Willie Banks, Dwight Gooden	.50
7	Kenny Lofton, Rickey Henderson	1.50
8	Keith Mitchell, Dave Henderson	.50
9	Kim Batiste, Barry Larkin	.50
10	Thurman Munson, Todd Hundley	1.00
11	Eddie Zosky, Cal Ripken Jr.	4.50
12	Todd Van Poppel, Nolan Ryan	4.50
13	Ryne Sandberg, Jim Thome	2.50
14	Dave Fleming, Bobby Murcer	.50
15	Royce Clayton, Ozzie Smith	2.50
16	Don Harris, Darryl Strawberry	.50
17	Alan Trammell, Chad Curtis	.50
18	Derek Bell, Dave Winfield	1.50

Rookies

Styled after the regular 1992 Pinnacle cards, this 30-card boxed set features the year's top rookies. The cards have a game-action photo which is borderless on the top and sides. Beneath the photo a team color-coded strip carries the player's name in gold foil, with a gold-bordered team logo at left. A black strip at bottom has the notation "1992 Rookie." Horizontal backs follow a similar design and include a bit of player information, Pinnacle's anti-counterfeiting strip and some gold-foil enhancements.

		NM/M
Complete Set (30):		2.00
Common Player:		.05
1	Luis Mercedes	.05
2	Scott Cooper	.05
3	Kenny Lofton	.25
4	John Doherty	.05
5	Pat Listach	.05
6	Andy Stankiewicz	.05
7	Derek Bell	.25
8	Gary DiSarcina	.05
9	Roberto Hernandez	.15
10	Joel Johnston	.05
11	Pat Mahomes	.05
12	Todd Van Poppel	.05
13	Dave Fleming	.05
14	Monty Fariss	.05
15	Gary Scott	.05
16	Moises Alou	.25
17	Todd Hundley	.25
18	Kim Batiste	.05
19	Denny Neagle	.05
20	Donovan Osborne	.05
21	Mark Wohlers	.05
22	Reggie Sanders	.10
23	Brian Williams	.05
24	Eric Karros	.25
25	Frank Seminara	.05
26	Royce Clayton	.05
27	Dave Nilsson	.05
28	Matt Stairs	.25
29	Chad Curtis	.25
30	Carlos Hernandez	.25

Slugfest

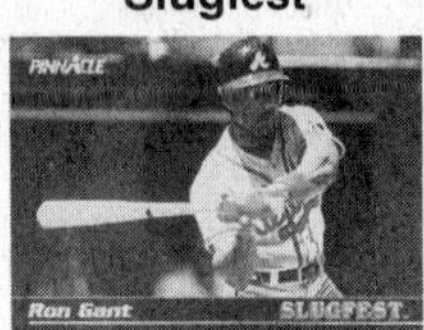

Each specially marked Slugfest jumbo pack of '92 Pinnacle contained one of these horizontal-format cards of the game's top hitters. The player's name is printed in gold foil at the bottom of the card, along with a red and white Slugfest logo. Backs, which are vertical, have a color player photo, a career summary and a few lifetime stats.

		NM/M
Complete Set (15):		15.00
Common Player:		.30
1	Cecil Fielder	.30
2	Mark McGwire	2.50
3	Jose Canseco	.65
4	Barry Bonds	3.00
5	Dave Justice	.30
6	Bobby Bonilla	.30
7	Ken Griffey Jr.	2.00
8	Ron Gant	.30
9	Ryne Sandberg	1.50
10	Ruben Sierra	.30
11	Frank Thomas	1.00
12	Will Clark	.30
13	Kirby Puckett	1.50
14	Cal Ripken, Jr.	3.00
15	Jeff Bagwell	1.00

Team Pinnacle

The most sought-after of the 1992 Pinnacle inserts is this 12-piece set of "two-headed" cards. An American and a National League superstar at each position are featured on each card, with two cards each for starting and relief pitchers. The ultra-realistic artwork of Chris Greco is featured on the cards, which were inserted into Series 1 foil packs.

		NM/M
Complete Set (12):		40.00
Common Player:		1.50
1	Roger Clemens, Ramon Martinez	8.00
2	Jim Abbott, Steve Avery	1.50
3	Benito Santiago, Ivan Rodriguez	3.00
4	Frank Thomas, Will Clark	3.00
5	Roberto Alomar, Ryne Sandberg	6.00
6	Robin Ventura, Matt Williams	1.50
7	Cal Ripken, Jr., Barry Larkin	10.00
8	Danny Tartabull, Barry Bonds	8.00
9	Brett Butler, Ken Griffey Jr.	8.00
10	Ruben Sierra, Dave Justice	1.50
11	Dennis Eckersley, Rob Dibble	1.50
12	Scott Radinsky, John Franco	1.50

Team 2000

Young stars projected to be the superstars of the 2000 season were chosen for this insert set found three at a time in jumbo packs. Cards #1-40 were included in Series 1 packaging, while cards #41-80 were inserted with Series 2 Pinnacle. Cards feature gold foil highlights on both front and back.

		NM/M
Complete Set (80):		3.00
Common Player:		.05
1	Mike Mussina	.30
2	Phil Plantier	.05
3	Frank Thomas	.50
4	Travis Fryman	.05
5	Kevin Appier	.05
6	Chuck Knoblauch	.05
7	Pat Kelly	.05
8	Ivan Rodriguez	.40
9	Dave Justice	.05
10	Jeff Bagwell	.50
11	Marquis Grissom	.05
12	Andy Benes	.05
13	Gregg Olson	.05
14	Kevin Morton	.05
15	Tim Naehring	.05
16	Dave Hollins	.05
17	Sandy Alomar Jr.	.05
18	Albert Belle	.05
19	Charles Nagy	.05
20	Brian McRae	.05
21	Larry Walker	.05
22	Delino DeShields	.05
23	Jeff Johnson	.05
24	Bernie Williams	.05
25	Jose Offerman	.05
26	Juan Gonzalez	.25
27	Juan Guzman	.05
28	Eric Anthony	.05
29	Brian Hunter	.05
30	John Smoltz	.05
31	Deion Sanders	.05
32	Greg Maddux	.75
33	Andujar Cedeno	.05
34	Royce Clayton	.05
35	Kenny Lofton	.05
36	Cal Eldred	.05
37	Jim Thome	.50
38	Gary DiSarcina	.05
39	Brian Jordan	.05
40	Chad Curtis	.05
41	Ben McDonald	.05
42	Jim Abbott	.05
43	Robin Ventura	.05
44	Milt Cuyler	.05
45	Gregg Jefferies	.05
46	Scott Radinsky	.05
47	Ken Griffey Jr.	1.00
48	Roberto Alomar	.15
49	Ramon Martinez	.05
50	Bret Barberie	.05
51	Ray Lankford	.05
52	Leo Gomez	.05
53	Tommy Greene	.05
54	Mo Vaughn	.05
55	Sammy Sosa	.75
56	Carlos Baerga	.05
57	Mark Lewis	.05
58	Tom Gordon	.05
59	Gary Sheffield	.25
60	Scott Erickson	.05
61	Pedro Munoz	.05
62	Tino Martinez	.05
63	Darren Lewis	.05
64	Dean Palmer	.05
65	John Olerud	.05
66	Steve Avery	.05
67	Pete Harnisch	.05
68	Luis Gonzalez	.05
69	Kim Batiste	.05
70	Reggie Sanders	.05
71	Luis Mercedes	.05
72	Todd Van Poppel	.05
73	Gary Scott	.05
74	Monty Fariss	.05
75	Kyle Abbott	.05
76	Eric Karros	.05
77	Mo Sanford	.05
78	Todd Hundley	.05
79	Reggie Jefferson	.05
80	Pat Mahomes	.05

Mickey Mantle

This boxed set highlighting the career of Mickey Mantle was issued in a reported edition of 180,000 sets. Fronts and backs feature an assortment of black-and-white, color and colorized photos. Fronts have gold-foil stamped highlights. Card backs have a few sentences about Mantle's life or career.

		NM/M
Complete Set (30):		20.00
Common Card:		1.00
1	Father and Son	1.00
2	High School	1.00
3	Commerce Comet	1.00
4	Spring Training	1.00
5	The Beginning	1.00
6	No. 6	1.00
7	The Rookie	1.00
8	Tape-Measure Shots	1.00
9	Shortstop	1.00
10	Outfield	1.00
11	Speed, Speed, Speed	1.00
12	Contracts	1.00
13	Three-time MVP	1.00
14	Triple Crown	1.00
15	Series Slam	1.00
16	Series Star	1.00
17	Switch Hitter	1.00
18	Fan Favorite	1.00
19	Milestones	1.00
20	Enthuiasm	1.00
21	Hitting	1.00
22	First Base	1.00
23	Courage	1.00
24	Mick & Stan (Musial)	1.00
25	Whitey & Yogi (Ford, Berra)	1.00
26	Mick & Billy (Martin)	1.00
27	Mick & Casey (Stengel)	1.00
28	Awards	1.00
29	Retirement	1.00
30	Cooperstown	1.00

1993 Pinnacle Promos

On six of the eight cards issued to premiere Pinnacle's '93 set, the difference between the promo version and the issued version is so slight it can easily go unnoticed - the "TM"

in the upper-right corner on front is larger on the promo than on the regular card. Promo cards #3 and 5 are easier to spot because the team logos on back of the promos are the old Expos and Mariners logos, rather than the new versions found on issued cards.

		NM/M
Complete Set (8):		10.00
Common Player:		1.25
1	Gary Sheffield	3.00
2	Cal Eldred	1.25
3	Larry Walker	1.25
4	Deion Sanders	1.50
5	Dave Fleming	1.25
6	Carlos Baerga	1.25
7	Bernie Williams	1.25
8	John Kruk	1.25

1993 Pinnacle

This set offers many of the same features which made the debut Pinnacle set so popular in 1992. Subsets are titled Rookies, Now & Then (which shows the player as he looked as a rookie and in 1993), Idols (active players and their heroes on the same card), Hometown Heroes (players who are playing with their hometown team), Draft Picks and Rookies. More than 100 rookies and 10 draft picks are featured. All regular cards have an action photo, a black border and the Pinnacle name in gold foil. Series 1 cards feature portraits of players on the two new expansion teams; Series 2 cards feature action shots of them. Team Pinnacle insert cards returned, while Rookie Team Pinnacle cards made their debut. Other insert sets are titled Team 2001, Slugfest and Tribute, which features five cards each of Nolan Ryan and George Brett.

		NM/M
Complete Set (620):		17.50
Common Player:		.05
Series 1 Pack (15):		.35
Series 1 Box (36):		8.00
Series 2 Pack (15):		.75
Series 2 Box (36):		20.00
1	Gary Sheffield	.30
2	Cal Eldred	.05
3	Larry Walker	.05
4	Deion Sanders	.05
5	Dave Fleming	.05
6	Carlos Baerga	.05
7	Bernie Williams	.05
8	John Kruk	.05
9	Jimmy Key	.05
10	Jeff Bagwell	.60
11	Jim Abbott	.05
12	Terry Steinbach	.05

No.	Player	Value
13	Bob Tewksbury	.05
14	Eric Karros	.05
15	Ryne Sandberg	.75
16	Will Clark	.05
17	Edgar Martinez	.05
18	Eddie Murray	.60
19	Andy Van Slyke	.05
20	Cal Ripken, Jr.	2.00
21	Ivan Rodriguez	.50
22	Barry Larkin	.05
23	Don Mattingly	.85
24	Gregg Jefferies	.05
25	Roger Clemens	.85
26	Cecil Fielder	.05
27	Kent Hrbek	.05
28	Robin Ventura	.05
29	Rickey Henderson	.60
30	Roberto Alomar	.15
31	Luis Polonia	.05
32	Andujar Cedeno	.05
33	Pat Listach	.05
34	Mark Grace	.05
35	Otis Nixon	.05
36	Felix Jose	.05
37	Mike Sharperson	.05
38	Dennis Martinez	.05
39	Willie McGee	.05
40	Kenny Lofton	.05
41	Randy Johnson	.60
42	Andy Benes	.05
43	Bobby Bonilla	.05
44	Mike Mussina	.50
45	Len Dykstra	.05
46	Ellis Burks	.05
47	Chris Sabo	.05
48	Jay Bell	.05
49	Jose Canseco	.40
50	Craig Biggio	.05
51	Wally Joyner	.05
52	Mickey Tettleton	.05
53	Tim Raines	.05
54	Brian Harper	.05
55	Rene Gonzales	.05
56	Mark Langston	.05
57	Jack Morris	.05
58	Mark McGwire	1.50
59	Ken Caminiti	.05
60	Terry Pendleton	.05
61	Dave Nilsson	.05
62	Tom Pagnozzi	.05
63	Mike Morgan	.05
64	Darryl Strawberry	.05
65	Charles Nagy	.05
66	Ken Hill	.05
67	Matt Williams	.05
68	Jay Buhner	.05
69	Vince Coleman	.05
70	Brady Anderson	.05
71	Fred McGriff	.05
72	Ben McDonald	.05
73	Terry Mulholland	.05
74	Randy Tomlin	.05
75	Nolan Ryan	2.00
76	Frank Viola	.05
77	Jose Rijo	.05
78	Shane Mack	.05
79	Travis Fryman	.05
80	Jack McDowell	.05
81	Mark Gubicza	.05
82	Matt Nokes	.05
83	Bert Blyleven	.05
84	Eric Anthony	.05
85	Mike Bordick	.05
86	John Olerud	.05
87	B.J. Surhoff	.05
88	Bernard Gilkey	.05
89	Shawon Dunston	.05
90	Tom Glavine	.30
91	Brett Butler	.05
92	Moises Alou	.05
93	Albert Belle	.05
94	Darren Lewis	.05
95	Omar Vizquel	.05
96	Dwight Gooden	.05
97	Gregg Olson	.05
98	Tony Gwynn	.75
99	Darren Daulton	.05
100	Dennis Eckersley	.50
101	Rob Dibble	.05
102	Mike Greenwell	.05
103	Jose Lind	.05
104	Julio Franco	.05
105	Tom Gordon	.05
106	Scott Livingstone	.05
107	Chuck Knoblauch	.05
108	Frank Thomas	.60
109	Melido Perez	.05
110	Ken Griffey Jr.	1.00
111	Harold Baines	.05
112	Gary Gaetti	.05
113	Pete Harnisch	.05
114	David Wells	.05
115	Charlie Leibrandt	.05
116	Ray Lankford	.05
117	Kevin Seitzer	.05
118	Robin Yount	.60
119	Lenny Harris	.05
120	Chris James	.05
121	Delino DeShields	.05
122	Kirt Manwaring	.05
123	Glenallen Hill	.05
124	Hensley Meulens	.05
125	Darrin Jackson	.05
126	Todd Hundley	.05
127	Dave Hollins	.05
128	Sam Horn	.05
129	Roberto Hernandez	.05
130	Vicente Palacios	.05
131	George Brett	.85
132	Dave Martinez	.05
133	Kevin Appier	.05
134	Pat Kelly	.05
135	Pedro Munoz	.05
136	Mark Carreon	.05
137	Lance Johnson	.05
138	Devon White	.05
139	Julio Valera	.05
140	Eddie Taubensee	.05
141	Willie Wilson	.05
142	Stan Belinda	.05
143	John Smoltz	.05
144	Darryl Hamilton	.05
145	Sammy Sosa	.75
146	Carlos Hernandez	.05
147	Tom Candiotti	.05
148	Mike Felder	.05
149	Rusty Meacham	.05
150	Ivan Calderon	.05
151	Pete O'Brien	.05
152	Erik Hanson	.05
153	Billy Ripken	.05
154	Kurt Stillwell	.05
155	Jeff Kent	.05
156	Mickey Morandini	.05
157	Randy Milligan	.05
158	Reggie Sanders	.05
159	Luis Rivera	.05
160	Orlando Merced	.05
161	Dean Palmer	.05
162	Mike Perez	.05
163	Scott Erikson	.05
164	Kevin McReynolds	.05
165	Kevin Maas	.05
166	Ozzie Guillen	.05
167	Rob Deer	.05
168	Danny Tartabull	.05
169	Lee Stevens	.05
170	Dave Henderson	.05
171	Derek Bell	.05
172	Steve Finley	.05
173	Greg Olson	.05
174	Geronimo Pena	.05
175	Paul Quantrill	.05
176	Steve Buechele	.05
177	Kevin Gross	.05
178	Tim Wallach	.05
179	Dave Valle	.05
180	Dave Silvestri	.05
181	Bud Black	.05
182	Henry Rodriguez	.05
183	Tim Teufel	.05
184	Mark McLemore	.05
185	Bret Saberhagen	.05
186	Chris Hoiles	.05
187	Ricky Jordan	.05
188	Don Slaught	.05
189	Mo Vaughn	.05
190	Joe Oliver	.05
191	Juan Gonzalez	.30
192	Scott Leius	.05
193	Milt Cuyler	.05
194	Chris Haney	.05
195	Ron Karkovice	.05
196	Steve Farr	.05
197	John Orton	.05
198	Kelly Gruber	.05
199	Ron Darling	.05
200	Ruben Sierra	.05
201	Chuck Finley	.05
202	Mike Moore	.05
203	Pat Borders	.05
204	Sid Bream	.05
205	Todd Zeile	.05
206	Rick Wilkins	.05
207	Jim Gantner	.05
208	Frank Castillo	.05
209	Dave Hansen	.05
210	Trevor Wilson	.05
211	Sandy Alomar, Jr.	.05
212	Sean Berry	.05
213	Tino Martinez	.05
214	Chito Martinez	.05
215	Dan Walters	.05
216	John Franco	.05
217	Glenn Davis	.05
218	Mariano Duncan	.05
219	Mike LaValliere	.05
220	Rafael Palmeiro	.50
221	Jack Clark	.05
222	Hal Morris	.05
223	Ed Sprague	.05
224	John Valentin	.05
225	Sam Militello	.05
226	Bob Wickman	.05
227	Damion Easley	.05
228	John Jaha	.05
229	Bob Ayrault	.05
230	Mo Sanford/ED	.05
231	Walt Weiss/ED	.05
232	Dante Bichette/ED	.05
233	Steve Decker/ED	.05
234	Jerald Clark/ED	.05
235	Bryan Harvey/ED	.05
236	Joe Girardi/ED	.05
237	Dave Magadan/ED	.05
238	David Nied (Rookie Prospect)	.05
239	Eric Wedge **RC** (Rookie Prospect)	.05
240	Rico Brogna (Rookie Prospect)	.05
241	J.T. Bruett (Rookie Prospect)	.05
242	Jonathan Hurst (Rookie Prospect)	.05
243	Bret Boone (Rookie Prospect)	.05
244	Manny Alexander (Rookie Prospect)	.05
245	Scooter Tucker (Rookie Prospect)	.05
246	Troy Neel (Rookie Prospect)	.05
247	Eddie Zosky (Rookie Prospect)	.05
248	Melvin Nieves (Rookie Prospect)	.05
249	Ryan Thompson (Rookie Prospect)	.05
250	Shawn Barton (Rookie Prospect)	.05
251	Ryan Klesko (Rookie Prospect)	.05
252	Mike Piazza (Rookie Prospect)	1.00
253	Steve Hosey (Rookie Prospect)	.05
254	Shane Reynolds (Rookie Prospect)	.05
255	Dan Wilson (Rookie Prospect)	.05
256	Tom Marsh (Rookie Prospect)	.05
257	Barry Manuel (Rookie Prospect)	.05
258	Paul Miller (Rookie Prospect)	.05
259	Pedro Martinez (Rookie Prospect)	.60
260	Steve Cooke (Rookie Prospect)	.05
261	Johnny Guzman (Rookie Prospect)	.05
262	Mike Butcher (Rookie Prospect)	.05
263	Bien Figueroa (Rookie Prospect)	.05
264	Rich Rowland (Rookie Prospect)	.05
265	Shawn Jeter (Rookie Prospect)	.05
266	Gerald Williams (Rookie Prospect)	.05
267	Derek Parks (Rookie Prospect)	.05
268	Henry Mercedes (Rookie Prospect)	.05
269	David Hulse **RC** (Rookie Prospect)	.05
270	Tim Pugh **RC** (Rookie Prospect)	.05
271	William Suero (Rookie Prospect)	.05
272	Ozzie Canseco (Rookie Prospect)	.05
273	Fernando Ramsey (Rookie Prospect)	.05
274	Bernardo Brito (Rookie Prospect)	.05
275	Dave Mlicki (Rookie Prospect)	.05
276	Tim Salmon (Rookie Prospect)	.05
277	Mike Raczka (Rookie Prospect)	.05
278	Ken Ryan **RC** (Rookie Prospect)	.05
279	Rafael Bournigal (Rookie Prospect)	.05
280	Wil Cordero (Rookie Prospect)	.05
281	Billy Ashley (Rookie Prospect)	.05
282	Paul Wagner (Rookie Prospect)	.05
283	Blas Minor (Rookie Prospect)	.05
284	Rick Trlicek (Rookie Prospect)	.05
285	Willie Greene (Rookie Prospect)	.05
286	Ted Wood (Rookie Prospect)	.05
287	Phil Clark (Rookie Prospect)	.05
288	Jesse Levis (Rookie Prospect)	.05
289	Tony Gwynn (Now & Then)	.40
290	Nolan Ryan (Now & Then)	1.00
291	Dennis Martinez (Now & Then)	.05
292	Eddie Murray (Now & Then)	.30
293	Robin Yount (Now & Then)	.30
294	George Brett (Now & Then)	.45
295	Dave Winfield (Now & Then)	.30
296	Bert Blyleven (Now & Then)	.05
297	Jeff Bagwell (Idols - Carl Yastrzemski)	.30
298	John Smoltz (Idols - Jack Morris)	.05
299	Larry Walker (Idols - Mike Bossy)	.05
300	Gary Sheffield (Idols - Barry Larkin)	.15
301	Ivan Rodriguez (Idols - Carlton Fisk)	.30
302	Delino DeShields (Idols - Malcolm X)	.05
303	Tim Salmon (Idols - Dwight Evans)	.05
304	Bernard Gilkey (Hometown Heroes)	.05
305	Cal Ripken, Jr. (Hometown Heroes)	1.00
306	Barry Larkin (Hometown Heroes)	.05
307	Kent Hrbek (Hometown Heroes)	.05
308	Rickey Henderson (Hometown Heroes)	.30
309	Darryl Strawberry (Hometown Heroes)	.05
310	John Franco (Hometown Heroes)	.05
311	Todd Stottlemyre	.05
312	Luis Gonzalez	.05
313	Tommy Greene	.05
314	Randy Velarde	.05
315	Steve Avery	.05
316	Jose Oquendo	.05
317	Rey Sanchez	.05
318	Greg Vaughn	.05
319	Orel Hershiser	.05
320	Paul Sorrento	.05
321	Royce Clayton	.05
322	John Vander Wal	.05
323	Henry Cotto	.05
324	Pete Schourek	.05
325	David Segui	.05
326	Arthur Rhodes	.05
327	Bruce Hurst	.05
328	Wes Chamberlain	.05
329	Ozzie Smith	.75
330	Scott Cooper	.05
331	Felix Fermin	.05
332	Mike Macfarlane	.05
333	Dan Gladden	.05
334	Kevin Tapani	.05
335	Steve Sax	.05
336	Jeff Montgomery	.05
337	Gary DiSarcina	.05
338	Lance Blankenship	.05
339	Brian Williams	.05
340	Duane Ward	.05
341	Chuck McElroy	.05
342	Joe Magrane	.05
343	Jaime Navarro	.05
344	Dave Justice	.05
345	Jose Offerman	.05
346	Marquis Grissom	.05
347	Bill Swift	.05
348	Jim Thome	.50
349	Archi Cianfrocco	.05
350	Anthony Young	.05
351	Leo Gomez	.05
352	Bill Gullickson	.05
353	Alan Trammell	.05
354	Dan Pasqua	.05
355	Jeff King	.05
356	Kevin Brown	.05
357	Tim Belcher	.05
358	Bip Roberts	.05
359	Brent Mayne	.05
360	Rheal Cormier	.05
361	Mark Guthrie	.05
362	Craig Grebeck	.05
363	Andy Stankiewicz	.05
364	Juan Guzman	.05
365	Bobby Witt	.05
366	Mark Portugal	.05
367	Brian McRae	.05
368	Mark Lemke	.05
369	Bill Wegman	.05
370	Donovan Osborne	.05
371	Derrick May	.05
372	Carl Willis	.05
373	Chris Nabholz	.05
374	Mark Lewis	.05
375	John Burkett	.05
376	Luis Mercedes	.05
377	Ramon Martinez	.05
378	Kyle Abbott	.05
379	Mark Wohlers	.05
380	Bob Walk	.05
381	Kenny Rogers	.05
382	Tim Naehring	.05
383	Alex Fernandez	.05
384	Keith Miller	.05
385	Mike Henneman	.05
386	Rick Aguilera	.05
387	George Bell	.05
388	Mike Gallego	.05
389	Howard Johnson	.05
390	Kim Batiste	.05
391	Jerry Browne	.05
392	Damon Berryhill	.05
393	Ricky Bones	.05
394	Omar Olivares	.05
395	Mike Harkey	.05
396	Pedro Astacio	.05
397	John Wetteland	.05
398	Rod Beck	.05
399	Thomas Howard	.05
400	Mike Devereaux	.05
401	Tim Wakefield	.05
402	Curt Schilling	.30
403	Zane Smith	.05
404	Bob Zupcic	.05
405	Tom Browning	.05
406	Tony Phillips	.05
407	John Doherty	.05
408	Pat Mahomes	.05
409	John Habyan	.05
410	Steve Olin	.05
411	Chad Curtis	.05
412	Joe Grahe	.05
413	John Patterson	.05
414	Brian Hunter	.05
415	Doug Henry	.05
416	Lee Smith	.05
417	Bob Scanlan	.05
418	Kent Mercker	.05
419	Mel Rojas	.05
420	Mark Whiten	.05
421	Carlton Fisk	.60
422	Candy Maldonado	.05
423	Doug Drabek	.05
424	Wade Boggs	.75
425	Mark Davis	.05
426	Kirby Puckett	.75
427	Joe Carter	.05
428	Paul Molitor	.60
429	Eric Davis	.05
430	Darryl Kile	.05
431	Jeff Parrett/ED	.05
432	Jeff Blauser	.05
433	Dan Plesac	.05
434	Andres Galarraga/ED	.05
435	Jim Gott	.05
436	Jose Mesa	.05
437	Ben Rivera	.05
438	Dave Winfield	.60
439	Norm Charlton	.05
440	Chris Bosio	.05
441	Wilson Alvarez	.05
442	Dave Stewart	.05
443	Doug Jones	.05
444	Jeff Russell	.05
445	Ron Gant	.05
446	Paul O'Neill	.05
447	Charlie Hayes/ED	.05
448	Joe Hesketh	.05
449	Chris Hammond	.05
450	Hipolito Pichardo	.05
451	Scott Radinsky	.05
452	Bobby Thigpen	.05
453	Xavier Hernandez	.05
454	Lonnie Smith	.05
455	Jamie Arnold **RC** (1st Draft Pick)	.05
456	B.J. Wallace (1st Draft Pick)	.05
457	Derek Jeter **RC** (Rookie Prospect)	10.00
458	Jason Kendall **RC** (Rookie Prospect)	.75
459	Rick Helling (Rookie Prospect)	.05
460	Derek Wallace **RC** (Rookie Prospect)	.05
461	Sean Lowe **RC** (Rookie Prospect)	.05
462	Shannon Stewart **RC** (Rookie Prospect)	.60
463	Benji Grigsby **RC** (Rookie Prospect)	.05
464	Todd Steverson **RC** (Rookie Prospect)	.05
465	Dan Serafini **RC** (Rookie Prospect)	.05
466	Michael Tucker (Rookie Prospect)	.05
467	Chris Roberts (Rookie Prospect)	.05
468	Pete Janicki **RC** (1st Draft Pick)	.05
469	Jeff Schmidt **RC** (1st Draft Pick)	.05
470	Don Mattingly (Now & Then)	.45
471	Cal Ripken, Jr. (Now & Then)	1.00
472	Jack Morris (Now & Then)	.05
473	Terry Pendleton (Now & Then)	.05
474	Dennis Eckersley (Now & Then)	.25
475	Carlton Fisk (Now & Then)	.30
476	Wade Boggs (Now & Then)	.35
477	Len Dykstra (Idols - Ken Stabler)	.05
478	Danny Tartabull (Idols - Jose Tartabull)	.05
479	Jeff Conine (Idols - Dale Murphy)	.10
480	Gregg Jefferies (Idols - Ron Cey)	.05
481	Paul Molitor (Idols - Harmon Killebrew)	.30
482	John Valentin (Idols - Dave Concepcion)	.05
483	Alex Arias (Idols - Dave Winfield)	.10
484	Barry Bonds (Hometown Heroes)	1.00
485	Doug Drabek (Hometown Heroes)	.05
486	Dave Winfield (Hometown Heroes)	.30
487	Brett Butler (Hometown Heroes)	.05
488	Harold Baines (Hometown Heroes)	.05
489	David Cone (Hometown Heroes)	.05
490	Willie McGee (Hometown Heroes)	.05
491	Robby Thompson	.05
492	Pete Incaviglia	.05
493	Manuel Lee	.05
494	Rafael Belliard	.05
495	Scott Fletcher	.05
496	Jeff Frye	.05
497	Andre Dawson	.25
498	Mike Scioscia	.05
499	Spike Owen	.05
500	Sid Fernandez	.05
501	Joe Orsulak	.05
502	Benito Santiago/ED	.05
503	Dale Murphy	.25
504	Barry Bonds	2.00
505	Jose Guzman	.05
506	Tony Pena	.05
507	Greg Swindell	.05
508	Mike Pagliarulo	.05
509	Lou Whitaker	.05
510	Greg Gagne	.05
511	Butch Henry/ED	.05
512	Jeff Brantley	.05
513	Jack Armstrong/ED	.05
514	Danny Jackson	.05
515	Junior Felix/ED	.05
516	Milt Thompson	.05
517	Greg Maddux	.75
518	Eric Young/ED	.05
519	Jody Reed	.05
520	Roberto Kelly	.05
521	Darren Holmes/ED	.05
522	Craig Lefferts	.05
523	Charlie Hough/ED	.05
524	Bo Jackson	.10
525	Bill Spiers	.05
526	Orestes Destrade/ED	.05
527	Greg Hibbard	.05
528	Roger McDowell	.05
529	Cory Snyder	.05
530	Harold Reynolds	.05
531	Kevin Reimer	.05
532	Rick Sutcliffe	.05
533	Tony Fernandez	.05
534	Tom Brunansky	.05
535	Jeff Reardon	.05
536	Chili Davis	.05
537	Bob Ojeda	.05
538	Greg Colbrunn	.05
539	Phil Plantier	.05
540	Brian Jordan	.05
541	Pete Smith	.05
542	Frank Tanana	.05
543	John Smiley	.05
544	David Cone	.05
545	Daryl Boston/ED	.05
546	Tom Henke	.05
547	Bill Krueger	.05
548	Freddie Benavides/ED	.05
549	Randy Myers	.05
550	Reggie Jefferson	.05
551	Kevin Mitchell	.05
552	Dave Stieb	.05
553	Bret Barberie/ED	.05
554	Tim Crews	.05
555	Doug Dascenzo	.05
556	Alex Cole/ED	.05
557	Jeff Innis	.05
558	Carlos Garcia	.05
559	Steve Howe	.05
560	Kirk McCaskill	.05
561	Frank Seminara	.05
562	Cris Carpenter/ED	.05
563	Mike Stanley	.05
564	Carlos Quintana	.05
565	Mitch Williams	.05
566	Juan Bell	.05
567	Eric Fox	.05
568	Al Leiter	.05
569	Mike Stanton	.05
570	Scott Kamieniecki	.05
571	Ryan Bowen/ED	.05
572	Andy Ashby/ED	.05
573	Bob Welch	.05
574	Scott Sanderson	.05
575	Joe Kmak (Rookie Prospect)	.05
576	Scott Pose (Rookie Prospect/ED)	.05
577	Ricky Gutierrez (Rookie Prospect)	.05
578	Mike Trombley (Rookie Prospect)	.05
579	Sterling Hitchcock **RC** (Rookie Prospect)	.10
580	Rodney Bolton (Rookie Prospect)	.05
581	Tyler Green (Rookie Prospect)	.05
582	Tim Costo (Rookie Prospect)	.05
583	Tim Laker **RC** (Rookie Prospect)	.05
584	Steve Reed **RC** (Rookie Prospect/ED)	.05
585	Tom Kramer **RC** (Rookie Prospect)	.05
586	Robb Nen (Rookie Prospect)	.05
587	Jim Tatum **RC** (Rookie Prospect)	.05
588	Frank Bolick (Rookie Prospect)	.05
589	Kevin Young (Rookie Prospect)	.05
590	Matt Whiteside **RC** (Rookie Prospect)	.05
591	Cesar Hernandez (Rookie Prospect)	.05
592	Mike Mohler **RC** (Rookie Prospect)	.05

#	Player	NM/M
593	Alan Embree (Rookie Prospect)	.05
594	Terry Jorgensen (Rookie Prospect)	.05
595	John Cummings **RC** (Rookie Prospect)	.05
596	Domingo Martinez (Rookie Prospect)	.05
597	Benji Gil (Rookie Prospect)	.05
598	Todd Pratt **RC** (Rookie Prospect)	.05
599	Rene Arocha **RC** (Rookie Prospect)	.05
600	Dennis Moeller (Rookie Prospect)	.05
601	Jeff Conine (Rookie Prospect/ED	.05
602	Trevor Hoffman (Rookie Prospect/ED	.05
603	Daniel Smith (Rookie Prospect)	.05
604	Lee Tinsley (Rookie Prospect)	.05
605	Dan Peltier (Rookie Prospect)	.05
606	Billy Brewer (Rookie Prospect)	.05
607	Matt Walbeck **RC** (Rookie Prospect)	.05
608	Richie Lewis (Rookie Prospect/ED)	.05
609	J.T. Snow **RC** (Rookie Prospect)	.40
610	Pat Gomez **RC** (Rookie Prospect)	.05
611	Phil Hiatt (Rookie Prospect)	.05
612	Alex Arias (Rookie Prospect/ED)	.05
613	Kevin Rogers (Rookie Prospect)	.05
614	Al Martin (Rookie Prospect)	.05
615	Greg Gohr (Rookie Prospect)	.05
616	Grame Lloyd **RC** (Rookie Prospect)	.05
617	Kent Bottenfield (Rookie Prospect)	.05
618	Chuck Carr (Rookie Prospect/ED)	.05
619	Darrell Sherman **RC** (Rookie Prospect)	.05
620	Mike Lansing **RC** (Rookie Prospect)	.15

Expansion Opening Day

This nine-card set features 18 players for the two N.L. expansion teams: Florida Marlins and Colorado Rockies. Each "two-headed" card shows a projected Opening Day starter for each team. Cards were available one per Series 2 hobby box. Complete sets were available through a special mail-in offer.

		NM/M
Complete Set (9):		2.50
Common Player:		.25
1	Charlie Hough, David Nied	.25
2	Benito Santiago, Joe Girardi	.40
3	Orestes Destrade, Andres Galarraga	.75
4	Bret Barberie, Eric Young	.25
5	Dave Magadan, Charlie Hayes	.25
6	Walt Weiss, Freddie Benevides	.25
7	Jeff Conine, Jerald Clark	.50
8	Scott Pose, Alex Cole	.25
9	Junior Felix, Dante Bichette	.40

Rookie Team Pinnacle

These 10 cards were randomly inserted into Series 2 packs. Rookie Team Pinnacle is printed in gold foil on both sides of the card. Cards are numbered 1 of 10, etc., and use the special Dufex process. Each card shows two players painted by artist Christopher Greco. Stated odds of finding a Rookie Team Pinnacle insert were one in 90 packs.

		NM/M
Complete Set (10):		20.00
Common Player:		1.50
1	Pedro Martinez, Mike Trombley	6.00
2	Kevin Rogers, Sterling Hitchcock	1.50
3	Mike Piazza, Jesse Levis	10.00
4	Ryan Klesko, J.T. Snow	1.50
5	John Patterson, Bret Boone	1.50
6	Domingo Martinez, Kevin Young	1.50
7	Wil Cordero, Manny Alexander	1.50
8	Steve Hosey, Tim Salmon	1.50
9	Ryan Thompson, Gerald Williams	1.50
10	Melvin Nieves, David Hulse	1.50

Slugfest

Baseball's top sluggers are featured in this 30-card insert set. Cards were available one per Series 2 jumbo pack. Slugfest is printed in gold foil on the card front.

		NM/M
Complete Set (30):		12.50
Common Player:		.25
1	Juan Gonzalez	.50
2	Mark McGwire	2.00
3	Cecil Fielder	.25
4	Joe Carter	.25
5	Fred McGriff	.25
6	Barry Bonds	2.50
7	Gary Sheffield	.50
8	Dave Hollins	.25
9	Frank Thomas	1.00
10	Danny Tartabull	.25
11	Albert Belle	.25
12	Ruben Sierra	.25
13	Larry Walker	.25
14	Jeff Bagwell	1.00
15	Dave Justice	.25
16	Kirby Puckett	1.25
17	John Kruk	.25
18	Howard Johnson	.25
19	Darryl Strawberry	.25
20	Will Clark	.25
21	Kevin Mitchell	.25
22	Mickey Tettleton	.25
23	Don Mattingly	1.50
24	Jose Canseco	.75
25	Sam Millitello	.25
26	Andre Dawson	.50
27	Ryne Sandberg	1.25
28	Ken Griffey Jr.	1.75
29	Carlos Baerga	.25
30	Travis Fryman	.25

Team Pinnacle

These cards were randomly inserted in Series 1 at a rate of about one in every 24 packs. Each card features two players painted by artist Christopher Greco. An eleventh card, featuring relief pitchers, was available only via a mail-in offer.

		NM/M
Complete Set (11):		40.00
Common Player:		1.50
1	Greg Maddux, Mike Mussina	10.00
2	Tom Glavine, John Smiley	2.00
3	Darren Daulton, Ivan Rodriguez	3.00
4	Fred McGriff, Frank Thomas	4.00
5	Delino DeShields, Carlos Baerga	1.50
6	Gary Sheffield, Edgar Martinez	2.00
7	Ozzie Smith, Pat Listach	8.00
8	Barry Bonds, Juan Gonzalez	15.00
9	Kirby Puckett, Andy Van Slyke	8.00
10	Larry Walker, Joe Carter	1.50
11	Rick Aguilera, Rob Dibble	1.50

Team 2001

This insert set features 30 players who are expected to be stars in the year 2001. Cards were randomly inserted into 27-card jumbo packs from Series 1.

		NM/M
Complete Set (30):		5.00
Common Player:		.05
1	Wil Cordero	.05
2	Cal Eldred	.05
3	Mike Mussina	.60
4	Chuck Knoblauch	.05
5	Melvin Nieves	.05
6	Tim Wakefield	.05
7	Carlos Baerga	.05
8	Bret Boone	.05
9	Jeff Bagwell	1.00
10	Travis Fryman	.05
11	Royce Clayton	.05
12	Delino DeShields	.05
13	Juan Gonzalez	.50
14	Pedro Martinez	1.00
15	Bernie Williams	.05
16	Billy Ashley	.05
17	Marquis Grissom	.05
18	Kenny Lofton	.05
19	Ray Lankford	.05
20	Tim Salmon	.05
21	Steve Hosey	.05
22	Charles Nagy	.05
23	Dave Fleming	.05
24	Reggie Sanders	.05
25	Sam Millitello	.05
26	Eric Karros	.05
27	Ryan Klesko	.05
28	Dean Palmer	.05
29	Ivan Rodriguez	.75
30	Sterling Hitchcock	.05

Tribute

These Hall of Famers each have five-card sets devoted to their career achievements. Each card commemorates a career milestone. Cards were random inserts in Series 2, about one every 24 packs. Fronts have a gold-foil stamped "Tribute" vertically at right.

		NM/M
Complete Set (10):		10.00
George Brett Card (1-5):		1.00
Nolan Ryan Card (6-10):		1.50
1	Kansas City Royalty (George Brett)	1.00
2	The Chase for .400 (George Brett)	1.00
3	Pine Tar Pandemonium - "The Bat"	1.00
4	MVP and a World Series, Too (George Brett)	1.00
5	3,000 or Bust (George Brett)	1.00
6	The Rookie (Nolan Ryan)	1.50
7	Angel of No Mercy (Nolan Ryan)	1.50
8	Astronomical Success (Nolan Ryan)	1.50
9	5,000 Ks (Nolan Ryan)	1.50
10	No-Hitter No. 7 (Nolan Ryan)	1.50

Cooperstown

This boxed set features "today's superstar players bound to become Cooperstown inductees." In standard 2-1/2" x 3-1/2" format, the cards feature on both front and back an action photo which is borderless at the top and sides. At bottom-center of each photo is a half-moon green and gold-foil "Cooperstown Card" logo. On front, the player's name is gold-foil stamped in a black bar at bottom. On back is a black box, again with the player's name in gold-foil, plus a few stats justifying the player's Hall of Fame potential. Pinnacle's trademark optical-variable anti-counterfeiting device is at the bottom. Cards are UV coated on both sides. A special edition of 1,000 of the Cooperstown sets was produced in Pinnacle's "Dufex" technology and distributed at the 1993 SCAI trade show. Other than being printed on foil, the cards are identical to the regular-issue Cooperstown cards. Each of the Pinnacle Cooperstown cards can also be found in a sample version which differs from the issued cards principally in the appearance on back of a large "PROMO" overprint.

		NM/M
Complete Set (30):		7.50
Common Player:		.25
Dufex:		25X
Promo:		30X
1	Nolan Ryan	2.00
2	George Brett	.85
3	Robin Yount	.65
4	Carlton Fisk	.65
5	Dale Murphy	.35
6	Dennis Eckersley	.50
7	Rickey Henderson	.65
8	Ryne Sandberg	.75
9	Ozzie Smith	.75
10	Dave Winfield	.65
11	Andre Dawson	.35
12	Kirby Puckett	.75
13	Wade Boggs	.75
14	Don Mattingly	.85
15	Barry Bonds	2.00
16	Will Clark	.25
17	Cal Ripken, Jr.	2.00
18	Roger Clemens	.85
19	Dwight Gooden	.25
20	Tony Gwynn	.75
21	Joe Carter	.25
22	Ken Griffey Jr.	1.00
23	Paul Molitor	.60
24	Frank Thomas	.60
25	Juan Gonzalez	.35
26	Barry Larkin	.25
27	Eddie Murray	.60
28	Cecil Fielder	.25
29	Roberto Alomar	.35
30	Mark McGwire	1.50

Joe DiMaggio

Sold in a special tin box in a limited edition of 200,000 sets, this set highlights the career of "The Yankee Clipper." Fronts feature black-and-white or colorized photos with a black border and gold-foil highlights. Backs feature a woodgrain center panel with a portion of DiMaggio's career recounted. The boxed set includes an "Authenticator" lens through which the name "DiMaggio" can be seen when placed over the optical-variable printing on back. Genuine DiMaggio autographed cards were randomly inserted into 9,000 sets.

		NM/M
Complete Set (30):		7.50
Common Card:		.35
1	An American Hero	.50
2	San Francisco Seals	.35
3	Seals Farewell	.35
4	First Game	.35
5	The Rookie	.35
6	Rookie All-Star (With Dizzy Dean.)	.45
7	Fan Favorite	.35
8	Teammates' Awe	.35
9	Classic Swing	.35
10	Joltin' Power	.35
11	Rapid Robert vs. Joltin' Joe (With Bob Feller.)	.45
12	The Complete Hitter	.35
13	Makin' It Look Easy	.35
14	Extra Swings	.35
15	The Run Producer	.35
16	Quiet Confidence	.35
17	Sticks 'N' Bones	.35
18	A Link to the Past (With Lou Gehrig.)	.50
19	The Center of Attention	.35
20	The DiMaggio Mystique	.35
21	Joe McCarthy (With Joe McCarthy.)	.35
22	World War II	.35
23	Fearless Baserunner	.35
24	The Summer of '41	.35
25	Career Statistics	.50
26	No. 45	.35
27	Chasing Ruth	.35
28	The Final Season	.35
29	Retirement	.35
30	Baseball's Greatest Living Player	.50

Joe DiMaggio Autographs

Eighteen hundred of each of five different insert cards were personally autographed by the Yankee Clipper and randomly inserted into the Joe DiMaggio box set tins at a rate of about one autograph per 22 sets. Fronts of the 2-1/8" x 3-1/2" cards have sepia artwork of DiMaggio at a particular stage of his career. In the wide white border at bottom is the autograph. Backs have a photo, part of a narrative about DiMaggio's career, and a serial number. A certificate of authenticity accompanies each signed card.

		NM/M
Complete Set (5):		850.00
1-5	Joe DiMaggio	175.00

Home Run Club

Pinnacle released this boxed set produced in a special metallic-foil printing process called "Dufex." Limited to 200,000 numbered sets, the cards are UV-coated and gold-foil stamped. The checklist includes 28 American League and 20 National League sluggers.

		NM/M
Complete Set (48):		6.00
Common Player:		.10
1	Juan Gonzalez	.40
2	Fred McGriff	.10
3	Cecil Fielder	.10
4	Barry Bonds	1.50
5	Albert Belle	.10
6	Gary Sheffield	.25
7	Joe Carter	.10
8	Mark McGwire	1.25
9	Darren Daulton	.10
10	Jose Canseco	.50
11	Dave Hollins	.10
12	Ryne Sandberg	.85
13	Ken Griffey Jr.	1.00
14	Larry Walker	.10
15	Rob Deer	.10
16	Andre Dawson	.25
17	Frank Thomas	.75
18	Mickey Tettleton	.10
19	Charlie Hayes	.10
20	Ron Gant	.10
21	Rickey Henderson	.75
22	Matt Williams	.10
23	Kevin Mitchell	.10
24	Robin Ventura	.10
25	Dean Palmer	.10
26	Mike Piazza	1.00
27	J.T. Snow	.10
28	Jeff Bagwell	.75
29	John Olerud	.10
30	Greg Vaughn	.10
31	Dave Justice	.10

32 Dave Winfield .75
33 Danny Tartabull .10
34 Eric Anthony .10
35 Eddie Murray .75
36 Jay Buhner .10
37 Derek Bell .10
38 Will Clark .10
39 Carlos Baerga .10
40 Mo Vaughn .10
41 Bobby Bonilla .10
42 Tim Salmon .10
43 Bo Jackson .10
44 Howard Johnson .10
45 Kent Hrbek .10
46 Ruben Sierra .10
47 Cal Ripken, Jr. 1.50
48 Travis Fryman .10

1994 Pinnacle Samples

Basically the same as the issued versions, these promo cards differ in the presence of a diagonal "SAMPLE" overprint on front and back. Cello-wrapped packs of hobby and retail versions were produced, with appropriate header cards.

NM/M
Complete Set (12): 10.00
Common Player: .50
2 Carlos Baerga .50
3 Sammy Sosa 2.00
5 John Olerud .75
7 Moises Alou .50
8 Steve Avery .50
10 Cecil Fielder .50
11 Greg Maddux 2.00
269 Jeff Granger .50
--- Jeff Granger (Museum) (Blank-back.) 1.00
--- Jeff Granger (Museum) (Black print on back.) 1.00
TR1 Paul Molitor (Tribute) 1.50
--- Hobby version header card .05
--- Retail version header card .05

1994 Pinnacle

Pinnacle's 1994 mid-priced brand features full bleed photos, gold-foil graphics and UV coating. On front, player and team names appear in a shield-and-bar motif in the lower-left corner. On horizontal backs, the front photo is reproduced as a subdued background photo, over which are printed recent stats and a few biographical details. A different player photo is featured at left, while the brand's optical-variable anti-counterfeiting device is at bottom center. Subsets include major award winners, Rookie Prospects and Draft Picks which are appropriately noted with gold-foil lettering on front. The issue was produced in two series of 270 cards each.

NM/M
Complete Set (540): 15.00
Common Player: .05
Artist's Proofs: 20X
Museums: 6X
Series 1 or 2 Pack (14): .75
Series 1 or 2 Box (24): 12.50
1 Frank Thomas .65
2 Carlos Baerga .05
3 Sammy Sosa .75
4 Tony Gwynn .75
5 John Olerud .05
6 Ryne Sandberg .75
7 Moises Alou .05
8 Steve Avery .05
9 Tim Salmon .05
10 Cecil Fielder .05
11 Greg Maddux .75
12 Barry Larkin .05
13 Mike Devereaux .05
14 Charlie Hayes .05
15 Albert Belle .05
16 Andy Van Slyke .05
17 Mo Vaughn .05
18 Brian McRae .05
19 Cal Eldred .05
20 Craig Biggio .05
21 Kirby Puckett .75
22 Derek Bell .05
23 Don Mattingly .85
24 John Burkett .05
25 Roger Clemens .85
26 Barry Bonds 2.00
27 Paul Molitor .65
28 Mike Piazza 1.00
29 Robin Ventura .05
30 Jeff Conine .05
31 Wade Boggs .75
32 Dennis Eckersley .50
33 Bobby Bonilla .05
34 Len Dykstra .05
35 Manny Alexander .05
36 Ray Lankford .05
37 Greg Vaughn .05
38 Chuck Finley .05
39 Todd Benzinger .05
40 Dave Justice .05
41 Rob Dibble .05
42 Tom Henke .05
43 David Nied .05
44 Sandy Alomar Jr. .05
45 Pete Harnisch .05
46 Jeff Russell .05
47 Terry Mulholland .05
48 Kevin Appier .05
49 Randy Tomlin .05
50 Cal Ripken, Jr. 2.00
51 Andy Benes .05
52 Jimmy Key .05
53 Kirt Manwaring .05
54 Kevin Tapani .05
55 Jose Guzman .05
56 Todd Stottlemyre .05
57 Jack McDowell .05
58 Orel Hershiser .05
59 Chris Hammond .05
60 Chris Nabholz .05
61 Ruben Sierra .05
62 Dwight Gooden .05
63 John Kruk .05
64 Omar Vizquel .05
65 Tim Naehring .05
66 Dwight Smith .05
67 Mickey Tettleton .05
68 J.T. Snow .05
69 Greg McMichael .05
70 Kevin Mitchell .05
71 Kevin Brown .05
72 Scott Cooper .05
73 Jim Thome .60
74 Joe Girardi .05
75 Eric Anthony .05
76 Orlando Merced .05
77 Felix Jose .05
78 Tommy Greene .05
79 Bernard Gilkey .05
80 Phil Plantier .05
81 Danny Tartabull .05
82 Trevor Wilson .05
83 Chuck Knoblauch .05
84 Rick Wilkins .05
85 Devon White .05
86 Lance Johnson .05
87 Eric Karros .05
88 Gary Sheffield .35
89 Wil Cordero .05
90 Ron Darling .05
91 Darren Daulton .05
92 Joe Orsulak .05
93 Steve Cooke .05
94 Darryl Hamilton .05
95 Aaron Sele .05
96 John Doherty .05
97 Gary DiSarcina .05
98 Jeff Blauser .05
99 John Smiley .05
100 Ken Griffey Jr. 1.00
101 Dean Palmer .05
102 Felix Fermin .05
103 Jerald Clark .05
104 Doug Drabek .05
105 Curt Schilling .30
106 Jeff Montgomery .05
107 Rene Arocha .05
108 Carlos Garcia .05
109 Wally Whitehurst .05
110 Jim Abbott .05
111 Royce Clayton .05
112 Chris Hoiles .05
113 Mike Morgan .05
114 Joe Magrane .05
115 Tom Candiotti .05
116 Ron Karkovice .05
117 Ryan Bowen .05
118 Rod Beck .05
119 John Wetteland .05
120 Terry Steinbach .05
121 Dave Hollins .05
122 Jeff Kent .05
123 Ricky Bones .05
124 Brian Jordan .05
125 Chad Kreuter .05
126 John Valentin .05
127 Billy Hathaway .05
128 Wilson Alvarez .05
129 Tino Martinez .05
130 Rodney Bolton .05
131 David Segui .05
132 Wayne Kirby .05
133 Eric Young .05
134 Scott Servais .05
135 Scott Radinsky .05
136 Bret Barberie .05
137 John Roper .05
138 Ricky Gutierrez .05
139 Bernie Williams .05
140 Bud Black .05
141 Jose Vizcaino .05
142 Gerald Williams .05
143 Duane Ward .05
144 Danny Jackson .05
145 Allen Watson .05
146 Scott Fletcher .05
147 Delino DeShields .05
148 Shane Mack .05
149 Jim Eisenreich .05
150 Troy Neel .05
151 Jay Bell .05
152 B.J. Surhoff .05
153 Mark Whiten .05
154 Mike Henneman .05
155 Todd Hundley .05
156 Greg Myers .05
157 Ryan Klesko .05
158 Dave Fleming .05
159 Mickey Morandini .05
160 Blas Minor .05
161 Reggie Jefferson .05
162 David Hulse .05
163 Greg Swindell .05
164 Roberto Hernandez .05
165 Brady Anderson .05
166 Jack Armstrong .05
167 Phil Clark .05
168 Melido Perez .05
169 Darren Lewis .05
170 Sam Horn .05
171 Mike Harkey .05
172 Juan Guzman .05
173 Bob Natal .05
174 Deion Sanders .05
175 Carlos Quintana .05
176 Mel Rojas .05
177 Willie Banks .05
178 Ben Rivera .05
179 Kenny Lofton .05
180 Leo Gomez .05
181 Roberto Mejia .05
182 Mike Perez .05
183 Travis Fryman .05
184 Ben McDonald .05
185 Steve Frey .05
186 Kevin Young .05
187 Dave Magadan .05
188 Bobby Munoz .05
189 Pat Rapp .05
190 Jose Offerman .05
191 Vinny Castilla .05
192 Ivan Calderon .05
193 Ken Caminiti .05
194 Benji Gil .05
195 Chuck Carr .05
196 Derrick May .05
197 Pat Kelly .05
198 Jeff Brantley .05
199 Jose Lind .05
200 Steve Buechele .05
201 Wes Chamberlain .05
202 Eduardo Perez .05
203 Bret Saberhagen .05
204 Gregg Jefferies .05
205 Darrin Fletcher .05
206 Kent Hrbek .05
207 Kim Batiste .05
208 Jeff King .05
209 Donovan Osborne .05
210 Dave Nilsson .05
211 Al Martin .05
212 Mike Moore .05
213 Sterling Hitchcock .05
214 Geronimo Pena .05
215 Kevin Higgins .05
216 Norm Charlton .05
217 Don Slaught .05
218 Mitch Williams .05
219 Derek Lilliquist .05
220 Armando Reynoso .05
221 Kenny Rogers .05
222 Doug Jones .05
223 Luis Aquino .05
224 Mike Oquist .05
225 Darryl Scott .05
226 Kurt Abbott .05
227 Andy Tomberlin .05
228 Norberto Martin .05
229 Pedro Castellano .05
230 Curtis Pride **RC** .05
231 Jeff McNeely .05
232 Scott Lydy .05
233 Darren Oliver .05
234 Danny Bautista .05
235 Butch Huskey .05
236 Chipper Jones .75
237 Eddie Zambrano .05
238 Jean Domingo .05
239 Javier Lopez .05
240 Nigel Wilson .05
241 Drew Denson **RC** .05
242 Raul Mondesi .05
243 Luis Ortiz .05
244 Manny Ramirez .65
245 Greg Blosser .05
246 Rondell White .05
247 Steve Karsay .05
248 Scott Stahoviak .05
249 Jose Valentin .05
250 Marc Newfield .05
251 Keith Kessinger .05
252 Carl Everett .05
253 John O'Donoghue .05
254 Turk Wendell .05
255 Scott Ruffcorn .05
256 Tony Tarasco .05
257 Andy Cook .05
258 Matt Mieske .05
259 Luis Lopez .05
260 Ramon Caraballo .05
261 Salomon Torres .05
262 Brooks Kieschnick **RC** .05
263 Daron Kirkreit **RC** .05
264 Bill Wagner **RC** .10
265 Matt Drews **RC** .05
266 Scott Christman .05
267 Torii Hunter **RC** 1.00
268 Jamey Wright **RC** .05
269 Jeff Granger .05
270 Trot Nixon **RC** 1.00
271 Randy Myers .05
272 Trevor Hoffman .05
273 Bob Wickman .05
274 Willie McGee .05
275 Hipolito Pichardo .05
276 Bobby Witt .05
277 Gregg Olson .05
278 Randy Johnson .65
279 Robb Nen .05
280 Paul O'Neill .05
281 Lou Whitaker .05
282 Chad Curtis .05
283 Doug Henry .05
284 Tom Glavine .30
285 Mike Greenwell .05
286 Roberto Kelly .05
287 Roberto Alomar .15
288 Charlie Hough .05
289 Alex Fernandez .05
290 Jeff Bagwell .65
291 Wally Joyner .05
292 Andujar Cedeno .05
293 Rick Aguilera .05
294 Darryl Strawberry .05
295 Mike Mussina .35
296 Jeff Gardner .05
297 Chris Gwynn .05
298 Matt Williams .05
299 Brent Gates .05
300 Mark McGwire 1.50
301 Jim Deshaies .05
302 Edgar Martinez .05
303 Danny Darwin .05
304 Pat Meares .05
305 Benito Santiago .05
306 Jose Canseco .40
307 Jim Gott .05
308 Paul Sorrento .05
309 Scott Kamieniecki .05
310 Larry Walker .05
311 Mark Langston .05
312 John Jaha .05
313 Stan Javier .05
314 Hal Morris .05
315 Robby Thompson .05
316 Pat Hentgen .05
317 Tom Gordon .05
318 Joey Cora .05
319 Luis Alicea .05
320 Andre Dawson .25
321 Darryl Kile .05
322 Jose Rijo .05
323 Luis Gonzalez .05
324 Billy Ashley .05
325 David Cone .05
326 Bill Swift .05
327 Phil Hiatt .05
328 Craig Paquette .05
329 Bob Welch .05
330 Tony Phillips .05
331 Archi Cianfrocco .05
332 Dave Winfield .65
333 David McCarty .05
334 Al Leiter .05
335 Tom Browning .05
336 Mark Grace .05
337 Jose Mesa .05
338 Mike Stanley .05
339 Roger McDowell .05
340 Damion Easley .05
341 Angel Miranda .05
342 John Smoltz .05
343 Jay Buhner .05
344 Bryan Harvey .05
345 Joe Carter .05
346 Dante Bichette .05
347 Jason Bere .05
348 Frank Viola .05
349 Ivan Rodriguez .60
350 Juan Gonzalez .35
351 Steve Finley .05
352 Mike Felder .05
353 Ramon Martinez .05
354 Greg Gagne .05
355 Ken Hill .05
356 Pedro Munoz .05
357 Todd Van Poppel .05
358 Marquis Grissom .05
359 Milt Cuyler .05
360 Reggie Sanders .05
361 Scott Erickson .05
362 Billy Hatcher .05
363 Gene Harris .05
364 Rene Gonzales .05
365 Kevin Rogers .05
366 Eric Plunk .05
367 Todd Zeile .05
368 John Franco .05
369 Brett Butler .05
370 Bill Spiers .05
371 Terry Pendleton .05
372 Chris Bosio .05
373 Orestes Destrade .05
374 Dave Stewart .05
375 Darren Holmes .05
376 Doug Strange .05
377 Brian Turang .05
378 Carl Willis .05
379 Mark McLemore .05
380 Bobby Jones .05
381 Scott Sanders .05
382 Kirk Rueter .05
383 Randy Velarde .05
384 Fred McGriff .05
385 Charles Nagy .05
386 Rich Amaral .05
387 Geronimo Berroa .05
388 Eric Davis .05
389 Ozzie Smith .75
390 Alex Arias .05
391 Brad Ausmus .05
392 Cliff Floyd .05
393 Roger Salkeld .05
394 Jim Edmonds .05
395 Jeromy Burnitz .05
396 Dave Staton .05
397 Rob Butler .05
398 Marcos Armas .05
399 Darrell Whitmore .05
400 Ryan Thompson .05
401 Ross Powell **RC** .05
402 Joe Oliver .05
403 Paul Carey .05
404 Bob Hamelin .05
405 Chris Turner .05
406 Nate Minchey .05
407 Lonnie Maclin **RC** .05
408 Harold Baines .05
409 Brian Williams .05
410 Johnny Ruffin .05
411 Julian Tavarez **RC** .05
412 Mark Hutton .05
413 Carlos Delgado .50
414 Chris Gomez .05
415 Mike Hampton .05
416 Alex Diaz .05
417 Jeffrey Hammonds .05
418 Jayhawk Owens .05
419 J.R. Phillips .05
420 Cory Bailey **RC** .05
421 Denny Hocking .05
422 Jon Shave .05
423 Damon Buford .05
424 Troy O'Leary .05
425 Tripp Cromer .05
426 Albie Lopez .05
427 Tony Fernandez .05
428 Ozzie Guillen .05
429 Alan Trammell .05
430 John Wasdin **RC** .05
431 Marc Valdes .05
432 Brian Anderson **RC** .20
433 Matt Brunson **RC** .05
434 Wayne Gomes **RC** .05
435 Jay Powell **RC** .05
436 Kirk Presley **RC** .05
437 Jon Ratliff **RC** .05
438 Derrek Lee **RC** 2.00
439 Tom Pagnozzi .05
440 Kent Mercker .05
441 Phil Leftwich **RC** .05
442 Jamie Moyer .05
443 John Flaherty .05
444 Mark Wohlers .05
445 Jose Bautista .05
446 Andres Galarraga .05
447 Mark Lemke .05
448 Tim Wakefield .05
449 Pat Listach .05
450 Rickey Henderson .65
451 Mike Gallego .05
452 Bob Tewksbury .05
453 Kirk Gibson .05
454 Pedro Astacio .05
455 Mike Lansing .05
456 Sean Berry .05
457 Bob Walk .05
458 Chili Davis .05
459 Ed Sprague .05
460 Kevin Stocker .05
461 Mike Stanton .05
462 Tim Raines .05
463 Mike Bordick .05
464 David Wells .05
465 Tim Laker .05
466 Cory Snyder .05
467 Alex Cole .05
468 Pete Incaviglia .05
469 Roger Pavlik .05
470 Greg W. Harris .05
471 Xavier Hernandez .05
472 Erik Hanson .05
473 Jesse Orosco .05
474 Greg Colbrunn .05
475 Harold Reynolds .05
476 Greg Harris .05
477 Pat Borders .05
478 Melvin Nieves .05
479 Mariano Duncan .05
480 Greg Hibbard .05
481 Tim Pugh .05
482 Bobby Ayala .05
483 Sid Fernandez .05
484 Tim Wallach .05
485 Randy Milligan .05
486 Walt Weiss .05
487 Matt Walbeck .05
488 Mike Macfarlane .05
489 Jerry Browne .05
490 Chris Sabo .05
491 Tim Belcher .05
492 Spike Owen .05
493 Rafael Palmeiro .60
494 Brian Harper .05
495 Eddie Murray .65
496 Ellis Burks .05
497 Karl Rhodes .05
498 Otis Nixon .05
499 Lee Smith .05
500 Bip Roberts .05
501 Pedro Martinez .65
502 Brian L. Hunter .05
503 Tyler Green .05
504 Bruce Hurst .05
505 Alex Gonzalez .05
506 Mark Portugal .05
507 Bob Ojeda .05
508 Dave Henderson .05
509 Bo Jackson .10
510 Bret Boone .05
511 Mark Eichhorn .05
512 Luis Polonia .05
513 Will Clark .05
514 Dave Valle .05
515 Dan Wilson .05
516 Dennis Martinez .05
517 Jim Leyritz .05
518 Howard Johnson .05
519 Jody Reed .05
520 Julio Franco .05
521 Jeff Reardon .05
522 Willie Greene .05
523 Shawon Dunston .05
524 Keith Mitchell .05
525 Rick Helling .05
526 Mark Kiefer .05
527 Chan Ho Park **RC** .75
528 Tony Longmire .05
529 Rich Becker .05
530 Tim Hyers .05
531 Darrin Jackson .05
532 Jack Morris .05
533 Rick White .05
534 Mike Kelly .05
535 James Mouton .05
536 Steve Trachsel .05
537 Tony Eusebio .05
538 Kelly Stinnett .05
539 Paul Spoljaric .05
540 Darren Dreifort .05

Artist's Proof

A specially designated version of the regular Pinnacle set, described as the first day's production of the first 1,000 of each card, was issued as a random pack insert. Cards feature a small gold-foil "Artist's Proof" rectangle embossed above the player/team name shield on front. In all other respects the cards are identical to the regular-issue versions.

NM/M
Complete Set (540): 250.00

Common Player:	1.50
Stars/Rookies:	20X

Museum Collection

Each card in the 1994 Pinnacle set was produced in a parallel "Museum Collection" version. The inserts were produced utilizing the company's Dufex foil-printing technology on front, with rays emanating from the Pinnacle logo. Backs are identical to the regular-issue version except for the substitution of a "1994 Museum Collection" logo for the optical-variable anti-counterfeiting bar at bottom-center. Museums were random package inserts, appearing at the rate of about once per four packs.

	NM/M
Complete Set (540):	225.00
Common Player:	1.00
Stars/Rookies:	6X

Rookie Team Pinnacle

The popular Rookie Team Pinnacle insert card tradition continued in 1994 with a series of nine "two-headed" cards featuring the top prospect from each league at each position. The cards again feature the ultra-realistic artwork of Chris Greco. Each side is enhanced with gold-foil presentations of the player's name, the Pinnacle logo and the Rookie Team Pinnacle logo. The inserts were packaged, on average, one per 90 packs of hobby foil only.

		NM/M
Complete Set (9):		12.00
Common Player:		.75
1	Carlos Delgado, Javier Lopez	2.50
2	Bob Hamelin, J.R. Phillips	.75
3	Jon Shave, Keith Kessinger	.75
4	Butch Huskey, Luis Ortiz	.75
5	Chipper Jones, Kurt Abbott	5.00
6	Rondell White, Manny Ramirez	3.00
7	Cliff Floyd, Jeffrey Hammonds	.75
8	Marc Newfield, Nigel Wilson	.75
9	Salomon Torres, Mark Hutton	.75

Run Creators

This insert set, exclusive to Pinnacle jumbo packaging, features the top 44 performers

of the previous season in the arcane statistic of "runs created." Fronts have an action photo on which the stadium background has been muted in soft-focus red or blue. The player's last name appears at right in gold foil; the logo, "The Run Creators" is in one of the lower corners. Backs are printed in teal with a color team logo at center, beneath the stats that earned the player's inclusion in the series. The player's runs created are in gold foil above the write-up. Cards are numbered with an "RC" prefix.

		NM/M
Complete Set (44):		17.50
Common Player:		.25
1	John Olerud	.25
2	Frank Thomas	1.00
3	Ken Griffey Jr.	3.00
4	Paul Molitor	1.00
5	Rafael Palmeiro	.75
6	Roberto Alomar	.35
7	Juan Gonzalez	.50
8	Albert Belle	.25
9	Travis Fryman	.25
10	Rickey Henderson	1.00
11	Tony Phillips	.25
12	Mo Vaughn	.25
13	Tim Salmon	.25
14	Kenny Lofton	.25
15	Carlos Baerga	.25
16	Greg Vaughn	.25
17	Jay Buhner	.25
18	Chris Hoiles	.25
19	Mickey Tettleton	.25
20	Kirby Puckett	1.50
21	Danny Tartabull	.25
22	Devon White	.25
23	Barry Bonds	4.00
24	Lenny Dykstra	.25
25	John Kruk	.25
26	Fred McGriff	.25
27	Gregg Jefferies	.25
28	Mike Piazza	3.00
29	Jeff Blauser	.25
30	Andres Galarraga	.25
31	Darren Daulton	.25
32	Dave Justice	.25
33	Craig Biggio	.25
34	Mark Grace	.25
35	Tony Gwynn	1.50
36	Jeff Bagwell	1.00
37	Jay Bell	.25
38	Marquis Grissom	.25
39	Matt Williams	.25
40	Charlie Hayes	.25
41	Dante Bichette	.25
42	Bernard Gilkey	.25
43	Brett Butler	.25
44	Rick Wilkins	.25

Team Pinnacle

The double-sided Team Pinnacle insert set features 18 of the top players in the game. They were inserted into Series 2 at a rate of one every 90 packs.

		NM/M
Complete Set (9):		35.00
Common Player:		1.50
1	Jeff Bagwell, Frank Thomas	4.00
2	Carlos Baerga, Robby Thompson	1.50
3	Matt Williams, Dean Palmer	1.50
4	Cal Ripken, Jr., Jay Bell	12.00
5	Ivan Rodriguez, Mike Piazza	6.00
6	Len Dykstra, Ken Griffey Jr.	8.00
7	Juan Gonzalez, Barry Bonds	10.00
8	Tim Salmon, Dave Justice	1.50
9	Greg Maddux, Jack McDowell	8.00

Tribute

A hobby-only insert set, found approximately one per 18 foil packs, this nine-card series honors players who reached significant season or career milestones or otherwise had special achievements in 1993. Fronts feature full-bleed action photos. At left is a black strip with "TRIBUTE" in gold foil. A colored strip at bottom has the player name in gold foil and a short description of why he is being feted beneath. The Pinnacle logo is in gold foil at top. The same gold-foil enhancements are found on back, along with a portrait photo. In a black box at bottom are details of the tribute. The Pinnacle optical-variable anti-counterfeiting device is at bottom center. Card numbers are prefixed with "TR."

		NM/M
Complete Set (18):		15.00
Common Player:		.25
1	Paul Molitor	1.00
2	Jim Abbott	.25
3	Dave Winfield	1.00
4	Bo Jackson	.35
5	Dave Justice	.25
6	Len Dykstra	.25
7	Mike Piazza	2.50
8	Barry Bonds	4.50
9	Randy Johnson	1.00
10	Ozzie Smith	1.50
11	Mark Whiten	.25
12	Greg Maddux	1.50
13	Cal Ripken, Jr.	4.50
14	Frank Thomas	1.00
15	Juan Gonzalez	.45
16	Roberto Alomar	.25
17	Ken Griffey Jr.	3.00
18	Lee Smith	.25

New Generation

Baseball's hottest rookies and second-year players were featured in this boxed set. Cards are typical Pinnacle quality with full-bleed action photos, UV coating and gold-foil stamping on front and back. A total of 100,000 sets was produced, with a suggested retail price of $9.95.

		NM/M
Complete Set (25):		5.00
Common Player:		.25
1	Tim Salmon	.25
2	Mike Piazza	2.00
3	Jason Bere	.25
4	Jeffrey Hammonds	.25
5	Aaron Sele	.25
6	Salomon Torres	.25
7	Wil Cordero	.25
8	Allen Watson	.25
9	J.T. Snow	.25
10	Cliff Floyd	.25
10a	Cliff Floyd (Overprinted "SAMPLE" card.)	.50
11	Jeff McNeely	.25
12	Butch Huskey	.25
13	J.R. Phillips	.25
14	Bobby Jones	.25
15	Javier Lopez	.25
16	Scott Ruffcorn	.25
17	Manny Ramirez	1.25
18	Carlos Delgado	1.00
19	Rondell White	.25
20	Chipper Jones	1.50
21	Billy Ashley	.25
22	Nigel Wilson	.25
23	Jeromy Burnitz	.25
24	Danny Bautista	.25
25	Darrell Whitmore	.25

Power Surge

The major leagues' heaviest hitters are featured in this boxed set. Cards are typical Pinnacle quality with gold-foil stamping, on front, UV coating on both sides and high-tech graphics. Fronts feature game-action photos while backs have smaller portrait and action photos on a marbled background, along with 1993 and career stats and a description of the player's power potential. Cards are numbered with a "PS" prefix. A total of 100,000 sets was produced.

		NM/M
Complete Set (25):		4.00
Common Player:		.25
1	Dave Justice	.25
2	Chris Hoiles	.25
3	Mo Vaughn	.25
4	Tim Salmon	.25
5	J.T. Snow	.25
6	Frank Thomas	.65
7	Sammy Sosa	.75
8	Rick Wilkins	.25
9	Robin Ventura	.25
10	Reggie Sanders	.25
11	Albert Belle	.25
12	Carlos Baerga	.25
12a	Carlos Baerga (Overprinted "SAMPLE" card.)	.50
13	Manny Ramirez	.65
14	Travis Fryman	.25
15	Gary Sheffield	.35
16	Jeff Bagwell	.65
17	Mike Piazza	1.00
18	Eric Karros	.25
19	Cliff Floyd	.25
20	Mark Whiten	.25
21	Phil Plantier	.25
22	Derek Bell	.25
23	Ken Griffey Jr.	1.00
24	Juan Gonzalez	.35
25	Dean Palmer	.25

The Naturals

The Naturals boxed set puts a game-action photo against a textured-foil background. Backs picture the player on a background of na-

ture photography, including lightning, blue skies and clouds. Pinnacle produced 100,000 sets, which come in a numbered, sealed box with a certificate of authenticity.

		NM/M
Complete Set (25):		6.00
Common Player:		.15
1	Frank Thomas	.50
2	Barry Bonds	1.50
3	Ken Griffey Jr.	1.00
4	Juan Gonzalez	.25
5	Dave Justice	.15
6	Albert Belle	.15
7	Kenny Lofton	.15
8	Roberto Alomar	.35
9	Tim Salmon	.15
10	Randy Johnson	.50
11	Kirby Puckett	.65
12	Tony Gwynn	.65
13	Fred McGriff	.15
14	Ryne Sandberg	.65
15	Greg Maddux	.65
16	Matt Williams	.15
17	Lenny Dykstra	.15
18	Gary Sheffield	.35
18a	Gary Sheffield (Overprinted "SAMPLE" card.)	.50
19	Mike Piazza	1.00
20	Dean Palmer	.15
21	Travis Fryman	.15
22	Carlos Baerga	.15
23	Cal Ripken, Jr.	1.50
24	John Olerud	.15
25	Roger Clemens	.75

1995 Pinnacle Series 1 Samples

This eight-card cello-wrapped sample set was sent to dealers to preview the 1995 Pinnacle Series 1 cards. The cards are identical to regular-issue Pinnacle cards except they carry a white diagonal "SAMPLE" notation on front and back.

		NM/M
Complete Set (9):		6.00
Common Player:		.50
16	Mickey Morandini	.50
22US	Wil Cordero (Upstart) (Card not included in most packs.)	2.00
119	Gary Sheffield	1.00
122	Ivan Rodriguez	1.50
132	Alex Rodriguez (Rookie)	3.00
208	Bo Jackson	.75
223	Jose Rijo	.50
224	Ryan Klesko	.50
----	Header card	.05

1995 Pinnacle

The 1995 Pinnacle set was produced in two series of 225 base cards each, plus inserts. Fronts have borderless photos with a large embossed gold foil "wave" at bottom containing the player's last

name and team logo. Horizontal backs have a portrait photo at left, an action photo at right and a few sentences about the player at center. Stats at the bottom offer previous year, career and career-best numbers. Subsets with the base cards include rookie specials in both Series 1 and 2 have a design featuring a green stripe at one side or bottom with the player's name in gold and a special round gold-foil logo. A similar design, with red stripes, is used for Series 1 cards featuring Draft Picks. In Series 2, a 30-card Swing Men subset has a blue vortex background design and special gold-foil identifier. Basic pack configurations offered 12-card ($2.49) and 15-card ($2.99) counts in both retail and hobby versions, each with some unique inserts.

		NM/M
Complete Set (450):		15.00
Common Player:		.10
Artist's Proofs:		10X
Museum Collection:		4X
Hobby Pack (12):		1.00
Hobby Wax Box (24):		15.00
Retail Pack (12):		1.00
Retail Wax Box (36):		20.00
1	Jeff Bagwell	.75
2	Roger Clemens	1.25
3	Mark Whiten	.10
4	Shawon Dunston	.10
5	Bobby Bonilla	.10
6	Kevin Tapani	.10
7	Eric Karros	.10
8	Cliff Floyd	.10
9	Pat Kelly	.10
10	Jeffrey Hammonds	.10
11	Jeff Conine	.10
12	Fred McGriff	.10
13	Chris Bosio	.10
14	Mike Mussina	.40
15	Danny Bautista	.10
16	Mickey Morandini	.10
17	Chuck Finley	.10
18	Jim Thome	.65
19	Luis Ortiz	.10
20	Walt Weiss	.10
21	Don Mattingly	1.25
22	Bob Hamelin	.10
23	Melido Perez	.10
24	Kevin Mitchell	.10
25	John Smoltz	.10
26	Hector Carrasco	.10
27	Pat Hentgen	.10
28	Derrick May	.10
29	Mike Kingery	.10
30	Chuck Carr	.10
31	Billy Ashley	.10
32	Todd Hundley	.10
33	Luis Gonzalez	.10
34	Marquis Grissom	.10
35	Jeff King	.10
36	Eddie Williams	.10
37	Tom Pagnozzi	.10
38	Chris Hoiles	.10
39	Sandy Alomar	.10
40	Mike Greenwell	.10
41	Lance Johnson	.10
42	Junior Felix	.10
43	Felix Jose	.10
44	Scott Leius	.10
45	Ruben Sierra	.10
46	Kevin Seitzer	.10
47	Wade Boggs	1.00
48	Reggie Jefferson	.10
49	Jose Canseco	.40
50	Dave Justice	.10
51	John Smiley	.10
52	Joe Carter	.10
53	Rick Wilkins	.10
54	Ellis Burks	.10
55	Dave Weathers	.10
56	Pedro Astacio	.10
57	Ryan Thompson	.10
58	James Mouton	.10

59	Mel Rojas	.10
60	Orlando Merced	.10
61	Matt Williams	.10
62	Bernard Gilkey	.10
63	J.R. Phillips	.10
64	Lee Smith	.10
65	Jim Edmonds	.10
66	Darrin Jackson	.10
67	Scott Cooper	.10
68	Ron Karkovice	.10
69	Chris Gomez	.10
70	Kevin Appier	.10
71	Bobby Jones	.10
72	Doug Drabek	.10
73	Matt Mieske	.10
74	Sterling Hitchcock	.10
75	John Valentin	.10
76	Reggie Sanders	.10
77	Wally Joyner	.10
78	Turk Wendell	.10
79	Wendell Hayes	.10
80	Bret Barberie	.10
81	Troy Neel	.10
82	Ken Caminiti	.10
83	Milt Thompson	.10
84	Paul Sorrento	.10
85	Trevor Hoffman	.10
86	Jay Bell	.10
87	Mark Portugal	.10
88	Sid Fernandez	.10
89	Charles Nagy	.10
90	Jeff Montgomery	.10
91	Chuck Knoblauch	.10
92	Jeff Frye	.10
93	Tony Gwynn	1.00
94	John Olerud	.10
95	David Nied	.10
96	Chris Hammond	.10
97	Edgar Martinez	.10
98	Kevin Stocker	.10
99	Jeff Fassero	.10
100	Curt Schilling	.30
101	Dave Clark	.10
102	Delino DeShields	.10
103	Leo Gomez	.10
104	Dave Hollins	.10
105	Tim Naehring	.10
106	Otis Nixon	.10
107	Ozzie Guillen	.10
108	Jose Lind	.10
109	Stan Javier	.10
110	Greg Vaughn	.10
111	Chipper Jones	1.00
112	Ed Sprague	.10
113	Mike Macfarlane	.10
114	Steve Finley	.10
115	Ken Hill	.10
116	Carlos Garcia	.10
117	Lou Whitaker	.10
118	Todd Zeile	.10
119	Gary Sheffield	.40
120	Ben McDonald	.10
121	Pete Harnisch	.10
122	Ivan Rodriguez	.65
123	Wilson Alvarez	.10
124	Travis Fryman	.10
125	Pedro Munoz	.10
126	Mark Lemke	.10
127	Jose Valentin	.10
128	Ken Griffey Jr.	1.50
129	Omar Vizquel	.10
130	Milt Cuyler	.10
131	Steve Traschel	.10
132	Alex Rodriguez	2.00
133	Garret Anderson	.10
134	Armando Benitez	.10
135	Shawn Green	.35
136	Jorge Fabregas	.10
137	Orlando Miller	.10
138	Rikkert Faneyte	.10
139	Ismael Valdes	.10
140	Jose Oliva	.10
141	Aaron Small	.10
142	Tim Davis	.10
143	Ricky Bottalacio	.10
144	Mike Matheny	.10
145	Roberto Petagine	.10
146	Fausto Cruz	.10
147	Bryce Florie	.10
148	Jose Lima	.10
149	John Hudek	.10
150	Duane Singleton	.10
151	John Mabry	.10
152	Robert Eenhoorn	.10
153	Jon Lieber	.10
154	Garey Ingram	.10
155	Paul Shuey	.10
156	Mike Lieberthal	.10
157	Steve Dunn	.10
158	Charles Johnson	.10
159	Ernie Young	.10
160	Jose Martinez	.10
161	Kurt Miller	.10
162	Joey Eischen	.10
163	Dave Stevens	.10
164	Brian Hunter	.10
165	Jeff Cirillo	.10
166	Mark Smith	.10
167	McKay Christensen **RC**	.10
168	C.J. Nitkowski	.10
169	Antone Williamson **RC**	.10
170	Paul Konerko	.15
171	Scott Elarton **RC**	.15
172	Jacob Shumate	.10
173	Terrence Long	.10
174	Mark Johnson **RC**	.10
175	Ben Grieve	.10
176	Jayson Peterson **RC**	.10
177	Checklist	.10
178	Checklist	.10
179	Checklist	.10
180	Checklist	.10
181	Brian Anderson	.10
182	Steve Buechele	.10
183	Mark Clark	.10
184	Cecil Fielder	.10
185	Steve Avery	.10
186	Devon White	.10
187	Craig Shipley	.10
188	Brady Anderson	.10
189	Kenny Lofton	.10
190	Alex Cole	.10
191	Brent Gates	.10
192	Dean Palmer	.10
193	Alex Gonzalez	.10
194	Steve Cooke	.10
195	Ray Lankford	.10
196	Mark McGwire	2.00
197	Marc Newfield	.10
198	Pat Rapp	.10
199	Darren Lewis	.10
200	Carlos Baerga	.10
201	Rickey Henderson	.75
202	Kurt Abbott	.10
203	Kirt Manwaring	.10
204	Cal Ripken Jr.	2.50
205	Darren Daulton	.10
206	Greg Colbrunn	.10
207	Darryl Hamilton	.10
208	Bo Jackson	.15
209	Tony Phillips	.10
210	Geronimo Berroa	.10
211	Rich Becker	.10
212	Tony Tarasco	.10
213	Karl Rhodes	.10
214	Phil Plantier	.10
215	J.T. Snow	.10
216	Mo Vaughn	.10
217	Greg Gagne	.10
218	Rickey Bones	.10
219	Mike Bordick	.10
220	Chad Curtis	.10
221	Royce Clayton	.10
222	Roberto Alomar	.15
223	Jose Rijo	.10
224	Ryan Klesko	.10
225	Mark Langston	.10
226	Frank Thomas	.75
227	Juan Gonzalez	.40
228	Ron Gant	.10
229	Javier Lopez	.10
230	Sammy Sosa	1.00
231	Kevin Brown	.10
232	Gary DiSarcina	.10
233	Albert Belle	.10
234	Jay Buhner	.10
235	Pedro Martinez	.75
236	Bob Tewksbury	.10
237	Mike Piazza	1.50
238	Darryl Kile	.10
239	Bryan Harvey	.10
240	Andres Galarraga	.10
241	Jeff Blauser	.10
242	Jeff Kent	.10
243	Bobby Munoz	.10
244	Greg Maddux	1.00
245	Paul O'Neill	.10
246	Lenny Dykstra	.10
247	Todd Van Poppel	.10
248	Bernie Williams	.05
249	Glenallen Hill	.10
250	Duane Ward	.10
251	Dennis Eckersley	.60
252	Pat Mahomes	.10
253	Rusty Greer (Photo actually Jeff Frye.)	.10
254	Roberto Kelly	.10
255	Randy Myers	.10
256	Scott Ruffcorn	.10
257	Robin Ventura	.10
258	Eduardo Perez	.10
259	Aaron Sele	.10
260	Paul Molitor	.75
261	Juan Guzman	.10
262	Darren Oliver	.10
263	Mike Stanley	.10
264	Tom Glavine	.30
265	Rico Brogna	.10
266	Craig Biggio	.10
267	Darrell Whitmore	.10
268	Jimmy Key	.10
269	Will Clark	.10
270	David Cone	.10
271	Brian Jordan	.10
272	Barry Bonds	2.50
273	Danny Tartabull	.10
274	Ramon Martinez	.10
275	Al Martin	.10
276	Fred McGriff (Swing Men)	.10
277	Carlos Delgado (Swing Men)	.25
278	Juan Gonzalez (Swing Men)	.20
279	Shawn Green (Swing Men)	.20
280	Carlos Baerga (Swing Men)	.10
281	Cliff Floyd (Swing Men)	.10
282	Ozzie Smith (Swing Men)	.50
283	Alex Rodriguez (Swing Men)	1.00
284	Kenny Lofton (Swing Men)	.10
285	Dave Justice (Swing Men)	.10
286	Tim Salmon (Swing Men)	.10
287	Manny Ramirez (Swing Men)	.40
288	Will Clark (Swing Men)	.10
289	Garret Anderson (Swing Men)	.10
290	Billy Ashley (Swing Men)	.10
291	Tony Gwynn (Swing Men)	.50
292	Raul Mondesi (Swing Men)	.10
293	Rafael Palmeiro (Swing Men)	.30
294	Matt Williams (Swing Men)	.10
295	Don Mattingly (Swing Men)	.60
296	Kirby Puckett (Swing Men)	.50
297	Paul Molitor (Swing Men)	.40
298	Albert Belle (Swing Men)	.10
299	Barry Bonds (Swing Men)	1.25
300	Mike Piazza (Swing Men)	.85
301	Jeff Bagwell (Swing Men)	.40
302	Frank Thomas (Swing Men)	.40
303	Chipper Jones (Swing Men)	.50
304	Ken Griffey Jr. (Swing Men)	.75
305	Cal Ripken Jr. (Swing Men)	1.25
306	Eric Anthony	.10
307	Todd Benzinger	.10
308	Jacob Brumfield	.10
309	Wes Chamberlain	.10
310	Tino Martinez	.10
311	Roberto Mejia	.10
312	Jose Offerman	.10
313	David Segui	.10
314	Eric Young	.10
315	Rey Sanchez	.10
316	Raul Mondesi	.10
317	Bret Boone	.10
318	Andre Dawson	.30
319	Brian McRae	.10
320	Dave Nilsson	.10
321	Moises Alou	.10
322	Don Slaught	.10
323	Dave McCarty	.10
324	Mike Huff	.10
325	Rick Aguilera	.10
326	Rod Beck	.10
327	Kenny Rogers	.10
328	Andy Benes	.10
329	Allen Watson	.10
330	Randy Johnson	.75
331	Willie Greene	.10
332	Hal Morris	.10
333	Ozzie Smith	1.00
334	Jason Bere	.10
335	Scott Erickson	.10
336	Dante Bichette	.10
337	Willie Banks	.10
338	Eric Davis	.10
339	Rondell White	.10
340	Kirby Puckett	1.00
341	Deion Sanders	.10
342	Eddie Murray	.75
343	Mike Harkey	.10
344	Joey Hamilton	.10
345	Roger Salkeld	.10
346	Wil Cordero	.10
347	John Wetteland	.10
348	Geronimo Pena	.10
349	Kirk Gibson	.10
350	Manny Ramirez	.75
351	William Van Landingham	.10
352	B.J. Surhoff	.10
353	Ken Ryan	.10
354	Terry Steinbach	.10
355	Bret Saberhagen	.10
356	John Jaha	.10
357	Joe Girardi	.10
358	Steve Karsay	.10
359	Alex Fernandez	.10
360	Salomon Torres	.10
361	John Burkett	.10
362	Derek Bell	.10
363	Tom Henke	.10
364	Gregg Jefferies	.10
365	Jack McDowell	.10
366	Andujar Cedeno	.10
367	Dave Winfield	.75
368	Carl Everett	.10
369	Danny Jackson	.10
370	Jeromy Burnitz	.10
371	Mark Grace	.10
372	Larry Walker	.10
373	Bill Swift	.10
374	Dennis Martinez	.10
375	Mickey Tettleton	.10
376	Mel Nieves	.10
377	Cal Eldred	.10
378	Orel Hershiser	.10
379	David Wells	.10
380	Gary Gaetti	.10
381	Tim Raines	.10
382	Barry Larkin	.10
383	Jason Jacome	.10
384	Tim Wallach	.10
385	Robby Thompson	.10
386	Frank Viola	.10
387	Dave Stewart	.10
388	Bip Roberts	.10
389	Ron Darling	.10
390	Carlos Delgado	.45
391	Tim Salmon	.10
392	Alan Trammell	.10
393	Kevin Foster	.10
394	Jim Abbott	.10
395	John Kruk	.10
396	Andy Van Slyke	.10
397	Dave Magadan	.10
398	Rafael Palmeiro	.65
399	Mike Devereaux	.10
400	Benito Santiago	.10
401	Brett Butler	.10
402	John Franco	.10
403	Matt Walbeck	.10
404	Terry Pendleton	.10
405	Chris Sabo	.10
406	Andrew Lorraine	.10
407	Dan Wilson	.10
408	Mike Lansing	.10
409	Ray McDavid	.10
410	Shane Andrews	.10
411	Tom Gordon	.10
412	Chad Ogea	.10
413	James Baldwin	.10
414	Russ Davis	.10
415	Ray Holbert	.10
416	Ray Durham	.10
417	Matt Nokes	.10
418	Rodney Henderson	.10
419	Gabe White	.10
420	Todd Hollandsworth	.10
421	Midre Cummings	.10
422	Harold Baines	.10
423	Troy Percival	.10
424	Joe Vitiello	.10
425	Andy Ashby	.10
426	Michael Tucker	.10
427	Mark Gubicza	.10
428	Jim Bullinger	.10
429	Jose Malave	.10
430	Pete Schourek	.10
431	Bobby Ayala	.10
432	Marvin Freeman	.10
433	Pat Listach	.10
434	Eddie Taubensee	.10
435	Steve Howe	.10
436	Kent Mercker	.10
437	Hector Fajardo	.10
438	Scott Kamieniecki	.10
439	Robb Nen	.10
440	Mike Kelly	.10
441	Tom Candiotti	.10
442	Albie Lopez	.10
443	Jeff Granger	.10
444	Rich Aude	.10
445	Luis Polonia	.10
446	A.L. Checklist (Frank Thomas)	.40
447	A.L. Checklist (Ken Griffey Jr.)	.65
448	N.L. Checklist (Mike Piazza)	.75
449	N.L. Checklist (Jeff Bagwell)	.40
450	Insert Checklist (Frank Thomas, Ken Griffey Jr., Mike Piazza, Jeff Bagwell)	.40

Artist's Proof

Said to represent the first 1,000 of each card printed, the Artist's Proof chase set is a parallel issue with a counterpart for each of the regular-issue cards. The proofs differ in the use of silver, rather than gold foil for front graphic highlights, and the inclusion of a rectangular silver-foil "ARTIST'S PROOF" logo on front. The AP inserts were reported seeded at an average rate of one per 26 packs.

	NM/M
Complete Set (450):	300.00
Common Player:	1.00
Stars/Rookies:	10X

Museum Collection

Pinnacle's Dufex foil-printing technology on the card fronts differentiates this parallel insert from the corresponding cards in the regular issue. Backs have a rectangular "1995 Museum Collection" logo at lower-left. Museum inserts are found at an average rate of one per four packs. Because of production difficulties, trade cards had to be issued in place of seven of the rookie cards in Series 2. Those redemption cards were valid only through Dec. 31, 1995.

	NM/M
Complete Set (450):	200.00
Common Player:	.50
Stars/Rookies:	4X
Redemption Card	.25

E.T.A. '95

This hobby-only chase set identifies six players picked to arrive in the major leagues for a 1995 debut. Both sides have borderless action photos on which the background has been subdued and posterized. Gold-foil headlines on each side of the card give the player's credentials. These inserts are found on average of once per 24 packs.

		NM/M
Complete Set (6):		5.00
Common Player:		.70
1	Ben Grieve	.75
2	Alex Ochoa	.75
3	Joe Vitiello	.75
4	Johnny Damon	3.00
5	Trey Beamon	.75
6	Brooks Kieschnick	.75

Gate Attraction

Series 2 jumbo packs are the exclusive source for this chase set. Printed on metallic foil, the cards have a color photo at top and a second photo at bottom that is shown in gold tones only. A "Gate Attraction" seal is in the lower-left corner. Backs have a large portrait photo on a color-streaked background, plus a few words about the player.

		NM/M
Complete Set (18):		25.00
Common Player:		.50
1	Ken Griffey Jr.	3.50
2	Frank Thomas	1.50
3	Cal Ripken Jr.	5.00
4	Jeff Bagwell	1.50
5	Mike Piazza	3.50
6	Barry Bonds	5.00
7	Kirby Puckett	2.00
8	Albert Belle	.50
9	Tony Gwynn	2.00
10	Raul Mondesi	.50
11	Will Clark	.50
12	Don Mattingly	2.75
13	Roger Clemens	2.75
14	Paul Molitor	1.50
15	Matt Williams	.50
16	Greg Maddux	2.00
17	Kenny Lofton	.50
18	Cliff Floyd	.50

New Blood

Both hobby and retail packs of Series 2 hide this insert set of young stars, at an average rate of one card per 90 packs. A player photo appears in the red and silver foil-printed background, and there is a color action photo in the foreground. Conventionally printed backs feature the same photos, but with their prominence reversed. A few words of text describe the player's star potential.

		NM/M
Complete Set (9):		10.00
Common Player:		.75
1	Alex Rodriguez	5.00
2	Shawn Green	1.50
3	Brian Hunter	.75
4	Garret Anderson	.75
5	Charles Johnson	.75
6	Chipper Jones	3.00
7	Carlos Delgado	1.50
8	Billy Ashley	.75
9	J.R. Phillips	.75

Performers

Series 1 jumbos were the only place to find this chase set. Fronts have a deep red background with a golden pyramid at center and a silver apex, all in foil printing. A color player action photo is in the center foreground. The reverse repeats the front photo in the background, in one color, and has a second color photo, along with a few words about the player.

	NM/M
Complete Set (18):	15.00

Common Player:		.35
1	Frank Thomas	2.00
2	Albert Belle	.35
3	Barry Bonds	3.50
4	Juan Gonzalez	1.00
5	Andres Galarraga	.35
6	Raul Mondesi	.35
7	Paul Molitor	2.00
8	Tim Salmon	.35
9	Mike Piazza	2.50
10	Gregg Jefferies	.35
11	Will Clark	.35
12	Greg Maddux	2.25
13	Manny Ramirez	2.00
14	Kirby Puckett	2.25
15	Shawn Green	1.25
16	Rafael Palmeiro	1.75
17	Paul O'Neill	.35
18	Jason Bere	.35

Red Hot

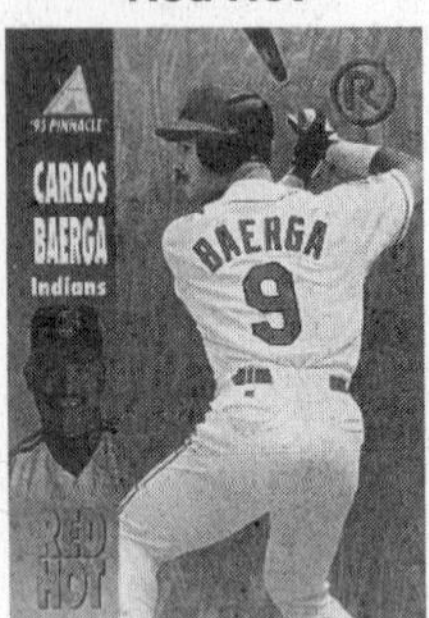

These Series 2 inserts are found at an average rate of one per 16 packs and feature top veteran stars. Fronts have a large action photo on right, over a background of foil-printed red and yellow flames. A vertical strip at left of graduated red tones has a player portrait photo and the "RED HOT" flame logo, again printed on foil. Backs are conventionally printed and have a black background with large flaming "RED HOT" letters and a color player photo.

		NM/M
Complete Set (25):		35.00
Common Player:		.75
1	Cal Ripken Jr.	5.50
2	Ken Griffey Jr.	4.00
3	Frank Thomas	1.50
4	Jeff Bagwell	1.50
5	Mike Piazza	4.00
6	Barry Bonds	5.50
7	Albert Belle	.75
8	Tony Gwynn	2.00
9	Kirby Puckett	2.00
10	Don Mattingly	2.50
11	Matt Williams	.75
12	Greg Maddux	2.00
13	Raul Mondesi	.75
14	Paul Molitor	1.50
15	Manny Ramirez	1.50
16	Joe Carter	.75
17	Will Clark	.75
18	Roger Clemens	2.50
19	Tim Salmon	.75
20	Dave Justice	.75
21	Kenny Lofton	.75
22	Deion Sanders	.75
23	Roberto Alomar	1.00
24	Cliff Floyd	.75
25	Carlos Baerga	.75

White Hot

Similar in format to the Red Hot inserts, and featuring the same players, the hobby-only White Hot cards are a chase set of a chase set. Seeded once per 36 packs on average (more than twice as scarce as the Red Hots), the White Hot cards have fronts totally printed in the Dufex process, with predominantly blue and white background colors, while the backs are highlighted by blue foil printing in the "WHITE HOT" background lettering on black background.

		NM/M
Complete Set (25):		140.00
Common Player:		2.50
1	Cal Ripken Jr.	16.00
2	Ken Griffey Jr.	13.50
3	Frank Thomas	8.00
4	Jeff Bagwell	8.00
5	Mike Piazza	13.50
6	Barry Bonds	16.00
7	Albert Belle	2.50
8	Tony Gwynn	10.00
9	Kirby Puckett	10.00
10	Don Mattingly	12.00
11	Matt Williams	2.50
12	Greg Maddux	10.00
13	Raul Mondesi	2.50
14	Paul Molitor	8.00
15	Manny Ramirez	8.00
16	Joe Carter	2.50
17	Will Clark	2.50
18	Roger Clemens	12.00
19	Tim Salmon	2.50
20	Dave Justice	2.50
21	Kenny Lofton	2.50
22	Deion Sanders	2.50
23	Roberto Alomar	3.50
24	Cliff Floyd	2.50
25	Carlos Baerga	2.50

Team Pinnacle

This nine-card Series 1 insert set becomes an 18-card challenge if the collector decides to hunt for both versions of each card. As in the past the Team Pinnacle cards picture National and American League counterparts at each position on different sides of the same card. In 1995 each card is printed with one side in Pinnacle's Dufex foil technology, and the other side conventionally printed. Thus card #1 can be found with Mike Mussina in Dufex and Greg Maddux conventionally printed, or with Maddux in Dufex and Mussina conventional. Team Pinnacle cards are found inserted at an average rate of only one per 90 packs. Card numbers have a "TP" prefix.

		NM/M
Complete Set (9):		35.00
Common Player:		1.50
1	Mike Mussina, Greg Maddux	8.00
2	Carlos Delgado, Mike Piazza	6.00
3	Frank Thomas, Jeff Bagwell	4.00
4	Roberto Alomar, Craig Biggio	3.00
5	Cal Ripken Jr., Ozzie Smith	12.00
6	Travis Fryman, Matt Williams	1.50
7	Ken Griffey Jr., Barry Bonds	10.00
8	Albert Belle, Dave Justice	1.50
9	Kirby Puckett, Tony Gwynn	8.00

Team Pinnacle Pin Trade Cards

In one of the hobby's first major attempts to cross-promote pin- and card-collecting, Series 2 Pinnacle packs offered

a special insert set of cards which could be redeemed for a collector's pin of the same player. Seeded at the rate of one per 48 regular packs and one per 36 jumbo packs, the pin redemption cards were valid until Nov. 15, 1995. Payment of $2 handling fee was required for redemption.

		NM/M
Complete Set (18):		40.00
Common Player:		.75
1	Greg Maddux	4.00
2	Mike Mussina	1.50
3	Mike Piazza	5.00
4	Carlos Delgado	1.50
5	Jeff Bagwell	3.00
6	Frank Thomas	3.00
7	Craig Biggio	.75
8	Roberto Alomar	1.00
9	Ozzie Smith	4.00
10	Cal Ripken Jr.	6.00
11	Matt Williams	.75
12	Travis Fryman	.75
13	Barry Bonds	6.00
14	Ken Griffey Jr.	5.00
15	Dave Justice	.75
16	Albert Belle	.75
17	Tony Gwynn	4.00
18	Kirby Puckett	4.00

Team Pinnacle Collector Pins

Redemption cards in Series 2 packs could be traded in (until Nov. 15, 1995) for an enameled pin of the player pictured on the trade card. Pins are about 1-3/8" x 1-1/4". A raised relief portrait of the player is at center with his name in pennants above and his team logo at bottom, along with the Pinnacle logo. Backs are gold-tone with a post-and-button style of pinback. The unnumbered pins are listed here in the same sequence as the redemption cards.

		NM/M
Complete Set (18):		135.00
Common Player:		5.00
(1)	Greg Maddux	10.00
(2)	Mike Mussina	6.00
(3)	Mike Piazza	15.00
(4)	Carlos Delgado	6.00
(5)	Jeff Bagwell	8.00
(6)	Frank Thomas	8.00
(7)	Craig Biggio	5.00
(8)	Roberto Alomar	6.00
(9)	Ozzie Smith	10.00
(10)	Cal Ripken Jr.	20.00
(11)	Matt Williams	5.00
(12)	Travis Fryman	5.00
(13)	Barry Bonds	20.00
(14)	Ken Griffey Jr.	15.00
(15)	Dave Justice	5.00
(16)	Albert Belle	5.00
(17)	Tony Gwynn	10.00
(18)	Kirby Puckett	10.00

Pin-Cards

Virtually nothing is known of this issue except that it is connected in some way to the Series 2 Pinnacle player pin issue. The front features portrait and action photos on a red background with gold-foil graphics. Backs have career highlights, a large color photo and a card

number with "PPC" prefix. To date only a single card is known.

Upstarts

The most dominant young players in the game were featured in this insert series. Cards are printed with most of the photo's background covered by the legs of a large blue-and-gold star device, which includes the team logo at its red center. A blue circular "'95 UPSTARTS" logo at bottom-left has the player name in gold. These cards are exclusive to Series 1, found at an average rate of one per eight packs.

		NM/M
Complete Set (30):		10.00
Common Player:		.15
1	Frank Thomas	1.50
2	Roberto Alomar	.30
3	Mike Piazza	2.50
4	Javier Lopez	.15
5	Albert Belle	.15
6	Carlos Delgado	.75
7	Rusty Greer	.15
8	Tim Salmon	.15
9	Raul Mondesi	.15
10	Juan Gonzalez	.75
11	Manny Ramirez	1.50
12	Sammy Sosa	2.00
13	Jeff Kent	.15
14	Melvin Nieves	.15
15	Rondell White	.15
16	Shawn Green	.75
17	Bernie Williams	.15
18	Aaron Sele	.15
19	Jason Bere	.15
20	Joey Hamilton	.15
21	Mike Kelly	.15
22	Wil Cordero	.15
23	Moises Alou	.15
24	Roberto Kelly	.15
25	Deion Sanders	.15
26	Steve Karsay	.15
27	Bret Boone	.15
28	Willie Greene	.15
29	Billy Ashley	.15
30	Brian Anderson	.15

FanFest

Pinnacle's sponsorship of the July 7-11 All-Star FanFest was marked with the issue of this set. Cards were distributed in two-card packs at various venues around the All-Star celebration in Arlington, Texas. Each card features the FanFest logo at lower-left on front, with the player's name and team logo in a stylized gold-foil baseball diamond diagram at lower-right. A full-bleed action photo comprises the rest of the front. Horizontal backs show a portrait photo of the player before a photo of The Ballpark at Arlington. The FanFast logo is repeated at bottom-center.

		NM/M
Complete Set (30):		7.50
Common Player:		.15
1	Cal Ripken Jr.	1.50
2	Roger Clemens	.75
3	Don Mattingly	.75
4	Albert Belle	.15
5	Kirby Puckett	.65
6	Cecil Fielder	.15
7	Kevin Appier	.15
8	Will Clark	.15
9	Juan Gonzalez	.25
10	Ivan Rodriguez	.45
11	Ken Griffey Jr.	1.00
12	Tim Salmon	.15
13	Frank Thomas	.50
14	Roberto Alomar	.20
15	Rickey Henderson	.50
16	Raul Mondesi	.15
17	Matt Williams	.15
18	Ozzie Smith	.65
19	Deion Sanders	.15
20	Tony Gwynn	.65
21	Greg Maddux	.65
22	Sammy Sosa	.65
23	Mike Piazza	1.00
24	Barry Bonds	1.50
25	Jeff Bagwell	.50
26	Len Dykstra	.15
27	Rico Brogna	.15
28	Larry Walker	.15
29	Gary Sheffield	.35
30	Wil Cordero	.15

1996 Pinnacle Samples

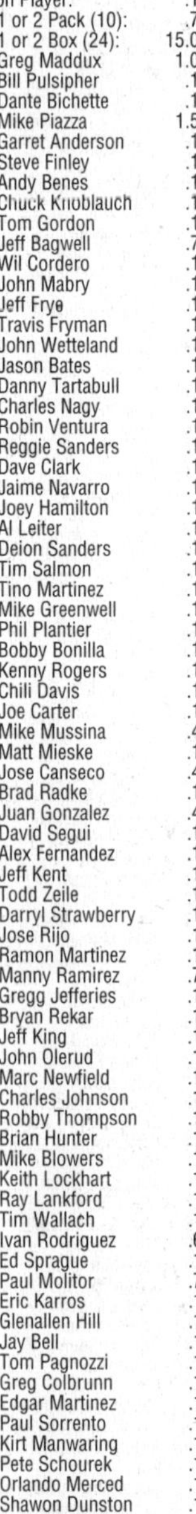

Pinnacle's 1996 issue was premiered with this nine-card sample set. The cards are virtually identical in format to the regular-issue cards, but feature a large white "SAMPLE" printed diagonally on front and back. The cards were sent to dealers and hobby media in a cello pack.

		NM/M
Complete Set (9):		5.00
Common Player:		.75
1	Greg Maddux	1.50
2	Bill Pulsipher	.75
3	Dante Bichette	.75
4	Mike Piazza	2.00
5	Garret Anderson	.75
165	Ruben Rivera	.75
168	Tony Clark	.75
2	Mo Vaughn (Pinnacle Power)	1.00
---	Header Card	.10

1996 Pinnacle

Pinnacle's 400-card regular-issue set has borderless front photos highlighted by prismatic gold-foil graphics in a triangle at bottom. Backs have another photo along with stats and data. Parallel Starburst and Starburst Artist's Proof sets

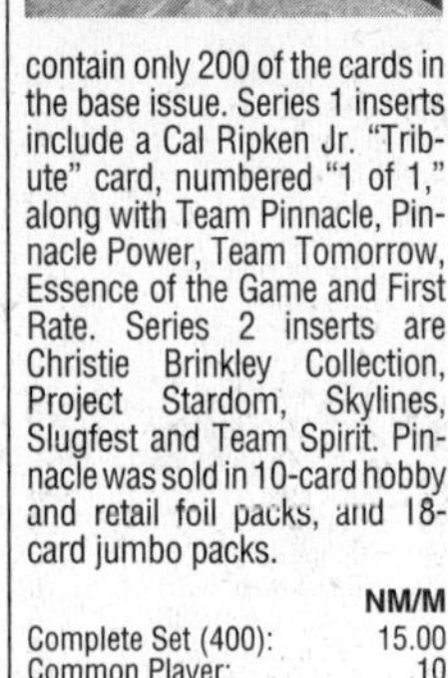

contain only 200 of the cards in the base issue. Series 1 inserts include a Cal Ripken Jr. "Tribute" card, numbered "1 of 1," along with Team Pinnacle, Pinnacle Power, Team Tomorrow, Essence of the Game and First Rate. Series 2 inserts are Christie Brinkley Collection, Project Stardom, Skylines, Slugfest and Team Spirit. Pinnacle was sold in 10-card hobby and retail foil packs, and 18-card jumbo packs.

		NM/M
Complete Set (400):		15.00
Common Player:		.10
Series 1 or 2 Pack (10):		.75
Series 1 or 2 Box (24):		15.00
1	Greg Maddux	1.00
2	Bill Pulsipher	.10
3	Dante Bichette	.10
4	Mike Piazza	1.50
5	Garret Anderson	.10
6	Steve Finley	.10
7	Andy Benes	.10
8	Chuck Knoblauch	.10
9	Tom Gordon	.10
10	Jeff Bagwell	.75
11	Wil Cordero	.10
12	John Mabry	.10
13	Jeff Frye	.10
14	Travis Fryman	.10
15	John Wetteland	.10
16	Jason Bates	.10
17	Danny Tartabull	.10
18	Charles Nagy	.10
19	Robin Ventura	.10
20	Reggie Sanders	.10
21	Dave Clark	.10
22	Jaime Navarro	.10
23	Joey Hamilton	.10
24	Al Leiter	.10
25	Deion Sanders	.10
26	Tim Salmon	.10
27	Tino Martinez	.10
28	Mike Greenwell	.10
29	Phil Plantier	.10
30	Bobby Bonilla	.10
31	Kenny Rogers	.10
32	Chili Davis	.10
33	Joe Carter	.10
34	Mike Mussina	.40
35	Matt Mieske	.10
36	Jose Canseco	.40
37	Brad Radke	.10
38	Juan Gonzalez	.40
39	David Segui	.10
40	Alex Fernandez	.10
41	Jeff Kent	.10
42	Todd Zeile	.10
43	Darryl Strawberry	.10
44	Jose Rijo	.10
45	Ramon Martinez	.10
46	Manny Ramirez	.75
47	Gregg Jefferies	.10
48	Bryan Rekar	.10
49	Jeff King	.10
50	John Olerud	.10
51	Marc Newfield	.10
52	Charles Johnson	.10
53	Robby Thompson	.10
54	Brian Hunter	.10
55	Mike Blowers	.10
56	Keith Lockhart	.10
57	Ray Lankford	.10
58	Tim Wallach	.10
59	Ivan Rodriguez	.65
60	Ed Sprague	.10
61	Paul Molitor	.75
62	Eric Karros	.10
63	Glenallen Hill	.10
64	Jay Bell	.10
65	Tom Pagnozzi	.10
66	Greg Colbrunn	.10
67	Edgar Martinez	.10
68	Paul Sorrento	.10
69	Kirt Manwaring	.10
70	Pete Schourek	.10
71	Orlando Merced	.10
72	Shawon Dunston	.10
73	Ricky Bottalico	.10
74	Brady Anderson	.10
75	Steve Ontiveros	.10
76	Jim Abbott	.10

77 Carl Everett .10
78 Mo Vaughn .10
79 Pedro Martinez .75
80 Harold Baines .10
81 Alan Trammell .10
82 Steve Avery .10
83 Jeff Cirillo .10
84 John Valentin .10
85 Bernie Williams .10
86 Andre Dawson .30
87 Dave Winfield .75
88 B.J. Surhoff .10
89 Jeff Blauser .10
90 Barry Larkin .10
91 Cliff Floyd .10
92 Sammy Sosa 1.00
93 Andres Galarraga .10
94 Dave Nilsson .10
95 James Mouton .10
96 Marquis Grissom .10
97 Matt Williams .10
98 John Jaha .10
99 Don Mattingly 1.25
100 Tim Naehring .10
101 Kevin Appier .10
102 Bobby Higginson .10
103 Andy Pettitte .25
104 Ozzie Smith 1.00
105 Kenny Lofton .10
106 Ken Caminiti .10
107 Walt Weiss .10
108 Jack McDowell .10
109 Brian McRae .10
110 Gary Gaetti .10
111 Curtis Goodwin .10
112 Dennis Martinez .10
113 Omar Vizquel .10
114 Chipper Jones 1.00
115 Mark Gubicza .10
116 Ruben Sierra .10
117 Eddie Murray .75
118 Chad Curtis .10
119 Hal Morris .10
120 Ben McDonald .10
121 Marty Cordova .10
122 Ken Griffey Jr. 1.50
123 Gary Sheffield .40
124 Charlie Hayes .10
125 Shawn Green .40
126 Jason Giambi .50
127 Mark Langston .10
128 Mark Whiten .10
129 Greg Vaughn .10
130 Mark McGwire 1.75
131 Hideo Nomo .40
132 Eric Karros, Raul Mondesi, Hideo Nomo, Mike Piazza .50
133 Jason Bere .10
134 Ken Griffey Jr. (The Naturals) .65
135 Frank Thomas (The Naturals) .40
136 Cal Ripken Jr. (The Naturals) 1.00
137 Albert Belle (The Naturals) .10
138 Mike Piazza (The Naturals) .65
139 Dante Bichette (The Naturals) .10
140 Sammy Sosa (The Naturals) .50
141 Mo Vaughn (The Naturals) .10
142 Tim Salmon (The Naturals) .10
143 Reggie Sanders (The Naturals) .10
144 Cecil Fielder (The Naturals) .10
145 Jim Edmonds (The Naturals) .10
146 Rafael Palmeiro (The Naturals) .10
147 Edgar Martinez (The Naturals) .10
148 Barry Bonds (The Naturals) 1.00
149 Manny Ramirez (The Naturals) .35
150 Larry Walker (The Naturals) .10
151 Jeff Bagwell (The Naturals) .35
152 Ron Gant (The Naturals) .10
153 Andres Galarraga (The Naturals) .10
154 Eddie Murray (The Naturals) .35
155 Kirby Puckett (The Naturals) .50
156 Will Clark (The Naturals) .10
157 Don Mattingly (The Naturals) .60
158 Mark McGwire (The Naturals) .75
159 Dean Palmer (The Naturals) .10
160 Matt Williams (The Naturals) .10
161 Fred McGriff (The Naturals) .10
162 Joe Carter (The Naturals) .10
163 Juan Gonzalez (The Naturals) .15
164 Alex Ochoa .10
165 Ruben Rivera .10
166 Tony Clark .10
167 Brian Barber .10
168 Matt Lawton .10
169 Terrell Wade .10
170 Johnny Damon .30
171 Derek Jeter 2.00
172 Phil Nevin .10
173 Robert Perez .10
174 C.J. Nitkowski .10
175 Joe Vitiello .10
176 Roger Cedeno .10
177 Ron Coomer .10
178 Chris Widger .10
179 Jimmy Haynes .10
180 Mike Sweeney **RC** .50
181 Howard Battle .10
182 John Wasdin .10
183 Jim Pittsley .10
184 Bob Wolcott .10
185 LaTroy Hawkins .10
186 Nigel Wilson .10
187 Dustin Hermanson .10
188 Chris Snopek .10
189 Mariano Rivera .15
190 Jose Herrera .10
191 Chris Stynes .10
192 Larry Thomas .10
193 David Bell .10
194 Frank Thomas (checklist) .40
195 Ken Griffey Jr. (checklist) .65
196 Cal Ripken Jr. (checklist) .75
197 Jeff Bagwell (checklist) .35
198 Mike Piazza (checklist) .60
199 Barry Bonds (checklist) .75
200 Garret Anderson, Chipper Jones (checklist) .25
201 Frank Thomas .75
202 Michael Tucker .10
203 Kirby Puckett 1.00
204 Alex Gonzalez .10
205 Tony Gwynn 1.00
206 Moises Alou .10
207 Albert Belle .10
208 Barry Bonds 2.00
209 Fred McGriff .10
210 Dennis Eckersley .65
211 Craig Biggio .10
212 David Cone .10
213 Will Clark .10
214 Cal Ripken Jr. 2.00
215 Wade Boggs 1.00
216 Pete Schourek .10
217 Darren Daulton .10
218 Carlos Baerga .10
219 Larry Walker .10
220 Denny Neagle .10
221 Jim Edmonds .10
222 Lee Smith .10
223 Jason Isringhausen .10
224 Jay Buhner .10
225 John Olerud .10
226 Jeff Conine .10
227 Dean Palmer .10
228 Jim Abbott .10
229 Raul Mondesi .10
230 Tom Glavine .35
231 Kevin Seitzer .10
232 Lenny Dykstra .10
233 Brian Jordan .10
234 Rondell White .10
235 Bret Boone .10
236 Randy Johnson .75
237 Paul O'Neill .10
238 Jim Thome .65
239 Edgardo Alfonzo .10
240 Terry Pendleton .10
241 Harold Baines .10
242 Roberto Alomar .20
243 Mark Grace .10
244 Derek Bell .10
245 Vinny Castilla .10
246 Cecil Fielder .10
247 Roger Clemens 1.25
248 Orel Hershiser .10
249 J.T. Snow .10
250 Rafael Palmeiro .65
251 Bret Saberhagen .10
252 Todd Hollandsworth .10
253 Ryan Klesko .10
254 Greg Maddux (Hardball Heroes) .50
255 Ken Griffey Jr. (Hardball Heroes) .65
256 Hideo Nomo (Hardball Heroes) .15
257 Frank Thomas (Hardball Heroes) .40
258 Cal Ripken Jr. (Hardball Heroes) 1.00
259 Jeff Bagwell (Hardball Heroes) .35
260 Barry Bonds (Hardball Heroes) 1.00
261 Mo Vaughn (Hardball Heroes) .10
262 Albert Belle (Hardball Heroes) .10
263 Sammy Sosa (Hardball Heroes) .50
264 Reggie Sanders (Hardball Heroes) .10
265 Mike Piazza (Hardball Heroes) .65
266 Chipper Jones (Hardball Heroes) .50
267 Tony Gwynn (Hardball Heroes) .50
268 Kirby Puckett (Hardball Heroes) .50
269 Wade Boggs (Hardball Heroes) .45
270 Will Clark (Hardball Heroes) .10
271 Gary Sheffield (Hardball Heroes) .10
272 Dante Bichette (Hardball Heroes) .10
273 Randy Johnson (Hardball Heroes) .35
274 Matt Williams (Hardball Heroes) .10
275 Alex Rodriguez (Hardball Heroes) .75
276 Tim Salmon (Hardball Heroes) .10
277 Johnny Damon (Hardball Heroes) .10
278 Manny Ramirez (Hardball Heroes) .35
279 Derek Jeter (Hardball Heroes) 1.00
280 Eddie Murray (Hardball Heroes) .35
281 Ozzie Smith (Hardball Heroes) .50
282 Garret Anderson (Hardball Heroes) .10
283 Raul Mondesi (Hardball Heroes) .10
284 Terry Steinbach .10
285 Carlos Garcia .10
286 Dave Justice .10
287 Eric Anthony .10
288 Benji Gil .10
289 Bob Hamelin .10
290 Dwayne Hosey .10
291 Andy Pettitte .25
292 Rod Beck .10
293 Shane Andrews .10
294 Julian Tavarez .10
295 Willie Greene .10
296 Ismael Valdes .10
297 Glenallen Hill .10
298 Troy Percival .10
299 Ray Durham .10
300 Jeff Conine (.300 Series) .10
301.8 Ken Griffey Jr. (.300 Series) .75
302 Will Clark (.300 Series) .10
303 Mike Greenwell (.300 Series) .10
304.9 Carlos Baerga (.300 Series) .10
305.3 Paul Molitor (.300 Series) .35
305.6 Jeff Bagwell (.300 Series) .35
306 Mark Grace (.300 Series) .10
307 Don Mattingly (.300 Series) .60
308 Hal Morris (.300 Series) .10
309 Butch Huskey .10
310 Ozzie Guillen .10
311 Erik Hanson .10
312 Kenny Lofton (.300 Series) .10
313 Edgar Martinez (.300 Series) .10
314 Kurt Abbott .10
315 John Smoltz .10
316 Ariel Prieto .10
317 Mark Carreon .10
318 Kirby Puckett (.300 Series) .50
319 Carlos Perez .10
320 Gary DiSarcina .10
321 Trevor Hoffman .10
322 Mike Piazza (.300 Series) .65
323 Frank Thomas (.300 Series) .40
324 Juan Acevedo .10
325 Bip Roberts .10
326 Javier Lopez .10
327 Benito Santiago .10
328 Mark Lewis .10
329 Royce Clayton .10
330 Tom Gordon .10
331 Ben McDonald .10
332 Dan Wilson .10
333 Ron Gant .10
334 Wade Boggs (.300 Series) .45
335 Paul Molitor .75
336 Tony Gwynn (.300 Series) .50
337 Sean Berry .10
338 Rickey Henderson .75
339 Wil Cordero .10
340 Kent Mercker .10
341 Kenny Rogers .10
342 Ryne Sandberg 1.00
343 Charlie Hayes .10
344 Andy Benes .10
345 Sterling Hitchcock .10
346 Bernard Gilkey .10
347 Julio Franco .10
348 Ken Hill .10
349 Russ Davis .10
350 Mike Blowers .10
351 B.J. Surhoff .10
352 Lance Johnson .10
353 Darryl Hamilton .10
354 Shawon Dunston .10
355 Rick Aguilera .10
356 Danny Tartabull .10
357 Todd Stottlemyre .10
358 Mike Bordick .10
359 Jack McDowell .10
360 Todd Zeile .10
361 Tino Martinez .10
362 Greg Gagne .10
363 Mike Kelly .10
364 Tim Raines .10
365 Ernie Young .10
366 Mike Stanley .10
367 Wally Joyner .10
368 Karim Garcia .10
369 Paul Wilson .10
370 Sal Fasano .10
371 Jason Schmidt .10
372 Livan Hernandez **RC** .25
373 George Arias .10
374 Steve Gibralter .10
375 Jermaine Dye .10
376 Jason Kendall .10
377 Brooks Kieschnick .10
378 Jeff Ware .10
379 Alan Benes .10
380 Rey Ordonez .10
381 Jay Powell .10
382 Osvaldo Fernandez **RC** .15
383 Wilton Guerrero **RC** .10
384 Eric Owens .10
385 George Williams .10
386 Chan Ho Park .10
387 Jeff Suppan .10
388 F.P. Santangelo **RC** .10
389 Terry Adams .10
390 Bob Abreu .10
391 Quinton McCracken **RC** .10
392 Mike Busby **RC** .10
393 Cal Ripken Jr. (Checklist) .75
394 Ken Griffey Jr. (Checklist) .60
395 Frank Thomas (Checklist) .40
396 Chipper Jones (Checklist) .50
397 Greg Maddux (Checklist) .50
398 Mike Piazza (Checklist) .65
399 Ken Griffey Jr., Frank Thomas, Cal Ripken Jr., Greg Maddux, Chipper Jones, Mike Piazza (Checklist) .50

Artist's Proof

AP is a parallel to the Starburst partial parallel of '96 Pinnacle. Like Starburst, the Artist's Proof cards are printed in Dufex technology on front, with the AP cards having the words "ARTIST'S PROOF" repeated throughout the background. AP backs are identical to Starburst. Stated insertion rate for the Artist's Proofs was one per 47 packs in hobby and one per 67 retail packs.

	NM/M
Common Artist's Proof:	2.00
Stars:	3X

Starburst

For 1996 Pinnacle abbreviated its parallel insert set to just half of the cards from the base issue. Only 200 select players are included in the Starburst Dufex-printed parallel set found on average of once per seven hobby packs and once per 10 retail packs.

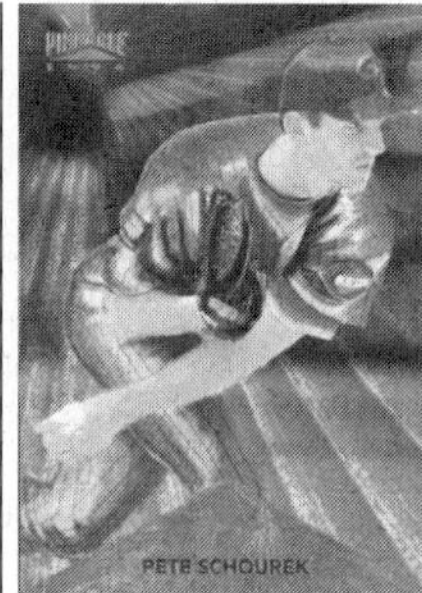

	NM/M
Complete Set (200):	150.00
Common Player:	.40
Common Artist's Proof:	.75
Artist's Proofs:	2X

1 Greg Maddux 3.00
2 Bill Pulsipher .40
3 Dante Bichette .40
4 Mike Piazza 4.00
5 Garret Anderson .40
6 Chuck Knoblauch .40
7 Jeff Bagwell 2.25
8 Wil Cordero .40
9 Travis Fryman .40
10 Reggie Sanders .40
11 Deion Sanders .40
12 Tim Salmon .40
13 Tino Martinez .40
14 Bobby Bonilla .40
15 Joe Carter .40
16 Mike Mussina 1.25
17 Jose Canseco 1.25
18 Manny Ramirez 2.25
19 Gregg Jefferies .40
20 Charles Johnson .40
21 Brian Hunter .40
22 Ray Lankford .40
23 Ivan Rodriguez 2.00
24 Paul Molitor 2.25
25 Eric Karros .40
26 Edgar Martinez .40
27 Shawon Dunston .40
28 Mo Vaughn .40
29 Pedro Martinez 2.25
30 Marty Cordova .40
31 Ken Caminiti .40
32 Gary Sheffield .75
33 Shawn Green .75
34 Cliff Floyd .40
35 Andres Galarraga .40
36 Matt Williams .40
37 Don Mattingly 3.50
38 Kevin Appier .40
39 Ozzie Smith 3.00
40 Kenny Lofton .40
41 Ken Griffey Jr. 4.00
42 Jack McDowell .40
43 Gary Gaetti .40
44 Dennis Martinez .40
45 Chipper Jones 3.00
46 Eddie Murray 2.25
47 Bernie Williams .40
48 Andre Dawson .60
49 Dave Winfield 2.25
50 B.J. Surhoff .40
51 Barry Larkin .40
52 Alan Trammell .40
53 Sammy Sosa 3.00
54 Hideo Nomo 1.00
55 Mark McGwire 4.50
56 Jay Bell .40
57 Juan Gonzalez 1.00
58 Chili Davis .40
59 Robin Ventura .40
60 John Mabry .40
61 Ken Griffey Jr. (Naturals) 2.00
62 Frank Thomas (Naturals) 1.25
63 Cal Ripken Jr. (Naturals) 3.00
64 Albert Belle (Naturals) .40
65 Mike Piazza (Naturals) 2.00
66 Dante Bichette (Naturals) .40
67 Sammy Sosa (Naturals) 1.50
68 Mo Vaughn (Naturals) .40
69 Tim Salmon (Naturals) .40
70 Reggie Sanders (Naturals) .40
71 Cecil Fielder (Naturals) .40
72 Jim Edmonds (Naturals) .40
73 Rafael Palmeiro (Naturals) .75
74 Edgar Martinez (Naturals) .40
75 Barry Bonds (Naturals) 3.00
76 Manny Ramirez (Naturals) 1.25
77 Larry Walker (Naturals) .40
78 Jeff Bagwell (Naturals) 1.25
79 Ron Gant (Naturals) .40
80 Andres Galarraga (Naturals) .40
81 Eddie Murray (Naturals) 1.25
82 Kirby Puckett (Naturals) 1.50
83 Will Clark (Naturals) .40
84 Don Mattingly (Naturals) 1.75
85 Mark McGwire (Naturals) 2.25
86 Dean Palmer (Naturals) .40
87 Matt Williams (Naturals) .40
88 Fred McGriff (Naturals) .40
89 Joe Carter (Naturals) .40
90 Juan Gonzalez (Naturals) .65
91 Alex Ochoa .40
92 Ruben Rivera .40
93 Tony Clark .40
94 Pete Schourek .40
95 Terrell Wade .40
96 Johnny Damon .65
97 Derek Jeter 6.00
98 Phil Nevin .40
99 Robert Perez .40
100 Dustin Hermanson .40
101 Frank Thomas 2.25
102 Michael Tucker .40
103 Kirby Puckett 3.00
104 Alex Gonzalez .40
105 Tony Gwynn 3.00
106 Moises Alou .40
107 Albert Belle .40
108 Barry Bonds 6.00
109 Fred McGriff .40
110 Dennis Eckersley 1.50
111 Craig Biggio .40
112 David Cone .40
113 Will Clark .40
114 Cal Ripken Jr. 6.00
115 Wade Boggs 3.00
116 Pete Schourek .40
117 Darren Daulton .40
118 Carlos Baerga .40
119 Larry Walker .40
120 Denny Neagle .40
121 Jim Edmonds .40
122 Lee Smith .40
123 Jason Isringhausen .40
124 Jay Buhner .40
125 John Olerud .40
126 Jeff Conine .40
127 Dean Palmer .40
128 Jim Abbott .40
129 Raul Mondesi .40
130 Tom Glavine .60
131 Kevin Seitzer .40
132 Lenny Dykstra .40
133 Brian Jordan .40
134 Rondell White .40
135 Bret Boone .40
136 Randy Johnson 2.25
137 Paul O'Neill .40
138 Jim Thome .75
139 Edgardo Alfonzo .40
140 Terry Pendleton .40
141 Harold Baines .40
142 Roberto Alomar .45
143 Mark Grace .40
144 Derek Bell .40
145 Vinny Castilla .40
146 Cecil Fielder .40
147 Roger Clemens 3.50
148 Orel Hershiser .40
149 J.T. Snow .40
150 Rafael Palmeiro 1.75
151 Bret Saberhagen .40
152 Todd Hollandsworth .40
153 Ryan Klesko .40
154 Greg Maddux (Hardball Heroes) 1.50
155 Ken Griffey Jr. (Hardball Heroes) 2.00
156 Hideo Nomo (Hardball Heroes) .65
157 Frank Thomas (Hardball Heroes) 1.25
158 Cal Ripken Jr. (Hardball Heroes) 3.00
159 Jeff Bagwell (Hardball Heroes) 1.25
160 Barry Bonds (Hardball Heroes) 3.00
161 Mo Vaughn (Hardball Heroes) .40
162 Albert Belle (Hardball Heroes) .40
163 Sammy Sosa (Hardball Heroes) 1.50
164 Reggie Sanders (Hardball Heroes) .40
165 Mike Piazza (Hardball Heroes) 2.00
166 Chipper Jones (Hardball Heroes) 1.50
167 Tony Gwynn (Hardball Heroes) 1.50
168 Kirby Puckett (Hardball Heroes) 1.50
169 Wade Boggs (Hardball Heroes) 1.25
170 Will Clark (Hardball Heroes) .40
171 Gary Sheffield (Hardball Heroes) .45
172 Dante Bichette (Hardball Heroes) .40

173 Randy Johnson (Hardball Heroes) 1.25
174 Matt Williams (Hardball Heroes) .40
175 Alex Rodriguez (Hardball Heroes) 4.50
176 Tim Salmon (Hardball Heroes) .40
177 Johnny Damon (Hardball Heroes) .40
178 Manny Ramirez (Hardball Heroes) 1.25
179 Derek Jeter (Hardball Heroes) 3.00
180 Eddie Murray (Hardball Heroes) 1.25
181 Ozzie Smith (Hardball Heroes) 1.50
182 Garret Anderson (Hardball Heroes) .40
183 Raul Mondesi (Hardball Heroes) .40
184 Jeff Conine (.300 Series) .40
185 Ken Griffey Jr. (.300 Series) 2.00
186 Will Clark (.300 Series) .40
187 Mike Greenwell (.300 Series) .40
188 Carlos Baerga (.300 Series) .40
189 Paul Molitor (.300 Series) 1.25
190 Jeff Bagwell (.300 Series) 1.25
191 Mark Grace (.300 Series) .40
192 Don Mattingly (.300 Series) 1.75
193 Hal Morris (.300 Series) .40
194 Kenny Lofton (.300 Series) .40
195 Edgar Martinez (.300 Series) .40
196 Kirby Puckett (.300 Series) 1.50
197 Mike Piazza (.300 Series) 2.00
198 Frank Thomas (.300 Series) 1.25
199 Wade Boggs (.300 Series) 1.25
200 Tony Gwynn (.300 Series) 1.50

Foil Series 2

The 200 cards from Series 2 were paralleled in a special foil edition which was sold at retail outlets only in five-card $2.99 packs. Fronts have a metallic foil background to differentiate them from the regular-issue Series 2 version.

NM/M
Complete Set (200): 15.00
Common Player: .20
Stars: 1.5X

Christie Brinkley Collection Promo

To promote its Brinkley-photographed insert cards in Series 2 Pinnacle, the company issued a card of the celebrity photographer. In the same format as the player inserts, the promo card has a gold-foil enhanced borderless glamor photo on front. The back repeats a detail of the front photo and has details of the insert series.

NM/M
Christie Brinkley 5.00

Christie Brinkley Collection

Supermodel Christie Brinkley took the photos for these 1996 Pinnacle Series 2 inserts. The cards capture players from

the 1995 World Series participants during a spring training photo session. Cards were seeded one per every 23 hobby packs or 32 retail packs.

NM/M
Complete Set (16): 15.00
Common Player: .75
1 Greg Maddux 3.50
2 Ryan Klesko .75
3 Dave Justice .75
4 Tom Glavine 1.50
5 Chipper Jones 3.50
6 Fred McGriff .75
7 Javier Lopez .75
8 Marquis Grissom .75
9 Jason Schmidt .75
10 Albert Belle .75
11 Manny Ramirez 2.25
12 Carlos Baerga .75
13 Sandy Alomar .75
14 Jim Thome 2.25
15 Julio Franco .75
16 Kenny Lofton .75

Essence of the Game

Essence of the Game is an 18-card insert set found only in hobby packs at a one per 23 packs rate in Series 1. Cards are printed on clear plastic with the front photo also appearing in an inverted fashion on back. Micro-etched Dufex printing technology is utilized on the front.

NM/M
Complete Set (18): 35.00
Common Player: .75
1 Cal Ripken Jr. 6.00
2 Greg Maddux 3.00
3 Frank Thomas 2.50
4 Matt Williams .75
5 Chipper Jones 3.00
6 Reggie Sanders .75
7 Ken Griffey Jr. 4.00
8 Kirby Puckett 3.00
9 Hideo Nomo 1.50
10 Mike Piazza 4.00
11 Jeff Bagwell 2.50
12 Mo Vaughn .75
13 Albert Belle .75
14 Tim Salmon .75
15 Don Mattingly 3.50
16 Will Clark .75
17 Eddie Murray 2.50
18 Barry Bonds 6.00

First Rate

Retail-exclusive First Rate showcases former first round draft picks playing in the majors. Printed in Dufex foil throughout, a red swirl pattern covers the left 2/3 of the front. Backs show the player again, within a large nu-

meral "1." These inserts are found at an average rate of one per 23 packs in Series 1.

NM/M
Complete Set (18): 40.00
Common Player: 1.25
1 Ken Griffey Jr. 5.00
2 Frank Thomas 2.50
3 Mo Vaughn 1.25
4 Chipper Jones 3.50
5 Alex Rodriguez 6.50
6 Kirby Puckett 3.50
7 Gary Sheffield 1.75
8 Matt Williams 1.25
9 Barry Bonds 7.50
10 Craig Biggio 1.25
11 Robin Ventura 1.25
12 Michael Tucker 1.25
13 Derek Jeter 7.50
14 Manny Ramirez 2.50
15 Barry Larkin 1.25
16 Shawn Green 1.75
17 Will Clark 1.25
18 Mark McGwire 6.50

Pinnacle Power

Pinnacle Power inserts are seeded at the rate of one per 47 packs in both hobby and retail Series 1. The sluggers are featured on a two-layered front. The bottom layer is silver Dufex foil with solid black on top; a color action photo of the player is at center, giving the card a die-cut appearance.

NM/M
Complete Set (20): 40.00
Common Player: 1.25
1 Frank Thomas 2.50
2 Mo Vaughn 1.25
2p Mo Vaughn (Promo) 1.50
3 Ken Griffey Jr. 4.50
4 Matt Williams 1.25
5 Barry Bonds 6.00
6 Reggie Sanders 1.25
7 Mike Piazza 4.50
8 Jim Edmonds 1.25
9 Dante Bichette 1.25
10 Sammy Sosa 3.50
11 Jeff Bagwell 2.50
12 Fred McGriff 1.25
13 Albert Belle 1.25
14 Tim Salmon 1.25
15 Joe Carter 1.25
16 Manny Ramirez 2.50
17 Eddie Murray 2.50
18 Cecil Fielder 1.25
19 Larry Walker 1.25
20 Juan Gonzalez 1.75

Project Stardom

These inserts feature young players on their way to stardom. The cards, which use Dufex technology, are seeded one per every 35 packs of Series 2 hobby packs.

NM/M
Complete Set (18): 35.00
Common Player: 1.00
1 Paul Wilson 1.00
2 Derek Jeter 8.50
3 Karim Garcia 1.00
4 Johnny Damon 2.75
5 Alex Rodriguez 7.50
6 Chipper Jones 6.50
7 Charles Johnson 1.00
8 Bob Abreu 1.25
9 Alan Benes 1.00
10 Richard Hidalgo 1.00
11 Brooks Kieschnick 1.00
12 Garret Anderson 1.00
13 Livan Hernandez 1.00
14 Manny Ramirez 5.00
15 Jermaine Dye 1.00
16 Todd Hollandsworth 1.00
17 Raul Mondesi 1.00
18 Ryan Klesko 1.00

Cal Ripken Tribute

A special Cal Ripken Tribute card was issued in Series 1 Pinnacle packs at a rate of 1:150. Front features an etched metallic foil background, a gold-foil facsimile autograph and a "2,131+ Consecutive Games Played" starburst. Back has a photo of the scoreboard on that historic occasion, and a photo of Ripken being driven around Camden Yards in a red Corvette. The card is numbered "1 of 1," but it is not unique.

NM/M
1 of 1 Cal Ripken Jr. 5.00

Skylines

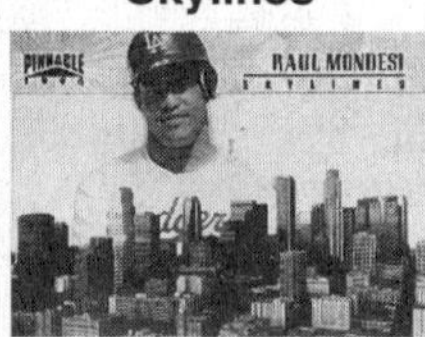

These inserts feature player portraits looming over the city skyline where they play their home games. Printed on a clear plastic stock, the cards were seeded one per every 29 Series 2 magazine packs, and one per 50 retail packs.

NM/M
Complete Set (18): 375.00
Common Player: 10.00
1 Ken Griffey Jr. 50.00
2 Frank Thomas 30.00
3 Greg Maddux 40.00
4 Cal Ripken Jr. 65.00
5 Albert Belle 10.00
6 Mo Vaughn 10.00
7 Mike Piazza 50.00
8 Wade Boggs 40.00
9 Will Clark 10.00
10 Barry Bonds 65.00
11 Gary Sheffield 10.00
12 Hideo Nomo 25.00
13 Tony Gwynn 40.00
14 Kirby Puckett 40.00
15 Chipper Jones 40.00
16 Jeff Bagwell 30.00
17 Manny Ramirez 30.00
18 Raul Mondesi 10.00

Slugfest

These Series 2 inserts feature the game's heaviest

hitters on all-foil Dufex cards. The cards were seeded one per every 35 retail packs.

NM/M
Complete Set (18): 40.00
Common Player: 1.25
1 Frank Thomas 2.75
2 Ken Griffey Jr. 4.00
3 Jeff Bagwell 2.75
4 Barry Bonds 5.00
5 Mo Vaughn 1.25
6 Albert Belle 1.25
7 Mike Piazza 4.00
8 Matt Williams 1.25
9 Dante Bichette 1.25
10 Sammy Sosa 3.00
11 Gary Sheffield 2.00
12 Reggie Sanders 1.25
13 Manny Ramirez 2.75
14 Eddie Murray 2.75
15 Juan Gonzalez 2.25
16 Dean Palmer 1.25
17 Rafael Palmeiro 2.75
18 Cecil Fielder 1.25

Team Pinnacle

Team Pinnacle inserts offer 18 players in a double-sided nine-card set. Each card can be found with Dufex printing on one side and regular gold-foil printing on the other. Inserted one per 72 packs of Series 1, Team Pinnacle pairs up an American League player and a National Leaguer at the same position on each card.

NM/M
Complete Set (9): 35.00
Common Player: 1.50
1 Frank Thomas, Jeff Bagwell 4.00
2 Chuck Knoblauch, Craig Biggio 1.50
3 Jim Thome, Matt Williams 3.00
4 Barry Larkin, Cal Ripken Jr. 12.00
5 Barry Bonds, Tim Salmon 10.00
6 Ken Griffey Jr., Reggie Sanders 8.00
7 Albert Belle, Sammy Sosa 6.00
8 Ivan Rodriguez, Mike Piazza 6.00
9 Greg Maddux, Randy Johnson 8.00

Team Spirit

One in every 72 Series 2 hobby packs or every 103 retail packs has one of these die-cut insert cards. Each card has a holographic baseball design behind an embossed glossy action photo of the player on a flat black background. Backs are conventionally printed.

NM/M
Complete Set (12): 45.00
Common Player: 1.25

1 Greg Maddux 4.00
2 Ken Griffey Jr. 5.00
3 Derek Jeter 8.00
4 Mike Piazza 5.00
5 Cal Ripken Jr. 8.00
6 Frank Thomas 2.75
7 Jeff Bagwell 2.75
8 Mo Vaughn 1.25
9 Albert Belle 1.25
10 Chipper Jones 4.00
11 Johnny Damon 1.50
12 Barry Bonds 8.00

Team Tomorrow

Team Tomorrow showcases young superstars on a horizontal Dufex design. While the player appears twice on the card front, the left side is merely a close-up of the same shot appearing on the right. These inserts are exclusive to Series 1 jumbo packs, found on average at the rate of one per 19 packs.

NM/M
Complete Set (10): 20.00
Common Player: .50
1 Ruben Rivera .50
2 Johnny Damon 1.00
3 Raul Mondesi .50
4 Manny Ramirez 3.00
5 Hideo Nomo 1.50
6 Chipper Jones 4.00
7 Garret Anderson .50
8 Alex Rodriguez 5.00
9 Derek Jeter 6.00
10 Karim Garcia .50

1996 Pinnacle/ Aficionado

Pinnacle's 1996 Aficionado set gives every card the look of maple woodgrain. The 200 regular issue cards include 160 cards in an antique-look sepia-tone finish. The horizontal front also has a rainbow holographic foil image of the player. The back has comparison statistics that show how the player compares with the league average at that position and the league average at that position in different eras. There are also 60 four-color cards, which include 25 rookie cards, and a 10-card Global Reach subset. This subset, which honors baseball's international flavor, features Aficionado's new heliogram printing process. Artist's Proof parallel cards, seeded about one per 35 packs, were also created. These cards mirror the regular issue and use a unique gold foil stamp. There were three insert sets: Slick Picks, Rivals and Magic Numbers.

		NM/M
Complete Set (200):		20.00
Common Player:		.10
Common Artist's Proof:		.50
Artist's Proof Stars:		8X
Pack (5):		1.50
Wax Box (16):		30.00
1	Jack McDowell	.10
2	Jay Bell	.10
3	Rafael Palmeiro	1.25
4	Wally Joyner	.10
5	Ozzie Smith	2.00
6	Mark McGwire	3.00
7	Kevin Seitzer	.10
8	Fred McGriff	.10
9	Roger Clemens	2.25
9s	Roger Clemens (Marked "SAMPLE.")	4.00
10	Randy Johnson	1.50
11	Cecil Fielder	.10
12	David Cone	.10
13	Chili Davis	.10
14	Andres Galarraga	.10
15	Joe Carter	.10
16	Ryne Sandberg	2.00
17	Paul O'Neill	.10
18	Cal Ripken Jr.	4.00
19	Wade Boggs	2.00
20	Greg Gagne	.10
21	Edgar Martinez	.10
22	Greg Maddux	2.00
23	Ken Caminiti	.10
24	Kirby Puckett	2.00
25	Craig Biggio	.10
26	Will Clark	.10
27	Ron Gant	.10
28	Eddie Murray	1.50
29	Lance Johnson	.10
30	Tony Gwynn	2.00
31	Dante Bichette	.10
32	Darren Daulton	.10
33	Danny Tartabull	.10
34	Jeff King	.10
35	Tom Glavine	.40
36	Rickey Henderson	1.50
37	Jose Canseco	1.00
38	Barry Larkin	.10
39	Dennis Martinez	.10
40	Ruben Sierra	.10
41	Bobby Bonilla	.10
42	Jeff Conine	.10
43	Lee Smith	.10
44	Charlie Hayes	.10
45	Walt Weiss	.10
46	Jay Buhner	.10
47	Kenny Rogers	.10
48	Paul Molitor	1.50
49	Hal Morris	.10
50	Todd Stottlemyre	.10
51	Mike Stanley	.10
52	Mark Grace	.10
53	Lenny Dykstra	.10
54	Andre Dawson	.25
55	Dennis Eckersley	1.25
56	Ben McDonald	.10
57	Ray Lankford	.10
58	Mo Vaughn	.10
59	Frank Thomas	1.50
60	Julio Franco	.10
61	Jim Abbott	.10
62	Greg Vaughn	.10
63	Marquis Grissom	.10
64	Tino Martinez	.10
65	Kevin Appier	.10
66	Matt Williams	.10
67	Sammy Sosa	2.00
68	Larry Walker	.10
69	Ivan Rodriguez	1.25
70	Eric Karros	.10
71	Bernie Williams	.10
72	Carlos Baerga	.10
73	Jeff Bagwell	1.50
74	Pete Schourek	.10
75	Ken Griffey Jr.	2.50
76	Bernard Gilkey	.10
77	Albert Belle	.10
78	Chuck Knoblauch	.10
79	John Smoltz	.10
80	Barry Bonds	4.00
81	Vinny Castilla	.10
82	John Olerud	.10
83	Mike Mussina	1.00
84	Alex Fernandez	.10
85	Shawon Dunston	.10
86	Travis Fryman	.10
87	Moises Alou	.10
88	Dean Palmer	.10
89	Gregg Jefferies	.10
90	Jim Thome	1.25
91	Dave Justice	.10
92	B.J. Surhoff	.10
93	Ramon Martinez	.10
94	Gary Sheffield	.40
95	Andy Benes	.10
96	Reggie Sanders	.10
97	Roberto Alomar	.35
98	Omar Vizquel	.10
99	Juan Gonzalez	.75
100	Robin Ventura	.10
101	Jason Isringhausen	.10
102	Greg Colbrunn	.10
103	Brian Jordan	.10
104	Shawn Green	.40
105	Brian Hunter	.10
106	Rondell White	.10
107	Ryan Klesko	.10
107s	Ryan Klesko (Marked "SAMPLE.")	1.00
108	Sterling Hitchcock	.10
109	Manny Ramirez	1.50
110	Bret Boone	.10
111	Michael Tucker	.10
112	Julian Tavarez	.10
113	Benji Gil	.10
114	Kenny Lofton	.10
115	Mike Kelly	.10
116	Ray Durham	.10
117	Trevor Hoffman	.10
118	Butch Huskey	.10
119	Phil Nevin	.10
120	Pedro Martinez	1.50
121	Wil Cordero	.10
122	Tim Salmon	.10
123	Jim Edmonds	.10
124	Mike Piazza	2.50
125	Rico Brogna	.10
126	John Mabry	.10
127	Chipper Jones	2.00
128	Johnny Damon	.35
129	Raul Mondesi	.10
130	Denny Neagle	.10
131	Marc Newfield	.10
132	Hideo Nomo	.75
133	Joe Vitiello	.10
134	Garret Anderson	.10
135	Dave Nilsson	.10
136	Alex Rodriguez	3.00
137	Russ Davis	.10
138	Frank Rodriguez	.10
139	Royce Clayton	.10
140	John Valentin	.10
141	Marty Cordova	.10
142	Alex Gonzalez	.10
143	Carlos Delgado	.75
144	Willie Greene	.10
145	Cliff Floyd	.10
146	Bobby Higginson	.10
147	J.T. Snow	.10
148	Derek Bell	.10
149	Edgardo Alfonzo	.10
150	Charles Johnson	.10
151	Hideo Nomo (Global Reach)	.60
152	Larry Walker (Global Reach)	.10
153	Bob Abreu (Global Reach)	.10
154	Karim Garcia (Global Reach)	.10
155	Dave Nilsson (Global Reach)	.10
156	Chan Ho Park (Global Reach)	.10
157	Dennis Martinez (Global Reach)	.10
158	Sammy Sosa (Global Reach)	1.25
159	Rey Ordonez (Global Reach)	.10
160	Roberto Alomar (Global Reach)	.10
161	George Arias	.10
162	Jason Schmidt	.10
163	Derek Jeter	4.00
164	Chris Snopek	.10
165	Todd Hollandsworth	.10
166	Sal Fasano	.10
167	Jay Powell	.10
168	Paul Wilson	.10
169	Jim Pittsley	.10
170	LaTroy Hawkins	.10
171	Bob Abreu	.10
172	Mike Grace **RC**	.10
173	Karim Garcia	.10
174	Richard Hidalgo	.10
175	Felipe Crespo	.10
176	Terrell Wade	.10
177	Steve Gibralter	.10
178	Jermaine Dye	.10
179	Alan Benes	.10
180	Wilton Guerrero **RC**	.10
181	Brooks Kieschnick	.10
182	Roger Cedeno	.10
183	Osvaldo Fernandez **RC**	.10
184	Matt Lawton **RC**	.50
185	George Williams	.10
186	Jimmy Haynes	.10
187	Mike Busby **RC**	.10
188	Chan Ho Park	.10
189	Marc Barcelo	.10
190	Jason Kendall	.10
191	Rey Ordonez	.10
192	Tyler Houston	.10
193	John Wasdin	.10
194	Jeff Suppan	.10
195	Jeff Ware	.10
196	Checklist	.10
197	Checklist	.10
198	Checklist	.10
199	Checklist	.10
200	Checklist	.10

First Pitch Previews

This parallel set differs from the regularly issued version in that there is a "FIRST PITCH / PREVIEW" label printed on the front on the end opposite the heliogram player portrait. Also, whereas on the regular cards, the player portrait is in silver metallic composition, the First Pitch Preview cards have the portrait in gold. These cards were most often obtained by visiting Pinnacle's site on the Internet and answering a trivia question.

	NM/M
Complete Set (200):	250.00
Common Player:	2.00

Magic Numbers

This insert set focuses on 10 of the game's best players, printing them on a wooden stock which carries the distinct grain and color of natural wood. The cards, seeded one every 72 packs, compares current players with others who have worn the same uniform number. Each card can also be found with a large black "SAMPLE" printed on back.

		NM/M
Complete Set (10):		15.50
Common Player:		.75
Samples:		1X
1	Ken Griffey Jr.	3.25
2	Greg Maddux	2.50
3	Frank Thomas	1.50
4	Mo Vaughn	.75
5	Jeff Bagwell	1.50
6	Chipper Jones	2.50
7	Albert Belle	.75
8	Cal Ripken Jr.	4.50
9	Matt Williams	.75
10	Sammy Sosa	2.50

Rivals

These inserts concentrate on the many matchups and rivalries that make baseball fun. Each card uses spot embossing. The cards are seeded one per every 24 packs.

		NM/M
Complete Set (24):		65.00
Common Player:		2.00
1	Ken Griffey Jr., Frank Thomas	4.00
2	Frank Thomas, Cal Ripken Jr.	4.50
3	Cal Ripken Jr., Mo Vaughn	4.00
4	Mo Vaughn, Ken Griffey Jr.	2.50
5	Ken Griffey Jr., Cal Ripken Jr.	5.00
6	Frank Thomas, Mo Vaughn	2.00
7	Cal Ripken Jr., Ken Griffey Jr.	5.00
8	Mo Vaughn, Frank Thomas	2.00
9	Ken Griffey Jr., Mo Vaughn	2.50
10	Frank Thomas, Ken Griffey Jr.	4.00
11	Cal Ripken Jr., Frank Thomas	4.50
12	Mo Vaughn, Cal Ripken Jr.	4.00
13	Mike Piazza, Jeff Bagwell	2.50
14	Jeff Bagwell, Barry Bonds	4.50
15	Jeff Bagwell, Mike Piazza	2.50
16	Tony Gwynn, Mike Piazza	3.00
17	Mike Piazza, Barry Bonds	5.00
18	Jeff Bagwell, Tony Gwynn	2.00
19	Barry Bonds, Mike Piazza	5.00
20	Tony Gwynn, Jeff Bagwell	2.00
21	Mike Piazza, Tony Gwynn	3.00
22	Barry Bonds, Jeff Bagwell	4.50
23	Tony Gwynn, Barry Bonds	4.50
24	Barry Bonds, Tony Gwynn	4.50

Slick Picks

This insert set pictures 32 of the best players in baseball on cards which use Spectroetch printing. Each card notes where that player was selected in the annual draft, emphasizing that there are numerous bargains available throughout the amateur draft. The cards were seeded one per 10 packs, making them the easiest to obtain of the set's insert cards.

		NM/M
Complete Set (32):		40.00
Common Player:		.50
1	Mike Piazza	2.50
2	Cal Ripken Jr.	4.00
3	Ken Griffey Jr.	2.50
4	Paul Wilson	.50
5	Frank Thomas	1.50
6	Mo Vaughn	.50
7	Barry Bonds	4.00
8	Albert Belle	.50
9	Jeff Bagwell	1.50
10	Dante Bichette	.50
11	Hideo Nomo	.75
12	Raul Mondesi	.50
13	Manny Ramirez	1.50
14	Greg Maddux	2.00
15	Tony Gwynn	2.00
16	Ryne Sandberg	2.00
17	Reggie Sanders	.50
18	Derek Jeter	4.00
19	Johnny Damon	.75
20	Alex Rodriguez	3.00
21	Ryan Klesko	.50
22	Jim Thome	1.50
23	Kenny Lofton	.50
24	Tino Martinez	.50
25	Randy Johnson	1.50
26	Wade Boggs	2.00
27	Juan Gonzalez	.75
28	Kirby Puckett	2.00
29	Tim Salmon	.50
30	Chipper Jones	2.00
31	Garret Anderson	.50
32	Eddie Murray	1.50

FanFest

In conjunction with its title sponsorship of baseball's All-Star FanFest, July 5-9 in Philadelphia, the company distributed two-card foil packs prior to and at the show. Fronts have a negative posterized image of Independence Hall as a backdrop for a player action photo. Textured gold-foil bottom corners hold a

team logo and a Liberty Bell silhouette with the player's position. The player name appears in gold foil above the FanFest logo at bottom center. Backs repeat the negative background and have another player photo, a few words about him and all the appropriate logos. The Darren Daulton card is in Sportflix technology as a tribute to the recently retired Phillies fan favorite. Card #31, Steve Carlton, was not distributed in packs. Cards of the Phillie Phanatic team mascot, the city's mayor and several other local dignitaries were produced and given to those persons.

		NM/M
Complete Set (30, No Carlton):		25.00
Common Player:		.50
1	Cal Ripken Jr.	4.00
2	Greg Maddux	2.00
3	Ken Griffey Jr.	2.50
4	Frank Thomas	1.50
5	Jeff Bagwell	1.50
6	Hideo Nomo	.75
7	Tony Gwynn	2.00
8	Albert Belle	.50
9	Mo Vaughn	.50
10	Mike Piazza	2.50
11	Dante Bichette	.50
12	Ryne Sandberg	2.00
13	Wade Boggs	2.00
14	Kirby Puckett	2.00
15	Ozzie Smith	2.00
16	Barry Bonds	4.00
17	Gary Sheffield	.75
18	Barry Larkin	.50
19	Kevin Seitzer	.50
20	Jay Bell	.50
21	Chipper Jones	2.00
22	Ivan Rodriguez	1.25
23	Cecil Fielder	.50
24	Manny Ramirez	1.50
25	Randy Johnson	1.50
26	Moises Alou	.50
27	Mark McGwire	3.00
28	Jason Isringhausen	.50
29	Joe Carter	.50
30	Darren Daulton (Sportflix)	1.50
31	Steve Carlton	10.00
---	Benjamin Franklin	5.00
---	Phillie Phanatic (Mascot)	5.00
---	Edward G. Rendell (Mayor)	3.00

FanFest Playing Cards

A special version of Pinnacle's FanFest cards was produced for construction of a large "house of cards" at the FanFest site. Following the event, some of the cards made their way into the hobby. Similar in format to the regular cards, the special issue was produced on textured playing-card stock in a 2-1/4" x 3-1/2" format with rounded corners. The playing cards lack the gold-foil found on regular cards and thus the player's name is nowhere to be found. Backs have a large gold-and-white Pinnacle logo on a black background. Cards are listed here using the numbering found on the regular version; the playing cards are unnumbered.

		NM/M
Complete Set (29):		300.00
Common Player:		10.00
(1)	Cal Ripken Jr.	30.00
(2)	Greg Maddux	17.50
(3)	Ken Griffey Jr.	20.00
(4)	Frank Thomas	15.00
(5)	Jeff Bagwell	15.00
(6)	Hideo Nomo	12.50
(7)	Tony Gwynn	17.50
(8)	Albert Belle	10.00
(9)	Mo Vaughn	10.00
(10)	Mike Piazza	20.00
(11)	Dante Bichette	10.00
(12)	Ryne Sandberg	17.50
(13)	Wade Boggs	17.50
(14)	Kirby Puckett	17.50
(15)	Ozzie Smith	17.50
(16)	Barry Bonds	30.00
(17)	Gary Sheffield	12.50
(18)	Barry Larkin	10.00
(19)	Kevin Seitzer	10.00
(20)	Jay Bell	10.00
(21)	Chipper Jones	17.50
(22)	Ivan Rodriguez	12.50
(23)	Cecil Fielder	10.00
(24)	Manny Ramirez	15.00
(25)	Randy Johnson	15.00
(26)	Moises Alou	10.00
(27)	Mark McGwire	25.00
(28)	Jason Isringhausen	10.00
(29)	Joe Carter	10.00

1997 Pinnacle

Pinnacle baseball consists of 200 base cards. Fronts have the player's name stamped within a foil baseball-diamond shape at the bottom of each card. Backs contain summaries of the players' 1996 and lifetime statistics. Included within the base set is a 30-card Rookies subset, a 12-card Clout subset and three checklists. Inserts include two parallel sets (Artist's Proof and Museum Collection), Passport to the Majors, Shades, Team Pinnacle, Cardfrontations, and Home/Away. Cards were sold in 10-card packs for $2.49 each.

		NM/M
Complete Set (200):		10.00
Common Player:		.05
Pack (10):		1.00
Wax Box (24):		12.50
Wax Retail Box (16):		10.00
1	Cecil Fielder	.05
2	Garret Anderson	.05
3	Charles Nagy	.05
4	Darryl Hamilton	.05
5	Greg Myers	.05
6	Eric Davis	.05
7	Jeff Frye	.05
8	Marquis Grissom	.05
9	Curt Schilling	.35
10	Jeff Fassero	.05
11	Alan Benes	.05
12	Orlando Miller	.05
13	Alex Fernandez	.05
14	Andy Pettitte	.25
15	Andre Dawson	.25
16	Mark Grudzielanek	.05
17	Joe Vitiello	.05
18	Juan Gonzalez	.40

#	Player	Price
19	Mark Whiten	.05
20	Lance Johnson	.05
21	Trevor Hoffman	.05
22	Marc Newfield	.05
23	Jim Eisenreich	.05
24	Joe Carter	.05
25	Jose Canseco	.30
26	Bill Swift	.05
27	Ellis Burks	.05
28	Ben McDonald	.05
29	Edgar Martinez	.05
30	Jamie Moyer	.05
31	Chan Ho Park	.05
32	Carlos Delgado	.50
33	Kevin Mitchell	.05
34	Carlos Garcia	.05
35	Darryl Strawberry	.05
36	Jim Thome	.60
37	Jose Offerman	.05
38	Ryan Klesko	.05
39	Ruben Sierra	.05
40	Devon White	.05
41	Brian Jordan	.05
42	Tony Gwynn	.75
43	Rafael Palmeiro	.50
44	Dante Bichette	.05
45	Scott Stahoviak	.05
46	Roger Cedeno	.05
47	Ivan Rodriguez	.50
48	Bob Abreu	.05
49	Darryl Kile	.05
50	Darren Dreifort	.05
51	Shawon Dunston	.05
52	Mark McGwire	1.50
53	Tim Salmon	.05
54	Gene Schall	.05
55	Roger Clemens	.85
56	Rondell White	.05
57	Ed Sprague	.05
58	Craig Paquette	.05
59	David Segui	.05
60	Jaime Navarro	.05
61	Tom Glavine	.35
62	Jeff Brantley	.05
63	Kimera Bartee	.05
64	Fernando Vina	.05
65	Eddie Murray	.65
66	Lenny Dykstra	.05
67	Kevin Elster	.05
68	Vinny Castilla	.05
69	Todd Greene	.05
70	Brett Butler	.05
71	Robby Thompson	.05
72	Reggie Jefferson	.05
73	Todd Hundley	.05
74	Jeff King	.05
75	Ernie Young	.05
76	Jeff Bagwell	.65
77	Dan Wilson	.05
78	Paul Molitor	.65
79	Kevin Seitzer	.05
80	Kevin Brown	.05
81	Ron Gant	.05
82	Dwight Gooden	.05
83	Todd Stottlemyre	.05
84	Ken Caminiti	.05
85	James Baldwin	.05
86	Jermaine Dye	.05
87	Harold Baines	.05
88	Pat Hentgen	.05
89	Frank Rodriguez	.05
90	Mark Johnson	.05
91	Jason Kendall	.05
92	Alex Rodriguez	1.50
93	Alan Trammell	.05
94	Scott Brosius	.05
95	Delino DeShields	.05
96	Chipper Jones	.75
97	Barry Bonds	2.00
98	Brady Anderson	.05
99	Ryne Sandberg	.75
100	Albert Belle	.05
101	Jeff Cirillo	.05
102	Frank Thomas	.65
103	Mike Piazza	1.00
104	Rickey Henderson	.65
105	Rey Ordonez	.05
106	Mark Grace	.05
107	Terry Steinbach	.05
108	Ray Durham	.05
109	Barry Larkin	.05
110	Tony Clark	.05
111	Bernie Williams	.05
112	John Smoltz	.05
113	Moises Alou	.05
114	Alex Gonzalez	.05
115	Rico Brogna	.05
116	Eric Karros	.05
117	Jeff Conine	.05
118	Todd Hollandsworth	.05
119	Troy Percival	.05
120	Paul Wilson	.05
121	Orel Hershiser	.05
122	Ozzie Smith	.75
123	Dave Hollins	.05
124	Ken Hill	.05
125	Rick Wilkins	.05
126	Scott Servais	.05
127	Fernando Valenzuela	.05
128	Mariano Rivera	.15
129	Mark Loretta	.05
130	Shane Reynolds	.05
131	Darren Oliver	.05
132	Steve Trachsel	.05
133	Darren Bragg	.05
134	Jason Dickson	.05
135	Darren Fletcher	.05
136	Gary Gaetti	.05
137	Joey Cora	.05
138	Terry Pendleton	.05
139	Derek Jeter	2.00
140	Danny Tartabull	.05
141	John Flaherty	.05
142	B.J. Surhoff	.05
143	Mark Sweeney	.05
144	Chad Mottola	.05
145	Andujar Cedeno	.05
146	Tim Belcher	.05
147	Mark Thompson	.05
148	Rafael Bournigal	.05
149	Marty Cordova	.05
150	Osvaldo Fernandez	.05
151	Mike Stanley	.05
152	Ricky Bottalico	.05
153	Donnie Wall	.05
154	Omar Vizquel	.05
155	Mike Mussina	.30
156	Brant Brown	.05
157	F.P. Santangelo	.05
158	Ryan Hancock	.05
159	Jeff D'Amico	.05
160	Luis Castillo	.05
161	Darin Erstad	.10
162	Ugueth Urbina	.05
163	Andruw Jones	.65
164	Steve Gibralter	.05
165	Robin Jennings	.05
166	Mike Cameron	.05
167	George Arias	.05
168	Chris Stynes	.05
169	Justin Thompson	.05
170	Jamey Wright	.05
171	Todd Walker	.05
172	Nomar Garciaparra	.75
173	Jose Paniagua	.05
174	Marvin Benard	.05
175	Rocky Coppinger	.05
176	Quinton McCracken	.05
177	Amaury Telemaco	.05
178	Neifi Perez	.05
179	Todd Greene	.05
180	Jason Thompson	.05
181	Wilton Guerrero	.05
182	Edgar Renteria	.05
183	Billy Wagner	.05
184	Alex Ochoa	.05
185	Billy McMillon	.05
186	Kenny Lofton	.05
187	Andres Galarraga (Clout)	.05
188	Chuck Knoblauch (Clout)	.05
189	Greg Maddux (Clout)	.75
190	Mo Vaughn (Clout)	.05
191	Cal Ripken Jr. (Clout)	2.00
192	Hideo Nomo (Clout)	.40
193	Ken Griffey Jr. (Clout)	1.00
194	Sammy Sosa (Clout)	.75
195	Jay Buhner (Clout)	.05
196	Manny Ramirez (Clout)	.65
197	Matt Williams (Clout)	.05
198	Andruw Jones (Checklist)	.30
199	Darin Erstad (Checklist)	.05
200	Trey Beamon (Checklist)	.05

Artist's Proofs

Artist's Proofs parallels for 1997 Pinnacle were issued in a "fractured" set form. That is, three levels of scarcity were created, with each card available in only one of those levels. For 125 of the players, bronze is the scarcity level; 50 of the players have a silver-level scarcity and 25 players are found in the top-shelf gold level, with a reported production of 300 each. Stated odds of finding an AP parallel were 1:47 in hobby and retail packs, and 1:55 in magazine packs.

	NM/M
Common Bronze (125):	1.00
Bronze Stars:	30X
Common Silver (50):	2.50
Silver Stars:	12X
Common Gold (25):	4.00
Gold Stars:	10X

Museum Collection

Each of the 200 cards in 1997 Pinnacle Series 1 was also issued in a graphically enhanced Museum Collection parallel set. The Museum cards utilize basically the same design as the regular-issue Pinnacle cards, but the front is printed in the company's Dufex gold-foil technology. On back, a small rectangular logo verifies the card's special status.

	NM/M
Complete Set (200):	100.00
Common Player:	1.00
Stars/Rookies:	6X

Cardfrontations

This hobby-only set was inserted every 23 packs of 1997 Pinnacle baseball. Fronts depict a player portrait imaged over a foil rainbow background. The same player is then pictured in action shots with the "Cardfrontation" logo in gold foil in the lower right half. The player's name appears in gold foil below the gold-foil team logo. Backs depict another player's portrait with text describing interaction between the two players. The cards are numbered as "x of 20."

		NM/M
	Complete Set (20):	35.00
	Common Player:	.50
1	Greg Maddux, Mike Piazza	3.00
2	Tom Glavine, Ken Caminiti	.75
3	Randy Johnson, Cal Ripken Jr.	5.00
4	Kevin Appier, Mark McGwire	4.00
5	Andy Pettitte, Juan Gonzalez	1.00
6	Pat Hentgen, Albert Belle	.50
7	Hideo Nomo, Chipper Jones	2.00
8	Ismael Valdes, Sammy Sosa	2.50
9	Mike Mussina, Manny Ramirez	1.50
10	David Cone, Jay Buhner	.50
11	Mark Wohlers, Gary Sheffield	.75
12	Alan Benes, Barry Bonds	5.00
13	Roger Clemens, Ivan Rodriguez	2.50
14	Mariano Rivera, Ken Griffey Jr.	3.00
15	Dwight Gooden, Frank Thomas	1.50
16	John Wetteland, Darin Erstad	.50
17	John Smoltz, Brian Jordan	.50
18	Kevin Brown, Jeff Bagwell	1.50
19	Jack McDowell, Alex Rodriguez	4.00
20	Charles Nagy, Bernie Williams	.50

Home/Away

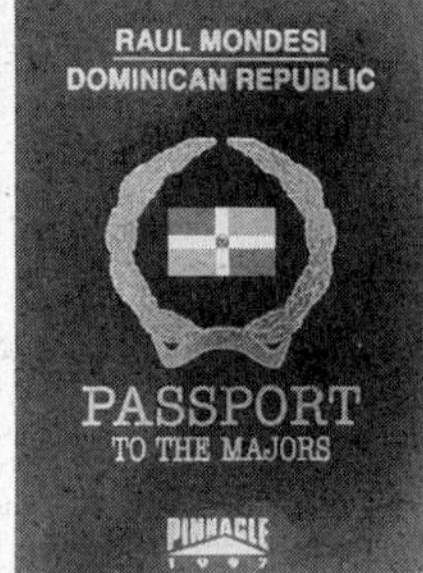

The 24-card, shirt-shaped, die-cut set was inserted every 33 retail packs. The background on front and back is a facsimile of the player's home or road jersey. A color action photo is on front with gold-foil graphics. Backs have a few words about the player.

#	Player	NM/M
	Complete Set (12):	65.00
	Common Player:	2.00
1	Chipper Jones	5.00
2	Ken Griffey Jr.	6.00
3	Mike Piazza	6.00
4	Frank Thomas	4.00
5	Jeff Bagwell	4.00
6	Alex Rodriguez	8.00
7	Barry Bonds	10.00
8	Mo Vaughn	2.00
9	Derek Jeter	10.00
10	Mark McGwire	8.00
11	Cal Ripken Jr.	10.00
12	Albert Belle	2.00

Passport to the Majors

The 25-card, regular-sized set was inserted every 36 packs of 1997 Pinnacle baseball. The cards fold out and resemble a mini passport.

#	Player	NM/M
	Complete Set (25):	55.00
	Common Player:	1.00
1	Greg Maddux	4.00
1s	Greg Maddux ("SAMPLE" overprint.)	4.00
2	Ken Griffey Jr.	6.00
3	Frank Thomas	3.00
4	Cal Ripken Jr.	10.00
5	Mike Piazza	6.00
6	Alex Rodriguez	7.50
7	Mo Vaughn	1.00
8	Chipper Jones	4.00
9	Roberto Alomar	1.00
10	Edgar Martinez	1.00
11	Javier Lopez	1.00
12	Ivan Rodriguez	2.50
13	Juan Gonzalez	1.50
14	Carlos Baerga	1.00
15	Sammy Sosa	4.00
16	Manny Ramirez	3.00
17	Raul Mondesi	1.00
18	Henry Rodriguez	1.00
19	Rafael Palmeiro	2.50
20	Rey Ordonez	1.00
21	Hideo Nomo	1.50
22	Makoto Suzuki	1.00
23	Chan Ho Park	1.00
24	Larry Walker	1.00
25	Ruben Rivera	1.00

Shades

This set was inserted every 23 retail packs of Pinnacle baseball. The horizontal cards are die-cut at the top of a pair of sunglasses whose lenses contain color portrait and action pictures of the player. The player face beneath the shades is printed on silver foil stock. Backs have a mirror-image of the front photos in the lenses and a baseball diamond in the background.

#	Player	NM/M
	Complete Set (10):	15.00
	Common Player:	.75
1	Ken Griffey Jr.	3.00
2	Juan Gonzalez	1.50
3	John Smoltz	.75
4	Gary Sheffield	1.00
5	Cal Ripken Jr.	5.00
6	Mo Vaughn	.75
7	Brian Jordan	.75
8	Mike Piazza	3.00
9	Frank Thomas	2.25
10	Alex Rodriguez	4.00

Team Pinnacle

This insert features top National League players from a position on one side with the best American League players on the other. One side of the card is in Dufex printing and there is actually two versions of each card, as either side can feature the Dufex foil. Team Pinnacle is inserted every 90 packs.

		NM/M
	Complete Set (10):	30.00
	Common Player:	1.50
1	Frank Thomas, Jeff Bagwell	4.00
2	Chuck Knoblauch, Eric Young	1.50
3	Ken Caminiti, Jim Thome	3.00
4	Alex Rodriguez, Chipper Jones	6.00
5	Mike Piazza, Ivan Rodriguez	5.00
6	Albert Belle, Barry Bonds	8.00
7	Ken Griffey Jr., Ellis Burks	6.00
8	Juan Gonzalez, Gary Sheffield	3.00
9	John Smoltz, Andy Pettitte	2.00
10	All Players	2.00

1997 New Pinnacle Samples

This group of sample cards was sent to dealers to introduce the New Pinnacle brand which took the place of a second series of Pinnacle in 1997. Cards are virtually identical to the issued versions except for the large diagonal black-and-white "SAMPLE" overprint on front and back.

#	Player	NM/M
	Complete Set (6):	7.50
	Common Player:	.50
2	Sammy Sosa	3.00
45	Mike Piazza	3.00
57	Jeff Bagwell	1.50
81	Alex Rodriguez	5.00
127	Ryan Klesko	.50
175	Andruw Jones	2.00

1997 New Pinnacle

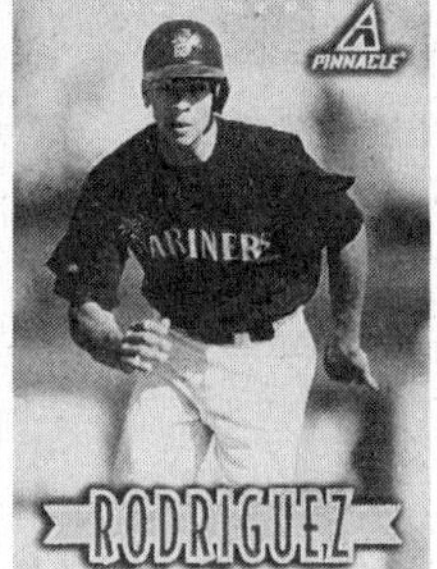

In lieu of a second series of Pinnacle Baseball, the company offered collectors New Pinnacle, a 200-card set sold in 10-card packs for $2.99. Two parallel versions of the 200-card set exist in Museum Collection and Artist's Proofs. Other inserts include Press Plates, Spellbound, Keeping the Pace and Interleague Encounter. Collectors who obtained four Press Plates of the same player's card back or front were eligible to win cash prizes.

#	Player	NM/M
	Complete Set (200):	12.50
	Common Player:	.05
	Common Museum:	1.00
	Museum Stars:	8X
	Common Red Artist's Proof:	1.00
	Red AP Stars:	10X
	Common Blue Artist's Proof:	3.00
	Blue AP Stars:	25X
	Common Green Artist's Proof:	6.00
	Green AP Stars:	35X
	Pack (10):	1.50
	Wax Box (18):	15.00
1	Ken Griffey Jr.	1.00
2	Sammy Sosa	.75
3	Greg Maddux	.75
4	Matt Williams	.05
5	Jason Isringhausen	.05
6	Gregg Jefferies	.05
7	Chili Davis	.05
8	Paul O'Neill	.05
9	Larry Walker	.05
10	Ellis Burks	.05
11	Cliff Floyd	.05
12	Albert Belle	.05
13	Javier Lopez	.05
14	David Cone	.05
15	Jose Canseco	.40
16	Todd Zeile	.05
17	Bernard Gilkey	.05
18	Andres Galarraga	.05
19	Chris Snopek	.05
20	Tim Salmon	.05
21	Roger Clemens	.85
22	Reggie Sanders	.05
23	John Jaha	.05
24	Andy Pettitte	.25
25	Kenny Lofton	.05
26	Robb Nen	.05
27	John Wetteland	.05
28	Bobby Bonilla	.05
29	Hideo Nomo	.40
30	Cecil Fielder	.05
31	Garret Anderson	.05
32	Pat Hentgen	.05
33	David Justice	.05
34	Billy Wagner	.05
35	Al Leiter	.05
36	Mark Wohlers	.05
37	Rondell White	.05
38	Charles Johnson	.05
39	Mark Grace	.05
40	Pedro Martinez	.65
41	Tom Goodwin	.05
42	Manny Ramirez	.65
43	Greg Vaughn	.05
44	Brian Jordan	.05
45	Mike Piazza	1.00
46	Roberto Hernandez	.05
47	Wade Boggs	.75
48	Scott Sanders	.05

49 Alex Gonzalez .05
50 Kevin Brown .05
51 Bob Higginson .05
52 Ken Caminiti .05
53 Derek Jeter 2.00
54 Carlos Baerga .05
55 Jay Buhner .05
56 Tim Naehring .05
57 Jeff Bagwell .65
58 Steve Finley .05
59 Kevin Appier .05
60 Jay Bell .05
61 Ivan Rodriguez .60
62 Terrell Wade .05
63 Rusty Greer .05
64 Juan Guzman .05
65 Fred McGriff .05
66 Tino Martinez .05
67 Ray Lankford .05
68 Juan Gonzalez .40
69 Ron Gant .05
70 Jack McDowell .05
71 Tony Gwynn .75
72 Joe Carter .05
73 Wilson Alvarez .05
74 Jason Giambi .60
75 Brian Hunter .05
76 Michael Tucker .05
77 Andy Benes .05
78 Brady Anderson .05
79 Ramon Martinez .05
80 Troy Percival .05
81 Alex Rodriguez 1.50
82 Jim Thome .60
83 Denny Neagle .05
84 Rafael Palmeiro .60
85 Jose Valentin .05
86 Marc Newfield .05
87 Mariano Rivera .15
88 Alan Benes .05
89 Jimmy Key .05
90 Joe Randa .05
91 Cal Ripken Jr. 2.00
92 Craig Biggio .05
93 Dean Palmer .05
94 Gary Sheffield .45
95 Ismael Valdez .05
96 John Valentin .05
97 Johnny Damon .35
98 Mo Vaughn .05
99 Paul Sorrento .05
100 Randy Johnson .65
101 Raul Mondesi .05
102 Roberto Alomar .20
103 Royce Clayton .05
104 Mark Grudzielanek .05
105 Wally Joyner .05
106 Wil Cordero .05
107 Will Clark .05
108 Chuck Knoblauch .05
109 Derek Bell .05
110 Henry Rodriguez .05
111 Edgar Renteria .05
112 Travis Fryman .05
113 Eric Young .05
114 Sandy Alomar Jr. .05
115 Darin Erstad .25
116 Barry Larkin .05
117 Barry Bonds 2.00
118 Frank Thomas .65
119 Carlos Delgado .50
120 Jason Kendall .05
121 Todd Hollandsworth .05
122 Jim Edmonds .05
123 Chipper Jones .75
124 Jeff Fassero .05
125 Deion Sanders .05
126 Matt Lawton .05
127 Ryan Klesko .05
128 Mike Mussina .40
129 Paul Molitor .65
130 Dante Bichette .05
131 Bill Pulsipher .05
132 Todd Hundley .05
133 J.T. Snow .05
134 Chuck Finley .05
135 Shawn Green .30
136 Charles Nagy .05
137 Willie Greene .05
138 Marty Cordova .05
139 Eddie Murray .65
140 Ryne Sandberg .75
141 Alex Fernandez .05
142 Mark McGwire 1.50
143 Eric Davis .05
144 Jermaine Dye .05
145 Ruben Sierra .05
146 Damon Buford .05
147 John Smoltz .05
148 Alex Ochoa .05
149 Moises Alou .05
150 Rico Brogna .05
151 Terry Steinbach .05
152 Jeff King .05
153 Carlos Garcia .05
154 Tom Glavine .35
155 Edgar Martinez .05
156 Kevin Elster .05
157 Darryl Hamilton .05
158 Jason Dickson .05
159 Kevin Orie .05
160 Bubba Trammell **RC** .25
161 Jose Guillen .05
162 Brant Brown .05
163 Wendell Magee .05
164 Scott Spiezio .05
165 Todd Walker .05
166 Rod Myers **RC** .05
167 Damon Mashore .05
168 Wilton Guerrero .05
169 Vladimir Guerrero .65
170 Nomar Garciaparra .75
171 Shannon Stewart .05
172 Scott Rolen .60
173 Bob Abreu .05
174 Danny Patterson **RC** .05
175 Andruw Jones .65
176 Brian Giles **RC** .50
177 Dmitri Young .05
178 Cal Ripken Jr. (East Meets West) 1.00
179 Chuck Knoblauch (East Meets West) .05
180 Alex Rodriguez (East Meets West) .75
181 Andres Galarraga (East Meets West) .05
182 Pedro Martinez (East Meets West) .35
183 Brady Anderson (East Meets West) .05
184 Barry Bonds (East Meets West) 1.00
185 Ivan Rodriguez (East Meets West) .30
186 Gary Sheffield (East Meets West) .05
187 Denny Neagle (East Meets West) .05
188 Mark McGwire (Aura) .75
189 Ellis Burks (Aura) .05
190 Alex Rodriguez (Aura) .75
191 Mike Piazza (Aura) .65
192 Barry Bonds (Aura) 1.00
193 Albert Belle (Aura) .05
194 Chipper Jones (Aura) .40
195 Juan Gonzalez (Aura) .20
196 Brady Anderson (Aura) .05
197 Frank Thomas (Aura) .35
198 Checklist (Vladimir Guerrero) .35
199 Checklist (Todd Walker) .05
200 Checklist (Scott Rolen) .30

Artist's Proof

This 200-card parallel set features a special AP seal and foil treatment and is fractured into three levels of scarcity - Red (125 cards), Blue (50 cards) and Green (25 cards). Cards were inserted at a rate of 1:39 packs. "Artist's Proof" is stamped along the lower edge.

	NM/M
Common Red Artist's Proof:	1.00
Red Artist's Proofs:	10X
Common Blue Artist's Proof:	3.00
Blue Artist's Proofs:	25X
Common Green Artist's Proof:	6.00
Green Artist's Proofs:	35X

Museum Collection

Dufex printing on gold-foil backgrounds differentiates the Musuem Collection parallel of New Pinnacle from the regular-issue cards. Museums were inserted at an average rate of one per nine packs.

	NM/M
Complete Set (200):	200.00
Common Player:	1.00
Stars/Rookies:	8X

Interleague Encounter

Inserted 1:240 packs, this 10-card set showcases 20 American League and National League rivals with the date of their first interleague match-up on double-sided mirror mylar cards.

		NM/M
Complete Set (10):		60.00
Common Player:		2.50
1	Albert Belle, Brian Jordan	2.50
2	Andruw Jones, Brady Anderson	4.50
3	Ken Griffey Jr., Tony Gwynn	7.50
4	Cal Ripken Jr., Chipper Jones	12.00
5	Mike Piazza, Ivan Rodriguez	7.50
6	Derek Jeter, Vladimir Guerrero	12.00
7	Greg Maddux, Mo Vaughn	6.00
8	Alex Rodriguez, Hideo Nomo	10.00
9	Juan Gonzalez, Barry Bonds	12.00
10	Frank Thomas, Jeff Bagwell	4.50

Keeping the Pace

Top sluggers who were considered candidates to break Roger Maris' single-season record of 61 home runs were featured in this insert set. Cards feature Dot Matrix holographic borders and backgrounds on front. Backs present career stats of an all-time great and project future numbers for the current player. The cards were inserted 1:89 packs.

		NM/M
Complete Set (18):		100.00
Common Player:		1.00
1	Juan Gonzalez	3.00
2	Greg Maddux	7.50
3	Ivan Rodriguez	4.50
4	Ken Griffey Jr.	12.00
5	Alex Rodriguez	13.50
6	Barry Bonds	15.00
7	Frank Thomas	6.00
8	Chuck Knoblauch	1.00
9	Derek Jeter	15.00
10	Roger Clemens	9.00
11	Kenny Lofton	1.00
12	Tony Gwynn	7.50
13	Troy Percival	1.00
14	Cal Ripken Jr.	15.00
15	Andy Pettitte	1.50
16	Hideo Nomo	3.00
17	Randy Johnson	6.00
18	Mike Piazza	12.00

Press Plates

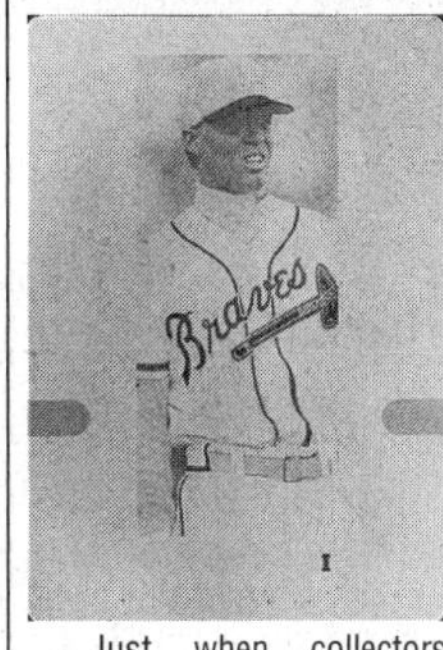

Just when collectors thought they had seen every type of insert card imaginable, New Pinnacle proved them wrong by cutting up and inserting into packs (about one per 1,250) the metal plates used to print the set. There are black, blue, red and yellow plates for the front and back of each card. Rather than touting the collector value of the plates, Pinnacle created a treasure hunt by offering $20,000-35,000 to anybody assembling a complete set of four plates for either the front or back of any card. The $35,000, which would have been awarded for completion prior to August 22, was unclaimed. The amount decreased to $20,000 for any set redeemed by the end of 1997.

Spellbound

Each of the 50 cards in this insert features a letter of the alphabet as the basic card design. The letters can be used to spell out the names of nine players featured in the set. Cards feature micro-etched foil and are inserted 1:19 packs. Cards of Griffey, Ripken and the Jones were inserted only in hobby packs; retail packs have cards of Belle, Thomas, Piazza and the Rodriguezes. Values shown are per card; multiply by number of cards to determine a player's set value.

		NM/M
Complete Set (50):		110.00
1-5AB	Albert Belle	1.00
1-6AJ	Andruw Jones	2.00
1-4AR	Alex Rodriguez	4.50
1-7CJ	Chipper Jones	2.50
1-6CR	Cal Ripken Jr.	6.00
1-5FT	Frank Thomas	2.00
1-5IR	Ivan Rodriguez	1.50
1-6KG	Ken Griffey Jr.	3.50
1-6MP	Mike Piazza	3.50

1997 Pinnacle Certified

This 150-card base features a mirror-like mylar finish and a peel-off protector on each card front. Backs feature the player's 1996 statistics against each opponent. There are four different parallel sets, each with varying degrees of scarcity: Certified Red (1:5), Mirror Red (1:99), Mirror Blue (1:199) and Mirror Gold (1:299). Other inserts include Lasting Impressions, Certified Team, and Certified Gold Team. Cards were sold in six-card packs for a suggested price of $4.99.

	NM/M
Complete Set (150):	30.00
Common Player:	.15
Common Certified Red:	1.00
Certified Red Stars:	5X
Common Mirror Red:	3.00
Mirror Red Stars:	12X
Common Mirror Blue:	4.00
Mirror Blue Stars:	15X
Common Mirror Gold:	7.50
Mirror Gold Stars:	35X
Jose Cruz Jr. Redemption:	2.00
Pack (6):	2.00
Wax Box (20):	35.00

1 Barry Bonds 3.00
2 Mo Vaughn .15
3 Matt Williams .15
4 Ryne Sandberg 1.25
5 Jeff Bagwell 1.00
6 Alan Benes .15
7 John Wetteland .15
8 Fred McGriff .15
9 Craig Biggio .15
10 Bernie Williams .15
11 Brian L. Hunter .15
12 Sandy Alomar Jr. .15
13 Ray Lankford .15
14 Ryan Klesko .15
15 Jermaine Dye .15
16 Andy Benes .15
17 Albert Belle .15
18 Tony Clark .15
19 Dean Palmer .15
20 Bernard Gilkey .15
21 Ken Caminiti .15
22 Alex Rodriguez 2.25
23 Tim Salmon .15
24 Larry Walker .15
25 Barry Larkin .15
26 Mike Piazza 1.50
27 Brady Anderson .15
28 Cal Ripken Jr. 3.00
29 Charles Nagy .15
30 Paul Molitor 1.00
31 Darin Erstad .25
32 Rey Ordonez .15
33 Wally Joyner .15
34 David Cone .15
35 Sammy Sosa 1.25
36 Dante Bichette .15
37 Eric Karros .15
38 Omar Vizquel .15
39 Roger Clemens 1.25
40 Joe Carter .15
41 Frank Thomas 1.00
42 Javier Lopez .15
43 Mike Mussina .45
44 Gary Sheffield .60
45 Tony Gwynn 1.25
46 Jason Kendall .15
47 Jim Thome .75
48 Andres Galarraga .15
49 Mark McGwire 2.25
50 Troy Percival .15
51 Derek Jeter 3.00
52 Todd Hollandsworth .15
53 Ken Griffey Jr. 1.50
54 Randy Johnson 1.00
55 Pat Hentgen .15
56 Rusty Greer .15
57 John Jaha .15
58 Kenny Lofton .15
59 Chipper Jones 1.25
60 Robb Nen .15
61 Rafael Palmeiro .75
62 Mariano Rivera .30
63 Hideo Nomo .50
64 Greg Vaughn .15
65 Ron Gant .15
66 Eddie Murray 1.00
67 John Smoltz .15
68 Manny Ramirez 1.00
69 Juan Gonzalez .50
70 F.P. Santangelo .15
71 Moises Alou .15
72 Alex Ochoa .15
73 Chuck Knoblauch .15
74 Raul Mondesi .15
75 J.T. Snow .15
76 Rickey Henderson 1.00
77 Bobby Bonilla .15
78 Wade Boggs 1.25
79 Ivan Rodriguez .75
80 Brian Jordan .15
81 Al Leiter .15
82 Jay Buhner .15
83 Greg Maddux 1.25
84 Edgar Martinez .15
85 Kevin Brown .15
86 Eric Young .15
87 Todd Hundley .15
88 Ellis Burks .15
89 Marquis Grissom .15
90 Jose Canseco .60
91 Henry Rodriguez .15
92 Andy Pettitte .45
93 Mark Grudzielanek .15
94 Dwight Gooden .15
95 Roberto Alomar .50
96 Paul Wilson .15
97 Will Clark .15
98 Rondell White .15
99 Charles Johnson .15
100 Jim Edmonds .15
101 Jason Giambi .60
102 Billy Wagner .15
103 Edgar Renteria .15
104 Johnny Damon .45
105 Jason Isringhausen .15
106 Andruw Jones 1.00
107 Jose Guillen .15
108 Kevin Orie .15
109 Brian Giles **RC** 1.25
110 Danny Patterson .15
111 Vladimir Guerrero 1.00
112 Scott Rolen .75
113 Damon Mashore .15
114 Nomar Garciaparra 1.25
115 Todd Walker .15
116 Wilton Guerrero .15
117 Bob Abreu .25
118 Brooks Kieschnick .15
119 Pokey Reese .15
120 Todd Greene .15
121 Dmitri Young .15
122 Raul Casanova .15
123 Glendon Rusch .15
124 Jason Dickson .15
125 Jorge Posada .15
126 Rod Myers **RC** .15
127 Bubba Trammell **RC** .40
128 Scott Spiezio .15
129 Hideki Irabu **RC** .40
130 Wendell Magee .15
131 Bartolo Colon .15
132 Chris Holt .15
133 Calvin Maduro .15
134 Ray Montgomery .15
135 Shannon Stewart .15
136 Ken Griffey Jr. (Certified Stars) 1.00
137 Vladimir Guerrero (Certified Stars) .50
138 Roger Clemens (Certified Stars) .75
139 Mark McGwire (Certified Stars) 1.25
140 Albert Belle (Certified Stars) .15
141 Derek Jeter (Certified Stars) 1.50
142 Juan Gonzalez (Certified Stars) .25
143 Greg Maddux (Certified Stars) .60
144 Alex Rodriguez (Certified Stars) 1.25
145 Jeff Bagwell (Certified Stars) .50
146 Cal Ripken Jr. (Certified Stars) 1.50
147 Tony Gwynn (Certified Stars) .60
148 Frank Thomas (Certified Stars) .50
149 Hideo Nomo (Certified Stars) .25
150 Andruw Jones (Certified Stars) .50

Red

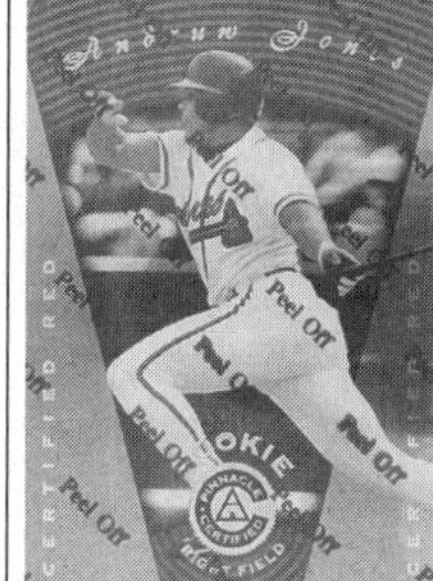

This parallel set features a red tint to the triangular mylar background left and right of the photo on front.

"CERTIFIED RED" is printed vertically on both edges. Backs are identical to regular Certified cards. A peel-off protection coating is on the front of the card. Cards were inserted 1:5 packs.

	NM/M
Common Certified Red:	1.00
Certified Red Stars:	5X

Mirror Red

This parallel set features a red design element on the front of each card. Cards were inserted 1:99 packs.

	NM/M
Common Mirror Red:	3.00
Mirror Red Stars:	12X

Mirror Blue

This parallel set features a blue design element on the front of each card. Cards were inserted 1:199 packs.

	NM/M
Common Mirror Blue:	4.00
Mirror Blue Stars:	15X

Mirror Gold

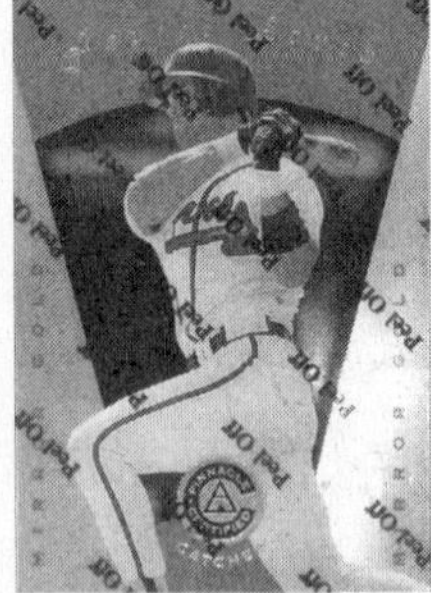

This parallel set features a holographic gold design on the front of each card. Cards were inserted 1:299 packs.

	NM/M
Common Mirror Gold:	7.50
Mirror Gold Stars:	35X

Mirror Black

The exact nature of these cards is undetermined. They may have been intentionally created and "secretly" seeded in packs as an insert or they may have been test cards which were mistakenly inserted. They are not marked in any fashion. The cards are said to reflect in bright green under direct light. It is commonly believed that each "Mirror Black" card exists in only a single piece, but that has not been verified. Neither is it confirmed that a Mirror Black parallel exists for each of the 151 cards in the base set. Even the most undistinguished player's card can sell for $100 or more due to the scarcity of the type.

	NM/M
Common Player:	100.00

Lasting Impression

This insert features an hour-glass die-cut design and a mirror mylar finish and pictures

some of baseball's top veteran stars. Backs are conventionally printed and include a color portrait photo and a few words about the player. Cards were inserted 1:19 packs.

		NM/M
Complete Set (20):		40.00
Common Player:		1.00
1	Cal Ripken Jr.	7.50
2	Ken Griffey Jr.	5.00
3	Mo Vaughn	1.00
4	Brian Jordan	1.00
5	Mark McGwire	6.00
6	Chuck Knoblauch	1.00
7	Sammy Sosa	3.00
8	Brady Anderson	1.00
9	Frank Thomas	2.00
10	Tony Gwynn	3.00
11	Roger Clemens	4.00
12	Alex Rodriguez	6.00
13	Paul Molitor	2.00
14	Kenny Lofton	1.00
15	John Smoltz	1.00
16	Roberto Alomar	1.50
17	Randy Johnson	2.00
18	Ryne Sandberg	3.00
19	Manny Ramirez	2.00
20	Mike Mussina	1.50

Team

The top 20 players in the game are honored on cards with frosted silver mylar printing. Cards were inserted 1:19 packs. A parallel version of this set, Certified Gold Team, has a gold mylar design with each card numbered to 500; while a super-premium parallel, Mirror Gold, is numbered to 25. Each card can also be found in a promo version overprinted "SAMPLE."

		NM/M
Complete Set (20):		30.00
Common Player:		.50
Gold:		3X
Mirror Gold:		15X
Sample:		1X
1	Frank Thomas	1.50
2	Jeff Bagwell	1.50
3	Derek Jeter	4.00
4	Chipper Jones	2.00
5	Alex Rodriguez	3.00
6	Ken Caminiti	.50
7	Cal Ripken Jr.	4.00
8	Mo Vaughn	.50
9	Ivan Rodriguez	1.00
10	Mike Piazza	2.50
11	Juan Gonzalez	.75
12	Barry Bonds	4.00
13	Ken Griffey Jr.	2.50
14	Andruw Jones	1.50
15	Albert Belle	.50
16	Gary Sheffield	.75
17	Andy Pettitte	.65
18	Hideo Nomo	.75
19	Greg Maddux	2.00
20	John Smoltz	.50

1997 Totally Certified Samples

This trio of promo cards previews the high-tech, all-numbered Totally Certified issue. The samples are similar in format to the issued versions except they carry a large, black "SAMPLE" overprint diagonally on front and back. Also, backs have a gold-foil "PROMO" instead of the individual serial number.

		NM/M
Complete Set (3):		5.00
Common Player:		1.00
18	Tony Clark (Platinum Red)	1.00
39	Roger Clemens (Platinum Blue)	3.00
41	Frank Thomas (Platinum Gold)	2.00

Platinum Red

Totally Certified doesn't have a true base set. Instead, the product consists of three different 150-card parallel sets. Packs consisted of three cards for $6.99 each. The first of three parallels is the Platinum Red set, inserted two per pack, and featuring micro-etched holographic mylar stock with red accents and foil stamping. Each card in the Red set is sequentially-numbered to 3,999.

		NM/M
Complete Set (150):		75.00
Common Player:		.25
Pack (3):		3.00
Wax Box (20):		45.00
1	Barry Bonds	4.00
2	Mo Vaughn	.25
3	Matt Williams	.25
4	Ryne Sandberg	2.00
5	Jeff Bagwell	1.25
6	Alan Benes	.25
7	John Wetteland	.25
8	Fred McGriff	.25
9	Craig Biggio	.25
10	Bernie Williams	.25
11	Brian Hunter	.25
12	Sandy Alomar Jr.	.25
13	Ray Lankford	.25
14	Ryan Klesko	.25
15	Jermaine Dye	.25
16	Andy Benes	.25
17	Albert Belle	.25
18	Tony Clark	.25
19	Dean Palmer	.25
20	Bernard Gilkey	.25
21	Ken Caminiti	.25
22	Alex Rodriguez	3.00
23	Tim Salmon	.25
24	Larry Walker	.25
25	Barry Larkin	.25
26	Mike Piazza	2.50
27	Brady Anderson	.25
28	Cal Ripken Jr.	4.00
29	Charles Nagy	.25
30	Paul Molitor	1.25
31	Darin Erstad	.35
32	Rey Ordonez	.25
33	Wally Joyner	.25
34	David Cone	.25
35	Sammy Sosa	2.00
36	Dante Bichette	.25
37	Eric Karros	.25
38	Omar Vizquel	.25
39	Roger Clemens	2.25
40	Joe Carter	.25
41	Frank Thomas	1.25
42	Javier Lopez	.25
43	Mike Mussina	.75
44	Gary Sheffield	.60
45	Tony Gwynn	2.00
46	Jason Kendall	.25
47	Jim Thome	1.00
48	Andres Galarraga	.25
49	Mark McGwire	3.00
50	Troy Percival	.25
51	Derek Jeter	4.00
52	Todd Hollandsworth	.25
53	Ken Griffey Jr.	2.50
54	Randy Johnson	1.25
55	Pat Hentgen	.25
56	Rusty Greer	.25
57	John Jaha	.25
58	Kenny Lofton	.25
59	Chipper Jones	2.00
60	Robb Nen	.25
61	Rafael Palmeiro	1.00
62	Mariano Rivera	.35
63	Hideo Nomo	.65
64	Greg Vaughn	.25
65	Ron Gant	.25
66	Eddie Murray	1.25
67	John Smoltz	.25
68	Manny Ramirez	1.25
69	Juan Gonzalez	.65
70	F.P. Santangelo	.25
71	Moises Alou	.25
72	Alex Ochoa	.25
73	Chuck Knoblauch	.25
74	Raul Mondesi	.25
75	J.T. Snow	.25
76	Rickey Henderson	1.25
77	Bobby Bonilla	.25
78	Wade Boggs	2.00
79	Ivan Rodriguez	1.00
80	Brian Jordan	.25
81	Al Leiter	.25
82	Jay Buhner	.25
83	Greg Maddux	2.00
84	Edgar Martinez	.25
85	Kevin Brown	.25
86	Eric Young	.25
87	Todd Hundley	.25
88	Ellis Burks	.25
89	Marquis Grissom	.25
90	Jose Canseco	.60
91	Henry Rodriguez	.25
92	Andy Pettitte	.50
93	Mark Grudzielanek	.25
94	Dwight Gooden	.25
95	Roberto Alomar	.35
96	Paul Wilson	.25
97	Will Clark	.25
98	Rondell White	.25
99	Charles Johnson	.25
100	Jim Edmonds	.25
101	Jason Giambi	.75
102	Billy Wagner	.25
103	Edgar Renteria	.25
104	Johnny Damon	.45
105	Jason Isringhausen	.25
106	Andruw Jones	1.25
107	Jose Guillen	.25
108	Kevin Orie	.25
109	Brian Giles **RC**	2.00
110	Danny Patterson	.25
111	Vladimir Guerrero	1.25
112	Scott Rolen	1.00
113	Damon Mashore	.25
114	Nomar Garciaparra	2.00
115	Todd Walker	.25
116	Wilton Guerrero	.25
117	Bob Abreu	.35
118	Brooks Kieschnick	.25
119	Pokey Reese	.25
120	Todd Greene	.25
121	Dmitri Young	.25
122	Raul Casanova	.25
123	Glendon Rusch	.25
124	Jason Dickson	.25
125	Jorge Posada	.25
126	Rod Myers	.25
127	Bubba Trammell	.25
128	Scott Spiezio	.25
129	Hideki Irabu	.25
130	Wendell Magee	.25
131	Bartolo Colon	.25
132	Chris Holt	.25
133	Calvin Maduro	.25
134	Ray Montgomery	.25
135	Shannon Stewart	.25
136	Ken Griffey Jr. (Certified Stars)	1.50
137	Vladimir Guerrero (Certified Stars)	.60
138	Roger Clemens (Certified Stars)	1.25
139	Mark McGwire (Certified Stars)	1.50
140	Albert Belle (Certified Stars)	.25
141	Derek Jeter (Certified Stars)	2.00
142	Juan Gonzalez (Certified Stars)	.30
143	Greg Maddux (Certified Stars)	1.00
144	Alex Rodriguez (Certified Stars)	1.50
145	Jeff Bagwell (Certified Stars)	.60
146	Cal Ripken Jr. (Certified Stars)	2.00
147	Tony Gwynn (Certified Stars)	1.00
148	Frank Thomas (Certified Stars)	.60
149	Hideo Nomo (Certified Stars)	.30
150	Andruw Jones (Certified Stars)	.60

Platinum Blue

Featuring blue accents and foil stamping, the Platinum Blue cards are sequentially numbered on back in gold foil to 1,999 and inserted per pack.

	NM/M
Complete Set (150):	200.00
Common Player:	1.00
Platinum Blue Stars:	1.5X

Platinum Gold

The most difficult to find of the Totally Certified cards, the Platinum Gold versions are sequentially-numbered to 30 per card and inserted 1:79 packs.

	NM/M
Common Player:	25.00
Platinum Gold Stars:	30X

1997 Pinnacle FanFest

As title sponsor for baseball's All-Star FanFest in Cleveland, July 4-8, Pinnacle issued a number of special cards including this set which was distributed in three-card cello packs both prior to and during the event. To help promote the event, six of the cards were issued with a schedule back, as well as the regular back design. Fronts have action photos highlighted at bottom by a stadium facade in gold foil. The FanFest logo is at bottom center. Backs feature a player portrait photo within a large star. Also on back are a few stats and personal data, a few words about the player and appropriate logos. Cards are numbered with an "FF" prefix and "of 21" following the number. Card #21 of the host team's Sandy Alomar, Jr., was not issued in packs. A redemption card, which could be traded in at area card shops for the Alomar card, was substituted.

		NM/M
Complete Set (21):		12.50
Common Player:		.25
FF1	Frank Thomas	.65
FF2	Jeff Bagwell	.65
FF3	Chuck Knoblauch	.25
FF4	Craig Biggio	.25
FF5	Alex Rodriguez	1.50
FF6	Chipper Jones	.75
FF7	Cal Ripken Jr.	1.50
FF8	Ken Caminiti	.25
FF9	Juan Gonzalez	.45
FF10	Barry Bonds	2.00
FF11	Ken Griffey Jr.	1.00
FF12	Andruw Jones	.65
FF13	Manny Ramirez	.65
FF14	Tony Gwynn	.75
FF15a	Ivan Rodriguez (Schedule back.)	2.50
FF15b	Ivan Rodriguez (Regular back.)	.50
FF16a	Mike Piazza (Schedule back.)	4.50
FF16b	Mike Piazza (Regular back.)	1.00
FF17a	Andy Pettitte (Schedule back.)	2.00
FF17b	Andy Pettitte (Regular back.)	.40
FF18a	Hideo Nomo (Schedule back.)	1.50
FF18b	Hideo Nomo (Regular back.)	.45
FF19a	Roger Clemens (Schedule back.)	4.00
FF19b	Roger Clemens (Regular back.)	.85
FF20a	Greg Maddux (Schedule back.)	3.50
FF20b	Greg Maddux (Regular back.)	.75
FF21	Sandy Alomar Jr.	2.50
----	Sandy Alomar Jr. (Trade-in card.)	.25

Larry Doby

Marking the 50th anniversary of the American League's integration, Pinnacle, title sponsor of baseball's All-Star FanFest, issued a special card of black A.L. pioneer Larry Doby, who debuted in 1947 with the Indians. FanFest and the All-Star Game were held in Cleveland in 1997, with Doby attending many of the functions. In the same format as its FanFest set of current players, the special Doby card has a black-and-white action photo on front, with gold-foil highlights at bottom. Back repeats the front photo within a star and offers some career notes and stats. The Doby card was given away to FanFest volunteer workers and laminated into identification badges for FanFest dealers.

	NM/M
Larry Doby	4.00

Personal Cards

Continuing a tradition begun a year earlier, Pinnacle, the title sponsor for baseball's FanFest, produced a series of cards for various local and media celebrities. The cards are in the same format as the FanFest player cards, with color photos on front and gold-foil highlights. Backs have a photo detail within a star design and a few words about the personality, along with stats such as Indians' games attended, popcorn consumed, etc. Cards are numbered with a PC prefix and are difficult to find because their distribution was controlled by the person pictured. Rick Manning was an Indians outfielder from 1975-83. Mike Hegan played in the American League from 1964-77; his father, Jim, was a staple behind the plate for the Indians between 1941-57. Six of the cards feature members of the Fox network which televised the 1997 All-Star Game.

		NM/M
Complete Set (12):		30.00
Common Player:		2.00
PC1	Macie McInnis (Fox)	2.00
PC2	Bill Martin (Fox)	2.00
PC3	Dick Gaddard (Fox)	2.00
PC4	Jack Corrigan (WUAB-TV)	2.00
PC5	Mike Hegan (WUAB-TV)	6.00
PC6	Rick Manning (Sports Channel)	5.00
PC7	John Sanders (Sports Channel)	2.00
PC8	Mayor Michael R. White	4.50
PC9	Wilma Smith (Fox)	2.00
PC10	Tim Taylor (Fox)	2.00
PC11	Robin Swoboda (Fox)	2.00
PC12	Slider (Mascot)	3.00

1997 Pinnacle Inside

The first baseball card set to be sold within a sealed tin can, Inside Baseball consists of a 150-card base set featuring both a color and black-and-white photo of the player on front. Included in the base set are 20 Rookies cards and three checklists. Inserts include the Club Edition and Diamond Edition parallel sets, Dueling Dugouts and Fortysomething. In addition, 24 different cans, each featuring a different player, were available. Cans containing one pack of 10 cards were sold for $2.99 each.

		NM/M
Complete Set (150):		15.00
Common Player:		.05
Common Club Edition:		.75
Club Edition Stars:		5X
Common Diamond Edition:		5.00
Diamond Edition Stars:		25X
Unopened Can (10):		2.00
Case Cans (48):		60.00
1	David Cone	.05
2	Sammy Sosa	1.00
3	Joe Carter	.05
4	Juan Gonzalez	.40
5	Hideo Nomo	.40
6	Moises Alou	.05
7	Marc Newfield	.05
8	Alex Rodriguez	2.00
9	Kimera Bartee	.05
10	Chuck Knoblauch	.05
11	Jason Isringhausen	.05
12	Jermaine Allensworth	.05
13	Frank Thomas	.75
14	Paul Molitor	.75
15	John Mabry	.05
16	Greg Maddux	1.00
17	Rafael Palmeiro	.65
18	Brian Jordan	.05
19	Ken Griffey Jr.	1.50
20	Brady Anderson	.05
21	Ruben Sierra	.05
22	Travis Fryman	.05
23	Cal Ripken Jr.	2.50
24	Will Clark	.05
25	Todd Hollandsworth	.05
26	Kevin Brown	.05
27	Mike Piazza	1.50
28	Craig Biggio	.05
29	Paul Wilson	.05
30	Andres Galarraga	.05
31	Chipper Jones	1.00
32	Jason Giambi	.65
33	Ernie Young	.05
34	Marty Cordova	.05
35	Albert Belle	.05
36	Roger Clemens	1.25
37	Ryne Sandberg	1.00
38	Henry Rodriguez	.05
39	Jay Buhner	.05
40	Raul Mondesi	.05
41	Jeff Fassero	.05
42	Edgar Martinez	.05
43	Trey Beamon	.05
44	Mo Vaughn	.05
45	Gary Sheffield	.40
46	Ray Durham	.05
47	Brett Butler	.05
48	Ivan Rodriguez	.65
49	Fred McGriff	.05
50	Dean Palmer	.05
51	Rickey Henderson	.75
52	Andy Pettitte	.30
53	Bobby Bonilla	.05
54	Shawn Green	.50
55	Tino Martinez	.05
56	Tony Gwynn	1.00
57	Tom Glavine	.35
58	Eric Young	.05
59	Kevin Appier	.05
60	Barry Bonds	2.50
61	Wade Boggs	1.00
62	Jason Kendall	.05
63	Jeff Bagwell	.75
64	Jeff Conine	.05
65	Greg Vaughn	.05
66	Eric Karros	.05
67	Manny Ramirez	.75
68	John Smoltz	.05
69	Terrell Wade	.05
70	John Wetteland	.05
71	Kenny Lofton	.05
72	Jim Thome	.65
73	Bill Pulsipher	.05
74	Darryl Strawberry	.05
75	Roberto Alomar	.25
76	Bobby Higginson	.05
77	James Baldwin	.05
78	Mark McGwire	2.00
79	Jose Canseco	.40
80	Mark Grudzielanek	.05
81	Ryan Klesko	.05
82	Javier Lopez	.05
83	Ken Caminiti	.05
84	Dave Nilsson	.05
85	Tim Salmon	.05
86	Cecil Fielder	.05
87	Derek Jeter	2.50
88	Garret Anderson	.05
89	Dwight Gooden	.05
90	Carlos Delgado	.50
91	Ugueth Urbina	.05
92	Chan Ho Park	.05
93	Eddie Murray	.75
94	Alex Ochoa	.05
95	Rusty Greer	.05
96	Mark Grace	.05
97	Pat Hentgen	.05
98	John Jaha	.05
99	Charles Johnson	.05
100	Jermaine Dye	.05
101	Quinton McCracken	.05
102	Troy Percival	.05
103	Shane Reynolds	.05
104	Rondell White	.05
105	Charles Nagy	.05
106	Alan Benes	.05
107	Tom Goodwin	.05
108	Ron Gant	.05
109	Dan Wilson	.05
110	Darin Erstad	.10
111	Matt Williams	.05
112	Barry Larkin	.05
113	Mariano Rivera	.15
114	Larry Walker	.05
115	Jim Edmonds	.05
116	Michael Tucker	.05
117	Todd Hundley	.05
118	Alex Fernandez	.05
119	J.T. Snow	.05
120	Ellis Burks	.05
121	Steve Finley	.05
122	Mike Mussina	.40
123	Curtis Pride	.05
124	Derek Bell	.05
125	Dante Bichette	.05
126	Terry Steinbach	.05
127	Randy Johnson	.75
128	Andruw Jones	.75
129	Vladimir Guerrero	.75
130	Ruben Rivera	.05
131	Billy Wagner	.05
132	Scott Rolen	.65
133	Rey Ordonez	.05
134	Karim Garcia	.05
135	George Arias	.05
136	Todd Greene	.05
137	Robin Jennings	.05
138	Raul Casanova	.05
139	Josh Booty	.05
140	Edgar Renteria	.05
141	Chad Mottola	.05
142	Dmitri Young	.05
143	Tony Clark	.05
144	Todd Walker	.05
145	Kevin Brown	.05
146	Nomar Garciaparra	1.00
147	Neifi Perez	.05
148	Derek Jeter, Todd Hollandsworth	.50
149	Pat Hentgen, John Smoltz	.05
150	Juan Gonzalez, Ken Caminiti	.05

Club Edition

A 150-card parallel set featuring a special silver foil design and "CLUB EDITION" notation on back, these cards were inserted 1:7 can of Inside.

	NM/M
Complete Club Edition Set (150):	300.00
Common Club Edition:	.75
Stars:	5X

Diamond Edition

A second parallel set, this time featuring a special die-cut design and gold holographic stamping. Cards were inserted 1:63 packs.

	NM/M
Common Diamond Edition:	5.00
Stars:	25X

Cans

In addition to the cards, collectors had the option of collecting the 24 different player cans which are the "packs" in which the cards were sold. About the size of a can of peas (3" diameter, 4-1/2" tall), the cans feature several color and black-and-white reproductions of the player's Inside card. The package had to be opened with a can opener to access the cards. Values shown are for empty cans which have been opened from the bottom; top-opened cans have little collectible value.

		NM/M
Complete Set (24):		10.00
Common Can:		.25
Sealed Cans:		2X
1	Ken Griffey Jr.	.75
2	Juan Gonzalez	.30
3	Frank Thomas	.40
4	Cal Ripken Jr.	1.50
5	Derek Jeter	1.50
6	Andruw Jones	.40
7	Alex Rodriguez	1.00
8	Mike Piazza	.75
9	Mo Vaughn	.25
10	Jeff Bagwell	.40
11	Ken Caminiti	.25
12	Andy Pettitte	.30
13	Barry Bonds	1.50
14	Mark McGwire	1.00
15	Ryan Klesko	.25
16	Manny Ramirez	.40
17	Ivan Rodriguez	.35
18	Chipper Jones	.50
19	Albert Belle	.25
20	Tony Gwynn	.50
21	Kenny Lofton	.25
22	Greg Maddux	.50
23	Hideo Nomo	.40
24	John Smoltz	.25

Dueling Dugouts

This 20-card insert set features a veteran player on one side, a rising star on the other, and a spinning wheel that reveals their respective achievements in various statistical categories. Cards were inserted 1:23 packs.

		NM/M
Complete Set (20):		65.00
Common Player:		1.25
1	Alex Rodriguez, Cal Ripken Jr.	10.00
2	Jeff Bagwell, Ken Caminiti	3.00
3	Barry Bonds, Albert Belle	10.00
4	Mike Piazza, Ivan Rodriguez	6.00
5	Chuck Knoblauch, Roberto Alomar	1.25
6	Ken Griffey Jr., Andruw Jones	6.00
7	Chipper Jones, Jim Thome	4.00
8	Frank Thomas, Mo Vaughn	3.00
9	Fred McGriff, Mark McGwire	7.50
10	Brian Jordan, Tony Gwynn	4.00
11	Barry Larkin, Derek Jeter	10.00
12	Kenny Lofton, Bernie Williams	1.25
13	Juan Gonzalez, Manny Ramirez	3.00
14	Will Clark, Rafael Palmeiro	2.50
15	Greg Maddux, Roger Clemens	4.50
16	John Smoltz, Andy Pettitte	1.25
17	Mariano Rivera, John Wetteland	1.25
18	Hideo Nomo, Mike Mussina	2.00
19	Todd Hollandsworth, Darin Erstad	1.25
20	Vladimir Guerrero, Karim Garcia	3.00

Fortysomething

The top home run hitters in the game are pictured in this 16-card set. Cards were inserted 1:47 packs.

		NM/M
Complete Set (16):		50.00
Common Player:		1.00
1	Juan Gonzalez	3.00
2	Barry Bonds	12.00
3	Ken Caminiti	1.00
4	Mark McGwire	10.00
5	Todd Hundley	1.00
6	Albert Belle	1.00
7	Ellis Burks	1.00
8	Jay Buhner	1.00
9	Brady Anderson	1.00
10	Vinny Castilla	1.00
11	Mo Vaughn	1.00
12	Ken Griffey Jr.	7.50
13	Sammy Sosa	6.50
14	Andres Galarraga	1.00
15	Gary Sheffield	2.00
16	Frank Thomas	5.00

Mint Collection

The 30-card Mint Collection set came in three-card packs that also contained two coins. Cards come in two versions: die-cut and foil. Three foil versions appear with Bronze as the "common." Silver (1:15) and Gold (1:48) parallels also appear. The coins that come with each pack arrive in brass, silver and gold and can be matched up with the corresponding player's die-cut card. Fronts feature a player action shot on the left side with a shadowed portrait at right. On the die-cut versions, the coin-size hole is in the lower-right; the foil team stamp for the common cards is in the same location. Backs are numbered as "x of 30" and deliver a short text.

		NM/M
Complete Set (30):		25.00
Common Player:		.25
Silver Cards:		4X
Gold Cards:		6X
Die-Cuts: 50 Percent		
Wax Box (24):		25.00
1	Ken Griffey Jr.	2.00
2	Frank Thomas	1.25
3	Alex Rodriguez	2.50
4	Cal Ripken Jr.	3.00
5	Mo Vaughn	.25
6	Juan Gonzalez	.60
7	Mike Piazza	2.00
8	Albert Belle	.25
9	Chipper Jones	1.50
10	Andruw Jones	1.25
11	Greg Maddux	1.50
12	Hideo Nomo	.60
13	Jeff Bagwell	1.25
14	Manny Ramirez	1.25
15	Mark McGwire	2.50
16	Derek Jeter	3.00
17	Sammy Sosa	1.50
18	Barry Bonds	3.00
19	Chuck Knoblauch	.25
20	Dante Bichette	.25
21	Tony Gwynn	1.50
22	Ken Caminiti	.25
23	Gary Sheffield	.60
24	Tim Salmon	.25
25	Ivan Rodriguez	1.00
26	Henry Rodriguez	.25
27	Barry Larkin	.25
28	Ryan Klesko	.25
29	Brian Jordan	.25
30	Jay Buhner	.25

Mint Collection Coins

Two coins from the 30-coin set were included in each three-card pack of 1997 Pinnacle Mint Collection. Brass coins are common while nickel-silver coins were inserted every 20 packs and gold-plated coins were inserted every 48 packs. Redemption cards for solid silver coins were found every 2,300 packs and a redemption card for a solid gold coin was inserted one per 47,200 packs. Only one of each 24K gold coin was produced. The front of the coins feature the player's portrait while the backs have a baseball diamond with "Limited Edition, Pinnacle Mint Collection 1997" printed.

		NM/M
Complete Set (30):		35.00
Common Brass Coin:		.25
Nickel Coins:		2X
Gold Plated Coins:		6X
Silver Coins:		20X
24K Gold Coins: Value Undetermined		
1	Ken Griffey Jr.	2.50
2	Frank Thomas	1.50
3	Alex Rodriguez	3.00
4	Cal Ripken Jr.	4.00
5	Mo Vaughn	.25
6	Juan Gonzalez	.75
7	Mike Piazza	2.50
8	Albert Belle	.25
9	Chipper Jones	2.00
10	Andruw Jones	1.50
11	Greg Maddux	2.00
12	Hideo Nomo	.75
13	Jeff Bagwell	1.50
14	Manny Ramirez	1.50
15	Mark McGwire	3.00
16	Derek Jeter	4.00
17	Sammy Sosa	2.00
18	Barry Bonds	4.00
19	Chuck Knoblauch	.25
20	Dante Bichette	.25
21	Tony Gwynn	2.00

22	Ken Caminiti	.25
23	Gary Sheffield	.65
24	Tim Salmon	.25
25	Ivan Rodriguez	1.00
26	Henry Rodriguez	.25
27	Barry Larkin	.25
28	Ryan Klesko	.25
29	Brian Jordan	.25
30	Jay Buhner	.25

1997 Pinnacle X-Press

The 150-card set features 115 base cards, a 22-card Rookies subset, 10 Peak Performers and three checklist cards. Each of the regular cards features a horizontal design with two photos of each player on front. Inserts include Swing for the Fences (regular player cards as well as base and booster cards that can be used to accumulate points for a sweepstakes), Men of Summer, Far & Away, Melting Pot, and Metal Works Silver and Gold redemptions. Cards were sold in eight-card packs for $1.99. X-Press Metal Works boxes were also available for $14.99 and contained a regular pack, one metal card and a master deck used to play the Swing for the Fences game.

		NM/M
Complete Set (150):		7.50
Common Player:		.05
Men of Summer:		4X
Pack (8):		.75
Wax Box (24):		10.00
1	Larry Walker	.05
2	Andy Pettitte	.30
3	Matt Williams	.05
4	Juan Gonzalez	.40
5	Frank Thomas	.75
6	Kenny Lofton	.05
7	Ken Griffey Jr.	1.25
8	Andres Galarraga	.05
9	Greg Maddux	1.00
10	Hideo Nomo	.40
11	Cecil Fielder	.05
12	Jose Canseco	.40
13	Tony Gwynn	1.00
14	Eddie Murray	.75
15	Alex Rodriguez	1.50
16	Mike Piazza	1.25
17	Ken Hill	.05
18	Chuck Knoblauch	.05
19	Ellis Burks	.05
20	Rafael Palmeiro	.65
21	Vinny Castilla	.05
22	Rusty Greer	.05
23	Chipper Jones	1.00
24	Rey Ordonez	.05
25	Mariano Rivera	.15
26	Garret Anderson	.05
27	Edgar Martinez	.05
28	Dante Bichette	.05
29	Todd Hundley	.05
30	Barry Bonds	2.00
31	Barry Larkin	.05
32	Derek Jeter	2.00
33	Marquis Grissom	.05
34	David Justice	.05
35	Ivan Rodriguez	.65
36	Jay Buhner	.05
37	Fred McGriff	.05
38	Brady Anderson	.05
39	Tony Clark	.05
40	Eric Young	.05
41	Charles Nagy	.05
42	Mark McGwire	1.50
43	Paul O'Neill	.05
44	Tino Martinez	.05
45	Ryne Sandberg	1.00
46	Bernie Williams	.05
47	Albert Belle	.05
48	Jeff Cirillo	.05
49	Tim Salmon	.05
50	Steve Finley	.05
51	Lance Johnson	.05
52	John Smoltz	.05
53	Javier Lopez	.05
54	Roger Clemens	1.00
55	Kevin Appier	.05
56	Ken Caminiti	.05
57	Cal Ripken Jr.	2.00
58	Moises Alou	.05
59	Marty Cordova	.05
60	David Cone	.05
61	Manny Ramirez	.75
62	Ray Durham	.05
63	Jermaine Dye	.05
64	Craig Biggio	.05
65	Will Clark	.05
66	Omar Vizquel	.05
67	Bernard Gilkey	.05
68	Greg Vaughn	.05
69	Wade Boggs	1.00
70	Dave Nilsson	.05
71	Mark Grace	.05
72	Dean Palmer	.05
73	Sammy Sosa	1.00
74	Mike Mussina	.30
75	Alex Fernandez	.05
76	Henry Rodriguez	.05
77	Travis Fryman	.05
78	Jeff Bagwell	.75
79	Pat Hentgen	.05
80	Gary Sheffield	.40
81	Jim Edmonds	.05
82	Darin Erstad	.10
83	Mark Grudzielanek	.05
84	Jim Thome	.65
85	Bobby Higginson	.05
86	Al Martin	.05
87	Jason Giambi	.50
88	Mo Vaughn	.05
89	Jeff Conine	.05
90	Edgar Renteria	.05
91	Andy Ashby	.05
92	Ryan Klesko	.05
93	John Jaha	.05
94	Paul Molitor	.75
95	Brian Hunter	.05
96	Randy Johnson	.75
97	Joey Hamilton	.05
98	Billy Wagner	.05
99	John Wetteland	.05
100	Jeff Fassero	.05
101	Rondell White	.05
102	Kevin Brown	.05
103	Andy Benes	.05
104	Raul Mondesi	.05
105	Todd Hollandsworth	.05
106	Alex Ochoa	.05
107	Bobby Bonilla	.05
108	Brian Jordan	.05
109	Tom Glavine	.35
110	Ron Gant	.05
111	Jason Kendall	.05
112	Roberto Alomar	.30
113	Troy Percival	.05
114	Michael Tucker	.05
115	Joe Carter	.05
116	Andruw Jones	.75
117	Nomar Garciaparra	1.00
118	Todd Walker	.05
119	Jose Guillen	.05
120	Bubba Trammell **RC**	.20
121	Wilton Guerrero	.05
122	Bob Abreu	.15
123	Vladimir Guerrero	.75
124	Dmitri Young	.05
125	Kevin Orie	.05
126	Glendon Rusch	.05
127	Brooks Kieschnick	.05
128	Scott Spiezio	.05
129	Brian Giles **RC**	.75
130	Jason Dickson	.05
131	Damon Mashore	.05
132	Wendell Magee	.05
133	Matt Morris	.05
134	Scott Rolen	.65
135	Shannon Stewart	.05
136	Deivi Cruz **RC**	.15
137	Hideki Irabu **RC**	.15
138	Larry Walker (Peak Performers)	.05
139	Ken Griffey Jr. (Peak Performers)	.65
140	Frank Thomas (Peak Performers)	.40
141	Ivan Rodriguez (Peak Performers)	.30
142	Randy Johnson (Peak Performers)	.40
143	Mark McGwire (Peak Performers)	.75
144	Tino Martinez (Peak Performers)	.05
145	Tony Clark (Peak Performers)	.05
146	Mike Piazza (Peak Performers)	.50
147	Alex Rodriguez (Peak Performers)	.75
148	Checklist (Roger Clemens)	.50
149	Checklist (Greg Maddux)	.45
150	Checklist (Hideo Nomo)	.20

Men of Summer

This parallel set of the 150 cards in the base X-Press issue differs in that the fronts are printed on foil backgrounds and the backs have a notation "MEN OF SUMMER" printed in gold vertically at top.

	NM/M
Complete Set (150):	50.00
Common Player:	.25
Stars:	3X

Far & Away

This 18-card insert highlights the top home run hitters in baseball and is printed with Dufex technology. Cards were inserted 1:19 packs.

		NM/M
Complete Set (18):		25.00
Common Player:		.50
1	Albert Belle	.50
2	Mark McGwire	4.50
3	Frank Thomas	1.75
4	Mo Vaughn	.50
5	Jeff Bagwell	1.75
6	Juan Gonzalez	1.00
7	Mike Piazza	3.50
8	Andruw Jones	1.75
9	Chipper Jones	2.50
10	Gary Sheffield	1.00
11	Sammy Sosa	2.50
12	Darin Erstad	.75
13	Jay Buhner	.50
14	Ken Griffey Jr.	3.50
15	Ken Caminiti	.50
16	Brady Anderson	.50
17	Manny Ramirez	1.75
18	Alex Rodriguez	4.50

Melting Pot

This insert showcases the talents of major leaguers from various countries. Fronts have color player photos on a background which combines shiny silver foil and textured foil in the design of the player's native flag. Backs have another photo and are ink-jet numbered in a white stripe at bottom in an edition of 500 each. Stated insertion rate was one per 288 packs. Each card can also be found in a promo card version overprinted "SAMPLE."

		NM/M
Complete Set (20):		110.00
Common Player:		1.50
Samples:		1X
1	Jose Guillen	1.50
2	Vladimir Guerrero	8.00
3	Andruw Jones	8.00
4	Larry Walker	1.50
5	Manny Ramirez	8.00
6	Ken Griffey Jr.	10.00
7	Alex Rodriguez	12.00
8	Frank Thomas	8.00
9	Juan Gonzalez	4.00
10	Ivan Rodriguez	6.00
11	Hideo Nomo	4.00
12	Rafael Palmeiro	6.00
13	Dave Nilsson	1.50
14	Nomar Garciaparra	9.00
15	Wilton Guerrero	1.50
16	Sammy Sosa	9.00
17	Edgar Renteria	1.50
18	Cal Ripken Jr.	16.00
19	Derek Jeter	16.00
20	Rey Ordonez	1.50

Metal Works

Each Home Plate Box of X-Press contains one heavy bronze Metal Works "card." The 2-3/8" x 3-1/2" slabs have a player portrait on front. Backs have a few words about the player. Redemption cards for silver-plated parallels were inserted 1:470 packs, while a silver slab was found 1:54 Home Plate Boxes. Silver Metal Works are serially numbered to 400 each. Gold-plated Metal Works were produced in an edition of 200 each, with redemption cards inserted 1:950 packs or one per 108 Home Plate Boxes.

		NM/M
Complete Set (20):		25.00
Common Player:		.50
Silver:		3X
Gold:		6X
1	Ken Griffey Jr.	2.00
2	Frank Thomas	1.00
3	Andruw Jones	1.00
4	Alex Rodriguez	2.50
5	Derek Jeter	3.00
6	Cal Ripken Jr.	3.00
7	Mike Piazza	2.00
8	Chipper Jones	1.50
9	Juan Gonzalez	.65
10	Greg Maddux	1.50
11	Tony Gwynn	1.50
12	Jeff Bagwell	1.00
13	Albert Belle	.50
14	Mark McGwire	2.50
15	Nomar Garciaparra	1.50
16	Mo Vaughn	.50
17	Andy Pettitte	.65
18	Manny Ramirez	1.00
19	Kenny Lofton	.50
20	Roger Clemens	1.75

Swing for the Fences

These inserts allowed collectors to play an interactive game based on the number of home runs hit by the home run champion of each league. Cards feature 60 different players and were inserted 1:2 packs. Base cards feature a number between 20-42 printed on them and are found one in every master deck. Booster cards feature a plus-or-minus point total (i.e. +7, -2) that can be used to add or subtract points to get to the winning home run total. Booster cards are found 1:2 packs. Collectors who accumulated the winning home run totals were eligible to win prizes ranging from autographs to a trip to the 1998 All-Star Game. The unnumbered cards are checklisted here in alphabetical order.

		NM/M
Complete Set (60):		20.00
Common Player:		.15
(1)	Sandy Alomar Jr.	.15
(2)	Moises Alou	.15
(3)	Brady Anderson	.15
(4)	Jeff Bagwell	1.00
(5)	Derek Bell	.15
(6)	Jay Bell	.15
(7)	Albert Belle	.15
(8)	Geronimo Berroa	.15
(9)	Dante Bichette	.15
(10)	Barry Bonds	2.50
(11)	Bobby Bonilla	.15
(12)	Jay Buhner	.15
(13)	Ellis Burks	.15
(14)	Ken Caminiti	.15
(15)	Jose Canseco	.40
(16)	Joe Carter	.15
(17)	Vinny Castilla	.15
(18)	Tony Clark	.15
(19)	Carlos Delgado	.50
(20)	Jim Edmonds	.15
(21)	Cecil Fielder	.15
(22)	Andres Galarraga	.15
(23)	Ron Gant	.15
(24)	Bernard Gilkey	.15
(25)	Juan Gonzalez	.50
(26)	Ken Griffey Jr. (AL WINNER)	4.00
(27)	Vladimir Guerrero	1.00
(28)	Todd Hundley	.15
(29)	John Jaha	.15
(30)	Andruw Jones	1.00
(31)	Chipper Jones	1.25
(32)	David Justice	.15
(33)	Jeff Kent	.15
(34)	Ryan Klesko	.15
(35)	Barry Larkin	.15
(36)	Mike Lieberthal	.15
(37)	Javy Lopez	.15
(38)	Edgar Martinez	.15
(39)	Tino Martinez	.15
(40)	Fred McGriff	.15
(41)	Mark McGwire (AL/NL WINNER)	4.00
(42)	Raul Mondesi	.15
(43)	Tim Naehring	.15
(44)	Dave Nillson	.15
(45)	Rafael Palmeiro	.75
(46)	Dean Palmer	.15
(47)	Mike Piazza	1.50
(48)	Cal Ripken Jr.	2.50
(49)	Henry Rodriguez	.15
(50)	Tim Salmon	.15
(51)	Gary Sheffield	.40
(52)	Sammy Sosa	1.25
(53)	Terry Steinbach	.15
(54)	Frank Thomas	1.00
(55)	Jim Thome	.75
(56)	Mo Vaughn	.15
(57)	Larry Walker (NL Winner)	1.25
(58)	Rondell White	.15
(59)	Matt Williams	.15
(60)	Todd Zeile	.15

Swing/Fences Gold

Collectors who correctly matched Swing for the Fences insert game cards of the final 1997 season American and National home run champions with proper point cards equal to the number of home runs each hit could exchange them for a random assortment of 10 upgraded cards featuring gold-foil highlights and a premium card stock. The first 1,000 redemptions received an autographed Andruw Jones gold card. The redemption period ended March 1, 1998.

	NM/M
Complete Set (60):	125.00
Common Player:	1.00
Stars:	4X
Andruw Jones Autograph:	25.00

1998 Pinnacle Samples

Six stars from its 1998 issue were issued in a promo card version with "SAMPLE" printed in large black letters diagonally on back. They were distributed in two-card cello packs.

		NM/M
Complete Set (6):		6.00
Common Player:		1.00
8	Nomar Garciaparra	2.00
9	Ken Griffey Jr.	2.00
24	Frank Thomas	1.25
33	Mike Piazza	2.00
56	Chipper Jones	1.50
72	Larry Walker	1.00

1998 Pinnacle

Pinnacle's 200-card base set features full-bleed photos on front. Three different backs were produced for each card #1-157: home stats, away stats and seasonal stats. The set also includes cards, 24 Rookies, six Field of Vision, 10 Goin' Jake cards and three checklists. Parallel sets include Artist's Proofs, Press Plates and Museum Collection. Inserts include Epix, Hit it Here, Spellbound and Uncut.

		NM/M
Complete Set (200):		12.50
Common Player:		.05
Pack (10):		1.00
Wax Box (18):		12.00
1	Tony Gwynn/AS	1.00
2	Pedro Martinez/AS	.75
3	Kenny Lofton/AS	.05
4	Curt Schilling/AS	.35
5	Shawn Estes/AS	.05
6	Tom Glavine/AS	.35
7	Mike Piazza/AS	1.50
8	Ray Lankford/AS	.05
9	Barry Larkin/AS	.05
10	Tony Womack/AS	.05
11	Jeff Blauser/AS	.05
12	Rod Beck/AS	.05
13	Larry Walker/AS	.05
14	Greg Maddux/AS	1.00
15	Mark Grace/AS	.05
16	Ken Caminiti/AS	.05
17	Bobby Jones/AS	.05
18	Chipper Jones/AS	1.00
19	Javier Lopez/AS	.05
20	Moises Alou/AS	.05
21	Royce Clayton/AS	.05
22	Darryl Kile/AS	.05
23	Barry Bonds/AS	2.50
24	Steve Finley/AS	.05
25	Andres Galarraga/AS	.05
26	Denny Neagle/AS	.05
27	Todd Hundley/AS	.05
28	Jeff Bagwell	.75
29	Andy Pettitte	.25
30	Darin Erstad	.15

31	Carlos Delgado	.50
32	Matt Williams	.05
33	Will Clark	.05
34	Vinny Castilla	.05
35	Brad Radke	.05
36	John Olerud	.05
37	Andruw Jones	.75
38	Jason Giambi	.50
39	Scott Rolen	.65
40	Gary Sheffield	.40
41	Jimmy Key	.05
42	Kevin Appier	.05
43	Wade Boggs	1.00
44	Hideo Nomo	.40
45	Manny Ramirez	.75
46	Wilton Guerrero	.05
47	Travis Fryman	.05
48	Chili Davis	.05
49	Jeromy Burnitz	.05
50	Craig Biggio	.05
51	Tim Salmon	.05
52	Jose Cruz Jr.	.05
53	Sammy Sosa	1.00
54	Hideki Irabu	.05
55	Chan Ho Park	.05
56	Robin Ventura	.05
57	Jose Guillen	.05
58	Deion Sanders	.05
59	Jose Canseco	.40
60	Jay Buhner	.05
61	Rafael Palmeiro	.65
62	Vladimir Guerrero	.75
63	Mark McGwire	2.00
64	Derek Jeter	2.50
65	Bobby Bonilla	.05
66	Raul Mondesi	.05
67	Paul Molitor	.75
68	Joe Carter	.05
69	Marquis Grissom	.05
70	Juan Gonzalez	.40
71	Kevin Orie	.05
72	Rusty Greer	.05
73	Henry Rodriguez	.05
74	Fernando Tatis	.05
75	John Valentin	.05
76	Matt Morris	.05
77	Ray Durham	.05
78	Geronimo Berroa	.05
79	Scott Brosius	.05
80	Willie Greene	.05
81	Rondell White	.05
82	Doug Drabek	.05
83	Derek Bell	.05
84	Butch Huskey	.05
85	Doug Jones	.05
86	Jeff Kent	.05
87	Jim Edmonds	.05
88	Mark McLemore	.05
89	Todd Zeile	.05
90	Edgardo Alfonzo	.05
91	Carlos Baerga	.05
92	Jorge Fabregas	.05
93	Alan Benes	.05
94	Troy Percival	.05
95	Edgar Renteria	.05
96	Jeff Fassero	.05
97	Reggie Sanders	.05
98	Dean Palmer	.05
99	J.T. Snow	.05
100	Dave Nilsson	.05
101	Dan Wilson	.05
102	Robb Nen	.05
103	Damion Easley	.05
104	Kevin Foster	.05
105	Jose Offerman	.05
106	Steve Cooke	.05
107	Matt Stairs	.05
108	Darryl Hamilton	.05
109	Steve Karsay	.05
110	Gary DiSarcina	.05
111	Dante Bichette	.05
112	Billy Wagner	.05
113	David Segui	.05
114	Bobby Higginson	.05
115	Jeffrey Hammonds	.05
116	Kevin Brown	.05
117	Paul Sorrento	.05
118	Mark Leiter	.05
119	Charles Nagy	.05
120	Danny Patterson	.05
121	Brian McRae	.05
122	Jay Bell	.05
123	Jamie Moyer	.05
124	Carl Everett	.05
125	Greg Colbrunn	.05
126	Jason Kendall	.05
127	Luis Sojo	.05
128	Mike Lieberthal	.05
129	Reggie Jefferson	.05
130	Cal Eldred	.05
131	Orel Hershiser	.05
132	Doug Glanville	.05
133	Willie Blair	.05
134	Neifi Perez	.05
135	Sean Berry	.05
136	Chuck Finley	.05
137	Alex Gonzalez	.05
138	Dennis Eckersley	.65
139	Kenny Rogers	.05
140	Troy O'Leary	.05
141	Roger Bailey	.05
142	Yamil Benitez	.05
143	Wally Joyner	.05
144	Bobby Witt	.05
145	Pete Schourek	.05
146	Terry Steinbach	.05
147	B.J. Surhoff	.05
148	Esteban Loaiza	.05
149	Heathcliff Slocumb	.05
150	Ed Sprague	.05
151	Gregg Jefferies	.05
152	Scott Erickson	.05
153	Jaime Navarro	.05
154	David Wells	.05
155	Alex Fernandez	.05
156	Tim Belcher	.05
157	Mark Grudzielanek	.05
158	Scott Hatteberg	.05
159	Paul Konerko	.15
160	Ben Grieve	.05
161	Abraham Nunez	.05
162	Shannon Stewart	.05
163	Jaret Wright	.05
164	Derrek Lee	.50
165	Todd Dunwoody	.05
166	Steve Woodard **RC**	.10
167	Ryan McGuire	.05
168	Jeremi Gonzalez	.05
169	Mark Kotsay	.05
170	Brett Tomko	.05
171	Bobby Estalella	.05
172	Livan Hernandez	.05
173	Todd Helton	.75
174	Garrett Stephenson	.05
175	Pokey Reese	.05
176	Tony Saunders	.05
177	Antone Williamson	.05
178	Bartolo Colon	.05
179	Karim Garcia	.05
180	Juan Encarnacion	.05
181	Jacob Cruz	.05
182	Alex Rodriguez (Field of Vision)	2.00
183	Cal Ripken Jr., Roberto Alomar (Field of Vision)	1.00
184	Roger Clemens (Field of Vision)	1.25
185	Derek Jeter (Field of Vision)	2.00
186	Frank Thomas (Field of Vision)	.75
187	Ken Griffey Jr. (Field of Vision)	1.50
188	Mark McGwire (Goin' Jake)	1.00
189	Tino Martinez (Goin' Jake)	.05
190	Larry Walker (Goin' Jake)	.05
191	Brady Anderson (Goin' Jake)	.05
192	Jeff Bagwell (Goin' Jake)	.75
193	Ken Griffey Jr. (Goin' Jake)	1.50
194	Chipper Jones (Goin' Jake)	1.00
195	Ray Lankford (Goin' Jake)	.05
196	Jim Thome (Goin' Jake)	.65
197	Nomar Garciaparra (Goin' Jake)	1.00
198	Checklist (1997 HR Contest)	.05
199	Checklist (1997 HR Contest Winner)	.05
200	Checklist (Overall View of the Park)	.05
9	Ken Griffey Jr./AS/OPS	2.00
24	Frank Thomas/AS/OPS	1.50

Artist's Proofs

Artist's Proofs is a 100-card partial parallel of the Pinnacle base set. The gold-foil Dufex cards were renumbered with a "PP" prefix and inserted one per 39 packs. A red AP seal appears on front.

		NM/M
Complete Set (100):		375.00
Common Artist's Proof:		1.50
1	Tony Gwynn/AS	12.50
2	Pedro Martinez/AS	10.00
3	Kenny Lofton/AS	1.50
4	Curt Schilling/AS	3.00
5	Shawn Estes/AS	1.50
6	Tom Glavine/AS	3.00
7	Mike Piazza/AS	16.00
8	Ray Lankford/AS	1.50
9	Barry Larkin/AS	1.50
10	Tony Womack/AS	1.50
11	Jeff Blauser/AS	1.50
12	Rod Beck/AS	1.50
13	Larry Walker/AS	1.50
14	Greg Maddux/AS	12.50
15	Mark Grace/AS	1.50
16	Ken Caminiti/AS	1.50
17	Bobby Jones/AS	1.50
18	Chipper Jones/AS	12.50
19	Javier Lopez/AS	1.50
20	Moises Alou/AS	1.50
21	Royce Clayton/AS	1.50
22	Darryl Kile/AS	1.50
23	Barry Bonds/AS	25.00
24	Steve Finley/AS	1.50
25	Andres Galarraga/AS	1.50
26	Denny Neagle/AS	1.50
27	Todd Hundley/AS	1.50
28	Jeff Bagwell	10.00
29	Andy Pettitte	2.50
30	Darin Erstad	2.00
31	Carlos Delgado	4.00
32	Matt Williams	1.50
33	Will Clark	1.50
34	Brad Radke	1.50
35	John Olerud	1.50
36	Andruw Jones	10.00
37	Scott Rolen	7.50
38	Gary Sheffield	3.00
39	Jimmy Key	1.50
40	Wade Boggs	12.50
41	Hideo Nomo	5.00
42	Manny Ramirez	10.00
43	Wilton Guerrero	1.50
44	Travis Fryman	1.50
45	Craig Biggio	1.50
46	Tim Salmon	1.50
47	Jose Cruz Jr.	1.50
48	Sammy Sosa	12.50
49	Hideki Irabu	1.50
50	Jose Guillen	1.50
51	Deion Sanders	1.50
52	Jose Canseco	4.00
53	Jay Buhner	1.50
54	Rafael Palmeiro	7.50
55	Vladimir Guerrero	10.00
56	Mark McGwire	20.00
57	Derek Jeter	25.00
58	Bobby Bonilla	1.50
59	Raul Mondesi	1.50
60	Paul Molitor	10.00
61	Joe Carter	1.50
62	Marquis Grissom	1.50
63	Juan Gonzalez	5.00
64	Dante Bichette	1.50
65	Shannon Stewart (Rookie)	1.50
66	Jaret Wright (Rookie)	1.50
67	Derrek Lee (Rookie)	6.00
68	Todd Dunwoody (Rookie)	1.50
69	Steve Woodard (Rookie)	1.50
70	Ryan McGuire (Rookie)	1.50
71	Jeremi Gonzalez (Rookie)	1.50
72	Mark Kotsay (Rookie)	1.50
73	Brett Tomko (Rookie)	1.50
74	Bobby Estalella (Rookie)	1.50
75	Livan Hernandez (Rookie)	1.50
76	Todd Helton (Rookie)	10.00
77	Garrett Stephenson (Rookie)	1.50
78	Pokey Reese (Rookie)	1.50
79	Tony Saunders (Rookie)	1.50
80	Antone Williamson (Rookie)	1.50
81	Bartolo Colon (Rookie)	1.50
82	Karim Garcia (Rookie)	1.50
83	Juan Encarnacion (Rookie)	1.50
84	Jacob Cruz (Rookie)	1.50
85	Alex Rodriguez (Field of Vision)	20.00
86	Cal Ripken Jr., Roberto Alomar (Field of Vision)	15.00
87	Roger Clemens (Field of Vision)	13.50
88	Derek Jeter (Field of Vision)	25.00
89	Frank Thomas (Field of Vision)	10.00
90	Ken Griffey Jr. (Field of Vision)	16.00
91	Mark McGwire (Goin' Jake)	20.00
92	Tino Martinez (Goin' Jake)	1.50
93	Larry Walker (Goin' Jake)	1.50
94	Brady Anderson (Goin' Jake)	1.50
95	Jeff Bagwell (Goin' Jake)	10.00
96	Ken Griffey Jr. (Goin' Jake)	16.00
97	Chipper Jones (Goin' Jake)	12.50
98	Ray Lankford (Goin' Jake)	1.50
99	Jim Thome (Goin' Jake)	7.50
100	Nomar Garciaparra (Goin' Jake)	12.50

Museum Collection

Museum Collection is a 100-card partial parallel of the Pinnacle base set. The silver-foil Dufex cards were renumbered with a "PP" prefix. Backs have a small "Musuem Collection" logo at bottom-center. The cards were inserted one per nine packs.

		NM/M
Complete Museum Set (100):		110.00
Common Museum:		.50
1	Tony Gwynn/AS	3.00
2	Pedro Martinez/AS	2.50
3	Kenny Lofton/AS	.50
4	Curt Schilling/AS	1.50
5	Shawn Estes/AS	.50
6	Tom Glavine/AS	1.50
7	Mike Piazza/AS	4.00
8	Ray Lankford/AS	.50
9	Barry Larkin/AS	.50
10	Tony Womack/AS	.50
11	Jeff Blauser/AS	.50
12	Rod Beck/AS	.50
13	Larry Walker/AS	.50
14	Greg Maddux/AS	3.00
15	Mark Grace/AS	.50
16	Ken Caminiti/AS	.50
17	Bobby Jones/AS	.50
18	Chipper Jones/AS	3.00
19	Javier Lopez/AS	.50
20	Moises Alou/AS	.50
21	Royce Clayton/AS	.50
22	Darryl Kile/AS	.50
23	Barry Bonds/AS	6.00
24	Steve Finley/AS	.50
25	Andres Galarraga/AS	.50
26	Denny Neagle/AS	.50
27	Todd Hundley/AS	.50
28	Jeff Bagwell	2.50
29	Andy Pettitte	1.00
30	Darin Erstad	1.00
31	Carlos Delgado	1.50
32	Matt Williams	.50
33	Will Clark	.50
34	Brad Radke	.50
35	John Olerud	.50
36	Andruw Jones	2.50
37	Scott Rolen	2.00
38	Gary Sheffield	1.50
39	Jimmy Key	.50
40	Wade Boggs	3.00
41	Hideo Nomo	1.25
42	Manny Ramirez	2.50
43	Wilton Guerrero	.50
44	Travis Fryman	.50
45	Craig Biggio	.50
46	Tim Salmon	.50
47	Jose Cruz Jr.	.50
48	Sammy Sosa	3.00
49	Hideki Irabu	.50
50	Jose Guillen	.50
51	Deion Sanders	.50
52	Jose Canseco	1.50
53	Jay Buhner	.50
54	Rafael Palmeiro	2.00
55	Vladimir Guerrero	2.50
56	Mark McGwire	5.00
57	Derek Jeter	6.00
58	Bobby Bonilla	.50
59	Raul Mondesi	.50
60	Paul Molitor	2.50
61	Joe Carter	.50
62	Marquis Grissom	.50
63	Juan Gonzalez	1.25
64	Dante Bichette	.50
65	Shannon Stewart (Rookie)	.50
66	Jaret Wright (Rookie)	.50
67	Derrek Lee (Rookie)	2.00
68	Todd Dunwoody (Rookie)	.50
69	Steve Woodard (Rookie)	.50
70	Ryan McGuire (Rookie)	.50
71	Jeremi Gonzalez (Rookie)	.50
72	Mark Kotsay (Rookie)	.50
73	Brett Tomko (Rookie)	.50
74	Bobby Estalella (Rookie)	.50
75	Livan Hernandez (Rookie)	.50
76	Todd Helton (Rookie)	2.50
77	Garrett Stephenson (Rookie)	.50
78	Pokey Reese (Rookie)	.50
79	Tony Saunders (Rookie)	.50
80	Antone Williamson (Rookie)	.50
81	Bartolo Colon (Rookie)	.50
82	Karim Garcia (Rookie)	.50
83	Juan Encarnacion (Rookie)	.50
84	Jacob Cruz (Rookie)	.50
85	Alex Rodriguez (Field of Vision)	5.00
86	Cal Ripken Jr., Roberto Alomar (Field of Vision)	3.50
87	Roger Clemens (Field of Vision)	2.50
88	Derek Jeter (Field of Vision)	6.00
89	Frank Thomas (Field of Vision)	2.50
90	Ken Griffey Jr. (Field of Vision)	4.00
91	Mark McGwire (Goin' Jake)	5.00
92	Tino Martinez (Goin' Jake)	.50
93	Larry Walker (Goin' Jake)	.50
94	Brady Anderson (Goin' Jake)	.50
95	Jeff Bagwell (Goin' Jake)	2.50
96	Ken Griffey Jr. (Goin' Jake)	4.00
97	Chipper Jones (Goin' Jake)	3.00
98	Ray Lankford (Goin' Jake)	.50
99	Jim Thome (Goin' Jake)	2.00
100	Nomar Garciaparra (Goin' Jake)	3.00

Power Packs Supers

Two dozen regular and subset (Goin' Jake, Field of Vision) cards from Pinnacle are paralleled in this super-size (3-1/2" x 5") version which was included along with 21 regular cards in a $5.99 "Power Pack." Other than being four times the size of the regular card, these supers differ only in their numbering which specifies "x of 24" on back. Each card can also be found in a promo version with a large black "SAMPLE" overprinted on back.

		NM/M
Complete Set (24):		30.00
Common Player:		.50
Samples:		1.5X
1	Alex Rodriguez (Field of Vision)	3.00
2	Cal Ripken Jr., Roberto Alomar (Field of Vision)	2.00
3	Roger Clemens (Field of Vision)	2.25
4	Derek Jeter (Field of Vision)	3.50
5	Frank Thomas (Field of Vision)	1.50
6	Ken Griffey Jr. (Field of Vision)	2.50
7	Mark McGwire (Goin' Jake)	3.00
8	Tino Martinez (Goin' Jake)	.50
9	Larry Walker (Goin' Jake)	.50
10	Brady Anderson (Goin' Jake)	.50
11	Jeff Bagwell (Goin' Jake)	1.50
12	Ken Griffey Jr. (Goin' Jake)	2.50
13	Chipper Jones (Goin' Jake)	2.00
14	Ray Lankford (Goin' Jake)	.50
15	Jim Thome (Goin' Jake)	1.00
16	Nomar Garciaparra (Goin' Jake)	2.00
17	Mike Piazza	2.50
18	Andruw Jones	1.50
19	Greg Maddux	2.00
20	Tony Gwynn	2.00
21	Larry Walker	.50
22	Jeff Bagwell	1.50
23	Chipper Jones	2.00
24	Scott Rolen	1.00

Epix

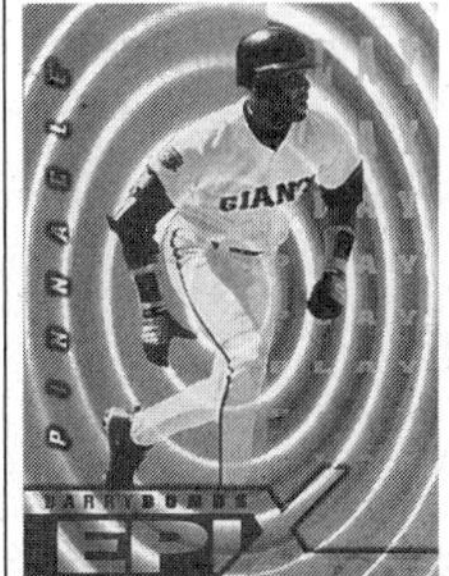

This cross-brand insert was included in Pinnacle, Score, Pinnacle Certified and Zenith. Twenty-four cards were seeded in Pinnacle packs (1:21). The four-tiered set highlights a memorable Game, Season, Moment and Play in a player's career. The holographic foil cards came in three colors: orange, purple and emerald.

		NM/M
Complete Set (24):		45.00
Common Player:		1.00
Purples:		2X
Emeralds:		4X
1	Ken Griffey Jr./G	3.00
2	Juan Gonzalez/G	1.25
3	Jeff Bagwell/G	2.00
4	Ivan Rodriguez/G	1.50
5	Nomar Garciaparra/G	2.50
6	Ryne Sandberg/G	2.50
7	Frank Thomas/S	2.00
8	Derek Jeter/S	5.00
9	Tony Gwynn/S	2.50
10	Albert Belle/S	1.00
11	Scott Rolen/S	1.50
12	Barry Larkin/S	1.00
13	Alex Rodriguez/M	4.00
14	Cal Ripken Jr./M	5.00
15	Chipper Jones/M	2.50
16	Roger Clemens/M	2.75
17	Mo Vaughn/M	1.00
18	Mark McGwire/M	4.00
19	Mike Piazza/P	3.00
20	Andruw Jones/P	2.00
21	Greg Maddux/P	2.50
22	Barry Bonds/P	5.00
23	Paul Molitor/P	2.00
24	Eddie Murray/P	2.00

Hit It Here

Hit it Here is seeded one per 17 packs. The micro-etched silver foil cards feature a color player photo with a red "Hit it Here" target at left. Each card has a serial number. If the pictured player hit for the cycle on Opening Day 1998, the collector with the correct serially numbered card would have won $1 million. Each card was also produced in a promo version without serial number and with a large black "SAMPLE" overprint on back.

		NM/M
Complete Set (10):		12.00
Common Player:		.50
Inserted 1:17		
Samples:		1X
1	Larry Walker	.50
2	Ken Griffey Jr.	2.00
3	Mike Piazza	2.00
4	Frank Thomas	1.50
5	Barry Bonds	3.00
6	Albert Belle	.50
7	Tino Martinez	.50
8	Mark McGwire	2.50
9	Juan Gonzalez	.75
10	Jeff Bagwell	1.00

Press Plates

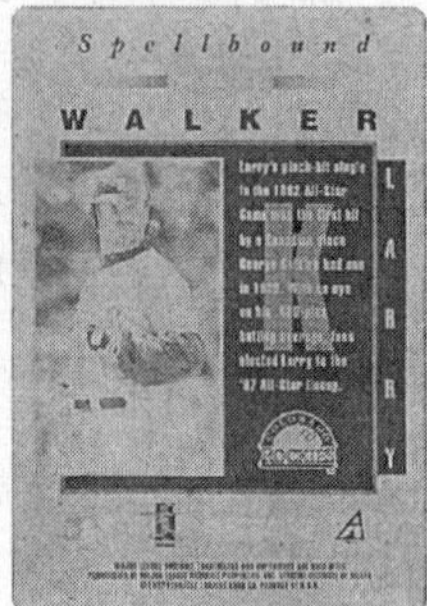

Pinnacle cut up and inserted into packs (about one per 1,250) the metal plates used to print the regular and insert cards in the set. There are black, blue, magenta and yellow plates for the front and back of each card. Because of their unique nature, establishment of catalog values isn't feasible.

	NM/M
Common Player:	50.00

Spellbound

Spellbound is a 50-card insert seeded one per 17 packs. Nine players are featured in the set. The cards feature a photo of the player with a letter from his first or last name in the background. Each player has enough cards to spell his first or last name or a nickname. Values shown are per card and should be multiplied by the number of cards in a player name to arrive at a value for a complete-player set.

		NM/M
Complete Set (50):		90.00
Common Card:		.75
Inserted 1:17		
1	Mark McGwire (M)	3.50
2	Mark McGwire (C)	3.50
3	Mark McGwire (G)	3.50
4	Mark McGwire (W)	3.50
5	Mark McGwire (I)	3.50
6	Mark McGwire (R)	3.50
7	Mark McGwire (E)	3.50
8	Roger Clemens (R)	2.50
9	Roger Clemens (O)	2.50
10	Roger Clemens (C)	2.50
11	Roger Clemens (K)	2.50
12	Roger Clemens (E)	2.50
13	Roger Clemens (T)	2.50
14	Frank Thomas (B)	1.50
15	Frank Thomas (I)	1.50
16	Frank Thomas (G)	1.50
17	Frank Thomas (H)	1.50
18	Frank Thomas (U)	1.50
19	Frank Thomas (R)	1.50
20	Frank Thomas (T)	1.50
21	Scott Rolen (R)	1.25
22	Scott Rolen (O)	1.25
23	Scott Rolen (L)	1.25
24	Scott Rolen (E)	1.25
25	Scott Rolen (N)	1.25
26	Ken Griffey Jr. (G)	3.00
27	Ken Griffey Jr. (R)	3.00
28	Ken Griffey Jr. (I)	3.00
29	Ken Griffey Jr. (F)	3.00
30	Ken Griffey Jr. (F)	3.00
31	Ken Griffey Jr. (E)	3.00
32	Ken Griffey Jr. (Y)	3.00
33	Larry Walker (W)	.75
34	Larry Walker (A)	.75
35	Larry Walker (L)	.75
36	Larry Walker (K)	.75
37	Larry Walker (E)	.75
38	Larry Walker (R)	.75
39	Nomar Garciaparra (N)	2.25
40	Nomar Garciaparra (O)	2.25
41	Nomar Garciaparra (M)	2.25
42	Nomar Garciaparra (A)	2.25
43	Nomar Garciaparra (R)	2.25
44	Cal Ripken Jr. (C)	4.50
45	Cal Ripken Jr. (A)	4.50
46	Cal Ripken Jr. (L)	4.50
47	Tony Gwynn (T)	2.25
48	Tony Gwynn (O)	2.25
49	Tony Gwynn (N)	2.25
50	Tony Gwynn (Y)	2.25

All-Star FanFest John Elway

The quarterback of the World's Champion Denver Broncos was featured on a card harkening back to his minor league baseball playing days. During the July 1998 All-Star FanFest in Denver, Pinnacle sold a special card of Elway, with proceeds benefiting the city's schools. Initial cost was $2 per card. Front has a black-and-white posed action photo with blue and white pinstriped backgrounds. Back has a ghosted photo of Elway in his Broncos uniform and provides details of his baseball career.

	NM/M
John Elway	3.00

Certified Mirrors

Among several card issues that were aborted by Pinnacle's bankruptcy in mid-1998, but that have leaked into the hobby market in dribs and drabs, are specimens of some of the intended mirror parallels for a Pinnacle Certified set. The majority of cards seen have been Mirror Reds, with a few Mirror Gold issues and even fewer Mirror Blues. Many cards are known in only a single example, and some commons have not yet been verified, though it is presumed that all cards among the first 99 numbers on the unissued Certified base set checklist will be found eventually.

		NM/M
Common Player:		15.00
1	Vladimir Guerrero	25.00
2	Andruw Jones	25.00
3	Paul Molitor	25.00
4	Jose Cruz Jr.	15.00
5	Edgar Martinez	15.00
6	Andy Pettitte	15.00
7	Darin Erstad	15.00
8	Barry Larkin	15.00
9	Derek Jeter	60.00
10	Rusty Greer	15.00
11	Brady Anderson	15.00
12	Tony Clark	15.00
13	Manny Ramirez	25.00
14	Jim Thome	20.00
15	Matt Williams	15.00
16	Ivan Rodriguez	20.00
17	Scott Rolen	20.00
18	Gary Sheffield	15.00
19	David Justice	15.00
20	Roberto Alomar	15.00
21	Ken Caminiti	15.00
22	Sammy Sosa	40.00
23	Albert Belle	15.00
24	Chuck Knoblauch	15.00
25	Mo Vaughn	15.00
26	Raul Mondesi	15.00
27	Tim Salmon	15.00
28	Bernie Williams	15.00
29	Tony Gwynn	25.00
30	Pedro Martinez	25.00
31	Roger Clemens	40.00
32	Craig Biggio	15.00
33	Randy Johnson	25.00
34	Tino Martinez	15.00
35	Chipper Jones	25.00
36	Kenny Lofton	15.00
37	Greg Maddux	25.00
38	Hideo Nomo	20.00
39	Andres Galarraga	15.00
40	Nomar Garciaparra	30.00
41	Juan Gonzalez	20.00
42	Mark McGwire	50.00
43	Mike Piazza	30.00
44	Jeff Bagwell	25.00
45	Barry Bonds	60.00
46	Larry Walker	15.00
47	Alex Rodriguez	60.00
48	Frank Thomas	30.00
49	Cal Ripken Jr.	75.00
50	Ken Griffey Jr.	50.00
51	Todd Walker	15.00
52	Jose Guillen	15.00
53	Vinny Castilla	15.00
54	Shannon Stewart	15.00
55	Jim Edmonds	15.00
56	Bobby Higginson	15.00
57	Jay Buhner	15.00
58	Mike Mussina	15.00
59	Todd Greene	15.00
60	Chan Ho Park	15.00
61	Livan Hernandez	15.00
62	Sandy Alomar Jr.	15.00
63	Fred McGriff	15.00
64	Travis Fryman	15.00
65	Jaret Wright	15.00
66	Bobby Bonilla	15.00
67	Moises Alou	15.00
68	Rafael Palmeiro	25.00
69	Charles Johnson	15.00
70	Ray Lankford	15.00
71	Kevin Brown	15.00
72	Neifi Perez	15.00
73	Rondell White	15.00
74	Bartolo Colon	15.00
75	Bob Abreu	15.00
76	Eric Young	15.00
77	Jason Giambi	20.00
78	Edgardo Alfonzo	15.00
79	Dante Bichette	15.00
80	Eric Karros	15.00
81	Matt Morris	15.00
82	Tom Glavine	15.00
83	Randy Hundley	15.00
84	Jason Dickson	15.00
85	Ryan Klesko	15.00
86	Mark Grace	15.00
87	Brett Tomko	15.00
88	Kevin Orie	15.00
89	Robin Ventura	15.00
90	Jose Canseco	15.00
91	Brian Jordan	15.00
92	Jason Kendall	15.00
93	Mike Cameron	15.00
94	Curt Schilling	20.00
95	Carlos Delgado	15.00
96	Garret Anderson	15.00
97	John Smoltz	15.00
98	Wade Boggs	25.00
99	Javy Lopez	15.00

1998 Pinnacle Inside

Pinnacle Inside features cards in a can. The 150 base cards have full-bleed photos on front with stats on the right and the player's name and position at bottom. The Club Edition parallel (1:7) is printed on silver foil board and the Diamond Edition parallel (1:67) is printed on prismatic foil board. Each pack of cards was packaged inside a collectible can. Inserts include Behind the Numbers and Stand Up Guys.

		NM/M
Complete Set (150):		12.00
Common Player:		.05
Club Edition (1:7):		4X
Diamond Edition (1:67):		10X
Can (10):		1.00
Box (48):		45.00
1	Darin Erstad	.15
2	Derek Jeter	2.50
3	Alex Rodriguez	2.00
4	Bobby Higginson	.05
5	Nomar Garciaparra	1.00
6	Kenny Lofton	.05
7	Ivan Rodriguez	.65
8	Cal Ripken Jr.	2.50
9	Todd Hundley	.05
10	Chipper Jones	1.00
11	Barry Larkin	.05
12	Roberto Alomar	.15
13	Mo Vaughn	.05
14	Sammy Sosa	1.00
15	Sandy Alomar Jr.	.05
16	Albert Belle	.05
17	Scott Rolen	.65
18	Pokey Reese	.05
19	Ryan Klesko	.05
20	Andres Galarraga	.05
21	Justin Thompson	.05
22	Gary Sheffield	.40
23	David Justice	.05
24	Ken Griffey Jr.	1.50
25	Andruw Jones	.75
26	Jeff Bagwell	.75
27	Vladimir Guerrero	.75
28	Mike Piazza	1.50
29	Chuck Knoblauch	.05
30	Rondell White	.05
31	Greg Maddux	1.00
32	Andy Pettitte	.20
33	Larry Walker	.05
34	Bobby Estalella	.05
35	Frank Thomas	.75
36	Tony Womack	.05
37	Tony Gwynn	1.00
38	Barry Bonds	2.50
39	Randy Johnson	.75
40	Mark McGwire	2.00
41	Juan Gonzalez	.40
42	Tim Salmon	.05
43	John Smoltz	.05
44	Rafael Palmeiro	.65
45	Mark Grace	.05
46	Mike Cameron	.05
47	Jim Thome	.65
48	Neifi Perez	.05
49	Kevin Brown	.05
50	Craig Biggio	.05
51	Bernie Williams	.05
52	Hideo Nomo	.40
53	Bob Abreu	.15
54	Edgardo Alfonzo	.05
55	Wade Boggs	1.00
56	Jose Guillen	.05
57	Ken Caminiti	.05
58	Paul Molitor	.75
59	Shawn Estes	.05
60	Edgar Martinez	.05
61	Livan Hernandez	.05
62	Ray Lankford	.05
63	Rusty Greer	.05
64	Jim Edmonds	.05
65	Tom Glavine	.35
66	Alan Benes	.05
67	Will Clark	.05
68	Garret Anderson	.05
69	Javier Lopez	.05
70	Mike Mussina	.35
71	Kevin Orie	.05
72	Matt Williams	.05
73	Bobby Bonilla	.05
74	Ruben Rivera	.05
75	Jason Giambi	.60
76	Todd Walker	.05
77	Tino Martinez	.05
78	Matt Morris	.05
79	Fernando Tatis	.05
80	Todd Greene	.05
81	Fred McGriff	.05
82	Brady Anderson	.05
83	Mark Kotsay	.05
84	Raul Mondesi	.05
85	Moises Alou	.05
86	Roger Clemens	1.25
87	Wilton Guerrero	.05
88	Shannon Stewart	.05
89	Chan Ho Park	.05
90	Carlos Delgado	.60
91	Jose Cruz Jr.	.05
92	Shawn Green	.35
93	Robin Ventura	.05
94	Reggie Sanders	.05
95	Orel Hershiser	.05
96	Dante Bichette	.05
97	Charles Johnson	.05
98	Pedro Martinez	.75
99	Mariano Rivera	.15
100	Joe Randa	.05
101	Jeff Kent	.05
102	Jay Buhner	.05
103	Brian Jordan	.05
104	Jason Kendall	.05
105	Scott Spiezio	.05
106	Desi Relaford	.05
107	Bernard Gilkey	.05
108	Manny Ramirez	.75
109	Tony Clark	.05
110	Eric Young	.05
111	Johnny Damon	.30
112	Glendon Rusch	.05
113	Ben Grieve	.05
114	Homer Bush	.05
115	Miguel Tejada	.25
116	Lou Collier	.05
117	Derrek Lee	.60
118	Jacob Cruz	.05
119	Raul Ibanez	.05
120	Ryan McGuire	.05
121	Antone Williamson	.05
122	Abraham Nunez	.05
123	Jeff Abbott	.05
124	Brett Tomko	.05
125	Richie Sexson	.05
126	Todd Helton	.75
127	Juan Encarnacion	.05
128	Richard Hidalgo	.05
129	Paul Konorko	.10
130	Brad Fullmer	.05
131	Jeremi Gonzalez	.05
132	Jaret Wright	.05
133	Derek Jeter (Inside Tips)	1.25
134	Frank Thomas (Inside Tips)	.40
135	Nomar Garciaparra (Inside Tips)	.50
136	Kenny Lofton (Inside Tips)	.05
137	Jeff Bagwell (Inside Tips)	.40
138	Todd Hundley (Inside Tips)	.05
139	Alex Rodriguez (Inside Tips)	1.00
140	Ken Griffey Jr. (Inside Tips)	.75
141	Sammy Sosa (Inside Tips)	.50
142	Greg Maddux (Inside Tips)	.50
143	Albert Belle (Inside Tips)	.05
144	Cal Ripken Jr. (Inside Tips)	1.25
145	Mark McGwire (Inside Tips)	1.00
146	Chipper Jones (Inside Tips)	.50
147	Charles Johnson (Inside Tips)	.05
148	Checklist (Ken Griffey Jr.)	.75
149	Checklist (Jose Cruz Jr.)	.05
150	Checklist (Larry Walker)	.05

Club Edition

This parallel set is virtually identical to the regular Inside cards, except for the addition of a "CLUB EDITION" notice to the right of the player's first name, and the use of gold foil highlights instead of silver on front.

	NM/M
Complete Set (150):	50.00
Common Player:	2.00
Stars:	4X
Inserted 1:7	

Diamond Edition

Diamond Edition cards parallel all 150 cards in Pinnacle Inside. The fronts have the insert name. These are printed on prismatic foil board and inserted one per 67 cans.

	NM/M
Common Card:	6.00
Stars:	10X
Inserted 1:67	

Behind the Numbers

Behind the Numbers is seeded one per 23 cans. Fronts feature an action photo printed in front of the player's number. The card is die-cut around the large metallic foil numerals. The back has a portrait photo and text explaining why the player wears that number.

		NM/M
Complete Set (20):		85.00
Common Player:		1.50
Inserted 1:23		
1	Ken Griffey Jr.	7.50
2	Cal Ripken Jr.	12.00
3	Alex Rodriguez	10.00
4	Jose Cruz Jr.	1.50
5	Mike Piazza	7.50
6	Nomar Garciaparra	5.50
7	Scott Rolen	2.50
8	Andruw Jones	4.00
9	Frank Thomas	4.00
10	Mark McGwire	10.00
11	Ivan Rodriguez	3.00
12	Greg Maddux	5.50
13	Roger Clemens	6.50
14	Derek Jeter	12.00
15	Tony Gwynn	5.50
16	Ben Grieve	1.50
17	Jeff Bagwell	4.00
18	Chipper Jones	5.50
19	Hideo Nomo	2.00
20	Sandy Alomar Jr.	1.50

Stand Up Guys

This 50-card insert was seeded one per can. Each card has a match; the two cards join together in the center to form a stand-up collectible featuring four Major League players. Each card can also be found in a promo edition with a large "SAMPLE" overprint.

	NM/M
Complete Set (50):	35.00
Common Card:	.25

Sample:		3X
1-A/B	Ken Griffey Jr., Cal Ripken Jr.	2.00
1-C/D	Tony Gwynn, Mike Piazza	1.25
2-A/B	Andruw Jones, Alex Rodriguez	1.50
2-C/D	Scott Rolen, Nomar Garciaparra	1.00
3-A/B	Andruw Jones, Greg Maddux	1.00
3-C/D	Javy Lopez, Chipper Jones	1.00
4-A/B	Jay Buhner, Randy Johnson	.75
4-C/D	Ken Griffey Jr., Alex Rodriguez	1.50
5-A/B	Frank Thomas, Jeff Bagwell	.75
5-C/D	Mark McGwire, Mo Vaughn	1.50
6-A/B	Nomar Garciaparra, Derek Jeter	2.00
6-C/D	Alex Rodriguez, Barry Larkin	1.50
7-A/B	Mike Piazza, Ivan Rodriguez	1.25
7-C/D	Charles Johnson, Javy Lopez	.25
8-A/B	Cal Ripken Jr., Chipper Jones	2.00
8-C/D	Ken Caminiti, Scott Rolen	.65
9-A/B	Jose Cruz Jr., Vladimir Guerrero	.75
9-C/D	Andruw Jones, Jose Guillen	.75
10-A/B	Larry Walker, Dante Bichette	.25
10-C/D	Ellis Burks, Neifi Perez	.25
11-A/B	Juan Gonzalez, Sammy Sosa	1.00
11-C/D	Vladimir Guerrero, Manny Ramirez	.75
12-A/B	Greg Maddux, Roger Clemens	1.00
12-C/D	Hideo Nomo, Randy Johnson	.75
13-A/B	Ben Grieve, Paul Konerko	.40
13-C/D	Jose Cruz Jr., Fernando Tatis	.25
14-A/B	Ryne Sandberg, Chuck Knoblauch	1.00
14-C/D	Roberto Alomar, Craig Biggio	.35
15-A/B	Cal Ripken Jr., Brady Anderson	2.00
15-C/D	Rafael Palmeiro, Roberto Alomar	.65
16-A/B	Darin Erstad, Jim Edmonds	.35
16-C/D	Tim Salmon, Garret Anderson	.25
17-A/B	Mike Piazza, Hideo Nomo	1.25
17-C/D	Raul Mondesi, Eric Karros	.25
18-A/B	Ivan Rodriguez, Juan Gonzalez	.65
18-C/D	Will Clark, Rusty Greer	.25
19-A/B	Derek Jeter, Bernie Williams	2.00
19-C/D	Tino Martinez, Andy Pettitte	.25
20-A/B	Kenny Lofton, Ken Griffey Jr.	1.25
20-C/D	Brady Anderson, Bernie Williams	.25
21-A/B	Paul Molitor, Eddie Murray	.75
21-C/D	Ryne Sandberg, Rickey Henderson	1.00
22-A/B	Tony Clark, Frank Thomas	.75
22-C/D	Jeff Bagwell, Mark McGwire	1.50
23-A/B	Manny Ramirez, Jim Thome	.75
23-C/D	David Justice, Sandy Alomar Jr.	.25
24-A/B	Barry Bonds, Albert Belle	2.00
24-C/D	Jeff Bagwell, Dante Bichette	.60
25-A/B	Ken Griffey Jr., Frank Thomas	1.25
25-C/D	Alex Rodriguez, Andruw Jones	1.50

Cans

Ten-card packs of Pinnacle Inside were packaged in collectible cans. The 24 cans featured a player photo or team logo. Cans were created to honor the Florida Marlins' world championship and the expansion Arizona and Tampa Bay teams. Gold parallel versions of the cans were found one every 47 cans. Values shown are for bottom-opened cans; cans opened from the top have little collectible value.

		NM/M
Complete Set (23):		15.00
Common Can:		.40
Gold Cans:		2X
1	Ken Griffey Jr.	1.25
2	Frank Thomas	.65
3	Alex Rodriguez	1.50
4	Andruw Jones	.65
5	Mike Piazza	1.25
6	Ben Grieve	.40
7	Hideo Nomo	.50
8	Vladimir Guerrero	.65
9	Roger Clemens	1.00
10	Tony Gwynn	.75
11	Mark McGwire	1.50
12	Cal Ripken Jr.	2.00
13	Jose Cruz Jr.	.40
14	Greg Maddux	.75
15	Chipper Jones	.75
16	Derek Jeter	2.00
17	Juan Gonzalez	.50
18	Nomar Garciaparra (AL ROY)	1.00
19	Scott Rolen (NL ROY)	.65
20	Florida Marlins World Series Winner	.40
21	Larry Walker (NL MVP)	.40
22	Tampa Bay Devil Rays	.40
23	Arizona Diamondbacks	.40

1998 Pinnacle Mint Collection

Mint Collection consists of 30 cards and 30 matching coins with numerous parallels of each. The cards come in four different versions. The base card features a player photo at left with a circular bronze foil team logo at right. The base cards were inserted one per hobby pack and two per retail pack. Die-cut versions removed the team logo and were inserted two per hobby and one per retail packs. Silver Mint Team (1:15 hobby, 1:23 retail) and Gold Mint Team (1:47 hobby, 1:71 retail) parallels were printed on silver foil and gold foil board, respectively.

		NM/M
Complete Set (30):		10.00
Common Die-Cut:		.25
Bronze (1:1H):		2X
Silver (1:15H):		5X
Gold (1:47):		12X
Pack (3+2):		1.00
Wax Box (24):		12.00
1	Jeff Bagwell	.65
2	Albert Belle	.25
3	Barry Bonds	2.00
4	Tony Clark	.25
5	Roger Clemens	1.00
6	Juan Gonzalez	.35
7	Ken Griffey Jr.	1.25
8	Tony Gwynn	.75
9	Derek Jeter	2.00
10	Randy Johnson	.65
11	Chipper Jones	.75
12	Greg Maddux	.75
13	Tino Martinez	.25
14	Mark McGwire	1.50
15	Hideo Nomo	.35
16	Andy Pettitte	.25
17	Mike Piazza	1.25
18	Cal Ripken Jr.	2.00
19	Alex Rodriguez	1.50
20	Ivan Rodriguez	.50
21	Sammy Sosa	.75
22	Frank Thomas	.65
23	Mo Vaughn	.25
24	Larry Walker	.25
25	Jose Cruz Jr.	.25
26	Nomar Garciaparra	.75
27	Vladimir Guerrero	.65
28	Livan Hernandez	.25
29	Andruw Jones	.65
30	Scott Rolen	.50

Coins

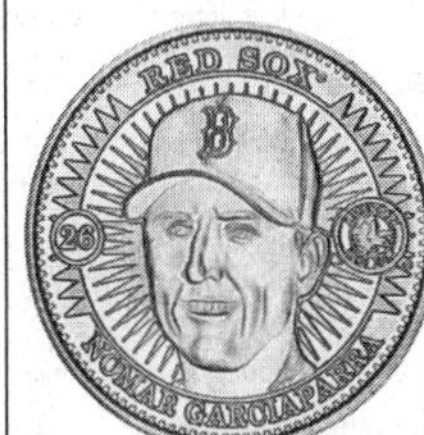

Two base coins were included in each pack of Mint Collection. The coins feature the player's image, name and number on the front along with his team's name and logo. The back has the Mint Collection logo. Seven parallels were included: Nickel-Silver (1:41), Brass Proof (numbered to 500), Nickel Proof (numbered to 250), Gold Proof (numbered to 100), Gold-Plated (1:199), Solid Silver (1:288 hobby, 1:960 retail) and Solid Gold by redemption (1-of-1).

		NM/M
Complete Set (30):		20.00
Common Brass Coin:		.25
Brass Proof (500):		5X
Nickel (1:41):		3X
Nickel Proof (250):		12X
Silver:		12X
Inserted 1:288 H, 1:960 R		
Gold Plated (1:199):		15X
Gold Proof (100):		20X
1	Jeff Bagwell	.75
2	Albert Belle	.25
3	Barry Bonds	2.00
4	Tony Clark	.25
5	Roger Clemens	1.00
6	Juan Gonzalez	.45
7	Ken Griffey Jr.	1.25
8	Tony Gwynn	1.00
9	Derek Jeter	2.00
10	Randy Johnson	.75
11	Chipper Jones	1.00
12	Greg Maddux	1.00
13	Tino Martinez	.25
14	Mark McGwire	1.50
15	Hideo Nomo	.45
16	Andy Pettitte	.35
17	Mike Piazza	1.25
18	Cal Ripken Jr.	2.00
19	Alex Rodriguez	1.50
20	Ivan Rodriguez	.65
21	Sammy Sosa	1.00
22	Frank Thomas	.75
23	Mo Vaughn	.25
24	Larry Walker	.25
25	Jose Cruz Jr.	.25
26	Nomar Garciaparra	1.00
27	Vladimir Guerrero	.75
28	Livan Hernandez	.25
29	Andruw Jones	.75
30	Scott Rolen	.65

Mint Gems

Mint Gems is a six-card insert printed on silver foil board. The cards were inserted 1:31

hobby packs and 1:47 retail. The oversized Mint Gems coins are twice the size of the regular coins. The six coins were inserted 1:31 hobby packs.

		NM/M
Complete Set (6)		20.00
Common Player:		2.00
Coins:		1X
1	Ken Griffey Jr.	6.00
2	Larry Walker	2.00
3	Roger Clemens	5.00
4	Pedro Martinez	4.00
5	Nomar Garciaparra	4.50
6	Scott Rolen	3.00

1998 Pinnacle Performers

Pinnacle Performers consists of a 150-card base set. The Peak Performers parallel adds silver foil to the base cards and was inserted 1:7. Inserts in the home run-themed product include Big Bang, Launching Pad, Player's Card and Power Trip.

		NM/M
Complete Set (150):		12.00
Common Player:		.05
Peak Performers (1:7):		2X
Pack (10):		1.00
Wax Box (24):		15.00
1	Ken Griffey Jr.	1.00
2	Frank Thomas	.65
3	Cal Ripken Jr.	1.50
4	Alex Rodriguez	1.25
5	Greg Maddux	.75
6	Mike Piazza	1.00
7	Chipper Jones	.75
8	Tony Gwynn	.75
9	Derek Jeter	1.50
10	Jeff Bagwell	.65
11	Juan Gonzalez	.35
12	Nomar Garciaparra	.75
13	Andruw Jones	.65
14	Hideo Nomo	.35
15	Roger Clemens	.85
16	Mark McGwire	1.25
17	Scott Rolen	.60
18	Vladimir Guerrero	.65
19	Barry Bonds	1.50
20	Darin Erstad	.15
21	Albert Belle	.05
22	Kenny Lofton	.05
23	Mo Vaughn	.05
24	Tony Clark	.05
25	Ivan Rodriguez	.60
26	Jose Cruz Jr.	.05
27	Larry Walker	.05
28	Jaret Wright	.05
29	Andy Pettitte	.25
30	Roberto Alomar	.20
31	Randy Johnson	.65
32	Manny Ramirez	.65
33	Paul Molitor	.65
34	Mike Mussina	.35
35	Jim Thome	.60
36	Tino Martinez	.05
37	Gary Sheffield	.45
38	Chuck Knoblauch	.05
39	Bernie Williams	.05
40	Tim Salmon	.05
41	Sammy Sosa	.75
42	Wade Boggs	.75
43	Will Clark	.05
44	Andres Galarraga	.05
45	Raul Mondesi	.05
46	Rickey Henderson	.65
47	Jose Canseco	.45
48	Pedro Martinez	.65
49	Jay Buhner	.05
50	Ryan Klesko	.05
51	Barry Larkin	.05
52	Charles Johnson	.05
53	Tom Glavine	.35
54	Edgar Martinez	.05
55	Fred McGriff	.05
56	Moises Alou	.05
57	Dante Bichette	.05
58	Jim Edmonds	.05
59	Mark Grace	.05
60	Chan Ho Park	.05
61	Justin Thompson	.05
62	John Smoltz	.05
63	Craig Biggio	.05
64	Ken Caminiti	.05
65	Richard Hidalgo	.05
66	Carlos Delgado	.50
67	David Justice	.05
68	J.T. Snow	.05
69	Jason Giambi	.50
70	Garret Anderson	.05
71	Rondell White	.05
72	Matt Williams	.05
73	Brady Anderson	.05
74	Eric Karros	.05
75	Javier Lopez	.05
76	Pat Hentgen	.05
77	Todd Hundley	.05
78	Ray Lankford	.05
79	Denny Neagle	.05
80	Sandy Alomar Jr.	.05
81	Jason Kendall	.05
82	Omar Vizquel	.05
83	Kevin Brown	.05
84	Kevin Appier	.05
85	Al Martin	.05
86	Rusty Greer	.05
87	Bobby Bonilla	.05
88	Shawn Estes	.05
89	Rafael Palmeiro	.60
90	Edgar Renteria	.05
91	Alan Benes	.05
92	Bobby Higginson	.05
93	Mark Grudzielanek	.05
94	Jose Guillen	.05
95	Neifi Perez	.05
96	Jeff Abbott	.05
97	Todd Walker	.05
98	Eric Young	.05
99	Brett Tomko	.05
100	Mike Cameron	.05
101	Karim Garcia	.05
102	Brian Jordan	.05
103	Jeff Suppan	.05
104	Robin Ventura	.05
105	Henry Rodriguez	.05
106	Shannon Stewart	.05
107	Kevin Orie	.05
108	Bartolo Colon	.05
109	Bob Abreu	.15
110	Vinny Castilla	.05
111	Livan Hernandez	.05
112	Derrek Lee	.50
113	Mark Kotsay	.05
114	Todd Greene	.05
115	Edgardo Alfonzo	.05
116	A.J. Hinch	.05
117	Paul Konerko	.15
118	Todd Helton	.65
119	Miguel Tejada	.20
120	Fernando Tatis	.05
121	Ben Grieve	.05
122	Travis Lee	.05
123	Kerry Wood	.25
124	Eli Marrero	.05
125	David Ortiz	.50
126	Juan Encarnacion	.05
127	Brad Fullmer	.05
128	Richie Sexson	.05
129	Aaron Boone	.05
130	Enrique Wilson	.05
131	Javier Valentin	.05
132	Abraham Nunez	.05
133	Ricky Ledee	.05
134	Carl Pavano	.05
135	Bobby Estalella	.05
136	Homer Bush	.05
137	Brian Rose	.05
138	Ken Griffey Jr. (Far and Away)	.50
139	Frank Thomas (Far and Away)	.35
140	Cal Ripken Jr. (Far and Away)	.75
141	Alex Rodriguez (Far and Away)	.65
142	Greg Maddux (Far and Away)	.40
143	Chipper Jones (Far and Away)	.40
144	Mike Piazza (Far and Away)	.50
145	Tony Gwynn (Far and Away)	.40
146	Derek Jeter (Far and Away)	.75
147	Jeff Bagwell (Far and Away)	.35
148	Checklist (Hideo Nomo)	.20
149	Checklist (Roger Clemens)	.45
150	Checklist (Greg Maddux)	.35

Peak Performers

This 150-card parallel set is printed on silver foil vs. the white cardboard stock used on regular-issue cards. The parallel set name is printed down the right side in gold letters. They were seeded one per seven packs.

	NM/M
Complete Set (150):	100.00
Common Player:	2.00
Stars:	6X
Inserted 1:7	

Big Bang

This 20-card insert features top power hitters. The micro-etched cards are sequentially numbered to 2,500. Each player has a Seasonal Outburst parallel, with a red overlay and numbered to that player's best seasonal home run total. Each card is also found in a promo edition with a large black "SAMPLE" overprinted on back.

		NM/M
Complete Set (20):		27.50
Common Player:		.50
Production 2,500 Sets		
Sample:		1X
1	Ken Griffey Jr.	2.50
2	Frank Thomas	1.50
3	Mike Piazza	2.50
4	Chipper Jones	2.00
5	Alex Rodriguez	3.00
6	Nomar Garciaparra	2.00
7	Jeff Bagwell	1.50
8	Cal Ripken Jr.	3.50
9	Albert Belle	.50
10	Mark McGwire	3.00
11	Juan Gonzalez	.75
12	Larry Walker	.50
13	Tino Martinez	.50
14	Jim Thome	1.00
15	Manny Ramirez	1.50
16	Barry Bonds	3.50
17	Mo Vaughn	.50
18	Jose Cruz Jr.	.50
19	Tony Clark	.50
20	Andruw Jones	1.50

Big Bang Seasonal Outburst

Season Outburst parallels the Big Bang insert. The cards have a red overlay and are sequentially numbered to each player's season-high home run total. Unnumbered versions of the cards, likely leaked into the market after Pinnacle went bankrupt in mid-1998, have been seen; their value is much lower than the issued version.

		NM/M
Complete Set (20):		500.00
Common Player:		10.00
#'d to player's 1997 HR total		
Unnumbered: 25 Percent		
1	Ken Griffey Jr./56	40.00
2	Frank Thomas/35	20.00
3	Mike Piazza/40	40.00
4	Chipper Jones/21	65.00
5	Alex Rodriguez/23	75.00
6	Nomar Garciaparra/30	40.00
7	Jeff Bagwell/43	20.00
8	Cal Ripken Jr./17	80.00
9	Albert Belle/30	10.00
10	Mark McGwire/58	65.00
11	Juan Gonzalez/42	12.50
12	Larry Walker/49	10.00
13	Tino Martinez /44	10.00
14	Jim Thome/40	15.00
15	Manny Ramirez/26	25.00
16	Barry Bonds/40	75.00
17	Mo Vaughn/35	10.00
18	Jose Cruz Jr./26	10.00
19	Tony Clark/32	10.00
20	Andruw Jones/18	25.00

Launching Pad

Launching Pad is a 20-card insert seeded one per nine packs. It features top sluggers on foil-on-foil cards with an outer space background.

		NM/M
Complete Set (20):		25.00
Common Player:		.50
Inserted 1:9		
1	Ben Grieve	.50
2	Ken Griffey Jr.	2.50
3	Derek Jeter	3.50
4	Frank Thomas	1.00
5	Travis Lee	.50
6	Vladimir Guerrero	1.00
7	Tony Gwynn	2.00
8	Jose Cruz Jr.	.50
9	Cal Ripken Jr.	3.50
10	Chipper Jones	2.00
11	Scott Rolen	.75
12	Andruw Jones	1.00
13	Ivan Rodriguez	.75
14	Todd Helton	1.00
15	Nomar Garciaparra	2.00
16	Mark McGwire	3.00
17	Gary Sheffield	.60
18	Bernie Williams	.50
19	Alex Rodriguez	3.00
20	Mike Piazza	2.50

Power Trip

This 10-card insert was seeded 1:21. Printed on silver foil, each card is sequentially-numbered to 10,000. Cards backs have details about one of the player's power-hitting highlights of the previous season.

		NM/M
Complete Set (10):		16.00
Common Player:		1.00
Production 10,000 Sets		
1	Frank Thomas	1.00
2	Alex Rodriguez	3.00
3	Nomar Garciaparra	1.50
4	Jeff Bagwell	1.00
5	Cal Ripken Jr.	4.00
6	Mike Piazza	2.00
7	Chipper Jones	1.50
8	Ken Griffey Jr.	2.00
9	Mark McGwire	3.00
10	Juan Gonzalez	1.00

Swing for the Fences

Pinnacle Performers included the "Swing for the Fences" sweepstakes. Fifty players were featured on cards with numbers on an all-red background. Fifty Home Run Points cards were also inserted, with each card featuring a point total on the front. Collectors who found the player cards of the AL and NL home run leaders, as well as enough point cards to match each of their season totals, were eligible to win prizes. A player or point card was inserted in each pack.

		NM/M
Complete Set (50):		24.00
Common Player:		.26
Inserted 1:1		
1	Brady Anderson	.25
2	Albert Belle	.25
3	Jay Buhner	.25
4	Jose Canseco	.50
5	Tony Clark	.25
6	Jose Cruz Jr.	.25
7	Jim Edmonds	.25
8	Cecil Fielder	.25
9	Travis Fryman	.25
10	Nomar Garciaparra	1.00
11	Juan Gonzalez	.40
12	Ken Griffey Jr.	1.50
13	David Justice	.25
14	Travis Lee	.25
15	Edgar Martinez	.25
16	Tino Martinez	.25
17	Rafael Palmeiro	.65
18	Manny Ramirez	.75
19	Cal Ripken Jr.	2.50
20	Alex Rodriguez	2.00
21	Tim Salmon	.25
22	Frank Thomas	.75
23	Jim Thome	.65
24	Mo Vaughn	.25
25	Bernie Williams	.25
26	Fred McGriff	.25
27	Jeff Bagwell	.75
28	Dante Bichette	.25
29	Barry Bonds	2.50
30	Ellis Burks	.25
31	Ken Caminiti	.25
32	Vinny Castilla	.25
33	Andres Galarraga	.25
34	Vladimir Guerrero	.75
35	Todd Helton	.75
36	Todd Hundley	.25
37	Andruw Jones	.75
38	Chipper Jones	1.00
39	Eric Karros	.25
40	Ryan Klesko	.25
41	Ray Lankford	.25
42	Mark McGwire	2.00
43	Raul Mondesi	.25
44	Mike Piazza	1.50
45	Scott Rolen	.65
46	Gary Sheffield	.50
47	Sammy Sosa	1.00
48	Larry Walker	.25
49	Matt Williams	.25
50	WILDCARD	.25

Swing/Fences Prize Cards

This set was evidently intended to be one of the prizes in Pinnacle's Swing for the Fences sweepstakes, but the cards were never officially dis-

tributed due to the company's midyear bankruptcy. Making their way out the back into hobby channels in later years, the cards feature action photos on a silver prismatic foil background. Unnumbered backs have the player's career home run totals versus each team.

		NM/M
Complete Set (10):		10.00
Common Player:		.50
(1)	Jeff Bagwell	1.00
(2)	Barry Bonds	3.00
(3)	Nomar Garciaparra	1.50
(4)	Juan Gonzalez	.50
(5)	Ken Griffey Jr.	2.00
(6)	Chipper Jones	1.50
(7)	Mark McGwire	2.50
(8)	Mike Piazza	1.50
(9)	Alex Rodriguez	2.50
(10)	Frank Thomas	1.00

1998 Pinnacle Plus

Pinnacle Plus consists of a 200-card base set. Five subsets are included: Field of Vision, Naturals, All-Stars, Devil Rays and Diamondbacks. Artist's Proof is a 60-card partial parallel of the base set, inserted 1:35 packs. Gold Artist's Proof cards are numbered to 100 and Mirror Artist's Proofs are 1-of-1 inserts. Inserts include Lasting Memories, Yardwork, A Piece of the Game, All-Star Epix, Team Pinnacle, Gold Team Pinnacle, Pinnabilia and Certified Souvenir.

		NM/M
Complete Set (200):		12.00
Common Player:		.05
Pack (10):		1.00
Wax Box (20):		12.00
1	Roberto Alomar/AS	.20
2	Sandy Alomar Jr./AS	.05
3	Brady Anderson/AS	.05
4	Albert Belle/AS	.05
5	Jeff Cirillo/AS	.05
6	Roger Clemens/AS	1.25
7	David Cone/AS	.05
8	Nomar Garciaparra/AS	1.00
9	Ken Griffey Jr./AS	1.50
10	Jason Dickson/AS	.05
11	Edgar Martinez/AS	.05
12	Tino Martinez/AS	.05
13	Randy Johnson/AS	.75
14	Mark McGwire/AS	2.00
15	David Justice/AS	.05
16	Mike Mussina/AS	.40
17	Chuck Knoblauch/AS	.05
18	Joey Cora/AS	.05
19	Pat Hentgen/AS	.05
20	Randy Myers/AS	.05
21	Cal Ripken Jr./AS	2.50
22	Mariano Rivera/AS	.15
23	Jose Rosado/AS	.05
24	Frank Thomas/AS	.75
25	Alex Rodriguez/AS	2.00
26	Justin Thompson/AS	.05
27	Ivan Rodriguez/AS	.65
28	Bernie Williams/AS	.05
29	Pedro Martinez	.75
30	Tony Clark	.05
31	Garret Anderson	.05
32	Travis Fryman	.05
33	Mike Piazza	1.50
34	Carl Pavano	.05
35	Kevin Millwood **RC**	1.00
36	Miguel Tejada	.20
37	Willie Blair	.05
38	Devon White	.05
39	Andres Galarraga	.05
40	Barry Larkin	.05
41	Al Leiter	.05
42	Moises Alou	.05
43	Eric Young	.05
44	John Jaha	.05
45	Bernard Gilkey	.05
46	Freddy Garcia	.05
47	Ruben Rivera	.05
48	Robb Nen	.05
49	Ray Lankford	.05
50	Kenny Lofton	.05
51	Joe Carter	.05
52	Jason McDonald	.05
53	Quinton McCracken	.05
54	Kerry Wood	.50
55	Mike Lansing	.05
56	Chipper Jones	1.00
57	Barry Bonds	2.50
58	Brad Fullmer	.05
59	Jeff Bagwell	.75
60	Rondell White	.05
61	Geronimo Berroa	.05
62	Magglio Ordonez **RC**	1.50
63	Dwight Gooden	.05
64	Brian Hunter	.05
65	Todd Walker	.05
66	Frank Catalanotto **RC**	.05
67	Tony Saunders	.05
68	Travis Lee	.05
69	Michael Tucker	.05
70	Reggie Sanders	.05
71	Derrek Lee	.50
72	Larry Walker	.05
73	Marquis Grissom	.05
74	Craig Biggio	.05
75	Kevin Brown	.05
76	J.T. Snow	.05
77	Eric Davis	.05
78	Jeff Abbott	.05
79	Jermaine Dye	.05
80	Otis Nixon	.05
81	Curt Schilling	.35
82	Enrique Wilson	.05
83	Tony Gwynn	1.00
84	Orlando Cabrera	.05
85	Ramon Martinez	.05
86	Greg Vaughn	.05
87	Alan Benes	.05
88	Dennis Eckersley	.65
89	Jim Thome	.65
90	Juan Encarnacion	.05
91	Jeff King	.05
92	Shannon Stewart	.05
93	Roberto Hernandez	.05
94	Raul Ibanez	.05
95	Darryl Kile	.05
96	Charles Johnson	.05
97	Rich Becker	.05
98	Hal Morris	.05
99	Ismael Valdes	.05
100	Orel Hershiser	.05
101	Mo Vaughn	.05
102	Aaron Boone	.05
103	Jeff Conine	.05
104	Paul O'Neill	.05
105	Tom Candiotti	.05
106	Wilson Alvarez	.05
107	Mike Stanley	.05
108	Carlos Delgado	.50
109	Tony Batista	.05
110	Dante Bichette	.05
111	Henry Rodriguez	.05
112	Karim Garcia	.05
113	Shane Reynolds	.05
114	Ken Caminiti	.05
115	Jose Silva	.05
116	Juan Gonzalez	.40
117	Brian Jordan	.05
118	Jim Leyritz	.05
119	Manny Ramirez	.75
120	Fred McGriff	.05
121	Brooks Kieschnick	.05
122	Sean Casey	.15
123	John Smoltz	.05
124	Rusty Greer	.05
125	Cecil Fielder	.05
126	Mike Cameron	.05
127	Reggie Jefferson	.05
128	Bobby Higginson	.05
129	Kevin Appier	.05
130	Robin Ventura	.05
131	Ben Grieve	.05
132	Wade Boggs	1.00
133	Jose Cruz Jr.	.05
134	Jeff Suppan	.05
135	Vinny Castilla	.05
136	Sammy Sosa	1.00
137	Mark Wohlers	.05
138	Jay Bell	.05
139	Brett Tomko	.05
140	Gary Sheffield	.40
141	Tim Salmon	.05
142	Jaret Wright	.05
143	Kenny Rogers	.05
144	Brian Anderson	.05
145	Darrin Fletcher	.05
146	John Flaherty	.05
147	Dmitri Young	.05
148	Andruw Jones	.75
149	Matt Williams	.05
150	Bobby Bonilla	.05
151	Mike Hampton	.05
152	Al Martin	.05
153	Mark Grudzielanek	.05
154	Dave Nilsson	.05
155	Roger Cedeno	.05
156	Greg Maddux	1.00
157	Mark Kotsay	.05
158	Steve Finley	.05
159	Wilson Delgado	.05
160	Ron Gant	.05
161	Jim Edmonds	.05
162	Jeff Blauser	.05
163	Dave Burba	.05
164	Pedro Astacio	.05
165	Livan Hernandez	.05
166	Neifi Perez	.05
167	Ryan Klesko	.05
168	Fernando Tatis	.05
169	Richard Hidalgo	.05
170	Carlos Perez	.05
171	Bob Abreu	.15
172	Francisco Cordova	.05
173	Todd Helton	.75
174	Doug Glanville	.05
175	Brian Rose	.05
176	Yamil Benitez	.05
177	Darin Erstad	.15
178	Scott Rolen	.60
179	John Wetteland	.05
180	Paul Sorrento	.05
181	Walt Weiss	.05
182	Vladimir Guerrero	.75
183	Ken Griffey Jr. (The Naturals)	.75
184	Alex Rodriguez (The Naturals)	1.00
185	Cal Ripken Jr. (The Naturals)	1.25
186	Frank Thomas (The Naturals)	.40
187	Chipper Jones (The Naturals)	.50
188	Hideo Nomo (The Naturals)	.20
189	Nomar Garciaparra (The Naturals)	.60
190	Mike Piazza (The Naturals)	1.00
191	Greg Maddux (The Naturals)	.50
192	Tony Gwynn (The Naturals)	.50
193	Mark McGwire (The Naturals)	1.00
194	Roger Clemens (The Naturals)	.65
195	Mike Piazza (Field of Vision)	.75
196	Mark McGwire (Field of Vision)	1.00
197	Chipper Jones (Field of Vision)	.50
198	Larry Walker (Field of Vision)	.05
199	Hideo Nomo (Field of Vision)	.20
200	Barry Bonds (Field of Vision)	1.25

Artist's Proofs

Artist's Proofs is a 60-card partial parallel of the Pinnacle Plus base set. The dot matrix hologram cards were inserted 1:35. Gold Artist's Proofs added a gold finish and are sequentially numbered to 100. Mirror Artist's Proofs are a "1-of-1" insert. Card numbers have an "AP" prefix.

		NM/M
Complete Set (60):		150.00
Common Player:		.75
Inserted 1:35		
Golds:		10X
Production 100 Sets		
1	Roberto Alomar/AS	1.50
2	Albert Belle/AS	.75
3	Roger Clemens/AS	8.00
4	Nomar Garciaparra/AS	7.50
5	Ken Griffey Jr./AS	10.00
6	Tino Martinez/AS	.75
7	Randy Johnson/AS	6.00
8	Mark McGwire/AS	12.50
9	David Justice/AS	.75
10	Chuck Knoblauch/AS	.75
11	Cal Ripken Jr./AS	15.00
12	Frank Thomas/AS	6.00
13	Alex Rodriguez/AS	12.50
14	Ivan Rodriguez/AS	5.00
15	Bernie Williams/AS	.75
16	Pedro Martinez	6.00
17	Tony Clark	.75
18	Mike Piazza	10.00
19	Miguel Tejada	1.00
20	Andres Galarraga	.75
21	Barry Larkin	.75
22	Kenny Lofton	.75
23	Chipper Jones	7.50
24	Barry Bonds	15.00
25	Brad Fullmer	.75
26	Jeff Bagwell	6.00
27	Todd Walker	.75
28	Travis Lee	.75
29	Larry Walker	.75
30	Craig Biggio	.75
31	Tony Gwynn	7.50
32	Jim Thome	5.00
33	Juan Encarnacion	.75
34	Mo Vaughn	.75
35	Karim Garcia	.75
36	Ken Caminiti	.75
37	Juan Gonzalez	3.00
38	Manny Ramirez	6.00
39	Fred McGriff	.75
40	Rusty Greer	.75
41	Bobby Higginson	.75
42	Ben Grieve	.75
43	Wade Boggs	7.50
44	Jose Cruz Jr.	.75
45	Sammy Sosa	7.50
46	Gary Sheffield	2.00
47	Tim Salmon	.75
48	Jaret Wright	.75
49	Andruw Jones	6.00
50	Matt Williams	.75
51	Greg Maddux	7.50
52	Jim Edmonds	.75
53	Livan Hernandez	.75
54	Neifi Perez	.75
55	Fernando Tatis	.75
56	Richard Hidalgo	.75
57	Todd Helton	6.00
58	Darin Erstad	1.50
59	Scott Rolen	5.00
60	Vladimir Guerrero	6.00

A Piece of the Game

Inserted 1:17 hobby packs (1:19 retail), this 10-card insert features baseball's top players on micro-etched foil cards.

		NM/M
Complete Set (10):		8.00
Common Player:		.50
Inserted 1:19		
1	Ken Griffey Jr.	1.00
2	Frank Thomas	.65
3	Alex Rodriguez	1.50
4	Chipper Jones	.75
5	Cal Ripken Jr.	2.00
6	Mike Piazza	1.00
7	Greg Maddux	.75
8	Juan Gonzalez	.50
9	Nomar Garciaparra	.75
10	Larry Walker	.50

Epix All-Star Moment

The All-Star Epix insert is part of the cross-brand Epix set. The cards honor the All-Star Game achievements of baseball's stars on cards with dot matrix holograms. All-Star Epix was seeded 1:21. Cards #1-12 were distributed in Score Rookie/Traded.

	NM/M
Complete Set (12):	25.00
Common Player:	1.00
Purples:	1.5X
Emeralds:	2.5X

Inserted 1:21

13	Alex Rodriguez	3.50
14	Cal Ripken Jr.	5.00
15	Chipper Jones	2.50
16	Roger Clemens	2.75
17	Mo Vaughn	1.00
18	Mark McGwire	3.50
19	Mike Piazza	3.00
20	Andruw Jones	2.00
21	Greg Maddux	2.50
22	Barry Bonds	5.00
23	Paul Molitor	2.00
24	Hideo Nomo	1.50

Lasting Memories

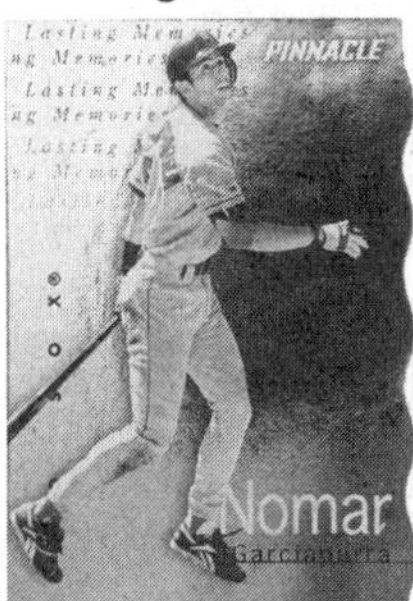

Lasting Memories is a 30-card insert seeded 1:5. Printed on foil board, the cards feature a player photo with a sky background.

		NM/M
Complete Set (30):		16.00
Common Player:		.25
Inserted 1:5		
1	Nomar Garciaparra	.75
2	Ken Griffey Jr.	1.00
3	Livan Hernandez	.25
4	Hideo Nomo	.40
5	Ben Grieve	.25
6	Scott Rolen	.50
7	Roger Clemens	.85
8	Cal Ripken Jr.	2.00
9	Mo Vaughn	.25
10	Frank Thomas	.65
11	Mark McGwire	1.50
12	Barry Larkin	.25
13	Matt Williams	.25
14	Jose Cruz Jr.	.25
15	Andruw Jones	.65
16	Mike Piazza	1.00
17	Jeff Bagwell	.65
18	Chipper Jones	.75
19	Juan Gonzalez	.40
20	Kenny Lofton	.25
21	Greg Maddux	.75
22	Ivan Rodriguez	.50
23	Alex Rodriguez	1.50
24	Derek Jeter	2.00
25	Albert Belle	.25
26	Barry Bonds	2.00
27	Larry Walker	.25
28	Sammy Sosa	.75
29	Tony Gwynn	.75
30	Randy Johnson	.65

Team Pinnacle

Team Pinnacle is a 15-card, double-sided insert. Printed on mirror-mylar, the cards were inserted 1:71. The hobby-only Gold Team Pinnacle parallel was inserted 1:199 packs.

		NM/M
Complete Set (15):		50.00
Common Player:		1.50
Inserted 1:71		
Golds:		2X
Inserted 1:199		
1	Mike Piazza, Ivan Rodriguez	6.00
2	Mark McGwire, Mo Vaughn	5.00
3	Roberto Alomar, Craig Biggio	2.00
4	Alex Rodriguez, Barry Larkin	8.00
5	Cal Ripken Jr., Chipper Jones	10.00
6	Ken Griffey Jr., Larry Walker	6.00
7	Juan Gonzalez, Tony Gwynn	4.00
8	Albert Belle, Barry Bonds	8.00
9	Kenny Lofton, Andruw Jones	3.00
10	Tino Martinez, Jeff Bagwell	3.00
11	Frank Thomas, Andres Galarraga	3.00
12	Roger Clemens, Greg Maddux	8.00
13	Pedro Martinez, Hideo Nomo	4.00
14	Nomar Garciaparra, Scott Rolen	5.00
15	Ben Grieve, Paul Konerko	1.50

Yardwork

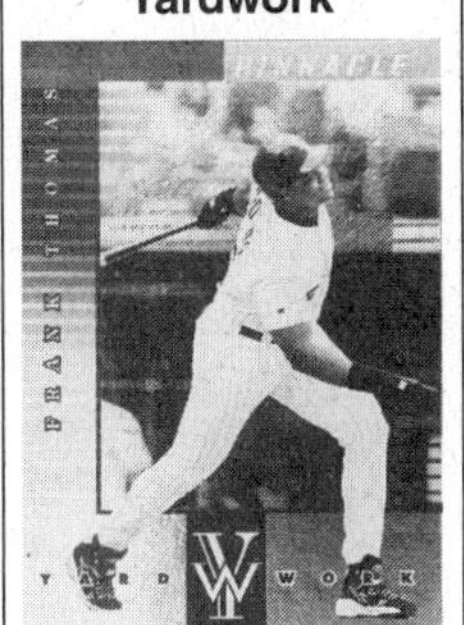

Yardwork is a 15-card insert seeded one per 19 packs. It features the top home run hitters in Major League Baseball.

		NM/M
Complete Set (15):		12.50
Common Player:		.35
Inserted 1:9		
1	Mo Vaughn	.35
2	Frank Thomas	.75
3	Albert Belle	.35
4	Nomar Garciaparra	1.00
5	Tony Clark	.35
6	Tino Martinez	.35
7	Ken Griffey Jr.	1.50
8	Juan Gonzalez	.60
9	Sammy Sosa	1.00
10	Jose Cruz Jr.	.35
11	Jeff Bagwell	.75
12	Mike Piazza	1.50
13	Larry Walker	.35
14	Mark McGwire	2.00
15	Barry Bonds	2.50

1998 Pinnacle Snapshots

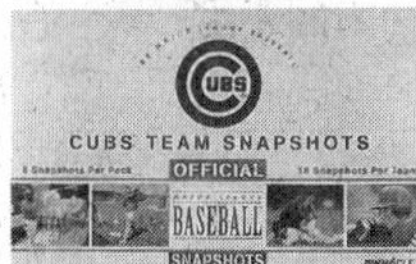

One of Pinnacle's last issues was a team-oriented presentation of large-format (4" x 6") cards called Snapshots. Like their namesake, the focus on this issue is on candid photos rather than posed portraits or game-action pictures. The cards are printed on thin high-gloss cardboard stock resembling photo paper. Fronts, many of them horizontally formatted, are borderless and have no graphic enhancement. Backs are lightly printed with Pinnacle and licensor logos and a card number expressed "x of 18." The player's name is nowhere to be found. Snapshots were sold regionally in single-team boxes of 25 packs with eight cards each.

Angels

		NM/M
Complete Set (18):		7.50
Common Player:		.50
1	Jason Dickson	.50
2	Gary DiSarcina	.50
3	Garret Anderson	.50
4	Shigetosi Hasegawa	.50
5	Ken Hill	.50
6	Todd Greene	.50
7	Tim Salmon	.75
8	Jim Edmonds	.60
9	Garret Anderson	.50
10	Dave Hollins	.50
11	Todd Greene	.50
12	Troy Percival	.50
13	Gary DiSarcina	.50
14	Cecil Fielder	.50
15	Darin Erstad	.75
16	Chuck Finley	.50
17	Jim Edmonds	.50
18	Jason Dickson	.50

Braves

		NM/M
Complete Set (18):		11.00
Common Player:		.50
1	Ryan Klesko	.50
2	Walt Weiss	.50
3	Tom Glavine	.75
4	Randall Simon	.50
5	John Smoltz	.50
6	Chipper Jones	1.50
7	Javier Lopez	.50
8	Greg Maddux	1.50
9	Andruw Jones	1.00
10	Michael Tucker	.50
11	Andres Galarraga	.50
12	Andres Galarraga	.50
13	Greg Maddux	1.50
14	Wes Helms	.50
15	Bruce Chen	.50
16	Denny Neagle	.50
17	Mark Wohlers	.50
18	Kevin Millwood	.60

Cardinals

		NM/M
Complete Set (18):		10.00
Common Player:		.50
1	Alan Benes	.50
2	Ron Gant	.50
3	Donovan Osborne	.50
4	Eli Marrero	.50
5	Mark McGwire	2.50
6	Delino DeShields	.50
7	Tom Pagnozzi	.50
8	Delino DeShields	.50
9	Mark McGwire	2.50
10	Royce Clayton	.50
11	Brian Jordan	.50
12	Ray Lankford	.50
13	Brian Jordan	.50
14	Matt Morris	.50
15	John Mabry	.50
16	Luis Ordaz	.50
17	Ron Gant	.50
18	Todd Stottlemyre	.50

Cubs

		NM/M
Complete Set (18):		9.00
Common Player:		.50
1	Mark Grace	.60
2	Manny Alexander	.50
3	Jeremi Gonzalez	.50
4	Brant Brown	.50
5	Mark Grace	.60
6	Lance Johnson	.50
7	Mark Clark	.50
8	Kevin Foster	.50
9	Brant Brown	.50
10	Kevin Foster	.50
11	Kevin Tapani	.50
12	Sammy Sosa	1.50
13	Sammy Sosa	1.50
14	Pat Cline	.50
15	Kevin Orie	.50
16	Steve Trachsel	.50
17	Lance Johnson	.50
18	Robin Jennings	.50

Devil Rays

		NM/M
Complete Set (18):		7.50
Common Player:		.50
1	Kevin Stocker	.50
2	Paul Sorrento	.50
3	John Flaherty	.50
4	Wade Boggs	1.50
5	Rich Butler	.50
6	Wilson Alvarez	.50
7	Bubba Trammell	.50
8	David Martinez	.50
9	Brooks Kieschnick	.50
10	Tony Saunders	.50
11	Esteban Yan	.50
12	Quinton McCracken	.50
13	Albie Lopez	.50
14	Roberto Hernandez	.50
15	Fred McGriff	.50
16	Bubba Trammell	.50
17	Brooks Kieschnick	.50
18	Fred McGriff	.50

Diamondbacks

		NM/M
Complete Set (18):		7.50
Common Player:		.50
1	Travis Lee	1.00
2	Matt Williams	.50
3	Jay Bell	.50
4	Devon White	.50
5	Andy Benes	.50
6	Tony Batista	.50
7	Jay Bell	.50
8	Edwin Diaz	.50
9	Devon White	.50
10	Bob Wolcott	.50
11	Karim Garcia	1.00
12	Yamil Benitez	.50
13	Jorge Fabregas	.50
14	Jeff Suppan	.50
15	Ben Ford	.50
16	Brian Anderson	.50
17	Travis Lee	1.00
18	Matt Williams	.50

Dodgers

		NM/M
Complete Set (18):		12.00
Common Player:		.50
1	Mike Piazza	2.50
2	Eric Karros	.50
3	Raul Mondesi	.50
4	Wilton Guerrero	.50
5	Darren Dreifort	.50
6	Roger Cedeno	.50
7	Todd Zeile	.50
8	Paul Konerko	.75
9	Todd Hollandsworth	.50
10	Ismael Valdes	.50
11	Hideo Nomo	1.00
12	Ramon Martinez	.50
13	Chan Ho Park	.75
14	Eric Young	.50
15	Dennis Reyes	.50
16	Eric Karros	.50
17	Mike Piazza	2.50
18	Raul Mondesi	.50

Indians

		NM/M
Complete Set (18):		7.50
Common Player:		.50
1	Manny Ramirez	1.50
2	Travis Fryman	.50
3	Jaret Wright	.50
4	Brian Giles	.50
5	Bartolo Colon	.50
6	Kenny Lofton	.50
7	David Justice	.50
8	Brian Giles	.50
9	Sandy Alomar Jr.	.50
10	Jose Mesa	.50
11	Jim Thome	1.00
12	Sandy Alomar Jr.	.50
13	Omar Vizquel	.50
14	Geronimo Berroa	.50
15	John Smiley	.50
16	Chad Ogea	.50
17	Charles Nagy	.50
18	Enrique Wilson	.50

Mariners

		NM/M
Complete Set (18):		12.00
Common Player:		.50
1	Alex Rodriguez	2.50
2	Jay Buhner	.50
3	Russ Davis	.50
4	Joey Cora	.50
5	Joey Cora	.50
6	Jay Buhner	.50
7	Ken Griffey Jr.	2.00
8	Raul Ibanez	.50
9	Rich Amaral	.50
10	Shane Monahan	.50
11	Alex Rodriguez	2.50
12	Dan Wilson	.50
13	Bob Wells	.50
14	Randy Johnson	1.00
15	Randy Johnson	1.00
16	Jeff Fassero	.50
17	Ken Cloude	.50
18	Edgar Martinez	.50

Mets

		NM/M
Complete Set (18):		7.50
Common Player:		.50
1	Rey Ordonez	.50
2	Todd Hundley	.50
3	Preston Wilson	.50
4	Rich Becker	.50
5	Bernard Gilkey	.50
6	Rey Ordonez	.50
7	Butch Huskey	.50
8	Carlos Baerga	.50
9	Edgardo Alfonzo	.50
10	Bill Pulsipher	.50
11	John Franco	.50
12	Todd Pratt	.50
13	Brian McRae	.50
14	Bobby Jones	.50
15	John Olerud	.50
16	Todd Hundley	.50
17	Jay Payton	.50
18	Paul Wilson	.50

Orioles

		NM/M
Complete Set (18):		12.50
Common Player:		.50
1	Cal Ripken Jr.	3.00
2	Rocky Coppinger	.50
3	Eric Davis	.50
4	Chris Hoiles	.50
5	Mike Mussina	.75
6	Joe Carter	.50
7	Rafael Palmeiro	1.00
8	B.J. Surhoff	.50
9	Jimmy Key	.50
10	Scott Erickson	.50
11	Armando Benitez	.50
12	Roberto Alomar	.65
13	Cal Ripken Jr.	3.00
14	Mike Bordick	.50
15	Roberto Alomar	.65
16	Jeffrey Hammonds	.50
17	Rafael Palmeiro	1.00
18	Brady Anderson	.50

Rangers

		NM/M
Complete Set (18):		9.00
Common Player:		.50
1	Ivan Rodriguez	1.00
2	Fernando Tatis	.50
3	Danny Patterson	.50
4	Will Clark	.66
5	Kevin Elster	.50
6	Rusty Greer	.50
7	Darren Oliver	.50
8	John Burkett	.50
9	Tom Goodwin	.50
10	Roberto Kelly	.50
11	Aaron Sele	.50
12	Rick Helling	.50
13	Mark McLemore	.50
14	Lee Stevens	.50
15	John Wetteland	.50
16	Will Clark	.65
17	Juan Gonzalez	.75
18	Roger Pavlik	.50

Red Sox

		NM/M
Complete Set (18):		9.00
Common Player:		.50
1	Tim Naehring	.50
2	Brian Rose	.50
3	Darren Bragg	.50
4	Pedro Martinez	1.00
5	Mo Vaughn	.50
6	Jim Leyritz	.50
7	Troy O'Leary	.50
8	Mo Vaughn	.50
9	Nomar Garciaparra	1.50
10	Michael Coleman	.50
11	Tom Gordon	.50
12	Tim Naehring	.50
13	Nomar Garciaparra	1.50
14	John Valentin	.50
15	Steve Avery	.50
16	Damon Buford	.50
17	Troy O'Leary	.50
18	Bret Saberhagen	.50

Rockies

		NM/M
Complete Set (18):		7.50
Common Player:		.50

1 Larry Walker .50
2 Pedro Astacio .50
3 Jamey Wright .50
4 Darryl Kile .50
5 Kirt Manwaring .50
6 Todd Helton 1.50
7 Mike Lansing .50
8 Neifi Perez .50
9 Dante Bichette .50
10 Derrick Gibson .50
11 Neifi Perez .50
12 Darryl Kile .50
13 Larry Walker .50
14 Roger Bailey .50
15 Ellis Burks .50
16 Dante Bichette .50
17 Derrick Gibson .50
18 Ellis Burks .50

Yankees

NM/M

Complete Set (18): 12.50
Common Player: .75
1 Andy Pettitte .75
2 Darryl Strawberry .50
3 Joe Girardi .50
4 Derek Jeter 3.00
5 Andy Pettitte .75
6 Tim Raines .50
7 Mariano Rivera .75
8 Tino Martinez .50
9 Derek Jeter 3.00
10 Hideki Irabu .50
11 Tino Martinez .50
12 David Cone .50
13 Bernie Williams .65
14 David Cone .50
15 Bernie Williams .65
16 Chuck Knoblauch .50
17 Paul O'Neill .50
18 David Wells .50

Sport Block

By manipulating the eight cubes of which this novelty is comprised, pictures of eight popular players and the team logo can be displayed. The cube measures 2-3/4" x 2-3/4" x 2-3/4".

NM/M

Complete Set (10): 20.00
Common Team: 3.00
(1) Anaheim Angels (Garret Anderson, Jason Dickson, Jim Edmonds, Darin Erstad, Chuck Finley, Todd Greene, Troy Percival, Tim Salmon, Angels Logo) 3.00
(2) Arizona Diamondbacks 3.00
(3) Atlanta Braves (Andres Galarraga, Tom Glavine, Andruw Jones, Chipper Jones, Ryan Klesko, Javier Lopez, Greg Maddux, John Smoltz, Braves Logo) 3.00
(4) Baltimore Orioles 3.00
(5) Boston Red Sox (Darren Bragg, Nomar Garciaparra, Reggie Jefferson, Jim Leyritz, Pedro Martinez, Troy O'Leary, John Valentin, Mo Vaughn, Red Sox Logo) 3.00
(6) Cleveland Indians 3.00
(7) Los Angeles Dodgers (Eric Karros, Paul Konerko, Ramon Martinez, Raul Mondesi, Hideo Nomo, Chan Ho Park, Mike Piazza, Ismael Valdes, Dodgers Logo) 3.00
(8) New York Yankees 3.00
(9) Seattle Mariners (Jay Buhner, Russ Davis, Jeff Fassero, Ken Griffey Jr., Randy Johnson, Edgar Martinez, Alex Rodriguez, Dan Wilson, Mariners Logo) 3.00
(10) Tampa Bay Devil Rays (Wilson Alvarez, Wade Boggs, Dave Martinez, Quinton McCracken, Fred McGriff, Tony Saunders, Paul Sorrento, Bubba Trammell, Devil Rays Logo) 3.00

Totally Certified Platinum Gold

Among several card issues that were aborted by Pinnacle's bankruptcy in mid-1998, but which have leaked into the hobby market in dribs and drabs, are 10 Totally Certified Platinum Gold cards that were intended to be random pack inserts in 1998 Certified. Each of the cards was produced in an edition of 30 serially numbered pieces. To date, confirmation of back-door release of the Platinum Red and Platinum Blue versions has not been made.

NM/M

Complete Set (10): 125.00
Common Player: 7.50
1 Vladimir Guerrero 15.00
2 Andruw Jones 12.00
3 Paul Molitor 15.00
4 Jose Cruz Jr. 7.50
5 Edgar Martinez 7.50
6 Andy Pettitte 9.00
7 Darin Erstad 9.00
8 Barry Larkin 7.50
9 Derek Jeter 40.00
10 Rusty Greer 7.50

1998 Team Pinnacle Baseball

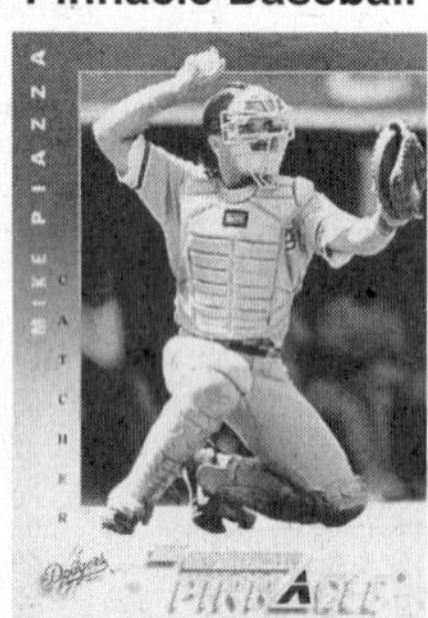

With each $30 membership in Pinnacle's collectors' club, "Team Pinnacle," the member received a litho tin box with 10 each special baseball, football and hockey cards, and a pack of unnumbered promo cards. In standard 2-1/2" x 3-1/2", cards have game-action photos on front, bordered in a dominant team color and enhanced with a gold-foil Team Pinnacle logo at bottom. Backs have portrait photos, a few personal details, career highlights and the player's uniform number ghosted in the background.

NM/M

Complete Set (10): 16.00
Common Player: 1.00
B1 Ken Griffey Jr. 2.00
B2 Frank Thomas 1.25
B3 Cal Ripken Jr. 3.00
B4 Alex Rodriguez 2.50
B5 Mike Piazza 2.00
B6 Derek Jeter 3.00
B7 Greg Maddux 1.50
B8 Chipper Jones 1.50
B9 Mark McGwire 2.50
B10 Juan Gonzalez 1.00
--- Cal Ripken Jr. (Unmarked sample.) 2.50

Team Pinnacle (Unissued)

This four-card set was reportedly created for distribution to members of the card company's "Team Pinnacle" but was never officially issued due to the manufacturer's bankruptcy. The 2-1/2" x 3-1/2" cards have game-action photos on front with a wide diagonal color stripe at top and a gold-foil "98 TEAM PINNACLE" logo at bottom. Backs have a color portrait photo along with some stats and highlights. The cards are unnumbered.

NM/M

Complete Set (4): 7.50
Common Player: 3.00
(1) John Elway (Football) 2.00
(2) Ken Griffey Jr. 2.00
(3) Derek Jeter 3.00
(4) Eric Lindros (Hockey) 2.00

Uncut

Advertised as the "BIGGEST CARD EVER!" these 13-3/8 x 18-5/8" cards are approximately 30 times larger than standard cards. Sold in individual cello bags with a suggested retail price of around $10, the cards are super-size replicas of the same players' cards found in the Field of Vision subset in regular 1998 Pinnacle. The giant cards have an etched metallic foil front not found on the regular cards. They are packaged with a die-cut cardboard backing which tends to bruise the edges or chip off small patches of ink.

NM/M

Complete Set (6): 20.00
Common Card: 3.00
182 Alex Rodriguez 6.00
183 Cal Ripken Jr., Roberto Alomar 4.50
184 Roger Clemens 3.50
185 Derek Jeter 7.50
186 Frank Thomas 3.00
186p Frank Thomas ("SAMPLE" on back.) 4.50
187 Ken Griffey Jr. 4.50

2004 Pitt Ohio Express 1979 Pirates

The purpose for which the Pennsylvania trucking company produced this card set, and the manner of their distribution, is unclear. The set commemorates the World Champion Pittsburgh Pirates of 1979. Fronts of the approximately 4-3/4" x 3-5/8" cards have large black-and-white portrait photos. Highlighted by gold graphics, the fronts also include a team logo, player name, position and uniform number. Backs have an ad for the trucking company.

NM/M

Complete Set (18): 20.00
Common Player: 2.00
(1) Matt Alexander 2.00
(2) Tony Bartirome 2.00
(3) Jim Bibby 2.00
(4) Mike Easler 2.00
(5) Grant Jackson 2.00
(6) Bruce Kison 2.00
(7) Lee Lacy 2.00
(8) Bill Madlock 3.00
(9) Omar Moreno 2.00
(10) Steve Nicosia 2.00
(11) Ed Ott 2.00
(12) Dave Parker 4.00
(13) Dave Roberts 2.00
(14) Don Robinson 2.00
(15) Jim Rooker 2.00
(16) Manny Sanguillen 3.00
(17) Chuck Tanner 2.00
(18) Kent Tekulve 2.00

1992 Pittsburgh Brewing Co. Roberto Clemente Tribute

The first 15,000 fans at Three Rivers Stadium on September 6 at a special promotional Clemente tribute night received this perforated pair of cards honoring the Pirates superstar. The 7" square panel has a pair of two-part cards. Each side has a 3-1/2" x 5-1/2" picture portion at top and a 1-1/2" tab at bottom, perforated for easy separation. The left side has a portrait of the Pirate great with his first name; at right is his last name and an action picture. Back of the portrait card has career stats; back of the action card has career highlights. Artwork on each card is by Tom Mosser. The sponsor logo is on back of each tab along with a quotation and copyright information.

NM/M

Complete Panel: 18.00
Complete Set (2): 15.00
#21 Roberto/Portrait 7.50
#21 Clemente/Action 7.50

1985 Pittsburgh Pirates Yearbook Cards

This 18-card set was issued on two nine-card perforated panels inserted into the Bucs' 1985 yearbook. Individual cards measure 2-1/2" x 3-1/2" and feature color photos surrounded by black and gold borders. The player's name, position and uniform number are printed in a white panel at bottom. Backs are in black-and-white and offer complete major and minor league stats, along with the logos of sponsor Cameron/Coca-Cola.

NM/M

Complete Set (18): 7.50
Common Player: .50
2 Jim Morrison .50
3 Johnny Ray .50
5 Bill Madlock .60
6 Tony Pena .50
7 Chuck Tanner .50
10 Tim Foli .50
13 Steve Kemp .50
15 George Hendrick .50
25 Jose DeLeon .50
27 Kent Tekulve .50
28 Sixto Lezcano .50
29 Rick Rhoden .50
30 Jason Thompson .50
36 Marvell Wynne .50
43 Don Robinson .50
45 John Candelaria .50
49 Larry McWilliams .50
51 Doug Frobel .50

1996 Pizza Hut

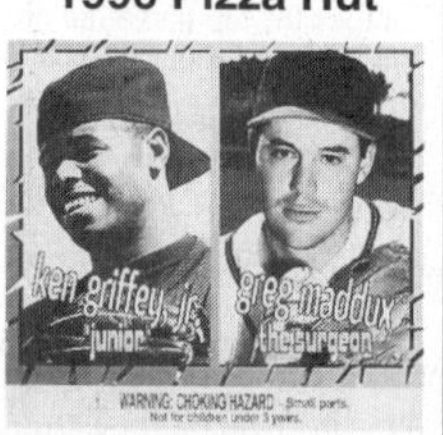

In conjunction with a foam bat/ball promotion, Pizza Hut issued a small set of small cards (2-1/2" x 2-1/4") featuring players involved in the endorsement. The player portrait photos on the cards are devoid of cap logos and surrounded by a rainbow border. Player names are in yellow with a nickname in red. A choking hazard warning is in black-and-white on bottom. Backs are printed in red and black and have career summaries, logos and copyright notice. The unnumbered cards are checklisted here alphabetically.

NM/M

Complete Set (4): 8.00
Common Card: 1.50
(1) Jeff Bagwell (Thumper), Orel Hershiser (Bulldawg) 1.50
(2) David Cone (Controller), Mike Piazza (Crusher) 3.00
(3) Ken Griffey Jr. (Junior), Greg Maddux (Surgeon) 3.00
(4) Randy Johnson (Big Unit), Mo Vaughn (Hit Dog) 1.50

2001 Playoff Absolute Memorabilia

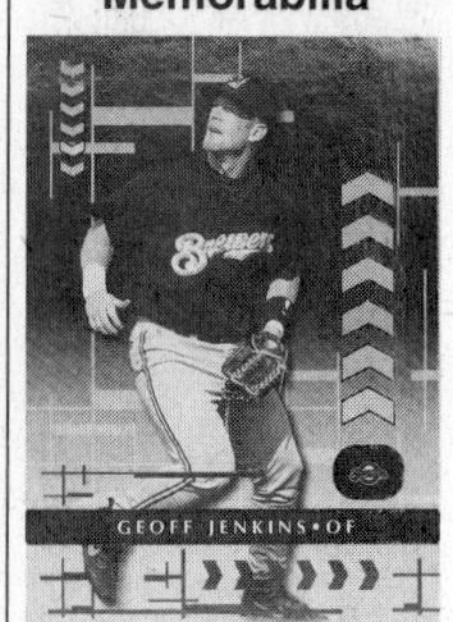

NM/M

Complete Set (200):
Common Player: .25
Common SP (151-200): 5.00
Production 700
Pack (6): 8.00
Box (18) w/baseball: 150.00
1 Alex Rodriguez 2.50
2 Barry Bonds 3.00
3 Cal Ripken Jr. 3.00
4 Chipper Jones 1.50
5 Derek Jeter 3.00
6 Troy Glaus 1.00
7 Frank Thomas 1.00
8 Greg Maddux 1.50
9 Ivan Rodriguez .75
10 Jeff Bagwell 1.00
11 Ryan Dempster .25
12 Todd Helton 1.00
13 Ken Griffey Jr. 2.00
14 Manny Ramirez 1.00
15 Mark McGwire 2.50
16 Mike Piazza 2.00
17 Nomar Garciaparra 2.00
18 Pedro Martinez 1.00
19 Randy Johnson 1.00
20 Rick Ankiel .25
21 Rickey Henderson 1.00
22 Roger Clemens 1.75
23 Sammy Sosa 2.00
24 Tony Gwynn 2.00
25 Vladimir Guerrero 1.00
26 Kazuhiro Sasaki .25
27 Roberto Alomar .50
28 Barry Zito .35
29 Pat Burrell .50
30 Harold Baines .25
31 Carlos Delgado .65
32 J.D. Drew .50
33 Jim Edmonds .25
34 Darin Erstad .50
35 Jason Giambi .75
36 Tom Glavine .50
37 Juan Gonzalez 1.00
38 Mark Grace .35
39 Shawn Green .50
40 Tim Hudson .50
41 Andruw Jones 1.00
42 David Justice .25
43 Jeff Kent .25
44 Barry Larkin .25
45 Rafael Furcal .25
46 Mike Mussina .50
47 Hideo Nomo 1.00
48 Rafael Palmeiro .75
49 Adam Piatt .25
50 Scott Rolen .75
51 Gary Sheffield .50
52 Bernie Williams .35
53 Bob Abreu .25
54 Edgardo Alfonzo .25
55 Edgar Renteria .25
56 Phil Nevin .25
57 Craig Biggio .25
58 Andres Galarraga .25
59 Edgar Martinez .25
60 Fred McGriff .25
61 Magglio Ordonez .25
62 Jim Thome .75
63 Matt Williams .25
64 Kerry Wood .65
65 Moises Alou .25
66 Brady Anderson .25
67 Garret Anderson .25
68 Russell Branyan .25
69 Tony Batista .25
70 Vernon Wells .25
71 Carlos Beltran .60
72 Adrian Beltre .25
73 Kris Benson .25
74 Lance Berkman .25
75 Kevin Brown .25
76 Dee Brown .25
77 Jeromy Burnitz .25
78 Timoniel Perez .25
79 Sean Casey .40
80 Luis Castillo .25
81 Eric Chavez .35
82 Jeff Cirillo .25
83 Bartolo Colon .25
84 David Cone .25
85 Freddy Garcia .25
86 Johnny Damon .40

87 Ray Durham .25
88 Jermaine Dye .25
89 Juan Encarnacion .25
90 Terrence Long .25
91 Carl Everett .25
92 Steve Finley .25
93 Cliff Floyd .25
94 Brad Fullmer .25
95 Brian Giles .25
96 Luis Gonzalez .35
97 Rusty Greer .25
98 Jeffrey Hammonds .25
99 Mike Hampton .25
100 Orlando Hernandez .25
101 Richard Hidalgo .25
102 Geoff Jenkins .25
103 Jacque Jones .25
104 Brian Jordan .25
105 Gabe Kapler .25
106 Eric Karros .25
107 Jason Kendall .25
108 Adam Kennedy .25
109 Deion Sanders .25
110 Ryan Klesko .25
111 Chuck Knoblauch .25
112 Paul Konerko .25
113 Carlos Lee .25
114 Kenny Lofton .25
115 Javy Lopez .25
116 Tino Martinez .25
117 Ruben Mateo .25
118 Kevin Millwood .25
119 Jimmy Rollins .25
120 Raul Mondesi .25
121 Trot Nixon .25
122 John Olerud .25
123 Paul O'Neill .25
124 Chan Ho Park .25
125 Andy Pettitte .35
126 Jorge Posada .25
127 Mark Quinn .25
128 Aramis Ramirez .25
129 Mariano Rivera .25
130 Tim Salmon .35
131 Curt Schilling .50
132 Richie Sexson .25
133 John Smoltz .25
134 J.T. Snow .25
135 Jay Payton .25
136 Shannon Stewart .25
137 B.J. Surhoff .25
138 Mike Sweeney .25
139 Fernando Tatis .25
140 Miguel Tejada .35
141 Jason Varitek .25
142 Greg Vaughn .25
143 Mo Vaughn .25
144 Robin Ventura .25
145 Jose Vidro .25
146 Omar Vizquel .25
147 Larry Walker .25
148 David Wells .25
149 Rondell White .25
150 Preston Wilson .25
151 Bud Smith **RC** 5.00
152 Cory Aldridge **RC** 5.00
153 Wilmy Caceres **RC** 5.00
154 Josh Beckett 6.00
155 Wilson Betemit **RC** 10.00
156 Jason Michaels **RC** 5.00
157 Albert Pujols **RC** 125.00
158 Andres Torres **RC** 5.00
159 Jack Wilson **RC** 8.00
160 Alex Escobar 5.00
161 Ben Sheets 5.00
162 Rafael Soriano **RC** 10.00
163 Nate Frese **RC** 5.00
164 Carlos Garcia **RC** 5.00
165 Brandon Larson **RC** 5.00
166 Alexis Gomez **RC** 8.00
167 Jason Hart 5.00
168 Nick Johnson 5.00
169 Donaldo Mendez **RC** 5.00
170 Christian Parker **RC** 5.00
171 Jackson Melian **RC** 5.00
172 Jack Cust 5.00
173 Adrian Hernandez **RC** 5.00
174 Joe Crede 5.00
175 Jose Mieses **RC** 5.00
176 Roy Oswalt 5.00
177 Eric Munson 5.00
178 Xavier Nady 5.00
179 Horacio Ramirez **RC** 8.00
180 Abraham Nunez 5.00
181 Jose Ortiz 5.00
182 Jeremy Owens **RC** 5.00
183 Claudio Vargas **RC** 5.00
184 Marcus Giles 5.00
185 Aubrey Huff 5.00
186 C.C. Sabathia 5.00
187 Adam Dunn 5.00
188 Adam Pettyjohn **RC** 5.00
189 Elpidio Guzman **RC** 5.00
190 Jay Gibbons **RC** 10.00
191 Wilkin Ruan **RC** 5.00
192 Tsuyoshi Shinjo **RC** 5.00
193 Alfonso Soriano 8.00
194 Corey Patterson 5.00
195 Ichiro Suzuki **RC** 75.00
196 Billy Sylvester **RC** 5.00
197 Juan Uribe **RC** 5.00
198 Johnny Estrada **RC** 8.00
199 Carlos Valderrama **RC** 5.00
200 Matt White **RC** 5.00

Ball Hoggs

NM/M

Common Player: 8.00
Production 75 unless noted.

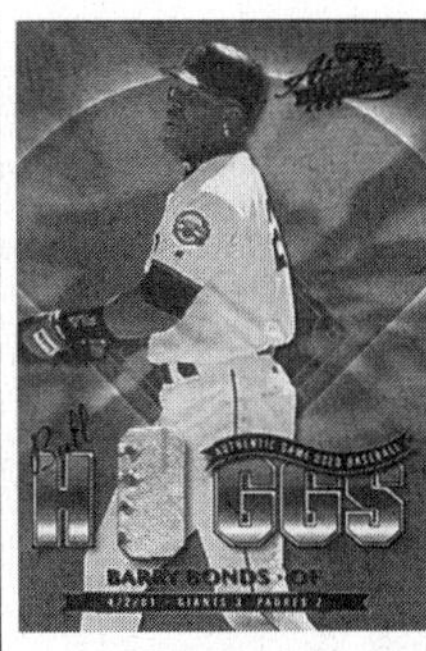

1 Vladimir Guerrero 15.00
2 Troy Glaus 10.00
3 Tony Gwynn 20.00
4 Cal Ripken/125 50.00
5 Todd Helton 15.00
6 Jacque Jones/125 8.00
7 Shawn Green/100 8.00
8 Ichiro Suzuki 85.00
9 Scott Rolen 15.00
10 Roger Clemens 30.00
11 Ken Griffey/25 50.00
14 Sammy Sosa 25.00
15 J.D. Drew 10.00
16 Barry Bonds/100 40.00
17 Pat Burrell 15.00
18 Mark McGwire/100 65.00
19 Mike Piazza 20.00
20 Magglio Ordonez/150 10.00
21 Miguel Tejada 10.00
22 Albert Pujols/100 150.00
23 Derek Jeter 40.00
24 Johnny Damon 15.00
25 Mike Sweeney 8.00
26 Ben Grieve 8.00
27 Jeff Kent 8.00
28 Andres Galarraga 8.00
29 Richie Sexson 10.00
30 Juan Encarnacion 8.00
31 Ruben Mateo 8.00
33 Manny Ramirez 15.00
35 Ivan Rodriguez 15.00
36 Darin Erstad 8.00
37 Carlos Delgado 10.00
38 Jeff Bagwell 15.00
39 Jermaine Dye 8.00
40 Jose Ortiz 8.00
41 Gary Sheffield 10.00
42 Eric Chavez 8.00
43 Mark Grace 15.00
44 Rafael Palmeiro 15.00
45 Tsuyoshi Shinjo/100 15.00
46 Terrence Long 8.00
47 Carlos Delgado/25 20.00
48 Frank Thomas 15.00
49 Chipper Jones/25 40.00
50 Jason Giambi 15.00

Ballpark Souvenirs

NM/M

Common Player: 4.00
Production 400 Sets
Doubles: 1-1.5X
Production 200 Sets
Triples: 1.5-2X
Production 75 Sets
Home Runs: 2-4X
Production 25 Sets

1 Barry Bonds 20.00
2 Cal Ripken Jr. 25.00
3 Pedro Martinez 10.00
4 Troy Glaus 6.00
5 Frank Thomas 8.00
6 Alex Rodriguez 10.00
7 Ivan Rodriguez 8.00
8 Jeff Bagwell 8.00
9 Mark McGwire 30.00
10 Todd Helton 8.00
11 Gary Sheffield 5.00
12 Manny Ramirez 8.00
13 Mike Piazza 10.00
14 Sammy Sosa 15.00
15 Preston Wilson 4.00
16 Tony Gwynn 8.00
17 Vladimir Guerrero 8.00
18 Carlos Delgado 6.00
19 Roberto Alomar 6.00
20 Todd Helton 8.00
21 Albert Pujols 50.00
22 Jason Giambi 8.00
23 Sammy Sosa 15.00
24 Ken Griffey Jr. 10.00
25 Darin Erstad 4.00
26 Mark McGwire 30.00
27 Carlos Delgado 6.00
28 Juan Gonzalez 8.00
29 Mike Sweeney 4.00
30 Alex Rodriguez 10.00
31 Roger Clemens 15.00
32 Tsuyoshi Shinjo 4.00
33 Ben Grieve 4.00
34 Jeff Kent 4.00
35 Vladimir Guerrero 8.00
36 Shawn Green 6.00
37 Rafael Palmeiro 6.00
38 Tony Gwynn 8.00
39 Scott Rolen 8.00
40 Ken Griffey Jr. 10.00
41 Albert Pujols 50.00
42 Barry Bonds 20.00
43 Mark Grace 8.00
44 Bernie Williams 6.00
45 Frank Thomas 8.00
46 Jermaine Dye 4.00
47 Mike Piazza 10.00
48 Chipper Jones 10.00
49 Richie Sexson 6.00
50 Magglio Ordonez 4.00

Boss Hoggs

NM/M

Production 25 Sets
4 Cal Ripken 80.00
6 Jacque Jones 15.00
7 Shawn Green 15.00
8 Ichiro Suzuki 100.00
9 Scott Rolen 20.00
11 Ken Griffey 50.00
14 Sammy Sosa 50.00
15 J.D. Drew 15.00
16 Barry Bonds 80.00
17 Pat Burrell 20.00
18 Mark McGwire 100.00
19 Mike Piazza 75.00
20 Magglio Ordonez 20.00
21 Miguel Tejada 20.00
23 Derek Jeter 85.00
24 Johnny Damon 15.00
25 Mike Sweeney 15.00
26 Ben Grieve 15.00
27 Jeff Kent 15.00
28 Andres Galarraga 15.00
29 Richie Sexson 20.00
30 Juan Encarnacion 15.00
31 Ruben Mateo 15.00
33 Manny Ramirez 20.00
35 Ivan Rodriguez 20.00
36 Darin Erstad 15.00
37 Carlos Delgado 20.00
38 Jeff Bagwell 20.00
39 Jermaine Dye 15.00
40 Jose Ortiz 15.00
42 Eric Chavez 15.00
43 Mark Grace 30.00
44 Rafael Palmeiro 30.00
45 Tsuyoshi Shinjo 20.00
46 Terrence Long 15.00
47 Carlos Delgado 20.00
48 Frank Thomas 25.00
50 Jason Giambi 25.00

Rookie Premiere Autographs

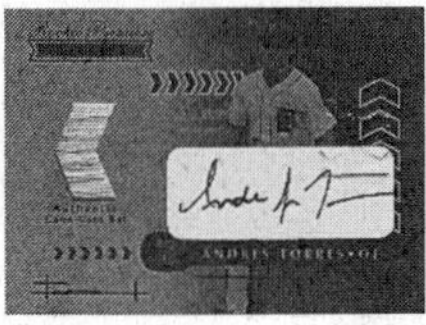

NM/M

Production 25 Sets
151 Bud Smith 15.00
152 Cory Aldridge 15.00
154 Josh Beckett 40.00
155 Wilson Betemit 15.00
157 Albert Pujols 500.00
158 Andres Torres 15.00
160 Alex Escobar 15.00
161 Ben Sheets 30.00
162 Rafael Soriano 30.00
164 Carlos Garcia 15.00
165 Brandon Larson 20.00
167 Jason Hart 15.00
168 Nick Johnson 25.00
169 Donaldo Mendez 15.00
170 Christian Parker 15.00
171 Jackson Melian 15.00
173 Adrian Hernandez 15.00
174 Joe Crede 15.00
175 Jose Mieses 15.00
176 Roy Oswalt 30.00
178 Xavier Nady 20.00
179 Horacio Ramirez 20.00
180 Abraham Nunez 15.00
181 Jose Ortiz 15.00
182 Jeremy Owens 15.00
183 Claudio Vargas 15.00
184 Marcus Giles 20.00
186 C.C. Sabathia 25.00
187 Adam Dunn 50.00
188 Adam Pettyjohn 15.00
190 Jay Gibbons 25.00
191 Wilkin Ruan 15.00
193 Alfonso Soriano 85.00
194 Corey Patterson 20.00
196 Billy Sylvester 15.00
197 Juan Uribe 15.00
198 Johnny Estrada 15.00
199 Carlos Valderrama 15.00
200 Matt White 15.00

Signing Bonus Baseballs

NM/M

Common Auto. Baseball: 15.00
Inserted 1:Box
Al Oliver/500 15.00
Andre Dawson/550 20.00
Barry Bonds/25 250.00
Bill Madlock/525 15.00
Bill Mazeroski/25 75.00
Billy Williams/325 20.00
Bob Feller/550 20.00
Bob Gibson/25 100.00
Bobby Doerr/300 25.00
Bobby Richardson/500 20.00
Boog Powell/500 20.00
Brian Jordan/25 40.00
Bucky Dent/500 15.00
Charles Johnson/25 40.00
Chipper Jones/25 100.00
Clete Boyer/500 20.00
Dale Murphy/25 80.00
Dave Concepcion/500 15.00
Dave Kingman/500 15.00
Don Larsen/200 40.00
Don Newcombe/500 15.00
Don Zimmer/500 15.00
Duke Snider/25 100.00
Earl Weaver/300 20.00
Enos Slaughter/525 20.00
Fergie Jenkins/1000 20.00
Frank Howard/500 20.00
Frank Robinson/25 100.00
Frank Thomas/25 85.00
Gary Carter/200 30.00
Gaylord Perry/1000 15.00
George Foster/500 15.00
George Kell/300 20.00
Goose Gossage/500 15.00
Greg Maddux/25 100.00
Hank Aaron/25 150.00
Hank Bauer/500 20.00
Harmon Killebrew/200 60.00
Henry Rodriguez/400 15.00
Herb Score/500 15.00
Hoyt Wilhelm/500 15.00
J.D. Drew/75 20.00
Javy Lopez/25 40.00
Jim Edmonds/25 50.00
Jim Palmer/500 20.00
Joe Pepitone/500 20.00
Johnny Bench/25 120.00
Johnny Podres/500 25.00
Juan Marichal/485 20.00
Kirby Puckett/25 100.00
Larry Doby/300 30.00
Lou Brock/25 75.00
Luis Tiant/500 15.00
Magglio Ordonez/200 25.00
Manny Ramirez/25 60.00
Maury Wills/500 20.00
Mike Schmidt/25 150.00
Minnie Minoso/1000 15.00
Monte Irvin/500 25.00
Moose Skowron/500 20.00
Nolan Ryan/25 200.00
Ozzie Smith/25 100.00
Phil Rizzuto/25 75.00
Ralph Kiner/100 40.00
Randy Johnson/25 100.00
Red Schoendienst/500 20.00
Reggie Jackson/25 80.00
Rickey Henderson/25 100.00
Robin Roberts/500 25.00
Roger Clemens/25 125.00
Rollie Fingers/575 20.00
Ryne Sandberg/25 100.00
Sean Casey/25 30.00
Stan Musial/25 100.00
Steve Carlton/25 75.00
Steve Garvey/1000 15.00
Todd Helton/25 50.00
Tom Glavine/25 50.00
Tom Seaver/25 75.00
Tommy John/1000 15.00
Tony Gwynn/25 75.00
Tony Perez/400 15.00
Wade Boggs/25 75.00
Warren Spahn/500 60.00
Whitey Ford/25 75.00
Willie Mays/25 150.00
Willie McCovey/25 60.00
Willie Stargell/25 75.00
Yogi Berra/25 75.00

Spectrum

Stars (1-150): No Pricing
Production 10
RK's (151-200): 2-4X
Production 25

Tools Of The Trade

NM/M

Common Player: 5.00
Jerseys (1-20):
Production 300
Bats (21-40):
Production 125
Batting Glove (41-45):
Production 50
Hat (46-50):
Production 100
Autographs: No Pricing
Production 25 Sets

1 Vladimir Guerrero 10.00
2 Troy Glaus 6.00
3 Tony Gwynn 10.00
4 Todd Helton 8.00
5 Scott Rolen 8.00
6 Roger Clemens 20.00
7 Pedro Martinez 10.00
8 Richie Sexson 6.00
9 Maggilo Ordonez 5.00
10 Ben Grieve 5.00
11 Jeff Bagwell 8.00
12 Edgar Martinez 5.00
13 Greg Maddux 25.00
15 Frank Thomas 10.00
16 Edgardo Alfonzo 5.00
17 Cal Ripken Jr. 40.00
18 Jose Vidro 5.00
19 Andruw Jones 8.00
21 Barry Bonds 50.00
22 Juan Gonzalez 8.00
23 Andruw Jones 8.00
24 Cal Ripken Jr. 60.00
25 Greg Maddux 30.00
26 Manny Ramirez 20.00
27 Roberto Alomar 8.00
28 Shawn Green 6.00
29 Edgardo Alfonzo 5.00
30 Rafael Palmeiro 10.00
31 Hideo Nomo 100.00
32 Andres Galarraga 6.00
33 Todd Helton 15.00
34 Darin Erstad 5.00
35 Ivan Rodriguez 15.00
36 Sean Casey 6.00
37 Vladimir Guerrero 20.00
39 Troy Glaus 8.00
40 Jeff Bagwell 10.00
41 Barry Bonds 100.00
42 Cal Ripken Jr. 125.00
43 Roberto Alomar 30.00
44 Sean Casey 20.00
45 Tony Gwynn 40.00
46 Bernie Williams 25.00
47 Barry Zito 25.00
49 Tom Glavine 25.00

2002 Playoff Absolute Memorabilia Samples

Selected issues of the September 2002 Beckett Baseball Card Monthly included a sample 2002 Playoff Absolute Memorabilia card rubber-cemented inside. The cards differ from the issued version only in the appearance on back of a (usually) silver-foil "SAMPLE" notation. Some cards were produced with the overprint in gold-foil, in much more limited quantities. The number of different players' cards involved in the promotion is unknown.

NM/M

Common Player: .10
Stars: 1.5-2X
Gold: 20X

2002 Playoff Absolute Memorabilia

NM/M

Complete Set (200):
Common Player: .50
Common RK/Prospect (151-200): 3.00
Production 1,000
Pack (6): 3.00
Box + 8 x 10: 140.00

1 David Eckstein .50
2 Darin Erstad .75
3 Troy Glaus 1.50
4 Garret Anderson .50
5 Tim Salmon .50
6 Curt Schilling 1.00
7 Randy Johnson 1.50
8 Luis Gonzalez .50
9 Mark Grace .60
10 Tom Glavine .75
11 Greg Maddux 2.00
12 Chipper Jones 2.00
13 Gary Sheffield .75
14 John Smoltz .50
15 Andruw Jones 1.50
16 Wilson Betemit .50
17 Tony Batista .50
18 Javier Vazquez .50
19 Scott Erickson .50
20 Josh Towers .50
21 Pedro J. Martinez 1.50
22 Johnny Damon .60
23 Manny Ramirez 1.50
24 Rickey Henderson 1.50
25 Trot Nixon .50
26 Nomar Garciaparra 2.50
27 Juan Cruz .50
28 Kerry Wood 1.25
29 Fred McGriff .50
30 Moises Alou .50
31 Sammy Sosa 2.50
32 Corey Patterson .50
33 Mark Buehrle .50
34 Keith Foulke .50
35 Frank Thomas 1.50
36 Kenny Lofton .50
37 Magglio Ordonez .50
38 Barry Larkin .50
39 Ken Griffey Jr. 2.50
40 Adam Dunn .75
41 Juan Encarnacion .50
42 Sean Casey .60
43 Bartolo Colon .50
44 C.C. Sabathia .50
45 Travis Fryman .50
46 Jim Thome 1.50
47 Omar Vizquel .50
48 Ellis Burks .50
49 Russell Branyan .50
50 Mike Hampton .50
51 Todd Helton 1.50
52 Jose Ortiz .50
53 Juan Uribe .50
54 Juan Pierre .50
55 Larry Walker .50
56 Mike Rivera .50
57 Robert Fick .50
58 Bobby Higginson .50
59 Josh Beckett .50
60 Richard Hidalgo .50
61 Cliff Floyd .50
62 Mike Lowell .50
63 Roy Oswalt .50
64 Morgan Ensberg .50
65 Jeff Bagwell 1.50
66 Craig Biggio .50
67 Lance Berkman .50
68 Carlos Beltran .75
69 Mike Sweeney .50
70 Neifi Perez .50
71 Kevin Brown .50
72 Hideo Nomo 1.50
73 Paul LoDuca .50
74 Adrian Beltre .60

75 Shawn Green .75
76 Eric Karros .50
77 Brad Radke .50
78 Corey Koskie .50
79 Doug Mientkiewicz .50
80 Torii Hunter .50
81 Jacque Jones .50
82 Ben Sheets .50
83 Richie Sexson .50
84 Geoff Jenkins .50
85 Tony Armas .50
86 Michael Barrett .50
87 Jose Vidro .50
88 Vladimir Guerrero 1.50
89 Roger Clemens 2.25
90 Derek Jeter 4.00
91 Bernie Williams .60
92 Jason Giambi 1.25
93 Jorge Posada .50
94 Mike Mussina .65
95 Andy Pettitte .65
96 Nick Johnson .50
97 Alfonso Soriano 1.25
98 Shawn Estes .50
99 Al Leiter .50
100 Mike Piazza 2.50
101 Roberto Alomar .75
102 Mo Vaughn .50
103 Jeromy Burnitz .50
104 Tim Hudson .65
105 Barry Zito .50
106 Mark Mulder .50
107 Eric Chavez .65
108 Miguel Tejada .65
109 Jeremy Giambi .50
110 Jermaine Dye .50
111 Mike Lieberthal .50
112 Scott Rolen 1.25
113 Pat Burrell .75
114 Brandon Duckworth .50
115 Bobby Abreu .50
116 Jason Kendall .50
117 Aramis Ramirez .50
118 Brian Giles .50
119 Pokey Reese .50
120 Phil Nevin .50
121 Ryan Klesko .50
122 Carlos Pena .50
123 Trevor Hoffman .50
124 Barry Bonds 4.00
125 Rich Aurilia .50
126 Jeff Kent .50
127 Tsuyoshi Shinjo .50
128 Ichiro Suzuki 2.00
129 Edgar Martinez .50
130 Freddy Garcia .50
131 Bret Boone .50
132 Matt Morris .50
133 Tino Martinez .50
134 Albert Pujols 3.00
135 J.D. Drew .75
136 Jim Edmonds .50
137 Gabe Kapler .50
138 Paul Wilson .50
139 Ben Grieve .50
140 Wade Miller .50
141 Chan Ho Park .50
142 Alex Rodriguez 3.00
143 Rafael Palmeiro 1.25
144 Juan Gonzalez 1.50
145 Ivan Rodriguez 1.25
146 Carlos Delgado .75
147 Jose Cruz Jr. .50
148 Shannon Stewart .50
149 Raul Mondesi .50
150 Vernon Wells .50
151 So Taguchi **RC** 8.00
152 Kazuhisa Ishii **RC** 8.00
153 Hank Blalock 6.00
154 Sean Burroughs 3.00
155 Geronimo Gil 3.00
156 Jon Rauch 3.00
157 Fernando Rodney 3.00
158 Miguel Asencio **RC** 3.00
159 Franklyn German **RC** 3.00
160 Luis Ugueto **RC** 3.00
161 Jorge Sosa **RC** 3.00
162 Felix Escalona **RC** 3.00
163 Colby Lewis 3.00
164 Mark Teixeira 5.00
165 Mark Prior 6.00
166 Francis Beltran **RC** 3.00
167 Joe Thurston 3.00
168 Earl Snyder **RC** 3.00
169 Takahito Nomura **RC** 3.00
170 Bill Hall 3.00
171 Marlon Byrd 3.00
172 Dave Williams 3.00
173 Yorvit Torrealba 3.00
174 Brandon Backe **RC** 3.00
175 Jorge de la Rosa **RC** 3.00
176 Brian Mallette **RC** 3.00
177 Rodrigo Rosario **RC** 3.00
178 Anderson Machado **RC** 3.00
179 Jorge Padilla **RC** 3.00
180 Allan Simpson **RC** 3.00
181 Doug DeVore **RC** 3.00
182 Steve Bechler **RC** 3.00
183 Raul Chavez 3.00
184 Tom Shearn **RC** 3.00
185 Ben Howard **RC** 3.00
186 Chris Baker **RC** 3.00
187 Travis Hughes **RC** 3.00
188 Kevin Mench 3.00
189 Drew Henson 3.00
190 Mike Moriarty **RC** 3.00
191 Corey Thurman **RC** 3.00
192 Bobby Hill 3.00
193 Steve Kent **RC** 3.00
194 Satoru Komiyama **RC** 3.00
195 Jason Lane 3.00
196 Angel Berroa 3.00
197 Brandon Puffer **RC** 3.00
198 Brian Fitzgerald **RC** 3.00
199 Rene Reyes **RC** 3.00
200 Hee Seop Choi 5.00

Spectrum

Stars (1-150): 3-5X
Production 100
SP's: 1-1.5X
Production 50

Absolutely Ink

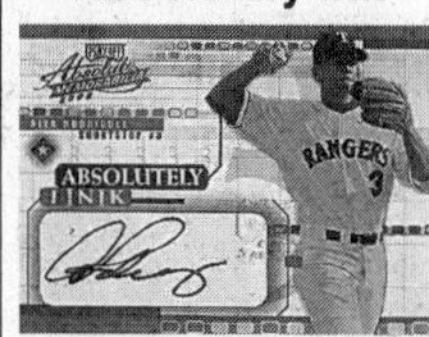

NM/M
Common Autograph: 5.00
Inserted 1:27
Gold Parallel #'d to 25 not priced.
Jsy Parallel #'d to Jsy # not priced.
Adrian Beltre 20.00
Alex Rodriguez/50 100.00
Ben Sheets 20.00
Bobby Doerr 15.00
Blaine Neal 5.00
Carlos Beltran 25.00
Carlos Pena 5.00
Corey Patterson/150 15.00
Dave Parker 10.00
David Justice/65 25.00
Don Mattingly/75 65.00
Duaner Sanchez 5.00
Eric Chavez/100 15.00
Freddy Garcia 10.00
Gary Carter 25.00
Ivan Rodriguez/50 40.00
J.D. Drew/100 20.00
Jack Cust 5.00
Jason Michaels 5.00
Jermaine Dye/125 10.00
Jose Vidro 8.00
Josh Towers 6.00
Kerry Wood/50 40.00
Kirby Puckett/50 75.00
Luis Gonzalez/75 25.00
Luis Rivera 5.00
Manny Ramirez/50 40.00
Marcus Giles 10.00
Mark Prior/100 30.00
Mark Teixeira/100 25.00
Marlon Byrd/250 15.00
Matt Ginter 5.00
Moises Alou/150 15.00
Nate Frese 5.00
Nick Johnson 5.00
Pablo Ozuna 5.00
Paul LoDuca/200 20.00
Richie Sexson 15.00
Roberto Alomar/100 40.00
Roy Oswalt/300 15.00
Ryan Klesko/75 15.00
Sean Casey/125 10.00
Shannon Stewart 8.00
So Taguchi 15.00
Terrence Long 8.00
Timoniel Perez 5.00
Tony Gwynn/50 60.00
Troy Glaus/300 15.00
Vladimir Guerrero/225 40.00
Wade Miller 15.00
Wilson Betemit 5.00

Signing Bonus

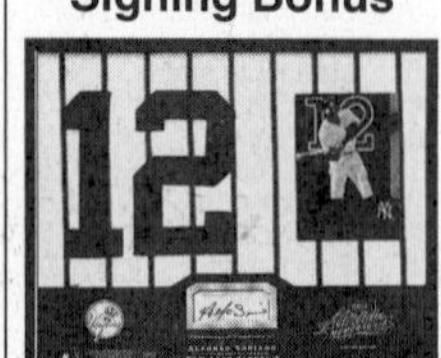

NM/M
Common Player:
Bobby Abreu/53 40.00
Roberto Alomar/100 50.00
Moises Alou/250 30.00
Carlos Beltran/50 50.00
Adrian Beltre/29 40.00
Adrian Beltre/150 30.00
Angel Berroa/50 20.00
Angel Berroa/100 20.00
Wilson Betemit/250 25.00
Hank Blalock/50 50.00
Hank Blalock/100 40.00
Lou Brock/100 60.00
Lou Brock/200 50.00
Kevin Brown/27 50.00
Kevin Brown/100 25.00
Kevin Brown/150 25.00
Mark Buehrle/56 60.00
Mark Buehrle/200 40.00
Marlon Byrd/61 25.00
Steve Carlton/100 50.00
Steve Carlton/150 40.00
Sean Casey/100 30.00
Eric Chavez/28 50.00
Juan Cruz/51 25.00
J.D. Drew/100 30.00
Brandon Duckworth/56 25.00
Brandon Duckworth/150 15.00
Adam Dunn/44 60.00
Jermaine Dye/100 40.00
Jermaine Dye/250 30.00
Morgan Ensberg/100 30.00
Cliff Floyd/200 25.00
Freddy Garcia/34 50.00
Freddy Garcia/125 25.00
Troy Glaus/50 65.00
Troy Glaus/100 40.00
Tom Glavine/200 60.00
Luis Gonzalez/125 30.00
Vladimir Guerrero/27 120.00
Vladimir Guerrero/150 80.00
Richard Hidalgo/100 20.00
Richard Hidalgo/135 20.00
Richard Hidalgo/150 20.00
Tim Hudson/50 60.00
Tim Hudson/100 40.00
Reggie Jackson/44 75.00
Nick Johnson/200 30.00
Andruw Jones/75 75.00
Al Kaline/250 60.00
Gabe Kapler/125 25.00
Gabe Kapler/175 25.00
Ryan Klesko/30 40.00
Jason Lane/100 30.00
Barry Larkin/50 60.00
Barry Larkin/100 50.00
Paul LoDuca/50 40.00
Fred Lynn/150 30.00
Fred Lynn/250 30.00
Greg Maddux/31 200.00
Edgar Martinez/150 50.00
Pedro J. Martinez/45 125.00
Don Mattingly/100 140.00
Willie McCovey/190 40.00
Willie McCovey/250 40.00
Wade Miller/52 25.00
Wade Miller/150 25.00
Wade Miller/250 20.00
Paul Molitor/75 50.00
Paul Molitor/100 40.00
Paul Molitor/125 40.00
Mark Mulder/40 35.00
Jose Ortiz/125 15.00
Roy Oswalt/44 40.00
Roy Oswalt/100 40.00
Jim Palmer/150 30.00
Jim Palmer/250 30.00
Dave Parker/150 25.00
Corey Patterson/250 25.00
Carlos Pena/150 15.00
Carlos Pena/250 15.00
Tony Perez/24 40.00
Tony Perez/250 25.00
Juan Pierre/75 25.00
Mark Prior/50 50.00
Mark Prior/75 40.00
Mark Prior/125 40.00
Kirby Puckett/34 125.00
Albert Pujols/100 250.00
Aramis Ramirez/50 50.00
Aramis Ramirez/125 40.00
Phil Rizzuto/10 265.00
Phil Rizzuto/250 70.00
Brooks Robinson/150 70.00
Brooks Robinson/250 60.00
Nolan Ryan/30 200.00
Nolan Ryan/34 200.00
Ryne Sandberg/50 150.00
Mike Schmidt/100 100.00
Richie Sexson/100 30.00
Ben Sheets/100 30.00
Ben Sheets/150 30.00
Alfonso Soriano/100 50.00
Shannon Stewart/100 25.00
Shannon Stewart/150 25.00
Mike Sweeney/100 30.00
So Taguchi/99 40.00
Mark Teixeira/23 65.00
Mark Teixeira/100 60.00
Miguel Tejada/40 60.00
Miguel Tejada/50 60.00
Frank Thomas/35 120.00
Javier Vazquez/125 25.00
Jose Vidro/150 20.00
Kerry Wood/34 75.00
Barry Zito/50 60.00

Team Tandems

NM/M
Complete Set (40): 80.00
Common Card: 1.00
Inserted 1:12
Golds: 2-3X
Inserted 1:72
1 Troy Glaus, Darin Erstad 1.50

2 Curt Schilling, Randy Johnson 3.00
3 Chipper Jones, Andruw Jones 3.00
4 Greg Maddux, Tom Glavine 4.00
5 Nomar Garciaparra, Manny Ramirez 6.00
6 Pedro J. Martinez, Trot Nixon 3.00
7 Kerry Wood, Sammy Sosa 5.00
8 Frank Thomas, Magglio Ordonez 2.00
9 Ken Griffey Jr., Barry Larkin 5.00
10 C.C. Sabathia, Jim Thome 2.50
11 Todd Helton, Larry Walker 2.00
12 Bobby Higginson, Shane Halter 1.00
13 Cliff Floyd, Brad Penny 1.00
14 Jeff Bagwell, Craig Biggio 2.00
15 Shawn Green, Adrian Beltre 1.50
16 Ben Sheets, Richie Sexson 1.50
17 Vladimir Guerrero, Jose Vidro 3.00
18 Mike Piazza, Roberto Alomar 5.00
19 Roger Clemens, Mike Mussina 6.00
20 Derek Jeter, Jason Giambi 8.00
21 Barry Zito, Tim Hudson 1.50
22 Eric Chavez, Miguel Tejada 1.50
23 Pat Burrell, Scott Rolen 3.00
24 Brian Giles, Aramis Ramirez 1.50
25 Ryan Klesko, Phil Nevin 1.50
26 Barry Bonds, Rich Aurilia 8.00
27 Ichiro Suzuki, Kazuhiro Sasaki 5.00
28 Albert Pujols, J.D. Drew 6.00
29 Alex Rodriguez, Ivan Rodriguez 6.00
30 Carlos Delgado, Shannon Stewart 1.50
31 Mo Vaughn, Roger Cedeno 1.00
32 Carlos Beltran, Mike Sweeney 1.50
33 Edgar Martinez, Bret Boone 1.50
34 Juan Gonzalez, Rafael Palmeiro 2.00
35 Johnny Damon, Rickey Henderson 1.50
36 Sean Casey, Adam Dunn 2.00
37 Jeff Kent, Tsuyoshi Shinjo 1.50
38 Lance Berkman, Richard Hidalgo 1.50
39 So Taguchi, Tino Martinez 1.50
40 Hideo Nomo, Kazuhisa Ishii 1.50

Team Tandems G-U

NM/M
Common Card: 5.00
Inserted 1:33
Golds: 2-3X
Production 50
1 Troy Glaus, Darin Erstad 8.00
2 Curt Schilling, Randy Johnson 10.00
3 Chipper Jones, Andruw Jones 10.00
4 Greg Maddux, Tom Glavine 20.00
5 Nomar Garciaparra, Manny Ramirez 25.00

6 Pedro J. Martinez, Trot Nixon 15.00
7 Kerry Wood, Sammy Sosa 15.00
8 Frank Thomas, Maggio Ordonez 10.00
9 Ken Griffey Jr., Barry Larkin 15.00
10 C.C. Sabathia, Jim Thome 15.00
11 Todd Helton, Larry Walker 8.00
12 Bobby Higginson, Shane Halter 8.00
13 Cliff Floyd, Brad Penny 5.00
14 Jeff Bagwell, Craig Biggio 15.00
15 Shawn Green, Adrian Beltre 8.00
16 Ben Sheets, Richie Sexson 8.00
17 Vladimir Guerrero, Jose Vidro 12.00
18 Mike Piazza, Roberto Alomar 15.00
19 Roger Clemens, Mike Mussina 50.00
20 Derek Jeter, Jason Giambi 30.00
21 Barry Zito, Tim Hudson 15.00
22 Eric Chavez, Miguel Tejada 10.00
23 Pat Burrell, Scott Rolen 15.00
24 Brian Giles, Aramis Ramirez 10.00
25 Ryan Klesko, Phil Nevin 8.00
26 Barry Bonds, Rich Aurilia 15.00
28 Albert Pujols, J.D. Drew 15.00
29 Alex Rodriguez, Ivan Rodriguez 15.00
30 Carlos Delgado, Shannon Stewart 8.00
31 Mo Vaughn, Roger Cedeno 5.00
32 Carlos Beltran, Mike Sweeney 8.00
33 Edgar Martinez, Bret Boone 8.00
34 Juan Gonzalez, Rafael Palmeiro 12.00
35 Johnny Damon, Rickey Henderson 10.00
36 Sean Casey, Adam Dunn 15.00
37 Jeff Kent, Tsuyoshi Shinjo 10.00
38 Lance Berkman, Richard Hidalgo 8.00
39 So Taguchi, Tino Martinez 15.00
40 Hideo Nomo, Kazuhisa Ishii 35.00

Team Quads

NM/M
Complete Set (20): 75.00
Common Card: 2.00
Inserted 1:18
Golds: 2X
Inserted 1:72
1 Troy Glaus, Darin Erstad, Garret Anderson, Troy Percival 2.00
2 Curt Schilling, Randy Johnson, Luis Gonzalez, Mark Grace 4.00
3 Chipper Jones, Andruw Jones, Greg Maddux, Tom Glavine 5.00
4 Nomar Garciaparra, Manny Ramirez, Trot Nixon, Pedro J. Martinez 6.00
5 Kerry Wood, Sammy Sosa, Fred McGriff, Moises Alou 6.00
6 Frank Thomas, Magglio Ordonez, Mark Buehrle, Kenny Lofton 3.00
7 Ken Griffey Jr., Barry Larkin, Juan Encarnacion, Sean Casey 6.00
8 C.C. Sabathia, Jim Thome, Bartolo Colon, Russell Branyan 4.00
9 Todd Helton, Larry Walker, Juan Pierre, Mike Hampton 2.50
10 Jeff Bagwell, Craig Biggio, Lance Berkman, Richard Hidalgo 3.00
11 Shawn Green, Adrian Beltre, Hideo Nomo, Paul LoDuca 2.00
12 Mike Piazza, Roberto Alomar, Mo Vaughn, Roger Cedeno 6.00
13 Roger Clemens, Derek Jeter, Jason Giambi, Mike Mussina 10.00
14 Barry Zito, Tim Hudson, Eric Chavez, Miguel Tejada 2.50
15 Pat Burrell, Scott Rolen, Bobby Abreu, Marlon Byrd 4.00
16 Bernie Williams, Jorge Posada, Alfonso Soriano, Andy Pettitte 3.00
17 Barry Bonds, Rich Aurilia, Tsuyoshi Shinjo, Jeff Kent 8.00
18 Ichiro Suzuki, Kazuhiro Sasaki, Bret Boone, Edgar Martinez 6.00
19 Albert Pujols, J.D. Drew, Jim Edmonds, Tino Martinez 8.00
20 Alex Rodriguez, Ivan Rodriguez, Juan Gonzalez, Rafael Palmeiro 8.00

Team Quads Game-Used

NM/M
Numbered to 100
Prime: No Pricing
Production 25
1 Troy Glaus, Darin Erstad, Garret Anderson, Troy Percival 25.00
2 Curt Schilling, Randy Johnson, Luis Gonzalez, Mark Grace 30.00
3 Chipper Jones, Andruw Jones, Greg Maddux, Tom Glavine 40.00
4 Nomar Garciaparra, Manny Ramirez, Trot Nixon, Pedro J. Martinez 50.00
5 Kerry Wood, Sammy Sosa, Fred McGriff, Moises Alou 35.00
6 Frank Thomas, Magglio Ordonez, Mark Buehrle, Kenny Lofton 25.00
8 C.C. Sabathia, Jim Thome, Bartolo Colon, Russell Branyan 40.00
9 Todd Helton, Larry Walker, Juan Pierre, Mike Hampton 30.00
10 Jeff Bagwell, Craig Biggio, Lance Berkman, Richard Hidalgo 30.00
11 Shawn Green, Adrian Beltre, Hideo Nomo, Paul LoDuca 40.00
12 Mike Piazza, Roberto Alomar, Mo Vaughn, Roger Cedeno 40.00
13 Roger Clemens, Derek Jeter, Jason Giambi, Mike Mussina 75.00

14 Barry Zito, Tim Hudson, Eric Chavez, Miguel Tejada 20.00
15 Pat Burrell, Scott Rolen, Bobby Abreu, Marlon Byrd 35.00
16 Bernie Williams, Jorge Posada, Alfonso Soriano, Andy Pettitte 30.00
17 Barry Bonds, Rich Aurilia, Tsuyoshi Shinjo, Jeff Kent 40.00
18 Ichiro Suzuki, Kazuhiro Sasaki, Bret Boone, Edgar Martinez 50.00
19 Albert Pujols, J.D. Drew, Jim Edmonds, Tino Martinez 40.00
20 Alex Rodriguez, Ivan Rodriguez, Juan Gonzalez, Rafael Palmeiro 40.00

Tools of the Trade

NM/M
Complete Set (95): 120.00
Common Player: 1.00
Inserted 1:9
Golds: 2-3X
Inserted 1:45
1 Mike Mussina 2.00
2 Rickey Henderson 2.00
3 Raul Mondesi 1.00
4 Nomar Garciaparra 6.00
5 Randy Johnson 3.00
6 Roger Clemens 6.00
7 Shawn Green 1.00
8 Todd Helton 2.00
9 Aramis Ramirez 1.50
10 Barry Larkin 1.50
11 Byung-Hyun Kim 1.00
12 C.C. Sabathia 1.00
13 Curt Schilling 2.50
14 Darin Erstad 1.50
15 Eric Karros 1.00
16 Freddy Garcia 1.00
17 Greg Maddux 4.00
18 Jason Kendall 1.00
19 Jim Thome 3.00
20 Juan Gonzalez 2.00
21 Kazuhiro Sasaki 1.00
22 Kerry Wood 3.00
23 Luis Gonzalez 1.50
24 Mark Mulder 1.00
25 Rich Aurilia 1.00
26 Ray Durham 1.00
27 Ben Grieve 1.00
28 Bret Boone 1.00
29 Edgar Martinez 1.00
30 Ivan Rodriguez 2.00
31 Jorge Posada 2.00
32 Mike Piazza 6.00
33 Pat Burrell 1.50
34 Robin Ventura 1.00
35 Trot Nixon 1.00
36 Adrian Beltre 1.00
37 Bernie Williams 1.50
38 Bobby Abreu 1.50
39 Carlos Delgado 1.50
40 Craig Biggio 1.50
41 Garret Anderson 1.50
42 Jermaine Dye 1.00
43 Johnny Damon 1.00
44 Tim Salmon 1.00
45 Tino Martinez 1.00
46 Fred McGriff 1.50
47 Gary Sheffield 1.00
48 Adam Dunn 2.00
49 Joe Mays 1.00
50 Kenny Lofton 1.00
51 Josh Beckett 1.50
52 Bud Smith 1.00
53 Johnny Estrada 1.00
54 Charles Johnson 1.00
55 Craig Wilson 1.00
56 Terrence Long 1.00
57 Andy Pettitte 1.50
58 Brian Giles 1.50
59 Juan Pierre 1.00
60 Cliff Floyd 1.00
61 Ivan Rodriguez 2.00
62 Andruw Jones 2.00
63 Lance Berkman 1.50
64 Mark Buehrle 1.00
65 Miguel Tejada 1.50
66 Wade Miller 1.00
67 Johnny Estrada 1.00
68 Tsuyoshi Shinjo 1.00
69 Scott Rolen 2.50
70 Roberto Alomar 2.00
71 Mark Grace 2.00
72 Larry Walker 1.50
73 Jim Edmonds 1.50
74 Jeff Kent 1.50
75 Frank Thomas 2.50
76 Carlos Beltran 1.50
77 Barry Zito 1.50
78 Alex Rodriguez 8.00
79 Troy Glaus 1.50
80 Ryan Klesko 1.00
81 Tom Glavine 1.50
82 Ben Sheets 1.50
83 Manny Ramirez 2.50
84 Shannon Stewart 1.00
85 Vladimir Guerrero 4.00
86 Chipper Jones 3.00
87 Jeff Bagwell 2.50
88 Richie Sexson 1.50
89 Sean Casey 1.50
90 Tim Hudson 1.50
91 J.D. Drew 1.50
92 Ivan Rodriguez 2.00
93 Magglio Ordonez 1.50
94 John Buck 1.00
95 Paul LoDuca 1.00

Tools of Trade G-U

NM/M
Common Player: 5.00
Jerseys #'d to 300.
Bats #'d to 250.
Shoes #'d to 150.
Shin Guard #'d to 150.
Glove #'d to 125.
Mask #'d to 100.
Hat #'d to 50.
Doubles #'d to 200.
Triples #'d to 75.
Quads #'d to 50.
1 Mike Mussina/Jsy 10.00
2 Rickey Henderson/Jsy 10.00
3 Raul Mondesi/Jsy 8.00
4 Nomar Garciaparra/Jsy 15.00
5 Randy Johnson/Jsy 10.00
6 Roger Clemens/Jsy 15.00
7 Shawn Green/Jsy 8.00
8 Todd Helton/Jsy 8.00
9 Aramis Ramirez/Jsy 8.00
10 Barry Larkin/Jsy 10.00
11 Byung-Hyun Kim/Jsy 5.00
12 C.C. Sabathia/Jsy 5.00
13 Curt Schilling/Jsy 10.00
14 Darin Erstad/Jsy 5.00
15 Eric Karros/Jsy 5.00
16 Freddy Garcia/Jsy 5.00
17 Greg Maddux/Jsy 15.00
18 Jason Kendall/Jsy 5.00
19 Jim Thome/Jsy 10.00
20 Juan Gonzalez/Jsy 8.00
21 Kazuhiro Sasaki/Jsy 5.00
22 Kerry Wood/Jsy 10.00
23 Luis Gonzalez/Jsy 8.00
24 Mark Mulder/Jsy 8.00
25 Rich Aurilia/Jsy 5.00
26 Ray Durham/Jsy 5.00
27 Ben Grieve/Jsy 5.00
28 Bret Boone/Jsy 5.00
29 Edgar Martinez/Jsy 8.00
30 Ivan Rodriguez/Jsy 10.00
31 Jorge Posada/Jsy 10.00
32 Mike Piazza/Jsy 15.00
33 Pat Burrell/Bat 8.00
34 Robin Ventura/Bat 5.00
35 Trot Nixon/Bat 8.00
36 Adrian Beltre/Bat 5.00
37 Bernie Williams/Bat 10.00
38 Bobby Abreu/Bat 8.00
39 Carlos Delgado/Bat 8.00
40 Craig Biggio/Bat 8.00
41 Garret Anderson/Bat 8.00
42 Jermaine Dye/Bat 5.00
43 Johnny Damon/Bat 8.00
44 Tim Salmon/Bat 8.00
45 Tino Martinez/Bat 10.00
46 Fred McGriff/Bat 8.00
47 Gary Sheffield/Bat 5.00
48 Adam Dunn/Shoe 15.00
49 Joe Mays/Shoe 8.00
50 Kenny Lofton/Shoe 10.00
51 Josh Beckett/Shoe 10.00
52 Bud Smith/Shoe 5.00
53 Johnny Estrada/Shin 10.00
54 Charles Johnson/Shin 8.00
55 Craig Wilson/Shin 15.00
56 Terrence Long/Glv 8.00
57 Andy Pettitte/Glv 15.00
58 Brian Giles/Glv 10.00
59 Juan Pierre/Glv 10.00
60 Cliff Floyd/Glv 10.00
61 Ivan Rodriguez/Glv 15.00
62 Andruw Jones/Hat 15.00
63 Lance Berkman/Hat 15.00
64 Mark Buehrle/Hat 10.00
65 Miguel Tejada/Hat 15.00
66 Wade Miller/Hat 10.00
67 Johnny Estrada/Shin 10.00
68 T. Shinjo/Bat/Shoe 15.00
69 S. Rolen/Bat/Jsy 20.00
70 R. Alomar/Bat/Shoe 20.00
71 M. Grace/Glv/Jsy 15.00
72 L. Walker/Jsy/Bat 10.00
73 J. Edmonds/Jsy/Bat 15.00
74 J. Kent/Jsy/Bat 10.00
75 F. Thomas/Jsy/Bat 15.00
76 C. Beltran/Jsy/Bat 10.00
77 B. Zito/Shoe/Jsy 10.00
78 A. Rodriguez/Jsy/Bat 25.00
79 T. Glaus/Dualjsy 15.00
80 R. Klesko/Bat/Glv 10.00
81 T. Glavine/Jsy/Shoe 20.00
82 B. Sheets/Bat/Jsy 10.00
83 M. Ramirez/Shoe/Glv/Jsy 25.00
84 S. Stewart/Hat/Jsy/Bat 15.00
85 V. Guerrero/Glv/Bat/Jsy 45.00
86 C. Jones/Glv/Bat/Jsy 40.00
87 J. Bagwell/Jsy/Hat/Bat 40.00
88 R. Sexson/Bat/Jsy/Glv/Shoe 40.00
89 S. Casey/Jsy/Hat/Shoe/Bat 30.00
90 T Hudson/Shoe/Hat/Glv/Jsy 30.00
91 JD Drew/Shoe/Jsy/Hat/Bat 40.00
92 I Rodriguez/Jsy/Mask/Chst/Glv 60.00
93 M Ordonez/Hat/Glv/Jsy/Shoe 40.00
94 J Buck/Glv/Chst/Shin/Msk 20.00
95 P LoDuca/Jsy/Chst/Shin/Msk 30.00

2002 Playoff Piece of the Game

NM/M
Complete Set (100):
Common Player: .50
Common SP (51-100): 5.00
Production 500
Pack (5): 15.00
Box (6): 75.00
1 Vladimir Guerrero 1.50
2 Troy Glaus 1.50
3 Ichiro Suzuki 2.50
4 Chipper Jones 2.00
5 Roberto Alomar .75
6 Scott Rolen 1.25
7 Randy Johnson 1.50
8 Roger Clemens 2.25
9 Nomar Garciaparra 2.50
10 Greg Maddux 2.00
11 Barry Bonds 4.00
12 Derek Jeter 4.00
13 Albert Pujols 3.00
14 Kerry Wood 1.25
15 Jim Thome 1.50
16 Manny Ramirez 1.50
17 Carlos Delgado .75
18 Magglio Ordonez .50
19 Torii Hunter .50
20 Garret Anderson .50
21 Eric Chavez .60
22 Rafael Palmeiro 1.25
23 Andruw Jones 1.50
24 Cliff Floyd .50
25 Sammy Sosa 2.50
26 Mike Mussina .60
27 Jeff Bagwell 1.50
28 Miguel Tejada .60
29 Curt Schilling .75
30 Tom Glavine .75
31 Frank Thomas 1.50
32 Jim Edmonds .50
33 Juan Gonzalez 1.50
34 Todd Helton 1.50
35 Shawn Green .75
36 Alfonso Soriano 1.25
37 Lance Berkman .50
38 Barry Zito .60
39 Ryan Klesko .50
40 Larry Walker .50
41 Craig Biggio .50
42 Luis Gonzalez .50
43 Ivan Rodriguez 1.25
44 J.D. Drew .75
45 Roy Oswalt .50
46 Jason Giambi 1.25
47 Brian Giles .50
48 Richie Sexson .50
49 Pat Burrell .75
50 Alex Rodriguez 3.00
51 So Taguchi **RC** 8.00
52 Allan Simpson **RC** 5.00
53 Oliver Perez **RC** 10.00
54 Ben Howard **RC** 5.00
55 Kirk Saarloos 5.00
56 Francis Beltran **RC** 5.00
57 Jorge Padilla **RC** 5.00
58 Brandon Puffer **RC** 5.00
59 Brian Mallette **RC** 5.00
60 Kyle Kane **RC** 5.00
61 Travis Driskill **RC** 5.00
62 Jeremy Lambert **RC** 5.00
63 Steve Kent **RC** 5.00
64 Julius Matos **RC** 5.00
65 Julio Mateo **RC** 5.00
66 Kazuhisa Ishii **RC** 8.00
67 Franklyn German **RC** 5.00
68 John Foster **RC** 5.00
69 Luis Ugueto **RC** 5.00
70 Shawn Sedlacek **RC** 5.00
71 Earl Snyder **RC** 5.00
72 Alex Pelaez **RC** 5.00
73 Victor Alvarez **RC** 5.00
74 Tom Shearn **RC** 5.00
75 Corey Thurman **RC** 5.00
76 Eric Junge **RC** 5.00
77 Hansel Izquierdo **RC** 5.00
78 Elio Serrano **RC** 5.00
79 J.J. Trujillo **RC** 5.00
80 Chris Snelling **RC** 6.00
81 Satoru Komiyama **RC** 5.00
82 Brandon Backe **RC** 5.00
83 Anderson Machado **RC** 5.00
84 Doug DeVore **RC** 5.00
85 Steve Bechler **RC** 5.00
86 John Ennis **RC** 5.00
87 Rodrigo Rosario **RC** 5.00
88 Jorge Sosa **RC** 5.00
89 Ken Huckaby **RC** 5.00
90 Mike Moriarty **RC** 5.00
91 Michael Crudale **RC** 5.00
92 Kevin Frederick **RC** 5.00
93 Aaron Guiel **RC** 5.00
94 Jose Rodriguez 5.00
95 Andy Shibilo **RC** 5.00
96 Deivis Santos 5.00
97 Felix Escalona **RC** 5.00
98 Miguel Asencio **RC** 5.00
99 Takahito Nomura **RC** 5.00
100 Cam Esslinger **RC** 5.00

Materials

NM/M
Common Materials (1-90): 4.00
Team Connections (91-95):
Production 500
Superstar Combos (96-100):
Production 250
Bronze Materials (1-90): 1-2X
Production 250
Bronze Team Connect. (91-95): 1.5-2X
Production 100
Bronze Combos (96-100): 2-3X
Production 50
Silver Materials (1-90): 1.5-2.5X
Production 150
Silver Tm. Connect. (91-95): 1.5-3X
Production 50
Silver Combos (96-100): No Pricing
Production 25
Gold Materials (1-90): 2-5X
Production 50
Gold Tm. Connect. (91-95): No Pricing
Production 25
Gold Combos (96-100):No Pricing
Production 10
Platinum Materials (1-90): No Pricing
Production 25
Platinum Tm Connect. (91-95): No Pricing
Production 10
Platinum Combos (96-100): No Pricing
Production 5
1 Adam Dunn/Bat 8.00
2 Adrian Beltre/Bat 4.00
3 Albert Pujols/Base 10.00
4 Alex Rodriguez/Jsy 12.00
5 Alex Rodriguez/Bat 12.00
6 Andruw Jones/Jsy 5.00
7 Andruw Jones/Bat 5.00
8 Barry Bonds/Base 15.00
9 Barry Larkin/Bat 5.00
10 Juan Gonzalez/Jsy 5.00
11 Bernie Williams/Bat 6.00
12 Carlos Delgado/Jsy 5.00
13 Chipper Jones/Jsy 10.00
14 Chipper Jones/Bat 10.00
15 Craig Biggio/Jsy 5.00
16 Craig Biggio/Bat 5.00
17 Cristian Guzman/Jsy 5.00
18 Curt Schilling/Jsy 6.00
19 Derek Jeter/Base 15.00
20 Edgar Martinez/Jsy 5.00
21 Edgardo Alfonzo/Jsy 4.00
22 Ellis Burks/Jsy 4.00
23 Frank Thomas/Bat 6.00
24 Freddy Garcia/Jsy 4.00
25 Greg Maddux/Jsy 10.00
26 Harmon Killebrew/Pants 15.00
27 Hideo Nomo/Jsy 12.00
28 Ichiro Suzuki/Base 15.00
29 Ivan Rodriguez/Jsy 8.00
30 Ivan Rodriguez/Bat 8.00
31 J.D. Drew/Bat 6.00
32 J.D. Drew/Jsy 6.00
33 Javy Lopez/Jsy 6.00
34 Jeff Bagwell/Jsy 6.00
35 Jim Edmonds/Jsy 6.00
36 Jim Edmonds/Bat 6.00
37 John Olerud/Bat 4.00
38 John Smoltz/Jsy 6.00
39 Jose Cruz Jr/Jsy 4.00
40 Jose Vidro/Jsy 4.00
41 Juan Gonzalez/Bat 6.00
42 Juan Pierre/Jsy 4.00
43 Ken Griffey Jr./Base 10.00
44 Kenny Lofton/Bat 4.00
45 Kerry Wood/Bat 8.00
46 Kevin Brown/Jsy 4.00
47 Lance Berkman/Jsy 6.00
48 Lance Berkman/Bat 6.00
49 Larry Walker/Jsy 5.00
50 Luis Gonzalez/Jsy 5.00
51 Magglio Ordonez/Jsy 5.00
52 Magglio Ordonez/Bat 5.00
53 Manny Ramirez/Jsy 8.00
54 Manny Ramirez/Bat 8.00
55 Vladimir Guerrero/Jsy 8.00
56 Mark Grace/Bat 8.00
57 Michael Barrett/Jsy 4.00
58 Miguel Tejada/Jsy 8.00
59 Mike Piazza/Jsy 12.00
60 Mike Piazza/Bat 12.00
61 Mike Schmidt/Bat 15.00
62 Mike Sweeney/Jsy 4.00
63 Nolan Ryan/Jsy 30.00
64 Nomar Garciaparra/Jsy 15.00
65 Paul LoDuca/Jsy 4.00
66 Rafael Palmeiro/Jsy 8.00
67 Rafael Palmeiro/Bat 8.00
68 Jose Canseco/Bat 8.00
69 Raul Mondesi/Jsy 4.00
70 Reggie Jackson/Bat 8.00
71 Rickey Henderson/Bat 8.00
72 Roberto Alomar/Bat 6.00
73 Robin Ventura/Jsy 4.00
74 Rod Carew/Bat 10.00
75 Roger Clemens/Jsy 15.00
76 Sammy Sosa/Base 10.00
77 Sean Casey/Jsy 5.00
78 Shannon Stewart/Jsy 4.00
79 Shawn Green/Jsy 6.00
80 Shawn Green/Bat 6.00
81 Tim Hudson/Jsy 6.00
82 Todd Helton/Bat 8.00
83 Tom Glavine/Jsy 6.00
84 Tony Gwynn/Jsy 10.00
85 Tony Gwynn/Jsy 10.00
86 Tony Gwynn/Bat 10.00
87 Troy Glaus/Jsy 6.00
88 Tsuyoshi Shinjo/Bat 4.00
89 Vladimir Guerrero/Jsy 8.00
90 Vladimir Guerrero/Bat 8.00
91 Nomar Garciaparra, Pedro J. Martinez 30.00
92 Randy Johnson, Curt Schilling 15.00
93 Andruw Jones, Chipper Jones 15.00
94 Todd Helton, Larry Walker 15.00
95 Jeff Bagwell, Craig Biggio 15.00
96 Alex Rodriguez 25.00
97 Greg Maddux 25.00
98 Mike Piazza 25.00
99 Lance Berkman 15.00
100 Vladimir Guerrero 20.00

LCS Programs

A perforated sheet of Piece of the Game cards was inserted into some of the programs sold for the American and National League Championship Series. The 8-1/2" x 11" sheet features eight player cards and a header card advertising the brand. Each 3-1/2" x 2-1/2" card is perforated on all sides and differs from the regularly issued version only in the card number on back. Sheet cards have either an "ALCS-" or "NLCS-" prefix to the number. Other programs could be found with similar sheets of Donruss Originals, Donruss Studio or Donruss Diamond Kings cards.

NM/M
Complete Sheet Set (2): 14.00
Common Player: .50
ALCS SHEET 7.00
17 Jim Thome 1.00
18 Garret Anderson .50
19 Alfonso Soriano 1.00
20 Nomar Garciaparra 2.50
21 Eric Chavez .60
22 Magglio Ordonez .50
23 Roger Clemens 2.25
24 Torii Hunter .50
--- Header Card .10
NLCS SHEET 7.00
9 Jeff Bagwell 1.50
10 Shawn Green .75
11 Vladimir Guerrero 1.50
12 Greg Maddux 2.00
13 Luis Gonzalez .50
14 Todd Helton 1.50
15 Richie Sexson .50
16 Chipper Jones 2.00
--- Header Card .10

2003 Playoff Absolute Memorabilia

NM/M
Complete Set (200):
Common Player: .50
Common SP (151-200): 3.00
Production 1,500
Pack (6): 3.00
Box (18 + Glass Plaque): 85.00
1 Nomar Garciaparra 2.50
2 Barry Bonds 4.00
3 Greg Maddux 2.00
4 Roger Clemens 3.00
5 Derek Jeter 4.00
6 Alex Rodriguez 3.00
7 Chipper Jones 2.00
8 Sammy Sosa 2.50
9 Alfonso Soriano 1.00
10 Albert Pujols 3.00
11 Adam Dunn 1.00
12 Tom Glavine .75
13 Pedro J. Martinez 1.50
14 Jim Thome 1.00
15 Hideo Nomo 1.50
16 Roberto Alomar .75
17 Barry Zito .65
18 Troy Glaus 1.50
19 Kerry Wood 1.00
20 Magglio Ordonez .50
21 Todd Helton 1.50
22 Craig Biggio .50
23 Roy Oswalt .50
24 Torii Hunter .50
25 Miguel Tejada .65
26 Tsuyoshi Shinjo .50
27 Scott Rolen 1.00
28 Rafael Palmeiro 1.00
29 Victor Martinez .75
30 Hank Blalock .75
31 Jason Lane .50
32 Junior Spivey .50
33 Gary Sheffield .75
34 Corey Patterson .50
35 Corky Miller .50
36 Brian Tallet .50
37 Cliff Lee .50
38 Jason Jennings .50
39 Kirk Saarloos .50
40 Wade Miller .50
41 Angel Berroa .50
42 Mike Sweeney .50
43 Paul LoDuca .50
44 A.J. Pierzynski .50
45 Drew Henson .50
46 Eric Chavez .65
47 Tim Hudson .75
48 Aramis Ramirez .50
49 Jack Wilson .50
50 Ryan Klesko .50
51 Antonio Perez .50
52 Dewon Brazelton .50
53 Mark Teixeira .75
54 Eric Hinske .50
55 Freddy Sanchez .50

56 Mike Rivera .50
57 Alfredo Amezaga .50
58 Cliff Floyd .50
59 Brandon Larson .50
60 Richard Hidalgo .50
61 Cesar Izturis .50
62 Richie Sexson .50
63 Michael Cuddyer .50
64 Javier Vazquez .50
65 Brandon Claussen .50
66 Carlos Rivera .50
67 Vernon Wells .50
68 Kenny Lofton .50
69 Aubrey Huff .50
70 Adam LaRoche .50
71 Jeff Baker .50
72 Jose Castillo .50
73 Joe Borchard .50
74 Walter Young .50
75 Jose Morban .50
76 Vinnie Chulk .50
77 Christian Parker .50
78 Mike Piazza 2.50
79 Ichiro Suzuki 2.50
80 Kazuhisa Ishii .50
81 Rickey Henderson 1.50
82 Ken Griffey Jr. 2.50
83 Jason Giambi .75
84 Randy Johnson 1.50
85 Curt Schilling .75
86 Manny Ramirez 1.50
87 Barry Larkin .50
88 Jeff Bagwell 1.50
89 Vladimir Guerrero 1.50
90 Mike Mussina .65
91 Juan Gonzalez 1.50
92 Andruw Jones 1.50
93 Frank Thomas 1.50
94 Sean Casey .50
95 Josh Beckett .50
96 Lance Berkman .50
97 Shawn Green .75
98 Bernie Williams .65
99 Pat Burrell .75
100 Edgar Martinez .50
101 Ivan Rodriguez 1.00
102 Jeremy Guthrie .50
103 Alexis Rios .50
104 Nic Jackson .50
105 Jason Anderson .50
106 Travis Chapman .50
107 Mac Suzuki .50
108 Toby Hall .50
109 Mark Prior 1.50
110 So Taguchi .50
111 Marlon Byrd .50
112 Garret Anderson .50
113 Luis Gonzalez .50
114 Jay Gibbons .50
115 Mark Buehrle .50
116 Wily Mo Pena .50
117 C.C. Sabathia .50
118 Ricardo Rodriguez .50
119 Robert Fick .50
120 Rodrigo Rosario .50
121 Alexis Gomez .50
122 Carlos Beltran 1.00
123 Joe Thurston .50
124 Ben Sheets .50
125 Jose Vidro .50
126 Nick Johnson .50
127 Mark Mulder .50
128 Bobby Abreu .50
129 Brian Giles .50
130 Brian Lawrence .50
131 Jeff Kent .50
132 Chris Snelling .50
133 Kevin Mench .50
134 Carlos Delgado .75
135 Orlando Hudson .50
136 Juan Cruz .50
137 Jim Edmonds .50
138 Geronimo Gil .50
139 Joe Crede .50
140 Wilson Valdez .50
141 Runelvys Hernandez .50
142 Nick Neugebauer .50
143 Takahito Nomura .50
144 Andres Galarraga .50
145 Mark Grace .65
146 Brandon Duckworth .50
147 Oliver Perez .50
148 Xavier Nady .50
149 Rafael Soriano .50
150 Ben Kozlowski .50
151 Prentice Redman **RC** 3.00
152 Craig Brazell **RC** 5.00
153 Nook Logan **RC** 4.00
154 Greg Aquino **RC** 3.00
155 Matt Kata **RC** 5.00
156 Ian Ferguson **RC** 3.00
157 Chien-Ming Wang **RC** 30.00
158 Beau Kemp **RC** 3.00
159 Alejandro Machado **RC** 3.00
160 Michael Hessman **RC** 3.00
161 Francisco Rosario **RC** 4.00
162 Pedro Liriano 3.00
163 Richard Fischer **RC** 3.00
164 Franklin Perez 3.00
165 Oscar Villarreal **RC** 3.00
166 Arnie Munoz **RC** 3.00
167 Tim Olson **RC** 4.00
168 Jose Contreras **RC** 5.00
169 Francisco Cruceta **RC** 4.00
170 Jeremy Bonderman 10.00
171 Jeremy Griffiths 3.00
172 John Webb 3.00
173 Phil Seibel **RC** 3.00
174 Aaron Looper **RC** 3.00
175 Brian Stokes **RC** 3.00
176 Guillermo Quiroz **RC** 4.00
177 Fernando Cabrera **RC** 3.00
178 Josh Hall **RC** 4.00
179 Diegomar Markwell **RC** 3.00
180 Andrew Brown **RC** 3.00
181 Doug Waechter **RC** 4.00
182 Felix Sanchez **RC** 3.00
183 Gerardo Garcia 3.00
184 Matt Bruback **RC** 3.00
185 Michel Hernandez **RC** 3.00
186 Rett Johnson **RC** 3.00
187 Ryan Cameron **RC** 3.00
188 Rob Hammock **RC** 4.00
189 Clint Barmes **RC** 10.00
190 Brandon Webb **RC** 10.00
191 Jon Leicester **RC** 3.00
192 Shane Bazzell **RC** 4.00
193 Joe Valentine **RC** 3.00
194 Josh Stewart **RC** 4.00
195 Pete LaForest **RC** 3.00
196 Shane Victorino **RC** 4.00
197 Terrmel Sledge **RC** 3.00
198 Lew Ford **RC** 5.00
199 Todd Wellemeyer **RC** 4.00
200 Hideki Matsui **RC** 10.00

Spectrum

Stars (1-150): 3-5X
Rookies (151-200): .75-2X
Production 100 Sets

Absolutely Ink

NM/M

Inserted 1:552
Blues: No Pricing
Production 10-25
Golds: No Pricing
Production 5-10
1 Vladimir Guerrero 50.00
6 Eric Hinske 15.00
8 Jose Vidro 8.00
16 Rodrigo Rosario 8.00
17 Brandon Claussen 20.00
18 Jermaine Dye 8.00
22 Mark Prior 50.00
24 Brian Lawrence 8.00
29 Barry Larkin 50.00
30 Drew Henson 40.00
36 Mark Teixeira 30.00
38 Roberto Alomar 30.00
39 Barry Zito 35.00

Glass Plaques

NM/M

One Per Box:
Roberto Alomar/Bat/Jsy/100 40.00
Roberto Alomar/Jsy/150 30.00
Jeff Bagwell/Bat/Jsy/100 40.00
Jeff Bagwell/Jsy/150 30.00
Ernie Banks/Jsy/150 40.00
Lance Berkman/Bat/Jsy/100 35.00
Lance Berkman/Jsy/150 25.00
Barry Bonds/Ball/Base/50 85.00
Barry Bonds/Ball/Base/100 75.00
Barry Bonds/Base/200 50.00
George Brett/Bat/Jsy/50 125.00
George Brett/Jsy/200 50.00
Pat Burrell/Bat/Jsy/100 35.00
Pat Burrell/Jsy/150 30.00
Steve Carlton/Auto./50 60.00
Steve Carlton/Bat/Jsy/100 40.00
Steve Carlton/Jsy/150 30.00
Roger Clemens/Glv/Jsy/50 150.00
Roger Clemens/Jsy/150 60.00
Roger Clemens/Glv/Jsy/50 150.00
Roger Clemens/Jsy/200 60.00
Roberto Clemente/Bat/Jsy/150 80.00
Roberto Clemente/Jsy/200 60.00
Jose Contreras/Jsy/Jsy/100 30.00
Jose Contreras/Jsy/150 25.00
Adam Dunn/Bat/Jsy/100 40.00
Adam Dunn/Jsy/150 30.00
Bob Feller/Auto./50 65.00
Bob Feller/Jsy/Jsy/50 50.00
Bob Feller/Jsy/100 30.00
Nomar Garciaparra/Bat/Jsy/100 65.00
Nomar Garciaparra/Jsy/200 55.00
Jason Giambi/Bat/Jsy/100 50.00
Jason Giambi/Jsy/150 40.00
Troy Glaus/Bat/Jsy/100 40.00
Troy Glaus/Jsy/150 35.00
Juan Gonzalez/Bat/Jsy/100 40.00
Juan Gonzalez/Jsy/150 30.00
Luis Gonzalez/Bat/Jsy/100 30.00
Luis Gonzalez/Jsy/150 25.00
Mark Grace/Auto./50 100.00
Mark Grace/Bat/Jsy/100 45.00
Mark Grace/Jsy/150 35.00
Shawn Green/Bat/Jsy/100 30.00
Shawn Green/Jsy/150 25.00
Ken Griffey Jr./Ball/Base/100 50.00
Ken Griffey Jr./Base/200 40.00
Vladimir Guerrero/Bat/Jsy/100 40.00
Vladimir Guerrero/Jsy/150 35.00
Tony Gwynn/Bat/Jsy/150 50.00
Tony Gwynn/Jsy/200 40.00
Todd Helton/Bat/Jsy/100 40.00
Todd Helton/Jsy/150 30.00
Rickey Henderson/Bat/Jsy/100 50.00
Rickey Henderson/Jsy/200 40.00
Tim Hudson/Auto./50 65.00
Tim Hudson/Hat/Jsy/100 30.00
Tim Hudson/Jsy/150 25.00
Torii Hunter/Auto./50 65.00
Torii Hunter/Hat/Jsy/100 40.00
Torii Hunter/Jsy/150 30.00
Kazuhisa Ishii/Bat/Jsy/100 30.00
Kazuhisa Ishii/Jsy/200 25.00
Derek Jeter/Ball/Base/150 60.00
Derek Jeter/Base/200 50.00
Randy Johnson/Bat/Jsy/100 50.00
Randy Johnson/Jsy/150 40.00
Andruw Jones/Bat/Jsy/100 35.00
Andruw Jones/Jsy/150 30.00
Chipper Jones/Bat/Jsy/100 40.00
Chipper Jones/Jsy/150 30.00
Al Kaline/Bat/Jsy/100 40.00
Al Kaline/Jsy/150 35.00
Barry Larkin/Auto./50 60.00
Barry Larkin/Bat/Jsy/100 40.00
Barry Larkin/Jsy/150 30.00
Greg Maddux/Bat/Jsy/100 50.00
Greg Maddux/Jsy/200 40.00
Pedro Martinez/Bat/Jsy/100 40.00
Pedro Martinez/Jsy/150 35.00
Hideki Matsui/Ball/Base/50 110.00
Hideki Matsui/Ball/Base/150 75.00
Hideki Matsui/Base/200 55.00
Don Mattingly/Bat/Jsy/100 65.00
Don Mattingly/Jsy/200 50.00
Mark Mulder/Auto./50 60.00
Mark Mulder/Jsy/150 25.00
Mark Mulder/Jsy/Jsy/100 30.00
Stan Musial/Bat/Jsy/150 65.00
Stan Musial/Jsy/200 60.00
Hideo Nomo/Bat/Jsy/50 60.00
Hideo Nomo/Bat/Jsy/100 40.00
Hideo Nomo/Jsy/200 30.00
Magglio Ordonez/Auto./50 50.00
Magglio Ordonez/Bat/Jsy/100 30.00
Magglio Ordonez/Jsy/150 25.00
Roy Oswalt/Auto./50 50.00
Roy Oswalt/Bat/Jsy/100 30.00
Roy Oswalt/Jsy/150 25.00
Rafael Palmeiro/Bat/Jsy/100 40.00
Rafael Palmeiro/Jsy/150 30.00
Mike Piazza/Bat/Jsy/50 75.00
Mike Piazza/Bat/Jsy/100 50.00
Mike Piazza/Jsy/200 40.00
Mark Prior/Bat/Jsy/100 60.00
Mark Prior/Jsy/150 40.00
Albert Pujols/Bat/Jsy/150 75.00
Albert Pujols/Jsy/150 60.00
Manny Ramirez/Bat/Jsy/100 40.00
Manny Ramirez/Jsy/150 30.00
Cal Ripken Jr./Bat/Jsy/150 90.00
Cal Ripken Jr./Jsy/200 70.00
Frank Robinson/Auto./50 65.00
Frank Robinson/Bat/Jsy/100 40.00
Frank Robinson/Jsy/150 30.00
Alex Rodriguez/Bat/Jsy/100 50.00
Alex Rodriguez/Jsy/200 40.00
Nolan Ryan/Jkt/Jsy/150 90.00
Nolan Ryan/Jsy/200 75.00
Nolan Ryan/Jsy/Jsy/100 100.00
Ryne Sandberg/Bat/Jsy/50 100.00
Ryne Sandberg/Jsy/200 65.00
Curt Schilling/Glv/Jsy/50 50.00
Curt Schilling/Jsy/150 30.00
Mike Schmidt/Bat/Jsy/100 70.00
Mike Schmidt/Jsy/200 50.00
Ozzie Smith/Bat/Jsy/150 65.00
Ozzie Smith/Jsy/150 50.00
Alfonso Soriano/Bat/Jsy/150 60.00
Alfonso Soriano/Jsy/150 50.00
Sammy Sosa/Bat/Jsy/150 50.00
Sammy Sosa/Jsy/200 40.00
Junior Spivey/Auto./50 50.00
Junior Spivey/Bat/Jsy/100 30.00
Junior Spivey/Jsy/150 25.00
Ichiro Suzuki/Ball/Base/50 80.00
Ichiro Suzuki/Ball/Base/150 60.00
Ichiro Suzuki/Base/200 40.00
Mark Teixeira/Bat/Jsy/100 40.00
Mark Teixeira/Jsy/150 30.00
Miguel Tejada/Auto./50 60.00
Miguel Tejada/Bat/Jsy/100 40.00
Miguel Tejada/Jsy/150 30.00
Frank Thomas/Bat/Jsy/100 40.00
Frank Thomas/Jsy/150 30.00
Bernie Williams/Bat/Jsy/100 40.00
Bernie Williams/Jsy/150 35.00
Kerry Wood/Auto./50 80.00
Kerry Wood/Bat/Jsy/100 45.00
Kerry Wood/Jsy/150 35.00
Barry Zito/Auto./50 75.00
Barry Zito/Hat/Jsy/100 40.00
Barry Zito/Jsy/150 30.00

Player's Collection - Bat

NM/M

Common Player: 4.00
Production 75 Sets
81 Alex Rodriguez 15.00
82 Alfonso Soriano 12.00
83 Barry Larkin 8.00
84 Roberto Alomar 8.00
85 Ivan Rodriguez 8.00
86 Jason Giambi 8.00
87 Jeff Bagwell 8.00
88 Juan Gonzalez 8.00
89 Larry Walker 4.00
90 Luis Gonzalez 4.00
91 Magglio Ordonez 6.00
92 Manny Ramirez 8.00
93 Marlon Byrd 4.00
94 Mike Piazza 12.00
95 Pat Burrell 8.00
96 Todd Helton 8.00
97 Rickey Henderson 8.00
98 Andruw Jones 8.00
99 Craig Biggio 4.00
100 Mark Prior 10.00

Player's Collection - Jersey

NM/M

Common Player: 4.00
Production 75 Sets
1 Adam Dunn 6.00
2 Adrian Beltre 4.00
3 Alex Rodriguez 15.00
4 Alfonso Soriano 12.00
5 Andruw Jones 8.00
6 Andy Pettitte 6.00
7 Barry Larkin 6.00
8 Barry Zito 6.00
9 Ben Grieve 4.00
10 Bernie Williams 8.00
11 Cal Ripken Jr. 40.00
12 Carlos Delgado 6.00
13 C.C. Sabathia 4.00
14 Chipper Jones 10.00
15 Craig Biggio 4.00
16 Curt Schilling 6.00
17 Alex Rodriguez 15.00
18 Frank Thomas 8.00
19 Freddy Garcia 4.00
20 Jay Bell 4.00
21 Roger Clemens 15.00
22 Tony Gwynn 10.00
23 Ivan Rodriguez 8.00
24 Jason Giambi 8.00
25 Jason Jennings 4.00
26 Jay Payton 4.00
27 J.D. Drew 5.00
28 Jeff Bagwell 8.00
29 Jeromy Burnitz 4.00
30 Jim Edmonds 6.00
31 Jim Thome 8.00
32 Joe Borchard 4.00
33 Joe Mays 4.00
34 John Olerud 5.00
35 David Wells 4.00
36 Juan Gonzalez 8.00
37 Kazuhiro Sasaki 4.00
38 Chan Ho Park 4.00
39 Kerry Wood 10.00
40 Kevin Brown 4.00
41 Lance Berkman 6.00
42 Larry Walker 4.00
43 Bret Boone 6.00
44 Magglio Ordonez 6.00
45 Manny Ramirez 8.00
46 Mark Mulder 6.00
47 Mark Prior 10.00
48 Matt Williams 4.00
49 Miguel Tejada 5.00
50 Mike Piazza 12.00
51 Nomar Garciaparra 15.00
52 Doug Davis 4.00
53 Paul Konerko 4.00
54 Paul LoDuca 4.00
55 Pedro J. Martinez 10.00
56 Preston Wilson 4.00
57 4.00
58 Marlon Byrd 4.00
59 Reggie Sanders 4.00
60 Richie Sexson 6.00
61 4.00
62 Rickey Henderson 8.00
63 Robert Person 4.00
64 4.00
65 Roger Clemens 15.00
66 Roy Oswalt 6.00
67 Ryan Klesko 4.00
68 Sammy Sosa 15.00
69 Shawn Green 6.00
70 Steve Finley 4.00
71 Terrence Long 4.00
72 Tim Hudson 6.00
73 Toby Hall 4.00
74 Todd Helton 8.00
75 Travis Lee 4.00
76 Troy Glaus 8.00
77 Tsuyoshi Shinjo 4.00
78 Vernon Wells 6.00
79 Vladimir Guerrero 8.00
80 Wes Helms 4.00

Rookie Materials Jersey Number

NM/M

Many not priced due to scarcity.
2 Yogi Berra/35 40.00
3 Vladimir Guerrero/27 35.00
4 Randy Johnson/51 25.00
5 Andruw Jones/25 25.00
10 Alfonso Soriano/33 35.00
13 Rafael Palmeiro/25 20.00

Rookie Materials Season

NM/M

Common Player: 5.00
Quantity produced listed
1 Stan Musial/42 75.00
2 Yogi Berra/47 40.00
3 Vladimir Guerrero/97 15.00
4 Randy Johnson/89 20.00
5 Andruw Jones/96 10.00
6 Jeff Kent/92 5.00
8 Hideo Nomo/95 20.00
9 Ivan Rodriguez/91 10.00
10 Alfonso Soriano/101 20.00
11 Scott Rolen/96 15.00
12 Juan Gonzalez/89 15.00
13 Rafael Palmeiro/86 15.00
14 Mike Schmidt/73 60.00
15 Cal Ripken Jr./82 75.00

Signing Bonus

Production 15 Sets
No Pricing

Spectrum Signatures

NM/M

Common Autograph: 6.00
Varying quantities produced
10 Albert Pujols/10 275.00
16 Roberto Alomar/15 100.00
17 Barry Zito/25 50.00
20 Magglio Ordonez/25 50.00
23 Roy Oswalt/25 30.00
24 Torii Hunter/25 40.00
29 Victor Martinez/100 30.00
30 Hank Blalock/50 30.00
32 Junior Spivey/50 15.00
34 Corey Patterson/50 20.00
35 Corky Miller/100 6.00
36 Brian Tallet/100 6.00
37 Cliff Lee/100 8.00
38 Jason Jennings/100 8.00
39 Kirk Saarloos/100 6.00
40 Wade Miller/50 15.00
41 Angel Berroa/100 10.00
42 Mike Sweeney/50 15.00
43 Paul LoDuca/50 20.00
44 A.J. Pierzynski/100 15.00
45 Drew Henson/50 25.00
47 Tim Hudson/50 40.00
51 Antonio Perez/25 8.00
52 Dewon Brazelton/50 15.00
53 Mark Teixeira/50 40.00
54 Eric Hinske/100 15.00
55 Freddy Sanchez/100 15.00
57 Alfredo Amezaga/100 10.00
59 Brandon Larson/100 8.00
60 Richard Hidalgo/100 10.00
62 Richie Sexson/25 30.00
63 Michael Cuddyer/100 15.00
68 Kenny Lofton/50 30.00
69 Aubrey Huff/100 15.00
70 Adam LaRoche/100 15.00
71 Jeff Baker/100 10.00
72 Jose Castillo/100 10.00
73 Joe Borchard/100 10.00
74 Walter Young/100 8.00
76 Vinnie Chulk/100 8.00
80 Kazuhisa Ishii/25 60.00
87 Barry Larkin/50 50.00
89 Vladimir Guerrero/50 50.00
92 Andruw Jones/25 60.00
95 Josh Beckett/100 25.00
100 Edgar Martinez/50 25.00
102 Jeremy Guthrie/100 15.00
103 Alexis Rios/100 20.00

104 Nic Jackson/100 8.00
105 Jason Anderson/100 8.00
106 Travis Chapman/100 8.00
107 Mac Suzuki/304 15.00
109 Mark Prior/50 30.00
111 Marlon Byrd/100 10.00
114 Jay Gibbons/100 10.00
118 Ricardo Rodriguez/100 10.00
119 Robert Fick/100 10.00
120 Rodrigo Rosario/250 8.00
121 Alexis Gomez/100 10.00
124 Ben Sheets/50 20.00
126 Nick Johnson/50 10.00
127 Mark Mulder/50 40.00
132 Chris Snelling/100 8.00
133 Kevin Mench/100 10.00
135 Orlando Hudson/50 15.00
139 Joe Crede/100 10.00
140 Wilson Valdez/25 10.00
141 Runelvys Hernandez/100 10.00
143 Takahito Nomura/47 15.00
147 Oliver Perez/50 15.00
148 Xavier Nady/100 12.00
150 Ben Kozlowski/100 8.00
151 Prentice Redman/250 10.00
152 Craig Brazell/250 10.00
153 Nook Logan/250 6.00
154 Greg Aquino/250 8.00
155 Matt Kata/250 15.00
156 Ian Ferguson/250 6.00
157 Chien-Ming Wang/250 200.00
158 Beau Kemp/250 6.00
159 Alejandro Machado/250 6.00
160 Michael Hessman/160 6.00
161 Francisco Rosario/250 6.00
162 Pedro Liriano/250 6.00
163 Richard Fischer/250 6.00
164 Franklin Perez/250 6.00
165 Oscar Villarreal/250 10.00
166 Arnie Munoz/250 6.00
167 Tim Olson/250 8.00
168 Jose Contreras/250 25.00
169 Francisco Cruceta/250 8.00
170 Jeremy Bonderman/250 40.00
171 Jeremy Griffiths/250 8.00
172 John Webb/250 6.00
173 Phil Seibel/250 6.00
174 Aaron Looper/250 6.00
175 Brian Stokes/250 6.00
176 Guillermo Quiroz/250 8.00
177 Fernando Cabrera/250 10.00
178 Josh Hall/250 10.00
179 Diegomar Markwell/250 6.00
180 Andrew Brown/250 8.00
181 Doug Waechter/250 8.00
182 Felix Sanchez/250 8.00
183 Gerardo Garcia/250 8.00
184 Matt Bruback/250 6.00
185 Michel Hernandez/250 6.00
186 Rett Johnson/250 10.00
187 Ryan Cameron/250 6.00
188 Rob Hammock/250 15.00
189 Clint Barmes/250 15.00
190 Brandon Webb/250 25.00
191 Jon Leicester/250 6.00
192 Shane Bazzell/250 10.00
193 Joe Valentine/250 8.00
194 Josh Stewart/250 15.00
195 Pete LaForest/250 8.00
196 Shane Victorino/250 8.00
197 Terrmel Sledge/250 6.00
198 Lew Ford/250 15.00
199 Todd Wellemeyer/250 10.00

Team Tandems

NM/M
Common Duo: 2.00
Inserted 1:48
Spectrums: 1-2X
Production 100 Sets
1 Mark Prior, Sammy Sosa 5.00
2 Vladimir Guerrero, Jose Vidro 3.00
3 Bernie Williams, Alfonso Soriano 6.00
4 Mike Sweeney, Carlos Beltran 2.00
5 Magglio Ordonez, Paul Konerko 2.00
6 Adam Dunn, Austin Kearns 3.00
7 Randy Johnson, Curt Schilling 4.00
8 Hideo Nomo, Kazuhisa Ishii 2.00
9 Pat Burrell, Bobby Abreu 3.00
10 Todd Helton, Larry Walker 2.00

Team Tandems Material

NM/M
Common Duo:
Quantity produced listed
Spectrums: No Pricing
Production 25 or 10
1 Mark Prior, Sammy Sosa/100 30.00
2 Vladimir Guerrero, Jose Vidro/100 10.00
3 Bernie Williams, Alfonso Soriano/100 20.00
4 Mike Sweeney, Carlos Beltran/100 6.00
5 Magglio Ordonez, Paul Konerko/100 6.00
6 Adam Dunn, Austin Kearns/100 15.00
7 Randy Johnson, Curt Schilling/100 15.00
8 Hideo Nomo, Kazuhisa Ishii/40 50.00
9 Pat Burrell, Bobby Abreu/40 20.00
10 Todd Helton, Larry Walker/100 8.00

Team Trios

NM/M
Common Trio: 5.00
Inserted 1:88
Spectrums: 1-2X
Production 50 Sets
1 Greg Maddux, Chipper Jones, Andruw Jones 8.00
2 Sammy Sosa, Mark Prior, Kerry Wood 8.00
3 Pedro Martinez, Nomar Garciaparra, Manny Ramirez 8.00
4 Jason Giambi, Roger Clemens, Alfonso Soriano 8.00
5 Alex Rodriguez, Rafael Palmeiro, Mark Teixeira 8.00
6 Mike Piazza, Roberto Alomar, Tsuyoshi Shinjo 6.00
7 Jeff Bagwell, Craig Biggio, Lance Berkman 5.00
8 Troy Glaus, Garret Anderson, Troy Percival 5.00
9 Miguel Tejada, Eric Chavez, Barry Zito 5.00
10 Luis Gonzalez, Randy Johnson, Curt Schilling 6.00

Team Trios Materials

NM/M
Quantity produced listed 5.00
Spectrums: No Pricing
Production 10 or 25
1 Greg Maddux, Chipper Jones, Andruw Jones/100 30.00
2 Sammy Sosa, Mark Prior, Kerry Wood/100 30.00
3 Pedro Martinez, Nomar Garciaparra, Manny Ramirez/50 50.00
4 Jason Giambi, Roger Clemens, Alfonso Soriano/100 40.00
5 Alex Rodriguez, Rafael Palmeiro, Mark Teixeira/100 25.00
6 Mike Piazza, Roberto Alomar, Tsuyoshi Shinjo/40 40.00
7 Jeff Bagwell, Craig Biggio, Lance Berkman/100 20.00
8 Troy Glaus, Garret Anderson, Troy Percival/40 25.00
9 Miguel Tejada, Eric Chavez, Barry Zito/100 20.00
10 Luis Gonzalez, Randy Johnson, Curt Schilling/100 25.00

Tools of the Trade

NM/M
Complete Set (110): 125.00
Common Player: 1.00
Inserted 1:5
1 Sammy Sosa 4.00

2 Nomar Garciaparra 5.00
3 Andruw Jones 1.50
4 Troy Glaus 1.00
5 Greg Maddux 4.00
6 Rickey Henderson 1.00
7 Alex Rodriguez 6.00
8 Manny Ramirez 1.50
9 Lance Berkman 1.00
10 Roger Clemens 5.00
11 Ivan Rodriguez 1.00
12 Kazuhisa Ishii 1.00
13 Alfonso Soriano 3.00
14 Austin Kearns 1.00
15 Mike Piazza 3.00
16 Curt Schilling 1.00
17 Jeff Bagwell 1.50
18 Todd Helton 1.50
19 Randy Johnson 2.00
20 Vladimir Guerrero 1.50
21 Kerry Wood 1.50
22 Rafael Palmeiro 1.50
23 Roy Oswalt 1.00
24 Chipper Jones 3.00
25 Pat Burrell 1.00
26 Jason Giambi 2.00
27 Pedro J. Martinez 2.00
28 Roberto Alomar 1.00
29 Shawn Green 1.00
30 Adam Dunn 1.00
31 Juan Gonzalez 1.50
32 Mark Prior 5.00
33 Hideo Nomo 1.00
34 Torii Hunter 1.00
35 Mark Teixeira 1.00
36 Craig Biggio 1.00
37 Rafael Palmeiro 1.00
38 Jeff Bagwell 1.50
39 Albert Pujols 6.00
40 Richie Sexson 1.00
41 Alex Rodriguez 6.00
42 Carlos Delgado 1.50
43 Frank Thomas 1.50
44 Sammy Sosa 4.00
45 Marlon Byrd 1.00
46 Mark Prior 5.00
47 Adrian Beltre 1.00
48 Tom Glavine 1.00
49 So Taguchi 1.00
50 Jeff Bagwell 1.50
51 Mike Sweeney 1.00
52 Luis Gonzalez 1.00
53 Chipper Jones 3.00
54 Jason Giambi 2.00
55 Miguel Tejada 1.00
56 Todd Helton 1.50
57 Andruw Jones 1.50
58 Mike Piazza 3.00
59 Manny Ramirez 1.50
60 Randy Johnson 2.00
61 Carlos Beltran 1.00
62 Victor Martinez 1.00
63 Orlando Hudson 1.00
64 Jeff Kent 1.00
65 Greg Maddux 4.00
66 Garret Anderson 1.00
67 Joe Thurston 1.00
68 Mark Teixeira 1.00
69 Kazuhisa Ishii 1.00
70 Austin Kearns 1.00
71 Pat Burrell 1.00
72 Joe Borchard 1.00
73 Josh Phelps 1.00
74 Travis Hafner 1.00
75 So Taguchi 1.00
76 Victor Martinez 1.00
77 Paul LoDuca 1.00
78 Bernie Williams 1.00
79 Josh Phelps 1.00
80 Marlon Byrd 1.00
81 Manny Ramirez 1.50
82 Jason Giambi 2.00
83 Jeff Bagwell 1.50
84 Sammy Sosa 4.00
85 Josh Phelps 1.00
86 Tim Hudson 1.00
87 Randy Johnson 2.00
88 Troy Glaus 1.00
89 Joe Thurston 1.00
90 Miguel Tejada 1.00
91 Adam Dunn 1.00
92 Magglio Ordonez 1.00
93 Mike Sweeney 1.00
94 Andruw Jones 1.50
95 Carlos Beltran 1.00
96 Joe Borchard 1.00
97 Austin Kearns 1.00
98 Richie Sexson 1.00
99 Mark Prior 5.00
100 Mark Teixeira 1.00
101 Ryan Klesko 1.00
102 Jason Jennings 1.00
103 Travis Hafner 1.00
104 Mark Buehrle 1.00
105 Eric Hinske 1.00
106 Rafael Palmeiro 1.00
107 Roy Oswalt 1.00
108 Kerry Wood 1.00
109 Brian Giles 1.00
110 Ivan Rodriguez 1.00

Tools of the Trade Materials

NM/M
Common Player: 3.00
Quantity produced listed
Spectrums: 1-2.5X
Production 10 to 50
1 Sammy Sosa/250 10.00
2 Nomar Garciaparra/250 10.00
3 Andruw Jones/250 5.00
4 Troy Glaus/250 5.00
5 Greg Maddux/250 10.00
6 Rickey Henderson/40 25.00
7 Alex Rodriguez/250 10.00
8 Manny Ramirez/250 6.00
9 Lance Berkman/250 4.00
10 Roger Clemens/250 10.00
11 Ivan Rodriguez/250 6.00
12 Kazuhisa Ishii/40 5.00
13 Alfonso Soriano/250 10.00
14 Austin Kearns/250 5.00
15 Mike Piazza/250 10.00
16 Curt Schilling/250 5.00
17 Jeff Bagwell/250 6.00
18 Todd Helton/250 6.00
19 Randy Johnson/250 6.00
20 Vladimir Guerrero/250 6.00
21 Kerry Wood/250 6.00
22 Rafael Palmeiro/250 6.00
23 Roy Oswalt/250 3.00
24 Chipper Jones/250 8.00
25 Pat Burrell/40 15.00
26 Jason Giambi/250 8.00
27 Pedro J. Martinez/250 8.00
28 Roberto Alomar/40 15.00
29 Shawn Green/250 3.00
30 Adam Dunn/250 5.00
31 Juan Gonzalez/40 15.00
32 Mark Prior/250 8.00
33 Hideo Nomo/250 8.00
34 Torii Hunter/250 5.00
35 Mark Teixeira/250 5.00
36 Craig Biggio/250 4.00
37 Rafael Palmeiro/250 5.00
38 Jeff Bagwell/250 5.00
39 Albert Pujols/200 12.00
40 Richie Sexson/250 4.00
41 Alex Rodriguez/250 10.00
42 Carlos Delgado/250 3.00
43 Frank Thomas/75 8.00
44 Sammy Sosa/250 10.00
45 Marlon Byrd/250 3.00
46 Mark Prior/250 8.00
47 Adrian Beltre/250 3.00
48 Tom Glavine/250 3.00
49 So Taguchi/250 3.00
50 Jeff Bagwell/250 5.00
51 Mike Sweeney/250 3.00
52 Luis Gonzalez/250 3.00
53 Chipper Jones/100 8.00
54 Jason Giambi/250 6.00
55 Miguel Tejada/250 4.00
56 Todd Helton/250 5.00
57 Andruw Jones/250 5.00
58 Mike Piazza/250 8.00
59 Manny Ramirez/250 6.00
60 Randy Johnson/250 6.00
61 Carlos Beltran/250 3.00
62 Victor Martinez/250 3.00
63 Orlando Hudson/250 3.00
64 Jeff Kent/250 3.00
65 Greg Maddux/250 8.00
66 Garret Anderson/150 4.00
67 Joe Thurston/250 3.00
68 Mark Teixeira/250 3.00
69 Kazuhisa Ishii/250 3.00
70 Austin Kearns/250 4.00
71 Pat Burrell/100 8.00
72 Joe Borchard/250 3.00
73 Josh Phelps/250 3.00
74 Travis Hafner/250 3.00
75 So Taguchi/125 3.00
76 Victor Martinez/125 5.00
77 Paul LoDuca/125 5.00
78 Bernie Williams/125 8.00
79 Josh Phelps/125 5.00
80 Marlon Byrd/125 5.00
81 Manny Ramirez/100 10.00
82 Jason Giambi/125 10.00
83 Jeff Bagwell/50 15.00
84 Sammy Sosa/125 20.00
85 Josh Phelps/125 5.00
86 Tim Hudson/125 5.00
87 Randy Johnson/125 10.00
88 Troy Glaus/125 8.00
89 Joe Thurston/125 4.00
90 Miguel Tejada/125 5.00
91 Adam Dunn/100 15.00
92 Magglio Ordonez/100 10.00
93 Mike Sweeney/100 10.00
94 Andruw Jones/100 15.00
95 Carlos Beltran/100 8.00
96 Joe Borchard/100 8.00
97 Austin Kearns/100 15.00
98 Richie Sexson/50 15.00
99 Mark Prior/50 50.00
100 Mark Teixeira/50 20.00
101 Ryan Klesko/50 10.00
102 Jason Jennings/50 10.00
103 Travis Hafner/50 10.00
104 Mark Buehrle/50 15.00
105 Eric Hinske/50 20.00
106 Rafael Palmeiro/50 40.00
107 Roy Oswalt/50 20.00
108 Kerry Wood/50 40.00
109 Brian Giles/50 15.00
110 Ivan Rodriguez/50 25.00

Total Bases

NM/M
Complete Set (30): 60.00
Common Player: 1.00
Inserted 1:16
1 Albert Pujols 6.00
2 Nomar Garciaparra 6.00
3 Jason Giambi 3.00
4 Miguel Tejada 1.00
5 Rafael Palmeiro 1.50
6 Sammy Sosa 5.00
7 Pat Burrell 1.50
8 Lance Berkman 1.00
9 Bernie Williams 1.50
10 Jim Thome 2.00
11 Carlos Beltran 1.00
12 Eric Chavez 1.00
13 Alex Rodriguez 6.00
14 Magglio Ordonez 1.00
15 Brian Giles 1.00
16 Alfonso Soriano 3.00
17 Shawn Green 1.00
18 Vladimir Guerrero 2.00
19 Garret Anderson 1.00
20 Todd Helton 2.00
21 Barry Bonds 8.00
22 Jeff Kent 1.00
23 Torii Hunter 1.00
24 Ichiro Suzuki 4.00
25 Derek Jeter 8.00
26 Chipper Jones 4.00
27 Jeff Bagwell 2.00
28 Mike Piazza 4.00
29 Rickey Henderson 1.50
30 Ken Griffey Jr. 4.00

Total Bases Materials 1B

NM/M
Common Player: 4.00
Quantity produced listed
1 Albert Pujols/109 12.00
2 Nomar Garciaparra/112 12.00
3 Jason Giambi/100 8.00
4 Miguel Tejada/140 4.00
5 Rafael Palmeiro/58 5.00
6 Sammy Sosa/90 15.00
7 Pat Burrell/87 8.00
8 Lance Berkman/90 4.00
9 Bernie Williams/146 6.00
10 Jim Thome/73 8.00
11 Carlos Beltran/94 4.00
12 Eric Chavez/93 4.00
13 Alex Rodriguez/101 15.00
14 Magglio Ordonez/103 4.00
15 Brian Giles/68 4.00
16 Alfonso Soriano/117 10.00
17 Shawn Green/92 4.00
18 Vladimir Guerrero/128 6.00
19 Garret Anderson/107 4.00
20 Todd Helton/109 6.00
21 Barry Bonds/70 20.00
22 Jeff Kent/114 4.00
23 Torii Hunter/92 6.00
24 Ichiro Suzuki/165 25.00
25 Derek Jeter/147 25.00
26 Chipper Jones/117 8.00
27 Jeff Bagwell/100 8.00
28 Mike Piazza/76 10.00
29 Rickey Henderson/28 40.00
30 Ken Griffey Jr./36 40.00

Total Bases Materials 2B

NM/M
Quantity produced listed
1 Albert Pujols/40 40.00
2 Nomar Garciaparra/56 25.00
3 Jason Giambi/34 15.00
4 Miguel Tejada/30 10.00
5 Rafael Palmeiro/34 15.00
7 Pat Burrell/39 10.00
8 Lance Berkman/35 8.00
9 Bernie Williams/37 15.00
11 Carlos Beltran/44 8.00
12 Eric Chavez/31 10.00
13 Alex Rodriguez/27 50.00
14 Magglio Ordonez/47 8.00
15 Brian Giles/37 8.00
16 Alfonso Soriano/51 25.00
17 Shawn Green/31 10.00
18 Vladimir Guerrero/37 15.00
19 Garret Anderson/56 8.00
20 Todd Helton/39 15.00
21 Barry Bonds/31 50.00
22 Jeff Kent/42 8.00
23 Torii Hunter/37 15.00
25 Derek Jeter/26 50.00
26 Chipper Jones/35 25.00
27 Jeff Bagwell/33 25.00
28 Mike Piazza/23 35.00

Total Bases Materials 3B

No pricing due to scarcity.

Total Bases Materials HR

NM/M
Quantity produced listed
1 Albert Pujols/34 40.00
3 Jason Giambi/41 20.00
4 Miguel Tejada/41 10.00
5 Rafael Palmeiro/43 15.00
6 Sammy Sosa/49 30.00
7 Pat Burrell/37 15.00
8 Lance Berkman/42 10.00
10 Jim Thome/52 15.00
11 Carlos Beltran/29 10.00
12 Eric Chavez/34 12.00
13 Alex Rodriguez/57 25.00
14 Magglio Ordonez/58 8.00
15 Brian Giles/38 8.00
16 Alfonso Soriano/39 30.00
17 Shawn Green/42 8.00
18 Vladimir Guerrero/39 15.00
19 Garret Anderson/29 15.00
20 Todd Helton/30 15.00
21 Barry Bonds/46 40.00
22 Jeff Kent/37 8.00
23 Torii Hunter/29 25.00
26 Chipper Jones/26 35.00
27 Jeff Bagwell/31 20.00
28 Mike Piazza/33 30.00

2003 Playoff Piece of the Game

NM/M
Common Player: 4.00
Pack (1): 12.00
Box (6): 60.00
1 Adam Dunn/Bat 8.00
2 Adam Dunn/Jsy 8.00
3 Adrian Beltre/Bat 6.00
4 Albert Pujols/Jsy 15.00
5 Albert Pujols/Bat 15.00
6 Alex Rodriguez/Bat 10.00
7 Alex Rodriguez/Blue Jsy 10.00
8 Alex Rodriguez/White Jsy 10.00
9 Alfonso Soriano/Bat 8.00
10 Alfonso Soriano/Gray Jsy 8.00
11 Alfonso Soriano/White Jsy 8.00
12 Brett Myers/Jsy 4.00
13 Andruw Jones/Jsy 6.00
14 Austin Kearns/Jsy 6.00
15 Barry Larkin/Jsy 6.00
16 Barry Zito/Jsy 6.00
17 Bernie Williams/Jsy 6.00
18 Brian Giles/Bat 4.00
19 Zach Day/Jsy 4.00
20 Carlos Beltran/Bat 8.00
21 Brandon Phillips/Bat 4.00
22 Carlos Lee/Bat 4.00
23 Casey Fossum/Jsy 4.00
24 Chipper Jones/Jsy 8.00
25 Marcus Giles/Jsy 4.00
26 Craig Biggio/Jsy 6.00
27 Curt Schilling/Jsy 8.00
28 Derek Jeter/Base 15.00
29 Edgar Martinez/Jsy 6.00
30 Eric Chavez/Jsy 6.00
31 Eric Hinske/Bat 4.00
32 Frank Thomas/190/Bat 8.00
33 Aubrey Huff/Jsy 4.00
34 Gary Carter/Jkt 8.00
35 Greg Maddux/Gray Jsy 8.00
36 Greg Maddux/White Jsy 8.00
37 Hideki Matsui/Base **RC** 15.00
38 Hideo Nomo/White Jsy 8.00
39 Rod Carew/Jkt 8.00
40 Ichiro Suzuki/Base 10.00
41 Ivan Rodriguez/Bat 8.00
42 Jason Giambi/Bat 6.00
43 Jason Giambi/Jsy 6.00

44 J.C. Romero/Jsy 4.00
45 Jason Giambi/White Jsy 6.00
46 Jeff Bagwell/Jsy 6.00
47 Josh Bard/Jsy 4.00
48 Jim Thome/Jsy 8.00
49 Jay Gibbons/Jsy 4.00
50 Jorge Posada/Jsy 6.00
51 Juan Gonzalez/Bat 6.00
52 Kazuhisa Ishii/Bat 4.00
53 George Brett/Bat 15.00
54 Kenny Lofton/Bat 4.00
55 Kerry Wood/Jsy 8.00
56 Kevin Brown/Jsy 4.00
57 Kirk Saarloos/Jsy 4.00
58 Lance Berkman/Jsy 5.00
59 Larry Walker/Jsy 4.00
60 Magglio Ordonez/Jsy 4.00
61 Manny Ramirez/Jsy 8.00
62 Mark Mulder/Jsy 4.00
63 Mark Prior/Jsy 8.00
64 Matt Williams/Jsy 4.00
65 Miguel Tejada/Jsy 6.00
66 Mike Mussina/Jsy 6.00
67 Mike Piazza/Bat 10.00
68 Mike Piazza/Black Jsy 10.00
69 Mike Piazza/White Jsy 10.00
70 Nomar Garciaparra/Bat 10.00
71 Nomar Garciaparra/Gray Jsy 10.00
72 Nomar Garciaparra/White Jsy 10.00
73 Paul LoDuca/Jsy 4.00
74 Pedro Martinez/Jsy 8.00
75 Rafael Palmeiro/Jsy 8.00
76 Randy Johnson/Gray Jsy 8.00
77 Randy Johnson/White Jsy 8.00
78 Rickey Henderson/Jsy 8.00
79 Roberto Alomar/Jsy 6.00
80 Rod Carew/Jkt 8.00
81 Roger Clemens/Gray Jsy 15.00
82 Roger Clemens/White Jsy 15.00
83 Cal Ripken Jr./Jsy 25.00
84 Roy Oswalt/Jsy 4.00
85 Jeremy Bonderman/Jsy 8.00
86 Ryne Sandberg/Bat 15.00
87 Sammy Sosa/Bat 12.00
88 Sammy Sosa/Grey Jsy 15.00
89 Sammy Sosa/White Jsy 15.00
90 Scott Rolen/Jsy 8.00
91 Frank Catalanotto/Jsy 4.00
92 Shawn Green/Jsy 5.00
93 Tim Hudson/Jsy 5.00
94 Todd Helton/Jsy 8.00
95 Tony Gwynn/Jsy 8.00
96 Torii Hunter/Jsy 6.00
97 Troy Glaus/Jsy 6.00
98 Runelvys Hernandez/Jsy 4.00
99 Vernon Wells/Jsy 4.00
100 Vladimir Guerrero/Jsy 8.00

Autographs

NM/M
Common Player:
Varying quantities produced
Prime Autos: No Pricing
Production 4-20
12 Brett Myers 10.00
18 Brian Giles/30 30.00
19 Zach Day 8.00
21 Brandon Phillips 10.00
22 Carlos Lee 12.00
23 Casey Fossum 10.00
25 Marcus Giles 15.00
29 Edgar Martinez/100 40.00
30 Eric Chavez/75 25.00
31 Eric Hinske 10.00
33 Aubrey Huff 10.00
41 Ivan Rodriguez/50 50.00
41 Ivan Rodriguez/75 40.00
44 J.C. Romero 8.00
47 Josh Bard 8.00
49 Jay Gibbons 10.00
51 Juan Gonzalez/50 50.00
57 Kirk Saarloos 8.00
62 Mark Mulder/100 25.00
63 Mark Prior/25 75.00
64 Matt Williams 15.00
73 Paul LoDuca 15.00
84 Roy Oswalt/50 25.00
85 Jeremy Bonderman 50.00
86 Ryne Sandberg/40 100.00
90 Scott Rolen/50 40.00
91 Frank Catalanotto 8.00
96 Torii Hunter/140 20.00
98 Runelvys Hernandez 10.00
100 Vladimir Guerrero/150 40.00

Prime Materials

No Pricing
Production 25 Sets

Bronze Materials

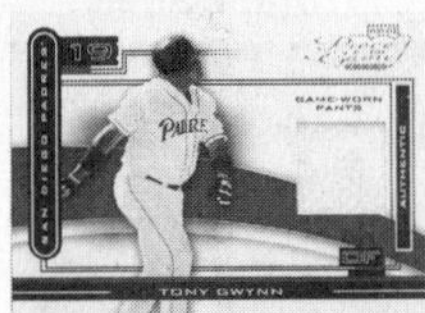

Cards (1-100): 1-1.5X
Production 150 Sets

Silver Materials

Cards (1-100): 1-2X
Production 75 Sets

Gold Materials

Cards (1-100): 1.5-2.5X
Production 50 Sets

Platinum Materials

No pricing due to scarcity.
Production 25 Sets

2003 Playoff Portraits Promos

To introduce its textured artwork issue, Playoff produced several types of promo cards. Two styles of white-bordered samples were issued; one has a blank-back and was distributed to dealers with ordering information, the other has a sample-marked back and was found one per box of Playoff Absolute. Otherwise unmarked promos with green top and bottom borders were distributed at All-Star FanFest, while similar promos with red top and bottom borders were handed out the Atlantic City National convention. Checklists for each of these styles are undetermined.

2003 Playoff Portraits Samples

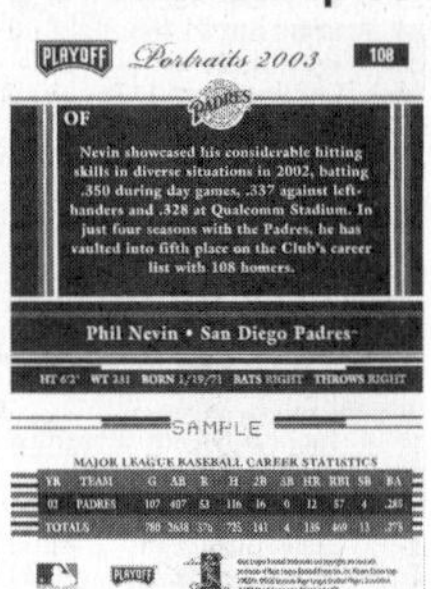

Each issue of the October 2003 Beckett Baseball Card Monthly included a sample 2003 Playoff Portraits card rubber-cemented inside. The cards differ from the issued version only in the appearance on back of a (usually) black dot-matrix printed "SAMPLE" notation. Some cards were produced with the overprint in silver, in much more limited quantities. The number of different players' cards involved in the promotion is unknown.

NM/M
Common Player: .10
Stars: 1.5-2X
Silvers: 10X

2003 Playoff Portraits

NM/M
Complete Set (144): 40.00
Common Player: .25
Pack (7): 4.00
Box (20): 60.00
1 Vladimir Guerrero 1.50
2 Luis Gonzalez .35
3 Andruw Jones 1.50
4 Manny Ramirez 1.50
5 Derek Jeter 4.00
6 Eric Hinske .25
7 Curt Schilling .45
8 Adam Dunn 1.00
9 Jason Jennings .25
10 Mike Piazza 2.50
11 Jason Giambi .75
12 Jeff Bagwell 1.50
13 Rickey Henderson 1.50
14 Randy Johnson 1.50
15 Roger Clemens 3.00
16 Troy Glaus 1.50
17 Hideo Nomo 1.50
18 Joe Borchard .25
19 Torii Hunter .25
20 Lance Berkman .25
21 Todd Helton 1.50
22 Mike Mussina .40
23 Vernon Wells .25
24 Pat Burrell .50
25 Ichiro Suzuki 2.50
26 Shawn Green .50
27 Frank Thomas 1.50
28 Barry Zito .40
29 Barry Bonds 4.00
30 Ken Griffey Jr. 2.50
31 Albert Pujols 3.00
32 Roberto Alomar .50
33 Barry Larkin .25
34 Tony Gwynn 2.00
35 Chipper Jones 2.00
36 Pedro J. Martinez 1.50
37 Juan Gonzalez 1.50
38 Greg Maddux 2.00
39 Tim Hudson .35
40 Sammy Sosa 2.50
41 Victor Martinez .50
42 Mark Buehrle .25
43 Austin Kearns .25
44 Kerry Wood 1.00
45 Nomar Garciaparra 2.50
46 Alfonso Soriano 1.00
47 Mark Prior 1.50
48 Richie Sexson .25
49 Mark Teixeira .75
50 Craig Biggio .25
51 Rafael Palmeiro 1.00
52 Carlos Beltran .75
53 Bernie Williams .35
54 Eric Chavez .35
55 Paul Konerko .35
56 Nolan Ryan 4.00
57 Mark Mulder .25
58 Miguel Tejada .35
59 Roy Oswalt .25
60 Jim Edmonds .25
61 Ryan Klesko .25
62 Cal Ripken Jr. 4.00
63 Josh Beckett .25
64 Kazuhisa Ishii .25
65 Alex Rodriguez 3.00
66 Mike Sweeney .25
67 C.C. Sabathia .25
68 Jose Vidro .25
69 Magglio Ordonez .25
70 Carlos Delgado .75
71 Jorge Posada .25
72 Bobby Abreu .25
73 Brian Giles .25
74 Kirby Puckett 2.00
75 Yogi Berra 1.00
76 Ryne Sandberg 2.00
77 Tom Glavine .45
78 Jim Thome 1.00
79 Chris Snelling .25
80 Drew Henson .25
81 Junior Spivey .25
82 Mike Schmidt 3.00
83 Jeff Kent .25
84 Stan Musial 2.00
85 Garret Anderson .25
86 Jose Contreras **RC** 3.00
87 Ivan Rodriguez 1.00
88 Hideki Matsui **RC** 6.00
89 Don Mattingly 3.00
90 Angel Berroa .25
91 George Brett 3.00
92 Jermaine Dye .25
93 John Olerud .25
94 Josh Phelps .25
95 Sean Casey .35
96 Larry Walker .25
97 Jason Lane .25
98 Travis Hafner .25
99 Terrence Long .25
100 Shannon Stewart .25
101 Richard Hidalgo .25
102 Joe Thurston .25
103 Ben Sheets .25
104 Orlando Cabrera .25
105 Aramis Ramirez .25
106 So Taguchi .25
107 Frank Robinson .75
108 Phil Nevin .25
109 Dennis Tankersley .25
110 J.D. Drew .50
111 Paul LoDuca .50
112 Ozzie Smith 2.00
113 Carlos Lee .25
114 Nick Johnson .25
115 Edgar Martinez .25
116 Hank Blalock .75
117 Orlando Hudson .25
118 Corey Patterson .25
119 Steve Carlton .50
120 Wade Miller .25
121 Adrian Beltre .75
122 Scott Rolen 1.00
123 Brian Lawrence .25
124 Rich Aurilia .25
125 Tsuyoshi Shinjo .25
126 John Buck .25
127 Marlon Byrd .25
128 Michael Cuddyer .25
129 Marshall McDougall .25
130 Travis Chapman .25
131 Jose Morban .25
132 Adam LaRoche .25
133 Jose Castillo .25
134 Walter Young .25
135 Jeff Baker .25
136 Jeremy Guthrie .25
137 Pedro J. Martinez .75
138 Randy Johnson .75
139 Alex Rodriguez 1.50
140 Hideo Nomo .50
141 Roger Clemens 1.00
142 Rickey Henderson .50
143 Jason Giambi .40
144 Mike Piazza 1.00

Artifacts Bronze

NM/M
Common Player: 4.00
Production 100 or less.
Silvers: 1-1.5X
Production 50 or less.
Golds: No Pricing
Production 25 or less.
Bronze Combos: 1-1.5X
Production 50 or less.
Silver Combos: No Pricing
Production 25 or less.
Gold Combos: No Pricing
Production 10 or less.
1 Vladimir Guerrero/100 8.00
2 Luis Gonzalez/100 5.00
3 Andruw Jones/100 8.00
4 Manny Ramirez/50 10.00
5 Derek Jeter/100 20.00
6 Eric Hinske/100 4.00
7 Curt Schilling/100 8.00
8 Adam Dunn/50 10.00
9 Jason Jennings/100 4.00
10 Mike Piazza/100 12.00
11 Jason Giambi/100 6.00
12 Jeff Bagwell/50 15.00
13 Rickey Henderson/50 20.00
14 Randy Johnson/100 8.00
15 Roger Clemens/100 20.00
16 Troy Glaus/100 6.00
17 Hideo Nomo/100 20.00
19 Torii Hunter/100 6.00
20 Lance Berkman/100 6.00
21 Todd Helton/50 15.00
22 Mike Mussina/100 8.00
23 Vernon Wells/100 4.00
24 Pat Burrell/100 6.00
25 Ichiro Suzuki/100 25.00
26 Shawn Green/100 6.00
27 Frank Thomas/100 10.00
28 Barry Zito/100 6.00
29 Barry Bonds/100 20.00
30 Ken Griffey Jr./100 15.00
31 Albert Pujols/100 20.00
32 Roberto Alomar/50 10.00
33 Barry Larkin/50 10.00
34 Tony Gwynn/100 15.00
35 Chipper Jones/100 10.00
36 Pedro Martinez/100 10.00
37 Juan Gonzalez/50 10.00
38 Greg Maddux/100 15.00
39 Tim Hudson/100 6.00
40 Sammy Sosa/100 20.00
41 Victor Martinez/100 8.00
42 Mark Buehrle/50 6.00
43 Austin Kearns/100 6.00
44 Kerry Wood/50 15.00
45 Nomar Garciaparra/100 15.00
46 Alfonso Soriano/100 10.00
47 Mark Prior/100 10.00
48 Richie Sexson/100 6.00
49 Mark Teixeira/50 8.00
50 Craig Biggio/50 8.00
51 Rafael Palmeiro/50 10.00
52 Carlos Beltran/50 10.00
53 Bernie Williams/50 10.00
54 Eric Chavez/100 6.00
55 Paul Konerko/100 4.00
56 Nolan Ryan/100 35.00
57 Mark Mulder/100 6.00
58 Miguel Tejada/100 6.00
59 Roy Oswalt/50 8.00
60 Jim Edmonds/50 8.00
61 Ryan Klesko/50 6.00
62 Cal Ripken Jr/100 40.00
63 Josh Beckett/100 6.00
64 Kazuhisa Ishii/50 6.00
65 Alex Rodriguez/100 15.00
66 Mike Sweeney/100 4.00
67 C.C. Sabathia/100 4.00
68 Jose Vidro/100 4.00
69 Magglio Ordonez/50 6.00
70 Carlos Delgado/50 8.00
71 Jorge Posada/100 8.00
72 Bobby Abreu/100 6.00
74 Kirby Puckett/50 30.00
75 Yogi Berra/50 25.00
76 Ryne Sandberg/50 40.00
77 Tom Glavine/50 8.00
78 Jim Thome/100 10.00
79 Chris Snelling/50 5.00
80 Drew Henson/50 10.00
81 Junior Spivey/50 8.00
82 Mike Schmidt/50 50.00
83 Jeff Kent/50 6.00
84 Stan Musial/100 30.00
85 Garret Anderson/50 8.00
87 Ivan Rodriguez/50 12.00
88 Hideki Matsui/100 25.00
89 Don Mattingly/100 30.00
90 Angel Berroa/100 4.00
91 George Brett/50 50.00
92 Jermaine Dye/50 4.00
93 John Olerud/100 4.00
94 Josh Phelps/50 4.00
95 Sean Casey/50 4.00
96 Larry Walker/50 8.00
97 Jason Lane/50 4.00
98 Travis Hafner/100 6.00
99 Terrence Long/50 4.00
100 Shannon Stewart/50 4.00
101 Richard Hidalgo/50 4.00
102 Joe Thurston/100 4.00
103 Ben Sheets/100 6.00
104 Orlando Cabrera/50 6.00
105 Aramis Ramirez/100 6.00
106 So Taguchi/50 5.00
107 Frank Robinson/50 12.00
109 Dennis Tankersley/100 4.00
110 J.D. Drew/100 6.00
111 Paul LoDuca/50 6.00
112 Ozzie Smith/50 40.00
113 Carlos Lee/100 4.00
114 Nick Johnson/100 4.00
115 Edgar Martinez/100 8.00
116 Hank Blalock/50 15.00
117 Orlando Hudson/100 4.00
118 Corey Patterson/100 6.00
119 Steve Carlton/50 10.00
120 Wade Miller/50 6.00
121 Adrian Beltre/50 8.00
122 Scott Rolen/50 20.00
123 Brian Lawrence/50 4.00
124 Rich Aurilia/50 4.00
125 Tsuyoshi Shinjo/50 8.00
126 John Buck/50 4.00
127 Marlon Byrd/100 4.00
128 Michael Cuddyer/50 4.00
130 Travis Chapman/100 4.00
131 Jose Morban/100 4.00
132 Adam LaRoche/100 4.00
133 Jose Castillo/100 4.00
134 Walter Young/100 4.00

Beige

Beige: 1-30X
Production 250 Sets

Bronze

Bronze: 2-4X
Production 100 Sets

Bronze Autographs

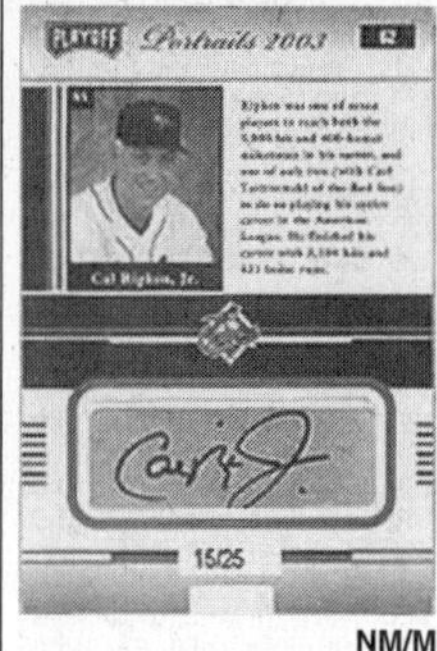

NM/M
Common Bronze Auto.:
Production 100 or less.
Silvers: 1-1.5X
Production 50 or less.
No Pricing for production 25 or less.
Golds: No Pricing
Production 25 or less.
1 Vladimir Guerrero/100 35.00
3 Andruw Jones/25 50.00
6 Eric Hinske/100 10.00
8 Adam Dunn/50 35.00
9 Jason Jennings/100 8.00
16 Troy Glaus/60 25.00
18 Joe Borchard/100 6.00
19 Torii Hunter/25 40.00
31 Albert Pujols/25 150.00
32 Roberto Alomar/100 35.00
33 Barry Larkin/95 25.00
34 Tony Gwynn/60 75.00
35 Chipper Jones/25 75.00
37 Juan Gonzalez/50 50.00
41 Victor Martinez/100 20.00
42 Mark Buehrle/100 10.00
44 Kerry Wood/40 40.00
47 Mark Prior/25 60.00
48 Richie Sexson/100 20.00
49 Mark Teixeira/25 40.00
50 Craig Biggio/25 40.00
56 Nolan Ryan/25 150.00
57 Mark Mulder/100 20.00
59 Roy Oswalt/40 25.00
61 Ryan Klesko/40 20.00
62 Cal Ripken Jr./25 150.00
67 C.C. Sabathia/50 15.00
72 Bobby Abreu/100 15.00
73 Brian Giles/50 15.00
74 Kirby Puckett/25 60.00
77 Tom Glavine/100 35.00
79 Chris Snelling/100 10.00
80 Drew Henson/25 40.00
81 Junior Spivey/100 10.00
82 Mike Schmidt/50 75.00
83 Jeff Kent/50 25.00
84 Stan Musial/50 65.00
85 Garret Anderson/25 30.00
86 Jose Contreras/50 40.00
89 Don Mattingly/50 90.00
90 Angel Berroa/100 10.00
92 Jermaine Dye/100 10.00
94 Josh Phelps/100 10.00
97 Jason Lane/100 8.00
98 Travis Hafner/100 12.00
99 Terrence Long/100 6.00
100 Shannon Stewart/100 8.00
101 Richard Hidalgo/25 20.00
102 Joe Thurston/100 8.00
103 Ben Sheets/100 15.00
105 Aramis Ramirez/40 15.00
106 So Taguchi/29 30.00
108 Phil Nevin/100 12.00
109 Dennis Tankersley/100 8.00
110 J.D. Drew/25 30.00
111 Paul LoDuca/100 15.00
113 Carlos Lee/100 10.00
114 Nick Johnson/100 10.00
115 Edgar Martinez/100 35.00
117 Orlando Hudson/100 8.00
118 Corey Patterson/100 15.00
119 Steve Carlton/25 40.00
120 Wade Miller/100 6.00
121 Adrian Beltre/25 30.00
122 Scott Rolen/100 30.00
123 Brian Lawrence/100 6.00
126 John Buck/100 6.00
127 Marlon Byrd/100 10.00
128 Michael Cuddyer/100 8.00
129 Marshall McDougall/100 6.00
130 Travis Chapman/100 6.00
131 Jose Morban/100 6.00
132 Adam LaRoche/100 12.00
133 Jose Castillo/100 6.00
134 Walter Young/100 6.00
135 Jeff Baker/100 6.00
136 Jeremy Guthrie/100 10.00

Silver Autographs

Production 50 or less.
Production 50 or less.

2003 Playoff Prestige Samples

Each issue of the July 2003 Beckett Baseball Card Monthly included a sample 2003 Playoff Prestige card rubber-cemented inside. The cards differ from the issued version only in the appearance on back of a (usually) silver-foil "SAMPLE" notation. Some cards were produced with the overprint in gold-foil, in much more limited quantities. The number of different players' cards involved in the promotion is unknown.

	NM/M
Common Player:	.10
Stars:	1.5-2X
Gold:	10X

2003 Playoff Prestige

	NM/M
Complete Set (200):	35.00
Common Player:	.15
Pack (6):	2.00
Box (24):	45.00

1 Darin Erstad .25
2 David Eckstein .15
3 Garret Anderson .15
4 Jarrod Washburn .15
5 Tim Salmon .25
6 Troy Glaus .75
7 Jay Gibbons .15
8 Marty Cordova .15
9 Melvin Mora .15
10 Rodrigo Lopez .15
11 Tony Batista .15
12 Cliff Floyd .15
13 Derek Lowe .15
14 Johnny Damon .30
15 Manny Ramirez .75
16 Nomar Garciaparra 1.50
17 Pedro J. Martinez .75
18 Rickey Henderson .75
19 Shea Hillenbrand .15
20 Carlos Lee .15
21 Frank Thomas .75
22 Magglio Ordonez .15
23 Mark Buehrle .15
24 Paul Konerko .15
25 C.C. Sabathia .15
26 Danys Baez .15
27 Ellis Burks .15
28 Travis Hafner .15
29 Omar Vizquel .15
30 Bobby Higginson .15
31 Carlos Pena .15
32 Mark Redman .15
33 Robert Fick .15
34 Steve Sparks .15
35 Carlos Beltran .50
36 Joe Randa .15
37 Mike Sweeney .15
38 Paul Byrd .15
39 Raul Ibanez .15
40 Runelvys Hernandez .15
41 Brad Radke .15
42 Corey Koskie .15
43 Cristian Guzman .15
44 David Ortiz .35
45 Doug Mientkiewicz .15
46 Dustan Mohr .15
47 Jacque Jones .15
48 Torii Hunter .15
49 Alfonso Soriano .75
50 Andy Pettitte .30
51 Bernie Williams .30
52 David Wells .15
53 Derek Jeter 2.00
54 Jason Giambi .50
55 Jeff Weaver .15
56 Jorge Posada .15
57 Mike Mussina .35
58 Roger Clemens 1.25
59 Barry Zito .25
60 David Justice .15
61 Eric Chavez .30
62 Jermaine Dye .15
63 Mark Mulder .15
64 Miguel Tejada .30
65 Ray Durham .15
66 Tim Hudson .30
67 Bret Boone .15
68 Chris Snelling .15
69 Edgar Martinez .15
70 Freddy Garcia .15
71 Ichiro Suzuki 1.50
72 Jamie Moyer .15
73 John Olerud .15
74 Kazuhiro Sasaki .15
75 Aubrey Huff .15
76 Joe Kennedy .15
77 Paul Wilson .15
78 Alex Rodriguez 1.75
79 Chan Ho Park .15
80 Hank Blalock .50
81 Ivan Rodriguez .65
82 Juan Gonzalez .75
83 Kevin Mench .15
84 Rafael Palmeiro .65
85 Carlos Delgado .40
86 Eric Hinske .15
87 Jose Cruz .15
88 Josh Phelps .15
89 Roy Halladay .15
90 Shannon Stewart .15
91 Vernon Wells .15
92 Curt Schilling .40
93 Junior Spivey .15
94 Luis Gonzalez .25
95 Mark Grace .25
96 Randy Johnson .75
97 Andruw Jones .75
98 Chipper Jones 1.00
99 Gary Sheffield .40
100 Greg Maddux 1.00
101 John Smoltz .15
102 Kevin Millwood .15
103 Mike Hampton .15
104 Corey Patterson .15
105 Fred McGriff .15
106 Kerry Wood .65
107 Mark Prior .75
108 Moises Alou .15
109 Sammy Sosa 1.50
110 Adam Dunn .50
111 Austin Kearns .15
112 Barry Larkin .15
113 Ken Griffey Jr. 1.50
114 Sean Casey .30
115 Jason Jennings .15
116 Jay Payton .15
117 Larry Walker .15
118 Todd Helton .75
119 A.J. Burnett .15
120 Josh Beckett .15
121 Juan Encarnacion .15
122 Mike Lowell .15
123 Craig Biggio .15
124 Daryle Ward .15
125 Jeff Bagwell .75
126 Lance Berkman .15
127 Roy Oswalt .15
128 Adrian Beltre .35
129 Hideo Nomo .75
130 Kazuhisa Ishii .15
131 Kevin Brown .15
132 Odalis Perez .15
133 Paul LoDuca .15
134 Shawn Green .35
135 Jeff Kent .15
136 Ben Sheets .15
137 Jeffrey Hammonds .15
138 Jose Hernandez .15
139 Richie Sexson .15
140 Bartolo Colon .15
141 Brad Wilkerson .15
142 Javier Vazquez .15
143 Jose Vidro .15
144 Michael Barrett .15
145 Vladimir Guerrero .75
146 Al Leiter .15
147 Mike Piazza 1.50
148 Mo Vaughn .15
149 Pedro Astacio .15
150 Roberto Alomar .40
151 Roger Cedeno .15
152 Tom Glavine .40
153 Bobby Abreu .15
154 Jimmy Rollins .25
155 Mike Lieberthal .15
156 Pat Burrell .35
157 Vicente Padilla .15
158 Jim Thome .65
159 Aramis Ramirez .15
160 Brian Giles .15
161 Jason Kendall .15
162 Josh Fogg .15
163 Kip Wells .15
164 Mark Kotsay .15
165 Oliver Perez .15
166 Phil Nevin .15
167 Ryan Klesko .15
168 Sean Burroughs .15
169 Trevor Hoffman .15
170 Barry Bonds 2.00
171 Benito Santiago .15
172 Reggie Sanders .15
173 Rich Aurilia .15
174 Russ Ortiz .15
175 Albert Pujols 1.75
176 J.D. Drew .25
177 Jim Edmonds .15
178 Matt Morris .15
179 Tino Martinez .15
180 Scott Rolen .65
181 Joe Borchard .15
182 Freddy Sanchez .15
183 Jose Contreras **RC** 3.00
184 Jeff Baker .15
185 Ryan Church .15
186 Mario Ramos .15
187 Corwin Malone .15
188 Jimmy Gobble .15
189 Jon Adkins .15
190 Tim Kalita .15
191 Nelson Castro .15
192 Colin Young .15
193 Luis Martinez .15
194 Todd Donovan .15
195 Jeremy Ward .15
196 Wilson Valdez .15
197 Hideki Matsui **RC** 6.00
198 Mitch Wylie .15
199 Adam Walker .15
200 Clifford Bartosh .15

X-tra Points

Stars (1-180):	4-8X
Production 150	
Prospects (181-200):	4-8X
Production 50	

Award Winners

	NM/M
Complete Set (15):	25.00
Common Player:	1.00
#'d to year of award	

1 Barry Zito 1.00
2 Barry Bonds 5.00
3 Randy Johnson 1.50
4 Roger Clemens 2.50
5 Ichiro Suzuki 3.00
6 Chipper Jones 2.00
7 Ken Griffey Jr. 3.00
8 Miguel Tejada 1.00
9 Greg Maddux 2.00
10 Jeff Bagwell 1.50
11 Rickey Henderson 1.50
12 Tom Glavine 1.00
13 Albert Pujols 4.00
14 Nomar Garciaparra 3.00
15 Derek Jeter 5.00

Connections

	NM/M
Complete Set (70):	90.00
Common Duo:	1.00
Inserted 1:8	
Century Connections:	3-6X
Production 100 Sets	

1 Troy Glaus, Garret Anderson 1.50
2 Troy Glaus, Tim Salmon 1.50
3 Randy Johnson, Curt Schilling 1.50
4 Matt Williams, Luis Gonzalez 1.00
5 Greg Maddux, John Smoltz 2.00
6 Andruw Jones, Chipper Jones 2.00
7 Greg Maddux, Kevin Millwood 2.00
8 Tony Batista, Geronimo Gil 1.00
9 Pedro J. Martinez, Nomar Garciaparra 3.00
10 Manny Ramirez, Nomar Garciaparra 3.00
11 Nomar Garciaparra, Rickey Henderson 3.00
12 Trot Nixon, Manny Ramirez 1.50
13 Kerry Wood, Mark Prior 1.00
14 Sammy Sosa, Fred McGriff 3.00
15 Sammy Sosa, Corey Patterson 3.00
16 Frank Thomas, Magglio Ordonez 1.50
17 Joe Borchard, Magglio Ordonez 1.00
18 Adam Dunn, Austin Kearns 1.00
19 Barry Larkin, Ken Griffey Jr. 3.00
20 Adam Dunn, Barry Larkin 1.00
21 Adam Dunn, Ken Griffey Jr. 3.00
22 Victor Martinez, Omar Vizquel 1.00
23 C.C. Sabathia, Victor Martinez 1.00
24 Larry Walker, Todd Helton 1.00
25 Carlos Pena, Robert Fick 1.00
26 Josh Beckett, Juan Encarnacion 1.00
27 Jeff Bagwell, Craig Biggio 1.50
28 Lance Berkman, Roy Oswalt 1.00
29 Lance Berkman, Jeff Bagwell 1.50
30 Mike Sweeney, Carlos Beltran 1.00
31 Mike Sweeney, Angel Berroa 1.00
32 Kazuhisa Ishii, Shawn Green 1.00
33 Adrian Beltre, Shawn Green 1.00
34 Kazuhisa Ishii, Hideo Nomo 1.50
35 Richie Sexson, Ben Sheets 1.00
36 Jacque Jones, Torii Hunter 1.00
37 Doug Mientkiewicz, David Ortiz 1.00
38 Vladimir Guerrero, Jose Vidro 1.50
39 Derek Jeter, Jason Giambi 5.00
40 Derek Jeter, Bernie Williams 5.00
41 Roger Clemens, Mike Mussina 2.50
42 Alfonso Soriano, Jorge Posada 1.50
43 Derek Jeter, Alfonso Soriano 5.00
44 Mike Piazza, Roberto Alomar 3.00
45 Mike Piazza, Mo Vaughn 3.00
46 Eric Chavez, Miguel Tejada 1.00
47 Mark Mulder, Barry Zito 1.00
48 Tim Hudson, Barry Zito 1.00
49 Pat Burrell, Bobby Abreu 1.00
50 Jim Thome, Pat Burrell 1.00
51 Jim Thome, Marlon Byrd 1.00
52 Brian Giles, Aramis Ramirez 1.00
53 Ryan Klesko, Phil Nevin 1.00
54 Barry Bonds, Benito Santiago 5.00
55 Jeff Kent, Rich Aurilia 1.00
56 Barry Bonds, Jeff Kent 5.00
57 Ichiro Suzuki, Kazuhiro Sasaki 3.00
58 Edgar Martinez, John Olerud 1.00
59 Albert Pujols, Scott Rolen 4.00
60 Jim Edmonds, J.D. Drew 1.00
61 Albert Pujols, Jim Edmonds 4.00
62 Dewon Brazelton, Joe Kennedy 1.00
63 Alex Rodriguez, Ivan Rodriguez 4.00
64 Juan Gonzalez, Rafael Palmeiro 1.50
65 Mark Teixeira, Hank Blalock 1.00
66 Alex Rodriguez, Juan Gonzalez 4.00
67 Alex Rodriguez, Juan Gonzalez 4.00
68 Shannon Stewart, Carlos Delgado 1.00
69 Josh Phelps, Eric Hinske 1.00
70 Vernon Wells, Roy Halladay 1.00

Material Connections

	NM/M
Common Duo:	4.00
Production 400 Sets	

1 Troy Glaus, Garret Anderson 8.00
2 Troy Glaus, Tim Salmon 8.00
4 Matt Williams, Luis Gonzalez 6.00
5 Greg Maddux, John Smoltz 12.00
6 Andruw Jones, Chipper Jones 12.00
7 Greg Maddux, Kevin Millwood 12.00
8 Tony Batista, Geronimo Gil 4.00
9 Pedro J. Martinez, Nomar Garciaparra 15.00
10 Manny Ramirez, Nomar Garciaparra 15.00
11 Nomar Garciaparra, Rickey Henderson 15.00
12 Trot Nixon, Manny Ramirez 10.00
13 Kerry Wood, Mark Prior 10.00
14 Sammy Sosa, Fred McGriff 10.00
15 Sammy Sosa, Corey Patterson 10.00
16 Frank Thomas, Magglio Ordonez 8.00
17 Joe Borchard, Magglio Ordonez 6.00
18 Adam Dunn, Austin Kearns 20.00
20 Adam Dunn, Barry Larkin 15.00
22 Victor Martinez, Omar Vizquel 4.00
23 C.C. Sabathia, Victor Martinez 6.00
24 Larry Walker, Todd Helton 8.00
26 Josh Beckett, Juan Encarnacion 8.00
27 Jeff Bagwell, Craig Biggio 10.00
28 Lance Berkman, Roy Oswalt 8.00
29 Lance Berkman, Jeff Bagwell 10.00
30 Mike Sweeney, Carlos Beltran 8.00
31 Mike Sweeney, Angel Berroa 4.00
32 Kazuhisa Ishii, Shawn Green 10.00
33 Adrian Beltre, Shawn Green 6.00
34 Kazuhisa Ishii, Hideo Nomo 25.00
35 Richie Sexson, Ben Sheets 8.00
36 Jacque Jones, Torii Hunter 10.00
37 Doug Mientkiewicz, David Ortiz 6.00
38 Vladimir Guerrero, Jose Vidro 10.00
39 Derek Jeter, Jason Giambi 15.00
40 Derek Jeter, Bernie Williams 15.00
41 Roger Clemens, Mike Mussina 20.00
42 Alfonso Soriano, Jorge Posada 10.00
43 Derek Jeter, Alfonso Soriano 20.00
44 Mike Piazza, Roberto Alomar 15.00
45 Mike Piazza, Mo Vaughn 10.00
46 Eric Chavez, Miguel Tejada 8.00
47 Mark Mulder, Barry Zito 10.00
48 Tim Hudson, Barry Zito 10.00
49 Pat Burrell, Bobby Abreu 8.00
50 Jim Thome, Pat Burrell 10.00
51 Jim Thome, Marlon Byrd 10.00
52 Brian Giles, Aramis Ramirez 6.00
53 Ryan Klesko, Phil Nevin 6.00
54 Barry Bonds, Benito Santiago 12.00
55 Jeff Kent, Rich Aurilia 5.00
56 Barry Bonds, Jeff Kent 12.00
57 Ichiro Suzuki, Kazuhiro Sasaki 25.00
58 Edgar Martinez, John Olerud 8.00
59 Albert Pujols, Scott Rolen 15.00
60 Jim Edmonds, J.D. Drew 8.00
61 Albert Pujols, Jim Edmonds 12.00
62 Dewon Brazelton, Joe Kennedy 8.00
63 Alex Rodriguez, Ivan Rodriguez 12.00
64 Juan Gonzalez, Rafael Palmeiro 8.00
65 Mark Teixeira, Hank Blalock 10.00
66 Alex Rodriguez, Juan Gonzalez 15.00
67 Alex Rodriguez, Juan Gonzalez 12.00
68 Shannon Stewart, Carlos Delgado 6.00
69 Josh Phelps, Eric Hinske 4.00
70 Vernon Wells, Roy Halladay 4.00

Diamond Heritage

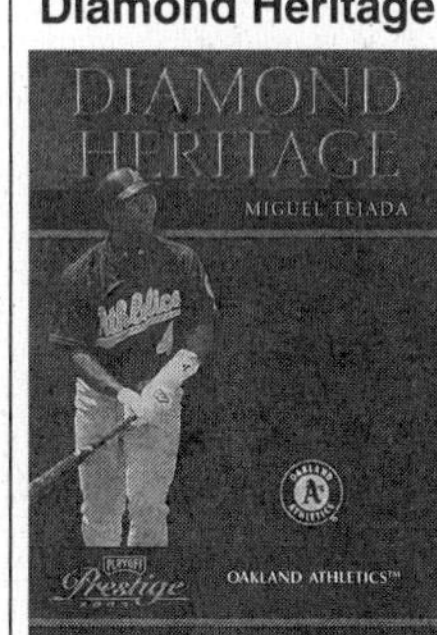

	NM/M
Complete Set (30):	35.00
Common Player:	1.00
Inserted 1:21	
Golds:	5-10X
Production 50 Sets	

1 Larry Walker 1.00
2 Troy Glaus 1.50
3 Magglio Ordonez 1.00
4 Roy Oswalt 1.00
5 Barry Zito 1.00
6 Nomar Garciaparra 3.00
7 Kerry Wood 1.25
8 Roger Clemens 2.50
9 Pedro J. Martinez 1.50
10 Mark Prior 1.00
11 Sammy Sosa 3.00
12 Randy Johnson 1.50
13 Greg Maddux 2.00
14 Manny Ramirez 1.50
15 Torii Hunter 1.00
16 Alex Rodriguez 4.00
17 Mike Piazza 3.00
18 Vladimir Guerrero 1.50
19 Ivan Rodriguez 1.25
20 Lance Berkman 1.00
21 Miguel Tejada 1.00
22 Chipper Jones 2.00
23 Todd Helton 1.50
24 Shawn Green 1.00
25 Scott Rolen 1.25
26 Adam Dunn 1.25
27 Jim Thome 1.25
28 Rafael Palmeiro 1.25
29 Eric Chavez 1.00
30 Andruw Jones 1.50

Diamond Heritage Materials

	NM/M
Common Player:	5.00
Production 200 unless noted.	
Autographs:	No Pricing
Production 15 to 25	

1 Larry Walker 6.00
2 Troy Glaus 6.00
3 Magglio Ordonez 5.00
4 Roy Oswalt 5.00
5 Barry Zito 8.00
6 Nomar Garciaparra 15.00
7 Kerry Wood 8.00
8 Roger Clemens 15.00
9 Pedro J. Martinez 10.00
10 Mark Prior 6.00
11 Sammy Sosa 15.00
12 Randy Johnson 10.00

13	Greg Maddux	10.00
14	Manny Ramirez	8.00
15	Torii Hunter	10.00
16	Alex Rodriguez/Bat/100	15.00
17	Mike Piazza/Bat/100	15.00
18	V. Guerrero/Bat/100	10.00
19	Ivan Rodriguez/Bat/100	10.00
20	Lance Berkman/Bat/100	8.00
21	Miguel Tejada/Bat/100	8.00
22	Chipper Jones/Bat/100	15.00
23	Todd Helton/Bat/100	10.00
24	Shawn Green/Bat/100	8.00
25	Scott Rolen/Bat/100	15.00
26	Adam Dunn/Bat/100	12.00
27	Jim Thome/Bat/100	10.00
28	Rafael Palmeiro/Bat/100	10.00
29	Eric Chavez/Bat/100	8.00
30	Andruw Jones/Bat/100	8.00

Diamond Heritage Material Autograph

Quantity produced listed

Draft Class Reunion

		NM/M
Complete Set (10):		20.00
Common Player:		1.00
Inserted 1:24		
1	Mike Piazza, John Olerud	3.00
2	Derek Jeter, Shannon Stewart	5.00
3	Alex Rodriguez, Torii Hunter	4.00
4	Nomar Garciaparra, Paul Konerko	3.00
5	Kerry Wood, Todd Helton	1.50
6	Eric Chavez, Billy Koch	1.00
7	Lance Berkman, Troy Glaus	1.50
8	Pat Burrell, Mark Mulder	1.50
9	Barry Zito, Jason Jennings	1.00
10	Mark Prior, Mark Teixeira	1.50

Infield/Outfield Tandems Material

		NM/M
Common Duo:		8.00
Production 100 Sets		
1	Troy Glaus, Garret Anderson	10.00
2	Mark Grace, Luis Gonzalez	10.00
3	Nomar Garciaparra, Manny Ramirez	20.00
4	Alfonso Soriano, Bernie Williams	15.00
5	Jeff Bagwell, Lance Berkman	15.00
6	Alex Rodriguez, Juan Gonzalez	15.00
7	Barry Larkin, Adam Dunn	15.00
8	Scott Rolen, Jim Edmonds	20.00
9	Todd Helton, Larry Walker	10.00
10	Adrian Beltre, Shawn Green	10.00
11	Jose Vidro, Vladimir Guerrero	12.00
12	Mike Sweeney, Carlos Beltran	10.00
13	Josh Phelps, Vernon Wells	8.00
14	Paul Konerko, Magglio Ordonez	10.00
15	Phil Nevin, Ryan Klesko	10.00

Inside The Numbers

		NM/M
Complete Set (25):		35.00
Common Player:		1.00
Production 2,002 Sets		
Die-Cuts:		10-25X
#'d to jersey number		
1	Roger Clemens	2.50
2	Greg Maddux	2.00
3	Miguel Tejada	1.00
4	Alex Rodriguez	4.00
5	Ichiro Suzuki	2.50
6	Sammy Sosa	3.00
7	Jim Thome	1.50
8	Derek Jeter	5.00
9	Randy Johnson	1.50
10	Barry Zito	1.00
11	Jason Giambi	1.50
12	Shawn Green	1.00
13	Curt Schilling	1.00
14	Albert Pujols	4.00
15	Vladimir Guerrero	1.50
16	Pedro J. Martinez	1.50
17	Alfonso Soriano	1.50
18	Barry Bonds	5.00
19	Magglio Ordonez	1.00
20	Chipper Jones	2.00
21	Pat Burrell	1.00
22	Luis Gonzalez	1.00
23	Jeff Bagwell	1.50
24	Garret Anderson	1.00
25	Larry Walker	1.00

League Leaders

		NM/M
Complete Set (15):		25.00
Common Player:		1.00
Production 2,002 Sets		
1	Manny Ramirez	2.00
2	Sammy Sosa	3.00
3	Alex Rodriguez	4.00
4	Alfonso Soriano	2.00
5	Vladimir Guerrero	2.00
6	Nomar Garciaparra	3.00
7	Johnny Damon	1.00
8	Alfonso Soriano	2.00
9	Barry Bonds	5.00
10	Barry Zito	1.00
11	Pedro J. Martinez	2.00
12	John Smoltz	1.00
13	Randy Johnson	2.00
14	Lance Berkman	1.00
15	Randy Johnson	2.00

League Leaders Materials

		NM/M
Common Player:		4.00
Production 250 Sets		
1	Manny Ramirez/Jsy	8.00
2	Sammy Sosa/Base	8.00
3	Alex Rodriguez/Jsy	10.00
4	Alfonso Soriano/Jsy	10.00
5	Vladimir Guerrero/Jsy	8.00
6	Nomar Garciaparra/Jsy	10.00
7	Johnny Damon/Bat	4.00
8	Alfonso Soriano/Jsy	10.00
9	Barry Bonds/Base	12.00
10	Barry Zito/Jsy	6.00
11	Pedro J. Martinez/Jsy	10.00
12	John Smoltz	6.00
13	Randy Johnson/Jsy	10.00
14	Lance Berkman/Jsy	6.00
15	Randy Johnson/Jsy	10.00

Player Collection

		NM/M
Common Player:		4.00
Production 325 Sets		
1	Adam Dunn	8.00
2	Adrian Beltre	6.00
3	Alex Rodriguez	20.00
4	Alfonso Soriano	10.00
5	Andruw Jones	8.00
6	Andy Pettitte	6.00
7	Barry Larkin	4.00
8	Barry Zito	4.00
9	Ben Grieve	4.00
10	Bernie Williams	4.00
11	Cal Ripken Jr.	25.00
12	Carlos Delgado	5.00
13	C.C. Sabathia	4.00
14	Chipper Jones	12.00
15	Craig Biggio	4.00
16	Curt Schilling	5.00
17	Alex Rodriguez	20.00
18	Frank Thomas	8.00
19	Freddy Garcia	4.00
20	Jay Bell	4.00
21	Roger Clemens	15.00
22	Tony Gwynn	12.00
23	Ivan Rodriguez	8.00
24	Jason Giambi	8.00
25	Jason Jennings	4.00
26	Jay Payton	4.00
27	J.D. Drew	6.00
28	Jeff Bagwell	8.00
29	Jeromy Burnitz	4.00
30	Jim Edmonds	4.00
31	Jim Thome	8.00
32	Joe Borchard	4.00
33	Joe Mays	4.00
34	John Olerud	4.00
35	David Wells	4.00
36	Juan Gonzalez	8.00
37	Kazuhiro Sasaki	4.00
38	Chan Ho Park	4.00
39	Kerry Wood	8.00
40	Kevin Brown	4.00
41	Lance Berkman	4.00
42	Larry Walker	4.00
43	Bret Boone	4.00
44	Magglio Ordonez	4.00
45	Manny Ramirez	8.00
46	Mark Mulder	4.00
47	Mark Prior	6.00
48	Matt Williams	4.00
49	Miguel Tejada	4.00
50	Mike Piazza	15.00
51	Nomar Garciaparra	15.00
52	Doug Davis	4.00
53	Paul Konerko	4.00
54	Paul LoDuca	4.00
55	Pedro J. Martinez	8.00
56	Preston Wilson	4.00
57	Rafael Palmeiro	8.00
58	Marlon Byrd	4.00
59	Reggie Sanders	4.00
60	Richie Sexson	4.00
61	Rickey Henderson	10.00
62	Rickey Henderson	10.00
63	Robert Person	4.00
64	Jeff Bagwell	8.00
65	Roger Clemens	15.00
66	Roy Oswalt	4.00
67	Ryan Klesko	4.00
68	Sammy Sosa	15.00
69	Shawn Green	5.00
70	Steve Finley	4.00
71	Terrence Long	4.00
72	Tim Hudson	4.00
73	Toby Hall	4.00
74	Todd Helton	8.00
75	Travis Lee	4.00
76	Troy Glaus	8.00
77	Tsuyoshi Shinjo	4.00
78	Vernon Wells	4.00
79	Vladimir Guerrero	8.00
80	Wes Helms	4.00
81	Alex Rodriguez	20.00
82	Alfonso Soriano	10.00
83	Barry Larkin	4.00
84	Roberto Alomar	5.00
85	Ivan Rodriguez	8.00
86	Jason Giambi	6.00
87	Jeff Bagwell	8.00
88	Juan Gonzalez	8.00
89	Larry Walker	4.00
90	Luis Gonzalez	4.00
91	Magglio Ordonez	4.00
92	Manny Ramirez	8.00
93	Marlon Byrd	4.00
94	Mike Piazza	15.00
95	Pat Burrell	6.00
96	Todd Helton	8.00
97	Rickey Henderson	10.00
98	Andruw Jones	8.00
99	Craig Biggio	4.00
100	Mark Prior	6.00

Signature Impressions

		NM/M
Varying quantities produced		
1	A.J. Pierzynski/50	20.00
2	Adam Dunn/25	60.00
3	Barry Zito/25	50.00
4	Bobby Abreu/20	30.00
5	Brandon Phillips/25	25.00
7	Don Mattingly/15	250.00
9	Eric Hinske/25	25.00
12	John Candelaria/50	15.00
16	Lance Berkman/25	30.00
18	Miguel Tejada/25	40.00
22	Roy Oswalt/25	30.00
27	Yogi Berra/15	100.00
28	Joe Kennedy/50	10.00
30	Lenny Dykstra/50	25.00
39	Toby Hall/50	10.00
40	Victor Martinez/25	45.00
46	Brian Giles/15	40.00
50	Jeremy Bonderman/100	35.00

Stars of MLB

		NM/M
Common Player:		5.00
Production 150 Sets		
Patches:		4-8X
Production 25 Sets		
Autographs:		No Pricing
Production 25		
Patch Autographs:		No Pricing
Production 5 to 10		
1	Roger Clemens	12.00
2	Randy Johnson	8.00
3	Sammy Sosa	12.00
4	Vladimir Guerrero	8.00
5	Lance Berkman	5.00
6	Alfonso Soriano	8.00
7	Alex Rodriguez	15.00
8	Roberto Alomar	6.00
9	Miguel Tejada	5.00
10	Pedro J. Martinez	8.00
11	Greg Maddux	10.00
12	Barry Zito	5.00
13	Magglio Ordonez	5.00
14	Chipper Jones	10.00
15	Manny Ramirez	8.00
16	Troy Glaus	8.00
17	Pat Burrell	6.00
18	Roy Oswalt	5.00
19	Mike Piazza	12.00
20	Nomar Garciaparra	12.00

2004 Playoff Absolute Memorabilia

		NM/M
Complete Set (250):		
Common Player (1-200):		1.50
Production 1,349		
Common Non-Auto. (201-250):		2.00
Production 1,000		
Common Auto. (201-250):		8.00
Production 500-700		
Pack (4):		40.00
Box (6):		185.00
1	Troy Glaus	2.00
2	Garret Anderson	2.00
3	Tim Salmon	2.00
4	Bartolo Colon	1.50
5	Troy Percival	1.50
6	Nolan Ryan/Angels	10.00
7	Vladimir Guerrero	4.00
8	Richie Sexson	2.00
9	Shea Hillenbrand	1.50
10	Luis Gonzalez	1.50
11	Brandon Webb	1.50
12	Randy Johnson	4.00
13	Robby Hammock	1.50
14	Edgar Gonzalez	1.50
15	Roberto Alomar	3.00
16	Andruw Jones	3.00
17	Chipper Jones	4.00
18	Dale Murphy	2.00
19	Rafael Furcal	1.50
20	J.D. Drew	2.00
21	Bubba Nelson	1.50
22	Julio Franco	1.50
23	Adam LaRoche	1.50
24	Michael Hessman	1.50
25	Warren Spahn	3.00
26	Jay Gibbons	1.50
27	Cal Ripken Jr.	10.00
28	Miguel Tejada	2.50
29	Adam Loewen	1.50
30	Rafael Palmeiro	3.00
31	Javy Lopez	2.00
32	Luis Matos	1.50
33	Jason Varitek	2.00
34	Carl Yastrzemski	3.00
35	Manny Ramirez	3.00
36	Trot Nixon	2.00
37	Curt Schilling	3.00
38	Pedro J. Martinez	4.00
39	Nomar Garciaparra	5.00
40	Luis Tiant	1.50
41	Kevin Youkilis	1.50
42	Michel Hernandez	1.50
43	Sammy Sosa	5.00
44	Greg Maddux	4.00
45	Kerry Wood	4.00
46	Mark Prior	4.00
47	Ernie Banks	4.00
48	Aramis Ramirez	2.00
49	Brendan Harris	1.50
50	Todd Wellemeyer	1.50
51	Frank Thomas	3.00
52	Magglio Ordonez	2.00
53	Carlos Lee	1.50
54	Joe Crede	1.50
55	Joe Borchard	1.50
56	Mark Buehrle	1.50
57	Sean Casey	2.00
58	Adam Dunn	2.50
59	Austin Kearns	2.00
60	Ken Griffey Jr.	5.00
61	Barry Larkin	2.00
62	Ryan Wagner	1.50
63	Jody Gerut	1.50
64	Jeremy Guthrie	1.50
65	Travis Hafner	2.00
66	Brian Tallet	1.50
67	Todd Helton	3.00
68	Preston Wilson	1.50
69	Jeff Baker	1.50
70	Clint Barmes	1.50
71	Joe Kennedy	1.50
72	Jack Morris	1.50
73	George Kell	1.50
74	Preston Larrison	1.50
75	Dmitri Young	1.50
76	Ivan Rodriguez	3.00
77	Dontrelle Willis	2.00
78	Josh Beckett	2.50
79	Miguel Cabrera	4.00
80	Mike Lowell	2.00
81	Luis Castillo	1.50
82	Juan Pierre	1.50
83	Jeff Bagwell	3.00
84	Jeff Kent	2.00
85	Craig Biggio	2.00
86	Lance Berkman	2.00
87	Andy Pettitte	2.00
88	Roy Oswalt	2.00
89	Chris Burke	1.50
90	Jason Lane	1.50
91	Roger Clemens	6.00
92	Mike Sweeney	1.50
93	Carlos Beltran	2.00
94	Angel Berroa	1.50
95	Juan Gonzalez	2.50
96	Ken Harvey	1.50
97	Byron Gettis	1.50
98	Alexis Gomez	1.50
99	Ian Ferguson	1.50
100	Duke Snider	3.00
101	Shawn Green	2.00
102	Hideo Nomo	2.00
103	Kazuhisa Ishii	1.50
104	Edwin Jackson	1.50
105	Fred McGriff	2.00
106	Hong-Chih Kou	1.50
107	Don Sutton **RC**	2.00
108	Rickey Henderson	2.00
109	Cesar Izturis	1.50
110	Robin Ventura	1.50
111	Paul LoDuca	1.50
112	Rickie Weeks	2.00
113	Scott Podsednik	2.00
114	Junior Spivey	1.50
115	Lyle Overbay	2.00
116	Tony Oliva	1.50
117	Jacque Jones	1.50
118	Shannon Stewart	1.50
119	Torii Hunter	2.00
120	Johan Santana	1.50
121	J.D. Durbin	1.50
122	Jason Kubel	1.50
123	Michael Cuddyer	1.50
124	Nick Johnson	1.50
125	Jose Vidro	1.50
126	Orlando Cabrera	1.50
127	Zach Day	1.50
128	Mike Piazza	5.00
129	Tom Glavine	2.00
130	Jae Weong Seo	1.50
131	Gary Carter	2.00
132	Phil Seibel	1.50
133	Edwin Almonte	1.50
134	Aaron Boone	1.50
135	Kenny Lofton	2.00
136	Don Mattingly	6.00
137	Jason Giambi	3.00
138	Alex Rodriguez/Yanks	8.00
139	Jorge Posada	2.00
140	Bernie Williams	2.00
141	Hideki Matsui	5.00
142	Mike Mussina	2.00
143	Mariano Rivera	2.00
144	Gary Sheffield	2.00
145	Derek Jeter	8.00
146	Chien-Ming Wang	1.50
147	Javier Vazquez	1.50
148	Jose Contreras	1.50
149	Whitey Ford	2.00
150	Kevin Brown	2.00
151	Eric Chavez	2.00
152	Barry Zito	2.00
153	Mark Mulder	2.00
154	Tim Hudson	2.00
155	Rich Harden	1.50
156	Eric Byrnes	1.50
157	Jim Thome	4.00
158	Bobby Abreu	2.00
159	Marlon Byrd	1.50
160	Lenny Dykstra	1.50
161	Steve Carlton	2.00
162	Ryan Howard	2.00
163	Bobby Hill	1.50
164	Jose Castillo	1.50
165	Jay Payton	1.50
166	Ryan Klesko	1.50
167	Brian Giles	1.50
168	Henri Stanley	1.50
169	Jason Schmidt	2.00
170	Jerome Williams	1.50
171	J.T. Snow	1.50
172	Bret Boone	2.00
173	Edgar Martinez	2.00
174	Ichiro Suzuki	5.00
175	Jamie Moyer	1.50
176	Rich Aurilia	1.50
177	Chris Snelling	1.50
178	Scott Rolen	4.00
179	Albert Pujols	6.00
180	Jim Edmonds	2.00
181	Stan Musial	4.00
182	Dan Haren	1.50
183	Red Schoendienst	1.50
184	Aubrey Huff	1.50
185	Delmon Young	1.50
186	Rocco Baldelli	2.00
187	Dewon Brazelton	1.50
188	Mark Teixeira	2.50
189	Hank Blalock	3.00
190	Nolan Ryan Ranger	10.00
191	Alfonso Soriano	4.00
192	Michael Young	1.50
193	Vernon Wells	1.50
194	Roy Halladay	2.00
195	Carlos Delgado	2.50
196	Dustin McGowan	1.50
197	Josh Phelps	1.50
198	Alexis Rios	1.50
199	Eric Hinske	1.50
200	Josh Towers	1.50
201	Kazuo Matsui/1,000 **RC**	5.00
202	Fernando Nieve AU/500 **RC**	8.00
203	Mike Rouse/1,000	3.00
204	Dennis Sarfate AU/500 **RC**	8.00
205	Josh Labandeira AU/500 **RC**	8.00
206	Chris Oxspring AU/500 **RC**	8.00
207	Alfredo Simon/1,000 **RC**	2.00
208	Cory Sullivan AU/500 **RC**	8.00
209	Ruddy Yan AU/500 **RC**	8.00
210	Jason Bartlett AU/500 **RC**	8.00
211	Akinori Otsuka/1,000 **RC**	5.00
212	Lincoln Holdzkom/1,000 **RC**	2.00
213	Justin Leone/1,000 **RC**	4.00
214	Jorge Sequea AU/500 **RC**	8.00
215	John Gall/1,000 RC **RC**	3.00
216	Jerome Gamble/1,000 RC **RC**	2.00
217	Tim Bittner AU/500 **RC**	8.00
218	Ronny Cedeno AU/500 **RC**	12.00
219	Justin Hampson/1,000 RC **RC**	2.00
220	Ryan Wing AU/500	8.00
221	Mariano Gomez AU/500 **RC**	8.00
222	Carlos Vasquez/1,000 **RC**	2.00
223	Casey Daigle AU/500 RC **RC**	8.00
224	Renyel Pinto AU/500 **RC**	8.00
225	Chris Shelton AU/500 **RC**	25.00
226	Mike Gosling AU/700	8.00
227	Aarom Baldiris AU/700 **RC**	8.00
228	Ramon Ramirez AU/700 **RC**	8.00
229	Roberto Novoa AU/500 **RC**	8.00
230	Sean Henn AU/500	10.00
231	Jamie Brown AU/500 **RC**	8.00
232	Nick Regilio AU/500 **RC**	8.00
233	David Crouthers AU/700	8.00
234	Greg Dobbs AU/500 **RC**	8.00
235	Angel Chavez AU/500 **RC**	8.00
236	Willy Taveras AU/500 **RC**	20.00
237	Justin Knoedler AU/500 **RC**	8.00
238	Ian Snell AU/700 **RC**	20.00
239	Jason Frasor AU/500 **RC**	8.00
240	Jerry Gil AU/500 **RC**	8.00
241	Carlos Hines AU/500 **RC**	8.00
242	Ivan Ochoa AU/500 **RC**	8.00
243	Jose Capellan AU/700 **RC**	10.00
244	Onil Joseph AU/700 **RC**	8.00
245	Hector Gimenez AU/700 **RC**	8.00
246	Shawn Hill AU/700 **RC**	8.00
247	Freddy Guzman AU/700 **RC**	8.00
248	Graham Koonce AU/500	8.00
249	Ronald Belisario AU/500 **RC**	8.00
250	Merkin Valdez AU/700 **RC**	8.00

Retail

Cards (1-200):	.15X
1-200 are not serial numbered	

Spectrum Silver

Stars (1-200): 1-2X
Gold Auto. (201-250): .25-.4X
Non-Auto. (201-250): 1X
Production 100 Sets

Spectrum Gold

Stars (1-200): 2-4X
Gold Auto. (201-250): .5X
Non-Auto. (201-250): 1-2X
Production 50 Sets

Spectrum Platinum

No Pricing
Production One Set

Absolutely Ink

NM/M

Quantity produced listed
Spectrum: .75-1.5X
Production 1-25
No pricing 15 or less.

1 Adam Dunn/100 25.00
2 Al Kaline/100 25.00
3 Alan Trammell/100 15.00
6 Andre Dawson/ Cubs/100 15.00
7 Andre Dawson/ Expos/100 15.00
8 Andruw Jones/50 25.00
9 Angel Berroa/50 10.00
10 Aramis Ramirez/50 25.00
11 Aubrey Huff/100 12.00
12 Austin Kearns/100 15.00
13 Barry Larkin/50 30.00
16 Bert Blyleven/100 15.00
17 Billy Williams/100 15.00
19 Bob Feller/100 20.00
20 Bob Gibson/25 35.00
21 Bobby Doerr/100 15.00
22 Brandon Webb/100 10.00
23 Brett Myers/50 15.00
24 Brooks Robinson/ 100 40.00
27 Carlos Beltran/100 30.00
28 Carlos Lee/100 10.00
31 Craig Biggio/50 25.00
33 Dale Murphy/100 25.00
34 Darryl Strawberry/ 100 15.00
35 Dave Concepcion/50 20.00
36 Dave Parker/50 15.00
38 Don Mattingly/100 60.00
39 Dontrelle Willis/100 20.00
40 Duke Snider/100 30.00
41 Dwight Gooden/100 15.00
42 Edgar Martinez/50 30.00
43 Eric Chavez/50 25.00
44 Ernie Banks/100 50.00
45 Fergie Jenkins/100 15.00
46 Frank Robinson/100 20.00
47 Frank Thomas/25 50.00
48 Fred Lynn/50 15.00
49 Fred McGriff/25 50.00
50 Garret Anderson/100 15.00
51 Gary Carter/ Expos/100 15.00
52 Gary Carter/Mets/100 15.00
53 Gary Sheffield/50 25.00
54 Gaylord Perry/100 15.00
57 Hank Blalock/100 25.00
58 Harold Baines/50 25.00
62 Jacque Jones/100 15.00
63 Jae Weong Seo/100 15.00
64 Jamie Moyer/25 25.00
65 Jason Varitek/50 35.00
66 Jay Gibbons/50 15.00
67 Jim Edmonds/25 35.00
68 Jim Palmer/100 20.00
69 Jim Rice/50 20.00
71 Johan Santana/50 40.00
72 Jorge Posada/50 40.00
73 Josh Beckett/25 40.00
74 Juan Gonzalez/25 40.00
75 Keith Hernandez/100 15.00
76 Kirby Puckett/25 60.00
77 Luis Tiant/100 15.00
78 Magglio Ordonez/100 15.00
81 Mark Grace/25 50.00
82 Mark Mulder/100 20.00
83 Mark Prior/100 40.00
84 Mark Teixeira/100 25.00
85 Marty Marion/100 15.00
86 Mike Lowell/25 25.00
90 Nolan Ryan/25 125.00
91 Orel Hershiser/100 30.00
92 Orlando Cepeda/100 15.00
97 Phil Niekro/100 15.00
99 Ralph Kiner/100 20.00
101 Red Schoendienst/ 100 15.00
103 Robin Roberts/50 25.00
104 Robin Ventura/100 15.00
106 Rocco Baldelli/25 30.00
109 Sammy Sosa/21 150.00
110 Sean Casey/23 25.00
111 Shannon Stewart/50 15.00
113 Stan Musial/100 60.00
114 Steve Carlton/50 40.00
115 Steve Garvey/100 15.00
117 Tommy John/100 15.00
118 Tony Gwynn/25 60.00
119 Tony Oliva/100 15.00
120 Torii Hunter/100 15.00
121 Trot Nixon/50 30.00
122 Troy Glaus/50 20.00
123 Vernon Wells/25 20.00
124 Vladimir Guerrero/ 100 35.00
125 Will Clark/100 35.00

Absolutely Ink Material

NM/M

Quantity produced listed
Prime: .5-1X
Production 1-25
No pricing 10 or less.

1 Adam Dunn/Jsy/100 30.00
2 Al Kaline/Pants/50 50.00
3 Alan Trammell/ Jsy/100 20.00
6 Andre Dawson/ Cubs Jsy/100 20.00
7 Andre Dawson/ Expos Jsy/100 20.00
9 Angel Berroa/Jsy/100 10.00
11 Aubrey Huff/Jsy/100 15.00
12 Austin Kearns/ Jsy/100 15.00
16 Bert Blyleven/Jsy/100 15.00
17 Billy Williams/ Jsy/100 25.00
19 Bob Feller/Jsy/100 25.00
21 Bobby Doerr/Jsy/100 25.00
22 Brandon Webb/ Jsy/50 15.00
23 Brett Myers/Jsy/100 15.00
24 Brooks Robinson/ Jsy/100 40.00
27 Carlos Beltran/ Jsy/100 40.00
28 Carlos Lee/Jsy/100 15.00
33 Dale Murphy/Jsy/100 30.00
34 Darryl Strawberry/ Jsy/100 20.00
35 Dave Concepcion/ Jsy/50 20.00
36 Dave Parker/Jsy/100 15.00
38 Don Mattingly/Jsy/50 75.00
39 Dontrelle Willis/ Jsy/20 25.00
41 Dwight Gooden/ Jsy/60 20.00
42 Edgar Martinez/ Jsy/100 30.00
44 Ernie Banks/Jsy/50 50.00
45 Fergie Jenkins/ Pants/100 15.00
46 Frank Robinson/ Jsy/50 40.00
48 Fred Lynn/Jsy/100 15.00
49 Fred McGriff/Jsy/20 60.00
50 Garret Anderson/ Jsy/100 15.00
51 Gary Carter/ Expos Jsy/100 20.00
52 Gary Carter/ Mets Jacket/100 20.00
53 Gary Sheffield/ Jsy/100 20.00
54 Gaylord Perry/ Jsy/100 15.00
57 Hank Blalock/ Jsy/100 30.00
58 Harold Baines/ Jsy/100 20.00
63 Jae Weong Seo/ Jsy/100 15.00
64 Jamie Moyer/Jsy/100 20.00
65 Jason Varitek/ Jsy/100 30.00
66 Jay Gibbons/Jsy/100 15.00
67 Jim Palmer/Jsy/100 25.00
69 Jim Rice/Jsy/100 20.00
70 Joe Carter/Jsy/50 20.00
71 Johan Santana/ Jsy/100 40.00
72 Jorge Posada/Jsy/15 75.00
75 Keith Hernandez/ Jsy/100 15.00
77 Luis Tiant Jsy/100 20.00
82 Mark Mulder/Jsy/20 40.00
85 Marty Marion/ Jsy/100 15.00
86 Mike Lowell/Jsy/60 20.00
92 Orlando Cepeda/ Bat/65 20.00
97 Phil Niekro/Jsy/25 25.00
99 Ralph Kiner/Bat/100 25.00
101 Red Schoendienst/ Jsy/60 20.00
103 Robin Roberts/ Hat/50 25.00
104 Robin Ventura/ Jsy/65 25.00
110 Sean Casey/Jsy/75 20.00
111 Shannon Stewart/ Jsy/100 15.00
114 Steve Carlton/Jsy/50 40.00
115 Steve Garvey/Bat/100 20.00
117 Tommy John/ Jsy/100 15.00
119 Tony Oliva/Jsy/100 20.00
120 Torii Hunter/Jsy/50 20.00
121 Trot Nixon/Jsy/100 30.00
124 Vladimir Guerrero/ Jsy/55 50.00
125 Will Clark/Jsy/100 40.00

Absolutely Ink Triple

No Pricing
Production 1-10
Prime: No Pricing
Production 1-5

Marks of Fame

NM/M

Production 100 Sets
Spectrum: 1-2X
Production 25 Sets

1 Nolan Ryan 15.00
2 Ernie Banks 6.00
3 Bob Feller 4.00
4 Duke Snider 5.00
5 Sammy Sosa 10.00
6 Whitey Ford 6.00
7 Steve Carlton 4.00
8 Tony Gwynn 8.00
9 Jim Bunning 4.00
10 Stan Musial 8.00
11 Cal Ripken Jr. 20.00
12 George Brett 15.00
13 Gary Carter 4.00
14 Jim Palmer 4.00
15 Gaylord Perry 4.00

Marks of Fame Signature

NM/M

Quantity produced listed
Spectrum: .75-1.5X
Production 1-25
No pricing 15 or less.

1 Nolan Ryan/50 120.00
2 Ernie Banks/50 50.00
3 Bob Feller/100 25.00
4 Duke Snider/100 25.00
5 Sammy Sosa/21 125.00
6 Whitey Ford/25 50.00
7 Steve Carlton/100 25.00
8 Tony Gwynn/25 75.00
9 Jim Bunning/100 20.00
10 Stan Musial/50 60.00
12 George Brett/25 100.00
13 Gary Carter/100 15.00
14 Jim Palmer/50 25.00
15 Gaylord Perry/100 15.00

Signature Club

NM/M

Quantity produced listed
2 Gary Sheffield/Bat/50 20.00
4 Will Clark/Bat/50 40.00
5 Ernie Banks/Bat/50 50.00

Signature Material

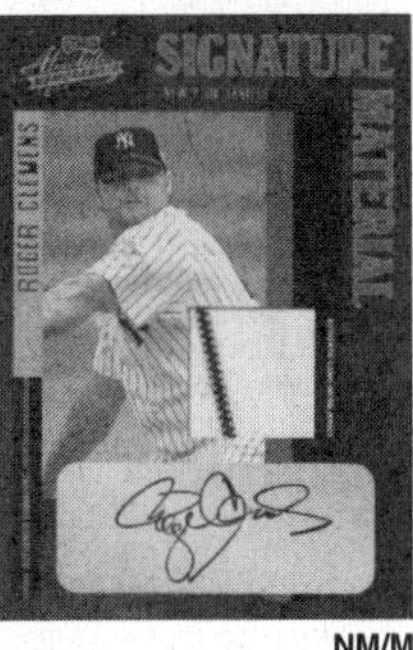

NM/M

Quantity produced listed
Prime: No Pricing
Production Five Sets
Combo: 1X
Production 25-50
Combo Prime: No Pricing
Production Five Sets

2 Gary Carter/Jsy/50 25.00
3 Dale Murphy/Jsy/50 35.00
4 Don Mattingly/ Jsy/25 100.00
5 Stan Musial/Jsy/25 100.00

Signature Spectrum Silver

NM/M

Quantity produced listed
1 Troy Glaus/34 25.00
2 Garret Anderson/100 15.00
6 Nolan Ryan/ Angels/25 150.00
7 Vladimir Guerrero/ 100 40.00
8 Richie Sexson/34 20.00
9 Shea Hillenbrand/100 10.00
11 Brandon Webb/100 10.00
13 Robby Hammock/ 250 10.00
14 Edgar Gonzalez/104 10.00
15 Roberto Alomar/32 50.00
16 Andruw Jones/50 20.00
18 Dale Murphy/100 25.00
19 Rafael Furcal/100 12.00
21 Bubba Nelson/250 10.00
22 Julio Franco/100 15.00
23 Adam LaRoche/100 10.00
24 Michael Hessman/ 250 10.00
26 Jay Gibbons/100 10.00
29 Adam Loewen/100 10.00
32 Luis Matos/100 10.00
33 Jason Varitek/50 35.00
36 Trot Nixon/100 20.00
40 Luis Tiant/100 15.00
41 Kevin Youkilis/25 40.00
42 Michel Hernandez/ 190 10.00
43 Sammy Sosa/21 150.00
45 Kerry Wood/50 40.00
46 Mark Prior/100 40.00
47 Ernie Banks/100 40.00
48 Aramis Ramirez/50 30.00
49 Brendan Harris/250 10.00
50 Todd Wellemeyer/ 250 10.00
51 Frank Thomas/50 40.00
52 Magglio Ordonez/ 100 20.00
53 Carlos Lee/100 15.00
54 Joe Crede/100 10.00
55 Joe Borchard/250 10.00
57 Sean Casey/50 20.00
58 Adam Dunn/100 25.00
59 Austin Kearns/100 15.00
61 Barry Larkin/50 30.00
62 Ryan Wagner/100 10.00
63 Jody Gerut/100 10.00
64 Jeremy Guthrie/50 10.00
65 Travis Hafner/50 20.00
66 Brian Tallet/250 10.00
68 Preston Wilson/100 10.00
69 Jeff Baker/50 10.00
70 Clint Barmes/250 10.00
71 Joe Kennedy/250 10.00
73 George Kell/100 15.00
74 Preston Larrison/250 10.00
77 Dontrelle Willis/100 20.00
78 Josh Beckett/25 35.00
79 Miguel Cabrera/100 35.00
80 Mike Lowell/25 25.00
81 Luis Castillo/50 10.00
83 Jeff Bagwell/50 40.00
85 Craig Biggio/50 30.00
86 Lance Berkman/25 40.00
87 Andy Pettitte/25 50.00
88 Roy Oswalt/25 25.00
89 Chris Burke/250 10.00
90 Jason Lane/231 10.00
93 Carlos Beltran/100 25.00
94 Angel Berroa/100 10.00
95 Juan Gonzalez/25 40.00
96 Ken Harvey/200 15.00
97 Byron Gettis/250 10.00
98 Alexis Gomez/250 10.00
99 Ian Ferguson/104 10.00
100 Duke Snider/100 25.00
103 Kazuhisa Ishii/25 40.00
104 Edwin Jackson/100 10.00
105 Fred McGriff/50 15.00
106 Hong-Chih Kuo/50 50.00
107 Don Sutton/100 15.00
109 Cesar Izturis/101 10.00
110 Robin Ventura/25 20.00
111 Paul LoDuca/50 20.00
112 Rickie Weeks/21 40.00
113 Scott Podsednik/100 15.00
114 Junior Spivey/89 10.00
115 Lyle Overbay/89 15.00
116 Tony Oliva/72 15.00
117 Jacque Jones/100 15.00
118 Shannon Stewart/100 10.00
119 Torii Hunter/100 15.00
120 Johan Santana/50 30.00
121 J.D. Durbin/250 10.00
122 Jason Kubel/250 20.00
123 Michael Cuddyer/225 10.00
124 Nick Johnson/25 15.00
125 Jose Vidro/25 15.00
126 Orlando Cabrera/25 20.00
127 Zach Day/100 10.00
130 Jae Weong Seo/100 10.00
131 Gary Carter/100 15.00
132 Phil Seibel/177 10.00
133 Edwin Almonte/250 10.00
136 Don Mattingly/100 50.00
139 Jorge Posada/50 40.00
144 Gary Sheffield/100 15.00
146 Chien-Ming Wang/50 150.00
147 Javier Vazquez/25 40.00
148 Jose Contreras/25 35.00
149 Whitey Ford/50 40.00
151 Eric Chavez/50 25.00
153 Mark Mulder/100 25.00
154 Tim Hudson/50 25.00
155 Rich Harden/100 15.00
156 Eric Byrnes/250 10.00
159 Marlon Byrd/100 10.00
160 Lenny Dykstra/100 15.00
161 Steve Carlton/100 25.00
162 Ryan Howard/250 75.00
163 Bobby Hill/250 10.00
164 Jose Castillo/100 10.00
165 Jay Payton/100 10.00
168 Henri Stanley/112 10.00
170 Jerome Williams/100 15.00
171 J.T. Snow/89 15.00
173 Edgar Martinez/50 30.00
175 Jamie Moyer/19 25.00
176 Rich Aurilia/25 15.00
177 Chris Snelling/177 10.00
178 Scott Rolen/100 30.00
180 Jim Edmonds/50 30.00
181 Stan Musial/100 60.00
182 Dan Haren/200 10.00
183 Red Schoendienst/ 100 15.00
184 Aubrey Huff/100 10.00
185 Delmon Young/100 20.00
186 Rocco Baldelli/50 20.00
187 Dewon Brazelton/50 15.00
188 Mark Teixeira/100 20.00
189 Hank Blalock/50 30.00
190 Nolan Ryan Rgr/25 125.00
192 Michael Young/100 25.00
194 Roy Halladay/50 20.00
196 Dustin McGowan/250 10.00
197 Josh Phelps/25 15.00
198 Alexis Rios/100 15.00
200 Josh Towers/158 10.00
202 Fernando Nieve/250 10.00
203 Mike Rouse/100 10.00
204 Dennis Sarfate/100 10.00
205 Josh Labandeira/250 10.00
206 Chris Oxspring/250 10.00
207 Alfredo Simon/100 10.00
208 Cory Sullivan/250 10.00
209 Ruddy Yan/250 10.00
210 Jason Bartlett/250 10.00
211 Akinori Otsuka/100 50.00
212 Lincoln Holdzkom/ 250 10.00
213 Justin Leone/250 20.00
214 Jorge Sequea/250 10.00
215 John Gall/50 25.00
217 Tim Bittner/250 10.00
219 Justin Hampson/250 10.00
220 Ryan Wing/250 10.00
221 Mariano Gomez/250 10.00
222 Carlos Vasquez/250 10.00
223 Casey Daigle/150 10.00
224 Renyel Pinto/250 15.00
225 Chris Shelton/250 35.00
229 Roberto Novoa/225 10.00
230 Sean Henn/250 10.00
231 Jamie Brown/200 10.00
232 Nick Regilio/250 10.00
234 Greg Dobbs/250 10.00
235 Angel Chavez/250 10.00
236 Willy Taveras/225 10.00
237 Justin Knoedler/225 10.00
239 Jason Frasor/225 10.00
240 Jerry Gil/225 10.00
241 Carlos Hines/225 10.00
242 Ivan Ochoa/250 10.00
248 Graham Koonce/250 10.00
249 Ronald Belisario/225 10.00

Signature Spectrum Gold

NM/M

Quantity produced listed
1 Troy Glaus/15 35.00
2 Garret Anderson/100 15.00
7 Vladimir Guerrero/25 60.00
8 Richie Sexson/15 25.00
9 Shea Hillenbrand/100 10.00
11 Brandon Webb/100 10.00
15 Roberto Alomar/25 50.00
18 Dale Murphy/100 25.00
19 Rafael Furcal/100 12.00
22 Julio Franco/25 20.00
23 Adam LaRoche/100 10.00
26 Jay Gibbons/100 10.00
29 Adam Loewen/100 10.00
32 Luis Matos/50 15.00
33 Jason Varitek/25 40.00
36 Trot Nixon/100 20.00
40 Luis Tiant/50 20.00
41 Kevin Youkilis/25 40.00
45 Kerry Wood/25 50.00
46 Mark Prior/100 40.00
47 Ernie Banks/100 40.00
52 Magglio Ordonez/100 15.00
53 Carlos Lee/100 15.00
54 Joe Crede/50 10.00
59 Austin Kearns/100 15.00
61 Barry Larkin/25 40.00
62 Ryan Wagner/50 10.00
63 Jody Gerut/100 10.00
64 Jeremy Guthrie/25 15.00
65 Travis Hafner/25 25.00
68 Preston Wilson/100 10.00
69 Jeff Baker/25 15.00
73 George Kell/100 15.00
79 Miguel Cabrera/100 35.00
81 Luis Castillo/25 15.00
83 Jeff Bagwell/25 50.00
87 Andy Pettitte/25 50.00
93 Carlos Beltran/100 25.00
94 Angel Berroa/100 10.00
100 Duke Snider/100 25.00
104 Edwin Jackson/50 15.00
106 Hong-Chih Kuo/25 75.00
107 Don Sutton/25 25.00
112 Rickie Weeks/24 40.00
113 Scott Podsednik/100 15.00
116 Tony Oliva/50 25.00
117 Jacque Jones/100 15.00
119 Torii Hunter/100 15.00
130 Jae Weong Seo/100 10.00
131 Gary Carter/100 15.00
136 Don Mattingly/100 50.00
139 Jorge Posada/25 50.00
144 Gary Sheffield/25 25.00
146 Chien-Ming Wang/ 25 180.00
153 Mark Mulder/100 25.00
155 Rich Harden/50 15.00
159 Marlon Byrd/100 10.00
160 Lenny Dykstra/100 15.00
161 Steve Carlton/50 40.00
164 Jose Castillo/50 15.00
165 Jay Payton/100 10.00
170 Jerome Williams/50 25.00
178 Scott Rolen/50 40.00
181 Stan Musial/100 60.00
182 Dan Haren/25 15.00
183 Red Schoendienst/ 100 15.00
184 Aubrey Huff/100 10.00
185 Delmon Young/100 20.00
187 Dewon Brazelton/25 15.00
188 Mark Teixeira/50 30.00
189 Hank Blalock/25 40.00
192 Michael Young/100 25.00
194 Roy Halladay/25 25.00
198 Alexis Rios/50 25.00
202 Fernando Nieve/100 10.00
205 Josh Labandeira/100 10.00
206 Chris Oxspring/100 15.00
208 Cory Sullivan/100 10.00
209 Ruddy Yan/100 10.00
210 Jason Bartlett/100 15.00
212 Lincoln Holdzkom/ 100 10.00
213 Justin Leone/100 20.00
214 Jorge Sequea/100 10.00
217 Tim Bittner/100 10.00
219 Justin Hampson/100 10.00
220 Ryan Wing/100 10.00
221 Mariano Gomez/100 10.00
222 Carlos Vasquez/100 10.00
224 Renyel Pinto/100 15.00
225 Chris Shelton/100 35.00
230 Sean Henn/100 10.00
232 Nick Regilio/100 10.00
234 Greg Dobbs/50 15.00
235 Angel Chavez/100 10.00
242 Ivan Ochoa/100 10.00
248 Graham Koonce/100 10.00

Team Tandem

NM/M

Production 250 Sets
Spectrum: 2-4X
Production 25 Sets

1 Vladimir Guerrero, Reggie Jackson 3.00
2 Dale Murphy, Chipper Jones 3.00
3 Gary Carter, Mike Piazza 4.00
4 Miguel Tejada, Cal Ripken Jr. 8.00
5 Gary Sheffield, Derek Jeter 6.00
6 Curt Schilling, Pedro J. Martinez 3.00

7 Roger Clemens, Andy Pettitte 5.00
8 Mike Sweeney, George Brett 6.00
9 Kazuhisa Ishii, Hideo Nomo 3.00
10 Austin Kearns, Adam Dunn 3.00
11 Miguel Cabrera, Dontrelle Willis 3.00
12 Don Mattingly, Derek Jeter 8.00
13 Barry Zito, Eric Chavez 2.00
14 Jim Thome, Mike Schmidt 4.00
15 Albert Pujols, Stan Musial 4.00
16 Nolan Ryan, Alex Rodriguez 8.00
17 Kerry Wood, Mark Prior 4.00
18 Rafael Palmeiro, Jay Gibbons 3.00
19 Nomar Garciaparra, Manny Ramirez 4.00
20 Ivan Rodriguez, Mike Piazza 4.00

Team Tandem Material

NM/M

Production 250 Sets
Prime: No Pricing
Production Five Sets
1 Reggie Jackson/Bat, Vladimir Guerrero/Bat 10.00
2 Chipper Jones/Jsy, Dale Murphy/Jsy 10.00
3 Gary Carter/Jsy, Mike Piazza/Jsy 10.00
4 Miguel Tejada/Bat, Cal Ripken Jr./Bat 25.00
5 Derek Jeter/Bat, Gary Sheffield/Bat 25.00
6 Curt Schilling/Bat, Pedro J. Martinez/Bat 10.00
7 Roger Clemens/Bat, Andy Pettitte/Bat 15.00
8 Mike Sweeney/Jsy, George Brett/Jsy 15.00
9 Kazuhisa Ishii/Jsy, Hideo Nomo/Jsy 10.00
10 Austin Kearns/Jsy, Adam Dunn/Jsy 10.00
11 Dontrelle Willis/Jsy, Miguel Cabrera/Jsy 10.00
12 Don Mattingly/Jsy, Derek Jeter/Jsy 35.00
13 Barry Zito/Jsy, Eric Chavez/Jsy 8.00
14 Jim Thome/Jsy, Mike Schmidt/Jsy 20.00
15 Albert Pujols/Jsy, Stan Musial/Jsy 40.00
16 Nolan Ryan/Jsy, Alex Rodriguez/Jsy 25.00
17 Mark Prior/Jsy, Kerry Wood/Jsy 15.00
18 Rafael Palmeiro/Jsy, Jay Gibbons/Jsy 10.00
19 Nomar Garciaparra/Jsy, Manny Ramirez/Jsy 15.00
20 Ivan Rodriguez/Jsy, Mike Piazza/Jsy 10.00

Team Trio

NM/M

Production 100 Sets
Spectrum: 1.5-2X
Production 25 Sets
1 Sammy Sosa, Kerry Wood, Mark Prior 10.00
2 Hank Blalock, Mark Teixeira, Alex Rodriguez 10.00
3 Vernon Wells, Roy Halladay, Carlos Delgado 4.00
4 Mike Mussina, Jorge Posada, Mariano Rivera 6.00
5 Shannon Stewart, Torii Hunter, Jacque Jones 4.00
6 Carlos Beltran, Mike Sweeney, Angel Berroa 4.00
7 Dontrelle Willis, Miguel Cabrera, Josh Beckett 6.00
8 Jeff Bagwell, Craig Biggio, Lance Berkman 6.00
9 Nomar Garciaparra, Pedro J. Martinez, Manny Ramirez 10.00
10 Shawn Green, Kazuhisa Ishii, Hideo Nomo 4.00
11 Mark Mulder, Barry Zito, Tim Hudson 4.00
12 Jim Edmonds, Scott Rolen, Albert Pujols 15.00
13 Cal Ripken Jr., Jay Gibbons, Rafael Palmeiro 20.00
14 Sammy Sosa, Mark Grace, Ryne Sandberg 10.00
15 Nolan Ryan, Roger Clemens, Randy Johnson 20.00

Team Trio Material

NM/M

Production 100 Sets
Prime: No Pricing
Production Five Sets
1 Sammy Sosa, Kerry Wood, Mark Prior 25.00
2 Hank Blalock, Mark Teixeira, Alex Rodriguez 15.00
3 Vernon Wells, Roy Halladay, Carlos Delgado 8.00
4 Mike Mussina, Jorge Posada, Mariano Rivera 25.00
5 Shannon Stewart, Torii Hunter, Jacque Jones 8.00
6 Carlos Beltran, Mike Sweeney, Angel Berroa 8.00
7 Dontrelle Willis, Miguel Cabrera, Josh Beckett 15.00
8 Jeff Bagwell, Craig Biggio, Lance Berkman 10.00
9 Nomar Garciaparra, Pedro J. Martinez, Manny Ramirez 20.00
10 Shawn Green, Kazuhisa Ishii, Hideo Nomo 10.00
11 Mark Mulder, Barry Zito, Tim Hudson 8.00
12 Jim Edmonds, Scott Rolen, Albert Pujols 25.00
13 Cal Ripken Jr., Jay Gibbons, Rafael Palmeiro 40.00
14 Sammy Sosa, Mark Grace, Ryne Sandberg 35.00
15 Nolan Ryan, Roger Clemens, Randy Johnson/25 80.00

Team Quad

NM/M

Production 100 Sets
Spectrum: 1.5-2X
Production 25 Sets
1 Jeff Kent, Lance Berkman, Craig Biggio, Jeff Bagwell 6.00
2 Nomar Garciaparra, Manny Ramirez, Pedro Martinez, Trot Nixon 10.00
3 Paul Konerko, Carlos Lee, Magglio Ordonez, Frank Thomas 6.00
4 John Smoltz, Chipper Jones, Andruw Jones, Rafael Furcal 6.00
5 Garret Anderson, Troy Percival, Troy Glaus, Darin Erstad 4.00
6 Steve Finley, Brandon Webb, Randy Johnson, Luis Gonzalez 6.00
7 Paul LoDuca, Hideo Nomo, Shawn Green, Kazuhisa Ishii 6.00
8 Larry Walker, Todd Helton, Jason Jennings, Preston Wilson 6.00
9 Dontrelle Willis, Brad Penny, Josh Beckett 4.00
10 Jose Reyes, Jae Weong Seo, Tom Glavine, Mike Piazza 10.00
11 Bernie Williams, Derek Jeter, Jason Giambi, Alfonso Soriano 15.00
12 Rich Harden, Tim Hudson, Barry Zito, Mark Mulder 4.00
13 Kevin Millwood, Marlon Byrd, Jim Thome, Bobby Abreu 8.00
14 Edgar Renteria, Jim Edmonds, Albert Pujols, Scott Rolen 10.00
15 Roger Clemens, Andy Pettitte, Wade Miller, Roy Oswalt 10.00

Team Quad Material

NM/M

Production 100 Sets
Prime: No Pricing
Production Five Sets
1 Jeff Kent, Lance Berkman, Craig Biggio, Jeff Bagwell 20.00
2 Nomar Garciaparra, Manny Ramirez, Pedro Martinez, Trot Nixon 35.00
3 Paul Konerko, Carlos Lee, Magglio Ordonez, Frank Thomas 20.00
4 John Smoltz, Chipper Jones, Andruw Jones, Rafael Furcal 20.00
5 Garret Anderson, Troy Percival, Troy Glaus, Darin Erstad 10.00
6 Steve Finley, Brandon Webb, Randy Johnson, Luis Gonzalez 20.00
7 Paul LoDuca, Hideo Nomo, Shawn Green, Kazuhisa Ishii 20.00
8 Larry Walker, Todd Helton, Jason Jennings, Preston Wilson 10.00
9 Dontrelle Willis, Brad Penny, Josh Beckett 20.00
10 Jose Reyes, Jae Weong Seo, Tom Glavine, Mike Piazza 20.00
11 Bernie Williams, Derek Jeter, Jason Giambi, Alfonso Soriano 40.00
12 Rich Harden, Tim Hudson, Barry Zito, Mark Mulder 10.00
13 Kevin Millwood, Marlon Byrd, Jim Thome, Bobby Abreu 20.00
14 Edgar Renteria, Jim Edmonds, Albert Pujols, Scott Rolen 40.00
15 Roger Clemens, Andy Pettitte, Wade Miller, Roy Oswalt 30.00

Tools of Trade Blue

NM/M

Common Player: 1.50
Production 250 Sets
Black: No Pricing
Production One Set
Blue Spectrum: 1-1.5X
Production 125 Sets
Green: 1-1.5X
Production 150 Sets
Green Spectrum: 2-3X
Production 50 Sets
Red: 1X
Production 200 Sets
Red Spectrum: 1-2X
Production 100 Sets
1 Adam Dunn/H 2.50
2 Adam Dunn/A 2.50
3 Alan Trammell 2.00
4 Albert Pujols/H 6.00
5 Albert Pujols/A 6.00
6 Alex Rodriguez 6.00
7 Alex Rodriguez 6.00
8 Alex Rodriguez 6.00
9 Alfonso Soriano 4.00
10 Andre Dawson 2.00
11 Andruw Jones/H 2.00
12 Andruw Jones/A 2.00
13 Andy Pettitte/H 2.00
14 Andy Pettitte/A 2.00
15 Angel Berroa 1.50
16 Aubrey Huff 1.50
17 Austin Kearns 2.00
18 Barry Zito 2.00
19 Barry Zito/A 2.00
20 Bernie Williams 2.00
21 Bobby Abreu 2.00
22 Brandon Webb 1.50
23 Cal Ripken Jr./H 8.00
24 Cal Ripken Jr./A 8.00
25 Cal Ripken Jr. 8.00
26 Carlos Beltran 2.00
27 Carlos Delgado/H 2.00
28 Carlos Delgado/A 2.00
29 Carlos Lee 1.50
30 Chipper Jones/H 3.00
31 Chipper Jones/A 3.00
32 Craig Biggio/H 2.00
33 Craig Biggio/A 2.00
34 Curt Schilling 2.00
35 Curt Schilling 2.00
36 Dale Murphy/H 2.00
37 Dale Murphy/A 2.00
38 Darryl Strawberry 1.50
39 Derek Jeter/H 8.00
40 Derek Jeter/A 8.00
41 Don Mattingly/H 8.00
42 Don Mattingly/A 8.00
43 Dontrelle Willis/H 2.00
44 Dontrelle Willis/A 2.00
45 Dwight Gooden 1.50
46 Edgar Martinez 1.50
47 Eric Chavez 2.00
48 Frank Thomas/A 2.00
49 Frank Thomas 2.00
50 Garret Anderson 2.00
51 Gary Carter 2.00
52 Gary Sheffield 2.00
53 George Brett/H 6.00
54 George Brett/A 6.00
55 Greg Maddux 4.00
56 Hank Blalock 2.00
57 Hideo Nomo 2.00
58 Ivan Rodriguez 2.00
59 Ivan Rodriguez 2.00
60 Jacque Jones 1.50
61 Jae Weong Seo 1.50
62 Jason Giambi 2.00
63 Jason Giambi 2.00
64 Javy Lopez 2.00
65 Jay Gibbons 1.50
66 Jeff Bagwell 2.00
67 Jeff Bagwell 2.00
68 Jeff Kent 1.50
69 Jim Edmonds 2.00
70 Jim Thome 3.00
71 Jorge Posada 2.00
72 Jose Canseco 2.00
73 Jose Reyes 2.00
74 Josh Beckett 2.00
75 Juan Gonzalez 2.00
76 Kazuhisa Ishii 1.50
77 Kerry Wood 3.00
78 Kerry Wood 3.00
79 Kirby Puckett 3.00
80 Lance Berkman 2.00
81 Lou Brock 2.00
82 Luis Castillo 1.50
83 Luis Gonzalez 1.50
84 Magglio Ordonez 1.50
85 Manny Ramirez 2.00
86 Manny Ramirez 2.00
87 Marcus Giles 1.50
88 Mark Grace 2.00
89 Mark Mulder 2.00
90 Mark Prior 4.00
91 Mark Prior 4.00
92 Mark Teixeira 2.00
93 Marlon Byrd 1.50
94 Miguel Cabrera 3.00
95 Miguel Tejada 2.00
96 Mike Lowell 2.00
97 Mike Mussina 2.00
98 Mike Mussina 2.00
99 Mike Piazza 4.00
100 Mike Piazza 4.00
101 Mike Piazza 4.00
102 Mike Schmidt 5.00
103 Mike Schmidt 5.00
104 Mike Sweeney 1.50
105 Nick Johnson 1.50
106 Nolan Ryan 8.00
107 Nolan Ryan 8.00
108 Nolan Ryan 8.00
109 Nomar Garciaparra 5.00
110 Nomar Garciaparra 5.00
111 Pat Burrell 2.00
112 Paul LoDuca 1.50
113 Pedro Martinez 3.00
114 Pedro Martinez 3.00
115 Preston Wilson 1.50
116 Rafael Palmeiro 2.00
117 Rafael Palmeiro 2.00
118 Randy Johnson 4.00
119 Randy Johnson 4.00
120 Richie Sexson 2.00
121 Rickey Henderson 2.00
122 Rickey Henderson 2.00
123 Rickey Henderson 2.00
124 Roberto Alomar 2.00
125 Rocco Baldelli 2.00
126 Rod Carew 2.00
127 Roger Clemens 6.00
128 Roger Clemens 6.00
129 Roy Halladay 2.00
130 Roy Oswalt 1.50
131 Ryne Sandberg 5.00
132 Sammy Sosa 5.00
133 Sammy Sosa 5.00
134 Sammy Sosa 5.00
135 Scott Rolen 4.00
136 Shawn Green 2.00
137 Steve Carlton 2.00
138 Tim Hudson 2.00
139 Todd Helton 2.00
140 Todd Helton 2.00
141 Tom Glavine 2.00
142 Tom Glavine 2.00
143 Tony Gwynn 4.00
144 Tony Gwynn 4.00
145 Torii Hunter 2.00
146 Trot Nixon 2.00
147 Troy Glaus 2.00
148 Vernon Wells 2.00
149 Vladimir Guerrero 4.00
150 Will Clark 3.00

Tools of Trade Signature Blue Spectrum

NM/M

Quantity produced listed
Black: No Pricing
Production One Set
Green: No Pricing
Production 1-10
Red: .75-1.5X
Production 1-50
No pricing 15 or less
3 Alan Trammell/100 15.00
10 Andre Dawson/100 15.00
15 Angel Berroa/100 8.00
16 Aubrey Huff/100 10.00
17 Austin Kearns/100 15.00
22 Brandon Webb/100 8.00
26 Carlos Beltran/100 20.00
29 Carlos Lee/100 15.00
36 Dale Murphy H/50 30.00
37 Dale Murphy A/50 30.00
38 Darryl Strawberry/50 20.00
41 Don Mattingly H/50 75.00
42 Don Mattingly A/50 75.00
43 Dontrelle Willis H/25 30.00
44 Dontrelle Willis A/25 30.00
45 Dwight Gooden/50 25.00
46 Edgar Martinez/25 50.00
48 Frank Thomas A/25 50.00
49 Frank Thomas/25 50.00
50 Garret Anderson/100 15.00
51 Gary Carter/100 15.00
60 Jacque Jones/50 20.00
61 Jae Weong Seo/25 25.00
65 Jay Gibbons/50 15.00
69 Jim Edmonds/25 35.00
71 Jorge Posada/25 40.00
73 Jose Reyes/25 25.00
75 Juan Gonzalez/20 40.00
77 Kerry Wood H/25 50.00
78 Kerry Wood/25 50.00
81 Lou Brock/100 25.00
84 Magglio Ordonez/50 20.00
87 Marcus Giles/50 20.00
88 Mark Grace/25 40.00
89 Mark Mulder/100 20.00
90 Mark Prior H/50 60.00
91 Mark Prior A/50 60.00
92 Mark Teixeira/50 30.00
93 Marlon Byrd/50 15.00
94 Miguel Cabrera/100 35.00
102 Mike Schmidt H/25 75.00
103 Mike Schmidt A/25 75.00
106 Nolan Ryan/25 125.00
107 Nolan Ryan/25 125.00
108 Nolan Ryan/25 125.00
112 Paul LoDuca/50 25.00
115 Preston Wilson/100 15.00
129 Roy Halladay/25 30.00
130 Roy Oswalt/25 25.00
135 Scott Rolen/50 40.00
137 Steve Carlton/50 30.00
143 Tony Gwynn A/25 60.00
144 Tony Gwynn/25 60.00
145 Torii Hunter/50 25.00
146 Trot Nixon/25 30.00
149 Vladimir Guerrero/25 65.00
150 Will Clark/50 50.00

Tools of Trade Material Signature Sing

NM/M

Quantity produced listed
Combo: 1-2X
Production 1-25
Combo Prime: No Pricing
Production 1-5
Trio: No Pricing
Production 1-10
Quad: No Pricing
Production 1-10
1 Adam Dunn/H/Jsy/25 50.00
2 Adam Dunn/A/Jsy/25 50.00
3 Alan Trammell/Jsy/25 50.00
10 Andre Dawson/Jsy/25 25.00
15 Angel Berroa/Jsy/50 15.00
17 Austin Kearns/Jsy/28 25.00
21 Bobby Abreu/Jsy/25 25.00
22 Brandon Webb/Jsy/25 20.00
26 Carlos Beltran/Jsy/15 50.00
29 Carlos Lee/Jsy/25 25.00
36 Dale Murphy/Jsy/25 40.00
37 Dale Murphy/Jsy/25 40.00
38 Darryl Strawberry/Jsy/39 20.00
43 Dontrelle Willis/Jsy/25 30.00
44 Dontrelle Willis/Jsy/25 30.00
45 Dwight Gooden/Jsy/16 35.00
50 Garret Anderson/Jsy/16 30.00
61 Jae Weong/Seo Jsy/25 20.00
71 Jorge Posada/Jsy/20 60.00
74 Josh Beckett/Jsy/21 40.00
82 Luis Castillo/Jsy/25 20.00
89 Mark Mulder/Jsy/20 40.00
93 Marlon Byrd/Jsy/29 20.00
94 Miguel Cabrera/Jsy/20 50.00
96 Mike Lowell/Jsy/19 30.00
112 Paul LoDuca/Jsy/50 25.00
115 Preston Wilson/Jsy/44 20.00
125 Rocco Baldelli/Jsy/25 30.00
129 Roy Halladay/Jsy/32 25.00
137 Steve Carlton/Jsy/25 50.00
145 Torii Hunter/Jsy/25 25.00
146 Trot Nixon/Jsy/25 50.00

Tools of Trade Material Combo

NM/M

Production 25-250
Single: No Pricing
Production 1-5
Combo Price Single: 2-4X
Production 1-25
Trio: 1-30X
Production 5-100
No pricing 15 or less.
Quad: 2-4X
Production 1-50
No pricing 15 or less.
Five: 3-5X
Production 10-25
Six: 3-6X
Production 5-25
1 Adam Dunn/Bat-Jsy/250 6.00
2 Adam Dunn/Bat-Jsy/250 6.00
3 Alan Trammell/Bat-Jsy/250 4.00
4 Albert Pujols/Bat-Jsy/250 20.00
5 Albert Pujols/Bat-Jsy/250 20.00
6 Alex Rodriguez/Bat-Jsy/250 10.00
7 Alex Rodriguez/Bat-Jsy/250 10.00
8 Alex Rodriguez/Bat-Jsy/250 10.00
9 Alfonso Soriano/Bat-Jsy/100 10.00
10 Andre Dawson/Bat-Jsy/250 5.00
11 Andruw Jones/Bat-Jsy/100 8.00
12 Andruw Jones/Bat-Jsy/250 8.00
13 Andy Pettitte/Bat-Jsy/100 10.00
14 Andy Pettitte/Bat-Jsy/100 10.00
15 Angel Berroa/Bat-Jsy/250 4.00
16 Aubrey Huff/Bat-Jsy/250 4.00
17 Austin Kearns/Bat-Jsy/250 6.00
18 Barry Zito/Bat-Jsy/250 6.00
19 Barry Zito/Bat-Jsy/250 6.00
20 Bernie Williams/Bat-Jsy/250 8.00
21 Bobby Abreu/Bat-Jsy/250 6.00
22 Brandon Webb/Bat-Jsy/250 4.00
23 Cal Ripken Jr./Bat-Jsy/250 30.00
24 Cal Ripken Jr./Bat-Jsy/250 30.00
25 Cal Ripken Jr./Bat-Jsy/250 30.00
26 Carlos Beltran/Bat-Jsy/250 6.00
27 Carlos Delgado/Bat-Jsy/250 6.00
28 Carlos Delgado/Bat-Jsy/250 6.00
29 Carlos Lee/Bat-Jsy/250 4.00
30 Chipper Jones/Bat-Jsy/250 10.00
31 Chipper Jones/Bat-Jsy/250 10.00
32 Craig Biggio/Bat-Jsy/250 6.00
33 Craig Biggio/Bat-Jsy/100 6.00
34 Curt Schilling/Bat-Jsy/250 8.00
35 Curt Schilling/Bat-Jsy/250 8.00
36 Dale Murphy/Bat-Jsy/250 8.00
37 Dale Murphy/Bat-Jsy/100 8.00
38 Darryl Strawberry/Bat-Jsy/250 4.00
39 Derek Jeter/Bat-Jsy/100 30.00
40 Derek Jeter/Bat-Jsy/100 30.00
41 Don Mattingly/Bat-Jsy/100 30.00
42 Don Mattingly/Bat-Jsy/100 30.00
43 Dontrelle Willis/Bat-Jsy/250 6.00
44 Dontrelle Willis/Bat-Jsy/250 6.00
45 Dwight Gooden/Bat-Jsy/250 6.00
46 Edgar Martinez/Bat-Jsy/250 6.00
47 Eric Chavez/Bat-Jsy/250 6.00
48 Frank Thomas/Bat-Jsy/250 10.00
49 Frank Thomas/Bat-Jsy/250 10.00
50 Garret Anderson/Bat-Jsy/250 6.00

51 Gary Carter/Bat-Jsy/250 6.00
52 Gary Sheffield/Bat-Jsy/250 6.00
53 George Brett/Bat-Jsy/250 20.00
54 George Brett/Bat-Jsy/250 20.00
55 Greg Maddux/Bat-Jsy/250 10.00
56 Hank Blalock/Bat-Jsy/250 8.00
57 Hideo Nomo/Bat-Jsy/250 10.00
58 Ivan Rodriguez/Bat-Jsy/250 8.00
59 Ivan Rodriguez/Bat-Jsy/250 8.00
60 Jacque Jones/Bat-Jsy/250 4.00
62 Jason Giambi/Bat-Jsy/250 8.00
63 Jason Giambi/Bat-Jsy/250 8.00
64 Javy Lopez/Bat-Jsy/250 6.00
65 Jay Gibbons/Bat-Jsy/250 4.00
66 Jeff Bagwell/Bat-Jsy/250 8.00
67 Jeff Bagwell/Bat-Jsy/250 8.00
68 Jeff Kent/Bat-Jsy/250 5.00
69 Jim Edmonds/Bat-Jsy/250 8.00
70 Jim Thome/Bat-Jsy/250 12.00
71 Jorge Posada/Bat-Jsy/250 8.00
72 Jose Canseco/Bat-Jsy/250 8.00
73 Jose Reyes/Bat-Jsy/250 8.00
74 Josh Beckett/Bat-Jsy/250 8.00
75 Juan Gonzalez/Bat-Jsy/250 8.00
76 Kazuhisa Ishii/Bat-Jsy/250 4.00
77 Kerry Wood/Bat-Jsy/250 10.00
78 Kerry Wood/Bat-Jsy/250 10.00
79 Kirby Puckett/Bat-Jsy/250 10.00
80 Lance Berkman/Bat-Jsy/250 6.00
81 Lou Brock/Bat-Jsy/250 8.00
82 Luis Castillo/Bat-Jsy/250 4.00
83 Luis Gonzalez/Bat-Jsy/250 4.00
84 Magglio Ordonez/Bat-Jsy/250 6.00
85 Manny Ramirez/Bat-Jsy/250 8.00
86 Manny Ramirez/Bat-Jsy/250 8.00
87 Marcus Giles/Bat-Jsy/25 10.00
88 Mark Grace/Bat-Jsy/250 8.00
89 Mark Mulder/Bat-Jsy/250 8.00
90 Mark Prior/Bat-Jsy/250 10.00
91 Mark Prior/Bat-Jsy/250 10.00
92 Mark Teixeira/Bat-Jsy/250 6.00
93 Marlon Byrd/Bat-Jsy/250 4.00
94 Miguel Cabrera/Bat-Jsy/250 10.00
95 Miguel Tejada/Bat-Jsy/250 6.00
96 Mike Lowell/Bat-Jsy/250 6.00
97 Mike Mussina/Jsy-Pants/250 8.00
98 Mike Mussina/Jsy-Jsy/250 8.00
99 Mike Piazza/Bat-Jsy/250 12.00
100 Mike Piazza/Bat-Jsy/250 12.00
101 Mike Piazza/Bat-Jsy/250 12.00
102 Mike Schmidt/Bat-Jsy/100 20.00
103 Mike Schmidt/Bat-Jsy/100 20.00
104 Mike Sweeney/Bat-Jsy/250 4.00
105 Nick Johnson/Bat-Jsy/250 4.00
106 Nolan Ryan/Jkt-Jsy/250 30.00
107 Nolan Ryan/Jkt-Jsy/250 30.00
108 Nolan Ryan/Jsy-Pants/250 30.00
109 Nomar Garciaparra/Bat-Jsy/250 15.00
110 Nomar Garciaparra/Bat-Jsy/250 15.00
111 Pat Burrell/Bat-Jsy/250 6.00
112 Paul LoDuca/Bat-Jsy/250 4.00
113 Pedro J. Martinez/Bat-Jsy/250 10.00
114 Pedro Martinez/Bat-Jsy/250 10.00
115 Preston Wilson/Bat-Jsy/250 4.00
116 Rafael Palmeiro/Bat-Jsy/250 8.00
117 Rafael Palmeiro/Bat-Jsy/250 8.00
118 Randy Johnson/Bat-Jsy/250 10.00
119 Randy Johnson/Bat-Jsy/250 10.00
120 Richie Sexson/Bat-Jsy/250 6.00
121 Rickey Henderson/Bat-Jsy/250 8.00
122 Rickey Henderson/Bat-Jsy/250 8.00
123 Rickey Henderson/Bat-Jsy/250 8.00
124 Roberto Alomar/Bat-Jsy/250 8.00
125 Rocco Baldelli/Bat-Jsy/250 6.00
126 Rod Carew/Bat-Jsy/250 8.00
127 Roger Clemens/Bat-Jsy/250 15.00
128 Roger Clemens/Bat-Jsy/250 15.00
129 Roy Halladay/Jsy-Jsy/250 4.00
130 Roy Oswalt/Bat-Jsy/250 6.00
131 Ryne Sandberg/Bat-Jsy/250 15.00
132 Sammy Sosa/Bat-Jsy/250 15.00
133 Sammy Sosa/Bat-Jsy/250 15.00
134 Sammy Sosa/Bat-Jsy/250 15.00
135 Scott Rolen/Bat-Jsy/250 10.00
136 Shawn Green/Bat-Jsy/250 6.00
137 Steve Carlton/Bat-Jsy/250 6.00
138 Tim Hudson/Bat-Jsy/250 6.00
139 Todd Helton/Bat-Jsy/250 8.00
140 Todd Helton/Bat-Jsy/250 8.00
141 Tom Glavine/Bat-Jsy/250 8.00
142 Tom Glavine/Bat-Jsy/250 8.00
143 Tony Gwynn/Bat-Jsy/250 12.00
144 Tony Gwynn/Bat-Jsy/250 12.00
145 Torii Hunter/Bat-Jsy/250 6.00
146 Trot Nixon/Bat-Jsy/250 8.00
147 Troy Glaus/Bat-Jsy/250 6.00
148 Vernon Wells/Bat-Jsy/250 4.00
149 Vladimir Guerrero/Bat-Jsy/250 10.00
150 Will Clark/Bat-Jsy/250 10.00

2004 Playoff Honors

NM/M

Complete Set (250):
Common Player (1-200): .15
Common SP (201-250): 3.00
Production 1,999
Common SP Auto. (226-250): 8.00
Pack (6): 5.00
Box (12): 55.00

1 Bartolo Colon .15
2 Garret Anderson .40
3 Tim Salmon .25
4 Troy Glaus .25
5 Vladimir Guerrero .75
6 Brandon Webb .15
7 Brian Bruney .15
8 Luis Gonzalez .25
9 Randy Johnson .75
10 Richie Sexson .40
11 Robby Hammock .15
12 Roberto Alomar .40
13 Shea Hillenbrand .15
14 Steve Finley .15
15 Adam LaRoche .15
16 Andruw Jones .50
17 Bubba Nelson .15
18 Chipper Jones .75
19 Dale Murphy .50
20 J.D. Drew .25
21 John Smoltz .25
22 Marcus Giles .15
23 Rafael Furcal .25
24 Warren Spahn .75
25 Greg Maddux 1.00
26 Adam Loewen .15
27 Cal Ripken Jr. 3.00
28 Javy Lopez .25
29 Jay Gibbons .15
30 Luis Matos .15
31 Miguel Tejada .40
32 Rafael Palmeiro .50
33 Bobby Doerr .15
34 Curt Schilling .50
35 Edwin Almonte .15
36 Jason Varitek .25
37 Kevin Youkilis .15
38 Manny Ramirez .50
39 Nomar Garciaparra 1.00
40 Pedro J. Martinez .75
41 Trot Nixon .25
42 Andre Dawson .25
43 Aramis Ramirez .40
44 Brendan Harris .15
45 Derrek Lee .25
46 Ernie Banks .75
47 Kerry Wood .75
48 Mark Prior 1.00
49 Ryne Sandberg 1.00
50 Sammy Sosa 1.50
51 Carlos Lee .15
52 Frank Thomas .50
53 Joe Borchard .15
54 Joe Crede .15
55 Magglio Ordonez .25
56 Adam Dunn .50
57 Austin Kearns .25
58 Barry Larkin .40
59 Brandon Larson .15
60 Ken Griffey Jr. 1.00
61 Ryan Wagner .15
62 Sean Casey .25
63 Bob Feller .25
64 Brian Tallet .15
65 C.C. Sabathia .15
66 Jeremy Guthrie .15
67 Jody Gerut .15
68 Clint Barmes .15
69 Jeff Baker .15
70 Joe Kennedy .15
71 Larry Walker .25
72 Preston Wilson .15
73 Todd Helton .50
74 Alan Trammell .25
75 Dmitri Young .15
76 Ivan Rodriguez .50
77 Jeremy Bonderman .15
78 Preston Larrison .15
79 Dontrelle Willis .25
80 Josh Beckett .50
81 Juan Pierre .15
82 Luis Castillo .15
83 Miguel Cabrera .75
84 Mike Lowell .25
85 Andy Pettitte .25
86 Chris Burke .15
87 Craig Biggio .25
88 Jeff Bagwell .50
89 Jeff Kent .25
90 Lance Berkman .25
91 Morgan Ensberg .15
92 Richard Hidalgo .15
93 Roger Clemens 1.50
94 Roy Oswalt .25
95 Angel Berroa .15
96 Byron Gettis .15
97 Carlos Beltran .40
98 George Brett 2.00
99 Juan Gonzalez .50
100 Mike Sweeney .15
101 Duke Snider .50
102 Edwin Jackson .15
103 Eric Gagne .50
104 Hideo Nomo .40
105 Hong-Chih Kuo .15
106 Kazuhisa Ishii .15
107 Paul LoDuca .15
108 Robin Ventura .15
109 Shawn Green .25
110 Junior Spivey .15
111 Rickie Weeks .25
112 Scott Podsednik .25
113 J.D. Durbin .15
114 Jacque Jones .15
115 Jason Kubel .25
116 Johan Santana .15
117 Shannon Stewart .15
118 Torii Hunter .15
119 Brad Wilkerson .15
120 Jose Vidro .15
121 Nick Johnson .15
122 Orlando Cabrera .15
123 Gary Carter .25
124 Jae Weong Seo .15
125 Lenny Dykstra .15
126 Mike Piazza 1.00
127 Tom Glavine .25
128 Alex Rodriguez 1.50
129 Bernie Williams .40
130 Chien-Ming Wang 1.00
131 Derek Jeter 2.00
132 Don Mattingly 1.50
133 Gary Sheffield .40
134 Hideki Matsui 1.50
135 Jason Giambi .50
136 Javier Vazquez .25
137 Jorge Posada .40
138 Jose Contreras .15
139 Kevin Brown .25
140 Mariano Rivera .40
141 Mike Mussina .40
142 Whitey Ford .50
143 Barry Zito .40
144 Eric Chavez .25
145 Mark Mulder .40
146 Rich Harden .15
147 Tim Hudson .25
148 Reggie Jackson .50
149 Rickey Henderson .50
150 Brett Myers .15
151 Bobby Abreu .25
152 Jim Thome .75
153 Kevin Millwood .25
154 Marlon Byrd .15
155 Mike Schmidt 1.50
156 Ryan Howard 3.00
157 Jack Wilson .15
158 Jason Kendall .15
159 Brian Giles .25
160 David Wells .15
161 Jay Payton .15
162 Phil Nevin .15
163 Ryan Klesko .15
164 Sean Burroughs .15
165 A.J. Pierzynski .15
166 J.T. Snow .15
167 Jason Schmidt .50
168 Jerome Williams .15
169 Will Clark .50
170 Bret Boone .15
171 Chris Snelling .15
172 Edgar Martinez .25
173 Ichiro Suzuki 1.50
174 Randy Winn .15
175 Rich Aurilia .15
176 Shigetoshi Hasegawa .15
177 Albert Pujols .15
178 Dan Haren .15
179 Edgar Renteria .25
180 Jim Edmonds .40
181 Matt Morris .15
182 Scott Rolen .75
183 Stan Musial 1.00
184 Aubrey Huff .15
185 Chad Gaudin .15
186 Delmon Young .25
187 Fred McGriff .25
188 Rocco Baldelli .15
189 Alfonso Soriano .75
190 Hank Blalock .50
191 Mark Teixeira .40
192 Nolan Ryan 2.00
193 Alexis Rios .15
194 Carlos Delgado .40
195 Dustin McGowan .15
196 Guillermo Quiroz .15
197 Josh Phelps .15
198 Roy Halladay .25
199 Vernon Wells .15
200 Vinnie Chulk .15
201 Jose Capellan/1999 **RC** 5.00
202 Kazuo Matsui/1999 **RC** 5.00
203 David Crouthers/1999 3.00
204 Akinori Otsuka/1999 **RC** 5.00
205 Nick Regilio/1999 **RC** 3.00
206 Justin Hampson/1999 **RC** 3.00
207 Lincoln Holdzkom/1999 **RC** 3.00
208 Jorge Sequea/1999 **RC** 3.00
209 Justin Leone/1999 **RC** 5.00
210 Renyel Pinto/1999 **RC** 3.00
211 Mariano Gomez/1999 **RC** 3.00
212 Onil Joseph Auto./1,000 **RC** 8.00
213 Josh Labandeira AU/1,000 **RC** 10.00
214 Cory Sullivan/1999 **RC** 3.00
215 Carlos Vasquez Auto./675 **RC** 8.00
216 Chris Shelton/1999 **RC** 8.00
217 Willy Taveras/1999 **RC** 6.00
218 John Gall/1999 **RC** 5.00
219 Jerry Gil/1999 **RC** 3.00
220 Jason Frasor/1999 **RC** 3.00
221 Justin Knoedler/1999 **RC** 3.00
222 Ronald Belisario/1999 **RC** 3.00
223 Mike Rouse/1999 3.00
224 Dennis Sarfate/1999 **RC** 3.00
225 Casey Daigle/1999 **RC** 3.00
226 Shingo Takatsu Auto./800 **RC** 10.00
227 Jason Bartlett Auto./800 **RC** 8.00
228 Alfredo Simon Auto./1,000 **RC** 8.00
229 Chris Oxspring/1999 **RC** 3.00
230 Fernando Nieve Auto./1,000 **RC** 8.00
231 Ruddy Yan Auto./800 **RC** 8.00
232 Ryan Wing/1999 3.00
233 Tim Bittner Auto./1,000 **RC** 8.00
234 Ramon Ramirez Auto./1,000 **RC** 8.00
235 Sean Henn Auto./1,000 8.00
236 Roberto Novoa **RC** 4.00
237 Jerome Gamble Auto./800 **RC** 8.00
238 Jamie Brown Auto./800 **RC** 8.00
239 Ian Snell Auto./800 **RC** 30.00
240 Freddy Guzman Auto./800 **RC** 8.00
241 Aarom Baldiris Auto./1,000 **RC** 8.00
242 Greg Dobbs/1999 **RC** 3.00
243 Ivan Ochoa/1999 **RC** 3.00
244 Angel Chavez Auto./800 **RC** 8.00
245 Merkin Valdez Auto./800 **RC** 10.00
246 Mike Gosling Auto./800 8.00
247 Carlos Hines Auto./800 **RC** 8.00
248 Graham Koonce Auto./1,000 10.00
249 William Bergolla Auto./1,000 **RC** 8.00
250 Hector Gimenez Auto./1,000 **RC** 8.00

Credits Bronze

Bronze (1-200): 3-6X
Bronze (201-250): .5-1X
Production 100 Sets

Credits Silver

Silver (1-200): 4-8X
Silver (201-250): No Pricing
Production 50 Sets

Credits Gold

Gold (1-200): 8-15X
Gold (201-250): No Pricing
Production 25 Sets

Credits Platinum

No Pricing
Production One Set

Awards

NM/M

Common Player: 2.00
Quantity produced listed
1 Phil Rizzuto/1950 3.00
2 Fred Lynn/1975 2.00
3 George Brett/1980 8.00
4 Cal Ripken Jr./1983 10.00
5 Don Mattingly/1985 8.00
6 Rickey Henderson/1990 3.00
7 Stan Musial/1943 5.00
8 Marty Marion/1944 3.00
9 Ernie Banks/1958 5.00
10 Sammy Sosa/1998 6.00
11 Terry Pendleton/1991 2.00
12 Ryne Sandberg/1984 6.00
13 Andre Dawson/1987 3.00
14 George Foster/1977 2.00
15 Dave Parker/1978 2.00
16 Keith Hernandez/1979 3.00
17 Mike Schmidt/1980 6.00
18 Dale Murphy/1982 3.00
19 Whitey Ford/1961 3.00
20 Roy Halladay/2003 2.00
21 Orel Hershiser/1988 2.00
22 Bob Feller/1940 3.00
23 Dwight Gooden/1985 2.00
24 Steve Carlton/1972 3.00
25 Randy Johnson/2002 4.00

Awards Signature

NM/M

Quantity produced listed
1 Phil Rizzuto/50 25.00
2 Fred Lynn/100 15.00
7 Stan Musial/50 50.00
8 Marty Marion/50 10.00
10 Sammy Sosa/21 125.00
11 Terry Pendleton/100 10.00
13 Andre Dawson/100 15.00
14 George Foster/100 10.00
15 Dave Parker/88 15.00
16 Keith Hernandez/100 20.00
19 Whitey Ford/50 25.00
20 Roy Halladay/25 25.00
21 Orel Hershiser/25 40.00
22 Bob Feller/100 15.00
23 Dwight Gooden/100 10.00

Champions

NM/M

Common Player: 2.00
Quantity produced listed
1 Stan Musial/1951 5.00
2 Warren Spahn/1958 3.00
3 Bob Gibson/1968 3.00
4 Mike Schmidt/1980 6.00
5 Dale Murphy/1982 4.00
6 Steve Carlton/1983 4.00
7 Will Clark/1988 4.00
8 Nolan Ryan/1990 10.00
9 Ryne Sandberg/1990 6.00
10 Roger Clemens/1990 8.00
11 George Brett/1990 8.00
12 Tony Gwynn/1997 5.00
13 Todd Helton/2000 3.00
14 Troy Glaus/2000 2.00
15 Sammy Sosa/2000 6.00
16 Pedro J. Martinez/2000 4.00
17 Mark Mulder/2001 2.00
18 Manny Ramirez/2002 3.00
19 Lance Berkman/2002 2.00
20 Alex Rodriguez/Rgr/2002 6.00

Champions Jersey

NM/M

Common Jersey: 5.00
Quantity produced listed
1 Stan Musial/100 30.00
2 Warren Spahn/100 10.00
3 Bob Gibson/100 10.00
4 Mike Schmidt/100 20.00
5 Dale Murphy/82 10.00
6 Steve Carlton/100 8.00
7 Will Clark/100 10.00
8 Nolan Ryan/100 25.00
9 Ryne Sandberg/100 20.00
10 Roger Clemens/100 15.00
11 George Brett/100 25.00
12 Tony Gwynn/250 10.00
13 Todd Helton/250 8.00
14 Troy Glaus/250 5.00
15 Sammy Sosa/250 15.00
16 Pedro J. Martinez/250 8.00
17 Mark Mulder/250 5.00
18 Manny Ramirez/250 8.00
19 Lance Berkman/250 5.00
20 Alex Rodriguez/250 10.00

Champions Signature

NM/M

Quantity produced listed
1 Stan Musial/50 50.00
3 Bob Gibson/50 25.00
7 Will Clark/50 40.00
8 Nolan Ryan/34 100.00

Champions Jersey Signature

No Pricing
Production Five Sets

Class Reunion

NM/M

Quantity produced listed
1 Eddie Murray, Gary Carter/2003 3.00
2 Carlton Fisk, Tony Perez/2000 3.00
3 Nolan Ryan, George Brett/1999 10.00
4 Rod Carew, Fergie Jenkins/1991 3.00
5 Joe Morgan, Jim Palmer/1990 3.00
6 Carl Yastrzemski, Johnny Bench/1989 5.00
7 Harmon Killebrew, Luis Aparicio/1984 3.00
8 Brooks Robinson, Juan Marichal/1983 3.00
9 Al Kaline, Duke Snider/1980 3.00
10 Roberto Clemente, Warren Spahn/1973 8.00
11 Mark Prior, Mark Teixeira/2001 3.00
12 Josh Beckett, Barry Zito/1999 3.00
13 Mark Mulder, Adam Dunn/1998 3.00
14 Vernon Wells, Lance Berkman/1997 3.00
15 Eric Chavez, Nick Johnson/1996 3.00
16 Kerry Wood, Roy Halladay/1995 4.00
17 Todd Helton, Carlos Beltran/1995 4.00
18 Derek Jeter, Jason Giambi/1992 8.00
19 Manny Ramirez, Shawn Green/1991 4.00
20 Chipper Jones, Mike Mussina/1990 4.00

Class Reunion Material

NM/M

Quantity produced listed

1 Eddie Murray/Jsy, Gary Carter/Jsy/100 15.00
2 Carlton Fisk/Jsy, Tony Perez/Bat/250 20.00
3 Nolan Ryan/Jsy, George Brett/Jsy/100 50.00
4 Rod Carew/Jsy, Fergie Jenkins/Pants/250 15.00
5 Joe Morgan/Jsy, Jim Palmer/Jsy/100 10.00
6 Carl Yastrzemski/Jsy, Johnny Bench/Jsy/250 30.00
7 Harmon Killebrew/Jsy, Luis Aparicio/Jsy/250 15.00
8 Brooks Robinson/Jsy, Juan Marichal/Jsy/100 15.00
9 Al Kaline/Jsy, Duke Snider/Jsy/25 35.00
10 Roger Clemens/Jsy, Warren Spahn/Jsy/100 80.00
11 Mark Prior/Jsy, Mark Teixeira/Jsy/250 10.00
12 Josh Beckett/Jsy, Barry Zito/Jsy/250 8.00
13 Mark Mulder/Jsy, Adam Dunn/Jsy/250 10.00
14 Vernon Wells/Jsy, Lance Berkman/Jsy/250 8.00
15 Eric Chavez/Jsy, Nick Johnson/Jsy/250 8.00
16 Kerry Wood/Jsy, Roy Halladay/Jsy/250 12.00
17 Todd Helton/Jsy, Carlos Beltran/Jsy/250 10.00
18 Derek Jeter/Jsy, Jason Giambi/Jsy/250 20.00
19 Manny Ramirez/Jsy, Shawn Green/Jsy/50 10.00
20 Chipper Jones/Jsy, Mike Mussina/Jsy/250 10.00

Game Day Souvenir

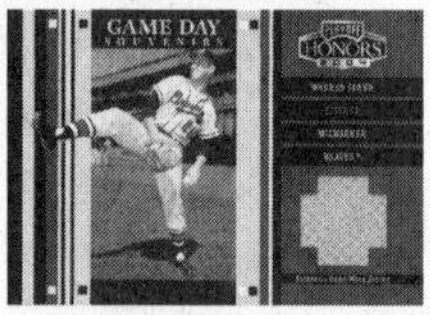

NM/M
2 Bob Gibson/Jsy/75 15.00
3 Frank Robinson/Bat/61 10.00
4 Tony Gwynn/Pants/99 20.00
5 Warren Spahn/Jsy/53 20.00
6 George Brett/Bat/77 25.00
7 Cal Ripken Jr./Hat/19 100.00
8 Frank Thomas/Bat/93 10.00
9 Sammy Sosa/Jsy/100 15.00
10 Harmon Killebrew/Bat/75 15.00

Game Day Souvenir Signature

No Pricing
Production Five Sets

Piece of the Game Bat

NM/M
1 Albert Pujols/250 15.00
2 Angel Berroa/250 4.00
3 Aubrey Huff/250 4.00
4 Barry Zito/250 6.00
5 Bobby Abreu/250 4.00
6 Carlos Beltran/250 4.00
7 Chipper Jones/250 8.00
8 Derek Jeter/250 20.00
9 Eric Chavez/150 6.00
10 Eric Hinske/50 6.00
11 Gary Sheffield/250 6.00
12 George Brett/250 15.00
13 Jay Gibbons/250 4.00
14 Jim Edmonds/250 6.00
15 Josh Beckett/250 6.00
16 Manny Ramirez/250 8.00
17 Mark Mulder/250 6.00
18 Marlon Byrd/250 4.00
19 Mike Lowell/250 4.00
20 Mike Schmidt/250 20.00
21 Nolan Ryan/250 20.00
22 Rafael Furcal/250 4.00
23 Randy Johnson/100 10.00
24 Rod Carew/250 8.00
25 Torii Hunter/250 4.00

Piece of the Game Bat Signature

No Pricing
Production 1-10

Piece of the Game Jersey

NM/M
Quantity produced listed
1 Albert Pujols/250 15.00
2 Angel Berroa/250 4.00
3 Aubrey Huff/250 4.00
4 Barry Zito/250 6.00
5 Bobby Abreu/250 4.00
6 Carlos Beltran/250 4.00
7 Chipper Jones/250 8.00
8 Derek Jeter/50 40.00
9 Eric Chavez/250 5.00
10 Eric Hinske/100 4.00
12 George Brett/250 15.00
13 Jay Gibbons/250 4.00
14 Jim Edmonds/250 6.00
15 Josh Beckett/250 4.00
16 Manny Ramirez/250 6.00
17 Mark Mulder/100 6.00
18 Marlon Byrd/250 4.00
19 Mike Lowell/250 4.00
20 Mike Schmidt/50 35.00
21 Nolan Ryan/100 25.00
22 Rafael Furcal/250 4.00
23 Randy Johnson/250 8.00
24 Rod Carew/100 8.00
25 Torii Hunter/250 4.00

Piece of the Game Jersey Signature

Quantity produced listed

Piece of the Game Combo

NM/M
1 Albert Pujols/Bat-Jsy/100 25.00
2 Angel Berroa/Bat-Pants/100 6.00
3 Aubrey Huff/Bat-Jsy/100 6.00
4 Barry Zito/Bat-Jsy/100 8.00
5 Bobby Abreu/Bat-Jsy/100 6.00
6 Carlos Beltran/Bat-Jsy/100 6.00
7 Chipper Jones/Bat-Jsy/100 10.00
8 Derek Jeter/Bat-Jsy/100 40.00
9 Eric Chavez/Bat-Jsy/50 8.00
10 Eric Hinske/Bat-Jsy/25 8.00
12 George Brett/Bat-Jsy/100 25.00
13 Jay Gibbons/Bat-Jsy/100 6.00
14 Jim Edmonds/Bat-Jsy/100 8.00
15 Josh Beckett/Bat-Jsy/100 6.00
16 Manny Ramirez/Bat-Jsy/100 10.00
17 Mark Mulder/Bat-Jsy/25 15.00
18 Marlon Byrd/Bat-Jsy/100 6.00
19 Mike Lowell/Bat-Jsy/100 6.00
20 Mike Schmidt/Bat-Jsy/50 50.00
21 Nolan Ryan/Bat-Jsy/100 35.00
22 Rafael Furcal/Bat-Jsy/100 6.00
23 Randy Johnson/Bat-Jsy/100 15.00
24 Rod Carew/Bat-Jsy/100 15.00
25 Torii Hunter/Bat-Jsy/100 8.00

Piece of the Game Combo Signature

No Pricing
Production 1-10

Prime Signature Autograph

NM/M
1 Garret Anderson/100 15.00
2 Rafael Palmeiro/50 40.00
3 Vladimir Guerrero/50 50.00
5 Dontrelle Willis/50 30.00
6 Miguel Cabrera/100 35.00
7 Shannon Stewart/100 10.00
9 Gary Sheffield/100 25.00
12 Tom Glavine/25 40.00
13 Brandon Webb/100 10.00
14 Carlos Lee/100 10.00
17 Magglio Ordonez/100 15.00
19 Andruw Jones/50 20.00
21 Sammy Sosa/50 100.00
22 Juan Gonzalez/50 25.00
23 Jeff Bagwell/25 50.00
24 Rickey Henderson/25 75.00
25 Mike Schmidt/50 60.00
26 Jim Rice/100 15.00
27 Billy Williams/100 15.00
28 Lou Brock/100 20.00
29 Robin Yount/25 75.00
30 Nolan Ryan/50 85.00
31 Darryl Strawberry/100 15.00
32 Cal Ripken Jr./25 200.00
33 Andre Dawson/100 15.00
34 Don Mattingly/50 75.00
35 Paul Molitor/25 50.00
36 Bo Jackson/50 75.00
37 Ernie Banks/50 50.00
38 Orel Hershiser/100 20.00
39 Mark Grace/50 40.00
40 Carlton Fisk/50 25.00

Prime Signature Autograph Bat

Quantity produced listed

Prime Signature Autograph Jersey

NM/M
Quantity produced listed
2 Rafael Palmeiro/25 75.00
6 Miguel Cabrera/20 75.00
7 Shannon Stewart/23 15.00
29 Robin Yount/19 75.00
31 Darryl Strawberry/25 25.00
34 Don Mattingly/23 100.00
39 Mark Grace/17 65.00

Prime Signature Insert

NM/M
Production 2,500 Sets
1 Garret Anderson 2.00
2 Rafael Palmeiro 3.00
3 Vladimir Guerrero 3.00
4 Alex Rodriguez 5.00
5 Dontrelle Willis 2.00
6 Miguel Cabrera 3.00
7 Shannon Stewart 2.00
8 Mike Piazza 4.00
9 Gary Sheffield 2.00
10 Ivan Rodriguez 3.00
11 Randy Johnson 3.00
12 Tom Glavine 2.00
13 Brandon Webb 2.00
14 Carlos Lee 2.00
15 Hideo Nomo 2.00
16 Mike Mussina 3.00
17 Magglio Ordonez 2.00
18 Austin Kearns 2.00
19 Andruw Jones 3.00
20 Mariano Rivera 3.00
21 Sammy Sosa 4.00
22 Juan Gonzalez 3.00
23 Jeff Bagwell 3.00
24 Rickey Henderson 3.00
25 Mike Schmidt 5.00
26 Jim Rice 2.00
27 Billy Williams 2.00
28 Lou Brock 2.00
29 Robin Yount 4.00
30 Nolan Ryan 8.00
31 Darryl Strawberry 2.00
32 Cal Ripken Jr. 10.00
33 Andre Dawson 2.00
34 Don Mattingly 8.00
35 Paul Molitor 3.00
36 Bo Jackson 3.00
37 Ernie Banks 4.00
38 Orel Hershiser 2.00
39 Mark Grace 3.00
40 Carlton Fisk 3.00

Quad Material

NM/M
Quantity produced listed
1 Matt Williams, Mark Grace, Will Clark, Keith Hernandez/100 60.00
2 Jason Giambi, Jim Thome, Carlos Delgado, Rafael Palmeiro/100 20.00
3 Albert Pujols, Ernie Banks, Jeff Bagwell, Jim Thome/100 50.00
4 Paul Molitor, Joe Morgan, Ryne Sandberg, Alfonso Soriano/50 50.00
5 Cal Ripken Jr., Derek Jeter, Alex Rodriguez, Nomar Garciaparra/100 75.00
6 Ozzie Smith, Robin Yount, Alan Trammell, Dave Concepcion/50 50.00
8 Johnny Bench, Carlton Fisk, Gary Carter, Mike Piazza/100 40.00
9 Todd Helton, Brian Giles, Edgar Renteria, Scott Rolen/25 40.00
10 Carlos Delgado, Alfonso Soriano, Alex Rodriguez, Troy Glaus/100 20.00
11 Harmon Killebrew, Reggie Jackson, Mike Schmidt, Sammy Sosa/100 65.00
12 Stan Musial, Rickey Henderson, Tony Gwynn, Lou Brock/25 80.00
13 Cal Ripken Jr., George Brett, Paul Molitor, Rod Carew/100 75.00
14 Sammy Sosa, Vladimir Guerrero, Manny Ramirez, Magglio Ordonez/100 40.00
15 Andruw Jones, Jim Edmonds, Torii Hunter, Vernon Wells/100 20.00
16 Chipper Jones, Shawn Green, Andruw Jones, Lance Berkman/100 20.00
17 Tony Gwynn, Dale Murphy, Kirby Puckett, Andre Dawson/100 40.00
19 Nolan Ryan, Roger Clemens, Kerry Wood, Josh Beckett/100 75.00
21 Dennis Eckersley, John Smoltz, Mariano Rivera, Lee Smith/100 40.00
22 Mike Mussina, Greg Maddux, Jack Morris, Bert Blyleven/100 40.00
23 Steve Carlton, Tom Glavine, Barry Zito, Andy Pettitte/100 20.00
24 Whitey Ford, Warren Spahn, Bob Feller, Juan Marichal/25 80.00
25 Nolan Ryan, Roger Clemens, Steve Carlton, Randy Johnson/100 80.00

Rookie Year Jersey Number

NM/M
1 Gary Carter/50 10.00
2 Robin Yount/50 30.00
3 Roger Clemens/25 40.00
4 Gary Sheffield/50 8.00
5 Mike Piazza/25 30.00
6 Hideo Nomo/25 30.00
7 Alex Rodriguez/50 20.00
8 Mark Prior/25 15.00
9 Dontrelle Willis/100 10.00
10 Angel Berroa/100 8.00

Rookie Year Jersey Signature

No Pricing
Production 1-10

Signature Bronze

NM/M
Quantity produced listed
2 Garret Anderson/100 15.00
5 Vladimir Guerrero/50 50.00
6 Brandon Webb/100 8.00
7 Brian Bruney/96 8.00
11 Robby Hammock/100 8.00
13 Shea Hillenbrand/100 10.00
15 Adam LaRoche/100 10.00
16 Andruw Jones/25 25.00
17 Bubba Nelson/100 8.00
22 Marcus Giles/100 15.00
23 Rafael Furcal/50 15.00
26 Adam Loewen/100 8.00
27 Cal Ripken Jr./25 150.00
29 Jay Gibbons/100 8.00
30 Luis Matos/100 8.00
33 Bobby Doerr/100 15.00
35 Edwin Almonte/99 8.00
36 Jason Varitek/50 30.00
37 Kevin Youkilis/100 15.00
42 Andre Dawson/100 15.00
43 Aramis Ramirez/25 25.00
44 Brendan Harris/100 8.00
45 Derrek Lee/100 20.00
46 Ernie Banks/25 60.00
47 Kerry Wood/25 50.00
48 Mark Prior/50 40.00
50 Sammy Sosa/50 125.00
51 Carlos Lee/100 10.00
52 Frank Thomas/25 50.00
53 Joe Borchard/100 8.00
54 Joe Crede/50 10.00
55 Magglio Ordonez/50 15.00
58 Barry Larkin/25 40.00
59 Brandon Larson/100 8.00
61 Ryan Wagner/100 8.00
63 Bob Feller/100 20.00
64 Brian Tallet/100 8.00
66 Jeremy Guthrie/100 8.00
67 Jody Gerut/100 10.00
68 Clint Barmes/100 8.00
69 Jeff Baker/25 20.00
72 Preston Wilson/100 15.00
74 Alan Trammell/100 15.00
78 Preston Larrison/100 8.00
79 Dontrelle Willis/25 30.00
83 Miguel Cabrera/100 40.00
85 Andy Pettitte/25 50.00
86 Chris Burke/100 8.00
88 Jeff Bagwell/25 50.00
91 Morgan Ensberg/100 10.00
96 Byron Gettis/100 8.00
97 Carlos Beltran/100 30.00
98 George Brett/25 100.00
101 Duke Snider/100 25.00
102 Edwin Jackson/100 10.00
105 Hong-Chih Kuo/100 25.00
106 Kazuhisa Ishii/25 40.00
107 Paul LoDuca/100 15.00
108 Robin Ventura/50 15.00
110 Junior Spivey/50 10.00
112 Scott Podsednik/100 15.00
113 J.D. Durbin/100 8.00
114 Jacque Jones/100 15.00
116 Johan Santana/100 25.00
117 Shannon Stewart/50 10.00
123 Gary Carter/100 15.00
125 Lenny Dykstra/100 15.00
130 Chien-Ming Wang/100 100.00
132 Don Mattingly/25 80.00
133 Gary Sheffield/50 25.00
137 Jorge Posada/50 25.00
142 Whitey Ford/50 25.00
145 Mark Mulder/100 15.00
146 Rich Harden/100 15.00
147 Tim Hudson/25 40.00
148 Reggie Jackson/25 50.00
149 Rickey Henderson/25 80.00
150 Brett Myers/100 8.00
154 Marlon Byrd/100 8.00
155 Mike Schmidt/50 60.00
156 Ryan Howard/100 80.00
161 Jay Payton/100 10.00
168 Jerome Williams/50 20.00
169 Will Clark/50 50.00
171 Chris Snelling/100 8.00
176 Shigetoshi Hasegawa/100 50.00
178 Dan Haren/100 10.00
180 Jim Edmonds/25 30.00
182 Scott Rolen/50 30.00
183 Stan Musial/50 60.00
184 Aubrey Huff/100 15.00
185 Chad Gaudin/100 8.00
186 Delmon Young/50 30.00
191 Mark Teixeira/50 25.00
192 Nolan Ryan/50 100.00
193 Alexis Rios/100 15.00
195 Dustin McGowan/100 10.00
196 Guillermo Quiroz/50 10.00
197 Josh Phelps/25 15.00
198 Roy Halladay/25 25.00
200 Vinnie Chulk/25 15.00
201 Jose Capellan/100 35.00
203 David Crouthers/100 8.00
204 Akinori Otsuka/100 35.00
205 Nick Regilio/100 8.00
206 Justin Hampson/100 8.00
207 Lincoln Holdzkom/100 8.00
208 Jorge Sequea/100 8.00
209 Justin Leone/100 15.00
210 Renyel Pinto/100 10.00
211 Mariano Gomez/100 8.00
214 Cory Sullivan/100 8.00
216 Chris Shelton/100 40.00
217 Willy Taveras/25 8.00
218 John Gall/100 15.00
222 Ronald Belisario/100 8.00
223 Mike Rouse/100 8.00
224 Dennis Sarfate/100 8.00

Signature Silver

Silver: .75-1.5X Bronze
Production 1-100
No pricing 25 or less.

Signature Gold

Gold: .75-1.5X Bronze
Production 1-50
No pricing 25 or less.

Signature Platinum

No Pricing
Production One Set

Signs of Greatness

NM/M
Quantity produced listed
1 Mark Prior/25 50.00
2 Scott Podsednik/25 25.00
4 Dontrelle Willis/25 30.00
5 Rocco Baldelli/20 40.00
6 Brandon Webb/25 20.00
7 Rich Harden/25 25.00
8 Miguel Cabrera/25 50.00
9 Josh Beckett/25 40.00
10 Mark Teixeira/25 40.00

Tandem Material

NM/M
Common Duo: 10.00
Quantity produced listed
1 Bo Jackson, Deion Sanders/100 30.00
2 Eddie Murray, Rafael Palmeiro/250 15.00
3 Alex Rodriguez, Dale Murphy/250 15.00
4 Carlton Fisk, Ivan Rodriguez/250 15.00
5 Rickey Henderson, Lou Brock/50 30.00
6 Sammy Sosa, Ernie Banks/250 25.00
7 Warren Spahn, Steve Carlton/100 15.00
8 Carl Yastrzemski, Darrell Evans/250 25.00
9 Keith Hernandez, Lenny Dykstra/250 10.00
10 Pee Wee Reese, Marty Marion/100 15.00
11 Hideo Nomo, Chipper Jones/250 15.00
12 Willie McCovey, Reggie Jackson/100 20.00
13 Mark Prior, Barry Zito/250 10.00
14 Cal Ripken Jr., Miguel Tejada/Bat/100 50.00
15 Roberto Clemente, Vladimir Guerrero/Bat/100 75.00
16 Gary Carter, Mike Piazza/250 15.00
17 Jim Rice, Fred Lynn/50 20.00
18 Willie Stargell, Keith Hernandez/250 15.00
19 Nomar Garciaparra, Mark Teixeira/100 20.00
20 Derek Jeter, Phil Rizzuto/50 50.00
21 Eric Chavez, Hank Blalock/100 10.00
22 Eric Davis, Darryl Strawberry/100 15.00
23 Rickey Henderson, Deion Sanders/100 30.00
24 Dave Parker, Austin Kearns/250 10.00
25 Luis Aparicio, Dave Concepcion/100 15.00
26 Rafael Palmeiro, Will Clark/100 25.00
27 Ryne Sandberg, Ozzie Smith/250 50.00
28 Alex Rodriguez M's, Jose Canseco/250 15.00
29 Sammy Sosa, Juan Gonzalez/250 15.00
30 Pedro J. Martinez, Juan Marichal/50 20.00
32 Dwight Gooden, Gary Sheffield/250 10.00
33 Lou Boudreau, Omar Vizquel/100 15.00
34 Mark Prior, Ron Santo Bat/100 30.00
35 Albert Pujols, Ken Boyer/250 25.00
36 Tom Seaver, Curt Schilling/250 15.00
37 Joe Morgan, Jeff Kent/250 10.00
38 Steve Garvey, Ozzie Smith/250 25.00
39 Mike Piazza, Ivan Rodriguez/250 15.00
40 Mike Schmidt, Jim Thome/100 25.00

2004 Playoff Prestige

NM/M
Complete Set (200): 35.00
Common Player: .15
Pack (6): 3.50
Box (24): 75.00
1 Bengie Molina .15
2 Garret Anderson .25

3 Jarrod Washburn .15
4 Scott Spiezio .15
5 Tim Salmon .25
6 Troy Glaus .40
7 Alex Cintron .15
8 Brandon Webb .25
9 Curt Schilling .50
10 Edgar Gonzalez .50
11 Luis Gonzalez .25
12 Randy Johnson .75
13 Steve Finley .15
14 Andruw Jones .50
15 Bubba Nelson .50
16 Chipper Jones 1.00
17 Gary Sheffield .40
18 Greg Maddux 1.00
19 Javy Lopez .40
20 John Smoltz .25
21 Marcus Giles .25
22 Rafael Furcal .25
23 Brian Roberts .15
24 Jason Johnson .15
25 Jay Gibbons .25
26 Luis Matos .15
27 Melvin Mora .15
28 Tony Batista .15
29 Bill Mueller .25
30 David Ortiz .40
31 Johnny Damon .25
32 Kevin Youkilis 1.00
33 Manny Ramirez .50
34 Nomar Garciaparra 1.50
35 Pedro Martinez .75
36 Trot Nixon .25
37 Aramis Ramirez .25
38 Brendan Harris .50
39 Carlos Zambrano .15
40 Corey Patterson .25
41 Kenny Lofton .25
42 Kerry Wood .75
43 Mark Prior 1.50
44 Sammy Sosa 1.50
45 Bartolo Colon .25
46 Carlos Lee .25
47 Esteban Loaiza .15
48 Frank Thomas .50
49 Joe Crede .15
50 Magglio Ordonez .40
51 Roberto Alomar .40
52 Adam Dunn .40
53 Austin Kearns .40
54 Josh Hall .15
55 Ken Griffey Jr. 1.00
56 Sean Casey .15
57 Micheal Nakamura .15
58 C.C. Sabathia .15
59 Casey Blake .15
60 Jody Gerut .15
61 Matt Lawton .15
62 Milton Bradley .15
63 Omar Vizquel .25
64 Jason Jennings .15
65 Jay Payton .25
66 Larry Walker .25
67 Preston Wilson .25
68 Todd Helton .50
69 Bobby Higginson .25
70 Carlos Pena .15
71 Dmitri Young .15
72 Jeremy Bonderman .15
73 Preston Larrison .50
74 Derrek Lee .40
75 Dontrelle Willis .40
76 Ivan Rodriguez .50
77 Josh Beckett .50
78 Juan Pierre .15
79 Miguel Cabrera .75
80 Mike Lowell .25
81 Chris Burke .15
82 Craig Biggio .25
83 Jeff Bagwell .50
84 Jeff Kent .25
85 Lance Berkman .40
86 Richard Hidalgo .25
87 Roy Oswalt .25
88 Aaron Guiel .15
89 Angel Berroa .15
90 Carlos Beltran .40
91 Jeremy Affeldt .15
92 Michael Sweeney .15
93 Runelvys Hernandez .15
94 Dave Roberts .15
95 Eric Gagne .40
96 Hideo Nomo .40
97 Kevin Brown .25
98 Paul Lo Duca .15
99 Shawn Green .40
100 Ben Sheets .25
101 Geoff Jenkins .40
102 Richie Sexson .40
103 Rickie Weeks 1.00
104 Scott Podsednik .50
105 J.D. Durbin .50
106 Jacque Jones .15
107 Jason Kubel .50
108 Shannon Stewart .15
109 Torii Hunter .40
110 Chad Cordero .50
111 Javier Vazquez .25
112 Jose Vidro .15
113 Livan Hernandez .15
114 Orlando Cabrera .25
115 Tony Armas Jr. .15
116 Vladimir Guerrero .75
117 Al Leiter .15
118 Cliff Floyd .15
119 Jae Weong So .15
120 Jose Reyes .50
121 Mike Piazza 1.00
122 Tom Glavine .25
123 Aaron Boone .15
124 Alfonso Soriano .75
125 Andy Pettitte .15
126 Derek Jeter .15
127 Hideki Matsui .15
128 Jason Giambi .15
129 Jorge Posada .50
130 Jose Contreras .25
131 Mike Mussina .50
132 Barry Zito .40
133 Eric Byrnes .15
134 Eric Chavez .40
135 Jose Guillen .15
136 Mark Mulder .40
137 Miguel Tejada .40
138 Ramon Hernandez .15
139 Rich Harden .15
140 Tim Hudson .40
141 Bobby Abreu .25
142 Brett Myers .15
143 Jim Thome .75
144 Kevin Millwood .40
145 Mike Lieberthal .15
146 Ryan Howard 1.50
147 Craig Wilson .15
148 Jack Wilson .15
149 Jason Kendall .15
150 Kip Wells .15
151 Reggie Sanders .15
152 Albert Pujols 1.50
153 Edgar Renteria .25
154 Jim Edmonds .40
155 Matt Morris .25
156 Scott Rolen .75
157 Tino Martinez .15
158 Woody Williams .15
159 Brian Giles .25
160 Freddy Guzman **RC** .50
161 Jake Peavy .15
162 Khalil Greene .50
163 Phil Nevin .15
164 Ryan Klesko .25
165 Ray Durham .15
166 Jason Schmidt .25
167 Jerome Williams .50
168 Jesse Foppert .15
169 Jose Cruz .15
170 Marquis Grissom .15
171 Merkin Valdez **RC** 1.50
172 Rich Aurilia .15
173 Bret Boone .25
174 Freddy Garcia .15
175 Ichiro Suzuki 1.50
176 Jamie Moyer .15
177 John Olerud .25
178 Mike Cameron .15
179 Randy Winn .15
180 Aubrey Huff .25
181 Carl Crawford .25
182 Chad Gaudin .50
183 Rocco Baldelli .50
184 Toby Hall .15
185 Travis Lee .15
186 Alex Rodriguez 1.50
187 Hank Blalock .40
188 John Thomson .15
189 Juan Gonzalez .50
190 Mark Teixeira .40
191 Michael Young .15
192 Rafael Palmeiro .50
193 Ramon Nivar .50
194 Carlos Delgado .50
195 Dustin McGowan .50
196 Frank Catalanotto .15
197 Vinnie Chulk .15
198 Orlando Hudson .15
199 Roy Halladay .40
200 Vernon Wells .25

Xtra Bases Black

Black (1-200): 4-8X
Production 75 Sets

Xtra Bases Black Autographs

No Pricing
Production 25 Sets

Xtra Bases Purple

Purple (1-200): 2-5X
Production 150 Sets

Xtra Bases Purple Autographs

NM/M

Production 100 Sets
10 Edgar Gonzalez 6.00
15 Bubba Nelson 8.00
32 Kevin Youkilis 15.00
38 Brendan Harris 8.00
57 Micheal Nakamura 6.00
73 Preston Larrison 6.00
79 Miguel Cabrera 35.00
81 Chris Burke 15.00
105 J.D. Durbin 10.00
107 Jason Kubel 8.00
146 Ryan Howard 75.00
193 Ramon Nivar 8.00
195 Dustin McGowan 10.00
198 Orlando Hudson 8.00

Xtra Bases Red Autographs

Complete Set:
Common Player:

Achievements

NM/M

1 Hideo Nomo/95 ROY 1.50
2 Don Mattingly/85 MVP 6.00
3 Roger Clemens/ 86 CY/MVP 6.00
4 Greg Maddux/95 CY 4.00
5 Stan Musial/43 MVP 4.00
6 Roberto Clemente/ 66 MVP 6.00
7 Derek Jeter/96 ROY 6.00
8 Albert Pujols/01 ROY 6.00
9 Cal Ripken Jr./91 MVP 8.00
10 George Brett/80 MVP 8.00
11 Carl Yastrzemski/ 67 MVP 4.00
12 Rickey Henderson/ 90 MVP 2.00
13 Sammy Sosa/98 MVP 5.00
14 Randy Johnson/02 CY 3.00
15 Bob Gibson/ 68 CY/MVP 3.00

Autographs

NM/M

Quantity produced listed
8 Brandon Webb/100 20.00
10 Edgar Gonzalez PROS/150 8.00
15 Bubba Nelson PROS/250 10.00
25 Jay Gibbons/50 20.00
32 Kevin Youkilis PROS/100 20.00
36 Trot Nixon/25 40.00
37 Aramis Ramirez/25 25.00
38 Brendan Harris PROS/400 8.00
49 Joe Crede/25 15.00
54 Josh Hall/25 15.00
57 Mike Nakamura/250 8.00
60 Jody Gerut/50 15.00
73 Preston Larrison PROS/250 8.00
75 Dontrelle Willis/25 40.00
79 Miguel Cabrera/100 30.00
81 Chris Burke PROS/250 10.00
93 Runelvys Hernandez/50 10.00
98 Paul Lo Duca/25 15.00
102 Richie Sexson/25 25.00
105 J.D. Durbin PROS/500 10.00
106 Jacque Jones/50 12.00
107 Jason Kubel PROS/400 8.00
108 Shannon Stewart/50 15.00
112 Jose Vidro/25 15.00
114 Orlando Cabrera/25 20.00
119 Jae Weong Seo/25 20.00
133 Eric Byrnes/50 15.00
136 Mark Mulder/25 20.00
139 Rich Harden/50 25.00
146 Ryan Howard PROS/400 75.00
193 Ramon Nivar PROS/100 8.00
195 Dustin McGowan PROS/100 10.00
197 Vinnie Chulk/112 8.00
198 Orlando Hudson/100 10.00

Changing Stripes

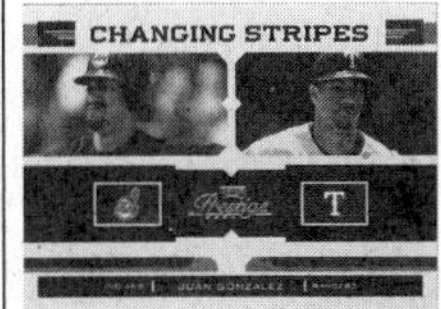

NM/M

Inserted 1:11
Foil: 1-2X
Production 150 Sets
Holofoil: 2-3X
Production 50 Sets
1 Rickey Henderson A-s-Yanks 4.00
2 Mike Mussina O's-Yanks 2.00
3 Jim Thome Indians-Phils 3.00
4 Hideo Nomo Sox-Dodgers 1.50
5 Scott Rolen Phils-Cards 3.00
6 Jason Giambi A-s-Yanks 3.00
7 Randy Johnson Astros-D'backs 3.00
8 Shawn Green Jays-Dodgers 1.50
9 Curt Schilling Phils-D'backs 2.00
10 Alex Rodriguez M's-Rangers 5.00
11 Greg Maddux Cubs-Braves 4.00
12 Randy Johnson M's-Astros 3.00
13 Hideo Nomo Dodgers-Mets 1.50
14 Juan Rodriguez Rgr-Marlins 2.00
15 Juan Gonzalez Indians-Rangers 2.00
16 Manny Ramirez Indians-Sox 2.00
17 Mike Piazza Dodgers-Mets 4.00
18 Nolan Ryan Angels-Astros 8.00
19 Nolan Ryan Astros-Rangers 8.00
20 Pedro Martinez Expos-Sox 3.00
21 Reggie Jackson Yanks-Angels 2.00
22 Roberto Alomar Mets-Sox 1.50
23 Rod Carew Twins-Angels 2.00
24 Roger Clemens Sox-Yanks 6.00
25 Sammy Sosa Sox-Cubs 5.00

Changing Stripes Dual Jersey

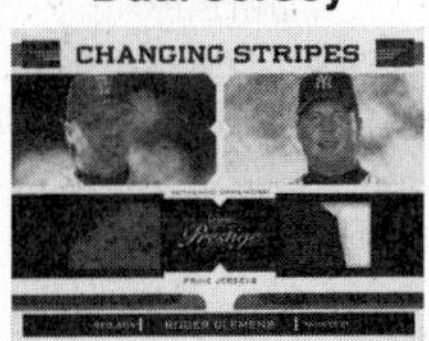

NM/M

Prodcution 150 Sets
Primes: No Pricing
Production 25 Sets
1 Rickey Henderson A's-Yanks 10.00
2 Mike Mussina O's-Yanks 8.00
3 Jim Thome Indians-Phils 10.00
4 Hideo Nomo Sox-Dodgers 15.00
5 Scott Rolen Phils-Cards 10.00
6 Jason Giambi A's-Yanks 12.00
7 Randy Johnson Astros-D'backs 10.00
8 Shawn Green Jays-Dodgers 6.00
9 Curt Schilling Phils-D'backs 8.00
10 Alex Rodriguez M's-Rangers 15.00
12 Randy Johnson M's-Astros 10.00
13 Hideo Nomo Dodgers-Mets 15.00
14 Ivan Rodriguez Rgr-Marlins 10.00
15 Juan Gonzalez Indians-Rangers 8.00
16 Manny Ramirez Indians-Sox 8.00
17 Mike Piazza Dodgers-Mets 10.00
18 Nolan Ryan Angels-Astros 30.00
19 Nolan Ryan Astrs-Rangers 30.00
20 Pedro Martinez Expos-Sox 10.00
22 Roberto Alomar Mets-Sox 8.00
23 Rod Carew Twins-Angels 12.00
24 Roger Clemens Sox-Yanks 15.00
25 Sammy Sosa Sox-Cubs 15.00

Connections

NM/M

Inserted 1:9
Foil: 1.5-2X
Production 100 Sets
Holofoil: No Pricing
Production 21 Sets
1 Derek Jeter, Alfonso Soriano 4.00
2 Greg Maddux, Chipper Jones 2.00
3 Albert Pujols, Scott Rolen 3.00
4 Randy Johnson, Curt Schilling 1.50
5 Nomar Garciaparra, Manny Ramirez 3.00
6 Alex Rodriguez, Mark Teixeira 3.00
7 Barry Zito, Tim Hudson .75
8 Sammy Sosa, Mark Prior 2.00
9 Derek Jeter, Jason Giambi 4.00
10 Roger Clemens, Mike Mussina 3.00
11 Mark Prior, Kerry Wood 2.00
12 Alex Rodriguez, Hank Blalock 3.00
13 Frank Thomas, Magglio Ordonez 1.00
14 Nomar Garciaparra, Pedro Martinez 3.00
15 Carlos Delgado, Vernon Wells 1.00
16 Miguel Tejada, Eric Chavez .75
17 Jeff Bagwell, Lance Berkman 1.00
18 Jim Thome, Bobby Abreu 1.50
19 Todd Helton, Preston Wilson 1.00
20 Vladimir Guerrero, Javier Vazquez 1.50

Connections Material

NM/M

Production 250 Sets
1 Derek Jeter/Bat, Alfonso Soriano/Bat 20.00
2 Greg Maddux/Bat, Chipper Jones/Jsy 12.00
3 Albert Pujols/Bat, Scott Rolen/Bat 15.00
4 Randy Johnson/Bat, Curt Schilling/Bat 10.00
5 Nomar Garciaparra/Bat, Manny Ramirez/Bat 10.00
6 Alex Rodriguez/Bat, Mark Teixeira/Bat 10.00
7 Barry Zito/Bat, Tim Hudson/Bat 10.00
8 Sammy Sosa/Bat, Mark Prior/Bat 15.00
9 Derek Jeter/Bat, Jason Giambi/Bat 20.00
10 Roger Clemens/Jsy, Mike Mussina/Bat 15.00
11 Mark Prior/Bat, Kerry Wood/Bat 10.00
12 Alex Rodriguez/Bat, Hank Blalock/Bat 10.00
13 Frank Thomas/Bat, Magglio Ordonez/Bat 8.00
14 Nomar Garciaparra/Bat, Pedro Martinez/Bat 15.00
15 Carlos Delgado/Bat, Vernon Wells/Bat 8.00
16 Miguel Tejada/Bat, Eric Chavez/Bat 8.00
17 Jeff Bagwell/Bat, Lance Berkman/Bat 10.00
18 Jim Thome/Jsy, Bobby Abreu/Bat 10.00
19 Todd Helton/Bat, Preston Wilson 8.00
20 Vladimir Guerrero/Bat, Javier Vazquez/Jsy 10.00

Diamond Heritage

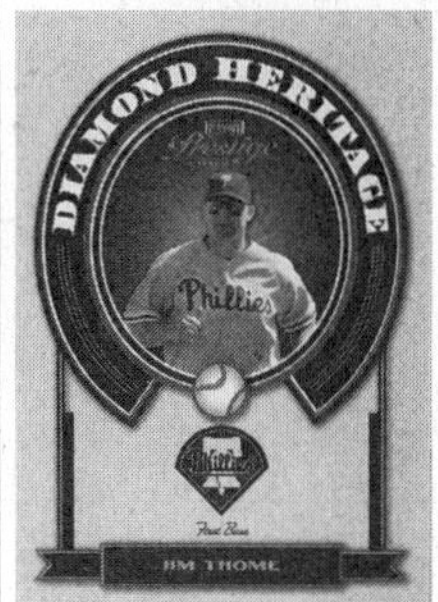

NM/M

Inserted 1:13
1 Mike Piazza 3.00
2 Greg Maddux 2.50
3 Nomar Garciaparra 3.00
4 Chipper Jones 2.00
5 Albert Pujols 4.00
6 Derek Jeter 5.00
7 Shawn Green .75
8 Alex Rodriguez 4.00
9 Jim Thome 2.00
10 Jason Giambi 1.50
11 Sammy Sosa 3.00
12 Hank Blalock 1.00
13 Garret Anderson .75
14 Manny Ramirez 1.50
15 Scott Rolen 1.50
16 Jeff Bagwell 1.50
17 Randy Johnson 2.00
18 Ichiro Suzuki 3.00
19 Ivan Rodriguez 1.50
20 Alfonso Soriano 1.50

Diamond Heritage Material

NM/M

Inserted 1:92
1 Mike Piazza/Bat 10.00
2 Greg Maddux/Bat 8.00
3 Nomar Garciaparra/ Bat 10.00
4 Chipper Jones/Jsy 8.00
5 Albert Pujols/Bat 15.00
6 Derek Jeter/Jsy 15.00
7 Shawn Green/Bat 5.00
8 Alex Rodriguez/Bat 10.00
9 Jim Thome/Jsy 8.00
10 Jason Giambi/Bat 8.00
11 Sammy Sosa/Bat 12.00
12 Hank Blalock/Bat 6.00
13 Garret Anderson/Bat 5.00
14 Manny Ramirez/Bat 6.00
15 Scott Rolen/Bat 6.00
16 Jeff Bagwell/Bat 6.00
17 Randy Johnson/Bat 8.00
19 Ivan Rodriguez/Bat 6.00
20 Alfonso Soriano/Bat 6.00

League Leaders Single

NM/M

Foil 2-3X
Production 100 Sets
Holofoil: No Pricing
Production 25 Sets

1 Alex Rodriguez/AL HR 3.00
2 Albert Pujols/NL Hit 3.00
3 Albert Pujols/NL Avg 3.00
4 Nomar Garciaparra/ AL Hit 2.00
5 Mark Prior/NL ERA 2.00
6 Pedro Martinez/ AL ERA 1.00
7 Kerry Wood/NL SO 1.00
8 Derek Jeter/AL Avg 3.00
9 Jason Giambi/AL BB 1.00
10 Roger Clemens/AL SO 2.00

League Leaders Single Material

NM/M
Production 250 Sets
1 Alex Rodriguez/Bat 10.00
2 Albert Pujols/Bat 15.00
3 Albert Pujols/Bat 15.00
4 Nomar Garciaparra/ Bat 10.00
5 Mark Prior/Jsy 10.00
6 Pedro Martinez/Jsy 8.00
7 Kerry Wood/Jsy 8.00
8 Derek Jeter/Jsy 15.00
9 Jason Giambi/Jsy 6.00
10 Roger Clemens/Jsy 12.00

League Leaders Double

NM/M
Production 500 Sets
Foil: 1-2X
Production 75 Sets
Holofoil: No Pricing
Production 10 Sets
1 Alex Rodriguez, Jim Thome HR 5.00
2 Mark Prior, Pedro Martinez ERA 4.00
3 Roger Clemens, Kerry Wood SO 5.00
4 Nomar Garciaparra, Albert Pujols Hit 5.00
5 Derek Jeter, Albert Pujols Avg 5.00

League Leaders Double Material

NM/M
Production 100 Sets
1 Alex Rodriguez/Bat, Jim Thome/Bat 20.00
2 Mark Prior/Jsy, Pedro Martinez/Jsy 15.00
3 Roger Clemens/Jsy, Kerry Wood/Jsy 20.00
4 Nomar Garciaparra/Bat, Albert Pujols/Bat 25.00
5 Derek Jeter/Jsy, Albert Pujols/Bat 25.00

League Leaders Quad

NM/M
Production 250 Sets
Foil: 1-2X
Production 50 Sets
Holofoil: No Pricing
Production Five Sets
1 Albert Pujols, Todd Helton, Edgar Renteria, Gary Sheffield 10.00
2 Derek Jeter, Manny Ramirez, Nomar Garciaparra, Ichiro Suzuki 10.00
3 Mark Prior, Curt Schilling, Nomar Garciaparra, Kevin Brown 8.00
4 Richie Sexson, Sammy Sosa, Albert Pujols, Jim Thome 10.00
5 Alex Rodriguez, Frank Thomas, Jason Giambi, Carlos Delgado 8.00

League Leaders Quad Material

NM/M
Production 50 Sets
1 Albert Pujols, Todd Helton, Edgar Renteria, Gary Sheffield 30.00
3 Mark Prior, Curt Schilling, Hideo Nomo, Kevin Brown 30.00
4 Richie Sexson, Sammy Sosa, Albert Pujols, Jim Thome 40.00
5 Alex Rodriguez, Frank Thomas, Jason Giambi, Carlos Delgado 35.00

Players Collection Jersey

NM/M
Inserted 1:79
Platinum: 1-2X
Production 50
1 Adam Dunn 5.00
2 Adam Dunn 5.00
3 Adam Dunn 5.00
4 Alex Rodriguez 10.00
5 Alex Rodriguez 10.00
6 Alex Rodriguez 10.00
7 Alex Rodriguez 10.00
8 Andruw Jones 6.00
9 Andruw Jones 6.00
10 Austin Kearns 6.00
11 Brandon Webb 4.00
12 C.C. Sabathia 4.00
13 Cal Ripken Jr. 25.00
14 Carlos Beltran 5.00
15 Carlos Delgado 6.00
16 Carlos Lee 4.00
17 Chipper Jones 8.00
18 Chipper Jones 8.00
19 Craig Biggio 4.00
20 Curt Schilling 6.00
21 David Wells 4.00
22 Don Mattingly 15.00
23 Dontrelle Willis 6.00
24 Frank Thomas 8.00
25 Frank Thomas 8.00
26 Fred McGriff 6.00
27 Garret Anderson 6.00
28 Gary Sheffield 6.00
29 Gary Sheffield 6.00
30 Greg Maddux 10.00
31 Hank Blalock 6.00
32 Hank Blalock 6.00
33 Hee Seop Choi 4.00
34 Hideo Nomo 8.00
35 Hideo Nomo 8.00
36 Hideo Nomo 8.00
37 Ivan Rodriguez 6.00
38 Ivan Rodriguez 6.00
39 Jason Giambi 6.00
40 Jim Edmonds 6.00
41 Jim Thome 8.00
42 John Olerud 4.00
43 John Smoltz 6.00
44 Josh Beckett 6.00
45 Josh Phelps 4.00
46 Juan Gonzalez 6.00
47 Juan Gonzalez 6.00
48 Kazuhisa Ishii 4.00
49 Lance Berkman 5.00
50 Larry Walker 5.00
51 Larry Walker 5.00
52 Luis Gonzalez 5.00
53 Magglio Ordonez 6.00
54 Magglio Ordonez 6.00
55 Manny Ramirez 6.00
56 Manny Ramirez 6.00
57 Mark Prior 8.00
58 Mark Prior 8.00
59 Mark Teixeira 6.00
60 Mike Mussina 6.00
61 Mike Piazza 8.00
62 Mike Piazza 8.00
63 Mike Piazza 8.00
64 Nomar Garciaparra 8.00
65 Nomar Garciaparra 8.00
66 Pat Burrell 6.00
67 Paul Konerko 5.00
68 Paul Lo Duca 5.00
69 Pedro Martinez 8.00
70 Rafael Furcal 5.00
71 Rafael Palmeiro 8.00
72 Rafael Palmeiro 8.00
73 Ramon Hernandez 4.00
74 Rickey Henderson 8.00
75 Rickey Henderson 8.00
76 Rickey Henderson 8.00
77 Roberto Alomar 6.00
78 Roberto Alomar 6.00
79 Robin Ventura 5.00
80 Roger Clemens 10.00
81 Roger Clemens 10.00
82 Roy Halladay 6.00
83 Sammy Sosa 12.00
84 Sammy Sosa 12.00
85 Sammy Sosa 12.00
86 Scott Rolen 8.00
87 Shannon Stewart 4.00
88 Shawn Green 5.00
89 Shawn Green 5.00
90 Shawn Green 5.00
91 Terrence Long 4.00
92 Tim Hudson 6.00
93 Todd Helton 8.00
94 Todd Helton 8.00
95 Tom Glavine 6.00
96 Tom Glavine 6.00
97 Torii Hunter 6.00
98 Vernon Wells 4.00
99 Vladimir Guerrero 8.00
100 Vladimir Guerrero 8.00

Prestigious Pros

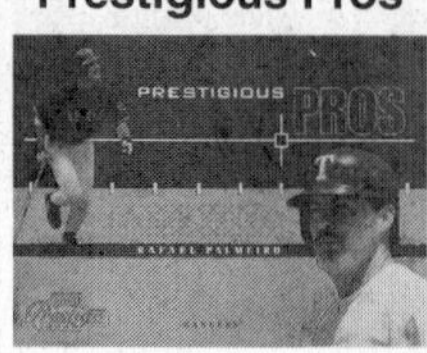

NM/M
Inserted 1:23
1 Mark Prior 3.00
2 Derek Jeter 5.00
3 Mike Mussina 1.50
4 Nomar Garciaparra 3.00
5 Roger Clemens 4.00
6 Jason Giambi 1.50
7 Randy Johnson 2.00
8 Rafael Palmeiro 1.50
9 Barry Zito 1.00
10 Pat Burrell 1.00

Stars of MLB

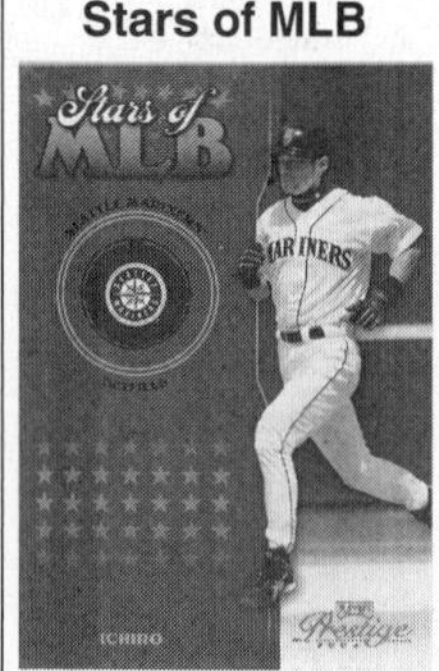

NM/M
Foil: 1-2X
Production 100 Sets
Holofoil: No Pricing
Prod. 25 Sets
1 Albert Pujols 6.00
2 Derek Jeter 8.00
3 Mike Piazza 4.00
4 Greg Maddux 4.00
5 Ichiro Suzuki 5.00
6 Nomar Garciaparra 5.00
7 Ivan Rodriguez 2.00
8 Randy Johnson 3.00
9 Alex Rodriguez 6.00
10 Sammy Sosa 5.00
11 Alfonso Soriano 3.00
12 Vladimir Guerrero 3.00
13 Jason Giambi 3.00
14 Mark Prior 4.00
15 Chipper Jones 3.00

Stars of MLB Jersey

NM/M
Production 250 Sets
Prime: 1-2X
Production 50
1 Albert Pujols 15.00
2 Derek Jeter 15.00
3 Mike Piazza 8.00
4 Greg Maddux 10.00
6 Nomar Garciaparra 8.00
7 Ivan Rodriguez 6.00
8 Randy Johnson 8.00
9 Alex Rodriguez 10.00
10 Sammy Sosa 12.00
11 Alfonso Soriano 8.00
12 Vladimir Guerrero 8.00
13 Jason Giambi 6.00
14 Mark Prior 10.00
15 Chipper Jones 8.00

Stars of MLB Jersey Autographs

NM/M
Quantity produced listed
14 Mark Prior/50 75.00

2004 Playoff Prime Cuts

NM/M
Complete Set (50): 150.00
Common Player: 1.50
Production 949 Sets
Box (1): 185.00
1 Roger Clemens 6.00
2 Nomar Garciaparra 6.00
3 Albert Pujols 6.00
4 Sammy Sosa 6.00
5 Greg Maddux 4.00
6 Jason Giambi 3.00
7 Hideo Nomo 1.50
8 Mike Piazza 4.00
9 Ichiro Suzuki 5.00
10 Jeff Bagwell 2.00
11 Derek Jeter 8.00
12 Manny Ramirez 2.00
13 Rickey Henderson 1.50
14 Alex Rodriguez 6.00
15 Troy Glaus 1.50
16 Mike Mussina 1.50
17 Kerry Wood 2.00
18 Kazuhisa Ishii 1.00
19 Hideki Matsui 8.00
20 Frank Thomas 2.00
21 Barry Bonds 8.00
22 Adam Dunn 1.50
23 Randy Johnson 3.00
24 Alfonso Soriano 3.00
25 Pedro J. Martinez 3.00
26 Andruw Jones 2.00
27 Mark Prior 4.00
28 Vladimir Guerrero 3.00
29 Chipper Jones 4.00
30 Todd Helton 2.00
31 Rafael Palmeiro 2.00
32 Mark Grace 2.00
33 Pedro J. Martinez 3.00
34 Randy Johnson 3.00
35 Randy Johnson 3.00
36 Roger Clemens 6.00
37 Roger Clemens 6.00
38 Alex Rodriguez 6.00
39 Greg Maddux 4.00
40 Mike Piazza 4.00
41 Mike Piazza 4.00
42 Hideo Nomo 1.50
43 Rickey Henderson 1.50
44 Rickey Henderson 1.50
45 Barry Bonds 8.00
46 Ivan Rodriguez 2.00
47 George Brett 6.00
48 Cal Ripken Jr. 8.00
49 Nolan Ryan 10.00
50 Don Mattingly 6.00

Century

Cards (1-50): 1-2X
Production 100 Sets
Century Gold: No Pricing
Production 10 Sets
Century Proof: No Pricing
Production One Set

Icons Material

NM/M
Varying quantities produced
4 Johnny Bench/50 35.00
5 Lefty Grove/25 75.00
6 Carlton Fisk/50 25.00
7 Mel Ott/25 75.00
8 Bob Feller/25 30.00
9 Jackie Robinson/25 75.00
10 Ted Williams/50 135.00
11 Roy Campanella/50 40.00
12 Stan Musial/50 40.00
13 Yogi Berra/50 40.00
14 Babe Ruth/25 750.00
15 Roberto Clemente/ 50 100.00
16 Warren Spahn/50 40.00
17 Ernie Banks/50 40.00
18 Eddie Mathews/50 35.00
19 Ryne Sandberg/50 40.00
20 Rod Carew/50 25.00
21 Duke Snider/50 25.00
22 Jim Palmer/50 20.00
24 Frank Robinson/50 20.00
25 Brooks Robinson/50 25.00
26 Harmon Killebrew/50 40.00
27 Carl Yastrzemski/50 40.00
28 Reggie Jackson/50 25.00
29 Mike Schmidt/50 40.00
30 Robin Yount/50 30.00
31 George Brett/50 40.00
32 Nolan Ryan/50 40.00
33 Kirby Puckett/50 40.00
34 Cal Ripken Jr./50 60.00
35 Don Mattingly/50 35.00
36 Tony Gwynn/19 65.00
37 Deion Sanders/19 45.00
38 Dave Winfield/19 40.00
39 Eddie Murray/19 60.00
40 Tom Seaver/19 50.00
41 Willie Stargell/19 50.00
42 Wade Boggs/19 50.00
43 Ozzie Smith/19 60.00
44 Willie McCovey/19 40.00
45 Reggie Jackson/19 40.00
46 Whitey Ford/19 40.00
47 Lou Brock/19 40.00
48 Lou Boudreau/19 30.00
49 Steve Carlton/19 45.00
50 Rod Carew/19 40.00
51 Bob Gibson/19 35.00
52 Thurman Munson/19 60.00
53 Roger Maris/19 80.00
54 Nolan Ryan/50 40.00
55 Nolan Ryan/50 40.00
56 Bo Jackson/19 50.00
57 Joe Morgan/19 30.00
58 Phil Rizzuto/19 35.00
59 Gary Carter/19 40.00
60 Paul Molitor/19 50.00
61 Don Drysdale/19 50.00
62 Jim "Catfish" Hunter/19 30.00
63 Fergie Jenkins/19 30.00
64 Pee Wee Reese/19 40.00
65 Dave Winfield/19 40.00
66 Wade Boggs/19 40.00
67 Lefty Grove/19 80.00
68 Rickey Henderson/19 45.00
69 Roger Clemens/19 50.00
70 Roger Clemens/19 50.00

Icons Material Signature

NM/M
Varying quantities produced
4 Johnny Bench/18 75.00
8 Bob Feller/45 50.00
12 Stan Musial/30 100.00
13 Yogi Berra/42 65.00
21 Duke Snider/35 50.00
26 Harmon Killebrew/ 30 100.00
33 Kirby Puckett/16 80.00
69 Roger Clemens/25 150.00

Icons Material Signature Prime

NM/M
Many not priced due to scarcity.
6 Carlton Fisk/50 60.00
11 Roy Campanella/1 (8/05 auction) 2,020
12 Stan Musial/20 120.00
16 Warren Spahn/25 90.00
17 Ernie Banks/50 70.00
19 Ryne Sandberg/50 100.00
20 Rod Carew/50 50.00
22 Jim Palmer/50 40.00
24 Frank Robinson/50 40.00
25 Brooks Robinson/50 60.00
26 Harmon Killebrew/ 20 100.00
27 Carl Yastrzemski/50 90.00
28 Reggie Jackson/50 60.00
29 Mike Schmidt/20 125.00
30 Robin Yount/50 75.00
31 George Brett/50 100.00
32 Nolan Ryan/50 120.00
33 Kirby Puckett/34 70.00
34 Cal Ripken Jr./50 150.00
35 Don Mattingly/50 100.00
36 Tony Gwynn/50 70.00
37 Deion Sanders/50 50.00
38 Dave Winfield/50 45.00
39 Eddie Murray/50 75.00
42 Wade Boggs/50 60.00
43 Ozzie Smith/50 75.00
44 Willie McCovey/50 50.00
45 Reggie Jackson/50 50.00
46 Whitey Ford/50 50.00
47 Lou Brock/25 50.00
48 Lou Boudreau/50 75.00
49 Steve Carlton/50 50.00
50 Rod Carew/50 40.00
51 Bob Gibson/50 70.00
54 Nolan Ryan/50 125.00
55 Nolan Ryan/50 125.00
56 Bo Jackson/50 60.00
57 Joe Morgan/50 35.00
58 Phil Rizzuto/50 45.00
59 Gary Carter/50 50.00
60 Paul Molitor/50 55.00
63 Fergie Jenkins/50 40.00
65 Dave Winfield/50 45.00
66 Wade Boggs/50 60.00
68 Rickey Henderson/50 85.00
69 Roger Clemens/25 150.00
70 Roger Clemens/50 120.00

Icons Material Combo Prime

NM/M
Varying quantities produced
6 Carlton Fisk/25 50.00
7 Mel Ott/25 85.00
11 Roy Campanella/25 70.00
15 Roberto Clemente/ 25 200.00
17 Ernie Banks/25 85.00
18 Eddie Mathews/25 50.00
19 Ryne Sandberg/25 80.00
20 Rod Carew/25 50.00
24 Frank Robinson/25 40.00
25 Brooks Robinson/25 50.00
27 Carl Yastrzemski/25 80.00
28 Reggie Jackson/25 50.00
29 Mike Schmidt/25 75.00
30 Robin Yount/25 60.00
31 George Brett/25 75.00
32 Nolan Ryan/25 75.00
33 Kirby Puckett/25 60.00
34 Cal Ripken Jr./25 120.00
35 Don Mattingly/25 70.00
36 Tony Gwynn/25 80.00
37 Deion Sanders/19 60.00
38 Dave Winfield/19 50.00
39 Eddie Murray/19 70.00
41 Willie Stargell/19 60.00
42 Wade Boggs/19 60.00
43 Ozzie Smith/19 70.00
44 Willie McCovey/19 50.00
45 Reggie Jackson/19 50.00
46 Whitey Ford/19 50.00
47 Lou Brock/19 50.00
48 Lou Boudreau/19 40.00
49 Steve Carlton/19 60.00
50 Rod Carew/19 50.00
52 Thurman Munson/19 70.00
53 Roger Maris/19 110.00
54 Nolan Ryan/19 75.00
55 Nolan Ryan/19 75.00
56 Bo Jackson/19 60.00
57 Joe Morgan/19 40.00
58 Phil Rizzuto/19 45.00
59 Gary Carter/19 50.00
60 Paul Molitor/19 60.00
63 Fergie Jenkins/19 40.00
64 Pee Wee Reese/19 50.00
65 Dave Winfield/19 50.00
66 Wade Boggs/19 50.00
69 Roger Clemens/19 50.00
70 Roger Clemens/19 60.00

Icons Signature

NM/M
Varying quantities produced
4 Johnny Bench/50 60.00
6 Carlton Fisk/50 40.00
8 Bob Feller/50 40.00
12 Stan Musial/50 65.00
13 Yogi Berra/50 50.00
16 Warren Spahn/25 100.00
17 Ernie Banks/50 60.00
19 Ryne Sandberg/50 70.00
21 Duke Snider/25 50.00
22 Jim Palmer/25 40.00
24 Frank Robinson/50 40.00
25 Brooks Robinson/50 50.00
26 Harmon Killebrew/25 75.00
27 Carl Yastrzemski/50 60.00
28 Reggie Jackson/50 50.00
29 Mike Schmidt/20 75.00
30 Robin Yount/25 65.00
31 George Brett/25 120.00
32 Nolan Ryan/50 110.00
33 Kirby Puckett/25 60.00
34 Cal Ripken Jr./25 200.00
35 Don Mattingly/50 85.00
36 Tony Gwynn/25 70.00
38 Dave Winfield/25 50.00
39 Eddie Murray/25 70.00
42 Wade Boggs/25 60.00
43 Ozzie Smith/25 75.00
44 Willie McCovey/25 50.00
45 Reggie Jackson/25 50.00

47 Lou Brock/25 50.00
48 Lou Boudreau/25 90.00
51 Bob Gibson/25 40.00
56 Bo Jackson/25 65.00
57 Joe Morgan/25 35.00
59 Gary Carter/25 45.00
60 Paul Molitor/25 55.00
65 Dave Winfield/25 50.00
66 Wade Boggs/25 60.00

Prime Cut Materials

NM/M
Varying quantities produced
1 Roger Clemens/150 40.00
2 Nomar Garciaparra/150 45.00
3 Albert Pujols/150 40.00
4 Sammy Sosa/150 40.00
5 Greg Maddux/150 40.00
6 Jason Giambi/125 40.00
7 Hideo Nomo/150 30.00
8 Mike Piazza/50 30.00
9 Ichiro Suzuki/25 60.00
10 Jeff Bagwell/25 35.00
11 Derek Jeter/25 50.00
12 Manny Ramirez/25 25.00
13 Rickey Henderson/50 30.00
14 Alex Rodriguez/25 60.00
15 Troy Glaus/25 30.00
17 Kerry Wood/25 40.00
18 Kazuhisa Ishii/25 30.00
19 Hideki Matsui/25 65.00
20 Frank Thomas/25 40.00
21 Barry Bonds/25 50.00
22 Adam Dunn/25 30.00
23 Randy Johnson/25 40.00
24 Alfonso Soriano/35 30.00
25 Pedro J. Martinez/25 40.00
26 Andruw Jones/25 30.00
27 Mark Prior/50 30.00
28 Vladimir Guerrero/25 40.00
29 Chipper Jones/25 40.00
30 Todd Helton/25 35.00
31 Rafael Palmeiro/25 40.00
32 Mark Grace/25 35.00
33 Pedro J. Martinez/25 40.00
34 Randy Johnson/25 40.00
35 Randy Johnson/25 40.00
36 Roger Clemens/50 45.00
38 Alex Rodriguez/25 60.00
40 Mike Piazza/50 30.00
42 Hideo Nomo/50 25.00
43 Rickey Henderson/50 30.00
44 Rickey Henderson/50 30.00
46 Ivan Rodriguez/25 30.00
47 George Brett/50 50.00
48 Cal Ripken Jr./50 65.00
49 Nolan Ryan/50 50.00
50 Don Mattingly/50 40.00

Prime Cut Material Signature

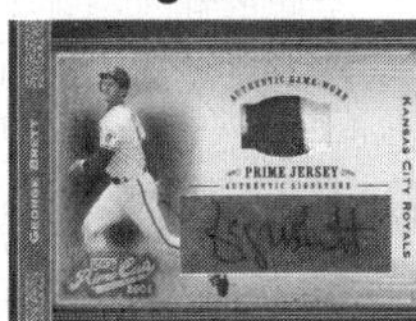

NM/M
Varying quantities produced
1 Roger Clemens/25 185.00
3 Albert Pujols/25 180.00
5 Greg Maddux/25 175.00
10 Jeff Bagwell/25 70.00
12 Manny Ramirez/25 60.00
13 Rickey Henderson/25 100.00
14 Alex Rodriguez/25 180.00
15 Troy Glaus/50 40.00
16 Mike Mussina/25 70.00
17 Kerry Wood/25 90.00
18 Kazuhisa Ishii/50 50.00
20 Frank Thomas/25 80.00
22 Adam Dunn/50 60.00
24 Alfonso Soriano/25 85.00
26 Andruw Jones/25 60.00
27 Mark Prior/50 75.00
28 Vladimir Guerrero/50 75.00
29 Chipper Jones/50 85.00
30 Todd Helton/50 60.00
31 Rafael Palmeiro/25 75.00
32 Mark Grace/50 70.00
36 Roger Clemens/25 185.00
38 Alex Rodriguez/25 180.00
44 Rickey Henderson/25 100.00
46 Ivan Rodriguez/25 60.00
47 George Brett/50 120.00
48 Cal Ripken Jr./50 200.00
49 Nolan Ryan/50 140.00
50 Don Mattingly/50 120.00

Material Combos

NM/M
Production 25 Sets
1 Roger Clemens 60.00
2 Nomar Garciaparra 50.00
3 Albert Pujols 80.00
4 Sammy Sosa 50.00
5 Greg Maddux 50.00
6 Jason Giambi 40.00
7 Hideo Nomo 30.00
8 Mike Piazza 40.00
9 Ichiro Suzuki 70.00
10 Jeff Bagwell 40.00
11 Derek Jeter 60.00
12 Manny Ramirez 30.00
13 Rickey Henderson 40.00
14 Alex Rodriguez 70.00
15 Troy Glaus 35.00
16 Mike Mussina 40.00
17 Kerry Wood 50.00
18 Kazuhisa Ishii 35.00
19 Hideki Matsui 75.00
20 Frank Thomas 45.00
21 Barry Bonds 60.00
22 Adam Dunn 35.00
23 Randy Johnson 50.00
24 Alfonso Soriano 40.00
25 Pedro J. Martinez 45.00
26 Andruw Jones 35.00
27 Mark Prior 40.00
28 Vladimir Guerrero 45.00
29 Chipper Jones 45.00
30 Todd Helton 40.00
31 Rafael Palmeiro 45.00
32 Mark Grace 40.00
33 Pedro J. Martinez 45.00
34 Randy Johnson 50.00
35 Randy Johnson 50.00
36 Roger Clemens 60.00
38 Alex Rodriguez 70.00
40 Mike Piazza 40.00
42 Hideo Nomo 25.00
43 Rickey Henderson 40.00
44 Rickey Henderson 40.00
46 Ivan Rodriguez 35.00
47 George Brett 85.00
48 Cal Ripken Jr. 140.00
49 Nolan Ryan 75.00
50 Don Mattingly 75.00

Signature

NM/M
Varying quantities produced
1 Roger Clemens/25 150.00
3 Albert Pujols/25 150.00
10 Jeff Bagwell/25 60.00
13 Rickey Henderson/25 80.00
14 Alex Rodriguez/25 150.00
15 Troy Glaus/25 35.00
16 Mike Mussina/25 60.00
17 Kerry Wood/25 80.00
18 Kazuhisa Ishii/25 40.00
20 Frank Thomas/25 70.00
22 Adam Dunn/25 50.00
24 Alfonso Soriano/25 75.00
26 Andruw Jones/25 50.00
27 Mark Prior/25 80.00
28 Vladimir Guerrero/25 60.00
29 Chipper Jones/25 75.00
31 Rafael Palmeiro/25 65.00
32 Mark Grace/25 60.00
36 Roger Clemens/25 150.00
37 Roger Clemens/25 150.00
38 Alex Rodriguez/25 150.00
43 Rickey Henderson/25 80.00
44 Rickey Henderson/25 80.00
46 Ivan Rodriguez/25 50.00
47 George Brett/25 120.00
48 Cal Ripken Jr./25 200.00
49 Nolan Ryan/25 125.00
50 Don Mattingly/25 100.00

Timeline Dual Achievement Material

NM/M
Varying quantities produced
3 Stan Musial, Ted Williams/19 175.00
4 George Brett, Mike Schmidt/19 75.00
5 Cal Ripken Jr., Dale Murphy/19 90.00
6 Mike Schmidt, Roger Clemens/19 65.00
10 George Brett, Nolan Ryan/19 100.00
12 Al Kaline, Duke Snider/19 50.00

Timeline Dual Achievement Material Signature

NM/M
Varying quantities produced
4 George Brett, Mike Schmidt/24 150.00
5 Cal Ripken Jr., Dale Murphy/25 200.00
6 Mike Schmidt, Roger Clemens/24 220.00
7 Babe Ruth, Ty Cobb/1 (4/04 auction) 18,000
10 George Brett, Nolan Ryan/25 220.00

Timeline Dual Achievement Material Prime

NM/M
Varying quantities produced
4 George Brett, Mike Schmidt/19 120.00
5 Cal Ripken Jr., Dale Murphy/19 120.00
6 Mike Schmidt, Roger Clemens/19 90.00
10 George Brett, Nolan Ryan/19 140.00

Timeline Dual Achievement Material Combo

No Pricing

Timeline Dual Achievement Signature

NM/M
Production 24 or 25
4 George Brett, Mike Schmidt/24 160.00
5 Cal Ripken Jr., Dale Murphy/25 180.00
6 Mike Schmidt, Roger Clemens/24 220.00
10 George Brett, Nolan Ryan/25 220.00
12 Al Kaline, Duke Snider/25 100.00

Timeline Dual League Leader Material

NM/M
Production 9 or 19
4 Jim Palmer, Steve Carlton/19 40.00
7 Nolan Ryan, Steve Carlton/19 70.00
8 Don Mattingly, Tony Gwynn/19 70.00
9 Nolan Ryan, Roger Clemens/19 80.00

Timeline Dual League Leader Material Prime

NM/M
Production 9 or 19
7 Nolan Ryan, Steve Carlton/19 80.00
8 Don Mattingly, Tony Gwynn/19 80.00
9 Nolan Ryan, Roger Clemens/19 100.00

Timeline Dual League Leader Material Signature

NM/M
Varying quantities produced
4 Jim Palmer, Steve Carlton/50 60.00
7 Nolan Ryan, Steve Carlton/25 200.00
8 Don Mattingly, Tony Gwynn/25 150.00
9 Nolan Ryan, Roger Clemens/25 350.00

Timeline Dual League Leader Signature

NM/M
Production 25 or 50
4 Jim Palmer, Steve Carlton/50 60.00
7 Nolan Ryan, Steve Carlton/25 180.00
8 Don Mattingly, Tony Gwynn/25 140.00
9 Nolan Ryan, Roger Clemens/25 300.00

Timeline Dual League Leader Mat Combo

NM/M
Production 9 or 19
7 Nolan Ryan, Steve Carlton/19 80.00
8 Don Mattingly, Tony Gwynn/19 80.00
9 Nolan Ryan, Roger Clemens/19 100.00

Timeline - Material

NM/M
Varying quantities produced
4 Ted Williams/50 140.00
5 Roy Campanella/50 30.00
6 Stan Musial/50 35.00
7 Yogi Berra/50 25.00
9 Roberto Clemente/50 85.00
12 Carl Yastrzemski/50 35.00
13 Mike Schmidt/50 30.00
14 George Brett/50 30.00
15 Nolan Ryan/50 35.00
16 Stan Musial/50 35.00
17 Ted Williams/50 140.00
18 Roberto Clemente/50 90.00
19 Greg Maddux/50 25.00
21 Robin Yount/50 20.00
22 Nolan Ryan/50 35.00
23 Ted Williams/50 140.00
24 George Brett/50 30.00
25 Yogi Berra/50 25.00
26 Rod Carew/50 20.00
27 Dale Murphy/25 40.00

Timeline Material Signature

NM/M
Varying quantities produced
6 Stan Musial/33 100.00
7 Yogi Berra/42 75.00
16 Stan Musial/38 100.00
25 Yogi Berra/42 75.00

Timeline Material Prime

NM/M
Varying quantities produced
5 Roy Campanella/25 40.00
10 Will Clark/25 50.00
12 Carl Yastrzemski/25 75.00
13 Mike Schmidt/25 50.00
14 George Brett/25 50.00
15 Nolan Ryan/25 50.00
19 Greg Maddux/25 40.00
21 Robin Yount/25 40.00
22 Nolan Ryan/25 50.00
24 George Brett/25 50.00
26 Rod Carew/25 40.00
27 Dale Murphy/25 40.00

Timeline Material Combo

NM/M
Varying quantities produced
10 Will Clark/19 60.00
12 Carl Yastrzemski/19 80.00
13 Mike Schmidt/19 60.00
14 George Brett/19 65.00
15 Nolan Ryan/19 100.00
19 Greg Maddux/19 50.00
21 Robin Yount/19 50.00
22 Nolan Ryan/19 100.00
24 George Brett/19 65.00
26 Rod Carew/19 40.00
27 Dale Murphy/19 50.00

Timeline Signature

NM/M
Varying quantities produced
6 Stan Musial/50 70.00
7 Yogi Berra/50 50.00
10 Will Clark/25 100.00
12 Carl Yastrzemski/50 80.00
13 Mike Schmidt/20 85.00
14 George Brett/25 90.00
15 Nolan Ryan/50 110.00
16 Stan Musial/50 70.00
19 Greg Maddux/31 120.00
21 Robin Yount/25 75.00
22 Nolan Ryan/50 110.00
24 George Brett/25 90.00
25 Yogi Berra/50 50.00
27 Dale Murphy/25 50.00

Timeline Material Signature Prime

NM/M
Varying quantities produced
10 Will Clark/50 75.00
12 Carl Yastrzemski/50 80.00
13 Mike Schmidt/20 120.00
14 George Brett/25 100.00
15 Nolan Ryan/50 125.00
19 Greg Maddux/50 125.00
21 Robin Yount/50 75.00
22 Nolan Ryan/50 125.00
24 George Brett/25 100.00

2004 Playoff Prime Cuts II

NM/M
Complete Set (100):
Common (1-91): 1.50
Common (92-100): 3.00
Production 699
Wood Box (One Pack): 150.00
1 Mark Prior 2.00
2 Derek Jeter 8.00
3 Eric Chavez 1.50
4 Carlos Delgado 1.50
5 Albert Pujols 8.00
6 Miguel Cabrera 2.00
7 Ivan Rodriguez 2.00
8 Javy Lopez 1.50
9 Hank Blalock 2.00
10 Chipper Jones 3.00
11 Gary Sheffield 2.00
12 Alfonso Soriano 3.00
13 Alex Rodriguez/Yanks 6.00
14 Edgar Renteria 1.50
15 Jim Edmonds 1.50
16 Garret Anderson 1.50
17 Lance Berkman 1.50
18 Brandon Webb 1.50
19 Mike Lowell 1.50
20 Mark Mulder 1.50
21 Sammy Sosa 5.00
22 Roger Clemens/Astros 8.00
23 Mark Teixeira 1.50
24 Manny Ramirez 3.00
25 Rafael Palmeiro 2.00
26 Ichiro Suzuki 6.00
27 Vladimir Guerrero 3.00
28 Austin Kearns 1.50
29 Troy Glaus 1.50
30 Ken Griffey Jr. 4.00
31 Greg Maddux 4.00
32 Roy Halladay 1.50
33 Roy Oswalt 1.50
34 Kerry Wood 3.00
35 Mike Mussina/Yanks 2.00
36 Michael Young 1.50
37 Juan Gonzalez 1.50
38 Curt Schilling 2.00
39 Shannon Stewart 1.50
40 Todd Helton 2.00
41 Larry Walker Cards 1.50
42 Mariano Rivera 1.50
43 Nomar Garciaparra 4.00
44 Adam Dunn 2.00
45 Pedro J. Martinez/Sox 3.00
46 Bernie Williams 1.50
47 Tom Glavine 2.00
48 Torii Hunter 1.50
49 David Ortiz 3.00
50 Frank Thomas 2.00
51 Randy Johnson/D'backs 3.00
52 Jason Giambi 1.50
53 Carlos Lee 1.50
54 Mike Sweeney 1.50
55 Hideki Matsui 6.00
56 Dontrelle Willis 1.50
57 Tim Hudson 1.50
58 Jose Vidro 1.50
59 Jeff Bagwell 2.00
60 Rocco Baldelli 1.50
61 Craig Biggio 1.50
62 Mike Piazza Mets 4.00
63 Magglio Ordonez 1.50
64 Hideo Nomo 1.50
65 Miguel Tejada 2.00
66 Vernon Wells 1.50
67 Barry Larkin 1.50
68 Jacque Jones 1.50
69 Scott Rolen 3.00
70 Jeff Kent 1.50
71 Steve Finley 1.50
72 Kazuo Matsui 6.00
73 Carlos Beltran 2.00
74 Shawn Green 1.50
75 Barry Zito 1.50
76 Aramis Ramirez 1.50
77 Paul LoDuca 1.50
78 Kazuhisa Ishii 1.50
79 Aubrey Huff 1.50
80 Jim Thome 3.00
81 Andy Pettitte Astros 1.50
82 Andruw Jones 1.50
83 Josh Beckett 1.50
84 Sean Casey 1.50
85 Alex Rodriguez/M's 6.00
86 Roger Clemens/Yanks 8.00
87 Mike Mussina/O's 2.00
88 Pedro Martinez/Dgr 3.00
89 Randy Johnson/Astros 3.00
90 Mike Piazza Dgr 4.00
91 Andy Pettitte Yanks 1.50
92 Cal Ripken Jr. 15.00
93 Dale Murphy 3.00
94 Don Mattingly 8.00
95 Gary Carter 3.00
96 George Brett 8.00
97 Nolan Ryan 10.00
98 Ozzie Smith 8.00
99 Steve Carlton 3.00
100 Tony Gwynn 6.00

Silver

Silver (1-91): 1-2X
Silver (92-100): 1-1.5X
Production 50 Sets

Gold

Gold (1-91): 2-4X
Gold (92-100): 1.5-2X
Production 25 Sets

Platinum

No Pricing
Production One Set

Icons

NM/M
Common Player: 4.00
Production 50 Sets
Gold: No Pricing
Production 10 Sets
Platinum: No Pricing
Production One Set
Silver: 1-1.5X
Production 25 Sets
1 Dale Murphy 6.00
2 Eddie Mathews 8.00
3 Brooks Robinson 6.00
4 Cal Ripken Jr. 25.00
5 Cal Ripken Jr. 25.00
6 Eddie Murray 8.00
7 Frank Robinson 4.00
8 Jim Palmer 4.00
9 Bobby Doerr 4.00
10 Carl Yastrzemski 10.00
11 Carlton Fisk 6.00
12 Dennis Eckersley 6.00
13 Luis Aparicio 4.00
14 Luis Tiant 4.00
15 Ted Williams 12.00
16 Wade Boggs 4.00
17 Duke Snider 6.00
18 Jackie Robinson 8.00
19 Pee Wee Reese 6.00
20 Burleigh Grimes 4.00
21 Nolan Ryan 20.00
22 Reggie Jackson 6.00
23 Rod Carew 6.00
24 Rod Carew 6.00
25 Billy Williams 4.00
26 Ernie Banks 8.00
27 Mark Grace 6.00
28 Ron Santo 4.00
29 Paul Molitor 6.00
30 Bo Jackson 8.00
31 Carlton Fisk 6.00
32 Johnny Bench 8.00
33 Tom Seaver 6.00
34 Tony Perez 4.00
35 Bob Feller 4.00
36 Lou Boudreau 4.00
37 Al Kaline 8.00
38 Alan Trammell 4.00
39 Ty Cobb 8.00
40 Don Sutton 4.00
41 Nolan Ryan 20.00
42 Roger Maris 8.00
43 Bo Jackson 8.00
44 George Brett 12.00
45 George Brett 12.00
46 Maury Wills 4.00
47 Warren Spahn 6.00
48 Robin Yount 10.00
49 Harmon Killebrew 8.00
50 Kirby Puckett 8.00
51 Paul Molitor 6.00
52 Andre Dawson 4.00
53 Mel Ott 6.00
54 Mel Ott 6.00
55 Duke Snider 6.00
56 Rickey Henderson 8.00
57 Tom Seaver 6.00
58 Babe Ruth 15.00
59 Babe Ruth 15.00
60 Jim "Catfish" Hunter 4.00
61 Dave Righetti 4.00
62 Dave Winfield 4.00
63 Don Mattingly 15.00
64 Don Mattingly 15.00
65 Lou Gehrig 10.00
66 Lou Gehrig 10.00
67 Phil Niekro 4.00
68 Phil Rizzuto 6.00
69 Reggie Jackson 6.00
70 Rickey Henderson 6.00
71 Roger Maris 8.00
72 Thurman Munson 8.00
73 Thurman Munson 8.00
74 Wade Boggs 6.00
75 Whitey Ford 6.00
76 Yogi Berra 8.00
77 Lefty Grove 4.00
78 Mike Schmidt 10.00
79 Mike Schmidt 10.00
80 Steve Carlton 4.00
81 Ralph Kiner 4.00
82 Roberto Clemente 15.00
83 Roberto Clemente 15.00
84 Dave Winfield 4.00
85 Rickey Henderson 6.00
86 Steve Garvey 4.00
87 Tony Gwynn 8.00
88 Tony Gwynn 8.00
89 Gaylord Perry 4.00
90 Joe Morgan 4.00
91 Juan Marichal 4.00
92 Steve Carlton 4.00
93 Will Clark 6.00
94 Willie McCovey 4.00
95 Bob Gibson 6.00
96 Lou Brock 6.00
97 Stan Musial 10.00
98 Fergie Jenkins 4.00
99 Nolan Ryan 20.00
100 Harmon Killebrew 8.00

Icons Material Combo

NM/M
Many not priced.
Prime: No Pricing
Production 1-10
4 Cal Ripken Jr./Bat-Jsy/25 75.00
5 Cal Ripken Jr./Jkt-Pants/25 75.00
6 Eddie Murray/Bat-Jsy/25 30.00

7 Frank Robinson/Bat-Jsy/20 20.00
10 Carl Yastrzemski/Bat-Jsy/25 40.00
11 Carlton Fisk/Bat-Jsy/25 25.00
15 Ted Williams/Bat-Jsy/25 100.00
17 Duke Snider/Jsy-Pants/25 25.00
18 Jackie Robinson/Jkt-Jsy/25 80.00
21 Nolan Ryan/Jkt-Jsy/25 50.00
22 Reggie Jackson/Hat-Jsy/25 25.00
23 Rod Carew/Bat-Jsy/25 25.00
24 Rod Carew/Jkt-Jsy/25 25.00
29 Paul Molitor/Jsy-Pants/25 25.00
31 Carlton Fisk/Bat-Jsy/25 25.00
33 Tom Seaver/Bat-Jsy/25 25.00
39 Ty Cobb/Bat-Pants/25 150.00
41 Nolan Ryan/Bat-Jsy/25 50.00
42 Roger Maris/Jsy-Pants/25 75.00
44 George Brett/Bat-Jsy/25 50.00
45 George Brett/Hat-Jsy/25 50.00
47 Warren Spahn/Jsy-Pants/25 30.00
48 Robin Yount/Bat-Jsy/19 50.00
49 Harmon Killebrew/Jsy-Jsy/25 40.00
53 Mel Ott/Bat-Jsy/25 50.00
54 Mel Ott/Bat-Pants/25 50.00
55 Duke Snider/Jsy/Pants/25 25.00
58 Babe Ruth/Bat-Jsy/25 300.00
59 Babe Ruth/Bat-Pants/25 300.00
65 Lou Gehrig/Bat-Jsy/25 200.00
66 Lou Gehrig/Bat-Pants/25 200.00
69 Reggie Jackson/Bat-Jsy/25 25.00
71 Roger Maris/Bat-Pants/25 60.00
72 Thurman Munson/Bat-Jsy/25 50.00
73 Thurman Munson/Bat-Pants/25 50.00
75 Whitey Ford/Jsy-Pants/16 40.00
78 Mike Schmidt/Bat-Jsy/20 50.00
79 Mike Schmidt/Hat-Jkt/20 50.00
82 Roberto Clemente/Bat-Jsy/21 150.00
83 Roberto Clemente/Bat-Hat/21 150.00
93 Will Clark/Bat-Jsy/22 30.00
94 Willie McCovey/Jsy-Jsy/25 25.00
99 Nolan Ryan/Jsy-Pants/25 50.00
100 Harmon Killebrew/Bat-Jsy/25 40.00

Icons Material Number

NM/M
Many not priced.
1 Dale Murphy/Jsy/25 20.00
3 Brooks Robinson/Jsy/25 20.00
4 Cal Ripken Jr./Jsy/25 60.00
5 Cal Ripken Jr./Jkt/25 60.00
6 Eddie Murray/Jsy/25 30.00
7 Frank Robinson/Jsy/25 10.00
8 Jim Palmer/Jsy/25 15.00
9 Bobby Doerr/Jsy/25 10.00
10 Carl Yastrzemski/Jsy/25 40.00
11 Carlton Fisk/Jsy/25 20.00
15 Ted Williams/Jsy/50 100.00
17 Duke Snider/Jsy/25 20.00
18 Jackie Robinson/Jkt/50 65.00
19 Pee Wee Reese/Jsy/25 20.00
20 Burleigh Grimes/Pants/25 50.00
21 Nolan Ryan/Jsy/25 40.00
22 Reggie Jackson/Jsy/25 2.00
23 Rod Carew/Jsy/25 20.00
24 Rod Carew/Jkt/25 20.00
25 Billy Williams/Jsy/25 10.00
26 Ernie Banks/Jsy/25 25.00
29 Paul Molitor/Pants/25 25.00
31 Carlton Fisk/Jsy/25 20.00
32 Johnny Bench/Jsy/25 30.00
33 Tom Seaver/Jsy/25 25.00
35 Bob Feller/Jsy/25 15.00
36 Lou Boudreau/Jsy/25 25.00
39 Ty Cobb/Pants/50 100.00
41 Nolan Ryan/Jsy/25 40.00
42 Roger Maris/Jsy/25 50.00
44 George Brett/Jsy/25 40.00
45 George Brett/Jsy/25 40.00
47 Warren Spahn/Jsy/25 25.00
48 Robin Yount/Jsy/25 30.00
49 Harmon Killebrew/Jsy/25 30.00
50 Kirby Puckett/Jsy/25 25.00
51 Paul Molitor/Jsy/25 20.00
53 Mel Ott/Jsy/25 40.00
54 Mel Ott/Pants/25 40.00
55 Duke Snider/Jsy/25 20.00
58 Babe Ruth/Jsy/25 300.00
59 Babe Ruth/Pants/50 180.00
60 Jim "Catfish" Hunter/Jsy/25 20.00
63 Don Mattingly/Jsy/25 40.00
64 Don Mattingly/Jkt/25 40.00
65 Lou Gehrig/Jsy/25 150.00
66 Lou Gehrig/Pants/50 100.00
68 Phil Rizzuto/Pants/25 20.00
69 Reggie Jackson/Jsy/25 20.00
71 Roger Maris/Pants/25 40.00
72 Thurman Munson/Jsy/50 35.00
73 Thurman Munson/Pants/50 35.00
77 Lefty Grove/Hat/25 120.00
78 Mike Schmidt/Jsy/20 40.00
79 Mike Schmidt/Jkt/20 40.00
82 Roberto Clemente/Jsy/21 100.00
83 Roberto Clemente/Hat/21 100.00
91 Juan Marichal/Jsy/25 15.00
93 Will Clark/Jsy/22 25.00
94 Willie McCovey/Jsy/25 20.00
95 Bob Gibson/Jsy/25 25.00
96 Lou Brock/Jkt/20 20.00
99 Nolan Ryan/Pants/25 40.00
100 Harmon Killebrew/Jsy/25 35.00

Icons Material Prime

No Pricing
Production 1-10

Icons Signature Century Silver

NM/M
1 Dale Murphy/25 40.00
3 Brooks Robinson/50 30.00
4 Cal Ripken Jr./25 180.00
5 Cal Ripken Jr./25 180.00
6 Eddie Murray/25 50.00
7 Frank Robinson/50 30.00
8 Jim Palmer/50 30.00
9 Bobby Doerr/25 30.00
10 Carl Yastrzemski/25 75.00
11 Carlton Fisk/27 40.00
12 Dennis Eckersley/43 30.00
13 Luis Aparicio/25 25.00
16 Wade Boggs/26 40.00
17 Duke Snider/50 30.00
21 Nolan Ryan/30 100.00
22 Reggie Jackson/25 50.00
23 Rod Carew/29 35.00
24 Rod Carew/29 35.00
25 Billy Williams/26 20.00
29 Paul Molitor/25 35.00
30 Bo Jackson/25 50.00
31 Carlton Fisk/25 40.00
32 Johnny Bench/50 30.00
33 Tom Seaver/25 40.00
34 Tony Perez/25 40.00
35 Bob Feller/25 30.00
37 Al Kaline/25 50.00
40 Don Sutton/20 20.00
41 Nolan Ryan/34 100.00
43 Bo Jackson/25 50.00
44 George Brett/25 100.00
45 George Brett/25 100.00
48 Robin Yount/19 65.00
49 Harmon Killebrew/50 40.00
51 Paul Molitor/50 30.00
55 Duke Snider/50 30.00
56 Rickey Henderson/24 60.00
57 Tom Seaver/25 40.00
62 Dave Winfield/31 35.00
63 Don Mattingly/50 60.00
64 Don Mattingly/50 60.00
67 Phil Niekro/35 20.00
68 Phil Rizzuto/25 40.00
69 Reggie Jackson/25 50.00
70 Rickey Henderson/24 60.00
75 Whitey Ford/25 50.00
76 Yogi Berra/25 50.00
78 Mike Schmidt/20 80.00
79 Mike Schmidt/20 80.00
80 Steve Carlton/32 30.00
81 Ralph Kiner/25 45.00
84 Dave Winfield/31 35.00
85 Rickey Henderson/24 60.00
87 Tony Gwynn/50 40.00
88 Tony Gwynn/50 40.00
89 Gaylord Perry/36 20.00
90 Joe Morgan/24 25.00
91 Juan Marichal/27 25.00
92 Steve Carlton/32 30.00
93 Will Clark/22 50.00
94 Willie McCovey/25 30.00
95 Bob Gibson/45 30.00
96 Lou Brock/50 30.00
97 Stan Musial/50 65.00
98 Fergie Jenkins/31 25.00
99 Nolan Ryan/34 100.00
100 Harmon Killebrew/50 40.00

Icons Signature Century Gold

NM/M
Many not priced.
1 Dale Murphy/25 40.00
3 Brooks Robinson/25 40.00
7 Frank Robinson/20 35.00
8 Jim Palmer/22 35.00
9 Bobby Doerr/25 30.00
17 Duke Snider/25 35.00
32 Johnny Bench/25 50.00
34 Tony Perez/24 40.00
35 Bob Feller/19 40.00
37 Al Kaline/25 50.00
43 Bo Jackson/16 75.00
49 Harmon Killebrew/25 50.00
51 Paul Molitor/25 35.00
55 Duke Snider/25 40.00
63 Don Mattingly/23 75.00
64 Don Mattingly/23 75.00
80 Steve Carlton/25 35.00
81 Ralph Kiner/25 45.00
87 Tony Gwynn/19 50.00
88 Tony Gwynn/19 50.00
92 Steve Carlton/25 35.00
95 Bob Gibson/25 40.00
96 Lou Brock/20 40.00
97 Stan Musial/25 90.00
100 Harmon Killebrew/25 50.00

Icons Signature Century Platinum

No Pricing
Production One Set

Icons Signature Material Combo

NM/M
Many not priced.
Prime: No Pricing
Production 1-10
1 Dale Murphy/Bat-Jsy/25 50.00
7 Frank Robinson/Bat-Jsy/20 45.00
8 Jim Palmer/Hat-Jsy/22 50.00
9 Bobby Doerr/Bat-Jsy/25 40.00
17 Duke Snider/Jsy-Pants/25 50.00
25 Billy Williams/Bat-Jsy/26 30.00
29 Paul Molitor/Jsy-Pants/25 50.00
34 Tony Perez/Bat-Fld Glv/24 50.00
48 Robin Yount/Bat-Jsy/19 100.00
49 Harmon Killebrew/Jsy-Jsy/25 80.00
51 Paul Molitor/Bat-Jsy/25 50.00
63 Don Mattingly/Bat-Jsy/23 100.00
64 Don Mattingly/Hat-Jkt/23 100.00
78 Mike Schmidt/Bat-Jsy/20 100.00
79 Mike Schmidt/Hat-Jkt/20 100.00
80 Steve Carlton/Fld Glv-Pants/32 50.00
87 Tony Gwynn/Fld Glv-Jsy/19 80.00
88 Tony Gwynn/Jsy-Pants/19 80.00
92 Steve Carlton/Bat/32 50.00
93 Will Clark/Bat-Jsy/22 75.00
98 Fergie Jenkins/Fld Glv-Hat/31 40.00

Icons Signautre Material Number

NM/M
Many not priced.
Prime: No Pricing
Production 1-10
7 Frank Robinson/Jsy/20 40.00
8 Jim Palmer/Jsy/22 40.00
9 Bobby Doerr/Jsy/25 30.00
11 Carlton Fisk/Jsy/27 40.00
12 Dennis Eckersley/Jsy/43 30.00
16 Wade Boggs/Jsy/26 40.00
21 Nolan Ryan/Jsy/30 100.00
22 Reggie Jackson/Jsy/44 50.00
25 Billy Williams/Jsy/26 25.00
27 Mark Grace/Jsy/17 45.00
35 Bob Feller/Jsy/19 30.00
40 Don Sutton/Jsy/20 25.00
41 Nolan Ryan/Jsy/34 100.00
43 Bo Jackson/Jsy/16 75.00
48 Robin Yount/Jsy/19 65.00
62 Dave Winfield/Pants/31 40.00
63 Don Mattingly/Jsy/23 80.00
64 Don Mattingly/Jkt/23 80.00
69 Reggie Jackson/Jsy/44 50.00
78 Mike Schmidt/Jsy/20 80.00
79 Mike Schmidt/Jkt/20 80.00
80 Steve Carlton/Pants/32 40.00
84 Dave Winfield/Jsy/31 40.00
87 Tony Gwynn/Jsy/19 75.00
88 Tony Gwynn/Jsy/19 75.00
89 Gaylord Perry/Jsy/36 20.00
91 Juan Marichal/Jsy/27 25.00
92 Steve Carlton/Jsy/32 40.00
93 Will Clark/Jsy/22 65.00
95 Bob Gibson/Jsy/45 35.00
96 Lou Brock/Jkt/20 40.00
98 Fergie Jenkins/Hat/31 25.00
99 Nolan Ryan/Pants/34 100.00

Material Combo

NM/M
Many not priced due to scarcity.
Prime: No Pricing
Production 1-9
1 Mark Prior/Hat-Jsy/22 20.00
12 Alfonso Soriano/Bat-Jsy/25 25.00
15 Jim Edmonds/Bat-Jsy/15 20.00
16 Garret Anderson/Bat-Jsy/16 15.00
21 Sammy Sosa/Bat-Jsy/21 40.00
22 Roger Clemens/Bat-Jsy/22 50.00
24 Manny Ramirez/Bat-Jsy/24 25.00
25 Rafael Palmeiro/Bat-Jsy/25 20.00
27 Vladimir Guerrero/Bat-Jsy/27 25.00
31 Greg Maddux/Bat-Jsy/31 40.00
35 Mike Mussina/Bat-Jsy/35 25.00
40 Todd Helton/Bat-Jsy/17 25.00
86 Roger Clemens/Fld Glv-Jsy/22 50.00
92 Cal Ripken Jr./Bat-Jsy/25 75.00
93 Dale Murphy/Bat-Jsy/25 20.00
94 Don Mattingly/Bat-Jsy/25 50.00
96 George Brett/Bat-Jsy/25 50.00
97 Nolan Ryan/Bat-Jkt/25 60.00
98 Ozzie Smith/Bat-Jsy/25 40.00

Material Number

NM/M
Most not priced.
Prime: No Pricing
Production 1-10
86 Roger Clemens/Jsy/25 40.00
92 Cal Ripken Jr./Jsy/25 60.00
93 Dale Murphy/Jsy/25 20.00
94 Don Mattingly/Jsy/25 40.00
96 George Brett/Jsy/25 40.00
97 Nolan Ryan/Jkt/25 50.00
98 Ozzie Smith/Jsy/25 30.00

Signature Century Silver

NM/M
Many not priced.
1 Mark Prior/22 30.00
6 Miguel Cabrera/24 40.00
9 Hank Blalock/25 40.00
11 Gary Sheffield/25 40.00
15 Jim Edmonds/25 40.00
16 Garret Anderson/25 25.00
17 Lance Berkman/25 30.00
20 Mark Mulder/20 25.00
21 Sammy Sosa/21 125.00
23 Mark Teixeira/40 40.00
24 Manny Ramirez/24 75.00
25 Rafael Palmeiro/25 50.00
31 Greg Maddux/31 100.00
34 Kerry Wood/34 50.00
35 Mike Mussina/35 40.00
37 Juan Gonzalez/22 40.00
44 Adam Dunn/44 30.00
49 David Ortiz/34 50.00
50 Frank Thomas/35 40.00
61 Craig Biggio/25 35.00
63 Magglio Ordonez/30 25.00
66 Vernon Wells/25 20.00
69 Scott Rolen/27 50.00
82 Andruw Jones/25 35.00
83 Josh Beckett/21 25.00
87 Mike Mussina/35 40.00
92 Cal Ripken Jr./25 175.00
93 Dale Murphy/25 40.00
94 Don Mattingly/23 75.00
95 Gary Carter/25 25.00
97 Nolan Ryan/34 100.00
99 Steve Carlton/32 30.00
100 Tony Gwynn/25 50.00

Signature Century Gold

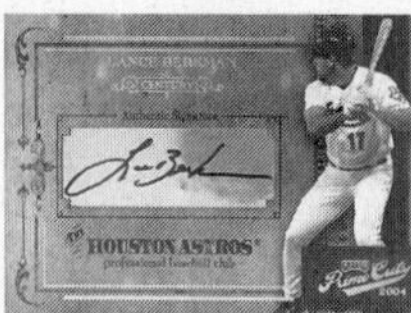

No Pricing
Production 1-17

Signature Century Platinum

No Pricing
Production One Set

Signature Material Combo

NM/M
Most not priced.
Prime: No Pricing
Production 1-9
1 Mark Prior/Hat-Jsy/22 50.00
20 Mark Mulder/Jsy-Jsy/20 35.00
40 Todd Helton/Bat-Jsy/17 75.00
83 Josh Beckett/Bat-Jsy/21 35.00
93 Dale Murphy/Bat-Jsy/25 50.00
94 Don Mattingly/Bat-Jsy/25 100.00

Signature Material Number

NM/M
Most not priced.
Prime: No Pricing
Production 1-9
1 Mark Prior/Jsy/22 40.00
17 Lance Berkman/Jsy/17 50.00
20 Mark Mulder/Jsy/20 25.00
40 Todd Helton/Jsy/17 60.00
57 Tim Hudson/Jsy/15 35.00
83 Josh Beckett/Jsy/21 25.00
94 Don Mattingly/Jsy/23 100.00
97 Nolan Ryan/Jkt/34 125.00
99 Steve Carlton/Jsy/32 40.00
100 Tony Gwynn/Jsy/19 80.00

Timeline

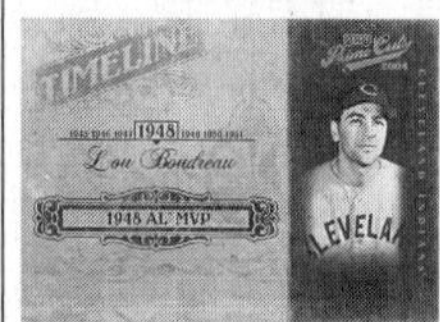

NM/M
Common Player: 4.00
Production 50 Sets
Century Gold: No Pricing
Production 10 Sets
Century Platinum: No Pricing
Production One Set
Century Silver: 1-1.5X
Production 25 Sets
1 Al Kaline 8.00
2 Alex Rodriguez 10.00
3 Andre Dawson 4.00
4 Babe Ruth 15.00
5 Barry Zito 4.00
6 Bob Feller 4.00
7 Bob Gibson 6.00
8 Bobby Doerr 4.00
9 Brooks Robinson 6.00
10 Cal Ripken Jr. 25.00
11 Carl Hubbell 4.00
12 Carl Yastrzemski 10.00
13 Carlton Fisk 6.00
14 Jim "Catfish" Hunter 6.00
15 Chipper Jones 8.00
16 Cy Young 6.00
17 Dale Murphy 6.00
18 Dave Parker 4.00
19 Dennis Eckersley 4.00
20 Don Drysdale 6.00
21 Don Mattingly 15.00
22 Duke Snider 6.00
23 Dwight Gooden 4.00
24 Early Wynn 4.00
25 Eddie Mathews 8.00
26 Eddie Murray 6.00
27 Enos Slaughter 4.00
28 Ernie Banks 8.00
29 Fergie Jenkins 4.00
30 Frank Robinson 6.00
31 Frank Thomas 8.00
32 Frankie Frisch 4.00
33 Fred Lynn 4.00
34 Gary Carter 4.00
35 Gaylord Perry 4.00
36 George Brett 15.00
37 Greg Maddux 10.00
38 Hal Newhouser 4.00
39 Harmon Killebrew 8.00
40 Honus Wagner 6.00
41 Hoyt Wilhelm 4.00
42 Ivan Rodriguez 8.00
43 Jackie Robinson 6.00
44 Jason Giambi 4.00
45 Jeff Bagwell 6.00
46 Jim Palmer 4.00
47 Jimmie Foxx 8.00
48 Joe Morgan 4.00
49 Johnny Bench 8.00
50 Johnny Mize 4.00
51 Jose Canseco 6.00
52 Juan Gonzalez 6.00
53 Juan Marichal 4.00
54 Keith Hernandez 4.00
55 Kirby Puckett 8.00
56 Lefty Grove 4.00
57 Lou Boudreau 4.00
58 Lou Brock 6.00
59 Lou Gehrig 10.00
60 Luis Aparicio 4.00
61 Marty Marion 4.00
62 Mel Ott 6.00
63 Miguel Tejada 6.00
64 Mike Schmidt 10.00
65 Nellie Fox 6.00
66 Nolan Ryan 15.00
67 Orel Hershiser 4.00
68 Orlando Cepeda 4.00
69 Paul Molitor 6.00
70 Pedro Martinez 8.00
71 Pee Wee Reese 6.00
72 Phil Niekro 4.00
73 Phil Rizzuto 6.00
74 Ralph Kiner 4.00
75 Randy Johnson 8.00
76 Red Schoendienst 4.00
77 Reggie Jackson 6.00
78 Rickey Henderson 6.00
79 Roberto Clemente 15.00
80 Robin Yount 10.00
81 Rod Carew 6.00
82 Roger Clemens 10.00
83 Roger Maris 10.00
84 Rogers Hornsby 6.00
85 Roy Campanella 8.00
86 Ozzie Smith 10.00
87 Sammy Sosa 10.00
88 Satchel Paige 6.00
89 Stan Musial 10.00
90 Steve Carlton 4.00
91 Ted Williams 10.00
92 Thurman Munson 8.00
93 Tom Seaver 6.00
94 Ty Cobb 10.00
95 Walter Johnson 6.00
96 Warren Spahn 8.00
97 Whitey Ford 6.00
98 Willie McCovey 6.00
99 Willie Stargell 6.00
100 Yogi Berra 8.00

Timeline Material Combo

NM/M
Quantity produced listed
4 Babe Ruth/Jsy-Jsy/25 350.00
7 Bob Gibson/Hat-Jsy/25 35.00
10 Cal Ripken Jr./Jkt-Jsy/25 75.00
13 Carlton Fisk/Bat-Jsy/27 25.00
14 Jim "Catfish" Hunter/Jsy-Jsy/27 25.00
17 Dale Murphy/Bat-Jsy/25 25.00
21 Don Mattingly/Btg Glv-Pants/25 50.00
25 Eddie Mathews/Bat-Jsy/41 40.00
26 Eddie Murray/Bat-Jsy/33 40.00
36 George Brett/Hat-Jsy/25 60.00
39 Harmon Killebrew/Bat-Jsy/25 50.00
43 Jackie Robinson/Jkt-Jsy/42 100.00
46 Jim Palmer/Hat-Jsy/22 20.00
47 Jimmie Foxx/Bat-Fld Glv/25 125.00
49 Johnny Bench/Bat-Jsy/25 40.00
58 Lou Brock/Bat-Jsy/20 25.00
59 Lou Gehrig/Jsy-Pants/25 250.00
62 Mel Ott/Jsy-Pants/25 50.00
64 Mike Schmidt/Bat-Jsy/20 60.00
66 Nolan Ryan/Jsy-Pants/25 60.00
68 Orlando Cepeda/Bat-Pants/25 20.00

71 Pee Wee Reese/ Bat-Jsy/25 30.00
77 Reggie Jackson/ Jsy-Jsy/25 30.00
79 Roberto Clemente/ Hat-Jsy/21 150.00
80 Robin Yount/ Bat-Jsy/19 50.00
81 Rod Carew/ Bat-Jsy/29 30.00
82 Roger Clemens/ Jsy-Jsy/21 40.00
83 Roger Maris/ Jsy-Pants/25 75.00
85 Roy Campanella/ Bat-Pants/39 35.00
86 Ozzie Smith/ Bat-Jsy/21 40.00
87 Sammy Sosa/ Bat-Jsy/21 40.00
90 Steve Carlton/ Hat-Jsy/32 20.00
91 Ted Williams/ Jsy-Jsy/25 140.00
92 Thurman Munson/ Jsy-Pants/10 50.00
94 Ty Cobb/ Bat-Pants/25 160.00
96 Warren Spahn/ Jsy-Jsy/21 40.00
98 Willie McCovey/ Bat-Jsy/25 25.00

Timeline Material Combo CY

Quantity produced listed

Timeline Material Number

NM/M

Quantity produced listed
4 Babe Ruth/Jsy/25 350.00
6 Bob Feller/Pants/19 25.00
7 Bob Gibson/Jsy/25 30.00
10 Cal Ripken Jr./Jsy/25 60.00
12 Carl Yastrzemski/ Jsy/25 40.00
13 Carlton Fisk/Jsy/27 25.00
14 Jim "Catfish" Hunter/Jsy/27 20.00
20 Don Drysdale/Jsy/25 40.00
22 Duke Snider/ Pants/25 25.00
24 Early Wynn/Jsy/24 15.00
25 Eddie Mathews/ Jsy/25 30.00
26 Eddie Murray/Jsy/25 25.00
28 Ernie Banks/Jsy/25 35.00
32 Frankie Frisch/Jkt/25 40.00
36 George Brett/Jsy/25 40.00
39 Harmon Killebrew/ Jsy/25 35.00
43 Jackie Robinson/ Jkt/42 60.00
46 Jim Palmer/Jsy/22 15.00
47 Jimmie Foxx/ Fld Glv/25 85.00
49 Johnny Bench/Jsy/25 25.00
53 Juan Marichal/Jsy/25 15.00
55 Kirby Puckett/Jsy/25 30.00
58 Lou Brock/Jsy/20 25.00
59 Lou Gehrig/Jsy/25 180.00
62 Mel Ott/Pants/25 40.00
64 Mike Schmidt/Jsy/20 50.00
66 Nolan Ryan/Jsy/25 50.00
68 Orlando Cepeda/ Pants/25 15.00
71 Pee Wee Reese/ Jsy/25 25.00
74 Ralph Kiner/Bat/25 25.00
77 Reggie Jackson/ Jsy/25 25.00
80 Robin Yount/Jsy/19 40.00
81 Rod Carew/Jsy/25 25.00
82 Roger Clemens/ Jsy/21 30.00
83 Roger Maris/Jsy/25 60.00
84 Rogers Hornsby/ Bat/25 75.00
85 Roy Campanella/ Pants/25 30.00
86 Ozzie Smith/Jsy/25 35.00
87 Sammy Sosa/Jsy/21 30.00
88 Satchel Paige/Jsy/25 75.00
90 Steve Carlton/Jsy/25 15.00
91 Ted Williams/Jsy/25 100.00
92 Thurman Munson/ Jsy/25 40.00
93 Tom Seaver/Pants/25 25.00
94 Ty Cobb/Pants/25 140.00
96 Warren Spahn/Jsy/21 35.00
98 Willie McCovey/Jsy/8 25.00

Timeline Material Position

NM/M

Quantity produced listed
4 Babe Ruth/Jsy/25 350.00
6 Bob Feller/Pants/19 25.00
7 Bob Gibson/Jsy/25 30.00
10 Cal Ripken Jr./Jsy/25 60.00
12 Carl Yastrzemski/ Jsy/25 40.00
13 Carlton Fisk/Jsy/27 25.00
14 Jim "Catfish" Hunter /Jsy/27 20.00
20 Don Drysdale/Jsy/25 40.00
22 Duke Snider/ Pants/25 25.00
24 Early Wynn/Jsy/24 15.00
25 Eddie Mathews/ Jsy/25 30.00
26 Eddie Murray/Jsy/25 25.00
28 Ernie Banks/Jsy/25 35.00
32 Frankie Frisch/Jkt/25 40.00
36 George Brett/Jsy/25 40.00
39 Harmon Killebrew/ Jsy/25 35.00
43 Jackie Robinson/ Jkt/42 60.00
46 Jim Palmer/Jsy/22 15.00
47 Jimmie Foxx/ Fld Glv/25 85.00
49 Johnny Bench/Jsy/25 25.00
53 Juan Marichal/Jsy/27 15.00
55 Kirby Puckett/Jsy/25 30.00
58 Lou Brock/Jsy/20 25.00
59 Lou Gehrig/Jsy/25 180.00
62 Mel Ott/Pants/25 40.00
64 Mike Schmidt/Jsy/20 50.00
66 Nolan Ryan/Jsy/25 50.00
68 Orlando Cepeda/ Pants/25 15.00
71 Pee Wee Reese/ Jsy/25 25.00
74 Ralph Kiner/Bat/25 25.00
77 Reggie Jackson/ Jsy/25 25.00
80 Robin Yount/Jsy/19 40.00
81 Rod Carew/Jsy/25 25.00
82 Roger Clemens/ Jsy/21 30.00
84 Rogers Hornsby/ Bat/25 75.00
86 Ozzie Smith/Jsy/25 35.00
87 Sammy Sosa/Jsy/21 30.00
88 Satchel Paige/ CO Jsy/25 75.00
90 Steve Carlton/Jsy/25 15.00
92 Thurman Munson/ Jsy/15 50.00
93 Tom Seaver/Pants/25 25.00
96 Warren Spahn/Jsy/21 35.00
98 Willie McCovey/ Jsy/25 25.00

Timeline Material Prime

No Pricing
Production 1-10

Timeline Material Quad

No Pricing
Production 1-25

Timeline Material Trio

NM/M

Most not priced.
Trio HOF: No Pricing
Production 1-9
Trio MVP: No Pricing
Production 1-10
Trio Stats: No Pricing
Production 1-15
10 Cal Ripken Jr./ Jkt-Jsy-Pants/25 100.00
17 Dale Murphy/ Bat-Jsy-Jsy/25 40.00
21 Don Mattingly/ Bat-Jkt-Pants/25 75.00
26 Eddie Murray/ Bat-Jsy-Shoe/25 85.00
80 Robin Yount/ Bat-Jsy-Jsy/19 70.00
82 Roger Clemens/ Bat-Jsy-Jsy/21 50.00

Timeline Signature Material Combo

NM/M

Most not priced.
7 Bob Gibson/ Hat-Jsy/25 50.00
8 Bobby Doerr/ Bat-Jsy/25 50.00
58 Lou Brock/ Bat-Jsy/20 50.00

Timeline Signautre Material Combo CY

NM/M

Most not priced.
7 Bob Gibson/ Hat-Jsy/25 50.00
46 Jim Palmer/ Hat-Jsy/22 50.00
90 Steve Carlton/ Hat-Jsy/32 50.00

Timeline Signature Material Number

NM/M

Most not priced.
6 Bob Feller/Pants/19 40.00
7 Bob Gibson/Jsy/25 50.00
8 Bobby Doerr/Jsy/25 40.00
21 Don Mattingly/ Pants/23 80.00
46 Jim Palmer/Jsy/22 40.00
53 Juan Marichal/Jsy/27 40.00
58 Lou Brock/Jsy/20 50.00
66 Nolan Ryan/Jsy/34 150.00
90 Steve Carlton/Jsy/32 40.00

Timeline Signature Material Position

NM/M

Most not priced.
6 Bob Feller/Pants/19 40.00
8 Bobby Doerr/Jsy/25 40.00
21 Don Mattingly/ Pants/23 80.00
46 Jim Palmer/Jsy/22 40.00
53 Juan Marichal/Jsy/27 40.00
58 Lou Brock/Jsy/20 50.00
66 Nolan Ryan/Jsy/34 150.00
67 Orel Hershiser/Jsy/25 30.00

Timeline Signature Material Prime

No Pricing
Production 1-9

Timeline Signature Material Quad

NM/M

Most not priced.
21 Don Mattingly/25 180.00

Timeline Signature Material Trio

NM/M

No Pricing
Production 1-9
Trio HOF: No Pricing
Production 1-9
Trio MVP: No Pricing
Production 1-8
Trio Stats: No Pricing
Production 1-9
91 Ted Williams/Bat-Jkt-Jsy/1 (2/06 Auction) 1,483

2005 Playoff Absolute Memorabilia

NM/M

Complete Set (100):
Common Player: .50
Retail: .3X
Retail doesn't have foil front.
Pack (4): 40.00
Box (4): 150.00
1 Andruw Jones .75
2 B.J. Upton .75
3 Jim Edmonds .75
4 Johan Santana 1.00
5 Jeff Bagwell .75
6 Derek Jeter 3.00
7 Eric Chavez .75
8 Albert Pujols 3.00
9 Craig Biggio .75
10 Hank Blalock .75
11 Chipper Jones 1.00
12 Jacque Jones .50
13 Alfonso Soriano 1.00
14 Carl Crawford .50
15 Ben Sheets .50
16 Garret Anderson .75
17 Luis Gonzalez .50
18 Andy Pettitte .75
19 Miguel Tejada .75
20 Carlos Delgado .75
21 Austin Kearns .50
22 Adrian Beltre .50
23 Rafael Palmeiro .75
24 Greg Maddux 2.00
25 Jason Bay .50
26 Jason Varitek .75
27 David Ortiz 1.00
28 Dontrelle Willis .75
29 Adam Dunn 1.00
30 Carlos Lee .50
31 Manny Ramirez 1.00
32 Rocco Baldelli .50
33 Jeff Kent .50
34 Jake Peavy .75
35 Vernon Wells .50
36 Ichiro Suzuki 2.00
37 C.C. Sabathia .50
38 Hideki Matsui 2.00
39 Gary Sheffield .75
40 Paul LoDuca .50
41 Vladimir Guerrero 1.00
42 Omar Vizquel .50
43 Lance Berkman .50
44 Shawn Green .50
45 Josh Beckett .50
46 Barry Zito .50
47 Roger Clemens 3.00
48 Sean Casey .50
49 Edgar Renteria .50
50 Mark Teixeira .75
51 Frank Thomas .75
52 Khalil Greene .50
53 Bobby Abreu .75
54 Rafael Furcal .50
55 Jose Vidro .50
56 Nomar Garciaparra 1.00
57 Melvin Mora .50
58 Trot Nixon .50
59 Magglio Ordonez .50
60 Michael Young .50
61 Richie Sexson .50
62 Alex Rodriguez 3.00
63 Tim Hudson .50
64 Todd Helton .75
65 Mike Lowell .50
66 Mark Mulder .50
67 Sammy Sosa 1.50
68 Mark Prior 1.00
69 Shannon Stewart .50
70 Miguel Cabrera 1.00
71 Troy Glaus .50
72 Scott Rolen 1.00
73 Ken Griffey Jr. 2.00
74 Mike Piazza 1.00
75 Roy Halladay .50
76 Larry Walker .75
77 Kerry Wood .75
78 Mike Mussina .75
79 Curt Schilling 1.00
80 Rich Harden .50
81 Victor Martinez .50
82 Roy Oswalt .50
83 Pedro Martinez 1.00
84 Tom Glavine .50
85 Randy Johnson 1.00
86 Ivan Rodriguez 1.00
87 Carlos Beltran .75
88 Torii Hunter .50
89 Hideo Nomo .50
90 Jim Thome 1.00
91 Aramis Ramirez .50
92 J.D. Drew .50
93 Javy Lopez .50
94 David Wright 2.00
95 Bobby Crosby .75
96 Jeff Niemann **RC** 3.00
97 Yuniesky Betancourt **RC** 3.00
98 Tadahito Iguchi **RC** 5.00
99 Philip Humber **RC** 3.00
100 Justin Verlander **RC** 5.00

Black

Black: 2-4X
Inserted 1:18 Retail

Blue

Blue: 1-2X
Inserted 1:3 Retail

Red

Red: 2-3X
Inserted 1:8 Retail

Spectrum Gold

No Pricing
Production 10 Sets

Spectrum Platinum

No Pricing
Production One Set

Spectrum Silver

Silver: 2-3X
Production 100 Sets

Absolutely Ink Swatch Single

NM/M

Production 5-50
1 Rafael Furcal/Jsy/50 15.00
3 Dale Murphy/Jsy/50 25.00
4 Duke Snider/ Pants/25 40.00
5 Bill Madlock/Bat/50 20.00
7 Bobby Crosby/Jsy/50 15.00
8 Cal Ripken Jr./ Jsy/25 140.00
9 Hank Blalock/Jsy/25 25.00
10 Vernon Wells/Jsy/50 20.00
11 Lyle Overbay/Jsy/50 15.00
13 Omar Vizquel/Jsy/50 25.00
15 Ben Sheets/Jsy/25 20.00
16 Aramis Ramirez/ Jsy/25 30.00
18 Travis Hafner/Jsy/50 20.00
19 Mike Lowell/Jsy/25 15.00
20 Frank Robinson/ Bat/50 30.00
22 Juan Gonzalez/ Jsy/50 25.00
27 Darryl Strawberry/ Jsy/50 20.00
28 Alexis Rios/Bat/50 15.00
30 Magglio Ordonez/ Jsy/50 15.00
31 Jay Gibbons/Jsy/50 15.00
32 Steve Carlton/Jsy/25 35.00
34 Kerry Wood/Jsy/25 35.00
36 Eric Chavez/Jsy/25 25.00
37 Keith Hernandez/ Jsy/50 15.00
38 Carlos Zambrano/ Jsy/50 25.00
39 Brett Myers/Jsy/50 15.00
40 Rich Harden/Jsy/50 20.00
41 Danny Kolb/Jsy/50 15.00
42 Mark Prior/Jsy/25 40.00
43 Joey Gathright/ Jsy/25 15.00
44 David Cone/Jsy/50 15.00
45 Carlos Lee/Jsy/50 20.00
47 Jack Morris/Jsy/50 20.00
48 Torii Hunter/Jsy/50 20.00
49 Garret Anderson/ Jsy/50 25.00
51 Dave Parker/Bat/50 20.00
52 C.C. Sabathia/Jsy/50 15.00
53 Dennis Eckersley/ Jsy/50 20.00
54 Barry Larkin/Jsy/25 40.00
55 Brandon Webb/ Pants/50 15.00
56 Sean Casey/Jsy/50 20.00
57 Johan Santana/ Jsy/50 40.00
58 Miguel Cabrera/ Jsy/50 40.00
59 Bert Blyleven/Jsy/50 15.00
60 Casey Kotchman/ Jsy/50 15.00
61 Dwight Gooden/ Jsy/50 20.00
62 Milton Bradley/ Jsy/50 15.00
63 John Kruk/Jsy/50 25.00
64 Michael Young/ Jsy/50 20.00
66 Robin Ventura/ Jsy/50 20.00
67 Tim Hudson/Jsy/25 30.00
68 Will Clark/Bat/50 40.00
69 Lew Ford/Jsy/50 15.00
70 Jody Gerut/Jsy/50 15.00
71 Don Sutton/Jsy/50 15.00
72 B.J. Upton/Bat/25 20.00
73 Austin Kearns/Jsy/50 15.00
77 Ryan Wagner/Jsy/50 15.00
78 Jermaine Dye/Jsy/50 15.00
80 Al Oliver/Jsy/50 15.00
81 Angel Berroa/ Pants/50 15.00
82 Edgar Renteria/ Jsy/50 20.00
83 Dennis Eckersley/ Jsy/25 25.00
84 Roy Oswalt/Jsy/50 20.00
86 Dave Righetti/Jsy/50 20.00
87 Aubrey Huff/Jsy/25 20.00
89 Jose Vidro/Jsy/50 15.00
90 Harold Baines/Jsy/50 15.00
93 Ken Harvey/Jsy/50 15.00
95 Jason Bay/Jsy/50 20.00
96 Dwight Evans/Jsy/50 30.00
97 Luis Tiant/Pants/50 15.00
98 Ron Santo/Bat/50 30.00
99 Brian Roberts/Jsy/50 40.00
100 Marty Marion/Jsy/50 15.00

Absolute Ink Swatch Single Spectrum

NM/M

Production 1-25
Prime: No Pricing
Production One Set
1 Rafael Furcal/Jsy/25 20.00
3 Dale Murphy/Jsy/25 35.00
5 Bill Madlock/Bat/25 25.00
7 Bobby Crosby/Jsy/25 20.00
11 Lyle Overbay/Jsy/25 15.00
13 Omar Vizquel/Jsy/25 25.00
18 Travis Hafner/Jsy/25 25.00
23 Mark Teixeira/Jsy/25 50.00
27 Darryl Strawberry/ Jsy/25 20.00
28 Alexis Rios/Bat/25 15.00
30 Magglio Ordonez/ Jsy/25 15.00
31 Jay Gibbons/Jsy/25 15.00
37 Keith Hernandez/ Jsy/25 20.00
38 Carlos Zambrano/ Jsy/25 30.00
39 Brett Myers/Jsy/25 15.00
40 Rich Harden/Jsy/25 25.00
41 Danny Kolb/Jsy/25 15.00
45 Carlos Lee/Jsy/25 20.00
47 Jack Morris/Jsy/25 20.00
51 Dave Parker/Bat/25 20.00
52 C.C. Sabathia/Jsy/25 20.00
55 Brandon Webb/ Pants/25 25.00
56 Sean Casey/Jsy/25 20.00
57 Johan Santana/ Jsy/25 50.00
58 Miguel Cabrera/ Jsy/25 50.00
59 Bert Blyleven/Jsy/25 20.00
60 Casey Kotchman/ Jsy/25 25.00
61 Dwight Gooden/ Jsy/25 25.00
62 Milton Bradley/ Jsy/25 20.00
63 John Kruk/Jsy/25 25.00
64 Michael Young/ Jsy/25 25.00
69 Lew Ford/Jsy/25 15.00
70 Jody Gerut/Jsy/25 15.00
71 Don Sutton/Jsy/25 20.00
73 Austin Kearns/Jsy/25 20.00
77 Ryan Wagner/Jsy/25 15.00
78 Jermaine Dye/Jsy/25 15.00
80 Al Oliver/Jsy/25 15.00
81 Angel Berroa/ Pants/25 15.00
89 Jose Vidro/Jsy/25 15.00
90 Harold Baines/Jsy/25 20.00
92 Mark Mulder/Jsy/25 25.00
93 Ken Harvey/Jsy/25 15.00
95 Jason Bay/Jsy/25 25.00
96 Dwight Evans/Jsy/25 40.00
97 Luis Tiant/Pants/25 15.00
98 Ron Santo/Bat/25 30.00
99 Brian Roberts/Jsy/25 40.00
100 Marty Marion/Jsy/25 25.00

Absolutely Ink Swatch Double

NM/M

Production 1-50
1 Rafael Furcal B-J/50 20.00
3 Dale Murphy B-J/50 30.00
7 Bobby Crosby B-J/50 20.00
8 Cal Ripken Jr. J-P/25 150.00
10 Vernon Wells J-J/25 20.00
11 Lyle Overbay J-J/50 15.00
13 Omar Vizquel J-J/50 25.00
16 Aramis Ramirez J-J/25 30.00
18 Travis Hafner BG-J/50 25.00
22 Juan Gonzalez B-J/25 25.00
23 Mark Teixeira FG-J/50 35.00
27 Darryl Strawberry J-J/50 20.00
30 Magglio Ordonez B-J/25 20.00
31 Jay Gibbons B-J/50 15.00
32 Steve Carlton FG-J/25 40.00
37 Keith Hernandez B-J/50 20.00
38 Carlos Zambrano J-J/25 25.00
39 Brett Myers J-J/50 15.00
41 Danny Kolb J-J/50 15.00
42 Mark Prior FG-J/25 40.00
43 Joey Gathright B-J/25 15.00
44 David Cone J-J/50 15.00
45 Carlos Lee FG-J/50 20.00
49 Garret Anderson J-J/25 25.00
51 Dave Parker B-J/25 25.00
52 C.C. Sabathia J-J/50 20.00
53 Dennis Eckersley A's J-P/50 20.00
55 Brandon Webb B-P/50 15.00
56 Sean Casey B-J/50 20.00
57 Johan Santana J-J/25 60.00
58 Miguel Cabrera J-J/50 40.00
59 Bert Blyleven J-J/50 15.00
60 Casey Kotchman B-J/50 20.00
62 Milton Bradley J-J/50 15.00
63 John Kruk J-J/50 25.00
64 Michael Young B-J/50 20.00
69 Lew Ford B-J/50 15.00
70 Jody Gerut B-J/50 15.00
71 Don Sutton J-J/50 15.00
73 Austin Kearns B-J/50 15.00
77 Ryan Wagner J-J/50 15.00
78 Jermaine Dye J-J/50 15.00
80 Al Oliver B-J/50 15.00
81 Angel Berroa B-P/50 15.00
82 Edgar Renteria J-J/50 20.00
84 Roy Oswalt FG-J/25 25.00
86 Dave Righetti J-J/50 20.00
87 Aubrey Huff H-J/25 20.00
89 Jose Vidro B-J/50 15.00
90 Harold Baines J-J/50 15.00
93 Ken Harvey J-J/50 15.00
95 Jason Bay B-J/50 20.00
96 Dwight Evans B-J/50 40.00
99 Brian Roberts J-J/50 40.00

Absolutely Ink Swatch Double Spectrum

NM/M

Production 1-25
Prime: No Pricing
Production One Set
1 Rafael Furcal B-J/25 20.00
3 Dale Murphy B-J/25 40.00
7 Bobby Crosby J-J/25 25.00
10 Vernon Wells J-J/25 20.00
11 Lyle Overbay J-J/25 15.00

18 Travis Hafner BG-J/25 30.00
27 Darryl Strawberry J-J/25 25.00
31 Jay Gibbons B-J/25 20.00
37 Keith Hernandez B-J/25 25.00
38 Carlos Zambrano J-J/25 30.00
39 Brett Myers J-J/25 15.00
41 Danny Kolb J-J/25 15.00
45 Carlos Lee FG-J/25 20.00
55 Brandon Webb B-P/25 25.00
59 Bert Blyleven J-J/25 15.00
60 Casey Kotchman B-J/25 25.00
62 Milton Bradley J-J/25 20.00
63 John Kruk J-J/25 25.00
64 Michael Young B-J/25 25.00
69 Lew Ford B-J/25 15.00
70 Jody Gerut B-J/25 15.00
71 Don Sutton J-J/25 20.00
73 Austin Kearns B-J/25 20.00
77 Ryan Wagner J-J/25 15.00
78 Jermaine Dye J-J/25 15.00
81 Angel Berroa B-P/25 15.00
89 Jose Vidro B-J/25 15.00
90 Harold Baines J-J/25 20.00
93 Ken Harvey J-J/25 15.00
95 Jason Bay B-J/25 25.00
96 Dwight Evans B-J/25 40.00
99 Brian Roberts J-J/25 40.00

Absolutely Ink Swatch Triple

NM/M
Production 1-75
1 Rafael Furcal/50 20.00
3 Dale Murphy/50 30.00
8 Cal Ripken Jr./25 160.00
9 Hank Blalock/25 30.00
13 Omar Vizquel/25 30.00
16 Aramis Ramirez/25 35.00
18 Travis Hafner/50 25.00
22 Juan Gonzalez/25 30.00
23 Mark Teixeira/75 40.00
27 Darryl Strawberry/50 20.00
31 Jay Gibbons/25 20.00
37 Keith Hernandez/25 25.00
45 Carlos Lee/50 20.00
49 Garret Anderson/25 30.00
52 C.C. Sabathia/25 20.00
53 Dennis Eckersley/50 25.00
55 Brandon Webb/50 20.00
56 Sean Casey/50 25.00
58 Miguel Cabrera/25 50.00
60 Casey Kotchman/50 25.00
64 Michael Young/75 25.00
69 Lew Ford/50 15.00
70 Jody Gerut/50 15.00
73 Austin Kearns/50 20.00
77 Ryan Wagner/50 15.00
78 Jermaine Dye/50 15.00
81 Angel Berroa/50 15.00
86 Dave Righetti/50 20.00
89 Jose Vidro/50 15.00
90 Harold Baines/50 20.00
95 Jason Bay/25 25.00
96 Dwight Evans/25 40.00

Absolute Ink Swatch Triple Spectrum

NM/M
Production 1-25
Prime: No Pricing
Production One Set
1 Rafael Furcal/25 20.00
3 Dale Murphy/25 40.00
18 Travis Hafner/25 25.00
23 Mark Teixeira/25 50.00
27 Darryl Strawberry/25 20.00
45 Carlos Lee/25 20.00
60 Casey Kotchman/25 25.00
64 Michael Young/25 30.00
69 Lew Ford/25 15.00
70 Jody Gerut/25 15.00
73 Austin Kearns/25 20.00
77 Ryan Wagner/25 15.00
78 Jermaine Dye/25 15.00
81 Angel Berroa/25 15.00
89 Jose Vidro/25 15.00
90 Harold Baines/25 20.00

Absolute Memorabilia Heroes

NM/M
Common Player: 1.50
Production 250 Sets
Spectrum: 1-2X
Production 50 Sets
Reverse Spectrum: 2-4X
Production 25 Sets
1 Billy Martin 3.00
2 Rickey Henderson 2.00
3 Alan Trammell 2.00
4 Lenny Dykstra 1.50
5 Jeff Bagwell 2.00
6 Steve Garvey 1.50
7 Jim "Catfish" Hunter 2.00
8 Cal Ripken Jr. 10.00
9 Reggie Jackson 3.00
10 Gary Sheffield 2.00
11 Edgar Martinez 1.50
12 Roberto Alomar 2.00
13 Luis Tiant 1.50
14 Jim Rice 2.00
15 Carlos Beltran 2.00
16 Hideo Nomo 2.00
17 Mark Grace 2.00
18 Joe Cronin 2.00
19 Tony Gwynn 3.00
20 Bo Jackson 3.00
21 Roger Clemens 5.00
22 Roger Clemens 5.00
23 Don Mattingly 5.00
24 Willie Mays 5.00
25 Andruw Jones 2.00
26 Andre Dawson 2.00
27 Carlton Fisk 2.00
28 Robin Yount 2.00
29 Joe Carter 1.50
30 Dale Murphy 2.00
31 Greg Maddux 3.00
32 Ichiro Suzuki 4.00
33 Jose Canseco 2.00
34 Nolan Ryan 8.00
35 Frank Thomas 2.00
36 Fred Lynn 1.50
37 Curt Schilling 2.00
38 Curt Schilling 2.00
39 Dave Parker 1.50
40 Randy Johnson 2.50
41 Randy Johnson 2.50
42 Vladimir Guerrero 2.50
43 Bernie Williams 1.50
44 Wade Boggs 2.00
45 Pedro Martinez 2.50
46 Andy Pettitte 1.50
47 Fergie Jenkins 2.00
48 Darryl Strawberry 1.50
49 Rafael Palmeiro 2.00
50 Albert Pujols 5.00

Heroes Swatch Double

NM/M
Production 25-50
Spectrum Prime: No Pricing
Production 1-25
1 Billy Martin J-P/50 25.00
2 Rickey Henderson B-J/50 10.00
3 Alan Trammell B-J/50 10.00
4 Lenny Dykstra B-J/50 8.00
5 Jeff Bagwell B-J/50 10.00
6 Steve Garvey B-J/50 8.00
7 Jim "Catfish" Hunter J-J/25 10.00
8 Cal Ripken Jr. J-P/50 40.00
9 Reggie Jackson JK-J/50 10.00
10 Gary Sheffield FG-J/50 8.00
11 Edgar Martinez J-J/50 8.00
12 Roberto Alomar J-J/50 8.00
13 Luis Tiant H-J/25 10.00
14 Jim Rice J-P/50 8.00
15 Carlos Beltran B-J/50 8.00
16 Hideo Nomo B-J/50 10.00
17 Mark Grace FG-J/50 10.00
18 Joe Cronin J-P/50 30.00
19 Tony Gwynn B-J/50 15.00
20 Bo Jackson B-J/50 10.00
21 Roger Clemens J-J/50 25.00
22 Roger Clemens J-J/50 25.00
23 Don Mattingly B-J/50 20.00
24 Willie Mays B-J/50 50.00
25 Andruw Jones B-J/50 8.00
26 Andre Dawson J-P/50 8.00
28 Robin Yount H-J/50 15.00
29 Joe Carter B-J/50 8.00
30 Dale Murphy B-J/50 10.00
31 Greg Maddux J-J/50 15.00
33 Jose Canseco H-J/50 10.00
34 Nolan Ryan B-J/50 30.00
35 Frank Thomas J-P/50 10.00
36 Fred Lynn B-J/50 8.00
37 Curt Schilling J-J/50 10.00
38 Curt Schilling J-J/50 10.00
39 Dave Parker B-J/50 8.00
40 Randy Johnson J-J/50 10.00
41 Randy Johnson B-J/25 10.00
42 Vladimir Guerrero J-J/50 10.00
43 Bernie Williams J-J/50 8.00
44 Wade Boggs B-J/50 10.00
45 Pedro Martinez J-J/50 10.00
46 Andy Pettitte J-J/50 8.00
47 Fergie Jenkins H-J/50 8.00
48 Darryl Strawberry J-P/50 8.00
49 Rafael Palmeiro B-J/50 10.00
50 Albert Pujols J-J/50 30.00

Heroes Autograph Swatch Double Spec Prime

No Pricing
Production 1-15
Triple: No Pricing
Production One Set

Heroes Swatch Triple

NM/M
Production 1-50
Spectrum Prime: No Pricing
Production 1-15
1 Billy Martin/25 35.00
2 Rickey Henderson/25 15.00
3 Alan Trammell/25 10.00
4 Lenny Dykstra/25 10.00
5 Jeff Bagwell/50 10.00
6 Steve Garvey/25 10.00
8 Cal Ripken Jr./25 50.00
9 Reggie Jackson/25 15.00
10 Gary Sheffield/50 10.00
11 Edgar Martinez/25 10.00
12 Roberto Alomar/50 10.00
14 Jim Rice/25 10.00
15 Carlos Beltran/25 15.00
16 Hideo Nomo/25 20.00
17 Mark Grace/25 15.00
18 Joe Cronin/25 40.00
19 Tony Gwynn/25 25.00
20 Bo Jackson/25 20.00
21 Roger Clemens/50 25.00
22 Roger Clemens/50 25.00
23 Don Mattingly/25 30.00
25 Andruw Jones/50 10.00
26 Andre Dawson/25 10.00
28 Robin Yount/25 60.00
31 Greg Maddux/50 15.00
34 Nolan Ryan/25 40.00
35 Frank Thomas/50 15.00
36 Fred Lynn/25 10.00
37 Curt Schilling/50 15.00
38 Curt Schilling/50 15.00
39 Dave Parker/25 10.00
42 Vladimir Guerrero/50 15.00
43 Bernie Williams/25 10.00
44 Wade Boggs/25 15.00
45 Pedro Martinez/50 15.00
46 Andy Pettitte/50 10.00
47 Fergie Jenkins/25 10.00
48 Darryl Strawberry/25 10.00
49 Rafael Palmeiro/50 15.00
50 Albert Pujols/50 40.00

Marks of Fame

NM/M
Common Player: 2.00
Production 150 Sets
Spectrum: 2-3X
Production 25 Sets
1 Bobby Doerr 2.00
2 Reggie Jackson 3.00
3 Harmon Killebrew 4.00
4 Duke Snider 3.00
5 Brooks Robinson 3.00
6 Al Kaline 4.00
7 Carlton Fisk 3.00
8 Willie Stargell 3.00
9 Enos Slaughter 2.00
10 Nolan Ryan 10.00
11 Luis Aparicio 2.00
12 Hoyt Wilhelm 2.00
13 Orlando Cepeda 2.00
14 Mike Schmidt 6.00
15 Frank Robinson 3.00
16 Whitey Ford 3.00
17 Don Sutton 2.00
18 Joe Morgan 2.00
19 Bob Feller 3.00
20 Lou Brock 3.00
21 Warren Spahn 4.00
22 Jim Palmer 2.00
23 Reggie Jackson 3.00
24 Willie Mays 8.00
25 George Brett 8.00
26 Billy Williams 2.00
27 Juan Marichal 2.00
28 Early Wynn 2.00
29 Rod Carew 3.00
30 Maury Wills 2.00
31 Fergie Jenkins 2.00
32 Steve Carlton 3.00
33 Eddie Murray 3.00
34 Kirby Puckett 3.00
35 Johnny Bench 4.00
36 Gaylord Perry 2.00
37 Gary Carter 2.00
38 Tony Perez 2.00
39 Tony Oliva 2.00
40 Luis Aparicio 2.00
41 Tom Seaver 3.00
42 Paul Molitor 3.00
43 Dennis Eckersley 2.00
44 Willie McCovey 3.00
45 Bob Gibson 3.00
46 Robin Roberts 2.00
47 Carl Yastrzemski 4.00
48 Ozzie Smith 4.00
49 Nolan Ryan 10.00
50 Stan Musial 6.00

Marks of Fame Autograph Swatch Single

NM/M
Production 5-125
1 Bobby Doerr/Pants/125 20.00
3 Harmon Killebrew/Jsy/50 40.00
4 Duke Snider/Jsy/25 40.00
5 Brooks Robinson/Jsy/125 30.00
6 Al Kaline/Bat/125 35.00
7 Carlton Fisk/Jkt/50 40.00
10 Nolan Ryan/Pants/50 80.00
11 Luis Aparicio/Jsy/125 20.00
13 Orlando Cepeda/Pants/50 25.00
14 Mike Schmidt/Jsy/50 60.00
15 Frank Robinson/Bat/125 30.00
16 Whitey Ford/Jsy/50 50.00
17 Don Sutton/Jsy/125 20.00
19 Bob Feller/Pants/125 30.00
20 Lou Brock/Jkt/125 30.00
22 Jim Palmer/Pants/50 25.00
26 Billy Williams/Jsy/50 25.00
27 Juan Marichal/Pants/125 25.00
29 Rod Carew/Jsy/50 35.00
31 Fergie Jenkins/Pants/125 20.00
32 Steve Carlton/Pants/125 25.00
35 Johnny Bench/Pants/50 50.00
36 Gaylord Perry/Jsy/125 15.00
37 Gary Carter/Pants/50 20.00
38 Tony Perez/Jsy/50 20.00
39 Tony Oliva/Jsy/125 25.00
40 Luis Aparicio/Bat/125 20.00
41 Tom Seaver/Pants/50 35.00
42 Paul Molitor/Pants/50 35.00
43 Dennis Eckersley/Jsy/125 20.00
44 Willie McCovey/Pants/50 35.00
46 Robin Roberts/Hat/50 35.00
48 Ozzie Smith/Pants/50 50.00
49 Nolan Ryan/Jkt/50 80.00
50 Stan Musial/Pants/50 60.00

Marks of Fame Swatch Double

NM/M
Production 1-50
Spectrum Prime: No Pricing
Production 1-25
1 Bobby Doerr/50 10.00
2 Reggie Jackson B-P/50 10.00
3 Harmon Killebrew B-J/50 15.00
4 Duke Snider J-P/25 15.00
5 Brooks Robinson B-J/50 15.00
7 Carlton Fisk B-JK/50 10.00
8 Willie Stargell B-J/50 10.00
9 Enos Slaughter J-J/50 10.00
10 Nolan Ryan J-P/50 25.00
11 Luis Aparicio B-J/50 8.00
12 Hoyt Wilhelm J-J/50 8.00
13 Orlando Cepeda B-P/50 10.00
14 Mike Schmidt B-J/50 20.00
15 Frank Robinson B-S/50 15.00
16 Whitey Ford J-J/25 15.00
17 Don Sutton J-J/50 8.00
18 Joe Morgan B-J/50 8.00
20 Lou Brock B-JK/50 10.00
21 Warren Spahn J-P/50 12.00
22 Jim Palmer H-P/50 10.00
23 Reggie Jackson B-J/50 10.00
24 Willie Mays B-J/25 50.00
26 Billy Williams J-J/50 8.00
27 Juan Marichal J-P/50 8.00
28 Early Wynn J-J/25 10.00
29 Rod Carew B-J/50 10.00
31 Fergie Jenkins FG-P/50 8.00
32 Steve Carlton B-P/50 8.00
33 Eddie Murray B-J/50 15.00
34 Kirby Puckett B-J/50 15.00
35 Johnny Bench B-J/50 15.00
36 Gaylord Perry J-J/50 8.00
37 Gary Carter B-J/50 8.00
39 Tony Oliva B-J/50 8.00
41 Tom Seaver J-P/50 15.00
42 Paul Molitor B-J/50 15.00
43 Dennis Eckersley J-J/50 10.00
44 Willie McCovey J-P/50 10.00
47 Carl Yastrzemski B-J/50 25.00
48 Ozzie Smith H-P/50 20.00
49 Nolan Ryan JK-J/50 25.00
50 Stan Musial B-P/50 30.00

Marks of Fame Autograph Swatch Double

NM/M
Production 1-75
Prime: No Pricing
Production 1-10
1 Bobby Doerr B-P/50 25.00
3 Harmon Killebrew B-J/50 40.00
4 Duke Snider J-P/25 40.00
5 Brooks Robinson B-J/25 40.00
7 Carlton Fisk B-JK/25 40.00
10 Nolan Ryan J-P/25 100.00
11 Luis Aparicio B-J/75 20.00
12 Hoyt Wilhelm J-J/25 25.00
13 Orlando Cepeda B-P/25 25.00
14 Mike Schmidt B-J/25 75.00
15 Frank Robinson B-S/25 50.00
16 Whitey Ford J-J/25 50.00
17 Don Sutton J-P/25 20.00
20 Lou Brock B-JK/25 50.00
22 Jim Palmer H-P/25 30.00
27 Juan Marichal J-P/25 25.00
29 Rod Carew B-J/25 40.00
31 Fergie Jenkins FG-P/25 20.00
32 Steve Carlton B-P/25 40.00
35 Johnny Bench B-J/25 50.00
36 Gaylord Perry J-J/25 20.00
37 Gary Carter B-J/25 25.00
38 Tony Perez FG-J/25 25.00
39 Tony Oliva B-J/75 20.00
41 Tom Seaver J-P/25 40.00
42 Paul Molitor B-J/25 35.00
43 Dennis Eckersley J-J/25 25.00
44 Willie McCovey J-P/25 40.00
48 Ozzie Smith H-P/25 50.00
49 Nolan Ryan JK-J/25 100.00
50 Stan Musial B-P/25 80.00

Marks of Fame Swatch Triple

NM/M
Production 1-25
Spectrum Prime: No Pricing
Production 1-15
1 Bobby Doerr/25 15.00
7 Carlton Fisk/25 15.00
8 Willie Stargell/25 15.00
10 Nolan Ryan/25 40.00
11 Luis Aparicio/25 12.00
12 Hoyt Wilhelm/25 10.00
14 Mike Schmidt/25 30.00
18 Joe Morgan/25 12.00
20 Lou Brock/25 15.00
21 Warren Spahn/25 50.00
23 Reggie Jackson/25 15.00
24 Willie Mays/25 60.00
27 Juan Marichal/25 12.00
29 Rod Carew/25 15.00
32 Steve Carlton/25 12.00
33 Eddie Murray/25 20.00
34 Kirby Puckett/25 20.00
35 Johnny Bench/25 20.00
37 Gary Carter/25 12.00
39 Tony Oliva/25 12.00
41 Tom Seaver/25 15.00
42 Paul Molitor/25 15.00
43 Dennis Eckersley/25 12.00
44 Willie McCovey/25 15.00
47 Carl Yastrzemski/25 35.00
48 Ozzie Smith/25 25.00
49 Nolan Ryan/25 40.00
50 Stan Musial/25 40.00

Marks of Fame Autograph Swatch Triple

No Pricing
Production 1-10
Prime: No Pricing
Production One Set

Team Tandems

NM/M
Common Card: 1.50
Production 250 Sets
Spectrum: .75-1.5X
Production 150 Sets
1 Mark Prior, Kerry Wood 2.00
2 Barry Zito, Tim Hudson 1.50
3 Curt Schilling, Pedro Martinez 2.50
4 Will Clark, Matt Williams 2.00
5 Bernie Williams, Jason Giambi 2.00
6 Vernon Wells, Roy Halladay 1.50
7 Josh Beckett, A.J. Burnett 1.50
8 Dale Murphy, Phil Niekro 2.00
9 Mike Schmidt, Steve Carlton 5.00
10 Tony Oliva, Harmon Killebrew 2.00
11 Robin Yount, Paul Molitor 2.50
12 Francisco Rodriguez, Troy Percival 1.50
13 Ben Sheets, Danny Kolb 1.50
14 Andruw Jones, Rafael Furcal 1.50
15 Todd Helton, Preston Wilson 1.50
16 Wade Boggs, Fred McGriff 2.00
17 Manny Ramirez, David Ortiz 2.50
18 Miguel Cabrera, Dontrelle Willis 2.00
19 Edgar Renteria, Scott Rolen 2.00
20 Carlos Beltran, Jeff Kent 2.00
21 Eric Davis, Deion Sanders 2.00
22 Frank Thomas, Paul Konerko 2.00
23 Mike Piazza, Al Leiter 3.00
24 Sean Burroughs, Ryan Klesko 1.50
25 Ken Harvey, Mike Sweeney 1.50
26 David Sanders, Hideki Matsui 4.00
27 Steve Carlton, Mark Buehrle 2.00
28 Gaylord Perry, Randy Johnson 2.00
29 Joe Morgan, Steve Carlton 2.00
30 Vladimir Guerrero, Orlando Cabrera 2.00
31 Scott Rolen, John Kruk 2.00
32 Aaron Boone, Dmitri Young 1.50
33 Rickey Henderson, Vladimir Guerrero 2.00
34 Charles Johnson, Cliff Floyd 1.50
35 Cal Ripken Jr., Rafael Palmeiro 8.00

Team Tandems Swatch Single

NM/M
Production 10-125
1 Mark Prior, Kerry Wood/125 6.00
2 Barry Zito, Tim Hudson/125 5.00
3 Curt Schilling, Pedro Martinez/125 8.00
4 Will Clark, Matt Williams/125 8.00
5 Bernie Williams, Jason Giambi/125 8.00
6 Vernon Wells, Roy Halladay/125 5.00
7 Josh Beckett, A.J. Burnett/125 5.00
8 Dale Murphy, Phil Niekro/125 15.00
9 Mike Schmidt, Steve Carlton/125 15.00
10 Tony Oliva, Harmon Killebrew/50 15.00
11 Robin Yount, Paul Molitor/125 15.00
12 Felix Rodriguez, Troy Percival/25 10.00
13 Ben Sheets, Danny Kolb/125 5.00
14 Andruw Jones, Rafael Furcal/125 5.00
15 Todd Helton, Preston Wilson/125 5.00
16 Wade Boggs, Fred McGriff/50 10.00
17 Manny Ramirez, David Ortiz/125 12.00
18 Miguel Cabrera, Dontrelle Willis/125 10.00
19 Edgar Renteria, Scott Rolen/125 10.00
20 Carlos Beltran, Jeff Kent Bat/125 8.00
21 Eric Davis Bat, Deion Sanders/125 8.00
22 Frank Thomas, Paul Konerko/50 10.00
23 Mike Piazza, Al Leiter/125 12.00
24 Sean Burroughs, Ryan Klesko/125 5.00
25 Ken Harvey, Mike Sweeney/125 5.00
26 Deion Sanders, Hideki Matsui/125 25.00
27 Steve Carlton, Mark Buehrle/50 8.00
28 Gaylord Perry, Randy Johnson/125 10.00
29 Joe Morgan, Steve Carlton/25 10.00
31 Scott Rolen, John Kruk/125 10.00

32 Aaron Boone, Dmitri Young/125 5.00
33 Rickey Henderson Hat, Vladimir Guerrero/25 15.00
34 Charles Johnson, Cliff Floyd/125 5.00
35 Cal Ripken Jr., Rafael Palmeiro/125 25.00

Team Tandems Swatch Single Spectrum

NM/M

Production 1-75
1 Mark Prior, Kerry Wood/75 6.00
2 Barry Zito, Tim Hudson/75 5.00
3 Curt Schilling, Pedro Martinez/75 10.00
4 Will Clark, M. Williams/75 8.00
5 Bernie Williams, Jason Giambi/75 5.00
6 Vernon Wells, Roy Halladay/75 5.00
7 Josh Beckett, A.J. Burnett/75 5.00
8 Dale Murphy, Phil Niekro/75 10.00
11 Robin Yount, Paul Molitor/75 15.00
13 Ben Sheets, Danny Kolb/75 5.00
14 Andruw Jones, Rafael Furcal/75 5.00
15 Todd Helton, Preston Wilson/75 5.00
17 Manny Ramirez, David Ortiz/75 10.00
18 Miguel Cabrera, Dontrelle Willis/75 8.00
19 Edgar Renteria, Scott Rolen/75 8.00
20 Carlos Beltran, Jeff Kent Bat/75 8.00
21 Eric Davis Bat, Deion Sanders/75 8.00
23 Mike Piazza, Al Leiter/75 10.00
24 Sean Burroughs, Ryan Klesko/75 5.00
25 Ken Harvey, Mike Sweeney/75 5.00
26 Deion Sanders, Hideki Matsui/75 25.00
28 Gaylord Perry, Randy Johnson/75 8.00
31 Scott Rolen, John Kruk/75 8.00
32 Aaron Boone, D. Young/75 5.00
34 Charles Johnson, Cliff Floyd/75 5.00
35 Cal Ripken Jr., Rafael Palmeiro/75 25.00

Team Tandems Swatch Double

NM/M

Production 1-125
Spectrum: 1-2X
Production 1-50
No pricing 20 or less.
1 Mark Prior, Kerry Wood/125 8.00
2 Barry Zito, Tim Hudson/125 8.00
3 Curt Schilling, Pedro Martinez/125 15.00
5 Bernie Williams, Jason Giambi/125 10.00
7 Josh Beckett, A.J. Burnett/125 8.00
8 Dale Murphy, Phil Niekro/125 20.00
10 Tony Oliva, Harmon Killebrew/50 30.00
11 Robin Yount, Paul Molitor/125 20.00
14 Andruw Jones, Rafael Furcal/125 8.00
15 Todd Helton, Preston Wilson/125 10.00
16 Wade Boggs, Fred McGriff/125 15.00
17 Manny Ramirez, David Ortiz/125 15.00
18 Miguel Cabrera, Dontrelle Willis/125 12.00
20 Carlos Beltran, Jeff Kent/50 12.00
21 Eric Davis, Deion Sanders/25 15.00
22 Frank Thomas, Paul Konerko/50 15.00
23 Mike Piazza, Al Leiter/125 20.00
24 Sean Burroughs, Ryan Klesko/50 10.00
26 Deion Sanders, Hideki Matsui/125 35.00
27 Steve Carlton, Mark Buehrle/50 12.00
29 Joe Morgan, Steve Carlton/25 15.00
33 Rickey Henderson, Vladimir Guerrero/50 15.00
34 Charles Johnson, Cliff Floyd/125 8.00
35 Cal Ripken Jr., Rafael Palmeiro/125 40.00

Team Trios

NM/M

Common Card:
Production 200 Sets
Spectrum: 1X
Production 125 Sets
1 Cal Ripken Jr., Jim Palmer, Eddie Murray 10.00
2 Roger Clemens, Wade Boggs, Evans 5.00
3 Rafael Palmeiro, Miguel Tejada, Javy Lopez 2.00
4 Carl Crawford, Rocco Baldelli, B.J. Upton 1.50
5 Mark Buehrle, Magglio Ordonez, Carlos Lee 1.50
6 Victor Martinez, Travis Hafner, Jody Gerut 1.50
7 Bobby Abreu, Brett Myers, Kevin Millwood 1.50
8 Sammy Sosa, Aramis Ramirez, Carlos Zambrano 3.00
9 Bo, George Brett, Carlos Beltran 5.00
10 Hideo Nomo, Adrian Beltre, Shawn Green 2.00
11 Wilson, Wilson, Jason Bay 1.50
12 Tom Seaver, Nolan Ryan, Dwight Gooden 8.00
13 David Dellucci, Laynce Nix, Kevin Mench 1.50
14 Alan Trammell, Morris, Gibson 2.00
15 M. Will, Grace, Randy Johnson 2.00
16 Dawson, Gary Carter, Tony Perez 2.00
17 Dale Murphy, John Kruk, Lenny Dykstra 2.00
18 B. Roberts, Ian Gibb, Larry Bigbie 1.50
19 Mike Lowell, Ivan Rodriguez, Brad Penny 2.00
20 Murray, Darryl Strawberry, Oliver 2.00
21 Darryl Strawberry, Rickey Henderson, Gary Sheffield 2.00
22 Roberto Alomar, Joe Crede, Durham 2.00
23 Jason Kendall, Giles, Aramis Ramirez 1.50
24 Delmon, Aubrey Huff, Tino 2.00
25 Jeff Bagwell, Cruz, Joe Morgan 2.00
26 Snow, Rich Aurilia, Jeff Kent 1.50
27 Jenkins, Nolan Ryan, Cordero 8.00
28 Lofton, Jim Thome, Roberto Alomar 3.00
29 Atkins, Todd Helton, Jennings 2.00
30 Gary Carter, Pedro, Randy Johnson 2.50

Team Trios Swatch Single

NM/M

Production 50 unless noted.
1 Cal Ripken Jr., Jim Palmer, Murray 40.00
2 Roger Clemens, Wade Boggs, Evans 25.00
3 Rafael Palmeiro, Miguel Tejada, Javy Lopez 12.00
4 Carl Crawford, Rocco Baldelli, B.J. Upton 10.00
5 Mark Buehrle, Magglio Ordonez, Carlos Lee 10.00
6 Victor Martinez, Travis Hafner, Jody Gerut 10.00
7 Bobby Abreu, Brett Myers, Kevin Millwood 10.00
8 Sammy Sosa, Aramis Ramirez, Carlos Zambrano 15.00
9 Bo, George Brett, Carlos Beltran 30.00
10 Hideo Nomo, Adrian Beltre, Shawn Green 15.00
11 Wilson, Wilson, Jason Bay 10.00
12 Tom Seaver, Nolan Ryan, Dwight Gooden 35.00
13 David Dellucci, Laynce Nix, Kevin Mench 8.00
14 Alan Trammell, Morris, Gibson 15.00
15 M. Will, Grace, Randy Johnson 15.00
16 Dawson, Gary Carter, Tony Perez 10.00
17 Dale Murphy, Tomas Kurka, Lenny Dykstra 20.00
18 Roberts, Ian Gibb, Larry Bigbie 15.00
19 Mike Lowell, Ivan Rodriguez, Brad Penny 10.00
20 Murray, Darryl Strawberry, Oliver 20.00
21 Darryl Strawberry, Rickey Henderson, Gary Sheffield 15.00
22 Roberto Alomar, Joe Crede, Durham 10.00
23 Jason Kendall, Giles, Aramis Ramirez 10.00
24 Delmon, Aubrey Huff, Tino 10.00
25 Jeff Bagwell, Cruz, Joe Morgan 12.00
26 Snow, Rich Aurilia, Jeff Kent 8.00
27 Jenkins, Nolan Ryan, Cordero 25.00
28 Lofton, Jim Thome, Roberto Alomar 20.00
29 Atkins, Todd Helton, Jennings 15.00
30 Gary Carter, Pedro, Randy Johnson 15.00

Team Trios Swatch Single Spectrum

NM/M

Production 10-50
Prime Black: No Pricing
Production 10 Sets
1 Cal Ripken Jr., Jim Palmer, Murray/50 40.00
2 Roger Clemens, Wade Boggs, Evans/50 30.00
4 Carl Crawford, Rocco Baldelli, B.J. Upton/50 10.00
5 Mark Buehrle, Magglio Ordonez, Carlos Lee/50 10.00
7 Bobby Abreu, Brett Myers, Kevin Millwood/50 10.00
8 Sammy Sosa, Aramis Ramirez, Carlos Zambrano/50 15.00
9 Bo, George Brett, Carlos Beltran/50 25.00
10 Hideo Nomo, Adrian Beltre, Shawn Green/50 15.00
11 Wilson, Wilson, Jason Bay/50 8.00
12 Tom Seaver, Nolan Ryan, Dwight Gooden/50 30.00
13 David Dellucci, Laynce Nix, Kevin Mench/50 10.00
14 Alan Trammell, Morris, Gibson/50 15.00
16 Dawson, Gary Carter, Tony Perez/50 10.00
17 Dale Murphy, Tomas Kurka, Lenny Dykstra/50 15.00
18 Roberts, Ian Gibb, Larry Bigbie/50 10.00
19 Mike Lowell, Ivan Rodriguez, Brad Penny/25 10.00
20 Murray, Darryl Strawberry, Oliver/50 20.00
21 Darryl Strawberry, Rickey Henderson, Gary Sheffield/50 15.00
22 Roberto Alomar, Joe Crede, Durham/50 10.00
24 Delmon, Aubrey Huff, Tino/50 10.00
25 Jeff Bagwell, Cruz, Joe Morgan/50 10.00
26 Snow, Rich Aurilia, Jeff Kent/50 8.00
27 Jenkins, Nolan Ryan, Cordero/50 25.00
28 Lofton, Jim Thome, Roberto Alomar/50 10.00
29 Atkins, Todd Helton, Jennings/50 10.00
30 Gary Carter, Pedro, Randy Johnson/50 15.00

Team Trios Swatch Double

NM/M

Production 25-100
Spectrum: .75-1.5X
Production 5-35
No pricing production 20 or less.
Prime Black: No Pricing
Production 5-10
1 Cal Ripken Jr., Jim Palmer, Murray/100 75.00
2 Roger Clemens, Wade Boggs, Evans/100 50.00
3 Rafael Palmeiro, Miguel Tejada, Javy Lopez/50 25.00
5 Mark Buehrle, Magglio Ordonez, Carlos Lee/100 15.00
6 Victor Martinez, Travis Hafner, Jody Gerut/50 20.00
9 Bo, George Brett, Carlos Beltran/100 40.00
10 Hideo Nomo, Adrian Beltre, Shawn Green/100 25.00
11 Wilson, Wilson, Jason Bay/100 15.00
12 Tom Seaver, Nolan Ryan, Dwight Gooden/100 50.00
14 Alan Trammell, Morris, Gibson/50 30.00
15 M. Will, Mark Grace, Randy Johnson/50 30.00
16 Dawson, Gary Carter, Tony Perez/100 20.00
19 Mike Lowell, Ivan Rodriguez, Brad Penny/50 25.00
20 Murray, Darryl Strawberry, Oliver/100 30.00
21 Darryl Strawberry, Rickey Henderson, Gary Sheffield/100 25.00
22 Roberto Alomar, Joe Crede, Durham/100 20.00
28 Lofton, Jim Thome, Roberto Alomar/25 40.00
29 Atkins, Todd Helton, Jennings/100 20.00
30 Gary Carter, Pedro, Randy Johnson/50 30.00

Team Quads

NM/M

Common Quad:
Production 150 Sets
Spectrum: 1X
Production 100 Sets
1 St. Louis Card Active 6.00
2 Cleveland Indians 2.00
3 California Angels 2.00
4 Boston Red Sox 5.00
5 New York Yanks Active 6.00
6 Atlanta Braves 3.00
7 Oakland A's 3.00
8 Anaheim Angels 3.00
9 Texas Rangers Active 2.00
10 Minnesota Twins Active 3.00
11 New York Mets 4.00
12 Houston Astros 5.00
13 San Diego Padres 4.00
14 Cincinnati Reds 2.00
15 Texas Rangers Retro 8.00
16 New York Yanks Retro 8.00
17 St. Louis Cards Retro 6.00
18 Pittsburgh Pirates 2.00
19 Chicago Cubs 4.00
20 Minnesota Twins Retro 3.00

Team Quads Swatch Single

NM/M

Production 25-100
1 St. Louis Card Active/100 25.00
2 Cleveland Indians/100 30.00
3 California Angels/100 15.00
4 Boston Red Sox/100 20.00
5 New York Yanks Active/100 30.00
6 Atlanta Braves/100 25.00
7 Oakland A's/100 10.00
8 Anaheim Angels/100 15.00
9 Texas Rangers Active/100 10.00
10 Minnesota Twins Active/25 25.00
11 New York Mets/100 20.00
12 Houston Astros/100 30.00
13 San Diego Padres/100 25.00
14 Cincinnati Reds/100 10.00
15 Texas Rangers Retro/100 30.00
16 New York Yanks Retro/100 50.00
17 St. Louis Cards Retro/25 50.00
18 Pittsburgh Pirates/100 15.00
19 Chicago Cubs/100 25.00
20 Minnesota Twins Retro/100 20.00

Team Quads Swatch Single Spectrum

NM/M

Production 10-35
Prime Black: No Pricing
Production 10 Sets
1 St. Louis Card Active/35 40.00
2 Cleveland Indians/35 50.00
3 California Angels/35 25.00
4 Boston Red Sox/35 30.00
5 New York Yanks Active/35 40.00
6 Atlanta Braves/35 40.00
7 Oakland A's/35 20.00
8 Anaheim Angels/35 25.00
9 Texas Rangers Active/35 20.00
11 New York Mets/35 30.00
12 Houston Astros/35 50.00
13 San Diego Padres/35 40.00
14 Cincinnati Reds/35 20.00
15 Texas Rangers Retro/35 40.00
16 New York Yanks Retro/35 75.00
18 Pittsburgh Pirates/35 20.00
19 Chicago Cubs/35 40.00
20 Minnesota Twins Retro/35 30.00

Team Quads Swatch Double

NM/M

Production 25-75
1 St. Louis Card Active/75 25.00
3 California Angels/75 30.00
4 Boston Red Sox/75 30.00
5 New York Yanks Active/25 75.00
6 Atlanta Braves/25 60.00
7 Oakland A's/75 20.00
8 Anaheim Angels/25 40.00
9 Texas Rangers Active/75 20.00
10 Minnesota Twins Active/25 40.00
11 New York Mets/75 30.00
12 Houston Astros/25 75.00
13 San Diego Padres/75 40.00
14 Cincinnati Reds/75 20.00
15 Texas Rangers Retro/75 50.00
18 Pittsburgh Pirates/75 20.00
20 Minnesota Twins Retro/75 30.00

Team Quads Swatch Double Spectrum

NM/M

Production 1-25
Prime Black: No Pricing
Production 1-5
1 St. Louis Card Active/25 40.00
3 California Angels/25 50.00
4 Boston Red Sox/25 60.00
9 Texas Rangers Active/25 30.00
11 New York Mets/25 50.00
13 San Diego Padres/25 60.00
14 Cincinnati Reds/25 30.00
15 Texas Rangers Retro/25 70.00

Team Six

NM/M

Common Card: 1.50
Production 100 Sets
Spectrum: 1-1.5X
Production 50 Sets
1 San Francisco Giants 8.00
2 Houston Astros 6.00
3 Cincinnati Reds 5.00
4 St. Louis Cardinals 8.00
5 New York Yankees 10.00
6 Chicago Cubs 6.00
7 Arizona Diamondbacks 1.50
8 Los Angeles Dodgers 6.00
9 Anaheim Angels 4.00
10 Boston Red Sox 8.00
11 Seattle Mariners 8.00
12 Chicago White Sox 4.00
13 Philadelphia Phillies 10.00
14 New York Mets 10.00
15 Atlanta Braves 4.00

Team Six Swatch Single

NM/M

Production 15-50
1 San Francisco Giants/50 80.00
2 Houston Astros/50 40.00
5 New York Yankees /50 60.00
6 Chicago Cubs/50 40.00
7 Arizona Diamondbacks/50 20.00
8 Los Angeles Dodgers/50 40.00
9 Anaheim Angels/50 30.00
10 Boston Red Sox/50 50.00
12 Chicago White Sox/50 30.00
13 Philadelphia Phillies/50 40.00
14 New York Mets/50 40.00
15 Atlanta Braves/50 40.00

Team Six Swatch Single Spectrum

NM/M

Production 5-25
Prime Black: No Pricing
Production Five Sets
1 San Francisco Giants/25 100.00
2 Houston Astros/25 50.00
5 New York Yankees/25 75.00
6 Chicago Cubs/25 50.00
7 Arizona Diamondbacks/25 25.00
8 Los Angeles Dodgers/25 50.00
10 Boston Red Sox/25 65.00
12 Chicago White Sox/25 40.00
13 Philadelphia Phillies/25 50.00
14 New York Mets/25 50.00
15 Atlanta Braves/25 50.00

Tools of the Trade Red

NM/M

Common Player:
Production 250 Sets
Black: 1-1.5X
Production 100 Sets
Blue: 1-1.5X
Production 150 Sets
Rev. Spectrum Red: 1-2X
Production 50 Sets
Rev. Spectrum Blue: No Pricing
Production 10 Sets
1 Ozzie Smith 5.00
2 Carlos Beltran 2.00
3 Dale Murphy 2.00
4 Paul Molitor 2.00
5 George Brett 6.00
6 Stan Musial 5.00
7 Ivan Rodriguez 2.00
8 Carl Yastrzemski 4.00
9 Reggie Jackson 2.00
10 Hideo Nomo 2.00
11 Gary Sheffield 2.00
12 Roberto Alomar 2.00
13 Pedro Martinez 2.00
14 Ernie Banks 3.00
15 Tim Hudson 1.50
16 Dwight Gooden 1.50
17 Lance Berkman 1.50
18 Darryl Strawberry 1.50
19 Larry Walker 1.50
20 Lou Brock 2.00
21 Roger Clemens 6.00
22 Paul LoDuca 1.50
23 Don Mattingly 6.00
24 Willie Mays 6.00
25 Rafael Palmeiro 2.00
26 Roy Oswalt 1.50
27 Vladimir Guerrero 3.00
28 Austin Kearns 1.50
29 Rod Carew 2.00
30 Nolan Ryan 8.00
31 Richie Sexson 2.00
32 Steve Carlton 2.00
33 Eddie Murray 3.00
34 Nolan Ryan 8.00
35 Mike Mussina 2.00
36 Sean Casey 1.50
37 Juan Gonzalez 1.50
38 Curt Schilling 2.00
39 Darryl Strawberry 1.50
40 Alfonso Soriano 3.00
41 Tom Seaver 3.00
42 Mike Schmidt 5.00
43 Todd Helton 2.00
44 Reggie Jackson 2.00
45 Shawn Green 1.50
46 Mike Mussina 2.00
47 Tom Glavine 1.50
48 Torii Hunter 1.50
49 Kerry Wood 2.00
50 Carlos Delgado 2.00
51 Randy Johnson 3.00
52 David Ortiz 3.00
53 Troy Glaus 2.00
54 Rickey Henderson 2.00
55 Craig Biggio 2.00
56 Brad Penny 1.50
57 Gary Carter 2.00
58 Andy Pettitte 1.50
59 Mark Prior 2.00
60 Kirby Puckett 3.00
61 Willie McCovey 3.00
62 Andre Dawson 2.00
63 Greg Maddux 4.00
64 Adrian Beltre 1.50
65 Andruw Jones 2.00
66 Juan Gonzalez 1.50
67 Frank Thomas 2.00
68 Victor Martinez 1.50

69 Randy Johnson 3.00
70 Andre Dawson 2.00
71 Adam Dunn 2.00
72 Carlton Fisk 2.00
73 Cal Ripken Jr. 8.00
74 Kenny Lofton 1.50
75 Barry Zito 1.50
76 Sammy Sosa 4.00
77 Deion Sanders 2.00
78 Tony Gwynn 3.00
79 Mike Piazza 4.00
80 Jeff Bagwell 2.00
81 Manny Ramirez 3.00
82 Carlos Beltran 2.00
83 Mark Grace 2.00
84 Robin Yount 4.00
85 Albert Pujols 6.00
86 Dontrelle Willis 2.00
87 Jim Thome 2.00
88 Magglio Ordonez 1.50
89 Miguel Tejada 2.00
90 Mark Teixeira 2.00
91 Gary Carter 2.00
92 Ivan Rodriguez 2.00
93 Jason Giambi 1.50
94 Rickey Henderson 2.00
95 Curt Schilling 2.00
96 Bobby Doerr 2.00
97 Chipper Jones 3.00
98 Eric Chavez 1.50
99 Johnny Bench 4.00
100 Harmon Killebrew 3.00

Tools of Trade Laundry Tag Prime Red

No Pricing
Production One Set

Tools of Trade Swatch Single Jumbo

NM/M
Production 1-100
Prime Red: No Pricing
Production 1-25
Reverse: 1-2X
Production 1-50
Prime Black: No Pricing
Production One Set
1 Ozzie Smith/25 30.00
2 Carlos Beltran/Jsy/50 10.00
3 Dale Murphy/Jsy/25 20.00
4 Paul Molitor/Jsy/25 25.00
6 Stan Musial/Pants/25 50.00
7 Ivan Rodriguez/Jsy/100 10.00
10 Hideo Nomo/Jsy/100 15.00
11 Gary Sheffield/Jsy/25 15.00
12 Roberto Alomar/Jsy/100 10.00
13 Pedro Martinez/Jsy/50 12.00
15 Tim Hudson/Jsy/100 10.00
17 Lance Berkman/Jsy/75 8.00
19 Larry Walker/Jsy/100 10.00
20 Lou Brock/Jkt/50 20.00
21 Roger Clemens/Jsy/50 30.00
23 Don Mattingly/Jsy/25 40.00
25 Rafael Palmeiro/Jsy/100 10.00
27 Vladimir Guerrero/Jsy/50 15.00
29 Rod Carew/Jsy/50 15.00
30 Nolan Ryan/Jsy/25 50.00
31 Richie Sexson/Jsy/100 10.00
33 Eddie Murray/Jsy/50 20.00
35 Mike Mussina/Jsy/50 12.00
36 Sean Casey/Jsy/100 8.00
37 Juan Gonzalez/Jsy/25 15.00
38 Curt Schilling/Jsy/100 15.00
39 Darryl Strawberry/Jsy/50 10.00
41 Tom Seaver/Jsy/50 15.00
42 Mike Schmidt/Jsy/25 40.00
43 Todd Helton/Jsy/50 10.00
45 Shawn Green/Jsy/100 8.00
47 Tom Glavine/Jsy/100 10.00
49 Kerry Wood/Jsy/50 10.00
51 R. John/Jsy/25 20.00
52 David Ortiz/Jsy/75 15.00
53 Troy Glaus/Jsy/100 10.00
54 Rickey Henderson/Jsy/25 15.00
55 Craig Biggio/Jsy/75 10.00
56 Brad Penny/Jsy/100 8.00
57 Gary Carter/Jsy/25 15.00
58 Andy Pettitte/Jsy/50 10.00
59 Mark Prior/Jsy/50 10.00
60 Kirby Puckett/Jsy/50 20.00
61 Willie McCovey/Jsy/50 15.00
63 Greg Maddux/Jsy/100 20.00
65 Andruw Jones/Jsy/100 10.00
68 Victor Martinez/Jsy/50 8.00
70 Andre Dawson/Jsy/50 10.00
72 Carlton Fisk/Jsy/100 10.00
73 Cal Ripken Jr./Jsy/100 35.00
74 Kenny Lofton/Hat/25 10.00
75 Barry Zito/Jsy/100 8.00
76 Sammy Sosa/Jsy/100 15.00
77 Deion Sanders/Jsy/25 20.00
78 Tony Gwynn/Jsy/100 20.00
79 Mike Piazza/Jsy/100 20.00
80 Jeff Bagwell/Jsy/100 10.00
83 Mark Grace/Jsy/50 15.00
84 Robin Yount/Jsy/50 20.00
85 Albert Pujols/Jsy/100 30.00
86 Dontrelle Willis/Jsy/50 10.00
89 Miguel Tejada/Jsy/100 12.00
90 Mark Teixeira/Jsy/25 15.00
92 Ivan Rodriguez/Jsy/100 10.00
93 Jason Giambi/Jsy/25 10.00
94 Rickey Henderson/Jsy/25 15.00
95 Curt Schilling/Jsy/50 10.00
96 Bobby Doerr/Pants/25 20.00
97 Chipper Jones/Jsy/25 20.00
98 Eric Chavez/Jsy/100 8.00
99 Johnny Bench/Jsy/25 25.00
100 Harmon Killebrew/Jsy/25 40.00

Tools of the Trade Swatch Double

NM/M
Production 1-150
Prime Red: No Pricing
Production 1-25
Prime Black: No Pricing
Production 1-25
1 Ozzie Smith B-P/50 15.00
2 Carlos Beltran J-S/50 8.00
3 Dale Murphy J-J/50 8.00
4 Paul Molitor J-P/150 8.00
5 George Brett B-H/25 25.00
6 Stan Musial B-P/25 30.00
7 Ivan Rodriguez J-J/150 8.00
8 Carl Yastrzemski B-J/25 30.00
9 Reggie Jackson J-J/50 10.00
10 Hideo Nomo J-P/150 10.00
11 Gary Sheffield H-J/25 8.00
12 Roberto Alomar B-J/150 8.00
13 Pedro Martinez J-P/150 8.00
15 Tim Hudson H-J/100 5.00
17 Lance Berkman B-J/150 5.00
19 Larry Walker J-J/150 5.00
20 Lou Brock B-JK/150 10.00
21 Roger Clemens B-J/150 15.00
22 Paul LoDuca B-J/50 5.00
23 Don Mattingly BG-P/50 20.00
24 Willie Mays B-P/25 50.00
25 Rafael Palmeiro B-J/150 8.00
27 Vladimir Guerrero B-J/150 8.00
29 Rod Carew JK-JK/150 8.00
30 Nolan Ryan B-JK/150 25.00
31 Richie Sexson H-J/150 8.00
32 Steve Carlton B-H/150 8.00
33 Eddie Murray B-J/150 10.00
34 Nolan Ryan B-J/150 25.00
35 Mike Mussina J-P/125 8.00
36 Sean Casey J-P/150 5.00
38 Curt Schilling J-J/150 8.00
39 Darryl Strawberry B-J/150 5.00
41 Tom Seaver J-P/150 10.00
42 Mike Schmidt B-J/150 15.00
43 Todd Helton B-J/150 8.00
45 Shawn Green B-J/150 5.00
47 Tom Glavine B-J/150 5.00
49 Kerry Wood FG-J/150 8.00
50 Carlos Delgado B-J/100 5.00
51 R. John J-P/150 8.00
52 David Ortiz B-J/150 8.00
53 Troy Glaus J-J/150 5.00
54 Rickey Henderson B-J/150 8.00
55 Craig Biggio B-J/150 5.00
56 Brad Penny FG-J/150 5.00
57 Gary Carter J-P/150 8.00
58 Andy Pettitte J-J/150 5.00
59 Mark Prior FG-J/150 5.00
60 Kirby Puckett B-FG/100 10.00
61 Willie McCovey J-P/150 10.00
63 Greg Maddux B-J/50 15.00
64 Adrian Beltre B-J/150 5.00
65 Andruw Jones B-J/150 8.00
67 Frank Thomas J-J/150 8.00
68 Victor Martinez CP-J/150 5.00
69 R. John J-P/150 8.00
71 Adam Dunn B-J/95 8.00
72 Carlton Fisk B-J/150 8.00
73 Cal Ripken Jr. J-P/150 25.00
74 Kenny Lofton B-H/150 5.00
75 Barry Zito J-J/150 5.00
76 Sammy Sosa B-J/150 10.00
77 Deion Sanders J-P/150 10.00
78 Tony Gwynn J-P/150 10.00
79 Mike Piazza J-P/150 10.00
80 Jeff Bagwell J-P/150 8.00
81 Manny Ramirez B-J/150 8.00
83 Mark Grace B-J/50 8.00
84 Robin Yount B-J/150 12.00
85 Albert Pujols B-J/150 20.00
86 Dontrelle Willis B-J/150 8.00
88 Magglio Ordonez B-S/150 5.00
89 Miguel Tejada H-J/150 8.00
90 Mark Teixeira FG-J/150 8.00
91 Gary Carter B-J/25 10.00
92 Ivan Rodriguez CP-J/150 8.00
93 Jason Giambi H-J/50 5.00
94 Rickey Henderson B-P/150 8.00
95 Curt Schilling J-J/150 8.00
96 Bobby Doerr B-P/150 8.00
97 Chipper Jones B-J/150 8.00
99 Johnny Bench B-P/150 10.00
100 Harmon Killebrew H-J/50 10.00

Tools of Trade Auto Swatch Double

NM/M
Production 1-75
Prime Red: .75-1.5X
Production 1-50
No pricing production 20 or less.
Prime Black: No Pricing
Production One Set
1 Ozzie Smith B-P/25 50.00
3 Dale Murphy J-J/50 30.00
4 Paul Molitor J-P/25 40.00
20 Lou Brock B-JK/50 40.00
22 Paul LoDuca B-J/25 25.00
36 Sean Casey J-P/50 20.00
37 Juan Gonzalez J-P/25 30.00
39 Darryl Strawberry B-J/50 25.00
41 Tom Seaver J-P/25 40.00
48 Torii Hunter B-J/40 25.00
56 Brad Penny FG-J/75 10.00
57 Gary Carter J-P/25 30.00
62 Andre Dawson B-J/50 25.00
64 Adrian Beltre B-J/50 25.00
66 Juan Gonzalez B-J/25 30.00
70 Andre Dawson J-P/50 25.00
73 Cal Ripken Jr. J-P/25 160.00
88 Magglio Ordoñez B-S/25 20.00
91 Gary Carter B-J/25 30.00
96 Bobby Doerr B-P/50 25.00
98 Eric Chavez B-J/25 25.00
100 Harmon Killebrew H-J/25 50.00

Tools/Trade Auto Swatch Double Reverse

NM/M
Production 1-75
20 Lou Brock B-JK/50 40.00
36 Sean Casey J-P/50 25.00
39 Darryl Strawberry B-J/75 20.00
48 Torii Hunter B-J/50 25.00
56 Brad Penny FG-J/50 12.00
62 Andre Dawson B-J/25 30.00
64 Adrian Beltre B-J/50 20.00
66 Juan Gonzalez B-J/25 30.00
70 Andre Dawson J-P/25 30.00

Tools of the Trade Swatch Triple

NM/M
Production 1-25
Prime Red: No Pricing
Production 1-25
Prime Black: No Pricing
Production 1-15
2 Carlos Beltran/25 15.00
3 Dale Murphy/25 15.00
4 Paul Molitor/25 20.00
5 George Brett/25 35.00
6 Stan Musial/25 40.00
7 Ivan Rodriguez/25 10.00
9 Reggie Jackson/25 15.00
10 Hideo Nomo/25 20.00
12 Roberto Alomar/25 10.00
13 Pedro Martinez/25 15.00
15 Tim Hudson/25 10.00
17 Lance Berkman/25 10.00
19 Larry Walker/25 10.00
21 Roger Clemens/25 30.00
22 Paul LoDuca/25 10.00
23 Don Mattingly/25 30.00
25 Rafael Palmeiro/25 15.00
27 Vladimir Guerrero/25 15.00
29 Rod Carew/25 15.00
30 Nolan Ryan/25 40.00
31 Richie Sexson/25 10.00
33 Eddie Murray/25 20.00
34 Nolan Ryan/25 40.00
36 Sean Casey/25 10.00
37 Juan Gonzalez/25 10.00
38 Curt Schilling/25 15.00
42 Mike Schmidt/25 30.00
43 Todd Helton/25 12.00
45 Shawn Green/25 10.00
47 Tom Glavine/25 10.00
49 Kerry Wood/25 15.00
50 Carlos Delgado/25 10.00
51 R. John/25 15.00
52 David Ortiz/25 15.00
53 Troy Glaus/25 10.00
54 Rickey Henderson/25 15.00
55 Craig Biggio/25 12.00
56 Brad Penny/25 10.00
57 Gary Carter/25 15.00
58 Andy Pettitte/25 10.00
59 Mark Prior/25 10.00
60 Kirby Puckett/25 20.00
63 Greg Maddux/25 25.00
64 Adrian Beltre/25 10.00
65 Andruw Jones/25 12.00
67 Frank Thomas/25 15.00
68 Victor Martinez/25 10.00
70 Andre Dawson/25 12.00
72 Carlton Fisk/25 15.00
73 Cal Ripken Jr./25 40.00
74 Kenny Lofton/25 10.00
75 Barry Zito/25 10.00
76 Sammy Sosa/25 15.00
77 Deion Sanders/25 20.00
78 Tony Gwynn/25 20.00
79 Mike Piazza/25 20.00
80 Jeff Bagwell/25 15.00
81 Manny Ramirez/25 15.00
83 Mark Grace/25 15.00
84 Robin Yount/25 20.00
85 Albert Pujols/25 40.00
86 Dontrelle Willis/25 15.00
88 Magglio Ordonez/25 10.00
89 Miguel Tejada/25 15.00
90 Mark Teixeira/25 12.00
91 Gary Carter/25 15.00
92 Ivan Rodriguez/25 10.00
93 Jason Giambi/25 10.00
94 Rickey Henderson/25 15.00
95 Curt Schilling/25 15.00
96 Bobby Doerr/25 15.00
97 Chipper Jones/25 15.00
98 Eric Chavez/25 10.00
99 Johnny Bench/25 20.00
100 Harmon Killebrew/25 30.00

Tools of Trade Autograph Swatch Triple

NM/M
Production 1-75
Prime Red: No Pricing
Production 1-25
Prime Black: No Pricing
Production One Set
2 Carlos Beltran/25 40.00
3 Dale Murphy/25 50.00
18 Darryl Strawberry/75 20.00
20 Lou Brock/50 40.00
36 Sean Casey/75 20.00
37 Juan Gonzalez/75 25.00
39 Darryl Strawberry/75 20.00
56 Brad Penny/25 20.00
57 Gary Carter/25 30.00
64 Adrian Beltre/25 25.00
66 Juan Gonzalez/50 25.00
70 Andre Dawson/75 25.00
73 Cal Ripken Jr./25 200.00
82 Carlos Beltran/25 40.00
91 Gary Carter/25 30.00
96 Bobby Doerr/25 30.00
100 Harmon Killebrew/25 60.00

Tools/Trade Autograph Swatch Triple Revers

NM/M
Production 1-50
18 Darryl Strawberry/50 25.00
20 Lou Brock/50 50.00
36 Sean Casey/25 25.00
37 Juan Gonzalez/25 30.00
39 Darryl Strawberry/50 25.00
70 Andre Dawson/50 25.00

Tools of the Trade Swatch Quad

NM/M
Production 1-100
Prime Red: No Pricing
Production 1-10
Prime Black: No Pricing
Production One Set
3 Dale Murphy/50 20.00
4 Paul Molitor/25 30.00
7 Ivan Rodriguez/50 15.00
8 Carl Yastrzemski/25 50.00
9 Reggie Jackson/100 20.00
10 Hideo Nomo/75 15.00
11 Gary Sheffield/30 15.00
12 Roberto Alomar/50 15.00
13 Pedro Martinez/50 20.00
14 Ernie Banks/25 40.00
15 Tim Hudson/50 10.00
17 Lance Berkman/65 10.00
19 Larry Walker/100 10.00
20 Lou Brock/50 20.00
21 Roger Clemens/25 40.00
22 Paul LoDuca/100 10.00
23 Don Mattingly/50 40.00
24 Willie Mays/25 80.00
25 Rafael Palmeiro/100 10.00
26 Roy Oswalt/30 15.00
27 Vladimir Guerrero/50 20.00
29 Rod Carew/75 15.00
31 Richie Sexson/100 10.00
33 Eddie Murray/100 15.00
36 Sean Casey/75 10.00
39 Darryl Strawberry/50 15.00
41 Tom Seaver/35 25.00
42 Mike Schmidt/50 40.00
43 Todd Helton/100 12.00
45 Shawn Green/100 10.00
46 Mike Mussina/25 20.00
50 Carlos Delgado/50 10.00
52 David Ortiz/90 30.00
53 Troy Glaus/50 12.00
54 Rickey Henderson/100 25.00
55 Craig Biggio/100 10.00
56 Brad Penny/25 15.00
57 Gary Carter/50 15.00
58 Andy Pettitte/50 15.00
59 Mark Prior/50 15.00
60 Kirby Puckett/50 25.00
64 Adrian Beltre/50 10.00
65 Andruw Jones/100 10.00
66 Juan Gonzalez/30 20.00
67 Frank Thomas/50 25.00
68 Victor Martinez/50 10.00
70 Andre Dawson/50 15.00
72 Carlton Fisk/26 25.00
73 Cal Ripken Jr./100 50.00
74 Kenny Lofton/100 10.00
75 Barry Zito/50 10.00
76 Sammy Sosa/100 15.00
78 Tony Gwynn/100 20.00
79 Mike Piazza/100 20.00
80 Jeff Bagwell/100 10.00
83 Mark Grace/50 20.00
85 Albert Pujols/50 60.00
86 Dontrelle Willis/50 10.00
88 Magglio Ordonez/50 10.00
89 Miguel Tejada/100 15.00
90 Mark Teixeira/100 15.00
91 Gary Carter/90 15.00
92 Ivan Rodriguez/50 15.00
93 Jason Giambi/25 15.00
94 Rickey Henderson/100 15.00
95 Curt Schilling/100 15.00
100 Harmon Killebrew/25 40.00

Tools of Trade Autograph Swatch Quad

NM/M
Production 1-25
Prime Red: No Pricing
Production 1-5
3 Dale Murphy/25 60.00
20 Lou Brock/25 80.00
23 Don Mattingly/25 120.00
36 Sean Casey/25 40.00
39 Darryl Strawberry/25 40.00
41 Tom Seaver/25 75.00
42 Mike Schmidt/25 100.00
56 Brad Penny/25 20.00
57 Gary Carter/25 40.00
73 Cal Ripken Jr./25 200.00
78 Tony Gwynn/25 75.00
88 Magglio Ordonez/25 30.00
91 Gary Carter/25 40.00
100 Harmon Killebrew/25 80.00

Tools/Trade Autograph Swatch Quad Reverse

No Pricing
Production 1-15

Tools of the Trade Swatch Five

NM/M
Production 1-50
Prime Red: No Pricing
Production 1-10
Prime Black: No Pricing
Production One Set
Reverse: No Pricing
Production 1-15
4 Paul Molitor/25 35.00
7 Ivan Rodriguez/25 25.00
12 Roberto Alomar/25 20.00
13 Pedro Martinez/25 30.00
15 Tim Hudson/25 25.00
17 Lance Berkman/25 20.00
22 Paul LoDuca/50 15.00
23 Don Mattingly/25 65.00
25 Rafael Palmeiro/25 25.00
26 Roy Oswalt/25 20.00
28 Austin Kearns/25 20.00
29 Rod Carew/25 40.00
31 Richie Sexson/50 15.00
33 Eddie Murray/25 50.00
36 Sean Casey/25 20.00
42 Mike Schmidt/25 70.00
43 Todd Helton/25 25.00
52 David Ortiz/50 35.00
53 Troy Glaus/25 20.00
54 Rickey Henderson/50 25.00
55 Craig Biggio/50 25.00
56 Brad Penny/45 15.00
57 Gary Carter/40 25.00
58 Andy Pettitte/25 25.00
59 Mark Prior/25 25.00
60 Kirby Puckett/25 50.00
64 Adrian Beltre/50 20.00
65 Andruw Jones/25 20.00
67 Frank Thomas/25 25.00
68 Victor Martinez/25 20.00
73 Cal Ripken Jr./50 75.00
76 Sammy Sosa/25 35.00
78 Tony Gwynn/50 40.00
79 Mike Piazza/25 50.00
80 Jeff Bagwell/50 25.00
82 Carlos Beltran/20 25.00
84 Robin Yount/25 40.00
88 Magglio Ordonez/25 20.00
89 Miguel Tejada/50 25.00
90 Mark Teixeira/50 20.00
91 Gary Carter/25 25.00
92 Ivan Rodriguez/25 25.00
94 Rickey Henderson/50 25.00
95 Curt Schilling/50 25.00

Tools of the Trade Swatch Six

NM/M
Production 1-50
Reverse: No Pricing
Production 1-10
Prime Red: No Pricing
Production 1-5
Prime Black: No Pricing
Production One Set
22 Paul LoDuca/50 20.00
31 Richie Sexson/50 20.00
52 David Ortiz/50 40.00
53 Troy Glaus/50 25.00
57 Gary Carter/25 35.00
59 Mark Prior/50 25.00
73 Cal Ripken Jr./50 85.00
76 Sammy Sosa/25 40.00
78 Tony Gwynn/50 40.00
79 Mike Piazza/50 40.00
80 Jeff Bagwell/50 25.00
90 Mark Teixeira/50 25.00
92 Ivan Rodriguez/25 30.00
94 Rickey Henderson/50 30.00

2005 Playoff Prestige

NM/M
Complete Set (200): 35.00
Common Player: .25
Hobby pack (8): 3.00
Hobby box (24): 65.00
1 Rafael Furcal .25
2 Derek Jeter 2.00
3 Edgar Renteria .40
4 Jeff Bagwell .50
5 Nomar Garciaparra 1.25
6 Melvin Mora .25
7 Craig Biggio .40
8 Brad Penny .25
9 Hank Blalock .50
10 Vernon Wells .25
11 Gary Sheffield .50
12 Jeff Kent .25
13 Carl Crawford .25
14 Paul Konerko .25
15 Carlos Beltran .50
16 Garret Anderson .40
17 Todd Helton .50
18 Javy Lopez .40
19 Mike Lowell .25
20 Robb Quinlan .25
21 Andy Pettitte .40
22 Roger Clemens 2.00
23 Mark Teixeira .50

24 Miguel Cabrera .75
25 Andruw Jones .40
26 Josh Beckett .40
27 Scott Rolen .75
28 J.J. Putz .25
29 Adrian Beltre .50
30 Magglio Ordonez .25
31 Mike Piazza 1.00
32 Danny Graves .25
33 Larry Walker .40
34 Kerry Wood .75
35 Mike Mussina .50
36 Joe Nathan .25
37 Chone Figgins .25
38 Curt Schilling .75
39 Brett Myers .25
40 Jae Weong Seo .25
41 Danny Kolb .25
42 Mariano Rivera .50
43 Francisco Cordero .25
44 Adam Dunn .50
45 Pedro Martinez .75
46 Frank Thomas .50
47 Tom Glavine .40
48 Torii Hunter .25
49 Ben Sheets .40
50 Shawn Green .25
51 Randy Johnson .75
52 C.C. Sabathia .25
53 Bobby Abreu .40
54 Octavio Dotel .25
55 Hideki Matsui 1.50
56 Mark Buehrle .25
57 Johan Santana .50
58 Brandon Inge .25
59 Dewon Brazelton .25
60 Ryan Wagner .25
61 Kevin Brown .25
62 Laynce Nix .25
63 Jason Bay .40
64 J.D. Drew .40
65 Jacque Jones .25
66 Jason Schmidt .40
67 Joe Kennedy .25
68 Miguel Tejada .50
69 Hideo Nomo .40
70 Michael Young .25
71 Lyle Overbay .25
72 Omar Vizquel .25
73 Johnny Estrada .25
74 Khalil Greene .40
75 Barry Zito .25
76 Wilson Valdez .25
77 Nick Green .25
78 Bucky Jacobsen .25
79 Keith Foulke .25
80 Sean Burroughs .25
81 Carlos Zambrano .40
82 Orlando Cabrera .25
83 Shigetoshi Hasegawa .25
84 Troy Glaus .40
85 Mike Sweeney .25
86 Jason Giambi .25
87 Derrek Lee .40
88 Carlos Delgado .40
89 Kazuo Matsui .25
90 Lew Ford .25
91 Akinori Otsuka .25
92 Bobby Crosby .25
93 Jose Reyes .40
94 Jose Vidro .25
95 Shingo Takatsu .25
96 Sean Casey .25
97 Tim Olson .25
98 Jeff Suppan .25
99 Rafael Palmeiro .50
100 Esteban Loaiza .25
101 Brian Roberts .25
102 Jack Wilson .25
103 Eric Chavez .40
104 Eric Milton .25
105 Albert Pujols 2.00
106 Jake Peavy .25
107 Ivan Rodriguez .50
108 Chad Cordero .25
109 Jody Gerut .25
110 Chipper Jones .75
111 Barry Larkin .40
112 Alfonso Soriano .75
113 Alex Rodriguez 1.50
114 Paul LoDuca .25
115 Jim Edmonds .40
116 Aramis Ramirez .40
117 Lance Berkman .40
118 Johnny Damon .75
119 Aubrey Huff .25
120 Mark Mulder .40
121 Sammy Sosa 1.50
122 Mark Prior .75
123 Shannon Stewart .25
124 Manny Ramirez .75
125 Jim Thome .75
126 Doug DeVore .25
127 Vladimir Guerrero .75
128 Ken Harvey .25
129 Jacob Cruz .25
130 Ken Griffey Jr. 1.00
131 Greg Maddux 1.00
132 Derek Lowe .25
133 Craig Monroe .25
134 David Ortiz .75
135 Dontrelle Willis .40
136 Tom Gordon .25
137 David Dellucci .25
138 Vance Wilson .25
139 Milton Bradley .25
140 Ichiro Suzuki 1.50
141 Victor Martinez .40
142 Wade Miller .25
143 Francisco Rodriguez .25
144 Roy Oswalt .40
145 Carlos Lee .25
146 Kazuhisa Ishii .25
147 Tim Hudson .40
148 Travis Hafner .25
149 Jermaine Dye .25
150 Steve Finley .25
151 Justin Verlander **RC** 1.50
152 Yadier Molina .25
153 Andy Green .25
154 Nick Swisher .25
155 Clint Nageotte .25
156 Grady Sizemore .50
157 Gavin Floyd .25
158 Josh Kroeger .25
159 Russ Adams .25
160 Jeff Baker .25
161 Dioner Navarro .25
162 Shawn Hill .25
163 Ryan Howard 1.00
164 Scott Proctor .25
165 Jason Kubel .25
166 Jose Lopez .25
167 Ryan Church .25
168 Yhency Brazoban .25
169 Jeff Francis .25
170 Angel Guzman .25
171 John Van Benschoten .25
172 Adrian Gonzalez .25
173 Casey Kotchman .25
174 David Wright .75
175 B.J. Upton .50
176 Dallas McPherson .50
177 Rene Rivera .25
178 Denny Bautista .25
179 Logan Kensing .25
180 Matt Peterson .25
181 Jeremy Reed .25
182 Jairo Garcia .25
183 Val Majewski .25
184 Victor Diaz .25
185 David Krynzel .25
186 Ron Cey .25
187 Bill Madlock .25
188 Dave Stewart .25
189 Billy Ripken .25
190 Gary Carter .50
191 Darryl Strawberry .25
192 Dave Parker .25
193 Ron Guidry .25
194 Gaylord Perry .25
195 Fred Lynn .25
196 Jack Morris .25
197 Steve Garvey .25
198 Andre Dawson .50
199 Nolan Ryan 2.50
200 Paul Molitor .75

Red Foil

Red Foil: 8-15X
Production 25 Sets

Xtra Bases Black

Black: 8-15X
Production 25 Sets

Xtra Bases Green

Green: 5-10X
Production 50 Sets

Xtra Bases Purple

Purple: 4-8X
Production 100 Sets

Xtra Bases Red

Red: 3-6X
Production 150 Sets

Autographs

NM/M
Common Autograph: 8.00
20 Robb Quinlan 8.00
28 J.J. Putz 8.00
58 Brandon Inge/SP 15.00
67 Joe Kennedy 8.00
76 Wilson Valdez 8.00
77 Nick Green 8.00
78 Bucky Jacobsen 10.00
97 Tim Olson 10.00
98 Jeff Suppan/SP 15.00
126 Doug DeVore 8.00
129 Jacob Cruz 8.00
133 Craig Monroe 10.00
138 Vance Wilson 8.00
153 Andy Green 8.00
164 Scott Proctor 8.00

Changing Stripes

NM/M
Complete Set (25): 25.00
Common Player: .75
Inserted 1:8
Foil: 2-3X
Production 100 Sets
Holo-Foil: 3-6X
Production 25 Sets
1 Ivan Rodriguez 1.00
2 Roger Clemens 4.00
3 Curt Schilling 1.50
4 Alex Rodriguez 4.00
5 Greg Maddux 2.00
6 Juan Gonzalez .75
7 Pedro Martinez 1.50
8 Roberto Alomar .75
9 Randy Johnson 1.50
10 Ken Griffey Jr. 2.00
11 Carlos Beltran 1.00
12 Andy Pettitte 1.00
13 Tom Glavine .75
14 Miguel Tejada 1.50
15 Alfonso Soriano 1.50
16 Shannon Stewart .75
17 Nomar Garciaparra 2.00
18 Jeff Kent .75
19 David Ortiz 1.50
20 Sean Casey .75
21 Rickey Henderson 1.00
22 Carlton Fisk 1.00
23 Phil Niekro .75
24 Dale Murphy 1.00
25 Reggie Jackson 1.50

Changing Stripes Mat. Dual Jersey

NM/M
Production 12-250
1 Ivan Rodriguez/250 10.00
2 Roger Clemens/50 20.00
3 Curt Schilling/250 12.00
6 Juan Gonzalez/250 8.00
7 Pedro Martinez/100 15.00
8 Roberto Alomar/250 10.00
9 Randy Johnson/100 15.00
11 Carlos Beltran/100 15.00
12 Andy Pettitte/250 10.00
13 Tom Glavine/50 15.00
14 Miguel Tejada/250 10.00
15 Alfonso Soriano/100 10.00
16 Shannon Stewart/100 8.00
19 David Ortiz/100 15.00
20 Sean Casey/50 10.00
21 Rickey Henderson/250 15.00
22 Carlton Fisk/250 15.00
23 Phil Niekro/250 8.00
24 Dale Murphy/250 15.00
25 Reggie Jackson/100 15.00

Connections

NM/M
Complete Set (25): 40.00
Common Duo: 1.50
Inserted 1:8
Foil: 2-3X
Production 100 Sets
Holo-Foil: 3-6X
Production 25 Sets
1 Josh Beckett, Dontrelle Willis 1.50
2 Andruw Jones, Chipper Jones 2.00
3 Kazuo Matsui, Jose Reyes 1.50
4 Bobby Abreu, Jim Thome 2.00
5 Jeff Bagwell, Lance Berkman 2.00
6 Roger Clemens, Roy Oswalt 4.00
7 Scott Rolen, Larry Walker 2.00
8 Albert Pujols, Jim Edmonds 4.00
9 Greg Maddux, Sammy Sosa 2.50
10 Mark Prior, Nomar Garciaparra 2.00
11 Barry Larkin, Sean Casey 1.50
12 Adrian Beltre, Shawn Green 1.50
13 Alex Rodriguez, Derek Jeter 6.00
14 Manny Ramirez, Jason Varitek 3.00
15 Miguel Tejada, Javy Lopez 2.00
16 B.J. Upton, Carl Crawford 1.50
17 Frank Thomas, Paul Konerko 2.00
18 Joe Mauer, Justin Morneau 2.00
19 Victor Martinez, Jody Gerut 1.50
20 Bobby Crosby, Barry Zito 1.50
21 Mark Teixeira, Hank Blalock 2.00
22 Reggie Jackson, Rod Carew 2.00
23 Rickey Henderson, Tony Gwynn 2.50
24 Tom Seaver, Johnny Bench 3.00
25 Don Mattingly, Dave Righetti 4.00

Connections Material Dual Bat

NM/M
Production 25-250
2 Andruw Jones, Chipper Jones/250 10.00
3 Kazuo Matsui, Jose Reyes/100 10.00
4 Bobby Abreu, Jim Thome/100 12.00
5 Jeff Bagwell, Lance Berkman/250 10.00
6 Roger Clemens, Roy Oswalt/250 15.00
10 Mark Prior, Nomar Garciaparra/100 10.00
11 Barry Larkin, Sean Casey/100 10.00
12 Shawn Green, Adrian Beltre/250 5.00
14 Jason Varitek, Manny Ramirez/100 15.00
15 Miguel Tejada, Javy Lopez/100 10.00
17 Frank Thomas, Paul Konerko/100 10.00
19 Victor Martinez, Jody Gerut/25 12.00
21 Mark Teixeira, Hank Blalock/100 10.00
22 Reggie Jackson, Rod Carew/100 10.00
23 Tony Gwynn, Rickey Henderson/250 15.00
24 Tom Seaver, Johnny Bench/250 15.00

Connections Material Dual Jersey

NM/M
Production 10-250
Prime: 1-2X
Production 10-25
No pricing 20 or less.
1 Josh Beckett, Dontrelle Willis/250 8.00
2 Andruw Jones, Chipper Jones/250 10.00
3 Kazuo Matsui, Jose Reyes/100 10.00
4 Bobby Abreu, Jim Thome/250 10.00
5 Jeff Bagwell, Lance Berkman/250 10.00
6 Roger Clemens, Roy Oswalt/250 15.00
8 Albert Pujols, Jim Edmonds/250 25.00
11 Barry Larkin, Sean Casey/50 15.00
12 Shawn Green, Adrian Beltre/250 8.00
14 Jason Varitek, Manny Ramirez/50 20.00
15 Miguel Tejada, Javy Lopez/50 12.00
17 Frank Thomas/Pants, Paul Konerko/250 10.00
20 Bobby Crosby, Barry Zito/250 10.00
21 Mark Teixeira, Hank Blalock/100 10.00
22 Reggie Jackson, Rod Carew/Jkt/250 12.00
23 Rickey Henderson, Tony Gwynn/250 15.00
24 Tom Seaver, Johnny Bench/Pants/100 15.00
25 Don Mattingly, Dave Righetti/250 20.00

Diamond Heritage

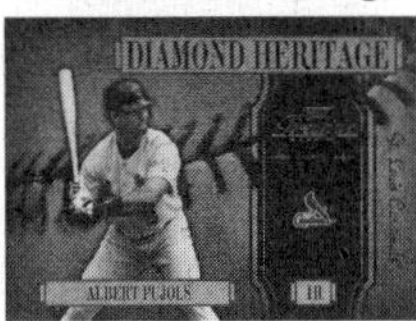

NM/M
Complete Set (15): 20.00
Common Player: .75
Inserted 1:12
1 Pedro Martinez 1.50
2 Mark Teixeira 1.00
3 Lance Berkman .75
4 Vladimir Guerrero 1.50
5 Albert Pujols 4.00
6 Roger Clemens 4.00
7 Manny Ramirez 1.50
8 Mike Piazza 2.00
9 Jim Thome 1.50
10 Mark Prior 1.00
11 Gary Sheffield .75
12 Sammy Sosa 2.50
13 Tim Hudson .75
14 Hideki Matsui 3.00
15 Jim Edmonds .75

Diamond Heritage Matieral Bat

NM/M
Production 100 Sets
1 Pedro Martinez 10.00
2 Mark Teixeira 10.00
3 Lance Berkman 5.00
4 Vladimir Guerrero 10.00
6 Roger Clemens 15.00
7 Manny Ramirez 10.00
8 Mike Piazza 10.00
9 Jim Thome 10.00
10 Mark Prior 8.00
11 Gary Sheffield 8.00
12 Sammy Sosa 10.00
13 Tim Hudson 5.00
14 Hideki Matsui 25.00
15 Jim Edmonds 8.00

Diamond Heritage Material Jersey

NM/M
Production 100 Sets
1 Pedro Martinez 10.00
2 Mark Teixeira 10.00
3 Lance Berkman 5.00
4 Vladimir Guerrero 10.00
5 Albert Pujols 25.00
6 Roger Clemens 15.00
7 Manny Ramirez 10.00
8 Mike Piazza 10.00
9 Jim Thome 10.00
10 Mark Prior 8.00
11 Gary Sheffield 8.00
12 Sammy Sosa 10.00
13 Tim Hudson 5.00
14 Hideki Matsui/Pants 25.00
15 Jim Edmonds 8.00

League Leaders Single

NM/M
Complete Set (10): 25.00
Inserted 1:21
Foil: 2-4X
Production 100 Sets
Holo-Foil: 4-8X
Production 25 Sets
1 Gary Sheffield 2.00
2 Ben Sheets 2.00
3 Adrian Beltre 2.00
4 Scott Rolen 3.00
5 George Brett 4.00
6 Johan Santana 3.00
7 Manny Ramirez 3.00
8 Cal Ripken Jr. 8.00
9 Carlos Zambrano 2.00
10 Tony Gwynn 4.00

League Leader Single Material Bat

NM/M
Production 250 Sets
1 Gary Sheffield 8.00
2 Ben Sheets 5.00
3 Adrian Beltre 5.00
5 George Brett 12.00
7 Manny Ramirez 10.00
8 Cal Ripken Jr. 25.00
10 Tony Gwynn 8.00

League Leaders Single Mat. Jersey

NM/M
Production 25-250
1 Gary Sheffield/250 8.00
2 Ben Sheets/250 5.00
3 Adrian Beltre/50 8.00
4 Scott Rolen/250 8.00
5 George Brett/250 15.00
6 Johan Santana/25 20.00
7 Manny Ramirez/250 8.00
8 Cal Ripken Jr./250 25.00
9 Carlos Zambrano/250 5.00
10 Tony Gwynn/250 8.00

League Leaders Double

NM/M
Complete Set (5): 15.00
Inserted 1:39
Foil: 2-3X
Production 100 Sets
Holo-Foil: 3-6X
Production 25 Sets
1 Tim Hudson, Roy Oswalt 2.00
2 Ivan Rodriguez, Todd Helton 3.00
3 Mark Teixeira, Jim Edmonds 2.00
4 Nolan Ryan, Roger Clemens 8.00
5 Sammy Sosa, Troy Glaus 3.00

League Leader Double Material Bat

NM/M
Production 250 Sets
1 Tim Hudson, Roy Oswalt 8.00
2 Ivan Rodriguez, Todd Helton 15.00
3 Mark Teixeira, Jim Edmonds 10.00
4 Nolan Ryan, Roger Clemens 25.00
5 Sammy Sosa, Troy Glaus 15.00

League Leaders Double Material Jersey

NM/M
Production 50-250
1 Tim Hudson, Roy Oswalt/100 10.00
2 Ivan Rodriguez, Todd Helton/50 15.00
3 Mark Teixeira, Jim Edmonds/250 15.00
4 Nolan Ryan, Roger Clemens/250 25.00
5 Sammy Sosa, Troy Glaus/250 15.00

League Leaders Quad

NM/M
Inserted 1:39
Foil: 1-2X
Production 100 Sets
Holo-Foil: 3-5X
Production 25 Sets
1 Wade Boggs, Paul Molitor, Alan Trammell, Kirby Puckett 4.00
2 Dale Murphy, Mike Schmidt, Gary Carter, Darryl Strawberry 6.00
3 Jose Canseco, Kirby Puckett, Will Clark, Darryl Strawberry 4.00
4 Pedro Martinez, Kevin Brown, Randy Johnson, Roger Clemens 6.00
5 Don Mattingly, Dave Parker, Eddie Murray, Dale Murphy 4.00

League Leaders Quad Material Bat

NM/M
Production 100 Sets
2 Dale Murphy, Mike Schmidt, Gary Carter, Darryl Strawberry 40.00
4 Pedro Martinez, Kevin Brown, Randy Johnson, Roger Clemens 50.00
5 Don Mattingly, Dave Parker, Eddie Murray, Dale Murphy 50.00

League Leaders Quad Material Jersey

NM/M
Production 100 Sets
1 Wade Boggs, Paul Molitor, Alan Trammell, Kirby Puckett 40.00
2 Dale Murphy, Mike Schmidt, Gary Carter, Darryl Strawberry 40.00
3 Jose Canseco, Kirby Puckett, Will Clark, Darryl Strawberry 40.00
4 Pedro Martinez, Kevin Brown, Randy Johnson, Roger Clemens 50.00
5 Don Mattingly, Dave Parker, Eddie Murray, Dale Murphy 50.00

Playoff Champions Combo Wild Card

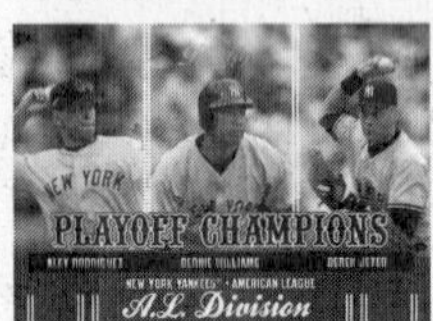

NM/M
Inserted 1:391
Division Combo: .75-1X
League Combo: .75-1X
World Series Combo: .75-1X
Redemption Deadline 4-15-06.
1 Andruw Jones, Johnny Estrada, Chipper Jones 10.00
2 Miguel Cabrera, Josh Beckett, Dontrelle Willis 10.00
3 Chad Cordero, Nick Johnson, Brad Wilkerson 5.00
4 Jim Thome, Bobby Abreu, Chase Utley 10.00
5 Mike Piazza, Kazuo Matsui, David Wright 10.00
6 Albert Pujols, Scott Rolen, Jim Edmonds 15.00
7 Kerry Wood, Mark Prior, Carlos Zambrano 8.00
8 Ben Sheets, Geoff Jenkins, Lyle Overbay 5.00
9 Kip Wells, Jack Wilson, Jason Bay 5.00
10 Austin Kearns, Adam Dunn, Ken Griffey Jr. 10.00
11 Roy Oswalt, Lance Berkman, Jeff Bagwell 10.00
12 Jason Jennings, Matt Holliday, Todd Helton 10.00
13 Eric Gagne, Jayson Werth, Milton Bradley 10.00
14 Alex Cintron, Brandon Webb, Luis Gonzalez 5.00
15 Jason Schmidt, Edgardo Alfonzo, Kirk Rueter 5.00
16 Khalil Greene, Jake Peavy, Trevor Hoffman 10.00
17 Manny Ramirez, Curt Schilling, David Ortiz 15.00
18 Miguel Tejada, Melvin Mora, Javy Lopez 8.00
19 Roy Halladay, Alexis Rios, Gabe Gross 5.00
20 Alex Rodriguez, Derek Jeter, Hideki Matsui 20.00
21 B.J. Upton, Scott Kazmir, Carl Crawford 10.00
22 Frank Thomas, Shingo Takatsu, Aaron Rowand 8.00
23 Victor Martinez, C.C. Sabathia, Travis Hafner 5.00
24 Torii Hunter, Johan Santana, Justin Morneau 10.00
25 Zack Greinke, Mike Sweeney, Ken Harvey 5.00
26 Ivan Rodriguez, Jeremy Bonderman, Carlos Guillen 8.00
27 Rich Harden, Bobby Crosby, Barry Zito 5.00
28 Bret Boone, Ichiro Suzuki, Jeremy Reed 12.00
29 Michael Young, Mark Teixeira, Hank Blalock 10.00
30 Vladimir Guerrero, Darin Erstad, Garret Anderson 10.00

Playoff Game Jersey Collection

Inserted 1:8 Retail

Prestigious Pros Blue

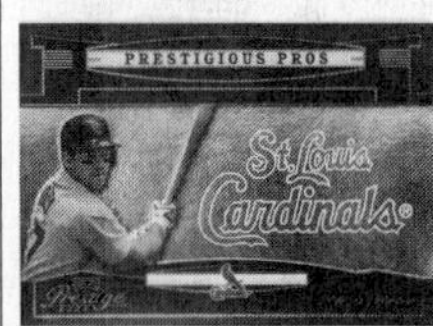

NM/M
Common Player: 1.00
Production 900 Sets
Black: No Pricing
Production 10 Sets
Bronze: 2-3X
Production 100 Sets
Gold: 2-4X
Production 50 Sets
Green: 1-2X
Production 350 Sets
Orange: 1-1.5X
Production 500 Sets
Platinum: 3-5X
Production 25 Sets
Purple: 1-2X
Production 200 Sets
Red: 1X
Production 70 Sets
Silver: 2-3X
Production 75 Sets
1 Ozzie Smith 3.00
2 Derek Jeter 6.00
3 Eric Chavez 1.00
4 Paul Molitor 2.00
5 Jeff Bagwell 1.50
6 Melvin Mora 1.00
7 Craig Biggio 1.00
8 Cal Ripken Jr. 8.00
9 Hank Blalock 1.50
10 Miguel Tejada 2.00
11 Jacque Jones 1.00
12 Alfonso Soriano 2.00
13 Omar Vizquel 1.00
14 Paul Konerko 1.00
15 Tim Hudson 1.00
16 Garret Anderson 1.00
17 Lance Berkman 1.00
18 Randy Johnson 2.00
19 Robin Yount 3.00
20 Mark Mulder 1.00
21 Sean Casey 1.00
22 Jim Palmer 1.50
23 Don Mattingly 5.00
24 Manny Ramirez 2.00
25 Rafael Palmeiro 1.50
26 Vernon Wells 1.00
27 Vladimir Guerrero 2.00
28 Ken Harvey 1.00
29 Rod Carew 1.50
30 Nolan Ryan 8.00
31 Mike Piazza 3.00
32 Steve Carlton 1.50
33 Miguel Cabrera 2.00
34 Kerry Wood 2.00
35 Mike Mussina 1.00
36 Gaylord Perry 1.00
37 Gary Sheffield 1.50
38 Curt Schilling 2.00
39 Don Sutton 1.00
40 Roger Clemens 6.00
41 Victor Martinez 1.00
42 Jason Giambi 1.00
43 Dennis Eckersley 1.00
44 Adam Dunn 1.50
45 Pedro Martinez 2.00
46 Tony Perez 1.00
47 Tom Glavine 1.00
48 Torii Hunter 1.00
49 Hideo Nomo 1.00
50 Scott Rolen 2.00
51 Ichiro Suzuki 5.00
52 C.C. Sabathia 1.00
53 George Brett 5.00
54 David Ortiz 2.00
55 Hideki Matsui 4.00
56 Nomar Garciaparra 4.00
57 Johan Santana 2.00
58 Phil Niekro 1.00
59 Dontrelle Willis 1.00
60 Magglio Ordonez 1.00
61 Livan Hernandez 1.00
62 Edgar Renteria 1.00
63 Todd Helton 1.50
64 Carlos Beltran 1.50
65 Sammy Sosa 4.00
66 Albert Pujols 6.00
67 Mike Lowell 1.00
68 Mark Prior 1.50
69 Ivan Rodriguez 1.50
70 Jake Peavy 1.00
71 Jim Thome 2.00
72 Mark Teixeira 1.50
73 Shawn Green 1.00
74 Rollie Fingers 1.00
75 Barry Zito 1.00
76 Jose Vidro 1.00
77 Ben Sheets 1.00
78 Roy Halladay 1.00
79 Frank Thomas 1.50
80 Chipper Jones 2.00
81 Jason Bay 1.00
82 Tony Gwynn 2.00
83 Shannon Stewart 1.00
84 Carl Crawford 1.00
85 Andruw Jones 1.00
86 Greg Maddux 3.00
87 Barry Larkin 1.00
88 Alex Rodriguez 5.00
89 Rickey Henderson 1.50
90 Troy Glaus 1.00
91 Roy Oswalt 1.00
92 Michael Young 1.00
93 Carlos Lee 1.00
94 Jim Edmonds 1.00
95 Fergie Jenkins 1.00
96 Paul LoDuca 1.00
97 Aubrey Huff 1.00
98 Ken Griffey Jr. 3.00
99 Carlos Delgado 1.50
100 Mike Schmidt 5.00

Prestigious Pros Material Bat Silver

NM/M
Production 5-50
No pricing 20 or less.
1 Ozzie Smith/50 25.00
3 Eric Chavez/25 10.00
4 Paul Molitor/50 12.00
5 Jeff Bagwell/50 10.00
7 Craig Biggio/25 15.00
8 Cal Ripken Jr./50 40.00
9 Hank Blalock/25 12.00
10 Miguel Tejada/25 12.00
14 Paul Konerko/25 8.00
15 Tim Hudson/25 10.00
16 Garret Anderson/25 10.00
17 Lance Berkman/50 8.00
18 Randy Johnson/25 20.00
19 Robin Yount/50 15.00
21 Sean Casey/25 10.00
23 Don Mattingly/50 25.00
25 Rafael Palmeiro/25 15.00
27 Vladimir Guerrero/25 20.00
28 Ken Harvey/25 8.00
29 Rod Carew/50 10.00
30 Nolan Ryan/50 35.00
31 Mike Piazza/25 20.00
32 Steve Carlton/50 8.00
34 Kerry Wood/25 15.00
35 Mike Mussina/25 15.00
37 Gary Sheffield/25 10.00
38 Curt Schilling/25 15.00
40 Roger Clemens/25 25.00
41 Victor Martinez/25 10.00
42 Jason Giambi/25 10.00
44 Adam Dunn/25 12.00
45 Pedro Martinez/25 15.00
46 Tony Perez/50 8.00
47 Tom Glavine/25 12.00
48 Torii Hunter/25 8.00
49 Hideo Nomo/25 25.00
50 Scott Rolen/25 20.00
53 George Brett/50 25.00
54 David Ortiz/50 12.00
55 Hideki Matsui/50 40.00
56 Nomar Garciaparra/25 20.00
58 Phil Niekro/50 8.00
60 Magglio Ordonez/50 8.00
62 Edgar Renteria/25 10.00
63 Todd Helton/25 15.00
64 Carlos Beltran/25 15.00
65 Sammy Sosa/50 15.00
67 Mike Lowell/25 10.00
68 Mark Prior/25 15.00
69 Ivan Rodriguez/50 10.00
71 Jim Thome/50 10.00
72 Mark Teixeira/50 10.00
73 Shawn Green/25 10.00
76 Jose Vidro/25 8.00
77 Ben Sheets/25 10.00
79 Frank Thomas/25 15.00
81 Jason Bay/25 10.00
82 Tony Gwynn/50 15.00
83 Shannon Stewart/25 8.00
85 Andruw Jones/25 10.00
87 Barry Larkin/50 10.00
89 Rickey Henderson/50 15.00
90 Troy Glaus/25 10.00
91 Roy Oswalt/25 10.00
92 Michael Young/25 10.00
93 Carlos Lee/25 10.00
94 Jim Edmonds/50 10.00
96 Paul LoDuca/25 10.00
99 Carlos Delgado/25 10.00
100 Mike Schmidt/50 25.00

Prestigious Pros Material Jersey Gold

NM/M
Production 5-50
No pricing 20 or less.
Platinum Patch: No Pricing
Production 5-10
1 Ozzie Smith/50 25.00
3 Eric Chavez/25 10.00
4 Paul Molitor/50 12.00
5 Jeff Bagwell/50 10.00
6 Melvin Mora/25 10.00
7 Craig Biggio/25 15.00
8 Cal Ripken Jr./50 40.00
10 Miguel Tejada/25 12.00
13 Omar Vizquel/25 15.00
14 Paul Konerko/25 8.00
15 Tim Hudson/25 10.00
17 Lance Berkman/50 8.00
18 Randy Johnson/25 20.00
19 Robin Yount/50 15.00
20 Mark Mulder/20 10.00
21 Sean Casey/25 10.00
22 Jim Palmer/50 8.00
23 Don Mattingly/50 25.00
26 Vernon Wells/25 8.00
27 Vladimir Guerrero/25 20.00
28 Ken Harvey/25 8.00
29 Rod Carew/50 10.00
30 Nolan Ryan/50 35.00
31 Mike Piazza/25 20.00
32 Steve Carlton/50 8.00
34 Kerry Wood/25 15.00
35 Mike Mussina/25 15.00
36 Gaylord Perry/50 8.00
37 Gary Sheffield/25 10.00
38 Curt Schilling/25 15.00
39 Don Sutton/50 8.00
40 Roger Clemens/25 25.00
41 Victor Martinez/25 10.00
42 Jason Giambi/25 10.00
43 Dennis Eckersley/50 10.00
45 Pedro Martinez/25 15.00
46 Tony Perez/50 8.00
49 Hideo Nomo/25 25.00
50 Scott Rolen/25 20.00
52 C.C. Sabathia/25 10.00
53 George Brett/50 25.00
55 Hideki Matsui/25 40.00
58 Phil Niekro/50 8.00
59 Dontrelle Willis/25 10.00
60 Magglio Ordonez/25 8.00
61 Livan Hernandez/25 8.00
62 Edgar Renteria/25 10.00
63 Todd Helton/25 15.00
65 Sammy Sosa/25 20.00
66 Albert Pujols/25 35.00
68 Mark Prior/25 10.00
71 Jim Thome/25 15.00
72 Mark Teixeira/25 12.00
73 Shawn Green/25 10.00
74 Rollie Fingers/50 8.00
77 Ben Sheets/25 10.00
78 Roy Halladay/25 10.00
79 Frank Thomas/25 15.00
80 Chipper Jones/25 15.00
81 Jason Bay/25 10.00
82 Tony Gwynn/50 15.00
84 Carl Crawford/25 10.00
85 Andruw Jones/25 10.00
86 Greg Maddux/25 20.00
87 Barry Larkin/25 12.00
89 Rickey Henderson/50 15.00
90 Troy Glaus/25 10.00
92 Michael Young/25 10.00
93 Carlos Lee/25 10.00
94 Jim Edmonds/25 12.00
95 Fergie Jenkins/50 10.00
97 Aubrey Huff/25 10.00
99 Carlos Delgado/25 10.00
100 Mike Schmidt/50 25.00

Prestigious Pros Signature Black

No Pricing
Production Five Sets

Signature Xtra Bases Black

No Pricing
Production 3-10

Signature Xtra Bases Purple

NM/M
Production 5-50
6 Melvin Mora/25 25.00
8 Brad Penny/50 10.00
13 Carl Crawford/25 25.00
20 Robb Quinlan/50 8.00
28 J.J. Putz/50 8.00
32 Danny Graves/50 10.00
36 Joe Nathan/50 25.00
37 Chone Figgins/50 10.00
39 Brett Myers/50 10.00
41 Danny Kolb/50 15.00
43 Francisco Cordero/50 10.00
52 C.C. Sabathia/25 25.00
54 Octavio Dotel/50 15.00
56 Mark Buehrle/25 20.00
58 Brandon Inge/50 15.00
59 Dewon Brazelton/50 10.00
60 Ryan Wagner/50 8.00
62 Laynce Nix/50 15.00
63 Jason Bay/50 15.00
65 Jacque Jones/25 20.00
67 Joe Kennedy/50 8.00
71 Lyle Overbay/25 20.00
73 Johnny Estrada/50 15.00
76 Wilson Valdez/50 8.00
77 Nick Green/50 8.00
78 Bucky Jacobsen/50 10.00
79 Keith Foulke/50 35.00
81 Carlos Zambrano/25 35.00
82 Orlando Cabrera/25 20.00
90 Lew Ford/50 15.00
92 Bobby Crosby/50 20.00
97 Tim Olson/50 8.00
98 Jeff Suppan/50 10.00
100 Esteban Loaiza/50 10.00
101 Brian Roberts/50 35.00
102 Jack Wilson/50 15.00
106 Jake Peavy/25 30.00
108 Chad Cordero/50 10.00
109 Jody Gerut/25 10.00
126 Doug DeVore/50 8.00
128 Ken Harvey/50 10.00
129 Jacob Cruz/50 8.00
133 Craig Monroe/50 10.00
136 Tom Gordon/50 15.00
137 David Dellucci/50 20.00
138 Vance Wilson/50 8.00
139 Milton Bradley/50 15.00
141 Victor Martinez/25 30.00
142 Wade Miller/50 15.00
145 Carlos Lee/25 20.00
148 Travis Hafner/50 15.00
149 Jermaine Dye/50 15.00
152 Yadier Molina/25 20.00
153 Andy Green/50 8.00
161 Dioner Navarro/50 12.00
162 Shawn Hill/50 8.00
164 Scott Proctor/50 10.00
165 Jason Kubel/50 15.00
168 Yhency Brazoban/50 10.00
170 Angel Guzman/50 15.00
172 Adrian Gonzalez/50 12.00
173 Casey Kotchman 15.00
187 Bill Madlock/25 20.00
189 Billy Ripken/25 10.00
190 Gary Carter/25 25.00
191 Darryl Strawberry/25 20.00
192 Dave Parker/25 25.00
195 Fred Lynn/25 20.00
196 Jack Morris/25 25.00
198 Andre Dawson/25 25.00

Stars of MLB

NM/M
Complete Set (15): 20.00
Common Player: 1.00
Inserted 1:12
Foil: 2-4X
Production 100 Sets
Holo-Foil: 4-8X
Production 25 Sets
1 Randy Johnson 3.00
2 Adrian Beltre 1.00
3 Eric Chavez 1.00
4 Mike Mussina 1.50
5 Todd Helton 2.00
6 Curt Schilling 2.00
7 Miguel Cabrera 3.00
8 Kerry Wood 2.50
9 David Ortiz 3.00
10 Michael Young 1.00
11 Mark Mulder 1.00
12 Victor Martinez 1.00
13 Johan Santana 2.00
14 Scott Rolen 3.00
15 Carlos Beltran 2.00

Stars of MLB Material Bat

NM/M
Production 50-100
1 Randy Johnson/100 10.00
2 Adrian Beltre/100 5.00
3 Eric Chavez/100 5.00
4 Mike Mussina/100 8.00
5 Todd Helton/100 8.00
6 Curt Schilling/100 10.00
7 Miguel Cabrera/100 8.00
8 Kerry Wood/100 10.00
9 David Ortiz/100 10.00
10 Michael Young/100 5.00
11 Mark Mulder/50 8.00
14 Scott Rolen/100 10.00
15 Carlos Beltran/100 8.00

Stars of MLB Signature Material Bat

NM/M
Production 10-50
2 Adrian Beltre/50 25.00
3 Eric Chavez/50 20.00
8 Kerry Wood/25 50.00
9 David Ortiz/50 40.00
10 Michael Young/50 25.00
15 Carlos Beltran/25 50.00

Stars of MLB Material Jersey

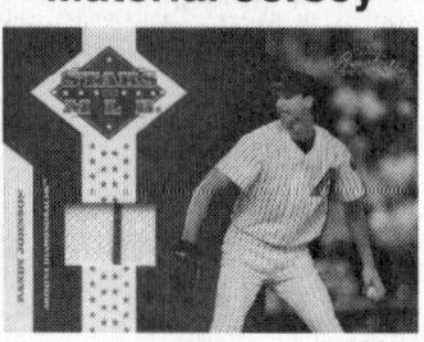

NM/M
Production 100 Sets
Prime: 1-2X
Production 25 Sets
1 Randy Johnson/Pants 10.00
2 Adrian Beltre 5.00
3 Eric Chavez 5.00
4 Mike Mussina 8.00
5 Todd Helton 8.00
6 Curt Schilling 10.00
7 Miguel Cabrera 10.00
8 Kerry Wood 10.00
9 David Ortiz 12.00
10 Michael Young 5.00
11 Mark Mulder 5.00
12 Victor Martinez 5.00
13 Johan Santana 10.00
14 Scott Rolen 10.00
15 Carlos Beltran 8.00

Stars of MLB Signature Material Jersey

NM/M
Production 10-50
Prime: No Pricing
Production Five Sets
2 Adrian Beltre/50 25.00
3 Eric Chavez/50 20.00
8 Kerry Wood/25 50.00
9 David Ortiz/50 40.00
10 Michael Young/50 25.00
12 Victor Martinez/50 20.00
13 Johan Santana/50 50.00
15 Carlos Beltran/25 50.00

2002 Poland Spring Boston Red Sox

This cello-wrapped stadium give-away set was sponsored by the team's bottled water concessionaire. Fronts have poses or action photos with team and sponsor logos in opposite corners. Backs have a U.S. flag ghost image in the background with a close-up repeat of the front photo. Personal data, '01 stats and career highlights appear along with the logos. The set is listed here by uniform number.

NM/M
Complete Set (24): 7.50

Common Player: .25
3 Grady Little .25
5 Nomar Garciaparra 2.00
7 Trot Nixon .50
10 Carlos Baerga .25
18 Johnny Damon .75
19 John Burkett .25
22 Tony Clark .25
23 Brian Daubach .25
24 Manny Ramirez 1.50
26 Lou Merloni .25
28 Doug Mirabelli .25
29 Shea Hillenbrand .25
30 Jose Offerman .25
32 Derek Lowe .25
33 Jason Varitek .25
34 Rich Garces .25
35 Rickey Henderson 1.50
37 Frank Castillo .25
41 Ugueth Urbina .25
44 Rolando Arrojo .25
45 Pedro Martinez 1.50
49 Tim Wakefield .25
--- Wally the Green Monster .25
--- Sponsor's Card .05

1985 Polaroid/J.C. Penney Indians

While the Cleveland Indians continued its four-year tradition of baseball card promotional game issues in 1985, the sponsor changed from Wheaties to Polaroid/J.C. Penney. The set features 30 player cards, a manager card and a group card of the coaching staff. Though produced in the "safety set" format - slightly oversize (2-13/16" by 4-1/8") with wide white borders - the Indians cards carry no safety message. Backs, once again numbered by uniform number, contain major and minor league stats.

NM/M
Complete Set (32): 9.00
Common Player: .50
2 Brett Butler .50
4 Tony Bernazard .50
8 Carmen Castillo .50
10 Pat Tabler .50
12 Benny Ayala .50
13 Ernie Camacho .50
14 Julio Franco .50
16 Jerry Willard .50
18 Pat Corrales .50
20 Otis Nixon .35
21 Mike Hargrove .50
22 Mike Fischlin .50
23 Chris Bando .50
24 George Vukovich .50
26 Brook Jacoby .50
27 Mel Hall .50
28 Bert Blyleven 1.00
29 Andre Thornton .30
30 Joe Carter .50
32 Rick Behenna .50
33 Roy Smith .50
35 Jerry Reed .50
36 Jamie Easterly .50
38 Dave Von Ohlen .50
41 Rich Thompson .50
43 Bryan Clark .50
44 Neal Heaton .50
48 Vern Ruhle .50
49 Jeff Barkley .50
50 Ramon Romero .50
54 Tom Waddell .50
--- Coaches (Bobby Bonds, Johnny Goryl, Don McMahon, Ed Napolean, Dennis Sommers) .50

1999 Pop Secret Detroit Tigers

This team set was sponsored by the snack food company and distributed at a pro-

motional game at Tiger Stadium. The 2-1/2" x 3-1/2" cards have color photos which are borderless at top, bottom and right. At left are black and blue vertical stripes with player identification. Backs have a color portrait photo, career stats and team and sponsor logos. The unnumbered cards are checklisted here alphabetically.

NM/M
Complete Set (26): 9.00
Common Player: .50
(1) Matt Anderson .50
(2) Brad Ausmus .50
(3) Willie Blair .50
(4) Doug Brocail .50
(5) Frank Catalanotto .50
(6) Tony Clark .50
(7) Deivi Cruz .50
(8) Damion Easley .50
(9) Juan Encarnacion .50
(10) Karim Garcia .50
(11) Seth Greisinger .50
(12) Bill Haselman .50
(13) Bobby Higginson .50
(14) Gregg Jefferies .50
(15) Todd Jones .50
(16) Gabe Kapler 1.00
(17) Masao Kida .50
(18) Dave Mlicki .50
(19) Brian Moehler .50
(20) C.J. Nitkowski .50
(21) Dean Palmer .50
(22) Larry Parrish .50
(23) Luis Polonia .50
(24) Justin Thompson .50
(25) Jeff Weaver .50
(26) The Corner (Tiger Stadium) .50

1990 Post Cereal

Post Cereal returned in 1990 with a 30-card set. Card fronts feature borders in white, red and blue, with the Post logo at top-left and the Major League Baseball logo at top-right. Backs show complete major league statistics; underneath is a facsimile autograph. The player photos do not display team logos. Cards were included three per box, inside Alpha-Bits cereal. An uncut sheet version of the set was also offered in a run of 5,000 serially numbered pieces.

NM/M
Complete Set (30): 4.00
Common Player: .10
Uncut Sheet: 15.00
1 Don Mattingly .75
2 Roger Clemens .75
3 Kirby Puckett .60
4 George Brett .75
5 Tony Gwynn .60
6 Ozzie Smith .60
7 Will Clark .10
8 Orel Hershiser .10
9 Ryne Sandberg .60
10 Darryl Strawberry .10
11 Nolan Ryan 1.50
12 Mark McGwire 1.00
13 Jim Abbott .10
14 Bo Jackson .20
15 Kevin Mitchell .10
16 Jose Canseco .35
17 Wade Boggs .60
18 Dale Murphy .20
19 Mark Grace .10
20 Mike Scott .10
21 Cal Ripken, Jr. 1.50
22 Pedro Guerrero .10
23 Ken Griffey Jr. .85
24 Eric Davis .10
25 Rickey Henderson .45
26 Robin Yount .45
27 Von Hayes .10
28 Alan Trammell .10
29 Dwight Gooden .10
30 Joe Carter .10

1991 Post Cereal

These superstar trading cards were inserted in several brands of Post's children's cereals. The cards were produced by Mike Schechter Associates, Inc. and are authorized by the Players Association, but not MLB, so team logos have been removed from the photos. Card backs feature statistics and a facsimile autograph.

NM/M
Complete Set (30): 4.00
Common Player: .10
1 Dave Justice .10
2 Mark McGwire .75
3 Will Clark .10
4 Jose Canseco .30
5 Vince Coleman .10
6 Sandy Alomar, Jr. .10
7 Darryl Strawberry .10
8 Len Dykstra .10
9 Gregg Jefferies .10
10 Tony Gwynn .50
11 Ken Griffey Jr. .75
12 Roger Clemens .65
13 Chris Sabo .10
14 Bobby Bonilla .10
15 Gary Sheffield .30
16 Ryne Sandberg .50
17 Nolan Ryan 1.00
18 Barry Larkin .10
19 Cal Ripken, Jr. 1.00
20 Jim Abbott .10
21 Barry Bonds 1.00
22 Mark Grace .10
23 Cecil Fielder .10
24 Kevin Mitchell .10
25 Todd Zeile .10
26 George Brett .65
27 Rickey Henderson .45
28 Kirby Puckett .50
29 Don Mattingly .65
30 Kevin Maas .10

Canadian

SÉRIE DES ÉTOILES 1991 SUPER STAR SERIES
BENITO SANTIAGO
SAN DIEGO PADRES DE SAN DIEGO

Specially-marked Post cereal boxes sold in Canada included one of 30 cards from a 1991 Super Star series. Cards are bilingual, and include player statistics and biographical information on the backs. The major league logos are airbrushed from the players' caps and uniforms. American Leaguers' cards have blue stripes above and below the photo on front and as a back border color; National Leaguers are in red.

NM/M
Complete Set (30): 10.00
Set in Album: 12.50
Common Player: .25
1 Delino DeShields .25
2 Tim Wallach .25
3 Andres Galarraga .25
4 Dave Magadan .25
5 Barry Bonds 2.00
6 Len Dykstra .25
7 Andre Dawson .35
8 Ozzie Smith .65
9 Will Clark .25
10 Chris Sabo .25
11 Eddie Murray .60
12 Dave Justice .25
13 Benito Santiago .25
14 Glenn Davis .25
15 Kelly Gruber .25
16 Dave Stieb .25
17 John Olerud .25
18 Roger Clemens .85
19 Cecil Fielder .25
20 Kevin Maas .25
21 Robin Yount .60
22 Cal Ripken, Jr. 2.00
23 Sandy Alomar .25
24 Rickey Henderson .60
25 Bobby Thigpen .25
26 Ken Griffey Jr. 1.00
27 Nolan Ryan 2.00
28 Dave Winfield .60
29 George Brett .75
30 Kirby Puckett .65

1992 Post Cereal

The addition of a back photo is notable on Post's 1992 set. Again packaged at the rate of three cards in specially marked boxes, a complete set was available via a mail-in offer. Front photos have a blue strip at top with the Post logo at upper-left. A red stripe at bottom has the player's name and the logo of the Major League Baseball Player's Association. The absence of a Major League Baseball logo, and the airbrushing of uniform logos on all photos identifies this set as the work of Mike Schechter Associates. Backs have a small photo at left, bordered in red. At right are biographical details, career stats and a facsimile autograph. The cards of 1991 Rookies of the Year Jeff Bagwell and Chuck Knoblauch are designated with a "Rookie Star" banner over the front photo.

NM/M
Complete Set (30): 3.00
Common Player: .10
1 Jeff Bagwell .35
2 Ryne Sandberg .45
3 Don Mattingly .50
4 Wally Joyner .10
5 Dwight Gooden .10
6 Chuck Knoblauch .10
7 Kirby Puckett .45
8 Ozzie Smith .45
9 Cal Ripken, Jr. .75
10 Darryl Strawberry .10
11 George Brett .50
12 Joe Carter .10
13 Cecil Fielder .10
14 Will Clark .10
15 Barry Bonds .75
16 Roger Clemens .50
17 Paul Molitor .35
18 Scott Erickson .10
19 Wade Boggs .45
20 Ken Griffey Jr. .60
21 Bobby Bonilla .10
22 Terry Pendleton .10
23 Barry Larkin .10
24 Frank Thomas .35
25 Jose Canseco .25
26 Tony Gwynn .45
27 Nolan Ryan .75
28 Howard Johnson .10
29 Dave Justice .10
30 Danny Tartabull .10

Canadian

SUPER STAR II 1992 SUPER-ETOILE II
DENNIS MARTINEZ
MONTREAL EXPOS DE MONTREAL

For the second year in a row Post Cereal of Canada issued a set of cards inserted in cereal boxes. The 1992 cards have a player photo on front (with airbrushed cap) and information on the reverse in both English and French. The back of the card also contains an action photo, which has a pop-up tab which when opened stands up, revealing a statistical base.

NM/M
Complete Set (18): 9.00
Common Player: .25
1 Dennis Martinez .25
2 Benito Santiago .25
3 Will Clark .25
4 Ryne Sandberg 1.00
5 Tim Wallach .25
6 Ozzie Smith 1.00
7 Darryl Strawberry .25
8 Brett Butler .25
9 Barry Bonds 2.00
10 Roger Clemens 1.25
11 Sandy Alomar .25
12 Cecil Fielder .25
13 Roberto Alomar .35
14 Kelly Gruber .25
15 Cal Ripken, Jr. 2.00
16 Jose Canseco .50
17 Kirby Puckett 1.00
18 Rickey Henderson .75

1993 Post Cereal

Post Cereal's 1993 Collectors Series cards feature a black border on the bottom and the right side, with the Post logo located at top right and the player's name, team and position along the bottom. Team logos have been air-brushed from the uniforms. Backs have a black background, a color player portrait photo, personal data, a career summary, 1992 and career stats, and a red strip with a white facsimile autograph. A special edition of 5,000 numbered uncut sheets was also produced.

NM/M
Complete Set (30): 3.00
Common Player: .10
Uncut Sheet: 10.00
1 Dave Fleming .10
2 Will Clark .10
3 Kirby Puckett .60
4 Roger Clemens .65
5 Fred McGriff .10
6 Eric Karros .10
7 Ken Griffey Jr. .75
8 Tony Gwynn .60
9 Cal Ripken, Jr. 1.25
10 Cecil Fielder .10
11 Gary Sheffield .25
12 Don Mattingly .65
13 Ryne Sandberg .60
14 Frank Thomas .50
15 Barry Bonds 1.25
16 Paul Molitor .50
17 Terry Pendleton .10
18 Darren Daulton .10
19 Mark McGwire 1.00
20 Nolan Ryan 1.25
21 Tom Glavine .30
22 Roberto Alomar .20
23 Juan Gonzalez .20
24 Bobby Bonilla .10
25 George Brett .60
26 Ozzie Smith .60
27 Andy Van Slyke .10
28 Barry Larkin .10
29 John Kruk .10
30 Robin Yount .50

Canadian

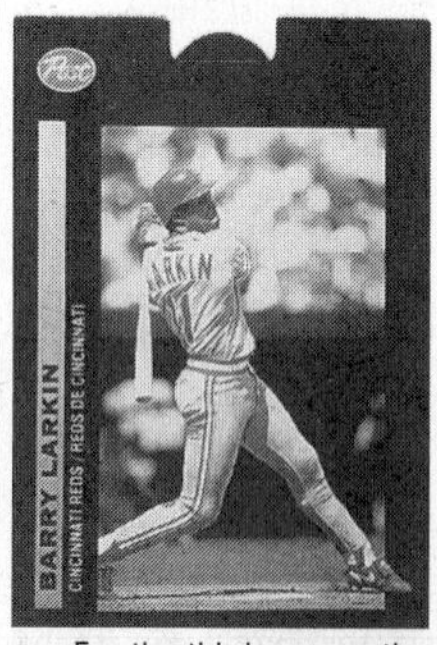

For the third consecutive year, Post Canada produced a set of cards. The 1993 set features a two-sided card with one side containing a special pop-up feature, much the same as their 1992 offering. There are 18 black-bordered and gold-lettered cards in the set. The cards were available in specially-marked boxes of cereal.

NM/M
Complete Set (18): 10.00
Common Player: .25
1 Pat Borders .25
2 Juan Guzman .25
3 Roger Clemens 1.25
4 Joe Carter .25
5 Roberto Alomar .35
6 Robin Yount .75
7 Cal Ripken, Jr. 3.00
8 Kirby Puckett 1.00
9 Ken Griffey Jr. 2.00
10 Darren Daulton .25
11 Andy Van Slyke .25
12 Bobby Bonilla .25
13 Larry Walker .25
14 Ryne Sandberg 1.00
15 Barry Larkin .25
16 Gary Sheffield .40
17 Ozzie Smith 1.00
18 Terry Pendleton .25

1994 Post Cereal

Post cereals' 1994 set was issued three cards at a time in cellophane packages in cereal boxes. A special edition of 5,000 numbered 15-1/2" x 20-1/2" uncut sheets was also produced.

		NM/M
Complete Set (30):		3.00
Common Player:		.10
Uncut Sheet:		15.00
1	Mike Piazza	.75
2	Don Mattingly	.65
3	Juan Gonzalez	.35
4	Kirby Puckett	.60
5	Gary Sheffield	.25
6	David Justice	.10
7	Jack McDowell	.10
8	Mo Vaughn	.10
9	Darren Daulton	.10
10	Bobby Bonilla	.10
11	Barry Bonds	1.00
12	Barry Larkin	.10
13	Tony Gwynn	.60
14	Mark Grace	.10
15	Ken Griffey Jr.	.75
16	Tom Glavine	.35
17	Cecil Fielder	.10
18	Roberto Alomar	.25
19	Mark Whiten	.10
20	Lenny Dykstra	.10
21	Frank Thomas	.45
22	Will Clark	.10
23	Andres Galarraga	.10
24	John Olerud	.10
25	Cal Ripken, Jr.	1.00
26	Tim Salmon	.10
27	Albert Belle	.10
28	Gregg Jefferies	.10
29	Jeff Bagwell	.45
30	Orlando Merced	.10

Canadian

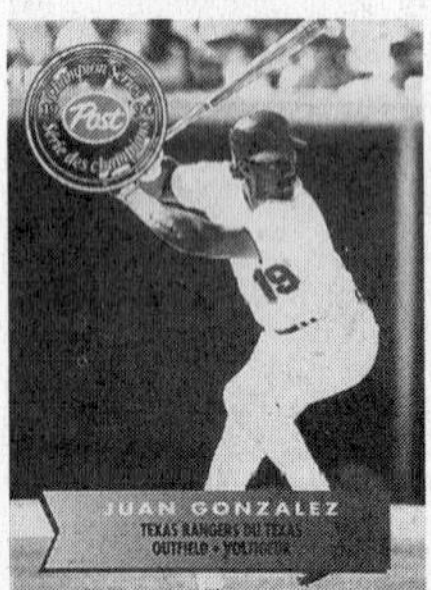

The emphasis was on Expos and Blue Jays players in the 1994 Post cereal cards issued in Canada. Several of the cards featured gold-foil stamping on the fronts. Like all contemporary Post cards, the uniform logos were air-brushed from the photos due to lack of licensing from Major League Baseball.

		NM/M
Complete Set (18):		12.00
Common Player:		.25
1	Joe Carter	1.00
2	Paul Molitor	.75
3	Roberto Alomar	.40
4	John Olerud	.25
5	Dave Stewart	.25
6	Juan Guzman	.25
7	Pat Borders	.25
8	Larry Walker	.25
9	Moises Alou	.25
10	Ken Griffey Jr.	1.50
11	Barry Bonds	2.50
12	Frank Thomas	.75
13	Cal Ripken, Jr.	2.50
14	Mike Piazza	1.50
15	Juan Gonzalez	.40
16	Lenny Dykstra	.25
17	David Justice	.25
18	Kirby Puckett	1.25

1995 Post Cereal

The 1995 Post Collector Series differs dramatically in format from the company's recent cereal-box insert issues. Each card measures 5" x 3-1/2" and is vertically scored at center to allow it to be folded. When folded, the front has a player action photo against a blue marbled background. On back is another photo, with career stats and highlights and a yellow facsimile autograph. In the center of the folded piece is a large game-action photo. All pictures have had the team logos removed for lack of a license by MLB. The cards are licensed by the Player Association. Complete sets of the '95 Post cards were available in a special cardboard display folder. Large quantities of the set made their way into dealer hands by 1998, and the value plummeted.

		NM/M
Complete Set (16):		2.50
Common Player:		.10
1	Wade Boggs	.60
2	Jeff Bagwell	.45
3	Greg Maddux	.60
4	Ken Griffey Jr.	.65
5	Roberto Alomar	.20
6	Kirby Puckett	.60
7	Tony Gwynn	.60
8	Cal Ripken Jr.	1.00
9	Matt Williams	.10
10	Dave Justice	.10
11	Barry Bonds	1.00
12	Mike Piazza	.65
13	Albert Belle	.10
14	Frank Thomas	.45
15	Len Dykstra	.10
16	Will Clark	.10
17	Barry Bonds	3.00
18	Cal Ripken Jr.	3.00

Canadian

Post cereals celebrated its fifth anniversary of baseball card production for the Canadian market by switching providers to Upper Deck, and issuing a high-quality album to house the 18-card set. Cards feature color action photos that are borderless at top, bottom and right. At left is a vertical black marbled panel with the player's name, team and position. An Upper Deck logo is at top-right; a Post anniversary logo at lower-left. Because the cards are licensed by the Major League Players Association, but not Major League Baseball, team logos have been airbrushed from photos. Backs have another player photo plus bilingual biographical data, career highlights and stats for the previous five seasons and lifetime. A ghost image of the front photo appears under the typography. As might be expected, the set's roster is especially rich in Expos and Blue Jays players.

		NM/M
Complete Set (18):		12.00
Common Player:		.50
Album:		6.00
1	Ken Griffey Jr.	2.00
2	Roberto Alomar	.35
3	Paul Molitor	.75
4	Devon White	.25
5	Moises Alou	.25
6	Ken Hill	.25
7	Paul O'Neill	.25
8	Joe Carter	.25
9	Kirby Puckett	1.50
10	Jimmy Key	.25
11	Frank Thomas	.75
12	David Cone	.25
13	Tony Gwynn	1.50
14	Matt Williams	.25
15	Jeff Bagwell	.75
16	Greg Maddux	1.50

2001 Post Collector's Series

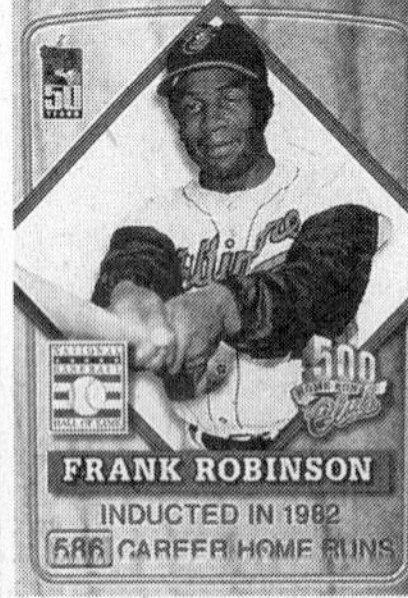

(See 2001 Topps/Post Collector's Series.)

2001 Post 500 Home Run Club

(See 2001 Topps/Post 500 Home Run Club for Checklist and values.)

2002 Post Collector's Series

(See 2002 Topps/Post Collector's Series.)

2003 Post MVP Action

(See 2003 Upper Deck/ Post MVP Action.)

1985 P.R.E. Pete Rose Set

This 120-card set traces the career of Pete Rose through the 1985 season. Many cards feature photos used on earlier Topps cards. Each card, and the box in which they were sold, says the set was "Designed by Topps Chewing Gum Inc." The set was distributed within the hobby by Renata Galasso and the copyright-holder is identified as "P.R.E." (Pete Rose Enterprises?). Besides the Topps photos, the cards include a number of original paintings by Ron Lewis, a few family-album type photos and some game-action shots of career highlights. Backs of the first three cards offer complete minor and major league stats through 1985. Cards #4-90 have a question and answer format on back and the final 30 cards in the set have a puzzle-back depicting many of Rose's Topps cards in full color. Single cards from the set are seldom offered in the market. A borderless version of card #1 was issued in an edition of 1,000, all cards being autographed.

	NM/M
Complete Set (120):	15.00
Single Card:	.25
Autographed #1:	35.00
1-120 Pete Rose	.25

1986 Provigo Expos

This 28-card set was issued in three-card panels of 7-1/2" x 3-3/8". Each card measures 2-1/2" x 3-3/8", and each panel includes two players and an advertising card. Panels are perforated to allow for separation, if desired. Card fronts have high quality game-action color photos with the player's name, uniform number and Expos and Provigo logos. Card backs include biographical information in both French and English and list the card's number within the set. There are 24 player, one manager and two coaches cards, along with a card of the Expos mascot, Youppi.

		NM/M
Complete Panel Set:		3.00
Complete Singles Set:		2.50
Common Panel:		.15
Common Single Player:		.10
Album:		5.00
Panel 1		.15
1	Hubie Brooks	.10
2	Dann Bilardello	.10
----	Checklist	.02
Panel 2		.15
3	Buck Rodgers	.10
4	Andy McGaffigan	.10
----	Album Offer	.02
Panel 3		.15
5	Mitch Webster	.10
6	Jim Wohlford	.10
----	Album Offer	.02
Panel 4		1.00
7	Tim Raines	.35
8	Jay Tibbs	.10
----	Album Offer	.02
Panel 5		.75
9	Andre Dawson	.50
10	Andres Galarraga	.35
----	Album Offer	.02
Panel 6		.30
11	Tim Wallach	.10
12	Dan Schatzeder	.10
----	Checklist	.02
Panel 7		.15
13	Jeff Reardon	.10
14	Expos' Coaching Staff (Larry Bearnarth, Joe Kerrigan, Bobby Winkles)	.10
----	Album Offer	.02
Panel 8		.15
15	Jason Thompson	.10
16	Bert Roberge	.10
----	$1 Expos Ticket Coupon	.02
Panel 9		.15
17	Al Newman	.10
18	Tim Burke	.10
----	Album Offer	.02
Panel 10		.15
19	Bryn Smith	.10
20	Wayne Krenchicki	.10
----	Album Offer	.02
Panel 11		.15
21	Joe Hesketh	.10
22	Herman Winningham	.10
----	Album Offer	.02
Panel 12		.15
23	Vance Law	.10
24	Floyd Youmans	.10
----	Album Offer	.02
Panel 13		.15
25	Jeff Parrett	.10
26	Mike Fitzgerald	.10
----	Album Offer	.02
Panel 14		.15
27	Youppi (Mascot)	.10
28	Expos' Coaching Staff (Ron Hansen, Ken Macha, Rick Renick)	.10
----	Album Offer	.02

Posters

This Provigo issue is much scarcer than the smaller card panels issued the same year. These posters measure about 9" x 14-7/8". A large (9" x 12-1/2") player portrait is separated from a bottom coupon panel. Backs are blank and can be found in red, white or blue. The player pictures have facsimile autographs and a white strip at bottom with identification, uniform number, team and sponsor logos and card number. Values shown are for complete poster/coupon combinations.

		NM/M
Complete Set (12):		20.00
Common Player:		2.00
1	Tim Raines	4.00
2	Bryn Smith	2.00
3	Hubie Brooks	2.00
4	Buck Rodgers	2.00
5	Mitch Webster	2.00
6	Joe Hesketh	2.00
7	Mike Fitzgerald	2.00
8	Andy McGaffigan	2.00
9	Andre Dawson	7.50
10	Tim Wallach	2.00
11	Jeff Reardon	2.00
12	Vance Law	2.00

1994 PruCare N.Y. Mets

Top names on the 1994 Mets are featured in this issue sponsored by PruCare, a division of Prudential Insurance, whose logo appears on front and back. Cards were issued in a nine-card panel, perforated for easy separation. Individual cards are 2-1/2" x 3-1/2". Fronts have color action photos surrounded by team-color frames and white borders. Backs are printed in orange and blue with personal data, 1993 stats and highlights and career major league stats. The unnumbered cards are checklisted here in alphabetical order.

		NM/M
Complete Sheet:		3.50
Complete Set (9):		3.00
Common Player:		.50
(1)	Bobby Bonilla	.50
(2)	Jeromy Burnitz	.50
(3)	John Franco	.50
(4)	Dwight Gooden	.50
(5)	Bud Harrelson	.50
(6)	Jeff Kent	.50
(7)	Kevin McReynolds	.50
(8)	Ryan Thompson	.50
(9)	Mookie Wilson	.50

1990 Publications International Stickers

Nolan Ryan

This large set was issued in the form of an album with pages of bound-in stickers which were to be removed and placed in the appropriately numbered spots. Arranged by team, the album's spaces have a trivia question about the player whose sticker belongs there. The 1-3/8" x 1-3/4" stickers are unnumbered and are listed here according to the number of their album space.

		NM/M
Complete Album:		20.00
Complete Sticker Set (648):		15.00
Common Player:		.05
(1)	Dave Anderson	.05
(2)	Tim Belcher	.05
(3)	Mike Davis	.05
(4)	Rick Dempsey	.05
(5)	Kirk Gibson	.05
(6)	Alfredo Griffin	.05
(7)	Jeff Hamilton	.05
(8)	Mickey Hatcher	.05
(9)	Orel Hershiser	.05
(10)	Ricky Horton	.05
(11)	Jay Howell	.05
(12)	Tim Leary	.05
(13)	Mike Marshall	.05
(14)	Eddie Murray	.60
(15)	Alejandro Pena	.05
(16)	Willie Randolph	.05
(17)	Mike Scoscia	.05
(18)	John Shelby	.05
(19)	Franklin Stubbs	.05
(20)	John Tudor	.05
(21)	Fernando Valenzuela	.05
(22)	Todd Benzinger	.05
(23)	Tom Browning	.05
(24)	Norm Charlton	.05
(25)	Kal Daniels	.05
(26)	Eric Davis	.05
(27)	Bo Diaz	.05
(28)	Rob Dibble	.05
(29)	John Franco	.05
(30)	Ken Griffey Sr.	.05
(31)	Lenny Harris	.05
(32)	Danny Jackson	.05
(33)	Barry Larkin	.05
(34)	Rick Mahler	.05
(35)	Ron Oester	.05
(36)	Paul O'Neill	.05
(37)	Jeff Reed	.05
(38)	Jose Rijo	.05

(39) Chris Sabo .05
(40) Kent Tekulve .05
(41) Manny Trillo .05
(42) Joel Youngblood .05
(43) Roberto Alomar .15
(44) Greg Booker .05
(45) Jack Clark .05
(46) Jerald Clark .05
(47) Mark Davis .05
(48) Tim Flannery .05
(49) Mark Grant .05
(50) Tony Gwynn .75
(51) Bruce Hurst .05
(52) John Kruk .05
(53) Dave Leiper .05
(54) Carmelo Martinez .05
(55) Mark Parent .05
(56) Dennis Rasmussen .05
(57) Randy Ready .05
(58) Benito Santiago .05
(59) Eric Show .05
(60) Garry Templeton .05
(61) Walt Terrell .05
(62) Ed Whitson .05
(63) Marvell Wynne .05
(64) Brett Butler .05
(65) Will Clark .05
(66) Kelly Downs .05
(67) Scott Garrelts .05
(68) Rich "Goose" Gossage .05
(69) Atlee Hammaker .05
(70) Tracy Jones .05
(71) Terry Kennedy .05
(72) Mike Krukow .05
(73) Mike LaCoss .05
(74) Craig Lefferts .05
(75) Candy Maldonado .05
(76) Kirt Manwaring .05
(77) Kevin Mitchell .05
(78) Donell Nixon .05
(79) Rick Reuschel .05
(80) Ernest Riles .05
(81) Don Robinson .05
(82) Chris Speier .05
(83) Robby Thompson .05
(84) Jose Uribe .05
(85) Juan Agosto .05
(86) Larry Andersen .05
(87) Kevin Bass .05
(88) Craig Biggio .05
(89) Ken Caminiti .05
(90) Jim Clancy .05
(91) Danny Darwin .05
(92) Glenn Davis .05
(93) Jim Deshaies .05
(94) Bill Doran .05
(95) Bob Forsch .05
(96) Billy Hatcher .05
(97) Bob Knepper .05
(98) Terry Puhl .05
(99) Rafael Ramirez .05
(100) Craig Reynolds .05
(101) Rick Rhoden .05
(102) Mike Scott .05
(103) Dave Smith .05
(104) Alex Trevino .05
(105) Gerald Young .05
(106) Jose Alvarez .05
(107) Paul Assenmacher .05
(108) Bruce Benedict .05
(109) Jeff Blauser .05
(110) Joe Boever .05
(111) Jody Davis .05
(112) Darrell Evans .05
(113) Ron Gant .05
(114) Tommy Gregg .05
(115) Dion James .05
(116) Derek Lilliquist .05
(117) Dale Murphy .20
(118) Gerald Perry .05
(119) Charlie Puleo .05
(120) John Russell .05
(121) Lonnie Smith .05
(122) Pete Smith .05
(123) Zane Smith .05
(124) John Smoltz .05
(125) Bruce Sutter .20
(126) Andres Thomas .05
(127) Rick Aguilera .05
(128) Gary Carter .60
(129) David Cone .05
(130) Ron Darling .05
(131) Lenny Dykstra .05
(132) Kevin Elster .05
(133) Sid Fernandez .05
(134) Dwight Gooden .05
(135) Keith Hernandez .05
(136) Gregg Jeffries .05
(137) Howard Johnson .05
(138) Dave Magadan .05
(139) Lee Mazzilli .05
(140) Roger McDowell .05
(141) Kevin McReynolds .05
(142) Randy Myers .05
(143) Bob Ojeda .05
(144) Mackey Sasser .05
(145) Darryl Strawberry .05
(146) Tim Teufel .05
(147) Mookie Wilson .05
(148) Rafael Belliard .05
(149) Barry Bonds 1.50
(150) Bobby Bonilla .05
(151) Sid Bream .05
(152) Benny Distefano .05
(153) Doug Drabek .05
(154) Brian Fisher .05
(155) Jim Gott .05
(156) Neal Heaton .05
(157) Bill Landrum .05
(158) Mike LaValliere .05
(159) Jose Lind .05
(160) Junior Ortiz .05
(161) Tom Prince .05
(162) Gary Redus .05
(163) R.J. Reynolds .05
(164) Jeff Robinson .05
(165) John Smiley .05
(166) Andy Van Slyke .05
(167) Bob Walk .05
(168) Glenn Wilson .05
(169) Hubie Brooks .05
(170) Tim Burke .05
(171) Mike Fitzgerald .05
(172) Tom Foley .05
(173) Andres Galarraga .05
(174) Kevin Gross .05
(175) Joe Hesketh .05
(176) Brian Holman .05
(177) Rex Hudler .05
(178) Wallace Johnson .05
(179) Mark Langston .05
(180) Dave Martinez .05
(181) Dennis Martinez .05
(182) Andy McGaffigan .05
(183) Otis Nixon .05
(184) Spike Owen .05
(185) Pascual Perez .05
(186) Tim Raines .05
(187) Nelson Santovenia .05
(188) Bryn Smith .05
(189) Tim Wallach .05
(190) Damon Berryhill .05
(191) Mike Bielecki .05
(192) Andre Dawson .20
(193) Shawon Dunston .05
(194) Mark Grace .05
(195) Darrin Jackson .05
(196) Paul Kilgus .05
(197) Vance Law .05
(198) Greg Maddux .75
(199) Pat Perry .05
(200) Jeff Pico .05
(201) Ryne Sandberg .75
(202) Scott Sanderson .05
(203) Calvin Schiraldi .05
(204) Dwight Smith .05
(205) Rick Sutcliffe .05
(206) Gary Varsho .05
(207) Jerome Walton .05
(208) Mitch Webster .05
(209) Curtis Wilkerson .05
(210) Mitch Williams .05
(211) Tom Brunansky .05
(212) Cris Carpenter .05
(213) Vince Coleman .05
(214) John Costello .05
(215) Danny Cox .05
(216) Ken Dayley .05
(217) Jose DeLeon .05
(218) Frank DiPino .05
(219) Pedro Guerrero .05
(220) Joe Magrane .05
(221) Greg Mathews .05
(222) Willie McGee .05
(223) Jose Oquendo .05
(224) Tom Pagnozzi .05
(225) Tony Pena .05
(226) Terry Pendleton .05
(227) Dan Quisenberry .05
(228) Ozzie Smith .75
(229) Scott Terry .05
(230) Milt Thompson .05
(231) Todd Worrell .05
(232) Steve Bedrosian .05
(233) Don Carman .05
(234) Darren Daulton .05
(235) Bob Dernier .05
(236) Marvin Freeman .05
(237) Greg Harris .05
(238) Von Hayes .05
(239) Tommy Herr .05
(240) Ken Howell .05
(241) Chris James .05
(242) Steve Jeltz .05
(243) Ron Jones .05
(244) Ricky Jordan .05
(245) Steve Lake .05
(246) Mike Maddux .05
(247) Larry McWilliams .05
(248) Jeff Parrett .05
(249) Juan Samuel .05
(250) Mike Schmidt .85
(251) Dickie Thon .05
(252) Floyd Youmans .05
(253) Bobby Bonilla/AS .05
(254) Will Clark/AS .05
(255) Eric Davis/AS .05
(256) Andre Dawson/AS .05
(257) Bill Doran/AS .05
(258) John Franco/AS .05
(259) Kirk Gibson/AS .05
(260) Dwight Gooden/AS .05
(261) Tony Gwynn/AS .35
(262) Keith Hernandez/AS .05
(263) Orel Hershiser/AS .05
(264) Danny Jackson/AS .05
(265) Howard Johnson/AS .05
(266) Barry Larkin/AS .05
(267) Joe Magrane/AS .05
(268) Kevin McReynolds/AS .05
(269) Tony Pena/AS .05
(270) Ryne Sandberg/AS .35
(271) Benito Santiago/AS .05
(272) Ozzie Smith/AS .35
(273) Darryl Strawberry/AS .05
(274) Todd Worrell/AS .05
(275) Harold Baines/AS .05
(276) George Bell/AS .05
(277) Wade Boggs/AS .35
(278) Bob Boone/AS .05
(279) Jose Canseco/AS .20
(280) Joe Carter/AS .05
(281) Roger Clemens/AS .40
(282) Dennis Eckersley/AS .25
(283) Tony Fernandez/AS .05
(284) Carlton Fisk/AS .30
(285) Julio Franco/AS .05
(286) Gary Gaetti/AS .05
(287) Mike Greenwell/AS .05
(288) Rickey Henderson/AS .30
(289) Teddy Higuera/AS .05
(289) Kent Hrbek/AS .05
(290) Don Mattingly/AS .40
(291) Kirby Puckett/AS .35
(292) Jeff Reardon/AS .05
(293) Harold Reynolds/AS .05
(294) Dave Stewart/AS .05
(295) Alan Trammell/AS .05
(297) Frank Viola/AS .05
(298) Dave Winfield/AS .30
(299) Todd Burns .05
(300) Greg Cadaret .05
(301) Jose Canseco .30
(302) Storm Davis .05
(303) Dennis Eckersley .45
(304) Mike Gallego .05
(305) Ron Hassey .05
(306) Dave Henderson .05
(307) Rick Honeycutt .05
(308) Stan Javier .05
(309) Carney Lansford .05
(310) Mark McGwire 1.25
(311) Mike Moore .05
(312) Dave Parker .05
(313) Eric Plunk .05
(314) Luis Polonia .05
(315) Terry Steinbach .05
(316) Dave Stewart .05
(317) Walt Weiss .05
(318) Bob Welch .05
(319) Curt Young .05
(320) Allan Anderson .05
(321) Wally Backman .05
(322) Doug Baker .05
(323) Juan Berenguer .05
(324) Randy Bush .05
(325) Jim Dwyer .05
(326) Gary Gaetti .05
(327) Greg Gagne .05
(328) Dan Gladden .05
(329) Brian Harper .05
(330) Kent Hrbek .05
(331) Gene Larkin .05
(332) Tim Laudner .05
(333) John Moses .05
(334) Al Newman .05
(335) Kirby Puckett .75
(336) Shane Rawley .05
(337) Jeff Reardon .05
(338) Steve Shields .05
(339) Frank Viola .05
(340) Gary Wayne .05
(341) Luis Aquino .05
(342) Floyd Bannister .05
(343) Bob Boone .05
(344) George Brett .85
(345) Bill Buckner .05
(346) Jim Eisenreich .05
(347) Steve Farr .05
(348) Tom Gordon .05
(349) Mark Gubicza .05
(350) Bo Jackson .10
(351) Charlie Leibrandt .05
(352) Mike Macfarlane .05
(353) Jeff Montgomery .05
(354) Bret Saberhagen .05
(355) Kevin Seitzer .05
(356) Kurt Stillwell .05
(357) Pat Tabler .05
(358) Danny Tartabull .05
(359) Gary Thurman .05
(360) Frank White .05
(361) Willie Wilson .05
(362) Jim Abbott .05
(363) Kent Anderson .05
(364) Tony Armas .05
(365) Dante Bichette .05
(366) Bert Blyleven .05
(367) Chili Davis .05
(368) Brian Downing .05
(369) Chuck Finley .05
(370) Willie Fraser .05
(371) Jack Howell .05
(372) Wally Joyner .05
(373) Kirk McCaskill .05
(374) Bob McClure .05
(375) Greg Minton .05
(376) Lance Parrish .05
(377) Dan Petry .05
(378) Johnny Ray .05
(379) Dick Schofield .05
(380) Claudell Washington .05
(381) Devon White .05
(382) Mike Witt .05
(383) Harold Baines .05
(384) Daryl Boston .05
(385) Ivan Calderon .05
(386) Carlton Fisk .60
(387) Dave Gallagher .05
(388) Ozzie Guillen .05
(389) Shawn Hillegas .05
(390) Barry Jones .05
(391) Ron Karkovice .05
(392) Eric King .05
(393) Ron Kittle .05
(394) Bill Long .05
(395) Steve Lyons .05
(396) Fred Manrique .05
(397) Donn Pall .05
(398) Dan Pasqua .05
(399) Melido Perez .05
(400) Jerry Reuss .05
(401) Bobby Thigpen .05
(402) Greg Walker .05
(403) Eddie Williams .05
(404) Buddy Bell .05
(405) Kevin Brown .05
(406) Steve Buechele .05
(407) Cecil Espy .05
(408) Scott Fletcher .05
(409) Julio Franco .05
(410) Cecilio Guante .05
(411) Jose Guzman .05
(412) Charlie Hough .05
(413) Pete Incaviglia .05
(414) Chad Kreuter .05
(415) Jeff Kunkel .05
(416) Rick Leach .05
(417) Jamie Moyer .05
(418) Rafael Palmeiro .50
(419) Geno Petralli .05
(420) Jeff Russell .05
(421) Nolan Ryan 1.50
(422) Ruben Sierra .05
(423) Jim Sundberg .05
(424) Bobby Witt .05
(425) Steve Balboni .05
(426) Scott Bankhead .05
(427) Scott Bradley .05
(428) Mickey Brantley .05
(429) Darnell Coles .05
(430) Henry Cotto .05
(431) Alvin Davis .05
(432) Mario Diaz .05
(433) Ken Griffey Jr. 1.00
(434) Erik Hanson .05
(435) Mike Jackson .05
(436) Jeffrey Leonard .05
(437) Edgar Martinez .05
(438) Tom Niedenfuer .05
(439) Jim Presley .05
(440) Jerry Reed .05
(441) Harold Reynolds .05
(442) Bill Swift .05
(443) Steve Trout .05
(444) Dave Valle .05
(445) Omar Vizquel .05
(446) Marty Barrett .05
(447) Mike Boddicker .05
(448) Wade Boggs .75
(449) Dennis "Oil Can" Boyd .05
(450) Ellis Burks .05
(451) Rick Cerone .05
(452) Roger Clemens .85
(453) Nick Esasky .05
(454) Dwight Evans .05
(455) Wes Gardner .05
(456) Rich Gedman .05
(457) Mike Greenwell .05
(458) Sam Horn .05
(459) Randy Kutcher .05
(460) Dennis Lamp .05
(461) Rob Murphy .05
(462) Jody Reed .05
(463) Jim Rice .10
(464) Lee Smith .05
(465) Mike Smithson .05
(466) Bob Stanley .05
(467) Doyle Alexander .05
(468) Dave Bergman .05
(469) Chris Brown .05
(470) Paul Gibson .05
(471) Mike Heath .05
(472) Mike Henneman .05
(473) Guillermo Hernandez .05
(474) Charles Hudson .05
(475) Chet Lemon .05
(476) Fred Lynn .05
(477) Keith Moreland .05
(478) Jack Morris .05
(479) Matt Nokes .05
(480) Gary Pettis .05
(481) Jeff Robinson .05
(482) Pat Sheridan .05
(483) Frank Tanana .05
(484) Alan Trammell .05
(485) Lou Whitaker .05
(486) Frank Williams .05
(487) Kenny Williams .05
(488) Don August .05
(489) Mike Birkbeck .05
(490) Chris Bosio .05
(491) Glenn Braggs .05
(492) Greg Brock .05
(493) Chuck Crim .05
(494) Rob Deer .05
(495) Mike Felder .05
(496) Jim Gantner .05
(497) Ted Higuera .05
(498) Joey Meyer .05
(499) Paul Mirabella .05
(500) Paul Molitor .60
(501) Juan Nieves .05
(502) Charlie O'Brien .05
(503) Dan Plesac .05
(504) Gary Sheffield .30
(505) B.J. Surhoff .05
(506) Dale Sveum .05
(507) Bill Wegman .05
(508) Robin Yount .60
(509) George Bell .05
(510) Pat Borders .05
(511) John Cerutti .05
(512) Rob Ducey .05
(513) Tony Fernandez .05
(514) Mike Flanagan .05
(515) Kelly Gruber .05
(516) Tom Henke .05
(517) Alexis Infante .05
(518) Jimmy Key .05
(519) Tom Lawless .05
(520) Manny Lee .05
(521) Al Leiter .05
(522) Nelson Liriano .05
(523) Fred McGriff .05
(524) Lloyd Moseby .05
(525) Rance Mulliniks .05
(526) Dave Steib .05
(527) Todd Stottlemyre .05
(528) Duane Ward .05
(529) Ernie Whitt .05
(530) Jesse Barfield .05
(531) Bob Brower .05
(532) John Candelaria .05
(533) Richard Dotson .05
(534) Lee Guetterman .05
(535) Mel Hall .05
(536) Andy Hawkins .05
(537) Rickey Henderson .60
(538) Roberto Kelly .05
(539) Dave LaPoint .05
(540) Don Mattingly .85
(541) Lance McCullers .05
(542) Mike Pagliarulo .05
(543) Clay Parker .05
(544) Ken Phelps .05
(545) Dave Righetti .05
(546) Rafael Santana .05
(547) Steve Sax .05
(548) Don Slaught .05
(549) Wayne Tolleson .05
(550) Dave Winfield .60
(551) Andy Allanson .05
(552) Keith Atherton .05
(553) Scott Bailes .05
(554) Bud Black .05
(555) Jerry Browne .05
(556) Tom Candiotti .05
(557) Joe Carter .05
(558) David Clark .05
(559) John Farrell .05
(560) Felix Fermin .05
(561) Brook Jacoby .05
(562) Doug Jones .05
(563) Oddibe McDowell .05
(564) Luis Medina .05
(565) Pete O'Brien .05
(566) Jesse Orosco .05
(567) Joel Skinner .05
(568) Cory Snyder .05
(569) Greg Swindell .05
(570) Rich Yett .05
(571) Mike Young .05
(572) Brady Anderson .05
(573) Jeff Ballard .05
(574) Jose Bautista .05
(575) Phil Bradley .05
(576) Mike Devereaux .05
(577) Kevin Hickey .05
(578) Brian Holton .05
(579) Bob Melvin .05
(580) Bob Milacki .05
(581) Gregg Olson .05
(582) Joe Orsulak .05
(583) Bill Ripken .05
(584) Cal Ripken Jr. 1.50
(585) Dave Schmidt .05
(586) Larry Sheets .05
(587) Mickey Tettleton .05
(588) Mark Thurmond .05
(589) Jay Tibbs .05
(590) Jim Traber .05
(591) Mark Williamson .05
(592) Craig Worthington .05
(593) Allan Anderson .05
(594) Ellis Burks .05
(595) Ken Griffey Jr. 1.00
(596) Bo Jackson .05
(597) Roberto Kelly .05
(598) Kirk McCaskill .05
(599) Fred McGriff .05
(600) Mark McGwire 1.25
(601) Bob Milacki .05
(602) Melido Perez .05
(603) Jeff Robinson .05
(604) Gary Sheffield .05
(605) Ruben Sierra .05
(606) Greg Swindell .05
(607) Roberto Alomar .15
(608) Tim Belcher .05
(609) Vince Coleman .05
(610) Kal Daniels .05
(611) Andres Galarraga .05
(612) Ron Gant .05
(613) Mark Grace .05
(614) Gregg Jeffries .05
(615) Ricky Jordan .05
(616) Jose Lind .05
(617) Kevin Mitchell .05
(618) Gerald Young .05
(619) Base .05
(620) Batting Helmets .05
(621) Bats .05
(622) Batting Gloves .05
(623) Los Angeles Dodgers .05
(624) Cincinnati Reds .05
(625) San Diego Padres .05
(626) San Francisco Giants .05
(627) Houston Astros .05
(628) Atlanta Braves .05
(629) New York Mets .05
(630) Pittsburgh Pirates .05
(631) Montreal Expos .05
(632) Chicago Cubs .05
(633) St. Louis Cardinals .05
(634) Philadelphia Phillies .05
(635) Oakland A's .05
(636) Minnesota Twins .05
(637) Kansas City Royals .05
(638) California Angels .05
(639) Chicago White Sox .05
(640) Texas Rangers .05
(641) Seattle Mariners .05
(642) Boston Red Sox .05
(643) Detroit Tigers .05
(644) Milwaukee Brewers .05
(645) Toronto Blue Jays .05
(646) New York Yankees .05
(647) Cleveland Indians .05
(648) Baltimore Orioles .05

1 Hottest Players Stickers

Established major league stars are featured in this set of large format (4-1/8" x 5-7/16") blank-back stickers. The stickers are printed four per sheet and were sold with a 36-page album for mounting. The album has player data, stats and highlights for each of the stars. Stickers have color action photos with a white frame at center. There is a red stripe at top of the frame and a blue stripe at bottom, which contains the player name. The unnumbered stickers are checklisted here in alphabetical order.

NM/M

Complete Set, W/Album (56): 4.00
Common Player: .05
(1) George Bell .05
(2) Wade Boggs .50
(3) Bobby Bonilla .05
(4) Jose Canseco .25
(5) Joe Carter .05
(6) Will Clark .05
(7) Roger Clemens .60
(8) Alvin Davis .05
(9) Eric Davis .05
(10) Glenn Davis .05
(11) Mark Davis .05
(12) Carlton Fisk .35
(13) John Franco .05
(14) Gary Gaetti .05
(15) Andres Galarraga .05
(16) Dwight Gooden .05
(17) Mark Grace .05
(18) Pedro Guerrero .05
(19) Tony Gwynn .50
(20) Rickey Henderson .35
(21) Orel Hershiser .05
(22) Bo Jackson .05
(23) Ricky Jordan .05
(24) Wally Joyner .05
(25) Don Mattingly .60
(26) Fred McGriff .05
(27) Kevin Mitchell .05
(28) Paul Molitor .35
(29) Dale Murphy .25
(30) Eddie Murray .35
(31) Kirby Puckett .50
(32) Tim Raines .05
(33) Harold Reynolds .05
(34) Cal Ripken Jr. 1.00
(35) Nolan Ryan 1.00
(36) Bret Saberhagen .05
(37) Ryne Sandberg .50
(38) Steve Sax .05
(39) Mike Scott .05
(40) Ruben Sierra .05
(41) Ozzie Smith .50
(42) John Smoltz .05
(43) Darryl Strawberry .05
(44) Greg Swindell .05
(45) Mickey Tettleton .05
(46) Alan Trammell .05
(47) Andy Van Slyke .05
(48) Lou Whitaker .05
(49) Devon White .05
(50) Robin Yount .35
(51) Dodger Stadium .05
(52) Jack Murphy Stadium .05

(53)	Shea Stadium	.05
(54)	Three Rivers Stadium	.05
(55)	Tiger Stadium	.05
(56)	Yankee Stadium	.05

Hottest Rookies Stickers

This set of large-format (4-1/8" x 5-7/16") stickers features the rookie crop of 1990 along with other young players who were not technically rookies in 1990. The stickers were sold four per sheet in complete sets which included a 36-page color album to mount the stamps. The album pages have personal data, career stats and highlights about each player. On the stickers, each action photo has a central frame in white with a blue stripe at top and a red stripe at bottom bearing the player name. Backs are, of course, blank. The set is checklisted here alphabetically.

		NM/M
Complete Set, W/Album (56):		4.00
Common Player:		.05
(1)	Jim Abbott	.05
(2)	Sandy Alomar	.05
(3)	Kent Anderson	.05
(4)	Eric Anthony	.05
(5)	Jeff Ballard	.05
(6)	Joey Belle	.15
(7)	Andy Benes	.05
(8)	Lance Blankenship	.05
(9)	Jeff Brantley	.05
(10)	Cris Carpenter	.05
(11)	Mark Carreon	.05
(12)	Dennis Cook	.05
(13)	Scott Coolbaugh	.05
(14)	Luis de los Santos	.05
(15)	Junior Felix	.05
(16)	Mark Gardner	.05
(17)	German Gonzalez	.05
(18)	Tom Gordon	.05
(19)	Ken Griffey Jr.	2.00
(20)	Marquis Grissom	.05
(21)	Charlie Hayes	.05
(22)	Gregg Jefferies	.05
(23)	Randy Johnson	1.00
(24)	Felix Jose	.05
(25)	Jeff King	.05
(26)	Randy Kramer	.05
(27)	Derek Lilliquist	.05
(28)	Greg Litton	.05
(29)	Kelly Mann	.05
(30)	Ramon Martinez	.05
(31)	Luis Medina	.05
(32)	Hal Morris	.05
(33)	Joe Oliver	.05
(34)	Gregg Olson	.05
(35)	Dean Palmer	.05
(36)	Carlos Quintana	.05
(37)	Kevin Ritz	.05
(38)	Deion Sanders	.05
(39)	Scott Scudder	.05
(40)	Steve Searcy	.05
(41)	Gary Sheffield	.25
(42)	Dwight Smith	.05
(43)	Sam Sosa	1.50
(44)	Greg Vaughn	.05
(45)	Robin Ventura	.05
(46)	Jerome Walton	.05
(47)	Dave West	.05
(48)	John Wetteland	.05
(49)	Eric Yelding	.05
(50)	Todd Zeile	.05
(51)	Dodger Stadium	.05
(52)	Jack Murphy Stadium	.05
(53)	Shea Stadium	.05
(54)	Three Rivers Stadium	.05
(55)	Tiger Stadium	.05
(56)	Yankee Stadium	.05

1993 Publix Florida Marlins

		NM/M
Complete Set (29):		10.00
Common Player:		.50
6	Rich Renteria	.50
8	Bret Barbarie	.50
09	Benito Santiago	.50
10	Gary Sheffield	1.50
11	Chris Hammond	.50
13	Bob Natal	.50
15	Rene Lachemann	.50
17	Darrell Whitmore	.50
19	Jeff Conine	.50
20	Greg Briley	.50
21	Chuck Carr	.50
22	Walt Weiss	.50
24	Richie Lewis	.50
26	Alex Arias	.50
27	Luis Aquino	.50
29	Henry Cotto	.50
30	Nigel Wilson	.50
31	Robb Nen	.50
34	Bryan Harvey	.50
39	Orestes Destrade	.50
42	Rich Rodriguez	.50
46	Ryan Bowen	.50
48	Pat Rapp	.50
49	Charlie Hough	.50
54	Matt Turner	.50
58	Joe Klink	.50
77	Jack Armstrong	.50
---	Marlins Coaches (Marcel Lachemann, Doug Rader, Vada Pinson, Frank Reberger, Cookie Rojas)	.50
---	Billy (Mascot)	.50
---	$1 Coke-Publix Coupon	.50

Q

1986 Quaker Oats

The Quaker Co., in conjunction with Topps, produced this 33-card set of current baseball stars for packaging in groups of three in Chewy Granola Bars packages. The cards are noted as the "1st Annual Collectors Edition." They are numbered and measure 2-1/2" x 3-1/2." Card fronts feature full-color player photos with the product name at the top and the player name, team and position below the photo. The complete set was offered via mail order by the Quaker Company.

		NM/M
Complete Set (33):		4.00
Common Player:		.05
1	Willie McGee	.05
2	Dwight Gooden	.05
3	Vince Coleman	.05
4	Gary Carter	.50
5	Jack Clark	.05
6	Steve Garvey	.15
7	Tony Gwynn	.65
8	Dale Murphy	.25
9	Dave Parker	.05
10	Tim Raines	.05
11	Pete Rose	1.00
12	Nolan Ryan	1.50
13	Ryne Sandberg	.65
14	Mike Schmidt	.75
15	Ozzie Smith	.65
16	Darryl Strawberry	.05
17	Fernando Valenzuela	.05
18	Don Mattingly	.75
19	Bret Saberhagen	.05
20	Ozzie Guillen	.05
21	Bert Blyleven	.05
22	Wade Boggs	.65
23	George Brett	.75
24	Darrell Evans	.05
25	Rickey Henderson	.50
26	Reggie Jackson	.75
27	Eddie Murray	.50
28	Phil Niekro	.25
29	Dan Quisenberry	.05
30	Jim Rice	.15
31	Cal Ripken, Jr.	1.50
32	Tom Seaver	.65
33	Dave Winfield	.50
----	Offer Card	.03

R

1993 Rainbow Foods Dave Winfield

Dave Winfield's return to Minnesota where he excelled in college sports was marked by the "Homecoming Collection," tracing the future Hall of Famer's career. The 2-1/2" x 3-1/2" cards have black-and-white or color photos on front and back. Each side also sports a special logo identifying the issue. Rainbow's logo appears on front, while that of a major food brand such as Kraft or Oscar Mayer appear on back, along with information about Winfield's career. Cards were sold in five-card packs with four blue-bordered cards and one gold-bordered parallel card.

		NM/M
Complete Set, Blue (10):		7.50
Common Player, Blue:		1.00
Gold:		2-3X
1	Dave Winfield (University of Minnesota Outfielder)	1.00
2	Dave Winfield (University of Minnesota Pitcher)	1.00
3	Dave Winfield (University of Minnesota Basketball Star)	1.00
4	Dave Winfield (San Diego Padres 1973-1980)	1.00
5	Dave Winfield (N.Y. Yankees 1981-1990)	1.00
6	Dave Winfield (California Angels 1990-1991)	1.00
7	Dave Winfield (Toronto Blue Jays 1992)	1.00
8	Dave Winfield (Minnesota Twins 1993-)	1.00
9	Dave Winfield (7-time Gold Glove Winner)	1.00
10	Dave Winfield (Pride of Minnesota)	1.00

2001 Rainbow Foods Minnesota Twins 10th Anniversary

As part of a three-game celebration of the 10th annivsary of the Twins 1991 World's Championship, Rainbow Foods sponsored a team-set card giveaway on June 29, distributing 10,000 sets. Fronts of the 2-1/2" x 3-1/2" cards have borderless game-action photos with an anniversary logo. Backs have team and sponsor logos and player career highlights on a baseball diamond design in color. The unnumbered cards are checklisted here in alphabetical order.

		NM/M
Complete Set (26):		9.00
Common Player:		.25
(1)	Rick Aguilera	.25
(2)	Steve Bedrosian	.25
(3)	Jarvis Brown	.25
(4)	Randy Bush	.25
(5)	Chili Davis	.25
(6)	Scott Erickson	.25
(7)	Greg Gagne	.25
(8)	Dan Gladden	.25
(9)	Mark Guthrie	.25
(10)	Brian Harper	.25
(11)	Kent Hrbek	.50
(12)	Tom Kelly	.25
(13)	Chuck Knoblauch	.25
(14)	Gene Larkin	.25
(15)	Terry Leach	.25
(16)	Scott Leius	.25
(17)	Shane Mack	.25
(18)	Jack Morris	.25
(19)	Al Newman	.25
(20)	Junior Ortiz	.25
(21)	Mike Pagliarulo	.25
(22)	Kirby Puckett	5.00
(23)	Paul Sorrento	.25
(24)	Kevin Tapani	.25
(25)	David West	.25
(26)	Carl Willis	.25

1989 Rainier Farms Super Stars Discs

This set is one of the scarcer late-1980s disc issues produced by Michael Schechter Associates for various local businesses. The bakery began distribution of the discs by placing them directly in the cello wrapper with a loaf of bread. This resulted in those cards being severely grease stained and often creased. It also resulted in problems with public health officials who halted the distribution. Since the bakery could not economically and sanitarily package the cards they dropped the promotion and sold the remainder cards into the hobby. Discs measure 2-3/4" in diameter and have a color player photo (with team logos airbrushed away) at center with a white border. A Rainier Farms Homestyle logo is at top in red and black. Backs are printed in dark blue and feature a few stats, biographical details and a card number.

		NM/M
Complete Set (20):		15.00
Common Player:		.60
1	Wally Joyner	.60
2	Wade Boggs	2.25
3	Ozzie Smith	2.25
4	Don Mattingly	2.50
5	Jose Canseco	1.25
6	Tony Gwynn	2.25
7	Eric Davis	.60
8	Kirby Puckett	2.25
9	Kevin Seitzer	.60
10	Darryl Strawberry	.60
11	Gregg Jefferies	.60
12	Mark Grace	.60
13	Matt Nokes	.60
14	Mark McGwire	3.50
15	Bobby Bonilla	.60
16	Roger Clemens	2.50
17	Frank Viola	.60
18	Orel Hershiser	.60
19	Dave Cone	.60
20	Kirk Gibson	.60

1984 Ralston Purina

This set, produced by Topps, features the game's top players. Photos on the 2-1/2" x 3-1/2" cards are all close-up poses. Topps' logo appears only on the card fronts, and the backs are completely different from Topps' regular issue of 1984, featuring a checkerboard look, coinciding with the well-known Ralston Purina logo. Cards are numbered with odd numbers for American Leaguers and even numbered cards for National Leaguers. Four cards were packed in boxes of Cookie Crisp and Donkey Kong Junior brand cereals, and the complete set was available via a mail-in offer in panel form.

		NM/M
Complete Set, Singles (33):		4.00
Complete Set, Panel		4.00
Common Player:		.05
1	Eddie Murray	.25
2	Ozzie Smith	.35
3	Ted Simmons	.05
4	Pete Rose	.75
5	Greg Luzinski	.05
6	Andre Dawson	.15
7	Dave Winfield	.25
8	Tom Seaver	.25
9	Jim Rice	.15
10	Fernando Valenzuela	.05
11	Wade Boggs	.35
12	Dale Murphy	.15
13	George Brett	.50
14	Nolan Ryan	1.00
15	Rickey Henderson	.25
16	Steve Carlton	.25
17	Rod Carew	.25
18	Steve Garvey	.15
19	Reggie Jackson	.50
20	Dave Concepcion	.05
21	Robin Yount	.25
22	Mike Schmidt	.50
23	Jim Palmer	.25
24	Bruce Sutter	.20
25	Dan Quisenberry	.05
26	Bill Madlock	.05
27	Cecil Cooper	.05
28	Gary Carter	.25
29	Fred Lynn	.05
30	Pedro Guerrero	.05
31	Ron Guidry	.05
32	Keith Hernandez	.05
33	Carlton Fisk	.25

1987 Ralston Purina

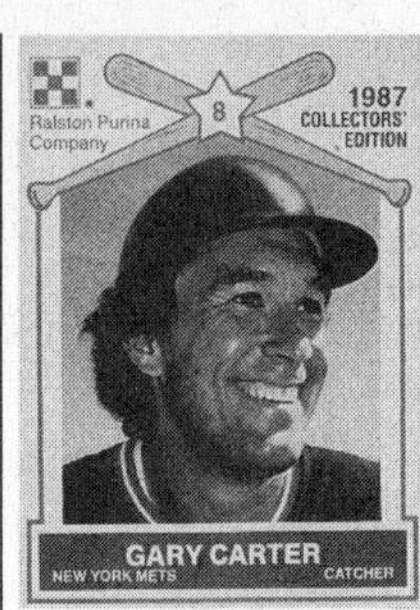

Ralston Purina, in conjunction with Mike Schechter Associates, issued this set in specially marked boxes of Cookie Crisp and Honey Graham Chex. Three cards, wrapped in cellophane, were inserted in each box. Fronts contain a full-color photo with the team insignia airbrushed away. Above the photo are two yellow crossed bats and a star, with the player's uniform number inside the star. Backs are gray with red printing and contain personal information and career major league statistics. As part of the promotion, the company advertised an uncut sheet of cards which was available by finding an "instant-winner" game card or sending $1 plus two non-winning cards. Cards on the uncut sheet are identical in design to the single cards, save the omission of the words "1987 Collectors Edition" in the upper-right corner.

		NM/M
Complete Set (15):		7.50
Common Player:		.25
1	Nolan Ryan	1.50
2	Steve Garvey	.35
3	Wade Boggs	.65
4	Dave Winfield	.50
5	Don Mattingly	.75
6	Don Sutton	.35
7	Dave Parker	.25
8	Eddie Murray	.50
9	Gary Carter	.50
10	Roger Clemens	.75
11	Fernando Valenzuela	.25
12	Cal Ripken Jr.	1.50
13	Ozzie Smith	.65
14	Mike Schmidt	.75
15	Ryne Sandberg	.65

Collectors' Sheet

Cards obtained from the mail-in redemption uncut sheet offer are identical to the cereal-box insert versions except that they lack the "1987 / COLLECTORS' / EDITION" legend at top-right.

		NM/M
Complete Panel:		8.00
Complete Singles Set (15):		5.00
Common Single Player:		.15
1	Nolan Ryan	1.00
2	Steve Garvey	.25
3	Wade Boggs	.50
4	Dave Winfield	.40
5	Don Mattingly	.65
6	Don Sutton	.30
7	Dave Parker	.15
8	Eddie Murray	.40
9	Gary Carter	.40
10	Roger Clemens	.65
11	Fernando Valenzuela	.15
12	Cal Ripken Jr.	1.00
13	Ozzie Smith	.50
14	Mike Schmidt	.65
15	Ryne Sandberg	.50

1989 Ralston Purina

Ralston Purina, in conjunction with Mike Schechter Associates, issued this "Superstars" set in 1989. As part of a late-spring and early-summer promotion, the standard-size cards were inserted, two per box, in specially-marked boxes of Crisp Crunch, Honey Nut O's, Fruit Rings and Frosted Flakes in most parts of the country. Ads on cereal boxes also offered complete sets through a mail-in offer. Fronts feature player portraits flanked by stars in all four corners. Backs include stats and player data. Team logos have been removed from the photos.

		NM/M
Complete Set (12):		3.00
Common Player:		.10
1	Ozzie Smith	.75
2	Andre Dawson	.20
3	Darryl Strawberry	.10
4	Mike Schmidt	1.00
5	Orel Hershiser	.10
6	Tim Raines	.10
7	Roger Clemens	1.00
8	Kirby Puckett	.75
9	George Brett	1.00
10	Alan Trammell	.10
11	Don Mattingly	1.00
12	Jose Canseco	.35

1990 Real Milk Mike Henneman

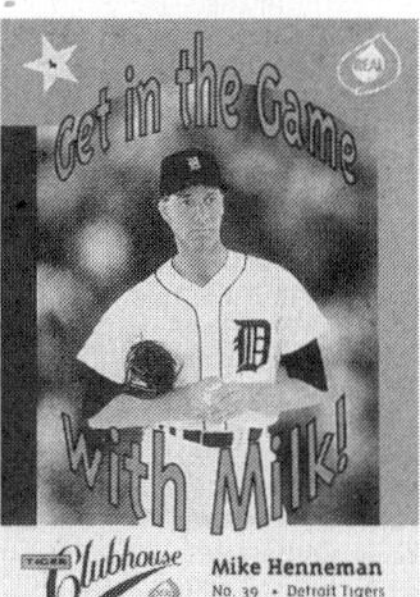

"Get in the Game" urges the headline on each of the cards in this collection featuring then-star Tiger relief pitcher Mike Henneman. The 2-1/2" x 3-1/2" cards have red, white and blue borders with a color photo at center. Backs are in red, black and white with Henneman's stats or career highlights. The set was available as a mail-in premium.

		NM/M
Complete Set (8):		6.00
Common Card:		.25
1	Mike Henneman (Drinking milk.)	2.00
2	Mike Henneman/ Pitching	2.00
3	Mike Henneman (In jacket.)	2.00
4	Mike Henneman (Rubbing up ball.)	2.00
5	Milk Carton	.25
6	Hand Holding Carton	.25
--	Title Card	.25
--	Tiger Clubhouse Membership Card	.25

1990 Red Apple Mariners Pin/ Cards

It is unknown whether the checklist presented here is complete. This combination promotional issue features a 2-1/2" x 3-13/16" baseball card separated by perforations from a 2-1/2" x 1-7/16" tab. The card portion has a color player photo with a large M's logo. The front of the tab is a coupon for a food product. On back the card has a black-and-white portrait photo along with player data and career highlights. The back of the tab has a Red Apple Markets logo. Attached to the tab is a color enameled pin of the player in action.

		NM/M
Common Player:		5.00
(1)	Alvin Davis	6.00
(2)	Ken Griffey Jr.	12.00
(3)	Harold Reynolds	6.00
(4)	David Valle	5.00

1982 Red Lobster Cubs

This 28-card set was co-sponsored by the team and a seafood restaurant chain for distribution at a 1982 Cubs promotional game. Card fronts are unbordered color photos, with player name, number, position and a superimposed facsimile autograph. The set includes 25 players on the 2-1/4" x 3-1/2" cards, along with a card for manager Lee Elia, an unnumbered card for the coaching staff and a team picture. Card backs have complete player statistics and a Red Lobster ad. Production was reported to be 15,000 sets.

		NM/M
Complete Set (28):		60.00
Common Player:		.50
1	Larry Bowa	.50
4	Lee Elia	.50
6	Keith Moreland	.50
7	Jody Davis	.50
10	Leon Durham	.50
15	Junior Kennedy	.50
17	Bump Wills	.50
18	Scot Thompson	.50
21	Jay Johnstone	.50
22	Bill Buckner	.50
23	Ryne Sandberg	50.00
24	Jerry Morales	.50
25	Gary Woods	.50
28	Steve Henderson	.50
29	Bob Molinaro	.50
31	Fergie Jenkins	2.00
33	Al Ripley	.50
34	Randy Martz	.50
36	Mike Proly	.50
37	Ken Kravec	.50
38	Willie Hernandez	.50
39	Bill Campbell	.50
41	Dick Tidrow	.50
46	Lee Smith	1.00
47	Doug Bird	.50
48	Dickie Noles	.50
---	Team Photo	.50
---	Coaching Staff (Billy Connors, Tom Harmon, Gordy MacKenzie, John Vukovich, Billy Williams)	.50

1991 Retort Negro League Legends, Series 1

MAXWELL "MAX" MANNING

One of the most extensive collectors' issues featuring former Negro League players was issued over a two-year period by Robert Retort Enterprises. Sold only in a boxed set with accompanying history book, the premiere issue featured 65 individual players, plus game-action and team photos. Fronts of the 3-1/2" x 5-1/2" cards feature sepia photos with a sepia border. Player identification is in the bottom border. Postcard style backs specify the teams on which the player appeared, have a card number and a serial number from within the edition of 10,000 sets.

		NM/M
Complete Set (100):		35.00
Common Player:		.50
1	Otha Bailey	.50
2	Harry Barnes	.50
3	Gene Benson	.50
4	Bill Beverly	.50
5	Charlie Biot	.50
6	Bob Boyd	.65
7	Allen Bryant	.50
8	Marlin Carter	.50
9	Bill Cash	.50
10	Jim Cohen	.50
11	Elliott Coleman	.50
12	Johnnie Cowan	.50
13	Jimmie Crutchfield	.65
14	Saul Davis	.50
15	Piper Davis	.65
16	Leon Day	2.00
17	Lou Dials	.75
18	Mahlon Duckett	.50
19	Felix Evans	.50
20	Rudy Fernandez	.50
21	Joe Fillmore	.50
22	George Giles	.50
23	Louis Gillis	.50
24	Stanley Glenn	.50
25	Willie Grace	.50
26	Wiley Griggs	.50
27	Albert Haywood	.50
28	Jimmy Hill	.50
29	Cowan Hyde	.50
30	Monte Irvin	1.50
31	Sam Jethroe	1.00
32	Connie Johnson	.65
33	Josh Johnson	.50
34	Clinton Jones	.50
35	Larry Kimbrough	.50
36	Clarence King	.50
37	Jim LaMarque	.50
38	Buck Leonard	2.00
39	Max Manning	.50
40	Verdell Mathis	.50
41	Nath McClinic	.50
42	Clinton McCord	.50
43	Clyde McNeal	.50
44	John Miles	.50
45	Buck O'Neil	2.00
46	Frank Pearson	.50
47	Art Pennington	.75
48	Nathan Peoples	.50
49	Andy Porter	.50
50	Ted Radcliffe	.50
51	Chico Renfroe	.50
52	Bobby Robinson	.50
53	Tommy Sampson	.50
54	Joe Scott	.50
55	Joe Burt Scott	.50
56	Herb Simpson	.50
57	Lonnie Summers	.50
58	Alfred Surratt	.50
59	Bob Thurman	.50
60	Harold Tinker	.50
61	Quincy Trouppe	.75
62	Edsall Walker	.50
63	Al Wilmore	.50
64	Artie Wilson	.75
65	Jim Zapp	.50
66	Grays vs. Stars 1937	.50
67	Grays vs. Eagles 1943	.50
68	Homestead Grays 1944	.50
69	Grays vs. Cuban Stars 1944	.50
70	Grays vs. Cubans 1944	.50
71	Grays vs. Eagles 1945	.50
72	Eagles Pitching Staff 1941	.50
73	Buckeyes Infield 1945	.50
74	Homestead Grays 1948	.50
75	Chicago Murderers Row 1943	.50
76	Indianapolis Clowns 1945	.50
77	East All-Stars 1937	.50
78	East All-Stars 1938	.50
79	East All-Stars 1939	.50
80	East All-Stars 1948	.50
81	West All-Stars 1948	.50
82	Homestead Grays 1931	.50
83	Homestead Grays 1938	.50
84	Pittsburgh Crawfords 1936	.50
85	Kansas City Monarchs 1934	.50
86	Kansas City Monarchs 1949	.50
87	Chicago American Giants 1941	.50
88	Chicago American Giants 1947	.50
89	Memphis Red Sox 1940	.50
90	Memphis Red Sox 1946	.50
91	Birmingham Black Barons 1946	.50
92	Birmingham Black Barons 1948	.50
93	Birmingham Black Barons 1950	.50
94	Harlem Globetrotters 1948	.50
95	Cleveland Buckeyes 1947	.50
96	Philadelphia Stars 1944	.50
97	Newark Eagles 1939	.50
98	Baltimore Elite Giants 1949	.50
99	Indianapolis Clowns 1943	.50
100	Cincinnati Tigers 1937	.50

1993 Retort Negro League Legends, Series 2

One of the most extensive collectors' issues featuring former Negro League players was issued over a two-year period by Robert Retort Enterprises. Sold only in a boxed set, the Series 2 issue features 41 individual players, plus game-action and team photos. Fronts of the 3-1/2" x 5-1/2" cards feature sepia photos with a white border. Player identification is in the bottom border, which also has space for autographing. Postcard style backs specify the teams on which the player appeared, have a card number and a serial number from within the edition of 10,000 sets.

		NM/M
Complete Set (100):		30.00
Common Player:		.50
1	Frank Barnes	.50
2	John Bissant	.50
3	Garnett Blair	.50
4	Jim "Fireball" Bolden	.50
5	Luther Branham	.50
6	Sherwood Brewer	.50
7	Jimmy Dean	.50
8	Frank Duncan, Jr.	.50
9	Wilmer Fields	.50
10	Harold Gordon	.50
11	Bill Greason	.50
12	Acie Griggs	.50
13	Napoleon Gulley	.75
14	Ray Haggins	.50
15	Wilmer Harris	.50
16	Bob Harvey	.50
17	Jehosie Heard	.65
18	Gordon Hopkins	.50
19	Herman Horn	.50
20	James Ivory	.50
21	Henry Kimbro	.75
22	Milford Laurent	.50
23	Ernest Long	.50
24	Frank Marsh	.50
25	Francis Matthews	.50
26	Jim McCurine	.50
27	John Mitchell	.50
28	Lee Moody	.50
29	Rogers Pierre	.50
30	Nathaniel Pollard	.50
31	Merle Porter	.50
32	William Powell	.50
33	Ulysses Redd	.50
34	Harry Rhodes	.50
35	DeWitt Smallwood	.50
36	Joseph Spencer	.50
37	Riley Stewart	.50
38	Earl Taborn	.50
39	Ron Teasley	.50
40	Joe Wiley	.50
41	Buck Leonard	2.00
42	Grays vs. Giants 1945	.50
43	Grays vs. Monarchs 1945	.50
44	Homestead Grays 1948	.50
45	Pittsburgh Crawfords 1928	.50
46	Pittsburgh Crawfords 1935	.50
47	Kansas City Monarchs 1942	.50
48	Buck O'Neil, William Dismukes	.50
49	Chicago American Giants 1942	.50
50	Nashville Elite Giants 1935	.50
51	Baltimore Elite Giants 1941	.50
52	Birmingham Black Barons 1948	.50
53	Birmingham Black Barons 1959	.50
54	Memphis Red Sox 1954	.50
55	Indianapolis ABCs 1923	.50
56	Harlem Globetrotters 1948	.50
57	Harlem Globetrotters 1948	.50
58	Bismarck Barons 1955	.50
59	Culican 1952	.50
60	Santurce 1947	.50
61	Pittsburgh Crawfords 1928	.50
62	Pittsburgh Crawfords 1932	.50
63	Pittsburgh Crawfords 1935	.50
64	Homestead Grays 1937	.50
65	Homestead Grays 1938	.50
66	Homestead Grays 1940	.50
67	Homestead Grays 1945	.50
68	Homestead Grays 1948	.50
69	Kansas City Monarchs 1932	.50
70	Kansas City Monarchs 1934	.50
71	Kansas City Monarchs 1941	.50
72	Kansas City Monarchs 1946	.50
73	Chicago American Giants 1950	.50
74	Memphis Red Sox 1949	.50
75	Birmingham Black Barons 1946	.50
76	Birmingham Black Barons 1948	.50
77	Birmingham Black Barons 1951	.50
78	Birmingham Black Barons 1954	.50
79	St. Louis Stars 1931	.50
80	Newark Dodgers 1935	.50
81	Brooklyn Eagles 1935	.50
82	Newark Eagles 1946	.50
83	Philadelphia Stars 1939	.50
84	Philadelphia Stars 1946	.50
85	Philadelphia Stars 1949	.50
86	Nashville Elite Giants 1935	.50
87	Baltimore Elite Giants 1939	.50
88	Baltimore Elite Giants 1949	.50
89	Cleveland Buckeyes 1947	.50
90	Cincinnati Tigers 1936	.50
91	Miami Ethiopian Clowns 1940	.50
92	Indianapolis Clowns 1944	.50
93	Indianapolis Clowns 1948	.50
94	New York Cubans 1943	.50
95	Harlem Globetrotters 1948	.50
96	House of David 1938	.50
97	E.T. Community 1926	.50
98	Bismarck Giants 1935	.50
99	American All-Stars 1945	.50
100	New York Stars 1949	.50

1988 Revco

This super-glossy boxed set of 33 standard-size cards was produced by Topps for exclusive distribution by Revco stores east of the Mississippi River. Card fronts feature a large blue Revco logo in the upper-left corner opposite a yellow and black boxed "Topps League Leader" label. Player photos are framed in black and orange with a diagonal player identification banner in the lower-right corner. Backs are horizontal, printed in red and black on white stock and include the player name, biographical data, batting/pitching stats and a brief career summary.

		NM/M
Complete Set (33):		4.00
Common Player:		.05
1	Tony Gwynn	.65
2	Andre Dawson	.25
3	Vince Coleman	.05
4	Jack Clark	.05
5	Tim Raines	.05
6	Tim Wallach	.05
7	Juan Samuel	.05
8	Nolan Ryan	1.50
9	Rick Sutcliffe	.05
10	Kent Tekulve	.05
11	Steve Bedrosian	.05
12	Orel Hershiser	.05
13	Rick Rueschel	.05
14	Fernando Valenzuela	.05
15	Bob Welch	.05
16	Wade Boggs	.50
17	Mark McGwire	1.00
18	George Bell	.05
19	Harold Reynolds	.05
20	Paul Molitor	.50
21	Kirby Puckett	.65
22	Kevin Seitzer	.05
23	Brian Downing	.05
24	Dwight Evans	.05
25	Willie Wilson	.05
26	Danny Tartabull	.05
27	Jimmy Key	.05
28	Roger Clemens	.75
29	Dave Stewart	.05
30	Mark Eichhorn	.05
31	Tom Henke	.05
32	Charlie Hough	.05
33	Mark Langston	.05

1996 Revco Cleveland Indians

This set is identified by a logo on front as the "1995 Award Winner Series," but its manner of distribution is unknown. Fronts of the 2-1/2" x 3-1/2" cards have action photos with mottled border. Backs have logos of the 1995 Indians A.L. Championship and of the sponsor, Revco drug stores. Listed on back are the awards earned by the player for the 1995 season. A uniform number also appears, where applicable.

		NM/M
Complete Set (12):		12.00
Common Player:		.50
(1)	Carlos Baerga	.50
(2)	Albert Belle	1.25
(3)	Mike Hargrove	.50
(4)	John Hart (GM)	.50
(5)	Orel Hershiser	1.00
(6)	Kenny Lofton	1.00
(7)	Jose Mesa	.50
(8)	Manny Ramirez	5.00
(9)	Julian Tavares	.50
(10)	Jim Thome	2.50
(11)	Omar Vizquel	1.00
(12)	Cleveland Indians (On-field celebration.)	.50

1985-86 RGI

Renata Galasso Inc.

1988 Rite Aid

This premiere edition was produced by Topps for distribution by Rite Aid discount drug stores in the Eastern U.S. The boxed set includes 33 standard-size full-color cards with at least one card for each major league team. Four cards in the set highlight MVPs from the 1987 season. Card fronts have white borders and carry a yellow "Team MVP's" header above the player photo which is bordered in red and blue. A large Rite Aid logo appears upper-left; the player's name appears bottom center. The numbered card backs are black on blue and white card stock in a horizontal layout containing the player name, biography and statistics.

		NM/M
Complete Set (33):		4.00
Common Player:		.05
1	Dale Murphy	.15
2	Andre Dawson	.15
3	Eric Davis	.05
4	Mike Scott	.05
5	Pedro Guerrero	.05
6	Tim Raines	.05
7	Darryl Strawberry	.05
8	Mike Schmidt	.65
9	Mike Dunne	.05
10	Jack Clark	.05
11	Tony Gwynn	.60
12	Will Clark	.05
13	Cal Ripken, Jr.	1.00
14	Wade Boggs	.60
15	Wally Joyner	.05
16	Harold Baines	.05
17	Joe Carter	.05
18	Alan Trammell	.05
19	Kevin Seitzer	.05
20	Paul Molitor	.50
21	Kirby Puckett	.60
22	Don Mattingly	.65
23	Mark McGwire	.75
24	Alvin Davis	.05
25	Ruben Sierra	.05
26	George Bell	.05
27	Jack Morris	.05
28	Jeff Reardon	.05
29	John Tudor	.05
30	Rick Rueschel	.05
31	Gary Gaetti	.05
32	Jeffrey Leonard	.05
33	Frank Viola	.05

1982 Roy Rogers N.Y. Yankees Lids

Members of the N.Y. Yankees (although in uniform which have the logos removed) are featured on these soft drink lids given away at Roy Rogers restaurants in the metropolitan area. Lids are 3-9/16" in diameter with a red plastic ring around a cardboard disc. At the center of the disc is a black-and-white player portrait photo. Player data appears in colored panels at the sides and in the white center section at bottom. The unnumbered lids are checklisted here in alphabetical order.

		NM/M
Complete Set (12):		35.00
Common Player:		2.50
(1)	Rick Cerone	2.50
(2)	Goose Gossage	3.50
(3)	Ken Griffey	2.50
(4)	Ron Guidry	3.00
(5)	Steve Kemp	2.50
(6)	Jerry Mumphrey	2.50
(7)	Graig Nettles	3.00
(8)	Lou Piniella	3.00
(9)	Willie Randolph	3.00
(10)	Andre Robertson	2.50
(11)	Roy Smalley	2.50
(12)	Dave Winfield	7.50

1993 Rolaids Cubs Relief Pitchers

The Chicago Cubs issued a four-card All-Time Cubs Relief Pitchers set as a giveaway at the September 4, 1993 game at Wrigley Field The four were selected by Cubs fans in a ballot conducted by Rolaids. The standard-sized cards have white borders with a color photo at center. Backs include the player's name, years he pitched for the Cubs, the Rolaids logo and an explanation of the card set's purpose.

		NM/M
Complete Set (4):		4.50
Common Player:		1.00
(1)	Randy Myers	1.00
(2)	Lee Smith	1.50
(3)	Bruce Sutter	2.50
(4)	Mitch Williams	1.00

1993 Nolan Ryan Topps Stickers

Twenty-seven of Nolan Ryan's Topps cards from 1968 through 1992 were reproduced, probably without authorization from Topps or Ryan, in a sticker format for regional distribution in Texas

Week #8

1981

1975

1990

area grocery stores. Printed just slightly smaller than the 2-1/2" x 3-1/2" cards, the stickers were issued in strips of three. When the front picture was peeled away, the back of the sticker could be used as a coupon for specific purchases. Stores known to have participated in the program include: Brookshire Bros., Budget Chopper, Minyards and Super S. Strips of three were generally offered on a weekly basis.

	NM/M
Complete Set, Strips (9):	30.00
Common Sticker:	2.00

1986 Safeway Houston Astros

Though not marked, these 6" x 9" color player photo were given away over the course of several weeks by area Safeway food stores. The pictures are player portraits in uniform, but without caps because they were licensed by the Players Union, but not MLB. The white-bordered pictures have a facsimile autograph and are blank-backed. Unnumbered, the pictures are checklisted here in alphabetical order.

		NM/M
Complete Set (16):		25.00
Common Player:		1.00
(1)	Alan Ashby	1.00
(2)	Kevin Bass	1.00
(3)	Jose Cruz	1.00
(4)	Glenn Davis	1.00
(5)	Bill Doran	1.00
(6)	Phil Garner	1.00
(7)	Billy Hatcher	1.00
(8)	Charlie Kerfeld	1.00
(9)	Bob Knepper	1.00
(10)	Aurelio Lopez	1.00
(11)	Terry Puhl	1.00
(12)	Craig Reynolds	1.00
(13)	Nolan Ryan	15.00
(14)	Mike Scott	1.00
(15)	Dickie Thon	1.00
(16)	Denny Walling	1.00

2005 Ryne Sandberg Jersey Retirement Day

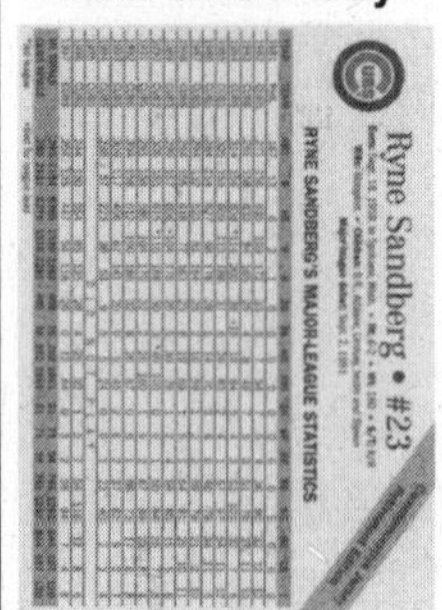

Stadium giveaway August 28.

	NM/M
Ryne Sandberg	6.00

1984 San Diego Padres Fire Safety

This set of 28 full-color 2-1/2" x 3-1/2" cards pictures Padres players, coaches, broadcasters and the Famous Chicken each posing with Smokey the Bear. Smokey's portrait and logo of the California and U.S. Forest Services are printed in the bottom border. Backs offer brief player information and a fire prevention tip. The cards were given away at a home game.

		NM/M
Complete Set (28):		7.00
Common Player:		.25
1	Garry Templeton	.25
2	Alan Wiggins	.25
4	Luis Salazar	.25
6	Steve Garvey	1.00
7	Kurt Bevacqua	.25
10	Doug Gwosdz	.25
11	Tim Flannery	.25
16	Terry Kennedy	.25
18	Kevin McReynolds	.25
19	Tony Gwynn	5.00
20	Bobby Brown	.25
30	Eric Show	.25
31	Ed Whitson	.25
35	Luis DeLeon	.25
38	Mark Thurmond	.25
42	Sid Monge	.25
43	Dave Dravecky	.25
48	Tim Lollar	.25
---	Smokey Logo Card	.25
---	The Chicken (Mascot)	.25
---	Dave Campbell (Broadcaster)	.25
---	Jerry Coleman (Broadcaster)	.25
---	Harry Dunlop	.25
---	Harold (Doug) Harvey (Umpire)	.25
---	Jack Krol (Coach)	.25
---	Jack McKeon (Vice President)	.25
---	Norm Sherry (Coach)	.25
---	Ozzie Virgil (Coach)	.25
---	Dick Williams (Manager)	.25

1986-87 San Diego Padres Fire Safety Flip Books

Differing from the contemporary fire safety issues of its time, the 1986-87 Padres promotional effort took the form of 24-page flip books, rather than cards. About 3-1/2" x 2-1/2", the multi-page black-and-white books offered photographic playing tips when the pictures were rapidly thumbed. When turned over, the books showed Smokey in action preventing forest fires. The 1987 books, McCullers and Santiago, are slightly larger, at about 4-1/2" x 2-3/4".

		NM/M
Complete Set (5):		25.00
Common Player:		4.00
(1)	Dave Dravecky	4.00
(2)	Tim Flannery	4.00
(3)	Tony Gwynn	15.00
(4)	Lance McCullers	4.00
(5)	Benito Santiago	4.00

1988 San Diego Padres Fire Safety

This oversized (3" x 5") set was produced in conjunction with the U.S. Forest Service as a fire prevention campaign promotion. A full-color player photo, framed by a thin white line, fills the card face. The player number, position and Smokey Bear logo appear at lower-right. Backs are printed in horizontal postcard format, with player info and a Smokey Bear cartoon on the left half of the card back. The set was available for purchase at the Padres Gift Shop. Cards of Candy Sierra and Larry Bowa were not officially released and are quite rare.

		NM/M
Complete Set (33):		45.00
Common Player:		.50
(1)	Shawn Abner	.50
(2)	Roberto Alomar	8.00
(3)	Sandy Alomar	3.00
(4)	Greg Booker	.50
(5)	Larry Bowa	15.00
(6)	Chris Brown	.50
(7)	Mark Davis	.50
(8)	Pat Dobson	.50
(9)	Tim Flannery	.50
(10)	Mark Grant	.50
(11)	Tony Gwynn	15.00
(12)	Andy Hawkins	.50
(13)	Stan Jefferson	.50
(14)	Jimmy Jones	.50
(15)	John Kruk	.50
(16)	Dave Leiper	.50
(17)	Shane Mack	.50
(18)	Carmelo Martinez	.50
(19)	Lance McCullers	.50
(20)	Keith Moreland	.50
(21)	Eric Nolte	.50
(22)	Amos Otis	.50
(23)	Mark Parent	.50
(24)	Randy Ready	.50
(25)	Greg Riddoch	.50
(26)	Benito Santiago	1.00
(27)	Eric Show	.50
(28)	Candy Sierra	10.00
(29)	Denny Sommers	.50
(30)	Garry Templeton	.50
(31)	Dickie Thon	.50
(32)	Ed Whitson	.50
(33)	Marvell Wynne	.50

1989 San Diego Padres Magazine/ S.D. Sports inserts

During the course of the 1989 season, a 24-card set sponsored by a local baseball card dealer was offered to collectors as an insert to the team's official game program, "Padres Magazine." The cards were offered in six panels of four cards. Each panel included a former Padres star and a career highlight. To complete the set, at least six copies of the $1.50 program had to be purchased. The 2-1/2" x 3-1/2" cards have color portrait photos on front. Backs have player identification and a career stats line, along with trivia about the player.

		NM/M
Complete Set (24):		15.00
Common Player:		.50
1	Jack McKeon	.50
2	Sandy Alomar Jr.	.50
3	Tony Gwynn	6.00
4	Willie McCovey	2.00
5	John Kruk	.50
6	Jack Clark	.50
7	Eric Show	.50
8	Rollie Fingers	1.50
9	The Alomars (Sandy Alomar, Roberto Alomar, Sandy Alomar Jr.)	.65
10	Carmelo Martinez	.50
11	Benito Santiago	.50
12	Nate Colbert	.50
13	Mark Davis	.50
14	Roberto Alomar	1.50
15	Tim Flannery	.50
16	Randy Jones	.50
17	Dennis Rasmussen	.50
18	Greg Harris	.50
19	Garry Templeton	.50
20	Steve Garvey	1.50
21	Bruce Hurst	.50
22	Ed Whitson	.50
23	Chris James	.50
24	Gaylord Perry	1.50

1990 San Diego Padres Magazine/ Unocal inserts

The first 24 cards in this set, sponsored by area Unocal service stations, were found in four-card panels bound into various issues of Padres Magazine, the team's official program. Sheets measure about 5" x 9" and the individual perforated cards are about 2-1/2" x 3-1/2". A coupon attached to the sheets could be redeemed at participating gas stations for cards #25-27. Fronts have color action photos with team logo at top and sponsor logo at lower-right. Black-and-white backs have player data, a line of career stats and highlights of his time with the Padres.

		NM/M
Complete Set (27):		15.00
Common Player:		.50
1	Tony Gwynn	5.00
2	Benito Santiago	.50
3	Mike Pagliarulo	.50
4	Dennis Rasmussen	.50
5	Eric Show	.50
6	Darrin Jackson	.50
7	Mark Parent	.50
8	Jerry Coleman, Rick Monday (Announcers)	.50
9	Andy Benes	.50
10	Roberto Alomar	2.50
11	Craig Lefferts	.50
12	Ed Whitson	.50
13	Calvin Schiraldi	.50
14	Garry Templeton	.50
15	Tony Gwynn	5.00
16	Bob Chandler, Ted Leitner (Announcers)	.50
17	Fred Lynn	.50
18	Jack Clark	.50
19	Mike Dunne	.50
20	Mark Grant	.50
21	Benito Santiago	.50
22	Sandy Alomar Sr., Pat Dobson, Amos Otis, Greg Riddoch, Denny Sommers	.50
23	Bruce Hurst	.50
24	Greg Harris	.50
25	Jack McKeon	1.00
26	Bip Roberts	1.00
27	Joe Carter	4.00

1991 San Diego Padres Magazine/ Rally's inserts

The first 24 cards of this set were issued as 5" x 8" perforated panels stapled into issues of "Padres Magazine." Due to substitutions dictated by player moves during the season (which also created Short-Printed cards) it would have been necessary to purchase six of the $2 programs to get the 27-card basic set. Cards #25-27 were only available at Rally's restaurants with a coupon attached to the magazine panels. Single cards measure about 2-1/2" x 3-1/2". Fronts have color portrait photos on a diamond background. Player name and position are in an orange banner at bottom. Team and sponsor logos appear in the upper corners on a dark blue background. Backs are in black-and-white with player identification, a line of career stats and highlights of his tenure in San Diego.

		NM/M
Complete Set (30):		27.50
Common Player:		.50
1	Greg Riddoch	.50
2	Dennis Rasmussen	.50
3	Thomas Howard	.50
4	Tom Lampkin	.50
5	Bruce Hurst	.50
6	Darrin Jackson	.50
7	Jerald Clark	.50
8	Shawn Abner	.50
9	Bip Roberts	.50
10	Marty Barrett	.50
11	Jim Vatcher	.50
12	Greg Gross	.50
13	Greg Harris	.50
14	Ed Whitson	.50
15a	Calvin Schiraldi/SP	1.50
15b	Jerald Clark	.50
16	Rich Rodriguez	.50
17	Larry Andersen	.50
18	Andy Benes	.50
19a	Wes Gardner/SP	1.50
19b	Bruce Hurst	.50
20	Paul Faries	.50
21	Craig Lefferts	.50
22	Tony Gwynn	8.00
23a	Jim Presley/SP	1.50
23b	Bip Roberts	.50
24	Fred McGriff	1.00
25	Gaylord Perry	2.00
26	Benito Santiago	1.50
27	Tony Fernandez	1.50

1992 San Diego Padres Fire Safety

The Padres issued a Smokey the Bear postcard set, sponsored by the U.S. Forest Service. Backs contain the usual fire safety messages, but they are also translated into Spanish. Fronts have full-bleed color photos with the player's name and position in orange in a dark blue box at bottom-center. A color Smokey logo appears in one of the upper corners. The unnumbered cards are checklisted here alphabetically.

		NM/M
Complete Set (36):		15.00
Common Player:		.25
(1)	Larry Andersen	.25
(2)	Oscar Azocar	.25
(3)	Andy Benes	.25
(4)	Dan Bilardello	.25
(5)	Jerald Clark	.25
(6)	Pat Clements	.25
(7)	Dave Eiland	.25
(8)	Tony Fernandez	.25
(9)	Tony Gwynn	6.00
(10)	Gene Harris	.25
(11)	Greg Harris	.25
(12)	Jeremy Hernandez	.25
(13)	Bruce Hurst	.25
(14)	Darrin Jackson	.25
(15)	Tom Lampkin	.25
(16)	Bruce Kimm	.25
(17)	Craig Lefferts	.25
(18)	Mike Maddux	.25
(19)	Fred McGriff	.25
(20)	Jose Melendez	.25
(21)	Randy Myers, Craig Shipley	.25
(22)	Gary Pettis	.25
(23)	Rob Picciolo	.25
(24)	Merv Rettenmund	.25
(25)	Greg Riddoch	.25
(26)	Mike Roarke	.25
(27)	Rich Rodriguez	.25
(28)	Benito Santiago	.25
(29)	Frank Seminara	.25
(30)	Gary Sheffield	2.00
(32)	Jim Snyder	.25
(33)	Dave Staton	.25
(34)	Kurt Stillwell	.25
(35)	Tim Teufel	.25
(36)	Kevin Ward	.25

Police

Anti-drug messages are featured on this safety set. The 2-1/2" x 3-1/2" cards have color action photos on front with wide white borders. Backs are horizontally formatted and feature a few player biographical notes, the D.A.R.E. logo and safety message. Unnumbered cards are checklisted here in alphabetical order. Cards #28-30 in this checklist were not distributed with the rest of the set and are scarcer.

		NM/M
Complete Set (30):		12.00
Common Player:		.25
(1)	Oscar Azocar	.25
(2)	Andy Benes	.25
(3)	Jerald Clark	.25
(4)	Jim Deshaies	.25
(5)	Dave Eiland	.25
(6)	Tony Fernandez	.25
(7)	Tony Gwynn	6.00
(8)	Greg W. Harris	.25
(9)	Bruce Hurst	.25
(10)	Darrin Jackson	.25
(11)	Tom Lampkin	.25
(12)	Fred McGriff	.25
(13)	Merv Rettenmund	.25
(14)	Greg Riddoch	.25
(15)	Benito Santiago	.25
(16)	Frank Seminara	.25
(17)	Gary Sheffield	1.00
(18)	Craig Shipley	.25
(19)	Phil Stephenson	.25
(20)	Kurt Stillwell	.25
(21)	Tim Teufel	.25
(22)	Dan Walters	.25
(23)	Kevin Ward	.25
(24)	Padres relievers (Larry Andersen, Mike Maddux, Jose Melendez, Rich Rodriguez, Tim Scott)	.25
(25)	Coaches (Bruce Kimm, Rob Picciolo, Merv Rettenmund, Mike Roarke, Jim Snyder)	.25
(26)	Bluepper (Mascot)	.25
(27)	Jack Murphy Stadium	.25
(28)	Craig Lefferts	1.00
(29)	Rob Picciolo	1.00
(30)	Fred McGriff, Tony Fernandez, Gary Sheffield, Tony Gwynn	2.00

1991 San Francisco Examiner A's

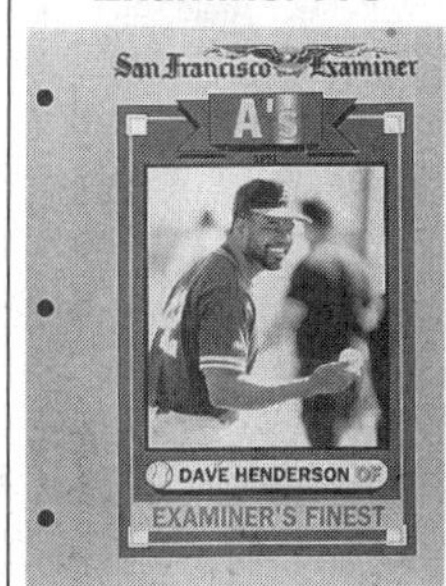

Evidently issued over the course of the season by the Bay Area daily newspaper, these large-format (8-3/8" x 10-7/8") cards are printed on light cardboard pre-punched for a three-ring binder. Color photos on the fronts are surrounded by team colors of green and yellow. The newspaper's logo appears in black at the top. Backs are in black-and-white with a portrait photo of the player, biographical data, major league stats and career highlights. The unnumbered cards are checklisted here alphabetically.

		NM/M
Complete Set (15):		45.00
Common Player:		2.00
(1)	Harold Baines	2.00
(2)	Jose Canseco	5.00
(3)	Dennis Eckersley	5.00
(4)	Mike Gallego	2.00
(5)	Dave Henderson	2.00
(6)	Rickey Henderson	6.00
(7)	Rick Honeycutt	2.00
(8)	Mark McGwire	10.00
(9)	Mike Moore	2.00
(10)	Gene Nelson	2.00
(11)	Eric Show	2.00
(12)	Terry Steinbach	2.00
(13)	Dave Stewart	2.00
(14)	Walt Weiss	2.00
(15)	Bob Welch	2.00

Giants

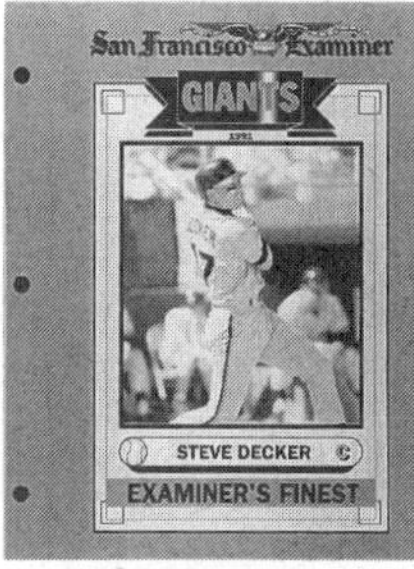

Evidently issued over the course of the season by the Bay Area daily newspaper, these large-format (8-3/8" x 10-7/8") cards are printed on light cardboard pre-punched for a three-ring binder. Color photos on the fronts are surrounded by team-color borders of orange and black on a gray background. The newspaper's logo appears in black at the top. Backs are in black-and-white with a portrait photo of the player, biographical data, major league stats and career highlights. The unnumbered cards are checklisted here alphabetically.

		NM/M
Complete Set (16):		35.00
Common Player:		2.00
(1)	Kevin Bass	2.00
(2)	Mike Benjamin	2.00
(3)	Bud Black	2.00
(4)	Jeff Brantley	2.00
(5)	John Burkett	2.00
(6)	Will Clark	4.00
(7)	Steve Decker	2.00
(8)	Scott Garrelts	2.00
(9)	Mike LaCoss	2.00
(10)	Willie McGee	2.00
(11)	Kevin Mitchell	2.00
(12)	Dave Righetti	2.00
(13)	Don Robinson	2.00
(14)	Robby Thompson	2.00
(15)	Jose Uribe	2.00
(16)	Matt Williams	4.00

2003 Ron Santo Jersey Retirement Card

This high-gloss, 2-1/2" x 3-1/2" card was a Wrigley Field giveaway on Sept. 23, 2003, on the occasion of the Cubs' retirement of the star third baseman's uniform number. The back has Santo's complete Major League stats.

	NM/M
Ron Santo	6.00

1989 SCD Baseball Card Price Guide Pocket Price Guides

Between its premiere issue of April 1988 and the September 1989 issue, SCD's monthly price guide magazine issued a gatefold player poster in each issue. Beginning with the October 1989 issue, panels of five (later six) repli-cards were stapled into the magazine in place of the posters. The

1989 repli-card series depicts contemporary players in the design of the 1964 Topps. Backs are in black-and-white with a photo of the player's rookie card and market advice pertaining to the player.

		NM/M
Complete Set (15):		6.00
Common Player:		.25
1	Mark McGwire	1.50
2	Bo Jackson	.35
3	Ken Griffey	1.50
4	Kevin Mitchell	.25
5	Ryne Sandberg	1.00
6	Will Clark	.25
7	Gregg Jefferies	.25
8	Gary Sheffield	.50
9	Fred McGriff	.25
10	Don Mattingly	1.00
11	Jim Abbott	.25
12	Mitch Williams	.25
13	Glenn Davis	.25
14	Ruben Sierra	.25
15	Robin Yount	.75

1990 SCD Baseball Card Price Guide Pocket Price Guides

For its first full year of inserting repli-cards in each issue, SCD Baseball Card Price Guide Monthly magazine rendered the game's stars and hot rookies in the style of 1957 Topps cards. Black, white and red backs have a photo of one of the player's other cards, personal data, current values of selected cards and market advice. Cards were printed on panels of five stapled into each month's issue.

		NM/M
Complete Set (60):		20.00
Common Player:		.25
1	Darryl Strawberry	.25
2	Wade Boggs	.75
3	Roger Clemens	1.00
4	Paul Molitor	.60
5	Craig Biggio	.25
6	Ruben Sierra	.25
7	Sandy Alomar Jr.	.25
8	Rickey Henderson	.60
9	Mark Langston	.25
10	Dwight Evans	.25
11	Ben McDonald	.25
12	Bo Jackson	.35
13	Don Mattingly	1.00
14	Todd Zeile	.25
15	Mike Greenwell	.25
16	Eric Anthony	.25
17	Dennis Eckersley	.50
18	Greg Vaughn	.25
19	Kevin Mitchell	.25
20	Ryne Sandberg	.75
21	Will Clark	.25
22	Robin Yount	.60
23	Kirby Puckett	.75
24	Andy Benes	.25
25	Wally Joyner	.25
26	Ozzie Smith	.75
27	John Olerud	.25
28	Devon White	.25
29	Alan Trammell	.25
30	Bobby Bonilla	.25
31	Jose Canseco	.40
32	Fred McGriff	.25
33	Mark Grace	.25
34	Ricky Jordan	.25
35	George Brett	1.00
36	Eric Davis	.25
37	Tony Gwynn	.75
38	Cal Ripken Jr.	2.00
39	Bret Saberhagen	.25
40	Howard Johnson	.25
41	Jerome Walton	.25
42	Mark McGwire	1.50
43	A.L. East Power Hitters (Mike Greenwell, Don Mattingly)	.50
44	Ken Griffey Jr.	1.25
45	Texas' Top Twirlers (Nolan Ryan, Mike Scott)	1.00
46	Barry Larkin	.25
47	Delino DeShields	.25
48	Roberto Alomar	.35
49	Frank Viola	.25
50	Kelly Gruber	.25
51	Michael Jordan	7.50
52	Glenn Davis	.25
53	Marquis Grissom	.25
54	Joe Carter	.25
55	Gregg Jefferies	.25
56	Gary Sheffield	.45
57	Cecil Fielder	.25
58	Matt Williams	.25
59	Ramon Martinez	.25
60	Len Dykstra	.25

1991 SCD Baseball Card Price Guide Pocket Price Guides

In its third year of including insert cards with each issue, the Price Guide chose the classic 1971 Topps design to showcase the game's top stars and hot rookies. The first five cards have red backgrounds on their backs, the rest are deep green. Backs have a black-and-white photo of one of the player's other cards, along with selected card value data. Also presented are some personal data and the editors' thoughts on each player's future market value.

		NM/M
Complete Set (60):		15.00
Common Player:		.25
1	Ryne Sandberg	.75
2	Bobby Thigpen	.25
3	Rickey Henderson	.65
4	Dwight Gooden	.25
5	Kevin Maas	.25
6	Ron Gant	.25
7	Frank Thomas	.65
8	Doug Drabek	.25
9	Bobby Bonilla	.25
10	Sandy Alomar Jr.	.25
11	Bob Welch	.25
12	Joe Carter	.25
13	Cecil Fielder	.25
14	Dave Justice	.25
15	Barry Bonds	2.00
16	Barry Larkin	.25
17	Ramon Martinez	.25
18	Ben McDonald	.25
19	Roger Clemens	1.00
20	Jose Canseco	.40
21	Will Clark	.25
22	Jeff Conine	.25
23	Chris Sabo	.25
24	Alan Trammell	.25
25	Howard Johnson	.25
26	Dale Murphy	.30
27	Gregg Jefferies	.25
28	Bo Jackson	.30
29	Craig Biggio	.25
30	Delino DeShields	.25

31	Rafael Palmeiro	.50
32	Robin Yount	.65
33	Mark McGwire	1.50
34	Kevin Mitchell	.25
35	George Brett	1.00
36	Tim Wallach	.25
37	Andre Dawson	.30
38	Kirby Puckett	.75
39	Matt Williams	.25
40	Wade Boggs	.75
41	Dave Winfield	.65
42	Don Mattingly	1.00
43	Carlton Fisk	.65
44	Dave Stewart	.25
45	Ken Griffey Jr.	1.25
46	Ruben Sierra	.25
47	George Bell	.25
48	Cal Ripken	2.00
49	Ellis Burks	.25
50	Roberto Alomar	.30
51	Tim Raines	.25
52	Mike Greenwell	.25
53	Benito Santiago	.25
54	Tom Glavine	.35
55	Scott Erickson	.25
56	Chuck Finley	.25
57	Julio Franco	.25
58	Paul Molitor	.65
59	Todd Van Poppel	.25
60	Mo Vaughn	.25

1992 BB Card Price Guide/Sports Card Price Guide

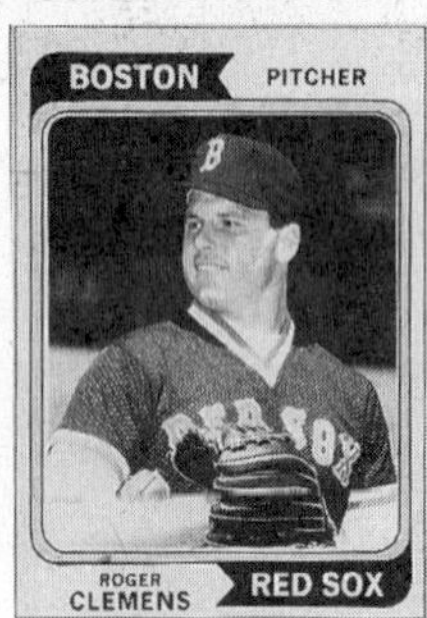

New collector focus on other team sports resulted in SCD's Baseball Card Price Guide Monthly changing its name to Sports Card Price Guide Monthly with its May 1992 issue. The title change was also reflected in the annual series of repli-cards stapled into each issue. For the first time football, basketball and hockey players joined the baseball stars. That change was effective with card #19. The '92 series utilized the design of Topps' 1974 baseball cards. Backs are printed in black, white and green and, as in previous years, include a photo of one of the player's cards along with selective current values and a market forecast. Only the set's baseball players are listed here.

		NM/M
Complete (Baseball) Set (56):		20.00
Common Player:		.25
1	Will Clark	.25
2	Albert Belle	.25
3	Luis Gonzalez	.25
4	Ramon Martinez	.25
5	Frank Thomas	.65
6	Travis Fryman	.25
7	Carlton Fisk	.65
8	Bo Jackson	.35
9	Chuck Knoblauch	.25
10	Ron Gant	.25
11	Jose Canseco	.45
12	Roger Clemens	1.00
13	Darren Lewis	.25
14	Kirby Puckett	.75
15	Tom Glavine	.35
16	Royce Clayton	.25
18	Ozzie Smith	.75
20	Robin Ventura	.25
21	Derek Bell	.25
23	Ryne Sandberg	.75
25	Andy Van Slyke	.25
26	Jim Abbott	.25
27	Ken Griffey Jr.	1.25
30	Jeff Bagwell	.65
32	Dwight Gooden	.25
33	Ruben Sierra	.25
35	David Justice	.25
36	Wade Boggs	.75
38	Barry Larkin	.25
39	Felix Jose	.25
40	Howard Johnson	.25
42	Fred McGriff	.25
44	Todd Van Poppel	.25
46	Brien Taylor	.25
48	Cal Ripken Jr.	2.00
50	Dave Winfield	.65
52	Juan Gonzalez	.40
53	Reggie Sanders	.25
57	Gary Sheffield	.45
58	Roberto Alomar	.40
59	Barry Bonds	2.00
60	Tom Glavine	.35
62	Kenny Lofton	.25
63	Joe Carter	.25
66	Paul Molitor	.65
67	Phil Plantier	.25
69	Mark McGwire	1.50
70	Nolan Ryan	2.00
72	Darryl Strawberry	.25
73	Pat Listach	.25
74	Dennis Eckersley	.50
75	Bobby Bonilla	.25
78	Delino DeShields	.25
80	Doug Drabek	.25
81	Deion Sanders	.25
84	Darren Daulton	.25

1993 Sports Card Pocket Price Guide

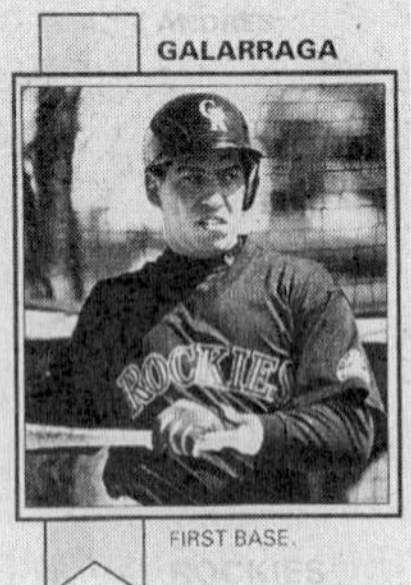

The final year of production of an annual repli-card insert set for the SCD price guide magazine combined stars and hot rookies from all four major team sports. Cards were produced in the style of Topps' 1973 football issue, with varying colored striped pennants down the left side of the front. Backs are printed in black, white and green (#1-8) and black, white and red (#9-104), and include a cartoon trivia question along with price guide and player data. The repli-cards were printed on sheets of eight stapled into the magazine's monthly issues. Only the baseball players are listed here.

		NM/M
Complete (Baseball) Set (54):		20.00
Common Player:		.25
1	Tyler Green	.25
3	Ozzie Smith	.75
5	Fred McGriff	.25
7	Marquis Grissom	.25
13	John Smoltz	.25
16	Ruben Sierra	.25
19	Roberto Alomar	.40
20	Gary Sheffield	.40
23	Carlos Baerga	.25
24	Robin Ventura	.25
25	Nigel Wilson	.25
26	David Nied	.25
27	Cal Ripken Jr.	2.00
28	Albert Belle	.25
34	Larry Walker	.25
37	Eric Karros	.25
38	Dwight Gooden	.25
39	Nolan Ryan	2.00
40	Juan Gonzalez	.45
41	Robin Yount	.65
44	Darryl Strawberry	.25
45	George Brett	1.00
46	Ray Lankford	.25
47	Kirby Puckett	.75
48	David Justice	.25
49	Travis Fryman	.25
50	Eddie Murray	.65
51	Tony Gwynn	.75
52	Jack McDowell	.25
57	Ryne Sandberg	.75
58	Deion Sanders	.25
61	Frank Thomas	.65
62	Carlton Fisk	.65
65	Tim Salmon	.25
66	Jeff Conine	.25
67	Benito Santiago	.25
68	Mike Piazza	1.50
70	Andres Galarraga	.25
71	Gregg Jefferies	.25
76	Joe Carter	.25
77	Rickey Henderson	.65
80	Barry Larkin	.25
82	Juan Gonzalez	.45
83	Gary Sheffield	.40
84	Will Clark	.25
89	Mark Grace	.25
90	Cliff Floyd	.25
91	Bobby Bonds Jr.	.25
92	Barry Bonds	2.00
94	Matt Williams	.25
97	Paul Molitor	.65
98	Ken Griffey Jr.	1.50
99	Steve Avery	.25
100	Kirby Puckett	.65

1989 Schafer's Bakery Super Stars Discs

(See 1989 Holsum for checklist and value information. Distributed in Michigan.)

1987 Schnucks St. Louis Cardinals

Sponsored by Schnucks food stores, and distributed at more than 50 locations around St. Louis, the company is not mentioned anywhere on these photos. The set of 6" x 9" photocards depicts the players without caps or other visible uniform logos in color photos against a plain blue backdrop. A facsimile autograph appears in the lower-left corner, with a Players Association logo at upper-left. Backs are blank. The unnumbered cards are checklisted here alphabetically. A Schnucks spokesman said about 50,000 of each picture were produced.

		NM/M
Complete Set (16):		14.00
Common Player:		.50
(1)	Jack Clark	.50
(2)	Vince Coleman	.75
(3)	Danny Cox	.50
(4)	Curt Ford	.50
(5)	Bob Forsch	.50
(6)	Tom Herr	.50
(7)	Whitey Herzog	.50
(8)	Ricky Horton	.50
(9)	Greg Mathews	.50
(10)	Willie McGee	.75
(11)	Jose Oquendo	.50
(12)	Tony Pena	.50
(13)	Terry Pendleton	.75
(14)	Ozzie Smith	6.00
(15)	John Tudor	.50
(16)	Todd Worrell	.50

1996 Schwebel's Stars Discs

Distributed in loaves of bread in the Youngstown, Ohio, area, the players in this disc set lean heavily towards Cleveland Indians. The 2-3/4" diameter discs were inserted into a special pocket in the bread wrapper to keep them from contact with the bread. Fronts have a purple-to-red graduated color scheme around the border, with a player

photo at center. Uniform logos have been removed from the photos because the discs are licensed only by the Players Union; they are a product of Mike Schechter Assoc. Backs are printed in purple with 1995 and career stats along with appropriate logos. A die-cut poster into which the discs could be inserted for display was also available.

		NM/M
Complete Set (20):		20.00
Common Player:		1.00
1	Jim Thome	1.50
2	Orel Hershiser	1.00
3	Greg Maddux	2.50
4	Charles Nagy	1.00
5	Omar Vizquel	1.00
6	Manny Ramirez	2.00
7	Dennis Martinez	1.00
8	Eddie Murray	2.00
9	Albert Belle	1.00
10	Fred McGriff	1.00
11	Jack McDowell	1.00
12	Kenny Lofton	1.00
13	Cal Ripken Jr.	4.00
14	Jose Mesa	1.00
15	Randy Johnson	2.00
16	Ken Griffey Jr.	3.00
17	Carlos Baerga	1.00
18	Frank Thomas	2.00
19	Sandy Alomar Jr.	1.00
20	Barry Bonds	4.00

1988 Score Promo Cards

While these Score promotional sample cards carry a 1988 copyright date on back, they were actually released to hobby dealers late in 1987. They can be easily differentiated from regular-issue 1988 cards by the use of zeros in the stats lines on back for 1987 and career figures. Most of the promos are otherwise identical to the issued versions of the same players. These were among the first promo cards to be widely distributed within the hobby.

		NM/M
Complete Set (6):		20.00
Common Player:		4.00
30	Mark Langston	4.00
48	Tony Pena	4.00
71	Keith Moreland	4.00
72	Barry Larkin	4.00
121	Dennis Boyd	4.00
149	Denny Walling	4.00

1988 Score Proofs

The first six cards in the eventual 1988 Score debut issue can also be found in proof versions intended to test various inks, finishes, etc. These cards are differentiated from regular issues (and promo cards) by the use of zeros in place of actual stats for 1987 and career on the backs.

		NM/M
Complete Set (6):		150.00
Common Player:		15.00
1	Don Mattingly	45.00
2	Wade Boggs	35.00
3	Tim Raines	15.00
4	Andre Dawson	25.00
5	Mark McGwire	60.00
6	Kevin Seitzer	15.00

1988 Score

A fifth member joined the group of nationally distributed baseball cards in 1988. Titled "Score," the cards are characterized by extremely sharp color photography and printing. Card backs are full-color also and carry a player portrait along with a brief biography, player data and statistics. The 660 cards in the set are standard 2-1/2" x 3-1/2" format. The fronts come with one of six different border colors which are equally divided at 110 cards per color. The Score set was produced by Major League Marketing, the same company that marketed the "triple-action" Sportflics card sets.

		NM/M
Unopened Fact. Set (660):		9.00
Complete Set (660):		6.00
Common Player:		.05
Pack:		.35
Wax Box:		9.00
Rack Pack (54):		.75
Rack Box (24):		12.00
1	Don Mattingly	.65
2	Wade Boggs	.50
3	Tim Raines	.05
4	Andre Dawson	.25
5	Mark McGwire	.75
6	Kevin Seitzer	.05
7	Wally Joyner	.05
8	Jesse Barfield	.05
9	Pedro Guerrero	.05
10	Eric Davis	.05
11	George Brett	.65
12	Ozzie Smith	.50
13	Rickey Henderson	.40
14	Jim Rice	.15
15	Matt Nokes **RC**	.05
16	Mike Schmidt	.65
17	Dave Parker	.05
18	Eddie Murray	.40
19	Andres Galarraga	.05
20	Tony Fernandez	.05
21	Kevin McReynolds	.05
22	B.J. Surhoff	.05
23	Pat Tabler	.05
24	Kirby Puckett	.50
25	Benny Santiago	.05
26	Ryne Sandberg	.50
27	Kelly Downs	.05
28	Jose Cruz	.05
29	Pete O'Brien	.05
30	Mark Langston	.05
31	Lee Smith	.05
32	Juan Samuel	.05
33	Kevin Bass	.05
34	R.J. Reynolds	.05
35	Steve Sax	.05
36	John Kruk	.05
37	Alan Trammell	.05
38	Chris Bosio	.05
39	Brook Jacoby	.05
40	Willie McGee	.05
41	Dave Magadan	.05
42	Fred Lynn	.05
43	Kent Hrbek	.05
44	Brian Downing	.05
45	Jose Canseco	.30
46	Jim Presley	.05
47	Mike Stanley	.05
48	Tony Pena	.05
49	David Cone	.05
50	Rick Sutcliffe	.05
51	Doug Drabek	.05
52	Bill Doran	.05
53	Mike Scioscia	.05
54	Candy Maldonado	.05
55	Dave Winfield	.40
56	Lou Whitaker	.05
57	Tom Henke	.05
58	Ken Gerhart	.05
59	Glenn Braggs	.05
60	Julio Franco	.05
61	Charlie Leibrandt	.05
62	Gary Gaetti	.05
63	Bob Boone	.05
64	Luis Polonia **RC**	.05
65	Dwight Evans	.05
66	Phil Bradley	.05
67	Mike Boddicker	.05
68	Vince Coleman	.05
69	Howard Johnson	.05
70	Tim Wallach	.05
71	Keith Moreland	.05
72	Barry Larkin	.05
73	Alan Ashby	.05
74	Rick Rhoden	.05
75	Darrell Evans	.05
76	Dave Stieb	.05
77	Dan Plesac	.05
78	Will Clark	.05
79	Frank White	.05
80	Joe Carter	.05
81	Mike Witt	.05
82	Terry Steinbach	.05
83	Alvin Davis	.05
84	Tom Herr	.05
85	Vance Law	.05
86	Kal Daniels	.05
87	Rick Honeycutt	.05
88	Alfredo Griffin	.05
89	Bret Saberhagen	.05
90	Bert Blyleven	.05
91	Jeff Reardon	.05
92	Cory Snyder	.05
93	Greg Walker	.05
94	Joe Magrane **RC**	.10
95	Rob Deer	.05
96	Ray Knight	.05
97	Casey Candaele	.05
98	John Cerutti	.05
99	Buddy Bell	.05
100	Jack Clark	.05
101	Eric Bell	.05
102	Willie Wilson	.05
103	Dave Schmidt	.05
104	Dennis Eckersley	.35
105	Don Sutton	.35
106	Danny Tartabull	.05
107	Fred McGriff	.05
108	Les Straker **RC**	.05
109	Lloyd Moseby	.05
110	Roger Clemens	.65
111	Glenn Hubbard	.05
112	Ken Williams **RC**	.05
113	Ruben Sierra	.05
114	Stan Jefferson	.05
115	Milt Thompson	.05
116	Bobby Bonilla	.05
117	Wayne Tolleson	.05
118	Matt Williams	.05
119	Chet Lemon	.05
120	Dale Sveum	.05
121	Dennis Boyd	.05
122	Brett Butler	.05
123	Terry Kennedy	.05
124	Jack Howell	.05
125	Curt Young	.05
126a	Dale Valle (First name incorrect.)	.25
126b	Dave Valle (Correct spelling.)	.05
127	Curt Wilkerson	.05
128	Tim Teufel	.05
129	Ozzie Virgil	.05
130	Brian Fisher	.05
131	Lance Parrish	.05
132	Tom Browning	.05
133a	Larry Anderson (Incorrect spelling.)	.25
133b	Larry Andersen (Correct spelling.)	.05
134a	Bob Brenley (Incorrect spelling.)	.25
134b	Bob Brenly (Correct spelling.)	.05
135	Mike Marshall	.05
136	Gerald Perry	.05
137	Bobby Meacham	.05
138	Larry Herndon	.05
139	Fred Manrique **RC**	.05
140	Charlie Hough	.05
141	Ron Darling	.05
142	Herm Winningham	.05
143	Mike Diaz	.05

144 Mike Jackson **RC** .05
145 Denny Walling .05
146 Rob Thompson .05
147 Franklin Stubbs .05
148 Albert Hall .05
149 Bobby Witt .05
150 Lance McCullers .05
151 Scott Bradley .05
152 Mark McLemore .05
153 Tim Laudner .05
154 Greg Swindell .05
155 Marty Barrett .05
156 Mike Heath .05
157 Gary Ward .05
158a Lee Mazilli (Incorrect spelling.) .25
158b Lee Mazzilli (Correct spelling.) .05
159 Tom Foley .05
160 Robin Yount .40
161 Steve Bedrosian .05
162 Bob Walk .05
163 Nick Esasky .05
164 Ken Caminiti **RC** .15
165 Jose Uribe .05
166 Dave Anderson .05
167 Ed Whitson .05
168 Ernie Whitt .05
169 Cecil Cooper .05
170 Mike Pagliarulo .05
171 Pat Sheridan .05
172 Chris Bando .05
173 Lee Lacy .05
174 Steve Lombardozzi .05
175 Mike Greenwell .05
176 Greg Minton .05
177 Moose Haas .05
178 Mike Kingery .05
179 Greg Harris .05
180 Bo Jackson .10
181 Carmelo Martinez .05
182 Alex Trevino .05
183 Ron Oester .05
184 Danny Darwin .05
185 Mike Krukow .05
186 Rafael Palmeiro .40
187 Tim Burke .05
188 Roger McDowell .05
189 Garry Templeton .05
190 Terry Pendleton .05
191 Larry Parrish .05
192 Rey Quinones .05
193 Joaquin Andujar .05
194 Tom Brunansky .05
195 Donnie Moore .05
196 Dan Pasqua .05
197 Jim Gantner .05
198 Mark Eichhorn .05
199 John Grubb .05
200 Bill Ripken **RC** .05
201 Sam Horn **RC** .05
202 Todd Worrell .05
203 Terry Leach .05
204 Garth Iorg .05
205 Brian Dayett .05
206 Bo Diaz .05
207 Craig Reynolds .05
208 Brian Holton .05
209 Marvelle Wynne (Marvell) .05
210 Dave Concepcion .05
211 Mike Davis .05
212 Devon White .05
213 Mickey Brantley .05
214 Greg Gagne .05
215 Oddibe McDowell .05
216 Jimmy Key .05
217 Dave Bergman .05
218 Calvin Schiraldi .05
219 Larry Sheets .05
220 Mike Easler .05
221 Kurt Stillwell .05
222 Chuck Jackson **RC** .05
223 Dave Martinez .05
224 Tim Leary .05
225 Steve Garvey .20
226 Greg Mathews .05
227 Doug Sisk .05
228 Dave Henderson .05
229 Jimmy Dwyer .05
230 Larry Owen .05
231 Andre Thornton .05
232 Mark Salas .05
233 Tom Brookens .05
234 Greg Brock .05
235 Rance Mulliniks .05
236 Bob Brower .05
237 Joe Niekro .05
238 Scott Bankhead .05
239 Doug DeCinces .05
240 Tommy John .05
241 Rich Gedman .05
242 Ted Power .05
243 Dave Meads **RC** .05
244 Jim Sundberg .05
245 Ken Oberkfell .05
246 Jimmy Jones .05
247 Ken Landreaux .05
248 Jose Oquendo .05
249 John Mitchell **RC** .05
250 Don Baylor .05
251 Scott Fletcher .05
252 Al Newman .05
253 Carney Lansford .05
254 Johnny Ray .05
255 Gary Pettis .05
256 Ken Phelps .05
257 Rick Leach .05
258 Tim Stoddard .05
259 Ed Romero .05
260 Sid Bream .05
261a Tom Neidenfuer (Incorrect spelling.) .25
261b Tom Niedenfuer (Correct spelling.) .05
262 Rick Dempsey .05
263 Lonnie Smith .05
264 Bob Forsch .05
265 Barry Bonds 1.00
266 Willie Randolph .05
267 Mike Ramsey .05
268 Don Slaught .05
269 Mickey Tettleton .05
270 Jerry Reuss .05
271 Marc Sullivan .05
272 Jim Morrison .05
273 Steve Balboni .05
274 Dick Schofield .05
275 John Tudor .05
276 Gene Larkin **RC** .05
277 Harold Reynolds .05
278 Jerry Browne .05
279 Willie Upshaw .05
280 Ted Higuera .05
281 Terry McGriff .05
282 Terry Puhl .05
283 Mark Wasinger **RC** .05
284 Luis Salazar .05
285 Ted Simmons .05
286 John Shelby .05
287 John Smiley **RC** .05
288 Curt Ford .05
289 Steve Crawford .05
290 Dan Quisenberry .05
291 Alan Wiggins .05
292 Randy Bush .05
293 John Candelaria .05
294 Tony Phillips .05
295 Mike Morgan .05
296 Bill Wegman .05
297a Terry Franconia (Incorrect spelling.) .25
297b Terry Francona (Correct spelling.) .05
298 Mickey Hatcher .05
299 Andres Thomas .05
300 Bob Stanley .05
301 Alfredo Pedrique **RC** .05
302 Jim Lindeman .05
303 Wally Backman .05
304 Paul O'Neill .05
305 Hubie Brooks .05
306 Steve Buechele .05
307 Bobby Thigpen .05
308 George Hendrick .05
309 John Moses .05
310 Ron Guidry .05
311 Bill Schroeder .05
312 Jose Nunez **RC** .05
313 Bud Black .05
314 Joe Sambito .05
315 Scott McGregor .05
316 Rafael Santana .05
317 Frank Williams .05
318 Mike Fitzgerald .05
319 Rick Mahler .05
320 Jim Gott .05
321 Mariano Duncan .05
322 Jose Guzman .05
323 Lee Guetterman .05
324 Dan Gladden .05
325 Gary Carter .40
326 Tracy Jones .05
327 Floyd Youmans .05
328 Bill Dawley .05
329 Paul Noce **RC** .05
330 Angel Salazar .05
331 Goose Gossage .10
332 George Frazier .05
333 Ruppert Jones .05
334 Billy Jo Robidoux .05
335 Mike Scott .05
336 Randy Myers .05
337 Bob Sebra .05
338 Eric Show .05
339 Mitch Williams .05
340 Paul Molitor .40
341 Gus Polidor .05
342 Steve Trout .05
343 Jerry Don Gleaton .05
344 Bob Knepper .05
345 Mitch Webster .05
346 John Morris .05
347 Andy Hawkins .05
348 Dave Leiper .05
349 Ernest Riles .05
350 Dwight Gooden .05
351 Dave Righetti .05
352 Pat Dodson .05
353 John Habyan .05
354 Jim Deshaies .05
355 Butch Wynegar .05
356 Bryn Smith .05
357 Matt Young .05
358 Tom Pagnozzi **RC** .05
359 Floyd Rayford .05
360 Darryl Strawberry .05
361 Sal Butera .05
362 Domingo Ramos .05
363 Chris Brown .05
364 Jose Gonzalez .05
365 Dave Smith .05
366 Andy McGaffigan .05
367 Stan Javier .05
368 Henry Cotto .05
369 Mike Birkbeck .05
370 Len Dykstra .05
371 Dave Collins .05
372 Spike Owen .05
373 Geno Petralli .05
374 Ron Karkovice .05
375 Shane Rawley .05
376 DeWayne Buice **RC** .05
377 Bill Pecota **RC** .05
378 Leon Durham .05
379 Ed Olwine .05
380 Bruce Hurst .05
381 Bob McClure .05
382 Mark Thurmond .05
383 Buddy Biancalana .05
384 Tim Conroy .05
385 Tony Gwynn .50
386 Greg Gross .05
387 Barry Lyons **RC** .05
388 Mike Felder .05
389 Pat Clements .05
390 Ken Griffey .05
391 Mark Davis .05
392 Jose Rijo .05
393 Mike Young .05
394 Willie Fraser .05
395 Dion James .05
396 Steve Shields **RC** .05
397 Randy St. Claire .05
398 Danny Jackson .05
399 Cecil Fielder .05
400 Keith Hernandez .05
401 Don Carman .05
402 Chuck Crim **RC** .05
403 Rob Woodward .05
404 Junior Ortiz .05
405 Glenn Wilson .05
406 Ken Howell .05
407 Jeff Kunkel .05
408 Jeff Reed .05
409 Chris James .05
410 Zane Smith .05
411 Ken Dixon .05
412 Ricky Horton .05
413 Frank DiPino .05
414 Shane Mack **RC** .05
415 Danny Cox .05
416 Andy Van Slyke .05
417 Danny Heep .05
418 John Cangelosi .05
419a John Christiansen (Incorrect spelling.) .25
419b John Christensen (Correct spelling.) .05
420 Joey Cora **RC** .05
421 Mike LaValliere .05
422 Kelly Gruber .05
423 Bruce Benedict .05
424 Len Matuszek .05
425 Kent Tekulve .05
426 Rafael Ramirez .05
427 Mike Flanagan .05
428 Mike Gallego .05
429 Juan Castillo .05
430 Neal Heaton .05
431 Phil Garner .05
432 Mike Dunne **RC** .05
433 Wallace Johnson .05
434 Jack O'Connor .05
435 Steve Jeltz .05
436 Donnell Nixon **RC** .05
437 Jack Lazorko .05
438 Keith Comstock **RC** .05
439 Jeff Robinson .05
440 Graig Nettles .05
441 Mel Hall .05
442 Gerald Young **RC** .05
443 Gary Redus .05
444 Charlie Moore .05
445 Bill Madlock .05
446 Mark Clear .05
447 Greg Booker .05
448 Rick Schu .05
449 Ron Kittle .05
450 Dale Murphy .25
451 Bob Dernier .05
452 Dale Mohorcic .05
453 Rafael Belliard .05
454 Charlie Puleo .05
455 Dwayne Murphy .05
456 Jim Eisenreich .05
457 David Palmer .05
458 Dave Stewart .05
459 Pascual Perez .05
460 Glenn Davis .05
461 Dan Petry .05
462 Jim Winn .05
463 Darrell Miller .05
464 Mike Moore .05
465 Mike LaCoss .05
466 Steve Farr .05
467 Jerry Mumphrey .05
468 Kevin Gross .05
469 Bruce Bochy .05
470 Orel Hershiser .05
471 Eric King .05
472 Ellis Burks **RC** .25
473 Darren Daulton .05
474 Mookie Wilson .05
475 Frank Viola .05
476 Ron Robinson .05
477 Bob Melvin .05
478 Jeff Musselman .05
479 Charlie Kerfeld .05
480 Richard Dotson .05
481 Kevin Mitchell .05
482 Gary Roenicke .05
483 Tim Flannery .05
484 Rich Yett .05
485 Pete Incaviglia .05
486 Rick Cerone .05
487 Tony Armas .05
488 Jerry Reed .05
489 Davey Lopes .05
490 Frank Tanana .05
491 Mike Loynd .05
492 Bruce Ruffin .05
493 Chris Speier .05
494 Tom Hume .05
495 Jesse Orosco .05
496 Robby Wine, Jr. **RC** .05
497 Jeff Montgomery **RC** .15
498 Jeff Dedmon .05
499 Luis Aguayo .05
500 Reggie Jackson (1968-75) .15
501 Reggie Jackson (1976) .15
502 Reggie Jackson (1977-81) .15
503 Reggie Jackson (1982-86) .15
504 Reggie Jackson (1987) .15
505 Billy Hatcher .05
506 Ed Lynch .05
507 Willie Hernandez .05
508 Jose DeLeon .05
509 Joel Youngblood .05
510 Bob Welch .05
511 Steve Ontiveros .05
512 Randy Ready .05
513 Juan Nieves .05
514 Jeff Russell .05
515 Von Hayes .05
516 Mark Gubicza .05
517 Ken Dayley .05
518 Don Aase .05
519 Rick Reuschel .05
520 Mike Henneman **RC** .10
521 Rick Aguilera .05
522 Jay Howell .05
523 Ed Correa .05
524 Manny Trillo .05
525 Kirk Gibson .05
526 Wally Ritchie **RC** .05
527 Al Nipper .05
528 Atlee Hammaker .05
529 Shawon Dunston .05
530 Jim Clancy .05
531 Tom Paciorek .05
532 Joel Skinner .05
533 Scott Garrelts .05
534 Tom O'Malley .05
535 John Franco .05
536 Paul Kilgus **RC** .05
537 Darrell Porter .05
538 Walt Terrell .05
539 Bill Long **RC** .05
540 George Bell .05
541 Jeff Sellers .05
542 Joe Boever **RC** .05
543 Steve Howe .05
544 Scott Sanderson .05
545 Jack Morris .05
546 Todd Benzinger **RC** .05
547 Steve Henderson .05
548 Eddie Milner .05
549 Jeff Robinson **RC** .05
550 Cal Ripken, Jr. 1.00
551 Jody Davis .05
552 Kirk McCaskill .05
553 Craig Lefferts .05
554 Darnell Coles .05
555 Phil Niekro .35
556 Mike Aldrete .05
557 Pat Perry .05
558 Juan Agosto .05
559 Rob Murphy .05
560 Dennis Rasmussen .05
561 Manny Lee .05
562 Jeff Blauser **RC** .10
563 Bob Ojeda .05
564 Dave Dravecky .05
565 Gene Garber .05
566 Ron Roenicke .05
567 Tommy Hinzo **RC** .05
568 Eric Nolte **RC** .05
569 Ed Hearn .05
570 Mark Davidson **RC** .05
571 Jim Walewander **RC** .05
572 Donnie Hill .05
573 Jamie Moyer .05
574 Ken Schrom .05
575 Nolan Ryan 1.00
576 Jim Acker .05
577 Jamie Quirk .05
578 Jay Aldrich **RC** .05
579 Claudell Washington .05
580 Jeff Leonard .05
581 Carmen Castillo .05
582 Daryl Boston .05
583 Jeff DeWillis **RC** .05
584 John Marzano **RC** .05
585 Bill Gullickson .05
586 Andy Allanson .05
587 Lee Tunnell .05
588 Gene Nelson .05
589 Dave LaPoint .05
590 Harold Baines .05
591 Bill Buckner .05
592 Carlton Fisk .40
593 Rick Manning .05
594 Doug Jones **RC** .10
595 Tom Candiotti .05
596 Steve Lake .05
597 Jose Lind **RC** .05
598 Ross Jones **RC** .05
599 Gary Matthews .05
600 Fernando Valenzuela .05
601 Dennis Martinez .05
602 Les Lancaster **RC** .05
603 Ozzie Guillen .05
604 Tony Bernazard .05
605 Chili Davis .05
606 Roy Smalley .05
607 Ivan Calderon .05
608 Jay Tibbs .05
609 Guy Hoffman .05
610 Doyle Alexander .05
611 Mike Bielecki .05
612 Shawn Hillegas **RC** .05
613 Keith Atherton .05
614 Eric Plunk .05
615 Sid Fernandez .05
616 Dennis Lamp .05
617 Dave Engle .05
618 Harry Spilman .05
619 Don Robinson .05
620 John Farrell **RC** .05
621 Nelson Liriano **RC** .05
622 Floyd Bannister .05
623 Randy Milligan **RC** .05
624 Kevin Elster **RC** .10
625 Jody Reed **RC** .05
626 Shawn Abner **RC** .05
627 Kirt Manwaring **RC** .10
628 Pete Stanicek **RC** .05
629 Rob Ducey **RC** .05
630 Steve Kiefer .05
631 Gary Thurman **RC** .05
632 Darrel Akerfelds **RC** .05
633 Dave Clark .05
634 Roberto Kelly **RC** .05
635 Keith Hughes **RC** .05
636 John Davis **RC** .05
637 Mike Devereaux **RC** .10
638 Tom Glavine **RC** 1.00
639 Keith Miller **RC** .05
640 Chris Gwynn **RC** .05
641 Tim Crews **RC** .05
642 Mackey Sasser **RC** .05
643 Vicente Palacios **RC** .05
644 Kevin Romine .05
645 Gregg Jefferies **RC** .25
646 Jeff Treadway **RC** .05
647 Ron Gant **RC** .25
648 Rookie Sluggers (Mark McGwire, Matt Nokes) .35
649 Speed and Power (Tim Raines, Eric Davis) .05
650 Game Breakers (Jack Clark, Don Mattingly) .25
651 Super Shortstops (Tony Fernandez, Cal Ripken, Jr., Alan Trammell) .25
652 Vince Coleman (Highlight) .05
653 Kirby Puckett (Highlight) .25
654 Benito Santiago (Highlight) .05
655 Juan Nieves (Highlight) .05
656 Steve Bedrosian (Highlight) .05
657 Mike Schmidt (Highlight) .30
658 Don Mattingly (Highlight) .30
659 Mark McGwire (Highlight) .35
660 Paul Molitor (Highlight) .20

Glossy

With production of a reported 5,000 sets, there is a significant premium attached to the glossy version of Score's debut baseball card issue. The specially packaged collector's edition features cards with a high-gloss front finish and was sold only as a complete set.

	NM/M
Complete Set (660):	65.00
Common Player:	.25
Stars:	15X

Box Panels

This 18-card set, produced by Major League Marketing and manufactured by Optigraphics, is the premiere box-bottom set issued under the Score trademark. The set features 1987 major league All-star players in full-color action poses, framed by a white border. A "1987 All-Star" banner (red or purple) curves above an orange player name block beneath the player photo. Card backs are printed in red, blue, gold and black and carry the card number, player name and position and league logo. Six colorful "Great Moments in Baseball" trivia cards are also included in this set.

	NM/M
Complete Panel Set:	7.50
Complete Singles Set (18):	7.50
Common Panel:	.50
Common Single Player:	.15
Panel 1	1.00
1 Terry Kennedy	.15
3 Willie Randolph	.15
15 Eric Davis	.15
Panel 2	4.50
3 Don Mattingly	1.00
5 Cal Ripken, Jr.	2.00
11 Jack Clark	.15
Panel 3	3.00
4 Wade Boggs	.75
9 Bret Saberhagen	.25
12 Ryne Sandberg	.75
Panel 4	2.50
6 George Bell	.15
13 Mike Schmidt	1.00
18 Mike Scott	.15
Panel 5	2.00
7 Rickey Henderson	.65
16 Andre Dawson	.25
17 Darryl Strawberry	.25
Panel 6	3.50
8 Dave Winfield	.65
10 Gary Carter	.65
14 Ozzie Smith	.75

Traded/Rookie

This 110-card set featuring rookies and traded veterans is similar in design to the 1988 Score set, except for a change in border color. Individual standard-size player cards (2-1/2" x 3-1/2") feature a bright orange border framing action photos highlighted by a thin white outline. The player name (in white) is centered in the bottom margin, flanked by three yellow stars lower left and a yellow Score logo lower right. The backs carry full-color player portraits on a cream-colored background, plus team name and logo, personal information and a purple stats chart that lists year-by-year and major league totals. A brief player profile follows the stats chart and, on some cards, information is included about the player's trade or acquisition. The boxed update set also includes 10 Magic Motion 3-D trivia cards. The cards are numbered with a "T" suffix.

	NM/M
Complete Set (110):	12.00
Common Player:	.05
1 Jack Clark	.05
2 Danny Jackson	.05
3 Brett Butler	.05
4 Kurt Stillwell	.05

5 Tom Brunansky .05
6 Dennis Lamp .05
7 Jose DeLeon .05
8 Tom Herr .05
9 Keith Moreland .05
10 Kirk Gibson .05
11 Bud Black .05
12 Rafael Ramirez .05
13 Luis Salazar .05
14 Goose Gossage .05
15 Bob Welch .05
16 Vance Law .05
17 Ray Knight .05
18 Dan Quisenberry .05
19 Don Slaught .05
20 Lee Smith .25
21 Rick Cerone .05
22 Pat Tabler .05
23 Larry McWilliams .05
24 Rick Horton .05
25 Graig Nettles .05
26 Dan Petry .05
27 Jose Rijo .05
28 Chili Davis .05
29 Dickie Thon .05
30 Mackey Sasser .05
31 Mickey Tettleton .05
32 Rick Dempsey .05
33 Ron Hassey .05
34 Phil Bradley .05
35 Jay Howell .05
36 Bill Buckner .05
37 Alfredo Griffin .05
38 Gary Pettis .05
39 Calvin Schiraldi .05
40 John Candelaria .05
41 Joe Orsulak .05
42 Willie Upshaw .05
43 Herm Winningham .05
44 Ron Kittle .05
45 Bob Dernier .05
46 Steve Balboni .05
47 Steve Shields .05
48 Henry Cotto .05
49 Dave Henderson .05
50 Dave Parker .05
51 Mike Young .05
52 Mark Salas .05
53 Mike Davis .05
54 Rafael Santana .05
55 Don Baylor .05
56 Dan Pasqua .05
57 Ernest Riles .05
58 Glenn Hubbard .05
59 Mike Smithson .05
60 Richard Dotson .05
61 Jerry Reuss .05
62 Mike Jackson .05
63 Floyd Bannister .05
64 Jesse Orosco .05
65 Larry Parrish .05
66 Jeff Bittiger **RC** .05
67 Ray Hayward **RC** .05
68 Ricky Jordan **RC** .05
69 Tommy Gregg **RC** .05
70 Brady Anderson **RC** .50
71 Jeff Montgomery .05
72 Darryl Hamilton **RC** .05
73 Cecil Espy **RC** .05
74 Greg Briley **RC** .05
75 Joey Meyer **RC** .05
76 Mike Macfarlane **RC** .05
77 Oswald Peraza **RC** .05
78 Jack Armstrong **RC** .05
79 Don Heinkel **RC** .05
80 Mark Grace **RC** 1.50
81 Steve Curry **RC** .05
82 Damon Berryhill **RC** .05
83 Steve Ellsworth **RC** .05
84 Pete Smith **RC** .05
85 Jack McDowell **RC** .25
86 Rob Dibble **RC** .05
87 Bryan Harvey **RC** .05
88 John Dopson **RC** .05
89 Dave Gallagher **RC** .05
90 Todd Stottlemyre **RC** .25
91 Mike Schooler **RC** .05
92 Don Gordon **RC** .05
93 Sil Campusano **RC** .05
94 Jeff Pico **RC** .05
95 Jay Buhner **RC** .75
96 Nelson Santovenia **RC** .05
97 Al Leiter **RC** .05
98 Luis Alicea **RC** .05
99 Pat Borders **RC** .05
100 Chris Sabo **RC** .25
101 Tim Belcher **RC** .05
102 Walt Weiss **RC** .05
103 Craig Biggio **RC** 6.00
104 Don August **RC** .05
105 Roberto Alomar **RC** 4.00
106 Todd Burns **RC** .05
107 John Costello **RC** .05
108 Melido Perez **RC** .05
109 Darrin Jackson **RC** .05
110 Orestes Destrade **RC** .05

Traded/Rookie Glossy

Among the scarcest of the major card companies' high-gloss collector's editions of the late 1980s is the 1988 Score Rookie/Traded issue. Production of the regular-finish set was limited in itself and the glossy version is more so, adding a significant premium value.

NM/M
Complete Set (110): 60.00
Common Player: .25
Stars: 3X

Young Superstar Series 1

This 40-card set of 2-1/2" x 3-1/2" cards is divided into five separate eight-card subsets. Similar to the company's regular issue, these cards are distinguished by excellent full-color photography on both front and back. The glossy player photos are centered on a white background and framed by a vivid blue and green border. A player name banner beneath the photo includes the name, position and uniform number. The card backs feature color player portraits beneath a hot pink player name/Score logo banner. Hot pink also frames the personal stats (in green), career stats (in black) and career biography (in blue). The backs also include quotes from well-known baseball authorities discussing player performance. This set was distributed via a write-in offer printed on 1988 Score 17-card package wrappers.

NM/M
Complete Set (40): 3.00
Common Player: .10
1 Mark McGwire 2.50
2 Benito Santiago .10
3 Sam Horn .10
4 Chris Bosio .10
5 Matt Nokes .10
6 Ken Williams .10
7 Dion James .10
8 B.J. Surhoff .10
9 Joe Magrane .10
10 Kevin Seitzer .10
11 Stanley Jefferson .10
12 Devon White .10
13 Nelson Liriano .10
14 Chris James .10
15 Mike Henneman .10
16 Terry Steinbach .10
17 John Kruk .10
18 Matt Williams .10
19 Kelly Downs .10
20 Bill Ripken .10
21 Ozzie Guillen .10
22 Luis Polonia .10
23 Dave Magadan .10
24 Mike Greenwell .10
25 Will Clark .10
26 Mike Dunne .10
27 Wally Joyner .10
28 Robby Thompson .10
29 Ken Caminiti .10
30 Jose Canseco .50
31 Todd Benzinger .10
32 Pete Incaviglia .10
33 John Farrell .10
34 Casey Candaele .10
35 Mike Aldrete .10
36 Ruben Sierra .10
37 Ellis Burks .10
38 Tracy Jones .10
39 Kal Daniels .10
40 Cory Snyder .10

Young Superstar Series 2

This set of 40 standard-size cards and five Magic trivia cards is part of a double series issued by Score. Each series is divided into five smaller sets of eight baseball cards and one trivia card. The design on both series is similar, except for border color. Series I has blue and green borders. Series II has red and blue borders framing full-color player photos. Backs carry color portrait photos and stats in a variety of colors. Young Superstar series were offered via a write-in offer on '88 Score wrappers. For each eight-card subset, collectors were instructed to send two Score wrappers and $1. Complete sets were offered by a number of hobby dealers nationwide.

NM/M
Complete Set (40): 4.00
Common Player: .10
1 Don Mattingly 1.00
2 Glenn Braggs .10
3 Dwight Gooden .10
4 Jose Lind .10
5 Danny Tartabull .10
6 Tony Fernandez .10
7 Julio Franco .10
8 Andres Galarraga .10
9 Bobby Bonilla .10
10 Eric Davis .10
11 Gerald Young .10
12 Barry Bonds 2.00
13 Jerry Browne .10
14 Jeff Blauser .10
15 Mickey Brantley .10
16 Floyd Youmans .10
17 Bret Saberhagen .10
18 Shawon Dunston .10
19 Len Dykstra .10
20 Darryl Strawberry .10
21 Rick Aguilera .10
22 Ivan Calderon .10
23 Roger Clemens 1.00
24 Vince Coleman .10
25 Gary Thurman .10
26 Jeff Treadway .10
27 Oddibe McDowell .10
28 Fred McGriff .10
29 Mark McLemore .10
30 Jeff Musselman .10
31 Mitch Williams .10
32 Dan Plesac .10
33 Juan Nieves .10
34 Barry Larkin .10
35 Greg Mathews .10
36 Shane Mack .10
37 Scott Bankhead .10
38 Eric Bell .10
39 Greg Swindell .10
40 Kevin Elster .10

1989 Score

This set of 660 cards plus 56 Magic Motion trivia cards is the second annual basic issue from Score. Full-color player photos highlight 651 individual players and nine season highlights, including the first Wrigley Field night game. Action photos are framed by thin brightly colored borders (green, cyan blue, purple, orange, red, royal blue) with a baseball diamond logo/player name beneath the photo. Full-color player close-ups (1-5/16" x 1-5/8") are printed on the pastel-colored backs, along with personal information, stats and career highlights. The cards measure 2-1/2" x 3-1/2".

NM/M
Unopened Fact. Set (660): 12.00
Complete Set (660): 9.00
Common Player: .05
Pack (16): .50
Wax Box (36): 10.00
1 Jose Canseco .25
2 Andre Dawson .25
3 Mark McGwire .65
4 Benny Santiago .05
5 Rick Reuschel .05
6 Fred McGriff .05
7 Kal Daniels .05
8 Gary Gaetti .05
9 Ellis Burks .05
10 Darryl Strawberry .05
11 Julio Franco .05
12 Lloyd Moseby .05
13 Jeff Pico **RC** .05
14 Johnny Ray .05
15 Cal Ripken, Jr. .75
16 Dick Schofield .05
17 Mel Hall .05
18 Bill Ripken .05
19 Brook Jacoby .05
20 Kirby Puckett .50
21 Bill Doran .05
22 Pete O'Brien .05
23 Matt Nokes .05
24 Brian Fisher .05
25 Jack Clark .05
26 Gary Pettis .05
27 Dave Valle .05
28 Willie Wilson .05
29 Curt Young .05
30 Dale Murphy .20
31 Barry Larkin .05
32 Dave Stewart .05
33 Mike LaValliere .05
34 Glenn Hubbard .05
35 Ryne Sandberg .50
36 Tony Pena .05
37 Greg Walker .05
38 Von Hayes .05
39 Kevin Mitchell .05
40 Tim Raines .05
41 Keith Hernandez .05
42 Keith Moreland .05
43 Ruben Sierra .05
44 Chet Lemon .05
45 Willie Randolph .05
46 Andy Allanson .05
47 Candy Maldonado .05
48 Sid Bream .05
49 Denny Walling .05
50 Dave Winfield .40
51 Alvin Davis .05
52 Cory Snyder .05
53 Hubie Brooks .05
54 Chili Davis .05
55 Kevin Seitzer .05
56 Jose Uribe .05
57 Tony Fernandez .05
58 Tim Teufel .05
59 Oddibe McDowell .05
60 Les Lancaster .05
61 Billy Hatcher .05
62 Dan Gladden .05
63 Marty Barrett .05
64 Nick Esasky .05
65 Wally Joyner .05
66 Mike Greenwell .05
67 Ken Williams .05
68 Bob Horner .05
69 Steve Sax .05
70 Rickey Henderson .40
71 Mitch Webster .05
72 Rob Deer .05
73 Jim Presley .05
74 Albert Hall .05
75a George Brett ("At age 33 ...") 1.00
75b George Brett ("At age 35 ...") .50
76 Brian Downing .05
77 Dave Martinez .05
78 Scott Fletcher .05
79 Phil Bradley .05
80 Ozzie Smith .50
81 Larry Sheets .05
82 Mike Aldrete .05
83 Darnell Coles .05
84 Len Dykstra .05
85 Jim Rice .15
86 Jeff Treadway .05
87 Jose Lind .05
88 Willie McGee .05
89 Mickey Brantley .05
90 Tony Gwynn .50
91 R.J. Reynolds .05
92 Milt Thompson .05
93 Kevin McReynolds .05
94 Eddie Murray .40
95 Lance Parrish .05
96 Ron Kittle .05
97 Gerald Young .05
98 Ernie Whitt .05
99 Jeff Reed .05
100 Don Mattingly .60
101 Gerald Perry .05
102 Vance Law .05
103 John Shelby .05
104 Chris Sabo .05
105 Danny Tartabull .05
106 Glenn Wilson .05
107 Mark Davidson .05
108 Dave Parker .05
109 Eric Davis .05
110 Alan Trammell .05
111 Ozzie Virgil .05
112 Frank Tanana .05
113 Rafael Ramirez .05
114 Dennis Martinez .05
115 Jose DeLeon .05
116 Bob Ojeda .05
117 Doug Drabek .05
118 Andy Hawkins .05
119 Greg Maddux .50
120 Cecil Fielder (Reversed negative.) .05
121 Mike Scioscia .05
122 Dan Petry .05
123 Terry Kennedy .05
124 Kelly Downs .05
125 Greg Gross .05
126 Fred Lynn .05
127 Barry Bonds .75
128 Harold Baines .05
129 Doyle Alexander .05
130 Kevin Elster .05
131 Mike Heath .05
132 Teddy Higuera .05
133 Charlie Leibrandt .05
134 Tim Laudner .05
135a Ray Knight (Photo reversed.) .40
135b Ray Knight (Correct photo.) .05
136 Howard Johnson .05
137 Terry Pendleton .05
138 Andy McGaffigan .05
139 Ken Oberkfell .05
140 Butch Wynegar .05
141 Rob Murphy .05
142 Rich Renteria **RC** .05
143 Jose Guzman .05
144 Andres Galarraga .05
145 Rick Horton .05
146 Frank DiPino .05
147 Glenn Braggs .05
148 John Kruk .05
149 Mike Schmidt .60
150 Lee Smith .05
151 Robin Yount .40
152 Mark Eichhorn .05
153 DeWayne Buice .05
154 B.J. Surhoff .05
155 Vince Coleman .05
156 Tony Phillips .05
157 Willie Fraser .05
158 Lance McCullers .05
159 Greg Gagne .05
160 Jesse Barfield .05
161 Mark Langston .05
162 Kurt Stillwell .05
163 Dion James .05
164 Glenn Davis .05
165 Walt Weiss .05
166 Dave Concepcion .05
167 Alfredo Griffin .05
168 Don Heinkel **RC** .05
169 Luis Rivera **RC** .05
170 Shane Rawley .05
171 Darrell Evans .05
172 Robby Thompson .05
173 Jody Davis .05
174 Andy Van Slyke .05
175 Wade Boggs .50
176 Garry Templeton .05
177 Gary Redus .05
178 Craig Lefferts .05
179 Carney Lansford .05
180 Ron Darling .05
181 Kirk McCaskill .05
182 Tony Armas .05
183 Steve Farr .05
184 Tom Brunansky .05
185 Bryan Harvey **RC** .05
186 Mike Marshall .05
187 Bo Diaz .05
188 Willie Upshaw .05
189 Mike Pagliarulo .05
190 Mike Krukow .05
191 Tommy Herr .05
192 Jim Pankovits .05
193 Dwight Evans .05
194 Kelly Gruber .05
195 Bobby Bonilla .05
196 Wallace Johnson .05
197 Dave Stieb .05
198 Pat Borders **RC** .05
199 Rafael Palmeiro .35
200 Dwight Gooden .05
201 Pete Incaviglia .05
202 Chris James .05
203 Marvell Wynne .05
204 Pat Sheridan .05
205 Don Baylor .05
206 Paul O'Neill .05
207 Pete Smith .05
208 Mark McLemore .05
209 Henry Cotto .05
210 Kirk Gibson .05
211 Claudell Washington .05
212 Randy Bush .05
213 Joe Carter .05
214 Bill Buckner .05
215 Bert Blyleven .05
216 Brett Butler .05
217 Lee Mazzilli .05
218 Spike Owen .05
219 Bill Swift .05
220 Tim Wallach .05
221 David Cone .05
222 Don Carman .05
223 Rich Gossage .05
224 Bob Walk .05
225 Dave Righetti .05
226 Kevin Bass .05
227 Kevin Gross .05
228 Tim Burke .05
229 Rick Mahler .05
230 Lou Whitaker .05
231 Luis Alicea **RC** .05
232 Roberto Alomar .25
233 Bob Boone .05
234 Dickie Thon .05
235 Shawon Dunston .05
236 Pete Stanicek .05
237 Craig Biggio .05
238 Dennis Boyd .05
239 Tom Candiotti .05
240 Gary Carter .40
241 Mike Stanley .05
242 Ken Phelps .05
243 Chris Bosio .05
244 Les Straker .05
245 Dave Smith .05
246 John Candelaria .05
247 Joe Orsulak .05
248 Storm Davis .05
249 Floyd Bannister .05
250 Jack Morris .05
251 Bret Saberhagen .05
252 Tom Niedenfuer .05
253 Neal Heaton .05
254 Eric Show .05
255 Juan Samuel .05
256 Dale Sveum .05
257 Jim Gott .05
258 Scott Garrelts .05
259 Larry McWilliams .05
260 Steve Bedrosian .05
261 Jack Howell .05
262 Jay Tibbs .05
263 Jamie Moyer .05
264 Doug Sisk .05
265 Todd Worrell .05
266 John Farrell .05
267 Dave Collins .05
268 Sid Fernandez .05
269 Tom Brookens .05
270 Shane Mack .05
271 Paul Kilgus .05
272 Chuck Crim .05
273 Bob Knepper .05
274 Mike Moore .05
275 Guillermo Hernandez .05
276 Dennis Eckersley .35
277 Graig Nettles .05
278 Rich Dotson .05
279 Larry Herndon .05
280 Gene Larkin .05
281 Roger McDowell .05
282 Greg Swindell .05
283 Juan Agosto .05
284 Jeff Robinson .05
285 Mike Dunne .05
286 Greg Mathews .05
287 Kent Tekulve .05
288 Jerry Mumphrey .05
289 Jack McDowell .05
290 Frank Viola .05
291 Mark Gubicza .05
292 Dave Schmidt .05
293 Mike Henneman .05
294 Jimmy Jones .05
295 Charlie Hough .05
296 Rafael Santana .05
297 Chris Speier .05
298 Mike Witt .05
299 Pascual Perez .05
300 Nolan Ryan .75
301 Mitch Williams .05
302 Mookie Wilson .05
303 Mackey Sasser .05
304 John Cerutti .05
305 Jeff Reardon .05
306 Randy Myers .05
307 Greg Brock .05
308 Bob Welch .05
309 Jeff Robinson .05
310 Harold Reynolds .05
311 Jim Walewander .05
312 Dave Magadan .05
313 Jim Gantner .05
314 Walt Terrell .05
315 Wally Backman .05
316 Luis Salazar .05
317 Rick Rhoden .05
318 Tom Henke .05
319 Mike Macfarlane .05
320 Dan Plesac .05
321 Calvin Schiraldi .05
322 Stan Javier .05
323 Devon White .05
324 Scott Bradley .05
325 Bruce Hurst .05

326 Manny Lee .05
327 Rick Aguilera .05
328 Bruce Ruffin .05
329 Ed Whitson .05
330 Bo Jackson .10
331 Ivan Calderon .05
332 Mickey Hatcher .05
333 Barry Jones **RC** .05
334 Ron Hassey .05
335 Bill Wegman .05
336 Damon Berryhill .05
337 Steve Ontiveros .05
338 Dan Pasqua .05
339 Bill Pecota .05
340 Greg Cadaret .05
341 Scott Bankhead .05
342 Ron Guidry .10
343 Danny Heep .05
344 Bob Brower .05
345 Rich Gedman .05
346 Nelson Santovenia **RC** .05
347 George Bell .05
348 Ted Power .05
349 Mark Grant .05
350a Roger Clemens (778 Wins) 2.00
350b Roger Clemens (78 Wins) .60
351 Bill Long .05
352 Jay Bell **RC** .05
353 Steve Balboni .05
354 Bob Kipper .05
355 Steve Jeltz .05
356 Jesse Orosco .05
357 Bob Dernier .05
358 Mickey Tettleton .05
359 Duane Ward **RC** .05
360 Darrin Jackson **RC** .05
361 Rey Quinones .05
362 Mark Grace .05
363 Steve Lake .05
364 Pat Perry .05
365 Terry Steinbach .05
366 Alan Ashby .05
367 Jeff Montgomery .05
368 Steve Buechele .05
369 Chris Brown .05
370 Orel Hershiser .05
371 Todd Benzinger .05
372 Ron Gant .05
373 Paul Assenmacher **RC** .05
374 Joey Meyer .05
375 Neil Allen .05
376 Mike Davis .05
377 Jeff Parrett **RC** .05
378 Jay Howell .05
379 Rafael Belliard .05
380 Luis Polonia .05
381 Keith Atherton .05
382 Kent Hrbek .05
383 Bob Stanley .05
384 Dave LaPoint .05
385 Rance Mulliniks .05
386 Melido Perez .05
387 Doug Jones .05
388 Steve Lyons .05
389 Alejandro Pena .05
390 Frank White .05
391 Pat Tabler .05
392 Eric Plunk **RC** .05
393 Mike Maddux **RC** .05
394 Allan Anderson **RC** .05
395 Bob Brenly .05
396 Rick Cerone .05
397 Scott Terry **RC** .05
398 Mike Jackson .05
399 Bobby Thigpen .05
400 Don Sutton .35
401 Cecil Espy .05
402 Junior Ortiz .05
403 Mike Smithson .05
404 Bud Black .05
405 Tom Foley .05
406 Andres Thomas .05
407 Rick Sutcliffe .05
408 Brian Harper .05
409 John Smiley .05
410 Juan Nieves .05
411 Shawn Abner .05
412 Wes Gardner **RC** .05
413 Darren Daulton .05
414 Juan Berenguer .05
415 Charles Hudson .05
416 Rick Honeycutt .05
417 Greg Booker .05
418 Tim Belcher .05
419 Don August .05
420 Dale Mohorcic .05
421 Steve Lombardozzi .05
422 Atlee Hammaker .05
423 Jerry Don Gleaton .05
424 Scott Bailes **RC** .05
425 Bruce Sutter .40
426 Randy Ready .05
427 Jerry Reed .05
428 Bryn Smith .05
429 Tim Leary .05
430 Mark Clear .05
431 Terry Leach .05
432 John Moses .05
433 Ozzie Guillen .05
434 Gene Nelson .05
435 Gary Ward .05
436 Luis Aguayo .05
437 Fernando Valenzuela .05
438 Jeff Russell .05
439 Cecilio Guante .05
440 Don Robinson .05
441 Rick Anderson **RC** .05
442 Tom Glavine .35
443 Daryl Boston .05
444 Joe Price .05
445 Stewart Cliburn .05
446 Manny Trillo .05
447 Joel Skinner .05
448 Charlie Puleo .05
449 Carlton Fisk .40
450 Will Clark .05
451 Otis Nixon .05
452 Rick Schu .05
453 Todd Stottlemyre .05
454 Tim Birtsas .05
455 Dave Gallagher **RC** .05
456 Barry Lyons .05
457 Fred Manrique .05
458 Ernest Riles .05
459 Doug Jennings **RC** .05
460 Joe Magrane .05
461 Jamie Quirk .05
462 Jack Armstrong **RC** .05
463 Bobby Witt .05
464 Keith Miller .05
465 Todd Burns **RC** .05
466 John Dopson **RC** .05
467 Rich Yett .05
468 Craig Reynolds .05
469 Dave Bergman .05
470 Rex Hudler .05
471 Eric King .05
472 Joaquin Andujar .05
473 Sil Campusano **RC** .05
474 Terry Mulholland **RC** .05
475 Mike Flanagan .05
476 Greg Harris .05
477 Tommy John .10
478 Dave Anderson .05
479 Fred Toliver .05
480 Jimmy Key .05
481 Donell Nixon .05
482 Mark Portugal **RC** .05
483 Tom Pagnozzi .05
484 Jeff Kunkel .05
485 Frank Williams .05
486 Jody Reed .05
487 Roberto Kelly .05
488 Shawn Hillegas .05
489 Jerry Reuss .05
490 Mark Davis .05
491 Jeff Sellers .05
492 Zane Smith .05
493 Al Newman **RC** .05
494 Mike Young .05
495 Larry Parrish .05
496 Herm Winningham .05
497 Carmen Castillo .05
498 Joe Hesketh .05
499 Darrell Miller .05
500 Mike LaCoss .05
501 Charlie Lea .05
502 Bruce Benedict .05
503 Chuck Finley **RC** .05
504 Brad Wellman **RC** .05
505 Tim Crews .05
506 Ken Gerhart .05
507a Brian Holton (Born: 1/25/65, Denver.) .15
507b Brian Holton (Born: 11/29/59, McKeesport.) .05
508 Dennis Lamp .05
509 Bobby Meacham .05
510 Tracy Jones .05
511 Mike Fitzgerald .05
512 Jeff Bittiger **RC** .05
513 Tim Flannery .05
514 Ray Hayward **RC** .05
515 Dave Leiper .05
516 Rod Scurry .05
517 Carmelo Martinez .05
518 Curtis Wilkerson .05
519 Stan Jefferson .05
520 Dan Quisenberry .05
521 Lloyd McClendon **RC** .05
522 Steve Trout .05
523 Larry Andersen .05
524 Don Aase .05
525 Bob Forsch .05
526 Geno Petralli .05
527 Angel Salazar .05
528 Mike Schooler **RC** .05
529 Jose Oquendo .05
530 Jay Buhner .05
531 Tom Bolton **RC** .05
532 Al Nipper .05
533 Dave Henderson .05
534 John Costello **RC** .05
535 Donnie Moore .05
536 Mike Laga .05
537 Mike Gallego .05
538 Jim Clancy .05
539 Joel Youngblood .05
540 Rick Leach .05
541 Kevin Romine .05
542 Mark Salas .05
543 Greg Minton .05
544 Dave Palmer .05
545 Dwayne Murphy .05
546 Jim Deshaies .05
547 Don Gordon **RC** .05
548 Ricky Jordan .05
549 Mike Boddicker .05
550 Mike Scott .05
551 Jeff Ballard **RC** .05
552a Jose Rijo (Uniform number #24 on card back.) .15
552b Jose Rijo (Uniform number #27 on card back.) .10
553 Danny Darwin .05
554 Tom Browning .05
555 Danny Jackson .05
556 Rick Dempsey .05
557 Jeffrey Leonard .05
558 Jeff Musselman .05
559 Ron Robinson .05
560 John Tudor .05
561 Don Slaught .05
562 Dennis Rasmussen .05
563 Brady Anderson .05
564 Pedro Guerrero .05
565 Paul Molitor .40
566 Terry Clark **RC** .05
567 Terry Puhl .05
568 Mike Campbell **RC** .05
569 Paul Mirabella .05
570 Jeff Hamilton **RC** .05
571 Oswald Peraza **RC** .05
572 Bob McClure .05
573 Jose Bautista **RC** .05
574 Alex Trevino .05
575 John Franco .05
576 Mark Parent **RC** .05
577 Nelson Liriano .05
578 Steve Shields .05
579 Odell Jones .05
580 Al Leiter .05
581 Dave Stapleton **RC** .05
582 1988 World Series (Jose Canseco, Kirk Gibson, Orel Hershiser, Dave Stewart) .10
583 Donnie Hill .05
584 Chuck Jackson .05
585 Rene Gonzales **RC** .05
586 Tracy Woodson **RC** .05
587 Jim Adduci **RC** .05
588 Mario Soto .05
589 Jeff Blauser .05
590 Jim Traber .05
591 Jon Perlman **RC** .05
592 Mark Williamson **RC** .05
593 Dave Meads .05
594 Jim Eisenreich .05
595a Paul Gibson **RC** (Player in background adjusting cup.) .25
595b Paul Gibson **RC** (Hand airbrushed away.) .05
596 Mike Birkbeck .05
597 Terry Francona .05
598 Paul Zuvella **RC** .05
599 Franklin Stubbs .05
600 Gregg Jefferies .05
601 John Cangelosi .05
602 Mike Sharperson **RC** .05
603 Mike Diaz .05
604 Gary Varsho **RC** .05
605 Terry Blocker **RC** .05
606 Charlie O'Brien **RC** .05
607 Jim Eppard **RC** .05
608 John Davis .05
609 Ken Griffey Sr. .05
610 Buddy Bell .05
611 Ted Simmons .05
612 Matt Williams .05
613 Danny Cox .05
614 Al Pedrique .05
615 Ron Oester .05
616 John Smoltz .05
617 Bob Melvin .05
618 Rob Dibble **RC** .10
619 Kirt Manwaring .05
620 Felix Fermin **RC** .05
621 Doug Dascenzo **RC** .05
622 Bill Brennan **RC** .05
623 Carlos Quintana **RC** .05
624 Mike Harkey **RC** .05
625 Gary Sheffield **RC** 1.25
626 Tom Prince **RC** .05
627 Steve Searcy **RC** .05
628 Charlie Hayes **RC** .05
629 Felix Jose **RC** .05
630 Sandy Alomar **RC** .50
631 Derek Lilliquist **RC** .05
632 Geronimo Berroa .05
633 Luis Medina **RC** .05
634 Tom Gordon **RC** .10
635 Ramon Martinez **RC** .25
636 Craig Worthington **RC** .05
637 Edgar Martinez **RC** .05
638 Chad Krueter **RC** .05
639 Ron Jones **RC** .05
640 Van Snider **RC** .05
641 Lance Blankenship **RC** .05
642 Dwight Smith **RC** .05
643 Cameron Drew **RC** .05
644 Jerald Clark **RC** .05
645 Randy Johnson **RC** 2.00
646 Norm Charlton **RC** .05
647 Todd Frohwirth **RC** .05
648 Luis de los Santos **RC** .05
649 Tim Jones **RC** .05
650 Dave West **RC** .05
651 Bob Milacki **RC** .05
652 1988 Highlight (Wrigley Field) .05
653 1988 Highlight (Orel Hershiser) .05
654a 1988 Highlight (Wade Boggs) ("...sixth consecutive seaason..." on back)) 2.00
654b 1988 Highlight (Wade Boggs) ("Season" corrected.) .10
655 1988 Highlight (Jose Canseco) .15
656 1988 Highlight (Doug Jones) .05
657 1988 Highlight (Rickey Henderson) .10
658 1988 Highlight (Tom Browning) .05
659 1988 Highlight (Mike Greenwell) .05
660 1988 Highlight (Joe Morgan (A.L. Win Streak)) .05

Rookie/Traded

Score issued its second consecutive traded set in 1989 to supplement and update its regular set. The 110-card traded set features the same basic card design as the regular 1989 Score set. The set consists of rookies and traded players pictured with correct teams. The set was sold by hobby dealers in a special box that included an assortment of "Magic Motion" trivia cards. Cards are numbered with a "T" suffix.

NM/M
Complete Set (110): 10.00
Common Player: .05
1 Rafael Palmeiro .35
2 Nolan Ryan 1.00
3 Jack Clark .05
4 Dave LaPoint .05
5 Mike Moore .05
6 Pete O'Brien .05
7 Jeffrey Leonard .05
8 Rob Murphy .05
9 Tom Herr .05
10 Claudell Washington .05
11 Mike Pagliarulo .05
12 Steve Lake .05
13 Spike Owen .05
14 Andy Hawkins .05
15 Todd Benzinger .05
16 Mookie Wilson .05
17 Bert Blyleven .05
18 Jeff Treadway .05
19 Bruce Hurst .05
20 Steve Sax .05
21 Juan Samuel .05
22 Jesse Barfield .05
23 Carmelo Castillo .05
24 Terry Leach .05
25 Mark Langston .05
26 Eric King .05
27 Steve Balboni .05
28 Len Dykstra .05
29 Keith Moreland .05
30 Terry Kennedy .05
31 Eddie Murray .45
32 Mitch Williams .05
33 Jeff Parrett .05
34 Wally Backman .05
35 Julio Franco .05
36 Lance Parrish .05
37 Nick Esasky .05
38 Luis Polonia .05
39 Kevin Gross .05
40 John Dopson .05
41 Willie Randolph .05
42 Jim Clancy .05
43 Tracy Jones .05
44 Phil Bradley .05
45 Milt Thompson .05
46 Chris James .05
47 Scott Fletcher .05
48 Kal Daniels .05
49 Steve Bedrosian .05
50 Rickey Henderson .45
51 Dion James .05
52 Tim Leary .05
53 Roger McDowell .05
54 Mel Hall .05
55 Dickie Thon .05
56 Zane Smith .05
57 Danny Heep .05
58 Bob McClure .05
59 Brian Holton .05
60 Randy Ready .05
61 Bob Melvin .05
62 Harold Baines .05
63 Lance McCullers .05
64 Jody Davis .05
65 Darrell Evans .05
66 Joel Youngblood .05
67 Frank Viola .05
68 Mike Aldrete .05
69 Greg Cadaret .05
70 John Kruk .05
71 Pat Sheridan .05
72 Oddibe McDowell .05
73 Tom Brookens .05
74 Bob Boone .05
75 Walt Terrell .05
76 Joel Skinner .05
77 Randy Johnson 1.50
78 Felix Fermin .05
79 Rick Mahler .05
80 Rich Dotson .05
81 Cris Carpenter **RC** .05
82 Bill Spiers **RC** .05
83 Junior Felix **RC** .05
84 Joe Girardi **RC** .05
85 Jerome Walton **RC** .05
86 Greg Litton **RC** .05
87 Greg Harris **RC** .05
88 Jim Abbott **RC** .05
89 Kevin Brown **RC** .05
90 John Wetteland **RC** .10
91 Gary Wayne **RC** .05
92 Rich Monteleone **RC** .05
93 Bob Geren **RC** .05
94 Clay Parker **RC** .05
95 Steve Finley **RC** .05
96 Gregg Olson **RC** .05
97 Ken Patterson **RC** .05
98 Ken Hill **RC** .05
99 Scott Scudder **RC** .05
100 Ken Griffey Jr. **RC** 6.00
101 Jeff Brantley **RC** .05
102 Donn Pall **RC** .05
103 Carlos Martinez **RC** .05
104 Joe Oliver **RC** .05
105 Omar Vizquel **RC** .25
106 Albert Belle **RC** 1.00
107 Kenny Rogers **RC** .10
108 Mark Carreon **RC** .05
109 Rolando Roomes **RC** .05
110 Pete Harnisch **RC** .05

Rising Stars

Similar in design to the Score Superstar set, this 100-card set showcased a host of rookies. Full-color action photos are surrounded by a bright blue border with a green inner highlight line. Backs display a full-color player portrait above his name and career highlights. The card number and player's rookie year are featured to the right. A "Rising Star" headline highlights the top border. The Score "Rising Star" set was marketed as a combination with a related magazine: "1988-89 Baseball's 100 Hottest Rookies." The set also includes six Magic Motion baseball trivia cards featuring "Rookies to Remember." The magazine/card sets were available at a select group of retailers.

NM/M
Complete Set (100): 5.00
Common Player: .10
1 Gregg Jefferies .10
2 Vicente Palacios .10
3 Cameron Drew .10
4 Doug Dascenzo .10
5 Luis Medina .10
6 Craig Worthington .10
7 Rob Ducey .10
8 Hal Morris .10
9 Bill Brennan .10
10 Gary Sheffield .25
11 Mike Devereaux .10
12 Hensley Meulens .10
13 Carlos Quintana .10
14 Todd Frohwirth .10
15 Scott Lusader .10
16 Mark Carreon .10
17 Torey Lovullo .10
18 Randy Velarde .10
19 Billy Bean .10
20 Lance Blankenship .10
21 Chris Gwynn .10
22 Felix Jose .10
23 Derek Lilliquist .10
24 Gary Thurman .10
25 Ron Jones .10
26 Dave Justice .10
27 Johnny Paredes .10
28 Tim Jones .10
29 Jose Gonzalez .10
30 Geronimo Berroa .10
31 Trevor Wilson .10
32 Morris Madden .10
33 Lance Johnson .10
34 Marvin Freeman .10
35 Jose Cecena .10
36 Jim Corsi .10
37 Rolando Roomes .10
38 Scott Medvin .10
39 Charlie Hayes .10
40 Edgar Martinez .10
41 Van Snider .10
42 John Fishel .10
43 Bruce Fields .10
44 Darryl Hamilton .10
45 Tom Prince .10
46 Kirt Manwaring .10
47 Steve Searcy .10
48 Mike Harkey .10
49 German Gonzalez .10
50 Tony Perezchica .10
51 Chad Kreuter .10
52 Luis de los Santos .10
53 Steve Curry .10
54 Greg Bailey .10
55 Ramon Martinez .10
56 Ron Tingley .10
57 Randy Kramer .10
58 Alex Madrid .10
59 Kevin Reimer .10
60 Dave Otto .10
61 Ken Patterson .10
62 Keith Miller .10
63 Randy Johnson 2.50
64 Dwight Smith .10
65 Eric Yelding .10
66 Bob Geren .10
67 Shane Turner .10
68 Tom Gordon .10
69 Jeff Huson .10
70 Marty Brown .10
71 Nelson Santovenia .10
72 Roberto Alomar 1.00
73 Mike Schooler .10
74 Pete Smith .10
75 John Costello .10
76 Chris Sabo .10
77 Damon Berryhill .10
78 Mark Grace .20
79 Melido Perez .10
80 Al Leiter .10
81 Todd Stottlemyre .10
82 Mackey Sasser .10
83 Don August .10
84 Jeff Treadway .10
85 Jody Reed .10
86 Mike Campbell .10
87 Ron Gant .10
88 Ricky Jordan .10
89 Terry Clark .10
90 Roberto Kelly .10
91 Pat Borders .10
92 Bryan Harvey .10
93 Joey Meyer .10
94 Tim Belcher .10
95 Walt Weiss .10
96 Dave Gallagher .10
97 Mike Macfarlane .10
98 Craig Biggio .10
99 Jack Armstrong .10
100 Todd Burns .10

Superstars

This 100-card set features full-color action photos of baseball's superstars, and six Magic Motion "Rookies to Remember" baseball trivia cards. Card fronts have a bright red border with a blue line inside highlighting the photo. The player ID is displayed in overlapping triangles of white, green, and yellow. The flip side features a full-color player close-up directly beneath a bright red "Superstar" headline. The set was marketed along with the magazine "1989 Baseball's 100 Hottest Players," at select retailers.

		NM/M
Complete Set (100):		6.00
Common Player:		.05
1	Jose Canseco	.35
2	David Cone	.05
3	Dave Winfield	.50
4	George Brett	.75
5	Frank Viola	.05
6	Cory Snyder	.05
7	Alan Trammell	.05
8	Dwight Evans	.05
9	Tim Leary	.05
10	Don Mattingly	.75
11	Kirby Puckett	.65
12	Carney Lansford	.05
13	Dennis Martinez	.05
14	Kent Hrbek	.05
15	Doc Gooden	.05
16	Dennis Eckersley	.40
17	Kevin Seitzer	.05
18	Lee Smith	.05
19	Danny Tartabull	.05
20	Gerald Perry	.05
21	Gary Gaetti	.05
22	Rick Reuschel	.05
23	Keith Hernandez	.05
24	Jeff Reardon	.05
25	Mark McGwire	.85
26	Juan Samuel	.05
27	Jack Clark	.05
28	Robin Yount	.50
29	Steve Bedrosian	.05
30	Kirk Gibson	.05
31	Barry Bonds	1.00
32	Dan Plesac	.05
33	Steve Sax	.05
34	Jeff Robinson	.05
35	Orel Hershiser	.05
36	Julio Franco	.05
37	Dave Righetti	.05
38	Bob Knepper	.05
39	Carlton Fisk	.50
40	Tony Gwynn	.65
41	Doug Jones	.05
42	Bobby Bonilla	.05
43	Ellis Burks	.05
44	Pedro Guerrero	.05
45	Rickey Henderson	.50
46	Glenn Davis	.05
47	Benny Santiago	.05
48	Greg Maddux	.65
49	Teddy Higuera	.05
50	Darryl Strawberry	.05
51	Ozzie Guillen	.05
52	Barry Larkin	.05
53	Tony Fernandez	.05
54	Ryne Sandberg	.65
55	Joe Carter	.05
56	Rafael Palmeiro	.40
57	Paul Molitor	.50
58	Eric Davis	.05
59	Mike Henneman	.05
60	Mike Scott	.05
61	Tom Browning	.05
62	Mark Davis	.05
63	Tom Henke	.05
64	Nolan Ryan	1.00
65	Fred McGriff	.05
66	Dale Murphy	.20
67	Mark Langston	.05
68	Bobby Thigpen	.05
69	Mark Gubicza	.05
70	Mike Greenwell	.05
71	Ron Darling	.05
72	Gerald Young	.05
73	Wally Joyner	.05
74	Andres Galarraga	.05
75	Danny Jackson	.05
76	Mike Schmidt	.75
77	Cal Ripken, Jr.	1.00
78	Alvin Davis	.05
79	Bruce Hurst	.05
80	Andre Dawson	.25
81	Bob Boone	.05
82	Harold Reynolds	.05
83	Eddie Murray	.50
84	Robby Thompson	.05
85	Will Clark	.05
86	Vince Coleman	.05
87	Doug Drabek	.05
88	Ozzie Smith	.65
89	Bob Welch	.05
90	Roger Clemens	.75
91	George Bell	.05
92	Andy Van Slyke	.05
93	Willie McGee	.05
94	Todd Worrell	.05
95	Tim Raines	.05
96	Kevin McReynolds	.05
97	John Franco	.05
98	Jim Gott	.05
99	Johnny Ray	.05
100	Wade Boggs	.65

Yankees

This team set was sponsored by National Westminster Bank and produced by

Score as an in-stadium promotion in 1989; distributed to fans attending the July 29 game at Yankee Stadium. The standard-size cards include a full-color player photo with a line drawing of the famous Yankee Stadium facade running along the top of the card. The player's name, "New York Yankees" and position appear below the photo. A second full-color photo is included on the back of the card, along with stats, data and a brief player profile. The set includes a special Thurman Munson commemorative card.

		NM/M
Complete Set (33):		4.00
Common Player:		.15
1	Don Mattingly	2.00
2	Steve Sax	.15
3	Alvaro Espinoza	.15
4	Luis Polonia	.15
5	Jesse Barfield	.15
6	Dave Righetti	.15
7	Dave Winfield	1.00
8	John Candelaria	.15
9	Wayne Tolleson	.15
10	Ken Phelps	.15
11	Rafael Santana	.15
12	Don Slaught	.15
13	Mike Pagliarulo	.15
14	Lance McCullers	.15
15	Dave LaPoint	.15
16	Dale Mohorcic	.15
17	Steve Balboni	.15
18	Roberto Kelly	.15
19	Andy Hawkins	.15
20	Mel Hall	.15
21	Tom Brookens	.15
22	Deion Sanders	.50
23	Richard Dotson	.15
24	Lee Guetterman	.15
25	Bob Geren	.15
26	Jimmy Jones	.15
27	Chuck Cary	.15
28	Ron Guidry	.25
29	Hal Morris	.15
30	Clay Parker	.15
31	Dallas Green	.15
32	Thurman Munson	1.00
33	Sponsor card	.05

Young Superstars Series 1

These standard-size cards (2-1/2" x 3-1/2") display color action photos with a high-gloss finish. Fronts feature a red and blue border surrounding the photo with the team logo in the lower right. A red band beneath the photo provides the setting for the player ID including name, position, and uniform number. Backs feature a red "Young Superstar" headline above a portrait photo. Above the headline appears the player's personal information and statistics in orange and black. To the right photo a condensed scouting report and career hightlights are revealed. The card number and related logos appear on the bottom portion. Five trivia cards featuring "A Year to Remember" accompanied the series. Each trivia card relates to a highlight from the past 56 years. This set was distributed via a write-in offer with Score card wrappers.

		NM/M
Complete Set (42):		3.00
Common Player:		.10
1	Gregg Jefferies	.10
2	Jody Reed	.10
3	Mark Grace	.10
4	Dave Gallagher	.10
5	Bo Jackson	.15
6	Jay Buhner	.10
7	Melido Perez	.10
8	Bobby Witt	.10
9	David Cone	.10
10	Chris Sabo	.10
11	Pat Borders	.10
12	Mark Grant	.10
13	Mike Macfarlane	.10
14	Mike Jackson	.10
15	Ricky Jordan	.10
16	Ron Gant	.10
17	Al Leiter	.10
18	Jeff Parrett	.10
19	Pete Smith	.10
20	Walt Weiss	.10
21	Doug Drabek	.10
22	Kirt Manwaring	.10
23	Keith Miller	.10
24	Damon Berryhill	.10
25	Gary Sheffield	.25
26	Brady Anderson	.10
27	Mitch Williams	.10
28	Roberto Alomar	.25
29	Bobby Thigpen	.10
30	Bryan Harvey	.10
31	Jose Rijo	.10
32	Dave West	.10
33	Joey Meyer	.10
34	Allan Anderson	.10
35	Rafael Palmeiro	.75
36	Tim Belcher	.10
37	John Smiley	.10
38	Mackey Sasser	.10
39	Greg Maddux	1.00
40	Ramon Martinez	.10
41	Randy Myers	.10
42	Scott Bankhead	.10

Young Superstars Series 2

Score followed up with a second series of Young Superstars in 1989. The second series also included 42 cards and featured the same design as the first series. The set was also distributed via a write-in offer with Score card wrappers.

		NM/M
Complete Set (42):		10.00
Common Player:		.10
1	Sandy Alomar	.10
2	Tom Gordon	.10
3	Ron Jones	.10
4	Todd Burns	.10
5	Paul O'Neill	.10
6	Gene Larkin	.10
7	Eric King	.10
8	Jeff Robinson	.10
9	Bill Wegman	.10
10	Cecil Espy	.10
11	Jose Guzman	.10
12	Kelly Gruber	.10
13	Duane Ward	.10
14	Mark Gubicza	.10
15	Norm Charlton	.10
16	Jose Oquendo	.10
17	Geronimo Berroa	.10
18	Ken Griffey Jr.	9.00
19	Lance McCullers	.10
20	Todd Stottlemyre	.10
21	Craig Worthington	.10
22	Mike Devereaux	.10
23	Tom Glavine	.50
24	Dale Sveum	.10
25	Roberto Kelly	.10
26	Luis Medina	.10
27	Steve Searcy	.10
28	Don August	.10
29	Shawn Hillegas	.10
30	Mike Campbell	.10
31	Mike Harkey	.10
32	Randy Johnson	1.00
33	Craig Biggio	.10
34	Mike Schooler	.10
35	Andres Thomas	.10
36	Jerome Walton	.10
37	Cris Carpenter	.10
38	Kevin Mitchell	.10
39	Eddie Williams	.10
40	Chad Kreuter	.10
41	Danny Jackson	.10
42	Kurt Stillwell	.10

Scoremasters

This unique 42-card boxed set from Score was reproduced from original artwork done by New York artist Jeffrey Rubin. The paintings are reproduced on a standard-size, white, glossy stock, and the set includes the top stars of the game, plus selected rookies.

		NM/M
Complete Set (42):		8.00
Common Player:		.10
1	Bo Jackson	.20
2	Jerome Walton	.10
3	Cal Ripken, Jr.	2.00
4	Mike Scott	.10
5	Nolan Ryan	2.00
6	Don Mattingly	1.00
7	Tom Gordon	.10
8	Jack Morris	.10
9	Carlton Fisk	.75
10	Will Clark	.10
11	George Brett	1.00
12	Kevin Mitchell	.10
13	Mark Langston	.10
14	Dave Stewart	.10
15	Dale Murphy	.30
16	Gary Gaetti	.10
17	Wade Boggs	.85
18	Eric Davis	.10
19	Kirby Puckett	.85
20	Roger Clemens	1.00
21	Orel Hershiser	.10
22	Mark Grace	.10
23	Ryne Sandberg	.85
24	Barry Larkin	.10
25	Ellis Burks	.10
26	Dwight Gooden	.10
27	Ozzie Smith	.85
28	Andre Dawson	.30
29	Julio Franco	.10
30	Ken Griffey Jr.	1.25
31	Ruben Sierra	.10
32	Mark McGwire	1.50
33	Andres Galarraga	.10
34	Joe Carter	.10
35	Vince Coleman	.10
36	Mike Greenwell	.10
37	Tony Gwynn	.85
38	Andy Van Slyke	.10
39	Gregg Jefferies	.10
40	Jose Canseco	.50
41	Dave Winfield	.75
42	Darryl Strawberry	.10

1990 Score Promos

To preview its 1990 baseball cards, Score pre-released the first 110 cards (#221-330) from its red-bordered series as samples. Subtle differences exist on most cards between the samples and the issued version; most easily spotted is that the samples have no statistics on the 1989 season or career lines. Many cards have different versions

of the career highlight write-ups on the back, as well. A handful of the sample cards were widely distributed to dealers and the hobby press, while others from the sheet were released more sparingly, creating inequities in the number of each card available. As few as two examples are known of some of the superstar cards, making them extremely expensive among the single-player specialists.

		NM/M
Common Player:		5.00
221	Steve Buechele	5.00
222	Jesse Barfield	5.00
223	Juan Berenguer	5.00
224	Andy McGaffigan	5.00
225	Pete Smith	5.00
226	Mike Witt	5.00
227	Jay Howell	5.00
228	Scott Bradley	5.00
229	Jerome Walton	5.00
230	Greg Swindell	5.00
231	Atlee Hammaker	5.00
232	Mike Devereaux	5.00
233	Ken Hill	5.00
234	Craig Worthington	5.00
235	Scott Terry	5.00
236	Brett Butler	5.00
237	Doyle Alexander	5.00
238	Dave Anderson	5.00
239	Bob Milacki	5.00
240	Dwight Smith	5.00
241	Otis Nixon	5.00
242	Pat Tabler	5.00
243	Derek Lilliquist	5.00
244	Danny Tartabull	5.00
245	Wade Boggs	65.00
246	Scott Garrelts	5.00
247	Spike Owen	5.00
248	Norm Charlton	5.00
249	Gerald Perry	5.00
250	Nolan Ryan	150.00
251	Kevin Gross	5.00
252	Randy Milligan	5.00
253	Mike LaCoss	5.00
254	Dave Bergman	5.00
255	Tony Gwynn	65.00
256	Felix Fermin	5.00
257	Greg W. Harris	5.00
258	Junior Felix	5.00
259	Mark Davis	5.00
260	Vince Coleman	5.00
261	Paul Gibson	5.00
262	Mitch Williams	5.00
263	Jeff Russell	5.00
264	Omar Vizquel	5.00
265	Andre Dawson	20.00
266	Storm Davis	5.00
267	Guillermo Hernandez	5.00
268	Mike Felder	5.00
269	Tom Candiotti	5.00
270	Bruce Hurst	5.00
271	Fred McGriff	5.00
272	Glenn Davis	5.00
273	John Franco	5.00
274	Rich Yett	5.00
275	Craig Biggio	5.00
276	Gene Larkin	5.00
277	Rob Dibble	5.00
278	Randy Bush	5.00
279	Kevin Bass	5.00
280	Bo Jackson	12.50
281	Wally Backman	5.00
282	Larry Andersen	5.00
283	Chris Bosio	5.00
284	Juan Agosto	5.00
285	Ozzie Smith	65.00
286	George Bell	5.00
287	Rex Hudler	5.00
288	Pat Borders	5.00
289	Danny Jackson	5.00
290	Carlton Fisk	30.00
291	Tracy Jones	5.00
292	Allan Anderson	5.00
293	Johnny Ray	5.00
294	Lee Guetterman	5.00
295	Paul O'Neill	5.00
296	Carney Lansford	5.00
297	Tom Brookens	5.00
298	Claudell Washington	5.00
299	Hubie Brooks	5.00
300	Will Clark	5.00
301	Kenny Rogers	5.00
302	Darrell Evans	5.00
303	Greg Briley	5.00
304	Donn Pall	5.00
305	Teddy Higuera	5.00
306	Dan Pasqua	5.00
307	Dave Winfield	30.00
308	Dennis Powell	5.00
309	Jose DeLeon	5.00
310	Roger Clemens	90.00
311	Melido Perez	5.00
312	Devon White	5.00
313	Dwight Gooden	5.00
314	Carlos Martinez	5.00
315	Dennis Eckersley	25.00
316	Clay Parker	5.00
317	Rick Honeycutt	5.00
318	Tim Laudner	5.00
319	Joe Carter	5.00
320	Robin Yount	30.00
321	Felix Jose	5.00
322	Mickey Tettleton	5.00
323	Mike Gallego	5.00
324	Edgar Martinez	5.00
325	Dave Henderson	5.00
326	Chili Davis	5.00
327	Steve Balboni	5.00
328	Jody Davis	5.00
329	Shawn Hillegas	5.00
330	Jim Abbott	5.00

1990 Score

The regular Score set increased to 704 cards in 1990. Included were a series of cards picturing first-round draft picks, an expanded subset of rookie cards, four World Series specials, five Highlight cards, and a 13-card "Dream Team" series featuring the game's top players pictured on old tobacco-style cards. For the first time in a Score set, team logos are displayed on the card fronts Card backs include a full-color portrait photo with player data. A one-paragraph write-up of each player was again provided by former Sports Illustrated editor Les Woodcock. The Score set was again distributed with "Magic Motion" trivia cards, this year using "Baseball's Most Valuable Players" as its theme.

		NM/M
Hobby Factory Set (714):		8.00
Retail Factory Set (704):		7.00
Complete Set (704):		6.00
Common Player:		.05
Plastic Pack (16):		.40
Plastic Wax Box (36):		9.00
1	Don Mattingly	.50
2	Cal Ripken, Jr.	1.00
3	Dwight Evans	.05
4	Barry Bonds	1.00
5	Kevin McReynolds	.05
6	Ozzie Guillen	.05
7	Terry Kennedy	.05
8	Bryan Harvey	.05
9	Alan Trammell	.05
10	Cory Snyder	.05
11	Jody Reed	.05
12	Roberto Alomar	.20
13	Pedro Guerrero	.05
14	Gary Redus	.05
15	Marty Barrett	.05
16	Ricky Jordan	.05
17	Joe Magrane	.05
18	Sid Fernandez	.05
19	Rich Dotson	.05
20	Jack Clark	.05
21	Bob Walk	.05
22	Ron Karkovice	.05
23	Lenny Harris **RC**	.05
24	Phil Bradley	.05
25	Andres Galarraga	.05
26	Brian Downing	.05
27	Dave Martinez	.05
28	Eric King	.05
29	Barry Lyons	.05

No.	Player	Value
30	Dave Schmidt	.05
31	Mike Boddicker	.05
32	Tom Foley	.05
33	Brady Anderson	.05
34	Jim Presley	.05
35	Lance Parrish	.05
36	Von Hayes	.05
37	Lee Smith	.05
38	Herm Winningham	.05
39	Alejandro Pena	.05
40	Mike Scott	.05
41	Joe Orsulak	.05
42	Rafael Ramirez	.05
43	Gerald Young	.05
44	Dick Schofield	.05
45	Dave Smith	.05
46	Dave Magadan	.05
47	Dennis Martinez	.05
48	Greg Minton	.05
49	Milt Thompson	.05
50	Orel Hershiser	.05
51	Bip Roberts	.05
52	Jerry Browne	.05
53	Bob Ojeda	.05
54	Fernando Valenzuela	.05
55	Matt Nokes	.05
56	Brook Jacoby	.05
57	Frank Tanana	.05
58	Scott Fletcher	.05
59	Ron Oester	.05
60	Bob Boone	.05
61	Dan Gladden	.05
62	Darnell Coles	.05
63	Gregg Olson	.05
64	Todd Burns	.05
65	Todd Benzinger	.05
66	Dale Murphy	.25
67	Mike Flanagan	.05
68	Jose Oquendo	.05
69	Cecil Espy	.05
70	Chris Sabo	.05
71	Shane Rawley	.05
72	Tom Brunansky	.05
73	Vance Law	.05
74	B.J. Surhoff	.05
75	Lou Whitaker	.05
76	Ken Caminiti	.05
77	Nelson Liriano	.05
78	Tommy Gregg	.05
79	Don Slaught	.05
80	Eddie Murray	.40
81	Joe Boever	.05
82	Charlie Leibrandt	.05
83	Jose Lind	.05
84	Tony Phillips	.05
85	Mitch Webster	.05
86	Dan Plesac	.05
87	Rick Mahler	.05
88	Steve Lyons	.05
89	Tony Fernandez	.05
90	Ryne Sandberg	.45
91	Nick Esasky	.05
92	Luis Salazar	.05
93	Pete Incaviglia	.05
94	Ivan Calderon	.05
95	Jeff Treadway	.05
96	Kurt Stillwell	.05
97	Gary Sheffield	.30
98	Jeffrey Leonard	.05
99	Andres Thomas	.05
100	Roberto Kelly	.05
101	Alvaro Espinoza **RC**	.05
102	Greg Gagne	.05
103	John Farrell	.05
104	Willie Wilson	.05
105	Glenn Braggs	.05
106	Chet Lemon	.05
107	Jamie Moyer	.05
108	Chuck Crim	.05
109	Dave Valle	.05
110	Walt Weiss	.05
111	Larry Sheets	.05
112	Don Robinson	.05
113	Danny Heep	.05
114	Carmelo Martinez	.05
115	Dave Gallagher	.05
116	Mike LaValliere	.05
117	Bob McClure	.05
118	Rene Gonzales	.05
119	Mark Parent	.05
120	Wally Joyner	.05
121	Mark Gubicza	.05
122	Tony Pena	.05
123	Carmen Castillo	.05
124	Howard Johnson	.05
125	Steve Sax	.05
126	Tim Belcher	.05
127	Tim Burke	.05
128	Al Newman	.05
129	Dennis Rasmussen	.05
130	Doug Jones	.05
131	Fred Lynn	.05
132	Jeff Hamilton	.05
133	German Gonzalez	.05
134	John Morris	.05
135	Dave Parker	.05
136	Gary Pettis	.05
137	Dennis Boyd	.05
138	Candy Maldonado	.05
139	Rick Cerone	.05
140	George Brett	.50
141	Dave Clark	.05
142	Dickie Thon	.05
143	Junior Ortiz	.05
144	Don August	.05
145	Gary Gaetti	.05
146	Kirt Manwaring	.05
147	Jeff Reed	.05
148	Jose Alvarez **RC**	.05
149	Mike Schooler	.05
150	Mark Grace	.05
151	Geronimo Berroa	.05
152	Barry Jones	.05
153	Geno Petralli	.05
154	Jim Deshaies	.05
155	Barry Larkin	.05
156	Alfredo Griffin	.05
157	Tom Henke	.05
158	Mike Jeffcoat **RC**	.05
159	Bob Welch	.05
160	Julio Franco	.05
161	Henry Cotto	.05
162	Terry Steinbach	.05
163	Damon Berryhill	.05
164	Tim Crews	.05
165	Tom Browning	.05
166	Frd Manrique	.05
167	Harold Reynolds	.05
168a	Ron Hassey (Uniform #27 on back.)	.05
168b	Ron Hassey (Uniform #24 on back.)	.50
169	Shawon Dunston	.05
170	Bobby Bonilla	.05
171	Tom Herr	.05
172	Mike Heath	.05
173	Rich Gedman	.05
174	Bill Ripken	.05
175	Pete O'Brien	.05
176a	Lloyd McClendon (Uniform number 1 on back.)	.50
176b	Lloyd McClendon (Uniform number 10 on back.)	.05
177	Brian Holton	.05
178	Jeff Blauser	.05
179	Jim Eisenreich	.05
180	Bert Blyleven	.05
181	Rob Murphy	.05
182	Bill Doran	.05
183	Curt Ford	.05
184	Mike Henneman	.05
185	Eric Davis	.05
186	Lance McCullers	.05
187	Steve Davis **RC**	.05
188	Bill Wegman	.05
189	Brian Harper	.05
190	Mike Moore	.05
191	Dale Mohorcic	.05
192	Tim Wallach	.05
193	Keith Hernandez	.05
194	Dave Righetti	.05
195a	Bret Saberhagen ("Joke" on card back.)	.10
195b	Bret Saberhagen ("Joker" on card back.)	.30
196	Paul Kilgus	.05
197	Bud Black	.05
198	Juan Samuel	.05
199	Kevin Seitzer	.05
200	Darryl Strawberry	.05
201	Dave Steib	.05
202	Charlie Hough	.05
203	Jack Morris	.05
204	Rance Mulliniks	.05
205	Alvin Davis	.05
206	Jack Howell	.05
207	Ken Patterson **RC**	.05
208	Terry Pendleton	.05
209	Craig Lefferts	.05
210	Kevin Brown **RC**	.05
211	Dan Petry	.05
212	Dave Leiper	.05
213	Daryl Boston	.05
214	Kevin Hickey **RC**	.05
215	Mike Krukow	.05
216	Terry Francona	.05
217	Kirk McCaskill	.05
218	Scott Bailes	.05
219	Bob Forsch	.05
220	Mike Aldrete	.05
221	Steve Buechele	.05
222	Jesse Barfield	.05
223	Juan Berenguer	.05
224	Andy McGaffigan	.05
225	Pete Smith	.05
226	Mike Witt	.05
227	Jay Howell	.05
228	Scott Bradley	.05
229	Jerome Walton **RC**	.05
230	Greg Swindell	.05
231	Atlee Hammaker	.05
232a	Mike Devereaux (RF)	.05
232b	Mike Devereaux (CF)	2.00
233	Ken Hill	.05
234	Craig Worthington	.05
235	Scott Terry	.05
236	Brett Butler	.05
237	Doyle Alexander	.05
238	Dave Anderson	.05
239	Bob Milacki	.05
240	Dwight Smith	.05
241	Otis Nixon	.05
242	Pat Tabler	.05
243	Derek Lilliquist	.05
244	Danny Tartabull	.05
245	Wade Boggs	.45
246	Scott Garrelts	.05
247	Spike Owen	.05
248	Norm Charlton	.05
249	Gerald Perry	.05
250	Nolan Ryan	1.00
251	Kevin Gross	.05
252	Randy Milligan	.05
253	Mike LaCoss	.05
254	Dave Bergman	.05
255	Tony Gwynn	.45
256	Felix Fermin	.05
257	Greg Harris	.05
258	Junior Felix **RC**	.05
259	Mark Davis	.05
260	Vince Coleman	.05
261	Paul Gibson	.05
262	Mitch Williams	.05
263	Jeff Russell	.05
264	Omar Vizquel	.05
265	Andre Dawson	.25
266	Storm Davis	.05
267	Guillermo Hernandez	.05
268	Mike Felder	.05
269	Tom Candiotti	.05
270	Bruce Hurst	.05
271	Fred McGriff	.05
272	Glenn Davis	.05
273	John Franco	.05
274	Rich Yett	.05
275	Craig Biggio	.05
276	Gene Larkin	.05
277	Rob Dibble	.05
278	Randy Bush	.05
279	Kevin Bass	.05
280a	Bo Jackson ("Watham" on back.)	.15
280b	Bo Jackson ("Wathan" on back.)	.50
281	Wally Backman	.05
282	Larry Andersen	.05
283	Chris Bosio	.05
284	Juan Agosto	.05
285	Ozzie Smith	.45
286	George Bell	.05
287	Rex Hudler	.05
288	Pat Borders	.05
289	Danny Jackson	.05
290	Carlton Fisk	.40
291	Tracy Jones	.05
292	Allan Anderson	.05
293	Johnny Ray	.05
294	Lee Guetterman	.05
295	Paul O'Neill	.05
296	Carney Lansford	.05
297	Tom Brookens	.05
298	Claudell Washington	.05
299	Hubie Brooks	.05
300	Will Clark	.05
301	Kenny Rogers	.05
302	Darrell Evans	.05
303	Greg Briley	.05
304	Donn Pall	.05
305	Teddy Higuera	.05
306	Dan Pasqua	.05
307	Dave Winfield	.40
308	Dennis Powell	.05
309	Jose DeLeon	.05
310	Roger Clemens	.50
311	Melido Perez	.05
312	Devon White	.05
313	Dwight Gooden	.05
314	Carlos Martinez **RC**	.05
315	Dennis Eckersley	.35
316	Clay Parker	.05
317	Rick Honeycutt	.05
318	Tim Laudner	.05
319	Joe Carter	.05
320	Robin Yount	.40
321	Felix Jose	.05
322	Mickey Tettleton	.05
323	Mike Gallego	.05
324	Edgar Martinez	.05
325	Dave Henderson	.05
326	Chili Davis	.05
327	Steve Balboni	.05
328	Jody Davis	.05
329	Shawn Hillegas	.05
330	Jim Abbott	.05
331	John Dopson	.05
332	Mark Williamson	.05
333	Jeff Robinson	.05
334	John Smiley	.05
335	Bobby Thigpen	.05
336	Garry Templeton	.05
337	Marvell Wynne	.05
338a	Ken Griffey Sr. (Uniform #25 on card back.)	.05
338b	Ken Griffey Sr. (Uniform #30 on card back.)	1.00
339	Steve Finley	.05
340	Ellis Burks	.05
341	Frank Williams	.05
342	Mike Morgan	.05
343	Kevin Mitchell	.05
344	Joel Youngblood	.05
345	Mike Greenwell	.05
346	Glenn Wilson	.05
347	John Costello	.05
348	Wes Gardner	.05
349	Jeff Ballard	.05
350	Mark Thurmond	.05
351	Randy Myers	.05
352	Shawn Abner	.05
353	Jesse Orosco	.05
354	Greg Walker	.05
355	Pete Harnisch	.05
356	Steve Farr	.05
357	Dave LaPoint	.05
358	Willie Fraser	.05
359	Mickey Hatcher	.05
360	Rickey Henderson	.40
361	Mike Fitzgerald	.05
362	Bill Schroeder	.05
363	Mark Carreon	.05
364	Ron Jones	.05
365	Jeff Montgomery	.05
366	Bill Krueger **RC**	.05
367	John Cangelosi	.05
368	Jose Gonzalez	.05
369	Greg Hibbard **RC**	.05
370	John Smoltz	.05
371	Jeff Brantley **RC**	.05
372	Frank White	.05
373	Ed Whitson	.05
374	Willie McGee	.05
375	Jose Canseco	.30
376	Randy Ready	.05
377	Don Aase	.05
378	Tony Armas	.05
379	Steve Bedrosian	.05
380	Chuck Finley	.05
381	Kent Hrbek	.05
382	Jim Gantner	.05
383	Mel Hall	.05
384	Mike Marshall	.05
385	Mark McGwire	.75
386	Wayne Tolleson	.05
387	Brian Holton	.05
388	John Wetteland	.05
389	Darren Daulton	.05
390	Rob Deer	.05
391	John Moses	.05
392	Todd Worrell	.05
393	Chuck Cary **RC**	.05
394	Stan Javier	.05
395	Willie Randolph	.05
396	Bill Buckner	.05
397	Robby Thompson	.05
398	Mike Scioscia	.05
399	Lonnie Smith	.05
400	Kirby Puckett	.45
401	Mark Langston	.05
402	Danny Darwin	.05
403	Greg Maddux	.45
404	Lloyd Moseby	.05
405	Rafael Palmeiro	.35
406	Chad Kreuter	.05
407	Jimmy Key	.05
408	Tim Birtsas	.05
409	Tim Raines	.05
410	Dave Stewart	.05
411	Eric Yelding **RC**	.05
412	Kent Anderson **RC**	.05
413	Les Lancaster	.05
414	Rick Dempsey	.05
415	Randy Johnson	.40
416	Gary Carter	.40
417	Rolando Roomes	.05
418	Dan Schatzeder	.05
419	Bryn Smith	.05
420	Ruben Sierra	.05
421	Steve Jeltz	.05
422	Ken Oberkfell	.05
423	Sid Bream	.05
424	Jim Clancy	.05
425	Kelly Gruber	.05
426	Rick Leach	.05
427	Len Dykstra	.05
428	Jeff Pico	.05
429	John Cerutti	.05
430	David Cone	.05
431	Jeff Kunkel	.05
432	Luis Aquino	.05
433	Ernie Whitt	.05
434	Bo Diaz	.05
435	Steve Lake	.05
436	Pat Perry	.05
437	Mike Davis	.05
438	Cecilio Guante	.05
439	Duane Ward	.05
440	Andy Van Slyke	.05
441	Gene Nelson	.05
442	Luis Polonia	.05
443	Kevin Elster	.05
444	Keith Moreland	.05
445	Roger McDowell	.05
446	Ron Darling	.05
447	Ernest Riles	.05
448	Mookie Wilson	.05
449a	Bill Spiers **RC** (66 missing for year of birth)	.50
449b	Bill Spiers **RC** (1966 for birth year)	.05
450	Rick Sutcliffe	.05
451	Nelson Santovenia	.05
452	Andy Allanson	.05
453	Bob Melvin	.05
454	Benny Santiago	.05
455	Jose Uribe	.05
456	Bill Landrum **RC**	.05
457	Bobby Witt	.05
458	Kevin Romine	.05
459	Lee Mazzilli	.05
460	Paul Molitor	.40
461	Ramon Martinez	.05
462	Frank DiPino	.05
463	Walt Terrell	.05
464	Bob Geren **RC**	.05
465	Rick Reuchel	.05
466	Mark Grant	.05
467	John Kruk	.05
468	Gregg Jefferies	.05
469	R.J. Reynolds	.05
470	Harold Baines	.05
471	Dennis Lamp	.05
472	Tom Gordon	.05
473	Terry Puhl	.05
474	Curtis Wilkerson	.05
475	Dan Quisenberry	.05
476	Oddibe McDowell	.05
477a	Zane Smith (Career ERA 3.93.)	.50
477b	Zane Smith	.05
478	Franklin Stubbs	.05
479	Wallace Johnson	.05
480	Jay Tibbs	.05
481	Tom Glavine	.35
482	Manny Lee	.05
483	Joe Hesketh	.05
484	Mike Bielecki	.05
485	Greg Brock	.05
486	Pascual Perez	.05
487	Kirk Gibson	.05
488	Scott Sanderson	.05
489	Domingo Ramos	.05
490	Kal Daniels	.05
491a	David Wells (Reversed negative on back photo.)	1.50
491b	David Wells (Corrected)	.05
492	Jerry Reed	.05
493	Eric Show	.05
494	Mike Pagliarulo	.05
495	Ron Robinson	.05
496	Brad Komminsk	.05
497	Greg Litton **RC**	.05
498	Chris James	.05
499	Luis Quinones **RC**	.05
500	Frank Viola	.05
501	Tim Teufel	.05
502	Terry Leach	.05
503	Matt Williams	.05
504	Tim Leary	.05
505	Doug Drabek	.05
506	Mariano Duncan	.05
507	Charlie Hayes	.05
508	Albert Belle	.05
509	Pat Sheridan	.05
510	Mackey Sasser	.05
511	Jose Rijo	.05
512	Mike Smithson	.05
513	Gary Ward	.05
514	Dion James	.05
515	Jim Gott	.05
516	Drew Hall **RC**	.05
517	Doug Bair	.05
518	Scott Scudder **RC**	.05
519	Rick Aguilera	.05
520	Rafael Belliard	.05
521	Jay Buhner	.05
522	Jeff Reardon	.05
523	Steve Rosenberg **RC**	.05
524	Randy Velarde **RC**	.05
525	Jeff Musselman	.05
526	Bill Long	.05
527	Gary Wayne **RC**	.05
528	Dave Johnson **RC**	.05
529	Ron Kittle	.05
530	Erik Hanson **RC**	.05
531	Steve Wilson **RC**	.05
532	Joey Meyer	.05
533	Curt Young	.05
534	Kelly Downs	.05
535	Joe Girardi	.05
536	Lance Blankenship	.05
537	Greg Mathews	.05
538	Donell Nixon	.05
539	Mark Knudson **RC**	.05
540	Jeff Wetherby **RC**	.05
541	Darrin Jackson	.05
542	Terry Mulholland	.05
543	Eric Hetzel **RC**	.05
544	Rick Reed **RC**	.05
545	Dennis Cook **RC**	.05
546	Mike Jackson	.05
547	Brian Fisher	.05
548	Gene Harris **RC**	.05
549	Jeff King **RC**	.05
550	Dave Dravecky (Salute)	.05
551	Randy Kutcher **RC**	.05
552	Mark Portugal	.05
553	Jim Corsi **RC**	.05
554	Todd Stottlemyre	.05
555	Scott Bankhead	.05
556	Ken Dayley	.05
557	Rick Wrona **RC**	.10
558	Sammy Sosa **RC**	3.00
559	Keith Miller	.05
560	Ken Griffey Jr.	.65
561a	Ryne Sandberg (Highlight, 3B on front.)	2.00
561b	Ryne Sandberg (Highlight, no position.)	.25
562	Billy Hatcher	.05
563	Jay Bell	.05
564	Jack Daugherty **RC**	.05
565	Rich Monteleone **RC**	.05
566	Bo Jackson (All-Star MVP)	.10
567	Tony Fossas **RC**	.05
568	Roy Smith **RC**	.05
569	Jaime Navarro **RC**	.05
570	Lance Johnson	.05
571	Mike Dyer **RC**	.05
572	Kevin Ritz **RC**	.05
573	Dave West	.05
574	Gary Mielke **RC**	.05
575	Scott Lusader **RC**	.05
576	Joe Oliver	.05
577	Sandy Alomar, Jr.	.05
578	Andy Benes	.05
579	Tim Jones	.05
580	Randy McCament **RC**	.05
581	Curt Schilling **RC**	.35
582	John Orton **RC**	.05
583a	Milt Cuyler **RC** (998 games)	1.00
583b	Milt Cuyler **RC** (98 games)	.05
584	Eric Anthony **RC**	.05
585	Greg Vaughn **RC**	.15
586	Deion Sanders	.05
587	Jose DeJesus **RC**	.05
588	Chip Hale **RC**	.05
589	John Olerud **RC**	.50
590	Steve Olin **RC**	.05
591	Marquis Grissom **RC**	.40
592	Moises Alou **RC**	.40
593	Mark Lemke **RC**	.05
594	Dean Palmer **RC**	.15
595	Robin Ventura	.05
596	Tino Martinez	.05
597	Mike Huff **RC**	.05
598	Scott Hemond **RC**	.05
599	Wally Whitehurst **RC**	.05
600	Todd Zeile **RC**	.15
601	Glenallen Hill **RC**	.05
602	Hal Morris **RC**	.05
603	Juan Bell **RC**	.05
604	Bobby Rose **RC**	.05
605	Matt Merullo **RC**	.05
606	Kevin Maas **RC**	.05
607	Randy Nosek **RC**	.05
608a	Billy Bates **RC** ("12 triples" mentioned in second-last line)	.05
608b	Billy Bates (Triples not mentioned.)	.75
609	Mike Stanton **RC**	.05
610	Goose Gozzo **RC**	.05
611	Charles Nagy **RC**	.40
612	Scott Coolbaugh **RC**	.05
613	Jose Vizcaino **RC**	.10
614	Greg Smith **RC**	.05
615	Jeff Huson **RC**	.05
616	Mickey Weston **RC**	.05
617	John Pawlowski **RC**	.05
618a	Joe Skalski **RC** (Uniform #27 on card back.)	.15
618b	Joe Skalski **RC** (Uniform #67 on card back.)	1.00
619	Bernie Williams **RC**	1.00
620	Shawn Holman **RC**	.05
621	Gary Eave **RC**	.05
622	Darrin Fletcher **RC**	.10
623	Pat Combs **RC**	.05
624	Mike Blowers **RC**	.05
625	Kevin Appier	.05
626	Pat Austin **RC**	.05
627	Kelly Mann **RC**	.05
628	Matt Kinzer **RC**	.05
629	Chris Hammond **RC**	.10
630	Dean Wilkins **RC**	.05
631	Larry Walker **RC**	.50
632	Blaine Beatty **RC**	.05
633a	Tom Barrett **RC** (Uniform #29 on card back.)	.05
633b	Tom Barrett **RC** (Uniform #14 on card back.)	1.00
634	Stan Belinda **RC**	.05
635	Tex Smith **RC**	.05
636	Hensley Meulens **RC**	.10
637	Juan Gonzalez **RC**	1.50
638	Lenny Webster **RC**	.10
639	Mark Gardner **RC**	.05
640	Tommy Greene **RC**	.05
641	Mike Hartley **RC**	.05
642	Phil Stephenson **RC**	.05
643	Kevin Mmahat **RC**	.05
644	Ed Whited **RC**	.05
645	Delino DeShields **RC**	.15
646	Kevin Blankenship **RC**	.05
647	Paul Sorrento **RC**	.05
648	Mike Roesler **RC**	.05
649	Jason Grimsley **RC**	.05
650	Dave Justice **RC**	1.00
651	Scott Cooper **RC**	.05
652	Dave Eiland **RC**	.05
653	Mike Munoz **RC**	.05
654	Jeff Fischer **RC**	.05
655	Terry Jorgenson **RC**	.05
656	George Canale **RC**	.05
657	Brian DuBois **RC**	.05
658	Carlos Quintana	.05
659	Luis de los Santos	.05
660	Jerald Clark	.05
661	Donald Harris **RC** (1st Round Pick)	.05
662	Paul Coleman **RC** (1st Round Pick)	.05
663	Frank Thomas **RC** (1st Round Pick)	2.00
664	Brent Mayne **RC** (1st Round Pick)	.10
665	Eddie Zosky **RC** (1st Round Pick)	.05
666	Steve Hosey **RC** (1st Round Pick)	.05
667	Scott Bryant **RC** (1st Round Pick)	.05
668	Tom Goodwin **RC** (1st Round Pick)	.10
669	Cal Eldred **RC** (1st Round Pick)	.10
670	Earl Cunningham **RC** (1st Round Pick)	.05
671	Alan Zinter **RC** (1st Round Pick)	.05
672	Chuck Knoblauch **RC** (1st Round Pick)	.40
672(a)	Chuck Knoblauch (3,000 autographed cards with a special hologram on back were inserted into 1992 rack packs)	10.00
673	Kyle Abbott **RC** (1st Round Pick)	.10
674	Roger Salkeld **RC** (1st Round Pick)	.05
675	Mo Vaughn **RC** (1st Round Pick)	.50

#	Player	NM/M
676	Kiki Jones **RC** (1st Round Pick)	.05
677	Tyler Houston **RC** (1st Round Pick)	.10
678	Jeff Jackson **RC** (1st Round Pick)	.05
679	Greg Gohr **RC** (1st Round Pick)	.05
680	Ben McDonald **RC** (1st Round Pick)	.15
681	Greg Blosser **RC** (1st Round Pick)	.05
682	Willie Green **RC** ((Greene) 1st Round Pick)	.05
683	Wade Boggs/DT	.25
684	Will Clark/DT	.05
685	Tony Gwynn/DT	.25
686	Rickey Henderson/DT	.20
687	Bo Jackson/DT	.15
688	Mark Langston/DT	.05
689	Barry Larkin/DT	.05
690	Kirby Puckett/DT	.25
691	Ryne Sandberg/DT	.25
692	Mike Scott/DT	.05
693	Terry Steinbach/DT	.05
694	Bobby Thigpen/DT	.05
695	Mitch Williams/DT	.05
696	Nolan Ryan (Highlight)	.40
697	Bo Jackson (FB/BB)	.25
698	Rickey Henderson (ALCS MVP)	.20
699	Will Clark (NLCS MVP)	.05
700	World Series Games 1-2	.05
701	Lights Out: Candlestick	.15
702	World Series Game 3	.05
703	World Series Wrap-up	.05
704	Wade Boggs (Highlight)	.25

Rookie Dream Team

This 10-card "Rookie Dream Team" set, in the same format as those found in the regular-issue 1990 Score, was available only in factory sets for the hobby trade. Factory sets for general retail outlets did not include these cards, nor were they available in Score packs. Cards carry a "B" prefix to their numbers.

		NM/M
Complete Set (10):		1.00
Common Player:		.10
1	A. Bartlett Giamatti	.10
2	Pat Combs	.10
3	Todd Zeile	.10
4	Luis de los Santos	.10
5	Mark Lemke	.10
6	Robin Ventura	.10
7	Jeff Huson	.10
8	Greg Vaughn	.10
9	Marquis Grissom	.10
10	Eric Anthony	.10

Traded

This 110-card set features players with new teams as well as 1990 Major League rookies. The cards feature full-color action photos framed in yellow with an orange border. The player's ID appears in green below the photo. The team logo is displayed next to the player's name. The card backs feature posed player photos and follow the style of the regular 1990 Score issue. The cards are numbered 1T-110T. Young hockey phenom Eric Lindros is featured trying out for the Toronto Blue Jays.

		NM/M
Complete Set (110):		4.00
Common Player:		.05
1	Dave Winfield	.75
2	Kevin Bass	.05
3	Nick Esasky	.05
4	Mitch Webster	.05
5	Pascual Perez	.05
6	Gary Pettis	.05
7	Tony Pena	.05
8	Candy Maldonado	.05
9	Cecil Fielder	.05
10	Carmelo Martinez	.05
11	Mark Langston	.05
12	Dave Parker	.05
13	Don Slaught	.05
14	Tony Phillips	.05
15	John Franco	.05
16	Randy Myers	.05
17	Jeff Reardon	.05
18	Sandy Alomar, Jr.	.05
19	Joe Carter	.05
20	Fred Lynn	.05
21	Storm Davis	.05
22	Craig Lefferts	.05
23	Pete O'Brien	.05
24	Dennis Boyd	.05
25	Lloyd Moseby	.05
26	Mark Davis	.05
27	Tim Leary	.05
28	Gerald Perry	.05
29	Don Aase	.05
30	Ernie Whitt	.05
31	Dale Murphy	.35
32	Alejandro Pena	.05
33	Juan Samuel	.05
34	Hubie Brooks	.05
35	Gary Carter	.75
36	Jim Presley	.05
37	Wally Backman	.05
38	Matt Nokes	.05
39	Dan Petry	.05
40	Franklin Stubbs	.05
41	Jeff Huson	.05
42	Billy Hatcher	.05
43	Terry Leach	.05
44	Phil Bradley	.05
45	Claudell Washington	.05
46	Luis Polonia	.05
47	Daryl Boston	.05
48	Lee Smith	.05
49	Tom Brunansky	.05
50	Mike Witt	.05
51	Willie Randolph	.05
52	Stan Javier	.05
53	Brad Komminsk	.05
54	John Candelaria	.05
55	Bryn Smith	.05
56	Glenn Braggs	.05
57	Keith Hernandez	.05
58	Ken Oberkfell	.05
59	Steve Jeltz	.05
60	Chris James	.05
61	Scott Sanderson	.05
62	Bill Long	.05
63	Rick Cerone	.05
64	Scott Bailes	.05
65	Larry Sheets	.05
66	Junior Ortiz	.05
67	Francisco Cabrera **RC**	.05
68	Gary DiSarcina **RC**	.05
69	Greg Olson **RC**	.05
70	Beau Allred **RC**	.05
71	Oscar Azocar **RC**	.05
72	Kent Mercker **RC**	.05
73	John Burkett **RC**	.05
74	Carlos Baerga **RC**	.05
75	Dave Hollins **RC**	.05
76	Todd Hundley **RC**	.25
77	Rick Parker **RC**	.05
78	Steve Cummings **RC**	.05
79	Bill Sampen **RC**	.05
80	Jerry Kutzler **RC**	.05
81	Derek Bell **RC**	.05
82	Kevin Tapani **RC**	.05
83	Jim Leyritz **RC**	.25
84	Ray Lankford **RC**	.25
85	Wayne Edwards **RC**	.05
86	Frank Thomas	2.00
87	Tim Naehring **RC**	.05
88	Willie Blair **RC**	.05
89	Alan Mills **RC**	.05
90	Scott Radinsky **RC**	.05
91	Howard Farmer **RC**	.05
92	Julio Machado **RC**	.05
93	Rafael Valdez **RC**	.05
94	Shawn Boskie **RC**	.05
95	David Segui **RC**	.05
96	Chris Hoiles **RC**	.05
97	D.J. Dozier **RC**	.05
98	Hector Villanueva **RC**	.05
99	Eric Gunderson **RC**	.05
100	Eric Lindros **RC**	1.00
101	Dave Otto **RC**	.05
102	Dana Kiecker **RC**	.05
103	Tim Drummond **RC**	.05
104	Mickey Pina **RC**	.05
105	Craig Grebeck **RC**	.05
106	Bernard Gilkey **RC**	.25
107	Tim Layana **RC**	.05
108	Scott Chiamparino **RC**	.05
109	Steve Avery **RC**	.05
110	Terry Shumpert **RC**	.05

Rising Stars

For the second consecutive year Score produced a 100-card "Rising Stars" set. The 1990 issue waas made available as a boxed set and also marketed with a related magazine like the 1989 issue. Magic Motion trivia cards featuring past MVP's accompany the card set. The cards feature full-color action photos on the front and portrait photos on the back.

		NM/M
Complete Set (100):		5.00
Common Player:		.05
1	Tom Gordon	.05
2	Jerome Walton	.05
3	Ken Griffey Jr.	1.25
4	Dwight Smith	.05
5	Jim Abbott	.05
6	Todd Zeile	.05
7	Donn Pall	.05
8	Rick Reed	.05
9	Joey Belle	.25
10	Gregg Jefferies	.05
11	Kevin Ritz	.05
12	Charlie Hayes	.05
13	Kevin Appier	.05
14	Jeff Huson	.05
15	Gary Wayne	.05
16	Eric Yelding	.05
17	Clay Parker	.05
18	Junior Felix	.05
19	Derek Lilliquist	.05
20	Gary Sheffield	.25
21	Craig Worthington	.05
22	Jeff Brantley	.05
23	Eric Hetzel	.05
24	Greg Harris	.05
25	John Wetteland	.05
26	Joe Oliver	.05
27	Kevin Maas	.05
28	Kevin Brown	.05
29	Mike Stanton	.05
30	Greg Vaughn	.05
31	Ron Jones	.05
32	Gregg Olson	.05
33	Joe Girardi	.05
34	Ken Hill	.05
35	Sammy Sosa	3.00
36	Geronimo Berroa	.05
37	Omar Vizquel	.05
38	Dean Palmer	.05
39	John Olerud	.05
40	Deion Sanders	.05
41	Randy Kramer	.05
42	Scott Lusader	.05
43	Dave Johnson	.05
44	Jeff Wetherby	.05
45	Eric Anthony	.05
46	Kenny Rogers	.05
47	Matt Winters	.05
48	Goose Gozzo	.05
49	Carlos Quintana	.05
50	Bob Geren	.05
51	Chad Kreuter	.05
52	Randy Johnson	.75
53	Hensley Meulens	.05
54	Gene Harris	.05
55	Bill Spiers	.05
56	Kelly Mann	.05
57	Tom McCarthy	.05
58	Steve Finley	.05
59	Ramon Martinez	.05
60	Greg Briley	.05
61	Jack Daugherty	.05
62	Tim Jones	.05
63	Doug Strange	.05
64	John Orton	.05
65	Scott Scudder	.05
66	Mark Gardner (Photo on back actually Steve Frey.)	.05
67	Mark Carreon	.05
68	Bob Milacki	.05
69	Andy Benes	.05
70	Carlos Martinez	.05
71	Jeff King	.05
72	Brad Arnsberg	.05
73	Rick Wrona	.05
74	Cris Carpenter	.05
75	Dennis Cook	.05
76	Pete Harnisch	.05
77	Greg Hibbard	.05
78	Ed Whited	.05
79	Scott Coolbaugh	.05
80	Billy Bates	.05
81	German Gonzalez	.05
82	Lance Blankenship	.05
83	Lenny Harris	.05
84	Milt Cuyler	.05
85	Erik Hanson	.05
86	Kent Anderson	.05
87	Hal Morris	.05
88	Mike Brumley	.05
89	Ken Patterson	.05
90	Mike Devereaux	.05
91	Greg Litton	.05
92	Rolando Roomes	.05
93	Ben McDonald	.05
94	Curt Schilling	.35
95	Jose DeJesus	.05
96	Robin Ventura	.05
97	Steve Searcy	.05
98	Chip Hale	.05
99	Marquis Grissom	.05
100	Luis de los Santos	.05

Superstars

The game's top 100 players are featured in this set. The card fronts feature full-color action photos and are similar in style to the past Score Superstar set. The set was marketed as a boxed set and with a special magazine devoted to baseball's 100 hottest players. Each set includes a series of Magic Motion cards honoring past MVP winners. The player cards measure 2-1/2" x 3-1/2".

		NM/M
Complete Set (100):		3.00
Common Player:		.05
1	Kirby Puckett	.50
2	Steve Sax	.05
3	Tony Gwynn	.50
4	Willie Randolph	.05
5	Jose Canseco	.25
6	Ozzie Smith	.50
7	Rick Reuschel	.05
8	Bill Doran	.05
9	Mickey Tettleton	.05
10	Don Mattingly	.60
11	Greg Swindell	.05
12	Bert Blyleven	.05
13	Dave Stewart	.05
14	Andres Galarraga	.05
15	Darryl Strawberry	.05
16	Ellis Burks	.05
17	Paul O'Neill	.05
18	Bruce Hurst	.05
19	Dave Smith	.05
20	Carney Lansford	.05
21	Robby Thompson	.05
22	Gary Gaetti	.05
23	Jeff Russell	.05
24	Chuck Finley	.05
25	Mark McGwire	.65
26	Alvin Davis	.05
27	George Bell	.05
28	Cory Snyder	.05
29	Keith Hernandez	.05
30	Will Clark	.05
31	Steve Bedrosian	.05
32	Ryne Sandberg	.50
33	Tom Browning	.05
34	Tim Burke	.05
35	John Smoltz	.05
36	Phil Bradley	.05
37	Bobby Bonilla	.05
38	Kirk McCaskill	.05
39	Dave Righetti	.05
40	Bo Jackson	.10
41	Alan Trammell	.05
42	Mike Moore	.05
43	Harold Reynolds	.05
44	Nolan Ryan	.75
45	Fred McGriff	.05
46	Brian Downing	.05
47	Brett Butler	.05
48	Mike Scioscia	.05
49	John Franco	.05
50	Kevin Mitchell	.05
51	Mark Davis	.05
52	Glenn Davis	.05
53	Barry Bonds	.75
54	Dwight Evans	.05
55	Terry Steinbach	.05
56	Dave Gallagher	.05
57	Roberto Kelly	.05
58	Rafael Palmeiro	.35
59	Joe Carter	.05
60	Mark Grace	.05
61	Pedro Guerrero	.05
62	Von Hayes	.05
63	Benny Santiago	.05
64	Dale Murphy	.25
65	John Smiley	.05
66	Cal Ripken, Jr.	.75
67	Mike Greenwell	.05
68	Devon White	.05
69	Ed Whitson	.05
70	Carlton Fisk	.40
71	Lou Whitaker	.05
72	Danny Tartabull	.05
73	Vince Coleman	.05
74	Andre Dawson	.25
75	Tim Raines	.05
76	George Brett	.60
77	Tom Herr	.05
78	Andy Van Slyke	.05
79	Roger Clemens	.60
80	Wade Boggs	.50
81	Wally Joyner	.05
82	Lonnie Smith	.05
83	Howard Johnson	.05
84	Julio Franco	.05
85	Ruben Sierra	.05
86	Dan Plesac	.05
87	Bobby Thigpen	.05
88	Kevin Seitzer	.05
89	Dave Steib	.05
90	Rickey Henderson	.40
91	Jeffrey Leonard	.05
92	Robin Yount	.40
93	Mitch Williams	.05
94	Orel Hershiser	.05
95	Eric Davis	.05
96	Mark Langston	.05
97	Mike Scott	.05
98	Paul Molitor	.40
99	Dwight Gooden	.05
100	Kevin Bass	.05

Yankees

For a second year, National Westminster Bank sponsored a Score-produced team set as a stadium promotion. The set features color player photos on front and back and is graphically enhanced by the team's traditional pinstripe motif. A tribute card to former Yankees infielder and manager Billy Martin, who was killed the previous Christmas, is included in the set. The set was given to fans attending the August 18 game.

		NM/M
Complete Set (32):		4.00
Common Player:		.15
1	Stump Merrill	.15
2	Don Mattingly	2.50
3	Steve Sax	.15
4	Alvaro Espinoza	.15
5	Jesse Barfield	.15
6	Roberto Kelly	.15
7	Mel Hall	.15
8	Claudell Washington	.15
9	Bob Geren	.15
10	Jim Leyritz	.15
11	Pascual Perez	.15
12	Dave LaPoint	.15
13	Tim Leary	.15
14	Mike Witt	.15
15	Chuck Cary	.15
16	Dave Righetti	.15
17	Lee Guetterman	.15
18	Andy Hawkins	.15
19	Greg Cadaret	.15
20	Eric Plunk	.15
21	Jimmy Jones	.15
22	Deion Sanders	.75
23	Jeff Robinson	.15
24	Matt Nokes	.15
25	Steve Balboni	.15
26	Wayne Tolleson	.15
27	Randy Velarde	.15
28	Rick Cerone	.15
29	Alan Mills	.15
30	Billy Martin	.30
31	Yankee Stadium	.15
32	All-Time Yankee Records	.15

Young Superstars Set 1

For the third consecutive year, Score produced Young Superstars boxed sets. The 1990 versions contain 42 player cards plus five Magic-Motion trivia cards. The cards are similar to previous Young Superstar sets, with action photography on the front and a glossy finish. Card backs have a color portrait, major league statistics and scouting reports. Besides the boxed set, cards from Set I were inserted into rack packs.

		NM/M
Complete Set (42):		2.00
Common Player:		.10
1	Bo Jackson	.25
2	Dwight Smith	.10
3	Joey Belle	.25
4	Gregg Olson	.10
5	Jim Abbott	.10
6	Felix Fermin	.10
7	Brian Holman	.10
8	Clay Parker	.10
9	Junior Felix	.10
10	Joe Oliver	.10
11	Steve Finley	.10
12	Greg Briley	.10
13	Greg Vaughn	.10
14	Bill Spiers	.10
15	Eric Yelding	.10
16	Jose Gonzalez	.10
17	Mark Carreon	.10
18	Greg Harris	.10
19	Felix Jose	.10
20	Bob Milacki	.10
21	Kenny Rogers	.10
22	Rolando Roomes	.10
23	Bip Roberts	.10
24	Jeff Brantley	.10
25	Jeff Ballard	.10
26	John Dopson	.10
27	Ken Patterson	.10
28	Omar Vizquel	.10
29	Kevin Brown	.10
30	Derek Lilliquist	.10
31	David Wells	.10
32	Ken Hill	.10
33	Greg Litton	.10
34	Rob Ducey	.10
35	Carlos Martinez	.10
36	John Smoltz	.10
37	Lenny Harris	.10
38	Charlie Hayes	.10
39	Tommy Gregg	.10
40	John Wetteland	.10
41	Jeff Huson	.10
42	Eric Anthony	.10

Young Superstars Set 2

Available only as a boxed set via a mail-order offer, Set II of 1990 Score Young Superstars is identical in format to Set I, with the exception that the graphic elements on the front of Set II cards are in red and green, while in Set I they are in blue and magenta.

		NM/M
Complete Set (42):		5.00
Common Player:		.10
1	Todd Zeile	.10
2	Ben McDonald	.10
3	Delino DeShields	.10
4	Pat Combs	.10
5	John Olerud	.10
6	Marquis Grissom	.10
7	Mike Stanton	.10
8	Robin Ventura	.10
9	Larry Walker	.10
10	Dante Bichette	.10
11	Jack Armstrong	.10
12	Jay Bell	.10
13	Andy Benes	.10
14	Joey Cora	.10
15	Rob Dibble	.10
16	Jeff King	.10
17	Jeff Hamilton	.10
18	Erik Hanson	.10
19	Pete Harnisch	.10
20	Greg Hibbard	.10
21	Stan Javier	.10
22	Mark Lemke	.10
23	Steve Olin	.10
24	Tommy Greene	.10
25	Sammy Sosa	4.00
26	Gary Wayne	.10
27	Deion Sanders	.10
28	Steve Wilson	.10
29	Joe Girardi	.10
30	John Orton	.10
31	Kevin Tapani	.10
32	Carlos Baerga	.10
33	Glenallen Hill	.10
34	Mike Blowers	.10
35	Dave Hollins	.10
36	Lance Blankenship	.10
37	Hal Morris	.10
38	Lance Johnson	.10
39	Chris Gwynn	.10
40	Doug Dascenzo	.10
41	Jerald Clark	.10
42	Carlos Quintana	.10

Sportflics 11th National Nolan Ryan

This two-fronted card is a unique souvenir given to those who participated in a special 1990 convention tour of the Optigraphics card manufacturing plant in Dallas. The card features Nolan Ryan on two of the company's best-known products, Score on one side, Sportflics on the other. Each side is similar to Ryan's regularly issued card in those sets, but carries logos or typography related to the 11th Annual National Sports Collectors Convention, held in nearby Arlington. Only 600 of the cards were reported produced.

	NM/M
Nolan Ryan	100.00

1991 Score Promos

To preview its 1991 baseball cards Score pre-released the 110 cards from its teal-

bordered series (cards #111-220) as samples. The main difference on most cards between the samples and the issued version is that the samples have no statistics on the 1990 season or career lines. Many cards have different career highlight write-ups on back, as well. A handful of the sample cards were widely distributed to dealers and the hobby press, while others from the sheet were released more sparingly. As few as two specimens are known of some superstar cards, driving up their prices among single-player specialty collectors.

		NM/M
Common Player:		5.00
111	Juan Berenguer	5.00
112	Mike Heath	5.00
113	Scott Bradley	5.00
114	Jack Morris	5.00
115	Barry Jones	5.00
116	Kevin Romine	5.00
117	Garry Templeton	5.00
118	Scott Sanderson	5.00
119	Roberto Kelly	5.00
120	George Brett	60.00
121	Oddibe McDowell	5.00
122	Jim Acker	5.00
123	Bill Swift	5.00
124	Eric King	5.00
125	Jay Buhner	5.00
126	Matt Young	5.00
127	Alvaro Espinoza	5.00
128	Greg Hibbard	5.00
129	Jeff M. Robinson	5.00
130	Mike Greenwell	5.00
131	Dion James	5.00
132	Donn Pall	5.00
133	Lloyd Moseby	5.00
134	Randy Velarde	5.00
135	Allan Anderson	5.00
136	Mark Davis	5.00
137	Eric Davis	5.00
138	Phil Stephenson	5.00
139	Felix Fermin	5.00
140	Pedro Guerrero	5.00
141	Charlie Hough	5.00
142	Mike Henneman	5.00
143	Jeff Montgomery	5.00
144	Lenny Harris	5.00
145	Bruce Hurst	5.00
146	Eric Anthony	5.00
147	Paul Assenmacher	5.00
148	Jesse Barfield	5.00
149	Carlos Quintana	5.00
150	Dave Stewart	5.00
151	Roy Smith	5.00
152	Paul Gibson	5.00
153	Mickey Hatcher	5.00
154	Jim Eisenreich	5.00
155	Kenny Rogers	5.00
156	Dave Schmidt	5.00
157	Lance Johnson	5.00
158	Dave West	5.00
159	Steve Balboni	5.00
160	Jeff Brantley	5.00
161	Craig Biggio	5.00
162	Brook Jacoby	5.00
163	Dan Gladden	5.00
164	Jeff Reardon	5.00
165	Mark Carreon	5.00
166	Mel Hall	5.00
167	Gary Mielke	5.00
168	Cecil Fielder	5.00
169	Darrin Jackson	5.00
170	Rick Aguilera	5.00
171	Walt Weiss	5.00
172	Steve Farr	5.00
173	Jody Reed	5.00
174	Mike Jeffcoat	5.00
175	Mark Grace	5.00
176	Larry Sheets	5.00
177	Bill Gullickson	5.00
178	Chris Gwynn	5.00
179	Melido Perez	5.00
180	Sid Fernandez	5.00
181	Tim Burke	5.00
182	Gary Pettis	5.00
183	Rob Murphy	5.00
184	Craig Lefferts	5.00
185	Howard Johnson	5.00
186	Ken Caminiti	5.00
187	Tim Belcher	5.00
188	Greg Cadaret	5.00
189	Matt Williams	5.00
190	Dave Magadan	5.00
191	Geno Petralli	5.00
192	Jeff D. Robinson	5.00
193	Jim Deshaies	5.00
194	Willie Randolph	5.00
195	George Bell	5.00
196	Hubie Brooks	5.00
197	Tom Gordon	5.00
198	Mike Fitzgerald	5.00
199	Mike Pagliarulo	5.00
200	Kirby Puckett	40.00
201	Shawon Dunston	5.00
202	Dennis Boyd	5.00
203	Junior Felix	5.00
204	Alejandro Pena	5.00
205	Pete Smith	5.00
206	Tom Glavine	20.00
207	Luis Salazar	5.00
208	John Smoltz	5.00
209	Doug Dascenzo	5.00
210	Tim Wallach	5.00
211	Greg Gagne	5.00
212	Mark Gubicza	5.00
213	Mark Parent	5.00
214	Ken Oberkfell	5.00
215	Gary Carter	30.00
216	Rafael Palmeiro	25.00
217	Tom Niedenfuer	5.00
218	Dave LaPoint	5.00
219	Jeff Treadway	5.00
220	Mitch Williams	5.00

1991 Score

Score introduced a two-series format in 1991. The first series includes cards 1-441. Score cards once again feature multiple border colors within the set, several subsets (Master Blaster, K-Man, Highlights and Riflemen), full-color action photos on the front and portraits on the flip side. Score eliminated display of the player's uniform number on the 1991 cards. Black-and-white Dream Team cards, plus Prospects and #1 Draft Picks highlight the 1991 set. The second series was released in February of 1991.

		NM/M
Unopened Fact. Set (900):		10.00
Complete Set (893):		6.00
Common Player:		.05
Series 1 or 2 Pack (16):		.25
Series 1 or 2 Box (36):		6.00
1	Jose Canseco	.25
2	Ken Griffey Jr.	.60
3	Ryne Sandberg	.50
4	Nolan Ryan	.75
5	Bo Jackson	.10
6	Bret Saberhagen	.05
7	Will Clark	.05
8	Ellis Burks	.05
9	Joe Carter	.05
10	Rickey Henderson	.40
11	Ozzie Guillen	.05
12	Wade Boggs	.50
13	Jerome Walton	.05
14	John Franco	.05
15	Ricky Jordan	.05
16	Wally Backman	.05
17	Rob Dibble	.05
18	Glenn Braggs	.05
19	Cory Snyder	.05
20	Kal Daniels	.05
21	Mark Langston	.05
22	Kevin Gross	.05
23	Don Mattingly	.55
24	Dave Righetti	.05
25	Roberto Alomar	.15
26	Robby Thompson	.05
27	Jack McDowell	.05
28	Bip Roberts	.05
29	Jay Howell	.05
30	Dave Steib	.05
31	Johnny Ray	.05
32	Steve Sax	.05
33	Terry Mulholland	.05
34	Lee Guetterman	.05
35	Tim Raines	.05
36	Scott Fletcher	.05
37	Lance Parrish	.05
38	Tony Phillips	.05
39	Todd Stottlemyre	.05
40	Alan Trammell	.05
41	Todd Burns	.05
42	Mookie Wilson	.05
43	Chris Bosio	.05
44	Jeffrey Leonard	.05
45	Doug Jones	.05
46	Mike Scott	.05
47	Andy Hawkins	.05
48	Harold Reynolds	.05
49	Paul Molitor	.40
50	John Farrell	.05
51	Danny Darwin	.05
52	Jeff Blauser	.05
53	John Tudor	.05
54	Milt Thompson	.05
55	Dave Justice	.05
56	Greg Olson **RC**	.05
57	Willie Blair **RC**	.05
58	Rick Parker **RC**	.05
59	Shawn Boskie	.05
60	Kevin Tapani	.05
61	Dave Hollins	.05
62	Scott Radinsky **RC**	.05
63	Francisco Cabrera	.05
64	Tim Layana **RC**	.05
65	Jim Leyritz	.05
66	Wayne Edwards	.05
67	Lee Stevens **RC**	.05
68	Bill Sampen **RC**	.05
69	Craig Grebeck **RC**	.05
70	John Burkett	.05
71	Hector Villanueva **RC**	.05
72	Oscar Azocar **RC**	.05
73	Alan Mills	.05
74	Carlos Baerga	.05
75	Charles Nagy	.05
76	Tim Drummond	.05
77	Dana Kiecker **RC**	.05
78	Tom Edens **RC**	.05
79	Kent Mercker	.05
80	Steve Avery	.05
81	Lee Smith	.05
82	Dave Martinez	.05
83	Dave Winfield	.40
84	Bill Spiers	.05
85	Dan Pasqua	.05
86	Randy Milligan	.05
87	Tracy Jones	.05
88	Greg Myers **RC**	.05
89	Keith Hernandez	.05
90	Todd Benzinger	.05
91	Mike Jackson	.05
92	Mike Stanley	.05
93	Candy Maldonado	.05
94	John Kruk	.05
95	Cal Ripken, Jr.	.75
96	Willie Fraser	.05
97	Mike Felder	.05
98	Bill Landrum	.05
99	Chuck Crim	.05
100	Chuck Finley	.05
101	Kirt Manwaring	.05
102	Jaime Navarro	.05
103	Dickie Thon	.05
104	Brian Downing	.05
105	Jim Abbott	.05
106	Tom Brookens	.05
107	Darryl Hamilton	.05
108	Bryan Harvey	.05
109	Greg Harris	.05
110	Greg Swindell	.05
111	Juan Berenguer	.05
112	Mike Heath	.05
113	Scott Bradley	.05
114	Jack Morris	.05
115	Barry Jones	.05
116	Kevin Romine	.05
117	Garry Templeton	.05
118	Scott Sanderson	.05
119	Roberto Kelly	.05
120	George Brett	.50
121	Oddibe McDowell	.05
122	Jim Acker	.05
123	Bill Swift	.05
124	Eric King	.05
125	Jay Buhner	.05
126	Matt Young	.05
127	Alvaro Espinoza	.05
128	Greg Hibbard	.05
129	Jeff Robinson	.05
130	Mike Greenwell	.05
131	Dion James	.05
132	Donn Pall	.05
133	Lloyd Moseby	.05
134	Randy Velarde	.05
135	Allan Anderson	.05
136	Mark Davis	.05
137	Eric Davis	.05
138	Phil Stephenson	.05
139	Felix Fermin	.05
140	Pedro Guerrero	.05
141	Charlie Hough	.05
142	Mike Henneman	.05
143	Jeff Montgomery	.05
144	Lenny Harris	.05
145	Bruce Hurst	.05
146	Eric Anthony	.05
147	Paul Assenmacher	.05
148	Jesse Barfield	.05
149	Carlos Quintana	.05
150	Dave Stewart	.05
151	Roy Smith	.05
152	Paul Gibson	.05
153	Mickey Hatcher	.05
154	Jim Eisenreich	.05
155	Kenny Rogers	.05
156	Dave Schmidt	.05
157	Lance Johnson	.05
158	Dave West	.05
159	Steve Balboni	.05
160	Jeff Brantley	.05
161	Craig Biggio	.05
162	Brook Jacoby	.05
163	Dan Gladden	.05
164	Jeff Reardon	.05
165	Mark Carreon	.05
166	Mel Hall	.05
167	Gary Mielke	.05
168	Cecil Fielder	.05
169	Darrin Jackson	.05
170	Rick Aguilera	.05
171	Walt Weiss	.05
172	Steve Farr	.05
173	Jody Reed	.05
174	Mike Jeffcoat	.05
175	Mark Grace	.05
176	Larry Sheets	.05
177	Bill Gullickson	.05
178	Chris Gwynn	.05
179	Melido Perez	.05
180	Sid Fernandez	.05
181	Tim Burke	.05
182	Gary Pettis	.05
183	Rob Murphy	.05
184	Craig Lefferts	.05
185	Howard Johnson	.05
186	Ken Caminiti	.05
187	Tim Belcher	.05
188	Greg Cadaret	.05
189	Matt Williams	.05
190	Dave Magadan	.05
191	Geno Petralli	.05
192	Jeff Robinson	.05
193	Jim Deshaies	.05
194	Willie Randolph	.05
195	George Bell	.05
196	Hubie Brooks	.05
197	Tom Gordon	.05
198	Mike Fitzgerald	.05
199	Mike Pagliarulo	.05
200	Kirby Puckett	.50
201	Shawon Dunston	.05
202	Dennis Boyd	.05
203	Junior Felix	.05
204	Alejandro Pena	.05
205	Pete Smith	.05
206	Tom Glavine	.35
207	Luis Salazar	.05
208	John Smoltz	.05
209	Doug Dascenzo	.05
210	Tim Wallach	.05
211	Greg Gagne	.05
212	Mark Gubicza	.05
213	Mark Parent	.05
214	Ken Oberkfell	.05
215	Gary Carter	.40
216	Rafael Palmeiro	.35
217	Tom Niedenfuer	.05
218	Dave LaPoint	.05
219	Jeff Treadway	.05
220	Mitch Williams	.05
221	Jose DeLeon	.05
222	Mike LaValliere	.05
223	Darrel Akerfelds	.05
224a	Kent Anderson ("Flachy" in first line.)	.05
224b	Kent Anderson ("Flashy" in first line.)	.05
225	Dwight Evans	.05
226	Gary Redus	.05
227	Paul O'Neill	.05
228	Marty Barrett	.05
229	Tom Browning	.05
230	Terry Pendleton	.05
231	Jack Armstrong	.05
232	Mike Boddicker	.05
233	Neal Heaton	.05
234	Marquis Grissom	.05
235	Bert Blyleven	.05
236	Curt Young	.05
237	Don Carman	.05
238	Charlie Hayes	.05
239	Mark Knudson	.05
240	Todd Zeile	.05
241	Larry Walker	.05
242	Jerald Clark	.05
243	Jeff Ballard	.05
244	Jeff King	.05
245	Tom Brunansky	.05
246	Darren Daulton	.05
247	Scott Terry	.05
248	Rob Deer	.05
249	Brady Anderson	.05
250	Len Dykstra	.05
251	Greg Harris	.05
252	Mike Hartley	.05
253	Joey Cora	.05
254	Ivan Calderon	.05
255	Ted Power	.05
256	Sammy Sosa	.50
257	Steve Buechele	.05
258	Mike Devereaux	.05
259	Brad Komminsk	.05
260	Teddy Higuera	.05
261	Shawn Abner	.05
262	Dave Valle	.05
263	Jeff Huson	.05
264	Edgar Martinez	.05
265	Carlton Fisk	.40
266	Steve Finley	.05
267	John Wetteland	.05
268	Kevin Appier	.05
269	Steve Lyons	.05
270	Mickey Tettleton	.05
271	Luis Rivera	.05
272	Steve Jeltz	.05
273	R.J. Reynolds	.05
274	Carlos Martinez	.05
275	Dan Plesac	.05
276	Mike Morgan	.05
277	Jeff Russell	.05
278	Pete Incaviglia	.05
279	Kevin Seitzer	.05
280	Bobby Thigpen	.05
281	Stan Javier	.05
282	Henry Cotto	.05
283	Gary Wayne	.05
284	Shane Mack	.05
285	Brian Holman	.05
286	Gerald Perry	.05
287	Steve Crawford	.05
288	Nelson Liriano	.05
289	Don Aase	.05
290	Randy Johnson	.40
291	Harold Baines	.05
292	Kent Hrbek	.05
293a	Les Lancaster ("Dallas Texas")	.05
293b	Les Lancaster ("Dallas, Texas")	.05
294	Jeff Musselman	.05
295	Kurt Stillwell	.05
296	Stan Belinda	.05
297	Lou Whitaker	.05
298	Glenn Wilson	.05
299	Omar Vizquel	.05
300	Ramon Martinez	.05
301	Dwight Smith	.05
302	Tim Crews	.05
303	Lance Blankenship	.05
304	Sid Bream	.05
305	Rafael Ramirez	.05
306	Steve Wilson	.05
307	Mackey Sasser	.05
308	Franklin Stubbs	.05
309	Jack Daugherty	.05
310	Eddie Murray	.40
311	Bob Welch	.05
312	Brian Harper	.05
313	Lance McCullers	.05
314	Dave Smith	.05
315	Bobby Bonilla	.05
316	Jerry Don Gleaton	.05
317	Greg Maddux	.50
318	Keith Miller	.05
319	Mark Portugal	.05
320	Robin Ventura	.05
321	Bob Ojeda	.05
322	Mike Harkey	.05
323	Jay Bell	.05
324	Mark McGwire	.65
325	Gary Gaetti	.05
326	Jeff Pico	.05
327	Kevin McReynolds	.05
328	Frank Tanana	.05
329	Eric Yelding	.05
330	Barry Bonds	.75
331	Brian McRae **RC**	.05
332	Pedro Munoz **RC**	.05
333	Daryl Irvine **RC**	.05
334	Chris Hoiles	.05
335	Thomas Howard **RC**	.05
336	Jeff Schulz **RC**	.05
337	Jeff Manto **RC**	.05
338	Beau Allred	.05
339	Mike Bordick **RC**	.10
340	Todd Hundley	.05
341	Jim Vatcher **RC**	.05
342	Luis Sojo **RC**	.05
343	Jose Offerman **RC**	.05
344	Pete Coachman **RC**	.05
345	Mike Benjamin **RC**	.05
346	Ozzie Canseco **RC**	.05
347	Tim McIntosh **RC**	.05
348	Phil Plantier **RC**	.05
349	Terry Shumpert **RC**	.05
350	Darren Lewis	.05
351	David Walsh **RC**	.05
352a	Scott Chiamparino **RC** (Bats: Left)	.05
352b	Scott Chiamparino **RC** (Bats: Right)	.05
353	Julio Valera **RC**	.05
354	Anthony Telford **RC**	.05
355	Kevin Wickander **RC**	.05
356	Tim Naehring **RC**	.05
357	Jim Poole **RC**	.05
358	Mark Whiten **RC**	.05
359	Terry Wells **RC**	.05
360	Rafael Valdez **RC**	.05
361	Mel Stottlemyre **RC**	.05
362	David Segui **RC**	.10
363	Paul Abbott	.05
364	Steve Howard **RC**	.05
365	Karl Rhodes **RC**	.10
366	Rafael Novoa **RC**	.05
367	Joe Grahe **RC**	.05
368	Darren Reed **RC**	.05
369	Jeff McKnight **RC**	.05
370	Scott Leius **RC**	.05
371	Mark Dewey **RC**	.05
372	Mark Lee **RC**	.05
373	Rosario Rodriguez **RC**	.05
374	Chuck McElroy **RC**	.05
375	Mike Bell **RC**	.05
376	Mickey Morandini **RC**	.05

377 Bill Haselman **RC** .05
378 Dave Pavlas **RC** .05
379 Derrick May .05
380 Jeromy Burnitz **RC** (1st Draft Pick) .25
381 Donald Peters **RC** (1st Draft Pick) .05
382 Alex Fernandez **RC** (1st Draft Pick) .05
383 Mike Mussina **RC** (1st Draft Pick) 1.00
384 Daniel Smith **RC** (1st Draft Pick) .05
385 Lance Dickson **RC** (1st Draft Pick) .10
386 Carl Everett **RC** (1st Draft Pick) .40
387 Thomas Nevers **RC** (1st Draft Pick) .05
388 Adam Hyzdu **RC** (1st Draft Pick) .05
389 Todd Van Poppel **RC** (1st Draft Pick) .10
390 Rondell White **RC** (1st Draft Pick) .30
391 Marc Newfield **RC** (1st Draft Pick) .05
392 Julio Franco/AS .05
393 Wade Boggs/AS .25
394 Ozzie Guillen/AS .05
395 Cecil Fielder/AS .05
396 Ken Griffey Jr./AS .30
397 Rickey Henderson/AS .20
398 Jose Canseco/AS .15
399 Roger Clemens/AS .30
400 Sandy Alomar,Jr./AS .05
401 Bobby Thigpen/AS .05
402 Bobby Bonilla (Master Blaster) .05
403 Eric Davis (Master Blaster) .05
404 Fred McGriff (Master Blaster) .05
405 Glenn Davis (Master Blaster) .05
406 Kevin Mitchell (Master Blaster) .05
407 Rob Dibble (K-Man) .05
408 Ramon Martinez (K-Man) .05
409 David Cone (K-Man) .05
410 Bobby Witt (K-Man) .05
411 Mark Langston (K-Man) .05
412 Bo Jackson (Rifleman) .10
413 Shawon Dunston (Rifleman) .05
414 Jesse Barfield (Rifleman) .05
415 Ken Caminiti (Rifleman) .05
416 Benito Santiago (Rifleman) .05
417 Nolan Ryan (Highlight) .40
418 Bobby Thigpen/HL .05
419 Ramon Martinez/HL .05
420 Bo Jackson/HL .10
421 Carlton Fisk/HL .20
422 Jimmy Key .05
423 Junior Noboa **RC** .05
424 Al Newman .05
425 Pat Borders .05
426 Von Hayes .05
427 Tim Teufel .05
428 Eric Plunk .05
429 John Moses .05
430 Mike Witt .05
431 Otis Nixon .05
432 Tony Fernandez .05
433 Rance Mulliniks .05
434 Dan Petry .05
435 Bob Geren .05
436 Steve Frey **RC** .05
437 Jamie Moyer .05
438 Junior Ortiz .05
439 Tom O'Malley .05
440 Pat Combs .05
441 Jose Canseco/DT .15
442 Alfredo Griffin .05
443 Andres Galarraga .05
444 Bryn Smith .05
445 Andre Dawson .25
446 Juan Samuel .05
447 Mike Aldrete .05
448 Ron Gant .05
449 Fernando Valenzuela .05
450 Vince Coleman .05
451 Kevin Mitchell .05
452 Spike Owen .05
453 Mike Bielecki .05
454 Dennis Martinez .05
455 Brett Butler .05
456 Ron Darling .05
457 Dennis Rasmussen .05
458 Ken Howell .05
459 Steve Bedrosian .05
460 Frank Viola .05
461 Jose Lind .05
462 Chris Sabo .05
463 Dante Bichette .05
464 Rick Mahler .05
465 John Smiley .05
466 Devon White .05
467 John Orton .05
468 Mike Stanton .05
469 Billy Hatcher .05
470 Wally Joyner .05
471 Gene Larkin .05
472 Doug Drabek .05
473 Gary Sheffield .30
474 David Wells .05
475 Andy Van Slyke .05
476 Mike Gallego .05
477 B.J. Surhoff .05
478 Gene Nelson .05
479 Mariano Duncan .05
480 Fred McGriff .05
481 Jerry Browne .05
482 Alvin Davis .05
483 Bill Wegman .05
484 Dave Parker .05
485 Dennis Eckersley .35
486 Erik Hanson .05
487 Bill Ripken .05
488 Tom Candiotti .05
489 Mike Schooler .05
490 Gregg Olson .05
491 Chris James .05
492 Pete Harnisch .05
493 Julio Franco .05
494 Greg Briley .05
495 Ruben Sierra .05
496 Steve Olin .05
497 Mike Fetters .05
498 Mark Williamson .05
499 Bob Tewksbury .05
500 Tony Gwynn .50
501 Randy Myers .05
502 Keith Comstock .05
503 Craig Worthington .05
504 Mark Eichhorn .05
505 Barry Larkin .05
506 Dave Johnson .05
507 Bobby Witt .05
508 Joe Orsulak .05
509 Pete O'Brien .05
510 Brad Arnsberg .05
511 Storm Davis .05
512 Bob Milacki .05
513 Bill Pecota .05
514 Glenallen Hill .05
515 Danny Tartabull .05
516 Mike Moore .05
517 Ron Robinson .05
518 Mark Gardner .05
519 Rick Wrona .05
520 Mike Scioscia .05
521 Frank Wills .05
522 Greg Brock .05
523 Jack Clark .05
524 Bruce Ruffin .05
525 Robin Yount .40
526 Tom Foley .05
527 Pat Perry .05
528 Greg Vaughn .05
529 Wally Whitehurst .05
530 Norm Charlton .05
531 Marvell Wynne .05
532 Jim Gantner .05
533 Greg Litton .05
534 Manny Lee .05
535 Scott Bailes .05
536 Charlie Leibrandt .05
537 Roger McDowell .05
538 Andy Benes .05
539 Rick Honeycutt .05
540 Dwight Gooden .05
541 Scott Garrelts .05
542 Dave Clark .05
543 Lonnie Smith .05
544 Rick Rueschel .05
545 Delino DeShields .05
546 Mike Sharperson .05
547 Mike Kingery .05
548 Terry Kennedy .05
549 David Cone .05
550 Orel Hershiser .05
551 Matt Nokes .05
552 Eddie Williams .05
553 Frank DiPino .05
554 Fred Lynn .05
555 Alex Cole **RC** .05
556 Terry Leach .05
557 Chet Lemon .05
558 Paul Mirabella .05
559 Bill Long .05
560 Phil Bradley .05
561 Duane Ward .05
562 Dave Bergman .05
563 Eric Show .05
564 Xavier Hernandez **RC** .05
565 Jeff Parrett .05
566 Chuck Cary .05
567 Ken Hill .05
568 Bob Welch .05
569 John Mitchell .05
570 Travis Fryman .05
571 Derek Lilliquist .05
572 Steve Lake .05
573 John Barfield **RC** .05
574 Randy Bush .05
575 Joe Magrane .05
576 Edgar Diaz .05
577 Casy Candaele .05
578 Jesse Orosco .05
579 Tom Henke .05
580 Rick Cerone .05
581 Drew Hall .05
582 Tony Castillo .05
583 Jimmy Jones .05
584 Rick Reed .05
585 Joe Girardi .05
586 Jeff Gray **RC** .05
587 Luis Polonia .05
588 Joe Klink **RC** .05
589 Rex Hudler .05
590 Kirk McCaskill .05
591 Juan Agosto .05
592 Wes Gardner .05
593 Rich Rodriguez **RC** .05
594 Mitch Webster .05
595 Kelly Gruber .05
596 Dale Mohorcic .05
597 Willie McGee .05
598 Bill Krueger .05
599 Bob Walk .05
600 Kevin Maas .05
601 Danny Jackson .05
602 Craig McMurtry .05
603 Curtis Wilkerson .05
604 Adam Peterson .05
605 Sam Horn .05
606 Tommy Gregg .05
607 Ken Dayley .05
608 Carmelo Castillo .05
609 John Shelby .05
610 Don Slaught .05
611 Calvin Schiraldi .05
612 Dennis Lamp .05
613 Andres Thomas .05
614 Jose Gonzales .05
615 Randy Ready .05
616 Kevin Bass .05
617 Mike Marshall .05
618 Daryl Boston .05
619 Andy McGaffigan .05
620 Joe Oliver .05
621 Jim Gott .05
622 Jose Oquendo .05
623 Jose DeJesus .05
624 Mike Brumley .05
625 John Olerud .05
626 Ernest Riles .05
627 Gene Harris .05
628 Jose Uribe .05
629 Darnell Coles .05
630 Carney Lansford .05
631 Tim Leary .05
632 Tim Hulett .05
633 Kevin Elster .05
634 Tony Fossas .05
635 Francisco Oliveras .05
636 Bob Patterson .05
637 Gary Ward .05
638 Rene Gonzales .05
639 Don Robinson .05
640 Darryl Strawberry .05
641 Dave Anderson .05
642 Scott Scudder .05
643 Reggie Harris **RC** .05
644 Dave Henderson .05
645 Ben McDonald .05
646 Bob Kipper .05
647 Hal Morris .05
648 Tim Birtsas .05
649 Steve Searcy .05
650 Dale Murphy .20
651 Ron Oester .05
652 Mike LaCoss .05
653 Ron Jones .05
654 Kelly Downs .05
655 Roger Clemens .55
656 Herm Winningham .05
657 Trevor Wilson .05
658 Jose Rijo .05
659 Dann Bilardello .05
660 Gregg Jefferies .05
661 Doug Drabek/AS .05
662 Randy Myers/AS .05
663 Benito Santiago/AS .05
664 Will Clark/AS .05
665 Ryne Sandberg/AS .25
666 Barry Larkin/AS .05
667 Matt Williams/AS .05
668 Barry Bonds/AS .35
669 Eric Davis .05
670 Bobby Bonilla/AS .05
671 Chipper Jones **RC** (1st Draft Pick) 1.50
672 Eric Christopherson **RC** (1st Draft Pick) .05
673 Robbie Beckett **RC** (1st Draft Pick) .05
674 Shane Andrews **RC** (1st Draft Pick) .15
675 Steve Karsay **RC** (1st Draft Pick) .10
676 Aaron Holbert **RC** (1st Draft Pick) .05
677 Donovan Osborne **RC** (1st Draft Pick) .05
678 Todd Ritchie **RC** (1st Draft Pick) .05
679 Ron Walden **RC** (1st Draft Pick) .05
680 Tim Costo **RC** (1st Draft Pick) .05
681 Dan Wilson **RC** (1st Draft Pick) .10
682 Kurt Miller **RC** (1st Draft Pick) .05
683 Mike Lieberthal **RC** (1st Draft Pick) .25
684 Roger Clemens (K-Man) .25
685 Dwight Gooden (K-Man) .05
686 Nolan Ryan (K-Man) .35
687 Frank Viola (K-Man) .05
688 Erik Hanson (K-Man) .05
689 Matt Williams (Master Blaster) .05
690 Jose Canseco (Master Blaster) .10
691 Darryl Strawberry (Master Blaster) .05
692 Bo Jackson (Master Blaster) .10
693 Cecil Fielder (Master Blaster) .05
694 Sandy Alomar, Jr. (Rifleman) .05
695 Cory Snyder (Rifleman) .05
696 Eric Davis (Rifleman) .05
697 Ken Griffey Jr. (Rifleman) .30
698 Andy Van Slyke (Rifleman) .05
699 Mark Langston, Mike Witt (No-hitter) .05
700 Randy Johnson (No-hitter) .20
701a Nolan Ryan (No-hitter) (White background on stat box.) 2.00
701b Nolan Ryan (No-hitter) (Blue background on stat box.) .35
702 Dave Stewart (No-hitter) .05
703 Fernando Valenzuela (No-hitter) .05
704 Andy Hawkins (No-hitter) .05
705 Melido Perez (No-hitter) .05
706 Terry Mulholland (No-hitter) .05
707 Dave Stieb (No-hitter) .05
708 Brian Barnes **RC** .05
709 Bernard Gilkey .05
710 Steve Decker **RC** .05
711 Paul Faries **RC** .05
712 Paul Marak **RC** .05
713 Wes Chamberlain **RC** .05
714 Kevin Belcher **RC** .05
715 Dan Boone **RC** .05
716 Steve Adkins **RC** .05
717 Geronimo Pena **RC** .05
718 Howard Farmer **RC** .05
719 Mark Leonard **RC** .05
720 Tom Lampkin .05
721 Mike Gardiner **RC** .05
722 Jeff Conine **RC** .25
723 Efrain Valdez **RC** .05
724 Chuck Malone **RC** .05
725 Leo Gomez **RC** .05
726 Paul McClellan **RC** .05
727 Mark Leiter **RC** .05
728 Rich DeLucia **RC** .05
729 Mel Rojas **RC** .05
730 Hector Wagner **RC** .05
731 Ray Lankford .05
732 Turner Ward **RC** .05
733 Gerald Alexander **RC** .05
734 Scott Anderson **RC** .05
735 Tony Perezchica **RC** .05
736 Jimmy Kremers **RC** .05
737a American Flag (SCORE 1991 copyright, unmarked promo.) .25
737b American Flag (1991 SCORE in copyright) .25
738 Mike York **RC** .05
739 Mike Rochford **RC** .05
740 Scott Aldred **RC** .05
741 Rico Brogna **RC** .05
742 Dave Burba **RC** .05
743 Ray Stephens **RC** .05
744 Eric Gunderson **RC** .05
745 Troy Afenir **RC** .05
746 Jeff Shaw **RC** .05
747 Orlando Merced **RC** .10
748 Omar Oliveras **RC** .05
749 Jerry Kutzler **RC** .05
750 Mo Vaughn .05
751 Matt Stark **RC** .05
752 Randy Hennis **RC** .05
753 Andujar Cedeno **RC** .05
754 Kelvin Torve **RC** .05
755 Joe Kraemer **RC** .05
756 Phil Clark **RC** .05
757 Ed Vosberg **RC** .05
758 Mike Perez **RC** .05
759 Scott Lewis **RC** .05
760 Steve Chitren **RC** .05
761 Ray Young **RC** .05
762 Andres Santana **RC** .05
763 Rodney McCray **RC** .05
764 Sean Berry **RC** .05
765 Brent Mayne .05
766 Mike Simms **RC** .05
767 Glenn Sutko **RC** .05
768 Gary Disarcina .05
769 George Brett (HL) .25
770 Cecil Fielder (HL) .05
771 Jim Presley .05
772 John Dopson .05
773 Bo Jackson (Breaker) .10
774 Brent Knackert **RC** .05
775 Bill Doran .05
776 Dick Schofield .05
777 Nelson Santovenia .05
778 Mark Guthrie **RC** .05
779 Mark Lemke .05
780 Terry Steinbach .05
781 Tom Bolton .05
782 Randy Tomlin **RC** .05
783 Jeff Kunkel .05
784 Felix Jose .05
785 Rick Sutcliffe .05
786 John Cerutti .05
787 Jose Vizcaino .05
788 Curt Schilling .35
789 Ed Whitson .05
790 Tony Pena .05
791 John Candelaria .05
792 Carmelo Martinez .05
793 Sandy Alomar, Jr. .05
794 Jim Neidlinger **RC** .05
795 Red's October (Barry Larkin, Chris Sabo) .10
796 Paul Sorrento .05
797 Tom Pagnozzi .05
798 Tino Martinez .05
799 Scott Ruskin **RC** .05
800 Kirk Gibson .05
801 Walt Terrell .05
802 John Russell .05
803 Chili Davis .05
804 Chris Nabholz **RC** .05
805 Juan Gonzalez .20
806 Ron Hassey .05
807 Todd Worrell .05
808 Tommy Greene .05
809 Joel Skinner .05
810 Benito Santiago .05
811 Pat Tabler .05
812 Scott Erickson **RC** .05
813 Moises Alou .05
814 Dale Sveum .05
815 Ryne Sandberg (Man of the Year) .25
816 Rick Dempsey .05
817 Scott Bankhead .05
818 Jason Grimsley .05
819 Doug Jennings .05
820 Tom Herr .05
821 Rob Ducey .05
822 Luis Quinones .05
823 Greg Minton .05
824 Mark Grant .05
825 Ozzie Smith .50
826 Dave Eiland .05
827 Danny Heep .05
828 Hensley Meulens .05
829 Charlie O'Brien .05
830 Glenn Davis .05
831 John Marzano .05
832 Steve Ontiveros .05
833 Ron Karkovice .05
834 Jerry Goff **RC** .05
835 Ken Griffey Sr. .05
836 Kevin Reimer **RC** .05
837 Randy Kutcher .05
838 Mike Blowers .05
839 Mike Macfarlane .05
840 Frank Thomas .40
841 Ken Griffey Sr., Ken Griffey Jr. .20
842 Jack Howell .05
843 Mauro Gozzo **RC** .05
844 Gerald Young .05
845 Zane Smith .05
846 Kevin Brown .05
847 Sil Campusano .05
848 Larry Andersen .05
849 Cal Ripken, Jr. (Franchise) .35
850 Roger Clemens (Franchise) .30
851 Sandy Alomar, Jr. (Franchise) .05
852 Alan Trammell (Franchise) .05
853 George Brett (Franchise) .25
854 Robin Yount (Franchise) .25
855 Kirby Puckett (Franchise) .25
856 Don Mattingly (Franchise) .30
857 Rickey Henderson (Franchise) .20
858 Ken Griffey Jr. (Franchise) .30
859 Ruben Sierra (Franchise) .05
860 John Olerud (Franchise) .05
861 Dave Justice (Franchise) .05
862 Ryne Sandberg (Franchise) .25
863 Eric Davis (Franchise) .05
864 Darryl Strawberry (Franchise) .05
865 Tim Wallach (Franchise) .05
866 Dwight Gooden (Franchise) .05
867 Len Dykstra (Franchise) .05
868 Barry Bonds (Franchise) .35
869 Todd Zeile (Franchise) .05
870 Benito Santiago (Franchise) .05
871 Will Clark (Franchise) .05
872 Craig Biggio (Franchise) .05
873 Wally Joyner (Franchise) .05
874 Frank Thomas (Franchise) .20
875 Rickey Henderson (MVP) .20
876 Barry Bonds (MVP) .35
877 Bob Welch (Cy Young) .05
878 Doug Drabek (Cy Young) .05
879 Sandy Alomar, Jr. (ROY) .05
880 Dave Justice (ROY) .05
881 Damon Berryhill .05
882 Frank Viola/DT .05
883 Dave Stewart/DT .05
884 Doug Jones/DT .05
885 Randy Myers/DT .05
886 Will Clark/DT .05
887 Roberto Alomar/DT .10
888 Barry Larkin/DT .05
889 Wade Boggs/DT .25
890 Rickey Henderson/DT .20
891 Kirby Puckett/DT .25
892 Ken Griffey Jr./DT .30
893 Benito Santiago/DT .05

Cooperstown

COOPERSTOWN CARD

NOLAN RYAN

This seven-card set was included as an insert in every factory set. The card fronts are white, with an oval-vignetted player portrait. The backs have green borders surrounding a yellow background which contains a summary of the player's career.

		NM/M
Complete Set (7):		3.50
Common Player:		.25
B1	Wade Boggs	.50
B2	Barry Larkin	.25
B3	Ken Griffey Jr.	1.00
B4	Rickey Henderson	.35
B5	George Brett	.75
B6	Will Clark	.25
D7	Nolan Ryan	1.50

Hot Rookies

These standard-size cards were inserted one per every 100-card 1991 Score blister pack. Action photos with white borders are featured on the front, and "Hot Rookie" is written in yellow at the top. The background is shaded from yellow to orange. The backs are numbered and each has a color mug shot and a career summary.

		NM/M
Complete Set (10):		2.50
Common Player:		.10
1	Dave Justice	.25
2	Kevin Maas	.10
3	Hal Morris	.10
4	Frank Thomas	1.50
5	Jeff Conine	.10
6	Sandy Alomar Jr.	.10
7	Ray Lankford	.10
8	Steve Decker	.10
9	Juan Gonzalez	.50
10	Jose Offerman	.10

Mickey Mantle

This special set recalls Mickey Mantle's career as a Yankee. Card fronts are glossy and have red and white borders. The card's caption appears at the bottom in a blue stripe. The backs have a photo and a summary of the caption, plus the card number and serial

number. Dealers and media members received the sets, which were limited to 5,000, in a fin-fold plastic wrapper. A total of 2,500 of the cards were numbered and autographed.

		NM/M
Complete Set (7):		35.00
Common Card:		7.50
Autographed Card:		575.00
1	The Rookie	9.00
2	Triple Crown	7.50
3	World Series	7.50
4	Going, Going, Gone	7.50
5	Speed and Grace	7.50
6	A True Yankee	7.50
7	Twilight	7.50

Traded

This 110-card set features players with new teams as well as 1991 Major League rookies. The cards are designed in the same style as the regular 1991 Score issue. The cards once again feature a "T" designation along with the card number. The complete set was sold at hobby shops in a special box.

		NM/M
Complete Set (110):		4.00
Common Player:		.05
1	Bo Jackson	.10
2	Mike Flanagan	.05
3	Pete Incaviglia	.05
4	Jack Clark	.05
5	Hubie Brooks	.05
6	Ivan Calderon	.05
7	Glenn Davis	.05
8	Wally Backman	.05
9	Dave Smith	.05
10	Tim Raines	.05
11	Joe Carter	.05
12	Sid Bream	.05
13	George Bell	.05
14	Steve Bedrosian	.05
15	Willie Wilson	.05
16	Darryl Strawberry	.05
17	Danny Jackson	.05
18	Kirk Gibson	.05
19	Willie McGee	.05
20	Junior Felix	.05
21	Steve Farr	.05
22	Pat Tabler	.05
23	Brett Butler	.05
24	Danny Darwin	.05
25	Mickey Tettleton	.05
26	Gary Carter	.50
27	Mitch Williams	.05
28	Candy Maldonado	.05
29	Otis Nixon	.05
30	Brian Downing	.05
31	Tom Candiotti	.05
32	John Candelaria	.05
33	Rob Murphy	.05
34	Deion Sanders	.05
35	Willie Randolph	.05
36	Pete Harnisch	.05
37	Dante Bichette	.05
38	Garry Templeton	.05
39	Gary Gaetti	.05
40	John Cerutti	.05
41	Rick Cerone	.05
42	Mike Pagliarulo	.05
43	Ron Hassey	.05
44	Roberto Alomar	.20
45	Mike Boddicker	.05
46	Bud Black	.05
47	Rob Deer	.05
48	Devon White	.05
49	Luis Sojo	.05
50	Terry Pendleton	.05
51	Kevin Gross	.05
52	Mike Huff	.05
53	Dave Righetti	.05
54	Matt Young	.05
55	Ernest Riles	.05
56	Bill Gullickson	.05
57	Vince Coleman	.05
58	Fred McGriff	.05
59	Franklin Stubbs	.05
60	Eric King	.05
61	Cory Snyder	.05
62	Dwight Evans	.05
63	Gerald Perry	.05
64	Eric Show	.05
65	Shawn Hillegas	.05
66	Tony Fernandez	.05
67	Tim Teufel	.05
68	Mitch Webster	.05
69	Mike Heath	.05
70	Chili Davis	.05
71	Larry Andersen	.05
72	Gary Varsho	.05
73	Juan Berenguer	.05
74	Jack Morris	.05
75	Barry Jones	.05
76	Rafael Belliard	.05
77	Steve Buechele	.05
78	Scott Sanderson	.05
79	Bob Ojeda	.05
80	Curt Schilling	.35
81	Brian Drahman **RC**	.05
82	Ivan Rodriguez **RC**	1.00
83	David Howard **RC**	.05
84	Heath Slocumb **RC**	.05
85	Mike Timlin **RC**	.05
86	Darryl Kile **RC**	.05
87	Pete Schourek **RC**	.05
88	Bruce Walton **RC**	.05
89	Al Osuna **RC**	.05
90	Gary Scott **RC**	.05
91	Doug Simons **RC**	.05
92	Chris Jones **RC**	.05
93	Chuck Knoblauch	.05
94	Dana Allison **RC**	.05
95	Erik Pappas **RC**	.05
96	Jeff Bagwell **RC**	2.50
97	Kirk Dressendorfer **RC**	.05
98	Freddie Benavides **RC**	.05
99	Luis Gonzalez **RC**	.50
100	Wade Taylor **RC**	.05
101	Ed Sprague **RC**	.05
102	Bob Scanlan **RC**	.05
103	Rick Wilkins **RC**	.05
104	Chris Donnels **RC**	.05
105	Joe Slusarski **RC**	.05
106	Mark Lewis **RC**	.05
107	Pat Kelly **RC**	.05
108	John Briscoe **RC**	.05
109	Luis Lopez **RC**	.05
110	Jeff Johnson **RC**	.05

Blue Jays

Sold as a special boxed issue including 40 player cards and five trivia cards, this set features the 1991 Blue Jays and their hosting of the 1991 All-Star Game. Cards carry a super-glossy front finish that features a player action photo in a home plate-shaped frame at center. Around the photo are blue and white border designs with the player's name and position at top, and Score and Blue Jays logos at bottom. Backs repeat the blue and white motif with a color player portrait, biographical notes, stats and career summary.

		NM/M
Complete Set (40):		7.00
Common Player:		.25
1	Joe Carter	.35
2	Tom Henke	.25
3	Jimmy Key	.25
4	Al Leiter	.25
5	Dave Steib	.25
6	Todd Stottlemyre	.35
7	Mike Timlin	.25
8	Duane Ward	.25
9	David Wells	.50
10	Frank Wills	.25
11	Pat Borders	.25
12	Greg Myers	.25
13	Roberto Alomar	2.50
14	Rene Gonzalez	.25
15	Kelly Gruber	.25
16	Manny Lee	.25
17	Rance Mulliniks	.25
18	John Olerud	1.00
19	Pat Tabler	.25
20	Derek Bell	.25
21	Jim Acker	.25
22	Rob Ducey	.25
23	Devon White	.35
24	Mookie Wilson	.25
25	Juan Guzman	.25
26	Ed Sprague	.25
27	Ken Dayley	.25
28	Tom Candiotti	.25
29	Candy Maldonado	.25
30	Eddie Zosky	.25
31	Steve Karsay	.25
32	Bob MacDonald	.25
33	Ray Giannelli	.25
34	Jerry Schunk	.25
35	Dave Weathers	.25
36	Cito Gaston	.25
37	Joe Carter/AS	.25
38	Jimmy Key/AS	.25
39	Roberto Alomar/AS	1.50
40	1991 All-Star Game	.25

FanFest/National

Two versions of this 10-card set were produced for distribution at the All-Star FanFest and the National Sports Collectors Convention. The appropriate venue is listed in a red stripe on back under the player career summary. Fronts have a color action photo against a background of pale green with blue ballplayer silhouettes and yellow baseballs. Backs repeat the player figure and baseball motif on a white background. A trapezoid at center has a player portrait photo, color team logo, biographical details and career highlights. At present neither version of these cards carries a premium over the other.

		NM/M
Complete Set (10):		2.00
Common Player:		.25
1	Ray Lankford	.25
2	Steve Decker	.25
3	Gary Scott	.25
4	Hensley Meulens	.25
5	Tim Naehring	.25
6	Mark Whiten	.25
7	Ed Sprague	.25
8	Charles Nagy	.25
9	Terry Shumpert	.25
10	Chuck Knoblauch	.25

"Life and Times of Nolan Ryan"

This four-card career highlights set was distributed with a series of four collector magazines. Cards feature color photos with Score and Texas Rangers logos in separate corners. A red stripe above the photo, or to its left, names the highlight; a blue stripe above or to the left of that has his name and position. Horizontally formatted backs have another color photo and a paragraph about the milestone.

		NM/M
Complete Set (4):		6.00
Common Player:		1.50
1	5,000th Career Strikeout (Nolan Ryan)	1.50
2	6th Career No-Hitter (Nolan Ryan)	1.50
3	300th Career Victory (Nolan Ryan)	1.50
4	7th Career No-Hitter (Nolan Ryan)	1.50

Rising Stars

Marketed along with 1990-91 "Baseball's Hottest Rookies" magazine, this 100-card set features top rookies and young players. The cards are similar in design to the Score Superstar set. The magazine/card sets were available to a select group of retailers.

		NM/M
Complete Set (100):		2.50
Common Player:		.05
1	Sandy Alomar,Jr.	.05
2	Tom Edens	.05
3	Terry Shumpert	.05
4	Shawn Boskie	.05
5	Steve Avery	.05
6	Deion Sanders	.05
7	John Burkett	.05
8	Stan Belinda	.05
9	Thomas Howard	.05
10	Wayne Edwards	.05
11	Rick Parker	.05
12	Randy Veres	.05
13	Alex Cole	.05
14	Scott Chaimparino	.05
15	Greg Olson	.05
16	Jose DeJesus	.05
17	Mike Blowers	.05
18	Jeff Huson	.05
19	Willie Blair	.05
20	Howard Farmer	.05
21	Larry Walker	.05
22	Scott Hemond	.05
23	Mel Stottlemyre	.05
24	Mark Whiten	.05
25	Jeff Schulz	.05
26	Gary Disarcina	.05
27	George Canale	.05
28	Dean Palmer	.05
29	Jim Leyritz	.05
30	Carlos Baerga	.05
31	Rafael Valdez	.05
32	Derek Bell	.05
33	Francisco Cabrera	.05
34	Chris Hoiles	.05
35	Craig Grebeck	.05
36	Scott Coolbaugh	.05
37	Kevin Wickander	.05
38	Marquis Grissom	.05
39	Chip Hale	.05
40	Kevin Maas	.05
41	Juan Gonzalez	.50
42	Eric Anthony	.05
43	Luis Sojo	.05
44	Paul Sorrento	.05
45	Dave Justice	.05
46	Oscar Azocar	.05
47	Charles Nagy	.05
48	Robin Ventura	.05
49	Reggie Harris	.05
50	Ben McDonald	.05
51	Hector Villanueva	.05
52	Kevin Tapani	.05
53	Brian Bohanon	.05
54	Tim Layana	.05
55	Delino DeShields	.05
56	Beau Allred	.05
57	Eric Gunderson	.05
58	Kent Mercker	.05
59	Juan Bell	.05
60	Glenallen Hill	.05
61	David Segui	.05
62	Alan Mills	.05
63	Mike Harkey	.05
64	Bill Sampen	.05
65	Greg Vaughn	.05
66	Alex Fernandez	.05
67	Mike Hartley	.05
68	Travis Fryman	.05
69	Dave Rohde	.05
70	Tom Lampkin	.05
71	Mark Gardner	.05
72	Pat Combs	.05
73	Kevin Appier	.05
74	Mike Fetters	.05
75	Greg Myers	.05
76	Steve Searcy	.05
77	Tim Naehring	.05
78	Frank Thomas	1.50
79	Todd Hundley	.05
80	Ed Vosburg	.05
81	Todd Zeile	.05
82	Lee Stevens	.05
83	Scott Radinsky	.05
84	Hensley Meulens	.05
85	Brian DuBois	.05
86	Steve Olin	.05
87	Julio Machado	.05
88	Jose Vizcaino	.05
89	Mark Lemke	.05
90	Felix Jose	.05
91	Wally Whitehurst	.05
92	Dana Kiecker	.05
93	Mike Munoz	.05
94	Adam Peterson	.05
95	Tim Drummond	.05
96	Dave Hollins	.05
97	Craig Wilson	.05
98	Hal Morris	.05
99	Jose Offerman	.05
100	John Olerud	.05

Rookies

This 40-card boxed set did not receive much attention in the hobby world, but features some of the top young players of 1991. The card fronts feature full-color action photos with a "Rookies" banner along the side border. The backs feature statistics and a player profile. This set was available through hobby dealers and is Score's first release of its kind.

		NM/M
Complete Set (40):		1.00
Common Player:		.05
1	Mel Rojas	.05
2	Ray Lankford	.05
3	Scott Aldred	.05
4	Turner Ward	.05
5	Omar Olivares	.05
6	Mo Vaughn	.05
7	Phil Clark	.05
8	Brent Mayne	.05
9	Scott Lewis	.05
10	Brian Barnes	.05
11	Bernard Gilkey	.05
12	Steve Decker	.05
13	Paul Marak	.05
14	Wes Chamberlain	.05
15	Kevin Belcher	.05
16	Steve Adkins	.05
17	Geronimo Pena	.05
18	Mark Leonard	.05
19	Jeff Conine	.05
20	Leo Gomez	.05
21	Chuck Malone	.05
22	Beau Allred	.05
23	Todd Hundley	.05
24	Lance Dickson	.05
25	Mike Benjamin	.05
26	Jose Offerman	.05
27	Terry Shumpert	.05
28	Darren Lewis	.05
29	Scott Chiamparino	.05
30	Tim Naehring	.05
31	David Segui	.05
32	Karl Rhodes	.05
33	Mickey Morandini	.05
34	Chuck McElroy	.05
35	Tim McIntosh	.05
36	Derrick May	.05
37	Rich DeLucia	.05
38	Tino Martinez	.05
39	Hensley Meulens	.05
40	Andujar Cedeno	.05

Superstars

This 100-card set features full-color action photos on the card fronts and posed shots on the flip sides. The set was marketed along with the magazine "1991 Baseball's Hottest Players." The cards feature red, white, and blue borders. The backs contain brief career highlights. The magazine/card set combo was available to select retailers.

		NM/M
Complete Set (100):		5.00
Common Player:		.05
1	Jose Canseco	.25
2	Bo Jackson	.10
3	Wade Boggs	.50
4	Will Clark	.05
5	Ken Griffey Jr.	.65
6	Doug Drabek	.05
7	Kirby Puckett	.50
8	Joe Orsulak	.05
9	Eric Davis	.05
10	Rickey Henderson	.40
11	Lenny Dykstra	.05
12	Ruben Sierra	.05
13	Paul Molitor	.40
14	Ron Gant	.05
15	Ozzie Guillen	.05
16	Ramon Martinez	.05
17	Edgar Martinez	.05
18	Ozzie Smith	.50
19	Charlie Hayes	.05
20	Barry Larkin	.05
21	Cal Ripken, Jr.	1.00
22	Andy Van Slyke	.05
23	Don Mattingly	.60
24	Dave Stewart	.05
25	Nolan Ryan	1.00
26	Barry Bonds	1.00
27	Gregg Olson	.05
28	Chris Sabo	.05
29	John Franco	.05
30	Gary Sheffield	.25
31	Jeff Treadway	.05
32	Tom Browning	.05
33	Jose Lind	.05
34	Dave Magadan	.05
35	Dale Murphy	.20
36	Tom Candiotti	.05
37	Willie McGee	.05
38	Robin Yount	.40
39	Mark McGwire	.75
40	George Bell	.05
41	Carlton Fisk	.40
42	Bobby Bonilla	.05
43	Randy Milligan	.05
44	Dave Parker	.05
45	Shawon Dunston	.05
46	Brian Harper	.05
47	John Tudor	.05
48	Ellis Burks	.05
49	Bob Welch	.05
50	Roger Clemens	.60
51	Mike Henneman	.05
52	Eddie Murray	.40
53	Kal Daniels	.05
54	Doug Jones	.05
55	Craig Biggio	.05
56	Rafael Palmeiro	.35
57	Wally Joyner	.05
58	Tim Wallach	.05
59	Bret Saberhagen	.05
60	Ryne Sandberg	.50
61	Benito Santiago	.05
62	Darryl Strawberry	.05
63	Alan Trammell	.05
64	Kelly Gruber	.05
65	Dwight Gooden	.05
66	Dave Winfield	.40
67	Rick Aguilera	.05
68	Dave Righetti	.05
69	Jim Abbott	.05
70	Frank Viola	.05

71	Fred McGriff	.05
72	Steve Sax	.05
73	Dennis Eckersley	.35
74	Cory Snyder	.05
75	Mackey Sasser	.05
76	Candy Maldonado	.05
77	Matt Williams	.05
78	Kent Hrbek	.05
79	Randy Myers	.05
80	Gregg Jefferies	.05
81	Joe Carter	.05
82	Mike Greenwell	.05
83	Jack Armstrong	.05
84	Julio Franco	.05
85	George Brett	.60
86	Howard Johnson	.05
87	Andre Dawson	.25
88	Cecil Fielder	.05
89	Tim Raines	.05
90	Chuck Finley	.05
91	Mark Grace	.05
92	Brook Jacoby	.05
93	Dave Steib	.05
94	Tony Gwynn	.50
95	Bobby Thigpen	.05
96	Roberto Kelly	.05
97	Kevin Seitzer	.05
98	Kevin Mitchell	.05
99	Dwight Evans	.05
100	Roberto Alomar	.20

1992 Score Promos

The six known Score promo cards differ from the issued versions in 1992 only in the lack of 1991 and career stats on the back and changes in the career summaries on some of the cards. The promos of Sandberg and Mack were distributed at a St. Louis baseball card show in November 1991, and are somewhat scarcer than the others.

		NM/M
Complete Set (6):		15.00
Common Player:		2.00
1	Ken Griffey Jr.	6.00
4	Dave Justice	2.00
122	Robin Ventura	2.00
200	Ryne Sandberg	5.00
241	Steve Avery	2.00
284	Shane Mack	2.00

1992 Score/ Pinnacle Promo Panels

Score debuted both its base-brand (Score) and premium-brand (Pinnacle) sets at one time in 1992 with this issue of four-card panels. Each panel measures 1/16" short each way of 5" x 7" and features Score cards in the upper-left and lower-right, with Pinnacle samples at upper-right and lower-left. Backs have a very light gray overprint, "FOR PROMOTIONAL PURPOSES ONLY NOT FOR RESALE." Cards cut from the panels would be otherwise indistinguishable from the issued versions. Panels are checklisted here alphabetically according to the lowest-numbered Score player. S prefix to the card number indicates Score, P is for Pinnacle. The prefixes do not appear on the cards.

		NM/M
Complete Set (25):		100.00
Common Panel:		3.00
(1)	S2 Nolan Ryan, S13 Lonnie Smith, P7 Willie McGee, P18 Terry Pendleton	15.00
(2)	S3 Will Clark, S12 Mark Langston, P8 Paul Molitor, P17 Devon White	4.50
(3)	S4 Dave Justice, S19 Mark Carreon, P1 Frank Thomas, P16 Dave Henderson	4.50
(4)	S5 Dave Henderson, S15 Roberto Alomar, P10 Ryne Sandberg, P20 Kirby Puckett	7.50
(5)	S9 Darryl Strawberry, S14 Jeff Montgomery, P6 Ozzie Smith, P11 Kevin Seitzer	5.00
(6)	S22 Chuck Crim, S33 Jimmy Jones, P27 Jay Buhner, P38 Robin Yount	4.50
(7)	S23 Don Mattingly, S32 Dave Winfield, P28 Matt Williams, P37 George Bell	10.00
(8)	S24 Dickie Thon, S39 Gary Gaetti, P21 Orel Hershiser, P36 Wes Chamberlain	3.00
(9)	S25 Ron Gant, S35 Andres Galarraga, P30 Alex Fernandez, P40 Bruce Hurst	3.00
(10)	S29 Melido Perez, S34 Kevin Gross, P26 Ellis Burks, P31 Albert Belle	3.00
(11)	S42 Rick Aguilera, S53 Doug Jones, P47 Bill Doran, P58 Ivan Calderon	3.00
(12)	S43 Mike Gallego, S52 Todd Zeile, P48 Jerald Clark, P57 Lenny Harris	3.00
(13)	S44 Eric Davis, S59 Randy Ready, P41 Harold Baines, P56 Walt Weiss	3.00
(14)	S45 George Bell, S55 Rafael Palmeiro, P50 Nolan Ryan, P60 George Brett	20.00
(15)	S49 David Wells, S54 Bob Walk, P46 Chili Davis, P51 Phil Plantier	3.00
(16)	S62 Jack McDowell, S73 Juan Samuel, P67 Dave Hollins, P78 John Olerud	3.00
(17)	S63 Jim Acker, S72 Carlton Fisk, P68 Kent Hrbek, P77 Dennis Martinez	3.00
(18)	S64 Jay Buhner, S79 Kirk McCaskill, P61 Gregg Olson, P76 Terry Steinbach	3.00
(19)	S65 Travis Fryman, S75 Andre Dawson, P70 Jeff Bagwell, P80 Darryl Strawberry	4.50
(20)	S69 Ken Caminiti, S74 Todd Stottlemyre, P66 Alex Cole, P71 Jim Gantner	3.00
(21)	S82 Alex Fernandez, S93 Shawn Hillegas, P87 Bill Gullickson, P98 Jose Guzman	3.00
(22)	S83 Ivan Calderon, S92 Ozzie Guillen, P88 Bernard Gilkey, P97 Omar Vizquel	3.00
(23)	S84 Brent Mayne, S99 Tom Bolton, P81 Gary Gaetti, P96 Doug Drabek	3.00
(24)	S85 Jody Reed, S95 Vince Coleman, P90 Kevin Maas, P100 Dave Justice	3.00
(25)	S89 Hensley Meulens, S94 Chili Davis, P86 David Howard, P91 Mark Lewis	3.00

1992 Score

Score used a two series format for the second consecutive year in 1992. Cards 1-442 are featured in the first series. Fronts feature full-color game action photos. Backs feature color head shots of the players, team logo and career stats. Several subsets are included in 1992, including a five-card Joe DiMaggio set. DiMaggio autographed cards were also inserted into random packs. Cards 736-772 can be found with or without a "Rookie Prospects" banner on the card front. Rack packs could be found with random inserts of 1991 Rookie of the Year Chuck Knoblauch's 1990 Score #1 Draft Pick card in a special autographed editon of 3,000. Factory sets contain 17 bonus cards not found in any other packaging.

		NM/M
Unopened Fact. Set (910):		7.50
Complete Set (893):		5.00
Common Player:		.05
Wax Pack (16):		.40
Wax Box (36):		7.50
1	Ken Griffey Jr.	.65
2	Nolan Ryan	1.00
3	Will Clark	.05
4	Dave Justice	.05
5	Dave Henderson	.05
6	Bret Saberhagen	.05
7	Fred McGriff	.05
8	Erik Hanson	.05
9	Darryl Strawberry	.05
10	Dwight Gooden	.05
11	Juan Gonzalez	.20
12	Mark Langston	.05
13	Lonnie Smith	.05
14	Jeff Montgomery	.05
15	Roberto Alomar	.20
16	Delino DeShields	.05
17	Steve Bedrosian	.05
18	Terry Pendleton	.05
19	Mark Carreon	.05
20	Mark McGwire	.75
21	Roger Clemens	.60
22	Chuck Crim	.05
23	Don Mattingly	.60
24	Dickie Thon	.05
25	Ron Gant	.05
26	Milt Cuyler	.05
27	Mike Macfarlane	.05
28	Dan Gladden	.05
29	Melido Perez	.05
30	Willie Randolph	.05
31	Albert Belle	.05
32	Dave Winfield	.40
33	Jimmy Jones	.05
34	Kevin Gross	.05
35	Andres Galarraga	.05
36	Mike Devereaux	.05
37	Chris Bosio	.05
38	Mike LaValliere	.05
39	Gary Gaetti	.05
40	Felix Jose	.05
41	Alvaro Espinoza	.05
42	Rick Aguilera	.05
43	Mike Gallego	.05
44	Eric Davis	.05
45	George Bell	.05
46	Tom Brunansky	.05
47	Steve Farr	.05
48	Duane Ward	.05
49	David Wells	.05
50	Cecil Fielder	.05
51	Walt Weiss	.05
52	Todd Zeile	.05
53	Doug Jones	.05
54	Bob Walk	.05
55	Rafael Palmeiro	.35
56	Rob Deer	.05
57	Paul O'Neill	.05
58	Jeff Reardon	.05
59	Randy Ready	.05
60	Scott Erickson	.05
61	Paul Molitor	.40
62	Jack McDowell	.05
63	Jim Acker	.05
64	Jay Buhner	.05
65	Travis Fryman	.05
66	Marquis Grissom	.05
67	Mike Harkey	.05
68	Luis Polonia	.05
69	Ken Caminiti	.05
70	Chris Sabo	.05
71	Gregg Olson	.05
72	Carlton Fisk	.40
73	Juan Samuel	.05
74	Todd Stottlemyre	.05
75	Andre Dawson	.25
76	Alvin Davis	.05
77	Bill Doran	.05
78	B.J. Surhoff	.05
79	Kirk McCaskill	.05
80	Dale Murphy	.25
81	Jose DeLeon	.05
82	Alex Fernandez	.05
83	Ivan Calderon	.05
84	Brent Mayne	.05
85	Jody Reed	.05
86	Randy Tomlin	.05
87	Randy Milligan	.05
88	Pascual Perez	.05
89	Hensley Meulens	.05
90	Joe Carter	.05
91	Mike Moore	.05
92	Ozzie Guillen	.05
93	Shawn Hillegas	.05
94	Chili Davis	.05
95	Vince Coleman	.05
96	Jimmy Key	.05
97	Billy Ripken	.05
98	Dave Smith	.05
99	Tom Bolton	.05
100	Barry Larkin	.05
101	Kenny Rogers	.05
102	Mike Boddicker	.05
103	Kevin Elster	.05
104	Ken Hill	.05
105	Charlie Leibrandt	.05
106	Pat Combs	.05
107	Hubie Brooks	.05
108	Julio Franco	.05
109	Vicente Palacios	.05
110	Kal Daniels	.05
111	Bruce Hurst	.05
112	Willie McGee	.05
113	Ted Power	.05
114	Milt Thompson	.05
115	Doug Drabek	.05
116	Rafael Belliard	.05
117	Scott Garrelts	.05
118	Terry Mulholland	.05
119	Jay Howell	.05
120	Danny Jackson	.05
121	Scott Ruskin	.05
122	Robin Ventura	.05
123	Bip Roberts	.05
124	Jeff Russell	.05
125	Hal Morris	.05
126	Teddy Higuera	.05
127	Luis Sojo	.05
128	Carlos Baerga	.05
129	Jeff Ballard	.05
130	Tom Gordon	.05
131	Sid Bream	.05
132	Rance Mulliniks	.05
133	Andy Benes	.05
134	Mickey Tettleton	.05
135	Rich DeLucia	.05
136	Tom Pagnozzi	.05
137	Harold Baines	.05
138	Danny Darwin	.05
139	Kevin Bass	.05
140	Chris Nabholz	.05
141	Pete O'Brien	.05
142	Jeff Treadway	.05
143	Mickey Morandini	.05
144	Eric King	.05
145	Danny Tartabull	.05
146	Lance Johnson	.05
147	Casey Candaele	.05
148	Felix Fermin	.05
149	Rich Rodriguez	.05
150	Dwight Evans	.05
151	Joe Klink	.05
152	Kevin Reimer	.05
153	Orlando Merced	.05
154	Mel Hall	.05
155	Randy Myers	.05
156	Greg Harris	.05
157	Jeff Brantley	.05
158	Jim Eisenreich	.05
159	Luis Rivera	.05
160	Cris Carpenter	.05
161	Bruce Ruffin	.05
162	Omar Vizquel	.05
163	Gerald Alexander	.05
164	Mark Guthrie	.05
165	Scott Lewis	.05
166	Bill Sampen	.05
167	Dave Anderson	.05
168	Kevin McReynolds	.05
169	Jose Vizcaino	.05
170	Bob Geren	.05
171	Mike Morgan	.05
172	Jim Gott	.05
173	Mike Pagliarulo	.05
174	Mike Jeffcoat	.05
175	Craig Lefferts	.05
176	Steve Finley	.05
177	Wally Backman	.05
178	Kent Mercker	.05
179	John Cerutti	.05
180	Jay Bell	.05
181	Dale Sveum	.05
182	Greg Gagne	.05
183	Donnie Hill	.05
184	Rex Hudler	.05
185	Pat Kelly	.05
186	Jeff Robinson	.05
187	Jeff Gray	.05
188	Jerry Willard	.05
189	Carlos Quintana	.05
190	Dennis Eckersley	.35
191	Kelly Downs	.05
192	Gregg Jefferies	.05
193	Darrin Fletcher	.05
194	Mike Jackson	.05
195	Eddie Murray	.40
196	Billy Landrum	.05
197	Eric Yelding	.05
198	Devon White	.05
199	Larry Walker	.05
200	Ryne Sandberg	.50
201	Dave Magadan	.05
202	Steve Chitren	.05
203	Scott Fletcher	.05
204	Dwayne Henry	.05
205	Scott Coolbaugh	.05
206	Tracy Jones	.05
207	Von Hayes	.05
208	Bob Melvin	.05
209	Scott Scudder	.05
210	Luis Gonzalez	.25
211	Scott Sanderson	.05
212	Chris Donnels	.05
213	Heath Slocumb	.05
214	Mike Timlin	.05
215	Brian Harper	.05
216	Juan Berenguer	.05
217	Mike Henneman	.05
218	Bill Spiers	.05
219	Scott Terry	.05
220	Frank Viola	.05
221	Mark Eichhorn	.05
222	Ernest Riles	.05
223	Ray Lankford	.05
224	Pete Harnisch	.05
225	Bobby Bonilla	.05
226	Mike Scioscia	.05
227	Joel Skinner	.05
228	Brian Holman	.05
229	Gilberto Reyes **RC**	.05
230	Matt Williams	.05
231	Jaime Navarro	.05
232	Jose Rijo	.05
233	Atlee Hammaker	.05
234	Tim Teufel	.05
235	John Kruk	.05
236	Kurt Stillwell	.05
237	Dan Pasqua	.05
238	Tim Crews	.05
239	Dave Gallagher	.05
240	Leo Gomez	.05
241	Steve Avery	.05
242	Bill Gullickson	.05
243	Mark Portugal	.05
244	Lee Guetterman	.05
245	Benny Santiago	.05
246	Jim Gantner	.05
247	Robby Thompson	.05
248	Terry Shumpert	.05
249	Mike Bell **RC**	.05
250	Harold Reynolds	.05
251	Mike Felder	.05
252	Bill Pecota	.05
253	Bill Krueger	.05
254	Alfredo Griffin	.05
255	Lou Whitaker	.05
256	Roy Smith	.05
257	Jerald Clark	.05
258	Sammy Sosa	.50
259	Tim Naehring	.05
260	Dave Righetti	.05
261	Paul Gibson	.05
262	Chris James	.05
263	Larry Andersen	.05
264	Storm Davis	.05
265	Jose Lind	.05
266	Greg Hibbard	.05
267	Norm Charlton	.05
268	Paul Kilgus	.05
269	Greg Maddux	.50
270	Ellis Burks	.05
271	Frank Tanana	.05
272	Gene Larkin	.05
273	Ron Hassey	.05
274	Jeff Robinson	.05
275	Steve Howe	.05
276	Daryl Boston	.05
277	Mark Lee	.05
278	Jose Segura **RC**	.05
279	Lance Blankenship	.05
280	Don Slaught	.05
281	Russ Swan	.05
282	Bob Tewksbury	.05
283	Geno Petralli	.05
284	Shane Mack	.05
285	Bob Scanlan	.05
286	Tim Leary	.05
287	John Smoltz	.05
288	Pat Borders	.05
289	Mark Davidson	.05
290	Sam Horn	.05
291	Lenny Harris	.05
292	Franklin Stubbs	.05
293	Thomas Howard	.05
294	Steve Lyons	.05
295	Francisco Oliveras	.05
296	Terry Leach	.05
297	Barry Jones	.05
298	Lance Parrish	.05
299	Wally Whitehurst	.05
300	Bob Welch	.05
301	Charlie Hayes	.05
302	Charlie Hough	.05
303	Gary Redus	.05
304	Scott Bradley	.05
305	Jose Oquendo	.05
306	Pete Incaviglia	.05
307	Marvin Freeman	.05
308	Gary Pettis	.05
309	Joe Slusarski	.05
310	Kevin Seitzer	.05
311	Jeff Reed	.05
312	Pat Tabler	.05
313	Mike Maddux	.05
314	Bob Milacki	.05
315	Eric Anthony	.05
316	Dante Bichette	.05
317	Steve Decker	.05
318	Jack Clark	.05
319	Doug Dascenzo	.05
320	Scott Leius	.05
321	Jim Lindeman	.05
322	Bryan Harvey	.05
323	Spike Owen	.05
324	Roberto Kelly	.05
325	Stan Belinda	.05
326	Joey Cora	.05
327	Jeff Innis	.05
328	Willie Wilson	.05
329	Juan Agosto	.05
330	Charles Nagy	.05
331	Scott Bailes	.05
332	Pete Schourek	.05
333	Mike Flanagan	.05
334	Omar Olivares	.05
335	Dennis Lamp	.05
336	Tommy Greene	.05
337	Randy Velarde	.05
338	Tom Lampkin	.05
339	John Russell	.05
340	Bob Kipper	.05
341	Todd Burns	.05
342	Ron Jones	.05
343	Dave Valle	.05
344	Mike Heath	.05
345	John Olerud	.05
346	Gerald Young	.05
347	Ken Patterson	.05
348	Les Lancaster	.05
349	Steve Crawford	.05
350	John Candelaria	.05
351	Mike Aldrete	.05
352	Mariano Duncan	.05
353	Julio Machado	.05
354	Ken Williams	.05
355	Walt Terrell	.05
356	Mitch Williams	.05
357	Al Newman	.05
358	Bud Black	.05
359	Joe Hesketh	.05
360	Paul Assenmacher	.05
361	Bo Jackson	.05
362	Jeff Blauser	.05
363	Mike Brumley	.05
364	Jim Deshaies	.05
365	Brady Anderson	.05
366	Chuck McElroy	.05
367	Matt Merullo	.05
368	Tim Belcher	.05
369	Luis Aquino	.05
370	Joe Oliver	.05
371	Greg Swindell	.05
372	Lee Stevens	.05
373	Mark Knudson	.05
374	Bill Wegman	.05
375	Jerry Don Gleaton	.05
376	Pedro Guerrero	.05
377	Randy Bush	.05
378	Greg Harris	.05
379	Eric Plunk	.05
380	Jose DeJesus	.05
381	Bobby Witt	.05
382	Curtis Wilkerson	.05
383	Gene Nelson	.05
384	Wes Chamberlain	.05
385	Tom Henke	.05
386	Mark Lemke	.05
387	Greg Briley	.05
388	Rafael Ramirez	.05
389	Tony Fossas	.05
390	Henry Cotto	.05
391	Tim Hulett	.05
392	Dean Palmer	.05
393	Glenn Braggs	.05
394	Mark Salas	.05
395	Rusty Meacham **RC**	.05
396	Andy Ashby **RC**	.10
397	Jose Melendez **RC**	.05
398	Warren Newson **RC**	.05
399	Frank Castillo **RC**	.05
400	Chito Martinez **RC**	.05
401	Bernie Williams	.05
402	Derek Bell	.05
403	Javier Ortiz **RC**	.05
404	Tim Sherrill **RC**	.05
405	Rob MacDonald **RC**	.05
406	Phil Plantier	.05
407	Troy Afenir	.05
408	Gino Minutelli **RC**	.05
409	Reggie Jefferson **RC**	.05
410	Mike Remlinger **RC**	.05
411	Carlos Rodriguez **RC**	.05
412	Joe Redfield **RC**	.05
413	Alonzo Powell **RC**	.05
414	Scott Livingstone **RC**	.05

415 Scott Kamieniecki **RC** .05
416 Tim Spehr **RC** .05
417 Brian Hunter **RC** .05
418 Ced Landrum **RC** .05
419 Bret Barberie **RC** .05
420 Kevin Morton **RC** .05
421 Doug Henry **RC** .05
422 Doug Piatt **RC** .05
423 Pat Rice **RC** .05
424 Juan Guzman .05
425 Nolan Ryan (No-Hit) .50
426 Tommy Greene (No-Hit) .05
427 Bob Milacki, Mike Flanagan, Mark Williamson, Gregg Olson (No-Hit) .05
428 Wilson Alvarez (No-Hit) .05
429 Otis Nixon (Highlight) .05
430 Rickey Henderson (Highlight) .20
431 Cecil Fielder/AS .05
432 Julio Franco/AS .05
433 Cal Ripken, Jr./AS .50
434 Wade Boggs/AS .25
435 Joe Carter/AS .05
436 Ken Griffey Jr./AS .35
437 Ruben Sierra/AS .05
438 Scott Erickson/AS .05
439 Tom Henke/AS .05
440 Terry Steinbach/AS .05
441 Rickey Henderson/DT .20
442 Ryne Sandberg/DT .30
443 Otis Nixon .05
444 Scott Radinsky .05
445 Mark Grace .05
446 Tony Pena .05
447 Billy Hatcher .05
448 Glenallen Hill .05
449 Chris Gwynn .05
450 Tom Glavine .35
451 John Habyan .05
452 Al Osuna .05
453 Tony Phillips .05
454 Greg Cadaret .05
455 Rob Dibble .05
456 Rick Honeycutt .05
457 Jerome Walton .05
458 Mookie Wilson .05
459 Mark Gubicza .05
460 Craig Biggio .05
461 Dave Cochrane .05
462 Keith Miller .05
463 Alex Cole .05
464 Pete Smith .05
465 Brett Butler .05
466 Jeff Huson .05
467 Steve Lake .05
468 Lloyd Moseby .05
469 Tim McIntosh .05
470 Dennis Martinez .05
471 Greg Myers .05
472 Mackey Sasser .05
473 Junior Ortiz .05
474 Greg Olson .05
475 Steve Sax .05
476 Ricky Jordan .05
477 Max Venable .05
478 Brian McRae .05
479 Doug Simons .05
480 Rickey Henderson .40
481 Gary Varsho .05
482 Carl Willis .05
483 Rick Wilkins .05
484 Donn Pall .05
485 Edgar Martinez .05
486 Tom Foley .05
487 Mark Williamson .05
488 Jack Armstrong .05
489 Gary Carter .40
490 Ruben Sierra .05
491 Gerald Perry .05
492 Rob Murphy .05
493 Zane Smith .05
494 Darryl Kile .05
495 Kelly Gruber .05
496 Jerry Browne .05
497 Darryl Hamilton .05
498 Mike Stanton .05
499 Mark Leonard .05
500 Jose Canseco .30
501 Dave Martinez .05
502 Jose Guzman .05
503 Terry Kennedy .05
504 Ed Sprague .05
505 Frank Thomas .40
506 Darren Daulton .05
507 Kevin Tapani .05
508 Luis Salazar .05
509 Paul Faries .05
510 Sandy Alomar, Jr. .05
511 Jeff King .05
512 Gary Thurman .05
513 Chris Hammond .05
514 Pedro Munoz **RC** .05
515 Alan Trammell .05
516 Geronimo Pena .05
517 Rodney McCray .05
518 Manny Lee .05
519 Junior Felix .05
520 Kirk Gibson .05
521 Darrin Jackson .05
522 John Burkett .05
523 Jeff Johnson .05
524 Jim Corsi .05
525 Robin Yount .40
526 Jamie Quirk .05
527 Bob Ojeda .05
528 Mark Lewis .05
529 Bryn Smith .05
530 Kent Hrbek .05
531 Dennis Boyd .05
532 Ron Karkovice .05
533 Don August .05
534 Todd Frohwirth .05
535 Wally Joyner .05
536 Dennis Rasmussen .05
537 Andy Allanson .05
538 Rich Gossage .05
539 John Marzano .05
540 Cal Ripken, Jr. 1.00
541 Bill Swift .05
542 Kevin Appier .05
543 Dave Bergman .05
544 Bernard Gilkey .05
545 Mike Greenwell .05
546 Jose Uribe .05
547 Jesse Orosco .05
548 Bob Patterson .05
549 Mike Stanley .05
550 Howard Johnson .05
551 Joe Orsulak .05
552 Dick Schofield .05
553 Dave Hollins .05
554 David Segui .05
555 Barry Bonds 1.00
556 Mo Vaughn .05
557 Craig Wilson .05
558 Bobby Rose .05
559 Rod Nichols .05
560 Len Dykstra .05
561 Craig Grebeck .05
562 Darren Lewis .05
563 Todd Benzinger .05
564 Ed Whitson .05
565 Jesse Barfield .05
566 Lloyd McClendon .05
567 Dan Plesac .05
568 Danny Cox .05
569 Skeeter Barnes .05
570 Bobby Thigpen .05
571 Deion Sanders .05
572 Chuck Knoblauch .05
573 Matt Nokes .05
574 Herm Winningham .05
575 Tom Candiotti .05
576 Jeff Bagwell .40
577 Brook Jacoby .05
578 Chico Walker .05
579 Brian Downing .05
580 Dave Stewart .05
581 Francisco Cabrera .05
582 Rene Gonzales .05
583 Stan Javier .05
584 Randy Johnson .40
585 Chuck Finley .05
586 Mark Gardner .05
587 Mark Whiten .05
588 Garry Templeton .05
589 Gary Sheffield .30
590 Ozzie Smith .50
591 Candy Maldonado .05
592 Mike Sharperson .05
593 Carlos Martinez .05
594 Scott Bankhead .05
595 Tim Wallach .05
596 Tino Martinez .05
597 Roger McDowell .05
598 Cory Snyder .05
599 Andujar Cedeno .05
600 Kirby Puckett .50
601 Rick Parker .05
602 Todd Hundley .05
603 Greg Litton .05
604 Dave Johnson .05
605 John Franco .05
606 Mike Fetters .05
607 Luis Alicea .05
608 Trevor Wilson .05
609 Rob Ducey .05
610 Ramon Martinez .05
611 Dave Burba .05
612 Dwight Smith .05
613 Kevin Maas .05
614 John Costello .05
615 Glenn Davis .05
616 Shawn Abner .05
617 Scott Hemond .05
618 Tom Prince .05
619 Wally Ritchie .05
620 Jim Abbott .05
621 Charlie O'Brien .05
622 Jack Daugherty .05
623 Tommy Gregg .05
624 Jeff Shaw .05
625 Tony Gwynn .50
626 Mark Leiter .05
627 Jim Clancy .05
628 Tim Layana .05
629 Jeff Schaefer .05
630 Lee Smith .05
631 Wade Taylor .05
632 Mike Simms .05
633 Terry Steinbach .05
634 Shawon Dunston .05
635 Tim Raines .05
636 Kirt Manwaring .05
637 Warren Cromartie .05
638 Luis Quinones .05
639 Greg Vaughn .05
640 Kevin Mitchell .05
641 Chris Hoiles .05
642 Tom Browning .05
643 Mitch Webster .05
644 Steve Olin .05
645 Tony Fernandez .05
646 Juan Bell .05
647 Joe Boever .05
648 Carney Lansford .05
649 Mike Benjamin .05
650 George Brett .60
651 Tim Burke .05
652 Jack Morris .05
653 Orel Hershiser .05
654 Mike Schooler .05
655 Andy Van Slyke .05
656 Dave Stieb .05
657 Dave Clark .05
658 Ben McDonald .05
659 John Smiley .05
660 Wade Boggs .50
661 Eric Bullock .05
662 Eric Show .05
663 Lenny Webster .05
664 Mike Huff .05
665 Rick Sutcliffe .05
666 Jeff Manto .05
667 Mike Fitzgerald .05
668 Matt Young .05
669 Dave West .05
670 Mike Hartley .05
671 Curt Schilling .35
672 Brian Bohanon .05
673 Cecil Espy .05
674 Joe Grahe .05
675 Sid Fernandez .05
676 Edwin Nunez .05
677 Hector Villanueva .05
678 Sean Berry .05
679 Dave Eiland .05
680 David Cone .05
681 Mike Bordick .05
682 Tony Castillo .05
683 John Barfield .05
684 Jeff Hamilton .05
685 Ken Dayley .05
686 Carmelo Martinez .05
687 Mike Capel .05
688 Scott Chiamparino .05
689 Rich Gedman .05
690 Rich Monteleone .05
691 Alejandro Pena .05
692 Oscar Azocar .05
693 Jim Poole .05
694 Mike Gardiner .05
695 Steve Buechele .05
696 Rudy Seanez .05
697 Paul Abbott .05
698 Steve Searcy .05
699 Jose Offerman .05
700 Ivan Rodriguez .35
701 Joe Girardi .05
702 Tony Perezchica .05
703 Paul McClellan .05
704 David Howard **RC** .05
705 Dan Petry .05
706 Jack Howell .05
707 Jose Mesa .05
708 Randy St. Claire .05
709 Kevin Brown .05
710 Ron Darling .05
711 Jason Grimsley .05
712 John Orton .05
713 Shawn Boskie .05
714 Pat Clements .05
715 Brian Barnes .05
716 Luis Lopez **RC** .05
717 Bob McClure .05
718 Mark Davis .05
719 Dann Billardello .05
720 Tom Edens .05
721 Willie Fraser .05
722 Curt Young .05
723 Neal Heaton .05
724 Craig Worthington .05
725 Mel Rojas .05
726 Daryl Irvine .05
727 Roger Mason .05
728 Kirk Dressendorfer .05
729 Scott Aldred .05
730 Willie Blair .05
731 Allan Anderson .05
732 Dana Kiecker .05
733 Jose Gonzalez .05
734 Brian Drahman .05
735 Brad Komminsk .05
736 Arthur Rhodes **RC** .10
737 Terry Mathews **RC** .05
738 Jeff Fassero **RC** .05
739 Mike Magnante **RC** .05
740 Kip Gross **RC** .05
741 Jim Hunter **RC** .05
742 Jose Mota **RC** .05
743 Joe Bitker .05
744 Tim Mauser **RC** .05
745 Ramon Garcia **RC** .05
746 Rod Beck **RC** .10
747 Jim Austin **RC** .05
748 Keith Mitchell **RC** .05
749 Wayne Rosenthal **RC** .05
750 Bryan Hickerson **RC** .05
751 Bruce Egloff **RC** .05
752 John Wehner **RC** .05
753 Darren Holmes **RC** .05
754 Dave Hansen .05
755 Mike Mussina .30
756 Anthony Young **RC** .05
757 Ron Tingley .05
758 Ricky Bones **RC** .05
759 Mark Wohlers **RC** .05
760 Wilson Alvarez **RC** .05
761 Harvey Pulliam **RC** .05
762 Ryan Bowen **RC** .05
763 Terry Bross **RC** .05
764 Joel Johnston **RC** .05
765 Terry McDaniel **RC** .05
766 Esteban Beltre **RC** .05
767 Rob Maurer **RC** .05
768 Ted Wood .05
769 Mo Sanford **RC** .05
770 Jeff Carter **RC** .05
771 Gil Heredia **RC** .05
772 Monty Fariss **RC** .05
773 Will Clark/AS .05
774 Ryne Sandberg/AS .25
775 Barry Larkin/AS .05
776 Howard Johnson/AS .05
777 Barry Bonds/AS .50
778 Brett Butler/AS .05
779 Tony Gwynn/AS .25
780 Ramon Martinez/AS .05
781 Lee Smith/AS .05
782 Mike Scioscia/AS .05
783 Dennis Martinez (Highlight) .05
784 Dennis Martinez (No-Hit) .05
785 Mark Gardner (No-Hit) .05
786 Bret Saberhagen (No-Hit) .05
787 Kent Mercker, Mark Wohlers, Alejandro Pena (No-Hit) .05
788 Cal Ripken (MVP) .50
789 Terry Pendleton (MVP) .05
790 Roger Clemens (CY) .35
791 Tom Glavine (CY) .05
792 Chuck Knoblauch (ROY) .05
793 Jeff Bagwell (ROY) .20
794 Cal Ripken, Jr. (Man of the Year) .50
795 David Cone (Highlight) .05
796 Kirby Puckett (Highlight) .25
797 Steve Avery (Highlight) .05
798 Jack Morris (Highlight) .05
799 Allen Watson **RC** .05
800 Manny Ramirez **RC** 2.00
801 Cliff Floyd **RC** .50
802 Al Shirley **RC** .05
803 Brian Barber **RC** .05
804 Jon Farrell **RC** .05
805 Brent Gates **RC** .05
806 Scott Ruffcorn **RC** .05
807 Tyrone Hill **RC** .05
808 Benji Gil **RC** .05
809 Aaron Sele **RC** .25
810 Tyler Green **RC** .05
811 Chris Jones .05
812 Steve Wilson .05
813 Cliff Young **RC** .05
814 Don Wakamatsu **RC** .05
815 Mike Humphreys **RC** .05
816 Scott Servais **RC** .05
817 Rico Rossy **RC** .05
818 John Ramos **RC** .05
819 Rob Mallicoat .05
820 Milt Hill **RC** .05
821 Carlos Garcia .05
822 Stan Royer .05
823 Jeff Plympton **RC** .05
824 Braulio Castillo **RC** .05
825 David Haas **RC** .05
826 Luis Mercedes **RC** .05
827 Eric Karros .05
828 Shawn Hare **RC** .05
829 Reggie Sanders .05
830 Tom Goodwin .05
831 Dan Gakeler **RC** .05
832 Stacy Jones **RC** .05
833 Kim Batiste **RC** .05
834 Cal Eldred .05
835 Chris George **RC** .05
836 Wayne Housie **RC** .05
837 Mike Ignasiak **RC** .05
838 Josias Manzanillo **RC** .05
839 Jim Olander **RC** .05
840 Gary Cooper **RC** .05
841 Royce Clayton .05
842 Hector Fajardo .05
843 Blaine Beatty .05
844 Jorge Pedre **RC** .05
845 Kenny Lofton .05
846 Scott Brosius .05
847 Chris Cron **RC** .05
848 Denis Boucher .05
849 Kyle Abbott .05
850 Bob Zupcic .05
851 Rheal Cormier **RC** .05
852 Jim Lewis **RC** .05
853 Anthony Telford .05
854 Cliff Brantley **RC** .05
855 Kevin Campbell **RC** .05
856 Craig Shipley **RC** .05
857 Chuck Carr .05
858 Tony Eusebio **RC** .10
859 Jim Thome .35
860 Vinny Castilla **RC** .30
861 Dann Howitt .05
862 Kevin Ward **RC** .05
863 Steve Wapnick **RC** .05
864 Rod Brewer .05
865 Todd Van Poppel .05
866 Jose Hernandez **RC** .05
867 Amalio Carreno **RC** .05
868 Calvin Jones **RC** .05
869 Jeff Gardner **RC** .05
870 Jarvis Brown **RC** .05
871 Eddie Taubensee **RC** .10
872 Andy Mota **RC** .05
873 Chris Haney (Front photo actually Scott Ruskin.) .05
874 Roberto Hernandez .05
875 Laddie Renfroe **RC** .05
876 Scott Cooper .05
877 Armando Reynoso **RC** .05
878 Ty Cobb (Memorabilia) .30
879 Babe Ruth (Memorabilia) .40
880 Honus Wagner (Memorabilia) .30
881 Lou Gehrig (Memorabilia) .30
882 Satchel Paige (Memorabilia) .35
883 Will Clark/DT .05
884 Cal Ripken, Jr./DT .50
885 Wade Boggs/DT .25
886 Kirby Puckett/DT .30
887 Tony Gwynn/DT .30
888 Craig Biggio/DT .05
889 Scott Erickson/DT .05
890 Tom Glavine/DT .10
891 Rob Dibble/DT .05
892 Mitch Williams/DT .05
893 Frank Thomas/DT .25

Joe DiMaggio

Colorized vintage photos are featured on the front and back of each of five Joe DiMaggio tribute cards which were issued as random inserts in 1992 Score Series 1 packs. It was reported at the time that 30,000 of each card were produced. A limited number (from an edition of 2,500) of each card were autographed.

		NM/M
Complete Set (5):		25.00
Common Card:		8.00
Autographed Card:		365.00
1	Joe DiMaggio (The Minors)	8.00
2	Joe DiMaggio (The Rookie)	8.00
3	Joe DiMaggio (The MVP)	8.00
4	Joe DiMaggio (The Streak)	8.00
5	Joe DiMaggio (The Legend)	8.00

Factory Set Inserts - Cooperstown

Available exclusively in factory sets, these bonus cards have posterized color portraits vignetted on a white background. Blue-bordered backs have a yellow "tombstone" at center with career highlights and a quote or two about the player.

		NM/M
Complete Set (4):		1.50
Common Player:		.50
B8	Carlton Fisk	.50
B9	Ozzie Smith	.75
B10	Dave Winfield	.50
B11	Robin Yount	.50

Factory Set Inserts - DiMaggio

Available exclusively in factory sets, these bonus cards honor Joe DiMaggio's career. Fronts have black-and-white photos with silver borders. Color backs have quotes from the Clipper or other ballplayers, plus detailed career highlights.

		NM/M
Complete Set (3):		4.00
Common Card:		1.25
B12	Joe DiMaggio (The Hard Hitter)	1.50
B13	Joe DiMaggio (The Stylish Fielder)	1.50
B14	Joe DiMaggio (The Championship Player)	1.50

Factory Set Inserts - World Series

Available exclusively in factory sets 17 bonus cards are divided into four subsets commemorating the 1991 World Series, potential Hall of Famers, the career of Joe DiMaggio and Carl Yastrzemski's 1967 Triple Crown season. Cards carry a "B" prefix to the card number.

		NM/M
Complete Set (7):		1.00
Common Card:		.15
1	World Series Game 1 (Greg Gagne)	.15
2	World Series Game 2 (Scott Leius)	.15
3	World Series Game 3 (David Justice, Brian Harper)	.15
4	World Series Game 4 (Lonnie Smith, Brian Harper)	.15
5	World Series Game 5 (David Justice)	.15
6	World Series Game 6 (Kirby Puckett)	1.00
7	World Series Game 7 (Gene Larkin)	.15

Factory Set Inserts - Yastrzemski

Available exclusively in factory sets, these bonus cards honor Carl Yastrzemski's 1967 Triple Crown season. Fronts have game-action photos with silver borders and a silver 25 Years logo. Color backs have quotes from Yaz or teammates, plus details of the season's highlights.

		NM/M
Complete Set (3):		2.00
Common Card:		1.00
B15	Carl Yastrzemski (The Impossible Dream)	1.00

B16 Carl Yastrzemski (The Triple Crown) 1.00
B17 Carl Yastrzemski (The World Series) 1.00

Hot Rookies

This 10-card rookie issue was produced as an insert in special blister packs of 1992 Score cards sold at retail outlets. Action photos on front and portraits on back are set against white backgrounds with orange highlights. Cards are standard 2-1/2" x 3-1/2".

		NM/M
Complete Set (10):		4.00
Common Player:		.50
1	Cal Eldred	.50
2	Royce Clayton	.50
3	Kenny Lofton	.75
4	Todd Van Poppel	.50
5	Scott Cooper	.50
6	Todd Hundley	.50
7	Tino Martinez	.75
8	Anthony Telford	.50
9	Derek Bell	.50
10	Reggie Jefferson	.50

Impact Players

Jumbo packs of 1992 Score Series 1 and 2 contained five of these special inserts labeled "90's Impact Players." Front action photos contrast with portrait photos on the backs, which are color-coded by team. Cards #1-45 were packaged with Series 1, cards #46-90 were included in Series 2 packs.

		NM/M
Complete Set (90):		3.00
Common Player:		.05
1	Chuck Knoblauch	.05
2	Jeff Bagwell	.50
3	Juan Guzman	.05
4	Milt Cuyler	.05
5	Ivan Rodriguez	.45
6	Rich DeLucia	.05
7	Orlando Merced	.05
8	Ray Lankford	.05
9	Brian Hunter	.05
10	Roberto Alomar	.25
11	Wes Chamberlain	.05
12	Steve Avery	.05
13	Scott Erickson	.05
14	Jim Abbott	.05
15	Mark Whiten	.05
16	Leo Gomez	.05
17	Doug Henry	.05
18	Brent Mayne	.05
19	Charles Nagy	.05
20	Phil Plantier	.05
21	Mo Vaughn	.05
22	Craig Biggio	.05
23	Derek Bell	.05
24	Royce Clayton	.05
25	Gary Cooper	.05
26	Scott Cooper	.05
27	Juan Gonzalez	.25
28	Ken Griffey Jr.	.75
29	Larry Walker	.05
30	John Smoltz	.05
31	Todd Hundley	.05
32	Kenny Lofton	.05
33	Andy Mota	.05
34	Todd Zeile	.05
35	Arthur Rhodes	.05
36	Jim Thome	.45
37	Todd Van Poppel	.05
38	Mark Wohlers	.05
39	Anthony Young	.05
40	Sandy Alomar Jr.	.05
41	John Olerud	.05
42	Robin Ventura	.05
43	Frank Thomas	.50
44	Dave Justice	.05
45	Hal Morris	.05
46	Ruben Sierra	.05
47	Travis Fryman	.05
48	Mike Mussina	.25
49	Tom Glavine	.35
50	Barry Larkin	.05
51	Will Clark	.05
52	Jose Canseco	.30
53	Bo Jackson	.10
54	Dwight Gooden	.05
55	Barry Bonds	1.00
56	Fred McGriff	.05
57	Roger Clemens	.65
58	Benito Santiago	.05
59	Darryl Strawberry	.05
60	Cecil Fielder	.05
61	John Franco	.05
62	Matt Williams	.05
63	Marquis Grissom	.05
64	Danny Tartabull	.05
65	Ron Gant	.05
66	Paul O'Neill	.05
67	Devon White	.05
68	Rafael Palmeiro	.45
69	Tom Gordon	.05
70	Shawon Dunston	.05
71	Rob Dibble	.05
72	Eddie Zosky	.05
73	Jack McDowell	.05
74	Len Dykstra	.05
75	Ramon Martinez	.05
76	Reggie Sanders	.05
77	Greg Maddux	.60
78	Ellis Burks	.05
79	John Smiley	.05
80	Roberto Kelly	.05
81	Ben McDonald	.05
82	Mark Lewis	.05
83	Jose Rijo	.05
84	Ozzie Guillen	.05
85	Lance Dickson	.05
86	Kim Batiste	.05
87	Gregg Olson	.05
88	Andy Benes	.05
89	Cal Eldred	.05
90	David Cone	.05

The Franchise

This four-card set, in both autographed and unautographed form, was a random insert in various premium packaging of Score's 1992 Series II cards. Each of the four cards was produced in an edition of 150,000, with 2,000 of each player's card being autographed and 500 of the triple-player card carrying the autographs of all three superstars.

		NM/M
Complete Set (4):		5.00
Common Player:		1.25
Musial Autograph:		80.00
Mantle Autograph:		450.00
Yastrzemski Autograph:		80.00
Triple Autograph:		1,100
1	Stan Musial	1.50
2	Mickey Mantle	2.50
3	Carl Yastrzemski	1.25
4	Stan Musial, Mickey Mantle, Carl Yastrzemski	1.50

Rookie & Traded

This 110-card set features traded players, free agents and top rookies from 1992. The cards are styled after the regular 1992 Score cards. Cards 80-110 feature the rookies. The set was released as a boxed set and was available only through hobby dealers.

		NM/M
Complete Set (110):		5.00
Common Player:		.05
1	Gary Sheffield	.20
2	Kevin Seitzer	.05
3	Danny Tartabull	.05
4	Steve Sax	.05
5	Bobby Bonilla	.05
6	Frank Viola	.05
7	Dave Winfield	.60
8	Rick Sutcliffe	.05
9	Jose Canseco	.45
10	Greg Swindell	.05
11	Eddie Murray	.60
12	Randy Myers	.05
13	Wally Joyner	.05
14	Kenny Lofton	.05
15	Jack Morris	.05
16	Charlie Hayes	.05
17	Pete Incaviglia	.05
18	Kevin Mitchell	.05
19	Kurt Stillwell	.05
20	Bret Saberhagen	.05
21	Steve Buechele	.05
22	John Smiley	.05
23	Sammy Sosa	3.00
24	George Bell	.05
25	Curt Schilling	.30
26	Dick Schofield	.05
27	David Cone	.05
28	Dan Gladden	.05
29	Kirk McCaskill	.05
30	Mike Gallego	.05
31	Kevin McReynolds	.05
32	Bill Swift	.05
33	Dave Martinez	.05
34	Storm Davis	.05
35	Willie Randolph	.05
36	Melido Perez	.05
37	Mark Carreon	.05
38	Doug Jones	.05
39	Gregg Jefferies	.05
40	Mike Jackson	.05
41	Dickie Thon	.05
42	Eric King	.05
43	Herm Winningham	.05
44	Derek Lilliquist	.05
45	Dave Anderson	.05
46	Jeff Reardon	.05
47	Scott Bankhead	.05
48	Cory Snyder	.05
49	Al Newman	.05
50	Keith Miller	.05
51	Dave Burba	.05
52	Bill Pecota	.05
53	Chuck Crim	.05
54	Mariano Duncan	.05
55	Dave Gallagher	.05
56	Chris Gwynn	.05
57	Scott Ruskin	.05
58	Jack Armstrong	.05
59	Gary Carter	.60
60	Andres Galarraga	.05
61	Ken Hill	.05
62	Eric Davis	.05
63	Ruben Sierra	.05
64	Darrin Fletcher	.05
65	Tim Belcher	.05
66	Mike Morgan	.05
67	Scott Scudder	.05
68	Tom Candiotti	.05
69	Hubie Brooks	.05
70	Kal Daniels	.05
71	Bruce Ruffin	.05
72	Billy Hatcher	.05
73	Bob Melvin	.05
74	Lee Guetterman	.05
75	Rene Gonzales	.05
76	Kevin Bass	.05
77	Tom Bolton	.05
78	John Wetteland	.05
79	Bip Roberts	.05
80	Pat Listach **RC**	.05
81	John Doherty **RC**	.05
82	Sam Militello **RC**	.05
83	Brian Jordan **RC**	.05
84	Jeff Kent **RC**	.10
85	Dave Fleming **RC**	.05
86	Jeff Tackett **RC**	.05
87	Chad Curtis **RC**	.05
88	Eric Fox	.05
89	Denny Neagle **RC**	.05
90	Donovan Osborne	.05
91	Carlos Hernandez **RC**	.05
92	Tim Wakefield **RC**	.05
93	Tim Salmon **RC**	.05
94	Dave Nilsson **RC**	.05
95	Mike Perez **RC**	.05
96	Pat Hentgen **RC**	.05
97	Frank Seminara **RC**	.05
98	Ruben Amaro Jr. **RC**	.05
99	Archi Cianfrocco **RC**	.05
100	Andy Stankiewicz **RC**	.05
101	Jim Bullinger **RC**	.05
102	Pat Mahomes **RC**	.05
103	Hipolito Pichardo **RC**	.05
104	Bret Boone **RC**	.05
105	John Vander Wal **RC**	.05
106	Vince Horsman **RC**	.05
107	James Austin **RC**	.05
108	Brian Williams **RC**	.05
109	Dan Walters **RC**	.05
110	Wil Cordero **RC**	.05

Procter & Gamble

In 1992 Score and Procter and Gamble combined to produce an 18-card All-Star set, reportedly two million cards making 101,000 sets offered to collectors originally for $1.49 along with proof of purchase from P & G products. Card fronts feature a color player action photo set against a background of blue star and pink-to-purple diagonal stripes (American Leaguers) or red star and green stripes (National Leaguers). Back designs include a color player portrait photo at upper-right, with personal data, career stats and highlights. Appropriate logos and card number complete the design, which is bordered in color striping similar to the front background.

		NM/M
Complete Set (18):		3.00
Common Player:		.10
1	Sandy Alomar Jr.	.10
2	Mark McGwire	.75
3	Roberto Alomar	.20
4	Wade Boggs	.50
5	Cal Ripken, Jr.	1.00
6	Kirby Puckett	.50
7	Ken Griffey Jr.	.65
8	Jose Canseco	.25
9	Kevin Brown	.10
10	Benito Santiago	.10
11	Fred McGriff	.10
12	Ryne Sandberg	.50
13	Terry Pendleton	.10
14	Ozzie Smith	.50
15	Barry Bonds	1.00
16	Tony Gwynn	.50
17	Andy Van Slyke	.10
18	Tom Glavine	.35

Rising Stars

Sold in a blister pack with a book and a handful of "Magic Motion" trivia cards this 100-

card set features baseball's top young players. Backs have a player portrait, a career summary and team, league and card company logos.

		NM/M
Complete Set (100):		3.00
Common Player:		.10
1	Milt Cuyler	.10
2	David Howard	.10
3	Brian Hunter	.10
4	Darryl Kile	.10
5	Pat Kelly	.10
6	Luis Gonzalez	.10
7	Mike Benjamin	.10
8	Eric Anthony	.10
9	Moises Alou	.10
10	Darren Lewis	.10
11	Chuck Knoblauch	.10
12	Geronimo Pena	.10
13	Jeff Plympton	.10
14	Bret Barberie	.10
15	Chris Haney	.10
16	Rick Wilkins	.10
17	Julio Valera	.10
18	Joe Slusarski	.10
19	Jose Melendez	.10
20	Pete Schourek	.10
21	Jeff Conine	.10
22	Paul Faries	.10
23	Scott Kamieniecki	.10
24	Bernard Gilkey	.10
25	Wes Chamberlain	.10
26	Charles Nagy	.10
27	Juan Guzman	.10
28	Heath Slocumb	.10
29	Eddie Taubensee	.10
30	Cedric Landrum	.10
31	Jose Offerman	.10
32	Andres Santana	.10
33	David Segui	.10
34	Bernie Williams	.10
35	Jeff Bagwell	1.50
36	Kevin Morton	.10
37	Kirk Dressendorfer	.10
38	Mike Fetters	.10
39	Darren Holmes	.10
40	Jeff Johnson	.10
41	Scott Aldred	.10
42	Kevin Ward	.10
43	Ray Lankford	.10
44	Terry Shumpert	.10
45	Wade Taylor	.10
46	Rob MacDonald	.10
47	Jose Mota	.10
48	Reggie Harris	.10
49	Mike Remlinger	.10
50	Mark Lewis	.10
51	Tino Martinez	.10
52	Ed Sprague	.10
53	Freddie Benavides	.10
54	Rich DeLucia	.10
55	Brian Drahman	.10
56	Steve Decker	.10
57	Scott Livingstone	.10
58	Mike Timlin	.10
59	Bob Scanlan	.10
60	Dean Palmer	.10
61	Frank Castillo	.10
62	Mark Leonard	.10
63	Chuck McElroy	.10
64	Derek Bell	.10
65	Andujar Cedeno	.10
66	Leo Gomez	.10
67	Rusty Meacham	.10
68	Dann Howitt	.10
69	Chris Jones	.10
70	Dave Cochrane	.10
71	Carlos Martinez	.10
72	Hensley Meulens	.10
73	Rich Reed	.10
74	Pedro Munoz	.10
75	Orlando Merced	.10
76	Chito Martinez	.10
77	Ivan Rodriguez	.75
78	Brian Barnes	.10
79	Chris Donnels	.10
80	Todd Hundley	.10
81	Gary Scott	.10
82	John Wehner	.10
83	Al Osuna	.10
84	Luis Lopez	.10
85	Brent Mayne	.10
86	Phil Plantier	.10
87	Joe Bitker	.10
88	Scott Cooper	.10
89	Chris Hammond	.10
90	Tim Sherrill	.10
91	Doug Simons	.10
92	Kip Gross	.10
93	Tim McIntosh	.10
94	Larry Casian	.10
95	Mike Dalton	.10
96	Lance Dickson	.10
97	Joe Grahe	.10
98	Glenn Sutko	.10
99	Gerald Alexander	.10
100	Mo Vaughn	.10

Rookies

A selection of 40 1992 rookie players is featured in this boxed set. Fronts have green borders with a red and white "1992 ROOKIE" notation printed vertically to the left of a game-action photo. Backs repeat the notation on a graduated blue background with a player portrait photo at top, biographical details and a career summary at center and appropriate logos at bottom.

		NM/M
Complete Set (40):		1.50
Common Player:		.05
1	Todd Van Poppel	.05
2	Kyle Abbott	.05
3	Derek Bell	.05
4	Jim Thome	.50
5	Mark Wohlers	.05
6	Todd Hundley	.05
7	Arthur Rhodes	.05
8	John Ramos	.05
9	Chris George	.05
10	Kenny Lofton	.05
11	Ted Wood	.05
12	Royce Clayton	.05
13	Scott Cooper	.05
14	Anthony Young	.05
15	Joel Johnston	.05
16	Andy Mota	.05
17	Lenny Webster	.05
18	Andy Ashby	.05
19	Jose Mota	.05
20	Tim McIntosh	.05
21	Terry Bross	.05
22	Harvey Pulliam	.05
23	Hector Fajardo	.05
24	Esteban Beltre	.05
25	Gary DiSarcina	.05
26	Mike Humphreys	.05
27	Jarvis Brown	.05
28	Gary Cooper	.05
29	Chris Donnels	.05
30	Monty Fariss	.05
31	Eric Karros	.05
32	Braulio Castillo	.05
33	Cal Eldred	.05
34	Tom Goodwin	.05
35	Reggie Sanders	.05
36	Scott Servais	.05
37	Kim Batiste	.05
38	Eric Wedge	.05
39	Willie Banks	.05
40	Mo Sanford	.05

Superstars

Available in a blister pack with a book and six "Magic Motion" trivia cards, this 100-card set spotlights the games top veteran stars.

		NM/M
Complete Set (100):		4.00
Common Player:		.05
1	Ken Griffey Jr.	.75
2	Scott Erickson	.05
3	John Smiley	.05
4	Rick Aguilera	.05
5	Jeff Reardon	.05
6	Chuck Finley	.05
7	Kirby Puckett	.50
8	Paul Molitor	.40
9	Dave Winfield	.40
10	Mike Greenwell	.05
11	Bret Saberhagen	.05
12	Pete Harnisch	.05
13	Ozzie Guillen	.05
14	Hal Morris	.05
15	Tom Glavine	.30
16	David Cone	.05
17	Edgar Martinez	.05
18	Willie McGee	.05
19	Jim Abbott	.05
20	Mark Grace	.05
21	George Brett	.65
22	Jack McDowell	.05
23	Don Mattingly	.65
24	Will Clark	.05
25	Dwight Gooden	.05
26	Barry Bonds	1.00
27	Rafael Palmeiro	.35
28	Lee Smith	.05
29	Wally Joyner	.05
30	Wade Boggs	.50
31	Tom Henke	.05
32	Mark Langston	.05
33	Robin Ventura	.05
34	Steve Avery	.05
35	Joe Carter	.05
36	Benito Santiago	.05
37	Dave Stieb	.05
38	Julio Franco	.05
39	Albert Belle	.05
40	Dale Murphy	.25
41	Rob Dibble	.05
42	Dave Justice	.05
43	Jose Rijo	.05
44	Eric Davis	.05
45	Terry Pendleton	.05
46	Kevin Maas	.05
47	Ozzie Smith	.50
48	Andre Dawson	.25
49	Sandy Alomar, Jr.	.05
50	Nolan Ryan	1.00
51	Frank Thomas	.40
52	Craig Biggio	.05
53	Doug Drabek	.05
54	Bobby Thigpen	.05
55	Darryl Strawberry	.05
56	Dennis Eckersley	.35
57	John Franco	.05
58	Paul O'Neill	.05
59	Scott Sanderson	.05
60	Dave Stewart	.05
61	Ivan Calderon	.05
62	Frank Viola	.05
63	Mark McGwire	.75
64	Kelly Gruber	.05
65	Fred McGriff	.05
66	Cecil Fielder	.05
67	Jose Canseco	.30
68	Howard Johnson	.05
69	Juan Gonzalez	.20
70	Tim Wallach	.05
71	John Olerud	.05
72	Carlton Fisk	.40
73	Otis Nixon	.05
74	Roger Clemens	.65
75	Ramon Martinez	.05
76	Ron Gant	.05
77	Barry Larkin	.05
78	Eddie Murray	.40
79	Vince Coleman	.05
80	Bobby Bonilla	.05
81	Tony Gwynn	.50
82	Roberto Alomar	.20
83	Ellis Burks	.05
84	Robin Yount	.40
85	Ryne Sandberg	.50
86	Len Dykstra	.05
87	Ruben Sierra	.05
88	George Bell	.05
89	Cal Ripken, Jr.	1.00
90	Danny Tartabull	.05
91	Gregg Olson	.05
92	Dave Henderson	.05
93	Kevin Mitchell	.05
94	Ben McDonald	.05
95	Matt Williams	.05
96	Roberto Kelly	.05
97	Dennis Martinez	.05
98	Kent Hrbek	.05
99	Felix Jose	.05
100	Rickey Henderson	.40

1993 Score Promos

Only close comparison with regularly issued versions can detect these unmarked promos. The promos feature

slightly different croppings of the pictures, situated higher than the normal version.

		NM/M
Complete Set (8):		15.00
Common Player:		1.00
1	Ken Griffey Jr.	4.00
3	Frank Thomas	2.00
4	Ryne Sandberg	3.00
6	Cal Ripken, Jr.	5.00
7	Roger Clemens	2.50
8	Bobby Bonilla	1.00
10	Darren Daulton	1.00
11	Travis Fryman	1.00

1993 Score

Score's 1993 cards have white borders surrounding color action photographs. The player's name is at the bottom of the card, while his team's name and position appears on the left side in a color band. Backs have color portraits, statistics and text. Subsets feature rookies, award winners, draft picks, highlights, World Series highlights, all-star caricatures, dream team players, and the Man of the Year (Kirby Puckett). Insert sets include: Boys of Summer, the Franchise and Stat Leaders, which feature Select's card design.

		NM/M
Complete Set (660):		15.00
Common Player:		.05
Pack (16):		.75
Wax Box (36):		17.50
1	Ken Griffey Jr.	.65
2	Gary Sheffield	.30
3	Frank Thomas	.40
4	Ryne Sandberg	.45
5	Larry Walker	.05
6	Cal Ripken, Jr.	1.00
7	Roger Clemens	.50
8	Bobby Bonilla	.05
9	Carlos Baerga	.05
10	Darren Daulton	.05
11	Travis Fryman	.05
12	Andy Van Slyke	.05
13	Jose Canseco	.30
14	Roberto Alomar	.15
15	Tom Glavine	.30
16	Barry Larkin	.05
17	Gregg Jefferies	.05
18	Craig Biggio	.05
19	Shane Mack	.05
20	Brett Butler	.05
21	Dennis Eckersley	.35
22	Will Clark	.05
23	Don Mattingly	.50
24	Tony Gwynn	.45
25	Ivan Rodriguez	.35
26	Shawon Dunston	.05
27	Mike Mussina	.30
28	Marquis Grissom	.05
29	Charles Nagy	.05
30	Len Dykstra	.05
31	Cecil Fielder	.05
32	Jay Bell	.05
33	B.J. Surhoff	.05
34	Bob Tewksbury	.05
35	Danny Tartabull	.05
36	Terry Pendleton	.05
37	Jack Morris	.05
38	Hal Morris	.05
39	Luis Polonia	.05
40	Ken Caminiti	.05
41	Robin Ventura	.05
42	Darryl Strawberry	.05
43	Wally Joyner	.05
44	Fred McGriff	.05
45	Kevin Tapani	.05
46	Matt Williams	.05
47	Robin Yount	.40
48	Ken Hill	.05
49	Edgar Martinez	.05
50	Mark Grace	.05
51	Juan Gonzalez	.20
52	Curt Schilling	.30
53	Dwight Gooden	.05
54	Chris Hoiles	.05
55	Frank Viola	.05
56	Ray Lankford	.05
57	George Brett	.50
58	Kenny Lofton	.05
59	Nolan Ryan	1.00
60	Mickey Tettleton	.05
61	John Smoltz	.05
62	Howard Johnson	.05
63	Eric Karros	.05
64	Rick Aguilera	.05
65	Steve Finley	.05
66	Mark Langston	.05
67	Bill Swift	.05
68	John Olerud	.05
69	Kevin McReynolds	.05
70	Jack McDowell	.05
71	Rickey Henderson	.40
72	Brian Harper	.05
73	Mike Morgan	.05
74	Rafael Palmeiro	.40
75	Dennis Martinez	.05
76	Tino Martinez	.05
77	Eddie Murray	.40
78	Ellis Burks	.05
79	John Kruk	.05
80	Gregg Olson	.05
81	Bernard Gilkey	.05
82	Milt Cuyler	.05
83	Mike LaValliere	.05
84	Albert Belle	.05
85	Bip Roberts	.05
86	Melido Perez	.05
87	Otis Nixon	.05
88	Bill Spiers	.05
89	Jeff Bagwell	.40
90	Orel Hershiser	.05
91	Andy Benes	.05
92	Devon White	.05
93	Willie McGee	.05
94	Ozzie Guillen	.05
95	Ivan Calderon	.05
96	Keith Miller	.05
97	Steve Buechele	.05
98	Kent Hrbek	.05
99	Dave Hollins	.05
100	Mike Bordick	.05
101	Randy Tomlin	.05
102	Omar Vizquel	.05
103	Lee Smith	.05
104	Leo Gomez	.05
105	Jose Rijo	.05
106	Mark Whiten	.05
107	Dave Justice	.05
108	Eddie Taubensee	.05
109	Lance Johnson	.05
110	Felix Jose	.05
111	Mike Harkey	.05
112	Randy Milligan	.05
113	Anthony Young	.05
114	Rico Brogna	.05
115	Bret Saberhagen	.05
116	Sandy Alomar, Jr.	.05
117	Terry Mulholland	.05
118	Darryl Hamilton	.05
119	Todd Zeile	.05
120	Bernie Williams	.05
121	Zane Smith	.05
122	Derek Bell	.05
123	Deion Sanders	.05
124	Luis Sojo	.05
125	Joe Oliver	.05
126	Craig Grebeck	.05
127	Andujar Cedeno	.05
128	Brian McRae	.05
129	Jose Offerman	.05
130	Pedro Munoz	.05
131	Bud Black	.05
132	Mo Vaughn	.05
133	Bruce Hurst	.05
134	Dave Henderson	.05
135	Tom Pagnozzi	.05
136	Erik Hanson	.05
137	Orlando Merced	.05
138	Dean Palmer	.05
139	John Franco	.05
140	Brady Anderson	.05
141	Ricky Jordan	.05
142	Jeff Blauser	.05
143	Sammy Sosa	.45
144	Bob Walk	.05
145	Delino DeShields	.05
146	Kevin Brown	.05
147	Mark Lemke	.05
148	Chuck Knoblauch	.05
149	Chris Sabo	.05
150	Bobby Witt	.05
151	Luis Gonzalez	.05
152	Ron Karkovice	.05
153	Jeff Brantley	.05
154	Kevin Appier	.05
155	Darrin Jackson	.05
156	Kelly Gruber	.05
157	Royce Clayton	.05
158	Chuck Finley	.05
159	Jeff King	.05
160	Greg Vaughn	.05
161	Geronimo Pena	.05
162	Steve Farr	.05
163	Jose Oquendo	.05
164	Mark Lewis	.05
165	John Wetteland	.05
166	Mike Henneman	.05
167	Todd Hundley	.05
168	Wes Chamberlain	.05
169	Steve Avery	.05
170	Mike Devereaux	.05
171	Reggie Sanders	.05
172	Jay Buhner	.05
173	Eric Anthony	.05
174	John Burkett	.05
175	Tom Candiotti	.05
176	Phil Plantier	.05
177	Doug Henry	.05
178	Scott Leius	.05
179	Kirt Manwaring	.05
180	Jeff Parrett	.05
181	Don Slaught	.05
182	Scott Radinsky	.05
183	Luis Alicea	.05
184	Tom Gordon	.05
185	Rick Wilkins	.05
186	Todd Stottlemyre	.05
187	Moises Alou	.05
188	Joe Grahe	.05
189	Jeff Kent	.05
190	Bill Wegman	.05
191	Kim Batiste	.05
192	Matt Nokes	.05
193	Mark Wohlers	.05
194	Paul Sorrento	.05
195	Chris Hammond	.05
196	Scott Livingstone	.05
197	Doug Jones	.05
198	Scott Cooper	.05
199	Ramon Martinez	.05
200	Dave Valle	.05
201	Mariano Duncan	.05
202	Ben McDonald	.05
203	Darren Lewis	.05
204	Kenny Rogers	.05
205	Manuel Lee	.05
206	Scott Erickson	.05
207	Dan Gladden	.05
208	Bob Welch	.05
209	Greg Olson	.05
210	Dan Pasqua	.05
211	Tim Wallach	.05
212	Jeff Montgomery	.05
213	Derrick May	.05
214	Ed Sprague	.05
215	David Haas	.05
216	Darrin Fletcher	.05
217	Brian Jordan	.05
218	Jaime Navarro	.05
219	Randy Velarde	.05
220	Ron Gant	.05
221	Paul Quantrill	.05
222	Damion Easley	.05
223	Charlie Hough	.05
224	Brad Brink **RC**	.05
225	Barry Manual **RC**	.05
226	Kevin Koslofski **RC**	.05
227	Ryan Thompson **RC**	.05
228	Mike Munoz **RC**	.05
229	Dan Wilson **RC**	.10
230	Peter Hoy **RC**	.05
231	Pedro Astacio **RC**	.10
232	Matt Stairs **RC**	.10
233	Jeff Reboulet **RC**	.05
234	Manny Alexander **RC**	.05
235	Willie Banks **RC**	.05
236	John Jaha **RC**	.05
237	Scooter Tucker **RC**	.05
238	Russ Springer **RC**	.05
239	Paul Miller **RC**	.05
240	Dan Peltier **RC**	.05
241	Ozzie Canseco **RC**	.05
242	Ben Rivera **RC**	.05
243	John Valentin **RC**	.05
244	Henry Rodriguez	.05
245	Derek Parks **RC**	.05
246	Carlos Garcia **RC**	.10
247	Tim Pugh **RC**	.05
248	Melvin Nieves **RC**	.05
249	Rich Amaral **RC**	.05
250	Willie Greene **RC**	.05
251	Tim Scott **RC**	.05
252	Dave Silvestri **RC**	.05
253	Rob Mallicoat **RC**	.05
254	Donald Harris **RC**	.05
255	Craig Colbert **RC**	.05
256	Jose Guzman	.05
257	Domingo Martinez **RC**	.05
258	William Suero **RC**	.05
259	Juan Guerrero **RC**	.05
260	J.T. Snow **RC**	.45
261	Tony Pena	.05
262	Tim Fortugno **RC**	.05
263	Tom Marsh **RC**	.05
264	Kurt Knudsen **RC**	.05
265	Tim Costo **RC**	.05
266	Steve Shifflett **RC**	.05
267	Billy Ashley **RC**	.05
268	Jerry Nielsen	.05
269	Pete Young **RC**	.05
270	Johnny Guzman **RC**	.05
271	Greg Colbrunn **RC**	.05
272	Jeff Nelson	.05
273	Kevin Young **RC**	.05
274	Jeff Frye	.05
275	J.T. Bruett **RC**	.05
276	Todd Pratt **RC**	.05
277	Mike Butcher **RC**	.05
278	John Flaherty **RC**	.05
279	John Patterson **RC**	.05
280	Eric Hillman **RC**	.05
281	Bien Figueros **RC**	.05
282	Shane Reynolds **RC**	.05
283	Rich Rowland **RC**	.05
284	Steve Foster **RC**	.05
285	Dave Mlicki **RC**	.05
286	Mike Piazza	.65
287	Mike Trombley **RC**	.05
288	Jim Pena **RC**	.05
289	Bob Ayrault **RC**	.05
290	Henry Mercedes **RC**	.05
291	Bob Wickman	.05
292	Jacob Brumfield **RC**	.05
293	David Hulse **RC**	.05
294	Ryan Klesko	.05
295	Doug Linton	.05
296	Steve Cooke	.05
297	Eddie Zosky	.05
298	Gerald Williams **RC**	.05
299	Jonathan Hurst **RC**	.05
300	Larry Carter **RC**	.05
301	William Pennyfeather **RC**	.05
302	Cesar Hernandez **RC**	.05
303	Steve Hosey **RC**	.05
304	Blas Minor **RC**	.05
305	Jeff Grotewold **RC**	.05
306	Bernardo Brito **RC**	.05
307	Rafael Bournigal **RC**	.05
308	Jeff Branson **RC**	.05
309	Tom Quinlan **RC**	.05
310	Pat Gomez **RC**	.05
311	Sterling Hitchcock **RC**	.10
312	Kent Bottenfield	.05
313	Alan Trammell	.05
314	Cris Colon **RC**	.05
315	Paul Wagner **RC**	.05
316	Matt Maysey **RC**	.05
317	Mike Stanton	.05
318	Rick Trlicek **RC**	.05
319	Kevin Rogers **RC**	.05
320	Mark Clark **RC**	.05
321	Pedro Martinez	.40
322	Al Martin **RC**	.05
323	Mike Macfarlane	.05
324	Rey Sanchez **RC**	.10
325	Roger Pavlik **RC**	.05
326	Troy Neel	.05
327	Kerry Woodson **RC**	.05
328	Wayne Kirby **RC**	.05
329	Ken Ryan **RC**	.05
330	Jesse Levis **RC**	.05
331	James Austin	.05
332	Dan Walters	.05
333	Brian Williams	.05
334	Wil Cordero	.05
335	Bret Boone	.05
336	Hipolito Pichardo	.05
337	Pat Mahomes	.05
338	Andy Stankiewicz	.05
339	Jim Bullinger	.05
340	Archi Cianfrocco	.05
341	Ruben Amaro Jr.	.05
342	Frank Seminara	.05
343	Pat Hentgen	.05
344	Dave Nilsson	.05
345	Mike Perez	.05
346	Tim Salmon	.05
347	Tim Wakefield **RC**	.10
348	Carlos Hernandez	.05
349	Donovan Osborne	.05
350	Denny Neagle	.05
351	Sam Militello	.05
352	Eric Fox	.05
353	John Doherty	.05
354	Chad Curtis	.05
355	Jeff Tackett	.05
356	Dave Fleming	.05
357	Pat Listach	.05
358	Kevin Wickander	.05
359	John VanderWal	.05
360	Arthur Rhodes	.05
361	Bob Scanlan	.05
362	Bob Zupcic	.05
363	Mel Rojas	.05
364	Jim Thome	.35
365	Bill Pecota	.05
366	Mark Carreon	.05
367	Mitch Williams	.05
368	Cal Eldred	.05
369	Stan Belinda	.05
370	Pat Kelly	.05
371	Pheal Cormier	.05
372	Juan Guzman	.05
373	Damon Berryhill	.05
374	Gary DiSarcina	.05
375	Norm Charlton	.05
376	Roberto Hernandez	.05
377	Scott Kamieniecki	.05
378	Rusty Meacham	.05
379	Kurt Stillwell	.05
380	Lloyd McClendon	.05
381	Mark Leonard	.05
382	Jerry Browne	.05
383	Glenn Davis	.05
384	Randy Johnson	.40
385	Mike Greenwell	.05
386	Scott Chiamparino	.05
387	George Bell	.05
388	Steve Olin	.05
389	Chuck McElroy	.05
390	Mark Gardner	.05
391	Rod Beck	.05
392	Dennis Rasmussen	.05
393	Charlie Leibrandt	.05
394	Julio Franco	.05
395	Pete Harnisch	.05
396	Sid Bream	.05
397	Milt Thompson	.05
398	Glenallen Hill	.05
399	Chico Walker	.05
400	Alex Cole	.05
401	Trevor Wilson	.05
402	Jeff Conine	.05
403	Kyle Abbott	.05
404	Tom Browning	.05
405	Jerald Clark	.05
406	Vince Horsman	.05
407	Kevin Mitchell	.05
408	Pete Smith	.05
409	Jeff Innis	.05
410	Mike Timlin	.05
411	Charlie Hayes	.05
412	Alex Fernandez	.05
413	Jeff Russell	.05
414	Jody Reed	.05
415	Mickey Morandini	.05
416	Darnell Coles	.05
417	Xavier Hernandez	.05
418	Steve Sax	.05
419	Joe Girardi	.05
420	Mike Fetters	.05
421	Danny Jackson	.05
422	Jim Gott	.05
423	Tim Belcher	.05
424	Jose Mesa	.05
425	Junior Felix	.05
426	Thomas Howard	.05
427	Julio Valera	.05
428	Dante Bichette	.05
429	Mike Sharperson	.05
430	Darryl Kile	.05
431	Lonnie Smith	.05
432	Monty Fariss	.05
433	Reggie Jefferson	.05
434	Bob McClure	.05
435	Craig Lefferts	.05
436	Duane Ward	.05
437	Shawn Abner	.05
438	Roberto Kelly	.05
439	Paul O'Neill	.05
440	Alan Mills	.05
441	Roger Mason	.05
442	Gary Pettis	.05
443	Steve Lake	.05
444	Gene Larkin	.05
445	Larry Anderson	.05
446	Doug Dascenzo	.05
447	Daryl Boston	.05
448	John Candelaria	.05
449	Storm Davis	.05
450	Tom Edens	.05
451	Mike Maddux	.05
452	Tim Naehring	.05
453	John Orton	.05
454	Joey Cora	.05
455	Chuck Crim	.05
456	Dan Plesac	.05
457	Mike Bielecki	.05
458	Terry Jorgensen **RC**	.05
459	John Habyan	.05
460	Pete O'Brien	.05
461	Jeff Treadway	.05
462	Frank Castillo	.05
463	Jimmy Jones	.05
464	Tommy Greene	.05
465	Tracy Woodson	.05
466	Rich Rodriguez	.05
467	Joe Hesketh	.05
468	Greg Myers	.05
469	Kirk McCaskill	.05
470	Ricky Bones	.05
471	Lenny Webster	.05
472	Francisco Cabrera	.05
473	Turner Ward	.05
474	Dwayne Henry	.05
475	Al Osuna	.05
476	Craig Wilson	.05
477	Chris Nabholz	.05
478	Rafael Belliard	.05
479	Terry Leach	.05
480	Tim Teufel	.05
481	Dennis Eckersley (Award Winner)	.15
482	Barry Bonds (Award Winner)	.50
483	Dennis Eckersley (Award Winner)	.15
484	Greg Maddux (Award Winner)	.25
485	Pat Listach (ROY)	.05
486	Eric Karros (ROY)	.05
487	Jamie Arnold **RC**	.05
488	B.J. Wallace	.05
489	Derek Jeter **RC**	8.00
490	Jason Kendall **RC**	.45
491	Rick Helling	.05
492	Derek Wallace **RC**	.05
493	Sean Lowe **RC**	.05
494	Shannon Stewart **RC**	.65
495	Benji Grigsby **RC**	.05
496	Todd Steverson **RC**	.05
497	Dan Serafini **RC**	.05
498	Michael Tucker	.05
499	Chris Roberts (Draft Pick)	.05

500 Pete Janicki **RC** (Draft Pick) .05
501 Jeff Schmidt **RC** .05
502 Edgar Martinez/AS .05
503 Omar Vizquel/AS .05
504 Ken Griffey Jr./AS .35
505 Kirby Puckett/AS .25
506 Joe Carter/AS .05
507 Ivan Rodriguez/AS .15
508 Jack Morris/AS .05
509 Dennis Eckersley/AS .15
510 Frank Thomas/AS .20
511 Roberto Alomar/AS .10
512 Mickey Morandini (Highlight) .05
513 Dennis Eckersley (Highlight) .15
514 Jeff Reardon (Highlight) .05
515 Danny Tartabull (Highlight) .05
516 Bip Roberts (Highlight) .05
517 George Brett (Highlight) .30
518 Robin Yount (Highlight) .20
519 Kevin Gross (Highlight) .05
520 Ed Sprague (World Series Highlight) .05
521 Dave Winfield (World Series Highlight) .20
522 Ozzie Smith/AS .25
523 Barry Bonds/AS .50
524 Andy Van Slyke/AS .05
525 Tony Gwynn/AS .25
526 Darren Daulton/AS .05
527 Greg Maddux/AS .25
528 Fred McGriff/AS .05
529 Lee Smith/AS .05
530 Ryne Sandberg/AS .25
531 Gary Sheffield/AS .10
532 Ozzie Smith/DT .25
533 Kirby Puckett/DT .25
534 Gary Sheffield/DT .10
535 Andy Van Slyke/DT .05
536 Ken Griffey Jr./DT .35
537 Ivan Rodriguez/DT .15
538 Charles Nagy/DT .05
539 Tom Glavine/DT .10
540 Dennis Eckersley/DT .15
541 Frank Thomas/DT .20
542 Roberto Alomar/DT .10
543 Sean Barry .05
544 Mike Schooler .05
545 Chuck Carr .05
546 Lenny Harris .05
547 Gary Scott .05
548 Derek Lilliquist .05
549 Brian Hunter .05
550 Kirby Puckett (MOY) .25
551 Jim Eisenreich .05
552 Andre Dawson .25
553 David Nied .05
554 Spike Owen .05
555 Greg Gagne .05
556 Sid Fernandez .05
557 Mark McGwire .75
558 Bryan Harvey .05
559 Harold Reynolds .05
560 Barry Bonds 1.00
561 Eric Wedge **RC** .05
562 Ozzie Smith .45
563 Rick Sutcliffe .05
564 Jeff Reardon .05
565 Alex Arias **RC** .05
566 Greg Swindell .05
567 Brook Jacoby .05
568 Pete Incaviglia .05
569 Butch Henry **RC** .05
570 Eric Davis .05
571 Kevin Seitzer .05
572 Tony Fernandez .05
573 Steve Reed **RC** .05
574 Cory Snyder .05
575 Joe Carter .05
576 Greg Maddux .45
577 Bert Blyleven .05
578 Kevin Bass .05
579 Carlton Fisk .40
580 Doug Drabek .05
581 Mark Gubicza .05
582 Bobby Thigpen .05
583 Chili Davis .05
584 Scott Bankhead .05
585 Harold Baines .05
586 Eric Young **RC** .15
587 Lance Parrish .05
588 Juan Bell .05
589 Bob Ojeda .05
590 Joe Orsulak .05
591 Benito Santiago .05
592 Wade Boggs .45
593 Robby Thompson .05
594 Erik Plunk .05
595 Hensley Meulens .05
596 Lou Whitaker .05
597 Dale Murphy .25
598 Paul Molitor .40
599 Greg W. Harris .05
600 Darren Holmes .05
601 Dave Martinez .05
602 Tom Henke .05
603 Mike Benjamin .05
604 Rene Gonzales .05
605 Roger McDowell .05
606 Kirby Puckett .45
607 Randy Myers .05
608 Ruben Sierra .05
609 Wilson Alvarez .05
610 Dave Segui .05
611 Juan Samuel .05
612 Tom Brunansky .05
613 Willie Randolph .05
614 Tony Phillips .05
615 Candy Maldonado .05
616 Chris Bosio .05
617 Bret Barberie .05
618 Scott Sanderson .05
619 Ron Darling .05
620 Dave Winfield .40
621 Mike Felder .05
622 Greg Hibbard .05
623 Mike Scioscia .05
624 John Smiley .05
625 Alejandro Pena .05
626 Terry Steinbach .05
627 Freddie Benavides .05
628 Kevin Reimer .05
629 Braulio Castillo .05
630 Dave Stieb .05
631 Dave Magadan .05
632 Scott Fletcher .05
633 Cris Carpenter .05
634 Kevin Maas .05
635 Todd Worrell .05
636 Rob Deer .05
637 Dwight Smith .05
638 Chito Martinez .05
639 Jimmy Key .05
640 Greg Harris .05
641 Mike Moore .05
642 Pat Borders .05
643 Bill Gullickson .05
644 Gary Gaetti .05
645 David Howard .05
646 Jim Abbott .05
647 Willie Wilson .05
648 David Wells .05
649 Andres Galarraga .05
650 Vince Coleman .05
651 Rob Dibble .05
652 Frank Tanana .05
653 Steve Decker .05
654 David Cone .05
655 Jack Armstrong .05
656 Dave Stewart .05
657 Billy Hatcher .05
658 Tim Raines .05
659 Walt Weiss .05
660 Jose Lind .05

Boys of Summer

These cards were available as inserts only in Score 35-card Super Packs, about one in every four packs. Borderless fronts have a color action photo of the player superimposed over the sun. The player's name is in black script in a green strip at bottom, along with a subset logo. On back is a player portrait, again with the sun as a background. Subset, company, team and major league logos are in color on the right, and there is a short career summary on the green background at bottom.

NM/M
Complete Set (30): 12.50
Common Player: .25
1 Billy Ashley .25
2 Tim Salmon .50
3 Pedro Martinez 4.00
4 Luis Mercedes .25
5 Mike Piazza 8.00
6 Troy Neel .25
7 Melvin Nieves .25
8 Ryan Klesko .25
9 Ryan Thompson .25
10 Kevin Young .25
11 Gerald Williams .25
12 Willie Greene .25
13 John Patterson .25
14 Carlos Garcia .25
15 Eddie Zosky .25
16 Sean Berry .25
17 Rico Brogna .25
18 Larry Carter .25
19 Bobby Ayala .25
20 Alan Embree .25
21 Donald Harris .25
22 Sterling Hitchcock .25
23 David Nied .25
24 Henry Mercedes .25
25 Ozzie Canseco .25
26 David Hulse .25
27 Al Martin .25
28 Dan Wilson .25
29 Paul Miller .25
30 Rich Rowland .25

Dream Team

This set which features most of the players in street clothes in sepia-toned photos on a white background, has gold-foil graphics and was available only via a mail-in offer.

NM/M
Complete Set (12): 5.00
Common Player: .25
1 Ozzie Smith 1.00
2 Kirby Puckett 1.00
3 Gary Sheffield .35
4 Andy Van Slyke .25
5 Ken Griffey Jr. 2.00
6 Ivan Rodriguez .60
7 Charles Nagy .25
8 Tom Glavine .35
9 Dennis Eckersley .60
10 Frank Thomas .75
11 Roberto Alomar .30
--- Header Card .05

The Franchise

These glossy inserts have full-bleed color action photos against a darkened background so that the player stands out. Cards could be found in 16-card packs only; odds of finding one are 1 in every 24 packs. The fronts have gold-foil highlights.

NM/M
Complete Set (28): 50.00
Common Player: .60
1 Cal Ripken, Jr. 12.00
2 Roger Clemens 6.00
3 Mark Langston .60
4 Frank Thomas 3.50
5 Carlos Baerga .60
6 Cecil Fielder .60
7 Gregg Jefferies .60
8 Robin Yount 3.50
9 Kirby Puckett 5.00
10 Don Mattingly 6.00
11 Dennis Eckersley 3.00
12 Ken Griffey Jr. 9.00
13 Juan Gonzalez 3.50
14 Roberto Alomar 1.50
15 Terry Pendleton .60
16 Ryne Sandberg 5.00
17 Barry Larkin .60
18 Jeff Bagwell 3.50
19 Brett Butler .60
20 Larry Walker .60
21 Bobby Bonilla .60
22 Darren Daulton .60
23 Andy Van Slyke .60
24 Ray Lankford .60
25 Gary Sheffield 1.50
26 Will Clark .60
27 Bryan Harvey .60
28 David Nied .60

Procter & Gamble Rookies

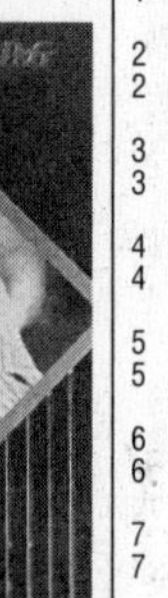

This set was available via a mail-in offer in the summer of 1993. Ten proofs of purchase were required along with a small amount of cash for postage. Fronts feature a player action photo in a diamond at center with the name, position and team logo in a home plate device at the bottom of the photo. At bottom center is a color photo of the player's home stadium, flanked by silver-foil stripes on a dark green background. Above the player photo are gold-foil Score and P&G logos on a dark green background. A center bar in gold foil has the word "ROOKIE" in green. Backs have a small player portrait photo at top against a dark green background. His name and position are in white at left and personal data at right. At center is a large color photo of the player's hometeam skyline, with the city name in gold type in a green stripe below. At bottom are complete major and minor league stats, MLB and MLBPA logos and the card number.

NM/M
Complete Set (10): 3.00
Common Player: .25
1 Wil Cordero .25
2 Pedro Martinez 2.00
3 Bret Boone .25
4 Melvin Nieves .25
5 Ryan Klesko .25
6 Ryan Thompson .25
7 Kevin Young .25
8 Willie Greene .25
9 Eric Wedge .25
10 David Nied .25

1994 Score Samples

Regular and Gold Rush versions of the first eight cards in the 1994 Score set were produced in a special promo version to familiarize buyers with the new issue. Cards have all zeroes in place of the 1993 stats and are overprinted on front and back with a diagonal black "SAMPLE." The samples were distributed in 11-card cello packs containing eight regular sample cards, one of the Gold Rush samples, a Barry Larkin Dream Team promo card and a header.

NM/M
Complete Set (18): 20.00
Common Player: .40
1 Barry Bonds 2.00
1 Barry Bonds (Gold Rush) 6.00
2 John Olerud .40
2 John Olerud (Gold Rush) 1.00
3 Ken Griffey Jr. 1.50
3 Ken Griffey Jr. (Gold Rush) 4.50
4 Jeff Bagwell 1.00
4 Jeff Bagwell (Gold Rush) 3.00
5 John Burkett .40
5 John Burkett (Gold Rush) 1.00
6 Jack McDowell .40
6 Jack McDowell (Gold Rush) 1.00
7 Albert Belle .50
7 Albert Belle (Gold Rush) 1.50
8 Andres Galarraga .40
8 Andres Galarraga (Gold Rush) 1.00
5 Barry Larkin/DT .50
-- Hobby Header Card .05
-- Retail Header Card .05

1994 Score

Score's 1994 set, with a new design and UV coating, was issued in two series of 330 cards each. The cards, which use more action photos than before, have dark blue borders with the player's name in a team color-coded strip at the bottom. A special Gold Rush card, done for each card in the set, is included in every pack. Series 1 includes American League checklists, which are printed on the backs of cards depicting panoramic views of each team's ballpark. Series 2 has the National League team checklists. Insert sets include Dream Team players, and National (Series 1 packs) and American League Gold Stars (Series 2 packs), which use the Gold Rush process and appear once every 18 packs.

NM/M
Complete Set (660): 15.00
Common Player: .05
Gold Rush: 2X
Pack (14): .75
Wax Box (36): 15.00
1 Barry Bonds 1.00
2 John Olerud .05
3 Ken Griffey Jr. .65
4 Jeff Bagwell .40
5 John Burkett .05
6 Jack McDowell .05
7 Albert Belle .05
8 Andres Galarraga .05
9 Mike Mussina .30
10 Will Clark .05
11 Travis Fryman .05
12 Tony Gwynn .50
13 Robin Yount .40
14 Dave Magadan .05
15 Paul O'Neill .05
16 Ray Lankford .05
17 Damion Easley .05
18 Andy Van Slyke .05
19 Brian McRae .05
20 Ryne Sandberg .50
21 Kirby Puckett .50
22 Dwight Gooden .05
23 Don Mattingly .60
24 Kevin Mitchell .05
25 Roger Clemens .60
26 Eric Karros .05
27 Juan Gonzalez .20
28 John Kruk .05
29 Gregg Jefferies .05
30 Tom Glavine .30
31 Ivan Rodriguez .35
32 Jay Bell .05
33 Randy Johnson .40
34 Darren Daulton .05
35 Rickey Henderson .40
36 Eddie Murray .40
37 Brian Harper .05
38 Delino DeShields .05
39 Jose Lind .05
40 Benito Santiago .05
41 Frank Thomas .40
42 Mark Grace .05
43 Roberto Alomar .20
44 Andy Benes .05
45 Luis Polonia .05
46 Brett Butler .05
47 Terry Steinbach .05
48 Craig Biggio .05
49 Greg Vaughn .05
50 Charlie Hayes .05
51 Mickey Tettleton .05
52 Jose Rijo .05
53 Carlos Baerga .05
54 Jeff Blauser .05
55 Leo Gomez .05
56 Bob Tewksbury .05
57 Mo Vaughn .05
58 Orlando Merced .05
59 Tino Martinez .05
60 Len Dykstra .05
61 Jose Canseco .25
62 Tony Fernandez .05
63 Donovan Osborne .05
64 Ken Hill .05
65 Kent Hrbek .05
66 Bryan Harvey .05
67 Wally Joyner .05
68 Derrick May .05
69 Lance Johnson .05
70 Willie McGee .05
71 Mark Langston .05
72 Terry Pendleton .05
73 Joe Carter .05
74 Barry Larkin .05
75 Jimmy Key .05
76 Joe Girardi .05
77 B.J. Surhoff .05
78 Pete Harnisch .05
79 Lou Whitaker .05
80 Cory Snyder .05
81 Kenny Lofton .05
82 Fred McGriff .05
83 Mike Greenwell .05
84 Mike Perez .05
85 Cal Ripken, Jr. 1.00
86 Don Slaught .05
87 Omar Vizquel .05
88 Curt Schilling .30
89 Chuck Knoblauch .05
90 Moises Alou .05
91 Greg Gagne .05
92 Bret Saberhagen .05
93 Ozzie Guillen .05
94 Matt Williams .05
95 Chad Curtis .05
96 Mike Harkey .05
97 Devon White .05
98 Walt Weiss .05
99 Kevin Brown .05
100 Gary Sheffield .25
101 Wade Boggs .50
102 Orel Hershiser .05
103 Tony Phillips .05
104 Andujar Cedeno .05
105 Bill Spiers .05
106 Otis Nixon .05
107 Felix Fermin .05
108 Bip Roberts .05
109 Dennis Eckersley .35
110 Dante Bichette .05
111 Ben McDonald .05
112 Jim Poole .05
113 John Dopson .05
114 Rob Dibble .05
115 Jeff Treadway .05
116 Ricky Jordan .05
117 Mike Henneman .05
118 Willie Blair .05
119 Doug Henry .05
120 Gerald Perry .05
121 Greg Myers .05
122 John Franco .05
123 Roger Mason .05
124 Chris Hammond .05
125 Hubie Brooks .05
126 Kent Mercker .05
127 Jim Abbott .05
128 Kevin Bass .05
129 Rick Aguilera .05
130 Mitch Webster .05
131 Eric Plunk .05
132 Mark Carreon .05
133 Dave Stewart .05
134 Willie Wilson .05
135 Dave Fleming .05
136 Jeff Tackett .05
137 Geno Petralli .05
138 Gene Harris .05
139 Scott Bankhead .05
140 Trevor Wilson .05
141 Alvaro Espinoza .05
142 Ryan Bowen .05
143 Mike Moore .05
144 Bill Pecota .05
145 Jaime Navarro .05
146 Jack Daugherty .05
147 Bob Wickman .05
148 Chris Jones .05
149 Todd Stottlemyre .05
150 Brian Williams .05
151 Chuck Finley .05

152	Lenny Harris	.05
153	Alex Fernandez	.05
154	Candy Maldonado	.05
155	Jeff Montgomery	.05
156	David West	.05
157	Mark Williamson	.05
158	Milt Thompson	.05
159	Ron Darling	.05
160	Stan Belinda	.05
161	Henry Cotto	.05
162	Mel Rojas	.05
163	Doug Strange	.05
164	Rene Arocha (1993 Rookie)	.05
165	Tim Hulett	.05
166	Steve Avery	.05
167	Jim Thome	.35
168	Tom Browning	.05
169	Mario Diaz	.05
170	Steve Reed (1993 Rookie)	.05
171	Scott Livingstone	.05
172	Chris Donnels	.05
173	John Jaha	.05
174	Carlos Hernandez	.05
175	Dion James	.05
176	Bud Black	.05
177	Tony Castillo	.05
178	Jose Guzman	.05
179	Torey Lovullo	.05
180	John Vander Wal	.05
181	Mike LaValliere	.05
182	Sid Fernandez	.05
183	Brent Mayne	.05
184	Terry Mulholland	.05
185	Willie Banks	.05
186	Steve Cooke (1993 Rookie)	.05
187	Brent Gates (1993 Rookie)	.05
188	Erik Pappas (1993 Rookie)	.05
189	Bill Haselman (1993 Rookie)	.05
190	Fernando Valenzuela	.05
191	Gary Redus	.05
192	Danny Darwin	.05
193	Mark Portugal	.05
194	Derek Lilliquist	.05
195	Charlie O'Brien	.05
196	Matt Nokes	.05
197	Danny Sheaffer	.05
198	Bill Gullickson	.05
199	Alex Arias (1993 Rookie)	.05
200	Mike Fetters	.05
201	Brian Jordan	.05
202	Joe Grahe	.05
203	Tom Candiotti	.05
204	Jeremy Stanton	.05
205	Mike Stanton	.05
206	David Howard	.05
207	Darren Holmes	.05
208	Rick Honeycutt	.05
209	Danny Jackson	.05
210	Rich Amaral (1993 Rookie)	.05
211	Blas Minor (1993 Rookie)	.05
212	Kenny Rogers	.05
213	Jim Leyritz	.05
214	Mike Morgan	.05
215	Dan Gladden	.05
216	Randy Velarde	.05
217	Mitch Williams	.05
218	Hipolito Pichardo	.05
219	Dave Burba	.05
220	Wilson Alvarez	.05
221	Bob Zupcic	.05
222	Francisco Cabrera	.05
223	Julio Valera	.05
224	Paul Assenmacher	.05
225	Jeff Branson	.05
226	Todd Frohwirth	.05
227	Armando Reynoso	.05
228	Rich Rowland (1993 Rookie)	.05
229	Freddie Benavides	.05
230	Wayne Kirby (1993 Rookie)	.05
231	Darryl Kile	.05
232	Skeeter Barnes	.05
233	Ramon Martinez	.05
234	Tom Gordon	.05
235	Dave Gallagher	.05
236	Ricky Bones	.05
237	Larry Andersen	.05
238	Pat Meares (1993 Rookie)	.05
239	Zane Smith	.05
240	Tim Leary	.05
241	Phil Clark	.05
242	Danny Cox	.05
243	Mike Jackson	.05
244	Mike Gallego	.05
245	Lee Smith	.05
246	Todd Jones (1993 Rookie)	.05
247	Steve Bedrosian	.05
248	Troy Neel	.05
249	Jose Bautista	.05
250	Steve Frey	.05
251	Jeff Reardon	.05
252	Stan Javier	.05
253	Mo Sanford (1993 Rookie)	.05
254	Steve Sax	.05
255	Luis Aquino	.05
256	Domingo Jean (1993 Rookie)	.05
257	Scott Servais	.05
258	Brad Pennington (1993 Rookie)	.05
259	Dave Hansen	.05
260	Goose Gossage	.05
261	Jeff Fassero	.05
262	Junior Ortiz	.05
263	Anthony Young	.05
264	Chris Bosio	.05
265	Ruben Amaro Jr.	.05
266	Mark Eichhorn	.05
267	Dave Clark	.05
268	Gary Thurman	.05
269	Les Lancaster	.05
270	Jamie Moyer	.05
271	Ricky Gutierrez (1993 Rookie)	.05
272	Greg Harris	.05
273	Mike Benjamin	.05
274	Gene Nelson	.05
275	Damon Berryhill	.05
276	Scott Radinsky	.05
277	Mike Aldrete	.05
278	Jerry DiPoto (1993 Rookie)	.05
279	Chris Haney	.05
280	Richie Lewis (1993 Rookie)	.05
281	Jarvis Brown	.05
282	Juan Bell	.05
283	Joe Klink	.05
284	Graeme Lloyd (1993 Rookie)	.05
285	Casey Candaele	.05
286	Bob MacDonald	.05
287	Mike Sharperson	.05
288	Gene Larkin	.05
289	Brian Barnes	.05
290	David McCarty (1993 Rookie)	.05
291	Jeff Innis	.05
292	Bob Patterson	.05
293	Ben Rivera	.05
294	John Habyan	.05
295	Rich Rodriguez	.05
296	Edwin Nunez	.05
297	Rod Brewer	.05
298	Mike Timlin	.05
299	Jesse Orosco	.05
300	Gary Gaetti	.05
301	Todd Benzinger	.05
302	Jeff Nelson	.05
303	Rafael Belliard	.05
304	Matt Whiteside	.05
305	Vinny Castilla	.05
306	Matt Turner	.05
307	Eduardo Perez	.05
308	Joel Johnston	.05
309	Chris Gomez	.05
310	Pat Rapp	.05
311	Jim Tatum	.05
312	Kirk Rueter	.05
313	John Flaherty	.05
314	Tom Kramer	.05
315	Mark Whiten (Highlights)	.05
316	Chris Bosio (Highlights)	.05
317	Orioles Checklist	.05
318	Red Sox Checklist	.05
319	Angels Checklist	.05
320	White Sox Checklist	.05
321	Indians Checklist	.05
322	Tigers Checklist	.05
323	Royals Checklist	.05
324	Brewers Checklist	.05
325	Twins Checklist	.05
326	Yankees Checklist	.05
327	Athletics Checklist	.05
328	Mariners Checklist	.05
329	Rangers Checklist	.05
330	Blue Jays Checklist	.05
331	Frank Viola	.05
332	Ron Gant	.05
333	Charles Nagy	.05
334	Roberto Kelly	.05
335	Brady Anderson	.05
336	Alex Cole	.05
337	Alan Trammell	.05
338	Derek Bell	.05
339	Bernie Williams	.05
340	Jose Offerman	.05
341	Bill Wegman	.05
342	Ken Caminiti	.05
343	Pat Borders	.05
344	Kirt Manwaring	.05
345	Chili Davis	.05
346	Steve Buechele	.05
347	Robin Ventura	.05
348	Teddy Higuera	.05
349	Jerry Browne	.05
350	Scott Kamieniecki	.05
351	Kevin Tapani	.05
352	Marquis Grissom	.05
353	Jay Buhner	.05
354	Dave Hollins	.05
355	Dan Wilson	.05
356	Bob Walk	.05
357	Chris Hoiles	.05
358	Todd Zeile	.05
359	Kevin Appier	.05
360	Chris Sabo	.05
361	David Segui	.05
362	Jerald Clark	.05
363	Tony Pena	.05
364	Steve Finley	.05
365	Roger Pavlik	.05
366	John Smoltz	.05
367	Scott Fletcher	.05
368	Jody Reed	.05
369	David Wells	.05
370	Jose Vizcaino	.05
371	Pat Listach	.05
372	Orestes Destrade	.05
373	Danny Tartabull	.05
374	Greg W. Harris	.05
375	Juan Guzman	.05
376	Larry Walker	.05
377	Gary DiSarcina	.05
378	Bobby Bonilla	.05
379	Tim Raines	.05
380	Tommy Greene	.05
381	Chris Gwynn	.05
382	Jeff King	.05
383	Shane Mack	.05
384	Ozzie Smith	.50
385	Eddie Zambrano **RC**	.05
386	Mike Devereaux	.05
387	Erik Hanson	.05
388	Scott Cooper	.05
389	Dean Palmer	.05
390	John Wetteland	.05
391	Reggie Jefferson	.05
392	Mark Lemke	.05
393	Cecil Fielder	.05
394	Reggie Sanders	.05
395	Darryl Hamilton	.05
396	Daryl Boston	.05
397	Pat Kelly	.05
398	Joe Orsulak	.05
399	Ed Sprague	.05
400	Eric Anthony	.05
401	Scott Sanderson	.05
402	Jim Gott	.05
403	Ron Karkovice	.05
404	Phil Plantier	.05
405	David Cone	.05
406	Robby Thompson	.05
407	Dave Winfield	.40
408	Dwight Smith	.05
409	Ruben Sierra	.05
410	Jack Armstrong	.05
411	Mike Felder	.05
412	Wil Cordero	.05
413	Julio Franco	.05
414	Howard Johnson	.05
415	Mark McLemore	.05
416	Pete Incaviglia	.05
417	John Valentin	.05
418	Tim Wakefield	.05
419	Jose Mesa	.05
420	Bernard Gilkey	.05
421	Kirk Gibson	.05
422	Dave Justice	.05
423	Tom Brunansky	.05
424	John Smiley	.05
425	Kevin Maas	.05
426	Doug Drabek	.05
427	Paul Molitor	.40
428	Darryl Strawberry	.05
429	Tim Naehring	.05
430	Bill Swift	.05
431	Ellis Burks	.05
432	Greg Hibbard	.05
433	Felix Jose	.05
434	Bret Barberie	.05
435	Pedro Munoz	.05
436	Darrin Fletcher	.05
437	Bobby Witt	.05
438	Wes Chamberlain	.05
439	Mackey Sasser	.05
440	Mark Whiten	.05
441	Harold Reynolds	.05
442	Greg Olson	.05
443	Billy Hatcher	.05
444	Joe Oliver	.05
445	Sandy Alomar Jr.	.05
446	Tim Wallach	.05
447	Karl Rhodes	.05
448	Royce Clayton	.05
449	Cal Eldred	.05
450	Rick Wilkins	.05
451	Mike Stanley	.05
452	Charlie Hough	.05
453	Jack Morris	.05
454	Jon Ratliff **RC**	.05
455	Rene Gonzales	.05
456	Eddie Taubensee	.05
457	Roberto Hernandez	.05
458	Todd Hundley	.05
459	Mike MacFarlane	.05
460	Mickey Morandini	.05
461	Scott Erickson	.05
462	Lonnie Smith	.05
463	Dave Henderson	.05
464	Ryan Klesko	.05
465	Edgar Martinez	.05
466	Tom Pagnozzi	.05
467	Charlie Leibrandt	.05
468	Brian Anderson **RC**	.10
469	Harold Baines	.05
470	Tim Belcher	.05
471	Andre Dawson	.25
472	Eric Young	.05
473	Paul Sorrento	.05
474	Luis Gonzalez	.05
475	Rob Deer	.05
476	Mike Piazza	.65
477	Kevin Reimer	.05
478	Jeff Gardner	.05
479	Melido Perez	.05
480	Darren Lewis	.05
481	Duane Ward	.05
482	Rey Sanchez	.05
483	Mark Lewis	.05
484	Jeff Conine	.05
485	Joey Cora	.05
486	Trot Nixon **RC**	.50
487	Kevin McReynolds	.05
488	Mike Lansing	.05
489	Mike Pagliarulo	.05
490	Mariano Duncan	.05
491	Mike Bordick	.05
492	Kevin Young	.05
493	Dave Valle	.05
494	Wayne Gomes **RC**	.05
495	Rafael Palmeiro	.35
496	Deion Sanders	.05
497	Rick Sutcliffe	.05
498	Randy Milligan	.05
499	Carlos Quintana	.05
500	Chris Turner	.05
501	Thomas Howard	.05
502	Greg Swindell	.05
503	Chad Kreuter	.05
504	Eric Davis	.05
505	Dickie Thon	.05
506	Matt Drews **RC**	.05
507	Spike Owen	.05
508	Rod Beck	.05
509	Pat Hentgen	.05
510	Sammy Sosa	.50
511	J.T. Snow	.05
512	Chuck Carr	.05
513	Bo Jackson	.10
514	Dennis Martinez	.05
515	Phil Hiatt	.05
516	Jeff Kent	.05
517	Brooks Kieschnick **RC**	.05
518	Kirk Presley **RC**	.05
519	Kevin Seitzer	.05
520	Carlos Garcia	.05
521	Mike Blowers	.05
522	Luis Alicea	.05
523	David Hulse	.05
524	Greg Maddux	.50
525	Gregg Olson	.05
526	Hal Morris	.05
527	Daron Kirkreit	.05
528	David Nied	.05
529	Jeff Russell	.05
530	Kevin Gross	.05
531	John Doherty	.05
532	Matt Brunson **RC**	.05
533	Dave Nilsson	.05
534	Randy Myers	.05
535	Steve Farr	.05
536	Billy Wagner **RC**	.10
537	Darnell Coles	.05
538	Frank Tanana	.05
539	Tim Salmon	.05
540	Kim Batiste	.05
541	George Bell	.05
542	Tom Henke	.05
543	Sam Horn	.05
544	Doug Jones	.05
545	Scott Leius	.05
546	Al Martin	.05
547	Bob Welch	.05
548	Scott Christman **RC**	.05
549	Norm Charlton	.05
550	Mark McGwire	.75
551	Greg McMichael	.05
552	Tim Costo	.05
553	Rodney Bolton	.05
554	Pedro Martinez	.40
555	Marc Valdes	.05
556	Darrell Whitmore	.05
557	Tim Bogar	.05
558	Steve Karsay	.05
559	Danny Bautista	.05
560	Jeffrey Hammonds	.05
561	Aaron Sele	.05
562	Russ Springer	.05
563	Jason Bere	.05
564	Billy Brewer	.05
565	Sterling Hitchcock	.05
566	Bobby Munoz	.05
567	Craig Paquette	.05
568	Bret Boone	.05
569	Dan Peltier	.05
570	Jeromy Burnitz	.05
571	John Wasdin **RC**	.05
572	Chipper Jones	.50
573	Jamey Wright **RC**	.05
574	Jeff Granger	.05
575	Jay Powell **RC**	.05
576	Ryan Thompson	.05
577	Lou Frazier	.05
578	Paul Wagner	.05
579	Brad Ausmus	.05
580	Jack Voigt	.05
581	Kevin Rogers	.05
582	Damon Buford	.05
583	Paul Quantrill	.05
584	Marc Newfield	.05
585	Derrek Lee **RC**	1.00
586	Shane Reynolds	.05
587	Cliff Floyd	.05
588	Jeff Schwarz	.05
589	Ross Powell **RC**	.05
590	Gerald Williams	.05
591	Mike Trombley	.05
592	Ken Ryan	.05
593	John O'Donoghue	.05
594	Rod Correia	.05
595	Darrell Sherman	.05
596	Steve Scarsone	.05
597	Sherman Obando	.05
598	Kurt Abbott	.05
599	Dave Telgheder	.05
600	Rick Trlicek	.05
601	Carl Everett	.05
602	Luis Ortiz	.05
603	Larry Luebbers **RC**	.05
604	Kevin Roberson	.05
605	Butch Huskey	.05
606	Benji Gil	.05
607	Todd Van Poppel	.05
608	Mark Hutton	.05
609	Chip Hale	.05
610	Matt Maysey	.05
611	Scott Ruffcorn	.05
612	Hilly Hathaway	.05
613	Allen Watson	.05
614	Carlos Delgado	.30
615	Roberto Mejia	.05
616	Turk Wendell	.05
617	Tony Tarasco	.05
618	Raul Mondesi	.05
619	Kevin Stocker	.05
620	Javier Lopez	.05
621	Keith Kessinger **RC**	.05
622	Bob Hamelin	.05
623	John Roper	.05
624	Len Dykstra (World Series)	.05
625	Joe Carter (World Series)	.05
626	Jim Abbott (Highlight)	.05
627	Lee Smith (Highlight)	.05
628	Ken Griffey Jr. (HL)	.35
629	Dave Winfield (Highlight)	.05
630	Darryl Kile (Highlight)	.05
631	Frank Thomas (MVP)	.25
632	Barry Bonds (MVP)	.50
633	Jack McDowell (Cy Young)	.05
634	Greg Maddux (Cy Young)	.25
635	Tim Salmon (ROY)	.05
636	Mike Piazza (ROY)	.40
637	Brian Turang **RC**	.05
638	Rondell White	.05
639	Nigel Wilson	.05
640	Torii Hunter **RC**	.75
641	Salomon Torres	.05
642	Kevin Higgins	.05
643	Eric Wedge	.05
644	Roger Salkeld	.05
645	Manny Ramirez	.40
646	Jeff McNeely	.05
647	Braves Checklist	.05
648	Cubs Checklist	.05
649	Reds Checklist	.05
650	Rockies Checklist	.05
651	Marlins Checklist	.05
652	Astros Checklist	.05
653	Dodgers Checklist	.05
654	Expos Checklist	.05
655	Mets Checklist	.05
656	Phillies Checklist	.05
657	Pirates Checklist	.05
658	Cardinals Checklist	.05
659	Padres Checklist	.05
660	Giants Checklist	.05

Gold Rush

Opting to include one insert card in each pack of its 1994 product, Score created a "Gold Rush" version of each card in its regular set. Gold Rush cards are basically the same as their counterparts with a few enhancements. Card fronts are printed on foil with a gold border and a Score Gold Rush logo in one of the upper corners. The background of the photo has been metalized, allowing the color player portion to stand out in sharp contrast. Backs are identical to the regular cards except for the appearance of a large Gold Rush logo under the typography.

	NM/M
Complete Set (660):	40.00
Common Player:	.15
Stars:	2X

Boys of Summer

A heavy emphasis on rookies and recent rookies is noted in this insert set. Released in two series, cards #1-30 are found in Series 1, with #31-60 packaged with Series 2. Fronts feature a color action photo on which the background has been rendered in a blurred watercolor effect. A hot-color aura separates the player from the background. The player's name appears vertically in gold foil. Backs have the background in reds and orange with a portrait-style player photo on one side and a large "Boys of Summer" logo on the other. A short description of the player's talents appears at center.

		NM/M
Complete Set (60):		25.00
Common Player:		.25
1	Jeff Conine	.25
2	Aaron Sele	.25
3	Kevin Stocker	.25
4	Pat Meares	.25
5	Jeromy Burnitz	.25
6	Mike Piazza	6.00
7	Allen Watson	.25
8	Jeffrey Hammonds	.25
9	Kevin Roberson	.25
10	Hilly Hathaway	.25
11	Kirk Reuter	.25
12	Eduardo Perez	.25
13	Ricky Gutierrez	.25
14	Domingo Jean	.25
15	David Nied	.25
16	Wayne Kirby	.25
17	Mike Lansing	.25
18	Jason Bere	.25
19	Brent Gates	.25
20	Javier Lopez	.25
21	Greg McMichael	.25
22	David Hulse	.25
23	Roberto Mejia	.25
24	Tim Salmon	.50
25	Rene Arocha	.25
26	Bret Boone	.25
27	David McCarty	.25
28	Todd Van Poppel	.25
29	Lance Painter	.25
30	Erik Pappas	.25
31	Chuck Carr	.25
32	Mark Hutton	.25
33	Jeff McNeely	.25
34	Willie Greene	.25
35	Nigel Wilson	.25
36	Rondell White	.25
37	Brian Turang	.25
38	Manny Ramirez	3.00
39	Salomon Torres	.25
40	Melvin Nieves	.25
41	Ryan Klesko	.25
42	Keith Kessinger	.25
43	Eric Wedge	.25
44	Bob Hamelin	.25
45	Carlos Delgado	2.50
46	Marc Newfield	.25
47	Raul Mondesi	.25
48	Tim Costo	.25
49	Pedro Martinez	3.00
50	Steve Karsay	.25
51	Danny Bautista	.25
52	Butch Huskey	.25
53	Kurt Abbott	.25
54	Darrell Sherman	.25
55	Damon Buford	.25
56	Ross Powell	.25
57	Darrell Whitmore	.25
58	Chipper Jones	5.00
59	Jeff Granger	.25
60	Cliff Floyd	.25

Dream Team

Score's 1994 "Dream Team," one top player at each position, was featured in a 10-card insert set. The stars were decked out in vintage uniforms and equipment for the photos. Green and black bars at top and bottom frame the photo, and all printing on the front is in gold

foil. Backs have a white background with green highlights. A color player portrait photo is featured, along with a brief justification for the player's selection to the squad. Cards are UV coated on both sides. Stated odds of finding a Dream Team insert were given as one per 72 packs.

		NM/M
Complete Set (10):		15.00
Common Player:		1.00
1	Mike Mussina	2.00
2	Tom Glavine	2.00
3	Don Mattingly	10.00
4	Carlos Baerga	1.00
5	Barry Larkin	1.00
6	Matt Williams	1.00
7	Juan Gonzalez	4.00
8	Andy Van Slyke	1.00
9	Larry Walker	1.00
10	Mike Stanley	1.00

Gold Stars

Limited to inclusion in hobby packs, Score's 60-card "Gold Stars" insert set features 30 National League players, found in Series I packs, and 30 American Leaguers inserted with Series II. Stated odds of finding a Gold Stars card were listed on the wrapper as one in 18 packs. A notation on the cards' back indicates that no more than 6,500 sets of Gold Stars were produced. The high-tech cards feature a color player action photo, the full-bleed background of which has been converted to metallic tones. Backs have a graduated gold background with a portrait-style color player photo.

		NM/M
Complete Set (60):		40.00
Common Player:		.25
1	Barry Bonds	6.00
2	Orlando Merced	.25
3	Mark Grace	.25
4	Darren Daulton	.25
5	Jeff Blauser	.25
6	Deion Sanders	.25
7	John Kruk	.25
8	Jeff Bagwell	2.50
9	Gregg Jefferies	.25
10	Matt Williams	.25
11	Andres Galarraga	.25
12	Jay Bell	.25
13	Mike Piazza	4.50
14	Ron Gant	.25
15	Barry Larkin	.25
16	Tom Glavine	.50
17	Len Dykstra	.25
18	Fred McGriff	.25
19	Andy Van Slyke	.25
20	Gary Sheffield	.75
21	John Burkett	.25
22	Dante Bichette	.25
23	Tony Gwynn	3.50
24	Dave Justice	.25
25	Marquis Grissom	.25
26	Bobby Bonilla	.25
27	Larry Walker	.25
28	Brett Butler	.25
29	Robby Thompson	.25
30	Jeff Conine	.25
31	Joe Carter	.25
32	Ken Griffey Jr.	4.50
33	Juan Gonzalez	1.25
34	Rickey Henderson	2.50
35	Bo Jackson	.35
36	Cal Ripken, Jr.	6.00
37	John Olerud	.25
38	Carlos Baerga	.25
39	Jack McDowell	.25
40	Cecil Fielder	.25
41	Kenny Lofton	.25
42	Roberto Alomar	1.00
43	Randy Johnson	2.50
44	Tim Salmon	.25
45	Frank Thomas	2.50
46	Albert Belle	.25
47	Greg Vaughn	.25
48	Travis Fryman	.25
49	Don Mattingly	4.00
50	Wade Boggs	3.50
51	Mo Vaughn	.25
52	Kirby Puckett	3.50
53	Devon White	.25
54	Tony Phillips	.25
55	Brian Harper	.25
56	Chad Curtis	.25
57	Paul Molitor	2.50
58	Ivan Rodriguez	2.00
59	Rafael Palmeiro	2.00
60	Brian McRae	.25

The Cycle

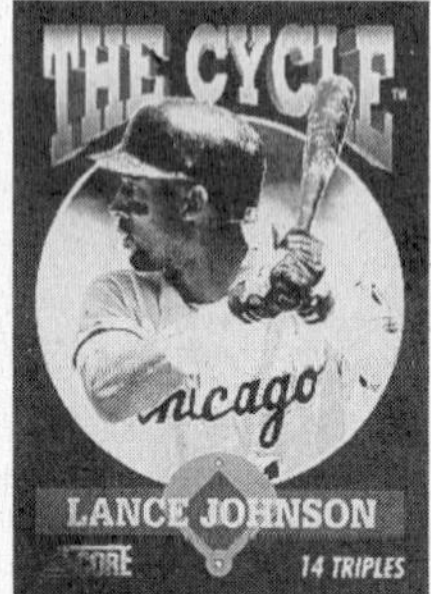

Leaders in the previous season's production of singles, doubles, triples and home runs are featured in this insert set which was packaged with Series II Score. Player action photos pop out of a circle at center and are surrounded by dark blue borders. "The Cycle" in printed in green at top. The player's name is in gold foil at bottom, printed over an infield diagram in a green strip. The stat which earned the player inclusion in the set is in gold foil at bottom right. On back are the rankings for the statistical category. Cards are numbered with a "TC" prefix.

		NM/M
Complete Set (20):		12.00
Common Player:		.50
1	Brett Butler	.50
2	Kenny Lofton	.50
3	Paul Molitor	2.00
4	Carlos Baerga	.50
5	Gregg Jefferies, Tony Phillips	.50
6	John Olerud	.50
7	Charlie Hayes	.50
8	Len Dykstra	.50
9	Dante Bichette	.50
10	Devon White	.50
11	Lance Johnson	.50
12	Joey Cora, Steve Finley	.50
13	Tony Fernandez	.50
14	David Hulse, Brett Butler	.50
15	Jay Bell, Brian McRae, Mickey Morandini	.50
16	Juan Gonzalez, Barry Bonds	4.00
17	Ken Griffey Jr.	4.00
18	Frank Thomas	2.50
19	Dave Justice	.50
20	Matt Williams, Albert Belle	.50

Cal Ripken, Jr.

Although the cards themselves do not indicate it, this issue was co-sponsored by Burger King and Coke, and distributed in BK restaurants in

the Baltimore-Washington area. Cards were available in three-card packs for 25 cents with the purchase of a Coke product. Each pack contains two regular cards and a gold card. Each of the nine cards could be found in a regular and gold version. Cards feature color photos with a semi-circular black border at top or left. "Score '94" appears in orange in one of the upper corners, along with an Orioles logo. Cal Ripken, Jr.'s name appears at the bottom. On the gold premium version, there is a gold-foil circle around the Orioles logo and Ripken's name appears in gold, rather than white. Backs have a smaller color photo, again meeting at a semi-circular edge with the black border at left and bottom. In the black are another Score logo, a card number, an Orioles logo, a headline and a few career details and/or stats. Cards are UV coated on each side. Several hundred of the cards were personally autographed by Ripken and distributed in a drawing.

		NM/M
Complete Set (9):		3.00
Complete Set, Gold (9):		6.00
Common Player:		.50
Common Card, Gold:		1.00
Autographed Card:		200.00
1	Double Honors	.50
1a	Double Honors/Gold	1.00
2	Perennial All-Star	.50
2a	Perennial All-Star/Gold	1.00
3	Peerless Power	.50
3a	Peerless Power/Gold	1.00
4	Fitness Fan	.50
4a	Fitness Fan/Gold	1.00
5	Prime Concerns	.50
5a	Prime Concerns/Gold	1.00
6	Home Run Club	.50
6a	Home Run Club/Gold	1.00
7	The Iron Man	.50
7a	The Iron Man/Gold	1.00
8	Heavy Hitter	.50
8a	Heavy Hitter/Gold	1.00
9	Gold Glover	.50
9a	Gold Glover/Gold	1.00

1994 Score Rookie/Traded Samples

To introduce the various types of card which would be included in the 1994 Score Rookie/Traded set, the company produced this sample set. Cards are virtually identical to the issued versions except for the overprint "SAMPLE" running diagonally on front and back. The Rafael Palmeiro "Changing Places" sample card does not feature the red foil logo found on issued cards.

		NM/M
Complete Set (11):		7.50
Common Player:		.50
1RT	Lee Smith	.50
2CP	Rafael Palmeiro (Changing Places)	2.00
2RT	Will Clark	.50
2SU	Manny Ramirez (Super Rookie)	2.50
3RT	Bo Jackson (Gold Rush)	1.00
4RT	Ellis Burks	.50
5RT	Eddie Murray	2.00
6RT	Delino DeShields	.50
102RT	Carlos Delgado	1.50
---	September Call-Up Winner Card	.10
---	Hobby Header Card	.10
---	Retail Header Card	.10

1994 Score Rookie/Traded

Score Rookie & Traded completed the 1994 baseball season with a 165-card update set. These were available in both retail and hobby packs. Score issued Super Rookies and Changing Places insert sets, as well as a Traded Redemption card and a parallel Gold Rush set. Basic cards features red front borders. Team logos are in a bottom corner in a gold polygon. One of the upper corners contains a green polygon with a gold Score logo. Most cards #71-163 feature a square multi-colored "Rookie '94" logo in a lower corner. Backs of all cards have a purple background. Traded players' card backs are vertical and contain two additional photos. Backs of the rookie cards are horizontal and feature a portrait photo at left. The "Rookie '94" logo is repeated in the upper-right corner. This is in reverse of the fronts, on which traded players have a single photo and rookie cards have both portrait and action photos. Card numbers have an "RT" prefix.

		NM/M
Complete Set (165):		5.00
Common Player:		.05
Gold Rush:		2X
Pack (10):		.40
Wax Box (36):		9.00
1	Will Clark	.05
2	Lee Smith	.05
3	Bo Jackson	.10
4	Ellis Burks	.05
5	Eddie Murray	1.00
6	Delino DeShields	.05
7	Erik Hanson	.05
8	Rafael Palmeiro	.75
9	Luis Polonia	.05
10	Omar Vizquel	.05
11	Kurt Abbott	.05
12	Vince Coleman	.05
13	Rickey Henderson	1.00
14	Terry Mulholland	.05
15	Greg Hibbard	.05
16	Walt Weiss	.05
17	Chris Sabo	.05
18	Dave Henderson	.05
19	Rick Sutcliffe	.05
20	Harold Reynolds	.05
21	Jack Morris	.05
22	Dan Wilson	.05
23	Dave Magadan	.05
24	Dennis Martinez	.05
25	Wes Chamberlain	.05
26	Otis Nixon	.05
27	Eric Anthony	.05
28	Randy Milligan	.05
29	Julio Franco	.05
30	Kevin McReynolds	.05
31	Anthony Young	.05
32	Brian Harper	.05
33	Lenny Harris	.05
34	Eddie Taubensee	.05
35	David Segui	.05
36	Stan Javier	.05
37	Felix Fermin	.05
38	Darrin Jackson	.05
39	Tony Fernandez	.05
40	Jose Vizcaino	.05
41	Willie Banks	.05
42	Brian Hunter	.05
43	Reggie Jefferson	.05
44	Junior Felix	.05
45	Jack Armstrong	.05
46	Bip Roberts	.05
47	Jerry Browne	.05
48	Marvin Freeman	.05
49	Jody Reed	.05
50	Alex Cole	.05
51	Sid Fernandez	.05
52	Pete Smith	.05
53	Xavier Hernandez	.05
54	Scott Sanderson	.05
55	Turner Ward	.05
56	Rex Hudler	.05
57	Deion Sanders	.05
58	Sid Bream	.05
59	Tony Pena	.05
60	Bret Boone	.05
61	Bobby Ayala	.05
62	Pedro Martinez	1.00
63	Howard Johnson	.05
64	Mark Portugal	.05
65	Roberto Kelly	.05
66	Spike Owen	.05
67	Jeff Treadway	.05
68	Mike Harkey	.05
69	Doug Jones	.05
70	Steve Farr	.05
71	Billy Taylor	.05
72	Manny Ramirez	1.00
73	Bob Hamelin	.05
74	Steve Karsay	.05
75	Ryan Klesko	.05
76	Cliff Floyd	.05
77	Jeffrey Hammonds	.05
78	Javier Lopez	.05
79	Roger Salkeld	.05
80	Hector Carrasco	.05
81	Gerald Williams	.05
82	Raul Mondesi	.05
83	Sterling Hitchcock	.05
84	Danny Bautista	.05
85	Chris Turner	.05
86	Shane Reynolds	.05
87	Rondell White	.05
88	Salomon Torres	.05
89	Turk Wendell	.05
90	Tony Tarasco	.05
91	Shawn Green	.65
92	Greg Colbrunn	.05
93	Eddie Zambrano	.05
94	Rich Becker	.05
95	Chris Gomez	.05
96	John Patterson	.05
97	Derek Parks	.05
98	Rich Rowland	.05
99	James Mouton	.05
100	Tim Hyers	.05
101	Jose Valentin	.05
102	Carlos Delgado	.65
103	Robert Esenhoorn	.05
104	John Hudek	.05
105	Domingo Cedeno	.05
106	Denny Hocking	.05
107	Greg Pirkl	.05
108	Mark Smith	.05
109	Paul Shuey	.05
110	Jorge Fabregas	.05
111	Rikkert Faneyte	.05
112	Rob Butler	.05
113	Darren Oliver	.05
114	Troy O'Leary	.05
115	Scott Brow	.05
116	Tony Eusebio	.05
117	Carlos Reyes	.05
118	J.R. Phillips	.05
119	Alex Diaz	.05
120	Charles Johnson	.05
121	Nate Minchey	.05
122	Scott Sanders	.05
123	Daryl Boston	.05
124	Joey Hamilton	.05
125	Brian Anderson	.05
126	Dan Miceli	.05
127	Tom Brunansky	.05
128	Dave Staton	.05
129	Mike Oquist	.05
130	John Mabry	.05
131	Norberto Martin	.05
132	Hector Fajardo	.05
133	Mark Hutton	.05
134	Fernando Vina	.05
135	Lee Tinsley	.05
136	Chan Ho Park **RC**	1.50
137	Paul Spoljaric	.05
138	Matias Carrillo	.05
139	Mark Kiefer	.05
140	Stan Royer	.05
141	Bryan Eversgerd	.05
142	Joe Hall	.05
144	Johnny Ruffin	.05
145	Alex Gonzalez	.05
146	Keith Lockhart	.05
147	Tom Marsh	.05
148	Tony Longmire	.05
149	Keith Mitchell	.05
150	Melvin Nieves	.05
151	Kelly Stinnett	.05
152	Miguel Jimenez	.05
153	Jeff Juden	.05
154	Matt Walbeck	.05
155	Marc Newfield	.05
156	Matt Mieske	.05
157	Marcus Moore	.05
158	Jose Lima **RC**	.25
159	Mike Kelly	.05
160	Jim Edmonds	.05
161	Steve Trachsel	.05
162	Greg Blosser	.05
163	Mark Acre	.05
164	AL Checklist	.05
165	NL Checklist	.05

Gold Rush

Each pack of Score Rookie and Traded cards included one Gold Rush parallel version of one of the set's cards. The insert cards feature fronts that are printed directly on gold foil and include a Gold Rush logo in an upper corner.

	NM/M
Complete Set (165):	15.00
Common Player:	.15
Stars:	2X

Changing Places

Changing Places documents the relocation of 10 veteran stars. Cards were inserted into one of every 36 retail or hobby packs. Fronts have a color photo of the player in his new uniform and are enhanced with red foil. Backs have a montage of color and black-and-white photos and a few words about the trade. Card numbers have a "CP" prefix.

		NM/M
Complete Set (10):		15.00
Common Player:		1.00
1	Will Clark	1.00
2	Rafael Palmeiro	4.00
3	Roberto Kelly	1.00
4	Bo Jackson	1.25
5	Otis Nixon	1.00
6	Rickey Henderson	5.00
7	Ellis Burks	1.00
8	Lee Smith	1.00
9	Delino DeShields	1.00
10	Deion Sanders	1.00

Super Rookies

Super Rookies is an 18-card set honoring baseball's brightest young stars. They appear only in hobby packs at a rate of one every 36 packs. Fronts are printed on foil, with a multi-colored border. Backs feature another photo, most of which is rendered in single-

color blocks, along with a few words about the player and a large Super Rookie logo. Cards are numbered with an "SU" prefix.

		NM/M
Complete Set (18):		15.00
Common Player:		1.00
1	Carlos Delgado	5.00
2	Manny Ramirez	5.00
3	Ryan Klesko	1.00
4	Raul Mondesi	1.00
5	Bob Hamelin	1.00
6	Steve Karsay	1.00
7	Jeffrey Hammonds	1.00
8	Cliff Floyd	1.00
9	Kurt Abbott	1.00
10	Marc Newfield	1.00
11	Javier Lopez	1.00
12	Rich Becker	1.00
13	Greg Pirkl	1.00
14	Rondell White	1.00
15	James Mouton	1.00
16	Tony Tarasco	1.00
17	Brian Anderson	1.00
18	Jim Edmonds	1.00

Redemption Card

The Score Rookie and Traded Redemption card was inserted at a rate of one every 240 packs. It gave collectors a chance to mail in for the best rookie in the annual September call-up: Alex Rodriguez.

	NM/M
September Call-Up Redemption Card (Expired)	2.00
Alex Rodriguez	400.00

1995 Score Samples

This cello-wrapped 10-card sample set of 1995 Score cards was sent to dealers to preview the issue. Cards are identical to the regular-issue versions except they have a diagonal white "SAMPLE" printed on front and back. The SAMPLE notice can be found on each card in either black or white, with the black version appearing to be somewhat less common.

		NM/M
Complete Set (10):		6.00
Common Player:		.50
2	Roberto Alomar	.75
4	Jose Canseco	1.00
5	Matt Williams	.50
5HG	Cal Ripken, Jr. (Hall of Gold)	2.50
8DP	McKay Christensen ('94 Draft Pick)	.50
221	Jeff Bagwell	1.25
223	Albert Belle	.50
224	Chuck Carr	.50
288	Jorge Fabreges (Rookie)	.50
	Header Card	.05

1995 Score

Score 1995 Baseball is composed of 605 cards, issued in two series; the first comprising 330 cards, the second, 275. Cards are identical to the regular-issue versions except they have a diagonal white "SAMPLE" printed on the front and back. The SAMPLE notice can be found on each card in either black or white, with the black version appearing to be somewhat less common. The player's name, position, and team logo is given in white letters on a blue strip across the bottom. Backs resemble the fronts, except with a smaller, portrait photo of the player, which leaves room for statistics and biographical information. Score had a parallel set of Gold Rush cards, along with several other series of inserts. Eleven players in Series 2 can be found in two team variations as a result of a redemption program for updated cards.

		NM/M
Complete Set (605):		13.50
Common Player:		.05
Gold Rush:		2X
Platinums:		3X
Series 1 or 2 Pack (12):		.75
Series 1 or 2 Box (36):		12.50
1	Frank Thomas	.50
2	Roberto Alomar	.15
3	Cal Ripken, Jr.	1.50
4	Jose Canseco	.30
5	Matt Williams	.05
6	Esteban Beltre	.05
7	Domingo Cedeno	.05
8	John Valentin	.05
9	Glenallen Hill	.05
10	Rafael Belliard	.05
11	Randy Myers	.05
12	Mo Vaughn	.05
13	Hector Carrasco	.05
14	Chili Davis	.05
15	Dante Bichette	.05
16	Darren Jackson	.05
17	Mike Piazza	.75
18	Junior Felix	.05
19	Moises Alou	.05
20	Mark Gubicza	.05
21	Bret Saberhagen	.05
22	Len Dykstra	.05
23	Steve Howe	.05
24	Mark Dewey	.05
25	Brian Harper	.05
26	Ozzie Smith	.60
27	Scott Erickson	.05
28	Tony Gwynn	.60
29	Bob Welch	.05
30	Barry Bonds	1.50
31	Leo Gomez	.05
32	Greg Maddux	.60
33	Mike Greenwell	.05
34	Sammy Sosa	.60
35	Darnell Coles	.05
36	Tommy Greene	.05
37	Will Clark	.05
38	Steve Ontiveros	.05
39	Stan Javier	.05
40	Bip Roberts	.05
41	Paul ONeill	.05
42	Bill Haselman	.05
43	Shane Mack	.05
44	Orlando Merced	.05
45	Kevin Seitzer	.05
46	Trevor Hoffman	.05
47	Greg Gagne	.05
48	Jeff Kent	.05
49	Tony Phillips	.05
50	Ken Hill	.05
51	Carlos Baerga	.05
52	Henry Rodriguez	.05
53	Scott Sanderson	.05
54	Jeff Conine	.05
55	Chris Turner	.05
56	Ken Caminiti	.05
57	Harold Baines	.05
58	Charlie Hayes	.05
59	Roberto Kelly	.05
60	John Olerud	.05
61	Tim Davis	.05
62	Rich Rowland	.05
63	Rey Sanchez	.05
64	Junior Ortiz	.05
65	Ricky Gutierrez	.05
66	Rex Hudler	.05
67	Johnny Ruffin	.05
68	Jay Buhner	.05
69	Tom Pagnozzi	.05
70	Julio Franco	.05
71	Eric Young	.05
72	Mike Bordick	.05
73	Don Slaught	.05
74	Goose Gossage	.05
75	Lonnie Smith	.05
76	Jimmy Key	.05
77	Dave Hollins	.05
78	Mickey Tettleton	.05
79	Luis Gonzalez	.05
80	Dave Winfield	.50
81	Ryan Thompson	.05
82	Felix Jose	.05
83	Rusty Meacham	.05
84	Darryl Hamilton	.05
85	John Wetteland	.05
86	Tom Brunansky	.05
87	Mark Lemke	.05
88	Spike Owen	.05
89	Shawon Dunston	.05
90	Wilson Alvarez	.05
91	Lee Smith	.05
92	Scott Kamieniecki	.05
93	Jacob Brumfield	.05
94	Kirk Gibson	.05
95	Joe Girardi	.05
96	Mike Macfarlane	.05
97	Greg Colbrunn	.05
98	Ricky Bones	.05
99	Delino DeShields	.05
100	Pat Meares	.05
101	Jeff Fassero	.05
102	Jim Leyritz	.05
103	Gary Redus	.05
104	Terry Steinbach	.05
105	Kevin McReynolds	.05
106	Felix Fermin	.05
107	Danny Jackson	.05
108	Chris James	.05
109	Jeff King	.05
110	Pat Hentgen	.05
111	Gerald Perry	.05
112	Tim Raines	.05
113	Eddie Williams	.05
114	Jamie Moyer	.05
115	Bud Black	.05
116	Chris Gomez	.05
117	Luis Lopez	.05
118	Roger Clemens	.65
119	Javier Lopez	.05
120	Dave Nilsson	.05
121	Karl Rhodes	.05
122	Rick Aguilera	.05
123	Tony Fernandez	.05
124	Bernie Williams	.05
125	James Mouton	.05
126	Mark Langston	.05
127	Mike Lansing	.05
128	Tino Martinez	.05
129	Joe Orsulak	.05
130	David Hulse	.05
131	Pete Incaviglia	.05
132	Mark Clark	.05
133	Tony Eusebio	.05
134	Chuck Finley	.05
135	Lou Frazier	.05
136	Craig Grebeck	.05
137	Kelly Stinnett	.05
138	Paul Shuey	.05
139	David Nied	.05
140	Billy Brewer	.05
141	Dave Weathers	.05
142	Scott Leius	.05
143	Brian Jordan	.05
144	Melido Perez	.05
145	Tony Tarasco	.05
146	Dan Wilson	.05
147	Rondell White	.05
148	Mike Henneman	.05
149	Brian Johnson	.05
150	Tom Henke	.05
151	John Patterson	.05
152	Bobby Witt	.05
153	Eddie Taubensee	.05
154	Pat Borders	.05
155	Ramon Martinez	.05
156	Mike Kingery	.05
157	Zane Smith	.05
158	Benito Santiago	.05
159	Matias Carrillo	.05
160	Scott Brosius	.05
161	Dave Clark	.05
162	Mark McLemore	.05
163	Curt Schilling	.30
164	J.T. Snow	.05
165	Rod Beck	.05
166	Scott Fletcher	.05
167	Bob Tewksbury	.05
168	Mike LaValliere	.05
169	Dave Hansen	.05
170	Pedro Martinez	.50
171	Kirk Rueter	.05
172	Jose Lind	.05
173	Luis Alicea	.05
174	Mike Moore	.05
175	Andy Ashby	.05
176	Jody Reed	.05
177	Darryl Kile	.05
178	Carl Willis	.05
179	Jeromy Burnitz	.05
180	Mike Gallego	.05
181	W. Van Landingham **RC**	.05
182	Sid Fernandez	.05
183	Kim Batiste	.05
184	Greg Myers	.05
185	Steve Avery	.05
186	Steve Farr	.05
187	Robb Nen	.05
188	Dan Pasqua	.05
189	Bruce Ruffin	.05
190	Jose Valentin	.05
191	Willie Banks	.05
192	Mike Aldrete	.05
193	Randy Milligan	.05
194	Steve Karsay	.05
195	Mike Stanley	.05
196	Jose Mesa	.05
197	Tom Browning	.05
198	John Vander Wal	.05
199	Kevin Brown	.05
200	Mike Oquist	.05
201	Greg Swindell	.05
202	Eddie Zambrano	.05
203	Joe Boever	.05
204	Gary Varsho	.05
205	Chris Gwynn	.05
206	David Howard	.05
207	Jerome Walton	.05
208	Danny Darwin	.05
209	Darryl Strawberry	.05
210	Todd Van Poppel	.05
211	Scott Livingstone	.05
212	Dave Fleming	.05
213	Todd Worrell	.05
214	Carlos Delgado	.40
215	Bill Pecota	.05
216	Jim Lindeman	.05
217	Rick White	.05
218	Jose Oquendo	.05
219	Tony Castillo	.05
220	Fernando Vina	.05
221	Jeff Bagwell	.50
222	Randy Johnson	.50
223	Albert Belle	.05
224	Chuck Carr	.05
225	Mark Leiter	.05
226	Hal Morris	.05
227	Robin Ventura	.05
228	Mike Munoz	.05
229	Jim Thome	.40
230	Mario Diaz	.05
231	John Doherty	.05
232	Bobby Jones	.05
233	Raul Mondesi	.05
234	Ricky Jordan	.05
235	John Jaha	.05
236	Carlos Garcia	.05
237	Kirby Puckett	.60
238	Orel Hershiser	.05
239	Don Mattingly	.65
240	Sid Bream	.05
241	Brent Gates	.05
242	Tony Longmire	.05
243	Robby Thompson	.05
244	Rick Sutcliffe	.05
245	Dean Palmer	.05
246	Marquis Grissom	.05
247	Paul Molitor	.50
248	Mark Carreon	.05
249	Jack Voight	.05
250	Greg McMichael (Photo on front is Mike Stanton.)	.05
251	Damon Berryhill	.05
252	Brian Dorsett	.05
253	Jim Edmonds	.05
254	Barry Larkin	.05
255	Jack McDowell	.05
256	Wally Joyner	.05
257	Eddie Murray	.50
258	Lenny Webster	.05
259	Milt Cuyler	.05
260	Todd Benzinger	.05
261	Vince Coleman	.05
262	Todd Stottlemyre	.05
263	Turner Ward	.05
264	Ray Lankford	.05
265	Matt Walbeck	.05
266	Deion Sanders	.05
267	Gerald Williams	.05
268	Jim Gott	.05
269	Jeff Frye	.05
270	Jose Rijo	.05
271	Dave Justice	.05
272	Ismael Valdes	.05
273	Ben McDonald	.05
274	Darren Lewis	.05
275	Graeme Lloyd	.05
276	Luis Ortiz	.05
277	Julian Tavarez	.05
278	Mark Dalesandro	.05
279	Brett Merriman	.05
280	Ricky Bottalico	.05
281	Robert Eenhoorn	.05
282	Rikkert Faneyte	.05
283	Mike Kelly	.05
284	Mark Smith	.05
285	Turk Wendell	.05
286	Greg Blosser	.05
287	Garey Ingram	.05
288	Jorge Fabregas	.05
289	Blaise Ilsley	.05
290	Joe Hall	.05
291	Orlando Miller	.05
292	Jose Lima	.05
293	Greg O'Halloran	.05
294	Mark Kiefer	.05
295	Jose Oliva	.05
296	Rich Becker	.05
297	Brian Hunter	.05
298	Dave Silvestri	.05
299	Armando Benitez **RC**	.10
300	Darren Dreifort	.05
301	John Mabry	.05
302	Greg Pirkl	.05
303	J.R. Phillips	.05
304	Shawn Green	.30
305	Roberto Petagine	.05
306	Keith Lockhart	.05
307	Jonathon Hurst	.05
308	Paul Spoljaric	.05
309	Mike Lieberthal	.05
310	Garret Anderson	.05
311	John Johnston	.05
312	Alex Rodriguez	1.50
313	Kent Mercker	.05
314	John Valentin	.05
315	Kenny Rogers	.05
316	Fred McGriff	.05
317	Atlanta Braves, Baltimore Orioles	.05
318	Chicago Cubs, Boston Red Sox	.05
319	Cincinnati Reds, California Angels	.05
320	Colorado Rockies, Chicago White Sox	.05
321	Cleveland Indians, Florida Marlins	.05
322	Houston Astros, Detroit Tigers	.05
323	Los Angels Dodgers, Kansas City Royals	.05
324	Montreal Expos, Milwaukee Brewers	.05
325	New York Mets, Minnesota Twins	.05
326	Philadelphia Phillies, New York Yankees	.05
327	Pittsburgh Pirates, Oakland Athletics	.05
328	San Diego Padres, Seattle Mariners	.05
329	San Francisco Giants, Texas Rangers	.05
330	St. Louis Cardinals, Toronto Blue Jays	.05
331	Pedro Munoz	.05
332	Ryan Klesko	.05
333a	Andre Dawson/Red Sox	.25
333b	Andre Dawson/Marlins	.35
334	Derrick May	.05
335	Aaron Sele	.05
336	Kevin Mitchell	.05
337	Steve Traschel	.05
338	Andres Galarraga	.05
339a	Terry Pendleton/Braves	.05
339b	Terry Pendleton/Marlins	.10
340	Gary Sheffield	.30
341	Travis Fryman	.05
342	Bo Jackson	.10
343	Gary Gaetti	.05
344a	Brett Butler/Dodgers	.05
344b	Brett Butler/Mets	.10
345	B. J. Surhoff	.05
346a	Larry Walker/Expos	.05
346b	Larry Walker/Rockies	.10
347	Kevin Tapani	.05
348	Rick Wilkins	.05
349	Wade Boggs	.60
350	Mariano Duncan	.05
351	Ruben Sierra	.05
352a	Andy Van Slyke/Pirates	.05
352b	Andy Van Slyke/Orioles	.10
353	Reggie Jefferson	.05
354	Gregg Jefferies	.05
355	Tim Naehring	.05
356	John Roper	.05
357	Joe Carter	.05
358	Kurt Abbott	.05
359	Lenny Harris	.05
360	Lance Johnson	.05
361	Brian Anderson	.05
362	Jim Eisenreich	.05
363	Jerry Browne	.05
364	Mark Grace	.05
365	Devon White	.05
366	Reggie Sanders	.05
367	Ivan Rodriguez	.40
368	Kirt Manwaring	.05
369	Pat Kelly	.05
370	Ellis Burks	.05
371	Charles Nagy	.05
372	Kevin Bass	.05
373	Lou Whitaker	.05
374	Rene Arocha	.05
375	Derrick Parks	.05
376	Mark Whiten	.05
377	Mark McGwire	1.00
378	Doug Drabek	.05
379	Greg Vaughn	.05
380	Al Martin	.05
381	Ron Darling	.05
382	Tim Wallach	.05
383	Alan Trammell	.05
384	Randy Velarde	.05
385	Chris Sabo	.05
386	Wil Cordero	.05
387	Darrin Fletcher	.05
388	David Segui	.05
389	Steve Buechele	.05
390	Otis Nixon	.05
391	Jeff Brantley	.05
392a	Chad Curtis/Angels	.05
392b	Chad Curtis/Tigers	.10
393	Cal Eldred	.05
394	Jason Bere	.05
395	Bret Barberie	.05
396	Paul Sorrento	.05
397	Steve Finley	.05
398	Cecil Fielder	.05
399	Eric Karros	.05
400	Jeff Montgomery	.05
401	Cliff Floyd	.05
402	Matt Mieske	.05
403	Brian Hunter	.05
404	Alex Cole	.05
405	Kevin Stocker	.05
406	Eric Davis	.05
407	Marvin Freeman	.05
408	Dennis Eckersley	.40
409	Todd Zeile	.05
410	Keith Mitchell	.05
411	Andy Benes	.05
412	Juan Bell	.05
413	Royce Clayton	.05
414	Ed Sprague	.05
415	Mike Mussina	.30
416	Todd Hundley	.05
417	Pat Listach	.05
418	Joe Oliver	.05
419	Rafael Palmeiro	.40
420	Tim Salmon	.05
421	Brady Anderson	.05
422	Kenny Lofton	.05
423	Craig Biggio	.05
424	Bobby Bonilla	.05
425	Kenny Rogers	.05
426	Derek Bell	.05
427a	Scott Cooper/Red Sox	.05
427b	Scott Cooper/Cardinals	.10
428	Ozzie Guillen	.05
429	Omar Vizquel	.05
430	Phil Plantier	.05
431	Chuck Knoblauch	.05
432	Darren Daulton	.05
433	Bob Hamelin	.05
434	Tom Glavine	.30
435	Walt Weiss	.05
436	Jose Vizcaino	.05
437	Ken Griffey Jr.	.75
438	Jay Bell	.05
439	Juan Gonzalez	.25
440	Jeff Blauser	.05
441	Rickey Henderson	.50
442	Bobby Ayala	.05
443a	David Cone/Royals	.05
443b	David Cone/Blue Jays	.10
444	Pedro Martinez	.05
445	Manny Ramirez	.50
446	Mark Portugal	.05
447	Damion Easley	.05
448	Gary DiSarcina	.05
449	Roberto Hernandez	.05
450	Jeffrey Hammonds	.05
451	Jeff Treadway	.05
452a	Jim Abbott/Yankees	.05
452b	Jim Abbott/White Sox	.10
453	Carlos Rodriguez	.05
454	Joey Cora	.05
455	Bret Boone	.05
456	Danny Tartabull	.05
457	John Franco	.05
458	Roger Salkeld	.05
459	Fred McGriff	.05
460	Pedro Astacio	.05
461	Jon Lieber	.05
462	Luis Polonia	.05
463	Geronimo Pena	.05
464	Tom Gordon	.05
465	Brad Ausmus	.05
466	Willie McGee	.05
467	Doug Jones	.05
468	John Smoltz	.05
469	Troy Neel	.05
470	Luis Sojo	.05
471	John Smiley	.05
472	Rafael Bournigal	.05
473	Billy Taylor	.05
474	Juan Guzman	.05
475	Dave Magadan	.05
476	Mike Devereaux	.05
477	Andujar Cedeno	.05
478	Edgar Martinez	.05
479	Troy Neel	.05
480	Allen Watson	.05
481	Ron Karkovice	.05

482 Joey Hamilton .05
483 Vinny Castilla .05
484 Kevin Gross .05
485 Bernard Gilkey .05
486 John Burkett .05
487 Matt Nokes .05
488 Mel Rojas .05
489 Craig Shipley .05
490 Chip Hale .05
491 Bill Swift .05
492 Pat Rapp .05
493a Brian McRae/Royals .05
493b Brian McRae/Cubs .10
494 Mickey Morandini .05
495 Tony Pena .05
496 Danny Bautista .05
497 Armando Reynoso .05
498 Ken Ryan .05
499 Billy Ripken .05
500 Pat Mahomes .05
501 Mark Acre .05
502 Geronimo Berroa .05
503 Norberto Martin .05
504 Chad Kreuter .05
505 Howard Johnson .05
506 Eric Anthony .05
507 Mark Wohlers .05
508 Scott Sanders .05
509 Pete Harnisch .05
510 Wes Chamberlain .05
511 Tom Candiotti .05
512 Albie Lopez .05
513 Denny Neagle .05
514 Sean Berry .05
515 Billy Hatcher .05
516 Todd Jones .05
517 Wayne Kirby .05
518 Butch Henry .05
519 Sandy Alomar Jr. .05
520 Kevin Appier .05
521 Robert Mejia .05
522 Steve Cooke .05
523 Terry Shumpert .05
524 Mike Jackson .05
525 Kent Mercker .05
526 David Wells .05
527 Juan Samuel .05
528 Salomon Torres .05
529 Duane Ward .05
530a Rob Dibble/Reds .05
530b Rob Dibble/White Sox .10
531 Mike Blowers .05
532 Mark Eichhorn .05
533 Alex Diaz .05
534 Dan Miceli .05
535 Jeff Branson .05
536 Dave Stevens .05
537 Charlie O'Brien .05
538 Shane Reynolds .05
539 Rich Amaral .05
540 Rusty Greer .05
541 Alex Arias .05
542 Eric Plunk .05
543 John Hudek .05
544 Kirk McCaskill .05
545 Jeff Reboulet .05
546 Sterling Hitchcock .05
547 Warren Newson .05
548 Bryan Harvey .05
549 Mike Huff .05
550 Lance Parrish .05
551 Ken Griffey Jr. (Hitters Inc.) .65
552 Matt Williams (Hitters Inc.) .05
553 Roberto Alomar (Hitters Inc.) .10
554 Jeff Bagwell (Hitters Inc.) .25
555 Dave Justice (Hitters Inc.) .05
556 Cal Ripken Jr. (Hitters Inc.) .75
557 Albert Belle (Hitters Inc.) .05
558 Mike Piazza (Hitters Inc.) .45
559 Kirby Puckett (Hitters Inc.) .35
560 Wade Boggs (Hitters Inc.) .30
561 Tony Gwynn (Hitters Inc.) .35
562 Barry Bonds (Hitters Inc.) .75
563 Mo Vaughn (Hitters Inc.) .05
564 Don Mattingly (Hitters Inc.) .40
565 Carlos Baerga (Hitters Inc.) .05
566 Paul Molitor (Hitters Inc.) .25
567 Raul Mondesi (Hitters Inc.) .05
568 Manny Ramirez (Hitters Inc.) .25
569 Alex Rodriguez (Hitters Inc.) .75
570 Will Clark (Hitters Inc.) .05
571 Frank Thomas (Hitters Inc.) .30
572 Moises Alou (Hitters Inc.) .05
573 Jeff Conine (Hitters Inc.) .05
574 Joe Ausanio .05
575 Charles Johnson .05
576 Ernie Young .05
577 Jeff Granger .05
578 Robert Perez .05
579 Melvin Nieves .05
580 Gar Finnvold .05
581 Duane Singleton .05
582 Chan Ho Park .05
583 Fausto Cruz .05
584 Dave Staton .05
585 Denny Hocking .05
586 Nate Minchey .05
587 Marc Newfield .05
588 Jayhawk Owens .05
589 Darren Bragg .05
590 Kevin King .05
591 Kurt Miller .05
592 Aaron Small .05
593 Troy O'Leary .05
594 Phil Stidham .05
595 Steve Dunn .05
596 Cory Bailey .05
597 Alex Gonzalez .05
598 Jim Bowie .05
599 Jeff Cirillo .05
600 Mark Hutton .05
601 Russ Davis .05
602 Checklist #331-400 .05
603 Checklist #401-469 .05
604 Checklist #470-537 .05
605 Checklist #538-605 .05
---- "You Trade 'em" Redemption Card (Expired Dec. 31, 1995.) .10

Gold Rush

Besides being collectible in their own right, the gold-foil printed parallel versions of the Score regular-issue cards could be collected into team sets and exchanged with a trade card for platinum versions. The deadline for redemption of Series I was July 1, 1995; Oct. 1, 1995, for Series II. Gold Rush cards were found either one or two per pack, depending on pack card count. Gold Rush versions exist for each card in the Score set and have fronts that are identical to the regular cards except they are printed on foil and have gold borders. Backs of the Gold Rush cards have a small rectangular "GOLD RUSH" logo overprinted.

NM/M
Complete Set (605): 35.00
Common Player: .10
Gold Rush Stars: 2X

Platinum Redemption Team Sets

This top of the line parallel set was only available by exchanging a complete Series 1 or Series 2 Gold Rush team set, along with a redemption card. Production of the Platinum sets was limited to 4,950 of each team in each series. Using the same photos and format as the regular issue and Gold Rush cards, the Platinum parallels have card fronts printed on silver prismatic foil. Backs are identical to the regular versions. Platinum series team sets were sent to collectors in specially printed plastic cases with a certificate of authenticity.

NM/M
Complete Set (587): 100.00
Complete Series 1 (316): 60.00
Complete Series 2 (271): 40.00
Common Player: .25
Platinum Stars: 3X

Airmail

Young ballplayers with a propensity for hitting the long ball are featured in this insert set found only in Series II jumbo packs. Cards have a player batting action photo set in sky-and-clouds background. A gold-foil stamp in the upper-left corner identifies the series. Backs have a background photo of sunset and dark clouds, with a player portrait photo in the foreground. A few stats and sentences describe the player's power hitting potential. Cards have an AM prefix to the number. Stated odds for insertion rate are an average of one Airmail chase card per 24 packs.

NM/M
Complete Set (18): 8.00
Common Player: .25
1 Bob Hamelin .25
2 John Mabry .25
3 Marc Newfield .25
4 Jose Oliva .25
5 Charles Johnson .25
6 Russ Davis .25
7 Ernie Young .25
8 Billy Ashley .25
9 Ryan Klesko .25
10 J.R. Phillips .25
11 Cliff Floyd .25
12 Carlos Delgado 1.50
13 Melvin Nieves .25
14 Raul Mondesi .25
15 Manny Ramirez 2.00
16 Mike Kelly .25
17 Alex Rodriguez 5.00
18 Rusty Greer .25

Double Gold Champions

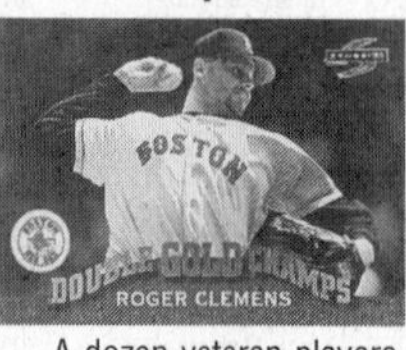

A dozen veteran players, who have won at least two of the game's top awards are designated as "Double Gold Champs," in this Series II hobby insert set. Fronts have horizontal action photos at top, with a speckled red border at bottom. Vertical backs have a portrait photo and a list of the major awards won by the player. Cards have a GC prefix to the number. These chase cards were reportedly inserted at an average rate of one per 36.

NM/M
Complete Set (12): 25.00
Common Player: .40
1 Frank Thomas 2.00
2 Ken Griffey Jr. 3.50
3 Barry Bonds 5.00
4 Tony Gwynn 2.50
5 Don Mattingly 3.00
6 Greg Maddux 2.50
7 Roger Clemens 3.00
8 Kenny Lofton .40
9 Jeff Bagwell 2.00
10 Matt Williams .40
11 Kirby Puckett 2.50
12 Cal Ripken Jr. 5.00

Draft Picks

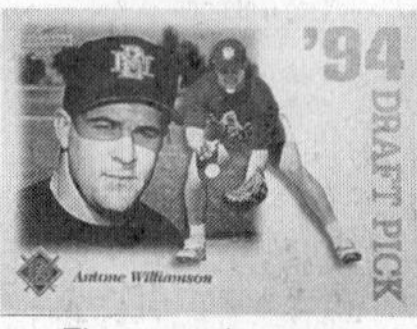

These cards were randomly included in 1995 Score hobby packs at a rate of one per every 36 packs. The cards showcase 18 of baseball's potential superstars and documented their professional beginnings. The card front has the player's team logo and name in the lower-right corner. "'94 Draft Pick" appears in the upper-right corner. The front also has a mug shot and an action shot of the player. The card back has a portrait and career summary and is numbered with a DP prefix.

NM/M
Complete Set (18): 4.00
Common Player: .50
1 McKay Christensen .50
2 Brett Wagner .50
3 Paul Wilson .50
4 C.J. Nitkowski .50
5 Josh Booty .50
6 Antone Williamson .50
7 Paul Konerko 1.50
8 Scott Elarton .50
9 Jacob Shumate .50
10 Terrence Long .50
11 Mark Johnson .50
12 Ben Grieve .50
13 Doug Million .50
14 Jayson Peterson .50
15 Dustin Hermanson .50
16 Matt Smith .50
17 Kevin Witt .50
18 Brian Buchanan .50

Dream Team Gold

The Major Leagues' top players at each position are featured in this Series I insert set. Fronts are printed entirely on rainbow holographic foil and feature a large and a small player action photo. Backs have a single-color version of one of the front photos as well as a color portrait photo in a circle at center, all in conventional printing technology. Card numbers have a DG prefix.

NM/M
Complete Set (12): 12.00
Common Player: .30
1 Frank Thomas 1.25
2 Roberto Alomar .50
3 Cal Ripken Jr. 4.00
4 Matt Williams .30
5 Mike Piazza 2.50
6 Albert Belle .30
7 Ken Griffey Jr. 2.50
8 Tony Gwynn 1.50
9 Paul Molitor 1.25
10 Jimmy Key .30
11 Greg Maddux 1.50
12 Lee Smith .30

Hall of Gold

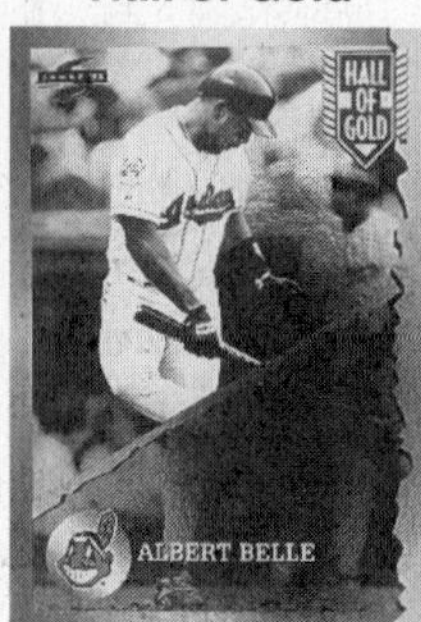

Hall of Gold inserts picture 110 of the top players on gold foil cards. Each card front has the Hall of Gold logo in an upper corner, plus a color action photo of the player, and his name and team logo at the bottom. The card back is numbered using an "HG" prefix and includes another color photo of the player, his team's name, his position, and a career summary. Cards were inserted one per every six regular 1995 Score packs and one per every two jumbo packs. Updated versions of five traded players were issued in Series II, available only via mail-in offer with a trade card found randomly inserted in packs.

NM/M
Complete Set (110): 25.00
Common Player: .10
1 Ken Griffey Jr. 1.25
2 Matt Williams .10
3 Roberto Alomar .25
4 Jeff Bagwell .75
5 Dave Justice .10
6 Cal Ripken Jr. 2.00
7 Randy Johnson .75
8 Barry Larkin .10
9 Albert Belle .10
10 Mike Piazza 1.25
11 Kirby Puckett 1.00
12 Moises Alou .10
13 Jose Canseco .45
14 Tony Gwynn 1.00
15 Roger Clemens 1.00
16 Barry Bonds 2.00
17 Mo Vaughn .10
18 Greg Maddux 1.00
19 Dante Bichette .10
20 Will Clark .10
21 Len Dykstra .10
22 Don Mattingly 1.00
23 Carlos Baerga .10
24 Ozzie Smith 1.00
25 Paul Molitor .75
26 Paul O'Neill .10
27 Deion Sanders .10
28 Jeff Conine .10
29 John Olerud .10
30 Jose Rijo .10
31 Sammy Sosa 1.00
32 Robin Ventura .10
33 Raul Mondesi .10
34 Eddie Murray .75
35 Marquis Grissom .10
36 Darryl Strawberry .10
37 Dave Nilsson .10
38 Manny Ramirez .75
39 Delino DeShields .10
40 Lee Smith .10
41 Alex Rodriguez 1.50
42 Julio Franco .10
43 Bret Saberhagen .10
44 Ken Hill .10
45 Roberto Kelly .10
46 Hal Morris .10
47 Jimmy Key .10
48 Terry Steinbach .10
49 Mickey Tettleton .10
50 Tony Phillips .10
51 Carlos Garcia .10
52 Jim Edmonds .10
53 Rod Beck .10
54 Shane Mack .10
55 Ken Caminiti .10
56 Frank Thomas .75
57 Kenny Lofton .10
58 Jack McDowell .10
59 Jason Bere .10
60 Joe Carter .10
61 Gary Sheffield .45
62 Andres Galarraga .10
63 Gregg Jefferies .10
64 Bobby Bonilla .10
65 Tom Glavine .35
66 John Smoltz .10
67 Fred McGriff .10
68 Craig Biggio .10
69 Reggie Sanders .10
70 Kevin Mitchell .10
71a Larry Walker/Expos .10
71b Larry Walker/Rockies .10
72 Carlos Delgado .50
73 Andujar Cedeno .10
74 Ivan Rodriguez .65
75 Ryan Klesko .10
76a John Kruk/Phillies .10
76b John Kruk/White Sox .10
77a Brian McRae/Royals .10
77b Brian McRae/Cubs .10
78 Tim Salmon .10
79 Travis Fryman .10
80 Chuck Knoblauch .10
81 Jay Bell .10
82 Cecil Fielder .10
83 Cliff Floyd .10
84 Ruben Sierra .10
85 Mike Mussina .45
86 Mark Grace .10
87 Dennis Eckersley .65
88 Dennis Martinez .10
89 Rafael Palmeiro .65
90 Ben McDonald .10
91 Dave Hollins .10
92 Steve Avery .10
93a David Cone/Royals .10
93b David Cone/Blue Jays .10
94 Darren Daulton .10
95 Bret Boone .10
96 Wade Boggs 1.00
97 Doug Drabek .10
98 Derek Bell .10
99 Jim Thome .65
100 Chili Davis .10
101 Jeffrey Hammonds .10
102 Rickey Henderson .75
103 Brett Butler .10
104 Tim Wallach .10
105 Wil Cordero .10
106 Mark Whiten .10
107 Bob Hamelin .10
108 Rondell White .10
109 Devon White .10
110a Tony Tarasco/Braves .10
110b Tony Tarasco/Expos .10
---- Redemption Trade Card (Expired Dec. 31, 1995.) .10

Rookie Dream Team

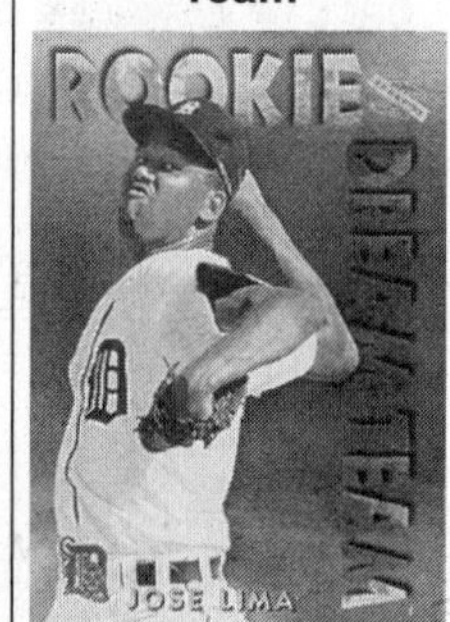

These Series 2 inserts feature a dozen of 1995's best rookie prospects. Fronts are printed on a silver-foil background. The words "ROOKIE DREAM TEAM" are formed of sky-and-cloud images within the letters. Horizontal backs repeat the motif and include another player photo in a vignette at center. Card numbers have an RDT prefix.

NM/M
Complete Set (12): 9.00
Common Player: .50
1 J.R. Phillips .50
2 Alex Gonzalez .50
3 Alex Rodriguez 6.00
4 Jose Oliva .50
5 Charles Johnson .50
6 Shawn Green 1.50
7 Brian Hunter .50
8 Garret Anderson .50
9 Julian Tavarez .50
10 Jose Lima .50
11 Armando Benitez .50
12 Ricky Bottalico .50

Rookie Greatness

This single-card insert set is the toughest pull among the 1995 Score chase cards. Honoring slugging Braves star Ryan Klesko, the card is inserted at the rate of one per 720 retail packs. An even scarcer autographed version of the card in an edition of just over 6,000 was also created for insertion into hobby packs.

		NM/M
RG1	Ryan Klesko	1.00
SG1	Ryan Klesko/Auto.	7.50

Score Rules

Series I jumbo packs were the only sources for "Score Rules" insert set of rookie and veteran stars. A color player photo at left has a team logo toward the bottom, beneath which is a gold-foil "tie tack" device with the league initials and position. At top-right is a baseball which appears to be dripping orange and green goop down the card. The player's last name is presented vertically with a sepia photo of the player within the letters. Backs repeat the green baseball and ooze motif, with three progressive color proof versions of the sepia front photo and a few sentences about the star. Cards are numbered with an "SR" prefix.

		NM/M
Complete Set (30):		30.00
Common Player:		.30
1	Ken Griffey Jr.	3.50
2	Frank Thomas	1.50
3	Mike Piazza	3.50
4	Jeff Bagwell	1.50
5	Alex Rodriguez	4.50
6	Albert Belle	.30
7	Matt Williams	.30
8	Roberto Alomar	.45
9	Barry Bonds	5.00
10	Raul Mondesi	.30
11	Jose Canseco	.60
12	Kirby Puckett	2.50
13	Fred McGriff	.30
14	Kenny Lofton	.30
15	Greg Maddux	2.50
16	Juan Gonzalez	.75
17	Cliff Floyd	.30
18	Cal Ripken, Jr.	5.00
19	Will Clark	.30
20	Tim Salmon	.30
21	Paul O'Neill	.30
22	Jason Bere	.30
23	Tony Gwynn	2.50
24	Manny Ramirez	1.50
25	Don Mattingly	3.00
26	Dave Justice	.30
27	Javier Lopez	.30
28	Ryan Klesko	.30
29	Carlos Delgado	.90
30	Mike Mussina	.60

Score Rules Supers

While colorful in the standard size, the Score Rules super-size cards found in special collectors kits are positively garish. The 7-1/2" x 10-1/2" cards are virtually identical to the Series 1 inserts, except that on back is a box with a serial number identifying the card from among an edition of 3,000. The Score Rules supers were available only in a collectors kit sold at large retail chains and came packaged with 26 Series 1 and 2 foil packs, a three-ring binder and 10 plastic sheets with a suggested retail price of around $25.

		NM/M
Complete Set (30):		60.00
Common Player:		.90
1	Ken Griffey Jr.	5.00
2	Frank Thomas	3.50
3	Mike Piazza	5.00
4	Jeff Bagwell	3.50
5	Alex Rodriguez	6.00
6	Albert Belle	.90
7	Matt Williams	.90
8	Roberto Alomar	1.25
9	Barry Bonds	7.50
10	Raul Mondesi	.90
11	Jose Canseco	2.50
12	Kirby Puckett	4.50
13	Fred McGriff	.90
14	Kenny Lofton	.90
15	Greg Maddux	4.50
16	Juan Gonzalez	2.00
17	Cliff Floyd	.90
18	Cal Ripken, Jr.	7.50
19	Will Clark	.90
20	Tim Salmon	.90
21	Paul O'Neill	.90
22	Jason Bere	.90
23	Tony Gwynn	4.50
24	Manny Ramirez	3.75
25	Don Mattingly	4.50
26	Dave Justice	.90
27	Javier Lopez	.90
28	Ryan Klesko	.90
29	Carlos Delgado	2.00
30	Mike Mussina	1.50

Ad Prize Cards

In a series of ads in hobby and public media, Score offered a pair of special cards as prizes in a mail-in offer. Cards feature the same basic design as 1995 Score, but are printed on platinum foil on front. Backs are conventionally printed with a portrait photo and a few words about the player.

		NM/M
Complete Set (2):		10.00
AD1	Alex Rodriguez	6.50
AD2	Ivan Rodriguez	3.50

1996 Score Samples

Score premiered its 1996 base brand offering with a cello pack of nine cards, including one of its new Dugout Collection inserts. The samples are virtually identical to the issued versions except that all 1995 and career stats are stated as zeros and the word "SAMPLE" is printed in white letters diagonally across front and back. Each of the cards can be found as a Dugout Collection version, making them eight times scarcer than the other samples.

		NM/M
Complete Set (16):		12.00
Common Player:		.50
3	Ryan Klesko	.50
3	Ryan Klesko (Dugout Collection)	1.00
4	Jim Edmonds	.50
4	Jim Edmonds (Dugout Collection)	1.00
5	Barry Larkin	.50
5	Barry Larkin (Dugout Collection)	1.00
6	Jim Thome	1.00
6	Jim Thome (Dugout Collection)	1.50
7	Raul Mondesi	.50
7	Raul Mondesi (Dugout Collection)	1.00
110	Derek Bell	.50
110	Derek Bell (Dugout Collection)	1.00
240	Derek Jeter	2.00
240	Derek Jeter (Dugout Collection)	4.50
241	Michael Tucker	.50
241	Michael Tucker (Dugout Collection)	1.00

1996 Score

Large, irregularly shaped action photos are featured on the fronts of the basic cards in the 1996 Score issue. Backs feature a portrait photo (in most cases) at left and a full slate of major and minor league stats at right, along with a few words about the player. Slightly different design details and a "ROOKIE" headline identify that subset within the regular issue. A wide variety of insert cards was produced, most of them exclusive to one type of packaging.

		NM/M
Complete Set (510):		15.00
Common Player:		.05
Wax Pack (10):		.45
Wax Box (36):		10.00
1	Will Clark	.05
2	Rich Becker	.05
3	Ryan Klesko	.05
4	Jim Edmonds	.05
5	Barry Larkin	.05
6	Jim Thome	.40
7	Raul Mondesi	.05
8	Don Mattingly	.65
9	Jeff Conine	.05
10	Rickey Henderson	.50
11	Chad Curtis	.05
12	Darren Daulton	.05
13	Larry Walker	.05
14	Carlos Garcia	.05
15	Carlos Baerga	.05
16	Tony Gwynn	.60
17	Jon Nunally	.05
18	Deion Sanders	.05
19	Mark Grace	.05
20	Alex Rodriguez	1.00
21	Frank Thomas	.50
22	Brian Jordan	.05
23	J.T. Snow	.05
24	Shawn Green	.30
25	Tim Wakefield	.05
26	Curtis Goodwin	.05
27	John Smoltz	.05
28	Devon White	.05
29	Brian Hunter	.05
30	Rusty Greer	.05
31	Rafael Palmeiro	.40
32	Bernard Gilkey	.05
33	John Valentin	.05
34	Randy Johnson	.50
35	Garret Anderson	.05
36	Rikkert Faneyte	.05
37	Ray Durham	.05
38	Bip Roberts	.05
39	Jaime Navarro	.05
40	Mark Johnson	.05
41	Darren Lewis	.05
42	Tyler Green	.05
43	Bill Pulsipher	.05
44	Jason Giambi	.40
45	Kevin Ritz	.05
46	Jack McDowell	.05
47	Felipe Lira	.05
48	Rico Brogna	.05
49	Terry Pendleton	.05
50	Rondell White	.05
51	Andre Dawson	.25
52	Kirby Puckett	.60
53	Wally Joyner	.05
54	B.J. Surhoff	.05
55	Chan Ho Park	.05
56	Greg Vaughn	.05
57	Roberto Alomar	.20
58	Dave Justice	.05
59	Kevin Seitzer	.05
60	Cal Ripken Jr.	1.50
61	Ozzie Smith	.60
62	Mo Vaughn	.05
63	Ricky Bones	.05
64	Gary DiSarcina	.05
65	Matt Williams	.05
66	Wilson Alvarez	.05
67	Lenny Dykstra	.05
68	Brian McRae	.05
69	Todd Stottlemyre	.05
70	Bret Boone	.05
71	Sterling Hitchcock	.05
72	Albert Belle	.05
73	Todd Hundley	.05
74	Vinny Castilla	.05
75	Moises Alou	.05
76	Cecil Fielder	.05
77	Brad Radke	.05
78	Quilvio Veras	.05
79	Eddie Murray	.50
80	James Mouton	.05
81	Pat Listach	.05
82	Mark Gubicza	.05
83	Dave Winfield	.50
84	Fred McGriff	.05
85	Darryl Hamilton	.05
86	Jeffrey Hammonds	.05
87	Pedro Munoz	.05
88	Craig Biggio	.05
89	Cliff Floyd	.05
90	Tim Naehring	.05
91	Brett Butler	.05
92	Kevin Foster	.05
93	Patrick Kelly	.05
94	John Smiley	.05
95	Terry Steinbach	.05
96	Orel Hershiser	.05
97	Darrin Fletcher	.05
98	Walt Weiss	.05
99	John Wetteland	.05
100	Alan Trammell	.05
101	Steve Avery	.05
102	Tony Eusebio	.05
103	Sandy Alomar	.05
104	Joe Girardi	.05
105	Rick Aguilera	.05
106	Tony Tarasco	.05
107	Chris Hammond	.05
108	Mike McFarlane	.05
109	Doug Drabek	.05
110	Derek Bell	.05
111	Ed Sprague	.05
112	Todd Hollandsworth	.05
113	Otis Nixon	.05
114	Keith Lockhart	.05
115	Donovan Osborne	.05
116	Dave Magadan	.05
117	Edgar Martinez	.05
118	Chuck Carr	.05
119	J.R. Phillips	.05
120	Sean Bergman	.05
121	Andujar Cedeno	.05
122	Eric Young	.05
123	Al Martin	.05
124	Ken Hill	.05
125	Jim Eisenreich	.05
126	Benito Santiago	.05
127	Ariel Prieto	.05
128	Jim Bullinger	.05
129	Russ Davis	.05
130	Jim Abbott	.05
131	Jason Isringhausen	.05
132	Carlos Perez	.05
133	David Segui	.05
134	Troy O'Leary	.05
135	Pat Meares	.05
136	Chris Hoiles	.05
137	Ismael Valdes	.05
138	Jose Oliva	.05
139	Carlos Delgado	.35
140	Tom Goodwin	.05
141	Bob Tewksbury	.05
142	Chris Gomez	.05
143	Jose Oquendo	.05
144	Mark Lewis	.05
145	Salomon Torres	.05
146	Luis Gonzalez	.05
147	Mark Carreon	.05
148	Lance Johnson	.05
149	Melvin Nieves	.05
150	Lee Smith	.05
151	Jacob Brumfield	.05
152	Armando Benitez	.05
153	Curt Schilling	.30
154	Javier Lopez	.05
155	Frank Rodriguez	.05
156	Alex Gonzalez	.05
157	Todd Worrell	.05
158	Benji Gil	.05
159	Greg Gagne	.05
160	Tom Henke	.05
161	Randy Myers	.05
162	Joey Cora	.05
163	Scott Ruffcorn	.05
164	William Van Landingham	.05
165	Tony Phillips	.05
166	Eddie Williams	.05
167	Bobby Bonilla	.05
168	Denny Neagle	.05
169	Troy Percival	.05
170	Billy Ashley	.05
171	Andy Van Slyke	.05
172	Jose Offerman	.05
173	Mark Parent	.05
174	Edgardo Alfonzo	.05
175	Trevor Hoffman	.05
176	David Cone	.05
177	Dan Wilson	.05
178	Steve Ontiveros	.05
179	Dean Palmer	.05
180	Mike Kelly	.05
181	Jim Leyritz	.05
182	Ron Karkovice	.05
183	Kevin Brown	.05
184	Jose Valentin **RC**	.05
185	Jorge Fabregas	.05
186	Jose Mesa	.05
187	Brent Mayne	.05
188	Carl Everett	.05
189	Paul Sorrento	.05
190	Pete Shourek	.05
191	Scott Kamieniecki	.05
192	Roberto Hernandez	.05
193	Randy Johnson (Radar Rating)	.25
194	Greg Maddux (Radar Rating)	.35
195	Hideo Nomo (Radar Rating)	.15
196	David Cone (Radar Rating)	.05
197	Mike Mussina (Radar Rating)	.15
198	Andy Benes (Radar Rating)	.05
199	Kevin Appier (Radar Rating)	.05
200	John Smoltz (Radar Rating)	.05
201	John Wetteland (Radar Rating)	.05
202	Mark Wohlers (Radar Rating)	.05
203	Stan Belinda	.05
204	Brian Anderson	.05
205	Mike Devereaux	.05
206	Mark Wohlers	.05
207	Omar Vizquel	.05
208	Jose Rijo	.05
209	Willie Blair	.05
210	Jamie Moyer	.05
211	Craig Shipley	.05
212	Shane Reynolds	.05
213	Chad Fonville	.05
214	Jose Vizcaino	.05
215	Sid Fernandez	.05
216	Andy Ashby	.05
217	Frank Castillo	.05
218	Kevin Tapani	.05
219	Kent Mercker	.05
220	Karim Garcia	.05
221	Chris Snopek	.05
222	Tim Unroe	.05
223	Johnny Damon	.25
224	LaTroy Hawkins	.05
225	Mariano Rivera	.10
226	Jose Alberro	.05
227	Angel Martinez	.05
228	Jason Schmidt	.05
229	Tony Clark	.05
230	Kevin Jordan	.05
231	Mark Thompson	.05
232	Jim Dougherty	.05
333	Roger Cedeno	.05
234	Ugueth Urbina	.05
235	Ricky Otero	.05
236	Mark Smith	.05
237	Brian Barber	.05
238	Marc Kroon	.05
239	Joe Rosselli	.05
240	Derek Jeter	1.50
241	Michael Tucker	.05
242	Joe Borowski **RC**	.05
243	Joe Vitiello	.05
244	Orlando Palmeiro	.05
245	James Baldwin	.05
246	Alan Embree	.05
247	Shannon Penn	.05
248	Chris Stynes	.05
249	Oscar Munoz	.05
250	Jose Herrera	.05
251	Scott Sullivan	.05
252	Reggie Williams	.05
253	Mark Grudzielanek	.05
254	Kevin Jordan	.05
255	Terry Bradshaw	.05
256	F.P. Santangelo **RC**	.05
257	Doug Johns	.05
258	George Williams	.05
259	Larry Thomas	.05
260	Rudy Pemberton	.05
261	Jim Pittsley	.05
262	Les Norman	.05
263	Ruben Rivera	.05
264	Cesar Devarez **RC**	.05
265	Gregg Zaun	.05
266	Eric Owens	.05
267	John Frascatore	.05
268	Shannon Stewart	.05
269	Checklist	.05
270	Checklist	.05
271	Checklist	.05
272	Checklist	.05
273	Checklist	.05
274	Checklist	.05
275	Checklist	.05
276	Greg Maddux	.60
277	Pedro Martinez	.50
278	Bobby Higginson	.05
279	Ray Lankford	.05
280	Shawon Dunston	.05
281	Gary Sheffield	.35
282	Ken Griffey Jr.	.75
283	Paul Molitor	.50
284	Kevin Appier	.05
285	Chuck Knoblauch	.05
286	Alex Fernandez	.05
287	Steve Finley	.05
288	Jeff Blauser	.05
289	Charles Johnson	.05
290	John Franco	.05
291	Mark Langston	.05
292	Bret Saberhagen	.05
293	John Mabry	.05
294	Ramon Martinez	.05
295	Mike Blowers	.05
296	Paul O'Neill	.05
297	Dave Nilsson	.05
298	Dante Bichette	.05
299	Marty Cordova	.05
300	Jay Bell	.05
301	Mike Mussina	.30
302	Ivan Rodriguez	.40
303	Jose Canseco	.30
304	Jeff Bagwell	.50
305	Manny Ramirez	.50
306	Dennis Martinez	.05
307	Charlie Hayes	.05
308	Joe Carter	.05
309	Travis Fryman	.05
310	Mark McGwire	1.00
311	Reggie Sanders	.05
312	Julian Tavarez	.05
313	Jeff Montgomery	.05
314	Andy Benes	.05
315	John Jaha	.05
316	Jeff Kent	.05
317	Mike Piazza	.75
318	Erik Hanson	.05
319	Kenny Rogers	.05
320	Hideo Nomo	.25
321	Gregg Jefferies	.05
322	Chipper Jones	.60
323	Jay Buhner	.05
324	Dennis Eckersley	.40
325	Kenny Lofton	.05
326	Robin Ventura	.05
327	Tom Glavine	.35
328	Tim Salmon	.05
329	Andres Galarraga	.05
330	Hal Morris	.05
331	Brady Anderson	.05
332	Chili Davis	.05
333	Roger Clemens	.65
334	Marquis Grissom	.05
335	Jeff (Mike) Greenwell	.05
336	Sammy Sosa	.60
337	Ron Gant	.05
338	Ken Caminiti	.05
339	Danny Tartabull	.05
340	Barry Bonds	1.50
341	Ben McDonald	.05
342	Ruben Sierra	.05
343	Bernie Williams	.05
344	Wil Cordero	.05
345	Wade Boggs	.60
346	Gary Gaetti	.05

#	Player	NM/M
347	Greg Colbrunn	.05
348	Juan Gonzalez	.25
349	Marc Newfield	.05
350	Charles Nagy	.05
351	Robby Thompson	.05
352	Roberto Petagine	.05
353	Darryl Strawberry	.05
354	Tino Martinez	.05
355	Eric Karros	.05
356	Cal Ripken Jr. (Star Struck)	.75
357	Cecil Fielder (Star Struck)	.05
358	Kirby Puckett (Star Struck)	.35
359	Jim Edmonds (Star Struck)	.05
360	Matt Williams (Star Struck)	.05
361	Alex Rodriguez (Star Struck)	.50
362	Barry Larkin (Star Struck)	.05
363	Rafael Palmeiro (Star Struck)	.20
364	David Cone (Star Struck)	.05
365	Roberto Alomar (Star Struck)	.10
366	Eddie Murray (Star Struck)	.25
367	Randy Johnson (Star Struck)	.20
368	Ryan Klesko (Star Struck)	.05
369	Raul Mondesi (Star Struck)	.05
370	Mo Vaughn (Star Struck)	.05
371	Will Clark (Star Struck)	.05
372	Carlos Baerga (Star Struck)	.05
373	Frank Thomas (Star Struck)	.30
374	Larry Walker (Star Struck)	.05
375	Garret Anderson (Star Struck)	.05
376	Edgar Martinez (Star Struck)	.05
377	Don Mattingly (Star Struck)	.40
378	Tony Gwynn (Star Struck)	.35
379	Albert Belle (Star Struck)	.05
380	Jason Isringhausen (Star Struck)	.05
381	Ruben Rivera (Star Struck)	.05
382	Johnny Damon (Star Struck)	.05
383	Karim Garcia (Star Struck)	.05
384	Derek Jeter (Star Struck)	.75
385	David Justice (Star Struck)	.05
386	Royce Clayton	.05
387	Mark Whiten	.05
388	Mickey Tettleton	.05
389	Steve Trachsel	.05
390	Danny Bautista	.05
391	Midre Cummings	.05
392	Scott Leius	.05
393	Manny Alexander	.05
394	Brent Gates	.05
395	Rey Sanchez	.05
396	Andy Pettitte	.20
397	Jeff Cirillo	.05
398	Kurt Abbott	.05
399	Lee Tinsley	.05
400	Paul Assenmacher	.05
401	Scott Erickson	.05
402	Todd Zeile	.05
403	Tom Pagnozzi	.05
404	Ozzie Guillen	.05
405	Jeff Frye	.05
406	Kirt Manwaring	.05
407	Chad Ogea	.05
408	Harold Baines	.05
409	Jason Bere	.05
410	Chuck Finley	.05
411	Jeff Fassero	.05
412	Joey Hamilton	.05
413	John Olerud	.05
414	Kevin Stocker	.05
415	Eric Anthony	.05
416	Aaron Sele	.05
417	Chris Bosio	.05
418	Michael Mimbs	.05
419	Orlando Miller	.05
420	Stan Javier	.05
421	Matt Mieske	.05
422	Jason Bates	.05
423	Orlando Merced	.05
424	John Flaherty	.05
425	Reggie Jefferson	.05
426	Scott Stahoviak	.05
427	John Burkett	.05
428	Rod Beck	.05
429	Bill Swift	.05
430	Scott Cooper	.05
431	Mel Rojas	.05
432	Todd Van Poppel	.05
433	Bobby Jones	.05
434	Mike Harkey	.05
435	Sean Berry	.05
436	Glenallen Hill	.05
437	Ryan Thompson	.05
438	Luis Alicea	.05
439	Esteban Loaiza	.05
440	Jeff Reboulet	.05
441	Vince Coleman	.05
442	Ellis Burks	.05
443	Allen Battle	.05
444	Jimmy Key	.05
445	Ricky Bottalico	.05
446	Delino DeShields	.05
447	Albie Lopez	.05
448	Mark Petkovsek	.05
449	Tim Raines	.05
450	Bryan Harvey	.05
451	Pat Hentgen	.05
452	Tim Laker	.05
453	Tom Gordon	.05
454	Phil Plantier	.05
455	Ernie Young	.05
456	Pete Harnisch	.05
457	Roberto Kelly	.05
458	Mark Portugal	.05
459	Mark Leiter	.05
460	Tony Pena	.05
461	Roger Pavlik	.05
462	Jeff King	.05
463	Bryan Rekar	.05
464	Al Leiter	.05
465	Phil Nevin	.05
466	Jose Lima	.05
467	Mike Stanley	.05
468	David McCarty	.05
469	Herb Perry	.05
470	Geronimo Berroa	.05
471	David Wells	.05
472	Vaughn Eshelman	.05
473	Greg Swindell	.05
474	Steve Sparks	.05
475	Luis Sojo	.05
476	Derrick May	.05
477	Joe Oliver	.05
478	Alex Arias	.05
479	Brad Ausmus	.05
480	Gabe White	.05
481	Pat Rapp	.05
482	Damon Buford	.05
483	Turk Wendell	.05
484	Jeff Brantley	.05
485	Curtis Leskanic	.05
486	Robb Nen	.05
487	Lou Whitaker	.05
488	Melido Perez	.05
489	Luis Polonia	.05
490	Scott Brosius	.05
491	Robert Perez	.05
492	Mike Sweeney **RC**	.50
493	Mark Loretta	.05
494	Alex Ochoa	.05
495	Matt Lawton **RC**	.10
496	Shawn Estes	.05
497	John Wasdin	.05
498	Marc Kroon	.05
499	Chris Snopek	.05
500	Jeff Suppan	.05
501	Terrell Wade	.05
502	Marvin Benard **RC**	.10
503	Chris Widger	.05
504	Quinton McCracken	.05
505	Bob Wolcott	.05
506	C.J. Nitkowski	.05
507	Aaron Ledesma	.05
508	Scott Hatteberg	.05
509	Jimmy Haynes	.05
510	Howard Battle	.05

Dugout Collection

The concept of a partial parallel set, including the stars and rookies, but not the journeymen and bench warmers, was initiated with Score's "Dugout Collection," with fewer than half of the cards from the regular series chosen for inclusion. The white borders of the regular cards are replaced with copper-foil and background printing is also done on foil in this special version. On back is a special "Dugout Collection '96" logo. Advertised insertion rate of the copper-version cards is one per three packs.

		NM/M
Complete Set (220):		60.00
Complete Series 1 (1-110):		30.00
Complete Series 2 (1-110):		30.00
Common Player:		.20
Artist's Proofs:		4X
1	Will Clark	.20
2	Rich Becker	.20
3	Ryan Klesko	.20
4	Jim Edmonds	.20
5	Barry Larkin	.20
6	Jim Thome	.65
7	Raul Mondesi	.20
8	Don Mattingly	1.25
9	Jeff Conine	.20
10	Rickey Henderson	.75
11	Chad Curtis	.20
12	Darren Daulton	.20
13	Larry Walker	.20
14	Carlos Baerga	.20
15	Tony Gwynn	1.00
16	Jon Nunnally	.20
17	Deion Sanders	.20
18	Mark Grace	.20
19	Alex Rodriguez	2.00
20	Frank Thomas	.75
21	Brian Jordan	.20
22	J.T. Snow	.20
23	Shawn Green	.50
24	Tim Wakefield	.20
25	Curtis Goodwin	.20
26	John Smoltz	.20
27	Devon White	.20
28	Brian Hunter	.20
29	Rusty Greer	.20
30	Rafael Palmeiro	.65
31	Bernard Gilkey	.20
32	John Valentin	.20
33	Randy Johnson	.75
34	Garret Anderson	.20
35	Ray Durham	.20
36	Bip Roberts	.20
37	Tyler Green	.20
38	Bill Pulsipher	.20
39	Jason Giambi	.50
40	Jack McDowell	.20
41	Rico Brogna	.20
42	Terry Pendleton	.20
43	Rondell White	.20
44	Andre Dawson	.35
45	Kirby Puckett	1.00
46	Wally Joyner	.20
47	B.J. Surhoff	.20
48	Randy Velarde	.20
49	Greg Vaughn	.20
50	Roberto Alomar	.30
51	David Justice	.20
52	Cal Ripken Jr.	3.00
53	Ozzie Smith	1.00
54	Mo Vaughn	.20
55	Gary DiSarcina	.20
56	Matt Williams	.20
57	Lenny Dykstra	.20
58	Bret Boone	.20
59	Albert Belle	.20
60	Vinny Castilla	.20
61	Moises Alou	.20
62	Cecil Fielder	.20
63	Brad Radke	.20
64	Quilvio Veras	.20
65	Eddie Murray	.75
66	Dave Winfield	.75
67	Fred McGriff	.20
68	Craig Biggio	.20
69	Cliff Floyd	.20
70	Tim Naehring	.20
71	John Wetteland	.20
72	Alan Trammell	.20
73	Steve Avery	.20
74	Rick Aguilera	.20
75	Derek Bell	.20
76	Todd Hollandsworth	.20
77	Edgar Martinez	.20
78	Mark Lemke	.20
79	Ariel Prieto	.20
80	Russ Davis	.20
81	Jim Abbott	.20
82	Jason Isringhausen	.20
83	Carlos Perez	.20
84	David Segui	.20
85	Troy O'Leary	.20
86	Ismael Valdes	.20
87	Carlos Delgado	.50
88	Lee Smith	.20
89	Javy Lopez	.20
90	Frank Rodriguez	.20
91	Alex Gonzalez	.20
92	Benji Gil	.20
93	Greg Gagne	.20
94	Randy Myers	.20
95	Bobby Bonilla	.20
96	Billy Ashley	.20
97	Andy Van Slyke	.20
98	Edgardo Alfonzo	.20
99	David Cone	.20
100	Dean Palmer	.20
101	Jose Mesa	.20
102	Karim Garcia	.20
103	Johnny Damon	.40
104	LaTroy Hawkins	.20
105	Mark Smith	.20
106	Derek Jeter	3.00
107	Michael Tucker	.20
108	Joe Vitiello	.20
109	Ruben Rivera	.20
110	Gregg Zaun	.20
1	Greg Maddux	1.00
2	Pedro Martinez	.75
3	Bobby Higginson	.20
4	Ray Lankford	.20
5	Shawon Dunston	.20
6	Gary Sheffield	.45
7	Ken Griffey Jr.	1.50
8	Paul Molitor	.75
9	Kevin Appier	.20
10	Chuck Knoblauch	.20
11	Alex Fernandez	.20
12	Steve Finley	.20
13	Jeff Blauser	.20
14	Charles Johnson	.20
15	John Franco	.20
16	Mark Langston	.20
17	Bret Saberhagen	.20
18	John Mabry	.20
19	Ramon Martinez	.20
20	Mike Blowers	.20
21	Paul O'Neill	.20
22	Dave Nilsson	.20
23	Dante Bichette	.20
24	Marty Cordova	.20
25	Jay Bell	.20
26	Mike Mussina	.40
27	Ivan Rodriguez	.65
28	Jose Canseco	.50
29	Jeff Bagwell	.75
30	Manny Ramirez	.75
31	Dennis Martinez	.20
32	Charlie Hayes	.20
33	Joe Carter	.20
34	Travis Fryman	.20
35	Mark McGwire	2.00
36	Reggie Sanders	.20
37	Julian Tavarez	.20
38	Jeff Montgomery	.20
39	Andy Benes	.20
40	John Jaha	.20
41	Jeff Kent	.20
42	Mike Piazza	1.50
43	Erik Hanson	.20
44	Kenny Rogers	.20
45	Hideo Nomo	.50
46	Gregg Jefferies	.20
47	Chipper Jones	1.00
48	Jay Buhner	.20
49	Dennis Eckersley	.65
50	Kenny Lofton	.20
51	Robin Ventura	.20
52	Tom Glavine	.30
53	Tim Salmon	.20
54	Andres Galarraga	.20
55	Hal Morris	.20
56	Brady Anderson	.20
57	Chili Davis	.20
58	Roger Clemens	1.25
59	Marquis Grissom	.20
60	Mike Greenwell	.20
61	Sammy Sosa	1.00
62	Ron Gant	.20
63	Ken Caminiti	.20
64	Danny Tartabull	.20
65	Barry Bonds	3.00
66	Ben McDonald	.20
67	Ruben Sierra	.20
68	Bernie Williams	.20
69	Wil Cordero	.20
70	Wade Boggs	1.00
71	Gary Gaetti	.20
72	Greg Colbrunn	.20
73	Juan Gonzalez	.50
74	Marc Newfield	.20
75	Charles Nagy	.20
76	Robby Thompson	.20
77	Roberto Petagine	.20
78	Darryl Strawberry	.20
79	Tino Martinez	.20
80	Eric Karros	.20
81	Cal Ripken Jr. (Star Struck)	1.50
82	Cecil Fielder (Star Struck)	.20
83	Kirby Puckett (Star Struck)	.50
84	Jim Edmonds (Star Struck)	.20
85	Matt Williams (Star Struck)	.20
86	Alex Rodriguez (Star Struck)	1.00
87	Barry Larkin (Star Struck)	.20
88	Rafael Palmeiro (Star Struck)	.40
89	David Cone (Star Struck)	.20
90	Roberto Alomar (Star Struck)	.25
91	Eddie Murray (Star Struck)	.40
92	Randy Johnson (Star Struck)	.40
93	Ryan Klesko (Star Struck)	.20
94	Raul Mondesi (Star Struck)	.20
95	Mo Vaughn (Star Struck)	.20
96	Will Clark (Star Struck)	.20
97	Carlos Baerga (Star Struck)	.20
98	Frank Thomas (Star Struck)	.45
99	Larry Walker (Star Struck)	.20
100	Garret Anderson (Star Struck)	.20
101	Edgar Martinez (Star Struck)	.20
102	Don Mattingly (Star Struck)	.60
103	Tony Gwynn (Star Struck)	.50
104	Albert Belle (Star Struck)	.20
105	Jason Isringhausen (Star Struck)	.20
106	Ruben Rivera (Star Struck)	.20
107	Johnny Damon (Star Struck)	.35
108	Karim Garcia (Star Struck)	.20
109	Derek Jeter (Star Struck)	1.50
110	David Justice (Star Struck)	.20

Dugout Collection Artist's Proofs

A parallel set within a parallel set, the Artist's Proof logo added to the copper-foil design of the Dugout Collection cards raises the odds of finding one to just once in 36 packs.

	NM/M
Complete Set (220):	300.00
Common Player:	1.00
Artist's Proof Stars:	4X

All-Stars

An exclusive insert found only in 20-card Series 2 jumbo packs at an average rate of one per nine packs, these inserts feature the game's top stars printed in a rainbow holographic-foil technology.

		NM/M
Complete Set (20):		13.50
Common Player:		.25
1	Frank Thomas	1.25
2	Albert Belle	.25
3	Ken Griffey Jr.	2.00
4	Cal Ripken Jr.	3.00
5	Mo Vaughn	.25
6	Matt Williams	.25
7	Barry Bonds	3.00
8	Dante Bichette	.25
9	Tony Gwynn	1.50
10	Greg Maddux	1.50
11	Randy Johnson	1.25
12	Hideo Nomo	.75
13	Tim Salmon	.25
14	Jeff Bagwell	1.25
15	Edgar Martinez	.25
16	Reggie Sanders	.25
17	Larry Walker	.25
18	Chipper Jones	1.50
19	Manny Ramirez	1.25
20	Eddie Murray	1.25

Big Bats

Gold-foil printing highlights cards of 20 of the game's top hitters found in this retail-

packaging exclusive insert set. Stated odds of picking a Big Bats card are one in 31 packs.

		NM/M
Complete Set (20):		12.50
Common Player:		.45
1	Cal Ripken Jr.	3.00
2	Ken Griffey Jr.	2.00
3	Frank Thomas	.75
4	Jeff Bagwell	.75
5	Mike Piazza	2.00
6	Barry Bonds	3.00
7	Matt Williams	.45
8	Raul Mondesi	.45
9	Tony Gwynn	1.25
10	Albert Belle	.45
11	Manny Ramirez	.75
12	Carlos Baerga	.45
13	Mo Vaughn	.45
14	Derek Bell	.45
15	Larry Walker	.45
16	Kenny Lofton	.45
17	Edgar Martinez	.45
18	Reggie Sanders	.45
19	Eddie Murray	.75
20	Chipper Jones	1.25

Diamond Aces

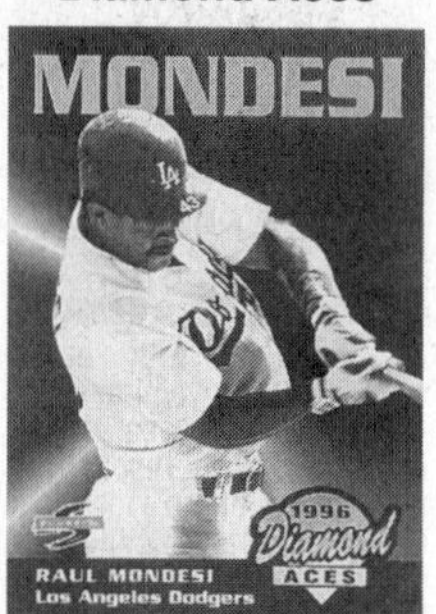

Thirty of the top veterans and young stars are included in this jumbo-only insert set, seeded at a rate of one per eight packs.

		NM/M
Complete Set (30):		25.00
Common Player:		.35
1	Hideo Nomo	.60
2	Brian Hunter	.35
3	Ray Durham	.35
4	Frank Thomas	1.00
5	Cal Ripken Jr.	3.50
6	Barry Bonds	3.50
7	Greg Maddux	1.25
8	Chipper Jones	1.25
9	Raul Mondesi	.35
10	Mike Piazza	2.00
11	Derek Jeter	3.50
12	Bill Pulsipher	.35
13	Larry Walker	.35
14	Ken Griffey Jr.	2.00
15	Alex Rodriguez	3.00
16	Manny Ramirez	1.00
17	Mo Vaughn	.35
18	Reggie Sanders	.35
19	Derek Bell	.35
20	Jim Edmonds	.35
21	Albert Belle	.35
22	Eddie Murray	1.00
23	Tony Gwynn	1.25
24	Jeff Bagwell	1.00
25	Carlos Baerga	.35
26	Matt Williams	.35
27	Garret Anderson	.35
28	Todd Hollandsworth	.35
29	Johnny Damon	.75
30	Tim Salmon	.35

Dream Team

The hottest player at each position is honored in the Dream Team insert set. Once again featured on holographic foil printing technology, the

cards are found in all types of Score packaging at a rate of once per 72 packs.

		NM/M
Complete Set (9):		15.00
Common Player:		.75
1	Cal Ripken Jr.	4.00
2	Frank Thomas	1.50
3	Carlos Baerga	.75
4	Matt Williams	.75
5	Mike Piazza	3.00
6	Barry Bonds	4.00
7	Ken Griffey Jr.	3.00
8	Manny Ramirez	1.50
9	Greg Maddux	2.00

Future Franchise

Future Franchise is the most difficult insert to pull from packs of Series 2, at the rate of once per 72 packs, on average. Sixteen young stars are showcased on holographic gold-foil printing in the set.

		NM/M
Complete Set (16):		20.00
Common Player:		.75
1	Jason Isringhausen	.75
2	Chipper Jones	2.50
3	Derek Jeter	5.00
4	Alex Rodriguez	4.00
5	Alex Ochoa	.75
6	Manny Ramirez	1.50
7	Johnny Damon	1.00
8	Ruben Rivera	.75
9	Karim Garcia	.75
10	Garret Anderson	.75
11	Marty Cordova	.75
12	Bill Pulsipher	.75
13	Hideo Nomo	1.00
14	Marc Newfield	.75
15	Charles Johnson	.75
16	Raul Mondesi	.75

Gold Stars

Appearing once in every 15 packs of Series 2, Gold Stars are labeled with a stamp in the upper-left corner. The set contains 30 top current stars printed on gold-foil and seeded at the average rate of one per 15 packs.

		NM/M
Complete Set (30):		20.00
Common Player:		.20
1	Ken Griffey Jr.	2.00
2	Frank Thomas	1.00
3	Reggie Sanders	.20
4	Tim Salmon	.20
5	Mike Piazza	2.00
6	Tony Gwynn	1.50
7	Gary Sheffield	.45
8	Matt Williams	.20
9	Bernie Williams	.20
10	Jason Isringhausen	.20
11	Albert Belle	.20
12	Chipper Jones	1.50
13	Edgar Martinez	.20
14	Barry Larkin	.20
15	Barry Bonds	3.00
16	Jeff Bagwell	1.00
17	Greg Maddux	1.50
18	Mo Vaughn	.20
19	Ryan Klesko	.20
20	Sammy Sosa	1.50
21	Darren Daulton	.20
22	Ivan Rodriguez	.75
23	Dante Bichette	.20
24	Hideo Nomo	.50
25	Cal Ripken Jr.	3.00
26	Rafael Palmeiro	.75
27	Larry Walker	.20
28	Carlos Baerga	.20
29	Randy Johnson	1.00
30	Manny Ramirez	1.00

Numbers Game

Some of the 1995 season's most impressive statistical accomplishments are featured in this chase set. Cards are enhanced with gold foil and found in all types of Score packs at an average rate of one per 15 packs.

		NM/M
Complete Set (30):		17.50
Common Player:		.15
1	Cal Ripken Jr	2.50
2	Frank Thomas	.75
3	Ken Griffey Jr.	1.50
4	Mike Piazza	1.50
5	Barry Bonds	2.50
6	Greg Maddux	1.00
7	Jeff Bagwell	.75
8	Derek Bell	.15
9	Tony Gwynn	1.00
10	Hideo Nomo	.50
11	Raul Mondesi	.15
12	Manny Ramirez	.75
13	Albert Belle	.15
14	Matt Williams	.15
15	Jim Edmonds	.15
16	Edgar Martinez	.15
17	Mo Vaughn	.15
18	Reggie Sanders	.15
19	Chipper Jones	1.00
20	Larry Walker	.15
21	Juan Gonzalez	.50
22	Kenny Lofton	.15
23	Don Mattingly	1.25
24	Ivan Rodriguez	.65
25	Randy Johnson	.75
26	Derek Jeter	2.50
27	J.T. Snow	.15
28	Will Clark	.15
29	Rafael Palmeiro	.65
30	Alex Rodriguez	2.00

Power Pace

Power Pace is exclusive to retail packs in Series 2, where they are found on average every 31 packs. Eighteen top power hitters are featured in this issue in a gold-foil design.

		NM/M
Complete Set (18):		24.00
Common Player:		.50
1	Mark McGwire	4.00
2	Albert Belle	.50
3	Jay Buhner	.50
4	Frank Thomas	1.50
5	Matt Williams	.50
6	Gary Sheffield	.75
7	Mike Piazza	3.00
8	Larry Walker	.50
9	Mo Vaughn	.50
10	Rafael Palmeiro	1.25
11	Dante Bichette	.50
12	Ken Griffey Jr.	3.00
13	Barry Bonds	5.00
14	Manny Ramirez	1.50
15	Sammy Sosa	2.00
16	Tim Salmon	.50
17	Dave Justice	.50
18	Eric Karros	.50

Reflexions

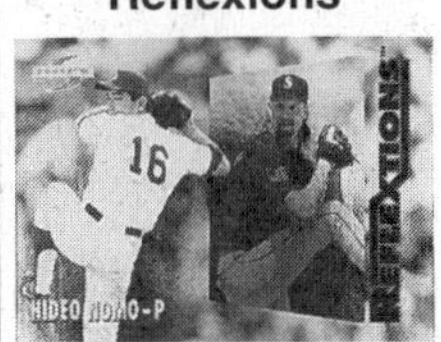

Appearing only in hobby packs this insert set pairs 20 veteran stars with 20 up-and-coming players in a foil-printed format. Odds of finding a Reflexions insert are stated as one per 31 packs.

		NM/M
Complete Set (20):		35.00
Common Player:		.45
1	Cal Ripken Jr., Chipper Jones	5.00
2	Ken Griffey Jr., Alex Rodriguez	4.50
3	Frank Thomas, Mo Vaughn	2.50
4	Kenny Lofton, Brian Hunter	.45
5	Don Mattingly, J.T. Snow	3.75
6	Manny Ramirez, Raul Mondesi	2.50
7	Tony Gwynn, Garret Anderson	3.75
8	Roberto Alomar, Carlos Baerga	.50
9	Andre Dawson, Larry Walker	.50
10	Barry Larkin, Derek Jeter	5.00
11	Barry Bonds, Reggie Sanders	5.00
12	Mike Piazza, Albert Belle	4.00
13	Wade Boggs, Edgar Martinez	3.75
14	David Cone, John Smoltz	.45
15	Will Clark, Jeff Bagwell	2.50
16	Mark McGwire, Cecil Fielder	4.50
17	Greg Maddux, Mike Mussina	3.75
18	Randy Johnson, Hideo Nomo	2.50
19	Jim Thome, Dean Palmer	2.00
20	Chuck Knoblauch, Craig Biggio	.45

Cal Ripken Tribute

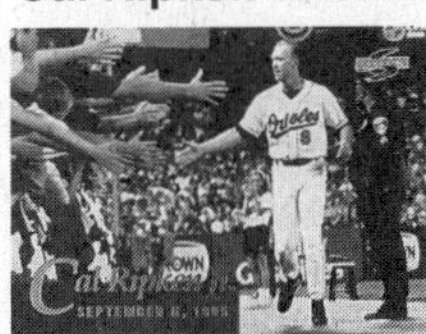

The toughest pick among the 1996 Score inserts is this special card marking Cal Ripken's 2,131st consecutive game. The insertion rate is one per 300 packs hobby and retail, one per 150 jumbo packs.

		NM/M
2131	Cal Ripken Jr. (Tribute)	4.00

Titantic Taters

One of the more creative names in the 1996 insert lineup, Titanic Taters are found one in

every 31 packs of Series 2 hobby. Gold-foil fronts feature 18 of the game's heaviest hitters.

		NM/M
Complete Set (18):		25.00
Common Player:		.60
1	Albert Belle	.60
2	Frank Thomas	2.00
3	Mo Vaughn	.60
4	Ken Griffey Jr.	3.00
5	Matt Williams	.60
6	Mark McGwire	3.50
7	Dante Bichette	.60
8	Tim Salmon	.60
9	Jeff Bagwell	2.00
10	Rafael Palmeiro	1.50
11	Mike Piazza	3.00
12	Cecil Fielder	.60
13	Larry Walker	.60
14	Sammy Sosa	2.50
15	Manny Ramirez	2.00
16	Gary Sheffield	.90
17	Barry Bonds	5.00
18	Jay Buhner	.60

1997 Score

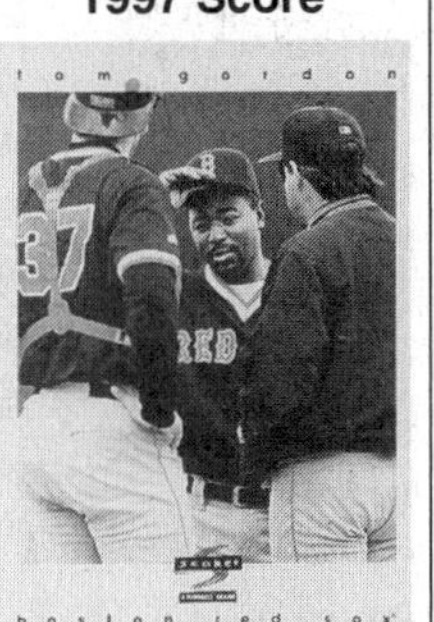

A total of 551 cards make up the base set, with 330 cards sold in Series I and 221 making up Series II. The basic card design features a color action photo surrounded by a white border. The player's name is above the photo, with the team name underneath. Backs feature text and statistics against a white background with the image of the team logo ghosted into the background. Two parallel insert sets - Artist's Proof and Showcase Series - were part of each series. Other inserts in Series I were Pitcher Perfect, The Franchise, The Glowing Franchise, Titanic Taters (retail exclusive), Stellar Season (magazine packs only), and The Highlight Zone (hobby exclusive). Series II inserts were Blastmasters, Heart of the Order and Stand and Deliver. Cards were sold in 10-card packs for 99 cents each.

		NM/M
Complete Set (551):		16.00
Factory Tin-Box Set (551):		17.50
Common Player:		.05
Showcase:		3X
Artist's Proofs:		10X
Premium Stocks:		3X
Wax Pack (10):		.50
Wax Box (36):		12.00
1	Jeff Bagwell	.50
2	Mickey Tettleton	.05
3	Johnny Damon	.25
4	Jeff Conine	.05
5	Bernie Williams	.05
6	Will Clark	.05
7	Ryan Klesko	.05
8	Cecil Fielder	.05
9	Paul Wilson	.05
10	Gregg Jefferies	.05
11	Chili Davis	.05
12	Albert Belle	.05
13	Ken Hill	.05
14	Cliff Floyd	.05
15	Jaime Navarro	.05
16	Ismael Valdes	.05
17	Jeff King	.05
18	Chris Bosio	.05
19	Reggie Sanders	.05
20	Darren Daulton	.05
21	Ken Caminiti	.05
22	Mike Piazza	.75
23	Chad Mottola	.05
24	Darin Erstad	.15
25	Dante Bichette	.05
26	Frank Thomas	.50
27	Ben McDonald	.05
28	Raul Casanova	.05
29	Kevin Ritz	.05
30	Garret Anderson	.05
31	Jason Kendall	.05
32	Billy Wagner	.05
33	David Justice	.05
34	Marty Cordova	.05
35	Derek Jeter	1.50
36	Trevor Hoffman	.05
37	Geronimo Berroa	.05
38	Walt Weiss	.05
39	Kirt Manwaring	.05
40	Alex Gonzalez	.05
41	Sean Berry	.05
42	Kevin Appier	.05
43	Rusty Greer	.05
44	Pete Incaviglia	.05
45	Rafael Palmeiro	.45
46	Eddie Murray	.50
47	Moises Alou	.05
48	Mark Lewis	.05
49	Hal Morris	.05
50	Edgar Renteria	.05
51	Rickey Henderson	.50
52	Pat Listach	.05
53	John Wasdin	.05
54	James Baldwin	.05
55	Brian Jordan	.05
56	Edgar Martinez	.05
57	Wil Cordero	.05
58	Danny Tartabull	.05
59	Keith Lockhart	.05
60	Rico Brogna	.05
61	Ricky Bottalico	.05
62	Terry Pendleton	.05
63	Bret Boone	.05
64	Charlie Hayes	.05
65	Marc Newfield	.05
66	Sterling Hitchcock	.05
67	Roberto Alomar	.15
68	John Jaha	.05
69	Greg Colbrunn	.05
70	Sal Fasano	.05
71	Brooks Kieschnick	.05
72	Pedro Martinez	.50
73	Kevin Elster	.05
74	Ellis Burks	.05
75	Chuck Finley	.05
76	John Olerud	.05
77	Jay Bell	.05
78	Allen Watson	.05
79	Darryl Strawberry	.05
80	Orlando Miller	.05
81	Jose Herrera	.05
82	Andy Pettitte	.20
83	Juan Guzman	.05
84	Alan Benes	.05
85	Jack McDowell	.05
86	Ugueth Urbina	.05
87	Rocky Coppinger	.05
88	Jeff Cirillo	.05
89	Tom Glavine	.35
90	Robby Thompson	.05
91	Barry Bonds	1.50
92	Carlos Delgado	.40
93	Mo Vaughn	.05
94	Ryne Sandberg	.65
95	Alex Rodriguez	1.00
96	Brady Anderson	.05
97	Scott Brosius	.05
98	Dennis Eckersley	.45
99	Brian McRae	.05
100	Rey Ordonez	.05
101	John Valentin	.05
102	Brett Butler	.05
103	Eric Karros	.05
104	Harold Baines	.05
105	Javier Lopez	.05
106	Alan Trammell	.05
107	Jim Thome	.45
108	Frank Rodriguez	.05
109	Bernard Gilkey	.05
110	Reggie Jefferson	.05
111	Scott Stahoviak	.05
112	Steve Gibralter	.05
113	Todd Hollandsworth	.05
114	Ruben Rivera	.05
115	Dennis Martinez	.05
116	Mariano Rivera	.10
117	John Smoltz	.05
118	John Mabry	.05
119	Tom Gordon	.05
120	Alex Ochoa	.05
121	Jamey Wright	.05
122	Dave Nilsson	.05
123	Bobby Bonilla	.05
124	Al Leiter	.05
125	Rick Aguilera	.05
126	Jeff Brantley	.05
127	Kevin Brown	.05
128	George Arias	.05
129	Darren Oliver	.05
130	Bill Pulsipher	.05
131	Roberto Hernandez	.05
132	Delino DeShields	.05
133	Mark Grudzielanek	.05
134	John Wetteland	.05
135	Carlos Baerga	.05
136	Paul Sorrento	.05
137	Leo Gomez	.05
138	Andy Ashby	.05
139	Julio Franco	.05
140	Brian Hunter	.05
141	Jermaine Dye	.05
142	Tony Clark	.05
143	Ruben Sierra	.05
144	Donovan Osborne	.05
145	Mark McLemore	.05
146	Terry Steinbach	.05
147	Bob Wells	.05
148	Chan Ho Park	.05
149	Tim Salmon	.05
150	Paul O'Neill	.05
151	Cal Ripken Jr.	1.50
152	Wally Joyner	.05
153	Omar Vizquel	.05
154	Mike Mussina	.30
155	Andres Galarraga	.05
156	Ken Griffey Jr.	.75
157	Kenny Lofton	.05
158	Ray Durham	.05
159	Hideo Nomo	.25
160	Ozzie Guillen	.05
161	Roger Pavlik	.05
162	Manny Ramirez	.50
163	Mark Lemke	.05
164	Mike Stanley	.05
165	Chuck Knoblauch	.05
166	Kimera Bartee	.05
167	Wade Boggs	.65
168	Jay Buhner	.05
169	Eric Young	.05
170	Jose Canseco	.30
171	Dwight Gooden	.05
172	Fred McGriff	.05
173	Sandy Alomar Jr.	.05
174	Andy Benes	.05
175	Dean Palmer	.05
176	Larry Walker	.05
177	Charles Nagy	.05
178	David Cone	.05
179	Mark Grace	.05
180	Robin Ventura	.05
181	Roger Clemens	.70
182	Bobby Witt	.05
183	Vinny Castilla	.05
184	Gary Sheffield	.35
185	Dan Wilson	.05
186	Roger Cedeno	.05
187	Mark McGwire	1.00
188	Darren Bragg	.05
189	Quinton McCracken	.05
190	Randy Myers	.05
191	Jeromy Burnitz	.05
192	Randy Johnson	.50
193	Chipper Jones	.65
194	Greg Vaughn	.05
195	Travis Fryman	.05
196	Tim Naehring	.05
197	B.J. Surhoff	.05
198	Juan Gonzalez	.25
199	Terrell Wade	.05
200	Jeff Frye	.05
201	Joey Cora	.05
202	Raul Mondesi	.05
203	Ivan Rodriguez	.45
204	Armando Reynoso	.05
205	Jeffrey Hammonds	.05
206	Darren Dreifort	.05
207	Kevin Seitzer	.05
208	Tino Martinez	.05
209	Jim Bruske	.05
210	Jeff Suppan	.05
211	Mark Carreon	.05
212	Wilson Alvarez	.05
213	John Burkett	.05
214	Tony Phillips	.05
215	Greg Maddux	.65
216	Mark Whiten	.05
217	Curtis Pride	.05
218	Lyle Mouton	.05
219	Todd Hundley	.05
220	Greg Gagne	.05
221	Rich Amaral	.05
222	Tom Goodwin	.05
223	Chris Hoiles	.05
224	Jayhawk Owens	.05
225	Kenny Rogers	.05
226	Mike Greenwell	.05
227	Mark Wohlers	.05
228	Henry Rodriguez	.05
229	Robert Perez	.05
230	Jeff Kent	.05
231	Darryl Hamilton	.05
232	Alex Fernandez	.05
233	Ron Karkovice	.05
234	Jimmy Haynes	.05
235	Craig Biggio	.05
236	Ray Lankford	.05
237	Lance Johnson	.05
238	Matt Williams	.05
239	Chad Curtis	.05
240	Mark Thompson	.05
241	Jason Giambi	.40
242	Barry Larkin	.05
243	Paul Molitor	.50
244	Sammy Sosa	.65
245	Kevin Tapani	.05

246 Marquis Grissom .05
247 Joe Carter .05
248 Ramon Martinez .05
249 Tony Gwynn .65
250 Andy Fox .05
251 Troy O'Leary .05
252 Warren Newson .05
253 Troy Percival .05
254 Jamie Moyer .05
255 Danny Graves .05
256 David Wells .05
257 Todd Zeile .05
258 Raul Ibanez .05
259 Tyler Houston .05
260 LaTroy Hawkins .05
261 Joey Hamilton .05
262 Mike Sweeney .05
263 Brant Brown .05
264 Pat Hentgen .05
265 Mark Johnson .05
266 Robb Nen .05
267 Justin Thompson .05
268 Ron Gant .05
269 Jeff D'Amico .05
270 Shawn Estes .05
271 Derek Bell .05
272 Fernando Valenzuela .05
273 Luis Castillo .05
274 Ray Montgomery .05
275 Ed Sprague .05
276 F.P. Santangelo .05
277 Todd Greene .05
278 Butch Huskey .05
279 Steve Finley .05
280 Eric Davis .05
281 Shawn Green .30
282 Al Martin .05
283 Michael Tucker .05
284 Shane Reynolds .05
285 Matt Mieske .05
286 Jose Rosado .05
287 Mark Langston .05
288 Ralph Milliard .05
289 Mike Lansing .05
290 Scott Servais .05
291 Royce Clayton .05
292 Mike Grace .05
293 James Mouton .05
294 Charles Johnson .05
295 Gary Gaetti .05
296 Kevin Mitchell .05
297 Carlos Garcia .05
298 Desi Relaford .05
299 Jason Thompson .05
300 Osvaldo Fernandez .05
301 Fernando Vina .05
302 Jose Offerman .05
303 Yamil Benitez .05
304 J.T. Snow .05
305 Rafael Bournigal .05
306 Jason Isringhausen .05
307 Bob Higginson .05
308 Nerio Rodriguez **RC** .05
309 Brian Giles **RC** .50
310 Andruw Jones .50
311 Billy McMillon .05
312 Arquimedez Pozo .05
313 Jermaine Allensworth .05
314 Luis Andujar .05
315 Angel Echevarria .05
316 Karim Garcia .05
317 Trey Beamon .05
318 Makoto Suzuki .05
319 Robin Jennings .05
320 Dmitri Young .05
321 Damon Mashore **RC** .05
322 Wendell Magee .05
323 Dax Jones **RC** .05
324 Todd Walker .05
325 Marvin Benard .05
326 Brian Raabe **RC** .05
327 Marcus Jensen .05
328 Checklist .05
329 Checklist .05
330 Checklist .05
331 Norm Charlton .05
332 Bruce Ruffin .05
333 John Wetteland .05
334 Marquis Grissom .05
335 Sterling Hitchcock .05
336 John Olerud .05
337 David Wells .05
338 Chili Davis .05
339 Mark Lewis .05
340 Kenny Lofton .05
341 Alex Fernandez .05
342 Ruben Sierra .05
343 Delino DeShields .05
344 John Wasdin .05
345 Dennis Martinez .05
346 Kevin Elster .05
347 Bobby Bonilla .05
348 Jaime Navarro .05
349 Chad Curtis .05
350 Terry Steinbach .05
351 Ariel Prieto .05
352 Jeff Kent .05
353 Carlos Garcia .05
354 Mark Whiten .05
355 Todd Zeile .05
356 Eric Davis .05
357 Greg Colbrunn .05
358 Moises Alou .05
359 Allen Watson .05
360 Jose Canseco .30
361 Matt Williams .05
362 Jeff King .05
363 Darryl Hamilton .05
364 Mark Clark .05
365 J.T. Snow .05
366 Kevin Mitchell .05
367 Orlando Miller .05
368 Rico Brogna .05
369 Mike James .05
370 Brad Ausmus .05
371 Darryl Kile .05
372 Edgardo Alfonzo .05
373 Julian Tavarez .05
374 Darren Lewis .05
375 Steve Karsay .05
376 Lee Stevens .05
377 Albie Lopez .05
378 Orel Hershiser .05
379 Lee Smith .05
380 Rick Helling .05
381 Carlos Perez .05
382 Tony Tarasco .05
383 Melvin Nieves .05
384 Benji Gil .05
385 Devon White .05
386 Armando Benitez .05
387 Bill Swift .05
388 John Smiley .05
389 Midre Cummings .05
390 Tim Belcher .05
391 Tim Raines .05
392 Todd Worrell .05
393 Quilvio Veras .05
394 Matt Lawton .05
395 Aaron Sele .05
396 Bip Roberts .05
397 Denny Neagle .05
398 Tyler Green .05
399 Hipolito Pichardo .05
400 Scott Erickson .05
401 Bobby Jones .05
402 Jim Edmonds .05
403 Chad Ogea .05
404 Cal Eldred .05
405 Pat Listach .05
406 Todd Stottlemyre .05
407 Phil Nevin .05
408 Otis Nixon .05
409 Billy Ashley .05
410 Jimmy Key .05
411 Mike Timlin .05
412 Joe Vitiello .05
413 Rondell White .05
414 Jeff Fassero .05
415 Rex Hudler .05
416 Curt Schilling .35
417 Rich Becker .05
418 William Van Landingham .05
419 Chris Snopek .05
420 David Segui .05
421 Eddie Murray .50
422 Shane Andrews .05
423 Gary DiSarcina .05
424 Brian Hunter .05
425 Willie Greene .05
426 Felipe Crespo .05
427 Jason Bates .05
428 Albert Belle .05
429 Rey Sanchez .05
430 Roger Clemens .70
431 Deion Sanders .05
432 Ernie Young .05
433 Jay Bell .05
434 Jeff Blauser .05
435 Lenny Dykstra .05
436 Chuck Carr .05
437 Russ Davis .05
438 Carl Everett .05
439 Damion Easley .05
440 Pat Kelly .05
441 Pat Rapp .05
442 David Justice .05
443 Graeme Lloyd .05
444 Damon Buford .05
445 Jose Valentin .05
446 Jason Schmidt .05
447 Dave Martinez .05
448 Danny Tartabull .05
449 Jose Vizcaino .05
450 Steve Avery .05
451 Mike Devereaux .05
452 Jim Eisenreich .05
453 Mark Leiter .05
454 Roberto Kelly .05
455 Benito Santiago .05
456 Steve Trachsel .05
457 Gerald Williams .05
458 Pete Schourek .05
459 Esteban Loaiza .05
460 Mel Rojas .05
461 Tim Wakefield .05
462 Tony Fernandez .05
463 Doug Drabek .05
464 Joe Girardi .05
465 Mike Bordick .05
466 Jim Leyritz .05
467 Erik Hanson .05
468 Michael Tucker .05
469 Tony Womack **RC** .10
470 Doug Glanville .05
471 Rudy Pemberton .05
472 Keith Lockhart .05
473 Nomar Garciaparra .65
474 Scott Rolen .40
475 Jason Dickson .05
476 Glendon Rusch .05
477 Todd Walker .05
478 Dmitri Young .05
479 Rod Myers **RC** .05
480 Wilton Guerrero .05
481 Jorge Posada .05
482 Brant Brown .05
483 Bubba Trammell **RC** .10
484 Jose Guillen .05
485 Scott Spiezio .05
486 Bob Abreu .10
487 Chris Holt .05
488 Deivi Cruz **RC** .15
489 Vladimir Guerrero .50
490 Julio Santana .05
491 Ray Montgomery .05
492 Kevin Orie .05
493 Todd Hundley (Goin' Yard) .05
494 Tim Salmon (Goin' Yard) .05
495 Albert Belle (Goin' Yard) .05
496 Manny Ramirez (Goin' Yard) .25
497 Rafael Palmeiro (Goin' Yard) .20
498 Juan Gonzalez (Goin' Yard) .15
499 Ken Griffey Jr. (Goin' Yard) .40
500 Andruw Jones (Goin' Yard) .25
501 Mike Piazza (Goin' Yard) .40
502 Jeff Bagwell (Goin' Yard) .25
503 Bernie Williams (Goin' Yard) .05
504 Barry Bonds (Goin' Yard) .65
505 Ken Caminiti (Goin' Yard) .05
506 Darin Erstad (Goin' Yard) .10
507 Alex Rodriguez (Goin' Yard) .50
508 Frank Thomas (Goin' Yard) .30
509 Chipper Jones (Goin' Yard) .35
510 Mo Vaughn (Goin' Yard) .05
511 Mark McGwire (Goin' Yard) .50
512 Fred McGriff (Goin' Yard) .05
513 Jay Buhner (Goin' Yard) .05
514 Jim Thome (Goin' Yard) .20
515 Gary Sheffield (Goin' Yard) .20
516 Dean Palmer (Goin' Yard) .05
517 Henry Rodriguez (Goin' Yard) .05
518 Andy Pettitte (Rock & Fire) .10
519 Mike Mussina (Rock & Fire) .10
520 Greg Maddux (Rock & Fire) .35
521 John Smoltz (Rock & Fire) .05
522 Hideo Nomo (Rock & Fire) .15
523 Troy Percival (Rock & Fire) .05
524 John Wetteland (Rock & Fire) .05
525 Roger Clemens (Rock & Fire) .40
526 Charles Nagy (Rock & Fire) .05
527 Mariano Rivera (Rock & Fire) .10
528 Tom Glavine (Rock & Fire) .15
529 Randy Johnson (Rock & Fire) .25
530 Jason Isringhausen (Rock & Fire) .05
531 Alex Fernandez (Rock & Fire) .05
532 Kevin Brown (Rock & Fire) .05
533 Chuck Knoblauch (True Grit) .05
534 Rusty Greer (True Grit) .05
535 Tony Gwynn (True Grit) .35
536 Ryan Klesko (True Grit) .05
537 Ryne Sandberg (True Grit) .35
538 Barry Larkin (True Grit) .05
539 Will Clark (True Grit) .05
540 Kenny Lofton (True Grit) .05
541 Paul Molitor (True Grit) .30
542 Roberto Alomar (True Grit) .10
543 Rey Ordonez (True Grit) .05
544 Jason Giambi (True Grit) .25
545 Derek Jeter (True Grit) .75
546 Cal Ripken Jr. (True Grit) .75
547 Ivan Rodriguez (True Grit) .25
548 Checklist (Ken Griffey Jr.) .35
549 Checklist (Frank Thomas) .25
550 Checklist (Mike Piazza) .40
551a Hideki Irabu/SP **RC** (English on back; factory sets/ retailpacks.) .25
551b Hideki Irabu/SP **RC** (Japanese back; Hobby Reserve packs.) .35

White Border Artist's Proofs

Specially marked Artist's Proof cards were random inserts in Series 1 retail packs. Like the regular-issue cards, they have white borders, so the gold-foil "ARTIST'S PROOF" logo on front may be overlooked. Only Series 1 (#1-330) are found in this style.

	NM/M
Complete Set (330):	150.00
Common Player:	.50
Artist's Proof Stars:	10X

Hobby Reserve

This is a hobby-only parallel version of Score Series 2, similar in concept to the Series 1 Premium Stock. Cards are identical to the regular Series 2 cards except for the addition of a gold Hobby Reserve foil seal on front.

	NM/M
Complete Set (221):	35.00
Common Player:	.10
Hobby Reserve Stars:	3X

Premium Stock

This is an upscale version of Score's regular Series 1 1997 issue, designated for hobby sales only. The cards are basically the same as the regular issue, except for the use of gray borders on front and an embossed gold-foil "Premium Stock" logo.

	NM/M
Complete Set (330):	17.50
Common Player:	.10
Premium Stock Stars:	3X

Reserve Collection

This was a hobby-only parallel version of Score Series 2, Cards are similar to regular Series 2 Score except for the use of a textured ray-like silver-foil background on front and a Reserve Collection underprint on back. Cards are numbered with an "HR" prefix. Average insertion rate was one per 11 packs.

	NM/M
Complete Set (221):	250.00
Common Player:	1.00
Reserve Collection Stars:	8X

Showcase

A silver metallic-foil background distinguishes the cards in this parallel set, inserted at a rate of about one per seven packs of both hobby and retail.

	NM/M
Complete Set (551):	200.00
Common Player:	.50
Showcase Stars:	3X

Showcase Artist's Proofs

This is a parallel of the Showcase parallel set covering all 551 cards of the base '97 Score set. The Artist's Proofs cards carry over the silver foil background of the Showcase cards on front with a rainbow-wave effect, and are marked with a round red "ARTIST'S PROOF" logo.

	NM/M
Common Player:	1.00
Showcase AP Stars:	10X

All-Star Fanfest

Highlighted with red foil and featuring participants in the 1996 All-Star Game, these inserts were a 1:29 seed in special retail boxes of Series 1 Score.

	NM/M
Complete Set (20):	15.00
Common Player:	.30

1	Frank Thomas	1.00
2	Jeff Bagwell	1.00
3	Chuck Knoblauch	.30
4	Ryne Sandberg	1.50
5	Alex Rodriguez	3.00
6	Chipper Jones	1.50
7	Jim Thome	.75
8	Ken Caminiti	.30
9	Albert Belle	.30
10	Tony Gwynn	1.50
11	Ken Griffey Jr.	2.00
12	Andruw Jones	1.00
13	Juan Gonzalez	.50
14	Brian Jordan	.30
15	Ivan Rodriguez	.75
16	Mike Piazza	2.00
17	Andy Pettitte	.30
18	John Smoltz	.30
19	John Wetteland	.30
20	Mark Wohlers	.30

Blast Masters

This set was inserted one per 35 Series 2 retail packs and every 23 hobby packs. The set displays the top power hitters in the game over a prismatic gold foil background. The word "Blast" is printed across the top, while "Master" is printed across the bottom, both in red. Backs are predominantly black with a color player photo at center.

		NM/M
Complete Set (18):		17.50
Common Player:		.25
1	Mo Vaughn	.25
2	Mark McGwire	2.25
3	Juan Gonzalez	.75
4	Albert Belle	.25
5	Barry Bonds	3.00
6	Ken Griffey Jr.	2.00
7	Andruw Jones	1.25
8	Chipper Jones	1.50
9	Mike Piazza	2.00
10	Jeff Bagwell	1.25
11	Dante Bichette	.25
12	Alex Rodriguez	2.25
13	Gary Sheffield	.60
14	Ken Caminiti	.25
15	Sammy Sosa	1.50
16	Vladimir Guerrero	1.25
17	Brian Jordan	.25
18	Tim Salmon	.25

Heart of the Order

This 36-card set was distributed in Series 2 retail and hobby packs, with cards 1-18 in retail (one per 23 packs) and cards 19-36 in hobby (one per 15). The cards are printed in a horizontal format, with some of the top hitters in the game included in the insert. Fronts are highlighted in red metallic foil. Backs have a color portrait photo and a few words about the player.

		NM/M
Complete Set (36):		35.00
Complete Retail Set (1-18):		20.00
Complete Hobby Set (19-36):		15.00
Common Player:		.50
1	Ivan Rodriguez	1.00
2	Will Clark	.50
3	Juan Gonzalez	.75
4	Frank Thomas	1.25
5	Albert Belle	.50
6	Robin Ventura	.50
7	Alex Rodriguez	3.00
8	Ken Griffey Jr.	2.50
9	Jay Buhner	.50
10	Roberto Alomar	.65
11	Rafael Palmeiro	1.00
12	Cal Ripken Jr.	4.00
13	Manny Ramirez	1.25
14	Matt Williams	.50
15	Jim Thome	.50
16	Derek Jeter	4.00
17	Wade Boggs	2.00
18	Bernie Williams	.50
19	Chipper Jones	2.00
20	Andruw Jones	1.25
21	Ryan Klesko	.50
22	Wilton Guerrero	.50
23	Mike Piazza	2.50
24	Raul Mondesi	.50
25	Tony Gwynn	2.00
26	Ken Caminiti	.50
27	Greg Vaughn	.50
28	Brian Jordan	.50
29	Ron Gant	.50
30	Dmitri Young	.50
31	Darin Erstad	.50
32	Jim Edmonds	.50
33	Tim Salmon	.50
34	Chuck Knoblauch	.50
35	Paul Molitor	1.25
36	Todd Walker	.50

Highlight Zone

Exclusive to 1997 Score Series 1 hobby packs are these Highlight Zone inserts, seeded one per every 35 packs. Within the 18-card set, card numbers 1-9 are in regular hobby packs, while numbers 10-18 are found only in premium stock packs.

		NM/M
Complete Set (18):		30.00
Common Player:		.60
1	Frank Thomas	1.50
2	Ken Griffey Jr.	3.00
3	Mo Vaughn	.60
4	Albert Belle	.60
5	Mike Piazza	3.00
6	Barry Bonds	4.50
7	Greg Maddux	2.25
8	Sammy Sosa	2.25
9	Jeff Bagwell	1.50
10	Alex Rodriguez	3.50
11	Chipper Jones	2.25
12	Brady Anderson	.60
13	Ozzie Smith	2.25
14	Edgar Martinez	.60
15	Cal Ripken Jr.	4.50
16	Ryan Klesko	.60
17	Randy Johnson	1.50
18	Eddie Murray	1.50

Andruw Jones Goin' Yard

This special card was a blister-pack topper on Series 2 jumbo retail packs. Jones' home run swing is featured on front with a background of the distances of his blasts. Back has details on Series 2 inserts and the Stand and Deliver promotion.

	NM/M
Andruw Jones	2.50

Pitcher Perfect

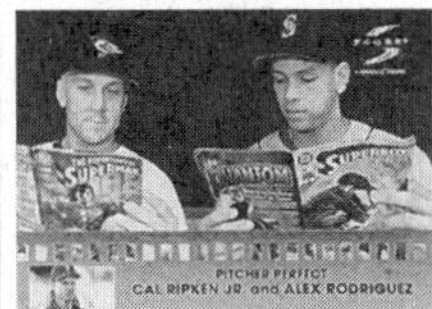

Seattle Mariners' star pitcher and accomplished photographer Randy Johnson makes his picks for the top talent in this 1997 Score Series 1 insert set. Fronts have player photos with a gold-foil filmstrip graphic at bottom featuring player names and a portrait of The Big Unit. Backs have additional color photos in a filmstrip design and a few words about the player.

		NM/M
Complete Set (15):		6.50
Common Player:		.15
1	Cal Ripken Jr.	2.00
2	Alex Rodriguez	1.25
3	Cal Ripken Jr., Alex Rodriguez	1.25
4	Edgar Martinez	.15
5	Ivan Rodriguez	.50
6	Mark McGwire	1.25
7	Tim Salmon	.15
8	Chili Davis	.15
9	Joe Carter	.15
10	Frank Thomas	.60
11	Will Clark	.15
12	Mo Vaughn	.15
13	Wade Boggs	.75
14	Ken Griffey Jr.	1.00
15	Randy Johnson	.60

Stand & Deliver

This 24-card insert was printed on a silver foil background, with the series name and team logo in gold foil across the bottom. Cards were found in Series 2 packs at the rate of one per 71 retail, one per 41 hobby. Card numbers 21-24 (Wild Card) were the winning group in a World Series contest, allowing the first 225 collectors that mailed in those four cards to receive a gold upgrade version of the set framed in glass. The gold cards have a gold foil background and red foil highlights.

		NM/M
Complete Set (24):		50.00
Common Player:		.50
Gold:		4X
1	Andruw Jones	3.00
2	Greg Maddux	4.00
3	Chipper Jones	4.00
4	John Smoltz	.50
5	Ken Griffey Jr.	5.00
6	Alex Rodriguez	6.00
7	Jay Buhner	.50
8	Randy Johnson	3.00
9	Derek Jeter	7.50
10	Andy Pettitte	.75
11	Bernie Williams	.50
12	Mariano Rivera	.50
13	Mike Piazza	5.00
14	Hideo Nomo	1.50
15	Raul Mondesi	.50
16	Todd Hollandsworth	.50
17	Manny Ramirez	3.00
18	Jim Thome	2.00
19	David Justice	.50
20	Matt Williams	.50
21	Juan Gonzalez	1.50
22	Jeff Bagwell	3.00
23	Cal Ripken Jr.	7.50
24	Frank Thomas	3.00

Stellar Season

These 1997 Score Series 1 inserts were seeded one per every 17 magazine packs.

		NM/M
Complete Set (18):		15.00
Common Player:		.50
1	Juan Gonzalez	.75
2	Chuck Knoblauch	.50
3	Jeff Bagwell	1.50
4	John Smoltz	.50
5	Mark McGwire	3.00
6	Ken Griffey Jr.	2.50
7	Frank Thomas	1.50
8	Alex Rodriguez	3.00
9	Mike Piazza	2.50
10	Albert Belle	.50
11	Roberto Alomar	.60
12	Sammy Sosa	2.00
13	Mo Vaughn	.50
14	Brady Anderson	.50
15	Henry Rodriguez	.50
16	Eric Young	.50
17	Gary Sheffield	.75
18	Ryan Klesko	.50

The Franchise

There were two versions made for these 1997 Score Series 1 inserts - regular and The Glowing Franchise, which has glow-in-the-dark highlights. The regular version is seeded one per 72 packs; glow-in-the-dark cards are seeded one per 240 packs. Each regular card can also be found in a promo version with a large, black "SAMPLE" on front and back.

		NM/M
Complete Set (9):		5.00
Common Player:		.15
Glowing:		2.5X
Samples:		2.5X
1	Ken Griffey Jr.	1.00
2	John Smoltz	.15
3	Cal Ripken Jr.	2.00
4	Chipper Jones	.75
5	Mike Piazza	1.00
6	Albert Belle	.15
7	Frank Thomas	.60
8	Sammy Sosa	.75
9	Roberto Alomar	.30

Titanic Taters

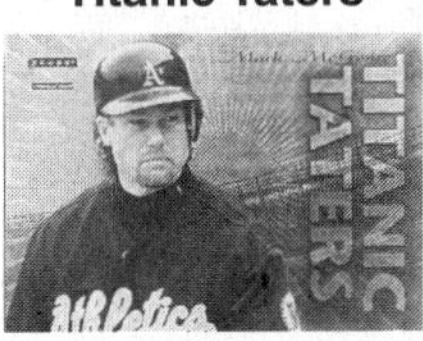

Some of the game's most powerful hitters are featured on these Series 1 inserts, found on average of one per 35 retail packs.

		NM/M
Complete Set (18):		25.00
Common Player:		.35
1	Mark McGwire	4.00
2	Mike Piazza	3.50
3	Ken Griffey Jr.	3.50
4	Juan Gonzalez	1.00
5	Frank Thomas	1.50
6	Albert Belle	.35
7	Sammy Sosa	2.50
8	Jeff Bagwell	1.50
9	Todd Hundley	.35
10	Ryan Klesko	.35
11	Brady Anderson	.35
12	Mo Vaughn	.35
13	Jay Buhner	.35
14	Chipper Jones	2.75
15	Barry Bonds	6.00
16	Gary Sheffield	.75
17	Alex Rodriguez	4.00
18	Cecil Fielder	.35

Team Collection

Team sets consisting of 15 players each were produced for 10 different teams. Each card is similar in design to the regular 1997 Score set except for a special foil stamping at the bottom of the card that corresponds with team colors. In a parallel "Platinum" version, seeded one per six packs, the background and team foil on front are replaced with silver prismatic foil. A top of the line parallel set, "Premier" utilizes gold foil highlights on fronts and is found one per 31 packs. Team Collection was sold in five-card, single-team packs with a suggested retail price of about $1.29. It was reported that 100 cases of each team were issued.

		NM/M
Complete Set (150):		30.00
Common Player:		.10
Platinums:		4X
Premiers:		15X
Braves Wax Box:		7.50
Orioles Wax Box:		6.00
Red Sox Wax Box:		6.00
White Sox Wax Box:		6.00
Indians Wax Box:		6.00
Rockies Wax Box:		5.00
Dodgers Wax Box:		6.00
Yankees Wax Box:		7.50
Mariners Wax Box:		7.50
Rangers Wax Box:		5.00
Atlanta Braves		5.00
1	Ryan Klesko	.10
2	David Justice	.10
3	Terry Pendleton	.10
4	Tom Glavine	.35
5	Javier Lopez	.10
6	John Smoltz	.10
7	Jermaine Dye	.10
8	Mark Lemke	.10
9	Fred McGriff	.10
10	Chipper Jones	1.50
11	Terrell Wade	.10
12	Greg Maddux	1.50
13	Mark Wohlers	.10
14	Marquis Grissom	.10
15	Andruw Jones	1.00
Baltimore Orioles		4.50
1	Rafael Palmeiro	.75
2	Eddie Murray	1.00
3	Roberto Alomar	.40
4	Rocky Coppinger	.10
5	Brady Anderson	.10
6	Bobby Bonilla	.10
7	Cal Ripken Jr.	2.50
8	Mike Mussina	.45
9	Nerio Rodriguez	.10
10	Randy Myers	.10
11	B.J. Surhoff	.10
12	Jeffrey Hammonds	.10
13	Chris Hoiles	.10
14	Jimmy Haynes	.10
15	David Wells	.10
Boston Red Sox		3.00
1	Wil Cordero	.10
2	Mo Vaughn	.10
3	John Valentin	.10
4	Reggie Jefferson	.10
5	Tom Gordon	.10
6	Mike Stanley	.10
7	Jose Canseco	.45
8	Roger Clemens	1.75
9	Darren Bragg	.10
10	Jeff Frye	.10
11	Jeff Suppan	.10
12	Mike Greenwell	.10
13	Arquimedez Pozo	.10
14	Tim Naehring	.10
15	Troy O'Leary	.10
Chicago White Sox		2.25
1	Frank Thomas	1.00
2	James Baldwin	.10
3	Danny Tartabull	.10
4	Jeff Darwin	.10
5	Harold Baines	.10
6	Roberto Hernandez	.10
7	Ray Durham	.10
8	Robin Ventura	.10
9	Wilson Alvarez	.10
10	Lyle Mouton	.10
11	Alex Fernandez	.10
12	Ron Karkovice	.10
13	Kevin Tapani	.10
14	Tony Phillips	.10
15	Mike Cameron	.10
Cleveland Indians		2.25
1	Albert Belle	.10
2	Jack McDowell	.10
3	Jim Thome	.75
4	Dennis Martinez	.10
5	Julio Franco	.10
6	Omar Vizquel	.10
7	Kenny Lofton	.10
8	Manny Ramirez	1.00
9	Sandy Alomar Jr.	.10
10	Charles Nagy	.10
11	Kevin Seitzer	.10
12	Mark Carreon	.10
13	Jeff Kent	.10
14	Danny Graves	.10
15	Brian Giles	.10
Colorado Rockies		1.75
1	Dante Bichette	.10
2	Kevin Ritz	.10
3	Walt Weiss	.10
4	Ellis Burks	.10
5	Jamey Wright	.10
6	Andres Galarraga	.10
7	Eric Young	.10
8	Larry Walker	.10
9	Vinny Castilla	.10
10	Quinton McCracken	.10
11	Armando Reynoso	.10
12	Jayhawk Owens	.10
13	Mark Thompson	.10
14	John Burke	.10
15	Bruce Ruffin	.10
Los Angeles Dodgers		4.00
1	Ismael Valdez	.10
2	Mike Piazza	2.00
3	Todd Hollandsworth	.10
4	Delino DeShields	.10
5	Chan Ho Park	.10
6	Roger Cedeno	.10
7	Raul Mondesi	.10
8	Darren Dreifort	.10
9	Jim Bruske	.10
10	Greg Gagne	.10
11	Chad Curtis	.10
12	Ramon Martinez	.10
13	Brett Butler	.10
14	Eric Karros	.10
15	Hideo Nomo	.50
New York Yankees		4.50
1	Bernie Williams	.10
2	Cecil Fielder	.10
3	Derek Jeter	2.50
4	Darryl Strawberry	.10
5	Andy Pettitte	.20
6	Ruben Rivera	.10
7	Mariano Rivera	.15
8	John Wetteland	.10
9	Paul O'Neill	.10
10	Wade Boggs	1.50
11	Dwight Gooden	.10
12	David Cone	.10
13	Tino Martinez	.10
14	Kenny Rogers	.10
15	Andy Fox	.10
Seattle Mariners		5.00
1	Chris Bosio	.10
2	Edgar Martinez	.10
3	Alex Rodriguez	2.25
4	Paul Sorrento	.10
5	Bob Wells	.10
6	Ken Griffey Jr.	2.00
7	Jay Buhner	.10
8	Dan Wilson	.10
9	Randy Johnson	1.00
10	Joey Cora	.10
11	Mark Whiten	.10
12	Rich Amaral	.10
13	Raul Ibanez	.10
14	Jamie Moyer	.10
15	Makoto Suzuki	.10
Texas Rangers		2.25
1	Mickey Tettleton	.10
2	Will Clark	.10
3	Ken Hill	.10
4	Rusty Greer	.10
5	Kevin Elster	.10
6	Darren Oliver	.10
7	Mark McLemore	.10
8	Roger Pavlik	.10
9	Dean Palmer	.10
10	Bobby Witt	.10
11	Juan Gonzalez	.50
12	Ivan Rodriguez	.75
13	Darryl Hamilton	.10
14	John Burkett	.10
15	Warren Newson	.10

Team Collection Platinum Team

Team sets consisting of 15 players each were produced for 10 different teams. Each card is similar in design to the regular 1997 Score set except for a special foil stamping at the bottom of the card that corresponds with team colors. In a parallel "Platinum" version, seeded one per six packs, the background and team foil on front are replaced with silver prismatic foil. Backs are overprinted in gold script, "Platinum Team." Team Collection was sold in five-card, single-team packs with a suggested retail price of about $1.29. It was reported that 100 cases of each team were issued.

	NM/M
Common Player:	2.00
Platinum Stars:	3X

Team Collection Premier Club

Team sets consisting of 15 players each were produced for 10 different teams. Each card is similar in design to the regular 1997 Score set except for a special foil stamping at the bottom of the card that corresponds with team colors. In a top of the line parallel "Premier Club" version, seeded one per 31 packs, the background and team foil on front are replaced with gold prismatic foil, and backs are overprinted "Premier Club" in gold script. Team Collection was sold in five-card, single-team packs with a suggested retail price of about $1.29. It was reported that 100 cases of each team were issued.

	NM/M
Common Player:	5.00
Premier Club Stars:	15X

1998 Score Samples

Half a dozen top stars were picked to introduce 1998 Score in this series of promo cards. Cards are virtually identical to the issued version except for the large black overprinted "SAMPLE" on back and the use of zeroes to replace 1997 stats.

		NM/M
Complete Set (6):		7.50
Common Player:		1.00
10	Alex Rodriguez	1.50
24	Mike Piazza	1.50
34	Ken Griffey Jr.	1.50
43	Cal Ripken Jr.	2.00
51	Chipper Jones	1.25
60	Carlos Delgado	1.00

1998 Score

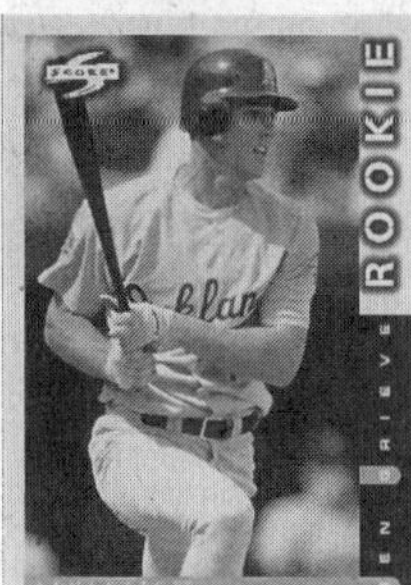

The cards in the 270-card base set feature a color photo inside a black and white border. The player's name is printed in the left border. The entire base set is paralleled in the silver-foil Showcase Series (1:5). The Artist's Proof partial parallel gives a prismatic foil treatment to 165 base cards and was seeded 1:23. Inserts included All-Stars, Complete Players and Epix.

		NM/M
Complete Set (270):		12.00
Common Player:		.05
Showcases:		3X
Artist's Proofs:		6X
Pack (10):		.75
Wax Box (36):		15.00
All-Star Edition Box (36/10):		10.00
Jumbo Pack (20):		1.00
Jumbo Box (24):		15.00
1	Andruw Jones	.50
2	Dan Wilson	.05
3	Hideo Nomo	.30
4	Chuck Carr	.05
5	Barry Bonds	1.50
6	Jack McDowell	.05
7	Albert Belle	.05
8	Francisco Cordova	.05
9	Greg Maddux	.65
10	Alex Rodriguez	1.00
11	Steve Avery	.05
12	Chuck McElroy	.05
13	Larry Walker	.05
14	Hideki Irabu	.05
15	Roberto Alomar	.20
16	Neifi Perez	.05
17	Jim Thome	.40
18	Rickey Henderson	.50
19	Andres Galarraga	.05
20	Jeff Fassero	.05
21	Kevin Young	.05
22	Derek Jeter	1.50
23	Andy Benes	.05
24	Mike Piazza	.75
25	Todd Stottlemyre	.05
26	Michael Tucker	.05
27	Denny Neagle	.05
28	Javier Lopez	.05
29	Aaron Sele	.05
30	Ryan Klesko	.05
31	Dennis Eckersley	.40
32	Quinton McCracken	.05
33	Brian Anderson	.05
34	Ken Griffey Jr.	.75
35	Shawn Estes	.05
36	Tim Wakefield	.05
37	Jimmy Key	.05
38	Jeff Bagwell	.50
39	Edgardo Alfonzo	.05
40	Mike Cameron	.05
41	Mark McGwire	1.00
42	Tino Martinez	.05
43	Cal Ripken Jr.	1.50
44	Curtis Goodwin	.05
45	Bobby Ayala	.05
46	Sandy Alomar Jr.	.05
47	Bobby Jones	.05
48	Omar Vizquel	.05
49	Roger Clemens	.70
50	Tony Gwynn	.65
51	Chipper Jones	.65
52	Ron Coomer	.05
53	Dmitri Young	.05
54	Brian Giles	.05
55	Steve Finley	.05
56	David Cone	.05
57	Andy Pettitte	.20
58	Wilton Guerrero	.05
59	Deion Sanders	.05
60	Carlos Delgado	.30
61	Jason Giambi	.30
62	Ozzie Guillen	.05
63	Jay Bell	.05
64	Barry Larkin	.05
65	Sammy Sosa	.65
66	Bernie Williams	.05
67	Terry Steinbach	.05
68	Scott Rolen	.40
69	Melvin Nieves	.05
70	Craig Biggio	.05
71	Todd Greene	.05
72	Greg Gagne	.05
73	Shigetosi Hasegawa	.05
74	Mark McLemore	.05
75	Darren Bragg	.05
76	Brett Butler	.05
77	Ron Gant	.05
78	Mike Difelice	.05
79	Charles Nagy	.05
80	Scott Hatteberg	.05
81	Brady Anderson	.05
82	Jay Buhner	.05
83	Todd Hollandsworth	.05
84	Geronimo Berroa	.05
85	Jeff Suppan	.05
86	Pedro Martinez	.50
87	Roger Cedeno	.05
88	Ivan Rodriguez	.40
89	Jaime Navarro	.05
90	Chris Hoiles	.05
91	Nomar Garciaparra	.65
92	Rafael Palmeiro	.40
93	Darin Erstad	.15
94	Kenny Lofton	.05
95	Mike Timlin	.05
96	Chris Clemons	.05
97	Vinny Castilla	.05
98	Charlie Hayes	.05
99	Lyle Mouton	.05
100	Jason Dickson	.05
101	Justin Thompson	.05
102	Pat Kelly	.05
103	Chan Ho Park	.05
104	Ray Lankford	.05
105	Frank Thomas	.50
106	Jermaine Allensworth	.05
107	Doug Drabek	.05
108	Todd Hundley	.05
109	Carl Everett	.05
110	Edgar Martinez	.05
111	Robin Ventura	.05
112	John Wetteland	.05
113	Mariano Rivera	.10
114	Jose Rosado	.05
115	Ken Caminiti	.05
116	Paul O'Neill	.05
117	Tim Salmon	.05
118	Eduardo Perez	.05
119	Mike Jackson	.05
120	John Smoltz	.05
121	Brant Brown	.05
122	John Mabry	.05
123	Chuck Knoblauch	.05
124	Reggie Sanders	.05
125	Ken Hill	.05
126	Mike Mussina	.25
127	Chad Curtis	.05
128	Todd Worrell	.05
129	Chris Widger	.05
130	Damon Mashore	.05
131	Kevin Brown	.05
132	Bip Roberts	.05
133	Tim Naehring	.05
134	Dave Martinez	.05
135	Jeff Blauser	.05
136	David Justice	.05
137	Dave Hollins	.05
138	Pat Hentgen	.05
139	Darren Daulton	.05
140	Ramon Martinez	.05
141	Raul Casanova	.05
142	Tom Glavine	.30
143	J.T. Snow	.05
144	Tony Graffanino	.05
145	Randy Johnson	.50
146	Orlando Merced	.05
147	Jeff Juden	.05
148	Darryl Kile	.05
149	Ray Durham	.05
150	Alex Fernandez	.05
151	Joey Cora	.05
152	Royce Clayton	.05
153	Randy Myers	.05
154	Charles Johnson	.05
155	Alan Benes	.05
156	Mike Bordick	.05
157	Heathcliff Slocumb	.05
158	Roger Bailey	.05
159	Reggie Jefferson	.05
160	Ricky Bottalico	.05
161	Scott Erickson	.05
162	Matt Williams	.05
163	Robb Nen	.05
164	Matt Stairs	.05
165	Ismael Valdes	.05
166	Lee Stevens	.05
167	Gary DiSarcina	.05
168	Brad Radke	.05
169	Mike Lansing	.05
170	Armando Benitez	.05
171	Mike James	.05
172	Russ Davis	.05
173	Lance Johnson	.05
174	Joey Hamilton	.05
175	John Valentin	.05
176	David Segui	.05
177	David Wells	.05
178	Delino DeShields	.05
179	Eric Karros	.05
180	Jim Leyritz	.05
181	Raul Mondesi	.05
182	Travis Fryman	.05
183	Todd Zeile	.05
184	Brian Jordan	.05
185	Rey Ordonez	.05
186	Jim Edmonds	.05
187	Terrell Wade	.05
188	Marquis Grissom	.05
189	Chris Snopek	.05
190	Shane Reynolds	.05
191	Jeff Frye	.05
192	Paul Sorrento	.05
193	James Baldwin	.05
194	Brian McRae	.05
195	Fred McGriff	.05
196	Troy Percival	.05
197	Rich Amaral	.05
198	Juan Guzman	.05
199	Cecil Fielder	.05
200	Willie Blair	.05
201	Chili Davis	.05
202	Gary Gaetti	.05
203	B.J. Surhoff	.05
204	Steve Cooke	.05
205	Chuck Finley	.05
206	Jeff Kent	.05
207	Ben McDonald	.05
208	Jeffrey Hammonds	.05
209	Tom Goodwin	.05
210	Billy Ashley	.05
211	Wil Cordero	.05
212	Shawon Dunston	.05
213	Tony Phillips	.05
214	Jamie Moyer	.05
215	John Jaha	.05
216	Troy O'Leary	.05
217	Brad Ausmus	.05
218	Garret Anderson	.05
219	Wilson Alvarez	.05
220	Kent Mercker	.05
221	Wade Boggs	.65
222	Mark Wohlers	.05
223	Kevin Appier	.05
224	Tony Fernandez	.05
225	Ugueth Urbina	.05
226	Gregg Jefferies	.05
227	Mo Vaughn	.05
228	Arthur Rhodes	.05
229	Jorge Fabregas	.05
230	Mark Gardner	.05
231	Shane Mack	.05
232	Jorge Posada	.05
233	Jose Cruz Jr.	.05
234	Paul Konerko	.15
235	Derrek Lee	.30
236	Steve Woodard **RC**	.15
237	Todd Dunwoody	.05
238	Fernando Tatis	.05
239	Jacob Cruz	.05
240	Pokey Reese **RC**	.25
241	Mark Kotsay	.05
242	Matt Morris	.05
243	Antone Williamson **RC**	.05
244	Ben Grieve	.05
245	Ryan McGuire	.05
246	Lou Collier **RC**	.05
247	Shannon Stewart	.05
248	Brett Tomko **RC**	.10
249	Bobby Estalella	.05
250	Livan Hernandez **RC**	.15
251	Todd Helton	.40
252	Jaret Wright	.05
253	Darryl Hamilton (Interleague Moments)	.05
254	Stan Javier (Interleague Moments)	.05
255	Glenallen Hill (Interleague Moments)	.05
256	Mark Gardner (Interleague Moments)	.05
257	Cal Ripken Jr. (Interleague Moments)	.75
258	Mike Mussina (Interleague Moments)	.15
259	Mike Piazza (Interleague Moments)	.45
260	Sammy Sosa (Interleague Moments)	.35
261	Todd Hundley (Interleague Moments)	.05
262	Eric Karros (Interleague Moments)	.05
263	Denny Neagle (Interleague Moments)	.05
264	Jeromy Burnitz (Interleague Moments)	.05
265	Greg Maddux (Interleague Moments)	.35
266	Tony Clark (Interleague Moments)	.05
267	Vladimir Guerrero (Interleague Moments)	.25
268	Checklist	.05
269	Checklist	.05
270	Checklist	.05

Artist's Proofs

This partial parallel reprinted 160 of the 270 cards in Score Baseball on a foil background with an Artist's Proof logo on the front. The cards were renumbered within the 160-card set and inserted one per 35 packs. Cards have a "PP" prefix to the number on back.

		NM/M
Complete Set (160):		125.00
Common Player:		.50
Inserted 1:35		
1	Andruw Jones	1.25
2	Dan Wilson	.50
3	Hideo Nomo	.75
4	Neifi Perez	.50
5	Jim Thome	1.00
6	Jeff Fassero	.50
7	Derek Jeter	4.00
8	Andy Benes	.50
9	Michael Tucker	.50
10	Ryan Klesko	.50
11	Dennis Eckersley	1.00
12	Jimmy Key	.50
13	Edgardo Alfonzo	.50
14	Mike Cameron	.50
15	Omar Vizquel	.50
16	Ron Coomer	.50
17	Dmitri Young	.50
18	Brian Giles	.50
19	Steve Finley	.50
20	Andy Pettitte	.75
21	Wilton Guerrero	.50
22	Deion Sanders	.50
23	Carlos Delgado	.75
24	Jason Giambi	.75
25	David Cone	.50
26	Jay Bell	.50
27	Sammy Sosa	2.00
28	Barry Larkin	.50
29	Scott Rolen	1.00
30	Todd Greene	.50
31	Bernie Williams	.50
32	Brett Butler	.50
33	Ron Gant	.50
34	Brady Anderson	.50
35	Craig Biggio	.50
36	Charles Nagy	.50
37	Jay Buhner	.50
38	Geronimo Berroa	.50
39	Jeff Suppan	.50
40	Rafael Palmeiro	1.00
41	Darin Erstad	.65
42	Mike Timlin	.50
43	Vinny Castilla	.50
44	Carl Everett	.50
45	Robin Ventura	.50
46	John Wetteland	.50
47	Paul O'Neill	.50
48	Tim Salmon	.50
49	Mike Jackson	.50
50	John Smoltz	.50
51	Brant Brown	.50
52	Reggie Sanders	.50
53	Ken Hill	.50
54	Todd Worrell	.50
55	Bip Roberts	.50
56	Tim Naehring	.50
57	Darren Daulton	.50
58	Ramon Martinez	.50
59	Raul Casanova	.50
60	J.T. Snow	.50
61	Jeff Juden	.50
62	Royce Clayton	.50
63	Charles Johnson	.50
64	Alan Benes	.50
65	Reggie Jefferson	.50
66	Ricky Bottalico	.50
67	Scott Erickson	.50
68	Matt Williams	.50
69	Robb Nen	.50
70	Matt Stairs	.50
71	Ismael Valdes	.50
72	Brad Radke	.50
73	Armando Benitez	.50
74	Russ Davis	.50
75	Lance Johnson	.50
76	Joey Hamilton	.50
77	John Valentin	.50
78	David Segui	.50
79	David Wells	.50
80	Eric Karros	.50
81	Raul Mondesi	.50
82	Travis Fryman	.50
83	Todd Zeile	.50
84	Brian Jordan	.50
85	Rey Ordonez	.50
86	Jim Edmonds	.50
87	Marquis Grissom	.50
88	Shane Reynolds	.50
89	Paul Sorrento	.50
90	Brian McRae	.50
91	Fred McGriff	.50
92	Troy Percival	.50
93	Juan Guzman	.50
94	Cecil Fielder	.50
95	Chili Davis	.50
96	B.J. Surhoff	.50
97	Chuck Finley	.50
98	Jeff Kent	.50
99	Ben McDonald	.50
100	Jeffrey Hammonds	.50
101	Tom Goodwin	.50
102	Wil Cordero	.50
103	Tony Phillips	.50
104	John Jaha	.50
105	Garret Anderson	.50
106	Wilson Alvarez	.50
107	Wade Boggs	2.00
108	Mark Wohlers	.50
109	Kevin Appier	.50
110	Mo Vaughn	.50
111	Ray Durham	.50
112	Alex Fernandez	.50
113	Barry Bonds	4.00
114	Albert Belle	.50
115	Greg Maddux	2.00
116	Alex Rodriguez	3.00
117	Larry Walker	.50
118	Roberto Alomar	.60
119	Andres Galarraga	.50
120	Mike Piazza	2.50
121	Denny Neagle	.50
122	Javier Lopez	.50
123	Ken Griffey Jr.	2.50
124	Shawn Estes	.50
125	Jeff Bagwell	1.25
126	Mark McGwire	3.00
127	Tino Martinez	.50
128	Cal Ripken Jr.	4.00
129	Sandy Alomar Jr.	.50
130	Bobby Jones	.50
131	Roger Clemens	2.25
132	Tony Gwynn	2.00
133	Chipper Jones	2.00
134	Orlando Merced	.50
135	Todd Stottlemyre	.50
136	Delino DeShields	.50
137	Pedro Martinez	1.25
138	Ivan Rodriguez	1.00
139	Nomar Garciaparra	2.00
140	Kenny Lofton	.50
141	Jason Dickson	.50
142	Justin Thompson	.50
143	Ray Lankford	.50
144	Frank Thomas	1.25
145	Todd Hundley	.50
146	Edgar Martinez	.50
147	Mariano Rivera	.50
148	Jose Rosado	.50
149	Ken Caminiti	.50
150	Chuck Knoblauch	.50
151	Mike Mussina	.65
152	Kevin Brown	.50
153	Jeff Blauser	.50
154	David Justice	.50
155	Pat Hentgen	.50
156	Tom Glavine	.65
157	Randy Johnson	1.25
158	Darryl Kile	.50
159	Joey Cora	.50
160	Randy Myers	.50

Showcase Series

This partial parallel reprinted 160 of the 270 cards in Score Baseball on silver foil. They were marked on the back and renumbered within the 160-card set. Showcase parallels were inserted one per seven packs. All Showcase Series cards except #1 have a "PP" prefix to the number.

		NM/M
Complete Set (160):		40.00
Common Player:		.25
Inserted 1:7		
1	Andruw Jones	.75
2	Dan Wilson	.25
3	Hideo Nomo	.40
4	Neifi Perez	.25
5	Jim Thome	.60
6	Jeff Fassero	.25
7	Derek Jeter	2.00
8	Andy Benes	.25
9	Michael Tucker	.25
10	Ryan Klesko	.25
11	Dennis Eckersley	.65
12	Jimmy Key	.25
13	Edgardo Alfonzo	.25
14	Mike Cameron	.25
15	Omar Vizquel	.25
16	Ron Coomer	.25
17	Dmitri Young	.25
18	Brian Giles	.25
19	Steve Finley	.25
20	Andy Pettitte	.40
21	Wilton Guerrero	.25
22	Deion Sanders	.25
23	Carlos Delgado	.50
24	Jason Giambi	.50
25	David Cone	.25
26	Jay Bell	.25
27	Sammy Sosa	1.00
28	Barry Larkin	.25
29	Scott Rolen	.60
30	Todd Greene	.25
31	Bernie Williams	.25
32	Brett Butler	.25
33	Ron Gant	.25
34	Brady Anderson	.25
35	Craig Biggio	.25
36	Charles Nagy	.25
37	Jay Buhner	.25
38	Geronimo Berroa	.25
39	Jeff Suppan	.25
40	Rafael Palmeiro	.65
41	Darin Erstad	.35
42	Mike Timlin	.25
43	Vinny Castilla	.25
44	Carl Everett	.25
45	Robin Ventura	.25
46	John Wetteland	.25
47	Paul O'Neill	.25
48	Tim Salmon	.25
49	Mike Jackson	.25
50	John Smoltz	.25
51	Brant Brown	.25
52	Reggie Sanders	.25
53	Ken Hill	.25
54	Todd Worrell	.25
55	Bip Roberts	.25
56	Tim Naehring	.25
57	Darren Daulton	.25
58	Ramon Martinez	.25
59	Raul Casanova	.25
60	J.T. Snow	.25
61	Jeff Juden	.25
62	Royce Clayton	.25
63	Charles Johnson	.25
64	Alan Benes	.25
65	Reggie Jefferson	.25
66	Ricky Bottalico	.25
67	Scott Erickson	.25
68	Matt Williams	.25
69	Robb Nen	.25
70	Matt Stairs	.25
71	Ismael Valdes	.25
72	Brad Radke	.25
73	Armando Benitez	.25
74	Russ Davis	.25
75	Lance Johnson	.25
76	Joey Hamilton	.25
77	John Valentin	.25
78	David Segui	.25
79	David Wells	.25
80	Eric Karros	.25
81	Raul Mondesi	.25
82	Travis Fryman	.25
83	Todd Zeile	.25
84	Brian Jordan	.25
85	Rey Ordonez	.25
86	Jim Edmonds	.25
87	Marquis Grissom	.25
88	Shane Reynolds	.25
89	Paul Sorrento	.25
90	Brian McRae	.25
91	Fred McGriff	.25
92	Troy Percival	.25
93	Juan Guzman	.25
94	Cecil Fielder	.25
95	Chili Davis	.25
96	B.J. Surhoff	.25
97	Chuck Finley	.25
98	Jeff Kent	.25
99	Ben McDonald	.25
100	Jeffrey Hammonds	.25
101	Tom Goodwin	.25
102	Wil Cordero	.25
103	Tony Phillips	.25
104	John Jaha	.25
105	Garret Anderson	.25
106	Wilson Alvarez	.25
107	Wade Boggs	1.00
108	Mark Wohlers	.25
109	Kevin Appier	.25
110	Mo Vaughn	.25
111	Ray Durham	.25
112	Alex Fernandez	.25
113	Barry Bonds	2.00
114	Albert Belle	.25
115	Greg Maddux	1.00
116	Alex Rodriguez	1.50
117	Larry Walker	.25
118	Roberto Alomar	.35
119	Andres Galarraga	.25
120	Mike Piazza	1.25
121	Denny Neagle	.25
122	Javier Lopez	.25
123	Ken Griffey Jr.	1.25

124 Shawn Estes .25
125 Jeff Bagwell .75
126 Mark McGwire 1.50
127 Tino Martinez .25
128 Cal Ripken Jr. 2.00
129 Sandy Alomar Jr. .25
130 Bobby Jones .25
131 Roger Clemens 1.00
132 Tony Gwynn 1.00
133 Chipper Jones 1.00
134 Orlando Merced .25
135 Todd Stottlemyre .25
136 Delino DeShields .25
137 Pedro Martinez .75
138 Ivan Rodriguez .65
139 Nomar Garciaparra 1.00
140 Kenny Lofton .25
141 Jason Dickson .25
142 Justin Thompson .25
143 Ray Lankford .25
144 Frank Thomas .75
145 Todd Hundley .25
146 Edgar Martinez .25
147 Mariano Rivera .25
148 Jose Rosado .25
149 Ken Caminiti .25
150 Chuck Knoblauch .25
151 Mike Mussina .40
152 Kevin Brown .25
153 Jeff Blauser .25
154 David Justice .25
155 Pat Hentgen .25
156 Tom Glavine .40
157 Randy Johnson .75
158 Darryl Kile .25
159 Joey Cora .25
160 Randy Myers .25

All Score Team

For its 10th anniversary Score selected an all-star team and issued this insert set. Cards have player action photos on a silver-foil background with an anniversary logo at bottom. Backs have a portrait photo and a career summary. The cards were inserted one per 35 packs.

NM/M
Complete Set (20): 15.00
Common Player: .25
Inserted 1:35
1 Mike Piazza 1.50
2 Ivan Rodriguez .65
3 Frank Thomas .75
4 Mark McGwire 2.00
5 Ryne Sandberg 1.00
6 Roberto Alomar .35
7 Cal Ripken Jr. 2.50
8 Barry Larkin .25
9 Paul Molitor .75
10 Travis Fryman .25
11 Kirby Puckett 1.00
12 Tony Gwynn 1.00
13 Ken Griffey Jr. 1.50
14 Juan Gonzalez .45
15 Barry Bonds 2.50
16 Andruw Jones .75
17 Roger Clemens 1.25
18 Randy Johnson .75
19 Greg Maddux 1.00
20 Dennis Eckersley .65

All Score Team - Gold

The purpose for which this variation of the regular All Score Team insert was created will likely remain unknown. A small number of the Gold version have turned up in the hobby market since Score's bankruptcy in mid-1998. This apparently premium version differs from the issued silver version only in its use of gold metallic foil background on front.

NM/M
Complete Set (20): 115.00
Common Player: 2.00
1 Mike Piazza 10.00
2 Ivan Rodriguez 5.00
3 Frank Thomas 6.00
4 Mark McGwire 12.00
5 Ryne Sandberg 7.50
6 Roberto Alomar 2.50
7 Cal Ripken Jr. 15.00
8 Barry Larkin 2.00
9 Paul Molitor 6.00
10 Travis Fryman 2.00
11 Kirby Puckett 7.50
12 Tony Gwynn 7.50
13 Ken Griffey Jr. 10.00
14 Juan Gonzalez 3.00
15 Barry Bonds 15.00
16 Andruw Jones 6.00
17 Roger Clemens 8.00
18 Randy Johnson 6.00
19 Greg Maddux 7.50
20 Dennis Eckersley 5.00

All Score Team Andruw Jones Autograph

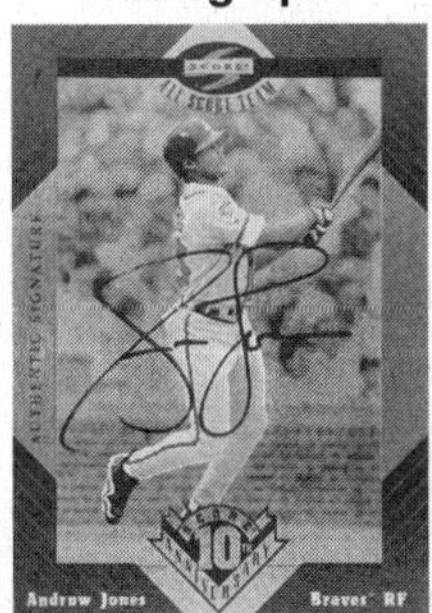

This special version of Jones' All Score Team was a prize in a random hobby-shop drawing. Instead of the silver foil seen on regular All Score Team inserts, this version has a gold-foil background and an "AUTHENTIC SIGNATURE" notation at right-center. Only 500 of the cards were produced.

NM/M
16 Andruw Jones 25.00

Complete Players

Complete Players is a 30-card insert featuring 10 players who can do it all. Each player had three cards displaying their variety of skills. The cards feature holographic foil highlights on fronts. Backs form a three-piece vertical picture of the player. The cards were inserted about one per 23 packs. Cards can be found with either gold or silver holographic foil. The gold version was found in packs of Score Team Collection at a 1:11 pack ratio. Because of these looser odds, the gold cards are valued lower than the silver.

NM/M
Complete Set (30): 75.00
Common Player: 1.00
Inserted 1:23
Golds: 75 Percent
1A Ken Griffey Jr. 3.25
1B Ken Griffey Jr. 3.25
1C Ken Griffey Jr. 3.25
2A Mark McGwire 3.75
2B Mark McGwire 3.75
2C Mark McGwire 3.75
3A Derek Jeter 5.00
3B Derek Jeter 5.00
3C Derek Jeter 5.00
4A Cal Ripken Jr. 5.00
4B Cal Ripken Jr. 5.00
4C Cal Ripken Jr. 5.00
5A Mike Piazza 3.25
5B Mike Piazza 3.25
5C Mike Piazza 3.25
6A Darin Erstad 1.00
6B Darin Erstad 1.00
6C Darin Erstad 1.00
7A Frank Thomas 2.00
7B Frank Thomas 2.00
7C Frank Thomas 2.00
8A Andruw Jones 2.00
8B Andruw Jones 2.00
8C Andruw Jones 2.00
9A Nomar Garciaparra 3.00
9B Nomar Garciaparra 3.00
9C Nomar Garciaparra 3.00
10A Manny Ramirez 2.00
10B Manny Ramirez 2.00
10C Manny Ramirez 2.00

Epix

Epix is a cross-brand insert, with 24 cards appearing in Score. The cards are printed on 20-point stock with holographic foil technology. The cards honor the top Play, Game, Season and Moment in a player's career and come in Orange, Purple and Emerald versions. Game cards were inserted 1:141, Plays 1:171, Seasons 1:437 and Moments 1:757.

NM/M
Common Card: .50
Purple: 2X
Emeralds: 3X
1 Ken Griffey Jr./P 2.50
2 Juan Gonzalez/P .75
3 Jeff Bagwell/P 1.25
4 Ivan Rodriguez/P 1.00
5 Nomar Garciaparra/P 2.00
6 Ryne Sandberg/P 1.50
7 Frank Thomas/G 1.25
8 Derek Jeter/G 3.50
9 Tony Gwynn/G 2.00
10 Albert Belle/G .50
11 Scott Rolen/G 1.00
12 Barry Larkin/G .50
13 Alex Rodriguez/S 6.00
14 Cal Ripken Jr./S 7.50
15 Chipper Jones/S 4.00
16 Roger Clemens/S 4.50
17 Mo Vaughn/S 1.50
18 Mark McGwire/S 6.00
19 Mike Piazza/M 8.00
20 Andruw Jones/M 4.00
21 Greg Maddux/M 6.00
22 Barry Bonds/M 12.00
23 Paul Molitor/M 4.00
24 Eddie Murray/M 4.00

First Pitch

These inserts were a 1:11 pack find in Score's All-Star edition. Fronts have portrait photos printed in the center of textured foil background of red and silver. The basic design is repeated on back, with career highlights and team logo instead of a photo.

NM/M
Complete Set (20): 25.00
Common Player: .50
Inserted 1:11 All-Star Edition.
1 Ken Griffey Jr. 2.00
2 Frank Thomas 1.25
3 Alex Rodriguez 2.50
4 Cal Ripken Jr. 3.25
5 Chipper Jones 1.50
6 Juan Gonzalez .75
7 Derek Jeter 3.25
8 Mike Piazza 2.00
9 Andruw Jones 1.25
10 Nomar Garciaparra 1.50
11 Barry Bonds 3.25
12 Jeff Bagwell 1.25
13 Scott Rolen 1.00
14 Hideo Nomo .75
15 Roger Clemens 1.75
16 Mark McGwire 2.50
17 Greg Maddux 1.50
18 Albert Belle .50
19 Ivan Rodriguez 1.00
20 Mo Vaughn .50

Andruw Jones Icon Order Card

This special card was the pack-topper on retail 27-card blister packs of 1998 Score. The front is identical to the regular Jones card in the set, but the back carries an ad for Pinnacle's Icon card display mail-in offer.

NM/M
Andruw Jones 2.50

Loaded Lineup

This insert series was packaged on average of one card per 45 packs of Score's All-Star edition. Fronts have action photos printed on a copper and silver textured metallic-foil background. Backs have a portrait photo, career highlights, the Loaded Lineup batting order and stats for the player's best season. Cards have an "LL" prefix to their number.

NM/M
Complete Set (10): 20.00
Common Player: .50
Inserted 1:45 All-Star Edition.
LL1 Chuck Knoblauch .50
LL2 Tony Gwynn 2.25
LL3 Frank Thomas 1.50
LL4 Ken Griffey Jr. 3.00
LL5 Mike Piazza 3.00
LL6 Barry Bonds 4.50
LL7 Cal Ripken Jr. 4.50
LL8 Paul Molitor 1.50
LL9 Nomar Garciaparra 2.25
LL10 Greg Maddux 2.25

New Season

Found only in Score All-Star Edition, at an average rate of one per 23 packs, this insert series mixes veteran stars with hot young players. Fronts have a large portrait photo. Horizontal backs have an action photo.

NM/M
Complete Set (15): 18.00
Common Player: .50
Inserted 1:23 All-Star Edition.
NS1 Kenny Lofton .50
NS2 Nomar Garciaparra 2.00
NS3 Todd Helton 1.00
NS4 Miguel Tejada .75
NS5 Jaret Wright .50
NS6 Alex Rodriguez 3.00
NS7 Vladimir Guerrero 1.25
NS8 Ken Griffey Jr. 2.50
NS9 Ben Grieve .50
NS10 Travis Lee .50
NS11 Jose Cruz Jr. .50
NS12 Paul Konerko .75
NS13 Frank Thomas 1.25
NS14 Chipper Jones 2.00
NS15 Cal Ripken Jr. 4.00

1998 Score Rookie & Traded

Score Rookie/Traded consists of a 270-card base set. The base cards have a white and gray border with the player's name on the left. Cards are printed on a slightly glossier stock. Cards #1-50 were short-printed and inserted at a rate of one per pack. Ten-card packs carried an SRP of 99 cents. The Showcase Series parallels 110 base cards and was inserted 1:7. Artist's Proofs is a 50-card partial parallel done on prismatic foil and inserted 1:35. Inserts included All-Star Epix, Complete Players and Star Gazing.

NM/M
Complete Set (270): 10.00
Common SP (1-50): .10
Common Player (51-270): .05
Artist's Proofs: 4X
Inserted 1:35
Paul Konerko Auto. (500): 15.00
Pack (10): .65
Wax Box (36): 15.00
Jumbo Pack (20): 1.50
Jumbo Box (24): 25.00
1 Tony Clark .10
2 Juan Gonzalez .35
3 Frank Thomas .60
4 Greg Maddux .75
5 Barry Larkin .10
6 Derek Jeter 1.50
7 Randy Johnson .60
8 Roger Clemens .85
9 Tony Gwynn .75
10 Barry Bonds 1.50
11 Jim Edmonds .10
12 Bernie Williams .10
13 Ken Griffey Jr. 1.00
14 Tim Salmon .10
15 Mo Vaughn .10
16 David Justice .10
17 Jose Cruz Jr. .10
18 Andruw Jones .60
19 Sammy Sosa .75
20 Jeff Bagwell .60
21 Scott Rolen .50
22 Darin Erstad .30
23 Andy Pettitte .35
24 Mike Mussina .40
25 Mark McGwire 1.25
26 Hideo Nomo .35
27 Chipper Jones .75
28 Cal Ripken Jr. 1.50
29 Chuck Knoblauch .10
30 Alex Rodriguez 1.25
31 Jim Thome .50
32 Mike Piazza 1.00
33 Ivan Rodriguez .50
34 Roberto Alomar .40
35 Nomar Garciaparra .75
36 Albert Belle .10
37 Vladimir Guerrero .60
38 Raul Mondesi .10
39 Larry Walker .10
40 Manny Ramirez .60
41 Tino Martinez .10
42 Craig Biggio .10
43 Jay Buhner .10
44 Kenny Lofton .10
45 Pedro Martinez .60
46 Edgar Martinez .10
47 Gary Sheffield .45
48 Jose Guillen .10
49 Ken Caminiti .10
50 Bobby Higginson .05
51 Alan Benes .05
52 Shawn Green .15
53 Ron Coomer .05
54 Charles Nagy .05
55 Steve Karsay .05
56 Matt Morris .05
57 Bobby Jones .05
58 Jason Kendall .05
59 Jeff Conine .05
60 Joe Girardi .05
61 Mark Kotsay .05
62 Eric Karros .05
63 Bartolo Colon .05
64 Mariano Rivera .10
65 Alex Gonzalez .05
66 Scott Spiezio .05
67 Luis Castillo .05
68 Joey Cora .05
69 Mark McLemore .05
70 Reggie Jefferson .05
71 Lance Johnson .05
72 Damian Jackson .05
73 Jeff D'Amico .05
74 David Ortiz .30
75 J.T. Snow .05
76 Todd Hundley .05
77 Billy Wagner .05
78 Vinny Castilla .05
79 Ismael Valdes .05
80 Neifi Perez .05
81 Derek Bell .05
82 Ryan Klesko .05
83 Rey Ordonez .05
84 Carlos Garcia .05
85 Curt Schilling .30
86 Robin Ventura .05
87 Pat Hentgen .05
88 Glendon Rusch .05
89 Hideki Irabu .05
90 Antone Williamson .05
91 Denny Neagle .05
92 Kevin Orie .05
93 Reggie Sanders .05
94 Brady Anderson .05
95 Andy Benes .05
96 John Valentin .05
97 Bobby Bonilla .05
98 Walt Weiss .05
99 Robin Jennings .05
100 Marty Cordova .05
101 Brad Ausmus .05
102 Brian Rose .05
103 Calvin Maduro .05
104 Raul Casanova .05
105 Jeff King .05
106 Sandy Alomar .05
107 Tim Naehring .05
108 Mike Cameron .05
109 Omar Vizquel .05
110 Brad Radke .05
111 Jeff Fassero .05
112 Deivi Cruz .05
113 Dave Hollins .05
114 Dean Palmer .05
115 Esteban Loaiza .05
116 Brian Giles .05
117 Steve Finley .05
118 Jose Canseco .30
119 Al Martin .05
120 Eric Young .05
121 Curtis Goodwin .05
122 Ellis Burks .05
123 Mike Hampton .05
124 Lou Collier .05
125 John Olerud .05
126 Ramon Martinez .05
127 Todd Dunwoody .05
128 Jermaine Allensworth .05
129 Eduardo Perez .05
130 Dante Bichette .05
131 Edgar Renteria .05
132 Bob Abreu .10
133 Rondell White .05
134 Michael Coleman .05
135 Jason Giambi .30
136 Brant Brown .05
137 Michael Tucker .05
138 Dave Nilsson .05
139 Benito Santiago .05
140 Ray Durham .05
141 Jeff Kent .05
142 Matt Stairs .05
143 Kevin Young .05
144 Eric Davis .05
145 John Wetteland .05
146 Esteban Yan .05
147 Wilton Guerrero .05
148 Moises Alou .05
149 Edgardo Alfonzo .05
150 Andy Ashby .05
151 Todd Walker .05
152 Jermaine Dye .05
153 Brian Hunter .05
154 Shawn Estes .05
155 Bernard Gilkey .05
156 Tony Womack .05

157	John Smoltz	.05
158	Delino DeShields	.05
159	Jacob Cruz	.05
160	Javier Valentin	.05
161	Chris Hoiles	.05
162	Garret Anderson	.05
163	Dan Wilson	.05
164	Paul O'Neill	.05
165	Matt Williams	.05
166	Travis Fryman	.05
167	Javier Lopez	.05
168	Ray Lankford	.05
169	Bobby Estalella	.05
170	Henry Rodriguez	.05
171	Quinton McCracken	.05
172	Jaret Wright	.05
173	Darryl Kile	.05
174	Wade Boggs	.65
175	Orel Hershiser	.05
176	B.J. Surhoff	.05
177	Fernando Tatis	.05
178	Carlos Delgado	.30
179	Jorge Fabregas	.05
180	Tony Saunders	.05
181	Devon White	.05
182	Dmitri Young	.05
183	Ryan McGuire	.05
184	Mark Bellhorn	.05
185	Joe Carter	.05
186	Kevin Stocker	.05
187	Mike Lansing	.05
188	Jason Dickson	.05
189	Charles Johnson	.05
190	Will Clark	.05
191	Shannon Stewart	.05
192	Johnny Damon	.20
193	Todd Greene	.05
194	Carlos Baerga	.05
195	David Cone	.05
196	Pokey Reese	.05
197	Livan Hernandez	.05
198	Tom Glavine	.25
199	Geronimo Berroa	.05
200	Darryl Hamilton	.05
201	Terry Steinbach	.05
202	Robb Nen	.05
203	Ron Gant	.05
204	Rafael Palmeiro	.40
205	Rickey Henderson	.40
206	Justin Thompson	.05
207	Jeff Suppan	.05
208	Kevin Brown	.05
209	Jimmy Key	.05
210	Brian Jordan	.05
211	Aaron Sele	.05
212	Fred McGriff	.05
213	Jay Bell	.05
214	Andres Galarraga	.05
215	Mark Grace	.05
216	Brett Tomko	.05
217	Francisco Cordova	.05
218	Rusty Greer	.05
219	Bubba Trammell	.05
220	Derrek Lee	.35
221	Brian Anderson	.05
222	Mark Grudzielanek	.05
223	Marquis Grissom	.05
224	Gary DiSarcina	.05
225	Jim Leyritz	.05
226	Jeffrey Hammonds	.05
227	Karim Garcia	.05
228	Chan Ho Park	.05
229	Brooks Kieschnick	.05
230	Trey Beamon	.05
231	Kevin Appier	.05
232	Wally Joyner	.05
233	Richie Sexson	.05
234	Frank Catalanotto **RC**	.15
235	Rafael Medina	.05
236	Travis Lee	.05
237	Eli Marrero	.05
238	Carl Pavano	.05
239	Enrique Wilson	.05
240	Richard Hidalgo	.05
241	Todd Helton	.40
242	Ben Grieve	.05
243	Mario Valdez	.05
244	Maggio Ordonez **RC**	.75
245	Juan Encarnacion	.05
246	Russell Branyan	.05
247	Sean Casey	.10
248	Abraham Nunez	.05
249	Brad Fullmer	.05
250	Paul Konerko	.20
251	Miguel Tejada	.15
252	Mike Lowell **RC**	.50
253	Ken Griffey Jr. (Spring Training)	.35
254	Frank Thomas (Spring Training)	.25
255	Alex Rodriguez (Spring Training)	.45
256	Jose Cruz Jr. (Spring Training)	.05
257	Jeff Bagwell (Spring Training)	.20
258	Chipper Jones (Spring Training)	.30
259	Mo Vaughn (Spring Training)	.05
260	Nomar Garciaparra (Spring Training)	.30
261	Jim Thome (Spring Training)	.05
262	Derek Jeter (Spring Training)	.50
263	Mike Piazza (Spring Training)	.45
264	Tony Gwynn (Spring Training)	.30
265	Scott Rolen (Spring Training)	.15
266	Andruw Jones (Spring Training)	.20
267	Cal Ripken Jr. (Spring Training)	.50
268	Checklist (Ken Griffey Jr.)	.30
269	Checklist (Cal Ripken Jr.)	.45
270	Checklist (Jose Cruz Jr.)	.05

Artist's Proofs

This partial parallel reprints 160 (the same cards as the Showcase Series) of the 270 cards in Score Rookie & Traded. The cards are printed on a foil surface and feature an Artist's Proof logo on front. The cards were renumbered within the 160-card set and inserted one per 35 packs.

	NM/M
Common Player:	1.00
AP Stars:	4X

Artist's Proofs 1 of 1

Printed on primatic gold metallic foil background and featuring a gold "001/001 One of One" seal on front, these were random inserts in hobby packs. More than one "1/1" from this issue are known for some players, probably having been produced for use as replacements for damaged cards pulled from packs, then entering the hobby with the company's demise in mid-1998.

	NM/M
Common Player:	40.00

Showcase Series

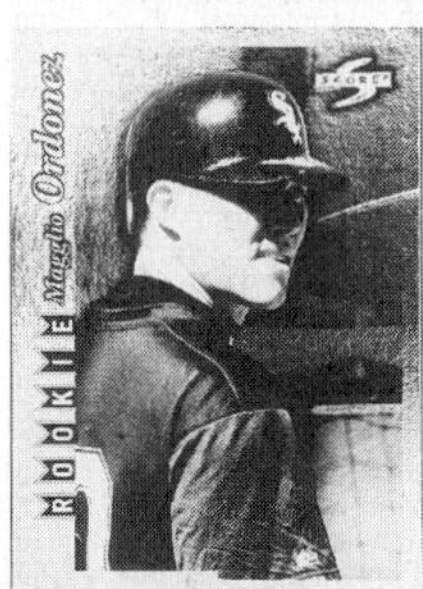

The Showcase Series is a partial parallel reprint of 160 of the 270 cards in Rookie & Traded. The cards are printed on a silver-foil surface, marked on the back and renumbered (with an "RTPP" prefix) within the 160-card set. Showcase parallels were inserted one per seven packs.

		NM/M
Complete Set (160):		10.00
Common Player:		.15
1	Tony Clark	.15
2	Juan Gonzalez	.30
3	Frank Thomas	.60
4	Greg Maddux	.75
5	Barry Larkin	.15
6	Derek Jeter	1.50
7	Randy Johnson	.60
8	Roger Clemens	.85
9	Tony Gwynn	.75
10	Barry Bonds	1.50
11	Jim Edmonds	.15
12	Bernie Williams	.15
13	Ken Griffey Jr.	1.00
14	Tim Salmon	.15
15	Mo Vaughn	.15
16	David Justice	.15
17	Jose Cruz Jr.	.15
18	Andruw Jones	.60
19	Sammy Sosa	.75
20	Jeff Bagwell	.60
21	Scott Rolen	.50
22	Darin Erstad	.25
23	Andy Pettitte	.30
24	Mike Mussina	.30
25	Mark McGwire	1.25
26	Hideo Nomo	.30
27	Chipper Jones	.75
28	Cal Ripken Jr.	1.50
29	Chuck Knoblauch	.15
30	Alex Rodriguez	1.25
31	Jim Thome	.50
32	Mike Piazza	1.00
33	Ivan Rodriguez	.50
34	Roberto Alomar	.25
35	Nomar Garciaparra	1.00
36	Albert Belle	.15
37	Vladimir Guerrero	.60
38	Raul Mondesi	.15
39	Larry Walker	.15
40	Manny Ramirez	.60
41	Tino Martinez	.15
42	Craig Biggio	.15
43	Jay Buhner	.15
44	Kenny Lofton	.15
45	Pedro Martinez	.60
46	Edgar Martinez	.15
47	Gary Sheffield	.40
48	Jose Guillen	.15
49	Ken Caminiti	.15
50	Bobby Higginson	.15
51	Alan Benes	.15
52	Shawn Green	.35
53	Matt Morris	.15
54	Jason Kendall	.15
55	Mark Kotsay	.15
56	Bartolo Colon	.15
57	Damian Jackson	.15
58	David Ortiz	.35
59	J.T. Snow	.15
60	Todd Hundley	.15
61	Neifi Perez	.15
62	Ryan Klesko	.15
63	Robin Ventura	.15
64	Pat Hentgen	.15
65	Antone Williamson	.15
66	Kevin Orie	.15
67	Brady Anderson	.15
68	Bobby Bonilla	.15
69	Brian Rose	.15
70	Sandy Alomar Jr.	.15
71	Mike Cameron	.15
72	Omar Vizquel	.15
73	Steve Finley	.15
74	Jose Canseco	.40
75	Al Martin	.15
76	Eric Young	.15
77	Ellis Burks	.15
78	Todd Dunwoody	.15
79	Dante Bichette	.15
80	Edgar Renteria	.15
81	Bobby Abreu	.15
82	Rondell White	.15
83	Michael Coleman	.15
84	Jason Giambi	.50
85	Wilton Guerrero	.15
86	Moises Alou	.15
87	Todd Walker	.15
88	Shawn Estes	.15
89	John Smoltz	.15
90	Jacob Cruz	.15
91	Javier Valentin	.15
92	Garret Anderson	.15
93	Paul O'Neill	.15
94	Matt Williams	.15
95	Travis Fryman	.15
96	Javier Lopez	.15
97	Ray Lankford	.15
98	Bobby Estalella	.15
99	Jaret Wright	.15
100	Wade Boggs	.75
101	Fernando Tatis	.15
102	Carlos Delgado	.50
103	Joe Carter	.15
104	Jason Dickson	.15
105	Charles Johnson	.15
106	Will Clark	.15
107	Shannon Stewart	.15
108	Todd Greene	.15
109	Pokey Reese	.15
110	Livan Hernandez	.15
111	Tom Glavine	.35
112	Rafael Palmeiro	.50
113	Justin Thompson	.15
114	Jeff Suppan	.15
115	Kevin Brown	.15
116	Brian Jordan	.15
117	Fred McGriff	.15
118	Andres Galarraga	.15
119	Mark Grace	.15
120	Rusty Greer	.15
121	Bubba Trammell	.15
122	Derrek Lee	.40
123	Brian Anderson	.15
124	Karim Garcia	.15
125	Chan Ho Park	.15
126	Richie Sexson	.15
127	Frank Catalanotto	.15
128	Rafael Medina	.15
129	Travis Lee	.15
130	Eli Marrero	.15
131	Carl Pavano	.15
132	Enrique Wilson	.15
133	Richard Hidalgo	.15
134	Todd Helton	.40
135	Ben Grieve	.15
136	Mario Valdez	.15
137	Magglio Ordonez	.25
138	Juan Encarnacion	.15
139	Russell Branyan	.15
140	Sean Casey	.25
141	Abraham Nunez	.15
142	Brad Fullmer	.15
143	Paul Konerko	.25
144	Miguel Tejada	.30
145	Mike Lowell	.15
146	Ken Griffey Jr. (Spring Training)	.50
147	Frank Thomas (Spring Training)	.35
148	Alex Rodriguez (Spring Training)	.65
149	Jose Cruz Jr. (Spring Training)	.15
150	Jeff Bagwell (Spring Training)	.35
151	Chipper Jones (Spring Training)	.40
152	Mo Vaughn (Spring Training)	.15
153	Nomar Garciaparra (Spring Training)	.40
154	Jim Thome (Spring Training)	.30
155	Derek Jeter (Spring Training)	.75
156	Mike Piazza (Spring Training)	.50
157	Tony Gwynn (Spring Training)	.40
158	Scott Rolen (Spring Training)	.25
159	Andruw Jones (Spring Training)	.35
160	Cal Ripken Jr. (Spring Training)	.75

Complete Players

Complete Players is a 30-card insert seeded one per 11 packs. The set highlights 10 players who can do it all on the field. Each player has three cards showcasing one of their talents. The cards feature holographic foil stamping. Each card can also be found in a promo version with a large, black "SAMPLE" overprinted on front and back.

		NM/M
Complete Set (30):		65.00
Common Player:		1.00
Inserted 1:11		
Samples:		1X
1A	Ken Griffey Jr.	3.50
1B	Ken Griffey Jr.	3.50
1C	Ken Griffey Jr.	3.50
2A	Larry Walker	1.00
2B	Larry Walker	1.00
2C	Larry Walker	1.00
3A	Alex Rodriguez	4.00
3B	Alex Rodriguez	4.00
3C	Alex Rodriguez	4.00
4A	Jose Cruz Jr.	1.00
4B	Jose Cruz Jr.	1.00
4C	Jose Cruz Jr.	1.00
5A	Jeff Bagwell	2.00
5B	Jeff Bagwell	2.00
5C	Jeff Bagwell	2.00
6A	Greg Maddux	2.75
6B	Greg Maddux	2.75
6C	Greg Maddux	2.75
7A	Ivan Rodriguez	1.75
7B	Ivan Rodriguez	1.75
7C	Ivan Rodriguez	1.75
8A	Roger Clemens	3.00
8B	Roger Clemens	3.00
8C	Roger Clemens	3.00
9A	Chipper Jones	2.75
9B	Chipper Jones	2.75
9C	Chipper Jones	2.75
10A	Hideo Nomo	1.50
10B	Hideo Nomo	1.50
10C	Hideo Nomo	1.50

Epix All-Star Moment

All-Star Epix is a 1:61 insert. The cards honor the top All-Star Game moments of 12 star players. The dot matrix hologram cards were printed in orange, purple and emerald versions. This series was continued with cards numbered 13-24 in Pinnacle Plus.

		NM/M
Complete Set (12):		25.00
Common Player:		1.00
Purples:		1.5X
Emeralds:		2.5X
1	Ken Griffey Jr.	4.00
2	Juan Gonzalez	1.50
3	Jeff Bagwell	2.50
4	Ivan Rodriguez	2.00
5	Nomar Garciaparra	3.00
6	Ryne Sandberg	3.00
7	Frank Thomas	2.50
8	Derek Jeter	5.00
9	Tony Gwynn	3.00
10	Albert Belle	1.00
11	Scott Rolen	2.00
12	Barry Larkin	1.00

Star Gazing

Printed on micro-etched foil board, Star Gazing features 20 top players and was seeded 1:35.

		NM/M
Complete Set (20):		12.00
Common Player:		.25
Inserted 1:35		
1	Ken Griffey Jr.	1.00
2	Frank Thomas	.60
3	Chipper Jones	.75
4	Mark McGwire	1.25
5	Cal Ripken Jr.	1.50
6	Mike Piazza	1.00
7	Nomar Garciaparra	.75
8	Derek Jeter	1.50
9	Juan Gonzalez	.35
10	Vladimir Guerrero	.60
11	Alex Rodriguez	1.25
12	Tony Gwynn	.75
13	Andruw Jones	.60
14	Scott Rolen	.40
15	Jose Cruz Jr.	.25
16	Mo Vaughn	.25
17	Bernie Williams	.25
18	Greg Maddux	.75
19	Tony Clark	.25
20	Ben Grieve	.25

1998 Score Team Collection

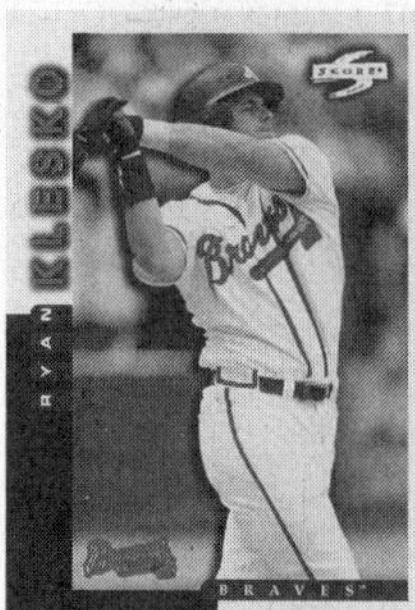

Team sets of 15 players each were produced for 10 different teams. Each card is similar in design to the regular 1998 Score set except for a special silver-foil team logo stamped at the bottom of the card. On back, this version has a "Team Collection" underprinted and each card is numbered "_ of 15." In a parallel "Platinum" version, seeded one per six packs, the front background is replaced with silver prismatic foil. A gold highlighted version of the three-card Complete Players inserts were found one per 11 packs. Team Collection was sold in five-card, single-team packs (32 per box).

		NM/M
Complete Set (150):		25.00
Common Player:		.10
ANAHEIM ANGELS		
	TEAM SET	2.00
1	Rickey Henderson	.60
2	Todd Greene	.10
3	Shigetoshi Hasegawa	.10
4	Darin Erstad	.20
5	Jason Dickson	.10
6	Tim Salmon	.10
7	Ken Hill	.10
8	Dave Hollins	.10
9	Gary DiSarcina	.10
10	Mike James	.10
11	Jim Edmonds	.10
12	Troy Percival	.10
13	Chuck Finley	.10
14	Tony Phillips	.10
15	Garret Anderson	.10
ATLANTA BRAVES TEAM SET		2.75
1	Andruw Jones	.60
2	Greg Maddux	.75
3	Michael Tucker	.10
4	Denny Naegle	.10
5	Javier Lopez	.10
6	Ryan Klesko	.10
7	Chipper Jones	.75
8	Kenny Lofton	.10
9	John Smoltz	.10
10	Jeff Blauser	.10
11	Tom Glavine	.30
12	Tony Graffanino	.10
13	Terrell Wade	.10
14	Fred McGriff	.10
15	Mark Wohlers	.10
BALTIMORE ORIOLES		
	TEAM SET	3.25
1	Roberto Alomar	.20
2	Jimmy Key	.10
3	Cal Ripken Jr.	1.75
4	Brady Anderson	.10
5	Geronimo Berroa	.10
6	Chris Hoiles	.10
7	Rafael Palmeiro	.50
8	Mike Mussina	.30
9	Randy Myers	.10
10	Mike Bordick	.10
11	Scott Erickson	.10
12	Armando Benitez	.10
13	B.J. Surhoff	.10
14	Jeffrey Hammonds	.10
15	Arthur Rhodes	.10
BOSTON RED SOX		
	TEAM SET	2.25
1	Steve Avery	.10

2 Aaron Sele .10
3 Tim Wakefield .10
4 Darren Bragg .10
5 Scott Hatteberg .10
6 Jeff Suppan .10
7 Nomar Garciaparra .75
8 Tim Naehring .10
9 Reggie Jefferson .10
10 John Valentin .10
11 Jeff Frye .10
12 Wil Cordero .10
13 Troy O'Leary .10
14 Mo Vaughn .10
15 Shane Mack .10

CHICAGO WHITE SOX

TEAM SET 2.00
1 Albert Belle .10
2 Chuck McElroy .10
3 Mike Cameron .10
4 Ozzie Guillen .10
5 Jaime Navarro .10
6 Chris Clemons .10
7 Lyle Mouton .10
8 Frank Thomas .60
9 Doug Drabek .10
10 Robin Ventura .10
11 Dave Martinez .10
12 Ray Durham .10
13 Chris Snopek .10
14 James Baldwin .10
15 Jorge Fabregas .10

CLEVELAND INDIANS

TEAM SET 1.25
1 Jack McDowell .10
2 Jim Thome .50
3 Brian Anderson .10
4 Sandy Alomar Jr. .10
5 Omar Vizquel .10
6 Brian Giles .10
7 Charles Nagy .10
8 Mike Jackson .10
9 David Justice .10
10 Jeff Juden .10
11 Matt Williams .10
12 Marquis Grissom .10
13 Tony Fernandez .10
14 Bartolo Colon .10
15 Jaret Wright .10

LOS ANGELES DODGERS

TEAM SET 2.75
1 Hideo Nomo .30
2 Mike Piazza 1.00
3 Wilton Guerrero .10
4 Greg Gagne .10
5 Brett Butler .10
6 Todd Hollandsworth .10
7 Roger Cedeno .10
8 Chan Ho Park .10
9 Todd Worrell .10
10 Ramon Martinez .10
11 Ismael Valdes .10
12 Eric Karros .10
13 Raul Mondesi .10
14 Todd Zeile .10
15 Billy Ashley .10

NEW YORK YANKEES

TEAM SET 3.25
1 Hideki Irabu .10
2 Derek Jeter 1.75
3 Tino Martinez .10
4 David Cone .10
5 Andy Pettitte .25
6 Bernie Williams .10
7 Charlie Hayes .10
8 Pat Kelly .10
9 Mariano Rivera .15
10 Paul O'Neill .10
11 Chad Curtis .10
12 David Wells .10
13 Cecil Fielder .10
14 Wade Boggs .75
15 Jorge Posada .10

SEATTLE MARINERS

TEAM SET 3.25
1 Dan Wilson .10
2 Alex Rodriguez 1.25
3 Jeff Fassero .10
4 Ken Griffey Jr. 1.00
5 Bobby Ayala .10
6 Jay Buhner .10
7 Mike Timlin .10
8 Edgar Martinez .10
9 Randy Johnson .60
10 Joey Cora .10
11 Heathcliff Slocumb .10
12 Russ Davis .10
13 Paul Sorrento .10
14 Rich Amaral .10
15 Jamie Moyer .10

ST. LOUIS CARDINALS

TEAM SET 2.25
1 Andy Benes .10
2 Todd Stottlemyre .10
3 Dennis Eckersley .45
4 Mark McGwire 1.25
5 Dmitri Young .10
6 Ron Gant .10
7 Mike Difelice .10
8 Ray Lankford .10
9 John Mabry .10
10 Royce Clayton .10
11 Alan Benes .10
12 Delino DeShields .10
13 Brian Jordan .10
14 Gary Gaetti .10
15 Matt Morris .10

Platinum

Each of the Team Collection cards was also issued in a Platinum Team version, inserted on average of one card per six packs. The front has a background of star-studded refractive silver foil and a "PLATINUM TEAM" designation at the right edge of the photo. That designation is repeated on back as an underprint.

NM/M
Common Player: .50
Stars: 4X

Complete Players

(See 1998 Score Complete Players.)

1996-97 Score Board All Sport PPF

Stars and prospects, Past, Present and Future (PPF), in the four major team sports are featued in this two series set whose issue spanned late 1996 and early 1997. Borderless action photos and gold-foil graphic highlights are featured on front. Another photo, stats and personal data can be found on back. Only the baseball players from the 200-card set are listed here. A gold parallel edition was also issued.

NM/M
Common Player: .10
Gold: 2X
Wax Pack (6): .65
Wax Box (18): 7.50
Wax Box (36): 15.00
21 Ryan Minor .10
60 Rey Ordonez .10
61 Todd Greene .10
62 Jermaine Dye .10
63 Karim Garcia .10
64 Todd Walker .10
65 Calvin Reese .10
66 Roger Cedeno .10
67 Ben Davis .10
68 Chad Hermansen .10
69 Vladimir Guerrero .50
70 Billy Wagner .10
94 Barry Bonds .50
95 Vladimir Guerrero .50
96 Livan Hernandez .10
160 Barry Bonds .50
161 Jay Payton .10
162 Jose Cruz Jr. .10
163 Richard Hidalgo .10
164 Bartolo Colon .10
165 Matt Drews .10
166 Kerry Wood .35
167 Ben Grieve .10
168 Wes Helms .10
169 Livan Hernandez .10
196 Todd Walker .10
197 Rey Ordonez .10
198 Todd Greene .10

Retro

Current and potential stars in the format of classic sports cards are featured in this Series 2 insert found at an announced rate of one per 35 packs. Only a single baseball player is included among the 10 cards in the set.

NM/M
R10 Rey Ordonez .50

Revivals

Current and potential stars in the format of classic sports cards are featured in this Series 1 insert found at an announced rate of one per 35 packs. Only a single baseball player is included among the 10 cards in the set.

NM/M
REV10 Barry Bonds 1.00

1997 Score Board Mickey Mantle Shoe Box Collection

Yet another collectors' issue of Mickey Mantle cards, the Score Board "Shoe Box Collection" offered packs containing two of the 75 Mantle cards or seven-card insert set, along with a genuine - usually a low-grade common - Topps card from 1951-69. Several designs of Mantle cards are featured in the set, including color photos as well as blue-and-white duotones. Five of the cards are printed with gold-foil backgrounds and die-cut. Cards #51-69 are short-printed at a ratio of about 1-to-3 with cards #1-50. Suggested retail price was $6.50 per pack.

NM/M
Complete Set (75): 60.00
Common Card: .75
1 Summary Of The Legend (Foil die-cut.) 3.00
1p Summary of the Legend (Promo Card) 3.00
2 Triple Crown 1956 .75
3 MVP 1956 .75
4 MVP 1957 .75
5 MVP 1962 .75
6 Uniform #6 (foil die-cut) 3.00
6p Uniform #6 (Promo Card) 3.00
7 Uniform #7 (foil die-cut) 3.00
7p Uniform #7 (Promo Card) 3.00
8 Gold Glove Winner .75
9 17-time All-Star .75
10 4-time HR Champion .75
11 World Series Records .75
12 The Dirty Dozen (Post-Seasons) .75
13 World Champion-1951 .75
14 World Champion-1952 .75
15 World Champion-1953 .75
16 World Champion-1956 .75
17 World Champion-1958 .75
18 World Champion-1961 .75
19 World Champion-1962 .75
20 Replacing A Legend .75
21 Casey On Mantle .75
22 Mickey & The Media .75
23 Family Man .75
24 Fan Favorite .75
25 Playing Injured .75
26 Clubhouse Leader .75
27 Team Leader .75
28 M & M Boys .75
29 Legendary Friendships .75
30 Time Out .75
31 Mantle Is Born .75
32 Mutt Mantle .75
33 Growing Up .75
34 5-tool player-Arm .75
35 5-tool player-Defense .75
36 5-tool player-Average .75
37 5-tool player-Speed .75
38 5-tool player-Power .75
39 First Homer .75
40 100th Homer .75
41 200th Homer .75
42 300th Homer .75
43 400th Homer .75
44 500th Homer .75
45 536 Career Homers .75
46 Yankee Stadium Blasts .75
47 Switch-hit Home Runs .75
48 565-ft. Home Run .75
49 Signs 1st Pro Contract .75
50 Mickey In The Minors .75
51 1951 Trading Card 3.00
52 1952 Trading Card 3.00
53 1953 Trading Card 3.00
54 1954 Trading Card 3.00
55 1955 Trading Card 3.00
56A 1956 Trading Card 3.00
56B 1956 Trading Card 3.00
57 1957 Trading Card 3.00
58 1958 Trading Card 3.00
59 1959 Trading Card 3.00
60 1960 Trading Card 3.00
61 1961 Trading Card 3.00
62 1962 Trading Card 3.00
63 1963 Trading Card 3.00
64 1964 Trading Card 3.00
65 1965 Trading Card 3.00
66 1966 Trading Card 3.00
67 1967 Trading Card 3.00
68 1968 Trading Card 3.00
69 1969 Trading Card 3.00
70 Number Retired By Yankees (Foil die-cut.) 3.00
70p Number Retired By Yankees (Promo Card) 3.00
71 Mickey Mantle Day/1965 .75
72 Mickey Mantle Day/1969 .75
73 Life After Baseball .75
74 Hall Of Fame Induction (Foil die-cut.) 3.00
74p Hall of Fame Induction (Promo Card) 3.00

Mickey Mantle Shoe Box Inserts

A set of seven insert cards, found on average of one per 16 packs, was part of the Mickey Mantle Shoe Box Collection. The inserts have a photo of Mantle on front, with blue metallic foil highlights. Contest rules on the back specify that the first seven persons to redeem a complete set of the seven insert cards will win a $7,000 Mantle phone card. All others redeeming the set of seven prior to July 7, 1998, received a $700 Mantle phone card. The #7 insert card was short-printed to limit the number of phone card winners.

NM/M
Complete Set (7): 70.00
Common Card: 6.00
$700 Phone Card: 115.00
$7,000 Phone Card: 850.00
1 Mickey Mantle Insert #1 6.00
2 Mickey Mantle Insert #2 6.00
3 Mickey Mantle Insert #3 6.00
4 Mickey Mantle Insert #4 6.00
5 Mickey Mantle Insert #5 25.00
6 Mickey Mantle Insert #6 6.00
7 Mickey Mantle Insert #7 (Short-Print) 40.00

Players Club

Seven baseball players are among the cards in this multi-sport issue. Card fronts feature borderless action photos from which uniform logos have been removed. The player's name and the city in which he plays are in gold-foil in a baseball strip at bottom. Backs have another photo, biographical data and stats, including projected 1998 figures. Only the baseball players in the set are listed here.

NM/M
Common Player: .25
3 Barry Bonds .50
7 Jose Cruz Jr. .25
17 Matt Drews .25
27 Wes Helms .25
37 Richard Hidalgo .25
48 Jay Payton .25
69 Kerry Wood .35

Players Club 1 Die-Cuts

Former #1 draft picks from all four major sports are included in this insert set. Highlighted in gold foil, cards are die-cut into the shape of a numeral 1. Backs have biographical information and stats. Cards are numbered with a "D" prefix. Only the baseball players are listed here. They were a 1:32 pack insert.

NM/M
D10 Jose Cruz Jr. 1.00
D11 Barry Bonds 5.00

Talk N' Sports

Insert phone cards with talk time worth up to $1,000, along with trivia contests to win memorabilia were among the incentives to purchase this four-sport issue. The base card set features 50 stars and prospects, all of whom are also found, along with a few other superstars, in the inserts. Fronts of the base cards have action photos on which uniform logos have been airbrushed away. Backs have a couple more photos, some player bio and stats. Only the baseball players from the set are listed here.

NM/M
Common Player: .10
40 Barry Bonds .50
41 Jay Payton .10
42 Todd Walker .10
43 Jose Cruz Jr. .10
44 Kerry Wood .30
45 Wes Helms .10

Talk N' Sports Essentials

See-through plastic and action photos are combined on this 1:20 pack insert. Only a single baseball player is included among the four-sport stars and prospects.

NM/M
E3 Barry Bonds 7.50

Visions Signings

Stars and prospects from all four major team sports are included in this issue. Fronts have borderless action photos with professional logos removed as necessary to meet licensing regulations. Front graphics feature holographic foil highlights. Backs have another photo along with stats, personal data and career notes. Cards were sold in five-card packs, each of which contained either an autographed card or an insert card. Only the seven baseball players from the 50-card set are listed here.

		NM/M
Common Player:		.25
Gold Parallel:		2X
1	Barry Bonds	1.50
5	Jose Cruz Jr.	.25
6	Ben Grieve	.25
7	Kerry Wood	.75
44	Wes Helms	.25
45	Richard Hidalgo	.25
46	Jay Payton	.25

Visions Signings Autographs

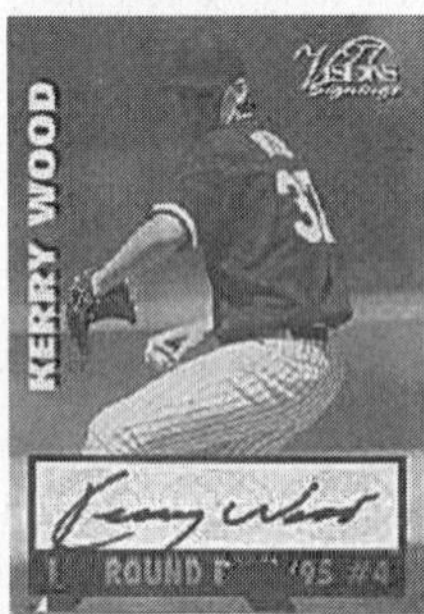

Each five-card pack of Score Board Vision Signings contained either an authentically autographed card or an insert card. Only the baseball players from the 63 autographed cards in the multi-sports set of stars and prospects are listed here. Barry Bonds autographs can be found on other companies' cards, with a Score Board authenticity seal.

		NM/M
9	Jose Cruz Jr.	2.00
20	Ben Grieve	2.00
21	Vladimir Guerrero	30.00
26	Wes Helms	2.00
27	Richard Hidalgo	2.00
34	Jason Kendall	2.00
44	Jay Payton	2.00
62	Paul Wilson	2.00
63	Kerry Wood	20.00
	Barry Bonds	45.00

Visions Signings Artistry

These specially printed cards were a one-in-six packs insert (regular version; 1:18 autographed) in five-card Visions Signings packs. Only a single baseball player is represented among the 20 cards in the set.

		NM/M
1	Jose Cruz Jr.	1.00
1	Jose Cruz Jr./Auto.	3.00

Autographed Collection

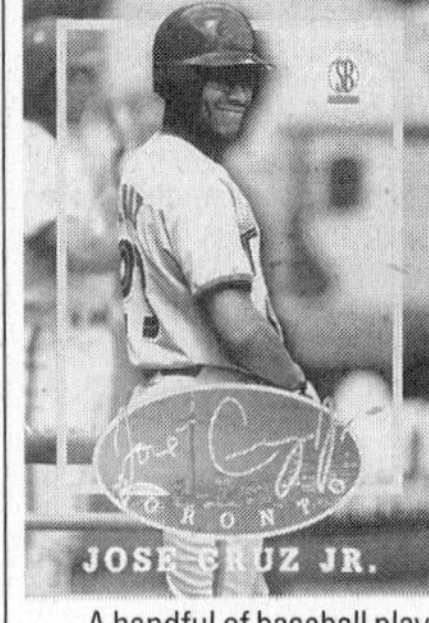

A handful of baseball players are among the four-sport stars and prospects in this set. Luring collectors was the presence of autographed cards at the rate of one per 4-1/2 packs, Blue Ribbon serially numbered autographs and memorabilia redemption cards (many of which became worthless when Score Board went bankrupt shortly after the set was issued). Because the cards are licensed only by the players, and not leagues, there are no uniform logos on the photos, nor mention of team names, only cities. Only the baseball players are listed here.

		NM/M
Common Player:		.25
3	J.D. Drew	1.50
11	Matt White	.25
12	Jay Payton	.25
23	Brandon Larson	.25
28	Jose Cruz Jr.	.25
49	Adrian Beltre	.50

Autographed Collection Strongbox

As part of a special $125 television offer, a parallel version of Score Board's Autographed Collection was offered featuring special inserts, autographs and memorabilia. The parallel cards are marked with an embossed "Strongbox" logo.

		NM/M
Common Player:		.25
3	J.D. Drew	2.00
11	Matt White	.50
12	Jay Payton	.50
23	Brandon Larson	.50
28	Jose Cruz Jr.	.50
49	Adrian Beltre	1.50

Autographed Collection Autographs

Authentically autographed cards were inserted in this issue at the rate of about four per 18-pack box. Cards have a round player photo at center with the signature in a white oval below. Backs have a congratulatory message. Only the baseball players among the four-sport stars and prospects are listed here. Cards are unnumbered.

	NM/M
Ben Grieve	2.00
Wes Helms	2.00
Jay Payton	2.00
Kerry Wood	20.00

Autographed Collection Blue Ribbon

These one-per-box inserts are similar in format to the autographed cards, but have a blue ribbon beneath the player photo on which the signature has been penned. Each card is individually serial numbered from within editions which vary from fewer than 100 to nearly 2,000. Only one baseball player was among the four-sport stars and prospects.

	NM/M
Jose Cruz Jr./1,600	3.00

Autographed Collection Sports City USA

Players whose teams share a common city are featured in this insert series, found on average one per nine packs. A parallel version, embossed "Strongbox" was issued in special $125 television-offer packages of Autographed Collection. The parallels are individually serial numbered to 600. Only cards with baseball players are listed here.

		NM/M
Common Card:		1.00
Embossed:		2X
SC3	Richard Hidalgo (Olajuwan, Drexler)	1.00
SC4	Kerry Wood (Pippen, Autry)	2.50
SC6	Adrian Beltre (Bryant)	1.50
SC7	J.D. Drew (Thomas, Staley)	2.50
SC12	Wes Helms (Hanspard, Gray)	1.00
SC14	Jay Payton (Barber, Van Horn)	1.00
SC15	Matt Drews (Westbrook, Pollard)	1.00

1981 Seattle Mariners Police

These 2-5/8" x 4-1/8" cards were co-sponsored by the Washington State Crime Prevention Assoc., Coca-Cola, Kiwanis and Ernst Home Centers. Fronts have a color photo, player name and position and a team logo. Card backs are printed in blue and red and offer a "Tip from the Mariners" along with the four sponsor logos.

		NM/M
Complete Set (16):		3.00
Common Player:		.25
1	Jeff Burroughs	.25
2	Floyd Bannister	.25
3	Glenn Abbott	.25
4	Jim Anderson	.25
5	Danny Meyer	.25
6	Dave Edler	.25
7	Julio Cruz	.25
8	Kenny Clay	.25
9	Lenny Randle	.25
10	Mike Parrott	.25
11	Tom Paciorek	.25
12	Jerry Narron	.25
13	Richie Zisk	.25
14	Maury Wills	.50
15	Joe Simpson	.25
16	Shane Rawley	.25

1993 Select Promos

Zeroes in the career stats line on the back of the card distinguish the promo cards for Score's premiere issue of its Select brand name. The promo cards were distributed to introduce dealers and collectors to the new mid-range set.

		NM/M
Complete Set (8):		12.00
Common Player:		1.00
22	Robin Yount	3.00
24	Don Mattingly	5.00
26	Sandy Alomar Jr.	1.00
41	Gary Sheffield	2.00
56	Brady Anderson	1.00
65	Rob Dibble	1.00
75	John Smiley	1.00
79	Mitch Williams	1.00

1993 Select Dufex Proofs

To test the Dufex textured foil printing technology which was used on its Stars, Rookies and Triple Crown insert sets, Select produced a very limited number of blank-back proof cards.

Select Rookies:	15X
Select Stars:	20X
Select Triple Crown:	20X

1993 Select

This 400-card set from Score is designed for the mid-priced card market. The card fronts feature green borders

on two sides of the card with the photo filling the remaining portion of the card front. The backs feature an additional photo, player information and statistics. Cards numbered 271-360 are devoted to rookies and draft picks.

		NM/M
Complete Set (405):		15.00
Common Player:		.05
Pack (15):		.75
Wax Box (36):		22.50
1	Barry Bonds	1.50
2	Ken Griffey Jr.	1.00
3	Will Clark	.05
4	Kirby Puckett	.75
5	Tony Gwynn	.75
6	Frank Thomas	.65
7	Tom Glavine	.35
8	Roberto Alomar	.25
9	Andre Dawson	.25
10	Ron Darling	.05
11	Bobby Bonilla	.05
12	Danny Tartabull	.05
13	Darren Daulton	.05
14	Roger Clemens	.85
15	Ozzie Smith	.75
16	Mark McGwire	1.25
17	Terry Pendleton	.05
18	Cal Ripken, Jr.	1.50
19	Fred McGriff	.05
20	Cecil Fielder	.05
21	Darryl Strawberry	.05
22	Robin Yount	.65
23	Barry Larkin	.05
24	Don Mattingly	.85
25	Craig Biggio	.05
26	Sandy Alomar Jr.	.05
27	Larry Walker	.05
28	Junior Felix	.05
29	Eddie Murray	.65
30	Robin Ventura	.05
31	Greg Maddux	.75
32	Dave Winfield	.65
33	John Kruk	.05
34	Wally Joyner	.05
35	Andy Van Slyke	.05
36	Chuck Knoblauch	.05
37	Tom Pagnozzi	.05
38	Dennis Eckersley	.60
39	Dave Justice	.05
40	Juan Gonzalez	.35
41	Gary Sheffield	.40
42	Paul Molitor	.65
43	Delino DeShields	.05
44	Travis Fryman	.05
45	Hal Morris	.05
46	Gregg Olson	.05
47	Ken Caminiti	.05
48	Wade Boggs	.75
49	Orel Hershiser	.05
50	Albert Belle	.05
51	Bill Swift	.05
52	Mark Langston	.05
53	Joe Girardi	.05
54	Keith Miller	.05
55	Gary Carter	.65
56	Brady Anderson	.05
57	Dwight Gooden	.05
58	Julio Franco	.05
59	Len Dykstra	.05
60	Mickey Tettleton	.05
61	Randy Tomlin	.05
62	B.J. Surhoff	.05
63	Todd Zeile	.05
64	Roberto Kelly	.05
65	Rob Dibble	.05
66	Leo Gomez	.05
67	Doug Jones	.05
68	Ellis Burks	.05
69	Mike Scioscia	.05
70	Charles Nagy	.05
71	Cory Snyder	.05
72	Devon White	.05
73	Mark Grace	.05
74	Luis Polonia	.05
75	John Smiley	.05
76	Carlton Fisk	.65
77	Luis Sojo	.05
78	George Brett	.85
79	Mitch Williams	.05
80	Kent Hrbek	.05
81	Jay Bell	.05
82	Edgar Martinez	.05
83	Lee Smith	.05
84	Deion Sanders	.05
85	Bill Gullickson	.05
86	Paul O'Neill	.05
87	Kevin Seitzer	.05
88	Steve Finley	.05
89	Mel Hall	.05
90	Nolan Ryan	1.50
91	Eric Davis	.05
92	Mike Mussina	.35
93	Tony Fernandez	.05
94	Frank Viola	.05
95	Matt Williams	.05
96	Joe Carter	.05
97	Ryne Sandberg	.75
98	Jim Abbott	.05
99	Marquis Grissom	.05
100	George Bell	.05
101	Howard Johnson	.05
102	Kevin Appier	.05
103	Dale Murphy	.20
104	Shane Mack	.05
105	Jose Lind	.05
106	Rickey Henderson	.65
107	Bob Tewksbury	.05
108	Kevin Mitchell	.05
109	Steve Avery	.05
110	Candy Maldonado	.05
111	Bip Roberts	.05
112	Lou Whitaker	.05
113	Jeff Bagwell	.65
114	Dante Bichette	.05
115	Brett Butler	.05
116	Melido Perez	.05
117	Andy Benes	.05
118	Randy Johnson	.65
119	Willie McGee	.05
120	Jody Reed	.05
121	Shawon Dunston	.05
122	Carlos Baerga	.05
123	Bret Saberhagen	.05
124	John Olerud	.05
125	Ivan Calderon	.05
126	Bryan Harvey	.05
127	Terry Mulholland	.05
128	Ozzie Guillen	.05
129	Steve Buechele	.05
130	Kevin Tapani	.05
131	Felix Jose	.05
132	Terry Steinbach	.05
133	Ron Gant	.05
134	Harold Reynolds	.05
135	Chris Sabo	.05
136	Ivan Rodriguez	.60
137	Eric Anthony	.05
138	Mike Henneman	.05
139	Robby Thompson	.05
140	Scott Fletcher	.05
141	Bruce Hurst	.05
142	Kevin Maas	.05
143	Tom Candiotti	.05
144	Chris Hoiles	.05
145	Mike Morgan	.05
146	Mark Whiten	.05
147	Dennis Martinez	.05
148	Tony Pena	.05
149	Dave Magadan	.05
150	Mark Lewis	.05
151	Mariano Duncan	.05
152	Gregg Jefferies	.05
153	Doug Drabek	.05
154	Brian Harper	.05
155	Ray Lankford	.05
156	Carney Lansford	.05
157	Mike Sharperson	.05
158	Jack Morris	.05
159	Otis Nixon	.05
160	Steve Sax	.05
161	Mark Lemke	.05
162	Rafael Palmeiro	.60
163	Jose Rijo	.05
164	Omar Vizquel	.05
165	Sammy Sosa	.75
166	Milt Cuyler	.05
167	John Franco	.05
168	Darryl Hamilton	.05
169	Ken Hill	.05
170	Mike Devereaux	.05
171	Don Slaught	.05
172	Steve Farr	.05
173	Bernard Gilkey	.05
174	Mike Fetters	.05
175	Vince Coleman	.05
176	Kevin McReynolds	.05
177	John Smoltz	.05
178	Greg Gagne	.05
179	Greg Swindell	.05
180	Juan Guzman	.05
181	Kal Daniels	.05
182	Rick Sutcliffe	.05
183	Orlando Merced	.05
184	Bill Wegman	.05
185	Mark Gardner	.05
186	Rob Deer	.05
187	Dave Hollins	.05
188	Jack Clark	.05
189	Brian Hunter	.05
190	Tim Wallach	.05
191	Tim Belcher	.05
192	Walt Weiss	.05
193	Kurt Stillwell	.05
194	Charlie Hayes	.05
195	Willie Randolph	.05
196	Jack McDowell	.05
197	Jose Offerman	.05
198	Chuck Finley	.05
199	Darrin Jackson	.05
200	Kelly Gruber	.05

201 John Wetteland .05
202 Jay Buhner .05
203 Mike LaValliere .05
204 Kevin Brown .05
205 Luis Gonzalez .05
206 Rick Aguilera .05
207 Norm Charlton .05
208 Mike Bordick .05
209 Charlie Leibrandt .05
210 Tom Brunansky .05
211 Tom Henke .05
212 Randy Milligan .05
213 Ramon Martinez .05
214 Mo Vaughn .05
215 Randy Myers .05
216 Greg Hibbard .05
217 Wes Chamberlain .05
218 Tony Phillips .05
219 Pete Harnisch .05
220 Mike Gallego .05
221 Bud Black .05
222 Greg Vaughn .05
223 Milt Thompson .05
224 Ben McDonald .05
225 Billy Hatcher .05
226 Paul Sorrento .05
227 Mark Gubicza .05
228 Mike Greenwell .05
229 Curt Schilling .35
230 Alan Trammell .05
231 Zane Smith .05
232 Bobby Thigpen .05
233 Greg Olson .05
234 Joe Orsulak .05
235 Joe Oliver .05
236 Tim Raines .05
237 Juan Samuel .05
238 Chili Davis .05
239 Spike Owen .05
240 Dave Stewart .05
241 Jim Eisenreich .05
242 Phil Plantier .05
243 Sid Fernandez .05
244 Dan Gladden .05
245 Mickey Morandini .05
246 Tino Martinez .05
247 Kirt Manwaring .05
248 Dean Palmer .05
249 Tom Browning .05
250 Brian McRae .05
251 Scott Leius .05
252 Bert Blyleven .05
253 Scott Erickson .05
254 Bob Welch .05
255 Pat Kelly .05
256 Felix Fermin .05
257 Harold Baines .05
258 Duane Ward .05
259 Bill Spiers .05
260 Jaime Navarro .05
261 Scott Sanderson .05
262 Gary Gaetti .05
263 Bob Ojeda .05
264 Jeff Montgomery .05
265 Scott Bankhead .05
266 Lance Johnson .05
267 Rafael Belliard .05
268 Kevin Reimer .05
269 Benito Santiago .05
270 Mike Moore .05
271 Dave Fleming .05
272 Moises Alou .05
273 Pat Listach .05
274 Reggie Sanders .05
275 Kenny Lofton .05
276 Donovan Osborne .05
277 Rusty Meacham .05
278 Eric Karros .05
279 Andy Stankiewicz .05
280 Brian Jordan .05
281 Gary DiSarcina .05
282 Mark Wohlers .05
283 Dave Nilsson .05
284 Anthony Young .05
285 Jim Bullinger .05
286 Derek Bell .05
287 Brian Williams .05
288 Julio Valera .05
289 Dan Walters .05
290 Chad Curtis .05
291 Michael Tucker .05
292 Bob Zupcic .05
293 Todd Hundley .05
294 Jeff Tackett .05
295 Greg Colbrunn .05
296 Cal Eldred .05
297 Chris Roberts .05
298 John Doherty .05
299 Denny Neagle .05
300 Arthur Rhodes .05
301 Mark Clark .05
302 Scott Cooper .05
303 Jamie Arnold **RC** .05
304 Jim Thome .60
305 Frank Seminara .05
306 Kurt Knudsen .05
307 Tim Wakefield .05
308 John Jaha .05
309 Pat Hentgen .05
310 B.J. Wallace .05
311 Roberto Hernandez .05
312 Hipolito Pichardo .05
313 Eric Fox .05
314 Willie Banks .05
315 Sam Militello .05
316 Vince Horsman .05
317 Carlos Hernandez .05
318 Jeff Kent .05
319 Mike Perez .05
320 Scott Livingstone .05
321 Jeff Conine .05
322 James Austin .05
323 John Vander Wal .05
324 Pat Mahomes .05
325 Pedro Astacio .05
326 Bret Boone .05
327 Matt Stairs .05
328 Damion Easley .05
329 Ben Rivera .05
330 Reggie Jefferson .05
331 Luis Mercedes .05
332 Kyle Abbott .05
333 Eddie Taubensee .05
334 Tim McIntosh .05
335 Phil Clark .05
336 Wil Cordero .05
337 Russ Springer .05
338 Craig Colbert .05
339 Tim Salmon .05
340 Braulio Castillo .05
341 Donald Harris .05
342 Eric Young .05
343 Bob Wickman .05
344 John Valentin .05
345 Dan Wilson .05
346 Steve Hosey .05
347 Mike Piazza 1.00
348 Willie Greene .05
349 Tom Goodwin .05
350 Eric Hillman .05
351 Steve Reed **RC** .05
352 Dan Serafini **RC** .05
353 Todd Steverson **RC** .05
354 Benji Grigsby .05
355 Shannon Stewart **RC** 1.00
356 Sean Lowe .05
357 Derek Wallace .05
358 Rick Helling .05
359 Jason Kendall **RC** 1.00
360 Derek Jeter **RC** 10.00
361 David Cone .05
362 Jeff Reardon .05
363 Bobby Witt .05
364 Jose Canseco .40
365 Jeff Russell .05
366 Ruben Sierra .05
367 Alan Mills .05
368 Matt Nokes .05
369 Pat Borders .05
370 Pedro Munoz .05
371 Danny Jackson .05
372 Geronimo Pena .05
373 Craig Lefferts .05
374 Joe Grahe .05
375 Roger McDowell .05
376 Jimmy Key .05
377 Steve Olin .05
378 Glenn Davis .05
379 Rene Gonzales .05
380 Manuel Lee .05
381 Ron Karkovice .05
382 Sid Bream .05
383 Gerald Williams .05
384 Lenny Harris .05
385 J.T. Snow **RC** .75
386 Dave Stieb .05
387 Kirk McCaskill .05
388 Lance Parrish .05
389 Craig Greback .05
390 Rick Wilkins .05
391 Manny Alexander .05
392 Mike Schooler .05
393 Bernie Williams .05
394 Kevin Koslofski .05
395 Willie Wilson .05
396 Jeff Parrett .05
397 Mike Harkey .05
398 Frank Tanana .05
399 Doug Henry .05
400 Royce Clayton .05
401 Eric Wedge .05
402 Derrick May .05
403 Carlos Garcia .05
404 Henry Rodriguez .05
405 Ryan Klesko .05

Aces

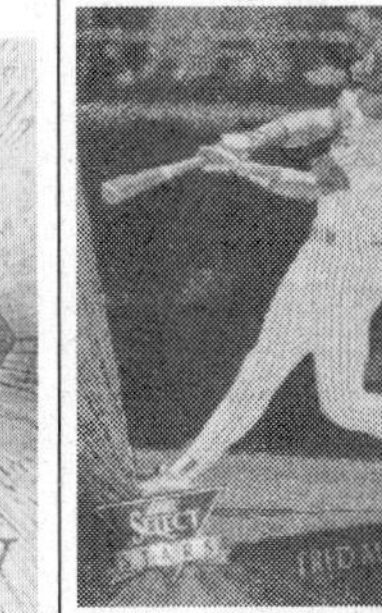

Cards from this set feature 24 of the top pitchers from 1992 and were included one per every 27-card Super Pack. The fronts have a picture of the player in action against an Ace card background. Backs have text and a portrait in the middle of a card suit for an Ace.

		NM/M
Complete Set (24):		20.00
Common Player:		1.00
1	Roger Clemens	6.00
2	Tom Glavine	3.00
3	Jack McDowell	1.00
4	Greg Maddux	4.50
5	Jack Morris	1.00
6	Dennis Martinez	1.00
7	Kevin Brown	1.00
8	Dwight Gooden	1.00
9	Kevin Appier	1.00
10	Mike Morgan	1.00
11	Juan Guzman	1.00
12	Charles Nagy	1.00
13	John Smiley	1.00
14	Ken Hill	1.00
15	Bob Tewksbury	1.00
16	Doug Drabek	1.00
17	John Smoltz	1.00
18	Greg Swindell	1.00
19	Bruce Hurst	1.00
20	Mike Mussina	2.00
21	Cal Eldred	1.00
22	Melido Perez	1.00
23	Dave Fleming	1.00
24	Kevin Tapani	1.00

Rookies

Top newcomers in 1992 are featured in this 21-card insert set. Cards were randomly inserted in 15-card hobby packs. The fronts, printed on metallic foil, have a Score Select Rookies logo on the front. The backs have text and a player portrait.

		NM/M
Complete Set (21):		4.00
Common Player:		.50
1	Pat Listach	.50
2	Moises Alou	.50
3	Reggie Sanders	.50
4	Kenny Lofton	.50
5	Eric Karros	.50
6	Brian Williams	.50
7	Donovan Osborne	.50
8	Sam Militello	.50
9	Chad Curtis	.50
10	Bob Zupcic	.50
11	Tim Salmon	1.50
12	Jeff Conine	.50
13	Pedro Astacio	.50
14	Arthur Rhodes	.50
15	Cal Eldred	.50
16	Tim Wakefield	.50
17	Andy Stankiewicz	.50
18	Wil Cordero	.50
19	Todd Hundley	.50
20	Dave Fleming	.50
21	Bret Boone	1.00

Stars

The top 24 players from 1992 are featured in this insert set. Cards were randomly inserted in 15-card retail packs. Fronts are printed on metallic foil.

		NM/M
Complete Set (24):		40.00
Common Player:		.60
1	Fred McGriff	.60
2	Ryne Sandberg	4.00
3	Ozzie Smith	4.00
4	Gary Sheffield	1.25
5	Darren Daulton	.60
6	Andy Van Slyke	.60
7	Barry Bonds	7.50
8	Tony Gwynn	4.00
9	Greg Maddux	4.00
10	Tom Glavine	1.00
11	John Franco	.60
12	Lee Smith	.60
13	Cecil Fielder	.60
14	Roberto Alomar	1.00
15	Cal Ripken, Jr.	7.50
16	Edgar Martinez	.60
17	Ivan Rodriguez	2.50
18	Kirby Puckett	4.00
19	Ken Griffey Jr.	6.00
20	Joe Carter	.60
21	Roger Clemens	4.50
22	Dave Fleming	.60
(22)	Dave Fleming (Blank-back sample card.)	1.00
23	Paul Molitor	3.00
(23)	Paul Molitor (Blank-back sample card.)	2.75
24	Dennis Eckersley	2.50

Stat Leaders

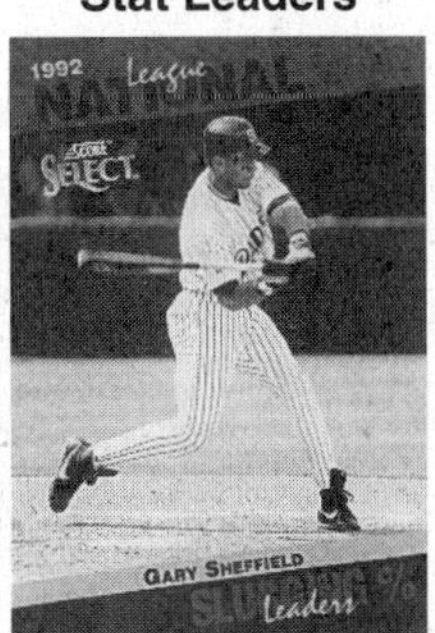

This 90-card set features 1992 American League and National League leaders in various statistical categories. Each card front indicates the league and the category in which the player finished at or near the top. The backs have a list of the leaders; the pictured player's name is in larger type size. Cards were inserted one per foil pack.

		NM/M
Complete Set (90):		8.00
Common Player:		.05
1	Edgar Martinez	.05
2	Kirby Puckett	.30
3	Frank Thomas	.25
4	Gary Sheffield	.15
5	Andy Van Slyke	.05
6	John Kruk	.05
7	Kirby Puckett	.30
8	Carlos Baerga	.05
9	Paul Molitor	.25
10	Andy Van Slyke, Terry Pendleton	.05
11	Ryne Sandberg	.30
12	Mark Grace	.05
13	Frank Thomas	.25
14	Don Mattingly	.35
15	Ken Griffey Jr.	.45
16	Andy Van Slyke	.05
17	Mariano Duncan, Jerald Clark, Ray Lankford	.05
18	Marquis Grissom, Terry Pendleton	.05
19	Lance Johnson	.05
20	Mike Devereaux	.05
21	Brady Anderson	.05
22	Deion Sanders	.05
23	Steve Finley	.05
24	Andy Van Slyke	.05
25	Juan Gonzalez	.15
26	Mark McGwire	.50
27	Cecil Fielder	.05
28	Fred McGriff	.05
29	Barry Bonds	.60
30	Gary Sheffield	.15
31	Cecil Fielder	.05
32	Joe Carter	.05
33	Frank Thomas	.25
34	Darren Daulton	.05
35	Terry Pendleton	.05
36	Fred McGriff	.05
37	Tony Phillips	.05
38	Frank Thomas	.25
39	Roberto Alomar	.15
40	Barry Bonds	.60
41	Dave Hollins	.05
42	Andy Van Slyke	.05
43	Mark McGwire	.50
44	Edgar Martinez	.05
45	Frank Thomas	.25
46	Barry Bonds	.60
47	Gary Sheffield	.15
48	Fred McGriff	.05
49	Frank Thomas	.25
50	Danny Tartabull	.05
51	Roberto Alomar	.15
52	Barry Bonds	.60
53	John Kruk	.05
54	Brett Butler	.05
55	Kenny Lofton	.05
56	Pat Listach	.05
57	Brady Anderson	.05
58	Marquis Grissom	.05
59	Delino DeShields	.05
60	Steve Finley, Bip Roberts	.05
61	Jack McDowell	.05
62	Kevin Brown	.05
63	Melido Perez	.05
64	Terry Mulholland	.05
65	Curt Schilling	.20
66	John Smoltz, Doug Drabek, Greg Maddux	.05
67	Dennis Eckersley	.20
68	Rick Aguilera	.05
69	Jeff Montgomery	.05
70	Lee Smith	.05
71	Randy Myers	.05
72	John Wetteland	.05
73	Randy Johnson	.25
74	Melido Perez	.05
75	Roger Clemens	.35
76	John Smoltz	.05
77	David Cone	.05
78	Greg Maddux	.30
79	Roger Clemens	.35
80	Kevin Appier	.05
81	Mike Mussina	.15
82	Bill Swift	.05
83	Bob Tewksbury	.05
84	Greg Maddux	.30
85	Kevin Brown	.05
86	Jack McDowell	.05
87	Roger Clemens	.35
88	Tom Glavine	.10
89	Ken Hill, Bob Tewksbury	.05
90	Dennis Martinez, Mike Morgan	.05

Triple Crown

This three-card set commemorates the Triple Crown seasons of Hall of Famers Mickey Mantle, Frank Robinson and Carl Yastrzemski. Cards were randomly inserted in 15-card hobby packs. Card fronts have a green metallic-look textured border, with the player's name at top in gold, and "Triple Crown" in gold at bottom. There are other silver and green highlights around the photo, which feature the player set against a metallized background. Dark green backs have a player photo and information on his Triple Crown season.

		NM/M
Complete Set (3):		35.00
Common Player:		10.00
1	Mickey Mantle	22.50
2	Frank Robinson	10.00
3	Carl Yastrzemski	12.50

1993 Select Rookie/Traded

Production of this 150-card set was limited to 1,950 numbered cases. Several future Hall of Famers and six dozen top rookies are featured in the set. Cards were available in packs rather than collated sets and include randomly inserted FX cards, which feature Nolan Ryan (two per 24-box case), Tim Salmon and Mike

Piazza (one per 576 packs) and All-Star Rookie Team members (one per 58 packs).

		NM/M
Complete Set (150):		11.00
Common Player:		.05
Pack (12):		1.25
Wax Box (24):		20.00
1	Rickey Henderson	.75
2	Rob Deer	.05
3	Tim Belcher	.05
4	Gary Sheffield	.35
5	Fred McGriff	.05
6	Mark Whiten	.05
7	Jeff Russell	.05
8	Harold Baines	.05
9	Dave Winfield	.75
10	Ellis Burks	.05
11	Andre Dawson	.25
12	Gregg Jefferies	.05
13	Jimmy Key	.05
14	Harold Reynolds	.05
15	Tom Henke	.05
16	Paul Molitor	.75
17	Wade Boggs	1.00
18	David Cone	.05
19	Tony Fernandez	.05
20	Roberto Kelly	.05
21	Paul O'Neill	.05
22	Jose Lind	.05
23	Barry Bonds	2.00
24	Dave Stewart	.05
25	Randy Myers	.05
26	Benito Santiago	.05
27	Tim Wallach	.05
28	Greg Gagne	.05
29	Kevin Mitchell	.05
30	Jim Abbott	.05
31	Lee Smith	.05
32	Bobby Munoz **RC**	.05
33	Mo Sanford **RC**	.05
34	John Roper	.05
35	David Hulse **RC**	.05
36	Pedro Martinez	.75
37	Chuck Carr **RC**	.05
38	Armando Reynoso **RC**	.10
39	Ryan Thompson	.05
40	Carlos Garcia **RC**	.05
41	Matt Whiteside	.05
42	Benji Gil	.05
43	Rodney Bolton **RC**	.05
44	J.T. Snow	.05
45	David McCarty	.05
46	Paul Quantrill **RC**	.05
47	Al Martin	.05
48	Lance Painter	.05
49	Lou Frazier **RC**	.05
50	Eduardo Perez	.05
51	Kevin Young	.05
52	Mike Trombley	.05
53	Sterling Hitchcock **RC**	.10
54	Tim Bogar **RC**	.05
55	Hilly Hathaway **RC**	.05
56	Wayne Kirby **RC**	.05
57	Craig Paquette **RC**	.05
58	Bret Boone	.05
59	Greg McMichael **RC**	.05
60	Mike Lansing **RC**	.35
61	Brent Gates	.05
62	Rene Arocha	.05
63	Ricky Gutierrez	.05
64	Kevin Rogers **RC**	.05
65	Ken Ryan **RC**	.05
66	Phil Hiatt	.05
67	Pat Meares **RC**	.05
68	Troy Neel	.05
69	Steve Cooke	.05
70	Sherman Obando **RC**	.05
71	Blas Minor **RC**	.05
72	Angel Miranda **RC**	.05
73	Tom Kramer **RC**	.05
74	Chip Hale **RC**	.05
75	Brad Pennington **RC**	.05
76	Graeme Lloyd **RC**	.05
77	Darrell Whitmore **RC**	.05
78	David Nied	.05
79	Todd Van Poppel	.05
80	Chris Gomez **RC**	.10
81	Jason Bere	.05
82	Jeffrey Hammonds	.05
83	Brad Ausmus **RC**	.10
84	Kevin Stocker	.05
85	Jeromy Burnitz	.05
86	Aaron Sele	.05
87	Roberto Mejia **RC**	.05
88	Kirk Rueter **RC**	.10

#	Player	NM/M
89	Kevin Roberson **RC**	.05
90	Allen Watson **RC**	.05
91	Charlie Leibrandt	.05
92	Eric Davis	.05
93	Jody Reed	.05
94	Danny Jackson	.05
95	Gary Gaetti	.05
96	Norm Charlton	.05
97	Doug Drabek	.05
98	Scott Fletcher	.05
99	Greg Swindell	.05
100	John Smiley	.05
101	Kevin Reimer	.05
102	Andres Galarraga	.05
103	Greg Hibbard	.05
104	Chris Hammond	.05
105	Darnell Coles	.05
106	Mike Felder	.05
107	Jose Guzman	.05
108	Chris Bosio	.05
109	Spike Owen	.05
110	Felix Jose	.05
111	Cory Snyder	.05
112	Craig Lefferts	.05
113	David Wells	.05
114	Pete Incaviglia	.05
115	Mike Pagliarulo	.05
116	Dave Magadan	.05
117	Charlie Hough	.05
118	Ivan Calderon	.05
119	Manuel Lee	.05
120	Bob Patterson	.05
121	Bob Ojeda	.05
122	Scott Bankhead	.05
123	Greg Maddux	1.00
124	Chili Davis	.05
125	Milt Thompson	.05
126	Dave Martinez	.05
127	Frank Tanana	.05
128	Phil Plantier	.05
129	Juan Samuel	.05
130	Eric Young	.05
131	Joe Orsulak	.05
132	Derek Bell	.05
133	Darrin Jackson	.05
134	Tom Brunansky	.05
135	Jeff Reardon	.05
136	Kevin Higgins **RC**	.05
137	Joel Johnston **RC**	.05
138	Rick Trlicek **RC**	.05
139	Richie Lewis **RC**	.05
140	Jeff Gardner **RC**	.05
141	Jack Voigt **RC**	.05
142	Rod Correia **RC**	.05
143	Billy Brewer **RC**	.05
144	Terry Jorgensen **RC**	.05
145	Rich Amaral **RC**	.05
146	Sean Berry **RC**	.05
147	Dan Peltier **RC**	.05
148	Paul Wagner **RC**	.05
149	Damon Buford **RC**	.05
150	Wil Cordero	.05

All-Star Rookies

These cards were randomly inserted into the Score Select Rookie/Traded packs, making them among the scarcest of the year's many "chase" cards. Card fronts feature metallic foil printing. Backs have a few words about the player. Stated odds of finding an All-Star Rookie Team insert card are one per 58 packs.

		NM/M
Complete Set (10):		30.00
Common Player:		1.00
1	Jeff Conine	1.00
2	Brent Gates	1.00
3	Mike Lansing	1.00
4	Kevin Stocker	1.00
5	Mike Piazza	25.00
6	Jeffrey Hammonds	1.00
7	David Hulse	1.00
8	Tim Salmon	2.00
9	Rene Arocha	1.00
10	Greg McMichael	1.00

Inserts

Three cards honoring the 1993 Rookies of the Year and retiring superstar Nolan Ryan were issued as random inserts

in the Select Rookie/Traded packs. Cards are printed with metallic foil front backgrounds. Stated odds of finding a Piazza or Salmon card are about one per 24-box case; Ryan cards are found on average two per case.

		NM/M
Complete Set (3):		60.00
Common Player:		6.00
1NR	Nolan Ryan	40.00
1ROY	Tim Salmon	6.00
2ROY	Mike Piazza	20.00

1994 Select Promos

To introduce its 1994 offering to dealers and collectors, Score Select created an eight-card promo set. Cards are identical in format to regular-issue cards with the exception of the word "SAMPLE" overprinted diagonally on front and back. The promos included five of the regular-run cards, a Rookie Prospect card and one each of its Rookie Surge '94 and Crown Contenders insert sets. The promos were cello-packaged with a header card describing the set and chase cards.

		NM/M
Complete Set (8):		7.50
Common Player:		.75
3	Paul Molitor	1.50
17	Kirby Puckett	2.50
19	Randy Johnson	1.50
24	John Kruk	.75
51	Jose Lind	.75
197	Ryan Klesko (Rookie Prospect)	1.00
1CC	Lenny Dykstra (Crown Contenders)	1.00
1RS	Cliff Floyd (Rookie Surge)	1.00
---	Header Card	.05

1994 Select

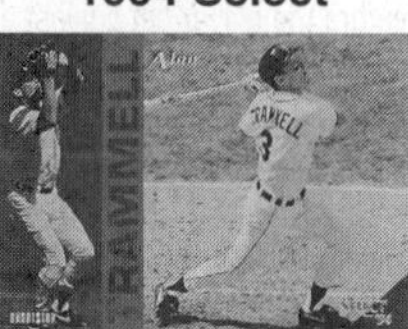

Both series of this premium brand from the Score/Pinnacle lineup offered 210 regular cards for a combined 420 cards, and seven insert sets. The announced press run for each series was 4,950 20-box cases. Cards have a horizontal format with a color action photo at right and a second photo at left done in a single team color-coded hue. The player's last name is dropped out of a vertical gold-foil strip between the two photos, with his first name in white at top-center. Backs are vertical with yet another color action photo at center. In a vertical bar at right, matching the color-coding on front and printed over the photo are 1993 and career stats, a "Select Stat," and a few sentences about the player. The appropriate logos and Pinnacle's optical-variable anti-counterfeiting device are at bottom-center. Thirty of the final 33 cards in the first series are a "1994 Rookie Prospect" subset, so noted in a special gold-foil logo on front.

		NM/M
Complete Set (420):		12.50
Common Player:		.05
Pack (12):		1.25
Wax Box (24):		16.00
1	Ken Griffey Jr.	1.50
2	Greg Maddux	1.00
3	Paul Molitor	.75
4	Mike Piazza	1.50
5	Jay Bell	.05
6	Frank Thomas	.75
7	Barry Larkin	.05
8	Paul O'Neill	.05
9	Darren Daulton	.05
10	Mike Greenwell	.05
11	Chuck Carr	.05
12	Joe Carter	.05
13	Lance Johnson	.05
14	Jeff Blauser	.05
15	Chris Hoiles	.05
16	Rick Wilkins	.05
17	Kirby Puckett	1.00
18	Larry Walker	.05
19	Randy Johnson	.75
20	Bernard Gilkey	.05
21	Devon White	.05
22	Randy Myers	.05
23	Don Mattingly	1.25
24	John Kruk	.05
25	Ozzie Guillen	.05
26	Jeff Conine	.05
27	Mike Macfarlane	.05
28	Dave Hollins	.05
29	Chuck Knoblauch	.05
30	Ozzie Smith	1.00
31	Harold Baines	.05
32	Ryne Sandberg	1.00
33	Ron Karkovice	.05
34	Terry Pendleton	.05
35	Wally Joyner	.05
36	Mike Mussina	.35
37	Felix Jose	.05
38	Derrick May	.05
39	Scott Cooper	.05
40	Jose Rijo	.05
41	Robin Ventura	.05
42	Charlie Hayes	.05
43	Jimmy Key	.05
44	Eric Karros	.05
45	Ruben Sierra	.05
46	Ryan Thompson	.05
47	Brian McRae	.05
48	Pat Hentgen	.05
49	John Valentin	.05
50	Al Martin	.05
51	Jose Lind	.05
52	Kevin Stocker	.05
53	Mike Gallego	.05
54	Dwight Gooden	.05
55	Brady Anderson	.05
56	Jeff King	.05
57	Mark McGwire	1.75
58	Sammy Sosa	1.00
59	Ryan Bowen	.05
60	Mark Lemke	.05
61	Roger Clemens	1.25
62	Brian Jordan	.05
63	Andres Galarraga	.05
64	Kevin Appier	.05
65	Don Slaught	.05
66	Mike Blowers	.05
67	Wes Chamberlain	.05
68	Troy Neel	.05
69	John Wetteland	.05
70	Joe Girardi	.05
71	Reggie Sanders	.05
72	Edgar Martinez	.05
73	Todd Hundley	.05
74	Pat Borders	.05
75	Roberto Mejia	.05
76	David Cone	.05
77	Tony Gwynn	1.00
78	Jim Abbott	.05
79	Jay Buhner	.05
80	Mark McLemore	.05
81	Wil Cordero	.05
82	Pedro Astacio	.05
83	Bob Tewksbury	.05
84	Dave Winfield	.75
85	Jeff Kent	.05
86	Todd Van Poppel	.05
87	Steve Avery	.05
88	Mike Lansing	.05
89	Len Dykstra	.05
90	Jose Guzman	.05
91	Brian Hunter	.05
92	Tim Raines	.05
93	Andre Dawson	.25
94	Joe Orsulak	.05
95	Ricky Jordan	.05
96	Billy Hatcher	.05
97	Jack McDowell	.05
98	Tom Pagnozzi	.05
99	Darryl Strawberry	.05
100	Mike Stanley	.05
101	Bret Saberhagen	.05
102	Willie Greene	.05
103	Bryan Harvey	.05
104	Tim Bogar	.05
105	Jack Voight	.05
106	Brad Ausmus	.05
107	Ramon Martinez	.05
108	Mike Perez	.05
109	Jeff Montgomery	.05
110	Danny Darwin	.05
111	Wilson Alvarez	.05
112	Kevin Mitchell	.05
113	David Nied	.05
114	Rich Amaral	.05
115	Stan Javier	.05
116	Mo Vaughn	.05
117	Ben McDonald	.05
118	Tom Gordon	.05
119	Carlos Garcia	.05
120	Phil Plantier	.05
121	Mike Morgan	.05
122	Pat Meares	.05
123	Kevin Young	.05
124	Jeff Fassero	.05
125	Gene Harris	.05
126	Bob Welch	.05
127	Walt Weiss	.05
128	Bobby Witt	.05
129	Andy Van Slyke	.05
130	Steve Cooke	.05
131	Mike Devereaux	.05
132	Joey Cora	.05
133	Bret Barberie	.05
134	Orel Hershiser	.05
135	Ed Sprague	.05
136	Shawon Dunston	.05
137	Alex Arias	.05
138	Archi Cianfrocco	.05
139	Tim Wallach	.05
140	Bernie Williams	.05
141	Karl Rhodes	.05
142	Pat Kelly	.05
143	Dave Magadan	.05
144	Kevin Tapani	.05
145	Eric Young	.05
146	Derek Bell	.05
147	Dante Bichette	.05
148	Geronimo Pena	.05
149	Joe Oliver	.05
150	Orestes Destrade	.05
151	Tim Naehring	.05
152	Ray Lankford	.05
153	Phil Clark	.05
154	David McCarty	.05
155	Tommy Greene	.05
156	Wade Boggs	1.00
157	Kevin Gross	.05
158	Hal Morris	.05
159	Moises Alou	.05
160	Rick Aguilera	.05
161	Curt Schilling	.35
162	Chip Hale	.05
163	Tino Martinez	.05
164	Mark Whiten	.05
165	Dave Stewart	.05
166	Steve Buechele	.05
167	Bobby Jones	.05
168	Darrin Fletcher	.05
169	John Smiley	.05
170	Cory Snyder	.05
171	Scott Erickson	.05
172	Kirk Rueter	.05
173	Dave Fleming	.05
174	John Smoltz	.05
175	Ricky Gutierrez	.05
176	Mike Bordick	.05
177	Chan Ho Park **RC**	1.00
178	Alex Gonzalez	.05
179	Steve Karsay	.05
180	Jeffrey Hammonds	.05
181	Manny Ramirez	.75
182	Salomon Torres	.05
183	Raul Mondesi	.05
184	James Mouton	.05
185	Cliff Floyd	.05
186	Danny Bautista	.05
187	Kurt Abbott **RC**	.05
188	Javier Lopez	.05
189	John Patterson	.05
190	Greg Blosser	.05
191	Bob Hamelin	.05
192	Tony Eusebio	.05
193	Carlos Delgado	.50
194	Chris Gomez	.05
195	Kelly Stinnett	.05
196	Shane Reynolds	.05
197	Ryan Klesko	.05
198	Jim Edmonds	.05
199	James Hurst	.05
200	Dave Staton	.05
201	Rondell White	.05
202	Keith Mitchell	.05
203	Darren Oliver	.05
204	Mike Matheny	.05
205	Chris Turner	.05
206	Matt Mieske	.05
207	N.L. Team Checklist	.05
208	N.L. Team Checklist	.05
209	A.L. Team Checklist	.05
210	A.L. Team Checklist	.05
211	Barry Bonds	2.00
212	Juan Gonzalez	.40
213	Jim Eisenreich	.05
214	Ivan Rodriguez	.65
215	Tony Phillips	.05
216	John Jaha	.05
217	Lee Smith	.05
218	Bip Roberts	.05
219	Dave Hansen	.05
220	Pat Listach	.05
221	Willie McGee	.05
222	Damion Easley	.05
223	Dean Palmer	.05
224	Mike Moore	.05
225	Brian Harper	.05
226	Gary DiSarcina	.05
227	Delino DeShields	.05
228	Otis Nixon	.05
229	Roberto Alomar	.30
230	Mark Grace	.05
231	Kenny Lofton	.05
232	Gregg Jefferies	.05
233	Cecil Fielder	.05
234	Jeff Bagwell	.75
235	Albert Belle	.05
236	Dave Justice	.05
237	Tom Henke	.05
238	Bobby Bonilla	.05
239	John Olerud	.05
240	Robby Thompson	.05
241	Dave Valle	.05
242	Marquis Grissom	.05
243	Greg Swindell	.05
244	Todd Zeile	.05
245	Dennis Eckersley	.65
246	Jose Offerman	.05
247	Greg McMichael	.05
248	Tim Belcher	.05
249	Cal Ripken, Jr.	2.00
250	Tom Glavine	.05
251	Luis Polonia	.05
252	Bill Swift	.05
253	Juan Guzman	.05
254	Rickey Henderson	.75
255	Terry Mulholland	.05
256	Gary Sheffield	.40
257	Terry Steinbach	.05
258	Brett Butler	.05
259	Jason Bere	.05
260	Doug Strange	.05
261	Kent Hrbek	.05
262	Graeme Lloyd	.05
263	Lou Frazier	.05
264	Charles Nagy	.05
265	Bret Boone	.05
266	Kirk Gibson	.05
267	Kevin Brown	.05
268	Matt Williams	.05
270	Greg Gagne	.05
271	Mariano Duncan	.05
272	Jeff Russell	.05
273	Eric Davis	.05
274	Shane Mack	.05
275	Jose Vizcaino	.05
276	Jose Canseco	.45
277	Roberto Hernandez	.05
278	Royce Clayton	.05
279	Carlos Baerga	.05
280	Pete Incaviglia	.05
281	Brent Gates	.05
282	Jeromy Burnitz	.05
283	Chili Davis	.05
284	Pete Harnisch	.05
285	Alan Trammell	.05
286	Eric Anthony	.05
287	Ellis Burks	.05
288	Julio Franco	.05
289	Jack Morris	.05
290	Erik Hanson	.05
291	Chuck Finley	.05
292	Reggie Jefferson	.05
293	Kevin McReynolds	.05
294	Greg Hibbard	.05
295	Travis Fryman	.05
296	Craig Biggio	.05
297	Kenny Rogers	.05
298	Dave Henderson	.05
299	Jim Thome	.50
300	Rene Arocha	.05
301	Pedro Munoz	.05
302	David Hulse	.05
303	Greg Vaughn	.05
304	Darren Lewis	.05
305	Deion Sanders	.05
306	Danny Tartabull	.05
307	Darryl Hamilton	.05
308	Andujar Cedeno	.05
309	Tim Salmon	.05
310	Tony Fernandez	.05
311	Alex Fernandez	.05
312	Roberto Kelly	.05
313	Harold Reynolds	.05
314	Chris Sabo	.05
315	Howard Johnson	.05
316	Mark Portugal	.05
317	Rafael Palmeiro	.65
318	Pete Smith	.05
319	Will Clark	.05
320	Henry Rodriguez	.05
321	Omar Vizquel	.05
322	David Segui	.05
323	Lou Whitaker	.05
324	Felix Fermin	.05
325	Spike Owen	.05
326	Darryl Kile	.05
327	Chad Kreuter	.05
328	Rod Beck	.05
329	Eddie Murray	.75
330	B.J. Surhoff	.05
331	Mickey Tettleton	.05
332	Pedro Martinez	.75
333	Roger Pavlik	.05
334	Eddie Taubensee	.05
335	John Doherty	.05
336	Jody Reed	.05
337	Aaron Sele	.05
338	Leo Gomez	.05
339	Dave Nilsson	.05
340	Rob Dibble	.05
341	John Burkett	.05
342	Wayne Kirby	.05
343	Dan Wilson	.05
344	Armando Reynoso	.05
345	Chad Curtis	.05
346	Dennis Martinez	.05
347	Cal Eldred	.05
348	Luis Gonzalez	.05
349	Doug Drabek	.05
350	Jim Leyritz	.05
351	Mark Langston	.05
352	Darrin Jackson	.05
353	Sid Fernandez	.05
354	Benito Santiago	.05
355	Kevin Seitzer	.05
356	Bo Jackson	.10
357	David Wells	.05
358	Paul Sorrento	.05
359	Ken Caminiti	.05
360	Eduardo Perez	.05
361	Orlando Merced	.05
362	Steve Finley	.05
363	Andy Benes	.05
364	Manuel Lee	.05
365	Todd Benzinger	.05
366	Sandy Alomar Jr.	.05
367	Rex Hudler	.05
368	Mike Henneman	.05
369	Vince Coleman	.05
370	Kirt Manwaring	.05
371	Ken Hill	.05
372	Glenallen Hill	.05
373	Sean Berry	.05
374	Geronimo Berroa	.05
375	Duane Ward	.05
376	Allen Watson	.05
377	Marc Newfield	.05
378	Dan Miceli	.05
379	Denny Hocking	.05
380	Mark Kiefer	.05
381	Tony Tarasco	.05
382	Tony Longmire	.05
383	Brian Anderson **RC**	.05
384	Fernando Vina	.05
385	Hector Carrasco	.05
386	Mike Kelly	.05
387	Greg Colbrunn	.05
388	Roger Salkeld	.05
389	Steve Trachsel	.05
390	Rich Becker	.05
391	Billy Taylor **RC**	.05
392	Rich Rowland	.05
393	Carl Everett	.05
394	Johnny Ruffin	.05
395	Keith Lockhart **RC**	.05
396	J.R. Phillips	.05
397	Sterling Hitchcock	.05
398	Jorge Fabregas	.05
399	Jeff Granger	.05
400	Eddie Zambrano **RC**	.05
401	Rikkert Faneyte **RC**	.05
402	Gerald Williams	.05
403	Joey Hamilton	.05
404	Joe Hall **RC**	.05
405	John Hudek **RC**	.05
406	Roberto Petagine	.05
407	Charles Johnson	.05
408	Mark Smith	.05
409	Jeff Juden	.05
410	Carlos Pulido **RC**	.05
411	Paul Shuey	.05
412	Rob Butler	.05
413	Mark Acre	.05
414	Greg Pirkl	.05
415	Melvin Nieves	.05
416	Tim Hyers **RC**	.05
417	N.L. Checklist	.05
418	N.L. Checklist	.05
419	A.L. Checklist	.05
420	A.L. Checklist	.05

Crown Contenders

Candidates for the major baseball annual awards are featured in this subset. Horizontal-format cards have a color player photo printed on a holographic foil background. Backs are vertically oriented with a player portrait photo and justification for the player's inclusion in the set. Cards are numbered with a "CC" prefix and feature a special optical-variable anti-counterfeiting device at bottom-center. According to stated odds of one card on average in every 24 packs it has been estimated that fewer than 12,000 of each Crown Contenders card was produced.

		NM/M
Complete Set (10):		12.50
Common Player:		.50
1	Len Dykstra	.50
2	Greg Maddux	1.75
3	Roger Clemens	2.00
4	Randy Johnson	1.50
5	Frank Thomas	1.50
6	Barry Bonds	3.00
7	Juan Gonzalez	1.00
8	John Olerud	.50
9	Mike Piazza	2.50
10	Ken Griffey Jr.	2.50

MVP

Paul Molitor was the 1994 Select MVP and is featured in this one card set. Molitor is pictured in front of three distinct foil designs across the rest of the card.

		NM/M
MVP1	Paul Molitor	5.00

Rookie of the Year

Carlos Delgado was the 1994 Select Rookie of the Year. Delgado is pictured on top of a glowing foil background with his initials in large capital letters in the background and Rookie of the Year printed across the bottom.

		NM/M
RY1	Carlos Delgado	7.50

Rookie Surge

Each series of 1994 Score Select offered a chase card set of nine top rookies. Fronts feature action photos set against a rainbow-colored metallic foil background. Backs have a portrait photo and a few words about the player. Cards are numbered with an "RS" prefix and were inserted at an average rate of one per 48 packs.

		NM/M
Complete Set (18):		10.00
Common Player:		.75
1	Cliff Floyd	.75
2	Bob Hamelin	.75
3	Ryan Klesko	.75
4	Carlos Delgado	3.00
5	Jeffrey Hammonds	.75
6	Rondell White	.75
7	Salomon Torres	.75
8	Steve Karsay	.75
9	Javier Lopez	.75
10	Manny Ramirez	3.00
11	Tony Tarasco	.75
12	Kurt Abbott	.75
13	Chan Ho Park	.75
14	Rich Becker	.75
15	James Mouton	.75
16	Alex Gonzalez	.75
17	Raul Mondesi	.75
18	Steve Trachsel	.75

Salute

With odds of finding one of these cards stated at one per 360 packs, it is estimated that only about 4,000 of each of this two-card chase set were produced.

		NM/M
Complete Set (2):		15.00
1	Cal Ripken, Jr.	12.50
2	Dave Winfield	5.00

Skills

Select Skills is a 10-card insert that was randomly inserted into every 24 packs. Ten specific skills were designated and matched with the player whom, in the opinion of Select officials, demonstrated that particular skill the best in baseball. Each card is printed on a foil background with the player name vertically on left side of the card and the skill that they are being featured for along the bottom.

		NM/M
Complete Set (10):		15.00
Common Player:		.75
1	Randy Johnson	3.00
2	Barry Larkin	.75
3	Len Dykstra	.75
4	Kenny Lofton	.75
5	Juan Gonzalez	1.50
6	Barry Bonds	6.00
7	Marquis Grissom	.75
8	Ivan Rodriguez	2.50
9	Larry Walker	.75
10	Travis Fryman	.75

1995 Select Samples

Pinnacle's hobby-only Select brand issue for 1995 was previewed with this four-

card cello-packed sample set. Three player cards are in the basic format of the regular-issue Select cards, except they have a large white "SAMPLE" printed diagonally across the front and back. The fourth card in the sample pack is a header card advertising the features of the issue.

		NM/M
Complete Set (4):		4.00
Common Player:		.50
34	Roberto Alomar	.50
37	Jeff Bagwell	.75
241	Alex Rodriguez	4.00
--	Header Card	.05

1995 Select

The 250 regular-issue cards in Pinnacle's mid-price brand feature three basic formats. Veteran players' cards are presented horizontally and feature an action photo at left. At right is a portrait in a trapezoidal gold-foil frame set against a team color-coordinated marbled background. The team logo beneath the portrait and the player's name below that are printed in gold foil. Backs feature a black-and-white photo with a few career highlights, 1994 and career stats, and a "Select Stat" printed in red. The colored marble effect is carried over from the front. The Select Rookie cards, which are grouped toward the end of the set, are vertical in format and feature a borderless player photo with a gold-foil band at bottom which includes the player name and team logo, along with waves of gold emanating from the logo. Backs have a small, narrow color photo at left, with a large sepia version of the same photo ghosted at center and overprinted with a career summary. At bottom are 1994 and career stats. Ending the set are a series of "Show Time" cards of top prospects. Cards feature large gold-foil "Show Time" and team logos at bottom, with a facsimile autograph printed above. The player photo is shown as if at a curtain raising, with spotlight effects behind. Backs repeat the curtain and spotlight motif and feature another player photo, with autograph above. Production of this hobby-only product was stated as 4,950 cases, which translates to about 110,000 of each regular-issue card. A special card (#251) of Hideo Nomo was added to the set later. It was not issued in foil packs, but distributed to dealers who had purchased Select cases.

		NM/M
Complete Set (251):		9.00
Common Player:		.05
Artist's Proofs:		10X
Pack (12):		1.50
Wax Box (24):		17.50
1	Cal Ripken Jr.	1.50
2	Robin Ventura	.05
3	Al Martin	.05
4	Jeff Frye	.05
5	Darryl Strawberry	.05
6	Chan Ho Park	.05
7	Steve Avery	.05
8	Bret Boone	.05
9	Danny Tartabull	.05
10	Dante Bichette	.05
11	Rondell White	.05
12	Dave McCarty	.05
13	Bernard Gilkey	.05
14	Mark McGwire	1.25
15	Ruben Sierra	.05
16	Wade Boggs	.75
17	Mike Piazza	1.00
18	Jeffrey Hammonds	.05
19	Mike Mussina	.35
20	Darryl Kile	.05
21	Greg Maddux	.75
22	Frank Thomas	.65
23	Kevin Appier	.05
24	Jay Bell	.05
25	Kirk Gibson	.05
26	Pat Hentgen	.05
27	Joey Hamilton	.05
28	Bernie Williams	.05
29	Aaron Sele	.05
30	Delino DeShields	.05
31	Danny Bautista	.05
32	Jim Thome	.45
33	Rikkert Faneyte	.05
34	Roberto Alomar	.20
35	Paul Molitor	.65
36	Allen Watson	.05
37	Jeff Bagwell	.65
38	Jay Buhner	.05
39	Marquis Grissom	.05
40	Jim Edmonds	.05
41	Ryan Klesko	.05
42	Fred McGriff	.05
43	Tony Tarasco	.05
44	Darren Daulton	.05
45	Marc Newfield	.05
46	Barry Bonds	1.50
47	Bobby Bonilla	.05
48	Greg Pirkl	.05
49	Steve Karsay	.05
50	Bob Hamelin	.05
51	Javier Lopez	.05
52	Barry Larkin	.05
53	Kevin Young	.05
54	Sterling Hitchcock	.05
55	Tom Glavine	.05
56	Carlos Delgado	.40
57	Darren Oliver	.05
58	Cliff Floyd	.05
59	Tim Salmon	.05
60	Albert Belle	.05
61	Salomon Torres	.05
62	Gary Sheffield	.35
63	Ivan Rodriguez	.50
64	Charles Nagy	.05
65	Eduardo Perez	.05
66	Terry Steinbach	.05
67	Dave Justice	.05
68	Jason Bere	.05
69	Dave Nilsson	.05
70	Brian Anderson	.05
71	Billy Ashley	.05
72	Roger Clemens	.85
73	Jimmy Key	.05
74	Wally Joyner	.05
75	Andy Benes	.05
76	Ray Lankford	.05
77	Jeff Kent	.05
78	Moises Alou	.05
79	Kirby Puckett	.75
80	Joe Carter	.05
81	Manny Ramirez	.65
82	J.R. Phillips	.05
83	Matt Mieske	.05
84	John Olerud	.05
85	Andres Galarraga	.05
86	Juan Gonzalez	.35
87	Pedro Martinez	.65
88	Dean Palmer	.05
89	Ken Griffey Jr.	1.00
90	Brian Jordan	.05
91	Hal Morris	.05
92	Lenny Dykstra	.05
93	Wil Cordero	.05
94	Tony Gwynn	.75
95	Alex Gonzalez	.05
96	Cecil Fielder	.05
97	Mo Vaughn	.05
98	John Valentin	.05
99	Will Clark	.05
100	Geronimo Pena	.05
101	Don Mattingly	.85
102	Charles Johnson	.05
103	Raul Mondesi	.05
104	Reggie Sanders	.05
105	Royce Clayton	.05
106	Reggie Jefferson	.05
107	Craig Biggio	.05
108	Jack McDowell	.05
109	James Mouton	.05
110	Mike Greenwell	.05
111	David Cone	.05
112	Matt Williams	.05
113	Garret Anderson	.05
114	Carlos Garcia	.05
115	Alex Fernandez	.05
116	Deion Sanders	.05
117	Chili Davis	.05
118	Mike Kelly	.05
119	Jeff Conine	.05
120	Kenny Lofton	.05
121	Rafael Palmeiro	.50
122	Chuck Knoblauch	.05
123	Ozzie Smith	.75
124	Carlos Baerga	.05
125	Brett Butler	.05
126	Sammy Sosa	.75
127	Ellis Burks	.05
128	Bret Saberhagen	.05
129	Doug Drabek	.05
130	Dennis Martinez	.05
131	Paul O'Neill	.05
132	Travis Fryman	.05
133	Brent Gates	.05
134	Rickey Henderson	.65
135	Randy Johnson	.65
136	Mark Langston	.05
137	Greg Colbrunn	.05
138	Jose Rijo	.05
139	Bryan Harvey	.05
140	Dennis Eckersley	.50
141	Ron Gant	.05
142	Carl Everett	.05
143	Jeff Granger	.05
144	Ben McDonald	.05
145	Kurt Abbott	.05
146	Jim Abbott	.05
147	Jason Jacome	.05
148	Rico Brogna	.05
149	Cal Eldred	.05
150	Rich Becker	.05
151	Pete Harnisch	.05
152	Roberto Petagine	.05
153	Jacob Brumfield	.05
154	Todd Hundley	.05
155	Roger Cedeno	.05
156	Harold Baines	.05
157	Steve Dunn	.05
158	Tim Belk	.05
159	Marty Cardova	.05
160	Russ Davis	.05
161	Jose Malave	.05
162	Brian Hunter	.05
163	Andy Pettitte	.20
164	Brooks Kieschnick	.05
165	Midre Cummings	.05
166	Frank Rodriguez	.05
167	Chad Mottola	.05
168	Brian Barber	.05
169	Tim Unroe	.05
170	Shane Andrews	.05
171	Kevin Flora	.05
172	Ray Durham	.05
173	Chipper Jones	.75
174	Butch Huskey	.05
175	Ray McDavid	.05
176	Jeff Cirillo	.05
177	Terry Pendleton	.05
178	Scott Ruffcorn	.05
179	Ray Holbert	.05
180	Joe Randa	.05
181	Jose Oliva	.05
182	Andy Van Slyke	.05
183	Albie Lopez	.05
184	Chad Curtis	.05
185	Ozzie Guillen	.05
186	Chad Ogea	.05
187	Dan Wilson	.05
188	Tony Fernandez	.05
189	John Smoltz	.05
190	Willie Greene	.05
191	Darren Lewis	.05
192	Orlando Miller	.05
193	Kurt Miller	.05
194	Andrew Lorraine	.05
195	Ernie Young	.05
196	Jimmy Haynes	.05
197	Raul Casanova **RC**	.05
198	Joe Vitiello	.05
199	Brad Woodall	.05
200	Juan Acevedo	.05
201	Michael Tucker	.05
202	Shawn Green	.35
203	Alex Rodriguez	1.25
204	Julian Tavarez	.05
205	Jose Lima	.05
206	Wilson Alvarez	.05
207	Rich Aude	.05
208	Armando Benitez	.05
209	Dwayne Hosey	.05
210	Gabe White	.05
211	Joey Eischen	.05
212	Bill Pulsipher	.05
213	Robby Thompson	.05
214	Toby Borland	.05
215	Rusty Greer	.05
216	Fausto Cruz	.05
217	Luis Ortiz	.05
218	Duane Singleton	.05
219	Troy Percival	.05
220	Gregg Jefferies	.05
221	Mark Grace	.05
222	Mickey Tettleton	.05
223	Phil Plantier	.05
224	Larry Walker	.05
225	Ken Caminiti	.05
226	Dave Winfield	.65
227	Brady Anderson	.05
228	Kevin Brown	.05
229	Andujar Cedeno	.05
230	Roberto Kelly	.05
231	Jose Canseco	.35
231	Scott Ruffcorn (Showtime)	.05
232	Billy Ashley (Showtime)	.05
234	J.R. Phillips (Showtime)	.05
235	Chipper Jones (Showtime)	.40
236	Charles Johnson (Showtime)	.05
237	Midre Cummings (Showtime)	.05
238	Brian Hunter (Showtime)	.05
239	Garret Anderson (Showtime)	.05
240	Shawn Green (Showtime)	.10
241	Alex Rodriguez (Showtime)	.65
242	Checklist #1 (Frank Thomas)	.35
243	Checklist #2 (Ken Griffey Jr.)	.50
244	Checklist #3 (Albert Belle)	.05
245	Checklist #4 (Cal Ripken Jr.)	.65
246	Checklist #5 (Barry Bonds)	.75
247	Checklist #6 (Raul Mondesi)	.05
248	Checklist #7 (Mike Piazza)	.65
249	Checklist #8 (Jeff Bagwell)	.30
250	Checklist #9 (Jeff Bagwell, Frank Thomas, Ken Griffey Jr., Mike Piazza)	.25
251	Hideo Nomo	.35

Artist's Proofs

Among the scarcest and most valuable of 1995's baseball card inserts are the Select Artist's Proof parallel set. While an AP card is found on average once per 24 packs, the limited print run of the basic Select set means that only about 475 of each of the 250 regular-issue cards in the Select set were made in this edition. The AP inserts have a gold-foil "ARTIST'S PROOF" line at bottom, and other gold-foil highlights are embossed, rather than merely stamped on, as on regular Select cards.

	NM/M
Complete Set (250):	100.00
Common Player:	1.00
AP Stars:	10X

Big Sticks

With fronts printed in what Pinnacle describes as "holographic Gold Rush technology," the Big Sticks chase card issue offers a dozen of the game's big hitters in action photos superimposed over their team's logo. Conventionally printed backs have another player photo, along with a summary of career highlights and description of the player's power potential. Stated odds of pulling a Big Sticks chase card are one per 48 packs, on average. Cards are numbered with a "BS" prefix.

	NM/M
Complete Set (12):	40.00
Common Player:	1.50

1	Frank Thomas	4.00
2	Ken Griffey Jr.	7.50
3	Cal Ripken Jr.	10.00
4	Mike Piazza	7.50
5	Don Mattingly	6.00
6	Will Clark	1.50
7	Tony Gwynn	5.00
8	Jeff Bagwell	4.00
9	Barry Bonds	10.00
10	Paul Molitor	4.00
11	Matt Williams	1.50
12	Albert Belle	1.50

Can't Miss

A mix of rookies and sophomore standouts, along with a few players of slightly longer service are presented in this chase set. Cards feature color player action photos printed on a metallic red background, with their last name in gold foil at lower-left. An umpire on the "Can't Miss" logo is at upper-left. Backs repeat the logo, have a tall, narrow player photo, a few biographical details and a paragraph of career summary. Cards are numbered with a "CM" prefix.

		NM/M
Complete Set (12):		10.00
Common Player:		.35
1	Cliff Floyd	.35
2	Ryan Klesko	.35
3	Charles Johnson	.35
4	Raul Mondesi	.35
5	Manny Ramirez	2.00
6	Billy Ashley	.35
7	Alex Gonzalez	.35
8	Carlos Delgado	.75
9	Garret Anderson	.35
10	Alex Rodriguez	5.00
11	Chipper Jones	3.00
12	Shawn Green	.75

Sure Shots

Ten of Select's picks for future stardom are featured in this chase set, the toughest find of any of the 1995 Select inserts, at an average rate of one per 90 packs. Card fronts feature player action photos set against a gold "Dufex" foil printed background with a Sure Shots logo vertically at left. Backs have a blue background with a few words about the player and a portrait photo at left. Cards are numbered with a "SS" prefix.

		NM/M
Complete Set (10):		10.00
Common Player:		1.00
1	Ben Grieve	1.00
2	Kevin Witt	1.00
3	Mark Farris	1.00
4	Paul Konerko	3.00
5	Dustin Hermanson	1.00
6	Ramon Castro	1.00
7	McKay Christensen	1.00
8	Brian Buchanan	1.00
9	Paul Wilson	1.00
10	Terrence Long	1.00

1995 Select Certified Samples

Pinnacle's hobby-only Select brand issue for 1995 was previewed with this four-card cello-packed sample set. Three player cards are in the basic format of the regular-issue Select cards, except they have a large "SAMPLE" printed diagonally across the front and back. The fourth card in the sample pack is a header card advertising the features of the issue.

		NM/M
Complete Set (8):		7.50
Common Player:		.50
2	Reggie Sanders	.50
10	Mo Vaughn	.50
39	Mike Piazza	2.00
50	Mark McGwire	2.50
75	Roberto Alomar	.65
89	Larry Walker	.50
110	Ray Durham	.50
3 of 12	Cal Ripken Jr. (Gold Team)	4.00

1995 Select Certified

The concepts of hobby-only distribution and limited production, which were the hallmarks of Pinnacle's Select brand, were carried a step further with the post-season release of Select Certified baseball. Printed on double-thick cardboard stock card fronts feature all metallic-foil printing protected by a double laminated gloss coat. Backs have key player stats against each team in the league. The final 44 cards in the set are distinguished with a special Rookie logo and with gold added to the silver foil in the photo background.

		NM/M
Complete Set (135):		10.00
Common Player:		.05
Mirror Gold Stars:		5X
Pack (6):		2.00
Wax Box (20):		25.00
1	Barry Bonds	2.50
2	Reggie Sanders	.05
3	Terry Steinbach	.05
4	Eduardo Perez	.05
5	Frank Thomas	.75
6	Wil Cordero	.05
7	John Olerud	.05
8	Deion Sanders	.05
9	Mike Mussina	.40
10	Mo Vaughn	.05
11	Will Clark	.05
12	Chili Davis	.05
13	Jimmy Key	.05
14	Eddie Murray	.75
15	Bernard Gilkey	.05
16	David Cone	.05
17	Tim Salmon	.05
19	Steve Ontiveros	.05
20	Andres Galarraga	.05
21	Don Mattingly	1.25
22	Kevin Appier	.05
23	Paul Molitor	.75
24	Edgar Martinez	.05
25	Andy Benes	.05
26	Rafael Palmeiro	.65
27	Barry Larkin	.05
28	Gary Sheffield	.25
29	Wally Joyner	.05
30	Wade Boggs	1.00
31	Rico Brogna	.05
32	Eddie Murray (Murray Tribute)	.40
33	Kirby Puckett	1.00
34	Bobby Bonilla	.05
35	Hal Morris	.05
36	Moises Alou	.05
37	Javier Lopez	.05
38	Chuck Knoblauch	.05
39	Mike Piazza	1.50
40	Travis Fryman	.05
41	Rickey Henderson	.75
42	Jim Thome	.60
43	Carlos Baerga	.05
44	Dean Palmer	.05
45	Kirk Gibson	.05
46	Bret Saberhagen	.05
47	Cecil Fielder	.05
48	Manny Ramirez	.75
49	Derek Bell	.05
50	Mark McGwire	2.00
51	Jim Edmonds	.05
52	Robin Ventura	.05
53	Ryan Klesko	.05
54	Jeff Bagwell	.75
55	Ozzie Smith	1.00
56	Albert Belle	.05
57	Darren Daulton	.05
58	Jeff Conine	.05
59	Greg Maddux	1.00
60	Lenny Dykstra	.05
61	Randy Johnson	.75
62	Fred McGriff	.05
63	Ray Lankford	.05
64	Dave Justice	.05
65	Paul O'Neill	.05
66	Tony Gwynn	1.00
67	Matt Williams	.05
68	Dante Bichette	.05
69	Craig Biggio	.05
70	Ken Griffey Jr.	1.50
71	J.T. Snow	.05
72	Cal Ripken Jr.	2.50
73	Jay Bell	.05
74	Joe Carter	.05
75	Roberto Alomar	.30
76	Benji Gil	.05
77	Ivan Rodriguez	.65
78	Raul Mondesi	.05
79	Cliff Floyd	.05
80	Eric Karros, Mike Piazza, Raul Mondesi (Dodger Dynasty)	.30
81	Royce Clayton	.05
82	Billy Ashley	.05
83	Joey Hamilton	.05
84	Sammy Sosa	1.00
85	Jason Bere	.05
86	Dennis Martinez	.05
87	Greg Vaughn	.05
88	Roger Clemens	1.25
89	Larry Walker	.05
90	Mark Grace	.05
91	Kenny Lofton	.05
92	Carlos Perez **RC**	.05
93	Roger Cedeno	.05
94	Scott Ruffcorn	.05
95	Jim Pittsley	.05
96	Andy Pettitte	.20
97	James Baldwin	.05
98	Hideo Nomo **RC**	1.50
99	Ismael Valdes	.05
100	Armando Benitez	.05
101	Jose Malave	.05
102	Bobby Higginson **RC**	.25
103	LaTroy Hawkins	.05
104	Russ Davis	.05
105	Shawn Green	.40
106	Joe Vitiello	.05
107	Chipper Jones	1.00
108	Shane Andrews	.05
109	Jose Oliva	.05
110	Ray Durham	.05
111	Jon Nunnally	.05
112	Alex Gonzalez	.05
113	Vaughn Eshelman	.05
114	Marty Cordova	.05
115	Mark Grudzielanek **RC**	.25
116	Brian Hunter	.05
117	Charles Johnson	.05
118	Alex Rodriguez	2.00
119	David Bell	.05
120	Todd Hollandsworth	.05
121	Joe Randa	.05
122	Derek Jeter	2.50
123	Frank Rodriguez	.05
124	Curtis Goodwin	.05
125	Bill Pulsipher	.05
126	John Mabry	.05
127	Julian Tavarez	.05
128	Edgardo Alfonzo	.05
129	Orlando Miller	.05
130	Juan Acevedo	.05
131	Jeff Cirillo	.05
132	Roberto Petagine	.05
133	Antonio Osuna	.05
134	Michael Tucker	.05
135	Garret Anderson	.05
2131	Cal Ripken Jr. (Consecutive Game Record)	1.00

Mirror Gold

Inserted at an average rate of one per nine packs, this parallel set is a gold-foil version of the regular Select Certified set. Backs have a "MIRROR GOLD" notation at bottom.

	NM/M
Complete Set (135):	150.00
Common Player:	1.00
Mirror Gold Stars:	5X

Checklists

The seven checklists issued with Select Certified are not numbered as part of the set. They are found one per foil pack and are printed on much thinner card stock than the regular-issue cards.

		NM/M
Complete Set (7):		2.00
Common Player:		.40
1	Ken Griffey Jr. (A.L., #3-41)	.50
2	Frank Thomas (A.L., #42-95)	.40
3	Cal Ripken Jr. (A.L., #96-135)	.65
4	Jeff Bagwell (N.L., #1-58)	.40
5	Mike Piazza (N.L., #59-92)	.50
6	Barry Bonds (N.L., #93-133)	.65
7	Manny Ramirez, Raul Mondesi (Chase Cards)	.40

Future

A striking new all-metal, brushed-foil printing technology was used in the production of this chase set of 10 rookie players with "unlimited future potential." Stated odds of finding a Certified Future insert card were one in 19 packs.

		NM/M
Complete Set (10):		10.00
Common Player:		.50
1	Chipper Jones	2.00
2	Curtis Goodwin	.50
3	Hideo Nomo	1.00
4	Shawn Green	1.00
5	Ray Durham	.50
6	Todd Hollandsworth	.50
7	Brian Hunter	.50
8	Carlos Delgado	1.00
9	Michael Tucker	.50
10	Alex Rodriguez	4.00

Gold Team

A dozen of the top position players in the league were selected for appearance in this insert set. Cards are printed in a special double-sided, all-gold Dufex technology. An action photo is featured on the front, a portrait on back. Odds of picking a Gold Team card were stated as one in 41 packs.

		NM/M
Complete Set (12):		40.00
Common Player:		2.00
1	Ken Griffey Jr.	7.50
2	Frank Thomas	4.00
3	Cal Ripken Jr.	10.00
4	Jeff Bagwell	4.00
5	Mike Piazza	7.50
6	Barry Bonds	10.00
7	Matt Williams	2.00
8	Don Mattingly	6.00
9	Will Clark	2.00
10	Tony Gwynn	5.00
11	Kirby Puckett	5.00
12	Jose Canseco	2.50

Potential Unlimited

Dufex printing with textured foil highlights and transparent inks is featured in this chase set, produced in an edition of 1,975, as witnessed by the numbering on card backs. Approximate odds of finding a Potential Unlimited card are one per 29 packs. A super-scarce edition of 903 cards each featuring "microetch" foil printing technology was issued at the rate of one per 70 packs.

		NM/M
Complete Set (20):		35.00
Common Player:		1.00
903s:		2.5X
1	Cliff Floyd	1.00
2	Manny Ramirez	4.50
3	Raul Mondesi	1.00
4	Scott Ruffcorn	1.00
5	Billy Ashley	1.00
6	Alex Gonzalez	1.00
7	Midre Cummings	1.00
8	Charles Johnson	1.00
9	Garret Anderson	1.00
10	Hideo Nomo	2.00
11	Chipper Jones	7.00
12	Curtis Goodwin	1.00
13	Frank Rodriguez	1.00
14	Shawn Green	2.00
15	Ray Durham	1.00
16	Todd Hollandsworth	1.00
17	Brian Hunter	1.00
18	Carlos Delgado	2.00
19	Michael Tucker	1.00
20	Alex Rodriguez	9.00

1996 Select

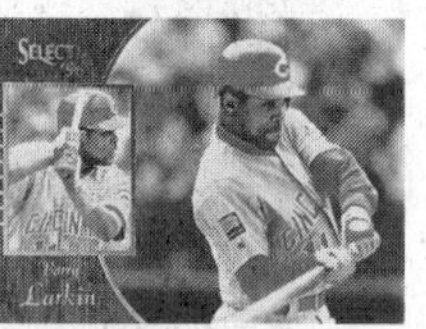

Select's 1996 baseball set has 200 cards in it, including 35 rookies, five checklists and 10 Lineup Leaders subset cards. All 200 cards are also reprinted as part of an Artist's Proof parallel set, using a holographic Artist's Proof logo. Cards were seeded one per every 35 packs; there were approximately 435 sets produced. Three insert sets were also created: Claim to Fame, En Fuego and Team Nucleus.

		NM/M
Complete Set (200):		9.00
Common Player:		.05
Artist's Proofs:		7X
Pack (10):		1.00
Wax Box (24):		16.00
1	Wade Boggs	1.00
2	Shawn Green	.35
3	Andres Galarraga	.05
4	Bill Pulsipher	.05
5	Chuck Knoblauch	.05
6	Ken Griffey Jr.	1.25
7	Greg Maddux	1.00
8	Manny Ramirez	.75
9	Ivan Rodriguez	.65
10	Tim Salmon	.05
11	Frank Thomas	.75
12	Jeff Bagwell	.75
13	Travis Fryman	.05
14	Kenny Lofton	.05
15	Matt Williams	.05
16	Jay Bell	.05
17	Ken Caminiti	.05
18	Ray Lankford	.05
19	Cal Ripken Jr.	2.00
20	Roger Clemens	1.00
21	Carlos Baerga	.05
22	Mike Piazza	1.25
23	Gregg Jefferies	.05
24	Reggie Sanders	.05
25	Rondell White	.05
26	Sammy Sosa	1.00
27	Kevin Appier	.05
28	Kevin Seitzer	.05
29	Gary Sheffield	.40
30	Mike Mussina	.35
31	Mark McGwire	1.50
32	Barry Larkin	.05
33	Marc Newfield	.05
34	Ismael Valdes	.05
35	Marty Cordova	.05
36	Albert Belle	.05
37	Johnny Damon	.35
38	Garret Anderson	.05
39	Cecil Fielder	.05
40	John Mabry	.05
41	Chipper Jones	1.00
42	Omar Vizquel	.05
43	Jose Rijo	.05
44	Charles Johnson	.05
45	Alex Rodriguez	1.50
46	Rico Brogna	.05
47	Joe Carter	.05
48	Mo Vaughn	.05
49	Moises Alou	.05
50	Raul Mondesi	.05
51	Robin Ventura	.05
52	Jim Thome	.60
53	Dave Justice	.05
54	Jeff King	.05
55	Brian Hunter	.05
56	Juan Gonzalez	.40
57	John Olerud	.05
58	Rafael Palmeiro	.65
59	Tony Gwynn	1.00
60	Eddie Murray	.75
61	Jason Isringhausen	.05
62	Dante Bichette	.05
63	Randy Johnson	.75
64	Kirby Puckett	1.00
65	Jim Edmonds	.05

66 David Cone .05
67 Ozzie Smith 1.00
68 Fred McGriff .05
69 Darren Daulton .05
70 Edgar Martinez .05
71 J.T. Snow .05
72 Butch Huskey .05
73 Hideo Nomo .40
74 Pedro Martinez .75
75 Bobby Bonilla .05
76 Jeff Conine .05
77 Ryan Klesko .05
78 Bernie Williams .05
79 Andre Dawson .25
80 Trevor Hoffman .05
81 Mark Grace .05
82 Benji Gil .05
83 Eric Karros .05
84 Pete Schourek .05
85 Edgardo Alfonzo .05
86 Jay Buhner .05
87 Vinny Castilla .05
88 Bret Boone .05
89 Ray Durham .05
90 Brian Jordan .05
91 Jose Canseco .40
92 Paul O'Neill .05
93 Chili Davis .05
94 Tom Glavine .30
95 Julian Tavarez .05
96 Derek Bell .05
97 Will Clark .05
98 Larry Walker .05
99 Denny Neagle .05
100 Alex Fernandez .05
101 Barry Bonds 2.00
102 Ben McDonald .05
103 Andy Pettitte .25
104 Tino Martinez .05
105 Sterling Hitchcock .05
106 Royce Clayton .05
107 Jim Abbott .05
108 Rickey Henderson .75
109 Ramon Martinez .05
110 Paul Molitor .75
111 Dennis Eckersley .65
112 Alex Gonzalez .05
113 Marquis Grissom .05
114 Greg Vaughn .05
115 Lance Johnson .05
116 Todd Stottlemyre .05
117 Jack McDowell .05
118 Ruben Sierra .05
119 Brady Anderson .05
120 Julio Franco .05
121 Brooks Kieshnick .05
122 Roberto Alomar .20
123 Greg Gagne .05
124 Wally Joyner .05
125 John Smoltz .05
126 John Valentin .05
127 Russ Davis .05
128 Joe Vitiello .05
129 Shawon Dunston .05
130 Frank Rodriguez .05
131 Charlie Hayes .05
132 Andy Benes .05
133 B.J. Surhoff .05
134 Dave Nilsson .05
135 Carlos Delgado .50
136 Walt Weiss .05
137 Mike Stanley .05
138 Greg Colbrunn .05
139 Mike Kelly .05
140 Ryne Sandberg 1.00
141 Lee Smith .05
142 Dennis Martinez .05
143 Bernard Gilkey .05
144 Lenny Dykstra .05
145 Danny Tartabull .05
146 Dean Palmer .05
147 Craig Biggio .05
148 Juan Acevedo .05
149 Michael Tucker .05
150 Bobby Higginson .05
151 Ken Griffey Jr. (Line Up Leaders) .65
152 Frank Thomas (Line Up Leaders) .45
153 Cal Ripken Jr. (Line Up Leaders) 1.00
154 Albert Belle (Line Up Leaders) .05
155 Mike Piazza (Line Up Leaders) .65
156 Barry Bonds (Line Up Leaders) 1.00
157 Sammy Sosa (Line Up Leaders) .60
158 Mo Vaughn (Line Up Leaders) .05
159 Greg Maddux (Line Up Leaders) .50
160 Jeff Bagwell (Line Up Leaders) .40
161 Derek Jeter 2.00
162 Paul Wilson .05
163 Chris Snopek .05
164 Jason Schmidt .05
165 Jimmy Haynes .05
166 George Arias .05
167 Steve Gibralter .05
168 Bob Wolcott .05
169 Jason Kendall .05
170 Gregg Zaun .05
171 Quinton McCracken .05
172 Alan Benes .05
173 Rey Ordonez .05
174 Ugueth Urbina .05
175 Osvaldo Fernandez **RC** .10
176 Marc Barcelo .05
177 Sal Fasano .05
178 Mike Grace **RC** .05
179 Chan Ho Park .05
180 Robert Perez .05
181 Todd Hollandsworth .05
182 Wilton Guerrero **RC** .05
183 John Wasdin .05
184 Jim Pittsley .05
185 LaTroy Hawkins .05
186 Jay Powell .05
187 Felipe Crespo .05
188 Jermaine Dye .05
189 Bob Abreu .05
190 Matt Luke **RC** .05
191 Richard Hidalgo .05
192 Karim Garcia .05
193 Tavo Alvarez .05
194 Andy Fox **RC** .05
195 Terrell Wade .05
196 Frank Thomas (Checklist) .40
197 Ken Griffey Jr. (Checklist) .65
198 Greg Maddux (Checklist) .50
199 Mike Piazza (Checklist) .65
200 Cal Ripken Jr. (Checklist) .75

Artist's Proofs

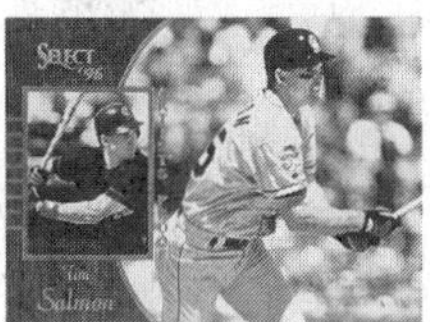

Approximately once per 35 packs, a card from this parallel chase set is encountered among 1996 Select. Reported production was 435 sets. The Artist's Proof cards are distinguished by a holographic logo testifying to their status on the front of the card.

	NM/M
Complete Set (200):	200.00
Common Player:	1.00
AP Stars:	7X

Claim to Fame

Twenty different stars are featured on these 1996 Select insert cards. Each card is numbered "1 of 2100" and uses an external die-cut design. The cards were seeded one per every 72 packs.

	NM/M
Complete Set (20):	45.00
Common Player:	.75
1 Cal Ripken Jr.	7.50
2 Greg Maddux	4.50
3 Ken Griffey Jr.	6.00
4 Frank Thomas	3.50
5 Mo Vaughn	.75
6 Albert Belle	.75
7 Jeff Bagwell	3.50
8 Sammy Sosa	4.50
8s Sammy Sosa (Overprinted "SAMPLE.")	2.50
9 Reggie Sanders	.75
10 Hideo Nomo	2.00
11 Chipper Jones	4.50
12 Mike Piazza	6.00
13 Matt Williams	.75
14 Tony Gwynn	4.50
15 Johnny Damon	1.50
16 Dante Bichette	.75
17 Kirby Puckett	4.50
18 Barry Bonds	7.50
19 Randy Johnson	3.50
20 Eddie Murray	3.50

En Fuego

ESPN announcer Dan Patrick is featured on his own card in this set, inspired by his

Sportscenter catch phrase "en fuego," which means "on fire." Patrick's teammate, Keith Olberman, wrote the card backs. The 25 cards, printed on all-foil Dufex stock, are seeded one per every 48 packs of 1996 Select baseball.

	NM/M
Complete Set (25):	35.00
Common Player:	.75
1 Ken Griffey Jr.	3.50
2 Frank Thomas	2.00
3 Cal Ripken Jr.	5.00
4 Greg Maddux	3.00
5 Jeff Bagwell	2.00
6 Barry Bonds	5.00
7 Mo Vaughn	.75
8 Albert Belle	.75
9 Sammy Sosa	3.00
10 Reggie Sanders	.75
11 Mike Piazza	3.50
12 Chipper Jones	3.00
13 Tony Gwynn	3.00
14 Kirby Puckett	3.00
15 Wade Boggs	3.00
16 Dan Patrick	.75
17 Gary Sheffield	1.25
18 Dante Bichette	.75
19 Randy Johnson	2.00
20 Matt Williams	.75
21 Alex Rodriguez	4.00
22 Tim Salmon	.75
23 Johnny Damon	1.25
24 Manny Ramirez	2.00
25 Hideo Nomo	1.25

Team Nucleus

This 1996 Select insert set pays tribute to the three top players from each Major League Baseball team; each card features the three teammates on it. The cards are printed on a clear plastic, utilizing a holographic micro-etched design. They are seeded one per every 18 packs.

	NM/M
Complete Set (28):	20.00
Common Player:	.50
1 Albert Belle, Manny Ramirez, Carlos Baerga	1.00
2 Ray Lankford, Brian Jordan, Ozzie Smith	1.25
3 Jay Bell, Jeff King, Denny Neagle	.50
4 Dante Bichette, Andres Galarraga, Larry Walker	.50
5 Mark McGwire, Mike Bordick, Terry Steinbach	1.75
6 Bernie Williams, Wade Boggs, David Cone	1.25
7 Joe Carter, Alex Gonzalez, Shawn Green	.50
8 Roger Clemens, Mo Vaughn, Jose Canseco	1.25
9 Ken Griffey Jr., Edgar Martinez, Randy Johnson	1.50
10 Gregg Jefferies, Darren Daulton, Lenny Dykstra	.50
11 Mike Piazza, Raul Mondesi, Hideo Nomo	1.50
12 Greg Maddux, Chipper Jones, Ryan Klesko	1.25
13 Cecil Fielder, Travis Fryman, Phil Nevin	.50
14 Ivan Rodriguez, Will Clark, Juan Gonzalez	1.00
15 Ryne Sandberg, Sammy Sosa, Mark Grace	1.50
16 Gary Sheffield, Charles Johnson, Andre Dawson	.60
17 Johnny Damon, Michael Tucker, Kevin Appier	.65
18 Barry Bonds, Matt Williams, Rod Beck	2.00
19 Kirby Puckett, Chuck Knoblauch, Marty Cordova	1.25
20 Cal Ripken Jr., Bobby Bonilla, Mike Mussina	2.00
21 Jason Isringhausen, Bill Pulsipher, Rico Brogna	.50
22 Tony Gwynn, Ken Caminiti, Marc Newfield	1.25
23 Tim Salmon, Garret Anderson, Jim Edmonds	.50
24 Moises Alou, Rondell White, Cliff Floyd	.50
25 Barry Larkin, Reggie Sanders, Bret Boone	.50
26 Jeff Bagwell, Craig Biggio, Derek Bell	1.00
27 Frank Thomas, Robin Ventura, Alex Fernandez	1.00
28 John Jaha, Greg Vaughn, Kevin Seitzer	.50

1996 Select Certified

This hobby-exclusive set has 144 cards in its regular issue, plus six parallel versions and two insert sets. The parallel sets are: Certified Red (one per five packs), Certified Blue (one per 50), Artist's Proofs (one per 12), Mirror Red (one per 100), Mirror Blue (one per 200), and Mirror Gold (one per 300). Breaking down the numbers, there are 1,800 Certified Red sets, 180 Certified Blue, 500 Artist's Proofs, 90 Mirror Red 45 Mirror Blue and 30 Mirror Gold sets. The insert sets are Interleague Preview cards and Select Few. Cards #135-144 are a "Pastime Power" subset.

	NM/M
Complete Set (144):	20.00
Common Player:	.15
Pack (6):	2.50
Wax Box (20):	40.00
1 Frank Thomas	1.25
2 Tino Martinez	.15
3 Gary Sheffield	.50
4 Kenny Lofton	.15
5 Joe Carter	.15
6 Alex Rodriguez	2.50
7 Chipper Jones	1.50
8 Roger Clemens	1.75
9 Jay Bell	.15
10 Eddie Murray	1.00
11 Will Clark	.15
12 Mike Mussina	.35
13 Hideo Nomo	.50
14 Andres Galarraga	.15
15 Marc Newfield	.15
16 Jason Isringhausen	.15
17 Randy Johnson	1.00
18 Chuck Knoblauch	.15
19 J.T. Snow	.15
20 Mark McGwire	2.50
21 Tony Gwynn	1.50
22 Albert Belle	.15
23 Gregg Jefferies	.15
24 Reggie Sanders	.15
25 Bernie Williams	.15
26 Ray Lankford	.15
27 Johnny Damon	.40
28 Ryne Sandberg	1.50
29 Rondell White	.15
30 Mike Piazza	2.00
31 Barry Bonds	3.00
32 Greg Maddux	1.50
33 Craig Biggio	.15
34 John Valentin	.15
35 Ivan Rodriguez	.75
36 Rico Brogna	.15
37 Tim Salmon	.15
38 Sterling Hitchcock	.15
39 Charles Johnson	.15
40 Travis Fryman	.15
41 Barry Larkin	.15
42 Tom Glavine	.35
43 Marty Cordova	.15
44 Shawn Green	.40
45 Ben McDonald	.15
46 Robin Ventura	.15
47 Ken Griffey Jr.	2.00
48 Orlando Merced	.15
49 Paul O'Neill	.15
50 Ozzie Smith	1.50
51 Manny Ramirez	1.00
52 Ismael Valdes	.15
53 Cal Ripken Jr.	3.00
54 Jeff Bagwell	1.00
55 Greg Vaughn	.15
56 Juan Gonzalez	.50
57 Raul Mondesi	.15
58 Carlos Baerga	.15
59 Sammy Sosa	1.50
60 Mike Kelly	.15
61 Edgar Martinez	.15
62 Kirby Puckett	1.50
63 Cecil Fielder	.15
64 David Cone	.15
65 Moises Alou	.15
66 Fred McGriff	.15
67 Mo Vaughn	.15
68 Edgardo Alfonzo	.15
69 Jim Thome	.75
70 Rickey Henderson	1.00
71 Dante Bichette	.15
72 Lenny Dykstra	.15
73 Benji Gil	.15
74 Wade Boggs	1.50
75 Jim Edmonds	.15
76 Michael Tucker	.15
77 Carlos Delgado	.65
78 Butch Huskey	.15
79 Billy Ashley	.15
80 Dean Palmer	.15
81 Paul Molitor	1.00
82 Ryan Klesko	.15
83 Brian Hunter	.15
84 Jay Buhner	.15
85 Larry Walker	.15
86 Mike Bordick	.15
87 Matt Williams	.15
88 Jack McDowell	.15
89 Hal Morris	.15
90 Brian Jordan	.15
91 Andy Pettitte	.35
92 Melvin Nieves	.15
93 Pedro Martinez	1.00
94 Mark Grace	.15
95 Garret Anderson	.15
96 Andre Dawson	.30
97 Ray Durham	.15
98 Jose Canseco	.50
99 Roberto Alomar	.30
100 Derek Jeter	3.00
101 Alan Benes	.15
102 Karim Garcia	.15
103 Robin Jennings **RC**	.15
104 Bob Abreu	.15
105 Sal Fasano (Livan Hernandez' name on front.)	.15
106 Steve Gibralter	.15
107 Jermaine Dye	.15
108 Jason Kendall	.15
109 Mike Grace **RC**	.15
110 Jason Schmidt	.15
111 Paul Wilson	.15
112 Rey Ordonez	.15
113 Wilton Guerrero **RC**	.15
114 Brooks Kieschnick	.15
115 George Arias	.15
116 Osvaldo Fernandez **RC**	.15
117 Todd Hollandsworth	.15
118 John Wasdin	.15
119 Eric Owens	.15
120 Chan Ho Park	.15
121 Mark Loretta	.15
122 Richard Hidalgo	.15
123 Jeff Suppan	.15
124 Jim Pittsley	.15
125 LaTroy Hawkins	.15
126 Chris Snopek	.15
127 Justin Thompson	.15
128 Jay Powell	.15
129 Alex Ochoa	.15
130 Felipe Crespo	.15
131 Matt Lawton **RC**	.15
132 Jimmy Haynes	.15
133 Terrell Wade	.15
134 Ruben Rivera	.15
135 Frank Thomas (Pastime Power)	.55
136 Ken Griffey Jr. (Pastime Power)	1.00
137 Greg Maddux (Pastime Power)	.65
138 Mike Piazza (Pastime Power)	.75
139 Cal Ripken Jr. (Pastime Power)	1.50
140 Albert Belle (Pastime Power)	.15
141 Mo Vaughn (Pastime Power)	.15
142 Chipper Jones (Pastime Power)	.65
143 Hideo Nomo (Pastime Power)	.25
144 Ryan Klesko (Pastime Power)	.15

Artist's Proofs

Only 500 cards each of this parallel issue were produced, seeded one in every dozen packs. The cards are identical to the regular-issue Select Certified except for the presence on front of a prismatic gold Artist's Proof logo.

	NM/M
Complete Set (144):	200.00
Common Player:	1.00
AP Stars:	7X

Red, Blue

These 1996 Select Certified insert cards were the most common of the parallel cards issued; they were seeded one per five packs. There were 1,800 Certified Red sets produced, with the number of Certified Blue sets at 180. Cards are essentially the same as regular-issue Select Certified except for the color of the foil background on front.

	NM/M
Common Red:	.50
Red Stars:	3X
Common Blue:	2.50
Blue Stars:	10X

Mirror Red, Blue, Gold

These 1996 Select Certified inserts are the scarcest of the set. Only 30 Mirror Gold sets were made, with 60 Mirror Blue sets and 90 Mirror Red. Due to the improbability of completing the collection, no complete set price is given.

	NM/M
Common Mirror Red:	6.00
Mirror Red Stars:	20X
Common Mirror Blue:	12.00
Mirror Blue Stars:	30X
Common Mirror Gold:	20.00
Mirror Gold Stars:	100X

Interleague Preview

These 1996 Select Certified insert cards feature 21 prospective matchups from interleague play's beginnings. The cards were seeded one per 42 packs. Each card can also be found in a promo version with a large, black "SAMPLE" overprint on front and back.

		NM/M
Complete Set (25):		45.00
Common Card:		.75
Promos:		1X
1	Ken Griffey Jr., Hideo Nomo	3.50
2	Greg Maddux, Mo Vaughn	3.00
3	Frank Thomas, Sammy Sosa	3.00
4	Mike Piazza, Jim Edmonds	3.50
5	Ryan Klesko, Roger Clemens	3.25
6	Derek Jeter, Rey Ordonez	4.50
7	Johnny Damon, Ray Lankford	1.00
8	Manny Ramirez, Reggie Sanders	2.50
9	Barry Bonds, Jay Buhner	4.50
10	Jason Isringhausen, Wade Boggs	3.00
11	David Cone, Chipper Jones	3.00
12	Jeff Bagwell, Will Clark	2.50
13	Tony Gwynn, Randy Johnson	3.00
14	Cal Ripken Jr., Tom Glavine	4.50
15	Kirby Puckett, Alan Benes	3.00
16	Gary Sheffield, Mike Mussina	1.00
17	Raul Mondesi, Tim Salmon	.75
18	Rondell White, Carlos Delgado	1.00
19	Cecil Fielder, Ryne Sandberg	3.00
20	Kenny Lofton, Brian Hunter	.75
21	Paul Wilson, Paul O'Neill	.75
22	Ismael Valdes, Edgar Martinez	.75
23	Matt Williams, Mark McGwire	4.00
24	Albert Belle, Barry Larkin	.75
25	Brady Anderson, Marquis Grissom	.75

Select Few

Eighteen top players are featured on these 1996 Select Certified inserts, which utilize holographic technology with a dot matrix hologram. Cards were seeded one per every 60 packs.

		NM/M
Complete Set (18):		40.00
Common Player:		1.00
1	Sammy Sosa	3.00
2	Derek Jeter	5.00
3	Ken Griffey Jr.	3.50
4	Albert Belle	1.00
5	Cal Ripken Jr.	5.00
6	Greg Maddux	3.00
7	Frank Thomas	2.50
8	Mo Vaughn	1.00
9	Chipper Jones	3.00
10	Mike Piazza	3.50
11	Ryan Klesko	1.00
12	Hideo Nomo	1.50
13	Alan Benes	1.00
14	Manny Ramirez	2.50
15	Gary Sheffield	2.00
16	Barry Bonds	5.00
17	Matt Williams	1.00
18	Johnny Damon	2.00

1997 Select Samples

The 1997 edition of Select was previewed with the issue of several regular-issue and Select Co., cards carrying a large black "SAMPLE" overprint on front and back. The Rodriguez sample, untrimmed and larger than standard size, was not distributed in three-card cello packs like the other cards. This checklist may not be complete.

		NM/M
Common Player:		1.00
3	Tony Gwynn	2.00
8	Frank Thomas	1.50
15	Paul Molitor	1.50
23	Greg Maddux	2.00
28	Javy Lopez	1.00
47	Ken Griffey Jr.	3.00
53	Alex Rodriguez	4.00
94	Will Clark	1.00

1997 Select

The Series 1 base set is made up of 150 cards printed on thick 16-point stock. Each card features a distinctive silver-foil treatment and either red (100 cards) or blue (50 cards) foil accent. Blue-foiled cards were short-printed at a ratio of 1:2 compared to the red-foil cards. Blue-foil cards are indicated with a (B) in the checklist. Subsets include 40 Rookies, eight Super Stars and two checklists. Inserts include two parallel sets, (Artist's Proof and Registered Gold), Tools of the Trade, Mirror Blue Tools of the Trade, and Rookie Revolution. The cards were sold only at hobby shops in six-card packs for $2.99 each. A high-number series was issued with each card bearing a "Select Company" notation.

		NM/M
Complete Set (200):		30.00
Series 1 (#1-150):		20.00
Common Red Player:		.10
Common Blue Player:		.25
Registered Golds:		2X
Artist's Proofs:		5X
High Series (#151-200):		10.00
Common High Series:		.25
Pack (6):		1.50
Wax Box (24):		25.00
1	Juan Gonzalez/B	2.00
2	Mo Vaughn/B	.25
3	Tony Gwynn	1.50
4	Manny Ramirez/B	2.00
5	Jose Canseco	.50
6	David Cone	.10
7	Chan Ho Park	.10
8	Frank Thomas/B	2.50
9	Todd Hollandsworth	.10
10	Marty Cordova	.10
11	Gary Sheffield/B	.75
12	John Smoltz/B	.25
13	Mark Grudzielanek	.10
14	Sammy Sosa/B	3.00
15	Paul Molitor	1.00
16	Kevin Brown	.10
17	Albert Belle/B	.25
18	Eric Young	.10
19	John Wetteland	.10
20	Ryan Klesko/B	.25
21	Joe Carter	.10
22	Alex Ochoa	.10
23	Greg Maddux/B	3.00
24	Roger Clemens/B	3.00
25	Ivan Rodriguez/B	1.50
26	Barry Bonds/B	5.00
27	Kenny Lofton/B	.25
28	Javy Lopez	.10
29	Hideo Nomo/B	1.00
30	Rusty Greer	.10
31	Rafael Palmeiro	.75
32	Mike Piazza/B	3.50
33	Ryne Sandberg	1.50
34	Wade Boggs	1.50
35	Jim Thome/B	1.50
36	Ken Caminiti/B	.25
37	Mark Grace	.10
38	Brian Jordan/B	.25
39	Craig Biggio	.10
40	Henry Rodriguez	.10
41	Dean Palmer	.10
42	Jason Kendall	.10
43	Bill Pulsipher	.10
44	Tim Salmon/B	.25
45	Marc Newfield	.10
46	Pat Hentgen	.10
47	Ken Griffey Jr./B	4.00
48	Paul Wilson	.10
49	Jay Buhner/B	.25
50	Rickey Henderson	1.00
51	Jeff Bagwell/B	2.00
52	Cecil Fielder	.10
53	Alex Rodriguez/B	4.00
54	John Jaha	.10
55	Brady Anderson/B	.25
56	Andres Galarraga	.10
57	Raul Mondesi	.10
58	Andy Pettitte	.30
59	Roberto Alomar/B	1.00
60	Derek Jeter/B	5.00
61	Charles Johnson	.10
62	Travis Fryman	.10
63	Chipper Jones/B	3.00
64	Edgar Martinez	.10
65	Bobby Bonilla	.10
66	Greg Vaughn	.10
67	Bobby Higginson	.10
68	Garret Anderson	.10
69	Chuck Knoblauch/B	.25
70	Jermaine Dye	.10
71	Cal Ripken Jr./B	5.00
72	Jason Giambi	.60
73	Trey Beamon	.10
74	Shawn Green	.35
75	Mark McGwire/B	4.00
76	Carlos Delgado	.60
77	Jason Isringhausen	.10
78	Randy Johnson/B	2.00
79	Troy Percival/B	.25
80	Ron Gant	.10
81	Ellis Burks	.10
82	Mike Mussina/B	1.00
83	Todd Hundley	.10
84	Jim Edmonds	.10
85	Charles Nagy	.10
86	Dante Bichette/B	.25
87	Mariano Rivera	.20
88	Matt Williams/B	.25
89	Rondell White	.10
90	Steve Finley	.10
91	Alex Fernandez	.10
92	Barry Larkin	.10
93	Tom Goodwin	.10
94	Will Clark	.10
95	Michael Tucker	.10
96	Derek Bell	.10
97	Larry Walker	.10
98	Alan Benes	.10
99	Tom Glavine	.35
100	Darin Erstad/B	.35
101	Andruw Jones/B	2.00
102	Scott Rolen	.65
103	Todd Walker/B	.25
104	Dmitri Young	.10
105	Vladimir Guerrero/B	2.00
106	Nomar Garciaparra	1.50
107	Danny Patterson **RC**	.10
108	Karim Garcia	.10
109	Todd Greene	.10
110	Ruben Rivera	.10
111	Raul Casanova	.10
112	Mike Cameron	.10
113	Bartolo Colon	.10
114	Rod Myers **RC**	.10
115	Todd Dunn	.10
116	Torii Hunter	.10
117	Jason Dickson	.10
118	Gene Kingsale **RC**	.10
119	Rafael Medina	.10
120	Raul Ibanez	.10
121	Bobby Henley **RC**	.10
122	Scott Spiezio	.10
123	Bobby Smith **RC**	.10
124	J.J. Johnson	.10
125	Bubba Trammell **RC**	.50
126	Jeff Abbott	.10
127	Neifi Perez	.10
128	Derrek Lee	.65
129	Kevin Brown **RC**	.10
130	Mendy Lopez	.10
131	Kevin Orie	.10
132	Ryan Jones	.10
133	Juan Encarnacion	.10
134	Jose Guillen/B	.25
135	Greg Norton	.10
136	Richie Sexson	.10
137	Jay Payton	.10
138	Bob Abreu	.15
139	Ronnie Belliard **RC**	.10
140	Wilton Guerrero/B	.25
141	Alex Rodriguez/B (Select Stars)	2.00
142	Juan Gonzalez/B (Select Stars)	.50
143	Ken Caminiti/B (Select Stars)	.25
144	Frank Thomas/B (Select Stars)	1.25
145	Ken Griffey Jr./B (Select Stars)	1.75
146	John Smoltz/B (Select Stars)	.25
147	Mike Piazza/B (Select Stars)	1.75
148	Derek Jeter/B (Select Stars)	3.00
149	Frank Thomas (Checklist)	.75
150	Ken Griffey Jr. (Checklist)	1.00
151	Jose Cruz Jr. **RC**	1.00
152	Moises Alou	.25
153	Hideki Irabu **RC**	.50
154	Glendon Rusch	.25
155	Ron Coomer	.25
156	Jeremi Gonzalez **RC**	.25
157	Fernando Tatis **RC**	.40
158	John Olerud	.25
159	Rickey Henderson	1.00
160	Shannon Stewart	.25
161	Kevin Polcovich	.25
162	Jose Rosado	.25
163	Ray Lankford	.25
164	David Justice	.25
165	Mark Kotsay **RC**	.50
166	Deivi Cruz **RC**	.50
167	Billy Wagner	.25
168	Jacob Cruz	.25
169	Matt Morris	.25
170	Brian Banks	.25
171	Brett Tomko	.25
172	Todd Helton	.75
173	Eric Young	.25
174	Bernie Williams	.25
175	Jeff Fassero	.25
176	Ryan McGuire	.25
177	Darryl Kile	.25
178	Kelvim Escobar **RC**	.50
179	Dave Nilsson	.25
180	Geronimo Berroa	.25
181	Livan Hernandez	.25
182	Tony Womack **RC**	.50
183	Deion Sanders	.25
184	Jeff Kent	.25
185	Brian Hunter	.25
186	Jose Malave	.25
187	Steve Woodard **RC**	.50
188	Brad Radke	.25
189	Todd Dunwoody	.25
190	Joey Hamilton	.25
191	Denny Naegle	.25
192	Bobby Jones	.25
193	Tony Clark	.25
194	Jaret Wright **RC**	.50
195	Matt Stairs	.25
196	Francisco Cordova	.25
197	Justin Thompson	.25
198	Pokey Reese	.25
199	Garrett Stephenson	.25
200	Carl Everett	.25

Artist's Proofs

Featuring a holographic foil background and special Artist's Proof logo on front, this parallel of the 150-card Series 1 Select was a random pack insert at an average pull rate of 1:71 for reds and 1:355 for blues.

	NM/M
Complete Set (150):	450.00
Common Red:	1.25
Red Stars:	5X
Common Blue:	2.50
Blue Stars:	1.5X

Company

Select Company was intended to be a one-per-pack parallel found in '97 high series. The cards have the front background photo replaced with textured silver metallic foil and "Select Company" printed vertically at right-center. While all high-number (151-200) cards have the "Select Company" notation erroneously printed on front, only those cards with silver-foil backgrounds are true parallels. All Select Company cards can also be found in a promo version with a large black "SAMPLE" overprinted on back.

	NM/M
Complete Set (200):	150.00
Common Player:	.50
Red Stars:	3X
Blue Stars:	1.5X
High-Series Stars:	1.5X
Samples:	10X

Registered Gold

This parallel insert set, like the regular issue, can be found with 100 red-foil and 50 blue-foil enhanced cards. They differ from the regular issue in the use of gold foil instead of silver on the right side of the front. Also, the inserts have "Registered Gold" printed vertically on the right side of the photo. Backs are identical to the regular issue. Red-foil Registered Gold cards are found on average of once every 11 packs; blue-foiled cards are a 1-in-47 pick.

	NM/M
Complete Set (150):	300.00
Common Red Gold:	.75
Common Blue Gold:	1.50
Registered Gold Stars:	2X

Autographs

Four top candidates for the 1997 Rookie of the Year Award - Wilton Guerrero, Jose Guillen, Andruw Jones and Todd Walker - each signed a limited number of their Select Rookie cards. Jones signed 2,500 cards while each of the other players signed 3,000 each.

		NM/M
Complete Set (4):		15.00
Common Autograph:		3.00
AU1	Wilton Guerrero	3.00
AU2	Jose Guillen	3.00
AU3	Andruw Jones	10.00
AU4	Todd Walker	3.00

Rookie Revolution

This 20-card insert highlights some of the top young stars in the game. Cards feature a silver micro-etched mylar design on front. Backs are sequentially numbered and contain a few words about the player. Odds of finding a card are 1:56 packs.

		NM/M
Complete Set (20):		21.00
Common Player:		.50
1	Andruw Jones	2.50
2	Derek Jeter	6.00
3	Todd Hollandsworth	.50
4	Edgar Renteria	.50
5	Jason Kendall	.50
6	Rey Ordonez	.50
7	F.P. Santangelo	.50
8	Jermaine Dye	.50
9	Alex Ochoa	.50
10	Vladimir Guerrero	2.50
11	Dmitri Young	.50
12	Todd Walker	.50
13	Scott Rolen	1.50
14	Nomar Garciaparra	3.50
15	Ruben Rivera	.50
16	Darin Erstad	1.00
17	Todd Greene	.50
18	Mariano Rivera	1.00
19	Trey Beamon	.50
20	Karim Garcia	.50

Tools of the Trade

A 25-card insert featuring a double-front design salutes a top veteran player on one side and a promising youngster on the other. Cards feature a silver-foil card stock with gold-foil stamping. Cards were inserted 1:9 packs. A parallel to this set - Blue Mirror Tools of the Trade - features blue-foil stock with an insert ratio of 1:240 packs.

		NM/M
Complete Set (25):		25.00
Common Player:		.40
Mirror Blues:		2.5X
1	Ken Griffey Jr., Andruw Jones	2.00
2	Greg Maddux, Andy Pettitte	1.50
3	Cal Ripken Jr., Chipper Jones	2.50
4	Mike Piazza, Jason Kendall	2.00
5	Albert Belle, Karim Garcia	.40
6	Mo Vaughn, Dmitri Young	.40
7	Juan Gonzalez, Vladimir Guerrero	1.00
8	Tony Gwynn, Jermaine Dye	1.50
9	Barry Bonds, Alex Ochoa	2.50
10	Jeff Bagwell, Jason Giambi	1.00
11	Kenny Lofton, Darin Erstad	.50
12	Gary Sheffield, Manny Ramirez	1.00
13	Tim Salmon, Todd Hollandsworth	.40
14	Sammy Sosa, Ruben Rivera	1.50
15	Paul Molitor, George Arias	1.00
16	Jim Thome, Todd Walker	.75
17	Wade Boggs, Scott Rolen	1.50
18	Ryne Sandberg, Chuck Knoblauch	1.50
19	Mark McGwire, Frank Thomas	2.25
20	Ivan Rodriguez, Charles Johnson	.75
21	Brian Jordan, Trey Beamon	.40
22	Roger Clemens, Troy Percival	1.75
23	John Smoltz, Mike Mussina	.65
24	Alex Rodriguez, Rey Ordonez	2.25
25	Derek Jeter, Nomar Garciaparra	2.50

1998 Select

Select was intended to be a four-tier, 100-player, 250-card base set based on the "Quasar System." One hundred players were to appear as one-star cards; two-star cards comprised a shortened checklist of 75 of those players, and so on through three- and four-star subsets. Besides an increase in player popularity, each level featured enhanced technical bells and whistles on the cards themselves. Each five-card $3.99 pack was to have three one-star cards and two two-star cards, unless one or more were replaced with three- or four-star cards or one of several insert series. The set was never officially released due to the mid-year collapse and subsequent bankruptcy of Select's parent firm, Pinnacle. Some cards, however, have made their way into the hobby market. Given the possibility that more - perhaps all - of the two-star cards may some day become available, the complete checklist is provided as originally formulated by Select. Values are shown only for those cards confirmed to exist.

	NM/M
Common Player:	10.00

Numbers

Five players from each of four major statistical categories were selected for inclusion in this all-numbered insert issue. Each player in the chase set was intended to have cards numbered to his 1997 performance in the category for which he was chosen. While distribution of the cards was halted by Pinnacle's bankruptcy, limited quantities of these insert cards have found their way into the hobby. Those cards seen thus far do not bear sequential numbers. The number of cards intended for each player is listed, although it is unknown how many of each player were actually released.

		NM/M
Complete Set (20):		1,150
Common Player:		20.00
1	Mark McGwire/58	225.00
2	Juan Gonzalez/42	40.00
3	Ken Griffey Jr./56	225.00
4	Jeff Bagwell/53	60.00
5	Andres Galarraga/41	40.00
6	Frank Thomas/347	30.00
7	Mike Piazza/362	100.00
8	Tony Gwynn/372	35.00
9	Larry Walker/366	20.00
10	Kenny Lofton/333	20.00
11	Barry Bonds/446	50.00
12	Chuck Knoblauch/390	20.00
13	Derek Jeter/370	150.00
14	Nomar Garciaparra/342	75.00
15	Chipper Jones/371	60.00
16	Pedro Martinez/305	40.00
17	Hideo Nomo/233	65.00
18	Randy Johnson/291	30.00
19	Roger Clemens/292	75.00
20	Greg Maddux/177	75.00

Jersey Numbers

Whatever the intended scope and manner of distribution for this parallel insert may never be known because Pinnacle's bankruptcy interrupted the issue. Only a few specimens have made their way into the hobby. The gold-foil highlighted cards were intended to be serially numbered on back to the extent of the player's uniform number.

		NM/M
116	Ken Griffey Jr./24	65.00

1998 Select Selected Samples

Selected promos were released in two-card cello packs prior to Pinnacle's bankruptcy. Fronts have color action photos on bright metallic-foil backgrounds was a large "S." Backs have a smaller version of the front photo along with career highlights and a large overprinted "SAMPLE."

		NM/M
Complete Set (10):		30.00
Common Player:		2.50
1	Vladimir Guerrero	4.00
2	Nomar Garciaparra	5.00
3	Ben Grieve	2.50
4	Travis Lee	2.50
5	Jose Cruz Jr.	2.50
6	Alex Rodriguez	6.00
7	Todd Helton	3.50
8	Derek Jeter	7.00
9	Scott Rolen	3.50
10	Jaret Wright	2.50

1998 Select Selected

Intended as a 1:23 pack insert for a set which was never released due to Pinnacle's bankruptcy, Selected cards later leaked out into the hobby market. Fronts have color action photos on bright metallic-foil backgrounds with a large "S." Backs have a smaller version of the front photo along with career highlights.

		NM/M
Complete Set (10):		135.00
Common Player:		10.00
1	Vladimir Guerrero	15.00
2	Nomar Garciaparra	20.00
3	Ben Grieve	10.00
4	Travis Lee	10.00
5	Jose Cruz Jr.	10.00
6	Alex Rodriguez	22.50
7	Todd Helton	12.50
8	Derek Jeter	25.00
9	Scott Rolen	12.50
10	Jaret Wright	10.00

2002 Select Rookies & Prospects Autographs

		NM/M
Common Player:		3.00
Retail-exclusive		
1	Abraham Nunez	5.00
2	Adam Bernero	3.00
3	Adam Pettyjohn	3.00

4	Alex Escobar	4.00
5	Allan Simpson	4.00
6	Andres Torres	3.00
7	Andy Pratt	4.00
8	Bert Snow	3.00
9	Bill Ortega	3.00
10	Billy Sylvester	3.00
11	Brad Voyles	3.00
12	Brandon Backe	3.00
13	Brent Abernathy	3.00
14	Brian Mallette	3.00
15	Brian Rogers	3.00
16	Cam Esslinger	3.00
17	Carlos Garcia	3.00
18	Carlos Valderrama	3.00
19	Cesar Izturis	6.00
20	Chad Durbin	3.00
21	Chris Baker	3.00
22	Claudio Vargas	3.00
23	Cory Aldridge	3.00
24	Craig Monroe	5.00
25	David Elder	3.00
26	David Brous	3.00
27	David Espinosa	3.00
28	Derrick Lewis	3.00
29	Elio Serrano	3.00
30	Elpidio Guzman	3.00
31	Eric Cyr	3.00
32	Eric Valent	4.00
33	Erik Bedard	5.00
34	Esix Snead	3.00
35	Francis Beltran	3.00
36	George Perez	3.00
37	Gene Altman	3.00
38	Greg Miller	4.00
39	Horacio Ramirez	3.00
40	Jason Hart	4.50
41	Jason Karnuth	3.00
42	Jason Romano	3.00
43	Jeff Deardorff	3.00
44	Jeremy Affeldt	3.00
45	Jeremy Lambert	3.00
46	John Ennis	3.00
47	John Grabow	3.00
48	Jose Cueto	3.00
49	Jose Mieses	3.00
50	Jose Ortiz	3.00
51	Josh Pearce	3.00
52	Josue Perez	3.00
53	Juan Diaz	3.00
54	Juan Pena	3.00
55	Keith Ginter	3.00
56	Kevin Frederick	3.00
57	Kevin Joseph	3.00
58	Kevin Olsen	3.00
60	Kris Keller	3.00
61	Larry Bigbie	3.00
62	Les Walrond	3.00
63	Luis Pineda	3.00
64	Luis Rivas	3.00
65	Luis Rivera	4.50
66	Luke Hudson	3.00
67	Marcus Giles	8.00
68	Mark Ellis	3.00
69	Martin Vargas	3.00
70	Matt Childers	3.00
71	Matt Guerrier	3.00
72	Matt Thornton	3.00
73	Matt White	3.00
74	Mike Penney	3.00
75	Nate Teut	3.00
76	Nick Maness	3.00
77	Orlando Woodards	3.00
78	Paul Phillips	3.00
79	Pedro Feliz	3.00
80	Ramon Vazquez	3.00
81	Raul Chavez	3.00
82	Reed Johnson	3.00
83	Ryan Freel	4.50
84	Ryan Jamison	3.00
85	Ryan Ludwick	3.00
86	Saul Rivera	3.00
87	Steve Bechler	3.00
88	Steve Green	3.00
89	Steve Smyth	3.00
90	Tike Redman	3.00
91	Tom Shearn	3.00
92	Tomas de la Rosa	3.00
93	Tony Cogan	3.00
94	Travis Hafner	25.00
95	Travis Hughes	3.00
96	Wilkin Ruan	3.00
97	Will Ohman	3.00
98	Wilmy Caceres	3.00
99	Wilson Guzman	3.00
100	Winston Abreu	3.00

1992 Sentry Robin Yount

At the Sept. 25, 1992, Brewers home game, the first 25,000 fans through the turnstile received a four-card set commemorating Robin Yount's 3,000th career hit. The 2-1/2" x 3-1/2" cards feature on front a gold-foil framed action photo set against a purple marbled border. Backs have a write-up about the career milestone hit and include the grocery store logo at bottom. The cards are unnumbered and were issued in a heavy paper wrapper.

		NM/M
Complete Set (4):		15.00
Common Card:		5.00
(1)	Hit #1, April 12, 1974 (Robin Yount)	5.00
(2)	Hit #1,000, Aug. 16, 1980 (Robin Yount)	5.00
(3)	Hit #2,000, Sept. 6, 1986 (Robin Yount)	5.00
(4)	Hit #3,000, Sept. 9, 1992 (Robin Yount)	5.00

1993 Sentry Brewers Memorable Moments

Fans at a special Brewer home game were given this set of team highlight cards. Fronts have a color photo of the highlight with a brief description and date printed in gold foil. The photo is framed in dark blue, which is also used for the border of the card. The territory between the photo and border is printed in light blue and includes the Brewers logo and "Memorable Moments" headline. Backs have a description of the action shown on front, and the sponsor's logo. Cards are numbered according to player uniform number printed on back.

		NM/M
Complete Set (4):		8.00
Common Card:		1.00
4	Paul Molitor	3.50
7	Dale Sveum	1.00
19	Robin Yount	3.50
20	Juan Nieves	1.00

1993 Sentry Milwaukee Brewers

This set of a dozen coupon/card combos was distributed at Milwaukee area Sentry grocery stores during the 1993 season. A new card was issued every week or two between

April 27 and September 28. Each piece measures 12-1/2" x 7" and has a 5" x 7" Brewer player photo attached to six perforated coupons, each of which has a postage stamp-size Brewer photo at lower-right. Backs are blank. Cards #11 and 12 were never officially issued and have blank coupons.

		NM/M
Complete Set (12):		7.00
Common Player:		.60
1	Pat Listach	.50
2	Tom Brunansky	.50
3	B.J. Surhoff	.50
4	Kevin Reimer	.50
5	Darryl Hamilton	.50
6	Greg Vaughn	.50
7	Robin Yount	4.00
8	Phil Garner	.50
9	Bill Spiers	.50
10	Dave Nilsson	.50
11	Bill Wegman	.50
12	Cal Eldred	.50

1994 Sentry Brewer Highlights

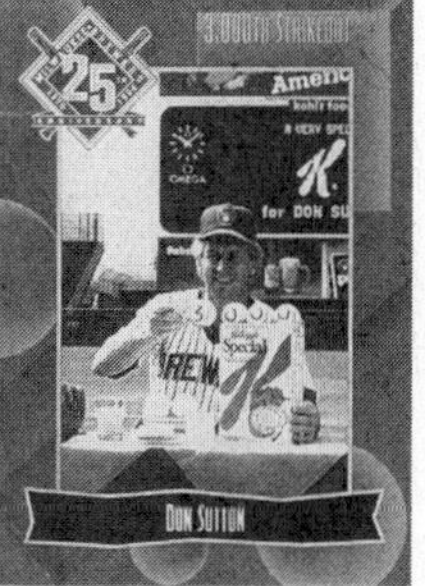

This eight-card set featuring highlights from Brewers history was issued in the team's 25th anniversary season. Sponsored by Sentry Foods, the cards were available on a one-per-week basis, attached to an 8-1/2" x 11" sheet of coupons, from May through August. (The last two cards were never officially issued due to the strike.) In standard 2-1/2" x 3-1/2", cards feature wide violet borders highlighted by green and gold geometric shapes. The team's 25th anniversary logo is at top-left, with the featured highlight at upper-right in gold. The player's name appears in white in a black ribbon beneath the color photo. Backs describe the highlight and are printed in blue and black. There is no sponsor's logo or card number. Cards are checklisted here alphabetically.

		NM/M
Complete Set (8):		14.00
Common Player:		1.00
(1)	Hank Aaron (Final Home Run)	5.00
(2)	Rollie Fingers (Cy Young/MVP Season)	1.50
(3)	Pat Listach (Rookie of the Year)	1.00
(4)	Paul Molitor (39-game Hitting Streak)	3.50
(5)	Juan Nieves (No-hitter)	1.00
(6)	Don Sutton (3,000th Strikeout)	1.00
(7)	Robin Yount (3,000 Hit)	3.50

(8)	Triumphant Trio (Jim Gantner, Paul Molitor, Robin Yount)	2.50

1983 7-11 Slurpee Coins

This first production of player coins by 7-Eleven stores was distributed only in the Los Angeles area. The test promotion, which awarded a coin to every purchaser of a large Slurpee drink, must have proved successful, as it was expanded nationally in subsequent years. Six California Angels and six Los Angeles Dodgers are included in the full-color set, with Angels players in red backgrounds and the Dodgers in blue. The 1-3/4" diameter plastic coins feature both an action and a portrait photo of the player, which can be alternately seen by moving the coin slightly from side to side. The 12 coin backs are numbered and include brief statistics and the company logo.

		NM/M
Complete Set (12):		6.00
Common Player:		.50
1	Rod Carew	2.00
2	Steve Sax	.50
3	Fred Lynn	.50
4	Pedro Guerrero	.50
5	Reggie Jackson	3.00
6	Dusty Baker	.50
7	Doug DeCinces	.50
8	Fernando Valenzuela	.50
9	Tommy John	.50
10	Rick Monday	.50
11	Bobby Grich	.50
12	Greg Brock	.50

1984 7-11 Slurpee Coins Central Region

The 7-Eleven/Slurpee coins were distributed nationally in 1984 with 60 different players in three regional issues of 24 pieces each. Coins of Brett, Dawson, Murphy, Murray, Schmidt and Yount were common to all three regions. The 1-3/4" diameter plastic coins feature an action and a portrait photo on front which change when the viewing angle is altered. Statistics and coin numbers are found on the backs, along with the 7-Eleven logo.

		NM/M
Complete Set (24):		7.50
Common Player:		.25
1	Andre Dawson	.40
2	Robin Yount	.75
3	Dale Murphy	.50
4	Mike Schmidt	1.25
5	George Brett	1.25
6	Eddie Murray	.75
7	Bruce Sutter	.65
8	Cecil Cooper	.25
9	Willie McGee	.25
10	Mike Hargrove	.25
11	Kent Hrbek	.25
12	Carlton Fisk	.75
13	Mario Soto	.25
14	Lonnie Smith	.25
15	Gary Carter	.75
16	Lou Whitaker	.25
17	Ron Kittle	.25
18	Paul Molitor	.75
19	Ozzie Smith	1.00
20	Fergie Jenkins	.40
21	Ted Simmons	.25
22	Pete Rose	1.50
23	LaMarr Hoyt	.25
24	Dan Quisenberry	.25

Eastern Region

		NM/M
Complete Set (24):		10.00
Common Player:		.25
1	Andre Dawson	.40
2	Robin Yount	.75
3	Dale Murphy	.50
4	Mike Schmidt	1.25
5	George Brett	1.25
6	Eddie Murray	.75
7	Dave Winfield	.75
8	Tom Seaver	.75
9	Mike Boddicker	.25
10	Wade Boggs	1.00
11	Bill Madlock	.25
12	Steve Carlton	.50
13	Dave Stieb	.25
14	Cal Ripken, Jr.	3.00
15	Jim Rice	.40
16	Ron Guidry	.25
17	Darryl Strawberry	.25
18	Tony Pena	.25
19	John Denny	.25
20	Tim Raines	.25
21	Rick Dempsey	.25
22	Rich Gossage	.25
23	Gary Matthews	.25
24	Keith Hernandez	.25

Western Region

		NM/M
Complete Set (24):		9.00
Common Player:		.25
1	Andre Dawcon	.40
2	Robin Yount	.75
3	Dale Murphy	.50
4	Mike Schmidt	1.25
5	George Brett	1.25
6	Eddie Murray	.75
7	Steve Garvey	.35
8	Rod Carew	.75
9	Fernando Valenzuela	.25
10	Bob Horner	.25
11	Buddy Bell	.25
12	Reggie Jackson	1.00
13	Nolan Ryan	2.00
14	Pedro Guerrero	.25
15	Atlee Hammaker	.25
16	Fred Lynn	.25
17	Terry Kennedy	.25
18	Dusty Baker	.25
19	Jose Cruz	.25
20	Steve Rogers	.25
21	Rickey Henderson	.75
22	Steve Sax	.25
23	Dickie Thon	.25
24	Matt Young	.25

Jumbo Coin

Dale Murphy, the MVP of the National League in 1983 was featured on a jumbo-format (4-1/2" diameter) "3D" disc distributed by 7-11 stores in conjunction with their Slurpee fountain drink. Like the smaller Slurpee coins, the photos on the disc change as the viewing angle is changed.

	NM/M
Dale Murphy	15.00

1985 7-11 Slurpee Coins Eastern Region

In 1985, the "Slurpee Disc" promotion was further expanded to a total of 94 full-color coins. The formats were very similar to the previous two years, but there were six different regional sets. Five of these regional series contain 16 coins, with a Detroit series totaling 14. The other five regions are: East, West, Great Lakes, Central and Southeast. The coins are again 1-1/4" in diameter, printed on plastic with double-image photos. All coins are numbered. No player appears in all regions, although several are in two or more.

		NM/M
Complete Set (16):		10.00
Common Player:		.25
1	Eddie Murray	1.00
2	George Brett	2.50
3	Steve Carlton	1.00
4	Jim Rice	.45
5	Dave Winfield	1.00
6	Mike Boddicker	.25
7	Wade Boggs	2.00
8	Dwight Evans	.25
9	Dwight Gooden	.25
10	Keith Hernandez	.25
11	Bill Madlock	.25
12	Don Mattingly	2.50
13	Dave Righetti	.25
14	Cal Ripken, Jr.	4.00
15	Juan Samuel	.25
16	Mike Schmidt	2.50

Great Lakes Region

		NM/M
Complete Set (16):		10.00
Common Player:		.25
1	Willie Hernandez	.25
2	George Brett	2.50
3	Dave Winfield	1.00
4	Eddie Murray	1.00
5	Bruce Sutter	.75
6	Harold Baines	.25
7	Bert Blyleven	.25
8	Leon Durham	.25
9	Chet Lemon	.25
10	Pete Rose	3.00
11	Ryne Sandberg	2.00
12	Tom Seaver	1.00
13	Mario Soto	.25
14	Rick Sutcliffe	.25
15	Alan Trammell	.25
16	Robin Yount	1.00

Southeastern Region

		NM/M
Complete Set (16):		7.50
Common Player:		.25
1	Dale Murphy	.75
2	Steve Carlton	1.00
3	Nolan Ryan	4.00
4	Bruce Sutter	.75
5	Dave Winfield	1.00
6	Steve Bedrosian	.25
7	Andre Dawson	.50
8	Kirk Gibson	.25
9	Fred Lynn	.25
10	Gary Matthews	.25
11	Phil Niekro	1.00
12	Tim Raines	.25
13	Darryl Strawberry	.25
14	Dave Stieb	.25
15	Willie Upshaw	.25
16	Lou Whitaker	.25

Southwest/Central Region

		NM/M
Complete Set (16):		10.00
Common Player:		.25
1	Nolan Ryan	4.00
2	George Brett	2.50
3	Dave Winfield	1.00
4	Mike Schmidt	2.50
5	Bruce Sutter	.75
6	Joaquin Andujar	.25
7	Willie Hernandez	.25
8	Wade Boggs	1.50
9	Gary Carter	1.00
10	Jose Cruz	.25
11	Kent Hrbek	.25
12	Reggie Jackson	1.50
13	Lance Parrish	.25
14	Terry Puhl	.25
15	Dan Quisenberry	.25
16	Ozzie Smith	1.50

Western Region

		NM/M
Complete Set (16):		7.50
Common Player:		.25
1	Mike Schmidt	2.50
2	Jim Rice	.45
3	Dale Murphy	.50
4	Eddie Murray	1.00
5	Dave Winfield	1.00
6	Rod Carew	1.00
7	Alvin Davis	.25
8	Steve Garvey	.35
9	Rich Gossage	.25
10	Pedro Guerrero	.25
11	Tony Gwynn	1.50
12	Rickey Henderson	1.00
13	Reggie Jackson	2.00
14	Jeff Leonard	.25
15	Alejandro Pena	.25
16	Fernando Valenzuela	.25

Tigers

		NM/M
Complete Set (14):		7.50
Common Player:		.75
1	Sparky Anderson	1.00
2	Darrell Evans	1.00
3	Kirk Gibson	1.00
4	Willie Hernandez	.75
5	Larry Herndon	.75
6	Chet Lemon	.75
7	Aurelio Lopez	.75
8	Jack Morris	.75
9	Lance Parrish	.75
10	Dan Petry	.75
11	Dave Rozema	.75
12	Alan Trammell	1.00
13	Lou Whitaker	1.00
14	Milt Wilcox	.75

Test Coins

These 3-D "Magic Motion" coins are identical to the regional issues in all aspects except size. These test coins are 2-1/4" diameter, an inch bigger than the issued versions.

		NM/M
Complete Set (3):		4.00
Common Player:		1.00
4	Mike Schmidt	2.50
5	Bruce Sutter	1.00
5	Dave Winfield	1.50

Jumbo Coins

World Series MVP Alan Trammell and Yankees slugger Dave Winfield were featured on jumbo-format (4-1/2" diameter) "3D" discs distributed by 7-11 stores in conjunction with their Slurpee fountain drink. Like the smaller Slurpee coins, the photos on the disc change as the viewing angle is changed.

		NM/M
Complete Set (2):		15.00
(1)	Alan Trammell	5.00
(2)	Dave Winfield	10.00

Twins

The Minnesota Twins, in co-operation with 7-Eleven and the Fire Marshall's Association, issued this set of 13 baseball fire safety cards. The card fronts feature full-color pictures of Twins players. A fire safety tip and short player history appear on the back. The cards were given out at all 7-Eleven stores in the state and at the Twins June 3 baseball game. Each fan received one baseball card with a poster which told how to collect the other cards in the set. Twelve cards feature players and the 13th card has an artist's rendering of Twins players on the front and a checklist of the set on the back. A group of 50,000 cards was distributed to fifth graders throughout the state by the fire departments.

		NM/M
Complete Set (13):		6.00
Common Player:		.35
1	Kirby Puckett	5.00
2	Frank Viola	.35
3	Mickey Hatcher	.35
4	Kent Hrbek	.35
5	John Butcher	.35
6	Roy Smalley	.35
7	Tom Brunansky	.35
8	Ron Davis	.35
9	Gary Gaetti	.35
10	Tim Teufel	.35
11	Mike Smithson	.35
12	Tim Laudner	.35
---	Checklist	.10

1986 7-11 Slurpee Coins Eastern Region

This marked the fourth year of production for these coins, issued with the purchase of a large Slurpee drink at 7-Eleven stores. Once again, there are different regional issues, with 16 coins issued for four different regions in 1986. The 1-3/4" diameter plastic coins each feature three different players' pictures, which can be seen alternately by tilting from side to side. Eight of the coins are the same in every region. Each coin is numbered on the back, along with brief player information.

		NM/M
Complete Set (16):		7.50
Common Coin:		.25
1	Dwight Gooden	.25
2	Batting Champs (Wade Boggs, George Brett, Pete Rose)	2.50
3	MVP's (Keith Hernandez, Don Mattingly, Cal Ripken, Jr.)	2.50
4	Slugging Champs (Harold Baines, Pedro Guerrero, Dave Parker)	.25
5	Home Run Champs (Dale Murphy, Jim Rice, Mike Schmidt)	2.00
6	Cy Young Winners (Ron Guidry, Bret Saberhagen, Fernando Valenzuela)	.25
7	Bullpen Aces (Rich Gossage, Dan Quisenberry, Bruce Sutter)	.50
8	Strikeout Kings (Steve Carlton, Nolan Ryan, Tom Seaver)	2.50
9	1985 Rookies (Steve Lyons, Rick Schu, Larry Sheets)	.25
10	Bullpen Aces (Jeff Reardon, Dave Righetti, Bob Stanley)	.25
11	Power Hitters (George Bell, Darryl Strawberry, Dave Winfield)	.75
12	Base Stealers (Rickey Henderson, Tim Raines, Juan Samuel)	.75
13	Home Run Hitters (Andre Dawson, Dwight Evans, Eddie Murray)	.75
14	Ace Pitchers (Mike Boddicker, Ron Darling, Dave Stieb)	.25
15	1985 Bullpen Rookies (Tim Burke, Brian Fisher, Roger McDowell)	.25
16	Sluggers (Jesse Barfield, Gary Carter, Fred Lynn)	.75

Mideastern Region

		NM/M
Complete Set (16):		7.50
Common Coin:		.25
1	Dwight Gooden	.25
2	Batting Champs (Wade Boggs, George Brett, Pete Rose)	2.50
3	MVP's (Keith Hernandez, Don Mattingly, Cal Ripken)	2.50
4	Slugging Champs (Harold Baines, Pedro Guerrero, Dave Parker)	.25
5	Home Run Champs (Dale Murphy, Jim Rice, Mike Schmidt)	2.00
6	Cy Young Winners (Ron Guidry, Bret Saberhagen, Fernando Valenzuela)	.25
7	Bullpen Aces (Rich Gossage, Dan Quisenberry, Bruce Sutter)	.50
8	Strikeout Kings (Steve Carlton, Nolan Ryan, Tom Seaver)	2.50
9	MVP's (Willie Hernandez, Ryne Sandberg, Robin Yount)	1.50
10	Ace Pitchers (Bert Blyleven, Jack Morris, Rick Sutcliffe)	.25
11	Bullpen Aces (Rollie Fingers, Bob James, Lee Smith)	.50
12	All-Star Catchers (Carlton Fisk, Lance Parrish, Tony Pena)	.75
13	1985 Rookies (Shawon Dunston, Ozzie Guillen, Ernest Riles)	.25
14	Star Outfielders (Brett Butler, Chet Lemon, Willie Wilson)	.25
15	Home Run Hitters (Tom Brunansky, Cecil Cooper, Darrell Evans)	.25
16	Big Hitters (Kirk Gibson, Paul Molitor, Greg Walker)	.75

Midwestern Region

		NM/M
Complete Set (16)		7.50
Common Coin:		.25
1	Dwight Gooden	.25
2	Batting Champs (Wade Boggs, George Brett, Pete Rose)	2.50
3	MVP's (Keith Hernandez, Don Mattingly, Cal Ripken, Jr.)	2.50
4	Slugging Champs (Harold Baines, Pedro Guerrero, Dave Parker)	.25
5	Home Run Champs (Dale Murphy, Jim Rice, Mike Schmidt)	2.00
6	Cy Young Winners (Ron Guidry, Bret Saberhagen, Fernando Valenzuela)	.25
7	Bullpen Aces (Rich Gossage, Dan Quisenberry, Bruce Sutter)	.50
8	Strikeout Kings (Steve Carlton, Nolan Ryan, Tom Seaver)	2.50
9	1985 Rookies (Vince Coleman, Glenn Davis, Oddibe McDowell)	.25
10	Gold Glovers (Buddy Bell, Ozzie Smith, Lou Whitaker)	1.00
11	Ace Pitchers (Mike Scott, Mario Soto, John Tudor)	.25
12	Bullpen Aces (Jeff Lahti, Ted Power, Dave Smith)	.25

13	Big Hitters (Jack Clark, Jose Cruz, Bob Horner)	.25
14	Star Second Basemen (Bill Doran, Tommy Herr, Ron Oester)	.25
15	1985 Rookie Pitchers (Tom Browning, Joe Hesketh, Todd Worrell)	.25
16	Top Switch-Hitters (Willie McGee, Jerry Mumphrey, Pete Rose)	2.00

Western Region

		NM/M
Complete Set (16):		7.50
Common Coin:		.25
1	Dwight Gooden	.25
2	Batting Champs (Wade Boggs, George Brett, Pete Rose)	2.50
3	MVP's (Keith Hernandez, Don Mattingly, Cal Ripken, Jr.)	2.50
4	Slugging Champs (Harold Baines, Pedro Guerrero, Dave Parker)	.25
5	Home Run Champs (Dale Murphy, Jim Rice, Mike Schmidt)	2.00
6	Cy Young Winners (Ron Guidry, Bret Saberhagen, Fernando Valenzuela)	.25
7	Bullpen Aces (Rich Gossage, Dan Quisenberry, Bruce Sutter)	.50
8	Strikeout Kings (Steve Carlton, Nolan Ryan, Tom Seaver)	2.50
9	Home Run Champs (Reggie Jackson, Dave Kingman, Gorman Thomas)	1.00
10	Batting Champs (Rod Carew, Tony Gwynn, Carney Lansford)	1.00
11	Sluggers (Phil Bradley, Mike Marshall, Graig Nettles)	.25
12	Ace Pitchers (Andy Hawkins, Orel Hershiser, Mike Witt)	.25
13	1985 Rookies (Chris Brown, Ivan Calderon, Mariano Duncan)	.25
14	Big Hitters (Steve Garvey, Bill Madlock, Jim Presley)	.25
15	Bullpen Aces (Jay Howell, Donnie Moore, Ed Nunez)	.25
16	1985 Bullpen Rookies (Karl Best, Stewart Cliburn, Steve Ontiveros)	.25

Jumbo Coin

Three of the game's top stars were featured on a jumbo-format (4-1/2" diameter) "3D" disc distributed by 7-11 stores in conjunction with their Slurpee fountain drink. Like the smaller Slurpee coins, the photos on the disc change as the viewing angle is changed.

	NM/M
Wade Boggs, George Brett, Pete Rose	10.00

1987 7-11 Slurpee Coins Eastern Region

Continuing with a tradition started in 1983, 7-Eleven stores offered a free "Super Star Sports Coin" with the purchase of a Slurpee drink. Five different regional sets of Slurpee coins were issued for 1987, a total of 75 coins. Each coin measures 1-3/4" in diameter and features a multiple image effect which allows three different pictures to be seen, depending on how the coin is tilted. The coin reverses contain career records and personal player information.

		NM/M
Complete Set (15):		7.50
Common Player:		.25
1	Gary Carter	1.00
2	Don Baylor	.25
3	Rickey Henderson	1.00
4	Lenny Dykstra	.25
5	Wade Boggs	1.50
6	Mike Pagliarulo	.25
7	Dwight Gooden	.25
8	Roger Clemens	2.00
9	Dave Righetti	.25
10	Keith Hernandez	.25
11	Pat Dodson	.25
12	Don Mattingly	2.00
13	Darryl Strawberry	.25
14	Jim Rice	.45
15	Dave Winfield	1.00

Great Lakes Region

		NM/M
Complete Set (16):		6.00
Common Player:		.25
1	Harold Baines	.25
2	Jody Davis	.25
3	John Cangelosi	.25
4	Shawon Dunston	.25
5	Dave Cochrane	.25
6	Leon Durham	.25
7	Carlton Fisk	1.50
8	Dennis Eckersley	1.00
9	Ozzie Guillen	.25
10	Gary Matthews	.25
11	Ron Karkovice	.25
12	Keith Moreland	.25
13	Bobby Thigpen	.25
14	Ryne Sandberg	2.50
15	Greg Walker	.25
16	Lee Smith	.25

Mideastern Region

		NM/M
Complete Set (16):		7.50
Common Player:		.25
1	Gary Carter	1.00
2	Marty Barrett	.25
3	Jody Davis	.25
4	Don Aase	.25
5	Lenny Dykstra	.25
6	Wade Boggs	1.50
7	Keith Moreland	.25
8	Mike Boddicker	.25
9	Dwight Gooden	.25
10	Roger Clemens	2.00
11	Ryne Sandberg	1.50
12	Eddie Murray	1.00
13	Keith Hernandez	.25
14	Jim Rice	.45
15	Lee Smith	.25
16	Cal Ripken, Jr.	4.00

Western Region

		NM/M
Complete Set (16):		2.00
Common Player:		.25
1	Doug DeCinces	.25
2	Mariano Duncan	.25
3	Wally Joyner	.25
4	Pedro Guerrero	.25
5	Kirk McCaskill	.25
6	Orel Hershiser	.25
7	Gary Pettis	.25
8	Mike Marshall	.25
9	Dick Schofield	.25
10	Steve Sax	.25
11	Don Sutton	1.00
12	Mike Scioscia	.25
13	Devon White	.25
14	Franklin Stubbs	.25
15	Mike Witt	.25
16	Fernando Valenzuela	.25

Tigers Coins

		NM/M
Complete Set (12):		6.00
Common Player:		.50
1	Darnell Coles	.50
2	Darrell Evans	.60
3	Kirk Gibson	.60
4	Willie Hernandez	.50
5	Larry Herndon	.50
6	Chet Lemon	.50
7	Dwight Lowry	.50
8	Jack Morris	.60
9	Dan Petry	.50
10	Frank Tanana	.50
11	Alan Trammell	.75
12	Lou Whitaker	.65

1991 7-11 Slurpee Coins Atlantic Region

After a three-year hiatus, "3-D" magic-motion coins returned to 7-11 stores in the form of regional sets produced by Score under the name Superstar Sports Coins and given away with the purchase of Slurpee fountain drinks. In the familiar 1-3/4" diameter, the discs have alternating portrait and action images on the front with the player name at top, the team at bottom, the uniform number at left and position at right. Each regional set has a different border color. Backs have 7-11 and Score logos along with career stats and a short career summary. The 120 coins in the sets feature 81 different major leaguers.

		NM/M
Complete Set (15):		7.50
Common Player:		.25
1	Glenn Davis	.25
2	Dwight Evans	.25
3	Leo Gomez	.25
4	Ken Griffey Jr.	1.50
5	Rickey Henderson	.75
6	Jose Canseco	.60
7	Dave Justice	.25
8	Ben McDonald	.25
9	Randy Milligan	.25
10	Gregg Olson	.25
11	Kirby Puckett	1.00
12	Bill Ripken	.25
13	Cal Ripken Jr.	2.50
14	Nolan Ryan	2.50
15	David Segui	.25

Florida Region

		NM/M
Complete Set (15):		10.00
Common Player:		.25
1	Barry Bonds	2.50
2	George Brett	1.50
3	Roger Clemens	1.50
4	Glenn Davis	.25
5	Alex Fernandez	.25
6	Cecil Fielder	.25
7	Ken Griffey Jr.	2.00
8	Dwight Gooden	.25
9	Dave Justice	.25
10	Barry Larkin	.25
11	Ramon Martinez	.25
12	Jose Offerman	.25
13	Kirby Puckett	1.00
14	Nolan Ryan	2.50
15	Terry Schumpert	.25

Metro Northeast Region

		NM/M
Complete Set (15):		9.00
Common Player:		.25
1	Wade Boggs	1.00
2	Barry Bonds	2.50
3	Roger Clemens	1.50
4	Len Dykstra	.25
5	Dwight Gooden	.25
6	Ken Griffey Jr.	2.00
7	Rickey Henderson	.75
8	Gregg Jefferies	.25
9	Roberto Kelly	.25
10	Kevin Maas	.25
11	Don Mattingly	1.50
12	Mickey Morandini	.25
13	Dale Murphy	.50
14	Darryl Strawberry	.25
15	Frank Viola	.25

Midwest

		NM/M
Complete Set (15):		6.00
Common Player:		.25
1	George Brett	1.50
2	Andre Dawson	.40
3	Cecil Fielder	.25
4	Carlton Fisk	.75
5	Travis Fryman	.25
6	Mark Grace	.25
7	Ken Griffey Jr.	2.00
8	Ozzie Guillen	.25
9	Alex Fernandez	.25
10	Ray Lankford	.25
11	Ryne Sandberg	1.00
12	Ozzie Smith	1.00
13	Bobby Thigpen	.25
14	Frank Thomas	.75
15	Alan Trammell	.25

Northern California Region

		NM/M
Complete Set (15):		9.00
Common Player:		.25
1	John Burkett	.25
2	Jose Canseco	.65
3	Will Clark	.25
4	Steve Decker	.25
5	Dennis Eckersley	.25
6	Ken Griffey Jr.	2.00
7	Rickey Henderson	.75
8	Nolan Ryan	3.00
9	Mark McGwire	2.50
10	Kevin Mitchell	.25
11	Terry Steinbach	.25
12	Dave Stewart	.25
13	Todd Van Poppel	.25
14	Bob Welch	.25
15	Matt Williams	.25

Northwest Region

		NM/M
Complete Set (15):		9.00
Common Player:		.25
1	George Brett	1.50
2	Jose Canseco	.60
3	Alvin Davis	.25
4	Ken Griffey Jr., Ken Griffey Sr.	1.00
5	Ken Griffey Jr.	2.00
6	Erik Hanson	.25
7	Rickey Henderson	.75
8	Ryne Sandberg	1.00
9	Randy Johnson	.75
10	Dave Justice	.25
11	Edgar Martinez	.25
12	Tino Martinez	.25
13	Harold Reynolds	.25
14	Nolan Ryan	3.00
15	Mike Schooler	.25

Southern California Region

		NM/M
Complete Set (15):		7.00
Common Player:		.25
1	Jim Abbott	.25
2	Jose Canseco	.60
3	Ken Griffey Jr.	2.00
4	Tony Gwynn	1.00
5	Orel Hershiser	.25
6	Eric Davis	.25
7	Wally Joyner	.25
8	Ramon Martinez	.25
9	Fred McGriff	.25
10	Eddie Murray	.75
11	Jose Offerman	.25
12	Nolan Ryan	3.00
13	Benito Santiago	.25
14	Darryl Strawberry	.25
15	Fernando Valenzuela	.25

Texas Region

		NM/M
Complete Set (15):		10.00
Common Player:		.25
1	Craig Biggio	.25
2	Barry Bonds	3.00
3	Jose Canseco	.50
4	Roger Clemens	1.50
5	Glenn Davis	.25
6	Julio Franco	.25
7	Juan Gonzalez	.50
8	Ken Griffey Jr.	2.00
9	Mike Scott	.25
10	Rafael Palmeiro	.75
11	Nolan Ryan	3.00
12	Ryne Sandberg	1.00
13	Ruben Sierra	.25
14	Todd Van Poppel	.25
15	Bobby Witt	.25

1992 7-11 Slurpee Superstar Action Coins

Score baseball 3-D coins returned to 7-11 stores on a very limited basis in 1992. A 26-piece set of the plastic coins (one for each major league team) was produced by Score in the familiar 1-3/4" diameter format. The coins feature a maroon border on which is printed in white the player's name, team, position and uniform number. At center is a 1-1/4" circle with "flasher" portrait and action photos of the player. Backs have a black border with the player name in yellow at the top, a few career stats, 7-11 and Score logos and a coin number in a pale yellow center circle. At bottom in green is "Superstar Action Coin."

		NM/M
Complete Set (26):		10.00
Common Player:		.25
1	Dwight Gooden	.25
2	Don Mattingly	1.00
3	Roger Clemens	1.00
4	Ivan Calderon	.25
5	Roberto Alomar	.40
6	Sandy Alomar, Jr.	.25
7	Andy Van Slyke	.25
8	Lenny Dykstra	.25
9	Cal Ripken, Jr.	2.00
10	Dave Justice	.25
11	Nolan Ryan	2.00
12	Craig Biggio	.25
13	Barry Larkin	.25
14	Ozzie Smith	.75
15	Ryne Sandberg	.75
16	Frank Thomas	.60
17	Robin Yount	.60
18	Kirby Puckett	.75
19	Cecil Fielder	.25
20	Will Clark	.25
21	Jose Canseco	.45
22	Jim Abbott	.25
23	Tony Gwynn	.75
24	Darryl Strawberry	.25
25	George Brett	1.00
26	Ken Griffey Jr.	1.50

2000 7-11 Slurpee Coins

Returning after a long hiatus, lenticular-motion player discs were once again affixed to the bottoms of Super Big Gulp and 32-oz. Slurpee cups at 20,000 convenience stores nationwide. A step up in quality from the "flicker image" coins of the 1980s, this generation was produced by Pacific Trading Cards and licensed by MLB and the Players Union. The 1-3/4" plastic discs have three photos at center with player identification at top and bottom; uniform numbers and logos are at the sides. On back, conventionally printed, is a color portrait photo, a few stats and vital data and appropriate copyright and licensing notices. There is one player coin from each major league team. An album was available to house the set.

		NM/M
Complete Set (30):		10.00
Common Player:		.25
Album:		3.00
In-Store Ad Sheet:		6.00
1	Tim Salmon	.25
2	Erubiel Durazo	.25
3	Chipper Jones	.65
4	Cal Ripken Jr.	2.00
5	Nomar Garciaparra	.65
6	Mark Grace	.25
7	Frank Thomas	.50
8	Sean Casey	.25
9	Manny Ramirez	.50
10	Larry Walker	.25
11	Dean Palmer	.25
12	Alex Gonzalez	.25
13	Jeff Bagwell	.50
14	Carlos Beltran	.45
15	Gary Sheffield	.40
16	Jeromy Burnitz	.25
17	Corey Koskie	.25
18	Vladimir Guerrero	.50
19	Mike Piazza	1.00
20	Roger Clemens	.75
21	Ben Grieve	.25
22	Scott Rolen	.45
23	Jason Kendall	.25
24	Mark McGwire	1.50
25	Tony Gwynn	.65
26	Jeff Kent	.25
27	Jay Buhner	.25
28	Jose Canseco	.40
29	Ivan Rodriguez	.45
30	Carlos Delgado	.45

1981 7-Up

These 5-1/2" x 8-1/2" color photocards are part of a multi-sport series. Fronts have a borderless photo, a facsimile autograph and, at lower-right, a 7-Up logo and slogan. Back is printed in black, red and green on white and features a career summary through the 1980 season, and a large version of the soda logo. Posters in 19" x 25" size were also issued.

		NM/M
Common Player:		3.00
(1)	George Brett	6.00
(3)	Dave Parker	3.00
(5)	Mike Schmidt	6.00

1984 7-Up Cubs

The Chicago Cubs and 7-Up issued this 28-card set featuring full-color game-action photos on a 2-1/4" x 3-1/2" borderless front. The backs have the player's stats and personal information. This was the third consecutive year the Cubs issued this type of set as a giveaway at a "Baseball Card Day" promotional game.

		NM/M
Complete Set (28):		13.50
Common Player:		.25
1	Larry Bowa	.25
6	Keith Moreland	.25
7	Jody Davis	.25
10	Leon Durham	.25
11	Ron Cey	.25
15	Ron Hassey	.25
18	Richie Hebner	.25
19	Dave Owen	.25
20	Bob Dernier	.25
21	Jay Johnstone	.25
23	Ryne Sandberg	9.00
24	Scott Sanderson	.25
25	Gary Woods	.25

27 Thad Bosley .25
28 Henry Cotto .25
34 Steve Trout .25
36 Gary Matthews .25
39 George Frazier .25
40 Rick Sutcliffe .25
41 Warren Brusstar .25
42 Rich Bordi .25
43 Dennis Eckersley 3.00
44 Dick Ruthven .25
46 Lee Smith .25
47 Rick Reuschel .25
49 Tim Stoddard .25
--- Jim Frey .25
--- Cubs Coaches (Ruben Amaro, Billy Connors, Johnny Oates, John Vukovich, Don Zimmer) .25

1985 7-Up Cubs

This was the second year a Chicago Cubs card set was released with 7-Up as the sponsor. The set has 28 unnumbered cards in the standard 2-1/2" x 3-1/2" size. They were distributed to fans attending the Cubs game on August 14 at Wrigley Field. They feature full-color game-action photos of the players. Card backs contain the player's professional stats.

NM/M
Complete Set (28): 10.00
Common Player: .25
1 Larry Bowa .25
6 Keith Moreland .25
7 Jody Davis .25
10 Leon Durham .25
11 Ron Cey .25
15 Davey Lopes .25
16 Steve Lake .25
18 Richie Hebner .25
20 Bob Dernier .25
21 Scott Sanderson .25
22 Billy Hatcher .25
23 Ryne Sandberg 7.50
24 Brian Dayett .25
25 Gary Woods .25
27 Thad Bosley .25
28 Chris Speier .25
31 Ray Fontenot .25
34 Steve Trout .25
36 Gary Matthews .25
39 George Frazier .25
40 Rick Sutcliffe .25
41 Warren Brusstar .25
42 Lary Sorensen .25
43 Dennis Eckersley 2.00
44 Dick Ruthven .25
46 Lee Smith .25
--- Jim Frey .25
--- Coaching Staff (Ruben Amaro, Billy Connors, Johnny Oates, John Vukovich, Don Zimmer) .25

1995 Skin Bracer

This three-card set was included in several packagings of Mennen skin care products for men. Three sepia-toned 3-1/2" x 2-1/2" cards feature great moments in post-season play. Fronts are trimmed in gold ink and feature the player's name in a green box. Backs are printed in black, green and gold and describe the highlight. Logos of the sponsor and Major League Baseball Players Alumni Association are also included on back. A related offer allowed collectors to purchase autographed 8" x 10" photos of the events for $7.99 each via a coupon.

NM/M
Complete Set (3): 6.00
Common Player: 2.00
(1) The Perfect Game (Don Larsen) 2.00
(2) The Series Ender (Bill Mazeroski) 2.00
(3) The Shot Heard 'Round the World (Bobby Thomson) 2.00

2001 Skippy Peanut Butter Derek Jeter

Specially marked jars Skippy Peanut Butter had a Derek Jeter "Digital Card" under the cap, enclosed in protective plastic. The 2-1/2" diameter discs are printed on thin cardboard and have portrait and action photos of the spokesman on front (Yankees team logos have been removed) along with a facsimile autograph and logos of Skippy and CyberAction. Backs are in red and blue with information on the company's website and a card title.

NM/M
Complete Set (4): 6.00
Common Card: 2.00
1 1,000 Hits Club/Btg (Derek Jeter) 2.00
2 1998 Runs Leader/Running (Derek Jeter) 2.00
3 Three Time All-Star/Leaping (Derek Jeter) 2.00
4 World Champion MVP/Throwing (Derek Jeter) 2.00

1995 SkyBox E-Motion Promo

To introduce its new super-premium baseball card line, SkyBox debuted a Cal Ripken promo card at the 1995 National Sports Collectors Convention. The card is virtually identical to Ripken's card in the regular issue, except for diagonal overprinting on each side which reads, "Promotional Sample."

NM/M
8 Cal Ripken Jr. (Class) 2.50

1995 SkyBox E-Motion

This is a super-premium debut issue from the newly merged Fleer/SkyBox company.

Printed on double-thick cardboard, card fronts have borderless photos marred by the presence of four gold-foil "viewfinder" corner marks. The player's last name and team are printed in gold foil near the bottom. On each card there is a large silver-foil word printed in block letters; either a nickname or an emotion or attribute associated with the player. Backs have two more player photos, 1994 and career stats and a few biographical bits. Eight-cards packs were issued with a suggested retail price of $4.99.

NM/M
Complete Set (200): 15.00
Common Player: .05
Pack (8): 1.00
Wax Box (36): 20.00
1 Brady Anderson .05
2 Kevin Brown .05
3 Curtis Goodwin .05
4 Jeffrey Hammonds .05
5 Den McDonald .05
6 Mike Mussina .35
7 Rafael Palmeiro .65
8 Cal Ripken Jr. 2.00
9 Jose Canseco .45
10 Roger Clemens 1.00
11 Vaughn Eshelman .05
12 Mike Greenwell .05
13 Erik Hanson .05
14 Tim Naehring .05
15 Aaron Sele .05
16 John Valentin .05
17 Mo Vaughn .05
18 Chili Davis .05
19 Gary DiSarcina .05
20 Chuck Finley .05
21 Tim Salmon .05
22 Lee Smith .05
23 J.T. Snow .05
24 Jim Abbott .05
25 Jason Bere .05
26 Ray Durham .05
27 Ozzie Guillen .05
28 Tim Raines .05
29 Frank Thomas .75
30 Robin Ventura .05
31 Carlos Baerga .05
32 Albert Belle .05
33 Orel Hershiser .05
34 Kenny Lofton .05
35 Dennis Martinez .05
36 Eddie Murray .75
37 Manny Ramirez .75
38 Julian Tavarez .05
39 Jim Thome .60
40 Dave Winfield .75
41 Chad Curtis .05
42 Cecil Fielder .05
43 Travis Fryman .05
44 Kirk Gibson .05
45 Bob Higginson **RC** .25
46 Alan Trammell .05
47 Lou Whitaker .05
48 Kevin Appier .05
49 Gary Gaetti .05
50 Jeff Montgomery .05
51 Jon Nunnally .05
52 Ricky Bones .05
53 Cal Eldred .05
54 Joe Oliver .05
55 Kevin Seitzer .05
56 Marty Cordova .05
57 Chuck Knoblauch .05
58 Kirby Puckett 1.00
59 Wade Boggs 1.00
60 Derek Jeter 2.00
61 Jimmy Key .05
62 Don Mattingly 1.00
63 Jack McDowell .05
64 Paul O'Neill .05
65 Andy Pettitte .30
66 Ruben Rivera .05
67 Mike Stanley .05
68 John Wetteland .05
69 Geronimo Berroa .05
70 Dennis Eckersley .65
71 Rickey Henderson .75
72 Mark McGwire 1.50
73 Steve Ontiveros .05
74 Ruben Sierra .05
75 Terry Steinbach .05
76 Jay Buhner .05
77 Ken Griffey Jr. 1.25
78 Randy Johnson .75
79 Edgar Martinez .05
80 Tino Martinez .05
81 Marc Newfield .05
82 Alex Rodriguez 1.50
83 Will Clark .05
84 Benji Gil .05
85 Juan Gonzalez .40
86 Rusty Greer .05
87 Dean Palmer .05
88 Ivan Rodriguez .65
89 Kenny Rogers .05
90 Roberto Alomar .30
91 Joe Carter .05
92 David Cone .05
93 Alex Gonzalez .05
94 Shawn Green .40
95 Pat Hentgen .05
96 Paul Molitor .75
97 John Olerud .05
98 Devon White .05
99 Steve Avery .05
100 Tom Glavine .35
101 Marquis Grissom .05
102 Chipper Jones 1.00
103 Dave Justice .05
104 Ryan Klesko .05
105 Javier Lopez .05
106 Greg Maddux 1.00
107 Fred McGriff .05
108 John Smoltz .05
109 Shawon Dunston .05
110 Mark Grace .05
111 Brian McRae .05
112 Randy Myers .05
113 Sammy Sosa 1.00
114 Steve Trachsel .05
115 Bret Boone .05
116 Ron Gant .05
117 Barry Larkin .05
118 Deion Sanders .05
119 Reggie Sanders .05
120 Pete Schourek .05
121 John Smiley .05
122 Jason Bates .05
123 Dante Bichette .05
124 Vinny Castilla .05
125 Andres Galarraga .05
126 Larry Walker .05
127 Greg Colbrunn .05
128 Jeff Conine .05
129 Andre Dawson .30
130 Chris Hammond .05
131 Charles Johnson .05
132 Gary Sheffield .45
133 Quilvio Veras .05
134 Jeff Bagwell .75
135 Derek Bell .05
136 Craig Biggio .05
137 Jim Dougherty .05
138 John Hudek .05
139 Orlando Miller .05
140 Phil Plantier .05
141 Eric Karros .05
142 Ramon Martinez .05
143 Raul Mondesi .05
144 Hideo Nomo **RC** 2.00
145 Mike Piazza 1.25
146 Ismael Valdes .05
147 Todd Worrell .05
148 Moises Alou .05
149 Yamil Benitez **RC** .05
150 Wil Cordero .05
151 Jeff Fassero .05
152 Cliff Floyd .05
153 Pedro Martinez .75
154 Carlos Perez **RC** .05
155 Tony Tarasco .05
156 Rondell White .05
157 Edgardo Alfonzo .05
158 Bobby Bonilla .05
159 Rico Brogna .05
160 Bobby Jones .05
161 Bill Pulsipher .05
162 Bret Saberhagen .05
163 Ricky Bottalico .05
164 Darren Daulton .05
165 Lenny Dykstra .05
166 Charlie Hayes .05
167 Dave Hollins .05
168 Gregg Jefferies .05
169 Michael Mimbs **RC** .05
170 Curt Schilling .35
171 Heathcliff Slocumb .05
172 Jay Bell .05
173 Micah Franklin **RC** .05
174 Mark Johnson **RC** .05
175 Jeff King .05
176 Al Martin .05
177 Dan Miceli .05
178 Denny Neagle .05
179 Bernard Gilkey .05
180 Ken Hill .05
181 Brian Jordan .05
182 Ray Lankford .05
183 Ozzie Smith 1.00
184 Andy Benes .05
185 Ken Caminiti .05
186 Steve Finley .05
187 Tony Gwynn 1.00
188 Joey Hamilton .05
189 Melvin Nieves .05
190 Scott Sanders .05
191 Rod Beck .05
192 Barry Bonds 2.00
193 Royce Clayton .05
194 Glenallen Hill .05
195 Darren Lewis .05
196 Mark Portugal .05
197 Matt Williams .05
198 Checklist .05
199 Checklist .05
200 Checklist .05

Masters

Ten of the game's top veterans are featured in this chase card set. A large close-up photo in a single team-related color in the background, with a color action photo in the foreground. Backs have a borderless color photo and a top to bottom color bar with some good words about the player. The Masters inserts are found at an average rate of one per eight packs.

NM/M
Complete Set (10): 12.00
Common Player: .50
1 Barry Bonds 2.50
2 Juan Gonzalez .65
3 Ken Griffey Jr. 2.00
4 Tony Gwynn 1.50
5 Kenny Lofton .50
6 Greg Maddux 1.50
7 Raul Mondesi .50
8 Cal Ripken Jr. 2.50
9 Frank Thomas 1.00
10 Matt Williams .50

N-Tense

A colored wave-pattern printed on metallic foil is the background for the action photo of one of baseball's top sluggers in this chase card set. A huge rainbow prismatic foil "N" appears in an upper corner. The player's name and team are at lower-right in gold foil. Backs are conventionally printed and repeat the front's patterned background, with another color player photo and a shaded box with a few career highlights.

NM/M
Complete Set (12): 16.00
Common Player: .50
1 Jeff Bagwell 2.00
2 Albert Belle .50
3 Barry Bonds 4.00
4 Cecil Fielder .50
5 Ron Gant .50
6 Ken Griffey Jr. 2.50
7 Mark McGwire 3.00
8 Mike Piazza 2.50
9 Manny Ramirez 2.00
10 Frank Thomas 2.00
11 Mo Vaughn .50
12 Matt Williams .50

Cal Ripken Jr. Timeless

A white background with a clockface and gold-foil "TIMELESS" logo are the standard elements of this insert tribute to Cal Ripken, Jr. Fronts also feature a large color photo and a smaller sepia photo contemporary to some phase of his career. The first 10 cards in the set chronicle Ripken's career through 1994. A special mail-in offer provided five more cards featuring highlights of his 1995 season.

NM/M
Complete Set (15): 20.00
Common Card: 1.50
1 High School Pitcher 1.50
2 Role Model 1.50
3 Rookie of the Year 1.50
4 1st MVP Season 1.50
5 95 Consecutive Errorless Games 1.50
6 All-Star MVP 1.50
7 Conditioning 1.50
8 Shortstop HR Record 1.50
9 Literacy Work 1.50
10 2000th Consecutive Game 1.50
11 All-Star Selection 2.25
12 Record-tying Game 2.25
13 Record-breaking Game 2.25
14 2,153 and Counting 2.25
15 Birthday 2.25

Rookies

A bold colored background with outline white letters repeating the word "ROOKIE" is the frame for the central action photo in this insert series. The top of the photo is vignetted with a white circle that has the player's name in gold at left, and his team in white at right. Backs repeat the front background and include a player portrait photo and a few sentences about his potential. Rookie inserts are found at an average rate of one per five packs.

NM/M
Complete Set (10): 6.50
Common Player: .25
1 Edgardo Alfonzo .25
2 Jason Bates .25
3 Marty Cordova .25
4 Ray Durham .25
5 Alex Gonzalez .25
6 Shawn Green .75
7 Charles Johnson .25
8 Chipper Jones 1.50
9 Hideo Nomo 1.00
10 Alex Rodriguez 3.00

1996 SkyBox E-Motion XL

Each card in SkyBox's 1996 E-Motion XL Baseball arrives on two layers of stock - a die-cut matte frame over a UV-coated card. The frames come in three colors - blue, green and maroon (but each player has only one color version). The 300-card set also includes four insert sets: Legion of Boom, D-Fense, N-Tense and Rare Breed.

		NM/M
Complete Set (300):		10.00
Common Player:		.05
Pack (7):		1.00
Wax Box (24):		20.00
1	Roberto Alomar	.15
2	Brady Anderson	.05
3	Bobby Bonilla	.05
4	Jeffrey Hammonds	.05
5	Chris Hoiles	.05
6	Mike Mussina	.30
7	Randy Myers	.05
8	Rafael Palmeiro	.50
9	Cal Ripken Jr.	2.00
10	B.J. Surhoff	.05
11	Jose Canseco	.25
12	Roger Clemens	1.00
13	Wil Cordero	.05
14	Mike Greenwell	.05
15	Dwayne Hosey	.05
16	Tim Naehring	.05
17	Troy O'Leary	.05
18	Mike Stanley	.05
19	John Valentin	.05
20	Mo Vaughn	.05
21	Jim Abbott	.05
22	Garret Anderson	.05
23	George Arias	.05
24	Chili Davis	.05
25	Jim Edmonds	.05
26	Chuck Finley	.05
27	Todd Greene	.05
28	Mark Langston	.05
29	Troy Percival	.05
30	Tim Salmon	.05
31	Lee Smith	.05
32	J.T. Snow	.05
33	Harold Baines	.05
34	Jason Bere	.05
35	Ray Durham	.05
36	Alex Fernandez	.05
37	Ozzie Guillen	.05
38	Darren Lewis	.05
39	Lyle Mouton	.05
40	Tony Phillips	.05
41	Danny Tartabull	.05
42	Frank Thomas	.60
43	Robin Ventura	.05
44	Sandy Alomar	.05
45	Carlos Baerga	.05
46	Albert Belle	.05
47	Julio Franco	.05
48	Orel Hershiser	.05
49	Kenny Lofton	.05
50	Dennis Martinez	.05
51	Jack McDowell	.05
52	Jose Mesa	.05
53	Eddie Murray	.60
54	Charles Nagy	.05
55	Manny Ramirez	.60
55p	Manny Ramirez (Overprinted "PROMOTIONAL SAMPLE.")	.60
56	Jim Thome	.45
57	Omar Vizquel	.05
58	Chad Curtis	.05
59	Cecil Fielder	.05
60	Travis Fryman	.05
61	Chris Gomez	.05
62	Felipe Lira	.05
63	Alan Trammell	.05
64	Kevin Appier	.05
65	Johnny Damon	.35
66	Tom Goodwin	.05
67	Mark Gubicza	.05
68	Jeff Montgomery	.05
69	Jon Nunnally	.05
70	Bip Roberts	.05
71	Ricky Bones	.05
72	Chuck Carr	.05
73	John Jaha	.05
74	Ben McDonald	.05
75	Matt Mieske	.05
76	Dave Nilsson	.05
77	Kevin Seitzer	.05
78	Greg Vaughn	.05
79	Rick Aguilera	.05
80	Marty Cordova	.05
81	Roberto Kelly	.05
82	Chuck Knoblauch	.05
83	Pat Meares	.05
84	Paul Molitor	.60
85	Kirby Puckett	.75
86	Brad Radke	.05
87	Wade Boggs	.75
88	David Cone	.05
89	Dwight Gooden	.05
90	Derek Jeter	2.00
91	Tino Martinez	.05
92	Paul O'Neill	.05
93	Andy Pettitte	.15
94	Tim Raines	.05
95	Ruben Rivera	.05
96	Kenny Rogers	.05
97	Ruben Sierra	.05
98	John Wetteland	.05
99	Bernie Williams	.05
100	Allen Battle	.05
101	Geronimo Berroa	.05
102	Brent Gates	.05
103	Doug Johns	.05
104	Mark McGwire	1.50
105	Pedro Munoz	.05
106	Ariel Prieto	.05
107	Terry Steinbach	.05
108	Todd Van Poppel	.05
109	Chris Bosio	.05
110	Jay Buhner	.05
111	Joey Cora	.05
112	Russ Davis	.05
113	Ken Griffey Jr.	1.25
114	Sterling Hitchcock	.05
115	Randy Johnson	.60
116	Edgar Martinez	.05
117	Alex Rodriguez	1.50
118	Paul Sorrento	.05
119	Dan Wilson	.05
120	Will Clark	.05
121	Juan Gonzalez	.30
122	Rusty Greer	.05
123	Kevin Gross	.05
124	Ken Hill	.05
125	Dean Palmer	.05
126	Roger Pavlik	.05
127	Ivan Rodriguez	.50
128	Mickey Tettleton	.05
129	Joe Carter	.05
130	Carlos Delgado	.40
131	Alex Gonzalez	.05
132	Shawn Green	.25
133	Erik Hanson	.05
134	Pat Hentgen	.05
135	Otis Nixon	.05
136	John Olerud	.05
137	Ed Sprague	.05
138	Steve Avery	.05
139	Jermaine Dye	.05
140	Tom Glavine	.35
141	Marquis Grissom	.05
142	Chipper Jones	.75
143	David Justice	.05
144	Ryan Klesko	.05
145	Javier Lopez	.05
146	Greg Maddux	.75
147	Fred McGriff	.05
148	Jason Schmidt	.05
149	John Smoltz	.05
150	Mark Wohlers	.05
151	Jim Bullinger	.05
152	Frank Castillo	.05
153	Kevin Foster	.05
154	Luis Gonzalez	.05
155	Mark Grace	.05
156	Brian McRae	.05
157	Jaime Navarro	.05
158	Rey Sanchez	.05
159	Ryne Sandberg	.75
160	Sammy Sosa	.75
161	Bret Boone	.05
162	Jeff Brantley	.05
163	Vince Coleman	.05
164	Steve Gibralter	.05
165	Barry Larkin	.05
166	Hal Morris	.05
167	Mark Portugal	.05
168	Reggie Sanders	.05
169	Pete Schourek	.05
170	John Smiley	.05
171	Jason Bates	.05
172	Dante Bichette	.05
173	Ellis Burks	.05
174	Vinny Castilla	.05
175	Andres Galarraga	.05
176	Kevin Ritz	.05
177	Bill Swift	.05
178	Larry Walker	.05
179	Walt Weiss	.05
180	Eric Young	.05
181	Kurt Abbott	.05
182	Kevin Brown	.05
183	John Burkett	.05
184	Greg Colbrunn	.05
185	Jeff Conine	.05
186	Chris Hammond	.05
187	Charles Johnson	.05
188	Terry Pendleton	.05
189	Pat Rapp	.05
190	Gary Sheffield	.25
191	Quilvio Veras	.05
192	Devon White	.05
193	Jeff Bagwell	.60
194	Derek Bell	.05
195	Sean Berry	.05
196	Craig Biggio	.05
197	Doug Drabek	.05
198	Tony Eusebio	.05
199	Mike Hampton	.05
200	Brian Hunter	.05
201	Derrick May	.05
202	Orlando Miller	.05
203	Shane Reynolds	.05
204	Mike Blowers	.05
205	Tom Candiotti	.05
206	Delino DeShields	.05
207	Greg Gagne	.05
208	Karim Garcia	.05
209	Todd Hollandsworth	.05
210	Eric Karros	.05
211	Ramon Martinez	.05
212	Raul Mondesi	.05
213	Hideo Nomo	.30
214	Chan Ho Park	.05
215	Mike Piazza	1.25
216	Ismael Valdes	.05
217	Todd Worrell	.05
218	Moises Alou	.05
219	Yamil Benitez	.05
220	Jeff Fassero	.05
221	Darrin Fletcher	.05
222	Cliff Floyd	.05
223	Pedro Martinez	.60
224	Carlos Perez	.05
225	Mel Rojas	.05
226	David Segui	.05
227	Rondell White	.05
228	Rico Brogna	.05
229	Carl Everett	.05
230	John Franco	.05
231	Bernard Gilkey	.05
232	Todd Hundley	.05
233	Jason Isringhausen	.05
234	Lance Johnson	.05
235	Bobby Jones	.05
236	Jeff Kent	.05
237	Rey Ordonez	.05
238	Bill Pulsipher	.05
239	Jose Vizcaino	.05
240	Paul Wilson	.05
241	Ricky Bottalico	.05
242	Darren Daulton	.05
243	Lenny Dykstra	.05
244	Jim Eisenreich	.05
245	Sid Fernandez	.05
246	Gregg Jefferies	.05
247	Mickey Morandini	.05
248	Benito Santiago	.05
249	Curt Schilling	.35
250	Mark Whiten	.05
251	Todd Zeile	.05
252	Jay Bell	.05
253	Carlos Garcia	.05
254	Charlie Hayes	.05
255	Jason Kendall	.05
256	Jeff King	.05
257	Al Martin	.05
258	Orlando Merced	.05
259	Dan Miceli	.05
260	Denny Neagle	.05
261	Alan Benes	.05
262	Andy Benes	.05
263	Royce Clayton	.05
264	Dennis Eckersley	.50
265	Gary Gaetti	.05
266	Ron Gant	.05
267	Brian Jordan	.05
268	Ray Lankford	.05
269	John Mabry	.05
270	Tom Pagnozzi	.05
271	Ozzie Smith	.75
272	Todd Stottlemyre	.05
273	Andy Ashby	.05
274	Brad Ausmus	.05
275	Ken Caminiti	.05
276	Steve Finley	.05
277	Tony Gwynn	.75
278	Joey Hamilton	.05
279	Rickey Henderson	.60
280	Trevor Hoffman	.05
281	Wally Joyner	.05
282	Jody Reed	.05
283	Bob Tewksbury	.05
284	Fernando Valenzuela	.05
285	Rod Beck	.05
286	Barry Bonds	2.00
287	Mark Carreon	.05
288	Shawon Dunston	.05
289	Osvaldo Fernandez **RC**	.10
290	Glenallen Hill	.05
291	Stan Javier	.05
292	Mark Leiter	.05
293	Kirt Manwaring	.05
294	Robby Thompson	.05
295	William Van Landingham	.05
296	Allen Watson	.05
297	Matt Williams	.05
298	Checklist	.05
299	Checklist	.05
300	Checklist	.05

XL D-Fense

Ten top defensive players are featured on these 1996 SkyBox E-Motion XL insert cards. The cards were seeded at a rate of one per every four packs.

		NM/M
Complete Set (10):		9.00
Common Player:		.50
1	Roberto Alomar	.65
2	Barry Bonds	3.50
3	Mark Grace	.50
4	Ken Griffey Jr.	2.50
5	Kenny Lofton	.50
6	Greg Maddux	1.50
7	Raul Mondesi	.50
8	Cal Ripken Jr.	3.50
9	Ivan Rodriguez	1.00
10	Matt Williams	.50

XL Legion of Boom

The top power hitters in baseball are featured on these 1996 SkyBox E-Motion XL insert cards. The cards, exclusive to hobby packs at a ratio of one per every 36 packs, have translucent card backs.

		NM/M
Complete Set (12):		27.50
Common Player:		2.00
1	Albert Belle	2.00
2	Barry Bonds	6.00
3	Juan Gonzalez	2.50
4	Ken Griffey Jr.	4.00
5	Mark McGwire	5.00
6	Mike Piazza	4.00
7	Manny Ramirez	3.00
8	Tim Salmon	2.00
9	Sammy Sosa	3.50
10	Frank Thomas	3.00
11	Mo Vaughn	2.00
12	Matt Williams	2.00

XL N-Tense

Ten top clutch performers are featured on these 1996 SkyBox E-Motion XL insert cards. The cards, which use an N-shaped die-cut design, were included one per every 12 packs.

		NM/M
Complete Set (10):		17.50
Common Player:		.50
1	Albert Belle	.50
2	Barry Bonds	3.50
3	Jose Canseco	1.00
4	Ken Griffey Jr.	3.00
5	Tony Gwynn	2.50
6	Randy Johnson	2.00
7	Greg Maddux	2.50
8	Cal Ripken Jr.	3.50
9	Frank Thomas	2.00
10	Matt Williams	.50

XL Rare Breed

These 1996 E-Motion XL inserts are the most difficult to find; they are seeded one per every 100 packs. The cards showcase top young stars on a 3-D lenticular-motion design.

		NM/M
Complete Set (10):		50.00
Common Player:		3.00
1	Garret Anderson	3.00
2	Marty Cordova	3.00
3	Brian Hunter	3.00
4	Jason Isringhausen	3.00
5	Charles Johnson	3.00
6	Chipper Jones	16.00
7	Raul Mondesi	3.00
8	Hideo Nomo	6.00
9	Manny Ramirez	12.00
10	Rondell White	3.00

1997 SkyBox E-X2000 Sample

To introduce its innovative high-tech premium brand, SkyBox released this promo card. It is identical in format to the issued version, except it carries a "SAMPLE" notation instead of a card number on back.

	NM/M
Alex Rodriguez	4.00

1997 SkyBox E-X2000

The premiere issue of E-X2000 consists of 100 base cards designed with "Sky-View" technology, utilizing a die-cut holofoil border and the player silhouetted in front of a transparent "window" featuring a variety of sky patterns. Inserts include two sequentially-numbered parallel sets - Credentials (1:50 packs) and Essential Credentials (1:200 packs) - as well as Emerald Autograph Exchange Cards, A Cut Above, Hall of Nothing, and Star Date. Cards were sold in two-card packs for $3.99 each.

		NM/M
Complete Set (100):		20.00
Common Player:		.15
Credentials Stars:		6X
Essential Credentials:		10X
Pack (2):		1.25
Wax Box (24):		20.00
1	Jim Edmonds	.15
2	Darin Erstad	.25
3	Eddie Murray	1.00
4	Roberto Alomar	.25
5	Brady Anderson	.15
6	Mike Mussina	.45
7	Rafael Palmeiro	.75
8	Cal Ripken Jr.	3.00
9	Steve Avery	.15
10	Nomar Garciaparra	1.50
11	Mo Vaughn	.15
12	Albert Belle	.15
13	Mike Cameron	.15
14	Ray Durham	.15
15	Frank Thomas	1.00
16	Robin Ventura	.15
17	Manny Ramirez	1.00
18	Jim Thome	.65
19	Matt Williams	.15
20	Tony Clark	.15
21	Travis Fryman	.15
22	Bob Higginson	.15
23	Kevin Appier	.15
24	Johnny Damon	.45
25	Jermaine Dye	.15
26	Jeff Cirillo	.15
27	Ben McDonald	.15
28	Chuck Knoblauch	.15
29	Paul Molitor	1.00
30	Todd Walker	.15
31	Wade Boggs	1.50
32	Cecil Fielder	.15
33	Derek Jeter	3.00
34	Andy Pettitte	.25
35	Ruben Rivera	.15
36	Bernie Williams	.15
37	Jose Canseco	.50
38	Mark McGwire	2.50
39	Jay Buhner	.15
40	Ken Griffey Jr.	2.00
41	Randy Johnson	1.00
42	Edgar Martinez	.15
43	Alex Rodriguez	2.50
44	Dan Wilson	.15
45	Will Clark	.40
46	Juan Gonzalez	.50
47	Ivan Rodriguez	.75
48	Joe Carter	.15
49	Roger Clemens	1.75
50	Juan Guzman	.15
51	Pat Hentgen	.15
52	Tom Glavine	.35
53	Andruw Jones	1.00
54	Chipper Jones	1.50
55	Ryan Klesko	.15
56	Kenny Lofton	.15
57	Greg Maddux	1.50
58	Fred McGriff	.15
59	John Smoltz	.15
60	Mark Wohlers	.15
61	Mark Grace	.15
62	Ryne Sandberg	1.50
63	Sammy Sosa	1.50
64	Barry Larkin	.15
65	Deion Sanders	.15
66	Reggie Sanders	.15
67	Dante Bichette	.15
68	Ellis Burks	.15
69	Andres Galarraga	.15
70	Moises Alou	.15
71	Kevin Brown	.15
72	Cliff Floyd	.15
73	Edgar Renteria	.15
74	Gary Sheffield	.50
75	Bob Abreu	.15
76	Jeff Bagwell	1.00
77	Craig Biggio	.15
78	Todd Hollandsworth	.15
79	Eric Karros	.15
80	Raul Mondesi	.15
81	Hideo Nomo	.50
82	Mike Piazza	2.00
83	Vladimir Guerrero	1.00
84	Henry Rodriguez	.15
85	Todd Hundley	.15
86	Rey Ordonez	.15
87	Alex Ochoa	.15
88	Gregg Jefferies	.15
89	Scott Rolen	.65
90	Jermaine Allensworth	.15
91	Jason Kendall	.15
92	Ken Caminiti	.15
93	Tony Gwynn	1.50
94	Rickey Henderson	1.00
95	Barry Bonds	3.00
96	J.T. Snow	.15
97	Dennis Eckersley	.75
98	Ron Gant	.15
99	Brian Jordan	.15
100	Ray Lankford	.15

Credentials

This parallel set features different colored foils from the base cards, as well as different

images on the "window." Cards are sequentially numbered on back within an issue of 299. Cards were inserted 1:50 packs.

	NM/M
Common Player:	1.00
Credentials Stars:	6X

Essential Credentials

A sequentially-numbered parallel set, found one per 200 packs, and limited to 99 total sets.

	NM/M
Common Player:	3.00
Essential Credentials Stars:	10X

A Cut Above

Some of the game's elite players are featured in this 1:288 pack insert that features a die-cut design resembling a saw blade. Printed on silver-foil stock, the player's name and Cut Above logo are embossed on front. On back is another color photo and a few words about the player.

		NM/M
Complete Set (10):		55.00
Common Player:		2.00
1	Frank Thomas	7.50
2	Ken Griffey Jr.	9.00
3	Alex Rodriguez	12.00
4	Albert Belle	2.00
5	Juan Gonzalez	4.00
6	Mark McGwire	10.00
7	Mo Vaughn	2.00
8	Manny Ramirez	7.50
9	Barry Bonds	12.00
10	Fred McGriff	2.00

Emerald Autograph Redemptions

Inserted 1:480 packs, these cards could be exchanged by mail prior to May 1, 1998 for autographed cards or memorabilia from one of six major leaguers.

		NM/M
Complete Set (6):		17.50
Common Player:		1.00
(1)	Darin Erstad	2.50
(2)	Todd Hollandsworth	1.00
(3)	Alex Ochoa	1.00
(4)	Alex Rodriguez	10.00
(5)	Scott Rolen	3.00
(6)	Todd Walker	1.00

Emerald Autographs

These authentically autographed versions of the players' E-X2000 cards were available (until May 1, 1998) by a mail-in exchange of redemption cards. The autographed cards are authenticated by the presence of an embossed SkyBox logo seal.

		NM/M
Complete Set (6):		75.00
Common Player:		3.00
2	Darin Erstad	12.00
30	Todd Walker	5.00
43	Alex Rodriguez	60.00
78	Todd Hollandsworth	3.00
86	Alex Ochoa	3.00
89	Scott Rolen	25.00

Hall or Nothing

This 20-card insert, featuring players who are candidates for the Hall of Fame, utilizes a die-cut design on plastic stock. Stately architectural details and brush bronze highlights frame the player picture on front. The player silhouette on back contains career information. Cards were inserted 1:20 packs.

		NM/M
Complete Set (20):		55.00
Common Player:		1.00
1	Frank Thomas	2.50
2	Ken Griffey Jr.	5.00
3	Eddie Murray	2.50
4	Cal Ripken Jr.	7.00
5	Ryne Sandberg	4.00
6	Wade Boggs	4.00
7	Roger Clemens	4.50
8	Tony Gwynn	4.00
9	Alex Rodriguez	6.00
10	Mark McGwire	6.00
11	Barry Bonds	7.00
12	Greg Maddux	4.00
13	Juan Gonzalez	1.25
14	Albert Belle	1.00
15	Mike Piazza	5.00
16	Jeff Bagwell	2.50
17	Dennis Eckersley	1.50
18	Mo Vaughn	1.00
19	Roberto Alomar	1.00
20	Kenny Lofton	1.00

Alex Rodriguez Jumbo

This 8" x 10" version of A-Rod's SkyBox E-X2000 card was given to dealers who ordered case quantities of the new product. The card is identical in design to the standard-sized issued version, but is numbered on back from within an edition of 3,000.

	NM/M
Alex Rodriguez	12.00

Star Date 2000

A 15-card set highlighting young stars that are likely to be the game's top players in the year 2000. Cards were inserted 1:9 packs.

		NM/M
Complete Set (15):		10.00
Common Player:		.40
1	Alex Rodriguez	2.00
2	Andruw Jones	1.25
3	Andy Pettitte	.60
4	Brooks Kieschnick	.40
5	Chipper Jones	1.50
6	Darin Erstad	.60
7	Derek Jeter	2.50
8	Jason Kendall	.40
9	Jermaine Dye	.40
10	Neifi Perez	.40
11	Scott Rolen	.90
12	Todd Hollandsworth	.40
13	Todd Walker	.40
14	Tony Clark	.40
15	Vladimir Guerrero	1.25

1998 SkyBox E-X2001 Sample

To preview its high-tech E-X2001 brand for 1998, SkyBox issued this sample card of A-Rod. Similar in format to the issued version, it is numbered "SAMPLE" on back and has a "PROMOTIONAL SAMPLE" overprint on back.

	NM/M
Alex Rodriguez	2.00

1998 SkyBox E-X2001

This super-premium set featured 100 players on a layered, die-cut design utilizing mirror-image silhouetted photography and etched holo-foil treatment over a clear, 20-point plastic card.

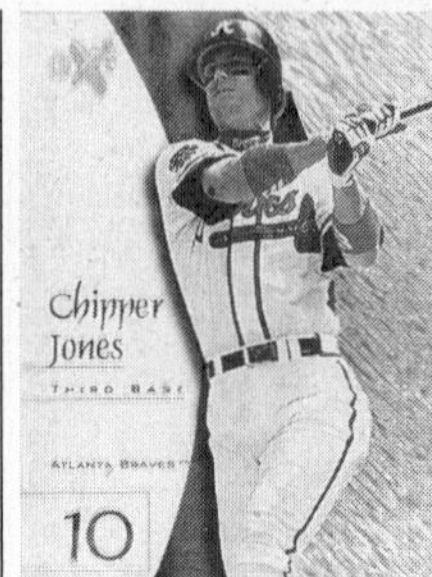

		NM/M
Complete Set (100):		25.00
Common Player:		.15
Pack (2):		1.50
Wax Box (24):		25.00
1	Alex Rodriguez	2.50
2	Barry Bonds	3.00
3	Greg Maddux	1.50
4	Roger Clemens	1.75
5	Juan Gonzalez	.50
6	Chipper Jones	1.50
7	Derek Jeter	3.00
8	Frank Thomas	1.00
9	Cal Ripken Jr.	3.00
10	Ken Griffey Jr.	2.00
11	Mark McGwire	2.50
12	Hideo Nomo	.50
13	Tony Gwynn	1.50
14	Ivan Rodriguez	.75
15	Mike Piazza	2.00
16	Roberto Alomar	.30
17	Jeff Bagwell	1.00
18	Andruw Jones	1.00
19	Albert Belle	.15
20	Mo Vaughn	.15
21	Kenny Lofton	.15
22	Gary Sheffield	.40
23	Tony Clark	.15
24	Mike Mussina	.30
25	Barry Larkin	.15
26	Moises Alou	.15
27	Brady Anderson	.15
28	Andy Pettitte	.25
29	Sammy Sosa	1.50
30	Raul Mondesi	.15
31	Andres Galarraga	.15
32	Chuck Knoblauch	.15
33	Jim Thome	.65
34	Craig Biggio	.15
35	Jay Buhner	.15
36	Rafael Palmeiro	.75
37	Curt Schilling	.35
38	Tino Martinez	.15
39	Pedro Martinez	1.00
40	Jose Canseco	.50
41	Jeff Cirillo	.15
42	Dean Palmer	.15
43	Tim Salmon	.15
44	Jason Giambi	.50
45	Bobby Higginson	.15
46	Jim Edmonds	.15
47	David Justice	.15
48	John Olerud	.15
49	Ray Lankford	.15
50	Al Martin	.15
51	Mike Lieberthal	.15
52	Henry Rodriguez	.15
53	Edgar Renteria	.15
54	Eric Karros	.15
55	Marquis Grissom	.15
56	Wilson Alvarez	.15
57	Darryl Kile	.15
58	Jeff King	.15
59	Shawn Estes	.15
60	Tony Womack	.15
61	Willie Greene	.15
62	Ken Caminiti	.15
63	Vinny Castilla	.15
64	Mark Grace	.15
65	Ryan Klesko	.15
66	Robin Ventura	.15
67	Todd Hundley	.15
68	Travis Fryman	.15
69	Edgar Martinez	.15
70	Matt Williams	.15
71	Paul Molitor	1.00
72	Kevin Brown	.15
73	Randy Johnson	1.00
74	Bernie Williams	.10
75	Manny Ramirez	1.00
76	Fred McGriff	.15
77	Tom Glavine	.35
78	Carlos Delgado	.60
79	Larry Walker	.15
80	Hideki Irabu	.15
81	Ryan McGuire	.15
82	Justin Thompson	.15
83	Kevin Orie	.15
84	Jon Nunnally	.15
85	Mark Kotsay	.15
86	Todd Walker	.15
87	Jason Dickson	.15
88	Fernando Tatis	.15
89	Karim Garcia	.15
90	Ricky Ledee	.15
91	Paul Konerko	.25
92	Jaret Wright	.15
93	Darin Erstad	.30
94	Livan Hernandez	.15
95	Nomar Garciaparra	1.50
96	Jose Cruz Jr.	.15
97	Scott Rolen	.65
98	Ben Grieve	.15
99	Vladimir Guerrero	1.00
100	Travis Lee	.15

Essential Credentials Future

Essential Credentials Future, along with Essential Credentials Now, paralleled all 100 cards in the base set. Production varied depending on the card number, with the exact production number of each player determined by subtracting his card number from 101. Number issued for each card is shown in parentheses.

		NM/M
Common Player:		5.00
1	Alex Rodriguez/100	55.00
2	Barry Bonds/99	60.00
3	Greg Maddux/98	40.00
4	Roger Clemens/97	45.00
5	Juan Gonzalez/96	15.00
6	Chipper Jones/95	40.00
7	Derek Jeter/94	55.00
8	Frank Thomas/93	35.00
9	Cal Ripken Jr./92	65.00
10	Ken Griffey Jr./91	45.00
11	Mark McGwire/90	55.00
12	Hideo Nomo/89	15.00
13	Tony Gwynn/88	25.00
14	Ivan Rodriguez/87	25.00
15	Mike Piazza/86	40.00
16	Roberto Alomar/85	15.00
17	Jeff Bagwell/84	25.00
18	Andruw Jones/83	25.00
19	Albert Belle/82	5.00
20	Mo Vaughn/81	5.00
21	Kenny Lofton/80	5.00
22	Gary Sheffield/79	12.00
23	Tony Clark/78	5.00
24	Mike Mussina/77	25.00
25	Barry Larkin/76	5.00
26	Moises Alou/75	5.00
27	Brady Anderson/74	5.00
28	Andy Pettitte/73	7.50
29	Sammy Sosa/72	40.00
30	Raul Mondesi/71	5.00
31	Andres Galarraga/70	6.00
32	Chuck Knoblauch/69	6.00
33	Jim Thome/68	20.00
34	Craig Biggio/67	6.00
35	Jay Buhner/66	6.00
36	Rafael Palmeiro/65	30.00
37	Curt Schilling/64	20.00
38	Tino Martinez/63	6.00
39	Pedro Martinez/62	32.50
40	Jose Canseco/61	30.00
41	Jeff Cirillo/60	6.00
42	Dean Palmer/59	6.00
43	Tim Salmon/58	7.50
44	Jason Giambi/57	25.00
45	Bobby Higginson/56	6.00
46	Jim Edmonds/55	6.00
47	David Justice/54	6.00
48	John Olerud/53	6.00
49	Ray Lankford/52	6.00
50	Al Martin/51	6.00
51	Mike Lieberthal/50	6.00
52	Henry Rodriguez/49	6.00
53	Edgar Renteria/48	6.00
54	Eric Karros/47	6.00
55	Marquis Grissom/46	6.00
56	Wilson Alvarez/45	6.00
57	Darryl Kile/44	6.00
58	Jeff King/43	6.00
59	Shawn Estes/42	6.00
60	Tony Womack/41	6.00
61	Willie Greene/40	6.00
62	Ken Caminiti/39	6.00
63	Vinny Castilla/38	6.00
64	Mark Grace/37	6.00
65	Ryan Klesko/36	6.00
66	Robin Ventura/35	6.00
67	Todd Hundley/34	6.00
68	Travis Fryman/33	6.00
69	Edgar Martinez/32	7.50
70	Matt Williams/31	7.50
71	Paul Molitor/30	45.00
72	Kevin Brown/29	7.50
73	Randy Johnson/28	40.00
74	Bernie Williams/27	20.00
75	Manny Ramirez/26	45.00
76	Fred McGriff/25	20.00
77	Tom Glavine/24	35.00
78	Carlos Delgado/23	35.00
79	Larry Walker/22	9.00
80	Hideki Irabu/21	9.00
81	Ryan McGuire/20	9.00
82	Justin Thompson/19	9.00
83	Kevin Orie/18	9.00
84	Jon Nunnally/17	9.00
85	Mark Kotsay/16	9.00

Essential Credentials Now

Essential Credentials Now parallels all 100 cards in the E-X2001 base set. Production for each card was limited to that player's card number, as shown in parentheses.

		NM/M
Common Player:		5.00
21	Kenny Lofton/21	10.00
22	Gary Sheffield/22	20.00
23	Tony Clark/23	10.00
24	Mike Mussina/24	30.00
25	Barry Larkin/25	10.00
26	Moises Alou/26	10.00
27	Brady Anderson/27	10.00
28	Andy Pettitte/28	15.00
29	Sammy Sosa/29	30.00
30	Raul Mondesi/30	10.00
31	Andres Galarraga/31	10.00
32	Chuck Knoblauch/32	10.00
33	Jim Thome/33	25.00
34	Craig Biggio/34	10.00
35	Jay Buhner/35	10.00
36	Rafael Palmeiro/36	25.00
37	Curt Schilling/37	20.00
38	Tino Martinez/38	10.00
39	Pedro Martinez/39	30.00
40	Jose Canseco/40	20.00
41	Jeff Cirillo/41	5.00
42	Dean Palmer/42	5.00
43	Tim Salmon/43	5.00
44	Jason Giambi/44	15.00
45	Bobby Higginson/45	5.00
46	Jim Edmonds/46	5.00
47	David Justice/47	5.00
48	John Olerud/48	5.00
49	Ray Lankford/49	5.00
50	Al Martin/50	5.00
51	Mike Lieberthal/51	5.00
52	Henry Rodriguez/52	5.00
53	Edgar Renteria/53	5.00
54	Eric Karros/54	5.00
55	Marquis Grissom/55	5.00
56	Wilson Alvarez/56	5.00
57	Darryl Kile/57	5.00
58	Jeff King/58	5.00
59	Shawn Estes/59	5.00
60	Tony Womack/60	5.00
61	Willie Greene/61	5.00
62	Ken Caminiti/62	5.00
63	Vinny Castilla/63	5.00
64	Mark Grace/64	5.00
65	Ryan Klesko/65	5.00
66	Robin Ventura/66	5.00
67	Todd Hundley/67	5.00
68	Travis Fryman/68	5.00
69	Edgar Martinez/69	5.00
70	Matt Williams/70	5.00
71	Paul Molitor/71	15.00
72	Kevin Brown/72	5.00
73	Randy Johnson/73	20.00
74	Bernie Williams/74	5.00
75	Manny Ramirez/75	20.00
76	Fred McGriff/76	5.00
77	Tom Glavine/77	12.00
78	Carlos Delgado/78	10.00
79	Larry Walker/79	5.00
80	Hideki Irabu/80	5.00
81	Ryan McGuire/81	5.00
82	Justin Thompson/82	5.00
83	Kevin Orie/83	5.00
84	Jon Nunnally/84	5.00
85	Mark Kotsay/85	5.00
86	Todd Walker/86	5.00
87	Jason Dickson/87	5.00
88	Fernando Tatis/88	5.00
89	Karim Garcia/89	5.00
90	Ricky Ledee/90	5.00
91	Paul Konerko/91	7.50
92	Jaret Wright/92	5.00
93	Darin Erstad/93	5.00
94	Livan Hernandez/94	5.00
95	Nomar Garciaparra/95	20.00
96	Jose Cruz Jr./96	5.00
97	Scott Rolen/97	10.00
98	Ben Grieve/98	5.00
99	Vladimir Guerrero/99	12.00
100	Travis Lee/100	5.00

Cheap Seat Treats

This 20-card die-cut insert arrived in the shape of a stadium seat. Inserted at one per 24 packs, Cheap Seat Treats included some of the top home run hitters and were numbered with a "CS" prefix.

		NM/M
Complete Set (20):		30.00
Common Player:		1.00
Inserted 1:24		
1	Frank Thomas	2.00
2	Ken Griffey Jr.	3.00

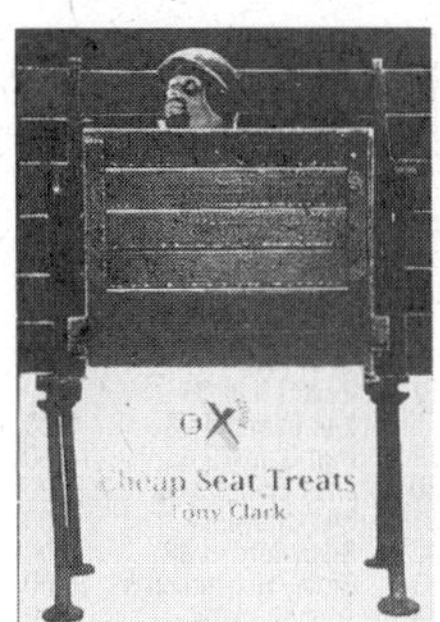

3	Mark McGwire	4.00
4	Tino Martinez	1.00
5	Larry Walker	1.00
6	Juan Gonzalez	1.50
7	Mike Piazza	3.00
8	Jeff Bagwell	2.00
9	Tony Clark	1.00
10	Albert Belle	1.00
11	Andres Galarraga	1.00
12	Jim Thome	1.50
13	Mo Vaughn	1.00
14	Barry Bonds	5.00
15	Vladimir Guerrero	2.00
16	Scott Rolen	1.25
17	Travis Lee	1.00
18	David Justice	1.00
19	Jose Cruz Jr.	1.00
20	Andruw Jones	2.00

Destination: Cooperstown

Destination: Cooperstown captures a mixture of rising young stars and top veterans on die-cut cards that were inserted one per 720 packs. Cards resemble a luggage tag and have a string through a hole at top. Fronts have an action photo, backs have a portrait. Cards are numbered with a "DC" prefix.

		NM/M
Complete Set (15):		375.00
Common Player:		8.00
Inserted 1:720		
1	Alex Rodriguez	40.00
2	Frank Thomas	20.00
3	Cal Ripken Jr.	50.00
4	Roger Clemens	30.00
5	Greg Maddux	25.00
6	Chipper Jones	25.00
7	Ken Griffey Jr.	35.00
8	Mark McGwire	40.00
9	Tony Gwynn	25.00
10	Mike Piazza	35.00
11	Jeff Bagwell	20.00
12	Jose Cruz Jr.	8.00
13	Derek Jeter	50.00
14	Hideo Nomo	10.00
15	Ivan Rodriguez	15.00

Signature 2001

Seventeen top young and future stars signed cards for Signature 2001 inserts in E-X2001. The cards featured the player over a blue and white, sky-like background, with an embossed SkyBox seal of authenticity. Backs were horizontal and also included a Certificate of Authenticity. These cards were unnumbered and inserted one per 60 packs.

		NM/M
Complete Set (17):		100.00
Common Player:		3.00
Inserted 1:60		
1	Ricky Ledee	3.00
2	Derrick Gibson	3.00
3	Mark Kotsay	3.00
4	Kevin Millwood	10.00
5	Brad Fullmer	3.00
6	Todd Walker	4.00
7	Ben Grieve	3.00
8	Tony Clark	3.00
9	Jaret Wright	4.00
10	Randall Simon	3.00
11	Paul Konerko	15.00
12	Todd Helton	15.00
13	David Ortiz	30.00
14	Alex Gonzalez	4.00
15	Bobby Estalella	3.00
16	Alex Rodriguez	50.00
17	Mike Lowell	10.00

Star Date 2001

Star Date 2001 displays 15 of the top rising stars on an acetate space/planet background with gold-foil printing on front. This insert was seeded one per 12 packs and was numbered with a "SD" suffix.

		NM/M
Complete Set (15):		5.00
Common Player:		.25
Inserted 1:12		
1	Travis Lee	.25
2	Jose Cruz Jr.	.25
3	Paul Konerko	1.00
4	Bobby Estalella	.25
5	Magglio Ordonez	1.00
6	Juan Encarnacion	.25
7	Richard Hidalgo	.25
8	Abraham Nunez	.25
9	Sean Casey	.50
10	Todd Helton	1.50
11	Brad Fullmer	.25
12	Ben Grieve	.25
13	Livan Hernandez	.25
14	Jaret Wright	.25
15	Todd Dunwoody	.25

Kerry Wood

In an effort to get rookie pitching phenom Kerry Wood into its E-X2001 set, SkyBox created a cardboard, rather than plastic, trade card and inserted it at a rate of one per 50 packs. The trade card could be exchanged by mail for a plastic version.

		NM/M
Complete Set (2):		2.00
---	Kerry Wood (Cardboard trade card.)	1.00
101	Kerry Wood (Plastic redemption card.)	4.00

1998 SkyBox Dugout Axcess Promo

This introduction to SkyBox's new brand is labeled front and back as a "PROMOTIONAL SAMPLE."

		NM/M
15	Alex Rodriguez	3.00

1998 SkyBox Dugout Axcess

Dugout Axcess was a 150-card set that attempted to provide collectors with an inside look at baseball. The cards were printed on "playing card" quality stock and used unique information and photography. The product arrived in 12-card packs with an Inside Axcess parallel set that was individually numbered to 50 sets. Six different inserts sets were available, including Double Header, Frequent Flyers, Dishwashers, Superheroes, Gronks and Autograph Redemptions.

		NM/M
Complete Set (150):		12.00
Common Player:		.05
Inside Axcess Stars:		25X
Production 50 Sets		
Pack (12):		1.00
Wax Box (36):		20.00
1	Travis Lee	.05
2	Matt Williams	.05
3	Andy Benes	.05
4	Chipper Jones	.75
5	Ryan Klesko	.05
6	Greg Maddux	.75
7	Sammy Sosa	.75
8	Henry Rodriguez	.05
9	Mark Grace	.05
10	Barry Larkin	.05
11	Bret Boone	.05
12	Reggie Sanders	.05
13	Vinny Castilla	.05
14	Larry Walker	.05
15	Darryl Kile	.05
16	Charles Johnson	.05
17	Edgar Renteria	.05
18	Gary Sheffield	.40
19	Jeff Bagwell	.65
20	Craig Biggio	.05
21	Moises Alou	.05
22	Mike Piazza	1.00
23	Hideo Nomo	.35
24	Raul Mondesi	.05
25	John Jaha	.05
26	Jeff Cirillo	.05
27	Jeromy Burnitz	.05
28	Mark Grudzielanek	.05
29	Vladimir Guerrero	.65
30	Rondell White	.05
31	Edgardo Alfonzo	.05
32	Rey Ordonez	.05
33	Bernard Gilkey	.05
34	Scott Rolen	.50
35	Curt Schilling	.35
36	Ricky Bottalico	.05
37	Tony Womack	.05
38	Al Martin	.05
39	Jason Kendall	.05
40	Ron Gant	.05
41	Mark McGwire	1.25
42	Ray Lankford	.05
43	Tony Gwynn	.75
44	Ken Caminiti	.05
45	Kevin Brown	.05
46	Barry Bonds	1.50
47	J.T. Snow	.05
48	Shawn Estes	.05
49	Jim Edmonds	.05
50	Tim Salmon	.05
51	Jason Dickson	.05
52	Cal Ripken Jr.	1.50
53	Mike Mussina	.35
54	Roberto Alomar	.20
55	Mo Vaughn	.05
56	Pedro Martinez	.65
57	Nomar Garciaparra	.75
58	Albert Belle	.05
59	Frank Thomas	.65
60	Robin Ventura	.05
61	Jim Thome	.60
62	Sandy Alomar Jr.	.05
63	Jaret Wright	.05
64	Bobby Higginson	.05
65	Tony Clark	.05
66	Justin Thompson	.05
67	Dean Palmer	.05
68	Kevin Appier	.05
69	Johnny Damon	.35
70	Paul Molitor	.65
71	Marty Cordova	.05
72	Brad Radke	.05
73	Derek Jeter	1.50
74	Bernie Williams	.05
75	Andy Pettitte	.25
76	Matt Stairs	.05
77	Ben Grieve	.05
78	Jason Giambi	.50
79	Randy Johnson	.65
80	Ken Griffey Jr.	1.00
81	Alex Rodriguez	1.25
82	Fred McGriff	.05
83	Wade Boggs	.75
84	Wilson Alvarez	.05
85	Juan Gonzalez	.35
86	Ivan Rodriguez	.50
87	Fernando Tatis	.05
88	Roger Clemens	.85
89	Jose Cruz Jr.	.05
90	Shawn Green	.30
91	Jeff Suppan (Little Dawgs)	.05
92	Eli Marrero (Little Dawgs)	.05
93	Mike Lowell RC (Little Dawgs)	.50
94	Ben Grieve (Little Dawgs)	.05
95	Cliff Politte (Little Dawgs)	.05
96	Rolando Arrojo RC (Little Dawgs)	.25
97	Mike Caruso (Little Dawgs)	.05
98	Miguel Tejada (Little Dawgs)	.15
99	Rod Myers (Little Dawgs)	.05
100	Juan Encarnacion (Little Dawgs)	.05
101	Enrique Wilson (Little Dawgs)	.05
102	Brian Giles (Little Dawgs)	.05
103	Magglio Ordonez RC (Little Dawgs)	1.00
104	Brian Rose (Little Dawgs)	.05
105	Ryan Jackson RC (Little Dawgs)	.05
106	Mark Kotsay (Little Dawgs)	.05
107	Desi Relaford (Little Dawgs)	.05
108	A.J. Hinch (Little Dawgs)	.05
109	Eric Milton (Little Dawgs)	.05
110	Ricky Ledee (Little Dawgs)	.05
111	Karim Garcia (Little Dawgs)	.05
112	Derrek Lee (Little Dawgs)	.60
113	Brad Fullmer (Little Dawgs)	.05
114	Travis Lee (Little Dawgs)	.05
115	Greg Norton (Little Dawgs)	.05
116	Rich Butler (Little Dawgs)	.05
117	Masato Yoshii RC (Little Dawgs)	.25
118	Paul Konerko (Little Dawgs)	.20
119	Richard Hidalgo (Little Dawgs)	.05
120	Todd Helton (Little Dawgs)	.60
121	Nomar Garciaparra (7th Inning Sketch)	.40
122	Scott Rolen (7th Inning Sketch)	.20
123	Cal Ripken Jr. (7th Inning Sketch)	.75
124	Derek Jeter (7th Inning Sketch)	.75
125	Mike Piazza (7th Inning Sketch)	.45
126	Tony Gwynn (7th Inning Sketch)	.40
127	Mark McGwire (7th Inning Sketch)	.65
128	Kenny Lofton (7th Inning Sketch)	.05
129	Greg Maddux (7th Inning Sketch)	.40
130	Jeff Bagwell (7th Inning Sketch)	.30
131	Randy Johnson (7th Inning Sketch)	.30
132	Alex Rodriguez (7th Inning Sketch)	.65
133	Mo Vaughn (Name Plates)	.05
134	Chipper Jones (Name Plates)	.40
135	Juan Gonzalez (Name Plates)	.15
136	Tony Clark (Name Plates)	.05
137	Fred McGriff (Name Plates)	.05
138	Roger Clemens (Name Plates)	.45
139	Ken Griffey Jr. (Name Plates)	.65
140	Ivan Rodriguez (Name Plates)	.25
141	Vinny Castilla (Trivia Card)	.05
142	Livan Hernandez (Trivia Card)	.05
143	Jose Cruz Jr. (Trivia Card)	.05
144	Andruw Jones (Trivia Card)	.30
145	Rafael Palmeiro (Trivia Card)	.50
146	Chuck Knoblauch (Trivia Card)	.05
147	Jay Buhner (Trivia Card)	.05
148	Andres Galarraga (Trivia Card)	.05
149	Frank Thomas (Trivia Card)	.35
150	Todd Hundley (Trivia Card)	.05

Inside Axcess

This 150-card parallel set was sequentially numbered to 50 sets, with each card containing a stamped logo on the front and serial numbering on the back.

	NM/M
Common Player:	4.00
Inside Axcess Stars:	25X

Autograph Redemption Cards

These scarce - one per 96 packs - inserts were redeemable (until March 31, 1999) for autographed baseballs or gloves from more than a dozen established stars and promising youngsters. Because the cards do not picture the player involved, having a generic photo of a person's arm signing an autograph, the exchange cards don't have tremendous collector value now that the redemption period has expired. The autographed balls and gloves would be valued according to supply and demand in the memorabilia marketplace.

		NM/M
Complete Set (15):		37.00
Common Card:		1.50
(1)	Jay Buhner/Ball	1.50
(2)	Roger Clemens/Ball	3.00
(3)	Jose Cruz Jr./Ball	2.25
(4)	Darin Erstad/Glv	4.50
(5)	Nomar Garciaparra/Ball	3.00
(6)	Tony Gwynn/Ball	2.75
(7)	Roberto Hernandez/Ball	1.50
(8)	Todd Hollandsworth/Glv	3.00
(9)	Greg Maddux/Ball	3.00
(10)	Alex Ochoa/Glv	3.00
(11)	Alex Rodriguez/Ball	4.00
(12)	Scott Rolen/Glv	4.50
(13)	Scott Rolen/Ball	2.50
(14)	Todd Walker/Glv	3.00
(15)	Tony Womack/Ball	1.50

Dishwashers

This 10-card set was a tribute to the game's best pitchers who "clean the home plate of opposing batters." Cards were inserted one per eight packs.

		NM/M
Complete Set (10):		7.00
Common Player:		.50
Inserted 1:8		
D1	Greg Maddux	2.00
D2	Kevin Brown	.50
D3	Pedro Martinez	1.00
D4	Randy Johnson	1.00
D5	Curt Schilling	.75
D6	John Smoltz	.50
D7	Darryl Kile	.50
D8	Roger Clemens	2.25
D9	Andy Pettitte	.60
D10	Mike Mussina	.65

Double Header

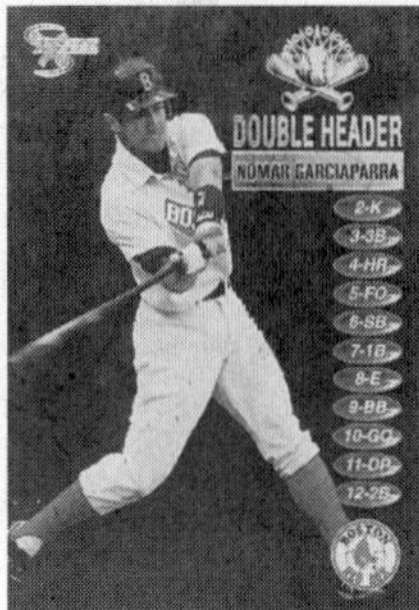

Double Header featured 20 players on cards that doubled as game pieces. The game instructions were on the card and required two dice to play. These were inserted at a rate of two per pack.

		NM/M
Complete Set (20):		2.00
Common Player:		.05
Inserted 2:1		
DH1	Jeff Bagwell	.15
DH2	Albert Belle	.05
DH3	Barry Bonds	.40
DH4	Derek Jeter	.40
DH5	Tony Clark	.05
DH6	Nomar Garciaparra	.20
DH7	Juan Gonzalez	.10
DH8	Ken Griffey Jr.	.25
DH9	Chipper Jones	.20
DH10	Kenny Lofton	.05
DH11	Mark McGwire	.30
DH12	Mo Vaughn	.05
DH13	Mike Piazza	.25
DH14	Cal Ripken Jr.	.40
DH15	Ivan Rodriguez	.10
DH16	Scott Rolen	.10
DH17	Frank Thomas	.15
DH18	Tony Gwynn	.20
DH19	Travis Lee	.05
DH20	Jose Cruz Jr.	.05

Frequent Flyers

The game's top 10 base stealers were included in Frequent Flyers. This insert was designed to look like airline frequent flyer cards and was inserted one per four packs. Fronts have player action photos on a metallic-foil background of a cloudy sky. Backs have a portrait photo and a few words about the player's base-stealing ability. Cards are numbered with an "FF" prefix.

		NM/M
Complete Set (10):		2.50
Common Player:		.25
Inserted 1:4		
FF1	Brian Hunter	.25
FF2	Kenny Lofton	.25
FF3	Chuck Knoblauch	.25
FF4	Tony Womack	.25
FF5	Marquis Grissom	.25
FF6	Craig Biggio	.25
FF7	Barry Bonds	2.00
FF8	Tom Goodwin	.25
FF9	Delino DeShields	.25
FF10	Eric Young	.25

Gronks

Gronks featured 10 of the top home run hitters and was a hobby exclusive insert. The name of the insert originated from shortstop Greg Gagne, and the cards were inserted in one per 72 packs.

		NM/M
Complete Set (10):		30.00
Common Player:		1.50
Inserted 1:72		
G1	Jeff Bagwell	3.50
G2	Albert Belle	1.50
G3	Juan Gonzalez	2.00
G4	Ken Griffey Jr.	6.00
G5	Mark McGwire	7.50
G6	Mike Piazza	6.00
G7	Frank Thomas	3.50
G8	Mo Vaughn	1.50
G9	Ken Caminiti	1.50
G10	Tony Clark	1.50

SuperHeroes

SuperHeroes combined 10 top superstars with the Marvel Comics superhero with whom they share a common trait in this 10-card insert set. Cards were inserted at a rate of one per 20 packs.

		NM/M
Complete Set (10):		10.00
Common Player:		.50
Inserted 1:20		
SH1	Barry Bonds	3.00
SH2	Andres Galarraga	.50
SH3	Ken Griffey Jr.	1.50
SH4	Chipper Jones	1.00
SH5	Andruw Jones	.75
SH6	Hideo Nomo	.60
SH7	Cal Ripken Jr.	3.00
SH8	Alex Rodriguez	2.00
SH9	Frank Thomas	.75
SH10	Mo Vaughn	.50

Todd Helton Autograph

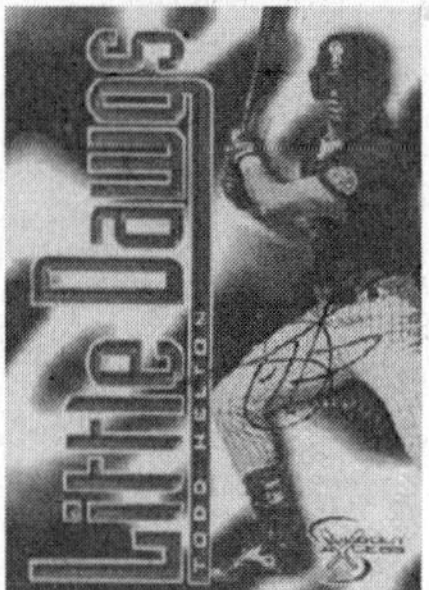

For use in various promotions, Fleer arranged to have Todd Helton autograph 800 of his SkyBox Dugout Axcess Little Dawgs subset cards. Besides the signature, the cards feature an embossed authentication logo.

		NM/M
120	Todd Helton	15.00

SportsFest

As part of its participation at SportsFest in Philadelphia in May 1998, SkyBox issued a special card of hometown hero Scott Rolen. The card was available only as a wrapper redemption at the show and was limited to 5,000. Front has an action photo of Rolen on a colorful background with the team and show logos at bottom. Back has a portrait photo and stats.

		NM/M
SF1	Scott Rolen	3.00

1999 SkyBox E-X Century

The 120-card base set features a clear plastic stock with the player name, logo and position stamped in holographic foil. Card backs have the featured player's vital information along with his '98 statistics and his major league totals. Cards 91-120 are part of a prospects subset and are short-printed seeded 1:2 packs. Three-card packs have a SRP of $5.99.

		NM/M
Complete Set (120):		35.00
Common Player:		.15
Common SP (91-120):		.60
Inserted 1:2		
Pack (3):		3.00
Wax Box (18):		40.00
1	Scott Rolen	.75
2	Nomar Garciaparra	1.50
3	Mike Piazza	2.00
4	Tony Gwynn	1.50
5	Sammy Sosa	1.50
6	Alex Rodriguez	2.50
7	Vladimir Guerrero	1.00
8	Chipper Jones	1.50
9	Derek Jeter	3.00
10	Kerry Wood	.50
11	Juan Gonzalez	.50
12	Frank Thomas	1.00
13	Mo Vaughn	.15
14	Greg Maddux	1.50
15	Jeff Bagwell	1.00
16	Mark McGwire	2.50
17	Ken Griffey Jr.	2.00
18	Roger Clemens	1.75
19	Cal Ripken Jr.	3.00
20	Travis Lee	.15
21	Todd Helton	.75
22	Darin Erstad	.30
23	Pedro Martinez	1.00
24	Barry Bonds	3.00
25	Andruw Jones	1.00
26	Larry Walker	.15
27	Albert Belle	.15
28	Ivan Rodriguez	.75
29	Magglio Ordonez	.25
30	Andres Galarraga	.15
31	Mike Mussina	.35
32	Randy Johnson	1.00
33	Tom Glavine	.35
34	Barry Larkin	.15
35	Jim Thome	.75
36	Gary Sheffield	.45
37	Bernie Williams	.15
38	Carlos Delgado	.60
39	Rafael Palmeiro	.75
40	Edgar Renteria	.15
41	Brad Fullmer	.15
42	David Wells	.15
43	Dante Bichette	.15
44	Jaret Wright	.15
45	Ricky Ledee	.15
46	Ray Lankford	.15
47	Mark Grace	.15
48	Jeff Cirillo	.15
49	Rondell White	.15
50	Jeromy Burnitz	.15
51	Sean Casey	.25
52	Rolando Arrojo	.15
53	Jason Giambi	.65
54	John Olerud	.15
55	Will Clark	.15
56	Raul Mondesi	.15
57	Scott Brosius	.15
58	Bartolo Colon	.15
59	Steve Finley	.15
60	Javy Lopez	.15
61	Tim Salmon	.15
62	Roberto Alomar	.30
63	Vinny Castilla	.15
64	Craig Biggio	.15
65	Jose Guillen	.15
66	Greg Vaughn	.15
67	Jose Canseco	.40
68	Shawn Green	.50
69	Curt Schilling	.35
70	Orlando Hernandez	.15
71	Jose Cruz Jr.	.15
72	Alex Gonzalez	.15
73	Tino Martinez	.15
74	Todd Hundley	.15
75	Brian Giles	.15
76	Cliff Floyd	.15
77	Paul O'Neill	.15
78	Ken Caminiti	.15
79	Ron Gant	.15
80	Juan Encarnacion	.15
81	Ben Grieve	.15
82	Brian Jordan	.15
83	Rickey Henderson	1.00
84	Tony Clark	.15
85	Shannon Stewart	.15
86	Robin Ventura	.15
87	Todd Walker	.15
88	Kevin Brown	.15
89	Moises Alou	.15
90	Manny Ramirez	1.00
91	Gabe Alvarez	.60
92	Jeremy Giambi	.60
93	Adrian Beltre	.75
94	George Lombard	.60
95	Ryan Minor	.60
96	Kevin Witt	.60
97	Scott Hunter **RC**	.60
98	Carlos Guillen	.60
99	Derrick Gibson	.60
100	Trot Nixon	.75
101	Troy Glaus	3.00
102	Armando Rios	.60
103	Preston Wilson	.60
104	Pat Burrell **RC**	3.00
105	J.D. Drew	1.50
106	Bruce Chen	.60
107	Matt Clement	.60
108	Carlos Beltran	1.50
109	Carlos Febles	.60
110	Rob Fick	.60
111	Russell Branyan	.60
112	Roosevelt Brown **RC**	.60
113	Corey Koskie	.60
114	Mario Encarnacion	.60
115	Peter Tucci **RC**	.60
116	Eric Chavez	.75
117	Gabe Kapler	.60
118	Marlon Anderson	.60
119	A.J. Burnett **RC**	.75
120	Ryan Bradley	.60
---	Checklist 1-96	.05
---	Checklist 97-120 Inserts	.05

Essential Credentials Future

A glossy silver design replaces the clear plastic portions seen on the base cards. Production varied depending on the card number, with the exact production number of each player determined by subtracting his card number from 121. Quantity issued is listed in parentheses.

		NM/M
Common Player:		5.00
1	Scott Rolen/120	10.00
2	Nomar Garciaparra/119	15.00
3	Mike Piazza/118	25.00
4	Tony Gwynn/117	20.00
5	Sammy Sosa/116	15.00
6	Alex Rodriguez/115	40.00
7	Vladimir Guerrero/114	15.00
8	Chipper Jones/113	20.00
9	Derek Jeter/112	50.00
10	Kerry Wood/111	10.00
11	Juan Gonzalez/110	10.00
12	Frank Thomas/109	25.00
13	Mo Vaughn/108	5.00
14	Greg Maddux/107	25.00
15	Jeff Bagwell/106	15.00
16	Mark McGwire/105	20.00
17	Ken Griffey Jr./104	25.00
18	Roger Clemens/103	25.00
19	Cal Ripken Jr./102	40.00
20	Travis Lee/101	5.00
21	Todd Helton/100	15.00
22	Darin Erstad/99	5.00
23	Pedro Martinez/98	15.00
24	Barry Bonds/97	40.00
25	Andruw Jones/96	10.00
26	Larry Walker/95	5.00
27	Albert Belle/94	5.00
28	Ivan Rodriguez/93	15.00
29	Magglio Ordonez/92	10.00
30	Andres Galarraga/91	5.00
31	Mike Mussina/90	10.00
32	Randy Johnson/89	20.00
33	Tom Glavine/88	15.00
34	Barry Larkin/87	8.00
35	Jim Thome/86	15.00
36	Gary Sheffield/85	15.00
37	Bernie Williams/84	5.00
38	Carlos Delgado/83	15.00
39	Rafael Palmeiro/82	10.00
40	Edgar Renteria/81	5.00
41	Brad Fullmer/80	5.00
42	David Wells/79	5.00
43	Dante Bichette/78	5.00
44	Jaret Wright/77	5.00
45	Ricky Ledee76	5.00
46	Ray Lankford/75	5.00
47	Mark Grace/74	8.00
48	Jeff Cirillo/73	5.00
49	Rondell White/72	5.00
50	Jeromy Burnitz/71	5.00
51	Sean Casey/70	5.00
52	Rolando Arrojo/69	5.00
53	Jason Giambi/68	10.00
54	John Olerud/67	5.00
55	Will Clark/66	8.00
56	Raul Mondesi/65	5.00
57	Scott Brosius/64	5.00
58	Bartolo Colon/63	5.00
59	Steve Finley/62	5.00
60	Javy Lopez/61	5.00
61	Tim Salmon/60	5.00
62	Roberto Alomar/59	10.00
63	Vinny Castilla/58	5.00
64	Craig Biggio/57	8.00
65	Jose Guillen/56	5.00
66	Greg Vaughn/55	5.00
67	Jose Canseco/54	10.00
68	Shawn Green/53	5.00
69	Curt Schilling/52	15.00
70	Orlando Hernandez/51	5.00
71	Jose Cruz Jr./50	5.00
72	Alex Gonzalez/49	5.00
73	Tino Martinez/48	8.00
74	Todd Hundley/47	5.00
75	Brian Giles/46	5.00
76	Cliff Floyd/45	5.00
77	Paul O'Neill/44	10.00
78	Ken Caminiti/43	5.00
79	Ron Gant/42	5.00
80	Juan Encarnacion/41	8.00
81	Ben Grieve/40	5.00
82	Brian Jordan/39	5.00
83	Rickey Henderson/38	15.00
84	Tony Clark/37	5.00
85	Shannon Stewart/36	5.00
86	Robin Ventura/35	5.00
87	Todd Walker/34	5.00
88	Kevin Brown/33	5.00
89	Moises Alou/32	10.00
90	Manny Ramirez/31	25.00
91	Gabe Alvarez/30	5.00
92	Jeremy Giambi/29	5.00
93	Adrian Beltre/28	8.00
94	George Lombard/27	5.00
95	Ryan Minor/26	5.00
96	Kevin Witt/25	5.00
97	Scott Hunter/24	5.00
98	Carlos Guillen/23	10.00
99	Derrick Gibson/22	5.00
100	Trot Nixon/22	8.00

Essential Credentials Now

Like Future, this is a parallel of the base set, with production of each card limited to that player's card number. These cards have a glossy gold look.

		NM/M
Common Player:		5.00
21	Todd Helton/21	15.00
22	Darin Erstad/22	5.00
23	Pedro Martinez/23	20.00
24	Barry Bonds/24	50.00
25	Andruw Jones/25	10.00
26	Larry Walker/26	8.00
27	Albert Belle/27	5.00
28	Ivan Rodriguez/28	10.00
29	Magglio Ordonez/29	10.00
30	Andres Galarraga/30	5.00
31	Mike Mussina/31	10.00
32	Randy Johnson/32	15.00
33	Tom Glavine/33	10.00
34	Barry Larkin/34	10.00
35	Jim Thome/35	10.00
36	Gary Sheffield/36	10.00
37	Bernie Williams/37	10.00
38	Carlos Delgado/38	10.00
39	Rafael Palmeiro/39	10.00
40	Edgar Renteria/40	10.00
41	Brad Fullmer/41	5.00
42	David Wells/42	5.00
43	Dante Bichette/43	5.00
44	Jaret Wright/44	5.00
45	Ricky Ledee/45	5.00
46	Ray Lankford/46	5.00
47	Mark Grace/47	8.00
48	Jeff Cirillo/48	5.00
49	Rondell White/49	5.00
50	Jeromy Burnitz/50	5.00
51	Sean Casey/51	5.00
52	Rolando Arrojo/52	5.00
53	Jason Giambi/53	10.00
54	John Olerud/54	5.00
55	Will Clark/55	8.00
56	Raul Mondesi/56	5.00
57	Scott Brosius/57	5.00
58	Bartolo Colon/58	5.00
59	Steve Finley/59	5.00
60	Javy Lopez/60	5.00
61	Tim Salmon/61	5.00
62	Roberto Alomar/62	8.00
63	Vinny Castilla/63	5.00
64	Craig Biggio/64	8.00
65	Jose Guillen/65	5.00
66	Greg Vaughn/66	5.00
67	Jose Canseco/67	10.00
68	Shawn Green/68	5.00
69	Curt Schilling/69	15.00
70	Orlando Hernandez/70	5.00
71	Jose Cruz Jr./71	5.00
72	Alex Gonzalez/72	5.00
73	Tino Martinez/73	8.00
74	Todd Hundley/74	5.00
75	Brian Giles/75	5.00
76	Cliff Floyd/76	5.00
77	Paul O'Neill/77	8.00
78	Ken Caminiti/78	5.00
79	Ron Gant/79	5.00
80	Juan Encarnacion/80	5.00
81	Ben Grieve/81	5.00
82	Brian Jordan/82	5.00
83	Rickey Henderson/83	10.00
84	Tony Clark/84	5.00
85	Shannon Stewart/85	5.00
86	Robin Ventura/86	5.00
87	Todd Walker/87	5.00
88	Kevin Brown/88	5.00
89	Moises Alou/89	8.00
90	Manny Ramirez/90	15.00
91	Gabe Alvarez/91	5.00
92	Jeremy Giambi/92	5.00
93	Adrian Beltre/93	5.00
94	George Lombard/94	5.00
95	Ryan Minor/95	5.00
96	Kevin Witt/96	5.00
97	Scott Hunter/97	5.00
98	Carlos Guillen/98	8.00
99	Derrick Gibson/99	5.00
100	Trot Nixon/100	5.00
101	Troy Glaus/101	8.00
102	Armando Rios/102	5.00
103	Preston Wilson/103	5.00
104	Pat Burrell/104	5.00
105	J.D. Drew/105	5.00
106	Bruce Chen/106	5.00
107	Matt Clement/107	5.00
108	Carlos Beltran/108	10.00
109	Carlos Febles/109	5.00
110	Rob Fick/110	5.00
111	Russell Branyan/111	5.00
112	Roosevelt Brown/112	5.00
113	Corey Koskie/113	5.00
114	Mario Encarnacion/114	5.00
115	Peter Tucci/115	5.00
116	Eric Chavez /116	8.00
117	Gabe Kapler/117	5.00
118	Marlon Anderson/118	5.00
119	A.J. Burnett/119	5.00
120	Ryan Bradley/120	5.00

Authen-Kicks

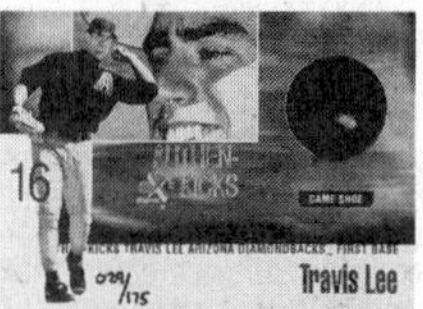

Authen-Kicks is a game-used insert that embeds game-worn shoe swatches from the featured player. Each is done in a horizontal format and is sequentially hand-numbered. The number of swatch cards differs from player to player, and is indicated here in parentheses. Autographed versions of two colors of J.D. Drew shoes were also produced.

		NM/M
Common Player:		4.00
(1)	J.D. Drew/160	8.00
(1ab)	J.D. Drew/Auto./8	75.00
(1ar)	J.D. Drew/Auto./8	75.00
(2)	Travis Lee/175	4.00
(3)	Kevin Millwood/160	6.00
(4)	Bruce Chen/205	4.00
(5)	Troy Glaus/205	10.00
(6)	Todd Helton/205	15.00
(7)	Ricky Ledee/180	4.00
(8)	Scott Rolen/205	15.00
(9)	Jeremy Giambi/205	4.00

E-X Quisite

15 of baseball's top young players are showcased, with a black background and interior die-cutting around the player image. These are seeded 1:18 packs.

NM/M
Complete Set (15): 15.00
Common Player: .50
Inserted 1:18
1 Troy Glaus 3.00
2 J.D. Drew 2.00
3 Pat Burrell 2.00
4 Russell Branyan .50
5 Kerry Wood 1.50
6 Eric Chavez 1.00
7 Ben Grieve .50
8 Gabe Kapler .50
9 Adrian Beltre 1.00
10 Todd Helton 4.00
11 Roosevelt Brown .50
12 Marlon Anderson .50
13 Jeremy Giambi .50
14 Magglio Ordonez 1.50
15 Travis Lee .50

Favorites for Fenway

This 20-card set pays tribute to one of baseball's favorite ballparks, Fenway Park the venue for the 1999 All-Star Game. These have a photo of the featured player with an image of Fenway Park in the background on a horizontal format. These are seeded 1:36 packs.

NM/M
Complete Set (20): 45.00
Common Player: 1.00
Inserted 1:36
1 Mo Vaughn 1.00
2 Nomar Garciaparra 2.00
3 Frank Thomas 2.00
4 Ken Griffey Jr. 3.00
5 Roger Clemens 2.50
6 Alex Rodriguez 4.00
7 Derek Jeter 5.00
8 Juan Gonzalez 1.50
9 Cal Ripken Jr. 5.00
10 Ivan Rodriguez 1.50
11 J.D. Drew 1.50
12 Barry Bonds 5.00
13 Tony Gwynn 2.00
14 Vladimir Guerrero 2.00
15 Chipper Jones 2.00
16 Kerry Wood 1.50
17 Mike Piazza 3.00
18 Sammy Sosa 2.00
19 Scott Rolen 1.50
20 Mark McGwire 4.00

Milestones of the Century

This 10-card set spotlights the top statistical performances from the 1998 season, sequentially numbered to that performance in a multi-layered design.

NM/M
Common Player: 5.00
Numbered to featured milestone.
1 Kerry Wood/20 15.00
2 Mark McGwire/70 20.00
3 Sammy Sosa/66 15.00
4 Ken Griffey Jr./350 15.00
5 Roger Clemens/98 25.00
6 Cal Ripken Jr./17 100.00
7 Alex Rodriguez/40 40.00
8 Barry Bonds/400 25.00
9 N.Y. Yankees/114 15.00
10 Travis Lee/98 5.00

1999 SkyBox Molten Metal

Distributed exclusively to the hobby, the 150-card set consists of three subsets: Metal Smiths, Heavy Metal and Supernatural. Metal Smiths (1-100) show baseball's top players, Heavy Metal (101-130) focus on power hitters and Supernatural (131-150) focus on rookies. Base cards feature silver foil stamping on a 24-point stock with holofoil and wet-laminate overlays. Molten Metal was released in six-card packs with a SRP of $4.99. A special version of the issue was sold only at the 20th Nat'l Sports Collectors Convention in Atlanta, July 19-24. The show version includes autograph redemption cards for show guests and a die-cut series of 30 current and former Braves favorites. Each of the show version cards has a small National Convention logo printed on back; they currently carry no premium.

NM/M
Complete Set (150): 35.00
Common Metalsmiths (1-100): .15
Inserted 4:1
Common Heavy Metal (101-130): .25
Inserted 1:1
Common Supernatural (131-150): .50
Inserted 1:2
Pack (6): 1.00
Wax Box (24): 20.00
1 Larry Walker .15
2 Jose Canseco .50
3 Brian Jordan .15
4 Rafael Palmeiro .65
5 Edgar Renteria .15
6 Dante Bichette .15
7 Mark Kotsay .15
8 Denny Neagle .15
9 Ellis Burks .15
10 Paul O'Neill .15
11 Miguel Tejada .30
12 Ken Caminiti .15
13 David Cone .15
14 Jason Kendall .15
15 Ruben Rivera .15
16 Todd Walker .15
17 Bobby Higginson .15
18 Derrek Lee .60
19 Rondell White .15
20 Pedro J. Martinez .75
21 Jeff Kent .15
22 Randy Johnson .75
23 Matt Williams .15
24 Sean Casey .25
25 Eric Davis .15
26 Ryan Klesko .15
27 Curt Schilling .35
28 Geoff Jenkins .15
29 Armand Abreu .15
30 Vinny Castilla .15
31 Will Clark .15
32 Ray Durham .15
33 Ray Lankford .15
34 Richie Sexson .15
35 Derrick Gibson .15
36 Mark Grace .15
37 Greg Vaughn .15
38 Bartolo Colon .15
39 Steve Finley .15
40 Chuck Knoblauch .15
41 Ricky Ledee .15
42 John Smoltz .15
43 Moises Alou .15
44 Jim Edmonds .15
45 Cliff Floyd .15
46 Javy Lopez .15
47 Jim Thome .65
48 J.T. Snow .15
49 Sandy Alomar Jr. .15
50 Andy Pettitte .25
51 Juan Encarnacion .15
52 Travis Fryman .15
53 Eli Marrero .15
54 Jeff Cirillo .15
55 Brady Anderson .15
56 Jose Cruz Jr. .15
57 Edgar Martinez .15
58 Garret Anderson .15
59 Paul Konerko .30
60 Eric Milton .15
61 Jason Giambi .45
62 Tom Glavine .35
63 Justin Thompson .15
64 Brad Fullmer .15
65 Marquis Grissom .15
66 Fernando Tatis .15
67 Carlos Beltran .45
68 Charles Johnson .15
69 Raul Mondesi .15
70 Richard Hildalgo .15
71 Barry Larkin .15
72 David Wells .15
73 Jay Buhner .15
74 Matt Clement .15
75 Eric Karros .15
76 Carl Pavano .15
77 Mariano Rivera .25
78 Livan Hernandez .15
79 A.J. Hinch .15
80 Tino Martinez .15
81 Rusty Greer .15
82 Jose Guillen .15
83 Robin Ventura .15
84 Kevin Brown .15
85 Chan Ho Park .15
86 John Olerud .15
87 Johnny Damon .35
88 Todd Hundley .15
89 Fred McGriff .15
90 Wade Boggs 1.00
91 Mike Cameron .15
92 Gary Sheffield .50
93 Rickey Henderson .75
94 Pat Hentgen .15
95 Omar Vizquel .15
96 Craig Biggio .15
97 Mike Caruso .15
98 Neifi Perez .15
99 Mike Mussina .50
100 Carlos Delgado .45
101 Andruw Jones (Heavy Metal) 1.00
102 Pat Burrell **RC** (Heavy Metal) 3.00
103 Orlando Hernandez (Heavy Metal) .25
104 Darin Erstad (Heavy Metal) .40
105 Roberto Alomar (Heavy Metal) .35
106 Tim Salmon (Heavy Metal) .25
107 Albert Belle (Heavy Metal) .25
108 Chad Allen **RC** (Heavy Metal) .25
109 Travis Lee (Heavy Metal) .25
110 Jesse Garcia **RC** (Heavy Metal) .25
111 Tony Clark (Heavy Metal) .25
112 Ivan Rodriguez (Heavy Metal) .75
113 Troy Glaus (Heavy Metal) 1.00
114 A.J. Burnett **RC** (Heavy Metal) 1.50
115 David Justice (Heavy Metal) .25
116 Adrian Beltre (Heavy Metal) .50
117 Eric Chavez (Heavy Metal) .35
118 Kenny Lofton (Heavy Metal) .25
119 Michael Barrett (Heavy Metal) .25
120 Jeff Weaver **RC** (Heavy Metal) 1.50
121 Manny Ramirez (Heavy Metal) 1.00
122 Barry Bonds (Heavy Metal) 2.00
123 Bernie Williams (Heavy Metal) .25
124 Freddy Garcia **RC** (Heavy Metal) 1.50
125 Scott Hunter **RC** (Heavy Metal) .25
126 Jeremy Giambi (Heavy Metal) .25
127 Masao Kida **RC** (Heavy Metal) .25
128 Todd Helton (Heavy Metal) 1.00
129 Mike Figga (Heavy Metal) .25
130 Mo Vaughn (Heavy Metal) .25
131 J.D. Drew (Supernaturals) .65
132 Cal Ripken Jr. (Supernaturals) 3.00
133 Ken Griffey Jr. (Supernaturals) 1.50
134 Mark McGwire (Supernaturals) 2.00
135 Nomar Garciaparra (Supernaturals) 1.00
136 Greg Maddux (Supernaturals) 1.00
137 Mike Piazza (Supernaturals) 1.50
138 Alex Rodriguez (Supernaturals) 2.00
139 Frank Thomas (Supernaturals) .85
140 Juan Gonzalez (Supernaturals) .65
141 Tony Gwynn (Supernaturals) 1.00
142 Derek Jeter (Supernaturals) 3.00
143 Chipper Jones (Supernaturals) 1.00
144 Scott Rolen (Supernaturals) .65
145 Sammy Sosa (Supernaturals) 1.00
146 Kerry Wood (Supernaturals) .50
147 Roger Clemens (Supernaturals) 1.25
148 Jeff Bagwell (Supernaturals) .75
149 Vladimir Guerrero (Supernaturals) .75
150 Ben Grieve (Supernaturals) .50

Fusion

Fusion is a 50-card partial parallel that is paralleled three times: Fusion, Sterling Fusion and Titanium Fusion. The three parallels consist of the two subsets Heavy Metal and Supernatural. Fusion Heavy Metals (1-30) are seeded 1:12 packs and Supernatural Fusions are seeded 1:24 packs. Fusions are laser die-cut with additional silver-foil stamping. Sterling Fusions are limited to 500 numbered sets with each card laser die-cut on a blue background with blue foil stamping. Titanium Fusions are limited to 50 sequentially numbered sets with gold background and enhanced with gold foil highlights.

NM/M
Complete Set (50): 100.00
Common Heavy Metal (1-30): 1.00
Inserted 1:12
Common Supernatural (31-50): 2.50
Inserted 1:24
Sterling (31-50): 1.5X
Production 500 Sets
Titanium (31-50): 6X
Production 50 Sets
1 Andruw Jones 4.00
2 Pat Burrell 2.00
3 Orlando Hernandez 1.00
4 Darin Erstad 1.50
5 Roberto Alomar 1.50
6 Tim Salmon 1.00
7 Albert Belle 1.00
8 Chad Allen 1.00
9 Travis Lee 1.00
10 Jesse Garcia 1.00
11 Tony Clark 1.00
12 Ivan Rodriguez 3.00
13 Troy Glaus 3.00
14 A.J. Burnett 1.00
15 David Justice 1.00
16 Adrian Beltre 1.50
17 Eric Chavez 1.50
18 Kenny Lofton 1.00
19 Michael Barrett 1.00
20 Jeff Weaver 1.00
21 Manny Ramirez 4.00
22 Barry Bonds 10.00
23 Bernie Williams 1.00
24 Freddy Garcia 1.00
25 Scott Hunter 1.00
26 Jeremy Giambi 1.00
27 Masao Kida 1.00
28 Todd Helton 3.00
29 Mike Figga 1.00
30 Mo Vaughn 1.00
31 J.D. Drew 2.00
32 Cal Ripken Jr. 10.00
33 Ken Griffey Jr. 6.00
34 Mark McGwire 7.50
35 Nomar Garciaparra 5.00
36 Greg Maddux 5.00
37 Mike Piazza 6.00
38 Alex Rodriguez 7.50
39 Frank Thomas 4.00
40 Juan Gonzalez 1.50
41 Tony Gwynn 5.00
42 Derek Jeter 10.00
43 Chipper Jones 5.00
44 Scott Rolen 3.00
45 Sammy Sosa 5.00
46 Kerry Wood 2.00
47 Roger Clemens 5.50
48 Jeff Bagwell 4.00
49 Vladimir Guerrero 4.00
50 Ben Grieve 1.00

Fusion - Sterling

Sterling Fusions are limited to 500 numbered sets with each card laser die-cut on a blue background with blue foil graphic highlights. A special version of the issue was sold only at the 20th Nat'l Sports Collectors Convention in Atlanta, July 19-24. Each of the show-version cards has a small National Convention logo printed on back; they currently carry no premium.

NM/M
Common Player: 1.50
Sterling Stars: 1.5X

Fusion - Titanium

Titanium Fusions are limited to 50 sequentially numbered sets with gold background and enhanced with gold foil highlights. A special version of the issue was sold only at the 20th Nat'l Sports Collectors Convention in Atlanta, July 19-24. Each of the show-version cards has a small National Convention logo printed on back; they currently carry no premium.

NM/M
Common Player: 4.00
Titanium Stars: 6X

Oh Atlanta!

This 30-card set features players who are either current or former Atlanta Braves like Chipper Jones and Dave Justice. These inserts are seeded one per pack and was produced

in conjunction with the 20th annual National Sports Collectors Convention in Atlanta.

NM/M
Complete Set (30): 30.00
Common Player: .60
Inserted 1:1
1 Kenny Lofton .60
2 Kevin Millwood .60
3 Bret Boone .60
4 Otis Nixon .60
5 Vinny Castilla .60
6 Brian Jordan .60
7 Chipper Jones 8.00
8 Dave Justice .60
9 Micah Bowie .60
10 Fred McGriff .60
11 Ron Gant .60
12 Andruw Jones 4.00
13 Kent Mercker .60
14 Greg McMichael .60
15 Steve Avery .60
16 Marquis Grissom .60
17 Jason Schmidt .60
18 Ryan Klesko .60
19 Charlie O'Brien .60
20 Terry Pendleton .60
21 Denny Neagle .60
22 Greg Maddux 8.00
23 Tom Glavine 1.50
24 Javy Lopez .60
25 John Rocker .60
26 Walt Weiss .60
27 John Smoltz .60
28 Michael Tucker .60
29 Odalis Perez .60
30 Andres Galarraga .60

Xplosion Sample

This sample card was issued to preview SkyBox's Xplosion metal inserts. Etched and printed on metal stock, the card is identical in format to the issued versions, except for sample notations on back.

NM/M
Kerry Wood 3.00

Xplosion

This is a 150-card parallel set, which is seeeded 1:2 packs. These are made of actual metal that have added etching and some foil stamping.

	NM/M
Complete Set (150):	300.00
Common Player:	1.00
Stars:	3X
Inserted 1:2	

1999 SkyBox Premium

The base set consists of 300 cards, base cards feature full bleed fronts with gold-foil stamped player and team names. Card backs have complete year-by-year stats along with a close-up photo. The Rookie subset (223-272) also have a short-printed parallel version as well. Different photos are used but they have the same card number and card back. The short-print versions are seeded 1:8 packs and have an action photo front while the non-seeded cards have a close-up photo.

	NM/M
Complete Set (300):	20.00
Complete Set w/SP's (350):	40.00
Common Player:	.10
Common SP (223-272):	.60
SP's inserted 1:8	
Star Rubies:	50X
Production 50 Sets	
SP Star Rubies:	15X
Production 15 Sets	
Pack (8):	1.50
Wax Box (24):	25.00

1 Alex Rodriguez 2.00
2 Sidney Ponson .10
3 Shawn Green .35
4 Dan Wilson .10
5 Rolando Arrojo .10
6 Roberto Alomar .30
7 Matt Anderson .10
8 David Segui .10
9 Alex Gonzalez .10
10 Edgar Renteria .10
11 Benito Santiago .10
12 Todd Stottlemyre .10
13 Rico Brogna .10
14 Troy Glaus .65
15 Al Leiter .10
16 Pedro J. Martinez .75
17 Paul O'Neill .10
18 Manny Ramirez .75
19 Scott Rolen .65
20 Curt Schilling .35
21 Bobby Abreu .15
22 Robb Nen .10
23 Andy Pettitte .25
24 John Wetteland .10
25 Bobby Bonilla .10
26 Darin Erstad .20
27 Shawn Estes .10
28 John Franco .10
29 Nomar Garciaparra 1.00
30 Rick Helling .10
31 David Justice .10
32 Chuck Knoblauch .10
33 Quinton McCracken .10
34 Kenny Rogers .10
35 Brian Giles .10
36 Armando Benitez .10
37 Trevor Hoffman .10
38 Charles Johnson .10
39 Travis Lee .10
40 Tom Glavine .35
41 Rondell White .10
42 Orlando Hernandez .10
43 Mickey Morandini .10
44 Darryl Kile .10
45 Greg Vaughn .10
46 Gregg Jefferies .10
47 Mark McGwire 2.00
48 Kerry Wood .40
49 Jeromy Burnitz .10
50 Ron Gant .10
51 Vinny Castilla .10
52 Doug Glanville .10
53 Juan Guzman .10
54 Dustin Hermanson .10
55 Jose Hernandez .10
56 Bob Higginson .10
57 A.J. Hinch .10
58 Randy Johnson .75
59 Eli Marrero .10
60 Rafael Palmeiro .65
61 Carl Pavano .10
62 Brett Tomko .10
63 Jose Guillen .10
64 Mike Lieberthal .10
65 Jim Abbott .10
66 Dante Bichette .10
67 Jeff Cirillo .10
68 Eric Davis .10
69 Delino DeShields .10
70 Steve Finley .10
71 Mark Grace .10
72 Jason Kendall .10
73 Jeff Kent .10
74 Desi Relaford .10
75 Ivan Rodriguez .65
76 Shannon Stewart .10
77 Geoff Jenkins .10
78 Ben Grieve .10
79 Cliff Floyd .10
80 Jason Giambi .50
81 Rod Beck .10
82 Derek Bell .10
83 Will Clark .10
84 David Dellucci .10
85 Joey Hamilton .10
86 Livan Hernandez .10
87 Barry Larkin .10
88 Matt Mantei .10
89 Dean Palmer .10
90 Chan Ho Park .10
91 Jim Thome .65
92 Miguel Tejada .20
93 Justin Thompson .10
94 David Wells .10
95 Bernie Williams .10
96 Jeff Bagwell .75
97 Derrek Lee .50
98 Devon White .10
99 Jeff Shaw .10
100 Brad Radke .10
101 Mark Grudzielanek .10
102 Javy Lopez .10
103 Mike Sirotka .10
104 Robin Ventura .10
105 Andy Ashby .10
106 Juan Gonzalez .40
107 Albert Belle .10
108 Andy Benes .10
109 Jay Buhner .10
110 Ken Caminiti .10
111 Roger Clemens 1.25
112 Mike Hampton .10
113 Pete Harnisch .10
114 Mike Piazza 1.50
115 J.T. Snow .10
116 John Olerud .10
117 Tony Womack .10
118 Todd Zeile .10
119 Tony Gwynn 1.00
120 Brady Anderson .10
121 Sean Casey .20
122 Jose Cruz Jr. .10
123 Carlos Delgado .50
124 Edgar Martinez .10
125 Jose Mesa .10
126 Shane Reynolds .10
127 John Valentin .10
128 Mo Vaughn .10
129 Kevin Young .10
130 Jay Bell .10
131 Aaron Boone .10
132 John Smoltz .10
133 Mike Stanley .10
134 Bret Saberhagen .10
135 Tim Salmon .10
136 Mariano Rivera .15
137 Ken Griffey Jr. 1.50
138 Jose Offerman .10
139 Troy Percival .10
140 Greg Maddux 1.00
141 Frank Thomas .75
142 Steve Avery .10
143 Kevin Millwood .10
144 Sammy Sosa 1.00
145 Larry Walker .10
146 Matt Williams .10
147 Mike Caruso .10
148 Todd Helton .65
149 Andruw Jones .75
150 Ray Lankford .10
151 Craig Biggio .10
152 Ugueth Urbina .10
153 Wade Boggs 1.00
154 Derek Jeter 2.50
155 Wally Joyner .10
156 Mike Mussina .30
157 Gregg Olson .10
158 Henry Rodriguez .10
159 Reggie Sanders .10
160 Fernando Tatis .10
161 Dmitri Young .10
162 Rick Aguilera .10
163 Marty Cordova .10
164 Johnny Damon .30
165 Ray Durham .10
166 Brad Fullmer .10
167 Chipper Jones 1.00
168 Bobby Smith .10
169 Omar Vizquel .10
170 Todd Hundley .10
171 David Cone .10
172 Royce Clayton .10
173 Ryan Klesko .10
174 Jeff Montgomery .10
175 Magglio Ordonez .10
176 Billy Wagner .10
177 Masato Yoshii .10
178 Jason Christiansen .10
179 Chuck Finley .10
180 Tom Gordon .10
181 Wilton Guerrero .10
182 Rickey Henderson .75
183 Sterling Hitchcock .10
184 Kenny Lofton .10
185 Tino Martinez .10
186 Fred McGriff .10
187 Matt Stairs .10
188 Neifi Perez .10
189 Bob Wickman .10
190 Barry Bonds 2.50
191 Jose Canseco .40
192 Damion Easley .10
193 Jim Edmonds .10
194 Juan Encarnacion .10
195 Travis Fryman .10
196 Tom Goodwin .10
197 Rusty Greer .10
198 Roberto Hernandez .10
199 B.J. Surhoff .10
200 Scott Brosius .10
201 Brian Jordan .10
202 Paul Konerko .20
203 Ismael Valdes .10
204 Eric Milton .10
205 Adrian Beltre .25
206 Tony Clark .10
207 Bartolo Colon .10
208 Cal Ripken Jr. 2.50
209 Moises Alou .10
210 Wilson Alvarez .10
211 Kevin Brown .10
212 Orlando Cabrera .10
213 Vladimir Guerrero .75
214 Jose Rosado .10
215 Raul Mondesi .10
216 Dave Nilsson .10
217 Carlos Perez .10
218 Jason Schmidt .10
219 Richie Sexson .10
220 Gary Sheffield .40
221 Fernando Vina .10
222 Todd Walker .10
223 Scott Sauerbeck **RC** .10
223 Scott Sauerbeck/SP **RC** .60
224 Pascual Matos **RC** .10
224 Pascual Matos/SP **RC** .60
225 Kyle Farnsworth **RC** .15
225 Kyle Farnsworth/SP **RC** .60
226 Freddy Garcia **RC** .75
226 Freddy Garcia/SP **RC** 1.50
227 David Lundquist **RC** .10
227 David Lundquist/SP **RC** .60
228 Jolbert Cabrera **RC** .10
228 Jolbert Cabrera/SP **RC** .60
229 Dan Perkins **RC** .10
229 Dan Perkins/SP **RC** .60
230 Warren Morris .10
230 Warren Morris/SP .60
231 Carlos Febles .10
231 Carlos Febles/SP .60
232 Brett Hinchliffe **RC** .10
232 Brett Hinchliffe/SP **RC** .60
233 Jason Phillips **RC** .10
233 Jason Phillips/SP **RC** .60
234 Glen Barker **RC** .10
234 Glen Barker/SP **RC** .60
235 Jose Macias **RC** .25
235 Jose Macias/SP **RC** 1.00
236 Joe Mays **RC** .10
236 Joe Mays/SP **RC** .60
237 Chad Allen **RC** .10
237 Chad Allen/SP **RC** .60
238 Miguel Del Toro **RC** .10
238 Miguel Del Toro/SP **RC** .60
239 Chris Singleton .10
239 Chris Singleton/SP .60
240 Jesse Garcia **RC** .10
240 Jesse Garcia/SP **RC** .60
241 Kris Benson .10
241 Kris Benson/SP .60
242 Clay Bellinger **RC** .10
242 Clay Bellinger/SP **RC** .60
243 Scott Williamson .10
243 Scott Williamson/SP .60
244 Masao Kida **RC** .10
244 Masao Kida/SP **RC** .60
245 Guillermo Garcia **RC** .10
245 Guillermo Garcia/SP **RC** .60
246 A.J. Burnett **RC** .25
246 A.J. Burnett/SP **RC** 1.50
247 Bo Porter **RC** .10
247 Bo Porter/SP **RC** .60
248 Pat Burrell **RC** 1.50
248 Pat Burrell/SP **RC** 4.00
249 Carlos Lee .50
249 Carlos Lee/SP 1.50
250 Jeff Weaver **RC** .50
250 Jeff Weaver/SP **RC** 1.50
251 Ruben Mateo .10
251 Ruben Mateo/SP .60
252 J.D. Drew .40
252 J.D. Drew/SP 2.00
253 Jeremy Giambi .10
253 Jeremy Giambi/SP .60
254 Gary Bennett **RC** .10
254 Gary Bennett/SP **RC** .60
255 Edwards Guzman **RC** .10
255 Edwards Guzman/SP **RC** .60
256 Ramon Martinez .10
256 Ramon Martinez/SP .60
257 Giomar Guevara **RC** .10
257 Giomar Guevara/SP **RC** .60
258 Joe McEwing **RC** .10
258 Joe McEwing/SP **RC** .60
259 Tom Davey **RC** .10
259 Tom Davey/SP **RC** .60
260 Gabe Kapler .10
260 Gabe Kapler/SP .60
261 Ryan Rupe **RC** .10
261 Ryan Rupe/SP **RC** .60
262 Kelly Dransfeldt **RC** .10
262 Kelly Dransfeldt/SP **RC** .60
263 Michael Barrett .10
263 Michael Barrett/SP .60
264 Eric Chavez .25
264 Eric Chavez/SP 1.00
265 Orber Moreno **RC** .10
265 Orber Moreno/SP **RC** .60
266 Marlon Anderson .10
266 Marlon Anderson/SP .60
267 Carlos Beltran .50
267 Carlos Beltran/SP 1.50
268 Doug Mientkiewicz .10
268 Doug Mientkiewicz/SP .60
269 Roy Halladay .10
269 Roy Halladay/SP .60
270 Torii Hunter .10
270 Torii Hunter/SP .60
271 Stan Spencer .10
271 Stan Spencer/SP .60
272 Alex Gonzalez .10
272 Alex Gonzalez/SP .60
273 Mark McGwire (Spring Fling) 1.00
274 Scott Rolen (Spring Fling) .30
275 Jeff Bagwell (Spring Fling) .40
276 Derek Jeter (Spring Fling) 1.50
277 Tony Gwynn (Spring Fling) .50
278 Frank Thomas (Spring Fling) .40
279 Sammy Sosa (Spring Fling) .50
280 Nomar Garciaparra (Spring Fling) .50
281 Cal Ripken Jr. (Spring Fling) 1.50
282 Albert Belle (Spring Fling) .10
283 Kerry Wood (Spring Fling) .20
284 Greg Maddux (Spring Fling) .50
285 Barry Bonds (Spring Fling) 1.50
286 Juan Gonzalez (Spring Fling) .25
287 Ken Griffey Jr. (Spring Fling) .75
288 Alex Rodriguez (Spring Fling) 1.00
289 Ben Grieve (Spring Fling) .10
290 Travis Lee (Spring Fling) .10
291 Mo Vaughn (Spring Fling) .10
292 Mike Piazza (Spring Fling) .85
293 Roger Clemens (Spring Fling) .60
294 J.D. Drew (Spring Fling) .20
295 Randy Johnson (Spring Fling) .40
296 Chipper Jones (Spring Fling) .50
297 Vladimir Guerrero (Spring Fling) .40
298 Checklist (Nomar Garciaparra) .40
299 Checklist (Ken Griffey Jr.) .50
300 Checklist (Mark McGwire) .60

Star Rubies

Star Rubies are a parallel of the base set and are limited to 50 sequentially numbered sets. SP Rookie parallels are limited to 15 numbered sets. Rubies feature a complete prism foil front with red-foil stamping.

Star Rubies:	50X
Production 50 Sets	
SP Star Rubies:	15X
Production 15 Sets	

Autographics

This 54-card autographed set feature an embossed SkyBox Seal of Authenticity stamp and are seeded 1:68 packs. Cards are commonly found signed in black ink. Blue-ink versions, serially numbered to 50 each, were also produced.

	NM/M
Common Player:	3.00
Inserted 1:68	
Blue Ink:	1.5X
Production 50 Sets	

Roberto Alomar 15.00
Paul Bako 3.00
Michael Barrett 8.00
Kris Benson 8.00
Micah Bowie 3.00
Roosevelt Brown 3.00
A.J. Burnett 8.00
Pat Burrell 15.00
Ken Caminiti 15.00
Royce Clayton 3.00
Edgard Clemente 3.00
Bartolo Colon 10.00
J.D. Drew 15.00
Damion Easley 5.00
Derrin Ebert 3.00
Mario Encarnacion 3.00
Juan Encarnacion 5.00
Troy Glaus 15.00
Tom Glavine 20.00
Juan Gonzalez/SP 50.00
Shawn Green 10.00
Wilton Guerrero 3.00
Jose Guillen 8.00
Tony Gwynn 30.00
Mark Harriger 3.00
Bobby Higginson 3.00
Todd Hollandsworth 3.00
Scott Hunter 3.00
Gabe Kapler 3.00
Scott Karl 3.00
Mike Kinkade 3.00
Ray Lankford 3.00
Barry Larkin 15.00
Matt Lawton 5.00
Ricky Ledee 3.00
Travis Lee 3.00
Eli Marrero 5.00
Ruben Mateo 3.00
Joe McEwing 3.00
Doug Mientkiewicz 4.00
Russ Ortiz 5.00
Jim Parque 3.00
Robert Person 3.00
Alex Rodriguez 80.00
Scott Rolen 20.00
Benj Sampson 3.00
Luis Saturria 3.00
Curt Schilling 35.00
David Segui 3.00
Fernando Tatis 3.00
Peter Tucci 3.00
Javier Vasquez 6.00
Robin Ventura 10.00
3.00
Checklist .05

Diamond Debuts

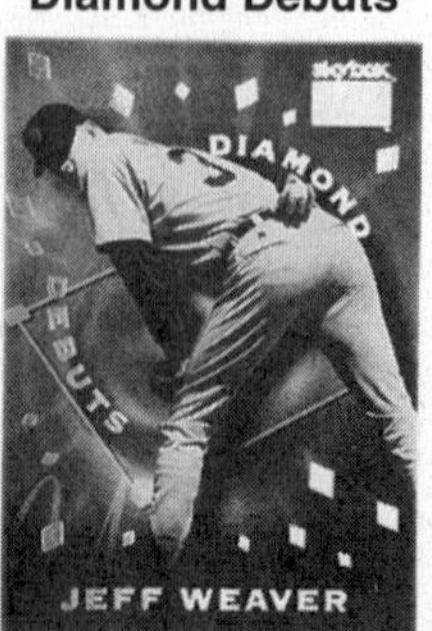

This 15-card set features the best rookies of 1999 on a silver rainbow holo-foil card stock. These are seeded 1:49 packs. Card backs are numbered with a "DD" suffix.

	NM/M
Complete Set (15):	17.50
Common Player:	2.00
Inserted 1:49	

1 Eric Chavez 3.00
2 Kyle Farnsworth 2.00
3 Ryan Rupe 2.00
4 Jeremy Giambi 2.00
5 Marlon Anderson 2.00
6 J.D. Drew 4.00
7 Carlos Febles 2.00
8 Joe McEwing 2.00
9 Jeff Weaver 2.00
10 Alex Gonzalez 2.00
11 Chad Allen 2.00
12 Michael Barrett 2.00
13 Gabe Kapler 2.00
14 Carlos Lee 2.00
15 Edwards Guzman 2.00

Intimidation Nation

This 15-card set highlights the top performers in baseball and features gold rainbow holo-foil stamping. These are limited to 99 sequentially numbered sets. Card backs are numbered with a "IN" suffix.

	NM/M
Complete Set (15):	280.00
Common Player:	12.00
Production 99 Sets	

1 Cal Ripken Jr. 40.00
2 Tony Gwynn 20.00
3 Nomar Garciaparra 20.00
4 Frank Thomas 15.00
5 Mike Piazza 25.00
6 Mark McGwire 30.00
7 Scott Rolen 12.00
8 Chipper Jones 20.00
9 Greg Maddux 20.00
10 Ken Griffey Jr. 25.00
11 Juan Gonzalez 12.00
12 Derek Jeter 40.00
13 J.D. Drew 12.00
14 Roger Clemens 22.50
15 Alex Rodriguez 30.00

Live Bats

This 15-card set spotlights baseball's top hitters and feature red foil stamping. Card backs are numbered with a "LB" suffix and are seeded 1:7 packs.

	NM/M
Complete Set (15):	10.00
Common Player:	.25
Inserted 1:7	

1 Juan Gonzalez .35
2 Mark McGwire 1.50
3 Jeff Bagwell .50
4 Frank Thomas .50
5 Mike Piazza 1.00
6 Nomar Garciaparra .75
7 Alex Rodriguez 1.50
8 Scott Rolen .40
9 Travis Lee .25
10 Tony Gwynn .75
11 Derek Jeter 2.00
12 Ben Grieve .25
13 Chipper Jones .75
14 Ken Griffey Jr. 1.00
15 Cal Ripken Jr. 2.00

Show Business

This 15-card set features some of the best players in the "show" on double foil-stamped card fronts. Card backs are numbered with a "SB" suffix and are seeded 1:70 packs.

		NM/M
Complete Set (15):		60.00
Common Player:		2.00
Inserted 1:70		
1	Mark McGwire	7.50
2	Tony Gwynn	5.00
3	Nomar Garciaparra	5.00
4	Juan Gonzalez	2.50
5	Roger Clemens	5.00
6	Chipper Jones	5.00
7	Cal Ripken Jr.	10.00
8	Alex Rodriguez	7.50
9	Orlando Hernandez	2.00
10	Greg Maddux	5.00
11	Mike Piazza	6.00
12	Frank Thomas	4.00
13	Ken Griffey Jr.	6.00
14	Scott Rolen	3.00
15	Derek Jeter	10.00

Soul of The Game

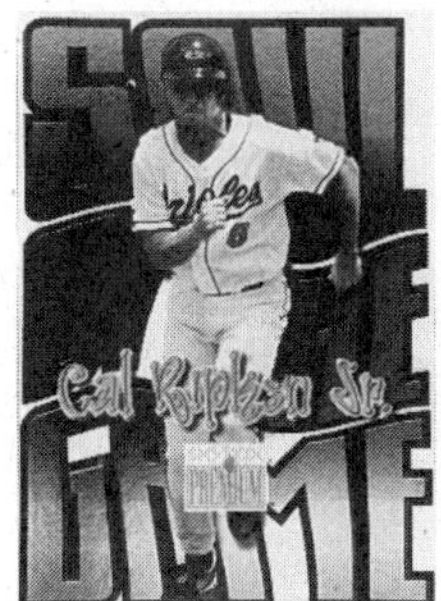

This 15-card set features rainbow foil stamping and the name Soul of the Game prominently stamped, covering the entire card behind the player photo. Card backs are numbered with a "SG" suffix and are seeded 1:14 packs.

		NM/M
Complete Set (15):		15.00
Common Player:		.60
Inserted 1:14		
1	Alex Rodriguez	2.00
2	Vladimir Guerrero	.90
3	Chipper Jones	1.25
4	Derek Jeter	2.50
5	Tony Gwynn	1.25
6	Scott Rolen	.60
7	Juan Gonzalez	.60
8	Mark McGwire	2.00
9	Ken Griffey Jr.	1.50
10	Jeff Bagwell	.90
11	Cal Ripken Jr.	2.50
12	Frank Thomas	.90
13	Mike Piazza	1.50
14	Nomar Garciaparra	1.25
15	Sammy Sosa	1.25

1999 SkyBox Thunder

Skybox Thunder consists of a 300-card base set with three parallels and six inserts. The base set is inserted at varying odds. In hobby packs, regular-player cards #1-140 come 4-5 per pack, veteran stars on cards #141-240 come two per pack, and superstars on cards #241-300 are seeded one per pack. For retail packs the odds were: #1-141 (3-4 per pack), #141-240 (two per pack), and #241-300 (one per pack). Parallels include Rave (numbered to 150 sets) and Super Rave (25 sets), which are both hobby exclusive. The Rant parallel set is retail exclusive (1:2).

		NM/M
Complete Set (300):		15.00
Common Player (1-240):		.05
Common Player (241-300):		.15
Raves:		15X
Production 150 Sets		
SuperRaves:		45X
Production 25 Sets		
Rants:		8X
Inserted 1:2 R		
Pack (8):		1.50
Wax Box (36):		25.00
1	John Smoltz	.05
2	Garret Anderson	.05
3	Matt Williams	.05
4	Daryle Ward	.05
5	Andy Ashby	.05
6	Miguel Tejada	.15
7	Dmitri Young	.05
8	Roberto Alomar	.25
9	Kevin Brown	.05
10	Eric Young	.05
11	Odalis Perez	.05
12	Preston Wilson	.05
13	Jeff Abbott	.05
14	Bret Boone	.05
15	Mendy Lopez	.05
16	B.J. Surhoff	.05
17	Steve Woodard	.05
18	Ron Coomer	.05
19	Rondell White	.05
20	Edgardo Alfonzo	.05
21	Kevin Millwood	.05
22	Jose Canseco	.45
23	Blake Stein	.05
24	Quilvio Veras	.05
25	Chuck Knoblauch	.05
26	David Segui	.05
27	Eric Davis	.05
28	Francisco Cordova	.05
29	Randy Winn	.05
30	Will Clark	.05
31	Billy Wagner	.05
32	Kevin Witt	.05
33	Jim Edmonds	.05
34	Todd Stottlemyre	.05
35	Shane Andrews	.05
36	Michael Tucker	.05
37	Sandy Alomar Jr.	.05
38	Neifi Perez	.05
39	Jaret Wright	.05
40	Devon White	.05
41	Edgar Renteria	.05
42	Shane Reynolds	.05
43	Jeff King	.05
44	Darren Dreifort	.05
45	Fernando Vina	.05
46	Marty Cordova	.05
47	Ugueth Urbina	.05
48	Bobby Bonilla	.05
49	Omar Vizquel	.05
50	Tom Gordon	.05
51	Ryan Christenson	.05
52	Aaron Boone	.05
53	Jamie Moyer	.05
54	Brian Giles	.05
55	Kevin Tapani	.05
56	Scott Brosius	.05
57	Ellis Burks	.05
58	Al Leiter	.05
59	Royce Clayton	.05
60	Chris Carpenter	.05
61	Bubba Trammell	.05
62	Tom Glavine	.35
63	Shannon Stewart	.05
64	Todd Zeile	.05
65	J.T. Snow	.05
66	Matt Clement	.05
67	Matt Stairs	.05
68	Ismael Valdes	.05
69	Todd Walker	.05
70	Jose Lima	.05
71	Mike Caruso	.05
72	Brett Tomko	.05
73	Mike Lansing	.05
74	Justin Thompson	.05
75	Damion Easley	.05
76	Derrek Lee	.50
77	Derek Bell	.05
78	Brady Anderson	.05
79	Charles Johnson	.05
80	Rafael Roque **RC**	.05
81	Corey Koskie	.05
82	Fernando Seguignol	.05
83	Jay Tessmer	.05
84	Jason Giambi	.50
85	Mike Lieberthal	.05
86	Jose Guillen	.05
87	Jim Leyritz	.05
88	Shawn Estes	.05
89	Ray Lankford	.05
90	Paul Sorrento	.05
91	Javy Lopez	.05
92	John Wetteland	.05
93	Sean Casey	.15
94	Chuck Finley	.05
95	Trot Nixon	.05
96	Ray Durham	.05
97	Reggie Sanders	.05
98	Bartolo Colon	.05
99	Henry Rodriguez	.05
100	Rolando Arrojo	.05
101	Geoff Jenkins	.05
102	Darryl Kile	.05
103	Mark Kotsay	.05
104	Craig Biggio	.05
105	Omar Daal	.05
106	Carlos Febles	.05
107	Eric Karros	.05
108	Matt Lawton	.05
109	Carl Pavano	.05
110	Brian McRae	.05
111	Mariano Rivera	.15
112	Jay Buhner	.05
113	Doug Glanville	.05
114	Jason Kendall	.05
115	Wally Joyner	.05
116	Jeff Kent	.05
117	Shane Monahan	.05
118	Eli Marrero	.05
119	Bobby Smith	.05
120	Shawn Green	.20
121	Kirk Rueter	.05
122	Tom Goodwin	.05
123	Andy Benes	.05
124	Ed Sprague	.05
125	Mike Mussina	.25
126	Jose Offerman	.05
127	Mickey Morandini	.05
128	Paul Konerko	.20
129	Denny Neagle	.05
130	Travis Fryman	.05
131	John Rocker	.05
132	Rob Fick **RC**	.05
133	Livan Hernandez	.05
134	Ken Caminiti	.05
135	Johnny Damon	.30
136	Jeff Kubenka	.05
137	Marquis Grissom	.05
138	Doug Mientkiewicz	.05
139	Dustin Hermanson	.05
140	Carl Everett	.05
141	Hideo Nomo	.40
142	Jorge Posada	.05
143	Rickey Henderson	.75
144	Robb Nen	.05
145	Ron Gant	.05
146	Aramis Ramirez	.05
147	Trevor Hoffman	.05
148	Bill Mueller	.05
149	Edgar Martinez	.05
150	Fred McGriff	.05
151	Rusty Greer	.05
152	Tom Evans	.05
153	Todd Greene	.05
154	Jay Bell	.05
155	Mike Lowell	.05
156	Orlando Cabrera	.05
157	Troy O'Leary	.05
158	Jose Hernandez	.05
159	Magglio Ordonez	.05
160	Barry Larkin	.05
161	David Justice	.05
162	Derrick Gibson	.05
163	Luis Gonzalez	.05
164	Alex Gonzalez	.05
165	Scott Elarton	.05
166	Dermal Brown	.05
167	Eric Milton	.05
168	Raul Mondesi	.05
169	Jeff Cirillo	.05
170	Benj Sampson	.05
171	John Olerud	.05
172	Andy Pettitte	.20
173	A.J. Hinch	.05
174	Rico Brogna	.05
175	Jason Schmidt	.05
176	Dean Palmer	.05
177	Matt Morris	.05
178	Quinton McCracken	.05
179	Rick Helling	.05
180	Walt Weiss	.05
181	Troy Percival	.05
182	Tony Batista	.05
183	Brian Jordan	.05
184	Jerry Hairston Jr.	.05
185	Bret Saberhagen	.05
186	Mark Grace	.05
187	Brian Simmons	.05
188	Pete Harnisch	.05
189	Kenny Lofton	.05
190	Vinny Castilla	.05
191	Bobby Higginson	.05
192	Joey Hamilton	.05
193	Cliff Floyd	.05
194	Andres Galarraga	.05
195	Chan Ho Park	.05
196	Jeromy Burnitz	.05
197	David Ortiz	.35
198	Wilton Guerrero	.05
199	Rey Ordonez	.05
200	Paul O'Neill	.05
201	Kenny Rogers	.05
202	Marlon Anderson	.05
203	Tony Womack	.05
204	Robin Ventura	.05
205	Russ Ortiz	.05
206	Mike Frank	.05
207	Fernando Tatis	.05
208	Miguel Cairo	.05
209	Ivan Rodriguez	.65
210	Carlos Delgado	.50
211	Tim Salmon	.15
212	Brian Anderson	.05
213	Ryan Klesko	.05
214	Scott Erickson	.05
215	Mike Stanley	.05
216	Brant Brown	.05
217	Rod Beck	.05
218	Guillermo Garcia **RC**	.05
219	David Wells	.05
220	Dante Bichette	.05
221	Armando Benitez	.05
222	Todd Dunwoody	.05
223	Kelvim Escobar	.05
224	Richard Hidalgo	.05
225	Angel Pena	.05
226	Ronnie Belliard	.05
227	Brad Radke	.05
228	Brad Fullmer	.05
229	Jay Payton	.05
230	Tino Martinez	.05
231	Scott Spiezio	.05
232	Bobby Abreu	.05
233	John Valentin	.05
234	Kevin Young	.05
235	Steve Finley	.05
236	David Cone	.05
237	Armando Rios	.05
238	Russ Davis	.05
239	Wade Boggs	1.00
240	Aaron Sele	.05
241	Jose Cruz Jr.	.15
242	George Lombard	.15
243	Todd Helton	.65
244	Andruw Jones	.75
245	Troy Glaus	.65
246	Manny Ramirez	.75
247	Ben Grieve	.15
247p	Ben Grieve ("PROMOTIONAL SAMPLE")	1.00
248	Richie Sexson	.15
249	Juan Encarnacion	.15
250	Randy Johnson	.75
251	Gary Sheffield	.45
252	Rafael Palmeiro	.65
253	Roy Halladay	.15
254	Mike Piazza	1.50
255	Tony Gwynn	1.00
256	Juan Gonzalez	.40
257	Jeremy Giambi	.15
258	Ben Davis	.15
259	Russ Branyan	.15
260	Pedro Martinez	.75
261	Frank Thomas	.75
262	Calvin Pickering	.15
263	Chipper Jones	1.00
264	Ryan Minor	.15
265	Roger Clemens	1.25
266	Sammy Sosa	1.00
267	Mo Vaughn	.15
268	Carlos Beltran	.50
269	Jim Thome	.65
270	Mark McGwire	2.00
271	Travis Lee	.15
272	Darin Erstad	.30
273	Derek Jeter	2.50
274	Greg Maddux	1.00
275	Ricky Ledee	.15
276	Alex Rodriguez	2.00
277	Vladimir Guerrero	.75
278	Greg Vaughn	.15
279	Scott Rolen	.60
280	Carlos Guillen	.15
281	Jeff Bagwell	.75
282	Bruce Chen	.15
283	Tony Clark	.15
284	Albert Belle	.05
285	Cal Ripken Jr.	2.50
286	Barry Bonds	2.50
287	Curt Schilling	.35
288	Eric Chavez	.30
289	Larry Walker	.15
290	Orlando Hernandez	.15
291	Moises Alou	.15
292	Ken Griffey Jr.	1.50
293	Kerry Wood	.50
294	Nomar Garciaparra	1.00
295	Gabe Kapler	.15
296	Bernie Williams	.05
297	Matt Anderson	.15
298	Adrian Beltre	.35
299	J.D. Drew	.40
300	Ryan Bradley	.15
		.05
---	Checklist 1-230	.05
---	Checklist 231-300 and Inserts	.05
---	Video Game Sweepstakes Form (Derek Jeter)	.05

Dial 1

Designed to look like a mobile phone, this insert set features 10 cards of long distance hitters. The format consists of black plastic cards with rounded corners.

		NM/M
Complete Set (10):		70.00
Common Player:		2.50
Inserted 1:300		
1D	Nomar Garciaparra	7.50
2D	Juan Gonzalez	3.40
3D	Ken Griffey Jr.	10.00
4D	Chipper Jones	7.50
5D	Mark McGwire	12.50
6D	Mike Piazza	10.00
7D	Manny Ramirez	6.00
8D	Alex Rodriguez	12.50
9D	Sammy Sosa	7.50
10D	Mo Vaughn	2.50

Rant

A retail-only parallel of the 300-card base set, Rant substitutes purple metallic foil highlights for the regular-issue's silver on front, and a has a "RANT" notation at upper-right on back, also in purple. The stated insertion rate for the parallel is one per two retail packs.

	NM/M
Common Player:	.50
Rant Stars:	8X

Todd Helton Autograph

An unknown number of Helton's regular card (#243) were autographed and received an embossed seal of authenticity for use in various promotional endeavors.

		NM/M
243	Todd Helton	15.00

Hip-No-Tized

This insert set consisted of 15 cards, featuring both hitters and pitchers. The cards were seeded one card in every 36 packs, and consist of mesmerizing patterned holo-foil stamping.

		NM/M
Complete Set (15):		20.00
Common Player:		1.25
Inserted 1:36		
1H	J.D. Drew	1.25
2H	Nomar Garciaparra	2.00
3H	Juan Gonzalez	1.25
4H	Ken Griffey Jr.	2.50
5H	Derek Jeter	4.00
6H	Randy Johnson	1.50
7H	Chipper Jones	2.00
8H	Mark McGwire	3.00
9H	Mike Piazza	2.50
10H	Cal Ripken Jr.	4.00
11H	Alex Rodriguez	3.00
12H	Sammy Sosa	2.00
13H	Frank Thomas	1.50
14H	Jim Thome	1.25
15H	Kerry Wood	1.25

In Depth

This insert set consists of 10 cards, featuring baseball's elite players. The cards are highlighted with gold rainbow holofoil and gold metallic ink. The insertion rate for this insert was one card in every 24 packs.

		NM/M
Complete Set (10):		17.50
Common Player:		1.00
Inserted 1:24		
1ID	Albert Belle	1.00
2ID	Barry Bonds	5.00
3ID	Roger Clemens	1.50
4ID	Juan Gonzalez	1.25
5ID	Ken Griffey Jr.	3.00
6ID	Mark McGwire	4.00
7ID	Mike Piazza	3.00
8ID	Sammy Sosa	2.50
9ID	Mo Vaughn	1.00
10ID	Kerry Wood	1.25

Turbo Charged

This 10-card insert set consisted of the top home run hitters. The players were featured on plastic see-through cards with rainbow holofoil.

		NM/M
Complete Set (10):		35.00
Common Player:		2.00
Inserted 1:72		
1TC	Jose Canseco	2.50
2TC	Juan Gonzalez	2.00
3TC	Ken Griffey Jr.	5.00
4TC	Vladimir Guerrero	3.00
5TC	Mark McGwire	6.00
6TC	Mike Piazza	5.00
7TC	Manny Ramirez	3.00
8TC	Alex Rodriguez	6.00

9TC Sammy Sosa 4.00
10TC Mo Vaughn 2.00

Unleashed

This insert set contained 15 cards designed to resemble a cereal box. The players featured included the best young talent in baseball. The cards were silver-foil stamped, and offered facsimile signatures of each player. One card was included with every six packs.

NM/M
Complete Set (15): 10.00
Common Player: .50
Inserted 1:6
1U Carlos Beltran 1.50
2U Adrian Beltre 1.00
3U Eric Chavez .75
4U J.D. Drew 1.00
5U Juan Encarnacion .50
6U Jeremy Giambi .50
7U Troy Glaus 2.00
8U Ben Grieve .50
9U Todd Helton 2.00
10U Orlando Hernandez .50
11U Gabe Kapler .50
12U Travis Lee .50
13U Calvin Pickering .50
14U Richie Sexson .50
15U Kerry Wood 1.00

www.Batterz.com

www.batterz.com is a 10-card insert set that was seeded one card per every 18 packs. The game's best hitters are in their own home site in this computer-inspired set.

NM/M
Complete Set (10): 12.00
Common Player: .50
Inserted 1:18
1WB J.D. Drew .60
2WB Nomar Garciaparra 1.00
3WB Ken Griffey Jr. 1.50
4WB Tony Gwynn 1.00
5WB Derek Jeter 3.00
6WB Mark McGwire 2.00
7WB Alex Rodriguez 2.00
8WB Scott Rolen .65
9WB Sammy Sosa 1.00
10WB Bernie Williams .50

2000 SkyBox National Covention Promos

Six-card cello packs of specially marked (printed logo in top corner) cards were distributed at the 2000 National Sports Collectors Convention in Anaheim, Calif., to promote Fleer's SkyBox brand. Cards are numbered "X of 6" on back.

NM/M
Complete Set (6): 8.00
Common Player: 1.25
1 Cal Ripken Jr. 2.00

2 Ken Griffey Jr. 1.25
3 Derek Jeter 2.00
4 Alex Rodriguez 1.50
5 Mark McGwire 1.50
6 Mike Piazza 1.25

2000 SkyBox

NM/M
Complete Set (250): 25.00
Comp. Set w/SPs (300): 60.00
Common Player: .10
Common SP (201-240): 1.00
Inserted 1:8
Common SP (241-250): .50
Inserted 1:12
Pack (10): 1.50
Wax Box (24): 30.00
1 Cal Ripken Jr. 2.00
2 Ivan Rodriguez .65
3 Chipper Jones 1.00
4 Dean Palmer .10
5 Devon White .10
6 Ugueth Urbina .10
7 Doug Glanville .10
8 Damian Jackson .10
9 Jose Canseco .40
10 Billy Koch .10
11 Brady Anderson .10
12 Vladimir Guerrero .75
13 Dan Wilson .10
14 Kevin Brown .10
15 Eddie Taubensee .10
16 Jose Lima .10
17 Greg Maddux 1.00
18 Manny Ramirez .75
19 Brad Fullmer .10
20 Ron Gant .10
21 Edgar Martinez .10
22 Pokey Reese .10
23 Jason Varitek .10
24 Neifi Perez .10
25 Shane Reynolds .10
26 Robin Ventura .10
27 Scott Rolen .65
28 Trevor Hoffman .10
29 John Valentin .10
30 Shannon Stewart .10
31 Troy Glaus .75
32 Kerry Wood .65
33 Jim Thome .65
34 Rafael Roque .10
35 Tino Martinez .10
36 Jeffrey Hammonds .10
37 Orlando Hernandez .10
38 Kris Benson .10
39 Fred McGriff .10
40 Brian Jordan .10
41 Trot Nixon .10
42 Matt Clement .10
43 Ray Durham .10
44 Johnny Damon .30
45 Todd Hollandsworth .10
46 Edgardo Alfonzo .10
47 Tim Hudson .25
48 Tony Gwynn 1.00
49 Barry Bonds 2.00
50 Andruw Jones .75
51 Pedro Martinez .75
52 Mike Hampton .10
53 Miguel Tejada .25
54 Kevin Young .10
55 J.T. Snow .10
56 Carlos Delgado .50
57 Bobby Howry .10
58 Andres Galarraga .10
59 Paul Konerko .20
60 Mike Cameron .10
61 Jeremy Giambi .10
62 Todd Hundley .10
63 Al Leiter .10
64 Matt Stairs .10
65 Edgar Renteria .10
66 Jeff Kent .10
67 John Wetteland .10
68 Nomar Garciaparra 1.25
69 Jeff Weaver .10
70 Matt Williams .10
71 Kyle Farnsworth .10
72 Brad Radke .10
73 Eric Chavez .25
74 J.D. Drew .25
75 Steve Finley .10
76 Pete Harnisch .10
77 Chad Kreuter .10
78 Todd Pratt .10
79 John Jaha .10
80 Armando Rios .10
81 Luis Gonzalez .25
82 Ryan Minor .10
83 Juan Gonzalez .75
84 Rickey Henderson .75
85 Jason Giambi .50
86 Shawn Estes .10
87 Chad Curtis .10
88 Jeff Cirillo .10
89 Juan Encarnacion .10
90 Tony Womack .10
91 Mike Mussina .35
92 Jeff Bagwell .75
93 Rey Ordonez .10
94 Joe McEwing .10
95 Robb Nen .10
96 Will Clark .10
97 Chris Singleton .10
98 Jason Kendall .10
99 Ken Griffey Jr. 1.25
100 Rusty Greer .10
101 Charles Johnson .10
102 Carlos Lee .10
103 Brad Ausmus .10
104 Preston Wilson .10
105 Ronnie Belliard .10
106 Mike Lieberthal .10
107 Alex Rodriguez 1.50
108 Jay Bell .10
109 Frank Thomas .75
110 Adrian Beltre .30
111 Ron Coomer .10
112 Ben Grieve .10
113 Darryl Kile .10
114 Erubiel Durazo .10
115 Magglio Ordonez .10
116 Gary Sheffield .40
117 Joe Mays .10
118 Fernando Tatis .10
119 David Wells .10
120 Tim Salmon .20
121 Troy O'Leary .10
122 Roberto Alomar .40
123 Damion Easley .10
124 Brant Brown .10
125 Carlos Beltran .45
126 Eric Karros .10
127 Geoff Jenkins .10
128 Roger Clemens 1.00
129 Warren Morris .10
130 Eric Owens .10
131 Jose Cruz Jr. .10
132 Mo Vaughn .10
133 Eric Young .10
134 Kenny Lofton .10
135 Marquis Grissom .10
136 A.J. Burnett .10
137 Bernie Williams .25
138 Javy Lopez .10
139 Jose Offerman .10
140 Sean Casey .25
141 Alex Gonzalez .10
142 Carlos Febles .10
143 Mike Piazza 1.25
144 Curt Schilling .35
145 Ben Davis .10
146 Rafael Palmeiro .65
147 Scott Williamson .10
148 Darin Erstad .25
149 Joe Girardi .10
150 Gerald Williams .10
151 Richie Sexson .10
152 Corey Koskie .10
153 Paul O'Neill .10
154 Chad Hermansen .10
155 Randy Johnson .75
156 Henry Rodriguez .10
157 Bartolo Colon .10
158 Tony Clark .10
159 Mike Lowell .10
160 Moises Alou .10
161 Todd Walker .10
162 Mariano Rivera .20
163 Mark McGwire 1.50
164 Roberto Hernandez .10
165 Larry Walker .10
166 Albert Belle .15
167 Barry Larkin .10
168 Rolando Arrojo .10
169 Mark Kotsay .10
170 Ken Caminiti .10
171 Dermal Brown .10
172 Michael Barrett .10
173 Jay Buhner .10
174 Ruben Mateo .10
175 Jim Edmonds .10
176 Sammy Sosa 1.25
177 Omar Vizquel .10
178 Todd Helton .75
179 Kevin Barker .10
180 Derek Jeter 2.00
181 Brian Giles .10
182 Greg Vaughn .10
183 Roy Halladay .10
184 Tom Glavine .35
185 Craig Biggio .10
186 Jose Vidro .10
187 Andy Ashby .10
188 Freddy Garcia .10
189 Garret Anderson .10
190 Mark Grace .20
191 Travis Fryman .10
192 Jeromy Burnitz .10
193 Jacque Jones .10
194 David Cone .10
195 Ryan Rupe .10
196 John Smoltz .10
197 Daryle Ward .10
198 Rondell White .10
199 Bobby Abreu .10
200 Justin Thompson .10
201 Norm Hutchins (Prospect) .10
201 Norm Hutchins/SP 1.00
202 Ramon Ortiz (Prospect) .10
202 Ramon Ortiz/SP 1.00
203 Dan Wheeler (Prospect) .10
203 Dan Wheeler/SP 1.00
204 Matt Riley (Prospect) .10
204 Matt Riley/SP 1.00
205 Steve Lomasney (Prospect) .10
205 Steve Lomasney/SP 1.00
206 Chad Meyers (Prospect) .10
206 Chad Meyers/SP 1.00
207 Gary Glover **RC** (Prospect) .20
207 Gary Glover/SP 1.00
208 Joe Crede (Prospect) .10
208 Joe Crede/SP 1.00
209 Kip Wells (Prospect) .10
209 Kip Wells/SP 1.00
210 Travis Dawkins (Prospect) .10
210 Travis Dawkins/SP 1.00
211 Denny Stark **RC** (Prospect) .20
211 Denny Stark/SP 1.00
212 Ben Petrick (Prospect) .10
212 Ben Petrick/SP 1.00
213 Eric Munson (Prospect) .10
213 Eric Munson/SP 1.00
214 Josh Beckett (Prospect) .25
214 Josh Beckett/SP 1.50
215 Pablo Ozuna (Prospect) .10
215 Pablo Ozuna/SP 1.00
216 Brad Penny (Prospect) .10
216 Brad Penny/SP 1.00
217 Julio Ramirez (Prospect) .10
217 Julio Ramirez/SP 1.00
218 Danny Peoples (Prospect) .10
218 Danny Peoples/SP 1.00
219 Wilfredo Rodriguez **RC** (Prospect) .10
219 Wilfredo Rodriguez/SP **RC** 1.00
220 Julio Lugo (Prospect) .10
220 Julio Lugo/SP 1.00
221 Mark Quinn (Prospect) .10
221 Mark Quinn/SP 1.00
222 Eric Gagne (Prospect) .10
222 Eric Gagne/SP 1.00
223 Chad Green (Prospect) .10
223 Chad Green/SP 1.00
224 Tony Armas Jr. (Prospect) .10
224 Tony Armas Jr./SP 1.00
225 Milton Bradley (Prospect) .10
225 Milton Bradley/SP 1.00
226 Rob Bell (Prospect) .10
226 Rob Bell/SP 1.00
227 Alfonso Soriano (Prospect) 1.00
227 Alfonso Soriano/SP 4.00
228 Wily Pena (Prospect) .10
228 Wily Pena/SP 1.00
229 Nick Johnson (Prospect) .10
229 Nick Johnson/SP 1.50
230 Ed Yarnall (Prospect) .10
230 Ed Yarnall/SP 1.00
231 Ryan Bradley (Prospect) .10
231 Ryan Bradley/SP 1.00
232 Adam Piatt (Prospect) .10
232 Adam Piatt/SP 1.00
233 Chad Harville (Prospect) .10
233 Chad Harville/SP 1.00
234 Alex Sanchez (Prospect) .10
234 Alex Sanchez/SP 1.00
235 Michael Coleman (Prospect) .10
235 Michael Coleman/SP 1.00
236 Pat Burrell (Prospect) .25
236 Pat Burrell/SP 1.50
237 Wascar Serrano **RC** (Prospect) .10
237 Wascar Serrano/SP **RC** 1.00
238 Rick Ankiel (Prospect) .10
238 Rick Ankiel/SP 1.00
239 Mike Lamb **RC** (Prospect) .10
239 Mike Lamb/SP **RC** 1.00
240 Vernon Wells (Prospect) .10
240 Vernon Wells/SP 1.00
241 Jorge Toca, Goefrey Tomlinson (Premium Pairs) .10
241 Jorge Toca, Goefrey Tomlinson/SP .50
242 Shea Hillenbrand, Josh Phelps **RC** (Premium Pairs) 2.00
242 Shea Hillenbrand, Josh Phelps/SP **RC** 4.00
243 Aaron Myette, Doug Davis (Premium Pairs) .10
243 Aaron Myette, Doug Davis/SP .50
244 Brett Laxton, Robert Ramsay (Premium Pairs) .10
244 Brett Laxton, Robert Ramsay/SP .50
245 B.J. Ryan, Corey Lee (Premium Pairs) .10
245 B.J. Ryan, Corey Lee/SP .50
246 Chris Haas, Wilton Veras (Premium Pairs) .10
246 Chris Haas, Wilton Veras/SP .50
247 Jimmy Anderson, Kyle Peterson (Premium Pairs) .10
247 Jimmy Anderson, Kyle Peterson/SP .50
248 Jason Dewey, Giuseppe Chiaramonte (Premium Pairs) .10
248 Jason Dewey, Giuseppe Chiaramonte/SP .50
249 Guillermo Mota, Orber Moreno (Premium Pairs) .10
249 Guillermo Mota, Orber Moreno/SP .50
250 Steve Cox, Julio Zuleta **RC** (Premium Pairs) .15
250 Steve Cox, Julio Zuleta/SP **RC** .50

Star Rubies

This parallel of the 250-card SkyBox base set shares the same format and photos. On front, however, the player identification and SkyBox logo are in red foil. On back, an SR has been added beneath the card number. Insertion rate was one per 12 packs.

NM/M
Complete Set (250): 200.00
Common Player (1-200): .50
Common SP Prospect (201-250): 3.00
Stars: 6X
Star SP's: 3X

Star Rubies Extreme

This parallel of the 250-card SkyBox base set shares the same format and photos. On front, however, the player identification and SkyBox logo are in red foil, and the metallic-foil background has an optical variable layer of stars. On back, an SRE has been added beneath the card number, as well as a strip with a red-foil serial number from within an edition of 50 cards each.

NM/M
Common Player (1-200): 3.00
Common SP Prospect (201-250): 4.50
Stars: 25X
Star SP's: 15X

Autographics

NM/M
Common Player: 5.00
Rick Ankiel 6.00
Michael Barrett 5.00
Josh Beckett 25.00
Rob Bell 5.00
Adrian Beltre 15.00
Peter Bergeron 5.00
Lance Berkman 15.00
Rico Brogna 5.00
Pat Burrell 20.00
Orlando Cabrera 15.00
Mike Cameron 8.00
Roger Cedeno 5.00
Eric Chavez 15.00
Bruce Chen 5.00
Johnny Damon 20.00
Ben Davis 5.00
Jason Dewey 5.00
Octavio Dotel 6.00
J.D. Drew 15.00
Erubiel Durazo 8.00
Jason Giambi 20.00
Doug Glanville 5.00
Troy Glaus 20.00
Alex Gonzalez 8.00
Shawn Green 15.00
Jason Grilli 5.00
Tony Gwynn 40.00
Mike Hampton 8.00
Tim Hudson 15.00
Norm Hutchins 5.00
John Jaha 5.00
Derek Jeter 100.00
D'Angelo Jimenez 5.00
Randy Johnson 60.00
Andruw Jones 20.00
Gabe Kapler 8.00
Jason Kendall 10.00
Adam Kennedy 8.00
Cesar King 5.00
Paul Konerko 8.00
Mark Kotsay 6.00
Carlos Lee 8.00
Mike Lieberthal 8.00
Steve Lomasney 5.00
Greg Maddux 60.00
Edgar Martinez 15.00
Aaron McNeal 5.00
Kevin Millwood 10.00
Raul Mondesi 8.00
Joe Nathan 5.00
Magglio Ordonez 15.00
Eric Owens 5.00
Rafael Palmeiro 25.00
Angel Pena 5.00
Wily Pena 15.00
Cal Ripken Jr. 85.00
Scott Rolen 20.00
Jimmy Rollins 15.00
B.J. Ryan 5.00
Tim Salmon 10.00
Chris Singleton 5.00
J.T. Snow 6.00
Mike Sweeney 8.00
Jose Vidro 8.00
Rondell White 8.00
Jaret Wright 5.00

E-Ticket

NM/M
Complete Set (14): 15.00
Common Player: .50
Inserted 1:4
Star Ruby: 4-8X
Production 100 Sets
1 Alex Rodriguez 2.50
2 Derek Jeter 3.00
3 Nomar Garciaparra 1.50
4 Cal Ripken Jr. 3.00
5 Sean Casey .50
6 Mark McGwire 2.50
7 Sammy Sosa 1.50
8 Ken Griffey Jr. 2.00
9 Tony Gwynn 1.50

10 Pedro Martinez 1.00
11 Chipper Jones 1.50
12 Vladimir Guerrero 1.00
13 Roger Clemens 1.75
14 Mike Piazza 2.00

Genuine Coverage

NM/M
Common Player: 8.00
Inserted 1:399
1 Troy Glaus 15.00
2 Cal Ripken Jr. 40.00
3 Alex Rodriguez 25.00
4 Mike Mussina 10.00
5 J.D. Drew 8.00
6 Robin Ventura 8.00
7 Matt Williams 8.00

Genuine Coverage HOBBY

NM/M
Common Player: 10.00
Inserted 1:144
1 Ivan Rodriguez 12.00
2 Jose Canseco 10.00
3 Frank Thomas 15.00
4 Manny Ramirez 15.00

Higher Level

NM/M
Complete Set (10): 20.00
Common Player: 1.00
Inserted 1:24
Star Ruby: 5-10X
Production 50 Sets
1 Cal Ripken Jr. 4.00
2 Derek Jeter 4.00
3 Nomar Garciaparra 2.00
4 Chipper Jones 2.00
5 Mike Piazza 2.50
6 Ivan Rodriguez 1.00
7 Ken Griffey Jr. 2.50
8 Sammy Sosa 2.00
9 Alex Rodriguez 3.00
10 Mark McGwire 3.00

Preeminence

NM/M
Complete Set (10): 15.00
Common Player: .50
Inserted 1:24
Star Ruby: 5-10X
Production 50 Sets
1 Pedro Martinez 1.25
2 Derek Jeter 4.00
3 Nomar Garciaparra 1.50
4 Alex Rodriguez 3.00
5 Mark McGwire 3.00
6 Sammy Sosa 1.50
7 Sean Casey .50
8 Mike Piazza 2.00
9 Chipper Jones 1.50
10 Ivan Rodriguez 1.00

SkyLines

NM/M
Complete Set (10): 10.00
Common Player: .50
Inserted 1:11
Star Ruby: 10-20X
Production 50 Sets
1 Cal Ripken Jr. 2.00
2 Mark McGwire 1.50
3 Alex Rodriguez 1.50
4 Sammy Sosa .75
5 Derek Jeter 2.00
6 Mike Piazza 1.00
7 Nomar Garciaparra .75
8 Chipper Jones .75
9 Ken Griffey Jr. 1.00
10 Manny Ramirez .50

Speed Merchants

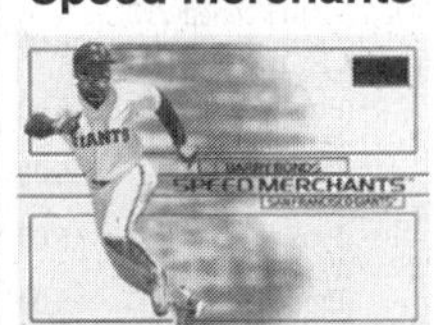

NM/M
Complete Set (10): 12.00
Common Player: .50
Inserted 1:8
Star Ruby: 3-6X
Production 100 Sets
1 Derek Jeter 3.00
2 Sammy Sosa 1.25
3 Nomar Garciaparra 1.25
4 Alex Rodriguez 2.50
5 Randy Johnson 1.00
6 Ken Griffey Jr. 1.50
7 Pedro Martinez 1.00
8 Pat Burrell .50
9 Barry Bonds 3.00
10 Mark McGwire 2.50

The Technique

NM/M
Complete Set (15): 20.00
Common Player: .50
Inserted 1:11
Star Ruby: 3-6X
Production 50 Sets
1 Alex Rodriguez 3.00
2 Tony Gwynn 1.50
3 Sean Casey .50
4 Mark McGwire 3.00
5 Sammy Sosa 1.50
6 Ken Griffey Jr. 2.00
7 Mike Piazza 2.00
8 Nomar Garciaparra 1.50
9 Derek Jeter 4.00
10 Vladimir Guerrero 1.00
11 Cal Ripken Jr. 4.00
12 Chipper Jones 1.50
13 Frank Thomas 1.00
14 Manny Ramirez 1.00
15 Jeff Bagwell 1.00

2000 SkyBox Dominion

NM/M
Complete Set (300): 20.00
Common Player: .10
Pack (10): 1.50

Wax Box (36): 30.00
1 Mark McGwire, Ken Griffey Jr. (League Leaders) .40
2 Mark McGwire, Manny Ramirez (League Leaders) .40
3 Larry Walker, Nomar Garciaparra (League Leaders) .25
4 Tony Womack, Brian Hunter (League Leaders) .10
5 Mike Hampton, Pedro Martinez (League Leaders) .20
6 Randy Johnson, Pedro Martinez (League Leaders) .20
7 Randy Johnson, Pedro Martinez (League Leaders) .20
8 Ugueth Urbina, Mariano Rivera (League Leaders) .10
9 Vinny Castilla (Highlights) .10
10 Orioles host Cuban National Team (Highlights) .10
11 Jose Canseco (Highlights) .10
12 Fernando Tatis (Highlights) .10
13 Robin Ventura (Highlights) .10
14 Roger Clemens (Highlights) .50
15 Jose Jimenez (Highlights) .10
16 David Cone (Highlights) .10
17 Mark McGwire (Highlights) .65
18 Cal Ripken Jr. (Highlights) .75
19 Tony Gwynn (Highlights) .30
20 Wade Boggs (Highlights) .25
21 Ivan Rodriguez (Highlights) .20
22 Chuck Finley (Highlights) .10
23 Eric Milton (Highlights) .10
24 Adrian Beltre (Highlights) .10
25 Brad Radke .10
26 Derek Bell .10
27 Garret Anderson .10
28 Ivan Rodriguez .40
29 Jeff Kent .10
30 Jeremy Giambi .10
31 John Franco .10
32 Jose Hernandez .10
33 Jose Offerman .10
34 Jose Rosado .10
35 Kevin Appier .10
36 Kris Benson .10
37 Mark McGwire 1.00
38 Matt Williams .10
39 Paul O'Neill .10
40 Rickey Henderson .50
41 Todd Greene .10
42 Russ Ortiz .10
43 Sean Casey .20
44 Tony Womack .10
45 Troy O'Leary .10
46 Ugueth Urbina .10
47 Tom Glavine .25
48 Mike Mussina .30
49 Carlos Febles .10
50 Jon Lieber .10
51 Juan Gonzalez .30
52 Matt Clement .10
53 Moises Alou .10
54 Ray Durham .10
55 Robb Nen .10
56 Tino Martinez .10
57 Troy Glaus .40
58 Curt Schilling .30
59 Mike Sweeney .10
60 Steve Finley .10
61 Roger Cedeno .10
62 Bobby Jones .10
63 John Smoltz .10
64 Darin Erstad .20
65 Carlos Delgado .35
66 Ray Lankford .10
67 Todd Stottlemyre .10
68 Andy Ashby .10
69 Bobby Abreu .15
70 Chuck Finley .10
71 Damion Easley .10
72 Dustin Hermanson .10
73 Frank Thomas .50
74 Kevin Brown .10
75 Kevin Millwood .10
76 Mark Grace .10
77 Matt Stairs .10
78 Mike Hampton .10
79 Omar Vizquel .10
80 Preston Wilson .10
81 Robin Ventura .10
82 Todd Helton .40
83 Tony Clark .10
84 Al Leiter .10
85 Alex Fernandez .10
86 Bernie Williams .10
87 Edgar Martinez .10
88 Edgar Renteria .10
89 Fred McGriff .10
90 Jermaine Dye .10
91 Joe McEwing .10
92 John Halama .10
93 Lee Stevens .10
94 Matt Lawton .10
95 Mike Piazza .75
96 Pete Harnisch .10
97 Scott Karl .10
98 Tony Fernandez .10
99 Sammy Sosa .60
100 Bobby Higginson .10
101 Tony Gwynn .60
102 J.D. Drew .20
103 Roberto Hernandez .10
104 Rondell White .10
105 David Nilsson .10
106 Shane Reynolds .10
107 Jaret Wright .10
108 Jeff Bagwell .50
109 Jay Bell .10
110 Kevin Tapani .10
111 Michael Barrett .10
112 Neifi Perez .10
113 Pat Hentgen .10
114 Roger Clemens .65
115 Travis Fryman .10
116 Aaron Sele .10
117 Eric Davis .10
118 Trevor Hoffman .10
119 Chris Singleton .10
120 Ryan Klesko .10
121 Scott Rolen .40
122 Jorge Posada .10
123 Abraham Nunez .10
124 Alex Gonzalez .10
125 B.J. Surhoff .10
126 Barry Bonds 1.50
127 Billy Koch .10
128 Billy Wagner .10
129 Brad Ausmus .10
130 Bret Boone .10
131 Cal Ripken Jr. 1.50
132 Chad Allen .10
133 Chris Carpenter .10
134 Craig Biggio .10
135 Dante Bichette .10
136 Dean Palmer .10
137 Derek Jeter 1.50
138 Ellis Burks .10
139 Freddy Garcia .10
140 Gabe Kapler .10
141 Greg Maddux .60
142 Greg Vaughn .10
143 Jason Kendall .10
144 Jim Parque .10
145 John Valentin .10
146 Jose Vidro .10
147 Ken Griffey Jr. .75
148 Kenny Lofton .10
149 Kenny Rogers .10
150 Kent Bottenfield .10
151 Chuck Knoblauch .10
152 Larry Walker .10
153 Manny Ramirez .50
154 Mickey Morandini .10
155 Mike Cameron .10
156 Mike Lieberthal .10
157 Mo Vaughn .10
158 Randy Johnson .50
159 Rey Ordonez .10
160 Roberto Alomar .20
161 Scott Williamson .10
162 Shawn Estes .10
163 Tim Wakefield .10
164 Tony Batista .10
165 Will Clark .10
166 Wade Boggs .60
167 David Cone .10
168 Doug Glanville .10
169 Jeff Cirillo .10
170 John Jaha .10
171 Mariano Rivera .20
172 Tom Gordon .10
173 Wally Joyner .10
174 Alex Gonzalez .10
175 Andruw Jones .50
176 Barry Larkin .10
177 Bartolo Colon .10
178 Brian Giles .10
179 Carlos Lee .10
180 Darren Dreifort .10
181 Eric Chavez .20
182 Henry Rodriguez .10
183 Ismael Valdes .10
184 Jason Giambi .40
185 John Wetteland .10
186 Juan Encarnacion .10
187 Luis Gonzalez .10
188 Reggie Sanders .10
189 Richard Hidalgo .10
190 Ryan Rupe .10
191 Sean Berry .10
192 Rick Helling .10
193 Randy Wolf .10
194 Cliff Floyd .10
195 Jose Lima .10
196 Chipper Jones .60
197 Charles Johnson .10
198 Nomar Garciaparra .60
199 Magglio Ordonez .10
200 Shawn Green .25
201 Travis Lee .10
202 Jose Canseco .35
203 Fernando Tatis .10
204 Bruce Aven .10
205 Johnny Damon .35
206 Gary Sheffield .25
207 Ken Caminiti .10
208 Ben Grieve .10
209 Sidney Ponson .10
210 Vinny Castilla .10
211 Alex Rodriguez 1.00
212 Chris Widger .10
213 Carl Pavano .10
214 J.T. Snow .10
215 Jim Thome .40
216 Kevin Young .10
217 Mike Sirotka .10
218 Rafael Palmeiro .40
219 Rico Brogna .10
220 Todd Walker .10
221 Todd Zelle .10
222 Brian Rose .10
223 Chris Fussell .10
224 Corey Koskie .10
225 Rich Aurilia .10
226 Geoff Jenkins .10
227 Pedro Martinez .50
228 Todd Hundley .10
229 Brian Jordan .10
230 Cristian Guzman .10
231 Raul Mondesi .10
232 Tim Hudson .20
233 Albert Belle .10
234 Andy Pettitte .25
235 Brady Anderson .10
236 Brian Bohannon .10
237 Carlos Beltran .35
238 Doug Mientkiewicz .10
239 Jason Schmidt .10
240 Jeff Zimmerman .10
241 John Olerud .10
242 Paul Byrd .10
243 Vladimir Guerrero .50
244 Warren Morris .10
245 Eric Karros .10
246 Jeff Weaver .10
247 Jeromy Burnitz .10
248 David Bell .10
249 Rusty Greer .10
250 Kevin Stocker .10
251 Shea Hillenbrand (Prospect) .15
252 Alfonso Soriano (Prospect) .50
253 Micah Bowie (Prospect) .10
254 Gary Matthews Jr. (Prospect) .10
255 Lance Berkman (Prospect) .10
256 Pat Burrell (Prospect) .25
257 Ruben Mateo (Prospect) .10
258 Kip Wells (Prospect) .10
259 Wilton Veras (Prospect) .10
260 Ben Davis (Prospect) .10
261 Eric Munson (Prospect) .10
262 Ramon Hernandez (Prospect) .10
263 Tony Armas Jr. (Prospect) .10
264 Erubiel Durazo (Prospect) .10
265 Chad Meyers (Prospect) .10
266 Rick Ankiel (Prospect) .10
267 Ramon Ortiz (Prospect) .10
268 Adam Kennedy (Prospect) .10
269 Vernon Wells (Prospect) .10
270 Chad Hermansen (Prospect) .10
271 Norm Hutchins, Trent Durrington (Prospects) .10
272 Gabe Molina, B.J. Ryan (Prospects) .10
273 Juan Pena, Tomokazu Ohka **RC** (Prospects) .25
274 Pat Daneker, Aaron Myette (Prospects) .15
275 Jason Rakers, Russell Branyan (Prospects) .10
276 Beiker Graterol, Dave Borkowski (Prospects) .10
277 Mark Quinn, Dan Reichert (Prospects) .10
278 Mark Redman, Jacque Jones (Prospects) .15
279 Ed Yarnall, Wily Pena (Prospects) .10
280 Chad Harville, Brett Laxton (Prospects) .10
281 Aaron Scheffer, Gil Meche (Prospects) .10
282 Jim Morris, Dan Wheeler (Prospects) .10
283 Danny Kolb, Kelly Dransfeldt (Prospects) .10
284 Peter Munro, Casey Blake (Prospects) .10
285 Rob Ryan, Byung-Hyun Kim (Prospects) .10
286 Derrin Ebert, Pascual Matos (Prospects) .10
287 Richard Barker, Kyle Farnsworth (Prospects) .10
288 Jason LaRue, Travis Dawkins (Prospects) .10
289 Chris Sexton, Edgard Clemente (Prospects) .10
290 Amaury Garcia, A.J. Burnett (Prospects) .10
291 Carlos Hernandez, Daryle Ward (Prospects) .10
292 Eric Gagne, Jeff Williams (Prospects) .10
293 Kyle Peterson, Kevin Barker (Prospects) .10
294 Fernando Seguignol, Guillermo Mota (Prospects) .10
295 Melvin Mora, Octavio Dotel (Prospects) .10
296 Anthony Shumaker, Cliff Politte (Prospects) .10
297 Yamid Haad, Jimmy Anderson (Prospects) .10
298 Rick Heiserman, Chad Hutchinson (Prospects) .10
299 Mike Darr, Wiki Gonzalez (Prospects) .10
300 Joe Nathan, Calvin Murray (Prospects) .10

Autographics

NM/M
Common Player: 5.00
Inserted 1:144
1 Rick Ankiel 6.00
2 Peter Bergeron 5.00
3 Wade Boggs 25.00
4 Barry Bonds 200.00
5 Pat Burrell 20.00
6 Miguel Cairo 5.00
7 Mike Cameron 8.00
8 Ben Davis 5.00
9 Russ Davis 5.00
10 Einar Diaz 5.00
11 Scott Elarton 5.00
12 Jeremy Giambi 5.00
13 Todd Greene 5.00
14 Vladimir Guerrero 25.00
15 Tony Gwynn 30.00
16 Bobby Howry 5.00
17 Tim Hudson 15.00
18 Randy Johnson 50.00
19 Andruw Jones 20.00
20 Jacque Jones 8.00
21 Jason LaRue 5.00
22 Matt Lawton 6.00
23 Greg Maddux 50.00
24 Pedro Martinez 50.00
25 Pokey Reese 5.00
26 Alex Rodriguez 75.00
27 Ryan Rupe 5.00
28 J.T. Snow 6.00
29 Jose Vidro 6.00
30 Tony Womack 6.00
31 Ed Yarnall 5.00
32 Kevin Young 5.00

Double Play

NM/M
Complete Set (10): 10.00
Common Player: 1.00
Inserted 1:9
Plus: 2-4X
Inserted 1:90
WarpTek: 10-20X
Inserted 1:900
1 Nomar Garciaparra 1.50
2 Pedro Martinez 1.25
3 Chipper Jones 1.50
4 Mark McGwire 2.50
5 Cal Ripken Jr. 3.00
6 Roger Clemens 1.75
7 Juan Gonzalez 1.00
8 Tony Gwynn 1.50
9 Sammy Sosa 1.50
10 Mike Piazza 2.00

Eye on October

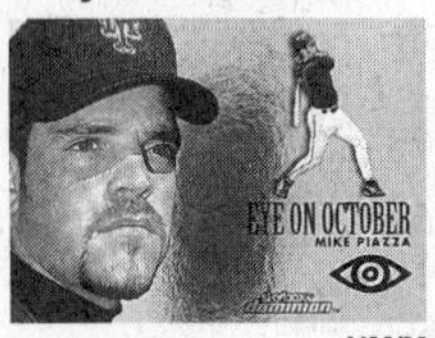

NM/M
Complete Set (15): 25.00
Common Player: 1.00
Inserted 1:24
Plus: 2-4X
Inserted 1:240
1 Ken Griffey Jr. 2.50
2 Mark McGwire 3.00
3 Derek Jeter 4.00
4 Juan Gonzalez 1.00
5 Chipper Jones 2.00
6 Sammy Sosa 2.00
7 Greg Maddux 2.00
8 Frank Thomas 1.50
9 Nomar Garciaparra 2.00
10 Shawn Green 1.00
11 Cal Ripken Jr. 4.00
12 Manny Ramirez 1.50
13 Scott Rolen 1.25
14 Mike Piazza 2.50
15 Alex Rodriguez 3.00

Hats Off

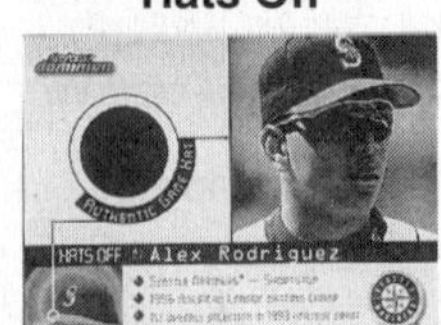

NM/M
Common Player: 15.00
Inserted 1:468 H
1 Wade Boggs 25.00
2 Barry Bonds 75.00
3 J.D. Drew 15.00
4 Shawn Green 15.00
5 Vladimir Guerrero 25.00
6 Randy Johnson 30.00
7 Andruw Jones 20.00
8 Greg Maddux 40.00
9 Pedro Martinez 25.00
10 Mike Mussina 15.00
11 Rafael Palmeiro 20.00
12 Alex Rodriguez 50.00
13 Scott Rolen 15.00
14 Tim Salmon 15.00
15 Robin Ventura 15.00

Milestones

NM/M
Common Player: 15.00
Inserted 1:1,999
1 Mark McGwire 60.00
2 Roger Clemens 40.00
3 Tony Gwynn 25.00
4 Wade Boggs 25.00
5 Cal Ripken Jr. 75.00
6 Jose Canseco 15.00

New Era

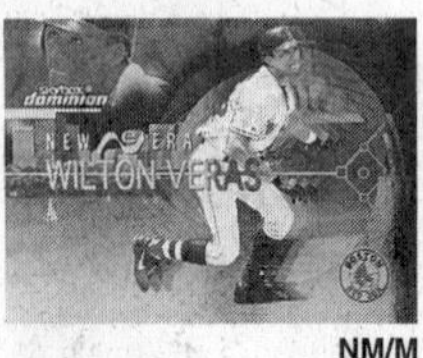

NM/M
Complete Set (20): 5.00
Common Player: .25
Inserted 1:3
Plus: 2-4X
Inserted 1:30
WarpTek: 5-10X
Inserted 1:300
1 Pat Burrell .75
2 Ruben Mateo .25
3 Wilton Veras .25
4 Eric Munson .25
5 Jeff Weaver .25
6 Tim Hudson .50
7 Carlos Beltran 1.00
8 Chris Singleton .25
9 Lance Berkman .25
10 Freddy Garcia .25
11 Erubiel Durazo .25
12 Randy Wolf .25
13 Shea Hillenbrand .25
14 Kip Wells .25
15 Alfonso Soriano 1.50
16 Rick Ankiel .25
17 Ramon Ortiz .25
18 Adam Kennedy .25
19 Vernon Wells .25
20 Chad Hermansen .25

2000 E-X

Released as a 90-card set the card fronts have a holo-foil card front, with the E-X logo and player name stamped in silver foil. Card backs have a player image, 1999 stats and the featured player's career totals.

NM/M
Complete Set (90): 80.00
Common Player: .25
Common Prospect (61-90): 3.00
Production 3,499 Sets
Pack: 2.75
Box: 50.00
1 Alex Rodriguez 2.50
2 Jeff Bagwell 1.00
3 Mike Piazza 2.00
4 Tony Gwynn 1.50
5 Ken Griffey Jr. 2.00
6 Juan Gonzalez .40
7 Vladimir Guerrero 1.00
8 Cal Ripken Jr. 3.00
9 Mo Vaughn .25
10 Chipper Jones 1.50
11 Derek Jeter 3.00
12 Nomar Garciaparra 1.50
13 Mark McGwire 2.50
14 Sammy Sosa 1.50
15 Pedro Martinez 1.00
16 Greg Maddux 1.50
17 Frank Thomas .75
18 Shawn Green .50
19 Carlos Beltran .50
20 Roger Clemens 1.75
21 Randy Johnson 1.00
22 Bernie Williams .25
23 Carlos Delgado .50
24 Manny Ramirez .75
25 Freddy Garcia .25
26 Barry Bonds 3.00
27 Tim Hudson .40
28 Larry Walker .25
29 Raul Mondesi .25
30 Ivan Rodriguez .65
31 Magglio Ordonez .25
32 Scott Rolen .65
33 Mike Mussina .40
34 J.D. Drew .40
35 Tom Glavine .50
36 Barry Larkin .25
37 Jim Thome .65
38 Erubiel Durazo .25
39 Curt Schilling .50
40 Orlando Hernandez .25
41 Rafael Palmeiro .65
42 Gabe Kapler .25
43 Mark Grace .25
44 Jeff Cirillo .25
45 Jeromy Burnitz .25
46 Sean Casey .35
47 Kevin Millwood .25
48 Vinny Castilla .25
49 Jose Canseco .50
50 Roberto Alomar .30
51 Craig Biggio .25
52 Preston Wilson .25
53 Jeff Weaver .25
54 Robin Ventura .25
55 Ben Grieve .25
56 Troy Glaus .65
57 Jacque Jones .25
58 Brian Giles .25
59 Kevin Brown .25
60 Todd Helton .65
61 Ben Petrick (Prospects) 3.00
62 Chad Hermansen (Prospects) 3.00
63 Kevin Barker (Prospects) 3.00
64 Matt LeCroy (Prospects) 3.00
65 Brad Penny (Prospects) 4.00
66 D.T. Cromer (Prospects) 3.00
67 Steve Lomasney (Prospects) 3.00
68 Cole Liniak (Prospects) 3.00
69 B.J. Ryan (Prospects) 3.00
70 Wilton Veras (Prospects) 3.00
71 Aaron McNeal **RC** (Prospects) 4.00
72 Nick Johnson (Prospects) 4.00
73 Adam Piatt (Prospects) 3.00
74 Adam Kennedy (Prospects) 3.00
75 Cesar King (Prospects) 3.00
76 Peter Bergeron (Prospects) 3.00
77 Rob Bell (Prospects) 3.00
78 Wily Pena (Prospects) 4.00
79 Ruben Mateo (Prospects) 3.00
80 Kip Wells (Prospects) 3.00
81 Alex Escobar (Prospects) 3.00
82 Danys Baez **RC** (Prospects) 5.00
83 Travis Dawkins (Prospects) 3.00
84 Mark Quinn (Prospects) 3.00
85 Jimmy Anderson (Prospects) 3.00
86 Rick Ankiel (Prospects) 4.00
87 Alfonso Soriano (Prospects) 5.00
88 Pat Burrell (Prospects) 4.00
89 Eric Munson (Prospects) 3.00
90 Josh Beckett (Prospects) 4.00

Autographics

NM/M
Common Player: 5.00
Inserted 1:24
Bob Abreu 15.00
Moises Alou 15.00
Rick Ankiel 6.00
Michael Barrett 5.00
Josh Beckett 25.00
Rob Bell 5.00
Adrian Beltre 15.00
Carlos Beltran 15.00
Wade Boggs 25.00
Barry Bonds 150.00
Kent Bottenfield 5.00
Milton Bradley 10.00
Pat Burrell 20.00
Chris Carpenter 20.00
Sean Casey 10.00
Eric Chavez 15.00
Will Clark 25.00
Johnny Damon 20.00
Mike Darr 5.00
Ben Davis 5.00
Russ Davis 5.00
Carlos Delgado 20.00
Jason Dewey 5.00
Octavio Dotel 5.00
J.D. Drew 15.00
Ray Durham 8.00
Damion Easley 6.00
Kelvim Escobar 6.00
Carlos Febles 6.00
Freddy Garcia 10.00
Jeremy Giambi 10.00
Todd Greene 5.00
Jason Grilli 5.00
Vladimir Guerrero 30.00
Tony Gwynn 40.00
Jerry Hairston Jr. 10.00
Mike Hampton 8.00
Todd Helton 20.00
Trevor Hoffman 10.00
Tim Hudson 15.00
John Jaha 5.00
Derek Jeter 100.00
D'Angelo Jimenez 5.00
Randy Johnson 60.00
Jason Kendall 10.00
Adam Kennedy 8.00
Cesar King 5.00
Paul Konerko 15.00
Mark Kotsay 6.00
Ray Lankford 6.00
Jason LaRue 6.00
Matt Lawton 10.00
Carlos Lee 8.00
Mike Lieberthal 8.00
Cole Liniak 5.00
Steve Lomasney 5.00
Jose Macias 5.00
Greg Maddux 60.00
Edgar Martinez 15.00
Pedro Martinez 75.00
Ruben Mateo 8.00
Gary Matthews Jr. 8.00
Aaron McNeal 5.00
Raul Mondesi 8.00
Orber Moreno 5.00
Warren Morris 5.00
Eric Munson 8.00
Heath Murray 5.00
Mike Mussina 30.00
Joe Nathan 5.00
Rafael Palmeiro 25.00
Jim Parque 6.00
Angel Pena 5.00
Wily Pena 10.00
Pokey Reese 6.00
Matt Riley 5.00
Cal Ripken Jr. 85.00
Alex Rodriguez 75.00
Scott Rolen 20.00
Jimmy Rollins 20.00
B.J. Ryan 5.00
Randall Simon 8.00
Chris Singleton 5.00
Alfonso Soriano 30.00
Shannon Stewart 10.00
Mike Sweeney 8.00
Miguel Tejada 20.00
Frank Thomas 25.00
Wilton Veras 5.00
Billy Wagner 12.00
Jeff Weaver 8.00
Rondell White 8.00
Scott Williamson 8.00
Randy Wolf 8.00
Jaret Wright 5.00
Ed Yarnall 5.00
Kevin Young 10.00

Essential Credentials Future

Production varied for these parallel inserts depending on the card number, with the exact production number for cards 1-60 determined by subtracting the card number from 61. Cards 61-90 are determined by subtracting the card number from 91. Quantity issued is listed in parantheses.

NM/M
Common Player: 10.00
1 Alex Rodriguez/60 75.00
2 Jeff Bagwell/59 30.00
3 Mike Piazza/58 50.00
4 Tony Gwynn/57 50.00
5 Ken Griffey Jr/56 50.00
6 Juan Gonzalez/55 15.00
7 Vladimir Guerrero/54 20.00
8 Cal Ripken Jr./53 85.00
9 Mo Vaughn/52 10.00
10 Chipper Jones/51 30.00
11 Derek Jeter/50 85.00
12 Nomar Garciaparra/49 45.00
13 Mark McGwire/48 75.00
14 Sammy Sosa/47 50.00
15 Pedro Martine/46 30.00
16 Greg Maddux/45 50.00
17 Frank Thomas/44 20.00
18 Shawn Green/43 10.00
19 Carlos Beltran/42 10.00
20 Roger Clemens/41 60.00
21 Randy Johnso/40 30.00
22 Bernie Williams/39 10.00
23 Carlos Delgado/38 15.00
24 Manny Ramirez/37 20.00
25 Freddy Garcia/36 10.00
26 Barry Bonds/35 90.00
27 Tim Hudson/34 20.00
28 Larry Walker/33 10.00
29 Raul Mondesi/32 10.00
30 Ivan Rodriguez/31 15.00
31 Magglio Ordonez/30 10.00
32 Scott Rolen/29 20.00
33 Mike Mussina/28 25.00
34 J.D. Drew/27 20.00
35 Tom Glavine/26 25.00
36 Barry Larkin/25 15.00
37 Jim Thome/24 30.00
38 Erubiel Durazo/23 15.00
39 Curt Schilling/22 25.00
40 Orlando Hernandez/21 15.00
41 Rafael Palmeiro/20 40.00
42 Gabe Kapler/19 15.00
43 Mark Grace/18 15.00
44 Jeff Cirillo/17 15.00
45 Jeromy Burnitz/16 15.00
46 Sean Casey/15 15.00
47 Kevin Millwood/14 20.00
48 Vinny Castilla/13 20.00
49 Jose Canseco/12 40.00
50 Roberto Alomar/11 50.00
51 Craig Biggio/10 50.00
61 Ben Petrick/30 (Prospects) 10.00
62 Chad Hermansen/29 (Prospects) 10.00
63 Kevin Barker/28 (Prospects) 10.00
64 Matt LeCroy/27 (Prospects) 10.00
65 Brad Penny/26 (Prospects) 10.00
66 D.T. Cromer/25 (Prospects) 10.00
67 Steve Lomasney/24 (Prospects) 10.00
68 Cole Liniak/23 (Prospects) 10.00
69 B.J. Ryan/22 (Prospects) 10.00
70 Wilton Veras21 (Prospects) 10.00
71 Aaron McNeal/20 (Prospects) 15.00
72 Nick Johnson/19 (Prospects) 25.00
73 Adam Piatt/18 (Prospects) 15.00
74 Adam Kennedy/17 (Prospects) 15.00
75 Cesar King/16 (Prospects) 15.00
76 Peter Bergeron/15 (Prospects) 15.00
77 Rob Bell/14 (Prospects) 15.00
78 Wily Pena/13 (Prospects) 15.00
79 Ruben Mateo/12 (Prospects) 15.00
80 Kip Wells/11 (Prospects) 15.00
81 Alex Escobar/10 (Prospects) 20.00

Essential Credentials Now

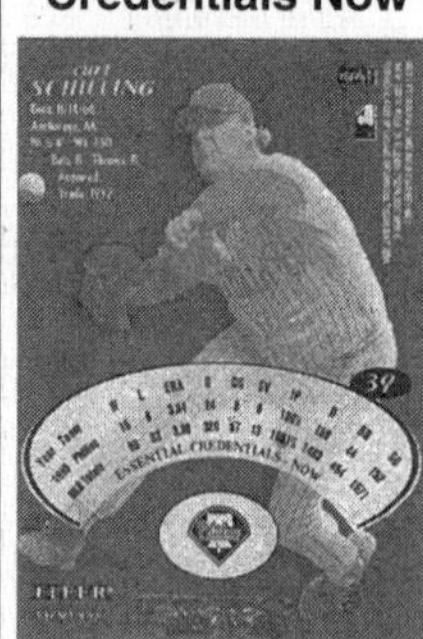

Like Future, this is a parallel of the base set, with the production of cards 1-60 limited to that player's card number. Production for cards 61-90 can be determined by subtracting 60 from the card number. Quantity issued is listed in parantheses.

NM/M
Common Player: 8.00
20 Roger Clemens/20 50.00
21 Randy Johnson /21 30.00
22 Bernie Williams/22 10.00
23 Carlos Delgado/23 25.00
24 Manny Ramirez/24 30.00
25 Freddy Garcia/25 10.00
26 Barry Bonds/26 75.00
27 Tim Hudson/27 15.00
28 Larry Walker/28 10.00
29 Raul Mondesi/29 10.00
30 Ivan Rodriguez/30 15.00
31 Magglio Ordonez/31 10.00
32 Scott Rolen/32 20.00
33 Mike Mussina/33 15.00
34 J.D. Drew/34 20.00
35 Tom Glavine/35 20.00
36 Barry Larkin/36 15.00
37 Jim Thome/37 25.00
38 Erubiel Durazo/38 8.00
39 Curt Schilling/39 20.00
40 Orlando Hernandez/40 8.00
41 Rafael Palmeiro/41 15.00
42 Gabe Kapler/42 8.00
43 Mark Grace/43 8.00
44 Jeff Cirillo/44 8.00
45 Jeromy Burnitz/45 8.00
46 Sean Casey/46 8.00
47 Kevin Millwood/47 8.00
48 Vinny Castilla/48 8.00
49 Jose Canseco/49 15.00
50 Roberto Alomar/50 12.00
51 Craig Biggio/51 15.00
52 Preston Wilson/52 8.00
53 Jeff Weaver/53 8.00
54 Robin Ventura/54 8.00
55 Ben Grieve/55 8.00
56 Troy Glaus/56 15.00
57 Jacque Jones/57 12.00
58 Brian Giles/58 8.00
59 Kevin Brown/59 8.00
60 Todd Helton/60 20.00
74 Adam Kennedy/14 (Prospects) 15.00
75 Cesar King/15 (Prospects) 15.00
76 Peter Bergeron/16 (Prospects) 15.00
77 Rob Bell/17 (Prospects) 15.00
78 Wily Pena/18 (Prospects) 15.00
79 Ruben Mateo/19 (Prospects) 15.00
80 Kip Wells/20 (Prospects) 15.00
81 Alex Escobar/21 (Prospects) 15.00
82 Danys Baez/22 (Prospects) 15.00
83 Travis Dawkins/23 (Prospects) 15.00
84 Mark Quinn/24 (Prospects) 15.00
85 Jimmy Anderson/25 (Prospects) 15.00
86 Rick Ankiel/26 (Prospects) 15.00
87 Alfonso Soriano/27 (Prospects) 60.00
88 Pat Burrell/28 (Prospects) 30.00
89 Eric Munson/29 (Prospects) 15.00
90 Josh Beckett/30 (Prospects) 20.00

E-Xceptional Red

Die-cut in a shape similar to an oval, these inserts have a cloth like feel with silver foil stamping with a red background. Card backs are numbered consecutively "1 Of 15XC" and so on. These are seeded 1:14 packs. Two parallels are also inserted: Blues are seeded 1:288 packs and Greens are limited to 999 serial numbered sets.

NM/M
Complete Set (15): 100.00
Common Player: 4.00
Inserted 1:14
Blue: 2-3X
Inserted 1:288
Green: 1-1.5X
Production 999 Sets
1 Ken Griffey Jr. 8.00
2 Derek Jeter 15.00
3 Nomar Garciaparra 6.00
4 Mark McGwire 10.00
5 Sammy Sosa 6.00
6 Mike Piazza 8.00
7 Alex Rodriguez 10.00
8 Cal Ripken Jr. 15.00
9 Chipper Jones 6.00
10 Pedro Martinez 4.00
11 Jeff Bagwell 4.00
12 Greg Maddux 6.00
13 Roger Clemens 7.00
14 Tony Gwynn 5.00
15 Frank Thomas 4.00

E-Xciting

Die-cut in the shape of a jersey card fronts have a holograpic appearance with silver foil stamping. These were seeded 1:24 packs. Card backs are numbered with an "XT" suffix.

NM/M
Complete Set (10): 25.00
Common Player: 1.00
Inserted 1:24
1 Mark McGwire 6.00
2 Ken Griffey Jr. 4.00
3 Randy Johnson 2.00
4 Sammy Sosa 3.00
5 Manny Ramirez 2.00
6 Jose Canseco 1.00
7 Derek Jeter 6.00
8 Scott Rolen 1.50
9 Juan Gonzalez 1.25
10 Barry Bonds 6.00

E-Xplosive

These inserts have a traditional format, with a holographic star like image in the background and "explosive" running down the top left side. Card backs are numbered with an "XP" suffix and are serial numbered on the bottom portion in an edition of 2,499 sets.

NM/M
Complete Set (20): 90.00
Common Player: 2.00
Production 2,499 Sets
1 Tony Gwynn 6.00
2 Alex Rodriguez 10.00
3 Pedro Martinez 5.00
4 Sammy Sosa 6.00
5 Cal Ripken Jr. 15.00
6 Adam Piatt 2.00
7 Pat Burrell 2.50
8 J.D. Drew 2.50
9 Mike Piazza 8.00
10 Shawn Green 2.50
11 Troy Glaus 4.00
12 Randy Johnson 5.00
13 Juan Gonzalez 2.50
14 Chipper Jones 6.00
15 Ivan Rodriguez 4.00
16 Nomar Garciaparra 6.00
17 Ken Griffey Jr. 8.00
18 Nick Johnson 2.50
19 Mark McGwire 10.00
20 Frank Thomas 5.00

Generation E-X

This 15-card set spotlights the top young players in the game and were seeded 1:8 packs. Card fronts have silver foil stamping over a background resembling a sky. These were seeded 1:8 packs. Card backs are numbered with a "GX" suffix.

NM/M
Complete Set (15): 20.00
Common Player: 1.00
Inserted 1:8
1 Rick Ankiel 1.00
2 Josh Beckett 1.50
3 Carlos Beltran 2.00
4 Pat Burrell 2.00
5 Freddy Garcia 1.00
6 Alex Rodriguez 5.00
7 Derek Jeter 6.00
8 Tim Hudson 1.50
9 Shawn Green 1.50
10 Eric Munson 1.00
11 Adam Piatt 1.00
12 Adam Kennedy 1.00
13 Nick Johnson 1.00
14 Alfonso Soriano 2.00
15 Nomar Garciaparra 4.00

Genuine Coverage

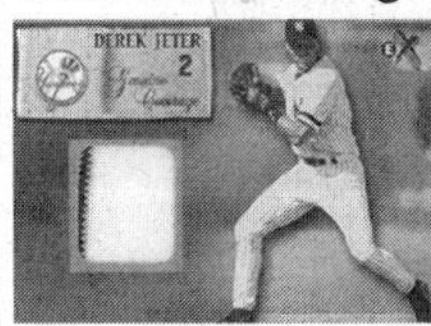

NM/M
Common Player: 5.00
Inserted 1:144
1 Alex Rodriguez 40.00
2 Tom Glavine 10.00
3 Cal Ripken Jr. 50.00
4 Edgar Martinez 5.00
5 Raul Mondesi 5.00
6 Carlos Beltran 5.00
7 Chipper Jones 25.00
8 Barry Bonds 50.00
9 Heath Murray 5.00
10 Tim Hudson 10.00
11 Mike Mussina 10.00
12 Derek Jeter 50.00

2004 SkyBox Autographics

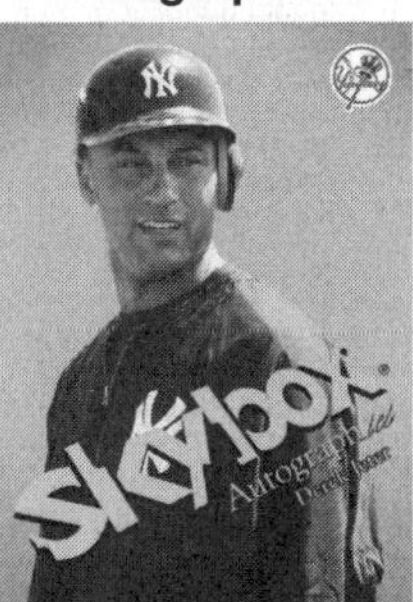

NM/M
Complete Set (100):
Common Player: .40
Hobby Box (4): 75.00
1 Albert Pujols 2.50
2 Richie Sexson .75
3 Scott Rolen 1.00
4 Rafael Palmeiro .75
5 Ichiro Suzuki 2.00
6 Craig Biggio .50
7 Todd Helton .75
8 Miguel Cabrera .75
9 Ken Griffey Jr. 1.50
10 Pat Burrell .50
11 Jose Reyes .50
12 Hideki Matsui 2.50
13 Geoff Jenkins .50
14 Mark Prior 2.00
15 Gary Sheffield .50
16 Nomar Garciaparra 2.00
17 Luis Gonzalez .50
18 Troy Glaus .50
19 Rocco Baldelli .75
20 Hank Blalock .50
21 Bret Boone .50
22 Mike Sweeney .40
23 Dmitri Young .40
24 Dontrelle Willis .50
25 Austin Kearns .50
26 Jason Kendall .40
27 Derek Jeter 3.00
28 Miguel Tejada .50
29 Torii Hunter .50
30 Sammy Sosa 2.00
31 Chipper Jones 1.50
32 Pedro J. Martinez 1.00
33 Curt Schilling .75
34 Roy Halladay .50
35 Jim Edmonds .50
36 Alex Rodriguez 2.50
37 Jason Schmidt .50
38 Jeff Bagwell .75
39 Omar Vizquel .40
40 Ivan Rodriguez .75
41 Magglio Ordonez .50
42 Jim Thome 1.00
43 Mike Piazza 2.00
44 Alfonso Soriano 1.00
45 Hideo Nomo .50
46 Kerry Wood 1.00
47 Greg Maddux 1.50
48 Tony Batista .40
49 Randy Johnson 1.00
50 Garret Anderson .50
51 Mark Teixeira .50
52 Carlos Delgado .75
53 Darin Erstad .50
54 Shawn Green .50
55 Josh Beckett .75
56 Lance Berkman .50
57 Adam Dunn .50
58 Brian Giles .50
59 Jason Giambi 1.00
60 Barry Zito .50
61 Vladimir Guerrero 1.00
62 Frank Thomas .75
63 Jay Gibbons .40
64 Manny Ramirez .75
65 Andruw Jones .75
66 Rickie Weeks 5.00
67 Chad Bentz **RC** 4.00
68 Bobby Crosby 4.00
69 Greg Dobbs **RC** 5.00
70 John Gall **RC** 3.00
71 Kazuo Matsui **RC** 20.00
72 Dallas McPherson 3.00
73 Brandon Watson 3.00
74 Jerry Gil **RC** 3.00
75 Garrett Atkins 3.00
76 Cory Sullivan **RC** 3.00
77 Khalil Greene 5.00
78 Shawn Hill **RC** 3.00
79 Graham Koonce 3.00
80 Chien-Ming Wang 3.00
81 Josh Labandeira **RC** 3.00
82 Jonny Gomes 3.00
83 Edwin Jackson 3.00
84 Alfredo Simon **RC** 4.00
85 Delmon Young 6.00
86 Jason Bartlett **RC** 5.00
87 Angel Chavez **RC** 3.00
88 Angel Guzman 3.00
89 Ryan Howard 3.00
90 Scott Hairston 3.00
91 Ronny Cedeno **RC** 3.00
92 Donald Kelly **RC** 3.00
93 Ivan Ochoa **RC** 3.00
94 Edwin Encarnacion 3.00
95 Byron Gettis 3.00
96 Kevin Youkilis 4.00
97 Grady Sizemore 3.00
98 Mariano Gomez **RC** 3.00
99 Hector Gimenez **RC** 3.00
100 Ruddy Yan **RC** 3.00

Insignia

Cards (1-65): 3-5X
Rookies (66-100): 1-2X
Production 150 Sets

Royal Insignia

No Pricing
Production 25 Sets

Autoclassics

NM/M
Complete Set (15): 25.00
Common Player: 1.50
Johnny Bench 4.00
Wade Boggs 2.00
Steve Carlton 2.00
Albert Chandler 1.50
Ty Cobb 4.00
Carlton Fisk 1.50
George Kelly 1.50
Sal Maglie 2.00
Bill Mazeroski 1.50
Jim Palmer 2.00
Nolan Ryan 6.00
Mike Schmidt 3.00
Joe Sewell 2.00
Duke Snider 3.00
Warren Spahn 4.00

Autographics Blue

NM/M
Common Player: 5.00
Silver: .75-1.5X
Production 100 Sets
Gold: 1.5-2X
Production 25 Sets
Purple: No Pricing
Production One Set
Garrett Atkins/175 5.00
Rocco Baldelli/255 15.00
Josh Beckett/100 25.00
Angel Berroa/182 10.00
Hank Blalock/205 15.00
A.J. Burnett/485 10.00
Marlon Byrd/240 8.00
Edwin Encarnacion/188 10.00
Eric Gagne/225 25.00
Jonny Gomes/265 15.00
Khalil Greene/190 25.00
Rich Harden/185 10.00
Dan Haren/176 10.00
Koyie Hill/240 5.00
Shea Hillenbrand/213 10.00
Ryan Howard/170 75.00
Tim Hudson/169 15.00
Aubrey Huff/296 10.00
Torii Hunter/215 10.00
Edwin Jackson/224 10.00
Bobby Jenks/307 10.00
Matt Kata/197 10.00
Austin Kearns/275 8.00
Graham Koonce/190 10.00
Barry Larkin/195 25.00
Dallas McPherson/179 8.00
Aaron Miles/140 10.00
Mark Mulder/186 15.00
Laynce Nix/185 8.00
Trot Nixon/210 15.00
Corey Patterson/220 12.00
Juan Pierre/220 15.00
Scott Podsednik/210 25.00
Albert Pujols/103 160.00
Jose Reyes/195 30.00
Juan Richardson/345 5.00
Gary Sheffield/210 20.00
Chris Snelling/200 5.00
Shannon Stewart/340 10.00
Cory Sullivan/170 5.00
Javier Vazquez/210 15.00
Billy Wagner/180 25.00
Chien-Ming Wang/195 100.00
Brandon Webb/310 12.00
Rickie Weeks/187 20.00
Dontrelle Willis/225 25.00
Kerry Wood/191 25.00
Delmon Young/205 25.00

Jerseygraphics Blue

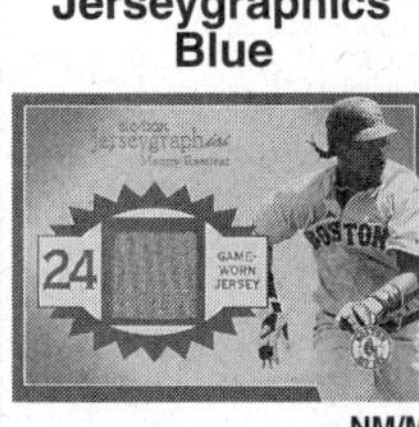

NM/M
Common Player: 4.00
Silver: 1-2X
Production 100 Sets
Gold: No Pricing
Production 25 Sets
Bobby Abreu 6.00
Rocco Baldelli 6.00
Josh Beckett 10.00
Lance Berkman 6.00
Craig Biggio 6.00
Hank Blalock 4.00
Pat Burrell 6.00
Miguel Cabrera 10.00
Carlos Delgado 6.00
Adam Dunn 8.00
Jim Edmonds 4.00
Darin Erstad 4.00
Nomar Garciaparra 8.00
Jason Giambi 8.00
Jay Gibbons 4.00
Troy Glaus 6.00
Shawn Green 4.00
Vladimir Guerrero 8.00
Roy Halladay 6.00
Todd Helton 8.00
Torii Hunter 6.00
Derek Jeter 15.00
Andruw Jones 8.00
Chipper Jones 10.00
Austin Kearns 4.00
Greg Maddux 15.00
Pedro J. Martinez 10.00
Kevin Millwood 4.00
Hideo Nomo 8.00
David Ortiz 10.00
Rafael Palmeiro 6.00
Mike Piazza 10.00
Mark Prior 6.00
Albert Pujols 15.00
Manny Ramirez 10.00
Jose Reyes 10.00
Alex Rodriguez 15.00
Ivan Rodriguez 6.00
Scott Rolen 8.00
Curt Schilling 6.00
Alfonso Soriano 8.00
Sammy Sosa 8.00
Mark Teixeira 8.00
Miguel Tejada 6.00
Frank Thomas 10.00
Jim Thome 8.00
Dontrelle Willis 4.00
Kerry Wood 4.00
Barry Zito 4.00

Prospects Endorsed

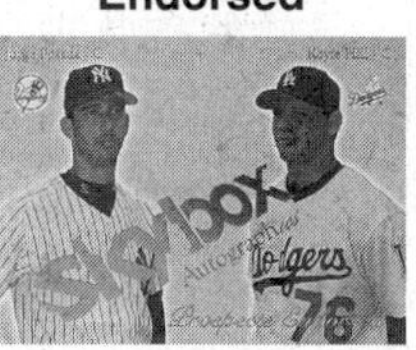

NM/M
Complete Set (15): 10.00
Common Duo: .50
1 Albert Pujols, Delmon Young 3.00
2 Eric Gagne, Bobby Jenks .50
3 Barry Larkin, Kazuo Matsui 2.00
4 Andruw Jones, Jonny Gomes 1.00
5 Hideo Nomo, Chien-Ming Wang .50
6 Gary Sheffield, Cory Sullivan .75
7 Billy Wagner, Ryan Howard 1.00
8 Jorge Posada, Koyie Hill .75
9 Curt Schilling, Ryan Wagner .75
10 Jose Reyes, Rickie Weeks 1.50
11 Alfonso Soriano, Matt Kata 1.50
12 Barry Zito, Rich Harden .75
13 Randy Johnson, Brandon Webb 1.50
14 Alex Rodriguez, Angel Berroa 3.00
15 Dontrelle Willis, Edwin Jackson .50

2004 SkyBox LE

NM/M
Complete Set (160):
Common Player (1-110): .25
Common SP (111-160): 4.00
Production 299 unless noted.
Pack (3): 5.00
Box (18): 80.00
1 Juan Pierre .25
2 Derek Jeter 3.00
3 Brandon Webb .25
4 Jeff Bagwell .75
5 Jason Schmidt .40
6 Marlon Byrd .25
7 Garret Anderson .50
8 Miguel Cabrera .75
9 Jose Reyes .50
10 Rocco Baldelli .50
11 Tony Batista .25
12 Carlos Beltran .50
13 Nomar Garciaparra 2.00
14 Shawn Green .50
15 Albert Pujols 2.50
16 Magglio Ordonez .50
17 Kip Wells .25
18 Andruw Jones .75
19 Ryan Wagner .25
20 Alex Rodriguez 3.00
21 Vernon Wells .50
22 Todd Helton .75
23 David Ortiz .25
24 Troy Glaus .50
25 Jim Thome 1.00
26 Greg Maddux 1.50
27 Roberto Alomar .50
28 Edgardo Alfonzo .25
29 Hee Seop Choi .25
30 Ken Griffey Jr. 1.50
31 Tim Hudson .50
32 Shannon Stewart .25
33 Ichiro Suzuki 2.00
34 Luis Gonzalez .50
35 Darin Erstad .50
36 Dmitri Young .25
37 Ivan Rodriguez .75
38 Scott Podsednik .50
39 Jose Vidro .25
40 Mark Prior 2.00
41 Mike Mussina .75
42 Gary Sheffield .50
43 Manny Ramirez .75
44 C.C. Sabathia .40
45 Curt Schilling .75
46 Scott Rolen 1.00
47 Hideo Nomo .50
48 Torii Hunter .50
49 Aubrey Huff .25
50 Javy Lopez .50
51 Austin Kearns .50
52 Mike Piazza 1.50
53 Sean Burroughs .25
54 Kerry Wood .75
55 Marquis Grissom .25
56 Preston Wilson .25
57 Angel Berroa .25
58 Jason Kendall .25
59 Rafael Palmeiro .75
60 Mike Lowell .40
61 Eric Chavez .50
62 Bartolo Colon .50
63 Adam Dunn .50
64 Pedro J. Martinez 1.00
65 Lance Berkman .50
66 Bret Boone .40
67 Eric Gagne .40
68 Vladimir Guerrero 1.00
69 Jay Gibbons .25
70 Larry Walker .40
71 Orlando Cabrera .40
72 Jorge Posada .50
73 Jamie Moyer .25
74 Carl Crawford .25
75 Hank Blalock .50
76 Josh Beckett .75
77 Jody Gerut .25
78 Kevin Brown .50
79 Sammy Sosa 2.00
80 Chipper Jones 1.00
81 Tom Glavine .50
82 Barry Zito .50
83 Edgar Renteria .50
84 Esteban Loaiza .25
85 Jason Giambi 1.00
86 Miguel Tejada .50
87 Randy Johnson 1.00
88 A.J. Burnett .25
89 Richie Sexson .75
90 Reggie Sanders .25
91 Carlos Delgado .75
92 Pat Burrell .50
93 Jacque Jones .25
94 Roy Oswalt .50
95 Frank Thomas .75
96 Melvin Mora .25
97 Jeremy Bonderman .25
98 Mike Sweeney .25
99 Brian Giles .50
100 Edgar Martinez .40
101 Mark Teixeira .50
102 Sean Casey .25
103 Javier Vazquez .50
104 Hideki Matsui 2.50
105 Jim Edmonds .40
106 Roy Halladay .50
107 Craig Biggio .40
108 Geoff Jenkins .50
109 Alfonso Soriano 1.00
110 Barry Larkin .50
111 Chris Bootcheck 4.00
112 Dallas McPherson/99 6.00
113 Matt Kata/99 6.00
114 Scott Hairston 4.00
115 Bobby Crosby 8.00
116 Adam Wainright/99 6.00
117 Daniel Cabrera 4.00
118 Kevin Youkilis 8.00
119 Ronny Cedeno **RC** 6.00
120 Ruddy Yan **RC** 4.00
121 Ryan Wing 4.00
122 William Bergolla **RC** 5.00
123 Edwin Encarnacion 4.00
124 Jonny Gomes 4.00
125 Garrett Atkins 4.00
126 Clint Barmes 4.00
127 Wilfredo Ledezma 4.00
128 Cody Ross 6.00
129 Josh Willingham/99 6.00
130 Chin-Hui Tsao 4.00
131 Hector Gimenez **RC** 6.00
132 David DeJesus 4.00
133 Jimmy Gobble 4.00
134 Edwin Jackson/99 6.00
135 Koyie Hill 4.00
136 Rickie Weeks/99 8.00
137 Graham Koonce 4.00
138 Rob Bowen 6.00
139 Shawn Hill **RC** 4.00

140 Craig Brazell 4.00
141 Mike Hessman 4.00
142 Jorge DePaula 4.00
143 Chien-Ming Wang/99 6.00
144 Rich Harden 4.00
145 Ryan Howard/99 6.00
146 Alfredo Simon **RC** 4.00
147 Ian Snell **RC** 6.00
148 Ryan Doumit 4.00
149 Khalil Greene/99 6.00
150 Angel Chavez **RC** 4.00
151 Dan Haren 6.00
152 Chris Snelling 4.00
153 Aaron Miles 4.00
154 John Gall **RC** 8.00
155 Chris Narveson 4.00
156 Delmon Young/99 8.00
157 Chad Gaudin 4.00
158 Gerald Laird 4.00
159 Alexis Rios 8.00
160 Jason Arnold 4.00

Artist's Proof

Cards (1-110): 3-6X
SP's (110-160): 1-1.5X
Production 50 Sets

Executive Proof

No Pricing
Production One Set

Gold Proof

Cards (1-110): 3-5X
SP's (111-160): 1X
Production 150 Sets

Photographer Proof

Cards (1-110): 6-12X
SP's (110-160): 2-3X
Production 25 Sets

History of the Draft Autographs

NM/M
Common Autograph: 10.00
Production 199 Sets
Draft Year: 1-1.25X
#'d to last 2 digits of draft year
Silver Proof: 1-1.5X
Production 50 Sets
Gold Proof: No Pricing
Production 10 Sets
Hank Blalock 10.00
A.J. Burnett 10.00
Marlon Byrd 10.00
Roy Halladay 20.00
Tim Hudson 15.00
Aubrey Huff 10.00
Torii Hunter 15.00
Austin Kearns 10.00
Mike Lowell 15.00
Corey Patterson 15.00
Juan Pierre 15.00
Scott Podsednik 20.00
Albert Pujols 125.00
Scott Rolen 25.00
Shannon Stewart 10.00
Javier Vazquez 10.00
Vernon Wells 15.00

History of the Draft Game-Used

NM/M
Common Player: 4.00
Numbered to last two digits of draft yr.
Silver Proof: 1-1.5X
Production 50 Sets
Gold Proof: No Pricing
Production 10 Sets
Garret Anderson 4.00
Josh Beckett 10.00
Carlos Beltran 8.00
Lance Berkman 6.00
Hank Blalock 4.00
Bret Boone 4.00
A.J. Burnett 4.00
Pat Burrell 4.00
Marlon Byrd 4.00
Eric Chavez 4.00
Adam Dunn 8.00
Darin Erstad 4.00
Nomar Garciaparra 8.00
Jason Giambi 8.00
Shawn Green 4.00
Roy Halladay 6.00
Todd Helton 8.00
Tim Hudson 6.00
Aubrey Huff 4.00
Torii Hunter 6.00
Derek Jeter 15.00
Chipper Jones 10.00
Austin Kearns 4.00
Mike Lowell 5.00
Mike Mussina 8.00
Corey Patterson 4.00
Juan Pierre 4.00
Scott Podsednik 4.00
Jorge Posada 8.00
Albert Pujols 20.00
Manny Ramirez 8.00
Alex Rodriguez 15.00
Scott Rolen 8.00
Jason Schmidt 4.00
Richie Sexson 6.00
Shannon Stewart 4.00
Javier Vazquez 4.00
Vernon Wells 6.00
Kerry Wood 6.00
Barry Zito 6.00

Jersey Proof

NM/M
Common Player: 4.00
Production 299 Sets
Silver Proof: 1.5-2X
Production 50 Sets
Gold Proof: No Pricing
Production 10 Sets
1 Troy Glaus 6.00
2 Curt Schilling 6.00
3 Randy Johnson 8.00
4 Brandon Webb 6.00
5 Gary Sheffield 6.00
6 Greg Maddux 15.00
7 Chipper Jones 10.00
8 David Ortiz 10.00
9 Nomar Garciaparra 15.00
10 Pedro J. Martinez 8.00
11 Manny Ramirez 8.00
12 Kerry Wood 6.00
13 Mark Prior 6.00
14 Sammy Sosa 10.00
15 Frank Thomas 8.00
16 Austin Kearns 4.00
17 Todd Helton 8.00
18 Preston Wilson 4.00
19 Juan Pierre 4.00
20 Josh Beckett 8.00
21 Ivan Rodriguez 6.00
22 Miguel Cabrera 8.00
23 Mike Lowell 6.00
24 Lance Berkman 6.00
25 Jeff Bagwell 8.00
26 Angel Berroa 4.00
27 Hideo Nomo 10.00
28 Eric Gagne 4.00
29 Scott Podsednik 10.00
30 Richie Sexson 6.00
31 Torii Hunter 6.00
32 Mike Piazza 10.00
33 Jose Reyes 10.00
34 Tom Glavine 6.00
35 Derek Jeter 25.00
36 Jorge Posada 6.00
37 Jason Giambi 8.00
38 Alfonso Soriano 8.00
39 Eric Chavez 4.00
40 Miguel Tejada 6.00
41 Jim Thome 8.00
42 Albert Pujols 15.00
43 Scott Rolen 8.00
44 Rocco Baldelli 6.00
45 Alex Rodriguez 15.00
46 Hank Blalock 6.00
47 Mark Teixeira 6.00
48 Rafael Palmeiro 6.00
49 Carlos Delgado 6.00
50 Roy Halladay 6.00

L.E.ague L.E.aders

NM/M
Complete Set (10): 10.00
Common Player: .50
Inserted 1:18
1LL Alex Rodriguez 3.00
2LL Jim Thome 1.50
3LL Albert Pujols 3.00
4LL Pedro J. Martinez 1.50
5LL Roy Halladay .75
6LL Jason Schmidt .50
7LL Kerry Wood 1.00
8LL Juan Pierre .50
9LL Preston Wilson .50
10LL Carlos Delgado 1.00

L.E.ague L.E.eaders Game-Used

NM/M
Common Player: 4.00
Production 75 Sets
Silver Proof: 1-1.5X
Production 50 Sets
Gold Proof: No Pricing
Production 10 Sets
Alex Rodriguez 15.00
Jim Thome 8.00

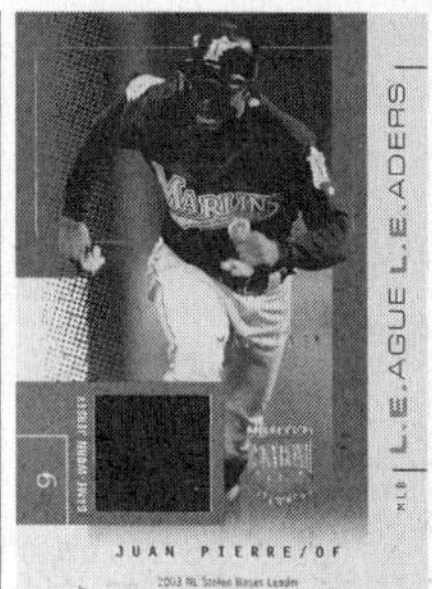

Albert Pujols 20.00
Pedro J. Martinez 10.00
Roy Halladay 6.00
Jason Schmidt 4.00
Kerry Wood 4.00
Juan Pierre 4.00
Preston Wilson 4.00
Carlos Delgado 6.00

Rare Form

NM/M
Common Player: 5.00
Inserted 1:288
1 Albert Pujols 20.00
2 Miguel Cabrera 5.00
3 Jim Thome 10.00
4 Derek Jeter 30.00
5 Nomar Garciaparra 15.00
6 Mike Piazza 15.00
7 Alex Rodriguez 20.00
8 Delmon Young 15.00
9 Chipper Jones 12.00
10 Rickie Weeks 10.00

Rare Form Autographs

NM/M
Common Autograph: 10.00
Production 299 Sets
Level 2: 1-1.5X
Production 99 Sets
Silver Proof: 1.5X
Production 50 Sets
Gold Proof: No Pricing
Production 10 Sets
Rocco Baldelli 25.00
Angel Berroa 15.00
Rich Harden 20.00
Edwin Jackson 20.00
Matt Kata 10.00
Dallas McPherson 15.00
Brandon Webb 15.00
Rickie Weeks 30.00
Delmon Young 30.00

Rare Form Game-Used Silver Proof

NM/M
Common Player: 5.00
Production 50 Sets
Gold Proof: No Pricing
Production 10 Sets
Rocco Baldelli 5.00
Miguel Cabrera 10.00
Nomar Garciaparra 15.00
Derek Jeter 25.00
Chipper Jones 12.00
Mike Piazza 15.00
Albert Pujols 25.00
Alex Rodriguez 20.00
Jim Thome 10.00

Rare Form Memorabilia Jersey Number

NM/M
Numbered to jersey number.
Most not priced due to scarcity.
Mike Piazza/31 30.00
Jim Thome/25 25.00

Sky's the Limit

NM/M
Complete Set (20): 20.00
Common Player: .50
Inserted 1:6
1SL Dontrelle Willis 1.00
2SL Rocco Baldelli 1.00
3SL Miguel Cabrera 1.00
4SL Mark Prior 3.00
5SL Hideki Matsui 4.00
6SL Kerry Wood 1.50
7SL Alfonso Soriano 1.50
8SL Ichiro Suzuki 2.50
9SL Brandon Webb .50
10SL Alex Rodriguez 3.00
11SL Barry Zito 1.00
12SL Hank Blalock 1.00
13SL Jose Reyes .75
14SL Torii Hunter .75
15SL Josh Beckett 1.00
16SL Manny Ramirez 1.00
17SL Andruw Jones 1.00
18SL Vladimir Guerrero 1.50
19SL Miguel Tejada .75
20SL Carlos Delgado 1.00

Sky's the Limit Game-Used

NM/M
Common Player: 4.00
Production 99 Sets
Silver Proof: 1X
Production 50 Sets
Gold Proof: No Pricing
Production 10 Sets
Rocco Baldelli 4.00
Josh Beckett 10.00
Hank Blalock 6.00
Miguel Cabrera 8.00
Carlos Delgado 6.00
Vladimir Guerrero 8.00
Torii Hunter 6.00
Andruw Jones 6.00
Mark Prior 6.00
Manny Ramirez 8.00
Jose Reyes 10.00
Alex Rodriguez 15.00
Alfonso Soriano 8.00
Miguel Tejada 6.00
Brandon Webb 6.00
Dontrelle Willis 4.00
Kerry Wood 4.00
Barry Zito 4.00

2005 SkyBox Autographics

NM/M
Complete Set (115):
Common Player (1-60): .15
Common (61-115): 1.50
Production 750
Pack (5): 8.00
Box (12): 85.00
1 Vladimir Guerrero .75
2 Garret Anderson .25
3 Troy Glaus .25
4 Shawn Green .25
5 Chipper Jones .75
6 Andruw Jones .40
7 Miguel Tejada .50
8 Melvin Mora .15
9 Manny Ramirez .75
10 Curt Schilling .75
11 Nomar Garciaparra .50
12 Mark Prior .50
13 Sammy Sosa 1.00
14 Frank Thomas .40
15 Paul Konerko .25
16 Adam Dunn .50
17 Ken Griffey Jr. 1.50
18 Victor Martinez .25
19 Travis Hafner .25
20 Todd Helton .50
21 Ivan Rodriguez .50
22 Carlos Guillen .15
23 Miguel Cabrera .75
24 Juan Pierre .15
25 Roger Clemens 2.00
26 Jeff Bagwell .50
27 Lance Berkman .25
28 Mike Sweeney .15
29 Eric Gagne .15
30 J.D. Drew .15
31 Ben Sheets .25
32 Lyle Overbay .15
33 Johan Santana .50
34 Torii Hunter .15
35 Mike Piazza 1.00
36 Pedro Martinez .75
37 Carlos Beltran .50
38 Derek Jeter 2.00
39 Alex Rodriguez 2.00
40 Hideki Matsui 1.50
41 Randy Johnson .75
42 Eric Chavez .25
43 Jim Thome .50
44 Craig Wilson .15
45 Khalil Greene .25
46 Jake Peavy .25
47 Jason Schmidt .15
48 Ichiro Suzuki 1.50
49 Adrian Beltre .25
50 Albert Pujols 2.00
51 Scott Rolen .50
52 Carl Crawford .15
53 Rocco Baldelli .15
54 Alfonso Soriano .50
55 Hank Blalock .25
56 Vernon Wells .15
57 Jose Vidro .15
58 David Ortiz .75
59 Bobby Abreu .25
60 Gary Sheffield .40
61 Nolan Ryan 15.00
62 Mike Schmidt 10.00
63 Johnny Bench 8.00
64 Lou Brock 3.00
65 Dennis Eckersley 2.00
66 Carlton Fisk 3.00
67 Bob Gibson 4.00
68 Reggie Jackson 4.00
69 Al Kaline 3.00
70 Bill Mazeroski 2.00
71 Willie McCovey 3.00
72 Jim Palmer 2.00
73 Phil Rizzuto 2.00
74 Warren Spahn 4.00
75 Brooks Robinson 3.00
76 Willie Stargell 3.00
77 Jim "Catfish" Hunter 2.00
78 Tony Perez 2.00
79 George Kell 2.00
80 Robin Yount 4.00
81 Fergie Jenkins 2.00
82 Tom Seaver 3.00
83 Eddie Mathews 3.00
84 Enos Slaughter 2.00
85 Pee Wee Reese 2.00
86 Harmon Killebrew 3.00
87 Eddie Murray 3.00
88 Orlando Cepeda 2.00
89 Billy Williams 2.00
90 Ralph Kiner 2.00
91 Ryan Raburn 1.50
92 Justin Morneau 2.00
93 Zack Greinke 1.50
94 David Aardsma 1.50
95 B.J. Upton 2.00
96 Gavin Floyd 1.50
97 David Wright 8.00
98 Russ Adams 1.50
99 Jose Lopez 2.00
100 Scott Kazmir 2.00
101 Mike Gosling 1.50
102 Jeff Keppinger 1.50
103 David Krynzel 1.50
104 Jeff Niemann **RC** 6.00
105 Ruben Gotay 1.50
106 Dioner Navarro 1.50
107 Nick Swisher 1.50
108 Yadier Molina 1.50
109 Joey Gathright 1.50
110 Jon Knott 1.50
111 J.D. Durbin 1.50
112 Andres Blanco 1.50
113 Charlton Jimerson 1.50
114 Sean Burnett 1.50
115 Justin Verlander **RC** 6.00

Insignia

Insignia (1-60): 2-3X
Insignia (61-115): 1X
Production 150 Sets

Royal Insignia

Royal Insignia (1-60): 4-6X
Royal Insignia (61-115): 1.5-2X
Production 25 Sets

1992 Snyder's Bread Washington Sports Heroes

This set was sponsored by Snyder's, a Northwest baker, and produced by Little Sun,

which had earlier done a number of amateur baseball card sets. Two baseball players are included in the set: Ryne Sandberg (in a high school football jersey) and John Olerud (pitching for WSU). Cards picture the athletes against a pine tree border photo. Backs are printed in blue and yellow on white and feature a summary of the athlete's days in Washington.

NM/M
Complete Set (8): 15.00
1 Ryne Sandberg 12.00
6 John Olerud 3.00

1995 Sonic/Coke Heroes of Baseball

In a promotion with the Sonic chain of Southern drive-in restaurants, Upper Deck issued a 20-card set of baseball greats. Cards featured vintage sepia photos on the front, with player biographies and stats on the back. The Coca-Cola and Sonic logos also appear on back.

NM/M
Complete Set (20): 5.00
Common Player: .25
1 Whitey Ford .25
2 Cy Young .25
3 Babe Ruth 1.50
4 Lou Gehrig 1.00
5 Mike Schmidt .35
6 Nolan Ryan 1.00
7 Robin Yount .25
8 Gary Carter .25
9 Tom Seaver .25
10 Reggie Jackson .25
11 Bob Gibson .25
12 Gil Hodges .25
13 Monte Irvin .25
14 Minnie Minoso .25
15 Willie Stargell .25
16 Al Kaline .25
17 Joe Jackson 1.50
18 Walter Johnson .25
19 Ty Cobb .50
20 Satchel Paige .25

1995 Sonic/Pepsi Baseball Greats

While some Sonic drive-in restaurants (basically a Southern chain) featured a baseball card promotion using Upper Deck cards with a Coca-Cola logo on back, other drive-ins in the chain featured a 12-card set sponsored by Pepsi. Cards have a red border on front and a color photo of a player on which team logos have been air-brushed away. Backs have career data and the Pepsi logo, along with that of the Major League Baseball Players Alumni, and are printed in red and blue. The cards were issued in three-card cello packs with a meal purchase. The unnumbered cards are checklisted here in alphabetical order.

		NM/M
Complete Set (12):		4.00
Common Player:		.25
(1)	Bert Campaneris	.25
(2)	George Foster	.25
(3)	Steve Garvey	.40
(4)	Fergie Jenkins	.25
(5)	Tommy John	.25
(6)	Harmon Killebrew	.75
(7)	Sparky Lyle	.25
(8)	Fred Lynn	.25
(9)	Joe Morgan	.60
(10)	Graig Nettles	.25
(11)	Warren Spahn	.75
(12)	Maury Wills	.25

1987 Sonshine Industries 19th Century Baseball

A. C. ANSON

There is no indication of the origins of this collectors' issue on the cards themselves. Fronts feature black-and-white reproductions of vintage woodcuts of the players with an ornate orange framework. Backs of the 2-1/2" x 3-1/2" cards are printed in black on blue-gray with lengthy biographical information. The unnumbered cards are checklisted here in alphabetical order.

		NM/M
Complete Set (20):		20.00
Common Player:		1.00
(1)	A.C. Anson	2.00
(2)	Cap Anson	2.00
(3)	D. Brouthers	1.00
(4)	Alexander Cartwright	1.50
(5)	Alexander Cartwright	1.50
(6)	L.N. David	1.00
(7)	Wes Fisler	1.00
(8)	F.E. Goldsmith	1.00
(9)	T.J. Keefe	1.00
(10)	M.J. Kelly	2.00
(11)	Robert T. Mathews	1.00
(12)	Wm. McLean	1.00
(13)	C.A. McVey	1.00
(14)	James Mutrie	1.00
(15)	Lipman Pike	1.50
(16)	John J. Smith	1.00
(17)	A.G. Spalding	1.50
(18)	M. Welch	1.50
(19)	N.E. Young	1.00
(20)	Going to the game	1.00

1995 South Carolina Athletic Hall of Fame

Sports stars from around the state were honored in this 108-card issue. Fronts feature borderless color or sepia photos with the S.C. Athletic Hall of Fame logo in an upper cor-

ner and a gold-foil seal at bottom-right. A colored stripe has the athlete's name in gold foil. On back are a few personal and career stats and highlights. Only the baseball players are listed here. Issue price of the set was $40.

		NM/M
Complete Set (108):		40.00
Common (Baseball) Player:		.50
5	Frank Howard	.75
6	Bobby Richardson	1.00
13	Shoeless Joe Jackson	4.00
27	Van Lingle Mungo	.50
35	Earl Wooten	.50
54	Marty Marion	.50
55	Frank Howard	.75
72	Jim Rice	.75
74	Danny Ford	.50
83	Lou Brissie	.50
84	Billy O'Dell	.50
97	Bobby Richardson	1.00
100	Frank Howard	.75

1993 SP

Upper Deck's first super-premium baseball card issue features 290 cards in the single-series set; 252 are individual player cards, while the remainder includes a Premier Prospects subset featuring top prospects (20 cards), 18 All-Stars and a Platinum Power insert set of 20 top home run hitters. Cards, which were available in 12-card foil packs, feature borderless color photos and UV coating on the front, plus a special logo using lenticular printing. Foil is also used intricately in the design. Backs have a large color photo and statistics. Cards are numbered and color-coded by team.

		NM/M
Complete Set (290):		75.00
Common Player:		.10
Pack (12):		10.00
Wax Box (24):		220.00
1	Roberto Alomar	.30
2	Wade Boggs	2.00
3	Joe Carter	.10
4	Ken Griffey Jr.	2.50
5	Mark Langston	.10
6	John Olerud	.10
7	Kirby Puckett	2.00
8	Cal Ripken, Jr.	4.00
9	Ivan Rodriguez	1.25
10	Barry Bonds	4.00
11	Darren Daulton	.10
12	Marquis Grissom	.10
13	Dave Justice	.10
14	John Kruk	.10
15	Barry Larkin	.10
16	Terry Mulholland	.10
17	Ryne Sandberg	2.00
18	Gary Sheffield	.10
19	Chad Curtis	.10
20	Chili Davis	.10
21	Gary DiSarcina	.10
22	Damion Easley	.10
23	Chuck Finley	.10
24	Luis Polonia	.10
25	Tim Salmon	.10
26	J.T. Snow **RC**	1.00
27	Russ Springer	.10
28	Jeff Bagwell	1.50
29	Craig Biggio	.10
30	Ken Caminiti	.10
31	Andujar Cedeno	.10
32	Doug Drabek	.10
33	Steve Finley	.10
34	Luis Gonzalez	.10
35	Pete Harnisch	.10
36	Darryl Kile	.10
37	Mike Bordick	.10
38	Dennis Eckersley	1.25
39	Brent Gates	.10
40	Rickey Henderson	1.50
41	Mark McGwire	3.00
42	Craig Paquette	.10
43	Ruben Sierra	.10
44	Terry Steinbach	.10
45	Todd Van Poppel	.10
46	Pat Borders	.10
47	Tony Fernandez	.10
48	Juan Guzman	.10
49	Pat Hentgen	.10
50	Paul Molitor	1.50
51	Jack Morris	.10
52	Ed Sprague	.10
53	Duane Ward	.10
54	Devon White	.10
55	Steve Avery	.10
56	Jeff Blauser	.10
57	Ron Gant	.10
58	Tom Glavine	.40
59	Greg Maddux	2.00
60	Fred McGriff	.10
61	Terry Pendleton	.10
62	Deion Sanders	.10
63	John Smoltz	.10
64	Cal Eldred	.10
65	Darryl Hamilton	.10
66	John Jaha	.10
67	Pat Listach	.10
68	Jaime Navarro	.10
69	Kevin Reimer	.10
70	B.J. Surhoff	.10
71	Greg Vaughn	.10
72	Robin Yount	1.50
73	Rene Arocha **RC**	.10
74	Bernard Gilkey	.10
75	Gregg Jefferies	.10
76	Ray Lankford	.10
77	Tom Pagnozzi	.10
78	Lee Smith	.10
79	Ozzie Smith	2.00
80	Bob Tewksbury	.10
81	Mark Whiten	.10
82	Steve Buechele	.10
83	Mark Grace	.10
84	Jose Guzman	.10
85	Derrick May	.10
86	Mike Morgan	.10
87	Randy Myers	.10
88	Kevin Roberson **RC**	.10
89	Sammy Sosa	2.00
90	Rick Wilkins	.10
91	Brett Butler	.10
92	Eric Davis	.10
93	Orel Hershiser	.10
94	Eric Karros	.10
95	Ramon Martinez	.10
96	Raul Mondesi	.10
97	Jose Offerman	.10
98	Mike Piazza	2.50
99	Darryl Strawberry	.10
100	Moises Alou	.10
101	Wil Cordero	.10
102	Delino DeShields	.10
103	Darrin Fletcher	.10
104	Ken Hill	.10
105	Mike Lansing **RC**	.40
106	Dennis Martinez	.10
107	Larry Walker	.10
108	John Wetteland	.10
109	Rod Beck	.10
110	John Burkett	.10
111	Will Clark	.10
112	Royce Clayton	.10
113	Darren Lewis	.10
114	Willie McGee	.10
115	Bill Swift	.10
116	Robby Thompson	.10
117	Matt Williams	.10
118	Sandy Alomar Jr.	.10
119	Carlos Baerga	.10
120	Albert Belle	.10
121	Reggie Jefferson	.10
122	Kenny Lofton	.10
123	Wayne Kirby	.10
124	Carlos Martinez	.10
125	Charles Nagy	.10
126	Paul Sorrento	.10
127	Rich Amaral	.10
128	Jay Buhner	.10
129	Norm Charlton	.10
130	Dave Fleming	.10
131	Erik Hanson	.10
132	Randy Johnson	1.50
133	Edgar Martinez	.10
134	Tino Martinez	.10
135	Omar Vizquel	.10
136	Bret Barberie	.10
137	Chuck Carr	.10
138	Jeff Conine	.10
139	Orestes Destrade	.10
140	Chris Hammond	.10
141	Bryan Harvey	.10
142	Benito Santiago	.10
143	Walt Weiss	.10
144	Darrell Whitmore **RC**	.10
145	Tim Bolger **RC**	.10
146	Bobby Bonilla	.10
147	Jeromy Burnitz	.10
148	Vince Coleman	.10
149	Dwight Gooden	.10
150	Todd Hundley	.10
151	Howard Johnson	.10
152	Eddie Murray	1.50
153	Bret Saberhagen	.10
154	Brady Anderson	.10
155	Mike Devereaux	.10
156	Jeffrey Hammonds	.10
157	Chris Hoiles	.10
158	Ben McDonald	.10
159	Mark McLemore	.10
160	Mike Mussina	.50
161	Gregg Olson	.10
162	David Segui	.10
163	Derek Bell	.10
164	Andy Benes	.10
165	Archi Cianfrocco	.10
166	Ricky Gutierrez	.10
167	Tony Gwynn	2.00
168	Gene Harris	.10
169	Trevor Hoffman	.10
170	Ray McDavid **RC**	.10
171	Phil Plantier	.10
172	Mariano Duncan	.10
173	Len Dykstra	.10
174	Tommy Greene	.10
175	Dave Hollins	.10
176	Pete Incaviglia	.10
177	Mickey Morandini	.10
178	Curt Schilling	.40
179	Kevin Stocker	.10
180	Mitch Williams	.10
181	Stan Belinda	.10
182	Jay Bell	.10
183	Steve Cooke	.10
184	Carlos Garcia	.10
185	Jeff King	.10
186	Orlando Merced	.10
187	Don Slaught	.10
188	Andy Van Slyke	.10
189	Kevin Young	.10
190	Kevin Brown	.10
191	Jose Canseco	.60
192	Julio Franco	.10
193	Benji Gil	.10
194	Juan Gonzalez	.75
195	Tom Henke	.10
196	Rafael Palmeiro	1.25
197	Dean Palmer	.10
198	Nolan Ryan	4.00
199	Roger Clemens	2.25
200	Scott Cooper	.10
201	Andre Dawson	.35
202	Mike Greenwell	.10
203	Carlos Quintana	.10
204	Jeff Russell	.10
205	Aaron Sele	.10
206	Mo Vaughn	.10
207	Frank Viola	.10
208	Rob Dibble	.10
209	Roberto Kelly	.10
210	Kevin Mitchell	.10
211	Hal Morris	.10
212	Joe Oliver	.10
213	Jose Rijo	.10
214	Bip Roberts	.10
215	Chris Sabo	.10
216	Reggie Sanders	.10
217	Dante Bichette	.10
218	Jerald Clark	.10
219	Alex Cole	.10
220	Andres Galarraga	.10
221	Joe Girardi	.10
222	Charlie Hayes	.10
223	Robert Mejia **RC**	.10
224	Armando Reynoso	.10
225	Eric Young	.10
226	Kevin Appier	.10
227	George Brett	2.25
228	David Cone	.10
229	Phil Hiatt	.10
230	Felix Jose	.10
231	Wally Joyner	.10
232	Mike Macfarlane	.10
233	Brian McRae	.10
234	Jeff Montgomery	.10
235	Rob Deer	.10
236	Cecil Fielder	.10
237	Travis Fryman	.10
238	Mike Henneman	.10
239	Tony Phillips	.10
240	Mickey Tettleton	.10
241	Alan Trammell	.10
242	David Wells	.10
243	Lou Whitaker	.10
244	Rick Aguilera	.10
245	Scott Erickson	.10
246	Brian Harper	.10
247	Kent Hrbek	.10
248	Chuck Knoblauch	.10
249	Shane Mack	.10
250	David McCarty	.10
251	Pedro Munoz	.10
252	Dave Winfield	1.50
253	Alex Fernandez	.10
254	Ozzie Guillen	.10
255	Bo Jackson	.20
256	Lance Johnson	.10
257	Ron Karkovice	.10
258	Jack McDowell	.10
259	Tim Raines	.10
260	Frank Thomas	1.50
261	Robin Ventura	.10
262	Jim Abbott	.10
263	Steve Farr	.10
264	Jimmy Key	.10
265	Don Mattingly	2.25
266	Paul O'Neill	.10
267	Mike Stanley	.10
268	Danny Tartabull	.10
269	Bob Wickman	.10
270	Bernie Williams	.10
271	Jason Bere	.10
272	Roger Cedeno **RC**	.50
273	Johnny Damon **RC**	12.00
274	Russ Davis **RC**	.25
275	Carlos Delgado	.75
276	Carl Everett	.10
277	Cliff Floyd	.10
278	Alex Gonzalez	.10
279	Derek Jeter **RC**	75.00
280	Chipper Jones	2.00
281	Javier Lopez	.10
282	Chad Mottola **RC**	.10
283	Marc Newfield	.10
284	Eduardo Perez	.10
285	Manny Ramirez	1.50
286	Todd Steverson **RC**	.10
287	Michael Tucker	.10
288	Allen Watson	.10
289	Rondell White	.10
290	Dmitri Young	.10

Platinum Power

This 20-card insert set features 20 of the game's top home run hitters. The top of each insert card features a special die cut treatment. Backs are numbered with a PP prefix.

		NM/M
Complete Set (20):		27.50
Common Player:		.50
1	Albert Belle	.50
2	Barry Bonds	5.00
3	Joe Carter	.50
4	Will Clark	.50
5	Darren Daulton	.50
6	Cecil Fielder	.50
7	Ron Gant	.50
8	Juan Gonzalez	1.00
9	Ken Griffey Jr.	3.00
10	Dave Hollins	.50
11	Dave Justice	.50
12	Fred McGriff	.50
13	Mark McGwire	5.00
14	Dean Palmer	.50
15	Mike Piazza	3.00
16	Tim Salmon	.50
17	Ryne Sandberg	2.50
18	Gary Sheffield	.75
19	Frank Thomas	2.00
20	Matt Williams	.50

Jumbos

These jumbo-size (8-1/2" x 11") versions of the players' 1993 SP cards were sold through Upper Deck Authenticated. Each player's jumbo card was produced in a limited edition of 1,000, except for Frank Thomas, whose jumbo card was an edition of 1,993. The jumbos were sold in heavy plastic screwdown holders.

		NM/M
Complete Set (5):		35.00
Common Player:		5.00
10	Barry Bonds	12.50
58	Tom Glavine	6.00
173	Lenny Dykstra	5.00
199	Roger Clemens	10.00
260	Frank Thomas	7.50

1994 SP Promo

Virtually identical to the issued version of Ken Griffey, Jr.'s card in the regular SP set (#105) this differs in the card number on the back (#24) and

the inclusion on front and back of the notice, "For Promotional Use Only."

		NM/M
24	Ken Griffey Jr.	3.00

1994 SP

The second edition of Upper Deck's top-shelf SP brand features each card with a front background printed on metallic foil; the first 20 cards in the set, a series of "Prospects," have front backgrounds of textured metallic foil. Backs are printed with standard processes and include a color player photo a few stats and typical copyright notice and logos. Each foil pack contains one card featuring a special die-cut treatment at top.

		NM/M
Complete Set (200):		100.00
Common Player:		.10
Die-Cut:		1-2X
Pack (8):		15.00
Wax Box (32):		450.00
1	Mike Bell **RC**	.10
2	D.J. Boston	.10
3	Johnny Damon	.45
4	Brad Fullmer **RC**	.75
5	Joey Hamilton	.10
6	Todd Hollandsworth	.10
7	Brian Hunter	.10
8	LaTroy Hawkins **RC**	.25
9	Brooks Kieschnick **RC**	.10
10	Derrek Lee **RC**	15.00
11	Trot Nixon **RC**	3.00
12	Alex Ochoa	.10
13	Chan Ho Park **RC**	1.50
14	Kirk Presley **RC**	.10
15	Alex Rodriguez **RC**	140.00
16	Jose Silva **RC**	.10
17	Terrell Wade **RC**	.10
18	Billy Wagner **RC**	1.00
19	Glenn Williams **RC**	.10
20	Preston Wilson	.10
21	Brian Anderson	.10
22	Chad Curtis	.10
23	Chili Davis	.10
24	Bo Jackson	.25
25	Mark Langston	.10
26	Tim Salmon	.10
27	Jeff Bagwell	1.00
28	Craig Biggio	.10
29	Ken Caminiti	.10
30	Doug Drabek	.10
31	John Hudek	.10
32	Greg Swindell	.10
33	Brent Gates	.10
34	Rickey Henderson	1.00
35	Steve Karsay	.10
36	Mark McGwire	2.50
37	Ruben Sierra	.10
38	Terry Steinbach	.10
39	Roberto Alomar	.30
40	Joe Carter	.10
41	Carlos Delgado	.50
42	Alex Gonzalez	.10
43	Juan Guzman	.10
44	Paul Molitor	1.00
45	John Olerud	.10

46	Devon White	.10
47	Steve Avery	.10
48	Jeff Blauser	.10
49	Tom Glavine	.35
50	Dave Justice	.10
51	Roberto Kelly	.10
52	Ryan Klesko	.10
53	Javier Lopez	.10
54	Greg Maddux	1.25
55	Fred McGriff	.10
56	Ricky Bones	.10
57	Cal Eldred	.10
58	Brian Harper	.10
59	Pat Listach	.10
60	B.J. Surhoff	.10
61	Greg Vaughn	.10
62	Bernard Gilkey	.10
63	Gregg Jefferies	.10
64	Ray Lankford	.10
65	Ozzie Smith	1.25
66	Bob Tewksbury	.10
67	Mark Whiten	.10
68	Todd Zeile	.10
69	Mark Grace	.10
70	Randy Myers	.10
71	Ryne Sandberg	1.25
72	Sammy Sosa	1.25
73	Steve Trachsel	.10
74	Rick Wilkins	.10
75	Brett Butler	.10
76	Delino DeShields	.10
77	Orel Hershiser	.10
78	Eric Karros	.10
79	Raul Mondesi	.10
80	Mike Piazza	2.00
81	Tim Wallach	.10
82	Moises Alou	.10
83	Cliff Floyd	.10
84	Marquis Grissom	.10
85	Pedro Martinez	1.00
86	Larry Walker	.10
87	John Wetteland	.10
88	Rondell White	.10
89	Rod Beck	.10
90	Barry Bonds	3.00
91	John Burkett	.10
92	Royce Clayton	.10
93	Billy Swift	.10
94	Robby Thompson	.10
95	Matt Williams	.10
96	Carlos Baerga	.10
97	Albert Belle	.10
98	Kenny Lofton	.10
99	Dennis Martinez	.10
100	Eddie Murray	1.00
101	Manny Ramirez	1.00
102	Eric Anthony	.10
103	Chris Bosio	.10
104	Jay Buhner	.10
105	Ken Griffey Jr.	2.00
106	Randy Johnson	1.00
107	Edgar Martinez	.10
108	Chuck Carr	.10
109	Jeff Conine	.10
110	Carl Everett	.10
111	Chris Hammond	.10
112	Bryan Harvey	.10
113	Charles Johnson	.10
114	Gary Sheffield	.45
115	Bobby Bonilla	.10
116	Dwight Gooden	.10
117	Todd Hundley	.10
118	Bobby Jones	.10
119	Jeff Kent	.10
120	Bret Saberhagen	.10
121	Jeffrey Hammonds	.10
122	Chris Hoiles	.10
123	Ben McDonald	.10
124	Mike Mussina	.40
125	Rafael Palmeiro	.75
126	Cal Ripken, Jr.	3.00
127	Lee Smith	.10
128	Derek Bell	.10
129	Andy Benes	.10
130	Tony Gwynn	1.25
131	Trevor Hoffman	.10
132	Phil Plantier	.10
133	Bip Roberts	.10
134	Darren Daulton	.10
135	Len Dykstra	.10
136	Dave Hollins	.10
137	Danny Jackson	.10
138	John Kruk	.10
139	Kevin Stocker	.10
140	Jay Bell	.10
141	Carlos Garcia	.10
142	Jeff King	.10
143	Orlando Merced	.10
144	Andy Van Slyke	.10
145	Paul Wagner	.10
146	Jose Canseco	.50
147	Will Clark	.10
148	Juan Gonzalez	.50
149	Rick Helling	.10
150	Dean Palmer	.10
151	Ivan Rodriguez	.75
152	Roger Clemens	1.50
153	Scott Cooper	.10
154	Andre Dawson	.30
155	Mike Greenwell	.10
156	Aaron Sele	.10
157	Mo Vaughn	.10
158	Bret Boone	.10
159	Barry Larkin	.10
160	Kevin Mitchell	.10
161	Jose Rijo	.10
162	Deion Sanders	.10
163	Reggie Sanders	.10
164	Dante Bichette	.10
165	Ellis Burks	.10
166	Andres Galarraga	.10
167	Charlie Hayes	.10
168	David Nied	.10
169	Walt Weiss	.10
170	Kevin Appier	.10
171	David Cone	.10
172	Jeff Granger	.10
173	Felix Jose	.10
174	Wally Joyner	.10
175	Brian McRae	.10
176	Cecil Fielder	.10
177	Travis Fryman	.10
178	Mike Henneman	.10
179	Tony Phillips	.10
180	Mickey Tettleton	.10
181	Alan Trammell	.10
182	Rick Aguilera	.10
183	Rich Becker	.10
184	Scott Erickson	.10
185	Chuck Knoblauch	.10
186	Kirby Puckett	1.25
187	Dave Winfield	1.00
188	Wilson Alvarez	.10
189	Jason Bere	.10
190	Alex Fernandez	.10
191	Julio Franco	.10
192	Jack McDowell	.10
193	Frank Thomas	1.00
194	Robin Ventura	.10
195	Jim Abbott	.10
196	Wade Boggs	1.25
197	Jimmy Key	.10
198	Don Mattingly	1.50
199	Paul O'Neill	.10
200	Danny Tartabull	.10

Die-Cut

Upper Deck SP Die-cuts are a 200-card parallel set inserted at the rate of one per foil pack. Each card has a die-cut top instead of the flat-top found on regular SP cards. Die-cuts also have a silver-foil Upper Deck hologram logo on back, in contrast to the gold-tone hologram found on regular SP; this is an effort to prevent fraudulent replication by any crook with a pair of scissors.

Holoview Blue

Holoview F/X Blue is a 38-card set utilizing Holoview printing technology, which uses 200 frames of video to produce a three-dimensional image on the bottom third of each card. The hologram is bordered in blue and there is a blue stripe running down the right side of the card. Backs are done with a blue background and feature a player photo over top of bold letters reading "Holoview FX." This insert could be found in one per five packs of SP baseball.

		NM/M
	Common Player:	1.50
1	Roberto Alomar	2.00
2	Kevin Appier	1.50
3	Jeff Bagwell	3.00
4	Jose Canseco	3.00
5	Roger Clemens	6.00
6	Carlos Delgado	2.00
7	Cecil Fielder	1.50
8	Cliff Floyd	1.50
9	Travis Fryman	1.50
10	Andres Galarraga	1.50
11	Juan Gonzalez	2.00
12	Ken Griffey Jr.	6.00
13	Tony Gwynn	4.00
14	Jeffrey Hammonds	1.50
15	Bo Jackson	3.00
16	Michael Jordan	15.00
17	Dave Justice	1.50
18	Steve Karsay	1.50
19	Jeff Kent	2.00
20	Brooks Kieschnick	1.50
21	Ryan Klesko	1.50
22	John Kruk	1.50
23	Barry Larkin	2.00
24	Pat Listach	1.50
25	Don Mattingly	5.00
26	Mark McGwire	8.00
27	Raul Mondesi	1.50
28	Trot Nixon	1.50
29	Mike Piazza	6.00
30	Kirby Puckett	4.00
31	Manny Ramirez	3.00
32	Cal Ripken, Jr.	10.00
33	Alex Rodriguez	60.00
34	Tim Salmon	1.50
35	Gary Sheffield	2.00
36	Ozzie Smith	4.00
37	Sammy Sosa	4.00
38	Andy Van Slyke	1.50

Holoview Blue Mismatches

Some Holoview Blue inserts are known on which the player photograph and data do not match the player shown in the horizontal hologram at bottom front.

Holoview Red

Holoview F/X Red is a parallel set to the Blue insert. Once again, this 38-card set utilizes Holoview printing technology. However, these cards have a red border surrounding the hologram and along the right side, as well as a red background on the back and a large "SPECIAL FX" under the player photo. Holoview red cards also have die-cut tops. Red cards are much scarcer than blue; the red being inserted once per 75 packs of SP baseball.

		NM/M
	Common Player:	12.00
1	Roberto Alomar	15.00
2	Kevin Appier	12.00
3	Jeff Bagwell	30.00
4	Jose Canseco	20.00
5	Roger Clemens	50.00
6	Carlos Delgado	20.00
7	Cecil Fielder	12.00
8	Cliff Floyd	12.00
9	Travis Fryman	12.00
10	Andres Galarraga	12.00
11	Juan Gonzalez	20.00
12	Ken Griffey Jr.	50.00
13	Tony Gwynn	40.00
14	Jeffrey Hammonds	12.00
15	Bo Jackson	20.00
16	Michael Jordan	120.00
17	Dave Justice	12.00
18	Steve Karsay	12.00
19	Jeff Kent	12.00
20	Brooks Kieschnick	12.00
21	Ryan Klesko	12.00
22	John Kruk	12.00
23	Barry Larkin	12.00
24	Pat Listach	12.00
25	Don Mattingly	45.00
26	Mark McGwire	60.00
27	Raul Mondesi	12.00
28	Trot Nixon	20.00
29	Mike Piazza	50.00
30	Kirby Puckett	40.00
31	Manny Ramirez	30.00
32	Cal Ripken, Jr.	80.00
33	Alex Rodriguez	1,200
34	Tim Salmon	12.00
35	Gary Sheffield	15.00
36	Ozzie Smith	40.00
37	Sammy Sosa	40.00
38	Andy Van Slyke	12.00

Alex Rodriguez Autographed Jumbo

This 3-1/2" x 5" version of A-Rod's SP rookie card was produced in an authentically autographed edition of 500. The card has serial numbers on front and back and a numbered UD Authenticated hologram sticker on front. The card was sold sealed in a heavy plastic holder and velour drawstring bag.

		NM/M
15	Alex Rodriguez	250.00

1995 SP

Foil highlights and die-cut specialty cards are once again featured in Upper Deck's premium-brand SP baseball card issue. The 207-card set opens with four die-cut tribute cards, followed by 20 Premier Prospect die-cuts printed on metallic foil backgrounds with copper-foil highlights. Three checklists follow, also die-cut. The regular player cards in the set are arranged in team-alphabetical order within league. Card fronts feature photos which are borderless at top, bottom and right. On the left is a gold-highlighted metallic foil border of blue for N.L., red for A.L. Backs have a large photo at top, with a few stats and career highlights at bottom, along with a gold infield-shaped hologram. The SP insert program consists of a "SuperbaFoil" parallel set, in which each card's normal foil highlights are replaced with silver foil; a 48-card Special F/X set utilizing holographic portraits, and, a 20-card Platinum Power set. The hobby-only SP was issued in eight-card foil packs with a $3.99 suggested retail price.

		NM/M
	Complete Set (207):	12.50
	Common Player:	.05
	Pack (8):	1.25
	Wax Box (32):	25.00
1	Cal Ripken Jr. (Salute)	2.00
2	Nolan Ryan (Salute)	2.00
3	George Brett (Salute)	1.25
4	Mike Schmidt (Salute)	1.25
5	Dustin Hermanson (Premier Prospects)	.05
6	Antonio Osuna (Premier Prospects)	.05
7	Mark Grudzielanek **RC** (Premier Prospects)	.35
8	Ray Durham (Premier Prospects)	.05
9	Ugueth Urbina (Premier Prospects)	.05
10	Ruben Rivera (Premier Prospects)	.05
11	Curtis Goodwin (Premier Prospects)	.05
12	Jimmy Hurst (Premier Prospects)	.05
13	Jose Malave (Premier Prospects)	.05
14	Hideo Nomo **RC** (Premier Prospects)	1.50
15	Juan Acevedo (Premier Prospects)	.05
16	Tony Clark (Premier Prospects)	.05
17	Jim Pittsley (Premier Prospects)	.05
18	Freddy Garcia **RC** (Premier Prospects)	.50
19	Carlos Perez **RC** (Premier Prospects)	.05
20	Raul Casanova **RC** (Premier Prospects)	.05
21	Quilvio Veras (Premier Prospects)	.05
22	Edgardo Alfonzo (Premier Prospects)	.05
23	Marty Cordova (Premier Prospects)	.05
24	C.J. Nitkowski (Premier Prospects)	.05
25	Checklist 1-69 (Wade Boggs)	.30
26	Checklist 70-138 (Dave Winfield)	.25
27	Checklist 139-207 (Eddie Murray)	.25
28	Dave Justice	.05
29	Marquis Grissom	.05
30	Fred McGriff	.05
31	Greg Maddux	1.00
32	Tom Glavine	.35
33	Steve Avery	.05
34	Chipper Jones	1.00
35	Sammy Sosa	1.00
36	Jaime Navarro	.05
37	Randy Myers	.05
38	Mark Grace	.05
39	Todd Zeile	.05
40	Brian McRae	.05
41	Reggie Sanders	.05
42	Ron Gant	.05
43	Deion Sanders	.05
44	Barry Larkin	.05
45	Bret Boone	.05
46	Jose Rijo	.05
47	Jason Bates	.05
48	Andres Galarraga	.05
49	Bill Swift	.05
50	Larry Walker	.05
51	Vinny Castilla	.05
52	Dante Bichette	.05
53	Jeff Conine	.05
54	John Burkett	.05
55	Gary Sheffield	.40
56	Andre Dawson	.30
57	Terry Pendleton	.05
58	Charles Johnson	.05
59	Brian L. Hunter	.05
60	Jeff Bagwell	.75
61	Craig Biggio	.05
62	Phil Nevin	.05
63	Doug Drabek	.05
64	Derek Bell	.05
65	Raul Mondesi	.05
66	Eric Karros	.05
67	Roger Cedeno	.05
68	Delino DeShields	.05
69	Ramon Martinez	.05
70	Mike Piazza	1.50
71	Billy Ashley	.05
72	Jeff Fassero	.05
73	Shane Andrews	.05
74	Wil Cordero	.05
75	Tony Tarasco	.05
76	Rondell White	.05
77	Pedro Martinez	.75
78	Moises Alou	.05
79	Rico Brogna	.05
80	Bobby Bonilla	.05
81	Jeff Kent	.05
82	Brett Butler	.05
83	Bobby Jones	.05
84	Bill Pulsipher	.05
85	Bret Saberhagen	.05
86	Gregg Jefferies	.05
87	Lenny Dykstra	.05
88	Dave Hollins	.05
89	Charlie Hayes	.05
90	Darren Daulton	.05
91	Curt Schilling	.35
92	Heathcliff Slocumb	.05
93	Carlos Garcia	.05
94	Denny Neagle	.05
95	Jay Bell	.05
96	Orlando Merced	.05
97	Dave Clark	.05
98	Bernard Gilkey	.05
99	Scott Cooper	.05
100	Ozzie Smith	1.00
100	Ken Griffey Jr. (Promo Card)	2.00
101	Tom Henke	.05
102	Ken Hill	.05
103	Brian Jordan	.05
104	Ray Lankford	.05
105	Tony Gwynn	1.00
106	Andy Benes	.05
107	Ken Caminiti	.05
108	Steve Finley	.05
109	Joey Hamilton	.05
110	Bip Roberts	.05
111	Eddie Williams	.05
112	Rod Beck	.05
113	Matt Williams	.05
114	Glenallen Hill	.05
115	Barry Bonds	2.50
116	Robby Thompson	.05
117	Mark Portugal	.05
118	Brady Anderson	.05
119	Mike Mussina	.35
120	Rafael Palmeiro	.65
121	Chris Hoiles	.05
122	Harold Baines	.05
123	Jeffrey Hammonds	.05
124	Tim Naehring	.05
125	Mo Vaughn	.05
126	Mike Macfarlane	.05
127	Roger Clemens	1.25
128	John Valentin	.05
129	Aaron Sele	.05
130	Jose Canseco	.50
131	J.T. Snow	.05
132	Mark Langston	.05
133	Chili Davis	.05
134	Chuck Finley	.05
135	Tim Salmon	.05
136	Tony Phillips	.05
137	Jason Bere	.05
138	Robin Ventura	.05
139	Tim Raines	.05
140a	Frank Thomas (5-yr. BA .326)	.75
140b	Frank Thomas (5-yr. BA .303)	.75
141	Alex Fernandez	.05
142	Jim Abbott	.05
143	Wilson Alvarez	.05
144	Carlos Baerga	.05
145	Albert Belle	.05
146	Jim Thome	.65
147	Dennis Martinez	.05
148	Eddie Murray	.75
149	Dave Winfield	.75
150	Kenny Lofton	.05
151	Manny Ramirez	.75
152	Chad Curtis	.05
153	Lou Whitaker	.05
154	Alan Trammell	.05
155	Cecil Fielder	.05
156	Kirk Gibson	.05
157	Michael Tucker	.05
158	Jon Nunnally	.05
159	Wally Joyner	.05
160	Kevin Appier	.05
161	Jeff Montgomery	.05
162	Greg Gagne	.05
163	Ricky Bones	.05
164	Cal Eldred	.05
165	Greg Vaughn	.05
166	Kevin Seitzer	.05
167	Jose Valentin	.05
168	Joe Oliver	.05
169	Rick Aguilera	.05
170	Kirby Puckett	1.00
171	Scott Stahoviak	.05
172	Kevin Tapani	.05
173	Chuck Knoblauch	.05
174	Rich Becker	.05
175	Don Mattingly	1.25
176	Jack McDowell	.05
177	Jimmy Key	.05
178	Paul O'Neill	.05
179	John Wetteland	.05
180	Wade Boggs	1.00
181	Derek Jeter	2.50
182	Rickey Henderson	.75

183 Terry Steinbach .05
184 Ruben Sierra .05
185 Mark McGwire 2.00
186 Todd Stottlemyre .05
187 Dennis Eckersley .65
188 Alex Rodriguez 2.00
189 Randy Johnson .75
190 Ken Griffey Jr. 1.50
191 Tino Martinez .05
192 Jay Buhner .05
193 Edgar Martinez .05
194 Mickey Tettleton .05
195 Juan Gonzalez .40
196 Benji Gil .05
197 Dean Palmer .05
198 Ivan Rodriguez .65
199 Kenny Rogers .05
200 Will Clark .05
201 Roberto Alomar .20
202 David Cone .05
203 Paul Molitor .75
204 Shawn Green .40
205 Joe Carter .05
206 Alex Gonzalez .05
207 Pat Hentgen .05

SuperbaFoil

This chase set parallels the 207 regular cards in the SP issue. Cards were found at the rate of one per eight-card foil pack. SuperbaFoil cards feature a silver-rainbow metallic foil in place of the gold, copper, red or blue foil highlights on regular-issue SP cards. On back, the SuperbaFoil inserts have a silver hologram instead of the gold version found on standard cards.

	NM/M
Complete Set (207):	30.00
Common Player:	.10
SuperbaFoil Stars:	1.5X

Platinum Power

This die-cut insert set features the game's top power hitters in color action photos set against a background of two-toned gold rays emanating from the SP logo at lower-right. Player name, team and position are printed in white in a black band at bottom. Backs repeat the golden ray effect in the background and have a color photo at center. Career and 1994 stats are presented. An infield-shaped gold foil hologram is at lower-right. Cards have a "PP" prefix. Stated odds of finding one of the 20 Platinum Power inserts are one per five packs.

	NM/M
Complete Set (20):	10.00
Common Player:	.20

1 Jeff Bagwell .75
2 Barry Bonds 2.00
3 Ron Gant .20
4 Fred McGriff .20
5 Raul Mondesi .20
6 Mike Piazza 1.25
7 Larry Walker .20
8 Matt Williams .20
9 Albert Belle .20
10 Cecil Fielder .20
11 Juan Gonzalez .40
12 Ken Griffey Jr. 1.25
13 Mark McGwire 1.50
14 Eddie Murray .75
15 Manny Ramirez .75
16 Cal Ripken Jr. 2.00
17 Tim Salmon .20
18 Frank Thomas .75
19 Jim Thome .65
20 Mo Vaughn .20

Special F/X

By far the preferred pick of the '95 SP insert program is the Special F/X set of 48. The cards have a color action photo on front, printed on a metallic foil background. A 3/4" square holographic portrait is printed on the front. Backs are printed in standard technology and include another photo and a few stats and career highlights. Stated odds of finding a Special F/X card are 1 per 75 packs, or about one per two boxes.

	NM/M
Complete Set (48):	200.00
Common Player:	2.00

1 Jose Canseco 6.00
2 Roger Clemens 20.00
3 Mo Vaughn 2.00
4 Tim Salmon 2.00
5 Chuck Finley 2.00
6 Robin Ventura 2.00
7 Jason Bere 2.00
8 Carlos Baerga 2.00
9 Albert Belle 2.00
10 Kenny Lofton 3.00
11 Manny Ramirez 8.00
12 Jeff Montgomery 2.00
13 Kirby Puckett 15.00
14 Wade Boggs 5.00
15 Don Mattingly 15.00
16 Cal Ripken Jr. 25.00
17 Ruben Sierra 2.00
18 Ken Griffey Jr. 20.00
19 Randy Johnson 8.00
20 Alex Rodriguez 25.00
21 Will Clark 5.00
22 Juan Gonzalez 4.00
23 Roberto Alomar 4.00
24 Joe Carter 3.00
25 Alex Gonzalez 2.00
26 Paul Molitor 6.00
27 Ryan Klesko 2.00
28 Fred McGriff 3.00
29 Greg Maddux 15.00
30 Sammy Sosa 10.00
31 Bret Boone 2.00
32 Barry Larkin 5.00
33 Reggie Sanders 2.00
34 Dante Bichette 2.00
35 Andres Galarraga 2.00
36 Charles Johnson 2.00
37 Gary Sheffield 5.00
38 Jeff Bagwell 6.00
39 Craig Biggio 4.00
40 Eric Karros 2.00
41 Billy Ashley 2.00
42 Raul Mondesi 2.00
43 Mike Piazza 10.00
44 Rondell White 2.00
45 Bret Saberhagen 2.00
46 Tony Gwynn 8.00
47 Melvin Nieves 2.00
48 Matt Williams 2.00

Griffey Gold Signature

A specially autographed version of Griffey's card from 1995 SP was made available from Upper Deck Authenticat-

ed. These cards are signed and numbered in gold ink from within an edition of 1,000.

		NM/M
190	Ken Griffey Jr.	65.00

1995 SP/ Championship

Championship was a version of Upper Deck's popular SP line designed for sale in retail outlets. The first 20 cards in the set are a "Diamond in the Rough" subset featuring hot rookies printed on textured metallic foil background. Regular player cards are arranged by team within league, alphabetically by city name. Each team set is led off with a "Pro Files" card of a star player; those card backs feature team season and post-season results. Each of the regular player cards has a borderless action photo on front, highlighted with a gold-foil SP Championship logo. The team name is in a blue-foil oval on National Leaguers' cards; red on American Leaguers. Backs have a portrait photo, a few stats and career highlights. Situated between the N.L. and A.L. cards in the checklist are a subset of 15 October Legends. A parallel set of cards with die-cut tops was inserted into the six-card foil packs at the rate of one per pack. A special card honoring Cal Ripken's consecutive-game record was issued as a super-scarce insert.

	NM/M
Complete Set (200):	25.00
Common Player:	.05
Die-Cuts:	1.5X
Wax Pack (6):	1.00
Wax Box (44):	30.00

1 Hideo Nomo **RC** (Diamonds in the Rough) 1.50
2 Roger Cedeno (Diamonds in the Rough) .05
3 Curtis Goodwin (Diamonds in the Rough) .05
4 Jon Nunnally (Diamonds in the Rough) .05
5 Bill Pulsipher (Diamonds in the Rough) .05
6 C.J. Nitkowski (Diamonds in the Rough) .05
7 Dustin Hermanson (Diamonds in the Rough) .05
8 Marty Cordova (Diamonds in the Rough) .05
9 Ruben Rivera (Diamonds in the Rough) .05
10 Ariel Prieto **RC** (Diamonds in the Rough) .05
11 Edgardo Alfonzo (Diamonds in the Rough) .05
12 Ray Durham (Diamonds in the Rough) .05
13 Quilvio Veras (Diamonds in the Rough) .05
14 Ugueth Urbina (Diamonds in the Rough) .05
15 Carlos Perez **RC** (Diamonds in the Rough) .05
16 Glenn Dishman **RC** (Diamonds in the Rough) .05
17 Jeff Suppan (Diamonds in the Rough) .05
18 Jason Bates (Diamonds in the Rough) .05
19 Jason Isringhausen (Diamonds in the Rough) .05
20 Derek Jeter (Diamonds in the Rough) 2.00
21 Fred McGriff (Major League ProFiles) .05
22 Marquis Grissom .05
23 Fred McGriff .05
24 Tom Glavine .35
25 Greg Maddux 1.00
26 Chipper Jones 1.00
27 Sammy Sosa (Major League ProFiles) .50
28 Randy Myers .05
29 Mark Grace .05
30 Sammy Sosa 1.00
31 Todd Zeile .05
32 Brian McRae .05
33 Ron Gant (Major League ProFiles) .05
34 Reggie Sanders .05
35 Ron Gant .05
36 Barry Larkin .05
37 Bret Boone .05
38 John Smiley .05
39 Larry Walker (Major League ProFiles) .05
40 Andres Galarraga .05
41 Bill Swift .05
42 Larry Walker .05
43 Vinny Castilla .05
44 Dante Bichette .05
45 Jeff Conine (Major League ProFiles) .05
46 Charles Johnson .05
47 Gary Sheffield .45
48 Andre Dawson .25
49 Jeff Conine .05
50 Jeff Bagwell (Major League ProFiles) .40
51 Phil Nevin .05
52 Craig Biggio .05
53 Brian L. Hunter .05
54 Doug Drabek .05
55 Jeff Bagwell .75
56 Derek Bell .05
57 Mike Piazza (Major League ProFiles) .65
58 Raul Mondesi .05
59 Eric Karros .05
60 Mike Piazza 1.25
61 Ramon Martinez .05
62 Billy Ashley .05
63 Rondell White (Major League ProFiles) .05
64 Jeff Fassero .05
65 Moises Alou .05
66 Tony Tarasco .05
67 Rondell White .05
68 Pedro Martinez .75
69 Bobby Jones (Major League ProFiles) .05
70 Bobby Bonilla .05
71 Bobby Jones .05
72 Bret Saberhagen .05
73 Darren Daulton (Major League ProFiles) .05
74 Darren Daulton .05
75 Gregg Jefferies .05
76 Tyler Green .05
77 Heathcliff Slocumb .05
78 Lenny Dykstra .05
79 Jay Bell (Major League ProFiles) .05
80 Denny Neagle .05
81 Orlando Merced .05
82 Jay Bell .05
83 Ozzie Smith (Major League ProFiles) .50
84 Ken Hill .05
85 Ozzie Smith 1.00
86 Bernard Gilkey .05
87 Ray Lankford .05
88 Tony Gwynn (Major League ProFiles) .50
89 Ken Caminiti .05
90 Tony Gwynn 1.00
91 Joey Hamilton .05
92 Bip Roberts .05
93 Deion Sanders (Major League ProFiles) .05
94 Glenallen Hill .05
95 Matt Williams .05
96 Barry Bonds 2.00
97 Rod Beck .05
98 Eddie Murray (Checklist) .35
99 Cal Ripken Jr. (Checklist) 1.00
100 Roberto Alomar (October Legends) .10
101 George Brett (October Legends) .60
102 Joe Carter (Ocober Legends) .05
103 Will Clark (October Legends) .05
104 Dennis Eckersley (October Legends) .40
105 Whitey Ford (October Legends) .40
106 Steve Garvey (October Legends) .05
107 Kirk Gibson (October Legends) .05
108 Orel Hershiser (October Legends) .05
109 Reggie Jackson (October Legends) .50
110 Paul Molitor (October Legends) .40
111 Kirby Puckett (October Legends) .50
112 Mike Schmidt (October Legends) .60
113 Dave Stewart (October Legends) .05
114 Alan Trammell (October Legends) .05
115 Cal Ripken Jr. (Major League ProFiles) 1.00
116 Brady Anderson .05
117 Mike Mussina .30
118 Rafael Palmeiro .65
119 Chris Hoiles .05
120 Cal Ripken Jr. 2.00
121 Mo Vaughn (Major League ProFiles) .05
122 Roger Clemens 1.25
123 Tim Naehring .05
124 John Valentin .05
125 Mo Vaughn .05
126 Tim Wakefield .05
127 Jose Canseco .40
128 Rick Aguilera .05
129 Chili Davis (Major League ProFiles) .05
130 Lee Smith .05
131 Jim Edmonds .05
132 Chuck Finley .05
133 Chili Davis .05
134 J.T. Snow .05
135 Tim Salmon .05
136 Frank Thomas (Major League ProFiles) .45
137 Jason Bere .05
138 Robin Ventura .05
139 Tim Raines .05
140 Frank Thomas .75
141 Alex Fernandez .05
142 Eddie Murray (Major League ProFiles) .40
143 Carlos Baerga .05
144 Eddie Murray .75
145 Albert Belle .05
146 Jim Thome .65
147 Dennis Martinez .05
148 Dave Winfield .75
149 Kenny Lofton .05
150 Manny Ramirez .75
151 Cecil Fielder (Major League ProFiles) .05
152 Lou Whitaker .05
153 Alan Trammell .05
154 Kirk Gibson .05
155 Cecil Fielder .05
156 Bobby Higginson **RC** .25
157 Kevin Appier (Major League ProFiles) .05
158 Wally Joyner .05
159 Jeff Montgomery .05
160 Kevin Appier .05
161 Gary Gaetti .05
162 Greg Gagne .05
163 Ricky Bones (Major League ProFiles) .05
164 Greg Vaughn .05
165 Kevin Seitzer .05
166 Ricky Bones .05
167 Kirby Puckett (Major League ProFiles) .50
168 Pedro Munoz .05
169 Chuck Knoblauch .05
170 Kirby Puckett 1.00
171 Don Mattingly (Major League ProFiles) .60
172 Wade Boggs 1.00
173 Paul O'Neill .05
174 John Wetteland .05
175 Don Mattingly 1.25
176 Jack McDowell .05
177 Mark McGwire (Major League ProFiles) .75
178 Rickey Henderson .75
179 Terry Steinbach .05
180 Ruben Sierra .05
181 Mark McGwire 1.50
182 Dennis Eckersley .05
183 Ken Griffey Jr. (Major League ProFiles) .65
184 Alex Rodriguez 1.50
185 Ken Griffey Jr. 1.25
186 Randy Johnson .75
187 Jay Buhner .05
188 Edgar Martinez .05
189 Will Clark (Major League ProFiles) .05
190 Juan Gonzalez .40
191 Benji Gil .05
192 Ivan Rodriguez .65
193 Kenny Rogers .05
194 Will Clark .05
195 Paul Molitor (Major League ProFiles) .40
196 Roberto Alomar .20
197 David Cone .05
198 Paul Molitor .75
199 Shawn Green .30
200 Joe Carter .05
CR1 Cal Ripken Jr. (2,131 games tribute) 5.00
CR1 Cal Ripken Jr. Die-Cut 7.50

Die-Cuts

Each of the 200 cards in the regular SP championship issue, plus the 20 insert cards, can also be found in a parallel chase card set with die-cut tops. One die-cut card was found in each six-card foil pack, making them five times scarcer than the regular cards. To prevent regular cards from being fraudulently cut, factory-issue die-cuts have the Upper Deck hologram on back in silver tone, rather than the gold holograms found on regular cards.

	NM/M
Complete Set (200):	50.00
Common Player:	.25
Die-Cut Stars:	1.5X

Classic Performances

Vintage action photos are featured in this chase set marking great post-season performances of modern times. The cards have a wide red strip at top with "CLASSIC PERFORMANCES" in gold-foil; the player's name, team and the SP Championship embossed logo at bottom are also in gold. Backs have a portrait photo and description of the highlight along with stats from that series. Regular Classic Performances cards are found at a stated rate of one per 15 foil packs, with die-cut versions in every 75 packs, on average. The die-cuts have silver UD holograms on back as opposed to the gold hologram found on regular versions of the chase cards.

	NM/M
Complete Set (10):	8.00

Common Player: .50
Complete Die-Cut Set (10): 16.00
Common Die-Cuts: 1.00
CP1 Reggie Jackson (Game 6 of '77 WS) .60
CP1 Reggie Jackson (Die-Cut) 2.00
CP2 Nolan Ryan (Game 3 of '69 WS) 4.00
CP2 Nolan Ryan (Die-Cut) 8.00
CP3 Kirk Gibson (Game 1 of '88 WS) .50
CP3 Kirk Gibson (Die-Cut) 1.00
CP4 Joe Carter (Game 6 of '93 WS) .50
CP4 Joe Carter (Die-Cut) 1.00
CP5 George Brett (Game 3 of '80 ALCS) 1.25
CP5 George Brett (Die-Cut) 2.50
CP6 Roberto Alomar (Game 4 of '92 ALCS) .50
CP6 Roberto Alomar (Die-Cut) 1.00
CP7 Ozzie Smith (Game 5 of '85 NLCS) .75
CP7 Ozzie Smith (Die-Cut) 2.00
CP8 Kirby Puckett (Game 6 of '91 WS) 1.25
CP8 Kirby Puckett (Die-Cut) 2.00
CP9 Bret Saberhagen (Game 7 of '85 WS) .50
CP9 Bret Saberhagen (Die-Cut) 1.00
CP10 Steve Garvey (Game 4 of '84 NLCS) .50
CP10 Steve Garvey (Die-Cut) 1.00

Destination: Fall Classic

Colored foil background printing and copper-foil graphic highlights are featured on this insert set picturing players who, for the most part, had yet to make a post-season appearance prior to 1995's expanded playoffs. Found at a stated average rate of one per 40 foil packs, the cards have short career summaries and another photo on back. A die-cut version of the cards was also issued, with a silver UD hologram on back rather than the gold found on the standard chase cards. The die-cut Fall Classic cards were inserted at a rate of one per 75 packs.

NM/M
Complete Set (9): 18.00
Common Player: 1.00
Complete Die-Cut Set (9): 36.00
Common Die-Cut: 2.00
1 Ken Griffey Jr. 3.00
1 Ken Griffey Jr. (Die-Cut) 6.00
2 Frank Thomas 2.00
2 Frank Thomas (Die-Cut) 4.00
3 Albert Belle 1.00
3 Albert Belle (Die-Cut) 2.00
4 Mike Piazza 3.00
4 Mike Piazza (Die-Cut) 6.00
5 Don Mattingly 2.75
5 Don Mattingly (Die-Cut) 5.50
6 Hideo Nomo 1.50
6 Hideo Nomo (Die-Cut) 2.00
7 Greg Maddux 2.50
7 Greg Maddux (Die-Cut) 5.00
8 Fred McGriff 1.00
8 Fred McGriff (Die-Cut) 2.00
9 Barry Bonds 5.00
9 Barry Bonds (Die-Cut) 8.00

Ripken Tribute Jumbo

A special super-size (3" x 5") version of the SP/Championship edition Cal Ripken Jr.

2,131 Games tribute card insert was created for sale by Upper Deck Authentic on home shopping programs. The card is die-cut and serially numbered on back from within an edition of 2,131 pieces.

NM/M
CR1 Cal Ripken Jr. 12.00

1996 SP FanFest Promos

To introduce its SP product, Upper Deck prepared an eight-card promo set for distribution at the All-Star FanFest in Philadelphia. The promos are identical in format to the issued versions except for the presence of a bright silver-foil FanFest logo in the lower-left corner of each card's front. The cards lack the overprint which has become standard on promo cards in the recent years.

NM/M
Complete Set (8): 8.00
Common Player: .60
1 Ken Griffey Jr. 1.50
2 Frank Thomas 1.00
3 Albert Belle .60
4 Mo Vaughn .60
5 Barry Bonds 2.50
6 Mike Piazza 1.50
7 Matt Williams .60
8 Sammy Sosa 1.25

1996 SP

This 188-card set, distributed through hobby-only channels, features tremendous photography, including two photos on the front, and six insert sets. The inserts sets are Heroes, Marquee Matchups Blue and Die-Cut Marquee Matchups Red, Holoview Special F/X Blue and Die-Cut Holoview Special F/X Red, and the continuation of the Cal Ripken Collection.

NM/M
Complete Set (188): 12.50
Common Player: .05
Pack (8): 1.25
Wax Box (30): 25.00
1 Rey Ordonez (Premier Prospects) .05
2 George Arias (Premier Prospects) .05
3 Osvaldo Fernandez **RC** (Premier Prospects) .25
4 Darin Erstad **RC** (Premier Prospects) 2.00
5 Paul Wilson (Premier Prospects) .05
6 Richard Hidalgo (Premier Prospects) .05
7 Bob Wolcott (Premier Prospects) .05
8 Jimmy Haynes (Premier Prospects) .05
9 Edgar Renteria (Premier Prospects) .05
10 Alan Benes (Premier Prospects) .05
11 Chris Snopek (Premier Prospects) .05
12 Billy Wagner (Premier Prospects) .05
13 Mike Grace **RC** (Premier Prospects) .05
14 Todd Greene (Premier Prospects) .05
15 Karim Garcia (Premier Prospects) .05
16 John Wasdin (Premier Prospects) .05
17 Jason Kendall (Premier Prospects) .05
18 Bob Abreu (Premier Prospects) .15
19 Jermaine Dye (Premier Prospects) .05
20 Jason Schmidt (Premier Prospects) .05
21 Javy Lopez .05
22 Ryan Klesko .05
23 Tom Glavine .35
24 John Smoltz .05
25 Greg Maddux 1.00
26 Chipper Jones 1.00
27 Fred McGriff .05
28 David Justice .05
29 Roberto Alomar .20
30 Cal Ripken Jr. 2.00
31 Jeffrey Hammonds .05
32 Bobby Bonilla .05
33 Mike Mussina .30
34 Randy Myers .05
35 Rafael Palmeiro .65
36 Brady Anderson .05
37 Tim Naehring .05
38 Jose Canseco .40
39 Roger Clemens 1.00
40 Mo Vaughn .05
41 Jose Valentin **RC** .05
42 Kevin Mitchell .05
43 Chili Davis .05
44 Garret Anderson .05
45 Tim Salmon .05
46 Chuck Finley .05
47 Mark Langston .05
48 Jim Abbott .05
49 J.T. Snow .05
50 Jim Edmonds .05
51 Sammy Sosa 1.00
52 Brian McRae .05
53 Ryne Sandberg 1.00
54 Mark Grace .05
55 Jaime Navarro .05
56 Harold Baines .05
57 Robin Ventura .05
58 Tony Phillips .05
59 Alex Fernandez .05
60 Frank Thomas .75
61 Ray Durham .05
62 Bret Boone .05
63 Barry Larkin .05
64 Pete Schourek .05
65 Reggie Sanders .05
66 John Smiley .05
67 Carlos Baerga .05
68 Jim Thome .65
69 Eddie Murray .75
70 Albert Belle .05
71 Dennis Martinez .05
72 Jack McDowell .05
73 Kenny Lofton .05
74 Manny Ramirez .75
75 Dante Bichette .05
76 Vinny Castilla .05
77 Andres Galarraga .05
78 Walt Weiss .05
79 Ellis Burks .05
80 Larry Walker .05
81 Cecil Fielder .05
82 Melvin Nieves .05
83 Travis Fryman .05
84 Chad Curtis .05
85 Alan Trammell .05
86 Gary Sheffield .45
87 Charles Johnson .05
88 Andre Dawson .30
89 Jeff Conine .05
90 Greg Colbrunn .05
91 Derek Bell .05
92 Brian Hunter .05
93 Doug Drabek .05
94 Craig Biggio .05
95 Jeff Bagwell .75
96 Kevin Appier .05
97 Jeff Montgomery .05
98 Michael Tucker .05
99 Bip Roberts .05
100 Johnny Damon .35
101 Eric Karros .05
102 Raul Mondesi .05
103 Ramon Martinez .05
104 Ismael Valdes .05
105 Mike Piazza 1.25
106 Hideo Nomo .40
107 Chan Ho Park .05
108 Ben McDonald .05
109 Kevin Seitzer .05
110 Greg Vaughn .05
111 Jose Valentin .05
112 Rick Aguilera .05
113 Marty Cordova .05
114 Brad Radke .05
115 Kirby Puckett 1.00
116 Chuck Knoblauch .05
117 Paul Molitor .75
118 Pedro Martinez .75
119 Mike Lansing .05
120 Rondell White .05
121 Moises Alou .05
122 Mark Grudzielanek .05
123 Jeff Fassero .05
124 Rico Brogna .05
125 Jason Isringhausen .05
126 Jeff Kent .05
127 Bernard Gilkey .05
128 Todd Hundley .05
129 David Cone .05
130 Andy Pettitte .25
131 Wade Boggs 1.00
132 Paul O'Neill .05
133 Ruben Sierra .05
134 John Wetteland .05
135 Derek Jeter 2.00
136 Geronimo Pena .05
137 Terry Steinbach .05
138 Ariel Prieto .05
139 Scott Brosius .05
140 Mark McGwire 1.50
141 Lenny Dykstra .05
142 Todd Zeile .05
143 Benito Santiago .05
144 Mickey Morandini .05
145 Gregg Jefferies .05
146 Denny Neagle .05
147 Orlando Merced .05
148 Charlie Hayes .05
149 Carlos Garcia .05
150 Jay Bell .05
151 Ray Lankford .05
152 Alan Benes .05
153 Dennis Eckersley .65
154 Gary Gaetti .05
155 Ozzie Smith 1.00
156 Ron Gant .05
157 Brian Jordan .05
158 Ken Caminiti .05
159 Rickey Henderson .75
160 Tony Gwynn 1.00
161 Wally Joyner .05
162 Andy Ashby .05
163 Steve Finley .05
164 Glenallen Hill .05
165 Matt Williams .05
166 Barry Bonds 2.00
167 William Van Landingham .05
168 Rod Beck .05
169 Randy Johnson .75
170 Ken Griffey Jr. 1.25
170p Ken Griffey Jr. (Unmarked promo; bio on back says, ". . .against Cleveland" as opposed to ". . . against the Indians.") 4.00
171 Alex Rodriguez 1.50
172 Edgar Martinez .05
173 Jay Buhner .05
174 Russ Davis .05
175 Juan Gonzalez .40
176 Mickey Tettleton .05
177 Will Clark .05
178 Ken Hill .05
179 Dean Palmer .05
180 Ivan Rodriguez .65
181 Carlos Delgado .50
182 Alex Gonzalez .05
183 Shawn Green .30
184 Erik Hanson .05
185 Joe Carter .05
186 Checklist (Hideo Nomo) .20
187 Checklist (Cal Ripken Jr.) 1.00
188 Checklist (Ken Griffey Jr.) .65

Baseball Heroes

This 1996 insert set is a continuation of the series which began in 1990. These cards, numbered 81-90, feature nine of today's top stars, plus a Ken Griffey Jr. header card (#81). The cards were seeded one per every 96 packs.

NM/M
Complete Set (10): 65.00

Common Player: 4.00
81 Ken Griffey Jr. Header 8.00
82 Frank Thomas 6.50
83 Albert Belle 4.00
84 Barry Bonds 12.00
85 Chipper Jones 8.00
86 Hideo Nomo 5.00
87 Mike Piazza 10.00
88 Manny Ramirez 6.50
89 Greg Maddux 8.00
90 Ken Griffey Jr. 10.00

Marquee Matchups Blue

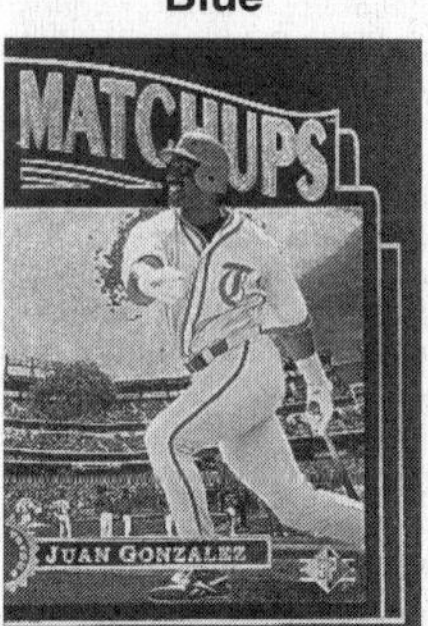

This 20-card Upper Deck SP insert set contains cards that allow collectors to match up the game's top players against each other, such as Greg Maddux against Cal Ripken Jr. The design and stadiums in the background match together when the two cards are next to each other. Blue versions are seeded one per five packs. Cards are numbered with a "MM" prefix.

NM/M
Complete Set (20): 15.00
Common Player: .50
1 Ken Griffey Jr. 2.00
2 Hideo Nomo .50
3 Derek Jeter 3.00
4 Rey Ordonez .50
5 Tim Salmon .50
6 Mike Piazza 1.50
7 Mark McGwire 1.50
8 Barry Bonds 2.00
9 Cal Ripken Jr. 3.00
10 Greg Maddux 1.50
11 Albert Belle .50
12 Barry Larkin 1.00
13 Jeff Bagwell .75
14 Juan Gonzalez .75
15 Frank Thomas 1.00
16 Sammy Sosa 1.00
17 Mike Mussina .75
18 Chipper Jones 1.00
19 Roger Clemens 2.00
20 Fred McGriff .50

Marquee Matchups Red

A parallel set to the blue Marquee Matchups, the red cards are found on average of one per 61 packs. Besides the red background printing, this version is distinguished from the more common blue version by the die-cutting around the top. Cards are numbered with a "MM" prefix.

NM/M
Common Player: 1.50
1 Ken Griffey Jr. 10.00
2 Hideo Nomo 2.00
3 Derek Jeter 15.00
4 Rey Ordonez 1.50
5 Tim Salmon 1.50
6 Mike Piazza 8.00
7 Mark McGwire 8.00
8 Barry Bonds 15.00
9 Cal Ripken Jr. 15.00
10 Greg Maddux 10.00
11 Albert Belle 1.50
12 Barry Larkin 4.00
13 Jeff Bagwell 4.00
14 Juan Gonzalez 3.00
15 Frank Thomas 5.00
16 Sammy Sosa 5.00
17 Mike Mussina 4.00
18 Chipper Jones 5.00
19 Roger Clemens 10.00
20 Fred McGriff 3.00

Ripken Collection

The last five cards of the Cal Ripken Jr. Collection, which began in Collector's Choice Series I, are featured in this Upper Deck SP product. These five cards, numbered 18-22, cover Ripken's early days, including his 1982 Rookie of the Year Award, his Major League debut, and photos of him playing third base. Ripken Collection inserts are found one per every 45 packs.

NM/M
Complete Set (5): 25.00
Common Card: 5.00
18-22 Cal Ripken Jr. 5.00

1996 SP SpecialFX

These 48 cards capture Upper Deck Holoview technology. Blue versions were seeded one per every five packs of 1996 Upper Deck SP baseball.

NM/M
Complete Set (48): 50.00
Common Player: .60
1 Greg Maddux 2.50
2 Eric Karros .60
3 Mike Piazza 3.00
4 Raul Mondesi .60
5 Hideo Nomo 1.00
6 Jim Edmonds .60
7 Jason Isringhausen .60
8 Jay Buhner .60
9 Barry Larkin .60
10 Ken Griffey Jr. 3.00

11	Gary Sheffield	1.25
12	Craig Biggio	.60
13	Paul Wilson	.60
14	Rondell White	.60
15	Chipper Jones	2.50
16	Kirby Puckett	2.50
17	Ron Gant	.60
18	Wade Boggs	2.50
19	Fred McGriff	.60
20	Cal Ripken Jr.	5.00
21	Jason Kendall	.60
22	Johnny Damon	.90
23	Kenny Lofton	.60
24	Roberto Alomar	1.00
25	Barry Bonds	5.00
26	Dante Bichette	.60
27	Mark McGwire	4.00
28	Rafael Palmeiro	1.50
29	Juan Gonzalez	1.00
30	Albert Belle	.60
31	Randy Johnson	1.75
32	Jose Canseco	1.25
33	Sammy Sosa	2.50
34	Eddie Murray	1.75
35	Frank Thomas	1.75
36	Tom Glavine	.90
37	Matt Williams	.60
38	Roger Clemens	2.75
39	Paul Molitor	1.75
40	Tony Gwynn	2.50
41	Mo Vaughn	.60
42	Tim Salmon	.60
43	Manny Ramirez	1.75
44	Jeff Bagwell	1.75
45	Edgar Martinez	.60
46	Rey Ordonez	.60
47	Osvaldo Fernandez	.60
48	Derek Jeter	5.00

Red

These 1996 Upper Deck SP red die-cut cards use Upper Deck's Holoview technology. They are scarcer than the blue versions; these being seeded one per every 75 packs.

		NM/M
Common Player:		3.00
Inserted 1:75		
1	Greg Maddux	20.00
2	Eric Karros	3.00
3	Mike Piazza	10.00
4	Raul Mondesi	3.00
5	Hideo Nomo	4.00
6	Jim Edmonds	4.00
7	Jason Isringhausen	4.00
8	Jay Buhner	3.00
9	Barry Larkin	5.00
10	Ken Griffey Jr.	20.00
11	Gary Sheffield	8.00
12	Craig Biggio	5.00
13	Paul Wilson	3.00
14	Rondell White	3.00
15	Chipper Jones	15.00
16	Kirby Puckett	20.00
17	Ron Gant	3.00
18	Wade Boggs	6.00
19	Fred McGriff	4.00
20	Cal Ripken Jr.	25.00
21	Jason Kendall	3.00
22	Johnny Damon	8.00
23	Kenny Lofton	4.00
24	Roberto Alomar	5.00
25	Barry Bonds	25.00
26	Dante Bichette	3.00
27	Mark McGwire	15.00
28	Rafael Palmeiro	6.00
29	Juan Gonzalez	5.00
30	Albert Belle	3.00
31	Randy Johnson	10.00
32	Jose Canseco	5.00
33	Sammy Sosa	10.00
34	Eddie Murray	8.00
35	Frank Thomas	10.00
36	Tom Glavine	10.00
37	Matt Williams	4.00
38	Roger Clemens	20.00
39	Paul Molitor	8.00
40	Tony Gwynn	10.00
41	Mo Vaughn	5.00
42	Tim Salmon	4.00
43	Manny Ramirez	10.00
44	Jeff Bagwell	8.00
45	Edgar Martinez	3.00
46	Rey Ordonez	3.00
47	Osvaldo Fernandez	3.00
48	Derek Jeter	25.00

1996 SPx

Upper Deck's 1996 SPx set has 60 players in it, which are each paralleled as a Gold version (one per every seven packs). Base cards feature a new look with a different perimeter die-cut design from those used in the past for basketball and football sets. A 10-card insert set, Bound for Glory, was also produced. Tribute cards were also made for Ken Griffey Jr. and Mike Piazza, with scarcer autographed versions also produced for each player.

		NM/M
Complete Set (60):		17.50
Common Player:		.15
Golds:		1.5X
Pack (1):		1.25
Wax Box (36):		25.00
1	Greg Maddux	1.50
2	Chipper Jones	1.50
3	Fred McGriff	.15
4	Tom Glavine	.50
5	Cal Ripken Jr.	3.00
6	Roberto Alomar	.50
7	Rafael Palmeiro	1.00
8	Jose Canseco	.65
9	Roger Clemens	1.75
10	Mo Vaughn	.15
11	Jim Edmonds	.15
12	Tim Salmon	.15
13	Sammy Sosa	1.50
14	Ryne Sandberg	1.50
15	Mark Grace	.15
16	Frank Thomas	1.25
17	Barry Larkin	.15
18	Kenny Lofton	.15
19	Albert Belle	.15
20	Eddie Murray	1.25
21	Manny Ramirez	1.25
22	Dante Bichette	.15
23	Larry Walker	.15
24	Vinny Castilla	.15
25	Andres Galarraga	.15
26	Cecil Fielder	.15
27	Gary Sheffield	.75
28	Craig Biggio	.15
29	Jeff Bagwell	1.25
30	Derek Bell	.15
31	Johnny Damon	.60
32	Eric Karros	.15
33	Mike Piazza	2.00
34	Raul Mondesi	.15
35	Hideo Nomo	.65
36	Kirby Puckett	1.50
37	Paul Molitor	1.25
38	Marty Cordova	.15
39	Rondell White	.15
40	Jason Isringhausen	.15
41	Paul Wilson	.15
42	Rey Ordonez	.15
43	Derek Jeter	3.00
44	Wade Boggs	1.50
45	Mark McGwire	2.50
46	Jason Kendall	.15
47	Ron Gant	.15
48	Ozzie Smith	1.50
49	Tony Gwynn	1.50
50	Ken Caminiti	.15
51	Barry Bonds	3.00
52	Matt Williams	.15
53	Osvaldo Fernandez **RC**	.25
54	Jay Buhner	.15
55	Ken Griffey Jr.	2.00
55p	Ken Griffey Jr. (Overprinted "For Promotional Use Only.")	2.00
56	Randy Johnson	1.25
57	Alex Rodriguez	2.50
58	Juan Gonzalez	.65
59	Joe Carter	.15
60	Carlos Delgado	.75

Bound for Glory

Some of baseball's best players are highlighted on these 1996 Upper Deck SPx insert cards. The cards were seeded one per every 24 packs. Fronts of the die-cut cards feature a color photograph on a background of silver-foil holographic portrait and action photos. Backs have another portrait photo, stats, career highlights and logos.

		NM/M
Complete Set (10):		18.00
Common Player:		1.00
1	Ken Griffey Jr.	3.00
2	Frank Thomas	1.50
3	Barry Bonds	4.00
4	Cal Ripken Jr.	4.00
5	Greg Maddux	2.00
6	Chipper Jones	2.00
7	Roberto Alomar	1.00
8	Manny Ramirez	1.50
9	Tony Gwynn	2.00
10	Mike Piazza	3.00

Ken Griffey Jr. Commemorative

Seattle Mariners' star Ken Griffey Jr. has this tribute card in Upper Deck's 1996 SPx set. The card was seeded one per every 75 packs. Autographed versions were also produced; these cards were seeded one per every 2,000 packs.

		NM/M
KG1	Ken Griffey Jr.	2.50
KGA1	Ken Griffey Jr./Auto.	100.00

Mike Piazza Tribute

Los Angeles Dodgers' star catcher Mike Piazza is featured on this 1996 Upper Deck SPx insert card. Normal versions of the card are found one per every 95 packs, making it scarcer than the Ken Griffey Jr. inserts. Autographed Piazza cards are seeded one per every 2,000 packs.

		NM/M
MP1	Mike Piazza	2.00
MP1	Mike Piazza/Auto.	125.00

1997 SP Sample

To preview its SP brand for 1997, Upper Deck issued a sample card of Ken Griffey Jr. Similar in format to the issued cards, the promo bears card number 1 and is overprinted "SAMPLE" on back.

		NM/M
1	Ken Griffey Jr.	3.00

1997 SP

The fifth anniversary edition of SP Baseball features 184 regular cards sold in eight-card packs for $4.39. Card fronts feature the player's name in gold foil-stamping at bottom. Team name and position are vertically at one edge. Backs have two more photos along with "Best Year" and career stats. Inserts include Marquee Matchups, Special FX, Inside Info, Baseball Heroes, Game Film, SPx Force, and Autographed Vintage SP cards.

		NM/M
Complete Set (184):		12.00
Common Player:		.05
Pack (8):		2.00
Wax Box (30):		45.00
1	Andruw Jones (Great Futures)	.75
2	Kevin Orie (Great Futures)	.05
3	Nomar Garciaparra (Great Futures)	1.00
4	Jose Guillen (Great Futures)	.05
5	Todd Walker (Great Futures)	.05
6	Derrick Gibson (Great Futures)	.05
7	Aaron Boone (Great Futures)	.05
8	Bartolo Colon (Great Futures)	.05
9	Derrek Lee (Great Futures)	.50
10	Vladimir Guerrero (Great Futures)	.75
11	Wilton Guerrero (Great Futures)	.05
12	Luis Castillo (Great Futures)	.05
13	Jason Dickson (Great Futures)	.05
14	Bubba Trammell **RC** (Great Futures)	.25
15	Jose Cruz Jr. **RC** (Great Futures)	.50
16	Eddie Murray	.75
17	Darin Erstad	.20
18	Garret Anderson	.05
19	Jim Edmonds	.05
20	Tim Salmon	.05
21	Chuck Finley	.05
22	John Smoltz	.05
23	Greg Maddux	1.00
24	Kenny Lofton	.05
25	Chipper Jones	1.00
26	Ryan Klesko	.05
27	Javier Lopez	.05
28	Fred McGriff	.05
29	Roberto Alomar	.20
30	Rafael Palmeiro	.65
31	Mike Mussina	.30
32	Brady Anderson	.05
33	Rocky Coppinger	.05
34	Cal Ripken Jr.	2.00
35	Mo Vaughn	.05
36	Steve Avery	.05
37	Tom Gordon	.05
38	Tim Naehring	.05
39	Troy O'Leary	.05
40	Sammy Sosa	1.00
41	Brian McRae	.05
42	Mel Rojas	.05
43	Ryne Sandberg	1.00
44	Mark Grace	.05
45	Albert Belle	.05
46	Robin Ventura	.05
47	Roberto Hernandez	.05
48	Ray Durham	.05
49	Harold Baines	.05
50	Frank Thomas	.75
51	Bret Boone	.05
52	Reggie Sanders	.05
53	Deion Sanders	.05
54	Hal Morris	.05
55	Barry Larkin	.05
56	Jim Thome	.65
57	Marquis Grissom	.05
58	David Justice	.05
59	Charles Nagy	.05
60	Manny Ramirez	.75
61	Matt Williams	.05
62	Jack McDowell	.05
63	Vinny Castilla	.05
64	Dante Bichette	.05
65	Andres Galarraga	.05
66	Ellis Burks	.05
67	Larry Walker	.05
68	Eric Young	.05
69	Brian L. Hunter	.05
70	Travis Fryman	.05
71	Tony Clark	.05
72	Bobby Higginson	.05
73	Melvin Nieves	.05
74	Jeff Conine	.05
75	Gary Sheffield	.40
76	Moises Alou	.05
77	Edgar Renteria	.05
78	Alex Fernandez	.05
79	Charles Johnson	.05
80	Bobby Bonilla	.05
81	Darryl Kile	.05
82	Derek Bell	.05
83	Shane Reynolds	.05
84	Craig Biggio	.05
85	Jeff Bagwell	.75
86	Billy Wagner	.05
87	Chili Davis	.05
88	Kevin Appier	.05
89	Jay Bell	.05
90	Johnny Damon	.35
91	Jeff King	.05
92	Hideo Nomo	.40
93	Todd Hollandsworth	.05
94	Eric Karros	.05
95	Mike Piazza	1.25
96	Ramon Martinez	.05
97	Todd Worrell	.05
98	Raul Mondesi	.05
99	Dave Nilsson	.05
100	John Jaha	.05
101	Jose Valentin	.05
102	Jeff Cirillo	.05
103	Jeff D'Amico	.05
104	Ben McDonald	.05
105	Paul Molitor	.75
106	Rich Becker	.05
107	Frank Rodriguez	.05
108	Marty Cordova	.05
109	Terry Steinbach	.05
110	Chuck Knoblauch	.05
111	Mark Grudzielanek	.05
112	Mike Lansing	.05
113	Pedro Martinez	.75
114	Henry Rodriguez	.05
115	Rondell White	.05
116	Rey Ordonez	.05
117	Carlos Baerga	.05
118	Lance Johnson	.05
119	Bernard Gilkey	.05
120	Todd Hundley	.05
121	John Franco	.05
122	Bernie Williams	.05
123	David Cone	.05
124	Cecil Fielder	.05
125	Derek Jeter	2.00
126	Tino Martinez	.05
127	Mariano Rivera	.15
128	Andy Pettitte	.15
129	Wade Boggs	1.00
130	Mark McGwire	1.50
131	Jose Canseco	.50
132	Geronimo Berroa	.05
133	Jason Giambi	.45
134	Ernie Young	.05
135	Scott Rolen	.65
136	Ricky Bottalico	.05
137	Curt Schilling	.35
138	Gregg Jefferies	.05
139	Mickey Morandini	.05
140	Jason Kendall	.05
141	Kevin Elster	.05
142	Al Martin	.05
143	Joe Randa	.05
144	Jason Schmidt	.05
145	Ray Lankford	.05
146	Brian Jordan	.05
147	Andy Benes	.05
148	Alan Benes	.05
149	Gary Gaetti	.05
150	Ron Gant	.05
151	Dennis Eckersley	.65
152	Rickey Henderson	.75
153	Joey Hamilton	.05
154	Ken Caminiti	.05
155	Tony Gwynn	1.00
156	Steve Finley	.05
157	Trevor Hoffman	.05
158	Greg Vaughn	.05
159	J.T. Snow	.05
160	Barry Bonds	2.00
161	Glenallen Hill	.05
162	William Van Landingham	.05
163	Jeff Kent	.05
164	Jay Buhner	.05
165	Ken Griffey Jr.	1.25
166	Alex Rodriguez	1.50
167	Randy Johnson	.75
168	Edgar Martinez	.05
169	Dan Wilson	.05
170	Ivan Rodriguez	.65
171	Roger Pavlik	.05
172	Will Clark	.05
173	Dean Palmer	.05
174	Rusty Greer	.05
175	Juan Gonzalez	.40
176	John Wetteland	.05
177	Joe Carter	.05
178	Ed Sprague	.05
179	Carlos Delgado	.45
180	Roger Clemens	1.00
181	Juan Guzman	.05
182	Pat Hentgen	.05
183	Ken Griffey Jr. (Checklist)	.65
184	Hideki Irabu **RC**	.25

Buy-Back Autographed Inserts

To celebrate the fifth anniversary of its premium SP brand, Upper Deck went into the hobby market to buy nearly 3,000 previous years' cards for a special insert program in 1997 SP packs. Various SP cards from 1993-96 issues and inserts were autographed by star players and a numbered holographic seal added on back. The number of each particular card signed ranged widely from fewer than 10 to more than 100. Numbers in parentheses in the checklist are the quantity reported signed for that card. All cards were inserted into foil packs except those of Mo Vaughn, which were a mail-in redemption.

		NM/M
Common Autograph:		7.50
4	Ken Griffey Jr./16	600.00
28	Jeff Bagwell/7	100.00
167	Tony Gwynn/17	250.00
280	Chipper Jones/34	110.00
PP9	Ken Griffey Jr./5	800.00
6	Todd Hollandsworth/167	7.50
15	Alex Rodriguez/94	1,200
105	Ken Griffey Jr./103	125.00
114	Gary Sheffield/130	25.00
130	Tony Gwynn/367	25.00
13	Tony Gwynn/31	150.00
35	Gary Sheffield/4	60.00
34	Chipper Jones/60	125.00
60	Jeff Bagwell/173	40.00
75	Gary Sheffield/221	20.00
105	Tony Gwynn/64	60.00
188	Alex Rodriguez/63	200.00
190	Ken Griffey Jr./38	200.00
195	Jay Buhner/57	15.00
1	Rey Ordonez/111	7.50
18	Gary Sheffield/58	30.00
26	Chipper Jones/102	50.00
40	Mo Vaughn/250	15.00
95	Jeff Bagwell/292	20.00
160	Tony Gwynn/20	200.00
170	Ken Griffey Jr./312	65.00
171	Alex Rodriguez/73	125.00
173	Jay Buhner/79	30.00
MM13	Jeff Bagwell/23	65.00
MM4	Rey Ordonez/40	15.00
8	Jay Buhner/27	30.00

Game Film

A 10-card insert utilizing pieces of actual game footage to highlight the top stars in the game. Only 500 of each card were available. Cards are numbered with a "GF" prefix.

		NM/M
Complete Set (10):		175.00
Common Player:		12.00
1	Alex Rodriguez	25.00
2	Frank Thomas	12.00
3	Andruw Jones	10.00
4	Cal Ripken Jr.	30.00

5 Mike Piazza 15.00
6 Derek Jeter 30.00
7 Mark McGwire 20.00
8 Chipper Jones 15.00
9 Barry Bonds 30.00
10 Ken Griffey Jr. 20.00

Griffey Baseball Heroes

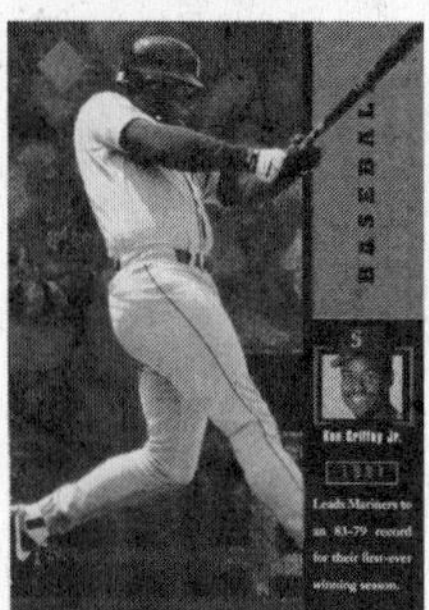

First started in 1990, this single-player insert continues with a salute to Ken Griffey Jr. Each card in the set is numbered to 2,000.

NM/M
Complete Set (10): 75.00
Common Griffey Jr.: 10.00
91-100 Ken Griffey Jr. 10.00

Inside Info

Each of the 25 cards in this insert feature a pull-out panel describing the player's major accomplishments. Both front and back are printed on metallic-foil stock. Cards were inserted one per box.

NM/M
Complete Set (25): 75.00
Common Player: 1.00
1 Ken Griffey Jr. 5.00
2 Mark McGwire 6.00
3 Kenny Lofton 1.00
4 Paul Molitor 3.00
5 Frank Thomas 3.00
6 Greg Maddux 3.50
7 Mo Vaughn 1.00
8 Cal Ripken Jr. 7.50
9 Jeff Bagwell 3.00
10 Alex Rodriguez 6.00
11 John Smoltz 1.00
12 Manny Ramirez 3.00
13 Sammy Sosa 3.50
14 Vladimir Guerrero 3.00
15 Albert Belle 1.00
16 Mike Piazza 5.00
17 Derek Jeter 7.50
18 Scott Rolen 2.00
19 Tony Gwynn 3.50
20 Barry Bonds 7.50
21 Ken Caminiti 1.00
22 Chipper Jones 3.50
23 Juan Gonzalez 1.50
24 Roger Clemens 4.00
25 Andruw Jones 3.00

Marquee Matchups

A 20-card die-cut set designed to highlight top inter-league matchups, when the matching cards are put together, a third player is highlighted in the background. Cards were inserted 1:5 packs and have an "MM" card-number prefix.

NM/M
Complete Set (20): 20.00
Common Player: .25
1 Ken Griffey Jr. 1.50
2 Andres Galarraga .25
3 Barry Bonds 3.00

4 Mark McGwire 2.00
5 Mike Piazza 1.50
6 Tim Salmon .25
7 Tony Gwynn 1.00
8 Alex Rodriguez 2.00
9 Chipper Jones 1.00
10 Derek Jeter 3.00
11 Manny Ramirez .75
12 Jeff Bagwell .75
13 Greg Maddux 1.00
14 Cal Ripken Jr. 3.00
15 Mo Vaughn .25
16 Gary Sheffield .45
17 Jim Thome .65
18 Barry Larkin .25
19 Frank Thomas .75
20 Sammy Sosa 1.00

1997 SP Special FX

Color 3-D motion portraits are front and center on these cards that also feature a die-cut design. The rest of the front includes color action photos printed on silver-foil stock. Backs have another color photo. One of the Alex Rodriguez cards (#49) features the 1996 die-cut design. Special FX were inserted 1:9 packs.

NM/M
Common Player: .75
1 Ken Griffey Jr. 6.00
2 Frank Thomas 3.00
3 Barry Bonds 8.00
4 Albert Belle .75
5 Mike Piazza 4.00
6 Greg Maddux 5.00
7 Chipper Jones 4.00
8 Cal Ripken Jr. 8.00
9 Jeff Bagwell 2.00
10 Alex Rodriguez 8.00
11 Mark McGwire 5.00
12 Kenny Lofton .75
13 Juan Gonzalez 1.50
14 Mo Vaughn .75
15 John Smoltz 1.00
16 Derek Jeter 8.00
17 Tony Gwynn 3.00
18 Ivan Rodriguez 2.00
19 Barry Larkin 1.00
20 Sammy Sosa 3.00
21 Mike Mussina 1.50
22 Gary Sheffield 2.00
23 Brady Anderson .75
24 Roger Clemens 6.00
25 Ken Caminiti .75
26 Roberto Alomar 1.50
27 Hideo Nomo 1.00
28 Bernie Williams 1.00
29 Todd Hundley .75
30 Manny Ramirez 3.00
31 Eric Karros .75
32 Tim Salmon .75
33 Jay Buhner .75
34 Andy Pettitte 1.50
35 Jim Thome 2.00
36 Ryne Sandberg 3.00
37 Matt Williams 1.00
38 Ryan Klesko .75
39 Jose Canseco 1.50
40 Paul Molitor 2.00
41 Eddie Murray 2.00
42 Darin Erstad .75
43 Todd Walker .75
44 Wade Boggs 2.50
45 Andruw Jones 2.00
46 Scott Rolen 2.00
47 Vladimir Guerrero 3.00
49 Alex Rodriguez (1996 design) 8.00

SPx Force

Each of the 10 cards in this set feature four different players. Cards are individually numbered to 500. In addition, a number of players signed 100 versions of their SPx Force cards that are also randomly inserted into packs.

NM/M
Complete Set (10): 60.00
Common Player: 6.00
1 Ken Griffey Jr., Jay Buhner, Andres Galarraga, Dante Bichette 7.50
2 Albert Belle, Brady Anderson, Mark McGwire, Cecil Fielder 9.00
3 Mo Vaughn, Ken Caminiti, Frank Thomas, Jeff Bagwell 6.00
4 Gary Sheffield, Sammy Sosa, Barry Bonds, Jose Canseco 12.00
5 Greg Maddux, Roger Clemens, John Smoltz, Randy Johnson 6.00
6 Alex Rodriguez, Derek Jeter, Chipper Jones, Rey Ordonez 12.00
7 Todd Hollandsworth, Mike Piazza, Raul Mondesi, Hideo Nomo 7.50
8 Juan Gonzalez, Manny Ramirez, Roberto Alomar, Ivan Rodriguez 6.00
9 Tony Gwynn, Wade Boggs, Eddie Murray, Paul Molitor 6.00
10 Andruw Jones, Vladimir Guerrero, Todd Walker, Scott Rolen 6.00

SPx Force Autographs

Ten players signed cards for this insert, which was serially numbered to 100. The cards were randomly seeded in packs except the Mo Vaughn card which was available by redemption.

NM/M
Common Player: 20.00
1 Ken Griffey Jr. 125.00
2 Albert Belle 25.00
3 Mo Vaughn 20.00
4 Gary Sheffield 25.00
5 Greg Maddux 100.00
6 Alex Rodriguez 160.00
7 Todd Hollandsworth 20.00
8 Roberto Alomar 30.00
9 Tony Gwynn 75.00
10 Andruw Jones 40.00

1997 SPx

Fifty cards, each featuring a perimeter die-cut design and a 3-D holoview photo, make up the SPx base set. Five different parallel sets - Steel (1:1 pack), Bronze (1:1), Silver (1:1), Gold (1:17) and Grand Finale (50 per card) - are found as inserts, as are Cornerstones of the Game, Bound for Glory and Bound for Glory Signature cards. Packs contain three cards and carried a suggested retail price of $5.99.

NM/M
Complete Set (50): 20.00
Common Player: .15
Steel: 1.5X
Bronze: 1.5X
Silver: 1.5X
Gold: 3X
Grand Finale: 4X
Pack (3): 2.00
Wax Box (18): 30.00
1 Eddie Murray 1.00
2 Darin Erstad .35
3 Tim Salmon .15
4 Andruw Jones 1.00
5 Chipper Jones 1.50
6 John Smoltz .15
7 Greg Maddux 1.50
8 Kenny Lofton .15
9 Roberto Alomar .30
10 Rafael Palmeiro .75
11 Brady Anderson .15
12 Cal Ripken Jr. 3.00
13 Nomar Garciaparra 1.50
14 Mo Vaughn .15
15 Ryne Sandberg 1.50
16 Sammy Sosa 1.50
17 Frank Thomas 1.00
18 Albert Belle .15
19 Barry Larkin .15
20 Deion Sanders .15
21 Manny Ramirez 1.00
22 Jim Thome .65
23 Dante Bichette .15
24 Andres Galarraga .15
25 Larry Walker .15
26 Gary Sheffield .50
27 Jeff Bagwell 1.00
28 Raul Mondesi .15
29 Hideo Nomo .50
30 Mike Piazza 2.00
31 Paul Molitor 1.00
32 Todd Walker .15
33 Vladimir Guerrero 1.00
34 Todd Hundley .15
35 Andy Pettitte .25
36 Derek Jeter 3.00
37 Jose Canseco .50
38 Mark McGwire 2.50
39 Scott Rolen .65
40 Ron Gant .15
41 Ken Caminiti .15
42 Tony Gwynn 1.50
43 Barry Bonds 3.00
44 Jay Buhner .15
45 Ken Griffey Jr. 2.00
45s Ken Griffey Jr. (Overprinted "SAMPLE" on back.) 2.00
46 Alex Rodriguez 2.50
47 Jose Cruz Jr. **RC** 1.00
48 Juan Gonzalez .50
49 Ivan Rodriguez .75
50 Roger Clemens 1.75

Bound for Glory

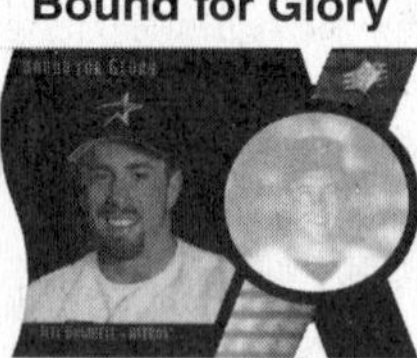

This 20-card insert utilizes holoview technology and is sequentially numbered to 1,500 per card.

NM/M
Complete Set (20): 60.00
Common Player: 1.00
1 Andruw Jones 3.00
2 Chipper Jones 4.00
3 Greg Maddux 4.00
4 Kenny Lofton 1.00
5 Cal Ripken Jr. 7.50
6 Mo Vaughn 1.00
7 Frank Thomas 3.00
8 Albert Belle 1.00
9 Manny Ramirez 3.00
10 Gary Sheffield 1.50
11 Jeff Bagwell 3.00
12 Mike Piazza 5.00
13 Derek Jeter 7.50
14 Mark McGwire 6.00
15 Tony Gwynn 4.00
16 Ken Caminiti 1.00
17 Barry Bonds 7.50
18 Alex Rodriguez 6.00
19 Ken Griffey Jr. 5.00
20 Juan Gonzalez 1.50

Bound for Glory Supreme Signatures

This five-card set featured autographs from the players and was sequentially numbered to 250.

NM/M
Complete Set (5): 250.00
Common Player: 30.00
1 Jeff Bagwell 40.00
2 Ken Griffey Jr. 120.00
3 Andruw Jones 40.00
4 Alex Rodriguez 160.00
5 Gary Sheffield 30.00

Cornerstones of the Game

A 20-card insert utilizing a double-front design highlighting 40 of the top players in the game. Each card is sequentially numbered to 500.

NM/M
Complete Set (10): 150.00
Common Player: 12.00
1 Ken Griffey Jr., Barry Bonds 25.00
2 Frank Thomas, Albert Belle 12.00
3 Chipper Jones, Greg Maddux 15.00
4 Tony Gwynn, Paul Molitor 15.00
5 Andruw Jones, Vladimir Guerrero 12.00
6 Jeff Bagwell, Ryne Sandberg 15.00
7 Mike Piazza, Ivan Rodriguez 20.00
8 Cal Ripken Jr., Eddie Murray 25.00
9 Mo Vaughn, Mark McGwire 20.00
10 Alex Rodriguez, Derek Jeter 25.00

1998 SP Authentic Sample

This card of Upper Deck spokesman Ken Griffey, Jr., was issued to preview the new SP Authentic line. Design is similar to the issued version but the sample displays different photos, a different the card number and the word "SAMPLE" printed in large letters on back.

NM/M
Ken Griffey Jr. 3.00

1998 SP Authentic

The SP Authentic base set consists of 198 cards, including the 30-card Future Watch subset and one checklist card. The base cards have a color photo inside a thick white border. Inserts include Chirography, Sheer Dominance and SP Authentics.

NM/M
Complete Set (198): 15.00
Common Player: .05
Pack (5): 2.00
Wax Box (24): 35.00
1 Travis Lee (Future Watch) .10
2 Mike Caruso (Future Watch) .05
3 Kerry Wood (Future Watch) .65
4 Mark Kotsay (Future Watch) .05
5 Magglio Ordonez **RC** (Future Watch) 5.00
6 Scott Elarton (Future Watch) .05
7 Carl Pavano (Future Watch) .10
8 A.J. Hinch (Future Watch) .05
9 Rolando Arrojo **RC** (Future Watch) .40
10 Ben Grieve (Future Watch) .05
11 Gabe Alvarez (Future Watch) .05
12 Mike Kinkade **RC** (Future Watch) .40
13 Bruce Chen (Future Watch) .05
14 Juan Encarnacion (Future Watch) .05
15 Todd Helton (Future Watch) .75
16 Aaron Boone (Future Watch) .05
17 Sean Casey (Future Watch) .15
18 Ramon Hernandez (Future Watch) .05
19 Daryle Ward (Future Watch) .05
20 Paul Konerko (Future Watch) .15
21 David Ortiz (Future Watch) .50
22 Derrek Lee (Future Watch) .50
23 Brad Fullmer (Future Watch) .05
24 Javier Vazquez (Future Watch) .05
25 Miguel Tejada (Future Watch) .15
26 David Dellucci (Future Watch) .05
27 Alex Gonzalez (Future Watch) .05
28 Matt Clement (Future Watch) .05
29 Eric Milton (Future Watch) .05
30 Russell Branyan (Future Watch) .05
31 Chuck Finley .05
32 Jim Edmonds .05
33 Darin Erstad .20
34 Jason Dickson .05
35 Tim Salmon .05
36 Cecil Fielder .05
37 Todd Greene .05
38 Andy Benes .05
39 Jay Bell .05
40 Matt Williams .05
41 Brian Anderson .05
42 Karim Garcia .05
43 Javy Lopez .05
44 Tom Glavine .35
45 Greg Maddux 1.50
46 Andruw Jones 1.00
47 Chipper Jones 1.50
48 Ryan Klesko .05
49 John Smoltz .05
50 Andres Galarraga .05
51 Rafael Palmeiro .75
52 Mike Mussina .30
53 Roberto Alomar .20
54 Joe Carter .05
55 Cal Ripken Jr. 3.00
56 Brady Anderson .05
57 Mo Vaughn .05

58 John Valentin .05
59 Dennis Eckersley .75
60 Nomar Garciaparra 1.50
61 Pedro J. Martinez 1.00
62 Jeff Blauser .05
63 Kevin Orie .05
64 Henry Rodriguez .05
65 Mark Grace .05
66 Albert Belle .05
67 Mike Cameron .05
68 Robin Ventura .05
69 Frank Thomas 1.00
70 Barry Larkin .05
71 Brett Tomko .05
72 Willie Greene .05
73 Reggie Sanders .05
74 Sandy Alomar Jr. .05
75 Kenny Lofton .05
76 Jaret Wright .05
77 David Justice .05
78 Omar Vizquel .05
79 Manny Ramirez 1.00
80 Jim Thome .75
81 Travis Fryman .05
82 Neifi Perez .05
83 Mike Lansing .05
84 Vinny Castilla .05
85 Larry Walker .05
86 Dante Bichette .05
87 Darryl Kile .05
88 Justin Thompson .05
89 Damion Easley .05
90 Tony Clark .05
91 Bobby Higginson .05
92 Brian L. Hunter .05
93 Edgar Renteria .05
94 Craig Counsell .05
95 Mike Piazza 2.00
96 Livan Hernandez .05
97 Todd Zeile .05
98 Richard Hidalgo .05
99 Moises Alou .05
100 Jeff Bagwell 1.00
101 Mike Hampton .05
102 Craig Biggio .05
103 Dean Palmer .05
104 Tim Belcher .05
105 Jeff King .05
106 Jeff Conine .05
107 Johnny Damon .30
108 Hideo Nomo .50
109 Raul Mondesi .05
110 Gary Sheffield .45
111 Ramon Martinez .05
112 Chan Ho Park .05
113 Eric Young .05
114 Charles Johnson .05
115 Eric Karros .05
116 Bobby Bonilla .05
117 Jeromy Burnitz .05
118 Carl Eldred .05
119 Jeff D'Amico .05
120 Marquis Grissom .05
121 Dave Nilsson .05
122 Brad Radke .05
123 Marty Cordova .05
124 Ron Coomer .05
125 Paul Molitor 1.00
126 Todd Walker .05
127 Rondell White .05
128 Mark Grudzielanek .05
129 Carlos Perez .05
130 Vladimir Guerrero 1.00
131 Dustin Hermanson .05
132 Butch Huskey .05
133 John Franco .05
134 Rey Ordonez .05
135 Todd Hundley .05
136 Edgardo Alfonzo .05
137 Bobby Jones .05
138 John Olerud .05
139 Chili Davis .05
140 Tino Martinez .05
141 Andy Pettitte .15
142 Chuck Knoblauch .05
143 Bernie Williams .05
144 David Cone .05
145 Derek Jeter 3.00
146 Paul O'Neill .05
147 Rickey Henderson 1.00
148 Jason Giambi .50
149 Kenny Rogers .05
150 Scott Rolen .75
151 Curt Schilling .35
152 Ricky Bottalico .05
153 Mike Lieberthal .05
154 Francisco Cordova .05
155 Jose Guillen .05
156 Jason Schmidt .05
157 Jason Kendall .05
158 Kevin Young .05
159 Delino DeShields .05
160 Mark McGwire 2.50
161 Ray Lankford .05
162 Brian Jordan .05
163 Ron Gant .05
164 Todd Stottlemyre .05
165 Ken Caminiti .05
166 Kevin Brown .05
167 Trevor Hoffman .05
168 Steve Finley .05
169 Wally Joyner .05
170 Tony Gwynn 1.50
171 Shawn Estes .05
172 J.T. Snow .05
173 Jeff Kent .05
174 Robb Nen .05
175 Barry Bonds 3.00
176 Randy Johnson 1.00
177 Edgar Martinez .05
178 Jay Buhner .05
179 Alex Rodriguez 2.50
180 Ken Griffey Jr. 2.00
181 Ken Cloude .05
182 Wade Boggs 1.50
183 Tony Saunders .05
184 Wilson Alvarez .05
185 Fred McGriff .05
186 Roberto Hernandez .05
187 Kevin Stocker .05
188 Fernando Tatis .05
189 Will Clark .05
190 Juan Gonzalez .50
191 Rusty Greer .05
192 Ivan Rodriguez .75
193 Jose Canseco .45
194 Carlos Delgado .50
195 Roger Clemens 1.75
196 Pat Hentgen .05
197 Randy Myers .05
198 Checklist (Ken Griffey Jr.) .85

Chirography

Chirography insert are seeded one per 25 packs. The featured player signed his cards in the white border at the bottom.

		NM/M
Common Card:		4.00
Inserted 1:25		
RA	Roberto Alomar	15.00
RB	Russell Branyan	4.00
SC	Sean Casey	10.00
TC	Tony Clark	4.00
RC	Roger Clemens/SP/400	80.00
JC	Jose Cruz Jr.	4.00
DE	Darin Erstad	7.50
NG	Nomar Garciaparra/SP/400	60.00
BG	Ben Grieve	4.00
KG	Ken Griffey Jr./SP/400	60.00
VG	Vladimir Guerrero	30.00
TG	Tony Gwynn/SP/850	30.00
TH	Todd Helton	15.00
LH	Livan Hernandez	6.00
CJ	Charles Johnson	6.00
AJ	Andruw Jones	17.50
CHIP	Chipper Jones/SP/800	30.00
PK	Paul Konerko	15.00
MK	Mark Kotsay	6.00
RL	Ray Lankford	6.00
TL	Travis Lee	6.00
PM	Paul Molitor/SP/800	20.00
MM	Mike Mussina	20.00
AR	Alex Rodriguez/SP/800	80.00
IR	Ivan Rodriguez	30.00
SR	Scott Rolen	20.00
GS	Gary Sheffield	15.00
MT	Miguel Tejada	20.00
JW	Jaret Wright	6.00
MV	Mo Vaughn/SP/800	12.50

Ken Griffey Jr. 300th HR Redemption

This 5" x 7" version of Ken Griffey Jr.'s SP Authentic card was issued as a redemption for one of the 1000 Trade Cards which were foil-pack inserts.

		NM/M
KG300	Ken Griffey Jr.	30.00

Jersey Swatch

These 5" x 7" redemption cards were issued in exchange for Trade Cards found as random foil-packs inserts. Fronts have a player action photo on a white background. Backs have a congratulatory message of authenticity. Sandwiched between is a swatch of that play-

er's uniform jersey. The large-format jersey cards were available in limited editions which are listed in parentheses, though all might not have been redeemed prior to the August 1, 1999, cut-off date.

		NM/M
Complete Set (6):		130.00
Common Player:		7.50
(1)	Jay Buhner/125	7.50
(2)	Ken Griffey Jr./125	50.00
(3)	Tony Gwynn/415	10.00
(4)	Greg Maddux/125	30.00
(5)	Alex Rodriguez /125	60.00
(6)	Gary Sheffield/125	12.00

Trade Cards

Cards which could be traded (prior to the Aug. 1, 1999 cut-off) for special cards and autographed memorabilia were inserted into SP Authentic foil packs at an announced rate of one per 291 packs. Trade cards have a white background on front with a color player action photo and the name of the redemption item. Backs gives details for redemption. In some cases, because of their insertion-rate rarity, the cards are worth more than the redemption items. The unnumbered cards are listed here alphabetically.

		NM/M
Common Card:		5.00
(1)	Roberto Alomar/Auto. Ball/100	15.00
(2)	Albert Belle/Auto. Ball/100	7.50
(3)	Jay Buhner/Jsy Card 125	5.00
(4)	Ken Griffey Jr./Auto. Glv/30	200.00
(5)	Ken Griffey Jr./Auto. Jsy/30	200.00
(6)	Ken Griffey Jr./Jsy Card 125	25.00
(7)	Ken Griffey Jr./Standee/200	15.00
(8)	Ken Griffey Jr./300th HR Card 1000	5.00
(9)	Tony Gwynn/Jsy Card 415	15.00
(10)	Brian Jordan/Auto. Ball/50	10.00
(11)	Greg Maddux/Jsey Card/125	20.00
(12)	Raul Mondesi/Auto. Ball/100	5.00
(13)	Alex Rodriguez/Jsy Card/125	40.00
(14)	Gary Sheffield/Jsy Card/125	5.00
(15)	Robin Ventura/Auto. Ball/50	10.00

Sheer Dominance

Sheer Dominance is a 42-card insert. The base set is inserted one per three packs. The Sheer Dominance Gold parallel is sequentially numbered to 2,000 and the Titanium parallel is numbered to 100. The cards feature a player photo inside a white border. The background color corresponds to the level of the insert.

		NM/M
Complete Set (42):		32.50
Common Player:		.25
Inserted 1:3		
Gold (2,000 Sets):		2X
Titanium (100 Sets):		12X
SD1	Ken Griffey Jr.	1.75
SD2	Rickey Henderson	1.00
SD3	Jaret Wright	.25
SD4	Craig Biggio	.25
SD5	Travis Lee	.25
SD6	Kenny Lofton	.25
SD7	Raul Mondesi	.25
SD8	Cal Ripken Jr.	2.50
SD9	Matt Williams	.25
SD10	Mark McGwire	2.00
SD11	Alex Rodriguez	2.00
SD12	Fred McGriff	.25
SD13	Scott Rolen	.75
SD14	Paul Molitor	1.00
SD15	Nomar Garciaparra	1.50
SD16	Vladimir Guerrero	1.00
SD17	Andruw Jones	1.00
SD18	Manny Ramirez	1.00
SD19	Tony Gwynn	1.50
SD20	Barry Bonds	2.50
SD21	Ben Grieve	.25
SD22	Ivan Rodriguez	.75
SD23	Jose Cruz Jr.	.25
SD24	Pedro J. Martinez	1.00
SD25	Chipper Jones	1.50
SD26	Albert Belle	.25
SD27	Todd Helton	.75
SD28	Paul Konerko	.35
SD29	Sammy Sosa	1.50
SD30	Frank Thomas	1.00
SD31	Greg Maddux	1.50
SD32	Randy Johnson	1.00
SD33	Larry Walker	.25
SD34	Roberto Alomar	.45
SD35	Roger Clemens	1.50
SD36	Mo Vaughn	.25
SD37	Jim Thome	.75
SD38	Jeff Bagwell	1.00
SD39	Tino Martinez	.25
SD40	Mike Piazza	1.75
SD41	Derek Jeter	2.50
SD42	Juan Gonzalez	.50

Sheer Dominance Gold

Identical in format and using the same photos as the Silver version, the scarcer Sheer Dominance Gold card differs on front in its use of a gold-metallic foil background within the white border. Backs of the gold version are individually serial numbered within an edition of 2,000 each.

	NM/M
Common Player:	.50
Gold Stars:	2X

Sheer Dominance Titanium

Sheer Dominance Titanium is a parallel of the 42-card Sheer Dominance insert. The cards are numbered to 100 and have a gray background with "Titanium" printed across it.

	NM/M
Common Player:	4.00
Titanium Stars:	12X

1998 SPx Finite Sample

This card was issued to promote SPx's all-numbered Finite issue. The serial number on the card's back is "0000/0000." The card is overprinted "SAMPLE" on back.

		NM/M
1	Ken Griffey Jr.	3.00

1998 SPx Finite

SPx Finite is an all-sequentially numbered set issued in two 180-card series. The Series 1 base set consists of five subsets: 90 regular cards (numbered to 9,000), 30 Star Focus (7,000), 30 Youth Movement (5,000), 20 Power Explosion (4,000) and 10 Heroes of the Game (2,000). The set is paralleled in the Radiance and Spectrum sets. Radiance regular cards are numbered to 4,500, Star Focus to 3,500, Youth Movement to 2,500, Power Explosion to 1,000 and Heroes of the Game to 100. Spectrum regular cards are numbered to 2,250, Star Focus to 1,750, Youth Movement to 1,250, Power Explosion to 50 and Heroes of the Game to 1. The Series 2 base set has 90 regular cards (numbered to 9,000), 30 Power Passion (7,000), 30 Youth Movement (5,000), 20 Tradewinds (4,000) and 10 Cornerstones of the Game (2,000). Series 2 also has Radiance and Spectrum parallels. Radiance regular cards are numbered to 4,500, Power Passion to 3,500, Youth Movement to 2,500, Tradewinds to 1,000 and Cornerstones of the Game to 100. Spectrum regular cards are numbered to 2,250, Power Passion to 1,750, Youth Movement to 1,250, Tradewinds to 50 and Cornerstones of the Game to 1. The 1-of-1 cards are not valued due to scarcity and fluctuating demand. The only insert is Home Run Hysteria.

		NM/M
Complete Set (360):		200.00
Common Youth Movement: (#1-30, 181-210):		.50
Radiance YM (2,500):		1.5X
Spectrum YM (1,250):		2X
Common Power Explosion: (#31-50):		.50
Radiance PE (1,000):		2X
Spectrum PE (50):		25X
Common Base Card (#51-140, 241-330):		.15
Radiance Base Card (4,500):		1X
Spectrum Base Card (2,250):		2X
Common Star Focus: (#141-170):		.35
Radiance SF (3,500):		1X
Spectrum SF (1,750):		2X
Common Heroes of the Game: (#171-180):		2.50
Radiance HG (100):		15X
Common Power Passion: (#211-240):		.50
Radiance PP (3,500)		1X
Spectrum PP (1,750)		2X
Common Tradewinds: (#331-350):		.75
Radiance TW (1,000)		2X
Spectrum TW (50):		25X
Common Cornerstones/Game: (#351-360):		2.50
Radiance CG (100):		15X
Pack (3):		2.00
Wax Box:		25.00
1	Nomar Garciaparra (Youth Movement)	3.00
2	Miguel Tejada (Youth Movement)	.75
3	Mike Cameron (Youth Movement)	.50
4	Ken Cloude (Youth Movement)	.50
5	Jaret Wright (Youth Movement)	.50
6	Mark Kotsay (Youth Movement)	.50
7	Craig Counsell (Youth Movement)	.50
8	Jose Guillen (Youth Movement)	.50
9	Neifi Perez (Youth Movement)	.50
10	Jose Cruz Jr. (Youth Movement)	.50
11	Brett Tomko (Youth Movement)	.50
12	Matt Morris (Youth Movement)	.50
13	Justin Thompson (Youth Movement)	.50
14	Jeremi Gonzalez (Youth Movement)	.50
15	Scott Rolen (Youth Movement)	1.50
16	Vladimir Guerrero (Youth Movement)	2.00
17	Brad Fullmer (Youth Movement)	.50
18	Brian Giles (Youth Movement)	.50
19	Todd Dunwoody (Youth Movement)	.50
20	Ben Grieve (Youth Movement)	.50
21	Juan Encarnacion (Youth Movement)	.50
22	Aaron Boone (Youth Movement)	.50
23	Richie Sexson (Youth Movement)	.50
24	Richard Hidalgo (Youth Movement)	.50
25	Andruw Jones (Youth Movement)	2.00
26	Todd Helton (Youth Movement)	1.50
27	Paul Konerko (Youth Movement)	.75
28	Dante Powell (Youth Movement)	.50
29	Elieser Marrero (Youth Movement)	.50
30	Derek Jeter (Youth Movement)	5.00
31	Mike Piazza (Power Explosion)	3.00
32	Tony Clark (Power Explosion)	.50
33	Larry Walker (Power Explosion)	.50
34	Jim Thome (Power Explosion)	1.50
35	Juan Gonzalez (Power Explosion)	1.00
36	Jeff Bagwell (Power Explosion)	2.00
37	Jay Buhner (Power Explosion)	.50
38	Tim Salmon (Power Explosion)	.50
39	Albert Belle (Power Explosion)	.50
40	Mark McGwire (Power Explosion)	4.00
41	Sammy Sosa (Power Explosion)	2.50
42	Mo Vaughn (Power Explosion)	.50
43	Manny Ramirez (Power Explosion)	2.00
44	Tino Martinez (Power Explosion)	.50
45	Frank Thomas (Power Explosion)	2.00
46	Nomar Garciaparra (Power Explosion)	2.50
47	Alex Rodriguez (Power Explosion)	4.00
48	Chipper Jones (Power Explosion)	2.50
49	Barry Bonds (Power Explosion)	5.00
50	Ken Griffey Jr. (Power Explosion)	3.00
51	Jason Dickson	.15
52	Jim Edmonds	.15
53	Darin Erstad	.35
54	Tim Salmon	.15
55	Chipper Jones	2.00
56	Ryan Klesko	.15
57	Tom Glavine	.35
58	Denny Neagle	.15
59	John Smoltz	.15
60	Javy Lopez	.15
61	Roberto Alomar	.30
62	Rafael Palmeiro	1.25
63	Mike Mussina	.35
64	Cal Ripken Jr.	4.00
65	Mo Vaughn	.15
66	Tim Naehring	.15
67	John Valentin	.15
68	Mark Grace	.15
69	Kevin Orie	.15
70	Sammy Sosa	2.50
71	Albert Belle	.15
72	Frank Thomas	1.50

#	Player	Price
73	Robin Ventura	.15
74	David Justice	.15
75	Kenny Lofton	.15
76	Omar Vizquel	.15
77	Manny Ramirez	1.50
78	Jim Thome	.65
79	Dante Bichette	.15
80	Larry Walker	.15
81	Vinny Castilla	.15
82	Ellis Burks	.15
83	Bobby Higginson	.15
84	Brian L. Hunter	.15
85	Tony Clark	.15
86	Mike Hampton	.15
87	Jeff Bagwell	1.50
88	Craig Biggio	.15
89	Derek Bell	.15
90	Mike Piazza	3.00
91	Ramon Martinez	.15
92	Raul Mondesi	.15
93	Hideo Nomo	.75
94	Eric Karros	.15
95	Paul Molitor	1.50
96	Marty Cordova	.15
97	Brad Radke	.15
98	Mark Grudzielanek	.15
99	Carlos Perez	.15
100	Rondell White	.15
101	Todd Hundley	.15
102	Edgardo Alfonzo	.15
103	John Franco	.15
104	John Olerud	.15
105	Tino Martinez	.15
106	David Cone	.15
107	Paul O'Neill	.15
108	Andy Pettitte	.25
109	Bernie Williams	.15
110	Rickey Henderson	1.50
111	Jason Giambi	.75
112	Matt Stairs	.15
113	Gregg Jefferies	.15
114	Rico Brogna	.15
115	Curt Schilling	.35
116	Jason Schmidt	.15
117	Jose Guillen	.15
118	Kevin Young	.15
119	Ray Lankford	.15
120	Mark McGwire	3.00
121	Delino DeShields	.15
122	Ken Caminiti	.15
123	Tony Gwynn	2.00
124	Trevor Hoffman	.15
125	Barry Bonds	4.00
126	Jeff Kent	.15
127	Shawn Estes	.15
128	J.T. Snow	.15
129	Jay Buhner	.15
130	Ken Griffey Jr.	2.50
131	Dan Wilson	.15
132	Edgar Martinez	.15
133	Alex Rodriguez	3.00
134	Rusty Greer	.15
135	Juan Gonzalez	.75
136	Fernando Tatis	.15
137	Ivan Rodriguez	1.00
138	Carlos Delgado	.75
139	Pat Hentgen	.15
140	Roger Clemens	2.25
141	Chipper Jones (Star Focus)	2.00
142	Greg Maddux (Star Focus)	2.00
143	Rafael Palmeiro (Star Focus)	1.25
144	Mike Mussina (Star Focus)	.65
145	Cal Ripken Jr. (Star Focus)	4.00
146	Nomar Garciaparra (Star Focus)	2.00
147	Mo Vaughn (Star Focus)	.35
148	Sammy Sosa (Star Focus)	2.00
149	Albert Belle (Star Focus)	.35
150	Frank Thomas (Star Focus)	1.50
151	Jim Thome (Star Focus)	1.25
152	Kenny Lofton (Star Focus)	.35
153	Manny Ramirez (Star Focus)	1.50
154	Larry Walker (Star Focus)	.35
155	Jeff Bagwell (Star Focus)	1.50
156	Craig Biggio (Star Focus)	.35
157	Mike Piazza (Star Focus)	2.50
158	Paul Molitor (Star Focus)	1.50
159	Derek Jeter (Star Focus)	4.00
160	Tino Martinez (Star Focus)	.35
161	Curt Schilling (Star Focus)	.50
162	Mark McGwire (Star Focus)	3.00
163	Tony Gwynn (Star Focus)	2.00
164	Barry Bonds (Star Focus)	4.00
165	Ken Griffey Jr. (Star Focus)	2.50
166	Randy Johnson (Star Focus)	1.50
167	Alex Rodriguez (Star Focus)	3.00
168	Juan Gonzalez (Star Focus)	.75
169	Ivan Rodriguez (Star Focus)	1.25
170	Roger Clemens (Star Focus)	2.25
171	Greg Maddux (Heroes of the Game)	3.00
172	Cal Ripken Jr. (Heroes of the Game)	6.50
173	Frank Thomas (Heroes of the Game)	2.00
174	Jeff Bagwell (Heroes of the Game)	2.00
175	Mike Piazza (Heroes of the Game)	4.00
176	Mark McGwire (Heroes of the Game)	5.00
177	Barry Bonds (Heroes of the Game)	6.50
178	Ken Griffey Jr. (Heroes of the Game)	4.00
179	Alex Rodriguez (Heroes of the Game)	5.00
180	Roger Clemens (Heroes of the Game)	3.25
181	Mike Caruso (Youth Movement)	.50
182	David Ortiz (Youth Movement)	1.00
183	Gabe Alvarez (Youth Movement)	.50
184	Gary Matthews Jr. (Youth Movement)	.50
185	Kerry Wood (Youth Movement)	1.25
186	Carl Pavano (Youth Movement)	.50
187	Alex Gonzalez (Youth Movement)	.50
188	Masato Yoshii (Youth Movement)	.50
189	Larry Sutton (Youth Movement)	.50
190	Russell Branyan (Youth Movement)	.50
191	Bruce Chen (Youth Movement)	.50
192	Rolando Arrojo (Youth Movement)	.50
193	Ryan Christenson (Youth Movement)	.50
194	Cliff Politte (Youth Movement)	.50
195	A.J. Hinch (Youth Movement)	.50
196	Kevin Witt (Youth Movement)	.50
197	Daryle Ward (Youth Movement)	.50
198	Corey Koskie (Youth Movement)	.50
199	Mike Lowell (Youth Movement)	.50
200	Travis Lee (Youth Movement)	.50
201	Kevin Millwood **RC** (Youth Movement)	1.00
202	Robert Smith (Youth Movement)	.50
203	Magglio Ordonez **RC** (Youth Movement)	10.00
204	Eric Milton (Youth Movement)	.50
205	Geoff Jenkins (Youth Movement)	.50
206	Rich Butler (Youth Movement)	.50
207	Mike Kinkade **RC** (Youth Movement)	.75
208	Braden Looper (Youth Movement)	.50
209	Matt Clement (Youth Movement)	.50
210	Derrek Lee (Youth Movement)	1.50
211	Randy Johnson (Power Passion)	1.50
212	John Smoltz (Power Passion)	.50
213	Roger Clemens (Power Passion)	2.25
214	Curt Schilling (Power Passion)	.75
215	Pedro J. Martinez (Power Passion)	1.50
216	Vinny Castilla (Power Passion)	.50
217	Jose Cruz Jr. (Power Passion)	.50
218	Jim Thome (Power Passion)	1.20
219	Alex Rodriguez (Power Passion)	3.00
220	Frank Thomas (Power Passion)	1.50
221	Tim Salmon (Power Passion)	.50
222	Larry Walker (Power Passion)	.50
223	Albert Belle (Power Passion)	.50
224	Manny Ramirez (Power Passion)	1.50
225	Mark McGwire (Power Passion)	3.00
226	Mo Vaughn (Power Passion)	.50
227	Andres Galarraga (Power Passion)	.50
228	Scott Rolen (Power Passion)	1.25
229	Travis Lee (Power Passion)	.50
230	Mike Piazza (Power Passion)	2.50
231	Nomar Garciaparra (Power Passion)	2.00
232	Andruw Jones (Power Passion)	1.50
233	Barry Bonds (Power Passion)	4.00
234	Jeff Bagwell (Power Passion)	1.50
235	Juan Gonzalez (Power Passion)	.75
236	Tino Martinez (Power Passion)	.50
237	Vladimir Guerrero (Power Passion)	1.50
238	Rafael Palmeiro (Power Passion)	1.25
239	Russell Branyan (Power Passion)	.50
240	Ken Griffey Jr. (Power Passion)	2.50
241	Cecil Fielder	.15
242	Chuck Finley	.15
243	Jay Bell	.15
244	Andy Benes	.15
245	Matt Williams	.15
246	Brian Anderson	.15
247	David Dellucci	.15
248	Andres Galarraga	.15
249	Andruw Jones	1.50
250	Greg Maddux	2.00
251	Brady Anderson	.15
252	Joe Carter	.15
253	Eric Davis	.15
254	Pedro J. Martinez	1.50
255	Nomar Garciaparra	2.00
256	Dennis Eckersley	1.25
257	Henry Rodriguez	.15
258	Jeff Blauser	.15
259	Jaime Navarro	.15
260	Ray Durham	.15
261	Chris Stynes	.15
262	Willie Greene	.15
263	Reggie Sanders	.15
264	Bret Boone	.15
265	Barry Larkin	.15
266	Travis Fryman	.15
267	Charles Nagy	.15
268	Sandy Alomar Jr.	.15
269	Darryl Kile	.15
270	Mike Lansing	.15
271	Pedro Astacio	.15
272	Damion Easley	.15
273	Joe Randa	.15
274	Luis Gonzalez	.15
275	Mike Piazza	2.50
276	Todd Zeile	.15
277	Edgar Renteria	.15
278	Livan Hernandez	.15
279	Cliff Floyd	.15
280	Moises Alou	.15
281	Billy Wagner	.15
282	Jeff King	.15
283	Hal Morris	.15
284	Johnny Damon	.35
285	Dean Palmer	.15
286	Tim Belcher	.15
287	Eric Young	.15
288	Bobby Bonilla	.15
289	Gary Sheffield	.60
290	Chan Ho Park	.15
291	Charles Johnson	.15
292	Jeff Cirillo	.15
293	Jeromy Burnitz	.15
294	Jose Valentin	.15
295	Marquis Grissom	.15
296	Todd Walker	.15
297	Terry Steinbach	.15
298	Rick Aguilera	.15
299	Vladimir Guerrero	1.50
300	Rey Ordonez	.15
301	Butch Huskey	.15
302	Bernard Gilkey	.15
303	Mariano Rivera	.25
304	Chuck Knoblauch	.15
305	Derek Jeter	4.00
306	Ricky Bottalico	.15
307	Bob Abreu	.15
308	Scott Rolen	1.25
309	Al Martin	.15
310	Jason Kendall	.15
311	Brian Jordan	.15
312	Ron Gant	.15
313	Todd Stottlemyre	.15
314	Greg Vaughn	.15
315	J. Kevin Brown	.15
316	Wally Joyner	.15
317	Robb Nen	.15
318	Orel Hershiser	.15
319	Russ Davis	.15
320	Randy Johnson	1.50
321	Quinton McCracken	.15
322	Tony Saunders	.15
323	Wilson Alvarez	.15
324	Wade Boggs	2.00
325	Fred McGriff	.15
326	Lee Stevens	.15
327	John Wetteland	.15
328	Jose Canseco	.60
329	Randy Myers	.15
330	Jose Cruz Jr.	.15
331	Matt Williams (Tradewinds)	.50
332	Andres Galarraga (Tradewinds)	.50
333	Walt Weiss (Tradewinds)	.50
334	Joe Carter (Tradewinds)	.50
335	Pedro J. Martinez (Tradewinds)	2.00
336	Henry Rodriguez (Tradewinds)	.50
337	Travis Fryman (Tradewinds)	.50
338	Darryl Kile (Tradewinds)	.50
339	Mike Lansing (Tradewinds)	.50
340	Mike Piazza (Tradewinds)	4.00
341	Moises Alou (Tradewinds)	.50
342	Charles Johnson (Tradewinds)	.50
343	Chuck Knoblauch (Tradewinds)	.50
344	Rickey Henderson (Tradewinds)	2.00
345	J. Kevin Brown (Tradewinds)	.50
346	Orel Hershiser (Tradewinds)	.50
347	Wade Boggs (Tradewinds)	3.00
348	Fred McGriff (Tradewinds)	.50
349	Jose Canseco (Tradewinds)	1.00
350	Gary Sheffield (Tradewinds)	1.00
351	Travis Lee (Cornerstones)	2.50
352	Nomar Garciaparra (Cornerstones)	5.00
353	Frank Thomas (Cornerstones)	4.00
354	Cal Ripken Jr. (Cornerstones)	10.00
355	Mark McGwire (Cornerstones)	8.00
356	Mike Piazza (Cornerstones)	6.00
357	Alex Rodriguez (Cornerstones)	8.00
358	Barry Bonds (Cornerstones)	10.00
359	Tony Gwynn (Cornerstones)	5.00
360	Ken Griffey Jr. (Cornerstones)	6.00

Home Run Hysteria

Home Run Hysteria is a 10-card insert in SPx Finite Series Two. The cards were sequentially numbered to 62.

		NM/M
Complete Set (10):		400.00
Common Player:		15.00
Production 62 Sets		
HR1	Ken Griffey Jr.	75.00
HR2	Mark McGwire	100.00
HR3	Sammy Sosa	60.00
HR4	Albert Belle	15.00
HR5	Alex Rodriguez	100.00
HR6	Greg Vaughn	15.00
HR7	Andres Galarraga	15.00
HR8	Vinny Castilla	15.00
HR9	Juan Gonzalez	25.00
HR10	Chipper Jones	60.00

1999 SP Authentic Sample

UD spokesman Ken Griffey Jr. is featured on the promo card for '99 SP Authentic. In the same format as the issued version, the sample card has different photos on

front and back, a different season summary on back and a large, black "SAMPLE" overprint on back.

		NM/M
1	Ken Griffey Jr.	3.00

1999 SP Authentic

SP Authentic was a 135-card set that sold in packs of five cards for $4.99. The set includes a 30-card Future Watch subset and a 15-card Season to Remember subset. Both subsets were shorted-printed, with each card sequentially numbered to 2,700. The insert lineup included Ernie Banks 500 Club "Piece of History" bat cards. Other insert sets included SP Chirography, The Home Run Chronicles, Epic Figures, Reflections, and SP Authentics.

		NM/M
Complete Set (135):		100.00
Common Player (1-90):		.10
Common Future Watch (91-120):		2.00
Production: (2,700)		
Common Season to Remember (121-135):		2.00
Production: (2,700)		
Pack (5):		3.50
Wax Box (24):		75.00
1	Mo Vaughn	.10
2	Jim Edmonds	.10
3	Darin Erstad	.25
4	Travis Lee	.10
5	Matt Williams	.10
6	Randy Johnson	1.50
7	Chipper Jones	1.75
8	Greg Maddux	1.75
9	Andruw Jones	1.50
10	Andres Galarraga	.10
11	Tom Glavine	.35
12	Cal Ripken Jr.	3.00
13	Brady Anderson	.10
14	Albert Belle	.10
15	Nomar Garciaparra	1.75
16	Donnie Sadler	.10
17	Pedro Martinez	1.50
18	Sammy Sosa	1.75
19	Kerry Wood	.60
20	Mark Grace	.10
21	Mike Caruso	.10
22	Frank Thomas	1.50
23	Paul Konerko	.20
24	Sean Casey	.20
25	Barry Larkin	.10
26	Kenny Lofton	.10
27	Manny Ramirez	1.50
28	Jim Thome	1.25
29	Bartolo Colon	.10
30	Jaret Wright	.10
31	Larry Walker	.10
32	Todd Helton	1.25
33	Tony Clark	.10
34	Dean Palmer	.10
35	Mark Kotsay	.10
36	Cliff Floyd	.10
37	Ken Caminiti	.10
38	Craig Biggio	.10
39	Jeff Bagwell	1.50
40	Moises Alou	.10
41	Johnny Damon	.35
42	Larry Sutton	.10
43	Kevin Brown	.10
44	Gary Sheffield	.40
45	Raul Mondesi	.10
46	Jeromy Burnitz	.10
47	Jeff Cirillo	.10
48	Todd Walker	.10
49	David Ortiz	.50
50	Brad Radtke	.10
51	Vladimir Guerrero	1.50
52	Rondell White	.10
53	Brad Fullmer	.10
54	Mike Piazza	2.00
55	Robin Ventura	.10
56	John Olerud	.10
57	Derek Jeter	3.00
58	Tino Martinez	.10
59	Bernie Williams	.10
60	Roger Clemens	1.75
61	Ben Grieve	.10
62	Miguel Tejada	.20
63	A.J. Hinch	.10
64	Scott Rolen	1.00
65	Curt Schilling	.35
66	Doug Glanville	.10
67	Aramis Ramirez	.10
68	Tony Womack	.10
69	Jason Kendall	.10
70	Tony Gwynn	1.75
71	Wally Joyner	.10
72	Greg Vaughn	.10
73	Barry Bonds	3.00
74	Ellis Burks	.10
75	Jeff Kent	.10
76	Ken Griffey Jr.	2.00
77	Alex Rodriguez	2.50
78	Edgar Martinez	.10
79	Mark McGwire	2.50
80	Eli Marrero	.10
81	Matt Morris	.10
82	Rolando Arrojo	.10
83	Quinton McCracken	.10
84	Jose Canseco	.50
85	Ivan Rodriguez	1.25
86	Juan Gonzalez	.75
87	Royce Clayton	.10
88	Shawn Green	.30
89	Jose Cruz Jr.	.10
90	Carlos Delgado	.60
91	Troy Glaus (Future Watch)	6.00
92	George Lombard (Future Watch)	2.00
93	Ryan Minor (Future Watch)	2.00
94	Calvin Pickering (Future Watch)	2.00
95	Jin Ho Cho (Future Watch)	2.00
96	Russ Branyon (Future Watch)	2.00
97	Derrick Gibson (Future Watch)	2.00
98	Gabe Kapler (Future Watch)	2.00
99	Matt Anderson (Future Watch)	2.00
100	Preston Wilson (Future Watch)	2.00
101	Alex Gonzalez (Future Watch)	2.00
102	Carlos Beltran (Future Watch)	6.00
103	Dee Brown (Future Watch)	2.00
104	Jeremy Giambi (Future Watch)	2.00
105	Angel Pena (Future Watch)	2.00
106	Geoff Jenkins (Future Watch)	2.00
107	Corey Koskie (Future Watch)	2.00
108	A.J. Pierzynski (Future Watch)	2.00
109	Michael Barrett (Future Watch)	2.00
110	Fernando Seguignol (Future Watch)	2.00
111	Mike Kinkade (Future Watch)	2.00
112	Ricky Ledee (Future Watch)	2.00
113	Mike Lowell (Future Watch)	2.00
114	Eric Chavez (Future Watch)	2.50
115	Matt Clement (Future Watch)	2.00
116	Shane Monahan (Future Watch)	2.00
117	J.D. Drew (Future Watch)	4.00
118	Bubba Trammell (Future Watch)	2.00
119	Kevin Witt (Future Watch)	2.00
120	Roy Halladay (Future Watch)	2.50
121	Mark McGwire (Season to Remember)	5.00
122	Mark McGwire, Sammy Sosa (Season to Remember)	4.00

123 Sammy Sosa (Season to Remember) 2.50
124 Ken Griffey Jr. (Season to Remember) 3.00
125 Cal Ripken Jr. (Season to Remember) 6.00
126 Juan Gonzalez (Season to Remember) 2.50
127 Kerry Wood (Season to Remember) 2.50
128 Trevor Hoffman (Season to Remember) 2.00
129 Barry Bonds (Season to Remember) 5.00
130 Alex Rodriguez (Season to Remember) 4.00
131 Ben Grieve (Season to Remember) 2.00
132 Tom Glavine (Season to Remember) 2.00
133 David Wells (Season to Remember) 2.00
134 Mike Piazza (Season to Remember) 3.00
135 Scott Brosius (Season to Remember) 2.00

Chirography

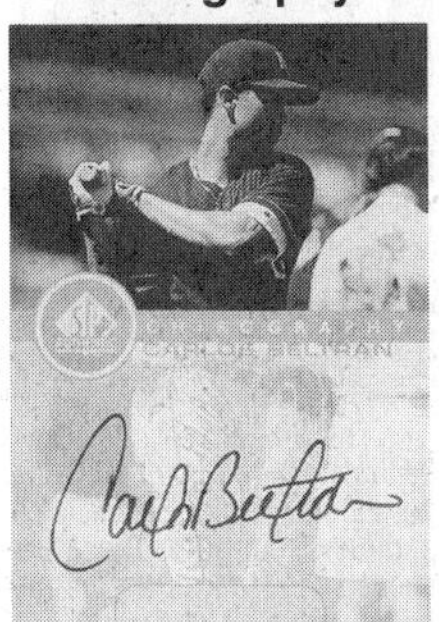

Baseball's top players and future stars are included in this 39-card autograph insert set. The set was split into Level 1 and Level 2 versions. Level 1 cards are not numbered and were inserted one card per 24 packs. Level 2 (gold) cards are sequentially numbered to the featured player's jersey number.

NM/M
Common Player: 4.00
Inserted 1:24
EC Eric Chavez 8.00
GK Gabe Kapler 4.00
GMj Gary Matthews Jr. 4.00
CP Calvin Pickering 4.00
CK Corey Koskie 6.00
SM Shane Monahan 4.00
RH Richard Hidalgo 4.00
MK Mike Kinkade 4.00
CB Carlos Beltran 35.00
AG Alex Gonzalez 4.00
BC Bruce Chen 4.00
MA Matt Anderson 4.00
RM Ryan Minor 4.00
RL Ricky Ledee 4.00
RR Ruben Rivera 4.00
BF Brad Fullmer 4.00
RB Russ Branyan 4.00
ML Mike Lowell 6.00
JG Jeremy Giambi 4.00
GL George Lombard 4.00
KW Kevin Witt 4.00
TW Todd Walker 4.00
SR Scott Rolen 20.00
KW Kerry Wood 25.00
BG Ben Grieve 4.00
JR Ken Griffey Jr. 75.00
CJ Chipper Jones 30.00
IR Ivan Rodriguez 25.00
TGl Troy Glaus 15.00
TL Travis Lee 4.00
VG Vladimir Guerrero 30.00
GV Greg Vaughn 4.00
JT Jim Thome 25.00
JD J.D. Drew 15.00
TH Todd Helton 15.00
GM Greg Maddux 75.00
NG Nomar Garciaparra 75.00
TG Tony Gwynn 30.00
CR Cal Ripken Jr. 125.00

Chirography Gold

These Chirography parallels can be identified by the gold tint on the card front and their sequential numbering; each featured player signed to his jersey number.

NM/M
Common Player: 5.00
Inserted 1:24
EC Eric Chavez/30 40.00
GK Gabe Kapler/51 10.00
GMj Gary Matthews Jr./68 5.00
CP Calvin Pickering/6 40.00
CK Corey Koskie/47 15.00
SM Shane Monahan/12 20.00
RH Richard Hidalgo/15 30.00
MK Mike Kinkade/33 10.00
CB Carlos Beltran/36 75.00
AG Alex Gonzalez/22 20.00
BC Bruce Chen/48 10.00
MA Matt Anderson/14 20.00
RM Ryan Minor/10 35.00
RL Ricky Ledee/38 10.00
RR Ruben Rivera/28 10.00
BF Brad Fullmer/20 10.00
RB Russ Branyan/66 10.00
ML Mike Lowell/60 15.00
JG Jeremy Giambi/15 20.00
GL George Lombard/26 10.00
KW Kevin Witt/6 20.00
TW Todd Walker/12 40.00
SR Scott Rolen/17 75.00
KW Kerry Wood/34 60.00
BG Ben Grieve/14 35.00
JR Ken Griffey Jr./24 250.00
CJ Chipper Jones/10 200.00
IR Ivan Rodriguez/7 125.00
TGl Troy Glaus/14 90.00
TL Travis Lee/16 35.00
VG Vladimir Guerrero/27 75.00
GV Greg Vaughn/23 10.00
JT Jim Thome/25 40.00
JD J.D. Drew/8 125.00
TH Todd Helton/17 75.00
GM Greg Maddux/31 150.00
NG Nomar Garciaparra/5 375.00
TG Tony Gwynn/19 125.00
CR Cal Ripken Jr./8 650.00

Epic Figures

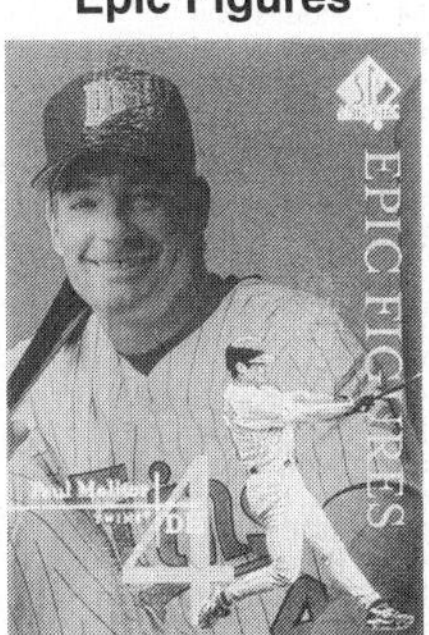

This 30-card set highlights baseball's biggest talents, including Mark McGwire and Derek Jeter. The card fronts have two photos, with the larger photo done with a shadow look in the background. Fronts also feature a holographic look, while the card backs feature the player's career highlights. These are seeded one per seven packs.

NM/M
Complete Set (30): 30.00
Common Player: .50
Inserted 1:7
E01 Mo Vaughn .50
E02 Travis Lee .50
E03 Andres Galarraga .50
E04 Andruw Jones 1.00
E05 Chipper Jones 1.25
E06 Greg Maddux 1.25
E07 Cal Ripken Jr. 3.00
E08 Nomar Garciaparra 1.25
E09 Sammy Sosa 1.25
E10 Frank Thomas 1.00
E11 Kerry Wood .60
E12 Kenny Lofton .50
E13 Manny Ramirez 1.00
E14 Larry Walker .50
E15 Jeff Bagwell 1.00
E16 Paul Molitor 1.00
E17 Vladimir Guerrero 1.00
E18 Derek Jeter 3.00
E19 Tino Martinez .50
E20 Mike Piazza 1.50
E21 Ben Grieve .50
E22 Scott Rolen .75
E23 Mark McGwire 2.00
E24 Tony Gwynn 1.25
E25 Barry Bonds 3.00
E26 Ken Griffey Jr. 1.50
E27 Alex Rodriguez 2.00
E28 J.D. Drew .65
E29 Juan Gonzalez .60
E30 Kevin Brown .50

Home Run Chronicles

This two-tiered 70-card set focuses on the amazing seasons of McGwire and Sammy Sosa. Other players help round out the 70-card set, but special emphasis has been placed on the duo. These are seeded one per pack. A die-cut version also exists, with each card serially numbered to 70.

NM/M
Complete Set (70): 50.00
Common Player: .15
Inserted 1:1
Die-Cuts: 10X
Production 70 Sets
HR01 Mark McGwire 1.50
HR02 Sammy Sosa 1.25
HR03 Ken Griffey Jr. 1.00
HR04 Mark McGwire 1.50
HR05 Mark McGwire 1.50
HR06 Albert Belle .15
HR07 Jose Canseco .30
HR08 Juan Gonzalez .45
HR09 Manny Ramirez .65
HR10 Rafael Palmeiro .50
HR11 Mo Vaughn .15
HR12 Carlos Delgado .45
HR13 Nomar Garciaparra .75
HR14 Barry Bonds 1.50
HR15 Alex Rodriguez 1.25
HR16 Tony Clark .15
HR17 Jim Thome .50
HR18 Edgar Martinez .15
HR19 Frank Thomas .65
HR20 Greg Vaughn .15
HR21 Vinny Castilla .15
HR22 Andres Galarraga .15
HR23 Moises Alou .15
HR24 Jeromy Burnitz .15
HR25 Vladimir Guerrero .65
HR26 Jeff Bagwell .65
HR27 Chipper Jones .75
HR28 Javier Lopez .15
HR29 Mike Piazza 1.00
HR30 Andruw Jones .65
HR31 Henry Rodriguez .15
HR32 Jeff Kent .15
HR33 Ray Lankford .15
HR34 Scott Rolen .50
HR35 Raul Mondesi .15
HR36 Ken Caminiti .15
HR37 J.D. Drew .40
HR38 Troy Glaus .50
HR39 Gabe Kapler .15
HR40 Alex Rodriguez 1.25
HR41 Ken Griffey Jr. 1.00
HR42 Sammy Sosa 1.25
HR43 Mark McGwire 1.50
HR44 Sammy Sosa 1.25
HR45 Mark McGwire 1.50
HR46 Vinny Castilla .15
HR47 Sammy Sosa 1.25
HR48 Mark McGwire 1.50
HR49 Sammy Sosa 1.25
HR50 Greg Vaughn .15
HR51 Sammy Sosa 1.25
HR52 Mark McGwire 1.50
HR53 Sammy Sosa 1.25
HR54 Mark McGwire 1.50
HR55 Sammy Sosa 1.25
HR56 Ken Griffey Jr. 1.00
HR57 Sammy Sosa 1.25
HR58 Mark McGwire 1.50
HR59 Sammy Sosa 1.25
HR60 Mark McGwire 1.50
HR61 Mark McGwire 2.50
HR62 Mark McGwire 2.50
HR63 Mark McGwire 1.50
HR64 Mark McGwire 1.50
HR65 Mark McGwire 1.50
HR66 Sammy Sosa 2.50
HR67 Mark McGwire 1.50
HR68 Mark McGwire 1.50
HR69 Mark McGwire 1.50
HR70 Mark McGwire 4.00

Home Run Chronicles Die-Cuts

Each of the 70 cards in the Home Run Chronicles insert set was also issued in a die-cut version. The die-cuts share the basic front and back design of the regular HR Chronicle cards but have portions of the upper-left and lower-right cut away. On back, each of the die-cuts features an ink-jetted serial number from within an edition of 70.

HR Chronicle Die-Cuts: 10X

Reflections

Dot Matrix technology is utilized to provide a unique look at 30 of the best players in the game. Card fronts are horizontal with two small and one large photo. These are seeded 1:23 packs.

NM/M
Complete Set (30): 60.00
Common Player: .75
Inserted 1:23
R01 Mo Vaughn .75
R02 Travis Lee .75
R03 Andres Galarraga .75
R04 Andruw Jones 2.50
R05 Chipper Jones 3.00
R06 Greg Maddux 3.00
R07 Cal Ripken Jr. 6.00
R08 Nomar Garciaparra 3.00
R09 Sammy Sosa 3.00
R10 Frank Thomas 2.50
R11 Kerry Wood 1.50
R12 Kenny Lofton .75
R13 Manny Ramirez 2.50
R14 Larry Walker .75
R15 Jeff Bagwell 2.50
R16 Paul Molitor 2.50
R17 Vladimir Guerrero 2.50
R18 Derek Jeter 6.00
R19 Tino Martinez .75
R20 Mike Piazza 3.50
R21 Ben Grieve .75
R22 Scott Rolen 2.00
R23 Mark McGwire 4.50
R24 Tony Gwynn 3.00
R25 Barry Bonds 6.00
R26 Ken Griffey Jr. 3.50
R27 Alex Rodriguez 4.50
R28 J.D. Drew 1.25
R29 Juan Gonzalez 1.25
R30 Roger Clemens 3.25

SP Authentics

These 1:864 pack inserts are redemption cards that could be redeemed for special pieces of memorabilia from either Ken Griffey Jr. or Mark McGwire. The redemption period ended March 1, 2000. Because of rarity any surviving unredeemed McGwire home run-game autographed tickets cannot be valued.

NM/M
Common Card: 10.00
(1) K.Griffey Jr./Auto. Ball/75 60.00
(2) Ken Griffey Jr./Glove/200 20.00
(3) K. Griffey Jr./HR Cel Card/346 10.00
(4) Ken Griffey Jr./Auto. Jsy/25 125.00
(5) K. Griffey Jr./Auto. Mini Helmet/75 80.00
(6) Ken Griffey Jr./SI Cover/200 15.00
(7) K. Griffey Jr./SI Cover Auto./75 75.00
(8) Ken Griffey Jr./Standee/300 10.00

500 Club Piece of History

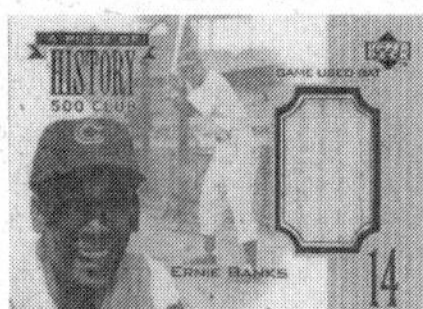

These cards feature a piece of game-used bat once swung by Ernie Banks. Approximately 350 cards exist. An autographed version of this card also exists, only 14 were produced.

NM/M
EB Ernie Banks 120.00
EB Ernie Banks/Auto./14 325.00

1999 SP Signature Edition

Even with one autograph per three-card pack, this single-series issue's price of $19.99 per pack shocked the hobby when it was introduced. Horizontal cards have a color or black-and-white photo at the left end with foil highlights and airbrushed geometric designs on a white background. Backs repeat the portrait portion of the front photo and add player data and some stats.

NM/M
Complete Set (180): 60.00
Common Player: .15
Pack (3): 20.00
Wax Box (12): 250.00
1 Nomar Garciaparra 2.00
2 Ken Griffey Jr. 2.50
3 J.D. Drew .50
4 Alex Rodriguez 3.00
5 Juan Gonzalez .60
6 Mo Vaughn .15
7 Greg Maddux 2.00
8 Chipper Jones 2.00
9 Frank Thomas 1.50
10 Vladimir Guerrero 1.50
11 Mike Piazza 2.50
12 Eric Chavez .25
13 Tony Gwynn 2.00
14 Orlando Hernandez .15
15 Pat Burrell **RC** 6.00
16 Darin Erstad .30
17 Greg Vaughn .15
18 Russ Branyan .15
19 Gabe Kapler .15
20 Craig Biggio .15
21 Troy Glaus 1.25
22 Pedro J. Martinez 1.50
23 Carlos Beltran .50
24 Derrek Lee .50
25 Manny Ramirez 1.50
26 Shea Hillenbrand **RC** 1.00
27 Carlos Lee .15
28 Angel Pena .15
29 Rafael Roque .15
30 Octavio Dotel .15
31 Jeromy Burnitz .15
32 Jeremy Giambi .15
33 Andruw Jones 1.50
34 Todd Helton 1.25
35 Scott Rolen 1.25
36 Jason Kendall .15
37 Trevor Hoffman .15
38 Barry Bonds 4.00
39 Ivan Rodriguez 1.25
40 Roy Halladay .15
41 Rickey Henderson 1.50
42 Ryan Minor .15
43 Brian Jordan .15
44 Alex Gonzalez .15
45 Raul Mondesi .15
46 Corey Koskie .15
47 Paul O'Neill .15
48 Todd Walker .15
49 Carlos Febles .15
50 Travis Fryman .15
51 Albert Belle .15
52 Travis Lee .15
53 Bruce Chen .15
54 Reggie Taylor .15
55 Jerry Hairston Jr. .15
56 Carlos Guillen .15
57 Michael Barrett .15
58 Jason Conti .15
59 Joe Lawrence .15
60 Jeff Cirillo .15
61 Juan Melo .15
62 Chad Hermansen .15
63 Ruben Mateo .15
64 Ben Davis .15
65 Mike Caruso .15
66 Jason Giambi .50
67 Jose Canseco .50
68 Chad Hutchinson **RC** .15
69 Mitch Meluskey .15
70 Adrian Beltre .25
71 Mark Kotsay .15
72 Juan Encarnacion .15
73 Dermal Brown .15
74 Kevin Witt .15
75 Vinny Castilla .15
76 Aramis Ramirez .15
77 Marlon Anderson .15
78 Mike Kinkade .15
79 Kevin Barker .15
80 Ron Belliard .15
81 Chris Haas .15
82 Bob Henley .15
83 Fernando Seguignol .15
84 Damon Minor .15
85 A.J. Burnett **RC** 1.00
86 Calvin Pickering .15
87 Mike Darr .15
88 Cesar King .15
89 Rob Bell .15
90 Derrick Gibson .15
91 Ober Moreno **RC** .15
92 Robert Fick .15
93 Doug Mientkiewicz **RC** .75
94 A.J. Pierzynski .15
95 Orlando Palmeiro .15
96 Sidney Ponson .15
97 Ivanon Coffie **RC** .15
98 Juan Pena **RC** 1.00
99 Mark Karchner .15
100 Carlos Castillo .15
101 Bryan Ward .15
102 Mario Valdez .15
103 Billy Wagner .15
104 Miguel Tejada .25
105 Jose Cruz Jr. .15
106 George Lombard .15
107 Geoff Jenkins .15
108 Ray Lankford .15
109 Todd Stottlemyre .15
110 Mike Lowell .15
111 Matt Clement .15
112 Scott Brosius .15
113 Preston Wilson .15
114 Bartolo Colon .15
115 Rolando Arrojo .15
116 Jose Guillen .15
117 Ron Gant .15
118 Ricky Ledee .15
119 Carlos Delgado .50
120 Abraham Nunez .15
121 John Olerud .15
122 Chan Ho Park .15
123 Brad Radke .15
124 Al Leiter .15
125 Gary Matthews Jr. .15
126 F.P. Santangelo .15
127 Brad Fullmer .15
128 Matt Anderson .15
129 A.J. Hinch .15
130 Sterling Hitchcock .15
131 Edgar Martinez .15
132 Fernando Tatis .15
133 Bobby Smith .15
134 Paul Konerko .25
135 Sean Casey .25
136 Donnie Sadler .15
137 Denny Neagle .15
138 Sandy Alomar .15
139 Mariano Rivera .25
140 Emil Brown .15
141 J.T. Snow .15
142 Eli Marrero .15
143 Rusty Greer .15
144 Johnny Damon .35
145 Damion Easley .15
146 Eric Milton .15
147 Rico Brogna .15
148 Ray Durham .15
149 Wally Joyner .15
150 Royce Clayton .15
151 David Ortiz .50
152 Wade Boggs 2.00
153 Ugueth Urbina .15
154 Richard Hidalgo .15
155 Bobby Abreu .15

156	Robb Nen	.15
157	David Segui	.15
158	Sean Berry	.15
159	Kevin Tapani	.15
160	Jason Varitek	.15
161	Fernando Vina	.15
162	Jim Leyritz	.15
163	Enrique Wilson	.15
164	Jim Parque	.15
165	Doug Glanville	.15
166	Jesus Sanchez	.15
167	Nolan Ryan	4.00
168	Robin Yount	.50
169	Stan Musial	1.00
170	Tom Seaver	.50
171	Mike Schmidt	1.00
172	Willie Stargell	.50
173	Rollie Fingers	.45
174	Willie McCovey	.50
175	Harmon Killebrew	.50
176	Eddie Mathews	.50
177	Reggie Jackson	1.00
178	Frank Robinson	.50
179	Ken Griffey Sr.	.15
180	Eddie Murray	1.50

Autographs

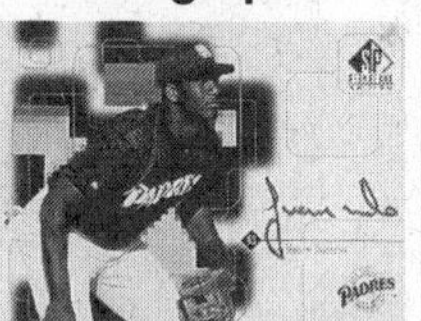

Authentically autographed cards of nearly 100 current stars, top prospects and Hall of Famers were featured as one-per-pack inserts in SP Signature Edition. Some players did not return their signed cards in time for pack inclusion and had to be obtained by returning an exchange card prior to the May 12, 2000, deadline.

		NM/M
Common Player:		3.00
Inserted 1:1		
BA	Bobby Abreu	10.00
SA	Sandy Alomar	5.00
MA	Marlon Anderson	4.00
KB	Kevin Barker	3.00
MB	Michael Barrett	4.00
RoB	Rob Bell	3.00
AB	Albert Belle	15.00
RBe	Ron Belliard	3.00
CBe	Carlos Beltran	50.00
ABe	Adrian Beltre	25.00
BB	Barry Bonds	180.00
RB	Russ Branyan	3.00
SB	Scott Brosius/SP	30.00
DB	Dermal Brown	3.00
EB	Emil Brown	3.00
AJB	A.J. Burnett (Exchange Card)	3.00
AJB	A.J. Burnett/Auto.	15.00
PB	Pat Burrell	12.50
JoC	Jose Canseco	30.00
MC	Mike Caruso	3.00
SC	Sean Casey (Exchange Card)	3.00
SC	Sean Casey/Auto.	15.00
VC	Vinny Castilla (Exchange Card)	3.00
VC	Vinny Castilla (Autographed)	8.00
CC	Carlos Castillo	3.00
EC	Eric Chavez	10.00
BC	Bruce Chen	3.00
JCi	Jeff Cirillo	3.00
RC	Royce Clayton	3.00
MCl	Matt Clement	6.00
IC	Ivanon Coffie	3.00
BCo	Bartolo Colon (Exchange Card)	3.00
BCo	Bartolo Colon/Auto.	8.00
JC	Jason Conti	3.00
JDa	Johnny Damon	25.00
BD	Ben Davis	3.00
CD	Carlos Delgado	15.00
OD	Octavio Dotel	3.00
JD	J.D. Drew	15.00
RD	Ray Durham	3.00
DEa	Damion Easley	3.00
JE	Juan Encarnacion	3.00
DE	Darin Erstad	8.00
CF	Carlos Febles	3.00
Rob	Robert Fick	3.00
Rol	Rollie Fingers	8.00
BF	Brad Fullmer	3.00
RGa	Ron Gant	8.00
NG	Nomar Garciaparra	75.00
JaG	Jason Giambi	20.00
DG	Derrick Gibson	3.00
DGl	Doug Glanville	3.00
TGl	Troy Glaus	15.00
AG	Alex Gonzalez	5.00
RGr	Rusty Greer	3.00
Jr.	Ken Griffey Jr.	80.00
1	Ken Griffey Jr. (Facsimile autographed "SAMPLE.")	15.00
Sr.	Ken Griffey Sr.	8.00
VG	Vladimir Guerrero	30.00
JG	Jose Guillen	8.00
TG	Tony Gwynn	35.00
CHa	Chris Haas	3.00
JHj	Jerry Hairston Jr.	4.00
RH	Roy Halladay	10.00
THe	Todd Helton	20.00
BH	Bob Henley	3.00
ED	Orlando Hernandez	40.00
CH	Chad Hermansen	3.00
ShH	Shea Hillenbrand	8.00
StH	Sterling Hitchcock	3.00
THo	Trevor Hoffman	5.00
CHu	Chad Hutchinson	3.00
RJ	Reggie Jackson/SP	40.00
GJ	Geoff Jenkins	5.00
AJ	Andruw Jones	20.00
CJ	Chipper Jones	40.00
WJ	Wally Joyner	8.00
GK	Gabe Kapler	3.00
MKa	Mark Karchner	3.00
JK	Jason Kendall	6.00
HK	Harmon Killebrew	40.00
CKi	Cesar King	3.00
MKi	Mike Kinkade	3.00
PK	Paul Konerko	10.00
CK	Corey Koskie	6.00
MK	Mark Kotsay	4.00
RL	Ray Lankford	5.00
JLa	Joe Lawrence	3.00
CL	Carlos Lee	10.00
DL	Derrek Lee	25.00
AL	Al Leiter	6.00
JLe	Jim Leyritz	6.00
GL	George Lombard	3.00
GM	Greg Maddux	80.00
Eli	Eli Marrero	3.00
EM	Edgar Martinez	20.00
PM	Pedro J. Martinez (Exchange Card)	5.00
PM	Pedro J. Martinez/ Auto.	100.00
RMa	Ruben Mateo (Exchange Card)	3.00
RMa	Ruben Mateo/Auto.	8.00
EMa	Eddie Mathews	60.00
GMj	Gary Matthews Jr.	3.00
WMc	Willie McCovey	35.00
JM	Juan Melo	3.00
MMe	Mitch Meluskey	3.00
DoM	Doug Mientkiewicz	6.00
EMi	Eric Milton	3.00
DaM	Damon Minor	3.00
RM	Ryan Minor	3.00
EMu	Eddie Murray	20.00
SM	Stan Musial	50.00
RN	Robb Nen	3.00
AN	Abraham Nunez	3.00
JO	John Olerud	10.00
PO	Paul O'Neill	17.50
DO	David Ortiz	35.00
OP	Orlando Palmeiro	3.00
JP	Jim Parque	3.00
AP	Angel Pena	3.00
MP	Mike Piazza (Exchange Card)	6.00
MP	Mike Piazza/Auto.	175.00
CP	Calvin Pickering	3.00
AJP	A.J. Pierzynski	5.00
SP	Sidney Ponson	8.00
BR	Brad Radke	4.00
ARa	Aramis Ramirez	10.00
MR	Manny Ramirez	50.00
MRi	Mariano Rivera	25.00
FR	Frank Robinson	25.00
AR	Alex Rodriguez	120.00
PG	Ivan Rodriguez	25.00
SR	Scott Rolen (Exchange Card)	3.00
SR	Scott Rolen/Auto.	25.00
RR	Rafael Roque	3.00
NR	Nolan Ryan	120.00
DS	Donnie Sadler	3.00
JS	Jesus Sanchez	3.00
MS	Mike Schmidt	60.00
TSe	Tom Seaver	35.00
DSe	David Segui	3.00
FS	Fernando Seguignol	3.00
BS	Bobby Smith	3.00
JT	J.T. Snow (Exchange Card)	3.00
JT	J.T. Snow/Auto.	6.00
POP	Willie Stargell (Exchange Card)	3.00
POP	Willie Stargell (Autographed)	40.00
TSt	Todd Stottlemyre	3.00
FTa	Fernando Tatis	3.00
RT	Reggie Taylor	3.00
MT	Miguel Tejada	20.00
FT	Frank Thomas	50.00
MV	Mario Valdez	3.00
JV	Jason Varitek	30.00
GV	Greg Vaughn	3.00
MO	Mo Vaughn	8.00
FV	Fernando Vina	3.00
BWa	Billy Wagner	10.00
TW	Todd Walker	3.00
BW	Bryan Ward	3.00
EW	Enrique Wilson	3.00
KW	Kevin Witt	3.00
RY	Robin Yount	40.00

Autographs Gold

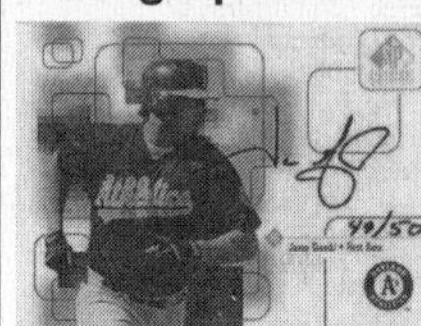

This parallel edition of the Signature Series Autographs features special gold graphic highlights on front and cards serially numbered within an edition of 50 each (except A.J. Burnett). Cards of 11 players were never signed, while cards of several others had to be obtained by sending in an exchange card, valid through May 12, 2000.

		NM/M
Common Player:		12.00
Production 50 Sets		
MA	Marlon Anderson	12.00
KB	Kevin Barker	12.00
MB	Michael Barrett	12.00
RoB	Rob Bell	12.00
AB	Albert Belle	20.00
RBe	Ron Belliard	12.00
CBe	Carlos Beltran	75.00
ABe	Adrian Beltre	40.00
CB	Craig Biggio (Unsigned)	3.00
BB	Barry Bonds	250.00
RB	Russ Branyan	12.00
DB	Dermal Brown	12.00
AJB	A.J. Burnett (Exchange Card)	4.00
AJB	A.J. Burnett (Autographed edition of 20.)	40.00
JB	Jeromy Burnitz (Unsigned)	3.00
PB	Pat Burrell	40.00
JoC	Jose Canseco	50.00
MC	Mike Caruso	12.00
VC	Vinny Castilla (Exchange Card)	3.00
VC	Vinny Castilla (Autographed)	20.00
CC	Carlos Castillo	12.00
EC	Eric Chavez	20.00
BC	Bruce Chen	12.00
JCi	Jeff Cirillo	12.00
JC	Jason Conti	12.00
MD	Mike Darr (Unsigned)	3.00
BD	Ben Davis	12.00
OD	Octavio Dotel	12.00
JD	J.D. Drew	30.00
JE	Juan Encarnacion	12.00
DE	Darin Erstad	20.00
CF	Carlos Febles	12.00
TF	Travis Fryman (Unsigned)	3.00
BF	Brad Fullmer	12.00
NG	Nomar Garciaparra	100.00
JaG	Jason Giambi	40.00
JeG	Jeremy Giambi (Unsigned)	3.00
DG	Derrick Gibson	12.00
DGl	Doug Glanville	12.00
TGl	Troy Glaus	30.00
AG	Alex Gonzalez	12.00
JG	Juan Gonzalez (Unsigned)	6.00
Jr.	Ken Griffey Jr.	150.00
Sr.	Ken Griffey Sr.	12.00
VG	Vladimir Guerrero	75.00
JG	Jose Guillen (Unsigned)	3.00
TG	Tony Gwynn	60.00
CHa	Chris Haas	12.00
JHj	Jerry Hairston Jr.	12.00
RH	Roy Halladay	25.00
THe	Todd Helton	30.00
RH	Rickey Henderson (Unsigned)	6.00
BH	Bob Henley	12.00
ED	Orlando Hernandez	25.00
CH	Chad Hermansen	12.00
ShH	Shea Hillenbrand	20.00
StH	Sterling Hitchcock	12.00
THo	Trevor Hoffman	30.00
CHu	Chad Hutchinson	12.00
GJ	Geoff Jenkins	12.00
AJ	Andruw Jones	40.00
CJ	Chipper Jones	80.00
BJ	Brian Jordan (Unsigned)	3.00
WJ	Wally Joyner	25.00
GK	Gabe Kapler	12.00
MKa	Mark Karchner	12.00
JK	Jason Kendall	20.00
CKi	Cesar King	12.00
MKi	Mike Kinkade	12.00
PK	Paul Konerko	15.00
CK	Corey Koskie	20.00
MK	Mark Kotsay	12.00
RL	Ray Lankford	12.00
JLa	Joe Lawrence	12.00
CL	Carlos Lee	25.00
DL	Derrek Lee	50.00
TL	Travis Lee (Unsigned)	4.00
AL	Al Leiter	12.00
JLe	Jim Leyritz	12.00
GL	George Lombard	12.00
GM	Greg Maddux	150.00
PM	Pedro Martinez (Exchange Card)	6.00
PM	Pedro Martinez/ Auto.	200.00
RMa	Ruben Mateo (Exchange Card)	3.00
RMa	Ruben Mateo (Autographed)	15.00
GMj	Gary Matthews Jr.	12.00
JM	Juan Melo	12.00
MMe	Mitch Meluskey	12.00
DoM	Doug Mientkiewicz	12.00
EMi	Eric Milton	12.00
DaM	Damon Minor	12.00
RM	Ryan Minor	12.00
PO	Paul O'Neill	30.00
DO	David Ortiz	75.00
OP	Orlando Palmeiro	12.00
AP	Angel Pena	12.00
MP	Mike Piazza (Exchange Card)	10.00
MP	Mike Piazza/Auto.	250.00
CP	Calvin Pickering	12.00
ARa	Aramis Ramirez	30.00
MR	Manny Ramirez	80.00
AR	Alex Rodriguez	185.00
PG	Ivan Rodriguez	45.00
SR	Scott Rolen (Exchange Card)	4.00
SR	Scott Rolen/Auto.	75.00
RR	Rafael Roque	12.00
DSe	David Segui	12.00
FS	Fernando Seguignol	12.00
BS	Bobby Smith	12.00
RT	Reggie Taylor	12.00
FT	Frank Thomas	70.00
MV	Mario Valdez	12.00
GV	Greg Vaughn	12.00
MO	Mo Vaughn	20.00
TW	Todd Walker	12.00
KW	Kevin Witt	12.00

Legendary Cuts

Each of the cards in this one-of-one insert series is unique, thus catalog values are impossible to assign.

No Pricing
Production One Set

500 Club Piece of History

		NM/M
MO	Mel Ott/350	100.00

1999 SPx

Formerly SPx Finite, this super-premium product showcases 80 of baseball's veteran players on regular cards and a 40-card rookie subset, which are serially numbered to 1,999. Two top rookies, J.D. Drew and Gabe Kapler autographed all 1,999 of their rookie subset cards. There are two parallels, SPx Radiance and SPx Spectrum. Radiance are serially numbered to 100 with Drew and Kapler signing all 100 of their cards. They are exclusive to Finite Radiance Hot Packs. Spectrums are limited to only one set and available only in Finite Spectrum Hot Packs. Packs consist of three cards with a S.R.P. of $5.99.

		NM/M
Complete Set (120):		100.00
Common Player:		.50
Common SPx Rookie (81-120):		2.00
Production 1,999 Sets		
Radiance (1-80):		7X
Radiance SP (81-120):		1.5X
Spectrum (1-of-1):		
Values Undetermined		
Pack (3):		3.00
Wax Box (18):		40.00
1	Mark McGwire #61	2.50
2	Mark McGwire #62	1.00
3	Mark McGwire #63	1.00
4	Mark McGwire #64	1.00
5	Mark McGwire #65	1.00
6	Mark McGwire #66	1.00
7	Mark McGwire #67	1.00
8	Mark McGwire #68	1.00
9	Mark McGwire #69	1.00
10	Mark McGwire #70	2.50
11	Mo Vaughn	.50
12	Darin Erstad	.75
13	Travis Lee	.50
14	Randy Johnson	1.50
15	Matt Williams	.50
16	Chipper Jones	2.00
17	Greg Maddux	2.00
18	Andruw Jones	1.50
19	Andres Galarraga	.50
20	Cal Ripken Jr.	4.00
21	Albert Belle	.50
22	Mike Mussina	.75
23	Nomar Garciaparra	2.00
24	Pedro Martinez	1.50
25	John Valentin	.50
26	Kerry Wood	1.00
27	Sammy Sosa	2.00
28	Mark Grace	.50
29	Frank Thomas	1.50
30	Mike Caruso	.50
31	Barry Larkin	.50
32	Sean Casey	.50
33	Jim Thome	1.25
34	Kenny Lofton	.50
35	Manny Ramirez	1.50
36	Larry Walker	.50
37	Todd Helton	1.25
38	Vinny Castilla	.50
39	Tony Clark	.50
40	Derrek Lee	1.00
41	Mark Kotsay	.50
42	Jeff Bagwell	1.50
43	Craig Biggio	.50
44	Moises Alou	.50
45	Larry Sutton	.50
46	Johnny Damon	1.00
47	Gary Sheffield	1.00
48	Raul Mondesi	.50
49	Jeromy Burnitz	.50
50	Todd Walker	.50
51	David Ortiz	1.00
52	Vladimir Guerrero	1.50
53	Rondell White	.50
54	Mike Piazza	2.50
55	Derek Jeter	4.00
56	Tino Martinez	.50
57	David Wells	.50
58	Ben Grieve	.50
59	A.J. Hinch	.50
60	Scott Rolen	1.25
61	Doug Glanville	.50
62	Aramis Ramirez	.50
63	Jose Guillen	.50
64	Tony Gwynn	2.00
65	Greg Vaughn	.50
66	Ruben Rivera	.50
67	Barry Bonds	4.00
68	J.T. Snow	.50
69	Alex Rodriguez	3.00
70	Ken Griffey Jr.	2.50
71	Jay Buhner	.50
72	Mark McGwire	3.00
73	Fernando Tatis	.50
74	Quinton McCracken	.50
75	Wade Boggs	2.00
76	Ivan Rodriguez	1.25
77	Juan Gonzalez	1.00
78	Rafael Palmeiro	1.25
79	Jose Cruz Jr.	.50
80	Carlos Delgado	1.00
81	Troy Glaus	5.00
82	Vladimir Nunez	2.00
83	George Lombard	2.00
84	Bruce Chen	2.00
85	Ryan Minor	2.00
86	Calvin Pickering	2.00
87	Jin Ho Cho	2.00
88	Russ Branyan	2.00
89	Derrick Gibson	2.00
90	Gabe Kapler/Auto	6.00
91	Matt Anderson	2.00
92	Robert Fick	2.00
93	Juan Encarnacion	2.00
94	Preston Wilson	2.00
95	Alex Gonzalez	2.00
96	Carlos Beltran	5.00
97	Jeremy Giambi	2.00
98	Dee Brown	2.00
99	Adrian Beltre	4.00
100	Alex Cora	2.00
101	Angel Pena	2.00
102	Geoff Jenkins	2.00
103	Ronnie Belliard	2.00
104	Corey Koskie	2.00
105	A.J. Pierzynski	2.00
106	Michael Barrett	2.00
107	Fernando Seguignol	2.00
108	Mike Kinkade	2.00
109	Mike Lowell	2.00
110	Ricky Ledee	2.00
111	Eric Chavez	3.00
112	Abraham Nunez	2.00
113	Matt Clement	2.00
114	Ben Davis	2.00
115	Mike Darr	2.00
116	Ramon Martinez	2.00
117	Carlos Guillen	2.00
118	Shane Monahan	2.00
119	J.D. Drew/Auto.	15.00
120	Kevin Witt	2.00

Dominance

This 20-card set showcases the most dominant MLB superstars, including Derek Jeter and Alex Rodriguez. These are seeded 1:17 packs and numbered with a FB prefix.

		NM/M
Complete Set (20):		35.00
Common Player:		1.00
Inserted 1:17		
1	Chipper Jones	2.00
2	Greg Maddux	2.00
3	Cal Ripken Jr.	4.00
4	Nomar Garciaparra	2.00
5	Mo Vaughn	1.00
6	Sammy Sosa	2.00
7	Albert Belle	1.00
8	Frank Thomas	1.50
9	Jim Thome	1.25
10	Jeff Bagwell	1.50
11	Vladimir Guerrero	1.50
12	Mike Piazza	2.50
13	Derek Jeter	4.00
14	Tony Gwynn	2.00
15	Barry Bonds	4.00
16	Ken Griffey Jr.	2.50
17	Alex Rodriguez	3.00
18	Mark McGwire	3.00
19	J.D. Drew	1.25
20	Juan Gonzalez	1.25

Power Explosion

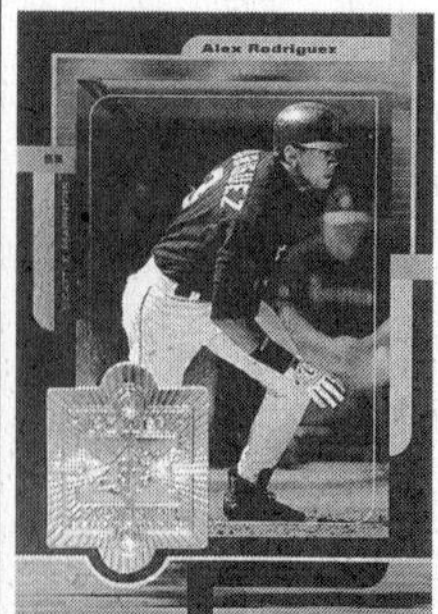

This 30-card set salutes the top power hitters in the game today, including Mark McGwire and Sammy Sosa. These are numbered with a PE prefix.

		NM/M
Complete Set (30):		15.00
Common Player:		.20
Inserted 1:3		
1	Troy Glaus	.65
2	Mo Vaughn	.20
3	Travis Lee	.20
4	Chipper Jones	1.00
5	Andres Galarraga	.20
6	Brady Anderson	.20
7	Albert Belle	.20
8	Nomar Garciaparra	1.00
9	Sammy Sosa	1.00
10	Frank Thomas	.75
11	Jim Thome	.65
12	Manny Ramirez	.75

13 Larry Walker .20
14 Tony Clark .20
15 Jeff Bagwell .75
16 Moises Alou .20
17 Ken Caminiti .20
18 Vladimir Guerrero .75
19 Mike Piazza 1.25
20 Tino Martinez .20
21 Ben Grieve .20
22 Scott Rolen .60
23 Greg Vaughn .20
24 Barry Bonds 2.00
25 Ken Griffey Jr. 1.25
26 Alex Rodriguez 1.50
27 Mark McGwire 1.50
28 J.D. Drew .35
29 Juan Gonzalez .45
30 Ivan Rodriguez .60

Premier Stars

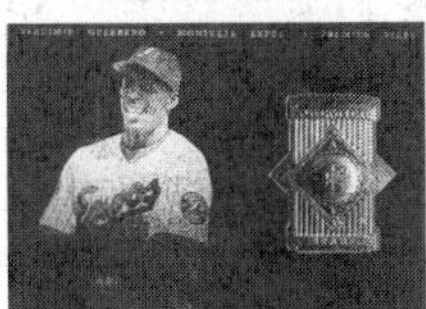

This 30-card set captures baseball's most dominant players, including Randy Johnson and Ken Griffey Jr. Featured on a rainbow-foil design, these are numbered with a PS prefix.

NM/M
Complete Set (30): 45.00
Common Player: 1.00
Inserted 1:17
1 Mark McGwire 3.00
2 Sammy Sosa 2.00
3 Frank Thomas 1.50
4 J.D. Drew 1.25
5 Kerry Wood 1.25
6 Moises Alou 1.00
7 Kenny Lofton 1.00
8 Jeff Bagwell 1.50
9 Tony Clark 1.00
10 Roberto Alomar 1.00
11 Cal Ripken Jr. 4.00
12 Derek Jeter 4.00
13 Mike Piazza 2.50
14 Jose Cruz Jr. 1.00
15 Chipper Jones 2.00
16 Nomar Garciaparra 2.00
17 Greg Maddux 2.00
18 Scott Rolen 1.25
19 Vladimir Guerrero 1.50
20 Albert Belle 1.00
21 Ken Griffey Jr. 2.50
22 Alex Rodriguez 3.00
23 Ben Grieve 1.00
24 Juan Gonzalez 1.25
25 Barry Bonds 4.00
26 Larry Walker 1.00
27 Tony Gwynn 2.00
28 Randy Johnson 1.50
29 Travis Lee 1.00
30 Mo Vaughn 1.00

Star Focus

This 30-card set focuses on the 30 brightest stars in the game. These are numbered with a SF prefix.

NM/M
Complete Set (30): 50.00
Common Player: .75
Inserted 1:8
1 Chipper Jones 2.25
2 Greg Maddux 2.25
3 Cal Ripken Jr. 4.50
4 Nomar Garciaparra 2.25
5 Mo Vaughn .75
6 Sammy Sosa 2.25
7 Albert Belle .75
8 Frank Thomas 1.50
9 Jim Thome 1.25
10 Kenny Lofton .75
11 Manny Ramirez 1.50
12 Larry Walker .75
13 Jeff Bagwell 1.50
14 Craig Biggio .75
15 Randy Johnson 1.50
16 Vladimir Guerrero 1.50
17 Mike Piazza 3.00
18 Derek Jeter 4.50
19 Tino Martinez .75
20 Bernie Williams .75
21 Curt Schilling 1.00
22 Tony Gwynn 2.25
23 Barry Bonds 4.50
24 Ken Griffey Jr. 3.00
25 Alex Rodriguez 4.00
26 Mark McGwire 4.00
27 J.D. Drew 1.00
28 Juan Gonzalez 1.00
29 Ivan Rodriguez 1.25
30 Ben Grieve .75

Winning Materials

This eight-card set includes a piece of the featured player's game-worn jersey and game-used bat on each card. These are seeded 1:251 packs.

NM/M
Complete Set (8): 90.00
Common Player: 5.00
Inserted 1:251
VC Vinny Castilla 5.00
JD J.D. Drew 7.50
JR Ken Griffey Jr. 20.00
VG Vladimir Guerrero 12.00
TG Tony Gwynn 15.00
TH Todd Helton 10.00
TL Travis Lee 5.00
IR Ivan Rodriguez 10.00

500 Club Piece of History

Each of these approximately 350 cards include a piece of game-used Louisville Slugger once swung by Wilie Mays. Mays also signed 24 of his Piece of History cards.

NM/M
WM Willie Mays/350 275.00
WM Willie Mays/Auto./24 1,700

2000 SP Authentic

The 135-card base set is composed of 90 regular cards, 30 Future Watch subset cards (serial numbered to 2,500) and 15 SP Superstars (serial numbered to 2,500). The regular cards have a gold foiled stamped line around the player image with a matte finished white border around the player image. The player name is stamped in gold foil in the top portion and the SP Authentic logo is stamped in silver foil. Card backs have a small photo, a brief career note and up to the past five seasons of complete statistics. Five-card packs carried a $4.99 SRP.

NM/M
Complete Set (135): 150.00
Common Player: .15
Common (91-105): 2.00
Production 2,500 Sets
Common (106-135): 2.00
Production 2,500 Sets
Pack (5): 3.00
Box (24): 60.00
1 Mo Vaughn .15
2 Troy Glaus .50
3 Jason Giambi .75
4 Tim Hudson .40
5 Eric Chavez .25
6 Shannon Stewart .15
7 Raul Mondesi .15
8 Carlos Delgado .50
9 Jose Canseco .50
10 Vinny Castilla .15
11 Greg Vaughn .15
12 Manny Ramirez 1.00
13 Roberto Alomar .40
14 Jim Thome .75
15 Richie Sexson .40
16 Alex Rodriguez 2.50
17 Fred Garcia .15
18 John Olerud .15
19 Albert Belle .25
20 Cal Ripken Jr. 3.00
21 Mike Mussina .50
22 Ivan Rodriguez .75
23 Gabe Kapler .15
24 Rafael Palmeiro .75
25 Nomar Garciaparra 1.00
26 Pedro Martinez 1.00
27 Carl Everett .15
28 Carlos Beltran .50
29 Jermaine Dye .15
30 Juan Gonzalez .50
31 Dean Palmer .15
32 Corey Koskie .15
33 Jacque Jones .15
34 Frank Thomas .75
35 Paul Konerko .40
36 Magglio Ordonez .25
37 Bernie Williams .40
38 Derek Jeter 2.50
39 Roger Clemens 2.00
40 Mariano Rivera .40
41 Jeff Bagwell .50
42 Craig Biggio .40
43 Jose Lima .15
44 Moises Alou .25
45 Chipper Jones 1.00
46 Greg Maddux 1.50
47 Andruw Jones 1.00
48 Kevin Millwood .15
49 Jeromy Burnitz .15
50 Geoff Jenkins .15
51 Mark McGwire 1.50
52 Fernando Tatis .15
53 J.D. Drew .25
54 Sammy Sosa 1.00
55 Kerry Wood .50
56 Mark Grace .25
57 Matt Williams .15
58 Randy Johnson 1.00
59 Erubiel Durazo .15
60 Gary Sheffield .50
61 Kevin Brown .15
62 Shawn Green .40
63 Vladimir Guerrero 1.00
64 Michael Barrett .15
65 Barry Bonds 2.50
66 Jeff Kent .25
67 Russ Ortiz .15
68 Preston Wilson .15
69 Mike Lowell .15
70 Mike Piazza 1.00
71 Mike Hampton .15
72 Robin Ventura .15
73 Edgardo Alfonzo .15
74 Tony Gwynn 1.50
75 Ryan Klesko .15
76 Trevor Hoffman .15
77 Scott Rolen 1.00
78 Bob Abreu .40
79 Mike Lieberthal .15
80 Curt Schilling .75
81 Jason Kendall .15
82 Brian Giles .15
83 Kris Benson .15
84 Ken Griffey Jr. 2.00
85 Sean Casey .25
86 Pokey Reese .15
87 Barry Larkin .40
88 Larry Walker .25
89 Todd Helton .75
90 Jeff Cirillo .15
91 Ken Griffey Jr. (SP Superstars) 4.00
92 Mark McGwire (SP Superstars) 4.00
93 Chipper Jones (SP Superstars) 3.00
94 Derek Jeter (SP Superstars) 6.00
95 Shawn Green (SP Superstars) 2.00
96 Pedro Martinez (SP Superstars) 4.00
97 Mike Piazza (SP Superstars) 4.00
98 Alex Rodriguez (SP Superstars) 5.00
99 Jeff Bagwell (SP Superstars) 2.50
100 Cal Ripken Jr. (SP Superstars) 6.00
101 Sammy Sosa (SP Superstars) 3.00
102 Barry Bonds (SP Superstars) 5.00
103 Jose Canseco (SP Superstars) 2.00
104 Nomar Garciaparra (SP Superstars) 4.00
105 Ivan Rodriguez (SP Superstars) 2.50
106 Rick Ankiel (Future Watch) 2.00
107 Pat Burrell (Future Watch) 2.50
108 Vernon Wells (Future Watch) 2.50
109 Nick Johnson (Future Watch) 2.00
110 Kip Wells (Future Watch) 2.00
111 Matt Riley (Future Watch) 2.00
112 Alfonso Soriano (Future Watch) 8.00
113 Josh Beckett (Future Watch) 4.00
114 Danys Baez **RC** (Future Watch) 6.00
115 Travis Dawkins (Future Watch) 2.50
116 Eric Gagne (Future Watch) 4.00
117 Mike Lamb **RC** (Future Watch) 4.00
118 Eric Munson (Future Watch) 2.50
119 Wilfredo Rodriguez **RC** (Future Watch) 2.00
120 Kazuhiro Sasaki **RC** (Future Watch) 3.00
121 Chad Hutchinson (Future Watch) 2.00
122 Peter Bergeron (Future Watch) 2.00
123 Wascar Serrano **RC** (Future Watch) 2.00
124 Tony Armas Jr. (Future Watch) 2.00
125 Ramon Ortiz (Future Watch) 2.00
126 Adam Kennedy (Future Watch) 2.00
127 Joe Crede (Future Watch) 5.00
128 Roosevelt Brown (Future Watch) 2.00
129 Mark Mulder (Future Watch) 2.50
130 Brad Penny (Future Watch) 2.00
131 Terrence Long (Future Watch) 2.00
132 Ruben Mateo (Future Watch) 2.00
133 Wily Mo Pena (Future Watch) 2.00
134 Rafael Furcal (Future Watch) 2.00
135 Mario Encarnacion (Future Watch) 2.00

Limited

A parallel to the 135-card base set these have "SP Limited" printed down the right side of the front and are serial numbered on the card front in an edition of 100 sets.

Cards (1-90): 4-8X
Cards (91-105): 2-3X
Cards (106-135): 1-2X
Production 100 Sets

Chirography

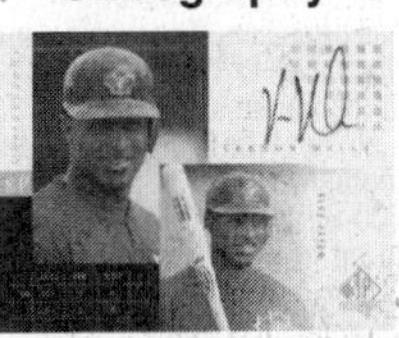

This autographed insert set has a horizontal format with two player images on the card front. The player signature appears in the top right portion over a silver, checkered background. The insert name and logo have a silver tint. Card backs are numbered with the featured players first and last initial. Chirographies are seeded 1:23 packs.

NM/M
Common Player: 5.00
Inserted 1:23
RA Rick Ankiel 8.00
CBe Carlos Beltran 30.00
BB Barry Bonds 200.00
PB Pat Burrell 15.00
JC Jose Canseco 25.00
SC Sean Casey 8.00
RC Roger Clemens 100.00
ED Erubiel Durazo 10.00
TGl Troy Glaus 20.00
VG Vladimir Guerrero 30.00
TG Tony Gwynn 40.00
DJ Derek Jeter 120.00
NJ Nick Johnson 10.00
CJ Chipper Jones 35.00
AJ Andruw Jones 25.00
SK Sandy Koufax 250.00
BP Ben Petrick 5.00
MQ Mark Quinn 5.00
MR Manny Ramirez 40.00
CR Cal Ripken Jr. 100.00
AR Alex Rodriguez 85.00
IR Ivan Rodriguez 30.00
SR Scott Rolen 30.00
AS Alfonso Soriano 30.00
MV Mo Vaughn 8.00
EY Ed Yarnall 5.00

Chirography Gold

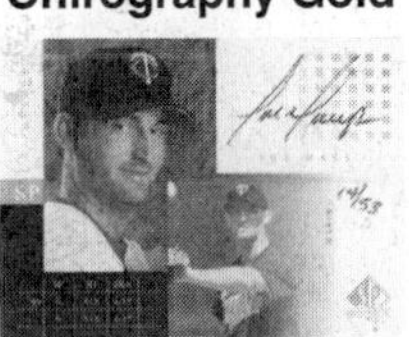

Golds use the same photos as the regular Chirography inserts and can be differentiated by the gold checkered background of the player signature in the upper right portion as well as the gold tint in the insert name and logo. Golds are also hand-numbered to the player's jersey number on the card front and are numbered with a "G" prefix on the card back before the players initials.

NM/M
Common Player:
RA Rick Ankiel/66 EXCH 50.00
CBe Carlos Beltran/15 65.00
BB Barry Bonds/25 300.00
PB Pat Burrell/33 EXCH 50.00
JC Jose Canseco/33 75.00
SC Sean Casey/21 65.00
RC Roger Clemens/22 300.00
ED Erubiel Durazo/44 25.00
VG Vladimir Guerrero/27 100.00
TG Tony Gwynn/19 200.00
NJ Nick Johnson/63 15.00
BP Ben Petrick/15 30.00
MR Manny Ramirez/24 EXCH 100.00
AS Alfonso Soriano/53 60.00
MV Mo Vaughn/42 25.00
EY Ed Yarnall/41 15.00

Joe DiMaggio Game Jersey

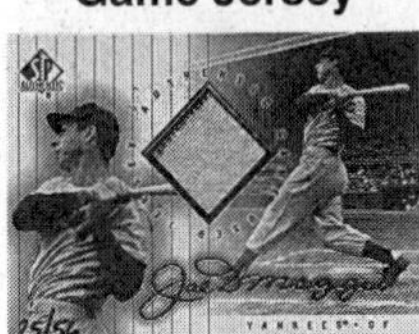

This is DiMaggio's first Game Jersey insert and has three different versions. The first is limited to 500 total cards, the second version is Gold and numbered to 56. The rarest version has a DiMaggio cut signature along with a piece of his game-used jersey and is limited to only five total cards.

NM/M
DiMaggio Jersey Card
JD Joe DiMaggio/Jsy/500 120.00
JD Joe DiMaggio/Jsy Gold/56 200.00

Midsummer Classics

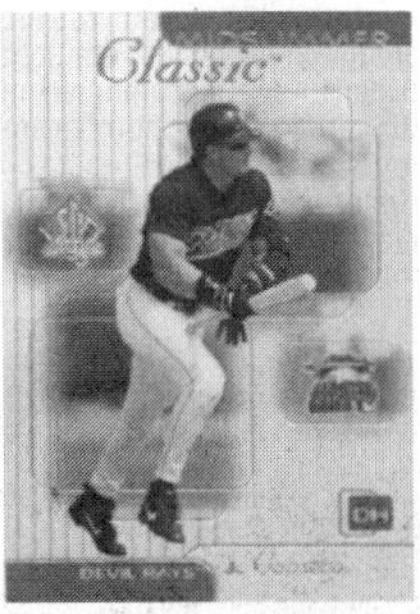

This 10-card set spotlights perennial All-Stars and has a silver holo-foiled front with gold foil etching and stamping. These are found 1:12 packs and are numbered on the card back with an "MC" prefix.

NM/M
Complete Set (10): 10.00
Common Player: .50
Inserted 1:12
1 Cal Ripken Jr. 3.00
2 Roger Clemens 1.75
3 Jeff Bagwell .75
4 Barry Bonds 3.00
5 Jose Canseco .50
6 Frank Thomas .75
7 Mike Piazza 2.00
8 Tony Gwynn 1.50
9 Juan Gonzalez .75
10 Greg Maddux 1.50

Premier Performers

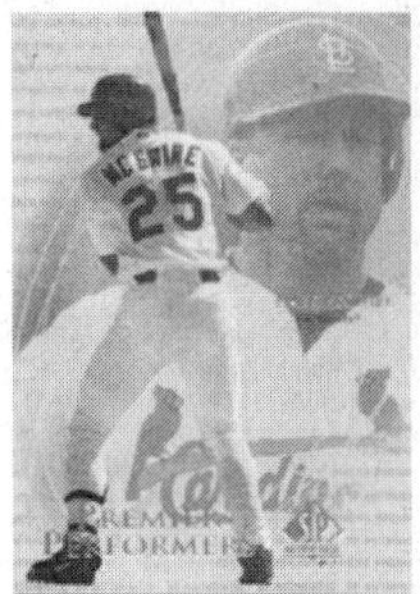

This 10-card set spotlights baseball's best on a silver holo-foiled card front with the player name, insert name and logo stamped in gold foil. Card backs are numbered with a "PP" prefix and are found 1:12 packs.

NM/M
Complete Set (10): 10.00
Common Player: .75
Inserted 1:12
1 Mark McGwire 2.00
2 Alex Rodriguez 2.50
3 Cal Ripken Jr. 3.00
4 Nomar Garciaparra 1.50
5 Ken Griffey Jr. 2.00
6 Chipper Jones 1.50
7 Derek Jeter 3.00
8 Ivan Rodriguez .75
9 Vladimir Guerrero .75
10 Sammy Sosa 1.50

SP Buyback

This autographed set features previously issued SP cards that were re-purchased by Upper Deck. The cards are autographed by the featured player and hand-numbered on the card front. The number autographed and released by Upper Deck is listed after the player name. Buybacks are found 1:95 packs.

NM/M
Common Player:
1 Jeff Bagwell Exch. 50.00
2 Craig Biggio '93/59 50.00
3 Craig Biggio '94/69 50.00
4 Craig Biggio '95/171 40.00
5 Craig Biggio '96/71 50.00
6 Craig Biggio '97/46 50.00
7 Craig Biggio '98/40 50.00
8 Craig Biggio '99/125 40.00
15 Barry Bonds '99/520 150.00
16 Jose Canseco '93/29 60.00
17 Jose Canseco '94/20 60.00
19 Jose Canseco '96/23 60.00
20 Jose Canseco '97/23 60.00
21 Jose Canseco '98/24 60.00
22 Jose Canseco '99/502 30.00
24 Sean Casey '99/139 20.00
25 Roger Clemens '93/68 85.00
26 Roger Clemens '94/60 85.00
27 Roger Clemens '95/68 85.00
28 Roger Clemens '96/68 85.00
30 Roger Clemens '98/25 200.00
31 Roger Clemens '99/134 75.00
32 Jason Giambi '97/34 50.00
33 Jason Giambi '98/25 50.00
34 Tom Glavine '93/99 40.00
35 Tom Glavine '94/107 40.00
36 Tom Glavine '95/97 40.00
37 Tom Glavine '96/42 50.00
38 Tom Glavine '98/40 50.00
39 Tom Glavine '99/138 40.00
40 Shawn Green '96/55 30.00
41 Shawn Green '99/530 20.00
42 Ken Griffey Jr. '96/12 275.00
47 Tony Gwynn '97/24 150.00
49 Tony Gwynn '99/129 50.00
50 Tony Gwynn '99/369 40.00
56 Derek Jeter '99/119 200.00
57 Randy Johnson '93/60 75.00
58 Randy Johnson '94/45 80.00
59 Randy Johnson '95/70 75.00
60 Randy Johnson '96/60 75.00
63 Randy Johnson '99/113 75.00
64 Andruw Jones Exch. 40.00
65 Chipper Jones Exch. 75.00
66 Kenny Lofton '94/100 25.00
67 Kenny Lofton '95/84 25.00
68 Kenny Lofton '96/34 40.00
69 Kenny Lofton '97/82 25.00
70 Kenny Lofton '98/21 40.00
71 Kenny Lofton '99/99 20.00
72 Javy Lopez '93/106 15.00
73 Javy Lopez '94/160 20.00
74 Javy Lopez '96/99 15.00
75 Javy Lopez '97/61 20.00
77 Greg Maddux '93/22 275.00
78 Greg Maddux '94/19 275.00
83 Greg Maddux '99/504 75.00
84 Paul O'Neill '93/110 25.00
85 Paul O'Neill '94/97 30.00
86 Paul O'Neill '95/142 25.00
87 Paul O'Neill '96/70 30.00
88 Paul O'Neill '98/23 40.00
89 Manny Ramirez/ Redemp 50.00
91 Cal Ripken Jr. '94/22 300.00
96 Cal Ripken Jr. '99/510 125.00
97 Alex Rodriguez Exch. 150.00
98 Ivan Rodriguez '93/29 100.00
100 Ivan Rodriguez '95/18 125.00
101 Ivan Rodriguez '96/22 125.00
103 Ivan Rodriguez '98/27 125.00
109 Frank Thomas '97/20 75.00
111 Frank Thomas '99/100 50.00
112 Greg Vaughn '93/79 20.00
113 Greg Vaughn '94/75 20.00
114 Greg Vaughn '95/155 15.00
115 Greg Vaughn '96/113 15.00
117 Greg Vaughn '99/527 10.00
118 Mo Vaughn '93/119 20.00
119 Mo Vaughn '94/96 20.00
120 Mo Vaughn '95/121 20.00
121 Mo Vaughn '96/114 20.00
122 Mo Vaughn '97/61 25.00
124 Mo Vaughn '99/537 15.00
125 Robin Ventura '93/59 25.00
126 Robin Ventura '94/49 25.00
127 Robin Ventura '95/125 20.00
128 Robin Ventura '96/55 25.00
129 Robin Ventura '97/44 30.00
130 Robin Ventura '98/28 35.00
131 Robin Ventura '99/370 15.00
133 Matt Williams '94/50 40.00
134 Matt Williams '95/137 40.00
135 Matt Williams '96/77 40.00
136 Matt Williams '97/54 40.00
137 Matt Williams '98/29 60.00
138 Matt Williams '99/529 15.00
139 Preston Wilson '94/249 15.00
140 Preston Wilson '99/195 15.00

SP Cornerstones

Printed on a silver holo-foiled card front a close-up image of the player appears in a baseball diamond shaped enclosed by gold foil etching. Another shadow image of the featured player appears in the background. The player name, insert name and logo are stamped in gold foil. These are seeded 1:23 packs and are numbered with a "C" prefix on the card back.

NM/M
Complete Set (7): 15.00
Common Player: 2.00
Inserted 1:23
1 Ken Griffey Jr. 2.00
2 Cal Ripken Jr. 4.00
3 Mike Piazza 2.00
4 Derek Jeter 4.00
5 Mark McGwire 3.00
6 Nomar Garciaparra 2.00
7 Sammy Sosa 2.00

SP Supremacy

This seven-card set has a silver foiled card front with the insert name and logo stamped in gold foil. The inserts are found on the average of 1:23 packs and are numbered with a "S" prefix.

NM/M
Complete Set (7): 8.00
Common Player: .75
Inserted 1:23
1 Alex Rodriguez 3.00
2 Shawn Green .75
3 Pedro Martinez 1.00
4 Chipper Jones 2.00
5 Tony Gwynn 2.00
6 Ivan Rodriguez 1.00
7 Jeff Bagwell 1.00

United Nations

Done on a horizontal format this 10-card set salutes the top international stars of the game. The featured player's country of origin flag is in the background of the player image. The card design features silver holofoil and silver foil etching and stamping. These are seeded 1:4 packs and are numbered with an "UN" prefix on the card back.

NM/M
Complete Set (10): 5.00
Common Player: .50
Inserted 1:4
1 Sammy Sosa (Dominican Rep.) 1.50
2 Ken Griffey Jr. (USA) 2.00
3 Orlando Hernandez (Cuba) .50
4 Andres Galarraga (Venezuela) .50
5 Kazuhiro Sasaki (Japan) .50
6 Larry Walker (Canada) .50
7 Vinny Castilla (Mexico) .50
8 Andruw Jones (Neth. Antilles) .75
9 Ivan Rodriguez (Puerto Rico) .75
10 Chan Ho Park (So. Korea) .50

3,000 Hit Club

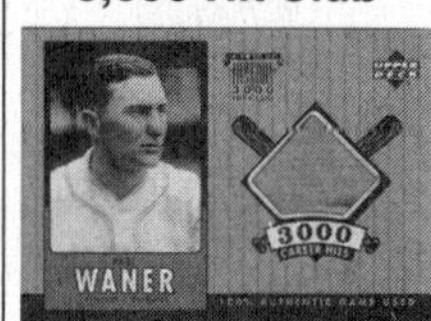

A continuation of Upper Deck's cross brand salute to players who have reached the magical 3,000 hit milestone. 350 game-used bat cards and five bat/cut signature combos were issued for each player.

NM/M
PW Paul Waner/Bat/350 50.00
TS Tris Speaker/ Bat/350 100.00

2000 SPx

The base set consists of 120-cards including 30 Rookie/Young Star subset cards which has three tiers. The first five are numbered to 1,000, the next 22 autographed and numbered to 1,500 and the final three are autographed and numbered to 500. Each base card has a holo-foiled front with the SPx logo, player name, team name stamped in gold foil.

NM/M
Complete Set (120): 400.00
Common Player: .15
Common Rookie (91-120): 10.00
Pack (4): 6.00
Box (18): 80.00
1 Troy Glaus .50
2 Mo Vaughn .15
3 Ramon Ortiz .15
4 Jeff Bagwell .75
5 Moises Alou .25
6 Craig Biggio .40
7 Jose Lima .15
8 Jason Giambi .75
9 John Jaha .15
10 Matt Stairs .15
11 Chipper Jones 1.00
12 Greg Maddux 1.50
13 Andres Galarraga .15
14 Andruw Jones 1.00
15 Jeromy Burnitz .15
16 Ron Belliard .15
17 Carlos Delgado .75
18 David Wells .15
19 Tony Batista .15
20 Shannon Stewart .15
21 Sammy Sosa 1.00
22 Mark Grace .50
23 Henry Rodriguez .15
24 Mark McGwire 2.00
25 J.D. Drew .25
26 Luis Gonzalez .25
27 Randy Johnson 1.00
28 Matt Williams .15
29 Steve Finley .15
30 Shawn Green .25
31 Kevin Brown .15
32 Gary Sheffield .50
33 Jose Canseco .50
34 Greg Vaughn .15
35 Vladimir Guerrero 1.00
36 Michael Barrett .15
37 Russ Ortiz .15
38 Barry Bonds 3.00
39 Jeff Kent .25
40 Richie Sexson .40
41 Manny Ramirez 1.00
42 Jim Thome 1.00
43 Roberto Alomar .50
44 Edgar Martinez .15
45 Alex Rodriguez 2.50
46 John Olerud .15
47 Alex Gonzalez .15
48 Cliff Floyd .15
49 Mike Piazza 1.50
50 Al Leiter .15
51 Robin Ventura .15
52 Edgardo Alfonzo .15
53 Albert Belle .15
54 Cal Ripken Jr. 3.00
55 B.J. Surhoff .15
56 Tony Gwynn 1.50
57 Trevor Hoffman .15
58 Brian Giles .15
59 Jason Kendall .15
60 Kris Benson .15
61 Bob Abreu .50
62 Scott Rolen 1.00
63 Curt Schilling .75
64 Mike Lieberthal .15
65 Sean Casey .25
66 Dante Bichette .15
67 Ken Griffey Jr. 2.00
68 Pokey Reese .15
69 Mike Sweeney .15
70 Carlos Febles .15
71 Ivan Rodriguez 1.00
72 Ruben Mateo .15
73 Rafael Palmeiro 1.00
74 Larry Walker .40
75 Todd Helton .75
76 Nomar Garciaparra 1.00
77 Pedro Martinez 1.00
78 Troy O'Leary .15
79 Jacque Jones .15
80 Corey Koskie .15
81 Juan Gonzalez .50
82 Dean Palmer .15
83 Juan Encarnacion .15
84 Frank Thomas 1.00
85 Magglio Ordonez .25
86 Paul Konerko .50
87 Bernie Williams .50
88 Derek Jeter 3.00
89 Roger Clemens 2.50
90 Orlando Hernandez .15
91 Vernon Wells AU-1,000 25.00
92 Rick Ankiel AU-1,000 35.00
93 Eric Chavez AU-1,000 20.00
94 Alfonso Soriano AU-1,000 50.00
95 Eric Gagne AU-1,000 25.00
96 Rob Bell AU-1,500 10.00
97 Matt Riley AU-1,500 10.00
98 Josh Beckett AU-1,500 90.00
99 Ben Petrick AU-1,500 10.00
100 Rob Ramsay AU-1,500 **RC** 10.00
101 Scott Williamson AU-1,500 10.00
102 Doug Davis AU-1,500 15.00
103 Eric Munson AU-1,500 10.00
104 Pat Burrell AU-500 30.00
105 Jim Morris AU-1,500 20.00
106 Gabe Kapler AU-500 15.00
107 Lance Berkman 1,500 20.00
108 Erubiel Durazo AU-1,500 15.00
109 Tim Hudson AU-1,500 30.00
110 Ben Davis AU-1,500 10.00
111 Nick Johnson AU-1,500 20.00
112 Octavio Dotel AU-1,500 10.00
113 Jerry Hairston Jr. 1,500 10.00
114 Ruben Mateo 1,500 10.00
115 Chris Singleton 1 ,500 10.00
116 Bruce Chen AU-1,500 10.00
117 Derrick Gibson AU-1,500 10.00
118 Carlos Beltran AU-500 100.00
119 Fred Garcia AU-500 10.00
120 Preston Wilson AU-500 15.00

Radiance

A parallel to the 120-card base set these are serially numbered to 100. A one-of-one Spectrum parallel of each base card is also randomly seeded.

NM/M
Stars (1-90): 4-8X
Common Young Star (91-120): 10.00
Production 100 Sets

Foundations

This 10-card set features a holo-foiled front with gold foil stamping. Three miniature action shots appear to the right of a close-up shot of the featured player. Card backs are numbered with an "F" prefix and inserted 1:32 packs.

NM/M
Complete Set (10): 15.00
Common Player: .50
Inserted 1:32
1 Ken Griffey Jr. 3.00
2 Nomar Garciaparra 3.00
3 Cal Ripken Jr. 4.00
4 Chipper Jones 2.00
5 Mike Piazza 3.00
6 Derek Jeter 4.00
7 Manny Ramirez 1.00
8 Jeff Bagwell 1.00
9 Tony Gwynn 2.00
10 Larry Walker .50

Heart of the Order

This 20-card set features a top hitter with his teams batting order to the left of his photo. The SPx logo and insert name are stamped in gold foil. Card backs are numbered with an "H" prefix and seeded 1:8 packs.

NM/M
Complete Set (20): 10.00
Common Player: .40
Inserted 1:8
1 Bernie Williams .50
2 Mike Piazza 2.00

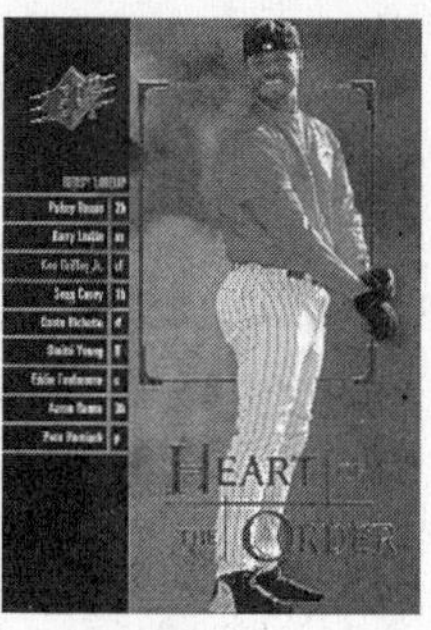

3 Ivan Rodriguez .75
4 Mark McGwire 2.50
5 Manny Ramirez 1.00
6 Ken Griffey Jr. 2.00
7 Matt Williams .40
8 Sammy Sosa 2.00
9 Mo Vaughn .40
10 Carlos Delgado .75
11 Brian Giles .40
12 Chipper Jones 1.50
13 Sean Casey .40
14 Tony Gwynn 1.50
15 Barry Bonds 3.00
16 Carlos Beltran .65
17 Scott Rolen .75
18 Juan Gonzalez 1.00
19 Larry Walker .40
20 Vladimir Guerrero 1.00

Highlight Heroes

This 10-card set has a horizontal format on a holo-foiled front with gold foil stamping. Card backs are numbered with an "HH" prefix and inserted 1:16 packs.

NM/M
Complete Set (10): 10.00
Common Player: .50
Inserted 1:16
1 Pedro Martinez 1.00
2 Ivan Rodriguez .75
3 Carlos Beltran .65
4 Nomar Garciaparra 2.00
5 Ken Griffey Jr. 2.00
6 Randy Johnson 1.00
7 Chipper Jones 1.50
8 Scott Williamson .50
9 Larry Walker .50
10 Mark McGwire 2.50

Power Brokers

This 20-card set has a horizontal format with the background of the player photo having a kaleidoscope effect. The SPx logo is stamped in gold foil. Card backs are numbered with an "PB" prefix and are inserted 1:8 packs.

NM/M
Complete Set (20): 10.00
Common Player: .25
Inserted 1:8
1 Rafael Palmeiro .75
2 Carlos Delgado .65
3 Ken Griffey Jr. 2.00
4 Matt Stairs .25
5 Mike Piazza 2.00
6 Vladimir Guerrero 1.00
7 Chipper Jones 1.50
8 Mark McGwire 2.50
9 Matt Williams .25
10 Juan Gonzalez 1.00
11 Shawn Green .50
12 Sammy Sosa 2.00
13 Brian Giles .25
14 Jeff Bagwell 1.00
15 Alex Rodriguez 2.50
16 Frank Thomas 1.00
17 Larry Walker .25
18 Albert Belle .25
19 Dean Palmer .25
20 Mo Vaughn .25

SPxcitement

This 20-card set features a holo-foiled front with gold foil stamping. Card backs are numbered with an "XC" prefix and are inserted 1:4 packs.

		NM/M
Complete Set (20):		15.00
Common Player:		.25
Inserted 1:4		
1	Nomar Garciaparra	1.25
2	Mark McGwire	1.50
3	Derek Jeter	2.00
4	Cal Ripken Jr.	2.00
5	Barry Bonds	2.00
6	Alex Rodriguez	1.50
7	Scott Rolen	.75
8	Pedro Martinez	.75
9	Sean Casey	.25
10	Sammy Sosa	1.25
11	Randy Johnson	.75
12	Ivan Rodriguez	.75
13	Frank Thomas	.75
14	Greg Maddux	1.00
15	Tony Gwynn	1.00
16	Ken Griffey Jr.	1.25
17	Carlos Beltran	.50
18	Mike Piazza	1.25
19	Chipper Jones	1.00
20	Craig Biggio	.25

SPx Signatures

These autographed inserts are seeded 1:112 packs.

		NM/M
Common Player:		15.00
Inserted 1:179		
JB	Jeff Bagwell	30.00
BB	Barry Bonds	150.00
JC	Jose Canseco	25.00
SC	Sean Casey	15.00
RC	Roger Clemens	125.00
KG	Ken Griffey Jr.	100.00
VG	Vladimir Guerrero	35.00
TG	Tony Gwynn	40.00
OH	Orlando Hernandez	40.00
DJ	Derek Jeter	125.00
CJ	Chipper Jones	40.00
MR	Manny Ramirez	40.00
CR	Cal Ripken Jr.	125.00
IR	Ivan Rodriguez	30.00
SR	Scott Rolen	30.00

Untouchable Talents

These inserts have a holo-foiled front and are numbered with an "UT" prefix. They are found on the average of 1:96 packs.

		NM/M
Complete Set (10):		30.00
Common Player:		1.50
Inserted 1:96		
1	Mark McGwire	8.00
2	Ken Griffey Jr.	6.00
3	Shawn Green	2.00
4	Ivan Rodriguez	2.50
5	Sammy Sosa	6.00
6	Derek Jeter	10.00
7	Sean Casey	1.50
8	Chipper Jones	4.50
9	Pedro Martinez	3.00
10	Vladimir Guerrero	3.00

Winning Materials

Five different tiers make up this memorabilia insert set with players having varying levels of their inserts in the set. Each insert has two pieces of memorabilia, combinations include Jersey/Bat, Jersey/Bat numbered to player's jersey number, Jersey/Cap, Jersey/Ball and Ball/Bat.

		NM/M
Common Bat/Jsy		6.00
AR	Alex Rodriguez/ Bat/Jsy	25.00
AR	Alex Rodriguez/ Cap/Jsy/100	40.00
AR	Alex Rodriguez/ Ball/Jsy/50	50.00
DJ	Derek Jeter/ Bat/Jsy	40.00
DJ	Derek Jeter/ Ball/Jsy/50	75.00
BB	Barry Bonds/ Bat/Jsy	30.00
BB	Barry Bonds/ Cap/Jsy/100	50.00
BB	Barry Bonds/ Ball/Jsy/Auto./25	350.00
JB	Jeff Bagwell/Bat/Jsy	8.00
JB	Jeff Bagwell/ Cap/Jsy/100	15.00
JB	Jeff Bagwell/ Ball/Jsy/50	25.00
KG	Ken Griffey Jr./ Bat/Jsy	20.00
KG	Ken Griffey Jr./ Ball/Jsy/50	50.00
KG	Ken Griffey Jr./ Jsy/Bat/Auto./24	225.00
TG	Tony Gwynn/Bat/Jsy	10.00
TG	Tony Gwynn/ Ball/Jsy/50	40.00
TG	Tony Gwynn/ Cap/Jsy/100	30.00
BW	Bernie Williams/ Bat/Jsy	8.00
EC	Eric Chavez/Bat/Jsy	8.00
EC	Eric Chavez/ Cap/Jsy/100	15.00
GM	Greg Maddux/Bat/Jsy	25.00
IR	Ivan Rodriguez/ Bat/Jsy	8.00
JC	Jose Canseco/Bat/Jsy	8.00
JL	Javy Lopez/Bat/Jsy	6.00
JL	Javy Lopez/ Cap/Jsy/100	8.00
MM	Mark McGwire/ Base/Ball/500	50.00
MR	Manny Ramirez/ Bat/Jsy	10.00
MW	Matt Williams/Bat/Jsy	6.00
PM	Pedro Martinez/ Cap/Jsy/100	25.00
PO	Paul O'Neill/Bat/Jsy	6.00
VG	Vladimir Guerrero/ Bat/Jsy	10.00
VG	Vladimir Guerrero/ Cap/Jsy/100	20.00
VG	Vladimir Guerrero/ Ball/Jsy/50	30.00
TG	Troy Glaus/Bat/Jsy	8.00

3,000 Hit Club

A continuation of Upper Deck's cross-brand insert program, this set pays tribute to Ty Cobb with three variations. The

collection includes 350 bat cards, three cut signatures and one bat/cut signature card.

		NM/M
TC-B	Ty Cobb/Bat/350	130.00

2001 SP Authentic Sample

Base cards in the forthcoming SP Authentic issue were previewed with this card. In a format identical to the regularly issued version, the promo card has a large black "SAMPLE" overprinted diagonally on back.

		NM/M
90	Ken Griffey Jr.	3.00

2001 SP Authentic

		NM/M
Common Player:		.25
Common SP (91-135):		4.00
Production 1,250		
Common SP (136-180):		2.00
Production 1,250		
Pack (5):		12.00
Box (24):		275.00
1	Troy Glaus	.50
2	Darin Erstad	.40
3	Jason Giambi	.75
4	Tim Hudson	.50
5	Eric Chavez	.40
6	Miguel Tejada	.50
7	Jose Ortiz	.25
8	Carlos Delgado	.75
9	Tony Batista	.25
10	Raul Mondesi	.25
11	Aubrey Huff	.25
12	Greg Vaughn	.25
13	Roberto Alomar	.50
14	Juan Gonzalez	.50
15	Jim Thome	.75
16	Omar Vizquel	.25
17	Edgar Martinez	.25
18	Fred Garcia	.25
19	Cal Ripken Jr.	3.00
20	Ivan Rodriguez	.75
21	Rafael Palmeiro	.75
22	Alex Rodriguez	2.00
23	Manny Ramirez	1.00
24	Pedro Martinez	1.00
25	Nomar Garciaparra	1.00
26	Mike Sweeney	.25
27	Jermaine Dye	.25
28	Bobby Higginson	.25
29	Dean Palmer	.25
30	Matt Lawton	.25
31	Eric Milton	.25
32	Frank Thomas	1.00
33	Magglio Ordonez	.25
34	David Wells	.25
35	Paul Konerko	.50
36	Derek Jeter	3.00
37	Bernie Williams	.50
38	Roger Clemens	2.00
39	Mike Mussina	.50
40	Jorge Posada	.50
41	Jeff Bagwell	.75
42	Richard Hidalgo	.25
43	Craig Biggio	.50
44	Greg Maddux	2.00
45	Chipper Jones	1.00
46	Andruw Jones	1.00
47	Rafael Furcal	.40
48	Tom Glavine	.50
49	Jeromy Burnitz	.25
50	Jeffrey Hammonds	.25
51	Mark McGwire	2.00
52	Jim Edmonds	.50
53	Rick Ankiel	.25
54	J.D. Drew	.40
55	Sammy Sosa	1.50
56	Corey Patterson	.25
57	Kerry Wood	.50
58	Randy Johnson	1.00
59	Luis Gonzalez	.40
60	Curt Schilling	.75
61	Gary Sheffield	.50
62	Shawn Green	.50
63	Kevin Brown	.25
64	Vladimir Guerrero	1.00
65	Jose Vidro	.25
66	Barry Bonds	3.00
67	Jeff Kent	.50
68	Livan Hernandez	.25
69	Preston Wilson	.25
70	Charles Johnson	.25
71	Ryan Dempster	.25
72	Mike Piazza	1.50
73	Al Leiter	.25
74	Edgardo Alfonzo	.25
75	Robin Ventura	.25
76	Tony Gwynn	1.50
77	Phil Nevin	.25
78	Trevor Hoffman	.25
79	Scott Rolen	1.00
80	Pat Burrell	.50
81	Bob Abreu	.40
82	Jason Kendall	.25
83	Brian Giles	.25
84	Kris Benson	.25
85	Ken Griffey Jr.	2.00
86	Barry Larkin	.50
87	Sean Casey	.40
88	Todd Helton	.75
89	Mike Hampton	.25
90	Larry Walker	.25
91	Ichiro Suzuki **RC** (Future Watch)	180.00
92	Wilson Betemit **RC** (Future Watch)	4.00
93	Adrian Hernandez **RC** (Future Watch)	4.00
94	Juan Uribe **RC** (Future Watch)	6.00
95	Travis Hafner **RC** (Future Watch)	50.00
96	Morgan Ensberg **RC** (Future Watch)	15.00
97	Sean Douglass **RC** (Future Watch)	4.00
98	Juan Diaz **RC** (Future Watch)	4.00
99	Erick Almonte **RC** (Future Watch)	4.00
100	Ryan Freel **RC** (Future Watch)	8.00
101	Elpidio Guzman **RC** (Future Watch)	4.00
102	Christian Parker **RC** (Future Watch)	4.00
103	Josh Fogg **RC** (Future Watch)	6.00
104	Bert Snow **RC** (Future Watch)	4.00
105	Horacio Ramirez **RC** (Future Watch)	8.00
106	Ricardo Rodriguez **RC** (Future Watch)	4.00
107	Tyler Walker **RC** (Future Watch)	4.00
108	Jose Mieses **RC** (Future Watch)	6.00
109	Billy Sylvester **RC** (Future Watch)	4.00
110	Martin Vargas **RC** (Future Watch)	4.00
111	Andres Torres **RC** (Future Watch)	4.00
112	Greg Miller **RC** (Future Watch)	4.00
113	Alexis Gomez **RC** (Future Watch)	4.00
114	Grant Balfour **RC** (Future Watch)	4.00
115	Henry Mateo **RC** (Future Watch)	4.00
116	Esix Snead **RC** (Future Watch)	4.00
117	Jackson Melian **RC** (Future Watch)	4.00
118	Nate Teut **RC** (Future Watch)	4.00
119	Tsuyoshi Shinjo **RC** (Future Watch)	4.00
120	Carlos Valderrama **RC** (Future Watch)	6.00
121	Johnny Estrada **RC** (Future Watch)	10.00
122	Jason Michaels **RC** (Future Watch)	4.00
123	William Ortega **RC** (Future Watch)	4.00
124	Jason Smith **RC** (Future Watch)	4.00
125	Brian Lawrence **RC** (Future Watch)	4.00
126	Albert Pujols **RC** (Future Watch)	450.00
127	Wilken Ruan **RC** (Future Watch)	4.00
128	Josh Towers **RC** (Future Watch)	6.00
129	Kris Keller **RC** (Future Watch)	4.00
130	Nick Maness **RC** (Future Watch)	4.00
131	Jack Wilson **RC** (Future Watch)	10.00
132	Brandon Duckworth **RC** (Future Watch)	4.00
133	Mike Penney **RC** (Future Watch)	4.00
134	Jay Gibbons **RC** (Future Watch)	10.00
135	Cesar Crespo **RC** (Future Watch)	4.00
136	Ken Griffey Jr. (SP Superstars)	8.00
137	Mark McGwire (SP Superstars)	8.00
138	Derek Jeter (SP Superstars)	10.00
139	Alex Rodriguez (SP Superstars)	10.00
140	Sammy Sosa (SP Superstars)	4.00
141	Carlos Delgado (SP Superstars)	3.00
142	Cal Ripken Jr. (SP Superstars)	12.00
143	Pedro Martinez (SP Superstars)	5.00
144	Frank Thomas (SP Superstars)	5.00
145	Juan Gonzalez (SP Superstars)	3.00
146	Troy Glaus (SP Superstars)	4.00
147	Jason Giambi (SP Superstars)	4.00
148	Ivan Rodriguez (SP Superstars)	4.00
149	Chipper Jones (SP Superstars)	5.00
150	Vladimir Guerrero (SP Superstars)	5.00
151	Mike Piazza (SP Superstars)	5.00
152	Jeff Bagwell (SP Superstars)	4.00
153	Randy Johnson (SP Superstars)	5.00
154	Todd Helton (SP Superstars)	4.00
155	Gary Sheffield (SP Superstars)	3.00
156	Tony Gwynn (SP Superstars)	5.00
157	Barry Bonds (SP Superstars)	10.00
158	Nomar Garciaparra (SP Superstars)	5.00
159	Bernie Williams (SP Superstars)	3.00
160	Greg Vaughn (SP Superstars)	2.00
161	David Wells (SP Superstars)	2.00
162	Roberto Alomar (SP Superstars)	3.00
163	Jermaine Dye (SP Superstars)	2.00
164	Rafael Palmeiro (SP Superstars)	4.00
165	Andruw Jones (SP Superstars)	4.00
166	Preston Wilson (SP Superstars)	2.00
167	Edgardo Alfonzo (SP Superstars)	2.00
168	Pat Burrell (SP Superstars)	3.00
169	Jim Edmonds (SP Superstars)	3.00
170	Mike Hampton (SP Superstars)	2.00
171	Jeff Kent (SP Superstars)	2.00
172	Kevin Brown (SP Superstars)	2.00
173	Manny Ramirez (SP Superstars)	5.00
174	Magglio Ordonez (SP Superstars)	2.00
175	Roger Clemens (SP Superstars)	8.00
176	Jim Thome (SP Superstars)	4.00
177	Barry Zito (SP Superstars)	2.00
178	Brian Giles (SP Superstars)	2.00
179	Rick Ankiel (SP Superstars)	2.00
180	Corey Patterson (SP Superstars)	2.00

Limited

Stars (1-90):	8-15X
SP (91-135):	1-2X
SP (136-180):	1-30X
Production 50 Sets	

Buyback Autographs

		NM/M
Inserted 1:144		
Some not priced due to scarcity.		
4	Ken Griffey/ '93 SP/34	125.00
105	Ken Griffey/ '94 SP/182	80.00
190	Ken Griffey/ '95 SP/116	80.00
170	Ken Griffey/ '96 SP/53	100.00
84	Ken Griffey/ '00 SP/333	70.00
188	Alex Rodriguez/ '95 SP Red/117	80.00
171	Alex Rodriguez/ '96 SP/72	100.00
16	Alex Rodriguez/ '00 SP/332	75.00
260	Frank Thomas/ '93 SP/79	40.00
193	Frank Thomas/ '94 SP/165	35.00
50	Frank Thomas/ '97 SP/34	75.00
34	Frank Thomas/ '00 SP/302	35.00
34	Chipper Jones/ '95 SP/118	40.00
26	Chipper Jones/ '96 SP/72	45.00
45	Chipper Jones/ '00 SP/303	30.00
132	Randy Johnson/ '93 SP/97	60.00
106	Randy Johnson/ '94 SP/146	40.00
189	Randy Johnson/ '95 SP/121	40.00
169	Randy Johnson/ '96 SP/78	50.00
58	Randy Johnson/ '00 SP/213	40.00
41	Carlos Delgado/ '94 SP/279	15.00
181	Carlos Delgado/ '96 SP/83	20.00
8	Carlos Delgado/ '00 SP/174	15.00
50	Jim Edmonds/ '96 SP/74	20.00
167	Tony Gwynn/ '93 SP/101	40.00
130	Tony Gwynn/ '94 SP/88	40.00
105	Tony Gwynn/ '95 SP/179	30.00
160	Tony Gwynn/ '96 SP/92	40.00
74	Tony Gwynn/ '00 SP/95	40.00
3	Jason Giambi/ '00 SP/290	30.00
9	Ivan Rodriguez/ '93 SP/89	40.00
180	Ivan Rodriguez/ '96 SP/64	40.00
22	Ivan Rodriguez/ '00 SP/163	30.00
47	Andruw Jones/ '00 SP/336	25.00
10	Barry Bonds/ '93 SP/75	180.00
90	Barry Bonds/ '94 SP/103	180.00
166	Barry Bonds/ '96 SP/49	180.00
65	Barry Bonds/ '00 SP/146	180.00
18	Gary Sheffield/ '93 SP/83	20.00
114	Gary Sheffield/ '94 SP/70	20.00
86	Gary Sheffield/ '96 SP/69	20.00
60	Gary Sheffield/ '00 SP/133	15.00

89 Sammy Sosa/ '93 SP/73 100.00
126 Cal Ripken/ '94 SP/99 100.00
1 Cal Ripken/ '95 SP/37 150.00
20 Cal Ripken/ '00 SP/266 100.00
89 Todd Helton/ '00 SP/194 25.00
4 Tim Hudson/ '00 SP/291 20.00
62 Shawn Green/ '00 SP/340 20.00
52 Fernando Tatis/ '00 SP/267 8.00
57 Matt Williams/ '00 SP/340 10.00
72 Robin Ventura/ '00 SP/340 10.00
2 Troy Glaus/ '00 SP/340 15.00
39 Roger Clemens/ '00 SP/145 100.00

Chirography

NM/M
Common Player: 5.00
Inserted 1:72
EA Edgardo Alfonzo 5.00
AB Albert Belle 15.00
CB Carlos Beltran 35.00
MB Milton Bradley 12.00
PB Pat Burrell 10.00
JC Jose Canseco 30.00
CD Carlos Delgado 12.00
DD Darren Dreifort/206 5.00
JD J.D. Drew 15.00
JE Jim Edmonds 20.00
DEr Darin Erstad 10.00
DEs David Espinosa 5.00
CF Cliff Floyd 10.00
RF Rafael Furcal/222 10.00
JG Jason Giambi 15.00
TrG Troy Glaus 15.00
LG Luis Gonzalez/271 15.00
SG Shawn Green/82 25.00
KG Ken Griffey Jr/126 80.00
ToG Tony Gwynn/76 40.00
RH Rick Helling/211 5.00
ToH Todd Helton/152 30.00
TiH Tim Hudson 15.00
RJ Randy Johnson/143 50.00
AJ Andruw Jones 20.00
CJ Chipper Jones/184 40.00
DJ David Justice 8.00
MK Mark Kotsay/228 5.00
TL Travis Lee/226 5.00
AlP Albert Pujols 550.00
CR Cal Ripken/109 125.00
AR Alex Rodriguez/229 100.00
DS Dane Sardinha 5.00
BS Ben Sheets 20.00
SS Sammy Sosa/76 100.00
MS Mike Sweeney 8.00
MV Mo Vaughn/103 8.00
RV Robin Ventura/92 10.00
DW David Wells 8.00
RW Rondell White 8.00
MW Matt Williams 8.00

Chirography Gold

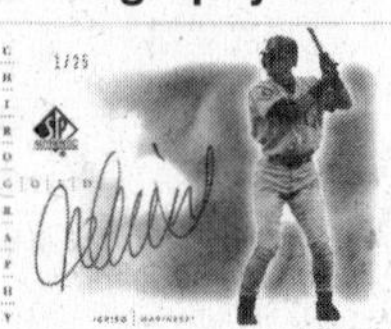

NM/M
Common Player:
AB Albert Belle/88 15.00
CD Carlos Delgado/25 50.00
DD Darren Dreifort/37 25.00
DES David Espinosa/79 15.00
KG Ken Griffey Jr./30 150.00
RH Rick Helling/32 15.00
RJ Randy Johnson/51 65.00
DJ David Justice/28 30.00
DS Dane Sardinha/50 15.00
MS Mike Sweeney/29 25.00
MV Mo Vaughn/42 15.00
DW David Wells/33 20.00

Cooperstown Calling Game Jersey

NM/M
Common Player: 5.00
Overall jersey odds 1:24.
JB Jeff Bagwell 8.00

WB Wade Boggs 8.00
GC Gary Carter 5.00
RC Roger Clemens 30.00
AD Andre Dawson 5.00
SG Steve Garvey 5.00
GG Goose Gossage 5.00
TG Tony Gwynn 10.00
RM Roger Maris/243 75.00
PM Pedro Martinez/SP 15.00
DM Don Mattingly 30.00
BM Bill Mazeroski 5.00
PM Paul Molitor 8.00
EM Eddie Murray 5.00
MP Mike Piazza/SP 25.00
KP Kirby Puckett 10.00
MR Manny Ramirez/SP 15.00
CR Cal Ripken Jr. 30.00
RS Ryne Sandberg 20.00
OS Ozzie Smith 10.00
DW Dave Winfield 5.00

Game Jersey

NM/M
Common Player: 5.00
Overall jersey odds 1:24
JD Joe DiMaggio/243 100.00
KG Ken Griffey Jr. 15.00
MM Mickey Mantle/243 150.00
AR Alex Rodriguez 15.00
GS Gary Sheffield 5.00
SS Sammy Sosa 10.00

Combo Game Jersey

NM/M
Overall jersey odds 1:24.
SD Sammy Sosa, Andre Dawson 25.00
RS Alex Rodriguez, Ozzie Smith 35.00
GD Ken Griffey Jr., Joe DiMaggio/98 120.00
SW Gary Sheffield, Dave Winfield 15.00
MD Mickey Mantle, Joe DiMaggio/98 300.00
MG Mickey Mantle, Ken Griffey /98 160.00

2001 SP Authentic Stars of Japan

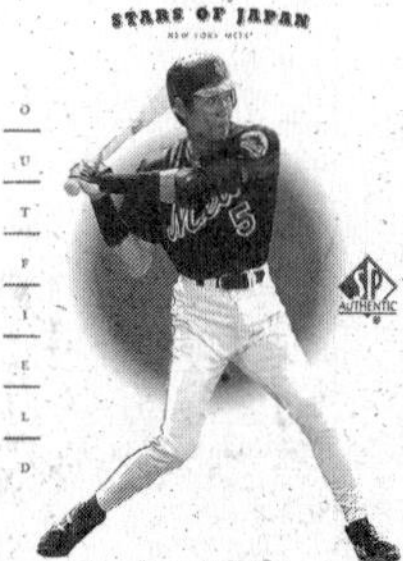

NM/M
Complete Set (30): 50.00
Common Player: 1.00
One pack/hobby box
RS1 Ichiro Suzuki, Tsuyoshi Shinjo 5.00
RS2 Shigetosi Hasegawa, Hideki Irabu 1.00
RS3 Tomokazu Ohka, Mac Suzuki 1.00
RS4 Tsuyoshi Shinjo, Hideki Irabu 1.00
RS5 Ichiro Suzuki, Hideo Nomo 5.00
RS6 Tsuyoshi Shinjo, Mac Suzuki 1.00
RS7 Tsuyoshi Shinjo, Kazuhiro Sasaki 1.00
RS8 Hideo Nomo, Tomokazu Ohka 1.50
RS9 Ichiro Suzuki, Mac Suzuki 5.00
RS10 Hideo Nomo, Shigetosi Hasegawa 1.50
RS11 Hideo Nomo, Masato Yoshii 1.50
RS12 Hideo Nomo, Hideki Irabu 1.50
RS13 Shigetosi Hasegawa, Kazuhiro Sasaki 1.00
RS14 Shigetosi Hasegawa, Mac Suzuki 1.00
RS15 Tsuyoshi Shinjo, Hideo Nomo 1.50
RS16 Tsuyoshi Shinjo, Tomokazu Ohka 1.00
RS17 Ichiro Suzuki, Kazuhiro Sasaki 5.00
RS18 Masato Yoshii, Hideki Irabu 1.00
RS19 Ichiro Suzuki, Tomokazu Ohka 5.00
RS20 Hideki Irabu, Kazuhiro Sasaki 1.00
RS21 Tsuyoshi Shinjo, Masato Yoshii 1.00
RS22 Ichiro Suzuki, Shigetosi Hasegawa 5.00
RS23 Mac Suzuki, Kazuhiro Sasaki 1.00
RS24 Ichiro Suzuki, Hideki Irabu 5.00
RS25 Tomokazu Ohka, Kazuhiro Sasaki 1.00
RS26 Tsuyoshi Shinjo, Shigetosi Hasegawa 1.00
RS27 Masato Yoshii, Kazuhiro Sasaki 1.00
RS28 Hideo Nomo, Kazuhiro Sasaki 1.50
RS29 Ichiro Suzuki, Masato Yoshii 5.00
RS30 Hideo Nomo, Ichiro Suzuki 5.00

Game Ball

NM/M
Common Player: 8.00
SH Shigetosi Hasegawa/ SP/30 15.00
HI Hideki Irabu 8.00
KS Kazuhiro Sasaki 10.00
TS Tsuyoshi Shinjo/ SP/50 20.00
IS Ichiro Suzuki 75.00
MY Masato Yoshii 10.00

Game Ball Gold

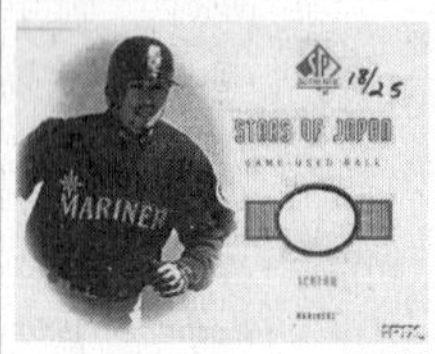

NM/M
Production 25 Sets
SH Shigetosi Hasegawa 40.00
HI Hideki Irabu 20.00
KS Kazuhiro Sasaki 40.00

Game Ball-Base Combos

NM/M
Inserted 1:576
HI-KS Hideki Irabu, Kazuhiro Sasaki/ SP/30 25.00
HN-KS Hideo Nomo, Kazuhiro Sasaki/ SP/50 75.00
HN-SH Hideo Nomo, Shigetosi Hasegawa 20.00
IS-KS Ichiro Suzuki, Kazuhiro Sasaki/ SP/30 120.00
IS-MY Ichiro Suzuki, Masato Yoshii 50.00
IS-SH Ichiro Suzuki, Shigetosi Hasegawa/ SP/72 75.00
IS-TS Ichiro Suzuki, Tsuyoshi Shinjo/ SP/40 125.00
MS-KS Mac Suzuki, Kazuhiro Sasaki/ SP/30 20.00
MY-KS Masato Yoshii, Kazuhiro Sasaki/ SP/30 25.00
SH-KS Shigetosi Hasegawa, Kazuhiro Sasaki/ SP/30 25.00
TO-KS Tomokazu Ohka, Kazuhiro Sasaki 20.00
TS-HI Tsuyoshi Shinjo, Hideki Irabu/SP/30 25.00
TS-KS Tsuyoshi Shinjo, Kazuhiro Sasaki/ SP/30 25.00
TS-SH Tsuyoshi Shinjo, Shigetosi Hasegawa/ SP/30 25.00

Game Ball-Base Combos Gold

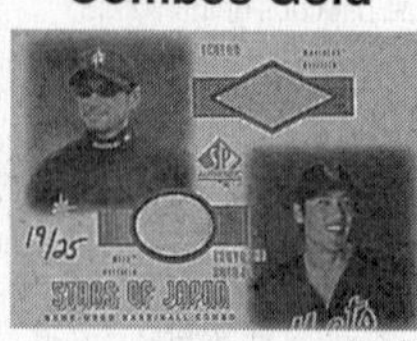

NM/M
Common Card: 20.00
Production 25 Sets
HI-KS Hideki Irabu, Kazuhiro Sasaki 25.00
HN-KS Hideo Nomo, Kazuhiro Sasaki 65.00
HN-SH Hideo Nomo, Shigetosi Hasegawa 65.00
IS-KS Ichiro Suzuki, Kazuhiro Sasaki 150.00
IS-MY Ichiro Suzuki, Masato Yoshii 150.00
IS-SH Ichiro Suzuki, Shigetosi Hasegawa 150.00
IS-TS Ichiro Suzuki, Tsuyoshi Shinjo 150.00
MS-KS Mac Suzuki, Kazuhiro Sasaki 20.00
MY-KS Masato Yoshii, Kazuhiro Sasaki 20.00
SH-KS Shigetosi Hasegawa, Kazuhiro Sasaki 20.00
TO-KS Tomokazu Ohka, Kazuhiro Sasaki 20.00
TS-HI Tsuyoshi Shinjo, Hideki Irabu 25.00
TS-KS Tsuyoshi Shinjo, Kazuhiro Sasaki 25.00
TS-SH Tsuyoshi Shinjo, Shigetosi Hasegawa 25.00

Game Ball-Base Trio

NM/M
Complete Set (1):
RS Kazuhiro Sasaki, Ichiro Suzuki, Hideo Nomo 175.00

Game Ball-Base Trio Gold

Production 25

Game Base

NM/M
Common Player: 15.00
SH Shigetosi Hasegawa/ SP/33 20.00
HI Hideki Irabu/SP/33 15.00
TO Tomokazu Ohka/ SP/33 15.00
KS Kazuhiro Sasaki/ SP/33 25.00
TS Tsuyoshi Shinjo/ SP/33 25.00
MS Mac Suzuki/SP/23 20.00
MY Masato Yoshii/SP/33 20.00

Game Base Gold

NM/M
Common Player: 25.00
Production 25 Sets
SH Shigetosi Hasegawa 25.00
HI Hideki Irabu 25.00
TO Tomokazu Ohka 25.00
KS Kazuhiro Sasaki 30.00
TS Tsuyoshi Shinjo 35.00
MS Mac Suzuki 25.00
MY Masato Yoshii 25.00

Game Bat Gold

NM/M
Common Player: 10.00
Production 25 Sets
HN Hideo Nomo 80.00
TS Tsuyoshi Shinjo 30.00
MY Masato Yoshii 10.00

Game Jersey

NM/M
Common Player: 5.00
Inserted 1:12
SH Shigetosi Hasegawa 5.00
HN Hideo Nomo 40.00
KS Kazuhiro Sasaki 8.00
TS Tsuyoshi Shinjo 8.00
IS Ichiro Suzuki/ SP/260 EXCH 100.00
MY Masato Yoshii 5.00

Game Jersey Gold

NM/M
Common Player: 10.00
Production 25 Sets
SH Shigetosi Hasegawa 10.00
HN Hideo Nomo 60.00
KS Kazuhiro Sasaki 15.00
TS Tsuyoshi Shinjo 15.00
MY Masato Yoshii 10.00

Game Jersey-Bat Combos

NM/M
Common Player: 15.00
HS Shigetosi Hasegawa, Tsuyoshi Shinjo 15.00
NN Hideo Nomo 60.00
SN Kazuhiro Sasaki, Hideo Nomo 40.00
SH Kazuhiro Sasaki, Shigetosi Hasegawa 15.00

Game Bat-Jersey Combo Gold

NM/M
Production 25 Sets
BB-HS Shigetosi Hasegawa, Tsuyoshi Shinjo 40.00

Game Bat

NM/M
Inserted 1:12
HN Hideo Nomo/SP/30 60.00
TS Tsuyoshi Shinjo/ SP/30 20.00
MY Masato Yoshii 5.00

Sultan of Swatch Jersey or Pants

NM/M
Quantity produced listed
SOS2 Babe Ruth/29 350.00
SOS3 Babe Ruth/94 300.00
SOS4 Babe Ruth/54 350.00
SOS5 Babe Ruth/59 350.00
SOS6 Babe Ruth/26 350.00
SOS7 Babe Ruth/27 350.00
SOS8 Babe Ruth/32 350.00
SOS9 Babe Ruth/20 350.00
SOS10 Babe Ruth/21 350.00
SOS11 Babe Ruth/23 350.00
SOS12 Babe Ruth/24 350.00
SOS13 Babe Ruth/26 350.00
SOS14 Babe Ruth/27 350.00
SOS15 Babe Ruth/28 350.00
SOS16 Babe Ruth/29 350.00
SOS17 Babe Ruth/30 350.00
SOS18 Babe Ruth/31 350.00
SOS19 Babe Ruth/33 350.00
SOS20 Babe Ruth/36 350.00
SOS21 Babe Ruth/48 350.00

Sultan of Swatch Jersey/Cut

No Pricing
Production One Set

2001 SP Game Bat

NM/M
Complete Set (90): 40.00
Common Player: .25
Pack (4): 10.00
Box (16): 150.00
1 Troy Glaus .50
2 Darin Erstad .50
3 Mo Vaughn .25
4 Jason Giambi .75
5 Ben Grieve .25
6 Eric Chavez .50
7 Carlos Delgado .75
8 Tony Batista .25
9 Shannon Stewart .25
10 Jose Cruz Jr. .25
11 Fred McGriff .25
12 Greg Vaughn .25
13 Roberto Alomar .50
14 Manny Ramirez 1.00
15 Jim Thome .75
16 Russ Branyan .25
17 Alex Rodriguez 2.00
18 John Olerud .25
19 Edgar Martinez .25
20 Cal Ripken Jr. 3.00
21 Albert Belle .25
22 Ivan Rodriguez .75
23 Rafael Palmeiro .50
24 Nomar Garciaparra 1.00
25 Carl Everett .25
26 Dante Bichette .25
27 Mike Sweeney .25
28 Jermaine Dye .25
29 Carlos Beltran .75
30 Juan Gonzalez .50
31 Dean Palmer .25
32 Bobby Higginson .25
33 Matt Lawton .25
34 Jacque Jones .25
35 Frank Thomas 1.00
36 Magglio Ordonez .25
37 Paul Konerko .50
38 Carlos Lee .40
39 Bernie Williams .50
40 Derek Jeter 3.00
41 Paul O'Neill .40
42 Jose Canseco .50
43 Ken Caminiti .25
44 Jeff Bagwell .75
45 Craig Biggio .40
46 Richard Hidalgo .25
47 Andruw Jones 1.00
48 Chipper Jones 1.00
49 Andres Galarraga .25
50 B.J. Surhoff .25
51 Jeromy Burnitz .25
52 Geoff Jenkins .25
53 Richie Sexson .40
54 Mark McGwire 2.50
55 Jim Edmonds .50
56 J.D. Drew .40
57 Fernando Tatis .25
58 Sammy Sosa 1.50
59 Mark Grace .50
60 Eric Young .25
61 Matt Williams .25
62 Luis Gonzalez .40
63 Steve Finley .25
64 Shawn Green .40
65 Gary Sheffield .50
66 Eric Karros .25
67 Vladimir Guerrero 1.00
68 Jose Vidro .25
69 Barry Bonds 3.00
70 Jeff Kent .40
71 Preston Wilson .25
72 Mike Lowell .25
73 Luis Castillo .25
74 Mike Piazza 1.50
75 Robin Ventura .25

76 Edgardo Alfonzo .25
77 Tony Gwynn 1.00
78 Eric Owens .25
79 Ryan Klesko .25
80 Scott Rolen .75
81 Bobby Abreu .50
82 Pat Burrell .50
83 Brian Giles .25
84 Jason Kendall .25
85 Aaron Boone .25
86 Ken Griffey Jr. 2.00
87 Barry Larkin .50
88 Todd Helton 1.00
89 Larry Walker .25
90 Jeffrey Hammonds .25

Big League Hit Parade

NM/M
Complete Set (6): 15.00
Common Player: 1.50
Inserted 1:15
1 Nomar Garciaparra 1.50
2 Ken Griffey Jr. 3.00
3 Sammy Sosa 2.00
4 Alex Rodriguez 4.00
5 Mark McGwire 4.00
6 Ivan Rodriguez 1.50

In the Swing

NM/M
Complete Set (15): 25.00
Common Player: 1.00
Inserted 1:7
1 Ken Griffey Jr. 2.50
2 Jim Edmonds 1.00
3 Carlos Delgado 1.00
4 Frank Thomas 1.50
5 Barry Bonds 4.00
6 Nomar Garciaparra 2.00
7 Gary Sheffield 1.00
8 Vladimir Guerrero 1.50
9 Alex Rodriguez 3.00
10 Todd Helton 1.50
11 Darin Erstad 1.00
12 Derek Jeter 4.00
13 Sammy Sosa 2.50
14 Mark McGwire 3.00
15 Jason Giambi 1.00

Lineup Time

NM/M
Complete Set (11): 20.00
Common Player: 1.00
Inserted 1:8
1 Mark McGwire 3.00
2 Roberto Alomar 1.00
3 Alex Rodriguez 3.00
4 Chipper Jones 2.00
5 Ivan Rodriguez 1.00
6 Ken Griffey Jr. 2.50
7 Sammy Sosa 2.50
8 Barry Bonds 4.00
9 Frank Thomas 1.50
10 Pedro Martinez 1.50
11 Derek Jeter 4.00

Piece of the Game

NM/M
Common Player: 4.00
Inserted 1:1
SP production 1,500 or fewer
Golds: 2-5X
Production 25 Sets
EA Edgardo Alfonzo/SP 10.00
RA Roberto Alomar 8.00
SA Sandy Alomar 4.00
RA Rick Ankiel 4.00
JB Jeff Bagwell/SP 15.00
TB Tony Batista 5.00
CB Carlos Beltran 5.00
JB Johnny Bench/SP 25.00
BB Barry Bonds 25.00
KB Kevin Brown/SP 10.00
PB Pat Burrell 8.00
JC Jose Canseco 6.00
WC Will Clark 8.00
CD Carlos Delgado 6.00
JoD Joe DiMaggio/SP 100.00
JD J.D. Drew 6.00
JE Jim Edmonds 6.00
DE Darin Erstad/SP 10.00
RF Rafael Furcal 6.00
BG Bob Gibson/SP 20.00
TGl Tom Glavine/SP 15.00
MG Mark Grace 8.00
SG Shawn Green 6.00
KG Ken Griffey Jr. 15.00
TGw Tony Gwynn 10.00
TH Todd Helton 8.00
TH Todd Hundley/SP 10.00
RJ Reggie Jackson/SP 20.00
RJ Randy Johnson 10.00
AJ Andruw Jones 8.00
CJ Chipper Jones 10.00
DJ David Justice 5.00
KL Kenny Lofton 4.00
GM Greg Maddux 15.00
EM Edgar Martinez 6.00
TM Tino Martinez 6.00
FM Fred McGriff/SP 10.00
PN Phil Nevin/SP 10.00
JO John Olerud 6.00
PO Paul O'Neill 6.00
MO Magglio Ordonez/SP 10.00
MQ Mark Quinn/SP 10.00
MR Manny Ramirez 8.00
CR Cal Ripken Jr./SP 40.00
AR Alex Rodriguez 10.00
IR Ivan Rodriguez 8.00
SR Scott Rolen 8.00
NR Nolan Ryan/SP 35.00
TS Tim Salmon/SP 10.00
GS Gary Sheffield 5.00
SS Sammy Sosa/SP 25.00
SS Shannon Stewart 4.00
FT Frank Thomas 8.00
GV Greg Vaughn 4.00
MV Mo Vaughn 4.00
RV Robin Ventura 4.00
BW Bernie Williams 6.00
MW Matt Williams 4.00
PW Preston Wilson 4.00

Piece of the Game Autograph

NM/M
Common Autograph: 30.00
Inserted 1:96
BB Barry Bonds 180.00
JC Jose Canseco 40.00
KG Ken Griffey Jr. 100.00
TGw Tony Gwynn 50.00
AJ Andruw Jones 30.00
AR Alex Rodriguez 120.00
NR Nolan Ryan 125.00
FT Frank Thomas 50.00

The Lumber Yard

NM/M
Complete Set (10): 15.00
Common Player: .50
Inserted 1:10
1 Jason Giambi 1.00
2 Chipper Jones 1.50
3 Carl Everett .50
4 Alex Rodriguez 3.00
5 Frank Thomas 1.50
6 Barry Bonds 4.00
7 Jeff Bagwell 1.50
8 Sammy Sosa 2.50
9 Carlos Delgado 1.00
10 Mike Piazza 2.50

Milestone

NM/M
Complete Set (96):
Common Player: .40
Common Rookie (91-96): 5.00
Production 500
Pack (4): 16.00
Box (10): 140.00
1 Troy Glaus .50
2 Darin Erstad .50
3 Jason Giambi .75
4 Jermaine Dye .40
5 Eric Chavez .50
6 Carlos Delgado .75
7 Raul Mondesi .40
8 Shannon Stewart .40
9 Greg Vaughn .40
10 Aubrey Huff .40
11 Juan Gonzalez .50
12 Roberto Alomar .50
13 Jim Thome .75
14 Omar Vizquel .40
15 Mike Cameron .40
16 Edgar Martinez .40
17 John Olerud .40
18 Bret Boone .40
19 Cal Ripken Jr. 3.00
20 Tony Batista .40
21 Alex Rodriguez 2.50
22 Ivan Rodriguez .75
23 Rafael Palmeiro .75
24 Manny Ramirez 1.00
25 Pedro Martinez 1.00
26 Nomar Garciaparra 1.00
27 Carl Everett .40
28 Mike Sweeney .40
29 Neifi Perez .40
30 Mark Quinn .40
31 Bobby Higginson .40
32 Tony Clark .40
33 Doug Mientkiewicz .40
34 Cristian Guzman .40
35 Joe Mays .40
36 David Ortiz 1.00
37 Frank Thomas 1.00
38 Magglio Ordonez .40
39 Carlos Lee .50
40 Alfonso Soriano 1.00
41 Bernie Williams .50
42 Derek Jeter 3.00
43 Roger Clemens 2.50
44 Jeff Bagwell 1.00
45 Richard Hidalgo .40
46 Moises Alou .40
47 Chipper Jones 1.00
48 Greg Maddux 2.00
49 Rafael Furcal .50
50 Andruw Jones 1.00
51 Jeromy Burnitz .40
52 Geoff Jenkins .40
53 Richie Sexson .50
54 Edgar Renteria .40
55 Mark McGwire 2.50
56 Jim Edmonds .50
57 J.D. Drew .50
58 Sammy Sosa 1.50
59 Bill Mueller .40
60 Luis Gonzalez .50
61 Randy Johnson 1.00
62 Gary Sheffield .50
63 Shawn Green .40
64 Kevin Brown .40
65 Vladimir Guerrero 1.00
66 Jose Vidro .40
67 Fernando Tatis .40
68 Barry Bonds 3.00
69 Jeff Kent .50
70 Rich Aurilia .40
71 Preston Wilson .40
72 Charles Johnson .40
73 Cliff Floyd .40
74 Mike Piazza 1.00
75 Matt Lawton .40
76 Edgardo Alfonzo .40
77 Tony Gwynn 1.50
78 Phil Nevin .40
79 Scott Rolen 1.00
80 Pat Burrell .50
81 Bobby Abreu .50
82 Brian Giles .40
83 Jason Kendall .40
84 Aramis Ramirez .50
85 Sean Casey .50
86 Ken Griffey Jr. 2.50
87 Barry Larkin .50
88 Todd Helton .75
89 Mike Hampton .40
90 Larry Walker .50
91 Ichiro Suzuki **RC** 70.00
92 Albert Pujols **RC** 180.00
93 Tsuyoshi Shinjo **RC** 5.00
94 Jack Wilson **RC** 8.00
95 Donaldo Mendez **RC** 5.00
96 Junior Spivey **RC** 8.00

Milestone Slugging Sensations

NM/M
Complete Set (12): 12.00
Common Player: .50
Inserted 1:5
SS1 Troy Glaus .50
SS2 Mark McGwire 2.50
SS3 Sammy Sosa 1.50
SS4 Juan Gonzalez .50
SS5 Barry Bonds 3.00
SS6 Jeff Bagwell .75
SS7 Jason Giambi .75
SS8 Ivan Rodriguez .75
SS9 Mike Piazza 1.50
SS10 Chipper Jones 1.00
SS11 Ken Griffey Jr. 2.00
SS12 Gary Sheffield .50

Milestone The Art of Hitting

NM/M
Complete Set (12): 10.00
Common Player: .50
Inserted 1:5
AH1 Tony Gwynn 1.50
AH2 Manny Ramirez 1.00
AH3 Todd Helton 1.00
AH4 Nomar Garciaparra 1.00
AH5 Vladimir Guerrero 1.00
AH6 Ichiro Suzuki 1.50
AH7 Darin Erstad .50
AH8 Alex Rodriguez 2.50
AH9 Carlos Delgado .75
AH10 Edgar Martinez .50
AH11 Luis Gonzalez .50
AH12 Barry Bonds 3.00

Milestone The Trophy Room

NM/M
Complete Set (6): 8.00
Common Player: 1.00
Inserted 1:10
TR1 Sammy Sosa 1.50
TR2 Jason Giambi 1.00
TR3 Todd Helton 1.00
TR4 Alex Rodriguez 2.50
TR5 Mark McGwire 2.50
TR6 Ken Griffey Jr. 2.00

Milestone P.O.A. Milestone Bat

NM/M
Common Player: 5.00
Golds: 3-5X
Production 35 Sets
JB Jeff Bagwell 8.00
BB Barry Bonds 20.00
RB Russell Branyan 5.00
JB Jeromy Burnitz 5.00
RC Roger Clemens 20.00
DE Darin Erstad 5.00
LG Luis Gonzalez 5.00
KG Ken Griffey Jr. 12.00
TH Todd Helton 8.00
Chj Chipper Jones 10.00
MP Mike Piazza 10.00
CR Cal Ripken Jr. 30.00
AR Alex Rodriguez 15.00
GS Gary Sheffield 5.00
SS Sammy Sosa 10.00
IS Ichiro Suzuki/203 80.00
FT Frank Thomas 8.00
JT Jim Thome 8.00

Milestone P.O.A. Autograph Bat

NM/M
Common Autograph: 15.00
Inserted 1:100
RB Russell Branyan 15.00
CD Carlos Delgado/97 35.00
JDr J.D. Drew 20.00
JDy Jermaine Dye 15.00
LG Luis Gonzalez 20.00
JK Jason Kendall 15.00
JK Jeff Kent/194 35.00
AR Alex Rodriguez/97 120.00
GS Gary Sheffield/194 40.00
IS Ichiro Suzuki/53 800.00
MT Miguel Tejada 40.00
JV Jose Vidro 15.00
PW Preston Wilson 15.00

Milestone P.O.A. BFH Bat

NM/M
Common Player: 5.00
Golds: 2-3X
Production 35 Sets
BB Barry Bonds 20.00
RC Roger Clemens/203 25.00
CD Carlos Delgado 5.00
JG Jason Giambi 5.00
KG Ken Griffey Jr. 15.00
TGw Tony Gwynn 15.00
GM Greg Maddux 12.00
EM Edgar Martinez 6.00
FM Fred McGriff 6.00
RP Rafael Palmeiro 8.00
MP Mike Piazza 10.00
CR Cal Ripken Jr. 30.00
AR Alex Rodriguez 15.00
IR Ivan Rodriguez 8.00
SS Sammy Sosa 10.00

Milestone P.O.A. Int. Conn. Bat

NM/M
Common Player: 5.00
Golds: 3-5X
Production 35 Sets
RA Roberto Alomar 6.00
AB Adrian Beltre 5.00
RF Rafael Furcal 5.00
JG Juan Gonzalez 6.00
AJ Andruw Jones 8.00
PM Pedro Martinez 10.00
HN Hideo Nomo/203 40.00
MO Magglio Ordonez 5.00
CP Chan Ho Park 5.00
JP Jorge Posada 10.00
AP Albert Pujols 70.00
MR Manny Ramirez 8.00
TS Tsuyoshi Shinjo 8.00
IS Ichiro Suzuki/273 80.00
MT Miguel Tejada 6.00
OV Omar Vizquel 5.00

Milestone P.O.A. Triple Bat

NM/M
Common Card: 15.00
Inserted 1:50
GRS Ken Griffey Jr., Alex Rodriguez, Sammy Sosa 40.00
JJF Chipper Jones, Andruw Jones, Rafael Furcal 15.00
RRP Alex Rodriguez, Ivan Rodriguez, Rafael Palmeiro 35.00
SGB Gary Sheffield, Shawn Green, Adrian Beltre 15.00
TVA Jim Thome, Omar Vizquel, Roberto Alomar 15.00
KGR Jason Kendall, Brian Giles, Aramis Ramirez 15.00
OJC Paul O'Neill, David Justice, Roger Clemens 35.00
CMG Roger Clemens, Greg Maddux, Tom Glavine 40.00
VSA Robin Ventura, Tsuyoshi Shinjo, Edgardo Alfonzo 15.00
OTA Magglio Ordonez, Frank Thomas, Sandy Alomar 15.00
PWS Kirby Puckett, Dave Winfield, Ozzie Smith 25.00
GRB Tony Gwynn, Cal Ripken Jr., Barry Bonds 60.00
GBM Ken Griffey Jr., Barry Bonds, Fred McGriff 35.00
SFR Alfonso Soriano, Rafael Furcal, Alex Ramirez 25.00

Milestone P.O.A. Quad Bat

NM/M
Common Card: 15.00
Inserted 1:50
TVAL Jim Thome, Omar Vizquel, Roberto Alomar, Kenny Lofton 25.00
RRPM Alex Rodriguez, Ivan Rodriguez, Rafael Palmeiro, Ruben Mateo 50.00
OJCP Paul O'Neill, David Justice, Roger Clemens, Jorge Posada 60.00
JJFM Chipper Jones, Andruw Jones, Rafael Furcal, Greg Maddux 40.00
PWSG Kirby Puckett, Dave Winfield, Ozzie Smith, Steve Garvey 30.00
GRSB Ken Griffey Jr., Alex Rodriguez, Sammy Sosa, Barry Bonds 80.00
SGBP Gary Sheffield, Shawn Green, Adrian Beltre, Chan Ho Park 15.00
GGRR Ken Griffey Jr., Ken Griffey Jr., Alex Rodriguez, Alex Rodriguez 65.00
GRBM Tony Gwynn, Cal Ripken Jr., Barry Bonds, Fred McGriff 70.00
TDTA Frank Thomas, Jermaine Dye, Jim Thome, Roberto Alomar 25.00
GHSK Luis Gonzalez, Todd Helton, Gary Sheffield, Jeff Kent 20.00

GDBS	Ken Griffey Jr., J.D. Drew, Jeromy Burnitz, Sammy Sosa	50.00
JVBW	Chipper Jones, Robin Ventura, Pat Burrell, Preston Wilson	30.00
RGGM	Alex Rodriguez, Troy Glaus, Jason Giambi, Edgar Martinez	40.00
ONRD	Paul O'Neill, Hideo Nomo, Cal Ripken Jr., Carlos Delgado	80.00

2001 SP Game-Used Edition

		NM/M
Common Player:		.50
Common SP (61-90):		5.00
Production 500		
Pack (3):		30.00
Box (6):		150.00
1	Garret Anderson	.50
2	Troy Glaus	1.00
3	Darin Erstad	.75
4	Jason Giambi	1.50
5	Tim Hudson	.75
6	Johnny Damon	2.00
7	Carlos Delgado	1.00
8	Greg Vaughn	.50
9	Juan Gonzalez	.75
10	Roberto Alomar	1.00
11	Jim Thome	1.50
12	Edgar Martinez	.50
13	Cal Ripken Jr.	5.00
14	Andres Galarraga	.50
15	Alex Rodriguez	4.00
16	Rafael Palmeiro	1.25
17	Ivan Rodriguez	1.50
18	Manny Ramirez	1.50
19	Nomar Garciaparra	1.50
20	Pedro Martinez	2.00
21	Jermaine Dye	.50
22	Dean Palmer	.50
23	Matt Lawton	.50
24	Frank Thomas	1.50
25	David Wells	.50
26	Magglio Ordonez	.50
27	Derek Jeter	5.00
28	Bernie Williams	.50
29	Roger Clemens	4.00
30	Jeff Bagwell	1.50
31	Richard Hidalgo	.50
32	Chipper Jones	2.00
33	Andruw Jones	1.50
34	Greg Maddux	3.00
35	Jeffrey Hammonds	.50
36	Mark McGwire	4.00
37	Jim Edmonds	.75
38	Sammy Sosa	2.00
39	Corey Patterson	.50
40	Randy Johnson	1.50
41	Luis Gonzalez	.75
42	Gary Sheffield	.75
43	Shawn Green	.75
44	Kevin Brown	.50
45	Vladimir Guerrero	1.50
46	Barry Bonds	5.00
47	Jeff Kent	.75
48	Preston Wilson	.50
49	Charles Johnson	.50
50	Mike Piazza	2.00
51	Edgardo Alfonzo	.50
52	Tony Gwynn	2.00
53	Scott Rolen	1.50
54	Pat Burrell	1.00
55	Brian Giles	.50
56	Jason Kendall	.50
57	Ken Griffey Jr.	3.00
58	Mike Hampton	.50
59	Todd Helton	1.50
60	Larry Walker	.75
61	Wilson Betemit **RC**	10.00
62	Travis Hafner **RC**	20.00
63	Ichiro Suzuki **RC**	60.00
64	Juan Diaz **RC**	5.00
65	Morgan Ensberg **RC**	15.00
66	Horacio Ramirez **RC**	10.00
67	Ricardo Rodriguez **RC**	5.00
68	Sean Douglass **RC**	5.00
69	Brandon Duckworth **RC**	5.00
70	Jackson Melian **RC**	5.00
71	Adrian Hernandez **RC**	5.00
72	Kyle Kessel **RC**	5.00
73	Jason Michaels **RC**	5.00
74	Esix Snead **RC**	5.00
75	Jason Smith **RC**	5.00
76	Tyler Walker **RC**	5.00
77	Juan Uribe **RC**	8.00
78	Adam Pettyjohn **RC**	5.00
79	Tsuyoshi Shinjo **RC**	5.00
80	Mike Penney **RC**	5.00
81	Josh Towers **RC**	8.00
82	Erick Almonte **RC**	5.00
83	Ryan Freel **RC**	8.00
84	Juan Pena	5.00
85	Albert Pujols **RC**	220.00
86	Henry Mateo **RC**	5.00
87	Greg Miller **RC**	5.00
88	Jose Mieses **RC**	5.00
89	Jack Wilson **RC**	10.00
90	Carlos Valderrama **RC**	5.00

Authentic Fabric Jersey

		NM/M
Common Player:		4.00
Inserted 1:1		
EA	Edgardo Alfonzo	4.00
RA	Roberto Alomar	6.00
RA	Rick Ankiel	4.00
TB	Tony Batista/SP	8.00
BB	Barry Bonds	25.00
KB	Kevin Brown	6.00
JB	Jeromy Burnitz	4.00
PB	Pat Burrell	6.00
JC(B)	Jose Canseco/BLC	8.00
JC(H)	Jose Canseco/Yanks	8.00
EC	Eric Chavez	6.00
JCi	Jeff Cirillo	4.00
RC	Roger Clemens	20.00
CD	Carlos Delgado/SP	10.00
JDi	Joe DiMaggio/SP/50	160.00
JDr	J.D. Drew	5.00
JDy	Jermaine Dye/SP	8.00
JE	Jim Edmonds	6.00
DE	Darin Erstad	5.00
JG	Jason Giambi	8.00
BG	Brian Giles SP	8.00
TGl	Troy Glaus	6.00
ToG	Tom Glavine	6.00
LG	Luis Gonzalez	6.00
MG	Mark Grace	8.00
SG	Shawn Green	6.00
KG(H)	Ken Griffey/Reds	12.00
KG(M)	Ken Griffey/M's	12.00
KG(R)	Ken Griffey/Reds	12.00
TGw	Tony Gwynn	10.00
MH	Mike Hampton	4.00
THe	Todd Helton	8.00
TrH	Trevor Hoffman	4.00
TH	Tim Hudson	6.00
AH	Aubrey Huff	4.00
JI	J. Isringhausen/SP	8.00
CJo	Charles Johnson	4.00
RJ	Randy Johnson	10.00
AJ	Andruw Jones	8.00
CJ	Chipper Jones	10.00
JK	Jason Kendall	4.00
JK	Jeff Kent	5.00
BL	Barry Larkin	6.00
AL	Al Leiter	4.00
KL	Kenny Lofton	4.00
TL	Terrence Long	4.00
GM	Greg Maddux	10.00
MM	Mickey Mantle/SP/50	250.00
RM	Roger Maris/SP	75.00
EM	Edgar Martinez	6.00
TM	Tino Martinez	5.00
FM	Fred McGriff	5.00
KM	Kevin Millwood	5.00
PN	Phil Nevin	4.00
JO	John Olerud	5.00
MO	Magglio Ordonez	6.00
AP	Adam Piatt	4.00
CR	Cal Ripken Jr.	25.00
MR	Mariano Rivera	6.00
AR(H)	Alex Rodriguez/Rangers	10.00
AR(M)	Alex Rodriguez/M's	10.00
IR	Ivan Rodriguez	8.00
SR	Scott Rolen	8.00
NR	Nolan Ryan/SP/50	50.00
TS	Tom Seaver/SP/50	30.00
GS	Gary Sheffield	5.00
SS(H)	Sammy Sosa	15.00
SS(R)	Sammy Sosa	15.00
FTa	Fernando Tatis	4.00
MT	Miguel Tejada	6.00
FTh	Frank Thomas	8.00
JT	Jim Thome	8.00
GV	Greg Vaughn	4.00
RV	Robin Ventura	4.00
JV	Jose Vidro	4.00
DW	David Wells/SP	8.00
MW	Matt Williams	5.00
PW	Preston Wilson	4.00
DY	Dmitri Young	4.00
TZ	Todd Zeile	4.00

2-Player Auth. Fabric Jersey

		NM/M
Common Card:		25.00
Production 50 Sets		
R-R	Alex Rodriguez, Ivan Rodriguez	50.00
M-D	Mickey Mantle, Joe DiMaggio	400.00
M-M	Mickey Mantle, Roger Maris	400.00
R-S	Nolan Ryan, Tom Seaver	100.00
B-C	Barry Bonds, Jose Canseco	70.00
S-G	Gary Sheffield, Shawn Green	25.00
J-J	Chipper Jones, Andruw Jones	40.00
C-W	Roger Clemens, Bernie Williams	40.00
J-R	Randy Johnson, Nolan Ryan	75.00
S-T	Sammy Sosa, Frank Thomas	35.00
G-S	Ken Griffey Jr., Sammy Sosa	50.00
G-R	Ken Griffey Jr., Alex Rodriguez	50.00
S-R	Sammy Sosa, Alex Rodriguez	40.00
H-G	Tim Hudson, Jason Giambi	30.00

3-Player Authentic Fabric Jersey

		NM/M
Production 25 Sets		
GRS	Ken Griffey Jr., Alex Rodriguez, Sammy Sosa	100.00
MJJ	Greg Maddux, Chipper Jones, Andruw Jones	80.00
JBS	Andruw Jones, Barry Bonds, Sammy Sosa	120.00
JSM	Randy Johnson, Tom Seaver, Greg Maddux	80.00

Authentic Fabric Jersey Autograph

		NM/M
Production 50 Sets		
EA	Edgardo Alfonzo	25.00
RA	Rick Ankiel	15.00
BB	Barry Bonds/50	200.00
JC	Jose Canseco	40.00
CD	Carlos Delgado/50	40.00
JDr	J.D. Drew/50	40.00
JG	Jason Giambi/50	40.00
TGl	Troy Glaus/50	50.00
KG	Ken Griffey Jr.	150.00
TH	Tim Hudson/50	50.00
RJ	Randy Johnson	100.00
AJ	Andruw Jones	50.00
CJ	Chipper Jones	80.00
CR	Cal Ripken/50	200.00
AR	Alex Rodriguez	150.00
IR	Ivan Rodriguez	75.00
NR	Nolan Ryan/50	200.00
TS	Tom Seaver/50	80.00
SS	Sammy Sosa/50	120.00
FTh	Frank Thomas	75.00
DW	David Wells/50	25.00

2001 SP Legendary Cuts

		NM/M
Complete Set (90):		25.00
Common Player:		.40
Pack (4):		16.00
Box (18):		250.00
1	Al Simmons	.40
2	Jimmie Foxx (Height, weight and birthplace incorrect.)	1.00
3	Mickey Cochrane	.40
4	Phil Niekro	.40
5	Eddie Mathews	1.00
6	Gary Matthews	.40
7	Hank Aaron	2.50
8	Joe Adcock	.40
9	Warren Spahn	.75
10	George Sisler	.40
11	Stan Musial	1.00
12	Dizzy Dean	.75
13	Frankie Frisch	.40
14	Harvey Haddix	.40
15	Johnny Mize	.40
16	Ken Boyer	.40
17	Rogers Hornsby	.75
18	Cap Anson	.40
19	Andre Dawson	.40
20	Billy Williams	.40
21	Billy Herman	.40
22	Hack Wilson	.40
23	Ron Santo	.40
24	Ryne Sandberg	1.50
25	Ernie Banks	1.50
26	Burleigh Grimes	.40
27	Don Drysdale	.75
28	Gil Hodges	.40
29	Jackie Robinson	2.00
30	Tommy Lasorda	.40
31	Pee Wee Reese	.40
32	Roy Campanella	.75
33	Tommy Davis	.40
34	Branch Rickey	.40
35	Leo Durocher	.75
36	Walt Alston	.40
37	Bill Terry	.40
38	Carl Hubbell	.40
39	Eddie Stanky	.40
40	George Kelly	.40
41	Mel Ott	.75
42	Juan Marichal	.40
43	Rube Marquard	.40
44	Travis Jackson	.40
45	Bob Feller	.40
46	Earl Averill	.40
47	Elmer Flick	.40
48	Ken Keltner	.40
49	Lou Boudreau	.40
50	Early Wynn	.40
51	Satchel Paige	1.50
52	Ron Hunt	.40
53	Tom Seaver	1.00
54	Richie Ashburn	.40
55	Mike Schmidt	1.00
56	Honus Wagner	1.00
57	Lloyd Waner	.40
58	Max Carey	.40
59	Paul Waner	.40
60	Roberto Clemente	2.50
61	Nolan Ryan	3.00
62	Bobby Doerr	.40
63	Carlton Fisk	.75
64	Joe Cronin	.40
65	Smokey Joe Wood	.40
66	Tony Conigliaro	.40
67	Edd Roush	.40
68	Johnny Vander Meer	.40
69	Walter Johnson	.75
70	Charlie Gehringer	.40
71	Al Kaline	1.00
72	Ty Cobb	2.00
73	Tony Oliva	.40
74	Luke Appling	.40
75	Minnie Minoso	.40
76	Nellie Fox	.40
77	Shoeless Joe Jackson	2.00
78	Babe Ruth	3.00
79	Bill Dickey	.40
80	Elston Howard	.40
81	Joe DiMaggio	2.50
82	Lefty Gomez	.40
83	Lou Gehrig	2.50
84	Mickey Mantle	3.00
85	Reggie Jackson	1.00
86	Roger Maris	1.00
87	Whitey Ford	.40
88	Waite Hoyt	.40
89	Yogi Berra	1.00
90	Casey Stengel	.40

Bat

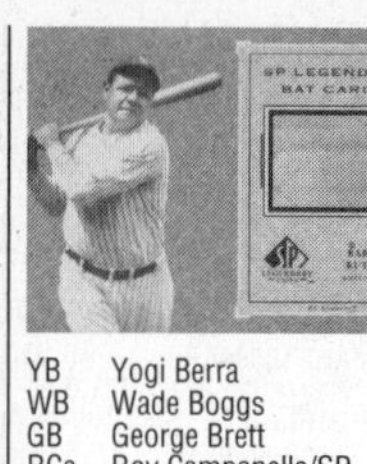

		NM/M
Common Player:		4.00
Inserted 1:18		
HA	Hank Aaron/SP	40.00
YB	Yogi Berra	10.00
WB	Wade Boggs	8.00
GB	George Brett	15.00
RCa	Roy Campanella/SP	40.00
RC	Rico Carty	4.00
RCl	Roberto Clemente	60.00
TC	Ty Cobb/SP	125.00
KC	Kiki Cuyler	8.00
TD	Tommy Davis/SP	40.00
AD	Andre Dawson	8.00
JD	Joe DiMaggio/SP	100.00
DD	Don Drysdale/SP	25.00
CF	Carlton Fisk	10.00
NF	Nellie Fox	10.00
JF	Jimmie Foxx	40.00
GH	Gil Hodges/SP	40.00
THo	Tommy Holmes (Photo on front is Eddie Mathews.)	8.00
RJ	Reggie Jackson	15.00
DJ	Davey Johnson	4.00
MM	Mickey Mantle/SP	120.00
RM	Roger Maris/SP	60.00
EM	Eddie Mathews	25.00
WMc	Willie McCovey	8.00
PM	Paul Molitor	15.00
MM	Manny Mota	4.00
MO	Mel Ott/SP	50.00
VP	Vada Pinson	4.00
JR	Jackie Robinson/SP	50.00
BR	Babe Ruth/SP	165.00
NR	Nolan Ryan/SP	40.00
RS	Ryne Sandberg	20.00
AS	Al Simmons/SP	25.00
BT	Bill Terry/SP	40.00
MW	Maury Wills	8.00
RY	Robin Yount	15.00

Combo Bat

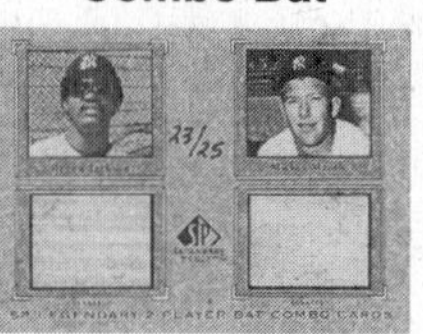

No pricing due to scarcity.
Production 25 Sets

Debut Bat

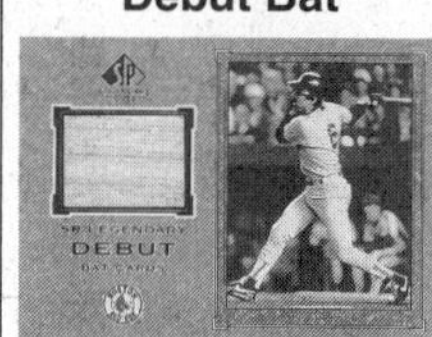

		NM/M
Common Player:		5.00
Inserted 1:18		
JA	Joe Adcock/SP	15.00
LA	Luke Appling/SP	25.00
RA	Richie Ashburn/SP	25.00
BB	Bobby Bonds	5.00
LB	Lou Boudreau	10.00
KB	Ken Boyer/SP	15.00
BB	Bill Buckner	5.00
MC	Mickey Cochrane	60.00
TC	Tony Conigliaro/SP	15.00
JC	Joe Cronin	10.00
BD	Bobby Doerr/SP	15.00
BF	Bob Feller/SP	15.00
BF	Bill Freehan	5.00
FF	Frankie Frisch/SP	15.00
CG	Charlie Gehringer	15.00
BH	Billy Herman/SP	15.00
WH	Willie Horton	6.00
EH	Elston Howard/SP	15.00
RH	Ron Hunt	5.00
JJ	Joe Jackson	300.00
GL	Greg Luzinski	5.00
GM	Gary Matthews	5.00
MM	Minnie Minoso/SP	15.00
TO	Tony Oliva	8.00
WP	Wes Parker	5.00
BR	Bobby Richardson/SP	15.00
SS	Steve Sax	5.00
GS	George Sisler	20.00
ES	Eddie Stanky	5.00
AT	Alan Trammell	5.00
PW	Paul Waner/SP	60.00
HW	Hack Wilson/SP	70.00
SY	Steve Yeager	5.00

Game Jersey

		NM/M
Common Player:		5.00
Inserted 1:18		
YB	Yogi Berra	15.00
WB	Wade Boggs	5.00
RC	Roberto Clemente	80.00
TC	Tony Conigliaro	8.00
BD	Bill Dickey	25.00
JD	Joe DiMaggio/SP	350.00
LD	Leo Durocher	8.00
WF	Whitey Ford	15.00
NF	Nellie Fox	8.00
JF	Jim Fregosi	5.00
GH	Gil Hodges	10.00
THo	Tommy Holmes	5.00
RJ	Reggie Jackson	15.00
TK	Ted Kluszewski	5.00
BL	Bob Lemon	5.00
VL	Vic Lombardi	5.00
MM	Mickey Mantle/SP	275.00
JM	Juan Marichal	10.00
RM	Roger Maris/SP	150.00
WM	Willie McCovey	10.00
JN	Joe Nuxhall	8.00
GP	Gaylord Perry	5.00
BR	Bobby Richardson	5.00
BRo	Brooks Robinson	15.00
BR	Babe Ruth/SP	600.00
NR	Nolan Ryan	40.00
TS	Tom Seaver/SP	100.00
CS	Casey Stengel	15.00
BT	Bobby Thomson	5.00
HW	Honus Wagner/SP	750.00
BW	Billy Williams	6.00
MW	Maury Wills	5.00
RY	Robin Yount	15.00

Signatures

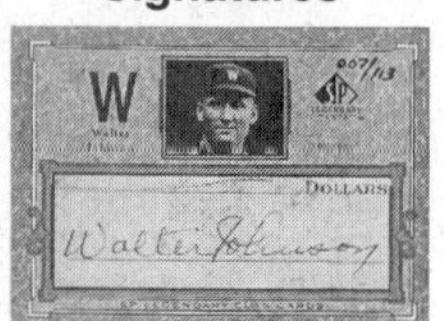

		NM/M
Inserted 1:252		
WA	Walt Alston/34	175.00
CA	Cap Anson/2 (11/01 Auction)	10,000
LA	Luke Appling/45	205.00
EA	Earl Averill/189	100.00
EB	E.G. Barrow/16	600.00
MC	Max Carey/73	145.00
TC	Ty Cobb/24	2,500
JC	Jocko Conlan/12	1,200
SC	Stanley Coveleski/42	315.00
JC	Joe Cronin/12	1,200
KC	Kiki Cuyler/6	4,000
DDe	Dizzy Dean/56	410.00
BD	Bill Dickey/28	275.00
JD	Joe DiMaggio/25	650.00
JD	Joe DiMaggio/50	400.00
JD	Joe DiMaggio/150	400.00
JD	Joe DiMaggio/275	350.00
DDr	Don Drysdale/12	1,500
LD	Leo Durocher/45	260.00
RF	Rick Ferrell/8	750.00
EF	Elmer Flick/22	400.00
NF	Nellie Fox/9	750.00
JF	Jimmie Foxx/16	2,500
FF	Ford Frick/21	750.00
FF	Frankie Frisch/3	3,500
LGe	Lou Gehrig/7	6,000
WG	Warren Giles/10	800.00
LGo	Lefty Gomez/85	195.00
BG	Burleigh Grimes/18	500.00
LG	Lefty Grove/34	600.00
HH	Harvey Haddix/4	3,000
BH	Bucky Harris/10	500.00
GH	Gabby Hartnett/32	380.00
BH	Billy Herman/88	140.00
GH	Gil Hodges/6	1,050
HH	Harry Hooper/14	800.00
WH	Waite Hoyt/38	245.00
CH	Carl Hubbell/30	375.00
TJ	Travis Jackson/35	225.00
JJ	Judy Johnson/9	650.00
WJ	Walter Johnson/113	510.00
CK	Charlie Keller/16	365.00
GK	George Kelly/52	140.00
KK	Ken Keltner/11	500.00
MK	Mark Koenig/30	275.00
BL	Bob Lemon/23	225.00
EL	Eddie Lopat/22	275.00
TL	Ted Lyons/59	185.00
SM	Sal Maglie/19	400.00
MM	Mickey Mantle/8	5,000
HM	Heinie Manush/50	185.00
RoM	Roger Maris/73	1,675
RuM	Rube Marquard/23	375.00
JMc	Joe McCarthy/40	340.00
JM	Joe Medwick/18	750.00
BM	Bob Meusel/23	400.00
JMi	Johnny Mize/84	160.00

MO	Mel Ott/8	4,000
SP	Satchel Paige/36	900.00
RP	Roger Peckinpaugh/45	200.00
VR	Vic Raschi/26	175.00
BRi	Branch Rickey/16	1,350
JR	Jackie Robinson/147	700.00
ER	Edd Roush/83	170.00
RR	Red Ruffing/5	2,250
BRu	Babe Ruth/7	9,000
GS	George Selkirk/15	450.00
JS	Joe Sewell/55	130.00
RS	Rip Sewell/39	155.00
BS	Bob Shawkey/39	165.00
CS	Casey Stengel/10	1,500
BT	Bill Terry/184	125.00
VM	Johnny Vander Meer/65	125.00
HW	Honus Wagner/24	2,200
BW	Bucky Walters/13	400.00
LW	Lloyd Waner/217	105.00
PW	Paul Waner/4	2,250
HW	Hack Wilson/4	6,000
JW	Smokey Joe Wood/43	215.00

2001 SPx Sample

To introduce the annual SPx brand, Upper Deck issued this sample card of spokesman Ken Griffey Jr. The card is in the same format as the later-issued version, but has a large red "SAMPLE" overprinted diagonally on back.

		NM/M
001	Ken Griffey Jr.	5.00

2001 SPx

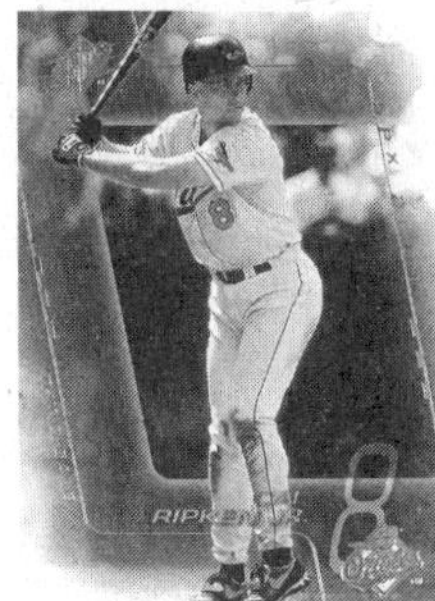

		NM/M
Complete Set (150):		
Common Player:		.25
Common Young Star (91-120):		4.00
Production 2,000		
Common Prospect Jersey (121-135):		6.00
Common Prosp. Auto. Jersey (136-150):		10.00
Pack (4):		12.00
Box (18):		200.00
1	Darin Erstad	.50
2	Troy Glaus	.50
3	Mo Vaughn	.25
4	Johnny Damon	1.00
5	Jason Giambi	.75
6	Tim Hudson	.50
7	Miguel Tejada	.50
8	Carlos Delgado	.75
9	Raul Mondesi	.25
10	Tony Batista	.25
11	Ben Grieve	.25
12	Greg Vaughn	.25
13	Juan Gonzalez	.75
14	Jim Thome	.75
15	Roberto Alomar	.50
16	John Olerud	.25
17	Edgar Martinez	.25
18	Albert Belle	.25
19	Cal Ripken Jr.	3.00
20	Ivan Rodriguez	.75
21	Rafael Palmeiro	.75
22	Alex Rodriguez	2.50
23	Nomar Garciaparra	1.50
24	Pedro J. Martinez	1.00
25	Manny Ramirez	1.00
26	Jermaine Dye	.25
27	Mark Quinn	.25
28	Carlos Beltran	.75
29	Tony Clark	.25
30	Bobby Higginson	.25
31	Eric Milton	.25
32	Matt Lawton	.25
33	Frank Thomas	1.00
34	Magglio Ordonez	.25
35	Ray Durham	.25
36	David Wells	.25
37	Derek Jeter	3.00
38	Bernie Williams	.50
39	Roger Clemens	2.00
40	David Justice	.25
41	Jeff Bagwell	.75
42	Richard Hidalgo	.25
43	Moises Alou	.40
44	Chipper Jones	1.00
45	Andruw Jones	1.00
46	Greg Maddux	2.00
47	Rafael Furcal	.50
48	Jeromy Burnitz	.25
49	Geoff Jenkins	.25
50	Mark McGwire	2.00
51	Jim Edmonds	.50
52	Rick Ankiel	.25
53	Edgar Renteria	.25
54	Sammy Sosa	1.50
55	Kerry Wood	.50
56	Rondell White	.25
57	Randy Johnson	1.00
58	Steve Finley	.25
59	Matt Williams	.25
60	Luis Gonzalez	.25
61	Kevin Brown	.25
62	Gary Sheffield	.50
63	Shawn Green	.50
64	Vladimir Guerrero	1.00
65	Jose Vidro	.25
66	Barry Bonds	3.00
67	Jeff Kent	.40
68	Livan Hernandez	.25
69	Preston Wilson	.25
70	Charles Johnson	.25
71	Cliff Floyd	.25
72	Mike Piazza	1.50
73	Edgardo Alfonzo	.25
74	Jay Payton	.25
75	Robin Ventura	.25
76	Tony Gwynn	1.50
77	Phil Nevin	.25
78	Ryan Klesko	.25
79	Scott Rolen	.75
80	Pat Burrell	.50
81	Bob Abreu	.50
82	Brian Giles	.25
83	Kris Benson	.25
84	Jason Kendall	.25
85	Ken Griffey Jr.	2.00
86	Barry Larkin	.50
87	Sean Casey	.40
88	Todd Helton	.75
89	Larry Walker	.25
90	Mike Hampton	.25
91	Billy Sylvester **RC**	4.00
92	Josh Towers **RC**	8.00
93	Zach Day **RC**	6.00
94	Martin Vargas **RC**	4.00
95	Adam Pettyjohn **RC**	4.00
96	Andres Torres **RC**	4.00
97	Kris Keller **RC**	4.00
98	Blaine Neal **RC**	4.00
99	Kyle Kessel **RC**	4.00
100	Greg Miller **RC**	4.00
101	Shawn Sonnier	4.00
102	Alexis Gomez **RC**	4.00
103	Grant Balfour **RC**	4.00
104	Henry Mateo **RC**	4.00
105	Wilkin Ruan **RC**	4.00
106	Nick Maness **RC**	4.00
107	Jason Michaels **RC**	4.00
108	Esix Snead **RC**	4.00
109	William Ortega **RC**	4.00
110	David Elder **RC**	4.00
111	Jackson Melian **RC**	4.00
112	Nate Teut **RC**	4.00
113	Jason Smith **RC**	4.00
114	Mike Penney **RC**	4.00
115	Jose Mieses **RC**	4.00
116	Juan Pena	4.00
117	Brian Lawrence **RC**	6.00
118	Jeremy Owens **RC**	4.00
119	Carlos Valderrama **RC**	4.00
120	Rafael Soriano **RC**	6.00
121	Horacio Ramirez **RC**	10.00
122	Ricardo Rodriguez **RC**	6.00
123	Juan Diaz **RC**	6.00
124	Donnie Bridges	6.00
125	Tyler Walker **RC**	6.00
126	Erick Almonte **RC**	6.00
127	Jesus Colome	6.00
128	Ryan Freel **RC**	8.00
129	Elpidio Guzman **RC**	6.00
130	Jack Cust	8.00
131	Eric Hinske **RC**	10.00
132	Josh Fogg **RC**	6.00
133	Juan Uribe **RC**	10.00
134	Bert Snow **RC**	6.00
135	Pedro Feliz	6.00
136	Wilson Betemit **RC**	25.00
137	Sean Douglass **RC**	10.00
138	Dernell Stenson	10.00
139	Brandon Inge	10.00
140	Morgan Ensberg **RC**	15.00
141	Brian Cole	10.00
142	Adrian Hernandez **RC**	10.00
143	Brandon Duckworth **RC**	10.00
144	Jack Wilson **RC**	15.00
145	Travis Hafner **RC**	75.00
146	Carlos Pena	20.00
147	Corey Patterson	15.00
148	Xavier Nady	10.00
149	Jason Hart	10.00
150	Ichiro Suzuki **RC**	750.00

Spectrum

Stars (1-90): 10-20X
SP's (91-120): 1-1.5X
Production 50 Sets

Foundations

		NM/M
Complete Set (12):		15.00
Common Player:		1.00
Inserted 1:8		
F1	Mark McGwire	3.00
F2	Jeff Bagwell	1.00
F3	Alex Rodriguez	3.00
F4	Ken Griffey Jr.	2.00
F5	Andruw Jones	1.00
F6	Cal Ripken Jr.	4.00
F7	Barry Bonds	4.00
F8	Derek Jeter	4.00
F9	Frank Thomas	1.00
F10	Sammy Sosa	2.00
F11	Tony Gwynn	1.50
F12	Vladimir Guerrero	1.50

SPXcitement

		NM/M
Complete Set (12):		15.00
Common Player:		.75
Inserted 1:8		
X1	Alex Rodriguez	3.00
X2	Jason Giambi	.75
X3	Ken Griffey Jr.	2.00
X4	Sammy Sosa	1.50
X5	Frank Thomas	1.00
X6	Todd Helton	1.00
X7	Mark McGwire	2.00
X8	Mike Piazza	1.50
X9	Derek Jeter	4.00
X10	Vladimir Guerrero	1.50
X11	Carlos Delgado	.75
X12	Chipper Jones	1.50

Untouchable Talents

		NM/M
Complete Set (6):		10.00
Inserted 1:15		
UT1	Ken Griffey Jr.	2.00
UT2	Mike Piazza	2.00
UT3	Mark McGwire	2.50
UT4	Alex Rodriguez	2.50
UT5	Sammy Sosa	1.50
UT6	Derek Jeter	3.00

Winning Materials Base

		NM/M
Common Duo:		40.00
Production 50		
Trios:		No Pricing
Production 25		
MG	Mark McGwire, Ken Griffey Jr.	40.00
MS	Mark McGwire, Sammy Sosa	50.00
MR	Mark McGwire, Alex Rodriguez	40.00
GJ	Nomar Garciaparra, Derek Jeter	50.00
TR	Frank Thomas, Alex Rodriguez	40.00
JG	Derek Jeter, Jason Giambi	40.00
PB	Mike Piazza, Barry Bonds	40.00
RJ	Alex Rodriguez, Derek Jeter	50.00
PM	Mike Piazza, Mark McGwire	40.00
JP	Derek Jeter, Mike Piazza	40.00
MGS	Mark McGwire, Ken Griffey Jr., Sammy Sosa	80.00
JRG	Derek Jeter, Alex Rodriguez, Nomar Garciaparra	100.00
PJW	Mike Piazza, Derek Jeter, Bernie Williams	80.00
BMS	Barry Bonds, Mark McGwire, Sammy Sosa	100.00
GJR	Ken Griffey Jr., Derek Jeter, Alex Rodriguez	100.00

Winning Materials Base/Ball

		NM/M
Common Player:		10.00
Production 250 Sets		
BB	Barry Bonds	50.00
NG	Nomar Garciaparra	20.00
KG	Ken Griffey Jr.	30.00
VG	Vladimir Guerrero	15.00
DJ	Derek Jeter	50.00
AJ	Andruw Jones	10.00
CJ	Chipper Jones	15.00
PM	Pedro Martinez	15.00
MM	Mark McGwire	75.00
MP	Mike Piazza	20.00
AR	Alex Rodriguez	20.00
SS	Sammy Sosa	20.00
FT	Frank Thomas	15.00

Winning Materials Jersey Combo

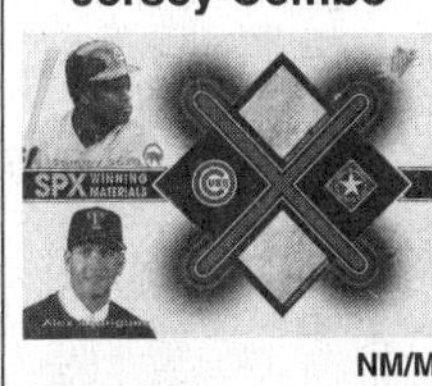

		NM/M
Common Duo:		25.00
Production 50		
Common Trio:		
Production 25		
KG-AR	Ken Griffey Jr., Alex Rodriguez	50.00
KG-BB	Ken Griffey Jr., Barry Bonds	50.00
KG-RJ	Ken Griffey Jr., Randy Johnson	50.00
CJ-DW	Chipper Jones, David Wells	25.00
BB-SS	Barry Bonds, Sammy Sosa	50.00
KG-JD	Ken Griffey Jr., Joe DiMaggio	180.00
KG-SS	Ken Griffey Jr., Sammy Sosa	50.00
SS-CD	Sammy Sosa, Carlos Delgado	25.00
SS-FT	Sammy Sosa, Frank Thomas	25.00
IR-AR	Ivan Rodriguez, Alex Rodriguez	40.00
AR-CR	Alex Rodriguez, Cal Ripken Jr.	60.00
AJ-CJ	Andruw Jones, Chipper Jones	25.00
KG-KG	Ken Griffey Jr., Ken Griffey Jr.	40.00
G-R-B	Ken Griffey Jr., Alex Rodriguez, Barry Bonds	100.00
S-G-C	Sammy Sosa, Ken Griffey Jr., Chipper Jones	60.00
B-G-J	Barry Bonds, Ken Griffey Jr., Andruw Jones	100.00
R-R-D	Alex Rodriguez, Ivan Rodriguez, Carlos Delgado	60.00
D-B-S	Carlos Delgado, Barry Bonds, Sammy Sosa	60.00
R-J-D	Cal Ripken Jr., Chipper Jones, Carlos Delgado	100.00

Winning Materials Jersey/Bat

		NM/M
Common Player:		8.00
Inserted 1:18		
RA	Rick Ankiel	8.00
BB1	Barry Bonds	25.00
BB2	Barry Bonds	25.00
CD	Carlos Delgado	10.00
JD	Joe DiMaggio	150.00
JE	Jim Edmonds	8.00
KG1	Ken Griffey Jr.	15.00
KG2	Ken Griffey Jr.	15.00
RJ1	Randy Johnson	15.00
RJ2	Randy Johnson	15.00
AJ1	Andruw Jones	10.00
AJ2	Andruw Jones	10.00
CJ1	Chipper Jones	15.00
CJ2	Chipper Jones	15.00
CR	Cal Ripken Jr.	40.00
AR1	Alex Rodriguez	15.00
AR2	Alex Rodriguez	15.00
IR1	Ivan Rodriguez	10.00
IR2	Ivan Rodriguez	10.00
SS	Sammy Sosa	15.00
FT	Frank Thomas	10.00

2002 SP Authentic

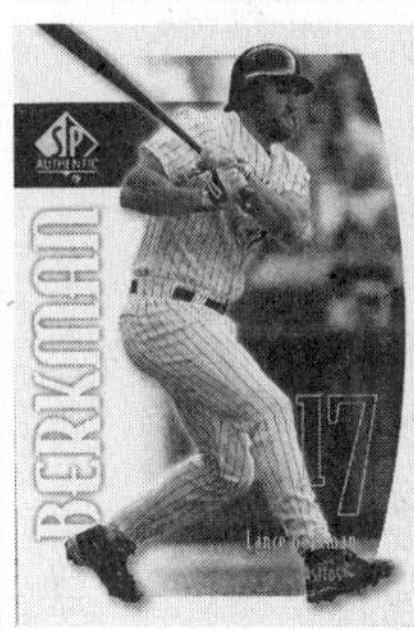

		NM/M
Complete Set (170):		
Common Player:		.25
Common SP (91-135):		4.00
Production 1,999		
Common SP Auto. (136-170):		10.00
Production 999		
Pack (5):		3.50
Box (24):		75.00
1	Troy Glaus	.50
2	Darin Erstad	.40
3	Barry Zito	.40
4	Eric Chavez	.40
5	Tim Hudson	.50
6	Miguel Tejada	.50
7	Carlos Delgado	.60
8	Shannon Stewart	.25
9	Ben Grieve	.25
10	Jim Thome	.75
11	C.C. Sabathia	.25
12	Ichiro Suzuki	2.00
13	Freddy Garcia	.25
14	Edgar Martinez	.25
15	Bret Boone	.25
16	Jeff Conine	.25
17	Alex Rodriguez	2.00
18	Juan Gonzalez	.50
19	Ivan Rodriguez	.75
20	Rafael Palmeiro	.75
21	Hank Blalock	.50
22	Pedro J. Martinez	1.00
23	Manny Ramirez	1.00
24	Nomar Garciaparra	1.00
25	Carlos Beltran	.75
26	Mike Sweeney	.25
27	Randall Simon	.25
28	Dmitri Young	.25
29	Bobby Higginson	.25
30	Corey Koskie	.25
31	Eric Milton	.25
32	Torii Hunter	.50
33	Joe Mays	.25
34	Frank Thomas	.75
35	Mark Buehrle	.40
36	Magglio Ordonez	.25
37	Kenny Lofton	.25
38	Roger Clemens	2.00
39	Derek Jeter	2.50
40	Jason Giambi	.75
41	Bernie Williams	.50
42	Alfonso Soriano	.75
43	Lance Berkman	.50
44	Roy Oswalt	.50
45	Jeff Bagwell	.75
46	Craig Biggio	.50
47	Chipper Jones	1.00
48	Greg Maddux	1.50
49	Gary Sheffield	.50
50	Andruw Jones	.75
51	Ben Sheets	.40
52	Richie Sexson	.50
53	Albert Pujols	2.50
54	Matt Morris	.25
55	J.D. Drew	.40
56	Sammy Sosa	1.00
57	Kerry Wood	.50
58	Corey Patterson	.25
59	Mark Prior	.75
60	Randy Johnson	.75
61	Luis Gonzalez	.40
62	Curt Schilling	.75
63	Shawn Green	.50
64	Kevin Brown	.25
65	Hideo Nomo	.75
66	Vladimir Guerrero	.75
67	Jose Vidro	.25
68	Barry Bonds	2.50
69	Jeff Kent	.40
70	Rich Aurilia	.25
71	Preston Wilson	.25
72	Josh Beckett	.40
73	Mike Lowell	.25
74	Roberto Alomar	.40
75	Mo Vaughn	.25
76	Jeromy Burnitz	.25
77	Mike Piazza	1.50
78	Sean Burroughs	.25
79	Phil Nevin	.25
80	Bobby Abreu	.50
81	Pat Burrell	.40
82	Scott Rolen	.75
83	Jason Kendall	.25
84	Brian Giles	.25
85	Ken Griffey Jr.	1.50
86	Adam Dunn	.75
87	Sean Casey	.40
88	Todd Helton	.75
89	Larry Walker	.25
90	Mike Hampton	.25
91	Brandon Puffer **RC**	4.00
92	Tom Shearn **RC**	4.00
93	Chris Baker **RC**	4.00
94	Gustavo Chacin **RC**	10.00
95	Joe Orloski **RC**	4.00
96	Mike Smith **RC**	4.00
97	John Ennis **RC**	4.00
98	John Foster **RC**	4.00
99	Kevin Gryboski **RC**	4.00
100	Brian Mallette **RC**	4.00
101	Takahito Nomura **RC**	4.00
102	So Taguchi **RC**	10.00
103	Jeremy Lambert **RC**	4.00
104	Jason Simontacchi **RC**	4.00
105	Jorge Sosa **RC**	4.00
106	Brandon Backe **RC**	8.00
107	P.J. Bevis **RC**	4.00
108	Jeremy Ward **RC**	4.00
109	Doug DeVore **RC**	4.00
110	Ron Chiavacci	4.00
111	Ron Calloway **RC**	4.00
112	Nelson Castro **RC**	4.00
113	Deivis Santos	4.00
114	Earl Snyder **RC**	4.00
115	Julio Mateo **RC**	4.00
116	J.J. Putz **RC**	4.00
117	Allan Simpson **RC**	4.00
118	Satoru Komiyama **RC**	4.00
119	Adam Walker **RC**	4.00
120	Oliver Perez **RC**	10.00
121	Clifford Bartosh **RC**	4.00
122	Todd Donovan **RC**	4.00
123	Elio Serrano **RC**	4.00
124	Peter Zamora **RC**	4.00
125	Mike Gonzalez **RC**	4.00
126	Travis Hughes **RC**	4.00
127	Jorge de la Rosa **RC**	4.00
128	Anastacio Martinez **RC**	4.00
129	Colin Young **RC**	4.00

130 Nate Field **RC** 4.00
131 Tim Kalita **RC** 4.00
132 Julius Matos **RC** 4.00
133 Terry Pearson **RC** 4.00
134 Kyle Kane **RC** 4.00
135 Mitch Wylie **RC** 4.00
136 Rodrigo Rosario **RC** 10.00
137 Franklyn German **RC** 10.00
138 Reed Johnson **RC** 15.00
139 Luis Martinez **RC** 10.00
140 Michael Crudale **RC** 10.00
141 Francis Beltran **RC** 10.00
142 Steve Kent **RC** 10.00
143 Felix Escalona **RC** 10.00
144 Jose Valverde **RC** 15.00
145 Victor Alvarez **RC** 10.00
146 Kazuhisa Ishii/ 249 **RC** 25.00
147 Jorge Nunez **RC** 10.00
148 Eric Good **RC** 10.00
149 Luis Ugueto **RC** 10.00
150 Matt Thornton 10.00
151 Wilson Valdez **RC** 10.00
152 Hansel Izquierdo/ 249 **RC** 25.00
153 Jaime Cerda **RC** 10.00
154 Mark Corey **RC** 10.00
155 Tyler Yates **RC** 10.00
156 Steve Bechler **RC** 10.00
157 Ben Howard/249 **RC** 20.00
158 Anderson Machado **RC** 15.00
159 Jorge Padilla **RC** 15.00
160 Eric Junge **RC** 10.00
161 Adrian Burnside **RC** 10.00
162 Josh Hancock **RC** 10.00
163 Chris Booker **RC** 10.00
164 Cam Esslinger **RC** 10.00
165 Rene Reyes **RC** 10.00
166 Aaron Cook **RC** 10.00
167 Juan Brito **RC** 10.00
168 Miguel Ascencio **RC** 10.00
169 Kevin Frederick **RC** 10.00
170 Edwin Almonte **RC** 10.00

Limited

Stars (1-90): 5-10X
Cards (91-135): .5-1X
Cards (136-170): .5-1X
Production 125 Sets
Golds (1-90): 10-20X
Golds (91-135): .75-1.5X
Golds (136-170): .75-1.5X
Production 50 Sets

Chirography

NM/M
Common Autograph: 10.00
Inserted 1:72
HB Hank Blalock/282 25.00
BB Barry Bonds/112 180.00
BBo Bret Boone/500 15.00
MB Milton Bradley/470 15.00
JB John Buck/427 10.00
MB Mark Buehrle/438 15.00
SB Sean Burroughs/275 15.00
AD Adam Dunn/348 30.00
DE Darin Erstad/80 15.00
CF Cliff Floyd/313 10.00
FG Freddy Garcia/456 15.00
JG Jason Giambi/244 25.00
TG Tom Glavine/376 25.00
AG Alex Graman/418 10.00
KG Ken Griffey Jr/238 100.00
TG Tony Gwynn/75 40.00
JL Jon Lieber/462 15.00
JM Joe Mays/469 15.00
MM Mark McGwire/50 300.00
DM Doug Mientkiewicz/ 478 15.00
AR Alex Rodriguez/391 90.00
CS C.C. Sabathia/442 15.00
RS Richie Sexson/483 15.00
SS Sammy Sosa/247 100.00
IS Ichiro Suzuki/78 350.00
MS Mike Sweeney/265 15.00
BZ Barry Zito/419 20.00

Chirography Gold

NM/M
Quantity produced listed
MB Mark Buehrle/56 25.00
AD Adam Dunn/44 40.00
CF Cliff Floyd/30 20.00
FG Freddy Garcia/34 35.00
TG Tom Glavine/47 50.00
AG Alex Graman/76 15.00
KG Ken Griffey Jr./30 200.00
JL Jon Lieber/32 20.00
CS C.C. Sabathia/52 20.00
MS Mike Sweeney/29 40.00
BZ Barry Zito/75 25.00

Excellence

NM/M
Production 25
AE-1 Ken Griffey Jr., Sammy Sosa, Cal Ripken Jr., Jason Giambi, Mark McGwire, Ichiro Suzuki 1,500

Future USA Watch

NM/M
Common Player: 5.00
Production 1,999 Sets
USA1 Chad Cordero 5.00
USA2 Philip Humber 10.00
USA3 Grant Johnson 5.00
USA4 Wes Littleton 5.00
USA5 Kyle Sleeth 10.00
USA6 Huston Street 15.00
USA7 Brad Sullivan 5.00
USA8 Bob Zimmermann 5.00
USA9 Abe Alvarez 5.00
USA10 Kyle Bakker 5.00
USA11 Landon Powell 5.00
USA12 Clint Sammons 5.00
USA13 Michael Aubrey 10.00
USA14 Aaron Hill 5.00
USA15 Conor Jackson 20.00
USA16 Eric Patterson 5.00
USA17 Dustin Pedroia 10.00
USA18 Rickie Weeks 25.00
USA19 Shane Costa 5.00
USA20 Mark Jurich 5.00
USA21 Sam Fuld 5.00
USA22 Carlos Quentin 20.00

Game Jerseys

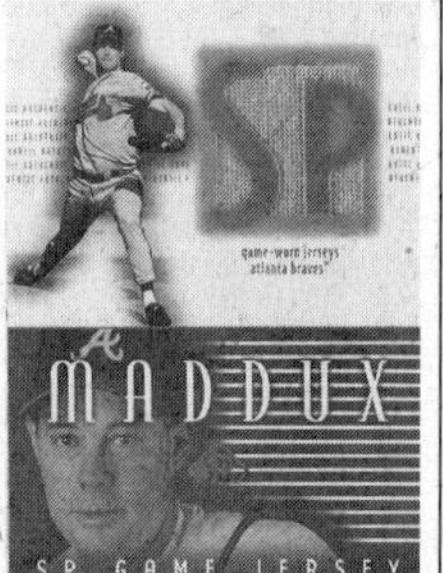

NM/M
Common Player: 5.00
Inserted 1:24
RA Roberto Alomar 8.00
JB Jeff Bagwell 10.00
JB Jeromy Burnitz/SP 5.00
RC Roger Clemens 15.00
CD Carlos Delgado 6.00
JE Jim Edmonds 8.00
DE Darin Erstad 8.00
JGi Jason Giambi 8.00
JGo Juan Gonzalez 8.00
SG Shawn Green 6.00
KG Ken Griffey Jr./95 40.00
TH Todd Helton 8.00
KI Kazuhisa Ishii 10.00
RJ Randy Johnson 10.00
AJ Andruw Jones 8.00
CJ Chipper Jones 10.00
JK Jason Kendall 5.00
GM Greg Maddux 10.00
MM Mark McGwire/SP 100.00
MO Magglio Ordonez 8.00
AP Andy Pettitte 10.00
MP Mike Piazza 15.00
MR Manny Ramirez 10.00
AR Alex Rodriguez 15.00
IR Ivan Rodriguez 8.00
SR Scott Rolen 10.00
CC C.C. Sabathia 5.00
CS Curt Schilling 10.00
GS Gary Sheffield 6.00
TS Tsuyoshi Shinjo 5.00
SS Sammy Sosa 15.00
IS Ichiro Suzuki/SP 50.00
JT Jim Thome 10.00
RV Robin Ventura 5.00
OV Omar Vizquel 5.00
BW Bernie Williams 8.00
PW Preston Wilson 5.00
BZ Barry Zito 6.00

Game Jersey Gold

NM/M
Quantity produced listed
KG Ken Griffey Jr./30 65.00
RJ Randy Johnson/51 25.00
GM Greg Maddux/31 50.00
MO Magglio Ordonez/30 15.00
AP Andy Pettitte/46 20.00
MP Mike Piazza/31 50.00
CC C.C. Sabathia/52 10.00
CS Curt Schilling/38 30.00
IS Ichiro Suzuki/51 85.00
BW Bernie Williams/51 20.00
PW Preston Wilson/44 10.00
BZ Barry Zito/75 10.00

Prospect Signatures

NM/M
Common Autograph: 5.00
Inserted 1:36
JC Jose Cueto 5.00
JDe Jeff Deardorff 5.00
JDi Jose Diaz 8.00
AG Alex Graman 8.00
MG Matt Guerrier 5.00
BH Bill Hall 15.00
KH Ken Huckaby 5.00
DM Dustan Mohr 5.00
XN Xavier Nady 8.00
MS Marco Scutaro 5.00
ST Steve Torrealba 6.00
DW Danny Wright 5.00

Big Mac Missing Link

Production 25 Sets

Signed SP Big Mac

NM/M
Quantity signed listed
MM6 Mark McGwire/70 250.00

Signs of Greatness

Only one example of this card exists. The card is actually a 3-1/2" x 2-1/2" folder. On front are pictures of the players and a 1/1 designation. On back is a certification of authenticity. Inside are cut signatures of each of the players.

NM/M
Babe Ruth, Joe DiMaggio, Mickey Mantle, Ken Griffey Jr., Sammy Sosa, (2/03 Auction) 30,000

2002 SP Legendary Cuts

NM/M
Complete Set (90): 30.00
Common Player: .40
Pack (4): 10.00
Box (12): 100.00
1 Al Kaline .75
2 Alvin Dark .40
3 Andre Dawson .75
4 Babe Ruth 3.00
5 Ernie Banks 1.00
6 Bob Lemon .40
7 Bobby Bonds .40
8 Carl Erskine .40
9 Carl Hubbell .40
10 Casey Stengel .40
11 Charlie Gehringer .40
12 Christy Mathewson .75
13 Dale Murphy .75
14 Dave Concepcion .40
15 Dave Parker .40
16 Dazzy Vance .40
17 Dizzy Dean .75
18 Don Baylor .40
19 Don Drysdale .75
20 Duke Snider 1.00
21 Earl Averill .40
22 Early Wynn .40
23 Edd Roush .40
24 Elston Howard .40
25 Ferguson Jenkins .75
26 Frank Crosetti .40
27 Frankie Frisch .40
28 Gaylord Perry .40
29 George Foster .40
30 George Kell .40
31 Gil Hodges .75
32 Hank Greenberg .75
33 Phil Niekro .40
34 Harvey Haddix .40
35 Harvey Kuenn .40
36 Honus Wagner 1.50
37 Jackie Robinson 2.00
38 Orlando Cepeda .40
39 Joe Adcock .40
40 Joe Cronin .40
41 Joe DiMaggio 2.50
42 Joe Morgan .75
43 Johnny Mize .40
44 Lefty Gomez .75
45 Lefty Grove .40
46 Jim Palmer .75
47 Lou Boudreau .40
48 Lou Gehrig 2.50
49 Luke Appling .40
50 Mark McGwire 2.00
51 Mel Ott .75
52 Mickey Cochrane .40
53 Mickey Mantle 3.00
54 Minnie Minoso .40
55 Brooks Robinson 1.00
56 Nellie Fox .40
57 Nolan Ryan 3.00
58 Rollie Fingers .40
59 Pee Wee Reese .40
60 Phil Rizzuto .75
61 Ralph Kiner .75
62 Ray Dandridge .40
63 Richie Ashburn .40
64 Robin Yount .75
65 Rocky Colavito .40
66 Roger Maris 2.00
67 Rogers Hornsby .75
68 Ron Santo .40
69 Ryne Sandberg 1.50
70 Stan Musial 1.50
71 Sam McDowell .40
72 Satchel Paige 1.00
73 Willie McCovey .40
74 Steve Garvey .40
75 Ted Kluszewski .40
76 Catfish Hunter .40
77 Terry Moore .40
78 Thurman Munson 1.00
79 Tom Seaver 1.00
80 Tommy John .40
81 Tony Gwynn 1.00
82 Tony Kubek .40
83 Tony Lazzeri .40
84 Ty Cobb 2.00
85 Wade Boggs 1.00
86 Waite Hoyt .40
87 Walter Johnson 1.00
88 Willie Stargell .75
89 Yogi Berra 1.00
90 Zack Wheat .40

Bat

NM/M
Common Player: 6.00
Inserted 1:8
DBa Don Baylor 6.00
YBe Yogi Berra/SP 20.00
BBo Bobby Bonds 6.00
RCo Rocky Colavito 12.00
ADa Alvin Dark 6.00
AnD Andre Dawson 8.00
GFo George Foster 6.00
NFo Nellie Fox 15.00
SGa Steve Garvey 6.00
HGr Hank Greenberg/SP 40.00
LGr Lefty Grove 15.00
TGw Tony Gwynn 12.00
EHo Elston Howard/SP 15.00
GKe George Kell 8.00
RKi Ralph Kiner 10.00
TKu Tonk (Tony) Kubek 8.00
TLa Tony Lazzeri 10.00
MMa Mickey Mantle/SP 120.00
RMa Roger Maris/SP 50.00
MMc Mark McGwire 60.00
JMi Johnny Mize 12.00
TMu Thurman Munson 25.00
DMu Dale Murphy 10.00
DPa Dave Parker 6.00
GPe Gaylord Perry 8.00
PWe Pee Wee Reese 10.00
CRi Cal Ripken Jr. 25.00
JaR Jackie Robinson/SP 50.00
BRu Babe Ruth/SP 150.00
NRy Nolan Ryan 30.00
RSa Ryne Sandberg 12.00
TSe Tom Seaver/SP 20.00
DSn Duke Snider 12.00
WSt Willie Stargell 8.00
RYo Robin Yount 10.00
EWy Early Wynn 8.00

Bat Barrel

NM/M
Many not priced due to scarcity.
BB-ADa Alvin Dark/4 800.00
BB-AnD Andre Dawson/4 750.00
BB-GFo George Foster/5 250.00
BB-LGr Lefty Grove/1 (8/03 Auction) 10,000
BB-TGw Tony Gwynn/11 650.00
BB-MMa Mickey Mantle/7 (8/04 Auction) 3,000
BB-MMc Mark McGwire/4 2,000
BB-JMi Johnny Mize/2 1,275
BB-DMu Dale Murphy/3 600.00
BB-PWe Pee Wee Reese/4 1,500
BB-BRu Babe Ruth/3 (8/05 Auction) 9,500
BB-NRy Nolan Ryan/9 1,500
BB-RSa Ryne Sandberg/3 2,250
BB-DSn Duke Snider/2 1,500
BB-RYo Robin Yount/8 750.00

Jersey

NM/M
Common Player: 6.00
Inserted 1:24
DBa Don Baylor 6.00
YBe Yogi Berra 20.00
BBo Bobby Bonds 6.00
FCr Frank Crosetti 10.00
AnD Andre Dawson 8.00
GFo George Foster 6.00
SGa Steve Garvey 8.00
MMa Mickey Mantle/SP 100.00
RMa Roger Maris 40.00
DPa Dave Parker 6.00
PWe Pee Wee Reese 12.00
JRo Jackie Robinson/SP 45.00
NRy Nolan Ryan 30.00
RSa Ryne Sandberg 25.00
TSe Tom Seaver 10.00

Signatures

NM/M
Quantity signed listed
JAd Joe Adcock/48 145.00
LAp Luke Appling/53 150.00
RAs Richie Ashburn/10 550.00
EAv Earl Averill/22 275.00
JBe Johnny Berardino/12 450.00
LBo Lou Boudreau/85 120.00
GBu Guy Bush/38 125.00
GCa George Case/36 180.00
HCh Happy Chandler/96 95.00
SCh Spud Chandler/17 350.00
TyC Ty Cobb/2 5,500
MCo Mickey Cochrane/2 5,000
JCo Johnny Cooney/64 75.00
SCo Stan Coveleski/85 150.00
JCr Joe Cronin/185 120.00
BDa Babe Dahlgren/51 180.00
RDa Ray Dandridge/179 85.00
DDe Dizzy Dean/4 2,000
JDi Joe DiMaggio/103 175.00
DDo Dick Donovan/23 200.00
TDo Taylor Douthit/60 165.00
DDr Don Drysdale/14 650.00
JDu Joe Dugan/39 140.00
BFa Bibb Falk/44 150.00
RFe Rick Ferrell/19 225.00
NFo Nellie Fox/1 (12/02 Auction) 3,100
FoF Ford Frick/1 (10/03 Auction) 4,000
LGe Lou Gehrig/3 (6/04 Auction) 7,500
CGe Charlie Gehringer/3 700.00
LGo Lefty Gomez/3 750.00
BGo Billy Goodman/53 140.00
HGr Hank Greenberg/94 425.00
LGr Lefty Grove/190 240.00
SHa Stan Hack/36 200.00
HHa Harvey Haddix/37 250.00
BHa Buddy Hassett/56 200.00
WHo Waite Hoyt/62 250.00
CHu Carl Hubbell/17 475.00
LJa Larry Jackson/37 125.00
NJa Newton "Bucky" Jacobs/44 150.00
EJo Earl Johnson/31 200.00
JJo Judy Johnson/86 150.00
WJo Walter Johnson/20 2,000
BKa Bob Kahle/53 150.00
WKa Willie Kamm/57 110.00
CKe Charlie Keller/29 280.00
KKe Ken Keltner/11 415.00
TKl Ted Kluszewski/23 300.00
MKo Mark Koenig/22 260.00
HKu Harvey Kuenn/23 230.00
CLa Cookie Lavagetto/22 200.00
BiL Billy Lee/40 150.00
BoL Bob Lemon/91 110.00
ELo Ed Lopat/58 150.00
SMa Sal Maglie/29 200.00
HMa Hank Majeski/21 300.00
MMa Mickey Mantle/2 (10/04 Auction) 6,000
ChrM Christy Mathewson/2 (5/03 Auction) 2,000
RMc Roy McMillan/18 250.00
JMi Johnny Mize/3 2,500
JMo Johnny Moore/22 250.00
TMo Terry Moore/86 95.00
ChM Chet Morgan/27 185.00
HNe Hal Newhouser/81 135.00
VRa Vic Raschi/98 110.00
PWe Pee Wee Reese/23 450.00
PRe Pete Reiser/73 140.00
RRe Rip Repulski/19 275.00
LRi Lance Richbourg/3 1,800
ORo Oscar Roettger/9 700.00
ERo Edd Roush/101 100.00
ERo2 Edd Roush/99 100.00
BRu Babe Ruth/3 (6/04 Auction) 12,500
BSc Bob Scheffing/19 200.00
WSc Willard Schmidt/10 350.00
HSc Hal Schumacher/17 300.00
BSe Bill Serena/16 275.00
JSe Joe Sewell/136 125.00
BSh Bob Shawkey/10 120.00
BSh Bill Sherdel/10 450.00
BSz Bill Shantz/17 300.00
WSt Willie Stargell/153 95.00
CSt Casey Stengel/8 750.00
BVe Bill Veeck/11 500.00
HWa Honus Wagner/6 (2/05 Auction) 5,000
BWa Bucky Walters/31 165.00
VWe Vic Wertz/17 300.00
ZWh Zack Wheat/127 150.00
PWi Pete Whisenant/13 300.00
EWy Early Wynn/4 1,650

Swatches

NM/M
Common Player: 6.00
Inserted 1:24
DBa Don Baylor 6.00
WBo Wade Boggs 8.00
FCr Frank Crosetti 8.00
DDr Don Drysdale 20.00
CEr Carl Erskine 8.00
TGw Tony Gwynn 10.00
FJe Ferguson Jenkins 8.00
TJo Tommy John 6.00
SMc Sam McDowell 6.00
MMi Minnie Minoso 8.00
JMo Joe Morgan 8.00
MOt Mel Ott 25.00
DPa Dave Parker 6.00
CRj Cal Ripken Jr. 25.00
RSa Ron Santo 10.00

2002 SPx

NM/M
Common Player: .25

Common SP (91-120): 4.00
Production 1,800
Common SP Auto. (121-150): 10.00
Common Star Swatch (151-190): 5.00
Production 800
Pack (4): 4.00
Box (18): 60.00

#	Player	NM/M
1	Troy Glaus	.50
2	Darin Erstad	.40
3	David Justice	.25
4	Tim Hudson	.50
5	Miguel Tejada	.75
6	Barry Zito	.40
7	Carlos Delgado	.50
8	Shannon Stewart	.25
9	Greg Vaughn	.25
10	Toby Hall	.25
11	Jim Thome	.75
12	C.C. Sabathia	.25
13	Ichiro Suzuki	2.00
14	Edgar Martinez	.25
15	Freddy Garcia	.25
16	Mike Cameron	.25
17	Jeff Conine	.25
18	Tony Batista	.25
19	Alex Rodriguez	2.00
20	Rafael Palmeiro	.75
21	Ivan Rodriguez	.75
22	Carl Everett	.25
23	Pedro J. Martinez	1.00
24	Manny Ramirez	1.00
25	Nomar Garciaparra	1.00
26	Johnny Damon	1.00
27	Mike Sweeney	.25
28	Carlos Beltran	.75
29	Dmitri Young	.25
30	Joe Mays	.25
31	Doug Mientkiewicz	.25
32	Cristian Guzman	.25
33	Corey Koskie	.25
34	Frank Thomas	.75
35	Magglio Ordonez	.25
36	Mark Buehrle	.25
37	Bernie Williams	.50
38	Roger Clemens	2.00
39	Derek Jeter	2.50
40	Jason Giambi	.50
41	Mike Mussina	.50
42	Lance Berkman	.50
43	Jeff Bagwell	.75
44	Roy Oswalt	.50
45	Greg Maddux	2.00
46	Chipper Jones	1.00
47	Andruw Jones	.75
48	Gary Sheffield	.50
49	Geoff Jenkins	.25
50	Richie Sexson	.50
51	Ben Sheets	.40
52	Albert Pujols	2.50
53	J.D. Drew	.40
54	Jim Edmonds	.50
55	Sammy Sosa	1.50
56	Moises Alou	.25
57	Kerry Wood	.50
58	Jon Lieber	.25
59	Fred McGriff	.40
60	Randy Johnson	.75
61	Luis Gonzalez	.35
62	Curt Schilling	.75
63	Kevin Brown	.25
64	Hideo Nomo	.50
65	Shawn Green	.40
66	Vladimir Guerrero	1.00
67	Jose Vidro	.25
68	Barry Bonds	2.50
69	Jeff Kent	.40
70	Rich Aurilia	.25
71	Cliff Floyd	.25
72	Josh Beckett	.40
73	Preston Wilson	.25
74	Mike Piazza	1.00
75	Mo Vaughn	.25
76	Jeromy Burnitz	.25
77	Roberto Alomar	.50
78	Phil Nevin	.25
79	Ryan Klesko	.25
80	Scott Rolen	.75
81	Bobby Abreu	.50
82	Jimmy Rollins	.50
83	Brian Giles	.25
84	Aramis Ramirez	.50
85	Ken Griffey Jr.	1.50
86	Sean Casey	.40
87	Barry Larkin	.50
88	Mike Hampton	.25
89	Larry Walker	.40
90	Todd Helton	.75
91	Ron Calloway **RC**	4.00
92	Joe Orloski **RC**	4.00
93	Anderson Machado **RC**	6.00
94	Eric Good **RC**	4.00
95	Reed Johnson **RC**	8.00
96	Brendan Donnelly **RC**	4.00
97	Chris Baker **RC**	4.00
98	Wilson Valdez **RC**	4.00
99	Scotty Layfield **RC**	4.00
100	P.J. Bevis **RC**	4.00
101	Edwin Almonte **RC**	4.00
102	Francis Beltran **RC**	4.00
103	Valentino Pasucci	4.00
104	Nelson Castro **RC**	4.00
105	Michael Crudale **RC**	4.00
106	Colin Young **RC**	4.00
107	Todd Donovan **RC**	4.00
108	Felix Escalona **RC**	4.00
109	Brandon Backe **RC**	8.00
110	Corey Thurman **RC**	4.00
111	Kyle Kane **RC**	4.00
112	Allan Simpson **RC**	4.00
113	Jose Valverde **RC**	4.00
114	Chris Booker **RC**	4.00
115	Brandon Puffer **RC**	4.00
116	John Foster **RC**	4.00
117	Clifford Bartosh **RC**	4.00
118	Gustavo Chacin **RC**	8.00
119	Steve Kent **RC**	4.00
120	Nate Field **RC**	4.00
121	Victor Alvarez **RC**	10.00
122	Steve Bechler **RC**	10.00
123	Adrian Burnside **RC**	10.00
124	Marlon Byrd	15.00
125	Jaime Cerda **RC**	10.00
126	Brandon Claussen	10.00
127	Mark Corey **RC**	10.00
128	Doug DeVore **RC**	10.00
129	Kazuhisa Ishii **RC**	40.00
130	John Ennis **RC**	10.00
131	Kevin Frederick **RC**	10.00
132	Josh Hancock **RC**	10.00
133	Ben Howard **RC**	10.00
134	Orlando Hudson	15.00
135	Hansel Izquierdo **RC**	10.00
136	Eric Junge **RC**	10.00
137	Austin Kearns	15.00
138	Victor Martinez	25.00
139	Luis Martinez **RC**	10.00
140	Danny Mota **RC**	10.00
141	Jorge Padilla **RC**	10.00
142	Andy Pratt **RC**	10.00
143	Rene Reyes **RC**	10.00
144	Rodrigo Rosario **RC**	10.00
145	Tom Shearn **RC**	10.00
146	So Taguchi **RC**	30.00
147	Dennis Tankersley	15.00
148	Matt Thornton	10.00
149	Jeremy Ward **RC**	10.00
150	Mitch Wylie **RC**	10.00
151	Pedro Martinez	8.00
152	Cal Ripken Jr.	25.00
153	Roger Clemens	15.00
154	Bernie Williams	6.00
155	Jason Giambi	8.00
156	Robin Ventura	5.00
157	Carlos Delgado	6.00
158	Frank Thomas	8.00
159	Magglio Ordonez	5.00
160	Jim Thome	10.00
161	Darin Erstad	5.00
162	Tim Salmon	5.00
163	Tim Hudson	5.00
164	Barry Zito	5.00
165	Ichiro Suzuki	30.00
166	Edgar Martinez	8.00
167	Alex Rodriguez	15.00
168	Ivan Rodriguez	8.00
169	Juan Gonzalez	6.00
170	Greg Maddux	12.00
171	Chipper Jones	10.00
172	Andruw Jones	8.00
173	Tom Glavine	6.00
174	Mike Piazza	15.00
175	Roberto Alomar	8.00
176	Scott Rolen	12.00
177	Sammy Sosa	15.00
178	Moises Alou	8.00
179	Ken Griffey Jr.	15.00
180	Jeff Bagwell	8.00
181	Jim Edmonds	6.00
182	J.D. Drew	5.00
183	Brian Giles	5.00
184	Randy Johnson	10.00
185	Curt Schilling	10.00
186	Luis Gonzalez	5.00
187	Todd Helton	8.00
188	Shawn Green	5.00
189	David Wells	5.00
190	Jeff Kent	5.00

SuperStar Swatch Silver

Jersey (151-190): .5-1X
Production 400

SuperStar Swatch Gold

Jersey (151-190): .75-1.5X
Production 150

Sweet Spot Bat Barrel

No Pricing

Winning Materials Ball/Patch Combo

No Pricing
Production 25 Sets

Winning Materials Base Combo

		NM/M
Common Card:		15.00
Production 200		
PE	Mike Piazza, Jim Edmonds	20.00
RJ	Alex Rodriguez, Derek Jeter	40.00
BG	Barry Bonds, Shawn Green	20.00
IM	Ichiro Suzuki, Edgar Martinez	50.00
SG	Sammy Sosa, Luis Gonzalez	25.00
GR	Troy Glaus, Alex Rodriguez	20.00
WJ	Bernie Williams, Derek Jeter	30.00
GS	Ken Griffey Jr., Sammy Sosa	30.00
PI	Albert Pujols, Ichiro Suzuki	60.00
SR	Kazuhiro Sasaki, Mariano Rivera	20.00

Winning Materials Base/Patch Combo

No Pricing
Production 25 Sets

Winning Materials Jersey Combo

		NM/M
Common Card:		8.00
Inserted 1:18		
AR	Alex Rodriguez, Ivan Rodriguez	20.00
GC	Ken Griffey Jr., Sean Casey/SP	20.00
BR	Jeff Bagwell, Alex Rodriguez	15.00
WG	Bernie Williams, Jason Giambi	10.00
JS	Randy Johnson, Curt Schilling	15.00
MJ	Greg Maddux, Chipper Jones	20.00
MC	Edgar Martinez, Mike Cameron	10.00
SP	Sammy Sosa, Corey Patterson	20.00
ED	Jim Edmonds, J.D. Drew	10.00
PA	Mike Piazza, Roberto Alomar	15.00
DH	Jermaine Dye, Tim Hudson	8.00
RA	Scott Rolen, Bobby Abreu	15.00
TO	Frank Thomas, Magglio Ordonez	15.00
HW	Mike Hampton, Larry Walker	8.00
TS	Jim Thome, C.C. Sabathia	15.00
GK	Shawn Green, Eric Karros	10.00
KG	Jason Kendall, Brian Giles	8.00
WP	David Wells, Jorge Posada	10.00
NM	Hideo Nomo, Pedro Martinez/SP	20.00
RP	Ivan Rodriguez, Chan Ho Park	10.00
LH	Al Leiter, Mike Hampton	8.00
BA	Jeromy Burnitz, Edgardo Alfonzo	8.00
DS	Carlos Delgado, Shannon Stewart	10.00
BG	Jeff Bagwell, Juan Gonzalez	10.00
GR	Juan Gonzalez, Ivan Rodriguez	10.00
VR	Omar Vizquel, Alex Rodriguez	15.00
SE	Aaron Sele, Darin Erstad	8.00
JJ	Chipper Jones, Andruw Jones	15.00
SH	Kazuhiro Sasaki, Shigetoshi Hasegawa	8.00

Winning Materials USA Jersey Combo

		NM/M
Common Card:		10.00
Production 150		
AH	Brent Abernathy, Orlando Hudson	8.00
BT	Sean Burroughs, Mark Teixeira	25.00
GB	Jason Giambi, Sean Burroughs	15.00
HD	Orlando Hudson, Jeff Deardorff	10.00
GT	Jason Giambi, Mark Teixeira	20.00
HOU	Roy Oswalt, Adam Everett	10.00
HP	Dustin Hermanson, Mark Prior	15.00
JC	Jacque Jones, Michael Cuddyer	10.00
KB	Austin Kearns, Sean Burroughs	15.00
KC	Austin Kearns, Michael Cuddyer	15.00
MG	Doug Mientkiewicz, Jason Giambi	15.00
MIN	Doug Mientkiewicz, Michael Cuddyer	10.00
MO	Matt Morris, Roy Oswalt	15.00
MP	Matt Morris, Mark Prior	15.00
AW	Matt Anderson, Jeff Weaver	10.00
MW	Matt Morris, Jeff Weaver	10.00
PB	Mark Prior, Dewon Brazelton	15.00
RE	Brian Roberts, Adam Everett	10.00
SD	Mark Kotsay, Sean Burroughs	10.00
TB	Brent Abernathy, Dewon Brazelton	10.00
TP	Mark Teixeira, Mark Prior	25.00
WB	Jeff Weaver, Dewon Brazelton	10.00
WH	Jeff Weaver, Dustin Hermanson	10.00

2003 SP Authentic

#	Player	NM/M
Complete Set (189):		
Common Player:		.25
Common Rk Archives (91-123):		1.00
Production 2,500		
Common Back to '93 (124-150):		1.50
Production 1,993		
Common Future Watch (150-180):		4.00
Production 2,003		
Pack (5):		3.50
Box (24):		70.00
1	Darin Erstad	.40
2	Garrett Anderson	.40
3	Troy Glaus	.50
4	Eric Chavez	.40
5	Barry Zito	.50
6	Miguel Tejada	.50
7	Eric Hinske	.25
8	Carlos Delgado	.50
9	Josh Phelps	.25
10	Ben Grieve	.25
11	Carl Crawford	.25
12	Omar Vizquel	.40
13	Matt Lawton	.25
14	C.C. Sabathia	.25
15	Ichiro Suzuki	1.50
16	John Olerud	.40
17	Freddy Garcia	.25
18	Jay Gibbons	.25
19	Tony Batista	.25
20	Melvin Mora	.25
21	Alex Rodriguez	2.00
22	Rafael Palmeiro	.50
23	Hank Blalock	.50
24	Nomar Garciaparra	1.00
25	Pedro J. Martinez	.75
26	Johnny Damon	.75
27	Mike Sweeney	.25
28	Carlos Febles	.25
29	Carlos Beltran	.50
30	Carlos Pena	.25
31	Eric Munson	.25
32	Bobby Higginson	.25
33	Torii Hunter	.40
34	Doug Mientkiewicz	.25
35	Jacque Jones	.25
36	Paul Konerko	.50
37	Bartolo Colon	.25
38	Magglio Ordonez	.40
39	Derek Jeter	2.00
40	Bernie Williams	.50
41	Jason Giambi	.50
42	Alfonso Soriano	.75
43	Roger Clemens	1.50
44	Jeff Bagwell	.50
45	Jeff Kent	.40
46	Lance Berkman	.40
47	Chipper Jones	.75
48	Andruw Jones	.50
49	Gary Sheffield	.50
50	Ben Sheets	.40
51	Richie Sexson	.50
52	Geoff Jenkins	.25
53	Jim Edmonds	.40
54	Albert Pujols	2.00
55	Scott Rolen	.75
56	Sammy Sosa	1.00
57	Kerry Wood	.75
58	Eric Karros	.25
59	Luis Gonzalez	.40
60	Randy Johnson	.75
61	Curt Schilling	.75
62	Fred McGriff	.40
63	Shawn Green	.40
64	Paul LoDuca	.25
65	Vladimir Guerrero	.75
66	Jose Vidro	.25
67	Barry Bonds	2.00
68	Rich Aurilia	.25
69	Edgardo Alfonzo	.25
70	Ivan Rodriguez	.50
71	Mike Lowell	.40
72	Derrek Lee	.50
73	Tom Glavine	.50
74	Mike Piazza	1.00
75	Roberto Alomar	.50
76	Ryan Klesko	.25
77	Phil Nevin	.25
78	Mark Kotsay	.25
79	Jim Thome	.75
80	Pat Burrell	.40
81	Bobby Abreu	.40
82	Jason Kendall	.40
83	Brian Giles	.40
84	Aramis Ramirez	.40
85	Austin Kearns	.40
86	Ken Griffey Jr.	1.00
87	Adam Dunn	.50
88	Larry Walker	.40
89	Todd Helton	.50
90	Preston Wilson	.40
91	Derek Jeter	6.00
92	Johnny Damon	3.00
93	Chipper Jones	3.00
94	Manny Ramirez	3.00
95	Trot Nixon	1.00
96	Alex Rodriguez	5.00
97	Chan Ho Park	1.00
98	Brad Fullmer	1.00
99	Billy Wagner	1.00
100	Hideo Nomo	2.00
101	Freddy Garcia	1.00
102	Darin Erstad	1.00
103	Jose Cruz Jr.	1.00
104	Nomar Garciaparra	4.00
105	Magglio Ordonez	1.50
106	Kerry Wood	2.00
107	Troy Glaus	1.50
108	J.D. Drew	1.00
109	Alfonso Soriano	3.00
110	Danys Baez	1.00
111	Kazuhiro Sasaki	1.00
112	Barry Zito	2.00
113	Brent Abernathy	1.00
114	Ben Diggins	1.00
115	Ben Sheets	2.00
116	Brad Wilkerson	1.00
117	Juan Pierre	1.00
118	Jon Rauch	1.00
119	Ichiro Suzuki	5.00
120	Albert Pujols	6.00
121	Mark Prior	2.00
122	Mark Teixeira	2.00
123	Kazuhisa Ishii	1.00
124	Troy Glaus	1.50
125	Randy Johnson	3.00
126	Curt Schilling	3.00
127	Chipper Jones	3.00
128	Greg Maddux	4.00
129	Nomar Garciaparra	3.00
130	Pedro J. Martinez	3.00
131	Sammy Sosa	3.00
132	Mark Prior	2.00
133	Ken Griffey Jr.	4.00
134	Adam Dunn	2.00
135	Jeff Bagwell	2.00
136	Vladimir Guerrero	3.00
137	Mike Piazza	4.00
138	Tom Glavine	1.50
139	Derek Jeter	8.00
140	Roger Clemens	6.00
141	Jason Giambi	2.00
142	Alfonso Soriano	3.00
143	Miguel Tejada	2.00
144	Barry Zito	1.50
145	Jim Thome	3.00
146	Barry Bonds	8.00
147	Ichiro Suzuki	5.00
148	Albert Pujols	8.00
149	Alex Rodriguez	6.00
150	Carlos Delgado	2.00
151	Richard Fischer **RC**	4.00
152	Brandon Webb **RC**	10.00
153	Rob Hammock **RC**	4.00
154	Matt Kata **RC**	4.00
155	Tim Olson **RC**	4.00
156	Oscar Villarreal **RC**	4.00
157	Michael Hessman **RC**	4.00
158	Daniel Cabrera **RC**	6.00
159	Jon Leicester **RC**	4.00
160	Todd Wellemeyer **RC**	4.00
161	Felix Sanchez **RC**	4.00
162	David Sanders **RC**	4.00
163	Josh Stewart **RC**	4.00
164	Arnie Munoz **RC**	4.00
165	Ryan Cameron **RC**	4.00
166	Clint Barmes **RC**	5.00
167	Josh Willingham **RC**	10.00
168		.25
169	Willie Eyre **RC**	4.00
170	Brent Hoard **RC**	4.00
171	Terrmel Sledge **RC**	4.00
172	Phil Seibel **RC**	4.00
173	Craig Brazell **RC**	4.00
174	Jeff Duncan **RC**	6.00
175		.25
176	Bernie Castro **RC**	4.00
177	Mike Nicolas **RC**	4.00
178	Rett Johnson **RC**	4.00
179	Bobby Madritsch **RC**	6.00
180	Chris Capuano **RC**	15.00
181	Hideki Matsui/Auto./500 **RC**	240.00
181	H. Matsui/Bronze/Auto./75	275.00
182	Jose Contreras/Auto./500 **RC**	35.00
183	Lew Ford/Auto./500 **RC**	15.00
184	Jeremy Griffiths/Auto./500	15.00
185	Guillermo Quiroz/Auto./500 **RC**	15.00
186	Alejandro Machado/Auto./500 **RC**	10.00
187	Francisco Cruceta/Auto./500 **RC**	15.00
188	Prentice Redman/Auto./500 **RC**	15.00
189	Shane Bazzell/Auto./500 **RC**	15.00

Simply Splendid

	NM/M
Complete Set (30):	200.00
Common Williams:	8.00
Production 406 Sets	
TW1-TW30 Ted Williams	8.00

Chirography

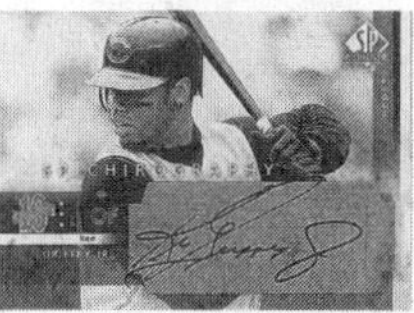
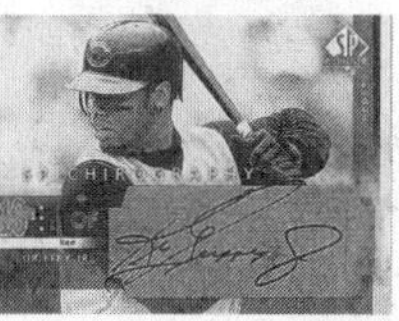

	NM/M
Common Autograph:	10.00

Varying quantities produced
Bronze Autos.: 1X
Production 100
Silver Autos.: 1-1.5X
Production 50
Gold Autos.: No Pricing
Production 10
GA1 Garret Anderson/245 15.00
BA Jeff Bagwell/175 50.00
JD Johnny Damon/245 35.00
AD Adam Dunn/170 25.00
JE2 Jim Edmonds/350 20.00
FL Cliff Floyd/125 12.00
FC Rafael Furcal/150 15.00
FG Freddy Garcia/345 15.00
GI Jason Giambi/250 15.00
GL Brian Giles/225 15.00
LG1 Luis Gonzalez/195 15.00
GJ Ken Griffey Jr./350 85.00
JR Ken Griffey Jr./350 85.00
TO Torii Hunter/245 15.00
KE Jason Kendall/145 10.00
MM Mark McGwire/50 275.00
MP Mark Prior/150 40.00
CR Cal Ripken Jr./250 100.00
RO Scott Rolen/345 35.00
TS Tim Salmon/350 20.00
RS Richie Sexson/245 15.00
SA Sammy Sosa/335 75.00
SO Sammy Sosa/335 75.00
IC Ichiro Suzuki/85 350.00
IS Ichiro Suzuki/75 350.00
SW Mike Sweeney/125 15.00
JT1 Jim Thome/250 35.00

Chirography Dodger Stars

NM/M
Common Autograph: 8.00
Bronze Autos.: 1X
Production 100
Silver Autos.: 1-1.5X
Production 50
Gold Autos.: No Pricing
Production 10
BB Bill Buckner/245 10.00
CE Ron Cey/345 15.00
SG Steve Garvey/320 20.00
JN Tommy John/170 15.00
DL Davey Lopes/245 8.00
DN Don Newcombe/345 15.00
BI Bill Russell/245 15.00
DS Duke Snider/345 30.00
SU Don Sutton/245 15.00
MW Maury Wills/320 10.00
SY Steve Yeager/345 15.00

Chirography Double

NM/M
Common Duo Auto: 40.00
FB Yogi Berra, Whitey Ford/75 150.00
FE Carlton Fisk, Dwight Evans/75 65.00
FM Carlton Fisk, Bill Mazeroski/75 40.00
GG Jason Giambi, Ken Griffey Jr. 125.00
GR Steve Garvey, Ron Cey/75 50.00
JI Ken Griffey Jr., Ichiro Suzuki 350.00
KR Tony Kubek, Bobby Richardson/75 80.00
KT Tom Seaver, Jerry Koosman/75 80.00
MG Don Mattingly, Jason Giambi/25 150.00
MS Mark McGwire, Sammy Sosa/15 500.00
SJ Sammy Sosa, Jason Giambi/25 125.00
WB Bill Buckner, Mookie Wilson/150 40.00

Chirography Flash Backs

NM/M
Common Autograph: 8.00
Bronze Autos.: 1X
Production 100
Silver Autos.: 1-1.5X
Production 50
Gold Autos.: No Pricing
No Pricing
JE1 Jim Edmonds/350 15.00
CF1 Cliff Floyd/350 8.00
JA Jason Giambi/350 15.00
BN Brian Giles/245 10.00
LA Luis Gonzalez/200 15.00
GM Ken Griffey Jr./350 80.00
MA Mark McGwire/245 280.00
SR Sammy Sosa/245 100.00

Chirography Hall of Famers

NM/M
Common Autograph: 15.00
Bronze Autos.: 1X
Production 100
Silver Autos.: 1-1.5X
Production 50
Gold Autos.: No Pricing
Production 10
JB1 Johnny Bench/350 40.00
GC1 Gary Carter/350 20.00
OC Orlando Cepeda/245 20.00
RF Rollie Fingers/170 15.00
CF Carlton Fisk/240 35.00
WF Whitey Ford/150 40.00
BG Bob Gibson/245 35.00
TP Tony Perez/320 20.00
RR Robin Roberts/170 30.00
NR Nolan Ryan/170 140.00
TS Tom Seaver/170 40.00
DS Duke Snider/250 30.00
DW2 Dave Winfield/350 25.00

Chirography Triple

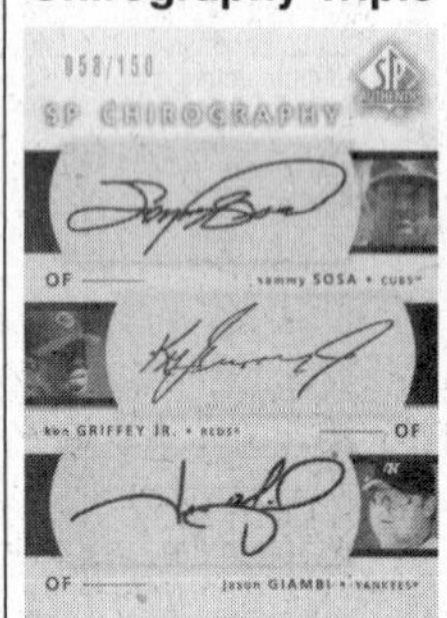

NM/M
Quantity produced listed
BKR Bobby Richardson, Yogi Berra, Tony Kubek/75 120.00
FCG Carlton Fisk, Gary Carter, Kirk Gibson/75 75.00
GIS Sammy Sosa, Ichiro Suzuki, Ken Griffey Jr./75 400.00
GLC Davey Lopes, Ron Cey, Steve Garvey/75 65.00
GRC Steve Garvey, Ron Cey, Bill Russell/75 60.00
GSG Sammy Sosa, Jason Giambi, Ken Griffey Jr./75 250.00
GSJ Ken Griffey Jr., Jason Giambi, Sammy Sosa/75 250.00
ISG Sammy Sosa, Jason Giambi, Ichiro Suzuki/75 300.00
SEA Tim Salmon, Garret Anderson, Darin Erstad/75 100.00
SKM Tom Seaver, Tug McGraw, Jerry Koosman/75 125.00

Chirography World Series Heroes

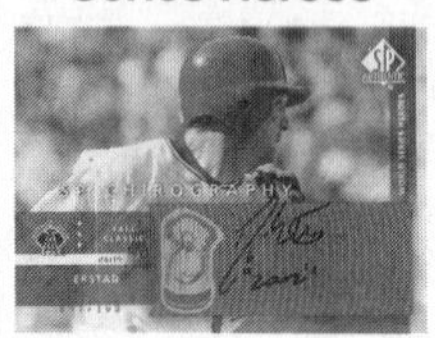

NM/M
Common Autograph: 10.00
Bronze Autos: 1X
Production 100
Silver Autos.: 1-1.5X
Production 50
Gold Autos.: No Pricing
Production 10
GA Garret Anderson/245 15.00
GC Gary Carter/345 20.00
DE Darin Erstad/245 15.00
CF Carlton Fisk/200 40.00
KG Kirk Gibson/145 15.00
GO Luis Gonzalez/225 15.00
GS Ken Griffey Sr./295 10.00
AJ1 Andruw Jones/350 20.00
DJ David Justice/170 20.00
JK Jerry Koosman/170 15.00
BM Bill Mazeroski/245 30.00
TM Tug McGraw/170 25.00
JP Jorge Posada/350 35.00
ER Edgar Renteria/220 15.00
CR Cal Ripken Jr./295 100.00
TI Tim Salmon/245 15.00
CS Curt Schilling/345 30.00

Chirography Yankee Stars

NM/M
Common Autograph: 10.00
Bronze Autos.: 1X
Production 100
Silver Autos.: 1-1.5X
Production 50
Gold Autos: No Pricing
Production 10
YB Yogi Berra/320 35.00
JB Jim Bouton/345 10.00
RC Roger Clemens/210 100.00
JG Jason Giambi/275 15.00
KS Ken Griffey Sr./350 10.00
TH Tommy Henrich/345 15.00
HK Ralph Houk/245 12.00
TJ Tommy John/245 15.00
TK Tony Kubek/345 20.00
SL Sparky Lyle/345 10.00
DM Don Mattingly/295 60.00
BR Bobby Richardson/320 20.00
ST Mel Stottlemyre/345 10.00
DW1 Dave Winfield/350 25.00

Chirography Young Stars

NM/M
Common Autograph: 6.00
Bronze Autos.: 1X
Production 100
Silver Autos.: 1-1.5X
Production 50
Gold Autos.: No Pricing
Production 10
HB Hank Blalock/245 25.00
BO Joe Borchard/245 8.00
SB Sean Burroughs/245 8.00
MB Marlon Byrd/245 8.00
HC Hee Seop Choi/245 20.00
DI1 Ben Diggins/350 8.00
DH Drew Henson/245 15.00
EH Eric Hinske/245 10.00
OH Orlando Hudson/245 15.00
JJ Jacque Jones/245 15.00
JJ1 Jimmy Journell/350 10.00
JL Jason Lane/245 6.00
JO Joe Mays/245 6.00
MI Doug Mientkiewicz/245 15.00
MY Brett Myers/245 10.00
CP Corey Patterson/245 15.00
PE Carlos Pena/245 10.00
OP Oliver Perez/245 10.00
JP Josh Phelps/245 8.00
BP1 Brandon Phillips/350 10.00
AP A.J. Pierzynski/245 15.00
FS1 Freddy Sanchez/350 15.00
TX Mark Teixeira/245 25.00
BZ Barry Zito/350 20.00

Splendid Jerseys

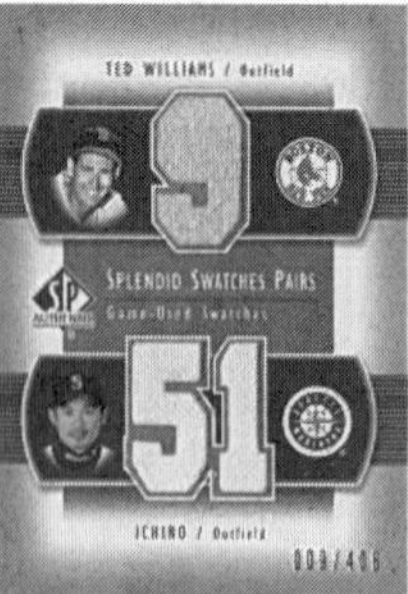

NM/M
Production 406 Sets
TW Mickey Mantle, Ted Williams 180.00
SJ-TW Ted Williams 100.00
TW-IS Ted Williams, Ichiro Suzuki 100.00
TW-JG Ted Williams, Jason Giambi 60.00
TW-KG Ted Williams, Ken Griffey Jr. 75.00
TW-MM Mark McGwire, Ted Williams 110.00
TW-SS Ted Williams, Sammy Sosa 80.00
TW-NM1 Ted Williams, Nomar Garciaparra 80.00
TW-NM2 Nomar Garciaparra, Ted Williams 80.00

Splendid Signatures

NM/M
Hand Numbered to five or three.

GA Nomar Garciaparra/406 100.00
TW-NM3 Ted Williams, Nomar Garciaparra/3 (10/03 Auction) 2,400

Spotlight "Godzilla"

Complete Set (15):
Common Matsui:
Production 500 Sets

Superstar Flashback

NM/M
Complete Set (60): 65.00
Common Player: 1.00
Production 2,003 Sets
SF1 Tim Salmon 1.00
SF2 Darin Erstad 1.00
SF3 Troy Glaus 1.50
SF4 Randy Johnson 2.00
SF5 Curt Schilling 1.50
SF6 Steve Finley 1.00
SF7 Greg Maddux 3.00
SF8 Chipper Jones 3.00
SF9 Andruw Jones 1.50
SF10 Gary Sheffield 1.00
SF11 Manny Ramirez 2.00
SF12 Pedro J. Martinez 2.00
SF13 Nomar Garciaparra 2.50
SF14 Sammy Sosa 3.00
SF15 Frank Thomas 1.50
SF16 Kerry Wood 1.50
SF17 Paul Konerko 1.00
SF18 Corey Patterson 1.00
SF19 Mark Prior 2.00
SF20 Ken Griffey Jr. 3.00
SF21 Adam Dunn 1.50
SF22 Larry Walker 1.00
SF23 Preston Wilson 1.00
SF24 Todd Helton 1.50
SF25 Ivan Rodriguez 1.50
SF26 Josh Beckett 1.00
SF27 Jeff Bagwell 1.50
SF28 Jeff Kent 1.00
SF29 Lance Berkman 1.00
SF30 Carlos Beltran 1.00
SF31 Shawn Green 1.50
SF32 Richie Sexson 1.00
SF33 Vladimir Guerrero 1.50
SF34 Mike Piazza 4.00
SF35 Roberto Alomar 1.50
SF36 Roger Clemens 4.00
SF37 Derek Jeter 6.00
SF38 Jason Giambi 1.50
SF39 Bernie Williams 1.50
SF40 Nick Johnson 1.00
SF41 Alfonso Soriano 3.00
SF42 Miguel Tejada 1.50
SF43 Eric Chavez 1.00
SF44 Barry Zito 1.50
SF45 Jim Thome 1.50
SF46 Pat Burrell 1.00
SF47 Marlon Byrd 1.00
SF48 Jason Kendall 1.00
SF49 Aramis Ramirez 1.50
SF50 Brian Giles 1.00
SF51 Phil Nevin 1.00
SF52 Barry Bonds 6.00
SF53 Ichiro Suzuki 4.00
SF54 Scott Rolen 2.00
SF55 J.D. Drew 1.00
SF56 Albert Pujols 6.00
SF57 Mark Teixeira 1.50
SF58 Hank Blalock 2.00
SF59 Carlos Delgado 1.50
SF60 Roy Halladay 1.00

500 Home Run Club

NM/M
Production 25

500HR Ted Williams, Barry Bonds, Mark McGwire, Sammy Sosa, Mickey Mantle 325.00

2003 SP Legendary Cuts

NM/M
Complete Set (130):
Common Player: .25
Common SP: 3.00
Production 1,299
Pack (4): 8.00
Box (12): 85.00
1 Luis Aparicio .25
2 Al Barlick .25
3 Al Lopez .25
4 Ernie Banks 1.00
5 Alexander Cartwright .25
6 Lou Brock .50
7 Babe Ruth/SP 10.00
8 Bill Dickey .50
9 Bill Mazeroski .25
10 Bob Feller .50
11 Billy Herman .25
12 Billy Williams .25
13 Bob Gibson/SP 4.00
14 Bob Lemon .25
15 Bobby Doerr .25
16 Branch Rickey .25
17 Gary Carter .50
18 Burleigh Grimes .25
19 Cap Anson .25
20 Carl Hubbell .25
21 Carlton Fisk .50
22 Casey Stengel .50
23 Charlie Gehringer .25
24 Chief Bender .25
25 Christy Mathewson/SP 5.00
26 Cy Young 1.00
27 Dave Winfield .50
28 Dazzy Vance .25
29 Dizzy Dean/SP 4.00
30 Don Drysdale/SP 4.00
31 Duke Snider/SP 4.00
32 Earl Averill .25
33 Earle Combs .25
34 Edd Roush .25
35 Earl Weaver .25
36 Eddie Collins .25
37 Eddie Plank .25
38 Elmer Flick .25
39 Enos Slaughter .25
40 Ernie Lombardi .25
41 Ford Frick .25
42 Jim "Catfish" Hunter .25
43 Frankie Frisch .25
44 Gabby Hartnett .25
45 George Kell .25
46 Early Wynn .25
47 Ferguson Jenkins .25
48 Al Kaline 1.00
49 Harmon Killebrew 1.00
50 Hal Newhouser .25
51 Hank Greenberg/SP 5.00
52 Harry Caray .25
53 Tommy Lasorda .25
54 Honus Wagner/SP 6.00
55 Hoyt Wilhelm/SP 3.00
56 Jackie Robinson/SP 6.00
57 Jim Bottomley .25
58 Jim Bunning/SP 3.00
59 Jimmie Foxx/SP 6.00
60 Eddie Mathews 1.00
61 Joe Cronin .25
62 Joe DiMaggio/SP 8.00
63 Joe McCarthy/SP 3.00
64 Joe Morgan/SP 3.00
65 Willie McCovey .50
66 Joe Tinker .25
67 Johnny Bench/SP 6.00
68 Johnny Evers/SP 3.00
69 Johnny Mize/SP 3.00
70 Josh Gibson/SP 5.00
71 Juan Marichal .50
72 Judy Johnson .25
73 Stan Musial 1.50
74 Kiki Cuyler .25
75 Larry Doby .75
76 Nap Lajoie .25
77 Larry MacPhail .25
78 Phil Niekro .25
79 Lefty Gomez/SP 3.00
80 Lefty Grove/SP 3.00
81 Leo Durocher/SP 3.00
82 Leon Day .25
83 Gaylord Perry/SP 3.00
84 Lou Boudreau .25
85 Lou Gehrig 3.00
86 Luke Appling .25
87 Max Carey .25
88 Mel Allen/SP 3.00
89 Mel Ott/SP 5.00
90 Mickey Cochrane .50
91 Mickey Mantle 4.00
92 Brooks Robinson 1.00
93 Monte Irvin .50
94 Nellie Fox .50
95 Nolan Ryan/SP 10.00
96 Ozzie Smith/SP 6.00
97 Mike Schmidt 2.00
98 Pee Wee Reese/SP 3.00
99 Phil Rizzuto .75
100 Ralph Kiner .50
101 Ray Dandridge .25
102 Richie Ashburn .25
103 Rick Ferrell .25
104 Roberto Clemente 2.00
105 Robin Roberts .25
106 Robin Yount 1.00
107 Rogers Hornsby .50
108 Rollie Fingers .25
109 Roy Campanella .50
110 Rube Marquard .25
111 Sam Crawford .25
112 Steve Carlton .50
113 Satchel Paige/SP 5.00
114 Sparky Anderson .25
115 Stan Coveleski .25
116 Red Schoendienst .25
117 Ted Williams 3.00
118 Tom Seaver 1.00
119 Tom Yawkey .25
120 Tony Lazzeri .25
121 Tony Perez .25
122 Tris Speaker .25
123 Ty Cobb 2.00
124 Waite Hoyt/SP 3.00
125 Walter Alston .25
126 Walter Johnson .75
127 Warren Spahn 1.00
128 Whitey Ford .75
129 Willie Stargell .50
130 Yogi Berra .75

Blue

Non SP's (1-130): 2-4X
SP's: 1-2X
Production 275 Sets

Green

No pricing due to scarcity.
Production 25 Sets

Autographs

NM/M
Common Player:
Inserted 1:196
Many not priced due to scarcity.
AL Alexander Cartwright/1 (6/05 Auction) 7,800
BG Burleigh Grimes/34 250.00
BI Billy Herman/30 150.00
BL Bob Lemon/34 150.00
BL1 Bob Lemon/41 150.00
CH Carl Hubbell/47 300.00
CH1 Carl Hubbell/63 300.00
EA Earl Averill/96 125.00
EC Earle Combs/45 150.00
ES Enos Slaughter/20 200.00
HC Harry Caray/29 225.00
HC1 Harry Caray/35 225.00
HG Hank Greenberg/30 375.00
JD Joe DiMaggio/50 375.00
JD1 Joe DiMaggio/28 400.00
LB Lou Boudreau/82 110.00
LB1 Lou Boudreau/49 120.00
LU Luke Appling/52 150.00
RM Rube Marquard/40 200.00

Autographs Blue

NM/M
Many not priced due to scarcity.
EA Earl Averill/50 125.00
HC1 Harry Caray/35 240.00
HN1 Hal Newhouser/B2B/29 125.00
JD1 Joe DiMaggio/40 375.00

Combo Cuts

No Pricing
Production One Set

Etched in Time

NM/M
Common Player: 3.00
Production 400 Sets
Etched 300: .5-1X
Production 300
Etched 175: .75-1.5X
Production 175
ME Mel Allen 3.00
RA Richie Ashburn 4.00
AB Al Barlick 3.00
LB Lou Boudreau 3.00
RO Roy Campanella 4.00
AC Alexander Cartwright 3.00
HC Harry Caray 3.00
RC Roberto Clemente 10.00
TC Ty Cobb 6.00
EC Eddie Collins 3.00
DD Dizzy Dean 3.00
JD Joe DiMaggio 8.00
DO Don Drysdale 3.00
LD Leo Durocher 3.00
JF Jimmie Foxx 5.00
LO Lou Gehrig 8.00
CG Charlie Gehringer 3.00
JG Josh Gibson 5.00
LG Lefty Gomez 3.00
HG Hank Greenberg 5.00
LE Lefty Grove 3.00
GH Gabby Hartnett 3.00
RH Rogers Hornsby 4.00
CH Carl Hubbell 3.00
TL Tony Lazzeri 3.00
EL Ernie Lombardi 3.00
MM Mickey Mantle 15.00
CM Christy Mathewson 8.00
JM Joe McCarthy 3.00
JO Johnny Mize 3.00
MO Mel Ott 4.00
SP Satchel Paige 5.00
PR Pee Wee Reese 3.00
JR Jackie Robinson 5.00
BR Babe Ruth 10.00
TS Tris Speaker 3.00
CS Casey Stengel 3.00
HW Honus Wagner 5.00
TW Ted Williams 8.00
CY Cy Young 5.00

Hall Marks Autographs

NM/M
Inserted 1:196
Many not priced due to scarcity.
Greens: No Pricing
Production 10
BD1 Bobby Doerr/Black/50 40.00
BM1 Bill Mazeroski/Black/50 40.00
CF1 Carlton Fisk/Black/50 50.00
CY1 Carl Yastrzemski/Black/45 75.00
DS1 Duke Snider/Black/50 40.00
GC1 Gary Carter/Black/50 30.00
GK1 George Kell/Black/50 20.00
JM1 Juan Marichal/Black/50 35.00
JO1 Joe Morgan/Black/75 30.00
LA1 Luis Aparicio/Black/45 30.00
MI1 Monte Irvin/Black/85 30.00
OS1 Ozzie Smith/Black/45 75.00
PR1 Phil Rizzuto/Black/50 40.00
RF1 Rollie Fingers/Black/99 20.00
RK1 Ralph Kiner/Black/50 30.00
RR1 Robin Roberts/Black/55 40.00
RY1 Robin Yount/Black/45 75.00
TP1 Tony Perez/Black/50 30.00
WS1 Warren Spahn/Black/35 70.00
YB1 Yogi Berra/Black/50 60.00

Historic Impressions

NM/M
Common Player: 3.00
Production 350 Sets
Golds: 1X
Production 200 Sets
Golds 75: 1.5-2X
Production 75
Silvers: 1X
Production 250 Sets
MA Mel Allen 3.00
RA Richie Ashburn 5.00
LB Lou Boudreau 3.00
RO Roy Campanella 5.00
AC Alexander Cartwright 3.00
HC Harry Caray 4.00
RC Roberto Clemente 15.00
TY Ty Cobb 8.00
MC Mickey Cochrane 5.00
EC Eddie Collins 3.00
DD Dizzy Dean 5.00
JD Joe DiMaggio 8.00
DO Don Drysdale 3.00
LD Leo Durocher 3.00
JF Jimmie Foxx 8.00
LO Lou Gehrig 10.00
CG Charlie Gehringer 3.00
LG Lefty Gomez 3.00
HG Hank Greenberg 6.00
LE Lefty Grove 6.00
GH Gabby Hartnett 3.00
RH Rogers Hornsby 6.00
CH Carl Hubbell 6.00
TL Tony Lazzeri 3.00
MM Mickey Mantle 25.00
CM Christy Mathewson 6.00
JO Joe McCarthy 3.00
JM Johnny Mize 3.00
MO Mel Ott 6.00
SP Satchel Paige 6.00
PR Pee Wee Reese 3.00
JR Jackie Robinson 8.00
BR Babe Ruth 15.00
ES Enos Slaughter 3.00
TS Tris Speaker 5.00
CS Casey Stengel 4.00
HW Honus Wagner 8.00
HO Hoyt Wilhelm 3.00
TW Ted Williams 15.00
CY Cy Young 8.00

Historic Lumber

NM/M
Common Player: 6.00
Inserted 1:12
BR Babe Ruth/Away/150 125.00
BR1 Babe Ruth/Home/150 125.00
CF Carlton Fisk R./Sox/50 15.00
CF1 Carlton Fisk W./Sox/50 15.00
CY Carl Yastrzemski/w/Bat/300 20.00
CY1 Carl Yastrzemski/w/Cap/350 20.00
CY2 Carl Yastrzemski/w/Helmet/350 20.00
DW Dave Winfield/Padres/350 10.00
DW1 Dave Winfield/Yanks/350 10.00
FR Frank Robinson/O's/300 10.00
FR1 Frank Robinson/Reds/350 10.00
FR2 Frank Robinson/Angels/350 10.00
GC Gary Carter/Mets/300 6.00
GC1 Gary Carter/Helmet Expos/100 6.00
GC2 Gary Carter/Cap Expos/100 6.00
HK Harmon Killebrew/350 10.00
JB Johnny Bench/w/Bat/350 10.00
JB1 Johnny Bench/Swing/350 10.00
JM Joe Morgan/Reds/350 6.00
JM1 Joe Morgan/Astros/350 6.00
MM Mickey Mantle/300 100.00
NR Nolan Ryan Rgr./225 25.00
OS Ozzie Smith/Cards/300 15.00
OS1 Ozzie Smith/Padres/350 15.00
RS Red Schoendienst/Look Right/165 6.00
RS1 Red Schoendienst/Look Left/165 6.00
SC Steve Carlton/350 8.00
TP Tony Perez/Swing/350 6.00
TP1 Tony Perez/Portrait/350 6.00
TS Tom Seaver/100 10.00
TW Ted Williams/w/3 Bats/150 75.00
TW1 Ted Williams/Portrait/150 75.00
WS Willie Stargell/Arms Down/150 8.00
WS1 Willie Stargell/Arms Up/150 8.00
YB Yogi Berra/Shout/350 10.00
YB1 Yogi Berra/w/Bat/350 10.00

Historic Lumber Green

NM/M
Common Player:
BR Babe Ruth/Away/75 140.00
BR1 Babe Ruth/Home/75 140.00
CY Carl Yastrzemski/w/Bat/125 25.00
CY1 Carl Yastrzemski/w/Cap/125 25.00
CY2 Carl Yastrzemski/w/Helmet/125 25.00
DW Dave Winfield/Padres/125 10.00
DW1 Dave Winfield/Yanks/125 10.00
FR Frank Robinson/O's/125 10.00
FR1 Frank Robinson/Reds/125 10.00
FR2 Frank Robinson/Angels/125 10.00
GC Gary Carter/Mets/125 6.00
GC1 Gary Carter/Helmet Expos/125 6.00
GC2 Gary Carter/Cap Expos/125 6.00
HK Harmon Killebrew/125 10.00
JB Johnny Bench/w/Bat/125 10.00
JB1 Johnny Bench/Swing/125 10.00
JM Joe Morgan/Reds/125 6.00
JM1 Joe Morgan/Astros/125 6.00
MM Mickey Mantle/75 120.00
NR Nolan Ryan/Astros/50 50.00
OS Ozzie Smith/Cards/125 20.00
OS1 Ozzie Smith/Padres/125 20.00
RS Red Schoendienst/Look Right/125 8.00
RS1 Red Schoendienst/Look Left/125 8.00
SC Steve Carlton/125 10.00
TP Tony Perez Swing/125 6.00
TP1 Tony Perez/Portrait/125 6.00
TS Tom Seaver/50 15.00
TW Ted Williams/w/3 Bats/75 75.00
TW1 Ted Williams/Portrait/75 75.00
WS Willie Stargell/Arms Down/125 10.00
WS1 Willie Stargell/Arms Up/125 10.00
YB Yogi Berra/Shout/125 10.00
YB1 Yogi Berra/w/Bat/125 10.00

Historic Swatches

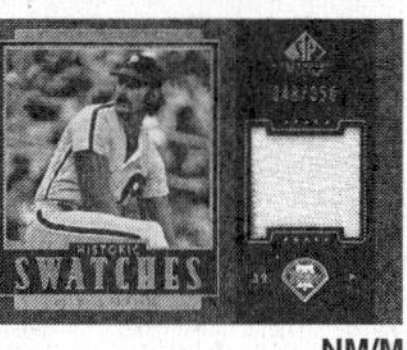

NM/M
Common Player: 5.00
Inserted 1:12
Blues: .75-1.5X
Production 50 Sets
Greens: .75-1X
Production 160 to 250
Purples: .75-1.5X
Production 75 to 150
BG Bob Gibson/CO/Jsy/350 10.00
BM Bill Mazeroski/Pants/50 15.00
BW Billy Williams/Jsy/190 5.00
CF Carlton Fisk/Pants/350 8.00
CM Christy Mathewson/Pants/300 100.00
CS Casey Stengel/Jsy/275 10.00
CY Carl Yastrzemski/Jsy/350 20.00
CY1 Carl Yastrzemski/Pants/350 20.00
DS Duke Snider/Jsy/350 10.00
DW1 Dave Winfield/Twins Jsy/300 8.00
FR Frank Robinson/O's Jsy/350 10.00
FR1 Frank Robinson/Angels Jsy/350 10.00
GC Gary Carter/Mets Jsy/350 5.00
GC1 Gary Carter/Expos Jsy/350 5.00
HW Honus Wagner/Pants/275 120.00
JB Johnny Bench/Jsy/150 10.00
JM Joe Morgan/Jsy/350 5.00
JN Juan Marichal/Pants/225 5.00
JN1 Juan Marichal/Jsy/48 5.00
LA Luis Aparicio/Jsy/230 5.00
LB Lou Boudreau/Jsy/265 5.00
MM Mickey Mantle/Pants/350 100.00
NR Nolan Ryan/Rgr. Pants/350 25.00
NR1 Nolan Ryan/Astro Pants/350 25.00
OS Ozzie Smith/Jsy/85 25.00
RF Rollie Fingers/Jsy/105 5.00
RY Robin Yount/Portrait/Jsy/350 10.00
RY1 Robin Yount/Swing/Jsy/350 10.00
SA Sparky Anderson/Jsy/350 5.00
SC Steve Carlton/Jsy/350 10.00
SM Stan Musial/Jsy/350 25.00
TC Ty Cobb/Pants/350 90.00
TP Tony Perez/Jsy/350 5.00
TS Tom Seaver/Jsy/350 10.00
TS1 Tom Seaver/Pants/350 10.00
TW Ted Williams/Jsy/250 85.00
WA Walter Alston/Look Left/Jsy/350 5.00
WA1 Walter Alston/Ahead/Jsy/350 5.00
WI Willie Stargell/Jsy/55 15.00
WS Warren Spahn/CO/Jsy/350 15.00
YB Yogi Berra/Jsy/300 10.00

2003 SPx

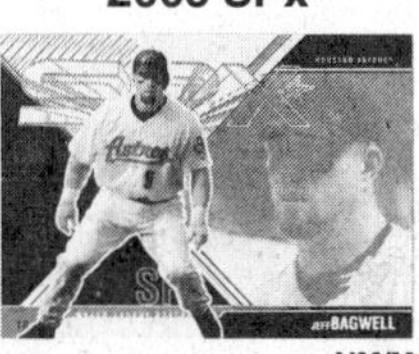

NM/M
Complete Set (178):
Common Player: .25
Common SP (126-160): 4.00
Production 999
Common Jsy Auto. (161-178): 10.00
Production 1,224 unless noted.
Pack (4): 6.00
Box (18): 90.00
1 Darin Erstad .50
2 Garret Anderson .50
3 Tim Salmon .50
4 Troy Glaus/SP 2.00
5 Luis Gonzalez .50
6 Randy Johnson 1.50
7 Curt Schilling 1.00
8 Lyle Overbay .25
9 Andruw Jones/SP 3.00
10 Gary Sheffield .75
11 Rafael Furcal .40
12 Greg Maddux 2.00
13 Chipper Jones/SP 3.00
14 Tony Batista .25
15 Rodrigo Lopez .25
16 Jay Gibbons .25
17 Byung-Hyun Kim .25
18 Johnny Damon 1.00
19 Derek Lowe .25
20 Nomar Garciaparra/SP 4.00
21 Pedro J. Martinez 1.50
22 Manny Ramirez/SP 4.00
23 Mark Prior 1.00
24 Kerry Wood .50
25 Corey Patterson .50
26 Sammy Sosa/SP 5.00
27 Moises Alou .50
28 Magglio Ordonez .50
29 Frank Thomas 1.00
30 Paul Konerko .50
31 Bartolo Colon .25
32 Adam Dunn 1.00
33 Austin Kearns .50
34 Aaron Boone .25
35 Ken Griffey Jr./SP 5.00
36 Omar Vizquel .50
37 C.C. Sabathia .25
38 Jason Davis .25
39 Travis Hafner .75
40 Brandon Phillips .25
41 Larry Walker .50
42 Preston Wilson .50
43 Jay Payton .25
44 Todd Helton .75
45 Carlos Pena .25
46 Eric Munson .25
47 Ivan Rodriguez 1.00
48 Josh Beckett .50
49 Alex Gonzalez .25
50 Roy Oswalt .50
51 Craig Biggio .50
52 Jeff Bagwell .75
53 Dontrelle Willis/SP 2.00
54 Mike Sweeney .25
55 Carlos Beltran 1.00
56 Brent Mayne .25
57 Hideo Nomo .75
58 Rickey Henderson .75
59 Adrian Beltre .50
60 Miguel Cabrera/SP 4.00
61 Kazuhisa Ishii .25
62 Ben Sheets .50
63 Richie Sexson .50
64 Torii Hunter/SP 2.00
65 Jacque Jones .25
66 Joe Mays .25
67 Corey Koskie .25
68 A.J. Pierzynski .25
69 Jose Vidro .25
70 Vladimir Guerrero/SP 4.00
71 Tom Glavine .50
72 Jose Reyes/SP 4.00
73 Aaron Heilman .25
74 Mike Piazza 2.00
75 Jorge Posada .75
76 Mike Mussina .75
77 Robin Ventura .25
78 Mariano Rivera .75
79 Roger Clemens/SP 6.00
80 Jason Giambi .75
81 Bernie Williams .75
82 Alfonso Soriano/SP 4.00
83 Derek Jeter 3.00
84 Miguel Tejada/SP 3.00
85 Eric Chavez .50
86 Tim Hudson .50
87 Barry Zito .50
88 Mark Mulder .50
89 Erubiel Durazo .25
90 Pat Burrell .50
91 Jim Thome/SP 3.00
92 Bobby Abreu .50
93 Brian Giles .50
94 Reggie Sanders/SP 2.00
95 Kenny Lofton .50
96 Ryan Klesko .25
97 Sean Burroughs .25
98 Edgardo Alfonzo .25
99 Rich Aurilia .25
100 Jose Cruz Jr. .25
101 Barry Bonds/SP 8.00
102 Mike Cameron .25
103 Kazuhiro Sasaki .25
104 Bret Boone .25
105 Ichiro Suzuki/SP 5.00
106 J.D. Drew .50
107 Jim Edmonds .50
108 Scott Rolen/SP 3.00
109 Matt Morris .25
110 Tino Martinez .25
111 Albert Pujols/SP 8.00
112 Damian Rolls .25
113 Carl Crawford .50
114 Rocco Baldelli/SP 2.00
115 Hank Blalock .50
116 Alex Rodriguez/SP 5.00
117 Kevin Mench .25
118 Rafael Palmeiro .75
119 Mark Teixeira .75
120 Shannon Stewart .25
121 Vernon Wells .50
122 Josh Phelps .25
123 Eric Hinske .25
124 Orlando Hudson .25
125 Carlos Delgado/SP 3.00
126 Jason Roach **RC** 4.00
127 Dan Haren 10.00
128 Luis Ayala **RC** 4.00
129 Bo Hart **RC** 4.00
130 Wilfredo Ledezma **RC** 4.00
131 Rick Roberts **RC** 4.00
132 Miguel Ojeda **RC** 4.00
133 Aquilino Lopez **RC** 4.00
134 Roger Deago **RC** 4.00
135 Arnie Munoz **RC** 4.00
136 Brent Hoard **RC** 4.00
137 Terrmel Sledge **RC** 4.00
138 Ryan Cameron **RC** 4.00
139 Prentice Redman **RC** 4.00
140 Clint Barmes **RC** 6.00
141 Jeremy Griffiths 4.00
142 Jon Leicester **RC** 4.00
143 Brandon Webb **RC** 15.00
144 Todd Wellemeyer **RC** 4.00
145 Felix Sanchez **RC** 4.00
146 Anthony Ferrari **RC** 4.00
147 Ian Ferguson **RC** 4.00
148 Micheal Nakamura **RC** 4.00
149 Lew Ford **RC** 8.00
150 Nate Bland **RC** 4.00
151 Dave Matranga **RC** 4.00
152 Edgar Gonzalez **RC** 4.00
153 Carlos Mendez **RC** 4.00
154 Jason Gilfillan **RC** 4.00
155 Mike Neu **RC** 4.00
156 Jason Shiell **RC** 4.00
157 Jeff Duncan **RC** 4.00
158 Oscar Villarreal **RC** 4.00
159 Diegomar Markwell **RC** 4.00
160 Joe Valentine **RC** 4.00
161 Hideki Matsui/864 **RC** 300.00
162 Jose Contreras/800 **RC** 20.00
163 Willie Eyre **RC** 10.00
164 Matt Bruback **RC** 10.00
165 Rett Johnson **RC** 15.00
166 Jeremy Griffiths 15.00
167 Francisco Cruceta **RC** 10.00
168 Fernando Cabrera **RC** 10.00
169 Jhonny Peralta 25.00
170 Shane Bazzell **RC** 10.00
171 Bobby Madritsch **RC** 20.00
172 Phil Seibel **RC** 10.00
173 Josh Willingham **RC** 20.00
174 Robby Hammock **RC** 10.00
175 Alejandro Machado **RC** 10.00
176 David Sanders **RC** 10.00
177 Matt Kata **RC** 15.00
178 Heath Bell **RC** 4.00

Spectrum

Stars (1-125) print run 51-99: 3-6X
Stars (1-125) p/r 26-50: 6-12X
Print run 25 or less not priced.
Numbered to jersey number.
SP's (126-160): .75-1.5X
Production 125

SPX Combos

NM/M
Common Duo: 20.00
Quantity produced listed
MJ Hideki Matsui, Derek Jeter/90 100.00
RC Nolan Ryan, Roger Clemens/90 120.00
SJ Curt Schilling, Randy Johnson/90 30.00
EG Darin Erstad, Troy Glaus/90 20.00
GC Greg Maddux, Chipper Jones/90 50.00
GS Jason Giambi, Alfonso Soriano/90 30.00
BK Jeff Bagwell, Jeff Kent/90 25.00
GD Ken Griffey Jr., Adam Dunn/90 50.00
GR Ken Griffey Jr., Sammy Sosa/90 50.00
SP Sammy Sosa, Rafael Palmeiro/90 40.00
MG Pedro Martinez, Nomar Garciaparra/90 40.00
RG Alex Rodriguez, Nomar Garciaparra/90 40.00
CM Jose Contreras, Pedro Martinez/90 40.00
FC Carlton Fisk, Gary Carter/90 30.00
RR Cal Ripken Jr., Scott Rolen/90 80.00
JJ Chipper Jones, Andruw Jones/90 30.00
PM Rafael Palmeiro, Fred McGriff/90 30.00
RT Alex Rodriguez, Miguel Tejada/90 30.00
SB Sammy Sosa, Barry Bonds/90 50.00
SN Ichiro Suzuki, Hideo Nomo/90 175.00
MS Hideki Matsui, Ichiro Suzuki/50 350.00
MW Mickey Mantle, Ted Williams/50 300.00
CC Jose Contreras, Roger Clemens/50 40.00
CL Cal Ripken Jr., Lou Gehrig/90 300.00
HJ Hideki Matsui, Jason Giambi/50 75.00
CA Cal Ripken Jr., Alex Rodriguez/50 150.00
IA Ichiro Suzuki, Albert Pujols/50 250.00

NI Hideo Nomo, Kazuhisa Ishii/50 50.00
MD Mickey Mantle, Derek Jeter/50 180.00
BT Barry Bonds, Ted Williams/50 180.00
BM Barry Bonds, Roger Maris/50 80.00
MB Mickey Mantle, Barry Bonds/50 150.00
PS Rafael Palmeiro, Sammy Sosa/90 40.00
RS Nolan Ryan, Tom Seaver/90 110.00

Stars

NM/M
Common Player: 20.00
Quantity produced listed
LB Lance Berkman/590 30.00
PB Pat Burrell/590 25.00
NM Nomar Garciaparra/195 80.00
JG Jason Giambi/315 30.00
TG Troy Glaus/490 25.00
LG Luis Gonzalez/790 20.00
KG Ken Griffey Jr./690 80.00
VG Vladimir Guerrero/390 50.00
CJ Chipper Jones/195 50.00
MP Mark Prior/490 40.00
CS Curt Schilling/490 40.00

Winning Materials

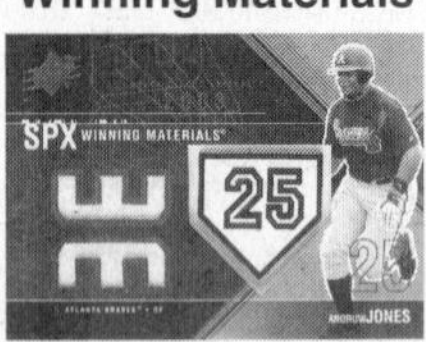

NM/M
Common Player: 5.00
Version 1 Production 375
Golds: 1X
Production 250
Version 2 Production 175
Golds: 1-2X
Production 50
RA1 Roberto Alomar 8.00
RA2 Roberto Alomar 10.00
JB1 Jeff Bagwell 6.00
JB2 Jeff Bagwell 8.00
LB1 Lance Berkman 5.00
LB2 Lance Berkman 5.00
PB1 Pat Burrell 6.00
PB2 Pat Burrell 8.00
RC1 Roger Clemens 15.00
RC2 Roger Clemens 15.00
CD1 Carlos Delgado 6.00
CD2 Carlos Delgado 8.00
RF1 Rafael Furcal 6.00
RF2 Rafael Furcal 8.00
JG1 Jason Giambi 8.00
JG2 Jason Giambi 8.00
TR1 Troy Glaus 6.00
TG2 Troy Glaus 8.00
TG1 Tom Glavine 5.00
TG2 Tom Glavine 6.00
LG1 Luis Gonzalez 5.00
LG2 Luis Gonzalez 5.00
SG1 Shawn Green 5.00
SG2 Shawn Green 5.00
KG1 Ken Griffey Jr. 15.00
KG2 Ken Griffey Jr. 15.00
VG1 Vladimir Guerrero 10.00
VG2 Vladimir Guerrero 12.00
TO1 Todd Helton 8.00
TH2 Todd Helton 10.00
TH1 Torii Hunter 8.00
RJ1 Randy Johnson 10.00
RJ2 Randy Johnson 12.00
AJ1 Andruw Jones 8.00
AJ2 Andruw Jones 8.00
CJ1 Chipper Jones 10.00
CJ2 Chipper Jones 15.00
JK1 Jeff Kent 5.00
JK2 Jeff Kent 5.00
GM1 Greg Maddux 15.00
GM2 Greg Maddux 15.00
MM2 Mickey Mantle 120.00
PM1 Pedro Martinez 10.00
PM2 Pedro Martinez 15.00
HM1 Hideki Matsui 30.00
HM2 Hideki Matsui 30.00
HN1 Hideo Nomo 15.00
HN2 Hideo Nomo 20.00
MP1 Mike Piazza 10.00
MP2 Mike Piazza 15.00
MA1 Mark Prior 10.00
MP2 Mark Prior 10.00
AP1 Albert Pujols 20.00
AP2 Albert Pujols 20.00
MR1 Manny Ramirez 10.00
MR2 Manny Ramirez 10.00
AR1 Alex Rodriguez 10.00
AR2 Alex Rodriguez 12.00
IR1 Ivan Rodriguez 8.00
IR2 Ivan Rodriguez 10.00
CS1 Curt Schilling 8.00
CS2 Curt Schilling 10.00
GS1 Gary Sheffield 6.00
GS2 Gary Sheffield 8.00
AS1 Alfonso Soriano 10.00
AS2 Alfonso Soriano 12.00
SS1 Sammy Sosa 10.00
SS2 Sammy Sosa 15.00
IS1 Ichiro Suzuki 25.00
IS2 Ichiro Suzuki 35.00
MT1 Miguel Tejada 6.00
MT2 Miguel Tejada 8.00
FT1 Frank Thomas 8.00
FT2 Frank Thomas 10.00
JT1 Jim Thome 8.00
JT2 Jim Thome 10.00
BW1 Bernie Williams 8.00
BW2 Bernie Williams 10.00
TW2 Ted Williams 80.00
TW2 Ted Williams/Gold/50 200.00
BZ1 Barry Zito 6.00
BZ2 Barry Zito 8.00

Young Stars

NM/M
Common Player: 8.00
Production 1,295 unless noted.
KA Kurt Ainsworth/1,460 8.00
RB Rocco Baldelli 20.00
JBa Josh Bard 8.00
HB Hank Blalock 20.00
SB Sean Burroughs 8.00
MD Michael Cuddyer/1,156 10.00
AD Adam Dunn 20.00
CG Chris George/1,260 8.00
EH Eric Hinske 8.00
JA Jason Jennings 8.00
NJ Nick Johnson 8.00
JJ Jacque Jones/1,260 12.00
AK Austin Kearns/964 15.00
MK Mike Kinkade 8.00
BM Brett Myers 8.00
RO Roy Oswalt 15.00
JP Josh Phelps 10.00
BP Brandon Phillips 10.00
KS Kirk Saarloos 8.00
MT Mark Teixeira 25.00

2004 SP Authentic

NM/M
Complete Set (191):
Common (1-90): .25
Common RC (91-132, 178-191): 4.00
Production 999
Common SP (133-177): 2.00
Production 999
Pack (5): 5.00
Box (24): 100.00
1 Bret Boone .25
2 Gary Sheffield .50
3 Rafael Palmeiro .75
4 Jorge Posada .50
5 Derek Jeter 3.00
6 Garret Anderson .50
7 Bartolo Colon .40
8 Kevin Brown .40
9 Shea Hillenbrand .25
10 Ryan Klesko .25
11 Bobby Abreu .50
12 Scott Rolen 1.00
13 Alfonso Soriano .75
14 Jason Giambi 1.00
15 Tom Glavine .50
16 Hideo Nomo .50
17 Johan Santana .75
18 Sammy Sosa 1.00
19 Rickie Weeks .50
20 Barry Zito .50
21 Kerry Wood .50
22 Austin Kearns .40
23 Shawn Green .40
24 Miguel Cabrera 1.00
25 Richard Hidalgo .25
26 Andruw Jones .75
27 Randy Wolf .25
28 David Ortiz 1.00
29 Roy Oswalt .50
30 Vernon Wells .50
31 Ben Sheets .50
32 Mike Lowell .25
33 Todd Helton .75
34 Jacque Jones .25
35 Mike Sweeney .25
36 Hank Blalock .50
37 Jason Schmidt .50
38 Jeff Kent .40
39 Josh Beckett .50
40 Manny Ramirez 1.00
41 Torii Hunter .50
42 Brian Giles .40
43 Javier Vazquez .25
44 Jim Edmonds .50
45 Dmitri Young .25
46 Preston Wilson .25
47 Jeff Bagwell .75
48 Pedro J. Martinez 1.00
49 Eric Chavez .40
50 Ken Griffey Jr. 2.00
51 Shannon Stewart .25
52 Rafael Furcal .40
53 Brandon Webb .25
54 Juan Pierre .25
55 Roger Clemens 2.00
56 Geoff Jenkins .25
57 Lance Berkman .50
58 Albert Pujols 3.00
59 Frank Thomas .75
60 Edgar Martinez .40
61 Tim Hudson .50
62 Eric Gagne .50
63 Richie Sexson .50
64 Corey Patterson .25
65 Nomar Garciaparra 1.00
66 Hideki Matsui 2.00
67 Mark Teixeira .75
68 Troy Glaus .50
69 Carlos Lee .40
70 Mike Mussina .75
71 Magglio Ordonez .50
72 Roy Halladay .50
73 Ichiro Suzuki 2.00
74 Randy Johnson 1.00
75 Luis Gonzalez .40
76 Mark Prior .75
77 Carlos Beltran .50
78 Ivan Rodriguez .75
79 Alex Rodriguez 2.50
80 Dontrelle Willis .50
81 Mike Piazza 1.00
82 Curt Schilling .75
83 Vladimir Guerrero 1.00
84 Greg Maddux 1.50
85 Jim Thome 1.00
86 Miguel Tejada .50
87 Carlos Delgado .50
88 Jose Reyes .75
89 Matt Morris .25
90 Mark Mulder .40
91 Angel Chavez **RC** 4.00
92 Brandon Medders **RC** 4.00
93 Carlos Vasquez **RC** 4.00
94 Chris Aguila **RC** 4.00
95 Colby Miller **RC** 4.00
96 David Crouthers 4.00
97 Dennis Sarfate **RC** 4.00
98 Donnie Kelly **RC** 4.00
99 Merkin Valdez **RC** 6.00
100 Eddy Rodriguez **RC** 4.00
101 Edwin Moreno **RC** 4.00
102 Enemencio Pacheco **RC** 4.00
103 Roberto Novoa **RC** 4.00
104 Greg Dobbs **RC** 4.00
105 Hector Gimenez **RC** 4.00
106 Ian Snell **RC** 10.00
107 Jake Woods 4.00
108 Jamie Brown **RC** 4.00
109 Jason Frasor **RC** 4.00
110 Jerome Gamble **RC** 4.00
111 Jerry Gil **RC** 6.00
112 Jesse Harper **RC** 4.00
113 Jorge Vasquez **RC** 4.00
114 Jose Capellan **RC** 6.00
115 Josh Labandeira **RC** 4.00
116 Justin Hampson **RC** 4.00
117 Justin Huisman **RC** 4.00
118 Justin Leone **RC** 6.00
119 Lincoln Holdzkom **RC** 4.00
120 Lino Urdaneta **RC** 4.00
121 Mike Gosling 4.00
122 Mike Johnston **RC** 4.00
123 Mike Rouse 4.00
124 Scott Proctor **RC** 4.00
125 Roman Colon **RC** 4.00
126 Ronny Cedeno **RC** 10.00
127 Ryan Meaux **RC** 4.00
128 Scott Dohmann **RC** 4.00
129 Sean Henn 6.00
130 Tim Bausher **RC** 4.00
131 Tim Bittner **RC** 4.00
132 William Bergolla **RC** 6.00
133 Rick Ferrell 2.00
134 Joe DiMaggio 6.00
135 Bob Feller 2.00
136 Ted Williams 6.00
137 Stan Musial 5.00
138 Larry Doby 2.00
139 Red Schoendienst 2.00
140 Enos Slaughter 2.00
141 Stan Musial 5.00
142 Mickey Mantle 8.00
143 Ted Williams 6.00
144 Mickey Mantle 8.00
145 Stan Musial 5.00
146 Tom Seaver 3.00
147 Willie McCovey 2.00
148 Bob Gibson 3.00
149 Frank Robinson 3.00
150 Joe Morgan 2.00
151 Billy Williams 2.00
152 Catfish Hunter 2.00
153 Joe Morgan 2.00
154 Joe Morgan 2.00
155 Mike Schmidt 5.00
156 Tommy Lasorda 2.00
157 Robin Yount 4.00
158 Nolan Ryan 8.00
159 John Franco 2.00
160 Nolan Ryan 8.00
161 Ken Griffey Jr. 4.00
162 Cal Ripken Jr. 8.00
163 Ken Griffey Jr. 5.00
164 Gary Sheffield 2.00
165 Fred McGriff 2.00
166 Hideo Nomo 2.00
167 Mike Piazza 4.00
168 Sandy Alomar Jr. 2.00
169 Roberto Alomar 2.00
170 Ted Williams 6.00
171 Pedro J. Martinez 4.00
172 Derek Jeter 8.00
173 Cal Ripken Jr. 8.00
174 Torii Hunter 2.00
175 Alfonso Soriano 3.00
176 Hank Blalock 2.00
177 Ichiro Suzuki 4.00
178 Orlando Rodriguez **RC** 4.00
179 Ramon Ramirez **RC** 4.00
180 Kazuo Matsui **RC** 6.00
181 Kevin Cave **RC** 4.00
182 John Gall **RC** 4.00
183 Freddy Guzman **RC** 4.00
184 Chris Oxspring **RC** 4.00
185 Rusty Tucker **RC** 4.00
186 Jorge Sequea **RC** 4.00
187 Carlos Hines **RC** 4.00
188 Luis Gonzalez 4.00
189 Ryan Wing 4.00
190 Jeff Bennett **RC** 4.00
191 Luis Gonzalez 4.00

Silver

Stars (1-90): 2-4X
Production 499
SP (91-132, 178-191): 1X
Production 249

Gold

Stars (1-90): 4-8X
Gold SP (91-132, 178-191): 2X
Production 99
Gold (133-177): 1-1.5X
Production 499

Chirography

NM/M
Bronze: 1X
Production 65
Bronze Duo Tone: 1X
Production 60
Gold: 1-1.5X
Production 40
Gold Duo Tone: No Pricing
Production 20
Silver: 1X
Production 60
Silver Duo Tone: 1.5-2X
Production 30
Duo Tone: 1X
Production 75
AB Bobby Abreu 15.00
GA Garret Anderson 15.00
RB Rocco Baldelli 20.00
JB Josh Beckett 20.00
CB Carlos Beltran 30.00
HB Hank Blalock 20.00
BB Bret Boone 20.00
MC Miguel Cabrera 40.00
EC Eric Chavez 20.00
DE Dennis Eckersley 30.00
WE Willie Eyre 8.00
EG Eric Gagne 30.00
JG Juan Gonzalez 20.00
KG Ken Griffey Jr. 120.00
TH Travis Hafner 15.00
HY Roy Halladay 20.00
HA Robby Hammock 10.00
BH Bo Hart 8.00
HE Runelvys Hernandez 8.00
HI Bobby Hill 10.00
DJ Derek Jeter 150.00
JJ Jacque Jones 15.00
AK Austin Kearns 15.00
CL Cliff Lee 15.00
AL Al Leiter 15.00
PL Paul LoDuca 15.00
JL Javy Lopez 15.00
ML Mike Lowell 15.00
EM Edgar Martinez 25.00
RO Roy Oswalt 20.00
PA Corey Patterson 15.00
PI Mike Piazza 125.00
CP Colin Porter 10.00
JP Jorge Posada 25.00
MP Mark Prior 30.00
HR Horacio Ramirez 15.00
JR Jose Reyes 35.00
CR Cal Ripken Jr. 100.00
JS Jae Weong Seo 15.00
BS Ben Sheets 20.00
SM John Smoltz 60.00
MT Mark Teixeira 25.00
JV Javier Vazquez 20.00
CW Chien-Ming Wang 125.00
RW Rickie Weeks 20.00
BW Brandon Webb 15.00
VW Vernon Wells 15.00
JW Jerome Williams 10.00
DW Dontrelle Willis 30.00
KW Kerry Wood 25.00
DY Delmon Young 25.00
BZ Barry Zito 20.00

Chirography Dual

NM/M
Common Duo: 40.00
Production 50 Sets
BC Bret Boone, Eric Chavez 50.00
BL Mike Lowell, Josh Beckett 50.00
BP Corey Patterson, Carlos Beltran 50.00
BT Hank Blalock, Mark Teixeira 50.00
EG Dennis Eckersley, Eric Gagne 50.00
HW Vernon Wells, Roy Halladay 40.00
JM Johnny Bench, Mike Piazza 200.00
KG Ken Griffey Jr., Austin Kearns 100.00
PB Yogi Berra, Jorge Posada 100.00
RR Alex Rodriguez, Cal Ripken Jr. 400.00
SG Ken Griffey Jr., Ichiro Suzuki 375.00
SM Stan Musial, Ozzie Smith 175.00
WC Miguel Cabrera, Dontrelle Willis 70.00
WJ Chien-Ming Wang, Derek Jeter 350.00
WR Nolan Ryan, Kerry Wood 225.00
WW Dontrelle Willis, Brandon Webb 50.00
YW Delmon Young, Rickie Weeks 50.00
ZC Eric Chavez, Barry Zito 50.00

Chirography Triple

NM/M
Production 25 Sets
BWR Kerry Wood, Nolan Ryan, Josh Beckett 250.00
FBB Johnny Bench, Carlton Fisk, Yogi Berra 300.00
GSM Bob Gibson, Stan Musial, Ozzie Smith 220.00
JVB Derek Jeter, Yogi Berra, Javier Vazquez 250.00
PRC Jose Reyes, Miguel Cabrera, Colin Porter 100.00
RBT Hank Blalock, Mark Teixeira, Alex Rodriguez 250.00
RRR Alex Rodriguez, Cal Ripken Jr., Phil Rizzuto 400.00
SJB Rocco Baldelli, Jacque Jones, Ichiro Suzuki 275.00
WLE Chien-Ming Wang, Willie Eyre, Cliff Lee 275.00
WPB Mark Prior, Josh Beckett, Brandon Webb 250.00
YYM Robin Yount, Carl Yastrzemski, Stan Musial 300.00
ZHO Barry Zito, Roy Oswalt, Roy Halladay 200.00

Chirography Quad

No Pricing
Production 10 Sets

Chirography Hall of Famers

NM/M
Production 40 Sets
Duo Tone: No Pricing
Production 25
LA Luis Aparicio 20.00
JB Johnny Bench 60.00
YB Yogi Berra 50.00
BD Bobby Doerr 30.00
DE Dennis Eckersley 30.00
CF Carlton Fisk 30.00
BG Bob Gibson 40.00
MI Monte Irvin 20.00
AK Al Kaline 50.00
HK Harmon Killebrew 65.00
RK Ralph Kiner 25.00
PM Paul Molitor 30.00
SM Stan Musial 100.00
TP Tony Perez 30.00
KP Kirby Puckett 100.00
PR Phil Rizzuto 40.00
RR Robin Roberts 40.00
BR Brooks Robinson 40.00
NR Nolan Ryan 120.00
MS Mike Schmidt 120.00
TS Tom Seaver 40.00
OS Ozzie Smith 65.00
DS Duke Snider 30.00
CY Carl Yastrzemski 75.00
RY Robin Yount 75.00

Future Watch Autograph

NM/M
Production 295 8.00
91 Angel Chavez 8.00
92 Brandon Medders 8.00
93 Carlos Vasquez 10.00
94 Chris Aguila 8.00
95 Colby Miller 10.00
96 David Crouthers 10.00
97 Dennis Sarfate 8.00
98 Donnie Kelly 10.00
99 Merkin Valdez 15.00
100 Eddy Rodriguez 15.00
101 Edwin Moreno 10.00
102 Enemencio Pacheco 10.00
103 Roberto Novoa 8.00
104 Greg Dobbs 8.00
105 Hector Gimenez 8.00
106 Ian Snell 30.00
107 Jake Woods 10.00
108 Jamie Brown 8.00
109 Jason Frasor 10.00
110 Jerome Gamble 8.00
111 Jerry Gil 12.00
112 Jesse Harper 8.00
113 Jorge Vasquez 12.00
114 Jose Capellan 10.00
115 Josh Labandeira 10.00
116 Justin Hampson 8.00
117 Justin Huisman 8.00
118 Justin Leone 15.00
119 Lincoln Holdzkom 8.00
120 Lino Urdaneta 10.00
121 Mike Gosling 10.00
122 Mike Johnston 10.00
123 Mike Rouse 10.00
124 Scott Proctor 15.00
125 Roman Colon 10.00
126 Ronny Cedeno 15.00
127 Ryan Meaux 10.00
128 Scott Dohmann 8.00
129 Sean Henn 15.00
130 Tim Bausher 10.00
131 Tim Bittner 8.00
132 William Bergolla 10.00
178 Orlando Rodriguez 10.00
179 Ramon Ramirez 10.00
181 Kevin Cave 10.00
182 John Gall 15.00
183 Freddy Guzman 10.00
184 Chris Oxspring 10.00
185 Rusty Tucker 10.00
186 Jorge Sequea 10.00
187 Carlos Hines 8.00
188 Luis Gonzalez 10.00
189 Ryan Wing 10.00
190 Jeff Bennett 10.00
191 Luis Gonzalez 10.00

USA Signature

NM/M

Production 445 Sets
Reds: 1.5X
Production 50
USA-1 Ernie Young 6.00
USA-2 Chris Burke 12.00
USA-3 Jesse Crain 15.00
USA-4 Justin Duchscherer 15.00
USA-5 J.D. Durbin 10.00
USA-6 Gerald Laird 10.00
USA-7 John Grabow 8.00
USA-8 Gabe Gross 15.00
USA-9 J.J. Hardy 15.00
USA-10 Jeremy Reed 15.00
USA-11 Graham Koonce 10.00
USA-12 Mike Lamb 10.00
USA-13 Justin Leone 15.00
USA-14 Ryan Madson 12.00
USA-15 Joe Mauer 40.00
USA-16 Todd Williams 6.00
USA-17 Horacio Ramirez 15.00
USA-18 Mike Rouse 15.00
USA-19 Jason Stanford 10.00
USA-20 John Van Benschoten 10.00
USA-21 Grady Sizemore 40.00

2004 SP Game Used Patch

NM/M

Complete Set (119):
Common (1-60): 2.00
Common (61-90): 2.00
Quantity produced listed
Common (91-119): 6.00
Production 375
Box (1:Pack): 125.00
1 Miguel Cabrera 4.00
2 Alex Rodriguez 10.00
3 Edgar Renteria 2.50
4 Juan Gonzalez 2.50
5 Mike Lowell 2.50
6 Andruw Jones 3.00
7 Eric Chavez 2.00
8 Jim Edmonds 2.00
9 Mike Piazza 5.00
10 Angel Berroa 2.00
11 Eric Gagne 3.00
12 Jody Gerut 2.00
13 Orlando Cabrera 2.00
14 Austin Kearns 2.00
15 Frank Thomas 3.00
16 Johan Santana 3.00
17 Randy Johnson 4.00
18 Preston Wilson 2.00
19 Garret Anderson 2.50
20 Jorge Posada 3.00
21 Rich Harden 2.00
22 Barry Zito 2.50
23 Gary Sheffield 3.00
24 Jose Reyes 3.00
25 Roy Halladay 2.50
26 Ben Sheets 2.00
27 Geoff Jenkins 2.00
28 Josh Beckett 3.00
29 Roy Oswalt 2.50
30 Bobby Abreu 2.50
31 Hank Blalock 2.50
32 Kerry Wood 2.50
33 Ryan Klesko 2.00
34 Rafael Furcal 2.00
35 Tom Glavine 2.50
36 Kevin Brown 2.50
37 Scott Rolen 3.00
38 Bret Boone 2.50
39 Ichiro Suzuki 6.00
40 Lance Berkman 3.00
41 Tim Hudson 2.50
42 Carlos Delgado 3.00
43 Ivan Rodriguez 3.00
44 Luis Gonzalez 2.00
45 Torii Hunter 2.00
46 Carlos Lee 2.00
47 Jacque Jones 2.00
48 Manny Ramirez 3.00
49 Troy Glaus 2.50
50 Corey Patterson 2.00
51 Jason Schmidt 2.50
52 Mark Mulder 2.00
53 Vernon Wells 2.00
54 Curt Schilling 4.00
55 Javy Lopez 2.50
56 Mark Prior 3.00
57 Dontrelle Willis 2.50
58 Derek Jeter 10.00
59 Jeff Bagwell 3.00
60 Marlon Byrd 2.00
61 Rafael Palmeiro/500 3.00
62 Kevin Millwood/165 2.00
63 Greg Maddux/273 6.00
64 Adam Dunn/400 3.00
65 Richie Sexson/469 3.00
66 Magglio Ordonez/567 2.00
67 Hideo Nomo/236 2.00
68 Albert Pujols/194 10.00
69 Rocco Baldelli/368 3.00
70 Mark Teixeira/86 4.00
71 Jason Giambi/660 3.00
72 Alfonso Soriano/230 4.00
73 Roger Clemens/300 8.00
74 Miguel Tejada/359 2.00
75 Jeff Kent/684 2.00
76 Bernie Williams/342 3.00
77 Sammy Sosa/470 6.00
78 Mike Mussina/641 3.00
79 Jim Thome/334 4.00
80 Brian Giles/506 2.00
81 Shawn Green/234 2.00
82 Mike Sweeney/340 2.00
83 John Smoltz/262 3.00
84 Carlos Beltran/319 3.00
85 Todd Helton/384 3.00
86 Nomar Garciaparra/372 4.00
87 Ken Griffey Jr./481 8.00
88 Chipper Jones/633 4.00
89 Vladimir Guerrero/226 4.00
90 Pedro Martinez/313 5.00
91 Brandon Medders **RC** 6.00
92 Colby Miller **RC** 6.00
93 David Crouthers 6.00
94 Dennis Sarfate **RC** 8.00
95 Donald Kelly **RC** 6.00
96 Alec Zumwalt **RC** 6.00
97 Chris Aguila **RC** 6.00
98 Greg Dobbs **RC** 6.00
99 Ian Snell **RC** 10.00
100 Jake Woods 6.00
101 Jamie Brown **RC** 6.00
102 Jason Frasor **RC** 6.00
103 Jerome Gamble **RC** 6.00
104 Jesse Harper **RC** 6.00
105 Josh Labandeira **RC** 6.00
106 Justin Hampson **RC** 6.00
107 Justin Huisman **RC** 6.00
108 Justin Leone **RC** 6.00
109 Lincoln Holdzkom **RC** 6.00
110 Mike Bumatay **RC** 6.00
111 Mike Gosling 6.00
112 Mike Johnston **RC** 6.00
113 Mike Rouse 6.00
114 Nick Regilio **RC** 6.00
115 Ryan Meaux **RC** 6.00
116 Scott Dohmann **RC** 6.00
117 Sean Henn 8.00
118 Tim Bausher **RC** 6.00
119 Tim Bittner **RC** 6.00

Logo Threads

No Pricing
Production One Set

Logo Threads Autograph

No Pricing
Production One Set

All-Star Patch Autograph

Production 10 Sets

All-Star Patch Auto-Dual

Production 10 Sets

All-Star Patch Gold

NM/M

Production 50 Sets
AP Albert Pujols 75.00
AR Alex Rodriguez 50.00
AS Alfonso Soriano 25.00
BZ Barry Zito 25.00
CD Carlos Delgado 20.00
CJ Chipper Jones 30.00
CS Curt Schilling 35.00
DJ Derek Jeter 85.00
EC Eric Chavez 20.00

FT Frank Thomas 30.00
GS Gary Sheffield 20.00
HE Todd Helton 25.00
HN Hideo Nomo 50.00
IS Ichiro Suzuki 80.00
JG Juan Gonzalez 20.00
JT Jim Thome 30.00
KG Ken Griffey Jr. 50.00
MP Mark Prior 30.00
SS Sammy Sosa 40.00
TH Tim Hudson 25.00
VW Vernon Wells 20.00

All-Star Patch Number

NM/M

Quantity produced listed
AJ Andruw Jones/25 30.00
AP Andy Pettitte/46 25.00
BZ Barry Zito/50 30.00
CD Carlos Delgado/25 25.00
CS Curt Schilling/38 30.00
FT Frank Thomas/35 40.00
GM Greg Maddux/31 50.00
IS Ichiro Suzuki/50 65.00
JG Juan Gonzalez/19 35.00
JP Jorge Posada/20 30.00
JT Jim Thome/25 30.00
KG Ken Griffey Jr./30 60.00
MM Mike Mussina/35 30.00
MO Magglio Ordonez/30 25.00
PM Pedro Martinez/45 35.00
RC Roger Clemens/22 50.00
RH Roy Halladay/32 25.00
RP Rafael Palmeiro/25 30.00
SG Shawn Green/15 30.00
SR Scott Rolen/27 35.00
SS Sammy Sosa/21 80.00

Famous Nicknames

NM/M

Quantity produced listed
BR Brooks Robinson/23 25.00
CR Cal Ripken Jr./21 140.00
CY Carl Yastrzemski/23 70.00
DM Don Mattingly/14 50.00
DS Darryl Strawberry/17 25.00
ES Duke Snider/18 45.00
FT Frank Thomas/14 40.00
GA Sparky Anderson/27 25.00
GC Gary Carter/19 30.00
HK Harmon Killebrew/22 50.00
JF Nellie Fox/19 120.00
JG Juan Gonzalez/15 35.00
JH "Catfish" Hunter/15 35.00
KG Ken Griffey Jr./15 80.00
LB Yogi Berra/19 50.00
MM Mike Mussina/13 35.00
NR Nolan Ryan/27 60.00
OC Orlando Cepeda/17 25.00
OS Ozzie Smith/19 60.00
PN Phil Niekro/24 25.00
RC Roger Clemens/20 60.00
RI Phil Rizzuto/13 50.00
RJ Randy Johnson/16 40.00
RY Robin Yount/20 40.00
TS Tom Seaver/20 60.00
SM Stan Musial/22 85.00
SS Sammy Sosa/15 50.00
WS Willie Stargell/21 40.00

Famous Nicknames Autograph

NM/M

Production 50 Sets
AD Andre Dawson 45.00
AR Alex Rodriguez 150.00
BM Bill Mazeroski 65.00
BR Brooks Robinson 60.00
DM Don Mattingly 120.00
FT Frank Thomas 70.00
HK Harmon Killebrew 70.00
HM Hideki Matsui 350.00
JB Jeff Bagwell 80.00
JG Juan Gonzalez 50.00
KG Ken Griffey Jr. 160.00
LJ Chipper Jones 80.00
MM Mike Mussina 60.00
NR Nolan Ryan 125.00
OS Ozzie Smith 90.00
PN Phil Niekro 45.00
RC Roger Clemens 150.00
RY Robin Yount 80.00
TS Tom Seaver 65.00
WI Dontrelle Willis 60.00

Hall of Fame Numbers

NM/M

Quantity produced listed
AJ Andruw Jones/25 30.00
BG Bob Gibson/45 35.00
BW Billy Williams/26 20.00
CD Carlos Delgado/25 25.00
CH Jim "Catfish" Hunter/27 40.00
CL Roger Clemens/22 50.00
CS Curt Schilling/38 25.00
DD Don Drysdale/50 35.00
DS Don Sutton/20 25.00
EG Eric Gagne/38 25.00
EM Eddie Mathews/41 50.00
FR Frank Robinson/20 25.00
FT Frank Thomas/35 40.00
GL Tom Glavine/47 25.00
GM Greg Maddux/31 45.00
GO Juan Gonzalez/35 35.00
GP Gaylord Perry/36 25.00
HE Todd Helton/17 35.00
IS Ichiro Suzuki/50 65.00
JC Jose Canseco/33 25.00
JG Jason Giambi/25 30.00
JI Jim Thome/25 30.00
JP Jim Palmer/22 35.00
KG Ken Griffey Jr./30 60.00
MA Juan Marichal/27 25.00
MP Mike Piazza/31 40.00
MR Manny Ramirez/24 30.00
MS Mike Schmidt/20 60.00
MZ Pedro Martinez/45 25.00
NR Nolan Ryan/34 70.00
OC Orlando Cepeda/30 20.00
PI Mark Prior/22 40.00
RC Roberto Clemente/21 200.00
RF Rollie Fingers/34 25.00
RH Rickey Henderson/25 40.00
RP Rafael Palmeiro/25 30.00
RY Robin Yount/19 45.00
SC Steve Carlton/32 30.00
SG Shawn Green/15 25.00
SR Scott Rolen/27 30.00
SS Sammy Sosa/21 50.00
TG Tony Gwynn/19 45.00
TH Tim Hudson/15 25.00
TS Tom Seaver/41 25.00
WB Wade Boggs/26 30.00
WS Warren Spahn/21 65.00

Hall of Fame Numbers Autograph

Production 10 Sets

Hall of Fame Numbers Auto Dual

Production 10 Sets

Historic Cut Signatures

Production One Set

Legendary Fabrics

NM/M

Production 50 unless noted. 20.00
BE Johnny Bench 25.00
BG Bob Gibson 30.00
BW Billy Williams 25.00
CH "Catfish" Hunter 25.00
CR Cal Ripken Jr. 60.00
CY Carl Yastrzemski/31 45.00
EM Eddie Mathews 35.00
FR Frank Robinson 25.00
GP Gaylord Perry 20.00
HK Harmon Killebrew 40.00
JC Jose Canseco 40.00
JM Joe Morgan 20.00
JT Joe Torre 25.00
LA Luis Aparicio 25.00
LD Leo Durocher 30.00
MS Mike Schmidt 40.00
NR Nolan Ryan 50.00
OC Orlando Cepeda 20.00
OS Ozzie Smith 35.00
PO Paul O'Neill 20.00
RF Rollie Fingers 20.00
RY Robin Yount 35.00
SC Steve Carlton 25.00
TS Tom Seaver 30.00
WS Warren Spahn 40.00

Legendary Fabrics Autograph Dual

NM/M

Production 25 unless noted.
AD Andre Dawson 60.00
BE Johnny Bench 90.00
BR Brooks Robinson 90.00
BW Billy Williams 65.00
CR Cal Ripken Jr. 275.00
CY Carl Yastrzemski/17 125.00
DE Dwight Evans 60.00
DM Don Mattingly 150.00
DS Don Sutton 65.00
FL Fred Lynn 70.00
FR Frank Robinson 75.00
GP Gaylord Perry 40.00
HK Harmon Killebrew 100.00
JC Jose Canseco 100.00
JM Joe Morgan 50.00
JP Jim Palmer 60.00
JT Joe Torre 70.00
KP Kirby Puckett 100.00
LA Luis Aparicio 70.00
LB Lou Brock/13 125.00
NR Nolan Ryan 200.00
OC Orlando Cepeda 50.00
OS Ozzie Smith 100.00
PM Paul Molitor 75.00
PO Paul O'Neill 70.00
RC Roger Clemens 150.00
RF Rollie Fingers 65.00
RY Robin Yount 120.00
SG Steve Garvey 60.00
ST Darryl Strawberry 65.00
TG Tony Gwynn 120.00
TS Tom Seaver 85.00
WB Wade Boggs 100.00
WI Maury Wills 50.00

Legendary Combo Cuts

Production One Set

Masters

NM/M

Quantity produced listed
AJ Andruw Jones/25 25.00
BE Josh Beckett/25 40.00
CD Carlos Delgado/25 25.00
CS Curt Schilling/38 25.00
FT Frank Thomas/35 30.00
GM Greg Maddux/31 45.00
GO Juan Gonzalez/19 30.00
HE Todd Helton/17 35.00
IS Ichiro Suzuki/50 65.00
JG Jason Giambi/25 30.00
JP Jorge Posada/20 30.00
JT Jim Thome/25 30.00
KG Ken Griffey Jr./30 60.00
MO Magglio Ordonez/30 20.00
MP Mark Prior/22 40.00
MR Manny Ramirez/24 25.00
PI Mike Piazza/31 40.00
PM Pedro Martinez/45 25.00
RC Roger Clemens/22 50.00
RH Roy Halladay/32 25.00
SG Shawn Green/15 25.00
SR Scott Rolen/27 30.00
SS Sammy Sosa/21 50.00
TH Tim Hudson/15 25.00

MVP Patch

NM/M

Production 25 Sets
AR Alex Rodriguez 60.00
BR Brooks Robinson 50.00
BW Bernie Williams 35.00
CJ Chipper Jones 40.00
CR Cal Ripken Jr. 90.00
CS Curt Schilling 35.00
DJ Derek Jeter 75.00
FT Frank Thomas 40.00
GA Garret Anderson 30.00
IS Ichiro Suzuki 75.00
IV Ivan Rodriguez 40.00
JB Josh Beckett 30.00
JG Jason Giambi 30.00
KG Ken Griffey Jr. 60.00
MP Mike Piazza 35.00
MT Miguel Tejada 40.00
PM Pedro Martinez 45.00
RC Roger Clemens 60.00
RJ Randy Johnson 40.00
SS Sammy Sosa 40.00
TG Troy Glaus 25.00

Premium Patch

NM/M

Production 50 unless noted.
AD Adam Dunn 30.00
AP Albert Pujols 50.00
AR Alex Rodriguez 50.00
AR1 Alex Rodriguez/Yankees 65.00
AS Alfonso Soriano/34 35.00
BE Josh Beckett 25.00
BW Bernie Williams 25.00
BZ Barry Zito 25.00
CD Carlos Delgado 25.00
CJ Chipper Jones 35.00
CS Curt Schilling 25.00
DJ Derek Jeter 60.00
DW Dontrelle Willis 20.00
EC Eric Chavez 20.00
FT Frank Thomas 40.00
GM Greg Maddux 40.00
GO Juan Gonzalez 25.00
HM Hideki Matsui/17 120.00
IR Ivan Rodriguez 30.00
IS Ichiro Suzuki 65.00
JB Jeff Bagwell 30.00
JG Jason Giambi 30.00
JP Jorge Posada 30.00
JT Jim Thome 30.00
KB Kevin Brown 20.00
KG Ken Griffey Jr. 50.00
MO Magglio Ordonez 20.00
MP Mark Prior 30.00
MR Manny Ramirez 30.00
MT Miguel Tejada 20.00
PI Mike Piazza 35.00
NR Nolan Ryan 50.00
PM Pedro Martinez 30.00
RC Roger Clemens 40.00
RH Roy Halladay 20.00
RI Mariano Rivera 30.00
RJ Randy Johnson 30.00
RP Rafael Palmeiro 30.00
SG Shawn Green 20.00
SR Scott Rolen 30.00
SS Sammy Sosa 35.00
TE Mark Teixeira 20.00
TG Tom Glavine 25.00
TH Tim Hudson 25.00

Premium Patch Autograph

NM/M

Production 50 unless noted.
AK Austin Kearns 45.00
AR Alex Rodriguez 150.00
BZ Barry Zito 60.00
CD Carlos Delgado 50.00
DW Dontrelle Willis 60.00
EC Eric Chavez 40.00
EG Eric Gagne 60.00
HM Hideki Matsui 350.00
IR Ivan Rodriguez 80.00
IS Ichiro Suzuki 300.00
KB Kevin Brown 45.00
KG Ken Griffey Jr. 160.00
MP Mark Prior 60.00
MT Miguel Tejada 50.00
NG Nomar Garciaparra/33 140.00
RC Roger Clemens 150.00
SG Shawn Green 50.00
TH Tim Hudson 50.00
TG Troy Glaus 50.00
VG Vladimir Guerrero 75.00

Significant Numbers

NM/M

Quantity produced listed
CR Cal Ripken Jr./21 120.00
CS Curt Schilling/16 40.00
CY Carl Yastrzemski/23 65.00
DS Darryl Strawberry/17 25.00
EM Eddie Mathews/17 50.00
FT Frank Thomas/14 50.00
GM Greg Maddux/18 50.00
GO Juan Gonzalez/15 40.00
GS Gary Sheffield/16 30.00
JB Jeff Bagwell/13 50.00
KG Ken Griffey Jr./15 75.00
NR Nolan Ryan/27 60.00
PO Paul O'Neill/17 25.00
RC Roger Clemens/20 50.00
RF Rollie Fingers/17 25.00
RJ Randy Johnson/16 35.00
RP Rafael Palmeiro/18 40.00
SN Duke Snider/18 50.00
SS Sammy Sosa/15 60.00
TG Tom Glavine/17 30.00
TS Tom Seaver/20 40.00

Significant Numbers Autograph

NM/M

Production 50 unless noted.
AR Alex Rodriguez 150.00
BA Bobby Abreu 40.00
BG Brian Giles 40.00
BW Bernie Williams 100.00
BZ Barry Zito 60.00
CD Carlos Delgado 50.00
CJ Chipper Jones 90.00
EC Eric Chavez 40.00
EG Eric Gagne 60.00
GM Greg Maddux 110.00
HE Todd Helton 60.00
GO Juan Gonzalez 50.00
HM Hideki Matsui 350.00
KB Kevin Brown 45.00
KG Ken Griffey Jr. 160.00
LB Lou Brock/16 60.00
LG Luis Gonzalez 50.00
MM Mike Mussina 60.00
MP Mike Piazza 185.00

MS Mike Schmidt 90.00
MT Miguel Tejada 50.00
NR Nolan Ryan 140.00
PB Pat Burrell 40.00
PO Paul O'Neill 65.00
PR Mark Prior 60.00
RA Roberto Alomar 60.00
RB Rocco Baldelli 55.00
RF Rollie Fingers 40.00
RO Roy Oswalt 60.00
RP Rafael Palmeiro 70.00
RS Ryne Sandberg 90.00
SG Shawn Green 50.00
TG Tom Glavine 60.00
TH Tim Hudson 50.00
VG Vladimir Guerrero 75.00

Significant Numbers Autograph Dual

NM/M
Production 25 unless noted.
AR Alex Rodriguez 200.00
BA Bobby Abreu 50.00
BG Brian Giles 50.00
BW Bernie Williams 120.00
BZ Barry Zito 80.00
CD Carlos Delgado 70.00
CJ Chipper Jones 100.00
DW Dontrelle Willis 60.00
EC Eric Chavez 65.00
EG Eric Gagne 80.00
GI Bob Gibson 100.00
GL Troy Glaus 70.00
GM Greg Maddux 140.00
HE Todd Helton 85.00
GO Juan Gonzalez 60.00
HM Hideki Matsui 500.00
KB Kevin Brown 65.00
KG Ken Griffey Jr. 200.00
KP Kirby Puckett 100.00
LB Lou Brock/14 85.00
LG Luis Gonzalez 50.00
MM Mike Mussina 80.00
MP Mike Piazza 200.00
MS Mike Schmidt 160.00
MT Miguel Tejada 50.00
NR Nolan Ryan 200.00
PB Pat Burrell 50.00
PO Paul O'Neill 80.00
RA Roberto Alomar 80.00
RF Rollie Fingers 65.00
RP Rafael Palmeiro 100.00
RS Ryne Sandberg 150.00
SG Shawn Green 60.00
TG Tom Glavine 80.00
TH Tim Hudson 75.00
VG Vladimir Guerrero 100.00
TO Tony Gwynn 120.00
TS Tom Seaver 85.00

Star Potential Patch

NM/M
Quantity produced listed
BW Brandon Webb/50 25.00
CP Corey Patterson/20 25.00
DW Dontrelle Willis/35 30.00
HA Roy Halladay/32 30.00
IS Ichiro Suzuki/50 65.00
HB Josh Beckett/21 30.00
LB Lance Berkman/17 30.00
MM Mark Mulder/20 30.00
MP Mark Prior/22 30.00
MT Mark Teixeira/23 25.00
RH Rich Harden/40 25.00
RO Roy Oswalt/44 25.00
RW Rickie Weeks/23 25.00
TG Troy Glaus/25 30.00
TH Tim Hudson/15 30.00

Stellar Combos

NM/M
Production 25 unless noted.
AD Derek Jeter, Alfonso Soriano 75.00
AJ Alex Rodriguez, Juan Gonzalez 50.00
AT Jim Thome, Bobby Abreu 40.00
BK Jeff Bagwell, Jeff Kent 30.00
BT Mark Teixeira, Hank Blalock 40.00
CA Roberto Alomar, Joe Carter 60.00
CO Roger Clemens, Roy Oswalt 60.00
CR Randy Johnson, Curt Schilling 40.00
DG Jason Giambi, Carlos Delgado 40.00
DK Austin Kearns, Adam Dunn 40.00
GH Eric Gagne, Trevor Hoffman 40.00
GT Greg Maddux, Tom Glavine 65.00
JJ Andruw Jones, Chipper Jones 50.00
KR Nolan Ryan, Jerry Koosman 100.00
LP Mike Piazza, Al Leiter 50.00
LS Fred Lynn, Ichiro Suzuki 75.00
MG Don Mattingly, Jason Giambi 80.00
MT Frank Thomas, Edgar Martinez 50.00
MY Paul Molitor, Robin Yount 60.00
NB Hideo Nomo, Kevin Brown 40.00
NY Alfonso Soriano, Jose Reyes 40.00
PC Mark Prior, Roger Clemens 60.00
PE Albert Pujols, Jim Edmonds 80.00
PM Mike Mussina, Andy Pettitte 50.00
PP Mike Piazza, Jorge Posada 60.00
PS Sammy Sosa, Rafael Palmeiro 50.00
RB Ivan Rodriguez, Josh Beckett 50.00
RJ Alex Rodriguez, Derek Jeter 100.00
RR Alex Rodriguez, Cal Ripken Jr. 180.00
RS Mike Schmidt, Brooks Robinson 85.00
SG Shawn Green, Duke Snider 40.00
SJ Randy Johnson, Gary Sheffield 40.00
SM Pedro Martinez, Curt Schilling 50.00
SR Nolan Ryan, Curt Schilling 75.00
TO Frank Thomas, Magglio Ordonez 60.00
WC Roger Clemens, David Wells 50.00
WH Larry Walker, Todd Helton 45.00
WS Sammy Sosa, Billy Williams 60.00
ZH Barry Zito, Tim Hudson 50.00
RJ Alex Rodriguez, Derek Jeter 100.00
RG Cal Ripken Jr., Lou Gehrig 350.00
SC Ty Cobb, Ichiro Suzuki 180.00

Team Threads

Production 10 unless noted.

Triple Authentic

Production 10

World Series Stars

NM/M
Production 50 unless noted.
AJ Andruw Jones 25.00
AP Andy Pettitte/15 40.00
AS Alfonso Soriano/15 35.00
BL Barry Larkin 25.00
BW Bernie Williams 25.00
CA Jose Canseco 30.00
CJ Chipper Jones 30.00
CS Curt Schilling 25.00
CY Carl Yastrzemski/31 50.00
DW Dontrelle Willis 20.00
GA Garret Anderson 25.00
GL Troy Glaus 30.00
GM Greg Maddux 40.00
HM Hideki Matsui/17 140.00
IR Ivan Rodriguez 30.00
JB Josh Beckett 25.00
JE Derek Jeter 60.00
JM Joe Morgan 25.00
JP Jorge Posada 30.00
JT Jim Thome 25.00
KB Kevin Brown 20.00
MM Mike Mussina/43 25.00
MP Mike Piazza 35.00
MR Mariano Rivera 30.00
MS Mike Schmidt 40.00
PM Paul Molitor 30.00
PO Paul O'Neill 20.00
RC Roger Clemens 40.00
RF Rollie Fingers 25.00
RJ Randy Johnson 30.00
TG Tom Glavine 25.00

World Series Stars Autograph

No Pricing
Production One Set

300 Win Club

Production 10 Sets

Autographed 300 Win Club

Production 10 Sets

500 HR Club

Production 10 Sets

Autographed 500 HR Club

Production 10 Sets

500 HR Club Triple Patches

Production 10 Sets

3000 Hit Club

Production 10 Sets

3000 Hit Club Autograph

Production 10 Sets

2004 SP Legendary Cuts

NM/M
Complete Set (126):
Common Player: .40
Pack (4): 12.00
Box (12): 120.00
1 Al Kaline 1.00
2 Al Lopez .40
3 Alan Trammell .40
4 Andre Dawson .40
5 Babe Ruth 3.00
6 Bert Campaneris .40
7 Bill Mazeroski .40
8 Bill Russell .40
9 Billy Williams .40
10 Bob Feller .50
11 Bob Gibson .75
12 Bob Lemon .40
13 Bobby Doerr .40
14 Brooks Robinson 1.00
15 Cal Ripken Jr. 3.00
16 Carl Yastrzemski 1.00
17 Carlton Fisk .40
18 Jim "Catfish" Hunter .40
19 Dale Murphy .40
20 Darryl Strawberry .40
21 Dave Concepcion .40
22 Dave Winfield .50
23 Dennis Eckersley .40
24 Denny McLain .40
25 Don Drysdale .50
26 Don Larsen .40
27 Don Mattingly 2.00
28 Don Sutton .40
29 Duke Snider 1.00
30 Dusty Baker .40
31 Dwight Gooden .40
32 Earl Weaver .40
33 Early Wynn .40
34 Eddie Mathews 1.00
35 Eddie Murray .75
36 Enos Slaughter .40
37 Ernie Banks 1.50
38 Fergie Jenkins .40
39 Frank Robinson .75
40 Fred Lynn .40
41 Gary Carter .50
42 Gaylord Perry .40
43 George Brett 2.00
44 George Foster .40
45 George Kell .40
46 Greg Luzinski .40
47 Hal Newhouser .40
48 Hank Greenberg 1.00
49 Harmon Killebrew 1.00
50 Honus Wagner 1.00
51 Hoyt Wilhelm .40
52 Jackie Robinson 1.50
53 Jim Bunning .40
54 Jim Palmer .75
55 Jimmie Foxx 1.00
56 Joe Carter .40
57 Joe DiMaggio 2.00
58 Joe Morgan .40
59 Joe Torre .40
60 Johnny Bench 1.00
61 Johnny Podres .40
62 John Roseboro .40
63 Johnny Sain .40
64 Juan Marichal .50
65 Keith Hernandez .40
66 Kirby Puckett .75
67 Kirk Gibson .40
68 Will Clark .50
69 Jim Rice .40
70 Larry Doby .40
71 Lou Boudreau .40
72 Lou Brock .50
73 Lou Gehrig 2.50
74 Lou Piniella .40
75 Luis Aparicio .40
76 Mark Grace .50
77 Mel Ott .40
78 Mickey Lolich .40
79 Mickey Mantle 3.00
80 Mike Greenwell .40
81 Mike Schmidt 2.00
82 Monte Irvin .40
83 Nellie Fox .50
84 Nolan Ryan 3.00
85 Orlando Cepeda .40
86 Ozzie Smith 1.00
87 Paul Molitor .75
88 Pee Wee Reese .40
89 Phil Niekro .40
90 Phil Rizzuto .75
91 Ralph Kiner .75
92 Red Rolfe .40
93 Red Schoendienst .40
94 Reggie Smith .40
95 Rich "Goose" Gossage .40
96 Richie Ashburn .40
97 Rick Ferrell .40
98 Elston Howard .40
99 Roberto Clemente 2.00
100 Robin Roberts .40
101 Robin Yount 1.00
102 Roger Maris 2.00
103 Rollie Fingers .40
104 Ron Santo .40
105 Roy Campanella .75
106 Ryne Sandberg 1.50
107 Sparky Anderson .40
108 Sparky Lyle .40
109 Stan Musial 2.00
110 Steve Carlton .50
111 Steve Garvey .40
112 Ted Williams 2.50
113 Thurman Munson 1.00
114 Tom Seaver 1.00
115 Tommy Henrich .40
116 Tommy Lasorda .40
117 Tony Gwynn 1.00
118 Tony Perez .40
119 Ty Cobb 1.50
120 Wade Boggs .50
121 Warren Spahn .75
122 Whitey Ford .75
123 Willie McCovey .40
124 Willie Randolph .40
125 Willie Stargell .50
126 Yogi Berra .75

All-Time Autos

NM/M
Production 50 Sets
LA Luis Aparicio 20.00
YB Yogi Berra 65.00
WB Wade Boggs 40.00
SC Steve Carlton 20.00
GC Gary Carter 25.00
JC Joe Carter 20.00
OC Orlando Cepeda 25.00
WC Will Clark 40.00
BD Bobby Doerr 20.00
DE Dennis Eckersley 20.00
RF Rollie Fingers 20.00
CF Carlton Fisk 30.00
WF Whitey Ford 40.00
TG Tony Gwynn 50.00
MI Monte Irvin 25.00
FJ Fergie Jenkins 20.00
AK Al Kaline 40.00
GK George Kell 25.00
HK Harmon Killebrew 40.00
FL Fred Lynn 15.00
MA Don Mattingly 60.00
BM Bill Mazeroski 50.00
WM Willie McCovey 40.00
MC Denny McLain 30.00
DM Dale Murphy 30.00
SM Stan Musial 80.00
DN Don Newcombe 25.00
PN Phil Niekro 20.00
TP Tony Perez 25.00
GP Gaylord Perry 20.00
JP Johnny Podres 20.00
CR Cal Ripken Jr. 125.00
RR Robin Roberts 30.00
NR Nolan Ryan 125.00
SA Ryne Sandberg 75.00
RS Red Schoendienst 25.00
TS Tom Seaver 50.00
DS Don Sutton 15.00
BW Billy Williams 20.00
MW Maury Willis 20.00
RY Robin Yount 75.00

Game Graphs

NM/M
Production 25 Sets
Gold: No Pricing
Production 10 Sets
LA Luis Aparicio 25.00
EB Ernie Banks 75.00
JB Johnny Bench 80.00
YB Yogi Berra 80.00
WB Wade Boggs 50.00
GB George Brett 100.00
LB Lou Brock 40.00
SC Steve Carlton 30.00
GC Gary Carter 35.00
JC Joe Carter 30.00
RF Rollie Fingers 25.00
CF Carlton Fisk 50.00
BG Bob Gibson 40.00
TG Tony Gwynn 65.00
AK Al Kaline 50.00
HK Harmon Killebrew 50.00
JM Juan Marichal 35.00
MA Don Mattingly 80.00
BM Bill Mazeroski 50.00
WM Willie McCovey 50.00
PM Paul Molitor 40.00
MO Joe Morgan 40.00
DM Dale Murphy 40.00
EM Eddie Murray 85.00
SM Stan Musial 100.00
PN Phil Niekro 30.00
KP Kirby Puckett 75.00
CR Cal Ripken Jr. 180.00
PR Phil Rizzuto 40.00
BR Brooks Robinson 50.00
FR Frank Robinson 40.00
NR Nolan Ryan 175.00
RS Ryne Sandberg 85.00
MS Mike Schmidt 80.00
TS Tom Seaver 60.00
OS Ozzie Smith 75.00
SN Duke Snider 50.00
DS Don Sutton 20.00
BW Billy Williams 25.00
DW Dave Winfield 30.00
CY Carl Yastrzemski 85.00
RY Robin Yount 85.00

Historic Patches

NM/M
Production 25 Sets
EB Ernie Banks 50.00
GB George Brett 60.00
DD Don Drysdale 40.00
BG Bob Gibson 25.00
TG Tony Gwynn 50.00
EM Eddie Mathews 30.00
SM Stan Musial 60.00
CR Cal Ripken Jr. 100.00
NR Nolan Ryan 75.00
TS Tom Seaver 50.00
DS Duke Snider 30.00
CY Carl Yastrzemski 60.00
RY Robin Yount 50.00

Historic Quads

No Pricing
Production 10 Sets

Historic Swatches

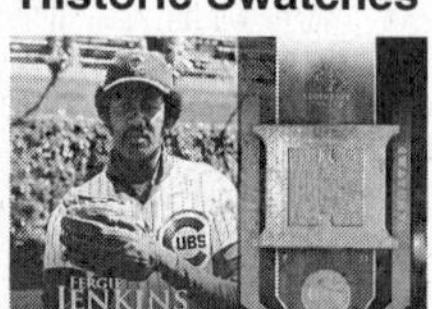

NM/M
Common Swatch: 4.00
Golds: 2X-3X
Production 25 Sets
AN Sparky Anderson 4.00
JB Johnny Bench/SP 10.00
GB George Brett 12.00
LB Lou Brock 8.00
GC Gary Carter 6.00
JC Joe Carter 6.00
DC Dave Concepcion 4.00
DD Don Drysdale 8.00
RF Rollie Fingers 6.00
CF Carlton Fisk 8.00
GF George Foster 4.00
SG Steve Garvey 4.00
CH Jim "Catfish" Hunter 6.00
FJ Fergie Jenkins 8.00
HK Harmon Killebrew 10.00
DL Don Larsen SP 10.00
ML Mickey Lolich 4.00
SL Sparky Lyle 4.00
MA Eddie Mathews 10.00
DM Don Mattingly 15.00
PM Paul Molitor 6.00
JM Joe Morgan 6.00
TM Thurman Munson 12.00
MU Dale Murphy 8.00
EM Eddie Murray/SP 10.00
SM Stan Musial 20.00
PN Phil Niekro 6.00
GP Gaylord Perry 6.00
JP Johnny Podres 6.00
KP Kirby Puckett 10.00
JR Jim Rice 8.00
CR Cal Ripken Jr. 20.00
BR Brooks Robinson 8.00
NR Nolan Ryan 20.00
TS Tom Seaver 8.00
OS Ozzie Smith 10.00
DS Don Sutton 4.00
HW Hoyt Wilhelm 4.00
DW Dave Winfield 6.00
RY Robin Yount 8.00

Legendary Cuts

NM/M
Quantity produced listed
WA Walter Alston/74 200.00
LU Luke Appling/108 150.00
RA Richie Ashburn/31 350.00
LB Lou Boudreau/199 125.00
EC Earle Combs/27 350.00
ST Stan Coveleski/102 150.00
RD Ray Dandridge/199 125.00
DD Dizzy Dean/33 650.00
BD Bill Dickey/82 250.00
JD Joe DiMaggio/111 500.00
DO Larry Doby/14 400.00
DR Don Drysdale/66 450.00
LD Leo Durocher/75 400.00
RF Rick Ferrell/44 160.00
WF Wes Ferrell/36 200.00
FF Frankie Frisch/57 450.00
CG Charlie Gehringer/171 200.00
LG Lefty Gomez/98 325.00
HG Hank Greenberg/37 500.00
BU Burleigh Grimes/83 200.00
GR Lefty Grove/75 375.00
GH Gabby Hartnett/19 475.00
BH Billy Herman/134 125.00
WH Waite Hoyt/106 200.00
CH Carl Hubbell/199 180.00
JH Jim "Catfish" Hunter/25 220.00
BJ "Indian" Bob Johnson/32 200.00
HK Harvey Kuenn/49 150.00
BL Bob Lemon/199 100.00
EL Ernie Lombardi/39 450.00
TL Ted Lyons/199 150.00
RU Rube Marquard/59 220.00
JM Joe Medwick/32 450.00
MI Johnny Mize/118 140.00
HN Hal Newhouser/51 140.00
KN Kid Nichols/4 2,500
SP Satchel Paige/28 1,325
GP George Pipgras/46 200.00
PR Pee Wee Reese/35 350.00
SR Sam Rice/28 500.00
ER Edd Roush/129 125.00
RR Red Ruffing/30 500.00
JS Joe Sewell/199 140.00
GS George Sisler/32 850.00
ES Enos Slaughter/147 125.00
WS Willie Stargell/39 220.00
WM Hoyt Wilhelm/115 100.00
SW "Smokey" Joe Wood/79 400.00
EW Early Wynn/54 200.00

Legendary Duels

NM/M
Production 25 Sets
BG George Brett, Rich "Goose" Gossage 40.00
DW Joe DiMaggio, Ted Williams 150.00
EG Dennis Eckersley, Kirk Gibson 25.00
FM Joe Morgan, Carlton Fisk 30.00
GL Bob Gibson, Mickey Lolich 30.00
MW Mickey Mantle, Ted Williams 200.00
PL Johnny Podres, Don Larsen 30.00
RM Juan Marichal, John Roseboro 25.00
RR Pee Wee Reese, Phil Rizzuto 35.00
SM Duke Snider, Mickey Mantle 125.00
SS Ryne Sandberg, Ozzie Smith 80.00
WB Ernie Banks, Honus Wagner 125.00

Legendary Duels Patch

No Pricing
Production 15 Sets

Legendary Duos

NM/M
Production 25 Sets
CM Joe Morgan, Dave Concepcion 20.00
DM Joe DiMaggio, Mickey Mantle 200.00
LB Yogi Berra, Don Larsen 60.00
MB Yogi Berra, Mickey Mantle 200.00
MM Mickey Mantle, Roger Maris 200.00
MY Paul Molitor, Robin Yount 30.00
PJ Jackie Robinson, Pee Wee Reese 75.00
RR Cal Ripken Jr., Brooks Robinson 65.00
RS Tom Seaver, Nolan Ryan 75.00
SC Roy Campanella, Duke Snider 40.00

SS Johnny Sain, Warren Spahn 40.00
WB Ernie Banks, Billy Williams 40.00

Legendary Duos Patch

No Pricing
Production 15 Sets

Legendary Sigs

NM/M
Production 50 Sets
LA Luis Aparicio 20.00
EB Ernie Banks 60.00
JB Johnny Bench 60.00
WB Wade Boggs 40.00
GC Gary Carter 25.00
JC Joe Carter 20.00
WC Will Clark 40.00
BD Bobby Doerr 20.00
DE Dennis Eckersley 25.00
BF Bob Feller 30.00
RF Rollie Fingers 20.00
BG Bob Gibson 35.00
TG Tony Gwynn 50.00
MI Monte Irvin 25.00
AK Al Kaline 40.00
GK George Kell 25.00
HK Harmon Killebrew 40.00
RK Ralph Kiner 30.00
FL Fred Lynn 15.00
JM Juan Marichal 30.00
MA Don Mattingly 60.00
WM Willie McCovey 40.00
MC Denny McLain 30.00
DM Dale Murphy 30.00
EM Eddie Murray 80.00
DN Don Newcombe 25.00
PA Jim Palmer 30.00
GP Gaylord Perry 20.00
JP Johnny Podres 20.00
CR Cal Ripken Jr. 125.00
PR Phil Rizzuto 25.00
RR Robin Roberts 30.00
BR Brooks Robinson 40.00
SA Ryne Sandberg 75.00
MS Mike Schmidt 60.00
RS Red Schoendienst 25.00
OS Ozzie Smith 65.00
SN Duke Snider 40.00
DS Don Sutton 15.00
MW Maury Wills 20.00
CY Carl Yastrzemski 75.00

Legendary Swatches

NM/M
Common Swatch: 4.00
Golds: No Pricing
Production 15 Sets
EB Ernie Banks/SP 15.00
JB Johnny Bench 10.00
YB Yogi Berra 12.00
WB Wade Boggs 6.00
GB George Brett 12.00
RC Roy Campanella 10.00
SC Steve Carlton 6.00
OC Orlando Cepeda 6.00
BD Bobby Doerr 8.00
DD Don Drysdale 8.00
CF Carlton Fisk 8.00
NF Nellie Fox 10.00
BG Bob Gibson 8.00
TG Tony Gwynn 10.00
EH Elston Howard 8.00
CH Jim "Catfish" Hunter 8.00
AK Al Kaline 10.00
HK Harmon Killebrew 10.00
MA Juan Marichal 8.00
EM Eddie Mathews 10.00
DM Don Mattingly 15.00
WM Willie McCovey 6.00
TM Thurman Munson 12.00
SM Stan Musial 15.00
TP Tony Perez 4.00
PO Johnny Podres 6.00
PR Pee Wee Reese 8.00
JR Jim Rice 8.00
CR Cal Ripken Jr. 20.00
RI Phil Rizzuto 10.00
FR Frank Robinson 6.00
NR Nolan Ryan 20.00
MS Mike Schmidt 15.00
TS Tom Seaver 8.00
DS Duke Snider 10.00
WS Warren Spahn 10.00
ST Willie Stargell 8.00
BW Billy Williams 4.00
DW Dave Winfield 6.00
CY Carl Yastrzemski 10.00
RY Robin Yount 8.00

Marked for the Hall

NM/M
Production 50 Sets
LA Luis Aparicio 20.00
EB Ernie Banks 60.00
JB Johnny Bench 60.00
YB Yogi Berra 65.00
GB George Brett 75.00
LB Lou Brock 30.00
SC Steve Carlton 20.00
GC Gary Carter 25.00
OC Orlando Cepeda 25.00
BD Bobby Doerr 20.00
BF Bob Feller 30.00
CF Carlton Fisk 35.00
WF Whitey Ford 40.00
BG Bob Gibson 35.00
AK Al Kaline 40.00
HK Harmon Killebrew 40.00
RK Ralph Kiner 30.00
MA Juan Marichal 30.00
BM Bill Mazeroski 50.00
WM Willie McCovey 40.00
PM Paul Molitor 40.00
JM Joe Morgan 35.00
EM Eddie Murray 80.00
SM Stan Musial 80.00
PN Phil Niekro 20.00
JP Jim Palmer 30.00
TP Tony Perez 25.00
GP Gaylord Perry 20.00
KP Kirby Puckett 60.00
PR Phil Rizzuto 25.00
RR Robin Roberts 30.00
BR Brooks Robinson 40.00
FR Frank Robinson 30.00
NR Nolan Ryan 125.00
MS Mike Schmidt 60.00
TS Tom Seaver 50.00
OS Ozzie Smith 65.00
DS Duke Snider 40.00
BW Billy Williams 20.00
DW Dave Winfield 30.00
CY Carl Yastrzemski 75.00
RY Robin Yount 75.00

Marks of Greatness

NM/M
Production 50 Sets
EB Ernie Banks 60.00
JB Johnny Bench 60.00
YB Yogi Berra 65.00
WB Wade Boggs 40.00
GB George Brett 75.00
LB Lou Brock 30.00
SC Steve Carlton 20.00
JC Joe Carter 20.00
OC Orlando Cepeda 25.00
WC Will Clark 40.00
RF Rollie Fingers 20.00
CF Carlton Fisk 35.00
WF Whitey Ford 40.00
BG Bob Gibson 35.00
TG Tony Gwynn 50.00
FJ Fergie Jenkins 20.00
AK Al Kaline 40.00
HK Harmon Killebrew 40.00
FL Fred Lynn 15.00
MA Don Mattingly 60.00
MC Denny McLain 30.00
PM Paul Molitor 40.00
JM Joe Morgan 35.00
DM Dale Murphy 30.00
SM Stan Musial 80.00
DN Don Newcombe 25.00
PN Phil Niekro 20.00
JP Jim Palmer 30.00
TP Tony Perez 25.00
KP Kirby Puckett 60.00
CR Cal Ripken Jr. 125.00
BR Brooks Robinson 40.00
FR Frank Robinson 30.00
NR Nolan Ryan 125.00
RS Ryne Sandberg 75.00
MS Mike Schmidt 60.00
TS Tom Seaver 50.00
OZ Ozzie Smith 65.00
DS Duke Snider 40.00
BW Billy Williams 20.00
DW Dave Winfield 30.00
RY Robin Yount 75.00

Significant Swatches

NM/M
Common Swatch: 4.00
Golds: 2-3X
Production 25 Sets
SA Sparky Anderson 4.00
EB Ernie Banks/SP 10.00
LB Lou Brock/SP 8.00
GC Gary Carter 4.00
JC Joe Carter 4.00
OC Orlando Cepeda 6.00
DC Dave Concepcion 4.00
BD Bobby Doerr 8.00
DD Don Drysdale 8.00
RF Rollie Fingers 6.00

CF Carlton Fisk 8.00
GF George Foster 4.00
SG Steve Garvey 4.00
CH Jim "Catfish" Hunter 8.00
FJ Fergie Jenkins 4.00
SL Sparky Lyle 4.00
RM Roger Maris 30.00
ED Eddie Mathews 10.00
MA Don Mattingly 15.00
BM Bill Mazeroski 8.00
WM Willie McCovey 6.00
PM Paul Molitor 6.00
TM Thurman Munson 12.00
DM Dale Murphy 8.00
EM Eddie Murray SP 8.00
PN Phil Niekro 6.00
TP Tony Perez 4.00
GP Gaylord Perry 6.00
JP Johnny Podres 6.00
CR Cal Ripken Jr. 20.00
FR Frank Robinson 6.00
NR Nolan Ryan 20.00
MS Mike Schmidt 15.00
TS Tom Seaver 8.00
SN Duke Snider 10.00
WS Warren Spahn 10.00
ST Willie Stargell 8.00
DS Don Sutton 4.00
HW Hoyt Wilhelm 4.00
DW Dave Winfield 6.00
CY Carl Yastrzemski 10.00
RY Robin Yount 8.00

Significant Trips

No Pricing
Production 15 Sets

Significant Trips Patch

No Pricing
Production 10 Sets

Ultimate Autographs

NM/M
Production 25 Sets
EB Ernie Banks 60.00
JB Johnny Bench 60.00
YB Yogi Berra 60.00
GB George Brett 90.00
LB Lou Brock 35.00
SC Steve Carlton 25.00
DE Dennis Eckersley 25.00
BF Bob Feller 35.00
WF Whitey Ford 40.00
BG Bob Gibson 40.00
MI Monte Irvin 30.00
FJ Fergie Jenkins 30.00
AK Al Kaline 50.00
GK George Kell 25.00
HK Harmon Killebrew 50.00
RK Ralph Kiner 40.00
MA Juan Marichal 30.00
DM Don Mattingly 75.00
BM Bill Mazeroski 40.00
PM Paul Molitor 40.00
JM Joe Morgan 35.00
EM Eddie Murray 80.00
SM Stan Musial 80.00
PA Jim Palmer 40.00
JP Johnny Podres 25.00
KP Kirby Puckett 70.00
PR Phil Rizzuto 35.00
BR Brooks Robinson 40.00
FR Frank Robinson 40.00
NR Nolan Ryan 120.00
SA Ryne Sandberg 80.00
MS Mike Schmidt 75.00
RS Red Schoendienst 25.00
TS Tom Seaver 50.00
OS Ozzie Smith 60.00
SN Duke Snider 50.00
DS Don Sutton 20.00
MW Maury Willis 25.00
DW Dave Winfield 30.00
CY Carl Yastrzemski 80.00
RY Robin Yount 60.00

Ultimate Swatches

NM/M
Common Swatch: 6.00
Golds: No Pricing
Production 10 Sets
EB Ernie Banks 12.00
JB Johnny Bench 10.00
YB Yogi Berra 12.00
WB Wade Boggs 6.00
GB George Brett 12.00
RC Roy Campanella 10.00
SC Steve Carlton 6.00
JD Joe DiMaggio/SP 75.00
DD Don Drysdale 8.00
NF Nellie Fox 12.00
BG Bob Gibson 8.00
HG Hank Greenberg 20.00
TG Tony Gwynn 10.00
CH Jim "Catfish" Hunter 6.00
HK Harmon Killebrew 10.00
MM Mickey Mantle/SP 125.00
MA Juan Marichal 8.00
RM Roger Maris 30.00
EM Eddie Mathews 10.00
DM Don Mattingly 15.00
WM Willie McCovey 6.00
TM Thurman Munson 10.00
SM Stan Musial 15.00
KP Kirby Puckett 10.00
PR Pee Wee Reese 8.00
CR Cal Ripken Jr. 20.00
BR Brooks Robinson 8.00
FR Frank Robinson 6.00
JR Jackie Robinson 40.00
NR Nolan Ryan 20.00
MS Mike Schmidt 15.00
TS Tom Seaver 10.00
OS Ozzie Smith 10.00
DS Duke Snider/SP 10.00
WS Warren Spahn 10.00
HW Honus Wagner/SP 140.00
BW Billy Williams 6.00
TW Ted Williams 60.00
DW Dave Winfield 6.00
CY Carl Yastrzemski 10.00
RY Robin Yount 8.00

2004 SP Prospects

NM/M
Complete Set (447):
Common SP (1-90): .50
1:Pack
Common Rookie (91-290): 1.00
Common Rookie Auto. (291-447): 8.00
Production 400 unless noted.
Overall Autos. 1:5
Pack (5): 9.00
Box (24): 200.00
1 Roger Clemens 3.00
2 Melvin Mora .50
3 Dontrelle Willis .50
4 Jose Vidro .50
5 Oliver Perez .50
6 Carlos Zambrano .50
7 Chipper Jones 1.00
8 Greg Maddux 1.50
9 Curt Schilling 1.00
10 Jose Reyes .75
11 David Ortiz 1.00
12 Mike Piazza 2.00
13 Jason Schmidt .50
14 Randy Johnson 1.00
15 Magglio Ordonez .50
16 Mike Mussina 1.00
17 Jake Peavy .50
18 Jim Edmonds .75
19 Ken Griffey Jr. 1.50
20 Jason Giambi .75
21 Mike Sweeney .50
22 Carlos Lee .50
23 Craig Wilson .50
24 Pedro Martinez 1.00
25 Bobby Abreu .50
26 Mike Lowell .50
27 Miguel Cabrera 1.00
28 Hank Blalock .50
29 Frank Thomas .75
30 Manny Ramirez 1.00
31 Mark Mulder .50
32 Scott Podsednik .50
33 Albert Pujols 3.00
34 Preston Wilson .50
35 Todd Helton .75
36 Victor Martinez .50
37 Kerry Wood .50
38 Carlos Beltran 1.00
39 Vernon Wells .50
40 Sammy Sosa 1.00
41 Pat Burrell .50
42 Tim Hudson .50
43 Eric Gagne .75
44 Jim Thome 1.00
45 Vladimir Guerrero 1.00
46 Travis Hafner .75
47 Rickie Weeks .50
48 Miguel Tejada .75
49 Ivan Rodriguez .75
50 J.D. Drew .50
51 Ben Sheets .50
52 Garret Anderson .50
53 Aubrey Huff .50
54 Nomar Garciaparra 1.00
55 Luis Gonzalez .50
56 Lance Berkman .50
57 Ichiro Suzuki 2.00
58 Torii Hunter .50
59 Adam Dunn .75
60 Mark Teixeira .75
61 Bret Boone .50
62 Roy Oswalt .50
63 Joe Mauer .75
64 Scott Rolen 1.00
65 Hideki Matsui 2.00
66 Richie Sexson .50
67 Jeff Kent .50
68 Barry Zito .50
69 C.C. Sabathia .50
70 Carlos Delgado .50
71 Gary Sheffield .75
72 Shawn Green .50
73 Jason Bay .50
74 Andruw Jones .75
75 Jeff Bagwell .75
76 Rafael Palmeiro .75
77 Alex Rodriguez 3.00
78 Adrian Beltre .50
79 Troy Glaus .50
80 Tom Glavine .50
81 Paul Konerko .50
82 Alfonso Soriano 1.00
83 Roy Halladay .50
84 Derek Jeter 3.00
85 Josh Beckett .50
86 Delmon Young .50
87 Brian Giles .50
88 Eric Chavez .50
89 Lyle Overbay .50
90 Mark Prior .75
91 Shawn Camp **RC** 1.00
92 Travis Smith 1.00
93 Juan Padilla **RC** 1.00
94 Brad Halsey **RC** 1.00
95 Scott Kazmir 6.00
96 Sam Narron **RC** 1.00
97 Frank Francisco **RC** 1.00
98 Mike Johnston **RC** 1.00
99 Sam McConnell **RC** 1.00
100 Josh Labandeira **RC** 1.00
101 Kazuhito Tadano **RC** 1.00
102 Hector Gimenez **RC** 1.00
103 David Aardsma **RC** 1.00
104 Charles Thomas **RC** 2.00
105 Ian Snell **RC** 2.50
106 Jeff Keppinger **RC** 3.00
107 Michael Vento **RC** 2.00
108 Jerry Gil **RC** 1.00
109 Marty McLeary **RC** 1.00
110 Donnie Kelly **RC** 1.00
111 Roman Colon **RC** 1.00
112 Travis Blackley **RC** 1.00
113 Edwardo Sierra **RC** 1.00
114 Chris Shelton **RC** 2.00
115 Bartolome Fortunato **RC** 1.00
116 Brandon Medders **RC** 1.00
117 Merkin Valdez **RC** 2.00
118 Carlos Vasquez **RC** 1.00
119 Shingo Takatsu **RC** 1.50
120 Aarom Baldiris **RC** 1.00
121 Chris Aguila **RC** 1.00
122 Jimmy Serrano **RC** 1.00
123 Mike Gosling 1.00
124 Brian Dallimore **RC** 1.00
125 Ronald Belisario **RC** 1.00
126 George Sherrill **RC** 1.00
127 Fernando Nieve **RC** 1.00
128 Abe Alvarez **RC** 1.50
129 Jeff Bennett **RC** 1.00
130 Ryan Meaux **RC** 1.00
131 Edwin Moreno **RC** 1.00
132 Jesse Crain **RC** 2.00
133 Scott Dohmann **RC** 1.00
134 Ronny Cedeno **RC** 1.00
135 Orlando Rodriguez **RC** 1.00
136 Mike Wuertz **RC** 1.00
137 Justin Hampson **RC** 1.00
138 Matt Treanor **RC** 1.00
139 Andy Green **RC** 1.00
140 Yadier Molina **RC** 2.50
141 Joe Nelson **RC** 1.00
142 Justin Lehr **RC** 1.00
143 Ryan Wing 1.00
144 Kevin Cave **RC** 1.50
145 Evan Rust **RC** 1.00
146 Mike Rouse 1.00
147 Lance Cormier **RC** 1.00
148 Eduardo Villacis **RC** 1.00
149 Justin Knoedler **RC** 1.00
150 Freddy Guzman **RC** 1.00
151 Casey Daigle **RC** 1.00
152 Joey Gathright **RC** 2.00
153 Tim Bittner **RC** 1.00
154 Scott Atchison **RC** 1.00
155 Ivan Ochoa **RC** 1.50
156 Lincoln Holdzkom **RC** 1.00
157 Onil Joseph **RC** 1.00
158 Jason Bartlett **RC** 1.00
159 Jon Knott **RC** 1.00
160 Jake Woods **RC** 1.00
161 Jerome Gamble **RC** 1.00
162 Sean Henn 1.50
163 Kazuo Matsui **RC** 1.50
164 Roberto Novoa **RC** 1.00
165 Eddy Rodriguez **RC** 1.00
166 Ramon Ramirez **RC** 1.00
167 Enemencio Pacheco **RC** 1.00
168 Chad Bentz **RC** 1.00
169 Chris Oxspring **RC** 1.00
170 Justin Leone **RC** 1.00
171 Joe Horgan **RC** 1.00
172 Jose Capellan **RC** 1.50
173 Greg Dobbs **RC** 1.00
174 Jason Frasor **RC** 1.50
175 Shawn Hill **RC** 1.00
176 Carlos Hines **RC** 1.00
177 John Gall **RC** 1.00
178 Steve Andrade **RC** 1.00
179 Scott Proctor **RC** 1.00
180 Rusty Tucker **RC** 1.00
181 David Crouthers 1.00
182 Franklyn Gracesqui **RC** 1.00
183 Justin Germano **RC** 1.00
184 Alfredo Simon **RC** 1.50
185 Jorge Sequea **RC** 1.00
186 Nick Regilio **RC** 1.00
187 Justin Huisman **RC** 1.00
188 Akinori Otsuka **RC** 1.50
189 Luis Gonzalez **RC** 1.00
190 Renyel Pinto **RC** 1.00
191 Josh LeBlanc **RC** 1.50
192 Devin Ivany **RC** 1.00
193 Chad Blackwell **RC** 1.50
194 Brandon Burgess **RC** 1.50
195 Cory Patton **RC** 1.50
196 Daniel Batz **RC** 1.50
197 Adam Russell **RC** 1.00
198 Jarrett Hoffpauir **RC** 1.50
199 Patrick Bryant **RC** 1.50
200 Sean Gamble **RC** 1.50
201 Jermaine Brock **RC** 1.50
202 Benjamin Zobrist **RC** 1.50
203 Cla Meredith **RC** 1.50
204 Derek Tharpe **RC** 1.00
205 Brad McCann **RC** 2.00
206 Justin Hedrick **RC** 1.00
207 Clint Sammons **RC** 2.50
208 Richard Steik **RC** 1.00
209 Fernando Perez **RC** 1.00
210 Mark Jecmen **RC** 1.00
211 Benjamin Harrison **RC** 1.00
212 Jason Quarles **RC** 1.00
213 William Layman **RC** 1.00
214 Koley Kolberg **RC** 1.00
215 Randy Dicken **RC** 1.00
216 Barry Richmond **RC** 1.00
217 Timothy Murphey **RC** 1.50
218 John Hardy **RC** 1.50
219 Sebastien Boucher **RC** 1.00
220 Andrew Alvarado **RC** 1.00
221 Patrick Perry **RC** 1.00
222 Jarod McAuliff **RC** 1.00
223 Jared Gaston **RC** 1.00
224 William Thompson **RC** 1.50
225 Lucas French **RC** 1.00
226 Brandon Parillo **RC** 1.00
227 Greg Goetz **RC** 1.00
228 David Haehnel **RC** 1.50
229 James Miller **RC** 1.00
230 Mark Roberts **RC** 1.00
231 Eric Ridener **RC** 1.00
232 Freddy Sandoval **RC** 1.00
234 Carlos Medero-Stullz **RC** 1.00
235 Matt Shepherd **RC** 1.00
236 Thomas Hubbard **RC** 1.00
238 Kyle Bono **RC** 1.50
239 Craig Moldrem **RC** 1.00
239 Brandon Timm **RC** 1.00
241 Mike Carp **RC** 2.50

No.	Player	Price
242	Joseph Muro **RC**	1.00
243	Derek Decarlo **RC**	1.50
244	Chris Niesel **RC**	1.50
245	Trevor Lawhorn **RC**	1.50
246	Joey Howell **RC**	1.00
247	Dustin Hahn **RC**	1.00
248	Jim Fasano **RC**	2.00
249	Hainley Statia **RC**	1.00
250	Brandon Conway **RC**	1.00
251	Christopher McConnell **RC**	2.00
252	Austin Shappi **RC**	1.50
253	Joey Metropoulos **RC**	2.00
254	David Nicholson **RC**	1.50
255	Ryan McCarthy **RC**	2.00
256	Michael Parisi **RC**	1.00
257	Andrew Macfarlane **RC**	1.00
258	Jeffery Dominguez **RC**	1.50
259	Troy Patton **RC**	4.00
260	Ryan Norwood **RC**	1.50
261	Chad Boyd **RC**	1.00
262	Grant Plumley **RC**	1.00
263	Jeffrey Katz **RC**	2.00
264	Cory Middleton **RC**	1.00
265	Andrew Moffitt **RC**	1.00
266	Jarrett Grube **RC**	1.00
267	Derek Hankins **RC**	1.00
268	Douglas Reinhardt **RC**	1.00
269	Duron Legrande **RC**	1.00
270	Steven Jackson **RC**	1.00
271	Brian Hall **RC**	2.00
272	Cory Wade **RC**	1.50
273	John Grogan **RC**	1.00
274	Robert Asanovich **RC**	1.50
275	Kevin Hart **RC**	1.50
276	Matt Guillory **RC**	1.00
277	Cliff Remole **RC**	1.00
278	David Trahan **RC**	1.00
279	Kristian Bell **RC**	1.00
280	Chris Westervelt **RC**	1.00
281	Garry Bakker **RC**	1.00
282	Jonny Ash **RC**	1.00
283	Ryan Phillips **RC**	1.00
284	Wes Letson **RC**	1.00
285	Jeff Landing **RC**	1.00
286	Mark Worrell **RC**	1.00
287	Sean Gallagher **RC**	5.00
288	Nick Blasi **RC**	1.00
289	Kevin Frandsen **RC**	2.00
290	Richard Mercado **RC**	1.00
291	Matt Bush **RC**	30.00
292	Mark Rogers **RC**	25.00
293	Homer Bailey **RC**	100.00
294	Chris Nelson **RC**	40.00
295	Thomas Diamond **RC**	30.00
296	Neil Walker **RC**	85.00
297	Bill Bray **RC**	15.00
298	David Purcey **RC**	25.00
299	Scott Elbert **RC**	60.00
300	Josh Fields **RC**	80.00
301	Chris Lambert **RC**	20.00
302	Trevor Plouffe **RC**	40.00
303	Greg Golson **RC**	25.00
304	Phillip Hughes **RC**	250.00
305	Kyle Waldrop **RC**	30.00
306	Richie Robnett/350 **RC**	30.00
307	Taylor Tankersley **RC**	20.00
308	Blake Dewitt **RC**	40.00
309	Eric Hurley **RC**	80.00
310	James Howell **RC**	20.00
311	Zachary Jackson **RC**	15.00
312	Justin Orenduff **RC**	20.00
313	Tyler Lumsden **RC**	25.00
314	Matt Fox/600 **RC**	10.00
315	Dan Putnam/450 **RC**	20.00
316	Jon Poterson **RC**	20.00
317	Gio Gonzalez **RC**	80.00
318	Jay Rainville/475 **RC**	25.00
319	Huston Street **RC**	40.00
320	Jeff Marquez **RC**	25.00
321	Eric Beattie/500 **RC**	20.00
322	Reid Brignac/325 **RC**	125.00
323	Yovani Gallardo **RC**	150.00
324	Justin Hoyman **RC**	20.00
325	Brandon Szymanski **RC**	25.00
326	Seth Smith/600 **RC**	35.00
327	Karl Herren/600 **RC**	20.00
328	Brian Bixler/600 **RC**	15.00
329	Wes Whisler/600 **RC**	15.00
330	Erick San Pedro **RC**	10.00
331	Billy Buckner **RC**	20.00
332	Jon Zeringue **RC**	20.00
333	Curtis Thigpen **RC**	20.00
334	Blake Johnson **RC**	15.00
335	Donny Lucy **RC**	10.00
336	Mike Ferris/600 **RC**	15.00
337	Anthony Swarzak/600 **RC**	30.00
338	Jason Jaramillo **RC**	15.00
339	Hunter Pence/600 **RC**	250.00
340	Dustin Pedroia **RC**	100.00
341	Grant Johnson **RC**	15.00
342	Kurt Suzuki **RC**	30.00
343	Jason Vargas/600 **RC**	25.00
344	Ray Liotta **RC**	20.00
346	Eric Campbell **RC**	40.00
347	Jeff Frazier **RC**	15.00
348	Gaby Hernandez **RC**	40.00
349	Wade Davis/600 **RC**	75.00
350	Josh Wahpepah **RC**	15.00
351	Scott Lewis **RC**	25.00
352	Jeff Fiorentino **RC**	15.00
353	Steven Register/600 **RC**	10.00
354	Michael Schlact **RC**	15.00
355	Eddie Prasch **RC**	15.00
356	Adam Lind **RC**	75.00
357	Ian Desmond **RC**	30.00
358	Josh Johnson/575 **RC**	15.00
359	Garrett Mock/600 **RC**	15.00
360	Danny Hill/600 **RC**	10.00
361	Cory Dunlap/600 **RC**	25.00
362	Grant Hansen/600 **RC**	12.00
363	Eric Haberer **RC**	15.00
364	Eduardo Morlan **RC**	20.00
365	James Happ/600 **RC**	15.00
366	Matt Tuiasosopo/600 **RC**	40.00
367	Jordan Parraz **RC**	20.00
368	Andrew Dobies **RC**	20.00
369	Mark Reed **RC**	30.00
370	Jason Windsor **RC**	30.00
371	Gregory Burns/600 **RC**	20.00
372	Christian Garcia/600 **RC**	25.00
373	John Bowker/575 **RC**	20.00
374	John Holt/550 **RC**	15.00
375	Daryl Jones **RC**	25.00
376	Colin Mahoney **RC**	10.00
377	Aaron Hathaway **RC**	15.00
378	Matt Spring **RC**	10.00
379	Josh Baker **RC**	10.00
380	Charles Lofgren **RC**	60.00
381	Rafael Gonzalez **RC**	15.00
382	Bradley Bergesen/575 **RC**	10.00
383	Brandon Boggs **RC**	15.00
384	Joseph Bauserman **RC**	15.00
385	Collin Balester/500 **RC**	40.00
386	James Moore **RC**	10.00
387	Robert Janssen **RC**	20.00
388	Luis Guerra **RC**	15.00
389	Lucas Harrell/550 **RC**	15.00
390	Donnie Smith/500 **RC**	15.00
391	Mark Robinson/525 **RC**	15.00
392	Louis Marson/550 **RC**	20.00
393	Robert Johnson/600 **RC**	10.00
394	Lou Santangelo/600 **RC**	12.00
395	Tommy Hottovy **RC**	10.00
396	Ryan Webb **RC**	15.00
397	Jamar Walton **RC**	15.00
398	Jason Jones **RC**	20.00
399	Clay Timpner/600 **RC**	15.00
400	James Parr **RC**	20.00
401	Sean Kazmar **RC**	20.00
402	Andrew Kown **RC**	15.00
403	Jacob McGee/600 **RC**	80.00
404	Mike Butia/600 **RC**	20.00
405	Paul Janish/500 **RC**	20.00
406	Matt Macri **RC**	25.00
407	Mike Nickeas/500 **RC**	15.00
408	Kyle Bloom/550 **RC**	10.00
409	Luis Rivera/500 **RC**	15.00
410	William Bunn/600 **RC**	15.00
411	Enrique Barrera **RC**	20.00
412	Ryan Klosterman **RC**	15.00
413	John Raglani/515 **RC**	15.00
414	Brandon Allen/500 **RC**	20.00
415	Andy Baldwin/600 **RC**	15.00
416	Mark Lowe **RC**	20.00
417	Mitch Einertson **RC**	20.00
418	Ryan Schroyer/600 **RC**	10.00
419	Brad Davis **RC**	15.00
420	Jesse Hoover/500 **RC**	15.00
421	Garrett Broshuis **RC**	15.00
422	Peter Pope **RC**	30.00
423	Brent Dlugach **RC**	15.00
424	Ryan Coultas **RC**	15.00
425	Ryan Royster **RC**	75.00
426	Stephen Chapman **RC**	15.00
427	Bryce Chamberlin **RC**	25.00
428	Joe Koshansky/550 **RC**	50.00
429	William Susdorf **RC**	15.00
430	A.J. Johnson **RC**	15.00
431	Jeremy Sowers **RC**	50.00
432	Justin Pekarek **RC**	15.00
433	Brett Smith **RC**	15.00
434	Matt Durkin **RC**	15.00
435	Daniel Barone **RC**	15.00
436	Scott Hyde **RC**	15.00
437	Thomas Everidge **RC**	25.00
444	Mark Trumbo **RC**	25.00
446	Eric Patterson **RC**	30.00
447	Mike Rozier **RC**	15.00

Gold

Gold (291-447): No Pricing
Production 10 Sets

Platinum

No Pricing
Production One Set

Draft Class

No Pricing
Production 10 Sets

Draft Duos

NM/M
Common Dual Autograph: 15.00

Production 175 Sets

LK	Adam Lind, Ryan Klosterman	40.00
BB	Bill Bray, Collin Balester	25.00
BI	Bill Bray, Ian Desmond	25.00
BM	William Buckner, James Moore	15.00
JH	James Howell, Josh Johnson	15.00
DB	Blake Dewitt, Daniel Batz	25.00
SJ	Brandon Szymanski, Paul Janish	25.00
SH	Brett Smith, Phillip Hughes	60.00
LS	Chris Lambert, Donnie Smith	15.00
LF	Chris Lambert, Mike Ferris	15.00
NS	Chris Nelson, Seth Smith	25.00
NM	Chris Nelson, Matt Macri	30.00
DG	Cory Dunlap, Luis Guerra	30.00
BN	Matt Bush, Chris Nelson	30.00
TH	Curtis Thigpen, Danny Hill	15.00
PT	Dan Putnam, Derek Tharpe	15.00
PJ	David Purcey, Robert Janssen	15.00
DZ	David Purcey, Zachary Jackson	20.00
LH	Donny Lucy, Grant Hansen	15.00
PD	Dustin Pedroia, Andrew Dobies	30.00
MR	Eduardo Morlan, Mark Robinson	15.00
PB	Eddie Prasch, Joseph Bauserman	20.00
EA	Eric Beattie, Andrew Kown	20.00
EJ	Eric Campbell, John Holt	25.00
EM	Eric Hurley, Mike Nickeas	25.00
PI	Erick San Pedro, Devin Ivany	15.00
HH	Gaby Hernandez, Aaron Hathaway	25.00
SK	Seth Smith, Joe Koshansky	30.00
GM	Gio Gonzalez, Timothy Murphey	25.00
BH	Matt Bush, Phillip Hughes	60.00
JR	Grant Johnson, Mark Reed	25.00
GH	Greg Golson, James Happ	20.00
GG	Greg Golson, Sean Gamble	15.00
BS	Homer Bailey, Brandon Szymanski	40.00
BG	Homer Bailey, Rafael Gonzalez	50.00
HJ	Hunter Pence, Jordan Parraz	80.00
SS	Huston Street, Kurt Suzuki	40.00
SW	Huston Street, Ryan Webb	30.00
HB	James Howell, Chad Blackwell	20.00
JM	Jason Jaramillo, Louis Marson	15.00
RS	Jay Rainville, Anthony Swarzak	20.00
JP	Jay Rainville, Patrick Bryant	20.00
FM	Jeff Frazier, Colin Mahoney	15.00
MS	Jeff Marquez, Brett Smith	20.00
MH	Jeff Marquez, Jesse Hoover	25.00
SL	Jeremy Sowers, Charles Lofgren	35.00
JS	Jeremy Sowers, Scott Lewis	25.00
JJ	Jon Poterson, Jason Jones	25.00
ZM	Jon Zeringue, Garrett Mock	20.00
FH	Josh Fields, Lucas Harrell	30.00
FW	Josh Fields, Wes Whisler	40.00
WB	Josh Wahpepah, Josh Baker	15.00
CL	Justin Hoyman, Jeremy Sowers	25.00
OJ	Justin Orenduff, Blake Johnson	25.00
OG	Justin Orenduff, Luis Guerra	20.00
HS	Karl Herren, Michael Schlact	20.00
WF	Kyle Waldrop, Matt Fox	20.00
KB	Kyle Waldrop, Patrick Bryant	25.00
RW	Richie Robnett, Jason Windsor	25.00
SR	Richie Robnett, Kurt Suzuki	25.00
RB	Mark Rogers, Josh Baker	30.00
RG	Mark Rogers, Yovani Gallardo	50.00
BK	Matt Bush, Sean Kazmar	25.00
WE	William Buckner, Enrique Barrera	15.00
WJ	William Buckner, James Howell	20.00
KH	Matt Durkin, Aaron Hathaway	20.00
NB	Neil Walker, Brian Bixler	25.00
NK	Neil Walker, Kyle Bloom	25.00
HG	Phillip Hughes, Christian Garcia	50.00
HP	Phillip Hughes, Jon Poterson	60.00
LA	Ray Liotta, Brandon Allen	25.00
BR	Reid Brignac, Ryan Royster	40.00
RP	Richie Robnett, Dan Putnam	25.00
RH	Richie Robnett, Huston Street	30.00
CO	Steven Register, Seth Smith	25.00
TD	Taylor Tankersley, Brad Davis	15.00
TV	Taylor Tankersley, Jason Vargas	20.00
BT	Thomas Diamond, Brandon Boggs	30.00
DH	Thomas Diamond, Eric Hurley	30.00
ED	Scott Elbert, Blake Dewitt	35.00
ER	Scott Elbert, John Raglani	25.00
PW	Trevor Plouffe, Kyle Waldrop	30.00
PR	Trevor Plouffe, Mark Robinson	25.00
LR	Tyler Lumsden, Adam Russell	15.00
LG	Tyler Lumsden, Gio Gonzalez	25.00
JB	William Buckner, Josh Johnson	20.00
BJ	Matt Bush, Daryl Jones	30.00
GW	Yovani Gallardo, Josh Wahpepah	40.00
JK	Zachary Jackson, Ryan Klosterman	15.00
DR	Blake Dewitt, John Raglani	25.00
GB	Homer Bailey, Greg Goetz	50.00
WR	Reid Brignac, Wade Davis	40.00
HM	Jeff Marquez, Phillip Hughes	60.00
PZ	Jordan Parraz, Benjamin Zobrist	25.00
RL	Luis Rivera, William Layman	15.00
EC	Eric Beattie, Collin Mahoney	15.00
JE	Jeff Frazier, Eric Beattie	15.00
BP	Matt Bush, Trevor Plouffe	30.00
CH	Ryan Coultas, Aaron Hathaway	15.00
SB	Jeremy Sowers, Homer Bailey	60.00
FB	Jeff Fiorentino, Bradley Bergesen	25.00
CF	Bryce Chamberlin, Jeff Fiorentino	20.00
RD	Cory Dunlap, John Raglani	20.00
ZP	Hunter Pence, Benjamin Zobrist	80.00

Draft Generations Triple Autograph

No Pricing
Production 25 Sets
No Pricing
Production 25 Sets

Draft Picks Autographs

NM/M
Common Autograph: 8.00
Golds: No Pricing
Production 10 Sets

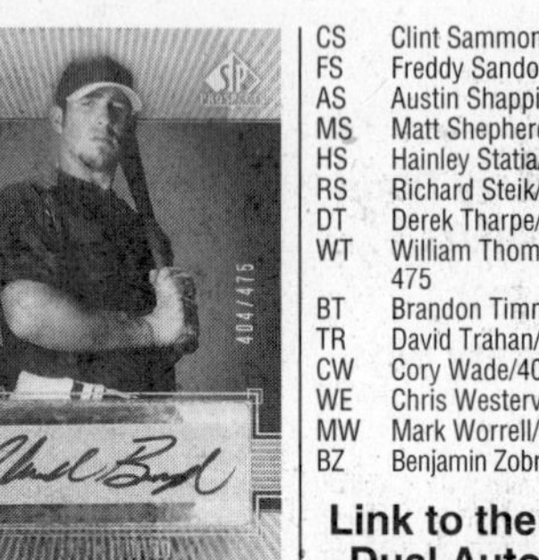

Platinum: No Pricing
Production One Set

AA	Andrew Alvarado/400	8.00
RA	Robert Asanovich/400	15.00
JA	Jonny Ash/400	15.00
GB	Garry Bakker/400	10.00
DB	Daniel Batz/400	10.00
KB	Kristian Bell/400	8.00
BL	Chad Blackwell/400	15.00
NB	Nick Blasi/400	15.00
BO	Kyle Bono/400	10.00
SB	Sebastien Boucher/325	15.00
CB	Chad Boyd/475	8.00
JB	Jermaine Brock/400	8.00
PB	Patrick Bryant/400	10.00
BB	Brandon Burgess/400	10.00
CA	Mike Carp/400	25.00
BC	Brandon Conway/400	8.00
DD	Derek Decarlo/400	10.00
RD	Randy Dicken/475	8.00
JD	Jeffery Dominguez/400	15.00
JF	Jim Fasano/400	15.00
KF	Kevin Frandsen/400	30.00
LF	Lucas French/400	15.00
SE	Sean Gallagher/400	50.00
SG	Sean Gamble/400	10.00
GA	Jared Gaston/400	10.00
GG	Greg Goetz/400	15.00
GR	John Grogan/475	10.00
JG	Jarrett Grube/400	8.00
MG	Matt Guillory/400	10.00
DA	David Haehnel/475	12.00
HA	Dustin Hahn/400	8.00
BH	Brian Hall/400	15.00
DH	Derek Hankins/400	8.00
JO	John Hardy/475	10.00
BE	Benjamin Harrison/387	20.00
KH	Kevin Hart/400	10.00
HE	Justin Hedrick/400	15.00
JH	Jarrett Hoffpauir/400	15.00
HO	Joey Howell/400	15.00
TH	Thomas Hubbard/400	10.00
DI	Devin Ivany/550	10.00
SJ	Steven Jackson/475	15.00
MJ	Mark Jecmen/600	8.00
JK	Jeffrey Katz/400	10.00
KK	Koley Kolberg/400	10.00
LA	Jeff Landing/400	10.00
TL	Trevor Lawhorn/475	10.00
WL	William Layman/400	8.00
JL	Josh LeBlanc/400	10.00
DL	Duron Legrande/400	8.00
LE	Wes Letson/400	10.00
MA	Andrew Macfarlane/400	8.00
MC	Jarod McAuliff/400	15.00
BM	Brad McCann/400	25.00
RM	Ryan McCarthy/400	15.00
CH	Christopher McConnell/400	25.00
ME	Carlos Medero-Stullz/400	8.00
RI	Richard Mercado/475	12.00
CL	Cla Meredith/400	25.00
JM	Joey Metropoulos/400	15.00
CM	Cory Middleton/400	20.00
MI	James Miller/475	12.00
AM	Andrew Moffitt/400	10.00
MO	Craig Molldrem/400	12.00
MU	Joseph Muro/400	8.00
TM	Timothy Murphey/400	10.00
DN	David Nicholson/475	10.00
CN	Chris Niesel/475	15.00
RN	Ryan Norwood/400	25.00
BP	Brandon Parillo/475	15.00
MP	Michael Parisi/475	15.00
CP	Cory Patton/400	15.00
TP	Troy Patton/400	85.00
FP	Fernando Perez/400	20.00
PP	Patrick Perry/475	15.00
RP	Ryan Phillips/400	15.00
GP	Grant Plumley/475	10.00
JQ	Jason Quarles/400	8.00
DR	Douglas Reinhardt/400	8.00
CR	Cliff Remole/400	15.00
BR	Barry Richmond/400	20.00
ER	Eric Ridener/475	10.00
MR	Mark Roberts/400	8.00
AR	Adam Russell/550	8.00
CS	Clint Sammons/400	15.00
FS	Freddy Sandoval/400	10.00
AS	Austin Shappi/475	15.00
MS	Matt Shepherd/400	10.00
HS	Hainley Statia/400	20.00
RS	Richard Steik/400	8.00
DT	Derek Tharpe/400	8.00
WT	William Thompson/475	10.00
BT	Brandon Timm/475	15.00
TR	David Trahan/400	10.00
CW	Cory Wade/400	15.00
WE	Chris Westervelt/400	15.00
MW	Mark Worrell/400	15.00
BZ	Benjamin Zobrist/600	25.00

Link to the Future Dual Autograph

NM/M
Common Dual Auto. 10.00
Production 100 Sets

BD	Adrian Beltre, Blake Dewitt	40.00
RF	Scott Rolen, Mike Ferris	40.00
JR	Andruw Jones, Richie Robnett	30.00
KB	Scott Kazmir, Reid Brignac	50.00
JB	Jason Kendall, Brian Bixler	20.00
SR	Ben Sheets, Mark Rogers	40.00
GP	Brian Giles, Dan Putnam	20.00
BG	Carlos Beltran, Greg Golson	30.00
SJ	Johan Santana, Jay Rainville	40.00
WT	Dontrelle Willis, Taylor Tankersley	15.00
JJ	Edwin Jackson, Blake Johnson	15.00
EJ	Eric Chavez, Josh Fields	40.00
QT	Guillermo Quiroz, Curtis Thigpen	10.00
KW	Jason Kendall, Neil Walker	40.00
VM	Javier Vazquez, Jeff Marquez	20.00
MP	Joe Mauer, Trevor Plouffe	50.00
SW	Johan Santana, Kyle Waldrop	40.00
VP	Javier Vazquez, Jon Poterson	20.00
GS	Ken Griffey Jr., Brandon Szymanski	75.00
WB	Kerry Wood, Homer Bailey	50.00
MS	Mike Mussina, Brett Smith	50.00
HS	Todd Helton, Seth Smith	30.00
GZ	Luis Gonzalez, Jon Zeringue	20.00
OH	Magglio Ordonez, Karl Herren	20.00
MB	Mark Mulder, Bill Bray	20.00
PJ	Mark Prior, Grant Johnson	40.00
CF	Matt Clement, Matt Fox	15.00
TN	Miguel Tejada, Chris Nelson	40.00
MH	Mike Mussina, Phillip Hughes	85.00
GB	Nomar Garciaparra, Matt Bush	80.00
PE	Odalis Perez, Scott Elbert	20.00
LS	Paul LoDuca, Erick San Pedro	20.00
HW	Rich Harden, Kyle Waldrop	25.00
CD	Roger Clemens, Thomas Diamond	100.00
RP	Alexis Rios, David Purcey	25.00
RE	Roy Oswalt, Eric Hurley	25.00
RL	Scott Rolen, Chris Lambert	40.00
TS	Tim Hudson, Huston Street	40.00
TJ	Tom Glavine, Jeremy Sowers	35.00
VD	Victor Martinez, Donny Lucy	25.00
BH	Angel Berroa, James Howell	15.00

Link to the Future Triple Autograph

NM/M
Common Triple Auto.
Production 50 Sets
BHH Hank Blalock, Eric Hurley, Benjamin Harrison 40.00
KBS Scott Kazmir, Reid Brignac, Matt Spring 75.00
SRB Ben Sheets, Mark Rogers, Josh Baker 50.00
JJB Edwin Jackson, Blake Johnson, Daniel Batz 20.00
SWM Johan Santana, Kyle Waldrop, Eduardo Morlan 60.00
VBB Jose Vidro, Bill Bray, Collin Balester 30.00
GSJ Ken Griffey Jr., Brandon Szymanski, Paul Janish 60.00
MSH Mike Mussina, Brett Smith, Jesse Hoover 50.00
OFA Magglio Ordonez, Josh Fields, Brandon Allen 30.00
PJR Mark Prior, Grant Johnson, Mark Reed 100.00
GHM Juan Gonzalez, James Howell, James Moore 40.00
HSW Rich Harden, Huston Street, Jason Windsor 50.00
GMZ Luis Gonzalez, Garrett Mock, Jon Zeringue 25.00
HRW Tim Hudson, Richie Robnett, Ryan Webb 60.00
GTR Vladimir Guerrero, Mark Trumbo, Luis Rivera 75.00

Link to the Past Dual Autograph

NM/M
Common Dual Autograph
Production 50 Sets
MB Bill Mazeroski, Brian Bixler 35.00
FL Carlton Fisk, Tyler Lumsden 35.00
WJ Dave Winfield, Zachary Jackson 35.00
BW Johnny Bench, Neil Walker 40.00
JD Jose Canseco, Dan Putnam 50.00
AS Billy Williams, Richie Robnett 40.00
RB Nolan Ryan, Homer Bailey 180.00
PD Gaylord Perry, Thomas Diamond 50.00
WR Wade Boggs, Reid Brignac 60.00
WB Whitey Ford, Brett Smith 30.00
WP Whitey Ford, Phillip Hughes 75.00
Common Dual Autograph
Production 50 Sets
MB Bill Mazeroski, Brian Bixler 35.00
FL Carlton Fisk, Tyler Lumsden 35.00
WJ Dave Winfield, Zachary Jackson 35.00
BW Johnny Bench, Neil Walker 40.00
JD Jose Canseco, Dan Putnam 50.00
AS Billy Williams, Richie Robnett 40.00
RB Nolan Ryan, Homer Bailey 180.00
PD Gaylord Perry, Thomas Diamond 50.00
WR Wade Boggs, Reid Brignac 60.00
WB Whitey Ford, Brett Smith 30.00
WP Whitey Ford, Phillip Hughes 75.00

National Honors

NM/M
Common Player: 4.00
Inserted 1:12
DB Daniel Bard 8.00
TB Travis Buck 8.00
JC Jeff Clement 8.00
BC Brent Cox 8.00
TC Trevor Crowe 4.00
JD Joey Devine 4.00
AG Alex Gordon 20.00
BH Brett Hayes 4.00
LH Luke Hochevar 8.00
SK Stephen Kahn 4.00
IK Ian Kennedy 8.00
JL Jed Lowrie 4.00
JM John Mayberry Jr. 8.00
MP Mike Pelfrey 15.00
CR Cesar Ramos 8.00
MR Mark Romanczuk 4.00
RR Ricky Romero 4.00
DS Drew Stubbs 8.00
TE Taylor Teagarden 6.00
TT Troy Tulowitzki 15.00
CV Chris Valaika 4.00
RZ Ryan Zimmerman 15.00

2004 SPx

NM/M
Complete Set (202):
Common Player: .25
Common SP (111-145): 3.00
Production 1,599
Common SP (146-154): 5.00
Production 499
Common SP (155-160): 8.00
Production 299
Common Jersey Auto. (161-202): 8.00
Production 799
Pack (4): 5.00
Box (18): 75.00
1 Alfonso Soriano 1.00
2 Todd Helton .75
3 Andruw Jones .75
4 Eric Gagne .50
5 Craig Wilson .25
6 Brian Giles .25
7 Miguel Tejada .50
8 Kevin Brown .25
9 Shawn Green .50
10 Ben Sheets .50
11 John Smoltz .50
12 Tim Hudson .50
13 Jason Schmidt .50
14 Paul Konerko .50
15 Randy Johnson 1.00
16 Roy Oswalt .50
17 Mike Lowell .25
18 Carlos Lee .50
19 Sean Burroughs .25
20 Edgar Renteria .50
21 Michael Young .25
22 Jose Vidro .25
23 Scott Rolen 1.00
24 Rafael Furcal .50
25 Tom Glavine .75
26 Scott Podsednik .25
27 Gary Sheffield .75
28 Eric Chavez .50
29 Mark Prior .75
30 Chipper Jones 1.00
31 Frank Thomas 1.00
32 Victor Martinez .50
33 Jake Peavy .50
34 Carlos Beltran 1.00
35 Roy Halladay .50
36 Mark Teixeira .75
37 Jacque Jones .25
38 Mike Sweeney .25
39 Troy Glaus .50
40 Pat Burrell .50
41 Ichiro Suzuki 2.00
42 Vladimir Guerrero 1.00
43 Bobby Abreu .50
44 Jim Edmonds .50
45 Garret Anderson .40
46 J.D. Drew .40
47 C.C. Sabathia .25
48 Joe Mauer .50
49 Phil Nevin .25
50 Hank Blalock .50
51 Carlos Zambrano .50
52 Mike Piazza 1.50
53 Manny Ramirez 1.00
54 Lance Berkman .50
55 Delmon Young .50
56 Nomar Garciaparra 1.00
57 Alex Rodriguez 2.50
58 Rickie Weeks .50
59 Adrian Beltre .50
60 Albert Pujols 2.50
61 Richie Sexson .50
62 Magglio Ordonez .50
63 Derrek Lee .75
64 Sammy Sosa 1.50
65 Jason Giambi .75
66 Curt Schilling 1.00
67 Jorge Posada .50
68 Rafael Palmeiro .75
69 Jeff Kent .50
70 Jose Reyes .50
71 David Ortiz 1.00
72 Aubrey Huff .25
73 Jim Thome 1.00
74 Andy Pettitte .50
75 Barry Zito .50
76 Carlos Delgado .50
77 Hideki Matsui 2.00
78 Sean Casey .25
79 Luis Gonzalez .25
80 Marcus Giles .25
81 Preston Wilson .25
82 Javy Lopez .25
83 Mark Mulder .50
84 Derek Jeter 2.50
85 Miguel Cabrera 1.00
86 Vernon Wells .50
87 Roger Clemens 2.50
88 Lyle Overbay .25
89 Bret Boone .25
90 Melvin Mora .25
91 Greg Maddux 2.00
92 Kerry Wood .50
93 Ivan Rodriguez .75
94 Pedro J. Martinez 1.00
95 Jeff Bagwell .75
96 Torii Hunter .50
97 Ken Griffey Jr. 2.00
98 Mike Mussina .75
99 Oliver Perez .25
100 Josh Beckett .50
101 Bob Gibson 4.00
102 Cal Ripken Jr. 8.00
103 Ted Williams 8.00
104 Nolan Ryan 8.00
105 Mickey Mantle 10.00
106 Ernie Banks 5.00
107 Joe DiMaggio 6.00
108 Stan Musial 5.00
109 Tom Seaver 4.00
110 Mike Schmidt 6.00
111 Jerry Gil **RC** 3.00
112 Dioner Navarro **RC** 8.00
113 Bartolome Fortunato **RC** 3.00
114 Carlos Hines **RC** 3.00
115 Franklyn Gracesqui **RC** 3.00
116 Aarom Baldiris **RC** 5.00
117 Casey Daigle **RC** 3.00
118 Joey Gathright **RC** 5.00
119 William Bergolla **RC** 3.00
120 Jeff Bennett **RC** 3.00
121 Lincoln Holdzkom **RC** 3.00
122 Jorge Vasquez **RC** 3.00
123 Donnie Kelly **RC** 3.00
124 Yadier Molina **RC** 8.00
125 Ryan Wing 3.00
126 Justin Germano **RC** 3.00
127 Freddy Guzman **RC** 3.00
128 Onil Joseph **RC** 3.00
129 Roman Colon **RC** 3.00
130 Roberto Novoa **RC** 5.00
131 Renyel Pinto **RC** 5.00
132 Evan Rust **RC** 3.00
133 Orlando Rodriguez **RC** 3.00
134 Edwardo Sierra **RC** 5.00
135 Mike Rose **RC** 3.00
136 Phil Stockman **RC** 3.00
137 Greg Dobbs **RC** 3.00
138 Brad Halsey **RC** 3.00
139 David Aardsma 5.00
140 Joe Hietpas **RC** 3.00
141 Josh Labandeira **RC** 3.00
142 Mariano Gomez **RC** 3.00
143 Jeff Bajenaru **RC** 3.00
144 Travis Blackley **RC** 3.00
145 Abe Alvarez 5.00
146 Ramon Ramirez **RC** 5.00
147 Edwin Moreno **RC** 5.00
148 Ronny Cedeno **RC** 8.00
149 Hector Gimenez **RC** 5.00
150 Carlos Vasquez **RC** 8.00
151 Jesse Crain 8.00
152 Logan Kensing **RC** 5.00
153 Sean Henn 5.00
154 Rusty Tucker **RC** 5.00
155 Justin Lehr **RC** 5.00
156 Ian Snell **RC** 15.00
157 Merkin Valdez **RC** 10.00
158 Scott Proctor **RC** 8.00
159 Jose Capellan **RC** 8.00
160 Kazuo Matsui **RC** 8.00
161 Chris Oxspring **RC** 8.00
162 Jimmy Serrano **RC** 10.00
163 Jeff Keppinger **RC** 35.00
164 Brandon Medders **RC** 8.00
165 Brian Dallimore **RC** 10.00
166 Chad Bentz **RC** 12.00
167 Chris Aguila **RC** 10.00
168 Chris Saenz **RC** 10.00
169 Frank Francisco **RC** 10.00
170 Colby Miller **RC** 12.00
171 David Crouthers 10.00
172 Charles Thomas **RC** 15.00
173 Dennis Sarfate **RC** 12.00
174 Lance Cormier **RC** 10.00
175 Joe Horgan **RC** 10.00
176 Fernando Nieve **RC** 10.00
177 Jake Woods 12.00
178 Matt Treanor **RC** 12.00
179 Jerome Gamble **RC** 15.00
180 John Gall **RC** 15.00
181 Jorge Sequea **RC** 10.00
182 Justin Hampson **RC** 10.00
183 Justin Huisman **RC** 15.00
184 Justin Knoedler **RC** 12.00
185 Justin Leone **RC** 15.00
186 Scott Atchison **RC** 12.00
187 Jon Knott **RC** 15.00
188 Kevin Cave **RC** 10.00
189 Jason Frasor **RC** 10.00
190 George Sherrill **RC** 12.00
191 Mike Gosling 10.00
192 Mike Johnston **RC** 10.00
193 Mike Rouse 10.00
194 Nick Regilio **RC** 10.00
195 Ryan Meaux **RC** 10.00
196 Scott Dohmann **RC** 15.00
197 Shawn Camp **RC** 10.00
198 Shawn Hill **RC** 10.00
199 Shingo Takatsu **RC** 15.00
200 Tim Bausher **RC** 10.00
201 Tim Bittner **RC** 10.00
202 Scott Kazmir 60.00

Master Player Prints

No Pricing
Production One Set

Spectrum

Stars (1-100): 5-10X
SP's (101-202): 2-3X
Production 25 Sets

Superscripts

NM/M
Common Player: 8.00
Inserted 1:18
JB Josh Beckett 20.00
MC Miguel Cabrera 25.00
EC Eric Chavez 15.00
BC Bobby Crosby 15.00
BF Bartolome Fortunato 10.00
NG Nomar Garciaparra/SP 80.00
MG Mariano Gomez 10.00
KG Ken Griffey Jr. 75.00
RH Rich Harden 15.00
SH Sean Henn 10.00
CH Carlos Hines 8.00
LH Lincoln Holdzkom 10.00
EJ Edwin Jackson 10.00
DJ Derek Jeter/SP 200.00
DK Donnie Kelly 8.00
LA Josh Labandeira 8.00
JL Justin Lehr 10.00
JM Joe Mauer 35.00
IO Ivan Ochoa 8.00
RO Roy Oswalt 20.00
MP Mark Prior 40.00
SP Scott Proctor 10.00
AP Albert Pujols/SP 240.00
RR Ramon Ramirez 12.00
JR Jose Reyes 35.00
CR Cal Ripken Jr./SP 125.00
RU Evan Rust 10.00
ES Edwardo Sierra 10.00
AS Alfredo Simon 10.00
IS Ian Snell 25.00
PS Phil Stockman 10.00
TE Miguel Tejada 35.00
MT Mark Teixeira 30.00
MV Merkin Valdez 12.00
CV Carlos Vasquez 10.00
VE Michael Vento 15.00
BW Brandon Webb 10.00
RW Rickie Weeks 15.00
DW Dontrelle Willis 25.00
DY Delmon Young 25.00

Swatch Supremecy Cut Signatures

No pricing due to scarcity.

Swatch Supremecy Signatures

NM/M
Common Player: 8.00
Production 999 unless noted.
Spectrum: 1.5-3X
Production 25 Sets
GA Garret Anderson/275 20.00
RB Rocco Baldelli 20.00
JB Josh Beckett 15.00
AB Angel Berroa 10.00
HB Hank Blalock 15.00
SB Sean Burroughs 10.00
MC Miguel Cabrera 30.00
EC Eric Chavez/275 20.00
CC Chad Cordero 10.00
BC Bobby Crosby 15.00
AE Adam Eaton 10.00
NG Nomar Garciaparra/275 60.00
MG Marcus Giles 15.00
GR Khalil Greene 25.00
KG Ken Griffey Jr./275 85.00
RH Rich Harden 20.00
DJ Derek Jeter/275 180.00
CK Casey Kotchman 20.00
CL Cliff Lee 10.00
DL Derrek Lee/275 30.00
JM Joe Mauer 40.00
RO Roy Oswalt 20.00
LO Lyle Overbay 15.00
CP Corey Patterson 20.00
JP Jake Peavy 35.00
SP Scott Podsednik 20.00
MP Mark Prior/275 40.00
AP Albert Pujols/275 240.00
HR Horacio Ramirez 10.00
JR Jose Reyes 35.00
CR Cal Ripken Jr./275 140.00
NR Nolan Ryan/275 120.00
BS Ben Sheets 20.00
MT Mark Teixeira 25.00
BW Brandon Webb 15.00
RW Rickie Weeks 15.00
DW Dontrelle Willis 25.00
JW Jerome Williams 15.00
MY Michael Young 15.00

Winning Materials

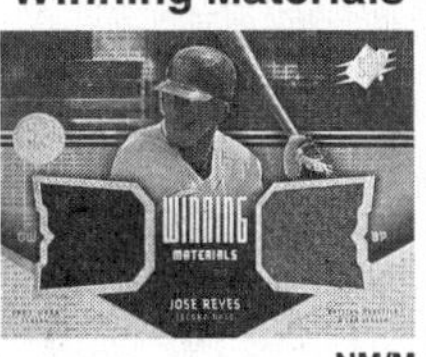

NM/M
Common Player: 8.00
Inserted 1:18
Spectrum: 2-3X
Production 25 Sets
JB Jeff Bagwell 10.00
BE Josh Beckett 10.00
HB Hank Blalock 10.00
KB Kevin Brown 10.00
EC Eric Chavez 8.00
RC Roger Clemens 20.00
CD Carlos Delgado 10.00
JG Jason Giambi 12.00
TG Troy Glaus 8.00
SG Shawn Green 8.00
VG Vladimir Guerrero 12.00
DJ Derek Jeter 35.00
CJ Chipper Jones 10.00
GM Greg Maddux 15.00
HM Hideki Matsui 30.00
MM Mike Mussina 10.00
RP Rafael Palmeiro 10.00
PI Mike Piazza 15.00
JP Jorge Posada 10.00
MP Mark Prior 10.00
AP Albert Pujols 30.00
MR Manny Ramirez 15.00
JR Jose Reyes 15.00
SR Scott Rolen 10.00
GS Gary Sheffield 10.00
SS Sammy Sosa 15.00
IS Ichiro Suzuki 30.00
TE Miguel Tejada 10.00
JT Jim Thome 12.00

2005 SP Collection

NM/M
Complete SPx Set (100): 25.00
Common Player: .25
Pack (5): 6.00
Box (20): 100.00
1 Aaron Harang .25
2 Aaron Rowand .25
3 Aaron Miles .25
4 Adrian Gonzalez .25
5 Alex Rios .25
6 Angel Berroa .25
7 B.J. Upton .25
8 Brandon Claussen .25
9 Andy Marte .25
10 Brandon Webb .25
11 Bronson Arroyo .25
12 Casey Kotchman .25
13 Cesar Izturis .25
14 Chad Cordero .25
15 Chad Tracy .25
16 Charles Thomas .25
17 Chase Utley .50
18 Chone Figgins .25
19 Chris Burke .25
20 Cliff Lee .25
21 Clint Barmes .25
22 Coco Crisp .25
23 Bill Hall .25
24 Dallas McPherson .25
25 Brad Halsey .25
26 Daniel Cabrera .25
27 Danny Haren .25
28 David Bush .25
29 David DeJesus .25
30 D.J. Houlton .25
31 Derek Jeter 3.00
32 Dewon Brazelton .25
33 Edwin Jackson .25
34 Brad Hawpe .25
35 Brandon Inge .25
36 Brett Myers .25
37 Garrett Atkins .25
38 Gavin Floyd .25
39 Grady Sizemore .50
40 Guillermo Mota .25
41 Carlos Guillen .25
42 Gustavo Chacin .25
43 Huston Street .25
44 Chris Duffy .25
45 J.D. Closser .25
46 J.J. Hardy .25
47 Jason Bartlett .25
48 Jason Dubois .25
49 Chris Shelton .25
50 Jason Lane .25
51 Jayson Werth .25
52 Jeff Baker .25
53 Jeff Francis .25
54 Jeremy Bonderman .25
55 Jeremy Reed .25
56 Jerome Williams .25
57 Jesse Crain .25
58 Chris Young .25
59 Jhonny Peralta .25
60 Joe Blanton .25
61 Joe Crede .25
62 Joel Pineiro .25
63 Joey Gathright .25
64 John Buck .25
65 Jonny Gomes .25
66 Jorge Cantu .25
67 Dan Johnson .25
68 Jose Valverde .25
69 Ervin Santana .25
70 Justin Morneau .50
71 Keiichi Yabu .25
72 Ken Griffey Jr. 2.00
73 Jason Repko .25
74 Kevin Youkilis .25
75 Koyie Hill .25
76 Laynce Nix .25
77 Luke Scott **RC** 1.00
78 Juan Rivera .25
79 Justin Duchscherer .25
80 Mark Teahen .25
81 Lance Niekro .25
82 Michael Cuddyer .25
83 Nick Swisher .25
84 Noah Lowry .25
85 Matt Holliday .50
86 Reed Johnson .25
87 Rich Harden .25
88 Robb Quinlan .25
89 Nick Johnson .25
90 Ryan Howard 1.00
91 Nook Logan .25
92 Steve Schmoll .25
93 Tadahito Iguchi .25
94 Willy Taveras .25
95 Wily Mo Pena .25
96 Xavier Nady .25
97 Yadier Molina .25
98 Yhency Brazoban .25
99 Ryan Freel .25
100 Zack Greinke .25
Complete SP Authentic Set (100): 25.00
Common Player: .25
1 A.J. Burnett .25
2 Aaron Rowand .25
3 Adam Dunn .75
4 Adrian Beltre .50
5 Adrian Gonzalez .25
6 Akinori Otsuka .25
7 Albert Pujols 3.00
8 Andre Dawson .50
9 Andruw Jones .50
10 Aramis Ramirez .50
11 Barry Larkin .50
12 Ben Sheets .50
13 Bo Jackson .50
14 Bobby Abreu .50
15 Bobby Crosby .50
16 Bronson Arroyo .25
17 Cal Ripken Jr. 4.00
18 Carl Crawford .25
19 Carlos Zambrano .50
20 Casey Kotchman .25
21 Cesar Izturis .25
22 Chone Figgins .25
23 Corey Patterson .25
24 Craig Biggio .50
25 Dale Murphy .50
26 Dallas McPherson .25
27 Danny Haren .25
28 Darryl Strawberry .25
29 David Ortiz 1.00
30 David Wright 1.00
31 Derek Jeter 3.00
32 Derrek Lee .50
33 Don Mattingly 1.50
34 Dwight Gooden .25
35 Edgar Renteria .50
36 Eric Chavez .50
37 Eric Gagne .25
38 Gary Sheffield .50
39 Gavin Floyd .25
40 Pedro Martinez 1.00
41 Greg Maddux 2.00
42 Hank Blalock .50
43 Huston Street .25
44 J.D. Drew .25
45 Jake Peavy .50
46 Jake Westbrook .25
47 Jason Bay .25
48 Austin Kearns .25

49 Jeremy Reed .25
50 Jim Rice .50
51 Jimmy Rollins .50
52 Joe Blanton .25
53 Joe Mauer .50
54 Johan Santana 1.00
55 John Smoltz .50
56 Johnny Estrada .25
57 Jose Reyes .50
58 Ken Griffey Jr. 2.00
59 Kerry Wood .50
60 Khalil Greene .50
61 Marcus Giles .25
62 Melvin Mora .25
63 Mark Grace .50
64 Mark Mulder .50
65 Mark Prior 1.00
66 Mark Teixeira .50
67 Matt Clement .25
68 Michael Young .25
69 Miguel Cabrera 1.00
70 Miguel Tejada .75
71 Mike Piazza 1.50
72 Mike Schmidt 2.00
73 Nolan Ryan 3.00
74 Oliver Perez .25
75 Nick Johnson .25
76 Paul Molitor .75
77 Rafael Palmeiro .50
78 Randy Johnson 1.00
79 Reggie Jackson 1.00
80 Rich Harden .25
81 Rickie Weeks .50
82 Robin Yount 1.00
83 Roger Clemens 3.00
84 Roy Oswalt .25
85 Ryan Howard 1.00
86 Ryne Sandberg 2.00
87 Scott Kazmir .25
88 Scott Rolen 1.00
89 Sean Burroughs .25
90 Sean Casey .25
91 Shingo Takatsu .25
92 Tim Hudson .50
93 Tony Gwynn 1.00
94 Torii Hunter .50
95 Travis Hafner .25
96 Victor Martinez .25
97 Vladimir Guerrero 1.00
98 Wade Boggs .50
99 Will Clark .50
100 Yadier Molina .25

SP Authentic Chirography

No Pricing
Production 15 Sets

SP Authentic Chirography Triple

No Pricing
Production Five Sets

SP Authentic Honors

NM/M
Common Player: 1.00
Production 299 Sets
JB Jason Bay 1.50
AB Adrian Beltre 1.50
WB Wade Boggs 1.50
BO Jeremy Bonderman 1.00
CA Miguel Cabrera 2.00
WC Will Clark 1.50
RC Roger Clemens 6.00
CC Carl Crawford 1.00
BC Bobby Crosby 1.50
MG Marcus Giles 1.00
DG Dwight Gooden 1.50
GR Khalil Greene 2.00
ZG Zack Greinke 1.00
KG Ken Griffey Jr. 4.00
TG Tony Gwynn 2.00
TH Travis Hafner 1.00
RH Rich Harden 1.00
BJ Bo Jackson 2.00
DJ Derek Jeter 6.00
SK Scott Kazmir 1.00
BL Barry Larkin 1.50
VM Victor Martinez 1.00
JM Joe Mauer 1.50
MC Dallas McPherson 1.00
PM Paul Molitor 2.00
MO Justin Morneau 1.00
DM Dale Murphy 1.50
DO David Ortiz 2.00
CP Corey Patterson 1.00
JP Jake Peavy 1.50
OP Oliver Perez 1.00
AP Albert Pujols 6.00
AR Aramis Ramirez 1.50
RE Jose Reyes 1.00
CR Cal Ripken Jr. 8.00
JR Jimmy Rollins 1.50
NR Nolan Ryan 6.00
RS Ryne Sandberg 4.00
JS Johan Santana 2.00
MS Mike Schmidt 4.00
BS Ben Sheets 1.50
SM John Smoltz 1.50
ST Shingo Takatsu 1.00
MT Mark Teixeira 1.50
TE Miguel Tejada 2.00
BU B.J. Upton 1.00
JW Jake Westbrook 1.00
DW David Wright 3.00
MY Michael Young 1.00
CZ Carlos Zambrano 1.50

SP Authentic Honors Jersey

NM/M
Common Player: 4.00
Production 130 Sets
JB Jason Bay 4.00
AB Adrian Beltre 6.00
WB Wade Boggs 8.00
BO Jeremy Bonderman 4.00
CA Miguel Cabrera 8.00
WC Will Clark 6.00
RC Roger Clemens 10.00
CC Carl Crawford 4.00
BC Bobby Crosby 4.00
MG Marcus Giles 4.00
DG Dwight Gooden 6.00
GR Khalil Greene 8.00
ZG Zack Greinke 4.00
KG Ken Griffey Jr. 15.00
TG Tony Gwynn 8.00
TH Travis Hafner 4.00
RH Rich Harden 4.00
BJ Bo Jackson 10.00
DJ Derek Jeter 15.00
SK Scott Kazmir 4.00
BL Barry Larkin 6.00
VM Victor Martinez 4.00
JM Joe Mauer 6.00
MC Dallas McPherson 4.00
PM Paul Molitor 8.00
MO Justin Morneau 4.00
DM Dale Murphy 8.00
DO David Ortiz 8.00
CP Corey Patterson 4.00
JP Jake Peavy 6.00
OP Oliver Perez 4.00
AP Albert Pujols 15.00
AR Aramis Ramirez 6.00
RE Jose Reyes 6.00
CR Cal Ripken Jr. 20.00
JR Jimmy Rollins 6.00
NR Nolan Ryan 15.00
RS Ryne Sandberg 10.00
JS Johan Santana 8.00
MS Mike Schmidt 8.00
BS Ben Sheets 4.00
SM John Smoltz 6.00
ST Shingo Takatsu 4.00
MT Mark Teixeira 6.00
TE Miguel Tejada 6.00
BU B.J. Upton 6.00
JW Jake Westbrook 4.00
DW David Wright 15.00
MY Michael Young 4.00
CZ Carlos Zambrano 6.00

SP Authentic Honors Signatures

No Pricing
Production Five Sets

SP Authentic Materials

NM/M
Common Player: 4.00
Production 199 Sets
Gold: 1X
Production 99 Sets
1 A.J. Burnett 4.00
2 Aaron Rowand 4.00
3 Adam Dunn 6.00
4 Adrian Beltre 6.00
5 Adrian Gonzalez 4.00
6 Akinori Otsuka 4.00
7 Albert Pujols 15.00
8 Andre Dawson 6.00
9 Andruw Jones 6.00
10 Aramis Ramirez 6.00
11 Barry Larkin 6.00
12 Ben Sheets 4.00
13 Bo Jackson 8.00
14 Bobby Abreu 4.00
15 Bobby Crosby 4.00
16 Bronson Arroyo 6.00
17 Cal Ripken Jr. 20.00
18 Carl Crawford 4.00
19 Carlos Zambrano 4.00
20 Casey Kotchman 4.00
21 Cesar Izturis 4.00
22 Chone Figgins 4.00
23 Corey Patterson 4.00
24 Craig Biggio 6.00
25 Dale Murphy 6.00
26 Dallas McPherson 4.00
27 Danny Haren 4.00
28 Darryl Strawberry 4.00
29 David Ortiz 8.00
30 David Wright 10.00
31 Derek Jeter 15.00
32 Derrek Lee 8.00
33 Don Mattingly 10.00
34 Dwight Gooden 4.00
35 Edgar Renteria 6.00
36 Eric Chavez 4.00
37 Eric Gagne 6.00
38 Gary Sheffield 6.00
39 Gavin Floyd 4.00
40 Pedro Martinez 8.00
41 Greg Maddux 10.00
42 Hank Blalock 4.00
43 Huston Street 6.00
44 J.D. Drew 4.00
45 Jake Peavy 6.00
46 Jake Westbrook 4.00
47 Jason Bay 4.00
48 Austin Kearns 4.00
49 Jeremy Reed 4.00
50 Jim Rice 6.00
51 Jimmy Rollins 6.00
52 Joe Blanton 4.00
53 Joe Mauer 6.00
54 Johan Santana 6.00
55 John Smoltz 6.00
56 Johnny Estrada 4.00
57 Jose Reyes 6.00
58 Ken Griffey Jr. 12.00
59 Kerry Wood 6.00
60 Khalil Greene 6.00
61 Marcus Giles 4.00
62 Melvin Mora 4.00
63 Mark Grace 6.00
64 Mark Mulder 4.00
65 Mark Prior 8.00
66 Mark Teixeira 6.00
67 Matt Clement 4.00
68 Michael Young 4.00
69 Miguel Cabrera 6.00
70 Miguel Tejada 6.00
71 Mike Piazza 8.00
72 Mike Schmidt 8.00
73 Nolan Ryan 15.00
74 Oliver Perez 4.00
75 Nick Johnson 4.00
76 Paul Molitor 8.00
77 Rafael Palmeiro 6.00
78 Randy Johnson 8.00
79 Reggie Jackson 8.00
80 Rich Harden 4.00
81 Rickie Weeks 6.00
82 Robin Yount 8.00
83 Roger Clemens 10.00
84 Roy Oswalt 6.00
85 Ryan Howard 15.00
86 Ryne Sandberg 8.00
87 Scott Kazmir 4.00
88 Scott Rolen 6.00
89 Sean Burroughs 4.00
90 Sean Casey 4.00
91 Shingo Takatsu 4.00
92 Tim Hudson 6.00
93 Tony Gwynn 8.00
94 Torii Hunter 6.00
95 Travis Hafner 4.00
96 Victor Martinez 4.00
97 Vladimir Guerrero 8.00
98 Wade Boggs 6.00
99 Will Clark 6.00
100 Yadier Molina 4.00

SP Authentic Signatures

NM/M
Production 25-550
Gold: No Pricing
Production 10 Sets
2 Aaron Rowand/550 20.00
3 Adam Dunn/25 20.00
4 Adrian Beltre/125 15.00
5 Adrian Gonzalez/550 10.00
6 Akinori Otsuka/475 15.00
8 Andre Dawson/125 15.00
10 Aramis Ramirez/475 15.00
11 Barry Larkin/125 20.00
12 Ben Sheets/350 12.00
15 Bobby Crosby/350 10.00
16 Bronson Arroyo/550 15.00
18 Carl Crawford/475 12.00
20 Casey Kotchman/550 8.00
21 Cesar Izturis/550 8.00
22 Chone Figgins/550 10.00
23 Corey Patterson/350 10.00
24 Craig Biggio/125 30.00
25 Dale Murphy/350 20.00
26 Dallas McPherson/550 10.00
27 Danny Haren/550 10.00
28 Darryl Strawberry/125 12.00
30 David Wright/350 60.00
31 Derek Jeter/150 140.00
32 Derrek Lee/350 15.00
34 Dwight Gooden/475 15.00
36 Eric Chavez/75 12.00
39 Gavin Floyd/550 8.00
43 Huston Street/550 25.00
45 Jake Peavy/475 15.00
46 Jake Westbrook/550 10.00
47 Jason Bay/475 12.00
48 Austin Kearns/75 10.00
49 Jeremy Reed/550 15.00
50 Jim Rice/350 15.00
52 Joe Blanton/550 10.00
53 Joe Mauer/350 20.00
57 Jose Reyes/475 35.00
60 Khalil Greene/350 20.00
62 Melvin Mora/475 12.00
64 Mark Mulder/350 15.00
66 Mark Teixeira/125 25.00
67 Matt Clement/350 20.00
68 Michael Young/475 15.00
69 Miguel Cabrera/125 25.00
74 Oliver Perez/475 15.00
75 Nick Johnson/550 10.00
84 Roy Oswalt/125 20.00
85 Ryan Howard/550 70.00
86 Ryne Sandberg/25 125.00
87 Scott Kazmir/475 15.00
89 Sean Burroughs/475 10.00
91 Shingo Takatsu/550 10.00

SP Authentic Signature Materials

No Pricing
Production 10 Sets

SP Collection of Stars

NM/M
Common Player: 1.00
Production 299 Sets
BR Bronson Arroyo 1.00
GA Garrett Atkins 1.00
JE Jeff Baker 1.00
BA Clint Barmes 1.00
JB Jason Bartlett 1.00
JA Jason Bay 1.00
BE Adrian Beltre 1.50
BL Joe Blanton 1.00
BO Jeremy Bonderman 1.00
YB Yhency Brazoban 1.00
CB Chris Burke 1.50
AB A.J. Burnett 1.00
DB David Bush 1.00
DC Daniel Cabrera 1.00
MC Miguel Cabrera 2.00
CA Jorge Cantu 1.00
GC Gustavo Chacin 1.00
RC Roger Clemens 6.00
JD J.D. Closser 1.00
CH Chad Cordero 1.00
JC Jesse Crain 1.00
CC Carl Crawford 1.00
CO Coco Crisp 1.00
DD David DeJesus 1.00
DU Jason Dubois 1.00
CD Chris Duffy 1.00
CF Chone Figgins 1.00
GF Gavin Floyd 1.00
JF Jeff Francis 1.00
RF Ryan Freel 1.00
JG Joey Gathright 1.00
GO Jonny Gomes 1.00
AG Adrian Gonzalez 1.00
GR Khalil Greene 2.00
ZG Zack Greinke 1.00
KG Ken Griffey Jr. 4.00
CG Carlos Guillen 1.00
TR Travis Hafner 1.00
BH Bill Hall 1.00
RH Rich Harden 1.50
DH Danny Haren 1.00
MH Matt Holliday 1.00
HO Ryan Howard 2.00
BI Brandon Inge 1.00
CI Cesar Izturis 1.00
EJ Edwin Jackson 1.00
DJ Derek Jeter 6.00
NJ Nick Johnson 1.00
RJ Reed Johnson 1.00
SK Scott Kazmir 1.00
CK Casey Kotchman 1.00
JL Jason Lane 1.00
LE Brandon League 1.00
CL Cliff Lee 1.00
GM Greg Maddux 4.00
AM Andy Marte 1.00
JM Joe Mauer 1.50
DM Dallas McPherson 1.00
YM Yadier Molina 1.00
MM Melvin Mora 1.00
MO Guillermo Mota 1.00
BM Brett Myers 1.00
DO David Ortiz 2.00
CP Corey Patterson 1.00
JP Jake Peavy 1.50
WM Wily Mo Pena 1.00
OP Oliver Perez 1.00
PI Joel Pineiro 1.00
MP Mark Prior 2.00
AP Albert Pujols 6.00
RQ Robb Quinlan 1.00
RA Aramis Ramirez 1.50
JR Jeremy Reed 1.00
RE Jose Reyes 1.50
RI Alex Rios 1.00
CR Cal Ripken Jr. 8.00
RO Jimmy Rollins 1.50
AR Aaron Rowand 1.00
JS Johan Santana 2.00
MS Mike Schmidt 4.00
LS Luke Scott 1.00
CS Chris Shelton 1.00
GS Grady Sizemore 1.50
SM John Smoltz 1.50
HS Huston Street 1.00
NS Nick Swisher 1.00
ST Shingo Takatsu 1.00
WT Willy Taveras 1.00
MT Mark Teahen 1.00
TE Mark Teixeira 1.50
MI Miguel Tejada 1.50
TH Charles Thomas 1.00
CT Chad Tracy 1.00
BU B.J. Upton 1.50
WE Jayson Werth 1.00
JW Jake Westbrook 1.00
DW David Wright 3.00
KY Kevin Youkilis 1.00
MY Michael Young 1.00
CZ Carlos Zambrano 1.50

SP Collection of Stars Jersey

NM/M
Production 130 Sets
BR Bronson Arroyo 4.00
GA Garrett Atkins 4.00
JE Jeff Baker 4.00
BA Clint Barmes 6.00
JB Jason Bartlett 4.00
JA Jason Bay 4.00
BE Adrian Beltre 6.00
BL Joe Blanton 4.00
BO Jeremy Bonderman 4.00
YB Yhency Brazoban 4.00
CB Chris Burke 4.00
AB A.J. Burnett 4.00
DB David Bush 4.00
DC Daniel Cabrera 4.00
MC Miguel Cabrera 8.00
CA Jorge Cantu 4.00
GC Gustavo Chacin 4.00
RC Roger Clemens 10.00
JD J.D. Closser 4.00
CH Chad Cordero 4.00
JC Jesse Crain 4.00
CC Carl Crawford 4.00
CO Coco Crisp 4.00
DD David DeJesus 4.00
DU Jason Dubois 4.00
CD Chris Duffy 6.00
CF Chone Figgins 4.00
GF Gavin Floyd 4.00
JF Jeff Francis 4.00
RF Ryan Freel 4.00
JG Joey Gathright 4.00
GO Jonny Gomes 6.00
AG Adrian Gonzalez 6.00
GR Khalil Greene 6.00
ZG Zack Greinke 4.00
KG Ken Griffey Jr. 15.00
CG Carlos Guillen 4.00
TR Travis Hafner 4.00
BH Bill Hall 4.00
RH Rich Harden 4.00
DH Danny Haren 4.00
MH Matt Holliday 8.00
HO Ryan Howard 15.00
BI Brandon Inge 4.00
CI Cesar Izturis 4.00
EJ Edwin Jackson 4.00
DJ Derek Jeter 15.00
NJ Nick Johnson 4.00
RJ Reed Johnson 4.00
SK Scott Kazmir 4.00
CK Casey Kotchman 4.00
JL Jason Lane 4.00
LE Brandon League 4.00
CL Cliff Lee 4.00
GM Greg Maddux 10.00
AM Andy Marte 4.00
JM Joe Mauer 6.00
DM Dallas McPherson 4.00
YM Yadier Molina 4.00
MM Melvin Mora 4.00
MO Guillermo Mota 4.00
BM Brett Myers 4.00
DO David Ortiz 8.00
CP Corey Patterson 4.00
JP Jake Peavy 6.00
WM Wily Mo Pena 4.00
OP Oliver Perez 4.00
PI Joel Pineiro 4.00
MP Mark Prior 6.00
AP Albert Pujols 15.00
RQ Robb Quinlan 4.00
RA Aramis Ramirez 6.00
JR Jeremy Reed 4.00
RE Jose Reyes 6.00
RI Alex Rios 4.00
CR Cal Ripken Jr. 20.00
RO Jimmy Rollins 6.00
AR Aaron Rowand 6.00
JS Johan Santana 8.00
MS Mike Schmidt 10.00
LS Luke Scott 4.00
CS Chris Shelton 4.00
GS Grady Sizemore 6.00
SM John Smoltz 6.00
HS Huston Street 6.00
NS Nick Swisher 4.00
ST Shingo Takatsu 4.00
WT Willy Taveras 4.00
MT Mark Teahen 4.00
TE Mark Teixeira 6.00
MI Miguel Tejada 6.00
TH Charles Thomas 4.00
CT Chad Tracy 4.00
BU B.J. Upton 4.00
WE Jayson Werth 4.00
JW Jake Westbrook 4.00
DW David Wright 10.00
KY Kevin Youkilis 4.00
CZ Carlos Zambrano 6.00

SP Collection of Stars Signatures

No Pricing
Production Five Sets

SPx Materials

NM/M
Common Player: 3.00
Production 199 Sets
Spectrum: 1X
Production 99 Sets
1 Aaron Harang 3.00
2 Aaron Rowand 5.00
3 Aaron Miles 3.00
4 Adrian Gonzalez 5.00
5 Alex Rios 3.00
6 Angel Berroa 3.00
7 B.J. Upton 5.00
8 Brandon Claussen 3.00
9 Andy Marte 3.00
10 Brandon Webb 5.00
11 Bronson Arroyo 5.00
12 Casey Kotchman 3.00
13 Cesar Izturis 3.00
14 Chad Cordero 3.00
15 Chad Tracy 3.00
16 Charles Thomas 3.00
17 Chase Utley 8.00
18 Chone Figgins 3.00
19 Chris Burke 5.00
20 Cliff Lee 3.00
21 Clint Barmes 5.00
22 Coco Crisp 3.00
23 Bill Hall 3.00
24 Dallas McPherson 3.00
25 Brad Halsey 3.00
26 Daniel Cabrera 3.00
27 Danny Haren 3.00
28 David Bush 3.00
29 David DeJesus 3.00
30 D.J. Houlton 3.00
31 Derek Jeter 20.00
32 Dewon Brazelton 3.00
33 Edwin Jackson 3.00
34 Brad Hawpe 3.00
35 Brandon Inge 3.00
36 Brett Myers 3.00
37 Garrett Atkins 3.00
38 Gavin Floyd 3.00
39 Grady Sizemore 10.00
40 Guillermo Mota 3.00
41 Carlos Guillen 3.00
42 Gustavo Chacin 3.00
43 Huston Street 5.00
44 Chris Duffy 3.00
45 J.D. Closser 3.00
46 J.J. Hardy 3.00
47 Jason Bartlett 3.00
48 Jason Dubois 3.00
49 Chris Shelton 3.00
50 Jason Lane 3.00
51 Jayson Werth 3.00
52 Jeff Baker 3.00
53 Jeff Francis 3.00
54 Jeremy Bonderman 3.00
55 Jeremy Reed 3.00
56 Jerome Williams 3.00
57 Jesse Crain 3.00
58 Chris Young 3.00
59 Jhonny Peralta 3.00
60 Joe Blanton 3.00
61 Joe Crede 3.00
62 Joel Pineiro 3.00
63 Joey Gathright 3.00
64 John Buck 3.00
65 Jonny Gomes 8.00
66 Jorge Cantu 8.00
67 Dan Johnson 3.00
68 Jose Valverde 3.00
69 Ervin Santana 3.00
70 Justin Morneau 5.00
71 Keiichi Yabu 5.00
72 Ken Griffey Jr. 15.00
73 Jason Repko 5.00
74 Kevin Youkilis 3.00
75 Koyie Hill 3.00
76 Laynce Nix 3.00
77 Luke Scott 3.00
78 Juan Rivera 3.00
79 Justin Duchscherer 3.00
80 Mark Teahen 3.00
81 Lance Niekro 3.00
82 Michael Cuddyer 3.00
83 Nick Swisher 3.00
84 Noah Lowry 3.00
85 Matt Holliday 8.00
86 Reed Johnson 3.00
87 Rich Harden 5.00
88 Robb Quinlan 3.00
89 Nick Johnson 3.00
90 Ryan Howard 20.00
91 Nook Logan 3.00
92 Steve Schmoll 3.00
93 Tadahito Iguchi 20.00
94 Willy Taveras 3.00
95 Wily Mo Pena 3.00
96 Xavier Nady 3.00
97 Yadier Molina 3.00
98 Yhency Brazoban 3.00
99 Ryan Freel 3.00
100 Zack Greinke 3.00

SPx Signatures

NM/M
Production 50-350
Spectrum: No Pricing
Production 10 Sets
Jersey Auto.: No Pricing
Production 10 Sets
1 Aaron Harang/350 8.00
2 Aaron Rowand/150 20.00
4 Adrian Gonzalez/225 15.00
6 Angel Berroa/150 8.00
7 B.J. Upton/50 12.00
8 Brandon Claussen/350 8.00
9 Andy Marte/350 10.00
11 Bronson Arroyo/350 20.00
12 Casey Kotchman/225 8.00
13 Cesar Izturis/150 8.00
14 Chad Cordero/350 10.00
15 Chad Tracy/350 10.00
16 Charles Thomas/350 5.00
17 Chase Utley/50 40.00
18 Chone Figgins/150 8.00
19 Chris Burke/350 15.00
20 Cliff Lee/225 10.00
21 Clint Barmes/350 12.00
22 Coco Crisp/225 15.00
23 Bill Hall/350 8.00
24 Dallas McPherson/150 10.00
25 Brad Halsey/350 8.00
26 Daniel Cabrera/350 15.00
27 Danny Haren/225 10.00
28 David Bush/350 10.00
29 David DeJesus/225 8.00
30 D.J. Houlton/350 8.00
31 Derek Jeter/50 150.00
32 Dewon Brazelton/225 8.00
33 Edwin Jackson/150 8.00
34 Brad Hawpe/350 8.00
35 Brandon Inge/350 10.00
36 Brett Myers/150 8.00
37 Garrett Atkins/350 15.00
38 Gavin Floyd/150 8.00
39 Grady Sizemore/350 40.00
40 Guillermo Mota/225 8.00
41 Carlos Guillen/150 8.00
42 Gustavo Chacin/350 10.00
43 Huston Street/350 25.00
44 Chris Duffy/225 15.00
45 J.D. Closser/350 8.00
46 J.J. Hardy/350 10.00
47 Jason Bartlett/350 8.00
48 Jason Dubois/350 10.00
50 Jason Lane/350 10.00
51 Jayson Werth/350 12.00
52 Jeff Baker/350 8.00
53 Jeff Francis/150 10.00
54 Jeremy Bonderman/50 20.00
55 Jeremy Reed/150 10.00
56 Jerome Williams/50 8.00
57 Jesse Crain/350 10.00
59 Jhonny Peralta/350 15.00
60 Joe Blanton/350 10.00
61 Joe Crede/350 25.00
62 Joel Pineiro/150 12.00
63 Joey Gathright/350 8.00
64 John Buck/350 8.00
65 Jonny Gomes/350 15.00
66 Jorge Cantu/350 15.00
67 Dan Johnson/350 15.00
68 Jose Valverde/350 8.00
69 Ervin Santana/350 15.00
71 Keiichi Yabu/350 25.00
73 Jason Repko/350 25.00
74 Kevin Youkilis/225 12.00
75 Koyie Hill/350 10.00
76 Laynce Nix/150 8.00
77 Luke Scott/350 40.00
78 Juan Rivera/225 8.00
79 Justin Duchscherer/350 10.00
80 Mark Teahen/350 8.00
81 Lance Niekro/350 10.00
82 Michael Cuddyer/350 8.00
84 Noah Lowry/150 15.00
85 Matt Holliday/225 25.00
86 Reed Johnson/350 8.00
88 Robb Quinlan/350 5.00
89 Nick Johnson/150 8.00
90 Ryan Howard/225 80.00
91 Nook Logan/350 8.00
92 Steve Schmoll/350 5.00
93 Tadahito Iguchi/50 200.00
95 Wily Mo Pena/150 8.00
96 Xavier Nady/150 10.00
98 Yhency Brazoban/350 8.00

SPx Superscripts Signatures

No Pricing
Production 15 Sets

SPx Superscripts Triple Signature

No Pricing
Production Five Sets

SPx Winning Materials Dual

No Pricing
Production 20 Sets
Dual Auto.: No Pricing
Production Five Sets

SPXtreme Stats

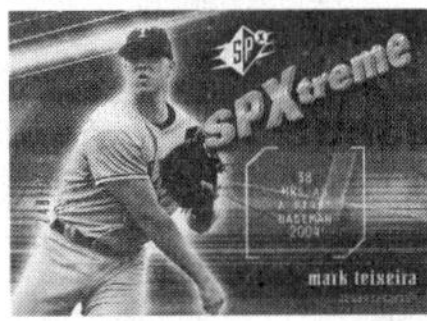

NM/M
Common Player: 1.00
Production 299 Sets
BA Bobby Abreu 1.50
AB Adrian Beltre 1.50
CB Craig Biggio 1.50
HB Hank Blalock 1.50
MC Miguel Cabrera 2.00
SC Sean Casey 1.00
EC Eric Chavez 1.00
RC Roger Clemens 6.00
CC Carl Crawford 1.00
BC Bobby Crosby 1.00
JD J.D. Drew 1.00
AD Adam Dunn 1.50
EG Eric Gagne 1.00
GR Khalil Greene 1.50
KG Ken Griffey Jr. 4.00
VG Vladimir Guerrero 2.00
TH Tim Hudson 1.50
HU Torii Hunter 1.00
DJ Derek Jeter 6.00
RJ Randy Johnson 2.00
AJ Andruw Jones 1.50
DL Derrek Lee 1.50
GM Greg Maddux 4.00
VM Victor Martinez 1.00
JM Joe Mauer 1.50
MO Melvin Mora 1.00
MM Mark Mulder 1.50
DO David Ortiz 2.00
RO Roy Oswalt 1.50
RP Rafael Palmeiro 1.50
CP Corey Patterson 1.00
JP Jake Peavy 1.50
OP Oliver Perez 1.00
PI Mike Piazza 3.00
MP Mark Prior 2.00
AP Albert Pujols 6.00
AR Aramis Ramirez 1.50
ER Edgar Renteria 1.00
JR Jose Reyes 1.00
SR Scott Rolen 2.00
SA Johan Santana 2.00
BS Ben Sheets 1.00
GS Gary Sheffield 1.50
SM John Smoltz 1.50
MT Mark Teixeira 1.50
TE Miguel Tejada 1.50
KW Kerry Wood 1.50
MY Michael Young 1.50
DW David Wright 3.00
CZ Carlos Zambrano 1.50

SPXtreme Stats Jersey

NM/M
BA Bobby Abreu 6.00
AB Adrian Beltre 6.00
CB Craig Biggio 6.00
HB Hank Blalock 4.00
MC Miguel Cabrera 8.00
SC Sean Casey 4.00
EC Eric Chavez 4.00
RC Roger Clemens 10.00
CC Carl Crawford 4.00
BC Bobby Crosby 4.00
JD J.D. Drew 4.00
AD Adam Dunn 6.00
EG Eric Gagne 4.00
GR Khalil Greene 6.00
KG Ken Griffey Jr. 15.00
VG Vladimir Guerrero 8.00
TH Tim Hudson 4.00
HU Torii Hunter 4.00
DJ Derek Jeter 15.00
RJ Randy Johnson 8.00
AJ Andruw Jones 6.00
DL Derrek Lee 6.00
GM Greg Maddux 10.00
VM Victor Martinez 4.00
JM Joe Mauer 6.00
MO Melvin Mora 4.00
MM Mark Mulder 4.00
DO David Ortiz 8.00
RO Roy Oswalt 4.00
RP Rafael Palmeiro 6.00
CP Corey Patterson 4.00
JP Jake Peavy 6.00
OP Oliver Perez 4.00
PI Mike Piazza 8.00
MP Mark Prior 6.00
AP Albert Pujols 15.00
AR Aramis Ramirez 6.00
ER Edgar Renteria 4.00
JR Jose Reyes 66.00
SR Scott Rolen 6.00
SA Johan Santana 8.00
BS Ben Sheets 4.00
GS Gary Sheffield 6.00
SM John Smoltz 6.00
MT Mark Teixeira 6.00
TE Miguel Tejada 6.00
KW Kerry Wood 6.00
DW David Wright 8.00
MY Michael Young 4.00
CZ Carlos Zambrano 6.00

SPXtreme Stats Signatures

No Pricing
Production Five Sets

2005 SP Legendary Cuts

NM/M
Complete Set (90): 25.00
Common Player: .25
Pack (4): 14.00
Box (12): 150.00
1 Al Kaline 1.00
2 Babe Ruth 3.00
3 Bill Mazeroski .25
4 Billy Williams .25
5 Bob Feller .50
6 Bob Gibson 1.00
7 Bob Lemon .25
8 Bobby Doerr .25
9 Brooks Robinson 1.00
10 Carl Yastrzemski 1.50
11 Carlton Fisk .75
12 Casey Stengel .50
13 Jim "Catfish" Hunter .25
14 Christy Mathewson 1.00
15 Cy Young .50
16 Dennis Eckersley .25
17 Dizzy Dean .50
18 Don Drysdale .25
19 Don Sutton .25
20 Duke Snider .75
21 Early Wynn .25
22 Eddie Mathews 1.00
23 Eddie Murray .75
24 Enos Slaughter .25
25 Ernie Banks 1.00
26 Fergie Jenkins .25
27 Frank Robinson 1.00
28 Gary Carter .25
29 Gaylord Perry .25
30 Reggie Jackson 1.00
31 George Kell .25
32 George Sisler .25
33 Hal Newhouser .25
34 Harmon Killebrew 1.00
35 Honus Wagner 1.00
36 Jackie Robinson .50
37 Jim Bunning .25
38 Jim Palmer .50
39 Jimmie Foxx .75
40 Joe DiMaggio 2.00
41 Joe Morgan .50
42 Johnny Bench 1.00
43 Johnny Mize .25
44 Juan Marichal .50
45 Kirby Puckett .75
46 Larry Doby .25
47 Lefty Grove .25
48 Lou Boudreau .25
49 Lou Brock .50
50 Lou Gehrig 2.00
51 Luis Aparicio .50
52 Mel Ott .50
53 Mickey Cochrane .25
54 Mickey Mantle 4.00
55 Mike Schmidt 1.50
56 Monte Irvin .50
57 Nolan Ryan 2.00
58 Orlando Cepeda .25
59 Ozzie Smith 1.00
60 Paul Molitor .50
61 Pee Wee Reese .25
62 Phil Niekro .25
63 Phil Rizzuto .50
64 Ralph Kiner .25
65 Red Schoendienst .25
66 Richie Ashburn .25
67 Rick Ferrell .25
68 Robin Roberts .25
69 Robin Yount 1.00
70 Rod Carew .50
71 Rogers Hornsby .50
72 Rollie Fingers .50
73 Roy Campanella .50
74 Ryne Sandberg 1.00
75 Satchel Paige 1.00
76 Stan Musial 1.00
77 Steve Carlton .25
78 Ted Williams 2.00
79 Thurman Munson 1.00
80 Tom Seaver 1.00
81 Tony Gwynn 1.00
82 Tony Perez .25
83 Ty Cobb 1.50
84 Wade Boggs .50
85 Walter Johnson 1.00
86 Warren Spahn 1.00
87 Whitey Ford 1.00
88 Willie McCovey .50
89 Willie Stargell .75
90 Yogi Berra 1.00

Holofoil

Holofoil: 3-5X
Production 50 Sets

Classic Careers

NM/M
Common Player: 2.00
Production 399 Sets
Gold: 1-2X
Production 75 Sets
Platinum: No Pricing
Production One Set
LA Luis Aparicio 2.00
HB Harold Baines 2.00
JB Jay Buhner 2.00
CA Jose Canseco 3.00
GC Gary Carter 2.00
OC Orlando Cepeda 2.00
JC Jack Clark 2.00
WC Will Clark 3.00
DC David Cone 2.00
AD Andre Dawson 2.00
BD Bobby Doerr 2.00
LD Lenny Dykstra 2.00
CE Carl Erskine 2.00
SF Sid Fernandez 2.00
CF Carlton Fisk 3.00
GF George Foster 2.00
BF Bill Freehan 2.00
DG Dwight Gooden 2.00
GG Rich "Goose" Gossage 2.00
MG Mark Grace 3.00
RG Ron Guidry 2.00
GU Don Gullett 2.00
KH Keith Hernandez 2.00
BH Bob Horner 2.00
FJ Fergie Jenkins 2.00
BL Barry Larkin 3.00
SL Sparky Lyle 2.00
BM Bill Madlock 2.00
DE Dennis Martinez 2.00
GM Gary Mathews 2.00
MA Don Mattingly 5.00
JM Jack Morris 2.00
MU Bobby Murcer 2.00
DM Dale Murphy 3.00
GN Graig Nettles 2.00
PN Phil Niekro 2.00
TO Tony Oliva 2.00
GP Gaylord Perry 2.00
JP Johnny Podres 2.00
TR Tim Raines 2.00
JR Jim Rice 2.00
CR Cal Ripken Jr. 8.00
AR Al Rosen 2.00
ST Dave Stewart 2.00
DS Darryl Strawberry 2.00
SU Bruce Sutter 2.00
DO Don Sutton 2.00
LT Luis Tiant 2.00
AV Andy Van Slyke 2.00
CY Carl Yastrzemski 4.00

Classic Careers Autograph

NM/M
Common Player: 15.00
Production 25 Sets
Gold: No Pricing
Production 10 Sets
Platinum: No Pricing
Production One Set
LA Luis Aparicio 20.00
HB Harold Baines 25.00
JB Jay Buhner 30.00
CA Jose Canseco 40.00
GC Gary Carter 20.00
OC Orlando Cepeda 30.00
JC Jack Clark 20.00
WC Will Clark 25.00
DC David Cone 20.00
AD Andre Dawson 20.00
BD Bobby Doerr 20.00
LD Lenny Dykstra 20.00
CE Carl Erskine 20.00
SF Sid Fernandez 15.00
CF Carlton Fisk 35.00
GF George Foster 25.00
BF Bill Freehan 25.00
DG Dwight Gooden 15.00
GG Rich "Goose" Gossage 20.00
MG Mark Grace 30.00
RG Ron Guidry 35.00
GU Don Gullett 15.00
KH Keith Hernandez 20.00
BH Bob Horner 15.00
FJ Fergie Jenkins 25.00
BL Barry Larkin 40.00
SL Sparky Lyle 20.00
BM Bill Madlock 20.00
DE Dennis Martinez 15.00
GM Gary Mathews 15.00
MA Don Mattingly 60.00
JM Jack Morris 20.00
MU Bobby Murcer 30.00
DM Dale Murphy 35.00
PN Phil Niekro 20.00
GN Graig Nettles 20.00
TO Tony Oliva 20.00
GP Gaylord Perry 20.00
JP Johnny Podres 15.00
TR Tim Raines 20.00
JR Jim Rice 25.00
CR Cal Ripken Jr. 125.00
AR Al Rosen 20.00
ST Dave Stewart 15.00
DS Darryl Strawberry 20.00
SU Bruce Sutter 25.00
DO Don Sutton 20.00
LT Luis Tiant 20.00
AV Andy Van Slyke 30.00
CY Carl Yastrzemski 50.00

Classic Careers Jersey

NM/M
Common Player: 4.00
Gold: 1X
Production 75 Sets
Platinum: No Pricing
Production One Set
LA Luis Aparicio 6.00
HB Harold Baines 6.00
JB Jay Buhner 6.00
CA Jose Canseco 8.00
GC Gary Carter 4.00
OC Orlando Cepeda 6.00
JC Jack Clark 4.00
WC Will Clark 6.00
DC David Cone 4.00
AD Andre Dawson 6.00
BD Bobby Doerr 6.00
LD Lenny Dykstra 6.00
CE Carl Erskine 6.00
SF Sid Fernandez 4.00
CF Carlton Fisk 6.00
GF George Foster 4.00
BF Bill Freehan 6.00
DG Dwight Gooden 4.00
GG Rich "Goose" Gossage 6.00
MG Mark Grace 8.00
RG Ron Guidry 6.00
GU Don Gullett 4.00
KH Keith Hernandez 4.00
BH Bob Horner 4.00
FJ Fergie Jenkins 6.00
BL Barry Larkin 6.00
SL Sparky Lyle 4.00
BM Bill Madlock 4.00
DE Dennis Martinez 4.00
GM Gary Mathews 4.00
MA Don Mattingly 12.00
JM Jack Morris 4.00
MU Bobby Murcer 4.00
DM Dale Murphy 8.00
PN Phil Niekro 4.00
GN Graig Nettles 4.00
TO Tony Oliva 4.00
GP Gaylord Perry 4.00
JP Johnny Podres 6.00
TR Tim Raines 4.00
JR Jim Rice 6.00
CR Cal Ripken Jr. 20.00
AR Al Rosen 6.00
ST Dave Stewart 4.00
DS Darryl Strawberry 6.00
SU Bruce Sutter 4.00
DO Don Sutton 4.00
LT Luis Tiant 4.00
AV Andy Van Slyke 4.00
CY Carl Yastrzemski 15.00

Classic Careers Jersey Autograph

NM/M
Production 25 Sets
Gold: No Pricing
Production 10 Sets
Platinum: No Pricing
Production One Set
LA Luis Aparicio 20.00
HB Harold Baines 25.00
JB Jay Buhner 30.00
GC Gary Carter 20.00
OC Orlando Cepeda 30.00
JC Jack Clark 20.00
WC Will Clark 25.00
DC David Cone 20.00
AD Andre Dawson 20.00
BD Bobby Doerr 20.00
LD Lenny Dykstra 20.00
CE Carl Erskine 20.00
SF Sid Fernandez 15.00
GF George Foster 25.00
BF Bill Freehan 25.00
DG Dwight Gooden 15.00
GG Rich "Goose" Gossage 20.00
MG Mark Grace 30.00
RG Ron Guidry 35.00
GU Don Gullett 15.00
KH Keith Hernandez 20.00
BH Bob Horner 15.00
FJ Fergie Jenkins 25.00
BL Barry Larkin 40.00
SL Sparky Lyle 20.00
BM Bill Madlock 20.00
DE Dennis Martinez 15.00
GM Gary Mathews 15.00
MA Don Mattingly 60.00
JM Jack Morris 20.00
MU Bobby Murcer 30.00
DM Dale Murphy 35.00
PN Phil Niekro 20.00
GN Graig Nettles 20.00
TO Tony Oliva 20.00
GP Gaylord Perry 20.00
JP Johnny Podres 15.00
TR Tim Raines 20.00
JR Jim Rice 25.00
CR Cal Ripken Jr. 125.00
AR Al Rosen 20.00
ST Dave Stewart 15.00
DS Darryl Strawberry 20.00
SU Bruce Sutter 25.00
DO Don Sutton 20.00
LT Luis Tiant 20.00
AV Andy Van Slyke 30.00
CY Carl Yastrzemski 50.00

Classic Careers Patch

NM/M
Production 50 Sets
Gold: No Pricing
Production 10 Sets
Platinum: No Pricing
Production One Set
HB Harold Baines 10.00
CA Jose Canseco 15.00
JC Jack Clark 10.00
WC Will Clark 20.00
DC David Cone 15.00
AD Andre Dawson 15.00
BD Bobby Doerr 15.00
LD Lenny Dykstra 15.00
SF Sid Fernandez 10.00
GF George Foster 10.00
BF Bill Freehan 12.00
DG Dwight Gooden 15.00
GG Rich "Goose" Gossage 12.00
MG Mark Grace 20.00
KH Keith Hernandez 12.00
BL Barry Larkin 25.00
DE Dennis Martinez 10.00
GM Gary Mathews 10.00
JM Jack Morris 10.00
GN Graig Nettles 10.00
GP Gaylord Perry 12.00
TR Tim Raines 10.00
JR Jim Rice 15.00
CR Cal Ripken Jr. 40.00
AV Andy Van Slyke 15.00
ST Dave Stewart 10.00
DS Darryl Strawberry 12.00

Classic Careers Patch Autograph

NM/M
Production 25 Sets
Gold: No Pricing
Production Five Sets
Platinum: No Pricing
Production One Set
HB Harold Baines 40.00
JB Jay Buhner 50.00
JC Jack Clark 35.00
WC Will Clark 40.00
DC David Cone 35.00
AD Andre Dawson 35.00
BD Bobby Doerr 35.00
LD Lenny Dykstra 35.00
SF Sid Fernandez 25.00
GF George Foster 40.00
BF Bill Freehan 40.00
DG Dwight Gooden 25.00
GG Rich "Goose" Gossage 35.00
MG Mark Grace 50.00
GU Don Gullett 25.00
KH Keith Hernandez 35.00
BL Barry Larkin 60.00
DE Dennis Martinez 25.00
GM Gary Mathews 25.00
JM Jack Morris 35.00
GN Graig Nettles 35.00
TO Tony Oliva 35.00
GP Gaylord Perry 30.00
TR Tim Raines 30.00
JR Jim Rice 40.00
CR Cal Ripken Jr. 200.00
ST Dave Stewart 25.00
DS Darryl Strawberry 30.00
AV Andy Van Slyke 40.00

Dual Legendary Cuts

Production 1-10

Glory Days

NM/M
Common Player: 2.00
Production 399 Sets
Gold: 1X-2X
Production 75 Sets
Platinum: No Pricing
Production One Set
HB Harold Baines 2.00
YB Yogi Berra 4.00
LB Lou Brock 2.00
JB Jay Buhner 2.00
CA Jose Canseco 3.00
JC Jack Clark 2.00
WC Will Clark 3.00
DC David Cone 2.00
AD Andre Dawson 2.00
BD Bobby Doerr 2.00
LD Lenny Dykstra 2.00
SF Sid Fernandez 2.00
WF Whitey Ford 3.00
GF George Foster 2.00
BF Bill Freehan 2.00
KG Kirk Gibson 2.00
DG Dwight Gooden 2.00
RG Ron Guidry 3.00
GU Don Gullett 2.00
TG Tony Gwynn 4.00
KH Keith Hernandez 2.00
BH Bob Horner 2.00
FJ Fergie Jenkins 2.00
BL Barry Larkin 3.00
SL Sparky Lyle 2.00
FL Fred Lynn 2.00

BM Bill Madlock 2.00
MA Juan Marichal 3.00
DE Dennis Martinez 2.00
GM Gary Mathews 2.00
PM Paul Molitor 4.00
JM Jack Morris 2.00
MU Bobby Murcer 2.00
DM Dale Murphy 3.00
GN Graig Nettles 2.00
TO Tony Oliva 2.00
JP Jim Palmer 3.00
TR Tim Raines 2.00
JR Jim Rice 2.00
CR Cal Ripken Jr. 8.00
AR Al Rosen 2.00
NR Nolan Ryan 8.00
RS Red Schoendienst 2.00
SN Duke Snider 3.00
ST Dave Stewart 2.00
DS Darryl Strawberry 2.00
BS Bruce Sutter 2.00
LT Luis Tiant 2.00
AV Andy Van Slyke 2.00
RY Robin Yount 4.00

Glory Days Autograph

NM/M
Common Player: 15.00
Production 25 Sets
Gold: No Pricing
Production 10 Sets
Platinum: No Pricing
Production One Set
HB Harold Baines 25.00
YB Yogi Berra 50.00
LB Lou Brock 30.00
JB Jay Buhner 30.00
CA Jose Canseco 40.00
JC Jack Clark 20.00
WC Will Clark 25.00
DC David Cone 20.00
AD Andre Dawson 20.00
BD Bobby Doerr 20.00
LD Lenny Dykstra 20.00
SF Sid Fernandez 15.00
WF Whitey Ford 40.00
GF George Foster 25.00
BF Bill Freehan 25.00
KG Kirk Gibson 20.00
DG Dwight Gooden 15.00
RG Ron Guidry 35.00
GU Don Gullett 15.00
TG Tony Gwynn 40.00
KH Keith Hernandez 20.00
BH Bob Horner 15.00
FJ Fergie Jenkins 25.00
BL Barry Larkin 40.00
SL Sparky Lyle 20.00
FL Fred Lynn 15.00
BM Bill Madlock 20.00
MA Juan Marichal 25.00
DE Dennis Martinez 15.00
GM Gary Mathews 15.00
PM Paul Molitor 40.00
JM Jack Morris 20.00
MU Bobby Murcer 20.00
DM Dale Murphy 35.00
GN Graig Nettles 20.00
TO Tony Oliva 20.00
JP Jim Palmer 25.00
TR Tim Raines 20.00
JR Jim Rice 25.00
CR Cal Ripken Jr. 125.00
AR Al Rosen 20.00
NR Nolan Ryan 100.00
RS Red Schoendienst 20.00
SN Duke Snider 40.00
ST Dave Stewart 15.00
DS Darryl Strawberry 20.00
BS Bruce Sutter 25.00
LT Luis Tiant 20.00
AV Andy Van Slyke 30.00
RY Robin Yount 50.00

Glory Days Jersey

NM/M
Common Player: 4.00
Gold: 1X
Production 75 Sets
Platinum: No Pricing
Production One Set
HB Harold Baines 6.00
YB Yogi Berra 10.00
LB Lou Brock 10.00
JB Jay Buhner 6.00
CA Jose Canseco 8.00
JC Jack Clark 4.00
WC Will Clark 6.00
DC David Cone 4.00
AD Andre Dawson 6.00
BD Bobby Doerr 6.00
LD Lenny Dykstra 4.00
SF Sid Fernandez 4.00
WF Whitey Ford 10.00
GF George Foster 4.00
BF Bill Freehan 6.00
KG Kirk Gibson 4.00
DG Dwight Gooden 4.00
RG Ron Guidry 6.00
GU Don Gullett 4.00
TG Tony Gwynn 8.00
KH Keith Hernandez 4.00
BH Bob Horner 4.00
FJ Fergie Jenkins 6.00
BL Barry Larkin 6.00
SL Sparky Lyle 4.00
FL Fred Lynn 4.00
BM Bill Madlock 4.00
MA Juan Marichal 6.00
DE Dennis Martinez 4.00
GM Gary Mathews 4.00
PM Paul Molitor 6.00
JM Jack Morris 4.00
MU Bobby Murcer 4.00
DM Dale Murphy 8.00
GN Graig Nettles 4.00
TO Tony Oliva 4.00
JP Jim Palmer 6.00
TR Tim Raines 4.00
JR Jim Rice 6.00
CR Cal Ripken Jr. 20.00
AR Al Rosen 6.00
NR Nolan Ryan 15.00
RS Red Schoendienst 4.00
SN Duke Snider 8.00
ST Dave Stewart 4.00
DS Darryl Strawberry 6.00
BS Bruce Sutter 4.00
LT Luis Tiant 4.00
AV Andy Van Slyke 4.00
RY Robin Yount 10.00

Glory Days Memorabilia Autograph

NM/M
Production 25 Sets
Gold: No Pricing
Production 10 Sets
Platinum: No Pricing
Production One Set
HB Harold Baines 25.00
YB Yogi Berra 50.00
JB Jay Buhner 30.00
JC Jack Clark 20.00
WC Will Clark 25.00
DC David Cone 20.00
AD Andre Dawson 20.00
BD Bobby Doerr 20.00
LD Lenny Dykstra 20.00
SF Sid Fernandez 15.00
WF Whitey Ford 40.00
GF George Foster 25.00
BF Bill Freehan 25.00
KG Kirk Gibson 20.00
DG Dwight Gooden 15.00
BG Ron Guidry 35.00
GU Don Gullett 15.00
TG Tony Gwynn 40.00
KH Keith Hernandez 20.00
BH Bob Horner 15.00
FJ Fergie Jenkins 25.00
BL Barry Larkin 40.00
SL Sparky Lyle 20.00
FL Fred Lynn 15.00
BM Bill Madlock 20.00
MA Juan Marichal 25.00
DE Dennis Martinez 15.00
GM Gary Mathews 15.00
PM Paul Molitor 40.00
JM Jack Morris 20.00
MU Bobby Murcer 25.00
DM Dale Murphy 35.00
GN Graig Nettles 20.00
TO Tony Oliva 20.00
JP Jim Palmer 25.00
TR Tim Raines 20.00
JR Jim Rice 25.00
AR Al Rosen 20.00
NR Nolan Ryan 100.00
RS Red Schoendienst 20.00
SN Duke Snider 40.00
ST Dave Stewart 15.00
DS Darryl Strawberry 20.00
BS Bruce Sutter 25.00
LT Luis Tiant 20.00
AV Andy Van Slyke 30.00
RY Robin Yount 50.00

Glory Days Patch

NM/M
Production 50 Sets
Gold: No Pricing
Production 10 Sets
Platinum: No Pricing
Production One Set
HB Harold Baines 10.00
JC Jack Clark 10.00
DC David Cone 15.00
AD Andre Dawson 15.00
BD Bobby Doerr 15.00
LD Lenny Dykstra 15.00
SF Sid Fernandez 10.00
GF George Foster 10.00
DG Dwight Gooden 15.00
KH Keith Hernandez 12.00
BH Bob Horner 10.00
FJ Fergie Jenkins 15.00
BL Barry Larkin 25.00
GM Gary Mathews 10.00
JM Jack Morris 10.00
DM Dale Murphy 20.00
GN Graig Nettles 10.00
JP Jim Palmer 15.00
TR Tim Raines 10.00
RS Red Schoendienst 15.00
DS Darryl Strawberry 12.00
BS Bruce Sutter 15.00
LT Luis Tiant 15.00
AV Andy Van Slyke 15.00

Glory Days Patch Autograph

NM/M
Production 25 Sets
Gold: No Pricing
Production Five Sets
Platinum: No Pricing
Production One Set
HB Harold Baines 40.00
JB Jay Buhner 50.00
JC Jack Clark 35.00
DC David Cone 35.00
AD Andre Dawson 35.00
BD Bobby Doerr 35.00
LD Lenny Dykstra 35.00
SF Sid Fernandez 25.00
GF George Foster 40.00
DG Dwight Gooden 25.00
KH Keith Hernandez 35.00
BH Bob Horner 25.00
FJ Fergie Jenkins 40.00
BL Barry Larkin 60.00
BM Bill Madlock 25.00
DE Dennis Martinez 25.00
GM Gary Mathews 25.00
JM Jack Morris 35.00
DM Dale Murphy 40.00
GN Graig Nettles 35.00
TO Tony Oliva 35.00
JP Jim Palmer 40.00
TR Tim Raines 30.00
JR Jim Rice 40.00
RS Red Schoendienst 30.00
DS Darryl Strawberry 30.00
BS Bruce Sutter 25.00
LT Luis Tiant 25.00
AV Andy Van Slyke 40.00

Historic Cuts

No Pricing
Production One Set

Historic Quads Autograph

No Pricing
Production Five Sets

Historic Quads Material

No Pricing
Production Five Sets
Patch: No Pricing
Production One Set

Lasting Legends

NM/M
Common Player: 2.00
Production 399 Sets
Gold: 1-2X
Production 75 Sets
Platinum: No Pricing
Production One Set
LA Luis Aparicio 2.00
EB Ernie Banks 4.00
BE Johnny Bench 4.00
YB Yogi Berra 4.00
WB Wade Boggs 3.00
LB Lou Brock 3.00
RC Rod Carew 3.00
SC Steve Carlton 2.00
GC Gary Carter 2.00
OC Orlando Cepeda 2.00
BD Bobby Doerr 2.00
DE Dennis Eckersley 2.00
RF Rollie Fingers 2.00
CF Carlton Fisk 3.00
WF Whitey Ford 3.00
BG Bob Gibson 3.00
DG Dwight Gooden 2.00
TG Tony Gwynn 3.00
KH Keith Hernandez 2.00
FJ Fergie Jenkins 2.00
AK Al Kaline 3.00
BL Barry Larkin 3.00
MA Juan Marichal 2.00
DM Don Mattingly 5.00
BM Bill Mazeroski 2.00
PM Paul Molitor 3.00
JM Joe Morgan 2.00
MU Dale Murphy 3.00
EM Eddie Murray 3.00
SM Stan Musial 4.00
PN Phil Niekro 2.00
GN Graig Nettles 2.00
JP Jim Palmer 3.00
TP Tony Perez 2.00
GP Gaylord Perry 2.00
KP Kirby Puckett 3.00
JR Jim Rice 2.00
CR Cal Ripken Jr. 8.00
BR Brooks Robinson 3.00
FR Frank Robinson 3.00
NR Nolan Ryan 6.00
SA Ryne Sandberg 4.00
MS Mike Schmidt 4.00
RS Red Schoendienst 3.00
OS Ozzie Smith 4.00
SN Duke Snider 3.00
BS Bruce Sutter 2.00
DS Don Sutton 2.00
CY Carl Yastrzemski 4.00
RY Robin Yount 4.00

Lasting Legends Autograph

NM/M
Common Player:
Production 25 Sets
Gold: No Pricing
Production 10 Sets
Platinum: No Pricing
Production One Set
LA Luis Aparicio 20.00
EB Ernie Banks 60.00
BE Johnny Bench 50.00
YB Yogi Berra 60.00
WB Wade Boggs 40.00
LB Lou Brock 25.00
RC Rod Carew 35.00
SC Steve Carlton 25.00
GC Gary Carter 25.00
OC Orlando Cepeda 25.00
BD Bobby Doerr 20.00
DE Dennis Eckersley 25.00
RF Rollie Fingers 20.00
CF Carlton Fisk 35.00
WF Whitey Ford 40.00
BG Bob Gibson 40.00
DG Dwight Gooden 15.00
TG Tony Gwynn 50.00
KH Keith Hernandez 20.00
FG Fergie Jenkins 25.00
AK Al Kaline 40.00
BL Barry Larkin 40.00
MA Juan Marichal 25.00
DM Don Mattingly 60.00
BM Bill Mazeroski 35.00
PM Paul Molitor 40.00
JM Joe Morgan 25.00
MU Dale Murphy 40.00
EM Eddie Murray 50.00
SM Stan Musial 60.00
GN Graig Nettles 20.00
PN Phil Niekro 25.00
JP Jim Palmer 25.00
TP Tony Perez 20.00
GP Gaylord Perry 20.00
KP Kirby Puckett 50.00
JR Jerry Rice 25.00
CR Cal Ripken Jr. 125.00
BR Brooks Robinson 40.00
FR Frank Robinson 25.00
NR Nolan Ryan 100.00
SA Ryne Sandberg 50.00
MS Mike Schmidt 50.00
RS Red Schoendienst 20.00
OS Ozzie Smith 60.00
SN Duke Snider 40.00
BS Bruce Sutter 25.00
DS Don Sutton 20.00
CY Carl Yastrzemski 50.00
RY Robin Yount 50.00

Lasting Legends Material

NM/M
Common Player: 4.00
Gold: 1-1.5X
Production 75 Sets
Platinum: No Pricing
Production One Set
LA Luis Aparicio 4.00
EB Ernie Banks 10.00
BE Johnny Bench 8.00
YB Yogi Berra 8.00
WB Wade Boggs 6.00
LB Lou Brock 6.00
RC Rod Carew 6.00
SC Steve Carlton 4.00
GC Gary Carter 4.00
OC Orlando Cepeda 4.00
BD Bobby Doerr 6.00
DE Dennis Eckersley 6.00
RF Rollie Fingers 4.00
CF Carlton Fisk 6.00
WF Whitey Ford 6.00
BG Bob Gibson 8.00
DG Dwight Gooden 4.00
TG Tony Gwynn 8.00
KH Keith Hernandez 4.00
FJ Fergie Jenkins 4.00
AK Al Kaline 10.00
BL Barry Larkin 6.00
MA Juan Marichal 6.00
DM Don Mattingly 10.00
BM Bill Mazeroski 6.00
PM Paul Molitor 6.00
JM Joe Morgan 4.00
MU Dale Murphy 6.00
EM Eddie Murray 6.00
SM Stan Musial 10.00
GN Graig Nettles 4.00
PN Phil Niekro 4.00
JP Jim Palmer 6.00
TP Tony Perez 4.00
GP Gaylord Perry 4.00
KP Kirby Puckett 8.00
JR Jim Rice 4.00
CR Cal Ripken Jr. 20.00
BR Brooks Robinson 6.00
FR Frank Robinson 6.00
NR Nolan Ryan 15.00
SA Ryne Sandberg 8.00
MS Mike Schmidt 10.00
RS Red Schoendienst 4.00
OS Ozzie Smith 8.00
SN Duke Snider 6.00
BS Bruce Sutter 4.00
DS Don Sutton 4.00
CY Carl Yastrzemski 15.00
RY Robin Yount 8.00

Lasting Legends Jersey Autograph

NM/M
Production 25 Sets
Gold: No Pricing
Production 10 Sets
Platinum: No Pricing
Production One Set
LA Luis Aparicio 20.00
EB Ernie Banks 60.00
BE Johnny Bench 50.00
YB Yogi Berra 60.00
WB Wade Boggs 40.00
LB Lou Brock 25.00
RC Rod Carew 40.00
SC Steve Carlton 25.00
GC Gary Carter 25.00
OC Orlando Cepeda 25.00
BD Bobby Doerr 20.00
DE Dennis Eckersley 25.00
RF Rollie Fingers 20.00
CF Carlton Fisk 40.00
WF Whitey Ford 40.00
BG Bob Gibson 40.00
DG Dwight Gooden 15.00
TG Tony Gwynn 50.00
KH Keith Hernandez 20.00
FG Fergie Jenkins 25.00
AK Al Kaline 50.00
BL Barry Larkin 40.00
MA Juan Marichal 25.00
DM Don Mattingly 60.00
BM Bill Mazeroski 40.00
PM Paul Molitor 40.00
JM Joe Morgan 25.00
MU Dale Murphy 40.00
SM Stan Musial 60.00
GN Graig Nettles 20.00
PN Phil Niekro 25.00
JP Jim Palmer 25.00
TP Tony Perez 20.00
GP Gaylord Perry 20.00
JR Jim Rice 25.00
CR Cal Ripken Jr. 140.00
BR Brooks Robinson 40.00
FR Frank Robinson 25.00
NR Nolan Ryan 100.00
SA Ryne Sandberg 50.00
MS Mike Schmidt 50.00
RS Red Schoendienst 20.00
OS Ozzie Smith 60.00
SN Duke Snider 40.00
BS Bruce Sutter 25.00
CY Carl Yastrzemski 50.00
RY Robin Yount 50.00

Lasting Legends Patch

NM/M
Production 50 Sets
Gold: No Pricing
Production 10 Sets
Platinum: No Pricing
Production One Set
WB Wade Boggs 20.00
LB Lou Brock 15.00
RC Rod Carew 15.00
SC Steve Carlton 15.00
GC Gary Carter 12.00
OC Orlando Cepeda 15.00
DE Dennis Eckersley 15.00
RF Rollie Fingers 10.00
CF Carlton Fisk 15.00
DG Dwight Gooden 10.00
KH Keith Hernandez 10.00
FJ Fergie Jenkins 15.00
BL Barry Larkin 25.00
MA Juan Marichal 15.00
JM Joe Morgan 15.00
PN Phil Niekro 15.00
JP Jim Palmer 15.00
TP Tony Perez 15.00
GP Gaylord Perry 12.00
KP Kirby Puckett 25.00
JR Jim Rice 15.00
BR Brooks Robinson 20.00
FR Frank Robinson 15.00
SA Ryne Sandberg 25.00
OS Ozzie Smith 25.00
BS Bruce Sutter 15.00
DS Don Sutton 12.00
RY Robin Yount 25.00

Lasting Legends Patch Autograph

NM/M
Production 25 Sets
Gold: No Pricing
Production Five Sets
Platinum: No Pricing
Production One Set
WB Wade Boggs 50.00
RC Rod Carew 50.00
SC Steve Carlton 35.00
GC Gary Carter 35.00
OC Orlando Cepeda 30.00
DE Dennis Eckersley 35.00
RF Rollie Fingers 25.00
DG Dwight Gooden 25.00
KH Keith Hernandez 25.00
FJ Fergie Jenkins 35.00
BL Barry Larkin 50.00
MA Juan Marichal 35.00
PM Paul Molitor 50.00
JM Joe Morgan 35.00
PN Phil Niekro 35.00
JP Jim Palmer 40.00
TP Tony Perez 30.00
GP Gaylord Perry 30.00
JR Jim Rice 35.00
BR Brooks Robinson 50.00
NR Nolan Ryan 140.00
SA Ryne Sandberg 80.00
OS Ozzie Smith 75.00
BS Bruce Sutter 30.00
RY Robin Yount 65.00

Legendary Cuts

NM/M
Production 1-108
LA Luke Appling/55 125.00
RI Richie Ashburn/83 150.00
EA Earl Averill/91 90.00
JB Cool Papa Bell/78 300.00
LB Lou Boudreau/99 100.00
MC Max Carey/84 140.00
HC Happy Chandler/39 125.00
JC Jocko Conlan/40 140.00
ST Stan Coveleski/71 140.00
CR Joe Cronin/76 140.00
RD Ray Dandridge/76 100.00
BD Bill Dickey/95 150.00
JD Joe DiMaggio/56 500.00
LD Larry Doby/32 200.00
DD Don Drysdale/50 200.00
DU Leo Durocher/57 150.00
FE Rick Ferrell/80 125.00
CF Carl Furillo/25 200.00
CG Charlie Gehringer/97 120.00
GO Lefty Gomez/68 150.00
HG Hank Greenberg/44 280.00
BU Burleigh Grimes/99 125.00
GR Lefty Grove/41 250.00
HA Chick Hafey/52 150.00
JH Jesse Haines/90 150.00
GH Gabby Hartnett/50 180.00
BH Billy Herman/99 90.00
WH Waite Hoyt/99 140.00
CH Carl Hubbell/99 150.00
HU Jim "Catfish" Hunter/65 140.00
JJ Jackie Jensen/48 180.00
JO Judy Johnson/39 150.00
CK Charlie Keller/98 140.00
HK Harvey Kuenn/33 165.00
BL Bob Lemon/108 100.00
LE Buck Leonard/71 140.00
LI Freddie Lindstrom/19 250.00
LO Ernie Lombardi/29 200.00
HM Heinie Manush/25 175.00
RU Rube Marquard/80 150.00
EM Eddie Mathews/80 150.00
RO Roy McMillan/23 140.00
MI Johnny Mize/90 125.00
HN Hal Newhouser/96 125.00
PR Pee Wee Reese/69 180.00
SR Sam Rice/41 180.00
ER Edd Roush/99 100.00
JS Joe Sewell/76 140.00
ES Enos Slaughter/99 100.00
WA Warren Spahn/92 140.00
WS Willie Stargell/63 165.00
CS Casey Stengel/61 250.00
BW Bucky Walters/34 150.00
JW Hoyt Wilhelm/48 100.00
EW Early Wynn/89 120.00

Legendary Cuts Material

NM/M
Production 75 unless noted.
Gold: No Pricing
Production 15 Sets
CA Roy Campanella 40.00
RC Roberto Clemente 80.00
TC Ty Cobb 140.00
CO Mickey Cochrane 50.00
CR Joe Cronin 15.00
DE Dizzy Dean 60.00
BD Bill Dickey 35.00
JD Joe DiMaggio 120.00
DD Don Drysdale 15.00
JF Jimmie Foxx 60.00
LG Lou Gehrig 175.00
HG Hank Greenberg 35.00
HO Gil Hodges 40.00
RH Rogers Hornsby 80.00
HU Jim "Catfish" Hunter 10.00
TK Ted Kluszewski 20.00
TL Tony Lazzeri 40.00
BL Bob Lemon 25.00
MM Mickey Mantle 150.00
RM Roger Maris 60.00
EM Eddie Mathews 40.00
CM Christy Mathewson 125.00
MI Johnny Mize 25.00
TM Thurman Munson 35.00
MO Mel Ott 50.00
SP Satchel Paige 75.00
PR Pee Wee Reese 25.00
JR Jackie Robinson 65.00
BR Babe Ruth 180.00
SI George Sisler 35.00
ES Enos Slaughter 15.00
WA Warren Spahn 40.00

CS Casey Stengel 40.00
HW Honus Wagner/22 140.00
JW Hoyt Wilhelm 15.00
TW Ted Williams 75.00
EW Early Wynn 10.00

Legendary Cuts Quad

No Pricing
Production One Set

Legendary Battery Cuts

NM/M
Production 6-99
SC Stan Coveleski/25 140.00
BD Bill Dickey/22 200.00
DD Don Drysdale/31 200.00
LG Lefty Gomez/77 160.00
JH Jesse Haines/28 200.00
WH Waite Hoyt/58 125.00
CH Carl Hubbell/99 140.00
HN Hal Newhouser/32 140.00
WS Warren Spahn/43 150.00
EW Early Wynn/32 125.00

Legendary Cornerstone Cuts

NM/M
Production 1-79
DC Dolph Camilli/79 120.00
RD Ray Dandridge/27 125.00
EM Eddie Mathews/50 150.00
JM Johnny Mize/46 150.00
WS Willie Stargell/36 150.00

Legendary Duels Material

NM/M
Production 25 Sets
Patch: No Pricing
Production 10 Sets
BM Ernie Banks, Stan Musial 50.00
CC Jose Canseco, Will Clark 40.00
DM Paul Molitor, Lenny Dykstra 25.00
EG Dennis Eckersley, Kirk Gibson 25.00
FB Carlton Fisk, Johnny Bench 25.00
FR George Foster, Jim Rice 15.00
JY Reggie Jackson, Carl Yastrzemski 40.00
MC Rod Carew, Paul Molitor 25.00
MH Don Mattingly, Keith Hernandez 35.00
SF Duke Snider, Whitey Ford 35.00
SG Ron Guidry, Don Sutton 15.00
SS Ozzie Smith, Ryne Sandberg 60.00
YS Mike Schmidt, Robin Yount 35.00

Legendary Duels Autograph

No Pricing
Production 15 Sets

Legendary Duos Material

NM/M
Production 25 Sets
Patch: No Pricing
Production 10 Sets
CO Tony Oliva, Rod Carew 20.00
ES Duke Snider, Carl Erskine 15.00
FB Yogi Berra, Whitey Ford 40.00
GS Ryne Sandberg, Mark Grace 50.00
JG Reggie Jackson, Ron Guidry 25.00
MB Joe Morgan, Johnny Bench 35.00
MY Robin Yount, Paul Molitor 40.00
RB Wade Boggs, Jim Rice 20.00
RC Will Clark, Cal Ripken Jr. 50.00
RM Cal Ripken Jr., Eddie Murray 50.00
RR Brooks Robinson, Frank Robinson 25.00
SC Mike Schmidt, Steve Carlton 30.00
SG Darryl Strawberry, Dwight Gooden 15.00

Legendary Duos Autograph

No Pricing
Production 15 Sets

Legendary Glovemen Cuts

NM/M
EA Earl Averill/39 120.00
CP Cool Papa Bell/29 350.00
MC Max Carey/50 140.00
JD Joe DiMaggio/75 400.00
ES Enos Slaughter/65 120.00

Middlemen Cuts

NM/M
Production 2-99
LA Luke Appling/32 150.00
LB Lou Boudreau/99 100.00
JC Joe Cronin/30 140.00
CG Charlie Gehringer/95 140.00
BH Billy Herman/90 90.00
PW Pee Wee Reese/39 200.00
JS Joe Sewell/76 140.00

Legendary Lineage

NM/M
Common Player: 2.00
Production 399 Sets
Gold: 1-2X
Production 75 Sets
Platinum: No Pricing
Production One Set
HB Harold Baines 2.00
JB Jay Buhner 2.00
CA Jose Canseco 3.00
SC Steve Carlton 2.00
JC Jack Clark 2.00
WC Will Clark 3.00
DC David Cone 2.00
AD Andre Dawson 2.00
BD Bobby Doerr 2.00
LD Lenny Dykstra 2.00
EC Dennis Eckersley 2.00
SF Sid Fernandez 2.00
BF Bill Freehan 2.00
DG Dwight Gooden 2.00
GG Rich "Goose" Gossage 2.00
MG Mark Grace 3.00
RG Ron Guidry 2.00
GU Don Gullett 2.00
TG Tony Gwynn 4.00
KH Keith Hernandez 2.00
BH Bob Horner 2.00
RJ Reggie Jackson 3.00
FJ Fergie Jenkins 2.00
BL Barry Larkin 3.00
SL Sparky Lyle 2.00
BM Bill Madlock 2.00
DE Dennis Martinez 2.00
GM Gary Matthews 2.00
MA Don Mattingly 5.00
PM Paul Molitor 3.00
JM Jack Morris 2.00
MU Bobby Murcer 2.00
DM Dale Murphy 3.00
GN Graig Nettles 2.00
TO Tony Oliva 2.00
JP Jim Palmer 3.00
KP Kirby Puckett 4.00
TR Tim Raines 2.00
JR Jim Rice 2.00
CR Cal Ripken Jr. 8.00
BR Brooks Robinson 3.00
AR Al Rosen 2.00
MS Mike Schmidt 5.00
OS Ozzie Smith 4.00
SN Duke Snider 3.00
DS Dave Stewart 2.00
ST Darryl Strawberry 2.00
SU Bruce Sutter 2.00
LT Luis Tiant 2.00
AV Andy Van Slyke 2.00

Legendary Lineage Autograph

NM/M
Common Player: 15.00
Production 25 Sets
Gold: No Pricing
Production 10 Sets
Platinum: No Pricing
Production One Set
HB Harold Baines 25.00
JB Jay Buhner 30.00
CA Jose Canseco 40.00
SC Steve Carlton 25.00
JC Jack Clark 20.00
WC Will Clark 25.00
DC David Cone 20.00
AD Andre Dawson 20.00
BD Bobby Doerr 20.00
LD Lenny Dykstra 20.00
EC Dennis Eckersley 25.00
SF Sid Fernandez 15.00
BF Bill Freehan 25.00
DG Dwight Gooden 15.00
GG Rich "Goose" Gossage 20.00
MG Mark Grace 30.00
RG Ron Guidry 35.00
GU Don Gullett 15.00
TG Tony Gwynn 40.00
KH Keith Hernandez 20.00
BH Bob Horner 15.00
RJ Reggie Jackson 40.00
FJ Fergie Jenkins 25.00
BL Barry Larkin 40.00
SL Sparky Lyle 20.00
BM Bill Madlock 20.00
DE Dennis Martinez 15.00
GM Gary Matthews 15.00
MA Don Mattingly 60.00
PM Paul Molitor 40.00
JM Jack Morris 20.00
MU Bobby Murcer 25.00
DM Dale Murphy 35.00
GN Graig Nettles 20.00
TO Tony Oliva 20.00
JP Jim Palmer 25.00
KP Kirby Puckett 50.00
TR Tim Raines 20.00
JR Jim Rice 25.00
CR Cal Ripken Jr. 125.00
BR Brooks Robinson 40.00
AR Al Rosen 20.00
MS Mike Schmidt 60.00
OS Ozzie Smith 50.00
SN Duke Snider 40.00
DS Dave Stewart 15.00
ST Darryl Strawberry 20.00
SU Bruce Sutter 25.00
LT Luis Tiant 20.00
AV Andy Van Slyke 30.00

Legendary Lineage Jersey

NM/M
Common Player: 4.00
Gold: 1-1.5X
Production 75 Sets
Platinum: No Pricing
Production One Set
HB Harold Baines 4.00
JB Jay Buhner 4.00
CA Jose Canseco 8.00
SC Steve Carlton 6.00
JC Jack Clark 4.00
WC Will Clark 6.00
DC David Cone 4.00
AD Andre Dawson 6.00
BD Bobby Doerr 6.00
LD Lenny Dykstra 4.00
EC Dennis Eckersley 6.00
SF Sid Fernandez 4.00
BF Bill Freehan 6.00
DG Dwight Gooden 4.00
GG Rich "Goose" Gossage 4.00
MG Mark Grace 8.00
RG Ron Guidry 4.00
GU Don Gullett 4.00
TG Tony Gwynn 8.00
KH Keith Hernandez 4.00
BH Bob Horner 4.00
RJ Reggie Jackson 8.00
FJ Fergie Jenkins 6.00
BL Barry Larkin 6.00
SL Sparky Lyle 4.00
BM Bill Madlock 4.00
DE Dennis Martinez 4.00
GM Gary Matthews 4.00
MA Don Mattingly 12.00
PM Paul Molitor 6.00
JM Jack Morris 4.00
MU Bobby Murcer 4.00
DM Dale Murphy 8.00
GN Graig Nettles 4.00
TO Tony Oliva 4.00
JP Jim Palmer 6.00
KP Kirby Puckett 8.00
TR Tim Raines 4.00
JR Jim Rice 6.00
CR Cal Ripken Jr. 20.00
BR Brooks Robinson 6.00
AR Al Rosen 6.00
MS Mike Schmidt 10.00
OS Ozzie Smith 8.00
SN Duke Snider 8.00
DS Dave Stewart 4.00
ST Darryl Strawberry 4.00
SU Bruce Sutter 4.00
LT Luis Tiant 4.00
AV Andy Van Slyke 4.00

Legendary Lineage Jersey Autograph

NM/M
Production 25 Sets
Gold: No Pricing
Production 10 Sets
Platinum: No Pricing
Production One Set
HB Harold Baines 25.00
JB Jay Buhner 30.00
CA Jose Canseco 40.00
SC Steve Carlton 25.00
JC Jack Clark 20.00
WC Will Clark 25.00
DC David Cone 20.00
AD Andre Dawson 20.00
BD Bobby Doerr 25.00
LD Lenny Dykstra 20.00
EC Dennis Eckersley 25.00
SF Sid Fernandez 15.00
BF Bill Freehan 25.00
DG Dwight Gooden 15.00
GG Rich "Goose" Gossage 20.00
MG Mark Grace 30.00
RG Ron Guidry 35.00
GU Don Gullett 15.00
TG Tony Gwynn 40.00
KH Keith Hernandez 20.00
BH Bob Horner 15.00
RJ Reggie Jackson 40.00
FJ Fergie Jenkins 25.00
BL Barry Larkin 40.00
SL Sparky Lyle 20.00
BM Bill Madlock 20.00
DE Dennis Martinez 15.00
GM Gary Matthews 15.00
MA Don Mattingly 60.00
PM Paul Molitor 40.00
JM Jack Morris 20.00
MU Bobby Murcer 25.00
DM Dale Murphy 35.00
GN Graig Nettles 20.00
TO Tony Oliva 20.00
JP Jim Palmer 25.00
KP Kirby Puckett 50.00
TR Tim Raines 20.00
JR Jim Rice 25.00
CR Cal Ripken Jr. 150.00
BR Brooks Robinson 40.00
AR Al Rosen 20.00
MS Mike Schmidt 60.00
OS Ozzie Smith 50.00
SN Duke Snider 40.00
DS Dave Stewart 20.00
ST Darryl Strawberry 20.00
SU Bruce Sutter 25.00
LT Luis Tiant 20.00
AV Andy Van Slyke 30.00

Legendary Lineage Patch

NM/M
Production 50 Sets
Gold: No Pricing
Production 10 Sets
Platinum: No Pricing
Production One Set
HB Harold Baines 10.00
JB Jay Buhner 15.00
JC Jack Clark 10.00
WC Will Clark 20.00
DC David Cone 15.00
AD Andre Dawson 15.00
BD Bobby Doerr 15.00
BF Bill Freehan 12.00
DG Dwight Gooden 15.00
GG Rich "Goose" Gossage 12.00
MG Mark Grace 20.00
TG Tony Gwynn 20.00
KH Keith Hernandez 12.00
BH Bob Horner 10.00
BL Barry Larkin 25.00
BM Bill Madlock 10.00
DE Dennis Martinez 10.00
JM Jack Morris 10.00
DM Dale Murphy 20.00
GN Graig Nettles 10.00
TR Tim Raines 10.00
CR Cal Ripken Jr. 40.00
MS Mike Schmidt 25.00
DS Dave Stewart 10.00
ST Darryl Strawberry 12.00
LT Luis Tiant 10.00
AV Andy Van Slyke 15.00

Legendary Lineage Patch Autograph

NM/M
Production 25 Sets
Gold: No Pricing
Production Five Sets
Platinum: No Pricing
Production One Set
HB Harold Baines 40.00
JB Jay Buhner 50.00
JC Jack Clark 35.00
WC Will Clark 40.00
DC David Cone 35.00
AD Andre Dawson 35.00
BD Bobby Doerr 35.00
BF Bill Freehan 40.00
DG Dwight Gooden 25.00
GG Rich "Goose" Gossage 35.00
MG Mark Grace 50.00
TG Tony Gwynn 70.00
KH Keith Hernandez 35.00
BH Bob Horner 25.00
BL Barry Larkin 60.00
BM Bill Madlock 25.00
DE Dennis Martinez 25.00
PM Paul Molitor 50.00
JM Jack Morris 35.00
DM Dale Murphy 40.00
GN Graig Nettles 35.00
TR Tim Raines 30.00
JR Jim Rice 40.00
CR Cal Ripken Jr. 200.00
MS Mike Schmidt 90.00
DS Dave Stewart 25.00
ST Darryl Strawberry 30.00
LT Luis Tiant 25.00
AV Andy Van Slyke 40.00

Significant Tips

No Pricing
Production 10 Sets
Patch: No Pricing
Production Five Sets

Significant Trips Autograph

No Pricing
Production 10 Sets

2006 SP Authentic

NM/M
Complete Set (300):
Common Player (1-100): .25
Common SP (101-200): 2.00
Production 899
Common Auto. (201-300): 8.00
Production 125-899
Pack (5): 5.00
Box (24): 110.00
1 Erik Bedard .25
2 Corey Patterson .25
3 Ramon Hernandez .25
4 Kris Benson .25
5 Miguel Batista .25
6 Orlando Hudson .25
7 Shawn Green .25
8 Jeff Francoeur .40
9 Marcus Giles .25
10 Edgar Renteria .25
11 Tim Hudson .40
12 Tim Wakefield .25
13 Mark Loretta .25
14 Kevin Youkilis .25
15 Mike Lowell .25
16 Coco Crisp .25
17 Tadahito Iguchi .25
18 Scott Podsednik .25
19 Jermaine Dye .25
20 Jose Contreras .25
21 Carlos Zambrano .40
22 Aramis Ramirez .40
23 Jacque Jones .25
24 Austin Kearns .25
25 Felipe Lopez .25
26 Brandon Phillips .25
27 Aaron Harang .25
28 Cliff Lee .25
29 Jhonny Peralta .25
30 Jason Michaels .25
31 Clint Barmes .25
32 Brad Hawpe .25
33 Aaron Cook .25
34 Kenny Rogers .25
35 Carlos Guillen .25
36 Brian Moehler .25
37 Andy Pettitte .40
38 Wandy Rodriguez .25
39 Morgan Ensberg .25
40 Preston Wilson .25
41 Mark Grudzielanek .25
42 Angel Berroa .25
43 Jeremy Affeldt .25
44 Zack Greinke .25
45 Orlando Cabrera .25
46 Garret Anderson .25
47 Ervin Santana .25
48 Derek Lowe .25
49 Nomar Garciaparra .75
50 J.D. Drew .25
51 Rafael Furcal .40
52 Rickie Weeks .40
53 Geoff Jenkins .25
54 Bill Hall .25
55 Chris Capuano .25
56 Derrick Turnbow .25
57 Justin Morneau .40
58 Michael Cuddyer .25
59 Luis Castillo .25
60 Hideki Matsui 1.00
61 Jason Giambi .50
62 Jorge Posada .50
63 Mariano Rivera .50
64 Billy Wagner .25
65 Carlos Delgado .50
66 Jose Reyes .75
67 Nick Swisher .40
68 Bobby Crosby .25
69 Frank Thomas .50
70 Ryan Howard 2.00
71 Pat Burrell .40
72 Jimmy Rollins .50
73 Craig Wilson .25
74 Freddy Sanchez .25
75 Sean Casey .25
76 Mike Piazza 1.00
77 Dave Roberts .25
78 Chris Young .25
79 Noah Lowry .25
80 Armando Benitez .25
81 Pedro Feliz .25
82 Jose Lopez .25
83 Adrian Beltre .25
84 Jamie Moyer .25
85 Jason Isringhausen .25
86 Jason Marquis .25
87 David Eckstein .25
88 Juan Encarnacion .25
89 Julio Lugo .25
90 Ty Wigginton .25
91 Jorge Cantu .25
92 Akinori Otsuka .25
93 Hank Blalock .40
94 Kevin Mench .25
95 Lyle Overbay .25
96 Shea Hillenbrand .25
97 B.J. Ryan .25
98 Tony Armas .25
99 Chad Cordero .25
100 Jose Guillen .25
101 Miguel Tejada 3.00
102 Brian Roberts 2.00
103 Melvin Mora 2.00
104 Brandon Webb 2.00
105 Chad Tracy 2.00
106 Luis Gonzalez 2.00
107 Andruw Jones 4.00
108 Chipper Jones 5.00
109 John Smoltz 3.00
110 Curt Schilling 4.00
111 Josh Beckett 3.00
112 David Ortiz 5.00
113 Manny Ramirez 4.00
114 Jason Varitek 4.00
115 Jim Thome 4.00
116 Paul Konerko 4.00
117 Javier Vazquez 2.00
118 Mark Prior 4.00
119 Derrek Lee 4.00
120 Greg Maddux 6.00
121 Ken Griffey Jr. 6.00
122 Adam Dunn 3.00
123 Bronson Arroyo 2.00
124 Travis Hafner 3.00
125 Victor Martinez 2.00
126 Grady Sizemore 3.00
127 C.C. Sabathia 2.00
128 Todd Helton 3.00
129 Matt Holliday 2.00
130 Garrett Atkins 2.00
131 Jeff Francis 2.00
132 Jeremy Bonderman 3.00
133 Ivan Rodriguez 4.00
134 Chris Shelton 2.00
135 Magglio Ordonez 2.00
136 Dontrelle Willis 3.00
137 Miguel Cabrera 5.00
138 Roger Clemens 8.00
139 Roy Oswalt 3.00
140 Lance Berkman 3.00
141 Reggie Sanders 2.00
142 Vladimir Guerrero 5.00
143 Bartolo Colon 2.00
144 Chone Figgins 2.00
145 Francisco Rodriguez 2.00
146 Brad Penny 2.00
147 Jeff Kent 3.00
148 Eric Gagne 2.00
149 Carlos Lee 2.00
150 Ben Sheets 2.00
151 Johan Santana 4.00
152 Torii Hunter 2.00
153 Joe Nathan 2.00
154 Alex Rodriguez 6.00
155 Derek Jeter 8.00
156 Randy Johnson 4.00
157 Johnny Damon 4.00
158 Mike Mussina 3.00
159 Pedro Martinez 4.00
160 Tom Glavine 3.00
161 David Wright 5.00
162 Carlos Beltran 4.00
163 Rich Harden 2.00
164 Barry Zito 3.00
165 Eric Chavez 2.00
166 Huston Street 2.00
167 Bobby Abreu 2.00
168 Chase Utley 3.00
169 Brett Myers 2.00
170 Jason Bay 3.00
171 Zachary Duke 2.00
172 Jake Peavy 3.00
173 Brian Giles 2.00
174 Khalil Greene 2.00
175 Trevor Hoffman 2.00
176 Jason Schmidt 2.00
177 Randy Winn 2.00
178 Omar Vizquel 2.00
179 Kenji Johjima 5.00
180 Ichiro Suzuki 6.00
181 Richie Sexson 3.00
182 Felix Hernandez 2.00
183 Albert Pujols 8.00
184 Chris Carpenter 3.00
185 Jim Edmonds 3.00
186 Scott Rolen 4.00
187 Carl Crawford 3.00
188 Scott Kazmir 2.00

No.	Player	Price
189	Jonny Gomes	2.00
190	Mark Teixeira	3.00
191	Michael Young	2.00
192	Kevin Millwood	2.00
193	Vernon Wells	3.00
194	Troy Glaus	3.00
195	Roy Halladay	2.00
196	Alex Rios	2.00
197	Nick Johnson	2.00
198	Livan Hernandez	2.00
199	Alfonso Soriano	4.00
200	Jose Vidro	2.00
201	Aaron Rakers/399 **(RC)**	10.00
202	Angel Pagan/399 **(RC)**	15.00
203	Ben Hendrickson/399 **(RC)**	10.00
204	Bobby Livingston/399 **(RC)**	8.00
205	Darrell Rasner/399 **(RC)**	10.00
206	Brian Bannister/399 **(RC)**	20.00
207	Brian Wilson/899 **RC**	15.00
208	Bobby Keppel/199 **(RC)**	8.00
209	Choo Freeman/399 **(RC)**	10.00
210	Chris Booker/899 **(RC)**	8.00
211	Chris Britton/399 **RC**	15.00
212	Chris Demaria/329 **RC**	12.00
213	Chris Resop/899 **(RC)**	8.00
214	Tony Gwynn Jr./399 **(RC)**	30.00
215	Eric Reed/399 **(RC)**	8.00
216	Fabio Castro/399 **RC**	15.00
217	Fernando Nieve/299 **(RC)**	10.00
218	Freddie Bynum/899 **(RC)**	10.00
219	Guillermo Quiroz/399 **(RC)**	8.00
220	Hong-Chih Kuo/899 **(RC)**	25.00
221	Ryan Theriot/399 **(RC)**	60.00
222	Jack Taschner/899 **(RC)**	8.00
223	Jason Bergmann/899 **RC**	15.00
224	Jason Hammel/899 **(RC)**	8.00
225	Jeff Harris/399 **RC**	8.00
226	Jeremy Accardo/399 **RC**	15.00
227	Ty Taubenheim/399 **RC**	15.00
228	Joel Zumaya/399 **(RC)**	25.00
229	John Koronka/399 **(RC)**	10.00
230	Erick Aybar/399 **(RC)**	15.00
231	Jordan Tata/399 **RC**	20.00
232	Russell Martin/399 **(RC)**	40.00
233	Josh Rupe/399 **(RC)**	10.00
234	Kevin Frandsen/399 **(RC)**	15.00
235	Martin Prado/399 **(RC)**	20.00
236	Matt Capps/399 **(RC)**	15.00
237	Agustin Montero/199 **(RC)**	10.00
238	Mike Thompson/399 **RC**	10.00
239	Nate McLouth/399 **(RC)**	15.00
240	Peter Moylan/399 **RC**	15.00
241	Reggie Abercrombie/399 **(RC)**	15.00
242	Carlos Quentin/399 **(RC)**	20.00
243	Ron Flores/399 **RC**	10.00
244	Ryan Shealy/399 **(RC)**	15.00
245	Mike Rouse/399 **(RC)**	10.00
246	Santiago Ramirez/399 **(RC)**	10.00
247	Clay Hensley/899 **(RC)**	15.00
248	Skip Schumaker/399 **(RC)**	15.00
249	Eliezer Alfonzo/899 **RC**	15.00
250	Steve Stemle/399 **RC**	10.00
251	Tim Hamulack/399 **(RC)**	12.00
252	Tony Pena/299 **(RC)**	10.00
253	Emiliano Fruto/899 **RC**	10.00
254	Wilbert Nieves/399 **(RC)**	15.00
255	Joey Devine/399 **RC**	15.00
256	Adam Wainwright/399 **(RC)**	25.00
257	Andre Ethier/399 **(RC)**	20.00
258	Ben Johnson/399 **(RC)**	10.00
259	Boone Logan/399 **RC**	10.00
260	Chris Denorfia/899 **(RC)**	10.00
261	Alay Soler/299 **RC**	15.00
262	Cody Ross/899 **(RC)**	10.00
263	Dave Gassner/399 **(RC)**	15.00
264	Fausto Carmona/399 **(RC)**	25.00
265	Jeremy Sowers/299 **(RC)**	15.00
266	Jason Kubel/399 **(RC)**	15.00
267	John Van Benschoten/399 **(RC)**	10.00
268	Jose Capellan/399 **(RC)**	10.00
269	Josh Wilson/399 **(RC)**	8.00
270	Kelly Shoppach/399 **(RC)**	10.00
271	Macay McBride/399 **(RC)**	15.00
272	Matt Cain/399 **(RC)**	25.00
273	Mike Jacobs/399 **(RC)**	15.00
274	Paul Maholm/399 **(RC)**	15.00
275	Chad Billingsley/399 **(RC)**	25.00
276	Ruddy Lugo/399 **(RC)**	15.00
277	Jon Lester/399 **(RC)**	30.00
278	Sean Marshall/383 **(RC)**	15.00
279	Melky Cabrera/399 **(RC)**	30.00
280	Yusmeiro Petit/399 **(RC)**	15.00
281	Anderson Hernandez/299 **(RC)**	10.00
282	Brian Anderson/699 **(RC)**	15.00
283	Cole Hamels/299 **(RC)**	50.00
284	Boof Bonser/299 **(RC)**	20.00
285	Dan Uggla/199 **(RC)**	30.00
286	Francisco Liriano/299 **(RC)**	30.00
287	Hanley Ramirez/199 **(RC)**	50.00
288	Ian Kinsler/299 **(RC)**	25.00
289	Jeremy Hermida/299 **(RC)**	20.00
290	Jonathan Papelbon/199 **(RC)**	60.00
291	Jered Weaver/199 **(RC)**	30.00
292	Josh Johnson/299 **(RC)**	15.00
293	Josh Willingham/199 **(RC)**	20.00
294	Justin Verlander/199 **(RC)**	60.00
295	Stephen Drew/299 **(RC)**	25.00
296	Prince Fielder/125 **(RC)**	125.00
297	Ryan Zimmerman/199 **(RC)**	50.00
298	Takashi Saito/283 **RC**	40.00
299	Taylor Buchholz/299 **(RC)**	10.00
300	Conor Jackson/299 **(RC)**	15.00

Rookie Signatures Platinum

No Pricing
Production One Set

By The Letter

		NM/M
Production 4-200		
JB	Jason Bay/110	50.00
JB2	Jason Bay/50	50.00
CB	Craig Biggio/55	125.00
BI	Chad Billingsley/75	40.00
HB	Hank Blalock/50	50.00
AB	A.J. Burnett/50	50.00
MC	Miguel Cabrera/35	85.00
EC	Eric Chavez/75	40.00
AD	Adam Dunn/50	60.00
MG	Marcus Giles/136	30.00
JG	Jonny Gomes/175	30.00
KH	Khalil Greene/75	40.00
KG	Ken Griffey Jr./25	200.00
KG2	Ken Griffey Jr./25	200.00
KG3	Ken Griffey Jr./25	200.00
KG4	Ken Griffey Jr./25	200.00
VG	Vladimir Guerrero/25	120.00
AG	Tony Gwynn Jr./150	50.00
CO	Cole Hamels/120	65.00
CH	Craig Hansen/30	50.00
DH	Danny Haren/180	35.00
JH	Jeremy Hermida/125	35.00
FH	Felix Hernandez/40	50.00
FH2	Felix Hernandez/75	50.00
MH	Matt Holliday/37	60.00
HU	Tim Hudson/50	40.00
TI	Tadahito Iguchi/20	120.00
HK	Howie Kendrick/75	50.00
IK	Ian Kinsler/125	50.00
DL	Derrek Lee/200	65.00
FL	Francisco Liriano/100	50.00
GM	Greg Maddux/25	140.00
GM2	Greg Maddux/25	140.00
VM	Victor Martinez/75	40.00
JM	Joe Mauer/25	75.00
MO	Justin Morneau/75	50.00
MM	Mark Mulder/50	40.00
JN	Joe Nathan/100	35.00
RO	Roy Oswalt/50	60.00
JP	Jonathan Papelbon/100	80.00
PE	Jake Peavy/100	40.00
HR	Hanley Ramirez/125	40.00
JR	Jose Reyes/75	65.00
AR	Alex Rios/100	50.00
CS	C.C. Sabathia/40	40.00
BS	Ben Sheets/125	35.00
SM	John Smoltz/75	75.00
JS	Jeremy Sowers/60	60.00
HS	Huston Street/75	40.00
NS	Nick Swisher/170	35.00
TE	Miguel Tejada/25	50.00
JT	Jim Thome/30	100.00
DU	Dan Uggla/100	40.00
BU	B.J. Upton/20	50.00
CU	Chase Utley/25	100.00
JW	Jered Weaver/40	60.00
RW	Rickie Weeks/100	50.00
WI	Josh Willingham/75	40.00
DW	Dontrelle Willis/150	40.00
MY	Michael Young/50	45.00
CZ	Carlos Zambrano/17	100.00
RZ	Ryan Zimmerman/17	120.00
JZ	Joel Zumaya/125	85.00

Chirography Dual Signatures

		NM/M
Production 25 Sets		
CE	Eric Reed, Cody Ross	25.00
FJ	Conor Jackson, Prince Fielder	40.00
GB	Khalil Greene, Josh Barfield	25.00
HA	Jeremy Hermida, Reggie Abercrombie	25.00
HK	Cole Hamels, Scott Kazmir	50.00
KH	Anderson Hernandez, Ian Kinsler	40.00
KS	Takashi Saito, Hong-Chih Kuo	180.00
LB	Francisco Liriano, Boof Bonser	50.00
MH	Rich Hill, Sean Marshall	60.00
MW	Josh Willingham, Victor Martinez	25.00
PB	Freddie Bynum, Angel Pagan	25.00
PG	Ken Griffey Jr., Albert Pujols	350.00
PO	Jake Peavy, Roy Oswalt	40.00
PP	Tony Pena, Martin Prado	30.00
RC	Hanley Ramirez, Miguel Cabrera	50.00
RR	Jose Reyes, Hanley Ramirez	50.00
SC	Jose Capellan, Ben Sheets	25.00
UH	Cole Hamels, Chase Utley	65.00
WS	Josh Wilson, Ryan Shealy	25.00

Chirography

		NM/M
Production 75 unless noted.		
AN	Brian Anderson	10.00
GA	Garret Anderson	15.00
BB	Brandon Backe	15.00
BA	Brian Bannister	25.00
DB	Denny Bautista	10.00
CB	Craig Biggio	60.00
BI	Chad Billingsley	25.00
HB	Hank Blalock	15.00
JB	Joe Blanton	15.00
BO	Boof Bonser	25.00
TB	Taylor Buchholz	8.00
MC	Matt Cain	30.00
JC	Jose Capellan	8.00
FC	Fausto Carmona	20.00
SC	Sean Casey	25.00
BC	Bobby Crosby	10.00
DD	David DeJesus	15.00
CD	Chris Denorfia	15.00
JD	Joey Devine	10.00
SD	Stephen Drew	30.00
JE	Johnny Estrada	10.00
AE	Andre Ethier	25.00
KF	Keith Foulke	20.00
JF	Jeff Francis	10.00
CF	Choo Freeman	8.00
DG	Dave Gassner	8.00
KG	Khalil Greene	30.00
GR	Ken Griffey Jr.	80.00
CG	Carlos Guillen	15.00
AG	Tony Gwynn Jr.	40.00
TH	Travis Hafner	20.00
CH	Cole Hamels	50.00
RH	Rich Harden	15.00
HA	Jeff Harris	10.00
JH	Jeremy Hermida	15.00
AH	Anderson Hernandez	10.00
FH	Felix Hernandez/25	40.00
CJ	Conor Jackson	15.00
DJ	Derek Jeter	160.00
JJ	Josh Johnson	15.00
JQ	Jacque Jones	10.00
SK	Scott Kazmir/25	20.00
IK	Ian Kinsler	25.00
CK	Casey Kotchman	15.00
JK	Jason Kubel	15.00
HK	Hong-Chih Kuo	60.00
CL	Cliff Lee	8.00
JL	Jon Lester	35.00
LI	Francisco Liriano	35.00
BL	Boone Logan	20.00
FL	Felipe Lopez	15.00
ML	Mark Loretta	10.00
PM	Paul Maholm	15.00
SM	Sean Marshall	20.00
VM	Victor Martinez	10.00
MM	Macay McBride	15.00
KM	Kevin Mench	15.00
JN	Joe Nathan	15.00
LO	Lyle Overbay/40	15.00
VP	Vicente Padilla	8.00
JP	Jonathan Papelbon	40.00
CP	Corey Patterson	10.00
TP	Tony Pena	8.00
WM	Wily Mo Pena	10.00
OP	Oliver Perez	20.00
YP	Yusmeiro Petit	15.00
MP	Mark Prior/55	20.00
HR	Hanley Ramirez	40.00
RE	Eric Reed	10.00
ER	Edgar Renteria	10.00
AR	Alex Rios	15.00
IR	Ivan Rodriguez	30.00
CR	Cody Ross	15.00
JR	Josh Rupe	10.00
CS	C.C. Sabathia	20.00
TS	Takashi Saito	50.00
BS	Ben Sheets	15.00
SH	Chris Shelton	15.00
KS	Kelly Shoppach	10.00
SO	Alay Soler	20.00
AS	Alfonso Soriano	40.00
JS	Jeremy Sowers	20.00
NS	Nick Swisher	20.00
FT	Frank Thomas	65.00
DU	Dan Uggla	25.00
CU	Chase Utley	50.00
VA	John Van Benschoten	15.00
JV	Jason Varitek	50.00
VE	Justin Verlander	40.00
AW	Adam Wainwright	30.00
WE	Jered Weaver	40.00
JW	Josh Willingham	15.00
DW	Dontrelle Willis	30.00
WI	Josh Wilson	10.00
KY	Kevin Youkilis	15.00
RZ	Ryan Zimmerman	40.00

Chirography Triple Signatures

No Pricing
Production 15 Sets

Sign of the Times

		NM/M
Production 75 Sets		
RA	Reggie Abercrombie	8.00
BA	Bobby Abreu	35.00
AN	Brian Anderson	10.00
BR	Brian Bannister	25.00
AB	Adrian Beltre	10.00
YB	Yuniesky Betancourt	15.00
BI	Chad Billingsley	25.00
BB	Boof Bonser	25.00
CB	Chris Booker	10.00
TB	Taylor Buchholz	8.00
ME	Melky Cabrera	25.00
MC	Miguel Cabrera	30.00
CA	Matt Cain	30.00
JC	Jose Capellan	8.00
FC	Fausto Carmona	8.00
CC	Carl Crawford	15.00
CD	Chris Demaria	15.00
DE	Chris Denorfia	15.00
JD	J.D. Drew	15.00
SD	Stephen Drew	30.00
AE	Andre Ethier	30.00
FR	Ron Flores	10.00
RF	Rafael Furcal	15.00
EG	Eric Gagne	20.00
DG	Dave Gassner	8.00
ZG	Zack Greinke	10.00
KG	Ken Griffey Jr.	80.00
VG	Vladimir Guerrero	50.00
JG	Jose Guillen	8.00
AG	Tony Gwynn Jr.	35.00
CH	Cole Hamels	50.00
JH	Jason Hammel	8.00
HA	Tim Hamulack	10.00
CY	Clay Hensley	10.00
HE	Jeremy Hermida	15.00
AH	Anderson Hernandez	8.00
RH	Ramon Hernandez	20.00
TH	Tim Hudson	15.00
JA	Conor Jackson	20.00
MJ	Mike Jacobs	15.00
DJ	Derek Jeter	160.00
BJ	Ben Johnson	10.00
JJ	Josh Johnson	20.00
RJ	Randy Johnson	50.00
AJ	Andruw Jones	25.00
JK	Jason Kendall	10.00
IK	Ian Kinsler	25.00
MK	Mark Kotsay	15.00
KU	Jason Kubel	15.00
CL	Carlos Lee	15.00
DL	Derrek Lee	25.00
FL	Francisco Liriano	35.00
BL	Boone Logan	20.00
LO	Derek Lowe	25.00
GM	Greg Maddux	140.00
PM	Paul Maholm	15.00
SM	Sean Marshall	20.00
RM	Russell Martin	20.00
JM	Joe Mauer	35.00
MA	Macay McBride	15.00
MO	Justin Morneau	25.00
MM	Mark Mulder	15.00
PA	Jonathan Papelbon	30.00
JP	Jake Peavy	20.00
TP	Tony Pena	8.00
PE	Joel Peralta	10.00
YP	Yusmeiro Petit	15.00
SP	Scott Podsednik	20.00
AR	Aramis Ramirez	20.00
HR	Hanley Ramirez	35.00
ER	Eric Reed	10.00
JR	Jose Reyes	40.00
SR	Scott Rolen	25.00
CR	Cody Ross	15.00
TS	Takashi Saito	50.00
CS	Curt Schilling	50.00
SS	Skip Schumaker	15.00
RS	Ryan Shealy	20.00
JS	John Smoltz	40.00
AS	Alay Soler	20.00
JY	Jeremy Sowers	20.00
ST	Steve Stemle	10.00
MT	Mark Teixeira	20.00
TE	Miguel Tejada	25.00
MI	Mike Thompson	10.00
DU	Dan Uggla	25.00
JV	John Van Benschoten	10.00
VE	Justin Verlander	40.00
AW	Adam Wainwright	30.00
JE	Jered Weaver	40.00
RW	Rickie Weeks	25.00
VW	Vernon Wells	20.00
JW	Josh Willingham	15.00
WI	Josh Wilson	10.00
RZ	Ryan Zimmerman	40.00

Sign of the Times Dual

		NM/M
Production 25 Sets		
BM	Nate McLouth, Jason Bay	25.00
CH	Jose Capellan, Ben Hendrickson	20.00
FW	Prince Fielder, Rickie Weeks	75.00
GP	Ken Griffey Jr., Albert Pujols	300.00
HD	Tim Hudson, Joey Devine	30.00
HF	Rich Harden, Ron Flores	20.00
KN	Michael Napoli, Howie Kendrick	40.00
LG	Dave Gassner, Francisco Liriano	30.00
MM	Sean Marshall, Greg Maddux	140.00
OB	Roy Oswalt, Taylor Buchholz	30.00
PB	Angel Pagan, Freddie Bynum	20.00
PT	Jake Peavy, Mike Thompson	20.00
RW	Josh Willingham, Hanley Ramirez	40.00
SC	Fausto Carmona, C.C. Sabathia	30.00
WM	Kendry Morales, Jered Weaver	40.00
ZH	Ryan Zimmerman, Brendan Harris	40.00

Signs of the Times Triple

No Pricing
Production 15 Sets

Heroes

		NM/M
Common Player:		.50
1	Albert Pujols	3.00
2	Andruw Jones	1.00
3	Aramis Ramirez	.75
4	Brian Roberts	.50
5	Carl Crawford	.75
6	Carlos Lee	.50
7	Vladimir Guerrero	1.00
8	Chris Carpenter	.75
9	Craig Biggio	.75
10	David Ortiz	1.50
11	David Wright	2.00
12	Derrek Lee	.75
13	Dontrelle Willis	.75
14	Felix Hernandez	.75
15	Garrett Atkins	.50
16	Grady Sizemore	.75
17	Huston Street	.50
18	Jake Peavy	.50
19	Jason Bay	.75
20	Joe Mauer	1.00
21	John Smoltz	.75
22	Jonny Gomes	.50
23	Jorge Cantu	.50
24	Ken Griffey Jr.	2.00
25	Marcus Giles	.50
26	Mark Teixeira	.75
27	Matt Cain	.75
28	Michael Young	.50
29	Miguel Cabrera	1.00
30	Johan Santana	1.00
31	Nick Swisher	.50
32	Prince Fielder	1.00
33	Joe Blanton	.50
34	Roy Oswalt	.75
35	Ryan Howard	3.00
36	Scott Kazmir	.50
37	Tadahito Iguchi	.50
38	Travis Hafner	.75
39	Victor Martinez	.50
40	Jose Reyes	1.00
41	Chris Carpenter, Albert Pujols	3.00
42	Albert Pujols, Miguel Cabrera	3.00
43	Andruw Jones, Ken Griffey Jr.	2.00
44	Derrek Lee, Aramis Ramirez	.75
45	Ryan Howard, Prince Fielder	3.00
46	Jake Peavy, Roy Oswalt	.75
47	Morgan Ensberg, Craig Biggio	.75
48	David Ortiz, Travis Hafner	1.50
49	Derek Jeter, David Wright	3.00
50	Derek Jeter, Ken Griffey Jr.	3.00
51	Derek Jeter, Michael Young	3.00
52	Scott Kazmir, Dontrelle Willis	.50
53	Jason Bay, Grady Sizemore	.75
54	Michael Young, Mark Teixeira	.75
55	Brian Roberts, Tadahito Iguchi	.50
56	Matt Cain, Felix Hernandez, Chien-Ming Wang	2.00
57	Mark Teixeira, Derrek Lee, Albert Pujols	3.00
58	Albert Pujols, Ken Griffey Jr., Miguel Cabrera	3.00
59	Marcus Giles, Andruw Jones, John Smoltz	1.00
60	Derrek Lee, Kerry Wood, Aramis Ramirez	1.00
61	Morgan Ensberg, David Wright, Aramis Ramirez	2.00
62	Carl Crawford, Jorge Cantu, Jonny Gomes	.50
63	Jake Peavy, Chris Carpenter, John Smoltz	1.00
64	Travis Hafner, Grady Sizemore, Victor Martinez	.75
65	Ryan Howard, Prince Fielder, David Ortiz	3.00
66	Chris Carpenter, John Smoltz, Jake Peavy, Dontrelle Willis	.75
67	Ken Griffey Jr., Derek Jeter, David Ortiz, Albert Pujols	3.00
68	David Ortiz, Andruw Jones, Derrek Lee, Mark Teixeira	1.50
69	Brian Roberts, Marcus Giles, Craig Biggio, Tadahito Iguchi	.50
70	Jason Bay, David Wright, Mark Teixeira, Miguel Cabrera	2.00

WBC Future Watch

		NM/M
Common Player:		3.00
Production 999 Sets		
1	Adrian Burnside	3.00
2	Gavin Fingleson	3.00
3	Bradley Harman	3.00
4	Brendan Kingman	3.00
5	Brett Roneberg	3.00
6	Paul Rutgers	3.00
7	Phil Stockman	3.00
8	Stubby Clapp	3.00
9	Steve Green	3.00
10	Pete LaForest	5.00
11	Adam Loewen	5.00
12	Ryan Radmanovich	3.00
13	Chenhao Li	3.00
14	Guangbiao Liu	3.00
15	Guogang Yang	3.00
16	Jingchao Wang	3.00
17	Lei Li	3.00
18	Lingfeng Sun	3.00
19	Nan Wang	3.00
20	Shuo Yang	3.00
21	Tao Bu	3.00
22	Wei Wang	3.00
23	Yi Feng	3.00
24	Chien-Ming Chiang	15.00
25	Yung-Chi Chen	20.00
26	Chia-Hsien Hseih	15.00

27 Chin-Lung Hu 15.00
28 En-Yu Lin 20.00
29 Wei-Lun Pan 10.00
30 Ariel Borrero 3.00
31 Yadel Marti 3.00
32 Yulieski Gourriel 20.00
33 Frederich Cepeda 3.00
34 Yadier Pedroso 3.00
35 Pedro Luis Lazo 3.00
36 Elier Sanchez 3.00
37 Norberto Gonzalez 3.00
38 Carlos Tabares 3.00
39 Eduardo Paret 3.00
40 Osmany Urrutia 3.00
41 Alexei Ramirez 3.00
42 Yoandy Garlobo 3.00
43 Vicyohandry Odelin 3.00
44 Michel Enriquez 3.00
45 Ormari Romero 3.00
46 Ariel Pestano 3.00
47 Francisco Liriano 5.00
48 Dustin Dellucchi 3.00
49 Tony Giarratano 3.00
50 Tom Gregorio 3.00
51 Mark Saccomanno 3.00
52 Takahiro Arai 8.00
53 Akinori Iwamura 20.00
54 Munenori Kawasaki 15.00
55 Nobuhiko Matsunaka 10.00
56 Daisuke Matsuzaka 100.00
57 Shinya Miyamoto 10.00
58 Tsuyoshi Nishioka 15.00
59 Tomoya Satozaki 8.00
60 Koji Uehara 15.00
61 Shunsuke Watanabe 15.00
62 Sadaharu Oh 20.00
63 Byung Kyu Lee 3.00
64 Ji Man Song 3.00
65 Jin Man Park 3.00
66 Jong Beom Lee 3.00
67 Jong Kook Kim 3.00
68 Min Han Son 3.00
69 Min Jae Kim 3.00
70 Seung-Yeop Lee 10.00
71 Luis A. Garcia 3.00
72 Mario Valenzuela 3.00
73 Sharnol Adriana 3.00
74 Rob Cordemans 3.00
75 Michael Duursma 3.00
76 Percy Isenia 3.00
77 Sidney de Jong 3.00
78 Dirk Klooster 3.00
79 Raylinoe Legito 3.00
80 Shairon Martis 5.00
81 Harvey Monte 3.00
82 Hainley Statia 3.00
83 Roger Deago 5.00
84 Audes De Leon 3.00
85 Freddy Herrera 3.00
86 Yoni Lasso 5.00
87 Orlando Miller 3.00
88 Len Picota 5.00
89 Federico Baez 3.00
90 Dicky Gonzalez 3.00
91 Josue Matos 3.00
92 Orlando Roman 3.00
93 Paul Bell 3.00
94 Kyle Botha 3.00
95 Jason Cook 3.00
96 Nicholás Dempsey 3.00
97 Victor Moreno 3.00
98 Ricardo Palma 3.00
99 Huston Street 3.00
100 Chase Utley 3.00

2006 SP Legendary Cuts

NM/M
Complete Set (200):
Common Player: .25
Common SP (101-200): 2.00
Production 550
Pack (4): 12.00
Box (12): 120.00
1 Juan Marichal .50
2 Monte Irvin .75
3 Will Clark .75
4 Willie McCovey .75
5 Eddie Gaedel .25
6 Ken Williams .25
7 Earl Battey .25
8 Rick Ferrell .25
9 Bob Gibson 1.00
10 Elmer Flick .25
11 Joe Medwick .25
12 Lou Brock .75
13 Ozzie Smith 1.00
14 Red Schoendienst .25
15 Stan Musial 2.00
16 Tony Oliva .50
17 Phil Niekro .25
18 Boog Powell .25
19 Brooks Robinson 1.00
20 Cal Ripken Jr. 3.00
21 Eddie Murray .75
22 Frank Robinson 1.00
23 Jim Palmer .50
24 Jocko Conlon .25
25 Carlton Fisk .50
26 Dwight Evans .25
27 Fred Lynn .25
28 Jim Rice .50
29 Ted Williams 2.00
30 Wade Boggs .75
31 Hugh Duffy .25
32 Kid Nichols .25
33 Johnny Vander Meer .25
34 Dolph Camilli .25
35 Carl Yastrzemski 1.00
36 Chick Hafey .25
37 Kirby Higbe .25
38 Pee Wee Reese .50
39 Pete Reiser .25
40 Don Sutton .25
41 Rod Carew .75
42 Andre Dawson .50
43 Billy Herman .25
44 Billy Williams .25
45 Charlie Root .25
46 Hack Wilson .25
47 Ernie Banks 1.00
48 Fergie Jenkins .50
49 Gabby Hartnett .25
50 Ken Hubbs .25
51 Kiki Cuyler .25
52 Mark Grace .25
53 Ryne Sandberg 1.50
54 Harold Newhouser .25
55 Charlie Robertson .25
56 Harold Baines .25
57 Luis Aparicio .25
58 Luke Appling .25
59 Nellie Fox .50
60 Ray Schalk .25
61 Red Faber .25
62 Sloppy Thurston .25
63 Freddie Lindstrom .25
64 Vern Kennedy .25
65 Barry Larkin .50
66 Bucky Walters .25
67 Dolf Luque .25
68 Al Campanis .25
69 Ernie Lombardi .25
70 George Foster .25
71 Joe Morgan .75
72 Johnny Bench 1.00
73 Ken Griffey Sr. .25
74 Ted Kluszewski .25
75 Tony Perez .50
76 Wally Post .25
77 Bob Feller .50
78 Bob Lemon .25
79 Earl Averill .25
80 Joe Sewell .25
81 Johnny Hodapp .25
82 Larry Doby .25
83 Lou Boudreau .25
84 Rocky Colavito .25
85 Stan Coveleski .25
86 Nap Lajoie .50
87 Al Kaline 1.00
88 Alan Trammell .50
89 Charlie Gehringer .25
90 Denny McLain .50
91 Hank Greenberg .50
92 Jack Morris .25
93 Mark Fidrych .25
94 Ray Boone .25
95 Rudy York .25
96 Buck Leonard .25
97 Bo Jackson 1.00
98 Zoilo Versalles .25
99 John Kruk .25
100 Don Drysdale .50
101 Cecil Cooper 2.00
102 Vic Wertz 2.00
103 Kirk Gibson 2.00
104 Maury Wills 2.00
105 Steve Garvey 2.00
106 Warren Spahn 5.00
107 Paul Molitor 4.00
108 Robin Yount 5.00
109 Rollie Fingers 3.00
110 Bob Allison 2.00
111 Kirby Puckett 6.00
112 Tim Raines 2.00
113 George Pipgras 2.00
114 Eddie Grant 2.00
115 Hoyt Wilhelm 2.00
116 Sal Maglie 2.00
117 Ron Santo 3.00
118 Wally Joyner 2.00
119 Tom Seaver 5.00
120 Tommie Agee 2.00
121 Harmon Killebrew 4.00
122 Bill Dickey 3.00
123 Early Wynn 2.00
124 Bobby Murcer 2.00
125 Bucky Dent 2.00
126 Dave Winfield 4.00
127 Don Larsen 4.00
128 Don Mattingly 8.00
129 Earle Combs 2.00
130 Ed Lopat 2.00
131 Elston Howard 4.00
132 Everett Scott 2.00
133 Rich "Goose" Gossage 2.00
134 Graig Nettles 2.00
135 Joe DiMaggio 8.00
136 Lou Piniella 2.00
137 Bill "Moose" Skowron 2.00
138 Phil Rizzuto 3.00
139 Red Ruffing 2.00
140 Reggie Jackson 4.00
141 Roger Maris 6.00
142 Ron Guidry 3.00
143 Tiny Bonham 2.00
144 Bruce Sutter 2.00
145 Tony Lazzeri 2.00
146 Waite Hoyt 2.00
147 Whitey Ford 4.00
148 Steve Sax 2.00
149 Yogi Berra 5.00
150 Enos Slaughter 2.00
151 Jim "Catfish" Hunter 2.00
152 Dennis Eckersley 3.00
153 Jose Canseco 3.00
154 Al Rosen 2.00
155 Al Simmons 2.00
156 Chief Bender 2.00
157 Cy Williams 2.00
158 Mike Schmidt 5.00
159 Richie Ashburn 2.00
160 Robin Roberts 3.00
161 Steve Carlton 3.00
162 Judy Johnson 2.00
163 Al Oliver 2.00
164 Bill Mazeroski 3.00
165 Dave Parker 3.00
166 Max Carey 2.00
167 Pie Traynor 3.00
168 Ralph Kiner 3.00
169 Roberto Clemente 10.00
170 Willie Stargell 4.00
171 Gaylord Perry 2.00
172 Tony Gwynn 5.00
173 Nolan Ryan 8.00
174 Joe Carter 2.00
175 Frank Howard 2.00
176 George Kell 2.00
177 Heinie Manush 2.00
178 Sam Rice 2.00
179 Babe Ruth 10.00
180 Casey Stengel 3.00
181 Christy Mathewson 4.00
182 Cy Young 4.00
183 Dizzy Dean 4.00
184 Eddie Mathews 5.00
185 George Sisler 3.00
186 Honus Wagner 5.00
187 Jackie Robinson 6.00
188 Jimmie Foxx 5.00
189 Johnny Mize 2.00
190 Lefty Gomez 2.00
191 Lou Gehrig 8.00
192 Mel Ott 3.00
193 Mickey Cochrane 3.00
194 Rogers Hornsby 4.00
195 Roy Campanella 5.00
196 Satchel Paige 5.00
197 Thurman Munson 5.00
198 Ty Cobb 6.00
199 Walter Johnson 3.00
200 Lefty Grove 3.00

Gold

Gold (101-200): 2-4X
Production 99 Sets

Legendary Materials

NM/M
Production 225 unless noted.
Tier 1: .75-1.5X
Production 50-199
Tier 2: 1-2X
Production 25-99
Tier 3: No Pricing
Production 5-15
HB Harold Baines 6.00
EB Ernie Banks 20.00
JB Johnny Bench 15.00
YB Yogi Berra 15.00
WB Wade Boggs 10.00
LB Lou Brock 10.00
LB2 Lou Brock 10.00
JC Jose Canseco 10.00
CW Rod Carew 10.00
SC Steve Carlton 8.00
SC2 Steve Carlton 8.00
WC Will Clark 10.00
WC2 Will Clark 10.00
RC Rocky Colavito 20.00
DC Dave Concepcion 6.00
CC Cecil Cooper 10.00
AD Andre Dawson 8.00
BD Bucky Dent 8.00
JD Joe DiMaggio/99 75.00
DE Dennis Eckersley 8.00
DE2 Dennis Eckersley 8.00
EV Dwight Evans 8.00
BF Bob Feller 10.00
RF Rollie Fingers 8.00
CF Carlton Fisk 10.00
GF George Foster 6.00
SG Steve Garvey 6.00
BG Bob Gibson 10.00
KI Kirk Gibson 10.00
GG Rich "Goose" Gossage 8.00
MG Mark Grace 10.00
KG Ken Griffey Sr. 6.00
GU Ron Guidry 10.00
TG Tony Gwynn 15.00
FH Frank Howard 8.00
BO Bo Jackson 15.00
RJ Reggie Jackson 10.00
FJ Fergie Jenkins 8.00
WJ Wally Joyner 10.00
AK Al Kaline 12.00
RK Ralph Kiner 10.00
JK John Kruk 8.00
BL Barry Larkin 8.00
DL Don Larsen 12.00
FL Fred Lynn 6.00
JU Juan Marichal 10.00
MA Don Mattingly 20.00
BM Bill Mazeroski 10.00
WM Willie McCovey 10.00
PM Paul Molitor 8.00
JO Joe Morgan 10.00
JM Jack Morris 6.00
MU Bobby Murcer 8.00
EM Eddie Murray 10.00
SM Stan Musial 20.00
GN Graig Nettles 10.00
PN Phil Niekro 8.00
PN2 Phil Niekro 8.00
TO Tony Oliva 8.00
AO Al Oliver 8.00
JP Jim Palmer 10.00
JP2 Jim Palmer 10.00
DP Dave Parker 8.00
TP Tony Perez 8.00
GP Gaylord Perry 8.00
GP2 Gaylord Perry 8.00
LP Lou Piniella 8.00
BP Boog Powell 8.00
KP Kirby Puckett 15.00
JR Jim Rice 8.00
CR Cal Ripken Jr. 25.00
PR Phil Rizzuto/99 10.00
RR Robin Roberts 10.00
RO Brooks Robinson/175 10.00
FR Frank Robinson 10.00
FR2 Frank Robinson 10.00
AR Al Rosen 8.00
BR Babe Ruth/99 225.00
NR Nolan Ryan 20.00
RS Ryne Sandberg 15.00
RN Ron Santo/125 12.00
RN2 Ron Santo/125 12.00
SS Steve Sax 6.00
MS Mike Schmidt 15.00
RE Red Schoendienst/99 12.00
TS Tom Seaver 12.00
SK Bill "Moose" Skowron 8.00
OS Ozzie Smith 15.00
BS Bruce Sutter 8.00
SU Don Sutton 8.00
JT Joe Torre 10.00
BW Billy Williams 8.00
MW Maury Wills 6.00
DW Dave Winfield 8.00
CY Carl Yastrzemski 15.00
RY Robin Yount 10.00
MW 6.00

Baseball Chronology

NM/M
Production 550 Sets
Platinum: 1.5-2X
Production 99 Sets
EB Ernie Banks 5.00
EB2 Ernie Banks 5.00
JB Johnny Bench 4.00
YB Yogi Berra 4.00
WB Wade Boggs 4.00
WB2 Wade Boggs 4.00
LB Lou Boudreau 2.00
LO Lou Brock 4.00
RC Roy Campanella 4.00
CA Rod Carew 3.00
SC Steve Carlton 3.00
SC2 Steve Carlton 3.00
JC Joe Carter 2.00
WC Will Clark 4.00
CL Roberto Clemente 10.00
TC Ty Cobb 6.00
TC2 Ty Cobb 6.00
MC Mickey Cochrane 3.00
CN Joe Cronin 2.00
AD Andre Dawson 3.00
DZ Dizzy Dean 3.00
BD Bucky Dent 2.00
JD Joe DiMaggio 8.00
DD Don Drysdale 3.00
DE Dennis Eckersley 3.00
BF Bob Feller 3.00
MF Mark Fidrych 2.00
RF Rollie Fingers 3.00
CF Carlton Fisk 3.00
WF Whitey Ford 4.00
JF Jimmie Foxx 5.00
JF2 Jimmie Foxx 5.00
SG Steve Garvey 2.00
LG Lou Gehrig 8.00
LG2 Lou Gehrig 8.00
BG Bob Gibson 4.00
KG Kirk Gibson 3.00
HG Hank Greenberg 3.00
TG Tony Gwynn 4.00
GH Gil Hodges 3.00
RH Rogers Hornsby 4.00
CH Jim "Catfish" Hunter 2.00
BO Bo Jackson 4.00
RJ Reggie Jackson 4.00
WJ Walter Johnson 4.00
AK Al Kaline 4.00
RK Ralph Kiner 2.00
NL Nap Lajoie 3.00
DL Don Larsen 3.00
BL Bob Lemon 2.00
FL Fred Lynn 2.00
RM Roger Maris 6.00
CM Christy Mathewson 4.00
DM Don Mattingly 6.00
BM Bill Mazeroski 3.00
WM Willie McCovey 3.00
JM Johnny Mize 2.00
PM Paul Molitor 3.00
JO Joe Morgan 3.00
TM Thurman Munson 5.00
EM Eddie Murray 3.00
SM Stan Musial 6.00
PN Phil Niekro 2.00
MO Mel Ott 3.00
SP Satchel Paige 5.00
GP Gaylord Perry 2.00
KP Kirby Puckett 5.00
PW Pee Wee Reese 3.00
RI Jim Rice 3.00
CR Cal Ripken Jr. 8.00
RO Brooks Robinson 4.00
FR Frank Robinson 4.00
JR Jackie Robinson 6.00
BR Babe Ruth 10.00
BR2 Babe Ruth 10.00
BR3 Babe Ruth 10.00
NR Nolan Ryan 8.00
NR2 Nolan Ryan 8.00
NR3 Nolan Ryan 8.00
RS Ryne Sandberg 5.00
MS Mike Schmidt 5.00
TS Tom Seaver 4.00
GS George Sisler 3.00
ES Enos Slaughter 2.00
OS Ozzie Smith 5.00
WS Warren Spahn 4.00
ST Willie Stargell 4.00
CS Casey Stengel 3.00
CS2 Casey Stengel 3.00
DS Don Sutton 2.00
AT Alan Trammell 3.00
HW Honus Wagner 5.00
HY Hoyt Wilhelm 2.00
BW Billy Williams 2.00
TW Ted Williams 8.00
TW2 Ted Williams 8.00
MW Maury Wills 2.00
YZ Carl Yastrzemski 4.00
CY Cy Young 3.00
RY Robin Yount 4.00

Baseball Chronology Materials

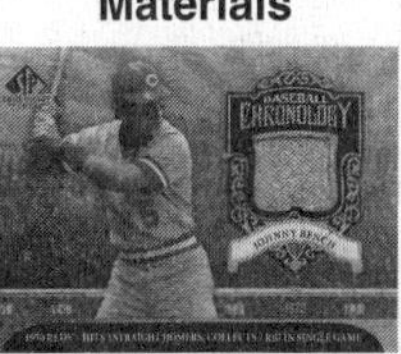

NM/M
Common Player:
EB Ernie Banks 15.00
EB2 Ernie Banks/SP 20.00
JB Johnny Bench 15.00
YB Yogi Berra 20.00
WB Wade Boggs 10.00
WB2 Wade Boggs 10.00
LB Lou Boudreau 12.00
LO Lou Brock 10.00
RC Roy Campanella 20.00
CA Rod Carew 10.00
SC Steve Carlton 8.00
SC2 Steve Carlton 8.00
JC Joe Carter 6.00
WC Will Clark 10.00
CL Roberto Clemente/SP 80.00
TC Ty Cobb/SP 150.00
TC2 Ty Cobb/SP 150.00
CN Joe Cronin 15.00
AD Andre Dawson 8.00
DZ Dizzy Dean SP 60.00
BD Bucky Dent 6.00
JD Joe DiMaggio/SP 75.00
DD Don Drysdale/SP 25.00
DE Dennis Eckersley 10.00
BF Bob Feller 10.00
MF Mark Fidrych 10.00
RF Rollie Fingers 8.00
CF Carlton Fisk 10.00
JF Jimmie Foxx/SP 40.00
JF2 Jimmie Foxx/SP 40.00
SG Steve Garvey 6.00
LG Lou Gehrig/SP 175.00
LG2 Lou Gehrig 175.00
BG Bob Gibson 10.00
HG Hank Greenberg 25.00
TG Tony Gwynn 12.00
GH Gil Hodges/SP 40.00
RH Rogers Hornsby/SP 50.00
CH Jim "Catfish" Hunter 10.00
BO Bo Jackson 12.00
RJ Reggie Jackson 12.00
AK Al Kaline 15.00
RK Ralph Kiner 12.00
DL Don Larsen 12.00
BL Bob Lemon 10.00
FL Fred Lynn 8.00
RM Roger Maris 30.00
CM Christy Mathewson/SP 240.00
DM Don Mattingly 15.00
BM Bill Mazeroski/SP 20.00
WM Willie McCovey 12.00
JM Johnny Mize 15.00
PM Paul Molitor 8.00
JO Joe Morgan 10.00
TM Thurman Munson 25.00
EM Eddie Murray 10.00
SM Stan Musial 20.00
PN Phil Niekro 8.00
MO Mel Ott/SP 35.00
SP Satchel Paige/SP 75.00
GP Gaylord Perry 8.00
KP Kirby Puckett 15.00
PW Pee Wee Reese 10.00
RI Jim Rice 8.00
CR Cal Ripken Jr. 25.00
RO Brooks Robinson 12.00
FR Frank Robinson 10.00
JR Jackie Robinson/SP 60.00
BR Babe Ruth/SP 250.00
BR2 Babe Ruth/SP 250.00
BR3 Babe Ruth/SP 250.00
NR Nolan Ryan 20.00
NR2 Nolan Ryan 20.00
NR3 Nolan Ryan 20.00
RS Ryne Sandberg 15.00
MS Mike Schmidt 12.00
TS Tom Seaver 15.00
GS George Sisler/SP 35.00
ES Enos Slaughter 15.00
OS Ozzie Smith 12.00
WS Warren Spahn 15.00
ST Willie Stargell 15.00
CS Casey Stengel 25.00
CS2 Casey Stengel/SP 35.00
DS Don Sutton 8.00
AT Alan Trammell 8.00
HW Honus Wagner/SP 160.00
HY Hoyt Wilhelm/SP 15.00
BW Billy Williams 8.00
TW Ted Williams 40.00
TW2 Ted Williams 40.00
MW Maury Wills 8.00
YZ Carl Yastrzemski 15.00
RY Robin Yount 12.00

When It Was A Game

NM/M
Production 550 Sets
Gold: 1.5-2X
Production 99 Sets
LA Luis Aparicio 2.00
HB Harold Baines 2.00
EB Ernie Banks 5.00
JB Johnny Bench 4.00
YB Yogi Berra 4.00
WB Wade Boggs 4.00
LB Lou Brock 4.00
CA Rod Carew 3.00
SC Steve Carlton 3.00

SC2 Steve Carlton 3.00
WC Will Clark 4.00
RC Roberto Clemente 10.00
MC Mickey Cochrane 3.00
CO Rocky Colavito 3.00
AD Andre Dawson 3.00
JD Joe DiMaggio 8.00
DD Don Drysdale 3.00
DE Dennis Eckersley 3.00
EV Dwight Evans 2.00
BF Bob Feller 3.00
RF Rollie Fingers 3.00
CF Carlton Fisk 3.00
WF Whitey Ford 4.00
JF Jimmie Foxx 5.00
SG Steve Garvey 2.00
LG Lou Gehrig 8.00
BG Bob Gibson 4.00
KI Kirk Gibson 3.00
GG Rich "Goose" Gossage 2.00
HG Hank Greenberg 3.00
KG Ken Griffey Sr. 2.00
GU Ron Guidry 3.00
TG Tony Gwynn 4.00
HO Rogers Hornsby 4.00
FH Frank Howard 2.00
RJ Reggie Jackson 4.00
FJ Fergie Jenkins 3.00
WJ Wally Joyner 2.00
AK Al Kaline 4.00
RK Ralph Kiner 2.00
JK John Kruk 2.00
DL Don Larsen 3.00
FL Fred Lynn 2.00
JU Juan Marichal 3.00
EM Eddie Mathews 3.00
MA Don Mattingly 6.00
BM Bill Mazeroski 3.00
WM Willie McCovey 3.00
DY Denny McLain 3.00
MZ Johnny Mize 2.00
PM Paul Molitor 3.00
JO Joe Morgan 3.00
JM Jack Morris 2.00
TM Thurman Munson 5.00
MU Bobby Murcer 2.00
ED Eddie Murray 3.00
SM Stan Musial 6.00
GN Graig Nettles 2.00
PN Phil Niekro 2.00
TO Tony Oliva 3.00
TO2 Tony Oliva 3.00
MO Mel Ott 3.00
SP Satchel Paige 5.00
JP Jim Palmer 3.00
DP Dave Parker 2.00
TP Tony Perez 2.00
GP Gaylord Perry 2.00
LP Lou Piniella 2.00
PS Johnny Podres 2.00
KP Kirby Puckett 5.00
TR Tim Raines 2.00
RI Jim Rice 3.00
CR Cal Ripken Jr. 8.00
PR Phil Rizzuto 3.00
RR Robin Roberts 2.00
RO Brooks Robinson 4.00
RO2 Brooks Robinson 4.00
FR Frank Robinson 4.00
FR2 Frank Robinson 4.00
JR Jackie Robinson 6.00
AR Al Rosen 2.00
BR Babe Ruth 10.00
NR Nolan Ryan 8.00
SA Ryne Sandberg 5.00
RN Ron Santo 3.00
MS Mike Schmidt 5.00
RS Red Schoendienst 2.00
TS Tom Seaver 4.00
GS George Sisler 3.00
SK Bill "Moose" Skowron 2.00
OS Ozzie Smith 5.00
BS Bruce Sutter 2.00
SU Don Sutton 2.00
JT Joe Torre 3.00
HW Honus Wagner 5.00
BW Billy Williams 2.00
MW Maury Wills 2.00
YZ Carl Yastrzemski 4.00
CY Cy Young 3.00
RY Robin Yount 4.00

When It Was A Game Used

NM/M
Production 75 unless noted.
LA Luis Aparicio/25 10.00
HB Harold Baines/25 10.00
EB Ernie Banks 20.00
JB Johnny Bench 15.00
YB Yogi Berra 20.00
WB Wade Boggs 10.00
LB Lou Brock/25 12.00
CA Rod Carew 12.00
SC Steve Carlton 10.00
SC2 Steve Carlton 10.00
WC Will Clark 12.00
RC Roberto Clemente 80.00
MC Mickey Cochrane/25 75.00
CO Rocky Colavito 25.00
AD Andre Dawson 10.00
JD Joe DiMaggio 80.00
DD Don Drysdale 15.00
DE Dennis Eckersley 10.00
EV Dwight Evans/25 15.00
BF Bob Feller 10.00
RF Rollie Fingers 10.00
CF Carlton Fisk 12.00
JF Jimmie Foxx 50.00
SG Steve Garvey 8.00
LG Lou Gehrig 140.00
BG Bob Gibson 12.00
KI Kirk Gibson 10.00
GG Rich "Goose" Gossage/25 10.00
HG Hank Greenberg 30.00
KG Ken Griffey Sr. 8.00
GU Ron Guidry 10.00
TG Tony Gwynn 15.00
HO Rogers Hornsby 50.00
FH Frank Howard/25 20.00
RJ Reggie Jackson/25 15.00
FJ Fergie Jenkins 10.00
WJ Wally Joyner 8.00
RK Ralph Kiner 10.00
JK John Kruk 10.00
DL Don Larsen 10.00
FL Fred Lynn 8.00
JU Juan Marichal 10.00
EM Eddie Mathews 15.00
MA Don Mattingly 15.00
BM Bill Mazeroski 25.00
WM Willie McCovey 10.00
MZ Johnny Mize 10.00
PM Paul Molitor 10.00
JO Joe Morgan 10.00
JM Jack Morris/25 10.00
TM Thurman Munson 25.00
MU Bobby Murcer 10.00
ED Eddie Murray 12.00
SM Stan Musial 25.00
GN Graig Nettles 10.00
PN Phil Niekro 10.00
TO Tony Oliva 10.00
TO2 Tony Oliva 10.00
MO Mel Ott 30.00
JP Jim Palmer 10.00
DP Dave Parker 8.00
TP Tony Perez 10.00
GP Gaylord Perry 10.00
LP Lou Piniella 10.00
KP Kirby Puckett 20.00
TR Tim Raines 10.00
RI Jim Rice 10.00
CR Cal Ripken Jr. 25.00
PR Phil Rizzuto/25 25.00
RR Robin Roberts 15.00
RO Brooks Robinson/25 20.00
RO2 Brooks Robinson/25 20.00
FR Frank Robinson 15.00
FR2 Frank Robinson 15.00
JR Jackie Robinson 50.00
AR Al Rosen 10.00
BR Babe Ruth/25 350.00
NR Nolan Ryan/25 30.00
SA Ryne Sandberg/25 20.00
RN Ron Santo 15.00
MS Mike Schmidt 20.00
RS Red Schoendienst 15.00
TS Tom Seaver 15.00
GS George Sisler 30.00
SK Bill "Moose" Skowron 10.00
OS Ozzie Smith 15.00
BS Bruce Sutter 10.00
SU Don Sutton 8.00
JT Joe Torre 10.00
BW Billy Williams 10.00
MW Maury Wills 10.00
YZ Carl Yastrzemski 15.00
RY Robin Yount 12.00

Place In History Signatures

NM/M
Production 99 unless noted.
LA Luis Aparicio 25.00
LA2 Luis Aparicio 25.00
HB Harold Baines/35 20.00
EB Ernie Banks/25 75.00
JB Johnny Bench/42 50.00
WB Wade Boggs/50 35.00
LB Lou Brock 25.00
LB2 Lou Brock 25.00
JC Jose Canseco 40.00
CA Rod Carew/50 25.00
SC Steve Carlton 25.00
SC2 Steve Carlton 25.00
WC Will Clark/92 25.00
WC2 Will Clark 25.00
CC Cecil Cooper 20.00
AD Andre Dawson 20.00
BD Bucky Dent 15.00
DE Dennis Eckersley 25.00
DE2 Dennis Eckersley 25.00
EV Dwight Evans 20.00
BF Bob Feller/35 40.00
RF Rollie Fingers/77 20.00
CF Carlton Fisk 30.00
WF Whitey Ford/35 60.00
GF George Foster/56 15.00
SG Steve Garvey 25.00
MG Mark Grace 25.00
KG Ken Griffey Sr. 15.00
TG Tony Gwynn/26 60.00
FH Frank Howard 25.00
BO Bo Jackson 50.00
RJ Reggie Jackson/25 60.00
FJ Fergie Jenkins 20.00
WJ Wally Joyner 25.00
BL Barry Larkin/49 40.00
FL Fred Lynn 15.00
JU Juan Marichal/29 35.00
MA Don Mattingly/50 100.00
BM Bill Mazeroski 35.00
MC Denny McLain/31 25.00
PM Paul Molitor 35.00
JO Joe Morgan/50 30.00
JM Jack Morris/82 20.00
SM Stan Musial/45 70.00
GN Graig Nettles 20.00
PN Phil Niekro/52 20.00
PN2 Phil Niekro/52 20.00
TO Tony Oliva 20.00
TO2 Tony Oliva 20.00
JP Jim Palmer 25.00
GP Gaylord Perry 20.00
GP2 Gaylord Perry 20.00
LP Lou Piniella 20.00
JY Johnny Podres/38 20.00
BP Boog Powell 20.00
KP Kirby Puckett 80.00
TR Tim Raines 25.00
JR Jim Rice 20.00
CR Cal Ripken Jr./50 140.00
PR Phil Rizzuto 40.00
RR Robin Roberts/55 25.00
BR Brooks Robinson/50 40.00
BR2 Brooks Robinson/50 40.00
FR Frank Robinson 40.00
FR2 Frank Robinson 40.00
AR Al Rosen 20.00
RO Ron Santo 60.00
RO2 Ron Santo 60.00
SS Steve Sax 20.00
MS Mike Schmidt/25 75.00
RD Red Schoendienst 35.00
TS Tom Seaver/55 50.00
SK Bill "Moose" Skowron 25.00
OS Ozzie Smith 50.00
BS Bruce Sutter 20.00
JT Joe Torre 40.00
BW Billy Williams 20.00
MW Maury Wills/96 20.00
CY Carl Yastrzemski 40.00
RY Robin Yount 40.00

Legendary Cuts

NM/M
Production 1-90
JA Joe Adcock/47 120.00
MA Mel Allen/67 175.00
WA Walter Alston/27 160.00
LA Luke Appling/84 100.00
RA Richie Ashburn/22 200.00
EA Earl Averill/50 100.00
EB Ed Barrow/35 250.00
RB Ray Boone/51 120.00
LB Lou Boudreau/86 100.00
DC Dolph Camilli/58 100.00
MC Max Carey/79 140.00
EC Earle Combs/65 200.00
ST Stan Coveleski/81 120.00
JO Joe Cronin/30 125.00
RD Ray Dandridge/35 100.00
DD Dizzy Dean/21 600.00
BD Bill Dickey/34 240.00
DR Don Drysdale/45 200.00
DU Joe Dugan/25 160.00
DL Leo Durocher/22 150.00
CG Charlie Gehringer/76 100.00
LG Lefty Gomez/44 125.00
HG Hank Greenberg/60 250.00
BG Burleigh Grimes/33 150.00
HE Billy Herman/87 100.00
WH Waite Hoyt/49 125.00
CH Jim "Catfish" Hunter/24 150.00
JJ Judy Johnson/40 150.00
HK Harvey Kuenn/89 120.00
BL Bob Lemon/77 80.00
LO Ernie Lombardi/25 160.00
EL Ed Lopat/32 140.00
EM Eddie Mathews/59 150.00
JM Joe McCarthy/67 180.00
ME Joe Medwick/82 180.00
MI Johnny Mize/90 140.00
WP Wally Post/66 120.00
PR Pee Wee Reese/47 160.00
SR Sam Rice/31 180.00
ER Edd Roush/90 80.00
RR Red Ruffing/72 200.00
JS Joe Sewell/83 120.00
WS Warren Spahn/52 140.00
CS Casey Stengel/35 300.00
PT Pie Traynor/26 500.00
BW Bucky Walters/52 120.00
WI Hoyt Wilhelm/47 100.00

Place In History Cut Signatures

NM/M
Production 1-98
BA Bob Allison/94 140.00
LA Luke Appling/94 100.00
EA Earl Averill/75 80.00
LB Lou Boudreau/88 100.00
HC Happy Chandler/61 100.00
CO Chuck Connors/25 450.00
JC Joe Cronin/30 125.00
RD Ray Dandridge/43 120.00
BD Bill Dickey/29 200.00
DL Leo Durocher/42 140.00
DU Joe Dugan/25 150.00
FF Ford Frick/30 150.00
CG Charlie Gehringer/57 120.00
WG Warren Giles/45 200.00
LG Lefty Gomez/30 125.00
HG Hank Greenberg/31 260.00
BG Burleigh Grimes/43 120.00
HI Kirby Higbe/59 140.00
JH Johnny Hodapp/26 125.00
DH Dick Howser/28 160.00
JJ Judy Johnson/20 180.00
VK Vern Kennedy/61 120.00
BL Bob Lemon/47 90.00
SM Sal Maglie/73 120.00
EM Eddie Mathews/34 150.00
JM Joe McCarthy/58 200.00
ME Joe Medwick/60 200.00
PR Pee Wee Reese/57 180.00
RE Pete Reiser/75 125.00
RO Charlie Robertson/42 150.00
ER Edd Roush/98 100.00
JS Joe Sewell/87 100.00
GS George Sisler/42 450.00
WS Warren Spahn/41 140.00
WI Hoyt Wilhelm/65 100.00
CW Cy Williams/29 180.00
EW Early Wynn/36 100.00

Dual Legendary Cuts

Production One Set

Quadruple Legendary Cuts

Production One Set

Historical Cut Signatures

Production One Set

Memorable Moments Swatch

NM/M
Common Player:
Production 225 Sets
JB Johnny Bench 15.00
CC Cesar Cedeno 8.00
RC Rocky Colavito 20.00
DC David Cone 8.00
CE Cecil Cooper 10.00
AD Andre Dawson 10.00
DE Dwight Evans 8.00
BF Bob Feller 12.00
RF Rollie Fingers 8.00
CF Carlton Fisk 10.00
GF George Foster 8.00
SG Steve Garvey 8.00
KG Kirk Gibson 10.00
GG Rich "Goose" Gossage 8.00
RG Ron Guidry 12.00
TG Tony Gwynn 12.00
BJ Bo Jackson 15.00
RJ Reggie Jackson 10.00
JK John Kruk 10.00
BL Barry Larkin 10.00
MA Juan Marichal 10.00
EM Eddie Mathews 15.00
DM Don Mattingly 20.00
JM Johnny Mize 15.00
MO Joe Morgan 10.00
BM Bobby Murcer 8.00
MU Eddie Murray 10.00
SM Stan Musial 20.00
PO Paul O'Neill 10.00
DP Dave Parker 8.00
GP Gaylord Perry 8.00
TR Tim Raines 8.00
PR Phil Rizzuto 10.00
RS Ron Santo 10.00
SS Steve Sax 8.00
MS Mike Schmidt 15.00
TS Tom Seaver 12.00
OS Ozzie Smith 15.00
BS Bruce Sutter 10.00
DS Don Sutton 8.00
RY Robin Yount 12.00

Memorable Moments Autograph

NM/M
Production 1-99
CC Cesar Cedeno/99 20.00
RC Rocky Colavito/25 80.00
DC David Cone/99 15.00
CE Cecil Cooper/99 20.00
AD Andre Dawson/99 20.00
DE Dwight Evans/25 20.00
BF Bob Feller/25 40.00
RF Rollie Fingers/47 20.00
CF Carlton Fisk/25 30.00
GF George Foster/25 20.00
SG Steve Garvey/25 35.00
KG Kirk Gibson/25 30.00
TG Tony Gwynn/25 75.00
BJ Bo Jackson/25 50.00
JK John Kruk/99 20.00
BL Barry Larkin/50 40.00
MA Juan Marichal/25 30.00
DM Don Mattingly/50 100.00
MO Joe Morgan/20 30.00
MU Eddie Murray/45 20.00
GP Gaylord Perry/99 20.00
TR Tim Raines/50 30.00
PR Phil Rizzuto/99 40.00
RS Ron Santo/25 65.00
TS Tom Seaver/44 40.00
OS Ozzie Smith/25 50.00
RY Robin Yount/25 60.00

When It Was a Game Cut Signature

NM/M
Production 2-99
JA Joe Adcock/18 150.00
LA Luke Appling/83 100.00
EA Earl Averill/67 80.00
EB Earl Battey/25 175.00
RB Ray Boone/68 120.00
LB Lou Boudreau/50 100.00
AC Al Campanis/30 250.00
MC Max Carey/71 140.00
HC Happy Chandler/64 100.00
SC Stan Coveleski/91 100.00
CR Joe Cronin/34 120.00
RD Ray Dandridge/75 120.00
JD Joe Dugan/30 150.00
DU Leo Durocher/25 160.00
RF Rick Ferrell/25 150.00
EF Elmer Flick/25 150.00
FF Ford Frick/30 150.00
CG Charlie Gehringer/64 120.00
LG Lefty Gomez/36 125.00
HG Hank Greenberg/21 260.00
BG Burleigh Grimes/56 140.00
HE Billy Herman/99 100.00
WH Waite Hoyt/70 100.00
CH Carl Hubbell/80 140.00
HU Jim "Catfish" Hunter/34 150.00
JJ Judy Johncon/20 180.00
VK Vern Kennedy/58 120.00
TK Ted Kluszewski/50 140.00
BL Bob Lemon/79 90.00
FL Freddie Lindstrom/25 200.00
EL Ernie Lombardi/24 150.00
LO Ed Lopat/28 140.00
SM Sal Maglie/68 120.00
EM Eddie Mathews/33 150.00
JM Joe McCarthy/51 200.00
ME Joe Medwick/57 200.00
MI Johnny Mize/70 120.00
GP George Pipgras/25 180.00
WP Wally Post/66 120.00
PR Pee Wee Reese/52 180.00
SR Sam Rice/33 175.00
ER Edd Roush/98 100.00
RR Red Ruffing/44 180.00
SE George Selkirk/175 175.00
JS Joe Sewell/78 100.00
GS George Sisler/37 450.00
WS Warren Spahn/78 125.00
ST Willie Stargell/27 160.00
JV Johnny Vander Meer/45 150.00
VW Vic Wertz/30 160.00
HW Hoyt Wilhelm/56 100.00
EW Early Wynn/40 100.00

2006 SPx

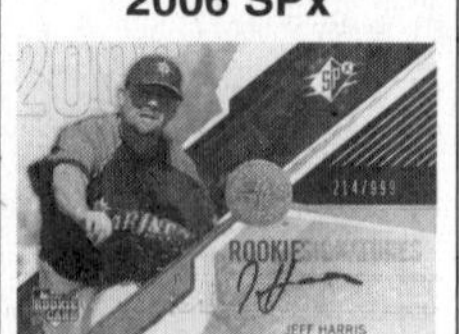

NM/M
Complete Set (160):
Common Player (1-100): .25
Common Auto. (101-160): 10.00
Production 190-999
Pack (4): 8.00
Box (18): 125.00
1 Luis Gonzalez .25
2 Chad Tracy .25
3 Brandon Webb .50
4 Andruw Jones 1.00
5 Chipper Jones 1.00
6 John Smoltz .75
7 Tim Hudson .50
8 Miguel Tejada .75
9 Brian Roberts .25
10 Ramon Hernandez .25
11 Curt Schilling 1.00
12 David Ortiz 1.50
13 Manny Ramirez 1.00
14 Jason Varitek 1.00
15 Josh Beckett .50
16 Greg Maddux 2.00
17 Derrek Lee .75
18 Mark Prior .75
19 Aramis Ramirez .50
20 Jim Thome .75
21 Paul Konerko .75
22 Scott Podsednik .25
23 Jose Contreras .25
24 Ken Griffey Jr. 2.00
25 Adam Dunn .75
26 Felipe Lopez .25
27 Travis Hafner .75
28 Victor Martinez .25
29 Grady Sizemore .75
30 Jhonny Peralta .25
31 Todd Helton .75
32 Garrett Atkins .25
33 Clint Barmes .25
34 Ivan Rodriguez .75
35 Chris Shelton .25
36 Jeremy Bonderman .50
37 Miguel Cabrera 1.00
38 Dontrelle Willis .50
39 Lance Berkman .50
40 Morgan Ensberg .25
41 Roy Oswalt .50
42 Reggie Sanders .25
43 Mike Sweeney .25
44 Vladimir Guerrero 1.00
45 Bartolo Colon .25
46 Chone Figgins .25
47 Nomar Garciaparra 1.00
48 Jeff Kent .50
49 J.D. Drew .25
50 Carlos Lee .50
51 Ben Sheets .50
52 Rickie Weeks .25
53 Johan Santana 1.00
54 Torii Hunter .50
55 Joe Mauer .50
56 Pedro Martinez 1.00
57 David Wright 2.00
58 Carlos Beltran .75
59 Carlos Delgado .75
60 Jose Reyes .75
61 Derek Jeter 3.00
62 Alex Rodriguez 3.00
63 Randy Johnson 1.00
64 Hideki Matsui 2.00
65 Gary Sheffield .75
66 Rich Harden .50
67 Eric Chavez .50
68 Huston Street .50
69 Bobby Crosby .25
70 Bobby Abreu .50
71 Ryan Howard 2.00
72 Chase Utley .75
73 Pat Burrell .50
74 Jason Bay .50
75 Sean Casey .25
76 Mike Piazza 1.00
77 Jake Peavy .50
78 Brian Giles .25
79 Milton Bradley .25
80 Omar Vizquel .25
81 Jason Schmidt .25
82 Ichiro Suzuki 2.00
83 Felix Hernandez .50
84 Richie Sexson .50
85 Albert Pujols 3.00
86 Chris Carpenter .75
87 Scott Rolen 1.00
88 Jim Edmonds .50
89 Carl Crawford .50
90 Jonny Gomes .25
91 Scott Kazmir .50
92 Mark Teixeira .75
93 Michael Young .50
94 Phil Nevin .25
95 Vernon Wells .25
96 Roy Halladay .50
97 Troy Glaus .50
98 Alfonso Soriano .75
99 Nick Johnson .25
100 Jose Vidro .25
101 Conor Jackson/999 **(RC)** 15.00
102 Jered Weaver/299 **(RC)** 40.00
103 Macay McBride/999 **(RC)** 10.00
104 Aaron Rakers/499 **(RC)** 15.00
105 Jonathan Papelbon/499 **(RC)** 50.00
106 Jason Bergmann/999 **RC** 15.00
107 Stephen Drew/350 **(RC)** 40.00
108 Chris Denorfia/999 **(RC)** 10.00
109 Kelly Shoppach/999 **(RC)** 15.00
110 Ryan Shealy/999 **(RC)** 15.00
111 Josh Wilson/999 **(RC)** 10.00
112 Brian Anderson/999 **(RC)** 10.00
113 Justin Verlander/749 **(RC)** 40.00
114 Jeremy Hermida/999 **(RC)** 15.00
115 Mike Jacobs/999 **(RC)** 15.00
116 Josh Johnson/999 **(RC)** 15.00
117 Hanley Ramirez/659 **(RC)** 30.00
118 Chris Resop/999 **(RC)** 10.00
119 Josh Willingham/999 **(RC)** 15.00

120 Cole Hamels/ 499 **(RC)** 50.00
121 Matt Cain/999 **(RC)** 30.00
122 Steve Stemle/999 **RC** 10.00
123 Tim Hamulack/ 999 **(RC)** 10.00
124 Choo Freeman/ 999 **(RC)** 10.00
125 Hong-Chih Kuo/ 999 **(RC)** 30.00
126 Cody Ross/999 **(RC)** 15.00
127 Jose Capellan /999 **(RC)** 10.00
128 Prince Fielder/ 190 **(RC)** 120.00
129 David Gassner/ 999 **(RC)** 10.00
130 Jason Kubel/ 999 **(RC)** 15.00
131 Francisco Liriano/ 299 **(RC)** 40.00
132 Anderson Hernandez/ 999 **(RC)** 10.00
133 Joey Devine/499 **RC** 15.00
134 Chris Booker/ 999 **(RC)** 10.00
135 Matt Capps/999 **(RC)** 15.00
136 Paul Maholm/ 999 **(RC)** 10.00
137 Nate McLouth/ 999 **(RC)** 10.00
138 John Van Benschoten/ 999 **(RC)** 10.00
139 Jeff Harris/999 **RC** 10.00
140 Ben Johnson/ 999 **(RC)** 10.00
141 Wilbert Nieves/ 999 **(RC)** 15.00
142 Guillermo Quiroz/ 999 **(RC)** 10.00
143 Josh Rupe/500 **(RC)** 15.00
144 Skip Schumaker/ 999 **(RC)** 15.00
145 Jack Taschner/ 999 **(RC)** 10.00
146 Adam Wainwright/ 999 **(RC)** 25.00
147 Alay Soler/499 **RC** 15.00
148 Kendry Morales/ 999 **(RC)** 15.00
149 Ian Kinsler/999 **(RC)** 20.00
150 Jason Hammel/ 999 **(RC)** 10.00
151 Chad Billingsley/ 499 **(RC)** 30.00
152 Boof Bonser/ 999 **(RC)** 20.00
153 Peter Moylan/999 **RC** 10.00
154 Chris Britton/999 **RC** 10.00
155 Takashi Saito/999 **RC** 30.00
156 Scott Dunn **(RC)** 10.00
157 Joel Zumaya/ 299 **(RC)** 25.00
158 Dan Uggla/999 **(RC)** 25.00
159 Taylor Buchholz/ 999 **(RC)** 10.00
160 Melky Cabrera/ 499 **(RC)** 40.00

Rookie Signature Printing Plates

No Pricing
Production one set per color.

Rookie Signature Platinum

No Pricing
Production One Set

Rookie Signature Gold

No Pricing
Production Five Sets

Spectrum

Stars (1-100): 2-3X
Inserted 1:3

Next in Line

NM/M
Common Player: 1.00
BA Brian Anderson 1.00
BB Brian Bannister 1.00
JB Josh Barfield 1.00
TB Taylor Buchholz 1.00
MC Matt Cain 1.50
RC Ryan Church 1.00
PF Prince Fielder 3.00
JH Jeremy Hermida 1.00
FH Felix Hernandez 1.50
RH Ryan Howard 3.00
TI Travis Ishikawa 1.00
CJ Conor Jackson 1.00
MJ Mike Jacobs 1.00
BJ Ben Johnson 1.00
IK Ian Kinsler 1.00
LE Jon Lester 3.00
FL Francisco Liriano 3.00
JL James Loney 1.00
SO Scott Olsen 1.00
JP Jonathan Papelbon 3.00
HR Hanley Ramirez 1.50
NM Alay Soler 1.00
JS Jeremy Sowers 1.00
HS Huston Street 1.00
DU Dan Uggla 1.00
JV Justin Verlander 3.00
AW Adam Wainwright 1.00
JE Jered Weaver 3.00
JW Josh Willingham 1.00
RZ Ryan Zimmerman 3.00

SPxciting Signatures

NM/M
Production 30 unless noted.
JA Jeremy Accardo 10.00
BA Brian Anderson 20.00
BY Jason Bay 30.00
BI Craig Biggio 40.00
CH Chad Billingsley 35.00
HB Hank Blalock 20.00
BR Chris Britton 15.00
MI Miguel Cabrera 40.00
MC Matt Cain 40.00
CA Matt Capps 15.00
RC Roger Clemens 165.00
CW Carl Crawford 30.00
SD Scott Dunn 10.00
EG Eric Gagne 35.00
GR Khalil Greene 30.00
KG Ken Griffey Jr. 100.00
HT Travis Hafner 25.00
HA Jason Hammel 15.00
TH Tim Hamulack 20.00
JH Jeff Harris 12.00
HE Jeremy Hermida 30.00
TR Trevor Hoffman 50.00
CJ Conor Jackson 20.00
KU Jason Kubel 25.00
HK Hong-Chih Kuo 180.00
CL Cliff Lee 15.00
PM Paul Maholm 15.00
VM Victor Martinez 20.00
MM Macay McBride 20.00
NM Nate McLouth 15.00
MU Mark Mulder 20.00
WN Wilbert Nieves 35.00
JP Jonathan Papelbon 100.00
CP Corey Patterson 20.00
PE Jake Peavy 25.00
OP Oliver Perez 15.00
HR Hanley Ramirez 40.00
CR Chris Resop 10.00
RO Cody Ross 30.00
TS Takashi Saito 140.00
SS Skip Schumaker 30.00
RS Ryan Shealy 20.00
KS Kelly Shoppach 25.00
DU Dan Uggla 75.00
JV John Van Benschoten 15.00
VE Justin Verlander 90.00
AW Adam Wainwright 50.00
JW Josh Willingham 20.00
WI Josh Wilson 15.00

SPxtra Info

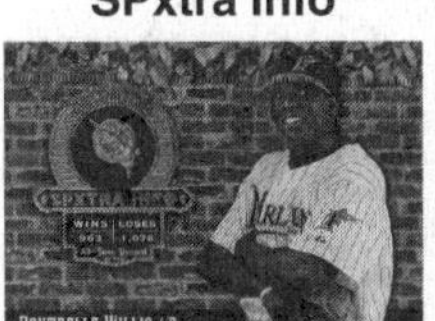

NM/M
Common Player: .50
BA Bobby Abreu .75
JB Jason Bay .75
EC Eric Chavez .50
CC Carl Crawford .75
BG Brian Giles .50
LG Luis Gonzalez .50
KG Ken Griffey Jr. 2.00
VG Vladimir Guerrero 1.00
TH Travis Hafner .75
HE Todd Helton .75
DJ Derek Jeter 3.00
NJ Nick Johnson .50
AJ Andruw Jones 1.00
JK Jeff Kent .50
CL Carlos Lee .75
DL Derrek Lee 1.00
PM Pedro Martinez 1.00
DO David Ortiz 1.50
RO Roy Oswalt .75
AP Albert Pujols 3.00
IR Ivan Rodriguez .75
RS Reggie Sanders .50
JS Johan Santana 1.00
SC Jason Schmidt .50
IS Ichiro Suzuki 2.00
TE Mark Teixeira .75
MT Miguel Tejada .75
JT Jim Thome 1.00
VW Vernon Wells .50
DW Dontrelle Willis .75

SPxtreme Team

NM/M
Common Player: .50
BA Bobby Abreu .75
JB Jason Bay .75
LB Lance Berkman .75
MC Miguel Cabrera 1.00
CC Chris Carpenter .75
CR Carl Crawford .75
CD Carlos Delgado .75
AD Adam Dunn .75
PF Prince Fielder 3.00
KG Ken Griffey Jr. 2.00
VG Vladimir Guerrero 1.00
HA Travis Hafner .75
RH Rich Harden .50
TH Todd Helton .75
HO Ryan Howard 2.00
DJ Derek Jeter 3.00
AJ Andruw Jones 1.00
JK Jeff Kent .50
PK Paul Konerko .75
CL Carlos Lee .75
DL Derrek Lee 1.00
PM Pedro Martinez 1.00
VM Victor Martinez .75
HM Hideki Matsui 2.00
DO David Ortiz 1.50
JP Jake Peavy .50
AP Albert Pujols 3.00
MR Manny Ramirez 1.00
JR Jose Reyes .75
AR Alex Rodriguez 3.00
JS Johan Santana 1.00
GS Grady Sizemore .75
AS Alfonso Soriano 1.00
IS Ichiro Suzuki 2.00
MT Mark Teixeira .75
TE Miguel Tejada .75
JT Jim Thome 1.00
VW Vernon Wells .75
DW David Wright 2.00
MY Michael Young .50

WBC All-World Team

NM/M
Common Player: .50
1 Brett Willemburg .50
2 Bradley Harman .50
3 Adam Stern 1.00
4 Jason Bay 1.00
5 Adam Loewen .50
6 Wei Wang 2.00
7 Yi Feng 1.00
8 Yung-Chi Chen 6.00
9 Chin-Lung Hu 6.00
10 Wei-Lun Pan 5.00
11 Yoandy Garlobo .50
12 Frederich Cepeda .50
13 Osmany Urrutia 1.00
14 Yulieski Gourriel 2.00
15 Yadel Marti .50
16 Pedro Luis Lazo .50
17 Adrian Beltre .50
18 David Ortiz 2.00
19 Albert Pujols 4.00
20 Bartolo Colon .50
21 Miguel Tejada 1.00
22 Mike Piazza 1.50
23 Jason Grilli 1.00
24 Nobuhiko Matsunaka 3.00
25 Tomoya Satozaki 3.00
26 Ichiro Suzuki 3.00
27 Hitoshi Tamura 3.00
28 Daisuke Matsuzaka 8.00
29 Koji Uehara 3.00
30 Jong Beom Lee .50
31 Seung-Yeop Lee .50
32 Jae Weong Seo .50
33 Min Han Son .50
34 Chan Ho Park .50
35 Jorge Cantu .50
36 Miguel Ojeda .50
37 Andruw Jones 1.00
38 Shairon Martis .50
39 Carlos Lee .75
40 Carlos Beltran 1.00
41 Javy Lopez .50
42 Javier Vazquez .50
43 Ken Griffey Jr. 3.00
44 Derek Jeter 4.00
45 Alex Rodriguez 4.00
46 Derrek Lee 1.50
47 Roger Clemens 3.00
48 Miguel Cabrera 1.50
49 Victor Martinez 1.50
50 Johan Santana 1.50

Winning Materials

NM/M
Common Player: 5.00
BA Bobby Abreu 6.00
JB Jason Bay 10.00
CB Carlos Beltran 10.00
MC Miguel Cabrera 10.00
FC Frederich Cepeda 5.00
HC Hee Seop Choi 10.00
RC Roger Clemens 15.00
JD Johnny Damon 10.00
CD Carlos Delgado 6.00
ME Michel Enriquez 5.00
MF Maikel Folch 5.00
YG Yulieski Gourriel 8.00
KG Ken Griffey Jr. 20.00
AI Akinori Iwamura 25.00
AJ Andruw Jones 8.00
MK Munenori Kawasaki 20.00
PL Pedro Luis Lazo 8.00
DL Derrek Lee 8.00
JL Jong Beom Lee 5.00
VM Victor Martinez 5.00
NM Nobuhiko Matsunaka 20.00
YM Yuneiski Maya 5.00
TN Tsuyoshi Nishioka 25.00
VO Vicyohandry Odelin 5.00
MO Michihiro Ogasawara 20.00
DO David Ortiz 15.00
EP Eduardo Paret 5.00
AP Ariel Pestano 5.00
MP Mike Piazza 15.00
PU Albert Pujols 20.00
AR Alex Rodriguez 20.00
JS Johan Santana 10.00
NS Naoyuki Shimizu 25.00
MS Min Han Son 8.00
AS Alfonso Soriano 10.00
IS Ichiro Suzuki 90.00
HT Hitoshi Tamura 20.00
MT Miguel Tejada 10.00
KU Koji Uehara 30.00
OU Osmany Urrutia 8.00
TW Tsuyoshi Wada 20.00
SW Shunsuke Watanabe 20.00

Winning Big Materials

NM/M
Production 5-55
BA Bobby Abreu/40 75.00
MA Moises Alou/53 50.00
JB Jason Bay/40 80.00
EB Erik Bedard/40 50.00
CB Carlos Beltran/40 75.00
AB Adrian Beltre/40 50.00
MC Miguel Cabrera/40 80.00
FC Frederich Cepeda/30 65.00
HC Hee Seop Choi/32 75.00
JD Johnny Damon/40 100.00
CD Carlos Delgado/40 65.00
ME Michel Enriquez/30 50.00
MF Maikel Folch/30 60.00
JF Jeff Francis/40 50.00
YG Yulieski Gourriel/30 100.00
AI Akinori Iwamura/30 275.00
AJ Andruw Jones/40 80.00
MK Munenori Kawasaki/30 350.00
PL Pedro Luis Lazo/30 80.00
CL Carlos Lee/40 60.00
DL Derrek Lee/40 75.00
JL Jong Beom Lee/20 75.00
WL Wei-Chu Lin/45 350.00
LO Javy Lopez/40 50.00
VM Victor Martinez/40 75.00
NM Nobuhiko Matsunaka/30 300.00
YM Yuneiski Maya/30 60.00
JM Justin Morneau/25 60.00
TN Tsuyoshi Nishioka/30 375.00
VO Vicyohandry Odelin/30 75.00
MO Michihiro Ogasawara/30 350.00
DO David Ortiz/30 150.00
WP Wei-Lun Pan/38 300.00
EP Eduardo Paret/30 50.00
PE Wily Mo Pena/60 50.00
AP Ariel Pestano/30 60.00
MP Mike Piazza/40 100.00
AR Alex Rios/55 50.00
IR Ivan Rodriguez/40 60.00
JS Johan Santana/40 75.00
NS Naoyuki Shimizu/30 250.00
AS Alfonso Soriano/40 90.00
HT Hitoshi Tamura/30 300.00
MT Miguel Tejada/40 60.00
KU Koji Uehara/30 300.00
OU Osmany Urrutia/30 65.00
JV Jason Varitek/40 120.00
TW Tsuyoshi Wada/30 250.00
SW Shunsuke Watanabe/30 260.00
BW Bernie Williams/40 75.00
GY Guogang Yang/52 50.00
CZ Carlos Zambrano/40 50.00

2007 SP Authentic

NM/M
Complete Set (162):
Common Player: .25
Common RC Letter Auto.: 15.00
Pack (5): 5.00
Box (24): 100.00
1 Chipper Jones 1.00
2 Andruw Jones .50
3 John Smoltz .50
4 Carlos Quentin .25
5 Randy Johnson 1.00
6 Brandon Webb .50
7 Alfonso Soriano 1.00
8 Derrek Lee .75
9 Aramis Ramirez .50
10 Carlos Zambrano .50
11 Ken Griffey Jr. 2.00
12 Adam Dunn .50
13 Josh Hamilton .50
14 Todd Helton .50
15 Jeff Francis .25
16 Matt Holliday .50
17 Hanley Ramirez 1.00
18 Dontrelle Willis .50
19 Miguel Cabrera 1.00
20 Lance Berkman .50
21 Roy Oswalt .50
22 Carlos Lee .50
23 Nomar Garciaparra .75
24 Derek Lowe .25
25 Juan Pierre .50
26 Rafael Furcal .50
27 Rickie Weeks .25
28 Prince Fielder 1.50
29 Ben Sheets .25
30 David Wright 1.50
31 Jose Reyes 1.00
32 Tom Glavine .50
33 Carlos Beltran .75
34 Cole Hamels .75
35 Jimmy Rollins .75
36 Ryan Howard 2.00
37 Jason Bay .50
38 Freddy Sanchez .25
39 Ian Snell .25
40 Jake Peavy .50
41 Greg Maddux 2.00
42 Trevor Hoffman .25
43 Matt Cain .50
44 Barry Zito .25
45 Ray Durham .25
46 Albert Pujols 3.00
47 Chris Carpenter .50
48 Jim Edmonds .50
49 Scott Rolen .50
50 Ryan Zimmerman .50
51 Felipe Lopez .25
52 Austin Kearns .25
53 Miguel Tejada .50
54 Erik Bedard .50
55 Daniel Cabrera .25
56 David Ortiz 1.00
57 Curt Schilling .75
58 Manny Ramirez 1.00
59 Jonathan Papelbon .75
60 Jim Thome .75
61 Paul Konerko .50
62 Bobby Jenks .25
63 Grady Sizemore 1.00
64 Victor Martinez .50
65 Travis Hafner .50
66 Ivan Rodriguez .75
67 Justin Verlander .50
68 Joel Zumaya .25
69 Jeremy Bonderman .50
70 Gil Meche .25
71 Mike Sweeney .25
72 Mark Teahen .25
73 Vladimir Guerrero 1.00
74 Howie Kendrick .25
75 Francisco Rodriguez .25
76 Johan Santana 1.00
77 Justin Morneau .50
78 Joe Mauer .50
79 Joe Nathan .25
80 Alex Rodriguez 3.00
81 Derek Jeter 3.00
82 Johnny Damon .75
83 Chien-Ming Wang 1.00
84 Rich Harden .25
85 Mike Piazza 1.00
86 Danny Haren .25
87 Ichiro Suzuki 2.00
88 Felix Hernandez .50
89 Kenji Johjima .25
90 Adrian Beltre .25
91 Carl Crawford .50
92 Scott Kazmir .50
93 Delmon Young .50
94 Michael Young .25
95 Mark Teixeira .50
96 Eric Gagne .25
97 Hank Blalock .25
98 Vernon Wells .50
99 Roy Halladay .50
100 Frank Thomas .75
101 Joaquin Arias/ 75 **(RC)** 15.00
102 Jeff Baker/ Redemp. **(RC)** 15.00
103 Michael Bourn/ 75 **(RC)** 20.00
104 Brian Burres/75 **(RC)** 20.00
105 Jared Burton/75 **RC** 20.00
106 Ryan Braun/50 **(RC)** 75.00
107 Yovani Gallardo/ 75 **(RC)** 60.00
107 Yovani Gallardo/ 35 **(RC)** 60.00
108 Hector Gimenez/ 75 **(RC)** 15.00
108 Hector Gimenez/ 50 **(RC)** 15.00
109 Alex Gordon/50 **RC** 60.00
110 Josh Hamilton/ 50 **(RC)** 30.00
110 Josh Hamilton/ 35 **(RC)** 30.00
111 Justin Hampson/ 50 **(RC)** 15.00
111 Justin Hampson/ 75 **(RC)** 15.00
112 Sean Henn/75 **(RC)** 20.00
113 Phil Hughes/ Redemp. **(RC)** 75.00
114 Kei Igawa/25 **RC** 60.00
115 Akinori Iwamura/ 20 **RC** 60.00
116 Mark Reynolds/ 75 **RC** 30.00
116 Mark Reynolds/ 35 **RC** 35.00
117 Homer Bailey/ 75 **(RC)** 40.00
117 Homer Bailey/ 50 **(RC)** 40.00
118 Kevin Kouzmanoff/ 75 **(RC)** 20.00
118 Kevin Kouzmanoff/ 40 **(RC)** 20.00
119 Adam Lind/75 **(RC)** 20.00
120 Carlos Gomez/75 **RC** 50.00
120 Carlos Gomez/50 **RC** 50.00
121 Glen Perkins/75 **(RC)** 20.00
121 Glen Perkins/50 **(RC)** 20.00
122 Rick Vanden Hurk/ 75 **RC** 20.00
122 Rick Vanden Hurk/ 35 **RC** 20.00
123 Brad Salmon/75 **RC** 15.00
124 Zack Segovia/75 **(RC)** 20.00
124 Zack Segovia/50 **(RC)** 20.00
125 Kurt Suzuki/75 **(RC)** 20.00
125 Kurt Suzuki/50 **(RC)** 20.00
126 Chris Stewart/ 75 **(RC)** 15.00
126 Chris Stewart/ 50 **(RC)** 15.00
127 Cesar Jimenez/75 **RC** 15.00
128 Ryan Sweeney/ 50 **(RC)** 20.00
128 Ryan Sweeney/ 40 **(RC)** 20.00
129 Troy Tulowitzki/ Redemp. **(RC)** 60.00
130 Chase Wright/75 **RC** 20.00
131 Delmon Young/ 20 **(RC)** 40.00
132 Tony Abreu/75 **(RC)** 20.00
132 Tony Abreu/50 **(RC)** 20.00
133 Brian Barden/75 **RC** 15.00
134 Curtis Thigpen/ 75 **(RC)** 20.00
134 Curtis Thigpen/ 40 **(RC)** 20.00
135 Jon Coutlangus/ 75 **(RC)** 15.00
135 Jon Coutlangus/ 55 **(RC)** 15.00
136 Kevin Cameron/ 75 **RC** 15.00
136 Kevin Cameron/ 50 **RC** 15.00
137 Billy Butler/75 **(RC)** 30.00
138 Alexi Casilla/75 **RC** 20.00
138 Alexi Casilla/50 **RC** 20.00
139 Kory Casto/75 **(RC)** 20.00
140 Matt Chico/75 **(RC)** 20.00
141 John Danks/75 **RC** 20.00
142 Andrew Miller/50 **RC** 40.00
143 Ben Francisco/ 75 **(RC)** 15.00
143 Ben Francisco/ 40 **(RC)** 15.00
144 Andy Gonzalez/75 **RC** 15.00
144 Andy Gonzalez/50 **RC** 15.00
145 Devern Hansack/ Redemp. **RC** 20.00
146 Mike Rabelo/75 **RC** 15.00

No.	Card	Price
147	Tim Lincecum/50 **RC**	75.00
147	Tim Lincecum/25 **RC**	75.00
148	Matt Lindstrom/75 **(RC)**	15.00
148	Matt Lindstrom/40 **(RC)**	15.00
149	Jay Marshall/75 **RC**	15.00
149	Jay Marshall/50 **RC**	15.00
150	Daisuke Matsuzaka/Redemp **RC**	350.00
151	Miguel Montero/75 **(RC)**	20.00
151	Miguel Montero/50 **(RC)**	20.00
152	Micah Owings/75 **(RC)**	35.00
153	Hunter Pence/75 **(RC)**	50.00
154	Brandon Wood/75 **(RC)**	20.00
155	Felix Pie/75 **(RC)**	20.00
155	Felix Pie/70 **(RC)**	20.00
156	Danny Putnam/75 **(RC)**	15.00
157	Andy LaRoche/50 **(RC)**	25.00
157	Andy LaRoche/40 **(RC)**	25.00
158	Jarrod Saltalamacchia/75 **(RC)**	30.00
158	Jarrod Saltalamacchia/25 **(RC)**	30.00
159	Doug Slaten/75 **RC**	20.00
160	Joe Smith/75 **RC**	20.00
161	Justin Upton/120 **RC**	80.00
162	Joba Chamberlain/60 **RC**	200.00

Authentic Power

No.	Card	NM/M
	Common Player:	.50
1	Adam Dunn	1.00
2	Albert Pujols	4.00
3	Alex Rodriguez	4.00
4	Alfonso Soriano	1.50
5	Andruw Jones	.75
6	Aramis Ramirez	.75
7	Bill Hall	.50
8	Carlos Beltran	1.00
9	Carlos Delgado	.75
10	Carlos Lee	.75
11	Chase Utley	1.50
12	Chipper Jones	1.50
13	Dan Uggla	.50
14	David Ortiz	1.50
15	David Wright	2.00
16	Derrek Lee	.75
17	Eric Chavez	.50
18	Frank Thomas	1.00
19	Garrett Atkins	.50
20	Gary Sheffield	1.00
21	Hideki Matsui	2.50
22	J.D. Drew	.50
23	Jason Bay	.75
24	Jason Giambi	1.00
25	Jeff Francoeur	1.50
26	Jermaine Dye	.50
27	Jim Thome	1.00
28	Justin Morneau	1.00
29	Ken Griffey Jr.	3.00
30	Lance Berkman	.75
31	Magglio Ordonez	.75
32	Manny Ramirez	1.00
33	Mark Teixeira	1.00
34	Matt Holliday	1.00
35	Miguel Cabrera	1.50
36	Miguel Tejada	.75
37	Mike Piazza	1.50
38	Nick Swisher	.75
39	Pat Burrell	.75
40	Paul Konerko	1.00
41	Prince Fielder	2.00
42	Richie Sexson	.75
43	Ryan Howard	2.50
44	Sammy Sosa	1.00
45	Todd Helton	1.00
46	Travis Hafner	.75
47	Troy Glaus	.75
48	Vernon Wells	.75
49	Victor Martinez	.75
50	Vladimir Guerrero	1.50

Authentic Speed

No.	Card	NM/M
	Common Player:	.50
1	Alex Rios	.75
2	Alex Rodriguez	4.00
3	Alfonso Soriano	1.50
4	B.J. Upton	.75
5	Bobby Abreu	.75
6	Brandon Phillips	.50
7	Brian Roberts	.75
8	Carl Crawford	.75
9	Carlos Beltran	1.00
10	Chase Utley	1.50
11	Chone Figgins	.75
12	Chris Burke	.50
13	Chris Duffy	.50
14	Coco Crisp	.50
15	Corey Patterson	.50
16	Dave Roberts	.50
17	David Wright	2.00
18	Derek Jeter	4.00
19	Edgar Renteria	.50
20	Eric Byrnes	.75
21	Felipe Lopez	.50
22	Gary Matthews	.50
23	Grady Sizemore	2.00
24	Hanley Ramirez	1.50
25	Ian Kinsler	.75
26	Ichiro Suzuki	3.00
27	Jacque Jones	.50
28	Jimmy Rollins	1.00
29	Johnny Damon	1.00
30	Jose Reyes	2.00
31	Juan Pierre	.50
32	Julio Lugo	.50
33	Kenny Lofton	.50
34	Luis Castillo	.50
35	Marcus Giles	.50
36	Melky Cabrera	1.00
37	Mike Cameron	.50
38	Orlando Cabrera	.75
39	Rafael Furcal	.75
40	Randy Winn	.50
41	Rickie Weeks	.50
42	Rocco Baldelli	.50
43	Ryan Freel	.50
44	Ryan Theriot	1.00
45	Scott Podsednik	.50
46	Shane Victorino	.50
47	Tadahito Iguchi	.50
48	Torii Hunter	.75
49	Vernon Wells	.75
50	Willy Taveras	.50

By The Letter Signatures

No.	Card	NM/M
	Common Player:	
1	Derek Jeter/redemp	250.00
2	Ken Griffey Jr./25	125.00
2	Ken Griffey Jr./20	125.00
4	Justin Verlander/25	50.00
4	Justin Verlander/15	50.00
5	Adrian Gonzalez/60	20.00
5	Adrian Gonzalez/50	20.00
8	Josh Beckett/15	100.00
10	Aramis Ramirez/25	50.00
11	Austin Kearns/50	15.00
12	B.J. Upton/25	35.00
12	B.J. Upton/15	35.00
13	Boof Bonser/75	15.00
13	Boof Bonser/50	15.00
14	Bronson Arroyo/75	20.00
15	Troy Tulowitzki/Redemp.	50.00
16	Felix Pie/75	25.00
17	Alex Gordon/25	60.00
18	Chris Duffy/Redemp.	15.00
19	Chris Young/75	20.00
19	Chris Young/50	20.00
20	Cliff Lee/75	20.00
20	Cliff Lee/50	20.00
21	Cole Hamels/25	50.00
21	Cole Hamels/15	50.00
22	Adam Lind/75	20.00
23	Akinori Iwamura/25	60.00
23	Akinori Iwamura/15	60.00
24	Dan Uggla/25	25.00
25	Danny Haren/25	30.00
26	David Ortiz/10	125.00
27	Felix Hernandez/10	75.00
28	Tony Gwynn Jr./Redemp.	25.00
29	Josh Hamilton/75	30.00
29	Josh Hamilton/50	30.00
30	Phil Hughes/redemp	65.00
31	Khalil Greene/25	30.00
32	Dontrelle Willis/25	30.00
32	Dontrelle Willis/20	30.00
33	Hanley Ramirez/50	35.00
33	Hanley Ramirez/25	35.00
34	Howie Kendrick/60	20.00
34	Howie Kendrick/50	20.00
35	Huston Street/50	20.00
35	Huston Street/25	20.00
36	Ian Kinsler/redmp	20.00
37	Jason Bay/50	25.00
37	Jason Bay/25	25.00
40	Joe Mauer/Redemp.	50.00
41	Jonathan Papelbon/40	50.00
42	Tim Lincecum/50	75.00
42	Tim Lincecum/40	75.00
43	Matt Cain/75	40.00
43	Matt Cain/40	40.00
44	Victor Martinez/25	40.00
46	Ryan Zimmerman/25	50.00
47	Stephen Drew/25	30.00
48	Travis Hafner/25	40.00
49	Josh Willingham/50	15.00
49	Josh Willingham/Redemp.	15.00
50	Torii Hunter/25	30.00
51	Billy Butler/50	30.00
52	Justin Morneau/25	40.00
52	Justin Morneau/15	40.00
53	Andy LaRoche/75	25.00
53	Andy LaRoche/60	25.00
53	Andy LaRoche/50	25.00
54	Brandon Wood/75	20.00
54	Brandon Wood/50	20.00
55	Hunter Pence/50	50.00
56	Devern Hansack/Redemp.	20.00
56	Devern Hansack/75	20.00
58	Derrek Lee/25	40.00
59	Prince Fielder/25	60.00
60	Kevin Kouzmanoff/50	20.00

Chirography Dual Signatures

No.	Card	NM/M
	Common Dual Auto:	25.00
CG	Eric Chavez, Alex Gordon/75	50.00
CL	Matt Cain, Tim Lincecum/175	80.00
DR	Stephen Drew, Hanley Ramirez/75	35.00
HD	Travis Hafner, Adam Dunn/75	30.00
HW	Danny Haren, Jered Weaver/175	30.00
KH	Scott Kazmir, Cole Hamels/175	40.00
MI	Daisuke Matsuzaka, Akinori Iwamura/75	300.00
ML	Andrew Miller, Tim Lincecum/175	100.00
MZ	Nicholas Markakis, Ryan Zimmerman/75	40.00
RJ	Cal Ripken Jr., Derek Jeter/75	200.00
VH	Justin Verlander, Felix Hernandez/175	50.00
WH	Vernon Wells, Torii Hunter/75	25.00
WK	Rickie Weeks, Ian Kinsler/175	25.00

Chirography Quad Signatures

Production Five Sets

Sign of the Times Dual Signatures

No.	Card	NM/M
	Common Dual Auto.:	20.00
BP	Josh Beckett, Jonathan Papelbon/75	120.00
CH	Eric Chavez, Rich Harden/75	20.00
CJ	Roger Clemens, Derek Jeter/75	200.00
CL	Matt Cain, Tim Lincecum/175	80.00
FL	Rafael Furcal, Andy LaRoche/175	20.00
GD	Ken Griffey Jr., Adam Dunn/75	100.00
HM	Travis Hafner, Victor Martinez/75	50.00
SW	Ben Sheets, Rickie Weeks/75	20.00
TK	Mark Teixeira, Ian Kinsler/75	20.00
UY	B.J. Upton, Delmon Young/75	35.00
VM	Justin Verlander, Andrew Miller/75	50.00

Sign of the Times Quad Signatures

Production Five Sets

Sign of the Times Triple Signatures

No Pricing

By The Letter RC Signatures Full Redm

No Pricing

By The Letter Signatures Full Redemption

No Pricing

Autograph Parallel

Production Five Sets

2007 SP Legendary Cuts

No.	Card	NM/M
	Complete Set (200):	
	Common Player (1-100):	.25
	Common SP (101-200):	3.00
	Production 550 Sets	
	Pack (4):	10.00
	Box (12):	100.00
1	Phil Niekro	.25
2	Brooks Robinson	1.00
3	Frank Robinson	1.00
4	Jim Palmer	.50
5	Cal Ripken Jr.	3.00
6	Warren Spahn	1.00
7	Cy Young	1.00
8	Carl Yastrzemski	1.00
9	Wade Boggs	1.00
10	Carlton Fisk	.50
11	Joe Cronin	.25
12	Bobby Doerr	.50
13	Roy Campanella	1.00
14	Pee Wee Reese	.25
15	Rod Carew	.75
16	Ernie Banks	1.00
17	Fergie Jenkins	.50
18	Billy Williams	.50
19	Gabby Hartnett	.25
20	Luis Aparicio	.25
21	Nellie Fox	.25
22	Luke Appling	.25
23	Joe Morgan	.50
24	Johnny Bench	1.00
25	Tony Perez	.50
26	George Foster	.25
27	Johnny Vander Meer	.25
28	Bob Feller	.50
29	Bob Lemon	.25
30	Lou Boudreau	.25
31	Early Wynn	.25
32	Charlie Gehringer	.25
33	George Kell	.25
34	Hal Newhouser	.25
35	Al Kaline	1.00
36	Ted Kluszewski	.25
38	Maury Wills	.25
39	Don Drysdale	.50
40	Don Sutton	.50
41	Eddie Mathews	1.00
42	Joe Adcock	.25
43	Paul Molitor	.75
44	Kirby Puckett	1.50
45	Harmon Killebrew	1.00
46	Monte Irvin	.50
47	Ralph Kiner	.50
48	Christy Mathewson	1.00
49	Hoyt Wilhelm	.25
50	Tom Seaver	1.00
51	Allie Reynolds	.25
52	Joe DiMaggio	2.00
53	Lou Gehrig	2.00
54	Babe Ruth	3.00
55	Casey Stengel	1.00
56	Phil Rizzuto	1.00
57	Thurman Munson	1.00
58	Johnny Mize	.50
59	Yogi Berra	1.00
61	Don Mattingly	1.00
62	Ray Dandridge	.25
63	Rollie Fingers	.50
64	Roberto Clemente	2.00
65	Reggie Jackson	1.00
66	Dennis Eckersley	.50
67	Robin Yount	1.00
68	Jimmie Foxx	1.00
69	Lefty Grove	.50
70	Richie Ashburn	.25
71	Jim Bunning	.25
72	Steve Carlton	.50
73	Robin Roberts	.50
74	Mike Schmidt	1.00
75	Willie Stargell	1.00
76	Ozzie Smith	1.00
77	Bill Mazeroski	.50
78	Honus Wagner	1.00
79	Pie Traynor	.25
80	Tony Gwynn	1.00
81	Willie McCovey	.50
82	Gaylord Perry	.25
83	Juan Marichal	.50
84	Orlando Cepeda	.50
85	Satchel Paige	1.00
86	George Sisler	.50
87	Ken Boyer	.25
88	Joe Medwick	.25
89	Travis Jackson	.25
90	Stan Musial	1.50
91	Dizzy Dean	1.00
92	Bob Gibson	1.00
93	Red Schoendienst	.50
94	Lou Brock	.75
95	Enos Slaughter	.25
96	Nolan Ryan	3.00
97	Smoky Burgess	.25
98	Mickey Vernon	.25
99	Vern Stephens	.25
100	Rick Ferrell	.25
101	Phil Niekro	3.00
102	Brooks Robinson	6.00
103	Frank Robinson	6.00
104	Jim Palmer	5.00
105	Cal Ripken Jr.	15.00
106	Warren Spahn	6.00
107	Cy Young	5.00
108	Nellie Fox	6.00
109	Carl Yastrzemski	6.00
110	Joe Sewell	4.00
111	Wade Boggs	5.00
112	Carlton Fisk	5.00
113	Jackie Robinson	8.00
114	Roy Campanella	6.00
115	Pee Wee Reese	5.00
116	Earl Averill	3.00
117	Rod Carew	5.00
118	Ernie Banks	5.00
119	Fergie Jenkins	3.00
120	Billy Williams	3.00
121	Al Lopez	3.00
122	Luis Aparicio	3.00
123	Luke Appling	3.00
124	Joe Morgan	5.00
125	Johnny Bench	6.00
126	Tony Perez	5.00
127	George Foster	3.00
128	Bob Feller	5.00
129	Bob Lemon	3.00
130	Larry Doby	5.00
132	George Kell	3.00
133	Hal Newhouser	3.00
134	Al Kaline	8.00
135	Ty Cobb	8.00
137	Buck Leonard	5.00
138	Maury Wills	3.00
139	Don Drysdale	5.00
140	Don Sutton	5.00
141	Eddie Mathews	6.00
142	Paul Molitor	5.00
143	Kirby Puckett	8.00
144	Harmon Killebrew	8.00
145	Monte Irvin	5.00
146	Mel Ott	5.00
147	Charlie Gehringer	5.00
148	Hoyt Wilhelm	3.00
149	Tom Seaver	6.00
150	Ted Kluszewski	3.00
151	Joe DiMaggio	8.00
152	Lou Gehrig	8.00
153	Babe Ruth	10.00
154	Casey Stengel	5.00
155	Phil Rizzuto	5.00
156	Thurman Munson	5.00
157	Johnny Mize	3.00
158	Yogi Berra	6.00
159	Roger Maris	6.00
160	Early Wynn	3.00
161	Bobby Doerr	5.00
162	Joe Cronin	5.00
163	Don Mattingly	8.00
164	Ray Dandridge	3.00
165	Rollie Fingers	3.00
166	Christy Mathewson	5.00
167	Reggie Jackson	5.00
168	Dennis Eckersley	3.00
169	Mickey Cochrane	3.00
170	Jimmie Foxx	5.00
171	Lefty Gomez	3.00
172	Jim Bunning	3.00
173	Steve Carlton	3.00
174	Robin Roberts	3.00
175	Richie Ashburn	5.00
176	Mike Schmidt	6.00
177	Ralph Kiner	3.00
178	Willie Stargell	5.00
179	Roberto Clemente	10.00
180	Bill Mazeroski	5.00
181	Honus Wagner	8.00
182	Pie Traynor	3.00
183	Tony Gwynn	5.00
184	Willie McCovey	3.00
185	Gaylord Perry	3.00
186	Juan Marichal	3.00
187	Orlando Cepeda	3.00
188	Satchel Paige	5.00
189	George Sisler	3.00
190	Rogers Hornsby	5.00
191	Stan Musial	8.00
192	Dizzy Dean	5.00
193	Bob Gibson	5.00
194	Red Schoendienst	5.00
195	Lou Brock	5.00
196	Enos Slaughter	3.00
197	Nolan Ryan	8.00
198	Mickey Vernon	3.00
199	Walter Johnson	5.00
200	Rick Ferrell	3.00

A Stitch In Time

No.	Card	NM/M
	Common Player:	5.00
BG	Bob Gibson	8.00
BR	Brooks Robinson	10.00
BW	Billy Williams	5.00
CR	Cal Ripken Jr.	20.00
DE	Dwight Evans	5.00
DM	Don Mattingly	10.00
EM	Eddie Murray	8.00
GP	Gaylord Perry	5.00
HK	Harmon Killebrew	10.00
JB	Johnny Bench	10.00
JR	Jim Rice	5.00
KP	Kirby Puckett	15.00
MS	Mike Schmidt	10.00
PM	Paul Molitor	8.00
RC	Rod Carew	8.00
RJ	Reggie Jackson	10.00
TG	Tony Gwynn	10.00

Cut Signatures

No.	Card	NM/M
	Production 1-133	
AB	Al Barlick/49	75.00
AH	Happy Chandler/44	75.00
AR	Allie Reynolds/40	150.00
BA	Bob Allison/31	90.00
BD	Bill Dickey/50	125.00
BG	Burleigh Grimes/52	125.00
BH	Babe Herman/99	100.00
BV	Bill Veeck/47	250.00
CA	Max Carey/40	80.00
CG	Charlie Gehringer/50	75.00
CH	Carl Hubbell/54	100.00
DC	Dolph Camilli/25	75.00
DI	Joe DiMaggio/52	400.00
DU	Leo Durocher/84	140.00
EA	Earl Averill/62	80.00
EL	Ed Lopat/66	100.00
EM	Eddie Mathews/69	125.00
ER	Edd Roush/50	60.00
ES	Enos Slaughter/47	80.00
EW	Early Wynn/40	100.00
FF	Ford Frick/88	140.00
FL	Freddy Lindstrom/45	200.00
GH	Gabby Hartnett/50	160.00
GP	George Pipgras/70	90.00
GR	Lefty Grove/66	220.00
HG	Hank Greenberg/59	200.00
HO	Gil Hodges/25	450.00
JA	Joe Adcock/49	100.00
JD	Joe Dugan/46	120.00
JO	Judy Johnson/54	150.00
JS	Joe Sewell/110	80.00
JV	Johnny Vander Meer/49	140.00
KB	Ken Boyer/19	275.00
LA	Luke Appling/92	80.00
LD	Larry Doby/50	100.00
MI	Johnny Mize/133	100.00
PR	Pee Wee Reese/39	160.00
RA	Richie Ashburn/50	150.00
RD	Ray Dandridge/50	85.00
RS	Ray Schalk/44	275.00
SC	Stan Coveleski/84	80.00
SW	Warren Spahn/95	100.00
WA	Walter Alston/48	140.00
WH	Waite Hoyt/79	90.00
WI	Hoyt Wilhelm/60	80.00
WS	Willie Stargell/71	180.00

Hall of Fame Cuts

No.	Card	NM/M
	Production 1-86	
AB	Al Barlick/44	100.00
BL	Bob Lemon/53	75.00
CG	Charlie Gehringer/65	85.00
CH	Carl Hubbell/31	100.00
EC	Earle Combs/27	250.00
ER	Edd Roush/65	80.00
GH	Gabby Hartnett/31	180.00
HN	Hal Newhouser/40	80.00
JC	Joe Cronin/86	90.00
LA	Luke Appling/45	80.00
LB	Lou Boudreau/30	80.00
WH	Waite Hoyt/33	100.00
WS	Warren Spahn/35	125.00

Historical Cuts

Production One Set

Inside the Numbers Cuts

No.	Card	NM/M
	Production 4-119	
BD	Bill Dickey/28	150.00
BH	Babe Herman/99	100.00
BL	Bob Lemon/75	75.00
CG	Charlie Gehringer/60	120.00
CH	Carl Hubbell/70	100.00
EA	Earl Averill/57	65.00
EL	Ernie Lombardi/52	200.00
EM	Eddie Mathews/70	125.00
ES	Enos Slaughter/69	80.00
EW	Early Wynn/34	100.00
FS	Fred Snodgrass/75	150.00
GH	Gabby Hartnett/50	160.00
GR	Lefty Grove/73	220.00
HG	Hank Greenberg/25	250.00
JC	Joe Cronin/29	100.00
JM	Joe Medwick/119	140.00
JV	Johnny Vander Meer/39	140.00
LA	Luke Appling/59	80.00
LG	Lefty Gomez/75	125.00
SC	Stan Coveleski/72	65.00
WH	Waite Hoyt/65	100.00
WI	Hoyt Wilhelm/55	80.00
WS	Warren Spahn/55	100.00

Legendary Americana

No.	Card	NM/M
	Common Card:	5.00
	Production 550 Sets	
1	George Washington Carver	5.00
3	Frederick Douglass	5.00
4	Crazy Horse	5.00
6	Abraham Lincoln	5.00
7	Thomas Edison	5.00
8	Andrew Carnegie	5.00
9	Eli Whitney	5.00
11	Davy Crockett	5.00
12	Robert E. Lee	5.00
13	John D. Rockefeller	5.00
14	Billy the Kid	5.00
15	Ulysses S. Grant	5.00
16	Kit Carson	5.00
19	Francis Scott Key	5.00
20	Franklin D. Roosevelt	5.00
21	Mark Twain	5.00
24	Alexander Graham Bell	5.00
27	Eleanor Roosevelt	5.00
28	John F. Kennedy	8.00
30	Frank Lloyd Wright	5.00
34	Henry Ford	5.00
35	Dwight D. Eisenhower	5.00
36	Daniel Boone	5.00
38	William Randolph Hearst	5.00
42	Wyatt Earp	5.00
47	Abner Doubleday	5.00
48	Harry S. Truman	5.00
49	Amelia Earhart	5.00
53	Orville Wright	5.00
55	Jack London	5.00
59	Andrew Jackson	5.00
60	Zachary Taylor	5.00
62	Jefferson Davis	5.00
63	Sitting Bull	10.00
64	Clara Barton	5.00
66	Booker T. Washington	5.00
68	Samuel F. B. Morse	5.00
69	Alexander Cartwright	5.00
72	Andrew Johnson	5.00
73	Rutherford B. Hayes	5.00

74 James A. Garfield 5.00
75 Chester Arthur 5.00
76 Grover Cleveland 5.00
78 William McKinley 5.00
79 William H. Taft 5.00
80 Woodrow Wilson 5.00
81 Warren G. Harding 5.00
82 Calvin Coolidge 5.00
83 Herbert Hoover 5.00
84 Lyndon B. Johnson 5.00
85 Richard M. Nixon 5.00
86 Gerald Ford 5.00
88 Ronald Reagan 5.00
92 Babe Ruth 10.00
93 Jackie Robinson 8.00

Legendary Dual Cuts

Production One Set

Legendary Materials

NM/M

Common Player: 5.00
Production 199 Sets
AO Al Oliver 5.00
BJ Bo Jackson 15.00
BL Barry Larkin 8.00
BS Bruce Sutter 5.00
BW Billy Williams 15.00
CA Roy Campanella 10.00
DD Don Drysdale 8.00
DE Dwight Evans 5.00
DP Dave Parker 5.00
DS Don Sutton 5.00
EC Dennis Eckersley 5.00
FJ Fergie Jenkins 5.00
FR Frank Robinson 10.00
GF George Foster 5.00
GG Rich "Goose" Gossage 5.00
HB Harold Baines 5.00
JP Jim Palmer 8.00
JT Joe Torre 10.00
KG Ken Griffey Sr. 5.00
LA Luis Aparicio 5.00
MA Bill Madlock 5.00
MG Mark Grace 10.00
PN Phil Niekro 5.00
PO Paul O'Neill 10.00
PW Pee Wee Reese 10.00
RA Roberto Alomar 10.00
RC Roberto Clemente 50.00
RF Rollie Fingers 8.00
RG Ron Guidry 20.00
RM Roger Maris 25.00
RS Ryne Sandberg 15.00
SC Red Schoendienst 10.00
TO Tony Oliva 8.00
TP Tony Perez 8.00
AD1 Andre Dawson 8.00
AD2 Andre Dawson 8.00
AK1 Al Kaline 15.00
AK2 Al Kaline 15.00
BR1 Brooks Robinson 15.00
BR2 Brooks Robinson 15.00
CF1 Carlton Fisk 10.00
CF2 Carlton Fisk 10.00
CR1 Cal Ripken Jr. 25.00
CR2 Cal Ripken Jr. 25.00
CY1 Carl Yastrzemski 15.00
CY2 Carl Yastrzemski 15.00
DM1 Don Mattingly 20.00
DM2 Don Mattingly 20.00
DW1 Dave Winfield 8.00
DW2 Dave Winfield 8.00
EM1 Eddie Murray 8.00
EM2 Eddie Murray 8.00
FL1 Fred Lynn 5.00
FL2 Fred Lynn 5.00
GP1 Gaylord Perry 5.00
GP2 Gaylord Perry 5.00
HK1 Harmon Killebrew 15.00
HK2 Harmon Killebrew 15.00
JB1 Johnny Bench 15.00
JB2 Johnny Bench 15.00
JM1 Jack Morris 5.00
JM2 Jack Morris 5.00
JR1 Jim Rice 8.00
J2 Jim Rice 8.00
KG1 Kirk Gibson 5.00
KG2 Kirk Gibson 5.00
KP1 Kirby Puckett 25.00
KP2 Kirby Puckett 25.00
LB1 Lou Brock 10.00
LB2 Lou Brock 10.00
MS1 Mike Schmidt 15.00
MS2 Mike Schmidt 15.00
NR1 Nolan Ryan 25.00
NR2 Nolan Ryan 25.00
OS1 Ozzie Smith 20.00
OS2 Ozzie Smith 20.00
PM1 Paul Molitor 8.00
PM2 Paul Molitor 8.00
RC1 Rod Carew 8.00
RC2 Rod Carew 8.00
RJ1 Reggie Jackson 10.00
RJ2 Reggie Jackson 10.00
RY1 Robin Yount 20.00
RY2 Robin Yount 20.00
SC1 Steve Carlton 8.00
SC2 Steve Carlton 8.00
SG1 Steve Garvey 5.00
SG2 Steve Garvey 5.00
TG1 Tony Gwynn 15.00
TG2 Tony Gwynn 15.00
WB1 Wade Boggs 8.00
WB2 Wade Boggs 8.00
WC1 Will Clark 8.00
WC2 Will Clark 8.00

Legendary Quad Cuts

Production One Set

Legendary Signatures

NM/M

Production 15-199
JT Joe Torre/99 40.00
KG Kirk Gibson/199 15.00
AD1 Andre Dawson/199 20.00
AD2 Andre Dawson/199 20.00
AK1 Al Kaline/199 25.00
AK2 Al Kaline/199 25.00
BF1 Bob Feller/199 20.00
BF2 Bob Feller/199 20.00
BF3 Bob Feller/189 20.00
BG1 Bob Gibson/50 25.00
BG2 Bob Gibson/50 25.00
BG3 Bob Gibson/40 25.00
BJ1 Bo Jackson/100 50.00
BJ2 Bo Jackson/100 50.00
BM1 Bill Mazeroski/189 30.00
BM2 Bill Mazeroski/199 30.00
BR1 Brooks Robinson/150 30.00
BR2 Brooks Robinson/140 30.00
BW1 Billy Williams/199 20.00
BW2 Billy Williams/189 20.00
CF1 Carlton Fisk/75 25.00
CF2 Carlton Fisk/75 25.00
CF3 Carlton Fisk/65 25.00
CR1 Cal Ripken Jr./99 100.00
CR2 Cal Ripken Jr./50 10.00
DM1 Don Mattingly/25 75.00
DM2 Don Mattingly/25 75.00
EB1 Ernie Banks/35 60.00
EB2 Ernie Banks/35 60.00
EM1 Eddie Murray/25 50.00
EM2 Eddie Murray/25 50.00
FJ1 Fergie Jenkins/125 20.00
FJ2 Fergie Jenkins/125 20.00
FJ3 Fergie Jenkins/125 20.00
FR1 Frank Robinson/50 25.00
FR2 Frank Robinson/50 25.00
FR3 Frank Robinson/40 25.00
GP1 Gaylord Perry/199 15.00
GP2 Gaylord Perry/199 15.00
HK1 Harmon Killebrew/100 75.00
HK2 Harmon Killebrew/90 75.00
JM1 Juan Marichal/199 20.00
JM2 Juan Marichal/199 20.00
JM3 Juan Marichal/189 20.00
JP1 Jim Palmer/199 20.00
JP2 Jim Palmer/199 20.00
JP3 Jim Palmer/199 20.00
LA1 Luis Aparicio/199 20.00
LA2 Luis Aparicio/186 20.00
MS1 Mike Schmidt/35 50.00
MS2 Mike Schmidt/35 50.00
MS3 Mike Schmidt/25 60.00
NR1 Nolan Ryan/25 100.00
NR2 Nolan Ryan/25 10.00
OS1 Ozzie Smith/100 40.00
OS2 Ozzie Smith/100 40.00
OS3 Ozzie Smith/100 40.00
PM1 Paul Molitor/100 25.00
PM2 Paul Molitor/90 25.00
RC1 Rod Carew/35 40.00
RC2 Rod Carew/35 40.00
RJ1 Reggie Jackson/25 60.00
RS1 Ryne Sandberg/25 60.00
RS2 Ryne Sandberg/25 60.00
RS3 Ryne Sandberg/25 60.00
RY1 Robin Yount/35 60.00
RY2 Robin Yount/35 60.00
RY3 Robin Yount/25 60.00
SC1 Steve Carlton/199 20.00
SC2 Steve Carlton/199 20.00
SC3 Steve Carlton/189 20.00
TP1 Tony Perez/199 20.00
TP2 Tony Perez/199 20.00
WB1 Wade Boggs/35 50.00
WB2 Wade Boggs/35 50.00
WB3 Wade Boggs/35 50.00
WC1 Will Clark/199 20.00
WC2 Will Clark/199 20.00
WM1 Willie McCovey/25 50.00
WM2 Willie McCovey/25 50.00

Legendary Team Cuts

Production One Set

Masterful Material

NM/M

Common Player: 5.00
AD Andre Dawson 5.00
BJ Bo Jackson 10.00
BL Barry Larkin 8.00
BM Bill Madlock 5.00
BR Brooks Robinson 8.00
BS Bruce Sutter 5.00
CF Carlton Fisk 8.00
CR Cal Ripken Jr. 20.00
CY Carl Yastrzemski 10.00
DE Dwight Evans 5.00
DM Don Mattingly 15.00
DP Dave Parker 5.00
DS Don Sutton 5.00
DW Dave Winfield 8.00
EM Eddie Mathews 10.00
FL Fred Lynn 5.00
FR Frank Robinson 8.00
GP Gaylord Perry 5.00
JB Johnny Bench 10.00
JR Jim Rice 5.00
KG Ken Griffey Sr. 5.00
KP Kirby Puckett 15.00
MS Mike Schmidt 10.00
MU Eddie Murray 8.00
NR Nolan Ryan 20.00
PM Paul Molitor 8.00
RJ Reggie Jackson 10.00
RS Ryne Sandberg 10.00
RY Robin Yount 10.00
SC Steve Carlton 8.00
SG Steve Garvey 5.00
TG Tony Gwynn 10.00
WB Wade Boggs 8.00
WC Will Clark 8.00
WM Willie McCovey 8.00
YB Yogi Berra 15.00

Material Cuts

No Pricing
Production 1-5

Material Signatures

No Pricing
Production 10 Sets

Quotation Cuts

NM/M

Production 1-109
BL Bob Lemon/80 75.00
CS Casey Stengel/36 275.00
HC Happy Chandler/44 75.00
JM Joe McCarthy/109 140.00
LB Lou Boudreau/28 60.00
MI Johnny Mize/45 80.00
RA Richie Ashburn/48 175.00
RD Ray Dandridge/72 90.00
SC Stan Coveleski/71 75.00
WA Walter Alston/31 80.00
WI Hoyt Wilhelm/37 90.00
WS Warren Spahn/60 100.00

Reel History Film Frame

NM/M

Cards are serial numbered 1/1
BR Babe Ruth 250.00
LG Lou Gehrig 200.00

Signature Cuts

Production One Set

When It Was A Game - Memorabilia

NM/M

Common Player: 5.00
AT Alan Trammell 5.00
BF Bob Feller 8.00
BG Bob Gibson 10.00
BM Bill Mazeroski 8.00
BW Billy Williams 5.00
CF Carlton Fisk 8.00
CY Carl Yastrzemski 10.00
DE Dennis Eckersley 5.00
DM Don Mattingly 15.00
DW Dave Winfield 8.00
EM Eddie Murray 8.00
FJ Fergie Jenkins 5.00
FL Fred Lynn 5.00
FR Frank Robinson 8.00
GP Gaylord Perry 5.00
HK Harmon Killebrew 10.00
JP Jim Palmer 8.00
JR Jim Rice 5.00
KG Kirk Gibson 5.00
KP Kirby Puckett 15.00
LB Lou Brock 8.00
MS Mike Schmidt 10.00
NR Nolan Ryan 20.00
PM Paul Molitor 8.00
PW Pee Wee Reese 10.00
RF Rollie Fingers 5.00
RJ Reggie Jackson 10.00
RM Roger Maris 25.00
RS Red Schoendienst 8.00
TG Tony Gwynn 10.00

2007 SPX

NM/M

Complete Set (150):
Common Player (1-100): .25
Common RC Auto. (101-150): 10.00
Pack (3): 20.00
Box (10): 180.00
1 Miguel Tejada .75
2 Brian Roberts .50
3 Melvin Mora .25
4 David Ortiz 1.00
5 Manny Ramirez 1.00
6 Jason Varitek .50
7 Curt Schilling 1.00
8 Jim Thome .75
9 Paul Konerko .50
10 Jermaine Dye .50
11 Travis Hafner .50
12 Victor Martinez .50
13 Grady Sizemore .75
14 C.C. Sabathia .50
15 Ivan Rodriguez .75
16 Magglio Ordonez .50
17 Carlos Guillen .25
18 Justin Verlander .75
19 Shane Costa .25
20 Emil Brown .25
21 Mark Teahen .25
22 Vladimir Guerrero 1.00
23 Jered Weaver .50
24 Juan Rivera .25
25 Justin Morneau .75
26 Joe Mauer .50
27 Torii Hunter .50
28 Johan Santana .75
29 Derek Jeter 3.00
30 Alex Rodriguez 3.00
31 Johnny Damon 1.00
32 Jason Giambi .75
33 Bobby Crosby .25
34 Nick Swisher .50
35 Eric Chavez .25
36 Ichiro Suzuki 2.00
37 Raul Ibanez .25
38 Richie Sexson .50
39 Carl Crawford .50
40 Rocco Baldelli .25
41 Scott Kazmir .50
42 Michael Young .50
43 Mark Teixeira .75
44 Ian Kinsler .25
45 Troy Glaus .50
46 Vernon Wells .50
47 Roy Halladay .50
48 Lyle Overbay .25
49 Brandon Webb .50
50 Conor Jackson .25
51 Stephen Drew .50
52 Chipper Jones 1.00
53 Andruw Jones .75
54 Adam LaRoche .25
55 John Smoltz .50
56 Derrek Lee .75
57 Aramis Ramirez .50
58 Carlos Zambrano .50
59 Ken Griffey Jr. 2.00
60 Adam Dunn .50
61 Aaron Harang .25
62 Todd Helton .75
63 Matt Holliday .50
64 Garrett Atkins .25
65 Miguel Cabrera 1.00
66 Hanley Ramirez .50
67 Dontrelle Willis .50
68 Lance Berkman .50
69 Roy Oswalt .50
70 Craig Biggio .50
71 J.D. Drew .25
72 Nomar Garciaparra 1.00
73 Rafael Furcal .50
74 Jeff Kent .50
75 Prince Fielder 1.00
76 Bill Hall .50
77 Rickie Weeks .50
78 Jose Reyes 1.00
79 David Wright 1.00
80 Carlos Delgado .75
81 Carlos Beltran .75
82 Ryan Howard 2.00
83 Chase Utley 1.00
84 Jimmy Rollins .50
85 Jason Bay .50
86 Freddy Sanchez .25
87 Zachary Duke .25
88 Trevor Hoffman .25
89 Adrian Gonzalez .50
90 Chris Young .25
91 Ray Durham .25
92 Omar Vizquel .25
93 Jason Schmidt .50
94 Albert Pujols 3.00
95 Scott Rolen .75
96 Jim Edmonds .50
97 Chris Carpenter .75
98 Alfonso Soriano .75
99 Ryan Zimmerman .50
100 Nick Johnson .25
101 Delmon Young **(RC)** 20.00
102 Andrew Miller **RC** 30.00
103 Troy Tulowitzki **(RC)** 35.00
104 Jeff Fiorentino **(RC)** 10.00
105 David Murphy **(RC)** 15.00
106 Tim Lincecum **RC** 160.00
107 Phil Hughes **(RC)** 75.00
108 Kevin Kouzmanoff **(RC)** 15.00
109 Adam Lind **(RC)** 15.00
110 Mark Reynolds **RC** 50.00
111 Kevin Hooper **(RC)** 10.00
112 Mitch Maier **RC** 10.00
113 Homer Bailey **(RC)** 50.00
114 Dennis Sarfate **(RC)** 10.00
115 Drew Anderson **(RC)** 10.00
116 Miguel Montero **(RC)** 10.00
117 Glen Perkins **(RC)** 10.00
118 Kevin Slowey **(RC)** 40.00
119 Tim Gradoville **RC** 10.00
120 Ryan Braun **(RC)** 120.00
121 Chris Narveson **(RC)** 10.00
122 Patrick Misch **(RC)** 10.00
123 Juan Salas **(RC)** 10.00
124 Beltran Perez **(RC)** 10.00
125 Joaquin Arias **(RC)** 10.00
126 Philip Humber **(RC)** 15.00
127 Kei Igawa **RC** 25.00
128 Daisuke Matsuzaka **RC** 300.00
129 Andy Cannizaro **RC** 10.00
130 Ubaldo Jimenez **(RC)** 10.00
131 Fred Lewis **(RC)** 15.00
132 Ryan Sweeney **(RC)** 10.00
133 Jeff Baker **(RC)** 10.00
134 Michael Bourn **(RC)** 15.00
135 Akinori Iwamura **RC** 30.00
136 Oswaldo Navarro **RC** 10.00
137 Hunter Pence **(RC)** 60.00
138 Jon Knott **(RC)** 10.00
139 Justin Hampson **(RC)** 10.00
140 Jeff Salazar **(RC)** 10.00
141 Juan Morillo **(RC)** 10.00
142 Delwyn Young **(RC)** 10.00
143 Brian Burres **(RC)** 10.00
144 Chris Stewart **RC** 10.00
145 Eric Stults **RC** 10.00
146 Carlos Maldonado **(RC)** 10.00
147 Angel Sanchez **RC** 10.00
148 Cesar Jimenez **RC** 10.00
149 Shawn Riggans **(RC)** 10.00
150 John Nelson **(RC)** 10.00

Printing Plates

No pricing
Production one set per color.

Spectrum

Spectrum (101-150): No Pricing
Production 25 Sets

Autofacts Preview

NM/M

Common Autograph: 10.00
1:Hobby Box
AI Akinori Iwamura 25.00
AL Adam Lind 15.00
AM Andrew Miller/SP 40.00
AS Angel Sanchez 10.00
BP Beltran Perez 10.00
BR Jeremy Brown 10.00
CM Carlos Maldonado 15.00
CN Chris Narveson 10.00
CR Cal Ripken Jr./SP 220.00
DS Dennis Sarfate 10.00
DW Dewayne Wise 10.00
DY Delmon Young 20.00
ES Eric Stults 10.00
FL Fred Lewis 15.00
GP Glen Perkins 10.00
JA Joaquin Arias 10.00
JB Jeff Baker 10.00
JH Justin Hampson 10.00
JK Jon Knott 15.00
JM Juan Morillo 10.00
JS Juan Salas 10.00
JW Jason Wood 10.00
KG Ken Griffey Jr./SP 80.00
KH Kevin Hooper 10.00
KI Kei Igawa 25.00
KK Kevin Kouzmanoff 15.00
MB Michael Bourn 15.00
MM Miguel Montero 10.00
PH Philip Humber 15.00
PM Patrick Misch 10.00
SA Jeff Salazar 10.00
SR Shawn Riggans 10.00
ST Chris Stewart 10.00
TT Troy Tulowitzki 25.00
YO Delwyn Young 10.00

Iron Man

NM/M

Common Ripken (1-100): 5.00
Production 699 Sets
Platinum: No Pricing
Production One Set
Printing Plates: No Pricing
Production One Set

Iron Man Memorabilia

NM/M

Common Ripken: 40.00
Production 25 Sets

Iron Man Autograph

Production One Set

Young Star Signatures

NM/M

Common Autograph: 10.00
Spectrum: 1-2X
Production 25 Sets
AE Andre Ethier 20.00
AG Adrian Gonzalez 20.00
AS Anibal Sanchez 10.00
BU B.J. Upton 20.00
CA Matt Cain/SP 20.00
CH Cole Hamels/SP 30.00
CQ Carlos Quentin 15.00
DJ Derek Jeter 125.00
DU Dan Uggla 20.00
DY Delmon Young 20.00
FH Felix Hernandez 25.00
FL Francisco Liriano 25.00
HA Rich Harden 15.00
HI Rich Hill/SP 20.00
HK Howie Kendrick 20.00
HR Hanley Ramirez 20.00
JB Jeremy Brown 10.00
JJ Josh Johnson 15.00
JL Jon Lester 25.00
JM Joe Mauer 25.00
JP Jonathan Papelbon 30.00
JR Jose Reyes 50.00
JS Jeremy Sowers 15.00
JV Justin Verlander 30.00
JW Jered Weaver/SP 20.00
JZ Joel Zumaya 20.00
KG Ken Griffey Jr. 75.00
KU Hong-Chih Kuo 25.00
LO James Loney 20.00
MO Justin Morneau 25.00
NM Nicholas Markakis 30.00
PH Philip Humber 15.00
RW Rickie Weeks 20.00
RZ Ryan Zimmerman 30.00
SD Stephen Drew 20.00
ST Scott Thorman 15.00
TT Troy Tulowitzki 30.00
WI Josh Willingham 15.00

Winning Materials Bronze 199

NM/M

Common player: 5.00
Gold 199: 1X
Silver 199: 1X
Production 199 Sets
Blue 175: 1X
Green 175: 1X
Production 175 Sets
Gold 99: 1-1.5X
Silver 99: 1-1.5X
Production 99 Sets
Dual Bronze: No Pricing
Production 25 Sets
Dual Gold: 1-1.5X
Dual Silver: 1-1.5X
Production 50 Sets
Dual Green: No Pricing
Production 15 Sets
AB A.J. Burnett 5.00
AD Adam Dunn 6.00
AE Andre Ethier 6.00
AJ Andruw Jones 8.00
AL Adam LaRoche 5.00
AP Albert Pujols 20.00
AR Aramis Ramirez 8.00
AS Anibal Sanchez 5.00
BA Bobby Abreu 6.00
BG Brian Giles 5.00
BL Joe Blanton 5.00
BM Brian McCann 5.00
BO Jeremy Bonderman 6.00
BR Brian Roberts 5.00
BS Ben Sheets 5.00
BU B.J. Upton 5.00
CA Miguel Cabrera 8.00
CB Craig Biggio 5.00
CC Chris Carpenter 8.00
CF Chone Figgins 5.00
CH Cole Hamels 10.00
CJ Chipper Jones 8.00
CL Roger Clemens 15.00
CN Robinson Cano 10.00
CR Carl Crawford 5.00
CU Chase Utley 10.00
CW Chien-Ming Wang 35.00
DJ Derek Jeter 20.00
DJ2 Derek Jeter 20.00
DL Derrek Lee 8.00
DO David Ortiz 10.00
DU Dan Uggla 5.00
DW Dontrelle Willis 5.00
EC Eric Chavez 5.00
FH Felix Hernandez 6.00
FL Francisco Liriano 5.00
FS Freddy Sanchez 5.00
FT Frank Thomas 8.00
GA Garrett Atkins 5.00
HA Travis Hafner 6.00
HE Todd Helton 8.00
HK Howie Kendrick 5.00
HN Rich Harden 5.00
HR Hanley Ramirez 8.00
HS Huston Street 5.00
IK Ian Kinsler 5.00
IR Ivan Rodriguez 8.00
JB Jason Bay 6.00
JE Jim Edmonds 5.00
JF Jeff Francoeur 8.00
JJ Josh Johnson 5.00
JL Chad Billingsley 5.00
JM Joe Mauer 8.00
JN Joe Nathan 5.00
JP Jake Peavy 5.00
JR Jose Reyes 10.00
JS Jeremy Sowers 5.00
JT Jim Thome 8.00
JV Justin Verlander 8.00
JW Jered Weaver 8.00
JZ Joel Zumaya 5.00
KG Ken Griffey Jr. 15.00
KG2 Ken Griffey Jr. 15.00
KH Khalil Greene 5.00
KU Hong-Chih Kuo 20.00
LE Jon Lester 8.00
LG Luis Gonzalez 5.00
MC Matt Cain 5.00
ME Melky Cabrera 6.00
MH Matt Holliday 8.00

MO Justin Morneau 8.00
MT Mark Teixeira 8.00
NM Nicholas Markakis 8.00
NS Nick Swisher 5.00
PA Jonathan Papelbon 15.00
PF Prince Fielder 10.00
PL Paul LoDuca 5.00
RC Cal Ripken Jr. 20.00
RI Alex Rios 5.00
RJ Randy Johnson 8.00
RO Roy Oswalt 6.00
RW Rickie Weeks 5.00
RZ Ryan Zimmerman 8.00
SA Alfonso Soriano 8.00
SD Stephen Drew 5.00
SH James Shields 5.00
SK Scott Kazmir 5.00
SM John Smoltz 8.00
SO Scott Olsen 5.00
SR Scott Rolen 8.00
TE Miguel Tejada 6.00
TG Tom Glavine 8.00
TH Trevor Hoffman 5.00
TO Torii Hunter 6.00
VG Vladimir Guerrero 8.00
VM Victor Martinez 5.00
WE David Wells 5.00
WI Josh Willingham 5.00
YB Yuniesky Betancourt 5.00

Winning Materials Patch Gold

NM/M

Common player: 10.00
Production 99 unless noted.
Patch Silver: 1X
Production 3-99
Patch Bronze: 1X
Production 50 Sets
Triple Patch: No Pricing
Production 25 Sets

AB A.J. Burnett 10.00
AD Adam Dunn 15.00
AE Andre Ethier 10.00
AJ Andruw Jones 15.00
AL Adam LaRoche 10.00
AP Albert Pujols 40.00
AR Aramis Ramirez 15.00
AS Anibal Sanchez/54 10.00
BA Bobby Abreu 15.00
BG Brian Giles 10.00
BL Joe Blanton 10.00
BM Brian McCann 10.00
BO Jeremy Bonderman 15.00
BR Brian Roberts 10.00
BS Ben Sheets 10.00
BU B.J. Upton 10.00
CA Miguel Cabrera 20.00
CB Craig Biggio 15.00
CC Chris Carpenter 20.00
CF Chone Figgins 10.00
CH Cole Hamels 20.00
CJ Chipper Jones 20.00
CL Roger Clemens 25.00
CN Robinson Cano 20.00
CR Carl Crawford 10.00
CU Chase Utley 20.00
CW Chien-Ming Wang 60.00
DJ Derek Jeter 40.00
DJ2 Derek Jeter 40.00
DL Derrek Lee 20.00
DO David Ortiz 20.00
DU Dan Uggla 10.00
DW Dontrelle Willis 10.00
EC Eric Chavez 10.00
FH Felix Hernandez 15.00
FL Francisco Liriano 15.00
FS Freddy Sanchez 10.00
FT Frank Thomas 20.00
GA Garrett Atkins 10.00
HA Travis Hafner 15.00
HE Todd Helton 20.00
HK Howie Kendrick/34 15.00
HN Rich Harden 10.00
HR Hanley Ramirez 20.00
HS Huston Street 10.00
IK Ian Kinsler 10.00
IR Ivan Rodriguez 20.00
JB Jason Bay 15.00
JE Jim Edmonds 10.00
JF Jeff Francoeur 20.00
JJ Josh Johnson 10.00
JL Chad Billingsley 10.00
JM Joe Mauer 20.00
JN Joe Nathan 10.00
JP Jake Peavy 10.00
JR Jose Reyes 25.00
JS Jeremy Sowers 10.00
JT Jim Thome 20.00
JW Jered Weaver 20.00
JZ Joel Zumaya 10.00
KG Ken Griffey Jr. 30.00
KG2 Ken Griffey Jr. 30.00
KH Khalil Greene 10.00
KU Hong-Chih Kuo 40.00
LE Jon Lester 20.00
LG Luis Gonzalez 10.00
MC Matt Cain 15.00
ME Melky Cabrera 20.00
MH Matt Holliday 20.00
MO Justin Morneau 15.00
MT Mark Teixeira 15.00
NM Nicholas Markakis 15.00
NS Nick Swisher 10.00
PA Jonathan Papelbon 30.00
PF Prince Fielder 20.00
PL Paul LoDuca 10.00
RC Cal Ripken Jr. 40.00
RI Alex Rios 10.00
RJ Randy Johnson 20.00
RO Roy Oswalt 15.00
RW Rickie Weeks 10.00
RZ Ryan Zimmerman 15.00
SA Alfonso Soriano 20.00
SD Stephen Drew 15.00
SH James Shields 10.00
SK Scott Kazmir 10.00
SM John Smoltz 20.00
SO Scott Olsen 10.00
SR Scott Rolen 15.00
TE Miguel Tejada 15.00
TG Tom Glavine 20.00
TH Trevor Hoffman 10.00
TO Torii Hunter 15.00
VG Vladimir Guerrero 20.00
VM Victor Martinez 10.00
WE David Wells 10.00
WI Josh Willingham 10.00
YB Yuniesky Betancourt 10.00

Winning Materials Triple Signatures

NM/M

Production 15-35 5.00
Platinum: No Pricing
Production 3-10

BR Brian Roberts/35 35.00
EC Eric Chavez/35 30.00
FH Felix Hernandez/35 50.00
GA Garrett Atkins/35 25.00
HA Travis Hafner/35 35.00
HK Howie Kendrick/35 30.00
JJ Josh Johnson/35 20.00
JM Joe Mauer/35 40.00
JP Jake Peavy/35 35.00
JR Jose Reyes/35 75.00
KU Hong-Chih Kuo/35 120.00
LE Jon Lester/35 40.00
TE Miguel Tejada/35 30.00
TG Tom Glavine/35 60.00

Winning Trios Gold

NM/M

Common Trio: 15.00
Production 75 Sets
Silver: 1X
Production 50 Sets
Bronze: 1-1.5X
Production 30 Sets
Patch: No Pricing
Production 8-25

1 Ken Griffey Jr., Derek Jeter, Albert Pujols 40.00
2 Josh Willingham, Hanley Ramirez, Dan Uggla 15.00
3 Josh Johnson, Dontrelle Willis, Anibal Sanchez 15.00
4 Travis Hafner, David Ortiz, Lance Berkman 25.00
5 Ben Sheets, Roy Oswalt, Jake Peavy 15.00
6 Ivan Rodriguez, Jeremy Bonderman, Justin Verlander 25.00
7 Jose Reyes, Stephen Drew, Hanley Ramirez 25.00
8 Miguel Cabrera, Ryan Zimmerman, B.J. Upton 20.00
9 Justin Verlander, Jonathan Papelbon, Jered Weaver 40.00
10 Randy Johnson, Derek Jeter, Bobby Abreu 40.00
11 Craig Biggio, Lance Berkman, Morgan Ensberg 15.00
12 Brian McCann, Jeff Francoeur, Adam LaRoche 30.00
13 Victor Martinez, Joe Mauer, Brian McCann 20.00
14 Carl Crawford, Grady Sizemore, Jose Reyes 30.00
15 Freddy Garcia, Carlos Zambrano, Johan Santana 20.00
16 Vladimir Guerrero, Bobby Abreu, Alfonso Soriano 20.00
17 Justin Morneau, Johan Santana, Joe Mauer 25.00
18 Carlos Delgado, Carlos Beltran, Jose Reyes 25.00
19 Andre Ethier, Chad Billingsley, Matthew Kemp 25.00
20 Jim Thome, Jermaine Dye, Tadahito Iguchi 20.00
21 Jimmy Rollins, Chase Utley, Aaron Rowand 30.00
22 Ivan Rodriguez, Maggio Ordonez, Curtis Granderson 20.00
23 Chris Carpenter, Scott Rolen, Albert Pujols 30.00
24 Carl Crawford, B.J. Upton, James Shields 15.00
25 Howie Kendrick, Mike Napoli, Jered Weaver 15.00
26 Ian Kinsler, Dan Uggla, Howie Kendrick 20.00
27 Miguel Tejada, Brian Roberts, Nicholas Markakis 15.00
28 Justin Verlander, Jered Weaver, Mike Pelfrey 20.00
30 Randy Johnson, Derek Lowe, Anibal Sanchez 15.00
31 Prince Fielder, Ryan Zimmerman, Dan Uggla 25.00
32 Trevor Hoffman, Joe Nathan, Huston Street 15.00
33 Vernon Wells, Alex Rios, A.J. Burnett 15.00
34 Ben Sheets, Rickie Weeks, Prince Fielder 20.00
35 Adrian Beltre, Felix Hernandez, Yuniesky Betancourt 15.00
36 Jeremy Bonderman, Justin Verlander, Joel Zumaya 20.00
37 Billy Wagner, Paul LoDuca, Jose Reyes 20.00
38 Victor Martinez, Jeremy Sowers, C.C. Sabathia 15.00
39 Conor Jackson, Brandon Webb, Stephen Drew 20.00
40 Justin Verlander, Felix Hernandez, Jered Weaver 20.00
41 Ken Griffey Jr., Frank Thomas, Ivan Rodriguez 20.00
42 Cal Ripken Jr., Derek Jeter, Jose Reyes 50.00

1993 Spectrum Diamond Club Promo Set

Ten Hall of Famers are featured in this promo card set. Fronts of the 2-1/2" x 3-1/2" cards have borderless player action or posed photos. The issuer's logo, player's name and striping are printed in gold. Backs have a color ghost-image photo of the player along with personal data and career summary. A box near the bottom indicates the set's serial number from within an edition of 10,000. A "Pure Gold" parallel edition of 5,000 each was also produced.

NM/M

Complete Set (10): 8.00
Common Player: 1.00
Pure Gold: 2X

1 Carl Yastrzemski 1.50
2 Johnny Bench (Numbered promo.) 1.00
-- Johnny Bench ("For Promotional Use Only" on back.) 1.00
3 Al Kaline 1.00
4 Ernie Banks 2.00
5 Catfish Hunter 1.00
6 Rod Carew 1.00
7 Mike Schmidt 2.00
8 Harmon Killebrew 1.00
9 Frank Robinson 1.50
10 Rollie Fingers 1.00

Diamond Club Red Sox

This collectors' issue features five stars of the Boston Red Sox from the 1940s-

1970s. Fronts have action photos on which uniform logos are eliminated. A pinstripe around the photo, the issuer's logo and player name are printed in gold. Size is standard 2-1/2" x 3-1/2". Horizontal backs have a color Fenway Park photo ghosted in the background. Player career highlights and stats are overprinted.

NM/M

Complete Set (5): 1.00
Common Player: .25

1 Carl Yastrzemski .50
2 Bobby Doerr .25
3 Dwight Evans .25
4 Fred Lynn .25
5 Luis Tiant .25

Legends of Baseball

This collectors' edition of 10 of baseball's greatest players was issued in two versions, with and without a gold facsimile autograph on the cards' fronts. The gold-signature cards were limited to an edition of 5,000 numbered cards of each player. Fronts have black-and-white photos with gold-foil graphic highlights. Backs have another photo subdued in the background with career history and stats and personal data overprinted in black. Copyright information is at bottom. Cards were issued in two series of five each and are checklisted here alphabetically.

NM/M

Complete Set (10): 7.50
Common Player: .50
Gold Signature: 2X

(1) Grover Alexander .50
(2) Ty Cobb .75
(3) Dizzy Dean .50
(4) Lou Gehrig 1.00
(5) Rogers Hornsby .50
(6) Satchel Paige .75
(7) Babe Ruth 2.00
(8) Casey Stengel .50
(9) Honus Wagner .75
(10) Cy Young .50

Nolan Ryan

Produced in the same format as its Legends of Baseball 10-card sets, this issue honors the career of Nolan Ryan. Each set comes with a numbered certificate of authenticity. There were 5,000 regular sets produced and 5,000 with gold-foil facsimile autographs

on fronts. Each card can also be found in a promotional overprinted version.

NM/M

Complete Set (10): 3.00
Common Card: .50
Gold: 2X
Promo: 2X

Nolan Ryan 23K

A "pure gold" background on front offsets the color action photo of Ryan in action (team logos have been removed for licensing reasons). Backs of the 2-1/2" x 3-1/2" cards have career highlights and stats. Each set was issued with a certificate of authenticity numbered from an edition of 10,000.

NM/M

Complete Set (3): 3.00
Common Card: 1.00

1-3 Nolan Ryan 1.00

1994 Spectrum 1969 Miracle Mets

The 1969 Miracle Mets card set, produced by Spectrum Holdings Group of Birmingham, Mich., was part of what the company called "an integrated memorabilia program, with the 1969 Mets card set as the centerpiece." The 70-card set measures the standard 2-1/2" x 3-1/2", with UV coating on both sides and gold foil on fronts. It was sold complete at $24.95, and limited to 25,000 sets. A reported 1,000 numbered sets were signed by all 25 living players, including Hall of Famer Tom Seaver and future Cooperstown resident Nolan Ryan.

NM/M

Complete Set (70): 20.00
Common Player: .25
Autographed Set: 500.00

1 Commemorative Card .25
2 Team Photo .25
3 Tom Seaver 4.00
4 Jerry Koosman .35
5 Tommie Agee .25
6 Bud Harrelson .25
7 Nolan Ryan 6.00
8 Jerry Grote .25
9 Ron Swoboda .25
10 Donn Clendenon .25
11 Art Shamsky .25
12 Tug McGraw .25
13 Ed Kranepool .25
14 Cleon Jones .25
15 Ron Taylor .25
16 Gary Gentry .25
17 Ken Boswell .25
18 Ed Charles .25
19 J.C. Martin .25
20 Al Weis .25
21 Jack DiLauro .25
22 Duffy Dyer .25
23 Wayne Garrett .25
24 Jim McAndrew .25
25 Rod Gaspar .25
26 Don Cardwell .25
27 Bob Pfeil .25
28 Cal Koonce .25
29 Gil Hodges 1.50
30 Yogi Berra 2.00
31 Joe Pignatano .25
32 Rube Walker .25
33 Eddie Yost .25
34 First-ever Met Game .25
35 Opening Day 1969 .25
36 Kranepool Breaks Home Run Record .25
37 Koosman Sets Club Strikeout Record .25
38 Mets Trade for Clendenon .25
39 Koosman's 23 Scoreless Innings .25
40 Mets Begin 7-Game Winning Streak .25
41 Mets vs. Division Leading Cubs .25
42 Seaver's Near Perfect Game .25
43 Mets Trail by 3-1/2 .25
44 All-Star Break .25
45 All-Star Game .25
46 Mets Sweep Atlanta .25
47 Mets Sweep Padres .25
48 Mets Defeat Cubs, Koosman Strikes Out 1 .25
49 Mets Defeat Cubs 1/2 Game Back .25
50 First Place! .25
51 Mets Continue Nine Game Winning Streak .25
52 Seaver Earns 22nd Victory .25
53 Mets Win, Carlton Strikes Out 19 .25
54 Koosman Pitches 15th Complete Game .25
55 Eastern Division Champs! .25
56 100th Victory .25
57 Final Game, Mets Prepare for Braves .25
58 N.L. Championship Series, Game 1 .25
59 N.L. Championship Series, Game 2 .25
60 N.L. Championship Series, Game 3 .25
61 World Series, Game 1 .25
62 World Series, Game 2 .25
63 World Series, Game 3 .25
64 World Series, Game 4 .25
65 World Series, Game 5 .25
66 World Champions .25
67 World Champions .25
68 World Champions .25
69 World Champions .25
---- Checklist .25

1986 Sportflics Prototype Cards

This six-card set was apparently produced as a prototype as part of the licensing process. Similar in format to the 1986 Sportflics issue the cards have stats through the 1984 season. The prototype cards are much rarer than the promo cards. The Schmidt, Sutter and Winfield cards are standard 2-1/2" x 3-1/2" in size while the DiMaggio card is 1-5/16" square and the MLB logo card is 1-3/4" x 2".

		NM/M
Complete Set (7):		175.00
Common Card:		2.00
(1)	Joe DiMaggio (Black-and-white.)	100.00
(2)	Mike Schmidt	20.00
(3)	Bruce Sutter	5.00
(4)	Dave Winfield (Biographical back.)	50.00
(5)	Dave Winfield (Statistical back.)	37.50
(6)	Mike Schmidt, Bruce Sutter, Dave Winfield (Blank-back.)	10.00
(7)	Major League Baseball Logo	2.00

1986 Sportflics Promo Cards

Though they carry stats only through 1984, and have a 1986 copyright date, these promo cards were issued late in 1985 to preview the "Triple Action Sportflics" concept. They were the first really widely distributed promo cards. Each of the promo cards differs slightly from the issued version. The RBI Sluggers card in the issued set, for instance, was #126 and pictured Gary Carter, George Foster and Al Oliver. In the regular set, Pete Rose's card was #50 while Tom Seaver was #25. The regular-issue 1986 Sportflics cards, of course, include complete 1985 stats on back. Promo cards were distributed in three-card cello packs.

		NM/M
Complete Set (3):		12.50
Common Player:		3.00
1	RBI Sluggers (Dale Murphy, Jim Rice, Mike Schmidt)	3.00
43	Pete Rose	10.00
45	Tom Seaver	4.00

1986 Sportflics

The premiere issue from Sportflics was distributed nationally by Amurol Division of Wrigley Gum Co. The three-phase "Magic Motion" cards depict three different photos per card, with each visible separately as the card is tilted. The 1986 issue features 200 full-color baseball cards plus 133 trivia cards. The cards are in the standard 2-1/2" x 3-1/2" size with the backs containing player stats and personal information. There are three different types of picture cards: 1) Tri-Star cards - 50 cards feature three players on one card; 2) Big Six cards - 10 cards which have six players in special categories; and 3) the Big Twelve card of 12 World Series players from the Kansas City Royals. The trivia cards are 1-3/4" x 2" and do not have player photos.

		NM/M
Unopened Factory Set (200):		10.00
Complete Set (200):		7.50
Common Player:		.10
Foil Pack (3+2):		.50
Foil Box (36):		9.00
1	George Brett	2.25
2	Don Mattingly	2.25
3	Wade Boggs	2.00
4	Eddie Murray	1.00
5	Dale Murphy	.65
6	Rickey Henderson	1.00
7	Harold Baines	.10
8	Cal Ripken, Jr.	3.00
9	Orel Hershiser	.10
10	Bret Saberhagen	.10
11	Tim Raines	.10
12	Fernando Valenzuela	.10
13	Tony Gwynn	2.00
14	Pedro Guerrero	.10
15	Keith Hernandez	.10
16	Ernest Riles	.10
17	Jim Rice	.20
18	Ron Guidry	.10
19	Willie McGee	.10
20	Ryne Sandberg	2.00
21	Kirk Gibson	.10
22	Ozzie Guillen	.10
23	Dave Parker	.10
24	Vince Coleman	.10
25	Tom Seaver	1.00
26	Brett Butler	.10
27	Steve Carlton	1.00
28	Gary Carter	1.00
29	Cecil Cooper	.10
30	Jose Cruz	.10
31	Alvin Davis	.10
32	Dwight Evans	.10
33	Julio Franco	.10
34	Damaso Garcia	.10
35	Steve Garvey	.60
36	Kent Hrbek	.10
37	Reggie Jackson	2.25
38	Fred Lynn	.10
39	Paul Molitor	1.00
40	Jim Presley	.10
41	Dave Righetti	.10
42a	Robin Yount (Yankees logo on back.)	85.00
42b	Robin Yount (Brewers logo.)	1.00
43	Nolan Ryan	3.00
44	Mike Schmidt	2.25
45	Lee Smith	.10
46	Rick Sutcliffe	.10
47	Bruce Sutter	.75
48	Lou Whitaker	.10
49	Dave Winfield	1.00
50	Pete Rose	2.50
51	N.L. MVPs (Steve Garvey, Pete Rose, Ryne Sandberg)	1.00
52	Slugging Stars (Harold Baines, George Brett, Jim Rice)	.35
53	No-Hitters (Phil Niekro, Jerry Reuss, Mike Witt)	.25
54	Big Hitters (Don Mattingly, Cal Ripken, Jr., Robin Yount)	2.00
55	Bullpen Aces (Goose Gossage, Dan Quisenberry, Lee Smith)	.10
56	Rookies of the Year (Pete Rose, Steve Sax, Darryl Strawberry)	1.00
57	A.L. MVPs (Don Baylor, Reggie Jackson, Cal Ripken, Jr.)	.50
58	Repeat Batting Champs (Bill Madlock, Dave Parker, Pete Rose)	.45
59	Cy Young Winners (Mike Flanagan, Ron Guidry, LaMarr Hoyt)	.10
60	Double Award Winners (Tom Seaver, Rick Sutcliffe, Fernando Valenzuela)	.20
61	Home Run Champs (Tony Armas, Reggie Jackson, Jim Rice)	.25
62	N.L. MVPs (Keith Hernandez, Dale Murphy, Mike Schmidt)	.40
63	A.L. MVPs (George Brett, Fred Lynn, Robin Yount)	.30
64	Comeback Players (Bert Blyleven, John Denny, Jerry Koosman)	.10
65	Cy Young Relievers (Rollie Fingers, Willie Hernandez, Bruce Sutter)	.10
66	Rookies of the Year (Andre Dawson, Bob Horner, Gary Matthews)	.20
67	Rookies of the Year (Carlton Fisk, Ron Kittle, Tom Seaver)	.25
68	Home Run Champs (George Foster, Dave Kingman, Mike Schmidt)	.25
69	Double Award Winners (Rod Carew, Cal Ripken, Jr., Pete Rose)	2.00
70	Cy Young Winners (Steve Carlton, Tom Seaver, Rick Sutcliffe)	.25
71	Top Sluggers (Reggie Jackson, Fred Lynn, Robin Yount)	.30
72	Rookies of the Year (Dave Righetti, Rick Sutcliffe, Fernando Valenzuela)	.10
73	Rookies of the Year (Fred Lynn, Eddie Murray, Cal Ripken, Jr.)	.50
74	Rookies of the Year (Rod Carew, Alvin Davis, Lou Whitaker)	.20
75	Batting Champs (Wade Boggs, Carney Lansford, Don Mattingly)	1.00
76	Jesse Barfield	.10
77	Phil Bradley	.10
78	Chris Brown	.10
79	Tom Browning	.10
80	Tom Brunansky	.10
81	Bill Buckner	.10
82	Chili Davis	.10
83	Mike Davis	.10
84	Rich Gedman	.10
85	Willie Hernandez	.10
86	Ron Kittle	.10
87	Lee Lacy	.10
88	Bill Madlock	.10
89	Mike Marshall	.10
90	Keith Moreland	.10
91	Graig Nettles	.10
92	Lance Parrish	.10
93	Kirby Puckett	2.00
94	Juan Samuel	.10
95	Steve Sax	.10
96	Dave Stieb	.10
97	Darryl Strawberry	.10
98	Willie Upshaw	.10
99	Frank Viola	.10
100	Dwight Gooden	.10
101	Joaquin Andujar	.10
102	George Bell	.10
103	Bert Blyleven	.10
104	Mike Boddicker	.10
105	Britt Burns	.10
106	Rod Carew	1.00
107	Jack Clark	.10
108	Danny Cox	.10
109	Ron Darling	.10
110	Andre Dawson	.45
111	Leon Durham	.10
112	Tony Fernandez	.10
113	Tom Herr	.10
114	Teddy Higuera	.10
115	Bob Horner	.10
116	Dave Kingman	.10
117	Jack Morris	.10
118	Dan Quisenberry	.10
119	Jeff Reardon	.10
120	Bryn Smith	.10
121	Ozzie Smith	2.00
122	John Tudor	.10
123	Tim Wallach	.10
124	Willie Wilson	.10
125	Carlton Fisk	1.00
126	RBI Sluggers (Gary Carter, George Foster, Al Oliver)	.10
127	Run Scorers (Keith Hernandez, Tim Raines, Ryne Sandberg)	.25
128	Run Scorers (Paul Molitor, Cal Ripken, Jr., Willie Wilson)	.50
129	No-Hitters (John Candelaria, Dennis Eckersley, Bob Forsch)	.25
130	World Series MVPs (Ron Cey, Rollie Fingers, Pete Rose)	.35
131	All-Star Game MVPs (Dave Concepcion, George Foster, Bill Madlock)	.10
132	Cy Young Winners (Vida Blue, John Denny, Fernando Valenzuela)	.10
133	Comeback Players (Doyle Alexander, Joaquin Andujar, Richard Dotson)	.10
134	Big Winners (John Denny, Tom Seaver, Rick Sutcliffe)	.10
135	Veteran Pitchers (Phil Niekro, Tom Seaver, Don Sutton)	.25
136	Rookies of the Year (Vince Coleman, Dwight Gooden, Alfredo Griffin)	.20
137	All-Star Game MVPs (Gary Carter, Steve Garvey, Fred Lynn)	.20
138	Veteran Hitters (Tony Perez, Pete Rose, Rusty Staub)	.50
139	Power Hitters (George Foster, Jim Rice, Mike Schmidt)	.30
140	Batting Champs (Bill Buckner, Tony Gwynn, Al Oliver)	.25
141	No-Hitters (Jack Morris, Dave Righetti, Nolan Ryan)	.50
142	No-Hitters (Vida Blue, Bert Blyleven, Tom Seaver)	.10
143	Strikeout Kings (Dwight Gooden, Nolan Ryan, Fernando Valenzuela)	1.25
144	Base Stealers (Dave Lopes, Tim Raines, Willie Wilson)	.10
145	RBI Sluggers (Tony Armas, Cecil Cooper, Eddie Murray)	.15
146	A.L. MVPs (Rod Carew, Rollie Fingers, Jim Rice)	.15
147	World Series MVPs (Rick Dempsey, Reggie Jackson, Alan Trammell)	.25
148	World Series MVPs (Pedro Guerrero, Darrell Porter, Mike Schmidt)	.20
149	ERA Leaders (Mike Boddicker, Ron Guidry, Rick Sutcliffe)	.10
150	Comeback Players (Reggie Jackson, Dave Kingman, Fred Lynn)	.20
151	Buddy Bell	.10
152	Dennis Boyd	.10
153	Dave Concepcion	.10
154	Brian Downing	.10
155	Shawon Dunston	.10
156	John Franco	.10
157	Scott Garrelts	.10
158	Bob James	.10
159	Charlie Leibrandt	.10
160	Oddibe McDowell	.10
161	Roger McDowell	.10
162	Mike Moore	.10
163	Phil Niekro	.75
164	Al Oliver	.10
165	Tony Pena	.10
166	Ted Power	.10
167	Mike Scioscia	.10
168	Mario Soto	.10
169	Bob Stanley	.10
170	Garry Templeton	.10
171	Andre Thornton	.10
172	Alan Trammell	.10
173	Doug DeCinces	.10
174	Greg Walker	.10
175	Don Sutton	.75
176	1985 Award Winners (Vince Coleman, Dwight Gooden, Ozzie Guillen, Don Mattingly, Willie McGee, Bret Saberhagen)	.50
177	1985 Hot Rookies (Stewart Cliburn, Brian Fisher, Joe Hesketh, Joe Orsulak, Mark Salas, Larry Sheets)	.10
178a	Future Stars (Jose Canseco **RC**, Mark Funderburk, Mike Greenwell, Steve Lombardozzi, Billy Joe Robidoux, Danny Tartabull)	2.00
178b	Future Stars (Jose Canseco, Mike Greenwell, Steve Lombardozzi, Billy Jo Robidoux, Danny Tartabull, Jim Wilson)	30.00
179	Gold Glove (George Brett, Ron Guidry, Keith Hernandez, Don Mattingly, Willie McGee, Dale Murphy)	1.00
180	.300 (Wade Boggs, George Brett, Rod Carew, Cecil Cooper, Don Mattingly, Willie Wilson)	1.00
181	.300 (Pedro Guerrero, Tony Gwynn, Keith Hernandez, Bill Madlock, Dave Parker, Pete Rose)	.50
182	1985 Milestones (Rod Carew, Phil Niekro, Pete Rose, Nolan Ryan, Tom Seaver, Matt Tallman)	1.50
183	1985 Triple Crown (Wade Boggs, Darrell Evans, Don Mattingly, Willie McGee, Dale Murphy, Dave Parker)	1.00
184	1985 HL (Wade Boggs, Dwight Gooden, Rickey Henderson, Don Mattingly, Willie McGee, John Tudor)	1.00
185	1985 20-Game Winners (Joaquin Andujar, Tom Browning, Dwight Gooden, Ron Guidry, Bret Saberhagen, John Tudor)	.10
186	World Series Champs (Steve Balboni, George Brett, Dane Iorg, Danny Jackson, Charlie Leibrandt, Darryl Motley, Dan Quisenberry, Bret Saberhagen, Lonnie Smith, Jim Sundberg, Frank White, Willie Wilson)	.40
187	Hubie Brooks	.10
188	Glenn Davis	.10
189	Darrell Evans	.10
190	Rich Gossage	.10
191	Andy Hawkins	.10
192	Jay Howell	.10
193	LaMarr Hoyt	.10
194	Davey Lopes	.10
195	Mike Scott	.10
196	Ted Simmons	.10
197	Gary Ward	.10
198	Bob Welch	.10
199	Mike Young	.10
200	Buddy Biancalana	.10

Decade Greats Sample Cards

To promote its Decade Greats set of current and former cards, Sportflics issued this two-card promo set. Card fronts are identical to the issued versions. Backs are printed in blue on white: "DECADE GREATS / SAMPLE CARD." The players are not identified on the cards.

		NM/M
Complete Set (2):		2.00
(1)	Dwight Gooden	1.00
(2)	Mel Ott	1.00

Decade Greats

This set, produced by Sportflics, features outstanding players, by position, from the 1930s to the 1980s by decades. The card fronts are

printed in sepia-toned photos or full-color with the Sportflics three-phase "Magic Motion" animation. The complete set contains 75 cards with 59 single player cards and 16 multi-player cards. Biographies appear on the card backs which are printed in full-color and color-coded by decade. The set was distributed only through hobby dealers and is in the popular 2-1/2" x 3-1/2" size.

		NM/M
Complete Set (75):		9.00
Common Player:		.10
1	Babe Ruth	2.00
2	Jimmie Foxx	.15
3	Lefty Grove	.10
4	Hank Greenberg	.25
5	Al Simmons	.10
6	Carl Hubbell	.10
7	Joe Cronin	.10
8	Mel Ott	.10
9	Lefty Gomez	.10
10	Lou Gehrig	1.25
11	Pie Traynor	.10
12	Charlie Gehringer	.10
13	Catchers (Mickey Cochrane, Bill Dickey, Gabby Hartnett)	.10
14	Pitchers (Dizzy Dean, Paul Derringer, Red Ruffing)	.10
15	Outfielders (Earl Averill, Joe Medwick, Paul Waner)	.10
16	Bob Feller	.40
17	Lou Boudreau	.10
18	Enos Slaughter	.15
19	Hal Newhouser	.10
20	Joe DiMaggio	1.25
21	Pee Wee Reese	.25
22	Phil Rizzuto	.15
23	Ernie Lombardi	.10
24	Infielders (Joe Cronin, George Kell, Johnny Mize)	.10
25	Ted Williams	1.25
26	Mickey Mantle	3.00
27	Warren Spahn	.15
28	Jackie Robinson	1.00
29	Ernie Banks	.20
30	Stan Musial	.75
31	Yogi Berra	.40
32	Duke Snider	.50
33	Roy Campanella	.50
34	Eddie Mathews	.15
35	Ralph Kiner	.15
36	Early Wynn	.10
37	Double Play Duo (Luis Aparicio, Nellie Fox)	.35
38	First Basemen (Gil Hodges, Ted Kluszewski, Mickey Vernon)	.25
40	Henry Aaron	.75
41	Frank Robinson	.20
42	Bob Gibson	.20
43	Roberto Clemente	1.75
44	Whitey Ford	.25
45	Brooks Robinson	.35
46	Juan Marichal	.15
47	Carl Yastrzemski	.40
48	First Basemen (Orlando Cepeda, Harmon Killebrew, Willie McCovey)	.15
49	Catchers (Bill Freehan, Elston Howard, Joe Torre)	.10
50	Willie Mays	.75
51	Outfielders (Al Kaline, Tony Oliva, Billy Williams)	.15
52	Tom Seaver	.40
53	Reggie Jackson	.50
54	Steve Carlton	.25
55	Mike Schmidt	.50
56	Joe Morgan	.15
57	Jim Rice	.15
58	Jim Palmer	.20
59	Lou Brock	.20
60	Pete Rose	1.00

61 Steve Garvey .25
62 Catchers (Carlton Fisk, Thurman Munson, Ted Simmons) .15
63 Pitchers (Vida Blue, Catfish Hunter, Nolan Ryan) .20
64 George Brett .50
65 Don Mattingly 1.00
66 Fernando Valenzuela .10
67 Dale Murphy .25
68 Wade Boggs .40
69 Rickey Henderson .40
70 Eddie Murray .40
71 Ron Guidry .10
72 Catchers (Gary Carter, Lance Parrish, Tony Pena) .15
73 Infielders (Cal Ripken, Jr., Lou Whitaker, Robin Yount) .35
74 Outfielders (Pedro Guerrero, Tim Raines, Dave Winfield) .15
75 Dwight Gooden .10

Rookies

The 1986 Rookies set offers 50 cards and features 47 individual rookie players. In addition, there are two Tri-Star cards; one highlights former Rookies of the Year and the other features three prominent players. There is one "Big Six" card featuring six superstars. The full-color photos on the 2-1/2" x 3-1/2" cards use Sportflics three-phase "Magic Motion" animation. The set was packaged in a collector box which also contained 34 trivia cards that measure 1-3/4" x 2". The set was distributed only by hobby dealers.

NM/M
Complete Set (50): 17.50
Common Player: .10
Complete Set (50): 17.50
Common Player: .10
1 John Kruk .10
2 Edwin Correa .10
3 Pete Incaviglia .10
4 Dale Sveum .10
5 Juan Nieves .10
6 Will Clark .25
7 Wally Joyner .25
8 Lance McCullers .10
9 Scott Bailes .10
10 Dan Plesac .10
11 Jose Canseco 1.50
12 Bobby Witt .10
13 Barry Bonds 15.00
14 Andres Thomas .10
15 Jim Deshaies .10
16 Ruben Sierra .10
17 Steve Lombardozzi .10
18 Cory Snyder .10
19 Reggie Williams .10
20 Mitch Williams .10
21 Glenn Braggs .10
22 Danny Tartabull .10
23 Charlie Kerfeld .10
24 Paul Assenmacher .10
25 Robby Thompson .10
26 Bobby Bonilla .10
27 Andres Galarraga .10
28 Billy Jo Robidoux .10
29 Bruce Ruffin .10
30 Greg Swindell .10
31 John Cangelosi .10
32 Jim Traber .10
33 Russ Morman .10
34 Barry Larkin .10
35 Todd Worrell .10
36 John Cerutti .10
37 Mike Kingery .10
38 Mark Eichhorn .10
39 Scott Bankhead .10
40 Bo Jackson .25
41 Greg Mathews .10
42 Eric King .10
43 Kal Daniels .10
44 Calvin Schiraldi .10
45 Mickey Brantley .10
46 Outstanding Rookie Seasons (Fred Lynn, Willie Mays, Pete Rose) .60
47 Outstanding Rookie Seasons (Dwight Gooden, Tom Seaver, Fernando Valenzuela) .25
48 Outstanding Rookie Seasons (Eddie Murray, Dave Righetti, Cal Ripken, Jr., Steve Sax, Darryl Strawberry, Lou Whitaker) .25
49 Kevin Mitchell .10
50 Mike Diaz .10

Dwight Gooden Discs

As the viewing angle changes on these 3-D simulated motion plastic discs, three different pictures of "Dr. K" can be seen, two action and one portrait. The discs are found in two diameters, 2-1/4" and 4-1/2". Fronts have team-color borders of blue with orange lettering. Backs are blank.

NM/M
Complete Set (2): 3.00
(1) Dwight Gooden (2-1/4") 1.00
(2) Dwight Gooden (4-1/2") 2.00

Jumbo Discs

A portrait and two action pictures of the players are featured in these large-format (4-1/2" diameter) "Magic Motion" discs. Fronts have the player's name below the photos, with a title above. Backs are printed in purple, red, black and white. Discs were available for $5 each with a paper coupon found in Sportflics packs.

NM/M
Complete Set (6): 13.50
Common Player: 1.50
(1) Wade Boggs 4.00
(2) Roger Clemens 5.00
(3) Wally Joyner 1.50
(4) Mickey Mantle 6.00
(5) Don Mattingly 5.00
(6) Dave Winfield 3.00
(1) Wade Boggs 1.00
(2) Roger Clemens 1.25
(3) Wally Joyner .40
(4) Mickey Mantle 2.00
(5) Don Mattingly 1.25
(6) Dave Winfield .75

1987 Sportflics

In its second year in the national market, Sportflics' basic issue was again a 200-card set of 2-1/2" x 3-1/2" "Magic Motion" cards, which offer three different photos on the same card, each visible in turn as the card is moved from top to bottom or side to side. Besides single-player cards, the '87 Sportflics set includes several three- and six-player

cards, though not as many as in the 1986 set. The card backs feature a small player portrait photo on the single-player cards, an innovation for 1987. The cards were issued with a series of 136 team logo trivia cards. Most cards exist in two variations, carrying 1986 or 1987 copyright dates on back.

NM/M
Factory Set (200+136): 12.00
Complete Set (200): 7.50
Common Player: .10
Foil Pack (3+2): .50
Foil Box (36): 10.00
1 Don Mattingly 1.25
2 Wade Boggs 1.00
3 Dale Murphy .50
4 Rickey Henderson .75
5 George Brett 1.25
6 Eddie Murray .75
7 Kirby Puckett 1.00
8 Ryne Sandberg 1.00
9 Cal Ripken, Jr. 2.00
10 Roger Clemens 1.25
11 Ted Higuera .10
12 Steve Sax .10
13 Chris Brown .10
14 Jesse Barfield .10
15 Kent Hrbek .10
16 Robin Yount .75
17 Glenn Davis .10
18 Hubie Brooks .10
19 Mike Scott .10
20 Darryl Strawberry .10
21 Alvin Davis .10
22 Eric Davis .10
23 Danny Tartabull .10
24a Cory Snyder (Pat Tabler photo on back.) 1.50
24b Cory Snyder (Pat Tabler photo on back.) (Facing front, 1/4 swing on front.) 1.50
24c Cory Snyder (Snyder photo on back.) (Facing to side.) .50
25 Pete Rose 1.50
26 Wally Joyner .10
27 Pedro Guerrero .10
28 Tom Seaver .75
29 Bob Knepper .10
30 Mike Schmidt 1.25
31 Tony Gwynn 1.00
32 Don Slaught .10
33 Todd Worrell .10
34 Tim Raines .10
35 Dave Parker .10
36 Bob Ojeda .10
37 Pete Incaviglia .10
38 Bruce Hurst .10
39 Bobby Witt .10
40 Steve Garvey .40
41 Dave Winfield .75
42 Jose Cruz .10
43 Orel Hershiser .10
44 Reggie Jackson .75
45 Chili Davis .10
46 Robby Thompson .10
47 Dennis Boyd .10
48 Kirk Gibson .10
49 Fred Lynn .10
50 Gary Carter .75
51 George Bell .10
52 Pete O'Brien .10
53 Ron Darling .10
54 Paul Molitor .75
55 Mike Pagliarulo .10
56 Mike Boddicker .10
57 Dave Righetti .10
58 Len Dykstra **RC** .10
59 Mike Witt .10
60 Tony Bernazard .10
61 John Kruk .10
62 Mike Krukow .10
63 Sid Fernandez .10
64 Gary Gaetti .10
65 Vince Coleman .10
66 Pat Tabler .10
67 Mike Scioscia .10
68 Scott Garrelts .10
69 Brett Butler .10
70 Bill Buckner .10
71a Dennis Rasmussen (John Montefusco photo on back; mustache.) .25
71b Dennis Rasmussen (Correct photo on back, no mustache.) .10
72 Tim Wallach .10
73 Bob Horner .10
74 Willie McGee .10
75 A.L. First Basemen (Wally Joyner, Don Mattingly, Eddie Murray) .50
76 Jesse Orosco .10
77 N.L. Relief Pitchers (Jeff Reardon, Dave Smith, Todd Worrell) .10
78 Candy Maldonado .10
79 N.L. Shortstops (Hubie Brooks, Shawon Dunston, Ozzie Smith) .10
80 A.L. Left Fielders (George Bell, Jose Canseco, Jim Rice) .25
81 Bert Blyleven .10
82 Mike Marshall .10
83 Ron Guidry .10
84 Julio Franco .10
85 Willie Wilson .10
86 Lee Lacy .10
87 Jack Morris .10
88 Ray Knight .10
89 Phil Bradley .10
90 Jose Canseco .60
91 Gary Ward .10
92 Mike Easler .10
93 Tony Pena .10
94 Dave Smith .10
95 Will Clark .10
96 Lloyd Moseby .10
97 Jim Rice .25
98 Shawon Dunston .10
99 Don Sutton .50
100 Dwight Gooden .10
101 Lance Parrish .10
102 Mark Langston .10
103 Floyd Youmans .10
104 Lee Smith .10
105 Willie Hernandez .10
106 Doug DeCinces .10
107 Ken Schrom .10
108 Don Carman .10
109 Brook Jacoby .10
110 Steve Bedrosian .10
111 A.L. Pitchers (Roger Clemens, Teddy Higuera, Jack Morris) .25
112 A.L. Second Basemen (Marty Barrett, Tony Bernazard, Lou Whitaker) .10
113 A.L. Shortstops (Tony Fernandez, Scott Fletcher, Cal Ripken, Jr.) .25
114 A.L. Third Basemen (Wade Boggs, George Brett, Gary Gaetti) .25
115 N.L. Third Basemen (Chris Brown, Mike Schmidt, Tim Wallach) .20
116 N.L. Second Basemen (Bill Doran, Johnny Ray, Ryne Sandberg) .10
117 N.L. Right Fielders (Kevin Bass, Tony Gwynn, Dave Parker) .10
118 Hot Rookie Prospects (David Clark, Pat Dodson, Ty Gainey, Phil Lombardi, Benito Santiago, Terry Steinbach **RC**) .25
119 1986 Season Highlights (Dave Righetti, Mike Scott, Fernando Valenzuela) .10
120 N.L. Pitchers (Dwight Gooden, Mike Scott, Fernando Valenzuela) .10
121 Johnny Ray .10
122 Keith Moreland .10
123 Juan Samuel .10
124 Wally Backman .10
125 Nolan Ryan 2.00
126 Greg Harris .10
127 Kirk McCaskill .10
128 Dwight Evans .10
129 Rick Rhoden .10
130 Bill Madlock .10
131 Oddibe McDowell .10
132 Darrell Evans .10
133 Keith Hernandez .10
134 Tom Brunansky .10
135 Kevin McReynolds .10
136 Scott Fletcher .10
137 Lou Whitaker .10
138 Carney Lansford .10
139 Andre Dawson .45
140 Carlton Fisk .75
141 Buddy Bell .10
142 Ozzie Smith 1.00
143 Dan Pasqua .10
144 Kevin Mitchell .10
145 Bret Saberhagen .10
146 Charlie Kerfeld .10
147 Phil Niekro .50
148 John Candelaria .10
149 Rich Gedman .10
150 Fernando Valenzuela .10
151 N.L. Catchers (Gary Carter, Tony Pena, Mike Scioscia) .10
152 N.L. Left Fielders (Vince Coleman, Jose Cruz, Tim Raines) .10
153 A.L. Right Fielders (Harold Baines, Jesse Barfield, Dave Winfield) .10
154 A.L. Catchers (Rich Gedman, Lance Parrish, Don Slaught) .10
155 N.L. Center Fielders (Kevin McReynolds, Dale Murphy, Eric Davis) .10
156 '86 Highlights (Jim Deshaies, Mike Schmidt, Don Sutton) .10
157 A.L. Speedburners (John Cangelosi, Rickey Henderson, Gary Pettis) .10
158 Hot Rookie Prospects (Randy Asadoor, Casey Candaele, Dave Cochrane, Rafael Palmeiro, Tim Pyznarski, Kevin Seitzer) .75
159 The Best of the Best (Roger Clemens, Dwight Gooden, Rickey Henderson, Don Mattingly, Dale Murphy, Eddie Murray) .75
160 Roger McDowell .10
161 Brian Downing .10
162 Bill Doran .10
163 Don Baylor .10
164 Alfredo Griffin .10
165 Don Aase .10
166 Glenn Wilson .10
167 Dan Quisenberry .10
168 Frank White .10
169 Cecil Cooper .10
170 Jody Davis .10
171 Harold Baines .10
172 Rob Deer .10
173 John Tudor .10
174 Larry Parrish .10
175 Kevin Bass .10
176 Joe Carter .10
177 Mitch Webster .10
178 Dave Kingman .10
179 Jim Presley .10
180 Mel Hall .10
181 Shane Rawley .10
182 Marty Barrett .10
183 Damaso Garcia .10
184 Bobby Grich .10
185 Leon Durham .10
186 Ozzie Guillen .10
187 Tony Fernandez .10
188 Alan Trammell .10
189 Jim Clancy .10
190 Bo Jackson .15
191 Bob Forsch .10
192 John Franco .10
193 Von Hayes .10
194 A.L. Relief Pitchers (Don Aase, Mark Eichhorn, Dave Righetti) .10
195 N.L. First Basemen (Will Clark, Glenn Davis, Keith Hernandez) .10
196 '86 Highlights (Roger Clemens, Joe Cowley, Bob Horner) .10
197 The Best of the Best (Wade Boggs, George Brett, Hubie Brooks, Tony Gwynn, Tim Raines, Ryne Sandberg) .75
198 A.L. Center Fielders (Rickey Henderson, Fred Lynn, Kirby Puckett) .50
199 N.L. Speedburners (Vince Coleman, Tim Raines, Eric Davis) .10
200 Steve Carlton .75

Rookie Discs

The 1987 Sportflics Rookie Discs set consists of seven discs which measure 4" in diameter. The front of the discs offer three "Magic Motion" photos in full color, encompassed by a blue border. The disc backs are printed in color and include the team logo, player statistics, biogra-

phy and the disc number. The set was issued with Cooperstown Timeless Trivia Cards.

NM/M
Complete Set (7): 8.00
Common Player: 1.00
1 Casey Candaele 1.00
2 Mark McGwire 6.00
3 Kevin Seitzer 1.00
4 Joe Magrane 1.00
5 Benito Santiago 1.00
6 Dave Magadan 1.00
7 Devon White 1.00

Rookie Prospects

The Rookie Prospects set consists of 10 cards in standard 2-1/2" x 3-1/2" size. The card fronts feature Sportflics' "Magic Motion" process. Card backs contain a player photo plus a short biography and player personal and statistical information. The set was offered in two separately wrapped mylar packs of five cards to hobby dealers purchasing cases of Sportflics' Team Preview set. Twenty-four packs of "Rookie Prospects" cards were included with each case.

NM/M
Complete Set (10): 4.00
Common Player: .25
1 Terry Steinbach .25
2 Rafael Palmeiro 3.00
3 Dave Magadan .25
4 Marvin Freeman .25
5 Brick Smith .25
6 B.J. Surhoff .25
7 John Smiley .25
8 Alonzo Powell .25
9 Benny Santiago .25
10 Devon White .25

Rookies

The Rookies set was issued in two boxed series of 25 cards. The first was released in July with the second series following in October. The cards, which are the standard 2-1/2" x 3-1/2", feature Sportflics' special "Magic Motion" process. The card fronts contain a full-color photo and present three different pictures, depending on how the card is held. The backs also contain a full-color photo along with player statistics and a biography.

		NM/M
Complete Set One (1-25):		4.00
Complete Set Two (26-50):		2.00
Common Player:		.10
1	Eric Bell	.10
2	Chris Bosio	.10
3	Bob Brower	.10
4	Jerry Browne	.10
5	Ellis Burks	.10
6	Casey Candaele	.10
7	Ken Gerhart	.10
8	Mike Greenwell	.10
9	Stan Jefferson	.10
10	Dave Magadan	.10
11	Joe Magrane	.10
12	Fred McGriff	.25
13	Mark McGwire	3.00
14	Mark McLemore	.10
15	Jeff Musselman	.10
16	Matt Nokes	.10
17	Paul O'Neill	.10
18	Luis Polonia	.10
19	Benny Santiago	.10
20	Kevin Seitzer	.10
21	John Smiley	.10
22	Terry Steinbach	.10
23	B.J. Surhoff	.10
24	Devon White	.10
25	Matt Williams	.25
26	DeWayne Buice	.10
27	Willie Fraser	.10
28	Bill Ripken	.10
29	Mike Henneman	.10
30	Shawn Hillegas	.10
31	Shane Mack	.10
32	Rafael Palmeiro	1.50
33	Mike Jackson	.10
34	Gene Larkin	.10
35	Jimmy Jones	.10
36	Gerald Young	.10
37	Ken Caminiti	.10
38	Sam Horn	.10
39	David Cone	.10
40	Mike Dunne	.10
41	Ken Williams	.10
42	John Morris	.10
43	Jim Lindeman	.10
44	Mike Stanley	.10
45	Les Straker	.10
46	Jeff Robinson	.10
47	Todd Benzinger	.10
48	Jeff Blauser	.10
49	John Marzano	.10
50	Keith Miller	.10

Superstar Discs

Released in three series of six discs, the Superstar Disc set features the special "Magic Motion" process. Each disc, which measures 4-1/2" in diameter, contains three different player photos, depending which way it is tilted. A red border, containing 11 stars, the player's name and uniform number, surrounds the photo. The backs have a turquoise border which carries the words "Superstar Disc Collector Series." The backs also include the team logo, player statistics, biography and the disc number. The discs were issued with 18 1-3/4" x 2-1/2" Cooperstown Timeless Trivia Cards.

		NM/M
Complete Set (18):		35.00
Common Player:		1.50
1	Jose Canseco	2.50
2	Mike Scott	1.50
3	Ryne Sandberg	3.50
4	Mike Schmidt	4.00
5	Dale Murphy	2.00
6	Fernando Valenzuela	1.50
7	Tony Gwynn	3.50
8	Cal Ripken, Jr.	6.00
9	Gary Carter	3.00
10	Cory Snyder	1.50
11	Kirby Puckett	3.50
12	George Brett	3.50
13	Keith Hernandez	1.50
14	Rickey Henderson	3.00
15	Tim Raines	1.50
16	Bo Jackson	2.00
17	Pete Rose	4.50
18	Eric Davis	1.50

Team Previews

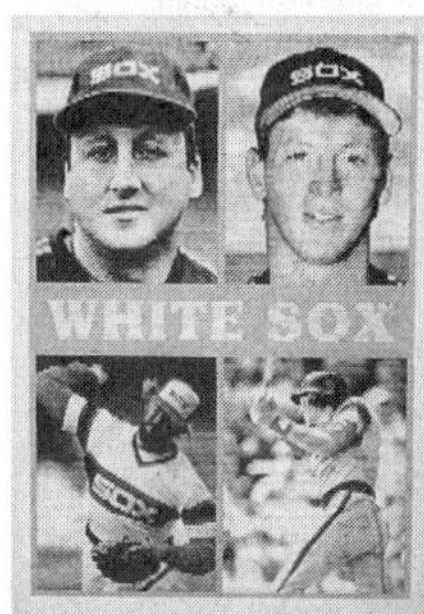

The 1987 Sportflics Team Preview set appeared to be a good idea, but never caught on with collectors. The intent of the set is to provide a preseason look at each of the 26 major league clubs. The card backs contain three categories of the team preview: Outlook, Newcomers to Watch and Summary. Using the "Magic Motion" process, 12 different players are featured on the card fronts. Four of the different player photos can be made visible at once. The cards, which measure 2-1/2" x 3-1/2", were issued with team logo/trivia cards in a specially designed box.

		NM/M
Complete Set (26):		15.00
Common Team:		.50
1	Texas Rangers (Scott Fletcher, Greg Harris, Charlie Hough, Pete Incaviglia, Mike Loynd, Oddibe McDowell, Pete O'Brien, Larry Parrish, Ruben Sierra, Don Slaught, Mitch Williams, Bobby Witt)	.50
2	New York Mets (Wally Backman, Gary Carter, Ron Darling, Lenny Dykstra, Sid Fernandez, Dwight Gooden, Keith Hernandez, Dave Magadan, Kevin McReynolds, Randy Myers, Bob Ojeda, Darryl Strawberry)	.75
3	Cleveland Indians (Tony Bernazard, Brett Butler, Tom Candiotti, Joe Carter, Julio Franco, Mel Hall, Brook Jacoby, Phil Niekro, Ken Schrom, Cory Snyder, Greg Swindell, Pat Tabler)	.50
4	Cincinnati Reds (Buddy Bell, Tom Browning, Kal Daniels, John Franco, Bill Gullickson, Tracy Jones, Barry Larkin, Rob Murphy, Paul O'Neill, Dave Parker, Pete Rose, Eric Davis)	1.00
5	Toronto Blue Jays (Jesse Barfield, George Bell, John Cerutti, Mark Eichhorn, Tony Fernandez, Tom Henke, Glenallen Hill, Jimmy Key, Fred McGriff, Lloyd Moseby, Dave Stieb, Willie Upshaw)	.50
6	Philadelphia Phillies (Steve Bedrosian, Don Carman, Marvin Freeman, Kevin Gross, Von Hayes, Shane Rawley, Bruce Ruffin, Juan Samuel, Mike Schmidt, Kent Tekulve, Milt Thompson, Glenn Wilson)	.75
7	New York Yankees (Rickey Henderson, Phil Lombardi, Don Mattingly, Mike Pagliarulo, Dan Pasqua, Willie Randolph, Dennis Rasmussen, Rick Rhoden, Dave Righetti, Joel Skinner, Bob Tewksbury, Dave Winfield)	1.25
8	Houston Astros (Kevin Bass, Jose Cruz, Glenn Davis, Jim Deshaies, Bill Doran, Ty Gainey, Charlie Kerfeld, Bob Knepper, Nolan Ryan, Mike Scott, Dave Smith, Robby Wine)	1.50
9	Boston Red Sox (Marty Barrett, Don Baylor, Wade Boggs, Dennis Boyd, Roger Clemens, Pat Dodson, Dwight Evans, Mike Greenwell, Dave Henderson, Bruce Hurst, Jim Rice, Calvin Schiraldi)	1.00
10	San Francisco Giants (Bob Brenly, Chris Brown, Will Clark, Chili Davis, Kelly Downs, Scott Garrelts, Mark Grant, Mike Krukow, Jeff Leonard, Candy Maldonado, Terry Mulholland, Robby Thompson)	.50
11	California Angels (John Candelaria, Doug DeCinces, Brian Downing, Ruppert Jones, Wally Joyner, Kirk McCaskill, Darrell Miller, Donnie Moore, Gary Pettis, Don Sutton, Devon White, Mike Witt)	.50
12	St. Louis Cardinals (Jack Clark, Vince Coleman, Danny Cox, Bob Forsch, Tom Herr, Joe Magrane, Willie McGee, Terry Pendleton, Ozzie Smith, John Tudor, Andy Van Slyke, Todd Worrell)	.75
13	Kansas City Royals (George Brett, Mark Gubicza, Bo Jackson, Charlie Leibrandt, Hal McRae, Dan Quisenberry, Bret Saberhagen, Kevin Seitzer, Lonnie Smith, Danny Tartabull, Frank White, Willie Wilson)	.75
14	Los Angeles Dodgers (Ralph Bryant, Mariano Duncan, Jose Gonzalez, Pedro Guerrero, Orel Hershiser, Mike Marshall, Steve Sax, Mike Scioscia, Franklin Stubbs, Fernando Valenzuela, Reggie Williams, Matt Young)	.50
15	Detroit Tigers (Darnell Coles, Darrell Evans, Kirk Gibson, Willie Hernandez, Eric King, Chet Lemon, Dwight Lowry, Jack Morris, Dan Petry, Frank Tanana, Alan Trammell, Lou Whitaker)	.50
16	San Diego Padres (Randy Asadoor, Steve Garvey, Tony Gwynn, Andy Hawkins, Jim Jones, John Kruk, Craig Lefferts, Shane Mack, Lance McCullers, Kevin Mitchell, Benny Santiago, Ed Wojna)	.75
17	Minnesota Twins (Bert Blyleven, Tom Brunansky, Gary Gaetti, Greg Gagne, Kent Hrbek, Joe Klink, Steve Lombardozzi, Kirby Puckett, Jeff Reardon, Mark Salas, Roy Smalley, Frank Viola)	.75
18	Pittsburgh Pirates (Barry Bonds, Bobby Bonilla, Sid Bream, Mike Diaz, Brian Fisher, Jim Morrison, Joe Orsulak, Bob Patterson, Tony Pena, Johnny Ray, R.J. Reynolds, John Smiley)	1.50
19	Milwaukee Brewers (Glenn Braggs, Rob Deer, Teddy Higuera, Paul Molitor, Juan Nieves, Dan Plesac, Tim Pyznarski, Ernest Riles, Billy Jo Robidoux, B.J. Surhoff, Dale Sveum, Robin Yount)	.75
20	Montreal Expos (Hubie Brooks, Tim Burke, Casey Candaele, Dave Collins, Mike Fitzgerald, Andres Galarraga, Billy Moore, Alonzo Powell, Randy St. Claire, Tim Wallach, Mitch Webster, Floyd Youmans)	.50
21	Baltimore Orioles (Don Aase, Eric Bell, Mike Boddicker, Ken Gerhardt, Terry Kennedy, Ray Knight, Lee Lacy, Fred Lynn, Eddie Murray, Cal Ripken, Jr., Larry Sheets, Jim Traber)	1.50
22	Chicago Cubs (Jody Davis, Shawon Dunston, Leon Durham, Dennis Eckersley, Greg Maddux, Dave Martinez, Keith Moreland, Jerry Mumphrey, Rafael Palmeiro, Ryne Sandberg, Scott Sanderson, Lee Smith)	1.00
23	Oakland Athletics (Jose Canseco, Mike Davis, Alfredo Griffin, Reggie Jackson, Carney Lansford, Mark McGwire, Dwayne Murphy, Rob Nelson, Tony Phillips, Jose Rijo, Terry Steinbach, Curt Young)	1.50
24	Atlanta Braves (Paul Assenmacher, Gene Garber, Tom Glavine, Ken Griffey, Glenn Hubbard, Dion James, Rick Mahler, Dale Murphy, Ken Oberkfell, David Palmer, Zane Smith, Andres Thomas)	.50
25	Seattle Mariners (Scott Bankhead, Phil Bradley, Scott Bradley, Mickey Brantley, Alvin Davis, Steve Fireovid, Mark Langston, Mike Moore, Donell Nixon, Ken Phelps, Jim Presley, Dave Valle)	.50
26	Chicago White Sox (Harold Baines, John Cangelosi, Dave Cochrane, Joe Cowley, Carlton Fisk, Ozzie Guillen, Ron Hassey, Bob James, Ron Karkovice, Russ Mormon, Bobby Thigpen, Greg Walker)	.50

4-in-1 Panels

These 4-in-1 player and team logo panels were given to dealers who made quantity purchases of Sportflics products. The player panels measure 4-7/8" x 6-7/8", making each of the four cards slightly smaller than the regular-issue versions. Otherwise the cards are identical to the standard version, right down to the card numbers. The team-logo panels correspond to the players on the player panels, but they are smaller, at 3-3/8" x 3-7/8". The logo cards have two views of each logo on front and on back display various team stats. Each of the panels carries a 1986 copyright.

		NM/M
Complete Set (8):		15.00
Common Panel:		1.00
(1)	1 Don Mattingly, 10 Roger Clemens, 30 Mike Schmidt, 34 Tim Raines	5.00
(2)	2 Wade Boggs, 6 Eddie Murray, 26 Wally Joyner, 150 Fernando Valenzuela	2.50
(3)	3 Dale Murphy, 31 Tony Gwynn, 97 Jim Rice, 133 Keith Hernandez	2.50
(4)	4 Rickey Henderson, 5 George Brett, 9 Cal Ripken Jr., 100 Dwight Gooden	6.50
(5)	Yankees, Expos, Red Sox, Phillies	1.00
(6)	Red Sox, Dodgers, Angels, Orioles	1.00
(7)	Braves, Mets, Red Sox, Padres	1.00
(8)	Mets, Orioles, Yankees, Royals	1.00

1988 Sportflics

The design of the 1988 Sportflics set differs greatly from the previous two years. Besides increasing the number of cards in the set to 225, Sportflics included the player name, team and uniform number on the card front. The triple-action color photos are surrounded by a red border. The backs are re-designed, also. Full-color action photos, plus extensive statistics and informative biographies are utilized. Three highlights cards and three rookie prospects card are included in the set. The cards are the standard 2-1/2" x 3-1/2".

		NM/M
Factory Set (225+136):		17.50
Complete Set (225):		10.00
Common Player:		.10
Foil Pack (3+2):		.50
Foil Box (36):		9.00
1	Don Mattingly	1.25
2	Tim Raines	.10
3	Andre Dawson	.25
4	George Bell	.10
5	Joe Carter	.10
6	Matt Nokes	.10
7	Dave Winfield	.75
8	Kirby Puckett	1.00
9	Will Clark	.10
10	Eric Davis	.10
11	Rickey Henderson	.75
12	Ryne Sandberg	1.00
13	Jesse Barfield	.10
14	Ozzie Guillen	.10
15	Bret Saberhagen	.10
16	Tony Gwynn	1.00
17	Kevin Seitzer	.10
18	Jack Clark	.10
19	Danny Tartabull	.10
20	Ted Higuera	.10
21	Charlie Leibrandt, Jr.	.10
22	Benny Santiago	.10
23	Fred Lynn	.10
24	Rob Thompson	.10
25	Alan Trammell	.10
26	Tony Fernandez	.10
27	Rick Sutcliffe	.10
28	Gary Carter	.75
29	Cory Snyder	.10
30	Lou Whitaker	.10
31	Keith Hernandez	.10
32	Mike Witt	.10
33	Harold Baines	.10
34	Robin Yount	.75
35	Mike Schmidt	1.25
36	Dion James	.10
37	Tom Candiotti	.10
38	Tracy Jones	.10
39	Nolan Ryan	2.00
40	Fernando Valenzuela	.10
41	Vance Law	.10
42	Roger McDowell	.10
43	Carlton Fisk	.75
44	Scott Garrelts	.10
45	Lee Guetterman	.10
46	Mark Langston	.10
47	Willie Randolph	.10
48	Bill Doran	.10
49	Larry Parrish	.10
50	Wade Boggs	1.00
51	Shane Rawley	.10
52	Alvin Davis	.10
53	Jeff Reardon	.10
54	Jim Presley	.10
55	Kevin Bass	.10
56	Kevin McReynolds	.10
57	B.J. Surhoff	.10
58	Julio Franco	.10
59	Eddie Murray	.75
60	Jody Davis	.10
61	Todd Worrell	.10
62	Von Hayes	.10
63	Billy Hatcher	.10
64	John Kruk	.10
65	Tom Henke	.10
66	Mike Scott	.10
67	Vince Coleman	.10
68	Ozzie Smith	1.00
69	Ken Williams	.10
70	Steve Bedrosian	.10
71	Luis Polonia	.10
72	Brook Jacoby	.10
73	Ron Darling	.10
74	Lloyd Moseby	.10
75	Wally Joyner	.10
76	Dan Quisenberry	.10
77	Scott Fletcher	.10
78	Kirk McCaskill	.10
79	Paul Molitor	.75
80	Mike Aldrete	.10
81	Neal Heaton	.10
82	Jeffrey Leonard	.10
83	Dave Magadan	.10
84	Danny Cox	.10
85	Lance McCullers	.10
86	Jay Howell	.10
87	Charlie Hough	.10
88	Gene Garber	.10
89	Jesse Orosco	.10
90	Don Robinson	.10
91	Willie McGee	.10
92	Bert Blyleven	.10
93	Phil Bradley	.10
94	Terry Kennedy	.10
95	Kent Hrbek	.10
96	Juan Samuel	.10
97	Pedro Guerrero	.10
98	Sid Bream	.10
99	Devon White	.10
100	Mark McGwire	1.50
101	Dave Parker	.10
102	Glenn Davis	.10
103	Greg Walker	.10
104	Rick Rhoden	.10
105	Mitch Webster	.10
106	Lenny Dykstra	.10
107	Gene Larkin	.10
108	Floyd Youmans	.10
109	Andy Van Slyke	.10
110	Mike Scioscia	.10
111	Kirk Gibson	.10
112	Kal Daniels	.10
113	Ruben Sierra	.10
114	Sam Horn	.10
115	Ray Knight	.10
116	Jimmy Key	.10
117	Bo Diaz	.10
118	Mike Greenwell	.10
119	Barry Bonds	2.00
120	Reggie Jackson	1.25
121	Mike Pagliarulo	.10
122	Tommy John	.10
123	Bill Madlock	.10
124	Ken Caminiti	.10
125	Gary Ward	.10
126	Candy Maldonado	.10
127	Harold Reynolds	.10
128	Joe Magrane	.10
129	Mike Henneman	.10
130	Jim Gantner	.10
131	Bobby Bonilla	.10
132	John Farrell	.10
133	Frank Tanana	.10
134	Zane Smith	.10
135	Dave Righetti	.10
136	Rick Reuschel	.10
137	Dwight Evans	.10
138	Howard Johnson	.10
139	Terry Leach	.10
140	Casey Candaele	.10
141	Tom Herr	.10
142	Tony Pena	.10
143	Lance Parrish	.10
144	Ellis Burks	.10
145	Pete O'Brien	.10
146	Mike Boddicker	.10
147	Buddy Bell	.10
148	Bo Jackson	.15
149	Frank White	.10
150	George Brett	1.25
151	Tim Wallach	.10
152	Cal Ripken, Jr.	2.00
153	Brett Butler	.10
154	Gary Gaetti	.10
155	Darryl Strawberry	.10
156	Alfredo Griffin	.10
157	Marty Barrett	.10
158	Jim Rice	.25
159	Terry Pendleton	.10
160	Orel Hershiser	.10
161	Larry Sheets	.10
162	Dave Stewart	.10
163	Shawon Dunston	.10
164	Keith Moreland	.10
165	Ken Oberkfell	.10
166	Ivan Calderon	.10
167	Bob Welch	.10
168	Fred McGriff	.10
169	Pete Incaviglia	.10
170	Dale Murphy	.25
171	Mike Dunne	.10

172 Chili Davis .10
173 Milt Thompson .10
174 Terry Steinbach .10
175 Oddibe McDowell .10
176 Jack Morris .10
177 Sid Fernandez .10
178 Ken Griffey .10
179 Lee Smith .10
180 1987 Highlights (Juan Nieves, Kirby Puckett, Mike Schmidt) .25
181 Brian Downing .10
182 Andres Galarraga .10
183 Rob Deer .10
184 Greg Brock .10
185 Doug DeCinces .10
186 Johnny Ray .10
187 Hubie Brooks .10
188 Darrell Evans .10
189 Mel Hall .10
190 Jim Deshaies .10
191 Dan Plesac .10
192 Willie Wilson .10
193 Mike LaValliere .10
194 Tom Brunansky .10
195 John Franco .10
196 Frank Viola .10
197 Bruce Hurst .10
198 John Tudor .10
199 Bob Forsch .10
200 Dwight Gooden .10
201 Jose Canseco .65
202 Carney Lansford .10
203 Kelly Downs .10
204 Glenn Wilson .10
205 Pat Tabler .10
206 Mike Davis .10
207 Roger Clemens 1.25
208 Dave Smith .10
209 Curt Young .10
210 Mark Eichhorn .10
211 Juan Nieves .10
212 Bob Boone .10
213 Don Sutton .50
214 Willie Upshaw .10
215 Jim Clancy .10
216 Bill Ripken .10
217 Ozzie Virgil .10
218 Dave Concepcion .10
219 Alan Ashby .10
220 Mike Marshall .10
221 '87 Highlights (Vince Coleman, Mark McGwire, Paul Molitor) .75
222 '87 Highlights (Steve Bedrosian, Don Mattingly, Benito Santiago) .40
223 Hot Rookie Prospects (Shawn Abner, Jay Buhner **RC**, Gary Thurman) .25
224 Hot Rookie Prospects (Tim Crews, John Davis, Vincente Palacios) .10
225 Hot Rookie Prospects (Keith Miller, Jody Reed, Jeff Treadway) .10

Gamewinners

This set of 25 standard-size cards (2-1/2" x 3-1/2"), featuring star players in the Sportflics patented 3-D Magic Motion design, was issued by Weiser Card Co. of Plainsboro, N.J., for use as a youth organizational fundraiser. (Weiser's president was former Yankees outfielder Bobby Murcer.) A limited number of sets was produced for test marketing in the Northwestern U.S., with plans for a 1989 set to be marketed nationwide. A green-and-yellow Gamewinners logo banner spans the upper border of the cards face, with a matching player name (with uniform number and position) below the full-color triple photo. The card backs carry large full-color player photos along with stats, personal information and career highlights.

NM/M
Complete Set (25): 7.50
Common Player: .25
1 Don Mattingly 1.50
2 Mark McGwire 3.50
3 Wade Boggs 1.25
4 Will Clark .25
5 Eric Davis .25
6 Willie Randolph .25
7 Dave Winfield .75
8 Rickey Henderson .75
9 Dwight Gooden .25
10 Benny Santiago .25
11 Keith Hernandez .25
12 Juan Samuel .25
13 Kevin Seitzer .25
14 Gary Carter .75
15 Darryl Strawberry .25
16 Rick Rhoden .25
17 Howard Johnson .25
18 Matt Nokes .25
19 Dave Righetti .25
20 Roger Clemens 1.50
21 Mike Schmidt 1.50
22 Kevin McReynolds .25
23 Mike Pagliarulo .25
24 Kevin Elster .25
25 Jack Clark .25

1989 Sportflics

This basic issue includes 225 standard-size player cards (2-1/2" x 3-1/2") and 153 trivia cards, all featuring the patented Magic Motion design. A five-card sub-set of "Tri-Star" cards features a mix of veterans and rookies. The card fronts feature a white outer border and double color inner border in one of six color schemes. The inner border color changes when the card is tilted and the bottom border carries a double stripe of colors. The player name appears in the top border, player position and uniform number appear, alternately, in the bottom border. The card backs contain crisp 1-7/8" by 1-3/4" player action shots, along with personal information, stats and career highlights. "The Unforgettables" trivia cards in this set salute members of the Hall of Fame.

NM/M
Factory Set (225+153): 17.50
Complete Set (225): 12.00
Common Player: .10
Foil Pack (3+2): .50
Foil Box (36): 10.00
1 Jose Canseco .60
2 Wally Joyner .10
3 Roger Clemens 1.25
4 Greg Swindell .10
5 Jack Morris .10
6 Mickey Brantley .10
7 Jim Presley .10
8 Pete O'Brien .10
9 Jesse Barfield .10
10 Frank Viola .10
11 Kevin Bass .10
12 Glenn Wilson .10
13 Chris Sabo .10
14 Fred McGriff .10
15 Mark Grace .20
16 Devon White .10
17 Juan Samuel .10
18 Lou Whitaker .10
19 Greg Walker .10
20 Roberto Alomar .20
21 Mike Schmidt 1.25
22 Benny Santiago .10
23 Dave Stewart .10
24 Dave Winfield .75
25 George Bell .10
26 Jack Clark .10
27 Doug Drabek .10
28 Ron Gant .10
29 Glenn Braggs .10
30 Rafael Palmeiro .65
31 Brett Butler .10
32 Ron Darling .10
33 Alvin Davis .10
34 Bob Walk .10
35 Dave Stieb .10
36 Orel Hershiser .10
37 John Farrell .10
38 Doug Jones .10
39 Kelly Downs .10
40 Bob Boone .10
41 Gary Sheffield .35
42 Doug Dascenzo .10
43 Chad Krueter .10
44 Ricky Jordan .10
45 Dave West .10
46 Danny Tartabull .10
47 Teddy Higuera .10
48 Gary Gaetti .10
49 Dave Parker .10
50 Don Mattingly 1.25
51 David Cone .10
52 Kal Daniels .10
53 Carney Lansford .10
54 Mike Marshall .10
55 Kevin Seitzer .10
56 Mike Henneman .10
57 Bill Doran .10
58 Steve Sax .10
59 Lance Parrish .10
60 Keith Hernandez .10
61 Jose Uribe .10
62 Jose Lind .10
63 Steve Bedrosian .10
64 George Brett 1.25
65 Kirk Gibson .10
66 Cal Ripken, Jr. 2.00
67 Mitch Webster .10
68 Fred Lynn .10
69 Eric Davis .10
70 Bo Jackson .15
71 Kevin Elster .10
72 Rick Reuschel .10
73 Tim Burke .10
74 Mark Davis .10
75 Claudell Washington .10
76 Lance McCullers .10
77 Mike Moore .10
78 Robby Thompson .10
79 Roger McDowell .10
80 Danny Jackson .10
81 Tim Leary .10
82 Bobby Witt .10
83 Jim Gott .10
84 Andy Hawkins .10
85 Ozzie Guillen .10
86 John Tudor .10
87 Todd Burns .10
88 Dave Gallagher .10
89 Jay Buhner .10
90 Gregg Jefferies .10
91 Bob Welch .10
92 Charlie Hough .10
93 Tony Fernandez .10
94 Ozzie Virgil .10
95 Andre Dawson .25
96 Hubie Brooks .10
97 Kevin McReynolds .10
98 Mike LaValliere .10
99 Terry Pendleton .10
100 Wade Boggs 1.00
101 Dennis Eckersley .65
102 Mark Gubicza .10
103 Frank Tanana .10
104 Joe Carter .10
105 Ozzie Smith 1.00
106 Dennis Martinez .10
107 Jeff Treadway .10
108 Greg Maddux 1.00
109 Bret Saberhagen .10
110 Dale Murphy .20
111 Rob Deer .10
112 Pete Incaviglia .10
113 Vince Coleman .10
114 Tim Wallach .10
115 Nolan Ryan 2.00
116 Walt Weiss .10
117 Brian Downing .10
118 Melido Perez .10
119 Terry Steinbach .10
120 Mike Scott .10
121 Tim Belcher .10
122 Mike Boddicker .10
123 Len Dykstra .10
124 Fernando Valenzuela .10
125 Gerald Young .10
126 Tom Henke .10
127 Dave Henderson .10
128 Dan Plesac .10
129 Chili Davis .10
130 Bryan Harvey .10
131 Don August .10
132 Mike Harkey .10
133 Luis Polonia .10
134 Craig Worthington .10
135 Joey Meyer .10
136 Barry Larkin .10
137 Glenn Davis .10
138 Mike Scioscia .10
139 Andres Galarraga .10
140 Doc Gooden .10
141 Keith Moreland .10
142 Kevin Mitchell .10
143 Mike Greenwell .10
144 Mel Hall .10
145 Rickey Henderson .75
146 Barry Bonds 2.00
147 Eddie Murray .75
148 Lee Smith .10
149 Julio Franco .10
150 Tim Raines .10
151 Mitch Williams .10
152 Tim Laudner .10
153 Mike Pagliarulo .10
154 Floyd Bannister .10
155 Gary Carter .75
156 Kirby Puckett 1.00
157 Harold Baines .10
158 Dave Righetti .10
159 Mark Langston .10
160 Tony Gwynn 1.00
161 Tom Brunansky .10
162 Vance Law .10
163 Kelly Gruber .10
164 Gerald Perry .10
165 Harold Reynolds .10
166 Andy Van Slyke .10
167 Jimmy Key .10
168 Jeff Reardon .10
169 Milt Thompson .10
170 Will Clark .10
171 Chet Lemon .10
172 Pat Tabler .10
173 Jim Rice .25
174 Billy Hatcher .10
175 Bruce Hurst .10
176 John Franco .10
177 Van Snider .10
178 Ron Jones .10
179 Jerald Clark .10
180 Tom Browning .10
181 Von Hayes .10
182 Bobby Bonilla .10
183 Todd Worrell .10
184 John Kruk .10
185 Scott Fletcher .10
186 Willie Wilson .10
187 Jody Davis .10
188 Kent Hrbek .10
189 Ruben Sierra .10
190 Shawon Dunston .10
191 Ellis Burks .10
192 Brook Jacoby .10
193 Jeff Robinson .10
194 Rich Dotson .10
195 Johnny Ray .10
196 Cory Snyder .10
197 Mike Witt .10
198 Marty Barrett .10
199 Robin Yount .75
200 Mark McGwire 1.50
201 Ryne Sandberg 1.00
202 John Candelaria .10
203 Matt Nokes .10
204 Dwight Evans .10
205 Darryl Strawberry .10
206 Willie McGee .10
207 Bobby Thigpen .10
208 B.J. Surhoff .10
209 Paul Molitor .75
210 Jody Reed .10
211 Doyle Alexander .10
212 Dennis Rasmussen .10
213 Kevin Gross .10
214 Kirk McCaskill .10
215 Alan Trammell .10
216 Damon Berryhill .10
217 Rick Sutcliffe .10
218 Don Slaught .10
219 Carlton Fisk .75
220 Allan Anderson .10
221 '88 Highlights (Wade Boggs, Jose Canseco, Mike Greenwell) .15
222 '88 Highlights (Tom Browning, Dennis Eckersley, Orel Hershiser) .20
223 Hot Rookie Prospects (Sandy Alomar, Gregg Jefferies, Gary Sheffield) .50
224 Hot Rookie Prospects (Randy Johnson, Ramon Martinez, Bob Milacki) .75
225 Hot Rookie Prospects (Geronimo Berroa, Cameron Drew, Ron Jones) .10

1990 Sportflics

The Sportflics set for 1990 again contains 225 cards. The cards feature the unique "Magic Motion" effect which displays either of two different photos depending on how the card is tilted. (Previous years' sets had used three photos per card.) The two-photo "Magic Motion" sequence is designed to depict sequential game-action, showing a batter following through on his swing, a pitcher completing his motion, etc. Sportflics also added a moving red and yellow "marquee" border on the cards to complement the animation effect. The player's name, which appears below the animation, remains stationary. The set includes 19 special rookie cards. The backs contain a color player photo, team logo, player information and stats. The cards were distributed in non-transparent mylar packs with small MVP trivia cards.

NM/M
Factory Set (225+153): 15.00
Complete Set (225): 12.00
Common Player: .10
Foil Pack (3+2): .75
Foil Box (36): 20.00
1 Kevin Mitchell .10
2 Wade Boggs 1.00
3 Cory Snyder .10
4 Paul O'Neill .10
5 Will Clark .10
6 Tony Fernandez .10
7 Ken Griffey Jr. 1.50
8 Nolan Ryan 2.00
9 Rafael Palmeiro .65
10 Jesse Barfield .10
11 Kirby Puckett 1.00
12 Steve Sax .10
13 Fred McGriff .10
14 Gregg Jefferies .10
15 Mark Grace .10
16 Devon White .10
17 Juan Samuel .10
18 Robin Yount .75
19 Glenn Davis .10
20 Jeffrey Leonard .10
21 Chili Davis .10
22 Craig Biggio .10
23 Jose Canseco .50
24 Derek Lilliquist .10
25 Chris Bosio .10
26 Dave Steib .10
27 Bobby Thigpen .10
28 Jack Clark .10
29 Kevin Ritz .10
30 Tom Gordon .10
31 Bryan Harvey .10
32 Jim Deshaies .10
33 Terry Steinbach .10
34 Tom Glavine .35
35 Bob Welch .10
36 Charlie Hayes .10
37 Jeff Reardon .10
38 Joe Orsulak .10
39 Scott Garrelts .10
40 Bob Boone .10
41 Scott Bankhead .10
42 Tom Henke .10
43 Greg Briley .10
44 Teddy Higuera .10
45 Pat Borders .10
46 Kevin Seitzer .10
47 Bruce Hurst .10
48 Ozzie Guillen .10
49 Wally Joyner .10
50 Mike Greenwell .10
51 Gary Gaetti .10
52 Gary Sheffield .30
53 Dennis Martinez .10
54 Ryne Sandberg 1.00
55 Mike Scott .10
56 Todd Benzinger .10
57 Kelly Gruber .10
58 Jose Lind .10
59 Allan Anderson .10
60 Robby Thompson .10
61 John Smoltz .10
62 Mark Davis .10
63 Tom Herr .10
64 Randy Johnson .75
65 Lonnie Smith .10
66 Pedro Guerrero .10
67 Jerome Walton .10
68 Ramon Martinez .10
69 Tim Raines .10
70 Matt Williams .10
71 Joe Oliver .10
72 Nick Esasky .10
73 Kevin Brown .10
74 Walt Weiss .10
75 Roger McDowell .10
76 Jose DeLeon .10
77 Brian Downing .10
78 Jay Howell .10
79 Jose Uribe .10
80 Ellis Burks .10
81 Sammy Sosa 7.50
82 Johnny Ray .10
83 Danny Darwin .10
84 Carney Lansford .10
85 Jose Oquendo .10
86 John Cerutti .10
87 Dave Winfield .75
88 Dave Righetti .10
89 Danny Jackson .10
90 Andy Benes .10
91 Tom Browning .10
92 Pete O'Brien .10
93 Roberto Alomar .20
94 Bret Saberhagen .10
95 Phil Bradley .10
96 Doug Jones .10
97 Eric Davis .10
98 Tony Gwynn 1.00
99 Jim Abbott .10
100 Cal Ripken, Jr. 2.00
101 Andy Van Slyke .10
102 Dan Plesac .10
103 Lou Whitaker .10
104 Steve Bedrosian .10
105 Dave Gallagher .10
106 Keith Hernandez .10
107 Duane Ward .10
108 Andre Dawson .35
109 Howard Johnson .10
110 Mark Langston .10
111 Jerry Browne .10
112 Alvin Davis .10
113 Sid Fernandez .10
114 Mike Devereaux .10
115 Benny Santiago .10
116 Bip Roberts .10
117 Craig Worthington .10
118 Kevin Elster .10
119 Harold Reynolds .10
120 Joe Carter .10
121 Brian Harper .10
122 Frank Viola .10
123 Jeff Ballard .10
124 John Kruk .10
125 Harold Baines .10
126 Tom Candiotti .10
127 Kevin McReynolds .10
128 Mookie Wilson .10
129 Danny Tartabull .10
130 Craig Lefferts .10
131 Jose DeJesus .10
132 John Orton .10
133 Curt Schilling .35
134 Marquis Grissom .10
135 Greg Vaughn .10
136 Brett Butler .10
137 Rob Deer .10
138 John Franco .10
139 Keith Moreland .10
140 Dave Smith .10
141 Mark McGwire 1.50
142 Vince Coleman .10
143 Barry Bonds 2.00
144 Mike Henneman .10
145 Doc Gooden .10
146 Darryl Strawberry .10
147 Von Hayes .10
148 Andres Galarraga .10
149 Roger Clemens 1.25
150 Don Mattingly 1.25
151 Joe Magrane .10
152 Dwight Smith .10
153 Ricky Jordan .10
154 Alan Trammell .10
155 Brook Jacoby .10
156 Lenny Dykstra .10
157 Mike LaValliere .10
158 Julio Franco .10
159 Joey Belle .25
160 Barry Larkin .10
161 Rick Reuschel .10
162 Nelson Santovenia .10
163 Mike Scioscia .10
164 Damon Berryhill .10
165 Todd Worrell .10
166 Jim Eisenreich .10
167 Ivan Calderon .10
168 Goose Gozzo .10
169 Kirk McCaskill .10
170 Dennis Eckersley .65
171 Mickey Tettleton .10
172 Chuck Finley .10
173 Dave Magadan .10
174 Terry Pendleton .10
175 Willie Randolph .10
176 Jeff Huson .10
177 Todd Zeile .10
178 Steve Olin .10
179 Eric Anthony .10
180 Scott Coolbaugh .10
181 Rick Sutcliffe .10
182 Tim Wallach .10
183 Paul Molitor .75
184 Roberto Kelly .10
185 Mike Moore .10
186 Junior Felix .10
187 Mike Schooler .10
188 Ruben Sierra .10
189 Dale Murphy .30
190 Dan Gladden .10
191 John Smiley .10
192 Jeff Russell .10
193 Bert Blyleven .10
194 Dave Stewart .10

195 Bobby Bonilla .10
196 Mitch Williams .10
197 Orel Hershiser .10
198 Kevin Bass .10
199 Tim Burke .10
200 Bo Jackson .15
201 David Cone .10
202 Gary Pettis .10
203 Kent Hrbek .10
204 Carlton Fisk .75
205 Bob Geren .10
206 Bill Spiers .10
207 Oddibe McDowell .10
208 Rickey Henderson .75
209 Ken Caminiti .10
210 Devon White .10
211 Greg Maddux 1.00
212 Ed Whitson .10
213 Carlos Martinez .10
214 George Brett 1.25
215 Gregg Olson .10
216 Kenny Rogers .10
217 Dwight Evans .10
218 Pat Tabler .10
219 Jeff Treadway .10
220 Scott Fletcher .10
221 Deion Sanders .15
222 Robin Ventura .10
223 Chip Hale .10
224 Tommy Greene .10
225 Dean Palmer .10

1994 Sportflics 2000 Promos

To reintroduce its "Magic Motion" baseball cards to the hobby (last produced by Score in 1990), Pinnacle Brands produced a three-card promo set which it sent to dealers along with a header card explaining the issue. In the same format as the regular issue, though some different photos were used, the promos feature on front what Sportflics calls "state-of-the-art lenticular technology" to create an action effect when the card is moved. Backs are produced by standard printing techniques and are gold-foil highlighted and UV-coated. Each of the promo cards has a large black "SAMPLE" overprinted diagonally across front and back.

NM/M

Complete Set (4): 5.00
Common Player: 1.00
1a Lenny Dykstra ("SAMPLE" front only.) 1.00
1b Lenny Dykstra ("SAMPLE" back and front.) 1.00
7 Javy Lopez (Shakers) 1.00
193 Greg Maddux (Starflics) 3.00
Header Card .25

1994 Sportflics 2000

The concept of "Magic Motion" baseball cards returned to the hobby in 1994 after a three-year hiatus. Pinnacle refined its "state-of-the-art lenticular technology" to produce cards which show alternating pictures when viewed from different angles on the basic cards, and to create a striking 3-D effect on its "Starflics" A.L. and N.L. All-Star team subset. Backs are conventionally printed, UV-coated and gold-foil highlighted, featuring a player photo and recent stats. Cards were sold in eight-card foil packs with a suggested retail price of $2.49.

NM/M

Complete Set (193): 15.00
Common Player: .10
Pack (8): .50
Wax Box (36): 15.00
1 Len Dykstra .10
2 Mike Stanley .10
3 Alex Fernandez .10
4 Mark McGuire (McGwire) 1.50
5 Eric Karros .10
6 Dave Justice .10
7 Jeff Bagwell .65
8 Darren Lewis .10
9 David McCarty .10
10 Albert Belle .10
11 Ben McDonald .10
12 Joe Carter .10
13 Benito Santiago .10
14 Rob Dibble .10
15 Roger Clemens .85
16 Travis Fryman .10
17 Doug Drabek .10
18 Jay Buhner .10
19 Orlando Merced .10
20 Ryan Klesko .10
21 Chuck Finley .10
22 Dante Bichette .10
23 Wally Joyner .10
24 Robin Yount .65
25 Tony Gwynn .75
26 Allen Watson .10
27 Rick Wilkins .10
28 Gary Sheffield .40
29 John Burkett .10
30 Randy Johnson .65
31 Roberto Alomar .25
32 Fred McGriff .10
33 Ozzie Guillen .10
34 Jimmy Key .10
35 Juan Gonzalez .35
36 Wil Cordero .10
37 Aaron Sele .10
38 Mark Langston .10
39 David Cone .10
40 John Jaha .10
41 Ozzie Smith .75
42 Kirby Puckett .75
43 Kenny Lofton .10
44 Mike Mussina .40
45 Ryne Sandberg .75
46 Robby Thompson .10
47 Bryan Harvey .10
48 Marquis Grissom .10
49 Bobby Bonilla .10
50 Dennis Eckersley .60
51 Curt Schilling .35
52 Andy Benes .10
53 Greg Maddux .75
54 Bill Swift .10
55 Andres Galarraga .10
56 Tony Phillips .10
57 Darryl Hamilton .10
58 Duane Ward .10
59 Bernie Williams .10
60 Steve Avery .10
61 Eduardo Perez .10
62 Jeff Conine .10
63 Dave Winfield .65
64 Phil Plantier .10
65 Ray Lankford .10
66 Robin Ventura .10
67 Mike Piazza 1.00
68 Jason Bere .10
69 Cal Ripken, Jr. 2.00
70 Frank Thomas .65
71 Carlos Baerga .10
72 Darryl Kile .10
73 Ruben Sierra .10
74 Gregg Jefferies .10
75 John Olerud .10
76 Andy Van Slyke .10
77 Larry Walker .10
78 Cecil Fielder .10
79 Andre Dawson .25
80 Tom Glavine .35
81 Sammy Sosa .75
82 Charlie Hayes .10
83 Chuck Knoblauch .10
84 Kevin Appier .10
85 Dean Palmer .10
86 Royce Clayton .10
87 Moises Alou .10
88 Ivan Rodriguez .60
89 Tim Salmon .10
90 Ron Gant .10
91 Barry Bonds 2.00
92 Jack McDowell .10
93 Alan Trammell .10
94 Dwight Gooden .10
95 Jay Bell .10
96 Devon White .10
97 Wilson Alvarez .10
98 Jim Thome .60
99 Ramon Martinez .10
100 Kent Hrbek .10
101 John Kruk .10
102 Wade Boggs .75
103 Greg Vaughn .10
104 Tom Henke .10
105 Brian Jordan .10
106 Paul Molitor .65
107 Cal Eldred .10
108 Deion Sanders .10
109 Barry Larkin .10
110 Mike Greenwell .10
111 Jeff Blauser .10
112 Jose Rijo .10
113 Pete Harnisch .10
114 Chris Hoiles .10
115 Edgar Martinez .10
116 Juan Guzman .10
117 Todd Zeile .10
118 Danny Tartabull .10
119 Chad Curtis .10
120 Mark Grace .10
121 J.T. Snow .10
122 Mo Vaughn .10
123 Lance Johnson .10
124 Eric Davis .10
125 Orel Hershiser .10
126 Kevin Mitchell .10
127 Don Mattingly .85
128 Darren Daulton .10
129 Rod Beck .10
130 Charles Nagy .10
131 Mickey Tettleton .10
132 Kevin Brown .10
133 Pat Hentgen .10
134 Terry Mulholland .10
135 Steve Finley .10
136 John Smoltz .10
137 Frank Viola .10
138 Jim Abbott .10
139 Matt Williams .10
140 Bernard Gilkey .10
141 Jose Canseco .45
142 Mark Whiten .10
143 Ken Griffey Jr. 1.00
144 Rafael Palmeiro .60
145 Dave Hollins .10
146 Will Clark .10
147 Paul O'Neill .10
148 Bobby Jones .10
149 Butch Huskey .10
150 Jeffrey Hammonds .10
151 Manny Ramirez .65
152 Bob Hamelin .10
153 Kurt Abbott .10
154 Scott Stahoviak .10
155 Steve Hosey .10
156 Salomon Torres .10
157 Sterling Hitchcock .10
158 Nigel Wilson .10
159 Luis Lopez .10
160 Chipper Jones .75
161 Norberto Martin .10
162 Raul Mondesi .10
163 Steve Karsay .10
164 J.R. Phillips .10
165 Marc Newfield .10
166 Mark Hutton .10
167 Curtis Pride .10
168 Carl Everett .10
169 Scott Ruffcorn .10
170 Turk Wendell .10
171 Jeff McNeely .10
172 Javier Lopez .10
173 Cliff Floyd .10
174 Rondell White .10
175 Scott Lydy .10
176 Frank Thomas/AS .35
177 Roberto Alomar/AS .20
178 Travis Fryman/AS .10
179 Cal Ripken, Jr./AS 1.00
180 Chris Hoiles/AS .10
181 Ken Griffey Jr./AS .60
182 Juan Gonzalez/AS .20
183 Joe Carter/AS .10
184 Jack McDowell/AS .10
185 Fred McGriff/AS .10
186 Robby Thompson/AS .10
187 Matt Williams/AS .10
188 Jay Bell/AS .10
189 Mike Piazza/AS .60
190 Barry Bonds/AS 1.00
191 Len Dykstra/AS .10
192 Dave Justice/AS .10
193 Greg Maddux/AS .45

Commemoratives

A pair of extra-rare commemorative chase cards was produced for the Sportflics 2000 set honoring Canada's veteran superstar Paul Molitor and its hottest rookie, Cliff Floyd. Cards, utilizing Magic Motion technology to alternate card-front pictures when the viewing angle changes, were inserted on average once in every 360 packs.

NM/M

Complete Set (2): 5.00
1 Paul Molitor 4.50
2 Cliff Floyd 1.25

Movers

A dozen top veteran ballplayers were featured in the "Movers" insert set produced for inclusion in retail packaging of Sportflics 2000. The inserts feature the same Magic Motion features as the regular cards, showing different images on the card front when the card is viewed from different angles. The UV-coated, gold-foil highlighted backs are printed conventionally. A special "Movers" logo is found on both front and back. Stated odds of finding a Movers card are one in 24 packs.

NM/M

Complete Set (12): 12.00
Common Player: .60
1 Gregg Jefferies .60
2 Ryne Sandberg 2.00
3 Cecil Fielder .60
4 Kirby Puckett 2.00
5 Tony Gwynn 2.00
6 Andres Galarraga .60
7 Sammy Sosa 2.00
8 Rickey Henderson 1.00
9 Don Mattingly 2.50
10 Joe Carter .60
11 Carlos Baerga .60
12 Len Dykstra .60

Shakers

Hobby packs are the exclusive source for this 12-card insert set of top rookies, found on average once every 24 packs. The chase cards utilize the Sportflics Magic Motion technology to create two different images on the card front when the card is viewed from different angles. Backs are printed conventionally but feature UV-coating and gold-foil highlights. The "Shakers" logo appears on both front and back.

NM/M

Complete Set (12): 12.00
Common Player: .60
1 Kenny Lofton .60
2 Tim Salmon .60
3 Jeff Bagwell 2.50
4 Jason Bere .60
5 Salomon Torres .60
6 Rondell White .60
7 Javier Lopez .60
8 Dean Palmer .60
9 Jim Thome 2.00
10 J.T. Snow .60
11 Mike Piazza 4.00
12 Manny Ramirez 2.50

1994 Sportflics 2000 Rookie/ Traded Promos

This nine-card set was issued to promote the Sportflics Rookie/Traded update set which was released as a hobby-only product. Cards are virtually identical to the corresponding cards in the R/T set except for the overprinted "SAMPLE" in white on front and back.

NM/M

Complete Set (9): 5.00
Common Player: 1.00
1 Will Clark 1.00
14 Bret Boone 1.00
20 Ellis Burks 1.00
25 Deion Sanders 1.00
62 Chris Turner 1.00
82 Tony Tarasco 1.00
102 Rich Becker 1.00
GG1 Gary Sheffield (Going, Going, Gone) 2.00
--- Header Card .25

1994 Sportflics 2000 Rookie/ Traded

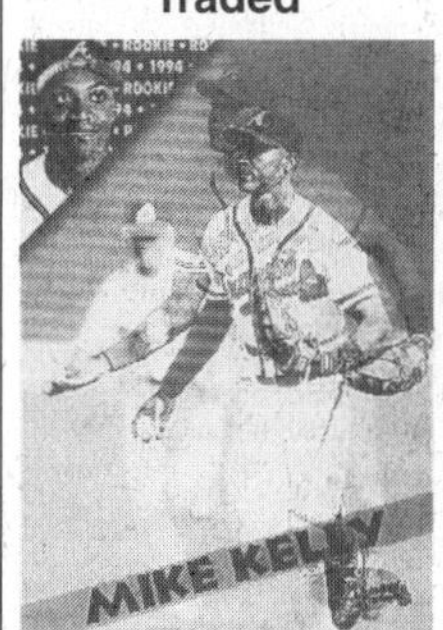

Each of the 150 regular cards in the Sportflics 2000 Rookie & Traded issue was also produced in a parallel chase card set designated on front with a black and gold "Artist's Proof" logo. Stated odds of finding an AP cards were one per 24 packs. Fewer than 1,000 or each AP card were reportedly produced.

NM/M

Complete Set (150): 20.00
Common Player: .10
Pack (5): 3.00
Wax Box (24): 60.00
1 Will Clark .10
2 Sid Fernandez .10
3 Joe Magrane .10
4 Pete Smith .10
5 Roberto Kelly .10
6 Delino DeShields .10
7 Brian Harper .10
8 Darrin Jackson .10
9 Omar Vizquel .10
10 Luis Polonia .10
11 Reggie Jefferson .10
12 Geronimo Berroa .10
13 Mike Harkey .10
14 Bret Boone .10
15 Dave Henderson .10
16 Pedro Martinez .75
17 Jose Vizcaino .10
18 Xavier Hernandez .10
19 Eddie Taubensee .10
20 Ellis Burks .10
21 Turner Ward .10
22 Terry Mulholland .10
23 Howard Johnson .10
24 Vince Coleman .10
25 Deion Sanders .10
26 Rafael Palmeiro .65
27 Dave Weathers .10
28 Kent Mercker .10
29 Gregg Olson .10
30 Cory Bailey .10
31 Brian Hunter .10
32 Garey Ingram .10
33 Daniel Smith .10
34 Denny Hocking .10
35 Charles Johnson .10
36 Otis Nixon .10
37 Hector Fajardo .10
38 Lee Smith .10
39 Phil Stidham .10
40 Melvin Nieves .10
41 Julio Franco .10
42 Greg Gohr .10
43 Steve Dunn .10
44 Tony Fernandez .10
45 Toby Borland .10
46 Paul Shuey .10
47 Shawn Hare .10
48 Shawn Green .50
49 Julian Tavarez **RC** .10
50 Ernie Young .10
51 Chris Sabo .10
52 Greg O'Halloran .10
53 Donnie Elliott .10
54 Jim Converse .10
55 Ray Holbert .10
56 Keith Lockhart .10
57 Tony Longmire .10
58 Jorge Fabregas .10
59 Ravelo Manzanillo .10
60 Marcus Moore .10
61 Carlos Rodriguez .10
62 Mark Portugal .10
63 Yorkis Perez .10
64 Dan Miceli .10
65 Chris Turner .10
66 Mike Oquist .10
67 Tom Quinlan .10
68 Matt Walbeck .10
69 Dave Staton .10
70 Bill Van Landingham **RC** .10
71 Dave Stevens .10
72 Domingo Cedeno .10
73 Alex Diaz .10
74 Darren Bragg .10
75 James Hurst .10
76 Alex Gonzalez .10
77 Steve Dreyer .10
78 Robert Eenhoorn .10
79 Derek Parks .10
80 Jose Valentin .10
81 Wes Chamberlain .10
82 Tony Tarasco .10
83 Steve Trachsel .10
84 Willie Banks .10
85 Rob Butler .10
86 Miguel Jimenez .10
87 Gerald Williams .10
88 Aaron Small .10
89 Matt Mieske .10
90 Tim Hyers .10
91 Eddie Murray .75
92 Dennis Martinez .10
93 Tony Eusebio .10
94 Brian Anderson **RC** .25
95 Blaise Ilsley .10
96 Johnny Ruffin .10
97 Carlos Reyes .10
98 Greg Pirkl .10
99 Jack Morris .10
100 John Mabry .10
101 Mike Kelly .10
102 Rich Becker .10
103 Chris Gomez .10
104 Jim Edmonds .10
105 Rich Rowland .10
106 Damon Buford .10
107 Mark Kiefer .10
108 Matias Carrillo .10
109 James Mouton .10
110 Kelly Stinnett .10
111 Billy Ashley .10
112 Fausto Cruz **RC** .10
113 Roberto Petagine .10
114 Joe Hall .10
115 Brian Johnson **RC** .10
116 Kevin Jarvis .10
117 Tim Davis .10
118 John Patterson .10
119 Stan Royer .10
120 Jeff Juden .10
121 Bryan Eversgerd .10
122 Chan Ho Park **RC** 1.00
123 Shane Reynolds .10
124 Danny Bautista .10
125 Rikkert Faneyte .10
126 Carlos Pulido .10
127 Mike Matheny .10
128 Hector Carrasco .10
129 Eddie Zambrano .10
130 Lee Tinsley .10
131 Roger Salkeld .10
132 Carlos Delgado 1.00
133 Troy O'Leary .10
134 Keith Mitchell .10
135 Lance Painter .10
136 Nate Minchey .10
137 Eric Anthony .10
138 Rafael Bournigal .10
139 Joey Hamilton .10
140 Bobby Munoz .10
141 Rex Hudler .10

142	Alex Cole	.10
143	Stan Javier	.10
144	Jose Oliva	.10
145	Tom Brunansky	.10
146	Greg Colbrunn	.10
147	Luis Lopez	.10
148	Alex Rodriguez **RC**	10.00
149	Darryl Strawberry	.10
150	Bo Jackson	.15

Artist's Proof

Each of the 150 regular cards in the Sportflics 2000 Rookie & Traded issue was also produced in a parallel chase set designated on front with a black and gold "Artist's Proof" logo. Stated odds of finding an AP card were one per 24 packs. Fewer than 1,000 of each AP card were reportedly produced.

	NM/M
Complete Set (150):	300.00
Common Player:	1.00
Stars:	25X
148 Alex Rodriguez:	

Going, Going, Gone

A dozen of the game's top home run hitters are featured in this insert set. On front, simulated 3-D action photos depict the player's swing for the fences. Backs have a portrait photo and information about the player's home run prowess. A crossed bats and "Going, Going Gone" logo appear on both front and back. Cards are numbered with a "GG" prefix. Stated odds of finding one of these inserts were once in 18 packs.

		NM/M
Complete Set (12):		10.00
Common Player:		.50
1	Gary Sheffield	.75
2	Matt Williams	.50
3	Juan Gonzalez	.90
4	Ken Griffey Jr.	2.00
5	Mike Piazza	2.00
6	Frank Thomas	1.50
7	Tim Salmon	.50
8	Barry Bonds	3.00
9	Fred McGriff	.50
10	Cecil Fielder	.50
11	Albert Belle	.50
12	Joe Carter	.50

Rookies of the Year

Sportflics' choices for Rookies of the Year were featured on this one-card insert set. Ryan Klesko (National League) and Manny Ramirez (American League) are shown on the card when viewed from different angles. Sportflics

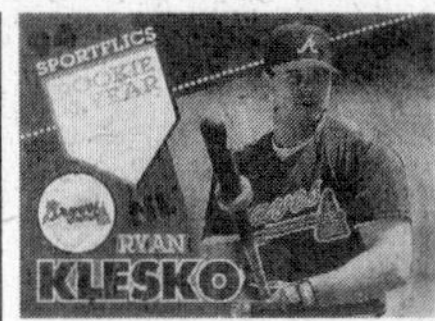

batted .000 in their guesses, however, as Raul Mondesi and Bob Hamelin were the actual R.O.Y. selections. This card was inserted at the average rate of once per 360 packs.

		NM/M
Complete Set (1):		
R01	Ryan Klesko, Manny Ramirez	3.00

3-D Rookies

Eighteen of 1994's premier rookies are featured in this insert set. Combining a 3-D look and Sportflics' "Magic Motion" technology, the horizontal-format Starflics rookie cards present a striking appearance. Backs feature a full-bleed color photo overprinted with gold foil. A notice on back gives the production run of the chase cards as "No more than 5,000 sets." Stated odds of finding a Starflics Rookie card were given as one per 36 packs. Cards are numbered with a "TR" prefix.

		NM/M
Complete Set (18):		65.00
Common Player:		2.00
1	John Hudek	2.00
2	Manny Ramirez	15.00
3	Jeffrey Hammonds	2.00
4	Carlos Delgado	7.50
5	Javier Lopez	2.00
6	Alex Gonzalez	2.00
7	Raul Mondesi	2.00
8	Bob Hamelin	2.00
9	Ryan Klesko	2.00
10	Brian Anderson	2.00
11	Alex Rodriguez	40.00
12	Cliff Floyd	2.00
13	Chan Ho Park	2.00
14	Steve Karsay	2.00
15	Rondell White	2.00
16	Shawn Green	6.00
17	Rich Becker	2.00
18	Charles Johnson	2.00

FanFest All-Stars

An American and a National League player at each position share the fronts of these "Magic Motion" cards. Cards were available by redeeming coupons acquired at various locations around the Pittsburgh All-Star FanFest celebration in July, 1994. Action photos of the players alternate on the fronts of the cards when the viewing angle is changed. The N.L. player's name appears at upper-left; the A.L. All-Star at lower-right. Backs have portrait photos of the players and a few stats and comments. The players' names, teams, position and card number are printed in gold foil, along with the notation "1 of 10,000." Cards are numbered with an "AS" prefix.

		NM/M
Complete Set (9):		25.00
Common Card:		2.50
1	Fred McGriff, Frank Thomas	3.00
2	Ryne Sandberg, Roberto Alomar	3.50
3	Matt Williams, Travis Fryman	2.50
4	Ozzie Smith, Cal Ripken Jr.	5.00
5	Mike Piazza, Ivan Rodriguez	4.00
6	Barry Bonds, Juan Gonzalez	5.00
7	Len Dykstra, Ken Griffey Jr.	4.00
8	Gary Sheffield, Kirby Puckett	3.50
9	Greg Maddux, Mike Mussina	3.50

1995 Sportflix Samples

This nine-card promo pack was sent to Pinnacle's dealer network to introduce its revamped (new logo, spelling) magic-motion card set for 1995. The sample cards are identical in format to the regular-issue Sportflix cards except that a large white "SAMPLE" is printed diagonally on front and back of the promos.

		NM/M
Complete Set (9):		20.00
Common Player:		2.00
3	Fred McGriff	2.00
20	Frank Thomas	3.50
105	Manny Ramirez	3.00
122	Cal Ripken Jr.	5.00
128	Roberto Alomar	2.25
152	Russ Davis (Rookie)	2.00
162	Chipper Jones (Rookie)	4.00
DE2	Matt Williams (Detonators)	2.00
----	Advertising Card	.10

1995 Sportflix

With only 170 cards in the set, only the biggest stars and hottest rookies (25 of them in a specially designed subset) are included in this simulated 3-D issue. Fronts feature two borderless action photos which are alternately visible as the card's viewing angle is changed. Backs are conventionally printed and have a portrait photo, a few career stats and a couple of sentences about the player. The basic packaging options for '95 Sportflix were five- and eight card foils at $1.89 and $2.99, respectively.

		NM/M
Complete Set (170):		13.50
Common Player:		.10
Artist's Proofs:		12X
Pack (5):		1.50
Wax Box (36):		30.00
1	Ken Griffey Jr.	1.25
2	Jeffrey Hammonds	.10
3	Fred McGriff	.10
4	Rickey Henderson	.75
5	Derrick May	.10
6	Robin Ventura	.10
7	Royce Clayton	.10
8	Paul Molitor	.75
9	Charlie Hayes	.10
10	David Nied	.10
11	Ellis Burks	.10
12	Bernard Gilkey	.10
13	Don Mattingly	1.00
14	Albert Belle	.10
15	Doug Drabek	.10
16	Tony Gwynn	1.00
17	Delino DeShields	.10
18	Bobby Bonilla	.10
19	Cliff Floyd	.10
20	Frank Thomas	.75
21	Raul Mondesi	.10
22	Dave Nilsson	.10
23	Todd Zeile	.10
24	Bernie Williams	.10
25	Kirby Puckett	1.00
26	David Cone	.10
27	Darren Daulton	.10
28	Marquis Grissom	.10
29	Randy Johnson	.75
30	Jeff Kent	.10
31	Orlando Merced	.10
32	Dave Justice	.10
33	Ivan Rodriguez	.65
34	Kirk Gibson	.10
35	Alex Fernandez	.10
36	Rick Wilkins	.10
37	Andy Benes	.10
38	Bret Saberhagen	.10
39	Billy Ashley	.10
40	Jose Rijo	.10
41	Matt Williams	.10
42	Lenny Dykstra	.10
43	Jay Bell	.10
44	Reggie Jefferson	.10
45	Greg Maddux	1.00
46	Gary Sheffield	.35
47	Bret Boone	.10
48	Jeff Bagwell	.75
49	Ben McDonald	.10
50	Eric Karros	.10
51	Roger Clemens	1.00
52	Sammy Sosa	1.00
53	Barry Bonds	2.00
54	Joey Hamilton	.10
55	Brian Jordan	.10
56	Wil Cordero	.10
57	Aaron Sele	.10
58	Paul O'Neill	.10
59	Carlos Garcia	.10
60	Mike Mussina	.40
61	John Olerud	.10
62	Kevin Appier	.10
63	Matt Mieske	.10
64	Carlos Baerga	.10
65	Ryan Klesko	.10
66	Jimmy Key	.10
67	James Mouton	.10
68	Tim Salmon	.10
69	Hal Morris	.10
70	Albie Lopez	.10
71	Dave Hollins	.10
72	Greg Colbrunn	.10
73	Juan Gonzalez	.40
74	Wally Joyner	.10
75	Bob Hamelin	.10
76	Brady Anderson	.10
77	Deion Sanders	.10
78	Javier Lopez	.10
79	Brian McRae	.10
80	Craig Biggio	.10
81	Kenny Lofton	.10
82	Cecil Fielder	.10
83	Mike Piazza	1.25
84	Rafael Palmeiro	.65
85	Jim Thome	.65
86	Ruben Sierra	.10
87	Mark Langston	.10
88	John Valentin	.10
89	Shawon Dunston	.10
90	Travis Fryman	.10
91	Chuck Knoblauch	.10
92	Dean Palmer	.10
93	Robby Thompson	.10
94	Barry Larkin	.10
95	Darren Lewis	.10
96	Andres Galarraga	.10
97	Tony Phillips	.10
98	Mo Vaughn	.10
99	Pedro Martinez	.75
100	Chad Curtis	.10
101	Brent Gates	.10
102	Pat Hentgen	.10
103	Rico Brogna	.10
104	Carlos Delgado	.50
105	Manny Ramirez	.75
106	Mike Greenwell	.10
107	Wade Boggs	1.00
108	Ozzie Smith	1.00
109	Rusty Greer	.10
110	Willie Greene	.10
111	Chili Davis	.10
112	Reggie Sanders	.10
113	Roberto Kelly	.10
114	Tom Glavine	.35
115	Moises Alou	.10
116	Dennis Eckersley	.65
117	Danny Tartabull	.10
118	Jeff Conine	.10
119	Will Clark	.10
120	Joe Carter	.10
121	Mark McGwire	1.50
122	Cal Ripken Jr.	2.00
123	Danny Jackson	.10
124	Phil Plantier	.10
125	Dante Bichette	.10
126	Jack McDowell	.10
127	Jose Canseco	.40
128	Roberto Alomar	.20
129	Rondell White	.10
130	Ray Lankford	.10
131	Ryan Thompson	.10
132	Ken Caminiti	.10
133	Gregg Jefferies	.10
134	Omar Vizquel	.10
135	Mark Grace	.10
136	Derek Bell	.10
137	Mickey Tettleton	.10
138	Wilson Alvarez	.10
139	Larry Walker	.10
140	Bo Jackson	.15
141	Alex Rodriguez	1.50
142	Orlando Miller	.10
143	Shawn Green	.35
144	Steve Dunn	.10
145	Midre Cummings	.10
146	Chan Ho Park	.10
147	Jose Oliva	.10
148	Armando Benitez	.10
149	J.R. Phillips	.10
150	Charles Johnson	.10
151	Garret Anderson	.10
152	Russ Davis	.10
153	Brian Hunter	.10
154	Ernie Young	.10
155	Marc Newfield	.10
156	Greg Pirkl	.10
157	Scott Ruffcorn	.10
158	Rikkert Faneyte	.10
159	Duane Singleton	.10
160	Gabe White	.10
161	Alex Gonzalez	.10
162	Chipper Jones	1.00
163	Mike Kelly	.10
164	Kurt Miller	.10
165	Roberto Petagine	.10
166	Checklist (Jeff Bagwell)	.40
167	Checklist (Mike Piazza)	.65
168	Checklist (Ken Griffey Jr.)	.65
169	Checklist (Frank Thomas)	.40
170	Checklist (Barry Bonds, Cal Ripken Jr.)	.75

Artist's Proofs

Each of the 170 cards in the regular Sportflix set can be found with a special tombstone shaped black-and-gold "Artist's Proof" seal designating it as one of a parallel edition of 700 cards each. Cards are otherwise identical to the regular-issue version. AP cards were inserted at an average rate of one per 36 packs.

	NM/M
Complete Set (170):	200.00
Common Player:	.75
Stars:	12X

Double Take

A see-through plastic background and A.L. and N.L. stars at the same position sharing the card with their shadows marks this chase set as the top of the line for '95

Sportflix. Found at an average rate of one per 48 packs, the Double Take inserts represent a new level in "magic motion" card technology.

		NM/M
Complete Set (12):		25.00
Common Player:		1.00
1	Frank Thomas, Jeff Bagwell	1.50
2	Will Clark, Fred McGriff	1.00
3	Roberto Alomar, Jeff Kent	1.00
4	Wade Boggs, Matt Williams	2.00
5	Cal Ripken Jr., Ozzie Smith	6.00
6	Alex Rodriguez, Wil Cordero	4.00
7	Carlos Delgado, Mike Piazza	3.00
8	Kenny Lofton, Dave Justice	1.00
9	Ken Griffey Jr., Barry Bonds	6.00
10	Albert Belle, Raul Mondesi	1.00
11	Kirby Puckett, Tony Gwynn	2.50
12	Jimmy Key, Greg Maddux	2.00

ProMotion

Twelve of baseball's biggest stars morph into team logos on a bright team-color background in this chase series. Backs have a portrait photo and a few words about the players. The ProMotion inserts are a one per 18 pack pick in jumbo packs only.

		NM/M
Complete Set (12):		30.00
Common Player:		1.50
1	Ken Griffey Jr.	4.00
2	Frank Thomas	2.50
3	Cal Ripken Jr.	5.00
4	Jeff Bagwell	2.50
5	Mike Piazza	4.00
6	Matt Williams	1.50
7	Albert Belle	1.50
8	Jose Canseco	2.00
9	Don Mattingly	3.50
10	Barry Bonds	5.00
11	Will Clark	1.50
12	Kirby Puckett	3.00

3D Detonators

With the players on a pedestal and fireworks in the background, this chase set lives up to its name, "Detonators." The cards feature a deep 3-D look on front. Backs have a close-up photo of the player in the pedestal's column. Detonator cards are pulled at an average rate of one per 16 packs.

	NM/M
Complete Set (9):	8.00
Common Player:	.40

1	Jeff Bagwell	1.00
2	Matt Williams	.40
3	Ken Griffey Jr.	1.50
4	Frank Thomas	1.25
5	Mike Piazza	1.50
6	Barry Bonds	2.00
7	Albert Belle	.40
8	Cliff Floyd	.40
9	Juan Gonzalez	.60

3D Hammer Team

Sledge hammers flying in formation through a cloud-studded sky are the background for this insert set featuring the game's heavy hitters. Backs have a portrait photo and a few words about the player's power hitting prowess. Hammer Team cards are picked on an average of once per four packs.

		NM/M
Complete Set (18):		7.50
Common Player:		.20
1	Ken Griffey Jr.	1.50
2	Frank Thomas	.65
3	Jeff Bagwell	.65
4	Mike Piazza	1.50
5	Cal Ripken Jr.	2.00
6	Albert Belle	.20
7	Barry Bonds	2.00
8	Don Mattingly	1.00
9	Will Clark	.20
10	Tony Gwynn	.75
11	Matt Williams	.20
12	Kirby Puckett	.75
13	Manny Ramirez	.65
14	Fred McGriff	.20
15	Juan Gonzalez	.35
16	Kenny Lofton	.20
17	Raul Mondesi	.20
18	Tim Salmon	.20

1995 Sportflix/UC3 Samples

To introduce the new technology it was bringing to the insert cards in the Sportflix UC3 issue, the company sent a sample of the Clear Shots insert, along with a header card describing the entire UC3 issue, to card dealers and the media in June 1995. A large, black, "SAMPLE" is overprinted diagonally on the front. A similarly marked Fred McGriff previewed the set's regular cards.

		NM/M
Complete Set (3):		5.00
3	Fred McGriff	2.00
CS8	Cliff Floyd	2.00
CS10	Alex Gonzalez	2.00
--	Header Card	.05

1995 Sportflix/UC3

Using advanced technology to create a premium 3-D card brand and inserts, UC3 offers three distinctly different card formats in the base 147-card set, plus a parallel set and three insert sets. All cards have borderless fronts and feature a heavy ribbed plastic top layer. The first 95 cards are veteran players in a horizontal format. A central action photo is flanked at left by a large gold glove (National Leaguers) or baseball (A.L.), and at right by a blue and green vista from which flies one (N.L.) or three (A.L.) baseballs. Player identification is in red at upper-left, the UC3 logo at lower-left. Backs have another color photo and a few stats set against a background of the team logo. Cards #96-122 are a vertical-format Rookie subset. Player photos are set against a purple and green vista with a large bat, ball and glove behind the player. His name is at upper-right; team logo at lower-right. Horizontal backs are similar to the other cards. The final 25 cards of the set are a subset titled, "In-Depth." These vertically formatted cards feature eye-popping graphics on front in which the main player photo almost jumps from the background. The only graphics are the player's name at left and the UC3 logo at upper-left. Backs have a portrait photo at top, bathed in golden rays. A team logo is at center and an outer space design at bottom. There is a short paragraph describing the player at right.

		NM/M
Complete Set (147):		12.50
Common Player:		.10
Artist's Proofs:		12X
Pack (5):		1.00
Wax Box (36):		25.00
1	Frank Thomas	.75
2	Wil Cordero	.10
3	John Olerud	.10
4	Deion Sanders	.10
5	Mike Mussina	.30
6	Mo Vaughn	.10
7	Will Clark	.10
8	Chili Davis	.10
9	Jimmy Key	.10
10	John Valentin	.10
11	Tony Tarasco	.10
12	Alan Trammell	.10
13	David Cone	.10
14	Tim Salmon	.10
15	Danny Tartabull	.10
16	Aaron Sele	.10
17	Alex Fernandez	.10
18	Barry Bonds	2.00
19	Andres Galarraga	.10
20	Don Mattingly	1.00
21	Kevin Appier	.10
22	Paul Molitor	.75
23	Omar Vizquel	.10
24	Andy Benes	.10
25	Rafael Palmeiro	.65
26	Barry Larkin	.10
27	Bernie Williams	.10
28	Gary Sheffield	.40
29	Wally Joyner	.10
30	Wade Boggs	1.00
31	Rico Brogna	.10
32	Ken Caminiti	.10
33	Kirby Puckett	1.00
34	Bobby Bonilla	.10
35	Hal Morris	.10
36	Moises Alou	.10
37	Jim Thome	.65
38	Chuck Knoblauch	.10
39	Mike Piazza	1.25
40	Travis Fryman	.10
41	Rickey Henderson	.75
42	Jack McDowell	.10
43	Carlos Baerga	.10
44	Gregg Jeffries	.10
45	Kirk Gibson	.10
46	Bret Saberhagen	.10
47	Cecil Fielder	.10
48	Manny Ramirez	.75
49	Marquis Grissom	.10
50	Dave Winfield	.75
51	Mark McGwire	1.50
52	Dennis Eckersley	.65
53	Robin Ventura	.10
54	Ryan Klesko	.10
55	Jeff Bagwell	.75
56	Ozzie Smith	1.00
57	Brian McRae	.10
58	Albert Belle	.10
59	Darren Daulton	.10
60	Jose Canseco	.40
61	Greg Maddux	1.00
62	Ben McDonald	.10
63	Lenny Dykstra	.10
64	Randy Johnson	.75
65	Fred McGriff	.10
66	Ray Lankford	.10
67	Dave Justice	.10
68	Paul O'Neill	.10
69	Tony Gwynn	1.00
70	Matt Williams	.10
71	Dante Bichette	.10
72	Craig Biggio	.10
73	Ken Griffey Jr.	1.25
74	Juan Gonzalez	.40
75	Cal Ripken Jr.	2.00
76	Jay Bell	.10
77	Joe Carter	.10
78	Roberto Alomar	.20
79	Mark Langston	.10
80	Dave Hollins	.10
81	Tom Glavine	.35
82	Ivan Rodriguez	.65
83	Mark Whiten	.10
84	Raul Mondesi	.10
85	Kenny Lofton	.10
86	Ruben Sierra	.10
87	Mark Grace	.10
88	Royce Clayton	.10
89	Billy Ashley	.10
90	Larry Walker	.10
91	Sammy Sosa	1.00
92	Jason Bere	.10
93	Bob Hamelin	.10
94	Greg Vaughn	.10
95	Roger Clemens	1.00
96	Scott Ruffcorn	.10
97	Hideo Nomo **RC**	1.50
98	Michael Tucker	.10
99	J.R. Phillips	.10
100	Roberto Petagine	.10
101	Chipper Jones	1.00
102	Armando Benitez	.10
103	Orlando Miller	.10
104	Carlos Delgado	.50
105	Jeff Cirillo	.10
106	Shawn Green	.30
107	Joe Rando	.10
108	Vaughn Eshelman	.10
109	Frank Rodriguez	.10
110	Russ Davis	.10
111	Todd Hollandsworth	.10
112	Mark Grudzielanek	.10
113	Jose Oliva	.10
114	Ray Durham	.10
115	Alex Rodriguez	1.50
116	Alex Gonzalez	.10
117	Midre Cummings	.10
118	Marty Cordova	.10
119	John Mabry	.10
120	Jason Jacome	.10
121	Joe Vitiello	.10
122	Charles Johnson	.10
123	Cal Ripken Jr. (In Depth)	1.00
124	Ken Griffey Jr. (In Depth)	.65
125	Frank Thomas (In Depth)	.40
126	Mike Piazza (In Depth)	.65
127	Matt Williams (In Depth)	.10
128	Barry Bonds (In Depth)	1.00
129	Greg Maddux (In Depth)	.50
130	Randy Johnson (In Depth)	.40
131	Albert Belle (In Depth)	.10
132	Will Clark (In Depth)	.10
133	Tony Gwynn (In Depth)	.50
134	Manny Ramirez (In Depth)	.40
135	Raul Mondesi (In Depth)	.10
136	Mo Vaughn (In Depth)	.10
137	Mark McGwire (In Depth)	.75
138	Kirby Puckett (In Depth)	.50
139	Don Mattingly (In Depth)	.60
140	Carlos Baerga (In Depth)	.10
141	Roger Clemens (In Depth)	.60
142	Fred McGriff (In Depth)	.10
143	Kenny Lofton (In Depth)	.10
144	Jeff Bagwell (In Depth)	.40
145	Larry Walker (In Depth)	.10
146	Joe Carter (In Depth)	.10
147	Rafael Palmeiro (In Depth)	.30

Artist's Proof

This chase set parallels the 147 regular cards in the UC3 set with a version on which a round, gold "ARTIST'S PROOF" seal is printed on the front of the card. The AP cards are found on the average of one per box (36 packs).

	NM/M
Complete Set (147):	200.00
Common Player:	.75
Stars:	12X

Clear Shots

Seeded at the rate of about one per 24 packs, the 12 cards in this chase set feature top rookies in a technologically advanced format. The left two-thirds of the card are clear plastic, the right third is blue (American League) or red-purple (N.L.). At center is a circle which features the player photos, portrait and action, depending on the viewing angle. Also changing with the viewpoint are the words "CLEAR" and "SHOT" at top-right, and team and UC3 logos at bottom-right. The player's last name is in black at lower-left and appears to change size as the card is moved. Backs have a gray strip vertically at left with the card number, manufacturer and licensor logos and copyright information. Card numbers have a "CS" prefix.

		NM/M
Complete Set (12):		12.00
Common Player:		.25
1	Alex Rodriguez	5.00
2	Shawn Green	.75
3	Hideo Nomo	1.25
4	Charles Johnson	.25
5	Orlando Miller	.25
6	Billy Ashley	.25
7	Carlos Delgado	1.50
8	Cliff Floyd	.25
9	Chipper Jones	4.00
10	Alex Gonzalez	.25
11	J.R. Phillips	.25
12	Michael Tucker	.25

Cyclone Squad

The most commonly encountered (one per four packs, on average) of the UC3 chase cards are the 20-card Cyclone Squad, featuring the game's top batsmen. Cards have a player in a batting pose set against a dark copper background with two golden pinwheels behind him which appear to spin when the card is moved. Horizontal backs have a green toned photo of the player in his follow-through swing, with shock waves radiating from the lower-left corner. Cards have a CS prefix.

		NM/M
Complete Set (20):		10.00
Common Player:		.25
1	Frank Thomas	.65
2	Ken Griffey Jr.	1.00
3	Jeff Bagwell	.65
4	Cal Ripken Jr.	2.00
5	Barry Bonds	2.00
6	Mike Piazza	1.00
7	Matt Williams	.25
8	Kirby Puckett	.75
9	Jose Canseco	.45
10	Will Clark	.25
11	Don Mattingly	.85
12	Albert Belle	.25
13	Tony Gwynn	.75
14	Raul Mondesi	.25
15	Bobby Bonilla	.25
16	Rafael Palmeiro	.60
17	Fred McGriff	.25
18	Tim Salmon	.25
19	Kenny Lofton	.25
20	Joe Carter	.25

In Motion

Found on an average of once per 18 packs, the cards in this chase set feature maximim motion. When the card is held almost vertically a small eight-piece jigsaw puzzle photo of the player is visible against a light blue background. As the card is moved toward a horizontal postion, the pieces appear to become large and move together until the picture fills most of the card. The player's name is in orange at lower-left, with manufacturer's logos at top. Horizontal backs have a green background, two color player photos and a few words of career highlights. The In Motion card numbers are preceded by an "IM" prefix.

		NM/M
Complete Set (10):		7.00
Common Player:		.25
1	Cal Ripken Jr.	1.50
2	Ken Griffey Jr.	1.00
3	Frank Thomas	.50
4	Mike Piazza	1.00
5	Barry Bonds	1.50
6	Matt Williams	.25
7	Kirby Puckett	.75
8	Greg Maddux	.75
9	Don Mattingly	.85
10	Will Clark	.25

1996 Sportflix

Distributed in only retail locations, this 1996 Sportflix set has 144 cards, including 24-card UC3 and 21-card Rookies subsets. The set also has a parallel set, Artist's Proof; these cards are seeded one per every 48 packs. Four insert sets were also produced: Double Take, Hit Parade, Power Surge and ProMotion.

		NM/M
Complete Set (144):		17.50
Common Player:		.10
Common Artist's Proof:		1.00
AP Stars:		12X
Pack (5):		1.00
Wax Box (36):		30.00
1	Wade Boggs	1.00
2	Tim Salmon	.10
3	Will Clark	.10
4	Dante Bichette	.10
5	Barry Bonds	2.00
6	Kirby Puckett	1.00
7	Albert Belle	.10
8	Greg Maddux	1.00
9	Tony Gwynn	1.00
10	Mike Piazza	1.25
11	Ivan Rodriguez	.65
12	Marty Cordova	.10
13	Frank Thomas	.75
14	Raul Mondesi	.10
15	Johnny Damon	.35
16	Mark McGwire	1.50
17	Lenny Dykstra	.10
18	Ken Griffey Jr.	1.25
19	Chipper Jones	1.00
20	Alex Rodriguez	1.50
21	Jeff Bagwell	.75
22	Jim Edmonds	.10
23	Edgar Martinez	.10
24	David Cone	.10
25	Tom Glavine	.35
26	Eddie Murray	.75
27	Paul Molitor	.75
28	Ryan Klesko	.10
29	Rafael Palmeiro	.65
30	Manny Ramirez	.75
31	Mo Vaughn	.10
32	Rico Brogna	.10
33	Marc Newfield	.10
34	J.T. Snow	.10
35	Reggie Sanders	.10
36	Fred McGriff	.10
37	Craig Biggio	.10
38	Jeff King	.10
39	Kenny Lofton	.10
40	Gary Gaetti	.10
41	Eric Karros	.10
42	Jason Isringhausen	.10
43	B.J. Surhoff	.10
44	Michael Tucker	.10
45	Gary Sheffield	.45
46	Chili Davis	.10
47	Bobby Bonilla	.10
48	Hideo Nomo	.40
49	Ray Durham	.10
50	Phil Nevin	.10
51	Randy Johnson	.75
52	Bill Pulsipher	.10
53	Ozzie Smith	1.00
54	Cal Ripken Jr.	2.00
55	Cecil Fielder	.10
56	Matt Williams	.10
57	Sammy Sosa	1.00
58	Roger Clemens	1.00
59	Brian Hunter	.10
60	Barry Larkin	.10
61	Charles Johnson	.10
62	Dave Justice	.10
63	Garret Anderson	.10
64	Rondell White	.10
65	Derek Bell	.10
66	Andres Galarraga	.10
67	Moises Alou	.10
68	Travis Fryman	.10

69 Pedro Martinez .75
70 Carlos Baerga .10
71 John Valentin .10
72 Larry Walker .10
73 Roberto Alomar .20
74 Mike Mussina .30
75 Kevin Appier .10
76 Bernie Williams .10
77 Ray Lankford .10
78 Gregg Jefferies .10
79 Robin Ventura .10
80 Kenny Rogers .10
81 Paul O'Neill .10
82 Mark Grace .10
83 Deion Sanders .10
84 Tino Martinez .10
85 Joe Carter .10
86 Pete Schourek .10
87 Jack McDowell .10
88 John Mabry .10
89 Darren Daulton .10
90 Jim Thome .65
91 Jay Buhner .10
92 Jay Bell .10
93 Kevin Seitzer .10
94 Jose Canseco .40
95 Juan Gonzalez .40
96 Jeff Conine .10
97 Chipper Jones (UC3) .50
98 Ken Griffey Jr. (UC3) .65
99 Frank Thomas (UC3) .40
100 Cal Ripken Jr. (UC3) 1.00
101 Albert Belle (UC3) .10
102 Mike Piazza (UC3) .65
103 Dante Bichette (UC3) .10
104 Sammy Sosa (UC3) .50
105 Mo Vaughn (UC3) .10
106 Tim Salmon (UC3) .10
107 Reggie Sanders (UC3) .10
108 Gary Sheffield (UC3) .25
109 Ruben Rivera (UC3) .10
110 Rafael Palmeiro (UC3) .35
111 Edgar Martinez (UC3) .10
112 Barry Bonds (UC3) 1.00
113 Manny Ramirez (UC3) .40
114 Larry Walker (UC3) .10
115 Jeff Bagwell (UC3) .40
116 Matt Williams (UC3) .10
117 Mark McGwire (UC3) .75
118 Johnny Damon (UC3) .30
119 Eddie Murray (UC3) .40
120 Jay Buhner (UC3) .10
121 Tim Unroe (Rookie) .10
122 Todd Hollandsworth (Rookie) .10
123 Tony Clark (Rookie) .10
124 Roger Cedeno (Rookie) .10
125 Jim Pittsley (Rookie) .10
126 Ruben Rivera (Rookie) .10
127 Bob Wolcott (Rookie) .10
128 Chan Ho Park (Rookie) .10
129 Chris Snopek (Rookie) .10
130 Alex Ochoa (Rookie) .10
131 Yamil Benitez (Rookie) .10
132 Jimmy Haynes (Rookie) .10
133 Dustin Hermanson (Rookie) .10
134 Shawn Estes (Rookie) .10
135 Howard Battle (Rookie) .10
136 Matt Lawton **RC** (Rookie) .25
137 Terrell Wade (Rookie) .10
138 Jason Schmidt (Rookie) .10
139 Derek Jeter (Rookie) 2.50
140 Shannon Stewart (Rookie) .10
141 Chris Stynes (Rookie) .10
142 Ken Griffey Jr. (Checklist) .65
143 Greg Maddux (Checklist) .50
144 Cal Ripken Jr. (Checklist) 1.00

Artist's Proofs

Artist's Proof parallels to 1996 Sportflix are a 1:48 find and are distinctively marked with an AP seal on front.

NM/M
Complete Set (144): 200.00
Common Player: 1.00
AP Stars: 12X

Double Take

These 1996 Sportflix insert cards each feature two players who are tops at a particular position. Tilting the card to change the angle of view brings each player into focus. The cards were seeded one per 22 packs.

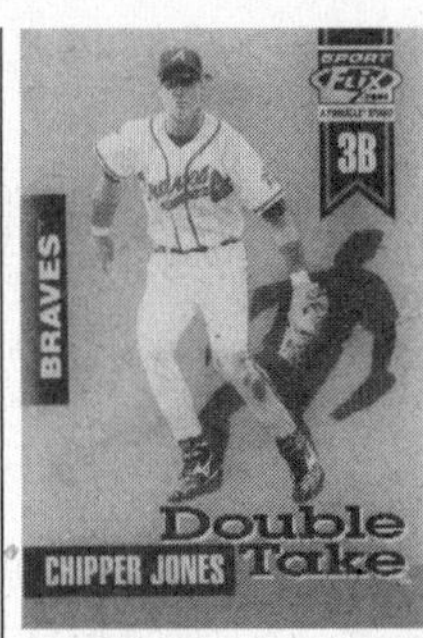

NM/M
Complete Set (12): 30.00
Common Player: 1.50
1 Barry Larkin, Cal Ripken Jr. 6.00
2 Roberto Alomar, Craig Biggio 1.50
3 Chipper Jones, Matt Williams 2.50
4 Ken Griffey Jr., Ruben Rivera 3.50
5 Greg Maddux, Hideo Nomo 3.00
6 Frank Thomas, Mo Vaughn 2.00
7 Mike Piazza, Ivan Rodriguez 3.50
8 Albert Belle, Barry Bonds 6.00
9 Alex Rodriguez, Derek Jeter 8.00
10 Kirby Puckett, Tony Gwynn 3.00
11 Manny Ramirez, Sammy Sosa 3.00
12 Jeff Bagwell, Rico Brogna 2.00

Hit Parade

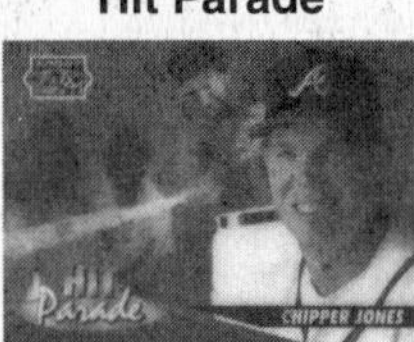

Sixteen of baseball's most productive hitters are featured on these inserts. Horizontal fronts have a player portrait at right. In the background is a lenticular-motion scene of a generic player swinging the bat. Backs have an action photo and a few career highlights. The cards were seeded one per every 35 packs.

NM/M
Complete Set (16): 24.00
Common Player: .50
1 Ken Griffey Jr. 2.50
2 Cal Ripken Jr. 4.00
3 Frank Thomas 1.50
4 Mike Piazza 2.50
5 Mo Vaughn .50
6 Albert Belle .50
7 Jeff Bagwell 1.50
8 Matt Williams .50
9 Sammy Sosa 2.00
9p Sammy Sosa (Overprinted "SAMPLE.") 2.00
10 Kirby Puckett 2.00
11 Dante Bichette .50
12 Gary Sheffield 1.00
13 Tony Gwynn 2.00
14 Wade Boggs 2.00
15 Chipper Jones 2.00
16 Barry Bonds 4.00

Power Surge

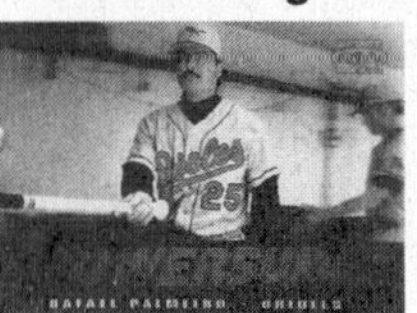

This 1996 Sportflix insert set showcases 24 sluggers on a clear 3-D parallel rendition of the UC3 subset in the main issue. These cards are seeded one per every 35 packs.

NM/M
Complete Set (24): 30.00
Common Player: .50
1 Chipper Jones 2.00
2 Ken Griffey Jr. 2.50
3 Frank Thomas 1.50
4 Cal Ripken Jr. 4.00
5 Albert Belle .50
6 Mike Piazza 2.50
7 Dante Bichette .50
8 Sammy Sosa 2.00
9 Mo Vaughn .50
10 Tim Salmon .50
11 Reggie Sanders .50
12 Gary Sheffield 1.00
13 Ruben Rivera .50
14 Rafael Palmeiro 1.25
15 Edgar Martinez .50
16 Barry Bonds 4.00
17 Manny Ramirez 1.50
18 Larry Walker .50
19 Jeff Bagwell 1.50
20 Matt Williams .50
21 Mark McGwire 3.00
22 Johnny Damon .90
23 Eddie Murray 1.50
24 Jay Buhner .50

ProMotion

These 1996 Sportflix inserts were seeded one per every 17 packs. The cards' "morphing" technology turns baseball equipment, such as bats, balls and gloves, into 20 of the top veteran superstars using multi-phase animation.

NM/M
Complete Set (20): 22.50
Common Player: .50
1 Cal Ripken Jr. 5.00
2 Greg Maddux 2.00
3 Mo Vaughn .50
4 Albert Belle .50
5 Mike Piazza 3.00
6 Ken Griffey Jr. 3.00
7 Frank Thomas 1.50
8 Jeff Bagwell 1.50
9 Hideo Nomo 1.00
10 Chipper Jones 2.00
11 Tony Gwynn 2.00
12 Don Mattingly 2.50
13 Dante Bichette .50
14 Matt Williams .50
15 Manny Ramirez 1.50
16 Barry Bonds 5.00
17 Reggie Sanders .50
18 Tim Salmon .50
19 Ruben Rivera .50
20 Garret Anderson .50

Rookie Supers

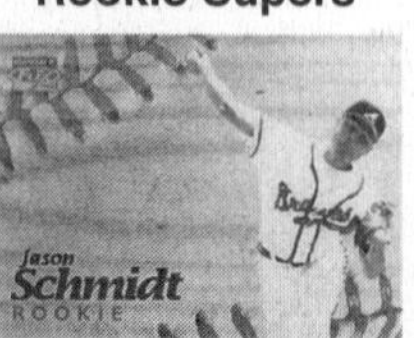

Eight of the young players included in the Sportflix Rookies subset are featured in an enlarged version which was issued one per retail box. The cards measure 3" x 5" and are numbered "X of 8," on back, but are otherwise identical to the smaller version.

NM/M
Complete Set (8): 12.50
Common player: 1.00
1 Jason Schmidt 1.00
2 Chris Snopek 1.00
3 Tony Clark 1.00
4 Todd Hollandsworth 1.00
5 Alex Ochoa 1.00
6 Derek Jeter 10.00
7 Howard Battle 1.00
8 Bob Wolcott 1.00

1981 Sporting News Conlon Collection

This set of 100 cards was sold directly into the hobby by The Sporting News in a slipcover case for $50. The blank-backed cards measure 4"x5" and feature a sepi-toned photo surrounded by a 1/4" white border. The photos were the first of several uses on baseball cards of TSN's archives of ballplayer photos taken by Charles Martin Conlon between 1915-1935. The paper's logo appears at the top of the card. At bottom are the player's or players' names(s), team at the time the photo was taken, and position or positions played for the season indicated. A card number appears at lower-right.

NM/M
Complete Set (100): 90.00
Common Player: 1.00
1 Ty Cobb 10.00
2 Hughie Jennings 1.00
3 Miller Huggins 1.00
4 Babe Ruth 12.50
5 Lou Gehrig 10.00
6 John McGraw 1.00
7 Bill Terry 1.00
8 Stan Baumgartner 1.00
9 Christy Mathewson 5.00
10 Grover Alexander 2.00
11 Tony Lazzeri 1.00
12 Frank Chance, Joe Tinker 2.00
13 Johnny Evers 1.00
14 Tris Speaker 2.00
15 Harry Hooper 1.00
16 Duffy Lewis 1.00
17 Joe Wood 1.00
18 Hugh Duffy 1.00
19 Rogers Hornsby 4.00
20 Earl Averill 1.00
21 Dizzy Dean 2.00
22 Daffy Dean 1.00
23 Frankie Frisch 1.00
24 Pepper Martin 1.00
25 Blondie Ryan 1.00
26 Hank Gowdy 1.00
27 Fred Merkle 1.00
28 Ernie Lombardi 1.00
29 Greasy Neale 1.00
30 Morris "Red" Badgro 1.00
31 Jim Thorpe 9.00
32 Roy Johnson 1.00
33 Bob Johnson 1.00
34 Mule Solters 1.00
35 Specs Toporcer 1.00
36 Jackie Hayes 1.00
37 Walter Johnson 5.00
38 Lefty Grove 1.00
39 Eddie Collins 1.00
40 Buck Weaver 7.50
41 Cozy Dolan 1.00
42 Emil Meusel 1.00
43 Bob Meusel 1.00
44 Lefty Gomez 1.00
45 Rube Marquard 1.00
46 Jeff Tesreau 1.00
47 Joe Heving 1.00
48 John Heving 1.00
49 Rick Ferrell 1.00
50 Wes Ferrell 1.00
51 Bill Wambsganss 1.00
52 Ben Chapman 1.00
53 Joe Sewell 1.00
54 Luke Sewell 1.00
55 Odell Hale 1.00
56 Sammy Hale 1.00
57 Earle Mack 1.00
58 Connie Mack 1.00
59 Rube Walberg 1.00
60 Mule Haas 1.00
61 Paul Waner 1.00
62 Lloyd Waner 1.00
63 Pie Traynor 1.00
64 Honus Wagner 2.00
65 Joe Cronin 1.00
66 Joe Harris 1.00
67 Dave Harris 1.00
68 Bucky Harris 1.00
69 Alex Gaston 1.00
70 Milt Gaston 1.00
71 Casey Stengel 1.00
72 Amos Rusie 1.00
73 Mickey Welch 1.00
74 Roger Bresnaham 1.00
75 Jesse Burkett 1.00
76 Harry Heilmann 1.00
77 Heinie Manush 1.00
78 Charlie Gehringer 1.00
79 Hank Greenberg 2.00
80 Jimmie Foxx 4.00
81 Al Simmons 1.00
82 Eddie Plank 1.00
83 George Sisler 1.00
84 Joe Medwick 1.00
85 Mel Ott 1.00
86 Hack Wilson 1.00
87 Jimmy Wilson 1.00
88 Chuck Klein 1.00
89 Gabby Hartnett 1.00
90 Henie Groh 1.00
91 Ping Bodie 1.00
92 Ted Lyons 1.00
93 Jack Quinn 1.00
94 Oscar Roettger 1.00
95 Wally Roettger 1.00
96 Bubbles Hargrave 1.00
97 Pinky Hargrave 1.00
98 Sam Crawford 1.00
99 Gee Walker 1.00
100 Homer Summa 1.00

1983 Sporting News Conlon Collection Prototypes

Unlike the issued cards which were in a large format, these prototypes are in standard 2-1/2" x 3-1/2" size. Fronts are printed in sepia. Black-and-white backs have player data, career summary and stats up to the date the photo was taken. Backs also have the TSN Conlon Collection logo and a Marketcom copyright.

NM/M
Complete Set (5): 7.50
Common Player: 2.00
83-1 Lewis (Hack) Wilson 2.00
83-2 Joe Cronin 2.00
82-3 Walter (Barney) Johnson 3.00
83-4 Paul (Daffy) Dean 2.00
83-5 Connie Mack 2.00

1983 Sporting News Conlon Collection

St. Louis
Commemorating 50th Anniversary Season
1933—1983
Year Of First Major League All-Star Game

This set was issued to mark the 50th anniversary of the first All-Star game in 1933. Besides the American and National League players who made up those teams, the set includes a group of all-stars from the Negro Leagues. The oversize (4-1/2" x 6-1/8") cards were sold only as complete sets. The cards feature sepia player photos on front, with a facsimile autograph and appropriate commemorative labeling. Black-and-white backs feature 1933 stats, an anecdote about the player, and the logos of appropriate parties in the set's marketing. The major leaguers' photos were the work of Charles M. Conlon, while the Black ballplayers' pictures were garnered from a variety of sources.

NM/M
Complete Set (60): 20.00
Common Player: .25
1 Jimmie Foxx .50
2 Heinie Manush .25
3 Lou Gehrig 2.50
4 Al Simmons .25
5 Charlie Gehringer .25
6 Luke Appling .25
7 Mickey Cochrane .25
8 Joe Kuhel .25
9 Bill Dickey .40
10 Pinky Higgins .25
11 Roy Johnson .25
12 Ben Chapman .25
13 Johnny Hodapp .25
14 Joe Cronin .25
15 Evar Swanson .25
16 Earl Averill .25
17 Babe Ruth 4.00
18 Tony Lazzeri .40
19 Alvin Crowder .25
20 Lefty Grove .25
21 Earl Whitehill .25
22 Lefty Gomez .25
23 Mel Harder .25
24 Tommy Bridges .25
25 Chuck Klein .25
26 Spud Davis .25
27 Riggs Stephenson .25
28 Tony Piet .25
29 Bill Terry .25
30 Wes Schulmerich .25
31a Pepper Martin (Teeth don't show.) .25
31b Pepper Martin (Teeth show.) .25
32 Arky Vaughan .25
33 Wally Berger .25
34 Rip Collins .25
35 Fred Lindstrom .25
36 Chick Fullis .25
37 Paul Waner .25
38 Johnny Frederick .25
39 Joe Medwick .25
40 Pie Traynor .25
41 Frank Frisch .25
42 Chick Hafey .25
43 Carl Hubbell .25
44 Guy Bush .25
45 Dizzy Dean .40
46 Hal Schumacher .25
47 Larry French .25
48 Lon Warneke .25
49 Cool Papa Bell .25
50 Oscar Charleston .25
51 Josh Gibson .50
52 Satchel Paige 1.00
53 Dave Malarcher .25
54 Pop Lloyd .25
55 Rube Foster .25
56 Buck Leonard .40
57 Smoky Joe Williams .40
58 Willie Wells .40
59 Judy Johnson .25
60 Martin DiHigo .25

1984 Sporting News Conlon Collection

This 60-card set, mostly Hall of Famers, was produced in conjunction with the Smithsonian Institution's "Baseball Immortals" photo exhibition of the work of Charles Martin Conlon. The oversize (4-1/2" x 6-1/8") cards have sepia-toned photos on front; backs are printed in black-and-white. The issue was initially sold only as a complete set.

		NM/M
Complete Set (60):		35.00
Common Player:		.25
1	Grover Cleveland Alexander	.60
2	Chief Bender	.25
3a	Fred Clarke (Jack Coombs front.)	1.50
3b	Fred Clarke (Correct front.)	.40
4	Ty Cobb	1.25
5	Ty Cobb	1.25
6	Ty Cobb	1.25
7	Ty Cobb	1.25
8	Mickey Cochrane	.25
9a	Jack Coombs (Fred Clarke front.)	1.50
9b	Jack Coombs (Correct front.)	.40
10	Charles & Margie Conlon	.25
11	Charles Conlon	.25
12	Joe Cronin	.25
13	Dizzy Dean	.60
14	Leo Durocher	.25
15	Jimmie Foxx	.40
16	The Gashouse Gang (Frank Frisch, Mike Gonzalez, Buzzy Wares)	.25
17	Lou Gehrig	1.75
18	Lou Gehrig	1.75
19	Lou Gehrig	1.75
20	Lou Gehrig	1.75
21	Charlie Gehringer	.25
22	Lefty Gomez	.25
23	Lefty Grove	.25
24	Bucky Harris	.25
25	Harry Heilmann	.25
26	Rogers Hornsby	.40
27	Waite Hoyt	.25
28	Carl Hubbell	.25
29	Miller Huggins	.25
30	Walter Johnson	.60
31	Bill Klem	.25
32	Connie Mack	.25
33	Heinie Manush	.25
34	Rube Marquard	.25
35	Pepper Martin	.25
36	Christy Mathewson	.60
37	Christy Mathewson	.60
38	Christy Mathewson	.60
39	Joe McCarthy	.25
40	John McGraw	.25
41	Fred Merkle	.25
42	Mel Ott	.25
43	Roger Peckinpaugh	.25
44	Herb Pennock	.25
45	Babe Ruth	2.25
46	Babe Ruth	2.25
47	Babe Ruth	2.25
48	Babe Ruth	2.25
49	Babe Ruth	2.25
50	Babe Ruth	2.25
51	Al Simmons	.25
52	Tris Speaker	.40
53	Casey Stengel	.25
54	Bill Terry	.25
55	Pie Traynor	.25
56	Rube Waddell	.25
57	Honus Wagner	1.00
58	Lloyd Waner, Paul Waner	.25
59	Paul Waner	.25
60	Hack Wilson	.25

1981 Sportrait Hall of Fame

This collectors' issue feature portrait art by Stan Sypulski in a blank-back 3-1/2" x 5" format. Portraits have a color frame line and are numbered.

		NM/M
Complete Set (25):		55.00
Common Player:		2.00
1	Honus Wagner	4.00
2	Miller Huggins	2.00
3	Babe Ruth	6.00
4	Connie Mack	2.00
5	Ty Cobb	5.00
6	Lou Gehrig	5.00
7	Eddie Collins	2.00
8	Chuck Klein	2.00
9	Ted Williams	5.00
10	Jimmy Foxx	3.00
11	Frank Baker	2.00
12	Nap Lajoie	2.00
13	Casey Stengel	2.00
14	Joe DiMaggio	5.00
15	Mickey Mantle	6.00
16	Frank Frisch	2.00
17	Bill Terry	2.00
18	Jackie Robinson	5.00
19	Sam Rice	2.00
20	Mickey Cochrane	2.00
21	George Sisler	2.00
22	Bob Feller	3.00
23	Walter Johnson	3.00
24	Tris Speaker	3.00
---	Checklist	2.00

1984 Sports Design Products Doug West

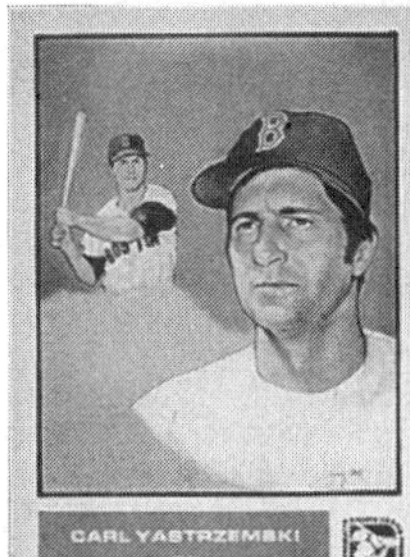

The art of Doug West is featured in portrait and action pictures on each card in this collectors set. The player art is on a blue background. In the white border at bottom a red box displays the player name and position in white. The producer's logo is in black at bottom-right. Backs are printed in red and blue on white with personal data, career summary and stats. Production was reported as 5,000 sets, including 250 uncut sheets. Issue price was about $10.

		NM/M
Complete Set (24):		15.00
Common Player:		.50
1	Jackie Robinson	1.25
2	Luis Aparicio	.50
3	Roberto Clemente	3.00
4	Mickey Mantle	5.00
5	Joe DiMaggio	3.00
6	Willie Stargell	.50
7	Brooks Robinson	.60
8	Ty Cobb	1.50
9	Don Drysdale	.50
10	Bob Feller	.50
11	Stan Musial	1.00
12	Al Kaline	.50
13	Willie Mays	1.75
14	Willie McCovey	.50
15	Thurman Munson	.75
16	Charlie Gehringer	.50
17	Eddie Mathews	.50
18	Carl Yastrzemski	.50
19	Warren Spahn	.50
20	Ted Williams	2.00
21	Ernie Banks	.60
22	Roy Campanella	.75
23	Harmon Killebrew	.50
24	Duke Snider	.75

1985 Sports Design Products Doug West

The art of Doug West is featured in portrait and action pictures on each card in this collectors' set. In the white border at bottom a blue box displays the player name and position in white. The producer's logo is in black at bottom-right. Backs are printed in red and blue on white with personal data, career summary and stats. Cards are numbered sequentially from the previous year's issue. Besides 5,000 complete sets (issued at $8), 250 uncut sheets were also sold.

		NM/M
Complete Set (24):		7.50
Common Player:		.25
25	Lou Gehrig	1.00
26	Hoyt Wilhelm	.25
27	Enos Slaughter	.25
28	Lou Brock	.25
29	Mickey Cochrane	.25
30	Gil Hodges	.50
31	Yogi Berra	.50
32	Carl Hubbell	.25
33	Hank Greenberg	.50
34	Casey Stengel	.25
35	Pee Wee Reese	.35
36	Ralph Kiner	.25
37	Satchel Paige	.50
38	Richie Ashburn	.35
39	Connie Mack	.25
40	Dick Groat	.25
41	Tony Oliva	.25
42	Honus Wagner	.40
43	Denny McLain	.25
44	Johnny Mize	.25
45	Bob Lemon	.25
46	Fergie Jenkins	.25
47	Babe Ruth	2.00
48	Ted Kluszewski	.35

1997 Sports Illustrated

Fleer teamed up with Sports Illustrated to produce a 180-card World Series Fever set. The regular set is divided into six different subsets: 96 Player Cards, 27 Fresh Faces, 18 Inside Baseball, 18 SIber Vision, 12 covers and 9 Newsmakers. Inserts included the Extra Edition parallel set, Great Shots, Cooperstown Collection and Autographed Mini-Cover Redemption Cards. Cards were sold in six-card packs for $1.99 each.

		NM/M
Complete Set (180):		20.00
Common Player:		.05
Extra Edition Stars:		8X
Pack (6):		1.25
Wax Box (24):		20.00
1	Bob Abreu (Fresh Faces)	.10
2	Jaime Bluma (Fresh Faces)	.05
3	Emil Brown (Fresh Faces)	.05
4	Jose Cruz, Jr. (Fresh Faces)	.05
5	Jason Dickson (Fresh Faces)	.05
6	Nomar Garciaparra (Fresh Faces)	1.00
7	Todd Greene (Fresh Faces)	.05
8	Vladimir Guerrero (Fresh Faces)	.75
9	Wilton Guerrero (Fresh Faces)	.05
10	Jose Guillen (Fresh Faces)	.05
11	Hideki Irabu (Fresh Faces)	.05
12	Russ Johnson (Fresh Faces)	.05
13	Andruw Jones (Fresh Faces)	.75
14	Damon Mashore (Fresh Faces)	.05
15	Jason McDonald (Fresh Faces)	.05
16	Ryan McGuire (Fresh Faces)	.05
17	Matt Morris (Fresh Faces)	.05
18	Kevin Orie (Fresh Faces)	.05
19	Dante Powell (Fresh Faces)	.05
20	Pokey Reese (Fresh Faces)	.05
21	Joe Roa (Fresh Faces)	.05
22	Scott Rolen (Fresh Faces)	.65
23	Glendon Rusch (Fresh Faces)	.05
24	Scott Spiezio (Fresh Faces)	.05
25	Bubba Trammell (Fresh Faces)	.05
26	Todd Walker (Fresh Faces)	.05
27	Jamey Wright (Fresh Faces)	.05
28	Ken Griffey Jr. (Season Highlights)	.75
29	Tino Martinez (Season Highlights)	.05
30	Roger Clemens (Season Highlights)	.65
31	Hideki Irabu (Season Highlights)	.05
32	Kevin Brown (Season Highlights)	.05
33	Chipper Jones, Cal Ripken Jr. (Season Highlights)	.65
34	Sandy Alomar (Season Highlights)	.05
35	Ken Caminiti (Season Highlights)	.05
36	Randy Johnson (Season Highlights)	.40
37	Andy Ashby (Inside Baseball)	.05
38	Jay Buhner (Inside Baseball)	.05
39	Joe Carter (Inside Baseball)	.05
40	Darren Daulton (Inside Baseball)	.05
41	Jeff Fassero (Inside Baseball)	.05
42	Andres Galarraga (Inside Baseball)	.05
43	Rusty Greer (Inside Baseball)	.05
44	Marquis Grissom (Inside Baseball)	.05
45	Joey Hamilton (Inside Baseball)	.05
46	Jimmy Key (Inside Baseball)	.05
47	Ryan Klesko (Inside Baseball)	.05
48	Eddie Murray (Inside Baseball)	.75
49	Charles Nagy (Inside Baseball)	.05
50	Dave Nilsson (Inside Baseball)	.05
51	Ricardo Rincon (Inside Baseball)	.05
52	Billy Wagner (Inside Baseball)	.05
53	Dan Wilson (Inside Baseball)	.05
54	Dmitri Young (Inside Baseball)	.05
55	Roberto Alomar (S.I.BER Vision)	.30
56	Sandy Alomar Jr. (S.I.BER Vision)	.05
57	Scott Brosius (S.I.BER Vision)	.05
58	Tony Clark (S.I.BER Vision)	.05
59	Carlos Delgado (S.I.BER Vision)	.45
60	Jermaine Dye (S.I.BER Vision)	.05
61	Darin Erstad (S.I.BER Vision)	.20
62	Derek Jeter (S.I.BER Vision)	1.00
63	Jason Kendall (S.I.BER Vision)	.05
64	Hideo Nomo (S.I.BER Vision)	.20
65	Rey Ordonez (S.I.BER Vision)	.05
66	Andy Pettitte (S.I.BER Vision)	.10
67	Manny Ramirez (S.I.BER Vision)	.75
68	Edgar Renteria (S.I.BER Vision)	.05
69	Shane Reynolds (S.I.BER Vision)	.05
70	Alex Rodriguez (S.I.BER Vision)	1.00
71	Ivan Rodriguez (S.I.BER Vision)	.65
72	Jose Rosado (S.I.BER Vision)	.05
73	John Smoltz	.05
74	Tom Glavine	.35
75	Greg Maddux	1.00
76	Chipper Jones	1.00
77	Kenny Lofton	.05
78	Fred McGriff	.05
79	Kevin Brown	.05
80	Alex Fernandez	.05
81	Al Leiter	.05
82	Bobby Bonilla	.05
83	Gary Sheffield	.40
84	Moises Alou	.05
85	Henry Rodriguez	.05
86	Mark Grudzielanek	.05
87	Pedro Martinez	.75
88	Todd Hundley	.05
89	Bernard Gilkey	.05
90	Bobby Jones	.05
91	Curt Schilling	.35
92	Ricky Bottalico	.05
93	Mike Lieberthal	.05
94	Sammy Sosa	1.00
95	Ryne Sandberg	1.00
96	Mark Grace	.05
97	Deion Sanders	.05
98	Reggie Sanders	.05
99	Barry Larkin	.05
100	Craig Biggio	.05
101	Jeff Bagwell	.75
102	Derek Bell	.05
103	Brian Jordan	.05
104	Ray Lankford	.05
105	Ron Gant	.05
106	Al Martin	.05
107	Kevin Elster	.05
108	Jermaine Allensworth	.05
109	Vinny Castilla	.05
110	Dante Bichette	.05
111	Larry Walker	.05
112	Mike Piazza	1.25
113	Eric Karros	.05
114	Todd Hollandsworth	.05
115	Raul Mondesi	.05
116	Hideo Nomo	.40
117	Ramon Martinez	.05
118	Ken Caminiti	.05
119	Tony Gwynn	1.00
120	Steve Finley	.05
121	Barry Bonds	2.00
122	J.T. Snow	.05
123	Rod Beck	.05
124	Cal Ripken Jr.	2.00
125	Mike Mussina	.30
126	Brady Anderson	.05
127	Bernie Williams	.05
128	Derek Jeter	2.00
129	Tino Martinez	.05
130	Andy Pettitte	.30
131	David Cone	.05
132	Mariano Rivera	.15
133	Roger Clemens	1.00
134	Pat Hentgen	.05
135	Juan Guzman	.05
136	Bob Higginson	.05
137	Tony Clark	.05
138	Travis Fryman	.05
139	Mo Vaughn	.05
140	Tim Naehring	.05
141	John Valentin	.05
142	Matt Williams	.05
143	David Justice	.05
144	Jim Thome	.65
145	Chuck Knoblauch	.05
146	Paul Molitor	.75
147	Marty Cordova	.05
148	Frank Thomas	.85
149	Albert Belle	.05
150	Robin Ventura	.05
151	John Jaha	.05
152	Jeff Cirillo	.05
153	Jose Valentin	.05
154	Jay Bell	.05
155	Jeff King	.05
156	Kevin Appier	.05
157	Ken Griffey Jr.	1.25
158	Alex Rodriguez	1.50
158p	Alex Rodriguez/OPS	1.50
159	Randy Johnson	.75
160	Juan Gonzalez	.40
161	Will Clark	.05
162	Dean Palmer	.05
163	Tim Salmon	.05
164	Jim Edmonds	.05
165	Jim Leyritz	.05
166	Jose Canseco	.40
167	Jason Giambi	.50
168	Mark McGwire	1.50
169	Barry Bonds (Classic Covers)	1.00
170	Alex Rodriguez (Classic Covers)	.75
171	Roger Clemens (Classic Covers)	.65
172	Ken Griffey Jr. (Classic Covers)	.65
173	Greg Maddux (Classic Covers)	.50
174	Mike Piazza (Classic Covers)	.65
175	Will Clark, Mark McGwire (Classic Covers)	1.00
176	Hideo Nomo (Classic Covers)	.20
177	Cal Ripken Jr. (Classic Covers)	1.00
178	Ken Griffey Jr., Frank Thomas (Classic Covers)	.50
179	Alex Rodriguez, Derek Jeter (Classic Covers)	1.50
180	John Wetteland (Classic Covers)	.05
---	Checklist (Jose Cruz Jr.)	.05

Extra Edition

Each of the regular cards in the premiere Fleer SI issue is also found in a parallel set designated on front in gold holographic foil as "Extra Edition." Backs of the cards carry a serial number from within a production of 500 of each card.

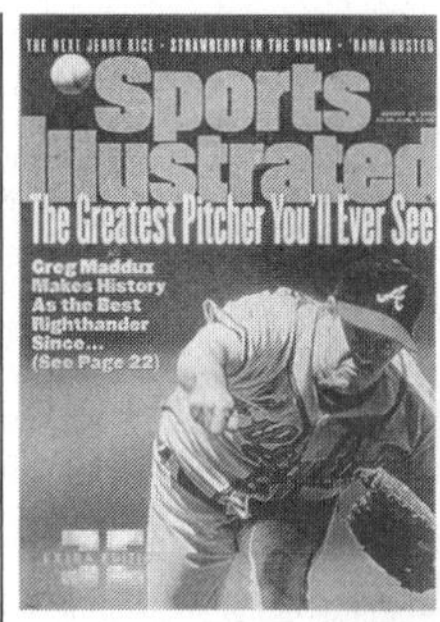

	NM/M
Complete Set (180):	150.00
Common Player:	1.00
Extra Edition Stars:	8X

Autographed Mini-Covers

Six different players autographed 250 magazine mini-covers that were available through randomly seeded redemption cards. The players who autographed cards were Hank Aaron, Willie Mays, Frank Robinson, Kirby Puckett, Cal Ripken Jr., and Alex Rodriguez.

	NM/M
Complete Set (6):	300.00
Common Player:	30.00
Alex Rodriguez	100.00
Cal Ripken Jr.	100.00
Kirby Puckett	80.00
Willie Mays	125.00
Frank Robinson	30.00
Hank Aaron	200.00

Box Topper

This special version of A-Rod's card was packaged one per box of foil packs. It was intended to be inserted into die-cuts on the box to create a sample display for the new issue. The card measures 2-1/2" x 4-1/16". The back is in black-and-white with instructions on how to insert the card into the box.

	NM/M
Alex Rodriguez	4.50

Cooperstown Collection

This 12-card insert (found 1:12 packs) lets collectors relive classic SI baseball covers with a description of each issue on the back.

		NM/M
Complete Set (12):		27.50
Common Player:		2.00
1	Hank Aaron	6.00
2	Yogi Berra	3.00
3	Lou Brock	2.00
4	Rod Carew	2.00
5	Juan Marichal	2.00
6	Al Kaline	2.50
7	Joe Morgan	2.00
8	Brooks Robinson	3.00
9	Willie Stargell	2.00
10	Kirby Puckett	4.00
11	Willie Mays	6.00
12	Frank Robinson	3.00

Great Shots

A 25-card insert, found one per pack, designed to highlight Sports Illustrated's classic photography. Each card in the set folds out to a 5" x 7" format to showcase a larger photo.

		NM/M
Complete Set (25):		10.00
Common Player:		.20
(1)	Roberto Alomar	.30
(2)	Andy Ashby	.20
(3)	Albert Belle	.20
(4)	Barry Bonds	2.00
(5)	Jay Buhner	.20
(6)	Vinny Castilla, Andres Galarraga	.20
(7)	Darren Daulton	.20
(8)	Juan Gonzalez	.40
(9)	Ken Griffey Jr.	1.25
(10)	Derek Jeter	2.00
(11)	Randy Johnson	.75
(12)	Chipper Jones	1.00
(13)	Eric Karros	.20
(14)	Ryan Klesko	.20
(15)	Kenny Lofton	.20
(16)	Greg Maddux	1.00
(17)	Mark McGwire	1.50
(18)	Mike Piazza	1.25
(19)	Cal Ripken Jr.	2.00
(20)	Alex Rodriguez	1.50
(21)	Ryne Sandberg	1.00
(22)	Deion Sanders	.30
(23)	John Smoltz	.20
(24)	Frank Thomas	.75
(25)	Mo Vaughn	.20

1998 Sports Illustrated Promo

This sample card was issued to preview the 1998 Sports Illustrated set presented by Fleer. The card is in the same format as the regular issue, but has a different card number and is overprinted "PROMOTIONAL SAMPLE" on front and back.

		NM/M
8	Cal Ripken Jr.	3.00

1998 Sports Illustrated

The second of three Sports Illustrated releases of 1998 from Fleer contained 200 cards and featured exclusive Sports Illustrated photography and commentary. Cards arrived in six-card packs and carried a Sports Illustrated logo in a top corner. The set included a Travis Lee One to Watch cards (#201) that was inserted just before going to press. Subsets included: Baseball's Best (129-148), One to Watch (149-176), and '97 in Review (177-200). Inserts sets include: Extra Edition and First Edition parallels, Autographs, Covers, Editor's Choice and Opening Day Mini Posters.

		NM/M
Complete Set (201):		20.00
Common Player:		.05
Pack (6):		1.50
Wax Box (24):		25.00
1	Edgardo Alfonzo	.05
2	Roberto Alomar	.20
3	Sandy Alomar	.05
4	Moises Alou	.05
5	Brady Anderson	.05
6	Garret Anderson	.05
7	Kevin Appier	.05
8	Jeff Bagwell	.75
9	Jay Bell	.05
10	Albert Belle	.05
11	Dante Bichette	.05
12	Craig Biggio	.05
13	Barry Bonds	2.00
14	Bobby Bonilla	.05
15	Kevin Brown	.05
16	Jay Buhner	.05
17	Ellis Burks	.05
18	Mike Cameron	.05
19	Ken Caminiti	.05
20	Jose Canseco	.45
21	Joe Carter	.05
22	Vinny Castilla	.05
23	Jeff Cirillo	.05
24	Tony Clark	.05
25	Will Clark	.05
26	Roger Clemens	1.00
27	David Cone	.05
28	Jose Cruz Jr.	.05
29	Carlos Delgado	.50
30	Jason Dickson	.05
31	Dennis Eckersley	.65
32	Jim Edmonds	.05
33	Scott Erickson	.05
34	Darin Erstad	.20
35	Shawn Estes	.05
36	Jeff Fassero	.05
37	Alex Fernandez	.05
38	Chuck Finley	.05
39	Steve Finley	.05
40	Travis Fryman	.05
41	Andres Galarraga	.05
42	Ron Gant	.05
43	Nomar Garciaparra	1.00
44	Jason Giambi	.50
45	Tom Glavine	.35
46	Juan Gonzalez	.40
47	Mark Grace	.05
48	Willie Green	.05
49	Rusty Greer	.05
50	Ben Grieve	.05
51	Ken Griffey Jr.	1.25
52	Mark Grudzielanek	.05
53	Vladimir Guerrero	.75
54	Juan Guzman	.05
55	Tony Gwynn	1.00
56	Joey Hamilton	.05
57	Rickey Henderson	.75
58	Pat Hentgen	.05
59	Livan Hernandez	.05
60	Bobby Higginson	.05
61	Todd Hundley	.05
62	Hideki Irabu	.05
63	John Jaha	.05
64	Derek Jeter	2.00
65	Charles Johnson	.05
66	Randy Johnson	.75
67	Andruw Jones	.75
68	Bobby Jones	.05
69	Chipper Jones	1.00
70	Brian Jordan	.05
71	David Justice	.05
72	Eric Karros	.05
73	Jeff Kent	.05
74	Jimmy Key	.05
75	Darryl Kile	.05
76	Jeff King	.05
77	Ryan Klesko	.05
78	Chuck Knoblauch	.05
79	Ray Lankford	.05
80	Barry Larkin	.05
81	Kenny Lofton	.05
82	Greg Maddux	1.00
83	Al Martin	.05
84	Edgar Martinez	.05
85	Pedro Martinez	.75
86	Tino Martinez	.05
87	Mark McGwire	1.50
88	Paul Molitor	.75
89	Raul Mondesi	.05
90	Jamie Moyer	.05
91	Mike Mussina	.30
92	Tim Naehring	.05
93	Charles Nagy	.05
94	Denny Neagle	.05
95	Dave Nilsson	.05
96	Hideo Nomo	.40
97	Rey Ordonez	.05
98	Dean Palmer	.05
99	Rafael Palmeiro	.65
100	Andy Pettitte	.30
101	Mike Piazza	1.25
102	Brad Radke	.05
103	Manny Ramirez	.75
104	Edgar Renteria	.05
105	Cal Ripken Jr.	2.00
106	Alex Rodriguez	1.50
106p	Alex Rodriguez ("PROMOTIONAL SAMPLE")	1.50
107	Henry Rodriguez	.05
108	Ivan Rodriguez	.65
109	Scott Rolen	.65
110	Tim Salmon	.05
111	Curt Schilling	.35
112	Gary Sheffield	.45
113	John Smoltz	.05
114	J.T. Snow	.05
115	Sammy Sosa	1.00
116	Matt Stairs	.05
117	Shannon Stewart	.05
118	Frank Thomas	.75
119	Jim Thome	.65
120	Justin Thompson	.05
121	Mo Vaughn	.05
122	Robin Ventura	.05
123	Larry Walker	.05
124	Rondell White	.05
125	Bernie Williams	.05
126	Matt Williams	.05
127	Tony Womack	.05
128	Jaret Wright	.05
129	Edgar Renteria (Baseball's Best)	.05
130	Kenny Lofton (Baseball's Best)	.05
131	Tony Gwynn (Baseball's Best)	.50
132	Mark McGwire (Baseball's Best)	.75
133	Craig Biggio (Baseball's Best)	.05
134	Charles Johnson (Baseball's Best)	.05
135	J.T. Snow (Baseball's Best)	.05
136	Ken Caminiti (Baseball's Best)	.05
137	Vladimir Guerrero (Baseball's Best)	.40
138	Jim Edmonds (Baseball's Best)	.05
139	Randy Johnson (Baseball's Best)	.40
140	Darryl Kile (Baseball's Best)	.05
141	John Smoltz (Baseball's Best)	.05
142	Greg Maddux (Baseball's Best)	.50
143	Andy Pettitte (Baseball's Best)	.05
144	Ken Griffey Jr. (Baseball's Best)	.65
145	Mike Piazza (Baseball's Best)	.65
146	Todd Greene (Baseball's Best)	.05
147	Vinny Castilla (Baseball's Best)	.05
148	Derek Jeter (Baseball's Best)	1.00
149	Robert Machado (One to Watch)	.05
150	Mike Gulan (One to Watch)	.05
151	Randall Simon (One to Watch)	.05
152	Michael Coleman (One to Watch)	.05
153	Brian Rose (One to Watch)	.05
154	Scott Eyre **RC** (One to Watch)	.05
155	Magglio Ordonez **RC** (One to Watch)	1.50
156	Todd Helton (One to Watch)	.65
157	Juan Encarnacion (One to Watch)	.05
158	Mark Kotsay (One to Watch)	.05
159	Josh Booty (One to Watch)	.05
160	Melvin Rosario **RC** (One to Watch)	.05
161	Shane Halter (One to Watch)	.05
162	Paul Konerko (One to Watch)	.25
163	Henry Blanco **RC** (One to Watch)	.05
164	Antone Williamson (One to Watch)	.05
165	Brad Fullmer (One to Watch)	.05
166	Ricky Ledee (One to Watch)	.05
167	Ben Grieve (One to Watch)	.05
168	Frank Catalanotto **RC** (One to Watch)	.25
169	Bobby Estalella (One to Watch)	.05
170	Dennis Reyes (One to Watch)	.05
171	Kevin Polcovich (One to Watch)	.05
172	Jacob Cruz (One to Watch)	.05
173	Ken Cloude (One to Watch)	.05
174	Eli Marrero (One to Watch)	.05
175	Fernando Tatis (One to Watch)	.05
176	Tom Evans (One to Watch)	.05
177	Carl Everett, Nomar Garciaparra (97 in Review)	.35
178	Eric Davis (97 in Review)	.05
179	Roger Clemens (97 in Review)	.60
180	Brett Butler, Eddie Murray (97 in Review)	.30
181	Frank Thomas (97 in Review)	.45
182	Curt Schilling (97 in Review)	.15
183	Jeff Bagwell (97 in Review)	.40
184	Mark McGwire, Ken Griffey Jr. (97 in Review)	.75
185	Kevin Brown (97 in Review)	.05
186	Marty Cordova, Ricardo Rincon (97 in Review)	.05
187	Charles Johnson (97 in Review)	.05
188	Hideki Irabu (97 in Review)	.05
189	Tony Gwynn (97 in Review)	.50
190	Sandy Alomar (97 in Review)	.05
191	Ken Griffey Jr. (97 in Review)	.65
192	Larry Walker (97 in Review)	.05
193	Roger Clemens (97 in Review)	.60
194	Pedro Martinez (97 in Review)	.40
195	Nomar Garciaparra (97 in Review)	.60
196	Scott Rolen (97 in Review)	.40
197	Brian Anderson (97 in Review)	.05
198	Tony Saunders (97 in Review)	.05
199	Florida Celebration (97 in Review)	.05
200	Livan Hernandez (97 in Review)	.05
201	Travis Lee/SP (One to Watch)	2.00

Extra Edition

Extra Edition is a 201-card parallel set that includes a holofoil stamp on the front and sequential numbering to 250 on the back. There is also a First Edition version of these that was identical on the front, but contains the text "The Only 1 of 1 First Edition" in purple lettering on the card back.

	NM/M
Common Player:	2.00
Extra Edition Stars:	8X

Autographs

This six-card insert features autographs of players. The Konerko and Grieve cards were available through redemptions until Nov. 1, 1999.

	NM/M
Common Player:	7.50
Lou Brock/500	40.00
Jose Cruz Jr./250	10.00
Rollie Fingers/500	10.00
Ben Grieve/250 (Exchange Card)	3.00
Ben Grieve (Signed Card)	7.50
Paul Konerko/250 (Exchange Card)	3.00
Paul Konerko (Signed Card)	20.00
Brooks Robinson/250	50.00

Covers

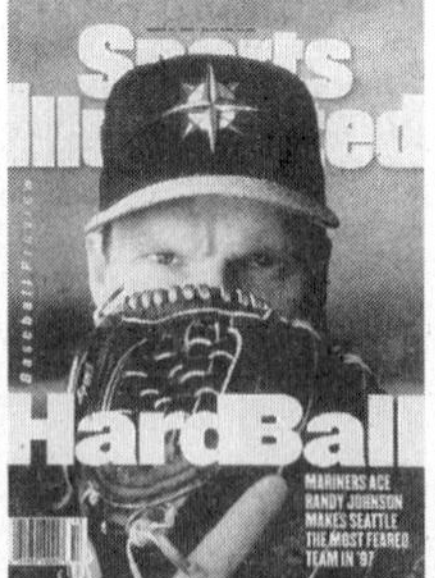

This 10-card insert set pictures actual Sports Illustrated covers on trading cards. The cards are numbered with a "C" prefix and inserted one per nine packs.

		NM/M
Complete Set (10):		15.00
Common Player:		1.00
Inserted 1:9		
1	Ken Griffey Jr., Mike Piazza	2.00
2	Derek Jeter	3.00
3	Ken Griffey Jr.	2.50
4	Cal Ripken Jr.	3.00
5	Manny Ramirez	1.50
6	Jay Buhner	1.00
7	Matt Williams	1.00
8	Randy Johnson	1.50
9	Deion Sanders	1.00
10	Jose Canseco	1.50

Editor's Choice

Editor's Choice includes 10 top players in 1998 as profiled by the editors of Sports Illustrated. Cards are numbered with an "EC" prefix and seeded one per 24 packs.

		NM/M
Complete Set (10):		20.00
Common Player:		1.00
Inserted 1:24		
1	Ken Griffey Jr.	3.00
2	Alex Rodriguez	4.00
3	Frank Thomas	1.50
4	Mark McGwire	4.00
5	Greg Maddux	2.00
6	Derek Jeter	5.00
7	Cal Ripken Jr.	5.00
8	Nomar Garciaparra	2.50
9	Jeff Bagwell	1.50
10	Jose Cruz Jr.	1.00

Mini-Posters

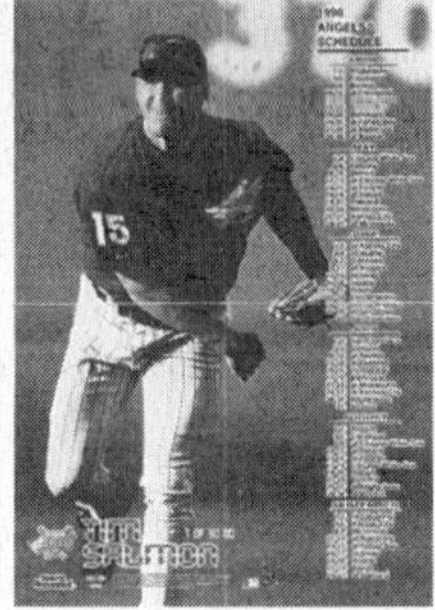

Thirty 5" x 7" mini-posters were available at a rate of one per pack. The posters took the top player or two from each team and added their 1998 schedule. Backs were blank so the cards are numbered on the front with an "OD" prefix.

		NM/M
Complete Set (30):		8.00
Common Player:		.10
Inserted 1:1		
1	Tim Salmon	.10
2	Travis Lee	.10
3	John Smoltz, Greg Maddux	.50
4	Cal Ripken Jr.	1.00
5	Nomar Garciaparra	.50
6	Sammy Sosa	.50
7	Frank Thomas	.45
8	Barry Larkin	.10
9	David Justice	.10
10	Larry Walker	.10
11	Tony Clark	.10
12	Livan Hernandez	.10
13	Jeff Bagwell	.45
14	Kevin Appier	.10
15	Mike Piazza	.65
16	Fernando Vina	.10
17	Chuck Knoblauch	.10
18	Vladimir Guerrero	.45
19	Rey Ordonez	.10
20	Bernie Williams	.10
21	Matt Stairs	.10
22	Curt Schilling	.30
23	Tony Womack	.10
24	Mark McGwire	.75
25	Tony Gwynn	.50
26	Barry Bonds	1.00
27	Ken Griffey Jr.	.65
28	Fred McGriff	.10
29	Juan Gonzalez, Alex Rodriguez	.50
30	Roger Clemens	.60

Then & Now

Then and Now was the first of three Sports Illustrated baseball releases in 1998. It contained 150 cards and sold

in six-card packs, with five cards and a mini-poster. Fronts carried photos of active and retired players, as well as rookies. There was only one subset - A Place in History (#37-53) - which compares statistics between current players and retired greats. The product arrived with an Extra Edition parallel set, Art of the Game, Autograph Redemptions, Covers and Great Shots inserts. There was also an Alex Rodriguez checklist / mini-poster seeded every 12th pack.

		NM/M
Complete Set (150):		15.00
Common Player:		.05
Extra Edition Stars:		6X
Production 500 Sets		
Pack (5):		1.00
Wax Box (24):		16.00
1	Luis Aparicio (Legends of the Game)	.05
2	Richie Ashburn (Legends of the Game)	.05
3	Ernie Banks (Legends of the Game)	.50
4	Yogi Berra (Legends of the Game)	.50
5	Lou Boudreau (Legends of the Game)	.05
6	Lou Brock (Legends of the Game)	.15
7	Jim Bunning (Legends of the Game)	.05
8	Rod Carew (Legends of the Game)	.15
9	Bob Feller (Legends of the Game)	.25
10	Rollie Fingers (Legends of the Game)	.05
11	Bob Gibson (Legends of the Game)	.15
12	Fergie Jenkins (Legends of the Game)	.05
13	Al Kaline (Legends of the Game)	.25
14	George Kell (Legends of the Game)	.05
15	Harmon Killebrew (Legends of the Game)	.25
16	Ralph Kiner (Legends of the Game)	.05
17	Tommy Lasorda (Legends of the Game)	.05
18	Juan Marichal (Legends of the Game)	.05
19	Eddie Mathews (Legends of the Game)	.25
20	Willie Mays (Legends of the Game)	1.00
21	Willie McCovey (Legends of the Game)	.05
22	Joe Morgan (Legends of the Game)	.15
23	Gaylord Perry (Legends of the Game)	.05
24	Kirby Puckett (Legends of the Game)	1.00
25	Pee Wee Reese (Legends of the Game)	.25
26	Phil Rizzuto (Legends of the Game)	.25
27	Robin Roberts (Legends of the Game)	.05
28	Brooks Robinson (Legends of the Game)	.35
29	Frank Robinson (Legends of the Game)	.35
30	Red Schoendienst (Legends of the Game)	.05
31	Enos Slaughter (Legends of the Game)	.05
32	Warren Spahn (Legends of the Game)	.25
33	Willie Stargell (Legends of the Game)	.15
34	Earl Weaver (Legends of the Game)	.05
35	Billy Williams (Legends of the Game)	.15
36	Early Wynn (Legends of the Game)	.05
37	Rickey Henderson (A Place in History)	.75
38	Greg Maddux (A Place in History)	1.00
39	Mike Mussina (A Place in History)	.40
40	Cal Ripken Jr. (A Place in History)	2.00
41	Albert Belle (A Place in History)	.05
42	Frank Thomas (A Place in History)	.75
43	Jeff Bagwell (A Place in History)	.75
44	Paul Molitor (A Place in History)	.75
45	Chuck Knoblauch (A Place in History)	.05
46	Todd Hundley (A Place in History)	.05
47	Bernie Williams (A Place in History)	.05
48	Tony Gwynn (A Place in History)	1.00
49	Barry Bonds (A Place in History)	2.00
50	Ken Griffey Jr. (A Place in History)	1.25
51	Randy Johnson (A Place in History)	.75
52	Mark McGwire (A Place in History)	1.50
53	Roger Clemens (A Place in History)	1.00
54	Jose Cruz Jr. (A Place in History)	.05
55	Roberto Alomar (Legends of Today)	.20
56	Sandy Alomar (Legends of Today)	.05
57	Brady Anderson (Legends of Today)	.05
58	Kevin Appier (Legends of Today)	.05
59	Jeff Bagwell (Legends of Today)	.75
60	Albert Belle (Legends of Today)	.05
61	Dante Bichette (Legends of Today)	.05
62	Craig Biggio (Legends of Today)	.05
63	Barry Bonds (Legends of Today)	2.00
64	Kevin Brown (Legends of Today)	.05
65	Jay Buhner (Legends of Today)	.05
66	Ellis Burks (Legends of Today)	.05
67	Ken Caminiti (Legends of Today)	.05
68	Jose Canseco (Legends of Today)	.50
69	Joe Carter (Legends of Today)	.05
70	Vinny Castilla (Legends of Today)	.05
71	Tony Clark (Legends of Today)	.05
72	Roger Clemens (Legends of Today)	1.00
73	David Cone (Legends of Today)	.05
74	Jose Cruz Jr. (Legends of Today)	.05
75	Jason Dickson (Legends of Today)	.05
76	Jim Edmonds (Legends of Today)	.05
77	Scott Erickson (Legends of Today)	.05
78	Darin Erstad (Legends of Today)	.20
79	Alex Fernandez (Legends of Today)	.05
80	Steve Finley (Legends of Today)	.05
81	Travis Fryman (Legends of Today)	.05
82	Andres Galarraga (Legends of Today)	.05
83	Nomar Garciaparra (Legends of Today)	1.00
84	Tom Glavine (Legends of Today)	.35
85	Juan Gonzalez (Legends of Today)	.40
86	Mark Grace (Legends of Today)	.05
87	Willie Greene (Legends of Today)	.05
88	Ken Griffey Jr. (Legends of Today)	1.25
89	Vladimir Guerrero (Legends of Today)	.75
90	Tony Gwynn (Legends of Today)	1.00
91	Livan Hernandez (Legends of Today)	.05
92	Bobby Higginson (Legends of Today)	.05
93	Derek Jeter (Legends of Today)	2.00
94	Charles Johnson (Legends of Today)	.05
95	Randy Johnson (Legends of Today)	.75
96	Andruw Jones (Legends of Today)	.75
97	Chipper Jones (Legends of Today)	1.00
98	David Justice (Legends of Today)	.05
99	Eric Karros (Legends of Today)	.05
100	Jason Kendall (Legends of Today)	.05
101	Jimmy Key (Legends of Today)	.05
102	Darryl Kile (Legends of Today)	.05
103	Chuck Knoblauch (Legends of Today)	.05
104	Ray Lankford (Legends of Today)	.05
105	Barry Larkin (Legends of Today)	.05
106	Kenny Lofton (Legends of Today)	.05
107	Greg Maddux (Legends of Today)	1.00
108	Al Martin (Legends of Today)	.05
109	Edgar Martinez (Legends of Today)	.05
110	Pedro Martinez (Legends of Today)	.75
111	Ramon Martinez (Legends of Today)	.05
112	Tino Martinez (Legends of Today)	.05
113	Mark McGwire (Legends of Today)	1.50
114	Raul Mondesi (Legends of Today)	.05
115	Matt Morris (Legends of Today)	.05
116	Charles Nagy (Legends of Today)	.05
117	Denny Neagle (Legends of Today)	.05
118	Hideo Nomo (Legends of Today)	.40
119	Dean Palmer (Legends of Today)	.05
120	Andy Pettitte (Legends of Today)	.25
121	Mike Piazza (Legends of Today)	1.25
122	Manny Ramirez (Legends of Today)	.75
123	Edgar Renteria (Legends of Today)	.05
124	Cal Ripken Jr. (Legends of Today)	2.00
125	Alex Rodriguez (Legends of Today)	1.50
126	Henry Rodriguez (Legends of Today)	.05
127	Ivan Rodriguez (Legends of Today)	.65
128	Scott Rolen (Legends of Today)	.65
129	Tim Salmon (Legends of Today)	.05
130	Curt Schilling (Legends of Today)	.35
131	Gary Sheffield (Legends of Today)	.45
132	John Smoltz (Legends of Today)	.05
133	Sammy Sosa (Legends of Today)	1.00
134	Frank Thomas (Legends of Today)	.75
135	Jim Thome (Legends of Today)	.65
136	Mo Vaughn (Legends of Today)	.05
137	Robin Ventura (Legends of Today)	.05
138	Larry Walker (Legends of Today)	.05
139	Bernie Williams (Legends of Today)	.05
140	Matt Williams (Legends of Today)	.05
141	Jaret Wright (Legends of Today)	.05
142	Michael Coleman (Legends of the Future)	.05
143	Juan Encarnacion (Legends of the Future)	.05
144	Brad Fullmer (Legends of the Future)	.05
145	Ben Grieve (Legends of the Future)	.05
146	Todd Helton (Legends of the Future)	.75
147	Paul Konerko (Legends of the Future)	.20
148	Derrek Lee (Legends of the Future)	.50
149	Magglio Ordonez **RC** (Legends of the Future)	1.50
150	Enrique Wilson (Legends of the Future)	.05
---	Alex Rodriguez (Checklist)	1.00

Then & Now Extra Edition

This 150-card set paralleled the base set and was distinguished by an "Extra Edition" foil stamp on the front. There were 500 sets of Extra Edition and the cards were individually numbered on the back.

	NM/M
Common Extra Edition:	1.00
Extra Edition Stars:	6X
Production 500 Sets	

Then & Now Art of the Game

Art of the Game was an eight-card insert featuring reproductions of original artwork of current and retired baseball stars done by eight popular sports artists. Cards are numbered with a "AG" prefix and inserted one per nine packs.

		NM/M
Complete Set (8):		11.00
Common Player:		1.00
Inserted 1:9		
1	It's Gone (Ken Griffey Jr.)	1.50
2	Alex Rodriguez	2.00
3	Mike Piazza	1.50
4	Brooks Robinson	1.00
5	David Justice/AS	1.00
6	Cal Ripken Jr.	3.00
7	The Prospect and the Prospector	1.00
8	Barry Bonds	3.00

Then & Now Autographs

Six autograph redemption cards were randomly inserted into packs of Then & Now and could be exchanged prior to Nov. 1, 1999. The signed cards were produced in the following quantities: Clemens 250, Gibson 500, Gwynn 250, Killebrew 500, Mays 250 and Rolen 150. Four of the six cards use the same fronts as the Covers insert; Gibson and Rolen cards each feature unique card fronts.

	NM/M
Common Autograph:	15.00
Redemption Cards: 10 Percent	
Bob Gibson/500	15.00
Tony Gwynn/250	35.00
Roger Clemens/250	120.00
Scott Rolen/150	20.00
Willie Mays/250	90.00
Harmon Killebrew/500	25.00

Then & Now Covers

This 12-card insert features color shots of six actual Sports Illustrated covers, including six current players and six retired players. The cards are numbered with a "C" prefix and were seeded one per 18 packs.

		NM/M
Complete Set (12):		22.00
Common Player:		1.00
Inserted 1:18		
1	Lou Brock (10/16/67)	1.00
2	Kirby Puckett (4/6/92)	2.50
3	Harmon Killebrew (4/8/63 - inside)	1.00
4	Eddie Mathews (8/16/54)	1.00
5	Willie Mays (5/22/72)	2.00
6	Frank Robinson (10/6/69)	1.00
7	Cal Ripken Jr. (9/11/95)	5.00
8	Roger Clemens (5/12/86)	2.50
9	Ken Griffey Jr. (10/16/95)	3.00
10	Mark McGwire (6/1/92)	4.00
11	Tony Gwynn (7/28/97)	2.50
12	Ivan Rodriguez (8/11/97)	1.50

Then & Now Great Shots!

This 25-card set featured 5" x 7" fold-out mini-posters using Sports Illustrated photos. Great Shots were inserted one per pack and contained a mix of retired and current players.

		NM/M
Complete Set (25):		7.50
Common Player:		.10
Inserted 1:1		
1	Ken Griffey Jr.	.65
2	Frank Thomas	.45
3	Alex Rodriguez	.75
4	Andruw Jones	.45
5	Chipper Jones	.50
6	Cal Ripken Jr.	1.00
7	Mark McGwire	.75
8	Derek Jeter	1.00
9	Greg Maddux	.50
10	Jeff Bagwell	.45
11	Mike Piazza	.65
12	Scott Rolen	.35
13	Nomar Garciaparra	.50
14	Jose Cruz Jr.	.10
15	Charles Johnson	.10
16	Fergie Jenkins	.10
17	Lou Brock	.10
18	Bob Gibson	.10
19	Harmon Killebrew	.10
20	Juan Marichal	.10
21	Brooks Robinson	.10
22	Rod Carew	.10
23	Yogi Berra	.25
24	Willie Mays	.50
25	Kirby Puckett	.50

Then & Now Road to Cooperstown

Road to Cooperstown features 10 current players who are having Hall of Fame careers. The insert name is printed across the back in bold, gold letters. Cards are numbered with a "RC" prefix and were inserted one per 24 packs.

		NM/M
Complete Set (10):		10.00
Common Player:		.75
Inserted 1:24		
1	Barry Bonds	2.50
2	Roger Clemens	1.25
3	Ken Griffey Jr.	1.50
4	Tony Gwynn	1.00
5	Rickey Henderson	.75
6	Greg Maddux	1.00
7	Paul Molitor	.75
8	Mike Piazza	1.50
9	Cal Ripken Jr.	2.50
10	Frank Thomas	.75

World Series Fever

The third and final Sports Illustrated release of 1998 contained 150 cards and focused on the World Series while recapping memorable moments from the season. The set also included many stars of tomorrow, like Kerry Wood, Orlando Hernandez, Ben Grieve and Travis Lee. Once again, all the photos were taken from Sports Illustrated archives. The set has two subsets - 10 Magnificent Moments and 20 Cover Collection. The set is paralleled twice in Extra and First Edition parallel sets, and has three insert sets - MVP Collection, Reggie Jackson's Picks and Autumn Excellence.

		NM/M
Complete Set (150):		10.00
Common Player:		.05
Pack (6):		1.00
Wax Box (24):		17.50
1	Mickey Mantle (Covers)	1.50

2 1957 World Series Preview (Covers) .15
3 1958 World Series Preview (Covers) .15
4 1959 World Series Preview (Covers) .15
5 1962 World Series (Covers) .10
6 Lou Brock (Covers) .10
7 Brooks Robinson (Covers) .25
8 Frank Robinson (Covers) .25
9 1974 World Series (Covers) .10
10 Reggie Jackson (Covers) .60
11 1985 World Series (Covers) .10
12 1987 World Series (Covers) .10
13 Orel Hershiser (Covers) .05
14 Rickey Henderson (Covers) .40
15 1991 World Series (Covers) .10
16 1992 World Series (Covers) .05
17 Joe Carter (Covers) .05
18 1995 World Series (Covers) .10
19 1996 World Series (Covers) .15
20 Edgar Renteria (Covers) .05
21 Bill Mazeroski (Magnificent Moments) .15
22 Joe Carter (Magnificent Moments) .05
23 Carlton Fisk (Magnificent Moments) .40
24 Bucky Dent (Magnificent Moments) .15
25 Mookie Wilson (Magnificent Moments) .05
26 Enos Slaughter (Magnificent Moments) .05
27 Mickey Lolich (Magnificent Moments) .05
28 Bobby Richardson (Magnificent Moments) .05
29 Kirk Gibson (Magnificent Moments) .05
30 Edgar Renteria (Magnificent Moments) .05
31 Albert Belle .05
32 Kevin Brown .05
33 Brian Rose .05
34 Ron Gant .05
35 Jeromy Burnitz .05
36 Andres Galarraga .05
37 Jim Edmonds .05
38 Jose Cruz Jr. .05
39 Mark Grudzielanek .05
40 Shawn Estes .05
41 Mark Grace .05
42 Nomar Garciaparra .50
43 Juan Gonzalez .20
44 Tom Glavine .25
45 Brady Anderson .05
46 Tony Clark .05
47 Jeff Cirillo .05
48 Dante Bichette .05
49 Ben Grieve .05
50 Ken Griffey Jr. .65
51 Edgardo Alfonzo .05
52 Roger Clemens .60
53 Pat Hentgen .05
54 Todd Helton .30
55 Andy Benes .05
56 Tony Gwynn .50
57 Andruw Jones .40
58 Bobby Higginson .05
59 Bobby Jones .05
60 Darryl Kile .05
61 Chan Ho Park .05
62 Charles Johnson .05
63 Rusty Greer .05
64 Travis Fryman .05
65 Derek Jeter 1.00
66 Jay Buhner .05
67 Chuck Knoblauch .05
68 David Justice .05
69 Brian Hunter .05
70 Eric Karros .05
71 Edgar Martinez .05
72 Chipper Jones .50
73 Barry Larkin .05
74 Mike Lansing .05
75 Craig Biggio .05
76 Al Martin .05
77 Barry Bonds 1.00
78 Randy Johnson .40
79 Ryan Klesko .05
80 Mark McGwire .75
81 Fred McGriff .05
82 Javy Lopez .05
83 Kenny Lofton .05
84 Sandy Alomar Jr. .05
85 Matt Morris .05
86 Paul Konerko .10
87 Ray Lankford .05
88 Kerry Wood .30
89 Roberto Alomar .20
90 Greg Maddux .50
91 Travis Lee .05
92 Moises Alou .05
93 Dean Palmer .05
94 Hideo Nomo .20
95 Ken Caminiti .05
96 Pedro Martinez .40
97 Raul Mondesi .05
98 Denny Neagle .05
99 Tino Martinez .05
100 Mike Mussina .20
101 Kevin Appier .05
102 Vinny Castilla .05
103 Jeff Bagwell .40
104 Paul O'Neill .05
105 Rey Ordonez .05
106 Vladimir Guerrero .40
107 Rafael Palmeiro .35
108 Alex Rodriguez .75
109 Andy Pettitte .15
110 Carl Pavano .05
111 Henry Rodriguez .05
112 Gary Sheffield .40
113 Curt Schilling .25
114 John Smoltz .05
115 Reggie Sanders .05
116 Scott Rolen .35
117 Mike Piazza .65
118 Manny Ramirez .40
119 Cal Ripken Jr. 1.00
120 Brad Radke .05
121 Tim Salmon .05
122 Brett Tomko .05
123 Robin Ventura .05
124 Mo Vaughn .05
125 A.J. Hinch .05
126 Derrek Lee .45
127 Orlando Hernandez **RC** .40
128 Aramis Ramirez .05
129 Frank Thomas .40
130 J.T. Snow .05
131 Magglio Ordonez **RC** 1.00
132 Bobby Bonilla .05
133 Marquis Grissom .05
134 Jim Thome .45
135 Justin Thompson .05
136 Matt Williams .05
137 Matt Stairs .05
138 Wade Boggs .50
139 Chuck Finley .05
140 Jaret Wright .05
141 Ivan Rodriguez .35
142 Brad Fullmer .05
143 Bernie Williams .05
144 Jason Giambi .30
145 Larry Walker .05
146 Tony Womack .05
147 Sammy Sosa .50
148 Rondell White .05
149 Todd Stottlemyre .05
150 Shane Reynolds .05

WS Fever Extra Edition

Extra Edition parallels the entire 150-card base set and is identified by a gold-foil stamp on the card front and sequential numbering to 98 sets on the back. World Series Fever also includes one-of-one parallel versions called First Edition. These have a purple-foil identifier on front, with the legend on back, "THE ONLY 1 OF 1 FIRST EDITION," also in purple foil.

NM/M

Common EE Player: 2.00
EE Stars: 15X
Production: 98 Sets
Common FE Player: 100.00
FE Stars: Values Undetermined
1 of 1

WS Fever Autumn Excellence

Autumn Excellence honors players with the most select World Series records. The 10-card set was seeded one per 24 packs, while rarer Gold versions were seeded one per 240 packs.

NM/M

Complete Set (10): 15.00

Common Player: .50
Inserted 1:24
Golds: 2X
Inserted 1:240
AE1 Willie Mays 2.50
AE2 Kirby Puckett 2.00
AE3 Babe Ruth 4.00
AE4 Reggie Jackson 1.50
AE5 Whitey Ford .50
AE6 Lou Brock .50
AE7 Mickey Mantle 4.00
AE8 Yogi Berra .75
AE9 Bob Gibson .50
AE10 Don Larsen 1.00

WS Fever Reggie Jackson Picks

Reggie Jackson's Picks contains top players that Jackson believes have what it takes to perform on center stage in the World Series. Fronts have a shot of the player with his name in the background, and a head shot of Reggie Jackson in the bottom right corner. These were numbered with a "RP" prefix and inserted one per 12 packs.

NM/M

Complete Set (15): 12.50
Common Player: .25
Inserted 1:12
1 Paul O'Neill .25
2 Barry Bonds 2.50
3 Ken Griffey Jr. 1.50
4 Juan Gonzalez .40
5 Greg Maddux 1.00
6 Mike Piazza 1.50
7 Larry Walker .25
8 Mo Vaughn .25
9 Roger Clemens 1.25
10 John Smoltz .25
11 Alex Rodriguez 2.00
12 Frank Thomas .75
13 Mark McGwire 2.00
14 Jeff Bagwell .75
15 Randy Johnson .75

WS Fever MVP Collection

This 10-card insert set features select MVPs from the World Series. Card fronts contain a shot of the player over a white border with the year in black letters and the insert and player's name in blue foil. MVP Collection inserts were seeded one per four packs and numbered with a "MC" prefix.

NM/M

Complete Set (10): 1.00
Common Player: .10
Inserted 1:4
1 Frank Robinson .25
2 Brooks Robinson .25
3 Willie Stargell .10
4 Bret Saberhagen .10
5 Rollie Fingers .10
6 Orel Hershiser .10
7 Paul Molitor .50
8 Tom Glavine .15
9 John Wetteland .10
10 Livan Hernandez .10

1999 Sports Illustrated

The Sports Illustrated set from Fleer consists of 180 base cards composed of 107 player cards, and four subsets. They include Team 2000, Postseason Review, Award Winners, and Season Highlights. Cards came in six-card packs with an SRP of $1.99. The set also includes five insert sets, along with hobby exclusive autographed J.D. Drew cards numbered to 250.

NM/M

Complete Set (180): 15.00
Common Player: .05
Wax Pack (6): 1.00
Hobby Box (24): 15.00
Retail Box (16): 10.00
1 Yankees (Postseason Review) .25
2 Scott Brosius (Postseason Review) .05
3 David Wells (Postseason Review) .05
4 Sterling Hitchcock (Postseason Review) .05
5 David Justice (Postseason Review) .05
6 David Cone (Postseason Review) .05
7 Greg Maddux (Postseason Review) .50
8 Jim Leyritz (Postseason Review) .05
9 Gary Gaetti (Postseason Review) .05
10 Mark McGwire (Award Winners) .75
11 Sammy Sosa (Award Winners) .50
12 Larry Walker (Award Winners) .05
13 Tony Womack (Award Winners) .05
14 Tom Glavine (Award Winners) .10
15 Curt Schilling (Award Winners) .10
16 Greg Maddux (Award Winners) .50
17 Trevor Hoffman (Award Winners) .05
18 Kerry Wood (Award Winners) .20
19 Tom Glavine (Award Winners) .10
20 Sammy Sosa (Award Winners) .50
21 Travis Lee (Season Highlights) .05
22 Roberto Alomar (Season Highlights) .05
23 Roger Clemens (Season Highlights) .60
24 Barry Bonds (Season Highlights) 1.00
25 Paul Molitor (Season Highlights) .45
26 Todd Stottlemyre (Season Highlights) .05
27 Chris Hoiles (Season Highlights) .05
28 Albert Belle (Season Highlights) .05
29 Tony Clark (Season Highlights) .05
30 Kerry Wood (Season Highlights) .20
31 David Wells (Season Highlights) .05
32 Dennis Eckersley (Season Highlights) .40
33 Mark McGwire (Season Highlights) .75
34 Cal Ripken Jr. (Season Highlights) 1.00
35 Ken Griffey Jr. (Season Highlights) .65
36 Alex Rodriguez (Season Highlights) .75
37 Craig Biggio (Season Highlights) .05
38 Sammy Sosa (Season Highlights) .50
39 Dennis Martinez (Season Highlights) .05
40 Curt Schilling (Season Highlights) .10
41 Orlando Hernandez (Season Highlights) .05
42 Troy Glaus, Ben Molina **RC**, Todd Greene ("Team" 2000) .45
43 Mitch Meluskey, Daryle Ward, Mike Grzanich ("Team" 2000) .05
44 Eric Chavez, Mike Neill, Steve Connelly **RC** ("Team" 2000) .10
45 Roy Halladay, Tom Evans, Kevin Witt ("Team" 2000) .05
46 George Lombard, Adam Butler, Bruce Chen ("Team" 2000) .05
47 Ronnie Belliard, Valerio de los Santos, Rafael Roque **RC** ("Team" 2000) .05
48 J.D. Drew, Placido Polanco, Mark Little **RC** ("Team" 2000) .50
49 Jason Maxwell, Jose Nieves **RC**, Jeremi Gonzalez ("Team" 2000) .05
50 Scott McClain, Kerry Robinson, Mike Duvall **RC** ("Team" 2000) .05
51 Ben Ford, Bryan Corey **RC**, Danny Klassen ("Team" 2000) .05
52 Angel Pena, Jeff Kubenka, Paul LoDuca ("Team" 2000) .05
53 Kirk Bullinger, Fernando Seguignol, Tim Young ("Team" 2000) .05
54 Ramon Martinez, Wilson Delgado, Armando Rios ("Team" 2000) .05
55 Russ Branyon, Jolbert Cabrera **RC**, Jason Rakers ("Team" 2000) .05
56 Carlos Guillen **RC**, David Holdridge **RC**, Giomar Guevara **RC** ("Team" 2000) .10
57 Alex Gonzalez, Joe Fontenot, Preston Wilson ("Team" 2000) .05
58 Mike Kinkade, Jay Payton, Masato Yoshii ("Team" 2000) .05
59 Willis Otanez, Ryan Minor, Calvin Pickering ("Team" 2000) .05
60 Ben Davis, Matt Clement, Stan Spencer ("Team" 2000) .05
61 Marlon Anderson, Mike Welch, Gary Bennett **RC** ("Team" 2000) .05
62 Abraham Nunez, Sean Lawrence **RC**, Aramis Ramirez ("Team" 2000) .05
63 Jonathan Johnson, Rob Sasser **RC**, Scott Sheldon **RC** ("Team" 2000) .05
64 Keith Glauber **RC**, Guillermo Garcia **RC**, Eddie Priest ("Team" 2000) .05
65 Brian Barkley, Jin Ho Cho, Donnie Sadler ("Team" 2000) .05
66 Derrick Gibson, Mark Strittmatter, Edgard Clemente **RC** ("Team" 2000) .05
67 Jeremy Giambi, Dermal Brown, Chris Hatcher **RC** ("Team" 2000) .05
68 Rob Fick **RC**, Gabe Kapler, Marino Santana ("Team" 2000) .10
69 Corey Koskie, A.J. Pierzynski, Benj Sampson ("Team" 2000) .05
70 Brian Simmons, Mark Johnson, Craig Wilson ("Team" 2000) .05
71 Ryan Bradley, Mike Lowell, Jay Tessmer ("Team" 2000) .05
72 Ben Grieve .05
73 Shawn Green .45
74 Rafael Palmeiro .65
75 Juan Gonzalez .40
76 Mike Piazza 1.25
77 Devon White .05
78 Jim Thome .65
79 Barry Larkin .05
80 Scott Rolen .65
81 Raul Mondesi .05
82 Jason Giambi .50
83 Jose Canseco .45
84 Tony Gwynn 1.00
85 Cal Ripken Jr. 2.00
86 Andy Pettitte .15
87 Carlos Delgado .50
88 Jeff Cirillo .05
89 Bret Saberhagen .05
90 John Olerud .05
91 Ron Coomer .05
92 Todd Helton .65
93 Ray Lankford .05
94 Tim Salmon .05
95 Fred McGriff .05
96 Matt Stairs .05
97 Ken Griffey Jr. 1.25
98 Chipper Jones 1.00
99 Mark Grace .05
100 Ivan Rodriguez .65
101 Jeromy Burnitz .05
102 Kenny Rogers .05
103 Kevin Millwood .05
104 Vinny Castilla .05
105 Jim Edmonds .05
106 Craig Biggio .05
107 Andres Galarraga .05
108 Sammy Sosa 1.00
109 Juan Encarnacion .05
110 Larry Walker .05
111 John Smoltz .05
112 Randy Johnson .75
113 Bobby Higginson .05
114 Albert Belle .05
115 Jaret Wright .05
116 Edgar Renteria .05
117 Andruw Jones .75
118 Barry Bonds 2.00
119 Rondell White .05
120 Jamie Moyer .05
121 Darin Erstad .20
122 Al Leiter .05
123 Mark McGwire 1.50
124 Mo Vaughn .05
125 Livan Hernandez .05
126 Jason Kendall .05
127 Frank Thomas .75
128 Denny Neagle .05
129 Johnny Damon .35
130 Derek Bell .05
131 Jeff Kent .05
132 Tony Womack .05
133 Trevor Hoffman .05
134 Gary Sheffield .40
135 Tino Martinez .05
136 Travis Fryman .05
137 Rolando Arrojo .05
138 Dante Bichette .05
139 Nomar Garciaparra 1.00
140 Moises Alou .05
141 Chuck Knoblauch .05
142 Robin Ventura .05
143 Scott Erickson .05
144 David Cone .05
145 Greg Vaughn .05
146 Wade Boggs 1.00
147 Mike Mussina .30
148 Tony Clark .05
149 Alex Rodriguez 1.50
150 Javy Lopez .05
151 Bartolo Colon .05
152 Derek Jeter 2.00
153 Greg Maddux 1.00
154 Kevin Brown .05
155 Curt Schilling .35
156 Jeff King .05
157 Bernie Williams .05
158 Roberto Alomar .20
159 Travis Lee .05
160 Kerry Wood .50

160p	Kerry Wood ("PROMOTIONAL SAMPLE")	1.00
161	Jeff Bagwell	.75
162	Roger Clemens	1.00
163	Matt Williams	.05
164	Chan Ho Park	.05
165	Damion Easley	.05
166	Manny Ramirez	.75
167	Quinton McCracken	.05
168	Todd Walker	.05
169	Eric Karros	.05
170	Will Clark	.05
171	Edgar Martinez	.05
172	Cliff Floyd	.05
173	Vladimir Guerrero	.75
174	Tom Glavine	.35
175	Pedro Martinez	.75
176	Chuck Finley	.05
177	Dean Palmer	.05
178	Omar Vizquel	.05
179	Checklist	.05
180	Checklist	.05

Diamond Dominators

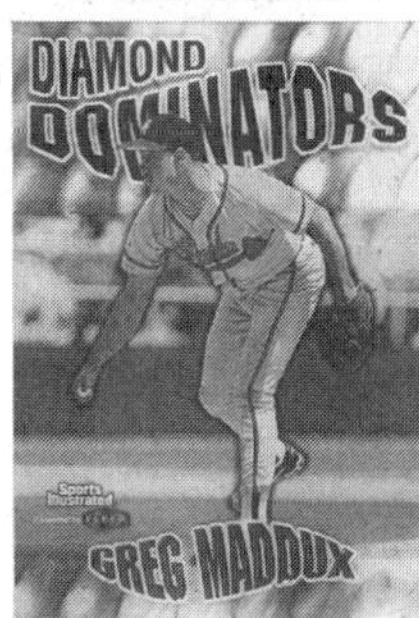

This 10-card insert set features five hitters and five pitchers on embossed cards. The hitters are seeded 1 in every 180 packs, while the pitchers are seeded 1 in every 90 packs.

		NM/M
Complete Set (10):		30.00
Common Player:		1.50
Pitchers inserted 1:90		
Hitters inserted 1:180		
1DD	Kerry Wood	1.50
2DD	Roger Clemens	3.00
3DD	Randy Johnson	2.00
4DD	Greg Maddux	2.50
5DD	Pedro Martinez	2.00
6DD	Ken Griffey Jr.	5.00
7DD	Sammy Sosa	2.50
8DD	Nomar Garciaparra	2.50
9DD	Mark McGwire	6.00
10DD	Alex Rodriguez	6.00

Fabulous 40s

This 13-card insert set consists of the players that hit 40 or more homers during the 1998 season. The cards are sculpture embossed and foil-stamped, with the player's home run total also on the card. One card comes with every 20 packs.

		NM/M
Complete Set (13):		9.00
Common Player:		.25
Inserted 1:20		
1FF	Mark McGwire	2.00
2FF	Sammy Sosa	1.25
3FF	Ken Griffey Jr.	1.50
4FF	Greg Vaughn	.25
5FF	Albert Belle	.25
6FF	Jose Canseco	.50
7FF	Vinny Castilla	.25
8FF	Juan Gonzalez	.50
9FF	Manny Ramirez	1.00
10FF	Andres Galarraga	.25
11FF	Rafael Palmeiro	.75
12FF	Alex Rodriguez	2.00
13FF	Mo Vaughn	.25

Fabulous 40s Extra

The insert set parallels the 13 cards in the Fabulous 40s set. The cards are hobby exclusive, highlighted with silver patterned holofoil. Each player's cards are hand-numbered to the total number of home runs he hit in 1998.

		NM/M
Common Player:		12.00
Numbered to amount of HRs.		
1FF	Mark McGwire/70	60.00
2FF	Sammy Sosa/66	40.00
3FF	Ken Griffey Jr./56	35.00
4FF	Greg Vaughn/50	12.00
5FF	Albert Belle/49	12.00
6FF	Jose Canseco/46	25.00
7FF	Vinny Castilla/46	12.00
8FF	Juan Gonzalez/45	20.00
9FF	Manny Ramirez/45	30.00
10FF	Andres Galarraga/44	12.00
11FF	Rafael Palmeiro/43	25.00
12FF	Alex Rodriguez/42	45.00
13FF	Mo Vaughn/40	12.00

Headliners

Headliners is a 25-card insert set that features silver foil stamped, team-color coded cards. One card comes with every four packs.

		NM/M
Complete Set (25):		10.00
Common Player:		.25
Inserted 1:4		
1H	Vladimir Guerrero	.40
2H	Randy Johnson	.40
3H	Mo Vaughn	.25
4H	Chipper Jones	.50
5H	Jeff Bagwell	.40
6H	Juan Gonzalez	.30
7H	Mark McGwire	.75
8H	Cal Ripken Jr.	1.00
9H	Frank Thomas	.40
10H	Manny Ramirez	.40
11H	Ken Griffey Jr.	.65
12H	Scott Rolen	.35
13H	Alex Rodriguez	.75
14H	Barry Bonds	1.00
15H	Roger Clemens	.55
16H	Darin Erstad	.30
17H	Nomar Garciaparra	.50
18H	Mike Piazza	.65
19H	Greg Maddux	.50
20H	Ivan Rodriguez	.35
21H	Derek Jeter	1.00
22H	Sammy Sosa	.50
23H	Andruw Jones	.40
24H	Pedro Martinez	.40
25H	Kerry Wood	.35

Ones To Watch

This 15-card insert set features the game's top rookies and young stars. The cards have 100 percent-foil background, and are team-color coded. One card was inserted in every 12 packs.

		NM/M
Complete Set (15):		5.00
Common Player:		.25
Inserted 1:12		
10W	J.D. Drew	.65
20W	Marlon Anderson	.25
30W	Roy Halladay	.35
40W	Ben Grieve	.25
50W	Todd Helton	.75
60W	Gabe Kapler	.25
70W	Troy Glaus	.75
80W	Ben Davis	.25
90W	Eric Chavez	.35
100W	Richie Sexson	.25
110W	Fernando Seguignol	.25
120W	Kerry Wood	.50
130W	Bobby Smith	.25
140W	Ryan Minor	.25
150W	Jeremy Giambi	.25
	J.D. Drew autograph (250)	15.00

Greats of the Game

The 90-card base set includes many legendary major-leaguers including Babe Ruth and Cy Young. Card fronts feature a full bleed photo with the player name across the bottom and Greats of the Game printed on the bottom left portion of the card. Card backs have the player's vital information, along with career statistics and a few career highlights. Seven-card packs were issued with a SRP of $15.

		NM/M
Complete Set (90):		12.00
Common Player:		.05
Pack (7):		15.00
Wax Box (12):		150.00
1	Jimmie Foxx	.25
2	Red Schoendienst	.05
3	Babe Ruth	3.00
4	Lou Gehrig	2.00
5	Mel Ott	.05
6	Stan Musial	.25
7	Mickey Mantle	3.00
8	Carl Yastrzemski	.15
9	Enos Slaughter	.05
10	Andre Dawson	.05
11	Luis Aparicio	.05
12	Ferguson Jenkins	.05
13	Christy Mathewson	.25
14	Ernie Banks	.15
15	Johnny Podres	.05
16	George Foster	.05
17	Jerry Koosman	.05
18	Curt Simmons	.05
19	Bob Feller	.05
20	Frank Robinson	.05
21	Gary Carter	.05
22	Frank Thomas	.05
23	Bill Lee	.05
24	Willie Mays	1.00
25	Tommie Agee	.05
26	Boog Powell	.05
27	Jimmy Wynn	.05
28	Sparky Lyle	.05
29	Bo Belinsky	.05
30	Maury Wills	.05
31	Bill Buckner	.05
32	Steve Carlton	.05
33	Harmon Killebrew	.05
34	Nolan Ryan	1.00
35	Randy Jones	.05
36	Robin Roberts	.05
37	Al Oliver	.05
38	Rico Petrocelli	.05
39	Dave Parker	.05
40	Eddie Mathews	.05
41	Earl Weaver	.05
42	Jackie Robinson	1.50
43	Lou Brock	.05
44	Reggie Jackson	.15
45	Bob Gibson	.05
46	Jeff Burroughs	.05
47	Jim Bouton	.05
48	Bob Forsch	.05
49	Ron Guidry	.05
50	Ty Cobb	2.00
51	Roy White	.05
52	Joe Rudi	.05
53	Moose Skowron	.05
54	Goose Gossage	.05
55	Ed Kranepool	.05
56	Paul Blair	.05
57	Kent Hrbek	.05
58	Orlando Cepeda	.05
59	Buck O'Neil	.05
60	Al Kaline	.05
61	Vida Blue	.05
62	Sam McDowell	.05
63	Jesse Barfield	.05
64	Dave Kingman	.05
65	Ron Santo	.05
66	Steve Garvey	.05
67	Gaylord Perry	.05
68	Darrell Evans	.05
69	Rollie Fingers	.05
70	Walter Johnson	.25
71	Al Hrabosky	.05
72	Mickey Rivers	.05
73	Mike Torrez	.05
74	Hank Bauer	.05
75	Tug McGraw	.05
76	David Clyde	.05
77	Jim Lonborg	.05
78	Clete Boyer	.05
79	Harry Walker	.05
80	Cy Young	.25
81	Bud Harrelson	.05
82	Paul Splittorff	.05
83	Bert Campaneris	.05
84	Joe Niekro	.05
85	Bob Horner	.05
86	Jerry Royster	.05
87	Tommy John	.05
88	Mark Fidrych	.05
89	Dick Williams	.05
90	Graig Nettles	.05

Greats/Game Autographs

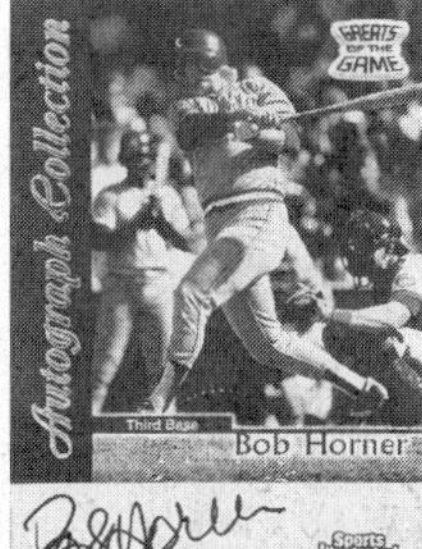

Each Greats of the Game pack has one autograph from the 80 card autograph checklist. Each card is autographed on the white portion on the bottom of the card, and is stamped "seal of authenticity." Card backs certify the autograph is authentic and "has been embossed with the Fleer Mark of Authenticity." The unnumbered cards are checklisted here in alphabetical order.

		NM/M
Common Player:		4.00
Inserted 1:1		
(1)	Tommie Agee	8.00
(2)	Luis Aparicio	12.00
(3)	Ernie Banks	25.00
(4)	Jesse Barfield	6.00
(5)	Hank Bauer	10.00
(6)	Bo Belinsky	6.00
(7)	Paul Blair	6.00
(8)	Vida Blue	10.00
(9)	Jim Bouton	10.00
(10)	Clete Boyer	10.00
(11)	Lou Brock	15.00
(12)	Bill Buckner	10.00
(13)	Jeff Burroughs	5.00
(14)	Bert Campaneris	8.00
(15)	Steve Carlton	20.00
(16)	Gary Carter	10.00
(17)	Orlando Cepeda	12.00
(18)	David Clyde	5.00
(19)	Andre Dawson	10.00
(20)	Darrell Evans	8.00
(21)	Bob Feller	15.00
(22)	Mark Fidrych	15.00
(23)	Rollie Fingers	10.00
(24)	Bob Forsch	6.00
(25)	George Foster	10.00
(26)	Steve Garvey	10.00
(27)	Bob Gibson	15.00
(28)	Goose Gossage	10.00
(29)	Ron Guidry	20.00
(30)	Bud Harrelson	10.00
(31)	Bob Horner	10.00
(32)	Al Hrabosky	8.00
(33)	Kent Hrbek	10.00
(34a)	Reggie Jackson	150.00
(34b)	Reggie Jackson ("Mr. October")	200.00
(34c)	Reggie Jackson ("HoF 93")	200.00
(35)	Ferguson Jenkins	10.00
(36)	Tommy John	8.00
(37)	Randy Jones	4.00
(38)	Al Kaline	25.00
(39)	Harmon Killebrew	25.00
(40)	Dave Kingman	8.00
(41)	Jerry Koosman	8.00
(42)	Ed Kranepool	8.00
(43)	Bill Lee	10.00
(44)	Jim Lonborg	5.00
(45)	Sparky Lyle	8.00
(46)	Eddie Mathews	60.00
(47)	Willie Mays	125.00
(48)	Sam McDowell	8.00
(49)	Tug McGraw	25.00
(50)	Stan Musial	100.00
(51)	Graig Nettles	10.00
(52)	Joe Niekro	8.00
(53)	Buck O'Neil	20.00
(54)	Al Oliver	10.00
(55)	Dave Parker	10.00
(56)	Gaylord Perry	10.00
(57)	Rico Petrocelli	10.00
(58)	Johnny Podres	20.00
(59)	Boog Powell	10.00
(60)	Mickey Rivers	8.00
(61)	Robin Roberts	20.00
(62)	Frank Robinson	20.00
(63)	Jerry Royster	4.00
(64)	Joe Rudi	8.00
(65)	Nolan Ryan	200.00
(66)	Ron Santo	15.00
(67)	Red Schoendienst	12.00
(68)	Curt Simmons	6.00
(69)	Moose Skowron	15.00
(70)	Enos Slaughter	20.00
(71)	Paul Splittorff	6.00
(72)	Frank Thomas	8.00
(73)	Mike Torrez	4.00
(74)	Harry Walker	4.00
(75)	Earl Weaver	10.00
(76)	Roy White	8.00
(77)	Dick Williams	10.00
(78)	Maury Wills	10.00
(79)	Jimmy Wynn	10.00
(80)	Carl Yastrzemski	50.00

Greats/Game Cover Collection

Each pack features one of the 50 chosen baseball covers from the Sports Illustrated archives. Card fronts are a reprint of the actual cover, while the backs give a brief description of the cover article and date of the magazine cover. Each card is numbered with a "C" suffix.

		NM/M
Complete Set (50):		25.00
Common Player:		.50
Inserted 1:1		
1	Johnny Podres	.50
2	Mickey Mantle	5.00
3	Stan Musial	.50
4	Eddie Mathews	.50
5	Frank Thomas	.50
6	Willie Mays	1.00
7	Red Schoendienst	.50
8	Luis Aparicio	.50
9	Mickey Mantle	3.00
10	Al Kaline	.50
11	Maury Wills	.50
12	Sam McDowell	.50
13	Harry Walker	.50
14	Carl Yastrzemski	.50
15	Carl Yastrzemski	.50
16	Lou Brock	.50
17	Ron Santo	.50
18	Reggie Jackson	.50
19	Frank Robinson	.50
20	Jerry Koosman	.50
21	Bud Harrelson	.50
22	Vida Blue	.50
23	Ferguson Jenkins	.50
24	Sparky Lyle	.50
25	Steve Carlton	.50
26	Bert Campaneris	.50
27	Jimmy Wynn	.50
28	Steve Garvey	.50
29	Nolan Ryan	1.00
30	Randy Jones	.50
31	Reggie Jackson	.50
32	Joe Rudi	.50
33	Reggie Jackson	.50
34	Dave Parker	.50
35	Mark Fidrych	.50
36	Earl Weaver	.50
37	Nolan Ryan	1.00
38	Steve Carlton	.50
39	Reggie Jackson	.50
40	Rollie Fingers	.50
41	Gary Carter	.50
42	Graig Nettles	.50
43	Gaylord Perry	.50
44	Kent Hrbek	.50
45	Gary Carter	.50
46	Steve Garvey	.50
47	Steve Carlton	.50
48	Nolan Ryan	1.00
49	Nolan Ryan	1.00
50	Mickey Mantle	3.00

Greats/Game Record Breakers

This 10-card set spotlights the top record breakers in the past century from Christy Mathewson to Nolan Ryan. Card fronts are full foiled with a oblong stamp on the bottom portion detailing the player's respective record. Card backs are numbered with a "RB" suffix and gives more detail on the featured player's record. These are seeded 1:12 packs. A Gold parallel is also randomly seeded 1:120 packs and have gold holo-foil.

		NM/M
Complete Set (10):		40.00
Common Player:		2.00
Inserted 1:12		
Golds:		6X
Inserted 1:120		
1	Mickey Mantle	8.00
2	Stan Musial	3.50
3	Babe Ruth	8.00
4	Christy Mathewson	2.00
5	Cy Young	2.00
6	Nolan Ryan	7.50
7	Jackie Robinson	6.00
8	Lou Gehrig	7.00
9	Ty Cobb	3.50
10	Walter Johnson	2.00

1989-91 Sports Illustrated For Kids

Beginning with its January 1989 issue and continuing for three years, the magazine "Sports Illustrated For Kids" produced a set of sportscards featuring many professional and amateur stars in more than a dozen sports. Generally issued in a nine-card panel, cards were perforated so they could be removed from the magazine and separated from each other. A variety of de-

signs and formats were used in that period. Only the pro baseball cards from the series are checklisted here.

		NM/M
Complete Set (60):		55.00
Common Player:		.50
5	Orel Hershiser	.50
11	Jose Canseco	1.00
20	Darryl Strawberry	.50
31	Mike Greenwell	.50
33	Tony Gwynn	2.00
35	Frank Viola	.50
37	Don Mattingly	2.25
43	Ozzie Smith	2.00
46	Rickey Henderson	1.50
48	Chris Sabo	.50
52	Andre Dawson	.75
56	Alan Trammell	.50
60	Roger Clemens	2.25
63	Andres Galarraga	.50
64	John Franco	.50
69	Cal Ripken Jr.	4.00
70	Will Clark	.50
75	Bo Jackson	.75
81	Nolan Ryan	4.00
90	Mike Schmidt	2.25
112	Kevin Mitchell	.50
121	Ryne Sandberg	2.00
127	Robin Yount	1.50
133	Dave Stewart	.50
140	Eric Davis	.50
144	Mike Scott	.50
146	Mark McGwire	3.00
151	Dwight Gooden	.50
158	Ken Griffey Jr.	2.50
162	George Brett	2.25
165	Ruben Sierra	.50
167	Kirby Puckett	2.00
171	Carlton Fisk	1.50
172	Fred McGriff	.50
176	Wade Boggs	2.00
178	Tim Raines	.50
181	Bobby Bonilla	.50
189	Kelly Gruber	.50
197	Dennis Eckersley	1.00
205	Cecil Fielder	.50
212	Jackie Robinson	2.00
216	Babe Ruth	3.00
229	Barry Bonds	4.00
240	Jose Rijo	.50
248	Sandy Alomar Jr.	.50
251	Ron Gant	.50
259	David Justice	.50
261	Bob Welch	.50
266	Doug Drabek	.50
268	Rafael Palmeiro	1.25
271	Paul Molitor	1.50
275	Bobby Thigpen	.50
279	Edgar Martinez	.50
282	Dave Winfield	1.50
283	Mark Grace	.50
288	Dwight Evans	.50
289	Dave Henderson	.50
294	Lee Smith	.50
303	Ramon Martinez	.50
321	Ty Cobb	1.50

1992-2000 Sports Illustrated For Kids

A new series, with cards numbered consecutively from #1, of magazine insert cards was begun with SI For Kids' in its January 1992 issue. Like the earlier series, cards are 2-1/2" x 3-1/2" inches and most often found as a nine-card panel, with each card perforated for removal from the magazine and separation from the other cards. As before, the cards feature a number of different designs, formats and back treatments. Backs usually include a few personal details and a trivia question. Only the cards of pro baseball players are checklisted here.

		NM/M
Complete Set (157):		150.00
Common Player:		.25
24	Terry Pendleton	.25
29	Kirby Puckett	2.00
36	Roger Clemens	2.25
40	Tom Glavine	.45
45	Frank Thomas	1.50
50	Jim Abbott	.25
54	Roberto Alomar	.35
64	Matt Williams	.25
68	Bobby Bonilla	.25
72	Chuck Finley	.25
75	Danny Tartabull	.25
81	Jack Morris	.25
86	Will Clark	.25
108	Lou Gehrig	2.50
121	Juan Gonzalez	.75
132	Cal Ripken Jr.	4.00
136	Jack McDowell	.25
144	Marquis Grissom	.25
145	Andy Van Slyke	.25
152	Dennis Eckersley	1.00
157	Barry Bonds	4.00
162	Greg Maddux	2.00
168	Nolan Ryan	4.00
170	Dave Winfield	1.50
173	Ken Griffey Jr.	2.50
178	Wade Boggs	2.00
185	Kirk Gibson	.25
187	Albert Belle	.25
190	John Burkett	.25
196	John Kruk	.25
199	Randy Johnson	1.50
204	Lou Whitaker	.25
212	Yogi Berra	.50
236	Lenny Dykstra	.25
244	Carlos Baerga	.25
254	Joe Carter	.25
266	Chuck Carr	.25
268	Julie Croteau (Colorado Silver Bullets)	.25
270	Michael Jordan	3.00
274	Andres Galarraga	.25
278	Jeff Bagwell	1.50
281	John Olerud	.25
288	Tony Gwynn	2.00
292	Gregg Jefferies	.25
297	Mo Vaughn	.25
298	Moises Alou	.25
305	Jimmy Key	.25
311	Mike Mussina	.40
313	Mike Piazza	2.50
320	Stan Musial	2.00
327	Matt Williams	.25
343	Frank Thomas (Boyhood photo.)	1.00
349	Michael Jordan (Boyhood photo.)	2.00
359	Kenny Lofton	.25
362	Raul Mondesi	.25
381	David Cone	.25
386	Brady Anderson	.25
390	Eric Karros	.25
391	Paul O'Neill	.25
398	Eddie Murray	1.50
402	Barry Larkin	.25
407	Edgar Martinez	.25
412	Mark McGwire	3.00
416	Albert Belle (Cartoon)	.25
430	Mark Grace	.25
433	Chuck Knoblauch	.25
447	Chipper Jones	2.00
451	Tom Glavine (Boyhood photo.)	.25
455	Cal Ripken Jr. (Boyhood photo.)	3.00
462	Jeff Conine	.25
470	Hideo Nomo	.75
475	Bernie Williams	.25
478	Craig Biggio	.25
485	Jose Mesa	.25
497	Roberto Alomar	.35
503	John Smoltz	.25
505	Henry Rodriguez	.25
513	Rey Ordonez	.25
516	Ellis Burks	.25
518	Ivan Rodriguez	1.25
543	Alex Rodriguez	3.00
553	Mo Vaughn	.25
561	Andy Pettitte	.35
562	Barry Bonds	4.00
582	Andruw Jones	1.50
570	Randy Johnson (April Fool card as L.A. Laker.)	1.50
572	Ken Griffey Jr. (April Fool card as Orlando Magic.)	2.50
588	Brian Jordan	.25
589	Derek Jeter	4.00
596	Juan Gonzalez	.75
598	Andres Galarraga	.25
608	Mark McGwire	3.00
611	Pat Hentgen	.25
627	Cal Ripken Jr. (Cartoon as Tin Man.)	4.00
634	Sandy Alomar Jr.	.25
641	Brady Anderson	.25
652	Jeff Bagwell	1.50
669	Larry Walker	.25
673	Roger Clemens	2.25
685	Frank Thomas	1.50
693	Denny Neagle	.25
695	Tony Gwynn	2.00
697	Mike Piazza	2.50
703	Kenny Lofton	.25
708	Moises Alou	.25
712	Dante Bichette	.25
720	John Wetteland	.25
721	Curt Schilling	.45
725	Nomar Garciaparra	2.00
734	Ken Griffey Jr. (Cartoon as The Cat in the Hat.)	2.50
737	Greg Maddux (Cartoon as Encyclopedia Brown.)	2.00
743	Sammy Sosa	2.00
749	David Wells	.25
No#	Mark McGwire (The Best of 1998)	2.50
758	Pedro Martinez	1.50
768	Ila Borders	.25
770	David Cone	.25
784	Mike Piazza (April Fool's - hockey player.)	2.50
790	Mark McGwire (April Fool's - Chicago Cub.)	3.00
795	Craig Biggio	.25
796	Tom Glavine	.45
802	Alex Rodriguez	3.00
804	Trevor Hoffman	.25
813	Rickey Henderson	1.50
815	Mo Vaughn	.25
817	Vinny Castilla	.25
820	John Smoltz	.25
825	Jose Canseco	.65
831	Matt Williams	.25
833	Derek Jeter	4.00
840	Ivan Rodriguez (As Darth Vader.)	1.25
841	Roger Clemens (As lion.)	2.25
846	Ken Caminiti (As Ghoul.)	.25
849	Roberto Alomar	.35
No#	Greg Maddux (Fall/Winter 1999)	2.00
No#	Ken Griffey Jr. (Fall/Winter 1999)	2.50
856	Randy Johnson	1.50
866	Babe Ruth	3.00
869	Mickey Mantle	5.00
870	Jackie Robinson	2.00
882	Mark McGwire (Kid photo.)	3.00
884	Mariano Rivera	.35
892	Billy the Marlin (Mascot)	.25
896	The Phillie Phanatic (Mascot)	.25
901	Kevin Millwood	.25
906	Manny Ramirez	1.50
910	Bernie Williams	.25
914	Larry Walker	.25
920	Ken Griffey Jr.	2.50
922	David Wells	.25
929	Chipper Jones	2.00
935	Carlos Beltran	.50
941	Vladimir Guerrero	1.50
945	Andres Galarraga	.25
953	Jason Kendall (As Pokemon's Ash Ketchum.)	.40
955	Pedro Martinez	1.50
962	Todd Helton	1.25

1996-98 Sports Illustrated For Kids Legends

Unlike the nine-card panels which appear in every issue of SI For Kids, the Legends series appeared sporadically as a four-card panel honoring the past greats of many sports. While designs vary from issue to issue, the format of the cards has remained a consistent 2-9/16" x 4". Only the baseball players are listed here.

		NM/M
Complete Set (7):		9.00
Common Player:		.25
45	Sadaharu Oh	1.00
52	Willie Mays	2.00
66	Mike Schmidt	1.50
(1)	Mickey Mantle	3.00
(2)	Bob Feller	.50
(3)	Lou Brock	.50
(4)	Honus Wagner	.50

1999 SI for Kids 10th Anniversary Sheet

Saluting Sports Illustrated for Kids on its 10th anniversary, Major League Baseball, the Players' Association and the four card licensees created a a special eight-card insert sheet which appears in the magazine's July 1999 issue. The sheet consists of nine 2-1/2" x 3-1/2" cards printed on thin cardboard and perforated for easy separation. The Fleer and Upper Deck cards are very similar to those companies' regular 1999 issues, except for the absence of foil printing and UV coating. The Topps and Pacific offerings are new designs. All player cards feature action photos on front along with card company and SI for Kids logos. Backs have another photo plus stats, biographical data and copyright notice.

		NM/M
Complete Sheet:		6.00
Complete Set (9):		5.00
Common Player:		.50
7	J.D. Drew (Fleer Tradition)	.50
49	Cal Ripken Jr. (Upper Deck)	1.00
205	Ken Griffey Jr. (Upper Deck)	.65
266	Sammy Sosa (SkyBox Thunder)	.65
---	Roger Clemens (Topps)	.50
---	Tony Gwynn (Pacific)	.50
---	Mark McGwire (Pacific)	.75
---	Mike Piazza (Topps)	.65
---	Sponsors' card	.10

2000-2005 Sports Illustrated for Kids

Beginning with its December 2000-dated edition, SI/Kids launched a new series of collectible sportscard inserts. Like earlier series, cards were inserted into the magazine as nine-card perforated sheets. Each card, if separated from the sheet, measures the standard 2-1/2" x 3-1/2". Fronts feature borderless color action photos with a Sports Illustrated for Kids logo in an upper corner. The athlete is identified in red and blue typography in a silver panel at bottom. Horizontal backs have a blue background. In a black box at right is a portrait photo and trivia question. A black box at bottom has recent and career stats. At top is player personal data; at center are career highlights. Only the baseball players from the multi-sport issue are listed here.

		NM/M
Complete Set (90):		55.00
Common Player:		.25
8	Gary Sheffield	.35
10	Carlos Delgado	.50
24	Jason Giambi	.50
30	Kazuhiro Sasaki	.25
34	Jeff Kent	.25
39	Randy Johnson	.75
40	Rafael Furcal	.25
50	Nomar Garciaparra	1.00
54	Darin Erstad	.35
57	Edgar Martinez	.25
62	Andruw Jones	.75
68	Edgardo Alfonzo	.25
72	Tim Hudson	.25
74	Barry Bonds	2.50
80	Juan Gonzalez	.40
85	Kevin Brown	.25
87	Luis Gonzalez	.25
92	Bret Boone	.25
98	Mike Hampton	.25
101	Mike Piazza	1.50
110	Alex Rodriguez	2.00
122	Sammy Sosa	1.00
131	Ichiro Suzuki	2.00
141	Curt Schilling	.35
144	Albert Pujols	2.00
152	Derek Jeter	2.50
157	Mariano Rivera	.25
162	Juan Pierre	.25
164	Robb Nen	.25
169	Jim Thome	.65
174	Ken Griffey Jr.	1.50
176	Hideo Nomo	.40
182	Pedro Martinez	.75
186	Tino Martinez	.25
191	Lance Berkman	.25
195	Omar Vizquel	.25
199	Tom Glavine	.35
207	Torii Hunter	.25
209	Luis Castillo	.25
216	Jorge Posada	.25
221	Barry Zito	.25
228	Manny Ramirez	.75
237	Troy Glaus	.65
246	Scott Rolen	.65
248	Alex Rodriguez	2.00
255	Eric Hinske	.25
257	John Smoltz	.25
267	Alfonso Soriano	.50
269	Derek Lowe	.25
271	Roy Oswalt	.25
276	Miguel Tejada	.25
339	Barry Bonds	2.50
347	Ivan Rodriguez	.65
352	Eric Gagne	.25
356	Hideki Matsui	2.00
361	Todd Helton	.65
366	Kerry Wood	.50
374	Carlos Delgado	.50
376	Tim Hudson	.25
381	Jim Thome	.65
383	Josh Beckett	.25
388	Andruw Jones	.75
393	Bill Mueller	.25
398	Sean Casey	.25
402	Dontrelle Willis	.25
408	Vladimir Guerrero	.75
410	Randy Johnson	.75
417	Ichiro Suzuki	2.00
422	Ben Sheets	.25
429	Eric Chavez	.25
430	Russ Ortiz	.25
442	Adrian Beltre	.35
447	Curt Schilling	.35
462	Jason Schmidt	.25
466	Adam Dunn	.40
470	Joe Nathan	.25
472	Jason Bay	.25
479	Roger Clemens	1.25
483	Melvin Mora	.25
488	Gary Sheffield	.25
490	C.C. Sabathia	.25
497	Miguel Cabrera	.25
505	Paul Konerko	.25
509	Pedro Martinez	.75
514	Derrek Lee	.50
521	Chris Carpenter	.25
523	Mark Teixeira	.25
527	Chad Cordero	.25
536	Tim Wakefield	.25
538	Carlos Lee	.25

2005- Sports Illustrated for Kids

Beginning with its December 2005-dated edition, SI/Kids launched a new series of collectible sportscard inserts. Like earlier series, cards were inserted into the magazine as nine-card perforated sheets. Each card, if separated from the sheet, measures the standard 2-1/2" x 3-1/2". Fronts feature color action photos, bordered in black, with a Sports Illustrated for Kids logo in in an upper corner. The athlete is identified in white and yellow typography at bottom. Horizontal backs have a blue background. At right is a portrait photo and trivia question. A black box at bottom has recent and career stats. At top is player personal data; at center are career highlights. Only the baseball players from the multi-sport issue are listed here.

		NM/M
Complete Set (12):		4.50
Common Player:		.25
5	Bartolo Colon	.25
7	Andruw Jones	.50
10	Roy Oswalt	.25
15	Alex Rodriguez	1.00
20	Jermaine Dye	.25
25	Jake Peavy	.25
30	David Ortiz	.50
34	Huston Street	.50
39	Chone Figgins	.25
40	Cliff Lee	.25
48	Dontrelle Willis	.25
53	Jim Edmonds	.25

1981 Spot-bilt George Brett

This one-card set was released in both 1981 and 1982 (see stats on back to differentiate) in boxes of turf baseball shoes, for which Brett served on the athletic advisory staff. Cards are standard 2-1/2" x 3-1/2". Despite the card number 5 on the back, there are no other players in the series. Brett wore uniform #5.

		NM/M
5	George Brett	2.50

1981 Squirt

These cards, issued in conjunction with Topps, were issued as two-card panels in eight-pack cartons of the soft drink. Individual cards measure the standard 2-1/2" x 3-1/2", while the vertical panels measure 2-1/2" x 10-1/2", with a promotional card reading "Free Topps 1981 Baseball Cards" attached. The promotional card is blank-backed, while the player card backs are similar to Topps' regular issue, though re-numbered for inclusion in this 33-card set. Most of the game's top players are included. There are only 22 different two-card panels, as card numbers 1-11 appear in two different bottom panel combinations. Card fronts feature a color player por-

trait photo within a baseball design, team and position designation, and the Squirt logo.

NM/M
Complete Panel Set (22): 20.00
Complete Singles Set (33): 20.00
Common Panel: .50
Common Player: .15
Panel (1) 2.00
1 George Brett 1.50
12 Garry Templeton .15
Panel (2) 2.00
1 George Brett 1.50
23 Jerry Mumphrey .15
Panel (3) .50
2 George Foster .15
13 Rick Burleson .15
Panel (4) .50
2 George Foster .15
24 Tony Armas .15
Panel (5) .50
3 Ben Oglivie .15
14 Dave Kingman .15
Panel (6) .50
3 Ben Oglivie .15
25 Fred Lynn .15
Panel (7) 1.50
4 Steve Garvey .50
15 Eddie Murray .75
Panel (8) .75
4 Steve Garvey .50
26 Ron LeFlore .15
Panel (9) 2.00
5 Reggie Jackson 1.50
16 Don Sutton .50
Panel (10) 2.00
5 Reggie Jackson 1.50
27 Steve Kemp .15
Panel (11) .75
6 Bill Buckner .15
17 Dusty Baker .15
Panel (12) 1.50
6 Bill Buckner .15
28 Rickey Henderson .75
Panel (13) .50
7 Jim Rice .25
18 Jack Clark .15
Panel (14) .50
7 Jim Rice .25
29 John Castino .15
Panel (15) 3.00
8 Mike Schmidt 1.50
19 Dave Winfield .75
Panel (16) 2.00
8 Mike Schmidt 1.50
30 Cecil Cooper .15
Panel (17) 2.50
9 Rod Carew 1.00
20 Johnny Bench 1.00
Panel (18) 1.00
9 Rod Carew 1.00
31 Bruce Bochte .15
Panel (19) .50
10 Dave Parker .15
21 Lee Mazzilli .15
Panel (20) .65
10 Dave Parker .15
32 Joe Charboneau .25
Panel (21) 3.00
11 Pete Rose 2.00
22 Al Oliver .15
Panel (22) 3.00
11 Pete Rose 2.00
33 Chet Lemon .15

1982 Squirt

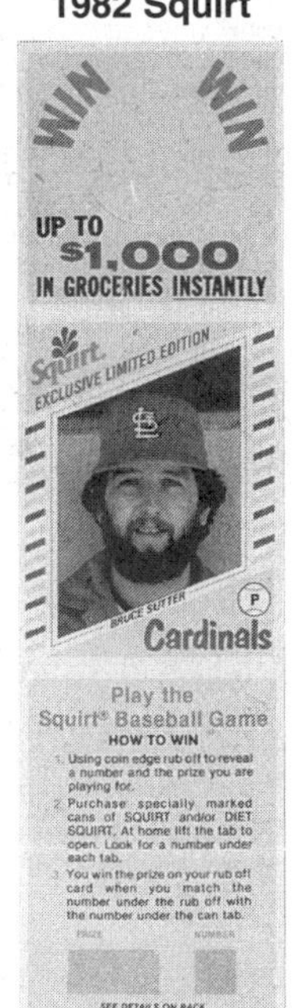

This set was again prepared in conjunction with Topps, but the 1982 Squirt cards are completely different from Topps' regular issue. Only 22 players are included in the full-color set, with the 2-1/2" x 3-1/2" player cards available on one- or two-player panels. Card panels come in four variations, with free grocery contest and scratch-off game cards taking one or two of the positions on the three-card panels. Card backs are numbered and list player statistics.

NM/M
Complete Set (22): 12.00
Common Player: .15
1 Cecil Cooper .15
2 Jerry Remy .15
3 George Brett 2.00
4 Alan Trammell .15
5 Reggie Jackson 2.00
6 Kirk Gibson .15
7 Dave Winfield .75
8 Carlton Fisk .75
9 Ron Guidry .15
10 Dennis Leonard .15
11 Rollie Fingers .60
12 Pete Rose 2.50
13 Phil Garner .15
14 Mike Schmidt 2.00
15 Dave Concepcion .15
16 George Hendrick .15
17 Andre Dawson .35
18 George Foster .15
19 Gary Carter .75
20 Fernando Valenzuela .15
21 Tom Seaver 1.00
22 Bruce Sutter .60

1996 St. Louis Browns Historical Society

This collectors issue honoring the 1944 American League Champion St. Louis Browns was issued in conjunction with a reunion of that team in 1996, sponsored by the St. Louis Browns Historical Society. Every player on the '44 team is included in the set, representing the first-ever baseball card for some of them. Fronts of the 2-5/8" x 3-3/4" cards feature color portraits by artist Ronnie Joyner. Shades of brown form the border. Backs are also printed in brown tones and include a cartoon, 1944 season and World Series stats, lifetime stats, personal data, a career summary and part of a team "Timeline" of the 1944 season. It was reported 2,500 sets were issued at $10 retail.

NM/M
Complete Set (36): 10.00
Common Player: .50
1 Team Logo Card .50
2 Don Gutteridge .50
3 Milt Byrnes .50
4 Al Hollingsworth .50
5 Willis Hudlin .50
6 Sig Jakucki .50
7 Nelson Potter .50
8 Len Schulte .50
9 Vern Stephens .50
10 Frank Demaree .50
11 Al Zarilla .50
12 Bob Muncrief .50
13 Steve Sundra .50
14 Jack Kramer .50
15 Lefty West .50
16 Denny Galehouse .50
17 Luke Sewell .50
18 Joe Schultz .50
19 George McQuinn .50
20 Ellis Clary .50
21 Babe Martin .50
22 Red Hayworth .50
23 Frank Mancuso .50
24 Tex Shirley .50
25 Mike Chartak .50
26 Mark Christman .50
27 Tom Hafey .50
28 Tom Turner .50
29 Floyd Baker .50
30 Mike Kreevich .50
31 George Caster .50
32 Gene Moore .50
33 Chet Laabs .50
34 Sam Zoldak .50
35 Hal Epps .50
36 Team Composite/ Checklist Card .50

1987 St. Louis Cardinals Fire Safety

Approximately 25,000 fans in attendance at Busch Stadium on August 24 received this set produced by the U.S. Forestry Service. The cards measure 4" x 6". Fronts feature a full-color photo set inside an oval frame. Only the player's last name appears on front. Backs carry the player's name, position and personal data plus a Smokey Bear cartoon fire prevention message.

NM/M
Complete Set (25): 6.00
Common Player: .25
1 Ray Soff .25
2 Todd Worrell .25
3 John Tudor .25
4 Pat Perry .25
5 Rick Horton .25
6 Dan Cox .25
7 Bob Forsch .25
8 Greg Mathews .25
9 Bill Dawley .25
10 Steve Lake .25
11 Tony Pena .25
12 Tom Pagnozzi .25
13 Jack Clark .25
14 Jim Lindeman .25
15 Mike Laga .25
16 Terry Pendleton .25
17 Ozzie Smith 3.50
18 Jose Oquendo .25
19 Tom Lawless .25
20 Tom Herr .25
21 Curt Ford .25
22 Willie McGee .25
23 Tito Landrum .25
24 Vince Coleman .25
25 Whitey Herzog .25

1988 St. Louis Cardinals Fire Safety

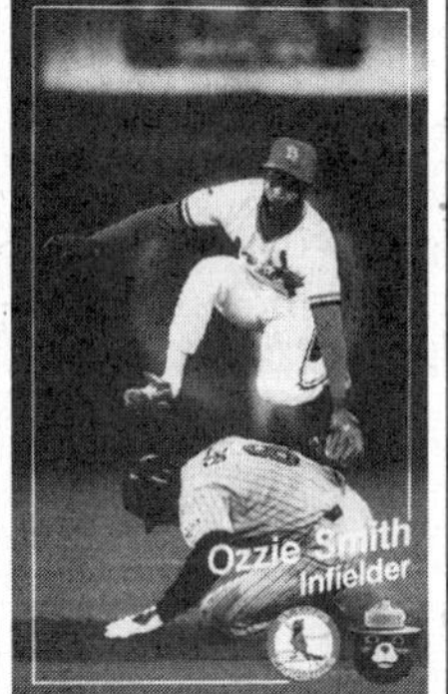

This set of oversized (3" x 5") cards features full-color action photos that fill the entire front. A thin white line frames the player photo. The player name, team logo and Smokey Bear picture logo are printed in the lower-right corner. Black-and-white backs contain player information and a Smokey Bear fire prevention cartoon. The sets were distributed to young St. Louis fans as part of a U.S. Forest Service fire prevention campaign. The National Association of State Foresters co-sponsored this set.

NM/M
Complete Set (25): 6.00
Common Player: .25
1 Whitey Herzog .25
2 Danny Cox .25
3 Ken Dayley .25
4 Jose DeLeon .25
5 Bob Forsch .25
6 Joe Magrane .25
7 Greg Mathews .25
8 Scott Terry .25
9 John Tudor .25
10 Todd Worrell .25
11 Steve Lake .25
12 Tom Pagnozzi .25
13 Tony Pena .25
14 Bob Horner .25
15 Tom Lawless .25
16 Jose Oquendo .25
17 Terry Pendleton .25
18 Ozzie Smith 3.50
19 Vince Coleman .25
20 Curt Ford .25
21 Willie McGee .25
22 Larry McWilliams .25
23 Steve Peters .25
24 Luis Alicea .25
25 Tom Brunansky .25

1989 St. Louis Cardinals Fire Safety

This set featuring action player photos was issued by the U.S. Forest Service to promote fire safety. The cards measure 4" x 6" and include the player's name, team logo and a small picture of Smokey Bear beneath the player photo.

NM/M
Complete Set (25): 6.00
Common Player: .25
(1) Tom Brunansky .25
(2) Cris Carpenter .25
(3) Vince Coleman .25
(4) John Costello .25
(5) Ken Dayley .25
(6) Jose DeLeon .25
(7) Frank DiPino .25
(8) Whitey Herzog .25
(9) Ken Hill .25
(10) Pedro Guerrero .25
(11) Tim Jones .25
(12) Jim Lindeman .25
(13) Joe Magrane .25
(14) Willie McGee .25
(15) John Morris .25
(16) Jose Oquendo .25
(17) Tom Pagnozzi .25
(18) Tony Pena .25
(19) Terry Pendleton .25
(20) Dan Quisenberry .25
(21) Ozzie Smith 3.50
(22) Scott Terry .25
(23) Milt Thompson .25
(24) Denny Walling .25
(25) Todd Worrell .25

1990 St. Louis Cardinals Fire Safety

Player photos dominate the fronts of this large-format (3" x 5") set sponsored by the U.S. Forest Service. Backs have a cartoon fire safety tip plus a few stats and personal data. The unnumbered cards are checklisted here in alphabetical order.

NM/M
Complete Set (27): 6.00
Common Player: .25
(1) Vince Coleman .25
(2) Dave Collins .25
(3) Danny Cox .25
(4) Ken Dayley .25
(5) Frank DiPino .25
(6) Jose DeLeon .25
(7) Pedro Guerrero .25
(8) Whitey Herzog .25
(9) Rick Horton .25
(10) Rex Hudler .25
(11) Tim Jones .25
(12) Joe Magrane .25
(13) Greg Mathews .25
(14) Willie McGee .25
(15) John Morris .25
(16) Tom Niedenfuer .25
(17) Jose Oquendo .25
(18) Tom Pagnozzi .25
(19) Terry Pendleton .25
(20) Bryn Smith .25
(21) Lee Smith .35
(22) Ozzie Smith 3.50
(23) Scott Terry .25
(24) Milt Thompson .25
(25) John Tudor .25
(26) Denny Walling .25
(27) Todd Zeile .25

1991 St. Louis Cardinals Police

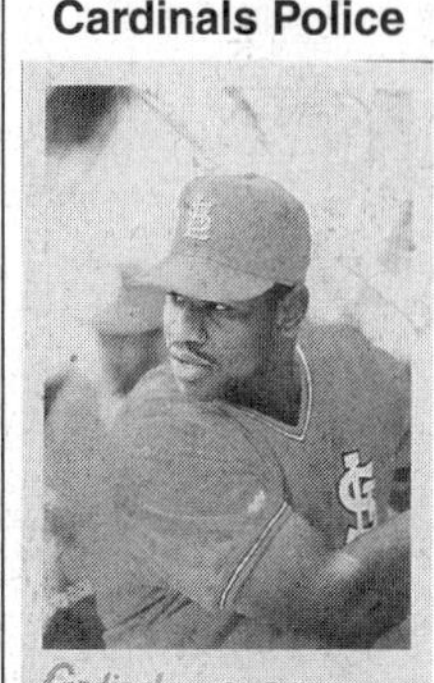

Color action photos are featured prominently on these large-format (2-5/8" x 4-1/16") cards. In the white border at bottom, the team name is printed in red, with the player name and uniform number printed in black. Backs feature a large cartoon safety message, career stats, some biographical data and the logos of the set's sponsors, Kansas City Life Insurance and the Greater St. Louis Law Enforcement Agencies. Backs are printed in red on white.

NM/M
Complete Set (24): 7.50
Common Player: .15
1 Ozzie Smith 5.00
7 Geronimo Pena .15
9 Joe Torre .50
10 Rex Hudler .15
11 Jose Oquendo .15
12 Craig Wilson .15
16 Ray Lankford .25
19 Tom Pagnozzi .15
21 Gerald Perry .15
23 Bernard Gilkey .15
25 Milt Thompson .15
27 Todd Zeile .25
28 Pedro Guerrero .15
29 Rich Gedman .15
34 Felix Jose .15
35 Frank DiPino .15
36 Bryn Smith .15
37 Scott Terry .15
38 Todd Worrell .15
39 Bob Tewksbury .15
43 Ken Hill .15
47 Lee Smith .25
48 Jose DeLeon .15
49 Juan Agosto .15

1992 St. Louis Cardinals Police

The Cardinals were the subject of this set given out at Busch Stadium on April 25. Sponsored by Kansas City Life Insurance and distributed by Greater St. Louis law enforcement agencies, the cards are 2-1/2" x 4", and contain a special logo on the front which commemorates the team's 100th anniversary.

NM/M
Complete Set (27): 7.50
Common Player: .25
1 Ozzie Smith 5.00
7 Geronimo Pena .25
9 Joe Torre .50
10 Rex Hudler .25
11 Jose Oquendo .25
12 Craig Wilson .25
16 Ray Lankford .25
19 Tom Pagnozzi .25
21 Gerald Perry .25
23 Bernard Gilkey .25
25 Milt Thompson .25
26 Omar Olivares .25
27 Todd Zeile .25
28 Pedro Guerrero .25
29 Rich Gedman .25
32 Joe Magrane .25
34 Felix Jose .25
36 Bryn Smith .25
37 Scott Terry .25
38 Todd Worrell .25
39 Bob Tewksbury .25
41 Andres Galarraga .25
44 Cris Carpenter .25
47 Lee Smith .30
48 Jose DeLeon .25
49 Juan Agosto .25
--- Checklist .25

1993 St. Louis Cardinals Police

This Cardinals/Kansas City Life police set features 2-5/8" x 4" cards with a blue border and

"Cardinals" printed in red at top. The team logo appears in the lower-left corner, while the player's name, position and number appear lower-right. Backs are printed in red on a white background with the player's biography and statistics listed above a safety message.

		NM/M
Complete Set (25):		7.50
Common Player:		.25
1	Ozzie Smith	5.00
3	Brian Jordan	.35
5	Stan Royer	.25
9	Joe Torre	.50
11	Jose Oquendo	.25
16	Ray Lankford	.25
18	Luis Alicea	.25
19	Tom Pagnozzi	.25
21	Geronimo Pena	.25
23	Bernard Gilkey	.25
25	Gregg Jefferies	.25
26	Rob Murphy	.25
27	Todd Zeile	.25
28	Gerald Perry	.25
29	Hector Villanueva	.25
31	Donovan Osborne	.25
33	Rod Brewer	.25
39	Bob Tewksbury	.25
42	Mike Perez	.25
43	Rene Arocha	.25
46	Ozzie Canseco	.25
47	Lee Smith	.25
52	Rheal Cormier	.25
54	Tracy Woodson	.25
---	Checklist	.25

1994 St. Louis Cardinals Police

An emphasis on border graphics marks the perennial Cardinals safety set for 1994. The 2-5/8" x 4" cards have a cream colored border. Near the left edge is a vertical red stripe with a team logo at top. Above the color photo at center is the team name. The player name and position are at lower-left. A baseball zooms out of the photo at lower-right carrying the uniform number. Backs are printed in red on white and feature a large cartoon safety message at center. Career stats and biographical data are at top. At bottom are sponsors' logos for the Kansas City Life Insurance Co., and Greater St. Louis Law Enforcement Agencies.

		NM/M
Complete Set (26):		7.50
Common Player:		.15
1	Ozzie Smith	5.00
3	Brian Jordan	.25
5	Stan Royer	.15
9	Joe Torre	.50
11	Jose Oquendo	.15
12	Erik Pappas	.15
16	Ray Lankford	.15
18	Luis Alicea	.15
19	Tom Pagnozzi	.15
21	Geronimo Pena	.15
22	Mark Whiten	.15
23	Bernard Gilkey	.15
25	Gregg Jefferies	.15
26	Omar Olivares	.15
27	Todd Zeile	.15
28	Gerald Perry	.15
34	Tom Urbani	.15
36	Paul Kilgus	.15
38	Allen Watson	.15
39	Bob Tewksbury	.15
40	Rick Sutcliffe	.15
42	Mike Perez	.15
43	Rene Arocha	.15
46	Rob Murphy	.15
48	Rich Batchelor	.15
52	Rheal Cormier	.15

1995 St. Louis Cardinals Police

In 1995, the Cardinals safety set was sponsored by Kansas City Life Insurance Co., and distributed by law enforcement agencies in the greater St. Louis area. The cards measure about 2-5/8" x 4" and feature action photos on front. The team name is scripted at bottom and the player's last name and "1995" are vertically at right. Backs have a few vital data, a career stats line, a safety message and sponsor's logo. Cards are listed here in alphabetical order.

		NM/M
Complete Set (12):		7.50
Common Player:		.50
(1)	Rene Arocha	.50
(2)	Scott Cooper	.50
(3)	Tripp Cromer	.50
(4)	Bernard Gilkey	.50
(5)	Tom Henke	.50
(6)	Ken Hill	.50
(7)	Danny Jackson	.50
(8)	Brian Jordan	.50
(9)	Ray Lankford	.50
(10)	Jose Oquendo	.50
(11)	Tom Pagnozzi	.50
(12)	Ozzie Smith	5.00

1996 St. Louis Cardinals Police

Once again for 1996, the Cardinals safety set was sponsored by Kansas City Life Insurance Co., and distributed by law enforcement agencies in the greater St. Louis area. The cards measure about 2-5/8" x 4" and feature action photos on front. The team name is vertically in a ghosted strip at left. At bottom, beneath a "torn" photo edge are the player's last name, uniform number and the team logo. Backs have a few vital data, a career stats line, a safety message and sponsor's logo.

		NM/M
Complete Set (26):		10.00
Common Player:		.25
1	Ozzie Smith	5.00
3	Brian Jordan	.25
5	Ron Gant	.25
8	Gary Gaetti	.25
10	Tony LaRussa	.25
12	Royce Clayton	.25
16	Ray Lankford	.25
19	Tom Pagnozzi	.25
22	Mike Gallego	.25
23	Mark Sweeney	.25
24	Tom Urbani	.25
29	Danny Jackson	.25
30	Todd Stottlemyre	.25
31	Donovan Osborne	.25
32	Rick Honeycutt	.25
33	T.J. Mathews	.25
36	Mike Morgan	.25
38	Pat Borders	.25
40	Andy Benes	.25
41	Alan Benes	.25
43	Dennis Eckersley	3.00
46	Mark Petkovsek	.25
47	John Mabry	.25
48	Tony Fossas	.25
51	Willie McGee	.25
---	Fredbird/Checklist (Mascot)	.25

1998 St. Louis Cardinals Police

Similar in format to those used in the preceding years, this safety issue is printed on a 2-1/4" x 4" format. Fronts have color action photos surrounded by busy borders in predominantly yellow and green. A blue strip at bottom has player name and uniform number and team logo. Backs are in red-and-white with a few biographical details and stats, a cartoon baseball figure, safety message and sponsors' credits. Cards are checklisted here by uniform number.

		NM/M
Complete Set (26):		8.00
Common Player:		.25
3	Brian Jordan	.25
5	Ron Gant	.25
7	Delino DeShields	.25
8	Gary Gaetti	.25
10	Tony LaRussa	.25
11	Royce Clayton	.25
13	David Howard	.25
16	Ray Lankford	.25
19	Tom Pagnozzi	.25
25	Mark McGwire	6.00
26	Eli Marrero	.25
28	Lance Painter	.25
30	Todd Stottlemyre	.25
35	Matt Morris	.25
37	Kent Bottenfield	.25
38	Manny Aybar	.25
41	Alan Benes	.25
43	Kent Mercker	.25
44	Jeff Brantley	.25
46	Mark Petkovsek	.25
47	John Mabry	.25
49	Tom Lampkin	.25
50	John Frascatore	.25
51	Willie McGee	.25
57	Curtis King	.25
	Fredbird (Mascot)	.25

2000 St. Louis Cardinals Police

The Cardinals issued this safety set to fans 15 and under at the April 22 game in Busch Stadium. The 2-5/8" x 4" cards have game-action color photos bordered in white. Backs are in red on white with a few bits of personal data, a cartoon safety message and the logo of sponsoring Kansas City Life Insurance, which provided the cards for distribution by the Metropolitan Chiefs and Sheriffs Assn. Cards are checklisted here by uniform number. The checklist of actually-issued cards does not correspond with the checklist on the Fredbird card due to the trades which sent away Kent Bottenfield, Joe McEwing, Brian McRae and Paul Spoljaric.

		NM/M
Complete Set (23):		6.00
Common Player:		.25
3	Edgar Renteria	.45
4	Fernando Vina	.25
5	Thomas Howard	.25
7	J.D. Drew	1.50
10	Tony LaRussa	.25
12	Shawon Dunston	.25
16	Ray Lankford	.25
21	Craig Paquette	.25
22	Mike Matheny	.25
23	Fernando Tatis	.25
24	Eric Davis	.25
25	Mark McGwire	3.00
26	Eli Marrero	.25
31	Alan Benes	.25
36	Scott Radinsky	.25
40	Andy Benes	.25
41	Pat Hentgen	.25
43	Dave Veres	.25
55	Garrett Stephenson	.25
57	Darryl Kile	.25
58	Heathcliff Slocumb	.25
66	Rick Ankiel	.25
	Fredbird/Checklist	.25

2001 St. Louis Cardinals Police

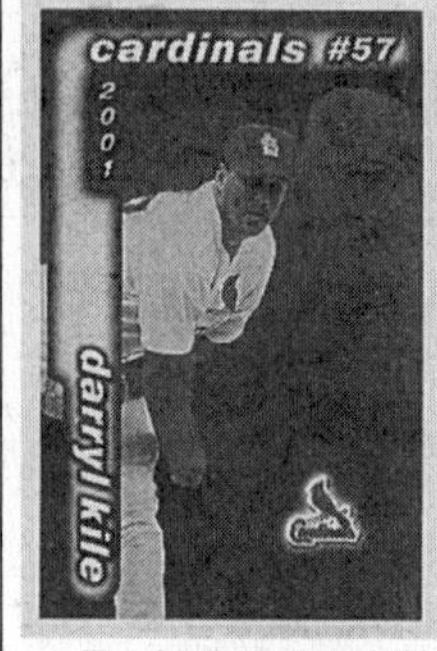

The Cardinals issued this safety set to fans attending a promotional game. The 2-5/8" x 4" cards have a game-action color photo on front. The same photo is enlarged, posterized and rendered in red as a background. A yellow stripe at left and top has player identification. Backs have a few bits of personal data, a cartoon safety message and the logo of sponsoring Kansas City Life Insurance, which provided the cards for distribution by the Metropolitan Chiefs and Sheriffs Assn. Cards are checklisted here alphabetically.

		NM/M
Complete Set (27):		5.00
Common Player:		.25
(1)	Rick Ankiel	.25
(2)	Alan Benes	.25
(3)	Andy Benes	.25
(4)	Bobby Bonilla	.25
(5)	Jack Buck (Broadcaster)	.25
(6)	Jason Christiansen	.25
(7)	J.D. Drew	.75
(8)	Jim Edmonds	.50
(9)	Dustin Hermanson	.35
(10)	Carlos Hernandez	.25
(11)	Mike James	.25
(12)	Darryl Kile	.25
(13)	Steve Kline	.25
(14)	Ray Lankford	.25
(15)	Tony LaRussa	.25
(16)	Mark McGwire	2.00
(17)	Eli Marrero	.25
(18)	Mike Matheny	.25
(19)	Matt Morris	.25
(20)	Craig Paquette	.25
(21)	Placido Polanco	.25
(22)	Edgar Renteria	.25
(23)	Larry Sutton	.25
(24)	Mike Timlin	.25
(25)	Dave Veres	.25
(26)	Fernando Vina	.25
(27)	Fredbird (Mascot)	.25

2002 St. Louis Cardinals Police

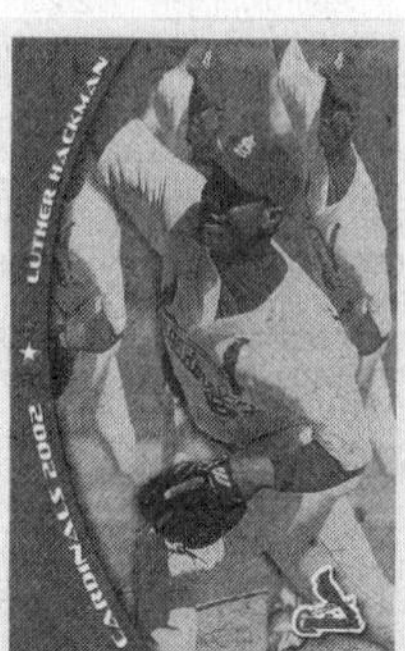

The Cardinals issued this safety set to fans attending a promotional game. The 2-5/8" x 4" cards have a game-action color photo on front. The same photo is vertically squeezed rendered in red and run three times as a background. A red arc at left has player identification. Backs have a few bits of personal data, a cartoon safety message and the logo of sponsoring Kansas City Life Insurance, which provided the cards for distribution by St. Louis area law enforcement agencies.

		NM/M
Complete Set (27):		5.00
Common Player:		.25
3	Edgar Renteria	.25
4	Fernando Vina	.25
5	Albert Pujols	3.00
7	J.D. Drew	.50
8	Mike DiFelice	.25
10	Tony LaRussa	.25
13	Kerry Robinson	.25
15	Jim Edmonds	.40
19	Woody Williams	.25
21	Tino Martinez	.25
22	Mike Matheny	.25
26	Eli Marrero	.25
27	Placido Polanco	.25
35	Matt Morris	.25
36	Gene Stechschulte	.25
40	Andy Benes	.25
43	Dave Veres	.25
44	Jason Isringhausen	.25
48	Mike Matthews	.25
49	Steve Kline	.25
50	Mike Timlin	.25
52	Bud Smith	.25
55	Garrett Stephenson	.25
57	Darryl Kile	.25
63	Luther Hackman	.25
66	Rick Ankiel	.25
---	Fredbird (Mascot)	.25

2003 St. Louis Cardinals Police

The Cardinals issued this safety set to fans 15 and under attending the May 18 game. The 2-5/8" x 4" cards have a game-action color photo on front along with a red and gold geometric lines design and player identification. Backs have a few bits of personal data, a cartoon safety message and the logo of sponsoring Kansas City Life Insurance, which provided the cards for distribution by St. Louis area law enforcement agencies.

		NM/M
Complete Set (26):		5.00
Common Player:		.25
0	Kerry Robinson	.35
3	Edgar Renteria	.25
4	Fernando Vina	.25
5	Albert Pujols	3.00
7	J.D. Drew	.50
8a	Joe Girardi	.25
8b	Dustin Hermanson (Should be 32.)	.25
10	Tony LaRussa	.25
13	Jeff Fassero	.25
15	Jim Edmonds	.50
16	Orlando Palmeiro	.25
19	Woody Williams	.25
21	Tino Martinez	.25
22	Mike Matheny	.25
26	Eli Marrero	.25
27	Scott Rolen	.50
30	Brett Tomko	.25
33	Eduardo Perez	.25
35	Matt Morris	.25
41	Miguel Cairo	.25
44	Jason Isringhausen	.25
46	Jason Simontacchi	.25
48	Russ Springer	.25
49	Steve Kline	.25
55	Garrett Stephenson	.25
---	Fredbird (Mascot)	.25

2004 St. Louis Cardinals Police

The Cardinals issued this safety set to 10,000 fans 15 and under attending the May 15 game. The 2-5/8" x 4" cards have a game-action color photo on front on a red, orange and black benday-dot background. Backs are printed in red, with a few bits of personal data, 2003 stats, a cartoon safety message and the logo of sponsoring Kansas City Life Insurance, which provided the cards for distribution by St. Louis area law enforcement agencies.

		NM/M
Complete Set (26):		5.00
Common Player:		.25
3	Edgar Renteria	.35
5	Albert Pujols	3.00
8	Marlon Anderson	.35
10	Tony LaRussa	.25
15	Jim Edmonds	.50
16	Reggie Sanders	.25
19	Woody Williams	.25
21	Jason Marquis	.25
22	Mike Matheny	.25
23	Cal Eldred	.25
27	Scott Rolen	.50
29	Chris Carpenter	.25
31	Bo Hart	.35
33	Mike Lincoln	.25
34	Steve Kline	.25
35	Matt Morris	.25
37	Jeff Suppan	.25
40a	Kiko Calero	.25
40b	Fredbird (Mascot)	.25
44	Jason Isringhausen	.25
46	Jason Simontacchi	.25
50a	Danny Haren	.25
50b	Julian Tavarez	.25
56	Ray King	.25
99	So Taguchi	.25
---	Busch Stadium 1966-2005	.25

2005 St. Louis Cardinals Police

The Cardinals issued this safety set to fans 15 and under attending the May 29 game. The 2-5/8" x 4" cards have a game-action color photo or portrait on front. Backs are printed in red, with a few bits of personal data, 2004 stats, a cartoon safety message and the logo of sponsoring Kansas City Life Insurance, which provided the cards for distribution by St. Louis area law enforcement agencies.

	NM/M
Complete Set (27):	8.00

Common Player: .25
3 Abraham Nunez .25
5 Albert Pujols 2.00
7 Hector Luna .25
8 Mark Grudzielanek .25
10 Tony LaRussa .25
15 Jim Edmonds 1.00
16 Reggie Sanders .25
21 Jason Marquis .25
22 David Eckstein .25
23 Cal Eldred .25
27 Scott Rolen 1.00
29 Chris Carpenter .25
30 Mark Mulder .50
32 Roger Cedeno .25
33 Larry Walker .50
35 Matt Morris .25
36 Mike Lincoln .25
37 Jeff Suppan .25
40 Bill Pulsipher .25
41 Yadier Molina .25
44 Jason Isringhausen .25
47 John Mabry .25
50 Julian Tavarez .25
56 Ray King .25
68 Carmen Cali .25
99 So Taguchi .25
--- Fredbird (Mascot) .25

1991 Stadium Club Promos

Topps' response to the upscale Leaf baseball card issue was a new brand labeled Stadium Club. To introduce the premium cards, a set of 50 promo cards was produced with single cards distributed to employees and candy companies. Production has been reported in the area of 600 of each card. The promos differ from the issued cards on front in that there are four horizontal gold-foil stripes on the promos, instead of three. The back of each promo card is identical, showing a 1986 Topps Traded Jose Canseco card. The unnumbered cards are checklisted here in alphabetical order.

NM/M
Complete Set (50): 150.00
Common Player: 2.50
(1) Allan Anderson 2.50
(2) Steve Balboni 2.50
(3) Jeff Ballard 2.50
(4) Jesse Barfield 2.50
(5) Andy Benes 2.50
(6) Bobby Bonilla 2.50
(7) Chris Bosio 2.50
(8) Daryl Boston 2.50
(9) Chuck Cary 2.50
(10) Pat Combs 2.50
(11) Delino DeShields 2.50
(12) Shawon Dunston 2.50
(13) Alvaro Espinoza 2.50
(14) Sid Fernandez 2.50
(15) Bob Geren 2.50
(16) Brian Holman 2.50
(17) Jay Howell 2.50
(18) Stan Javier 2.50
(19) Dave Johnson 2.50
(20) Howard Johnson 2.50
(21) Kevin Maas 2.50
(22) Shane Mack 2.50
(23) Joe Magrane 2.50
(24) Denny Martinez 2.50
(25) Don Mattingly 30.00
(26) Ben McDonald 2.50
(27) Eddie Murray 15.00
(28) Matt Nokes 2.50
(29) Greg Olson 2.50
(30) Gregg Olson 2.50
(31) Jose Oquendo 2.50
(32) Tony Phillips 2.50
(33) Rafael Ramirez 2.50
(34) Dennis Rasmussen 2.50
(35) Billy Ripken 2.50
(36) Nolan Ryan 65.00
(37) Bill Sampen 2.50
(38) Steve Sax 2.50
(39) Mike Scioscia 2.50
(40) David Segui 2.50
(41) Zane Smith 2.50
(42) B.J. Surhoff 2.50
(43) Bobby Thigpen 2.50
(44) Alan Trammell 2.50
(45) Fernando Valenzuela 2.50
(46) Andy Van Slyke 2.50
(47) Hector Villanueva 2.50
(48) Larry Walker 2.50
(49) Walt Weiss 2.50
(50) Bob Welch 2.50

1991 Stadium Club

One of the most popular sets of 1991, this 600-card issue was released in two 300-card series. The cards were available in foil packs only. No factory sets were available. The cards feature borderless high gloss photos on the front and a player evaluation and card photo on the back. Each card can be found with two different letters preceding the copyright cymbol on back. A special Stadium Club membership package was made available for $29.95 with 10 proof of purchase seals from wrappers.

NM/M
Complete Set (600): 20.00
Common Player: .05
Series 1 or 2 Pack (13): .60
Series 1 or 2 Box (36): 15.00
1 Dave Stewart .05
2 Wally Joyner .05
3 Shawon Dunston .05
4 Darren Daulton .05
5 Will Clark .05
6 Sammy Sosa 1.00
7 Dan Plesac .05
8 Marquis Grissom .05
9 Erik Hanson .05
10 Geno Petralli .05
11 Jose Rijo .05
12 Carlos Quintana .05
13 Junior Ortiz .05
14 Bob Walk .05
15 Mike Macfarlane .05
16 Eric Yelding .05
17 Bryn Smith .05
18 Bip Roberts .05
19 Mike Scioscia .05
20 Mark Williamson .05
21 Don Mattingly 1.00
22 John Franco .05
23 Chet Lemon .05
24 Tom Henke .05
25 Jerry Browne .05
26 Dave Justice .05
27 Mark Langston .05
28 Damon Berryhill .05
29 Kevin Bass .05
30 Scott Fletcher .05
31 Moises Alou .05
32 Dave Valle .05
33 Jody Reed .05
34 Dave West .05
35 Kevin McReynolds .05
36 Pat Combs .05
37 Eric Davis .05
38 Bret Saberhagen .05
39 Stan Javier .05
40 Chuck Cary .05
41 Tony Phillips .05
42 Lee Smith .05
43 Tim Teufel .05
44 Lance Dickson .05
45 Greg Litton .05
46 Teddy Higuera .05
47 Edgar Martinez .05
48 Steve Avery .05
49 Walt Weiss .05
50 David Segui .05
51 Andy Benes .05
52 Karl Rhodes .05
53 Neal Heaton .05
54 Dan Gladden .05
55 Luis Rivera .05
56 Kevin Brown .05
57 Frank Thomas .75
58 Terry Mulholland .05
59 Dick Schofield .05
60 Ron Darling .05
61 Sandy Alomar, Jr. .05
62 Dave Stieb .05
63 Alan Trammell .05
64 Matt Nokes .05
65 Lenny Harris .05
66 Milt Thompson .05
67 Storm Davis .05
68 Joe Oliver .05
69 Andres Galarraga .05
70 Ozzie Guillen .05
71 Ken Howell .05
72 Garry Templeton .05
73 Derrick May .05
74 Xavier Hernandez .05
75 Dave Parker .05
76 Rick Aguilera .05
77 Robby Thompson .05
78 Pete Incaviglia .05
79 Bob Welch .05
80 Randy Milligan .05
81 Chuck Finley .05
82 Alvin Davis .05
83 Tim Naehring .05
84 Jay Bell .05
85 Joe Magrane .05
86 Howard Johnson .05
87 Jack McDowell .05
88 Kevin Seitzer .05
89 Bruce Ruffin .05
90 Fernando Valenzuela .05
91 Terry Kennedy .05
92 Barry Larkin .05
93 Larry Walker .05
94 Luis Salazar .05
95 Gary Sheffield .45
96 Bobby Witt .05
97 Lonnie Smith .05
98 Bryan Harvey .05
99 Mookie Wilson .05
100 Dwight Gooden .05
101 Lou Whitaker .05
102 Ron Karkovice .05
103 Jesse Barfield .05
104 Jose DeJesus .05
105 Benito Santiago .05
106 Brian Holman .05
107 Rafael Ramirez .05
108 Ellis Burks .05
109 Mike Bielecki .05
110 Kirby Puckett 1.00
111 Terry Shumpert .05
112 Chuck Crim .05
113 Todd Benzinger .05
114 Brian Barnes .05
115 Carlos Baerga .05
116 Kal Daniels .05
117 Dave Johnson .05
118 Andy Van Slyke .05
119 John Burkett .05
120 Rickey Henderson .75
121 Tim Jones .05
122 Daryl Irvine .05
123 Ruben Sierra .05
124 Jim Abbott .05
125 Daryl Boston .05
126 Greg Maddux 1.00
127 Von Hayes .05
128 Mike Fitzgerald .05
129 Wayne Edwards .05
130 Greg Briley .05
131 Rob Dibble .05
132 Gene Larkin .05
133 David Wells .05
134 Steve Balboni .05
135 Greg Vaughn .05
136 Mark Davis .05
137 Dave Rohde .05
138 Eric Show .05
139 Bobby Bonilla .05
140 Dana Kiecker .05
141 Gary Pettis .05
142 Dennis Boyd .05
143 Mike Benjamin .05
144 Luis Polonia .05
145 Doug Jones .05
146 Al Newman .05
147 Alex Fernandez .05
148 Bill Doran .05
149 Kevin Elster .05
150 Len Dykstra .05
151 Mike Gallego .05
152 Tim Belcher .05
153 Jay Buhner .05
154 Ozzie Smith 1.00
155 Jose Canseco .50
156 Gregg Olson .05
157 Charlie O'Brien .05
158 Frank Tanana .05
159 George Brett 1.00
160 Jeff Huson .05
161 Kevin Tapani .05
162 Jerome Walton .05
163 Charlie Hayes .05
164 Chris Bosio .05
165 Chris Sabo .05
166 Lance Parrish .05
167 Don Robinson .05
168 Manuel Lee .05
169 Dennis Rasmussen .05
170 Wade Boggs 1.00
171 Bob Geren .05
172 Mackey Sasser .05
173 Julio Franco .05
174 Otis Nixon .05
175 Bert Blyleven .05
176 Craig Biggio .05
177 Eddie Murray .75
178 Randy Tomlin .05
179 Tino Martinez .05
180 Carlton Fisk .75
181 Dwight Smith .05
182 Scott Garrelts .05
183 Jim Gantner .05
184 Dickie Thon .05
185 John Farrell .05
186 Cecil Fielder .05
187 Glenn Braggs .05
188 Allan Anderson .05
189 Kurt Stillwell .05
190 Jose Oquendo .05
191 Joe Orsulak .05
192 Ricky Jordan .05
193 Kelly Downs .05
194 Delino DeShields .05
195 Omar Vizquel .05
196 Mark Carreon .05
197 Mike Harkey .05
198 Jack Howell .05
199 Lance Johnson .05
200 Nolan Ryan 2.00
201 John Marzano .05
202 Doug Drabek .05
203 Mark Lemke .05
204 Steve Sax .05
205 Greg Harris .05
206 B.J. Surhoff .05
207 Todd Burns .05
208 Jose Gonzalez .05
209 Mike Scott .05
210 Dave Magadan .05
211 Dante Bichette .05
212 Trevor Wilson .05
213 Hector Villanueva .05
214 Dan Pasqua .05
215 Greg Colbrunn .05
216 Mike Jeffcoat .05
217 Harold Reynolds .05
218 Paul O'Neill .05
219 Mark Guthrie .05
220 Barry Bonds 2.00
221 Jimmy Key .05
222 Billy Ripken .05
223 Tom Pagnozzi .05
224 Bo Jackson .10
225 Sid Fernandez .05
226 Mike Marshall .05
227 John Kruk .05
228 Mike Fetters .05
229 Eric Anthony .05
230 Ryne Sandberg 1.00
231 Carney Lansford .05
232 Melido Perez .05
233 Jose Lind .05
234 Darryl Hamilton .05
235 Tom Browning .05
236 Spike Owen .05
237 Juan Gonzalez .40
238 Felix Fermin .05
239 Keith Miller .05
240 Mark Gubicza .05
241 Kent Anderson .05
242 Alvaro Espinoza .05
243 Dale Murphy .20
244 Orel Hershiser .05
245 Paul Molitor .75
246 Eddie Whitson .05
247 Joe Girardi .05
248 Kent Hrbek .05
249 Bill Sampen .05
250 Kevin Mitchell .05
251 Mariano Duncan .05
252 Scott Bradley .05
253 Mike Greenwell .05
254 Tom Gordon .05
255 Todd Zeile .05
256 Bobby Thigpen .05
257 Gregg Jefferies .05
258 Kenny Rogers .05
259 Shane Mack .05
260 Zane Smith .05
261 Mitch Williams .05
262 Jim DeShaies .05
263 Dave Winfield .75
264 Ben McDonald .05
265 Randy Ready .05
266 Pat Borders .05
267 Jose Uribe .05
268 Derek Lilliquist .05
269 Greg Brock .05
270 Ken Griffey Jr. 1.25
271 Jeff Gray .05
272 Danny Tartabull .05
273 Dennis Martinez .05
274 Robin Ventura .05
275 Randy Myers .05
276 Jack Daugherty .05
277 Greg Gagne .05
278 Jay Howell .05
279 Mike LaValliere .05
280 Rex Hudler .05
281 Mike Simms .05
282 Kevin Maas .05
283 Jeff Ballard .05
284 Dave Henderson .05
285 Pete O'Brien .05
286 Brook Jacoby .05
287 Mike Henneman .05
288 Greg Olson .05
289 Greg Myers .05
290 Mark Grace .05
291 Shawn Abner .05
292 Frank Viola .05
293 Lee Stevens .05
294 Jason Grimsley .05
295 Matt Williams .05
296 Ron Robinson .05
297 Tom Brunansky .05
298 Checklist .05
299 Checklist .05
300 Checklist .05
301 Darryl Strawberry .05
302 Bud Black .05
303 Harold Baines .05
304 Roberto Alomar .20
305 Norm Charlton .05
306 Gary Thurman .05
307 Mike Felder .05
308 Tony Gwynn 1.00
309 Roger Clemens 1.00
310 Andre Dawson .25
311 Scott Radinsky .05
312 Bob Melvin .05
313 Kirk McCaskill .05
314 Pedro Guerrero .05
315 Walt Terrell .05
316 Sam Horn .05
317 Wes Chamberlain **RC** .05
318 Pedro Munoz **RC** .05
319 Roberto Kelly .05
320 Mark Portugal .05
321 Tim McIntosh .05
322 Jesse Orosco .05
323 Gary Green .05
324 Greg Harris .05
325 Hubie Brooks .05
326 Chris Nabholz .05
327 Terry Pendleton .05
328 Eric King .05
329 Chili Davis .05
330 Anthony Telford .05
331 Kelly Gruber .05
332 Dennis Eckersley .65
333 Mel Hall .05
334 Bob Kipper .05
335 Willie McGee .05
336 Steve Olin .05
337 Steve Buechele .05
338 Scott Leius .05
339 Hal Morris .05
340 Jose Offerman .05
341 Kent Mercker .05
342 Ken Griffey .05
343 Pete Harnisch .05
344 Kirk Gibson .05
345 Dave Smith .05
346 Dave Martinez .05
347 Atlee Hammaker .05
348 Brian Downing .05
349 Todd Hundley .05
350 Candy Maldonado .05
351 Dwight Evans .05
352 Steve Searcy .05
353 Gary Gaetti .05
354 Jeff Reardon .05
355 Travis Fryman .05
356 Dave Righetti .05
357 Fred McGriff .05
358 Don Slaught .05
359 Gene Nelson .05
360 Billy Spiers .05
361 Lee Guetterman .05
362 Darren Lewis .05
363 Duane Ward .05
364 Lloyd Moseby .05
365 John Smoltz .05
366 Felix Jose .05
367 David Cone .05
368 Wally Backman .05
369 Jeff Montgomery .05
370 Rich Garces .05
371 Billy Hatcher .05
372 Bill Swift .05
373 Jim Eisenreich .05
374 Rob Ducey .05
375 Tim Crews .05
376 Steve Finley .05
377 Jeff Blauser .05
378 Willie Wilson .05
379 Gerald Perry .05
380 Jose Mesa .05
381 Pat Kelly .05
382 Matt Merullo .05
383 Ivan Calderon .05
384 Scott Chiamparino .05
385 Lloyd McClendon .05
386 Dave Bergman .05
387 Ed Sprague .05
388 Jeff Bagwell **RC** 3.00
389 Brett Butler .05
390 Larry Andersen .05
391 Glenn Davis .05
392 Alex Cole (Photo is Otis Nixon.) .05
393 Mike Heath .05
394 Danny Darwin .05
395 Steve Lake .05
396 Tim Layana .05
397 Terry Leach .05
398 Bill Wegman .05
399 Mark McGwire 1.50
400 Mike Boddicker .05
401 Steve Howe .05
402 Bernard Gilkey .05
403 Thomas Howard .05
404 Rafael Belliard .05
405 Tom Candiotti .05
406 Rene Gonzalez .05
407 Chuck McElroy .05
408 Paul Sorrento .05
409 Randy Johnson .75
410 Brady Anderson .05
411 Dennis Cook .05
412 Mickey Tettleton .05
413 Mike Stanton .05
414 Ken Oberkfell .05
415 Rick Honeycutt .05
416 Nelson Santovenia .05
417 Bob Tewksbury .05
418 Brent Mayne .05
419 Steve Farr .05
420 Phil Stephenson .05
421 Jeff Russell .05
422 Chris James .05
423 Tim Leary .05
424 Gary Carter .75
425 Glenallen Hill .05
426 Matt Young .05
427 Sid Bream .05
428 Greg Swindell .05
429 Scott Aldred .05
430 Cal Ripken, Jr. 2.00
431 Bill Landrum .05
432 Ernie Riles .05
433 Danny Jackson .05
434 Casey Candaele .05
435 Ken Hill .05
436 Jaime Navarro .05
437 Lance Blankenship .05
438 Randy Velarde .05
439 Frank DiPino .05
440 Carl Nichols .05
441 Jeff Robinson .05
442 Deion Sanders .05
443 Vincente Palacios .05
444 Devon White .05
445 John Cerutti .05
446 Tracy Jones .05
447 Jack Morris .05
448 Mitch Webster .05
449 Bob Ojeda .05
450 Oscar Azocar .05
451 Luis Aquino .05
452 Mark Whiten .05
453 Stan Belinda .05
454 Ron Gant .05
455 Jose DeLeon .05
456 Mark Salas .05
457 Junior Felix .05
458 Wally Whitehurst .05
459 Phil Plantier **RC** .05
460 Juan Berenguer .05
461 Franklin Stubbs .05
462 Joe Boever .05
463 Tim Wallach .05
464 Mike Moore .05
465 Albert Belle .05
466 Mike Witt .05
467 Craig Worthington .05
468 Jerald Clark .05
469 Scott Terry .05
470 Milt Cuyler .05
471 John Smiley .05
472 Charles Nagy .05
473 Alan Mills .05
474 John Russell .05
475 Bruce Hurst .05
476 Andujar Cedeno .05
477 Dave Eiland .05
478 Brian McRae **RC** .10
479 Mike LaCoss .05
480 Chris Gwynn .05
481 Jamie Moyer .05
482 John Olerud .05
483 Efrain Valdez .05
484 Sil Campusano .05
485 Pascual Perez .05
486 Gary Redus .05
487 Andy Hawkins .05
488 Cory Snyder .05
489 Chris Hoiles .05
490 Ron Hassey .05
491 Gary Wayne .05
492 Mark Lewis .05
493 Scott Coolbaugh .05
494 Gerald Young .05
495 Juan Samuel .05
496 Willie Fraser .05
497 Jeff Treadway .05
498 Vince Coleman .05
499 Cris Carpenter .05
500 Jack Clark .05
501 Kevin Appier .05
502 Rafael Palmeiro .65
503 Hensley Meulens .05
504 George Bell .05
505 Tony Pena .05
506 Roger McDowell .05
507 Luis Sojo .05
508 Mike Schooler .05
509 Robin Yount .75
510 Jack Armstrong .05
511 Rick Cerone .05
512 Curt Wilkerson .05
513 Joe Carter .05
514 Tim Burke .05
515 Tony Fernandez .05
516 Ramon Martinez .05
517 Tim Hulett .05
518 Terry Steinbach .05
519 Pete Smith .05
520 Ken Caminiti .05
521 Shawn Boskie .05
522 Mike Pagliarulo .05
523 Tim Raines .05
524 Alfredo Griffin .05
525 Henry Cotto .05
526 Mike Stanley .05
527 Charlie Leibrandt .05
528 Jeff King .05
529 Eric Plunk .05

530 Tom Lampkin .05
531 Steve Bedrosian .05
532 Tom Herr .05
533 Craig Lefferts .05
534 Jeff Reed .05
535 Mickey Morandini .05
536 Greg Cadaret .05
537 Ray Lankford .05
538 John Candelaria .05
539 Rob Deer .05
540 Brad Arnsberg .05
541 Mike Sharperson .05
542 Jeff Robinson .05
543 Mo Vaughn .05
544 Jeff Parrett .05
545 Willie Randolph .05
546 Herm Winningham .05
547 Jeff Innis .05
548 Chuck Knoblauch .05
549 Tommy Greene .05
550 Jeff Hamilton .05
551 Barry Jones .05
552 Ken Dayley .05
553 Rick Dempsey .05
554 Greg Smith .05
555 Mike Devereaux .05
556 Keith Comstock .05
557 Paul Faries .05
558 Tom Glavine .35
559 Craig Grebeck .05
560 Scott Erickson .05
561 Joel Skinner .05
562 Mike Morgan .05
563 Dave Gallagher .05
564 Todd Stottlemyre .05
565 Rich Rodriguez .05
566 Craig Wilson **RC** .05
567 Jeff Brantley .05
568 Scott Kamieniecki .05
569 Steve Decker .05
570 Juan Agosto .05
571 Tommy Gregg .05
572 Kevin Wickander .05
573 Jamie Quirk .05
574 Jerry Don Gleaton .05
575 Chris Hammond .05
576 Luis Gonzalez **RC** 1.00
577 Russ Swan .05
578 Jeff Conine **RC** .50
579 Charlie Hough .05
580 Jeff Kunkel .05
581 Darrel Akerfelds .05
582 Jeff Manto .05
583 Alejandro Pena .05
584 Mark Davidson .05
585 Bob MacDonald .05
586 Paul Assenmacher .05
587 Dan Wilson .05
588 Tom Bolton .05
589 Brian Harper .05
590 John Habyan .05
591 John Orton .05
592 Mark Gardner .05
593 Turner Ward .05
594 Bob Patterson .05
595 Edwin Nunez .05
596 Gary Scott .05
597 Scott Bankhead .05
598 Checklist .05
599 Checklist .05
600 Checklist .05

Charter Members

Charter members of Topps Stadium Club received a package which included a 50-card multi-sport set unavailable in any other fashion. Cards are similar in format to S.C. regular issues, with full-bleed photos on front, UV coating and gold-foil highlights. This special edition has a gold foil "Charter Member" notation at the bottom of each card front. Backs have a simulated newspaper page describing a career highlight. The cards are unnumbered and the checklist here includes only the baseball cards from the set.

NM/M
Complete Set (50): 12.50
Common Player: .15
(1) Sandy Alomar, Jr. .15
(2) George Brett 1.00
(3) Barry Bonds 2.50
(4) Ellis Burks .15
(5) Eric Davis .15
(6) Delino DeShields .15
(7) Doug Drabek .15
(8) Cecil Fielder .15
(9) Carlton Fisk .50
(10) Ken Griffey Jr., Ken Griffey Sr. 1.50
(11) Billy Hatcher .15
(12) Andy Hawkins .15
(13) Rickey Henderson (A.L. MVP) .50
(14) Rickey Henderson (A.L. base-stealing leader.) .50
(15) Randy Johnson .50
(16) Dave Justice .15
(17) Mark Langston, Mike Witt .15
(18) Kevin Maas .15
(19) Ramon Martinez .15
(20) Willie McGee .15
(21) Terry Mulholland .15
(22) Jose Offerman .15
(23) Melido Perez .15
(24) Nolan Ryan (No-hitter.) 2.50
(25) Nolan Ryan (300th win) 2.50
(26) Ryne Sandberg .75
(27) Dave Stewart .15
(28) Dave Stieb .15
(29) Bobby Thigpen .15
(30) Fernando Valenzuela .15
(31) Frank Viola .15
(32) Bob Welch .15

Members Only

Each member of Topps Stadium Club during 1991 received three packages of multi-sport cards bearing a special design and stamped "Members Only" in gold foil on the front. Cards followed the basic Stadium Club format of full-bleed action photos on front. Backs have a facsimile newspaper page - the "Stadium Club Herald" - which gives details of a career highlight. Cards are unnumbered and the baseball-only checklist here is arranged alphabetically.

NM/M
Complete Set (30): 9.00
Common Player: .15
(1) A.L. Home Run Leaders (Jose Canseco, Cecil Fielder) .15
(2) Wilson Alvarez .15
(3) Andy Ashby .15
(4) Jeff Bagwell 1.00
(5) Braves no-hitter (Kent Mercker, Mark Wohlers, Alejandro Pena) .15
(6) Roger Clemens .75
(7) David Cone .15
(8) Carlton Fisk .50
(9) Julio Franco .15
(10) Tom Glavine .35
(11) Tommy Greene .15
(12) Pete Harnisch .15
(13) Rickey Henderson (All-time theft leader.) .50
(14) Rickey Henderson (11th time A.L. theft leader) .50
(15) Howard Johnson .15
(16) Chuck Knoblauch .15
(17) Ray Lankford .15
(18) Denny Martinez .15
(19) Paul Molitor .50
(20) Jack Morris .15
(21) Orioles No-Hitter (Bob Milacki, Mike Flanagan, Mark Williamson, Gregg Olson, Chris Hoiles) .15
(22) Terry Pendleton (N.L. leading hitter) .15
(23) Terry Pendleton (MVP) .15
(24) Jeff Reardon .15
(25) Cal Ripken, Jr. 2.50
(26) Nolan Ryan (7th no-hitter) 2.50
(27) Nolan Ryan (22nd 100-K season) 2.50
(28) Bret Saberhagen .15
(29) Robby Thompson .15
(30) Dave Winfield .50

Nolan Ryan Bronze

One of the premiums included with charter membership in the Topps Stadium Club was a bronze replica of the Nolan Ryan card from the Charter Member's card set. The replica measures 2-1/2" x 3-1/2" and reproduces both front and back of the Ryan card on a 10-oz. metal slab.

NM/M
Nolan Ryan/Bronze 15.00

1992 Stadium Club

This 900-card set was released in three 100-card series. Like the 1991 issue, the cards feature borderless high-gloss photos on the front. The flip sides feature the player's first Topps card and a player evaluation. Topps released updated cards in the third series for traded player and free agents. Several players appear on two cards. Special Members Choice cards are included in the set. Series III features special inserts of the last three number one draft picks: Phil Nevin, Brien Taylor and Chipper Jones.

NM/M
Complete Set (900): 20.00
Common Player: .05
Series 1, 2, 3 Pack (15): .75
Series 1, 2, 3 Box (36): 15.00
1 Cal Ripken, Jr. 1.50
2 Eric Yelding .05
3 Geno Petralli .05
4 Wally Backman .05
5 Milt Cuyler .05
6 Kevin Bass .05
7 Dante Bichette .05
8 Ray Lankford .05
9 Mel Hall .05
10 Joe Carter .05
11 Juan Samuel .05
12 Jeff Montgomery .05
13 Glenn Braggs .05
14 Henry Cotto .05
15 Deion Sanders .05
16 Dick Schofield .05
17 David Cone .05
18 Chili Davis .05
19 Tom Foley .05
20 Ozzie Guillen .05
21 Luis Salazar .05
22 Terry Steinbach .05
23 Chris James .05
24 Jeff King .05
25 Carlos Quintana .05
26 Mike Maddux .05
27 Tommy Greene .05
28 Jeff Russell .05
29 Steve Finley .05
30 Mike Flanagan .05
31 Darren Lewis .05
32 Mark Lee .05
33 Willie Fraser .05
34 Mike Henneman .05
35 Kevin Maas .05
36 Dave Hansen .05
37 Erik Hanson .05
38 Bill Doran .05
39 Mike Boddicker .05
40 Vince Coleman .05
41 Devon White .05
42 Mark Gardner .05
43 Scott Lewis .05
44 Juan Berenguer .05
45 Carney Lansford .05
46 Curt Wilkerson .05
47 Shane Mack .05
48 Bip Roberts .05
49 Greg Harris .05
50 Ryne Sandberg .75
51 Mark Whiten .05
52 Jack McDowell .05
53 Jimmy Jones .05
54 Steve Lake .05
55 Bud Black .05
56 Dave Valle .05
57 Kevin Reimer .05
58 Rich Gedman .05
59 Travis Fryman .05
60 Steve Avery .05
61 Francisco de la Rosa .05
62 Scott Hemond .05
63 Hal Morris .05
64 Hensley Meulens .05
65 Frank Castillo .05
66 Gene Larkin .05
67 Jose DeLeon .05
68 Al Osuna .05
69 Dave Cochrane .05
70 Robin Ventura .05
71 John Cerutti .05
72 Kevin Gross .05
73 Ivan Calderon .05
74 Mike Macfarlane .05
75 Stan Belinda .05
76 Shawn Hillegas .05
77 Pat Borders .05
78 Jim Vatcher .05
79 Bobby Rose .05
80 Roger Clemens .85
81 Craig Worthington .05
82 Jeff Treadway .05
83 Jamie Quirk .05
84 Randy Bush .05
85 Anthony Young .05
86 Trevor Wilson .05
87 Jaime Navarro .05
88 Les Lancaster .05
89 Pat Kelly .05
90 Alvin Davis .05
91 Larry Andersen .05
92 Rob Deer .05
93 Mike Sharperson .05
94 Lance Parrish .05
95 Cecil Espy .05
96 Tim Spehr .05
97 Dave Stieb .05
98 Terry Mulholland .05
99 Dennis Boyd .05
100 Barry Larkin .05
101 Ryan Bowen .05
102 Felix Fermin .05
103 Luis Alicea .05
104 Tim Hulett .05
105 Rafael Belliard .05
106 Mike Gallego .05
107 Dave Righetti .05
108 Jeff Schaefer .05
109 Ricky Bones .05
110 Scott Erickson .05
111 Matt Nokes .05
112 Bob Scanlan .05
113 Tom Candiotti .05
114 Sean Berry .05
115 Kevin Morton .05
116 Scott Fletcher .05
117 B.J. Surhoff .05
118 Dave Magadan .05
119 Bill Gullickson .05
120 Marquis Grissom .05
121 Lenny Harris .05
122 Wally Joyner .05
123 Kevin Brown .05
124 Braulio Castillo .05
125 Eric King .05
126 Mark Portugal .05
127 Calvin Jones .05
128 Mike Heath .05
129 Todd Van Poppel .05
130 Benny Santiago .05
131 Gary Thurman .05
132 Joe Girardi .05
133 Dave Eiland .05
134 Orlando Merced .05
135 Joe Orsulak .05
136 John Burkett .05
137 Ken Dayley .05
138 Ken Hill .05
139 Walt Terrell .05
140 Mike Scioscia .05
141 Junior Felix .05
142 Ken Caminiti .05
143 Carlos Baerga .05
144 Tony Fossas .05
145 Craig Grebeck .05
146 Scott Bradley .05
147 Kent Mercker .05
148 Derrick May .05
149 Jerald Clark .05
150 George Brett .85
151 Luis Quinones .05
152 Mike Pagliarulo .05
153 Jose Guzman .05
154 Charlie O'Brien .05
155 Darren Holmes .05
156 Joe Boever .05
157 Rich Monteleone .05
158 Reggie Harris .05
159 Roberto Alomar .20
160 Robby Thompson .05
161 Chris Hoiles .05
162 Tom Pagnozzi .05
163 Omar Vizquel .05
164 John Candelaria .05
165 Terry Shumpert .05
166 Andy Mota .05
167 Scott Bailes .05
168 Jeff Blauser .05
169 Steve Olin .05
170 Doug Drabek .05
171 Dave Bergman .05
172 Eddie Whitson .05
173 Gilberto Reyes .05
174 Mark Grace .05
175 Paul O'Neill .05
176 Greg Cadaret .05
177 Mark Williamson .05
178 Casey Candaele .05
179 Candy Maldonado .05
180 Lee Smith .05
181 Harold Reynolds .05
182 Dave Justice .05
183 Lenny Webster .05
184 Donn Pall .05
185 Gerald Alexander .05
186 Jack Clark .05
187 Stan Javier .05
188 Ricky Jordan .05
189 Franklin Stubbs .05
190 Dennis Eckersley .60
191 Danny Tartabull .05
192 Pete O'Brien .05
193 Mark Lewis .05
194 Mike Felder .05
195 Mickey Tettleton .05
196 Dwight Smith .05
197 Shawn Abner .05
198 Jim Leyritz .05
199 Mike Devereaux .05
200 Craig Biggio .05
201 Kevin Elster .05
202 Rance Mulliniks .05
203 Tony Fernandez .05
204 Allan Anderson .05
205 Herm Winningham .05
206 Tim Jones .05
207 Ramon Martinez .05
208 Teddy Higuera .05
209 John Kruk .05
210 Jim Abbott .05
211 Dean Palmer .05
212 Mark Davis .05
213 Jay Buhner .05
214 Jesse Barfield .05
215 Kevin Mitchell .05
216 Mike LaValliere .05
217 Mark Wohlers .05
218 Dave Henderson .05
219 Dave Smith .05
220 Albert Belle .05
221 Spike Owen .05
222 Jeff Gray .05
223 Paul Gibson .05
224 Bobby Thigpen .05
225 Mike Mussina .30
226 Darrin Jackson .05
227 Luis Gonzalez .05
228 Greg Briley .05
229 Brent Mayne .05
230 Paul Molitor .65
231 Al Leiter .05
232 Andy Van Slyke .05
233 Ron Tingley .05
234 Bernard Gilkey .05
235 Kent Hrbek .05
236 Eric Karros .05
237 Randy Velarde .05
238 Andy Allanson .05
239 Willie McGee .05
240 Juan Gonzalez .35
241 Karl Rhodes .05
242 Luis Mercedes .05
243 Billy Swift .05
244 Tommy Gregg .05
245 David Howard .05
246 Dave Hollins .05
247 Kip Gross .05
248 Walt Weiss .05
249 Mackey Sasser .05
250 Cecil Fielder .05
251 Jerry Browne .05
252 Doug Dascenzo .05
253 Darryl Hamilton .05
254 Dann Bilardello .05
255 Luis Rivera .05
256 Larry Walker .05
257 Ron Karkovice .05
258 Bob Tewksbury .05
259 Jimmy Key .05
260 Bernie Williams .05
261 Gary Wayne .05
262 Mike Simms .05
263 John Orton .05
264 Marvin Freeman .05
265 Mike Jeffcoat .05
266 Roger Mason .05
267 Edgar Martinez .05
268 Henry Rodriguez .05
269 Sam Horn .05
270 Brian McRae .05
271 Kirt Manwaring .05
272 Mike Bordick .05
273 Chris Sabo .05
274 Jim Olander .05
275 Greg Harris .05
276 Dan Gakeler .05
277 Bill Sampen .05
278 Joel Skinner .05
279 Curt Schilling .35
280 Dale Murphy .25
281 Lee Stevens .05
282 Lonnie Smith .05
283 Manuel Lee .05
284 Shawn Boskie .05
285 Kevin Seitzer .05
286 Stan Royer .05
287 John Dopson .05
288 Scott Bullett .05
289 Ken Patterson .05
290 Todd Hundley .05
291 Tim Leary .05
292 Brett Butler .05
293 Gregg Olson .05
294 Jeff Brantley .05
295 Brian Holman .05
296 Brian Harper .05
297 Brian Bohanon .05
298 Checklist 1-100 .05
299 Checklist 101-200 .05
300 Checklist 201-300 .05
301 Frank Thomas .65
302 Lloyd McClendon .05
303 Brady Anderson .05
304 Julio Valera .05
305 Mike Aldrete .05
306 Joe Oliver .05
307 Todd Stottlemyre .05
308 Rey Sanchez .05
309 Gary Sheffield .35
310 Andujar Cedeno .05
311 Kenny Rogers .05
312 Bruce Hurst .05
313 Mike Schooler .05
314 Mike Benjamin .05
315 Chuck Finley .05
316 Mark Lemke .05
317 Scott Livingstone .05
318 Chris Nabholz .05
319 Mike Humphreys .05
320 Pedro Guerrero .05
321 Willie Banks .05
322 Tom Goodwin .05
323 Hector Wagner .05
324 Wally Ritchie .05
325 Mo Vaughn .05
326 Joe Klink .05
327 Cal Eldred .05
328 Daryl Boston .05
329 Mike Huff .05
330 Jeff Bagwell .65
331 Bob Milacki .05
332 Tom Prince .05
333 Pat Tabler .05
334 Ced Landrum .05
335 Reggie Jefferson .05
336 Mo Sanford .05
337 Kevin Ritz .05
338 Gerald Perry .05
339 Jeff Hamilton .05
340 Tim Wallach .05
341 Jeff Huson .05
342 Jose Melendez .05
343 Willie Wilson .05
344 Mike Stanton .05
345 Joel Johnston .05
346 Lee Guetterman .05
347 Francisco Olivares .05
348 Dave Burba .05
349 Tim Crews .05
350 Scott Leius .05
351 Danny Cox .05
352 Wayne Housie .05
353 Chris Donnels .05
354 Chris George .05
355 Gerald Young .05
356 Roberto Hernandez .05
357 Neal Heaton .05
358 Todd Frohwirth .05
359 Jose Vizcaino .05
360 Jim Thome .60
361 Craig Wilson .05
362 Dave Haas .05
363 Billy Hatcher .05
364 John Barfield .05
365 Luis Aquino .05
366 Charlie Leibrandt .05
367 Howard Farmer .05
368 Bryn Smith .05
369 Mickey Morandini .05
370 Jose Canseco (Members Choice, should have been #597.) .35
371 Jose Uribe .05
372 Bob MacDonald .05
373 Luis Sojo .05
374 Craig Shipley .05

#	Player	Price
375	Scott Bankhead	.05
376	Greg Gagne	.05
377	Scott Cooper	.05
378	Jose Offerman	.05
379	Billy Spiers	.05
380	John Smiley	.05
381	Jeff Carter	.05
382	Heathcliff Slocumb	.05
383	Jeff Tackett	.05
384	John Kiely	.05
385	John Vander Wal	.05
386	Omar Olivares	.05
387	Ruben Sierra	.05
388	Tom Gordon	.05
389	Charles Nagy	.05
390	Dave Stewart	.05
391	Pete Harnisch	.05
392	Tim Burke	.05
393	Roberto Kelly	.05
394	Freddie Benavides	.05
395	Tom Glavine	.35
396	Wes Chamberlain	.05
397	Eric Gunderson	.05
398	Dave West	.05
399	Ellis Burks	.05
400	Ken Griffey Jr.	1.00
401	Thomas Howard	.05
402	Juan Guzman	.05
403	Mitch Webster	.05
404	Matt Merullo	.05
405	Steve Buechele	.05
406	Danny Jackson	.05
407	Felix Jose	.05
408	Doug Piatt	.05
409	Jim Eisenreich	.05
410	Bryan Harvey	.05
411	Jim Austin	.05
412	Jim Poole	.05
413	Glenallen Hill	.05
414	Gene Nelson	.05
415	Ivan Rodriguez	.60
416	Frank Tanana	.05
417	Steve Decker	.05
418	Jason Grimsley	.05
419	Tim Layana	.05
420	Don Mattingly	.85
421	Jerome Walton	.05
422	Rob Ducey	.05
423	Andy Benes	.05
424	John Marzano	.05
425	Gene Harris	.05
426	Tim Raines	.05
427	Bret Barberie	.05
428	Harvey Pulliam	.05
429	Cris Carpenter	.05
430	Howard Johnson	.05
431	Orel Hershiser	.05
432	Brian Hunter	.05
433	Kevin Tapani	.05
434	Rick Reed	.05
435	Ron Witmeyer	.05
436	Gary Gaetti	.05
437	Alex Cole	.05
438	Chito Martinez	.05
439	Greg Litton	.05
440	Julio Franco	.05
441	Mike Munoz	.05
442	Erik Pappas	.05
443	Pat Combs	.05
444	Lance Johnson	.05
445	Ed Sprague	.05
446	Mike Greenwell	.05
447	Milt Thompson	.05
448	Mike Magnante	.05
449	Chris Haney	.05
450	Robin Yount	.65
451	Rafael Ramirez	.05
452	Gino Minutelli	.05
453	Tom Lampkin	.05
454	Tony Perezchica	.05
455	Dwight Gooden	.05
456	Mark Guthrie	.05
457	Jay Howell	.05
458	Gary DiSarcina	.05
459	John Smoltz	.05
460	Will Clark	.05
461	Dave Otto	.05
462	Rob Maurer	.05
463	Dwight Evans	.05
464	Tom Brunansky	.05
465	Shawn Hare **RC**	.05
466	Geronimo Pena	.05
467	Alex Fernandez	.05
468	Greg Myers	.05
469	Jeff Fassero	.05
470	Len Dykstra	.05
471	Jeff Johnson	.05
472	Russ Swan	.05
473	Archie Corbin	.05
474	Chuck McElroy	.05
475	Mark McGwire	1.25
476	Wally Whitehurst	.05
477	Tim McIntosh	.05
478	Sid Bream	.05
479	Jeff Juden	.05
480	Carlton Fisk	.65
481	Jeff Plympton	.05
482	Carlos Martinez	.05
483	Jim Gott	.05
484	Bob McClure	.05
485	Tim Teufel	.05
486	Vicente Palacios	.05
487	Jeff Reed	.05
488	Tony Phillips	.05
489	Mel Rojas	.05
490	Ben McDonald	.05
491	Andres Santana	.05
492	Chris Beasley	.05
493	Mike Timlin	.05
494	Brian Downing	.05
495	Kirk Gibson	.05
496	Scott Sanderson	.05
497	Nick Esasky	.05
498	Johnny Guzman **RC**	.05
499	Mitch Williams	.05
500	Kirby Puckett	.75
501	Mike Harkey	.05
502	Jim Gantner	.05
503	Bruce Egloff	.05
504	Josias Manzanillo	.05
505	Delino DeShields	.05
506	Rheal Cormier	.05
507	Jay Bell	.05
508	Rich Rowland	.05
509	Scott Servais	.05
510	Terry Pendleton	.05
511	Rich DeLucia	.05
512	Warren Newson	.05
513	Paul Faries	.05
514	Kal Daniels	.05
515	Jarvis Brown	.05
516	Rafael Palmeiro	.60
517	Kelly Downs	.05
518	Steve Chitren	.05
519	Moises Alou	.05
520	Wade Boggs	.75
521	Pete Schourek	.05
522	Scott Terry	.05
523	Kevin Appier	.05
524	Gary Redus	.05
525	George Bell	.05
526	Jeff Kaiser	.05
527	Alvaro Espinoza	.05
528	Luis Polonia	.05
529	Darren Daulton	.05
530	Norm Charlton	.05
531	John Olerud	.05
532	Dan Plesac	.05
533	Billy Ripken	.05
534	Rod Nichols	.05
535	Joey Cora	.05
536	Harold Baines	.05
537	Bob Ojeda	.05
538	Mark Leonard	.05
539	Danny Darwin	.05
540	Shawon Dunston	.05
541	Pedro Munoz	.05
542	Mark Gubicza	.05
543	Kevin Baez	.05
544	Todd Zeile	.05
545	Don Slaught	.05
546	Tony Eusebio	.05
547	Alonzo Powell	.05
548	Gary Pettis	.05
549	Brian Barnes	.05
550	Lou Whitaker	.05
551	Keith Mitchell	.05
552	Oscar Azocar	.05
553	Stu Cole	.05
554	Steve Wapnick	.05
555	Derek Bell	.05
556	Luis Lopez	.05
557	Anthony Telford	.05
558	Tim Mauser	.05
559	Glenn Sutko	.05
560	Darryl Strawberry	.05
561	Tom Bolton	.05
562	Cliff Young	.05
563	Bruce Walton	.05
564	Chico Walker	.05
565	John Franco	.05
566	Paul McClellan	.05
567	Paul Abbott	.05
568	Gary Varsho	.05
569	Carlos Maldonado	.05
570	Kelly Gruber	.05
571	Jose Oquendo	.05
572	Steve Frey	.05
573	Tino Martinez	.05
574	Bill Haselman	.05
575	Eric Anthony	.05
576	John Habyan	.05
577	Jeffrey McNeely	.05
578	Chris Bosio	.05
579	Joe Grahe	.05
580	Fred McGriff	.05
581	Rick Honeycutt	.05
582	Matt Williams	.05
583	Cliff Brantley	.05
584	Rob Dibble	.05
585	Skeeter Barnes	.05
586	Greg Hibbard	.05
587	Randy Milligan	.05
588	Checklist 301-400	.05
589	Checklist 401-500	.05
590	Checklist 501-600	.05
591	Frank Thomas (Members Choice)	.35
592	Dave Justice (Members Choice)	.05
593	Roger Clemens (Members Choice)	.45
594	Steve Avery (Members Choice)	.05
595	Cal Ripken, Jr. (Members Choice)	.75
596	Barry Larkin (Members Choice)	.05
597	Not issued (See #370)	.05
598	Will Clark (Members Choice)	.05
599	Cecil Fielder (Members Choice)	.05
600	Ryne Sandberg (Members Choice)	.40
601	Chuck Knoblauch (Members Choice)	.05
602	Dwight Gooden (Members Choice)	.05
603	Ken Griffey Jr. (Members Choice)	.65
604	Barry Bonds (Members Choice)	.75
605	Nolan Ryan (Members Choice)	.75
606	Jeff Bagwell (Members Choice)	.35
607	Robin Yount (Members Choice)	.30
608	Bobby Bonilla (Members Choice)	.05
609	George Brett (Members Choice)	.50
610	Howard Johnson (Members Choice)	.05
611	Esteban Beltre	.05
612	Mike Christopher	.05
613	Troy Afenir	.05
614	Mariano Duncan	.05
615	Doug Henry	.05
616	Doug Jones	.05
617	Alvin Davis	.05
618	Craig Lefferts	.05
619	Kevin McReynolds	.05
620	Barry Bonds	1.50
621	Turner Ward	.05
622	Joe Magrane	.05
623	Mark Parent	.05
624	Tom Browning	.05
625	John Smiley	.05
626	Steve Wilson	.05
627	Mike Gallego	.05
628	Sammy Sosa	.75
629	Rico Rossy	.05
630	Royce Clayton	.05
631	Clay Parker	.05
632	Pete Smith	.05
633	Jeff McKnight	.05
634	Jack Daugherty	.05
635	Steve Sax	.05
636	Joe Hesketh	.05
637	Vince Horsman	.05
638	Eric King	.05
639	Joe Boever	.05
640	Jack Morris	.05
641	Arthur Rhodes	.05
642	Bob Melvin	.05
643	Rick Wilkins	.05
644	Scott Scudder	.05
645	Bip Roberts	.05
646	Julio Valera	.05
647	Kevin Campbell	.05
648	Steve Searcy	.05
649	Scott Kamieniecki	.05
650	Kurt Stillwell	.05
651	Bob Welch	.05
652	Andres Galarraga	.05
653	Mike Jackson	.05
654	Bo Jackson	.10
655	Sid Fernandez	.05
656	Mike Bielecki	.05
657	Jeff Reardon	.05
658	Wayne Rosenthal	.05
659	Eric Bullock	.05
660	Eric Davis	.05
661	Randy Tomlin	.05
662	Tom Edens	.05
663	Rob Murphy	.05
664	Leo Gomez	.05
665	Greg Maddux	.75
666	Greg Vaughn	.05
667	Wade Taylor	.05
668	Brad Arnsberg	.05
669	Mike Moore	.05
670	Mark Langston	.05
671	Barry Jones	.05
672	Bill Landrum	.05
673	Greg Swindell	.05
674	Wayne Edwards	.05
675	Greg Olson	.05
676	Bill Pulsipher **RC**	.05
677	Bobby Witt	.05
678	Mark Carreon	.05
679	Patrick Lennon	.05
680	Ozzie Smith	.75
681	John Briscoe	.05
682	Matt Young	.05
683	Jeff Conine	.05
684	Phil Stephenson	.05
685	Ron Darling	.05
686	Bryan Hickerson	.05
687	Dale Sveum	.05
688	Kirk McCaskill	.05
689	Rich Amaral	.05
690	Danny Tartabull	.05
691	Donald Harris	.05
692	Doug Davis	.05
693	John Farrell	.05
694	Paul Gibson	.05
695	Kenny Lofton	.05
696	Mike Fetters	.05
697	Rosario Rodriguez	.05
698	Chris Jones	.05
699	Jeff Manto	.05
700	Rick Sutcliffe	.05
701	Scott Bankhead	.05
702	Donnie Hill	.05
703	Todd Worrell	.05
704	Rene Gonzales	.05
705	Rick Cerone	.05
706	Tony Pena	.05
707	Paul Sorrento	.05
708	Gary Scott	.05
709	Junior Noboa	.05
710	Wally Joyner	.05
711	Charlie Hayes	.05
712	Rich Rodriguez	.05
713	Rudy Seanez	.05
714	Jim Bullinger	.05
715	Jeff Robinson	.05
716	Jeff Branson	.05
717	Andy Ashby	.05
718	Dave Burba	.05
719	Rich Gossage	.05
720	Randy Johnson	.65
721	David Wells	.05
722	Paul Kilgus	.05
723	Dave Martinez	.05
724	Denny Neagle	.05
725	Andy Stankiewicz	.05
726	Rick Aguilera	.05
727	Junior Ortiz	.05
728	Storm Davis	.05
729	Don Robinson	.05
730	Ron Gant	.05
731	Paul Assenmacher	.05
732	Mark Gardiner	.05
733	Milt Hill	.05
734	Jeremy Hernandez	.05
735	Ken Hill	.05
736	Xavier Hernandez	.05
737	Gregg Jefferies	.05
738	Dick Schofield	.05
739	Ron Robinson	.05
740	Sandy Alomar	.05
741	Mike Stanley	.05
742	Butch Henry	.05
743	Floyd Bannister	.05
744	Brian Drahman	.05
745	Dave Winfield	.65
746	Bob Walk	.05
747	Chris James	.05
748	Don Prybylinski	.05
749	Dennis Rasmussen	.05
750	Rickey Henderson	.65
751	Chris Hammond	.05
752	Bob Kipper	.05
753	Dave Rohde	.05
754	Hubie Brooks	.05
755	Bret Saberhagen	.05
756	Jeff Robinson	.05
757	Pat Listach **RC**	.05
758	Bill Wegman	.05
759	John Wetteland	.05
760	Phil Plantier	.05
761	Wilson Alvarez	.05
762	Scott Aldred	.05
763	Armando Reynoso **RC**	.05
764	Todd Benzinger	.05
765	Kevin Mitchell	.05
766	Gary Sheffield	.35
767	Allan Anderson	.05
768	Rusty Meacham	.05
769	Rick Parker	.05
770	Nolan Ryan	1.50
771	Jeff Ballard	.05
772	Cory Snyder	.05
773	Denis Boucher	.05
774	Jose Gonzales	.05
775	Juan Guerrero	.05
776	Ed Nunez	.05
777	Scott Ruskin	.05
778	Terry Leach	.05
779	Carl Willis	.05
780	Bobby Bonilla	.05
781	Duane Ward	.05
782	Joe Slusarski	.05
783	David Segui	.05
784	Kirk Gibson	.05
785	Frank Viola	.05
786	Keith Miller	.05
787	Mike Morgan	.05
788	Kim Batiste	.05
789	Sergio Valdez	.05
790	Eddie Taubensee	.05
791	Jack Armstrong	.05
792	Scott Fletcher	.05
793	Steve Farr	.05
794	Dan Pasqua	.05
795	Eddie Murray	.65
796	John Morris	.05
797	Francisco Cabrera	.05
798	Mike Perez	.05
799	Ted Wood	.05
800	Jose Rijo	.05
801	Danny Gladden	.05
802	Arci Cianfrocco	.05
803	Monty Fariss	.05
804	Roger McDowell	.05
805	Randy Myers	.05
806	Kirk Dressendorfer	.05
807	Zane Smith	.05
808	Glenn Davis	.05
809	Torey Lovullo	.05
810	Andre Dawson	.25
811	Bill Pecota	.05
812	Ted Power	.05
813	Willie Blair	.05
814	Dave Fleming	.05
815	Chris Gwynn	.05
816	Jody Reed	.05
817	Mark Dewey	.05
818	Kyle Abbott	.05
819	Tom Henke	.05
820	Kevin Seitzer	.05
821	Al Newman	.05
822	Tim Sherrill	.05
823	Chuck Crim	.05
824	Darren Reed	.05
825	Tony Gwynn	.75
826	Steve Foster	.05
827	Steve Howe	.05
828	Brook Jacoby	.05
829	Rodney McCray	.05
830	Chuck Knoblauch	.05
831	John Wehner	.05
832	Scott Garrelts	.05
833	Alejandro Pena	.05
834	Jeff Parrett	.05
835	Juan Bell	.05
836	Lance Dickson	.05
837	Darryl Kile	.05
838	Efrain Valdez	.05
839	Bob Zupcic **RC**	.05
840	George Bell	.05
841	Dave Gallagher	.05
842	Tim Belcher	.05
843	Jeff Shaw	.05
844	Mike Fitzgerald	.05
845	Gary Carter	.65
846	John Russell	.05
847	Eric Hillman **RC**	.05
848	Mike Witt	.05
849	Curt Wilkerson	.05
850	Alan Trammell	.05
851	Rex Hudler	.05
852	Michael Walkden **RC**	.05
853	Kevin Ward	.05
854	Tim Naehring	.05
855	Bill Swift	.05
856	Damon Berryhill	.05
857	Mark Eichhorn	.05
858	Hector Villanueva	.05
859	Jose Lind	.05
860	Denny Martinez	.05
861	Bill Krueger	.05
862	Mike Kingery	.05
863	Jeff Innis	.05
864	Derek Lilliquist	.05
865	Reggie Sanders	.05
866	Ramon Garcia	.05
867	Bruce Ruffin	.05
868	Dickie Thon	.05
869	Melido Perez	.05
870	Ruben Amaro	.05
871	Alan Mills	.05
872	Matt Sinatro	.05
873	Eddie Zosky	.05
874	Pete Incaviglia	.05
875	Tom Candiotti	.05
876	Bob Patterson	.05
877	Neal Heaton	.05
878	Terrel Hansen **RC**	.05
879	Dave Eiland	.05
880	Von Hayes	.05
881	Tim Scott	.05
882	Otis Nixon	.05
883	Herm Winningham	.05
884	Dion James	.05
885	Dave Wainhouse	.05
886	Frank DiPino	.05
887	Dennis Cook	.05
888	Jose Mesa	.05
889	Mark Leiter	.05
890	Willie Randolph	.05
891	Craig Colbert	.05
892	Dwayne Henry	.05
893	Jim Lindeman	.05
894	Charlie Hough	.05
895	Gil Heredia	.05
896	Scott Chiamparino	.05
897	Lance Blankenship	.05
898	Checklist 601-700	.05
899	Checklist 701-800	.05
900	Checklist 801-900	.05

First Draft Picks

Issued as inserts with Stadium Club Series 3, this three-card set features the No. 1 draft picks of 1990-92. Fronts have a full-bleed photo with S.C. logo and player name in the lower-right corner. At bottom-left in a red strip is a gold-foil stamping, "#1 Draft Pick of the '90's." An orange circle at upper-right has the year the player was the No. 1 choice. The basic red-and-black back has a color photo, a few biographical and draft details and a gold facsimile autograph among other gold-foil highlights.

		NM/M
Complete Set (3):		4.50
Common Player:		.25
1	Chipper Jones	4.00
2	Brien Taylor	.25
3	Phil Nevin	.25

Master Photos

Uncropped versions of the photos which appear on regular Stadium Club cards are featured on these large-format (5" x 7") cards. The photos are set against a white background and trimmed with holographic foil. Backs are blank and the cards are unnumbered. Members of Topps' Stadium Club received a Master Photo in their members' packs for 1992. The cards were also available as inserts in special boxes of Stadium Club cards sold at Wal-Mart stores.

		NM/M
Complete Set (15):		20.00
Common Player:		.50
(1)	Wade Boggs	2.25
(2)	Barry Bonds	4.00
(3)	Jose Canseco	1.00
(4)	Will Clark	.50
(5)	Cecil Fielder	.50
(6)	Dwight Gooden	.50
(7)	Ken Griffey Jr.	3.00
(8)	Rickey Henderson	2.00
(9)	Lance Johnson	.50
(10)	Cal Ripken, Jr.	4.00
(11)	Nolan Ryan	4.00
(12)	Deion Sanders	.50
(13)	Darryl Strawberry	.50
(14)	Danny Tartabull	.50
(15)	Frank Thomas	2.00

East Coast National

In conjunction with its appearance at the August 1992 East Coast National card show, Topps distributed 22,000 five-card cello packs of its 1992 Stadium Club series bearing a special gold-foil show commemorative overprint. The cards are in all other respects identical to regular issue '92 S.C. Only 100 cards from Series III can be found with the overprint. Production of each card thus totals 1,100.

		NM/M
Complete Set (100):		40.00
Common Player:		.60
601	Chuck Knoblauch (Members Choice)	.60
602	Dwight Gooden (Members Choice)	.60
603	Ken Griffey Jr. (Members Choice)	6.00
604	Barry Bonds (Members Choice)	6.50
605	Nolan Ryan (Members Choice)	7.50

No.	Player	NM/M
606	Jeff Bagwell (Members Choice)	2.50
607	Robin Yount (Members Choice)	2.50
608	Bobby Bonilla (Members Choice)	.60
609	George Brett (Members Choice)	5.50
610	Howard Johnson (Members Choice)	.60
611	Esteban Beltre	.60
612	Mike Christopher	.60
613	Troy Afenir	.60
619	Kevin McReynolds	.60
620	Barry Bonds	7.50
622	Joe Magrane	.60
623	Mark Parent	.60
626	Steve Wilson	.60
629	Rico Rossy	.60
631	Clay Parker	.60
633	Jeff McKnight	.60
637	Vince Horsman	.60
638	Eric King	.60
639	Joe Boever	.60
641	Arthur Rhodes	.60
647	Kevin Campbell	.60
653	Mike Jackson	.60
661	Randy Tomlin	.60
665	Greg Maddux	3.00
668	Brad Arnsberg	.60
671	Barry Jones	.60
672	Bill Landrum	.60
673	Greg Swindell	.60
676	Bill Pulsipher	.60
679	Patrick Lennon	.60
681	John Briscoe	.60
684	Phil Stephenson	.60
685	Ron Darling	.60
686	Bryan Hickerson	.60
688	Kirk McCaskill	.60
689	Rich Amaral	.60
692	Doug Davis	.60
693	John Farrell	.60
700	Rick Sutcliffe	.60
704	Rene Gonzalez	.60
713	Rudy Seanez	.60
714	Jim Bullinger	.60
716	Jeff Branson	.60
717	Andy Ashby	.60
725	Andy Stankiewicz	.60
733	Milt Hill	.60
739	Ron Robinson	.60
742	Butch Henry	.60
747	Chris James	.60
749	Dennis Rasmussen	.60
753	Dave Rohde	.60
757	Pat Listach	.60
758	Bill Wegman	.60
763	Armando Reynoso	.60
765	Kevin Mitchell	.60
766	Gary Sheffield	.90
769	Rick Parker	.60
771	Jeff Ballard	.60
772	Cory Snyder	.60
774	Jose Gonzalez	.60
775	Juan Guerrero	.60
776	Edwin Nunez	.60
778	Terry Leach	.60
782	Joe Slusarski	.60
784	Kirk Gibson	.60
788	Kim Batiste	.60
802	Arci Cianfrocco	.60
806	Kirk Dressendorfer	.60
807	Zane Smith	.60
814	Dave Fleming	.60
815	Chris Gwynn	.60
817	Mark Dewey	.60
819	Tom Henke	.60
822	Tim Sherrill	.60
826	Steve Foster	.60
831	John Wehner	.60
832	Scott Garrelts	.60
840	George Bell	.60
841	Dave Gallagher	.60
846	John Russell	.60
847	Eric Hillman	.60
852	Michael Walkden	.60
855	Bill Swift	.60
864	Derek Lilliquist	.60
876	Bob Patterson	.60
878	Terrel Hansen	.60
881	Tim Scott	.60
886	Frank DiPino	.60
891	Craig Colbert	.60
892	Dwayne Henry	.60
893	Jim Lindeman	.60
895	Gil Heredia	.60
898	Checklist 601-700	.05
899	Checklist 701-800	.05
900	Checklist 801-900	.05

National Convention

To promote its Stadium Club baseball card brand to dealers, Topps distributed sample cards during the National Sports Collectors Convention in Atlanta, Ga. The sample cards are regular-issue S.C. cards which have received a gold-foil overprint of the 1992 National logo. Only 100 cards from the third series can be found with the overprint. Only 5,000 four-card packs were distributed, thus only 200 of each card were made.

		NM/M
Complete Set (100):		135.00
Common Player:		1.50
616	Doug Jones	1.50
617	Alvin Davis	1.50
618	Craig Lefferts	1.50
621	Turner Ward	1.50
625	John Smiley	1.50
627	Mike Gallego	1.50
630	Royce Clayton	1.50
634	Jack Daugherty	1.50
635	Steve Sax	1.50
636	Joe Hesketh	1.50
643	Rick Wilkins	1.50
644	Scott Scudder	1.50
645	Bip Roberts	1.50
650	Kurt Stillwell	1.50
652	Andres Galarraga	1.50
657	Jeff Reardon	1.50
660	Eric Davis	1.50
662	Tom Edens	1.50
675	Greg Olson	1.50
678	Mark Carreon	1.50
680	Ozzie Smith	15.00
682	Matt Young	1.50
690	Danny Tartabull	1.50
691	Donald Harris	1.50
695	Kenny Lofton	1.50
697	Rosario Rodriguez	1.50
701	Scott Bankhead	1.50
705	Rick Cerone	1.50
706	Tony Pena	1.50
709	Junior Noboa	1.50
710	Wally Joyner	1.50
711	Charlie Hayes	1.50
712	Rich Rodriguez	1.50
721	David Wells	1.50
723	Dave Martinez	1.50
726	Rick Aguilera	1.50
727	Junior Ortiz	1.50
729	Don Robinson	1.50
730	Ron Gant	1.50
731	Paul Assenmacher	1.50
732	Mark Gardiner	1.50
735	Ken Hill	1.50
736	Xavier Hernandez	1.50
737	Gregg Jefferies	1.50
740	Sandy Alomar, Jr.	1.50
741	Mike Stanley	1.50
744	Brian Drahman	1.50
746	Bob Walk	1.50
751	Chris Hammond	1.50
759	John Wetteland	1.50
760	Phil Plantier	1.50
761	Wilson Alvarez	1.50
773	Denis Boucher	1.50
777	Scott Ruskin	1.50
779	Carl Willis	1.50
783	David Segui	1.50
786	Keith Miller	1.50
790	Eddie Taubensee	1.50
791	Jack Armstrong	1.50
792	Scott Fletcher	1.50
793	Steve Farr	1.50
794	Dan Pasqua	1.50
797	Francisco Cabrera	1.50
798	Mike Perez	1.50
801	Danny Gladden	1.50
803	Monty Fariss	1.50
804	Roger McDowell	1.50
805	Randy Myers	1.50
808	Glenn Davis	1.50
809	Torey Lovullo	1.50
816	Jody Reed	1.50
825	Tony Gwynn	15.00
827	Steve Howe	1.50
828	Brook Jacoby	1.50
829	Rodney McCray	1.50
830	Chuck Knoblauch	1.50
835	Juan Bell	1.50
836	Lance Dickson	1.50
837	Darryl Kile	1.50
842	Tim Belcher	1.50
843	Jeff Shaw	1.50
844	Mike Fitzgerald	1.50
845	Gary Carter	6.00
850	Alan Trammell	1.50
851	Rex Hudler	1.50
856	Damon Berryhill	1.50
857	Mark Eichhorn	1.50
858	Hector Villanueva	1.50
860	Denny Martinez	1.50
865	Reggie Sanders	1.50
869	Melido Perez	1.50
874	Pete Incaviglia	1.50
875	Tom Candiotti	1.50
877	Neal Heaton	1.50
879	Dave Eiland	1.50
882	Otis Nixon	1.50
883	Herm Winningham	1.50
884	Dion James	1.50
887	Dennis Cook	1.50
894	Charlie Hough	1.50

Members Only

A multi-sport set of 50 cards was sent in four installments to members of Topps' Stadium Club as part of their 1992 benefits package. Cards are similar in format to regular. Stadium Club cards, 2-1/2" x 3-1/2", UV coated on front. Fronts have a special gold foil "Members Only" logo on front. Backs have a stadium scoreboard design with details of a career highlight. The unnumbered cards (baseball only) are checklisted here alphabetically.

		NM/M
Complete Set (36):		18.00
Common Player:		.15
(1)	Carlos Baerga	.15
(2)	Wade Boggs	1.00
(3)	Barry Bonds	2.50
(4)	Bret Boone	.15
(5)	Pat Borders	.15
(6)	George Brett	1.00
(7)	George Brett (3,000 hits)	1.00
(8)	Jim Bullinger	.15
(9)	Gary Carter	.75
(10)	Andujar Cedeno	.15
(11)	Roger Clemens, Matt Young	.45
(12)	Dennis Eckersley (Cy Young Award)	.60
(13)	Dennis Eckersley (MVP)	.60
(14)	Dave Eiland	.15
(15)	Dwight Gooden, Gary Sheffield	.25
(16)	Ken Griffey Jr.	1.50
(17)	Kevin Gross	.15
(18)	Bo Jackson	.25
(19)	Eric Karros	.15
(20)	Pat Listach	.15
(21)	Greg Maddux	1.00
(22)	Fred McGriff, Gary Sheffield	.25
(23)	Mickey Morandini	.15
(24)	Jack Morris	.15
(25)	Eddie Murray	.75
(26)	Eddie Murray	.75
(27)	Bip Roberts	.15
(28)	Nolan Ryan (27 seasons)	2.50
(29)	Nolan Ryan (1993 finale)	2.50
(30)	Lee Smith	.15
(31)	Ozzie Smith (2,000 hits)	1.00
(32)	Ozzie Smith (7,000 assists)	1.00
(33)	Ozzie Smith (stolen base record)	1.00
(34)	Bobby Thigpen	.15
(35)	Dave Winfield	.75
(36)	Robin Yount	.75

SkyDome

This 200-card special Stadium Club set from Topps was uniquely packaged in a plastic replica of the Toronto SkyDome, the home of the 1991 All-Star Game. Featured in the set are members of Team USA, All-Stars, draft picks, top prospects and eight cards from the World Series between the Twins and Braves. The cards are styled much like the regular Stadium Club cards. Some cards have been found with incorrect gold-foil identifiers as well as the correct version.

		NM/M
Unopened Factory Set (200):		15.00
Complete Set (200):		10.00
Common Player:		.05
1	Terry Adams RC	.05
2	Tommy Adams	.05
3	Rick Aguilera	.05
4	Ron Allen	.05
5	Roberto Alomar/AS	.20
6	Sandy Alomar	.05
7	Greg Anthony	.05
8	James Austin	.05
9	Steve Avery	.05
10	Harold Baines	.05
11	Brian Barber RC	.05
12	Jon Barnes	.05
13	George Bell	.05
14	Doug Bennett	.05
15	Sean Bergman	.05
16	Craig Biggio	.05
17	Bill Bliss	.05
18	Wade Boggs/AS	.60
19	Bobby Bonilla/AS	.05
20	Russell Brock	.05
21	Tarrik Brock	.05
22	Tom Browning	.05
23	Brett Butler	.05
24	Ivan Calderon	.05
25	Joe Carter	.05
26	Joe Caruso	.05
27	Dan Cholowsky	.05
28	Will Clark/AS	.05
29	Roger Clemens/AS	.65
30	Shawn Curran	.05
31	Chris Curtis	.05
32	Chili Davis	.05
33	Andre Dawson	.25
34	Joe DeBerry	.05
35	John Dettmer	.05
36	Rob Dibble	.05
37	John Donati RC	.05
38	Dave Doorneweerd	.05
39	Darren Dreifort	.05
40	Mike Durant	.05
41	Chris Durkin	.05
42	Dennis Eckersley	.40
43	Brian Edmondson RC	.05
44	Vaughn Eshelman RC	.05
45	Shawn Estes RC	.50
46	Jorge Fabregas RC	.10
47	Jon Farrell	.05
48	Cecil Fielder/AS	.05
49	Carlton Fisk	.50
50	Tim Flannelly	.05
51	Cliff Floyd RC	.50
52	Julio Franco	.05
53	Greg Gagne	.05
54	Chris Gambs RC	.05
55	Ron Gant	.05
56	Brent Gates	.05
57	Dwayne Gerald	.05
58	Jason Giambi	1.50
59	Benji Gil RC	.05
60	Mark Gipner	.05
61	Danny Gladden	.05
62	Tom Glavine	.35
63	Jimmy Gonzalez	.05
64	Jeff Granger	.05
65	Dan Grapenthien	.05
66	Dennis Gray	.05
67	Shawn Green RC	2.00
68	Tyler Green	.05
69	Todd Greene	.05
70	Ken Griffey Jr./AS	.75
71	Kelly Gruber	.05
72	Ozzie Guillen	.05
73	Tony Gwynn/AS	.60
74	Shane Halter	.05
75	Jeffrey Hammonds	.05
76	Larry Hanlon	.05
77	Pete Harnisch	.05
78	Mike Harrison	.05
79	Bryan Harvey	.05
80	Scott Hatteberg	.05
81	Rick Helling	.05
82	Dave Henderson	.05
83	Rickey Henderson/AS	.50
84	Tyrone Hill	.05
85	Todd Hollandsworth RC	.10
86	Brian Holliday	.05
87	Terry Horn	.05
88	Jeff Hostetler	.05
89	Kent Hrbek	.05
90	Mark Hubbard	.05
91	Charles Johnson	.05
92	Howard Johnson	.05
93	Todd Johnson	.05
94	Bobby Jones RC	.10
95	Dan Jones	.05
96	Felix Jose	.05
97	Dave Justice	.05
98	Jimmy Key	.05
99	Marc Kroom RC	.05
100	John Kruk	.05
101	Mark Langston	.05
102	Barry Larkin	.05
103	Mike LaValliere	.05
104a	Scott Leius (1991 N.L. All-Star - Error)	.05
104b	Scott Leius (1991 World Series - Correct)	.25
105	Mark Lemke	.05
106	Donnie Leshnock	.05
107	Jimmy Lewis	.05
108	Shawn Livesy	.05
109	Ryan Long	.05
110	Trevor Mallory	.05
111	Denny Martinez	.05
112	Justin Mashore	.05
113	Jason McDonald	.05
114	Jack McDowell	.05
115	Tom McKinnon	.05
116	Billy McKinnon	.05
117	Buck McNabb RC	.05
118	Jim Mecir	.05
119	Dan Melendez	.05
120	Shawn Miller RC	.05
121	Trever Miller	.05
122	Paul Molitor	.50
123	Vincent Moore	.05
124	Mike Morgan	.05
125	Jack Morris (World Series)	.05
126	Jack Morris/AS	.05
127	Sean Mulligan	.05
128	Eddie Murray	.50
129	Mike Neill	.05
130	Phil Nevin	.05
131	Mark O'Brien	.05
132	Alex Ochoa RC	.05
133	Chad Ogea RC	.05
134	Greg Olson	.05
135	Paul O'Neill	.05
136a	Jared Osentowski (1991 World Series - Error)	.05
136b	Jared Osentowski (Draft Pick - Correct)	.25
137	Mike Pagliarulo	.05
138	Rafael Palmeiro	.40
139	Rodney Pedraza	.05
140	Tony Phillips	.05
141	Scott Pisciotta RC	.05
142	Chris Pritchott	.05
143	Jason Pruitt	.05
144a	Kirby Puckett (1991 N.L. All-Star - Error)	.60
144b	Kirby Puckett (1991 World Series - Correct)	3.00
145	Kirby Puckett/AS	.60
146	Manny Ramirez RC	5.00
147	Eddie Ramos	.05
148	Mark Ratekin	.05
149	Jeff Reardon	.05
150	Sean Rees	.05
151	Calvin Reese RC	.50
152	Desmond Relaford RC	.10
153	Eric Richardson	.05
154	Cal Ripken, Jr./AS	1.50
155	Chris Roberts	.05
156	Mike Robertson	.05
157	Steve Rodriguez	.05
158	Mike Rossiter	.05
159	Scott Ruffcorn	.05
160a	Chris Sabo (1991 World Series - Error)	.05
160b	Chris Sabo (1991 N.L. All-Star - Correct)	.25
161	Juan Samuel	.05
162	Ryne Sandberg/AS	.60
163	Scott Sanderson	.05
164	Benito Santiago	.05
165	Gene Schall RC	.05
166	Chad Schoenvogel	.05
167	Chris Seelbach RC	.05
168	Aaron Sele RC	.50
169	Basil Shabazz	.05
170	Al Shirley RC	.05
171	Paul Shuey	.05
172	Ruben Sierra	.05
173	John Smiley	.05
174	Lee Smith	.05
175	Ozzie Smith	.60
176	Tim Smith	.05
177	Zane Smith	.05
178	John Smoltz	.05
179	Scott Stahoviak	.05
180	Kennie Steenstra	.05
181	Kevin Stocker	.05
182	Chris Stynes RC	.05
183	Danny Tartabull	.05
184	Brien Taylor	.05
185	Todd Taylor	.05
186	Larry Thomas	.05
187a	Ozzie Timmons RC	.05
187b	David Tuttle (Should be #188.)	.05
188	Not issued	.05
189	Andy Van Slyke	.05
190a	Frank Viola (1991 World Series - Error)	.05
190b	Frank Viola (1991 N.L. All-Star - Correct)	.25
191	Michael Walkden	.05
192	Jeff Ware	.05
193	Allen Watson RC	.05
194	Steve Whitaker	.05
195a	Jerry Willard (1991 Draft Pick - Error)	.05
195b	Jerry Willard (1991 World Series - Correct)	.25
196	Craig Wilson	.05
197	Chris Wimmer	.05
198	Steve Wojciechowski RC	.05
199	Joel Wolfe	.05
200	Ivan Zweig	.05

1993 Stadium Club

Topps' premium set for 1993 was issued in three series, two 300-card series and a final series of 150. Boxes contained 24 packs this year, compared to 36 in the past. Packs had 14 cards and an insert card. Each box had a 5" x 7" Master Photo card.

		NM/M
Complete Set (750):		25.00
Common Player:		.05
First Day:		8X
Pack (15):		.75
Wax Box (24):		10.00
1	Pat Borders	.05
2	Greg Maddux	.85
3	Daryl Boston	.05
4	Bob Ayrault	.05
5	Tony Phillips	.05
6	Damion Easley	.05
7	Kip Gross	.05
8	Jim Thome	.65
9	Tim Belcher	.05
10	Gary Wayne	.05
11	Sam Militello	.05
12	Mike Magnante	.05
13	Tim Wakefield	.05
14	Tim Hulett	.05
15	Rheal Cormier	.05
16	Juan Guerrero	.05
17	Rich Gossage	.05
18	Tim Laker	.05
19	Darrin Jackson	.05
20	Jack Clark	.05
21	Roberto Hernandez	.05
22	Dean Palmer	.05
23	Harold Reynolds	.05
24	Dan Plesac	.05
25	Brent Mayne	.05
26	Pat Hentgen	.05
27	Luis Sojo	.05
28	Ron Gant	.05
29	Paul Gibson	.05
30	Bip Roberts	.05
31	Mickey Tettleton	.05
32	Randy Velarde	.05
33	Brian McRae	.05
34	Wes Chamberlain	.05
35	Wayne Kirby	.05
36	Rey Sanchez	.05
37	Jesse Orosco	.05
38	Mike Stanton	.05
39	Royce Clayton	.05
40	Cal Ripken, Jr.	2.50
41	John Dopson	.05
42	Gene Larkin	.05
43	Tim Raines	.05
44	Randy Myers	.05
45	Clay Parker	.05
46	Mike Scioscia	.05
47	Pete Incaviglia	.05
48	Todd Van Poppel	.05
49	Ray Lankford	.05
50	Eddie Murray	.75
51	Barry Bonds	2.50
52	Gary Thurman	.05
53	Bob Wickman	.05
54	Joey Cora	.05
55	Kenny Rogers	.05
56	Mike Devereaux	.05
57	Kevin Seitzer	.05
58	Rafael Belliard	.05
59	David Wells	.05
60	Mark Clark	.05
61	Carlos Baerga	.05
62	Scott Brosius	.05
63	Jeff Grotewold	.05
64	Rick Wrona	.05
65	Kurt Knudsen	.05
66	Lloyd McClendon	.05
67	Omar Vizquel	.05
68	Jose Vizcaino	.05
69	Rob Ducey	.05
70	Casey Candaele	.05
71	Ramon Martinez	.05
72	Todd Hundley	.05
73	John Marzano	.05

No.	Player	Value
74	Derek Parks	.05
75	Jack McDowell	.05
76	Tim Scott	.05
77	Mike Mussina	.40
78	Delino DeShields	.05
79	Chris Bosio	.05
80	Mike Bordick	.05
81	Rod Beck	.05
82	Ted Power	.05
83	John Kruk	.05
84	Steve Shifflett	.05
85	Danny Tartabull	.05
86	Mike Greenwell	.05
87	Jose Melendez	.05
88	Craig Wilson	.05
89	Melvin Nieves	.05
90	Ed Sprague	.05
91	Willie McGee	.05
92	Joe Orsulak	.05
93	Jeff King	.05
94	Dan Pasqua	.05
95	Brian Harper	.05
96	Joe Oliver	.05
97	Shane Turner	.05
98	Lenny Harris	.05
99	Jeff Parrett	.05
100	Luis Polonia	.05
101	Kent Bottenfield	.05
102	Albert Belle	.05
103	Mike Maddux	.05
104	Randy Tomlin	.05
105	Andy Stankiewicz	.05
106	Rico Rossy	.05
107	Joe Hesketh	.05
108	Dennis Powell	.05
109	Derrick May	.05
110	Pete Harnisch	.05
111	Kent Mercker	.05
112	Scott Fletcher	.05
113	Rex Hudler	.05
114	Chico Walker	.05
115	Rafael Palmeiro	.65
116	Mark Leiter	.05
117	Pedro Munoz	.05
118	Jim Bullinger	.05
119	Ivan Calderon	.05
120	Mike Timlin	.05
121	Rene Gonzales	.05
122	Greg Vaughn	.05
123	Mike Flanagan	.05
124	Mike Hartley	.05
125	Jeff Montgomery	.05
126	Mike Gallego	.05
127	Don Slaught	.05
128	Charlie O'Brien	.05
129a	Jose Offerman (Home: (Blank))	2.00
129b	Jose Offerman (Home: S.P. de MACORIS, D.R.)	.05
130	Mark Wohlers	.05
131	Eric Fox	.05
132	Doug Strange	.05
133	Jeff Frye	.05
134	Wade Boggs	.85
135	Lou Whitaker	.05
136	Craig Grebeck	.05
137	Rich Rodriguez	.05
138	Jay Bell	.05
139	Felix Fermin	.05
140	Denny Martinez	.05
141	Eric Anthony	.05
142	Roberto Alomar	.20
143	Darren Lewis	.05
144	Mike Blowers	.05
145	Scott Bankhead	.05
146	Jeff Reboulet	.05
147	Frank Viola	.05
148	Bill Pecota	.05
149	Carlos Hernandez	.05
150	Bobby Witt	.05
151	Sid Bream	.05
152	Todd Zeile	.05
153	Dennis Cook	.05
154	Brian Bohanon	.05
155	Pat Kelly	.05
156	Milt Cuyler	.05
157	Juan Bell	.05
158	Randy Milligan	.05
159	Mark Gardner	.05
160	Pat Tabler	.05
161	Jeff Reardon	.05
162	Ken Patterson	.05
163	Bobby Bonilla	.05
164	Tony Pena	.05
165	Greg Swindell	.05
166	Kirk McCaskill	.05
167	Doug Drabek	.05
168	Franklin Stubbs	.05
169	Ron Tingley	.05
170	Willie Banks	.05
171	Sergio Valdez	.05
172	Mark Lemke	.05
173	Robin Yount	.75
174	Storm Davis	.05
175	Dan Walters	.05
176	Steve Farr	.05
177	Curt Wilkerson	.05
178	Luis Alicea	.05
179	Russ Swan	.05
180	Mitch Williams	.05
181	Wilson Alvarez	.05
182	Carl Willis	.05
183	Craig Biggio	.05
184	Sean Berry	.05
185	Trevor Wilson	.05
186	Jeff Tackett	.05
187	Ellis Burks	.05
188	Jeff Branson	.05
189	Matt Nokes	.05
190	John Smiley	.05
191	Danny Gladden	.05
192	Mike Boddicker	.05
193	Roger Pavlik	.05
194	Paul Sorrento	.05
195	Vince Coleman	.05
196	Gary DiSarcina	.05
197	Rafael Bournigal	.05
198	Mike Schooler	.05
199	Scott Ruskin	.05
200	Frank Thomas	.75
201	Kyle Abbott	.05
202	Mike Perez	.05
203	Andre Dawson	.25
204	Bill Swift	.05
205	Alejandro Pena	.05
206	Dave Winfield	.75
207	Andujar Cedeno	.05
208	Terry Steinbach	.05
209	Chris Hammond	.05
210	Todd Burns	.05
211	Hipolito Pichardo	.05
212	John Kiely	.05
213	Tim Teufel	.05
214	Lee Guetterman	.05
215	Geronimo Pena	.05
216	Brett Butler	.05
217	Bryan Hickerson	.05
218	Rick Trlicek	.05
219	Lee Stevens	.05
220	Roger Clemens	1.25
221	Carlton Fisk	.75
222	Chili Davis	.05
223	Walt Terrell	.05
224	Jim Eisenreich	.05
225	Ricky Bones	.05
226	Henry Rodriguez	.05
227	Ken Hill	.05
228	Rick Wilkins	.05
229	Ricky Jordan	.05
230	Bernard Gilkey	.05
231	Tim Fortugno	.05
232	Geno Petralli	.05
233	Jose Rijo	.05
234	Jim Leyritz	.05
235	Kevin Campbell	.05
236	Al Osuna	.05
237	Pete Smith	.05
238	Pete Schourek	.05
239	Moises Alou	.05
240	Donn Pall	.05
241	Denny Neagle	.05
242	Dan Peltier	.05
243	Scott Scudder	.05
244	Juan Guzman	.05
245	Dave Burba	.05
246	Rick Sutcliffe	.05
247	Tony Fossas	.05
248	Mike Munoz	.05
249	Tim Salmon	.05
250	Rob Murphy	.05
251	Roger McDowell	.05
252	Lance Parrish	.05
253	Cliff Brantley	.05
254	Scott Leius	.05
255	Carlos Martinez	.05
256	Vince Horsman	.05
257	Oscar Azocar	.05
258	Craig Shipley	.05
259	Ben McDonald	.05
260	Jeff Brantley	.05
261	Damon Berryhill	.05
262	Joe Grahe	.05
263	Dave Hansen	.05
264	Rich Amaral	.05
265	Tim Pugh **RC**	.05
266	Dion James	.05
267	Frank Tanana	.05
268	Stan Belinda	.05
269	Jeff Kent	.05
270	Bruce Ruffin	.05
271	Xavier Hernandez	.05
272	Darrin Fletcher	.05
273	Tino Martinez	.05
274	Benny Santiago	.05
275	Scott Radinsky	.05
276	Mariano Duncan	.05
277	Kenny Lofton	.05
278	Dwight Smith	.05
279	Joe Carter	.05
280	Tim Jones	.05
281	Jeff Huson	.05
282	Phil Plantier	.05
283	Kirby Puckett	.85
284	Johnny Guzman	.05
285	Mike Morgan	.05
286	Chris Sabo	.05
287	Matt Williams	.05
288	Checklist 1-100	.05
289	Checklist 101-200	.05
290	Checklist 201-300	.05
291	Dennis Eckersley (Members Choice)	.30
292	Eric Karros (Members Choice)	.05
293	Pat Listach (Members Choice)	.05
294	Andy Van Slyke (Members Choice)	.05
295	Robin Ventura (Members Choice)	.05
296	Tom Glavine (Members Choice)	.05
297	Juan Gonzalez (Members Choice)	.20
298	Travis Fryman (Members Choice)	.05
299	Larry Walker (Members Choice)	.05
300	Gary Sheffield (Members Choice)	.20
301	Chuck Finley	.05
302	Luis Gonzalez	.05
303	Darryl Hamilton	.05
304	Bien Figueroa	.05
305	Ron Darling	.05
306	Jonathan Hurst	.05
307	Mike Sharperson	.05
308	Mike Christopher	.05
309	Marvin Freeman	.05
310	Jay Buhner	.05
311	Butch Henry	.05
312	Greg Harris	.05
313	Darren Daulton	.05
314	Chuck Knoblauch	.05
315	Greg Harris	.05
316	John Franco	.05
317	John Wehner	.05
318	Donald Harris	.05
319	Benny Santiago	.05
320	Larry Walker	.05
321	Randy Knorr	.05
322	Ramon D. Martinez **RC**	.05
323	Mike Stanley	.05
324	Bill Wegman	.05
325	Tom Candiotti	.05
326	Glenn Davis	.05
327	Chuck Crim	.05
328	Scott Livingstone	.05
329	Eddie Taubensee	.05
330	George Bell	.05
331	Edgar Martinez	.05
332	Paul Assenmacher	.05
333	Steve Hosey	.05
334	Mo Vaughn	.05
335	Bret Saberhagen	.05
336	Mike Trombley	.05
337	Mark Lewis	.05
338	Terry Pendleton	.05
339	Dave Hollins	.05
340	Jeff Conine	.05
341	Bob Tewksbury	.05
342	Billy Ashley	.05
343	Zane Smith	.05
344	John Wetteland	.05
345	Chris Hoiles	.05
346	Frank Castillo	.05
347	Bruce Hurst	.05
348	Kevin McReynolds	.05
349	Dave Henderson	.05
350	Ryan Bowen	.05
351	Sid Fernandez	.05
352	Mark Whiten	.05
353	Nolan Ryan	2.50
354	Rick Aguilera	.05
355	Mark Langston	.05
356	Jack Morris	.05
357	Rob Deer	.05
358	Dave Fleming	.05
359	Lance Johnson	.05
360	Joe Millette	.05
361	Wil Cordero	.05
362	Chito Martinez	.05
363	Scott Servais	.05
364	Bernie Williams	.05
365	Pedro Martinez	.75
366	Ryne Sandberg	.85
367	Brad Ausmus	.05
368	Scott Cooper	.05
369	Rob Dibble	.05
370	Walt Weiss	.05
371	Mark Davis	.05
372	Orlando Merced	.05
373	Mike Jackson	.05
374	Kevin Appier	.05
375	Esteban Beltre	.05
376	Joe Slusarski	.05
377	William Suero	.05
378	Pete O'Brien	.05
379	Alan Embree	.05
380	Lenny Webster	.05
381	Eric Davis	.05
382	Duane Ward	.05
383	John Habyan	.05
384	Jeff Bagwell	.75
385	Ruben Amaro	.05
386	Julio Valera	.05
387	Robin Ventura	.05
388	Archi Cianfrocco	.05
389	Skeeter Barnes	.05
390	Tim Costo	.05
391	Luis Mercedes	.05
392	Jeremy Hernandez	.05
393	Shawon Dunston	.05
394	Andy Van Slyke	.05
395	Kevin Maas	.05
396	Kevin Brown	.05
397	J.T. Bruett	.05
398	Darryl Strawberry	.05
399	Tom Pagnozzi	.05
400	Sandy Alomar	.05
401	Keith Miller	.05
402	Rich DeLucia	.05
403	Shawn Abner	.05
404	Howard Johnson	.05
405	Mike Benjamin	.05
406	Roberto Mejia **RC**	.05
407	Mike Butcher	.05
408	Deion Sanders	.05
409	Todd Stottlemyre	.05
410	Scott Kamieniecki	.05
411	Doug Jones	.05
412	John Burkett	.05
413	Lance Blankenship	.05
414	Jeff Parrett	.05
415	Barry Larkin	.05
416	Alan Trammell	.05
417	Mark Kiefer	.05
418	Gregg Olson	.05
419	Mark Grace	.05
420	Shane Mack	.05
421	Bob Walk	.05
422	Curt Schilling	.25
423	Erik Hanson	.05
424	George Brett	1.25
425	Reggie Jefferson	.05
426	Mark Portugal	.05
427	Ron Karkovice	.05
428	Matt Young	.05
429	Troy Neel	.05
430	Hector Fajardo	.05
431	Dave Righetti	.05
432	Pat Listach	.05
433	Jeff Innis	.05
434	Bob MacDonald	.05
435	Brian Jordan	.05
436	Jeff Blauser	.05
437	Mike Myers **RC**	.05
438	Frank Seminara	.05
439	Rusty Meacham	.05
440	Greg Briley	.05
441	Derek Lilliquist	.05
442	John Vander Wal	.05
443	Scott Erickson	.05
444	Bob Scanlan	.05
445	Todd Frohwirth	.05
446	Tom Goodwin	.05
447	William Pennyfeather	.05
448	Travis Fryman	.05
449	Mickey Morandini	.05
450	Greg Olson	.05
451	Trevor Hoffman	.05
452	Dave Magadan	.05
453	Shawn Jeter	.05
454	Andres Galarraga	.05
455	Ted Wood	.05
456	Freddie Benavides	.05
457	Junior Felix	.05
458	Alex Cole	.05
459	John Orton	.05
460	Eddie Zosky	.05
461	Dennis Eckersley	.65
462	Lee Smith	.05
463	John Smoltz	.05
464	Ken Caminiti	.05
465	Melido Perez	.05
466	Tom Marsh	.05
467	Jeff Nelson	.05
468	Jesse Levis	.05
469	Chris Nabholz	.05
470	Mike Mcfarlane	.05
471	Reggie Sanders	.05
472	Chuck McElroy	.05
473	Kevin Gross	.05
474	Matt Whiteside **RC**	.05
475	Cal Eldred	.05
476	Dave Gallagher	.05
477	Len Dykstra	.05
478	Mark McGwire	2.00
479	David Segui	.05
480	Mike Henneman	.05
481	Bret Barberie	.05
482	Steve Sax	.05
483	Dave Valle	.05
484	Danny Darwin	.05
485	Devon White	.05
486	Eric Plunk	.05
487	Jim Gott	.05
488	Scooter Tucker	.05
489	Omar Oliveres	.05
490	Greg Myers	.05
491	Brian Hunter	.05
492	Kevin Tapani	.05
493	Rich Monteleone	.05
494	Steve Buechele	.05
495	Bo Jackson	.10
496	Mike LaValliere	.05
497	Mark Leonard	.05
498	Daryl Boston	.05
499	Jose Canseco	.45
500	Brian Barnes	.05
501	Randy Johnson	.75
502	Tim McIntosh	.05
503	Cecil Fielder	.05
504	Derek Bell	.05
505	Kevin Koslofski	.05
506	Darren Holmes	.05
507	Brady Anderson	.05
508	John Valentin	.05
509	Jerry Browne	.05
510	Fred McGriff	.05
511	Pedro Astacio	.05
512	Gary Gaetti	.05
513	John Burke **RC**	.05
514	Dwight Gooden	.05
515	Thomas Howard	.05
516	Darrell Whitmore **RC**	.05
517	Ozzie Guillen	.05
518	Darryl Kile	.05
519	Rich Rowland	.05
520	Carlos Delgado	.50
521	Doug Henry	.05
522	Greg Colbrunn	.05
523	Tom Gordon	.05
524	Ivan Rodriguez	.65
525	Kent Hrbek	.05
526	Eric Young	.05
527	Rod Brewer	.05
528	Eric Karros	.05
529	Marquis Grissom	.05
530	Rico Brogna	.05
531	Sammy Sosa	1.00
532	Bret Boone	.05
533	Luis Rivera	.05
534	Hal Morris	.05
535	Monty Fariss	.05
536	Leo Gomez	.05
537	Wally Joyner	.05
538	Tony Gwynn	.85
539	Mike Williams	.05
540	Juan Gonzalez	.40
541	Ryan Klesko	.05
542	Ryan Thompson	.05
543	Chad Curtis	.05
544	Orel Hershiser	.05
545	Carlos Garcia	.05
546	Bob Welch	.05
547	Vinny Castilla	.05
548	Ozzie Smith	.85
549	Luis Salazar	.05
550	Mark Guthrie	.05
551	Charles Nagy	.05
552	Alex Fernandez	.05
553	Mel Rojas	.05
554	Orestes Destrade	.05
555	Mark Gubicza	.05
556	Steve Finley	.05
557	Don Mattingly	1.25
558	Rickey Henderson	.75
559	Tommy Greene	.05
560	Arthur Rhodes	.05
561	Alfredo Griffin	.05
562	Will Clark	.05
563	Bob Zupcic	.05
564	Chuck Carr	.05
565	Henry Cotto	.05
566	Billy Spiers	.05
567	Jack Armstrong	.05
568	Kurt Stillwell	.05
569	David McCarty	.05
570	Joe Vitiello	.05
571	Gerald Williams	.05
572	Dale Murphy	.25
573	Scott Aldred	.05
574	Bill Gullickson	.05
575	Bobby Thigpen	.05
576	Glenallen Hill	.05
577	Dwayne Henry	.05
578	Calvin Jones	.05
579	Al Martin	.05
580	Ruben Sierra	.05
581	Andy Benes	.05
582	Anthony Young	.05
583	Shawn Boskie	.05
584	Scott Pose **RC**	.05
585	Mike Piazza	1.50
586	Donovan Osborne	.05
587	James Austin	.05
588	Checklist 301-400	.05
589	Checklist 401-500	.05
590	Checklist 501-600	.05
591	Ken Griffey Jr. (Members Choice)	.75
592	Ivan Rodriguez (Members Choice)	.40
593	Carlos Baerga (Members Choice)	.05
594	Fred McGriff (Members Choice)	.05
595	Mark McGwire (Members Choice)	1.00
596	Roberto Alomar (Members Choice)	.10
597	Kirby Puckett (Members Choice)	.45
598	Marquis Grissom (Members Choice)	.05
599	John Smoltz (Members Choice)	.05
600	Ryne Sandberg (Members Choice)	.45
601	Wade Boggs	.85
602	Jeff Reardon	.05
603	Billy Ripken	.05
604	Bryan Harvey	.05
605	Carlos Quintana	.05
606	Greg Hibbard	.05
607	Ellis Burks	.05
608	Greg Swindell	.05
609	Dave Winfield	.75
610	Charlie Hough	.05
611	Chili Davis	.05
612	Jody Reed	.05
613	Mark Williamson	.05
614	Phil Plantier	.05
615	Jim Abbott	.05
616	Dante Bichette	.05
617	Mark Eichhorn	.05
618	Gary Sheffield	.45
619	Richie Lewis **RC**	.05
620	Joe Girardi	.05
621	Jaime Navarro	.05
622	Willie Wilson	.05
623	Scott Fletcher	.05
624	Bud Black	.05
625	Tom Brunansky	.05
626	Steve Avery	.05
627	Paul Molitor	.75
628	Gregg Jefferies	.05
629	Dave Stewart	.05
630	Javier Lopez	.05
631	Greg Gagne	.05
632	Bobby Kelly	.05
633	Mike Fetters	.05
634	Ozzie Canseco	.05
635	Jeff Russell	.05
636	Pete Incaviglia	.05
637	Tom Henke	.05
638	Chipper Jones	1.00
639	Jimmy Key	.05
640	Dave Martinez	.05
641	Dave Stieb	.05
642	Milt Thompson	.05
643	Alan Mills	.05
644	Tony Fernandez	.05
645	Randy Bush	.05
646	Joe Magrane	.05
647	Ivan Calderon	.05
648	Jose Guzman	.05
649	John Olerud	.05
650	Tom Glavine	.25
651	Julio Franco	.05
652	Armando Reynoso	.05
653	Felix Jose	.05
654	Ben Rivera	.05
655	Andre Dawson	.25
656	Mike Harkey	.05
657	Kevin Seitzer	.05
658	Lonnie Smith	.05
659	Norm Charlton	.05
660	Dave Justice	.05
661	Fernando Valenzuela	.05
662	Dan Wilson	.05
663	Mark Gardner	.05
664	Doug Dascenzo	.05
665	Greg Maddux	.85
666	Harold Baines	.05
667	Randy Myers	.05
668	Harold Reynolds	.05
669	Candy Maldonado	.05
670	Al Leiter	.05
671	Jerald Clark	.05
672	Doug Drabek	.05
673	Kirk Gibson	.05
674	Steve Reed **RC**	.05
675	Mike Felder	.05
676	Ricky Gutierrez	.05
677	Spike Owen	.05
678	Otis Nixon	.05
679	Scott Sanderson	.05
680	Mark Carreon	.05
681	Troy Percival	.05
682	Kevin Stocker	.05
683	Jim Converse **RC**	.05
684	Barry Bonds	2.50
685	Greg Gohr	.05
686	Tim Wallach	.05
687	Matt Mieske	.05
688	Robby Thompson	.05
689	Brien Taylor	.05
690	Kirt Manwaring	.05
691	Mike Lansing **RC**	.25
692	Steve Decker	.05
693	Mike Moore	.05
694	Kevin Mitchell	.05
695	Phil Hiatt	.05
696	Tony Tarasco **RC**	.05
697	Benji Gil	.05
698	Jeff Juden	.05
699	Kevin Reimer	.05
700	Andy Ashby	.05
701	John Jaha	.05
702	Tim Bogar **RC**	.05
703	David Cone	.05
704	Willie Greene	.05
705	David Hulse **RC**	.05
706	Cris Carpenter	.05
707	Ken Griffey Jr.	1.50
708	Steve Bedrosian	.05
709	Dave Nilsson	.05
710	Paul Wagner	.05
711	B.J. Surhoff	.05
712	Rene Arocha **RC**	.05
713	Manny Lee	.05
714	Brian Williams	.05
715	Sherman Obando **RC**	.05
716	Terry Mulholland	.05
717	Paul O'Neill	.05
718	David Nied	.05
719	J.T. Snow **RC**	.50
720	Nigel Wilson	.05
721	Mike Bielecki	.05
722	Kevin Young	.05
723	Charlie Leibrandt	.05
724	Frank Bolick	.05
725	Jon Shave **RC**	.05
726	Steve Cooke	.05
727	Domingo Martinez **RC**	.05
728	Todd Worrell	.05
729	Jose Lind	.05
730	Jim Tatum **RC**	.05
731	Mike Hampton	.05
732	Mike Draper	.05
733	Henry Mercedes	.05
734	John Johnstone **RC**	.05
735	Mitch Webster	.05
736	Russ Springer	.05
737	Rob Natal	.05
738	Steve Howe	.05
739	Darrell Sherman **RC**	.05
740	Pat Mahomes	.05
741	Alex Arias	.05
742	Damon Buford	.05
743	Charlie Hayes	.05
744	Guillermo Velasquez	.05
745	Checklist 601-750	.05
746	Frank Thomas (Members Choice)	.40
747	Barry Bonds (Members Choice)	1.50
748	Roger Clemens (Members Choice)	.50
749	Joe Carter (Members Choice)	.05
750	Greg Maddux (Members Choice)	.45

1st Day Production

Inserted at the rate of about one per box, with an estimated production of 2,000 apiece, 1st Day Production cards are a parallel of 1993 TSC on which an embossed silver holographic foil logo has been added. Because of the considerably higher value of the 1st Day parallels, collectors should be aware that fakes can be created by cutting the logo off a common player's card and attaching it to a superstar card.

	NM/M
Common Player:	1.00
1st Day Stars:	8X

Series 1 Inserts

Four bonus cards were produced as special inserts in Series I Stadium Club packs. Two of the full-bleed, gold-foil enhanced cards honor Robin Yount and George Brett for achieving the 3,000-hit mark, while the other two commemorate the first picks in the 1993 expansion draft by the Colorado Rockies (David Nied) and Marlins (Nigel Wilson).

		NM/M
Complete Set (4):		3.00
Common Player:		.25
1	Robin Yount (3,000 hits)	1.00
2	George Brett (3,000 hits)	2.00
3	David Nied (#1 pick)	.25
4	Nigel Wilson (#1 pick)	.25

Series 2 Inserts

Cross-town and regional rivals were featured in this four-card insert set found, on average, one per 24 packs of Series II Stadium Club. Each of the two-faced cards is typical S.C. quality with gold-foil stamping and UV coating front and back.

		NM/M
Complete Set (4):		5.00
Common Card:		1.50
1	Pacific Terrific (Will Clark, Mark McGwire)	2.00
2	Broadway Stars (Dwight Gooden, Don Mattingly)	1.50
3	Second City Sluggers (Ryne Sandberg, Frank Thomas)	1.50
4	Pacific Terrific (Ken Griffey Jr., Darryl Strawberry)	1.50

Series 3 Inserts

Team "firsts" - first game, first pitch, first batter, etc. - for the 1993 expansion Florida Marlins and Colorado Rockies are featured on this pair of inserts found in Series III Stadium Club packs. Fronts featured game-action photos with the player's name in gold foil. On back is a stadium scene with the team first overprinted in black. At top the team name and Stadium Club logo are in gold foil.

		NM/M
Complete Set (2):		.50
Common Player:		.25
1	David Nied	.25
2	Charlie Hough	.25

Master Photos

Each box of 1993 Stadium Club packs included one Master Photo premium insert. Prize cards good for three Master Photos in a mail-in offer were also included in each of the three series. The 5" x 7" Master Photos feature wide white borders and a large Stadium Club logo at top, highlighted by prismatic foil. The same foil is used as a border for a larger-format version of the player's regular S.C. card at the center of the Master Photo. A "Members Only" version of each of the 1993 Master Photos was available as a premium with the purchase of a Members Only Stadium Club set. the Members Only Master Photos have a gold-foil seal in the upper-right corner.

		NM/M
Complete Set (30):		15.00
Common Player:		.20
Series 1		
(1)	Carlos Baerga	.20
(2)	Delino DeShields	.20
(3)	Brian McRae	.20
(4)	Sam Militello	.20
(5)	Joe Oliver	.20
(6)	Kirby Puckett	1.50
(7)	Cal Ripken Jr.	4.00
(8)	Bip Roberts	.20
(9)	Mike Scioscia	.20
(10)	Rick Sutcliffe	.20
(11)	Danny Tartabull	.20
(12)	Tim Wakefield	.20
Series 2		
(13)	George Brett	3.00
(14)	Jose Canseco	.50
(15)	Will Clark	.20
(16)	Travis Fryman	.20
(17)	Dwight Gooden	.20
(18)	Mark Grace	.30
(19)	Rickey Henderson	1.00
(20)	Mark McGwire	2.50
(21)	Nolan Ryan	4.00
(22)	Ruben Sierra	.20
(23)	Darryl Strawberry	.20
(24)	Larry Walker	.20
Series 3		
(25)	Barry Bonds	5.00
(26)	Ken Griffey Jr.	2.50
(27)	Greg Maddux	2.00
(28)	David Nied	.20
(29)	J.T. Snow	.20
(30)	Brien Taylor	.20
Redemption Card:		3X

Members Only

A special version of the Topps' 1993 Stadium Club set was made available exclusively to members of the company's Stadium Club program. The set is a parallel of the regular-issue SC set (plus insert) on which a gold-foil "Members Only" shield logo has been added to the card front. In all other respects the cards are identical to the regular SC issue. Production was a reported 12,000 sets.

	NM/M
Complete Set (750):	100.00
Common Player:	.50
Members Only Stars:	8X

Members Only Baseball

As a benefit of membership in Topps' Stadium Club, each member received a 59-card set in four separate shipments. The cards featured highlights of the 1993 baseball, hockey, football and basketball seasons. Besides the 28 baseball player cards checklisted here there were nine football cards, six hockey card and 16 basketball cards. Each sport's cards came separately in a heat-sealed cello wrap in a special box. Cards were typical S.C. quality, featuring full-bleed action photos on the front, with the Stadium Club log and player name enhanced with gold-foil stamping and a gold-foil "Members Only" notice beneath the player's name. Backs feature a parti-color background with a colorized, stylized player figure at right. At left is the story of the player's season or career highlight. The cards are unnumbered and are checklisted alphabetically.

		NM/M
Complete Set (28):		9.00
Common Player:		.10
(1)	Jim Abbott	.10
(2)	Barry Bonds	2.50
(3)	Chris Bosio	.10
(4)	George Brett	.75
(5)	Jay Buhner	.10
(6)	Joe Carter (3 HR in game 5th time)	.10
(7)	Joe Carter (World Series-winning HR)	.10
(8)	Carlton Fisk	.60
(9)	Travis Fryman	.10
(10)	Mark Grace	.20
(11)	Ken Griffey Jr.	1.50
(12)	Darryl Kile	.10
(13)	Darren Lewis	.10
(14)	Greg Maddux	.65
(15)	Jack McDowell	.10
(16)	Paul Molitor	.60
(17)	Eddie Murray	.60
(18)	Mike Piazza (Rookie catcher HR record)	1.50
(19)	Mike Piazza (N.L. Rookie of the Year)	1.50
(20)	Kirby Puckett	.65
(21)	Jeff Reardon	.10
(22)	Tim Salmon	.20
(23)	Curt Schilling	.35
(24)	Lee Smith	.10
(25)	Dave Stewart	.10
(26)	Frank Thomas	.60
(27)	Mark Whiten	.10
(28)	Dave Winfield	.60

Special

Though the packaging and the cards themselves identify this 200-card set as a 1992 issue, it was not released until 1993 and is thought of by the hobby at large as a 1993 set. The set is sold in a plastic replica of Jack Murphy Stadium in San Diego, venue for the 1993 All-Star Game. Fifty-six of the cards feature players from that contest and are so identified by a line of gold-foil on the card front and an All-Star logo on back. Twenty-five members of the 1992 Team U.S.A. Olympic baseball squad are also included in the set, with appropriate logos and notations front and back. There are 19 cards depicting action and stars of the 1992 League Championships and World Series. The other 100 cards in the set are 1992 draft picks. All cards have the same basic format as the regular-issue 1992 Topps Stadium Club cards, full-bleed photos on front and back, UV coating on both sides and gold-foil highlights on front. Besides the 200 standard-size cards, the Special Edition set included a dozen "Master Photos," 5" x 7" white-bordered premium cards.

		NM/M
Unopened Set (200):		45.00
Complete Set (200):		40.00
Common Player:		.05
1	Dave Winfield	.75
2	Juan Guzman	.05
3	Tony Gwynn	.85
4	Chris Roberts	.05
5	Benny Santiago	.05
6	Sherard Clinkscales	.05
7	Jonathan Nunnally **RC**	.05
8	Chuck Knoblauch	.05
9	Bob Wolcott **RC**	.05
10	Steve Rodriguez	.05
11	Mark Williams **RC**	.05
12	Danny Clyburn **RC**	.05
13	Darren Dreifort	.05
14	Andy Van Slyke	.05
15	Wade Boggs	.85
16	Scott Patton	.05
17	Gary Sheffield	.45
18	Ron Villone	.05
19	Roberto Alomar	.20
20	Marc Valdes	.05
21	Daron Kirkreit	.05
22	Jeff Granger	.05
23	Levon Largusa	.05
24	Jimmy Key	.05
25	Kevin Pearson	.05
26	Michael Moore	.05
27	Preston Wilson **RC**	1.00
28	Kirby Puckett	.85
29	Tim Crabtree **RC**	.05
30	Bip Roberts	.05
31	Kelly Gruber	.05
32	Tony Fernandez	.05
33	Jason Angel	.05
34	Calvin Murray	.05
35	Chad McConnell	.05
36	Jason Moler	.05
37	Mark Lemke	.05
38	Tom Knauss	.05
39	Larry Mitchell	.05
40	Doug Mirabelli	.05
41	Everett Stull II	.05
42	Chris Wimmer	.05
43	Dan Serafini **RC**	.05
44	Ryne Sandberg	.85
45	Steve Lyons	.05
46	Ryan Freeburg	.05
47	Ruben Sierra	.05
48	David Mysel	.05
49	Joe Hamilton	.05
50	Steve Rodriguez	.05
51	Tim Wakefield	.05
52	Scott Gentile	.05
53	Doug Jones	.05
54	Willie Brown	.05
55	Chad Mottola **RC**	.05
56	Ken Griffey Jr.	1.50
57	Jon Lieber **RC**	.50
58	Denny Martinez	.05
59	Joe Petcka	.05
60	Benji Simonton	.05
61	Brett Backlund	.05
62	Damon Berryhill	.05
63	Juan Guzman	.05
64	Doug Hecker	.05
65	Jamie Arnold	.05
66	Bob Tewksbury	.05
67	Tim Leger	.05
68	Todd Etler	.05
69	Lloyd McClendon	.05
70	Kurt Ehmann	.05
71	Rick Magdaleno	.05
72	Tom Pagnozzi	.05
73	Jeffrey Hammonds	.05
74	Joe Carter	.05
75	Chris Holt	.05
76	Charles Johnson	.05
77	Bob Walk	.05
78	Fred McGriff	.05
79	Tom Evans	.05
80	Scott Klingenbeck	.05
81	Chad McConnell	.05
82	Chris Eddy	.05
83	Phil Nevin	.05
84	John Kruk	.05
85	Tony Sheffield	.05
86	John Smoltz	.05
87	Trevor Humphry	.05
88	Charles Nagy	.05
89	Sean Runyan	.05
90	Mike Gulan	.05
91	Darren Daulton	.05
92	Otis Nixon	.05
93	Nomar Garciaparra	8.00
94	Larry Walker	.05
95	Hut Smith	.05
96	Rick Helling	.05
97	Roger Clemens	1.00
98	Ron Gant	.05
99	Kenny Felder	.05
100	Steve Murphy	.05
101	Mike Smith	.05
102	Terry Pendleton	.05
103	Tim Davis	.05
104	Jeff Patzke	.05
105	Craig Wilson	.05
106	Tom Glavine	.35
107	Mark Langston	.05
108	Mark Thompson	.05
109	Eric Owens **RC**	.05
110	Keith Johnson	.05
111	Robin Ventura	.05
112	Ed Sprague	.05
113	Jeff Schmidt **RC**	.05
114	Don Wengert	.05
115	Craig Biggio	.05
116	Kenny Carlyle	.05
117	Derek Jeter **RC**	30.00
118	Manuel Lee	.05
119	Jeff Haas	.05
120	Roger Bailey	.05
121	Sean Lowe	.05
122	Rick Aguilera	.05
123	Sandy Alomar	.05
124	Derek Wallace	.05
125	B.J. Wallace	.05
126	Greg Maddux	.85
127	Tim Moore	.05
128	Lee Smith	.05
129	Todd Steverson	.05
130	Chris Widger	.05
131	Paul Molitor	.75
132	Chris Smith	.05
133	Chris Gomez **RC**	.05
134	Jimmy Baron	.05
135	John Smoltz	.05
136	Pat Borders	.05
137	Donnie Leshnock	.05
138	Gus Gandarillos	.05
139	Will Clark	.05
140	Ryan Luzinski **RC**	.05
141	Cal Ripken, Jr.	2.50
142	B.J. Wallace	.05
143	Trey Beamon **RC**	.05
144	Norm Charlton	.05
145	Mike Mussina	.30
146	Billy Owens	.05
147	Ozzie Smith	.85
148	Jason Kendall **RC**	1.00
149	Mike Matthews **RC**	.05
150	David Spykstra	.05
151	Benji Grigsby	.05
152	Sean Smith	.05
153	Mark McGwire	2.00
154	David Cone	.05
155	Shon Walker **RC**	.05
156	Jason Giambi	.50
157	Jack McDowell	.05
158	Paxton Briley	.05
159	Edgar Martinez	.05
160	Brian Sackinsky	.05
161	Barry Bonds	2.50
162	Roberto Kelly	.05
163	Jeff Alkire	.05
164	Mike Sharperson	.05
165	Jamie Taylor	.05
166	John Saffer	.05
167	Jerry Browne	.05
168	Travis Fryman	.05
169	Brady Anderson	.05
170	Chris Roberts	.05
171	Lloyd Peever	.05
172	Francisco Cabrera	.05
173	Ramiro Martinez	.05
174	Jeff Alkire	.05
175	Ivan Rodriguez	.65
176	Kevin Brown	.05
177	Chad Roper	.05
178	Rod Henderson	.05
179	Dennis Eckersley	.65
180	Shannon Stewart **RC**	1.00
181	DeShawn Warren	.05
182	Lonnie Smith	.05
183	Willie Adams	.05
184	Jeff Montgomery	.05
185	Damon Hollins	.05
186	Byron Matthews	.05
187	Harold Baines	.05
188	Rick Greene	.05
189	Carlos Baerga	.05
190	Brandon Cromer	.05
191	Roberto Alomar	.20
192	Rich Ireland	.05
193	Steve Montgomery	.05
194	Brant Brown	.05
195	Ritchie Moody	.05
196	Michael Tucker	.05
197	Jason Varitek **RC**	6.00
198	David Manning	.05
199	Marquis Riley	.05
200	Jason Giambi	.60

Special Master Photos

Each 1993 Stadium Club Special (Jack Murphy Stadium) set included 12 Master Photos replicating cards from the set. There were nine All-Stars, two '92 rookies and a Team USA player among the Master Photos. Gold-tone prismatic foil highlights the 5" x 7" cards, decorating the large logo at top and separating the card photo from the wide white border. Backs have Stadium Club and MLB logos and copyright information printed in black. The unnumbered cards are checklisted here in alphabetical order.

		NM/M
Complete Set (12):		5.00
Common Player:		.20
(1)	Sandy Alomar	.20
(2)	Tom Glavine	.65
(3)	Ken Griffey Jr.	2.00
(4)	Tony Gwynn	1.50
(5)	Chuck Knoblauch	.20
(6)	Chad Mottola	.20
(7)	Kirby Puckett	1.50
(8)	Chris Roberts	.20
(9)	Ryne Sandberg	1.50
(10)	Gary Sheffield	.40
(11)	Larry Walker	.20
(12)	Preston Wilson	.20

Team Sets

This special edition of Stadium Club cards consists of 16 separate team sets of 30 cards each. Each blister-packed team set was priced around $6 and sold exclusively at Wal-Mart. Fronts of the UV coated cards have a player photo that is is borderless at the top, bottom and left. At right is a green stripe, at top of which is a partial baseball design and some other striping in gold-foil. Backs are basically green, with a light blue box at lower-right containing personal information and stats, along with the S.C. logo. A player photo is at upper-left, with his name superimposed on a bat. Cards are checklisted here within team set. Several of the Braves cards were authentically autographed as pack-toppers on specially marked sets.

		NM/M
Complete Set (480):		30.00
Common Player:		.10
ATLANTA BRAVES		
	Team Set:	3.00
1	Tom Glavine	.35
2	Bill Pecota	.10
3	David Justice	.10
4	Mark Lemke	.10
5	Jeff Blauser	.10
6	Ron Gant	.10
7	Greg Olson	.10
8	Francisco Cabrera	.10
9	Chipper Jones	1.00
9a	Chipper Jones/Auto.	20.00
10	Steve Avery	.10
11	Kent Mercker	.10
12	John Smoltz	.10
12a	John Smoltz (Autographed)	6.00
13	Pete Smith	.10
14	Damon Berryhill	.10
15	Sid Bream	.10
16	Otis Nixon	.10
17	Mike Stanton	.10
18	Greg Maddux	1.00
19	Jay Howell	.10
20	Rafael Belliard	.10
21	Terry Pendleton	.10
22	Deion Sanders	.15
23	Brian Hunter	.10
24	Marvin Freeman	.10
25	Mark Wohlers	.10
26	Ryan Klesko	.10
26a	Ryan Klesko/Auto.	4.00
27a	Javy Lopez/Auto.	4.00
27	Javy Lopez	.10
28	Melvin Nieves	.10
29	Tony Tarasco	.10
30	Ramon Caraballo	.10
CHICAGO CUBS		
	Team Set:	2.50
1	Ryne Sandberg	1.50
2	Sammy Sosa	1.50
3	Greg Hibbard	.10
4	Candy Maldonado	.10
5	Willie Wilson	.10
6	Dan Plesac	.10
7	Steve Buechele	.10
8	Mark Grace	.25
9	Shawon Dunston	.10
10	Steve Lake	.10
11	Dwight Smith	.10
12	Derrick May	.10
13	Paul Assenmacher	.10
14	Mike Harkey	.10
15	Lance Dickson	.10
16	Randy Myers	.10
17	Mike Morgan	.10
18	Chuck McElroy	.10
19	Jose Guzman	.10
20	Jose Vizcaino	.10
21	Frank Castillo	.10
22	Bob Scanlon	.10
23	Rick Wilkins	.10
24	Rey Sanchez	.10
25	Phil Dauphin	.10
26	Jim Bullinger	.10
27	Jessie Hollins	.10
28	Matt Walbeck	.10
29	Fernando Ramsey	.10
30	Jose Bautista	.10
CALIFORNIA ANGELS		
	Team Set:	1.50
1	J.T. Snow	.25
2	Chuck Crim	.10
3	Chili Davis	.10
4	Mark Langston	.10
5	Ron Tingley	.10
6	Eduardo Perez	.10
7	Scott Sanderson	.10
8	Jorge Fabregas	.10
9	Troy Percival	.10
10	Rod Carreia	.10
11	Greg Myers	.10
12	Steve Frey	.10
13	Tim Salmon	.25
14	Scott Lewis	.10
15	Rene Gonzales	.10
16	Chuck Finley	.10
17	John Orton	.10
18	Joe Grahe	.10
19	Luis Polonia	.10
20	John Farrell	.10
21	Damion Easley	.10
22	Gene Nelson	.10
23	Chad Curtis	.10
24	Russ Springer	.10
25	De Shawn Warren	.10
26	Darryl Scott	.10
27	Gary DiSarcina	.10
28	Jerry Nielson	.10
29	Torey Lovullo	.10
30	Julio Valera	.10
CHICAGO WHITE SOX		
	Team Set:	2.50
1	Frank Thomas	1.00
2	Bo Jackson	.25
3	Rod Bolton	.10
4	Dave Stieb	.10
5	Tim Raines	.10
6	Joey Cora	.10
7	Warren Newson	.10
8	Roberto Hernandez	.10
9	Brandon Wilson	.10
10	Wilson Alvarez	.10
11	Dan Pasqua	.10
12	Ozzie Guillen	.10
13	Robin Ventura	.25
14	Craig Grebeck	.10
15	Lance Johnson	.10
16	Carlton Fisk	.75
17	Ron Karkovice	.10
18	Jack McDowell	.10
19	Scott Radinsky	.10
20	Bobby Thigpen	.10
21	Donn Pall	.10
22	George Bell	.10
23	Alex Fernandez	.10
24	Mike Huff	.10
25	Jason Bere	.10
26	Johnny Ruffin	.10
27	Ellis Burks	.10
28	Kirk McCaskill	.10
29	Terry Leach	.10
30	Shawn Gilbert	.10
COLORADO ROCKIES		
	Team Set:	1.50
1	David Nied	.10
2	Quinton McCracken	.10
3	Charlie Hayes	.10
4	Bryn Smith	.10
5	Dante Bichette	.10
6	Alex Cole	.10
7	Scott Aldred	.10
8	Roberto Mejia	.10
9	Jeff Parrett	.10
10	Joe Girardi	.10
11	Andres Galarraga	.10
12	Daryl Boston	.10
13	Jerald Clark	.10
14	Gerald Young	.10
15	Bruce Ruffin	.10
16	Rudy Seanez	.10
17	Darren Holmes	.10
18	Andy Ashby	.10
19	Chris Jones	.10
20	Mark Thompson	.10
21	Freddie Benavides	.10
22	Eric Wedge	.10
23	Vinny Castilla	.10
24	Butch Henry	.10
25	Jim Tatum	.10
26	Steve Reed	.10
27	Eric Young	.10
28	Danny Sheaffer	.10
29	Roger Bailey	.10
30	Brad Ausmus	.10
FLORIDA MARLINS		
	Team Set:	1.50
1	Nigel Wilson	.10
2	Bryan Harvey	.10
3	Bob McClure	.10
4	Alex Arias	.10
5	Walt Weiss	.10
6	Charlie Hough	.10
7	Scott Chiamparino	.10
8	Junior Felix	.10
9	Jack Armstrong	.10
10	Dave Magadan	.10
11	Cris Carpenter	.10
12	Benny Santiago	.10
13	Jeff Conine	.10
14	Jerry Don Gleaton	.10
15	Steve Decker	.10
16	Ryan Bowen	.10
17	Ramon Martinez	.10
18	Bret Barberie	.10
19	Monty Fariss	.10
20	Trevor Hoffman	.25
21	Scott Pose	.10
22	Mike Myers	.10
23	Geronimo Berroa	.10
24	Darrell Whitmore	.10
25	Chuck Carr	.10
26	Dave Weathers	.10
27	Matt Turner	.10
28	Jose Martinez	.10
29	Orestes Destrade	.10
30	Carl Everett	.10
HOUSTON ASTROS		
	Team Set:	1.50
1	Doug Drabek	.10
2	Eddie Taubensee	.10
3	James Mouton	.10
4	Ken Caminiti	.10
5	Chris James	.10
6	Jeff Juden	.10
7	Eric Anthony	.10
8	Jeff Bagwell	1.00
9	Greg Swindell	.10
10	Steve Finley	.10
11	Al Osuna	.10
12	Gary Mota	.10
13	Scott Servais	.10
14	Craig Biggio	.50
15	Doug James	.10
16	Rob Mallicoat	.10
17	Darryl Kile	.10
18	Kevin Bass	.10
19	Pete Harnisch	.10
20	Andujar Cedeno	.10
21	Brian Hunter	.10
22	Brian Williams	.10
23	Chris Donnels	.10
24	Xavier Hernandez	.10
25	Todd Jones	.10
26	Luis Gonzalez	.10
27	Rick Parker	.10
28	Casey Candaele	.10
29	Tony Eusebio	.10
30	Mark Portugal	.10
KANSAS CITY ROYALS		
	Team Set:	1.50
1	George Brett	1.00
2	Mike MacFarlane	.10
3	Tom Gordon	.15
4	Wally Joyner	.10
5	Kevin Appier	.10
6	Phil Hiatt	.10
7	Keith Miller	.10
8	Hipolito Pichardo	.10
9	Chris Gwynn	.10
10	Jose Lind	.10
11	Mark Gubicza	.10
12	Dennis Rasmussen	.10
13	Mike Magnante	.10
14	Joe Vitiello	.10
15	Kevin McReynolds	.10
16	Greg Gagne	.10
17	David Cone	.15
18	Brent Mayne	.10
19	Jeff Montgomery	.10
20	Joe Randa	.10
21	Felix Jose	.10
22	Bill Sampen	.10
23	Curt Wilkerson	.10
24	Mark Gardner	.10
25	Brian McRae	.10
26	Hubie Brooks	.10
27	Chris Eddy	.10
28	Harvey Pulliam	.10
29	Rusty Meacham	.10
30	Danny Miceli	.10
LOS ANGELES DODGERS		
	Team Set:	3.00
1	Darryl Strawberry	.10
2	Pedro Martinez	.75
3	Jody Reed	.10
4	Carlos Hernandez	.10
5	Kevin Gross	.10
6	Mike Piazza	1.50
7	Jim Gott	.10
8	Eric Karros	.10
9	Mike Sharperson	.10
10	Ramon Martinez	.10
11	Tim Wallach	.10
12	Pedro Astacio	.10
13	Lenny Harris	.10
14	Brett Butler	.10
15	Raul Mondesi	.10
16	Todd Worrell	.10
17	Jose Offerman	.10
18	Mitch Webster	.10
19	Tom Candiotti	.10
20	Eric Davis	.10
21	Michael Moore	.10
22	Billy Ashley	.10
23	Orel Hershiser	.15
24	Roger Cedeno	.10
25	Roger McDowell	.10
26	Mike James	.10
27	Steve Wilson	.10
28	Todd Hollandsworth	.10
29	Cory Snyder	.10
30	Todd Williams	.10
NEW YORK YANKEES		
	Team Set:	2.50
1	Don Mattingly	1.25
2	Jim Abbott	.10
3	Matt Nokes	.10
4	Danny Tartabull	.10
5	Wade Boggs	1.00
6	Melido Perez	.10
7	Steve Farr	.10
8	Kevin Maas	.10
9	Randy Velarde	.10
10	Mike Humphreys	.10
11	Mike Gallego	.10
12	Mike Stanley	.10
13	Jimmy Key	.10
14	Paul O'Neill	.10
15	Spike Owen	.10
16	Pat Kelly	.10
17	Sterling Hitchcock	.10
18	Mike Witt	.10
19	Scott Kamieniecki	.10
20	John Habyan	.10
21	Bernie Williams	.20
22	Brien Taylor	.10
23	Rich Monteleone	.10
24	Mark Hutton	.10
25	Robert Eenhoorn	.10
26	Gerald Williams	.10
27	Sam Militello	.10
28	Bob Wickman	.10
29	Andy Stankiewicz	.10
30	Domingo Jean	.10
OAKLAND A'S		
	Team Set:	3.00
1	Dennis Eckersley	.75
2	Lance Blankenship	.10
3	Mike Mohler	.10
4	Jerry Browne	.10
5	Kevin Seitzer	.10
6	Storm Davis	.10
7	Mark McGwire	2.00
8	Rickey Henderson	.75
9	Terry Steinbach	.10
10	Ruben Sierra	.10
11	Dave Henderson	.10
12	Bob Welch	.10
13	Rick Honeycutt	.10
14	Ron Darling	.10
15	Joe Boever	.10
16	Bobby Witt	.10
17	Izzy Molina	.10
18	Mike Bordick	.10
19	Brent Gates	.10
20	Shawn Hillegas	.10
21	Scott Hammond	.10
22	Todd Van Poppel	.10
23	Johnny Guzman	.10
24	Scott Lydy	.10
25	Scott Baker	.10
26	Todd Revenig	.10
27	Scott Brosius	.10
28	Troy Neel	.10
29	Dale Sveum	.10
30	Mike Neill	.10
PHILADELPHIA PHILLIES		
	Team Set:	1.50
1	Darren Daulton	.10
2	Larry Anderson	.10
3	Kyle Abbott	.10
4	Chad McConnell	.10
5	Danny Jackson	.10
6	Kevin Stocker	.10
7	Jim Eisenreich	.10
8	Mickey Morandini	.10
9	Bob Ayrault	.10
10	Doug Lindsey	.10
11	Dave Hollins	.10
12	Dave West	.10
13	Wes Chamberlain	.10
14	Curt Schilling	.35
15	Len Dykstra	.10
16	Trevor Humphry	.10
17	Terry Mulholland	.10
18	Gene Schall	.10
19	Mike Lieberthal	.15
20	Ben Rivera	.10
21	Mariano Duncan	.10
22	Pete Incaviglia	.10
23	Ron Blazier	.10
24	Jeff Jackson	.10
25	Jose DeLeon	.10
26	Ron Lockett	.10
27	Tommy Greene	.10
28	Milt Thompson	.10
29	Mitch Williams	.10
30	John Kruk	.10
ST. LOUIS CARDINALS		
	Team Set:	1.50
1	Ozzie Smith	1.00
2	Rene Arocha	.10
3	Bernard Gilkey	.10
4	Jose Oquendo	.10
5	Mike Perez	.10
6	Tom Pagnozzi	.10
7	Rod Brewer	.10
8	Joe Magrane	.10
9	Todd Zeile	.10
10	Bob Tewksbury	.10
11	Darrel Deak	.10
12	Gregg Jefferies	.10
13	Lee Smith	.25
14	Ozzie Canseco	.10
15	Tom Urbani	.10
16	Donovan Osborne	.10
17	Ray Lankford	.10
18	Rheal Cormier	.10
19	Allen Watson	.10
20	Geronimo Pena	.10
21	Rob Murphy	.10
22	Tracy Woodson	.10
23	Basil Shabazz	.10
24	Omar Olivares	.10
25	Brian Jordan	.10
26	Les Lancaster	.10
27	Sean Lowe	.10
28	Hector Villanueva	.10
29	Brian Barber	.10
30	Aaron Holbert	.10
SAN FRANCISCO GIANTS		
	Team Set:	2.50
1	Barry Bonds	2.00
2	Dave Righetti	.10
3	Matt Williams	.10
3a	Matt Williams/Auto.	10.00
4	Royce Clayton	.10
5	Salomon Torres	.10
6	Kirt Manwaring	.10
7	J.R. Phillips	.10
8	Kevin Rogers	.10
9	Will Clark	.10
10	John Burkett	.10
11	Willie McGee	.10
12	Rod Beck	.10
13	Jeff Reed	.10
14	Jeff Brantley	.10
15	Steve Hosey	.10
16	Chris Hancock	.10
17	Adell Davenport	.10
18	Mike Jackson	.10
19	Dave Martinez	.10
20	Bill Swift	.10
21	Steve Scarsone	.10
22	Trevor Wilson	.10
23	Mark Carreon	.10
24	Bud Black	.10
25	Darren Lewis	.10
26	Dan Carlson	.10
27	Craig Colbert	.10
28	Greg Brummet	.10
29	Bryan Hickerson	.10
30	Robby Thompson	.10
SEATTLE MARINERS		
	Team Set:	3.00
1	Ken Griffey Jr.	1.50
2	Desi Realford	.10
3	Dave Weinhouse	.10
4	Rich Amaral	.10
5	Brian Deak	.10
6	Bret Boone	.10
7	Bill Haselman	.10
8	Dave Fleming	.10
9	Fernando Vina	.10
10	Greg Litton	.10
11	Mackey Sasser	.10
12	Lee Tinsley	.10
13	Norm Charlton	.10
14	Russ Swan	.10
15	Brian Holman	.10
16	Randy Johnson	.75
17	Erik Hanson	.10
18	Tino Martinez	.10
19	Marc Newfield	.10
20	Dave Valle	.10
21	John Cummings	.10
22	Mike Hampton	.10
23	Jay Buhner	.10
24	Edgar Martinez	.10
25	Omar Vizquel	.10
26	Pete O'Brien	.10
27	Brian Turang	.10
28	Chris Bosio	.10
29	Mike Felder	.10
30	Shawn Estes	.10
TEXAS RANGERS		
	Team Set:	5.00
1	Nolan Ryan	2.50
2	Ritchie Moody	.10
3	Matt Whiteside	.10
4	David Hulse	.10
5	Roger Pavlik	.10
6	Dan Smith	.10
7	Donald Harris	.10
8	Butch Davis	.10
9	Benji Gil	.10
10	Ivan Rodriguez	.65
11	Dean Palmer	.10
12	Jeff Huson	.10
13	Rob Mauer	.10
14	Gary Redus	.10
15	Doug Dascenzo	.10
16	Charlie Liebrandt	.10
17	Tom Henke	.10
18	Manuel Lee	.10
19	Kenny Rogers	.10
20	Kevin Brown	.10
21	Juan Gonzalez	.50
22	Geno Petralli	.10
23	John Russell	.10
24	Robb Nen	.10
25	Julio Franco	.10
26	Rafael Palmeiro	.65
27	Todd Burns	.10
28	Jose Canseco	.50
29	Billy Ripken	.10
30	Dan Peltier	.10

Ultra Pro

Special packages of plastic sheets and sleeves carrying the "Topps Stadium Club UltraPro" brand name included one of 10 special Stadium Club cards of Barry Bonds, Bobby Bonds and/or Willie Mays. Cards are typical UV coated, gold-foil quality, but because the cards were not licensed by Major League Baseball, team logos were removed from the photos.

		NM/M
Complete Set (10):		7.00
Common Card:		.50
1	Barry Bonds, Willie Mays, Bobby Bonds	.50
2	Willie Mays	1.00
3	Bobby Bonds	.50
4	Barry Bonds	1.00
5	Barry Bonds, Bobby Bonds	.50
6	Willie Mays	1.00
7	Barry Bonds (Business suit.)	1.00
8	Willie Mays, Bobby Bonds	1.00
9	Willie Mays	1.00
10	Barry Bonds (Tuxedo)	1.00

1994 Stadium Club Pre-production

These sample cards introducing the 1994 Stadium Club set differ from their regular-issue counterparts only in the inclusion of a line of type vertically on the back-right, "Pre-Production Sample."

		NM/M
Complete Set (9):		5.00
Common Player:		.50
6	Al Martin	.50
15	Junior Ortiz	.50
36	Tim Salmon	.75
56	Jerry Spradlin	.50
122	Tom Pagnozzi	.50
123	Ron Gant	.50
125	Dennis Eckersley	1.50
135	Jose Lind	.50
238	Barry Bonds	4.00

1994 Stadium Club

Issued in three series to a total of 720 cards, Topps' mid-price brand features a hip look and a wide range of insert specials. The regular cards feature a borderless photo with the player's name presented in a unique typewriter/label maker style at bottom. The player's last name and Topps Stadium Club logo at top are in red foil. Backs feature another player photo, some personal data and a headlined career summary. Various stats and skills rankings complete the data. Subsets within the issue include cards annotated with Major League debut dates, 1993 awards won, home run club cards, cards featuring two or three players, and Final Tribute cards for George Brett and Nolan Ryan.

	NM/M
Complete Set (720):	20.00
Common Player:	.05
1st Day:	8X
Golden Rainbow:	2X
Series 1, 2, 3 Pack (12):	1.00
Series 1, 2, 3 Wax Box (24):	15.00

1 Robin Yount .65
2 Rick Wilkins .05
3 Steve Scarsone .05
4 Gary Sheffield .40
5 George Brett 1.00
6 Al Martin .05
7 Joe Oliver .05
8 Stan Belinda .05
9 Denny Hocking .05
10 Roberto Alomar .20
11 Luis Polonia .05
12 Scott Hemond .05
13 Joey Reed .05
14 Mel Rojas .05
15 Junior Ortiz .05
16 Harold Baines .05
17 Brad Pennington .05
18 Jay Bell .05
19 Tom Henke .05
20 Jeff Branson .05
21 Roberto Mejia .05
22 Pedro Munoz .05
23 Matt Nokes .05
24 Jack McDowell .05
25 Cecil Fielder .05
26 Tony Fossas .05
27 Jim Eisenreich .05
28 Anthony Young .05
29 Chuck Carr .05
30 Jeff Treadway .05
31 Chris Nabholz .05
32 Tom Candiotti .05
33 Mike Maddux .05
34 Nolan Ryan 2.00
35 Luis Gonzalez .05
36 Tim Salmon .05
37 Mark Whiten .05
38 Roger McDowell .05
39 Royce Clayton .05
40 Troy Neel .05
41 Mike Harkey .05
42 Darrin Fletcher .05
43 Wayne Kirby .05
44 Rich Amaral .05
45 Robb Nen .05
46 Tim Teufel .05
47 Steve Cooke .05
48 Jeff McNeely .05
49 Jeff Montgomery .05
50 Skeeter Barnes .05
51 Scott Stahoviak .05
52 Pat Kelly .05
53 Brady Anderson .05
54 Mariano Duncan .05
55 Brian Bohanon .05
56 Jerry Spradlin .05
57 Ron Karkovice .05
58 Jeff Gardner .05
59 Bobby Bonilla .05
60 Tino Martinez .05
61 Todd Benzinger .05
62 Steve Trachsel **RC** .25
63 Brian Jordan .05
64 Steve Bedrosian .05
65 Brent Gates .05
66 Shawn Green .35
67 Sean Berry .05
68 Joe Klink .05
69 Fernando Valenzuela .05
70 Andy Tomberlin .05
71 Tony Pena .05
72 Eric Young .05
73 Chris Gomez .05
74 Paul O'Neill .05
75 Ricky Gutierrez .05
76 Brad Holman .05
77 Lance Painter .05
78 Mike Butcher .05
79 Sid Bream .05
80 Sammy Sosa .75
81 Felix Fermin .05
82 Todd Hundley .05
83 Kevin Higgins .05
84 Todd Pratt .05
85 Ken Griffey Jr. 1.25
86 John O'Donoghue .05
87 Rick Renteria .05
88 John Burkett .05
89 Jose Vizcaino .05
90 Kevin Seitzer .05
91 Bobby Witt .05
92 Chris Turner .05
93 Omar Vizquel .05
94 Dave Justice .05
95 David Segui .05
96 Dave Hollins .05
97 Doug Strange .05
98 Jerald Clark .05
99 Mike Moore .05
100 Joey Cora .05
101 Scott Kamieniecki .05
102 Andy Benes .05
103 Chris Bosio .05
104 Rey Sanchez .05
105 John Jaha .05
106 Otis Nixon .05
107 Rickey Henderson .65
108 Jeff Bagwell .65
109 Gregg Jefferies .05
110 Topps Trios (Roberto Alomar, Paul Molitor, John Olerud) .25
111 Topps Trios (Ron Gant, David Justice, Fred McGriff) .05
112 Topps Trios (Juan Gonzalez, Rafael Palmeiro, Dean Palmer) .25
113 Greg Swindell .05
114 Bill Haselman .05
115 Phil Plantier .05
116 Ivan Rodriguez .60
117 Kevin Tapani .05
118 Mike LaValliere .05
119 Tim Costo .05
120 Mickey Morandini .05
121 Brett Butler .05
122 Tom Pagnozzi .05
123 Ron Gant .05
124 Damion Easley .05
125 Dennis Eckersley .60
126 Matt Mieske .05
127 Cliff Floyd .05
128 Julian Tavarez **RC** .05
129 Arthur Rhodes .05
130 Dave West .05
131 Tim Naehring .05
132 Freddie Benavides .05
133 Paul Assenmacher .05
134 David McCarty .05
135 Jose Lind .05
136 Reggie Sanders .05
137 Don Slaught .05
138 Andujar Cedeno .05
139 Rob Deer .05
140 Mike Piazza 1.25
141 Moises Alou .05
142 Tom Foley .05
143 Benny Santiago .05
144 Sandy Alomar .05
145 Carlos Hernandez .05
146 Luis Alicea .05
147 Tom Lampkin .05
148 Ryan Klesko .05
149 Juan Guzman .05
150 Scott Servais .05
151 Tony Gwynn .75
152 Tim Wakefield .05
153 David Nied .05
154 Chris Haney .05
155 Danny Bautista .05
156 Randy Velarde .05
157 Darrin Jackson .05
158 J.R. Phillips **RC** .05
159 Greg Gagne .05
160 Luis Aquino .05
161 John Vander Wal .05
162 Randy Myers .05
163 Ted Power .05
164 Scott Brosius .05
165 Len Dykstra .05
166 Jacob Brumfield .05
167 Bo Jackson .10
168 Eddie Taubensee .05
169 Carlos Baerga .05
170 Tim Bogar .05
171 Jose Canseco .50
172 Greg Blosser .05
173 Chili Davis .05
174 Randy Knorr .05
175 Mike Perez .05
176 Henry Rodriguez .05
177 Brian Turang **RC** .05
178 Roger Pavlik .05
179 Aaron Sele .05
180 Tale of 2 Players (Fred McGriff, Gary Sheffield) .05
181 Tale of 2 Players (J.T. Snow, Tim Salmon) .05
182 Roberto Hernandez .05
183 Jeff Reboulet .05
184 John Doherty .05
185 Danny Sheaffer .05
186 Bip Roberts .05
187 Denny Martinez .05
188 Darryl Hamilton .05
189 Eduardo Perez .05
190 Pete Harnisch .05
191 Rick Gossage .05
192 Mickey Tettleton .05
193 Lenny Webster .05
194 Lance Johnson .05
195 Don Mattingly 1.00
196 Gregg Olson .05
197 Mark Gubicza .05
198 Scott Fletcher .05
199 Jon Shave .05
200 Tim Mauser .05
201 Jeromy Burnitz .05
202 Rob Dibble .05
203 Will Clark .05
204 Steve Buechele .05
205 Brian Williams .05
206 Carlos Garcia .05
207 Mark Clark .05
208 Rafael Palmeiro .60
209 Eric Davis .05
210 Pat Meares .05
211 Chuck Finley .05
212 Jason Bere .05
213 Gary DiSarcina .05
214 Tony Fernandez .05
215 B.J. Surhoff .05
216 Lee Guetterman .05
217 Tim Wallach .05
218 Kirt Manwaring .05
219 Albert Belle .05
220 Dwight Gooden .05
221 Archi Cianfrocco .05
222 Terry Mulholland .05
223 Hipolito Pichardo .05
224 Kent Hrbek .05
225 Craig Grebeck .05
226 Todd Jones .05
227 Mike Bordick .05
228 John Olerud .05
229 Jeff Blauser .05
230 Alex Arias .05
231 Bernard Gilkey .05
232 Denny Neagle .05
233 Pedro Borbon **RC** .05
234 Dick Schofield .05
235 Matias Carrillo .05
236 Juan Bell .05
237 Mike Hampton .05
238 Barry Bonds 2.00
239 Cris Carpenter .05
240 Eric Karros .05
241 Greg McMichael .05
242 Pat Hentgen .05
243 Tim Pugh .05
244 Vinny Castilla .05
245 Charlie Hough .05
246 Bobby Munoz .05
247 Kevin Baez .05
248 Todd Frohwirth .05
249 Charlie Hayes .05
250 Mike Macfarlane .05
251 Danny Darwin .05
252 Ben Rivera .05
253 Dave Henderson .05
254 Steve Avery .05
255 Tim Belcher .05
256 Dan Plesac .05
257 Jim Thome .60
258 Albert Belle (35+ HR Hitter) .05
259 Barry Bonds (35+ HR Hitter) 1.00
260 Ron Gant (35+ HR Hitter) .05
261 Juan Gonzalez (35+ HR Hitter) .20
262 Ken Griffey Jr. (35+ HR Hitter) .65
263 Dave Justice (35+ HR Hitter) .05
264 Fred McGriff (35+ HR Hitter) .05
265 Rafael Palmeiro (35+ HR Hitter) .20
266 Mike Piazza (35+ HR Hitter) .65
267 Frank Thomas (35+ HR Hitter) .35
268 Matt Williams (35+ HR Hitter) .05
269a Checklist 1-135 .05
269b Checklist 271-408 .05
270a Checklist 136-270 .05
270b Checklist 409-540 .05
271 Mike Stanley .05
272 Tony Tarasco .05
273 Teddy Higuera .05
274 Ryan Thompson .05
275 Rick Aguilera .05
276 Ramon Martinez .05
277 Orlando Merced .05
278 Guillermo Velasquez .05
279 Mark Hutton .05
280 Larry Walker .05
281 Kevin Gross .05
282 Jose Offerman .05
283 Jim Leyritz .05
284 Jamie Moyer .05
285 Frank Thomas .65
286 Derek Bell .05
287 Derrick May .05
288 Dave Winfield .65
289 Curt Schilling .35
290 Carlos Quintana .05
291 Bob Natal .05
292 David Cone .05
293 Al Osuna .05
294 Bob Hamelin .05
295 Chad Curtis .05
296 Danny Jackson .05
297 Bob Welch .05
298 Felix Jose .05
299 Jay Buhner .05
300 Joe Carter .05
301 Kenny Lofton .05
302 Kirk Rueter **RC** .15
303 Kim Batiste .05
304 Mike Morgan .05
305 Pat Borders .05
306 Rene Arocha .05
307 Ruben Sierra .05
308 Steve Finley .05
309 Travis Fryman .05
310 Zane Smith .05
311 Willie Wilson .05
312 Trevor Hoffman .05
313 Terry Pendleton .05
314 Salomon Torres .05
315 Robin Ventura .05
316 Randy Tomlin .05
317 Dave Stewart .05
318 Mike Benjamin .05
319 Matt Turner .05
320 Manny Ramirez .65
321 Kevin Young .05
322 Ken Caminiti .05
323 Joe Girardi .05
324 Jeff McKnight .05
325 Gene Harris .05
326 Devon White .05
327 Darryl Kile .05
328 Craig Paquette .05
329 Cal Eldred .05
330 Bill Swift .05
331 Alan Trammell .05
332 Armando Reynoso .05
333 Brent Mayne .05
334 Chris Donnels .05
335 Darryl Strawberry .05
336 Dean Palmer .05
337 Frank Castillo .05
338 Jeff King .05
339 John Franco .05
340 Kevin Appier .05
341 Lance Blankenship .05
342 Mark McLemore .05
343 Pedro Astacio .05
344 Rich Batchelor .05
345 Ryan Bowen .05
346 Terry Steinbach .05
347 Troy O'Leary .05
348 Willie Blair .05
349 Wade Boggs .75
350 Tim Raines .05
351 Scott Livingstone .05
352 Rod Carreia .05
353 Ray Lankford .05
354 Pat Listach .05
355 Milt Thompson .05
356 Miguel Jimenez .05
357 Marc Newfield .05
358 Mark McGwire 1.50
359 Kirby Puckett .75
360 Kent Mercker .05
361 John Kruk .05
362 Jeff Kent .05
363 Hal Morris .05
364 Edgar Martinez .05
365 Dave Magadan .05
366 Dante Bichette .05
367 Chris Hammond .05
368 Bret Saberhagen .05
369 Billy Ripken .05
370 Bill Gullickson .05
371 Andre Dawson .35
372 Bobby Kelly .05
373 Cal Ripken, Jr. 2.00
374 Craig Biggio .05
375 Dan Pasqua .05
376 Dave Nilsson .05
377 Duane Ward .05
378 Greg Vaughn .05
379 Jeff Fassero .05
380 Jerry Dipoto .05
381 John Patterson .05
382 Kevin Brown .05
383 Kevin Roberson .05
384 Joe Orsulak .05
385 Hilly Hathaway .05
386 Mike Greenwell .05
387 Orestes Destrade .05
388 Mike Gallego .05
389 Ozzie Guillen .05
390 Raul Mondesi .05
391 Scott Lydy .05
392 Tom Urbani .05
393 Wil Cordero .05
394 Tony Longmire .05
395 Todd Zeile .05
396 Scott Cooper .05
397 Ryne Sandberg .75
398 Ricky Bones .05
399 Phil Clark .05
400 Orel Hershiser .05
401 Mike Henneman .05
402 Mark Lemke .05
403 Mark Grace .05
404 Ken Ryan .05
405 John Smoltz .05
406 Jeff Conine .05
407 Greg Harris .05
408 Doug Drabek .05
409 Dave Fleming .05
410 Danny Tartabull .05
411 Chad Kreuter .05
412 Brad Ausmus .05
413 Ben McDonald .05
414 Barry Larkin .05
415 Bret Barberie .05
416 Chuck Knoblauch .05
417 Ozzie Smith .75
418 Ed Sprague .05
419 Matt Williams .05
420 Jeremy Hernandez .05
421 Jose Bautista .05
422 Kevin Mitchell .05
423 Manuel Lee .05
424 Mike Devereaux .05
425 Omar Olivares .05
426 Rafael Belliard .05
427 Richie Lewis .05
428 Ron Darling .05
429 Shane Mack .05
430 Tim Hulett .05
431 Wally Joyner .05
432 Wes Chamberlain .05
433 Tom Browning .05
434 Scott Radinsky .05
435 Rondell White .05
436 Rod Beck .05
437 Rheal Cormier .05
438 Randy Johnson .65
439 Pete Schourek .05
440 Mo Vaughn .05
441 Mike Timlin .05
442 Mark Langston .05
443 Lou Whitaker .05
444 Kevin Stocker .05
445 Ken Hill .05
446 John Wetteland .05
447 J.T. Snow .05
448 Erik Pappas .05
449 David Hulse .05
450 Darren Daulton .05
451 Chris Hoiles .05
452 Bryan Harvey .05
453 Darren Lewis .05
454 Andres Galarraga .05
455 Joe Hesketh .05
456 Jose Valentin .05
457 Dan Peltier .05
458 Joe Boever .05
459 Kevin Rogers .05
460 Craig Shipley .05
461 Alvaro Espinoza .05
462 Wilson Alvarez .05
463 Cory Snyder .05
464 Candy Maldonado .05
465 Blas Minor .05
466 Rod Bolton .05
467 Kenny Rogers .05
468 Greg Myers .05
469 Jimmy Key .05
470 Tony Castillo .05
471 Mike Stanton .05
472 Deion Sanders .05
473 Tito Navarro .05
474 Mike Gardiner .05
475 Steve Reed .05
476 John Roper .05
477 Mike Trombley .05
478 Charles Nagy .05
479 Larry Casian .05
480 Eric Hillman .05
481 Bill Wertz .05
482 Jeff Schwarz .05
483 John Valentin .05
484 Carl Willis .05
485 Gary Gaetti .05
486 Bill Pecota .05
487 John Smiley .05
488 Mike Mussina .35
489 Mike Ignasiak **RC** .05
490 Billy Brewer .05
491 Jack Voigt .05
492 Mike Munoz .05
493 Lee Tinsley .05
494 Bob Wickman .05
495 Roger Salkeld .05
496 Thomas Howard .05
497 Mark Davis .05
498 Dave Clark .05
499 Turk Wendell .05
500 Rafael Bournigal .05
501 Chip Hale .05
502 Matt Whiteside .05
503 Brian Koelling .05
504 Jeff Reed .05
505 Paul Wagner .05
506 Torey Lovullo .05
507 Curtis Leskanic .05
508 Derek Lilliquist .05
509 Joe Magrane .05
510 Mackey Sasser .05
511 Lloyd McClendon .05
512 Jayhawk Owens **RC** .05
513 Woody Williams **RC** .05
514 Gary Redus .05
515 Tim Spehr .05
516 Jim Abbott .05
517 Lou Frazier .05
518 Erik Plantenberg .05
519 Tim Worrell .05
520 Brian McRae .05
521 Chan Ho Park **RC** 1.00
522 Mark Wohlers .05
523 Geronimo Pena .05
524 Andy Ashby .05
525 Tale of 2 Players (Tim Raines, Andre Dawson) .05
526 Tale of 2 Players (Paul Molitor, Dave Winfield) .40
527 Joe Carter (RBI Leader) .05
528 Frank Thomas (HR Leader) .35
529 Ken Griffey Jr. (TB Leader) .65
530 Dave Justice (HR Leader) .05
531 Gregg Jefferies (AVG Leader) .05
532 Barry Bonds (HR Leader) 1.00
533 John Kruk (Quick Start) .05
534 Roger Clemens (Quick Start) .50
535 Cecil Fielder (Quick Start) .05
536 Ruben Sierra (Quick Start) .05
537 Tony Gwynn (Quick Start) .40
538 Tom Glavine (Quick Start) .10
541 Ozzie Smith (Career Leader) .40
542 Eddie Murray (Career Leader) .30
543a Lee Smith (Career Leader) .05
543b Lonnie Smith (should be #643) .05
544 Greg Maddux .75
545 Denis Boucher .05
546 Mark Gardner .05
547 Bo Jackson .10
548 Eric Anthony .05
549 Delino DeShields .05
550 Turner Ward .05
551 Scott Sanderson .05
552 Hector Carrasco .05
553 Tony Phillips .05
554 Melido Perez .05
555 Mike Felder .05
556 Jack Morris .05
557 Rafael Palmeiro .60
558 Shane Reynolds .05
559 Pete Incaviglia .05
560 Greg Harris .05
561 Matt Walbeck .05
562 Todd Van Poppel .05
563 Todd Stottlemyre .05
564 Ricky Bones .05
565 Mike Jackson .05
566 Kevin McReynolds .05
567 Melvin Nieves .05
568 Juan Gonzalez .35
569 Frank Viola .05
570 Vince Coleman .05
571 Brian Anderson **RC** .25
572 Omar Vizquel .05
573 Bernie Williams .05
574 Tom Glavine .35
575 Mitch Williams .05
576 Shawon Dunston .05
577 Mike Lansing .05
578 Greg Pirkl .05
579 Sid Fernandez .05
580 Doug Jones .05
581 Walt Weiss .05
582 Tim Belcher .05
583 Alex Fernandez .05
584 Alex Cole .05
585 Greg Cadaret .05
586 Bob Tewksbury .05
587 Dave Hansen .05
588 Kurt Abbott **RC** .25
589 Rick White **RC** .05
590 Kevin Bass .05
591 Geronimo Berroa .05
592 Jaime Navarro .05
593 Steve Farr .05
594 Jack Armstrong .05
595 Steve Howe .05
596 Jose Rijo .05
597 Otis Nixon .05
598 Robby Thompson .05
599 Kelly Stinnett .05
600 Carlos Delgado .50
601 Brian Johnson **RC** .05
602 Gregg Olson .05
603 Jim Edmonds .05
604 Mike Blowers .05
605 Lee Smith .05
606 Pat Rapp .05
607 Mike Magnante .05
608 Karl Rhodes .05
609 Jeff Juden .05
610 Rusty Meacham .05
611 Pedro Martinez .65
612 Todd Worrell .05
613 Stan Javier .05
614 Mike Hampton .05
615 Jose Guzman .05
616 Xavier Hernandez .05
617 David Wells .05
618 John Habyan .05
619 Chris Nabholz .05
620 Bobby Jones .05
621 Chris James .05
622 Ellis Burks .05
623 Erik Hanson .05
624 Pat Meares .05
625 Harold Reynolds .05
626 Bob Hamelin (Rookie Rocker) .05

627	Manny Ramirez (Rookie Rocker)	.30
628	Ryan Klesko (Rookie Rocker)	.05
629	Carlos Delgado (Rookie Rocker)	.30
630	Javier Lopez (Rookie Rocker)	.05
631	Steve Karsay (Rookie Rocket)	.05
632	Rick Helling (Rookie Rocket)	.05
633	Steve Trachsel (Rookie Rocket)	.05
634	Hector Carrasco (Rookie Rocket)	.05
635	Andy Stankiewicz	.05
636	Paul Sorrento	.05
637	Scott Erickson	.05
638	Chipper Jones	.75
639	Luis Polonia	.05
640	Howard Johnson	.05
641	John Dopson	.05
642	Jody Reed	.05
644	Mark Portugal	.05
645	Paul Molitor	.65
646	Paul Assenmacher	.05
647	Hubie Brooks	.05
648	Gary Wayne	.05
649	Sean Berry	.05
650	Roger Clemens	1.00
651	Brian Hunter	.05
652	Wally Whitehurst	.05
653	Allen Watson	.05
654	Rickey Henderson	.65
655	Sid Bream	.05
656	Dan Wilson	.05
657	Ricky Jordan	.05
658	Sterling Hitchcock	.05
659	Darrin Jackson	.05
660	Junior Felix	.05
661	Tom Brunansky	.05
662	Jose Vizcaino	.05
663	Mark Leiter	.05
664	Gil Heredia	.05
665	Fred McGriff	.05
666	Will Clark	.05
667	Al Leiter	.05
668	James Mouton	.05
669	Billy Bean	.05
670	Scott Leius	.05
671	Bret Boone	.05
672	Darren Holmes	.05
673	Dave Weathers	.05
674	Eddie Murray	.65
675	Felix Fermin	.05
676	Chris Sabo	.05
677	Billy Spiers	.05
678	Aaron Sele	.05
679	Juan Samuel	.05
680	Julio Franco	.05
681	Heathcliff Slocumb	.05
682	Denny Martinez	.05
683	Jerry Browne	.05
684	Pedro A. Martinez **RC**	.05
685	Rex Hudler	.05
686	Willie McGee	.05
687	Andy Van Slyke	.05
688	Pat Mahomes	.05
689	Dave Henderson	.05
690	Tony Eusebio	.05
691	Rick Sutcliffe	.05
692	Willie Banks	.05
693	Alan Mills	.05
694	Jeff Treadway	.05
695	Alex Gonzalez	.05
696	David Segui	.05
697	Rick Helling	.05
698	Bip Roberts	.05
699	Jeff Cirillo **RC**	.25
700	Terry Mulholland	.05
701	Marvin Freeman	.05
702	Jason Bere	.05
703	Javier Lopez	.05
704	Greg Hibbard	.05
705	Tommy Greene	.05
706	Marquis Grissom	.05
707	Brian Harper	.05
708	Steve Karsay	.05
709	Jeff Brantley	.05
710	Jeff Russell	.05
711	Bryan Hickerson	.05
712	Jim Pittsley **RC**	.05
713	Bobby Ayala	.05
714	John Smoltz (Fantastic Finisher)	.05
715	Jose Rijo (Fantastic Finisher)	.05
716	Greg Maddux (Fantastic Finisher)	.40
717	Matt Williams (Fantastic Finisher)	.05
718	Frank Thomas (Fantastic Finisher)	.35
719	Ryne Sandberg (Fantastic Finisher)	.40
720	Checklist	.05

Golden Rainbow

Found at the rate of one per pack, Stadium Club "Golden Rainbow" cards were issued for each of the 720 cards in the regular set. These inserts are distinguished by the use of gold prismatic foil high-

lights for the S.C. logo and box with the player's last name, instead of the red foil found on regular S.C. cards.

	NM/M
Complete Set (720):	60.00
Common Player:	.25
Stars:	2X

1st Day Issue

A special silver-foil embossment designating "1st Day Issue" was placed on fewer than 2,000 of each of the 720 regular cards in the '94 Stadium Club set. Inserted at the rate of one per 24 foil packs and one per 15 jumbo packs, the cards are otherwise identical to the regular TSC cards.

	NM/M
Common Player:	1.00
Stars:	8X

Dugout Dirt

Cartoons of some of baseball's top stars are featured on the backs of this 12-card insert set. Fronts are virtually identical in format to regular S.C. cards, except the logo and box with the player's last name are in gold-foil, rather than red. Stated odds of finding a Dugout Dirt insert card were one per six packs, on average. Cards can also be found with a gold "Members Only" seal on front.

		NM/M
Complete Set (12):		5.00
Common Player:		.25
1	Mike Piazza (Catch of the Day)	1.00
2	Dave Winfield (The Road to 3,000)	.65
3	John Kruk (From Coal Mine to Gold Mine)	.25
4	Cal Ripken, Jr. (On Track)	2.00
5	Jack McDowell (Chin Music)	.25
6	Barry Bonds (The Bonds Market)	2.00
7	Ken Griffey Jr./AS (Gold Gloves)	1.00
8	Tim Salmon (The Salmon Run)	.25
9	Frank Thomas (Big Hurt)	.65
10	Jeff Kent (Super Kent)	.25
11	Randy Johnson (High Heat)	.65
12	Darren Daulton (Daulton's Gym)	.25

Finest

This insert set was included only in Series III packs of Topps Stadium Club, at the rate of one card per six packs, on average. Cards utilize Topps Finest technology and feature a player action photo on front, set against a red-and-gold sunburst background. Backs have a player portrait photo, a few stats and appropriate logos. Cards can also be found with a "Members Only" logo on front.

		NM/M
Complete Set (10):		11.00
Common Player:		.50
1	Jeff Bagwell	1.25
2	Albert Belle	.50
3	Barry Bonds	3.00
4	Juan Gonzalez	.75
5	Ken Griffey Jr.	2.00
6	Marquis Grissom	.50
7	David Justice	.50
8	Mike Piazza	2.00
9	Tim Salmon	.50
10	Frank Thomas	1.50

Finest Jumbo

Found only as a one per tub insert in special Wal-Mart repackaging of baseball packs, these 5" x 7" versions of the Series III Stadium Club inserts are identical to the smaller version. Cards utilize Topps Finest technology and feature a player action photo on front, set against a red-and-gold sunburst background. Backs have a player portrait photo, a few stats and appropriate logos.

		NM/M
Complete Set (10):		30.00
Common Player:		2.00
1	Jeff Bagwell	4.00
2	Albert Belle	2.00
3	Barry Bonds	6.50
4	Juan Gonzalez	3.00
5	Ken Griffey Jr.	5.00
6	Marquis Grissom	2.00
7	David Justice	2.00
8	Mike Piazza	5.00
9	Tim Salmon	2.00
10	Frank Thomas	4.00

Super Teams

Super Team cards were issued for each of the 28 major league teams and inserted at the rate of one per 24 regular packs and one per 15 jumbo packs. At the end of the 1995 season (the promotion was carried over when the 1994 season was ended prematurely by the players' strike), persons holding Super Team cards of the division winners, league champions and World Champions could redeem the cards for prizes. Division winning team cards could be redeemed for a set of 10 S.C. cards of that team with a special division winner embossed logo. League champion cards could be redeemed for a set of 10 Master Photos of the team with a special league logo embossed. Persons with a Super Team card of the eventual World Series champion could trade the card in for a complete set of Stadium Club cards embossed with a World's Champion logo. Each of the Super Team cards features a small group of players on the front with the Super Team Card and S.C. logos in gold foil, and the team name in prismatic foil. Backs contain redemption rules. A version of the Super Team cards was distributed with "Members Only" sets containing such an indicia on front and team roster on back.

		NM/M
Complete Set (28):		25.00
Common Team:		.70
Expired Jan. 31, 1996.		
1	Atlanta Braves	5.00
2	Chicago Cubs	.70
3	Cincinnati Reds	1.25
4	Colorado Rockies	1.00
5	Florida Marlins	.70
6	Houston Astros	1.00
7	Los Angeles Dodgers	1.75
8	Montreal Expos	1.00
9	New York Mets	.70
10	Philadelphia Phillies	.70
11	Pittsburgh Pirates	.70
12	St. Louis Cardinals	.70
13	San Diego Padres	.70
14	San Francisco Giants	1.25
15	Baltimore Orioles	1.25
16	Boston Red Sox	1.00
17	California Angels	.70
18	Chicago White Sox	1.50
19	Cleveland Indians	2.00
20	Detroit Tigers	.70
21	Kansas City Royals	1.00
22	Milwaukee Brewers	.70
23	Minnesota Twins	1.00
24	New York Yankees	1.50
25	Oakland Athletics	1.00
26	Seattle Mariners	2.00
27	Texas Rangers	1.00
28	Toronto Blue Jays	1.00

Members Only

This special gold-seal embossed version of the 1994 Topps Stadium Club set was available by a mail-in offer to club members for $230. The set includes all regular Stadium Club cards from Series I, II and III, along with the Dugout Dirt, Finest, and Super Teams insert cards. The Super Team cards, which were not eligible for the contest, have team rosters on

back, rather than contest rules. All other cards are identical to the regular-issue S.C. cards except for the present of the 1/2" round gold-foil "Members Only" seal beneath or alongside of the red-foil Topps Stadium Club logo on front. There are two different checklists each numbered 269 and 270. Only 5,000 sets were produced.

	NM/M
Complete Set (770):	150.00
Common Player:	.50
Stars:	8X

Members Only Baseball

Available for purchase by Topps Stadium Club members as a 50-card boxed set (football and basketball sets were also available), this issue features top stars, performances and career highlights from the 1993 season. Cards feature borderless action photos on front with the Topps logo and player's last name in gold-foil. Backs are horizontal and feature a black background on which the player's achievement is detailed in blue and gold. A second player photo appears on the card back. Cards #46-50 were produced in the Topps Finest-style foil-printing technology.

		NM/M
Complete Set (50):		6.00
Common Player:		.10
1	Juan Gonzalez	.25
2	Tom Henke	.10
3	John Kruk	.10
4	Paul Molitor	.50
5	Dave Justice	.10
6	Rafael Palmeiro	.45
7	John Smoltz	.10
8	Matt Williams	.10
9	John Olerud	.10
10	Mark Grace	.10
11	Joe Carter	.10
12	Wilson Alvarez	.10
13	Lenny Dykstra	.10
14	Kevin Appier	.10
15	Andres Galarraga	.10
16	Mark Langston	.10
17	Ken Griffey Jr.	.75
18	Albert Belle	.10
19	Gregg Jefferies	.10
20	Duane Ward	.10
21	Jack McDowell	.10
22	Randy Johnson	.50
23	Tom Glavine	.35
24	Barry Bonds	1.50
25	Chuck Carr	.10
26	Ron Gant	.10
27	Kenny Lofton	.10
28	Mike Piazza	.75
29	Frank Thomas	.55
30	Fred McGriff	.10
31	Bryan Harvey	.10
32	John Burkett	.10
33	Roberto Alomar	.20
34	Cecil Fielder	.10
35	Marquis Grissom	.10
36	Randy Myers	.10
37	Tony Phillips	.10
38	Rickey Henderson	.50
39	Luis Polonia	.10
40	Jose Rijo	.10
41	Jeff Montgomery	.10
42	Greg Maddux	.60
43	Tony Gwynn	.60
44	Rod Beck	.10
45	Carlos Baerga	.10
46	Wil Cordero	.10
47	Tim Salmon	.10
48	Mike Lansing	.10
49	J.T. Snow	.10
50	Jeff Conine	.10

Superstar Sampler

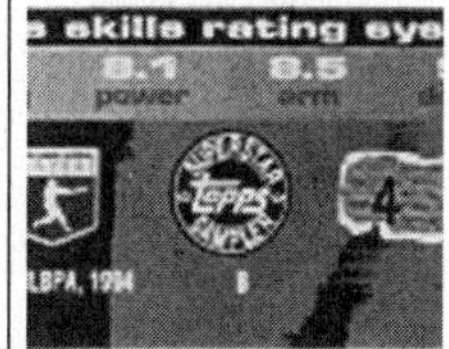

A small, round black-and-white "Topps Superstar Sampler" logo printed on the back is all that distinguishes these cards from regular-issue S.C. cards. This version of 45 of the top stars from the Stadium Club set was issued only in three-card cello packs inserted into 1994 Topps retail factory sets. The packs also contained the same player's cards from the Bowman and Finest sets, similarly marked.

		NM/M
Complete Set (45):		275.00
Common Player:		2.00
4	Gary Sheffield	3.00
10	Roberto Alomar	4.00
24	Jack McDowell	2.00
25	Cecil Fielder	2.00
36	Tim Salmon	2.00
59	Bobby Bonilla	2.00
85	Ken Griffey Jr.	20.00
94	Dave Justice	2.00
108	Jeff Bagwell	12.00
109	Gregg Jefferies	2.00
127	Cliff Floyd	2.00
140	Mike Piazza	20.00
151	Tony Gwynn	12.50
165	Len Dykstra	2.00
169	Carlos Baerga	2.00
171	Jose Canseco	8.00
195	Don Mattingly	15.00
203	Will Clark	2.00
208	Rafael Palmeiro	10.00
219	Albert Belle	2.00
228	John Olerud	2.00
238	Barry Bonds	30.00
280	Larry Walker	2.00
285	Frank Thomas	12.00
300	Joe Carter	2.00
320	Manny Ramirez	12.00
359	Kirby Puckett	12.50
373	Cal Ripken Jr.	30.00
390	Raul Mondesi	2.00
397	Ryne Sandberg	12.50
403	Mark Grace	2.00
414	Barry Larkin	2.00
419	Matt Williams	2.00
438	Randy Johnson	12.00
440	Mo Vaughn	2.00
450	Darren Daulton	2.00
454	Andres Galarraga	2.00
544	Greg Maddux	12.50
568	Juan Gonzalez	6.00
574	Tom Glavine	3.00
645	Paul Molitor	12.00
650	Roger Clemens	15.00
665	Fred McGriff	2.00
687	Andy Van Slyke	2.00
706	Marquis Grissom	2.00

Team Series

Only 12 of the 28 major league teams are included in this special issue marketed in both team-set blister packs and foil packs at Wal-Mart stores around the country. Card fronts feature a player action photo bordered in the lower-right corner by a dark green mottled effect. The player's name, team and "Team Stadium Club" logo are in gold foil. Backs have a second player photo set against a back-

ground in mottled shades of green. There are a few stats and player biographical details.

	NM/M
Complete Set (360):	25.00
Common Player:	.10
Wax Box (24):	15.00

#	Player	NM/M
1	Barry Bonds	3.50
2	Royce Clayton	.10
3	Kirt Manwaring	.10
4	J.R. Phillips	.10
5	Robby Thompson	.10
6	Willie McGee	.10
7	Steve Hosey	.10
8	Dave Burba	.10
9	Steve Scarsone	.10
10	Salomon Torres	.10
11	Bryan Hickerson	.10
12	Mike Benjamin	.10
13	Mark Carreon	.10
14	Rich Monteleone	.10
15	Dave Martinez	.10
16	Bill Swift	.10
17	Jeff Reed	.10
18	John Patterson	.10
19	Darren Lewis	.10
20	Mark Portugal	.10
21	Trevor Wilson	.10
22	Matt Williams	.10
23	Kevin Rogers	.10
24	Luis Mercedes	.10
25	Mike Jackson	.10
26	Steve Frey	.10
27	Tony Menendez	.10
28	John Burkett	.10
29	Todd Benzinger	.10
30	Rod Beck	.10
31	Greg Maddux	1.50
32	Steve Avery	.10
33	Milt Hill	.10
34	Charlie O'Brien	.10
35	John Smoltz	.10
36	Jarvis Brown	.10
37	Dave Gallagher	.10
38	Ryan Klesko	.10
39	Kent Mercker	.10
40	Terry Pendleton	.10
41	Ron Gant	.10
42	Pedro Borbon	.10
43	Steve Bedrosian	.10
44	Ramon Caraballo	.10
45	Tyler Houston	.10
46	Mark Lemke	.10
47	Fred McGriff	.10
48	Jose Oliva	.10
49	David Justice	.10
50	Chipper Jones	1.50
51	Tony Tarasco	.10
52	Javy Lopez	.10
53	Mark Wohlers	.10
54	Deion Sanders	.10
55	Greg McMichael	.10
56	Tom Glavine	.35
57	Bill Pecota	.10
58	Mike Stanton	.10
59	Rafael Belliard	.10
60	Jeff Blauser	.10
61	Bryan Harvey	.10
62	Bret Barberie	.10
63	Rick Renteria	.10
64	Chris Hammond	.10
65	Pat Rapp	.10
66	Nigel Wilson	.10
67	Gary Sheffield	.30
68	Jerry Browne	.10
69	Charlie Hough	.10
70	Orestes Destrade	.10
71	Mario Diaz	.10
72	Ryan Bowen	.10
73	Carl Everett	.10
74	Richie Lewis	.10
75	Bob Natal	.10
76	Rich Rodriguez	.10
77	Darrell Whitmore	.10
78	Matt Turner	.10
79	Benny Santiago	.10
80	Robb Nen	.10
81	Dave Magadan	.10
82	Brian Drahman	.10
83	Mark Gardner	.10
84	Chuck Carr	.10
85	Alex Arias	.10
86	Kurt Abbott	.10
87	Joe Klink	.10
88	Jeff Mutis	.10
89	Dave Weathers	.10
90	Jeff Conine	.10
91	Andres Galarraga	.10
92	Vinny Castilla	.10
93	Roberto Mejia	.10
94	Darrell Sherman	.10
95	Mike Harkey	.10
96	Danny Sheaffer	.10
97	Pedro Castellano	.10
98	Walt Weiss	.10
99	Greg Harris	.10
100	Jayhawk Owens	.10
101	Bruce Ruffin	.10
102	Mike Munoz	.10
103	Armando Reynoso	.10
104	Eric Young	.10
105	Dante Bichette	.10
106	Marvin Freeman	.10
107	Joe Girardi	.10
108	Kent Bottenfield	.10
109	Howard Johnson	.10
110	Nelson Liriano	.10
111	David Nied	.10
112	Steve Reed	.10
113	Eric Wedge	.10
114	Charlie Hayes	.10
115	Ellis Burks	.10
116	Willie Blair	.10
117	Darren Holmes	.10
118	Curtis Leskanic	.10
119	Lance Painter	.10
120	Jim Tatum	.10
121	Frank Thomas	1.00
122	Jack McDowell	.10
123	Ron Karkovice	.10
124	Mike LaValliere	.10
125	Scott Radinsky	.10
126	Robin Ventura	.10
127	Scott Ruffcorn	.10
128	Steve Sax	.10
129	Roberto Hernandez	.10
130	Jose DeLeon	.10
131	Rod Bolton	.10
132	Wilson Alvarez	.10
133	Craig Grebeck	.10
134	Lance Johnson	.10
135	Kirk McCaskill	.10
136	Tim Raines	.10
137	Jeff Schwarz	.10
138	Warren Newson	.10
139	Norberto Martin	.10
140	Mike Huff	.10
141	Ozzie Guillen	.10
142	Alex Fernandez	.10
143	Joey Cora	.10
144	Jason Bere	.10
145	James Baldwin	.10
146	Esteban Beltre	.10
147	Julio Franco	.10
148	Matt Merullo	.10
149	Dan Pasqua	.10
150	Darrin Jackson	.10
151	Joe Carter	.10
152	Danny Cox	.10
153	Roberto Alomar	.20
154	Woody Williams	.10
155	Duane Ward	.10
156	Ed Sprague	.10
157	Domingo Martinez	.10
158	Pat Hentgen	.10
159	Shawn Green	.30
160	Dick Schofield	.10
161	Paul Molitor	1.00
162	Darnell Coles	.10
163	Willie Canate	.10
164	Domingo Cedeno	.10
165	Pat Borders	.10
166	Greg Cadaret	.10
167	Tony Castillo	.10
168	Carlos Delgado	.45
169	Scott Brow	.10
170	Juan Guzman	.10
171	Al Leiter	.10
172	John Olerud	.10
173	Todd Stottlemyre	.10
174	Devon White	.10
175	Paul Spoljaric	.10
176	Randy Knorr	.10
177	Huck Flener **RC**	.10
178	Rob Butler	.10
179	Dave Stewart	.10
180	Mike Timlin	.10
181	Don Mattingly	2.00
182	Mark Hutton	.10
183	Mike Gallego	.10
184	Jim Abbott	.10
185	Paul Gibson	.10
186	Scott Kamieniecki	.10
187	Sam Horn	.10
188	Melido Perez	.10
189	Randy Velarde	.10
190	Gerald Williams	.10
191	Dave Silvestri	.10
192	Jim Leyritz	.10
193	Steve Howe	.10
194	Russ Davis	.10
195	Paul Assenmacher	.10
196	Pat Kelly	.10
197	Mike Stanley	.10
198	Bernie Williams	.10
199	Paul O'Neill	.10
200	Donn Pall	.10
201	Xavier Hernandez	.10
202	James Austin	.10
203	Sterling Hitchcock	.10
204	Wade Boggs	1.50
205	Jimmy Key	.10
206	Matt Nokes	.10
207	Terry Mulholland	.10
208	Luis Polonia	.10
209	Danny Tartabull	.10
210	Bob Wickman	.10
211	Len Dykstra	.10
212	Kim Batiste	.10
213	Tony Longmire	.10
214	Bobby Munoz	.10
215	Pete Incaviglia	.10
216	Doug Jones	.10
217	Mariano Duncan	.10
218	Jeff Juden	.10
219	Milt Thompson	.10
220	Dave West	.10
221	Roger Mason	.10
222	Tommy Greene	.10
223	Larry Andersen	.10
224	Jim Eisenreich	.10
225	Dave Hollins	.10
226	John Kruk	.10
227	Todd Pratt	.10
228	Ricky Jordan	.10
229	Curt Schilling	.35
230	Mike Williams	.10
231	Heathcliff Slocumb	.10
232	Ben Rivera	.10
233	Mike Lieberthal	.10
234	Mickey Morandini	.10
235	Danny Jackson	.10
236	Kevin Foster	.10
237	Darren Daulton	.10
238	Wes Chamberlain	.10
239	Tyler Green	.10
240	Kevin Stocker	.10
241	Juan Gonzalez	.50
242	Rick Honeycutt	.10
243	Bruce Hurst	.10
244	Steve Dreyer	.10
245	Brian Bohanon	.10
246	Benji Gil	.10
247	Jon Shave	.10
248	Manuel Lee	.10
249	Donald Harris	.10
250	Jose Canseco	.50
251	David Hulse	.10
252	Kenny Rogers	.10
253	Jeff Huson	.10
254	Dan Peltier	.10
255	Mike Scioscia	.10
256	Jack Armstrong	.10
257	Rob Ducey	.10
258	Will Clark	.10
259	Cris Carpenter	.10
260	Kevin Brown	.10
261	Jeff Frye	.10
262	Jay Howell	.10
263	Roger Pavlik	.10
264	Gary Redus	.10
265	Ivan Rodriguez	.75
266	Matt Whiteside	.10
267	Doug Strange	.10
268	Billy Ripken	.10
269	Dean Palmer	.10
270	Tom Henke	.10
271	Cal Ripken Jr.	3.50
272	Mark McLemore	.10
273	Sid Fernandez	.10
274	Sherman Obando	.10
275	Paul Carey	.10
276	Mike Oquist	.10
277	Alan Mills	.10
278	Harold Baines	.10
279	Mike Mussina	.30
280	Arthur Rhodes	.10
281	Kevin McGehee	.10
282	Mark Eichhorn	.10
283	Damon Buford	.10
284	Ben McDonald	.10
285	David Segui	.10
286	Brad Pennington	.10
287	Jamie Moyer	.10
288	Chris Hoiles	.10
289	Mike Cook	.10
290	Brady Anderson	.10
291	Chris Sabo	.10
292	Jack Voigt	.10
293	Jim Poole	.10
294	Jeff Tackett	.10
295	Rafael Palmeiro	.75
296	Alex Ochoa	.10
297	John O'Donoghue	.10
298	Tim Hulett	.10
299	Mike Devereaux	.10
300	Manny Alexander	.10
301	Ozzie Smith	1.50
302	Omar Olivares	.10
303	Rheal Cormier	.10
304	Donovan Osborne	.10
305	Mark Whiten	.10
306	Todd Zeile	.10
307	Geronimo Pena	.10
308	Brian Jordan	.10
309	Luis Alicea	.10
310	Ray Lankford	.10
311	Stan Royer	.10
312	Bob Tewksbury	.10
313	Jose Oquendo	.10
314	Steve Dixon	.10
315	Rene Arocha	.10
316	Bernard Gilkey	.10
317	Gregg Jefferies	.10
318	Rob Murphy	.10
319	Tom Pagnozzi	.10
320	Mike Perez	.10
321	Tom Urbani	.10
322	Allen Watson	.10
323	Erik Pappas	.10
324	Paul Kilgus	.10
325	John Habyan	.10
326	Rod Brewer	.10
327	Rich Batchelor	.10
328	Tripp Cromer	.10
329	Gerald Perry	.10
330	Les Lancaster	.10
331	Ryne Sandberg	1.50
332	Derrick May	.10
333	Steve Buechele	.10
334	Willie Banks	.10
335	Larry Luebbers	.10
336	Tommy Shields	.10
337	Eric Yelding	.10
338	Rey Sanchez	.10
339	Mark Grace	.10
340	Jose Bautista	.10
341	Frank Castillo	.10
342	Jose Guzman	.10
343	Rafael Novoa	.10
344	Karl Rhodes	.10
345	Steve Trachsel	.10
346	Rick Wilkins	.10
347	Sammy Sosa	1.50
348	Kevin Roberson	.10
349	Mark Parent	.10
350	Randy Myers	.10
351	Glenallen Hill	.10
352	Lance Dickson	.10
353	Shawn Boskie	.10
354	Shawon Dunston	.10
355	Dan Plesac	.10
356	Jose Vizcaino	.10
357	Willie Wilson	.10
358	Turk Wendell	.10
359	Mike Morgan	.10
360	Jim Bullinger	.10

Team Series 1st Day Issue

Each of the cards in the Stadium Club Team Series can be found with a speial embossed silver-foil "1st Day Issue" seal on front. Cards are otherwise identical to the regular issue.

	NM/M
Complete Set (360):	200.00
Common Player:	.50
Stars:	8X

Team Series Finest

One player from each of the 12 teams in the Stadium Club Team Series issue was printed in a chromium-metallic technology reminiscent of Topps Finest cards. These special cards are labeled "Team Stadium Club Finest." Other than the printing, the cards are in the same format as the rest of the issue.

	NM/M
Complete Set (12):	12.00
Common Player:	.50

#	Player	NM/M
1	Roberto Alomar	.50
2	Barry Bonds	3.00
3	Len Dykstra	.50
4	Andres Galarraga	.50
5	Juan Gonzalez	.50
6	Dave Justice	.50
7	Don Mattingly	2.00
8	Cal Ripken Jr.	3.00
9	Ryne Sandberg	1.50
10	Gary Sheffield	.65
11	Ozzie Smith	1.50
12	Frank Thomas	1.00

1995 Stadium Club

Topps' upscale brand was issued for 1995 in three series of, respectively, 270, 225 and 135 cards. Fronts have borderless color photos with a gold-foil device at bottom holding the team logo. Also in gold are the player's name at bottom and the Stadium Club logo at top. Backs have another player photo at left with a pair of computer-enhanced close-ups above it. At right are bar graphs detailing the player's '94 stats and his skills rankings. A number of specially designed subsets - "Best Seat in the House, Cover Story, MLB Debut," etc., are spread throughout the issue, which also includes a full slate of chase cards depending on the series and packaging.

	NM/M
Complete Set (630):	25.00
Common Player:	.05
Common First Day Production:	.50
First Day Stars:	7X
Series 1 or 2 Pack (14):	1.25
Series 1 or 2 Wax Box (24):	20.00
Series 3 Pack (13):	1.25
Series 3 Wax Box (24):	20.00

#	Player	NM/M
1	Cal Ripken Jr.	2.50
2	Bo Jackson	.10
3	Bryan Harvey	.05
4	Curt Schilling	.35
5	Bruce Ruffin	.05
6	Travis Fryman	.05
7	Jim Abbott	.05
8	David McCarty	.05
9	Gary Gaetti	.05
10	Roger Clemens	1.25
11	Carlos Garcia	.05
12	Lee Smith	.05
13	Bobby Ayala	.05
14	Charles Nagy	.05
15	Lou Frazier	.05
16	Rene Arocha	.05
17	Carlos Delgado	.50
18	Steve Finley	.05
19	Ryan Klesko	.05
20	Cal Eldred	.05
21	Rey Sanchez	.05
22	Ken Hill	.05
23	Benny Santiago	.05
24	Julian Tavarez	.05
25	Jose Vizcaino	.05
26	Andy Benes	.05
27	Mariano Duncan	.05
28	Checklist A	.05
29	Shawon Dunston	.05
30	Rafael Palmeiro	.65
31	Dean Palmer	.05
32	Andres Galarraga	.05
33	Joey Cora	.05
34	Mickey Tettleton	.05
35	Barry Larkin	.05
36	Carlos Baerga	.05
37	Orel Hershiser	.05
38	Jody Reed	.05
39	Paul Molitor	.75
40	Jim Edmonds	.05
41	Bob Tewksbury	.05
42	John Patterson	.05
43	Ray McDavid	.05
44	Zane Smith	.05
45	Bret Saberhagen	.05
46	Greg Maddux	1.00
47	Frank Thomas	.75
48	Carlos Baerga	.05
49	Billy Spiers	.05
50	Stan Javier	.05
51	Rex Hudler	.05
52	Denny Hocking	.05
53	Todd Worrell	.05
54	Mark Clark	.05
55	Hipilito Pichardo	.05
56	Bob Wickman	.05
57	Raul Mondesi	.05
58	Steve Cooke	.05
59	Rod Beck	.05
60	Tim Davis	.05
61	Jeff Kent	.05
62	John Valentin	.05
63	Alex Arias	.05
64	Steve Reed	.05
65	Ozzie Smith	1.00
66	Terry Pendleton	.05
67	Kenny Rogers	.05
68	Vince Coleman	.05
69	Tom Pagnozzi	.05
70	Roberto Alomar	.20
71	Darrin Jackson	.05
72	Dennis Eckersley	.65
73	Jay Buhner	.05
74	Darren Lewis	.05
75	Dave Weathers	.05
76	Matt Walbeck	.05
77	Brad Ausmus	.05
78	Danny Bautista	.05
79	Bob Hamelin	.05
80	Steve Traschel	.05
81	Ken Ryan	.05
82	Chris Turner	.05
83	David Segui	.05
84	Ben McDonald	.05
85	Wade Boggs	1.00
86	John Vander Wal	.05
87	Sandy Alomar	.05
88	Ron Karkovice	.05
89	Doug Jones	.05
90	Gary Sheffield	.40
91	Ken Caminiti	.05
92	Chris Bosio	.05
93	Kevin Tapani	.05
94	Walt Weiss	.05
95	Erik Hanson	.05
96	Ruben Sierra	.05
97	Nomar Garciaparra	1.00
98	Terrence Long	.05
99	Jacob Shumate	.05
100	Paul Wilson	.05
101	Kevin Witt	.05
102	Paul Konerko	.15
103	Ben Grieve	.05
104	Mark Johnson **RC**	.05
105	Cade Gaspar **RC**	.05
106	Mark Farris	.05
107	Dustin Hermanson	.05
108	Scott Elarton **RC**	.15
109	Doug Million	.05
110	Matt Smith	.05
111	Brian Buchanan **RC**	.05
112	Jayson Peterson **RC**	.05
113	Bret Wagner	.05
114	C.J. Nitkowski	.05
115	Ramon Castro **RC**	.05
116	Rafael Bournigal	.05
117	Jeff Fassero	.05
118	Bobby Bonilla	.05
119	Ricky Gutierrez	.05
120	Roger Pavlik	.05
121	Mike Greenwell	.05
122	Deion Sanders	.05
123	Charlie Hayes	.05
124	Paul O'Neill	.05
125	Jay Bell	.05
126	Royce Clayton	.05
127	Willie Banks	.05
128	Mark Wohlers	.05
129	Todd Jones	.05
130	Todd Stottlemyre	.05
131	Will Clark	.05
132	Wilson Alvarez	.05
133	Chili Davis	.05
134	Dave Burba	.05
135	Chris Hoiles	.05
136	Jeff Blauser	.05
137	Jeff Reboulet	.05
138	Bret Saberhagen	.05
139	Kirk Rueter	.05
140	Dave Nilsson	.05
141	Pat Borders	.05
142	Ron Darling	.05
143	Derek Bell	.05
144	Dave Hollins	.05
145	Juan Gonzalez	.40
146	Andre Dawson	.25
147	Jim Thome	.65
148	Larry Walker	.05
149	Mike Piazza	1.50
150	Mike Perez	.05
151	Steve Avery	.05
152	Dan Wilson	.05
153	Andy Van Slyke	.05
154	Junior Felix	.05
155	Jack McDowell	.05
156	Danny Tartabull	.05
157	Willie Blair	.05
158	William Van Landingham	.05
159	Robb Nen	.05
160	Lee Tinsley	.05
161	Ismael Valdes	.05
162	Juan Guzman	.05
163	Scott Servais	.05
164	Cliff Floyd	.05
165	Allen Watson	.05
166	Eddie Taubensee	.05
167	Scott Hemond	.05
168	Jeff Tackett	.05
169	Chad Curtis	.05
170	Rico Brogna	.05
171	Luis Polonia	.05
172	Checklist B	.05
173	Lance Johnson	.05
174	Sammy Sosa	1.00
175	Mike MacFarlane	.05
176	Darryl Hamilton	.05
177	Rick Aguilera	.05
178	Dave West	.05
179	Mike Gallego	.05
180	Marc Newfield	.05
181	Steve Buechele	.05
182	David Wells	.05
183	Tom Glavine	.35
184	Joe Girardi	.05

185 Craig Biggio .05
186 Eddie Murray .75
187 Kevin Gross .05
188 Sid Fernandez .05
189 John Franco .05
190 Bernard Gilkey .05
191 Matt Williams .05
192 Darrin Fletcher .05
193 Jeff Conine .05
194 Ed Sprague .05
195 Eduardo Perez .05
196 Scott Livingstone .05
197 Ivan Rodriguez .65
198 Orlando Merced .05
199 Ricky Bones .05
200 Javier Lopez .05
201 Miguel Jimenez .05
202 Terry McGriff .05
203 Mike Lieberthal .05
204 David Cone .05
205 Todd Hundley .05
206 Ozzie Guillen .05
207 Alex Cole .05
208 Tony Phillips .05
209 Jim Eisenreich .05
210 Greg Vaughn .05
211 Barry Larkin .05
212 Don Mattingly 1.00
213 Mark Grace .05
214 Jose Canseco .50
215 Joe Carter .05
216 David Cone .05
217 Sandy Alomar .05
218 Al Martin .05
219 Roberto Kelly .05
220 Paul Sorrento .05
221 Tony Fernandez .05
222 Stan Belinda .05
223 Mike Stanley .05
224 Doug Drabek .05
225 Todd Van Poppel .05
226 Matt Mieske .05
227 Tino Martinez .05
228 Andy Ashby .05
229 Midre Cummings .05
230 Jeff Frye .05
231 Hal Morris .05
232 Jose Lind .05
233 Shawn Green .30
234 Rafael Belliard .05
235 Randy Myers .05
236 Frank Thomas .45
237 Darren Daulton .05
238 Sammy Sosa .65
239 Cal Ripken Jr. 1.00
240 Jeff Bagwell .40
241 Ken Griffey Jr. 1.50
242 Brett Butler .05
243 Derrick May .05
244 Pat Listach .05
245 Mike Bordick .05
246 Mark Langston .05
247 Randy Velarde .05
248 Julio Franco .05
249 Chuck Knoblauch .05
250 Bill Gullickson .05
251 Dave Henderson .05
252 Bret Boone .05
253 Al Martin .05
254 Armando Benitez .05
255 Wil Cordero .05
256 Al Leiter .05
257 Luis Gonzalez .05
258 Charlie O'Brien .05
259 Tim Wallach .05
260 Scott Sanders .05
261 Tom Henke .05
262 Otis Nixon .05
263 Darren Daulton .05
264 Manny Ramirez .75
265 Bret Barberie .05
266 Mel Rojas .05
267 John Burkett .05
268 Brady Anderson .05
269 John Roper .05
270 Shane Reynolds .05
271 Barry Bonds 2.50
272 Alex Fernandez .05
273 Brian McRae .05
274 Todd Zeile .05
275 Greg Swindell .05
276 Johnny Ruffin .05
277 Troy Neel .05
278 Eric Karros .05
279 John Hudek .05
280 Thomas Howard .05
281 Joe Carter .05
282 Mike Devereaux .05
283 Butch Henry .05
284 Reggie Jefferson .05
285 Mark Lemke .05
286 Jeff Montgomery .05
287 Ryan Thompson .05
288 Paul Shuey .05
289 Mark McGwire 2.00
290 Bernie Williams .05
291 Mickey Morandini .05
292 Scott Leius .05
293 David Hulse .05
294 Greg Gagne .05
295 Moises Alou .05
296 Geronimo Berroa .05
297 Eddie Zambrano .05
298 Alan Trammell .05
299 Don Slaught .05
300 Jose Rijo .05
301 Joe Ausanio .05
302 Tim Raines .05
303 Melido Perez .05
304 Kent Mercker .05
305 James Mouton .05
306 Luis Lopez .05
307 Mike Kingery .05
308 Willie Greene .05
309 Cecil Fielder .05
310 Scott Kamieniecki .05
311 Mike Greenwell (Best Seat in the House) .05
312 Bobby Bonilla (Best Seat in the House) .05
313 Andres Galarraga (Best Seat in the House) .05
314 Cal Ripken Jr. (Best Seat in the House) 1.25
315 Matt Williams (Best Seat in the House) .05
316 Tom Pagnozzi (Best Seat in the House) .05
317 Len Dykstra (Best Seat in the House) .05
318 Frank Thomas (Best Seat in the House) .40
319 Kirby Puckett (Best Seat in the House) .50
320 Mike Piazza (Best Seat in the House) 1.00
321 Jason Jacome .05
322 Brian Hunter .05
323 Brent Gates .05
324 Jim Converse .05
325 Damion Easley .05
326 Dante Bichette .05
327 Kurt Abbott .05
328 Scott Cooper .05
329 Mike Henneman .05
330 Orlando Miller .05
331 John Kruk .05
332 Jose Oliva .05
333 Reggie Sanders .05
334 Omar Vizquel .05
335 Devon White .05
336 Mike Morgan .05
337 J.R. Phillips .05
338 Gary DiSarcina .05
339 Joey Hamilton .05
340 Randy Johnson .75
341 Jim Leyritz .05
342 Bobby Jones .05
343 Jaime Navarro .05
344 Bip Roberts .05
345 Steve Karsay .05
346 Kevin Stocker .05
347 Jose Canseco .50
348 Bill Wegman .05
349 Rondell White .05
350 Mo Vaughn .05
351 Joe Orsulak .05
352 Pat Meares .05
353 Albie Lopez .05
354 Edgar Martinez .05
355 Brian Jordan .05
356 Tommy Greene .05
357 Chuck Carr .05
358 Pedro Astacio .05
359 Russ Davis .05
360 Chris Hammond .05
361 Gregg Jefferies .05
362 Shane Mack .05
363 Fred McGriff .05
364 Pat Rapp .05
365 Bill Swift .05
366 Checklist .05
367 Robin Ventura .05
368 Bobby Witt .05
369 Karl Rhodes .05
370 Eddie Williams .05
371 John Jaha .05
372 Steve Howe .05
373 Leo Gomez .05
374 Hector Fajardo .05
375 Jeff Bagwell .75
376 Mark Acre .05
377 Wayne Kirby .05
378 Mark Portugal .05
379 Jesus Tavarez .05
380 Jim Lindeman .05
381 Don Mattingly 1.25
382 Trevor Hoffman .05
383 Chris Gomez .05
384 Garret Anderson .05
385 Bobby Munoz .05
386 Jon Lieber .05
387 Rick Helling .05
388 Marvin Freeman .05
389 Juan Castillo .05
390 Jeff Cirillo .05
391 Sean Berry .05
392 Hector Carrasco .05
393 Mark Grace .05
394 Pat Kelly .05
395 Tim Naehring .05
396 Greg Pirkl .05
397 John Smoltz .05
398 Robby Thompson .05
399 Rick White .05
400 Frank Thomas .75
401 Jeff Conine (Cover Story) .05
402 Jose Valentin (Cover Story) .05
403 Carlos Baerga (Cover Story) .05
404 Rick Aguilera (Cover Story) .05
405 Wilson Alvarez (Cover Story) .05
406 Juan Gonzalez (Cover Story) .20
407 Barry Larkin (Cover Story) .05
408 Ken Hill (Cover Story) .05
409 Chuck Carr (Cover Story) .05
410 Tim Raines (Cover Story) .05
411 Bryan Eversgerd .05
412 Phil Plantier .05
413 Josias Manzanillo .05
414 Roberto Kelly .05
415 Rickey Henderson .75
416 John Smiley .05
417 Kevin Brown .05
418 Jimmy Key .05
419 Wally Joyner .05
420 Roberto Hernandez .05
421 Felix Fermin .05
422 Checklist .05
423 Greg Vaughn .05
424 Ray Lankford .05
425 Greg Maddux 1.00
426 Mike Mussina .30
427 Geronimo Pena .05
428 David Nied .05
429 Scott Erickson .05
430 Kevin Mitchell .05
431 Mike Lansing .05
432 Brian Anderson .05
433 Jeff King .05
434 Ramon Martinez .05
435 Kevin Seitzer .05
436 Salomon Torres .05
437 Brian Hunter .05
438 Melvin Nieves .05
439 Mike Kelly .05
440 Marquis Grissom .05
441 Chuck Finley .05
442 Len Dykstra .05
443 Ellis Burks .05
444 Harold Baines .05
445 Kevin Appier .05
446 Dave Justice .05
447 Darryl Kile .05
448 John Olerud .05
449 Greg McMichael .05
450 Kirby Puckett 1.00
451 Jose Valentin .05
452 Rick Wilkins .05
453 Arthur Rhodes .05
454 Pat Hentgen .05
455 Tom Gordon .05
456 Tom Candiotti .05
457 Jason Bere .05
458 Wes Chamberlain .05
459 Greg Colbrunn .05
460 John Doherty .05
461 Kevin Foster .05
462 Mark Whiten .05
463 Terry Steinbach .05
464 Aaron Sele .05
465 Kirt Manwaring .05
466 Darren Hall .05
467 Delino DeShields .05
468 Andujar Cedeno .05
469 Billy Ashley .05
470 Kenny Lofton .05
471 Pedro Munoz .05
472 John Wetteland .05
473 Tim Salmon .05
474 Denny Neagle .05
475 Tony Gwynn 1.00
476 Vinny Castilla .05
477 Steve Dreyer .05
478 Jeff Shaw .05
479 Chad Ogea .05
480 Scott Ruffcorn .05
481 Lou Whitaker .05
482 J.T. Snow .05
483 Rich Rowland .05
484 Dennis Martinez .05
485 Pedro Martinez .75
486 Rusty Greer .05
487 Dave Fleming .05
488 John Dettmer .05
489 Albert Belle .05
490 Ravelo Manzanillo .05
491 Henry Rodriguez .05
492 Andrew Lorraine .05
493 Dwayne Hosey .05
494 Mike Blowers .05
495 Turner Ward .05
496 Fred McGriff (Extreme Corps) .05
497 Sammy Sosa (Extreme Corps) .50
498 Barry Larkin (Extreme Corps) .05
499 Andres Galarraga (Extreme Corps) .05
500 Gary Sheffield (Extreme Corps) .15
501 Jeff Bagwell (Extreme Corps) .40
502 Mike Piazza (Extreme Corps) 1.00
503 Moises Alou (Extreme Corps) .05
504 Bobby Bonilla (Extreme Corps) .05
505 Darren Daulton (Extreme Corps) .05
506 Jeff King (Extreme Corps) .05
507 Ray Lankford (Extreme Corps) .05
508 Tony Gwynn (Extreme Corps) .50
509 Barry Bonds (Extreme Corps) 1.25
510 Cal Ripken Jr. (Extreme Corps) 1.25
511 Mo Vaughn (Extreme Corps) .05
512 Tim Salmon (Extreme Corps) .05
513 Frank Thomas (Extreme Corps) .45
514 Albert Belle (Extreme Corps) .05
515 Cecil Fielder (Extreme Corps) .05
516 Kevin Appier (Extreme Corps) .05
517 Greg Vaughn (Extreme Corps) .05
518 Kirby Puckett (Extreme Corps) .50
519 Paul O'Neill (Extreme Corps) .05
520 Ruben Sierra (Extreme Corps) .05
521 Ken Griffey Jr. (Extreme Corps) .75
522 Will Clark (Extreme Corps) .05
523 Joe Carter (Extreme Corps) .05
524 Antonio Osuna .05
525 Glenallen Hill .05
526 Alex Gonzalez .05
527 Dave Stewart .05
528 Ron Gant .05
529 Jason Bates .05
530 Mike Macfarlane .05
531 Esteban Loaiza .05
532 Joe Randa .05
533 Dave Winfield .75
534 Danny Darwin .05
535 Pete Harnisch .05
536 Joey Cora .05
537 Jaime Navarro .05
538 Marty Cordova .05
539 Andujar Cedeno .05
540 Mickey Tettleton .05
541 Andy Van Slyke .05
542 Carlos Perez **RC** .05
543 Chipper Jones 1.00
544 Tony Fernandez .05
545 Tom Henke .05
546 Pat Borders .05
547 Chad Curtis .05
548 Ray Durham .05
549 Joe Oliver .05
550 Jose Mesa .05
551 Steve Finley .05
552 Otis Nixon .05
553 Jacob Brumfield .05
554 Bill Swift .05
555 Quilvio Veras .05
556 Hideo Nomo **RC** 1.50
557 Joe Vitiello .05
558 Mike Perez .05
559 Charlie Hayes .05
560 Brad Radke **RC** .25
561 Darren Bragg .05
562 Orel Hershiser .05
563 Edgardo Alfonzo .05
564 Doug Jones .05
565 Andy Pettitte .25
566 Benito Santiago .05
567 John Burkett .05
568 Brad Clontz .05
569 Jim Abbott .05
570 Joe Rosselli .05
571 Mark Grudzielanek **RC** .25
572 Dustin Hermanson .05
573 Benji Gil .05
574 Mark Whiten .05
575 Mike Ignasiak .05
576 Kevin Ritz .05
577 Paul Quantrill .05
578 Andre Dawson .25
579 Jerald Clark .05
580 Frank Rodriguez .05
581 Mark Kiefer .05
582 Trevor Wilson .05
583 Gary Wilson **RC** .05
584 Andy Stankiewicz .05
585 Felipe Lira .05
586 Mike Mimbs **RC** .05
587 Jon Nunnally .05
588 Tomas Perez **RC** .05
589 Checklist .05
590 Todd Hollandsworth .05
591 Roberto Petagine .05
592 Mariano Rivera .15
593 Mark McLemore .05
594 Bobby Witt .05
595 Jose Offerman .05
596 Jason Christiansen .05
597 Jeff Manto .05
598 Jim Dougherty .05
599 Juan Acevedo .05
600 Troy O'Leary .05
601 Ron Villone .05
602 Tripp Cromer .05
603 Steve Scarsone .05
604 Lance Parrish .05
605 Ozzie Timmons .05
606 Ray Holbert .05
607 Tony Phillips .05
608 Phil Plantier .05
609 Shane Andrews .05
610 Heathcliff Slocumb .05
611 Bobby Higginson **RC** .25
612 Bob Tewksbury .05
613 Terry Pendleton .05
614 Scott Cooper (Trans-Action) .05
615 John Wetteland (Trans-Action) .05
616 Ken Hill (Trans-Action) .05
617 Marquis Grissom (Trans-Action) .05
618 Larry Walker (Trans-Action) .05
619 Derek Bell (Trans-Action) .05
620 David Cone (Trans-Action) .05
621 Ken Caminiti (Trans-Action) .05
622 Jack McDowell (Trans-Action) .05
623 Vaughn Eshelman (Trans-Action) .05
624 Brian McRae (Trans-Action) .05
625 Gregg Jefferies (Trans-Action) .05
626 Kevin Brown (Trans-Action) .05
627 Lee Smith (Trans-Action) .05
628 Tony Tarasco (Trans-Action) .05
629 Brett Butler (Trans-Action) .05
630 Jose Canseco (Trans-Action) .35

1st Day Pre-Production

Stadium Club 1st Day Pre-production cards were randomly packed into one every 36 packs of Topps Series I baseball. The set of nine cards is only found in hobby packs.

NM/M

Complete Set (9): 7.50
Common Player: .50
29 Shawon Dunston .50
39 Paul Molitor 1.50
79 Bob Hamelin .50
96 Ruben Sierra .50
131 Will Clark .50
149 Mike Piazza 3.00
153 Andy Van Slyke .50
166 Jeff Tackett .50
197 Ivan Rodriguez 1.00

1st Day Issue

Series II hobby packs of Topps baseball featured a chase set of Stadium Club 1st Day Issue cards, #1-270. The FDI cards have a small gold embossed seal on front. Cards were seeded on an average of one per six packs. Ten FDI cards were also randomly inserted in each Factory set.

NM/M

Common Player: .50
Stars: 7X

Clear Cut

Among the most technically advanced of 1995's insert cards is the Clear Cut chase set found in Series I and II packs. Cards feature a color player action photo printed on see-through plastic. There is a rainbow-hued trapezoid behind the player with an overall background tinted in blue, green and gold. The player's name is in white in a vertical blue bar at right. Backs have a few stats and data in a blue bar vertically at left. Each of the cards can also be found in a version with the round Members Only seal embossed into the plastic at lower-left.

NM/M

Complete Set (28): 20.00
Common Player: .65
1 Mike Piazza 3.00
2 Ruben Sierra .65
3 Tony Gwynn 2.50
4 Frank Thomas 2.00
5 Fred McGriff .65
6 Rafael Palmeiro 1.50
7 Bobby Bonilla .65
8 Chili Davis .65
9 Hal Morris .65
10 Jose Canseco 1.00
11 Jay Bell .65
12 Kirby Puckett 2.50
13 Gary Sheffield 1.00
14 Bob Hamelin .65
15 Jeff Bagwell 2.00
16 Albert Belle .65
17 Sammy Sosa 2.50
18 Ken Griffey Jr. 3.00
19 Todd Zeile .65
20 Mo Vaughn .65
21 Moises Alou .65
22 Paul O'Neill .65
23 Andres Galarraga .65
24 Greg Vaughn .65
25 Len Dykstra .65
26 Joe Carter .65
27 Barry Bonds 4.50
28 Cecil Fielder .65

Crunch Time

Series 1 rack packs were the exclusive provenance of these cards featuring baseball's top run creators. Fronts are printed on rainbow prismatic foil. The central color action photo is repeated as an enlarged background photo, along with a team logo. At bottom in gold foil are the player name and Crunch Time logo. Backs have a positive and a negative image of the same photo as background to a pie chart and stats relative to the player's runs-created stats.

NM/M

Complete Set (20): 15.00
Common Player: 1.00
1 Jeff Bagwell 2.50
2 Kirby Puckett 3.00
3 Frank Thomas 2.50
4 Albert Belle 1.00
5 Julio Franco 1.00
6 Jose Canseco 1.50
7 Paul Molitor 2.50
8 Joe Carter 1.00
9 Ken Griffey Jr. 4.00
10 Larry Walker 1.00
11 Dante Bichette 1.00
12 Carlos Baerga 1.00
13 Fred McGriff 1.00
14 Ruben Sierra 1.00
15 Will Clark 1.00
16 Moises Alou 1.00
17 Rafael Palmeiro 2.00
18 Travis Fryman 1.00
19 Barry Bonds 5.00
20 Cal Ripken Jr. 5.00

Crystal Ball

Multi-colored swirls around a clear central circle with the player's photo, all printed on foil, are the front design for this Series 3 insert. Backs have a portrait photo in a floating crystal ball image at one side. At the other end are year-by-year minor league stats and a few words about each of the player's seasons. This insert was also produced in an edition of 4,000 bearing a gold-foil "Members Only" seal, sold in complete Stadium Club Members Only factory sets.

		NM/M
Complete Set (15):		15.00
Common Player:		.75
1	Chipper Jones	5.00
2	Dustin Hermanson	.75
3	Ray Durham	.75
4	Phil Nevin	.75
5	Billy Ashley	.75
6	Shawn Green	2.50
7	Jason Dates	.75
8	Benji Gil	.75
9	Marty Cordova	.75
10	Quilvio Veras	.75
11	Mark Grudzielanek	.75
12	Ruben Rivera	.75
13	Bill Pulsipher	.75
14	Derek Jeter	7.50
15	LaTroy Hawkins	.75

Power Zone

The performance in several parks around the league is chronicled on the back of these Series 3 inserts. Fronts are printed on foil and feature a player swinging into an exploding asteroid. His name is printed vertically down one side in prismatic glitter foil. Backs also have a portrait photo and a baseball with a weird red and green vapor trail. A special edition of 4,000 each of these inserts was included with the purchase of Stadium Club Members Only factory sets; those cards have an embossed gold-foil seal on front.

		NM/M
Complete Set (12):		9.00
Common Player:		.50
1	Jeff Bagwell	1.00
2	Albert Belle	.50
3	Barry Bonds	3.00
4	Joe Carter	.50
5	Cecil Fielder	.50
6	Andres Galarraga	.50
7	Ken Griffey Jr.	2.00
8	Paul Molitor	1.00
9	Fred McGriff	.50
10	Rafael Palmeiro	.75
11	Frank Thomas	1.00
12	Matt Williams	.50

Ring Leaders

With a background that looks like an explosion at a jewelry factory, these cards feature players who have won championship, All-Star or other award rings. Fronts are

foil-printed with a player action photo on a background of flying rings and stars, and, - for some reason - an attacking eagle. Backs repeat the background motif, have a player portrait in an oval frame at top-left, photos of some of his rings and a list of rings won. Cards were random inserts in both Series 1 and 2; complete sets could also be won in Stadium Club's phone card insert contest. A version with the Members Only gold seal was also issued for each.

		NM/M
Complete Set (40):		70.00
Common Player:		.75
1	Jeff Bagwell	3.00
2	Mark McGwire	7.50
3	Ozzie Smith	4.00
4	Paul Molitor	3.00
5	Darryl Strawberry	.75
6	Eddie Murray	3.00
7	Tony Gwynn	4.00
8	Jose Canseco	2.00
9	Howard Johnson	.75
10	Andre Dawson	1.25
11	Matt Williams	.75
12	Tim Raines	.75
13	Fred McGriff	.75
14	Ken Griffey Jr.	6.00
15	Gary Sheffield	2.00
16	Dennis Eckersley	2.50
17	Kevin Mitchell	.75
18	Will Clark	.75
19	Darren Daulton	.75
20	Paul O'Neill	.75
21	Julio Franco	.75
22	Albert Belle	.75
23	Juan Gonzalez	1.50
24	Kirby Puckett	4.00
25	Joe Carter	.75
26	Frank Thomas	3.00
27	Cal Ripken Jr.	9.00
28	John Olerud	.75
29	Ruben Sierra	.75
30	Barry Bonds	9.00
31	Cecil Fielder	.75
32	Roger Clemens	5.00
33	Don Mattingly	5.00
34	Terry Pendleton	.75
35	Rickey Henderson	3.00
36	Dave Winfield	3.00
37	Edgar Martinez	.75
38	Wade Boggs	4.00
39	Willie McGee	.75
40	Andres Galarraga	.75

Ring Leaders Phone Cards

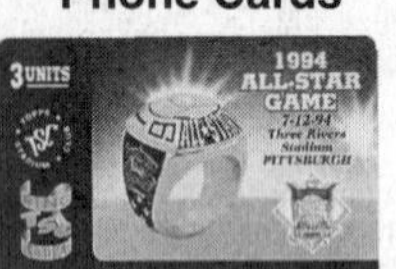

An interactive contest carrying through the "Ring Leaders" insert card set theme featured randomly inserted phone cards picturing All-Star Game players' rings. The 2-1/8" x 3-3/8" plastic cards could be found in regular, silver and gold editions. By using the card for a long distance call, the holder could determine if it was a further winner. Regular card winners received a set of Stadium Club Ring Leaders insert cards. Winners on a silver card received a complete set of the 13 different phone cards in all three versions. Gold card winners received the genuine All-Star ring pictured on the card. Approximately 217,000 phone cards were inserted in the program; odds of finding a regular card were about one per 40 packs; silver, one per 237 packs, and, gold, one per 2,955 packs. Cards picturing the 1988 and 1989 All-Star rings were not issued. Phone cards with the number panel on back scratched off are worth 50 percent of the values quoted.

		NM/M
Complete Set, Regular (13):		10.00
Complete Set, Silver (13):		25.00
Complete Set, Gold (13):		50.00
Common Card, Regular:		1.00
Common Card, Silver:		2.50
Common Card, Gold:		5.00
(1)	1980 All-Star Game, Los Angeles	1.00
(1s)	1980 All-Star Game, Los Angeles/Silver	2.50
(1g)	1980 All-Star Game, Los Angeles/Gold	5.00
(2)	1981 All-Star Game, Cleveland	1.00
(2s)	1981 All-Star Game, Cleveland/Silver	2.50
(2g)	1981 All-Star Game, Cleveland/Gold	5.00
(3)	1982 All-Star Game, Montreal	1.00
(3s)	1982 All-Star Game, Montreal/Silver	2.50
(3g)	1982 All-Star Game, Montreal/Gold	5.00
(4)	1983 All-Star Game, Chicago A.L.	1.00
(4s)	1983 All-Star Game, Chicago A.L./Silver	2.50
(4g)	1983 All-Star Game, Chicago A.L./Gold	5.00
(5)	1984 All-Star Game, San Francisco	1.00
(5s)	1984 All-Star Game, San Francisco/Silver	2.50
(5g)	1984 All-Star Game, San Francisco/Gold	5.00
(6)	1985 All-Star Game, Minneapolis	1.00
(6s)	1985 All-Star Game, Minneapolis/Silver	2.50
(6g)	1985 All-Star Game, Minneapolis/Gold	5.00
(7)	1986 All-Star Game, Houston	1.00
(7s)	1986 All-Star Game, Houston/Silver	2.50
(7g)	1986 All-Star Game, Houston/Gold	5.00
(8)	1987 All-Star Game, Oakland	1.00
(8s)	1987 All-Star Game, Oakland/Silver	2.50
(8g)	1987 All-Star Game, Oakland/Gold	5.00
(9)	1990 All-Star Game, Chicago N.L.	1.00
(9s)	1990 All-Star Game Chicago N.L./Silver	2.50
(9g)	1990 All-Star Game, Chicago N.L./Gold	5.00
(10)	1991 All-Star Game, Toronto	1.00
(10s)	1991 All-Star Game, Toronto/Silver	2.50
(10g)	1991 All-Star Game, Toronto/Gold	5.00
(11)	1992 All-Star Game, San Diego	1.00
(11s)	1992 All-Star Game, San Diego/Silver	2.50
(11g)	1992 All-Star Game, San Diego/Gold	5.00
(12)	1993 All-Star Game, Baltimore	1.00
(12s)	1993 All-Star Game, Baltimore/Silver	2.50
(12g)	1993 All-Star Game, Baltimore/Gold	5.00
(13)	1994 All-Star Game, Pittsburgh	1.00
(13s)	1994 All-Star Game, Pittsburgh/Silver	2.50
(13g)	1994 All-Star Game, Pittsburgh/Gold	5.00

Super Skills

These random hobby pack inserts in both Series 1 and 2 are printed on rainbow prismatic foil which features as a background an enlarged version of the front photo. The S.C. and Super Skills logos are printed in gold foil in opposite corners, while the player's name is in blue at bottom-right. Backs repeat the enlarged background image of a close-up foreground photo, while a few words about the player's particular specialties are in white at left. Each card can also be found in a version featuring the Members Only gold-foil seal on front.

		NM/M
Complete Set (20):		30.00
Common Player:		.75
1	Roberto Alomar	1.00
2	Barry Bonds	10.00
3	Jay Buhner	.75
4	Chuck Carr	.75
5	Don Mattingly	5.00
6	Raul Mondesi	.75
7	Tim Salmon	.75
8	Deion Sanders	.75
9	Devon White	.75
10	Mark Whiten	.75
11	Ken Griffey Jr.	7.50
12	Marquis Grissom	.75
13	Paul O'Neill	.75
14	Kenny Lofton	.75
15	Larry Walker	.75
16	Scott Cooper	.75
17	Barry Larkin	.75
18	Matt Williams	.75
19	John Wetteland	.75
20	Randy Johnson	2.50

Virtual Reality

A partial parallel set found one per foil pack, two per rack pack, these cards share the basic front and back with the corresponding card in the regular S.C. issue. On front, however, is a "Virtual Reality" seal around the team logo at bottom (gold foil in Series 1, silver-foil in Series 2). Backs differ in that instead of actual 1994 season stats, they present a bar graph of computer projected stats representing a full 162-game season instead of the strike-shortened reality. Each of these inserts can also be found in a version bearing the round gold- (Series 1) or silver-foil (Series 2) Members Only seal on the front.

		NM/M
Complete Set (270):		35.00
Common Player:		.10
1	Cal Ripken Jr.	2.50
2	Travis Fryman	.10
3	Jim Abbott	.10
4	Gary Gaetti	.10
5	Roger Clemens	1.25
6	Carlos Garcia	.10
7	Lee Smith	.10
8	Bobby Ayala	.10
9	Charles Nagy	.10
10	Rene Arocha	.10
11	Carlos Delgado	.50
12	Steve Finley	.10
13	Ryan Klesko	.10
14	Cal Eldred	.10
15	Rey Sanchez	.10
16	Ken Hill	.10
17	Jose Vizcaino	.10
18	Andy Benes	.10
19	Shawon Dunston	.10
20	Rafael Palmeiro	.65
21	Dean Palmer	.10
22	Joey Cora	.10
23	Mickey Tettleton	.10
24	Barry Larkin	.10
25	Carlos Baerga	.10
26	Orel Hershiser	.10
27	Jody Reed	.10
28	Paul Molitor	.75
29	Jim Edmonds	.10
30	Bob Tewksbury	.10
31	Ray McDavid	.10
32	Stan Javier	.10
33	Todd Worrell	.10
34	Bob Wickman	.10
35	Raul Mondesi	.10
36	Rod Beck	.10
37	Jeff Kent	.10
38	John Valentin	.10
39	Ozzie Smith	1.00
40	Terry Pendleton	.10
41	Kenny Rogers	.10
42	Vince Coleman	.10
43	Roberto Alomar	.20
44	Darrin Jackson	.10
45	Dennis Eckersley	.65
46	Jay Buhner	.10
47	Dave Weathers	.10
48	Danny Bautista	.10
49	Bob Hamelin	.10
50	Steve Trachsel	.10
51	Ben McDonald	.10
52	Wade Boggs	1.00
53	Sandy Alomar	.10
54	Ron Karkovice	.10
55	Doug Jones	.10
56	Gary Sheffield	.40
57	Ken Caminiti	.10
58	Kevin Tapani	.10
59	Ruben Sierra	.10
60	Bobby Bonilla	.10
61	Deion Sanders	.10
62	Charlie Hayes	.10
63	Paul O'Neill	.10
64	Jay Bell	.10
65	Todd Jones	.10
66	Todd Stottlemyre	.10
67	Will Clark	.10
68	Wilson Alvarez	.10
69	Chili Davis	.10
70	Chris Hoiles	.10
71	Bret Saberhagen	.10
72	Dave Nilsson	.10
73	Derek Bell	.10
74	Juan Gonzalez	.40
75	Andre Dawson	.30
76	Jim Thome	.65
77	Larry Walker	.10
78	Mike Piazza	1.50
79	Dan Wilson	.10
80	Junior Felix	.10
81	Jack McDowell	.10
82	Danny Tartabull	.10
83	William Van Landingham	.10
84	Robb Nen	.10
85	Ismael Valdes	.10
86	Juan Guzman	.10
87	Cliff Floyd	.10
88	Rico Brogna	.10
89	Luis Polonia	.10
90	Lance Johnson	.10
91	Sammy Sosa	1.00
92	Dave West	.10
93	Tom Glavine	.35
94	Joe Girardi	.10
95	Craig Biggio	.10
96	Eddie Murray	.75
97	Kevin Gross	.10
98	John Franco	.10
99	Matt Williams	.10
100	Darrin Fletcher	.10
101	Jeff Conine	.10
102	Ed Sprague	.10
103	Ivan Rodriguez	.65
104	Orlando Merced	.10
105	Ricky Bones	.10
106	David Cone	.10
107	Todd Hundley	.10
108	Alex Cole	.10
109	Tony Phillips	.10
110	Jim Eisenreich	.10
111	Paul Sorrento	.10
112	Mike Stanley	.10
113	Doug Drabek	.10
114	Matt Mieske	.10
115	Tino Martinez	.10
116	Midre Cummings	.10
117	Hal Morris	.10
118	Shawn Green	.40
119	Randy Myers	.10
120	Ken Griffey Jr.	1.50
121	Brett Butler	.10
122	Julio Franco	.10
123	Chuck Knoblauch	.10
124	Bret Boone	.10
125	Wil Cordero	.10
126	Luis Gonzalez	.10
127	Tim Wallach	.10
128	Scott Sanders	.10
129	Tom Henke	.10
130	Otis Nixon	.10
131	Darren Daulton	.10
132	Manny Ramirez	.75
133	Bret Barberie	.10
134	Brady Anderson	.10
135	Shane Reynolds	.10
136	Barry Bonds	2.50
137	Alex Fernandez	.10
138	Brian McRae	.10
139	Todd Zeile	.10
140	Greg Swindell	.10
141	Troy Neel	.10
142	Eric Karros	.10
143	John Hudek	.10
144	Joe Carter	.10
145	Mike Devereaux	.10
146	Butch Henry	.10
147	Mark Lemke	.10
148	Jeff Montgomery	.10
149	Ryan Thompson	.10
150	Bernie Williams	.10
151	Scott Leius	.10
152	Greg Gagne	.10
153	Moises Alou	.10
154	Geronimo Berroa	.10
155	Alan Trammell	.10
156	Don Slaught	.10
157	Jose Rijo	.10
158	Tim Raines	.10
159	Melido Perez	.10
160	Kent Mercker	.10
161	James Mouton	.10
162	Luis Lopez	.10
163	Mike Kingery	.10
164	Cecil Fielder	.10
165	Scott Kamieniecki	.10
166	Brent Gates	.10
167	Jason Jacome	.10
168	Dante Bichette	.10
169	Kurt Abbott	.10
170	Mike Henneman	.10
171	John Kruk	.10
172	Jose Oliva	.10
173	Reggie Sanders	.10
174	Omar Vizquel	.10
175	Devon White	.10
176	Mark McGwire	2.00
177	Gary DiSarcina	.10
178	Joey Hamilton	.10
179	Randy Johnson	.75
180	Jim Leyritz	.10
181	Bobby Jones	.10
182	Bip Roberts	.10
183	Jose Canseco	.40
184	Mo Vaughn	.10
185	Edgar Martinez	.10
186	Tommy Greene	.10
187	Chuck Carr	.10
188	Pedro Astacio	.10
189	Shane Mack	.10
190	Fred McGriff	.10
191	Pat Rapp	.10
192	Bill Swift	.10
193	Robin Ventura	.10
194	Bobby Witt	.10
195	Steve Howe	.10
196	Leo Gomez	.10
197	Hector Fajardo	.10
198	Jeff Bagwell	.75
199	Rondell White	.10
200	Don Mattingly	1.25
201	Trevor Hoffman	.10
202	Chris Gomez	.10
203	Bobby Munoz	.10
204	Marvin Freeman	.10
205	Sean Berry	.10
206	Mark Grace	.10
207	Pat Kelly	.10
208	Eddie Williams	.10
209	Frank Thomas	.75
210	Bryan Eversgerd	.10
211	Phil Plantier	.10
212	Roberto Kelly	.10
213	Rickey Henderson	.75
214	John Smiley	.10
215	Kevin Brown	.10
216	Jimmy Key	.10
217	Wally Joyner	.10
218	Roberto Hernandez	.10
219	Felix Fermin	.10
220	Greg Vaughn	.10
221	Ray Lankford	.10
222	Greg Maddux	1.00
223	Mike Mussina	.30
224	David Nied	.10
225	Scott Erickson	.10
226	Kevin Mitchell	.10
227	Brian Anderson	.10
228	Jeff King	.10
229	Ramon Martinez	.10
230	Kevin Seitzer	.10
231	Marquis Grissom	.10
232	Chuck Finley	.10
233	Len Dykstra	.10
234	Ellis Burks	.10
235	Harold Baines	.10
236	Kevin Appier	.10
237	Dave Justice	.10
238	Darryl Kile	.10
239	John Olerud	.10
240	Greg McMichael	.10
241	Kirby Puckett	1.00
242	Jose Valentin	.10
243	Rick Wilkins	.10
244	Pat Hentgen	.10
245	Tom Gordon	.10
246	Tom Candiotti	.10
247	Jason Bere	.10
248	Wes Chamberlain	.10
249	Jeff Cirillo	.10
250	Kevin Foster	.10
251	Mark Whiten	.10
252	Terry Steinbach	.10
253	Aaron Sele	.10
254	Kirt Manwaring	.10
255	Delino DeShields	.10
256	Andujar Cedeno	.10
257	Kenny Lofton	.10
258	John Wetteland	.10
259	Tim Salmon	.10
260	Denny Neagle	.10
261	Tony Gwynn	1.00
262	Lou Whitaker	.10
263	J.T. Snow	.10
264	Dennis Martinez	.10
265	Pedro Martinez	.75
266	Rusty Greer	.10
267	Dave Fleming	.10
268	John Dettmer	.10

269	Albert Belle	.10
270	Henry Rodriguez	.10

VR Extremist

A huge silver-blue metallic baseball separates the player from the background of the photo in this Series 2 insert found only in rack packs. A blue sky and clouds provides the front border. The player rises out of the clouds in a back photo in the foreground of which are some pie-in-the-sky stats. The metallic baseball is also repeated on the back, with the player's name in orange script on the sweet spot. Each card was also issued in the Members Only boxed set in a version with a round silver-foil Members Only seal on front. Cards are numbered with a "VRE" prefix.

		NM/M
Complete Set (10):		25.00
Common Player:		1.50
1	Barry Bonds	7.50
2	Ken Griffey Jr.	6.00
3	Jeff Bagwell	3.50
4	Albert Belle	1.50
5	Frank Thomas	3.50
6	Tony Gwynn	4.50
7	Kenny Lofton	1.50
8	Deion Sanders	1.50
9	Ken Hill	1.50
10	Jimmy Key	1.50

Super Team Division Winners

Persons who saved 1994 Topps Stadium Club Super Team cards for the 1995 divisional winners in Major League Baseball's new playoff format were able to redeem them for a set of 10 SC cards of that team's players with a special gold-foil division series logo on front. The cards are otherwise identical to the regular-issue '95 SC versions. Included in the cello-wrapped team set was a Super Team card with the gold logo on front and a white "REDEEMED" across the back.

		NM/M
Complete Set (66):		25.00
Common Player:		.15
Atlanta Braves Team Set		7.00
1	Atlanta Braves Super Team	.30
19	Ryan Klesko	.15
128	Mark Wohlers	.15
151	Steve Avery	.15
183	Tom Glavine	.60
200	Javy Lopez	.15
393	Fred McGriff	.15
397	John Smoltz	.15
425	Greg Maddux	3.00
446	David Justice	.15
543	Chipper Jones	3.00
Boston Red Sox Team Set		4.50
16	Boston Red Sox Super Team	.30
10	Roger Clemens	3.25
62	John Valentin	.15
121	Mike Greenwell	.15
160	Lee Tinsley	.15
347	Jose Canseco	1.25
350	Mo Vaughn	.15
395	Tim Naehring	.15
464	Aaron Sele	.15
530	Mike MacFarlane	.15
600	Troy O'Leary	.15
Cincinnati Red Team Set		1.50
3	Cincinnati Reds Super Team	.30
35	Barry Larkin	.15
231	Hal Morris	.15
252	Bret Boone	.15
280	Thomas Howard	.15
300	Jose Rijo	.15
333	Reggie Sanders	.15
392	Hector Carrasco	.15
416	John Smiley	.15
528	Ron Gant	.15
566	Benito Santiago	.15
Cleveland Indians Team Set		4.50
19	Cleveland Indians Super Team	2.00
36	Carlos Baerga	.15
147	Jim Thome	1.50
186	Eddie Murray	2.00
264	Manny Ramirez	2.00
334	Omar Vizquel	.15
470	Kenny Lofton	.15
484	Dennis Martinez	.15
489	Albert Belle	.15
550	Jose Mesa	.15
562	Orel Hershiser	.15
Los Angeles Dodgers Team Set		7.00
7	Los Angeles Dodgers Super Team	.30
57	Raul Mondesi	.15
149	Mike Piazza	4.00
161	Ismael Valdez	.15
242	Brett Butler	.15
259	Tim Wallach	.15
278	Eric Karros	.15
434	Ramon Martinez	.15
456	Tom Candiotti	.15
467	Delino DeShields	.15
556	Hideo Nomo	1.00
Seattle Mariners Team Set		6.50
26	Seattle Mariners Super Team	.30
73	Jay Buhner	.15
92	Chris Bosio	.15
152	Dan Wilson	.15
227	Tino Martinez	.15
241	Ken Griffey Jr.	4.00
340	Randy Johnson	2.00
354	Edgar Martinez	.15
421	Felix Fermin	.15
494	Mike Blowers	.15
536	Joey Cora	.15

League Champion Master Photos

Persons who held onto Braves and Indians Super Team insert cards from the 1994 Stadium Club issue could redeem them following the 1995 season for special Master Photos team sets of the League Champions. Each team set included 10 player cards and a Super Team card with special gold-foil League Champion logos on the fronts. The player cards are in 5" x 7" format with the player's 1995 SC card in the center of a blue background. Backs are in black-and-white with a card number and appropriate logos and copyright. The Super Team card is 2-1/2" x 3-1/2" with a white "REDEEMED" notice overprinted on back.

		NM/M
Complete Set (22):		15.00
Common Player:		.35
Atlanta Braves Team Set		9.00
1	Steve Avery	.40
2	Tom Glavine	.75
3	Chipper Jones	3.00
4	David Justice	.40
5	Ryan Klesko	.40
6	Javy Lopez	.40
7	Greg Maddux	3.00
8	Fred McGriff	.40
9	John Smoltz	.40
10	Mark Wohlers	.40
1	Atlanta Braves Super Team	.40
Cleveland Indians Team Set		7.50
11	Carlos Baerga	.40
12	Albert Belle	.40
13	Orel Hershiser	.40
14	Kenny Lofton	.40
15	Dennis Martinez	.40
16	Jose Mesa	.40
17	Eddie Murray	2.50
18	Manny Ramirez	2.50
19	Jim Thome	2.00
20	Omar Vizquel	.40
19	Cleveland Indians Super Team	.40

World Series Winners

Persons who redeemed a 1994 Stadium Club Atlanta Braves Super Team insert following the Tribe's 1995 World Series victory received a set of 1995 Stadium Club cards, each of which bears a gold-foil World's Series logo on front. The cards are otherwise identical to the regular-issue SC cards. The prize "set" contains only 585 cards, a note sent with the set explains 45 of the TSC cards - #496-523 (the Extreme Corps subset) and cards #614-630 (the Trans-Action subset) were not printed in the parallel version.

	NM/M
Complete Set (585):	40.00
Common Player:	.25
Stars:	3X

Members Only

A special version of all of the regular cards from Stadium Club Series I-III, as well as many of the insert sets was offered to members of Topps' Stadium Club. Virtually identical to the regular S.C. cards, the specially boxed set differs in the presence on each card front of an embossed round 1/2" gold-foil "Members Only" seal. Even the plastic Clear Cut inserts have the members' seal embossed directly into the plastic. The edition was limited to 4,000 sets.

	NM/M
Complete Set (630):	150.00
Common Player:	.25
Stars:	6X
Inserts: 50-100 Percent	

Members Only Baseball

This boxed set was sold exclusively through the newsletter for Topps Stadium Club members. Cards feature noteworthy performances and achievements of the 1994 baseball season. Borderless card fronts have a player action photo on which the background has been quartered in colors of blue, green, orange and magenta. The Members Only logo, and player name and position are presented in gold foil. Backs have another player photo at left and a description of the highlight printed in white on a blue background at right. Both front and back of each card are UV coated. The final five cards in the set are printed in Topps Finest technology and feature the company's choice of the top rookies of 1994.

		NM/M
Complete Set (50):		9.00
Common Player:		.20
1	Moises Alou	.20
2	Jeff Bagwell	.75
3	Albert Belle	.20
4	Andy Benes	.20
5	Dante Bichette	.20
6	Craig Biggio	.20
7	Wade Boggs	1.00
8	Barry Bonds	3.00
9	Brett Butler	.20
10	Jose Canseco	.50
11	Joe Carter	.20
12	Vince Coleman	.20
13	Jeff Conine	.20
14	Cecil Fielder	.20
15	John Franco	.20
16	Julio Franco	.20
17	Travis Fryman	.20
18	Andres Galarraga	.20
19	Ken Griffey Jr.	1.50
20	Marquis Grissom	.20
21	Tony Gwynn	1.00
22	Ken Hill	.20
23	Randy Johnson	.75
24	Lance Johnson	.20
25	Jimmy Key	.20
26	Chuck Knoblauch	.20
27	Ray Lankford	.20
28	Darren Lewis	.20
29	Kenny Lofton	.20
30	Greg Maddux	1.00
31	Fred McGriff	.20
32	Kevin Mitchell	.20
33	Paul Molitor	.75
34	Hal Morris	.20
35	Paul O'Neill	.20
36	Rafael Palmeiro	.65
37	Tony Phillips	.20
38	Mike Piazza	1.50
39	Kirby Puckett	1.00
40	Cal Ripken Jr.	3.00
41	Deion Sanders	.20
42	Lee Smith	.20
43	Frank Thomas	.75
44	Larry Walker	.20
45	Matt Williams	.20
46	Manny Ramirez (Rookie Picks)	1.00
47	Joey Hamilton (Rookie Picks)	.20
48	Raul Mondesi (Rookie Picks)	.20
49	Bob Hamelin (Rookie Picks)	.20
50	Ryan Klesko (Rookie Picks)	.20

1996 Stadium Club

Consisting of 450 cards in a pair of 225-card series, Stadium Club continued Topps' 1996 tribute to Mickey Mantle with 19 Retrospective inserts. Cards feature full-bleed photos with gold-foil graphic highlights. Backs offer a TSC Skills Matrix along with another player photo, some biographical data and stats. Team TSC is the only subset with 45 cards each in Series 1 and 2. Stadium Club was issued in retail and hobby packs, with inserts found at differing ratios in each type of packaging.

		NM/M
Complete Set (450):		25.00
Common Player:		.05
Series 1 or 2 Pack (10):		1.00
Series 1 or 2 Wax Box (24):		20.00
1	Hideo Nomo (Extreme Player)	.40
2	Paul Molitor	.75
3	Garret Anderson (Extreme Player)	.05
4	Jose Mesa (Extreme Player)	.05
5	Vinny Castilla (Extreme Player)	.05
6	Mike Mussina (Extreme Player)	.30
7	Ray Durham (Extreme Player)	.05
8	Jack McDowell (Extreme Player)	.05
9	Juan Gonzalez (Extreme Player)	.40
10	Chipper Jones (Extreme Player)	1.00
11	Deion Sanders (Extreme Player)	.05
12	Rondell White (Extreme Player)	.05
13	Tom Henke (Extreme Player)	.05
14	Derek Bell (Extreme Player)	.05
15	Randy Myers (Extreme Player)	.05
16	Randy Johnson (Extreme Player)	.75
17	Len Dykstra (Extreme Player)	.05
18	Bill Pulsipher (Extreme Player)	.05
19	Greg Colbrunn	.05
20	David Wells	.05
21	Chad Curtis (Extreme Player)	.05
22	Roberto Hernandez (Extreme Player)	.05
23	Kirby Puckett (Extreme Player)	1.00
24	Joe Vitiello	.05
25	Roger Clemens (Extreme Player)	1.25
26	Al Martin	.05
27	Chad Ogea	.05
28	David Segui	.05
29	Joey Hamilton	.05
30	Dan Wilson	.05
31	Chad Fonville (Extreme Player)	.05
32	Bernard Gilkey (Extreme Player)	.05
33	Kevin Seitzer	.05
34	Shawn Green (Extreme Player)	.35
35	Rick Aguilera (Extreme Player)	.05
36	Gary DiSarcina	.05
37	Jaime Navarro	.05
38	Doug Jones	.05
39	Brent Gates	.05
40	Dean Palmer (Extreme Player)	.05
41	Pat Rapp	.05
42	Tony Clark	.05
43	Bill Swift	.05
44	Randy Velarde	.05
45	Matt Williams (Extreme Player)	.05
46	John Mabry	.05
47	Mike Fetters	.05
48	Orlando Miller	.05
49	Tom Glavine (Extreme Player)	.35
50	Delino DeShields (Extreme Player)	.05
51	Scott Erickson	.05
52	Andy Van Slyke	.05
53	Jim Bullinger	.05
54	Lyle Mouton	.05
55	Bret Saberhagen	.05
56	Benito Santiago (Extreme Player)	.05
57	Dan Miceli	.05
58	Carl Everett	.05
59	Rod Beck (Extreme Player)	.05
60	Phil Nevin	.05
61	Jason Giambi	.50
62	Paul Menhart	.05
63	Eric Karros (Extreme Player)	.05
64	Allen Watson	.05
65	Jeff Cirillo	.05
66	Lee Smith (Extreme Player)	.05
67	Sean Berry	.05
68	Luis Sojo	.05
69	Jeff Montgomery (Extreme Player)	.05
70	Todd Hundley (Extreme Player)	.05
71	John Burkett	.05
72	Mark Gubicza	.05
73	Don Mattingly (Extreme Player)	1.25
74	Jeff Brantley	.05
75	Matt Walbeck	.05
76	Steve Parris	.05
77	Ken Caminiti (Extreme Player)	.05
78	Kirt Manwaring	.05
79	Greg Vaughn	.05
80	Pedro Martinez (Extreme Player)	.75
81	Benji Gil	.05
82	Heathcliff Slocumb (Extreme Player)	.05
83	Joe Girardi (Extreme Player)	.05
84	Sean Bergman	.05
85	Matt Karchner	.05
86	Butch Huskey	.05
87	Mike Morgan	.05
88	Todd Worrell (Extreme Player)	.05
89	Mike Bordick	.05
90	Bip Roberts (Extreme Player)	.05
91	Mike Hampton	.05
92	Troy O'Leary	.05
93	Wally Joyner	.05
94	Dave Stevens	.05
95	Cecil Fielder (Extreme Player)	.05
96	Wade Boggs (Extreme Player)	1.00
97	Hal Morris	.05
98	Mickey Tettleton (Extreme Player)	.05
99	Jeff Kent (Extreme Player)	.05
100	Denny Martinez	.05
101	Luis Gonzalez (Extreme Player)	.05
102	John Jaha	.05
103	Javy Lopez (Extreme Player)	.05
104	Mark McGwire (Extreme Player)	2.00
105	Ken Griffey Jr. (Extreme Player)	1.50
106	Darren Daulton (Extreme Player)	.05
107	Bryan Rekar	.05
108	Mike Macfarlane (Extreme Player)	.05
109	Gary Gaetti (Extreme Player)	.05
110	Shane Reynolds (Extreme Player)	.05
111	Pat Meares	.05
112	Jason Schmidt	.05
113	Otis Nixon	.05
114	John Franco (Extreme Player)	.05
115	Marc Newfield	.05
116	Andy Benes (Extreme Player)	.05
117	Ozzie Guillen	.05
118	Brian Jordan (Extreme Player)	.05
119	Terry Pendleton (Extreme Player)	.05
120	Chuck Finley (Extreme Player)	.05
121	Scott Stahoviak	.05
122	Sid Fernandez	.05

123 Derek Jeter (Extreme Player) 3.00
124 John Smiley (Extreme Player) .05
125 David Bell .05
126 Brett Butler (Extreme Player) .05
127 Doug Drabek (Extreme Player) .05
128 J.T. Snow (Extreme Player) .05
129 Joe Carter (Extreme Player) .05
130 Dennis Eckersley (Extreme Player) .65
131 Marty Cordova (Extreme Player) .05
132 Greg Maddux (Extreme Player) 1.00
133 Tom Goodwin .05
134 Andy Ashby .05
135 Paul Sorrento (Extreme Player) .05
136 Ricky Bones .05
137 Shawon Dunston (Extreme Player) .05
138 Moises Alou (Extreme Player) .05
139 Mickey Morandini .05
140 Ramon Martinez (Extreme Player) .05
141 Royce Clayton (Extreme Player) .05
142 Brad Ausmus .05
143 Kenny Rogers (Extreme Player) .05
144 Tim Naehring (Extreme Player) .05
145 Chris Gomez (Extreme Player) .05
146 Bobby Bonilla (Extreme Player) .05
147 Wilson Alvarez .05
148 Johnny Damon (Extreme Player) .35
149 Pat Hentgen .05
150 Andres Galarraga (Extreme Player) .05
151 David Cone (Extreme Player) .05
152 Lance Johnson (Extreme Player) .05
153 Carlos Garcia .05
154 Doug Johns .05
155 Midre Cummings .05
156 Steve Sparks .05
157 Sandy Martinez **RC** .05
158 William Van Landingham .05
159 Dave Justice (Extreme Player) .05
160 Mark Grace (Extreme Player) .05
161 Robb Nen (Extreme Player) .05
162 Mike Greenwell (Extreme Player) .05
163 Brad Radke .05
164 Edgardo Alfonzo .05
165 Mark Leiter .05
166 Walt Weiss .05
167 Mel Rojas (Extreme Player) .05
168 Bret Boone (Extreme Player) .05
169 Ricky Bottalico .05
170 Bobby Higginson .05
171 Trevor Hoffman .05
172 Jay Bell (Extreme Player) .05
173 Gabe White .05
174 Curtis Goodwin .05
175 Tyler Green .05
176 Roberto Alomar (Extreme Player) .20
177 Sterling Hitchcock .05
178 Ryan Klesko (Extreme Player) .05
179 Donne Wall **RC** .05
180 Brian McRae .05
181 Will Clark (Team TSC) .05
182 Frank Thomas (Team TSC) .60
183 Jeff Bagwell (Team TSC) .60
184 Mo Vaughn (Team TSC) .05
185 Tino Martinez (Team TSC) .05
186 Craig Biggio (Team TSC) .05
187 Chuck Knoblauch (Team TSC) .05
188 Carlos Baerga (Team TSC) .05
189 Quilvio Veras (Team TSC) .05
190 Luis Alicea (Team TSC) .05
191 Jim Thome (Team TSC) .40
192 Mike Blowers (Team TSC) .05
193 Robin Ventura (Team TSC) .05
194 Jeff King (Team TSC) .05
195 Tony Phillips (Team TSC) .05
196 John Valentin (Team TSC) .05
197 Barry Larkin (Team TSC) .05
198 Cal Ripken Jr. (Team TSC) 2.00
199 Omar Vizquel (Team TSC) .05
200 Kurt Abbott (Team TSC) .05
201 Albert Belle (Team TSC) .05
202 Barry Bonds (Team TSC) 2.00
203 Ron Gant (Team TSC) .05
204 Dante Bichette (Team TSC) .05
205 Jeff Conine (Team TSC) .05
206 Jim Edmonds (Team TSC) .05
207 Stan Javier (Team TSC) .05
208 Kenny Lofton (Team TSC) .05
209 Ray Lankford (Team TSC) .05
210 Bernie Williams (Team TSC) .05
211 Jay Buhner (Team TSC) .05
212 Paul O'Neill (Team TSC) .05
213 Tim Salmon (Team TSC) .05
214 Reggie Sanders (Team TSC) .05
215 Manny Ramirez (Team TSC) .60
216 Mike Piazza (Team TSC) 1.50
217 Mike Stanley (Team TSC) .05
218 Tony Eusebio (Team TSC) .05
219 Chris Hoiles (Team TSC) .05
220 Ron Karkovice (Team TSC) .05
221 Edgar Martinez (Team TSC) .05
222 Chili Davis (Team TSC) .05
223 Jose Canseco (Team TSC) .35
224 Eddie Murray (Team TSC) .60
225 Geronimo Berroa (Team TSC) .05
226 Chipper Jones (Team TSC) .75
227 Garret Anderson (Team TSC) .05
228 Marty Cordova (Team TSC) .05
229 Jon Nunnally (Team TSC) .05
230 Brian Hunter (Team TSC) .05
231 Shawn Green (Team TSC) .20
232 Ray Durham (Team TSC) .05
233 Alex Gonzalez (Team TSC) .05
234 Bobby Higginson (Team TSC) .05
235 Randy Johnson (Team TSC) .60
236 Al Leiter (Team TSC) .05
237 Tom Glavine (Team TSC) .10
238 Kenny Rogers (Team TSC) .05
239 Mike Hampton (Team TSC) .05
240 David Wells (Team TSC) .05
241 Jim Abbott (Team TSC) .05
242 Denny Neagle (Team TSC) .05
243 Wilson Alvarez (Team TSC) .05
244 John Smiley (Team TSC) .05
245 Greg Maddux (Team TSC) .75
246 Andy Ashby (Team TSC) .05
247 Hideo Nomo (Team TSC) .30
248 Pat Rapp (Team TSC) .05
249 Tim Wakefield (Team TSC) .05
250 John Smoltz (Team TSC) .05
251 Joey Hamilton (Team TSC) .05
252 Frank Castillo (Team TSC) .05
253 Denny Martinez (Team TSC) .05
254 Jaime Navarro (Team TSC) .05
255 Karim Garcia (Team TSC) .05
256 Bob Abreu (Team TSC) .05
257 Butch Huskey (Team TSC) .05
258 Ruben Rivera (Team TSC) .05
259 Johnny Damon (Team TSC) .20
260 Derek Jeter (Team TSC) 2.00
261 Dennis Eckersley (Team TSC) .50
262 Jose Mesa (Team TSC) .05
263 Tom Henke (Team TSC) .05
264 Rick Aguilera (Team TSC) .05
265 Randy Myers (Team TSC) .05
266 John Franco (Team TSC) .05
267 Jeff Brantley (Team TSC) .05
268 John Wetteland (Team TSC) .05
269 Mark Wohlers (Team TSC) .05
270 Rod Beck (Team TSC) .05
271 Barry Larkin .05
272 Paul O'Neill .05
273 Bobby Jones .05
274 Will Clark .05
275 Steve Avery .05
276 Jim Edmonds .05
277 John Olerud .05
278 Carlos Perez .05
279 Chris Hoiles .05
280 Jeff Conine .05
281 Jim Eisenreich .05
282 Jason Jacome .05
283 Ray Lankford .05
284 John Wasdin .05
285 Frank Thomas .75
286 Jason Isringhausen .05
287 Glenallen Hill .05
288 Esteban Loaiza .05
289 Bernie Williams .05
290 Curtis Leskanic .05
291 Scott Cooper .05
292 Curt Schilling .35
293 Eddie Murray .75
294 Rick Krivda .05
295 Domingo Cedeno .05
296 Jeff Fassero .05
297 Albert Belle .05
298 Craig Biggio .05
299 Fernando Vina .05
300 Edgar Martinez .05
301 Tony Gwynn 1.00
302 Felipe Lira .05
303 Mo Vaughn .05
304 Alex Fernandez .05
305 Keith Lockhart .05
306 Roger Pavlik .05
307 Lee Tinsley .05
308 Omar Vizquel .05
309 Scott Servais .05
310 Danny Tartabull .05
311 Chili Davis .05
312 Cal Eldred .05
313 Roger Cedeno .05
314 Chris Hammond .05
315 Rusty Greer .05
316 Brady Anderson .05
317 Ron Villone .05
318 Mark Carreon .05
319 Larry Walker .05
320 Pete Harnisch .05
321 Robin Ventura .05
322 Tim Belcher .05
323 Tony Tarasco .05
324 Juan Guzman .05
325 Kenny Lofton .05
326 Kevin Foster .05
327 Wil Cordero .05
328 Troy Percival .05
329 Turk Wendell .05
330 Thomas Howard .05
331 Carlos Baerga .05
332 B.J. Surhoff .05
333 Jay Buhner .05
334 Andujar Cedeno .05
335 Jeff King .05
336 Dante Bichette .05
337 Alan Trammell .05
338 Scott Leius .05
339 Chris Snopek .05
340 Roger Bailey .05
341 Jacob Brumfield .05
342 Jose Canseco .50
343 Rafael Palmeiro .65
344 Quilvio Veras .05
345 Darrin Fletcher .05
346 Carlos Delgado .50
347 Tony Eusebio .05
348 Ismael Valdes .05
349 Terry Steinbach .05
350 Orel Hershiser .05
351 Kurt Abbott .05
352 Jody Reed .05
353 David Howard .05
354 Ruben Sierra .05
355 John Ericks .05
356 Buck Showalter .05
357 Jim Thome .65
358 Geronimo Berroa .05
359 Robby Thompson .05
360 Jose Vizcaino .05
361 Jeff Frye .05
362 Kevin Appier .05
363 Pat Kelly .05
364 Ron Gant .05
365 Luis Alicea .05
366 Armando Benitez .05
367 Rico Brogna .05
368 Manny Ramirez .75
369 Mike Lansing .05
370 Sammy Sosa 1.00
371 Don Wengert .05
372 Dave Nilsson .05
373 Sandy Alomar .05
374 Joey Cora .05
375 Larry Thomas .05
376 John Valentin .05
377 Kevin Ritz .05
378 Steve Finley .05
379 Frank Rodriguez .05
380 Ivan Rodriguez .65
381 Alex Ochoa .05
382 Mark Lemke .05
383 Scott Brosius .05
384 James Mouton .05
385 Mark Langston .05
386 Ed Sprague .05
387 Joe Oliver .05
388 Steve Ontiveros .05
389 Rey Sanchez .05
390 Mike Henneman .05
391 Jose Valentin **RC** .05
392 Tom Candiotti .05
393 Damon Buford .05
394 Erik Hanson .05
395 Mark Smith .05
396 Pete Schourek .05
397 John Flaherty .05
398 Dave Martinez .05
399 Tommy Greene .05
400 Gary Sheffield .45
401 Glenn Dishman .05
402 Barry Bonds 3.00
403 Tom Pagnozzi .05
404 Todd Stottlemyre .05
405 Tim Salmon .05
406 John Hudek .05
407 Fred McGriff .05
408 Orlando Merced .05
409 Brian Barber .05
410 Ryan Thompson .05
411 Mariano Rivera .10
412 Eric Young .05
413 Chris Bosio .05
414 Chuck Knoblauch .05
415 Jamie Moyer .05
416 Chan Ho Park .05
417 Mark Portugal .05
418 Tim Raines .05
419 Antonio Osuna .05
420 Todd Zeile .05
421 Steve Wojciechowski .05
422 Marquis Grissom .05
423 Norm Charlton .05
424 Cal Ripken Jr. 3.00
425 Gregg Jefferies .05
426 Mike Stanton .05
427 Tony Fernandez .05
428 Jose Rijo .05
429 Jeff Bagwell .75
430 Raul Mondesi .05
431 Travis Fryman .05
432 Ron Karkovice .05
433 Alan Benes .05
434 Tony Phillips .05
435 Reggie Sanders .05
436 Andy Pettitte .25
437 Matt Lawton **RC** .25
438 Jeff Blauser .05
439 Michael Tucker .05
440 Mark Loretta .05
441 Charlie Hayes .05
442 Mike Piazza 1.50
443 Shane Andrews .05
444 Jeff Suppan .05
445 Steve Rodriguez .05
446 Mike Matheny .05
447 Trenidad Hubbard .05
448 Denny Hocking .05
449 Mark Grudzielanek .05
450 Joe Randa .05

Mickey Mantle "Cereal Box" Set

This factory-set version of TSC was packaged in boxes which resembled single-serving cereal boxes. The cards are identical to the regular TSC version except for the use of silver-foil, rather than gold-foil, highlights on front.

NM/M
Unopened Set: 30.00
Common Player: .10

Extreme Player

A special interactive version of 179 players' cards in 1996 Stadium Club was issued as an insert set across Series 1 and 2. Specially stamped with an "Extreme Player" logo in bronze (1 per 12 packs average), silver (1:24) or gold (1:48), the cards have backs which detail a contest by which the player's on-field performance was used to rank each by position. At season's end, cards of the winning players at each position could be redeemed for special prizes. The contest cards do not have card numbers on back and are numbered here based on the regular version.

NM/M
Complete Bronze Set (179): 40.00
Common Bronze: .10
Silvers: 1.5X
Golds: 2.5X
1 Hideo Nomo .50
3 Garret Anderson .10
4 Jose Mesa .10
5 Vinny Castilla .10
6 Mike Mussina .30
7 Ray Durham .10
8 Jack McDowell .10
9 Juan Gonzalez .50
10 Chipper Jones 1.50
11 Deion Sanders .10
12 Rondell White .10
13 Tom Henke .10
14 Derek Bell .10
15 Randy Myers .10
16 Randy Johnson 1.00
17 Len Dykstra .10
18 Bill Pulsipher .10
21 Chad Curtis .10
22 Roberto Hernandez .10
23 Kirby Puckett 1.50
25 Roger Clemens 1.75
31 Chad Fonville .10
32 Bernard Gilkey .10
34 Shawn Green .35
35 Rick Aguilera .10
40 Dean Palmer .10
45 Matt Williams .10
49 Tom Glavine .35
50 Delino DeShields .10
56 Benito Santiago .10
59 Rod Beck .10
63 Eric Karros .10
66 Lee Smith .10
69 Jeff Montgomery .10
70 Todd Hundley .10
73 Don Mattingly 1.75
77 Ken Caminiti .10
80 Pedro Martinez 1.00
82 Heathcliff Slocumb .10
83 Joe Girardi .10
88 Todd Worrell .10
90 Bip Roberts .10
95 Cecil Fielder .10
96 Wade Boggs 1.50
98 Mickey Tettleton .10
99 Jeff Kent .10
101 Luis Gonzalez .10
103 Javier Lopez .10
104 Mark McGwire 3.00
105 Ken Griffey Jr. 2.00
106 Darren Daulton .10
108 Mike Macfarlane .10
109 Gary Gaetti .10
110 Shane Reynolds .10
114 John Franco .10
116 Andy Benes .10
118 Brian Jordan .10
119 Terry Pendleton .10
120 Chuck Finley .10
123 Derek Jeter 4.00
124 John Smiley .10
126 Brett Butler .10
127 Doug Drabek .10
128 J.T. Snow .10
129 Joe Carter .10
130 Dennis Eckersley .75
131 Marty Cordova .10
132 Greg Maddux 1.50
135 Paul Sorrento .10
137 Shawon Dunston .10
138 Moises Alou .10
140 Ramon Martinez .10
141 Royce Clayton .10
143 Kenny Rogers .10
144 Tim Naehring .10
145 Chris Gomez .10
146 Bobby Bonilla .10
148 Johnny Damon .40
150 Andres Galarraga .10
151 David Cone .10
152 Lance Johnson .10
159 Dave Justice .10
160 Mark Grace .10
161 Robb Nen .10
162 Mike Greenwell .10
167 Mel Rojas .10
168 Bret Boone .10
172 Jay Bell .10
176 Roberto Alomar .25
178 Ryan Klesko .10
271 Barry Larkin .10
272 Paul O'Neill .10
274 Will Clark .10
275 Steve Avery .10
276 Jim Edmonds .10
277 John Olerud .10
279 Chris Hoiles .10
280 Jeff Conine .10
283 Ray Lankford .10
285 Frank Thomas 1.00
286 Jason Isringhausen .10
287 Glenallen Hill .10
289 Bernie Williams .10
290 Eddie Murray 1.00
296 Jeff Fassero .10
297 Albert Belle .10
298 Craig Biggio .10
300 Edgar Martinez .10
301 Tony Gwynn 1.50
303 Mo Vaughn .10
304 Alex Fernandez .10
308 Omar Vizquel .10
310 Danny Tartabull .10
316 Brady Anderson .10
319 Larry Walker .10
321 Robin Ventura .10
325 Kenny Lofton .10
327 Wil Cordero .10
328 Troy Percival .10
331 Carlos Baerga .10
333 Jay Buhner .10
335 Jeff King .10
336 Dante Bichette .10
337 Alan Trammell .10
342 Jose Canseco .50
343 Rafael Palmeiro .75
344 Quilvio Veras .10
345 Darrin Fletcher .10
347 Tony Eusebio .10
348 Ismael Valdes .10
349 Terry Steinbach .10
350 Orel Hershiser .10
351 Kurt Abbott .10
354 Ruben Sierra .10
357 Jim Thome .75
358 Geronimo Berroa .10
359 Robby Thompson .10
360 Jose Vizcaino .10
362 Kevin Appier .10
364 Ron Gant .10
367 Rico Brogna .10
368 Manny Ramirez 1.00
370 Sammy Sosa 1.50
373 Sandy Alomar .10
378 Steve Finley .10
380 Ivan Rodriguez .75
382 Mark Lemke .10
385 Mark Langston .10
386 Ed Sprague .10
388 Steve Ontiveros .10
392 Tom Candiotti .10
394 Erik Hanson .10
396 Pete Schourek .10
400 Gary Sheffield .35
402 Barry Bonds 4.00
403 Tom Pagnozzi .10
404 Todd Stottlemyre .10
405 Tim Salmon .10
407 Fred McGriff .10
408 Orlando Merced .10
412 Eric Young .10
414 Chuck Knoblauch .10
417 Mark Portugal .10
418 Tim Raines .10
420 Todd Zeile .10
422 Marquis Grissom .10
423 Norm Charlton .10
424 Cal Ripken Jr. 4.00
425 Gregg Jefferies .10
428 Jose Rijo .10
429 Jeff Bagwell 1.00
430 Raul Mondesi .10
431 Travis Fryman .10
434 Tony Phillips .10
435 Reggie Sanders .10
436 Andy Pettitte .25
438 Jeff Blauser .10
441 Charlie Hayes .10
442 Mike Piazza 2.00

Extreme Player - Bronze Winner

Ten-card sets of these special bronze-foil highlighted cards were the prize for those who redeemed bronze statistical winners' cards from the Stadium Club Extreme Player interactive series. Backs have statistical ratings pertinent to the game and scoring rules. Cards have an "EW" prefix to the number. The same photos and back design were used in different technologies in the bronze, silver and gold winners cards.

		NM/M
Complete Set (10):		6.00
Common Player:		.40
1	Greg Maddux	1.50
2	Mike Piazza	2.00
3	Andres Galarraga	.40
4	Chuck Knoblauch	.40
5	Ken Caminiti	.40
6	Barry Larkin	.40
7	Barry Bonds	3.00
8	Ken Griffey Jr.	2.00
9	Gary Sheffield	.75
10	Todd Worrell	.40

Extreme Player - Silver Winner

Ten-card sets of these Finest technology cards were the prize for those who redeemed statistical winners' cards from the Stadium Club Extreme Player interactive series. Backs have statistical ratings pertinent to the game and scoring rules. Cards have an "EW" prefix to the number.

		NM/M
Complete Set (10):		17.50
Common Player:		.75
1	Greg Maddux	3.00
2	Mike Piazza	4.00
3	Andres Galarraga	.75
4	Chuck Knoblauch	.75
5	Ken Caminiti	.75
6	Barry Larkin	.75
7	Barry Bonds	5.00
8	Ken Griffey Jr.	4.00
9	Gary Sheffield	1.50
10	Todd Worrell	.75

Extreme Player - Gold Winner

One of these large (2-3/4" x 3-3/4"), heavy, acrylic-coated bronze refractor cards was the prize for those who redeemed the same player's gold statistical winners' card from the Stadium Club Extreme Player interactive series. Backs have statistical ratings pertinent to the game and scoring rules. Cards have an "EW" prefix to the number. The same photos and back design were used in different technologies in the bronze, silver and gold winners cards.

		NM/M
Complete Set (10):		45.00
Common Player:		2.00
1	Greg Maddux	8.00
2	Mike Piazza	10.00
3	Andres Galarraga	2.00
4	Chuck Knoblauch	2.00
5	Ken Caminiti	2.00
6	Barry Larkin	2.00
7	Barry Bonds	15.00
8	Ken Griffey Jr.	10.00
9	Gary Sheffield	3.50
10	Todd Worrell	2.00

Bash & Burn

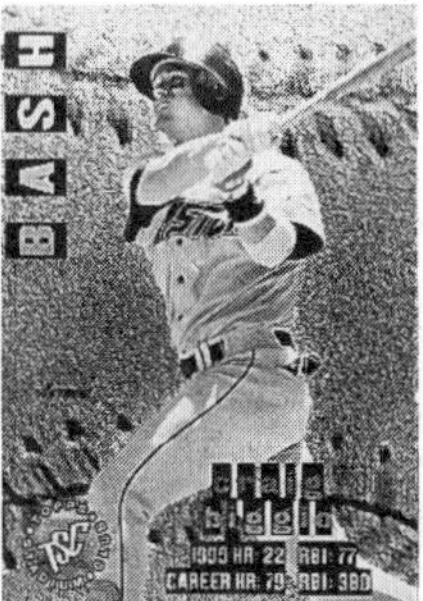

Inserted in one per 24 retail packs and one per 48 hobby packs of Series II, Bash & Burn includes 10 players on double-fronted cards. Both sides are foil-etched with the Bash side highlighting home runs and runs batted in for 1995 and career, and the Burn side featured stolen base and runs scored leaders for 1995 and career. Cards are numbered with a "B&B" prefix.

		NM/M
Complete Set (10):		10.00
Common Player:		.75
1	Sammy Sosa	3.50
2	Barry Bonds	6.00
3	Reggie Sanders	.75
4	Craig Biggio	.75
5	Raul Mondesi	.75
6	Ron Gant	.75
7	Ray Lankford	.75
8	Glenallen Hill	.75
9	Chad Curtis	.75
10	John Valentin	.75

Mickey Mantle Retrospective

Following the success of the Mantle reprints in Topps baseball, Stadium Club produced a series of 19 Mickey Mantle Retrospective inserts; nine black-and-white cards in Series 1 and 10 color cards in Series 2. The cards chronicle Mantle's career and provide insights from baseball contemporaries. The Mantle cards are found on an average of once per 24 Series 1 packs and once per 12 Series 2 packs. Cards are numbered with an "MM" prefix.

		NM/M
Complete Set (19):		35.00
Common Series 1:		4.00
Common Series 2:		2.00
1	Mickey Mantle/1950 (minor league)	4.00
2	Mickey Mantle/1951	4.00
3	Mickey Mantle/1951	4.00
4	Mickey Mantle/1953	4.00
5	Mickey Mantle/1954 (W/ Yogi Berra.)	4.00
6	Mickey Mantle/1956	4.00
7	Mickey Mantle/1957	4.00
8	Mickey Mantle/1958 (W/ Casey Stengel.)	4.00
9	Mickey Mantle/1959	4.00
10	Mickey Mantle/1960 (W/ Elston Howard.)	2.00
11	Mickey Mantle/1961	2.00
12	Mickey Mantle/1961 (W/ Roger Maris.)	4.00
13	Mickey Mantle/1962	2.00
14	Mickey Mantle/1963	2.00
15	Mickey Mantle/1964	2.00
16	Mickey Mantle	2.00
17	Mickey Mantle/1968	2.00
18	Mickey Mantle/1969	2.00
19	Mickey Mantle (In Memoriam)	3.50

Mega Heroes

Ten heroic players are matched with a comic book-style illustration depicting their nicknames in the Mega Heroes insert set. Printed on foilboard in a defraction technology, the cards are found, on average, once per 48 Series 1 hobby packs and twice as often in retail packs.

		NM/M
Complete Set (10):		10.00
Common Player:		1.00
1	Frank Thomas	1.50
2	Ken Griffey Jr.	3.00
3	Hideo Nomo	1.25
4	Ozzie Smith	1.75
5	Will Clark	1.00
6	Jack McDowell	1.00
7	Andres Galarraga	1.00
8	Roger Clemens	2.00
9	Deion Sanders	1.00
10	Mo Vaughn	1.00

Metalists

Eight players who have won two or more major awards in their careers are featured in this Series II insert. Cards are printed on foilboard and feature intricate laser-cut designs that depict the player's face. Metalist inserts are found one per 96 retail and one per 48 hobby packs, on average. Cards are numbered with a "M" prefix.

		NM/M
Complete Set (8):		12.00
Common Player:		1.00
1	Jeff Bagwell	1.25
2	Barry Bonds	3.50
3	Jose Canseco	1.00
4	Roger Clemens	2.50
5	Dennis Eckersley	1.00
6	Greg Maddux	2.00
7	Cal Ripken Jr.	3.50
8	Frank Thomas	1.25

Midsummer Matchups

These inserts salute 1995 National League and American League All-Stars on back-to-back etched-foil cards. Players are matched by position in the 10-card set. Average insertion rate is one per 48 hobby packs and one per 24 retail packs in Series 1. Cards are numbered with an "M" prefix.

		NM/M
Complete Set (10):		20.00
Common Player:		1.00
1	Hideo Nomo, Randy Johnson	2.00
2	Mike Piazza, Ivan Rodriguez	4.00
3	Fred McGriff, Frank Thomas	2.00
4	Craig Biggio, Carlos Baerga	1.00
5	Vinny Castilla, Wade Boggs	2.50
6	Barry Larkin, Cal Ripken Jr.	5.00
7	Barry Bonds, Albert Belle	5.00
8	Len Dykstra, Kenny Lofton	1.00
9	Tony Gwynn, Kirby Puckett	3.00
10	Ron Gant, Edgar Martinez	1.00

Power Packed

Topps' Power Matrix technology is used to showcase 15 of the biggest, strongest players in this Series 2 insert set. Card backs feature a diagram of the player's home park with baseball graphics measuring his home runs during the 1995 season. The inserts are a one in 48 packs pick, on average, both hobby and retail. Cards are numbered with a "PP" prefix.

		NM/M
Complete Set (15):		15.00
Common Player:		1.00
1	Albert Belle	1.00
2	Mark McGwire	4.00
3	Jose Canseco	1.75
4	Mike Piazza	3.00
5	Ron Gant	1.00
6	Ken Griffey Jr.	3.00
7	Mo Vaughn	1.00
8	Cecil Fielder	1.00
9	Tim Salmon	1.00
10	Frank Thomas	2.50
11	Juan Gonzalez	1.50
12	Andres Galarraga	1.00
13	Fred McGriff	1.00
14	Jay Buhner	1.00
15	Dante Bichette	1.00

Power Streak

The best power hitters in baseball are featured in Power Matrix technology on these

Series I inserts. Average insertion rate is one per 24 hobby and 48 retail packs. Cards are numbered with a "PS" prefix.

		NM/M
Complete Set (15):		20.00
Common Player:		1.00
1	Randy Johnson	2.00
2	Hideo Nomo	1.25
3	Albert Belle	1.00
4	Dante Bichette	1.00
5	Jay Buhner	1.00
6	Frank Thomas	2.00
7	Mark McGwire	4.00
8	Rafael Palmeiro	1.50
9	Mo Vaughn	1.00
10	Sammy Sosa	3.00
11	Larry Walker	1.00
12	Gary Gaetti	1.00
13	Tim Salmon	1.00
14	Barry Bonds	5.00
15	Jim Edmonds	1.00

Prime Cuts

The purest swings in baseball are the focus on these laser-cut, defraction-foil inserts found in Series 1 packs at an average rate of one per 36 hobby and 72 retail packs. Cards are numbered with a "PC" prefix.

		NM/M
Complete Set (8):		20.00
Common Player:		1.50
1	Albert Belle	1.50
2	Barry Bonds	6.00
3	Ken Griffey Jr.	4.00
4	Tony Gwynn	3.00
5	Edgar Martinez	1.50
6	Rafael Palmeiro	2.00
7	Mike Piazza	4.00
8	Frank Thomas	2.50

TSC Awards

TSC Awards insert cards allowed Topps' experts to honor best performances, newcomer, comeback, etc. The cards are found in Series 2 packs at an average rate of one per 24 retail and 48 hobby packs.

		NM/M
Complete Set (10):		15.00
Common Player:		.50
1	Cal Ripken Jr.	5.00
2	Albert Belle	.60
3	Tom Glavine	1.00
4	Jeff Conine	.50
5	Ken Griffey Jr.	4.00
6	Hideo Nomo	1.25
7	Greg Maddux	3.00
8	Chipper Jones	3.00
9	Randy Johnson	2.00
10	Jose Mesa	.50

Members Only

For the fourth year Topps offered a special edition of its high-end Stadium Club issue to members of its mail-order family. Each of the regular and insert cards was stamped with a gold- or silver-foil "MEMBERS ONLY" seal. The '96 edition was the scarcest ever produced, with only 750 sets offered at $200. Single "Members Only" cards paralleling the regular-issue Stadium Club cards sell for a premium while the M.O. versions of the inserts usually sell at par or even a discount from the issued cards.

	NM/M
Complete Set (660):	150.00
Common Player:	.50
Stars:	6X
Inserts: 50-100 Percent	

Members Only Baseball

This 50-card boxed set was offered to members of Topps Stadium Club at about $15 retail. The first 45 cards in the set represent Topps' choice of 1995's top players in each league. The final five cards, printed in Topps Finest technology, honor hot rookies. The basic cards feature borderless action photos on which the background has been posterized and darkened to make the color photo stand out in the foreground. A gold-foil strip at bottom has the player name and position; a "Members Only" logo is in gold foil in an upper corner. Horizontal backs once again have much of the photo background darkened with a close-up photo at right and a few sentences about the player at left. "Member's Choice" Finest rookie cards have a stylized baseball diamond in red tones as background to the action photos. Backs have a large red-shaded baseball with player write-up at bottom and - honest - a pea-green portrait photo at upper-left. Each of the Finest cards has a peel-off protective layer on front.

		NM/M
Complete Set (50):		6.00
Common Player:		.10
1	Carlos Baerga	.10
2	Derek Bell	.10
3	Albert Belle	.10
4	Dante Bichette	.10
5	Craig Biggio	.10
6	Wade Boggs	.65
7	Barry Bonds	1.50
8	Jay Buhner	.10
9	Vinny Castilla	.10
10	Jeff Conine	.10
11	Jim Edmonds	.10
12	Steve Finley	.10
13	Andres Galarraga	.10
14	Mark Grace	.10
15	Tony Gwynn	.65
16	Lance Johnson	.10
17	Randy Johnson	.50
18	Eric Karros	.10
19	Chuck Knoblauch	.10
20	Barry Larkin	.10
21	Kenny Lofton	.10
22	Greg Maddux	.65
23	Edgar Martinez	.10
24	Tino Martinez	.10
25	Mark McGwire	1.00
26	Brian McRae	.10
27	Jose Mesa	.10
28	Eddie Murray	.50
29	Mike Mussina	.30
30	Randy Myers	.10
31	Hideo Nomo	.25
32	Rafael Palmeiro	.50
33	Tony Phillips	.10
34	Mike Piazza	.75
35	Kirby Puckett	.65
36	Manny Ramirez	.50
37	Tim Salmon	.10
38	Reggie Sanders	.10
39	Sammy Sosa	.65
40	Frank Thomas	.50
41	Jim Thome	.45
42	John Valentin	.10
43	Mo Vaughn	.10
44	Quilvio Veras	.10
45	Larry Walker	.10
46	Hideo Nomo (Finest)	.50
47	Marty Cordova (Finest)	.50
48	Chipper Jones (Finest)	1.50
49	Garret Anderson (Finest)	.50
50	Andy Pettitte (Finest)	.50

1997 Stadium Club Pre-Production

These specially marked promo cards were issued in a cello wrapper.

		NM/M
Complete Set (3):		4.00
Common Player:		1.00
PP1	Chipper Jones	3.00
PP2	Kenny Lofton	1.00
PP3	Gary Sheffield	1.50

1997 Stadium Club

Stadium Club totalled 390 cards in 1997, issued in two series of 195 cards each. In Series 1 (Feb.), cards #181-195 are a rookie subset called TSC 2000. In Series 2 (April), cards #376-390 form a subset called Stadium Slugger. Each of these subsets was short-printed and inserted about one per two packs. TSC is printed on an improved 20-point stock with Topps' Super Color process.

		NM/M
Complete Set (390):		35.00
Common Player:		.05
Series 1 or 2 Pack (9):		1.50
Series 1 or 2 Wax Box (24):		27.50
1	Chipper Jones	1.50
2	Gary Sheffield	.50
3	Kenny Lofton	.05
4	Brian Jordan	.05
5	Mark McGwire	2.50
6	Charles Nagy	.05
7	Tim Salmon	.05
8	Cal Ripken Jr.	3.00
9	Jeff Conine	.05
10	Paul Molitor	1.00
11	Mariano Rivera	.15
12	Pedro Martinez	1.00
13	Jeff Bagwell	1.00
14	Bobby Bonilla	.05
15	Barry Bonds	3.00
16	Ryan Klesko	.05
17	Barry Larkin	.05
18	Jim Thome	.65
19	Jay Buhner	.05
20	Juan Gonzalez	.50
21	Mike Mussina	.30
22	Kevin Appier	.05
23	Eric Karros	.05
24	Steve Finley	.05
25	Ed Sprague	.05
26	Bernard Gilkey	.05
27	Tony Phillips	.05
28	Henry Rodriguez	.05
29	John Smoltz	.05
30	Dante Bichette	.05
31	Mike Piazza	2.00
32	Paul O'Neill	.05
33	Billy Wagner	.05
34	Reggie Sanders	.05
35	John Jaha	.05
36	Eddie Murray	1.00
37	Eric Young	.05
38	Roberto Hernandez	.05
39	Pat Hentgen	.05
40	Sammy Sosa	1.50
41	Todd Hundley	.05
42	Mo Vaughn	.05
43	Robin Ventura	.05
44	Mark Grudzielanek	.05
45	Shane Reynolds	.05
46	Andy Pettitte	.25
47	Fred McGriff	.05
48	Rey Ordonez	.05
49	Will Clark	.05
50	Ken Griffey Jr.	2.00
51	Todd Worrell	.05
52	Rusty Greer	.05
53	Mark Grace	.05
54	Tom Glavine	.35
55	Derek Jeter	3.00
56	Rafael Palmeiro	.75
57	Bernie Williams	.05
58	Marty Cordova	.05
59	Andres Galarraga	.05
60	Ken Caminiti	.05
61	Garret Anderson	.05
62	Denny Martinez	.05
63	Mike Greenwell	.05
64	David Segui	.05
65	Julio Franco	.05
66	Rickey Henderson	1.00
67	Ozzie Guillen	.05
68	Pete Harnisch	.05
69	Chan Ho Park	.05
70	Harold Baines	.05
71	Mark Clark	.05
72	Steve Avery	.05
73	Brian Hunter	.05
74	Pedro Astacio	.05
75	Jack McDowell	.05
76	Gregg Jefferies	.05
77	Jason Kendall	.05
78	Todd Walker	.05
79	B.J. Surhoff	.05
80	Moises Alou	.05
81	Fernando Vina	.05
82	Darryl Strawberry	.05
83	Jose Rosado	.05
84	Chris Gomez	.05
85	Chili Davis	.05
86	Alan Benes	.05
87	Todd Hollandsworth	.05
88	Jose Vizcaino	.05
89	Edgardo Alfonzo	.05
90	Ruben Rivera	.05
91	Donovan Osborne	.05
92	Doug Glanville	.05
93	Gary DiSarcina	.05
94	Brooks Kieschnick	.05
95	Bobby Jones	.05
96	Raul Casanova	.05
97	Jermaine Allensworth	.05
98	Kenny Rogers	.05
99	Mark McLemore	.05
100	Jeff Fassero	.05
101	Sandy Alomar	.05
102	Chuck Finley	.05
103	Eric Owens	.05
104	Billy McMillon	.05
105	Dwight Gooden	.05
106	Sterling Hitchcock	.05
107	Doug Drabek	.05
108	Paul Wilson	.05
109	Chris Snopek	.05
110	Al Leiter	.05
111	Bob Tewksbury	.05
112	Todd Greene	.05
113	Jose Valentin	.05
114	Delino DeShields	.05
115	Mike Bordick	.05
116	Pat Meares	.05
117	Mariano Duncan	.05
118	Steve Trachsel	.05
119	Luis Castillo	.05
120	Andy Benes	.05
121	Donne Wall	.05
122	Alex Gonzalez	.05
123	Dan Wilson	.05
124	Omar Vizquel	.05
125	Devon White	.05
126	Darryl Hamilton	.05
127	Orlando Merced	.05
128	Royce Clayton	.05
129	William Van Landingham	.05
130	Terry Steinbach	.05
131	Jeff Blauser	.05
132	Jeff Cirillo	.05
133	Roger Pavlik	.05
134	Danny Tartabull	.05
135	Jeff Montgomery	.05
136	Bobby Higginson	.05
137	Mike Grace	.05
138	Kevin Elster	.05
139	Brian Giles **RC**	1.00
140	Rod Beck	.05
141	Ismael Valdes	.05
142	Scott Brosius	.05
143	Mike Fetters	.05
144	Gary Gaetti	.05
145	Mike Lansing	.05
146	Glenallen Hill	.05
147	Shawn Green	.35
148	Mel Rojas	.05
149	Joey Cora	.05
150	John Smiley	.05
151	Marvin Benard	.05
152	Curt Schilling	.35
153	Dave Nilsson	.05
154	Edgar Renteria	.05
155	Joey Hamilton	.05
156	Carlos Garcia	.05
157	Nomar Garciaparra	2.00
158	Kevin Ritz	.05
159	Keith Lockhart	.05
160	Justin Thompson	.05
161	Terry Adams	.05
162	Jamey Wright	.05
163	Otis Nixon	.05
164	Michael Tucker	.05
165	Mike Stanley	.05
166	Ben McDonald	.05
167	John Mabry	.05
168	Troy O'Leary	.05
169	Mel Nieves	.05
170	Bret Boone	.05
171	Mike Timlin	.05
172	Scott Rolen	.75
173	Reggie Jefferson	.05
174	Neifi Perez	.05
175	Brian McRae	.05
176	Tom Goodwin	.05
177	Aaron Sele	.05
178	Benny Santiago	.05
179	Frank Rodriguez	.05
180	Eric Davis	.05
181	Andruw Jones (TSC 2000)	.75
182	Todd Walker (TSC 2000)	.15
183	Wes Helms (TSC 2000)	.15
184	Nelson Figueroa **RC** (TSC 2000)	.15
185	Vladimir Guerrero (TSC 2000)	.75
186	Billy McMillon (TSC 2000)	.15
187	Todd Helton (TSC 2000)	.65
188	Nomar Garciaparra (TSC 2000)	2.00
189	Katsuhiro Maeda (TSC 2000)	.15
190	Russell Branyan (TSC 2000)	.15
191	Glendon Rusch (TSC 2000)	.15
192	Bartolo Colon (TSC 2000)	.15
193	Scott Rolen (TSC 2000)	.50
194	Angel Echevarria (TSC 2000)	.15
195	Bob Abreu (TSC 2000)	.20
196	Greg Maddux	1.50
197	Joe Carter	.05
198	Alex Ochoa	.05
199	Ellis Burks	.05
200	Ivan Rodriguez	.75
201	Marquis Grissom	.05
202	Trevor Hoffman	.05
203	Matt Williams	.05
204	Carlos Delgado	.50
205	Ramon Martinez	.05
206	Chuck Knoblauch	.05
207	Juan Guzman	.05
208	Derek Bell	.05
209	Roger Clemens	1.75
210	Vladimir Guerrero	1.00
211	Cecil Fielder	.05
212	Hideo Nomo	.50
213	Frank Thomas	1.00
214	Greg Vaughn	.05
215	Javy Lopez	.05
216	Raul Mondesi	.05
217	Wade Boggs	1.50
218	Carlos Baerga	.05
219	Tony Gwynn	1.50
220	Tino Martinez	.05
221	Vinny Castilla	.05
222	Lance Johnson	.05
223	David Justice	.05
224	Rondell White	.05
225	Dean Palmer	.05
226	Jim Edmonds	.05
227	Albert Belle	.05
228	Alex Fernandez	.05
229	Ryne Sandberg	1.50
230	Jose Mesa	.05
231	David Cone	.05
232	Troy Percival	.05
233	Edgar Martinez	.05
234	Jose Canseco	.50
235	Kevin Brown	.05
236	Ray Lankford	.05
237	Karim Garcia	.05
238	J.T. Snow	.05
239	Dennis Eckersley	.75
240	Roberto Alomar	.35
241	John Valentin	.05
242	Ron Gant	.05
243	Geronimo Berroa	.05
244	Manny Ramirez	1.00
245	Travis Fryman	.05
246	Denny Neagle	.05
247	Randy Johnson	1.00
248	Darin Erstad	.15
249	Mark Wohlers	.05
250	Ken Hill	.05
251	Larry Walker	.05
252	Craig Biggio	.05
253	Brady Anderson	.05
254	John Wetteland	.05
255	Andruw Jones	1.00
256	Turk Wendell	.05
257	Jason Isringhausen	.05
258	Jaime Navarro	.05
259	Sean Berry	.05
260	Albie Lopez	.05
261	Jay Bell	.05
262	Bobby Witt	.05
263	Tony Clark	.05
264	Tim Wakefield	.05
265	Brad Radke	.05
266	Tim Belcher	.05
267	Mark Lewis	.05
268	Roger Cedeno	.05
269	Tim Naehring	.05
270	Kevin Tapani	.05
271	Joe Randa	.05
272	Randy Myers	.05
273	Dave Burba	.05
274a	Mike Sweeney	.05
274b	Tom Pagnozzi (Should be #374.)	.05
275	Danny Graves	.05
276	Chad Mottola	.05
277	Ruben Sierra	.05
278	Norm Charlton	.05
279	Scott Servais	.05
280	Jacob Cruz	.05
281	Mike Macfarlane	.05
282	Rich Becker	.05
283	Shannon Stewart	.05
284	Gerald Williams	.05
285	Jody Reed	.05
286	Jeff D'Amico	.05
287	Walt Weiss	.05
288	Jim Leyritz	.05
289	Francisco Cordova	.05
290	F.P. Santangelo	.05
291	Scott Erickson	.05
292	Hal Morris	.05
293	Ray Durham	.05
294	Andy Ashby	.05
295	Darryl Kile	.05
296	Jose Paniagua	.05
297	Mickey Tettleton	.05
298	Joe Girardi	.05
299	Rocky Coppinger	.05
300	Bob Abreu	.05
301	John Olerud	.05
302	Paul Shuey	.05
303	Jeff Brantley	.05
304	Bob Wells	.05
305	Kevin Seitzer	.05
306	Shawon Dunston	.05
307	Jose Herrera	.05
308	Butch Huskey	.05
309	Jose Offerman	.05
310	Rick Aguilera	.05
311	Greg Gagne	.05
312	John Burkett	.05
313	Mark Thompson	.05
314	Alvaro Espinoza	.05
315	Todd Stottlemyre	.05
316	Al Martin	.05
317	James Baldwin	.05
318	Cal Eldred	.05
319	Sid Fernandez	.05
320	Mickey Morandini	.05
321	Robb Nen	.05
322	Mark Lemke	.05
323	Pete Schourek	.05
324	Marcus Jensen	.05
325	Rich Aurilia	.05
326	Jeff King	.05
327	Scott Stahoviak	.05
328	Ricky Otero	.05
329	Antonio Osuna	.05
330	Chris Hoiles	.05
331	Luis Gonzalez	.05
332	Wil Cordero	.05
333	Johnny Damon	.35
334	Mark Langston	.05
335	Orlando Miller	.05
336	Jason Giambi	.50
337	Damian Jackson	.05
338	David Wells	.05
339	Bip Roberts	.05
340	Matt Ruebel	.05
341	Tom Candiotti	.05
342	Wally Joyner	.05
343	Jimmy Key	.05
344	Tony Batista	.05
345	Paul Sorrento	.05
346	Ron Karkovice	.05
347	Wilson Alvarez	.05
348	John Flaherty	.05
349	Rey Sanchez	.05
350	John Vander Wal	.05
351a	Jermaine Dye	.05
351b	Brant Brown (Should be #361.)	.05
352	Mike Hampton	.05
353	Greg Colbrunn	.05
354	Heathcliff Slocumb	.05
355	Ricky Bottalico	.05
356	Marty Janzen	.05
357	Orel Hershiser	.05
358	Rex Hudler	.05
359	Amaury Telemaco	.05
360	Darrin Fletcher	.05
361	Not Issued - See #351	.05
362	Russ Davis	.05
363	Allen Watson	.05
364	Mike Lieberthal	.05
365	Dave Stevens	.05
366	Jay Powell	.05
367	Tony Fossas	.05
368	Bob Wolcott	.05
369	Mark Loretta	.05
370	Shawn Estes	.05
371	Sandy Martinez	.05
372	Wendell Magee Jr.	.05
373	John Franco	.05
374	Not Issued - See #274	.05
375	Willie Adams	.05
376	Chipper Jones (Stadium Sluggers)	2.00
377	Mo Vaughn (Stadium Sluggers)	.15
378	Frank Thomas (Stadium Sluggers)	1.50
379	Albert Belle (Stadium Sluggers)	.15
380	Andres Galarraga (Stadium Sluggers)	.15
381	Gary Sheffield (Stadium Sluggers)	.85
382	Jeff Bagwell (Stadium Sluggers)	1.50
383	Mike Piazza (Stadium Sluggers)	3.00
384	Mark McGwire (Stadium Sluggers)	3.00
385	Ken Griffey Jr. (Stadium Sluggers)	2.50
386	Barry Bonds (Stadium Sluggers)	3.50
387	Juan Gonzalez (Stadium Sluggers)	.40
388	Brady Anderson (Stadium Sluggers)	.15
389	Ken Caminiti (Stadium Sluggers)	.15
390	Jay Buhner (Stadium Sluggers)	.15

Co-Signers

Each series of Stadium Club included five different Co-Signers, with an insertion ratio of one per 168 hobby packs. These double-sided cards featured authentic autographs from each star, one per side.

		NM/M
Complete Set (10):		200.00
Common Card:		5.00
CO1	Andy Pettitte, Derek Jeter	100.00
CO2	Paul Wilson, Todd Hundley	5.00
CO3	Jermaine Dye, Mark Wohlers	6.00
CO4	Scott Rolen, Gregg Jefferies	15.00
CO5	Todd Hollandsworth, Jason Kendall	8.00
CO6	Alan Benes, Robin Ventura	8.00
CO7	Eric Karros, Raul Mondesi	15.00
CO8	Rey Ordonez, Nomar Garciaparra	45.00
CO9	Rondell White, Marty Cordova	6.00
CO10	Tony Gwynn, Karim Garcia	30.00

Firebrand Redemption

Because of production problems with its "Laser-Etched Wood" technology, Stadium Club was unable to package the Firebrand insert cards with the rest of the issue. Instead, a redemption card was substituted. The redemption card pictures the Firebrand card on its horizontal front; the back has details for exchanging the redemption card for the actual wood-printed, die-cut version. The exchange offer ended Sept. 30, 1997.

		NM/M
Complete Set (12):		15.00
Common Player:		.60
F1	Jeff Bagwell	1.25
F2	Albert Belle	.60
F3	Barry Bonds	4.00
F4	Andres Galarraga	.60
F5	Ken Griffey Jr.	2.50
F6	Brady Anderson	.60
F7	Mark McGwire	3.25
F8	Chipper Jones	2.00
F9	Frank Thomas	1.25
F10	Mike Piazza	2.50
F11	Mo Vaughn	.60
F12	Juan Gonzalez	.85

Firebrand

This 12-card insert was found only in packs sold at retail chains. Cards were inserted 1:36 packs. The hortizontal format cards are printed on thin wood stock, die-cut at top. Fronts are trimmed in gold foil. Cards are numbered with a "F" prefix.

		NM/M
Complete Set (12):		25.00
Common Player:		1.00
1	Jeff Bagwell	2.50
2	Albert Belle	1.00
3	Barry Bonds	6.50
4	Andres Galarraga	1.00
5	Ken Griffey Jr.	4.50
6	Brady Anderson	1.00
7	Mark McGwire	5.50
8	Chipper Jones	3.50
9	Frank Thomas	2.50
10	Mike Piazza	4.50
11	Mo Vaughn	1.00
12	Juan Gonzalez	1.50

Instavision

Instavision features holographic cards with exciting moments from the 1996 playoffs and World Series. Inserted one per 24 hobby packs and one per 36 retail packs, these cards are printed horizontally on plastic stock. Cards carry an "I" prefix, with the first 10 found in Series 1 and the final 12 in Series 2.

	NM/M
Complete Set (22):	10.00

Common Player:		.35
11	Eddie Murray	.75
12	Paul Molitor	.75
13	Todd Hundley	.35
14	Roger Clemens	1.50
15	Barry Bonds	3.00
16	Mark McGwire	2.00
17	Brady Anderson	.35
18	Barry Larkin	.35
19	Ken Caminiti	.35
110	Hideo Nomo	.45
111	Bernie Williams	.35
112	Juan Gonzalez	.45
113	Andy Pettitte	.45
114	Albert Belle	.35
115	John Smoltz	.35
116	Brian Jordan	.35
117	Derek Jeter	3.00
118	Ken Caminiti	.35
119	John Wetteland	.35
120	Brady Anderson	.35
121	Andruw Jones	.75
122	Jim Leyritz	.35

Millennium

Millennium was a 40-card insert that was released with 20 cards in Series I and Series II. The set featured 40 top prospects and rookies on a silver foil, holographic front, with a Future Forecast section on the back. Cards carried an "M" prefix and were numbered consecutively M1-M40. Millennium inserts were found every 24 hobby packs and every 36 retail packs.

		NM/M
Complete Set (40):		12.50
Common Player:		.25
1	Derek Jeter	5.00
2	Mark Grudzielanek	.25
3	Jacob Cruz	.25
4	Ray Durham	.25
5	Tony Clark	.25
6	Chipper Jones	2.50
7	Luis Castillo	.25
8	Carlos Delgado	.50
9	Brant Brown	.25
10	Jason Kendall	.25
11	Alan Benes	.25
12	Rey Ordonez	.25
13	Justin Thompson	.25
14	Jermaine Allensworth	.25
15	Brian Hunter	.25
16	Marty Cordova	.25
17	Edgar Renteria	.25
18	Karim Garcia	.25
19	Todd Greene	.25
20	Paul Wilson	.25
21	Andruw Jones	1.50
22	Todd Walker	.25
23	Alex Ochoa	.25
24	Bartolo Colon	.25
25	Wendell Magee Jr.	.25
26	Jose Rosado	.25
27	Katsuhiro Maeda	.25
28	Bob Abreu	.25
29	Brooks Kieschnick	.25
30	Derrick Gibson	.25
31	Mike Sweeney	.25
32	Jeff D'Amico	.25
33	Chad Mottola	.25
34	Chris Snopek	.25
35	Jaime Bluma	.25
36	Vladimir Guerrero	1.50
37	Nomar Garciaparra	2.50
38	Scott Rolen	1.25
39	Dmitri Young	.25
40	Neifi Perez	.25

Patent Leather

Patent Leather featured 13 of the top gloves in baseball on a leather, die-cut card. The cards carry a "PL" prefix and are inerted one per 36 retail packs.

		NM/M
Complete Set (13):		25.00
Common Player:		1.00
1	Ivan Rodriguez	3.00
2	Ken Caminiti	1.00
3	Barry Bonds	6.00
4	Ken Griffey Jr.	5.00
5	Greg Maddux	4.00
6	Craig Biggio	1.00
7	Andres Galarraga	1.00
8	Kenny Lofton	1.00
9	Barry Larkin	1.00
10	Mark Grace	1.00
11	Rey Ordonez	1.00
12	Roberto Alomar	1.25
13	Derek Jeter	6.00

Pure Gold

Pure Gold featured 20 of the top players in baseball on gold, embossed foil cards. Cards carry a "PG" prefix and were inserted every 72 hobby packs and every 108 retail packs. The first 10 cards were in Series I packs, while the final 10 cards are exclusive to Series II.

		NM/M
Complete Set (20):		60.00
Common Player:		1.25
1	Brady Anderson	1.25
2	Albert Belle	1.25
3	Dante Bichette	1.25
4	Barry Bonds	12.00
5	Jay Buhner	1.25
6	Tony Gwynn	6.00
7	Chipper Jones	6.00
8	Mark McGwire	9.00
9	Gary Sheffield	2.25
10	Frank Thomas	4.50
11	Juan Gonzalez	2.50
12	Ken Caminiti	1.25
13	Kenny Lofton	1.25
14	Jeff Bagwell	4.50
15	Ken Griffey Jr.	7.50
16	Cal Ripken Jr.	12.00
17	Mo Vaughn	1.25
18	Mike Piazza	7.50
19	Derek Jeter	12.00
20	Andres Galarraga	1.25

TSC Matrix

TSC Matrix consists of 120 cards from Series I and II reprinted with Power Matrix technology. In each Series, 60 of the 190 cards were selected for inclusion in TSC Matrix and inserted every 12 hobby packs and every 18 retail packs. Each insert carries the TSC Matrix logo in a top corner of the card.

		NM/M
Complete Set (120):		70.00
Common Player:		.50
1	Chipper Jones	2.50
2	Gary Sheffield	1.00
3	Kenny Lofton	.50
4	Brian Jordan	.50
5	Mark McGwire	4.25
6	Charles Nagy	.50
7	Tim Salmon	.50
8	Cal Ripken Jr.	5.00
9	Jeff Conine	.50
10	Paul Molitor	1.75
11	Mariano Rivera	.65
12	Pedro Martinez	1.75
13	Jeff Bagwell	1.75
14	Bobby Bonilla	.50
15	Barry Bonds	5.00
16	Ryan Klesko	.50
17	Barry Larkin	.50
18	Jim Thome	1.50
19	Jay Buhner	.50
20	Juan Gonzalez	1.00
21	Mike Mussina	.75
22	Kevin Appier	.50
23	Eric Karros	.50
24	Steve Finley	.50
25	Ed Sprague	.50
26	Bernard Gilkey	.50
27	Tony Phillips	.50
28	Henry Rodriguez	.50
29	John Smoltz	.50
30	Dante Bichette	.50
31	Mike Piazza	3.25
32	Paul O'Neill	.50
33	Billy Wagner	.50
34	Reggie Sanders	.50
35	John Jaha	.50
36	Eddie Murray	1.75
37	Eric Young	.50
38	Roberto Hernandez	.50
39	Pat Hentgen	.50
40	Sammy Sosa	2.50
41	Todd Hundley	.50
42	Mo Vaughn	.50
43	Robin Ventura	.50
44	Mark Grudzielanek	.50
45	Shane Reynolds	.50
46	Andy Pettitte	.65
47	Fred McGriff	.50
48	Rey Ordonez	.50
49	Will Clark	.50
50	Ken Griffey Jr.	3.25
51	Todd Worrell	.50
52	Rusty Greer	.50
53	Mark Grace	.50
54	Tom Glavine	.75
55	Derek Jeter	5.00
56	Rafael Palmeiro	1.50
57	Bernie Williams	.50
58	Marty Cordova	.50
59	Andres Galarraga	.50
60	Ken Caminiti	.50
196	Greg Maddux	2.50
197	Joe Carter	.50
198	Alex Ochoa	.50
199	Ellis Burks	.50
200	Ivan Rodriguez	1.50
201	Marquis Grissom	.50
202	Trevor Hoffman	.50
203	Matt Williams	.50
204	Carlos Delgado	1.25
205	Ramon Martinez	.50
206	Chuck Knoblauch	.50
207	Juan Guzman	.50
208	Derek Bell	.50
209	Roger Clemens	3.00
210	Vladimir Guerrero	1.75
211	Cecil Fielder	.50
212	Hideo Nomo	1.00
213	Frank Thomas	1.75
214	Greg Vaughn	.50
215	Javy Lopez	.50
216	Raul Mondesi	.50
217	Wade Boggs	2.50
218	Carlos Baerga	.50
219	Tony Gwynn	2.50
220	Tino Martinez	.50
221	Vinny Castilla	.50
222	Lance Johnson	.50
223	David Justice	.50
224	Rondell White	.50
225	Dean Palmer	.50
226	Jim Edmonds	.50
227	Albert Belle	.50
228	Alex Fernandez	.50
229	Ryne Sandberg	2.50
230	Jose Mesa	.50
231	David Cone	.50
232	Troy Percival	.50
233	Edgar Martinez	.50
234	Jose Canseco	1.25
235	Kevin Brown	.50
236	Ray Lankford	.50
237	Karim Garcia	.50
238	J.T. Snow	.50
239	Dennis Eckersley	1.50
240	Roberto Alomar	.75
241	John Valentin	.50
242	Ron Gant	.50
243	Geronimo Berroa	.50
244	Manny Ramirez	1.75
245	Travis Fryman	.50
246	Denny Neagle	.50
247	Randy Johnson	1.75
248	Darin Erstad	.65
249	Mark Wohlers	.50
250	Ken Hill	.50
251	Larry Walker	.50
252	Craig Biggio	.50
253	Brady Anderson	.50
254	John Wetteland	.50
255	Andruw Jones	1.75

Members Only

Production was reported at just 750 complete sets of these specially marked Stadium Club cards and inserts. Sold only as complete sets through Topps' Stadium Club program, each card differs from the regular-issue TSC version only in the presence of a subdued "MEMBERS ONLY" repeated all across the cards' backs. Star players' cards sell for a significant premium over regular-issue TSC version; inserts, depending on the scarcity of the regular version, usually sell for a significant discount in the Members Only version.

	NM/M
Complete Set:	250.00
Common Player:	.50
Stars:	5X
Inserts: 50-100 Percent	

Members Only Baseball

This boxed set was available only to members of Topps' Stadium Club for a price of $15, which included a year's membership in the club. Fronts feature action photos with a 2-1/2" circle behind the player, a gold-foil Members Only seal and the player's name, also in gold-foil. Backs feature another photo and a career summary on a red background which has the Members Only seal in a repeating pattern. Cards #51-55 are rookie stars and are printed in Topps Finest technologies.

		NM/M
Complete Set (55):		12.00
Common Player:		.10
1	Brady Anderson	.10
2	Carlos Baerga	.10
3	Jeff Bagwell	.75
4	Albert Belle	.10
5	Dante Bichette	.10
6	Craig Biggio	.10
7	Wade Boggs	1.00
8	Barry Bonds	2.50
9	Jay Buhner	.10
10	Ellis Burks	.10
11	Ken Caminiti	.10
12	Jose Canseco	.50
13	Joe Carter	.10
14	Roger Clemens	1.25
15	Jeff Conine	.10
16	Andres Galarraga	.10
17	Ron Gant	.10
18	Juan Gonzalez	.40
19	Mark Grace	.10
20	Ken Griffey Jr.	1.50
21	Tony Gwynn	1.00
22	Pat Hentgen	.10
23	Todd Hollandsworth	.10
24	Todd Hundley	.10
25	Derek Jeter	2.50
26	Randy Johnson	.75
27	Chipper Jones	1.00
28	Ryan Klesko	.10
29	Chuck Knoblauch	.10
30	Barry Larkin	.10
31	Kenny Lofton	.10
32	Greg Maddux	1.00
33	Mark McGwire	2.00
34	Paul Molitor	.75
35	Raul Mondesi	.10
36	Hideo Nomo	.40
37	Rafael Palmeiro	.65
38	Mike Piazza	1.50
39	Manny Ramirez	.75
40	Cal Ripken Jr.	2.50
41	Ivan Rodriguez	.65
42	Tim Salmon	.10
43	Gary Sheffield	.45
44	John Smoltz	.10
45	Sammy Sosa	1.00
46	Frank Thomas	.75
47	Jim Thome	.65
48	Mo Vaughn	.10
49	Bernie Williams	.10
50	Matt Williams	.10
51	Darin Erstad (Finest)	1.00
52	Vladimir Guerrero (Finest)	2.50
53	Andruw Jones (Finest)	2.00
54	Scott Rolen (Finest)	1.00
55	Todd Walker (Finest)	1.00

1998 Stadium Club

Stadium Club was issued in two series for 1998, with 200 odd-numbered cards in Series 1 and 200 even-numbered cards in Series 2. Retail packs contain six cards and carried an SRP of $2; hobby packs have nine cards and an SRP of $3 and HTA packs offered 15 cards at an SRP of $5. Three subsets were included: Future Stars (361-379) and Draft Picks (381-399), both being odd-numbered, and Traded (356-400) being even-numbered. Inserts in Series 1 include: First Day Issue parallels (retail), One of a Kind parallels (hobby), Printing Plates parallels (HTA), Bowman Previews, Co-Signers (hobby), In the Wings, Never Comprimise, and Triumvirates (retail). Inserts in Series 2 include: First Day Issue parallels (retail), One of a Kind parallels (hobby), Printing Plates parallels (HTA), Bowman Prospect Previews, Co-Signers (hobby), Playing with Passion, Royal Court and Triumvirates (retail).

		NM/M
Complete Set (400):		30.00
Common Player:		.05
Hobby Pack (10):		1.50
Retail Pack (7):		1.50
Home Team Adv. Pack (16):		4.00
Hobby Box (24):		30.00
1	Chipper Jones	1.00
2	Frank Thomas	.75
3	Vladimir Guerrero	.75
4	Ellis Burks	.05
5	John Franco	.05
6	Paul Molitor	.75
7	Rusty Greer	.05
8	Todd Hundley	.05
9	Brett Tomko	.05
10	Eric Karros	.05
11	Mike Cameron	.05
12	Jim Edmonds	.05
13	Bernie Williams	.05
14	Denny Neagle	.05
15	Jason Dickson	.05
16	Sammy Sosa	1.00
17	Brian Jordan	.05
18	Jose Vidro	.05
19	Scott Spiezio	.05
20	Jay Buhner	.05
21	Jim Thome	.65
22	Sandy Alomar	.05
23	Devon White	.05
24	Roberto Alomar	.20
25	John Flaherty	.05
26	John Wetteland	.05
27	Willie Greene	.05
28	Gregg Jefferies	.05
29	Johnny Damon	.35
30	Barry Larkin	.05
31	Chuck Knoblauch	.05
32	Mo Vaughn	.05
33	Tony Clark	.05
34	Marty Cordova	.05
35	Vinny Castilla	.05
36	Jeff King	.05
37	Reggie Jefferson	.05
38	Mariano Rivera	.15
39	Jermaine Allensworth	.05
40	Livan Hernandez	.05
41	Heathcliff Slocumb	.05
42	Jacob Cruz	.05
43	Barry Bonds	2.50
44	Dave Magadan	.05
45	Chan Ho Park	.05
46	Jeremi Gonzalez	.05
47	Jeff Cirillo	.05
48	Delino DeShields	.05
49	Craig Biggio	.05
50	Benito Santiago	.05
51	Mark Clark	.05
52	Fernando Vina	.05
53	F.P. Santangelo	.05
54	Pep Harris **RC**	.05
55	Edgar Renteria	.05
56	Jeff Bagwell	.75
57	Jimmy Key	.05
58	Bartolo Colon	.05
59	Curt Schilling	.35
60	Steve Finley	.05
61	Andy Ashby	.05
62	John Burkett	.05
63	Orel Hershiser	.05
64	Pokey Reese	.05
65	Scott Servais	.05
66	Todd Jones	.05
67	Javy Lopez	.05
68	Robin Ventura	.05
69	Miguel Tejada	.15
70	Raul Casanova	.05
71	Reggie Sanders	.05
72	Edgardo Alfonzo	.05
73	Dean Palmer	.05
74	Todd Stottlemyre	.05
75	David Wells	.05
76	Troy Percival	.05
77	Albert Belle	.05
78	Pat Hentgen	.05
79	Brian Hunter	.05
80	Richard Hidalgo	.05
81	Darren Oliver	.05
82	Mark Wohlers	.05
83	Cal Ripken Jr.	2.50
84	Hideo Nomo	.40
85	Derrek Lee	.50
86	Stan Javier	.05
87	Rey Ordonez	.05
88	Randy Johnson	.75
89	Jeff Kent	.05
90	Brian McRae	.05
91	Manny Ramirez	.75
92	Trevor Hoffman	.05
93	Doug Glanville	.05
94	Todd Walker	.05
95	Andy Benes	.05
96	Jason Schmidt	.05
97	Mike Matheny	.05
98	Tim Naehring	.05
99	Jeff Blauser	.05
100	Jose Rosado	.05
101	Roger Clemens	1.25
102	Pedro Astacio	.05
103	Mark Bellhorn	.05
104	Paul O'Neill	.05
105	Darin Erstad	.15
106	Mike Lieberthal	.05
107	Wilson Alvarez	.05
108	Mike Mussina	.30
109	George Williams	.05
110	Cliff Floyd	.05
111	Shawn Estes	.05
112	Mark Grudzielanek	.05
113	Tony Gwynn	1.00
114	Alan Benes	.05
115	Terry Steinbach	.05
116	Greg Maddux	1.00
117	Andy Pettitte	.25
118	Dave Nilsson	.05
119	Deivi Cruz	.05
120	Carlos Delgado	.50
121	Scott Hatteberg	.05
122	John Olerud	.05
123	Moises Alou	.05
124	Garret Anderson	.05
125	Royce Clayton	.05
126	Dante Powell	.05

127 Tom Glavine .35
128 Gary DiSarcina .05
129 Terry Adams .05
130 Raul Mondesi .05
131 Dan Wilson .05
132 Al Martin .05
133 Mickey Morandini .05
134 Rafael Palmeiro .65
135 Juan Encarnacion .05
136 Jim Pittsley .05
137 Magglio Ordonez **RC** 1.00
138 Will Clark .05
139 Todd Helton .65
140 Kelvim Escobar .05
141 Esteban Loaiza .05
142 John Jaha .05
143 Jeff Fassero .05
144 Harold Baines .05
145 Butch Huskey .05
146 Pat Meares .05
147 Brian Giles .05
148 Ramiro Mendoza .05
149 John Smoltz .05
150 Felix Martinez .05
151 Jose Valentin .05
152 Brad Rigby .05
153 Ed Sprague .05
154 Mike Hampton .05
155 Mike Lansing .05
156 Ray Lankford .05
157 Bobby Bonilla .05
158 Bill Mueller .05
159 Jeffrey Hammonds .05
160 Charles Nagy .05
161 Rich Loiselle .05
162 Al Leiter .05
163 Larry Walker .05
164 Chris Hoiles .05
165 Jeff Montgomery .05
166 Francisco Cordova .05
167 James Baldwin .05
168 Mark McLemore .05
169 Kevin Appier .05
170 Jamey Wright .05
171 Nomar Garciaparra 1.00
172 Matt Franco .05
173 Armando Benitez .05
174 Jeromy Burnitz .05
175 Ismael Valdes .05
176 Lance Johnson .05
177 Paul Sorrento .05
178 Rondell White .05
179 Kevin Elster .05
180 Jason Giambi .50
181 Carlos Baerga .05
182 Russ Davis .05
183 Ryan McGuire .05
184 Eric Young .05
185 Ron Gant .05
186 Manny Alexander .05
187 Scott Karl .05
188 Brady Anderson .05
189 Randall Simon .05
190 Tim Belcher .05
191 Jaret Wright .05
192 Dante Bichette .05
193 John Valentin .05
194 Darren Bragg .05
195 Mike Sweeney .05
196 Craig Counsell .05
197 Jaime Navarro .05
198 Todd Dunn .05
199 Ken Griffey Jr. 1.50
200 Juan Gonzalez .40
201 Billy Wagner .05
202 Tino Martinez .05
203 Mark McGwire 2.00
204 Jeff D'Amico .05
205 Rico Brogna .05
206 Todd Hollandsworth .05
207 Chad Curtis .05
208 Tom Goodwin .05
209 Neifi Perez .05
210 Derek Bell .05
211 Quilvio Veras .05
212 Greg Vaughn .05
213 Roberto Hernandez .05
214 Arthur Rhodes .05
215 Cal Eldred .05
216 Bill Taylor .05
217 Todd Greene .05
218 Mario Valdez .05
219 Ricky Bottalico .05
220 Frank Rodriguez .05
221 Rich Becker .05
222 Roberto Duran .05
223 Ivan Rodriguez .65
224 Mike Jackson .05
225 Deion Sanders .05
226 Tony Womack .05
227 Mark Kotsay .05
228 Steve Trachsel .05
229 Ryan Klesko .05
230 Ken Cloude .05
231 Luis Gonzalez .05
232 Gary Gaetti .05
233 Michael Tucker .05
234 Shawn Green .35
235 Ariel Prieto .05
236 Kirt Manwaring .05
237 Omar Vizquel .05
238 Matt Beech .05
239 Justin Thompson .05
240 Bret Boone .05
241 Derek Jeter 2.50
242 Ken Caminiti .05
243 Jay Bell .05
244 Kevin Tapani .05
245 Jason Kendall .05
246 Jose Guillen .05
247 Mike Bordick .05
248 Dustin Hermanson .05
249 Darrin Fletcher .05
250 Dave Hollins .05
251 Ramon Martinez .05
252 Hideki Irabu .05
253 Mark Grace .05
254 Jason Isringhausen .05
255 Jose Cruz Jr. .05
256 Brian Johnson .05
257 Brad Ausmus .05
258 Andruw Jones .75
259 Doug Jones .05
260 Jeff Shaw .05
261 Chuck Finley .05
262 Gary Sheffield .45
263 David Segui .05
264 John Smiley .05
265 Tim Salmon .05
266 J.T. Snow Jr. .05
267 Alex Fernandez .05
268 Matt Stairs .05
269 B.J. Surhoff .05
270 Keith Foulke .05
271 Edgar Martinez .05
272 Shannon Stewart .05
273 Eduardo Perez .05
274 Wally Joyner .05
275 Kevin Young .05
276 Eli Marrero .05
277 Brad Radke .05
278 Jamie Moyer .05
279 Joe Girardi .05
280 Troy O'Leary .05
281 Aaron Sele .05
282 Jose Offerman .05
283 Scott Erickson .05
284 Sean Berry .05
285 Shigetosi Hasegawa .05
286 Felix Heredia .05
287 Willie McGee .05
288 Alex Rodriguez 2.00
289 Ugueth Urbina .05
290 Jon Lieber .05
291 Fernando Tatis .05
292 Chris Stynes .05
293 Bernard Gilkey .05
294 Joey Hamilton .05
295 Matt Karchner .05
296 Paul Wilson .05
297 Mel Nieves .05
298 Kevin Millwood **RC** .75
299 Quinton McCracken .05
300 Jerry DiPoto .05
301 Jermaine Dye .05
302 Travis Lee .05
303 Ron Coomer .05
304 Matt Williams .05
305 Bobby Higginson .05
306 Jorge Fabregas .05
307 Hal Morris .05
308 Jay Bell .05
309 Joe Randa .05
310 Andy Benes .05
311 Sterling Hitchcock .05
312 Jeff Suppan .05
313 Shane Reynolds .05
314 Willie Blair .05
315 Scott Rolen .65
316 Wilson Alvarez .05
317 David Justice .05
318 Fred McGriff .05
319 Bobby Jones .05
320 Wade Boggs 1.00
321 Tim Wakefield .05
322 Tony Saunders .05
323 David Cone .05
324 Roberto Hernandez .05
325 Jose Canseco .45
326 Kevin Stocker .05
327 Gerald Williams .05
328 Quinton McCracken .05
329 Mark Gardner .05
330 Ben Grieve (Prime Rookie) .05
331 Kevin Brown .05
332 Mike Lowell **RC** (Prime Rookie) 1.00
333 Jed Hansen .05
334 Abraham Nunez (Prime Rookie) .05
335 John Thomson .05
336 Derrek Lee (Prime Rookie) .05
337 Mike Piazza 1.50
338 Brad Fullmer (Prime Rookie) .05
339 Ray Durham .05
340 Kerry Wood (Prime Rookie) .50
341 Kevin Polcovich **RC** .05
342 Russ Johnson (Prime Rookie) .05
343 Darryl Hamilton .05
344 David Ortiz (Prime Rookie) .45
345 Kevin Orie .05
346 Sean Casey (Prime Rookie) .25
347 Juan Guzman .05
348 Ruben Rivera (Prime Rookie) .05
349 Rick Aguilera .05
350 Bobby Estalella (Prime Rookie) .05
351 Bobby Witt .05
352 Paul Konerko (Prime Rookie) .25
353 Matt Morris .05
354 Carl Pavano (Prime Rookie) .05
355 Todd Zeile .05
356 Kevin Brown (Transaction) .05
357 Alex Gonzalez .05
358 Chuck Knoblauch (Transaction) .05
359 Joey Cora .05
360 Mike Lansing (Transaction) .05
361 Adrian Beltre (Future Stars) .45
362 Dennis Eckersley (Transaction) .65
363 A.J. Hinch (Future Stars) .05
364 Kenny Lofton (Transaction) .05
365 Alex Gonzalez (Future Stars) .05
366 Henry Rodriguez (Transaction) .05
367 Mike Stoner **RC** (Future Stars) .05
368 Darryl Kile (Transaction) .05
369 Carl Pavano (Future Stars) .05
370 Walt Weiss (Transaction) .05
371 Kris Benson (Future Stars) .05
372 Cecil Fielder (Transaction) .05
373 Dermal Brown (Future Stars) .05
374 Rod Beck (Transaction) .05
375 Eric Milton (Future Stars) .05
376 Travis Fryman (Transaction) .05
377 Preston Wilson (Future Stars) .10
378 Chili Davis (Transaction) .05
379 Travis Lee (Future Stars) .10
380 Jim Leyritz (Transaction) .05
381 Vernon Wells (Draft Picks) .05
382 Joe Carter (Transaction) .05
383 J.J. Davis (Draft Picks) .05
384 Marquis Grissom (Transaction) .05
385 Mike Cuddyer **RC** (Draft Picks) .50
386 Rickey Henderson (Transaction) .75
387 Chris Enochs **RC** (Draft Picks) .10
388 Andres Galarraga (Transaction) .05
389 Jason Dellaero (Draft Picks) .05
390 Robb Nen (Transaction) .05
391 Mark Mangum (Draft Picks) .05
392 Jeff Blauser (Transaction) .05
393 Adam Kennedy (Draft Picks) .05
394 Bob Abreu (Transaction) .05
395 Jack Cust **RC** (Draft Picks) 1.00
396 Jose Vizcaino (Transaction) .05
397 Jon Garland (Draft Picks) .05
398 Pedro Martinez (Transaction) .75
399 Aaron Akin (Draft Picks) .05
400 Jeff Conine (Transaction) .05

First Day Issue

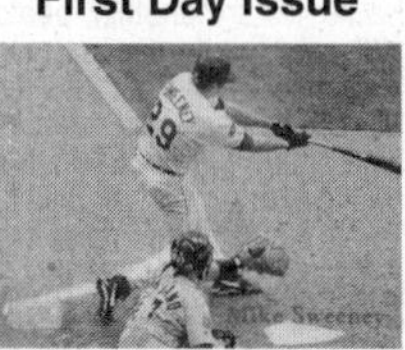

	NM/M
Common Player:	2.00
Stars:	10X
Production 200 Sets	

One of a Kind

This hobby-only parallel set includes all 400 cards from Series 1 and 2 printed on a silver mirrorboard stock. Cards are sequentially numbered to

150 and inserted one per 21 Series 1 packs and one per 24 Series 2 packs.

	NM/M
Common Player:	2.00
Stars:	12X
Production 150 Sets	

Bowman Preview

This Series I insert gave collectors a sneak peak at Bowman's 50th anniversary set, with 10 top veterans displayed on the 1998 Bowman design. The cards were inserted one per 12 packs and numbered with a "BP" prefix.

		NM/M
Complete Set (10):		10.00
Common Player:		.25
Inserted 1:12		
BP1	Nomar Garciaparra	1.00
BP2	Scott Rolen	.65
BP3	Ken Griffey Jr.	1.50
BP4	Frank Thomas	.75
BP5	Larry Walker	.25
BP6	Mike Piazza	1.50
BP7	Chipper Jones	1.00
BP8	Tino Martinez	.25
BP9	Mark McGwire	2.00
BP10	Barry Bonds	2.50

Bowman Prospect Preview

Bowman Prospect Previews were inserted into Series 2 retail and hobby packs at a rate of one per 12 and HTA packs at one per four. The 10-card insert previews the upcoming 1998 Bowman set and includes top prospects that were expected to make an impact in 1998.

		NM/M
Complete Set (10):		3.00
Common Player:		.25
Inserted 1:12		
BP1	Ben Grieve	.25
BP2	Brad Fullmer	.25
BP3	Ryan Anderson	.25
BP4	Mark Kotsay	.25
BP5	Bobby Estalella	.25
BP6	Juan Encarnacion	.25
BP7	Todd Helton	2.00
BP8	Mike Lowell	.25
BP9	A.J. Hinch	.25
BP10	Richard Hidalgo	.25

Co-Signers

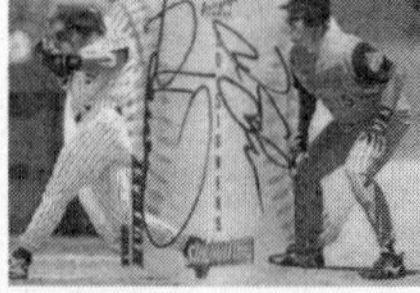

Co-Signers were inserted into both Series 1 and 2 hobby and HTA packs. The complete set is 36 cards, each featuring two top players along with both autographs. They were available in three levels of scarcity: Series 1 Group A 1:4,372 hobby and 1:2,623 HTA; Series 1 Group B 1:1,457 hobby and HTA 1:874; Series 1 Group C 1:121 hobby and 1:73 HTA; Series 2 Group A 1:4,702 hobby and 1:2,821 HTA; Series 2 Group B 1:1,567 hobby and 1:940 HTA, Series 2 Group C 1:1,131 hobby and 1:78 HTA. Some cards are known that bear fake autographs, despite having the Topps seal of authenticity. Those cards are believed to have been released in unsigned form in an unauthorized manner, and then signed with counterfeit signatures.

		NM/M
Common Card:		10.00
Group A 1:4,372		
Group B 1:1,457		
Group C 1:121		
CS1	Nomar Garciaparra, Scott Rolen/A	120.00
CS2	Nomar Garciaparra, Derek Jeter/B	250.00
CS3	Nomar Garciaparra, Eric Karros/C	60.00
CS4	Scott Rolen, Derek Jeter/C	100.00
CS5	Scott Rolen, Eric Karros/B	40.00
CS6	Derek Jeter, Eric Karros/A	150.00
CS7	Travis Lee, Jose Cruz Jr./B	15.00
CS8	Travis Lee, Mark Kotsay/C	10.00
CS9	Travis Lee, Paul Konerko/A	25.00
CS10	Jose Cruz Jr., Mark Kotsay/A	25.00
CS11	Jose Cruz Jr., Paul Konerko/C	12.00
CS12	Mark Kotsay, Paul Konerko/B	20.00
CS13	Tony Gwynn, Larry Walker/A	120.00
CS14	Tony Gwynn, Mark Grudzielanek/C	30.00
CS15	Tony Gwynn, Andres Galarraga/B	60.00
CS16	Larry Walker, Mark Grudzielanek/B	40.00
CS17	Larry Walker, Andres Galarraga/C	30.00
CS18	Mark Grudzielanek, Andres Galarraga/A	25.00
CS19	Sandy Alomar, Roberto Alomar/A	75.00
CS20	Sandy Alomar, Andy Pettitte/C	20.00
CS21	Sandy Alomar, Tino Martinez/B	40.00
CS22	Roberto Alomar, Andy Pettitte/B	50.00
CS23	Roberto Alomar, Tino Martinez/C	25.00
CS24	Andy Pettitte, Tino Martinez/A	75.00
CS25	Tony Clark, Todd Hundley/A	25.00
CS26	Tony Clark, Tim Salmon/B	30.00
CS27	Tony Clark, Robin Ventura/C	10.00
CS28	Todd Hundley, Tim Salmon/C	15.00
CS29	Todd Hundley, Robin Ventura/B	12.00
CS30	Tim Salmon, Robin Ventura/A	50.00
CS31	Roger Clemens, Randy Johnson/B	175.00
CS32	Roger Clemens, Jaret Wright/A	140.00
CS33	Roger Clemens, Matt Morris/C	100.00
CS34	Randy Johnson, Jaret Wright/C	50.00
CS35	Randy Johnson, Matt Morris/A	85.00
CS36	Jaret Wright, Matt Morris/B	20.00

In the Wings

In the Wings was a Series I insert found every 36 packs. It included 15 future stars on uniluster technology.

		NM/M
Complete Set (15):		6.00
Common Player:		.50

Inserted 1:36		
W1	Juan Encarnacion	.50
W2	Brad Fullmer	.50
W3	Ben Grieve	.50
W4	Todd Helton	3.00
W5	Richard Hidalgo	.50
W6	Russ Johnson	.50
W7	Paul Konerko	.75
W8	Mark Kotsay	.50
W9	Derrek Lee	1.00
W10	Travis Lee	.50
W11	Eli Marrero	.50
W12	David Ortiz	.75
W13	Randall Simon	.50
W14	Shannon Stewart	.50
W15	Fernando Tatis	.50

Never Compromise

Never Compromise was a 20-card insert found in packs of Series I. Cards were inserted one per 12 packs and numbered with a "NC" prefix.

		NM/M
Complete Set (20):		10.00
Common Player:		.15
Inserted 1:12		
NC1	Cal Ripken Jr.	2.00
NC2	Ivan Rodriguez	.50
NC3	Ken Griffey Jr.	1.00
NC4	Frank Thomas	.60
NC5	Tony Gwynn	.75
NC6	Mike Piazza	1.00
NC7	Randy Johnson	.60
NC8	Greg Maddux	.75
NC9	Roger Clemens	.85
NC10	Derek Jeter	2.00
NC11	Chipper Jones	.75
NC12	Barry Bonds	2.00
NC13	Larry Walker	.15
NC14	Jeff Bagwell	.60
NC15	Barry Larkin	.15
NC16	Ken Caminiti	.15
NC17	Mark McGwire	1.50
NC18	Manny Ramirez	.60
NC19	Tim Salmon	.15
NC20	Paul Molitor	.60

Playing with Passion

This Series II insert displayed 10 players with a strong desire to win. The cards are numbered with a "P" prefix.

		NM/M
Complete Set (10):		10.00
Common Player:		.35
Inserted 1:12		
P1	Bernie Williams	.35
P2	Jim Edmonds	.35
P3	Chipper Jones	1.00
P4	Cal Ripken Jr.	3.00
P5	Craig Biggio	.35
P6	Juan Gonzalez	.45
P7	Alex Rodriguez	2.25
P8	Tino Martinez	.35
P9	Mike Piazza	1.50
P10	Ken Griffey Jr.	1.50

Printing Plates

Inserted only in Home Team Advantage boxes at a rate of approximately one per 90 packs were the actual aluminum plates used to print the fronts of the base cards. Unlike some printing plate issues, the plates used for the card backs were not inserted. Each card's plate can be found in four different colors: Cyan, magenta, yellow and black. Because of their unique nature, pricing of individual player's plates cannot be provided.

	NM/M
Common Player:	25.00

Royal Court

Fifteen players were showcased on uniluster technology for this Series II insert. The set is broken up into 10 Kings (veterans) and five Princes (rookies) and inserted one per 36 packs.

		NM/M
Complete Set (15):		15.00
Common Player:		.50
Inserted 1:36		
RC1	Ken Griffey Jr.	2.00
RC2	Frank Thomas	1.25
RC3	Mike Piazza	2.00
RC4	Chipper Jones	1.50
RC5	Mark McGwire	2.50
RC6	Cal Ripken Jr.	3.00
RC7	Jeff Bagwell	1.25
RC8	Barry Bonds	3.00
RC9	Juan Gonzalez	.85
RC10	Alex Rodriguez	2.50
RC11	Travis Lee	.50
RC12	Paul Konerko	.75
RC13	Todd Helton	1.00
RC14	Ben Grieve	.50
RC15	Mark Kotsay	.50

Screen Plays Sound Chips

One of the packs in each Home Team Advantage box of TSC "Odd Series" cards contained this special "card" commemorating the home run hit by Cal Ripken, Jr. in his historic 2,131st game on Sept. 6, 1995. The item is 3-1/2" x 2-1/2" x 3/8" deep. Glued to the top is a magic motion card showing Ripken hitting the blast. When a corner of the card is squeezed, a sound chip replays the radio call of the home run by Jon Miller and President Bill Clinton. The top of the package opens to reveal a newspaper-like presentation with a picture of Ripken, details of his home run and the technology used to produce the item.

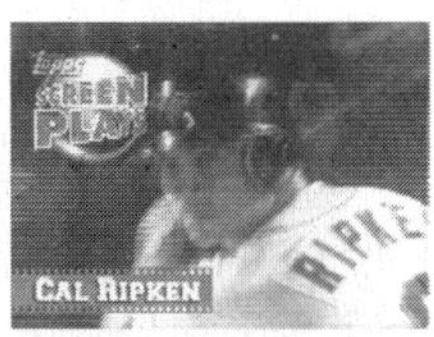

		NM/M
SC1	Cal Ripken Jr.	5.00

Triumvirate

Triumvirates were included in both series of Stadium Club and were available only in retail packs. Series 1 has 24 players, with three players from eight different teams, while Series 2 has 30 players, with three players from 10 different positions. The cards are all die-cut and fit together to form three-card panels. Three different versions of each card were available - Luminous (regular) versions were seeded one per 48 packs, Luminescent versions were seeded one per 192 packs and Illuminator versions were seeded one per 384 packs.

		NM/M
Complete Set (54):		70.00
Complete Series 1 (24):		30.00
Complete Series 2 (30):		40.00
Common Player:		.50
Luminous 1:48		
Luminescents 1:192:		1.5X
Illuminators 1:384:		2.5X
T1a	Chipper Jones	2.50
T1b	Andruw Jones	2.00
T1c	Kenny Lofton	.50
T2a	Derek Jeter	5.00
T2b	Bernie Williams	.50
T2c	Tino Martinez	.50
T3a	Jay Buhner	.50
T3b	Edgar Martinez	.50
T3c	Ken Griffey Jr.	3.00
T4a	Albert Belle	.50
T4b	Robin Ventura	.50
T4c	Frank Thomas	2.00
T5a	Brady Anderson	.50
T5b	Cal Ripken Jr.	5.00
T5c	Rafael Palmeiro	1.50
T6a	Mike Piazza	3.00
T6b	Raul Mondesi	.50
T6c	Eric Karros	.50
T7a	Vinny Castilla	.50
T7b	Andres Galarraga	.50
T7c	Larry Walker	.50
T8a	Jim Thome	1.50
T8b	Manny Ramirez	2.00
T8c	David Justice	.50
T9a	Mike Mussina	.75
T9b	Greg Maddux	2.50
T9c	Randy Johnson	2.00
T10a	Mike Piazza	3.00
T10b	Sandy Alomar	.50
T10c	Ivan Rodriguez	1.50
T11a	Mark McGwire	4.00
T11b	Tino Martinez	.50
T11c	Frank Thomas	2.00
T12a	Roberto Alomar	.75
T12b	Chuck Knoblauch	.50
T12c	Craig Biggio	.50
T13a	Cal Ripken Jr.	5.00
T13b	Chipper Jones	2.50
T13c	Ken Caminiti	.50
T14a	Derek Jeter	5.00
T14b	Nomar Garciaparra	2.50
T14c	Alex Rodriguez	4.00
T15a	Barry Bonds	5.00
T15b	David Justice	.50
T15c	Albert Belle	.50
T16a	Bernie Williams	.50
T16b	Ken Griffey Jr.	3.00
T16c	Ray Lankford	.50
T17a	Tim Salmon	.50
T17b	Larry Walker	.50
T17c	Tony Gwynn	2.50
T18a	Paul Molitor	2.00
T18b	Edgar Martinez	.50
T18c	Juan Gonzalez	1.00

1999 Stadium Club

Released in two series, base cards feature a full bleed design on 20-pt. stock with an embossed holographic logo. Draft Pick, Prospect and Series 2 Future Star subset cards are short-printed, seeded in every three packs. Card backs have 1998 statistics and personal information. Hobby packs consist of six cards with an S.R.P. of $2.

		NM/M
Complete Set (355):		40.00
Complete Series 1 (170):		20.00
Complete Series 2 (185):		20.00
Common Player:		.05
Common SP (141-160; 336-355):		.50
Inserted 1:3		
Pack (6):		1.25
Wax Box (24):		25.00
1	Alex Rodriguez	2.00
2	Chipper Jones	1.50
3	Rusty Greer	.05
4	Jim Edmonds	.05
5	Ron Gant	.05
6	Kevin Polcovich	.05
7	Darryl Strawberry	.05
8	Bill Mueller	.05
9	Vinny Castilla	.05
10	Wade Boggs	1.50
11	Jose Lima	.05
12	Darren Dreifort	.05
13	Jay Bell	.05
14	Ben Grieve	.05
15	Shawn Green	.35
16	Andres Galarraga	.05
17	Bartolo Colon	.05
18	Francisco Cordova	.05
19	Paul O'Neill	.05
20	Trevor Hoffman	.05
21	Darren Oliver	.05
22	John Franco	.05
23	Eli Marrero	.05
24	Roberto Hernandez	.05
25	Craig Biggio	.05
26	Brad Fullmer	.05
27	Scott Erickson	.05
28	Tom Gordon	.05
29	Brian Hunter	.05
30	Raul Mondesi	.05
31	Rick Reed	.05
32	Jose Canseco	.50
33	Robb Nen	.05
34	Turner Ward	.05
35	Bret Boone	.05
36	Jose Offerman	.05
37	Matt Lawton	.05
38	David Wells	.05
39	Bob Abreu	.10
40	Jeromy Burnitz	.05
41	Deivi Cruz	.05
42	Mike Cameron	.05
43	Rico Brogna	.05
44	Dmitri Young	.05
45	Chuck Knoblauch	.05
46	Johnny Damon	.35
47	Brian Meadows	.05
48	Jeremi Gonzalez	.05
49	Gary DiSarcina	.05
50	Frank Thomas	1.00
51	F.P. Santangelo	.05
52	Tom Candiotti	.05
53	Shane Reynolds	.05
54	Rod Beck	.05
55	Rey Ordonez	.05
56	Todd Helton	.75
57	Mickey Morandini	.05
58	Jorge Posada	.05
59	Mike Mussina	.30
60	Bobby Bonilla	.05
61	David Segui	.05
62	Brian McRae	.05
63	Fred McGriff	.05
64	Brett Tomko	.05
65	Derek Jeter	2.50
66	Sammy Sosa	1.50
67	Kenny Rogers	.05
68	Dave Nilsson	.05
69	Eric Young	.05
70	Mark McGwire	2.00
71	Kenny Lofton	.05
72	Tom Glavine	.35
73	Joey Hamilton	.05
74	John Valentin	.05
75	Mariano Rivera	.15
76	Ray Durham	.05
77	Tony Clark	.05
78	Livan Hernandez	.05
79	Rickey Henderson	1.00
80	Vladimir Guerrero	1.00
81	J.T. Snow Jr.	.05
82	Juan Guzman	.05
83	Darryl Hamilton	.05
84	Matt Anderson	.05
85	Travis Lee	.05
86	Joe Randa	.05
87	Dave Dellucci	.05
88	Moises Alou	.05
89	Alex Gonzalez	.05
90	Tony Womack	.05
91	Neifi Perez	.05
92	Travis Fryman	.05
93	Masato Yoshii	.05
94	Woody Williams	.05
95	Ray Lankford	.05
96	Roger Clemens	1.50
97	Dustin Hermanson	.05
98	Joe Carter	.05
99	Jason Schmidt	.05
100	Greg Maddux	1.50
101	Kevin Tapani	.05
102	Charles Johnson	.05
103	Derrek Lee	.50
104	Pete Harnisch	.05
105	Dante Bichette	.05
106	Scott Brosius	.05
107	Mike Caruso	.05
108	Eddie Taubensee	.05
109	Jeff Fassero	.05
110	Marquis Grissom	.05
111	Jose Hernandez	.05
112	Chan Ho Park	.05
113	Wally Joyner	.05
114	Bobby Estalella	.05
115	Pedro Martinez	1.00
116	Shawn Estes	.05
117	Walt Weiss	.05
118	John Mabry	.05
119	Brian Johnson	.05
120	Jim Thome	.65
121	Bill Spiers	.05
122	John Olerud	.05
123	Jeff King	.05
124	Tim Belcher	.05
125	John Wetteland	.05
126	Tony Gwynn	1.50
127	Brady Anderson	.05
128	Randy Winn	.05
129	Devon White	.05
130	Eric Karros	.05
131	Kevin Millwood	.05
132	Andy Benes	.05
133	Andy Ashby	.05
134	Ron Comer	.05
135	Juan Gonzalez	.50
136	Randy Johnson	1.00
137	Aaron Sele	.05
138	Edgardo Alfonzo	.05
139	B.J. Surhoff	.05
140	Jose Vizcaino	.05
141	Chad Moeller **RC** (Prospect)	.75
142	Mike Zwicka **RC** (Prospect)	.50
143	Angel Pena (Prospect)	.50
144	Nick Johnson **RC** (Prospect)	2.00
145	Giuseppe Chiaramonte **RC** (Prospect)	.50
146	Kit Pellow **RC** (Prospect)	.50
147	Clayton Andrews **RC** (Prospect)	.50
148	Jerry Hairston Jr. **RC** (Prospect)	.75
149	Jason Tyner **RC** (Draft Pick)	.50
150	Chip Ambres **RC** (Draft Pick)	.50
151	Pat Burrell **RC** (Draft Pick)	2.00
152	Josh McKinley **RC** (Draft Pick)	.75
153	Choo Freeman **RC** (Draft Pick)	.75
154	Rick Elder **RC** (Draft Pick)	.50
155	Eric Valent **RC** (Draft Pick)	.75
156	Jeff Winchester **RC** (Draft Pick)	.50
157	Mike Nannini **RC** (Draft Pick)	.50
158	Mamon Tucker **RC** (Draft Pick)	.50
159	Nate Bump **RC** (Draft Pick)	.50
160	Andy Brown **RC** (Draft Pick)	.50
161	Troy Glaus (Future Star)	1.00
162	Adrian Beltre (Future Star)	.45
163	Mitch Meluskey (Future Star)	.05
164	Alex Gonzalez (Future Star)	.05
165	George Lombard (Future Star)	.05
166	Eric Chavez (Future Star)	.25
167	Ruben Mateo (Future Star)	.05
168	Calvin Pickering (Future Star)	.05
169	Gabe Kapler (Future Star)	.05
170	Bruce Chen (Future Star)	.05
171	Darin Erstad	.15
172	Sandy Alomar	.05
173	Miguel Cairo	.05
174	Jason Kendall	.05
175	Cal Ripken Jr.	2.50
176	Darryl Kile	.05
177	David Cone	.05
178	Mike Sweeney	.05
179	Royce Clayton	.05
180	Curt Schilling	.25
181	Barry Larkin	.05
182	Eric Milton	.05
183	Ellis Burks	.05
184	A.J. Hinch	.05
185	Garret Anderson	.05
186	Sean Bergman	.05
187	Shannon Stewart	.05
188	Bernard Gilkey	.05
189	Jeff Blauser	.05
190	Andruw Jones	1.00
191	Omar Daal	.05
192	Jeff Kent	.05
193	Mark Kotsay	.05
194	Dave Burba	.05
195	Bobby Higginson	.05
196	Hideki Irabu	.05
197	Jamie Moyer	.05
198	Doug Glanville	.05
199	Quinton McCracken	.05
200	Ken Griffey Jr.	1.75
201	Mike Lieberthal	.05
202	Carl Everett	.05
203	Omar Vizquel	.05
204	Mike Lansing	.05
205	Manny Ramirez	1.00
206	Ryan Klesko	.05
207	Jeff Montgomery	.05
208	Chad Curtis	.05
209	Rick Helling	.05
210	Justin Thompson	.05
211	Tom Goodwin	.05
212	Todd Dunwoody	.05
213	Kevin Young	.05
214	Tony Saunders	.05
215	Gary Sheffield	.45
216	Jaret Wright	.05
217	Quilvio Veras	.05
218	Marty Cordova	.05
219	Tino Martinez	.05
220	Scott Rolen	.75
221	Fernando Tatis	.05
222	Damion Easley	.05
223	Aramis Ramirez	.05
224	Brad Radke	.05
225	Nomar Garciaparra	1.50
226	Magglio Ordonez	.05
227	Andy Pettitte	.20
228	David Ortiz	.45
229	Todd Jones	.05
230	Larry Walker	.05
231	Tim Wakefield	.05
232	Jose Guillen	.05
233	Gregg Olson	.05
234	Ricky Gutierrez	.05
235	Todd Walker	.05
236	Abraham Nunez	.05
237	Sean Casey	.15
238	Greg Norton	.05
239	Bret Saberhagen	.05
240	Bernie Williams	.05
241	Tim Salmon	.05
242	Jason Giambi	.50
243	Fernando Vina	.05
244	Darrin Fletcher	.05
245	Greg Vaughn	.05
246	Dennis Reyes	.05
247	Hideo Nomo	.50
248	Reggie Sanders	.05
249	Mike Hampton	.05
250	Kerry Wood	.50
251	Ismael Valdes	.05
252	Pat Hentgen	.05
253	Scott Spiezio	.05
254	Chuck Finley	.05
255	Troy Glaus	.75
256	Bobby Jones	.05
257	Wayne Gomes	.05
258	Rondell White	.05
259	Todd Zeile	.05
260	Matt Williams	.05
261	Henry Rodriguez	.05
262	Matt Stairs	.05
263	Jose Valentin	.05
264	David Justice	.05
265	Javy Lopez	.05
266	Matt Morris	.05
267	Steve Trachsel	.05
268	Edgar Martinez	.05
269	Al Martin	.05
270	Ivan Rodriguez	.75
271	Carlos Delgado	.50
272	Mark Grace	.05
273	Ugueth Urbina	.05
274	Jay Buhner	.05
275	Mike Piazza	1.75
276	Rick Aguilera	.05
277	Javier Valentin	.05
278	Brian Anderson	.05
279	Cliff Floyd	.05
280	Barry Bonds	2.50
281	Troy O'Leary	.05
282	Seth Greisinger	.05
283	Mark Grudzielanek	.05
284	Jose Cruz Jr.	.05
285	Jeff Bagwell	1.00
286	John Smoltz	.05
287	Jeff Cirillo	.05
288	Richie Sexson	.05
289	Charles Nagy	.05
290	Pedro Martinez	1.00
291	Juan Encarnacion	.05
292	Phil Nevin	.05
293	Terry Steinbach	.05
294	Miguel Tejada	.15
295	Dan Wilson	.05
296	Chris Peters	.05
297	Brian Moehler	.05
298	Jason Christiansen	.05
299	Kelly Stinnett	.05
300	Dwight Gooden	.05
301	Randy Velarde	.05
302	Kirt Manwaring	.05
303	Jeff Abbott	.05
304	Dave Hollins	.05
305	Kerry Ligtenberg	.05
306	Aaron Boone	.05
307	Carlos Hernandez	.05
308	Mike DiFelice	.05
309	Brian Meadows	.05
310	Tim Bogar	.05
311	Greg Vaughn (Transaction)	.05
312	Brant Brown (Transaction)	.05
313	Steve Finley (Transaction)	.05
314	Bret Boone (Transaction)	.05
315	Albert Belle (Transaction)	.05
316	Robin Ventura (Transaction)	.05
317	Eric Davis (Transaction)	.05
318	Todd Hundley (Transaction)	.05
319	Jose Offerman (Transaction)	.05
320	Kevin Brown (Transaction)	.05
321	Denny Neagle (Transaction)	.05
322	Brian Jordan (Transaction)	.05
323	Brian Giles (Transaction)	.05
324	Bobby Bonilla (Transaction)	.05
325	Roberto Alomar (Transaction)	.20
326	Ken Caminiti (Transaction)	.05
327	Todd Stottlemyre (Transaction)	.05
328	Randy Johnson (Transaction)	1.00
329	Luis Gonzalez (Transaction)	.05
330	Rafael Palmeiro (Transaction)	.75
331	Devon White (Transaction)	.05
332	Will Clark (Transaction)	.05
333	Dean Palmer (Transaction)	.05
334	Gregg Jefferies (Transaction)	.05
335	Mo Vaughn (Transaction)	.05
336	Brad Lidge **RC** (Draft Pick)	2.00
337	Chris George **RC** (Draft Pick)	.75
338	Austin Kearns **RC** (Draft Pick)	1.50
339	Matt Belisle **RC** (Draft Pick)	.75
340	Nate Cornejo **RC** (Draft Pick)	.75
341	Matt Holliday **RC** (Draft Pick)	5.00
342	J.M. Gold **RC** (Draft Pick)	.50

343	Matt Roney **RC** (Draft Pick)	.50
344	Seth Etherton **RC** (Draft Pick)	.75
345	Adam Everett **RC** (Draft Pick)	.75
346	Marlon Anderson (Future Star)	.50
347	Ron Belliard (Future Star)	.50
348	Fernando Seguignol (Future Star)	.50
349	Michael Barrett (Future Star)	.50
350	Dernell Stenson (Future Star)	.50
351	Ryan Anderson (Future Star)	.50
352	Ramon Hernandez (Future Star)	.50
353	Jeremy Giambi (Future Star)	.50
354	Ricky Ledee (Future Star)	.50
355	Carlos Lee (Future Star)	1.00

First Day Issue

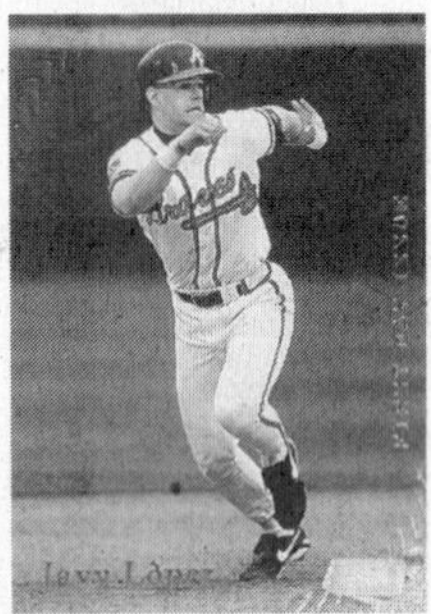

A parallel of the 355-card set inserted exclusively in retail packs, Series I (1-170) are serially numbered to 170 at a rate of 1:75 packs. Series 2 (171-355) are serially numbered to 200 and inserted at a rate of 1:60 packs.

	NM/M
Common Player:	2.00
Stars:	8X
SP Stars:	4X

One of a Kind

This insert set parallels the 355-card base set. Cards feature a mirrorboard look and are serially numbered to 150. Inserted exclusively in hobby packs, insertion rate for Series 1 is 1:53 and Series 2 is 1:48 packs.

	NM/M
Common Player:	2.00
Stars:	8X
SP Stars:	4X

Autographs

This 10-card autographed set was issued in Series 1 and 2 with five players signing in each series. Available exclusively in retail chains, Series 1 autographs were seeded 1:1,107 packs, while series 2 were inserted in every 877 packs. Each autograph is marked with the Topps Certified Autograph Issue stamp. Card numbers have an "SCA" prefix.

		NM/M
Common Player:		10.00
Inserted 1:1,107		
1	Alex Rodriguez	75.00
2	Chipper Jones	30.00
3	Barry Bonds	150.00
4	Tino Martinez	25.00
5	Ben Grieve	10.00
6	Juan Gonzalez	15.00
7	Vladimir Guerrero	30.00
8	Albert Belle	15.00
9	Kerry Wood	25.00
10	Todd Helton	20.00

Chrome

This 40-card set was inserted in Series 1 and 2 packs, with 1-20 in first series packs and 21-40 in Series 2. Chrome appropriately utilizes chromium technology. Card numbers have an "SCC" prefix.

		NM/M
Complete Set (40):		45.00
Common Player:		.50
Inserted 1:24		
Refractors:		2X
Inserted 1:96		
1	Nomar Garciaparra	2.00
2	Kerry Wood	1.00
3	Jeff Bagwell	1.50
4	Ivan Rodriguez	1.25
5	Albert Belle	.50
6	Gary Sheffield	1.00
7	Andruw Jones	1.50
8	Kevin Brown	.50
9	David Cone	.50
10	Darin Erstad	.75
11	Manny Ramirez	1.50
12	Larry Walker	.50
13	Mike Piazza	2.50
14	Cal Ripken Jr.	4.00
15	Pedro Martinez	1.50
16	Greg Vaughn	.50
17	Barry Bonds	4.00
18	Mo Vaughn	.50
19	Bernie Williams	.50
20	Ken Griffey Jr.	2.50
21	Alex Rodriguez	3.00
22	Chipper Jones	2.00
23	Ben Grieve	.50
24	Frank Thomas	1.50
25	Derek Jeter	4.00
26	Sammy Sosa	2.00
27	Mark McGwire	3.00
28	Vladimir Guerrero	1.50
29	Greg Maddux	2.00
30	Juan Gonzalez	.75
31	Troy Glaus	1.25
32	Adrian Beltre	1.25
33	Mitch Meluskey	.50
34	Alex Gonzalez	.50
35	George Lombard	.50
36	Eric Chavez	.75
37	Ruben Mateo	.50
38	Calvin Pickering	.50
39	Gabe Kapler	.50
40	Bruce Chen	.50

Co-Signers

Co-Signers feature two autographs on each card and also for the first time includes one level of four autographs per card. Co-Signers are grouped into categories A, B, C and D. Group A Co-Signers are autographed by four players, while B-D are signed by two players. Each card features the Topps Certified Autograph Issue stamp.

		NM/M
Common Group A:		90.00
Inserted 1:18,085		
Common Group B:		20.00
Inserted 1:9043		
Common Group C:		9.00
Inserted 1:3014		
Common Group D:		6.00
Inserted 1:254		
CS1	Ben Grieve, Richie Sexson/D	15.00
CS2	Todd Helton, Troy Glaus/D	50.00
CS3	Alex Rodriguez, Scott Rolen/D	85.00
CS4	Derek Jeter, Chipper Jones/D	150.00
CS5	Cliff Floyd, Eli Marrero/D	6.00
CS6	Jay Buhner, Kevin Young/D	8.00
CS7	Ben Grieve, Troy Glaus/C	40.00
CS8	Todd Helton, Richie Sexson/C	40.00
CS9	Alex Rodriguez, Chipper Jones/C	125.00
CS10	Derek Jeter, Scott Rolen/C	125.00
CS11	Cliff Floyd, Kevin Young/C	10.00
CS12	Jay Buhner, Eli Marrero/B	10.00
CS13	Ben Grieve, Todd Helton/B	50.00
CS14	Richie Sexson, Troy Glaus/B	40.00
CS15	Alex Rodriguez, Derek Jeter/B	350.00
CS16	Chipper Jones, Scott Rolen/B	150.00
CS17	Cliff Floyd, Jay Buhner/B	15.00
CS18	Eli Marrero, Kevin Young/B	20.00
CS19	Ben Grieve, Todd Helton, Richie Sexson, Troy Glaus/A	180.00
CS20	Alex Rodriguez, Derek Jeter, Chipper Jones, Scott Rolen/A	2,500
CS21	Cliff Floyd, Jay Buhner, Eli Marrero, Kevin Young/A	100.00
CS22	Edgardo Alfonzo, Jose Guillen/D	15.00
CS23	Mike Lowell, Ricardo Rincon/D	10.00
CS24	Juan Gonzalez, Vinny Castilla/D	20.00
CS25	Moises Alou, Roger Clemens/D	60.00
CS26	Scott Spezio, Tony Womack/D	10.00
CS27	Fernando Vina, Quilvio Veras/D	10.00
CS28	Edgardo Alfonzo, Ricardo Rincon/C	10.00
CS29	Jose Guillen, Mike Lowell/C	10.00
CS30	Juan Gonzalez, Moises Alou/C	25.00
CS31	Roger Clemens, Vinny Castilla/C	85.00
CS32	Scott Spezio, Fernando Vina/C	10.00
CS33	Tony Womack, Quilvio Veras/B	20.00
CS34	Edgardo Alfonzo, Mike Lowell/B	30.00
CS35	Jose Guillen, Ricardo Rincon/B	30.00
CS36	Juan Gonzalez, Roger Clemens/B	135.00
CS37	Moises Alou, Vinny Castilla/B	30.00
CS38	Scott Spezio, Quilvio Veras/B	20.00
CS39	Tony Womack, Fernando Vina/B	20.00
CS40	Edgardo Alfonzo, Jose Guillen, Mike Lowell, Ricardo Rincon/A	90.00
CS41	Juan Gonzalez, Moises Alou, Roger Clemens, Vinny Castilla/A	900.00
CS42	Scott Spezio, Tony Womack, Fernando Vina, Quilvio Veras/A	90.00

Never Compromise

Topps selected players who bring hard work and devotion to the field every game. The first 10 cards in the set are inserted in Series 1 packs while the remaining 10 are seeded in Series 2 at a rate of 1:12 packs.

		NM/M
Complete Set (20):		10.00
Common Player:		.25
Inserted 1:12		
NC1	Mark McGwire	1.00
NC2	Sammy Sosa	.65
NC3	Ken Griffey Jr.	.75
NC4	Greg Maddux	.65
NC5	Barry Bonds	1.50
NC6	Alex Rodriguez	1.00
NC7	Darin Erstad	.35
NC8	Roger Clemens	.65
NC9	Nomar Garciaparra	.65
NC10	Derek Jeter	1.50
NC11	Cal Ripken Jr.	1.50
NC12	Mike Piazza	.75
NC13	Greg Vaughn	.25
NC14	Andres Galarraga	.25
NC15	Vinny Castilla	.25
NC16	Jeff Bagwell	.50
NC17	Chipper Jones	.65
NC18	Eric Chavez	.35
NC19	Orlando Hernandez	.25
NC20	Troy Glaus	.40

Printing Plates

Inserted only in Home Team Advantage boxes at a rate of approximately one per 175 packs were the actual aluminum plates used to print the fronts of the base cards. Unlike some printing plate issues, the plates used for the card backs were not inserted. Each card's plate can be found in four different colors: Cyan, magenta, yellow and black. Because of their unique nature, pricing of individual player's plates cannot be provided.

	NM/M
Common Player:	25.00

Triumvirate

Three of these inserts "fuse" together to form a set of three cards, forming a Triumvirate. 48 players, 24 from each series, are available in three different technologies, Luminous, Luminescent and Illuminator.

	NM/M
Complete Set (48):	75.00
Common Player:	.50
Inserted 1:36	
Luminescents:	1.5X
Inserted 1:144	

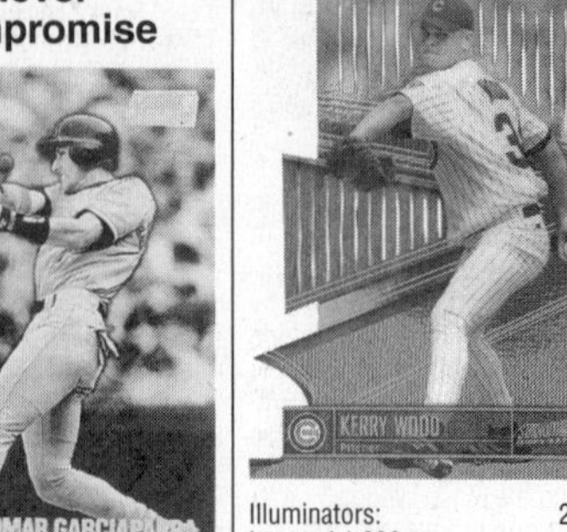

Illuminators:		2.5X
Inserted 1:288		
T1A	Greg Vaughn	.50
T1B	Ken Caminiti	.50
T1C	Tony Gwynn	2.50
T2A	Andruw Jones	2.00
T2B	Chipper Jones	2.50
T2C	Andres Galarraga	.50
T3A	Jay Buhner	.50
T3B	Ken Griffey Jr.	3.00
T3C	Alex Rodriguez	4.00
T4A	Derek Jeter	6.00
T4B	Tino Martinez	.50
T4C	Bernie Williams	.50
T5A	Brian Jordan	.50
T5B	Ray Lankford	.50
T5C	Mark McGwire	4.00
T6A	Jeff Bagwell	2.00
T6B	Craig Biggio	.50
T6C	Randy Johnson	2.00
T7A	Nomar Garciaparra	2.50
T7B	Pedro Martinez	2.00
T7C	Mo Vaughn	.50
T8A	Mark Grace	.50
T8B	Sammy Sosa	2.50
T8C	Kerry Wood	1.00
T9A	Alex Rodriguez	4.00
T9B	Nomar Garciaparra	2.50
T9C	Derek Jeter	6.00
T10A	Todd Helton	1.50
T10B	Travis Lee	.50
T10C	Pat Burrell	1.50
T11A	Greg Maddux	2.50
T11B	Kerry Wood	1.00
T11C	Tom Glavine	.75
T12A	Chipper Jones	2.50
T12B	Vinny Castilla	.50
T12C	Scott Rolen	1.50
T13A	Juan Gonzalez	1.00
T13B	Ken Griffey Jr.	3.00
T13C	Ben Grieve	.50
T14A	Sammy Sosa	3.00
T14B	Vladimir Guerrero	2.00
T14C	Barry Bonds	6.00
T15A	Frank Thomas	2.00
T15B	Jim Thome	1.50
T15C	Tino Martinez	.50
T16A	Mark McGwire	4.00
T16B	Andres Galarraga	.50
T16C	Jeff Bagwell	2.00

Video Replay

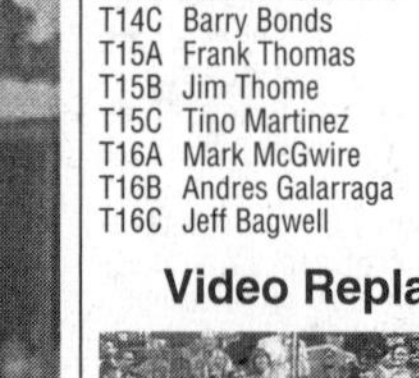

Utilizing lenticular technology, these inserts capture highlights, such as McGwire's 70th home run, from the '98 season. By tilting the card, successive images show the selected highlight almost come to life. Video Replays are in inserted in Series 2 packs at a rate of 1:12.

		NM/M
Complete Set (5):		4.50
Common Player:		.75
Inserted 1:12		
VR1	Mark McGwire	1.50
VR2	Sammy Sosa	1.00
VR3	Ken Griffey Jr.	1.25
VR4	Kerry Wood	.75
VR5	Alex Rodriguez	1.50

Photography

The photos used on some Stadium Club Series 1 cards was available as a special issue in the format of a framed 11" x 14" color photo. The borderless action photos could be ordered from a form found in TSC packs. With a $4 shipping charge, the initial cost per picture was $23.99. The numbers here are as given on the order form.

		NM/M
Complete Set (10):		200.00
Common Player:		20.00
1	Alex Rodriguez	20.00
65	Derek Jeter	20.00
66	Sammy Sosa	20.00
135	Juan Gonzalez	20.00
NC1	Mark McGwire	20.00
NC3	Ken Griffey Jr.	20.00
SCA5	Ben Grieve	20.00
SCC1	Nomar Garciaparra	20.00
SCC2	Kerry Wood	20.00
SCC13	Mike Piazza	20.00

2000 Stadium Club

Released in one series, the base set consists of 250 cards, embossed and printed on 20-pt. stock with silver holo-foil stamping. Card backs have a small photo, with the player's vital information and 1999 season statistical breakdown. The 20-card Draft Pick subset (#231-250) are short-printed, seeded 1:5 packs.

		NM/M
Complete Set (250):		80.00
Common Player:		.15
Common SP (201-250):		2.00
Inserted 1:5		
Pack (6):		1.50
Wax Box (24):		30.00
1	Nomar Garciaparra	1.25
2	Brian Jordan	.15
3	Mark Grace	.25
4	Jeromy Burnitz	.15
5	Shane Reynolds	.15
6	Alex Gonzalez	.15
7	Jose Offerman	.15
8	Orlando Hernandez	.15
9	Mike Caruso	.15
10	Tony Clark	.15
11	Sean Casey	.25
12	Johnny Damon	.25
13	Dante Bichette	.15
14	Kevin Young	.15
15	Juan Gonzalez	.75
16	Chipper Jones	1.00
17	Quilvio Veras	.15
18	Trevor Hoffman	.15
19	Roger Cedeno	.15
20	Ellis Burks	.15
21	Richie Sexson	.15
22	Gary Sheffield	.40
23	Delino DeShields	.15
24	Wade Boggs	1.00
25	Ray Lankford	.15
26	Kevin Appier	.15
27	Roy Halladay	.15
28	Harold Baines	.15
29	Todd Zeile	.15
30	Barry Larkin	.15
31	Ron Coomer	.15
32	Jorge Posada	.15
33	Magglio Ordonez	.15
34	Brian Giles	.15
35	Jeff Kent	.15
36	Henry Rodriguez	.15
37	Fred McGriff	.15
38	Shawn Green	.50
39	Derek Bell	.15
40	Ben Grieve	.15
41	Dave Nilsson	.15
42	Mo Vaughn	.15
43	Rondell White	.15
44	Doug Glanville	.15
45	Paul O'Neill	.15
46	Carlos Lee	.15
47	Vinny Castilla	.15
48	Mike Sweeney	.15
49	Rico Brogna	.15
50	Alex Rodriguez	1.50
51	Luis Castillo	.15
52	Kevin Brown	.15
53	Jose Vidro	.15
54	John Smoltz	.15
55	Garret Anderson	.15
56	Matt Stairs	.15
57	Omar Vizquel	.15
58	Tom Goodwin	.15

59 Scott Brosius .15
60 Robin Ventura .15
61 B.J. Surhoff .15
62 Andy Ashby .15
63 Chris Widger .15
64 Tim Hudson .40
65 Javy Lopez .15
66 Tim Salmon .25
67 Warren Morris .15
68 John Wetteland .15
69 Gabe Kapler .15
70 Bernie Williams .30
71 Rickey Henderson .75
72 Andruw Jones .75
73 Eric Young .15
74 Bob Abreu .15
75 David Cone .15
76 Rusty Greer .15
77 Ron Belliard .15
78 Troy Glaus .75
79 Mike Hampton .15
80 Miguel Tejada .30
81 Jeff Cirillo .15
82 Todd Hundley .15
83 Roberto Alomar .40
84 Charles Johnson .15
85 Rafael Palmeiro .65
86 Doug Mientkiewicz .15
87 Mariano Rivera .25
88 Neifi Perez .15
89 Jermaine Dye .15
90 Ivan Rodriguez .65
91 Jay Buhner .15
92 Pokey Reese .15
93 John Olerud .15
94 Brady Anderson .15
95 Manny Ramirez .75
96 Keith Osik .15
97 Mickey Morandini .15
98 Matt Williams .15
99 Eric Karros .15
100 Ken Griffey Jr. 1.25
101 Bret Boone .15
102 Ryan Klesko .15
103 Craig Biggio .15
104 John Jaha .15
105 Vladimir Guerrero .75
106 Devon White .15
107 Tony Womack .15
108 Marvin Benard .15
109 Kenny Lofton .15
110 Preston Wilson .15
111 Al Leiter .15
112 Reggie Sanders .15
113 Scott Williamson .15
114 Deivi Cruz .15
115 Carlos Beltran .50
116 Ray Durham .15
117 Ricky Ledee .15
118 Torii Hunter .15
119 John Valentin .15
120 Scott Rolen .65
121 Jason Kendall .15
122 Dave Martinez .15
123 Jim Thome .65
124 David Bell .15
125 Jose Canseco .45
126 Jose Lima .15
127 Carl Everett .15
128 Kevin Millwood .15
129 Bill Spiers .15
130 Omar Daal .15
131 Miguel Cairo .15
132 Mark Grudzielanek .15
133 David Justice .15
134 Russ Ortiz .15
135 Mike Piazza 1.25
136 Brian Meadows .15
137 Tony Gwynn 1.00
138 Cal Ripken Jr. 2.00
139 Kris Benson .15
140 Larry Walker .15
141 Cristian Guzman .15
142 Tino Martinez .25
143 Chris Singleton .15
144 Lee Stevens .15
145 Rey Ordonez .15
146 Russ Davis .15
147 J.T. Snow Jr. .15
148 Luis Gonzalez .25
149 Marquis Grissom .15
150 Greg Maddux 1.00
151 Fernando Tatis .15
152 Jason Giambi .50
153 Carlos Delgado .50
154 Joe McEwing .15
155 Raul Mondesi .15
156 Rich Aurilia .15
157 Alex Fernandez .15
158 Albert Belle .25
159 Pat Meares .15
160 Mike Lieberthal .15
161 Mike Cameron .15
162 Juan Encarnacion .15
163 Chuck Knoblauch .15
164 Pedro Martinez .75
165 Randy Johnson .75
166 Shannon Stewart .15
167 Jeff Bagwell .75
168 Edgar Renteria .15
169 Barry Bonds 2.00
170 Steve Finley .15
171 Brian Hunter .15
172 Tom Glavine .35
173 Mark Kotsay .15
174 Tony Fernandez .15
175 Sammy Sosa 1.25
176 Geoff Jenkins .15
177 Adrian Beltre .15
178 Jay Bell .15
179 Mike Bordick .15
180 Ed Sprague .15
181 Dave Roberts .15
182 Greg Vaughn .15
183 Brian Daubach .15
184 Damion Easley .15
185 Carlos Febles .15
186 Kevin Tapani .15
187 Frank Thomas .75
188 Roger Clemens 1.00
189 Mike Benjamin .15
190 Curt Schilling .40
191 Edgardo Alfonzo .15
192 Mike Mussina .40
193 Todd Helton .75
194 Todd Jones .15
195 Dean Palmer .15
196 John Flaherty .15
197 Derek Jeter 2.00
198 Todd Walker .15
199 Brad Ausmus .15
200 Mark McGwire 1.50
201 Erubiel Durazo (Future Stars) 2.00
202 Nick Johnson (Future Stars) 2.50
203 Ruben Mateo (Future Stars) 2.00
204 Lance Berkman (Future Stars) 2.50
205 Pat Burrell (Future Stars) 3.00
206 Pablo Ozuna (Future Stars) 2.00
207 Roosevelt Brown (Future Stars) 2.00
208 Alfonso Soriano (Future Stars) 4.00
209 A.J. Burnett (Future Stars) 2.00
210 Rafael Furcal (Future Stars) 2.00
211 Scott Morgan (Future Stars) 2.00
212 Adam Piatt (Future Stars) 2.00
213 Dee Brown (Future Stars) 2.00
214 Corey Patterson (Future Stars) 2.50
215 Mickey Lopez (Future Stars) 2.00
216 Rob Ryan (Future Stars) 2.00
217 Sean Burroughs (Future Stars) 2.00
218 Jack Cust (Future Stars) 2.00
219 John Patterson (Future Stars) 2.00
220 Kit Pellow (Future Stars) 2.00
221 Chad Hermansen (Future Stars) 2.00
222 Daryle Ward (Future Stars) 2.00
223 Jayson Werth (Future Stars) 2.00
224 Jason Standridge (Future Stars) 2.00
225 Mark Mulder (Future Stars) 2.50
226 Peter Bergeron (Future Stars) 2.00
227 Willi Mo Pena (Future Stars) 2.00
228 Aramis Ramirez (Future Stars) 2.00
229 John Sneed **RC** (Future Stars) 2.00
230 Wilton Veras (Future Stars) 2.00
231 Josh Hamilton (Draft Picks) 2.00
232 Eric Munson (Draft Picks) 2.00
233 Bobby Bradley **RC** (Draft Picks) 2.00
234 Larry Bigbie **RC** (Draft Picks) 2.00
235 B.J. Garbe **RC** (Draft Picks) 2.00
236 Brett Myers **RC** (Draft Picks) 6.00
237 Jason Stumm **RC** (Draft Picks) 2.00
238 Corey Myers **RC** (Draft Picks) 2.00
239 Ryan Christianson **RC** (Draft Picks) 2.00
240 David Walling (Draft Picks) 2.00
241 Josh Girdley (Draft Picks) 2.00
242 Omar Ortiz (Draft Picks) 2.00
243 Jason Jennings (Draft Picks) 2.00
244 Kyle Snyder **RC** (Draft Picks) 2.00
245 Jay Gehrke (Draft Picks) 2.00
246 Mike Paradis **RC** (Draft Picks) 2.00
247 Chance Caple **RC** (Draft Picks) 2.00
248 Ben Christiansen **RC** (Draft Picks) 2.00
249 Brad Baker **RC** (Draft Picks) 2.00
250 Rick Asadoorian **RC** (Draft Picks) 2.00
--- Checklist (Nomar Garciaparra) .25

First Day Issue

Identifiable by the "First Day Issue" stamp, this retail exclusive parallel set is limited to 150 sequentially numbered sets.

Stars: 5-10X
Short-prints: 2-3X
Production 150 Sets R

One of a Kind

This 250-card set is a parallel to the base set, is hobby exclusive and limited to 150 serially numbered sets.

Stars: 5-10X
Short-prints: 2-3X
Production 150 Sets H

Bats of Brilliance

This insert set focused on 10 of baseball's top hitters. Card fronts have a silver foil border over a black backdrop. Backs highlight the player's statistics from 1999 and his career statistics. They are numbered with a "BB" prefix and are seeded 1:12 packs. A die-cut parallel is also randomly seeded 1:60 packs.

NM/M
Complete Set (10): 10.00
Common Player: .50
Inserted 1:12
1 Mark McGwire 2.50
2 Sammy Sosa 1.50
3 Jose Canseco .50
4 Jeff Bagwell .75
5 Ken Griffey Jr. 1.50
6 Nomar Garciaparra 1.50
7 Mike Piazza 1.50
8 Alex Rodriguez 2.50
9 Vladimir Guerrero .75
10 Chipper Jones 1.50

Capture The Action

This 20-card set is divided into categories of Rookies, Stars, and Legends. These were seeded 1:12 packs and have the insert title, player name and logo stamped in silver foil. They are numbered with a "CA" prefix on the backs. A hobby-exclusive parallel version was also available, serially numbered to 100 and featuring a replica of the actual photo slide used to create the card.

NM/M
Complete Set (20): 20.00
Common Player: .50
Inserted 1:12
Game View Stars: 3-6X
Production 100 Sets H
1 Josh Hamilton .50
2 Pat Burrell .75
3 Erubiel Durazo .50
4 Alfonso Soriano 1.00
5 A.J. Burnett .50
6 Alex Rodriguez 3.00
7 Sean Casey .50
8 Derek Jeter 4.00
9 Vladimir Guerrero 1.00
10 Nomar Garciaparra 2.00
11 Mike Piazza 2.00
12 Ken Griffey Jr. 2.00
13 Sammy Sosa 2.00
14 Juan Gonzalez 1.00
15 Mark McGwire 3.00
16 Ivan Rodriguez .75
17 Barry Bonds 4.00
18 Wade Boggs 1.50
19 Tony Gwynn 1.50
20 Cal Ripken Jr. 4.00

Co-Signers

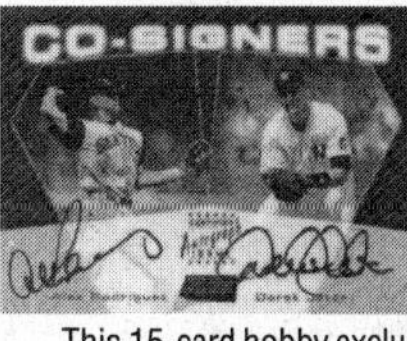

This 15-card hobby exclusive set features two signatures on the card front, with the Topps "Certified Autograph Issue" stamp as well as the Topps 3M sticker to ensure its authenticity. The cards are divided into three groupings with the following odds: Group A - 1:10,184; Group B - 1:5,092; and Group C - 1:508.

NM/M
Common Card: 15.00
Group A 1:10,184
Group B 1:5,092
Group C 1:508
1 Alex Rodriguez, Derek Jeter 400.00
2 Derek Jeter, Omar Vizquel 150.00
3 Alex Rodriguez, Rey Ordonez 100.00
4 Derek Jeter, Rey Ordonez 150.00
5 Omar Vizquel, Alex Rodriguez 100.00
6 Rey Ordonez, Omar Vizquel 15.00
7 Wade Boggs, Robin Ventura 30.00
8 Randy Johnson, Mike Mussina 90.00
9 Pat Burrell, Magglio Ordonez 40.00
10 Chad Hermansen, Pat Burrell 20.00
11 Magglio Ordonez, Chad Hermansen 20.00
12 Josh Hamilton, Corey Myers 20.00
13 B.J. Garbe, Josh Hamilton 20.00
14 Corey Myers, B.J. Garbe 15.00
15 Tino Martinez, Fred McGriff 60.00

Lone Star Signatures

This 16-card autographed set features the Topps "Certified Autograph Issue" stamp to verify its authenticity. The cards are divided into four groupings with the following odds: Group 1, 1:1,979 hobby; Group 2, 1:2,374 hobby; Group 3, 1:1,979; and Group 4, 1:424 hobby.

NM/M
Common Player: 8.00
Group 1 1:1,979
Group 2 1:2,374
Group 3 1:1,979
Group 4 1:424
1 Derek Jeter 100.00
2 Alex Rodriguez 100.00
3 Wade Boggs 25.00
4 Robin Ventura 15.00
5 Randy Johnson 60.00
6 Mike Mussina 25.00
7 Tino Martinez 35.00
8 Fred McGriff 25.00
9 Omar Vizquel 15.00
10 Rey Ordonez 8.00
11 Pat Burrell 15.00
12 Chad Hermansen 8.00
13 Magglio Ordonez 10.00
14 Josh Hamilton 20.00
15 Corey Myers 8.00
16 B.J. Garbe 8.00

Onyx Extreme

This 10-card set features black styrene technology with silver foil stamping and are seeded 1:12 packs. A die-cut parallel is also randomly inserted 1:60 hobby packs.

NM/M
Complete Set (10): 10.00
Common Player: .40
Inserted 1:12
Die-cuts: 2-3X
Inserted 1:60
1 Ken Griffey Jr. 1.50
2 Derek Jeter 3.00
3 Vladimir Guerrero 1.00
4 Nomar Garciaparra 1.50
5 Barry Bonds 3.00
6 Alex Rodriguez 2.50
7 Sammy Sosa 1.50
8 Ivan Rodriguez .75
9 Larry Walker .40
10 Andruw Jones 1.00

Printing Plates

Inserted only in Home Team boxes at a rate of approximately one per 100 packs were the actual aluminum plates used to print the fronts of the base cards. Unlike some printing plate issues, the plates used for the card backs were not inserted. Each card's plate can be found in four different colors: Cyan, magenta, yellow and black. Because of their unique nature, pricing of individual player's plates cannot be provided.

NM/M
Common Player: 60.00

Scenes

Available only in hobby and Home Team Advantage boxes, these broaden the view of the featured player and have a format sized 2-1/2" x 4-11/16". These are boxtoppers, seeded one per box.

NM/M
Complete Set (9): 10.00
Common Player: .50
Inserted 1:Box
1 Mark McGwire 2.50
2 Alex Rodriguez 2.50
3 Cal Ripken Jr. 3.00
4 Sammy Sosa 2.00
5 Derek Jeter 3.00
6 Ken Griffey Jr. 2.00
7 Raul Mondesi .50
8 Chipper Jones 1.50
9 Nomar Garciaparra 2.00

Souvenirs

These memorabilia inserts feature die-cut technology that incorporates an actual piece of a game-used uniform. Each card back contains the Topps 3M sticker to ensure its authenticity. The insert rate is 2:339 hobby packs and 2:136 HTA packs.

NM/M
Complete Set (3): 35.00
Common Player: 8.00
Inserted 2:339
1 Wade Boggs 20.00
2 Randy Johnson 20.00
3 Robin Ventura 8.00

3 X 3

Ten groups of three top-notch players are arranged by position on three different laser-cut technologies. The three players can be "fused" together to form one oversize card. The three versions are Luminous (1:18), Luminescent (1:72) and Illuminator (1:144).

NM/M
Complete Set (30): 40.00
Common Player: .75
Inserted 1:18
Luminescent: 2X
Inserted 1:72
Illuminator: 3-4X
Inserted 1:144
1A Randy Johnson 1.50
1B Pedro Martinez 1.50
1C Greg Maddux 2.00
2A Mike Piazza 3.00
2B Ivan Rodriguez 1.25
2C Mike Lieberthal .75
3A Mark McGwire 4.50
3B Jeff Bagwell 1.50
3C Sean Casey .75
4A Craig Biggio .75
4B Roberto Alomar 1.00
4C Jay Bell .75
5A Chipper Jones 2.00
5B Matt Williams .75
5C Robin Ventura .75
6A Alex Rodriguez 4.50
6B Derek Jeter 6.00
6C Nomar Garciaparra 3.00
7A Barry Bonds 6.00
7B Luis Gonzalez 1.00
7C Dante Bichette .75
8A Ken Griffey Jr. 3.00
8B Bernie Williams 1.00
8C Andruw Jones 1.50
9A Manny Ramirez 1.50

9B Sammy Sosa 3.00
9C Juan Gonzalez 1.50
10A Jose Canseco 1.00
10B Frank Thomas 1.50
10C Rafael Palmeiro 1.00

2000 Stadium Club Chrome Preview

This 20-card set features Topps Chromium technology, previewing the debut of Stadium Club Chrome, a later release. The insertion odds are 1:24 packs. A Refractor parallel version is also available seeded 1:120 packs.

NM/M
Complete Set (20): 40.00
Common Player: 1.00
Inserted 1:24
Refractors: 2-3X
Inserted 1:120

1 Nomar Garciaparra 3.00
2 Juan Gonzalez 1.50
3 Chipper Jones 2.00
4 Alex Rodriguez 4.50
5 Ivan Rodriguez 1.25
6 Manny Ramirez 1.50
7 Ken Griffey Jr. 3.00
8 Vladimir Guerrero 1.50
9 Mike Piazza 3.00
10 Pedro Martinez 2.00
11 Jeff Bagwell 1.50
12 Barry Bonds 6.00
13 Sammy Sosa 3.00
14 Derek Jeter 6.00
15 Mark McGwire 4.50
16 Erubiel Durazo 1.00
17 Nick Johnson 1.00
18 Pat Burrell 1.00
19 Alfonso Soriano 1.50
20 Adam Piatt 1.00

2000 Stadium Club Chrome

The 250-card base set uses the same photography and is identical to 2000 Stadium Club besides the utilization of Chromium technology. Five-card packs had a $4 SRP.

NM/M
Complete Set (250): 40.00
Common Player: .15
Pack (11): 1.50
Wax Box (36): 40.00

1 Nomar Garciaparra 1.50
2 Brian Jordan .15
3 Mark Grace .25
4 Jeromy Burnitz .15
5 Shane Reynolds .15
6 Alex Gonzalez .15
7 Jose Offerman .15
8 Orlando Hernandez .15
9 Mike Caruso .15
10 Tony Clark .15
11 Sean Casey .25
12 Johnny Damon .25
13 Dante Bichette .15
14 Kevin Young .15
15 Juan Gonzalez .75
16 Chipper Jones 1.00
17 Quilvio Veras .15
18 Trevor Hoffman .15
19 Roger Cedeno .15
20 Ellis Burks .15
21 Richie Sexson .15
22 Gary Sheffield .45
23 Delino DeShields .15
24 Wade Boggs 1.00
25 Ray Lankford .15
26 Kevin Appier .15
27 Roy Halladay .15
28 Harold Baines .15
29 Todd Zeile .15
30 Barry Larkin .15
31 Ron Coomer .15
32 Jorge Posada .15
33 Magglio Ordonez .15
34 Brian Giles .15
35 Jeff Kent .15
36 Henry Rodriguez .15
37 Fred McGriff .15
38 Shawn Green .50
39 Derek Bell .15
40 Ben Grieve .15
41 Dave Nilsson .15
42 Mo Vaughn .15
43 Rondell White .15
44 Doug Glanville .15
45 Paul O'Neill .15
46 Carlos Lee .15
47 Vinny Castilla .15
48 Mike Sweeney .15
49 Rico Brogna .15
50 Alex Rodriguez 2.50
51 Luis Castillo .15
52 Kevin Brown .15
53 Jose Vidro .15
54 John Smoltz .15
55 Garret Anderson .15
56 Matt Stairs .15
57 Omar Vizquel .15
58 Tom Goodwin .15
59 Scott Brosius .15
60 Robin Ventura .15
61 B.J. Surhoff .15
62 Andy Ashby .15
63 Chris Widger .15
64 Tim Hudson .40
65 Javy Lopez .15
66 Tim Salmon .25
67 Warren Morris .15
68 John Wetteland .15
69 Gabe Kapler .15
70 Bernie Williams .25
71 Rickey Henderson .75
72 Andruw Jones .75
73 Eric Young .15
74 Bobby Abreu .15
75 David Cone .15
76 Rusty Greer .15
77 Ron Belliard .15
78 Troy Glaus .75
79 Mike Hampton .15
80 Miguel Tejada .30
81 Jeff Cirillo .15
82 Todd Hundley .15
83 Roberto Alomar .35
84 Charles Johnson .15
85 Rafael Palmeiro .65
86 Doug Mientkiewicz .15
87 Mariano Rivera .25
88 Neifi Perez .15
89 Jermaine Dye .15
90 Ivan Rodriguez .65
91 Jay Buhner .15
92 Pokey Reese .15
93 John Olerud .15
94 Brady Anderson .15
95 Manny Ramirez .75
96 Keith Osik .15
97 Mickey Morandini .15
98 Matt Williams .15
99 Eric Karros .15
100 Ken Griffey Jr. 1.50
101 Bret Boone .15
102 Ryan Klesko .15
103 Craig Biggio .15
104 John Jaha .15
105 Vladimir Guerrero .75
106 Devon White .15
107 Tony Womack .15
108 Marvin Benard .15
109 Kenny Lofton .15
110 Preston Wilson .15
111 Al Leiter .15
112 Reggie Sanders .15
113 Scott Williamson .15
114 Deivi Cruz .15
115 Carlos Beltran .50
116 Ray Durham .15
117 Ricky Ledee .15
118 Torii Hunter .15
119 John Valentin .15
120 Scott Rolen .65
121 Jason Kendall .15
122 Dave Martinez .15
123 Jim Thome .65
124 David Bell .15
125 Jose Canseco .50
126 Jose Lima .15
127 Carl Everett .15
128 Kevin Millwood .15
129 Bill Spiers .15
130 Omar Daal .15
131 Miguel Cairo .15
132 Mark Grudzielanek .15
133 David Justice .15
134 Russ Ortiz .15
135 Mike Piazza 1.50
136 Brian Meadows .15
137 Tony Gwynn 1.00
138 Cal Ripken Jr. 3.00
139 Kris Benson .15
140 Larry Walker .15
141 Cristian Guzman .15
142 Tino Martinez .15
143 Chris Singleton .15
144 Lee Stevens .15
145 Rey Ordonez .15
146 Russ Davis .15
147 J.T. Snow Jr. .15
148 Luis Gonzalez .25
149 Marquis Grissom .15
150 Greg Maddux 1.00
151 Fernando Tatis .15
152 Jason Giambi .50
153 Carlos Delgado .50
154 Joe McEwing .15
155 Raul Mondesi .15
156 Rich Aurilia .15
157 Alex Fernandez .15
158 Albert Belle .25
159 Pat Meares .15
160 Mike Lieberthal .15
161 Mike Cameron .15
162 Juan Encarnacion .15
163 Chuck Knoblauch .15
164 Pedro Martinez .75
165 Randy Johnson .75
166 Shannon Stewart .15
167 Jeff Bagwell .75
168 Edgar Renteria .15
169 Barry Bonds 3.00
170 Steve Finley .15
171 Brian Hunter .15
172 Tom Glavine .40
173 Mark Kotsay .15
174 Tony Fernandez .15
175 Sammy Sosa 1.50
176 Geoff Jenkins .15
177 Adrian Beltre .45
178 Jay Bell .15
179 Mike Bordick .15
180 Ed Sprague .15
181 Dave Roberts .15
182 Greg Vaughn .15
183 Brian Daubach .15
184 Damion Easley .15
185 Carlos Febles .15
186 Kevin Tapani .15
187 Frank Thomas .75
188 Roger Clemens 1.25
189 Mike Benjamin .15
190 Curt Schilling .40
191 Edgardo Alfonzo .15
192 Mike Mussina .45
193 Todd Helton .75
194 Todd Jones .15
195 Dean Palmer .15
196 John Flaherty .15
197 Derek Jeter 3.00
198 Todd Walker .15
199 Brad Ausmus .15
200 Mark McGwire 2.50
201 Erubiel Durazo (Future Stars) .15
202 Nick Johnson (Future Stars) .15
203 Ruben Mateo (Future Stars) .15
204 Lance Berkman (Future Stars) .15
205 Pat Burrell (Future Stars) .65
206 Pablo Ozuna (Future Stars) .15
207 Roosevelt Brown (Future Stars) .15
208 Alfonso Soriano (Future Stars) 1.00
209 A.J. Burnett (Future Stars) .15
210 Rafael Furcal (Future Stars) .15
211 Scott Morgan (Future Stars) .15
212 Adam Piatt (Future Stars) .15
213 Dee Brown (Future Stars) .15
214 Corey Patterson (Future Stars) .15
215 Mickey Lopez (Future Stars) .15
216 Rob Ryan (Future Stars) .15
217 Sean Burroughs (Future Stars) .15
218 Jack Cust (Future Stars) .15
219 John Patterson (Future Stars) .15
220 Kit Pellow (Future Stars) .15
221 Chad Hermansen (Future Stars) .15
222 Daryle Ward (Future Stars) .15
223 Jayson Werth (Future Stars) .15
224 Jason Standridge (Future Stars) .15
225 Mark Mulder (Future Stars) .15
226 Peter Bergeron (Future Stars) .15
227 Willi Mo Pena (Future Stars) .15
228 Aramis Ramirez (Future Stars) .15
229 John Sneed (Future Stars) .15
230 Wilton Veras (Future Stars) .15
231 Josh Hamilton (Draft Picks) .15
232 Eric Munson (Draft Picks) .15
233 Bobby Bradley **RC** (Draft Picks) 1.00
234 Larry Bigbie **RC** (Draft Picks) 1.00
235 B.J. Garbe **RC** (Draft Picks) 1.00
236 Brett Myers **RC** (Draft Picks) 4.00
237 Jason Stumm **RC** (Draft Picks) 1.00
238 Corey Myers **RC** (Draft Picks) 1.00
239 Ryan Christianson **RC** (Draft Picks) 1.00
240 David Walling (Draft Picks) .15
241 Josh Girdley (Draft Picks) .15
242 Omar Ortiz (Draft Picks) .15
243 Jason Jennings (Draft Picks) .15
244 Kyle Snyder (Draft Picks) .15
245 Jay Gehrke (Draft Picks) .15
246 Mike Paradis (Draft Picks) .15
247 Chance Caple **RC** (Draft Picks) 1.00
248 Ben Christensen **RC** (Draft Picks) 1.00
249 Brad Baker **RC** (Draft Picks) 1.00
250 Rick Asadoorian **RC** (Draft Picks) 1.00

Refractor

A parallel to the 250-card base set these utilize Refractor technology and have a mirror sheen to them when held up to a light source. "Refractor" is also written under the card number on the card back. Refractors are seeded 1:12 packs.

Stars: 2-4X
Rookies: 1-2X
Inserted 1:12

First Day Issue

A parallel to the 250-card base set. Card fronts are identical besides "First Day Issue" printed three times over the player name and Stadium Club Chrome logo. Card backs are serial numbered in an edition of 100. A Refractor First Day Issue parallel is also randomly inserted, limited to 25 serial-numbered sets.

Stars: 4-8X
Rookies: 1-30X
Production 100 Sets
Refractor: 25-40X
Rookies: 5-10X
Production 25 Sets

Capture The Action

This 20-card set is divided into three groups: Rookies, Stars and Legends. Card backs are numbered with a "CA" prefix. These are found 1:18 packs. A Refractor parallel version is also randomly seeded 1:90 packs and also have "Refractor" written under the card number on the back.

NM/M
Complete Set (20): 40.00
Common Player: 1.00
Inserted 1:18
Refractors: 2-3X
Inserted 1:90

1 Josh Hamilton 1.00
2 Pat Burrell 1.50
3 Erubiel Durazo 1.00
4 Alfonso Soriano 1.50
5 A.J. Burnett 1.00
6 Alex Rodriguez 5.00
7 Sean Casey 1.00
8 Derek Jeter 6.00
9 Vladimir Guerrero 1.50
10 Nomar Garciaparra 3.00
11 Mike Piazza 3.00
12 Ken Griffey Jr. 3.00
13 Sammy Sosa 3.00
14 Juan Gonzalez 1.50
15 Mark McGwire 5.00
16 Ivan Rodriguez 1.50
17 Barry Bonds 6.00
18 Wade Boggs 2.00
19 Tony Gwynn 2.00
20 Cal Ripken Jr. 6.00

Clear Shots

Printed on a clear, acetate stock this 10-card insert set will depict the front of the player on the card front and the back on the card back. Card backs are numbered with a "CS" prefix. Clear Shots are inserted 1:24 packs. A die-cut Refractor parallel version is also randomly seeded 1:120 packs.

NM/M
Complete Set (10): 10.00
Common Player: .50
Inserted 1:24
Refractor: 2-3X
Inserted 1:120

1 Derek Jeter 4.00
2 Bernie Williams .50
3 Roger Clemens 2.50
4 Chipper Jones 2.00
5 Greg Maddux 2.00
6 Andruw Jones 1.00
7 Juan Gonzalez 1.00
8 Manny Ramirez 1.00
9 Ken Griffey Jr. 3.00
10 Josh Hamilton .50

Eyes of the Game

Printed on a clear, acetate stock this 10-card set focuses on the facial expression of the featured player. Two images are on the front with the background image a close-up shot of the player's facial expression. These were seeded 1:16. Card backs are numbered with an "EG" prefix. A Refractor parallel is randomly inserted in 1:80 packs and has "Refractor" written under the card number on the back.

NM/M
Complete Set (10): 10.00
Common Player: .50
Inserted 1:16
Refractors: 2-3X
Inserted 1:80

1 Randy Johnson 1.00
2 Mike Piazza 1.50
3 Nomar Garciaparra 1.50
4 Mark McGwire 2.50
5 Alex Rodriguez 2.50
6 Derek Jeter 3.00
7 Tony Gwynn 1.00
8 Sammy Sosa 1.50
9 Larry Walker .50
10 Ken Griffey Jr. 1.50

True Colors

This 10-card set focuses on players Topps deemed that performed best when the game's on the line. These were inserted 1:32 and are numbered with a "TC" prefix on the card back. A Refractor parallel is randomly inserted 1:160 packs.

NM/M
Complete Set (10): 15.00
Common Player: 1.00
Inserted 1:32
Refractors: 2-3X
Inserted 1:160

1 Sammy Sosa 2.00
2 Nomar Garciaparra 2.00
3 Alex Rodriguez 3.00
4 Derek Jeter 4.00
5 Mark McGwire 3.00
6 Chipper Jones 1.50
7 Mike Piazza 2.00
8 Ken Griffey Jr. 2.00
9 Manny Ramirez 1.00
10 Vladimir Guerrero 1.00

Visionaries

This 20-card set spotlights young prospects who are deemed destined for stardom. Card backs are numbered with a "V" prefix. These are found 1:18 packs. A Refractor parallel version is also seeded 1:90 packs. "Refractor" is written under the card number on the back.

NM/M
Complete Set (20): 17.50

Common Player: 1.00
Inserted 1:18
Refractors: 2X
Inserted 1:90
1 Alfonso Soriano 3.00
2 Josh Hamilton 1.00
3 A.J. Burnett 1.50
4 Pat Burrell 2.50
5 Ruben Salazar 1.00
6 Aaron Rowand 1.00
7 Adam Piatt 1.00
8 Nick Johnson 1.00
9 Rafael Furcal 1.00
10 Jack Cust 1.00
11 Corey Patterson 1.00
12 Sean Burroughs 1.50
13 Pablo Ozuna 1.00
14 Dee Brown 1.00
15 John Patterson 1.00
16 Willi Mo Pena 1.00
17 Mark Mulder 1.00
18 Eric Munson 1.00
19 Alex Escobar 1.00
20 Rob Ryan 1.00

2001 Stadium Club

NM/M
Complete Set (200): 65.00
Common Player: .15
Common SP: 1.50
Inserted 1:6
Pack (7): 2.00
Box (24): 35.00
1 Nomar Garciaparra 1.25
2 Chipper Jones 1.00
3 Jeff Bagwell .75
4 Chad Kreuter .15
5 Randy Johnson .75
6 Mike Hampton .15
7 Barry Larkin .15
8 Bernie Williams .30
9 Chris Singleton .15
10 Larry Walker .15
11 Brad Ausmus .15
12 Ron Coomer .15
13 Edgardo Alfonzo .15
14 Delino DeShields .15
15 Tony Gwynn 1.00
16 Andruw Jones .75
17 Raul Mondesi .15
18 Troy Glaus .75
19 Ben Grieve .15
20 Sammy Sosa 1.25
21 Fernando Vina .15
22 Jeromy Burnitz .15
23 Jay Bell .15
24 Pete Harnisch .15
25 Barry Bonds 2.00
26 Eric Karros .15
27 Alex Gonzalez .15
28 Mike Lieberthal .15
29 Juan Encarnacion .15
30 Derek Jeter 2.00
31 Bruce Aven .15
32 Eric Milton .15
33 Aaron Boone .15
34 Roberto Alomar .40
35 John Olerud .15
36 Orlando Cabrera .15
37 Shawn Green .45
38 Roger Cedeno .15
39 Garret Anderson .15
40 Jim Thome .65
41 Gabe Kapler .15
42 Mo Vaughn .15
43 Sean Casey .25
44 Preston Wilson .15
45 Javy Lopez .15
46 Ryan Klesko .15
47 Ray Durham .15
48 Dean Palmer .15
49 Jorge Posada .15
50 Alex Rodriguez 1.50
51 Tom Glavine .40
52 Ray Lankford .15
53 Jose Canseco .40
54 Tim Salmon .25
55 Cal Ripken Jr. 2.00
56 Bob Abreu .15
57 Robin Ventura .15
58 Damion Easley .15
59 Paul O'Neill .15
60 Ivan Rodriguez .65
61 Carl Everett .15
62 Doug Glanville .15
63 Jeff Kent .15
64 Jay Buhner .15
65 Cliff Floyd .15
66 Rick Ankiel .15
67 Mark Grace .25
68 Brian Jordan .15
69 Craig Biggio .15
70 Carlos Delgado .50
71 Brad Radke .15
72 Greg Maddux 1.00
73 Al Leiter .15
74 Pokey Reese .15
75 Todd Helton .75
76 Mariano Rivera .25
77 Shane Spencer .15
78 Jason Kendall .15
79 Chuck Knoblauch .15
80 Scott Rolen .65
81 Jose Offerman .15
82 J.T. Snow Jr. .15
83 Pat Meares .15
84 Quilvio Veras .15
85 Edgar Renteria .15
86 Luis Matos .15
87 Adrian Beltre .15
88 Luis Gonzalez .25
89 Rickey Henderson .75
90 Brian Giles .15
91 Carlos Febles .15
92 Tino Martinez .15
93 Magglio Ordonez .15
94 Rafael Furcal .15
95 Mike Mussina .30
96 Gary Sheffield .40
97 Kenny Lofton .15
98 Fred McGriff .15
99 Ken Caminiti .15
100 Mark McGwire 1.50
101 Tom Goodwin .15
102 Mark Grudzielanek .15
103 Derek Bell .15
104 Mike Lowell .15
105 Jeff Cirillo .15
106 Orlando Hernandez .15
107 Jose Valentin .15
108 Warren Morris .15
109 Mike Williams .15
110 Gregg Zaun .15
111 Jose Vidro .15
112 Omar Vizquel .15
113 Vinny Castilla .15
114 Gregg Jefferies .15
115 Kevin Brown .15
116 Shannon Stewart .15
117 Marquis Grissom .15
118 Manny Ramirez .75
119 Albert Belle .15
120 Bret Boone .15
121 Johnny Damon .25
122 Juan Gonzalez .75
123 David Justice .15
124 Jeffrey Hammonds .15
125 Ken Griffey Jr. 1.25
126 Mike Sweeney .15
127 Tony Clark .15
128 Todd Zeile .15
129 Mark Johnson .15
130 Matt Williams .15
131 Geoff Jenkins .15
132 Jason Giambi .50
133 Steve Finley .15
134 Derrek Lee .15
135 Royce Clayton .15
136 Joe Randa .15
137 Rafael Palmeiro .65
138 Kevin Young .15
139 Curt Schilling .40
140 Vladimir Guerrero .75
141 Greg Vaughn .15
142 Jermaine Dye .15
143 Roger Clemens 1.00
144 Denny Hocking .15
145 Frank Thomas .75
146 Carlos Beltran .50
147 Eric Young .15
148 Pat Burrell .50
149 Pedro Martinez .75
150 Mike Piazza 1.25
151 Adrian Gonzalez .50
152 Adam Johnson .15
153 Luis Montanez **RC** 1.50
154 Mike Stodolka .15
155 Phil Dumatrait .15
156 Sean Burnett 1.50
157 Dominic Rich **RC** 1.50
158 Adam Wainwright .50
159 Scott Thorman .15
160 Scott Heard .25
161 Chad Petty **RC** 1.50
162 Matt Wheatland 2.00
163 Brad Digby .15
164 Rocco Baldelli 1.00
165 Grady Sizemore 1.00
166 Brian Sellier **RC** 1.50
167 Rick Brosseau **RC** 1.50
168 Shawn Fagan **RC** 1.50
169 Sean Smith 1.50
170 Chris Bass **RC** 1.50
171 Corey Patterson (Future Stars) .25
172 Sean Burroughs (Future Stars) .25
173 Ben Petrick (Future Stars) .15
174 Mike Glendenning (Future Stars) .15
175 Barry Zito (Future Stars) .50
176 Milton Bradley (Future Stars) .15
177 Bobby Bradley (Future Stars) .15
178 Jason Hart (Future Stars) .15
179 Ryan Anderson (Future Stars) .15
180 Ben Sheets (Future Stars) .25
181 Adam Everett (Future Stars) .15
182 Alfonso Soriano (Future Stars) .75
183 Josh Hamilton (Future Stars) .25
184 Eric Munson (Future Stars) .15
185 Chin-Feng Chen (Future Stars) .25
186 Tim Christman **RC** 1.50
187 J.R. House 2.00
188 Brandon Parker **RC** 1.50
189 Sean Fesh **RC** 1.50
190 Joel Pieniero **RC** 2.00
191 Oscar Ramirez **RC** 1.50
192 Alex Santos **RC** 1.50
193 Eddy Reyes **RC** 1.50
194 Mike Jacobs **RC** 1.50
195 Erick Almonte **RC** 2.00
196 Brandon Claussen **RC** 2.00
197 Kris Keller **RC** 1.50
198 Wilson Betemit **RC** 1.50
199 Andy Phillips **RC** 1.50
200 Adam Pettyjohn **RC** 1.50
--- Derek Jeter (Checklist) .25

Beam Team

NM/M
Complete Set (30): 100.00
Common Player: 1.50
Production 500 Sets
1 Sammy Sosa 6.00
2 Mark McGwire 8.00
3 Vladimir Guerrero 3.00
4 Chipper Jones 4.50
5 Manny Ramirez 3.00
6 Derek Jeter 10.00
7 Alex Rodriguez 8.00
8 Cal Ripken Jr. 10.00
9 Ken Griffey Jr. 6.00
10 Greg Maddux 4.50
11 Barry Bonds 10.00
12 Pedro Martinez 3.00
13 Nomar Garciaparra 6.00
14 Randy Johnson 3.00
15 Frank Thomas 3.00
16 Ivan Rodriguez 2.50
17 Jeff Bagwell 3.00
18 Mike Piazza 6.00
19 Todd Helton 3.00
20 Shawn Green 2.00
21 Juan Gonzalez 3.00
22 Larry Walker 1.50
23 Tony Gwynn 4.50
24 Pat Burrell 2.00
25 Rafael Furcal 1.50
26 Corey Patterson 1.50
27 Chin-Feng Chen 1.50
28 Sean Burroughs 1.50
29 Ryan Anderson 1.50
30 Josh Hamilton 4.00

Capture The Action

NM/M
Complete Set (15): 15.00
Common Player: 1.00
Inserted 1:8
1 Cal Ripken Jr. 3.00
2 Alex Rodriguez 2.50
3 Mike Piazza 2.00
4 Mark McGwire 2.50
5 Greg Maddux 1.50
6 Derek Jeter 3.00
7 Chipper Jones 1.50
8 Pedro Martinez 1.00
9 Ken Griffey Jr. 2.00
10 Nomar Garciaparra 2.00
11 Randy Johnson 1.00
12 Sammy Sosa 2.00
13 Vladimir Guerrero 1.00
14 Barry Bonds 3.00
15 Ivan Rodriguez 1.00

Capture The Action Game View

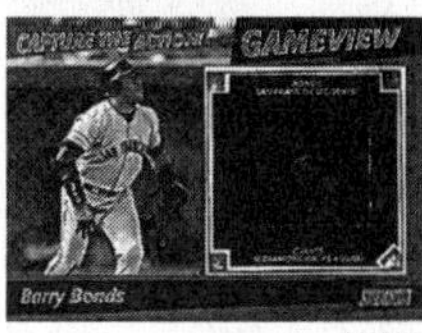

NM/M
Common Player: 10.00
Production 100 Sets
1 Cal Ripken Jr. 30.00
2 Alex Rodriguez 25.00
3 Mike Piazza 20.00
4 Mark McGwire 25.00
5 Greg Maddux 15.00
6 Derek Jeter 30.00
7 Chipper Jones 15.00
8 Pedro Martinez 10.00
9 Ken Griffey Jr. 20.00
10 Nomar Garciaparra 20.00
11 Randy Johnson 10.00
12 Sammy Sosa 20.00
13 Vladimir Guerrero 10.00
14 Barry Bonds 30.00
15 Ivan Rodriguez 10.00

Co-Signers

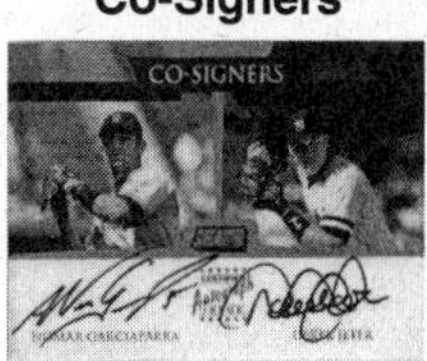

NM/M
Common Duo: 15.00
Inserted 1:1,117
1 Nomar Garciaparra, Derek Jeter 400.00
2 Roberto Alomar, Edgardo Alfonzo 50.00
3 Rick Ankiel, Kevin Millwood 15.00
4 Chipper Jones, Troy Glaus 65.00
5 Magglio Ordonez, Bobby Abreu 20.00
6 Adam Piatt, Sean Burroughs 20.00
7 Corey Patterson, Nick Johnson 40.00
8 Adrian Gonzalez, Rocco Baldelli 40.00
9 Adam Johnson, Mike Stodolka 15.00

Diamond Pearls

NM/M
Complete Set (20): 20.00
Common Player: .65
Inserted 1:8
1 Ken Griffey Jr. 2.00
2 Alex Rodriguez 2.50
3 Derek Jeter 3.00
4 Chipper Jones 1.50
5 Nomar Garciaparra 2.00
6 Vladimir Guerrero 1.00
7 Jeff Bagwell 1.00
8 Cal Ripken Jr. 3.00
9 Sammy Sosa 2.00
10 Mark McGwire 2.50
11 Frank Thomas 1.00
12 Pedro Martinez 1.00
13 Manny Ramirez 1.00
14 Randy Johnson 1.00
15 Barry Bonds 3.00
16 Ivan Rodriguez .75
17 Greg Maddux 1.50
18 Mike Piazza 2.00
19 Todd Helton 1.00
20 Shawn Green .65

Game-Used Cards

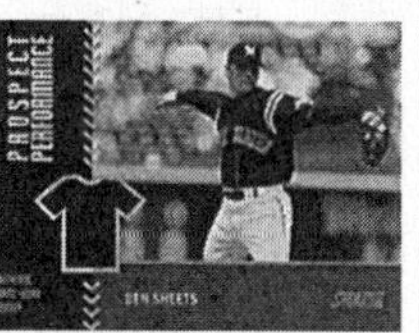

NM/M
Common Player: 5.00
Inserted 1:285
1 Chin-Feng Chen 20.00
2 Bobby Bradley 5.00
3 Tomokazu Ohka 5.00
4 Kurt Ainsworth 5.00
5 Craig Anderson 5.00
6 Josh Hamilton 10.00
7 Felipe Lopez 5.00
8 Ryan Anderson 5.00
9 Alex Escobar 5.00
10 Ben Sheets 8.00
11 Ntema Ndungidi 5.00
12 Eric Munson 5.00
13 Aaron Myette 5.00
14 Jack Cust 5.00
15 Julio Zuleta 5.00
16 Corey Patterson 10.00
17 Carlos Pena 5.00
18 Marcus Giles 5.00
19 Travis Wilson 5.00
20 Barry Zito 8.00

King of the Hill

NM/M
Complete Set (5): 30.00
Common Player: 3.00
Inserted 1:21
1 Pedro Martinez 10.00
2 Randy Johnson 10.00
3 Greg Maddux 15.00
4 Rick Ankiel 3.00
5 Kevin Brown 3.00

Lone Star Signatures

NM/M
Common Player: 6.00
Inserted 1:196
1 Nomar Garciaparra 100.00
2 Derek Jeter 120.00
3 Edgardo Alfonzo 20.00
4 Roberto Alomar 40.00
5 Magglio Ordonez 20.00
6 Bobby Abreu 40.00
7 Chipper Jones 40.00
8 Troy Glaus 30.00
9 Nick Johnson 15.00
10 Adam Piatt 6.00
11 Sean Burroughs 8.00
12 Corey Patterson 15.00
13 Rick Ankiel 6.00
14 Kevin Millwood 10.00
15 Adrian Gonzalez 15.00
16 Adam Johnson 6.00
17 Rocco Baldelli 25.00
18 Mike Stodolka 6.00

Play at the Plate

NM/M
Common Player: 10.00
Inserted 1:11
1 Mark McGwire 20.00
2 Sammy Sosa 15.00
3 Vladimir Guerrero 8.00
4 Ken Griffey Jr. 15.00
5 Mike Piazza 15.00
6 Chipper Jones 10.00
7 Barry Bonds 25.00
8 Alex Rodriguez 20.00
9 Jeff Bagwell 8.00
10 Nomar Garciaparra 15.00

Souvenirs

NM/M
Common Player: 4.00
1 Scott Rolen/Bat 8.00
2 Larry Walker/Bat 5.00
3 Rafael Furcal/Bat 5.00
4 Darin Erstad/Bat 5.00
5 Mike Sweeney/Jsy 4.00
6 Matt Lawton/Jsy 4.00
7 Jose Vidro/Jsy 4.00
8 Pat Burrell/Jsy 6.00

2001 Stadium Club Super Teams

These scarce exchange cards were seeded at an average rate of about one per 875 packs of TSC Hobby and Retail and one per 340 packs of Home Team Advantage. Prior to the cards' redemption deadline which expired Dec. 1, 2001, they could be entered into drawings for various prizes including specially marked card sets, game tickets, autographs, etc.

NM/M
Common Card: 1.00
STP1 Anaheim Angels (Troy Glaus) 2.00
STP2 Houston Astros (Jeff Bagwell) 2.00
STP3 Oakland A's (Jason Giambi) 1.25
STP4 Toronto Blue Jays (Carlos Delgado) 1.00
STP5 Atlanta Braves (Chipper Jones) 2.50
STP6 Milwaukee Brewers (Geoff Jenkins) 1.00
STP7 St. Louis Cardinals (Mark McGwire) 4.00
STP8 Chicago Cubs (Sammy Sosa) 3.00
STP9 Tampa Bay Devil Rays (Greg Vaughn) 1.00
STP10 Arizona Diamondbacks (Luis Gonzalez) 1.00
STP11 L.A. Dodgers (Shawn Green) 1.00
STP12 Montreal Expos (Vladimir Guerrero) 1.50
STP13 S.F. Giants (Barry Bonds) 5.00
STP14 Cleveland Indians (Roberto Alomar) 1.00
STP15 Seattle Mariners (Alex Rodriguez) 4.00
STP16 Florida Marlins (Preston Wilson) 1.00
STP17 N.Y. Mets (Mike Piazza) 3.00
STP18 Baltimore Orioles (Mike Mussina) 1.00
STP19 S.D. Padres (Tony Gwynn) 2.00
STP20 Philadelphia Phillies (Scott Rolen) 1.25
STP21 Pittsburgh Pirates (Jason Kendall) 1.00
STP22 Texas Rangers (Ivan Rodriguez) 1.25
STP23 Boston Red Sox (Nomar Garciaparra) 3.00
STP24 Cincinnati Reds (Ken Griffey Jr.) 3.00
STP25 Colorado Rockies (Todd Helton) 1.50
STP26 K.C. Royals (Mike Sweeney) 1.00
STP27 Detroit Tigers (Juan Gonzalez) 1.50
STP28 Minnesota Twins (Brad Radke) 1.00
STP29 Chicago White Sox (Frank Thomas) 1.50
STP30 N.Y. Yankees (Derek Jeter) 5.00

2002 Stadium Club Relic Edition

NM/M
Complete Set (125):
Common Player: .15
Common SP (101-125): 5.00
Production 2,999
Pack (6): 1.50
Box (24): 30.00
1 Pedro Martinez .75
2 Derek Jeter 2.00
3 Chipper Jones 1.00
4 Roberto Alomar .40

5 Albert Pujols 1.50
6 Bret Boone .15
7 Alex Rodriguez 1.50
8 Jose Cruz .15
9 Mike Hampton .15
10 Vladimir Guerrero .75
11 Jim Edmonds .25
12 Luis Gonzalez .25
13 Jeff Kent .15
14 Mike Piazza 1.25
15 Ben Sheets .15
16 Tsuyoshi Shinjo .15
17 Pat Burrell .40
18 Jermaine Dye .15
19 Rafael Furcal .15
20 Randy Johnson .75
21 Carlos Delgado .50
22 Roger Clemens 1.00
23 Eric Chavez .25
24 Nomar Garciaparra 1.25
25 Ivan Rodriguez .65
26 Juan Gonzalez .75
27 Reggie Sanders .15
28 Jeff Bagwell .75
29 Kazuhiro Sasaki .15
30 Larry Walker .15
31 Ben Grieve .15
32 David Justice .15
33 David Wells .15
34 Kevin Brown .15
35 Miguel Tejada .25
36 Jorge Posada .15
37 Javy Lopez .15
38 Cliff Floyd .15
39 Carlos Lee .15
40 Manny Ramirez .75
41 Jim Thome .65
42 Pokey Reese .15
43 Scott Rolen .65
44 Richie Sexson .15
45 Dean Palmer .15
46 Rafael Palmeiro .65
47 Alfonso Soriano .75
48 Craig Biggio .15
49 Troy Glaus .75
50 Andruw Jones .75
51 Ichiro Suzuki 1.50
52 Kenny Lofton .15
53 Hideo Nomo .75
54 Magglio Ordonez .15
55 Brad Penny .15
56 Omar Vizquel .15
57 Mike Sweeney .15
58 Gary Sheffield .25
59 Ken Griffey Jr. 1.25
60 Curt Schilling .40
61 Bobby Higginson .15
62 Terrence Long .15
63 Moises Alou .15
64 Sandy Alomar .15
65 Cristian Guzman .15
66 Sammy Sosa 1.25
67 Jose Vidro .15
68 Edgar Martinez .15
69 Jason Giambi .50
70 Mark McGwire 1.50
71 Barry Bonds 2.00
72 Greg Vaughn .15
73 Phil Nevin .15
74 Jason Kendall .15
75 Greg Maddux 1.00
76 Jeromy Burnitz .15
77 Mike Mussina .40
78 Johnny Damon .25
79 Shawn Green .40
80 Jimmy Rollins .25
81 Edgardo Alfonzo .15
82 Barry Larkin .15
83 Raul Mondesi .15
84 Preston Wilson .15
85 Mike Lieberthal .15
86 J.D. Drew .40
87 Ryan Klesko .15
88 David Segui .15
89 Derek Bell .15
90 Bernie Williams .40
91 Doug Mientkiewicz .15
92 Rich Aurilia .15
93 Ellis Burks .15
94 Placido Polanco .15
95 Darin Erstad .25
96 Brian Giles .15
97 Geoff Jenkins .15
98 Kerry Wood .65
99 Mariano Rivera .40
100 Todd Helton .75
101 Adam Dunn 15.00
102 Grant Balfour 5.00
103 Jae Weong Seo 5.00
104 Hank Blalock 8.00
105 Chris George 5.00
106 Jack Cust 5.00
107 Juan Cruz 5.00
108 Adrian Gonzalez 8.00
109 Nick Johnson 5.00
110 Jeff Devanon **RC** 5.00
111 Juan Diaz 5.00
112 Brandon Duckworth 5.00
113 Jason Lane 5.00
114 Seung Jun Song 5.00
115 Morgan Ensberg 5.00
116 Marlyn Tisdale **RC** 5.00
117 Jason Botts **RC** 5.00
118 Henry Pichardo **RC** 5.00
119 John Rodriguez **RC** 5.00
120 Mike Peeples **RC** 5.00
121 Rob Bowen **RC** 5.00
122 Jeremy Affeldt 5.00
123 Jorge Buret **RC** 5.00
124 Manny Ravelo **RC** 5.00
125 Eudy Lajara **RC** 5.00

All-Star Relics

NM/M
Common Player: 5.00
RA Roberto Alomar 7.50
MA Moises Alou 5.00
BB Barry Bonds 40.00
BRB Bret Boone 5.00
MC Mike Cameron 5.00
SC Sean Casey 7.50
CF Cliff Floyd 5.00
BG Brian Giles 5.00
JG Juan Gonzalez 12.00
LG3 Luis Gonzalez 5.00
CG Cristian Guzman 5.00
TG Tony Gwynn 15.00
MH Mike Hampton 5.00
TH Todd Helton 12.00
RJ Randy Johnson 12.00
CJ Chipper Jones 15.00
JK Jeff Kent 5.00
RK Ryan Klesko 5.00
EM Edgar Martinez 5.00
ERM Eric Milton 5.00
JO John Olerud 5.00
MO Magglio Ordonez 5.00
MP Mike Piazza 20.00
JP Jorge Posada 5.00
AP Albert Pujols 30.00
MR Manny Ramirez 12.00
IR Ivan Rodriguez 10.00
KS Kazuhiro Sasaki 5.00
MS Mike Sweeney 5.00
LW Larry Walker 5.00

Chasing 500-500

NM/M
Common Player:
BB1 Barry Bonds/Dual 40.00
BB2 Barry Bonds/Jsy/600 30.00
BB3 Barry Bonds/Mult/200 75.00

Passport to the Majors

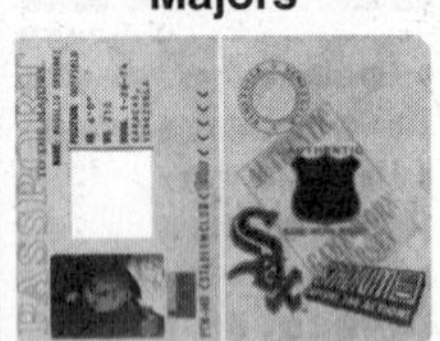

NM/M
Common Player: 5.00
Jsy 1:84
Bat 1:795
BA Bobby Abreu/400 6.00
EA Edgardo Alfonzo 5.00
RA Roberto Alomar 6.00
WB Wilson Betemit/325 5.00
BC Bartolo Colon 5.00
RF Rafael Furcal 5.00
AG Andres Galarraga 5.00
JG Juan Gonzalez 8.00
SH Shigetoshi Hasegawa 5.00
AJ Andruw Jones 8.00
CL Carlos Lee 5.00
JL Javy Lopez 5.00
PM Pedro Martinez 10.00
RM Raul Mondesi 5.00
MO Magglio Ordonez 5.00
RP Rafael Palmeiro 8.00
CP Chan Ho Park 5.00
AP Albert Pujols/450 40.00
MR Manny Ramirez 10.00
IR Ivan Rodriguez 10.00
KS Kazuhiro Sasaki 5.00
TS Tsuyoshi Shinjo/400 6.00
AS Alfonso Soriano/400 10.00
MT Miguel Tejada/375 6.00
LW Larry Walker 5.00

Reel Time

NM/M
Complete Set (20): 25.00
Common Player: .50
Inserted 1:8
RT1 Luis Gonzalez .50

RT2 Derek Jeter 4.00
RT3 Ken Griffey Jr. 2.50
RT4 Alex Rodriguez 3.00
RT5 Barry Bonds 4.00
RT6 Ichiro Suzuki 2.50
RT7 Carlos Delgado 1.00
RT8 Manny Ramirez 1.50
RT9 Mike Piazza 2.50
RT10 Mark McGwire 3.00
RT11 Todd Helton 1.50
RT12 Vladimir Guerrero 1.50
RT13 Jim Thome 1.50
RT14 Rich Aurilia .50
RT15 Bret Boone .50
RT16 Roberto Alomar .75
RT17 Jason Giambi 1.00
RT18 Chipper Jones 2.00
RT19 Albert Pujols 3.00
RT20 Sammy Sosa 2.50

Stadium Shots

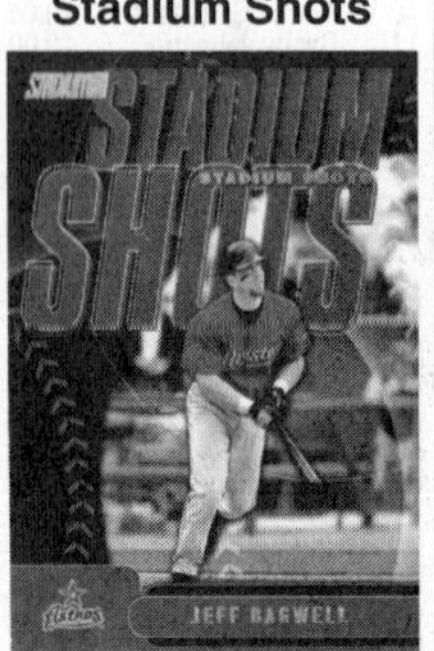

NM/M
Complete Set (10): 15.00
Common Player: 1.00
Inserted 1:12
SS1 Sammy Sosa 2.00
SS2 Manny Ramirez 1.50
SS3 Jason Giambi 1.00
SS4 Mike Piazza 2.00
SS5 Barry Bonds 4.00
SS6 Ken Griffey Jr. 2.00
SS7 Juan Gonzalez 1.50
SS8 Jeff Bagwell 1.50
SS9 Jim Thome 1.00
SS10 Mark McGwire 3.00

Stadium Slices Barrel

NM/M
Common Player: 15.00
BB Barry Bonds 75.00
LG Luis Gonzalez 15.00
AP Albert Pujols 75.00
IR Ivan Rodriguez 35.00
BW Bernie Williams 25.00

Stadium Slices Handle

NM/M
Common Player: 15.00
BB Barry Bonds 50.00
LG Luis Gonzalez 15.00
AP Albert Pujols 50.00
IR Ivan Rodriguez 20.00
BW Bernie Williams 15.00

Stadium Slices Trademar

NM/M
Common Player: 15.00
BB Barry Bonds 60.00
LG Luis Gonzalez 15.00
AP Albert Pujols 60.00
IR Ivan Rodriguez 20.00
BW Bernie Williams 15.00

World Champions Relics

NM/M
Common Player: 4.00
Jersey 1:106
Bat 1:94
Pants 1:795
Spikes 1:38,400
RA Roberto Alomar 15.00
MA Moises Alou 8.00
DB Don Baylor 8.00
JB Johnny Bench 20.00
BB Bert Blyleven 8.00
WB Wade Boggs 15.00
BRB Bob Boone 4.00
GB George Brett 50.00
SB Scott Brosius 10.00
AB Al Bumbry 4.00
JC1 Jose Canseco 15.00
JC2 Jose Canseco 15.00
GC1 Gary Carter 15.00
GC2 Gary Carter 15.00
JC Joe Carter 10.00
RC Ron Cey 10.00
CC Chris Chambliss 8.00
DC Dave Concepcion 8.00
ED Eric Davis 10.00
BD Bucky Dent 8.00
GF George Foster 8.00
PG Phil Garner 4.00
KG1 Kirk Gibson 10.00
KG2 Kirk Gibson 10.00
TG Tom Glavine 15.00
KG Ken Griffey Sr. 10.00
RH Rickey Henderson/50 80.00
GH George Hendrick 6.00
KH Keith Hernandez 15.00
WH Willie Hernandez 8.00
OH Orel Hershiser 10.00
RJ Reggie Jackson 15.00
CWJ Chipper Jones 15.00
DJ David Justice 8.00
CK Chuck Knoblauch 4.00
AL Al Leiter 8.00
DL Davey Lopes 8.00
JL Javy Lopez 8.00
GL Greg Luzinski 6.00
GM Greg Maddux 30.00
BM Bill Madlock 8.00
TLM Tino Martinez 15.00
HM Hal McCrae 8.00
FM Fred McGriff 10.00
PM Paul Molitor 15.00
TM Thurman Munson 50.00
EM1 Eddie Murray 15.00
EM2 Eddie Murray 15.00
JO John Olerud 6.00
PO Paul O'Neill 15.00
DP Dave Parker 10.00
TP Tony Perez 10.00
LVP Lou Pinella 8.00
JP Jorge Posada 10.00
KP Kirby Puckett 20.00
WR Willie Randolph 10.00
MJS Mike Schmidt 50.00
MS Mike Scoscia 10.00
OS Ozzie Smith 30.00
JS John Smoltz 10.00
ES Ed Sprague 4.00
WS Willie Stargell 15.00
AT Alan Trammell 10.00
LW Lou Whitaker 10.00
BW Bernie Williams 15.00
MW Mookie Wilson 10.00
DW Dave Winfield 10.00
FV Fernando Valenzuela 8.00
JV Jose Vizcaino 4.00

2003 Stadium Club

NM/M
Complete Set (125): 30.00
Common Player: .15
Hobby Pack (6): 1.50
Hobby Box (24): 30.00
1 Rafael Furcal .15
2 Randy Winn .15
3 Eric Chavez .25
4 Fernando Vina .15
5 Pat Burrell .25
6 Derek Jeter 2.00
7 Ivan Rodriguez .65
8 Eric Hinske .15
9 Roberto Alomar .40
10 Tony Batista .15
11 Jacque Jones .15
12 Alfonso Soriano .75
13 Omar Vizquel .15
14 Paul Konerko .25
15 Shawn Green .45
16 Garret Anderson .15
17 Darin Erstad .25
18 Johnny Damon .25
19 Juan Gonzalez .75
20 Luis Gonzalez .25
21 Sean Burroughs .15
22 Mark Prior .75
23 Javier Vazquez .15
24 Shannon Stewart .15
25 Jay Gibbons .15
26 A.J. Pierzynski .15
27 Vladimir Guerrero .75
28 Austin Kearns .25
29 Shea Hillenbrand .15
30 Magglio Ordonez .15
31 Mike Cameron .15
32 Tim Salmon .25
33 Brian Jordan .15
34 Moises Alou .15
35 Rich Aurilia .15
36 Nick Johnson .15
37 Junior Spivey .15
38 Curt Schilling .40
39 Jose Vidro .15
40 Orlando Cabrera .15
41 Jeff Bagwell .75
42 Mo Vaughn .15
43 Luis Castillo .15
44 Vicente Padilla .15
45 Pedro J. Martinez .75
46 John Olerud .15
47 Tom Glavine .40
48 Torii Hunter .15
49 J.D. Drew .25
50 Alex Rodriguez 1.50
51 Randy Johnson .75
52 Richie Sexson .15
53 Jimmy Rollins .25
54 Cristian Guzman .15
55 Tim Hudson .25
56 Mark Buehrle .15
57 Paul LoDuca .15
58 Aramis Ramirez .25
59 Todd Helton .75
60 Lance Berkman .15
61 Josh Beckett .25
62 Bret Boone .15
63 Miguel Tejada .35
64 Nomar Garciaparra 1.25
65 Albert Pujols 1.50
66 Chipper Jones 1.00
67 Scott Rolen .65
68 Kerry Wood .65
69 Jorge Posada .15
70 Ichiro Suzuki 1.50
71 Jeff Kent .15
72 David Eckstein .15
73 Phil Nevin .15
74 Brian Giles .15
75 Barry Zito .25
76 Andruw Jones .50
77 Jim Thome .65
78 Robert Fick .15
79 Rafael Palmeiro .65
80 Barry Bonds 2.00
81 Gary Sheffield .40
82 Jim Edmonds .25
83 Kazuhisa Ishii .15
84 Jose Hernandez .15
85 Jason Giambi .40
86 Mark Mulder .15
87 Roger Clemens 1.00
88 Troy Glaus .75
89 Carlos Delgado .50
90 Mike Sweeney .15
91 Ken Griffey Jr. 1.25
92 Manny Ramirez .75
93 Ryan Klesko .15
94 Larry Walker .15
95 Adam Dunn .65
96 Raul Ibanez .15
97 Preston Wilson .15
98 Roy Oswalt .15
99 Sammy Sosa 1.25
100 Mike Piazza 1.25
101 Jose Reyes .50
102 Ed Rogers .15
103 Hank Blalock .75
104 Mark Teixeira .65
105 Orlando Hudson .15
106 Drew Henson .25
107 Joe Mauer .75
108 Carl Crawford .15
109 Marlon Byrd .15
110 Jason Stokes .15
111 Miguel Cabrera .50
112 Wilson Betemit .15
113 Jerome Williams .15
114 Walter Young .15
115 Juan Camacho **RC** .15
116 Chris Duncan **RC** 3.00
117 Franklin Gutierrez **RC** 3.00
118 Adam LaRoche .50
119 Manuel Ramirez **RC** .50
120 Il Kim **RC** .50
121 Wayne Lydon **RC** .50
122 Daryl Clark **RC** .50
123 Sean Pierce .15
124 Andy Marte **RC** 3.00
125 Matthew Peterson **RC** .75

Photographer's Proof

Stars (1-100): 4-8X
Cards (101-125): 2-4X
Production 299 Sets

Royal Gold

Stars: 1-30X
Inserted 1:1

Beam Team

NM/M
Complete Set (20): 50.00
Common Player: 1.00
Inserted 1:12
BT1 Larry Walker 1.00
BT2 Miguel Tejada 1.50
BT3 Ichiro Suzuki 5.00
BT4 Sammy Sosa 5.00
BT5 Ivan Rodriguez 2.50
BT6 Alex Rodriguez 6.00
BT7 Mike Piazza 5.00
BT8 Jeff Kent 1.00
BT9 Chipper Jones 4.00
BT10 Derek Jeter 8.00
BT11 Todd Helton 3.00
BT12 Vladimir Guerrero 3.00
BT13 Shawn Green 1.50
BT14 Brian Giles 1.00
BT15 Jason Giambi 2.00
BT16 Nomar Garciaparra 5.00
BT17 Adam Dunn 2.00
BT18 Carlos Delgado 1.50
BT19 Barry Bonds 8.00
BT20 Lance Berkman 1.00

Born In The USA

NM/M
Common Player: 5.00
Jerseys Inserted 1:52
Bats Inserted 1:76
RA Rich Aurilia/Jsy 5.00
JB Jeff Bagwell/Jsy 12.00
CB Craig Biggio/Jsy 8.00
BB Bret Boone/Jsy 5.00
AB A.J. Burnett/Jsy 5.00
JNB Jeromy Burnitz/Bat 6.00
PB Pat Burrell/Bat 10.00
SB Sean Burroughs/Bat 6.00
EC Eric Chavez/Jsy 6.00
TC Tony Clark/Bat 5.00
JD Johnny Damon/Bat 8.00
JDD J.D. Drew/Bat 6.00
AD Adam Dunn/Bat 12.00
JE Jim Edmonds/Jsy 8.00
CF Cliff Floyd/Bat 5.00
BF Brad Fullmer/Bat 5.00
NG Nomar Garciaparra/Bat 20.00
LG Luis Gonzalez/Bat 6.00

MG	Mark Grace/Jsy	12.00
SG	Shawn Green/Bat	6.00
TJH	Toby Hall	5.00
JH	Josh Hamilton/Bat	8.00
TH	Todd Helton/Bat	8.00
RH	Rickey Henderson/ Bat	15.00
RJ	Randy Johnson/Bat	12.00
CJ	Chipper Jones/Jsy	12.00
RK	Ryan Klesko/Bat	5.00
PK	Paul Konerko/Bat	8.00
BL	Barry Larkin/Jsy	10.00
TRL	Travis Lee/Bat	5.00
TL	Terrence Long/Jsy	5.00
GM	Greg Maddux/Jsy	15.00
TM	Tino Martinez/Bat	10.00
WM	Willie Mays/Bat	40.00
EM	Eric Milton/Jsy	6.00
JO	John Olerud/Jsy	6.00
CP	Corey Patterson/Bat	8.00
MP	Mike Piazza/Jsy	15.00
AR	Alex Rodriguez/Bat	15.00
SR	Scott Rolen/Bat	15.00
RS	Richie Sexson/Bat	6.00
GS	Gary Sheffield/Bat	8.00
JS	John Smoltz/Jsy	6.00
FT	Frank Thomas/Bat	8.00
JT	Jim Thome/Jsy	15.00
MV	Mo Vaughn/Bat	6.00
RV	Robin Ventura/Bat	8.00
MW	Matt Williams/Bat	8.00
PW	Preston Wilson/Jsy	5.00
KW	Kerry Wood/Bat	10.00

Clubhouse Exclusive

		NM/M
Jersey Inserted 1:488		
Jersey & Bat 1:2,073		
Jersey, Bat & Spikes 1:2,750		
CE1	Albert Pujols/Jsy	15.00
CE2	Albert Pujols/Bat/Jsy	35.00
CE3	Albert Pujols/ Jsy/Bat/Spike	100.00

Co-Signers

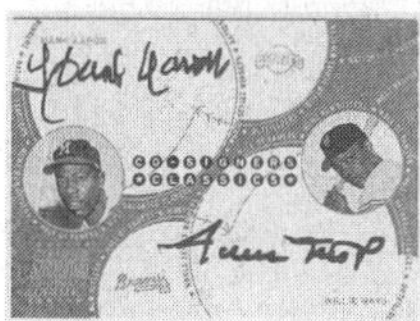

		NM/M
HTA Exclusive		
MI	Masanori Murakami, Kazuhisa Ishii	180.00
AM	Hank Aaron, Willie Mays	400.00

License To Drive

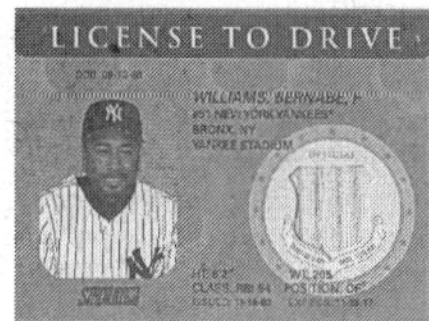

		NM/M
Common Player:		6.00
Inserted 1:98		
RA	Roberto Alomar	8.00
MA	Moises Alou	6.00
AB	Adrian Beltre	8.00
LB	Lance Berkman	6.00
EC	Eric Chavez	6.00
AD	Adam Dunn	8.00
NG	Nomar Garciaparra	15.00
JG	Juan Gonzalez	8.00
LG	Luis Gonzalez	6.00
SG	Shawn Green	8.00
TH	Todd Helton	10.00
AJ	Andruw Jones	10.00
CJ	Chipper Jones	12.00
TM	Tino Martinez	6.00
RP	Rafael Palmeiro	8.00
MP	Mike Piazza	15.00
AP	Albert Pujols	25.00
ANR	Aramis Ramirez	6.00
AR	Alex Rodriguez	20.00
IR	Ivan Rodriguez	8.00
SR	Scott Rolen	10.00
GS	Gary Sheffield	8.00
FT	Frank Thomas	10.00
LW	Larry Walker	6.00
BW	Bernie Williams	6.00

MLB Match-Ups

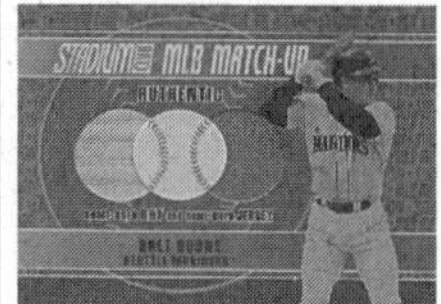

		NM/M
Inserted 1:485		
BB	Bret Boone	15.00
TH	Todd Helton	15.00
AJ	Andruw Jones	12.00
GM	Greg Maddux	30.00
AP	Albert Pujols	30.00

Stadium Shots

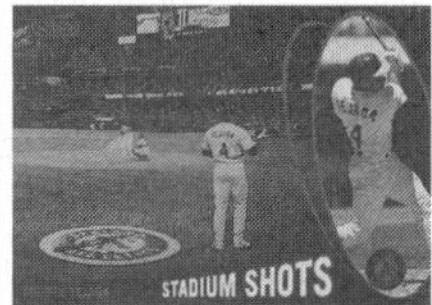

		NM/M
Complete Set (10):		25.00
Common Player:		1.00
Inserted 1:24		
SS1	Lance Berkman	1.00
SS2	Barry Bonds	6.00
SS3	Jason Giambi	2.50
SS4	Shawn Green	1.50
SS5	Vladimir Guerrero	3.00
SS6	Paul Konerko	1.00
SS7	Mike Piazza	4.50
SS8	Alex Rodriguez	6.00
SS9	Sammy Sosa	4.50
SS10	Jim Thome	2.00

Stadium Slices Handle

		NM/M
Common Player:		5.00
Inserted 1:237		
Trademarks:		1-1.5X
Inserted 1:415		
Barrels:		1.5-2X
Inserted 1:550		
RA	Roberto Alomar	15.00
CD	Carlos Delgado	8.00
NG	Nomar Garciaparra	20.00
TH	Todd Helton	10.00
AJ	Andruw Jones	8.00
RP	Rafael Palmeiro	10.00
MP	Mike Piazza	15.00
AP	Albert Pujols	20.00
AR	Alex Rodriguez	15.00
GS	Gary Sheffield	10.00

World Stage

		NM/M
Common Player:		5.00
Jerseys Inserted 1:118		
Bats Inserted 1:809		
AB	Adrian Beltre/Jsy	6.00
KI	Kazuhisa Ishii/Jsy	5.00
BK	Byung-Hyun Kim/Jsy	5.00
HN	Hideo Nomo/Bat	20.00
AP	Albert Pujols/Jsy	15.00
IR	Ivan Rodriguez/Jsy	8.00
KS	Kazuhiro Sasaki/Jsy	5.00
TS	Tsuyoshi Shinjo/Bat	5.00
AS	Alfonso Soriano/Bat	15.00
MT	Miguel Tejada/Jsy	8.00

1983 Star '83

Star's first baseball card issue was a 15-card tribute to Mike Schmidt, subtitled "Ten Years of Excellence." On the cards' fronts, Schmidt is shown in various posed and game-action photos, surrounded by a red border. Backs tell his story in words and num-

bers. The cards are the standard 2-1/2" x 3-1/2" and were sold only as complete sets through hobby dealers. Single cards are not listed because the sets are seldom broken for individual card sales.

	NM/M
Complete Set:	6.00

1984 Star '84

Star broadened the selection of its single-player collectors' issues in 1984 and adopted a new design which it used with little variation for several years. Most cards were issued in panels of three, perforated for easy separation. Each set has posed and game-action photos surrounded by colorful borders. Team logos are in a circle at lower-left; "Star '84" is in an inset at the photo's upper-right. Backs within a set feature stats, career highlights personal information and, sometimes, puzzle pieces.

		NM/M
1-24	George Brett	7.50
1-24	Steve Carlton	6.00
1-36	Steve Garvey (7,500 Sets)	3.50
1-36	Darryl Strawberry	2.00
1-24	Carl Yastrzemski (Not issued in panels.)	4.00
1-24	Carl Yastrzemski (First card autographed, edition of 500.)	20.00

1985 Star Nolan Ryan Promo

Issued to promote a set that was never issued, this promo card has on back logos and copyright information for an NBA issue.

	NM/M
Nolan Ryan	15.00

1985 Star '85

Star maintained the basic format of 1984 for its sole single-player issue of 1985. The 36-card set of Reggie Jackson has portrait and action photos surrounded by colorful borders. The logo of the A's, Orioles or Yankees appears in a circle at lower-left on front, with a "Star '85" logo at upper-right. Backs have a mix of stats, personal data and career highlights. Cards were issued in a dozen three-card panels, perforated between the cards. Production was reported as 6,000 sets, with 500 of them signed and numbered by Jackson.

	NM/M
Complete Set (36):	5.00

1986 Star Promos

Several of the 1986 Star single-player series were introduced with the issue of a promo cards, different on their backs, but otherwise similar in appearance to the regular cards.

		NM/M
Complete Set (7):		55.00
Common Player:		2.50
(1)	Rod Carew (Ad back.)	1.50
(2)	Don Mattingly (White card.) (Blank back.)	2.50
(3)	Don Mattingly (Yellow sticker.) (Blank back.)	3.00
(4)	Dale Murphy (Ad back.)	3.50
(5)	Jim Rice (Blank back.)	2.50
(6)	Nolan Ryan (Ad back.)	15.00
(7)	Tom Seaver (Name on back.)	2.00

1986 Star '86

The basic format of previous years' issues was retained for Star's single-player sets of 1986. Player poses and game-action photos are presented on the front, bordered in a bright color usually associated with the player's team. In standard 2-1/2" x 3-1/2" size, the cards have a circle at lower-left with the player's name - first only or first and last. At top-right, infringing on the photo is the notation, "Star '86". Backs have stats, career highlights, personal data or puzzle pieces. Most sets were issued in three-card perforated panels. Some of the player sets can also be found in a glossy edition and/or a blank-back sticker version. Single cards are seldom offered and are not listed here.

		NM/M
1-24	Wade Boggs	2.00
1-24	Wade Boggs (Glossy set.)	2.00
(1-24)	Wade Boggs (Sticker set.)	2.00
1-15	Jose Canseco (Not issued in panels.)	3.00
1-15	Jose Canseco (Autographed, edition of 500.)	17.50
1-15	Jose Canseco (Glossy set.)	3.00
(1-15)	Jose Canseco (Sticker set.)	1.50
1-24	Rod Carew	1.50
1-15	Wally Joyner (Not issued in panels.)	1.00
1-15	Wally Joyner (Autographed, edition of 500.)	15.00
1-15	Wally Joyner (Glossy set.)	1.50
(1-15)	Wally Joyner (Sticker set.)	2.50
1-24	Don Mattingly	5.00
1-24	Don Mattingly (Glossy set.)	7.50
(1-24)	Don Mattingly (Sticker set.)	5.00
1-24	Dale Murphy	5.00
1-20	Jim Rice (Four-card panels.)	1.00
1-20	Jim Rice/Auto. (Edition of 500.)	40.00
1-20	Jim Rice (Glossy set.)	1.50
(1-20)	Jim Rice (Sticker set.)	1.50
1-24	Nolan Ryan (4,000 Sets)	9.00
1-24	Tom Seaver (8,000 Sets)	3.50

1987 Star Promos

Most of Star's single-player sets issued for 1987 were preceded by the issue of blank-backed promo cards in a nearly identical format to the issued version.

		NM/M
Complete Set (6):		8.75
Common Player:		1.00
(1)	Steve Carlton	2.50
(2)	Gary Carter	2.00
(3)	Roger Clemens	4.00
(4)	Keith Hernandez	1.00
(5)	Tim Raines	1.00
(6)	Fernando Valenzuela	1.00

1987 Star '87

The single-player sets issued by Star in 1987 retain the basic format used since 1984. Standard size (2-1/2" x 3-1/2") cards were printed singly, rather than in panels, but the design remained virtually unchanged. Posed and action photos are surrounded by a colorful border which protrudes into the photo at upper-right with the logo "Star '87." At lower-left is a circle with the player's first name, or, in the case of Fernando Valenzuela, the team logo. Backs have stats, personal data or career highlights. Sets were also issued in a limited glossy version and/or as blank-back stickers. Single cards are usually not sold, so are not listed here.

		NM/M
		17.50
(1-5)	Wade Boggs, Jose Canseco (Unnumbered)	3.00
(1-5)	Wade Boggs, Jose Canseco (Glossy set.) (Unnumbered)	4.50
1-14	Steve Carlton (Glossy version only.)	3.50
1-14	Gary Carter	2.00
1-14	Gary Carter (Glossy set.)	2.25
(1-10)	Gary Carter (Sticker set.) (Different photos.)	2.50
1-12	Roger Clemens (8,500 Regular Sets; 500 Autographed)	2.00
1-12	Roger Clemens (Glossy; 1,000 Sets)	2.50
(1-5)	Roger Clemens (Update) (Unnumbered)	3.00
(1-5)	Roger Clemens (Update, glossy.) (Unnumbered)	4.50
1-13	Keith Hernandez (8,500 Regular Sets, 500 Autographed)	1.25
1-13	Keith Hernandez (Glossy; 1,000 Sets)	2.25
(1-6)	Don Mattingly (Unnumbered, five blank-back cards, one w/ 1986 stats.)	3.00
(1-6)	Don Mattingly (Glossy) (Unnumbered, five cards blank-back, one w/1986 stats.)	4.50
1-12	Tim Raines (8,500 Regular Sets; 500 Autographed)	1.00
1-12	Tim Raines (Glossy; 1,000 Sets)	1.50
1-13	Fernando Valenzuela (8,500 Regular Sets, 500 Autographed)	1.50
1-13	Fernando Valenzuela (Glossy; 1,000 Sets)	2.25
(1-10)	Fernando Valenzuela (Sticker set.) (Different photos.)	2.50

1988-89 Star Promos

The lengthy series of 11-card sets issued by Star in 1988-89 in the company's "new" format included one promo card for nearly every player's set. The promos are blank-backed but otherwise similar in design to the regular cards.

		NM/M
Complete Set (40):		32.50
Common Player:		.75
(1)	Alomar Brothers (Roberto Alomar)	.75
(2)	Sandy Alomar Jr. (Alomar Brothers)	.75
(3)	Sandy Alomar Jr.	.75
(4)	Wade Boggs	2.00
(5)	Jose Canseco (Blue borders.)	1.50
(6)	Jose Conseco (Canseco) (Yellow borders.)	1.50
(7)	Jose Canseco (Bay Bombers Series)	1.50
(8)	Will Clark (Purple/Yellow)	1.50
(9)	Will Clark (Clark/Mitchell set, gold borders.)	.75
(10)	Will Clark (Bay Bombers Series)	1.50
(11)	David Cone	.75
(12)	Dwight Gooden	.75
(13)	Tom Gordon	.75
(14)	Mark Grace (1,300 Issued)	1.00
(15)	Mike Greenwell (Blue borders.)	.75
(16)	Mike Greenwell (Pink borders.)	.75
(17)	Ken Griffey Jr. (White-back set, blue/white borders.)	2.50
(18)	Ken Griffey Jr. (Yellow-back set, yellow borders.)	3.50
(19)	Orel Hershiser	.75
(20)	Sam Horn	.75

(21) Bo Jackson .75
(22) Gregg Jefferies (Blue-border set, orange borders.) .75
(23) Gregg Jefferies (Orange-border set, dark blue borders, misspelled Greg.) .75
(24) Gregg Jefferies (Pink-border set, light blue borders, misspelled Greg.) .75
(25) Ricky Jordan .75
(26) Don Mattingly 2.00
(27) Kevin McReynolds .75
(28) Kevin Mitchell (Clark/Mitchell set, gold borders.) .75
(29) Kevin Mitchell (Orange borders.) .75
(30) Matt Nokes (Yellow borders, glossy.) .75
(31) Kirby Puckett 1.75
(32) Nolan Ryan 2.50
(33) Benito Santiago .75
(34) Gary Sheffield .75
(35) Darryl Strawberry (Blue-border set, pink borders.) .75
(36) Darryl Strawberry (Purple-border set, orange borders.) .75
(37) Alan Trammell .75
(38) Robin Ventura .75
(39) Jerome Walton (Regular set, borders in two shades of blue.) .75
(40) Jerome Walton (Glossy set, solid blue borders, portrait.) .75

1988-1989 Star

Late in 1988 Star introduced a new format for its single-player card sets, which it carried forward into 1989. Sets were standardized at 11 cards in the 2-1/2" x 3-1/2" format. Fronts feature posed and game-action photos that are bordered by graduating shades of a particular color, or two different colors, going from dark at top to light at bottom, or vice versa. (The first Gregg Jefferies set is an exception, having the same shade of blue on all borders.) Backs may be printed in any of a variety of colors on white, yellow, pink or green backgrounds. Stats, personal data, career highlights and team logos are found on back. Sets may carry either a 1988 or 1989 copyright date. Because the sets are seldom broken up for singles sales, individual cards are not listed here. The number of player sets for which glossy versions were issued is uncertain. Existing glossy sets should retail for 2-5X the regular version, depending on player popularity.

NM/M
1-11 Alomar Brothers (Roberto Alomar, Sandy Alomar Jr.) 1.50
1-11 Sandy Alomar Jr. 1.50
1-11 Bay Bombers Series (Jose Canseco (Solid green borders.) 3.00
1-11 Bay Bombers Series (Will Clark (Solid orange borders.)) 1.75
1-11 Wade Boggs (Solid red borders.) 4.00
1-11 Jose Canseco (Error set - "Conseco.") 5.00
1-11 Jose Canseco (Correct, dark green borders, white name.) 3.00
1-11 Jose Canseco (Correct, light green borders, green name.) 3.00
1-11 Will Clark 3.00
1-11 Will Clark, Kevin Mitchell 1.50
1-11 David Cone 1.50
1-11 Dwight Gooden 1.50
1-11 Tom Gordon 1.50
1-11 Mark Grace (Solid orange borders; 6,500 sets.) 1.00
1-11 Mark Grace/Auto. (500 sets.) 5.00
1-11 Mike Greenwell (Purple borders.) 1.50
1-11 Mike Greenwell (Red borders.) 1.50
1-11 Ken Griffey Jr. (White backs.) 7.50
1-11 Ken Griffey Jr. (Yellow backs, different photos.) 7.50
1-11 Orel Hershiser (8,000 Regular Sets) 1.50
1-11 Orel Hershiser (Glossy - 250 sets.) 2.25
1-11 Sam Horn (Solid blue borders; 4,000 sets.) 1.00
1-11 Sam Horn (Glossy - 1,000 sets.) 1.50
1-11 Bo Jackson 1.50
1-11 Gregg Jefferies (Blue borders; 8,000 sets.) 1.50
1-11 Gregg Jefferies (Orange borders.) 1.50
1-11 Gregg Jefferies (Pink borders.) 1.50
1-11 Ron Jones 1.00
1-11 Ricky Jordan (8,000 Sets) 1.00
1-11 Ricky Jordan (Glossy - 250 sets.) 2.00
1-11 Ricky Jones/Auto. (500 sets.) 3.00
1-11 Kevin McReynolds (8,000 Sets) 1.50
1-11 Kevin McReynolds (Glossy - 250 sets.) 2.25
1-11 Kevin Mitchell 1.50
1-11 Matt Nokes (3,500 sets, each bag serial numbered) 1.25
1-11 Kirby Puckett 4.50
--- Pete Rose (Blank-back, Reds.) 15.00
1-11 Nolan Ryan (Pink backs only.) 6.00
1-11 Benito Santiago 1.50
1-11 Gary Sheffield 1.50
1-11 Darryl Strawberry (Blue borders.) 1.00
1-11 Darryl Strawberry (Purple borders.) 1.00
1-11 Alan Trammell (#4 Misspelled Trammel) 1.50
1-11 Robin Ventura 1.50
1-11 Jerome Walton 1.50
1-11 Jerome Walton (Glossy, borders one shade of blue.) 1.50

1988-92 Star Ad Cards

These cards were distributed to give dealers and collectors basic information about Star's baseball issues. Fronts look like contemporary Star cards, but most (not all) have the notation "Ad Card" beneath the city name at lower-right. Backs have an advertising message with general information except for Horn and Jefferies, whose ads are specific to ordering those player sets. Some cards exist in both regular and glossy finish. Except for the 1992s, the Ad Cards are undated and some of the dates on this possibly incomplete checklist are only best estimates. The unnumbered cards are checklisted here alphabetically.

NM/M
Complete Set (45): 70.00
Common Player: 1.50
(1) Sandy Alomar Jr./1989 (Regular gray.) 1.50
(1g) Sandy Alomar Jr./1989 (Glossy gray.) 1.50
(2) Steve Avery/1992 (Plastic red/blue.) 1.50
(3) Jeff Bagwell/1992 (Plastic orange/green.) 1.50
(4) Wade Boggs/1989 (Regular pink.) 3.25
(5) Bobby Bonilla/1991 (Regular purple.) 1.50
(5g) Bobby Bonilla/1991 (Glossy purple.) 1.50
(6) Will Clark/1988 (Regular green.) 1.50
(6g) Will Clark/1988 (Glossy green.) 1.50
(7) Roger Clemens/1988 (Regular) 2.50
(8) Eric Davis/1989 (Glossy red.) 1.50
(9) Ken Griffey Jr./1989 (Regular purple.) 3.50
(10) Ken Griffey Jr./1990 (Regular green.) 2.50
(10g) Ken Griffey Jr./1990 (Glossy green.) 3.50
(11) Rickey Henderson/1991 (Regular green/yellow.) 1.50
(11g) Rickey Henderson/1991 (Glossy green/yellow.) 1.50
(12) Keith Hernandez/1989 (Regular orange.) 1.50
(13) Orel Hershiser/1989 (Regular purple.) 1.50
(14) Sam Horn/1989 (Regular purple.) 1.50
(15) Bo Jackson/1990 (Regular blue.) 1.50
(16) Bo Jackson/1992 (Regular green.) 1.50
(17) Gregg Jefferies/1988 (Regular blue.) 1.50
(18) Howard Johnson/1990 (Regular orange.) 1.50
(19) David Justice/1992 (Plastic blue/yellow.) 1.50
(20) Eric Karros/1992 (Glossy white.) 1.50
(21) Barry Larkin/1990 (Regular red.) 1.50
(22) Kevin Maas/1990 (Regular white.) 1.50
(23) Don Mattingly/1988 (Regular green.) 3.50
(24) Don Mattingly/1989 (Regular blue.) 3.50
(25) Don Mattingly/1989 (Regular gray.) 3.50
(26) Kevin Mitchell/1990 (Regular white/black.) 1.50
(27) Phil Plantier/1992 (Plastic blue/purple.) 1.50
(28) Kirby Puckett/1989 (Regular red.) 6.50
(29) Kirby Puckett/1992 (Plastic purple/blue.) 3.25
(30) Cal Ripken Jr./1992 (Regular black/orange.) 3.50
(31) Reggie Sanders/1992 (Glossy white.) 1.50
(32) Benito Santiago/1990 (Regular purple.) 1.50
(33) Mike Scott/1989 (Regular green.) 1.50
(34) Darryl Strawberry/1991 (Regular red.) 1.50
(35g) Frank Thomas/1991 (Glossy blue/red.) 3.25
(35p) Frank Thomas/1991 (Plastic blue/red.) 3.25
(36) Frank Thomas/1992 (Plastic red/yellow.) 3.25
(37) Alan Trammell/1989 (Glossy blue.) 1.50
(38) Robin Ventura/1990 (Glossy gold.) 3.25
(39) Jerome Walton/1990 (Regular blue/red.) 1.50

1988-89 Star Gold Edition

This 180-card set was released from late 1988 into 1989 (though all cards bear 1988 copyright date) in a format matching the regular-issue player sets of the 1988-89 issue. Eighteen single-player sets of 10 cards each are included. The high quality photographs on front feature a special gold embossing. The cards devoted to each player are noted by number in the corresponding listings. Single cards are not checklisted because the issue is usually sold only as complete single-player sets. Fifteen hundred of each set were produced, plus 300 black-bordered, blank-back "promo" cards of each player.

NM/M
Complete Set (180): 22.50
Common Player Set (10): 1.00
Complete Promo Set: 32.50
Common Promo Card: 1.50
1-10 Gregg Jefferies 1.00
Gregg Jefferies (Promo card.) 1.50
11-20 Sam Horn 1.00
Sam Horn (Promo card.) 1.50
21-30 Don Mattingly 6.00
Don Mattingly (Promo card.) 7.50
31-40 Matt Nokes 1.00
Matt Nokes (Promo card.) 1.50
41-50 Darryl Strawberry 1.00
Darryl Strawberry (Promo card.) 1.50
51-60 Will Clark 2.00
Will Clark (Promo card.) 3.00
61-70 Wade Boggs 3.00
Wade Boggs (Promo card.) 3.00
71-80 Mark Grace 1.50
Mark Grace (Promo card.) 2.00
81-90 Bo Jackson 1.00
Bo Jackson (Promo card.) 1.50
91-100 Jose Canseco 2.00
Jose Canseco (Promo card.) 3.00
101-110 Eric Davis 1.00
Eric Davis (Promo card.) 1.50
110-119 Orel Hershiser (#120 Misnumbered #110) 1.00
Orel Hershiser (Promo card.) 1.50
121-130 Mike Greenwell 1.00
Mike Greenwell (Promo card.) 1.50
131-140 Dave Winfield 2.00
Dave Winfield (Promo card.) 3.00
141-150 Alan Trammell 1.00
Alan Trammell (Promo card.) 1.50
151-160 Roger Clemens 4.00
Roger Clemens (Promo card.) 3.50
161-170 Kirby Puckett 2.50
Kirby Puckett (Promo card.) 3.50
171-180 Kevin Seitzer 1.00
Kevin Seitzer (Promo card.) 1.50

1988-89 Star Nova Edition

With production limited to just 500 sets and 40 promo cards of each player, these are the most limited of the regular Star issues of 1989. Cards follow the format of the regular-issue Star single-player sets of the 1988-89 issue. Each of the nine-card player sets is listed here in alphabetical order. Single cards are not listed because complete player sets are seldom broken for individual card sales. The Nova promo cards have blue borders at the top and red at bottom. Cards #109-117 were not issued. Ryne Sandberg cards #154-161 have his name misspelled Sanberg on front and back.

NM/M
Complete Set (153): 85.00
Common Player Set (9): 3.00
Complete Promo Card Set (17): 225.00
Common Promo Card: 7.50
1-9 Mike Greenwell 3.00
Mike Greenwell (Promo card.) 7.50
10-18 Darryl Strawberry 3.00
Darryl Strawberry (Promo card.) 7.50
19-27 Don Mattingly 11.00
Don Mattingly (Promo card.) 30.00
28-36 Eric Davis 3.00
Eric Davis (Promo) 7.50
37-45 Jose Canseco 7.50
Jose Canseco (Promo card.) 22.50
46-54 Sandy Alomar Jr. 3.00
Sandy Alomar Jr. (Promo card.) 7.50
55-63 Kirby Puckett 9.00
Kirby Puckett (Promo card.) 25.00
64-72 Orel Hershiser 3.00
Orel Hershiser (Promo card.) 7.50
73-81 Wade Boggs 7.50
Wade Boggs (Promo card.) 17.50
82-90 Rickey Henderson 5.00
Rickey Henderson (Promo card.) 9.00
91-99 Will Clark 3.50
Will Clark (Promo card.) 15.00
100-108 Bo Jackson 3.50
Bo Jackson (Promo card.) 12.50
118-126 Ken Griffey Jr. 15.00
Ken Griffey Jr. (Promo card.) 30.00
127-135 Mike Schmidt 11.00
Mike Schmidt (Promo card.) 30.00
136-144 Gary Sheffield 3.50
Gary Sheffield (Promo card.) 9.00
145-153 Cal Ripken Jr. 12.50
Cal Ripken Jr. (Promo card.) 35.00
154-162 Ryne Sandberg 7.50
Ryne Sandberg (Promo card.) 20.00

1988 Star Platinum Edition

Twelve single-player sets make up the 1988 Star Platinum series. Ten cards were devoted to each player. While the cards were sold as individual player sets, they were numbered contiguously. Fronts feature color photos with various colorful borders (by player), highlighted in silver foil. No single card prices are quoted because the cards are usually sold only as complete player sets. One thousand sets of each player were issued, along with 200 gold-bordered promo cards per player.

NM/M
Complete Set (120): 27.50
Common Player Set (10): 1.50
Complete Promo Set (12): 32.50
Common Promo Player: 2.00
1-10 Don Mattingly 6.00
Don Mattingly (Promo card.) 10.00
11-20 Dwight Gooden 1.50
Dwight Gooden (Promo card.) 2.00
21-30 Roger Clemens 3.50
Roger Clemens (Promo card.) 3.50
31-40 Mike Schmidt 3.50
Mike Schmidt (Promo card.) 4.00
41-50 Wade Boggs 2.50
Wade Boggs (Promo card.) 3.00
51-60 Mark McGwire 6.00
Mark McGwire (Promo card.) 5.00
61-70 Andre Dawson 1.50
Andre Dawson (Promo card.) 2.50
71-80 Jose Canseco 2.50
Jose Canseco (Promo card.) 4.00
81-90 Eric Davis 1.50
Eric Davis (Promo card.) 2.00
91-100 George Brett 5.00
George Brett/Throwing (Promo card.) 4.00
101-110 Darryl Strawberry 1.50
Darryl Strawberry (Promo card.) (Blue uniform.) 2.00
111-120 Dale Murphy 1.50
Dale Murphy (Promo card.) 2.00

1988-89 Star Platinum

Fourteen of baseball's top players are featured in 10-card single-player sets within this issue. Cards #21-30 were devoted to Gregg Jefferies, but a contract dispute prevented their release. While sold as single-player sets, the cards are numbered contiguously. Card numbers are provided for each player in the checklist below. Single cards are not checklisted because the issue is generally sold only as complete player sets. A thousand sets of each player were produced, along with 200 promo cards of each player. The cards follow the format of the regular-issue Star 1988-89 player sets.

NM/M
Complete Set (140): 17.50
Common Player Set (10): 1.00
Complete Promo Set (14): 22.50
Common Promo Card: 1.50
1-10 Jose Canseco 2.00
Jose Canseco (Promo card.) 2.00
11-20 Mike Greenwell 1.00
Mike Greenwell (Promo card.) 1.50
31-40 Wade Boggs 2.50
Wade Boggs (Promo card.) 3.00
41-50 Don Mattingly 3.25
Don Mattingly (Promo card.) 3.75
51-60 Kirby Puckett 2.50
Kirby Puckett (Promo card.) 3.00
61-70 Dwight Gooden 1.00

	Dwight Gooden (Promo card.)	1.50
71-80	Alan Trammell	1.00
	Alan Trammell (Promo card.)	1.50
81-90	Darryl Strawberry	1.00
	Darryl Strawberry (Promo card.) (White uniform.)	1.50
91-100	Orel Hershiser	1.00
	Orel Hershiser (Promo card.)	1.50
101-110	Will Clark	1.50
	Will Clark (Promo card.)	2.50
111-120	Roger Clemens	2.00
	Roger Clemens (Promo card.)	3.50
121-130	Eric Davis	1.00
	Eric Davis (Promo card.)	1.50
131-140	George Brett	3.00
	George Brett/Btg (Promo card.)	3.50
141-150	Frank Viola	1.00
	Frank Viola (Promo card.)	1.50

1988-89 Star Silver Edition

This 90-card issue features 10 single-player sets. Only Only 2,000 serial numbered sets were printed (plus 400 "promo" cards of each player, featuring black borders fading to white at the middle). Single-card values are not quoted because the player sets are seldom broken for individual card sales. Cards follow the format of the regular-issue 1988-89 Star player sets.

		NM/M
	Complete Set (90):	35.00
	Common Player Set:	1.50
	Complete Promo Card Set (10):	37.50
	Common Promo Card:	3.00
1-9	Ken Griffey Jr.	17.50
	Ken Griffey Jr. (Promo card.)	9.00
10-18	Wade Boggs	5.00
	Wade Boggs (Promo card.)	6.00
19-27	Ricky Jordan	1.50
	Ricky Jordan (Promo card.)	3.00
28-36	Mike Greenwell	1.50
	Mike Greenwell (Promo card.)	3.00
37-45	Sandy Alomar Jr.	1.50
	Sandy Alomar Jr. (Promo card.)	3.00
46-54	Mike Schmidt	6.00
	Mike Schmidt (Promo card.)	7.50
55-63	Gary Sheffield	2.25
	Gary Sheffield (Promo card.)	3.00
64-72	Will Clark	2.25
	Will Clark (Promo card.)	3.50
73-81	Ron Jones	1.50
	Ron Jones (Promo card.)	3.00
82-90	Kirby Puckett	6.00
	Kirby Puckett (Promo card.)	6.00

1988 Star '88 Promos

Most of the Star '88 single- and dual-player card sets also had a promo card issued; blank-backed but otherwise nearly identical to the regular cards.

		NM/M
	Complete Set (23):	35.00
	Common Player:	1.00
(1)	George Bell	1.00
(2)	Wade Boggs	2.00
(3)	Wade Boggs, Tony Gwynn	1.50
(4)	Gary Carter	1.50
(5)	Will Clark	1.50
(6)	Roger Clemens, Dwight Gooden	1.50
(7)	Eric Davis	1.00
(8)	Andre Dawson	1.50
(9)	Dwight Gooden	1.00
(10)	Tony Gwynn	2.00
(11)	Bo Jackson	1.50
(12)	Don Mattingly	3.00
(13)	Don Mattingly, Mike Schmidt	1.75
(14)	Mark McGwire (Yellow-border set, green-border promo.)	4.00
(15)	Mark McGwire (Aqua-border set, yellow-border promo.)	2.50
(16)	Mark McGwire (Green-border set, white-border promo.)	4.00
(17)	Eddie Murray	2.00
(18)	Cal Ripken Jr.	3.50
(19)	Mike Schmidt	2.50
(20)	Mike Scott	1.00
(21)	Kevin Seitzer	1.00
(22)	Cory Snyder	1.00
(23)	Dave Winfield	2.50

1988 Star '88

For the fifth straight year Star utilized the same basic format for its single-player card sets of 1988. Fronts have player posed and game-action photos surrounded by a brightly colored border. Pushing into the top-right of the photo is a "Star '88" logo. A circle at the lower-left contains the player name or logo. Backs have stats, personal data, career highlights or a checklist. Single cards are not listed here because sets are seldom broken. Many player sets were also issued in a more limited glossy edition, and some sets were produced with the first card authentically autographed.

		NM/M
1-11	George Bell (7,500 Sets)	1.50
(1-10)	George Bell (Sticker set.)	2.00
1-11	Wade Boggs (10,000 Sets)	2.50
1-11	Wade Boggs (#1 Autographed)	25.00
1-11	Wade Boggs (Glossy - 1,000 sets.)	4.00
1-11	Wade Boggs, Tony Gwynn	2.50
1-11	Gary Carter (6,000 Sets)	2.00
1-11	Gary Carter (Glossy - 1,000 sets.)	3.00
1-11	Will Clark (7,500 Sets)	1.75
1-11	Will Clark (#1 Autographed)	15.00
1-11	Roger Clemens, Dwight Gooden	2.00
1-12	Eric Davis	1.50
1-12	Eric Davis (Glossy - 1,000 sets.)	1.50
1-11	Eric Davis, Mark McGwire	2.25
1-11	Andre Dawson (4,500 Sets)	1.50
1-11	Andre Dawson (Glossy - 1,000 sets.)	2.50
1-11	Andre Dawson/Auto. (500 sets.)	12.50
1-12	Dwight Gooden (5,600 Sets)	1.50
1-12	Dwight Gooden (Glossy - 1,000 sets.)	2.25
1-12	Dwight Gooden/Auto. (400 sets.)	10.00
1-11	Tony Gwynn (5,000 Sets)	2.50
1-11	Tony Gwynn (Glossy - 1,000 sets.)	4.50
1-11	Tony Gwynn/Auto. (500 sets.)	15.00
1-16	Bo Jackson (Set includes four blank-back cards as Auburn football player; 6,000 sets.)	3.00
1-16	Bo Jackson (Glossy - 1,000 sets.)	4.50
1-11	Don Mattingly (Card #3 exists with fielding or batting pose, 10,000 sets.)	6.00
1-11	Don Mattingly (Glossy - 1,000 sets.)	7.00
1-11	Don Mattingly, Mike Schmidt (2,000 Sets)	4.00
1-11	Don Mattingly, Mike Schmidt (Glossy - 1,000 sets.)	4.50
1-12	Mark McGwire (Yellow borders; 12,000 sets.)	3.50
1-12	Mark McGwire (Yellow borders; glossy - 1,000 sets.)	4.50
1-12	Mark McGwire/Auto. (Yellow borders; 500 sets.)	50.00
1-11	Mark McGwire (Aqua borders.)	7.50
1-11	Mark McGwire (Green borders; 6,000 sets.)	3.50
1-11	Mark McGwire (Green borders; glossy - 1,000 sets.)	5.00
1-12	Eddie Murray (Glossy version only.)	2.00
1-12	Cal Ripken Jr.	6.00
1-12	Mike Schmidt (Glossy version only.)	4.00
1-11	Mike Scott	1.50
1-11	Kevin Seitzer (6,000 Sets)	1.50
1-11	Kevin Seitzer (Glossy - 1,000 sets.)	2.25
1-11	Cory Snyder (8,500 Sets)	1.50
1-11	Cory Snyder (Glossy - 1,000 sets.)	2.25
1-11	Cory Snyder/Auto. (500 sets.)	5.00
(1-8)	Cory Snyder (Sticker set; 4,000 sets.)	2.00
1-12	Dave Winfield (5,000 Sets)	2.00
1-12	Dave Winfield (Glossy - 1,000 sets.)	3.00
1-12	Dave Winfield/Auto. (500 sets.)	16.00
(1-10)	Dave Winfield (Sticker set; 3,000.)	2.00

1989-90 Star Rookies

Two-card "sets" of each of 12 promising players were produced in an edition of 10,000 each as an exclusive for a New York comic book dealer. Cards have player photos on front with a few stats on back. Cards #1-12 have borders of red and gold and backs printed in red and tan. The 1990 cards, #13-24, are bordered in purple and yellow with backs printed in purple on yellow. All cards have 1989 copyright dates. Unlike most other contemporary Star sets, no glossy or promo cards were made.

		NM/M
	Complete Set (24):	2.50
	Common Player:	.15
1	Eric Anthony	.15
2	Eric Anthony	.15
3	Mark Lewis	.15
4	Mark Lewis	.15
5	Pete Rose, Jr.	.25
6	Pete Rose, Jr.	.25
7	Robin Ventura	.40
8	Robin Ventura	.40
9	Beau Allred	.15
10	Beau Allred	.15
11	Pat Combs	.15
12	Pat Combs	.15
13	Deion Sanders	.25
14	Deion Sanders	.25
15	Bob Hamelin	.15
16	Bob Hamelin	.15
17	Andy Benes	.20
18	Andy Benes	.20
19	Bam Bam Muelens	.15
20	Bam Bam Meulens	.15
21	Trey McCoy	.15
22	Trey McCoy	.15
23	Sandy Alomar Jr.	.25
24	Sandy Alomar Jr.	.25

1990-91 Star Promos

Most of the 1990-91 series of Star player sets feature a promo card in the same format. They are blank-backed and have the word "Promo" on front beneath the city name. Regular and glossy promos exist for most cards.

		NM/M
	Complete Set (44):	75.00
	Common Player:	1.50
(1)	Jim Abbott	1.50
(2)	Andy Benes	1.50
(3)	Barry Bonds (Correct)	6.00
(4)	Bobby Bonds (Photo actually Barry.)	6.00
(5)	Bobby Bonilla	1.50
(6)	Jose Canseco (Blue borders, from purple set.)	1.50
(7)	Jose Canseco (Orange borders, from yellow set.)	1.50
(8)	Jose Canseco (Green borders, from yellow set.)	1.50
(9)	Will Clark (Black borders.)	1.50
(10)	Will Clark (Purple)	1.50
(11)	Will Clark (Orange, from Clark/Grace set.)	1.50
(12)	Mark Davis	1.50
(13)	Cecil Fielder (Purple, from blue set.)	1.50
(14)	Cecil Fielder (Yellow glossy, from blue set.)	12.50
(15)	Ken Griffey Jr. (Purple, from blue set.)	2.25
(16)	Ken Griffey Jr. (Blue on yellow, from blue set.)	1.50
(17)	Ken Griffey Jr. (Red, batting with "S" on helmet, from yellow set.)	1.50
(18)	Ken Griffey Jr. (Red, no "S" on helmet, from aqua Jr./Sr. set.)	2.25
(19)	Ken Griffey Jr. (Red on yellow, from red Jr./Sr. set.)	2.25
(20)	Ken Griffey Sr. (Blue, from aqua set.)	1.50
(21)	Ken Griffey Sr. (Yellow, from red set.)	1.50
(22)	Rickey Henderson (Blue, 1990.)	1.50
(23)	Rickey Henderson/Running (Green, 1990.)	1.50
(24)	Rickey Henderson/Btg (Green, 1991.)	1.50
(25)	Bo Jackson/Running	1.50
(26)	Bo Jackson/Portrait	1.50
(27)	Bo Jackson (Diamond Terror, yellow.)	1.50
(28)	David Justice	1.50
(29)	Barry Larkin	1.50
(30)	Kevin Maas	1.50
(31)	Ben McDonald	1.50
(32)	Kevin Mitchell	1.50
(33)	Gregg Olson	1.50
(34)	Cal Ripken Jr.	3.00
(35)	Nolan Ryan (Blue, from Rangers set.)	4.00
(36)	Nolan Ryan (Yellow, from all-team set.)	3.00
(37)	Bret Saberhagen	1.50
(38)	Ryne Sandberg	1.50
(39)	Darryl Strawberry	1.50
(40)	Frank Thomas	1.50
(41)	Jerome Walton	1.50
(42)	Matt Williams	1.50
(43)	Robin Yount (Brown on yellow, from Mitchell/Yount set.)	1.50
(44)	Robin Yount (Blue on yellow.)	1.50

1990-91 Star

Issued as single-player sets over the two-year span these sets maintain a design continuity despite the fact some have a 1990 copyright line on back and some have a 1991 date. Fronts of all cards have posed and game-action photos which are bordered in a single bright color, by player. That border color is darkest at top and bottom and fades to white at the center. Backs are printed in one of several colors on white cardboard and feature personal data, stats, career highlights, checklists and team logos. Single cards are not listed because sets are seldom broken for individual card sales. Glossy versions are known for most, but not all, player sets.

		NM/M
1-11	Jim Abbott	1.50
1-11	Andy Benes	1.50
1-11	Barry Bonds (Error, cards #2-11 say "Bobby Bonds.")	9.00
1-11	Barry Bonds (Corrected)	9.00
1-11	Bobby Bonilla	1.50
1-11	Jose Canseco (Purple borders.)	1.50
1-11	Jose Canseco (Yellow borders.)	1.50
1-11	Will Clark	1.50
1-11	Will Clark, Mark Grace	1.50
1-11	Cecil Fielder (Blue borders.)	1.50
1-11	Cecil Fielder (Orange borders.)	1.50
1-11	Ken Griffey Jr. (Blue borders.)	3.00
1-11	Ken Griffey Jr. (Yellow borders.)	2.00
1-11	Ken Griffey Jr., Ken Griffey Sr. (Aqua borders.)	2.00
1-11	Ken Griffey Jr., Ken Griffey Sr. (Red borders.)	2.00
1-11	Rickey Henderson/1990	4.00
1-11	Rickey Henderson (Glossy - 250 sets.)	4.50
1-11	Rickey Henderson/1991	4.00
1-11	Bo Jackson	1.50
1-11	Bo Jackson, Barry Larkin (Diamond Terror)	1.50
1	Howard Johnson (Autographed card numbered to 400.)	5.00
1-11	Dave Justice	1.50
1-11	Dave Justice, Kevin Maas	1.50
1-11	Barry Larkin	1.50
1-11	Kevin Maas	1.50
1-11	Ben McDonald	1.50
1-11	Kevin Mitchell, Robin Yount	1.50
1-11	Cal Ripken Jr.	6.00
1-11	Nolan Ryan (Card #1 pitching, all Rangers photos.)	2.50
1-11	Nolan Ryan (Card #1 portrait, all four teams.)	2.50
1-11	Bret Saberhagen, Mark Davis	1.50
1-11	Ryne Sandberg	2.00
1-11	Ryne Sandberg (Glossy)	10.00
1-11	Darryl Strawberry	1.50
1-11	Frank Thomas	1.50
1-11	Jerome Walton, Gregg Olson	1.50
1-11	Matt Williams	1.50
1-11	Robin Yount	1.50

1990-93 Star "Career Stats"

These unnumbered cards are not part of any Star sets. They share a common design of two-color graduated borders on front, with color photos both front and back. The words "Career Stats" are prominently displayed on both front and back. Some players were sold in both autographed and unautographed versions, while some are known only in one version or the other.

		NM/M
	Complete Set (26):	65.00
	Common Player:	1.50
(1)	Ken Griffey Jr./1990	3.50
(2)	Barry Bonds/1991	4.00
(2a)	Barry Bonds/Auto./1991	15.00
(3)	Bobby Bonilla/1991	1.50
(4)	Scott Erickson/1991	1.50
(4a)	Scott Erickson/Auto./1991	3.00
(5)	Chuck Knoblauch/1991	1.50
(5a)	Chuck Knoblauch/Auto./1991	3.00
(6)	Frank Thomas/1991	3.00
(6a)	Frank Thomas/Auto./1991	10.00
(6g)	Frank Thomas/1991 (Glossy)	3.00
(7)	Matt Williams/1991	1.50
(7a)	Matt Williams/Auto./1991	3.00
(8)	Jeff Bagwell/1992	2.00
(9a)	Pat Kelly/Auto./1992	3.00
(10a)	Mark Lewis/Auto./1992	3.00
(11a)	John Olerud/Auto./1992	3.00
(12)	Jim Abbott/1993	1.50
(12a)	Jim Abbott/Auto./1993	3.00
(13)	Bret Barberie/1993	1.50
(13a)	Bret Barberie/Auto./1993	3.00
(14)	Andy Benes/1993	1.50
(14a)	Andy Benes/Auto./1993	3.00
(15)	Rickey Henderson/1993	2.00
(16a)	Eric Karros/Auto./1993	3.00
(17)	Ryan Klesko/1993	1.50
(18)	Kevin Mass/1993 (Maas)	1.50
(19)	Dean Palmer/1993	1.50

1990-91 Star Gold Edition

Only 1,500 of each nine-card, single-player set was produced in Star's 1990-91 Gold Edition. Single cards are not listed or priced because the issue is almost exclusively traded in complete player sets. Cards were numbered contiguously as noted in the alpha-

betical checklist presented here. Suggested retail price at issue was $15-20 per set. An edition of 300 gray-bordered promo cards was issued for each player.

		NM/M
	Complete Set (180):	40.00
	Common Player Set:	1.50
	Complete Promo Set (20):	50.00
	Common Promo Card:	2.00
(1)	Wade Boggs (#136-144)	2.25
(1)	Wade Boggs (Promo card.)	4.00
(2)	Bobby Bonilla (#145-153)	1.50
(2)	Bobby Bonilla (Promo card.)	2.00
(3)	Jose Canseco (#19-27)	2.25
(3)	Jose Canseco (Promo card.)	3.00
(4)	Will Clark (#64-72)	2.25
(4)	Will Clark (Promo card.)	3.00
(5)	Dwight Gooden (#109-117)	1.50
(5)	Dwight Gooden (Promo card.)	2.00
(6)	Mark Grace (#154-162)	1.50
(6)	Mark Grace (Promo card.)	2.00
(7)	Ken Griffey Jr. (#10-18)	7.50
(7)	Ken Griffey Jr. (Promo card.)	10.00
(8)	Rickey Henderson (#82-90)	3.00
(8)	Rickey Henderson (Promo card.)	4.00
(9)	Bo Jackson (#1-9)	1.50
(9)	Bo Jackson (Promo card.)	2.00
(10)	Howard Johnson (#163-171)	1.50
(10)	Howard Johnson (Promo card.)	2.00
(11)	David Justice (#118-126)	1.50
(11)	David Justice (Promo card.)	2.00
(12)	Barry Larkin (#91-99)	1.50
(12)	Barry Larkin (Promo card.)	2.00
(13)	Kevin Maas (#127-135)	1.50
(13)	Kevin Maas (Promo card.)	2.00
(14)	Don Mattingly (#100-108)	4.50
(14)	Don Mattingly (Promo card.)	6.00
(15)	Kirby Puckett (#55-63)	4.00
(15)	Kirby Puckett (Promo card.)	6.00
(16)	Tim Raines (#37-45)	1.50
(16)	Tim Raines (Promo card.)	2.00
(17)	Cal Ripken Jr. (#73-81)	7.50
(17)	Cal Ripken Jr. (Promo card.)	10.00
(18)	Ryne Sandberg (#46-54)	3.00
(18)	Ryne Sandberg (Promo card.)	4.00
(19)	Darryl Strawberry (#172-180)	1.50
(19)	Darryl Strawberry (Promo card.)	2.00
(20)	Robin Ventura (#28-36)	1.50
(20)	Robin Ventura (Promo card.)	2.00

1990-91 Star Nova Edition

With just 500 of each nine-card single-player set produced, the Nova Edition was Star's top of the line in 1990. Player sets are listed alphabetically. Single cards are not listed because sets are seldom broken. Each set is also represented by an issue of 100 promo cards, featuring black borders at top and yellow at bottom.

		NM/M
	Complete Set (180):	50.00
	Common Player Set:	2.25
	Complete Promo Set (20):	65.00
	Common Promo Card:	3.00
(1)	Wade Boggs (#28-36)	5.00
(1)	Wade Boggs (Promo card.)	6.00
(2)	Jose Canseco (#55-63)	3.75
(2)	Jose Canseco (Promo card.)	5.00
(3)	Joe Carter (#118-126)	2.25
(3)	Joe Carter (Promo card.)	3.00
(4)	Will Clark (#46-54)	3.00
(4)	Will Clark (Promo card.)	4.00
(5)	Roger Clemens (#109-117)	6.50
(5)	Roger Clemens (Promo card.)	7.50
(6)	Glenn Davis (#127-135)	2.25
(6)	Glenn Davis (Promo card.)	3.00
(7)	Len Dykstra (#163-171)	2.25
(7)	Len Dykstra (Promo card.)	3.00
(8)	Cecil Fielder (#154-162)	2.25
(8)	Cecil Fielder (Promo card.)	3.00
(9)	Ken Griffey Jr. (#172-180)	7.50
(9)	Ken Griffey Jr. (Promo card.)	10.00
(10)	Rickey Henderson (#73-81)	3.00
(10)	Rickey Henderson (Promo card.)	4.00
(11)	Bo Jackson (#64-72)	2.25
(11)	Bo Jackson (Promo card.)	3.00
(12)	Howard Johnson (#37-45)	2.25
(12)	Howard Johnson (Promo card.)	3.00
(13)	Barry Larkin (#100-108)	2.25
(13)	Barry Larkin (Promo card.)	3.00
(14)	Don Mattingly (#1-9)	6.50
(14)	Don Mattingly (Promo card.)	9.00
(15)	Kevin Mitchell (#145-153)	2.25
(15)	Kevin Mitchell (Promo card.)	3.00
(16)	Nolan Ryan (#19-27)	7.50
(16)	Nolan Ryan (Promo card.)	10.00
(17)	Ryne Sandberg (#136-144)	5.00
(17)	Ryne Sandberg (Promo card.)	6.00
(18)	Dave Stewart (#91-99)	2.25
(18)	Dave Stewart (Promo card.)	3.00
(19)	Darryl Strawberry (#82-90)	2.25
(19)	Darryl Strawberry (Promo card.)	3.00
(20)	Robin Yount (#10-18)	2.25
(20)	Robin Yount (Promo card.)	3.00

1990-91 Star Platinum Edition

The stars in Star's Platinum Edition were featured in nine-card sets with production of 1,000 each (plus 200 black-bordered promo cards of each player). Suggested retail price at the time of issue was about $20. The player sets are checklisted here in alphabetical order. Single cards are not listed because the sets are almost never broken up. Cards are numbered contiguously as noted in the alphabetical checklisted.

		NM/M
	Complete Set (180):	40.00
	Common Player Set:	1.50
	Complete Promo Set (21):	50.00
	Common Promo Card:	2.00
(1)	Jim Abbott (#19-27)	1.50
(1)	Jim Abbott (Promo card.)	2.00
(2)	Wade Boggs (#145-153)	3.00
(2)	Wade Boggs (Promo card.)	4.00
(3)	Jose Canseco (#91-99)	3.50
(3)	Jose Canseco (Promo card.)	4.00
(4)	Will Clark (#1-9)	2.50
(4)	Will Clark (Promo card.)	4.00
(5)	Roger Clemens (#46-54)	3.50
(5)	Roger Clemens (Promo card.)	7.50
(6)	Eric Davis (#55-63)	1.50
(6)	Eric Davis (Promo card.)	2.00
(7)	Dwight Gooden (#82-90)	1.50
(7)	Dwight Gooden (Promo card.)	2.00
(8)	Mark Grace (#172-180) (#172 says "Silver Series")	2.25
(8)	Mark Grace (Promo card.)	3.00
(9)	Mike Greenwell (#64-72)	1.50
(9)	Mike Greenwell (Promo card.)	2.00
(10)	Ken Griffey Jr. (#100 108)	7.00
(10)	Ken Griffey Jr. (Promo card.)	8.00
(11)	Tony Gwynn (#28-36)	4.50
(11)	Tony Gwynn (Promo card.)	6.00
(12)	Bo Jackson (#136-144)	1.50
(12)	Bo Jackson (Promo card.)	2.00
(13)	Howard Johnson (#109-117)	1.50
(13)	Howard Johnson (Promo card.)	2.00
(14)	Don Mattingly (#73-81)	5.00
(14)	Don Mattingly (Promo card.)	7.00
(15)	Kevin Mitchell (#10-18)	1.50
(15)	Kevin Mitchell/Btg (Promo card.)	2.00
(16)	Kevin Mitchell (#154-162)	1.50
(16)	Kevin Mitchell/Running (Promo card.)	2.00
(17)	Kirby Puckett (#37-45)	4.50
(17)	Kirby Puckett (Promo card.)	6.00
(18)	Ryne Sandberg (#163-171)	3.00
(18)	Ryne Sandberg (Promo card.)	4.00
(19)	Darryl Strawberry (#118-126)	1.50
(19)	Darryl Strawberry (Promo card.)	2.00
(20)	Matt Williams (#127-135)	1.50
(20)	Matt Williams (Promo card.)	2.00

1990-91 Star Silver Edition

Many of 1990's biggest stars are represented in nine-card single-player sets within Star Co.'s Silver Edition. Production of each silver-foil trimmed set was limited to 2,000. Because single cards are seldom offered, only complete player sets are priced. Cards are numbered contiguously as noted in the alphabetical checklist presented here. Retail price at issue was $10-15. Each player is also represented by an issue of 400 black-bordered promo cards.

		NM/M
	Complete Set (180):	17.50
	Common Player Set:	.75
	Complete Promo Set:	22.50
	Common Promo Card:	1.00
(1)	Jim Abbott (#1-9)	.75
(1)	Jim Abbott (Promo card.)	1.00
(2)	Sandy Alomar Jr. (#55-63)	.75
(2)	Sandy Alomar Jr. (Promo card.)	1.00
(3)	Andy Benes (#19-27)	.75
(3)	Andy Benes (Promo card.)	1.00
(4)	Barry Bonds (#172-180)	3.00
(4)	Barry Bonds (Promo card.)	4.00
(5)	Bobby Bonilla (#154-162)	.75
(5)	Bobby Bonilla (Promo card.)	1.00
(6)	Jose Canseco (#127-135)	1.25
(6)	Jose Canseco (Promo card.)	1.50
(7)	Will Clark (#73-81)	1.25
(7)	Will Clark (Promo card.)	1.50
(8)	Delino DeShields (#145-153)	.75
(8)	Delino DeShields (Promo card.)	1.00
(9)	Tom Gordon (#37-45)	.75
(9)	Tom Gordon (Promo card.)	1.00
(10)	Mark Grace (#10-18)	1.25
(10)	Mark Grace (Promo card.)	1.50
(11)	Ken Griffey Jr. (#91-99)	3.50
(11)	Ken Griffey Jr. (Promo card.)	5.00
(12)	Mike Harkey (#163-171)	.75
(12)	Mike Harkey (Promo card.)	1.00
(13)	Wally Joyner (#28-36)	.75
(13)	Wally Joyner (Promo card.)	1.00
(14)	David Justice (#118-126)	.75
(14)	David Justice (Promo card.)	1.00
(15)	Kevin Maas (#109-117)	.75
(15)	Kevin Maas (Promo card.)	1.00
(16)	Don Mattingly (#136-144)	2.50
(16)	Don Mattingly (Promo card.)	3.00
(17)	Ben McDonald (#100-108)	.75
(17)	Ben McDonald (Promo card.)	1.00
(18)	Benito Santiago (#64-72)	.75
(18)	Benito Santiago (Promo card.)	1.00
(19)	Alan Trammell (#46-54) (All cards misspelled "Allan.")	.75
(19)	Alan Trammell (Promo card.)	1.00
(20)	Jerome Walton (#82-90)	.75
(20)	Jerome Walton (Promo card.)	1.00

1990 Star Sophomore Stars

This special six-card set was distributed only at the 1990 Arlington 11th National Sports Collectors Convention. The set came polybagged with a DC comic book in exchange for a $2 donation to the Arthritis Foundation. The 2-1/2" x 3-1/2" cards feature a border that changes from dark blue at the top to red at the bottom. Backs are printed in blue-on-white and include team and MLB logos along with major and minor league career stats. Production was reported as 10,000 sets.

		NM/M
	Complete Set (6):	4.50
	Common Player:	.15
1	Ken Griffey Jr. (Batting cage.)	2.00
2	Ken Griffey Jr./Sitting	2.00
3	Gary Sheffield/Portrait	.30
4	Gary Sheffield/Btg	.30
5	Jerome Walton/Portrait	.15
6	Jerome Walton/Btg	.15

1991 Star

A common design is again shared by the single-player card sets released by Star for 1991. Cards feature posed and action photos on front with borders that graduate from one color at top to another at bottom (yellow to blue; green to gray, etc.). The player name is at left beneath the photo, his city at right and the card name beneath that. Backs are printed in one of several colors on white stock and feature personal data, stats, career highlights, checklist or team logo. Each set was also produced in a high-gloss version, which carries a 4-5X premium today. Single cards are not listed here because player sets are seldom broken for individual card sales. All promo cards except Clemens have a solid-color border.

		NM/M
	Complete Set (88):	10.00
	Common Player Set:	1.25
	Complete Promo Set (6):	11.00
	Common Promo Card:	1.50
1-11	Roger Clemens	1.50
	Roger Clemens (Promo card.)	2.50
1-11	Rickey Henderson	1.50
1-11	Bo Jackson	1.25
	Bo Jackson (Promo card.)	1.50
1-11	Pat Kelly (Glossy version only.)	1.25
	Pat Kelly (Promo card.)	1.50
1-11	Cal Ripken Jr.	2.50
	Cal Ripken Jr. (Promo card.)	3.25
1-11	Nolan Ryan	2.00
	Nolan Ryan (Promo card.)	3.25
1-11	Darryl Strawberry	1.25
1-11	Frank Thomas (Glossy version only.)	2.50
	Frank Thomas (Promo card.)	3.00

All-Stars

This Star issue is comprised of 500 sets and 100 promo cards of each player. (Except Jackson who has 200.) The checklist is arranged alphabetically.

		NM/M
	Complete Set (135):	80.00
	Common Player Set:	3.75
	Complete Promo Set (15):	110.00
	Common Promo Card:	5.00
(1)	Wade Boggs (#109-117)	7.50
(1)	Wade Boggs (Promo card.)	10.00
(2)	Jose Canseco (#37-45)	7.50
(2)	Jose Canseco (Promo card.)	10.00
(3)	Roger Clemens (#64-72)	7.50
(3)	Roger Clemens (Promo card.)	10.00
(4)	Lenny Dykstra (#91-99)	3.75
(4)	Lenny Dykstra (Promo card.)	5.00
(5)	Cecil Fielder (#118-126)	3.75
(5)	Cecil Fielder (Promo card.)	5.00
(6)	Dwight Gooden (#82-90)	3.75
(6)	Dwight Gooden (Promo card.)	5.00
(7)	Ken Griffey Jr. (#1-9)	10.00
(7)	Ken Griffey Jr. (Promo card.)	15.00
(8)	Rickey Henderson (#19-27)	7.50
(8)	Rickey Henderson (Promo card.)	10.00
(9)	Bo Jackson (#46-54)	3.75
(9)	Bo Jackson (Promo card.)	5.00
(10)	Don Mattingly (#73-81)	9.00
(10)	Don Mattingly (Promo card.)	12.00
(11)	Kirby Puckett (#100-108)	7.50
(11)	Kirby Puckett (Promo card.)	12.00
(12)	Cal Ripken Jr. (#55-63)	9.00
(12p)	Cal Ripken Jr. (#55-63) (Plastic test issue.)	12.00
(12)	Cal Ripken Jr. (Promo card.)	12.00
(12p)	Cal Ripken Jr. (Promo card.) (Plastic)	16.00
(13)	Nolan Ryan (#10-18)	9.00
(13)	Nolan Ryan (Promo card.)	12.00
(14)	Ryne Sandberg (#28-36)	7.50
(14)	Ryne Sandberg (Promo card.)	10.00

Diamond Series

Production of these nine-card, single-player sets was limited to 2,000 of each (plus 400 promo cards each), with a suggested retail price at issue of $25. Players in the edition are listed here in alphabetical order. Cards are numbered contiguously throughout the issue, as noted in the alpha-order listings here. Single cards are not priced because the sets are seldom broken up.

		NM/M
	Complete Set (126):	22.50
	Common Player Set:	1.00
	Complete Promo Set:	27.50
	Common Promo Card:	1.50
(1)	Barry Bonds (#10-18)	5.00
(1)	Barry Bonds (Promo card.)	5.00
(2)	Bobby Bonilla (#46-54)	1.00
(2)	Bobby Bonilla (Promo card.)	1.50

No.	Player	NM/M
(3)	Jose Canseco (#37-45)	2.00
(3)	Jose Canseco (Promo card.)	2.50
(4)	Roger Clemens (#64-72)	2.50
(4)	Roger Clemens (Promo card.)	2.50
(5)	Cecil Fielder (#118-126)	1.00
(5)	Cecil Fielder (Promo card.)	1.50
(6)	Ken Griffey Jr. (#55-63)	3.50
(6)	Ken Griffey Jr. (Promo card.)	5.00
(7)	Tony Gwynn (#100-108)	1.75
(7)	Tony Gwynn (Promo card.)	2.50
(8)	Bo Jackson (#1-9)	1.00
(8)	Bo Jackson (Promo card.)	1.50
(9)	Don Mattingly (#19-27)	5.00
(9)	Don Mattingly (Promo card.)	6.00
(10)	Kirby Puckett (#82-90)	2.50
(10)	Kirby Puckett (Promo card.)	6.00
(11)	Cal Ripken Jr. (#28-36)	7.50
(11)	Cal Ripken Jr. (Promo card.)	3.50
(12)	Nolan Ryan (#109-117)	6.00
(12)	Nolan Ryan (Promo card.)	7.50
(13)	Darryl Strawberry (#73-81)	1.00
(13)	Darryl Strawberry (Promo card.)	1.50
(14)	Frank Thomas (#91-99)	2.25
(14)	Frank Thomas (Promo card.)	3.00

Gold Edition

Only 1,500 of each nine-card, single-player set was produced - along with 300 promo cards of each player - in Star's 1991 Gold Edition. Cards are numbered contiguously throughout the issue, as noted in the alphabetical checklist shown here. Single cards are not listed or priced because the issue is almost exclusively traded in complete-player sets.

No.	Player	NM/M
	Complete Set (144):	40.00
	Common Player Set:	2.00
	Complete Promo Set (16):	40.00
	Common Promo Card:	2.00
(1)	Albert Belle (#118-126)	2.00
(1)	Albert Belle (Promo card.)	2.00
(2)	Barry Bonds (#73-81)	7.00
(2)	Barry Bonds (Promo card.)	7.00
(3)	Bobby Bonilla (#127-135)	2.00
(3)	Bobby Bonilla (Promo card.)	2.00
(4)	Jose Canseco (#55-63)	3.00
(4)	Jose Canseco (Promo card.)	3.00
(5)	Will Clark (#28-36)	2.00
(5)	Will Clark (Promo card.)	2.00
(6)	Roger Clemens (#64-72)	6.00
(6)	Roger Clemens (Promo card.)	6.00
(7)	Ken Griffey Jr. (#19-27)	5.00
(7)	Ken Griffey Jr. (Promo card.)	5.00
(8)	Bo Jackson (#37-45)	2.00
(8)	Bo Jackson (Promo card.)	2.00
(9)	David Justice (#82-90)	2.00
(9)	David Justice (Promo card.)	2.00
(10)	Don Mattingly (#91-99)	6.00
(10)	Don Mattingly (Promo card.)	6.00
(11)	Fred McGriff (#136-144)	2.00
(11)	Fred McGriff (Promo card.)	2.00
(12)	Kirby Puckett (#1-9)	4.50
(12)	Kirby Puckett (Promo card.)	4.50
(13)	Nolan Ryan (#109-117)	6.00
(13)	Nolan Ryan (Promo card.)	6.00
(14)	Ryne Sandberg (#10-18)	4.00
(14)	Ryne Sandberg (Promo card.)	4.00
(15)	Darryl Strawberry (#46-54)	2.00
(15)	Darryl Strawberry (Promo card.)	2.00
(16)	Frank Thomas (#100-108)	3.00
(16)	Frank Thomas (Promo card.)	3.00

Home Run Series

With a suggested retail price at issue of $25 or so, and an edition limit of 1,500 each of the single-player, nine-card sets (plus 300 promo cards of each player), these are among the scarcer of the 1991 Star issues. Numbers on individual player cards run contiguously throughout the issue and are noted in the alphabetical checklist. Because sets are seldom available as singles, individual cards are not listed here.

No.	Player	NM/M
	Complete Set (126):	65.00
	Common Player Set:	3.75
	Complete Promo Set (14):	85.00
	Common Promo Card:	5.00
(1)	Wade Boggs (#91-99)	5.50
(1)	Wade Boggs (Promo card.)	7.50
(2)	Barry Bonds (#64-72)	9.00
(2)	Barry Bonds (Promo card.)	12.00
(3)	Bobby Bonilla (#10-18)	3.75
(3)	Bobby Bonilla (Promo card.)	5.00
(4)	Jose Canseco (#1-9)	5.50
(4)	Jose Canseco (Promo card.)	7.50
(5)	Dwight Gooden (#73-81)	3.75
(5)	Dwight Gooden (Promo card.)	5.00
(6)	Ken Griffey Jr. (#37-45)	5.00
(6)	Ken Griffey Jr. (Promo card.)	7.50
(7)	Rickey Henderson (#19-27)	6.00
(7)	Rickey Henderson (Promo card.)	8.00
(8)	Bo Jackson (#82-90)	3.00
(8)	Bo Jackson (Promo card.)	4.50
(9)	Don Mattingly (#46-54)	9.00
(9)	Don Mattingly (Promo card.)	10.00
(10)	Cal Ripken Jr. (#109-117)	9.00
(10)	Cal Ripken Jr. (Promo card.)	12.00
(11)	Nolan Ryan (#55-63)	9.00
(11)	Nolan Ryan (Promo card.)	12.00
(12)	Ryne Sandberg (#100-108)	7.50
(12)	Ryne Sandberg (Promo card.)	7.50
(13)	Darryl Strawberry (#28-36)	3.75
(13)	Darryl Strawberry (Promo card.)	5.00
(14)	Frank Thomas (#118-126)	7.50
(14)	Frank Thomas (Promo card.)	10.00

Millennium Edition

As the name suggests, production of each of these nine-card, single-player sets was pegged at 1,000 (plus 200 promo cards of each player). Suggested retail price at issue was about $30. Cards are numbered contiguously throughout the issue, as noted in the alphabetical checklist (part of each Ripken and Gooden set are misnumbered). Individual cards are not listed or priced because the sets are almost never broken down for singles sales.

No.	Player	NM/M
	Complete Set (126):	50.00
	Common Player Set:	1.50
	Complete Promo Set (14):	50.00
	Common Promo Card:	1.50
(1)	Wade Boggs (#55-63)	7.50
(1)	Wade Boggs (Promo card.)	7.50
(2)	Will Clark (#46-54)	3.00
(2)	Will Clark (Promo card.)	3.00
(3)	Cecil Fielder (#109-117)	1.50
(3)	Cecil Fielder (Promo card.)	1.50
(4)	Dwight Gooden (#10-14, 78-81)	1.50
(4)	Dwight Gooden (Promo card.)	1.50
(5)	Ken Griffey Jr. (#91-99)	6.00
(5)	Ken Griffey Jr. (Promo card.)	6.00
(6)	Howard Johnson (#64-72)	1.50
(6)	Howard Johnson (Promo card.)	1.50
(7)	Dave Justice (#100-108)	1.50
(7)	David Justice (Promo card.)	1.50
(8)	Kevin Maas (#82-90)	1.50
(8)	Kevin Maas (Promo card.)	1.50
(9)	Don Mattingly (#37-45)	7.50
(9)	Don Mattingly (Promo card.)	7.50
(10)	Kirby Puckett (#19-27)	7.50
(10)	Kirby Puckett (Promo card.)	7.50
(11)	Cal Ripken Jr. (#15-18, 73-77)	7.50
(11)	Cal Ripken Jr. (Promo card.)	7.50
(12)	Ryne Sandberg (#28-36)	6.00
(12)	Ryne Sandberg (Promo card.)	6.00
(13)	Frank Thomas (#118-126)	6.00
(13)	Frank Thomas (Promo card.)	6.00
(14)	Robin Yount (#1-9)	3.00
(14)	Robin Yount (Promo card.)	3.00

Nova Edition

Production of these nine-card, single-player sets was limited to 500 of each (plus 100 promo cards of each player). Sets are checklisted here in alphabetical order. Individual cards are numbered contiguously throughout the issue, as noted. Single cards are not priced because sets are seldom broken up for sale of individual cards.

No.	Player	NM/M
	Complete Set (144):	60.00
	Common Player Set:	2.50
	Complete Promo Set (16):	60.00
	Common Promo Card:	2.50
(1)	Wade Boggs (#82-90)	6.00
(1)	Wade Boggs (Promo card.)	6.00
(2)	Jose Canseco (#55-63)	5.00
(2)	Jose Canseco (Promo card.)	5.00
(3)	Vince Coleman (#127-135)	2.50
(3)	Vince Coleman (Promo card.)	2.50
(4)	Cecil Fielder (#136-144)	2.50
(4)	Cecil Fielder (Promo card.)	2.50
(5)	Dwight Gooden (#10-18)	2.50
(5)	Dwight Gooden (Promo card.)	2.50
(6)	Ken Griffey Jr. (#91-99)	7.50
(6)	Ken Griffey Jr. (Promo card.)	7.50
(7)	Tony Gwynn (#100-108)	5.00
(7)	Tony Gwynn (Promo card.)	5.00
(8)	Rickey Henderson (#1-9)	5.00
(8)	Rickey Henderson (Promo card.)	5.00
(9)	Bo Jackson (#28-36)	2.50
(9)	Bo Jackson (Promo card.)	2.50
(10)	Howard Johnson (#118-126)	2.50
(10)	Howard Johnson (Promo card.)	2.50
(11)	Don Mattingly (#64-72)	7.50
(11)	Don Mattingly (Promo card.)	7.50
(12)	Kirby Puckett (#109-117)	5.00
(12)	Kirby Puckett (Promo card.)	5.00
(13)	Cal Ripken Jr. (#46-54)	9.00
(13)	Cal Ripken Jr. (Promo card.)	9.00
(14)	Nolan Ryan (#19-27)	10.00
(14)	Nolan Ryan (Promo card.)	10.00
(15)	Ryne Sandberg (#73-81)	6.00
(15)	Ryne Sandberg (Promo card.)	6.00
(16)	Darryl Strawberry (#37-45)	2.50
(16)	Darryl Strawberry (Promo card.)	2.50

Platinum Edition

These nine-card, single-player sets were produced in an edition of 1,000 each (plus 200 promo cards per player). Sets are checklisted here alphabetically, with individual card numbers shown for each player. Single cards are not listed because the sets are seldom offered as singles.

No.	Player	NM/M
	Complete Set (108):	45.00
	Common Player Set:	2.00
	Complete Promo Set (14):	60.00
	Common Promo Card:	2.50
(1)	Wade Boggs (#109-117)	5.00
(1)	Wade Boggs (Promo card.)	5.00
(2)	Barry Bonds (#28-36)	5.00
(2)	Barry Bonds (Promo card.)	7.50
(3)	Bobby Bonilla (#73-81)	2.00
(3)	Bobby Bonilla (Promo card.)	2.50
(4)	Jose Canseco (#19-27)	5.00
(4)	Jose Canseco (Promo card.)	6.00
(5)	Will Clark (#118-126)	3.75
(5)	Will Clark (Promo card.)	5.00
(6)	Roger Clemens (#10-18)	6.00
(6)	Roger Clemens (Promo card.)	8.00
(7)	Mark Grace (#1-9)	2.00
(7)	Mark Grace (Promo card.)	2.50
(8)	Ken Griffey Jr. (#55-63)	3.75
(8)	Ken Griffey Jr. (Promo card.)	6.00
(9)	Rickey Henderson (#46-54)	3.75
(9)	Rickey Henderson (Promo card.)	5.00
(10)	Kevin Maas (#37-45)	2.00
(10)	Kevin Maas (Promo card.)	2.50
(11)	Don Mattingly (#82-90)	6.00
(11)	Don Mattingly (Promo card.)	6.50
(12)	Cal Ripken Jr. (#91-99)	7.50
(12)	Cal Ripken Jr. (Promo card.)	10.00
(13)	Nolan Ryan (#64-72)	7.50
(13)	Nolan Ryan (Promo card.)	10.00
(14)	Frank Thomas (#100-108)	3.75
(14)	Frank Thomas (Promo card.)	5.00

Cal Ripken Promo Set

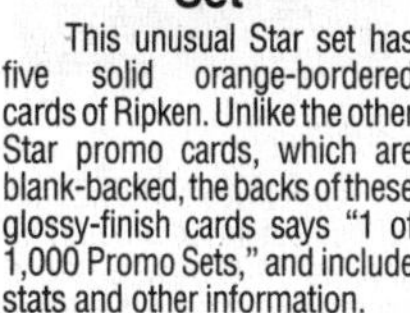

This unusual Star set has five solid orange-bordered cards of Ripken. Unlike the other Star promo cards, which are blank-backed, the backs of these glossy-finish cards says "1 of 1,000 Promo Sets," and include stats and other information.

No.	Player	NM/M
1-5	Cal Ripken Jr.	10.00

Rookie Guild Prototypes

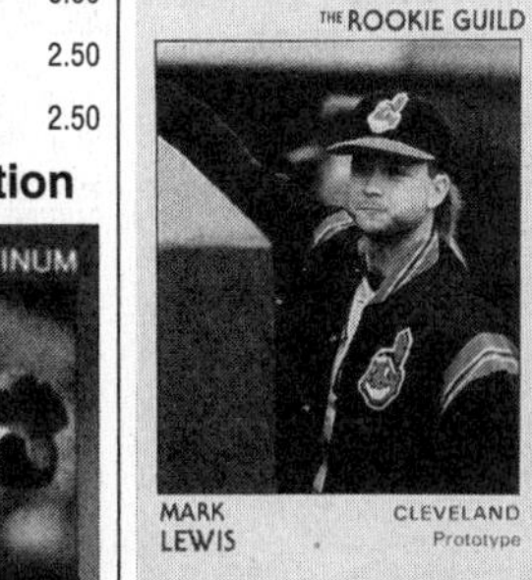

Labeled as "Prototype" cards, these unnumbered blank-back cards can be found in a confusing variety of regular, glossy and plastic finish for the six players in the Rookie Guild set. Only those cards confirmed to exist are listed here.

No.	Player	NM/M
	Complete Set, Regular (3):	4.00
	Complete Set, Glossy (3):	6.00
	Complete Set, Plastic (4):	8.00
(1g)	Jeff Bagwell (Glossy)	2.00
(1p)	Jeff Bagwell (Plastic)	2.50
(2)	Albert Belle	1.50
(3g)	Juan Gonzalez (Glossy)	2.00
(3p)	Juan Gonzalez (Plastic)	2.50
(4a)	Chris Knoblauch (Chuck)	2.50
(4bp)	Chuck Knoblauch (Plastic)	2.00
(5)	Mark Lewis	1.00
(6g)	Frank Thomas (Glossy)	3.75
(6p)	Frank Thomas (Plastic)	4.50

Rookie Guild Promos

A confusing variety of regular, glossy and plastic finish promo cards were issued in different combinations for the six players in Star's 1991 Rookie Guild issue. The blank-back, unnumbered cards are checklisted here in alphabetical order. Only those cards confirmed to have been issued are listed.

No.	Player	NM/M
	Complete Set, Regular (3):	4.00
	Complete Set, Glossy (6):	12.50
	Complete Set, Plastic (4):	9.00
(1g)	Jeff Bagwell (Glossy)	2.25
(1p)	Jeff Bagwell (Plastic)	2.50
(2)	Albert Belle	1.50
(2g)	Albert Belle (Glossy)	3.00
(3g)	Juan Gonzalez (Glossy)	2.25
(3p)	Juan Gonzalez (Plastic)	2.50
(4a)	Chris Knoblauch (Chuck)	1.75
(4ag)	Chris Knoblauch (Chuck) (Glossy)	3.25
(4bp)	Chuck Knoblauch (Plastic)	2.00
(5)	Mark Lewis	.70
(5g)	Mark Lewis (Glossy)	1.50
(6g)	Frank Thomas (Glossy)	2.50
(6p)	Frank Thomas (Plastic)	3.25

Rookie Guild

Late in the 1991 baseball season, Star introduced yet another series of single-player card sets. The emphasis was on young stars in 11-card sets. Most player sets were produced in some combination of regular and glossy finish, or glossy and plastic finish. Each player was also represented with some combination of 1,000 each promotional (border other than white) and prototype cards and 50 glossy and/or plastic promo cards. Single cards are not listed because sets are seldom broken for individual card sales.

No.	Player	NM/M
	Common Player Set, Regular:	1.00
	Common Player Set, Glossy:	1.50
	Common Player Set, Plastic:	4.00
(1)	Albert Belle (#1-11)	1.00
(1g)	Albert Belle (Glossy)	3.00
(2a)	Chris Knoblauch (Chuck)	3.00
(2ag)	Chris Knoblauch (Chuck) (Glossy)	4.50
(2bg)	Chuck Knoblauch (#12-22) (Glossy only.)	1.50
(3)	Mark Lewis (#23-33)	1.00
(3g)	Mark Lewis (Glossy)	3.00
(4g)	Frank Thomas (#33-44)(Glossy)	1.75
(4p)	Frank Thomas (Plastic)	5.00
(5g)	Juan Gonzalez (#45-55) (Glossy)	1.50
(5p)	Juan Gonzalez (Plastic)	4.00
(6g)	Jeff Bagwell (#56-66) (Glossy)	1.50
(6p)	Jeff Bagwell (Plastic)	4.00

1991 Star Silver Edition

Two thousand of each nine-card player set was produced in Star's silver-enhanced set, along with 400 promo cards of each player. Players are listed here in alphabetical order. Indi-

vidual cards are not listed because the sets are seldom offered as singles.

NM/M
Complete Set (126): 35.00
Common Player Set: 1.50
Complete Promo Set (15): 45.00
Common Promo Card: 2.00
(1) Wade Boggs (#10-18) 4.00
(1) Wade Boggs (Promo card.) 4.00
(2) Bobby Bonilla (#37-45) 1.50
(2) Bobby Bonilla (Promo card.) 2.00
(3) Jose Canseco (#109-117) 3.00
(3) Jose Canseco (Promo card.) 4.00
(4) Vince Coleman (#1-9) 1.50
(4) Vince Coleman (Promo card.) 2.00
(5) Dwight Gooden (#73-81) 1.50
(5) Dwight Gooden (Promo card.) 2.00
(6) Ken Griffey Jr. (#91-99) 6.00
(6) Ken Griffey Jr. (Promo card.) 8.00
(7) Tony Gwynn (#46-54) 4.00
(7) Tony Gwynn (Promo card.) 5.00
(8) Rickey Henderson (#82-90) 3.00
(8) Rickey Henderson (Promo card.) 4.00
(9) Bo Jackson (#100-108) 1.50
(9) Bo Jackson (Promo card.) 2.00
(10) Kevin Maas (#28-36) 1.50
(10) Kevin Maas (Promo card.) 2.00
(11) Don Mattingly (#19-27) 4.50
(11) Don Mattingly (Promo card.) 6.00
(12) Nolan Ryan (#55-63) 6.00
(12) Nolan Ryan (Promo card.) 8.00
(13) Ryne Sandberg (#64-72) 4.00
(13) Ryne Sandberg (Promo card.) 5.00
(14) Frank Thomas (#118-126) 3.75
(14) Frank Thomas (Promo card.) 5.00
(15) Albert Belle (Promo card only, produced in error.) 3.00

Stellar Edition

The same players who appear in other Star sets for 1991 are repackaged into this edition of 500 sets of each player. One hundred promo cards of each player were also issued.

NM/M
Complete Set (126): 50.00
Common Player Set: 2.00
Complete Promo Set (14): 65.00
Common Promo Card: 2.50
(1) Bobby Bonilla (#55-63) 2.00
(1) Bobby Bonilla (Promo card.) 2.50
(2) Will Clark (#37-45) 5.00
(2) Will Clark (Promo card.) 5.00
(3) Roger Clemens (#10-18) 6.50
(3) Roger Clemens (Promo card.) 8.00
(4) Vince Coleman (#73-81) 2.00
(4) Vince Coleman (Promo card.) 2.50
(5) Ken Griffey Jr. (#1-9) 7.50
(5) Ken Griffey Jr. (Promo card.) 10.00
(6) Tony Gwynn (#46-54) 5.00
(6) Tony Gwynn (Promo card.) 6.50
(7) Rickey Henderson (#118-126) 5.00
(7) Rickey Henderson (Promo card.) 6.50
(8) Howard Johnson (#100-108) 2.00
(8) Rickey Henderson (Promo card.) 2.50
(9) Don Mattingly (#109-117) 6.00
(9) Don Mattingly (Promo card.) 8.00
(10) Kirby Puckett (#64-72) 6.00
(10) Kirby Puckett (Promo card.) 6.00
(11) Cal Ripken Jr. (#82-90) 7.50
(11) Cal Ripken Jr. (Promo card.) 8.00
(12) Nolan Ryan (#19-27) 7.50
(12) Nolan Ryan (Promo card.) 8.00
(13) Ryne Sandberg (#91-99) 6.00
(13) Ryne Sandberg (Promo card.) 6.50
(14) Robin Yount (#28-36) 4.50
(14) Robin Yount (Promo card.) 5.00

1991 Star The Future

A few players who had not yet been included among the flood of 1991 Star issues joined the others in this post-season issue. Production was put at 1,000 nine-card sets per player, plus 200 promo cards of each. Players are listed here in alphabetical order. Individual cards are not listed because the sets are usually never sold as singles.

NM/M
Complete Set (90): 15.00
Common Player Set: 1.50
Complete Promo Set (10): 20.00
Common Promo Card: 2.00
(1) Jeff Bagwell (#28-36) 3.00
(1) Jeff Bagwell (Promo card.) 4.00
(2) Albert Belle (#55-63) 2.00
(2) Albert Belle (Promo card.) 2.75
(3) Scott Erickson (#82-90) 1.50
(3) Scott Erickson (Promo card.) 2.00
(4) Juan Gonzalez (#1-9) 2.25
(4) Juan Gonzalez (Promo card.) 3.50
(5) Pat Kelly (#10-18) 1.50
(5) Pat Kelly (Promo card.) 2.00
(6) Mark Lewis (#73-81) 1.50
(6) Mark Lewis (Promo card.) 2.00
(7) Ramon Martinez (#46-54) 1.50
(7) Ramon Martinez (Promo card.) 2.00
(8) Brian McRae (#64-72) 1.50
(8) Brian McRae (Promo card.) 2.00
(9) Frank Thomas (#37-45) 3.50
(9) Frank Thomas (Promo card.) 5.00
(10) Mo Vaughn (#19-27) 1.50
(10) Mo Vaughn (Promo card.) 2.00

Star '92

Though labeled "Star '92" on front, these single-player 11-card sets were produced in 1991. Fronts feature borders which fade from one color at top to gray at the bottom. The

photos at center are a mix of poses and game-action shots. Backs have a small color portrait photo - the same on all cards within a set - at upper-left. Stats, personal data, highlights, checklists and team logos are printed in color on yellow cardboard. The cards carry a 1991 copyright line at bottom center. Each set can be found in a glossy version, which carries a premium of 2X.

NM/M
Complete Set (22): 5.00
Common Player Set: 2.50
Complete Promo Set (2): 4.00
Common Promo Card: 2.00
1-11 Scott Erickson 1.50
Scott Erickson (Promo card.) 2.00
1-11 Todd Van Poppel 1.50
Todd Van Poppel (Promo card.) 2.00

1992 Star '92

Utilizing a design introduced the previous year, the Star '92 single-player card sets produced in 1992 are printed on cardboard laminated with thin high-gloss plastic surfaces front and back. Each player's cards are bordered with a single bright color at top which fades to gray at bottom. Photos are a mix of poses and game-action shots. Backs have a yellow background with a small color portrait (the same throughout the player's set) at upper-left. Stats, personal data, career highlights, checklist or team logo are printed in colored ink. The cards carry a 1992 copyright date and each set has a large capital letter in the lower-right corner. It is not known whether sets were issued for the letters missing in the checklist below, though prototype cards are known for some. Production was reported as 4,000 of each player set and 800 of each promo and prototype card. Only confirmed cards are listed. Single cards are not listed because sets are seldom broken for individual card sales.

NM/M
Common Player Set: 1.00
Common Promo Card: 1.75
Common Prototype Card: 1.75
A1-11 Jeff Bagwell 2.00
Jeff Bagwell (Promo card.) 3.00
Jeff Bagwell (Prototype) 3.00
B1-11 Albert Belle 1.50
Albert Belle (Promo) 2.00
C1-11 Ron Gant 1.00
Ron Gant (Promo card.) 1.75
Ron Gant (Prototype) 1.75
D1-11 Bo Jackson 1.00
Bo Jackson (Promo card.) 1.75
Bo Jackson (Prototype) 1.75
E1-11 Dave Justice 1.00
David Justice (Promo card.) 1.75
David Justice (Prototype) 1.75
F1-11 Chuck Knoblauch 1.00
Chuck Knoblauch (Promo card.) 1.75
Chuck Knoblauch (Prototype) 1.75
G1-11 Kirby Puckett 2.50
Kirby Puckett (Promo card.) 3.25
Kirby Puckett (Prototype) 3.25
H1-11 Ryne Sandberg 2.50
Ryne Sandberg (Promo) 3.25
Ryne Sandberg (Prototype) 3.25
I1-11 Steve Avery 1.00
Steve Avery (Promo) 1.75
Steve Avery (Prototype) 1.75
J1-11 Phil Plantier 1.00
Phil Plantier (Promo) 1.75
K Wade Boggs (Prototype) 3.25
M1-11 Will Clark 1.50
Will Clark (Promo card.) 3.25
N1-11 Ken Griffey Jr. 5.00
Ken Griffey Jr. (Promo card.) 6.25
Ken Griffey Jr. (Prototype) 6.25
O Cal Ripken Jr. (Prototype) 3.75
P Nolan Ryan (Prototype, regular finish.) 4.50
Nolan Ryan (Plastic prototype.) 6.00
R Frank Thomas (Prototype) 4.50
S Bobby Bonilla (Prototype) 1.75
T Kevin Mitchell (Prototype) 1.75
U1-11 Danny Tartabull 1.00
Danny Tartabull (Promo card.) 1.75
V1-11 Dean Palmer 1.00
Dean Palmer (Promo) 1.75
Dean Palmer (Prototype) 1.75

Gold Edition

The 12 players in Star's 1992 Gold Edition are represented in an issue of 750 sets each, plus 150 promo cards. The checklist is arranged alphabetically. Single cards are not listed because sets are not often broken up for individual card sales.

NM/M
Complete Set (108): 55.00
Common Player Set: 3.00
Complete Promo Set (12): 75.00
Common Promo Card: 5.00
(1) Steve Avery (#91-99) 3.00
(1) Steve Avery (Promo card.) 5.00
(2) Jose Canseco (#19-27) 6.00
(2) Jose Canseco (Promo card.) 8.00
(3) Will Clark (#28-36) 5.00
(3) Will Clark (Promo card.) 8.00
(4) Ken Griffey Jr. (#82-90) 9.00
(4) Ken Griffey Jr. (Promo card.) 12.00
(5) Bo Jackson (#46-54) 3.00
(5) Bo Jackson (Promo card.) 4.00
(6) David Justice (#10-18) 3.50
(6) David Justice (Promo card.) 5.00
(7) Don Mattingly (#1-9) 7.50
(7) Don Mattingly (Promo card.) 10.00
(8) Cal Ripken Jr. (#64-72) 9.00
(8) Cal Ripken Jr. (Promo card.) 12.00
(9) Nolan Ryan (#37-45) 9.00
(9) Nolan Ryan (Promo card.) 12.00
(10) Ryne Sandberg (#55-63) 6.00
(10) Ryne Sandberg (Promo card.) 8.00
(11) Darryl Strawberry (#100-108) 3.50
(11) Darryl Strawberry (Promo card.) 5.00
(12) Frank Thomas (#73-81) 7.50
(12) Frank Thomas (Promo card.) 10.00

Millenium Edition

Star's Millenium Edition for 1992 included an issue of 750 sets and 150 promo cards for each of 12 players, listed alphabetically in the checklist here. Single cards are not listed because player sets are seldom broken for individual card sales.

NM/M
Complete Set (108): 70.00
Common Player Set: 4.00
Complete Promo Set (12): 95.00
Common Promo Card: 5.00
(1) Wade Boggs (#100-108) 7.50
(1) Wade Boggs (Promo card.) 10.00
(2) Jose Canseco (#10-18) 7.50
(2) Jose Canseco (Promo card.) 10.00
(3) Roger Clemens (#28-36) 7.50
(3) Roger Clemens (Promo card.) 10.00
(4) Ken Griffey Jr. (#1-9) 10.00
(4) Ken Griffey Jr. (Promo card.) 12.50
(5) Bo Jackson (#82-90) 4.00
(5) Bo Jackson (Promo card.) 5.00
(6) David Justice (#73-81) 4.00
(6) David Justice (Promo card.) 5.00
(7) Don Mattingly (#37-45) 9.00
(7) Don Mattingly (Promo card.) 12.00
(8) Kirby Puckett (#91-99) 9.00
(8) Kirby Puckett (Promo card.) 12.00
(9) Cal Ripken Jr. (#19-27) 10.00
(9) Cal Ripken Jr. (Promo card.) 12.50
(10) Nolan Ryan (#55-63) 10.00
(10) Nolan Ryan (Promo card.) 12.50
(11) Ryne Sandberg (#46-54) 7.50
(11) Ryne Sandberg (Promo card.) 10.00
(12) Frank Thomas (#64-72) 9.00
(12) Frank Thomas (Promo card.) 12.00

Nova Edition

These nine-card, single-player sets were limited to an edition of 500 for each player, plus 100 promo cards. Numbering errors occurred on the Avery and Strawberry cards. The former were supposed to be numbered 10-18; the latter 64-72

NM/M
Complete Set (108): 75.00
Common Player Set: 4.50
Complete Promo Set: 100.00
Common Promo Card: 6.00
(1) Nolan Ryan (#1-9) 12.50
(1) Nolan Ryan (Promo card.) 15.00
(2) Steve Avery (#10-14, 69-72) 4.50
(2) Steve Avery (Promo card.) 6.00
(3) Frank Thomas (#19-27) 9.00
(3) Frank Thomas (Promo card.) 12.00
(4) Don Mattingly (#28-36) 12.50
(4) Don Mattingly (Promo card.) 15.00
(5) Ken Griffey Jr. (#37-45) 12.50
(5) Ken Griffey Jr. (Promo card.) 15.00
(6) David Justice (#46-54) 4.50
(6) David Justice (Promo card.) 6.00
(7) Ryne Sandberg (#55-63) 9.00
(7) Ryne Sandberg (Promo card.) 12.00
(8) Darryl Strawberry (#64-68, 15-18) 4.50
(8) Darryl Strawberry (Promo card.) 6.00
(9) Cal Ripken Jr. (#73-81) 12.50
(9) Cal Ripken Jr. (Promo card.) 15.00
(10) Bo Jackson (#82-90) 4.50
(10) Bo Jackson (Promo card.) 6.00
(11) Jose Canseco (#91-99) 7.50
(11) Jose Canseco (Promo card.) 10.00
(12) Roger Clemens (#100-108) 9.00
(12) Roger Clemens (Promo card.) 12.00

Platinum Edition

A dozen established stars are featured in the '92 Star Platinum issue, each in nine-card sets, contiguously numbered. One thousand sets of each player were issued, along with 200 promo cards. The cards are listed here in alphabetical order. Single cards are not listed because the player sets are not often broken up for individual sales.

NM/M
Complete Set (108): 50.00
Common Player Set: 2.50
Complete Promo Set (12): 65.00
Common Promo Card: 3.00
(1) Jeff Bagwell (#55-63) 5.00
(1) Jeff Bagwell (Promo card.) 6.00
(2) Jose Canseco (#73-81) 5.00
(2) Jose Canseco (Promo card.) 6.50
(3) Will Clark (#100-108) 5.00
(3) Will Clark (Promo card.) 4.00
(4) Roger Clemens (#91-99) 5.00
(4) Roger Clemens (Promo card.) 6.50
(5) Ken Griffey Jr. (#37-45) 7.50
(5) Ken Griffey Jr. (Promo card.) 10.00
(6) Bo Jackson (#28-36) 2.50
(6) Bo Jackson (Promo card.) 3.00
(7) David Justice (#10-18) 2.50
(7) David Justice (Promo card.) 3.00
(8) Don Mattingly (#64-72) 7.50
(8) Don Mattingly (Promo card.) 10.00
(9) Cal Ripken Jr. (#46-54) 7.50
(9) Cal Ripken Jr. (Promo card.) 10.00
(10) Nolan Ryan (#82-90) 7.50
(10) Nolan Ryan (Promo card.) 10.00
(11) Ryne Sandberg (#1-9) 5.00
(11) Ryne Sandberg (Promo card.) 6.50
(12) Frank Thomas (#19-27) 6.00
(12) Frank Thomas (Promo card.) 8.00

Rookie Guild

Each of the four players in the '92 Rookie Guild issue is represented by an 11-card set, a promo card and a gold preview card. The first 10 cards in each player's set have blue borders, while the last card has white borders. Cards are seldom available as singles since the sets are rarely broken up.

		NM/M
Complete Set (44):		6.00
Complete Promo Set:		8.00
Complete Preview Set:		12.00
1-11	Reggie Sanders	1.50
	Reggie Sanders (Promo card.)	2.00
	Reggie Sanders (Gold preview.)	3.00
12-22	Phil Plantier	1.50
	Phil Plantier (Promo card.)	2.00
	Phil Plantier (Gold preview.)	3.00
23-33	Dean Palmer	1.50
	Dean Palmer (Promo card.)	2.00
	Dean Palmer (Gold preview.)	3.00
34-44	Eric Karros	1.50
	Eric Karros (Promo card.)	2.00
	Eric Karros (Gold preview.)	3.00
	Eric Karros (Ad card.)	3.00

Silver Edition

Nearly the same line-up as found in other special edition Star nine-card player sets is found in the silver version. Announced production was 1,000 sets of each player along with 200 promo cards. The cards are listed here in alphabetical order. Single cards are not listed because the player sets are not often broken up for individual sales.

		NM/M
Complete Set (108):		40.00
Common Player Set:		3.00
Complete Promo Set (12):		55.00
Common Promo Card:		4.00
(1)	Jeff Bagwell (#46-54)	4.50
(1)	Jeff Bagwell (Promo card.)	6.00
(2)	Jose Canseco (#64-72)	4.50
(2)	Jose Canseco (Promo card.)	5.00
(3)	Will Clark (#1-9)	4.50
(3)	Will Clark (Promo card.)	4.00
(4)	Ken Griffey Jr. (#28-36)	6.00
(4)	Ken Griffey Jr. (Promo card.)	8.00
(5)	Bo Jackson (#37-45)	3.00
(5)	Bo Jackson (Promo card.)	4.00
(6)	David Justice (#19-27)	3.00
(6)	David Justice (Promo card.)	4.00
(7)	Don Mattingly (#100-108)	6.00
(7)	Don Mattingly (Promo card.)	8.00
(8)	Cal Ripken Jr. (#82-90)	6.00
(8)	Cal Ripken Jr. (Promo card.)	8.00
(9)	Nolan Ryan (#73-81)	6.00
(9)	Nolan Ryan (Promo card.)	8.00
(10)	Ryne Sandberg (#10-18)	6.00
(10)	Ryne Sandberg (Promo card.)	7.50
(11)	Darryl Strawberry (#91-99)	3.00
(11)	Darryl Strawberry (Promo card.)	4.00
(12)	Frank Thomas (#55-63)	5.00
(12)	Frank Thomas (Promo card.)	6.00

Stellar Edition

Among the scarcer of Star's 1992 single-player, nine-card sets, the Stellar Edition was produced in an issue of 500 sets and 100 promo cards of each player, contiguously numbered. The cards are listed here in alphabetical order. Single cards are not listed because the player sets are not often broken up for individual sales.

		NM/M
Complete Set (108):		65.00
Common Player Set:		4.50
Complete Promo Set (12):		90.00
Common Promo Card:		6.00
(1)	Jeff Bagwell (#19-27)	6.00
(1)	Jeff Bagwell (Promo card.)	10.00
(2)	Jose Canseco (#100-108)	7.50
(2)	Jose Canseco (Promo card.)	7.50
(3)	Will Clark (#37-45)	6.00
(3)	Will Clark (Promo card.)	6.00
(4)	Roger Clemens (#10-18)	7.50
(4)	Roger Clemens (Promo card.)	10.00
(5)	Ken Griffey Jr. (#55-63)	7.50
(5)	Ken Griffey Jr. (Promo card.)	12.00
(6)	Bo Jackson (#73-81)	4.50
(6)	Bo Jackson (Promo card.)	6.00
(7)	David Justice (#64-72)	4.50
(7)	David Justice (Promo card.)	6.00
(8)	Don Mattingly (#91-99)	9.00
(8)	Don Mattingly (Promo card.)	12.00
(9)	Cal Ripken Jr. (#46-54)	9.00
(9)	Cal Ripken Jr. (Promo card.)	12.00
(10)	Nolan Ryan (#82-90)	9.00
(10)	Nolan Ryan (Promo card.)	12.00
(11)	Ryne Sandberg (#28-36)	7.50
(11)	Ryne Sandberg (Promo card.)	10.00
(12)	Frank Thomas (#1-9)	7.50
(12)	Frank Thomas (Promo card.)	10.00

The Kid

This five-card set was reportedly produced in an edition of 1,000 as a value-added with Star's porcelain statue of Ken Griffey, Jr. One card set was given with the purchase of five statues at $125 each. No promo cards or glossy version were issued.

		NM/M
Complete Set (5):		50.00
1-5	Ken Griffey Jr.	10.00

1993 Star '93 Andy Benes

It is unknown whether the usual 11-card set was produced for this continuation of the Star single-player series, or whether this represents a promotional card. In format similar to the Star '92 issues, the card has a red top border which morphs to yellow at bottom. Back repeats a detail of the front photo and has career stats printed in red on a yellow background. There is a 1993 copyright date, but no card number. The card does not have the high-gloss plastic coating found on the earlier series.

	NM/M
Andy Benes	2.00
Andy Benes (Auto. w/COA.)	3.00

1995 Star Cal Ripken, Jr.

A major design fault apparently prevented this issue from being widely circulated. Each of the 80 cards in the boxed set has an extraneous comma between "Cal" and "Ripken." That fatal flaw aside, the set does a creditable job of detailing Ripken's major league career through his record 2,131st consecutive game in 1995. Glossy card fronts have color photos at center with orange and brown graphic highlights. Each card has him identified as "Cal, Ripken, Jr." at bottom, below which there is a card title. Backs have a baseball at center with career highlights, stats, personal information or trivia. The name error is repeated in orange script at bottom. The set was fully licensed by Ripken and Major League Baseball.

	NM/M
Complete Boxed Set (80):	10.00
Common Card:	.25

1989 Starline Prototypes

Prior to its first major baseball card issue, Starline produced six variations of a prototype issue. The seven-card sets feature game-action photos on the front, surrounded by colorful borders and with a combination of up to three logos in the bottom border. Cards were produced with just the Starline logo, with the Starline and Coca-Cola logos and with the card company and soft drink logos in conjunction with those of McDonald's, 7-11, Burger King or Dominos pizza. Backs repeat the logos at bottom, along with that of Major League Baseball. At top is a color player photo, along with biographical data, complete major and minor league stats and career highlights. The unnumbered cards are checklisted here alphabetically.

		NM/M
Complete Set (7):		45.00
Common Player:		6.00
(1)	Eric Davis	6.00
(2)	Mark Grace	6.00
(3)	Tony Gwynn	10.00
(4)	Gregg Jefferies	6.00
(5)	Don Mattingly	12.00
(6)	Mark McGwire	13.50
(7)	Darryl Strawberry	6.00

1990 Starline

Five-card cello packs of this Coca-Cola sponsored issue were given away with the purchase of dinner and a soft drink at Long John Silver fish restaurants. Cards feature game-action photos on front, bordered in team colors. Backs repeat the team-color scheme and feature a portrait photo along with major league stats and career highlights. Most of the players had two or more cards in the 40-card issue. A header card in each pack offered a 2' x 3' poster of one of 18 players in set for $3.99.

		NM/M
Complete Set (40):		3.00
Common Player:		.10
1	Don Mattingly	.40
2	Mark Grace	.10
3	Eric Davis	.10
4	Tony Gwynn	.30
5	Bobby Bonilla	.10
6	Wade Boggs	.30
7	Frank Viola	.10
8	Ruben Sierra	.10
9	Mark McGwire	.50
10	Alan Trammell	.10
11	Mark McGwire	.50
12	Gregg Jefferies	.10
13	Nolan Ryan	.60
14	John Smoltz	.10
15	Glenn Davis	.10
16	Mark Grace	.10
17	Wade Boggs	.30
18	Frank Viola	.10
19	Bret Saberhagen	.10
20	Chris Sabo	.10
21	Darryl Strawberry	.10
22	Wade Boggs	.30
23	Tim Raines	.10
24	Alan Trammell	.10
25	Chris Sabo	.10
26	Nolan Ryan	.60
27	Mark McGwire	.50
28	Don Mattingly	.40
29	Tony Gwynn	.30
30	Glenn Davis	.10
31	Bobby Bonilla	.10
32	Gregg Jefferies	.10
33	Ruben Sierra	.10
34	John Smoltz	.10
35	Don Mattingly	.40
36	Bret Saberhagen	.10
37	Darryl Strawberry	.10
38	Eric Davis	.10
39	Tim Raines	.10
40	Mark Grace	.10
---	Header Card/ Poster Offer	.05

1990 Starline Americana

Several baseball players were among the subjects featured in a set of "Americana" quiz cards. The 2-1/2" x 3-1/2" cards are printed in full-color front and back. Backs repeat the front photo in miniature and provide "Historical Highlights" along with a trivia question and the answer to the question on another card.

		NM/M
237	Jackie Robinson	2.00
245	Babe Ruth	2.00

1991 Starline Prototypes

These sample cards were produced for submission to baseball licensing authorities for approval, and to prospective sponsors. Only 60 of each card were reported produced. Card fronts have color action photos and a team logo set against a black background. The player's name appears in white and red at top and along the side. Backs have a smaller player photo at upper-right. All of the prototypes have back stats and biography of Nolan Ryan, with a gray diagonal "PROTOTYPE" across them. The Starline, MLB and Players' Associations logo appear across the bottom.

		NM/M
Complete Set (5):		50.00
Common Player:		10.00
(1)	George Bell	10.00
(2)	Bobby Bonilla	10.00
(3)	Roger Clemens	20.00
(4)	Tim Raines	10.00
(5)	Darryl Strawberry	10.00

1983 Starliner Stickers

This unauthorized collector's issue is based on 16 of the cards issued by Dexter Press in 1967 as Coca-Cola premiums. In July 1983, a Midwestern card dealer produced these stickers by reprinting the 5-1/2" x 7" Dexter Press cards in 2-7/16" x 3-1/4" format and eliminating the white border. The stickers can be found with either white ("Mactac Starliner") or tan ("Tuchdown Splitless") paper on back. By the early 1990s, the story of the true origins of these stickers had been largely forgotten within the hobby and some dealers were charging between $10-50 apiece for them. The unnumbered stickers are checklisted here in alphabetical order. Production of the white-back stickers was reported at 2,000 sets, with Mantle and Rose double printed.

		NM/M
Complete Set (16):		40.00
Common Player:		1.00
(1)	Hank Aaron	7.50
(2)	Ernie Banks	1.50
(3)	Roberto Clemente	10.00
(4)	Rocky Colavito	1.00
(5)	Al Kaline	1.50
(6)	Harmon Killebrew	1.00
(7)	Mickey Mantle/DP	20.00
(8)	Willie Mays	7.50
(9)	Willie McCovey	1.00
(10)	Joe Morgan	1.00
(11)	Jim Palmer	1.00
(12)	Brooks Robinson	1.00
(13)	Frank Robinson	1.00
(14)	Pete Rose (DP)	7.50
(15)	Willie Stargell	1.00
(16)	Carl Yastrzemski	1.50

1988 Starting Lineup Talking Baseball

Measuring 2-5/8" x 3", these cards were part of the Starting Lineup Talking Baseball game produced by Kenner Parker Toys Inc. The electronic game, with a computer memory and keyboard to respond to a particular baseball game situation, retailed for more than $100. However, several hobby dealers sold the cards separately from the game. The set includes seven instruction cards that do not picture players.

		NM/M
Complete Set (42):		25.00
Common Player:		.25
11a	Terry Kennedy	.25
11b	Gary Carter	1.25
12a	Carlton Fisk	1.25
12b	Steve Sax	.25
13a	Eddie Murray	1.25
13b	Jack Clark	.25
14a	Don Mattingly	2.50
14b	Keith Hernandez	.25
15a	Willie Randolph	.25
15b	Buddy Bell	.25
16a	Cal Ripken	4.00
16b	Ryne Sandberg	2.00
17a	Lou Whitaker	.25
17b	Ozzie Smith	2.00
18a	Wade Boggs	2.00
18b	Dale Murphy	.75
19a	George Brett	2.50
19b	Mike Schmidt	2.50
20a	Alan Trammell	.25
20b	Eric Davis	.25
21a	Kirby Puckett	2.00
21b	Tony Gwynn	2.00
22a	George Bell	.25
22b	Darryl Strawberry	.25
23a	Rickey Henderson	1.25
23b	Tim Raines	.25
24a	Dave Winfield	1.25
24b	Andre Dawson	.75
25a	Jack Morris	.25
25b	Mike Scott	.25
26a	Robin Yount	1.25
26b	Jody Davis	.25
27a	Roger Clemens	2.50
27b	Todd Worrell	.25
28a	Bret Saberhagen	.25
28b	Fernando Valenzuela	.25
29a	Dave Righetti	.25
29b	Dwight Gooden	.25
30a	Dan Quisenberry	.25
30b	Nolan Ryan	4.00
---	American League Checklist	.25
---	National League Checklist	.25

Team Sets

Similar in format to the cards issued with the Parker Brothers game, these accessory cards could be pur-

chased in groups of three team sets. The team-set cards share the format (2-5/8" x 3") and design of the boxed-set cards, but differ in that the player portraits are presented as colored drawings rather than photos. Because the issue was licensed only by the Players Union, and not MLB, the caps have no team logos. Backs are in black-and-white. Each team set has 20 player cards (the Indians have only 19) plus a batting order/checklist card. Several players appear in more than one set as a result of trades. The cards are checklisted here alphabetically within team.

NM/M
Complete Set (545): 60.00
Common Player: .10
Atlanta Braves Team Set: 4.00
(1) Jim Acker .10
(2) Paul Assenmacher .10
(3) Jeff Blauser .10
(4) Jeff Dedmon .10
(5) Ron Gant .10
(6) Tom Glavine .75
(7) Ken Griffey .10
(8) Albert Hall .10
(9) Glenn Hubbard .10
(10) Dion James .10
(11) Rick Mahler .10
(12) Dale Murphy 1.00
(13) Ken Oberkfell .10
(14) Gerald Perry .10
(15) Gary Roenicke .10
(16) Paul Runge .10
(17) Ted Simmons .10
(18) Pete Smith .10
(19) Andres Thomas .10
(20) Ozzie Virgil .10
(21) Batting Order/Checklist .05
Baltimore Orioles
Team Set: 12.00
(1) Eric Bell .10
(2) Mike Boddicker .10
(3) Jim Dwyer .10
(4) Ken Gerhart .10
(5) Rene Gonzalez .10
(6) Terry Kennedy .10
(7) Ray Knight .10
(8) Lee Lacy .10
(9) Fred Lynn .10
(10) Eddie Murray 3.00
(11) Tom Niedenfuer .10
(12) Billy Ripkin (Ripken) .10
(13) Cal Ripken Jr. 7.50
(14) Dave Schmidt .10
(15) Larry Sheets .10
(16) Pete Stanicek .10
(17) Mark Thurmond .10
(18) Ron Washington .10
(19) Mark Williamson .10
(20) Mike Young .10
(21) Batting Order/Checklist .05
Boston Red Sox Team Set: 7.50
(1) Marty Barrett .10
(2) Todd Benzinger .10
(3) Wade Boggs 4.00
(4) Dennis Boyd .10
(5) Ellis Burks .10
(6) Roger Clemens 4.50
(7) Dwight Evans .10
(8) Wes Gardner .10
(9) Rich Gedman .10
(10) Mike Greenwell .10
(11) Sam Horn .10
(12) Bruce Hurst .10
(13) John Marzano .10
(14) Spike Owen .10
(15) Jody Reed .10
(16) Jim Rice .35
(17) Ed Romero .10
(18) Kevin Romine .10
(19) Lee Smith .10
(20) Bob Stanley .10
(21) Batting Order/Checklist .05
California Angels Team Set: 2.25
(1) Tony Armas .10
(2) Bob Boone .10
(3) Bill Buckner .10
(4) DeWayne Buice .10
(5) Brian Downing .10
(6) Chuck Finley .10
(7) Willie Fraser .10
(8) George Hendrick .10
(9) Jack Howell .10
(10) Ruppert Jones .10
(11) Wally Joyner .10
(12) Kirk McCaskill .10
(13) Mark McLemore .10
(14) Darrell Miller .10
(15) Greg Minton .10
(16) Gary Pettis .10
(17) Johnny Ray .10
(18) Dick Schofield .10
(19) Devon White .10
(20) Mike Witt .10
(21) Batting Order/Checklist .05
Chicago Cubs Team Set: 6.00
(1) Jody Davis .10
(2) Andre Dawson .35
(3) Bob Dernier .10
(4) Frank DiPino .10
(5) Shawon Dunston .10
(6) Leon Durham .10
(7) Dave Martinez .10
(8) Keith Moreland .10
(9) Jamie Moyer .10
(10) Jerry Mumphrey .10
(11) Paul Noce .10
(12) Rafael Palmeiro 2.50
(13) Luis Quinones .10
(14) Ryne Sandberg 4.00
(15) Scott Sanderson .10
(16) Calvin Schiraldi .10
(17) Lee Smith .10
(18) Jim Sundberg .10
(19) Rick Sutcliffe .10
(20) Manny Trillo .10
(21) Batting Order/Checklist .05
Chicago White Sox
Team Set: 4.00
(1) Harold Baines .10
(2) Floyd Bannister .10
(3) Daryl Boston .10
(4) Ivan Calderon .10
(5) Jose DeLeon .10
(6) Rich Dotson .10
(7) Carlton Fisk 3.00
(8) Ozzie Guillen .10
(9) Jerry Hairston Sr. .10
(10) Donnie Hill .10
(11) Dave LaPoint .10
(12) Steve Lyons .10
(13) Fred Manrique .10
(14) Dan Pasqua .10
(15) Gary Redus .10
(16) Mark Salas .10
(17) Ray Searage .10
(18) Bobby Thigpen .10
(19) Greg Walker .10
(20) Ken Williams .10
(21) Batting Order/Checklist .05
Cincinnati Reds Team Set: 2.25
(1) Buddy Bell .10
(2) Tom Browning .10
(3) Dave Collins .10
(4) Dave Concepcion .10
(5) Kal Daniels .10
(6) Eric Davis .10
(7) Bo Diaz .10
(8) Nick Esasky .10
(9) John Franco .10
(10) Terry Francona .10
(11) Tracy Jones .10
(12) Barry Larkin .10
(13) Rob Murphy .10
(14) Paul O'Neill .10
(15) Dave Parker .10
(16) Ted Power .10
(17) Dennis Rasmussen .10
(18) Kurt Stillwell .10
(19) Jeff Treadway .10
(20) Frank Williams .10
(21) Batting Order/Checklist .05
Cleveland Indians Team Set: 2.25
(1) Andy Allanson .10
(2) Scott Bailes .10
(3) Chris Bando .10
(4) Jay Bell .10
(5) Brett Butler .10
(6) Tom Candiotti .10
(7) Joe Carter .10
(8) Carmen Castillo .10
(9) Dave Clark .10
(10) John Farrell .10
(11) Julio Franco .10
(12) Mel Hall .10
(13) Tom Hinzo .10
(14) Brook Jacoby .10
(15) Doug Jones .10
(16) Junior Noboa .10
(17) Ken Schrom .10
(18) Cory Snyder .10
(19) Pat Tabler .10
(20) Batting Order/Checklist .05
Detroit Tigers Team Set: 2.25
(1) Doyle Alexander .10
(2) Dave Bergman .10
(3) Tom Brookens .10
(4) Darrell Evans .10
(5) Kirk Gibson .10
(6) Mike Heath .10
(7) Mike Henneman .10
(8) Willie Hernandez .10
(9) Larry Herndon .10
(10) Eric King .10
(11) Ray Knight .10
(12) Chet Lemon .10
(13) Bill Madlock .10
(14) Jack Morris .10
(15) Jim Morrison .10
(16) Matt Nokes .10
(17) Pat Sheridan .10
(18) Frank Tanana .10
(19) Alan Trammell .10
(20) Lou Whitaker .10
(21) Batting Order/Checklist .05
Houston Astros Team Set: 6.00
(1) Juan Agosto .10
(2) Larry Anderson .10
(3) Alan Ashby .10
(4) Kevin Bass .10
(5) Ken Caminiti .10
(6) Jose Cruz .10
(7) Danny Darwin .10
(8) Glenn Davis .10
(9) Bill Doran .10
(10) Billy Hatcher .10
(11) Jim Pankovitz .10
(12) Terry Puhl .10
(13) Rafael Ramirez .10
(14) Craig Reynolds .10
(15) Nolan Ryan 7.50
(16) Mike Scott .10
(17) Dave Smith .10
(18) Marc Sullivan .10
(19) Dennis Walling .10
(20) Eric Young .10
(21) Batting Order/Checklist .05
Kansas City Royals
Team Set: 6.00
(1) Steve Balboni .10
(2) George Brett 4.50
(3) Jim Eisenreich .10
(4) Gene Garber .10
(5) Jerry Don Gleaton .10
(6) Mark Gubicza .10
(7) Bo Jackson .50
(8) Charlie Leibrandt .10
(9) Mike Macfarlane .10
(10) Larry Owen .10
(11) Bill Pecota .10
(12) Jamie Quirk .10
(13) Dan Quisenberry .10
(14) Bret Saberhagen .10
(15) Kevin Seitzer .10
(16) Kurt Stillwell .10
(17) Danny Tartabull .10
(18) Gary Thurman .10
(19) Frank White .10
(20) Willie Wilson .10
(21) Batting Order/Checklist .05
Los Angeles Dodgers
Team Set: 2.50
(1) Dave Anderson .10
(2) Mike Davis .10
(3) Mariano Duncan .10
(4) Kirk Gibson .10
(5) Alfredo Griffin .10
(6) Pedro Guerrero .10
(7) Mickey Hatcher .10
(8) Orel Hershiser .10
(9) Glenn Hoffman .10
(10) Brian Holton .10
(11) Mike Marshall .10
(12) Jesse Orosco .10
(13) Alejandro Pena .10
(14) Steve Sax .10
(15) Mike Scioscia .10
(16) John Shelby .10
(17) Franklin Stubbs .10
(18) Don Sutton 2.00
(19) Alex Trevino .10
(20) Fernando Valenzuela .10
(21) Batting Order/Checklist .05
Milwaukee Brewers
Team Set: 6.00
(1) Chris Bosio .10
(2) Glenn Braggs .10
(3) Greg Brock .10
(4) Juan Castillo .10
(5) Chuck Crim .10
(6) Rob Deer .10
(7) Mike Felder .10
(8) Jim Gantner .10
(9) Teddy Higuera .10
(10) Steve Kiefer .10
(11) Paul Molitor 3.00
(12) Juan Nieves .10
(13) Dan Plesac .10
(14) Ernie Riles .10
(15) Billy Jo Robidoux .10
(16) Bill Schroeder .10
(17) B.J. Surhoff .10
(18) Dale Sveum .10
(19) Bill Wegman .10
(20) Robin Yount 3.00
(21) Batting Order/Checklist .05
Minnesota Twins Team Set: 6.00
(1) Don Baylor .10
(2) Juan Berenguer .10
(3) Bert Blyleven .10
(4) Tom Brunansky .10
(5) Randy Bush .10
(6) Mark Davidson .10
(7) Gary Gaetti .10
(8) Greg Gagne .10
(9) Dan Gladden .10
(10) Kent Hrbek .10
(11) Gene Larkin .10
(12) Tim Laudner .10
(13) Steve Lombardozzi .10
(14) Al Newman .10
(15) Kirby Puckett 4.00
(16) Jeff Reardon .10
(17) Dan Schatzeder .10
(18) Roy Smalley .10
(19) Les Straker .10
(20) Frank Viola .10
(21) Batting Order/Checklist .05
Montreal Expos Team Set: 9.00
(1) Hubie Brooks .10
(2) Tim Burke .10
(3) Casey Candaele .10
(4) Mike Fitzgerald .10
(5) Tom Foley .10
(6) Andres Galarraga .10
(7) Neal Heaton .10
(8) Randy Johnson 7.50
(9) Vance Law .10
(10) Bob McClure .10
(11) Andy McGaffigan .10
(12) Dennis Powell .10
(13) Tim Raines .10
(14) Jeff Reed .10
(15) Luis Rivera .10
(16) Bryn Smith .10
(17) Tim Wallach .10
(18) Mitch Webster .10
(19) Herm Winningham .10
(20) Floyd Youmans .10
(21) Batting Order/Checklist .05
New York Mets Team Issue: 4.00
(1) Bill Almon .10
(2) Wally Backman .10
(3) Gary Carter 3.00
(4) David Cone .10
(5) Ron Darling .10
(6) Lenny Dykstra .10
(7) Sid Fernandez .10
(8) Dwight Gooden .10
(9) Keith Hernandez .10
(10) Howard Johnson .10
(11) Barry Lyons .10
(12) Dave Magadan .10
(13) Lee Mazzilli .10
(14) Roger McDowell .10
(15) Kevin McReynolds .10
(16) Jesse Orosco .10
(17) Rafael Santana .10
(18) Darryl Strawberry .10
(19) Tim Teufel .10
(20) Mookie Wilson .10
(21) Batting Order/Checklist .05
New York Yankees
Team Set: 9.00
(1) Rick Cerone .10
(2) Jack Clark .10
(3) Pat Clements .10
(4) Mike Easler .10
(5) Ron Guidry .10
(6) Rickey Henderson 3.00
(7) Tommy John .10
(8) Don Mattingly 4.50
(9) Bobby Meacham .10
(10) Mike Pagliarulo .10
(11) Willie Randolph .10
(12) Rick Rhoden .10
(13) Dave Righetti .10
(14) Jerry Royster .10
(15) Don Slaught .10
(16) Tim Stoddard .10
(17) Wayne Tolleson .10
(18) Gary Ward .10
(19) Claudell Washington .10
(20) Dave Winfield 3.00
(21) Batting Order/Checklist .05
Oakland A's Team Set: 15.00
(1) Tony Bernazard .10
(2) Jose Canseco 1.50
(3) Mike Davis .10
(4) Dennis Eckersley 2.00
(5) Mike Gallego .10
(6) Alfredo Griffin .10
(7) Rickey Henderson 3.00
(8) Reggie Jackson 4.50
(9) Carney Lansford .10
(10) Mark McGwire 6.00
(11) Gene Nelson .10
(12) Steve Ontiveros .10
(13) Dave Parker .10
(14) Tony Phillips .10
(15) Luis Polonia .10
(16) Terry Steinbach .10
(17) Dave Stewart .10
(18) Mickey Tettleton .10
(19) Bob Welch .10
(20) Curt Young .10
(21) Batting Order/Checklist .05
Philadelphia Phillies
Team Set: 5.00
(1) Luis Aguayo .10
(2) Steve Bedrosian .10
(3) Phil Bradley .10
(4) Jeff Calhoun .10
(5) Don Carman .10
(6) Darren Daulton .10
(7) Bob Dernier .10
(8) Greg Gross .10
(9) Von Hayes .10
(10) Chris James .10
(11) Steve Jeltz .10
(12) Lance Parrish .10
(13) Shane Rawley .10
(14) Bruce Ruffin .10
(15) Juan Samuel .10
(16) Mike Schmidt 4.50
(17) Rick Schu .10
(18) Kent Tekulve .10
(19) Milt Thompson .10
(20) Glenn Wilson .10
(21) Batting Order/Checklist .05
Pittsburgh Pirates Team Set: 9.00
(1) Rafael Belliard .10
(2) Barry Bonds 7.50
(3) Bobby Bonilla .10
(4) Sid Bream .10
(5) John Cangelosi .10
(6) Darnell Coles .10
(7) Mike Diaz .10
(8) Doug Drabek .10
(9) Mike Dunne .10
(10) Felix Fermin .10
(11) Brian Fisher .10
(12) Jim Gott .10
(13) Mike LaValliere .10
(14) Jose Lind .10
(15) Junior Ortiz .10
(16) Al Pedrique .10
(17) R.J. Reynolds .10
(18) Jeff Robinson .10
(19) John Smiley .10
(20) Andy Van Slyke .10
(21) Batting Order/Checklist .05
San Diego Padres Team Set: 5.00
(1) Shawn Abner .10
(2) Roberto Alomar .25
(3) Bobby Brown .10
(4) Joey Cora .10
(5) Mark Davis .10
(6) Tim Flannery .10
(7) Goose Gossage .10
(8) Mark Grant .10
(9) Tony Gwynn 4.00
(10) Stan Jefferson .10
(11) John Kruk .10
(12) Shane Mack .10
(13) Carmelo Martinez .10
(14) Lance McCullers .10
(15) Randy Ready .10
(16) Benito Santiago .10
(17) Eric Show .10
(18) Garry Templeton .10
(19) Ed Whitson .10
(20) Marvell Wynne .10
(21) Batting Order/Checklist .05
San Francisco Giants
Team Set: 2.50
(1) Mike Aldrete .10
(2) Bob Brenly .10
(3) Brett Butler .10
(4) Will Clark .10
(5) Chili Davis .10
(6) Dave Dravecky .10
(7) Scott Garrelts .10
(8) Atlee Hammaker .10
(9) Craig Lefferts .10
(10) Jeffrey Leonard .10
(11) Candy Maldonado .10
(12) Bob Melvin .10
(13) Kevin Mitchell .10
(14) Rick Reuschel .10
(15) Don Robinson .10
(16) Chris Speier .10
(17) Chris Spielman .10
(18) Robby Thompson .10
(19) Jose Uribe .10
(20) Matt Williams .10
(21) Batting Order/Checklist .05
Seattle Mariners Team Set: 2.25
(1) Phil Bradley .10
(2) Scott Bradley .10
(3) Mickey Brantley .10
(4) Mike Campbell .10
(5) Henry Cotto .10
(6) Alvin Davis .10
(7) Mike Kingery .10
(8) Mark Langston .10
(9) Mike Moore .10
(10) John Moses .10
(11) Donell Nixon .10
(12) Ed Nunez .10
(13) Ken Phelps .10
(14) Jim Presley .10
(15) Rey Quinones .10
(16) Jerry Reed .10
(17) Harold Reynolds .10
(18) Dave Valle .10
(19) Bill Wilkinson .10
(20) Glenn Wilson .10
(21) Batting Order/Checklist .05
St. Louis Cardinals
Team Set: 4.50
(1) Greg Booker .10
(2) Jack Clark .10
(3) Vince Coleman .10
(4) Danny Cox .10
(5) Ken Dayley .10
(6) Curt Ford .10
(7) Tom Herr .10
(8) Bob Horner .10
(9) Ricky Horton .10
(10) Lance Johnson .10
(11) Steve Lake .10
(12) Jim Lindeman .10
(13) Greg Mathews .10
(14) Willie McGee .10
(15) Jose Oquendo .10
(16) Tony Pena .10
(17) Terry Pendleton .10
(18) Ozzie Smith 4.00
(19) John Tudor .10
(20) Todd Worrell .10
(21) Batting Order/Checklist .05
Texas Rangers Team Set: 2.25
(1) Jerry Browne .10
(2) Bob Brower .10
(3) Steve Buechele .10
(4) Scott Fletcher .10
(5) Juan Guzman .10
(6) Charlie Hough .10
(7) Pete Incaviglia .10
(8) Oddibe McDowell .10
(9) Dale Mohorcic .10
(10) Pete O'Brien .10
(11) Tom O'Malley .10
(12) Larry Parrish .10
(13) Geno Petralli .10
(14) Jeff Russell .10
(15) Ruben Sierra .10
(16) Don Slaught .10
(17) Mike Stanley .10
(18) Curt Wilkerson .10
(19) Mitch Williams .10
(20) Bobby Witt .10
(21) Batting Order/Checklist .05
Toronto Blue Jays Team Set: 2.25
(1) Jesse Barfield .10
(2) George Bell .10
(3) Juan Beniquez .10
(4) Jim Clancy .10
(5) Mark Eichhorn .10
(6) Tony Fernandez .10
(7) Cecil Fielder .10
(8) Tom Henke .10
(9) Garth Iorg .10
(10) Jimmy Key .10
(11) Rick Leach .10
(12) Manny Lee .10
(13) Nelson Liriano .10
(14) Fred McGriff .10
(15) Lloyd Moseby .10
(16) Rance Mulliniks .10
(17) Jeff Musselman .10
(18) Dave Steib .10
(19) Willie Upshaw .10
(20) Ernie Whitt .10
(21) Batting Order/Checklist .05

1995 Stouffer's Legends of Baseball

To promote its French bread frozen pizza, this Nestle's subsidiary issued a series of five three-dimensional cards featuring current and future Hall of Famers. The 2-1/2" x 3-1/2" cards have a die-cut action photo on front connected to a tab at the card top. When the tab is pulled, the player figure stands up. The back of the card has another player photo and a few career highlights. Because the promotion was licensed only by individuals, and not Major League Baseball, uniform and cap logos have been air-brushed off the photos.

NM/M
Complete Set (6): 4.00
Common Player: 1.00
1 Yogi Berra 2.00
1a Yogi Berra/Auto. 20.00
2 Gary Carter 1.50
3 Don Drysdale 2.00
4 Bob Feller 2.00
5 Willie Stargell 2.00

1983 Stuart Expos

This set of Montreal Expos players and coaches was issued by a Montreal area baking company for inclusion in packages of snack cakes. The 30 cards feature full-color player photos, with the player name, number and team logo also on the card fronts. The backs list brief player biographies in both English and French. Twenty-five players are pictured on the 2-1/2" x 3-1/2" cards.

		NM/M
Complete Set (30):		10.00
Common Player:		.25
1	Bill Virdon	.25
2	Woodie Fryman	.25
3	Vern Rapp	.25
4	Andre Dawson	2.00
5	Jeff Reardon	.35
6	Al Oliver	.50
7	Doug Flynn	.25
8	Gary Carter	5.00
9	Tim Raines	1.00
10	Steve Rogers	.25
11	Billy DeMars	.25
12	Tim Wallach	.25
13	Galen Cisco	.25
14	Terry Francona	.25
15	Bill Gullickson	.25
16	Ray Burris	.25
17	Scott Sanderson	.25
18	Warren Cromartie	.25
19	Jerry White	.25
20	Bobby Ramos	.25
21	Jim Wolhford	.25
22	Dan Schatzeder	.25
23	Charlie Lea	.25
24	Bryan Little	.25
25	Mel Wright	.25
26	Tim Blackwell	.25
27	Chris Speier	.25
28	Randy Lerch	.25
29	Bryn Smith	.25
30	Brad Mills	.25

1984 Stuart Expos

For the second year in a row, Stuart Cakes issued a full-color card set of the Montreal Expos. The 2-1/2" x 3-1/2" cards again list the player name and number along with the team and company logos on the card fronts. The backs are bilingual with biographical information in both English and French. The 40-card set was issued in two series. Card numbers 21-40, issued late in the summer, are more difficult to find than the first 20 cards. The 40 cards include players, the manager, coaches and team mascot.

		NM/M
Complete Set (40):		15.00
Common Player (1-20):		.25
Common Player (21-40):		.35
Album:		6.00
1	Youppi! (Mascot)	.25
2	Bill Virdon	.25
3	Billy DeMars	.25
4	Galen Cisco	.25
5	Russ Nixon	.25
6	Felipe Alou	.75
7	Dan Schatzeder	.25
8	Charlie Lea	.25
9	Bobby Ramos	.25
10	Bob James	.25
11	Andre Dawson	2.00
12	Gary Lucas	.25
13	Jeff Reardon	.35
14	Tim Wallach	.35
15	Gary Carter	5.00
16	Bill Gullickson	.25
17	Pete Rose	6.00
18	Terry Francona	.25
19	Steve Rogers	.25
20	Tim Raines	1.00
21	Bryn Smith	.25
22	Greg Harris	.35
23	David Palmer	.35
24	Jim Wohlford	.35
25	Miguel Dilone	.35
26	Mike Stenhouse	.35
27	Chris Speier	.35
28	Derrel Thomas	.35
29	Doug Flynn	.35
30	Bryan Little	.35
31	Argenis Salazar	.35
32	Mike Fuentes	.35
33	Joe Kerrigan	.35
34	Andy McGaffigan	.35
35	Fred Breining	.35
36	Expos 1983 All-Stars (Gary Carter, Andre Dawson, Tim Raines, Steve Rogers)	.75
37	Co-Players Of The Year (Andre Dawson, Tim Raines)	.75
38	Expos' Coaching Staff (Felipe Alou, Galen Cisco, Billy DeMars, Joe Kerrigan, Russ Nixon, Bill Virdon)	.35
39	Team Photo	.50
40	Checklist	.10

1987 Stuart

Twenty-eight four-part folding panels make up the 1987 Stuart Super Stars set, which was issued only in Canada. Three player cards and a sweepstakes entry form card comprise each panel. All 26 major league teams are included with the Montreal Expos and Toronto Blue Jays being represented twice. The cards, which are full color and measure 2-1/2" x 3-1/2", are written in both English and French. The card backs contain the player's previous year's statistics. All team insignias have been airbrushed away.

		NM/M
Complete Panel Set (28):		15.00
Complete Singles Set (84):		10.00
Common Panel:		.35
Common Single Player:		.05
Panel (New York Mets)		.60
1a	Gary Carter	.50
1b	Keith Hernandez	.05
1c	Darryl Strawberry	.05
Panel (Atlanta Braves)		.60
2a	Bruce Benedict	.05
2b	Ken Griffey	.05
2c	Dale Murphy	.25
Panel (Chicago Cubs)		.50
3a	Jody Davis	.05
3b	Andre Dawson	.35
3c	Leon Durham	.05
Panel (Cincinnati Reds)		.50
4a	Buddy Bell	.05
4b	Eric Davis	.05
4c	Dave Parker	.05
Panel (Houston Astros)		1.75
5a	Glenn Davis	.05
5b	Nolan Ryan	.75
5c	Mike Scott	.05
Panel (Los Angeles Dodgers)		.35
6a	Pedro Guerrero	.05
6b	Mike Marshall	.05
6c	Fernando Valenzuela	.05
Panel (Montreal Expos)		1.00
7a	Tim Raines	.25
7b	Tim Wallach	.10
7c	Mitch Webster	.10
Panel (Montreal Expos)		.75
8a	Hubie Brooks	.10
8b	Bryn Smith	.10
8c	Floyd Youmans	.10
Panel (Philadelphia Phillies)		1.25
9a	Shane Rawley	.05
9b	Juan Samuel	.05
9c	Mike Schmidt	.60
Panel (Pittsburgh Pirates)		.35
10a	Jim Morrison	.05
10b	Johnny Ray	.05
10c	R.J. Reynolds	.05
Panel (St. Louis Cardinals)		1.00
11a	Jack Clark	.05
11b	Vince Coleman	.05
11c	Ozzie Smith	.50
Panel (San Diego Padres)		1.00
12a	Steve Garvey	.15
12b	Tony Gwynn	.50
12c	John Kruk	.05
Panel (San Francisco Giants)		.35
13a	Chili Davis	.05
13b	Jeffrey Leonard	.05
13c	Robbie Thompson	.05
Panel (Baltimore Orioles)		2.50
14a	Fred Lynn	.05
14b	Eddie Murray	.50
14c	Cal Ripken, Jr.	1.00
Panel (Boston Red Sox)		1.75
15a	Don Baylor	.05
15b	Wade Boggs	.50
15c	Roger Clemens	.60
Panel (California Angels)		.40
16a	Doug DeCinces	.05
16b	Wally Joyner	.05
16c	Mike Witt	.05
Panel (Chicago White Sox)		.70
17a	Harold Baines	.05
17b	Carlton Fisk	.50
17c	Ozzie Guillen	.05
Panel (Cleveland Indians)		.35
18a	Joe Carter	.05
18b	Julio Franco	.05
18c	Pat Tabler	.05
Panel (Detroit Tigers)		.35
19a	Kirk Gibson	.05
19b	Jack Morris	.05
19c	Alan Trammell	.05
Panel (Kansas City Royals)		1.25
20a	George Brett	.50
20b	Bret Saberhagen	.05
20c	Willie Wilson	.05
Panel (Milwaukee Brewers)		1.50
21a	Cecil Cooper	.05
21b	Paul Molitor	.40
21c	Robin Yount	.40
Panel (Minnesota Twins)		.70
22a	Tom Brunansky	.05
22b	Kent Hrbek	.05
22c	Kirby Puckett	.50
Panel (New York Yankees)		2.50
23a	Rickey Henderson	.40
23b	Don Mattingly	.60
23c	Dave Winfield	.40
Panel (Oakland A's)		1.00
24a	Jose Canseco	.35
24b	Alfredo Griffin	.05
24c	Carney Lansford	.05
Panel (Seattle Mariners)		.35
25a	Phil Bradley	.05
25b	Alvin Davis	.05
25c	Mark Langston	.05
Panel (Texas Rangers)		.35
26a	Pete Incaviglia	.05
26b	Pete O'Brien	.05
26c	Larry Parrish	.05
Panel (Toronto Blue Jays)		.75
27a	Jesse Barfield	.10
27b	George Bell	.10
27c	Tony Fernandez	.10
Panel (Toronto Blue Jays)		.75
28a	Lloyd Moseby	.10
28b	Dave Stieb	.10
28c	Ernie Whitt	.10

1991 Studio Preview

Each 1991 Donruss set packaged for the retail trade included a pack of four cards previewing the debut Studio set. The cards are in the same format as the regular set, 2-1/2" x 3-1/2" with evocative black-and-white photos bordered in maroon on front, and a biographical write-up on the back.

		NM/M
Complete Set (18):		5.00
Common Player:		.50
1	Juan Bell	.50
2	Roger Clemens	3.00
3	Dave Parker	.50
4	Tim Raines	.50
5	Kevin Seitzer	.50
6	Teddy Higuera	.50
7	Bernie Williams	.50
8	Harold Baines	.50
9	Gary Pettis	.50
10	Dave Justice	.50
11	Eric Davis	.50
12	Andujar Cedeno	.50
13	Tom Foley	.50
14	Dwight Gooden	.50
15	Doug Drabek	.50
16	Steve Decker	.50
17	Joe Torre	.75
18	Header Card	.10

1991 Studio

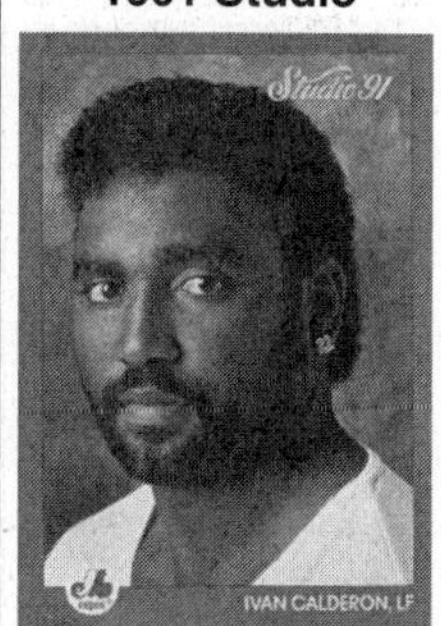

Donruss introduced this 264-card set in 1991. The cards feature maroon borders surrounding black and white posed player photos. The card backs are printed in black and white and feature personal data, career highlights, hobbies and interests and the player's hero. The cards were released in foil packs only and feature a special Rod Carew puzzle.

		NM/M
Complete Set (264):		7.50
Common Player:		.05
Foil Pack (10):		.50
Foil Box (48):		12.50
1	Glenn Davis	.05
2	Dwight Evans	.05
3	Leo Gomez	.05
4	Chris Hoiles	.05
5	Sam Horn	.05
6	Ben McDonald	.05
7	Randy Milligan	.05
8	Gregg Olson	.05
9	Cal Ripken, Jr.	1.00
10	David Segui	.05
11	Wade Boggs	.40
12	Ellis Burks	.05
13	Jack Clark	.05
14	Roger Clemens	.45
15	Mike Greenwell	.05
16	Tim Naehring	.05
17	Tony Pena	.05
18	Phil Plantier **RC**	.05
19	Jeff Reardon	.05
20	Mo Vaughn	.05
21	Jimmy Reese	.05
22	Jim Abbott	.05
23	Bert Blyleven	.05
24	Chuck Finley	.05
25	Gary Gaetti	.05
26	Wally Joyner	.05
27	Mark Langston	.05
28	Kirk McCaskill	.05
29	Lance Parrish	.05
30	Dave Winfield	.30
31	Alex Fernandez	.05
32	Carlton Fisk	.30
33	Scott Fletcher	.05
34	Greg Hibbard	.05
35	Charlie Hough	.05
36	Jack McDowell	.05
37	Tim Raines	.05
38	Sammy Sosa	.40
39	Bobby Thigpen	.05
40	Frank Thomas	.30
41	Sandy Alomar	.05
42	John Farrell	.05
43	Glenallen Hill	.05
44	Brook Jacoby	.05
45	Chris James	.05
46	Doug Jones	.05
47	Eric King	.05
48	Mark Lewis	.05
49	Greg Swindell	.05
50	Mark Whiten	.05
51	Milt Cuyler	.05
52	Rob Deer	.05
53	Cecil Fielder	.05
54	Travis Fryman	.05
55	Bill Gullickson	.05
56	Lloyd Moseby	.05
57	Frank Tanana	.05
58	Mickey Tettleton	.05
59	Alan Trammell	.05
60	Lou Whitaker	.05
61	Mike Boddicker	.05
62	George Brett	.45
63	Jeff Conine	.05
64	Warren Cromartie	.05
65	Storm Davis	.05
66	Kirk Gibson	.05
67	Mark Gubicza	.05
68	Brian McRae **RC**	.05
69	Bret Saberhagen	.05
70	Kurt Stillwell	.05
71	Tim McIntosh	.05
72	Candy Maldonado	.05
73	Paul Molitor	.30
74	Willie Randolph	.05
75	Ron Robinson	.05
76	Gary Sheffield	.20
77	Franklin Stubbs	.05
78	B.J. Surhoff	.05
79	Greg Vaughn	.05
80	Robin Yount	.30
81	Rick Aguilera	.05
82	Steve Bedrosian	.05
83	Scott Erickson	.05
84	Greg Gagne	.05
85	Dan Gladden	.05
86	Brian Harper	.05
87	Kent Hrbek	.05
88	Shane Mack	.05
89	Jack Morris	.05
90	Kirby Puckett	.40
91	Jesse Barfield	.05
92	Steve Farr	.05
93	Steve Howe	.05
94	Roberto Kelly	.05
95	Tim Leary	.05
96	Kevin Maas	.05
97	Don Mattingly	.45
98	Hensley Meulens	.05
99	Scott Sanderson	.05
100	Steve Sax	.05
101	Jose Canseco	.20
102	Dennis Eckersley	.25
103	Dave Henderson	.05
104	Rickey Henderson	.30
105	Rick Honeycutt	.05
106	Mark McGwire	.75
107	Dave Stewart	.05
108	Eric Show	.05
109	Todd Van Poppel **RC**	.05
110	Bob Welch	.05
111	Alvin Davis	.05
112	Ken Griffey Jr.	.50
113	Ken Griffey Sr.	.05
114	Erik Hanson	.05
115	Brian Holman	.05
116	Randy Johnson	.30
117	Edgar Martinez	.05
118	Tino Martinez	.05
119	Harold Reynolds	.05
120	David Valle	.05
121	Kevin Belcher	.05
122	Scott Chiamparino	.05
123	Julio Franco	.05
124	Juan Gonzalez	.20
125	Rich Gossage	.05
126	Jeff Kunkel	.05
127	Rafael Palmeiro	.25
128	Nolan Ryan	1.00
129	Ruben Sierra	.05
130	Bobby Witt	.05
131	Roberto Alomar	.10
132	Tom Candiotti	.05
133	Joe Carter	.05
134	Ken Dayley	.05
135	Kelly Gruber	.05
136	John Olerud	.05
137	Dave Stieb	.05
138	Turner Ward	.05
139	Devon White	.05
140	Mookie Wilson	.05
141	Steve Avery	.05
142	Sid Bream	.05
143	Nick Esasky	.05
144	Ron Gant	.05
145	Tom Glavine	.20
146	Dave Justice	.05
147	Kelly Mann	.05
148	Terry Pendleton	.05
149	John Smoltz	.05
150	Jeff Treadway	.05
151	George Bell	.05
152	Shawn Boskie	.05
153	Andre Dawson	.20
154	Lance Dickson	.05
155	Shawon Dunston	.05
156	Joe Girardi	.05
157	Mark Grace	.05
158	Ryne Sandberg	.40
159	Gary Scott	.05
160	Dave Smith	.05
161	Tom Browning	.05
162	Eric Davis	.05
163	Rob Dibble	.05
164	Mariano Duncan	.05
165	Chris Hammond	.05
166	Billy Hatcher	.05
167	Barry Larkin	.05
168	Hal Morris	.05
169	Paul O'Neill	.05
170	Chris Sabo	.05
171	Eric Anthony	.05
172	Jeff Bagwell **RC**	1.50
173	Craig Biggio	.05
174	Ken Caminitti	.05
175	Jim Deshaies	.05
176	Steve Finley	.05
177	Pete Harnisch	.05
178	Darryl Kile	.05
179	Curt Schilling	.20
180	Mike Scott	.05
181	Brett Butler	.05
182	Gary Carter	.30
183	Orel Hershiser	.05
184	Ramon Martinez	.05
185	Eddie Murray	.30
186	Jose Offerman	.05
187	Bob Ojeda	.05
188	Juan Samuel	.05
189	Mike Scioscia	.05
190	Darryl Strawberry	.05
191	Moises Alou	.05
192	Brian Barnes	.05
193	Oil Can Boyd	.05
194	Ivan Calderon	.05
195	Delino DeShields	.05
196	Mike Fitzgerald	.05
197	Andres Galarraga	.05
198	Marquis Grissom	.05
199	Bill Sampen	.05
200	Tim Wallach	.05
201	Daryl Boston	.05
202	Vince Coleman	.05
203	John Franco	.05
204	Dwight Gooden	.05
205	Tom Herr	.05
206	Gregg Jefferies	.05
207	Howard Johnson	.05
208	Dave Magadan	.05
209	Kevin McReynolds	.05
210	Frank Viola	.05
211	Wes Chamberlain	.05
212	Darren Daulton	.05
213	Len Dykstra	.05
214	Charlie Hayes	.05
215	Ricky Jordan	.05
216	Steve Lake	.05
217	Roger McDowell	.05
218	Mickey Morandini	.05
219	Terry Mulholland	.05
220	Dale Murphy	.15
221	Jay Bell	.05
222	Barry Bonds	1.00
223	Bobby Bonilla	.05
224	Doug Drabek	.05
225	Bill Landrum	.05
226	Mike LaValliere	.05
227	Jose Lind	.05
228	Don Slaught	.05
229	John Smiley	.05
230	Andy Van Slyke	.05
231	Bernard Gilkey	.05
232	Pedro Guerrero	.05
233	Rex Hudler	.05
234	Ray Lankford	.05
235	Joe Magrane	.05
236	Jose Oquendo	.05
237	Lee Smith	.05
238	Ozzie Smith	.40
239	Milt Thompson	.05
240	Todd Zeile	.05
241	Larry Andersen	.05
242	Andy Benes	.05
243	Paul Faries	.05
244	Tony Fernandez	.05
245	Tony Gwynn	.40
246	Atlee Hammaker	.05
247	Fred McGriff	.05
248	Bip Roberts	.05
249	Benito Santiago	.05
250	Ed Whitson	.05
251	Dave Anderson	.05
252	Mike Benjamin	.05
253	John Burkett	.05
254	Will Clark	.05
255	Scott Garrelts	.05
256	Willie McGee	.05
257	Kevin Mitchell	.05
258	Dave Righetti	.05
259	Matt Williams	.05
260	Black & Decker (Bud Black, Steve Decker)	.10
261	Checklist	.03
262	Checklist	.03
263	Checklist	.03
---	Header Card	.03

1992 Studio Preview

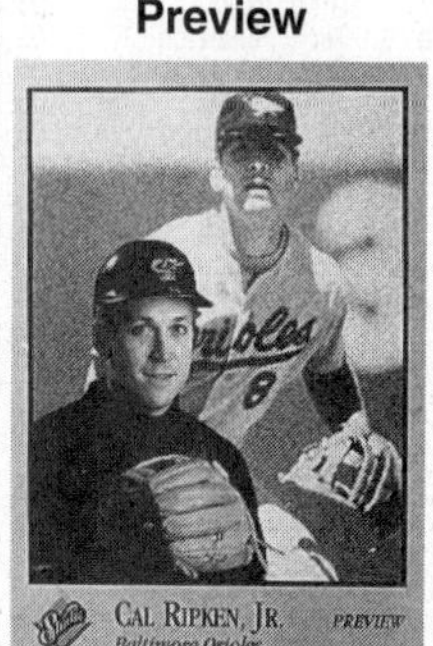

To introduce its 1992 Studio brand, Leaf produced 22 preview cards in format virtually identical to the issued versions of the same cards. The only differences are the appearance of the word "PREVIEW" in the lower-right corner of the card front, in place of the player's position, and the number "X of 22 / Preview Card" on the back where regular cards have the card number in the upper-right corner. The cards were distributed on a very limited basis to members of the Donruss dealers' network.

		NM/M
Complete Set (22):		75.00
Common Player:		1.50
1	Ruben Sierra	1.50
2	Kirby Puckett	6.00
3	Ryne Sandberg	6.00
4	John Kruk	1.50
5	Cal Ripken, Jr.	12.00
6	Robin Yount	4.50
7	Dwight Gooden	1.50
8	David Justice	1.50
9	Don Mattingly	7.50
10	Wally Joyner	1.50
11	Will Clark	1.50
12	Rob Dibble	1.50
13	Roberto Alomar	2.50
14	Wade Boggs	6.00
15	Barry Bonds	12.00
16	Jeff Bagwell	4.50
17	Mark McGwire	9.00
18	Frank Thomas	6.00
19	Brett Butler	1.50
20	Ozzie Smith	6.00
21	Jim Abbott	1.50
22	Tony Gwynn	6.00

1992 Studio

Donruss introduced the Studio line in 1991 and released another 264-card set entitled Leaf Studio for 1992. The cards feature a color player closeup with a large, rough-textured black-and-white photo of the player in the background. Tan borders surround the photos. The cards were only released in foil packs. Special Heritage insert cards featuring top players in vintage uniforms could be found in foil and jumbo packs.

		NM/M
Complete Set (264):		8.00
Common Player:		.05
Pack (10):		.65
Wax Box (48):		15.00
1	Steve Avery	.05
2	Sid Bream	.05
3	Ron Gant	.05
4	Tom Glavine	.25
5	Dave Justice	.05
6	Mark Lemke	.05
7	Greg Olson	.05
8	Terry Pendleton	.05
9	Deion Sanders	.05
10	John Smoltz	.05
11	Doug Dascenzo	.05
12	Andre Dawson	.25
13	Joe Girardi	.05
14	Mark Grace	.05
15	Greg Maddux	.50
16	Chuck McElroy	.05
17	Mike Morgan	.05
18	Ryne Sandberg	.50
19	Gary Scott	.05
20	Sammy Sosa	.50
21	Norm Charlton	.05
22	Rob Dibble	.05
23	Barry Larkin	.05
24	Hal Morris	.05
25	Paul O'Neill	.05
26	Jose Rijo	.05
27	Bip Roberts	.05
28	Chris Sabo	.05
29	Reggie Sanders	.05
30	Greg Swindell	.05
31	Jeff Bagwell	.45
32	Craig Biggio	.05
33	Ken Caminiti	.05
34	Andujar Cedeno	.05
35	Steve Finley	.05
36	Pete Harnisch	.05
37	Butch Henry	.05
38	Doug Jones	.05
39	Darryl Kile	.05
40	Eddie Taubensee	.05
41	Brett Butler	.05
42	Tom Candiotti	.05
43	Eric Davis	.05
44	Orel Hershiser	.05
45	Eric Karros	.05
46	Ramon Martinez	.05
47	Jose Offerman	.05
48	Mike Scioscia	.05
49	Mike Sharperson	.05
50	Darryl Strawberry	.05
51	Bret Barbarie	.05
52	Ivan Calderon	.05
53	Gary Carter	.45
54	Delino DeShields	.05
55	Marquis Grissom	.05
56	Ken Hill	.05
57	Dennis Martinez	.05
58	Spike Owen	.05
59	Larry Walker	.05
60	Tim Wallach	.05
61	Bobby Bonilla	.05
62	Tim Burke	.05
63	Vince Coleman	.05
64	John Franco	.05
65	Dwight Gooden	.05
66	Todd Hundley	.05
67	Howard Johnson	.05
68	Eddie Murray	.45
69	Bret Saberhagen	.05
70	Anthony Young	.05
71	Kim Batiste	.05
72	Wes Chamberlain	.05
73	Darren Daulton	.05
74	Mariano Duncan	.05
75	Len Dykstra	.05
76	John Kruk	.05
77	Mickey Morandini	.05
78	Terry Mulholland	.05
79	Dale Murphy	.20
80	Mitch Williams	.05
81	Jay Bell	.05
82	Barry Bonds	1.00
83	Steve Buechele	.05
84	Doug Drabek	.05
85	Mike LaValliere	.05
86	Jose Lind	.05
87	Denny Neagle	.05
88	Randy Tomlin	.05
89	Andy Van Slyke	.05
90	Gary Varsho	.05
91	Pedro Guerrero	.05
92	Rex Hudler	.05
93	Brian Jordan	.05
94	Felix Jose	.05
95	Donovan Osborne	.05
96	Tom Pagnozzi	.05
97	Lee Smith	.05
98	Ozzie Smith	.50
99	Todd Worrell	.05
100	Todd Zeile	.05
101	Andy Benes	.05
102	Jerald Clark	.05
103	Tony Fernandez	.05
104	Tony Gwynn	.50
105	Greg Harris	.05
106	Fred McGriff	.05
107	Benito Santiago	.05
108	Gary Sheffield	.30
109	Kurt Stillwell	.05
110	Tim Teufel	.05
111	Kevin Bass	.05
112	Jeff Brantley	.05
113	John Burkett	.05
114	Will Clark	.05
115	Royce Clayton	.05
116	Mike Jackson	.05
117	Darren Lewis	.05
118	Bill Swift	.05
119	Robby Thompson	.05
120	Matt Williams	.05
121	Brady Anderson	.05
122	Glenn Davis	.05
123	Mike Devereaux	.05
124	Chris Hoiles	.05
125	Sam Horn	.05
126	Ben McDonald	.05
127	Mike Mussina	.25
128	Gregg Olson	.05
129	Cal Ripken, Jr.	1.00
130	Rick Sutcliffe	.05
131	Wade Boggs	.50
132	Roger Clemens	.60
133	Greg Harris	.05
134	Tim Naehring	.05
135	Tony Pena	.05
136	Phil Plantier	.05
137	Jeff Reardon	.05
138	Jody Reed	.05
139	Mo Vaughn	.05
140	Frank Viola	.05
141	Jim Abbott	.05
142	Hubie Brooks	.05
143	Chad Curtis **RC**	.05
144	Gary DiSarcina	.05
145	Chuck Finley	.05
146	Bryan Harvey	.05
147	Von Hayes	.05
148	Mark Langston	.05
149	Lance Parrish	.05
150	Lee Stevens	.05
151	George Bell	.05
152	Alex Fernandez	.05
153	Greg Hibbard	.05
154	Lance Johnson	.05
155	Kirk McCaskill	.05
156	Tim Raines	.05
157	Steve Sax	.05
158	Bobby Thigpen	.05
159	Frank Thomas	.45
160	Robin Ventura	.05
161	Sandy Alomar, Jr.	.05
162	Jack Armstrong	.05
163	Carlos Baerga	.05
164	Albert Belle	.05
165	Alex Cole	.05
166	Glenallen Hill	.05
167	Mark Lewis	.05
168	Kenny Lofton	.05
169	Paul Sorrento	.05
170	Mark Whiten	.05
171	Milt Cuyler (Color photo is Lou Whitaker.)	.05
172	Rob Deer	.05
173	Cecil Fielder	.05
174	Travis Fryman	.05
175	Mike Henneman	.05
176	Tony Phillips	.05
177	Frank Tanana	.05
178	Mickey Tettleton	.05
179	Alan Trammell	.05
180	Lou Whitaker	.05
181	George Brett	.60
182	Tom Gordon	.05
183	Mark Gubicza	.05
184	Gregg Jefferies	.05
185	Wally Joyner	.05
186	Brent Mayne	.05
187	Brian McRae	.05
188	Kevin McReynolds	.05
189	Keith Miller	.05
190	Jeff Montgomery	.05
191	Dante Bichette	.05
192	Ricky Bones	.05
193	Scott Fletcher	.05
194	Paul Molitor	.45
195	Jaime Navarro	.05
196	Franklin Stubbs	.05
197	B.J. Surhoff	.05
198	Greg Vaughn	.05
199	Bill Wegman	.05
200	Robin Yount	.45
201	Rick Aguilera	.05
202	Scott Erickson	.05
203	Greg Gagne	.05
204	Brian Harper	.05
205	Kent Hrbek	.05
206	Scott Leius	.05
207	Shane Mack	.05
208	Pat Mahomes	.05
209	Kirby Puckett	.50
210	John Smiley	.05
211	Mike Gallego	.05
212	Charlie Hayes	.05
213	Pat Kelly	.05
214	Roberto Kelly	.05
215	Kevin Maas	.05
216	Don Mattingly	.60
217	Matt Nokes	.05
218	Melido Perez	.05
219	Scott Sanderson	.05
220	Danny Tartabull	.05
221	Harold Baines	.05
222	Jose Canseco	.30
223	Dennis Eckersley	.35
224	Dave Henderson	.05
225	Carney Lansford	.05
226	Mark McGwire	.75
227	Mike Moore	.05
228	Randy Ready	.05
229	Terry Steinbach	.05
230	Dave Stewart	.05
231	Jay Buhner	.05
232	Ken Griffey Jr.	.65
233	Erik Hanson	.05
234	Randy Johnson	.45
235	Edgar Martinez	.05
236	Tino Martinez	.05
237	Kevin Mitchell	.05
238	Pete O'Brien	.05
239	Harold Reynolds	.05
240	David Valle	.05
241	Julio Franco	.05
242	Juan Gonzalez	.25
243	Jose Guzman	.05
244	Rafael Palmeiro	.35
245	Dean Palmer	.05
246	Ivan Rodriguez	.35
247	Jeff Russell	.05
248	Nolan Ryan	1.00
249	Ruben Sierra	.05
250	Dickie Thon	.05
251	Roberto Alomar	.20
252	Derek Bell	.05
253	Pat Borders	.05
254	Joe Carter	.05
255	Kelly Gruber	.05
256	Juan Guzman	.05
257	Jack Morris	.05
258	John Olerud	.05
259	Devon White	.05
260	Dave Winfield	.45
261	Checklist	.05
262	Checklist	.05
263	Checklist	.05
264	History Card	.05

Heritage

Superstars of 1992 were photographed in vintage-style uniforms in this 14-card insert set found in packages of Studio's 1992 issue. Cards #1-8 could be found in standard foil packs while #9-14 were inserted in Studio jumbos. Cards featured a sepia-tone photo bordered in turquoise

and highlighted with copper foil. Cards carry a "BC" prefix to the card number on back.

		NM/M
Complete Set (14):		6.00
Common Player:		.50
1	Ryne Sandberg	1.00
2	Carlton Fisk	.75
3	Wade Boggs	1.00
4	Jose Canseco	.65
5	Don Mattingly	1.25
6	Darryl Strawberry	.50
7	Cal Ripken, Jr.	1.50
8	Will Clark	.50
9	Andre Dawson	.50
10	Andy Van Slyke	.50
11	Paul Molitor	.75
12	Jeff Bagwell	.75
13	Darren Daulton	.50
14	Kirby Puckett	1.00

1993 Studio Promos

Though unmarked as such, a pair of promo cards was produced in advance of '93 Studio. At first glance the cards appear identical to the same players' issued versions, but there are noticeable cropping differences. On the back of the Thomas card, the promo has a smaller projection of his face, with much more of his hair showing at top and the last line of type about even with the bottom of his nose. The issued card shows almost no hair at top and has the last line even with his top lip. The Sandberg cropping difference appears on front. On the promo his right ear is well clear of the left border; on the issued version his ear touches the border.

		NM/M
Complete Set (2):		6.00
Common Player:		2.00
139	Frank Thomas	2.00
176	Ryne Sandberg	5.00

1993 Studio

This 220-card set features full-bleed photos. The player's portrait appears against one of several backgrounds featuring his team's uniform. His signature and the Studio logo are printed in gold foil. Backs have an extreme closeup partial portrait of the player and insights into his personality.

		NM/M
Complete Set (220):		15.00
Common Player:		.05
Pack (12):		.75
Wax Box (36):		12.50
1	Dennis Eckersley	.35
2	Chad Curtis	.05
3	Eric Anthony	.05
4	Roberto Alomar	.20
5	Steve Avery	.05
6	Cal Eldred	.05
7	Bernard Gilkey	.05
8	Steve Buechele	.05
9	Brett Butler	.05
10	Terry Mulholland	.05
11	Moises Alou	.05
12	Barry Bonds	1.00
13	Sandy Alomar Jr.	.05
14	Chris Bosio	.05
15	Scott Sanderson	.05
16	Bobby Bonilla	.05
17	Brady Anderson	.05
18	Derek Bell	.05
19	Wes Chamberlain	.05
20	Jay Bell	.05
21	Kevin Brown	.05
22	Roger Clemens	.60
23	Roberto Kelly	.05
24	Dante Bichette	.05
25	George Brett	.60
26	Rob Deer	.05
27	Brian Harper	.05
28	George Bell	.05
29	Jim Abbott	.05
30	Dave Henderson	.05
31	Wade Boggs	.50
32	Chili Davis	.05
33	Ellis Burks	.05
34	Jeff Bagwell	.40
35	Kent Hrbek	.05
36	Pat Borders	.05
37	Cecil Fielder	.05
38	Sid Bream	.05
39	Greg Gagne	.05
40	Darryl Hamilton	.05
41	Jerald Clark	.05
42	Mark Grace	.05
43	Barry Larkin	.05
44	John Burkett	.05
45	Scott Cooper	.05
46	Mike Lansing **RC**	.25
47	Jose Canseco	.30
48	Will Clark	.05
49	Carlos Garcia	.05
50	Carlos Baerga	.05
51	Darren Daulton	.05
52	Jay Buhner	.05
53	Andy Benes	.05
54	Jeff Conine	.05
55	Mike Devereaux	.05
56	Vince Coleman	.05
57	Terry Steinbach	.05
58	J.T. Snow **RC**	.40
59	Greg Swindell	.05
60	Devon White	.05
61	John Smoltz	.05
62	Todd Zeile	.05
63	Rick Wilkins	.05
64	Tim Wallach	.05
65	John Wetteland	.05
66	Matt Williams	.05
67	Paul Sorrento	.05
68	David Valle	.05
69	Walt Weiss	.05
70	John Franco	.05
71	Nolan Ryan	1.00
72	Frank Viola	.05
73	Chris Sabo	.05
74	David Nied	.05
75	Kevin McReynolds	.05
76	Lou Whitaker	.05
77	Dave Winfield	.40
78	Robin Ventura	.05
79	Spike Owen	.05
80	Cal Ripken, Jr.	1.00
81	Dan Walter	.05
82	Mitch Williams	.05
83	Tim Wakefield	.05
84	Rickey Henderson	.40
85	Gary DiSarcina	.05
86	Craig Biggio	.05
87	Joe Carter	.05
88	Ron Gant	.05
89	John Jaha	.05
90	Gregg Jefferies	.05
91	Jose Guzman	.05
92	Eric Karros	.05
93	Wil Cordero	.05
94	Royce Clayton	.05
95	Albert Belle	.05
96	Ken Griffey Jr.	.65
97	Orestes Destrade	.05
98	Tony Fernandez	.05
99	Leo Gomez	.05
100	Tony Gwynn	.50
101	Len Dykstra	.05
102	Jeff King	.05
103	Julio Franco	.05
104	Andre Dawson	.25
105	Randy Milligan	.05
106	Alex Cole	.05
107	Phil Hiatt	.05
108	Travis Fryman	.05
109	Chuck Knoblauch	.05
110	Bo Jackson	.10
111	Pat Kelly	.05
112	Bret Saberhagen	.05
113	Ruben Sierra	.05
114	Tim Salmon	.05
115	Doug Jones	.05
116	Ed Sprague	.05
117	Terry Pendleton	.05
118	Robin Yount	.40
119	Mark Whiten	.05
120	Checklist	.05
121	Sammy Sosa	.50
122	Darryl Strawberry	.05
123	Larry Walker	.05
124	Robby Thompson	.05
125	Carlos Martinez	.05
126	Edgar Martinez	.05
127	Benito Santiago	.05
128	Howard Johnson	.05
129	Harold Reynolds	.05
130	Craig Shipley	.05
131	Curt Schilling	.30
132	Andy Van Slyke	.05
133	Ivan Rodriguez	.35
134	Mo Vaughn	.05
135	Bip Roberts	.05
136	Charlie Hayes	.05
137	Brian McRae	.05
138	Mickey Tettleton	.05
139	Frank Thomas	.40
140	Paul O'Neill	.05
141	Mark McGwire	.75
142	Damion Easley	.05
143	Ken Caminiti	.05
144	Juan Guzman	.05
145	Tom Glavine	.25
146	Pat Listach	.05
147	Lee Smith	.05
148	Derrick May	.05
149	Ramon Martinez	.05
150	Delino DeShields	.05
151	Kirt Manwaring	.05
152	Reggie Jefferson	.05
153	Randy Johnson	.40
154	Dave Magadan	.05
155	Dwight Gooden	.05
156	Chris Hoiles	.05
157	Fred McGriff	.05
158	Dave Hollins	.05
159	Al Martin	.05
160	Juan Gonzalez	.20
161	Mike Greenwell	.05
162	Kevin Mitchell	.05
163	Andres Galarraga	.05
164	Wally Joyner	.05
165	Kirk Gibson	.05
166	Pedro Munoz	.05
167	Ozzie Guillen	.05
168	Jimmy Key	.05
169	Kevin Seitzer	.05
170	Luis Polonia	.05
171	Luis Gonzalez	.05
172	Paul Molitor	.40
173	Dave Justice	.05
174	B.J. Surhoff	.05
175	Ray Lankford	.05
176	Ryne Sandberg	.50
177	Jody Reed	.05
178	Marquis Grissom	.05
179	Willie McGee	.05
180	Kenny Lofton	.05
181	Junior Felix	.05
182	Jose Offerman	.05
183	John Kruk	.05
184	Orlando Merced	.05
185	Rafael Palmeiro	.35
186	Billy Hatcher	.05
187	Joe Oliver	.05
188	Joe Girardi	.05
189	Jose Lind	.05
190	Harold Baines	.05
191	Mike Pagliarulo	.05
192	Lance Johnson	.05
193	Don Mattingly	.60
194	Doug Drabek	.05
195	John Olerud	.05
196	Greg Maddux	.50
197	Greg Vaughn	.05
198	Tom Pagnozzi	.05
199	Willie Wilson	.05
200	Jack McDowell	.05
201	Mike Piazza	.65
202	Mike Mussina	.30
203	Charles Nagy	.05
204	Tino Martinez	.05
205	Charlie Hough	.05
206	Todd Hundley	.05
207	Gary Sheffield	.30
208	Mickey Morandini	.05
209	Don Slaught	.05
210	Dean Palmer	.05
211	Jose Rijo	.05
212	Vinny Castilla	.05
213	Tony Phillips	.05
214	Kirby Puckett	.50
215	Tim Raines	.05
216	Otis Nixon	.05
217	Ozzie Smith	.50
218	Jose Vizcaino	.05
219	Randy Tomlin	.05
220	Checklist	.05

Heritage

All types of 1993 Leaf Studio packs were candidates for having one of 12 Heritage cards inserted in them. The fronts feature the player posing in an old-time uniform, framed in turquoise with copper highlights. The backs have a mug shot surrounded by an ornate frame and describe the uniform on the front. Team trivia is also included.

	NM/M
Complete Set (12):	12.00

Common Player:		.50
1	George Brett	2.00
2	Juan Gonzalez	.75
3	Roger Clemens	2.00
4	Mark McGwire	4.00
5	Mark Grace	.50
6	Ozzie Smith	1.50
7	Barry Larkin	.50
8	Frank Thomas	1.00
9	Carlos Baerga	.50
10	Eric Karros	.50
11	J.T. Snow	.50
12	John Kruk	.50

Silhouettes

These insert cards were randomly included in jumbo packs only. The card fronts feature a ghosted image of the player against an action silhouette on a gray background. The player's name is in bronze foil at bottom. Backs have a player action photo and description of career highlights.

		NM/M
Complete Set (10):		7.00
Common Player:		.15
1	Frank Thomas	.65
2	Barry Bonds	3.00
3	Jeff Bagwell	.65
4	Juan Gonzalez	.40
5	Travis Fryman	.15
6	J.T. Snow	.15
7	John Kruk	.15
8	Jeff Blauser	.15
9	Mike Piazza	2.00
10	Nolan Ryan	3.00

Superstars on Canvas

Ten players are featured on these insert cards, which were available in hobby and retail packs. The cards show player portraits which mix photography and artwork.

		NM/M
Complete Set (10):		8.00
Common Player:		.25
1	Ken Griffey Jr.	1.50
2	Jose Canseco	.60
3	Mark McGwire	2.00
4	Mike Mussina	.50
5	Joe Carter	.25
6	Frank Thomas	1.00
7	Darren Daulton	.25
8	Mark Grace	.25
9	Andres Galarraga	.25
10	Barry Bonds	2.50

Frank Thomas

This five-card set is devoted to Frank Thomas. Cards were randomly included in all types of 1993 Leaf Studio packs. Topics covered on the cards include Thomas' childhood, his baseball memories, his family, his performance and being a role model.

		NM/M
Complete Set (5):		5.00
Common Card:		1.00
1	Childhood	1.00
2	Baseball Memories	1.00
3	Importance of Family	1.00
4	Performance	1.00
5	On Being a Role Model	1.00

1994 Studio Samples

To introduce its "locker-room look" issue for 1994, Leaf's Studio brand produced this three-star sample set and distributed it to its hobby dealer network. The cards are basically the same as the regular-issue cards of those players except for the addition of a "Promotional Sample" overprinted diagonally on front and back. The "Up Close" biographies on the cards' backs are different between the promos and the regular cards and there is a slight difference in front photo cropping on the Gonzalez card.

		NM/M
Complete Set (3):		6.00
83	Barry Bonds	3.00
154	Juan Gonzalez	1.00
209	Frank Thomas	2.00

1994 Studio

Studio baseball from Donruss returned in mid-August, 1994, with a three-time MVP spokesman, several jazzy and short-printed inserts subsets and a reduced overall production figure that represents a sharp drop from 1993. Barry Bonds is the MVP whose mug adorns Studio counter boxes and advertisements. According to Donruss officials, production was limited to 8,000 cases of 20 boxes each, which represents a

35 percent decrease from 1993 and works out to about 315,000 of each card. Only 2,000 cases were earmarked for retail distribution and no jumbo packs were produced. Studio 1994 features 220 cards issued in one series, once again with close-up personal portraits of the top stars in the game. Each card is foil-stamped with a borderless design and UV coating front and back. The front of the card features the player in the foreground with his locker in the background. As in the previous three Studio offerings, the backs of the cards contain personal information about the players.

		NM/M
Complete Set (220):		7.50
Common Player:		.05
Pack (12):		.45
Wax Box (36):		10.00
1	Dennis Eckersley	.45
2	Brent Gates	.05
3	Rickey Henderson	.55
4	Mark McGwire	1.00
5	Troy Neel	.05
6	Ruben Sierra	.05
7	Terry Steinbach	.05
8	Chad Curtis	.05
9	Chili Davis	.05
10	Gary DiSarcina	.05
11	Damion Easley	.05
12	Bo Jackson	.10
13	Mark Langston	.05
14	Eduardo Perez	.05
15	Tim Salmon	.05
16	Jeff Bagwell	.55
17	Craig Biggio	.05
18	Ken Caminiti	.05
19	Andujar Cedeno	.05
20	Doug Drabek	.05
21	Steve Finley	.05
22	Luis Gonzalez	.05
23	Darryl Kile	.05
24	Roberto Alomar	.20
25	Pat Borders	.05
26	Joe Carter	.05
27	Carlos Delgado	.40
28	Pat Hentgen	.05
29	Paul Molitor	.55
30	John Olerud	.05
31	Ed Sprague	.05
32	Devon White	.05
33	Steve Avery	.05
34	Tom Glavine	.25
35	David Justice	.05
36	Roberto Kelly	.05
37	Ryan Klesko	.05
38	Javier Lopez	.05
39	Greg Maddux	.60
40	Fred McGriff	.05
41	Terry Pendleton	.05
42	Ricky Bones	.05
43	Darryl Hamilton	.05
44	Brian Harper	.05
45	John Jaha	.05
46	Dave Nilsson	.05
47	Kevin Seitzer	.05
48	Greg Vaughn	.05
49	Turner Ward	.05
50	Bernard Gilkey	.05
51	Gregg Jefferies	.05
52	Ray Lankford	.05
53	Tom Pagnozzi	.05
54	Ozzie Smith	.60
55	Bob Tewksbury	.05
56	Mark Whiten	.05
57	Todd Zeile	.05
58	Steve Buechele	.05
59	Shawon Dunston	.05
60	Mark Grace	.05
61	Derrick May	.05
62	Tuffy Rhodes	.05
63	Ryne Sandberg	.60
64	Sammy Sosa	.60
65	Rick Wilkins	.05
66	Brett Butler	.05
67	Delino DeShields	.05
68	Orel Hershiser	.05
69	Eric Karros	.05
70	Raul Mondesi	.05
71	Jose Offerman	.05
72	Mike Piazza	.75
73	Tim Wallach	.05
74	Moises Alou	.05
75	Sean Berry	.05
76	Wil Cordero	.05
77	Cliff Floyd	.05
78	Marquis Grissom	.05
79	Ken Hill	.05
80	Larry Walker	.05
81	John Wetteland	.05
82	Rod Beck	.05
83	Barry Bonds	1.50
84	Royce Clayton	.05
85	Darren Lewis	.05
86	Willie McGee	.05
87	Bill Swift	.05
88	Robby Thompson	.05
89	Matt Williams	.05
90	Sandy Alomar Jr.	.05
91	Carlos Baerga	.05
92	Albert Belle	.05
93	Kenny Lofton	.05
94	Eddie Murray	.55
95	Manny Ramirez	.55
96	Paul Sorrento	.05
97	Jim Thome	.45
98	Rich Amaral	.05
99	Eric Anthony	.05
100	Jay Buhner	.05
101	Ken Griffey Jr.	.75
102	Randy Johnson	.55
103	Edgar Martinez	.05
104	Tino Martinez	.05
105	Kurt Abbott **RC**	.05
106	Bret Barberie	.05
107	Chuck Carr	.05
108	Jeff Conine	.05
109	Chris Hammond	.05
110	Bryan Harvey	.05
111	Benito Santiago	.05
112	Gary Sheffield	.30
113	Bobby Bonilla	.05
114	Dwight Gooden	.05
115	Todd Hundley	.05
116	Bobby Jones	.05
117	Jeff Kent	.05
118	Kevin McReynolds	.05
119	Bret Saberhagen	.05
120	Ryan Thompson	.05
121	Harold Baines	.05
122	Mike Devereaux	.05
123	Jeffrey Hammonds	.05
124	Ben McDonald	.05
125	Mike Mussina	.25
126	Rafael Palmeiro	.45
127	Cal Ripken, Jr.	1.50
128	Lee Smith	.05
129	Brad Ausmus	.05
130	Derek Bell	.05
131	Andy Benes	.05
132	Tony Gwynn	.60
133	Trevor Hoffman	.05
134	Scott Livingstone	.05
135	Phil Plantier	.05
136	Darren Daulton	.05
137	Mariano Duncan	.05
138	Len Dykstra	.05
139	Dave Hollins	.05
140	Pete Incaviglia	.05
141	Danny Jackson	.05
142	John Kruk	.05
143	Kevin Stocker	.05
144	Jay Bell	.05
145	Carlos Garcia	.05
146	Jeff King	.05
147	Al Martin	.05
148	Orlando Merced	.05
149	Don Slaught	.05
150	Andy Van Slyke	.05
151	Kevin Brown	.05
152	Jose Canseco	.40
153	Will Clark	.05
154	Juan Gonzalez	.30
155	David Hulse	.05
156	Dean Palmer	.05
157	Ivan Rodriguez	.45
158	Kenny Rogers	.05
159	Roger Clemens	.65
160	Scott Cooper	.05
161	Andre Dawson	.25
162	Mike Greenwell	.05
163	Otis Nixon	.05
164	Aaron Sele	.05
165	John Valentin	.05
166	Mo Vaughn	.05
167	Bret Boone	.05
168	Barry Larkin	.05
169	Kevin Mitchell	.05
170	Hal Morris	.05
171	Jose Rijo	.05
172	Deion Sanders	.05
173	Reggie Sanders	.05
174	John Smiley	.05
175	Dante Bichette	.05
176	Ellis Burks	.05
177	Andres Galarraga	.05
178	Joe Girardi	.05
179	Charlie Hayes	.05
180	Roberto Mejia	.05
181	Walt Weiss	.05
182	David Cone	.05
183	Gary Gaetti	.05
184	Greg Gagne	.05
185	Felix Jose	.05
186	Wally Joyner	.05
187	Mike Macfarlane	.05
188	Brian McRae	.05
189	Eric Davis	.05
190	Cecil Fielder	.05
191	Travis Fryman	.05
192	Tony Phillips	.05
193	Mickey Tettleton	.05
194	Alan Trammell	.05
195	Lou Whitaker	.05
196	Kent Hrbek	.05
197	Chuck Knoblauch	.05
198	Shane Mack	.05
199	Pat Meares	.05
200	Kirby Puckett	.60
201	Matt Walbeck	.05
202	Dave Winfield	.55
203	Wilson Alvarez	.05
204	Alex Fernandez	.05
205	Julio Franco	.05
206	Ozzie Guillen	.05
207	Jack McDowell	.05
208	Tim Raines	.05
209	Frank Thomas	.55
210	Robin Ventura	.05
211	Jim Abbott	.05
212	Wade Boggs	.60
213	Pat Kelly	.05
214	Jimmy Key	.05
215	Don Mattingly	.65
216	Paul O'Neill	.05
217	Mike Stanley	.05
218	Danny Tartabull	.05
219	Checklist	.05
220	Checklist	.05

Editor's Choice

Printed in similitude to a strip of color slide film, each of the cards in this insert set feature a complete player photo at center, with partial "frames" at top and bottom. Printed on acetate, the back of the card shows a reversed image of the front. Stated odds of finding an Editor's Choice insert card are about one per box of 36 packs.

		NM/M
Complete Set (8):		12.00
Common Player:		.50
1	Barry Bonds	3.00
2	Frank Thomas	1.50
3	Ken Griffey Jr.	2.50
4	Andres Galarraga	.50
5	Juan Gonzalez	.75
6	Tim Salmon	.50
7	Paul O'Neill	.50
8	Mike Piazza	2.50

Heritage

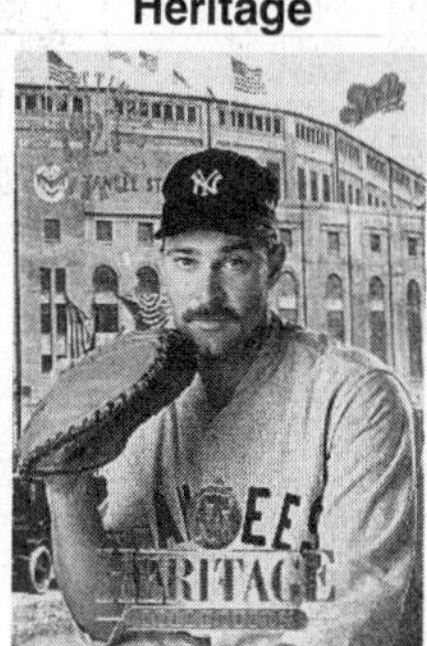

Besides picturing today's players in vintage uniforms, the 1994 Studio Heritage inserts have the player portraits set against sepia-toned photos of old ballparks. Fronts are enhanced by copper-foil logos and by a round device at upper-left containing the player's name, team and year represented. Backs have a second color player photo and a short write-up about the team represented. Unlike the other cards in the set, the Heritage cards are printed on a porous cardboard stock to enhance the image of antiquity. Stated odds of finding a Heritage Collection insert card are one in nine packs.

		NM/M
Complete Set (8):		9.00
Common Player:		.50
1	Barry Bonds	4.00
2	Frank Thomas	1.50
3	Joe Carter	.50
4	Don Mattingly	3.00
5	Ryne Sandberg	2.00
6	Javier Lopez	.50
7	Gregg Jefferies	.50
8	Mike Mussina	.65

Silver Stars

Each of the 10 players in this insert set was produced in an edition of 10,000 cards. Printed on acetate, fronts feature action photos set against a clear plastic background with a silver-foil seal at bottom. Within the player silhouette on back, a second photo is printed. The back also features a black-and-white version of the seal, including the card's unique serial number. Stated odds of picking a Silver Series Star are one per 60 packs, on average.

		NM/M
Complete Set (10):		35.00
Common Player:		1.50
1	Tony Gwynn	3.50
2	Barry Bonds	7.50
3	Frank Thomas	2.50
4	Ken Griffey Jr.	4.50
5	Joe Carter	1.50
6	Mike Piazza	4.50
7	Cal Ripken, Jr.	7.50
8	Greg Maddux	3.50
9	Juan Gonzalez	2.00
10	Don Mattingly	4.00

Gold Stars

The scarcest of the 1994 Studio chase cards, only 5,000 cards of each of the 10 players were produced. Printed on acetate, fronts feature an action photo set against a clear plastic background. At bottom is a large gold-foil seal. Backs have another player photo, within the silhouette of the front photo, and a black-and-white version of the seal, including the card's unique serial number. According to the series wrapper, odds of finding a Gold Series Star card are one in 120 packs.

		NM/M
Complete Set (10):		80.00

Common Player: 4.50
1 Tony Gwynn 9.00
2 Barry Bonds 16.00
3 Frank Thomas 7.50
4 Ken Griffey Jr. 12.50
5 Joe Carter 4.50
6 Mike Piazza 12.50
7 Cal Ripken, Jr. 16.00
8 Greg Maddux 9.00
9 Juan Gonzalez 5.00
10 Don Mattingly 10.00

1995 Studio

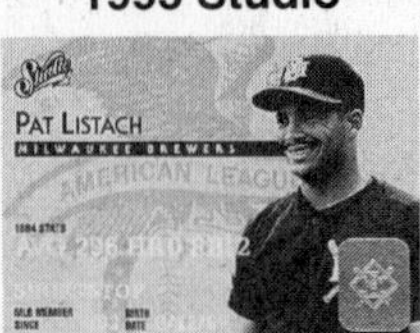

Known since its inception as a brand name for its innovative design, Studio did not disappoint in 1995, unveiling a baseball card with a credit card look. In horizontal format the cards feature embossed stats and data on front, plus a team logo hologram. Backs have a color player photo, facsimile autograph and simulated magnetic data strip to carry through the credit card impression.

NM/M
Complete Set (200): 25.00
Common Player: .05
Pack (5): 1.00
Wax Box (36): 20.00
1 Frank Thomas .75
2 Jeff Bagwell .75
3 Don Mattingly 1.25
4 Mike Piazza 1.50
5 Ken Griffey Jr. 1.50
6 Greg Maddux 1.00
7 Barry Bonds 2.50
8 Cal Ripken Jr. 2.50
9 Jose Canseco .40
10 Paul Molitor .75
11 Kenny Lofton .05
12 Will Clark .05
13 Tim Salmon .05
14 Joe Carter .05
15 Albert Belle .05
16 Roger Clemens 1.25
17 Roberto Alomar .30
18 Alex Rodriguez 2.00
19 Raul Mondesi .05
20 Deion Sanders .05
21 Juan Gonzalez .40
22 Kirby Puckett 1.00
23 Fred McGriff .05
24 Matt Williams .05
25 Tony Gwynn 1.00
26 Cliff Floyd .05
27 Travis Fryman .05
28 Shawn Green .30
29 Mike Mussina .35
30 Bob Hamelin .05
31 Dave Justice .05
32 Manny Ramirez .75
33 David Cone .05
34 Marquis Grissom .05
35 Moises Alou .05
36 Carlos Baerga .05
37 Barry Larkin .05
38 Robin Ventura .05
39 Mo Vaughn .05
40 Jeffrey Hammonds .05
41 Ozzie Smith 1.00
42 Andres Galarraga .05
43 Carlos Delgado .50
44 Lenny Dykstra .05
45 Cecil Fielder .05
46 Wade Boggs 1.00
47 Gregg Jefferies .05
48 Randy Johnson .75
49 Rafael Palmeiro .65
50 Craig Biggio .05
51 Steve Avery .05
52 Ricky Bottalico .05
53 Chris Gomez .05
54 Carlos Garcia .05
55 Brian Anderson .05
56 Wilson Alvarez .05
57 Roberto Kelly .05
58 Larry Walker .05
59 Dean Palmer .05
60 Rick Aguilera .05
61 Javy Lopez .05
62 Shawon Dunston .05
63 William Van Landingham .05
64 Jeff Kent .05
65 David McCarty .05
66 Armando Benitez .05
67 Brett Butler .05
68 Bernard Gilkey .05
69 Joey Hamilton .05
70 Chad Curtis .05
71 Dante Bichette .05
72 Chuck Carr .05
73 Pedro Martinez .75
74 Ramon Martinez .05
75 Rondell White .05
76 Alex Fernandez .05
77 Dennis Martinez .05
78 Sammy Sosa 1.00
79 Bernie Williams .05
80 Lou Whitaker .05
81 Kurt Abbott .05
82 Tino Martinez .05
83 Willie Greene .05
84 Garret Anderson .05
85 Jose Rijo .05
86 Jeff Montgomery .05
87 Mark Langston .05
88 Reggie Sanders .05
89 Rusty Greer .05
90 Delino DeShields .05
91 Jason Bere .05
92 Lee Smith .05
93 Devon White .05
94 John Wetteland .05
95 Luis Gonzalez .05
96 Greg Vaughn .05
97 Lance Johnson .05
98 Alan Trammell .05
99 Bret Saberhagen .05
100 Jack McDowell .05
101 Trevor Hoffman .05
102 Dave Nilsson .05
103 Bryan Harvey .05
104 Chuck Knoblauch .05
105 Bobby Bonilla .05
106 Hal Morris .05
107 Mark Whiten .05
108 Phil Plantier .05
109 Ryan Klesko .05
110 Greg Gagne .05
111 Ruben Sierra .05
112 J.R. Phillips .05
113 Terry Steinbach .05
114 Jay Buhner .05
115 Ken Caminiti .05
116 Gary DiSarcina .05
117 Ivan Rodriguez .65
118 Bip Roberts .05
119 Jay Bell .05
120 Ken Hill .05
121 Mike Greenwell .05
122 Rick Wilkins .05
123 Rickey Henderson .75
124 Dave Hollins .05
125 Terry Pendleton .05
126 Rich Becker .05
127 Billy Ashley .05
128 Derek Bell .05
129 Dennis Eckersley .65
130 Andujar Cedeno .05
131 John Jaha .05
132 Chuck Finley .05
133 Steve Finley .05
134 Danny Tartabull .05
135 Jeff Conine .05
136 Jon Lieber .05
137 Jim Abbott .05
138 Steve Traschel .05
139 Bret Boone .05
140 Charles Johnson .05
141 Mark McGwire 2.00
142 Eddie Murray .75
143 Doug Drabek .05
144 Steve Cooke .05
145 Kevin Seitzer .05
146 Rod Beck .05
147 Eric Karros .05
148 Tim Raines .05
149 Joe Girardi .05
150 Aaron Sele .05
151 Robby Thompson .05
152 Chan Ho Park .05
153 Ellis Burks .05
154 Brian McRae .05
155 Jimmy Key .05
156 Rico Brogna .05
157 Ozzie Guillen .05
158 Chili Davis .05
159 Darren Daulton .05
160 Chipper Jones 1.00
161 Walt Weiss .05
162 Paul O'Neill .05
163 Al Martin .05
164 John Valentin .05
165 Tim Wallach .05
166 Scott Erickson .05
167 Ryan Thompson .05
168 Todd Zeile .05
169 Scott Cooper .05
170 Matt Mieske .05
171 Allen Watson .05
172 Brian Hunter .05
173 Kevin Stocker .05
174 Cal Eldred .05
175 Tony Phillips .05
176 Ben McDonald .05
177 Mark Grace .05
178 Midre Cummings .05
179 Orlando Merced .05
180 Jeff King .05
181 Gary Sheffield .40
182 Tom Glavine .35
183 Edgar Martinez .05
184 Steve Karsay .05
185 Pat Listach .05
186 Wil Cordero .05
187 Brady Anderson .05
188 Bobby Jones .05
189 Andy Benes .05
190 Ray Lankford .05
191 John Doherty .05
192 Wally Joyner .05
193 Jim Thome .65
194 Royce Clayton .05
195 John Olerud .05
196 Steve Buechele .05
197 Harold Baines .05
198 Geronimo Berroa .05
199 Checklist .05
200 Checklist .05

Gold

The chase cards in 1995 Studio are plastic versions of some of the regular cards. The round-cornered plastic format of the inserts gives them an even greater similitude to credit cards. The first 50 numbers in the regular set are reproduced in a parallel Studio Gold plastic version, found one per pack, except for those packs which have a platinum card.

NM/M
Complete Set (50): 25.00
Common Player: .15
1 Frank Thomas 1.00
2 Jeff Bagwell 1.00
3 Don Mattingly 1.75
4 Mike Piazza 2.00
5 Ken Griffey Jr. 2.00
6 Greg Maddux 1.50
7 Barry Bonds 3.00
8 Cal Ripken Jr. 3.00
9 Jose Canseco .50
10 Paul Molitor 1.00
11 Kenny Lofton .15
12 Will Clark .15
13 Tim Salmon .15
14 Joe Carter .15
15 Albert Belle .15
16 Roger Clemens 1.75
17 Roberto Alomar .35
18 Alex Rodriguez 2.50
19 Raul Mondesi .15
20 Deion Sanders .15
21 Juan Gonzalez .50
22 Kirby Puckett 1.50
23 Fred McGriff .15
24 Matt Williams .15
25 Tony Gwynn 1.50
26 Cliff Floyd .15
27 Travis Fryman .15
28 Shawn Green .40
29 Mike Mussina .35
30 Bob Hamelin .15
31 Dave Justice .15
32 Manny Ramirez 1.00
33 David Cone .15
34 Marquis Grissom .15
35 Moises Alou .15
36 Carlos Baerga .15
37 Barry Larkin .15
38 Robin Ventura .15
39 Mo Vaughn .15
40 Jeffrey Hammonds .15
41 Ozzie Smith 1.50
42 Andres Galarraga .15
43 Carlos Delgado .50
44 Lenny Dykstra .15
45 Cecil Fielder .15
46 Wade Boggs 1.50
47 Gregg Jefferies .15
48 Randy Johnson 1.00
49 Rafael Palmeiro .75
50 Craig Biggio .15

Platinum

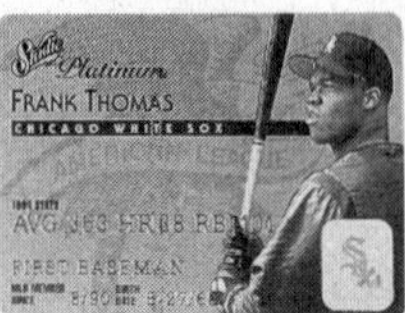

Found at the rate of one per 10 packs, Studio Platinum cards are silver-toned plastic versions of the first 25 cards from the regular set.

NM/M
Complete Set (25): 25.00
Common Player: .50
1 Frank Thomas 2.00
2 Jeff Bagwell 2.00
3 Don Mattingly 3.25
4 Mike Piazza 3.50
5 Ken Griffey Jr. 3.50
6 Greg Maddux 3.00
7 Barry Bonds 5.00
8 Cal Ripken Jr. 5.00
9 Jose Canseco 1.00
10 Paul Molitor 2.00
11 Kenny Lofton .50
12 Will Clark .50
13 Tim Salmon .50
14 Joe Carter .50
15 Albert Belle .50
16 Roger Clemens 3.25
17 Roberto Alomar .75
18 Alex Rodriguez 4.00
19 Raul Mondesi .50
20 Deion Sanders .50
21 Juan Gonzalez 1.00
22 Kirby Puckett 3.00
23 Fred McGriff .50
24 Matt Williams .50
25 Tony Gwynn 3.00

1996 Studio

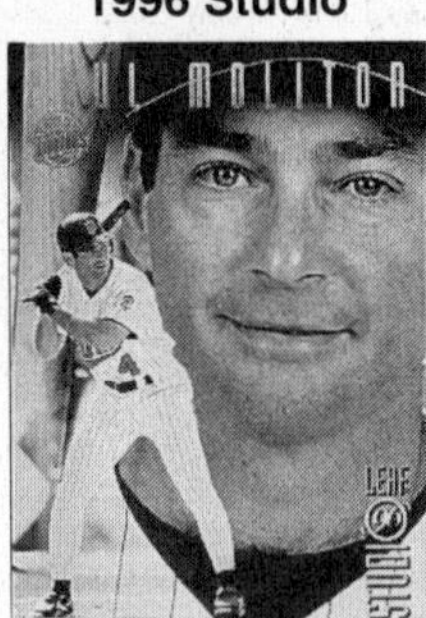

The 1996 Studio set is the first Donruss product to be released under the Pinnacle Brands flagship. The 150-card set has three parallel sets - Bronze Press Proofs (2,000 sets), Silver Press Proofs (found only in magazine packs, 100 sets), and Gold Press Proofs (500 sets). Three insert sets were also made - Hit Parade, Masterstrokes and Stained Glass Stars.

NM/M
Complete Set (150): 9.00
Common Player: .05
Bronze Press Proofs: 3X
Gold Press Proofs: 7X
Silver Press Proofs: 25X
Pack (7): 1.25
Wax Box (24): 20.00
1 Cal Ripken Jr. 1.50
2 Alex Gonzalez .05
3 Roger Cedeno .05
4 Todd Hollandsworth .05
5 Gregg Jefferies .05
6 Ryne Sandberg .65
7 Eric Karros .05
8 Jeff Conine .05
9 Rafael Palmeiro .45
10 Bip Roberts .05
11 Roger Clemens .70
12 Tom Glavine .30
13 Jason Giambi .40
14 Rey Ordonez .05
15 Chan Ho Park .05
16 Vinny Castilla .05
17 Butch Huskey .05
18 Greg Maddux .65
19 Bernard Gilkey .05
20 Marquis Grissom .05
21 Chuck Knoblauch .05
22 Ozzie Smith .65
23 Garret Anderson .05
24 J.T. Snow .05
25 John Valentin .05
26 Barry Larkin .05
27 Bobby Bonilla .05
28 Todd Zeile .05
29 Roberto Alomar .20
30 Ramon Martinez .05
31 Jeff King .05
32 Dennis Eckersley .45
33 Derek Jeter 1.50
34 Edgar Martinez .05
35 Geronimo Berroa .05
36 Hal Morris .05
37 Troy Percival .05
38 Jason Isringhausen .05
39 Greg Vaughn .05
40 Robin Ventura .05
41 Craig Biggio .05
42 Will Clark .05
43 Sammy Sosa .65
44 Bernie Williams .05
45 Kenny Lofton .05
46 Wade Boggs .65
47 Javy Lopez .05
48 Reggie Sanders .05
49 Jeff Bagwell .55
50 Fred McGriff .05
51 Charles Johnson .05
52 Darren Daulton .05
53 Jose Canseco .40
54 Cecil Fielder .05
55 Hideo Nomo .30
56 Tim Salmon .05
57 Carlos Delgado .40
58 David Cone .05
59 Tim Raines .05
60 Lyle Mouton .05
61 Wally Joyner .05
62 Bret Boone .05
63 Raul Mondesi .05
64 Gary Sheffield .35
65 Alex Rodriguez 1.00
66 Russ Davis .05
67 Checklist .05
68 Marty Cordova .05
69 Ruben Sierra .05
70 Jose Mesa .05
71 Matt Williams .05
72 Chipper Jones .65
73 Randy Johnson .55
74 Kirby Puckett .65
75 Jim Edmonds .05
76 Barry Bonds 1.50
77 David Segui .05
78 Larry Walker .05
79 Jason Kendall .05
80 Mike Piazza .75
81 Brian Hunter .05
82 Julio Franco .05
83 Jay Bell .05
84 Kevin Seitzer .05
85 John Smoltz .05
86 Joe Carter .05
87 Ray Durham .05
88 Carlos Baerga .05
89 Ron Gant .05
90 Orlando Merced .05
91 Lee Smith .05
92 Pedro Martinez .55
93 Frank Thomas .55
94 Al Martin .05
95 Chad Curtis .05
96 Eddie Murray .55
97 Rusty Greer .05
98 Jay Buhner .05
99 Rico Brogna .05
100 Todd Hundley .05
101 Moises Alou .05
102 Chili Davis .05
103 Ismael Valdes .05
104 Mo Vaughn .05
105 Juan Gonzalez .30
106 Mark Grudzielanek .05
107 Derek Bell .05
108 Shawn Green .30
109 David Justice .05
110 Paul O'Neill .05
111 Kevin Appier .05
112 Ray Lankford .05
113 Travis Fryman .05
114 Manny Ramirez .55
115 Brooks Kieschnick .05
116 Ken Griffey Jr. .75
117 Jeffrey Hammonds .05
118 Mark McGwire 1.00
119 Denny Neagle .05
120 Quilvio Veras .05
121 Alan Benes .05
122 Rondell White .05
123 Osvaldo Fernandez **RC** .20
124 Andres Galarraga .05
125 Johnny Damon .35
126 Lenny Dykstra .05
127 Jason Schmidt .05
128 Mike Mussina .30
129 Ken Caminiti .05
130 Michael Tucker .05
131 LaTroy Hawkins .05
132 Checklist .05
133 Delino DeShields .05
134 Dave Nilsson .05
135 Jack McDowell .05
136 Joey Hamilton .05
137 Dante Bichette .05
138 Paul Molitor .55
139 Ivan Rodriguez .45
140 Mark Grace .05
141 Paul Wilson .05
142 Orel Hershiser .05
143 Albert Belle .05
144 Tino Martinez .05
145 Tony Gwynn .65
146 George Arias .05
147 Brian Jordan .05
148 Brian McRae .05
149 Rickey Henderson .55
150 Ryan Klesko .05

Press Proofs

The basic 150-card 1996 Studio set was also produced in three parallel press proof versions. Each is basically identical to the regular-issue cards except for appropriately colored foil highlights on front and a notation of edition size in the circle around the portrait photo on back. Bronze press proofs were issued in an edition of 2,000 each and were inserted at an average rate of one per six packs. Gold press proofs were

an edition of 500 with an average insertion rate of one per 24 packs. The silver press proofs were inserted only into magazine packs and limited to just 100 cards of each.

NM/M
Common Player, Bronze: .50
Bronze Stars: 3X
Common Player, Gold: 1.00
Gold Stars: 7X
Common Player, Silver: 4.00
Silver Stars: 25X

Hit Parade

These die-cut inserts resemble an album with half of the record pulled out of the sleeve. Hit Parade cards, which feature top long ball hitters, were seeded one per every 36 packs. The cards were individually numbered up to 7,500. Each card can also be found in a sample version which has a "XXXX/5000" serial number on back.

NM/M
Complete Set (10): 10.00
Common Player: .75
1 Tony Gwynn 1.50
2 Ken Griffey Jr. 2.00
3 Frank Thomas 1.00
4 Jeff Bagwell 1.00
5 Kirby Puckett 1.50
6 Mike Piazza 2.00
7 Barry Bonds 2.50
8 Albert Belle .75
9 Tim Salmon .75
10 Mo Vaughn .75

Masterstrokes

Only 5,000 each of these 1996 Studio insert cards were made. The cards simulate oil painting detail on an embossed canvas-feel front. Backs are glossy and individually serial numbered. They are found on average of once per 70 packs. Sample versions of each card overprinted as such on the back and numbered "PROMO/5000" were also issued.

NM/M
Complete Set (8): 30.00
Common Player: 4.00
Samples: 75 Percent
1 Tony Gwynn 6.00
2 Mike Piazza 8.00

3 Jeff Bagwell 4.00
4 Manny Ramirez 4.00
5 Cal Ripken Jr. 12.00
6 Frank Thomas 4.00
7 Ken Griffey Jr. 8.00
8 Greg Maddux 6.00

Stained Glass Stars

Twelve superstars are featured on these clear, die-cut plastic cards which resemble stained glass windows. These 1996 Studio inserts were seeded one per every 30 packs.

NM/M
Complete Set (12): 24.00
Common Player: 1.00
1 Cal Ripken Jr. 5.00
2 Ken Griffey Jr. 3.50
3 Frank Thomas 2.00
4 Greg Maddux 2.50
5 Chipper Jones 2.50
6 Mike Piazza 3.50
7 Albert Belle 1.00
8 Jeff Bagwell 2.00
9 Hideo Nomo 1.50
10 Barry Bonds 5.00
11 Manny Ramirez 2.00
12 Kenny Lofton 1.00

1997 Studio

Innovations in both product and packaging marked the seventh annual issue of Donruss' Studio brand. As in the past, the 165 cards in the base set rely on high-quality front photos to bring out the players' personalities. For '97, the photos are set against a background of variously shaded gray horizontal stripes. Backs have a second player photo, often an action shot, along with a short career summary. The "pack" for '97 Studio is something totally new to the hobby. An 8-1/2" x 12" cardboard envelope, complete with a zip strip opener in the style of an express-mail envelope, contains a cello pack of five standard-size cards plus either an 8" x 10" Studio Portrait card or an 8" x 10" version of the Master Strokes insert. Suggested retail price at issue was $2.49 per pack. Regular-size Master Strokes cards are one of several insert series which includes silver and gold press proofs and die-cut plastic Hard Hats.

NM/M
Complete Set (165): 17.50
Common Player: .05
Silver Press Proofs: 4X
Gold Press Proofs: 8X
Pack (5): 3.00
Wax Box (18): 40.00
1 Frank Thomas .65
2 Gary Sheffield .45
3 Jason Isringhausen .05
4 Ron Gant .05
5 Andy Pettitte .25
6 Todd Hollandsworth .05
7 Troy Percival .05
8 Mark McGwire 1.50
9 Barry Larkin .05
10 Ken Caminiti .05
11 Paul Molitor .65
12 Travis Fryman .05
13 Kevin Brown .05
14 Robin Ventura .05
15 Andres Galarraga .05
16 Ken Griffey Jr. 1.00
17 Roger Clemens .85
18 Alan Benes .05
19 David Justice .05
20 Damon Buford .05
21 Mike Piazza 1.00
22 Ray Durham .05
23 Billy Wagner .05
24 Dean Palmer .05
25 David Cone .05
26 Ruben Sierra .05
27 Henry Rodriguez .05
28 Ray Lankford .05
29 Jamey Wright .05
30 Brady Anderson .05
31 Tino Martinez .05
32 Manny Ramirez .65
33 Jeff Conine .05
34 Dante Bichette .05
35 Jose Canseco .50
36 Mo Vaughn .05
37 Sammy Sosa .75
38 Mark Grudzielanek .05
39 Mike Mussina .35
40 Bill Pulsipher .05
41 Ryne Sandberg .75
42 Rickey Henderson .65
43 Alex Rodriguez 1.50
44 Eddie Murray .65
45 Ernie Young .05
46 Joey Hamilton .05
47 Wade Boggs .75
48 Rusty Greer .05
49 Carlos Delgado .50
50 Ellis Burks .05
51 Cal Ripken Jr. 2.00
52 Alex Fernandez .05
53 Wally Joyner .05
54 James Baldwin .05
55 Juan Gonzalez .35
56 John Smoltz .05
57 Omar Vizquel .05
58 Shane Reynolds .05
59 Barry Bonds 2.00
60 Jason Kendall .05
61 Marty Cordova .05
62 Charles Johnson .05
63 John Jaha .05
64 Chan Ho Park .05
65 Jermaine Allensworth .05
66 Mark Grace .05
67 Tim Salmon .05
68 Edgar Martinez .05
69 Marquis Grissom .05
70 Craig Biggio .05
71 Bobby Higginson .05
72 Kevin Seitzer .05
73 Hideo Nomo .35
74 Dennis Eckersley .60
75 Bobby Bonilla .05
76 Dwight Gooden .05
77 Jeff Cirillo .05
78 Brian McRae .05
79 Chipper Jones .75
80 Jeff Fassero .05
81 Fred McGriff .05
82 Garret Anderson .05
83 Eric Karros .05
84 Derek Bell .05
85 Kenny Lofton .05
86 John Mabry .05
87 Pat Hentgen .05
88 Greg Maddux .75
89 Jason Giambi .45
90 Al Martin .05
91 Derek Jeter 2.00
92 Rey Ordonez .05
93 Will Clark .05
94 Kevin Appier .05
95 Roberto Alomar .30
96 Joe Carter .05
97 Bernie Williams .05
98 Albert Belle .05
99 Greg Vaughn .05
100 Tony Clark .05
101 Matt Williams .05
102 Jeff Bagwell .65
103 Reggie Sanders .05
104 Mariano Rivera .15
105 Larry Walker .05
106 Shawn Green .30
107 Alex Ochoa .05
108 Ivan Rodriguez .60
109 Eric Young .05
110 Javier Lopez .05
111 Brian Hunter .05
112 Raul Mondesi .05
113 Randy Johnson .65
114 Tony Phillips .05
115 Carlos Garcia .05
116 Moises Alou .05
117 Paul O'Neill .05
118 Jim Thome .60
119 Jermaine Dye .05
120 Wilson Alvarez .05
121 Rondell White .05
122 Michael Tucker .05
123 Mike Lansing .05
124 Tony Gwynn .75
125 Ryan Klesko .05
126 Jim Edmonds .05
127 Chuck Knoblauch .05
128 Rafael Palmeiro .60
129 Jay Buhner .05
130 Tom Glavine .35
131 Julio Franco .05
132 Cecil Fielder .05
133 Paul Wilson .05
134 Deion Sanders .05
135 Alex Gonzalez .05
136 Charles Nagy .05
137 Andy Ashby .05
138 Edgar Renteria .05
139 Pedro Martinez .65
140 Brian Jordan .05
141 Todd Hundley .05
142 Marc Newfield .05
143 Darryl Strawberry .05
144 Dan Wilson .05
145 Brian Giles **RC** .50
146 Bartolo Colon .05
147 Shannon Stewart .05
148 Scott Spiezio .05
149 Andruw Jones .65
150 Karim Garcia .05
151 Vladimir Guerrero .65
152 George Arias .05
153 Brooks Kieschnick .05
154 Todd Walker .05
155 Scott Rolen .60
156 Todd Greene .05
157 Dmitri Young .05
158 Ruben Rivera .05
159 Trey Beamon .05
160 Nomar Garciaparra .75
161 Bob Abreu .05
162 Darin Erstad .15
163 Ken Griffey Jr. (Checklist) .50
164 Frank Thomas (Checklist) .35
165 Alex Rodriguez (Checklist) .75

Press Proofs

Each of the 165 cards in the base set of '97 Studio was also produced in a pair of Press Proof versions as random pack inserts. Fronts of the Press Proofs have either silver or gold holographic foil replacing the silver foil graphics found on regular cards, as well as foil strips down each side. Backs are identical to the regular issue. The silver Press Proofs were issued in an edition of 1,500 of each player; the golds are limited to 500 of each.

NM/M
Common Player, Silver: .50
Silver Stars: 4X
Common Player, Gold: 1.00
Gold Stars: 8X

Hard Hats

Die-cut plastic is used to represent a player's batting helmet in this set of '97 Studio inserts. A player action photo appears in the foreground with his name and other graphic elements in silver foil. Backs feature a small portrait photo, short career summary and a serial number from within the edition of 5,000 of each card.

NM/M
Complete Set (24): 50.00
Common Player: 1.50
1 Ivan Rodriguez 3.00
2 Albert Belle 1.50
3 Ken Griffey Jr. 6.00
4 Chuck Knoblauch 1.50
5 Frank Thomas 4.00
6 Cal Ripken Jr. 8.00
7 Todd Walker 1.50
8 Alex Rodriguez 7.00
9 Jim Thome 3.00
10 Mike Piazza 6.00
11 Barry Larkin 1.50
12 Chipper Jones 5.00
13 Derek Jeter 8.00
14 Jermaine Dye 1.50
15 Jason Giambi 2.00
16 Tim Salmon 1.50
17 Brady Anderson 1.50
18 Rondell White 1.50
19 Bernie Williams 1.50
20 Juan Gonzalez 2.00
21 Karim Garcia 1.50
22 Scott Rolen 3.00
23 Darin Erstad 2.00
24 Brian Jordan 1.50

Master Strokes

The look and feel of a painting on canvas is the effect presented by '97 Studio's Master Strokes inserts. Card fronts feature unique player action art and are highlighted by gold-foil graphics. Each card has a facsimile autograph on front. UV-coated backs are team-color coordinated and have a few sentences about the player. Gold-foil serial numbering identifies the card from an edition of 2,000 of each player.

NM/M
Complete Set (24): 120.00
Common Player: 2.00
1 Derek Jeter 12.00
2 Jeff Bagwell 4.50
3 Ken Griffey Jr. 8.00
4 Barry Bonds 12.00
5 Frank Thomas 4.50
6 Andy Pettitte 2.25
7 Mo Vaughn 2.00
8 Alex Rodriguez 10.00
9 Andruw Jones 4.50
10 Kenny Lofton 2.00
11 Cal Ripken Jr. 12.00
12 Greg Maddux 6.00
13 Manny Ramirez 4.50
14 Mike Piazza 8.00
14p Mike Piazza (Promo) 3.50
15 Vladimir Guerrero 4.50
16 Albert Belle 2.00
17 Chipper Jones 6.00
18 Hideo Nomo 2.50
19 Sammy Sosa 6.00
20 Tony Gwynn 6.00
21 Gary Sheffield 2.50
22 Mark McGwire 10.00
23 Juan Gonzalez 2.50
24 Paul Molitor 4.50

Master Strokes 8x10

The look and feel of a painting on canvas is the effect presented by the 8" x 10" version of '97 Studio's Master Strokes inserts. Card fronts feature unique player action art and are highlighted by gold-foil graphics. Each card has a facsimile autograph on front. UV-coated backs are team-color coordinated and

have a few sentences about the player. Gold-foil serial numbering identifies the card from an edition of 5,000 of each player - making the super-size version more than twice as common as the 2-1/2" x 3-1/2" version.

NM/M
Complete Set (24): 45.00
Common Player: .75
1 Derek Jeter 5.00
2 Jeff Bagwell 2.00
3 Ken Griffey Jr. 3.00
4 Barry Bonds 5.00
5 Frank Thomas 2.00
6 Andy Pettitte 1.00
7 Mo Vaughn .75
8 Alex Rodriguez 4.00
9 Andruw Jones 2.00
10 Kenny Lofton .75
11 Cal Ripken Jr. 5.00
12 Greg Maddux 2.50
13 Manny Ramirez 2.00
14 Mike Piazza 3.00
15 Vladimir Guerrero 2.00
16 Albert Belle .75
17 Chipper Jones 2.50
18 Hideo Nomo 1.50
19 Sammy Sosa 2.50
20 Tony Gwynn 2.50
21 Gary Sheffield 1.50
22 Mark McGwire 4.00
23 Juan Gonzalez 1.50
24 Paul Molitor 2.00

Portraits

Perhaps the most innovative feature of '97 Studio is the 8" x 10" Portrait cards which come one per pack (except when a pack contains a Master Strokes 8x10). Virtually identical to the player's regular-size Studio card, the jumbo version has the word "PORTRAIT" in black beneath the team name on front. Backs have different card numbers than the same player's card in the regular set. The Portrait cards are produced with a special UV coating on front to facilitate autographing. Pre-autographed cards of three youngsters in the series were included as random pack inserts.

NM/M
Complete Set (24): 10.00
Common Player: .25
1 Ken Griffey Jr. 1.00
1s Frank Thomas (Overprinted "SAMPLE.") .75
2 Frank Thomas .65
3 Alex Rodriguez 1.50
4 Andruw Jones .65
5 Cal Ripken Jr. 2.00
6 Greg Maddux .75
7 Mike Piazza 1.00
8 Chipper Jones .75
9 Albert Belle .25
10 Derek Jeter 2.00
11 Juan Gonzalez .45
12 Todd Walker .25
12a Todd Walker (Autographed edition of 1,250.) 10.00
13 Mark McGwire 1.50
14 Barry Bonds 2.00
15 Jeff Bagwell .65
16 Manny Ramirez .65
17 Kenny Lofton .25
18 Mo Vaughn .25
19 Hideo Nomo .45
20 Tony Gwynn .75
21 Vladimir Guerrero .65
21a Vladimir Guerrero (Autographed edition of 500.) 30.00
22 Gary Sheffield .45
23 Ryne Sandberg .75
24 Scott Rolen .50
24a Scott Rolen (Autographed edition of 1,000.) 12.00

Portrait Collection

In a departure from traditional sportscard marketing, the 1997 Studio program offered a pair of specially framed editions directly to consumers. The offer was made in a color brochure found in about half the packs advertising the "Portrait Collection." The offer includes one standard-size card and an 8" x 10" Portrait or Master card similar to those in the regular issue. These cards differ from the regular issue in that they are trimmed in platinum holographic foil, individually hand-numbered and signed by the photographer. The cards were sold framed with a metal plaque, also numbered, attesting to the limited-edition status. The framed Studio Portrait piece was produced in an edition of 500 of each player; the Master Strokes piece was limited to 100 for each player on the checklist. The former was issued at $159; the latter at $299.

NM/M
Complete Set, Studio Portrait (24): 2,850
Complete Set, Master Strokes (24): 5,250
Common Plaque, Studio Portrait: 125.00
Common Plaque, Master Strokes: 225.00
P1 Ken Griffey Jr. 125.00
P2 Frank Thomas 125.00
P3 Alex Rodriquez 125.00
P4 Andruw Jones 125.00
P5 Cal Ripken Jr. 125.00
P6 Greg Maddux 125.00
P7 Mike Piazza 125.00
P8 Chipper Jones 125.00
P9 Albert Belle 125.00
P10 Derek Jeter 125.00
P11 Juan Gonzalez 125.00
P12 Todd Walker 125.00
P13 Mark McGwire 125.00
P14 Barry Bonds 125.00
P15 Jeff Bagwell 125.00
P16 Manny 125.00
P17 Kenny Lofton 125.00
P18 Mo Vaughn 125.00
P19 Hideo Nomo 125.00
P20 Tony Gwynn 125.00
P21 Vladimir Guerrero 125.00
P22 Gary Sheffield 125.00
P23 Ryne Sandberg 125.00
P24 Scott Rolen 125.00
M1 Derek Jeter 225.00
M2 Jeff Bagwell 225.00
M3 Ken Griffey Jr. 225.00
M4 Barry Bonds 225.00
M5 Frank Thomas 225.00
M6 Andy Pettitte 225.00
M7 Mo Vaughn 225.00
M8 Alex Rodriguez 225.00
M9 Andruw Jones 225.00
M10 Kenny Lofton 225.00
M11 Cal Ripken Jr. 225.00
M12 Greg Maddux 225.00
M13 Manny Ramirez 225.00
M14 Mike Piazza 225.00
M15 Vladimir Guerrero 225.00
M16 Albert Belle 225.00
M17 Chipper Jones 225.00
M18 Hideo Nomo 225.00
M19 Sammy Sosa 225.00
M20 Tony Gwynn 225.00
M21 Gary Sheffield 225.00
M22 Mark McGwire 225.00
M23 Juan Gonzalez 225.00
M24 Paul Molitor 225.00

1998 Studio

The Donruss Studio base set consists of 220 regular-sized cards and 36 8-x-10 portraits. The base cards feature a posed photo with an action

shot in the background, surrounded by a white border. Silver Studio Proofs (numbered to 1,000) and Gold Studio Proofs (300) parallel the regular-size base set. Inserts included Freeze Frame, Hit Parade and Masterstrokes.

		NM/M
Complete Set (220):		25.00
Common Player:		.05
Silver Proofs:		3X
Gold Proofs:		6X
Pack (7 Cards+8x10):		2.00
Wax Box (18):		20.00
1	Tony Clark	.05
2	Jose Cruz Jr.	.05
3	Ivan Rodriguez	.65
4	Mo Vaughn	.05
5	Kenny Lofton	.05
6	Will Clark	.05
7	Barry Larkin	.05
8	Jay Bell	.05
9	Kevin Young	.05
10	Francisco Cordova	.05
11	Justin Thompson	.05
12	Paul Molitor	.75
13	Jeff Bagwell	.75
14	Jose Canseco	.45
15	Scott Rolen	.65
16	Wilton Guerrero	.05
17	Shannon Stewart	.05
18	Hideki Irabu	.05
19	Michael Tucker	.05
20	Joe Carter	.05
21	Gabe Alvarez	.05
22	Ricky Ledee	.05
23	Karim Garcia	.05
24	Eli Marrero	.05
25	Scott Elarton	.05
26	Mario Valdez	.05
27	Ben Grieve	.05
28	Paul Konerko	.15
29	Esteban Yan **RC**	.05
30	Esteban Loaiza	.05
31	Delino DeShields	.05
32	Bernie Williams	.05
33	Joe Randa	.05
34	Randy Johnson	.75
35	Brett Tomko	.05
36	Todd Erdos **RC**	.05
37	Bobby Higginson	.05
38	Jason Kendall	.05
39	Ray Lankford	.05
40	Mark Grace	.05
41	Andy Pettitte	.25
42	Alex Rodriguez	2.00
43	Hideo Nomo	.45
44	Sammy Sosa	1.00
45	J.T. Snow	.05
46	Jason Varitek	.05
47	Vinny Castilla	.05
48	Neifi Perez	.05
49	Todd Walker	.05
50	Mike Cameron	.05
51	Jeffrey Hammonds	.05
52	Deivi Cruz	.05
53	Brian Hunter	.05
54	Al Martin	.05
55	Ron Coomer	.05
56	Chan Ho Park	.05
57	Pedro Martinez	.75
58	Darin Erstad	.15
59	Albert Belle	.05
60	Nomar Garciaparra	1.00
61	Tony Gwynn	1.00
62	Mike Piazza	1.50
63	Todd Helton	.65
64	David Ortiz	.45
65	Todd Dunwoody	.05
66	Orlando Cabrera	.05
67	Ken Cloude	.05
68	Andy Benes	.05
69	Mariano Rivera	.15
70	Cecil Fielder	.05
71	Brian Jordan	.05
72	Darryl Kile	.05
73	Reggie Jefferson	.05
74	Shawn Estes	.05
75	Bobby Bonilla	.05
76	Denny Neagle	.05
77	Robin Ventura	.05
78	Omar Vizquel	.05
79	Craig Biggio	.05
80	Moises Alou	.05
81	Garret Anderson	.05
82	Eric Karros	.05
83	Dante Bichette	.05
84	Charles Johnson	.05
85	Rusty Greer	.05
86	Travis Fryman	.05
87	Fernando Tatis	.05
88	Wilson Alvarez	.05
89	Carl Pavano	.05
90	Brian Rose	.05
91	Geoff Jenkins	.05
92	Magglio Ordonez **RC**	1.50
93	David Segui	.05
94	David Cone	.05
95	John Smoltz	.05
96	Jim Thome	.65
97	Gary Sheffield	.45
98	Barry Bonds	2.50
99	Andres Galarraga	.05
100	Brad Fullmer	.05
101	Bobby Estalella	.05
102	Enrique Wilson	.05
103	Frank Catalanotto **RC**	.25
104	Mike Lowell **RC**	1.00
105	Kevin Orie	.05
106	Matt Morris	.05
107	Pokey Reese	.05
108	Shawn Green	.35
109	Tony Womack	.05
110	Ken Caminiti	.05
111	Roberto Alomar	.20
112	Ken Griffey Jr.	1.50
113	Cal Ripken Jr.	2.50
114	Lou Collier	.05
115	Larry Walker	.05
116	Fred McGriff	.05
117	Jim Edmonds	.05
118	Edgar Martinez	.05
119	Matt Williams	.05
120	Ismael Valdes	.05
121	Bartolo Colon	.05
122	Jeff Cirillo	.05
123	Steve Woodard **RC**	.25
124	Kevin Millwood **RC**	1.00
125	Derrick Gibson	.05
126	Jacob Cruz	.05
127	Russell Branyan	.05
128	Sean Casey	.15
129	Derrek Lee	.50
130	Paul O'Neill	.05
131	Brad Radke	.05
132	Kevin Appier	.05
133	John Olerud	.05
134	Alan Benes	.05
135	Todd Greene	.05
136	Carlos Mendoza **RC**	.05
137	Wade Boggs	1.00
138	Jose Guillen	.05
139	Tino Martinez	.05
140	Aaron Boone	.05
141	Abraham Nunez	.05
142	Preston Wilson	.05
143	Randall Simon	.05
144	Dennis Reyes	.05
145	Mark Kotsay	.05
146	Richard Hidalgo	.05
147	Travis Lee	.05
148	Hanley Frias **RC**	.05
149	Ruben Rivera	.05
150	Rafael Medina	.05
151	Dave Nilsson	.05
152	Curt Schilling	.35
153	Brady Anderson	.05
154	Carlos Delgado	.50
155	Jason Giambi	.45
156	Pat Hentgen	.05
157	Tom Glavine	.35
158	Ryan Klesko	.05
159	Chipper Jones	1.00
160	Juan Gonzalez	.45
161	Mark McGwire	2.00
162	Vladimir Guerrero	.75
163	Derek Jeter	2.50
164	Manny Ramirez	.75
165	Mike Mussina	.30
166	Rafael Palmeiro	.65
167	Henry Rodriguez	.05
168	Jeff Suppan	.05
169	Eric Milton	.05
170	Scott Spiezio	.05
171	Wilson Delgado	.05
172	Bubba Trammell	.05
173	Ellis Burks	.05
174	Jason Dickson	.05
175	Butch Huskey	.05
176	Edgardo Alfonzo	.05
177	Eric Young	.05
178	Marquis Grissom	.05
179	Lance Johnson	.05
180	Kevin Brown	.05
181	Sandy Alomar Jr.	.05
182	Todd Hundley	.05
183	Rondell White	.05
184	Javier Lopez	.05
185	Damian Jackson	.05
186	Raul Mondesi	.05
187	Rickey Henderson	.75
188	David Justice	.05
189	Jay Buhner	.05
190	Jaret Wright	.05
191	Miguel Tejada	.25
192	Ron Wright	.05
193	Livan Hernandez	.05
194	A.J. Hinch	.05
195	Richie Sexson	.05
196	Bob Abreu	.05
197	Luis Castillo	.05
198	Michael Coleman	.05
199	Greg Maddux	1.00
200	Frank Thomas	.75
201	Andruw Jones	.75
202	Roger Clemens	1.25
203	Tim Salmon	.05
204	Chuck Knoblauch	.05
205	Wes Helms	.05
206	Juan Encarnacion	.05
207	Russ Davis	.05
208	John Valentin	.05
209	Tony Saunders	.05
210	Mike Sweeney	.05
211	Steve Finley	.05
212	David Dellucci **RC**	.25
213	Edgar Renteria	.05
214	Jeremi Gonzalez	.05
215	Checklist (Jeff Bagwell)	.40
216	Checklist (Mike Piazza)	1.00
217	Checklist (Greg Maddux)	.50
218	Checklist (Cal Ripken Jr.)	1.25
219	Checklist (Frank Thomas)	.45
220	Checklist (Ken Griffey Jr.)	.75

Silver Proofs

This parallel set includes all 220 cards in Studio baseball. Cards are identified by a silver holographic strip around the borders. Silver versions are limited to 1,000 sets.

	NM/M
Common Player:	1.00
Silver Stars:	3X

Gold Proofs

Gold proofs is a parallel of the 220-card base set. Card fronts feature gold holo-foil highlights. Backs are sequentially numbered to 300 each.

	NM/M
Common Player:	3.00
Stars:	6X

Autographs

Three top rookies signed a number of 8x10s for this product. Cards have a Donruss "Authentic Signature" stamp on front.

		NM/M
1	Travis Lee/500	20.00
2	Todd Helton/1,000	20.00
3	Ben Grieve/1,000	10.00

Freeze Frame

Freeze Frame is a 30-card insert sequentially numbered to 5,000. The cards are designed to look like a piece of film with a color action photo. The first 500 of each card are die-cut.

		NM/M
Complete Set (30):		75.00
Common Player:		1.25
Production 4,500 Sets		
Die-Cuts:		1.5X
Production 500 Sets		
1	Ken Griffey Jr.	5.00
2	Derek Jeter	7.50
3	Ben Grieve	1.25
4	Cal Ripken Jr.	7.50
5	Alex Rodriguez	6.00
6	Greg Maddux	4.00
7	David Justice	1.25
8	Mike Piazza	5.00
9	Chipper Jones	4.00
10	Randy Johnson	3.00
11	Jeff Bagwell	3.00
12	Nomar Garciaparra	4.00
13	Andruw Jones	3.00
14	Frank Thomas	3.00
15	Scott Rolen	2.50
16	Barry Bonds	7.50
17	Kenny Lofton	1.25
18	Ivan Rodriguez	2.50
19	Chuck Knoblauch	1.25
20	Jose Cruz Jr.	1.25
21	Bernie Williams	1.25
22	Tony Gwynn	4.00
23	Juan Gonzalez	2.00
24	Gary Sheffield	2.25
25	Roger Clemens	4.50
26	Travis Lee	1.25
27	Brad Fullmer	1.25
28	Tim Salmon	1.25
29	Raul Mondesi	1.25
30	Roberto Alomar	2.00

Hit Parade

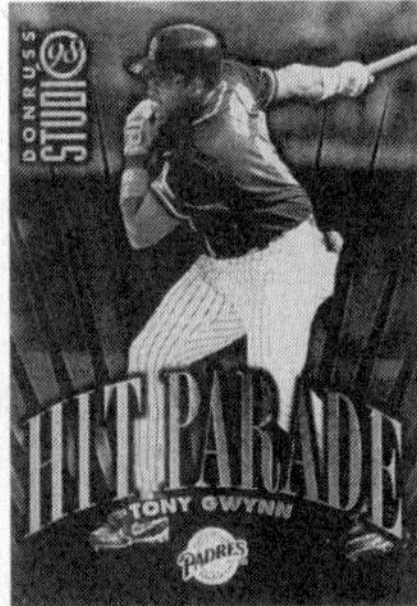

These 20 cards are printed on micro-etched foil board. This set honors baseball's top hitters and is sequentially numbered to 5,000.

		NM/M
Complete Set (20):		30.00
Common Player:		1.00
Production 5,000 Sets		
1	Tony Gwynn	2.50
2	Larry Walker	1.00
3	Mike Piazza	3.00
4	Frank Thomas	2.00
5	Manny Ramirez	2.00
6	Ken Griffey Jr.	3.00
7	Todd Helton	1.50
8	Vladimir Guerrero	2.00
9	Albert Belle	1.00
10	Jeff Bagwell	2.00
11	Juan Gonzalez	1.25
12	Jim Thome	1.50
13	Scott Rolen	1.50
14	Tino Martinez	1.00
15	Mark McGwire	4.00
16	Barry Bonds	5.00
17	Tony Clark	1.00
18	Mo Vaughn	1.00
19	Darin Erstad	1.25
20	Paul Konerko	1.25

Masterstrokes

Printed on a canvas-like material, these 20 cards are numbered to 1,000.

		NM/M
Complete Set (20):		95.00
Common Player:		2.00
Production 1,000 Sets		
Samples:		3X
1	Travis Lee	2.00
2	Kenny Lofton	2.00
3	Mo Vaughn	2.00
4	Ivan Rodriguez	3.50
5	Roger Clemens	6.50
6	Mark McGwire	10.00
7	Hideo Nomo	2.50
8	Andruw Jones	4.50
9	Nomar Garciaparra	6.00
10	Juan Gonzalez	2.50
11	Jeff Bagwell	4.50
12	Derek Jeter	12.50
13	Tony Gwynn	6.00
14	Chipper Jones	6.00
15	Mike Piazza	7.50
16	Greg Maddux	6.00
17	Alex Rodriguez	10.00
18	Cal Ripken Jr.	12.50
19	Frank Thomas	4.50
20	Ken Griffey Jr.	7.50

Sony MLB 99

Twenty Sony MLB '99 sweepstakes cards were inserted one per two Studio packs. The fronts feature a color action shot and the backs have sweepstakes rules and a MLB '99 tip.

		NM/M
Complete Set (20):		8.00
Common Player:		.15
1	Cal Ripken Jr.	1.50
2	Nomar Garciaparra	.75
3	Barry Bonds	1.50
4	Mike Mussina	.35
5	Pedro Martinez	.60
6	Derek Jeter	1.50
7	Andruw Jones	.60
8	Kenny Lofton	.15
9	Gary Sheffield	.45
10	Raul Mondesi	.15
11	Jeff Bagwell	.60
12	Tim Salmon	.15
13	Tom Glavine	.35
14	Ben Grieve	.15
15	Matt Williams	.15
16	Juan Gonzalez	.35
17	Mark McGwire	1.00
18	Bernie Williams	.15
19	Andres Galarraga	.15
20	Jose Cruz Jr.	.15

8x10 Portraits Samples

Sample versions of the 8x10 cards which would be found in '98 Studio packs were also issued. They are identical in format to the issued cards, with UV coating and silver-foil graphics on fronts. Backs have a large black "SAMPLE" overprinted diagonally.

		NM/M
001	Travis Lee	2.00
002	Todd Helton	3.00

8x10 Portraits

One Studio 8-x-10 was included in each pack. The cards were blown-up versions of the regular-size base cards, which were inserted seven per pack. The large portraits are paralleled in the Gold Proofs set, which adds gold holo-foil to the cards. Gold Proofs are numbered to 300.

		NM/M
Complete Set (36):		65.00
Common Player:		.50
Inserted 1:1		
1	Travis Lee	.50
2	Todd Helton	1.50
3	Ben Grieve	.50
4	Paul Konerko	.65
5	Jeff Bagwell	2.00
6	Derek Jeter	7.00
7	Ivan Rodriguez	1.50
8	Cal Ripken Jr.	7.00
9	Mike Piazza	4.00
10	Chipper Jones	3.00
11	Frank Thomas	2.00
12	Tony Gwynn	3.00
13	Nomar Garciaparra	3.00
14	Juan Gonzalez	1.00
15	Greg Maddux	3.00
16	Hideo Nomo	1.00
17	Scott Rolen	1.50
18	Barry Bonds	7.00
19	Ken Griffey Jr.	4.00
20	Alex Rodriguez	5.00
21	Roger Clemens	3.50
22	Mark McGwire	5.00
23	Jose Cruz Jr.	.50
24	Andruw Jones	2.00
25	Tino Martinez	.50
26	Mo Vaughn	.50
27	Vladimir Guerrero	2.00
28	Tony Clark	.50
29	Andy Pettitte	.65
30	Jaret Wright	.50
31	Paul Molitor	2.00
32	Darin Erstad	.65
33	Larry Walker	.50
34	Chuck Knoblauch	.50
35	Barry Larkin	.50
36	Kenny Lofton	.50

8x10 Portraits Gold Proofs

This parallel of the 8x10 base set adds gold holo-foil treatments to the 36 cards, which are sequentially numbered to 300 and randomly inserted in packs.

	NM/M
Common Player:	5.00
Stars:	6X

1995 Summit Samples

Nine-card cello packs of Summit cards, including "Big Bang" inserts, were released to dealers to debut the new Score brand. Cards are specially marked as promotional samples.

		NM/M
Complete Set (9):		5.00
Common Player:		.50
10	Barry Larkin	.50
11	Albert Belle	.50
79	Cal Ripken Jr.	3.00
80	David Cone	.50

125	Alex Gonzalez (Rookie)	.50
130	Charles Johnson (Rookie)	.50
BB12	Jose Canseco (Big Bang)	1.00
BB17	Fred McGriff (Big Bang)	.50
---	Information Card	.05

1995 Summit

A late-season release, Summit introduced the Score label to a premium brand card. Printed on extra heavy cardboard stock and UV coated on both sides the veteran player cards (#1-111) feature horizontal or vertical action photos with the player's name and team logo printed in gold-foil on front. Backs have a player portrait photo along with his 1994 stats in monthly charted form. The rookie cards subset (#112-173) have a large black "ROOKIE" on top-front while the back has a short career summary instead of stats. Other subsets include "BAT SPEED" (#174-188), honoring top hitters, and "SPECIAL DELIVERY" (#189-193), featuring top pitchers. Each are designated on front with special gold-foil logos. Seven checklists close out the regular 200-card set. The Summit issued featured a four-tiered chase card program, including a parallel "Nth Degree" set. Summit was a hobby-only issue sold in 7-card foil packs.

		NM/M
Complete Set (200):		10.00
Common Player:		.05
Pack (7):		1.00
Wax Box (24):		12.50
1	Ken Griffey Jr.	1.00
2	Alex Fernandez	.05
3	Fred McGriff	.05
4	Ben McDonald	.05
5	Rafael Palmeiro	.60
6	Tony Gwynn	.75
7	Jim Thome	.60
8	Ken Hill	.05
9	Barry Bonds	2.00
10	Barry Larkin	.05
11	Albert Belle	.05
12	Billy Ashley	.05
13	Matt Williams	.05
14	Andy Benes	.05
15	Midre Cummings	.05
16	J.R. Phillips	.05
17	Edgar Martinez	.05
18	Manny Ramirez	.65
19	Jose Canseco	.40
20	Chili Davis	.05
21	Don Mattingly	.85
22	Bernie Williams	.05
23	Tom Glavine	.35
24	Robin Ventura	.05
25	Jeff Conine	.05
26	Mark Grace	.05
27	Mark McGwire	1.50
28	Carlos Delgado	.45
29	Greg Colbrunn	.05
30	Greg Maddux	.75
31	Craig Biggio	.05
32	Kirby Puckett	.75
33	Derek Bell	.05
34	Lenny Dykstra	.05
35	Tim Salmon	.05
36	Deion Sanders	.05
37	Moises Alou	.05
38	Ray Lankford	.05
39	Willie Greene	.05
40	Ozzie Smith	.75
41	Roger Clemens	.85
42	Andres Galarraga	.05
43	Gary Sheffield	.35
44	Sammy Sosa	.75
45	Larry Walker	.05
46	Kevin Appier	.05
47	Raul Mondesi	.05
48	Kenny Lofton	.05
49	Darryl Hamilton	.05
50	Roberto Alomar	.20
51	Hal Morris	.05
52	Cliff Floyd	.05
53	Brent Gates	.05
54	Rickey Henderson	.65
55	John Olerud	.05
56	Gregg Jefferies	.05
57	Cecil Fielder	.05
58	Paul Molitor	.65
59	Bret Boone	.05
60	Greg Vaughn	.05
61	Wally Joyner	.05
62	Jeffrey Hammonds	.05
63	James Mouton	.05
64	Omar Vizquel	.05
65	Wade Boggs	.75
66	Terry Steinbach	.05
67	Wil Cordero	.05
68	Joey Hamilton	.05
69	Rico Brogna	.05
70	Darren Daulton	.05
71	Chuck Knoblauch	.05
72	Bob Hamelin	.05
73	Carl Everett	.05
74	Joe Carter	.05
75	Dave Winfield	.65
76	Bobby Bonilla	.05
77	Paul O'Neill	.05
78	Javier Lopez	.05
79	Cal Ripken Jr.	2.00
80	David Cone	.05
81	Bernard Gilkey	.05
82	Ivan Rodriguez	.60
83	Dean Palmer	.05
84	Jason Bere	.05
85	Will Clark	.05
86	Scott Cooper	.05
87	Royce Clayton	.05
88	Mike Piazza	1.00
89	Ryan Klesko	.05
90	Juan Gonzalez	.35
91	Travis Fryman	.05
92	Frank Thomas	.65
93	Eduardo Perez	.05
94	Mo Vaughn	.05
95	Jay Bell	.05
96	Jeff Bagwell	.65
97	Randy Johnson	.65
98	Jimmy Key	.05
99	Dennis Eckersley	.60
100	Carlos Baerga	.05
101	Eddie Murray	.65
102	Mike Mussina	.30
103	Brian Anderson	.05
104	Jeff Cirillo	.05
105	Dante Bichette	.05
106	Bret Saberhagen	.05
107	Jeff Kent	.05
108	Ruben Sierra	.05
109	Kirk Gibson	.05
110	Reggie Sanders	.05
111	Dave Justice	.05
112	Benji Gil	.05
113	Vaughn Eshelman	.05
114	Carlos Perez **RC**	.05
115	Chipper Jones	.75
116	Shane Andrews	.05
117	Orlando Miller	.05
118	Scott Ruffcorn	.05
119	Jose Oliva	.05
120	Joe Vitiello	.05
121	Jon Nunnally	.05
122	Garret Anderson	.05
123	Curtis Goodwin	.05
124	Mark Grudzielanek **RC**	.25
125	Alex Gonzalez	.05
126	David Bell	.05
127	Dustin Hermanson	.05
128	Dave Nilsson	.05
129	Wilson Heredia	.05
130	Charles Johnson	.05
131	Frank Rodriguez	.05
132	Alex Ochoa	.05
133	Alex Rodriguez	1.50
134	Bobby Higginson **RC**	.25
135	Edgardo Alfonzo	.05
136	Armando Benitez	.05
137	Rich Aude	.05
138	Tim Naehring	.05
139	Joe Randa	.05
140	Quilvio Veras	.05
141	Hideo Nomo **RC**	1.00
142	Ray Holbert	.05
143	Michael Tucker	.05
144	Chad Mottola	.05
145	John Valentin	.05
146	James Baldwin	.05
147	Esteban Loaiza	.05
148	Marty Cordova	.05
149	Juan Acevedo **RC**	.05
150	Tim Unroe **RC**	.05
151	Brad Clontz	.05
152	Steve Rodriguez	.05
153	Rudy Pemberton	.05
154	Ozzie Timmons	.05
155	Ricky Otero	.05
156	Allen Battle	.05
157	Joe Roselli	.05
158	Roberto Petagine	.05
159	Todd Hollandsworth	.05
160	Shannon Penn	.05
161	Antonio Osuna	.05
162	Russ Davis	.05
163	Jason Giambi	.40
164	Terry Bradshaw	.05
165	Ray Durham	.05
166	Todd Steverson	.05
167	Tim Belk	.05
168	Andy Pettitte	.25
169	Roger Cedeno	.05
170	Jose Parra	.05
171	Scott Sullivan	.05
172	LaTroy Hawkins	.05
173	Jeff McCurry	.05
174	Ken Griffey Jr. (Bat Speed)	.50
175	Frank Thomas (Bat Speed)	.30
176	Cal Ripken Jr. (Bat Speed)	1.00
177	Jeff Bagwell (Bat Speed)	.30
178	Mike Piazza (Bat Speed)	.50
179	Barry Bonds (Bat Speed)	1.00
180	Matt Williams (Bat Speed)	.05
181	Don Mattingly (Bat Speed)	.45
182	Will Clark (Bat Speed)	.05
183	Tony Gwynn (Bat Speed)	.40
184	Kirby Puckett (Bat Speed)	.40
185	Jose Canseco (Bat Speed)	.25
186	Paul Molitor (Bat Speed)	.30
187	Albert Belle (Bat Speed)	.05
188	Joe Carter (Bat Speed)	.05
189	Greg Maddux (Special Delivery)	.40
190	Roger Clemens (Special Delivery)	.45
191	David Cone (Special Delivery)	.05
192	Mike Mussina (Special Delivery)	.15
193	Randy Johnson (Special Delivery)	.30
194	Checklist (Frank Thomas)	.30
195	Checklist (Ken Griffey Jr.)	.50
196	Checklist (Cal Ripken Jr.)	.75
197	Checklist (Jeff Bagwell)	.30
198	Checklist (Mike Piazza)	.50
199	Checklist (Barry Bonds)	.75
200	Checklist (Mo Vaughn, Matt Williams)	.05

Big Bang

The game's top sluggers are featured in this insert set. The front is printed on prismatic metallic foil, a process which Score calls "Spectroetch," with large and small action photos. Backs are conventionally printed and have a large photo with a career highlight printed beneath. The toughest of the Summit chase cards, these are found on the average of once every two boxes (72 packs). Cards are numbered with a "BB" prefix.

		NM/M
Complete Set (20):		45.00
Common Player:		1.00
1	Ken Griffey Jr.	6.00
2	Frank Thomas	3.25
3	Cal Ripken Jr.	8.00
4	Jeff Bagwell	3.25
5	Mike Piazza	6.00
6	Barry Bonds	8.00
7	Matt Williams	1.00
8	Don Mattingly	4.50
9	Will Clark	1.00
10	Tony Gwynn	4.00
11	Kirby Puckett	4.00
12	Jose Canseco	2.00
13	Paul Molitor	3.25
14	Albert Belle	1.00
15	Joe Carter	1.00
16	Rafael Palmeiro	3.00
17	Fred McGriff	1.00
18	Dave Justice	1.00
19	Tim Salmon	1.00
20	Mo Vaughn	1.00

New Age

Printed on metallic foil in a horizontal format, the New Age inserts were seeded at a rate of about one per 18 packs. Red and silver colors predominate on front, while the backs are printed in standard technology and feature a second photo and career summary.

		NM/M
Complete Set (15):		10.00
Common Player:		.25
1	Cliff Floyd	.25
2	Manny Ramirez	2.00
3	Raul Mondesi	.25
4	Alex Rodriguez	5.00
5	Billy Ashley	.25
6	Alex Gonzalez	.25
7	Michael Tucker	.25
8	Charles Johnson	.25
9	Carlos Delgado	1.00
10	Benji Gil	.25
11	Chipper Jones	3.00
12	Todd Hollandsworth	.25
13	Frank Rodriguez	.25
14	Shawn Green	.60
15	Ray Durham	.25

Nth Degree

A prismatic foil background differentiates the Nth Degree parallel inserts from the Summit base cards. Nth Degree inserts are found on a 1:4 pack ratio.

	NM/M
Complete Set (200):	50.00
Common Player:	.25
Stars:	2X

21 Club

Metallic foil printing on front and back distinguishes this set of chase cards. A large red-foil "21 / CLUB" logo on each side identifies the theme of this set as players who professed to be that age during the 1955 baseball season. The players are pictured in action pose on front and a portrait on back. On average the 21 Club cards are seeded one per box (36 packs). Cards are numbered with a "TC" prefix.

		NM/M
Complete Set (9):		4.00
Common Player:		.50
1	Bob Abreu	.65
2	Pokey Reese	.50
3	Edgardo Alfonzo	.50
4	Jim Pittsley	.50
5	Ruben Rivera	.50
6	Chan Ho Park	.50
7	Julian Tavarez	.50
8	Ismael Valdes	.50
9	Dmitri Young	.50

1996 Summit

Pinnacle's 1996 Summit baseball has 200 cards, including 35 rookies, four checklists and 10 Deja Vu subset cards. Each card is also reprinted in three parallel versions - Above and Beyond (one per seven packs), Artist's Proofs (one in 36) and a retail-only silver foil-bordered version. Above and Beyond cards use an all-prismatic foil design; Artist's Proof cards have holographic foil stamping. Five insert sets were produced: Big Bang; Mirage (a parallel set to Big Bang); Hitters, Inc.; Ballparks; and Positions (found one per every 50 magazine packs).

		NM/M
Complete Set (200):		10.00
Common Player:		.05
Pack (7):		1.25
Wax Box (18):		15.00
1	Mike Piazza	1.25
2	Matt Williams	.05
3	Tino Martinez	.05
4	Reggie Sanders	.05
5	Ray Durham	.05
6	Brad Radke	.05
7	Jeff Bagwell	.65
8	Ron Gant	.05
9	Lance Johnson	.05
10	Kevin Seitzer	.05
11	Dante Bichette	.05
12	Ivan Rodriguez	.60
13	Jim Abbott	.05
14	Greg Colbrunn	.05
15	Rondell White	.05
16	Shawn Green	.40
17	Gregg Jefferies	.05
18	Omar Vizquel	.05
19	Cal Ripken Jr.	2.00
20	Mark McGwire	1.50
21	Wally Joyner	.05
22	Chili Davis	.05
23	Jose Canseco	.40
24	Royce Clayton	.05
25	Jay Bell	.05
26	Travis Fryman	.05
27	Jeff King	.05
28	Todd Hundley	.05
29	Joe Vitiello	.05
30	Russ Davis	.05
31	Mo Vaughn	.05
32	Raul Mondesi	.05
33	Ray Lankford	.05
34	Mike Stanley	.05
35	B.J. Surhoff	.05
36	Greg Vaughn	.05
37	Todd Stottlemyre	.05
38	Carlos Delgado	.50
39	Kenny Lofton	.05
40	Hideo Nomo	.35
41	Sterling Hitchcock	.05
42	Pete Schourek	.05
43	Edgardo Alfonzo	.05
44	Ken Hill	.05
45	Ken Caminiti	.05
46	Bobby Higginson	.05
47	Michael Tucker	.05
48	David Cone	.05
49	Cecil Fielder	.05
50	Brian Hunter	.05
51	Charles Johnson	.05
52	Bobby Bonilla	.05
53	Eddie Murray	.65
54	Kenny Rogers	.05
55	Jim Edmonds	.05
56	Trevor Hoffman	.05
57	Kevin Mitchell	.05
58	Ruben Sierra	.05
59	Benji Gil	.05
60	Juan Gonzalez	.35
61	Larry Walker	.05
62	Jack McDowell	.05
63	Shawon Dunston	.05
64	Andy Benes	.05
65	Jay Buhner	.05
66	Rickey Henderson	.65
67	Alex Gonzalez	.05
68	Mike Kelly	.05
69	Fred McGriff	.05
70	Ryne Sandberg	.75
71	Ernie Young	.05
72	Kevin Appier	.05
73	Moises Alou	.05
74	John Jaha	.05
75	J.T. Snow	.05
76	Jim Thome	.60
77	Kirby Puckett	.75
78	Hal Morris	.05
79	Robin Ventura	.05
80	Ben McDonald	.05
81	Tim Salmon	.05
82	Albert Belle	.05
83	Marquis Grissom	.05
84	Alex Rodriguez	1.50
85	Manny Ramirez	.65
86	Ken Griffey Jr.	1.25
87	Sammy Sosa	.75
88	Frank Thomas	.65
89	Lee Smith	.05
90	Marty Cordova	.05
91	Greg Maddux	.75
92	Lenny Dykstra	.05
93	Butch Huskey	.05
94	Garret Anderson	.05
95	Mike Bordick	.05
96	Dave Justice	.05
97	Chad Curtis	.05
98	Carlos Baerga	.05
99	Jason Isringhausen	.05
100	Gary Sheffield	.35
101	Roger Clemens	1.00
102	Ozzie Smith	.75
103	Ramon Martinez	.05
104	Paul O'Neill	.05
105	Will Clark	.05
106	Tom Glavine	.35
107	Barry Bonds	2.00
108	Barry Larkin	.05
109	Derek Bell	.05
110	Randy Johnson	.65
111	Jeff Conine	.05
112	John Mabry	.05
113	Julian Tavarez	.05
114	Gary DiSarcina	.05
115	Andres Galarraga	.05
116	Marc Newfield	.05
117	Frank Rodriguez	.05
118	Brady Anderson	.05
119	Mike Mussina	.30
120	Orlando Merced	.05
121	Melvin Nieves	.05
122	Brian Jordan	.05
123	Rafael Palmeiro	.60
124	Johnny Damon	.35
125	Wil Cordero	.05
126	Chipper Jones	.75
127	Eric Karros	.05
128	Darren Daulton	.05
129	Vinny Castilla	.05
130	Joe Carter	.05
131	Bernie Williams	.05
132	Bernard Gilkey	.05
133	Bret Boone	.05
134	Tony Gwynn	.75
135	Dave Nilsson	.05
136	Ryan Klesko	.05
137	Paul Molitor	.65
138	John Olerud	.05
139	Craig Biggio	.05
140	John Valentin	.05
141	Chuck Knoblauch	.05
142	Edgar Martinez	.05
143	Rico Brogna	.05
144	Dean Palmer	.05
145	Mark Grace	.05
146	Roberto Alomar	.20
147	Alex Fernandez	.05
148	Andre Dawson	.25
149	Wade Boggs	.75
150	Mark Lewis	.05
151	Gary Gaetti	.05
152	Paul Wilson, Roger Clemens (Deja Vu)	.45
153	Rey Ordonez, Ozzie Smith (Deja Vu)	.35
154	Derek Jeter, Cal Ripken Jr. (Deja Vu)	1.00
155	Alan Benes, Andy Benes (Deja Vu)	.05
156	Jason Kendall, Mike Piazza (Deja Vu)	.75
157	Ryan Klesko, Frank Thomas (Deja Vu)	.30

158	Johnny Damon, Ken Griffey Jr. (Deja Vu)	.65
159	Karim Garcia, Sammy Sosa (Deja Vu)	.40
160	Raul Mondesi, Tim Salmon (Deja Vu)	.05
161	Chipper Jones, Matt Williams (Deja Vu)	.40
162	Rey Ordonez	.05
163	Bob Wolcott	.05
164	Brooks Kieschnick	.05
165	Steve Gibralter	.05
166	Bob Abreu	.05
167	Gregg Zaun	.05
168	Tavo Alvarez	.05
169	Sal Fasano	.05
170	George Arias	.05
171	Derek Jeter	2.00
172	Livan Hernandez **RC**	.25
173	Alan Benes	.05
174	George Williams	.05
175	John Wasdin	.05
176	Chan Ho Park	.05
177	Paul Wilson	.05
178	Jeff Suppan	.05
179	Quinton McCracken	.05
180	Wilton Guerrero **RC**	.05
181	Eric Owens	.05
182	Felipe Crespo	.05
183	LaTroy Hawkins	.05
184	Jason Schmidt	.05
185	Terrell Wade	.05
186	Mike Grace **RC**	.05
187	Chris Snopek	.05
188	Jason Kendall	.05
189	Todd Hollandsworth	.05
190	Jim Pittsley	.05
191	Jermaine Dye	.05
192	Mike Busby **RC**	.05
193	Richard Hidalgo	.05
194	Tyler Houston	.05
195	Jimmy Haynes	.05
196	Karim Garcia	.05
197	Ken Griffey Jr. (Checklist)	.50
198	Frank Thomas (Checklist)	.30
199	Greg Maddux (Checklist)	.40
200	Cal Ripken Jr. (Checklist)	1.00

Artist's Proof

Holographic-foil highlights and an "ARTIST'S PROOF" notation on the front photo distinguish the cards in this parallel edition. The AP cards are found once per 36 packs.

	NM/M
Complete Set (200):	100.00
Common Player:	1.00
Stars:	8X

Foil

This parallel issue was an exclusive in Summit seven-card magazine retail packaging. The black borders of the regular Summit versions have been replaced on these cards by silver foil.

	NM/M
Complete Set (200):	30.00
Common Player:	.25
Stars:	3X

Above & Beyond

These 200 insert cards parallel Pinnacle's 1996 Summit set, using all-prismatic foil for each card. The cards were seeded one per every four packs.

	NM/M
Complete Set (200):	50.00
Common Player:	.25
Stars:	3X

Ballparks

These 18 cards feature images of players superimposed over their respective teams' ballparks. The cards were seeded one per every 18 packs of 1996 Pinnacle Summit baseball and are serially within an edition of 8,000 each.

		NM/M
Complete Set (18):		45.00
Common Player:		1.00
1	Cal Ripken Jr.	7.50
2	Albert Belle	1.00
3	Dante Bichette	1.00
4	Mo Vaughn	1.00
5	Ken Griffey Jr.	6.00
6	Derek Jeter	7.50
7	Juan Gonzalez	1.50
8	Greg Maddux	4.00
9	Frank Thomas	3.00
10	Ryne Sandberg	4.00
11	Mike Piazza	6.00
12	Johnny Damon	1.50
13	Barry Bonds	7.50
14	Jeff Bagwell	3.00
15	Paul Wilson	1.00
16	Tim Salmon	1.00
17	Kirby Puckett	4.00
18	Tony Gwynn	4.00

Big Bang

Sixteen of the biggest hitters are featured on these 1996 Pinnacle Summit insert cards. The cards, seeded one per every 72 packs, use Spectroetched backgrounds with foil highlights.

		NM/M
Complete Set (16):		60.00
Common Player:		1.50
1	Frank Thomas	4.00
2	Ken Griffey Jr.	7.50
3	Albert Belle	1.50
4	Mo Vaughn	1.50
5	Barry Bonds	12.00
6	Cal Ripken Jr.	12.00
7	Jeff Bagwell	4.00
8	Mike Piazza	7.50
9	Ryan Klesko	1.50
10	Manny Ramirez	4.00
11	Tim Salmon	1.50
12	Dante Bichette	1.50
13	Sammy Sosa	6.00
14	Raul Mondesi	1.50
15	Chipper Jones	6.00
16	Garret Anderson	1.50

Big Bang Mirage

These 16 cards form a parallel version to Summit's Big Bang inserts. The cards use an innovative technology that creates a floating background behind the player's image. By holding the card in direct sunlight or under an incandescent bulb, a collector can see three dimensions and a floating baseball that seems to levitate in the background. Mirage cards are serially numbered in an edition of 600 each.

		NM/M
Complete Set (16):		115.00
Common Player:		3.50
1	Frank Thomas	10.00
2	Ken Griffey Jr.	15.00
3	Albert Belle	3.50
4	Mo Vaughn	3.50
5	Barry Bonds	20.00
6	Cal Ripken Jr.	20.00
7	Jeff Bagwell	10.00
8	Mike Piazza	15.00
9	Ryan Klesko	3.50
10	Manny Ramirez	10.00
11	Tim Salmon	3.50
12	Dante Bichette	3.50
13	Sammy Sosa	12.50
14	Raul Mondesi	3.50
15	Chipper Jones	12.50
16	Garret Anderson	3.50

Hitters, Inc.

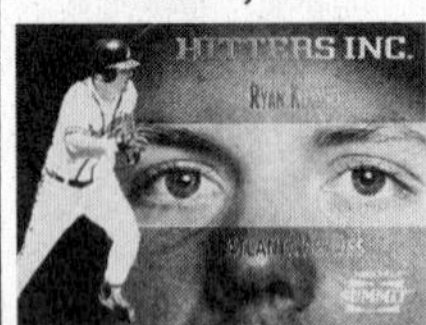

This 1996 Pinnacle Summit set honors 16 top hitters. The cards, seeded one per 36 packs, put an embossed highlight on an enlarged photo of the player's eyes. Backs are serially numbered within an edition of 4,000 each.

		NM/M
Complete Set (16):		40.00
Common Player:		1.25
1	Tony Gwynn	4.00
2	Mo Vaughn	1.25
3	Tim Salmon	1.25
4	Ken Griffey Jr.	5.00
5	Sammy Sosa	4.00
6	Frank Thomas	3.00
7	Wade Boggs	4.00
8	Albert Belle	1.25
9	Cal Ripken Jr.	8.00
10	Manny Ramirez	3.00
11	Ryan Klesko	1.25
11p	Ryan Klesko (Overprinted "SAMPLE.")	1.25
12	Dante Bichette	1.25
13	Mike Piazza	5.00
14	Chipper Jones	4.00
15	Ryne Sandberg	4.00
16	Matt Williams	1.25

Positions

This insert issue features top players at each position. It is an exclusive magazine pack

find, seeded about one per 50 packs. Fronts have action photos of three top players at the position on a baseball infield background at top. Close-ups of those photos appear at bottom, separated by a gold-foil strip. Backs have narrow action photos of each player, a few stats and a serial number from within an edition of 1,500 each.

		NM/M
Complete Set (9):		100.00
Common Card:		6.00
1	Jeff Bagwell, Mo Vaughn, Frank Thomas (First Base)	10.00
2	Roberto Alomar, Craig Biggio, Chuck Knoblauch (Second Base)	6.00
3	Matt Williams, Jim Thome, Chipper Jones (Third Base)	12.50
4	Barry Larkin, Cal Ripken Jr., Alex Rodriguez (Short Stop)	20.00
5	Mike Piazza, Ivan Rodriguez, Charles Johnson (Catcher)	15.00
6	Hideo Nomo, Greg Maddux, Randy Johnson (Pitcher)	12.50
7	Barry Bonds, Albert Belle, Ryan Klesko (Left Field)	20.00
8	Johnny Damon, Jim Edmonds, Ken Griffey Jr. (Center Field)	15.00
9	Manny Ramirez, Gary Sheffield, Sammy Sosa (Right Field)	12.50

1981 Sunbeam Bakery Discs

(See 1981 MSA/Peter Pan Sunbeam Bakery Discs.)

1987 Sun Foods Milwaukee Brewers

Though they are nowhere identified on the cards, Sun Foods was the sponsor of this team set, issuing four cards per week. Measuring 6" x 9", the cards were licensed only by the Players' Association and so do not feature team uniform logos. Bare-headed players are photographed against a blue background with a black facsimile autograph at bottom. An MLBPA logo appears in the upper-left. Backs are blank. The unnumbered cards are checklisted here in alphabetical order.

		NM/M
Complete Set (16):		15.00
Common Player:		.50
(1)	Glenn Braggs	.50
(2)	Greg Brock	.50
(3)	Mark Clear	.50
(4)	Cecil Cooper	.50
(5)	Rob Deer	.50
(6)	Jim Gantner	.50
(7)	Ted Higuera	.50
(8)	Paul Molitor	5.00
(9)	Juan Nieves	.50
(10)	Dan Plesac	.50
(11)	Billy Jo Robidoux	.50
(12)	Bill Schroeder	.50
(13)	B.J. Surhoff	.50
(14)	Dale Sveum	.50
(15)	Bill Wegman	.50
(16)	Robin Yount	5.00

2001 Sunoco Dream Team

Twenty-four former stars are depicted two per card on this "Dream Team" set. Horizontal format cards have action photos (or in the case of two cards, Jim Trusilo artwork) with a city name at top and player names at left and right. A gold-foil Sunoco Dream Team logo is at lower-right. Backs have career stats and highlights, a card title, Sunoco, Coca-Cola and MLB Players Alumni logos. Cards were available in three-card packs for 49 cents with a gasoline or Coke purchase.

		NM/M
Complete Set (12):		5.00
Common Card:		.50
1	Game Seven Slams (Bill Mazeroski, Willie Stargell)	1.00
2	Philly Phenoms (Mike Schmidt, Steve Carlton)	1.50
3	Red Hot Heroes (Tony Perez, Joe Morgan)	1.00
4	Bronx Legends (Yogi Berra, Don Mattingly)	1.50
5	Outstanding O's (Jim Palmer, Frank Robinson)	1.00
6	Dynamic Duo (Carlton Fisk, Luis Tiant)	1.00
7	Beantown Beginnings (Fred Lynn, Jim Rice)	1.00
8	Tiger Tough (Sparky Anderson, Al Kaline)	1.00
9	Whiz Kids (Robin Roberts, Richie Ashburn (artwork)	1.00
10	Amazin' Championships (Tug McGraw, Gary Carter)	1.00
11	Top of the Tribe (Lou Boudreau, Bob Feller (artwork)	1.00
12	In Tribute (Roger Maris, Catfish Hunter)	1.50

1994 SuperSlam

An innovative issued felled by the 1994 baseball strike, SuperSlams are a 5-1/2" x 7-1/2" tent-fold display card. Front and back have a gridded silver metallic background. At center on front is a 3-3/4" x 5-1/4" color photo on which is superimposed a 3-D action pose of the player. Backs have extensive "This is my life" biographical information about the player. The cards are skip-numbered. Promo cards of Jack McDowell were issued with either silver or gold background. Cards were sold for $7.95 apiece with reported production between 2,000 and 50,000, depending on player.

		NM/M
Complete Set (18):		60.00
Common Player:		2.50
3	Greg Maddux	5.00
4	Fred McGriff	2.50
5	Moises Alou	2.50
19	Roberto Alomar	3.00
27	Cal Ripken Jr.	8.00
28	Roger Clemens	5.50
40	Mike Piazza	6.00
42	Barry Bonds	8.00
47	Tony Gwynn	5.00
53	Rickey Henderson	4.00
58	Tim Salmon	2.50
60	Ken Griffey Jr.	6.00
65	Juan Gonzalez	3.00
67	Jeff Bagwell	4.00
83	Albert Belle	2.50
84	Kenny Lofton	2.50
90	Kirby Puckett	5.00
95	Frank Thomas	4.00
P1	Jack McDowell/Gold	2.50
P2	Jack McDowell/Silver	2.50

1982 Superstar

A second series of Superstar collector cards was produced in 1982. Similar in format to the 1980 issue, they also feature black-and-white photos. Surrounding graphics on the second series are in red, white and blue. Backs are numbered from 45-90 in continuation of the first series and contain career narratives. Many players are again featured on multiple cards, and the second series contains sports stars other than baseball players. Issue price was again $3.50.

		NM/M
Complete Set (45):		10.00
Common Player:		.40
46	Duke Snider	.40
47	Al Kaline	.40
48	Stan Musial	.60
49	Frank Robinson	.40
50	Jim Brown	.80
51	Bobby Orr	.60
52	Roger Staubach	.40
53	Honus Wagner	.40
54	Willie Mays	.80
55	Roy Campanella	.40
56	Mickey Mantle	2.50
57	Hank Aaron	.80
58	Ernie Banks	.60
59	Babe Ruth, Lou Gehrig	1.50
60	Ted Williams	.80
61	Babe Ruth	1.50
62	Lou Gehrig	.80
63	Sandy Koufax	.80
64	Fran Tarkenton	.40
65	Gordie Howe	.60
66	Roberto Clemente	1.25
67	Ty Cobb	.60
68	Lou Brock	.40
69	Joe Namath	.60
70	O.J. Simpson	.60
71	Whitey Ford	.40

#	Player	NM/M
72	Jackie Robinson	.80
73	Bill Russell	.60
74	Johnny Unitas	.40
75	Bobby Hull	.60
76	Bob Cousy	.60
77	Walter Johnson	.40
78	Satchel Paige	.50
79	Joe DiMaggio	1.25
80	Yogi Berra	.40
81	Jerry West	.60
82	Rod Gilbert	.60
83	Sadaharu Oh	.40
84	Wilt Chamberlain	.60
85	Frank Gifford	.40
86	Casey Stengel	.40
87	Eddie Mathews	.40
88	Hank Aaron, Sandy Koufax	.80
89	Ted Williams, Mickey Mantle	1.25
90	Casey Stengel, Mickey Mantle	1.50

1987 Super Stars Discs

Produced by Mike Schecter Associates, the Super Stars disc set was released as part of a promotion for various brands of iced tea mixes in many parts of the country. Among the brands participating in the promotion were Acme, Alpha Beta, Bustelo, Key, King Kullen, Lady Lee, Our Own, and Weis. The discs were issued in three-part folding panels with each disc measuring 2-1/2" in diameter. Fronts feature a full-color photo inside a bright yellow border. Two player discs were included in each panel along with a coupon disc offering either an uncut press sheet of the set or a facsimile autographed ball. Because the series was licensed only by the players' union, and not MLB, cap logos were removed.

#		NM/M
	Complete Panel Set (10):	7.50
	Complete Singles Set (20):	4.50
	Common Panel:	.25
	Common Single Player:	.10
	Panel (1)	1.00
1	Darryl Strawberry	.10
2	Roger Clemens	.50
	Panel (2)	.25
3	Ron Darling	.10
4	Keith Hernandez	.10
	Panel (3)	1.00
5	Tony Pena	.10
6	Don Mattingly	.50
	Panel (4)	.75
7	Eric Davis	.10
8	Gary Carter	.25
	Panel (5)	.75
9	Dave Winfield	.25
10	Wally Joyner	.10
	Panel (6)	1.00
11	Mike Schmidt	.50
12	Robby Thompson	.10
	Panel (7)	2.00
13	Wade Boggs	.35
14	Cal Ripken Jr.	.75
	Panel (8)	1.00
15	Dale Murphy	.25
16	Tony Gwynn	.35
	Panel (9)	1.00
17	Jose Canseco	.20
18	Rickey Henderson	.25
	Panel (10)	.25
19	Lance Parrish	.10
20	Leo Righetti	.10

1988 Super Stars Discs

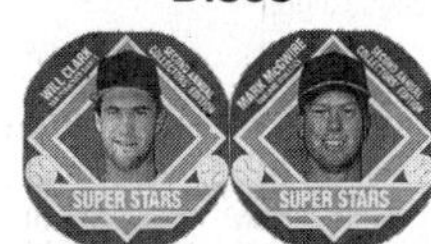

The "Second Annual Collector's Edition" of Super Stars discs is similar to the 1987 issue. A set of 20 discs (2-1/2" diameter) featuring full-color player photos was inserted in specially marked cannisters of iced tea and fruit drinks. Each triple-fold insert consists of two player discs and one redemption card. Player discs are bright blue, yellow, red and green with a diamond design framing the player portrait. The player name appears upper left, the set logo appears upper right. Personalized disc series were issued for Tetley, Weis, Key Food and A&P supermarkets (untitled series were also sold at Lucky, Skaggs, Alpha Beta, Acme King Kullen, Laneco and Krasdale stores). The series name (i.e. Weis Winners) is printed below the player photo. Backs are in red with a few personal data and stats. Because the discs are licensed only through the players' union, cap logos have been airbrushed off the photos.

#		NM/M
	Complete Panel Set (10):	7.50
	Complete Singles Set (20):	4.50
	Common Panel:	.25
	Common Single Player:	.10
	Panel (1)	2.00
1	Wade Boggs	.50
9	Roger Clemens	.60
	Panel (2)	1.25
3	Don Mattingly	.60
13	Dave Magadan	.10
	Panel (3)	1.50
4	Mark McGwire	.65
10	Will Clark	.10
	Panel (4)	.25
5	Matt Nokes	.10
11	Vince Coleman	.10
	Panel (5)	.25
8	Kevin Seitzer	.10
2	Ellis Burks	.10
	Panel (6)	1.25
12	Eric Davis	.10
6	Kirby Puckett	.50
	Panel (7)	.25
15	Benito Santiago	.10
20	Fernando Valenzuela	.10
	Panel (8)	1.50
16	Mike Schmidt	.60
14	Dale Murphy	.25
	Panel (9)	.25
17	Darryl Strawberry	.10
10	Dwight Gooden	.10
	Panel (10)	.25
18	Steve Bedrosian	.10
7	Billy Ripken	.10

1989 Super Stars Discs

The third annual series of Super Stars perforated disc folders again offered two players and an offer for a a facsimile autographed baseball or an uncut sheet of discs. The 2-3/4" diameter discs have a yellow border with a red star at center. A player portrait photo is in the star. Backs are printed in black and have a few previous season stats and biographical bits. As in previous years, the discs were produced by Michael Schechter Associates, which does business only with the Players Union, precluding the use of MLB logos on the player photos.

#		NM/M
	Complete Panel Set (10):	9.00
	Complete Singles Set (20):	5.00
	Common Panel:	.25
	Common Player:	.10
	Panel (1)	1.25
1	Don Mattingly	.50
2	David Cone	.10
	Panel (2)	2.00
3	Mark McGwire	.65
4	Will Clark	.10
	Panel (3)	.25
5	Darryl Strawberry	.10
6	Dwight Gooden	.10
	Panel (4)	2.00
7	Wade Boggs	.45
8	Roger Clemens	.50
	Panel (5)	.25
9	Benito Santiago	.10
10	Orel Hershiser	.10
	Panel (6)	1.25
11	Eric Davis	.10
12	Kirby Puckett	.45
	Panel (7)	1.25
13	Dave Winfield	.40
14	Andre Dawson	.25
	Panel (8)	2.00
15	Steve Bedrosian	.10
16	Cal Ripken Jr.	.75
	Panel (9)	1.00
17	Andy Van Slyke	.10
18	Jose Canseco	.35
	Panel (10)	.75
19	Jose Oquendo	.10
20	Dale Murphy	.25

1990 Super Stars Discs

In its fourth annual edition the Super Stars discs continued the three-piece perforated folder format. Each panel consists of two player discs and a disc offering a 1990-1991 calendar at the center of an uncut sheet of the discs. Discs have a red border with a player portrait photo in the center of a tombstone-shaped yellow frame. A few 1989 stats and biographical notes are printed in black on the back. Because the discs are licensed only by the players' union, and not Major League Baseball, the player photos have had team logos excised.

#		NM/M
	Complete Panel Set (10):	9.00
	Complete Set, Singles (20):	4.50
	Common Panel:	.25
	Common Player:	.10
	Panel (1)	.50
1	Will Clark	.10
2	Howard Johnson	.10
	Panel (2)	1.00
3	Chris Sabo	.10
4	Jose Canseco	.40
	Panel (3)	.50
5	Bo Jackson	.15
6	Kevin Mitchell	.10
	Panel (4)	2.25
7	Wade Boggs	.50
8	Ken Griffey Jr.	.65
	Panel (5)	.25
9	George Bell	.10
10	Dwight Gooden	.10
	Panel (6)	1.00
11	Bobby Bonilla	.10
12	Ryne Sandberg	.50
	Panel (7)	2.00
13	Kirby Puckett	.50
14	Don Mattingly	.60
	Panel (8)	1.50
15	Mark McGwire	.75
16	Frank Viola	.10
	Panel (9)	.25
17	Bret Saberhagen	.10
18	Mike Greenwell	.10
	Panel (10)	2.00
19	Steve Sax	.10
20	Nolan Ryan	1.00

1989 Swell Baseball Greats

Collectors Marketing Corp. handled the distribution of Philadelphia Gum Company's debut "old-timers" set. Most cards featured color photos, though some of the older players were represented in sepia shots. Red-and-white backs featured career stats, a baseball biography and a few vital statistics.

#		NM/M
	Complete Set (135):	12.00
	Common Player:	.15
	Wax Pack (10):	.65
	Wax Box (36):	15.00
1	Babe Ruth	3.50
2	Ty Cobb	1.50
3	Walter Johnson	.75
4	Honus Wagner	.75
5	Cy Young	.75
6	Joe Adcock	.15
7	Jim Bunning	.15
8	Orlando Cepeda	.15
9	Harvey Kuenn	.15
10	Catfish Hunter	.15
11	Johnny VanderMeer	.15
12	Tony Oliva	.15
13	Harvey Haddix (Reversed negative.)	.15
14	Dick McAuliffe	.15
15	Lefty Grove	.15
16	Bo Belinski	.15
17	Claude Osteen	.15
18	Doc Medich	.15
19	Del Ennis	.15
20	Rogers Hornsby	.40
21	Bob Buhl	.15
22	Phil Nickro	.15
23	Don Zimmer	.15
24	Greg Luzinski	.15
25	Lou Gehrig	2.50
26	Ken Singleton	.15
27	Bob Allison	.15
28	Ed Kranepool	.15
29	Manny Sanguillen	.15
30	Luke Appling	.15
31	Ralph Terry	.15
32	Smoky Burgess	.15
33	Gil Hodges	.40
34	Harry Walker	.15
35	Edd Roush	.15
36	Ron Santo	.15
37	Jim Perry	.15
38	Jose Morales	.15
39	Stan Bahnsen	.15
40	Al Kaline	.40
41	Mel Harder	.15
42	Ralph Houk	.15
43	Jack Billingham	.15
44	Carl Erskine	.15
45	Hoyt Wilhelm	.15
46	Dick Radatz	.15
47	Roy Sievers	.15
48	Jim Lonborg	.15
49	Bobby Richardson	.25
50	Whitey Ford	.40
51	Roy Face	.15
52	Tom Tresh	.15
53	Joe Nuxhall	.15
54	Mickey Vernon	.15
55	Johnny Mize	.15
56	Scott McGregor	.15
57	Billy Pierce	.15
58	Dave Giusti	.15
59	Minnie Minoso	.15
60	Early Wynn	.15
61	Jose Cardenal	.15
62	Sam Jethroe	.15
63	Sal Bando	.15
64	Elrod Hendricks	.15
65	Enos Slaughter	.15
66	Jim Bouton	.15
67	Bill Mazeroski	.25
68	Tony Kubek	.25
69	Joe Black	.15
70	Harmon Killebrew	.40
71	Sam McDowell	.15
72	Bucky Dent	.15
73	Virgil Trucks	.15
74	Andy Pafko	.15
75	Bob Feller	.40
76	Tito Francona	.15
77	Al Dark	.15
78	Larry Dierker	.15
79	Nellie Briles	.15
80	Lou Boudreau	.15
81	Wally Moon	.15
82	Hank Bauer	.15
83	Jim Piersall	.15
84	Jim Grant	.15
85	Richie Ashburn	.15
86	Bob Friend	.15
87	Ken Keltner	.15
88	Jim Kaat	.15
89	Dean Chance	.15
90	Al Lopez	.15
91	Dick Groat	.15
92	Johnny Blanchard	.15
93	Chuck Hinton	.15
94	Clete Boyer	.15
95	Steve Carlton	.40
96	Tug McGraw	.15
97	Mickey Lolich	.15
98	Earl Weaver	.15
99	Sal Maglie	.15
100	Ted Williams	2.25
101	Allie Reynolds (Photo actually Marius Russo.)	.15
102	Gene Woodling (Photo actually Irv Noren.)	.15
103	Moe Drabowsky	.15
104	Mickey Stanley	.15
105	Jim Palmer	.15
106	Bill Freehan	.15
107	Bob Robertson	.15
108	Walt Dropo	.15
109	Jerry Koosman	.15
110	Bobby Doerr	.15
111	Phil Rizzuto	.40
112	Don Kessinger	.15
113	Milt Pappas	.15
114	Herb Score	.15
115	Larry Doby	.15
116	Glenn Beckert	.15
117	Andre Thornton	.15
118	Gary Matthews	.15
119	Bill Virdon	.15
120	Billy Williams	.15
121	Johnny Sain	.15
122	Don Newcombe	.15
123	Rico Petrocelli	.15
124	Dick Bosman	.15
125	Roberto Clemente	3.00
126	Rocky Colavito	.15
127	Wilbur Wood	.15
128	Duke Sims	.15
129	Ken Holtzman	.15
130	Casey Stengel	.15
131	Bobby Shantz	.15
132	Del Crandall	.15
133	Bobby Thomson	.15
134	Brooks Robinson	.40
135	Checklist	.15

1990 Swell Baseball Greats

In its second year of "old-timers" set production, Swell moved its "Baseball Greats" banner to the card front, above a color player photo. Where color photos were unavailable, sepia pictures were used. Backs were virtually identical to the previous year, with a line of lifetime stats, a career highlights write-up and a few bits of personal data. Also nearly identical is player selection within the 135-card set.

#		NM/M
	Complete Set (135):	12.00
	Common Player:	.15
	Wax Pack (10):	.75
	Wax Box (36):	12.50
1	Tom Seaver	.50
2	Hank Aaron	2.50
3	Mickey Cochrane	.15
4	Rod Carew	.15
5	Carl Yastrzemski	.40
6	Dizzy Dean	.50
7	Sal Bando	.15
8	Whitey Ford	.40
9	Bill White	.15
10	Babe Ruth	3.50
11	Robin Roberts	.15
12	Warren Spahn	.15
13	Billy Williams	.15
14	Joe Garagiola	.40
15	Ty Cobb	1.50
16	Boog Powell	.15
17	Tom Tresh	.15
18	Luke Appling	.15
19	Tommie Agee	.15
20	Roberto Clemente	3.00
21	Bobby Thomson	.15
22	Charlie Keller	.15
23	George Bamberger	.15
24	Eddie Lopat	.15
25	Lou Gehrig	2.50
26	Manny Mota	.15
27	Steve Stone	.15
28	Orlando Cepeda	.15
29	Al Bumbry	.15
30	Grover Alexander	.15
31	Lou Boudreau	.15
32	Herb Score	.15
33	Harry Walker	.15
34	Deron Johnson	.15
35	Edd Roush	.15
36	Carl Erskine	.15
37	Ken Forsch	.15
38	Sal Maglie	.15
39	Al Rosen	.15
40	Casey Stengel	.15
41	Cesar Cedeno	.15
42	Roy White	.15
43	Larry Doby	.15
44	Rod Kanehl	.15
45	Tris Speaker	.40
46	Ralph Garr	.15
47	Andre Thornton	.15
48	Frankie Crosetti	.15
49	Dick Groat	.15
50	Honus Wagner	.75
51	Rogers Hornsby	.40
52	Ken Brett	.15
53	Lenny Randle	.15
54	Enos Slaughter	.15
55	Mel Ott	.15
56	Rico Petrocelli	.15
57	Walt Dropo	.15
58	Bob Grich	.15
59	Billy Herman	.15
60	Bob Feller	.40
61	Davey Johnson	.15
62	Don Drysdale	.15
63	Larry Sorensen	.15
64	Ron Santo	.15
65	Eddie Mathews	.15
66	Gaylord Perry	.15
67	Lee May	.15
68	Johnnie LeMaster	.15
69	Don Kessinger	.15
70	Lefty Grove	.15
71	Lou Brock	.15
72	Don Cardwell	.15
73	Harvey Haddix	.15
74	Frank Torre	.15
75	Walter Johnson	.75
76	Don Newcombe	.15
77	Marv Throneberry	.15
78	Jim Northrup	.15
79	Fritz Peterson	.15
80	Ralph Kiner	.15
81	Mickey Lolich	.15
82	Donn Clendenon	.15
83	Pete Vuckovich	.15
84	Lefty Gomez	.15
85	Monte Irvin	.15
86	Rick Ferrell	.15
87	Tommy Hutton	.15
88	Julio Cruz	.15
89	Vida Blue	.15
90	Johnny Mize	.15
91	Rusty Staub	.15
92	Jimmy Piersall	.15
93	Bill Mazeroski	.15
94	Lee Lacy	.15
95	Ernie Banks	.40
96	Bobby Doerr	.15
97	George Foster	.15
98	Eric Soderholm	.15
99	Johnny VanderMeer	.15
100	Cy Young	.75
101	Jimmie Foxx	.40
102	Clete Boyer	.15
103	Steve Garvey	.15
104	Johnny Podres	.15
105	Yogi Berra	.40
106	Bill Monbouquette	.15
107	Milt Pappas	.15
108	Dave LaRoche	.15
109	Elliott Maddox	.15
110	Steve Carlton	.15
111	Bud Harrelson	.15
112	Mark Littell	.15
113	Frank J. Thomas	.15
114	Bill Robinson	.15
115	Satchel Paige	.75
116	John Denny	.15
117	Clyde King	.15
118	Billy Sample	.15
119	Rocky Colavito	.15
120	Bob Gibson	.15
121	Bert Campaneris	.15
122	Mark Fidrych	.15
123	Ed Charles	.15
124	Jim Lonborg	.15
125	Ted Williams	2.50
126	Manny Sanguillen	.15
127	Matt Keough	.15
128	Vern Ruhle	.15
129	Bob Skinner	.15
130	Joe Torre	.15
131	Ralph Houk	.15
132	Gil Hodges	.40
133	Ralph Branca	.15
134	Christy Mathewson	.75
135	Checklist	.15

1991 Swell Baseball Greats

The last of three "old-timers" sets issued by Philadelphia Gum Co., this 150-card set was marketed by Impel. Cards are 2-1/2" x 3-1/2" and feature red and yellow borders around color player photos. In

the case of some older players, sepia-toned photos are used instead of color. Backs are printed in red and black and include career stats and a few vital statistics.

		NM/M
Complete Set (150):		17.50
Common Player:		.15
Wax Pack (10):		.75
Wax Box (36):		15.00
1	Tommie Agee	.15
2	Matty Alou	.15
3	Luke Appling	.15
4	Richie Ashburn	.15
5	Ernie Banks	.40
6	Don Baylor	.15
7	Buddy Bell	.15
8	Yogi Berra	.40
9	Joe Black	.15
10	Vida Blue	.15
11	Bobby Bonds	.15
12	Lou Boudreau	.15
13	Lou Brock	.15
14	Ralph Branca	.15
15	Bobby Brown	.15
16	Lou Burdette	.15
17	Steve Carlton	.25
18	Rico Carty	.15
19	Jerry Coleman	.15
20	Frankie Crosetti	.15
21	Julio Cruz	.15
22	Alvin Dark	.15
23	Doug DeCinces	.15
24	Larry Doby	.15
25	Bobby Doerr	.15
26	Don Drysdale	.15
27	Carl Erskine	.15
28	Elroy Face	.15
29	Rick Ferrell	.15
30	Rollie Fingers	.15
31	Joe Garagiola	.40
32	Steve Garvey	.15
33	Bob Gibson	.15
34	Mudcat Grant	.15
35	Dick Groat	.15
36	Jerry Grote	.15
37	Toby Harrah	.15
38	Bud Harrelson	.15
39	Billy Herman	.15
40	Ken Holtzman	.15
41	Willie Horton	.15
42	Ralph Houk	.15
43	Al Hrabosky	.15
44	Monte Irvin	.15
45	Fergie Jenkins	.15
46	Davey Johnson	.15
47	George Kell	.15
48	Charlie Keller	.15
49	Harmon Killebrew	.25
50	Ralph Kiner	.15
51	Clyde King	.15
52	Dave Kingman	.15
53	Al Kaline	.40
54	Clem Labine	.15
55	Vern Law	.15
56	Mickey Lolich	.15
57	Jim Lonborg	.15
58	Eddie Lopat	.15
59	Sal Maglie	.15
60	Bill Mazeroski	.25
61	Johnny VanderMeer	.15
62	Johnny Mize	.15
63	Manny Mota	.15
64	Wally Moon	.15
65	Rick Monday	.15
66	Tom Tresh	.15
67	Graig Nettles	.15
68	Don Newcombe	.15
69	Milt Pappas	.15
70	Gaylord Perry	.15
71	Rico Petrocelli	.15
72	Jimmy Piersall	.15
73	Johnny Podres	.15
74	Boog Powell	.15
75	Bobby Richardson	.25
76	Vern Ruhle	.15
77	Robin Roberts	.15
78	Al Rosen	.15
79	Billy Sample	.15
80	Manny Sanguillen	.15
81	Ron Santo	.15
82	Herb Score	.15
83	Bobby Shantz	.15
84	Enos Slaughter	.15
85	Eric Soderholm	.15
86	Warren Spahn	.15
87	Rusty Staub	.15
88	Bobby Thomson	.15
89	Marv Throneberry	.15
90	Luis Tiant	.15
91	Frank Torre	.15
92	Joe Torre	.25
93	Bill Virdon	.15
94	Harry Walker	.15
95	Earl Weaver	.15
96	Bill White	.15
97	Roy White	.15
98	Billy Williams	.15
99	Dick Williams	.15
100	Ted Williams	2.50
101	Gene Woodling	.15
102	Hank Aaron	2.50
103	Rod Carew	.15
104	Cesar Cedeno	.15
105	Orlando Cepeda	.15
106	Willie Mays	2.50
107	Tom Seaver	.40
108	Carl Yastrzemski	.40
109	Clete Boyer	.15
110	Bert Campaneris	.15
111	Walt Dropo	.15
112	George Foster	.15
113	Phil Garner	.15
114	Harvey Kuenn	.15
115	Don Kessinger	.15
116	Rocky Colavito	.15
117	Bobby Murcer	.15
118	Mel Parnell	.15
119	Ken Reitz	.15
120	Earl Wilson	.15
121	Wilbur Wood	.15
122	Ed Yost	.15
123	Jim Bouton	.15
124	Babe Ruth	3.50
125	Lou Gehrig	2.50
126	Honus Wagner	.75
127	Ty Cobb	1.50
128	Grover C. Alexander	.15
129	Lefty Gomez	.15
130	Walter Johnson	.75
131	Gil Hodges	.40
132	Roberto Clemente	3.00
133	Satchel Paige	.75
134	Edd Roush	.15
135	Cy Young	.75
136	Casey Stengel	.15
137	Rogers Hornsby	.40
138	Dizzy Dean	.50
139	Lefty Grove	.15
140	Tris Speaker	.40
141	Christy Mathewson	.75
142	Mickey Cochrane	.15
143	Jimmie Foxx	.40
144	Mel Ott	.25
145	Bob Feller	.25
146	Brooks Robinson	.40
147	Eddie Mathews	.15
148	Pie Traynor	.15
149	Thurman Munson	.25
150	Checklist	.15

2003 Sycuan Casino-Resort Tony Gwynn

This series of 3-1/2" x 5" cards commemorating the career of Padres icon Tony Gwynn was issued on a one-per-month basis between April-September by a San Diego area tribal entertainment complex. Cards are UV coated and feature silver-foil highlights on front. Posed or action photos are framed in dark green. Backs have a ghosted photo of the player, a few sentences about him and logos of the team and casino.

		NM/M
Complete Set (6):		50.00
Common Card:		10.00
1	Tony Gwynn (Twenty Great Years)	10.00
2	Tony Gwynn (Eight Batting Titles)	10.00
3	Tony Gwynn (Five Gold Gloves)	10.00
4	Tony Gwynn (3,000th Hit)	10.00
5	Tony Gwynn (Hitting Machine)	10.00
6	Tony Gwynn (Last At Bat)	10.00

T

1988 T & M Sports Umpires

The first umpires to be featured on baseball cards since the 1955 Bowman set are the arbiters included in this boxed set issued T & M and licensed by the umps' union. Cards have posed photos framed in red (American League) green (National League) with a black border on front. The correct league logo is in a lower corner. The umpire's uniform number and name are in white at bottom. The back has a blue background with personal data, career summary, service record and card number, along with licensor logos.

		NM/M
Complete Set (64):		5.00
Common Card:		.15
1	Doug Harvey	.15
2	Lee Weyer	.15
3	Billy Williams	.15
4	John Kibler	.15
5	Bob Engel	.15
6	Harry Wendelstedt	.15
7	Larry Barnett	.15
8	Don Denkinger	.15
9	Dave Phillips	.15
10	Larry McCoy	.15
11	Bruce Froemming	.15
12	John McSherry	.15
13	Jim Evans	.15
14	Frank Pulli	.15
15	Joe Brinkman	.15
16	Terry Tata	.15
17	Paul Runge	.15
18	Dutch Rennert	.15
19	Nick Bremigan	.15
20	Jim McKean	.15
21	Terry Cooney	.15
22	Rich Garcia	.15
23	Dale Ford	.15
24	Al Clark	.15
25	Greg Kosc	.15
26	Jim Quick	.15
27	Ed Montague	.15
28	Jerry Crawford	.15
29	Steve Palermo	.15
30	Durwood Merrill	.15
31	Ken Kaiser	.15
32	Vic Voltaggio	.15
33	Mike Reilly	.15
34	Eric Gregg	.15
35	Ted Hendry	.15
36	Joe West	.15
37	Dave Pallone	.15
38	Fred Brocklander	.15
39	John Shulock	.15
40	Derryl Cousins	.15
41	Charlie Williams	.15
42	Rocky Roe	.15
43	Randy Marsh	.15
44	Bob Davidson	.15
45	Drew Coble	.15
46	Tim McClelland	.15
47	Dan Morrison	.15
48	Rick Reed	.15
49	Steve Rippley	.15
50	John Hirschbeck	.15
51	Mark Johnson	.15
52	Gerry Davis	.15
53	Dana DeMuth	.15
54	Larry Young	.15
55	Tim Welke	.15
56	Greg Bonin	.15
57	Tom Hallion	.15
58	Dale Scott	.15
59	Tim Tschida	.15
60	Dick Stello	.15
61	1987 All-Star Game (Derryl Cousins, Bob Davidson, Don Denkinger, Dick Stello, Vic Voltaggio, Joe West)	.15
62	1987 World Series (Ken Kaiser, Greg Kosc, John McSherry, Dave Phillips, Terry Tata, Lee Weyer)	.15
63	Jocko Conlan	.30
64	Checklist	.15

1989 T & M Sports Senior League

The 120-card 1989-90 T&M Sports Senior League set features a full-color photo of the player on the front on a borderless card. A red stripe separates the photo from the black bottom with the player's name, team logo and position. The cards are printed on heavy, white cardboard stock and sold as a boxed set. The backs have a red border across the top and bio and career notes, along with a summary of the player's career. Included in the set are eight static-cling puzzle pieces which, when put together, show a drawing of a prominent player from each team.

		NM/M
Complete Set (120):		4.00
Common Player:		.05
1	Curt Flood (Commissioner)	.10
2	Willie Aikens	.05
3	Gary Allenson	.05
4	Stan Bahnsen	.05
5	Alan Bannister	.05
6	Juan Beniquez	.05
7	Jim Bibby	.05
8	Paul Blair	.05
9	Vida Blue	.10
10	Bobby Bonds	.15
11	Pedro Borbon	.05
12	Clete Boyer	.05
13	Gates Brown	.05
14	Al Bumbry	.05
15	Sal Butera	.05
16	Bert Campaneris	.10
17	Bill Campbell	.05
18	Bernie Carbo	.05
19	Dave Cash	.05
20	Cesar Cedeno	.05
21	Gene Clines	.05
22	Dave Collins	.05
23	Cecil Cooper	.05
24	Doug Corbett	.05
25	Al Cowens	.05
26	Jose Cruz	.05
27	Mike Cuellar	.10
28	Pat Dobson	.05
29	Dick Drago	.05
30	Dan Driessen	.05
31	Jamie Easterly	.05
32	Juan Eichelberger	.05
33	Dock Ellis	.05
34	Ed Figueroa	.05
35	Rollie Fingers	.50
36	George Foster	.15
37	Oscar Gamble	.05
38	Wayne Garland	.05
39	Wayne Garrett	.05
40	Ross Grimsley	.05
41	Jerry Grote	.05
42	Johnny Grubb	.05
43	Mario Guerrero	.05
44	Toby Harrah	.05
45	Steve Henderson	.05
46	George Hendrick	.05
47	Butch Hobson	.05
48	Roy Howell	.05
49	Al Hrabosky	.05
50	Clint Hurdle	.05
51	Garth Iorg	.05
52	Tim Ireland	.05
53	Grant Jackson	.05
54	Ron Jackson	.05
55	Ferguson Jenkins	.50
56	Odell Jones	.05
57	Mike Kekich	.05
58	Steve Kemp	.05
59	Dave Kingman	.10
60	Bruce Kison	.05
61	Lee Lacy	.05
62	Rafael Landestoy	.05
63	Ken Landreaux	.05
64	Tito Landrum	.05
65	Dave LaRoche	.05
66	Bill Lee	.05
67	Ron LeFlore	.05
68	Dennis Leonard	.05
69	Bill Madlock	.10
70	Mickey Mahler	.05
71	Rick Manning	.05
72	Tippy Martinez	.05
73	Jon Matlack	.05
74	Bake McBride	.05
75	Steve McCarty	.05
76	Hal McRae	.10
77	Dan Meyer	.05
78	Felix Millan	.05
79	Paul Mirabella	.05
80	Omar Moreno	.05
81	Jim Morrison	.05
82	Graig Nettles	.05
83	Al Oliver	.10
84	Amos Otis	.05
85	Tom Paciorek	.05
86	Lowell Plamer	.05
87	Pat Putnam	.05
88	Lenny Randle	.05
89	Ken Reitz	.05
90	Gene Richards	.05
91	Mickey Rivers	.05
92	Leon Roberts	.05
93	Joe Sambito	.05
94	Rodney Scott	.05
95	Bob Shirley	.05
96	Jim Slaton	.05
97	Elias Sosa	.05
98	Fred Stanley	.05
99	Bill Stein	.05
100	Rennie Stennett	.05
101	Sammy Stewart	.05
102	Tim Stoddard	.05
103	Champ Summers	.05
104	Derrell Thomas	.05
105	Luis Tiant	.10
106	Bobby Tolan	.05
107	Bill Travers	.05
108	Tom Underwood	.05
109	Rick Waits	.05
110	Ron Washington	.05
111	U.L. Washington	.05
112	Earl Weaver	.25
113	Jerry White	.05
114	Milt Wilcox	.05
115	Dick Williams	.05
116	Walt Williams	.05
117	Rick Wise	.05
118	Favorite Suns (Luis Tiant, Cesar Cedeno)	.05
119	Home Run Legends (George Foster, Bobby Bonds)	.05
120	Sunshine Skippers (Earl Weaver, Dick Williams)	.25

Umpires

A second edition of umpires' cards from T & M was also sold as a boxed set. Fronts of the 2-1/2" x 3-1/2" cards have color photos which are borderless at top and sides. At bottom is a strip with the ump's name and uniform number at right and league logo at left. Backs have personal data and a career summary, along with logos of MLB and the Umpires' Association.

		NM/M
Complete Set (63):		7.50
Common Card:		.15
1	Doug Harvey	.25
2	John Kibler	.15
3	Bob Engel	.15
4	Harry Wendelstedt	.15
5	Larry Barnett	.15
6	Don Denkinger	.15
7	Dave Phillips	.15
8	Larry McCoy	.15
9	Bruce Froemming	.15
10	John McSherry	.20
11	Jim Evans	.15
12	Frank Pulli	.15
13	Joe Brinkman	.15
14	Terry Tata	.15
15	Nick Bremigan	.15
16	Jim McKean	.15
17	Paul Runge	.15
18	Dutch Rennert	.15
19	Terry Cooney	.15
20	Rich Garcia	.15
21	Dale Ford	.15
22	Al Clark	.15
23	Greg Kosc	.15
24	Jim Quick	.15
25	Ed Montague	.15
26	Jerry Crawford	.15
27	Steve Palermo	.35
28	Durwood Merrill	.15
29	Ken Kaiser	.20
30	Vic Voltaggio	.15
31	Mike Reilly	.15
32	Eric Gregg	.25
33	Ted Hendry	.15
34	Joe West	.15
35	Dave Pallone	.25
36	Fred Brocklander	.15
37	John Shulock	.15
38	Derryl Cousins	.15
39	Charlie Williams	.15
40	Rocky Roe	.15
41	Randy Marsh	.15
42	Bob Davidson	.15
43	Drew Coble	.15
44	Tim McClelland	.15
45	Dan Morrison	.15
46	Rick Reed	.15
47	Steve Ripley	.15
48	John Hirschbeck	.15
49	Mark Johnson	.15
50	Gerry Davis	.15
51	Dana DeMuth	.15
52	Larry Young	.15
53	Tim Welke	.15
54	Greg Bonin	.15
55	Tom Hallion	.15
56	Dale Scott	.15
57	Tim Tschida	.15
58	Gary Darling	.15
59	Mark Hirschbeck	.15
60	All-Star Crew	.15
61	World Series Crew	.15
62	Lee Weyer	.15
63	Tom Connolly, Bill Klem	.25

1990 T & M Sports Umpires

Puzzle piece inserts and a send-away premium card offer are featured in the 1990 umpires set. Card fronts have action photos of the arbiters with league insignia in a home plate-shaped frame in a lower corner. Above the photo, the umpire's name and uniform number are printed in a banner. Backs have biographical data, a baseball rules trivia question and the logos of MLB and the Major League Umpires Association. Card #71, Hall of Fame umpire Al Barlick, was only available by sending in the four puzzle pieces overprinted with the National League logo.

		NM/M
Complete Set (70, No Barlick.):		6.00
Common Card:		.10
1	Doug Harvey	.10
2	John Kibler	.10
3	Bob Engel	.10
4	Harry Wendelstedt	.10
5	Larry Barnett	.10
6	Don Denkinger	.10
7	Dave Phillips	.10
8	Larry McCoy	.10
9	Bruce Froemming	.10
10	John McSherry	.10
11	Jim Evans	.10
12	Frank Pulli	.10

13 Joe Brinkman .10
14 Terry Tata .10
15 Jim McKean .10
16 Dutch Rennert .10
17 Paul Runge .10
18 Terry Cooney .10
19 Rich Garcia .10
20 Dale Ford .10
21 Al Clark .10
22 Greg Kosc .10
23 Jim Quick .10
24 Eddie Montague .10
25 Jerry Crawford .10
26 Steve Palermo .10
27 Durwood Merrill .10
28 Ken Kaiser .10
29 Vic Voltaggio .10
30 Mike Reilly .10
31 Eric Gregg .10
32 Ted Hendry .10
33 Joe West .10
34 Fred Brocklander .10
35 John Shulock .10
36 Derryl Cousins .10
37 Charlie Williams .10
38 Rocky Roe .10
39 Randy Marsh .10
40 Bob Davidson .10
41 Drew Coble .10
42 Tim McClelland .10
43 Dan Morrison .10
44 Rick Reed .10
45 Steve Rippley .10
46 John Hirschbeck .10
47 Mark Johnson .10
48 Gerry Davis .10
49 Dana DeMuth .10
50 Larry Young .10
51 Tim Welke .10
52 Greg Bonin .10
53 Tom Hallion .10
54 Dale Scott .10
55 Tim Tschida .10
56 Gary Darling .10
57 Mark Hirschbeck .10
58 Jerry Layne .10
59 Jim Joyce .10
60 Bill Hohn .10
61 All-Star Game .10
62 World Series .10
63 Nick Bremigan .10
64 The Runges (Ed Runge, Paul Runge) .10
65 A. Bartlett Giamatti .10
66 Puzzle Piece #1 .10
66a Puzzle Piece #1 (W/N.L. logo on back.) .10
67 Puzzle Piece #2 .10
67a Puzzle Piece #3 (N.L. logo.) .10
68 Puzzle Piece #3 .10
68a Puzzle Piece #3 (N.L. logo.) .10
69 Puzzle Piece #4 .10
69a Puzzle piece #4 (N.L. logo.) .10
70 Checklist .05
71 Al Barlick 4.00

1990 Target Dodgers

Virtually every player who appeared in the uniform of the Brooklyn or Los Angeles Dodgers between 1890-1990 was included in this 1,100-card issue. Quality of the photo varies wildly from sharp to barely identifiable. Cards measure 2-1/16" x 3" and are perforated on two, three or four sides, depending where they were positioned on the 15-card perforated sheets in which the cards were distributed at various Dodgers home games. Player photos are in dark blue and white, bordered in speckled blue. Name and position appear in black in a light blue banner at top. At lower-left is the Dodgers 100th anniversary logo, with the Target stores logo at lower-right. On back the player's name and position reappear at top, with the logos below and the card number in a banner at bottom. Cards were numbered roughly alphabetically, though many are out of order. Some cards have duplicated numbers and there were some numbers skipped in the issue. All back printing is in blue on white. Career major league stats and the years in which the player was with the Dodgers are also noted on back. According to figures released by the team, production was to be about 50,000 sets.

NM/M

Complete Set (1,103): 150.00
Common Player: .25
1 Bert Abbey .25
2 Cal Abrams .50
3 Hank Aguirre .25
4 Eddie Ainsmith .25
5 Ed Albosta .25
6 Luis Alcaraz .25
7 Doyle Alexander .25
8 Dick Allen 2.50
9 Frank Allen .25
10 Johnny Allen .25
11 Mel Almada 1.25
12 Walter Alston 1.25
13 Ed Amelung .25
14 Sandy Amoros 1.25
15 Dave Anderson .25
16 Ferrell Anderson .25
17 John Anderson .25
18 Stan Andrews .25
19 Bill Antonello .25
20 Jimmy Archer .25
21 Bob Aspromonte .25
22 Rick Auerbach .25
23 Charlie Babb .25
24 Johnny Babich .25
25 Bob Bailey .25
26 Bob Bailor .25
27 Dusty Baker 1.25
28 Tom Baker .25
29 Dave Bancroft .25
30 Dan Bankhead .75
31 Jack Banta .25
32 Jim Barbieri .25
33 Red Barkley .25
34 Jesse Barnes .25
35 Rex Barney .75
36 Billy Barnie .25
37 Bob Barrett .25
38 Jim Baxes .25
39 Billy Bean .25
40 Boom Boom Beck .25
41 Joe Beckwith .25
42 Hank Behrman .25
43 Mark Belanger .25
44 Wayne Belardi .25
45 Tim Belcher .25
46 George Bell .25
47 Ray Benge .25
48 Moe Berg 4.00
49 Bill Bergen .25
50 Ray Berres .25
51 Don Bessent .25
52 Steve Bilko .25
53 Jack Billingham .25
54 Babe Birrer .25
55 Del Bissonette .25
56 Joe Black 1.25
57 Lu Blue .25
58 George Boehler .25
59 Sammy Bohne 1.50
60 John Boiling .25
61 Ike Boone .25
62 Frenchy Bordagaray .25
63 Ken Boyer 1.25
64 Buzz Boyle .25
65 Mark Bradley .25
66 Bobby Bragan .25
67 Ralph Branca 1.25
68 Ed Brandt .25
69 Sid Bream .25
70 Marv Breeding .25
71 Tom Brennan .25
72 William Brennan .25
73 Rube Bressler .25
74 Ken Brett .25
75 Jim Brewer .25
76 Tony Brewer .25
77 Rocky Bridges .25
78 Greg Brock .25
79 Dan Brouthers .25
80 Eddie Brown .25
81 Elmer Brown .25
82 Lindsay Brown .25
83 Lloyd Brown .25
84 Mace Brown .25
85 Tommy Brown .25
86 Pete Browning .25
87 Ralph Bryant .25
88 Jim Bucher .25
89 Bill Buckner 1.25
90 Jim Bunning 1.25
91 Jack Burdock .25
92 Glenn Burke .25
93 Buster Burrell .25
94 Larry Burright .25
95 Doc Bushong .25
96 Max Butcher .25
97 Johnny Butler .25
98 Enos Cabell .25
99 Leon Cadore .25
100 Bruce Caldwell .25
101 Dick Calmus .25
102 Dolf Camilli .25
103 Doug Camilli .25
104 Roy Campanella 9.00
105 Al Campanis .25
106 Jim Campanis .25
107A Leo Callahan .25
107B Gilly Campbell .25
108 Jimmy Canavan .25
109 Chris Cannizzaro .25
110 Guy Cantrell .25
111 Ben Cantwell .25
112 Andy Carey .25
113 Max Carey .25
114 Tex Carleton .25
115 Ownie Carroll .25
116 Bob Caruthers .25
117 Doc Casey .25
118 Hugh Casey .25
119 Bobby Castillo .25
120 Cesar Cedeno .25
121 Ron Cey 1.25
122 Ed Chandler .25
123 Ben Chapman .25
124 Larry Cheney .25
125 Bob Chipman .25
126 Chuck Churn .25
127 Gino Cimoli .50
128 Moose Clabaugh .25
129 Bud Clancy .25
130 Bob Clark .25
131 Watty Clark .25
132 Alta Cohen .25
133 Rocky Colavito 5.00
134 Jackie Collum .25
135 Chuck Connors 5.00
136 Jack Coombs .25
137 Johnny Cooney .25
138 Tommy Corcoran .25
139 Pop Corkhill .25
140 John Corriden .25
141 Pete Coscarart .25
142 Wes Covington .25
143 Billy Cox 1.25
144 Roger Craig .75
145 Cannonball Crane .25
146 Willie Crawford .25
147 Tim Crews .25
148 John Cronin .25
149 Lave Cross .25
150 Bill Crouch .25
151 Don Crow .25
152 Henry Cruz .25
153 Tony Cuccinello .25
154 Roy Cullenbine .25
155 George Culver .25
156 Nick Cullop .25
157 George Cutshaw .25
158 Kiki Cuyler .25
159 Bill Dahlen .25
160 Babe Dahlgren .25
161 Jack Dalton .25
162 Tom Daly .25
163 Cliff Dapper .25
164 Bob Darnell .25
165 Bobby Darwin .25
166 Jake Daubert .25
167 Vic Davalillo .25
168 Curt Davis .25
169 Mike Davis .25
170 Ron Davis .25
171 Tommy Davis 1.25
172 Willie Davis 1.25
173 Pea Ridge Day .25
174 Tommy Dean .25
175 Hank DeBerry .25
176 Art Decatur .25
177 Raoul Dedeaux .25
178 Ivan DeJesus .25
179 Don Demeter .25
180 Gene DeMontreville .25
181 Rick Dempsey .25
182 Eddie Dent .25
183 Mike Devereaux .25
184 Carlos Diaz .25
185 Dick Dietz .25
186 Pop Dillon .25
187 Bill Doak .25
188 John Dobbs .25
189 George Dockins .25
190 Cozy Dolan .25
191 Patsy Donovan .25
192 Wild Bill Donovan .25
193 Mickey Doolan .25
194 Jack Doscher .25
195 Phil Douglas .25
196 Snooks Dowd .25
197 Al Downing .25
198 Red Downs .25
199 Jack Doyle .25
200 Solly Drake .25
201 Tom Drake .25
202 Chuck Dressen .75
203 Don Drysdale 5.00
204 Clise Dudley .25
205 Mariano Duncan .25
206 Jack Dunn .25
207 Bull Durham .25
208 Leo Durocher 1.25
209 Billy Earle .25
210 George Earnshaw .25
211 Ox Eckhardt .25
212 Bruce Edwards .25
213 Hank Edwards .25
214 Dick W. Egan .25
215 Harry Eisenstat .25
216 Kid Elberfeld .25
217 Jumbo Elliot .25
218 Don Elston .25
219 Gil English .25
220 Johnny Enzmann .25
221 Al Epperly .25
222 Carl Erskine 1.25
223 Tex Erwin .25
224 Cecil Espy .25
225 Chuck Essegian .25
226 Dude Esterbrook .25
227 Red Evans .25
228 Bunny Fabrique .25
229 Jim Fairey .25
230 Ron Fairly 1.25
231 George Fallon .25
232 Turk Farrell .25
233 Duke Farrel .25
234 Jim Faulkner .25
235 Alex Ferguson .25
236 Joe Ferguson .25
237 Chico Fernandez .25
238 Sid Fernandez .25
239 Al Ferrara .25
240 Wes Ferrell .25
241 Lou Fette .25
242 Chick Fewster .25
243 Jack Fimple .25
244 Neal "Mickey" Finn .25
245 Bob Fisher .25
246 Freddie Fitzsimmons .25
247 Tim Flood .25
248 Jake Flowers .25
249 Hod Ford .25
250 Terry Forster .75
251 Alan Foster .25
252 Jack Fournier .25
253 Dave Foutz .25
254 Art Fowler .25
255 Fred Frankhouse .25
256 Herman Franks .25
257 Johnny Frederick .25
258 Larry French .25
259 Lonny Frey .25
260 Pepe Frias .25
261 Charlie Fuchs .25
262 Carl Furillo 4.00
263 Len Gabrielson .25
264 Augie Galan .25
265 Joe Gallagher .25
266 Phil Gallivan .25
267 Balvino Galvez .25
268 Mike Garman .25
269 Phil Garner .25
270 Steve Garvey 2.50
271 Ned Garvin .25
272 Hank Gastright .25
273 Sid Gautreaux .25
274 Jim Gentile .25
275 Greek George .25
276 Ben Geraghty .25
277 Gus Getz .25
278 Bob Giallombardo .25
279 Kirk Gibson 1.25
280 Charlie Gilbert .25
281 Jim Gilliam 1.25
282 Al Gionfriddo .50
283 Tony Giuliani .25
284 Al Glossop .25
285 John Gochnaur .25
286 Jim Golden .25
287 Dave Goltz .25
288 Jose Gonzalez .25
289 Johnny Gooch .25
290 Ed Goodson .25
291 Bill Grabarkewitz .25
292 Jack Graham .25
293 Mudcat Grant .25
294 Dick Gray .25
295 Kent Greenfield .25
296 Hal Gregg .25
297 Alfredo Griffin .25
298 Mike Griffin .25
299 Derrell Griffith .25
300 Tommy Griffith .25
301 Burleigh Grimes .25
302 Lee Grissom .25
303 Jerry Grote .25
304 Pedro Guerrero .75
305 Brad Gulden .25
306 Ad Gumbert .25
307 Chris Gwynn .25
308 Bert Haas .25
309 John Hale .25
310 Tom Haller .25
311 Bill Hallman .25
312 Jeff Hamilton .25
313 Luke Hamlin .25
314 Ned Hanlon .25
315 Gerald Hannahs .25
316 Charlie Hargreaves .25
317 Tim Harkness .25
318 Harry Harper .25
319 Joe Harris .25
320 Lenny Harris .25
321 Bill F. Hart .25
322 Buddy Hassett .25
323 Mickey Hatcher .25
324 Joe Hatten .25
325 Phil Haugstad .25
326 Brad Havens .25
327 Ray Hayworth .25
328 Ed Head .25
329 Danny Heep .25
330 Fred Heimach .25
331 Harvey Hendrick .25
332 Weldon Henley .25
333 Butch Henline .25
334 Dutch Henry .25
335 Roy Henshaw .25
336 Babe Herman .75
337 Billy Herman .75
338 Gene Hermanski .25
339 Enzo Hernandez .25
340 Art Herring .25
341 Orel Hershiser 1.25
342 Dave J. Hickman .25
343 Jim Hickman .25
344 Kirby Higbe .25
345 Andy High .25
346 George Hildebrand .25
347 Hunkey Hines .25
348 Don Hoak .75
349 Oris Hockett .25
350 Gil Hodges 5.00
351 Glenn Hoffman .25
352 Al Hollingsworth .25
353 Tommy Holmes .25
354 Brian Holton .25
355 Rick Honeycutt .25
356 Burt Hooton .25
357 Gail Hopkins .25
358 Johnny Hopp .25
359 Charlie Hough .75
360 Frank Howard 1.25
361 Steve Howe .75
362 Dixie Howell .25
363 Harry Howell .25
364 Jay Howell .25
365 Ken Howell .25
366 Waite Hoyt .25
367 Johnny Hudson .25
368 Jim J. Hughes .25
369 Jim R. Hughes .25
370 Mickey Hughes .25
371 John Hummel .25
372 Ron Hunt .25
373 Willard Hunter .25
374 Ira Hutchinson .25
375 Tom Hutton .25
376 Charlie Irwin .25
377 Fred Jacklitsch .25
378 Randy Jackson .25
379 Merwin Jacobson .25
380 Cleo James .25
381 Hal Janvrin .25
382 Roy Jarvis .25
383 George Jeffcoat .25
384 Jack Jenkins .25
385 Hughie Jennings .25
386 Tommy John 1.25
387 Lou Johnson .25
388 Fred Ivy Johnston .25
389 Jimmy Johnston .25
390 Jay Johnstone .75
391 Fielder Jones .25
392 Oscar Jones .25
393 Tim Jordan .25
394 Spider Jorgensen .25
395 Von Joshua .25
396 Bill Joyce .25
397 Joe Judge .25
398 Alex Kampouris .25
399 Willie Keeler .25
400 Mike Kekich .25
401 John Kelleher .25
402 Frank Kellert .25
403 Joe Kelley .25
404 George Kelly .25
405 Bob Kennedy .25
406 Brickyard Kennedy .25
407 John Kennedy .25
409 Newt Kimball .25
410 Clyde King .25
411 Enos Kirkpatrick .25
412 Frank Kitson .25
413 Johnny Klippstein .25
414 Elmer Klumpp .25
415 Len Koenecke .25
416 Ed Konetchy .25
417 Andy Kosco .25
418 Sandy Koufax 15.00
419 Ernie Koy .25
420 Charlie Kress .25
421 Bill Krueger .25
422 Ernie Krueger .25
423 Clem Labine .75
424 Candy LaChance .25
425 Lee Lacy .25
426 Lerrin LaGrow .25
427 Bill Lamar .25
428 Wayne LaMaster .25
429 Ray Lamb .25
430 Rafael Landestoy .25
431 Ken Landreaux .25
432 Tito Landrum .25
433 Norm Larker .75
434 Lyn Lary .25
435 Tom Lasorda 1.25
436 Cookie Lavagetto .25
437 Rudy Law .25
438 Tony Lazzeri .25
439 Tim Leary .25
440 Bob Lee .25
441 Hall Lee .25
442 Leron Lee .25
443 Jim Lefebvre .25
444 Ken Lehman .25
445 Don LeJohn .25
446 Steve Lembo .25
447 Ed Lennox .25
448 Dutch Leonard .25
449 Jeffery Leonard .25
450 Sam Leslie .25
451 Dennis Lewallyn .25
452 Bob Lillis .25
453 Jim Lindsey .25
454 Fred Lindstrom .25
455 Billy Loes .50
456 Bob Logan .25
457 Bill Lohrman .25
459 Vic Lombardi .25
460 Davey Lopes .75
461 Al Lopez .25
462 Ray Lucas .25
464 Harry Lumley .25
465 Don Lund .25
466 Dolf Luque .25
467 Jim Lyttle .25
468 Max Macon .25
469 Bill Madlock .75
470 Lee Magee .25
471 Sal Maglie .75
472 George Magoon .25
473 Duster Mails .25
474 Candy Maldonado .25
475 Tony Malinosky .25
476 Lew Malone .25
477 Al Mamaux .25
478 Gus Mancuso .25
479 Charlie Manuel .25
480 Heinie Manush .25
481 Rabbit Maranville .25
482 Juan Marichal 2.50
483 Rube Marquard .25
484 Bill Marriott .25
485 Buck Marrow .25
486 Mike A. Marshall .75
487 Mike G. Marshall .75
488 Morrie Martin .25
489 Ramon Martinez 1.25
490 Teddy Martinez .25
491 Earl Mattingly .25
492 Len Matuszek .25
493 Gene Mauch .25
494 Al Maul .25
495 Carmen Mauro .25
496 Alvin McBean .25
497 Bill McCarren .25
498 Jack McCarthy .25
499 Tommy McCarthy .25
500 Lew McCarty .25
501 Mike J. McCormick .25
502 Judge McCreedie .25
503 Tom McCreery .25
504 Danny McDevitt .25
505 Chappie McFarland .25
506 Joe McGinnity .25
507 Bob McGraw .25
508 Deacon McGuire .25
509 Bill McGunnigle .25
510 Harry McIntyre .25
511 Cal McLish .25
512 Ken McMullen .25
513 Dough McWeeny .25
514 Joe Medwick .25
515 Rube Melton .25
516 Fred Merkle .25
517 Orlando Mercado .25
518 Andy Messersmith .25
519 Irish Meusel .25
520 Benny Meyer .25
521 Russ Meyer .25
522 Chief Meyers .25
523 Gene Michael .25
524 Pete Mikkelsen .25
525 Eddie Miksis .25
526 Johnny Miljus .25
527 Bob Miller .25
528 Larry Miller .25
529 Otto Miller .25
530 Ralph Miller .25
531 Walt Miller .25
532 Wally Millies .25
533 Bob Milliken .25
534 Buster Mills .25
535 Paul Minner .25
536 Bobby Mitchell .25
537 Clarence Mitchell .25
538 Dale Mitchell .25
539 Fred Mitchell .25
540 Johnny Mitchell .25
541 Joe Moeller .25
542 Rick Monday .75
543 Wally Moon .75
544 Cy Moore .25
545 Dee Moore .25
546 Eddie Moore .25
547 Gene Moore .25
548 Randy Moore .25
549 Ray Moore .25
550 Jose Morales .25
551 Bobby Morgan .25
552 Eddie Morgan .25
553 Mike Morgan .25
554 Johnny Morrison .25
555 Walt Moryn .25
556 Ray Moss .25
557 Manny Mota .75
558 Joe Mulvey .25
559 Van Lingle Mungo .25
560 Les Munns .25
561 Mike Munoz .25
562 Simmy Murch .25
563 Eddie Murray 4.00

564 Hy Myers .25
565 Sam Nahem .25
566 Earl Naylor .25
567 Charlie Neal .75
568 Ron Negray .25
569 Bernie Neis .25
570 Rocky Nelson .25
571 Dick Nen .25
572 Don Newcombe 2.50
573 Bobo Newsom .25
574 Doc Newton .25
575 Tom Niedenfuer .25
576 Otho Nitcholas .25
577 Al Nixon .25
578 Jerry Nops .25
579 Irv Noren .25
580 Fred Norman .25
581 Bill North .25
582 Johnny Oates .25
583 Bob O'Brien .25
584 John O'Brien .25
585 Lefty O'Doul .25
586 Joe Oeschger .25
587 Al Oliver .75
588 Nate Oliver .25
589 Luis Olmo .25
590 Ivy Olson .25
591 Mickey O'Neil .25
592 Joe Orengo .25
593 Jesse Orosco .25
594 Frank O'Rourke .25
595 Jorge Orta .25
596 Phil Ortega .25
597 Claude Osteen .25
598 Fritz Ostermueller .25
599 Mickey Owen .25
600 Tom Paciorek .25
601 Don Padgett .25
602 Andy Pafko .75
603 Erv Palica .25
604 Ed Palmquist .25
605 Wes Parker .25
606 Jay Partridge .25
607 Camilo Pascual .25
608 Kevin Pasley .25
609 Dave Patterson .25
610 Harley Payne .25
611 Johnny Peacock .25
612 Hal Peck .25
613 Stu Pederson .25
614 Alejandro Pena .25
615 Jose Pena .25
616 Jack Perconte .25
617 Charlie Perkins .25
618 Ron Perranoski .50
619 Jim Peterson .25
620 Jesse Petty .25
621 Jeff Pfeffer .25
622 Babe Phelps .25
623 Val Picinich .25
624 Joe Pignatano .25
625 George Pinckney .25
626 Ed Pipgras .25
627 Bud Podbielan .25
628 Johnny Podres .75
629 Boots Poffenberger .25
630 Nick Polly .25
631 Paul Popovich .25
632 Bill Posedel .25
633 Boog Powell .50
634 Dennis Powell .25
635 Paul Ray Powell .25
636 Ted Power .25
637 Tot Pressnell .25
638 John Purdin .25
639 Jack Quinn .25
640 Marv Rackley .25
641 Jack Radtke .25
642 Pat Ragan .25
643 Ed Rakow .25
644 Bob Ramazzotti .25
645 Willie Ramsdell .25
646 Mike James Ramsey .25
647 Mike Jeffery Ramsey .25
648 Willie Randolph .25
649 Doug Rau .25
650 Lance Rautzhan .25
651 Howie Reed .25
652 Pee Wee Reese 9.00
653 Phil Regan .25
654 Bill Reidy .25
655 Bobby Reis .25
656 Pete Reiser .75
657 Rip Repulski .25
658 Ed Reulbach .25
659 Jerry Reuss .50
660 R.J. Reynolds .25
661 Billy Rhiel .25
662 Rick Rhoden .25
663 Paul Richards .25
664 Danny Richardson .25
665 Pete Richert .25
666 Harry Riconda .25
667 Joe Riggert .25
668 Lew Riggs .25
669 Jimmy Ripple .25
670 Lou Ritter .25
671 German Rivera .25
672 Johnny Rizzo .25
673 Jim Roberts .25
674 Earl Robinson .25
675 Frank Robinson 5.00
676 Jackie Robinson 15.00
677a Wilbert Robinson .25
677b Sergio Robles .25
678 Rich Rodas .25
679 Ellie Rodriguez .25
680 Preacher Roe .75
681 Ed Roebuck .25
682 Ron Roenicke .25
683 Oscar Roettger .25
684 Lee Rogers .25
685 Packy Rogers .25
686 Stan Rojek .25
687 Vicente Romo .25
688 Johnny Roseboro .75
689 Goody Rosen .25
690 Don Ross .25
691 Ken Rowe .25
692 Schoolboy Rowe .25
693 Luther Roy .25
694 Jerry Royster .50
695 Nap Rucker .25
696 Dutch Ruether .25
697 Bill Russell .75
698 Jim Russell .25
699 John Russell .25
700 Johnny Rutherford .25
701 John Ryan .25
702 Rosy Ryan .25
703 Mike Sandlock .25
704 Ted Savage .25
705 Dave Sax .25
706 Steve Sax .75
707 Bill Sayles .25
708 Bill Schardt .25
709 Johnny Schmitz .25
710 Dick Schofield .25
711 Howie Schultz .25
712 Ferdie Schupp .25
713 Mike Scioscia .75
714 Dick Scott .25
715 Tom Seats .25
716 Jimmy Sebring .25
717 Larry See .25
718 Dave Sells .25
719 Greg Shanahan .25
720 Mike Sharperson .25
721 Joe Shaute .25
722 Merv Shea .25
723 Jimmy Sheckard .25
724 Jack Sheehan .25
725 John Shelby .25
726 Vince Sherlock .25
727 Larry Sherry .75
728 Norm Sherry .75
729 Bill Shindle .25
730 Craig Shipley .25
731 Bart Shirley .25
732 Steve Shirley .25
733 Burt Shotton .25
734 George Shuba .50
735 Dick Siebert .25
736 Joe Simpson .25
737 Duke Sims .25
738 Bill Singer .25
739 Fred Sington .25
740 Ted Sizemore .25
741 Frank Skaff .25
742 Bill Skowron 1.25
743 Gordon Slade .25
744 Dwain Lefty Sloat .25
745 Charley Smith .25
746 Dick Smith .25
747 George Smith .25
748 Germany Smith .25
749 Jack Smith .25
750 Reggie Smith .75
751 Sherry Smith .25
752 Harry Smythe .25
753 Duke Snider 9.00
754 Eddie Solomon .25
755 Elias Sosa .25
756 Daryl Spencer .25
757 Roy Spencer .25
758 Karl Spooner .50
759 Eddie Stack .25
760 Tuck Stainback .25
761 George Stallings .25
762 Jerry Standaert .25
763 Don Stanhouse .25
764 Eddie Stanky .25
765 Dolly Stark .25
766 Jigger Statz .25
767 Casey Stengel 1.25
768 Jerry Stephenson .25
769 Ed Stevens .25
770 Dave Stewart .75
771 Stuffy Stewart .25
772 Bob Stinson .25
773 Milt Stock .25
774 Harry Stovey .25
775 Mike Strahler .25
776 Sammy Strang .25
777 Elmer Stricklett .25
778 Joe Stripp .25
779 Dick Stuart .50
780 Franklin Stubbs .25
781 Bill Sudakis .25
782 Clyde Sukeforth .25
783 Billy Sullivan .25
784 Tom Sunkel .25
785 Rick Sutcliffe .75
786 Don Sutton 4.00
787 Bill Swift .25
788 Vito Tamulis .25
789 Danny Taylor .25
790 Harry Taylor .25
791 Zack Taylor .25
792 Chuck Templeton .25
793 Wayne Terwilliger .25
794 Wayne Terwilliger .25
795 Derrel Thomas .25
796 Fay Thomas .25
797 Gary Thomasson .25
798 Don Thompson .25
799 Fresco Thompson .25
800 Tim Thompson .25
801 Hank Thormahlen .25
802 Sloppy Thurston .25
803 Cotton Tierney .25
804 Al Todd .25
805 Bert Tooley .25
806 Jeff Torborg .25
807 Dick Tracewski .25
808 Nick Tremark .25
809 Alex Trevino .25
810 Tommy Tucker .25
811 John Tudor .25
812 Mike Vail .25
813 Rene Valdes (Valdez) .25
814 Bobby Valentine .25
815 Fernando Valenzuela .75
816 Elmer Valo .25
817 Dazzy Vance .75
818 Sandy Vance .25
819 Chris Van Cuyk .25
820 Ed VandeBerg .25
821 Arky Vaughan .75
822 Zoilo Versalles .25
823 Joe Vosmik .25
824 Ben Wade .25
825 Dixie Walker .50
826 Rube Walker .50
827 Stan Wall .25
828 Lee Walls .25
829 Danny Walton .25
830 Lloyd Waner .25
831 Paul Waner .25
832 Chuck Ward .25
833 John Monte Ward .25
834 Preston Ward .25
835 Jack Warner .25
836 Tommy Warren .25
837 Carl Warwick .25
838 Jimmy Wasdell .25
839 Ron Washington .25
840 George Watkins .25
841 Hank Webb .25
842 Les Webber .25
843 Gary Weiss .25
844 Bob Welch .75
845 Brad Wellman .25
846 John Werhas .25
847 Max West .25
848 Gus Weyhing .25
849 Mack Wheat .25
850 Zack Wheat .25
851 Ed Wheeler .25
852 Larry White .25
853 Myron White .25
854 Terry Whitfield .25
855 Dick Whitman .25
856 Possum Whitted .25
857 Kemp Wicker .25
858 Hoyt Wilhelm .75
859 Kaiser Wilhelm .25
860 Nick Willhite .25
861 Dick Williams .75
862 Reggie Williams .25
863 Stan Williams .25
864 Woody Williams .25
865 Maury Wills .75
866 Hack Wilson .75
867 Robert Wilson .25
868 Gordon Windhorn .25
869 Jim Winford .25
870 Lave Winham .25
871 Tom Winsett .25
872 Hank Winston .25
873 Whitey Witt .25
874 Pete Wojey .25
875 Tracy Woodson .25
876 Clarence Wright .25
877 Glenn Wright .25
878 Ricky Wright .25
879 Whit Wyatt .25
880 Jimmy Wynn .25
881 Joe Yeager .25
882 Steve Yeager .25
883 Matt Young .25
884 Tom Zachary .25
885 Pat Zachry .25
886 Geoff Zahn .25
887 Don Zimmer .75
888 Morrie Aderholt .25
889 Raleigh Aitchison .25
890 Whitey Alperman .25
891 Orlando Alvarez .25
892 Pat Ankenman .25
893 Ed Appleton .25
894 Doug Baird .25
895 Lady Baldwin .25
896 Win Ballou .25
897 Bob Barr .25
898 Boyd Bartley .25
899 Eddie Basinski .25
900 Erve Beck .25
901 Ralph Birkofer .25
903 Joe Bradshaw .25
904 Bruce Brubaker .25
905 Oyster Burns .25
906 John Butler .25
908 Kid Carsey .25
909 Pete Cassidy .25
910 Tom Catterson .25
911 Glenn Chapman .25
912 Paul Chervinko .25
913 George Cisar .25
914 Wally Clement .25
915 Bill Collins .25
916 Chuck Corgan .25
917 Dick Cox .25
918 George Crable .25
919 Sam Crane .25
920 Cliff Curtis .25
921 Fats Dantonio .25
922 Con Daily .25
923 Jud Daley .25
924 Jake Daniel .25
925 Kal Daniels .25
926 Dan Daub .25
927 Lindsay Deal .25
928 Artie Dede .25
929 Pat Deisel .25
930 Bert Delmas .25
931 Rube Dessau .25
932 Leo Dickerman .25
933 John Douglas .25
934 Red Downey .25
935 Carl Doyle .25
936 John Duffie .25
937 Dick Durning .25
938 Red Durrett .25
939 Mal Eason .25
940 Charlie Ebbetts .75
941 Rube Ehardt .25
942 Rowdy Elliot .25
943 Bones Ely .25
944 Woody English .25
945 Roy Evans .25
946 Gus Felix .25
947 Bill Fischer .25
948 Jeff Fischer .25
949 Chauncey Fisher .25
950 Tom Fitzsimmons .25
951 Darrin Fletcher .25
952 Wes Flowers .25
953 Howard Freigau .25
954 Nig Fuller .25
955 John Gaddy .25
956 Welcome Gaston .25
957 Frank Gatins .25
958 Pete Gilbert .25
959 Wally Wilbert .25
960 Carden Gillenwater .25
961 Roy Gleason .25
962 Harvey Green .25
963 Nelson Greene .25
964 John Grim .25
965 Dan Griner .25
967 Bill Hall .25
968 Johnny Hall .25
970 Pat Hanifin .25
971 Bill Harris .25
972 Bill W. Hart .25
973 Chris Hartje .25
974 Mike Hartley .25
975 Gil Hatfield .25
976 Chris Haughey .25
977 Hugh Hearne .25
978 Mike Hechinger .25
979 Jake Hehl .25
980 Bob Higgins .25
981 Still Bill Hill .25
982 Shawn Hillegas .25
983 Wally Hood .25
984 Lefty Hopper .25
985 Ricky Horton .25
986 Ed Householder .25
987 Bill Hubbell .25
988 Al Humphrey .25
989 Bernie Hungling .25
990 George Hunter .25
991 Pat Hurley .25
992 Joe Hutcheson .25
993 Roy Hutson .25
994 Bert Inks .25
995 Dutch Jordan .25
997 Frank Kane .25
998 Chet Kehn .25
999 Maury Kent .25
1000 Tom Kinslow .25
1001 Fred Kipp .25
1002 Joe Klugman .25
1003 Elmer Knetzer .25
1004 Barney Koch .25
1005 Jim Korwan .25
1006 Joe Koukalik .25
1007 Lou Koupal .25
1008 Joe Kustus .25
1009 Frank Lamanske .25
1010 Tacks Latimer .25
1011 Bill Leard .25
1012 Phil Lewis .25
1013 Mickey Livingston .25
1014 Dick Loftus .25
1015 Charlie Loudenslager .25
1016 Tom Lovett .25
1017 Charlie Malay .25
1018 Mal Mallett .25
1019 Ralph Mauriello .25
1020 Bill McCabe .25
1021 Gene McCann .25
1022 Mike McCormick .25
1023 Terry McDermott .25
1024 John McDougal .25
1025 Pryor McElveen .25
1026 Dan McGann .25
1027 Pat McGlothin .25
1028 Doc McJames .25
1029 Kit McKenna .25
1030 Sadie McMahon .25
1032 Tommy McMillan .25
1033 Glenn Mickens .25
1034 Don Miles .25
1035 Hack Miller .25
1036 John Miller .25
1037 Lemmie Miller .25
1038 George Mohart .25
1039 Gary Moore .25
1040 Herbie Moran .25
1041 Earl Mossor .25
1042 Glen Moulder .25
1043 Billy Mullen .25
1044 Hub Northen .25
1045 Curly Onis .25
1046 Tiny Osbourne .25
1047 Jim Pastorius .25
1048 Art Parks .25
1049 Chink Outen .25
1050 Jimmy Pattison .25
1051 Norman Pitt .25
1052 Doc Reisling .25
1053 Gilberto Reyes .25
1055 Lou Rochelli .25
1056 Jim Romano .25
1057 Max Rosenfeld .25
1058 Andy Rush .25
1059 Jack Ryan .25
1060 Jack Savage .25
1062 Ray Schmandt .25
1063 Henry Schmidt .25
1064 Charlie Schmutz .25
1065 Joe Schultz .25
1066 Ray Searage .25
1067 Elmer Sexauer .25
1068 George Sharrott .25
1069 Tommy Sheehan .25
1071 George Shoch .25
1072 Broadway Aleck Smith .25
1073 Hap Smith .25
1074 Red Smith .25
1075 Tony Smith .25
1076 Gene Snyder .25
1077 Denny Sothern .25
1078 Bill Steele .25
1080 Farmer Steelman .25
1081 Dutch Stryker .25
1082 Tommy Tatum .25
1084 Adonis Terry .25
1085 Ray Thomas .25
1086 George Treadway .25
1087 Overton Tremper .25
1088 Ty Tyson .25
1089 Rube Vickers .25
1090 Jose Vizcaino .25
1091 Bull Wagner .25
1092 Butts Wagner .25
1093 Rube Ward .25
1094 John Wetteland .25
1095 Eddie Wilson .25
1096 Tex Wilson .25
1097 Zeke Wrigley .25
1099 Rube Yarrison .25
1100 Earl Yingling .25
1101 Chink Zachary .25
1102 Lefty Davis .25
1103 Bob Hall .25
1104 Darby O'Brien .25
1105 Larry LeJeune .25

1989 Taystee Kansas City Royals

The 1989 Royals are featured on this set of discs distributed by a K.C. area bakery. The 2-3/4" discs have color player photos at center. The team logo has been airbrushed off the caps because the issue was licensed only by the players, and not by Major League Baseball. In the white border is the issuer's logo in red at top, player identification at bottom in a yellow banner and "AL STARS" in blue stars at each side. Backs are printed in blue with player data, 1988 stats and copyright information.

		NM/M
Complete Set (12):		9.00
Common Player:		.50
1	George Brett	4.00
2	Kevin Seitzer	.50
3	Pat Tabler	.50
4	Danny Tartabull	.50
5	Willie Wilson	.75
6	Bo Jackson	1.00
7	Frank White	.50
8	Kurt Stillwell	.50
9	Mark Gubicza	.50
10	Charlie Leibrandt	.50
11	Bret Saberhagen	.75
12	Steve Farr	.50

1981 TCMA The 1960's, Series 2

A second series of cards depicting major and minor league players of the 1960s was produced by TCMA in 1981. The cards continued in the same 2-1/2" x 3-1/2" format as the earlier series. Fronts are unadorned color photos, backs have player identification, data and career summary printed in green on white. The numbering of the cards continues at #294, where the first series concluded, but only about one-third the quantity was produced of this series, compared with the first series.

		NM/M
Complete Set (189):		75.00
Common Player:		.50
294	Fritzie Brickell	.50
295	Craig Anderson	.50
296	Cliff Cook	.50
297	Pumpsie Green	.50
298	Choo Choo Coleman	.50
299	Don Buford	.50
300	Sparky Anderson	1.00
301	John Anderson	.50
302	Ted Beard	.50
303	Mickey Mantle, Roger Maris	15.00
304	Gene Freese	.50
305	Don Wilkinson	.50
306	Walter Alston	1.00
307	George Bamberger	.50
308	Nelson Briles	.50
309	Dave Baldwin	.50
310	Bob Bailey	.50
311	Paul Blair	.50
312	Ken Boswell	.50
313	Sam Bowens	.50
314	Ray Barker	.50
315	Tommie Agee, Gil Hodges	.50
316	Elmer Valo	.50
317	Ken Walters	.50
318	Joel Horlen	.50
320	Charlie Maxwell	.50
321	Joe Foy	.50
322	Tommie Agee, Cleon Jones, Ron Swoboda	.50
323	Paul Foytack	.50
324	Ron Fairly	.50
325	Wilbur Wood	.50
327	Felix Mantilla	.50
328a	Ed Bouchee	.50
328b	Don Wilson	.50
329	Sandy Valdespino	.50
330	Al Ferrera	.50
331	Jose Tartabull	.50
332	Dick Kenworthy	.50
333	Don Pavletich	.50
334	Jim Fairey	.50
335	Rico Petrocelli	.50
336	Gary Roggenburk	.50
337	Rick Reichardt	.50
338	Ken McMullen	.50
339	Dooley Womack	.50
340	Joe Moock	.50
341	Lou Brock	1.00
342	Hector Torres	.50
343	Ted Savage	.50
344	Hobie Landrith	.50
345	Ed Lopat	.50
346	Mel Nelson	.50
347	Mickey Lolich	.50
348	Al Lopez	1.00
349	Frederico Olivo	.50
350	Bob Moose	.50
351	Bill McCool	.50
352	Ernie Bowman	.50
353	Tom McCraw	.50
354	Sam Mele	.50
355	Len Boehmer	.50
356	Hank Aaron	9.00
357	Ron Hunt	.50
358	Luis Aparicio	1.00
359	Gene Mauch	.50
360	Barry Moore	.50

361 John Buzhardt .50
362 Spring Training (St. Louis Cardinals) .50
363 Duke Snider 3.00
364 Billy Martin 1.00
365 Wes Parker .50
366 Dick Stuart .50
367 Glenn Beckert .50
368 Ollie Brown .50
369 Stan Bahnsen .50
370 Lee Bales .50
371 Johnny Keane .50
372 Wally Moon .50
373 Larry Miller .50
374 Fred Newman .50
375 John Orsino .50
376 Joe Pactwa .50
377 John O'Donoghue .50
378 Jim Ollom .50
379 Ray Oyler .50
380 Ron Nischwitz .50
381 Ron Paul .50
382 Yogi Berra, John Blanchard, Roger Maris 2.00
383 Jim McKnight .50
384 Gene Michael .50
385 Dave May .50
386 Tim McCarver 1.00
387 Larry Mason .50
388 Don Hoak .50
389 Nate Oliver .50
390 Phil Ortega .50
391 Billy Madden .50
392 John Miller .50
393 Danny Murtaugh .50
394 Nelson Mathews .50
395 Red Schoendienst 1.00
396 Roger Nelson .50
397 Tom Matchick .50
398 Dennis Musgraves .50
399 Tommy Harper .50
400 Fracis Peters .50
401 Tony Pierce .50
402 Billy Williams 1.00
403 Dave Boswell .50
404 Ray Washburn .50
405 Al Worthington .50
406 Jesus Alou .50
407 Yogi Berra, Gil Hodges, Joe Pignatano, Eddie Yost 1.00
408 Wally Bunker .50
409 Jim Brenneman .50
410 Bobby Bragan .50
411 Cal McLish .50
412 Curt Blefary .50
413 Jim Bethke .50
414 Infield 1964 (St. Louis Cardinals) .50
415 Richie Allen 1.00
416 Larry Brown .50
417 Mike Andrews .50
418 Don Mossi .50
419 J.C. Martin .50
420 Dick Rusteck .50
421 Elly Rodriguez .50
422 Casey Stengel 1.00
423 Gil Hodges, Ed Vargo .50
424 Johnny Briggs .50
425 Bud Harrelson, Al Weis .50
426 Doc Edwards .50
427 Joe Hague .50
428 Lee Elia .50
429 Billy Moran .50
431 Pete Mikkelsen .50
432a Al Moran (should be #430) .50
432b Aurelio Monteagudo .50
433 Ken MacKenzie .50
434 Dick Egan .50
435 Al McBean .50
436 Mike Ferraro .50
437 Gary Wagner .50
438 Jerry Grote, J.C. Martin .50
439 Ted Kluszewski 1.00
440 Jerry Johnson .50
441 Ross Moschitto .50
442 Zoilo Versalles .50
443 Dennis Ribant .50
444 Ted Williams 9.00
445 Steve Whitaker .50
446 Frank Bertaina .50
447 Bo Belinsky .50
448 Joe Moeller .50
449 Don Shaw, Ron Taylor .50
450 Al Downing, Whitey Ford, Fritz Peterson, Mel Stottlemyre 1.00
451 Jack Tracy .50
452 Tony Curry .50
453 Roy White .50
454 Jim Bunning 1.00
455 Ralph Houk .50
456 Bobby Shantz .50
457 Bill Rigney .50
458 Roger Repoz .50
459 Robin Roberts, Bob Turley .50
460 Gordon Richardson .50
461 Dick Tracewski .50
462 Thad Tillotson .50
463 Larry Osborne .50
464 Larry Burright .50
465 Alan Foster .50
466 Ron Taylor .50
467 Fred Talbot .50
468 Bob Miller .50
469 Frank Tepedino .50
470 Danny Frisella .50
471 Cecil Perkins .50
472 Danny Napoleon .50
473 John Upham .50
474 Yogi Berra, Elston Howard, Mickey Mantle, Roger Maris, Bill Skowron 6.00
475 Al Weis .50
476 Rich Beck .50
477 Clete Boyer, Tony Kubek, Joe Pepitone, Bobby Richardson 3.00
478 Jack Fisher .50
479 Archie Moore .50
480 Roger Craig .50
481 Frank Crosetti, Mike Hegan, Ralph Houk, Wally Moses .50
482 Roger Craig, Gil Hodges, Clem Labine, Cookie Lavagetto .50

1959 Chicago White Sox

The A.L. Champion Chicago White Sox are featured in this collectors' issue. The 2-1/2" x 3-1/2" cards have black-and-white player photos with dark blue borders. Backs are in black-and-white with a few bits of player data, career information, 1959 and lifetime stats, along with a TCMA copyright line.

		NM/M
Complete Set (45):		45.00
Common Player:		1.00
1	Earl Torgeson	1.00
2	Nellie Fox	5.00
3	Luis Aparicio	5.00
4	Bubba Phillips	1.00
5	Jim McAnany	1.00
6	Jim Landis	1.00
7	Al Smith	1.00
8	Sherman Lollar	1.00
9	Billy Goodman	1.00
10	Jim Rivera	1.00
11	Sammy Esposito	1.00
12	Norm Cash	2.50
13	Johnny Romano	1.00
14	Johnny Callison	1.00
15	Harry Simpson	1.00
16	Ted Kluszewski	4.00
17	Del Ennis	1.00
18	Earl Battey	1.00
19	Larry Doby	4.00
20	Ron Jackson	1.00
21	Ray Boone	1.00
22	Lou Skizas	1.00
23	Joe Hicks	1.00
24	Don Mueller	1.00
25	J.C. Martin	1.00
26	Cam Carreon	1.00
27	Early Wynn	3.00
28	Bob Shaw	1.00
29	Billy Pierce	1.50
30	Turk Lown	1.00
31	Dick Donovan	1.00
32	Gerry Staley	1.00
33	Barry Latman	1.00
34	Ray Moore	1.00
35	Rudy Arias	1.00
36	Joe Stanka	1.00
37	Ken McBride	1.00
38	Don Rudolph	1.00
39	Claude Raymond	1.00
40	Gary Peters	1.00
41	Al Lopez	1.50
42	Don Gutteridge	1.00
43	Ray Berres	1.00
44	Tony Cuccinello	1.00
45	John Cooney	1.00

1962 San Francisco Giants

The National League Champions for 1962 are featured in this collector's edition card set. The 2-1/2" x 3-1/2" cards have orange borders on

front, around black-and-white player photos. Backs are in black-and-white with personal data, career information and 1982 stats.

		NM/M
Complete Set (35):		45.00
Common Player:		1.00
1	Alvin Dark	1.00
2	Whitey Lockman	1.00
3	Larry Jansen	1.00
4	Wes Westrum	1.00
5	Ed Bailey	1.00
6	Tom Haller	1.00
7	Harvey Kuenn	1.00
8	Willie Mays	15.00
9	Felipe Alou	1.50
10	Orlando Cepeda	4.00
11	Chuck Hiller	1.00
12	Jose Pagan	1.00
13	Jim Davenport	1.00
14	Willie McCovey	4.00
15	Matty Alou	1.00
16	Manny Mota	1.50
17	Ernie Bowman	1.00
18	Carl Boles	1.00
19	John Orsino	1.00
20	Joe Pignatano	1.00
21	Gaylord Perry	2.50
22	Jim Duffalo	1.00
23	Dick LeMay	1.00
24	Bob Garibaldi	1.00
25	Bobby Bolin	1.00
26	Don Larsen	1.25
27	Mike McCormick	1.00
28	Stu Miller	1.00
29	Jack Sanford	1.00
30	Billy O'Dell	1.00
31	Juan Marichal	2.50
32	Billy Pierce	1.00
33	Dick Phillips	1.00
34	Cap Peterson	1.00
35	Bob Nieman	1.00

1982 TCMA Baseball's Greatest Hitters

Baseball's hit kings of the past are featured in this collectors set. Fronts of the 2-1/2" x 3-1/2" cards have a color or black-and-white photo surrounded by a colored frame. Backs are in black-and-white with a career summary, lifetime stats and Major League Baseball licensee logo.

		NM/M
Complete Set (45):		8.00
Common Player:		.25
1	Ted Williams	1.00
2	Stan Musial	1.00
3	Joe DiMaggio	2.00
4	Roberto Clemente	2.00
5	Jackie Robinson	1.00
6	Willie Mays	1.00
7	Lou Brock	.25
8	Al Kaline	.25
9	Richie Ashburn	.25
10	Tony Oliva	.25
11	Harvey Kuenn	.25
12	Mickey Vernon	.25
13	Tommy Davis	.25
14	Ty Cobb	.75
15	Rogers Hornsby	.25
16	Joe Jackson	2.00
17	Willie Keeler	.25
18	Tris Speaker	.25
19	Babe Ruth	2.50
20	Harry Heilmann	.25
21	Bill Terry	.25
22	George Sisler	.25
23	Lou Gehrig	1.00
24	Nap Lajoie	.25
25	Riggs Stephenson	.25
26	Al Simmons	.25
27	Cap Anson	.25
28	Paul Waner	.25
29	Eddie Collins	.25
30	Heinie Manush	.25
31	Honus Wagner	.50
32	Earle Combs	.25
33	Sam Rice	.25
34	Charlie Gehringer	.25
35	Chick Hafey	.25
36	Zack Wheat	.25
37	Frank Frisch	.25
38	Bill Dickey	.25
39	Ernie Lombardi	.25
40	Joe Cronin	.25
41	Lefty O'Doul	.25
42	Luke Appling	.25
43	Ferris Fain	.25
44	Arky Vaughan	.25
45	Joe Medwick	.25

Baseball's Greatest Pitchers

The best pitchers who were no longer active are featured in this collectors issue. Color or black-and-white photos are presented at center of the 2-1/2" x 3-1/2" cards, with a colored frame surrounding the title, name and position. Backs are printed in dark blue and have a career summary and lifetime stats.

		NM/M
Complete Set (45):		6.00
Common Player:		.25
1	Bob Feller	.35
2	Bob Lemon	.25
3	Whitey Ford	.75
4	Joe Page	.25
5	Wilbur Wood	.25
6	Robin Roberts	.25
7	Warren Spahn	.25
8	Sandy Koufax	3.00
9	Juan Marichal	.25
10	Don Newcombe	.25
11	Hoyt Wilhelm	.25
12	Roy Face	.25
13	Allie Reynolds	.25
14	Don Drysdale	.25
15	Bob Gibson	.25
16	Cy Young	.25
17	Walter Johnson	.25
18	Grover Alexander	.25
19	Jack Chesbro	.25
20	Lefty Gomez	.25
21	Wes Ferrell	.25
22	Hal Newhouser	.25
23	Early Wynn	.25
24	Denny McLain	.25
25	Catfish Hunter	.25
26	Jim Lonborg	.25
27	Frank Lary	.25
28	Red Ruffing	.25
29	Lefty Grove	.25
30	Herb Pennock	.25
31	Satchel Paige	1.50
32	Iron Man McGinnity	.25
33	Christy Mathewson	.50
34	Mordecai Brown	.25
35	Eppa Rixey	.25
36	Dizzy Dean	.40
37	Carl Hubbell	.25
38	Dazzy Vance	.25
39	Jim Bunning	.25
40	Smokey Joe Wood	.25
41	Freddie Fitzsimmons	.25
42	Rube Waddell	.25
43	Addie Joss	.25
44	Burleigh Grimes	.25
45	Chief Bender	.25

Baseball's Greatest Sluggers

The heaviest hitters in baseball history are featured in this collectors issue. The 2-1/2" x 3-1/2" cards have color or black-and-white photos on front framed in red or green and bordered in white. Backs have a few personal data, career stats and career summary along with a logo indicating licensing by Major League Baseball, all in black-and-white, or blue-and-white. Cards can be found printed on either white or gray cardboard.

		NM/M
Complete Set (45):		8.00
Common Player:		.25
1	Harmon Killebrew	.25
2	Roger Maris	.50
3	Mickey Mantle	3.00
4	Hank Aaron	1.50
5	Ralph Kiner	.25
6	Willie McCovey	.25
7	Eddie Mathews	.25
8	Ernie Banks	.50
9	Duke Snider	.50
10	Frank Howard	.25
11	Ted Kluszewski	.25
12	Frank Robinson	.25
13	Billy Williams	.25
14	Gil Hodges	.50
15	Yogi Berra	.50
16	Richie Allen	.25
17	Joe Adcock	.25
18	Babe Ruth	2.50
19	Lou Gehrig	2.00
20	Jimmie Foxx	.25
21	Rogers Hornsby	.25
22	Ted Williams	1.50
23	Hack Wilson	.25
24	Al Simmons	.25
25	John Mize	.25
26	Chuck Klein	.25
27	Hank Greenberg	.25
28	Babe Herman	.25
29	Norm Cash	.25
30	Rudy York	.25
31	Gavvy Cravath	.25
32	Mel Ott	.25
33	Orlando Cepeda	.25
34	Dolf Camilli	.25
35	Frank Baker	.25
36	Larry Doby	.25
37	Jim Gentile	.25
38	Harry Davis	.25
39	Rocco Colavito	.25
40	Cy Williams	.25
41	Roy Sievers	.25
42	Boog Powell	.25
43	Willie Mays	1.50
44	Joe DiMaggio	2.00
45	Earl Averill	.25

Great Players of the 1950's & 60's: Series 1

These large-format (3-3/4" x 5-3/4") cards have white-bordered color poses on front, with no extraneous graphics. Backs have a black-and-white head shot of the player with lifetime stats, career highlights and personal data in a red border.

		NM/M
Complete Set (20):		15.00
Common Player:		.60
1	Roberto Clemente	3.00
2	Sandy Koufax	2.50
3	Phil Rizzuto	1.00
4	Bob Feller	.60
5	Duke Snider	1.00
6	Hank Aaron	2.50
7	Eddie Mathews	.60
8	Roy Campanella	1.50
9	Willie Mays	2.50
10	Robin Roberts	.60
11	Nelson Fox	.60
12	Early Wynn	.60
13	Ted Williams	2.50
14	Warren Spahn	.60
15	Jackie Robinson	2.00
16	Joe DiMaggio	2.50
17	Frank Robinson	.60
18	Yogi Berra	1.25
19	Mickey Mantle	3.50
20	Stan Musial	2.00

"1952" Bowman

A find of player paintings evidently intended for use in Bowman's 1952 baseball card set allowed TCMA to produce this collectors' issue of 15 Bowman "high numbers that never were." The 2-1/8" x 3-1/8" cards approximate the size of the originals. Fronts have only the color picture with a white border around; the facsimile signatures found on original 1952 Bowmans are not present. Backs are printed in red and black and have layout and style similar to the 1952 cards, along with a 1982 TCMA copyright. The issue was numbered consecutively from #253, beginning where the original issue ended.

		NM/M
Complete Set (15):		12.00
Common Player:		1.00
253	Bob Kennedy	1.00
254	Barney McCosky	1.00
255	Chris Van Cuyk	1.00
256	Morrie Martin	1.00
257	Jim Wilson	1.00
258	Bob Thorpe	1.00
259	Bill Henry	1.00
260	Bob Addis	1.00
261	Terry Moore	1.00
262	Joe Dobson	1.00
263	Jack Merson	1.00
264	Virgil Trucks	1.00
265	Johnny Hopp	1.00
266	Cookie Lavagetto	1.00
267	George Shuba	1.00

1983 TCMA All-Time Athletics

This was one of several early 1980s collectors issues from TCMA depicting an All-Time team. The 2-1/2" x 3-1/2" cards have black-and-white photos on front with red graphics. Backs are printed in blue and offer personal data, a career summary and lifetime stats.

	NM/M
Complete Set (12):	12.00
Common Player:	.75

1 Jimmie Foxx 1.50
2 Eddie Collins 1.25
3 Frank Baker 1.25
4 Jack Barry .75
5 Al Simmons 1.25
6 Mule Haas .75
7 Bing Miller .75
8 Mickey Cochrane 1.25
9 Chief Bender 1.25
10 Lefty Grove 1.25
11 John Wyatt .75
12 Connie Mack 1.25

All-Time Cardinals

A picked team of Cardinal greats through the 1970s is featured on this collectors' issue. The 2-1/2" x 3-1/2" cards have black-and-white photos on front, with the set title printed in red in the white bottom border. Backs have player data and a career summary printed in purple on gray or blue on white.

NM/M
Complete Set (12): 18.00
Common Player: 1.00
1 Jim Bottomley 1.00
2 Rogers Hornsby 1.25
3 Ken Boyer 1.50
4 Marty Marion 1.00
5 Ducky Medwick 1.00
6 Chick Hafey 1.00
7 Stan Musial 6.00
8 Tim McCarver 1.25
9 Robert "Bob" Gibson 1.50
10 Harry Brecheen 1.00
11 Alpha Brazle 1.00
12 Red Schoendienst 1.25

All-Time Pirates

This was one of several early 1980s collectors' issues from TCMA depicting an All-Time team. The 2-1/2" x 3-1/2" cards have black-and-white photos on front with blue graphics. Backs are printed in blue and offer personal data, a career summary and lifetime stats.

NM/M
Complete Set (12): 12.00
Common Player: 1.00
1 Willie Stargell 2.00
2 Bill Mazeroski 2.00
3 Pie Traynor 1.00
4 Honus Wagner 2.00
5 Roberto Clemente 6.00
6 Lloyd Waner, Paul Waner 1.50
7 Ralph Kiner 1.00
8 Manny Sanguillen 1.00
9 Deacon Phillippe 1.00
10 Bob Veale 1.00
11 Elroy Face 1.00
12 Danny Murtaugh 1.00

Play Ball Postcards

These 5-1/2" x 3-1/2" postcards have vintage photos in sepia with white borders and player identification on front. The postcard-style backs have a write-up about the team represented.

NM/M
Complete Set (18): 25.00
Common Card: 2.00
1 1949 Indians (Lou Boudreau, Joe Gordon) 2.00
2 1948 Red Sox (Murrell Jones, Bobby Doerr, Junior Stephens, Johnny Pesky) 2.00
3 1948 Red Sox (Sam Mele, Ted Williams, Stan Spence, Dom DiMaggio) 4.00
4 1948 Yankees (Joe DiMaggio, Johnny Lindell, Charlie Keller, Tommy Henrich) 5.00
5 Pittsburgh 1947 (Happy Chandler, Hank Greenberg) 2.00
6 1948 Phillies (Eddie Miller, Emil Verban) 2.00
7 1948 Cardinals (Howie Pollett, Red Munger, Murry Dickson, Harry Brecheen, Ken Burkhart) 2.00
8 1948 Braves (Warren Spahn, Johnny Sain) 2.50
9 1948 Braves (Alvin Dark, Eddie Stanky) 2.00
10 1948 Braves (Bob Elliott, Tommy Holmes) 2.00
11 1941 Yankees Team Photo 3.00
12 1943 Yankees Team Photo 3.00
13 1947 Yankees Team Photo 3.00
14 1948 Spring Training (Yankees) (Eddie Lopat, Spec Shea, Vic Raschi, Red Embree, Bill Bevens) 3.00
15 1948 A's (Lou Brissie, Connie Mack) 2.00
16 1948 Tigers (Ted Gray, Hal Newhouser, Virgil Trucks, Art Houtteman, Fred Hutchinson, Dizzy Trout) 2.00
17 Yankees (Phil Rizzuto, Joe Gordon) 3.00
18 1944 Browns (Ellis Clary, Floyd Baker, Vern Stephens, Mark Christman, Don Gutteridge, George McQuinn) 2.00

50 Years of Yankees All-Stars

Yankees' players who participated in the first 50 years of All-Star Games (1933-1983) are featured in this collectors' issue. The 2-3/4" x 3-1/2" cards feature on front the art of Robert Stephen Simon.

NM/M
Complete Set (50): 12.50
Common Player: .40
1 Checklist (Mickey Mantle) 1.25
2 Luis Arroyo .40
3 Hank Bauer .40
4 Yogi Berra .75
5 Tommy Byrne .40
6 Spud Chandler .40
7 Ben Chapman .40
8 Jim Coates .40
9 Bill Dickey .50
10 Joe DiMaggio 3.00
11 Al Downing .40
12 Ryne Duren .40
13 Whitey Ford .75
14 Whitey Ford .75
15 Lou Gehrig 3.00
16 Lefty Gomez .40
17 Bob Grim .40
18 Tommy Henrich .40
19 Elston Howard .40
20 Catfish Hunter .40
21 Billy Johnson .40
22 Charlie Keller .40
23 Johnny Kucks .40
24 Ed Lopat .40
25 Sparky Lyle .40
26 Mickey Mantle 4.00
27 Roger Maris .75
28 Billy Martin .50
29 Johnny Mize .50
30 Bobby Murcer .40
31 Irv Noren .40
32 Joe Pepitone .40
33 Fritz Peterson .40
34 Vic Raschi .40
35 Allie Reynolds .40
36 Bobby Richardson .40
37 Phil Rizzuto .75
38 Marius Russo .40
39 Babe Ruth 3.50
40 Johnny Sain .40
41 George Selkirk .40
42 Bobby Shantz .40
43 Spec Shea .40
44 Moose Skowron .40
45 Casey Stengel .60
46 Mel Stottlemyre .40
47 Ralph Terry .40
48 Tom Tresh .40
49 Bob Turley .40
50 Roy White .40

1936-1939 Yankee Dynasty

Many of the players who participated in one or more of the Yankees' four consecutive World Champion seasons in the late 1930s are included in this collectors' edition. Cards are 2-3/4" x 4" and feature black-and-white photos on front. In the white borders at top and bottom, the set name and player identification are printed in blue. Backs have stats for each season and are printed in black-and-white on a brown background. This set is a virtual reprint of the set made in 1974, with two player cards added. The unnumbered cards are checklisted here alphabetically.

NM/M
Complete Set (56): 45.00
Common Player: 1.00
(1) "Poison Ivy" Andrews 1.00
(2) Joe Beggs 1.00
(3) Marv Breuer 1.00
(4) Johnny Broaca 1.00
(5) "Jumbo" Brown 1.00
(6) "Spud" Chandler 1.00
(7) Ben Chapman 1.00
(8) Earle Combs 1.00
(9) Frankie Crosetti 1.00
(10) "Babe" Dahlgren 1.00
(11) Bill Dickey 1.50
(12) Joe DiMaggio 8.00
(13) Atley Donald 1.00
(14) Wes Ferrell 1.00
(15) Artie Fletcher 1.00
(16) Joe Gallagher 1.00
(17) Lou Gehrig 8.00
(18) Joe Glenn 1.00
(19) "Lefty" Gomez 1.00
(20) Joe Gordon 1.00
(21) "Bump" Hadley 1.00
(22) Don Heffner 1.00
(23) Tommy Henrich 1.00
(24) Oral Hildebrand 1.00
(25) Myril Hoag 1.00
(26) Roy Johnson 1.00
(27) Arndt Jorgens 1.00
(28) Charlie Keller 1.00
(29) Ted Kleinhans 1.00
(30) Billy Knickerbocker 1.00
(31) Tony Lazzeri 1.00
(32) Frank Makosky 1.00
(33) "Pat" Malone 1.00
(34) Johnny Murphy 1.00
(35) "Monty" Pearson 1.00
(36) "Jake" Powell 1.00
(37) "Red" Rolfe 1.00
(38) "Buddy" Rosar 1.00
(39) "Red" Ruffing 1.00
(40) Marius Russo 1.00
(41) "Jack" Saltzgaver 1.00
(42) Paul Schreiber 1.00
(43) Johnny Schulte 1.00
(44) Bob Seeds 1.00
(45) "Twinkletoes" Selkirk 1.00
(46) Lee Stine 1.00
(47) Steve Sundra 1.00
(48) "Sandy" Vance 1.00
(49) Dixie Walker 1.00
(50) Kemp Wicker 1.00
(51) Joe McCarthy, Jacob Ruppert 1.00
(52) Joe DiMaggio, Frank Crosetti, Tony Lazzeri, Bill Dickey, Lou Gehrig, Jake Powell, George Selkirk 3.00
(53) Lou Gehrig, Joe DiMaggio 5.00
(54) Gehrig Hits Another 5.00
(55) Red Rolfe, Tony Lazzeri, Lou Gehrig, Frank Crosetti 3.00
(56) World Champions - 1936 3.00

1942-46 St. Louis Cardinals

This set is a virtual reissue of the 1975 set, except for some minor changes in player selection, the use of a slightly smaller (2-1/2" x 3-1/2") format, gray cardboard backs instead of white and which include biographical information as well as stats and the appearance on a black line around the black-and-white player photos. Highlight printing on front is again in red. This version of the set includes card numbers.

NM/M
Complete Set (68): 24.00
Common Player: .25
1 Jimmy Brown .25
2 Jeff Cross .25
3 Lou Klein .25
4 Danny Litwhiler .25
5 Sam Narron .25
6 Estel Crabtree .25
7 Buzzy Wares .25
8 Ken O'Dea .25
9 Buddy Blattner .25
10 Erv Dusak .25
11 Ray Sanders .25
12 Harry Walker .25
13 Coaker Triplett .25
14 Stan Musial 4.00
15 Walker Cooper .25
16 Whitey Kurowski .25
17 Enos Slaughter 1.50
18 Terry Moore .35
19 Johnny Hopp .25
20 Creepy Crespi .25
21 Marty Marion .50
22 Debs Garms .25
23 Frank Demaree .25
24 George Fallon .25
25 Buster Adams .25
26 Emil Verban .25
27 Augie Bergamo .50
28 Pepper Martin .50
29 Mike Gonzalez .50
30 Leo Durocher, Eddie Dyer .50
31 Red Schoendienst 1.50
32 Del Rice .25
33 Joe Garagiola 2.00
34 Dick Sisler .25
35 Clyde Kluttz .25
36 Bill Endicott .25
37 Nippy Jones .25
38 Walt Sessi .25
39 Del Wilber .25
40 Mort Cooper .25
41 John Beazley .25
42 Howie Krist .25
43 Max Lanier .25
44 Harry Grumbert (Gumbert) .25
45 Howie Pollet .25
46 Ernie White .25
47 Murray Dickson (Murry) .25
48 Lon Warneke .25
49 Bill Lohrman .25
50 Clyde Shoun .25
51 Red Munger .25
52 Harry Brecheen .25
53 Al Brazle .25
54 Bud Byerly .25
55 Ted Wilks .25
56 Fred Schmidt .25
57 Al Jurisich .25
58 Red Barrett .25
59 Ken Burkhart .25
60 Blix Donnelly .25
61 Johnny Grodzicki .25
62 Billy Southworth .25
63 Eddie Dyer .25
64 Red Ruffing, Johnny Beazley .25
65 Stan Musial, Billy Southworth, Johnny Hopp 1.00
66 Sportsman's Park (5" x 3-1/2") 2.00
67 1942 St. Louis Cardinals (5" x 3-1/2") 2.00
68 Stan Musial, Billy Southworth, Ray Sanders 1.00

1942 Play Ball

Between 1983-85, TCMA produced eight sets of collectors' cards resurrecting the Play Ball brand name which had been active in the field from 1939-41. The TCMA sets attempt to replicate the style and substance of the earlier Play Ball cards as if the company had continued production through World War II and the end of the 1940s. The "1942" set features sepia-toned photos on front, with black graphics. Backs are printed on gray stock in blue ink. Size approximates the original Play Balls at 2-1/2" x 3-1/4".

NM/M
Complete Set (45): 30.00
Common Player: 1.50
1 Joe Gordon 1.50
2 Joe DiMaggio 6.50
3 Bill Dickey 2.00
4 Joe McCarthy 1.50
5 Tex Hughson 1.50
6 Ted Williams 5.00
7 Walt Judnich 1.50
8 Vern Stephens 1.50
9 Denny Galehouse 1.50
10 Lou Boudreau 1.50
11 Ken Keltner 1.50
12 Jim Bagby 1.50
13 Rudy York 1.50
14 Barney McCosky 1.50
15 Schoolboy Rowe 1.50
16 Luke Appling 1.50
17 Taft Wright 1.50
18 Ted Lyons 1.50
19 Mickey Vernon 1.50
20 George Case 1.50
21 Bobo Newsom 1.50
22 Bob Johnson 1.50
23 Buddy Blair 1.50
24 Pete Suder 1.50
25 Terry Moore 1.50
26 Stan Musial 5.00
27 Marty Marion 1.50
28 Pee Wee Reese 3.50
29 Arky Vaughan 1.50
30 Larry French 1.50
31 Johnny Mize 2.00
32 Mel Ott 2.00
33 Willard Marshall 1.50
34 Carl Hubbell 2.00
35 Frank McCormick 1.50
36 Linus Frey 1.50
37 Bob Elliott 1.50
38 Vince DiMaggio 1.50
39 Al Lopez 1.50
40 Stan Hack 1.50
41 Lou Novikoff 1.50
42 Casey Stengel 2.00
43 Tommy Holmes 1.50
44 Ron Northey 1.50
45 Rube Melton 1.50

1943 Play Ball

Between 1983-85, TCMA produced eight sets of collectors' cards resurrecting the Play Ball brand name which had been active in the field from 1939-41. The TCMA sets attempt to replicate the style and substance of the earlier Play Ball cards as if the company had continued production through World War II and the end of the 1940s. The "1943" set features sepia-toned photos on front, with black graphics. Backs are printed on gray stock in purple ink. Size approximates the original Play Balls at 2-1/2" x 3-1/4".

NM/M
Complete Set (45): 25.00
Common Player: 1.50
1 Spud Chandler 1.50
2 Frank Crosetti 1.50
3 Johnny Lindell 1.50
4 Emil "Dutch" Leonard 1.50
5 Stan Spence 1.50
6 Ray Mack 1.50
7 Hank Edwards 1.50
8 Al Smith 1.50
9 Mike Tresh 1.50
10 Don Kolloway 1.50
11 Orval Grove 1.50
12 Doc Cramer 1.50
13 Pinky Higgins 1.50
14 Dick Wakefield 1.50
15 Harland Clift (Harlond) 1.50
16 Chet Laabs 1.50
17 George McQuinn 1.50
18 Tony Lupien 1.50
19 Oscar Judd 1.50
20 Roy Partee 1.50
21 Lum Harris 1.50
22 Roger Wolf 1.50
23 Dick Siebert 1.50
24 Walker Cooper 1.50
25 Mort Cooper 1.50
26 Whitey Kurowski 1.50
27 Eddie Miller 1.50
28 Elmer Riddle 1.50
29 Bucky Walters 1.50
30 Whitlow Wyatt 1.50
31 Dolf Camilli 1.50
32 Elbie Fletcher 1.50
33 Frank Gustine 1.50
34 Rip Sewell 1.50
35 Phil Cavarretta 1.50
36 Bill "Swish" Nicholson 1.50
37 Peanuts Lowrey 1.50
38 Phil Masi 1.50
39 Al Javery 1.50
40 Jim Tobin 1.50
41 Glen Stewart 1.50
42 Mickey Livingston 1.50
43 Ace Adams 1.50
44 Joe Medwick 2.50
45 Sid Gordon 1.50

1944 Play Ball

Between 1983-85, TCMA produced eight sets of collectors' cards resurrecting the Play Ball brand name which had been active in the field from 1939-41. The TCMA sets attempt to replicate the style and substance of the earlier Play Ball cards as if the company had continued production through World War II and the end of the 1940s. The "1944" set features black-and-white photos on front, with blue graphics. Backs are printed on gray stock in black ink. Size approximates the original Play Balls at 2-1/2" x 3-1/4".

		NM/M
Complete Set (45):		25.00
Common Player:		1.50
1	Don Gutteridge	1.50
2	Mark Christman	1.50
3	Mike Kreevich	1.50
4	Jimmy Outlaw	1.50
5	Paul Richards	1.50
6	Hal Newhouser	2.50
7	Bud Metheny	1.50
8	Mike Garbark	1.50
9	Hersh Martin	1.50
10	Bob Johnson	1.50
11	Mike Ryba	1.50
12	Oris Hockett	1.50
13	Ed Klieman	1.50
14	Ford Garrison	1.50
15	Irv Hall	1.50
16	Ed Busch	1.50
17	Ralph Hogdin	1.50
18	Thurman Tucker	1.50
19	Bill Dietrich	1.50
20	Rick Ferrell	2.00
21	John Sullivan	1.50
22	Mickey Haefner	1.50
23	Ray Sanders	1.50
24	Johnny Hopp	1.50
25	Ted Wilks	1.50
26	John Barrett	1.50
27	Jim Russell	1.50
28	Nick Strincevich	1.50
29	Eric Tipton	1.50
30	Jim Konstanty	1.50
31	Gee Walker	1.50
32	Dom Dellessandro	1.50
33	Bob Chipman	1.50
34	Hank Wyse	1.50
35	Phil Weintraub	1.50
36	George Hausmann	1.50
37	Bill Voiselle	1.50
38	Whitey Wietelmann	1.50
39	Clyde Kluttz	1.50
40	Connie Ryan	1.50
41	Eddie Stanky	1.50
42	Augie Galan	1.50
43	Mickey Owen	1.50
44	Charlie Schanz	1.50
45	Bob Finley	1.50

1945 Play Ball

Between 1983-85, TCMA produced eight sets of collectors' cards resurrecting the Play Ball brand name which had been active in the field from 1939-41. The TCMA sets attempt to replicate the style and substance of the earlier Play Ball cards as if the company had continued production through World War II and the end of the 1940s. The "1945" set features black-and-white photos on front, with blue graphics. Backs are printed on gray stock in black ink. Size approximates the original Play Balls at 2-1/2" x 3-1/4".

		NM/M
Complete Set (45):		25.00
Common Player:		1.50
1	Eddie Mayo	1.50
2	Dizzy Trout	1.50
3	Roy Cullenbine	1.50
4	Joe Kuhel	1.50
5	George Binks	1.50
6	Roger Wolff	1.50
7	Gene Moore	1.50
8	Frank Mancuso	1.50
9	Bob Muncrief	1.50
10	Tuck Stainback	1.50
11	Bill Bevens	1.50
12	Snuffy Stirnweiss	1.50
13	Don Ross	1.50
14	Felix Mackiewicz	1.50
15	Jeff Heath	1.50
16	John Dickshot	1.50
17	Ed Lopat	2.00
18	Skeeter Newsom (Newsome)	1.50
19	Eddie Lake	1.50
20	John Lazor	1.50
21	Hal Peck	1.50
22	Al Brancato	1.50
23	Paul Derringer	1.50
24	Stan Hack	1.50
25	Len Merullo	1.50
26	Emil Verban	1.50
27	Ken O'Dea	1.50
28	Red Barrett	1.50
29	Eddie Basinski	1.50
30	Dixie Walker	1.50
31	Goody Rosen	1.50
32	Preacher Roe	1.50
33	Pete Coscarat	1.50
34	Frankie Frisch	2.50
35	Napoleon Reyes	1.50
36	Dan Gardella	1.50
37	Buddy Kerr	1.50
38	Dick Culler	1.50
39	Tommy Holmes	1.50
40	Al Libke	1.50
41	Howie Fox	1.50
42	Johnny Riddle	1.50
43	Andy Seminick	1.50
44	Andy Karl	1.50
45	Rene Monteguedo	1.50

1984 TCMA American League All-Stars

The American League "players who compiled the greatest All-Star Game Records" are included in this collectors' edition - one at each position. In standard 2-1/2" x 3-1/2" size, the cards have black-and-white photos with blue frames. Backs have career All-Star Game stats and a copyright line. The unnumbered cards are listed here in alphabetical order.

		NM/M
Complete Set (9):		6.00
Common Player:		.25
(1)	Lou Boudreau	.25
(2)	Rocky Colavito	.50
(3)	Bill Dickey	.50
(4)	Nellie Fox	.50
(5)	Jimmie Foxx	.50
(6)	Mel Harder	.25
(7)	Al Kaline	1.00
(8)	Brooks Robinson	1.00
(9)	Ted Williams	2.50

Roberto Clemente

This one-card set was produced in the same format as the four-card 1984 Hall of Fame Induction set and was probably printed on the same sheet in the same quantity (fewer than 500). Front has a black-and-white photo, back has lifetime stats.

	NM/M
Roberto Clemente	7.50

Great Players of the 1950's & 60's: Series 2

These large-format (3-3/4" x 5-3/4") cards have color photos bordered in white with a green stripe at bottom bearing the player (or team) name. Backs have a black-and-white head shot of the player, his identification, personal data, career

stats and a short biography, all framed in blue with decorative top corners.

		NM/M
Complete Set (33):		75.00
Common Player:		2.00
1	Brooks Robinson	6.00
2	Al Kaline	6.00
3	Tony Oliva	2.00
4	Frank Howard	2.00
5	Richie Ashburn	6.00
6	Harmon Killebrew	6.00
7	George Kell	6.00
8	Larry Doby	6.00
9	Ernie Banks	7.50
10	Maury Wills	4.00
11	Roger Maris	10.00
12	Al Rosen	2.00
13	Willie McCovey	6.00
14	Luis Aparicio	6.00
15	Ron Santo	4.00
16	Harvey Kuenn	2.00
17	Lou Brock	6.00
18	1960 Pittsburgh Pirates (Murtaugh on back)	7.50
19	1966 N.Y. Yankees (Westrum on back)	7.50
20	1950 Philadelphia Phillies (Sawyer on back)	6.00
21	1955 Brooklyn Dodgers (Alston on back)	7.50
22	1957 Milwaukee Braves (Haney on back)	7.50
23	Bob Gibson	6.00
24	Don Drysdale	6.00
25	Whitey Ford	6.00
26	Mickey Mantle, Roger Maris, Mrs. Babe Ruth	7.50
27	Harmon Killebrew, Willie Mays, Mickey Mantle	10.00
28	Willie Mays, Don Drysdale	7.50
29	1961 Yankees, Manager and Coaches	7.50
30	1964 Mets, Manager and Coaches	6.00
31	Ken Boyer, Stan Musial, Red Schoendienst	3.50
32	1952 Giants Pitching Staff	2.00
33	Vada Pinson	2.00

Hall of Fame Induction

While the production of Induction cards in the larger format continued for several years, TCMA's issue of standard 2-1/2" x 3-1/2" format cards was exclusive to 1984. The black-and-white cards have lifetime stats on back. It is reported that fewer than 500 sets were made.

		NM/M
Complete Set (4):		20.00
Common Player:		4.00
(1)	Luis Aparicio	6.00
(2)	Don Drysdale	8.00
(3)	Rick Ferrell	4.00
(4)	Harmon Killebrew	8.00

Hall of Fame Induction 8x10s

For four years TCMA produced 8" x 10" cards for the current inductees to the Baseball Hall of Fame. There are no TCMA markings on the cards, which were distributed by Baseball Nostalgia of Cooperstown, N.Y. The cards are blank-backed and unnumbered. They were printed in black-and-white in 1984, 1986-1987; the 1985 cards are blue-and-white. Only 500 of each card were issued.

		NM/M
Complete Set (18):		250.00
Common Player:		15.00
(1)	Luis Aparicio	15.00
(2)	Don Drysdale	15.00
(3)	Rick Ferrell	15.00
(4)	Harmon Killebrew	15.00
(5)	Pee Wee Reese	20.00
(6)	Composite (Luis Aparicio, Don Drysdale, Rick Ferrell, Harmon Killebrew, Pee Wee Reese)	20.00
(7)	Lou Brock	15.00
(8)	Enos Slaughter	15.00
(9)	Hoyt Wilhelm	15.00
(10)	Composite (Lou Brock, Enos Slaughter, Arky Vaughn (Vaughan), Hoyt Wilhelm)	20.00
(11)	Bobby Doerr	15.00
(12)	Willie McCovey	15.00
(13)	Composite (Bobby Doerr, Ernie Lombardi, Willie McCovey)	20.00
(14)	50th Anniversary Composite (Ty Cobb, Walter Johnson, Christy Mathewson, Babe Ruth, Honus Wagner (Edition of 300.)	75.00
(15)	Ray Dandridge	15.00
(16)	Jim "Catfish" Hunter	15.00
(17)	Billy Williams	15.00
(18)	Composite (Ray Dandridge, Jim "Catfish" Hunter, Billy Williams)	15.00

National League All-Stars

The National League "players who compiled the greatest All-Star Game Records" are included in this collectors' edition - one at each position. In standard 2-1/2" x 3-1/2" size, the cards have black-and-white photos with red frames. Backs have career All-Star Game stats and a copyright line. The unnumbered cards are listed here in alphabetical order.

		NM/M
Complete Set (9):		6.00
Common Player:		.25
(1)	Ernie Banks	1.00
(2)	Ken Boyer	.25
(3)	Roberto Clemente	2.50
(4)	Dick Groat	.25
(5)	Billy Herman	.25
(6)	Ernie Lombardi	.25
(7)	Juan Marichal	.25
(8)	Willie Mays	2.00
(9)	Stan Musial	1.00

Bruce Stark Postcards

Color artwork by Bruce Stark is featured on these 3-3/4" x 5-3/4" postcards.

		NM/M
Complete Set (5):		9.00
Common Player:		1.25
BS1	Joe DiMaggio	4.50
BS2	Ted Williams	3.00
BS3	Ted Kluzewski (Kluszewski)	1.75
BS4	Mickey Vernon	1.25
BS5	Stan Musial	2.50

1946 Play Ball

Between 1983-85, TCMA produced eight sets of collectors' cards resurrecting the Play Ball brand name which had been active in the field from 1939-41. The TCMA sets attempt to replicate the style and substance of the earlier Play Ball cards as if the company had continued production through World War II and the end of the 1940s. The "1946" set features black-and-white photos on front, with green graphics. Backs are printed on white stock in black ink. Size approximates the originals at 2-1/2" x 3-1/4".

		NM/M
Complete Set (45):		20.00
Common Player:		1.00
1	Dom DiMaggio	1.25
2	Boo Ferriss	1.00
3	Johnny Pesky	1.00
4	Hank Greenberg	2.00
5	George Kell	1.00
6	Virgil Trucks	1.00
7	Phil Rizzuto	1.75
8	Charlie Keller	1.25
9	Tommy Henrich	1.25
10	Cecil Travis	1.00
11	Al Evans	1.00
12	Buddy Lewis	1.00
13	Edgar Smith	1.00
14	Dario Lodigiani	1.00
15	Earl Caldwell	1.00
16	Jim Hegan	1.00
17	Bob Feller	1.75
18	John Berardino	1.25
19	Jack Kramer	1.00
20	John Lucadello	1.00
21	Hank Majeski	1.00
22	Elmer Valo	1.00
23	Buddy Rosar	1.00
24	Red Schoendienst	1.25
25	Dick Sisler	1.00
26	John Beazley	1.00
27	Vic Lombardi	1.00
28	Dick Whitman	1.00
29	Carl Furillo	1.75
30	Bill Jurges	1.00
31	Marv Rickert	1.00
32	Clyde McCullough	1.00
33	Johnny Hopp	1.00
34	Mort Cooper	1.00
35	Johnny Sain	1.25
36	Del Ennis	1.00
37	Roy Hughes	1.00
38	Bert Haas	1.00
39	Grady Hatton	1.00
40	Ed Bahr	1.00
41	Billy Cox	1.00
42	Lee Handley	1.00
43	Bill Rigney	1.00
44	Babe Young	1.00
45	Buddy Blattner	1.00

1985 TCMA Cy Young Award Winners

This polybagged set of 2-1/2" x 3-1/2" cards is formatted on two perforated strips. Fronts have color photos with orange borders while backs detail the player's CY season(s). The header card presents the history of the award. The unnumbered cards are listed here alphabetically.

		NM/M
Complete Set (10):		6.00
Common Player:		.25
(1)	Don Drysdale	.75
(2)	Whitey Ford	1.50
(3)	Bob Gibson	.50
(4)	Catfish Hunter	.40
(5)	Sandy Koufax	4.00
(6)	Vern Law	.25
(7)	Sparky Lyle	.25
(8)	Denny McLain	.35
(9)	Jim Palmer	.50
(10a)	Warren Spahn (Boston Braves)	.50
(10b)	Warren Spahn (Milwaukee Braves)	.50

Home Run Champs

This polybagged set of 2-1/2" x 3-1/2" cards is formatted on two perforated strips. Fronts have color photos with reddish-brown borders while backs detail the player's slugging prowess. The header cards presents the history of the award. The unnumbered cards are listed here alphabetically.

		NM/M
Complete Set (10):		6.00
Common Player:		.30
(1)	Hank Aaron	1.50
(2)	Orlando Cepeda	.60
(3)	Joe DiMaggio	2.00
(4)	Larry Doby	.60
(5)	Ralph Kiner	.60
(6)	Eddie Mathews	.60
(7)	Willie McCovey	.60
(8)	Al Rosen	.30
(9)	Duke Snider	.60
(10)	Ted Williams	1.50

Most Valuable Players - A.L.

This polybagged set of 2-1/2" x 3-1/2" cards is formatted on two perforated strips. Fronts have color photos with green borders while backs detail the player's MVP season(s). The header card presents the history of the award. The unnumbered cards are listed here alphabetically.

		NM/M
Complete Set (10):		9.00
Common Player:		.40
(1)	Richie Allen	.40
(2)	Yogi Berra	.75
(3)	Elston Howard	.40
(4)	Jackie Jensen	.40
(5)	Harmon Killebrew	.75
(6)	Mickey Mantle	4.00
(7)	Roger Maris	1.50
(8)	Boog Powell	.40
(9)	Brooks Robinson	.75
(10)	Carl Yastrzemski	1.25

Most Valuable Players - N.L.

This polybagged set of 2-1/2" x 3-1/2" cards is formatted on two perforated strips. Fronts have color photos with blue borders while backs detail the player's MVP season(s). The header card presents the history of the award. The unnumbered cards are listed here alphabetically.

		NM/M
Complete Set (10):		9.00
Common Player:		.40
(1)	Ernie Banks	1.00
(2)	Johnny Bench	1.00
(3)	Roy Campanella	.90
(4)	Roberto Clemente	3.00
(5)	Dick Groat	.40
(6)	Willie Mays	2.50
(7)	Stan Musial	1.50
(8)	Frank Robinson	1.00
(9)	Willie Stargell	.75
(10)	Maury Wills	.40

N.Y. Mets Postcards

A certain sameness of poses, generally belt-to-cap, marks the cards in this color player postcard issue produced by TCMA for team issue. The 3-1/2" x 5-1/2" cards have borderless color photos with a glossy finish and no extraneous graphics. Backs have a large, light blue team logo at left, with player ID at top and a line of 1984 stats at

bottom. A TCMA copyright line is vertically at center. The postcard indicia at right includes a card number at the bottom of the stamp box; the number is preceded by an "NYM85-" prefix.

		NM/M
Complete Set (40):		12.50
Common Player:		.50
1	Davey Johnson	.75
2	Vern Hoscheit	.50
3	Bill Robinson	.50
4	Mel Stottlemyre	.75
5	Bobby Valentine	.50
6	Bruce Berenyi	.50
7	Jeff Bettendorf	.50
8	Ron Darling	.50
9	Sid Fernandez	.50
10	Brent Gaff	.50
11	Wes Gardner	.50
12	Dwight Gooden	1.50
13	Tom Gorman	.50
14	Ed Lynch	.50
15	Jesse Orosco	.50
16	Calvin Schiraldi	.50
17	Doug Sisk	.50
18	Gary Carter	2.00
19	John Gibbons	.50
20	Ronn Reynolds	.50
21	Wally Backman	.50
22	Kelvin Chapman	.50
23	Ron Gardenhire	.50
24	Keith Hernandez	1.00
25	Howard Johnson	.75
26	Ray Knight	.75
27	Kevin Mitchell	.50
28	Terry Blocker	.50
29	Rafael Santana	.50
30	Billy Beane	.50
31	John Christensen	.50
32	Len Dykstra	1.00
33	George Foster	1.00
34	Danny Heep	.50
35	Darryl Strawberry	1.00
36	Mookie Wilson	.75
37	Jeff Bittiger	.50
38	Clint Hurdle	.50
39	Laschelle Tarver	.50
40	Roger McDowell	.50

N.Y. Yankees Postcards

In 1985-86, TCMA produced color player postcard sets for the two New York teams. The 1985 Yankees set is 3-1/2" x 5-1/2" with borderless color poses on front. Backs have a light blue Yankees logo at left. Player identification and data is at top-left with 1984 stats at bottom. A TCMA copyright lines is vertically at center. Cards are numbered in the stamp box NYY85-1 through NYY85-40.

		NM/M
Complete Set (40):		12.50
Common Player:		.50
1	Yogi Berra	1.75
2	Mark Connor	.50
3	Stump Merrill	.50
4	Gene Michael	.50
5	Lou Piniella	.75
6	Jeff Torborg	.50
7	Mike Armstrong	.50
8	Rich Bordi	.50
9	Clay Christensen	.50
10	Joe Cowley	.50
11	Jim Deshaies	.50
12	Ron Guidry	.75
13	John Montefusco	.50
14	Dale Murray	.50
15	Phil Niekro	1.00
16	Alfonso Pulido	.50
17	Dennis Rasmussen	.50
18	Dave Righetti	.50
19	Bob Shirley	.50
20	Ed Whitson	.50
21	Scott Bradley	.50
22	Ron Hassey	.50
23	Butch Wynegar	.50
24	Dale Berra	.50
25	Billy Sample	.50
26	Rex Hudler	.50
27	Don Mattingly	3.00
28	Bobby Meacham	.50
29	Mike Pagliarulo	.50
30	Willie Randolph	.75
31	Andre Robertson	.50
32	Henry Cotto	.50
33	Don Baylor	.75
34	Ken Griffey	.50
35	Rickey Henderson	2.00
36	Vic Mata	.50
37	Omar Moreno	.50
38	Dan Pasqua	.50
39	Dave Winfield	2.00
40	Brian Fisher	.50

Photo Classics Postcards

Teammate pairings and other groupings are featured in this collector's issue set of black-and-white postcards. In 3-1/2" x 5-1/2" format, the postcard-style backs identify the players on front.

		NM/M
Complete Set (40):		45.00
Common Card:		1.00
1	Warren Spahn, Johnny Sain	1.50
2	Jackie Robinson	3.00
3	President Eisenhower w/ Yankees	1.50
4	Babe Ruth	4.00
5	Joe McCarthy, Lou Gehrig, Joe DiMaggio	2.00
6	Bob Feller	1.50
7	Johnny Lindell, Johnny Murphy	1.00
8	Babe Ruth, Claire Ruth	1.50
9	Babe Ruth, Joe Cook	1.50
10	Bobo Newsom	1.00
11	Johnny Antonelli, Robin Roberts	1.00
12	Joe Adcock, Eddie Mathews	1.50
13	Al Lopez, Mike Garcia, Bob Lemon, Early Wynn	2.00
14	Gil McDougald, Roy Campanella	1.50
15	Ralph Branca, Bobby Thomson	2.00
16	Lou Gehrig	2.50
17	Johnny Mize, Bill Rigney, Mel Ott	1.50
18	Spider Jorgensen, Pee Wee Reese, Eddie Stanky, Jackie Robinson	2.00
19	Tommy Holmes, Earl Torgeson, Jeff Heath, Connie Ryan, Billy Southworth	1.00
20	Ted Williams, Bobby Doerr, Dom DiMaggio, Vern Stephens	1.50
21	Chuck Schilling, Carl Yastrzemski	1.50
22	Roger Maris, Mickey Mantle	3.00
23	Rogers Hornsby, Gil McDougald	1.00
24	Jim Gentile, Gus Triandos	1.00
25	Bobby Avila, Willie Mays	1.50
26	Joe Garagiola, Ralph Kiner	1.00
27	Jim Gentile, Willie Mays	1.50
28	Red Schoendienst, Marty Marion	1.00
29	Charlie Keller	1.00
30	House of David Team	1.00
31	Harvey Kuenn, Al Kaline	1.50
32	Hank Sauer	1.00
33	Enos Slaughter	1.00
34	Stan Musial	2.00
35	Willie Mays	2.00
36	William Bendix, Babe Ruth	1.50
37	Whitey Lockman, Davey Williams, Hank Thompson, Alvin Dark, Don Mueller, Willie Mays, Monte Irvin, Wes Westrum	1.00
38	Pete Runnels, Vic Wertz	1.00
39	Stan Musial	2.00
40	Dom DiMaggio	1.00

Rookies of the Year

This polybagged set of 2-1/2" x 3-1/2" cards is formatted on two perforated strips. Fronts have color photos while backs detail the player's ROY season. The header card presents the history of the award. The unnumbered cards are listed here alphabetically.

		NM/M
Complete Set (10):		6.00
Common Player:		.25
(1)	Tommy Agee	.25
(2)	Luis Aparicio	.50
(3)	Frank Howard	.25
(4)	Harvey Kuenn	.25
(5)	Thurman Munson	3.00
(6)	Don Newcombe	.25
(7)	Tony Oliva	.25
(8)	Jackie Robinson	3.00
(9)	Herb Score	.25
(10)	Billy Williams	.50

1947 Play Ball

Between 1983-85, TCMA produced eight sets of collectors' cards resurrecting the Play Ball brand name which had been active in the field from 1939-41. The TCMA sets attempt to replicate the style and substance of the earlier Play Ball cards as if the company had continued production through World War II and the end of the 1940s. The "1947" set features black-and-white photos on front, with green graphics. Backs are printed on white stock in black ink. Size approximates the originals at 2-1/2" x 3-1/4".

		NM/M
Complete Set (45):		30.00
Common Player:		1.00
1	Hal Wagner	1.00
2	Jake Jones	1.00
3	Bobby Doerr	1.00
4	Fred Hutchinson	1.00
5	Bob Swift	1.00
6	Pat Mullin	1.00
7	Joe Page	1.00
8	Allie Reynolds	1.00
9	Billy Johnson	1.00
10	Early Wynn	1.00
11	Eddie Yost	1.00
12	Floyd Baker	1.00
13	Dave Philley	1.00
14	George Dickey	1.00
15	Dale Mitchell	1.00
16	Bob Lemon	1.00
17	Jerry Witte	1.00
18	Paul Lehner	1.00
19	Sam Zoldak	1.00
20	Sam Chapman	1.00
21	Eddie Joost	1.00
22	Ferris Fain	1.00
23	Erv Dusak	1.00
24	Joe Garagiola	1.00
25	Vernal "Nippy" Jones	1.00
26	Bobby Bragan	1.00
27	Jackie Robinson	6.00
28	Spider Jorgensen	1.00
29	Bob Scheffing	1.00
30	Johnny Schmitz	1.00
31	Doyle Lade	1.00
32	Earl Torgeson	1.00
33	Warren Spahn	1.00
34	Walt Lanfranconi	1.00
35	Johnny Wyrostek	1.00
36	Oscar Judd	1.00
37	Ewell Blackwell	1.00
38	Ed Lukon	1.00
39	Denny Zientara	1.00
40	Gene Woodling	1.00
41	Ernie Bonham	1.00
42	Hank Greenberg	3.00
43	Bobby Thomson	1.00
44	Jack "Lucky" Lohrke	1.00
45	Dave Koslo	1.00

1948 Play Ball

Between 1983-85, TCMA produced eight sets of collectors' cards resurrecting the Play Ball brand name which had been active in the field from 1939-41. The TCMA sets attempt to replicate the style and substance of the earlier Play Ball cards as if the company had continued production through World War II and the end of the 1940s. The "1948" set features black-and-white photos on front, with red graphics. Backs are printed on white stock in black ink. Size approximates the originals at 2-1/2" x 3-1/4".

		NM/M
Complete Set (45):		50.00
Common Player:		1.00
1	Murry Dickson	1.00
2	Enos Slaughter	1.50
3	Don Lang	1.00
4	Joe Hatten	1.00
5	Gil Hodges	2.00
6	Gene Hermanski	1.00
7	Eddie Waitkus	1.00
8	Jess Dobernic	1.00
9	Andy Pafko	1.00
10	Vern Bickford	1.00
11	Mike McCormick	1.00
12	Harry Walker	1.00
13	Putsy Caballero	1.00
14	Hubert "Dutch" Leonard	1.00
15	Frankie Baumholtz	1.00
16	Ted Kluszewski	1.50
17	Virgil Stallcup	1.00
18	Bob Chesnes	1.00
19	Ted Beard	1.00
20	Wes Westrum	1.00
21	Clint Hartung	1.00
22	Whitey Lockman	1.00
23	Billy Goodman	1.00
24	Jack Kramer	1.00
25	Mel Parnell	1.00
26	George Vico	1.00
27	Walter "Hoot" Evers	1.00
28	Vic Wertz	1.00
29	Yogi Berra	2.00
30	Joe DiMaggio	8.00
31	Tommy Byrne	1.00
32	Al Kozar	1.00
33	Jake Early	1.00
34	Gil Coan	1.00
35	Pat Seerey	1.00
36	Ralph Hodgin	1.00
37	Allie Clark	1.00
38	Gene Bearden	1.00
39	Steve Gromek	1.00
40	Al Zarilla	1.00
41	Fred Sanford	1.00
42	Les Moss	1.00
43	Don White	1.00
44	Carl Scheib	1.00
45	Lou Brissie	1.00

1949 Play Ball

Between 1983-85, TCMA produced eight sets of collectors' cards resurrecting the Play Ball brand name which had been active in the field from 1939-41. The TCMA sets attempt to replicate the style and substance of the earlier Play Ball cards as if the company had continued production through World War II and the end of the 1940s. The "1949" set features black-and-white photos on front, with red graphics. Backs are printed on white stock in black ink. Size approximates the originals at 2-1/2" x 3-1/4".

		NM/M
Complete Set (45):		40.00
Common Player:		1.00
1	Al Brazle	1.00
2	Harry Brecheen	1.00
3	Howie Pollett	1.00
4	Cal Abrams	1.00
5	Ralph Branca	1.00
6	Duke Snider	2.50
7	Charlie Grimm	1.00
8	Clarence Maddern	1.00
9	Hal Jeffcoat	1.00
10	Johnny Antonelli	1.00
11	Alvin Dark	1.00
12	Nelson Potter	1.00
13	Granny Hamner	1.00
14	Willie Jones	1.00
15	Robin Roberts	1.50
16	Lloyd Merriman	1.00
17	Bobby Adams	1.00
18	Herman Wehmeier	1.00
19	Ralph Kiner	1.00
20	Dino Restelli	1.00
21	Larry Jansen	1.00
22	Sheldon Jones	1.00
23	Red Webb	1.00
24	Vern Stephens	1.00
25	Tex Hughson	1.00
26	Ellis Kinder	1.00
27	Neil Berry	1.00
28	Johnny Groth	1.00
29	Art Houtteman	1.00
30	Hank Bauer	1.00
31	Vic Raschi	1.00
32	Bobby Brown	1.00
33	Joe Haynes	1.00
34	Eddie Robinson	1.00
35	Sam Dente	1.00
36	Herb Adams	1.00
37	Don Wheeler	1.00
38	Randy Gumpert	1.00
39	Ray Boone	1.00
40	Larry Doby	1.50
41	Jack Graham	1.00
42	Bob Dillinger	1.00
43	Dick Kokos	1.00
44	Wally Moses	1.00
45	Mike Guerra	1.00

1986 TCMA All Time Teams

Similar to TCMA sets of 1980-83, these sets feature 11 all-time great players and a manager from each team. In standard 2-1/2" x 3-1/2" format, most of the cards utilize black-and-white player photos, though some more recent stars are pictured in color. Several decorative borders, varying by team, surround the front photos. On most team sets there is an "All Time" designation at top, with the player name and (usually) position at bottom. Backs are fairly uniform, printed in blue, and offering a few biographical details and career highlights. Besides hobby sales, these old-timers' sets were also sold in several major retails chains, originally priced at about $4.

All Time Angels

		NM/M
Complete Set (12):		4.50
Common Player:		.50
1-ANG	Rod Carew	2.00
2-ANG	Sandy Alomar	.50
3-ANG	Jim Fregosi	.50
4-ANG	Dave Chalk	.50
5-ANG	Leon Wagner	.50
6-ANG	Albie Pearson	.50
7-ANG	Rick Reichardt	.50
8-ANG	Bob Rodgers	.50
9-ANG	Dean Chance	.50
10-ANG	Clyde Wright	.50
11-ANG	Bob Lee	.50
12-ANG	Bill Rigney	.50

All Time Astros

		NM/M
Complete Set (12):		6.00
Common Player:		.50
1-AST	Bob Watson	.50
2-AST	Joe Morgan	1.75
3-AST	Roger Metzger	.50
4-AST	Doug Rader	.50
5-AST	Jimmy Wynn	.70
6-AST	Cesar Cedeno	.70
7-AST	Rusty Staub	.70
8-AST	Johnny Edwards	.50
9-AST	J.R. Richard	.80
10-AST	Dave Roberts	.50
11-AST	Fred Gladding	.50
12-AST	Bill Virdon	.50

All Time Blue Jays

		NM/M
Complete Set (12):		5.00
Common Player:		.50
1-BLU	John Mayberry	.50
2-BLU	Bob Bailor	.50
3-BLU	Luis Gomez	.50
4-BLU	Roy Howell	.50
5-BLU	Otto Velez	.50
6-BLU	Rick Bosetti	.50
7-BLU	Al Woods	.50
8-BLU	Rick Cerone	.50
9-BLU	Dave Lemanczyk	.50
10-BLU	Tom Underwood	.50
11-BLU	Joey McLaughlin	.50
12-BLU	Bobby Cox	.75

All Time Boston/ Milwaukee Braves

		NM/M
Complete Set (12):		7.50
Common Player:		.50
1B	Joe Adcock	.70
2B	Felix Millan	.50
3B	Rabbit Maranville	.50
4B	Eddie Mathews	2.00
5B	Hank Aaron	6.00
6B	Wally Berger	.50
7B	Tommy Holmes	.50
8B	Del Crandall	.50
9B	Warren Spahn	2.00

10B Charles "Kid" Nichols .50
11B Cecil Upshaw .50
12B Fred Haney .50

All Time Brewers

NM/M
Complete Set (12): 6.00
Common Player: .50
1-BRE George Scott .75
2-BRE Pedro Garcia .50
3-BRE Tim Johnson .50
4-BRE Don Money .50
5-BRE Sixto Lezcano .50
6-BRE John Briggs .50
7-BRE Dave May .50
8-BRE Darrell Porter .50
9-BRE Jim Colborn .50
10-BRE Mike Caldwell .50
11-BRE Rollie Fingers 1.50
12-BRE Harvey Kuenn .50

All Time Expos

NM/M
Complete Set (12): 5.00
Common Player: .50
1-EXP Ron Fairly .50
2-EXP Dave Cash .50
3-EXP Tim Foley .50
4-EXP Bob Bailey .50
5-EXP Ken Singleton .75
6-EXP Ellis Valentine .50
7-EXP Rusty Staub .75
8-EXP John Bateman .50
9-EXP Steve Rogers .50
10-EXP Woodie Fryman .50
11-EXP Mike Marshall .50
12-EXP Jim Fanning .50

All Time Indians

NM/M
Complete Set (12): 7.00
Common Player: .50
1-IND Hal Trosky .50
2-IND Nap Lajoie .50
3-IND Lou Boudreau .50
4-IND Al Rosen .50
5-IND Joe Jackson 6.00
6-IND Tris Speaker .75
7-IND Larry Doby 1.00
8-IND Jim Hegan .50
9-IND Cy Young 1.00
10-IND Sam McDowell .60
11-IND Ray Narleski .50
12-IND Al Lopez .50

All Time Mariners

NM/M
Complete Set (12): 5.00
Common Player: .50
1-MAR Pat Putnam .50
2-MAR Larry Milbourne .50
3-MAR Todd Cruz .50
4-MAR Bill Stein .50
5-MAR Leon Roberts .50
6-MAR Leroy Stanton .50
7-MAR Dan Meyer .50
8-MAR Bob Stinson .50
9-MAR Glenn Abbott .50
10-MAR John Montague .50
11-MAR Bryan Clark .50
12-MAR Rene Lachemann .50

All Time Mets

NM/M
Complete Set (12): 7.50
Common Player: .50
1M Ed Kranepool .50
2M Ron Hunt .50
3M Bud Harrelson .75
4M Wayne Garrett .50
5M Cleon Jones .75
6M Tommie Agee .75
7M Rusty Staub 1.00
8M Jerry Grote .50
9M Gary Gentry .50
10M Jerry Koosman .75
11M Tug McGraw .75
12M Gil Hodges 2.00

All Time Oakland A's

NM/M
Complete Set (12): 7.00
Common Player: .50
1-ATH Gene Tenace .50
2-ATH Dick Green .50
3-ATH Bert Campaneris .75
4-ATH Sal Bando .50
5-ATH Joe Rudi .75
6-ATH Rick Monday .50
7-ATH Bill North .50
8-ATH Dave Duncan .50
9-ATH Jim "Catfish" Hunter 1.50
10-ATH Ken Holtzman .50
11-ATH Rollie Fingers 1.50
12-ATH Alvin Dark .50

All Time Orioles

NM/M
Complete Set (12): 14.00
Common Player: .50
1BA Hoyt Wilhelm .50
2BA Hank Bauer .50
3BA Jim Palmer 2.00
4BA Dave McNally .50
5BA Paul Blair .50
6BA Gus Triandos .50
7BA Frank Robinson 3.00
8BA Ken Singleton .50
9BA Luis Aparicio 2.50
10BA Brooks Robinson 4.00
11BA John "Boog" Powell 1.00
12BA Dave Johnson .50

All Time Padres

NM/M
Complete Set (12): 6.00
Common Player: .50
1-PAD Nate Colbert .50
2-PAD Tito Fuentes .50
3-PAD Enzo Hernandez .50
4-PAD Dave Roberts .50
5-PAD Gene Richards .50
6-PAD Ollie Brown .50
7-PAD Clarence Gaston .50
8-PAD Fred Kendall .50
9-PAD Gaylord Perry 1.50
10-PAD Randy Jones .50
11-PAD Rollie Fingers 1.50
12-PAD Preston Gomez .50

All Time Phillies

NM/M
Complete Set (12): 7.00
Common Player: .35
1PP Chuck Klein .50
2PP Richie Ashburn 3.00
3PP Del Ennis .35
4PP Spud Davis .35
5PP Grover Alexander .50
6PP Chris Short .35
7PP Jim Konstanty .35
8PP Danny Ozark .35
9PP Larry Bowa .35
10PP Richie Allen 1.00
11PP Don Hurst .35
12PP Tony Taylor .35

All Time Pirates

NM/M
Complete Set (12): 14.00
Common Player: .50
1-PIR Willie Stargell 2.50
2-PIR Bill Mazeroski 2.50
3-PIR Honus Wagner 2.50
4-PIR Pie Traynor .50
5-PIR Ralph Kiner .75
6-PIR Paul Waner .50
7-PIR Roberto Clemente 5.00
8-PIR Manny Sanguillen .50
9-PIR Vic Willis .50
10-PIR Wilbur Cooper .50
11-PIR Roy Face .50
12-PIR Danny Murtaugh .50

All Time Rangers

NM/M
Complete Set (12): 6.00
Common Player: .50
1-RAN Gaylord Perry 2.00
2-RAN Jon Matlack .50
3-RAN Jim Kern .50
4-RAN Billy Hunter .50
5-RAN Mike Hargrove .75
6-RAN Bump Wills .50
7-RAN Toby Harrah .75
8-RAN Lenny Randle .50
9-RAN Al Oliver .75
10-RAN Mickey Rivers .50
11-RAN Jeff Burroughs .50
12-RAN Dick Billings .50

All Time Reds

NM/M
Complete Set (12): 9.00
Common Player: .50
1CR Clay Carroll .50
2CR Bill McKechnie .50
3CR Paul Derringer .50
4CR Eppa Rixey .50
5CR Frank Robinson 2.50
6CR Vada Pinson 1.00
7CR Leo Cardenas .50
8CR Heinie Groh .50
9CR Ted Kluszewski 2.00
10CR Joe Morgan 1.50
11CR Edd Roush .50
12CR Johnny Bench 3.00

All Time Red Sox

NM/M
Complete Set (12): 10.00
Common Player: .50
1BRS Sammy White .50
2BRS Lefty Grove .50
3BRS Cy Young 1.00
4BRS Jimmie Foxx 1.00
5BRS Bobby Doerr .50
6BRS Joe Cronin .50
7BRS Frank Malzone .50
8BRS Ted Williams 6.00
9BRS Carl Yastrzemski 4.00
10BRS Tris Speaker 1.00
11BRS Dick Radatz .50
12BRS Dick Williams .50

All Time Royals

NM/M
Complete Set (12): 5.00
Common Player: .50
1-ROY John Mayberry .50
2-ROY Cookie Rojas .50
3-ROY Fred Patek .50
4-ROY Paul Schall .50
5-ROY Lou Piniella 1.00
6-ROY Amos Otis .50
7-ROY Tom Poquette .50
8-ROY Ed Kirkpatrick .50
9-ROY Steve Busby .50
10-ROY Paul Splittorff .50
11-ROY Mark Littell .50
12-ROY Jim Frey .50

All Time Twins

NM/M
Complete Set (12): 9.00
Common Player: .50
1-TWI Harmon Killebrew 2.50
2-TWI Rod Carew 4.00
3-TWI Zoilo Versalles .50
4-TWI Cesar Tovar .50
5-TWI Bob Allison .50
6-TWI Larry Hisle .50
7-TWI Tony Oliva .50
8-TWI Earl Battey .50
9-TWI Jim Perry .50
10-TWI Jim Kaat .75
11-TWI Allan Worthington .50
12-TWI Sam Mele .50

N.Y. Mets Postcards

For a second, and final, year TCMA produced a set of color player postcards for the Mets. The 3-1/2" x 5-1/2" cards have borderless player poses on their glossy fronts; there are no other graphic elements. Backs have a large, light blue team 25th anniversary logo at left, with player ID above and a line of 1985 stats below. There is a TCMA copyright line vertically at center. Among the post-card indicia at right, a card number prefixed with "NYM86-" appears within the stamp box. Cards were sold only as complete sets, for $7.95.

NM/M
Complete Set (40): 7.50
Common Player: .50
1 Rick Aguilera .50
2 Bruce Berenyi .50
3 Ron Darling .50
4 Sid Fernandez .50
5 Dwight Gooden .75
6 Tom Gorman .50
7 Ed Lynch .50
8 Roger McDowell .50
9 Randy Myers .60
10 Bob Ojeda .50
11 Jesse Orosco .50
12 Doug Sisk .50
13 Gary Carter 2.00
14 John Gibbons .50
15 Barry Lyons .50
16 Wally Backman .50
17 Ron Gardenhire .50
18 Keith Hernandez .75
19 Howard Johnson .75
20 Ray Knight .75
21 Kevin Mitchell .50
22 Rafael Santana .50
23 Tim Teufel .50
24 Lenny Dykstra .75
25 George Foster .75
26 Danny Heep .50
27 Mel Stottlemyre .50
28 Darryl Strawberry .75
29 Mookie Wilson .75
31 Randy Nieman .50
32 Ed Hearn .50
33 Stan Jefferson .50
34 Bill Robinson .50
35 Shawn Abner .50
36 Terry Blocker .50
37 Davey Johnson .50
38 Bud Harrelson .50
39 Vern Hoscheit .50
40 Greg Pavlick .50
43 Tim Corcoran .50

N.Y. Yankees Postcards

For a second consecutive year, TCMA produced a set of color player postcards for team issue. Similar in format to the 1985 cards, the 1986 version is in 3-1/2" x 5-1/2" format. Fronts have borderless color poses with no other graphics and a high-gloss finish. Backs have a Yankee logo in light blue at left and (usually) a line of 1985 stats at lower-left. Player ID is at upper left. A TCMA copyright line is vertically at center. Among the postcard indicia at right is a card number within the stamp box; cards are skip-numbered with an "NYY86-" prefix; there are two #18. The cards were sold only as complete sets, for $7.95.

NM/M
Complete Set (40): 9.00
Common Player: .50
1 Tommy John 1.00
2 Brad Arnsburg (Arnsberg) .50
3 All Holland (Al) .50
4 Mike Armstrong .50
5 Marty Bystrom .50
6 Doug Drabek .50
7 Brian Fisher .50
8 Stump Merrill .50
9 Ron Guidry .75
10 Joe Niekro .50
12 Dennis Rasmussen .50
13 Dave Righetti .50
14 Rod Scurry .50
15 Bob Shirley .50
16 Bob Tewksbury .50
17 Ed Whitson .50
18a Britt Burns .50
18b Gene Michael .50
19 Butch Wynegar .50
20 Ron Hassey .50
21 Dale Berra .50
22 Jeff Torborg .50
23 Mike Fischlin .50
24 Don Mattingly 3.00
25 Bobby Meacham .50
26 Mike Pagliarulo .50
27 Willie Randolph .75
28 Andre Robertson .50
29 Roy White .75
31 Henry Cotto .50
32 Ken Griffey .50
33 Rickey Henderson 2.00
34 Vic Mata .50
35 Dan Pasqua .50
36 Dave Winfield 2.00
37 Gary Roenicke .50
38 Lou Piniella .75
39 Joe Altobelli .50
40 Sammy Ellis .50
45 Mike Easler .50

Premium Autographs

This three-card set was made available with the purchase of other items from TCMA. The 2-1/2" x 3-1/2" cards have a glossy front finish and each card is personally autographed by the player depicted. Backs have a message about card collecting from the player and 1985 stats, along with TCMA advertising.

NM/M
Complete Set (3): 175.00
Common Player: 45.00
(1) Gary Carter 60.00
(2) Tony Gwynn 90.00
(3) Bret Saberhagen 30.00

Simon's Super Stars

The paintings of sports artist Robert Stephen Simon are reproduced in an unusually sized (2-13/16" x 3-1/2") card issue marketed to collectors. Fronts have color pictures with no extraneous graphics, bordered in white. Backs, printed in blue and white, have biographical and career information.

NM/M
Complete Set (50): 35.00
Common Player: .50
1 Carl Erskine .50
2 Babe Ruth, Henry Aaron 1.50
3 Ted Williams 1.50
4 Mickey Mantle 2.00
5 Gil Hodges .75
6 Roberto Clemente 1.50
7 Mickey Mantle 2.00
8 Walter Johnson .50
9 N.Y. Yankees Stars 1.50
10 Carl Yastrzemski, Ted Williams 1.50
11 Mickey Mantle 2.00
12 Harmon Killebrew .50
13 Warren Spahn .50
14 Ralph Kiner, Babe Ruth 1.00
15 Bob Gibson .50
16 Pee Wee Reese .50
17 Billy Martin .50
18 Joe DiMaggio, Mickey Mantle 2.00
19 Phil Rizzuto .50
20 Sandy Koufax 1.00
21 Jackie Robinson 1.00
22 Don Drysdale .50
23 Mickey Mantle 2.00
24 Mickey Mantle 2.00
25 Joe DiMaggio 1.50
26 Robin Roberts .50
27 Lou Brock .50
28 Lou Gehrig 1.50
29 Willie Mays 1.00
30 Brooks Robinson .50
31 Thurman Munson .50
32 Roger Maris 1.00
33 Jim Palmer .50
34 Stan Musial .75
35 Roy Campanella .50
36 Joe Pepitone .50
37 Ebbetts Field .50
38 Honus Wagner .50
39 Yogi Berra .50
40 Eddie Mathews .50
41 Carl Yastrzemski .50
42 Babe Ruth 1.50
43 Babe Ruth 1.50
44 Pete Reiser .50
45 Don Larsen .50
46 Ernie Banks .50
47 Casey Stengel .50
48 Jackie Robinson 1.00
49 Duke Snider .50
50 Checklist (Duke Snider) .50

1987 TCMA All Time N.Y. Yankees

Essentially a reprint of its 1980 team set, this TCMA collectors issue can be distinguished by the presence on back of a Major League Baseball logo. The earlier set has a TCMA date line on back. Fronts of the 2-1/2" x 3-1/2" cards have black-and-white player photos with an ornate blue frame and white border. Backs are in black-and-white and include the All Time team roster.

NM/M
Complete Set (12): 33.00
Common Player: .35
1 Lou Gehrig 7.00
2 Tony Lazzeri .50
3 Red Rolfe .40
4 Phil Rizzuto 1.25
5 Babe Ruth 7.50
6 Mickey Mantle 9.00
7 Joe DiMaggio 7.00
8 Bill Dickey .70
9 Rod Ruffing .40
10 Whitey Ford 1.25
11 Johnny Murphy .40
12 Casey Stengel .60

Baseball's Greatest Teams

Ten of the greatest line-ups in baseball history are featured in this collectors' series. Each of the nine-card team sets features a different front design while backs share a common format offering player biographical details. The earlier teams picture players in black-and-white photos, while the later sets have color photos. Original issue price was about $1 per set, retail.

NM/M
Complete Set (90): 70.00
Common Team Set (9): 4.50
Common Player: .25
1907 Chicago Cubs
Team Set 4.50
1 Harry Steinfeldt .25
2 Three-Finger Brown .25
3 Ed Reulbach .25
4 Johnny Kling .25
5 Orvie Overall .25
6 Joe Tinker .75
7 Wildfire Schulte .25
8 Frank Chance .75
9 Johnny Evers .75
1927 N.Y. Yankees
Team Set 20.00
1 Miller Huggins .25
2 Herb Pennock .25
3 Tony Lazzeri .25
4 Waite Hoyt .25
5 Wilcy Moore .25
6 Earle Combs .25
7 Bob Meusel .25
8 Lou Gehrig 6.00
9 Babe Ruth 9.00
1934 St. Louis Cardinals
Team Set 4.50
1 Dizzy Dean 1.50
2 Daffy Dean .60
3 Pepper Martin .50
4 Rip Collins .25
5 Frank Frisch .50
6 Leo Durocher .50
7 Ducky Medwick .25
8 Tex Carleton .25
9 Spud Davis .25
1946 Boston Red Sox
Team Set 7.50
1 Joe Cronin .25
2 Rudy York .25
3 Bobby Doerr .25
4 Johnny Pesky .25
5 Dom DiMaggio .60
6 Ted Williams 4.50
7 Boo Ferriss .25
8 Tex Hughson .25
9 Mickey Harris .25
1950 Philadelphia Phillies
Team Set 4.50
1 Eddie Sawyer .25
2 Curt Simmons .25
3 Jim Konstanty .50
4 Eddie Waitkus .25
5 Granny Hamner .25
6 Del Ennis .25
7 Richie Ashburn .60
8 Dick Sisler .25
9 Robin Roberts .60
1955 Brooklyn Dodgers
Team Set 7.50
1 Duke Snider, Walt Alston .75
2 Roy Campanella 1.50
3 Jackie Robinson 3.00
4 Carl Furillo .60
5 Gil Hodges .75
6 Pee Wee Reese, Jim Gilliam .75
7 Don Newcombe .60
8 Ed Roebuck, Clem Labine .50
9 Carl Erskine .50
1957 Milwaukee Braves
Team Set 7.50
1 Hank Aaron 4.50
2 Eddie Mathews .60
3 Bob Hazle .25
4 Johnny Logan .25
5 Red Schoendienst .50
6 Wes Covington .25
7 Lew Burdette .35
8 Warren Spahn .60
9 Bob Buhl .25
1960 Pittsburgh Pirates
Team Set 7.50
1 Dick Stuart .25
2 Bill Mazeroski .75
3 Dick Groat .35
4 Roberto Clemente 6.00
5 Bob Skinner .25
6 Smoky Burgess .35
7 Roy Face .25
8 Bob Friend .25
9 Vernon Law .35
1961 N.Y. Yankees
Team Set 20.00
1 Bill Skowron .50
2 Mickey Mantle 10.00
3 Bobby Richardson .50
4 Tony Kubek .50
5 Elston Howard .50
6 Yogi Berra 2.25
7 Whitey Ford 2.25
8 Roger Maris 4.50
9 Ralph Houk .25
1969 N.Y. Mets Team Set 4.50
1 Ed Kranepool .35
2 Bud Harrelson .35
3 Cleon Jones, Tommie Agee, Ron Swoboda .25
4 Jerry Koosman .25
5 Gary Gentry .25
6 Tug McGraw .35
7 Ron Taylor .25
8 Jerry Grote .25
9 Ken Boswell .25

1996 Team Metal Ken Griffey Jr.

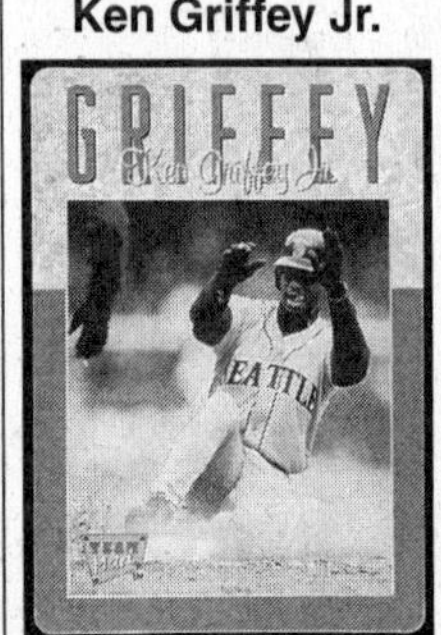

CUI, the parent firm of the company that produces Metallic Images sports and non-sports cards, created this set of metal cards for sale in large retail chains. The four cards come packaged in a lithographed steel box about the size and shape of a Band-aid tin. The 2-5/8" x 3-9/16" cards have a blue and teal background with a color game-action photo at center. Backs have rolled metal edges with a photo at left. A few sentences about the player are printed at right. Logos and copyright data are at bottom. Issue price of the four-card set was just under $10.

NM/M
Complete Set (4): 7.50
Common Card: 2.00
1 Ken Griffey Jr. (Home run trot.) 2.00
2 Ken Griffey Jr./Sliding 2.00
3 Ken Griffey Jr. (Batting follow-through.) 2.00
4 Ken Griffey Jr. (Batting follow-through.) 2.00

Cal Ripken, Jr.

CUI, the parent firm of the company that produces Metallic Impressions sports and non-sports cards, created this set of metal cards for sale in large retail chains. The four cards come packaged in a lithographed steel box about the size and shape of a Band-aid tin. The 2-5/8" x 3-9/16" cards have a green and orange background with a color game-action photo at center. Backs have rolled metal edges with a photo at left. A few sentences about the player are printed at right. Logos and copyright data are at bottom. Issue price of the four-card set was just under $10.

NM/M
Complete Set (4): 7.50
Common Card: 2.00
1 Cal Ripken Jr./Btg (Black jersey.) 2.00
2 Cal Ripken Jr. (Batting follow-through.) 2.00
3 Cal Ripken Jr./Fldg 2.00
4 Cal Ripken Jr./Btg (White jersey.) 2.00

1996 Team Out! Game

This baseball card game is sold as a boxed set containing 37 of the 91 different player cards, plus an assortment of 23 of the 10 cartoon "action" cards used to play the game. Cards are 2-1/4" x 3-1/2" with rounded corners and glossy surfaces. Backs have a close-up photo of a baseball with product and licensor logos and copyright information. Fronts of the player photo cards are bordered in black; the cartoon action cards have red or blue borders. The unnumbered cards are checklisted here in alphabetical order.

NM/M
Complete Set (101): 40.00
Common Player: .25
(1) Roberto Alomar .35
(2) Brady Anderson .25
(3) Kevin Appier .25
(4) Carlos Baerga .25
(5) Jeff Bagwell 1.50
(6) Albert Belle .25
(7) Dante Bichette .25
(8) Craig Biggio .25
(9) Wade Boggs 2.00
(10) Barry Bonds 3.00
(11) Kevin Brown .25
(12) Jay Buhner .25
(13) Ellis Burks .25
(14) Ken Caminiti .25
(15) Joe Carter .25
(16) Vinny Castilla .25
(17) Jeff Cirillo .25
(18) Will Clark .25
(19) Jeff Conine .25
(20) Joey Cora .25
(21) Marty Cordova .25
(22) Eric Davis .25
(23) Ray Durham .25
(24) Jim Edmonds .25
(25) Cecil Fielder .25
(26) Travis Fryman .25
(27) Jason Giambi .60
(28) Bernard Gilkey .25
(29) Tom Glavine .45
(30) Juan Gonzalez .75
(31) Mark Grace .25
(32) Ken Griffey Jr. 2.25
(33) Marquis Grissom .25
(34) Mark Grudzielanek .25
(35) Ozzie Guillen .25
(36) Tony Gwynn 2.00
(37) Bobby Higginson .25
(38) Todd Hundley .25
(39) Derek Jeter 3.00
(40) Lance Johnson .25
(41) Randy Johnson 1.50
(42) Chipper Jones 2.00
(43) Brian Jordan .25
(44) Wally Joyner .25
(45) Jason Kendall .25
(46) Chuck Knoblauch .25
(47) Ray Lankford .25
(48) Mike Lansing .25
(49) Barry Larkin .25
(50) Kenny Lofton .25
(51) Javier Lopez .25
(52) Mike MacFarlane .25
(53) Greg Maddux 2.00
(54) Al Martin .25
(55) Brian McRae .25
(56) Mark McGwire 2.50
(57) Raul Mondesi .25
(58) Denny Neagle .25
(59) Hideo Nomo .75
(60) John Olerud .25
(61) Rey Ordonez .25
(62) Troy Percival .25
(63) Mike Piazza 2.25
(64) Andy Pettitte .35
(65) Manny Ramirez 1.50
(66) Cal Ripken Jr. 3.00
(67) Alex Rodriguez 2.50
(68) Ivan Rodriguez 1.00
(69) Ryne Sandberg 2.00
(70) Tim Salmon .25
(71) Benito Santiago .25
(72) Kevin Seitzer .25
(73) Scott Servais .25
(74) Gary Sheffield .60
(75) Ozzie Smith 2.00
(76) John Smoltz .25
(77) Sammy Sosa 2.00
(78) Mike Stanley .25
(79) Terry Steinbach .25
(80) Frank Thomas 1.50
(81) Steve Trachsel .25
(82) Jose Valentin .25
(83) Mo Vaughn .25
(84) Jose Vizcaino .25
(85) Robin Ventura .25
(86) Larry Walker .25
(87) Walt Weiss .25
(88) Bernie Williams .25
(89) Matt Williams .25
(90) Eric Young .25
(91) Todd Zeile .25
(92) Double Play (Roberto Alomar (Cartoon)) .25
(93) Free Agent Acquisition (Barry Bonds (Cartoon) 1.50
(94) No Trade - Infield (Mark McGwire, Ozzie Smith, Mo Vaughn (Cartoon) .75
(95) No Trade - Outfield (Albert Belle, Raul Mondesi (Cartoon) .25
(96) Out! (Mike Piazza, Matt Williams (Cartoon) .75
(97) Pitcher Bombed (Cartoon) .25
(98) Pitcher Stays (Greg Maddux (Cartoon) 1.00
(99) Safe! (Frank Thomas (Cartoon) .75
(100) Trade - Infield (Cal Ripken Jr., Alex Rodriguez (Cartoon) .75
(101) Trade - Outfield (Ken Griffey Jr., Sammy Sosa (Cartoon) .65

1988 Tetley Tea Discs

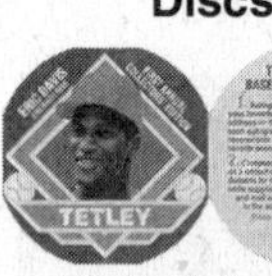

The Tetley iced tea discs are virtually identical in format to the 1988 Baseball Super Stars discs, but are labeled "FIRST ANNUAL COLLECTORS' EDITION," rather than Second and appear to have slight differences in the player pairs which make up each folder. Values for these can be extrapolated by combining the values of individual discs shown under the 1988 Baseball Super Stars listing.

1989 Tetley Tea Discs

The Tetley iced tea discs are virtually identical in format to the 1989 Baseball Super Stars discs, but are labeled "SECOND ANNUAL COLLECTORS' EDITION." The tri-fold panels were distributed in canisters of iced tea mix in the East.

1990 Tetley Tea Discs

The Tetley iced tea discs are virtually identical in format to the 1990 Baseball Super Stars discs, but are labeled "THIRD ANNUAL COLLECTORS' EDITION." The tri-fold panels were distributed in canisters of iced tea mix in the East.

1986 Texas Gold Ice Cream Reds

One of the last regional baseball card sets produced during the 1986 season was a 28-card team set sponsored by a Cincinnati-area ice cream company and given to fans attending the September 19 game. Photos on the 2-1/2" x 3-1/2" cards are game-action shots, and include three different cards of playing manager Pete Rose. The set is also notable for the inclusion of first cards of some of the Reds' young prospects.

NM/M
Complete Set (28): 16.00
Common Player: .50
6 Bo Diaz .50
9 Max Venable .50
11 Kurt Stillwell .50
12 Nick Esasky .50
13 Dave Concepcion .75
14a Pete Rose (Commemorative) 4.00
14b Pete Rose (Infield) 6.00
14c Pete Rose (Manager) 4.00
16 Ron Oester .50
20 Eddie Milner .50
22 Sal Butera .50
24 Tony Perez 1.50
25 Buddy Bell .75
28 Kal Daniels .50
29 Tracy Jones .50
31 John Franco .50
32 Tom Browning .50
33 Ron Robinson .50
34 Bill Gullickson .50
36 Mario Soto .50
39 Dave Parker .75
40 John Denny .50
44 Eric Davis 1.00
45 Chris Welsh .50
48 Ted Power .50
49 Joe Price .50
--- Reds Coaches (Scott Breeden, Billy Demars, Tommy Helms, Bruce Kimm, Jim Lett, George Scherger) .50
--- Logo/Coupon Card .20

1987 Texas Rangers Fire Safety

Co-sponsored by the team, U.S. and Texas Forest Services, the set was given out to fans at special promotions at Arlington Stadium. Cards measure 4-1/4" x 6" and feature color action photos. Backs contain brief player personal information along with a Smokey the Bear wildfire prevention message. Cards of Mike Mason and Tom Paciorek were withdrawn from the sets given out by the Rangers and are quite scarce.

NM/M
Complete Set (32): 45.00
Common Player: .30
1 Charlie Hough .30
2 Greg Harris .30
3 Jose Guzman .30
4 Mike Mason 20.00
5 Dale Mohorcic .30
6 Bobby Witt .30
7 Mitch Williams .30
8 Geno Petralli .30
9 Don Slaught .30
10 Darrell Porter .30
11 Steve Beuchele .30
12 Pete O'Brien .30
13 Scott Fletcher .30
14 Tom Paciorek 20.00
15 Pete Incaviglia .30
16 Oddibe McDowell .30
17 Ruben Sierra .30

18 Larry Parrish .30
19 Bobby Valentine .30
20 Tom House .30
21 Tom Robson .30
22 Edwin Correa .30
23 Mike Stanley .30
24 Joe Ferguson .30
25 Art Howe .30
26 Bob Brower .30
27 Mike Loynd .30
28 Curtis Wilkerson .30
29 Tim Foli .30
30 Dave Oliver .30
31 Jerry Browne .30
32 Jeff Russell .30

1988 Texas Rangers Fire Safety

This oversized (3-1/2" x 5") set was distributed to Rangers' fans at Smokey Bear Game Day on August 7. Fronts feature full-color action photos framed in an oval blue and red border on a white background. A nameplate above the photo identifies the player and a "Wildfire Prevention" logo is printed beneath the photo. Rangers (left) and Smokey (right) logos fill the upper corners of the card face. The card backs are black-and-white and include player info, U.S. and Texas Forest Service logos, and fire prevention tips.

NM/M
Complete Set (21): 5.00
Common Player: .30
1 Tom O'Malley .30
2 Pete O'Brien .30
3 Geno Petralli .30
4 Pete Incaviglia .30
5 Oddibe McDowell .30
6 Dale Mohorcic .30
7 Bobby Witt .30
8 Bobby Valentine .30
9 Ruben Sierra .30
10 Scott Fletcher .30
11 Mike Stanley .30
12 Steve Buechele .30
13 Charlie Hough .30
14 Larry Parrish .30
15 Jerry Browne .30
16 Bob Brower .30
17 Jeff Russell .30
18 Edwin Correa .30
19 Mitch Williams .30
20 Jose Guzman .30
21 Curtis Wilkerson .30

1989 Texas Rangers Fire Safety

Given away at a Rangers home game in 1989, this large-format (4-1/4" x 6") set features player portrait photos within an oval frame on a white border. The team logo is at upper-left; Smokey the Bear at upper-right. Backs have minimal biographical data and stats and a cartoon fire prevention tip. The unnumbered cards are checklisted here alphabetically.

NM/M
Complete Set (34): 20.00
Common Player: .25
(1) Darrel Akerfelds .25
(2) Brad Arnsberg .25
(3) Buddy Bell .25
(4) Kevin Brown .25
(5) Steve Buechele .25
(6) Dick Egan .25
(7) Cecil Espy .25
(8) Scott Fletcher .25
(9) Julio Franco .25
(10) Cecilio Guante .25
(11) Jose Guzman .25
(12) Drew Hall .25
(13) Toby Harrah .25
(14) Charlie Hough .25
(15) Tom House .25
(16) Pete Incaviglia .25
(17) Chad Kreuter .25
(18) Jeff Kunkel .25
(19) Rick Leach .25
(20) Davey Lopes .25
(21) Craig McMurtry .25
(22) Jamie Moyer .25
(23) Dave Oliver .25
(24) Rafael Palmeiro 2.00
(25) Geno Petralli .25
(26) Tom Robson .25
(27) Kenny Rogers .25
(28) Jeff Russell .25
(29) Nolan Ryan 15.00
(30) Ruben Sierra .25
(31) Mike Stanley .25
(32) Jim Sundberg .25
(33) Bobby Valentine .25
(34) Bobby Witt .25

1990 Texas Rangers Fire Safety

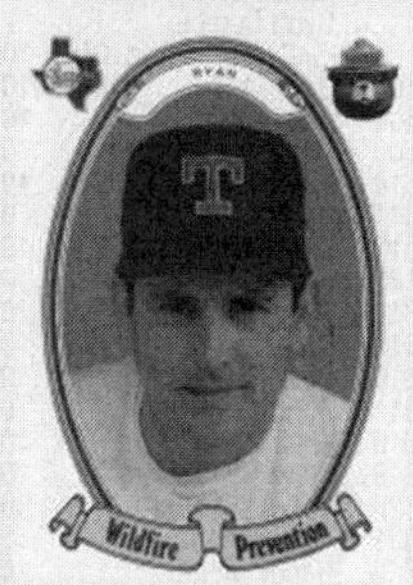

This stadium giveaway set is identical in design to the 1989 issue, but at 3-1/2" x 5", is slightly smaller. Backs have a cartoon fire safety tip and a bit of player personal data.

NM/M
Complete Set (24): 30.00
Common Player: .50
(1) Harold Baines .50
(2) Brian Bohannon .50
(3) Thad Bosley .50
(4) Kevin Brown .75
(5) Jack Daugherty .50
(6) Cecil Espy .50
(7) Julio Franco .75
(8) Jeff Huson .50
(9) Pete Incaviglia .50
(10) Mike Jeffcoat .50
(11) Chad Kreuter .50
(12) Jeff Kunkel .50
(13) Gary Mielke .50
(14) Jamie Moyer .50
(15) Rafael Palmeiro 3.00
(16) Gary Pettis .50
(17) Kenny Rogers .50
(18) Jeff Russell .50
(19) John Russell .50
(20) Nolan Ryan 25.00
(21) Ruben Sierra .50
(22) Bobby Valentine .50
(23) Bobby Witt .50
(24) Arlington Stadium 1.00

1983 Thorn Apple Valley Cubs

This set of 27 cards was issued in conjuction with a "Baseball Card Day" promotion at Wrigley Field in 1983. Thorn Apple Valley was the meat company which produced the hot dogs sold at the ballpark. The cards feature borderless color photos with the player's name, uniform number (also the card's number in the checklist) and an abbreviation for their position. Card backs feature annual statistics. Of the 27 cards, which measure 2-1/4" x 3-1/2", 25 feature players, one is a team card, and one features the manager and coaches.

NM/M
Complete Set (27): 25.00
Common Player: .50
1 Larry Bowa .50
6 Keith Moreland .50
7 Jody Davis .50
10 Leon Durham .50
11 Ron Cey .50
16 Steve Lake .50
20 Thad Bosley .50
21 Jay Johnstone .50
22 Bill Buckner 1.00
23 Ryne Sandberg 15.00
24 Jerry Morales .50
25 Gary Woods .50
27 Mel Hall .50
29 Tom Veryzer .50
30 Chuck Rainey .50
31 Fergie Jenkins 4.00
32 Craig Lefferts .50
33 Joe Carter 2.00
34 Steve Trout .50
36 Mike Proly .50
39 Bill Campbell .50
41 Warren Brusstar .50
44 Dick Ruthven .50
46 Lee Smith 1.50
48 Dickie Noles .50
--- Coaching Staff (Ruben Amaro, Billy Connors, Duffy Dyer, Lee Elia, Fred Koenig, John Vukovich) .50
--- Team Photo .50

1994 Tombstone Pizza

'94 TOMBSTONE SUPER-PRO SERIES
Mike Greenwell
BOSTON RED SOX

Score produced a special 30-card set which could be obtained by eating a lot of frozen pizzas (one card per pizza) or by sending in a dollar and five proofs of purchase. Titled "'94 Tombstone Super-Pro Series," the cards are black-bordered and UV coated on front and back. Because the set is licensed only by the Players Union and not by Major League Baseball, the uniform logos on the front action photos and back portraits have been airbrushed away. Cards feature the Tombstone logo on both front and back. Backs have recent and career stats, a facsimile autograph and a card number.

NM/M
Complete Set (30): 4.00
Common Player: .25
1 Jeff Bagwell .50
2 Jay Bell .25
3 Barry Bonds 1.50
4 Bobby Bonilla .25
5 Andres Galarraga .25
6 Mark Grace .25
7 Marquis Grissom .25
8 Tony Gwynn .65
9 Bryan Harvey .25
10 Gregg Jefferies .25
11 David Justice .25
12 John Kruk .25
13 Barry Larkin .25
14 Greg Maddux .65
15 Mike Piazza .75
16 Jim Abbott .25
17 Albert Belle .25
18 Cecil Fielder .25
19 Juan Gonzalez .35
20 Mike Greenwell .25
21 Ken Griffey Jr. .75
22 Jack McDowell .25
23 Jeff Montgomery .25
24 John Olerud .25
25 Kirby Puckett .65
26 Cal Ripken, Jr. 1.50
27 Tim Salmon .25
28 Ruben Sierra .25
29 Frank Thomas .50
30 Robin Yount .50

1995 Tombstone Pizza

Tombstone's second annual baseball card issue was available either singly in frozen pizza packages, or as a 30-card boxed set via a mail-in offer. Cards feature action player photos on front and portrait photos on back; both have had uniform logos airbrushed for lack of a MLB license. There is a graduated red to black border on each side. On front at lower-right are the player and team name and the Tombstone logo. Backs have biographical data, recent stats and career highlights. At bottom is a card number and the Players Association logo.

NM/M
Complete Set (30): 4.00
Common Player: .25
1 Frank Thomas .50
2 David Cone .25
3 Bob Hamelin .25
4 Jeff Bagwell .50
5 Greg Maddux .65
6 Raul Mondesi .25
7 Chili Davis .25
8 Cecil Fielder .25
9 Ken Griffey Jr. .75
10 Jimmy Key .25
11 Kenny Lofton .25
12 Paul Molitor .50
13 Kirby Puckett .65
14 Cal Ripken Jr. 1.50
15 Ivan Rodriguez .40
16 Kevin Seitzer .25
17 Ruben Sierra .25
18 Mo Vaughn .25
19 Moises Alou .25
20 Barry Bonds 1.50
21 Jeff Conine .25
22 Lenny Dykstra .25
23 Andres Galarraga .25
24 Tony Gwynn .65
25 Barry Larkin .25
26 Fred McGriff .25
27 Orlando Merced .25
28 Bret Saberhagen .25
29 Ozzie Smith .65
30 Sammy Sosa .65

1981 Topps

This is another 726-card set of 2-1/2" x 3-1/2" cards from Topps. The cards have the usual color photo with all cards from the same team sharing the same color borders. Player names appear under the photo with team and position on a baseball cap at lower-left. The Topps logo returned in a small baseball in the lower-right. Card backs include the usual stats along with a headline and a cartoon if there was room. Specialty cards include previous season record-breakers, highlights of the playoffs and World Series, along with the final appearance of team cards. Eleven cards on each of the six press sheets were double-printed.

NM/M
Complete Set (726): 45.00
Common Player: .10
Wax Pack (15): 3.00
Wax Box (36): 85.00
Cello Pack (28): 3.00
Cello Box (24): 75.00
Rack Pack (48): 6.00
Rack Box (24): 120.00
Vending Box (500): 40.00
1 Batting Leaders (George Brett, Bill Buckner) .75
2 Home Run Leaders (Reggie Jackson, Ben Oglivie, Mike Schmidt) .75
3 RBI Leaders (Cecil Cooper, Mike Schmidt) .25
4 Stolen Base Leaders (Rickey Henderson, Ron LeFlore) .50
5 Victory Leaders (Steve Carlton, Steve Stone) .15
6 Strikeout Leaders (Len Barker, Steve Carlton) .15
7 ERA Leaders (Rudy May, Don Sutton) .10
8 Leading Firemen (Rollie Fingers, Tom Hume, Dan Quisenberry) .10
9 Pete LaCock/DP .10
10 Mike Flanagan .10
11 Jim Wohlford/DP .10
12 Mark Clear .10
13 Joe Charboneau **RC** .50
14 John Tudor **RC** .20
15 Larry Parrish .10
16 Ron Davis .10
17 Cliff Johnson .10
18 Glenn Adams .10
19 Jim Clancy .10
20 Jeff Burroughs .10
21 Ron Oester .10
22 Danny Darwin .10
23 Alex Trevino .10
24 Don Stanhouse .10
25 Sixto Lezcano .10
26 U.L. Washington .10
27 Champ Summers/DP .10
28 Enrique Romo .10
29 Gene Tenace .10
30 Jack Clark .10
31 Checklist 1-121/DP .10
32 Ken Oberkfell .10
33 Rick Honeycutt .10
34 Aurelio Rodriguez .10
35 Mitchell Page .10
36 Ed Farmer .10
37 Gary Roenicke .10
38 Win Remmerswaal .10
39 Tom Veryzer .10
40 Tug McGraw .10
41 Rangers Future Stars (Bob Babcock, John Butcher, Jerry Don Gleaton) .10
42 Jerry White/DP .10
43 Jose Morales .10
44 Larry McWilliams .10
45 Enos Cabell .10
46 Rick Bosetti .10
47 Ken Brett .10
48 Dave Skaggs .10
49 Bob Shirley .10
50 Dave Lopes .10
51 Bill Robinson/DP .10
52 Hector Cruz .10
53 Kevin Saucier .10
54 Ivan DeJesus .10
55 Mike Norris .10
56 Buck Martinez .10
57 Dave Roberts .10
58 Joel Youngblood .10
59 Dan Petry .10
60 Willie Randolph .10
61 Butch Wynegar .10
62 Joe Pettini .10
63 Steve Renko/DP .10
64 Brian Asselstine .10
65 Scott McGregor .10
66 Royals Future Stars (Manny Castillo, Tim Ireland, Mike Jones) .10
67 Ken Kravec .10
68 Matt Alexander/DP .10
69 Ed Halicki .10
70 Al Oliver/DP .10
71 Hal Dues .10
72 Barry Evans/DP .10
73 Doug Bair .10
74 Mike Hargrove .10
75 Reggie Smith .10
76 Mario Mendoza .10
77 Mike Barlow .10
78 Steve Dillard .10
79 Bruce Robbins .10
80 Rusty Staub .15
81 Dave Stapleton .10
82 Astros Future Stars (Danny Heep, Alan Knicely, Bobby Sprowl/DP) .10
83 Mike Proly .10
84 Johnnie LeMaster .10
85 Mike Caldwell .10
86 Wayne Gross .10
87 Rick Camp .10
88 Joe Lefebvre .10
89 Darrell Jackson .10
90 Bake McBride .10
91 Tim Stoddard/DP .10
92 Mike Easler .10
93 Ed Glynn/DP .10
94 Harry Spilman/DP .10
95 Jim Sundberg .10
96 A's Future Stars (Dave Beard, Ernie Camacho **RC**, Pat Dempsey) .10
97 Chris Speier .10
98 Clint Hurdle .10
99 Eric Wilkins .10
100 Rod Carew 2.00
101 Benny Ayala .10
102 Dave Tobik .10
103 Jerry Martin .10
104 Terry Forster .10
105 Jose Cruz .10
106 Don Money .10
107 Rich Wortham .10
108 Bruce Benedict .10
109 Mike Scott .10
110 Carl Yastrzemski 2.00
111 Greg Minton .10
112 White Sox Future Stars (Rusty Kuntz, Fran Mullins, Leo Sutherland) .10
113 Mike Phillips .10
114 Tom Underwood .10
115 Roy Smalley .10
116 Joe Simpson .10
117 Pete Falcone .10
118 Kurt Bevacqua .10
119 Tippy Martinez .10
120 Larry Bowa .10
121 Larry Harlow .10
122 John Denny .10
123 Al Cowens .10
124 Jerry Garvin .10
125 Andre Dawson 1.50
126 Charlie Leibrandt **RC** .40
127 Rudy Law .10
128 Gary Allenson/DP .10
129 Art Howe .10
130 Larry Gura .10
131 Keith Moreland **RC** .20
132 Tommy Boggs .10
133 Jeff Cox .10
134 Steve Mura .10
135 Gorman Thomas .10
136 Doug Capilla .10
137 Hosken Powell .10
138 Rich Dotson/DP **RC** .20
139 Oscar Gamble .10
140 Bob Forsch .10
141 Miguel Dilone .10
142 Jackson Todd .10
143 Dan Meyer .10
144 Allen Ripley .10
145 Mickey Rivers .10
146 Bobby Castillo .10
147 Dale Berra .10
148 Randy Niemann .10
149 Joe Nolan .10
150 Mark Fidrych .15
151 Claudell Washington/DP .10
152 John Urrea .10
153 Tom Poquette .10
154 Rick Langford .10
155 Chris Chambliss .10
156 Bob McClure .10

157 John Wathan .10
158 Fergie Jenkins 1.00
159 Brian Doyle .10
160 Garry Maddox .10
161 Dan Graham .10
162 Doug Corbett .10
163 Billy Almon .10
164 Lamarr Hoyt (LaMarr) **RC** .15
165 Tony Scott .10
166 Floyd Bannister .10
167 Terry Whitfield .10
168 Don Robinson/DP .10
169 John Mayberry .10
170 Ross Grimsley .10
171 Gene Richards .10
172 Gary Woods .10
173 Bump Wills .10
174 Doug Rau .10
175 Dave Collins .10
176 Mike Krukow .10
177 Rick Peters .10
178 Jim Essian/DP .10
179 Rudy May .10
180 Pete Rose 5.00
181 Elias Sosa .10
182 Bob Grich .10
183 Dick Davis/DP .10
184 Jim Dwyer .10
185 Dennis Leonard .10
186 Wayne Nordhagen .10
187 Mike Parrott .10
188 Doug DeCinces .10
189 Craig Swan .10
190 Cesar Cedeno .10
191 Rick Sutcliffe .10
192 Braves Future Stars (Terry Harper **RC**, Ed Miller, Rafael Ramirez **RC**) .10
193 Pete Vuckovich .10
194 Rod Scurry **RC** .10
195 Rich Murray .10
196 Duffy Dyer .10
197 Jim Kern .10
198 Jerry Dybzinski .10
199 Chuck Rainey .10
200 George Foster .10
201 Johnny Bench (Record Breaker) .45
202 Steve Carlton (Record Breaker) .25
203 Bill Gullickson (Record Breaker) .10
204 Ron LeFlore, Rodney Scott (Record Breaker) .10
205 Pete Rose (Record Breaker) 1.50
206 Mike Schmidt (Record Breaker) 1.00
207 Ozzie Smith (Record Breaker) 1.00
208 Willie Wilson (Record Breaker) .10
209 Dickie Thon/DP .10
210 Jim Palmer 1.50
211 Derrel Thomas .10
212 Steve Nicosia .10
213 Al Holland **RC** .10
214 Angels Future Stars (Ralph Botting, Jim Dorsey, John Harris) .10
215 Larry Hisle .10
216 John Henry Johnson .10
217 Rich Hebner .10
218 Paul Splittorff .10
219 Ken Landreaux .10
220 Tom Seaver 2.00
221 Bob Davis .10
222 Jorge Orta .10
223 Roy Lee Jackson .10
224 Pat Zachry .10
225 Ruppert Jones .10
226 Manny Sanguillen/DP .10
227 Fred Martinez .10
228 Tom Paciorek .10
229 Rollie Fingers 1.00
230 George Hendrick .10
231 Joe Beckwith .10
232 Mickey Klutts .10
233 Skip Lockwood .10
234 Lou Whitaker .10
235 Scott Sanderson .10
236 Mike Ivie .10
237 Charlie Moore .10
238 Willie Hernandez .10
239 Rick Miller/DP .10
240 Nolan Ryan 5.00
241 Checklist 122-242/DP .10
242 Chet Lemon .10
243 Sal Butera .10
244 Cardinals Future Stars (Tito Landrum **RC**, Al Olmsted, Andy Rincon) .10
245 Ed Figueroa .10
246 Ed Ott/DP .10
247 Glenn Hubbard/DP .10
248 Joey McLaughlin .10
249 Larry Cox .10
250 Ron Guidry .15
251 Tom Brookens .10
252 Victor Cruz .10
253 Dave Bergman .10
254 Ozzie Smith 3.00
255 Mark Littell .10
256 Bombo Rivera .10
257 Rennie Stennett .10
258 Joe Price **RC** .10
259 Mets Future Stars (Juan Berenguer, Hubie Brooks **RC**, Mookie Wilson **RC**) .75
260 Ron Cey .10
261 Rickey Henderson 4.50
262 Sammy Stewart .10
263 Brian Downing .10
264 Jim Norris .10
265 John Candelaria .10
266 Tom Herr .10
267 Stan Bahnsen .10
268 Jerry Royster .10
269 Ken Forsch .10
270 Greg Luzinski .10
271 Bill Castro .10
272 Bruce Kimm .10
273 Stan Papi .10
274 Craig Chamberlain .10
275 Dwight Evans .10
276 Dan Spillner .10
277 Alfredo Griffin .10
278 Rick Sofield .10
279 Bob Knepper .10
280 Ken Griffey .10
281 Fred Stanley .10
282 Mariners Future Stars (Rick Anderson, Greg Biercevicz, Rodney Craig) .10
283 Billy Sample .10
284 Brian Kingman .10
285 Jerry Turner .10
286 Dave Frost .10
287 Lenn Sakata .10
288 Bob Clark .10
289 Mickey Hatcher .10
290 Bob Boone/DP .10
291 Aurelio Lopez .10
292 Mike Squires .10
293 Charlie Lea **RC** .15
294 Mike Tyson/DP .10
295 Hal McRae .10
296 Bill Nahorodny/DP .10
297 Bob Bailor .10
298 Buddy Solomon .10
299 Elliott Maddox .10
300 Paul Molitor 2.00
301 Matt Keough .10
302 Dodgers Future Stars (Jack Perconte **RC**, Mike Scioscia **RC**, Fernando Valenzuela **RC**) 2.00
303 Johnny Oates .10
304 John Castino .10
305 Ken Clay .10
306 Juan Beniquez/DP .10
307 Gene Garber .10
308 Rick Manning .10
309 Luis Salazar **RC** .10
310 Vida Blue/DP .10
311 Freddie Patek .10
312 Rick Rhoden .10
313 Luis Pujols .10
314 Rich Dauer .10
315 Kirk Gibson **RC** 5.00
316 Craig Minetto .10
317 Lonnie Smith .10
318 Steve Yeager .10
319 Rowland Office .10
320 Tom Burgmeier .10
321 Leon Durham **RC** .15
322 Neil Allen .10
323 Jim Morrison/DP .10
324 Mike Willis .10
325 Ray Knight .10
326 Biff Pocoroba .10
327 Moose Haas .10
328 Twins Future Stars (Dave Engle **RC**, Greg Johnston, Gary Ward) .15
329 Joaquin Andujar .10
330 Frank White .10
331 Dennis Lamp .10
332 Lee Lacy (DP) .10
333 Sid Monge .10
334 Dane Iorg .10
335 Rick Cerone .10
336 Eddie Whitson .10
337 Lynn Jones .10
338 Checklist 243-363 .10
339 John Ellis .10
340 Bruce Kison .10
341 Dwayne Murphy .10
342 Eric Rasmussen/DP .10
343 Frank Taveras .10
344 Byron McLaughlin .10
345 Warren Cromartie .10
346 Larry Christenson/DP .10
347 Harold Baines **RC** 4.00
348 Bob Sykes .10
349 Glenn Hoffman .10
350 J.R. Richard .10
351 Otto Velez .10
352 Dick Tidrow/DP .10
353 Terry Kennedy .10
354 Mario Soto .10
355 Bob Horner .10
356 Padres Future Stars (George Stablein, Craig Stimac, Tom Tellmann) .10
357 Jim Slaton .10
358 Mark Wagner .10
359 Tom Hausman .10
360 Willie Wilson .10
361 Joe Strain .10
362 Bo Diaz .10
363 Geoff Zahn .10
364 Mike Davis **RC** .10
365 Graig Nettles/DP .15
366 Mike Ramsey .10
367 Denny Martinez .10
368 Leon Roberts .10
369 Frank Tanana .10
370 Dave Winfield 2.00
371 Charlie Hough .10
372 Jay Johnstone .10
373 Pat Underwood .10
374 Tom Hutton .10
375 Dave Concepcion .10
376 Ron Reed .10
377 Jerry Morales .10
378 Dave Rader .10
379 Lary Sorensen .10
380 Willie Stargell 2.00
381 Cubs Future Stars (Carlos Lezcano, Steve Macko, Randy Martz) .10
382 Paul Mirabella **RC** .10
383 Eric Soderholm/DP .10
384 Mike Sadek .10
385 Joe Sambito .10
386 Dave Edwards .10
387 Phil Niekro 1.00
388 Andre Thornton .10
389 Marty Pattin .10
390 Cesar Geronimo .10
391 Dave Lemanczyk/DP .10
392 Lance Parrish .10
393 Broderick Perkins .10
394 Woodie Fryman .10
395 Scot Thompson .10
396 Bill Campbell .10
397 Julio Cruz .10
398 Ross Baumgarten .10
399 Orioles Future Stars (Mike Boddicker **RC**, Mark Corey, Floyd Rayford **RC**) .20
400 Reggie Jackson 3.00
401 A.L. Championships (Royals Sweep Yankees) .50
402 N.L. Championships (Phillies Squeak Past Astros) .25
403 World Series (Phillies Beat Royals In 6) .25
404 World Series Summary (Phillies Win First World Series) .25
405 Nino Espinosa .10
406 Dickie Noles .10
407 Ernie Whitt .10
408 Fernando Arroyo .10
409 Larry Herndon .10
410 Bert Campaneris .10
411 Terry Puhl .10
412 Britt Burns **RC** .10
413 Tony Bernazard .10
414 John Pacella/DP .10
415 Ben Oglivie .10
416 Gary Alexander .10
417 Dan Schatzeder .10
418 Bobby Brown .10
419 Tom Hume .10
420 Keith Hernandez .10
421 Bob Stanley .10
422 Dan Ford .10
423 Shane Rawley .10
424 Yankees Future Stars (Tim Lollar, Bruce Robinson, Dennis Werth) .10
425 Al Bumbry .10
426 Warren Brusstar .10
427 John D'Acquisto .10
428 John Stearns .10
429 Mick Kelleher .10
430 Jim Bibby .10
431 Dave Roberts .10
432 Len Barker .10
433 Rance Mulliniks .10
434 Roger Erickson .10
435 Jim Spencer .10
436 Gary Lucas .10
437 Mike Heath/DP .10
438 John Montefusco .10
439 Denny Walling .10
440 Jerry Reuss .10
441 Ken Reitz .10
442 Ron Pruitt .10
443 Jim Beattie/DP .10
444 Garth Iorg .10
445 Ellis Valentine .10
446 Checklist 364-484 .10
447 Junior Kennedy/DP .10
448 Tim Corcoran .10
449 Paul Mitchell .10
450 Dave Kingman/DP .10
451 Indians Future Stars (Chris Bando, Tom Brennan, Sandy Wihtol) .10
452 Renie Martin .10
453 Rob Wilfong/DP .10
454 Andy Hassler .10
455 Rick Burleson .10
456 Jeff Reardon **RC** 1.50
457 Mike Lum .10
458 Randy Jones .10
459 Greg Gross .10
460 Rich Gossage .10
461 Dave McKay .10
462 Jack Brohamer .10
463 Milt May .10
464 Adrian Devine .10
465 Bill Russell .10
466 Bob Molinaro .10
467 Dave Stieb .10
468 Johnny Wockenfuss .10
469 Jeff Leonard .10
470 Manny Trillo .10
471 Mike Vail .10
472 Dyar Miller (DP) .10
473 Jose Cardenal .10
474 Mike LaCoss .10
475 Buddy Bell .10
476 Jerry Koosman .10
477 Luis Gomez .10
478 Juan Eichelberger .10
479 Expos Future Stars (Bobby Pate **RC**, Tim Raines **RC**, Roberto Ramos **RC**) 3.00
480 Carlton Fisk 2.00
481 Bob Lacey/DP .10
482 Jim Gantner .10
483 Mike Griffin .10
484 Max Venable/DP .10
485 Garry Templeton .10
486 Marc Hill .10
487 Dewey Robinson .10
488 Damaso Garcia **RC** .10
489 John Littlefield (Photo actually Mark Riggins.) .10
490 Eddie Murray 2.00
491 Gordy Pladson .10
492 Barry Foote .10
493 Dan Quisenberry .10
494 Bob Walk **RC** .20
495 Dusty Baker .15
496 Paul Dade .10
497 Fred Norman .10
498 Pat Putnam .10
499 Frank Pastore .10
500 Jim Rice .25
501 Tim Foli/DP .10
502 Giants Future Stars (Chris Bourjos, Al Hargesheimer, Mike Rowland) .10
503 Steve McCatty .10
504 Dale Murphy .75
505 Jason Thompson .10
506 Phil Huffman .10
507 Jamie Quirk .10
508 Rob Dressler .10
509 Pete Mackanin .10
510 Lee Mazzilli .10
511 Wayne Garland .10
512 Gary Thomasson .10
513 Frank LaCorte .10
514 George Riley .10
515 Robin Yount 2.00
516 Doug Bird .10
517 Richie Zisk .10
518 Grant Jackson .10
519 John Tamargo/DP .10
520 Steve Stone .10
521 Sam Mejias .10
522 Mike Colbern .10
523 John Fulgham .10
524 Willie Aikens .10
525 Mike Torrez .10
526 Phillies Future Stars (Marty Bystrom, Jay Loviglio, Jim Wright) .10
527 Danny Goodwin .10
528 Gary Matthews .10
529 Dave LaRoche .10
530 Steve Garvey .75
531 John Curtis .10
532 Bill Stein .10
533 Jesus Figueroa .10
534 Dave Smith **RC** .10
535 Omar Moreno .10
536 Bob Owchinko/DP .10
537 Ron Hodges .10
538 Tom Griffin .10
539 Rodney Scott .10
540 Mike Schmidt/DP 3.00
541 Steve Swisher .10
542 Larry Bradford/DP .10
543 Terry Crowley .10
544 Rich Gale .10
545 Johnny Grubb .10
546 Paul Moskau .10
547 Mario Guerrero .10
548 Dave Goltz .10
549 Jerry Remy .10
550 Tommy John .20
551 Pirates Future Stars (Vance Law **RC**, Tony Pena **RC**, Pascual Perez **RC**) .75
552 Steve Trout .10
553 Tim Blackwell .10
554 Bert Blyleven .10
555 Cecil Cooper .10
556 Jerry Mumphrey .10
557 Chris Knapp .10
558 Barry Bonnell .10
559 Willie Montanez .10
560 Joe Morgan 2.00
561 Dennis Littlejohn .10
562 Checklist 485-605 .10
563 Jim Kaat .15
564 Ron Hassey/DP .10
565 Burt Hooton .10
566 Del Unser .10
567 Mark Bomback .10
568 Dave Revering .10
569 Al Williams/DP .10
570 Ken Singleton .10
571 Todd Cruz .10
572 Jack Morris .10
573 Phil Garner .10
574 Bill Caudill .10
575 Tony Perez 1.00
576 Reggie Cleveland .10
577 Blue Jays Future Stars (Luis Leal, Brian Milner, Ken Schrom **RC**) .10
578 Bill Gullickson **RC** .20
579 Tim Flannery .10
580 Don Baylor .15
581 Roy Howell .10
582 Gaylord Perry 1.00
583 Larry Milbourne .10
584 Randy Lerch .10
585 Amos Otis .10
586 Silvio Martinez .10
587 Jeff Newman .10
588 Gary Lavelle .10
589 Lamar Johnson .10
590 Bruce Sutter 1.00
591 John Lowenstein .10
592 Steve Comer .10
593 Steve Kemp .10
594 Preston Hanna/DP .10
595 Butch Hobson .10
596 Jerry Augustine .10
597 Rafael Landestoy .10
598 George Vukovich/DP .10
599 Dennis Kinney .10
600 Johnny Bench 2.00
601 Don Aase .10
602 Bobby Murcer .10
603 John Verhoeven .10
604 Rob Picciolo .10
605 Don Sutton 1.00
606 Reds Future Stars (Bruce Berenyi, Geoff Combe, Paul Householder/DP) .10
607 Dave Palmer .10
608 Greg Pryor .10
609 Lynn McGlothen .10
610 Darrell Porter .10
611 Rick Matula (DP) .10
612 Duane Kuiper .10
613 Jim Anderson .10
614 Dave Rozema .10
615 Rick Dempsey .10
616 Rick Wise .10
617 Craig Reynolds .10
618 John Milner .10
619 Steve Henderson .10
620 Dennis Eckersley 1.00
621 Tom Donohue .10
622 Randy Moffitt .10
623 Sal Bando .10
624 Bob Welch .10
625 Bill Buckner .10
626 Tigers Future Stars (Dave Steffen, Jerry Ujdur, Roger Weaver) .10
627 Luis Tiant .10
628 Vic Correll .10
629 Tony Armas .10
630 Steve Carlton 2.00
631 Ron Jackson .10
632 Alan Bannister .10
633 Bill Lee .10
634 Doug Flynn .10
635 Bobby Bonds .10
636 Al Hrabosky .10
637 Jerry Narron .10
638 Checklist 606 .10
639 Carney Lansford .10
640 Dave Parker .10
641 Mark Belanger .10
642 Vern Ruhle .10
643 Lloyd Moseby **RC** .20
644 Ramon Aviles/DP .10
645 Rick Reuschel .10
646 Marvis Foley .10
647 Dick Drago .10
648 Darrell Evans .10
649 Manny Sarmiento .10
650 Bucky Dent .10
651 Pedro Guerrero .10
652 John Montague .10
653 Bill Fahey .10
654 Ray Burris .10
655 Dan Driessen .10
656 Jon Matlack .10
657 Mike Cubbage/DP .10
658 Milt Wilcox .10
659 Brewers Future Stars (John Flinn, Ed Romero, Ned Yost) .10
660 Gary Carter 2.00
661 Orioles Team (Earl Weaver) .25
662 Red Sox Team (Ralph Houk) .20
663 Angels Team (Jim Fregosi) .10
664 White Sox Team (Tony LaRussa) .25
665 Indians Team (Dave Garcia) .10
666 Tigers Team (Sparky Anderson) .25
667 Royals Team (Jim Frey) .10
668 Brewers Team (Bob Rodgers) .10
669 Twins Team (John Goryl) .10
670 Yankees Team (Gene Michael) .15
671 A's Team (Billy Martin) .25
672 Mariners Team (Maury Wills) .20
673 Rangers Team (Don Zimmer) .20
674 Blue Jays Team (Bobby Mattick) .10
675 Braves Team (Bobby Cox) .25
676 Cubs Team (Joe Amalfitano) .10
677 Reds Team (John McNamara) .10
678 Astros Team (Bill Virdon) .10
679 Dodgers Team (Tom Lasorda) .25
680 Expos Team (Dick Williams) .20
681 Mets Team (Joe Torre) .25
682 Phillies Team (Dallas Green) .15
683 Pirates Team (Chuck Tanner) .10
684 Cardinals Team (Whitey Herzog) .15
685 Padres Team (Frank Howard) .20
686 Giants Team (Dave Bristol) .10
687 Jeff Jones .10
688 Kiko Garcia .10
689 Red Sox Future Stars (Bruce Hurst **RC**, Keith MacWhorter, Reid Nichols **RC**) .30
690 Bob Watson .10
691 Dick Ruthven .10
692 Lenny Randle .10
693 Steve Howe **RC** .20
694 Bud Harrelson/DP .10
695 Kent Tekulve .10
696 Alan Ashby .10
697 Rick Waits .10
698 Mike Jorgensen .10
699 Glenn Abbott .10
700 George Brett 3.50
701 Joe Rudi .10
702 George Medich .10
703 Alvis Woods .10
704 Bill Travers/DP .10
705 Ted Simmons .10
706 Dave Ford .10
707 Dave Cash .10
708 Doyle Alexander .10
709 Alan Trammell/DP .10
710 Ron LeFlore/DP .10
711 Joe Ferguson .10
712 Bill Bonham .10
713 Bill North .10
714 Pete Redfern .10
715 Bill Madlock .10
716 Glenn Borgmann .10
717 Jim Barr/DP .10
718 Larry Biittner .10
719 Sparky Lyle .10
720 Fred Lynn .10
721 Toby Harrah .10
722 Joe Niekro .10
723 Bruce Bochte .10
724 Lou Piniella .15
725 Steve Rogers .10
726 Rick Monday .10

Traded

The 132 cards in this extension set are numbered from 727 to 858, technically making them a high-numbered series of the regular Topps set. The set was not packaged in gum packs, but rather sold in a specially designed red box through baseball card dealers only. The set features not only mid-season trades, but also single-player rookie cards of some of the hottest prospects. The cards measure 2-1/2" x 3-1/2".

		NM/M
Complete Set (132):		15.00
Common Player:		.10
727	Danny Ainge **RC**	2.00
728	Doyle Alexander	.10
729	Gary Alexander	.10
730	Billy Almon	.10
731	Joaquin Andujar	.10
732	Bob Bailor	.10
733	Juan Beniquez	.10
734	Dave Bergman	.10
735	Tony Bernazard	.10
736	Larry Biittner	.10
737	Doug Bird	.10
738	Bert Blyleven	.25
739	Mark Bomback	.10
740	Bobby Bonds	.15
741	Rick Bosetti	.10
742	Hubie Brooks	.10
743	Rick Burleson	.10
744	Ray Burris	.10
745	Jeff Burroughs	.10
746	Enos Cabell	.10
747	Ken Clay	.10
748	Mark Clear	.10
749	Larry Cox	.10
750	Hector Cruz	.10
751	Victor Cruz	.10
752	Mike Cubbage	.10
753	Dick Davis	.10
754	Brian Doyle	.10
755	Dick Drago	.10
756	Leon Durham	.10
757	Jim Dwyer	.10
758	Dave Edwards	.10
759	Jim Essian	.10
760	Bill Fahey	.10
761	Rollie Fingers	1.00
762	Carlton Fisk	2.00
763	Barry Foote	.10
764	Ken Forsch	.10
765	Kiko Garcia	.10
766	Cesar Geronimo	.10
767	Gary Gray	.10
768	Mickey Hatcher	.10
769	Steve Henderson	.10
770	Marc Hill	.10
771	Butch Hobson	.10
772	Rick Honeycutt	.10
773	Roy Howell	.10
774	Mike Ivie	.10
775	Roy Lee Jackson	.10
776	Cliff Johnson	.10
777	Randy Jones	.10
778	Ruppert Jones	.10
779	Mick Kelleher	.10
780	Terry Kennedy	.10
781	Dave Kingman	.10
782	Bob Knepper	.10
783	Ken Kravec	.10
784	Bob Lacey	.10
785	Dennis Lamp	.10
786	Rafael Landestoy	.10
787	Ken Landreaux	.10
788	Carney Lansford	.10
789	Dave LaRoche	.10
790	Joe Lefebvre	.10
791	Ron LeFlore	.10
792	Randy Lerch	.10
793	Sixto Lezcano	.10
794	John Littlefield	.10
795	Mike Lum	.10
796	Greg Luzinski	.10
797	Fred Lynn	.10
798	Jerry Martin	.10
799	Buck Martinez	.10
800	Gary Matthews	.10
801	Mario Mendoza	.10
802	Larry Milbourne	.10
803	Rick Miller	.10
804	John Montefusco	.10
805	Jerry Morales	.10
806	Jose Morales	.10
807	Joe Morgan	2.00
808	Jerry Mumphrey	.10
809	Gene Nelson **RC**	.10
810	Ed Ott	.10
811	Bob Owchinko	.10
812	Gaylord Perry	1.00
813	Mike Phillips	.10
814	Darrell Porter	.10
815	Mike Proly	.10
816	Tim Raines	3.00
817	Lenny Randle	.10
818	Doug Rau	.10
819	Jeff Reardon	.10
820	Ken Reitz	.10
821	Steve Renko	.10
822	Rick Reuschel	.10
823	Dave Revering	.10
824	Dave Roberts	.10
825	Leon Roberts	.10
826	Joe Rudi	.10
827	Kevin Saucier	.10
828	Tony Scott	.10
829	Bob Shirley	.10
830	Ted Simmons	.10
831	Lary Sorensen	.10
832	Jim Spencer	.10
833	Harry Spilman	.10
834	Fred Stanley	.10
835	Rusty Staub	.25
836	Bill Stein	.10
837	Joe Strain	.10
838	Bruce Sutter	1.00
839	Don Sutton	1.00
840	Steve Swisher	.10
841	Frank Tanana	.10
842	Gene Tenace	.10
843	Jason Thompson	.10
844	Dickie Thon	.10
845	Bill Travers	.10
846	Tom Underwood	.10
847	John Urrea	.10
848	Mike Vail	.10
849	Ellis Valentine	.10
850	Fernando Valenzuela	2.00
851	Pete Vuckovich	.10
852	Mark Wagner	.10
853	Bob Walk	.10
854	Claudell Washington	.10
855	Dave Winfield	4.00
856	Geoff Zahn	.10
857	Richie Zisk	.10
858	Checklist 727-858	.05

Team Card Sheet

Via a special mail-in offer, uncut sheets of team cards from the 1981 Topps issue were made available to collectors.

	NM/M
Team Card Sheet	20.00

Giant Photo Cards

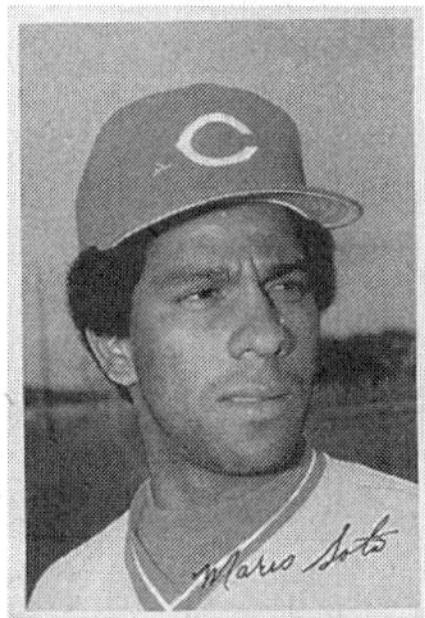

Once again testing the popularity of large-format cards, Topps issued 4-7/8" x 6-7/8" cards in two different sets. The team-set cards feature a large color photo, facsimile autograph and white border on the front. Backs have the player's name, team, position and a checklist at the bottom. The 102 cards were sold in limited areas corresponding to the teams' geographic home. Cards were sold in one-card wax packs with 36 packs per box. Boxes contained either the cards of a single team, or of two teams from the same city or state. It was also possible to order the whole set by mail. Ten teams are involved in the issue, with the number of players from each team ranging from 6 to 12.

		NM/M
Complete Set (102):		25.00
Common Player:		.25
Angels-Dodgers Wax Box:		6.00
Astros-Rangers Wax Box:		7.50
Cubs-White Sox Wax Box:		6.00
Mets-Yankees Wax Box:		9.00
Phillies Wax Box:		9.00
Reds Wax Box:		7.50
Red Sox Wax Box:		7.50
(1)	Tom Burgmeier	.25
(2)	Dennis Eckersley	1.00
(3)	Dwight Evans	.35
(4)	Carlton Fisk	1.00
(5)	Glenn Hoffman	.25
(6)	Carney Lansford	.25
(7)	Tony Perez	1.00
(8)	Jim Rice	.75
(9)	Bob Stanley	.25
(10)	Dave Stapleton	.25
(11)	Frank Tanana	.25
(12)	Carl Yastrzemski	1.50
(1)	Don Baylor	.35
(2)	Rick Burleson	.25
(3)	Rod Carew	1.00
(4)	Bobby Grich	.35
(5)	Butch Hobson	.25
(6)	Fred Lynn	.35
(1)	Tim Blackwell	.25
(2)	Bill Buckner	.35
(3)	Ivan DeJesus	.25
(4)	Leon Durham	.25
(5)	Dave Kingman	.40
(6)	Mike Krukow	.25
(7)	Ken Reitz	.25
(8)	Rick Reuschel	.25
(9)	Mike Tyson	.25
(1)	Britt Burns	.25
(2)	Rich Dotson	.25
(3)	Ed Farmer	.25
(4)	Lamar Johnson	.25
(5)	Ron LeFlore	.25
(6)	Chet Lemon	.25
(7)	Bob Molinaro	.25
(8)	Jim Morrison	.25
(9)	Wayne Nordhagen	.25
(1)	Johnny Bench	1.00
(2)	Dave Collins	.25
(3)	Dave Concepcion	.25
(4)	Dan Driessen	.25
(5)	George Foster	.35
(6)	Ken Griffey	.35
(7)	Tom Hume	.25
(8)	Ray Knight	.25
(9)	Joe Nolan	.25
(10)	Ron Oester	.25
(11)	Tom Seaver	1.00
(12)	Mario Soto	.25
(1)	Cesar Cedeno	.25
(2)	Jose Cruz	.25
(3)	Art Howe	.25
(4)	Terry Puhl	.25
(5)	Nolan Ryan	3.00
(6)	Don Sutton	1.00
(1)	Dusty Baker	.35
(2)	Ron Cey	.25
(3)	Steve Garvey	.75
(4)	Burt Hooton	.25
(5)	Steve Howe	.25
(6)	Davey Lopes	.25
(7)	Rick Monday	.25
(8)	Jerry Reuss	.25
(9)	Bill Russell	.25
(10)	Reggie Smith	.25
(11)	Bob Welch	.25
(12)	Steve Yeager	.25
(1)	Neil Allen	.25
(2)	Doug Flynn	.25
(3)	Lee Mazzilli	.25
(4)	Rusty Staub	.40
(5)	Alex Taveras	.25
(6)	Alex Trevino	.25
(1)	Rick Cerone	.25
(2)	Bucky Dent	.35
(3)	Rich Gossage	.50
(4)	Ron Guidry	.35
(5)	Reggie Jackson	1.50
(6)	Tommy John	.35
(7)	Ruppert Jones	.25
(8)	Rudy May	.25
(9)	Graig Nettles	.25
(10)	Willie Randolph	.25
(11)	Bob Watson	.25
(12)	Dave Winfield	1.00
(1)	Bob Boone	.35
(2)	Larry Bowa	.25
(3)	Steve Carlton	1.00
(4)	Greg Luzinski	.25
(5)	Garry Maddox	.25
(6)	Bake McBride	.25
(7)	Tug McGraw	.35
(8)	Pete Rose	3.00
(9)	Dick Ruthven	.25
(10)	Mike Schmidt	2.00
(11)	Manny Trillo	.25
(12)	Del Unser	.25
(1)	Buddy Bell	.25
(2)	Jon Matlack	.25
(3)	Al Oliver	.35
(4)	Mickey Rivers	.25
(5)	Jim Sundberg	.25
(6)	Bump Wills	.25

National 5x7 Photos

This set is the other half of Topps' efforts with large cards in 1981. Measuring 4-7/8" x 6-7/8", the National photo issue was limited to 15 cards. They were sold in areas not covered by the team-set issues. The set includes 10 cards which carry the same photos found in the team sets, but with no checklist on the backs. Five cards are unique to the National set: Brett, Cooper, Palmer, Parker and Simmons.

		NM/M
Complete Set (15):		4.00
Common Player:		.15
(1)	Buddy Bell	.15
(2)	Johnny Bench	.50
(3)	George Brett	.75
(4)	Rod Carew	.50
(5)	Cecil Cooper	.15
(6)	Steve Garvey	.35
(7)	Rich Gossage	.15
(8)	Reggie Jackson	.60
(9)	Jim Palmer	.50
(10)	Dave Parker	.15
(11)	Jim Rice	.30
(12)	Pete Rose	1.00
(13)	Mike Schmidt	.75
(14)	Tom Seaver	.50
(15)	Ted Simmons	.15

Mets Magic Memories

Celebrating 20 years of N.Y. Mets baseball, the team issued a set of "Magic Memories" cards. Topps produced 20,000 each of the 6-7/8" x 4-7/8" cards. The cards were individually cello wrapped. Cards #1-2 were distributed at the team's August 27 game; cards #3-4 at the September 22 contest. The first card is a sepia team photo of the 1962 Mets. Card #2-3 are color team photos from 1969 and 1973. The team photo cards have player stats on back. The fourth card depicts four of the Mets managers on front, with biographies on back.

		NM/M
Complete Set (4):		24.00
Common Player:		6.00
1	1962 Mets Team Photo	6.00
2	1969 Mets Team Photo	6.00
3	1973 Mets Team Photo	6.00
4	New York Mets Managers (Casey Stengel, Gil Hodges, Yogi Berra, Joe Torre)	12.00

Scratchoffs

Sold as a separate issue with bubble gum, this 108-card set was issued in three-card panels that measure 3-1/4" x 5-1/4". Each individual card measures 1-13/16" x 3-1/4" and contains a small player photo alongside a series of black dots designed to be scratched off as part of a baseball game. Cards of National League players have a green background, while American League players have a red background. While there are 108 different players in the set, there are 144 possible panel combinations. An intact panel of three cards is valued approximately 20-25 percent more the sum of the individual cards.

		NM/M
Complete Set (108):		10.00
Common Player:		.15
Wax Pack:		.75
Wax Box (36):		15.00
1	George Brett	1.00
2	Cecil Cooper	.15
3	Reggie Jackson	.50
4	Al Oliver	.15
5	Fred Lynn	.15
6	Tony Armas	.15
7	Ben Oglivie	.15
8	Tony Perez	.25
9	Eddie Murray	.25
10	Robin Yount	.25
11	Steve Kemp	.15
12	Joe Charboneau	.25
13	Jim Rice	.20
14	Lance Parrish	.15
15	John Mayberry	.15
16	Richie Zisk	.15
17	Ken Singleton	.15
18	Rod Carew	.25
19	Rick Manning	.15
20	Willie Wilson	.15
21	Buddy Bell	.15
22	Dave Revering	.15
23	Tom Paciorek	.15
24	Champ Summers	.15
25	Carney Lansford	.15
26	Lamar Johnson	.15
27	Willie Aikens	.15
28	Rick Cerone	.15
29	Al Bumbry	.15
30	Bruce Bochte	.15
31	Mickey Rivers	.15
32	Mike Hargrove	.15
33	John Castino	.15
34	Chet Lemon	.15
35	Paul Molitor	.25
36	Willie Randolph	.15
37	Rick Burleson	.15
38	Alan Trammell	.15
39	Rickey Henderson	.25
40	Dan Meyer	.15
41	Ken Landreaux	.15
42	Damaso Garcia	.15
43	Roy Smalley	.15
44	Otto Velez	.15
45	Sixto Lezcano	.15
46	Toby Harrah	.15
47	Frank White	.15
48	Dave Stapleton	.15
49	Steve Stone	.15
50	Jim Palmer	.25
51	Larry Gura	.15
52	Tommy John	.15
53	Mike Norris	.15
54	Ed Farmer	.15
55	Bill Buckner	.15
56	Steve Garvey	.20
57	Reggie Smith	.15
58	Bake McBride	.15
59	Dave Parker	.15
60	Mike Schmidt	1.00
61	Bob Horner	.15
62	Pete Rose	2.00
63	Ted Simmons	.15
64	Johnny Bench	.25
65	George Foster	.15
66	Gary Carter	.25
67	Keith Hernandez	.15
68	Ozzie Smith	.35
69	Dave Kingman	.15
70	Jack Clark	.15
71	Dusty Baker	.15
72	Dale Murphy	.20
73	Ron Cey	.15
74	Greg Luzinski	.15
75	Lee Mazzilli	.15
76	Gary Matthews	.15
77	Cesar Cedeno	.15
78	Warren Cromartie	.15
79	Steve Henderson	.15
80	Ellis Valentine	.15
81	Mike Easler	.15
82	Garry Templeton	.15
83	Jose Cruz	.15
84	Dave Collins	.15
85	George Hendrick	.15
86	Gene Richards	.15
87	Terry Whitfield	.15
88	Terry Puhl	.15
89	Larry Parrish	.15
90	Andre Dawson	.20
91	Ken Griffey	.15
92	Dave Lopes	.15
93	Doug Flynn	.15
94	Ivan DeJesus	.15
95	Dave Concepcion	.15
96	John Stearns	.15
97	Jerry Mumphrey	.15
98	Jerry Martin	.15
99	Art Howe	.15
100	Omar Moreno	.15
101	Ken Reitz	.15
102	Phil Garner	.15
103	Jerry Reuss	.15
104	Steve Carlton	.25
105	Jim Bibby	.15
106	Steve Rogers	.15
107	Tom Seaver	.25
108	Vida Blue	.15

Stickers

The 262 stickers in this full-color set measure 1-15/16" x 2-9/16" and are numbered on both the front and back. They were produced for Topps by the Panini Co., of Italy. The set includes a series of "All-Star" stickers printed on silver or gold "foil." An album to house the stickers was also available.

		NM/M
Complete Set (262):		9.00
Common Player:		.05
Sticker Album:		2.00
Wax Pack (5):		.40
Wax Box (100):		15.00
1	Steve Stone	.05
2	Tommy John, Mike Norris	.05
3	Rudy May	.05
4	Mike Norris	.05
5	Len Barker	.05
6	Mike Norris	.05
7	Dan Quisenberry	.05
8	Rich Gossage	.05
9	George Brett	.30
10	Cecil Cooper	.05
11	Reggie Jackson, Ben Oglivie	.05
12	Gorman Thomas	.05
13	Cecil Cooper	.05
14	George Brett, Ben Oglivie	.05
15	Rickey Henderson	.25
16	Willie Wilson	.05
17	Bill Buckner	.05
18	Keith Hernandez	.05
19	Mike Schmidt	.30
20	Bob Horner	.05
21	Mike Schmidt	.30
22	George Hendrick	.05
23	Ron LeFlore	.05
24	Omar Moreno	.05
25	Steve Carlton	.20
26	Joe Niekro	.05
27	Don Sutton	.20
28	Steve Carlton	.20
29	Steve Carlton	.20
30	Nolan Ryan	.50
31	Rollie Fingers, Tom Hume	.05
32	Bruce Sutter	.20
33	Ken Singleton	.05
34	Eddie Murray	.25
35	Al Bumbry	.05
36	Rich Dauer	.05
37	Scott McGregor	.05
38	Rick Dempsey	.05
39	Jim Palmer	.25
40	Steve Stone	.05
41	Jim Rice	.15
42	Fred Lynn	.05
43	Carney Lansford	.05
44	Tony Perez	.25
45	Carl Yastrzemski	.25
46	Carlton Fisk	.25
47	Dave Stapleton	.05
48	Dennis Eckersley	.20
49	Rod Carew	.25
50	Brian Downing	.05
51	Don Baylor	.05
52	Rick Burleson	.05
53	Bobby Grich	.05
54	Butch Hobson	.05
55	Andy Hassler	.05
56	Frank Tanana	.05
57	Chet Lemon	.05
58	Lamar Johnson	.05
59	Wayne Nordhagen	.05
60	Jim Morrison	.05
61	Bob Molinaro	.05
62	Rich Dotson	.05
63	Britt Burns	.05
64	Ed Farmer	.05
65	Toby Harrah	.05
66	Joe Charboneau	.25
67	Miguel Dilone	.05
68	Mike Hargrove	.05
69	Rick Manning	.05
70	Andre Thornton	.05
71	Ron Hassey	.05
72	Len Barker	.05
73	Lance Parrish	.05
74	Steve Kemp	.05
75	Alan Trammell	.05
76	Champ Summers	.05
77	Rick Peters	.05
78	Kirk Gibson	.05
79	Johnny Wockenfuss	.05
80	Jack Morris	.05

81 Willie Wilson .05
82 George Brett .30
83 Frank White .05
84 Willie Aikens .05
85 Clint Hurdle .05
86 Hal McRae .05
87 Dennis Leonard .05
88 Larry Gura .05
89 American League Pennant Winner (Kansas City Royals Team) .05
90 American League Pennant Winner (Kansas City Royals Team) .05
91 Paul Molitor .25
92 Ben Oglivie .05
93 Cecil Cooper .05
94 Ted Simmons .05
95 Robin Yount .25
96 Gorman Thomas .05
97 Mike Caldwell .05
98 Moose Haas .05
99 John Castino .05
100 Roy Smalley .05
101 Ken Landreaux .05
102 Butch Wynegar .05
103 Ron Jackson .05
104 Jerry Koosman .05
105 Roger Erickson .05
106 Doug Corbett .05
107 Reggie Jackson .30
108 Willie Randolph .05
109 Rick Cerone .05
110 Bucky Dent .05
111 Dave Winfield .25
112 Ron Guidry .10
113 Rich Gossage .05
114 Tommy John .10
115 Rickey Henderson .25
116 Tony Armas .05
117 Dave Revering .05
118 Wayne Gross .05
119 Dwayne Murphy .05
120 Jeff Newman .05
121 Rick Langford .05
122 Mike Norris .05
123 Bruce Bochte .05
124 Tom Paciorek .05
125 Dan Meyer .05
126 Julio Cruz .05
127 Richie Zisk .05
128 Floyd Bannister .05
129 Shane Rawley .05
130 Buddy Bell .05
131 Al Oliver .05
132 Mickey Rivers .05
133 Jim Sundberg .05
134 Bump Wills .05
135 Jon Matlack .05
136 Danny Darwin .05
137 Damaso Garcia .05
138 Otto Velez .05
139 John Mayberry .05
140 Alfredo Griffin .05
141 Alvis Woods .05
142 Dave Stieb .05
143 Jim Clancy .05
144 Gary Matthews .05
145 Bob Horner .05
146 Dale Murphy .25
147 Chris Chambliss .05
148 Phil Niekro .20
149 Glenn Hubbard .05
150 Rick Camp .05
151 Dave Kingman .05
152 Bill Caudill .05
153 Bill Buckner .05
154 Barry Foote .05
155 Mike Tyson .05
156 Ivan DeJesus .05
157 Rick Reuschel .05
158 Ken Reitz .05
159 George Foster .05
160 Johnny Bench .25
161 Dave Concepcion .05
162 Dave Collins .05
163 Ken Griffey .05
164 Dan Driessen .05
165 Tom Seaver .25
166 Tom Hume .05
167 Cesar Cedeno .05
168 Rafael Landestoy .05
169 Jose Cruz .05
170 Art Howe .05
171 Terry Puhl .05
172 Joe Sambito .05
173 Nolan Ryan .50
174 Joe Niekro .05
175 Dave Lopes .05
176 Steve Garvey .15
177 Ron Cey .05
178 Reggie Smith .05
179 Bill Russell .05
180 Burt Hooton .05
181 Jerry Reuss .05
182 Dusty Baker .05
183 Larry Parrish .05
184 Gary Carter .25
185 Rodney Scott .05
186 Ellis Valentine .05
187 Andre Dawson .20
188 Warren Cromartie .05
189 Chris Speier .05
190 Steve Rogers .05
191 Lee Mazzilli .05
192 Doug Flynn .05
193 Steve Henderson .05
194 John Stearns .05
195 Joel Youngblood .05
196 Frank Taveras .05
197 Pat Zachry .05
198 Neil Allen .05
199 Mike Schmidt .30
200 Pete Rose .50
201 Larry Bowa .05
202 Bake McBride .05
203 Bob Boone .05
204 Garry Maddox .05
205 Tug McGraw .05
206 Steve Carlton .20
207 National League Pennant Winner (Philadelphia Phillies Team) .05
208 National League Pennant Winner (Philadelphia Phillies Team) .05
209 Phil Garner .05
210 Dave Parker .05
211 Omar Moreno .05
212 Mike Easler .05
213 Bill Madlock .05
214 Ed Ott .05
215 Willie Stargell .25
216 Jim Bibby .05
217 Garry Templeton .05
218 Sixto Lezcano .05
219 Keith Hernandez .05
220 George Hendrick .05
221 Bruce Sutter .20
222 Ken Oberkfell .05
223 Tony Scott .05
224 Darrell Porter .05
225 Gene Richards .05
226 Broderick Perkins .05
227 Jerry Mumphrey .05
228 Luis Salazar .05
229 Jerry Turner .05
230 Ozzie Smith .30
231 John Curtis .05
232 Rick Wise .05
233 Terry Whitfield .05
234 Jack Clark .05
235 Darrell Evans .05
236 Larry Herndon .05
237 Milt May .05
238 Greg Minton .05
239 Vida Blue .05
240 Eddie Whitson .05
241 Cecil Cooper .05
242 Willie Randolph .05
243 George Brett .30
244 Robin Yount .25
245 Reggie Jackson .30
246 Al Oliver .05
247 Willie Wilson .05
248 Rick Cerone .05
249 Steve Stone .05
250 Tommy John .10
251 Rich Gossage .05
252 Steve Garvey .15
253 Phil Garner .05
254 Mike Schmidt .30
255 Garry Templeton .05
256 George Hendrick .05
257 Dave Parker .05
258 Cesar Cedeno .05
259 Gary Carter .25
260 Jim Bibby .05
261 Steve Carlton .20
262 Tug McGraw .05

Thirst Break Comics

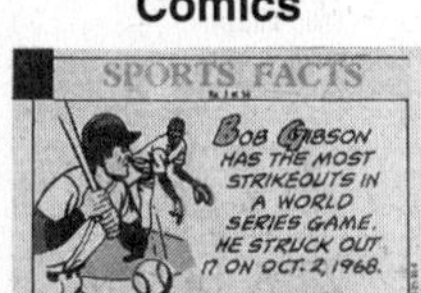

These 2-1/2" x 1-5/8" wax paper comics were the wrapper for Thirst Break Gum, a Topps test issue distributed to parts of Ohio and Pennsylvania. Each orange foil pack contained five comics (labeled as "Sport Facts") which were folded and wrapped around five soft gum pieces. A total of 56 different comics were produced, 20 of which were baseball players. The great majority of comics found today are slightly wrinkled and stained by the gum, but are usually considered to be in Near Mint condition.

NM/M
Complete (Baseball) Set (20):
Common Player: 1.00
Wax Pack (1): 4.00
Wax Box (48): 110.00
1 Shortest Game .50
2 Lefty Gomez 1.00
3 Bob Gibson 1.00
4 Hoyt Wilhelm 1.00
5 Babe Ruth 5.00
6 Toby Harrah 1.00
7 Carl Hubbell 1.00
8 Harvey Haddix 1.00
9 Steve Carlton 1.50
10 Nolan Ryan, Tom Seaver, Steve Carlton 3.50
11 Lou Brock 1.00
12 Mickey Mantle 6.00
13 Tom Seaver 2.50
14 Don Drysdale 1.00
15 Billy Williams 1.00
20 Christy Mathewson 1.00
21 Hank Aaron 4.00
22 Ron Blomberg 1.00
23 Joe Nuxhall 1.00
24 Reggie Jackson 3.00

1982 Topps

At 792 cards, this was the largest issue produced up to that time, eliminating the need for double-printed cards. The 2-1/2" x 3-1/2" cards feature a front color photo with a pair of stripes down the left side. Under the player's photo are found his name, team and position. A facsimile autograph runs across the front of the picture. Specialty cards include great performances of the previous season, All-Stars, statistical leaders and "In Action" cards (indicated by "IA" in listings below). Managers and hitting/pitching leaders have cards, while rookies are shown as "Future Stars" on group cards.

NM/M
Unopened Fact. Set (792): 180.00
Complete Set (792): 70.00
Common Player: .10
Wax Pack (15): 5.00
Wax Box (36): 140.00
Cello Pack (28): 6.00
Cello Box (24): 130.00
Rack Pack (51): 8.00
Rack Box (24): 210.00
Vending Box (500): 60.00
1 Steve Carlton (1981 Highlight) .25
2 Ron Davis (1981 Highlight) .10
3 Tim Raines (1981 Highlight) .10
4 Pete Rose (1981 Highlight) .75
5 Nolan Ryan (1981 Highlight) 3.00
6 Fernando Valenzuela (1981 Highlight) .10
7 Scott Sanderson .10
8 Rich Dauer .10
9 Ron Guidry .15
10 Ron Guidry/IA .10
11 Gary Alexander .10
12 Moose Haas .10
13 Lamar Johnson .10
14 Steve Howe .10
15 Ellis Valentine .10
16 Steve Comer .10
17 Darrell Evans .10
18 Fernando Arroyo .10
19 Ernie Whitt .10
20 Garry Maddox .10
21 Orioles Future Stars (Bob Bonner **RC**, Cal Ripken, Jr. **RC**, Jeff Schneider **RC**) 50.00
22 Jim Beattie .10
23 Willie Hernandez .10
24 Dave Frost .10
25 Jerry Remy .10
26 Jorge Orta .10
27 Tom Herr .10
28 John Urrea .10
29 Dwayne Murphy .10
30 Tom Seaver 1.50
31 Tom Seaver/IA 1.00
32 Gene Garber .10
33 Jerry Morales .10
34 Joe Sambito .10
35 Willie Aikens .10
36 Rangers Batting/Pitching Leaders (George Medich, Al Oliver) .10
37 Dan Graham .10
38 Charlie Lea .10
39 Lou Whitaker .10
40 Dave Parker .10
41 Dave Parker/IA .10
42 Rick Sofield .10
43 Mike Cubbage .10
44 Britt Burns .10
45 Rick Cerone .10
46 Jerry Augustine .10
47 Jeff Leonard .10
48 Bobby Castillo .10
49 Alvis Woods .10
50 Buddy Bell .10
51 Chicago Cubs Future Stars (Jay Howell **RC**, Carlos Lezcano **RC**, Ty Waller **RC**) .40
52 Larry Andersen .10
53 Greg Gross .10
54 Ron Hassey .10
55 Rick Burleson .10
56 Mark Littell .10
57 Craig Reynolds .10
58 John D'Acquisto .10
59 Rich Gedman **RC** .10
60 Tony Armas .10
61 Tommy Boggs .10
62 Mike Tyson .10
63 Mario Soto .10
64 Lynn Jones .10
65 Terry Kennedy .10
66 Astros Batting/Pitching Leaders (Art Howe, Nolan Ryan) .75
67 Rich Gale .10
68 Roy Howell .10
69 Al Williams .10
70 Tim Raines .50
71 Roy Lee Jackson .10
72 Rick Auerbach .10
73 Buddy Solomon .10
74 Bob Clark .10
75 Tommy John .20
76 Greg Pryor .10
77 Miguel Dilone .10
78 George Medich .10
79 Bob Bailor .10
80 Jim Palmer 1.00
81 Jim Palmer/IA .30
82 Bob Welch .10
83 Yankees Future Stars (Steve Balboni **RC**, Andy McGaffigan **RC**, Andre Robertson **RC**) .15
84 Rennie Stennett .10
85 Lynn McGlothen .10
86 Dane Iorg .10
87 Matt Keough .10
88 Biff Pocoroba .10
89 Steve Henderson .10
90 Nolan Ryan 4.00
91 Carney Lansford .10
92 Brad Havens .10
93 Larry Hisle .10
94 Andy Hassler .10
95 Ozzie Smith 2.00
96 Royals Batting/Pitching Leaders (George Brett, Larry Gura) .35
97 Paul Moskau .10
98 Terry Bulling .10
99 Barry Bonnell .10
100 Mike Schmidt 3.00
101 Mike Schmidt/IA 1.50
102 Dan Briggs .10
103 Bob Lacey .10
104 Rance Mulliniks .10
105 Kirk Gibson .10
106 Enrique Romo .10
107 Wayne Krenchicki .10
108 Bob Sykes .10
109 Dave Revering .10
110 Carlton Fisk 1.50
111 Carlton Fisk/IA .65
112 Billy Sample .10
113 Steve McCatty .10
114 Ken Landreaux .10
115 Gaylord Perry 1.00
116 Jim Wohlford .10
117 Rawly Eastwick .10
118 Expos Future Stars (Terry Francona **RC**, Brad Mills **RC**, Bryn Smith **RC**) .20
119 Joe Pittman .10
120 Gary Lucas .10
121 Ed Lynch .10
122 Jamie Easterly .10
123 Danny Goodwin .10
124 Reid Nichols .10
125 Danny Ainge 1.00
126 Braves Batting/Pitching Leaders (Rick Mahler, Claudell Washington) .10
127 Lonnie Smith .10
128 Frank Pastore .10
129 Checklist 1-132 .10
130 Julio Cruz .10
131 Stan Bahnsen .10
132 Lee May .10
133 Pat Underwood .10
134 Dan Ford .10
135 Andy Rincon .10
136 Lenn Sakata .10
137 George Cappuzzello .10
138 Tony Pena .10
139 Jeff Jones .10
140 Ron LeFlore .10
141 Indians Future Stars (Chris Bando, Tom Brennan, Von Hayes **RC**) .20
142 Dave LaRoche .10
143 Mookie Wilson .10
144 Fred Breining .10
145 Bob Horner .10
146 Mike Griffin .10
147 Denny Walling .10
148 Mickey Klutts .10
149 Pat Putnam .10
150 Ted Simmons .10
151 Dave Edwards .10
152 Ramon Aviles .10
153 Roger Erickson .10
154 Dennis Werth .10
155 Otto Velez .10
156 A's Batting/Pitching Leaders (Rickey Henderson, Steve McCatty) .10
157 Steve Crawford .10
158 Brian Downing .10
159 Larry Biittner .10
160 Luis Tiant .10
161 Batting Leaders (Carney Lansford, Bill Madlock) .10
162 Home Run Leaders (Tony Armas, Dwight Evans, Bobby Grich, Eddie Murray, Mike Schmidt) .25
163 RBI Leaders (Eddie Murray, Mike Schmidt) .40
164 Stolen Base Leaders (Rickey Henderson, Tim Raines) .35
165 Victory Leaders (Denny Martinez, Steve McCatty, Jack Morris, Tom Seaver, Pete Vuckovich) .10
166 Strikeout Leaders (Len Barker, Fernando Valenzuela) .10
167 ERA Leaders (Steve McCatty, Nolan Ryan) 1.50
168 Leading Relievers (Rollie Fingers, Bruce Sutter) .15
169 Charlie Leibrandt .10
170 Jim Bibby .10
171 Giants Future Stars (Bob Brenly **RC**, Chili Davis **RC**, Bob Tufts **RC**) 2.00
172 Bill Gullickson .10
173 Jamie Quirk .10
174 Dave Ford .10
175 Jerry Mumphrey .10
176 Dewey Robinson .10
177 John Ellis .10
178 Dyar Miller .10
179 Steve Garvey .75
180 Steve Garvey/IA .30
181 Silvio Martinez .10
182 Larry Herndon .10
183 Mike Proly .10
184 Mick Kelleher .10
185 Phil Niekro 1.00
186 Cardinals Batting/Pitching Leaders (Bob Forsch, Keith Hernandez) .10
187 Jeff Newman .10
188 Randy Martz .10
189 Glenn Hoffman .10
190 J.R. Richard .05
191 Tim Wallach **RC** 2.00
192 Broderick Perkins .10
193 Darrell Jackson .10
194 Mike Vail .10
195 Paul Molitor 1.50
196 Willie Upshaw .10
197 Shane Rawley .10
198 Chris Speier .10
199 Don Aase .10
200 George Brett 3.00
201 George Brett/IA 2.00
202 Rick Manning .10
203 Blue Jays Future Stars (Jesse Barfield **RC**, Brian Milner, Boomer Wells) .50
204 Gary Roenicke .10
205 Neil Allen .10
206 Tony Bernazard .10
207 Rod Scurry .10
208 Bobby Murcer .10
209 Gary Lavelle .10
210 Keith Hernandez .10
211 Dan Petry .10
212 Mario Mendoza .10
213 Dave Stewart **RC** 4.00
214 Brian Asselstine .10
215 Mike Krukow .10
216 White Sox Batting/Pitching Leaders (Dennis Lamp, Chet Lemon) .10
217 Bo McLaughlin .10
218 Dave Roberts .10
219 John Curtis .10
220 Manny Trillo .10
221 Jim Slaton .10
222 Butch Wynegar .10
223 Lloyd Moseby .10
224 Bruce Bochte .10
225 Mike Torrez .10
226 Checklist 133-264 .10
227 Ray Burris .10
228 Sam Mejias .10
229 Geoff Zahn .10
230 Willie Wilson .10
231 Phillies Future Stars (Mark Davis **RC**, Bob Dernier **RC**, Ozzie Virgil **RC**) .20
232 Terry Crowley .10
233 Duane Kuiper .10
234 Ron Hodges .10
235 Mike Easler .10
236 John Martin .10
237 Rusty Kuntz .10
238 Kevin Saucier .10
239 Jon Matlack .10
240 Bucky Dent .10
241 Bucky Dent/IA .10
242 Milt May .10
243 Bob Owchinko .10
244 Rufino Linares .10
245 Ken Reitz .10
246 Mets Batting/Pitching Leaders (Hubie Brooks, Mike Scott) .10
247 Pedro Guerrero .10
248 Frank LaCorte .10
249 Tim Flannery .10
250 Tug McGraw .10
251 Fred Lynn .10
252 Fred Lynn/IA .10
253 Chuck Baker .10
254 George Bell **RC** 1.00
255 Tony Perez 1.00
256 Tony Perez/IA .10
257 Larry Harlow .10
258 Bo Diaz .10
259 Rodney Scott .10
260 Bruce Sutter 1.00
261 Tigers Future Stars (Howard Bailey, Marty Castillo, Dave Rucker) .10
262 Doug Bair .10
263 Victor Cruz .10
264 Dan Quisenberry .10
265 Al Bumbry .10
266 Rick Leach .10
267 Kurt Bevacqua .10
268 Rickey Keeton .10
269 Jim Essian .10
270 Rusty Staub .15
271 Larry Bradford .10
272 Bump Wills .10
273 Doug Bird .10
274 Bob Ojeda **RC** .50
275 Bob Watson .10
276 Angels Batting/Pitching Leaders (Rod Carew, Ken Forsch) .25
277 Terry Puhl .10
278 John Littlefield .10
279 Bill Russell .10
280 Ben Oglivie .10
281 John Verhoeven .10
282 Ken Macha .10
283 Brian Allard .10
284 Bob Grich .10
285 Sparky Lyle .10
286 Bill Fahey .10
287 Alan Bannister .10
288 Garry Templeton .10
289 Bob Stanley .10
290 Ken Singleton .10
291 Pirates Future Stars (Vance Law, Bob Long, Johnny Ray **RC**) .15
292 Dave Palmer .10
293 Rob Picciolo .10
294 Mike LaCoss .10
295 Jason Thompson .10
296 Bob Walk .10
297 Clint Hurdle .10
298 Danny Darwin .10
299 Steve Trout .10
300 Reggie Jackson 2.00
301 Reggie Jackson/IA 1.50
302 Doug Flynn .10
303 Bill Caudill .10
304 Johnnie LeMaster .10
305 Don Sutton 1.00
306 Don Sutton/IA .20
307 Randy Bass .10
308 Charlie Moore .10
309 Pete Redfern .10
310 Mike Hargrove .10
311 Dodgers Batting/Pitching Leaders (Dusty Baker, Burt Hooton) .10
312 Lenny Randle .10
313 John Harris .10
314 Buck Martinez .10
315 Burt Hooton .10
316 Steve Braun .10
317 Dick Ruthven .10
318 Mike Heath .10
319 Dave Rozema .10
320 Chris Chambliss .10
321 Chris Chambliss/IA .10
322 Garry Hancock .10
323 Bill Lee .10

324 Steve Dillard .10
325 Jose Cruz .10
326 Pete Falcone .10
327 Joe Nolan .10
328 Ed Farmer .10
329 U.L. Washington .10
330 Rick Wise .10
331 Benny Ayala .10
332 Don Robinson .10
333 Brewers Future Stars (Frank DiPino **RC**, Marshall Edwards, Chuck Porter) .10
334 Aurelio Rodriguez .10
335 Jim Sundberg .10
336 Mariners Batting/Pitching Leaders (Glenn Abbott, Tom Paciorek) .10
337 Pete Rose/AS 1.50
338 Dave Lopes/AS .10
339 Mike Schmidt/AS 1.00
340 Dave Concepcion/AS .10
341 Andre Dawson/AS .25
342a George Foster (All-Star no autograph) 2.00
342b George Foster (All-Star autograph on front) .10
343 Dave Parker/AS .10
344 Gary Carter/AS .60
345 Fernando Valenzuela/AS .10
346 Tom Seaver/AS .75
347 Bruce Sutter/AS .50
348 Derrel Thomas .10
349 George Frazier .10
350 Thad Bosley .10
351 Reds Future Stars (Scott Brown, Geoff Combe, Paul Householder) .10
352 Dick Davis .10
353 Jack O'Connor .10
354 Roberto Ramos .10
355 Dwight Evans .10
356 Denny Lewallyn .10
357 Butch Hobson .10
358 Mike Parrott .10
359 Jim Dwyer .10
360 Len Barker .10
361 Rafael Landestoy .10
362 Jim Wright .10
363 Bob Molinaro .10
364 Doyle Alexander .10
365 Bill Madlock .10
366 Padres Batting/Pitching Leaders (Juan Eichelberger, Luis Salazar) .10
367 Jim Kaat .10
368 Alex Trevino .10
369 Champ Summers .10
370 Mike Norris .10
371 Jerry Don Gleaton .10
372 Luis Gomez .10
373 Gene Nelson **RC** .10
374 Tim Blackwell .10
375 Dusty Baker .15
376 Chris Welsh .10
377 Kiko Garcia .10
378 Mike Caldwell .10
379 Rob Wilfong .10
380 Dave Stieb .10
381 Red Sox Future Stars (Bruce Hurst, Dave Schmidt, Julio Valdez) .25
382 Joe Simpson .10
383a Pascual Perez (no position on front) 20.00
383b Pascual Perez ("Pitcher" on front) .10
384 Keith Moreland .10
385 Ken Forsch .10
386 Jerry White .10
387 Tom Veryzer .10
388 Joe Rudi .10
389 George Vukovich .10
390 Eddie Murray 1.50
391 Dave Tobik .10
392 Rick Bosetti .10
393 Al Hrabosky .10
394 Checklist 265-396 .10
395 Omar Moreno .10
396 Twins Batting/Pitching Leaders (Fernando Arroyo, John Castino) .10
397 Ken Brett .10
398 Mike Squires .10
399 Pat Zachry .10
400 Johnny Bench 1.50
401 Johnny Bench/IA .45
402 Bill Stein .10
403 Jim Tracy .10
404 Dickie Thon .10
405 Rick Reuschel .10
406 Al Holland .10
407 Danny Boone .10
408 Ed Romero .10
409 Don Cooper .10
410 Ron Cey .10
411 Ron Cey (In Action) .10
412 Luis Leal .10
413 Dan Meyer .10
414 Elias Sosa .10
415 Don Baylor .15
416 Marty Bystrom .10
417 Pat Kelly .10
418 Rangers Future Stars (John Butcher, Bobby Johnson, Dave Schmidt **RC**) .10
419 Steve Stone .10
420 George Hendrick .10
421 Mark Clear .10
422 Cliff Johnson .10
423 Stan Papi .10
424 Bruce Benedict .10
425 John Candelaria .10
426 Orioles Batting/Pitching Leaders (Eddie Murray, Sammy Stewart) .25
427 Ron Oester .10
428 Lamarr Hoyt (LaMarr) .10
429 John Wathan .10
430 Vida Blue .10
431 Vida Blue/IA .10
432 Mike Scott .10
433 Alan Ashby .10
434 Joe Lefebvre .10
435 Robin Yount 1.50
436 Joe Strain .10
437 Juan Berenguer .10
438 Pete Mackanin .10
439 Dave Righetti **RC** .75
440 Jeff Burroughs .10
441 Astros Future Stars (Danny Heep, Billy Smith, Bobby Sprowl) .10
442 Bruce Kison .10
443 Mark Wagner .10
444 Terry Forster .10
445 Larry Parrish .10
446 Wayne Garland .10
447 Darrell Porter .10
448 Darrell Porter/IA .10
449 Luis Aguayo **RC** .10
450 Jack Morris .10
451 Ed Miller .10
452 Lee Smith **RC** 4.00
453 Art Howe .10
454 Rick Langford .10
455 Tom Burgmeier .10
456 Cubs Batting & Pitching Ldrs. (Bill Buckner, Randy Martz) .10
457 Tim Stoddard .10
458 Willie Montanez .10
459 Bruce Berenyi .10
460 Jack Clark .10
461 Rich Dotson .10
462 Dave Chalk .10
463 Jim Kern .10
464 Juan Bonilla .10
465 Lee Mazzilli .10
466 Randy Lerch .10
467 Mickey Hatcher .10
468 Floyd Bannister .10
469 Ed Ott .10
470 John Mayberry .10
471 Royals Future Stars (Atlee Hammaker **RC**, Mike Jones, Darryl Motley) .15
472 Oscar Gamble .10
473 Mike Stanton .10
474 Ken Oberkfell .10
475 Alan Trammell .10
476 Brian Kingman .10
477 Steve Yeager .10
478 Ray Searage .10
479 Rowland Office .10
480 Steve Carlton 1.50
481 Steve Carltonr/IA .40
482 Glenn Hubbard .10
483 Gary Woods .10
484 Ivan DeJesus .10
485 Kent Tekulve .10
486 Yankees Batting & Pitching Ldrs. (Tommy John, Jerry Mumphrey) .10
487 Bob McClure .10
488 Ron Jackson .10
489 Rick Dempsey .10
490 Dennis Eckersley 1.00
491 Checklist 397-528 .10
492 Joe Price .10
493 Chet Lemon .10
494 Hubie Brooks .10
495 Dennis Leonard .10
496 Johnny Grubb .10
497 Jim Anderson .10
498 Dave Bergman .10
499 Paul Mirabella .10
500 Rod Carew 1.50
501 Rod Carew (In Action) .40
502 Braves Future Stars (Steve Bedrosian **RC**, Brett Butler **RC**, Larry Owen) 2.00
503 Julio Gonzalez .10
504 Rick Peters .10
505 Graig Nettles .10
506 Graig Nettles/IA .10
507 Terry Harper .10
508 Jody Davis **RC** .15
509 Harry Spilman .10
510 Fernando Valenzuela .10
511 Ruppert Jones .10
512 Jerry Dybzinski .10
513 Rick Rhoden .10
514 Joe Ferguson .10
515 Larry Bowa .10
516 Larry Bowa/IA .10
517 Mark Brouhard .10
518 Garth Iorg .10
519 Glenn Adams .10
520 Mike Flanagan .10
521 Billy Almon .10
522 Chuck Rainey .10
523 Gary Gray .10
524 Tom Hausman .10
525 Ray Knight .10
526 Expos Batting & Pitching Ldrs. (Warren Cromartie, Bill Gullickson) .10
527 John Henry Johnson .10
528 Matt Alexander .10
529 Allen Ripley .10
530 Dickie Noles .10
531 A's Future Stars (Rich Bordi, Mark Budaska, Kelvin Moore) .10
532 Toby Harrah .10
533 Joaquin Andujar .10
534 Dave McKay .10
535 Lance Parrish .10
536 Rafael Ramirez .10
537 Doug Capilla .10
538 Lou Piniella .10
539 Vern Ruhle .10
540 Andre Dawson .75
541 Barry Evans .10
542 Ned Yost .10
543 Bill Robinson .10
544 Larry Christenson .10
545 Reggie Smith .10
546 Reggie Smith/IA .10
547 Rod Carew/AS .25
548 Willie Randolph/AS .10
549 George Brett/AS 1.50
550 Bucky Dent/AS .10
551 Reggie Jackson/AS .75
552 Ken Singleton/AS .10
553 Dave Winfield/AS .60
554 Carlton Fisk/AS .25
555 Scott McGregor/AS .10
556 Jack Morris/AS .10
557 Rich Gossage/AS .10
558 John Tudor .10
559 Indians Batting & Pitching Ldrs. (Bert Blyleven, Mike Hargrove) .10
560 Doug Corbett .10
561 Cardinals Future Stars (Glenn Brummer, Luis DeLeon, Gene Roof) .10
562 Mike O'Berry .10
563 Ross Baumgarten .10
564 Doug DeCinces .10
565 Jackson Todd .10
566 Mike Jorgensen .10
567 Bob Babcock .10
568 Joe Pettini .10
569 Willie Randolph .10
570 Willie Randolphr/IA .10
571 Glenn Abbott .10
572 Juan Beniquez .10
573 Rick Waits .10
574 Mike Ramsey .10
575 Al Cowens .10
576 Giants Batting & Pitching Ldrs. (Vida Blue, Milt May) .10
577 Rick Monday .10
578 Shooty Babitt .10
579 Rick Mahler **RC** .10
580 Bobby Bonds .10
581 Ron Reed .10
582 Luis Pujols .10
583 Tippy Martinez .10
584 Hosken Powell .10
585 Rollie Fingers 1.00
586 Rollie Fingersr/IA .15
587 Tim Lollar .10
588 Dale Berra .10
589 Dave Stapleton .10
590 Al Oliver .10
591 Al Oliverr/IA .10
592 Craig Swan .10
593 Billy Smith .10
594 Renie Martin .10
595 Dave Collins .10
596 Damaso Garcia .10
597 Wayne Nordhagen .10
598 Bob Galasso .10
599 White Sox Future Stars (Jay Loviglio, Reggie Patterson, Leo Sutherland) .10
600 Dave Winfield 1.50
601 Sid Monge .10
602 Freddie Patek .10
603 Rich Hebner .10
604 Orlando Sanchez .10
605 Steve Rogers .10
606 Blue Jays Batting & Pitching Ldrs. (John Mayberry, Dave Stieb) .10
607 Leon Durham .10
608 Jerry Royster .10
609 Rick Sutcliffe .10
610 Rickey Henderson 1.50
611 Joe Niekro .10
612 Gary Ward .10
613 Jim Gantner .10
614 Juan Eichelberger .10
615 Bob Boone .10
616 Bob Boone/IA .10
617 Scott McGregor .10
618 Tim Foli .10
619 Bill Campbell .10
620 Ken Griffey .10
621 Ken Griffey/IA .10
622 Dennis Lamp .10
623 Mets Future Stars (Ron Gardenhire, Terry Leach **RC**, Tim Leary **RC**) .20
624 Fergie Jenkins 1.00
625 Hal McRae .10
626 Randy Jones .10
627 Enos Cabell .10
628 Bill Travers .10
629 Johnny Wockenfuss .10
630 Joe Charboneau .10
631 Gene Tenace .10
632 Bryan Clark .10
633 Mitchell Page .10
634 Checklist 529-660 .10
635 Ron Davis .10
636 Phillies Batting & Pitching Ldrs. (Steve Carlton, Pete Rose) .50
637 Rick Camp .10
638 John Milner .10
639 Ken Kravec .10
640 Cesar Cedeno .10
641 Steve Mura .10
642 Mike Scioscia .10
643 Pete Vuckovich .10
644 John Castino .10
645 Frank White .10
646 Frank White/IA .10
647 Warren Brusstar .10
648 Jose Morales .10
649 Ken Clay .10
650 Carl Yastrzemski 1.50
651 Carl Yastrzemski/IA .65
652 Steve Nicosia .10
653 Angels Future Stars (Tom Brunansky **RC**, Luis Sanchez **RC**, Daryl Sconiers **RC**) .40
654 Jim Morrison .10
655 Joel Youngblood .10
656 Eddie Whitson .10
657 Tom Poquette .10
658 Tito Landrum .10
659 Fred Martinez .10
660 Dave Concepcion .10
661 Dave Concepcion/IA .10
662 Luis Salazar .10
663 Hector Cruz .10
664 Dan Spillner .10
665 Jim Clancy .10
666 Tigers Batting & Pitching Ldrs. (Steve Kemp, Dan Petry) .10
667 Jeff Reardon .15
668 Dale Murphy .75
669 Larry Milbourne .10
670 Steve Kemp .10
671 Mike Davis .10
672 Bob Knepper .10
673 Keith Drumright .10
674 Dave Goltz .10
675 Cecil Cooper .10
676 Sal Butera .10
677 Alfredo Griffin .10
678 Tom Paciorek .10
679 Sammy Stewart .10
680 Gary Matthews .10
681 Dodgers Future Stars (Mike Marshall **RC**, Ron Roenicke **RC**, Steve Sax **RC**) .75
682 Jesse Jefferson .10
683 Phil Garner .10
684 Harold Baines .05
685 Bert Blyleven .10
686 Gary Allenson .10
687 Greg Minton .10
688 Leon Roberts .10
689 Lary Sorensen .10
690 Dave Kingman .10
691 Dan Schatzeder .10
692 Wayne Gross .10
693 Cesar Geronimo .10
694 Dave Wehrmeister .10
695 Warren Cromartie .10
696 Pirates Batting & Pitching Ldrs. (Bill Madlock, Buddy Solomon) .10
697 John Montefusco .10
698 Tony Scott .10
699 Dick Tidrow .10
700 George Foster .10
701 George Foster/IA .10
702 Steve Renko .10
703 Brewers Batting & Pitching Ldrs. (Cecil Cooper, Pete Vuckovich) .10
704 Mickey Rivers .10
705 Mickey Rivers/IA .10
706 Barry Foote .10
707 Mark Bomback .10
708 Gene Richards .10
709 Don Money .10
710 Jerry Reuss .10
711 Mariners Future Stars (Dave Edler **RC**, Dave Henderson **RC**, Reggie Walton **RC**) .25
712 Denny Martinez .10
713 Del Unser .10
714 Jerry Koosman .10
715 Willie Stargell 1.50
716 Willie Stargell/IA .30
717 Rick Miller .10
718 Charlie Hough .10
719 Jerry Narron .10
720 Greg Luzinski .10
721 Greg Luzinski/IA .10
722 Jerry Martin .10
723 Junior Kennedy .10
724 Dave Rosello .10
725 Amos Otis .10
726 Amos Otis/IA .10
727 Sixto Lezcano .10
728 Aurelio Lopez .10
729 Jim Spencer .10
730 Gary Carter 1.50
731 Padres Future Stars (Mike Armstrong, Doug Gwosdz, Fred Kuhaulua) .10
732 Mike Lum .10
733 Larry McWilliams .10
734 Mike Ivie .10
735 Rudy May .10
736 Jerry Turner .10
737 Reggie Cleveland .10
738 Dave Engle .10
739 Joey McLaughlin .10
740 Dave Lopes .10
741 Dave Lopes/IA .10
742 Dick Drago .10
743 John Stearns .10
744 Mike Witt **RC** .25
745 Bake McBride .10
746 Andre Thornton .10
747 John Lowenstein .10
748 Marc Hill .10
749 Bob Shirley .10
750 Jim Rice .20
751 Rick Honeycutt .10
752 Lee Lacy .10
753 Tom Brookens .10
754 Joe Morgan 1.50
755 Joe Morgan/IA .25
756 Reds Batting & Pitching Ldrs. (Ken Griffey, Tom Seaver) .25
757 Tom Underwood .10
758 Claudell Washington .10
759 Paul Splittorff .10
760 Bill Buckner .10
761 Dave Smith .10
762 Mike Phillips .10
763 Tom Hume .10
764 Steve Swisher .10
765 Gorman Thomas .10
766 Twins Future Stars (Lenny Faedo **RC**, Kent Hrbek **RC**, Tim Laudner **RC**) 2.00
767 Roy Smalley .10
768 Jerry Garvin .10
769 Richie Zisk .10
770 Rich Gossage .10
771 Rich Gossage/IA .10
772 Bert Campaneris .10
773 John Denny .10
774 Jay Johnstone .10
775 Bob Forsch .10
776 Mark Belanger .10
777 Tom Griffin .10
778 Kevin Hickey .10
779 Grant Jackson .10
780 Pete Rose 3.50
781 Pete Rose/IA 2.00
782 Frank Taveras .10
783 Greg Harris **RC** .10
784 Milt Wilcox .10
785 Dan Driessen .10
786 Red Sox Batting & Pitching Ldrs. (Carney Lansford, Mike Torrez) .10
787 Fred Stanley .10
788 Woodie Fryman .10
789 Checklist 661-792 .10
790 Larry Gura .10
791 Bobby Brown .10
792 Frank Tanana .10

"Blackless"

Whether through faulty pre-production work or the simple fact that the black ink may have run dry during printing, exactly half of the 1982 Topps cards can be found in a "blackless" version. All cards on the set's A, B and C press sheets can be found blackless. On regular player's cards the lack of black printing is most obvious in the absence of the facsimile autograph on front. The thin black pinstripe around the player photo is also missing on those cards. On cards in which the position was supposed to be printed in black, it will be missing on these variations. All-Star cards affected by this error will be missing the player's name. It is estimated fewer than 100 of each "blackless" card were released. Originally cards from the A and B sheets were found in metro New York, while the C cards turned up most often in the Midwest. Cards from the C sheet are much scarcer than those from the A and B sheets, although limited collector demand for full sets has kept prices in relative parity.

		NM/M
Complete Set (396):		5,500
Common Player:		12.50
8	Rich Dauer	12.50
9	Ron Guidry	20.00
10	Ron Guidry/IA	12.50
11	Gary Alexander	12.50
12	Moose Haas	12.50
13	Lamar Johnson	12.50
14	Steve Howe	12.50
17	Darrell Evans	12.50
18	Fernando Arroyo	12.50
20	Garry Maddox	12.50
24	Dave Frost	12.50
26	Jorge Orta	12.50
28	John Urrea	12.50
31	Tom Seaver/IA	22.50
35	Willie Aikens	12.50
37	Dan Graham	12.50
38	Charlie Lea	12.50
39	Lou Whitaker	12.50
40	Dave Parker	12.50
42	Rick Sofield	12.50
48	Bobby Castillo	12.50
49	Alvis Woods	12.50
50	Buddy Bell	12.50
52	Larry Andersen	12.50
54	Ron Hassey	12.50
55	Rick Burleson	12.50
60	Tony Armas	12.50
64	Lynn Jones	12.50
65	Terry Kennedy	12.50
67	Rich Gale	12.50
68	Roy Howell	12.50
70	Tim Raines	12.50
71	Roy Lee Jackson	12.50
72	Rick Auerbach	12.50
73	Buddy Solomon	12.50
74	Bob Clark	12.50
77	Miguel Dilone	12.50
78	George Medich	12.50
80	Jim Palmer	40.00
81	Jim Palmer/IA	15.00
84	Rennie Stennett	12.50
87	Matt Keough	12.50
88	Biff Pocoroba	12.50
89	Steve Henderson	12.50
90	Nolan Ryan	425.00
91	Carney Lansford	12.50
92	Brad Havens	12.50
94	Andy Hassler	12.50
95	Ozzie Smith	60.00
98	Terry Bulling	12.50
99	Barry Bonnell	12.50
100	Mike Schmidt	185.00
101	Mike Schmidt/IA	130.00
105	Kirk Gibson	12.50
107	Wayne Krenchicki	12.50
109	Dave Revering	12.50
110	Carlton Fisk	45.00
112	Billy Sample	12.50
113	Steve McCatty	12.50
114	Ken Landreaux	12.50
115	Gaylord Perry	35.00
116	Jim Wohlford	12.50
117	Rawly Eastwick	12.50
119	Joe Pittman	12.50
120	Gary Lucas	12.50
122	Jamie Easterley	12.50
123	Danny Goodwin	12.50
125	Danny Ainge	22.50
127	Lonnie Smith	12.50
128	Frank Pastore	12.50
130	Julio Cruz	12.50
131	Stan Bahnsen	12.50
132	Lee May	12.50
134	Dan Ford	12.50
135	Andy Rincon	12.50
136	Lenn Sakata	12.50
137	George Cappuzzello	12.50
138	Tony Pena	12.50
140	Ron LeFlore	12.50
143	Mookie Wilson	12.50
147	Denny Walling	12.50
150	Ted Simmons	12.50
155	Otto Velez	12.50
157	Steve Crawford	12.50
158	Brian Downing	12.50

159	Larry Biittner	12.50
160	Luis Tiant	12.50
170	Jim Bibby	12.50
172	Bill Gullickson	12.50
173	Jamie Quirk	12.50
174	Dave Ford	12.50
175	Jerry Mumphrey	12.50
177	John Ellis	12.50
178	Dyar Miller	12.50
179	Steve Garvey	30.00
181	Silvio Martinez	12.50
183	Mike Proly	12.50
185	Phil Niekro	35.00
189	Glenn Hoffman	12.50
190	J.R. Richard	12.50
192	Broderick Perkins	12.50
198	Chris Speier	12.50
200	George Brett	150.00
201	George Brett/IA	55.00
204	Gary Roenicke	12.50
209	Gary Lavelle	12.50
210	Keith Hernandez	12.50
211	Dan Petry	12.50
212	Mario Mendoza	12.50
215	Mike Krukow	12.50
220	Manny Trillo	12.50
221	Jim Slaton	12.50
222	Butch Wynegar	12.50
223	Lloyd Moseby	12.50
224	Bruce Bochte	12.50
225	Mike Torrez	12.50
228	Sam Mejias	12.50
230	Willie Wilson	12.50
232	Terry Crowley	12.50
233	Duane Kuiper	12.50
234	Ron Hodges	12.50
235	Mike Easler	12.50
237	Rusty Kuntz	12.50
238	Kevin Saucier	12.50
239	Jon Matlack	12.50
240	Bucky Dent	12.50
241	Bucky Dent/IA	12.50
245	Ken Reitz	12.50
247	Pedro Guerrero	12.50
251	Fred Lynn	12.50
255	Tony Perez	35.00
256	Tony Perez/IA	12.50
257	Larry Harlow	12.50
258	Bo Diaz	12.50
259	Rodney Scott	12.50
260	Bruce Sutter	35.00
262	Doug Bair	12.50
264	Dan Quisenberry	12.50
265	Al Bumbry	12.50
267	Kurt Bevacqua	12.50
270	Rusty Staub	15.00
272	Bump Wills	12.50
275	Bob Watson	12.50
278	John Littlefield	12.50
280	Ben Oglivie	12.50
281	John Verhoeven	12.50
282	Ken Macha	12.50
283	Brian Allard	12.50
285	Sparky Lyle	12.50
287	Alan Bannister	12.50
288	Garry Templeton	12.50
289	Bob Stanley	12.50
290	Ken Singleton	12.50
297	Clint Hurdle	12.50
299	Steve Trout	12.50
300	Reggie Jackson	65.00
302	Doug Flynn	12.50
305	Don Sutton	30.00
307	Randy Bass	12.50
308	Charlie Moore	12.50
310	Mike Hargrove	12.50
312	Lenny Randle	12.50
313	John Harris	12.50
315	Burt Hooton	12.50
317	Dick Ruthven	12.50
323	Bill Lee	12.50
324	Steve Dillard	12.50
325	Jose Cruz	12.50
328	Ed Farmer	12.50
329	U.L. Washington	12.50
330	Rick Wise	12.50
332	Don Robinson	12.50
334	Aurelio Rodriguez	12.50
335	Jim Sundberg	12.50
339	Mike Schmidt/AS	130.00
340	Dave Concepcion/AS	12.50
341	Andre Dawson/AS	15.00
342	George Foster/AS	12.50
343	Dave Parker/AS	12.50
344	Gary Carter/AS	15.00
345	Fernando Valenzuela/AS	12.50
349	George Frazier	12.50
352	Dick Davis	12.50
354	Roberto Ramos	12.50
355	Dwight Evans	12.50
357	Butch Hobson	12.50
359	Jim Dwyer	12.50
360	Len Barker	12.50
363	Bob Molinaro	12.50
365	Bill Madlock	12.50
370	Mike Norris	12.50
380	Dave Stieb	12.50
382	Joe Simpson	12.50
385	Ken Forsch	12.50
387	Tom Veryzer	12.50
388	Joe Rudi	12.50
390	Eddie Murray	45.00
397	Ken Brett	12.50
398	Mike Squires	12.50
399	Pat Zachry	12.50
400	Johnny Bench	50.00
406	Al Holland	12.50
409	Don Cooper	12.50
412	Luis Leal	12.50
413	Dan Meyer	12.50
415	Don Baylor	12.50
417	Pat Kelly	12.50
419	Steve Stone	12.50
420	George Hendrick	12.50
421	Mark Clear	12.50
422	Cliff Johnson	12.50
423	Stan Papi	12.50
424	Bruce Benedict	12.50
425	John Candelaria	12.50
430	Vida Blue	12.50
440	Jeff Burroughs	12.50
442	Bruce Kison	12.50
443	Mark Wagner	12.50
445	Larry Parrish	12.50
446	Wayne Garland	12.50
448	Darrell Porter/IA	12.50
450	Jack Morris	12.50
451	Ed Miller	12.50
459	Bruce Berenyi	12.50
460	Jack Clark	12.50
461	Rich Dotson	12.50
462	Dave Chalk	12.50
463	Jim Kern	12.50
464	Juan Bonilla	12.50
465	Lee Mazzilli	12.50
467	Mickey Hatcher	12.50
468	Floyd Bannister	12.50
472	Oscar Gamble	12.50
475	Alan Trammell	12.50
476	Brian Kingman	12.50
477	Steve Yeager	12.50
480	Steve Carlton	35.00
481	Steve Carlton/IA	15.00
484	Ivan DeJesus	12.50
490	Dennis Eckersley	35.00
492	Joe Price	12.50
493	Chet Lemon	12.50
494	Hubie Brooks	12.50
495	Dennis Leonard	12.50
496	Johnny Grubb	12.50
498	Dave Bergman	12.50
499	Paul Mirabella	12.50
500	Rod Carew	45.00
501	Rod Carew/IA	15.00
503	Julio Gonzalez	12.50
507	Terry Harper	12.50
510	Fernando Valenzuela	17.50
511	Ruppert Jones	12.50
512	Jerry Dybzinski	12.50
515	Larry Bowa	12.50
518	Garth Iorg	12.50
519	Glenn Adams	12.50
520	Mike Flanagan	12.50
521	Bill Almon	12.50
523	Gary Gray	12.50
524	Tom Hausman	12.50
532	Toby Harrah	12.50
534	Dave McKay	12.50
536	Rafael Ramirez	12.50
540	Andre Dawson	30.00
541	Barry Evans	12.50
542	Ned Yost	12.50
543	Bill Robinson	12.50
547	Rod Carew/AS	25.00
548	Willie Randolph/AS	12.50
549	George Brett/AS	150.00
550	Bucky Dent/AS	15.00
551	Reggie Jackson/AS	30.00
552	Ken Singleton/AS	12.50
553	Dave Winfield/AS	25.00
554	Carlton Fisk/AS	25.00
555	Scott McGregor/AS	12.50
556	Jack Morris/AS	12.50
557	Rich Gossage/AS	12.50
560	Doug Corbett	12.50
563	Ross Baumgarten	12.50
564	Doug DeCinces	12.50
565	Jackson Todd	12.50
567	Bob Babcock	12.50
568	Joe Pettini	12.50
569	Willie Randolph	12.50
573	Rick Waits	12.50
574	Mike Ramsey	12.50
575	Al Cowens	12.50
579	Rick Mahler	12.50
580	Bobby Bonds	12.50
581	Ron Reed	12.50
582	Luis Pujols	12.50
585	Rollie Fingers	35.00
588	Dale Berra	12.50
590	Al Oliver	12.50
594	Renie Martin	12.50
600	Dave Winfield	50.00
601	Sid Monge	12.50
602	Freddie Patek	12.50
603	Richie Hebner	12.50
608	Jerry Royster	12.50
610	Rickey Henderson	150.00
611	Joe Niekro	12.50
612	Gary Ward	12.50
613	Jim Gantner	12.50
615	Bob Boone	12.50
616	Bob Boone/IA	12.50
622	Dennis Lamp	12.50
624	Fergie Jenkins	35.00
625	Hal McRae	12.50
626	Randy Jones	12.50
627	Enos Cabell	12.50
629	Johnny Wockenfuss	12.50
630	Joe Charboneau	25.00
632	Bryan Clark	12.50
635	Ron Davis	12.50
637	Rick Camp	12.50
640	Cesar Cedeno	12.50
645	Frank White	12.50
646	Frank White/IA	12.50
648	Jose Morales	12.50
649	Ken Clay	12.50
654	Jim Morrison	12.50
655	Joel Youngblood	12.50
656	Eddie Whitson	12.50
661	Dave Concepcion/IA	12.50
663	Hector Cruz	12.50
664	Dan Spillner	12.50
665	Jim Clancy	12.50
668	Dale Murphy	35.00
669	Larry Milbourne	12.50
670	Steve Kemp	12.50
672	Bob Knepper	12.50
675	Cecil Cooper	12.50
677	Alfredo Griffin	12.50
678	Tom Paciorek	12.50
684	Harold Baines	12.50
685	Bert Blyleven	12.50
686	Gary Allenson	12.50
690	Dave Kingman	12.50
691	Dan Schatzeder	12.50
694	Dave Wehrmeister	12.50
695	Warren Cromartie	12.50
700	George Foster	12.50
702	Steve Renko	12.50
704	Mickey Rivers	12.50
705	Mickey Rivers/IA	12.50
706	Barry Foote	12.50
707	Mark Bomback	12.50
708	Gene Richards	12.50
710	Jerry Reuss	12.50
713	Del Unser	12.50
715	Willie Stargell	45.00
716	Willie Stargell/IA	15.00
718	Charlie Hough	12.50
720	Greg Luzinski	12.50
721	Greg Luzinski/IA	12.50
722	Jerry Martin	12.50
724	Dave Rosello	12.50
725	Amos Otis	12.50
730	Gary Carter	45.00
735	Rudy May	12.50
737	Reggie Cleveland	12.50
738	Dave Engle	12.50
739	Joey McLaughlin	12.50
740	Dave Lopes	12.50
741	Dave Lopes/IA	12.50
742	Dick Drago	12.50
743	John Stearns	12.50
745	Bake McBride	12.50
747	John Lowenstein	12.50
748	Marc Hill	12.50
751	Rick Honeycutt	12.50
753	Tom Brookens	12.50
754	Joe Morgan	45.00
757	Tom Underwood	12.50
760	Bill Buckner	12.50
761	Dave Smith	12.50
764	Steve Swisher	12.50
765	Gorman Thomas	12.50
767	Roy Smalley	12.50
768	Jerry Garvin	12.50
769	Richie Zisk	12.50
771	Rich Gossage/IA	12.50
775	Bob Forsch	12.50
776	Mark Belanger	12.50
777	Tom Griffin	12.50
778	Kevin Hickey	12.50
780	Pete Rose	225.00
781	Pete Rose/IA	100.00
782	Frank Taveras	12.50
784	Milt Wilcox	12.50
788	Woodie Fryman	12.50
790	Larry Gura	12.50
792	Frank Tanana	12.50

Traded

Topps released its second straight 132-card Traded set in September of 1982. Again, the 2-1/2" x 3-1/2" cards feature not only players who had been traded during the season, but also promising rookies who were given their first individual cards. The cards follow the basic design of the regular issues, but have their backs printed in red rather than the regular-issue green. As in 1981, the cards were not available in normal retail outlets and could only be purchased through regular baseball card dealers. Unlike the previous year, the cards are numbered 1-132 with the letter "T" following the number.

		NM/M
Complete Set (132):		175.00
Common Player:		.10
1T	Doyle Alexander	.10
2T	Jesse Barfield	.10
3T	Ross Baumgarten	.10
4T	Steve Bedrosian	.10
5T	Mark Belanger	.10
6T	Kurt Bevacqua	.10
7T	Tim Blackwell	.10
8T	Vida Blue	.10
9T	Bob Boone	.30
10T	Larry Bowa	.10
11T	Dan Briggs	.10
12T	Bobby Brown	.10
13T	Tom Brunansky	.10
14T	Jeff Burroughs	.10
15T	Enos Cabell	.10
16T	Bill Campbell	.10
17T	Bobby Castillo	.10
18T	Bill Caudill	.10
19T	Cesar Cedeno	.10
20T	Dave Collins	.10
21T	Doug Corbett	.10
22T	Al Cowens	.10
23T	Chili Davis	.50
24T	Dick Davis	.10
25T	Ron Davis	.10
26T	Doug DeCinces	.10
27T	Ivan DeJesus	.10
28T	Bob Dernier	.10
29T	Bo Diaz	.10
30T	Roger Erickson	.10
31T	Jim Essian	.10
32T	Ed Farmer	.10
33T	Doug Flynn	.10
34T	Tim Foli	.10
35T	Dan Ford	.10
36T	George Foster	.10
37T	Dave Frost	.10
38T	Rich Gale	.10
39T	Ron Gardenhire	.10
40T	Ken Griffey	.10
41T	Greg Harris	.10
42T	Von Hayes	.10
43T	Larry Herndon	.10
44T	Kent Hrbek	2.00
45T	Mike Ivie	.10
46T	Grant Jackson	.10
47T	Reggie Jackson	5.00
48T	Ron Jackson	.10
49T	Fergie Jenkins	2.00
50T	Lamar Johnson	.10
51T	Randy Johnson	.10
52T	Jay Johnstone	.10
53T	Mick Kelleher	.10
54T	Steve Kemp	.10
55T	Junior Kennedy	.10
56T	Jim Kern	.10
57T	Ray Knight	.10
58T	Wayne Krenchicki	.10
59T	Mike Krukow	.10
60T	Duane Kuiper	.10
61T	Mike LaCoss	.10
62T	Chet Lemon	.10
63T	Sixto Lezcano	.10
64T	Dave Lopes	.10
65T	Jerry Martin	.10
66T	Renie Martin	.10
67T	John Mayberry	.10
68T	Lee Mazzilli	.10
69T	Bake McBride	.10
70T	Dan Meyer	.10
71T	Larry Milbourne	.10
72T	Eddie Milner **RC**	.10
73T	Sid Monge	.10
74T	John Montefusco	.10
75T	Jose Morales	.10
76T	Keith Moreland	.10
77T	Jim Morrison	.10
78T	Rance Mulliniks	.10
79T	Steve Mura	.10
80T	Gene Nelson	.10
81T	Joe Nolan	.10
82T	Dickie Noles	.10
83T	Al Oliver	.10
84T	Jorge Orta	.10
85T	Tom Paciorek	.10
86T	Larry Parrish	.10
87T	Jack Perconte	.10
88T	Gaylord Perry	2.00
89T	Rob Picciolo	.10
90T	Joe Pittman	.10
91T	Hosken Powell	.10
92T	Mike Proly	.10
93T	Greg Pryor	.10
94T	Charlie Puleo **RC**	.10
95T	Shane Rawley	.10
96T	Johnny Ray	.10
97T	Dave Revering	.10
98T	Cal Ripken, Jr.	140.00
99T	Allen Ripley	.10
100T	Bill Robinson	.10
101T	Aurelio Rodriguez	.10
102T	Joe Rudi	.10
103T	Steve Sax	.50
104T	Dan Schatzeder	.10
105T	Bob Shirley	.10
106T	Eric Show **RC**	.10
107T	Roy Smalley	.10
108T	Lonnie Smith	.10
109T	Ozzie Smith	20.00
110T	Reggie Smith	.10
111T	Lary Sorensen	.10
112T	Elias Sosa	.10
113T	Mike Stanton	.10
114T	Steve Stroughter	.10
115T	Champ Summers	.10
116T	Rick Sutcliffe	.10
117T	Frank Tanana	.10
118T	Frank Taveras	.10
119T	Garry Templeton	.10
120T	Alex Trevino	.10
121T	Jerry Turner	.10
122T	Ed Vande Berg **RC**	.10
123T	Tom Veryzer	.10
124T	Ron Washington	.10
125T	Bob Watson	.10
126T	Dennis Werth	.10
127T	Eddie Whitson	.10
128T	Rob Wilfong	.10
129T	Bump Wills	.10
130T	Gary Woods	.10
131T	Butch Wynegar	.10
132T	Checklist 1-132	.10

Team Leaders Sheet

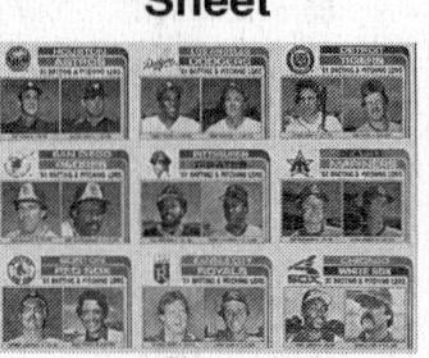

Available via a special mail-in offer, this 10-1/2" x 23" uncut sheet contained the 26 team batting and pitching leaders cards plus a card offering Topps collectors boxes. The team leader cards are identical to those issued in packs.

	NM/M
Team Leaders Sheet	10.00

Insert Stickers

85
WILLIE STARGELL
1st Base
ALBUMS COMING SOON!
SAVE THIS STICKER . . . and place it in your new 1982 Topps Baseball Sticker Album. Albums and ALL stickers are sold where Topps Baseball cards are available.
IT'S Topps FOR SPORTS
© 1982 TOPPS CHEWING GUM, INC.

This 48-player set is actually an abbreviated version of the regular 1982 Topps sticker set with different backs. Used to promote the 1982 sticker set, Topps inserted these stickers in its baseball card wax packs. They are identical to the regular 1982 stickers, except for the backs, which advertise that the Topps sticker album will be "Coming Soon." The 48 stickers retain the same numbers used in the regular sticker set, resulting in the smaller set being skip-numbered.

		NM/M
Complete Set (48):		3.00
Common Player:		.05
17	Chris Chambliss	.05
21	Bruce Benedict	.05
25	Leon Durham	.05
29	Bill Buckner	.05
33	Dave Collins	.05
37	Dave Concepcion	.05
41	Nolan Ryan	1.00
45	Bob Knepper	.05
49	Ken Landreaux	.05
53	Burt Hooton	.05
57	Andre Dawson	.15
61	Gary Carter	.25
65	Joel Youngblood	.05
69	Ellis Valentine	.05
73	Garry Maddox	.05
77	Bob Boone	.05
81	Omar Moreno	.05
85	Willie Stargell	.25
89	Ken Oberkfell	.05
93	Darrell Porter	.05
97	Juan Eichelberger	.05
101	Luis Salazar	.05
105	Enos Cabell	.05
109	Larry Herndon	.05
143	Scott McGregor	.05
148	Mike Flanagan	.05
151	Mike Torrez	.05
156	Carney Lansford	.05
161	Fred Lynn	.05
166	Rich Dotson	.05
171	Tony Bernazard	.05
176	Bo Diaz	.05
181	Alan Trammell	.05
186	Milt Wilcox	.05
191	Dennis Leonard	.05
196	Willie Aikens	.05
201	Ted Simmons	.05
206	Hosken Powell	.05
211	Roger Erickson	.05
215	Graig Nettles	.05
216	Reggie Jackson	.45
221	Rickey Henderson	.25
226	Cliff Johnson	.05
231	Jeff Burroughs	.05
236	Tom Paciorek	.05
241	Pat Putnam	.05
246	Lloyd Moseby	.05
251	Barry Bonnell	.05

Stickers

The 1982 Topps sticker set is complete at 260 stickers and includes another series of "foil" All-Stars. The stickers measure 1-15/16" x 2-9/16" and feature full-color photos surrounded by a red border for American League players or a blue border for National League players. They are numbered on both the front and back and were designed to be mounted in a special album.

		NM/M
Complete Set (260):		7.50
Common Player:		.05
Sticker Album:		2.00
Wax Pack (5):		.25
Wax Box (100):		15.00
1	Bill Madlock	.05
2	Carney Lansford	.05
3	Mike Schmidt	.30
4	Tony Armas, Dwight Evans, Bobby Grich, Eddie Murray	.05
5	Mike Schmidt	.30
6	Eddie Murray	.25
7	Tim Raines	.05
8	Rickey Henderson	.25
9	Tom Seaver	.25
10	Denny Martinez, Steve McCatty, Jack Morris, Pete Vuckovich	.05
11	Fernando Valenzuela	.05
12	Len Barker	.05
13	Nolan Ryan	.50
14	Steve McCatty	.05
15	Bruce Sutter	.20
16	Rollie Fingers	.20
17	Chris Chambliss	.05
18	Bob Horner	.05
19	Dale Murphy	.15
20	Phil Niekro	.20
21	Bruce Benedict	.05
22	Claudell Washington	.05
23	Glenn Hubbard	.05
24	Rick Camp	.05
25	Leon Durham	.05
26	Ken Reitz	.05
27	Dick Tidrow	.05
28	Tim Blackwell	.05
29	Bill Buckner	.05
30	Steve Henderson	.05
31	Mike Krukow	.05
32	Ivan DeJesus	.05
33	Dave Collins	.05
34	Ron Oester	.05
35	Johnny Bench	.25
36	Tom Seaver	.25
37	Dave Concepcion	.05
38	Ken Griffey	.05
39	Ray Knight	.05
40	George Foster	.05
41	Nolan Ryan	.50
42	Terry Puhl	.05
43	Art Howe	.05
44	Jose Cruz	.05
45	Bob Knepper	.05
46	Craig Reynolds	.05

47 Cesar Cedeno .05
48 Alan Ashby .05
49 Ken Landreaux .05
50 Fernando Valenzuela .05
51 Ron Cey .05
52 Dusty Baker .05
53 Burt Hooton .05
54 Steve Garvey .15
55 Pedro Guerrero .05
56 Jerry Reuss .05
57 Andre Dawson .20
58 Chris Speier .05
59 Steve Rogers .05
60 Warren Cromartie .05
61 Gary Carter .25
62 Tim Raines .05
63 Scott Sanderson .05
64 Larry Parrish .05
65 Joel Youngblood .05
66 Neil Allen .05
67 Lee Mazzilli .05
68 Hubie Brooks .05
69 Ellis Valentine .05
70 Doug Flynn .05
71 Pat Zachry .05
72 Dave Kingman .05
73 Garry Maddox .05
74 Mike Schmidt .30
75 Steve Carlton .25
76 Manny Trillo .05
77 Bob Boone .05
78 Pete Rose .40
79 Gary Matthews .05
80 Larry Bowa .05
81 Omar Moreno .05
82 Rick Rhoden .05
83 Bill Madlock .05
84 Mike Easler .05
85 Willie Stargell .25
86 Jim Bibby .05
87 Dave Parker .05
88 Tim Foli .05
89 Ken Oberkfell .05
90 Bob Forsch .05
91 George Hendrick .05
92 Keith Hernandez .05
93 Darrell Porter .05
94 Bruce Sutter .20
95 Sixto Lezcano .05
96 Garry Templeton .05
97 Juan Eichelberger .05
98 Broderick Perkins .05
99 Ruppert Jones .05
100 Terry Kennedy .05
101 Luis Salazar .05
102 Gary Lucas .05
103 Gene Richards .05
104 Ozzie Smith .30
105 Enos Cabell .05
106 Jack Clark .05
107 Greg Minton .05
108 Johnnie LeMaster .05
109 Larry Herndon .05
110 Milt May .05
111 Vida Blue .05
112 Darrell Evans .05
113 Len Barker .05
114 Julio Cruz .05
115 Billy Martin .05
116 Tim Raines .05
117 Pete Rose .40
118 Bill Stein .05
119 Fernando Valenzuela .05
120 Carl Yastrzemski .25
121 Pete Rose .40
122 Manny Trillo .05
123 Mike Schmidt .30
124 Dave Concepcion .05
125 Andre Dawson .20
126 George Foster .05
127 Dave Parker .05
128 Gary Carter .25
129 Steve Carlton .25
130 Bruce Sutter .20
131 Rod Carew .25
132 Jerry Remy .05
133 George Brett .30
134 Rick Burleson .05
135 Dwight Evans .05
136 Ken Singleton .05
137 Dave Winfield .25
138 Carlton Fisk .25
139 Jack Morris .05
140 Rich Gossage .05
141 Al Bumbry .05
142 Doug DeCinces .05
143 Scott McGregor .05
144 Ken Singleton .05
145 Eddie Murray .25
146 Jim Palmer .20
147 Rich Dauer .05
148 Mike Flanagan .05
149 Jerry Remy .05
150 Jim Rice .15
151 Mike Torrez .05
152 Tony Perez .25
153 Dwight Evans .05
154 Mark Clear .05
155 Carl Yastrzemski .25
156 Carney Lansford .05
157 Rick Burleson .05
158 Don Baylor .10
159 Ken Forsch .05
160 Rod Carew .25
161 Fred Lynn .05
162 Bob Grich .05
163 Dan Ford .05
164 Butch Hobson .05
165 Greg Luzinski .05
166 Rich Dotson .05
167 Billy Almon .05
168 Chet Lemon .05
169 Steve Trout .05
170 Carlton Fisk .25
171 Tony Bernazard .05
172 Ron LeFlore .05
173 Bert Blyleven .05
174 Andre Thornton .05
175 Jorge Orta .05
176 Bo Diaz .05
177 Toby Harrah .05
178 Len Barker .05
179 Rick Manning .05
180 Mike Hargrove .05
181 Alan Trammell .05
182 Al Cowens .05
183 Jack Morris .05
184 Kirk Gibson .05
185 Steve Kemp .05
186 Milt Wilcox .05
187 Lou Whitaker .05
188 Lance Parrish .05
189 Willie Wilson .05
190 George Brett .30
191 Dennis Leonard .05
192 John Wathan .05
193 Frank White .05
194 Amos Otis .05
195 Larry Gura .05
196 Willie Aikens .05
197 Ben Oglivie .05
198 Rollie Fingers .20
199 Cecil Cooper .05
200 Paul Molitor .20
201 Ted Simmons .05
202 Pete Vuckovich .05
203 Robin Yount .25
204 Gorman Thomas .05
205 Rob Wilfong .05
206 Hosken Powell .05
207 Roy Smalley .05
208 Butch Wynegar .05
209 John Castino .05
210 Doug Corbett .05
211 Roger Erickson .05
212 Mickey Hatcher .05
213 Dave Winfield .25
214 Tommy John .10
215 Graig Nettles .05
216 Reggie Jackson .25
217 Rich Gossage .05
218 Rick Cerone .05
219 Willie Randolph .05
220 Jerry Mumphrey .05
221 Rickey Henderson .25
222 Mike Norris .05
223 Jim Spencer .05
224 Tony Armas .05
225 Matt Keough .05
226 Cliff Johnson .05
227 Dwayne Murphy .05
228 Steve McCatty .05
229 Richie Zisk .05
230 Lenny Randle .05
231 Jeff Burroughs .05
232 Bruce Bochte .05
233 Gary Gray .05
234 Floyd Bannister .05
235 Julio Cruz .05
236 Tom Paciorek .05
237 Danny Darwin .05
238 Buddy Bell .05
239 Al Oliver .05
240 Jim Sundberg .05
241 Pat Putnam .05
242 Steve Comer .05
243 Mickey Rivers .05
244 Bump Wills .05
245 Damaso Garcia .05
246 Lloyd Moseby .05
247 Ernie Whitt .05
248 John Mayberry .05
249 Otto Velez .05
250 Dave Stieb .05
251 Barry Bonnell .05
252 Alfredo Griffin .05
253 1981 N.L. Championship (Gary Carter) .10
254 1981 A.L. Championship (Mike Heath, Larry Milbourne) .05
255 1981 World Champions (Los Angeles Dodgers Team) .05
256 1981 World Champions (Los Angeles Dodgers Team) .05
257 1981 World Series - Game 3 (Fernando Valenzuela) .05
258 1981 World Series - Game 4 (Steve Garvey) .10
259 1981 World Series - Game 5 (Jerry Reuss, Steve Yeager) .05
260 1981 World Series - Game 6 (Pedro Guerrero) .05

1983 Topps

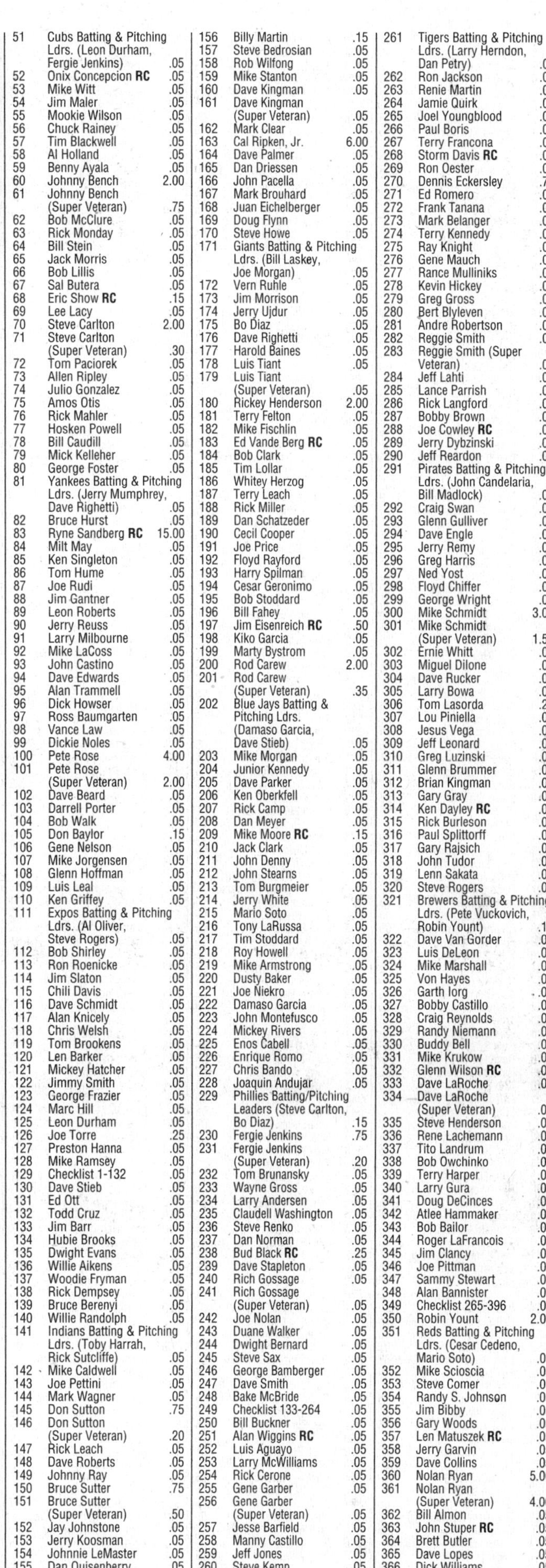

The 1983 Topps set totals 792 cards. Missing among the regular 2-1/2" x 3-1/2" cards are some form of future stars cards, as Topps was saving them for the now-established late season "Traded" set. The 1983 cards carry a large color photo as well as a smaller color photo on the front, quite similar in design to the 1963 set. Team colors frame the card, which, at the bottom, have the player's name, position and team. At the upper right-hand corner is a Topps Logo. The backs are horizontal and include statistics, personal information and 1982 highlights. Specialty cards include record-breaking performances, league leaders, All-Stars, numbered checklists "Team Leaders" and "Super Veteran" cards which are horizontal with a current and first-season picture of the honored player.

	NM/M
Complete Set (792):	60.00
Common Player:	.05
Wax Pack (15):	3.00
Wax Box (36):	110.00
Crimp-End Test Pack (15):	4.00
Crimp-end Test Box (36):	110.00
Cello Pack (28):	5.00
Cello Box (24):	125.00
Rack Pack (51):	7.50
Rack Box (24):	175.00
Vending Box (500):	65.00

1 Tony Armas (Record Breaker) .05
2 Rickey Henderson (Record Breaker) .75
3 Greg Minton (Record Breaker) .05
4 Lance Parrish (Record Breaker) .05
5 Manny Trillo (Record Breaker) .05
6 John Wathan (Record Breaker) .05
7 Gene Richards .05
8 Steve Balboni .05
9 Joey McLaughlin .05
10 Gorman Thomas .05
11 Billy Gardner .05
12 Paul Mirabella .05
13 Larry Herndon .05
14 Frank LaCorte .05
15 Ron Cey .05
16 George Vukovich .05
17 Kent Tekulve .05
18 Kent Tekulve (Super Veteran) .05
19 Oscar Gamble .05
20 Carlton Fisk 2.00
21 Orioles Batting & Pitching Ldrs. (Eddie Murray, Jim Palmer) .25
22 Randy Martz .05
23 Mike Heath .05
24 Steve Mura .05
25 Hal McRae .05
26 Jerry Royster .05
27 Doug Corbett .05
28 Bruce Bochte .05
29 Randy Jones .05
30 Jim Rice .15
31 Bill Gullickson .05
32 Dave Bergman .05
33 Jack O'Connor .05
34 Paul Householder .05
35 Rollie Fingers .75
36 Rollie Fingers (Super Veteran) .15
37 Darrell Johnson .05
38 Tim Flannery .05
39 Terry Puhl .05
40 Fernando Valenzuela .05
41 Jerry Turner .05
42 Dale Murray .05
43 Bob Dernier .05
44 Don Robinson .05
45 John Mayberry .05
46 Richard Dotson .05
47 Dave McKay .05
48 Lary Sorensen .05
49 Willie McGee **RC** 1.50
50 Bob Horner .05
51 Cubs Batting & Pitching Ldrs. (Leon Durham, Fergie Jenkins) .05
52 Onix Concepcion **RC** .05
53 Mike Witt .05
54 Jim Maler .05
55 Mookie Wilson .05
56 Chuck Rainey .05
57 Tim Blackwell .05
58 Al Holland .05
59 Benny Ayala .05
60 Johnny Bench 2.00
61 Johnny Bench (Super Veteran) .75
62 Bob McClure .05
63 Rick Monday .05
64 Bill Stein .05
65 Jack Morris .05
66 Bob Lillis .05
67 Sal Butera .05
68 Eric Show **RC** .15
69 Lee Lacy .05
70 Steve Carlton 2.00
71 Steve Carlton (Super Veteran) .30
72 Tom Paciorek .05
73 Allen Ripley .05
74 Julio Gonzalez .05
75 Amos Otis .05
76 Rick Mahler .05
77 Hosken Powell .05
78 Bill Caudill .05
79 Mick Kelleher .05
80 George Foster .05
81 Yankees Batting & Pitching Ldrs. (Jerry Mumphrey, Dave Righetti) .05
82 Bruce Hurst .05
83 Ryne Sandberg **RC** 15.00
84 Milt May .05
85 Ken Singleton .05
86 Tom Hume .05
87 Joe Rudi .05
88 Jim Gantner .05
89 Leon Roberts .05
90 Jerry Reuss .05
91 Larry Milbourne .05
92 Mike LaCoss .05
93 John Castino .05
94 Dave Edwards .05
95 Alan Trammell .05
96 Dick Howser .05
97 Ross Baumgarten .05
98 Vance Law .05
99 Dickie Noles .05
100 Pete Rose 4.00
101 Pete Rose (Super Veteran) 2.00
102 Dave Beard .05
103 Darrell Porter .05
104 Bob Walk .05
105 Don Baylor .15
106 Gene Nelson .05
107 Mike Jorgensen .05
108 Glenn Hoffman .05
109 Luis Leal .05
110 Ken Griffey .05
111 Expos Batting & Pitching Ldrs. (Al Oliver, Steve Rogers) .05
112 Bob Shirley .05
113 Ron Roenicke .05
114 Jim Slaton .05
115 Chili Davis .05
116 Dave Schmidt .05
117 Alan Knicely .05
118 Chris Welsh .05
119 Tom Brookens .05
120 Len Barker .05
121 Mickey Hatcher .05
122 Jimmy Smith .05
123 George Frazier .05
124 Marc Hill .05
125 Leon Durham .05
126 Joe Torre .25
127 Preston Hanna .05
128 Mike Ramsey .05
129 Checklist 1-132 .05
130 Dave Stieb .05
131 Ed Ott .05
132 Todd Cruz .05
133 Jim Barr .05
134 Hubie Brooks .05
135 Dwight Evans .05
136 Willie Aikens .05
137 Woodie Fryman .05
138 Rick Dempsey .05
139 Bruce Berenyi .05
140 Willie Randolph .05
141 Indians Batting & Pitching Ldrs. (Toby Harrah, Rick Sutcliffe) .05
142 Mike Caldwell .05
143 Joe Pettini .05
144 Mark Wagner .05
145 Don Sutton .75
146 Don Sutton (Super Veteran) .20
147 Rick Leach .05
148 Dave Roberts .05
149 Johnny Ray .05
150 Bruce Sutter .75
151 Bruce Sutter (Super Veteran) .50
152 Jay Johnstone .05
153 Jerry Koosman .05
154 Johnnie LeMaster .05
155 Dan Quisenberry .05
156 Billy Martin .15
157 Steve Bedrosian .05
158 Rob Wilfong .05
159 Mike Stanton .05
160 Dave Kingman .05
161 Dave Kingman (Super Veteran) .05
162 Mark Clear .05
163 Cal Ripken, Jr. 6.00
164 Dave Palmer .05
165 Dan Driessen .05
166 John Pacella .05
167 Mark Brouhard .05
168 Juan Eichelberger .05
169 Doug Flynn .05
170 Steve Howe .05
171 Giants Batting & Pitching Ldrs. (Bill Laskey, Joe Morgan) .05
172 Vern Ruhle .05
173 Jim Morrison .05
174 Jerry Ujdur .05
175 Bo Diaz .05
176 Dave Righetti .05
177 Harold Baines .05
178 Luis Tiant .05
179 Luis Tiant (Super Veteran) .05
180 Rickey Henderson 2.00
181 Terry Felton .05
182 Mike Fischlin .05
183 Ed Vande Berg **RC** .05
184 Bob Clark .05
185 Tim Lollar .05
186 Whitey Herzog .05
187 Terry Leach .05
188 Rick Miller .05
189 Dan Schatzeder .05
190 Cecil Cooper .05
191 Joe Price .05
192 Floyd Rayford .05
193 Harry Spilman .05
194 Cesar Geronimo .05
195 Bob Stoddard .05
196 Bill Fahey .05
197 Jim Eisenreich **RC** .50
198 Kiko Garcia .05
199 Marty Bystrom .05
200 Rod Carew 2.00
201 Rod Carew (Super Veteran) .35
202 Blue Jays Batting & Pitching Ldrs. (Damaso Garcia, Dave Stieb) .05
203 Mike Morgan .05
204 Junior Kennedy .05
205 Dave Parker .05
206 Ken Oberkfell .05
207 Rick Camp .05
208 Dan Meyer .05
209 Mike Moore **RC** .15
210 Jack Clark .05
211 John Denny .05
212 John Stearns .05
213 Tom Burgmeier .05
214 Jerry White .05
215 Mario Soto .05
216 Tony LaRussa .05
217 Tim Stoddard .05
218 Roy Howell .05
219 Mike Armstrong .05
220 Dusty Baker .05
221 Joe Niekro .05
222 Damaso Garcia .05
223 John Montefusco .05
224 Mickey Rivers .05
225 Enos Cabell .05
226 Enrique Romo .05
227 Chris Bando .05
228 Joaquin Andujar .05
229 Phillies Batting/Pitching Leaders (Steve Carlton, Bo Diaz) .15
230 Fergie Jenkins .75
231 Fergie Jenkins (Super Veteran) .20
232 Tom Brunansky .05
233 Wayne Gross .05
234 Larry Andersen .05
235 Claudell Washington .05
236 Steve Renko .05
237 Dan Norman .05
238 Bud Black **RC** .25
239 Dave Stapleton .05
240 Rich Gossage .05
241 Rich Gossage (Super Veteran) .05
242 Joe Nolan .05
243 Duane Walker .05
244 Dwight Bernard .05
245 Steve Sax .05
246 George Bamberger .05
247 Dave Smith .05
248 Bake McBride .05
249 Checklist 133-264 .05
250 Bill Buckner .05
251 Alan Wiggins **RC** .05
252 Luis Aguayo .05
253 Larry McWilliams .05
254 Rick Cerone .05
255 Gene Garber .05
256 Gene Garber (Super Veteran) .05
257 Jesse Barfield .05
258 Manny Castillo .05
259 Jeff Jones .05
260 Steve Kemp .05
261 Tigers Batting & Pitching Ldrs. (Larry Herndon, Dan Petry) .05
262 Ron Jackson .05
263 Renie Martin .05
264 Jamie Quirk .05
265 Joel Youngblood .05
266 Paul Boris .05
267 Terry Francona .05
268 Storm Davis **RC** .05
269 Ron Oester .05
270 Dennis Eckersley .75
271 Ed Romero .05
272 Frank Tanana .05
273 Mark Belanger .05
274 Terry Kennedy .05
275 Ray Knight .05
276 Gene Mauch .05
277 Rance Mulliniks .05
278 Kevin Hickey .05
279 Greg Gross .05
280 Bert Blyleven .05
281 Andre Robertson .05
282 Reggie Smith .05
283 Reggie Smith (Super Veteran) .05
284 Jeff Lahti .05
285 Lance Parrish .05
286 Rick Langford .05
287 Bobby Brown .05
288 Joe Cowley **RC** .05
289 Jerry Dybzinski .05
290 Jeff Reardon .05
291 Pirates Batting & Pitching Ldrs. (John Candelaria, Bill Madlock) .05
292 Craig Swan .05
293 Glenn Gulliver .05
294 Dave Engle .05
295 Jerry Remy .05
296 Greg Harris .05
297 Ned Yost .05
298 Floyd Chiffer .05
299 George Wright .05
300 Mike Schmidt 3.00
301 Mike Schmidt (Super Veteran) 1.50
302 Ernie Whitt .05
303 Miguel Dilone .05
304 Dave Rucker .05
305 Larry Bowa .05
306 Tom Lasorda .25
307 Lou Piniella .05
308 Jesus Vega .05
309 Jeff Leonard .05
310 Greg Luzinski .05
311 Glenn Brummer .05
312 Brian Kingman .05
313 Gary Gray .05
314 Ken Dayley **RC** .05
315 Rick Burleson .05
316 Paul Splittorff .05
317 Gary Rajsich .05
318 John Tudor .05
319 Lenn Sakata .05
320 Steve Rogers .05
321 Brewers Batting & Pitching Ldrs. (Pete Vuckovich, Robin Yount) .10
322 Dave Van Gorder .05
323 Luis DeLeon .05
324 Mike Marshall .05
325 Von Hayes .05
326 Garth Iorg .05
327 Bobby Castillo .05
328 Craig Reynolds .05
329 Randy Niemann .05
330 Buddy Bell .05
331 Mike Krukow .05
332 Glenn Wilson **RC** .05
333 Dave LaRoche .05
334 Dave LaRoche (Super Veteran) .05
335 Steve Henderson .05
336 Rene Lachemann .05
337 Tito Landrum .05
338 Bob Owchinko .05
339 Terry Harper .05
340 Larry Gura .05
341 Doug DeCinces .05
342 Atlee Hammaker .05
343 Bob Bailor .05
344 Roger LaFrancois .05
345 Jim Clancy .05
346 Joe Pittman .05
347 Sammy Stewart .05
348 Alan Bannister .05
349 Checklist 265-396 .05
350 Robin Yount 2.00
351 Reds Batting & Pitching Ldrs. (Cesar Cedeno, Mario Soto) .05
352 Mike Scioscia .05
353 Steve Comer .05
354 Randy S. Johnson .05
355 Jim Bibby .05
356 Gary Woods .05
357 Len Matuszek **RC** .05
358 Jerry Garvin .05
359 Dave Collins .05
360 Nolan Ryan 5.00
361 Nolan Ryan (Super Veteran) 4.00
362 Bill Almon .05
363 John Stuper **RC** .05
364 Brett Butler .05
365 Dave Lopes .05
366 Dick Williams .05

367 Bud Anderson .05
368 Richie Zisk .05
369 Jesse Orosco .05
370 Gary Carter 2.00
371 Mike Richardt .05
372 Terry Crowley .05
373 Kevin Saucier .05
374 Wayne Krenchicki .05
375 Pete Vuckovich .05
376 Ken Landreaux .05
377 Lee May .05
378 Lee May (Super Veteran) .05
379 Guy Sularz .05
380 Ron Davis .05
381 Red Sox Batting & Pitching Ldrs. (Jim Rice, Bob Stanley) .05
382 Bob Knepper .05
383 Ozzie Virgil .05
384 Dave Dravecky **RC** .50
385 Mike Easler .05
386 Rod Carew /AS .35
387 Bob Grich /AS .05
388 George Brett/AS 1.50
389 Robin Yount/AS .60
390 Reggie Jackson/AS 1.00
391 Rickey Henderson/AS .50
392 Fred Lynn/AS .05
393 Carlton Fisk/AS .35
394 Pete Vuckovich/AS .05
395 Larry Gura/AS .05
396 Dan Quisenberry/AS .05
397 Pete Rose/AS 2.00
398 Manny Trillo/AS .05
399 Mike Schmidt/AS 1.50
400 Dave Concepcion/AS .05
401 Dale Murphy/AS .20
402 Andre Dawson/AS .35
403 Tim Raines/AS .05
404 Gary Carter/AS .35
405 Steve Rogers/AS .05
406 Steve Carlton/AS .30
407 Bruce Sutter/AS .25
408 Rudy May .05
409 Marvis Foley .05
410 Phil Niekro .75
411 Phil Niekro (Super Veteran) .25
412 Rangers Batting & Pitching Ldrs. (Buddy Bell, Charlie Hough) .05
413 Matt Keough .05
414 Julio Cruz .05
415 Bob Forsch .05
416 Joe Ferguson .05
417 Tom Hausman .05
418 Greg Pryor .05
419 Steve Crawford .05
420 Al Oliver .05
421 Al Oliver (Super Veteran) .05
422 George Cappuzzello .05
423 Tom Lawless **RC** .05
424 Jerry Augustine .05
425 Pedro Guerrero .05
426 Earl Weaver .25
427 Roy Lee Jackson .05
428 Champ Summers .05
429 Eddie Whitson .05
430 Kirk Gibson .05
431 Gary Gaetti **RC** .75
432 Porfirio Altamirano .05
433 Dale Berra .05
434 Dennis Lamp .05
435 Tony Armas .05
436 Bill Campbell .05
437 Rick Sweet .05
438 Dave LaPoint **RC** .05
439 Rafael Ramirez .05
440 Ron Guidry .20
441 Astros Batting & Pitching Ldrs. (Ray Knight, Joe Niekro) .05
442 Brian Downing .05
443 Don Hood .05
444 Wally Backman **RC** .05
445 Mike Flanagan .05
446 Reid Nichols .05
447 Bryn Smith .05
448 Darrell Evans .05
449 Eddie Milner **RC** .05
450 Ted Simmons .05
451 Ted Simmons (Super Veteran) .05
452 Lloyd Moseby .05
453 Lamar Johnson .05
454 Bob Welch .05
455 Sixto Lezcano .05
456 Lee Elia .05
457 Milt Wilcox .05
458 Ron Washington .05
459 Ed Farmer .05
460 Roy Smalley .05
461 Steve Trout .05
462 Steve Nicosia .05
463 Gaylord Perry .75
464 Gaylord Perry (Super Veteran) .20
465 Lonnie Smith .05
466 Tom Underwood .05
467 Rufino Linares .05
468 Dave Goltz .05
469 Ron Gardenhire .05
470 Greg Minton .05
471 Royals Batting & Pitching Ldrs. (Vida Blue, Willie Wilson) .05
472 Gary Allenson .05
473 John Lowenstein .05
474 Ray Burris .05
475 Cesar Cedeno .05
476 Rob Picciolo .05
477 Tom Niedenfuer **RC** .05
478 Phil Garner .05
479 Charlie Hough .05
480 Toby Harrah .05
481 Scot Thompson .05
482 Tony Gwynn **RC** 25.00
483 Lynn Jones .05
484 Dick Ruthven .05
485 Omar Moreno .05
486 Clyde King .05
487 Jerry Hairston Sr. .05
488 Alfredo Griffin .05
489 Tom Herr .05
490 Jim Palmer 1.50
491 Jim Palmer (Super Veteran) .20
492 Paul Serna .05
493 Steve McCatty .05
494 Bob Brenly .05
495 Warren Cromartie .05
496 Tom Veryzer .05
497 Rick Sutcliffe .05
498 Wade Boggs **RC** 15.00
499 Jeff Little .05
500 Reggie Jackson 2.00
501 Reggie Jackson (Super Veteran) .75
502 Braves Batting & Pitching Ldrs. (Dale Murphy, Phil Niekro) .20
503 Moose Haas .05
504 Don Werner .05
505 Garry Templeton .05
506 Jim Gott **RC** .25
507 Tony Scott .05
508 Tom Filer .05
509 Lou Whitaker .05
510 Tug McGraw .05
511 Tug McGraw (Super Veteran) .05
512 Doyle Alexander .05
513 Fred Stanley .05
514 Rudy Law .05
515 Gene Tenace .05
516 Bill Virdon .05
517 Gary Ward .05
518 Bill Laskey .05
519 Terry Bulling .05
520 Fred Lynn .05
521 Bruce Benedict .05
522 Pat Zachry .05
523 Carney Lansford .05
524 Tom Brennan .05
525 Frank White .05
526 Checklist 397-528 .05
527 Larry Biittner .05
528 Jamie Easterly .05
529 Tim Laudner .05
530 Eddie Murray 2.00
531 Athletics Batting & Pitching Ldrs. (Rickey Henderson, Rick Langford) .15
532 Dave Stewart .05
533 Luis Salazar .05
534 John Butcher .05
535 Manny Trillo .05
536 Johnny Wockenfuss .05
537 Rod Scurry .05
538 Danny Heep .05
539 Roger Erickson .05
540 Ozzie Smith 2.00
541 Britt Burns .05
542 Jody Davis .05
543 Alan Fowlkes .05
544 Larry Whisenton .05
545 Floyd Bannister .05
546 Dave Garcia .05
547 Geoff Zahn .05
548 Brian Giles .05
549 Charlie Puleo **RC** .05
550 Carl Yastrzemski 2.00
551 Carl Yastrzemski (Super Veteran) .50
552 Tim Wallach .05
553 Denny Martinez .05
554 Mike Vail .05
555 Steve Yeager .05
556 Willie Upshaw .05
557 Rick Honeycutt .05
558 Dickie Thon .05
559 Pete Redfern .05
560 Ron LeFlore .05
561 Cardinals Batting & Pitching Ldrs. (Joaquin Andujar, Lonnie Smith) .05
562 Dave Rozema .05
563 Juan Bonilla .05
564 Sid Monge .10
565 Bucky Dent .05
566 Manny Sarmiento .05
567 Joe Simpson .05
568 Willie Hernandez .05
569 Jack Perconte .05
570 Vida Blue .05
571 Mickey Klutts .05
572 Bob Watson .05
573 Andy Hassler .05
574 Glenn Adams .05
575 Neil Allen .05
576 Frank Robinson .25
577 Luis Aponte .05
578 David Green .05
579 Rich Dauer .05
580 Tom Seaver 2.00
581 Tom Seaver (Super Veteran) .50
582 Marshall Edwards .05
583 Terry Forster .05
584 Dave Hostetler .05
585 Jose Cruz .05
586 Frank Viola **RC** 1.50
587 Ivan DeJesus .05
588 Pat Underwood .05
589 Alvis Woods .05
590 Tony Pena .05
591 White Sox Batting & Pitching Ldrs. (LaMarr Hoyt, Greg Luzinski) .05
592 Shane Rawley .05
593 Broderick Perkins .05
594 Eric Rasmussen .05
595 Tim Raines .05
596 Randy S. Johnson .05
597 Mike Proly .05
598 Dwayne Murphy .05
599 Don Aase .05
600 George Brett 3.00
601 Ed Lynch .05
602 Rich Gedman .05
603 Joe Morgan 2.00
604 Joe Morgan (Super Veteran) .35
605 Gary Roenicke .05
606 Bobby Cox .05
607 Charlie Leibrandt .05
608 Don Money .05
609 Danny Darwin .05
610 Steve Garvey .50
611 Bert Roberge .05
612 Steve Swisher .05
613 Mike Ivie .05
614 Ed Glynn .05
615 Garry Maddox .05
616 Bill Nahorodny .05
617 Butch Wynegar .05
618 LaMarr Hoyt .05
619 Keith Moreland .05
620 Mike Norris .05
621 Mets Batting & Pitching Ldrs. (Craig Swan, Mookie Wilson) .05
622 Dave Edler .05
623 Luis Sanchez .05
624 Glenn Hubbard .05
625 Ken Forsch .05
626 Jerry Martin .05
627 Doug Bair .05
628 Julio Valdez .05
629 Charlie Lea .05
630 Paul Molitor 2.00
631 Tippy Martinez .05
632 Alex Trevino .05
633 Vicente Romo .05
634 Max Venable .05
635 Graig Nettles .05
636 Graig Nettles (Super Veteran) .05
637 Pat Corrales .05
638 Dan Petry .05
639 Art Howe .05
640 Andre Thornton .05
641 Billy Sample .05
642 Checklist 529-660 .05
643 Bump Wills .05
644 Joe Lefebvre .05
645 Bill Madlock .05
646 Jim Essian .05
647 Bobby Mitchell .05
648 Jeff Burroughs .05
649 Tommy Boggs .05
650 George Hendrick .05
651 Angels Batting & Pitching Ldrs. (Rod Carew, Mike Witt) .05
652 Butch Hobson .05
653 Ellis Valentine .05
654 Bob Ojeda .05
655 Al Bumbry .05
656 Dave Frost .05
657 Mike Gates .05
658 Frank Pastore .05
659 Charlie Moore .05
660 Mike Hargrove .05
661 Bill Russell .05
662 Joe Sambito .05
663 Tom O'Malley .05
664 Bob Molinaro .05
665 Jim Sundberg .05
666 Sparky Anderson .25
667 Dick Davis .05
668 Larry Christenson .05
669 Mike Squires .05
670 Jerry Mumphrey .05
671 Lenny Faedo .05
672 Jim Kaat .10
673 Jim Kaat (Super Veteran) .05
674 Kurt Bevacqua .05
675 Jim Beattie .05
676 Biff Pocoroba .05
677 Dave Revering .05
678 Juan Beniquez .05
679 Mike Scott .05
680 Andre Dawson .60
681 Dodgers Batting & Pitching Ldrs. (Pedro Guerrero, Fernando Valenzuela) .05
682 Bob Stanley .05
683 Dan Ford .05
684 Rafael Landestoy .05
685 Lee Mazzilli .05
686 Randy Lerch .05
687 U.L. Washington .05
688 Jim Wohlford .05
689 Ron Hassey .05
690 Kent Hrbek .05
691 Dave Tobik .05
692 Denny Walling .05
693 Sparky Lyle .05
694 Sparky Lyle (Super Veteran) .05
695 Ruppert Jones .05
696 Chuck Tanner .05
697 Barry Foote .05
698 Tony Bernazard .05
699 Lee Smith .05
700 Keith Hernandez .05
701 Batting Leaders (Al Oliver, Willie Wilson) .05
702 Home Run Leaders (Reggie Jackson, Dave Kingman, Gorman Thomas) .15
703 Runs Batted In Leaders (Hal McRae, Dale Murphy, Al Oliver) .05
704 Stolen Base Leaders (Rickey Henderson, Tim Raines) .10
705 Victory Leaders (Steve Carlton, LaMarr Hoyt) .05
706 Strikeout Leaders (Floyd Bannister, Steve Carlton) .05
707 Earned Run Average Leaders (Steve Rogers, Rick Sutcliffe) .05
708 Leading Firemen (Dan Quisenberry, Bruce Sutter) .10
709 Jimmy Sexton .05
710 Willie Wilson .05
711 Mariners Batting & Pitching Ldrs. (Jim Beattie, Bruce Bochte) .05
712 Bruce Kison .05
713 Ron Hodges .05
714 Wayne Nordhagen .05
715 Tony Perez 1.50
716 Tony Perez (Super Veteran) .05
717 Scott Sanderson .05
718 Jim Dwyer .05
719 Rich Gale .05
720 Dave Concepcion .05
721 John Martin .05
722 Jorge Orta .05
723 Randy Moffitt .05
724 Johnny Grubb .05
725 Dan Spillner .05
726 Harvey Kuenn .05
727 Chet Lemon .05
728 Ron Reed .05
729 Jerry Morales .05
730 Jason Thompson .05
731 Al Williams .05
732 Dave Henderson .05
733 Buck Martinez .05
734 Steve Braun .05
735 Tommy John .20
736 Tommy John (Super Veteran) .05
737 Mitchell Page .05
738 Tim Foli .05
739 Rick Ownbey .05
740 Rusty Staub .05
741 Rusty Staub (Super Veteran) .05
742 Padres Batting & Pitching Ldrs. (Terry Kennedy, Tim Lollar) .05
743 Mike Torrez .05
744 Brad Mills .05
745 Scott McGregor .05
746 John Wathan .05
747 Fred Breining .05
748 Derrel Thomas .05
749 Jon Matlack .05
750 Ben Oglivie .05
751 Brad Havens .05
752 Luis Pujols .05
753 Elias Sosa .05
754 Bill Robinson .05
755 John Candelaria .05
756 Russ Nixon .05
757 Rick Manning .05
758 Aurelio Rodriguez .05
759 Doug Bird .05
760 Dale Murphy .60
761 Gary Lucas .05
762 Cliff Johnson .05
763 Al Cowens .05
764 Pete Falcone .05
765 Bob Boone .05
766 Barry Bonnell .05
767 Duane Kuiper .05
768 Chris Speier .05
769 Checklist 661-792 .05
770 Dave Winfield 2.00
771 Twins Batting & Pitching Ldrs. (Bobby Castillo, Kent Hrbek) .05
772 Jim Kern .05
773 Larry Hisle .05
774 Alan Ashby .05
775 Burt Hooton .05
776 Larry Parrish .05
777 John Curtis .05
778 Rich Hebner .05
779 Rick Waits .05
780 Gary Matthews .05
781 Rick Rhoden .05
782 Bobby Murcer .05
783 Bobby Murcer (Super Veteran) .05
784 Jeff Newman .05
785 Dennis Leonard .05
786 Ralph Houk .05
787 Dick Tidrow .05
788 Dane Iorg .05
789 Bryan Clark .05
790 Bob Grich .05
791 Gary Lavelle .05
792 Chris Chambliss .05

Traded

These 2-1/2" x 3-1/2" cards mark a continuation of the traded set introduced in 1981. The 132 cards retain the basic design of the year's regular issue, with their numbering being 1-132 with the "T" suffix. Cards in the set include traded players, new managers and promising rookies. Sold only through dealers, the set was in heavy demand as it contained the first cards of Darryl Strawberry, Ron Kittle, Julio Franco, and Mel Hall. While some of those cards were very hot in 1983, it seems likely that some of the rookies may not live up to their initial promise.

NM/M
Complete Set (132): 20.00
Common Player: .05
1T Neil Allen .05
2T Bill Almon .05
3T Joe Altobelli .05
4T Tony Armas .05
5T Doug Bair .05
6T Steve Baker .05
7T Floyd Bannister .05
8T Don Baylor .25
9T Tony Bernazard .05
10T Larry Biittner .05
11T Dann Bilardello .05
12T Doug Bird .05
13T Steve Boros .05
14T Greg Brock **RC** .05
15T Mike Brown .05
16T Tom Burgmeier .05
17T Randy Bush **RC** .05
18T Bert Campaneris .05
19T Ron Cey .05
20T Chris Codiroli **RC** .05
21T Dave Collins .05
22T Terry Crowley .05
23T Julio Cruz .05
24T Mike Davis .05
25T Frank DiPino .05
26T Bill Doran **RC** .05
27T Jerry Dybzinski .05
28T Jamie Easterly .05
29T Juan Eichelberger .05
30T Jim Essian .05
31T Pete Falcone .05
32T Mike Ferraro .05
33T Terry Forster .05
34T Julio Franco **RC** 3.00
35T Rich Gale .05
36T Kiko Garcia .05
37T Steve Garvey 1.00
38T Johnny Grubb .05
39T Mel Hall **RC** .05
40T Von Hayes .05
41T Danny Heep .05
42T Steve Henderson .05
43T Keith Hernandez .15
44T Leo Hernandez .05
45T Willie Hernandez .05
46T Al Holland .05
47T Frank Howard .05
48T Bobby Johnson .05
49T Cliff Johnson .05
50T Odell Jones .05
51T Mike Jorgensen .05
52T Bob Kearney .05
53T Steve Kemp .05
54T Matt Keough .05
55T Ron Kittle **RC** .05
56T Mickey Klutts .05
57T Alan Knicely .05
58T Mike Krukow .05
59T Rafael Landestoy .05
60T Carney Lansford .05
61T Joe Lefebvre .05
62T Bryan Little .05
63T Aurelio Lopez .05
64T Mike Madden .05
65T Rick Manning .05
66T Billy Martin .25
67T Lee Mazzilli .05
68T Andy McGaffigan .05
69T Craig McMurtry **RC** .05
70T John McNamara .05
71T Orlando Mercado .05
72T Larry Milbourne .05
73T Randy Moffitt .05
74T Sid Monge .05
75T Jose Morales .05
76T Omar Moreno .05
77T Joe Morgan 4.00
78T Mike Morgan .05
79T Dale Murray .05
80T Jeff Newman .05
81T Pete O'Brien **RC** .05
82T Jorge Orta .05
83T Alejandro Pena **RC** .05
84T Pascual Perez .05
85T Tony Perez 1.00
86T Broderick Perkins .05
87T Tony Phillips **RC** .15
88T Charlie Puleo .05
89T Pat Putnam .05
90T Jamie Quirk .05
91T Doug Rader .05
92T Chuck Rainey .05
93T Bobby Ramos .05
94T Gary Redus .05
95T Steve Renko .05
96T Leon Roberts .05
97T Aurelio Rodriguez .05
98T Dick Ruthven .05
99T Daryl Sconiers .05
100T Mike Scott .05
101T Tom Seaver 6.00
102T John Shelby **RC** .05
103T Bob Shirley .05
104T Joe Simpson .05
105T Doug Sisk **RC** .05
106T Mike Smithson **RC** .05
107T Elias Sosa .05
108T Darryl Strawberry **RC** 10.00
109T Tom Tellmann .05
110T Gene Tenace .05
111T Gorman Thomas .05
112T Dick Tidrow .05
113T Dave Tobik .05
114T Wayne Tolleson **RC** .05
115T Mike Torrez .05
116T Manny Trillo .05
117T Steve Trout .05
118T Lee Tunnell **RC** .05
119T Mike Vail .05
120T Ellis Valentine .05
121T Tom Veryzer .05
122T George Vukovich .05
123T Rick Waits .05
124T Greg Walker **RC** .05
125T Chris Welsh .05
126T Len Whitehouse .05
127T Eddie Whitson .05
128T Jim Wohlford .05
129T Matt Young **RC** .05
130T Joel Youngblood .05
131T Pat Zachry .05
132T Checklist 1-132 .05

Traded Steve Carlton Bronze

The first in a series of 1/4-size metal replicas of Topps star cards was issued to dealers who purchased cases of 1983 Topps Traded sets. Each detail of the 1983 Steve Carlton card is reproduced on the 1-1/4" x 1-3/4" bronze metal mini-card, right down to the stats.

		NM/M
70	Steve Carlton	6.00

1982 League Leaders Sheet

The leaders in various major statistical categories in 1982 are featured on this 7-1/2" x 10-1/2" blank-back sheet. Most of the cards on the sheet are identical to the players' regular 1983 Topps cards except for a white strip at upper-left identifying their statistical accomplishment. Reggie Jackson and Gorman Thomas who shared the A.L. home run record for 1982 share a card on this sheet. Available via a mail-in offer, huge quantities of these sheets are readily available.

	NM/M
Uncut Sheet: Willie Wilson, Reggie Jackson, Gorman Thomas, Al Oliver, LaMarr Hoyt, Steve Carlton, Dan Quisenberry, Dave Kingman, Bruce Sutter	1.00

All-Star Glossy Set of 40

This set was a "consolation prize" in a scratch-off contest in regular packs of 1983 cards. The 2-1/2" x 3-1/2" cards have a large color photo surrounded by a yellow frame on the front. In very small type on a white border is printed the player's name. Backs carry the player's name, team, position and the card number along with a Topps identification. A major feature is that the surface of the front is glossy, which most collectors find very attractive. With many top stars, the set is a popular one, but the price has not moved too far above the issue price.

		NM/M
Complete Set (40):		3.00
Common Player:		.05
1	Carl Yastrzemski	.25
2	Mookie Wilson	.05
3	Andre Thornton	.05
4	Keith Hernandez	.05
5	Robin Yount	.25
6	Terry Kennedy	.05
7	Dave Winfield	.25
8	Mike Schmidt	.50
9	Buddy Bell	.05
10	Fernando Valenzuela	.05
11	Rich Gossage	.05
12	Bob Horner	.05
13	Toby Harrah	.05
14	Pete Rose	.75
15	Cecil Cooper	.05
16	Dale Murphy	.15
17	Carlton Fisk	.25
18	Ray Knight	.05
19	Jim Palmer	.25
20	Gary Carter	.25
21	Richard Zisk	.05
22	Dusty Baker	.05
23	Willie Wilson	.05
24	Bill Buckner	.05
25	Dave Stieb	.05
26	Bill Madlock	.05
27	Lance Parrish	.05
28	Nolan Ryan	1.00
29	Rod Carew	.25
30	Al Oliver	.05
31	George Brett	.50
32	Jack Clark	.05
33	Rickey Henderson	.25
34	Dave Concepcion	.05
35	Kent Hrbek	.05
36	Steve Carlton	.25
37	Eddie Murray	.25
38	Ruppert Jones	.05
39	Reggie Jackson	.30
40	Bruce Sutter	.20

Foldouts

Another Topps test issue, these 3-1/2" x 5-5/16" cards were printed in booklets like souvenir postcards. Each of the booklets have a theme of currently playing statistical leaders in a specific category such as home runs. The cards feature a color player photo on each side. A black strip at the bottom gives the player's name, position and team along with statistics in the particular category. A facsimile autograph crosses the photograph. Booklets carry nine cards, with eight having players on both sides and one doubling as the back cover, for a total of 17 cards per booklet. There are 85 cards in the set, although some players appear in more than one category. Naturally, most of the players pictured are stars. Even so, the set is a problem as it seems to be most valuable when complete and unseparated, so the cards are difficult to display.

		NM/M
Complete Set (5):		9.00
Common Folder:		3.00
1	Pitching Leaders (Vida Blue, Bert Blyleven, Steve Carlton, Fergie Jenkins, Tommy John, Jim Kaat, Jerry Koosman, Joe Niekro, Phil Niekro, Jim Palmer, Gaylord Perry, Jerry Reuss, Nolan Ryan, Tom Seaver, Paul Splittorff, Don Sutton, Mike Torrez)	6.00
2	Home Run Leaders (Johnny Bench, Ron Cey, Darrell Evans, George Foster, Reggie Jackson, Dave Kingman, Greg Luzinski, John Mayberry, Rick Monday, Joe Morgan, Bobby Murcer, Graig Nettles, Tony Perez, Jim Rice, Mike Schmidt, Rusty Staub, Carl Yastrzemski)	4.50
3	Batting Leaders (George Brett, Rod Carew, Cecil Cooper, Steve Garvey, Ken Griffey, Pedro Guerrero, Keith Hernandez, Dane Iorg, Fred Lynn, Bill Madlock, Bake McBride, Al Oliver, Dave Parker, Jim Rice, Pete Rose, Lonnie Smith, Willie Wilson)	4.50
4	Relief Aces (Tom Burgmeier, Bill Campbell, Ed Farmer, Rollie Fingers, Terry Forster, Gene Garber, Rich Gossage, Jim Kern, Gary Lavelle, Tug McGraw, Greg Minton, Randy Moffitt, Dan Quisenberry, Ron Reed, Elias Sosa, Bruce Sutter, Kent Tekulve)	3.00
5	Stolen Base Leaders (Don Baylor, Larry Bowa, Al Bumbry, Rod Carew, Cesar Cedeno, Dave Concepcion, Jose Cruz, Julio Cruz, Rickey Henderson, Ron LeFlore, Davey Lopes, Garry Maddox, Omar Moreno, Joe Morgan, Amos Otis, Mickey Rivers, Willie Wilson)	3.00

Stickers

Topps increased the number of stickers in its set to 330 in 1983, but retained the same 1-15/16" x 2-9/16" size. The stickers are again numbered on both the front and back. Similar in style to previous sticker issues, the set includes 28 "foil" stickers, and various special stickers highlighting the 1982 season, playoffs and World Series. An album was also available.

		NM/M
Complete Set (330):		15.00
Common Player:		.05
Sticker Album:		2.00
Wax Pack (5):		.25
Wax Box (100):		16.00
1	Hank Aaron	1.00
2	Babe Ruth	2.00
3	Willie Mays	1.00
4	Frank Robinson	.15
5	Reggie Jackson	.50
6	Carl Yastrzemski	.25
7	Johnny Bench	.25
8	Tony Perez	.25
9	Lee May	.05
10	Mike Schmidt	.50
11	Dave Kingman	.05
12	Reggie Smith	.05
13	Graig Nettles	.05
14	Rusty Staub	.05
15	Willie Wilson	.05
16	LaMarr Hoyt	.05
17	Reggie Jackson, Gorman Thomas	.10
18	Floyd Bannister	.05
19	Hal McRae	.05
20	Rick Sutcliffe	.05
21	Rickey Henderson	.25
22	Dan Quisenberry	.05
23	Jim Palmer	.25
24	John Lowenstein	.05
25	Mike Flanagan	.05
26	Cal Ripken, Jr.	1.00
27	Rich Dauer	.05
28	Ken Singleton	.05
29	Eddie Murray	.25
30	Rick Dempsey	.05
31	Carl Yastrzemski	.25
32	Carney Lansford	.05
33	Jerry Remy	.05
34	Dennis Eckersley	.20
35	Dave Stapleton	.05
36	Mark Clear	.05
37	Jim Rice	.15
38	Dwight Evans	.05
39	Rod Carew	.25
40	Don Baylor	.10
41	Reggie Jackson	.50
42	Geoff Zahn	.05
43	Bobby Grich	.05
44	Fred Lynn	.05
45	Bob Boone	.05
46	Doug DeCinces	.05
47	Tom Paciorek	.05
48	Britt Burns	.05
49	Tony Bernazard	.05
50	Steve Kemp	.05
51	Greg Luzinski	.05
52	Harold Baines	.05
53	LaMarr Hoyt	.05
54	Carlton Fisk	.25
55	Andre Thornton	.05
56	Mike Hargrove	.05
57	Len Barker	.05
58	Toby Harrah	.05
59	Dan Spillner	.05
60	Rick Manning	.05
61	Rick Sutcliffe	.05
62	Ron Hassey	.05
63	Lance Parrish	.05
64	John Wockenfuss	.05
65	Lou Whitaker	.05
66	Alan Trammell	.05
67	Kirk Gibson	.05
68	Larry Herndon	.05
69	Jack Morris	.05
70	Dan Petry	.05
71	Frank White	.05
72	Amos Otis	.05
73	Willie Wilson	.05
74	Dan Quisenberry	.05
75	Hal McRae	.05
76	George Brett	.60
77	Larry Gura	.05
78	John Wathan	.05
79	Rollie Fingers	.20
80	Cecil Cooper	.05
81	Robin Yount	.25
82	Ben Oglivie	.05
83	Paul Molitor	.25
84	Gorman Thomas	.05
85	Ted Simmons	.05
86	Pete Vuckovich	.05
87	Gary Gaetti	.05
88	Kent Hrbek	.05
89	John Castino	.05
90	Tom Brunansky	.05
91	Bobby Mitchell	.05
92	Gary Ward	.05
93	Tim Laudner	.05
94	Ron Davis	.05
95	Willie Randolph	.05
96	Roy Smalley	.05
97	Jerry Mumphrey	.05
98	Ken Griffey	.05
99	Dave Winfield	.25
100	Rich Gossage	.05
101	Butch Wynegar	.05
102	Ron Guidry	.05
103	Rickey Henderson	.25
104	Mike Heath	.05
105	Dave Lopes	.05
106	Rick Langford	.05
107	Dwayne Murphy	.05
108	Tony Armas	.05
109	Matt Keough	.05
110	Dan Meyer	.05
111	Bruce Bochte	.05
112	Julio Cruz	.05
113	Floyd Bannister	.05
114	Gaylord Perry	.20
115	Al Cowens	.05
116	Richie Zisk	.05
117	Jim Essian	.05
118	Bill Caudill	.05
119	Buddy Bell	.05
120	Larry Parrish	.05
121	Danny Darwin	.05
122	Bucky Dent	.05
123	Johnny Grubb	.05
124	George Wright	.05
125	Charlie Hough	.05
126	Jim Sundberg	.05
127	Dave Stieb	.05
128	Willie Upshaw	.05
129	Alfredo Griffin	.05
130	Lloyd Moseby	.05
131	Ernie Whitt	.05
132	Jim Clancy	.05
133	Barry Bonnell	.05
134	Damaso Garcia	.05
135	Jim Kaat	.05
136	Jim Kaat	.05
137	Greg Minton	.05
138	Greg Minton	.05
139	Paul Molitor	.20
140	Paul Molitor	.20
141	Manny Trillo	.05
142	Manny Trillo	.05
143	Joel Youngblood	.05
144	Joel Youngblood	.05
145	Robin Yount	.20
146	Robin Yount	.20
147	Willie McGee	.05
148	Darrell Porter	.05
149	Darrell Porter	.05
150	Robin Yount	.20
151	Bruce Benedict	.05
152	Bruce Benedict	.05
153	George Hendrick	.05
154	Bruce Benedict	.05
155	Doug DeCinces	.05
156	Paul Molitor	.20
157	Charlie Moore	.05
158	Fred Lynn	.05
159	Rickey Henderson	.25
160	Dale Murphy	.15
161	Willie Wilson	.05
162	Jack Clark	.05
163	Reggie Jackson	.50
164	Andre Dawson	.15
165	Dan Quisenberry	.05
166	Bruce Sutter	.20
167	Robin Yount	.25
168	Ozzie Smith	.25
169	Frank White	.05
170	Phil Garner	.05
171	Doug DeCinces	.05
172	Mike Schmidt	.50
173	Cecil Cooper	.05
174	Al Oliver	.05
175	Jim Palmer	.25
176	Steve Carlton	.25
177	Carlton Fisk	.25
178	Gary Carter	.25
179	Joaquin Andujar	.05
180	Ozzie Smith	.25
181	Cecil Cooper	.05
182	Darrell Porter	.05
183	Darrell Porter	.05
184	Mike Caldwell	.05
185	Mike Caldwell	.05
186	Ozzie Smith	.25
187	Bruce Sutter	.20
188	Keith Hernandez	.05
189	Dane Iorg	.05
190	Dane Iorg	.05
191	Tony Armas	.05
192	Tony Armas	.05
193	Lance Parrish	.05
194	Lance Parrish	.05
195	John Wathan	.05
196	John Wathan	.05
197	Rickey Henderson	.20
198	Rickey Henderson	.20
199	Rickey Henderson	.20
200	Rickey Henderson	.20
201	Rickey Henderson	.20
202	Rickey Henderson	.20
203	Steve Carlton	.20
204	Steve Carlton	.20
205	Al Oliver	.05
206	Dale Murphy, Al Oliver	.05
207	Dave Kingman	.05
208	Steve Rogers	.05
209	Bruce Sutter	.20
210	Tim Raines	.05
211	Dale Murphy	.15
212	Chris Chambliss	.05
213	Gene Garber	.05
214	Bob Horner	.05
215	Glenn Hubbard	.05
216	Claudell Washington	.05
217	Bruce Benedict	.05
218	Phil Niekro	.20
219	Leon Durham	.05
220	Jay Johnstone	.05
221	Larry Bowa	.05
222	Keith Moreland	.05
223	Bill Buckner	.05
224	Fergie Jenkins	.20
225	Dick Tidrow	.05
226	Jody Davis	.05
227	Dave Concepcion	.05
228	Dan Driessen	.05
229	Johnny Bench	.25
230	Ron Oester	.05
231	Cesar Cedeno	.05
232	Alex Trevino	.05
233	Tom Seaver	.25
234	Mario Soto	.05
235	Nolan Ryan	1.00
236	Art Howe	.05
237	Phil Garner	.05
238	Ray Knight	.05
239	Terry Puhl	.05
240	Joe Niekro	.05
241	Alan Ashby	.05
242	Jose Cruz	.05
243	Steve Garvey	.15
244	Ron Cey	.05
245	Dusty Baker	.05
246	Ken Landreaux	.05
247	Jerry Reuss	.05
248	Pedro Guerrero	.05
249	Bill Russell	.05
250	Fernando Valenzuela	.05
251	Al Oliver	.05
252	Andre Dawson	.15
253	Tim Raines	.05
254	Jeff Reardon	.05
255	Gary Carter	.25
256	Steve Rogers	.05
257	Tim Wallach	.05
258	Chris Speier	.05
259	Dave Kingman	.05
260	Bob Bailor	.05
261	Hubie Brooks	.05
262	Craig Swan	.05
263	George Foster	.05
264	John Stearns	.05
265	Neil Allen	.05
266	Mookie Wilson	.05
267	Steve Carlton	.20
268	Manny Trillo	.05
269	Gary Matthews	.05
270	Mike Schmidt	.50
271	Ivan DeJesus	.05
272	Pete Rose	.75
273	Bo Diaz	.05
274	Sid Monge	.05
275	Bill Madlock	.05
276	Jason Thompson	.05
277	Don Robinson	.05
278	Omar Moreno	.05
279	Dale Berra	.05
280	Dave Parker	.05
281	Tony Pena	.05
282	John Candelaria	.05
283	Lonnie Smith	.05
284	Bruce Sutter	.20
285	George Hendrick	.05
286	Tom Herr	.05
287	Ken Oberkfell	.05
288	Ozzie Smith	.25
289	Bob Forsch	.05
290	Keith Hernandez	.05
291	Garry Templeton	.05
292	Broderick Perkins	.05
293	Terry Kennedy	.05
294	Gene Richards	.05
295	Ruppert Jones	.05
296	Tim Lollar	.05
297	John Montefusco	.05
298	Sixto Lezcano	.05
299	Greg Minton	.05
300	Jack Clark	.05
301	Milt May	.05
302	Reggie Smith	.05
303	Joe Morgan	.25
304	John LeMaster	.05
305	Darrell Evans	.05
306	Al Holland	.05
307	Jesse Barfield	.05
308	Wade Boggs	.60
309	Tom Brunansky	.05
310	Storm Davis	.05
311	Von Hayes	.05
312	Dave Hostetler	.05
313	Kent Hrbek	.05
314	Tim Laudner	.05
315	Cal Ripken, Jr.	1.00
316	Andre Robertson	.05
317	Ed Vande Berg	.05
318	Glenn Wilson	.05
319	Chili Davis	.05
320	Bob Dernier	.05
321	Terry Francona	.05
322	Brian Giles	.05
323	David Green	.05
324	Atlee Hammaker	.05
325	Bill Laskey	.05
326	Willie McGee	.05
327	Johnny Ray	.05
328	Ryne Sandberg	.75
329	Steve Sax	.05
330	Eric Show	.05

Stickers Boxes

These eight cards were printed on the back panels of 1983 Topps sticker boxes, one card per box. The blank-backed cards measure the standard 2-1/2" x 3-1/2" and feature a full-color photo with the player's name at the top. The rest of the back panel advertises the sticker album, while the front of the box has an action photo of Reggie Jackson. The boxes are numbered on the front. Prices in the checklist that follows are for complete boxes.

		NM/M
Complete Set (8):		6.50
Common Player:		.75
1	Fernando Valenzuela	.75
2	Gary Carter	1.00
3	Mike Schmidt	1.50
4	Reggie Jackson	1.25
5	Jim Palmer	.75
6	Rollie Fingers	.75
7	Pete Rose	2.00
8	Rickey Henderson	1.00

1952 Reprint Set

The first of several reprint/retro sets in different sports issued by Topps, the 402-card reprinting of its classic 1952 baseball card set was controversial at the time of issue, but has since gained

hobby acceptance and market value. To avoid possible confusion of the reprints for originals, the reprints were done in the now-standard 2-1/2" x 3-1/2" format instead of the original 2-5/8" x 3-3/4". Backs, printed in red, carry a line "Topps 1952 Reprint Series" at bottom, though there is no indication of the year of reprinting. Fronts have a semi-gloss finish, which also differs from the originals. Because of inability to come to terms with five of the players from the original 1952 Topps set, they were not included in the reprint series. Those cards which weren't issued are: #20 Billy Loes, #22 Dom DiMaggio, #159 Saul Rogovin, #196 Solly Hemus, and #289 Tommy Holmes. The '52 reprints were available only as a complete boxed set with a retail price of about $40 at issue.

NM/M
Complete Sealed Boxed Set: 175.00
Complete Set (402): 150.00
Common Player: .25
Minor Stars: .35
Typical Hall of Famers: 2.00
Superstar Hall of Famers: 8.00
311 Mickey Mantle 30.00
407 Eddie Mathews (Sample card.) 8.00

1984 Topps

Another 792-card regular set from Topps. For the second straight year, the 2-1/2" x 3-1/2" cards featured a color action photo on the front along with a small portrait photo in the lower-left. The team name runs in big letters down the left side, while the player's name and position appear under the action photo. Backs have a team logo in the upper-right, along with statistics, personal information and a few highlights, all in a hard-to-read red and purple coloring. Specialty cards include past season highlights, team leaders, statistical leaders, All-Stars, active career leaders and numbered checklists. Again, promising rookies were saved for the traded set. The six 132-card uncut sheets which comprise the set were made available to collectors at about $30 for the set.

NM/M
Complete Set (792): 40.00
Common Player: .05
Wax Pack (15): 2.00
Wax Box (36): 50.00
Cello Pack (28): 2.50
Cello Box (24): 50.00
Rack Pack (54+1): 3.50
Rack Box (24): 60.00
Vending Box (500): 20.00

1 Steve Carlton (1983 Highlight) .25
2 Rickey Henderson (1983 Highlight) .25
3 Dan Quisenberry (1983 Highlight) .05
4 Steve Carlton, Gaylord Perry, Nolan Ryan (1983 Highlight) .50
5 Bob Forsch, Dave Righetti, Mike Warren (1983 Highlight) .05
6 Johnny Bench, Gaylord Perry, Carl Yastrzemski (1983 Highlight) .25
7 Gary Lucas .05
8 Don Mattingly **RC** 15.00
9 Jim Gott .05
10 Robin Yount 1.00
11 Twins Batting & Pitching Leaders (Kent Hrbek, Ken Schrom) .05
12 Billy Sample .05
13 Scott Holman .05
14 Tom Brookens .05
15 Burt Hooton .05
16 Omar Moreno .05
17 John Denny .05
18 Dale Berra .05
19 Ray Fontenot **RC** .05
20 Greg Luzinski .05
21 Joe Altobelli .05
22 Bryan Clark .05
23 Keith Moreland .05
24 John Martin .05
25 Glenn Hubbard .05
26 Bud Black .05
27 Daryl Sconiers .05
28 Frank Viola .05
29 Danny Heep .05
30 Wade Boggs 3.00
31 Andy McGaffigan .05
32 Bobby Ramos .05
33 Tom Burgmeier .05
34 Eddie Milner .05
35 Don Sutton .65
36 Denny Walling .05
37 Rangers Batting & Pitching Leaders (Buddy Bell, Rick Honeycutt) .05
38 Luis DeLeon .05
39 Garth Iorg .05
40 Dusty Baker .05
41 Tony Bernazard .05
42 Johnny Grubb .05
43 Ron Reed .05
44 Jim Morrison .05
45 Jerry Mumphrey .05
46 Ray Smith .05
47 Rudy Law .05
48 Julio Franco .05
49 John Stuper .05
50 Chris Chambliss .05
51 Jim Frey .05
52 Paul Splittorff .05
53 Juan Beniquez .05
54 Jesse Orosco .05
55 Dave Concepcion .05
56 Gary Allenson .05
57 Dan Schatzeder .05
58 Max Venable .05
59 Sammy Stewart .05
60 Paul Molitor 1.00
61 Chris Codiroli **RC** .05
62 Dave Hostetler .05
63 Ed Vande Berg .05
64 Mike Scioscia .05
65 Kirk Gibson .05
66 Astros Batting & Pitching Leaders (Jose Cruz, Nolan Ryan) .25
67 Gary Ward .05
68 Luis Salazar .05
69 Rod Scurry .05
70 Gary Matthews .05
71 Leo Hernandez .05
72 Mike Squires .05
73 Jody Davis .05
74 Jerry Martin .05
75 Bob Forsch .05
76 Alfredo Griffin .05
77 Brett Butler .05
78 Mike Torrez .05
79 Rob Wilfong .05
80 Steve Rogers .05
81 Billy Martin .15
82 Doug Bird .05
83 Richie Zisk .05
84 Lenny Faedo .05
85 Atlee Hammaker .05
86 John Shelby **RC** .05
87 Frank Pastore .05
88 Rob Picciolo .05
89 Mike Smithson **RC** .05
90 Pedro Guerrero .05
91 Dan Spillner .05
92 Lloyd Moseby .05
93 Bob Knepper .05
94 Mario Ramirez .05
95 Aurelio Lopez .05
96 Royals Batting & Pitching Leaders (Larry Gura, Hal McRae) .05
97 LaMarr Hoyt .05
98 Steve Nicosia .05
99 Craig Lefferts **RC** .25
100 Reggie Jackson 1.50
101 Porfirio Altamirano .05
102 Ken Oberkfell .05
103 Dwayne Murphy .05
104 Ken Dayley .05
105 Tony Armas .05
106 Tim Stoddard .05
107 Ned Yost .05
108 Randy Moffitt .05
109 Brad Wellman .05
110 Ron Guidry .05
111 Bill Virdon .05
112 Tom Niedenfuer .05
113 Kelly Paris .05
114 Checklist 1-132 .05
115 Andre Thornton .05
116 George Bjorkman .05
117 Tom Veryzer .05
118 Charlie Hough .05
119 Johnny Wockenfuss .05
120 Keith Hernandez .05
121 Pat Sheridan **RC** .05
122 Cecilio Guante **RC** .05
123 Butch Wynegar .05
124 Damaso Garcia .05
125 Britt Burns .05
126 Braves Batting & Pitching Leaders (Craig McMurtry, Dale Murphy) .05
127 Mike Madden .05
128 Rick Manning .05
129 Bill Laskey .05
130 Ozzie Smith 2.00
131 Batting Leaders (Wade Boggs, Bill Madlock) .25
132 Home Run Leaders (Jim Rice, Mike Schmidt) .25
133 RBI Leaders (Cecil Cooper, Dale Murphy, Jim Rice) .10
134 Stolen Base Leaders (Rickey Henderson, Tim Raines) .25
135 Victory Leaders (John Denny, LaMarr Hoyt) .05
136 Strikeout Leaders (Steve Carlton, Jack Morris) .05
137 Earned Run Average Leaders (Atlee Hammaker, Rick Honeycutt) .05
138 Leading Firemen (Al Holland, Dan Quisenberry) .05
139 Bert Campaneris .05
140 Storm Davis .05
141 Pat Corrales .05
142 Rich Gale .05
143 Jose Morales .05
144 Brian Harper **RC** .20
145 Gary Lavelle .05
146 Ed Romero .05
147 Dan Petry .05
148 Joe Lefebvre .05
149 Jon Matlack .05
150 Dale Murphy .50
151 Steve Trout .05
152 Glenn Brummer .05
153 Dick Tidrow .05
154 Dave Henderson .05
155 Frank White .05
156 Athletics Batting & Pitching Leaders (Tim Conroy, Rickey Henderson) .15
157 Gary Gaetti .05
158 John Curtis .05
159 Darryl Cias .05
160 Mario Soto .05
161 Junior Ortiz **RC** .05
162 Bob Ojeda .05
163 Lorenzo Gray .05
164 Scott Sanderson .05
165 Ken Singleton .05
166 Jamie Nelson .05
167 Marshall Edwards .05
168 Juan Bonilla .05
169 Larry Parrish .05
170 Jerry Reuss .05
171 Frank Robinson .25
172 Frank DiPino .05
173 Marvell Wynne **RC** .05
174 Juan Berenguer .05
175 Graig Nettles .05
176 Lee Smith .05
177 Jerry Hairston Sr. .05
178 Bill Krueger .05
179 Buck Martinez .05
180 Manny Trillo .05
181 Roy Thomas .05
182 Darryl Strawberry .25
183 Al Williams .05
184 Mike O'Berry .05
185 Sixto Lezcano .05
186 Cardinals Batting & Pitching Leaders (Lonnie Smith, John Stuper) .05
187 Luis Aponte .05
188 Bryan Little .05
189 Tim Conroy **RC** .05
190 Ben Oglivie .05
191 Mike Boddicker .05
192 Nick Esasky **RC** .05
193 Darrell Brown .05
194 Domingo Ramos .05
195 Jack Morris .05
196 Don Slaught **RC** .05
197 Garry Hancock .05
198 Bill Doran **RC** .05
199 Willie Hernandez .05
200 Andre Dawson .60
201 Bruce Kison .05
202 Bobby Cox .05
203 Matt Keough .05
204 Bobby Meacham **RC** .05
205 Greg Minton .05
206 Andy Van Slyke **RC** .75
207 Donnie Moore .05
208 Jose Oquendo **RC** .05
209 Manny Sarmiento .05
210 Joe Morgan 1.00
211 Rick Sweet .05
212 Broderick Perkins .05
213 Bruce Hurst .05
214 Paul Householder .05
215 Tippy Martinez .05
216 White Sox Batting & Pitching Leaders (Richard Dotson, Carlton Fisk) .05
217 Alan Ashby .05
218 Rick Waits .05
219 Joe Simpson .05
220 Fernando Valenzuela .05
221 Cliff Johnson .05
222 Rick Honeycutt .05
223 Wayne Krenchicki .05
224 Sid Monge .05
225 Lee Mazzilli .05
226 Juan Eichelberger .05
227 Steve Braun .05
228 John Rabb .05
229 Paul Owens .05
230 Rickey Henderson 1.00
231 Gary Woods .05
232 Tim Wallach .05
233 Checklist 133-264 .05
234 Rafael Ramirez .05
235 Matt Young **RC** .05
236 Ellis Valentine .05
237 John Castino .05
238 Reid Nichols .05
239 Jay Howell .05
240 Eddie Murray 1.00
241 Billy Almon .05
242 Alex Trevino .05
243 Pete Ladd .05
244 Candy Maldonado **RC** .05
245 Rick Sutcliffe .05
246 Mets Batting & Pitching Leaders (Tom Seaver, Mookie Wilson) .25
247 Onix Concepcion .05
248 Bill Dawley **RC** .05
249 Jay Johnstone .05
250 Bill Madlock .05
251 Tony Gwynn 4.00
252 Larry Christenson .05
253 Jim Wohlford .05
254 Shane Rawley .05
255 Bruce Benedict .05
256 Dave Geisel .05
257 Julio Cruz .05
258 Luis Sanchez .05
259 Sparky Anderson .15
260 Scott McGregor .05
261 Bobby Brown .05
262 Tom Candiotti **RC** .25
263 Jack Fimple .05
264 Doug Frobel .05
265 Donnie Hill **RC** .05
266 Steve Lubratich .05
267 Carmelo Martinez **RC** .05
268 Jack O'Connor .05
269 Aurelio Rodriguez .05
270 Jeff Russell **RC** .05
271 Moose Haas .05
272 Rick Dempsey .05
273 Charlie Puleo .05
274 Rick Monday .05
275 Len Matuszek .05
276 Angels Batting & Pitching Leaders (Rod Carew, Geoff Zahn) .10
277 Eddie Whitson .05
278 Jorge Bell .05
279 Ivan DeJesus .05
280 Floyd Bannister .05
281 Larry Milbourne .05
282 Jim Barr .05
283 Larry Biittner .05
284 Howard Bailey .05
285 Darrell Porter .05
286 Lary Sorensen .05
287 Warren Cromartie .05
288 Jim Beattie .05
289 Randy S. Johnson .05
290 Dave Dravecky .05
291 Chuck Tanner .05
292 Tony Scott .05
293 Ed Lynch .05
294 U.L. Washington .05
295 Mike Flanagan .05
296 Jeff Newman .05
297 Bruce Berenyi .05
298 Jim Gantner .05
299 John Butcher .05
300 Pete Rose 5.00
301 Frank LaCorte .05
302 Barry Bonnell .05
303 Marty Castillo .05
304 Warren Brusstar .05
305 Roy Smalley .05
306 Dodgers Batting & Pitching Leaders (Pedro Guerrero, Bob Welch) .05
307 Bobby Mitchell .05
308 Ron Hassey .05
309 Tony Phillips .05
310 Willie McGee .05
311 Jerry Koosman .05
312 Jorge Orta .05
313 Mike Jorgensen .05
314 Orlando Mercado .05
315 Bob Grich .05
316 Mark Bradley .05
317 Greg Pryor .05
318 Bill Gullickson .05
319 Al Bumbry .05
320 Bob Stanley .05
321 Harvey Kuenn .05
322 Ken Schrom .05
323 Alan Knicely .05
324 Alejandro Pena **RC** .05
325 Darrell Evans .05
326 Bob Kearney .05
327 Ruppert Jones .05
328 Vern Ruhle .05
329 Pat Tabler **RC** .05
330 John Candelaria .05
331 Bucky Dent .05
332 Kevin Gross **RC** .05
333 Larry Herndon .05
334 Chuck Rainey .05
335 Don Baylor .15
336 Mariners Batting & Pitching Leaders (Pat Putnam, Matt Young) .05
337 Kevin Hagen .05
338 Mike Warren .05
339 Roy Lee Jackson .05
340 Hal McRae .05
341 Dave Tobik .05
342 Tim Foli .05
343 Mark Davis .05
344 Rick Miller .05
345 Kent Hrbek .05
346 Kurt Bevacqua .05
347 Allan Ramirez .05
348 Toby Harrah .05
349 Bob L. Gibson .05
350 George Foster .05
351 Russ Nixon .05
352 Dave Stewart .05
353 Jim Anderson .05
354 Jeff Burroughs .05
355 Jason Thompson .05
356 Glenn Abbott .05
357 Ron Cey .05
358 Bob Dernier .05
359 Jim Acker **RC** .05
360 Willie Randolph .05
361 Dave Smith .05
362 David Green .05
363 Tim Laudner .05
364 Scott Fletcher **RC** .05
365 Steve Bedrosian .05
366 Padres Batting & Pitching Leaders (Dave Dravecky, Terry Kennedy) .05
367 Jamie Easterly .05
368 Hubie Brooks .05
369 Steve McCatty .05
370 Tim Raines .05
371 Dave Gumpert .05
372 Gary Roenicke .05
373 Bill Scherrer .05
374 Don Money .05
375 Dennis Leonard .05
376 Dave Anderson **RC** .05
377 Danny Darwin .05
378 Bob Brenly .05
379 Checklist 265-396 .05
380 Steve Garvey .45
381 Ralph Houk .05
382 Chris Nyman .05
383 Terry Puhl .05
384 Lee Tunnell **RC** .05
385 Tony Perez 1.00
386 George Hendrick/AS .05
387 Johnny Ray/AS .05
388 Mike Schmidt/AS .75
389 Ozzie Smith/AS .50
390 Tim Raines/AS .05
391 Dale Murphy/AS .20
392 Andre Dawson/AS .25
393 Gary Carter/AS .30
394 Steve Rogers/AS .05
395 Steve Carlton/AS .25
396 Jesse Orosco/AS .05
397 Eddie Murray/AS .40
398 Lou Whitaker/AS .05
399 George Brett/AS .75
400 Cal Ripken, Jr./AS 4.00
401 Jim Rice/AS .05
402 Dave Winfield/AS .30
403 Lloyd Moseby/AS .05
404 Ted Simmons/AS .05
405 LaMarr Hoyt/AS .05
406 Ron Guidry/AS .05
407 Dan Quisenberry/AS .05
408 Lou Piniella .05
409 Juan Agosto **RC** .05
410 Claudell Washington .05
411 Houston Jimenez .05
412 Doug Rader .05
413 Spike Owen **RC** .05
414 Mitchell Page .05
415 Tommy John .15
416 Dane Iorg .05
417 Mike Armstrong .05
418 Ron Hodges .05
419 John Henry Johnson .05
420 Cecil Cooper .05
421 Charlie Lea .05
422 Jose Cruz .05
423 Mike Morgan .05
424 Dann Bilardello .05
425 Steve Howe .05
426 Orioles Batting & Pitching Leaders (Mike Boddicker, Cal Ripken, Jr.) .50
427 Rick Leach .05
428 Fred Breining .05
429 Randy Bush **RC** .05
430 Rusty Staub .05
431 Chris Bando .05
432 Charlie Hudson **RC** .05
433 Rich Hebner .05
434 Harold Baines .05
435 Neil Allen .05
436 Rick Peters .05
437 Mike Proly .05
438 Biff Pocoroba .05
439 Bob Stoddard .05
440 Steve Kemp .05
441 Bob Lillis .05
442 Byron McLaughlin .05
443 Benny Ayala .05
444 Steve Renko .05
445 Jerry Remy .05
446 Luis Pujols .05
447 Tom Brunansky .05
448 Ben Hayes .05
449 Joe Pettini .05
450 Gary Carter 1.00
451 Bob Jones .05
452 Chuck Porter .05
453 Willie Upshaw .05
454 Joe Beckwith .05
455 Terry Kennedy .05
456 Cubs Batting & Pitching Leaders (Fergie Jenkins, Keith Moreland) .05
457 Dave Rozema .05
458 Kiko Garcia .05
459 Kevin Hickey .05
460 Dave Winfield 1.00
461 Jim Maler .05
462 Lee Lacy .05
463 Dave Engle .05
464 Jeff Jones .05
465 Mookie Wilson .05
466 Gene Garber .05
467 Mike Ramsey .05
468 Geoff Zahn .05
469 Tom O'Malley .05
470 Nolan Ryan 6.00
471 Dick Howser .05
472 Mike Brown .05
473 Jim Dwyer .05
474 Greg Bargar .05
475 Gary Redus **RC** .05
476 Tom Tellmann .05
477 Rafael Landestoy .05
478 Alan Bannister .05
479 Frank Tanana .05
480 Ron Kittle **RC** .05
481 Mark Thurmond **RC** .05
482 Enos Cabell .05
483 Fergie Jenkins .65
484 Ozzie Virgil .05
485 Rick Rhoden .05
486 Yankees Batting & Pitching Leaders (Don Baylor, Ron Guidry) .05
487 Ricky Adams .05
488 Jesse Barfield .05
489 Dave Von Ohlen .05
490 Cal Ripken, Jr. 6.00
491 Bobby Castillo .05
492 Tucker Ashford .05
493 Mike Norris .05
494 Chili Davis .05
495 Rollie Fingers .65
496 Terry Francona .05
497 Bud Anderson .05
498 Rich Gedman .05
499 Mike Witt .05
500 George Brett 2.00
501 Steve Henderson .05
502 Joe Torre .05
503 Elias Sosa .05
504 Mickey Rivers .05
505 Pete Vuckovich .05
506 Ernie Whitt .05
507 Mike LaCoss .05
508 Mel Hall .05
509 Brad Havens .05
510 Alan Trammell .05
511 Marty Bystrom .05
512 Oscar Gamble .05
513 Dave Beard .05
514 Floyd Rayford .05
515 Gorman Thomas .05
516 Expos Batting & Pitching Leaders (Charlie Lea, Al Oliver) .05
517 John Moses .05
518 Greg Walker **RC** .05
519 Ron Davis .05
520 Bob Boone .05
521 Pete Falcone .05

522	Dave Bergman	.05
523	Glenn Hoffman	.05
524	Carlos Diaz	.05
525	Willie Wilson	.05
526	Ron Oester	.05
527	Checklist 397-528	.05
528	Mark Brouhard	.05
529	Keith Atherton **RC**	.05
530	Dan Ford	.05
531	Steve Boros	.05
532	Eric Show	.05
533	Ken Landreaux	.05
534	Pete O'Brien	.05
535	Bo Diaz	.05
536	Doug Bair	.05
537	Johnny Ray	.05
538	Kevin Bass	.05
539	George Frazier	.05
540	George Hendrick	.05
541	Dennis Lamp	.05
542	Duane Kuiper	.05
543	Craig McMurtry **RC**	.05
544	Cesar Geronimo	.05
545	Bill Buckner	.05
546	Indians Batting & Pitching Leaders (Mike Hargrove, Lary Sorensen)	.05
547	Mike Moore	.05
548	Ron Jackson	.05
549	Walt Terrell **RC**	.05
550	Jim Rice	.15
551	Scott Ullger	.05
552	Ray Burris	.05
553	Joe Nolan	.05
554	Ted Power **RC**	.05
555	Greg Brock	.05
556	Joey McLaughlin	.05
557	Wayne Tolleson	.05
558	Mike Davis	.05
559	Mike Scott	.05
560	Carlton Fisk	1.00
561	Whitey Herzog	.05
562	Manny Castillo	.05
563	Glenn Wilson	.05
564	Al Holland	.05
565	Leon Durham	.05
566	Jim Bibby	.05
567	Mike Heath	.05
568	Pete Filson	.05
569	Bake McBride	.05
570	Dan Quisenberry	.05
571	Bruce Bochy	.05
572	Jerry Royster	.05
573	Dave Kingman	.05
574	Brian Downing	.05
575	Jim Clancy	.05
576	Giants Batting & Pitching Leaders (Atlee Hammaker, Jeff Leonard)	.05
577	Mark Clear	.05
578	Lenn Sakata	.05
579	Bob James	.05
580	Lonnie Smith	.05
581	Jose DeLeon **RC**	.05
582	Bob McClure	.05
583	Derrel Thomas	.05
584	Dave Schmidt	.05
585	Dan Driessen	.05
586	Joe Niekro	.05
587	Von Hayes	.05
588	Milt Wilcox	.05
589	Mike Easler	.05
590	Dave Stieb	.05
591	Tony LaRussa	.05
592	Andre Robertson	.05
593	Jeff Lahti	.05
594	Gene Richards	.05
595	Jeff Reardon	.05
596	Ryne Sandberg	3.00
597	Rick Camp	.05
598	Rusty Kuntz	.05
599	Doug Sisk **RC**	.05
600	Rod Carew	1.00
601	John Tudor	.05
602	John Wathan	.05
603	Renie Martin	.05
604	John Lowenstein	.05
605	Mike Caldwell	.05
606	Blue Jays Batting & Pitching Leaders (Lloyd Moseby, Dave Stieb)	.05
607	Tom Hume	.05
608	Bobby Johnson	.05
609	Dan Meyer	.05
610	Steve Sax	.05
611	Chet Lemon	.05
612	Harry Spilman	.05
613	Greg Gross	.05
614	Len Barker	.05
615	Garry Templeton	.05
616	Don Robinson	.05
617	Rick Cerone	.05
618	Dickie Noles	.05
619	Jerry Dybzinski	.05
620	Al Oliver	.05
621	Frank Howard	.05
622	Al Cowens	.05
623	Ron Washington	.05
624	Terry Harper	.05
625	Larry Gura	.05
626	Bob Clark	.05
627	Dave LaPoint	.05
628	Ed Jurak	.05
629	Rick Langford	.05
630	Ted Simmons	.05
631	Denny Martinez	.05
632	Tom Foley	.05
633	Mike Krukow	.05
634	Mike Marshall	.05
635	Dave Righetti	.05
636	Pat Putnam	.05
637	Phillies Batting & Pitching Leaders (John Denny, Gary Matthews)	.05
638	George Vukovich	.05
639	Rick Lysander	.05
640	Lance Parrish	.05
641	Mike Richardt	.05
642	Tom Underwood	.05
643	Mike Brown	.05
644	Tim Lollar	.05
645	Tony Pena	.05
646	Checklist 529-660	.05
647	Ron Roenicke	.05
648	Len Whitehouse	.05
649	Tom Herr	.05
650	Phil Niekro	.65
651	John McNamara	.05
652	Rudy May	.05
653	Dave Stapleton	.05
654	Bob Bailor	.05
655	Amos Otis	.05
656	Bryn Smith	.05
657	Thad Bosley	.05
658	Jerry Augustine	.05
659	Duane Walker	.05
660	Ray Knight	.05
661	Steve Yeager	.05
662	Tom Brennan	.05
663	Johnnie LeMaster	.05
664	Dave Stegman	.05
665	Buddy Bell	.05
666	Tigers Batting & Pitching Leaders (Jack Morris, Lou Whitaker)	.05
667	Vance Law	.05
668	Larry McWilliams	.05
669	Dave Lopes	.05
670	Rich Gossage	.05
671	Jamie Quirk	.05
672	Ricky Nelson	.05
673	Mike Walters	.05
674	Tim Flannery	.05
675	Pascual Perez	.05
676	Brian Giles	.05
677	Doyle Alexander	.05
678	Chris Speier	.05
679	Art Howe	.05
680	Fred Lynn	.05
681	Tom Lasorda	.15
682	Dan Morogiello	.05
683	Marty Barrett **RC**	.05
684	Bob Shirley	.05
685	Willie Aikens	.05
686	Joe Price	.05
687	Roy Howell	.05
688	George Wright	.05
689	Mike Fischlin	.05
690	Jack Clark	.05
691	Steve Lake **RC**	.05
692	Dickie Thon	.05
693	Alan Wiggins	.05
694	Mike Stanton	.05
695	Lou Whitaker	.05
696	Pirates Batting & Pitching Leaders (Bill Madlock, Rick Rhoden)	.05
697	Dale Murray	.05
698	Marc Hill	.05
699	Dave Rucker	.05
700	Mike Schmidt	2.00
701	NL Active Career Batting Leaders (Bill Madlock, Dave Parker, Pete Rose)	.25
702	NL Active Career Hit Leaders (Tony Perez, Pete Rose, Rusty Staub)	.25
703	NL Active Career Home Run Leaders (Dave Kingman, Tony Perez, Mike Schmidt)	.15
704	NL Active Career RBI Leaders (Al Oliver, Tony Perez, Rusty Staub)	.05
705	NL Active Career Stolen Bases Leaders (Larry Bowa, Cesar Cedeno, Joe Morgan)	.05
706	NL Active Career Victory Leaders (Steve Carlton, Fergie Jenkins, Tom Seaver)	.05
707	NL Active Career Strikeout Leaders (Steve Carlton, Nolan Ryan, Tom Seaver)	.35
708	NL Active Career ERA Leaders (Steve Carlton, Steve Rogers, Tom Seaver)	.05
709	NL Active Career Save Leaders (Gene Garber, Tug McGraw, Bruce Sutter)	.10
710	AL Active Career Batting Leaders (George Brett, Rod Carew, Cecil Cooper)	.25
711	AL Active Career Hit Leaders (Bert Campaneris, Rod Carew, Reggie Jackson)	.15
712	AL Active Career Home Run Leaders (Reggie Jackson, Greg Luzinski, Graig Nettles)	.15
713	AL Active Career RBI Leaders (Reggie Jackson, Graig Nettles, Ted Simmons)	.15
714	AL Active Career Stolen Bases Leaders (Bert Campaneris, Dave Lopes, Omar Moreno)	.05
715	AL Active Career Victory Leaders (Tommy John, Jim Palmer, Don Sutton)	.05
716	AL Active Strikeout Leaders (Bert Blyleven, Jerry Koosman, Don Sutton)	.05
717	AL Active Career ERA Leaders (Rollie Fingers, Ron Guidry, Jim Palmer)	.05
718	AL Active Career Save Leaders (Rollie Fingers, Rich Gossage, Dan Quisenberry)	.05
719	Andy Hassler	.05
720	Dwight Evans	.05
721	Del Crandall	.05
722	Bob Welch	.05
723	Rich Dauer	.05
724	Eric Rasmussen	.05
725	Cesar Cedeno	.05
726	Brewers Batting & Pitching Leaders (Moose Haas, Ted Simmons)	.05
727	Joel Youngblood	.05
728	Tug McGraw	.05
729	Gene Tenace	.05
730	Bruce Sutter	.75
731	Lynn Jones	.05
732	Terry Crowley	.05
733	Dave Collins	.05
734	Odell Jones	.05
735	Rick Burleson	.05
736	Dick Ruthven	.05
737	Jim Essian	.05
738	Bill Schroeder **RC**	.05
739	Bob Watson	.05
740	Tom Seaver	1.00
741	Wayne Gross	.05
742	Dick Williams	.05
743	Don Hood	.05
744	Jamie Allen	.05
745	Dennis Eckersley	.65
746	Mickey Hatcher	.05
747	Pat Zachry	.05
748	Jeff Leonard	.05
749	Doug Flynn	.05
750a	Jim Palmer	1.00
750b	Jim Palmer (Missing 1980-82 losses on back.)	3.00
750c	Jim Palmer (Missing 1979-83 losses on back.)	4.00
751	Charlie Moore	.05
752	Phil Garner	.05
753	Doug Gwosdz	.05
754	Kent Tekulve	.05
755	Garry Maddox	.05
756	Reds Batting & Pitching Leaders (Ron Oester, Mario Soto)	.05
757	Larry Bowa	.05
758	Bill Stein	.05
759	Richard Dotson	.05
760	Bob Horner	.05
761	John Montefusco	.05
762	Rance Mulliniks	.05
763	Craig Swan	.05
764	Mike Hargrove	.05
765	Ken Forsch	.05
766	Mike Vail	.05
767	Carney Lansford	.05
768	Champ Summers	.05
769	Bill Caudill	.05
770	Ken Griffey	.05
771	Billy Gardner	.05
772	Jim Slaton	.05
773	Todd Cruz	.05
774	Tom Gorman	.05
775	Dave Parker	.05
776	Craig Reynolds	.05
777	Tom Paciorek	.05
778	Andy Hawkins **RC**	.05
779	Jim Sundberg	.05
780	Steve Carlton	1.00
781	Checklist 661-792	.05
782	Steve Balboni	.05
783	Luis Leal	.05
784	Leon Roberts	.05
785	Joaquin Andujar	.05
786	Red Sox Batting & Pitching Leaders (Wade Boggs, Bob Ojeda)	.25
787	Bill Campbell	.05
788	Milt May	.05
789	Bert Blyleven	.05
790	Doug DeCinces	.05
791	Terry Forster	.05
792	Bill Russell	.05

Tiffany

In 1984 Topps introduced a specially boxed, limited edition version of its baseball card set. Sold only through hobby dealers, the cards differed from regular-issue 1984 Topps cards in their use of white cardboard stock and the application of a high-gloss finish to the front of the card. Production was limited to a reported 10,000 sets. The nickname "Tiffany" was coined by collectors to identify the glossy collectors edition.

		NM/M
Unopened Set (792):		175.00
Complete Set (792):		95.00
Common Player:		.15
Stars:		6X
8	Don Mattingly	80.00

Traded

The popular Topps Traded set returned for its fourth year in 1984 with another 132-card set. The 2-1/2" x 3-1/2" cards have an identical design to the regular Topps cards except that the back cardboard is white and card numbers carry a "T" suffix. As before, the set was sold only through hobby dealers. Also as before, players who changed teams, new managers and promising rookies are included in the set. A glossy-finish "Tiffany" version of the set was also issued.

		NM/M
Complete Set (132):		17.50
Common Player:		.05
1T	Willie Aikens	.05
2T	Luis Aponte	.05
3T	Mike Armstrong	.05
4T	Bob Bailor	.05
5T	Dusty Baker	.15
6T	Steve Balboni	.05
7T	Alan Bannister	.05
8T	Dave Beard	.05
9T	Joe Beckwith	.05
10T	Bruce Berenyi	.05
11T	Dave Bergman	.05
12T	Tony Bernazard	.05
13T	Yogi Berra	.25
14T	Barry Bonnell	.05
15T	Phil Bradley	.05
16T	Fred Breining	.05
17T	Bill Buckner	.05
18T	Ray Burris	.05
19T	John Butcher	.05
20T	Brett Butler	.05
21T	Enos Cabell	.05
22T	Bill Campbell	.05
23T	Bill Caudill	.05
24T	Bob Clark	.05
25T	Bryan Clark	.05
26T	Jaime Cocanower	.05
27T	Ron Darling **RC**	.50
28T	Alvin Davis **RC**	.05
29T	Ken Dayley	.05
30T	Jeff Dedmon	.05
31T	Bob Dernier	.05
32T	Carlos Diaz	.05
33T	Mike Easler	.05
34T	Dennis Eckersley	1.50
35T	Jim Essian	.05
36T	Darrell Evans	.05
37T	Mike Fitzgerald **RC**	.05
38T	Tim Foli	.05
39T	George Frazier	.05
40T	Rich Gale	.05
41T	Barbaro Garbey	.05
12T	Dwight Gooden **RC**	3.00
43T	Rich Gossage	.05
44T	Wayne Gross	.05
45T	Mark Gubicza **RC**	.25
46T	Jackie Gutierrez	.05
47T	Mel Hall	.05
48T	Toby Harrah	.05
49T	Ron Hassey	.05
50T	Rich Hebner	.05
51T	Willie Hernandez	.05
52T	Ricky Horton **RC**	.05
53T	Art Howe	.05
54T	Dane Iorg	.05
55T	Brook Jacoby **RC**	.05
56T	Mike Jeffcoat **RC**	.05
57T	Dave Johnson	.05
58T	Lynn Jones	.05
59T	Ruppert Jones	.05
60T	Mike Jorgensen	.05
61T	Bob Kearney	.05
62T	Jimmy Key **RC**	.50
63T	Dave Kingman	.05
64T	Jerry Koosman	.05
65T	Wayne Krenchicki	.05
66T	Rusty Kuntz	.05
67T	Rene Lachemann	.05
68T	Frank LaCorte	.05
69T	Dennis Lamp	.05
70T	Mark Langston **RC**	.50
71T	Rick Leach	.05
72T	Craig Lefferts	.05
73T	Gary Lucas	.05
74T	Jerry Martin	.05
75T	Carmelo Martinez	.05
76T	Mike Mason **RC**	.05
77T	Gary Matthews	.05
78T	Andy McGaffigan	.05
79T	Larry Milbourne	.05
80T	Sid Monge	.05
81T	Jackie Moore	.05
82T	Joe Morgan	2.00
83T	Graig Nettles	.05
84T	Phil Niekro	1.00
85T	Ken Oberkfell	.05
86T	Mike O'Berry	.05
87T	Al Oliver	.05
88T	Jorge Orta	.05
89T	Amos Otis	.05
90T	Dave Parker	.05
91T	Tony Perez	1.00
92T	Gerald Perry **RC**	.05
93T	Gary Pettis **RC**	.05
94T	Rob Picciolo	.05
95T	Vern Rapp	.05
96T	Floyd Rayford	.05
97T	Randy Ready **RC**	.05
98T	Ron Reed	.05
99T	Gene Richards	.05
100T	Jose Rijo **RC**	.25
101T	Jeff Robinson **RC**	.05
102T	Ron Romanick **RC**	.05
103T	Pete Rose	7.50
104T	Bret Saberhagen **RC**	3.00
105T	Juan Samuel **RC**	.05
106T	Scott Sanderson	.05
107T	Dick Schofield **RC**	.05
108T	Tom Seaver	3.00
109T	Jim Slaton	.05
110T	Mike Smithson	.05
111T	Lary Sorensen	.05
112T	Tim Stoddard	.05
113T	Champ Summers	.05
114T	Jim Sundberg	.05
115T	Rick Sutcliffe	.05
116T	Craig Swan	.05
117T	Tim Teufel **RC**	.05
118T	Derrel Thomas	.05
119T	Gorman Thomas	.05
120T	Alex Trevino	.05
121T	Manny Trillo	.05
122T	John Tudor	.05
123T	Tom Underwood	.05
124T	Mike Vail	.05
125T	Tom Waddell	.05
126T	Gary Ward	.05
127T	Curt Wilkerson	.05
128T	Frank Williams **RC**	.05
129T	Glenn Wilson	.05
130T	Johnny Wockenfuss	.05
131T	Ned Yost	.05
132T	Checklist 1-132	.05

Traded Tiffany

Following up on its inaugural Tiffany collectors' edition, Topps produced a special glossy version of its Traded set for 1984, as well. Cards in this special boxed set differ from regular Traded cards only in the use of white cardboard stock with a high-gloss finish coat on front.

	NM/M
Complete Set (132):	35.00
Common Player:	.25
Stars:	2X

Traded Darryl Strawberry Bronze

This 1/4-size metal replica of Strawberry's first-ever Topps card was issued to dealers who purchased cases of 1984 Topps Traded sets. Each detail of the 1983 Topps Traded Strawberry card is reproduced on the 1-1/4" x 1-3/4" bronze metal mini-card, right down to the stats.

		NM/M
108T	Darryl Strawberry	3.00

Proofs

Though still small in terms of actual numbers, the quantity of 1984 Topps proofs from the "A" sheet which have made their way into the hobby is relatively large. More precisely, 66 cards (half a production press sheet) are frequently seen in proof version. Like other true proofs, they are blank-backed but these have a very discernible difference from the issued 1984 Topps cards. On the proofs, the portrait photo at lower-left is completely within the black frame of the box. On issued cards, the cap extends above the box border. On the proofs, portrait photos of Steve Carlton and Gary Matthews are found on each other's cards and Manny Trillo is pictured in an Indians uniform, rather than the Expos livery on which he appears in the regularly issued version. Single proofs in the market have been cut from half-sheets.

		NM/M
Uncut Sheet (66):		650.00
Complete Set, Singles (66):		800.00
Common Player:		10.00
(1)	Buddy Bell	10.00
(2)	Wade Boggs	50.00
(3)	Bob Boone	12.50
(4)	Greg Brock	10.00
(5)	Hubie Brooks	10.00
(6)	Steve Carlton (Inset photo Gary Matthews.)	150.00
(7)	Gary Carter	20.00
(8)	Cecil Cooper	10.00
(9)	Andre Dawson	20.00
(10)	Storm Davis	10.00
(11)	Doug DeCinces	10.00
(12)	Ivan DeJesus	10.00
(13)	Rick Dempsey	10.00
(14)	Dwight Evans	10.00
(15)	Rollie Fingers	20.00
(16)	Carlton Fisk	50.00
(17)	Ken Forsch	10.00
(18)	George Foster	10.00
(19)	Julio Franco	10.00
(20)	Jim Gantner	10.00
(21)	Damaso Garcia	10.00
(22)	Ken Griffey	12.50
(23)	Alfredo Griffin	10.00
(24)	Bill Gullickson	10.00
(25)	Moose Haas	10.00
(26)	Rickey Henderson	50.00
(27)	Kent Hrbek	12.50
(28)	Reggie Jackson	50.00
(29)	Roy Lee Jackson	10.00
(30)	Cliff Johnson	10.00
(31)	Ron Kittle	10.00
(32)	Charlie Lea	10.00
(33)	Luis Leal	10.00
(34)	Bill Madlock	10.00
(35)	Buck Martinez	10.00
(36)	Gary Matthews (Inset photo is Steve Carlton.)	75.00
(37)	Willie McGee	12.50
(38)	Greg Minton	10.00
(39)	Paul Molitor	30.00
(40)	Joe Morgan	30.00
(41)	Lloyd Moseby	10.00
(42)	Rance Mulliniks	10.00
(43)	Graig Nettles	10.00
(44)	Al Oliver	15.00
(45)	Lou Piniella	15.00
(46)	Bobby Ramos	10.00
(47)	Johnny Ray	10.00

(48)	Jeff Reardon	10.00
(49)	Jim Rice	20.00
(50)	Andre Robertson	10.00
(51)	Nolan Ryan	300.00
(52)	Scott Sanderson	10.00
(53)	Steve Sax	10.00
(54)	Dan Schatzeder	10.00
(55)	Tom Seaver	60.00
(56)	Lee Smith	15.00
(57)	Don Sutton	20.00
(58)	Jason Thompson	10.00
(59)	Alan Trammell	15.00
(60)	Manny Trillo (Indians)	100.00
(61)	Willie Upshaw	10.00
(62)	Fernando Valenzuela	15.00
(63)	Tim Wallach	10.00
(64)	Ernie Whitt	10.00
(65)	Glenn Wilson	10.00
(66)	Robin Yount	30.00

All-Star Glossy Set of 22

These 2-1/2" x 3-1/2" cards were a result of the success of Topps' efforts the previous year with glossy cards on a mail-in basis. The set is divided evenly between the two leagues. Each All-Star Game starter for both leagues, the managers and the honorary team captains have an All-Star Glossy card. Cards feature a large color photo on the front with an All-Star banner across the top and the league emblem in the lower-left. Player identification appears below the photo. Backs have a name, team, position and card number along with the phrase "1983 All-Star Game Commemorative Set." The '84 Glossy All-Stars were distributed one card per rack pack.

		NM/M
Complete Set (22):		4.00
Common Player:		.10
1	Harvey Kuenn	.10
2	Rod Carew	.50
3	Manny Trillo	.10
4	George Brett	1.00
5	Robin Yount	.50
6	Jim Rice	.25
7	Fred Lynn	.10
8	Dave Winfield	.50
9	Ted Simmons	.10
10	Dave Stieb	.10
11	Carl Yastrzemski	.50
12	Whitey Herzog	.10
13	Al Oliver	.10
14	Steve Sax	.10
15	Mike Schmidt	1.00
16	Ozzie Smith	.50
17	Tim Raines	.10
18	Andre Dawson	.25
19	Dale Murphy	.25
20	Gary Carter	.50
21	Mario Soto	.10
22	Johnny Bench	.50

All-Star Glossy Set of 40

For the second straight year in 1984, Topps produced a 40-card All-Star "Collector's Edition" set as a "consolation prize" for its sweepstakes game. By collecting game cards and sending them in with a bit of cash, the collector could receive one of eight different five-card series. As the previous year, the 2-1/2" x 3-1/2" cards feature a nearly full-

frame color photo on its glossy finish front. Backs are printed in red and blue.

		NM/M
Complete Set (40):		6.00
Common Player:		.10
1	Pete Rose	1.00
2	Lance Parrish	.10
3	Steve Rogers	.10
4	Eddie Murray	.40
5	Johnny Ray	.10
6	Rickey Henderson	.40
7	Atlee Hammaker	.10
8	Wade Boggs	.50
9	Gary Carter	.40
10	Jack Morris	.10
11	Darrell Evans	.10
12	George Brett	1.00
13	Bob Horner	.10
14	Ron Guidry	.10
15	Nolan Ryan	1.50
16	Dave Winfield	.40
17	Ozzie Smith	.50
18	Ted Simmons	.10
19	Bill Madlock	.10
20	Tony Armas	.10
21	Al Oliver	.10
22	Jim Rice	.25
23	George Hendrick	.10
24	Dave Stieb	.10
25	Pedro Guerrero	.10
26	Rod Carew	.40
27	Steve Carlton	.40
28	Dave Righetti	.10
29	Darryl Strawberry	.10
30	Lou Whitaker	.10
31	Dale Murphy	.25
32	LaMarr Hoyt	.10
33	Jesse Orosco	.10
34	Cecil Cooper	.10
35	Andre Dawson	.25
36	Robin Yount	.40
37	Tim Raines	.10
38	Dan Quisenberry	.10
39	Mike Schmidt	1.00
40	Carlton Fisk	.40

Cereal Series

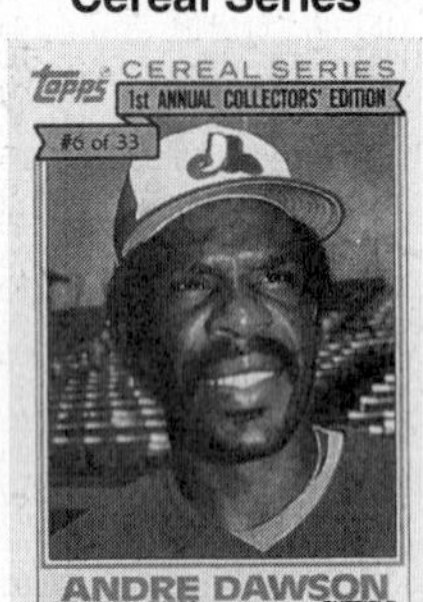

The Topps-produced 1984 Cereal Series set is identical to the Ralston Purina set from the same year in nearly all aspects. On the card fronts the words "Ralston Purina Company" were replaced by "Cereal Series" and Topps logos were substituted for Ralston checkerboard logos. The set is comprised of 33 cards, each measuring 2-1/2" x 3-1/2." The cards were inserted in unmarked boxes of Chex brand cereals.

		NM/M
Complete Set (33):		4.00
Common Player:		.05
1	Eddie Murray	.25
2	Ozzie Smith	.30
3	Ted Simmons	.05
4	Pete Rose	.75
5	Greg Luzinski	.05
6	Andre Dawson	.15
7	Dave Winfield	.25
8	Tom Seaver	.25
9	Jim Rice	.15
10	Fernando Valenzuela	.05
11	Wade Boggs	.30
12	Dale Murphy	.15
13	George Brett	.50
14	Nolan Ryan	1.00
15	Rickey Henderson	.25
16	Steve Carlton	.25
17	Rod Carew	.25
18	Steve Garvey	.15
19	Reggie Jackson	.35
20	Dave Concepcion	.05
21	Robin Yount	.25
22	Mike Schmidt	.50
23	Jim Palmer	.25
24	Bruce Sutter	.20
25	Dan Quisenberry	.05
26	Bill Madlock	.05
27	Cecil Cooper	.05
28	Gary Carter	.25
29	Fred Lynn	.05
30	Pedro Guerrero	.05
31	Ron Guidry	.05
32	Keith Hernandez	.05
33	Carlton Fisk	.25

"Darryl Palmer"

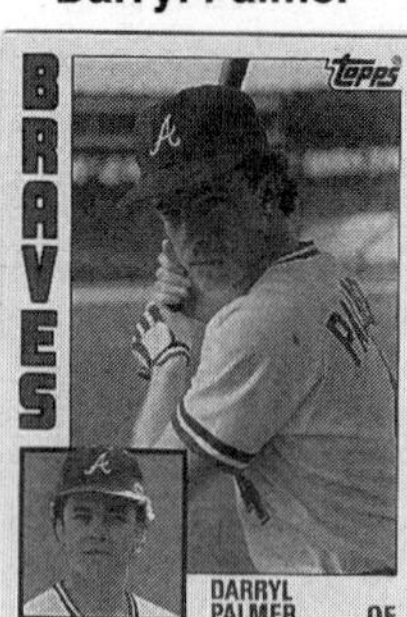

For use as a prop in the 1985 movie "The Slugger's Wife," Topps produced this 1984-style card of actor Michael O'Keefe as Darryl Palmer. (O'Keefe is better remembered as caddy Danny Noonan is "Caddyshack.") Front and back are in the '84T format, complete with personal data, stats and Topps copyrights.

		NM/M
801	Darryl Palmer	15.00

Gallery of Immortals

The Gallery of Immortals bronze and silver replicas were the first metal miniature set from Topps and the start of an annual tradition (in 1985, the name was changed to Gallery of Champions). Each mini is an exact one-quarter scale replica of the featured player's 1984 Topps baseball card, both front and back, in minute detail. The three-dimensional metal cards were packaged in a velvet-lined case that bears the title of the set in gold-embossed letters. A certificate of authenticity is included with each set. A Tom Seaver pewter metal mini-card was given as a premium to dealers who purchsed sets. Issue price was about $100 for the cased bronze set, $500 for the silver edition of 1,000.

		NM/M
Complete Bronze Set (12):		40.00
Complete Silver Set (12):		190.00
(1b)	George Brett/Bronze	12.50
(1s)	George Brett/Silver	45.00
(2b)	Rod Carew/Bronze	6.00
(2s)	Rod Carew/Silver	15.00
(3b)	Steve Carlton/Bronze	6.00
(3s)	Steve Carlton/Silver	15.00
(4b)	Rollie Fingers/Bronze	4.00
(4s)	Rollie Fingers/Silver	12.50
(5b)	Steve Garvey/Bronze	4.00
(5s)	Steve Garvey/Silver	12.50
(6b)	Reggie Jackson/ Bronze	7.50
(6s)	Reggie Jackson/ Silver	17.50
(7b)	Joe Morgan/Bronze	5.00
(7s)	Joe Morgan/Silver	12.50
(8b)	Jim Palmer/Bronze	5.00
(8s)	Jim Palmer/Silver	12.50
(9b)	Pete Rose/Bronze	20.00
(9s)	Pete Rose/Silver	50.00
(10b)	Nolan Ryan/Bronze	25.00
(10s)	Nolan Ryan/Silver	60.00
(11b)	Mike Schmidt/Bronze	12.50
(11s)	Mike Schmidt/Silver	45.00
(12b)	Tom Seaver/Bronze	6.00
(12s)	Tom Seaver/Silver	15.00
(12p)	Tom Seaver/Pewter	15.00

"Pewter" Gallery Ingots

All of the Topps Gallery of Immortals (1984) and Gallery of Champions (1985-1989) miniature ingots have been counterfeited in a pewter or pot metal alloy designed to look like the genuine silver pieces. The fakes are cast, rather than die-struck, have a porous surface upon magnification and sometimes the casting seam is visible despite the filing done to remove it. These are often sold on eBay as "pewter." Topps did did make one genuine pewter piece each year 1984-1991, as an ordering incentive; they are listed within each year's Gallery checklist.

Rub Downs

This set consists of 32 "Rub Down" sheets featuring 112 different players. Each sheet measures 2-3/8" x 3-15/16" and includes small, color baseball player figures along with bats, balls and gloves. The pictures can be transferred to another surface by rubbing the paper backing. The sheets, which were sold as a separate issue, are somewhat reminiscent of earlier tattoo sets issued by Topps. The sheets are not numbered.

		NM/M
Complete Set (32):		7.50
Common Sheet:		.50
Pack (2):		.50
Box (36):		9.00
(1)	Steve Bedrosian, Bruce Benedict, Tony Armas, Harold Baines, Lonnie Smith	.50
(2)	Chris Chambliss, Bob Horner, Don Baylor, George Hendrick, Ron Kittle, Johnnie LeMaster	.50
(3)	Glenn Hubbard, Rafael Ramirez, Buddy Bell, Ray Knight, Lloyd Moseby	.50
(4)	Craig McMurtry, Bruce Benedict, Atlee Hammaker, Frank White	.50
(5)	Wade Boggs, Rick Dempsey, Keith Hernandez	.75
(6)	George Brett, Andre Dawson, Paul Molitor, Alan Wiggins	1.00
(7)	Tom Brunansky, Pedro Guerrero, Darryl Strawberry	.50
(8)	Bill Buckner, Rich Gossage, Dave Stieb, Rick Sutcliffe	.50
(9)	Rod Carew, Carlton Fisk, Johnny Ray, Matt Young	.60
(10)	Steve Carlton, Bob Horner, Dan Quisenberry	.60
(11)	Gary Carter, Phil Garner, Ron Guidry	.60
(12)	Ron Cey, Steve Kemp, Greg Luzinski, Kent Tekulve	.50
(13)	Chris Chambliss, Dwight Evans, Julio Franco	.50
(14)	Jack Clark, Damaso Garcia, Hal McRae, Lance Parrish	.50
(15)	Dave Concepcion, Cecil Cooper, Fred Lynn, Jesse Orosco	.50
(16)	Jose Cruz, Gary Matthews, Jack Morris, Jim Rice	.50
(17)	Ron Davis, Kent Hrbek, Tom Seaver	.60
(18)	John Denny, Carney Lansford, Mario Soto, Lou Whitaker	.50
(19)	Leon Durham, Dave Lopes, Steve Sax	.50
(20)	George Foster, Gary Gaetti, Bobby Grich, Gary Redus	.50
(21)	Steve Garvey, Bill Russell, Jerry Remy, George Wright	.50
(22)	Moose Haas, Bruce Sutter, Dickie Thon, Andre Thornton	.50
(23)	Toby Harrah, Pat Putnam, Tim Raines, Mike Schmidt	1.00
(24)	Rickey Henderson, Dave Righetti, Pete Rose	1.00
(25)	Steve Henderson, Bill Madlock, Alan Trammell	.50
(26)	LaMarr Hoyt, Larry Parrish, Nolan Ryan	1.50
(27)	Reggie Jackson, Eric Show, Jason Thompson	.60
(28)	Tommy John, Terry Kennedy, Eddie Murray, Ozzie Smith	.60
(29)	Jeff Leonard, Dale Murphy, Ken Singleton, Dave Winfield	.60
(30)	Craig McMurtry, Cal Ripken, Steve Rogers, Willie Upshaw	1.50
(31)	Ben Oglivie, Jim Palmer, Darrell Porter	.50
(32)	Tony Pena, Fernando Valenzuela, Robin Yount	.60

Stickers

The largest sticker set issued by Topps, the 1984 set consists of 386 stickers, each measuring 1-15/16" x 2-9/16". The full color photos have stars in each of the corners and are numbered on both the front and the back. The back includes information about the sticker album and a promotion to order stickers through the mail. The back of the album is a tribute to Carl Yastrzemski,

including a large photo and reproductions of his 1960-1983 cards in miniature.

		NM/M
Complete Set (386):		12.00
Common Player:		.05
Sticker Album:		3.00
Box (35):		6.00
1	Steve Carlton	.25
2	Steve Carlton	.25
3	Rickey Henderson	.25
4	Rickey Henderson	.25
5	Fred Lynn	.05
6	Fred Lynn	.05
7	Greg Luzinski	.05
8	Greg Luzinski	.05
9	Dan Quisenberry	.05
10	Dan Quisenberry	.05
11	1983 Championship (LaMarr Hoyt)	.05
12	1983 Championship (Mike Flanagan)	.05
13	1983 Championship (Mike Boddicker)	.05
14	1983 Championship (Tito Landrum)	.05
15	1983 Championship (Steve Carlton)	.10
16	1983 Championship (Fernando Valenzuela)	.05
17	1983 Championship (Charlie Hudson)	.05
18	1983 Championship (Gary Matthews)	.05
19	1983 World Series (John Denny)	.05
20	1983 World Series (John Lowenstein)	.05
21	1983 World Series (Jim Palmer)	.10
22	1983 World Series (Benny Ayala)	.05
23	1983 World Series (Rick Dempsey)	.05
24	1983 World Series (Cal Ripken)	.50
25	1983 World Series (Sammy Stewart)	.05
26	1983 World Series (Eddie Murray)	.10
27	Dale Murphy	.15
28	Chris Chambliss	.05
29	Glenn Hubbard	.05
30	Bob Horner	.05
31	Phil Niekro	.20
32	Claudell Washington	.05
33	Rafael Ramirez	.05
34	Bruce Benedict	.05
35	Gene Garber	.05
36	Pascual Perez	.05
37	Jerry Royster	.05
38	Steve Bedrosian	.05
39	Keith Moreland	.05
40	Leon Durham	.05
41	Ron Cey	.05
42	Bill Buckner	.05
43	Jody Davis	.05
44	Lee Smith	.05
45	Ryne Sandberg	.30
46	Larry Bowa	.05
47	Chuck Rainey	.05
48	Fergie Jenkins	.20
49	Dick Ruthven	.05
50	Jay Johnstone	.05
51	Mario Soto	.05
52	Gary Redus	.05
53	Ron Oester	.05
54	Cesar Cedeno	.05
55	Dan Driessen	.05
56	Dave Concepcion	.05
57	Dann Bilardello	.05
58	Joe Price	.05
59	Tom Hume	.05
60	Eddie Milner	.05
61	Paul Householder	.05
62	Bill Scherrer	.05
63	Phil Garner	.05
64	Dickie Thon	.05
65	Jose Cruz	.05
66	Nolan Ryan	.60
67	Terry Puhl	.05
68	Ray Knight	.05
69	Joe Niekro	.05
70	Jerry Mumphrey	.05
71	Bill Dawley	.05
72	Alan Ashby	.05
73	Denny Walling	.05

74 Frank DiPino .05
75 Pedro Guerrero .05
76 Ken Landreaux .05
77 Bill Russell .05
78 Steve Sax .05
79 Fernando Valenzuela .05
80 Dusty Baker .05
81 Jerry Reuss .05
82 Alejandro Pena .05
83 Rick Monday .05
84 Rick Honeycutt .05
85 Mike Marshall .05
86 Steve Yeager .05
87 Al Oliver .05
88 Steve Rogers .05
89 Jeff Reardon .05
90 Gary Carter .25
91 Tim Raines .05
92 Andre Dawson .15
93 Manny Trillo .05
94 Tim Wallach .05
95 Chris Speier .05
96 Bill Gullickson .05
97 Doug Flynn .05
98 Charlie Lea .05
99 Bill Madlock .05
100 Wade Boggs .25
101 Mike Schmidt .40
102a Jim Rice .15
102b Reggie Jackson .25
103 Hubie Brooks .05
104 Jesse Orosco .05
105 George Foster .05
106 Tom Seaver .25
107 Keith Hernandez .05
108 Mookie Wilson .05
109 Bob Bailor .05
110 Walt Terrell .05
111 Brian Giles .05
112 Jose Oquendo .05
113 Mike Torrez .05
114 Junior Ortiz .05
115 Pete Rose .50
116 Joe Morgan .25
117 Mike Schmidt .40
118 Gary Matthews .05
119 Steve Carlton .20
120 Bo Diaz .05
121 Ivan DeJesus .05
122 John Denny .05
123 Garry Maddox .05
124 Von Hayes .05
125 Al Holland .05
126 Tony Perez .25
127 John Candelaria .05
128 Jason Thompson .05
129 Tony Pena .05
130 Dave Parker .05
131 Bill Madlock .05
132 Kent Tekulve .05
133 Larry McWilliams .05
134 Johnny Ray .05
135 Marvell Wynne .05
136 Dale Berra .05
137 Mike Easler .05
138 Lee Lacy .05
139 George Hendrick .05
140 Lonnie Smith .05
141 Willie McGee .05
142 Tom Herr .05
143 Darrell Porter .05
144 Ozzie Smith .40
145 Bruce Sutter .20
146 Dave LaPoint .05
147 Neil Allen .05
148 Ken Oberkfell .05
149 David Green .05
150 Andy Van Slyke .05
151 Garry Templeton .05
152 Juan Bonilla .05
153 Alan Wiggins .05
154 Terry Kennedy .05
155 Dave Dravecky .05
156 Steve Garvey .10
157 Bobby Brown .05
158 Ruppert Jones .05
159 Luis Salazar .05
160 Tony Gwynn .40
161 Gary Lucas .05
162 Eric Show .05
163 Darrell Evans .05
164 Gary Lavelle .05
165 Atlee Hammaker .05
166 Jeff Leonard .05
167 Jack Clark .05
168 Johnny LeMaster .05
169 Duane Kuiper .05
170 Tom O'Malley .05
171 Chili Davis .05
172 Bill Laskey .05
173 Joel Youngblood .05
174 Bob Brenly .05
175 Atlee Hammaker .05
176 Rick Honeycutt .05
177 John Denny .05
178 LaMarr Hoyt .05
179 Tim Raines .05
180 Dale Murphy .25
181 Andre Dawson .15
182 Steve Rogers .05
183 Gary Carter .25
184 Steve Carlton .25
185 George Hendrick .05
186 Johnny Ray .05
187 Ozzie Smith .40
188 Mike Schmidt .40
189 Jim Rice .15
190 Dave Winfield .25
191 Lloyd Moseby .05
192 LaMarr Hoyt .05
193 Ted Simmons .05
194 Ron Guidry .05
195 Eddie Murray .25
196 Lou Whitaker .05
197 Cal Ripken, Jr. .60
198 George Brett .40
199 Dale Murphy .15
200a Cecil Cooper .05
200b Jim Rice .15
201 Tim Raines .05
202 Rickey Henderson .25
203 Eddie Murray .25
204 Cal Ripken .60
205 Gary Roenicke .05
206 Ken Singleton .05
207 Scott McGregor .05
208 Tippy Martinez .05
209 John Lowenstein .05
210 Mike Flanagan .05
211 Jim Palmer .20
212 Dan Ford .05
213 Rick Dempsey .05
214 Rich Dauer .05
215 Jerry Remy .05
216 Wade Boggs .25
217 Jim Rice .15
218 Tony Armas .05
219 Dwight Evans .05
220 Bob Stanley .05
221 Dave Stapleton .05
222 Rich Gedman .05
223 Glenn Hoffman .05
224 Dennis Eckersley .20
225 John Tudor .05
226 Bruce Hurst .05
227 Rod Carew .25
228 Bobby Grich .05
229 Doug DeCinces .05
230 Fred Lynn .05
231 Reggie Jackson .25
232 Tommy John .05
233 Luis Sanchez .05
234 Bob Boone .05
235 Bruce Kison .05
236 Brian Downing .05
237 Ken Forsch .05
238 Rick Burleson .05
239 Dennis Lamp .05
240 LaMarr Hoyt .05
241 Richard Dotson .05
242 Harold Baines .05
243 Carlton Fisk .25
244 Greg Luzinski .05
245 Rudy Law .05
246 Tom Paciorek .05
247 Floyd Bannister .05
248 Julio Cruz .05
249 Vance Law .05
250 Scott Fletcher .05
251 Toby Harrah .05
252 Pat Tabler .05
253 Gorman Thomas .05
254 Rick Sutcliffe .05
255 Andre Thornton .05
256 Bake McBride .05
257 Alan Bannister .05
258 Jamie Easterly .05
259 Lary Sorenson .05
260 Mike Hargrove .05
261 Bert Blyleven .05
262 Ron Hassey .05
263 Jack Morris .05
264 Larry Herndon .05
265 Lance Parrish .05
266 Alan Trammell .05
267 Lou Whitaker .05
268 Aurelio Lopez .05
269 Dan Petry .05
270 Glenn Wilson .05
271 Chet Lemon .05
272 Kirk Gibson .05
273 Enos Cabell .05
274 Johnny Wockenfuss .05
275 George Brett .40
276 Willie Aikens .05
277 Frank White .05
278 Hal McRae .05
279 Dan Quisenberry .05
280 Willie Wilson .05
281 Paul Splitorff .05
282 U.L. Washington .05
283 Bud Black .05
284 John Wathan .05
285 Larry Gura .05
286 Pat Sheridan .05
287a Rusty Staub .05
287b Dave Righetti .05
288a Bob Forsch .05
288b Mike Warren .05
289 Al Holland .05
290 Dan Quisenberry .05
291 Cecil Cooper .05
292 Moose Haas .05
293 Ted Simmons .05
294 Paul Molitor .25
295 Robin Yount .25
296 Ben Oglivie .05
297 Tom Tellmann .05
298 Jim Gantner .05
299 Rick Manning .05
300 Don Sutton .20
301 Charlie Moore .05
302 Jim Slaton .05
303 Gary Ward .05
304 Tom Brunansky .05
305 Kent Hrbek .05
306 Gary Gaetti .05
307 John Castino .05
308 Ken Schrom .05
309 Ron Davis .05
310 Lenny Faedo .05
311 Darrell Brown .05
312 Frank Viola .05
313 Dave Engle .05
314 Randy Bush .05
315 Dave Righetti .05
316 Rich Gossage .05
317 Ken Griffey .05
318 Ron Guidry .05
319 Dave Winfield .25
320 Don Baylor .10
321 Butch Wynegar .05
322 Omar Moreno .05
323 Andre Robertson .05
324 Willie Randolph .05
325 Don Mattingly .60
326 Graig Nettles .05
327 Rickey Henderson .25
328 Carney Lansford .05
329 Jeff Burroughs .05
330 Chris Codiroli .05
331 Dave Lopes .05
332 Dwayne Murphy .05
333 Wayne Gross .05
334 Bill Almon .05
335 Tom Underwood .05
336 Dave Beard .05
337 Mike Heath .05
338 Mike Davis .05
339 Pat Putnam .05
340 Tony Bernazard .05
341 Steve Henderson .05
342 Richie Zisk .05
343 Dave Henderson .05
344 Al Cowens .05
345 Bill Caudill .05
346 Jim Beattie .05
347 Ricky Nelson .05
348 Roy Thomas .05
349 Spike Owen .05
350 Jamie Allen .05
351 Buddy Bell .05
352 Billy Sample .05
353 George Wright .05
354 Larry Parrish .05
355 Jim Sundberg .05
356 Charlie Hough .05
357 Pete O'Brien .05
358 Wayne Tolleson .05
359 Danny Darwin .05
360 Dave Stewart .05
361 Mickey Rivers .05
362 Bucky Dent .05
363 Willie Upshaw .05
364 Damaso Garcia .05
365 Lloyd Moseby .05
366 Cliff Johnson .05
367 Jim Clancy .05
368 Dave Stieb .05
369 Alfredo Griffin .05
370 Barry Bonnell .05
371 Luis Leal .05
372 Jesse Barfield .05
373 Ernie Whitt .05
374 Rance Mulliniks .05
375 Mike Boddicker .05
376 Greg Brock .05
377 Bill Doran .05
378 Nick Esasky .05
379 Julio Franco .05
380 Mel Hall .05
381 Bob Kearney .05
382 Ron Kittle .05
383 Carmelo Martinez .05
384 Craig McMurtry .05
385 Darryl Strawberry .05
386 Matt Young .05

Stickers Boxes

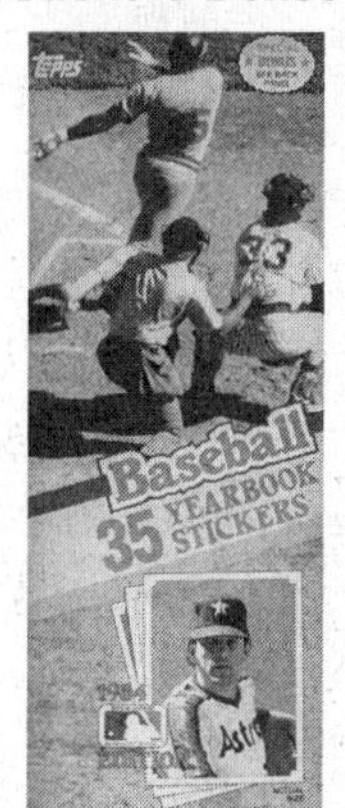

For the second straight year, Topps printed baseball cards on the back of its sticker boxes. The 1984 set, titled "The Super Bats" features 24 hitting leaders. The cards are blank-backed and measure 2-1/2" x 3-1/2". Two cards were printed on each of 12 different boxes. The player's name appears inside a bat above his photo. Prices listed are for complete boxes.

		NM/M
Complete Set (12):		8.50
Common Player:		.75
1	Al Oliver, Lou Whitaker	.75
2	Ken Oberkfell, Ted Simmons	.75
3	Hal McRae, Alan Wiggins	.75
4	Lloyd Moseby, Tim Raines	.75
5	Lonnie Smith, Willie Wilson	.75
6	Keith Hernandez, Robin Yount	1.00
7	Wade Boggs, Johnny Ray	1.00
8	Willie McGee, Ken Singleton	.75
9	Ray Knight, Alan Trammell	.75
11	Rod Carew, George Hendrick	1.00
12	Bill Madlock, Eddie Murray	1.00
13	Jose Cruz, Cal Ripken, Jr.	3.00

Super

A new generation in Topps' experiments to market large-format cards, these 4-7/8" x 6-7/8" cards were sold in single-card plastic-wrap packs with a complete set being 30 cards. Other than their size and the change in card number on the back, there is nothing to distinguish the Supers from the regular 1984 Topps cards of the same players. One plus is that the players are all big name stars, and are likely to remain in demand.

		NM/M
Complete Set (30):		10.00
Common Player:		.25
Wax Pack (1):		.50
Wax Box (36):		9.00
1	Cal Ripken, Jr.	3.00
2	Dale Murphy	.40
3	LaMarr Hoyt	.25
4	John Denny	.25
5	Jim Rice	.40
6	Mike Schmidt	1.00
7	Wade Boggs	.60
8	Bill Madlock	.25
9	Dan Quisenberry	.25
10	Al Holland	.25
11	Ron Kittle	.25
12	Darryl Strawberry	.35
13	George Brett	1.00
14	Bill Buckner	.25
15	Carlton Fisk	.50
16	Steve Carlton	.50
17	Ron Guidry	.25
18	Gary Carter	.50
19	Rickey Henderson	.50
20	Andre Dawson	.40
21	Reggie Jackson	.75
22	Steve Garvey	.30
23	Fred Lynn	.25
24	Pedro Guerrero	.25
25	Eddie Murray	.50
26	Keith Hernandez	.25
27	Dave Winfield	.50
28	Nolan Ryan	3.00
29	Robin Yount	.50
30	Fernando Valenzuela	.25

"1977" Topps Dale Murphy Aluminum

Authorized by Topps to be issued in 1984 as a fund raiser for Huntington's Disease research, this aluminum card is a full size replica of 1977 Topps card #476, Dale Murphy's rookie card. Front features rather crude black etchings of the player portraits found on the cardboard version, while back reproduces the biographical data and includes a serial number. The cards were originally sold for $10.

		NM/M
476	Rookie Catchers (Gary Alexander, Rick Cerone, Dale Murphy, Kevin Pasley)	10.00

7-Eleven/Pepsi Sheets

This test issue was reportedly limited to locations in the Midwest. About 28-1/2" x 43" the sheets have 128 regular '84 Topps cards and a 5" x 7" panel at lower-right with the sponsors' logos.

NM/M
10.00

1985 Topps

Holding the line at 792 cards, Topps initiated major design changes in its 2-1/2" x 3-1/2" cards in 1985. The use of two photos on the front was discontinued in favor of one large photo. The Topps logo appears in the upper-left corner. At bottom is a diagonal box with the team name. It joins a team logo, and below that point runs the player's position and name. The backs feature statistics, biographical information and a trivia question. Some interesting specialty sets were introduced in 1985, including the revival of the father/son theme from 1976, a subset of the 1984 U.S. Olympic Baseball Team members and a set featuring #1 draft choices since the inception of the baseball draft in 1965. Large numbers of uncut sheets were made available within the hobby, originally selling around $60 for a set of six.

		NM/M
Unopened Fact. Set (792):		140.00
Complete Set (792):		70.00
Common Player:		.05
Wax Pack (15):		4.50
Wax Box (36):		150.00
Cello Pack (28):		6.50
Cello Box (24):		150.00
Rack Pack (51+1):		9.00
Rack Box (24):		180.00
Vending Box (500):		60.00
1	Carlton Fisk (Record Breaker)	.25
2	Steve Garvey (Record Breaker)	.05
3	Dwight Gooden (Record Breaker)	.05
4	Cliff Johnson (Record Breaker)	.05
5	Joe Morgan (Record Breaker)	.10
6	Pete Rose (Record Breaker)	.50
7	Nolan Ryan (Record Breaker)	1.50
8	Juan Samuel **RC** (Record Breaker)	.05
9	Bruce Sutter (Record Breaker)	.10
10	Don Sutton (Record Breaker)	.05
11	Ralph Houk	.05
12	Dave Lopes	.05
13	Tim Lollar	.05
14	Chris Bando	.05
15	Jerry Koosman	.05
16	Bobby Meacham	.05
17	Mike Scott	.05
18	Mickey Hatcher	.05
19	George Frazier	.05
20	Chet Lemon	.05
21	Lee Tunnell	.05
22	Duane Kuiper	.05
23	Bret Saberhagen	.05
24	Jesse Barfield	.05
25	Steve Bedrosian	.05
26	Roy Smalley	.05
27	Bruce Berenyi	.05
28	Dann Bilardello	.05
29	Odell Jones	.05
30	Cal Ripken, Jr.	4.00
31	Terry Whitfield	.05
32	Chuck Porter	.05
33	Tito Landrum	.05
34	Ed Nunez **RC**	.05
35	Graig Nettles	.05
36	Fred Breining	.05
37	Reid Nichols	.05
38	Jackie Moore	.05
39	Johnny Wockenfuss	.05
40	Phil Niekro	.60
41	Mike Fischlin	.05
42	Luis Sanchez	.05
43	Andre David	.05
44	Dickie Thon	.05
45	Greg Minton	.05
46	Gary Woods	.05
47	Dave Rozema	.05
48	Tony Fernandez **RC**	.05
49	Butch Davis	.05
50	John Candelaria	.05
51	Bob Watson	.05
52	Jerry Dybzinski	.05
53	Tom Gorman	.05
54	Cesar Cedeno	.05
55	Frank Tanana	.05
56	Jim Dwyer	.05
57	Pat Zachry	.05
58	Orlando Mercado	.05
59	Rick Waits	.05
60	George Hendrick	.05
61	Curt Kaufman	.05
62	Mike Ramsey	.05
63	Steve McCatty	.05
64	Mark Bailey **RC**	.05
65	Bill Buckner	.05
66	Dick Williams	.05
67	Rafael Santana **RC**	.05
68	Von Hayes	.05
69	Jim Winn **RC**	.05
70	Don Baylor	.10
71	Tim Laudner	.05
72	Rick Sutcliffe	.05
73	Rusty Kuntz	.05
74	Mike Krukow	.05
75	Willie Upshaw	.05
76	Alan Bannister	.05
77	Joe Beckwith	.05
78	Scott Fletcher	.05
79	Rick Mahler	.05
80	Keith Hernandez	.05
81	Lenn Sakata	.05
82	Joe Price	.05
83	Charlie Moore	.05
84	Spike Owen	.05
85	Mike Marshall	.05
86	Don Aase	.05
87	David Green	.05
88	Bryn Smith	.05
89	Jackie Gutierrez	.05
90	Rich Gossage	.05
91	Jeff Burroughs	.05
92	Paul Owens	.05

93 Don Schulze **RC** .05
94 Toby Harrah .05
95 Jose Cruz .05
96 Johnny Ray .05
97 Pete Filson .05
98 Steve Lake .05
99 Milt Wilcox .05
100 George Brett 3.00
101 Jim Acker .05
102 Tommy Dunbar .05
103 Randy Lerch .05
104 Mike Fitzgerald .05
105 Ron Kittle .05
106 Pascual Perez .05
107 Tom Foley .05
108 Darnell Coles **RC** .05
109 Gary Roenicke .05
110 Alejandro Pena .05
111 Doug DeCinces .05
112 Tom Tellmann .05
113 Tom Herr .05
114 Bob James .05
115 Rickey Henderson .75
116 Dennis Boyd **RC** .05
117 Greg Gross .05
118 Eric Show .05
119 Pat Corrales .05
120 Steve Kemp .05
121 Checklist 1-132 .05
122 Tom Brunansky .05
123 Dave Smith .05
124 Rich Hebner .05
125 Kent Tekulve .05
126 Ruppert Jones .05
127 Mark Gubicza .05
128 Ernie Whitt .05
129 Gene Garber .05
130 Al Oliver .05
131 Father - Son (Buddy Bell, Gus Bell) .05
132 Father - Son (Dale Berra, Yogi Berra) .10
133 Father - Son (Bob Boone, Ray Boone) .05
134 Father - Son (Terry Francona, Tito Francona) .05
135 Father - Son (Bob Kennedy, Terry Kennedy) .05
136 Father - Son (Bill Kunkel, Jeff Kunkel **RC**) .05
137 Father - Son (Vance Law, Vern Law) .05
138 Father - Son (Dick Schofield, Dick Schofield, Jr.) .05
139 Father - Son (Bob Skinner, Joel Skinner) .05
140 Father - Son (Roy Smalley, Jr., Roy Smalley III) .05
141 Father - Son (Dave Stenhouse, Mike Stenhouse) .05
142 Father - Son (Dizzy Trout, Steve Trout) .05
143 Father - Son (Ozzie Virgil, Ozzie Virgil) .05
144 Ron Gardenhire .05
145 Alvin Davis .05
146 Gary Redus .05
147 Bill Swaggerty .05
148 Steve Yeager .05
149 Dickie Noles .05
150 Jim Rice .15
151 Moose Haas .05
152 Steve Braun .05
153 Frank LaCorte .05
154 Argenis Salazar **RC** .05
155 Yogi Berra .10
156 Craig Reynolds .05
157 Tug McGraw .05
158 Pat Tabler .05
159 Carlos Diaz .05
160 Lance Parrish .05
161 Ken Schrom .05
162 Benny Distefano **RC** .05
163 Dennis Eckersley .60
164 Jorge Orta .05
165 Dusty Baker .05
166 Keith Atherton .05
167 Rufino Linares .05
168 Garth Iorg .05
169 Dan Spillner .05
170 George Foster .05
171 Bill Stein .05
172 Jack Perconte .05
173 Mike Young **RC** .05
174 Rick Honeycutt .05
175 Dave Parker .05
176 Bill Schroeder .05
177 Dave Von Ohlen .05
178 Miguel Dilone .05
179 Tommy John .10
180 Dave Winfield .75
181 Roger Clemens 25.00
182 Tim Flannery .05
183 Larry McWilliams .05
184 Carmen Castillo **RC** .05
185 Al Holland .05
186 Bob Lillis .05
187 Mike Walters .05
188 Greg Pryor .05
189 Warren Brusstar .05
190 Rusty Staub .05
191 Steve Nicosia .05
192 Howard Johnson .05
193 Jimmy Key .05
194 Dave Stegman .05
195 Glenn Hubbard .05
196 Pete O'Brien .05
197 Mike Warren .05
198 Eddie Milner .05
199 Denny Martinez .05
200 Reggie Jackson 2.00
201 Burt Hooton .05
202 Gorman Thomas .05
203 Bob McClure .05
204 Art Howe .05
205 Steve Rogers .05
206 Phil Garner .05
207 Mark Clear .05
208 Champ Summers .05
209 Bill Campbell .05
210 Gary Matthews .05
211 Clay Christiansen .05
212 George Vukovich .05
213 Billy Gardner .05
214 John Tudor .05
215 Bob Brenly .05
216 Jerry Don Gleaton .05
217 Leon Roberts .05
218 Doyle Alexander .05
219 Gerald Perry .05
220 Fred Lynn .05
221 Ron Reed .05
222 Hubie Brooks .05
223 Tom Hume .05
224 Al Cowens .05
225 Mike Boddicker .05
226 Juan Beniquez .05
227 Danny Darwin .05
228 Dion James **RC** .05
229 Dave LaPoint .05
230 Gary Carter .75
231 Dwayne Murphy .05
232 Dave Beard .05
233 Ed Jurak .05
234 Jerry Narron .05
235 Garry Maddox .05
236 Mark Thurmond .05
237 Julio Franco .05
238 Jose Rijo .05
239 Tim Teufel .05
240 Dave Stieb .05
241 Jim Frey .05
242 Greg Harris .05
243 Barbaro Garbey .05
244 Mike Jones .05
245 Chili Davis .05
246 Mike Norris .05
247 Wayne Tolleson .05
248 Terry Forster .05
249 Harold Baines .05
250 Jesse Orosco .05
251 Brad Gulden .05
252 Dan Ford .05
253 Sid Bream **RC** .10
254 Pete Vuckovich .05
255 Lonnie Smith .05
256 Mike Stanton .05
257 Brian Little (Bryan) .05
258 Mike Brown .05
259 Gary Allenson .05
260 Dave Righetti .05
261 Checklist 133-264 .05
262 Greg Booker **RC** .05
263 Mel Hall .05
264 Joe Sambito .05
265 Juan Samuel **RC** .05
266 Frank Viola .05
267 Henry Cotto **RC** .05
268 Chuck Tanner .05
269 Doug Baker **RC** .05
270 Dan Quisenberry .05
271 Tim Foli (#1 Draft Pick) .05
272 Jeff Burroughs (#1 Draft Pick) .05
273 Bill Almon (#1 Draft Pick) .05
274 Floyd Bannister (#1 Draft Pick) .05
275 Harold Baines (#1 Draft Pick) .10
276 Bob Horner (#1 Draft Pick) .10
277 Al Chambers (#1 Draft Pick) .05
278 Darryl Strawberry (#1 Draft Pick) .30
279 Mike Moore **RC** (#1 Draft Pick) .05
280 Shawon Dunston **RC** (#1 Draft Pick) .40
281 Tim Belcher **RC** (#1 Draft Pick) .30
282 Shawn Abner **RC** (#1 Draft Pick) .05
283 Fran Mullins .05
284 Marty Bystrom .05
285 Dan Driessen .05
286 Rudy Law .05
287 Walt Terrell .05
288 Jeff Kunkel **RC** .05
289 Tom Underwood .05
290 Cecil Cooper .05
291 Bob Welch .05
292 Brad Komminsk **RC** .05
293 Curt Young **RC** .05
294 Tom Nieto **RC** .05
295 Joe Niekro .05
296 Ricky Nelson .05
297 Gary Lucas .05
298 Marty Barrett .05
299 Andy Hawkins .05
300 Rod Carew .75
301 John Montefusco .05
302 Tim Corcoran .05
303 Mike Jeffcoat **RC** .05
304 Gary Gaetti .05
305 Dale Berra .05
306 Rick Reuschel .05
307 Sparky Anderson .10
308 John Wathan .05
309 Mike Witt .05
310 Manny Trillo .05
311 Jim Gott .05
312 Marc Hill .05
313 Dave Schmidt .05
314 Ron Oester .05
315 Doug Sisk .05
316 John Lowenstein .05
317 Jack Lazorko **RC** .05
318 Ted Simmons .05
319 Jeff Jones .05
320 Dale Murphy .35
321 Ricky Horton **RC** .05
322 Dave Stapleton .05
323 Andy McGaffigan .05
324 Bruce Bochy .05
325 John Denny .05
326 Kevin Bass .05
327 Brook Jacoby .05
328 Bob Shirley .05
329 Ron Washington .05
330 Leon Durham .05
331 Bill Laskey .05
332 Brian Harper .05
333 Willie Hernandez .05
334 Dick Howser .05
335 Bruce Benedict .05
336 Rance Mulliniks .05
337 Billy Sample .05
338 Britt Burns .05
339 Danny Heep .05
340 Robin Yount .75
341 Floyd Rayford .05
342 Ted Power .05
343 Bill Russell .05
344 Dave Henderson .05
345 Charlie Lea .05
346 Terry Pendleton **RC** .75
347 Rick Langford .05
348 Bob Boone .05
349 Domingo Ramos .05
350 Wade Boggs 1.00
351 Juan Agosto .05
352 Joe Morgan .75
353 Julio Solano .05
354 Andre Robertson .05
355 Bert Blyleven .05
356 Dave Meier .05
357 Rich Bordi .05
358 Tony Pena .05
359 Pat Sheridan .05
360 Steve Carlton .75
361 Alfredo Griffin .05
362 Craig McMurtry .05
363 Ron Hodges .05
364 Richard Dotson .05
365 Danny Ozark .05
366 Todd Cruz .05
367 Keefe Cato .05
368 Dave Bergman .05
369 R.J. Reynolds **RC** .05
370 Bruce Sutter .65
371 Mickey Rivers .05
372 Roy Howell .05
373 Mike Moore .05
374 Brian Downing .05
375 Jeff Reardon .05
376 Jeff Newman .05
377 Checklist 265-396 .05
378 Alan Wiggins .05
379 Charles Hudson .05
380 Ken Griffey .05
381 Roy Smith .05
382 Denny Walling .05
383 Rick Lysander .05
384 Jody Davis .05
385 Jose DeLeon .05
386 Dan Gladden **RC** .30
387 Buddy Biancalana **RC** .05
388 Bert Roberge .05
389 Rod Dedeaux (Team USA) .05
390 Sid Akins **RC** (Team USA) .05
391 Flavio Alfaro (Team USA) .05
392 Don August **RC** (Team USA) .05
393 Scott Bankhead **RC** (Team USA) .10
394 Bob Caffrey **RC** (Team USA) .05
395 Mike Dunne **RC** (Team USA) .05
396 Gary Green **RC** (Team USA) .05
397 John Hoover (Team USA) .05
398 Shane Mack **RC** (Team USA) .10
399 John Marzano **RC** (Team USA) .05
400 Oddibe McDowell **RC** (Team USA) .05
401 Mark McGwire **RC** (Team USA) 20.00
402 Pat Pacillo **RC** (Team USA) .05
403 Cory Snyder **RC** (Team USA) .30
404 Billy Swift **RC** (Team USA) .40
405 Tom Veryzer .05
406 Len Whitehouse .05
407 Bobby Ramos .05
408 Sid Monge .05
409 Brad Wellman .05
410 Bob Horner .05
411 Bobby Cox .05
412 Bud Black .05
413 Vance Law .05
414 Gary Ward .05
415 Ron Darling .05
416 Wayne Gross .05
417 John Franco **RC** .50
418 Ken Landreaux .05
419 Mike Caldwell .05
420 Andre Dawson .50
421 Dave Rucker .05
422 Carney Lansford .05
423 Barry Bonnell .05
424 Al Nipper **RC** .05
425 Mike Hargrove .05
426 Verne Ruhle .05
427 Mario Ramirez .05
428 Larry Andersen .05
429 Rick Cerone .05
430 Ron Davis .05
431 U.L. Washington .05
432 Thad Bosley .05
433 Jim Morrison .05
434 Gene Richards .05
435 Dan Petry .05
436 Willie Aikens .05
437 Al Jones .05
438 Joe Torre .10
439 Junior Ortiz .05
440 Fernando Valenzuela .05
441 Duane Walker .05
442 Ken Forsch .05
443 George Wright .05
444 Tony Phillips .05
445 Tippy Martinez .05
446 Jim Sundberg .05
447 Jeff Lahti .05
448 Derrel Thomas .05
449 Phil Bradley **RC** .10
450 Steve Garvey .25
451 Bruce Hurst .05
452 John Castino .05
453 Tom Waddell .05
454 Glenn Wilson .05
455 Bob Knepper .05
456 Tim Foli .05
457 Cecilio Guante .05
458 Randy S. Johnson .05
459 Charlie Leibrandt .05
460 Ryne Sandberg 1.00
461 Marty Castillo .05
462 Gary Lavelle .05
463 Dave Collins .05
464 Mike Mason **RC** .05
465 Bob Grich .05
466 Tony LaRussa .10
467 Ed Lynch .05
468 Wayne Krenchicki .05
469 Sammy Stewart .05
470 Steve Sax .05
471 Pete Ladd .05
472 Jim Essian .05
473 Tim Wallach .05
474 Kurt Kepshire .05
475 Andre Thornton .05
476 Jeff Stone **RC** .05
477 Bob Ojeda .05
478 Kurt Bevacqua .05
479 Mike Madden .05
480 Lou Whitaker .05
481 Dale Murray .05
482 Harry Spilman .05
483 Mike Smithson .05
484 Larry Bowa .05
485 Matt Young .05
486 Steve Balboni .05
487 Frank Williams **RC** .05
488 Joel Skinner **RC** .05
489 Bryan Clark .05
490 Jason Thompson .05
491 Rick Camp .05
492 Dave Johnson .05
493 Orel Hershiser **RC** 2.00
494 Rich Dauer .05
495 Mario Soto .05
496 Donnie Scott .05
497 Gary Pettis .05
498 Ed Romero .05
499 Danny Cox **RC** .05
500 Mike Schmidt 2.00
501 Dan Schatzeder .05
502 Rick Miller .05
503 Tim Conroy .05
504 Jerry Willard .05
505 Jim Beattie .05
506 Franklin Stubbs **RC** .05
507 Ray Fontenot .05
508 John Shelby .05
509 Milt May .05
510 Kent Hrbek .05
511 Lee Smith .05
512 Tom Brookens .05
513 Lynn Jones .05
514 Jeff Cornell .05
515 Dave Concepcion .05
516 Roy Lee Jackson .05
517 Jerry Martin .05
518 Chris Chambliss .05
519 Doug Rader .05
520 LaMarr Hoyt .05
521 Rick Dempsey .05
522 Paul Molitor .75
523 Candy Maldonado .05
524 Rob Wilfong .05
525 Darrell Porter .05
526 Dave Palmer .05
527 Checklist 397-528 .05
528 Bill Krueger .05
529 Rich Gedman .05
530 Dave Dravecky .05
531 Joe Lefebvre .05
532 Frank DiPino .05
533 Tony Bernazard .05
534 Brian Dayett **RC** .05
535 Pat Putnam .05
536 Kirby Puckett 10.00
537 Don Robinson .05
538 Keith Moreland .05
539 Aurelio Lopez .05
540 Claudell Washington .05
541 Mark Davis .05
542 Don Slaught .05
543 Mike Squires .05
544 Bruce Kison .05
545 Lloyd Moseby .05
546 Brent Gaff .05
547 Pete Rose 1.50
548 Larry Parrish .05
549 Mike Scioscia .05
550 Scott McGregor .05
551 Andy Van Slyke .05
552 Chris Codiroli .05
553 Bob Clark .05
554 Doug Flynn .05
555 Bob Stanley .05
556 Sixto Lezcano .05
557 Len Barker .05
558 Carmelo Martinez .05
559 Jay Howell .05
560 Bill Madlock .05
561 Darryl Motley .05
562 Houston Jimenez .05
563 Dick Ruthven .05
564 Alan Ashby .05
565 Kirk Gibson .05
566 Ed Vande Berg .05
567 Joel Youngblood .05
568 Cliff Johnson .05
569 Ken Oberkfell .05
570 Darryl Strawberry .10
571 Charlie Hough .05
572 Tom Paciorek .05
573 Jay Tibbs **RC** .05
574 Joe Altobelli .05
575 Pedro Guerrero .05
576 Jaime Cocanower .05
577 Chris Speier .05
578 Terry Francona .05
579 Ron Romanick **RC** .05
580 Dwight Evans .05
581 Mark Wagner .05
582 Ken Phelps **RC** .05
583 Bobby Brown .05
584 Kevin Gross .05
585 Butch Wynegar .05
586 Bill Scherrer .05
587 Doug Frobel .05
588 Bobby Castillo .05
589 Bob Dernier .05
590 Ray Knight .05
591 Larry Herndon .05
592 Jeff Robinson **RC** .05
593 Rick Leach .05
594 Curt Wilkerson **RC** .05
595 Larry Gura .05
596 Jerry Hairston Sr. .05
597 Brad Lesley .05
598 Jose Oquendo .05
599 Storm Davis .05
600 Pete Rose 3.00
601 Tom Lasorda .10
602 Jeff Dedmon **RC** .05
603 Rick Manning .05
604 Daryl Sconiers .05
605 Ozzie Smith 1.00
606 Rich Gale .05
607 Bill Almon .05
608 Craig Lefferts .05
609 Broderick Perkins .05
610 Jack Morris .05
611 Ozzie Virgil .05
612 Mike Armstrong .05
613 Terry Puhl .05
614 Al Williams .05
615 Marvell Wynne .05
616 Scott Sanderson .05
617 Willie Wilson .05
618 Pete Falcone .05
619 Jeff Leonard .05
620 Dwight Gooden .50
621 Marvis Foley .05
622 Luis Leal .05
623 Greg Walker .05
624 Benny Ayala .05
625 Mark Langston .05
626 German Rivera .05
627 Eric Davis **RC** 1.00
628 Rene Lachemann .05
629 Dick Schofield .05
630 Tim Raines .05
631 Bob Forsch .05
632 Bruce Bochte .05
633 Glenn Hoffman .05
634 Bill Dawley .05
635 Terry Kennedy .05
636 Shane Rawley .05
637 Brett Butler .05
638 Mike Pagliarulo **RC** .10
639 Ed Hodge .05
640 Steve Henderson .05
641 Rod Scurry .05
642 Dave Owen .05
643 Johnny Grubb .05
644 Mark Huismann **RC** .05
645 Damaso Garcia .05
646 Scot Thompson .05
647 Rafael Ramirez .05
648 Bob Jones .05
649 Sid Fernandez **RC** .05
650 Greg Luzinski .05
651 Jeff Russell .05
652 Joe Nolan .05
653 Mark Brouhard .05
654 Dave Anderson .05
655 Joaquin Andujar .05
656 Chuck Cottier .05
657 Jim Slaton .05
658 Mike Stenhouse .05
659 Checklist 529-660 .05
660 Tony Gwynn 1.00
661 Steve Crawford .05
662 Mike Heath .05
663 Luis Aguayo .05
664 Steve Farr **RC** .05
665 Don Mattingly 3.00
666 Mike LaCoss .05
667 Dave Engle .05
668 Steve Trout .05
669 Lee Lacy .05
670 Tom Seaver .75
671 Dane Iorg .05
672 Juan Berenguer .05
673 Buck Martinez .05
674 Atlee Hammaker .05
675 Tony Perez .75
676 Albert Hall **RC** .05
677 Wally Backman .05
678 Joey McLaughlin .05
679 Bob Kearney .05
680 Jerry Reuss .05
681 Ben Oglivie .05
682 Doug Corbett .05
683 Whitey Herzog .05
684 Bill Doran .05
685 Bill Caudill .05
686 Mike Easler .05
687 Bill Gullickson .05
688 Len Matuszek .05
689 Luis DeLeon .05
690 Alan Trammell .05
691 Dennis Rasmussen **RC** .05
692 Randy Bush .05
693 Tim Stoddard .05
694 Joe Carter .05
695 Rick Rhoden .05
696 John Rabb .05
697 Onix Concepcion .05
698 Jorge Bell .05
699 Donnie Moore .05
700 Eddie Murray .75
701 Eddie Murray/AS .40
702 Damaso Garcia/AS .05
703 George Brett/AS .50
704 Cal Ripken, Jr./AS 1.50
705 Dave Winfield/AS .40
706 Rickey Henderson/AS .40
707 Tony Armas/AS .05
708 Lance Parrish/AS .05
709 Mike Boddicker/AS .05
710 Frank Viola/AS .05
711 Dan Quisenberry/AS .05
712 Keith Hernandez/AS .05
713 Ryne Sandberg/AS .40
714 Mike Schmidt/AS .75
715 Ozzie Smith/AS .50
716 Dale Murphy/AS .15
717 Tony Gwynn/AS .75
718 Jeff Leonard/AS .05
719 Gary Carter/AS .40
720 Rick Sutcliffe/AS .05
721 Bob Knepper/AS .05
722 Bruce Sutter/AS .30
723 Dave Stewart .05
724 Oscar Gamble .05
725 Floyd Bannister .05
726 Al Bumbry .05
727 Frank Pastore .05
728 Bob Bailor .05
729 Don Sutton .60
730 Dave Kingman .05
731 Neil Allen .05
732 John McNamara .05
733 Tony Scott .05
734 John Henry Johnson .05
735 Garry Templeton .05
736 Jerry Mumphrey .05
737 Bo Diaz .05
738 Omar Moreno .05
739 Ernie Camacho .05
740 Jack Clark .05
741 John Butcher .05
742 Ron Hassey .05
743 Frank White .05
744 Doug Bair .05
745 Buddy Bell .05
746 Jim Clancy .05
747 Alex Trevino .05
748 Lee Mazzilli .05
749 Julio Cruz .05
750 Rollie Fingers .60
751 Kelvin Chapman .05
752 Bob Owchinko .05
753 Greg Brock .05
754 Larry Milbourne .05
755 Ken Singleton .05
756 Rob Picciolo .05

757	Willie McGee	.05
758	Ray Burris	.05
759	Jim Fanning	.05
760	Nolan Ryan	4.00
761	Jerry Remy	.05
762	Eddie Whitson	.05
763	Kiko Garcia	.05
764	Jamie Easterly	.05
765	Willie Randolph	.05
766	Paul Mirabella	.05
767	Darrell Brown	.05
768	Ron Cey	.05
769	Joe Cowley	.05
770	Carlton Fisk	.75
771	Geoff Zahn	.05
772	Johnnie LeMaster	.05
773	Hal McRae	.05
774	Dennis Lamp	.05
775	Mookie Wilson	.05
776	Jerry Royster	.05
777	Ned Yost	.05
778	Mike Davis	.05
779	Nick Esasky	.05
780	Mike Flanagan	.05
781	Jim Gantner	.05
782	Tom Niedenfuer	.05
783	Mike Jorgensen	.05
784	Checklist 661-792	.05
785	Tony Armas	.05
786	Enos Cabell	.05
787	Jim Wohlford	.05
788	Steve Comer	.05
789	Luis Salazar	.05
790	Ron Guidry	.10
791	Ivan DeJesus	.05
792	Darrell Evans	.05

Tiffany

In its second year of producing a high-gloss collectors' edition of its regular baseball card set, Topps cut production to a reported 5,000 sets. Other than the use of white cardboard stock and the glossy front coating, the cards in this specially boxed set are identical to regular 1985 Topps cards.

		NM/M
Complete Unopened Set (792):		500.00
Complete Set, Opened (792):		325.00
Common Player:		.25
Stars:		4X
181	Roger Clemens	150.00
401	Mark McGwire	80.00

Traded

Topps continued the annual Traded set tradition with another 132-card set. The 2-1/2" x 3-1/2" cards follow the pattern of being virtually identical in design to the regular cards of that year. Sold only through hobby dealers, the set features traded veterans and promising rookies. A glossy-finish "Tiffany" edition of the set was also issued. Cards are numbered with a "T" suffix.

		NM/M
Complete Set (132):		10.00
Common Player:		.05
Wax Test Pack (8):		10.00
Wax Test Wax Box (36):		150.00
1	Don Aase	.05
2	Bill Almon	.05
3	Benny Ayala	.05
4	Dusty Baker	.25
5	George Bamberger	.05
6	Dale Berra	.05
7	Rich Bordi	.05
8	Daryl Boston **RC**	.05
9	Hubie Brooks	.05
10	Chris Brown **RC**	.05
11	Tom Browning **RC**	.05
12	Al Bumbry	.05
13	Ray Burris	.05
14	Jeff Burroughs	.05
15	Bill Campbell	.05
16	Don Carman **RC**	.05
17	Gary Carter	1.50
18	Bobby Castillo	.05
19	Bill Caudill	.05
20	Rick Cerone	.05
21	Bryan Clark	.05
22	Jack Clark	.05
23	Pat Clements **RC**	.05
24	Vince Coleman **RC**	.50
25	Dave Collins	.05
26	Danny Darwin	.05
27	Jim Davenport	.05
28	Jerry Davis	.05
29	Brian Dayett	.05
30	Ivan DeJesus	.05
31	Ken Dixon	.05
32	Mariano Duncan **RC**	.05
33	John Felske	.05
34	Mike Fitzgerald	.05
35	Ray Fontenot	.05
36	Greg Gagne **RC**	.05
37	Oscar Gamble	.05
38	Scott Garrelts **RC**	.05
39	Bob L. Gibson	.05
40	Jim Gott	.05
41	David Green	.05
42	Alfredo Griffin	.05
43	Ozzie Guillen **RC**	3.00
44	Eddie Haas	.05
45	Terry Harper	.05
46	Toby Harrah	.05
47	Greg Harris	.05
48	Ron Hassey	.05
49	Rickey Henderson	2.50
50	Steve Henderson	.05
51	George Hendrick	.05
52	Joe Hesketh **RC**	.05
53	Teddy Higuera **RC**	.05
54	Donnie Hill	.05
55	Al Holland	.05
56	Burt Hooton	.05
57	Jay Howell	.05
58	Ken Howell **RC**	.05
59	LaMarr Hoyt	.05
60	Tim Hulett **RC**	.05
61	Bob James	.05
62	Steve Jeltz **RC**	.05
63	Cliff Johnson	.05
64	Howard Johnson	.05
65	Ruppert Jones	.05
66	Steve Kemp	.05
67	Bruce Kison	.05
68	Alan Knicely	.05
69	Mike LaCoss	.05
70	Lee Lacy	.05
71	Dave LaPoint	.05
72	Gary Lavelle	.05
73	Vance Law	.05
74	Johnnie LeMaster	.05
75	Sixto Lezcano	.05
76	Tim Lollar	.05
77	Fred Lynn	.05
78	Billy Martin	.25
79	Ron Mathis	.05
80	Len Matuszek	.05
81	Gene Mauch	.05
82	Oddibe McDowell	.05
83	Roger McDowell **RC**	.05
84	John McNamara	.05
85	Donnie Moore	.05
86	Gene Nelson	.05
87	Steve Nicosia	.05
88	Al Oliver	.05
89	Joe Orsulak **RC**	.05
90	Rob Picciolo	.05
91	Chris Pittaro	.05
92	Jim Presley **RC**	.05
93	Rick Reuschel	.05
94	Bert Roberge	.05
95	Bob Rodgers	.05
96	Jerry Royster	.05
97	Dave Rozema	.05
98	Dave Rucker	.05
99	Vern Ruhle	.05
100	Paul Runge **RC**	.05
101	Mark Salas **RC**	.05
102	Luis Salazar	.05
103	Joe Sambito	.05
104	Rick Schu **RC**	.05
105	Donnie Scott	.05
106	Larry Sheets **RC**	.05
107	Don Slaught	.05
108	Roy Smalley	.05
109	Lonnie Smith	.05
110	Nate Snell	.05
111	Chris Speier	.05
112	Mike Stenhouse	.05
113	Tim Stoddard	.05
114	Jim Sundberg	.05
115	Bruce Sutter	1.00
116	Don Sutton	.50
117	Kent Tekulve	.05
118	Tom Tellmann	.05
119	Walt Terrell	.05
120	Mickey Tettleton **RC**	1.00
121	Derrel Thomas	.05
122	Rich Thompson	.05
123	Alex Trevino	.05
124	John Tudor	.05
125	Jose Uribe **RC**	.05
126	Bobby Valentine	.05
127	Dave Von Ohlen	.05
128	U.L. Washington	.05
129	Earl Weaver	.30
130	Eddie Whitson	.05
131	Herm Winningham **RC**	.05
132	Checklist 1-132	.05

Traded Tiffany

This specially boxed collectors version of the Topps Traded sets features cards that differ only in the use of a high-gloss finish coat on the fronts.

	NM/M
Complete Set (132):	35.00
Common Player:	.25
Stars:	4X

Traded Pete Rose Bronze

This 1/4-size metal replica was issued to dealers who purchased cases of 1985 Topps Traded sets. Each detail of the 1985 Topps Pete Rose card is reproduced on the 1-3/4" x 1-3/4" bronze metal mini-card, right down to the stats.

		NM/M
600	Pete Rose	10.00

All-Star Glossy Set of 22

This was the second straight year for this set of 22 cards featuring the starting players, honorary captains and managers in the All-Star Game. The set is virtually identical to that of the previous year in design with a color photo, All-Star banner, league emblem, and player ID on the front. Fronts have a high-gloss finish. The cards were available as inserts in Topps rack packs.

		NM/M
Complete Set (22):		5.00
Common Player:		.10
1	Paul Owens	.10
2	Steve Garvey	.30
3	Ryne Sandberg	.50
4	Mike Schmidt	1.00
5	Ozzie Smith	.50
6	Tony Gwynn	.50
7	Dale Murphy	.30
8	Darryl Strawberry	.10
9	Gary Carter	.40
10	Charlie Lea	.10
11	Willie McCovey	.30
12	Joe Altobelli	.10
13	Rod Carew	.40
14	Lou Whitaker	.10
15	George Brett	1.00
16	Cal Ripken, Jr.	1.50
17	Dave Winfield	.40
18	Chet Lemon	.10
19	Reggie Jackson	.50
20	Lance Parrish	.10
21	Dave Stieb	.10
22	Hank Greenberg	.25

All-Star Glossy Set of 40

Similar to previous years' glossy sets, the 1985 All-Star "Collector's Edition" set of 40 could be obtained through the mail in eight five-card subsets. To obtain the 2-1/2" x 3-1/2" cards, collectors had to accumulate sweepstakes insert cards from Topps packs, and pay 75¢ postage and handling. Under the circumstances, the complete set of 40 cards was not inexpensive.

		NM/M
Complete Set (40):		8.00
Common Player:		.10
1	Dale Murphy	.30
2	Jesse Orosco	.10
3	Bob Brenly	.10
4	Mike Boddicker	.10
5	Dave Kingman	.10
6	Jim Rice	.20
7	Frank Viola	.10
8	Alvin Davis	.10
9	Rick Sutcliffe	.10
10	Pete Rose	2.00
11	Leon Durham	.10
12	Joaquin Andujar	.10
13	Keith Hernandez	.10
14	Dave Winfield	.40
15	Reggie Jackson	.50
16	Alan Trammell	.10
17	Bert Blyleven	.10
18	Tony Armas	.10
19	Rich Gossage	.10
20	Jose Cruz	.10
21	Ryne Sandberg	.50
22	Bruce Sutter	.30
23	Mike Schmidt	1.00
24	Cal Ripken, Jr.	3.00
25	Dan Petry	.10
26	Jack Morris	.10
27	Don Mattingly	1.00
28	Eddie Murray	.40
29	Tony Gwynn	.50
30	Charlie Lea	.10
31	Juan Samuel	.10
32	Phil Niekro	.30
33	Alejandro Pena	.10
34	Harold Baines	.10
35	Dan Quisenberry	.10
36	Gary Carter	.40
37	Mario Soto	.10
38	Dwight Gooden	.10
39	Tom Brunansky	.10
40	Dave Stieb	.10

All-Time Record Holders

(See 1985 Woolworth and 1987 and Boardwalk Baseball.)

Gallery of Champions

This second annual metallic miniatures issue honors 12 award winners from the previous season (MVP, Cy Young, Rookie of Year, Fireman, etc.). Each mini is an exact reproduction at one-quarter scale of the player's 1985 Topps card, both front and back. The sets (editions of 1,000) were issued in a specially-designed velvet-like case. A Dwight Gooden pewter replica was given as a premium to dealers who bought the sets.

		NM/M
Complete Bronze Set (12):		60.00
Complete Silver Set (12):		280.00
(1b)	Tony Armas/Bronze	3.00
(1s)	Tony Armas/Silver	10.00
(2b)	Alvin Davis/Bronze	3.00
(2s)	Alvin Davis/Silver	10.00
(3b)	Dwight Gooden/ Bronze	5.00
(3s)	Dwight Gooden/ Silver	15.00
(3p)	Dwight Gooden/ Pewter	6.00
(4b)	Tony Gwynn/Bronze	15.00
(4s)	Tony Gwynn/Silver	50.00
(5b)	Willie Hernandez/ Bronze	3.00
(5s)	Willie Hernandez/ Silver	10.00
(6b)	Don Mattingly/ Bronze	30.00
(6s)	Don Mattingly/Silver	75.00
(7b)	Dale Murphy/Bronze	10.00
(7s)	Dale Murphy/Silver	45.00
(8b)	Dan Quisenberry/ Bronze	3.00
(8s)	Dan Quisenberry/ Silver	10.00
(9b)	Ryne Sandberg/ Bronze	15.00
(9s)	Ryne Sandberg/ Silver	50.00
(10b)	Mike Schmidt/Bronze	25.00
(10s)	Mike Schmidt/Silver	60.00
(11b)	Rick Sutcliffe/Bronze	3.00
(11s)	Rick Sutcliffe/Silver	10.00
(12b)	Bruce Sutter/Bronze	6.00
(12s)	Bruce Sutter/Silver	20.00

Minis

Never released for public sale, quantities of these enigmatic cards nevertheless reached the hobby market. Smaller than the standard 2-1/2" x 3-1/2" Topps cards, the "mini" version measures 2-3/8" x 3-9/32", 10% smaller than regular cards. Printed in Canada, the minis use a whiter cardboard stock than the regular '85 Topps, making the color printing more vibrant. The minis were the result of a test of new printing equipment by O-Pee-Chee, Topps' Canadian licensee. Only 132 of the 792 cards in the '85 Topps set are found in mini version. Only about 100 of each mini card are known, including about 15% blank-backs.

		NM/M
Complete Set (132):		1,500
Common Player:		5.00
Blank-backs: 50 Percent		
12	Dave Lopes	5.00
15	Jerry Koosman	5.00
17	Mike Scott	5.00
25	Steve Bedrosian	5.00
44	Dickie Thon	5.00
65	Bill Buckner	5.00
68	Von Hayes	5.00
72	Rick Sutcliffe	5.00
75	Willie Upshaw	5.00
82	Joe Price	5.00
88	Bryn Smith	5.00
91	Jeff Burroughs	5.00
95	Jose Cruz	5.00
96	Johnny Ray	5.00
109	Gary Roenicke	5.00
113	Tom Herr	5.00
114	Bob James	5.00
117	Greg Gross	5.00
120	Steve Kemp	5.00
121	Checklist 1-132	3.00
128	Ernie Whitt	5.00
148	Steve Yaeger	5.00
150	Jim Rice	15.00
151	Moose Haas	5.00
154	Argenis Salazar	5.00
156	Craig Reynolds	5.00
160	Lance Parrish	5.00
165	Dusty Baker	5.00
170	George Foster	5.00
178	Miguel Dilone	5.00
185	Al Holland	5.00
190	Rusty Staub	5.00
198	Eddie Milner	5.00
201	Burt Hooton	5.00
205	Steve Rogers	5.00
209	Bill Campbell	5.00
210	Gary Matthews	5.00
218	Doyle Alexander	5.00
222	Hubie Brooks	5.00
223	Tom Hume	5.00
225	Mike Boddicker	5.00
229	Dave LaPoint	5.00
230	Gary Carter	45.00
235	Garry Maddox	5.00
236	Mark Thurmond	5.00
237	Julio Franco	5.00
239	Tim Teufel	5.00
248	Terry Forster	5.00
250	Jesse Orosco	5.00
251	Brad Gulden	5.00
255	Lonnie Smith	5.00
261	Checklist 133-264	3.00
263	Mel Hall	5.00
266	Frank Viola	5.00
287	Walt Terrell	5.00
306	Rick Reuschel	5.00
310	Manny Trillo	5.00
313	Dave Schmidt	5.00
325	John Denny	5.00
330	Leon Durham	5.00
333	Willie Hernandez	5.00
340	Robin Yount	45.00
343	Bill Russell	5.00
345	Charlie Lea	5.00
352	Joe Morgan	45.00
355	Bert Blyleven	5.00
358	Tony Pena	5.00
360	Steve Carlton	45.00
362	Craig McMurtry	5.00
375	Jeff Reardon	5.00
379	Charles Hudson	5.00
415	Ron Darling	5.00
445	Tippy Martinez	5.00
446	Jim Sundberg	5.00
450	Steve Garvey	7.50
452	John Castino	5.00
464	Mike Mason	5.00
470	Steve Sax	5.00
485	Matt Young	5.00
487	Frank Williams	5.00
489	Bryan Clark	5.00
491	Rick Camp	5.00
495	Mario Soto	5.00
500	Mike Schmidt	250.00
501	Dan Schatzeder	5.00
504	Jerry Willard	5.00
511	Lee Smith	5.00
515	Dave Concepcion	5.00
520	LaMarr Hoyt	5.00
526	Dave Palmer	5.00
530	Dave Dravecky	5.00
538	Keith Moreland	5.00
545	Lloyd Moseby	5.00
551	Andy Van Slyke	5.00
554	Doug Flynn	5.00
556	Sixto Lezcano	5.00
560	Bill Madlock	5.00
563	Dick Ruthven	5.00
566	Ed Vande Berg	5.00
568	Cliff Johnson	5.00
569	Ken Oberkfell	5.00
575	Pedro Guerrero	5.00
580	Dwight Evans	5.00
589	Bob Dernier	5.00
592	Jeff Robinson	5.00
603	Rick Manning	5.00
608	Craig Lefferts	5.00
610	Jack Morris	5.00
613	Terry Puhl	5.00
615	Marvell Wynne	5.00
619	Jeff Leonard	5.00
625	Mark Langston	5.00
630	Tim Raines	5.00
634	Bill Dawley	5.00
670	Tom Seaver	45.00
673	Buck Martinez	5.00
674	Atlee Hammaker	5.00
685	Bill Caudill	5.00
700	Eddie Murray	45.00
725	Floyd Bannister	5.00
729	Don Sutton	10.00

731	Neil Allen	5.00
736	Jerry Mumphrey	5.00
748	Lee Mazzilli	5.00
753	Greg Brock	5.00
755	Ken Singleton	5.00
757	Willie McGee	5.00
760	Nolan Ryan	650.00
762	Eddie Whitson	5.00
775	Mookie Wilson	5.00
780	Mike Flanagan	5.00
782	Tom Niedenfuer	5.00

Rub Downs

Similar in size and design to the Rub Downs of the previous year, the 1985 set again consisted of 32 unnumbered sheets featuring 112 different players. The set was sold by Topps as a separate issue.

		NM/M
Complete Set (32):		5.00
Common Sheet:		.25
Pack (2):		.50
Wax Box (36):		7.50
(1)	Tony Armas, Harold Baines, Lonnie Smith	.25
(2)	Don Baylor, George Hendrick, Ron Kittle, Johnnie LeMaster	.25
(3)	Buddy Bell, Tony Gwynn, Lloyd Moseby	.75
(4)	Bruce Benedict, Atlee Hammaker, Frank White	.25
(5)	Mike Boddicker, Rod Carew, Carlton Fisk, Johnny Ray	.60
(6)	Wade Boggs, Rick Dempsey, Keith Hernandez	.60
(7)	George Brett, Andre Dawson, Paul Molitor, Alan Wiggins	1.00
(8)	Tom Brunansky, Pedro Guerrero, Darryl Strawberry	.25
(9)	Bill Buckner, Tim Raines, Ryne Sandberg, Mike Schmidt	1.00
(10)	Steve Carlton, Bob Horner, Dan Quisenberry	.60
(11)	Gary Carter, Phil Garner, Ron Guidry	.60
(12)	Jack Clark, Damaso Garcia, Hal McRae, Lance Parrish	.25
(13)	Dave Concepcion, Cecil Cooper, Fred Lynn, Jesse Orosco	.25
(14)	Jose Cruz, Jack Morris, Jim Rice, Rick Sutcliffe	.25
(15)	Alvin Davis, Steve Kemp, Greg Luzinski, Kent Tekulve	.25
(16)	Ron Davis, Kent Hrbek, Juan Samuel	.25
(17)	John Denny, Carney Lansford, Mario Soto, Lou Whitaker	.25
(18)	Leon Durham, Willie Hernandez, Steve Sax	.25
(19)	Dwight Evans, Julio Franco, Dwight Gooden	.25
(20)	George Foster, Gary Gaetti, Bobby Grich, Gary Redus	.25
(21)	Steve Garvey, Jerry Remy, Bill Russell, George Wright	.25
(22)	Kirk Gibson, Rich Gossage, Don Mattingly, Dave Stieb	1.00
(23)	Moose Haas, Bruce Sutter, Dickie Thon, Andre Thornton	.25
(24)	Rickey Henderson, Dave Righetti, Pete Rose	1.50
(25)	Steve Henderson, Bill Madlock, Alan Trammell	.25
(26)	LaMarr Hoyt, Larry Parrish, Nolan Ryan	2.00
(27)	Reggie Jackson, Eric Show, Jason Thompson	.75
(28)	Terry Kennedy, Eddie Murray, Tom Seaver, Ozzie Smith	.75
(29)	Mark Langston, Ben Oglivie, Darrell Porter	.25
(30)	Jeff Leonard, Gary Matthews, Dale Murphy, Dave Winfield	.60
(31)	Craig McMurtry, Cal Ripken, Jr., Steve Rogers, Willie Upshaw	2.00
(32)	Tony Pena, Fernando Valenzuela, Robin Yount	.60

Stickers

Topps went to a larger size for its stickers in 1985. Produced by Panini, each of the 376 stickers measures 2-1/8" x 3" and is numbered on both the front and the back. The backs contain either an offer to obtain an autographed team ball or a poster. An album was also available.

		NM/M
Complete Set (376):		12.50
Common Player:		.05
Sticker Album:		2.00
Pack (5):		.25
Box (100):		15.00
1	Steve Garvey	.15
2	Steve Garvey	.15
3	Dwight Gooden	.05
4	Dwight Gooden	.05
5	Joe Morgan	.30
6	Joe Morgan	.30
7	Don Sutton	.30
8	Don Sutton	.30
9	1984 A.L. Championships (Jack Morris)	.05
10	1984 A.L. Championships (Milt Wilcox)	.05
11	1984 A.L. Championships (Kirk Gibson)	.05
12	1984 N.L. Championships (Gary Matthews)	.05
13	1984 N.L. Championships (Steve Garvey)	.05
14	1984 N.L. Championships (Steve Garvey)	.05
15	1984 World Series (Jack Morris)	.05
16	1984 World Series (Kurt Bevacqua)	.05
17	1984 World Series (Milt Wilcox)	.05
18	1984 World Series (Alan Trammell)	.05
19	1984 World Series (Kirk Gibson)	.05
20	1984 World Series (Alan Trammell)	.05
21	1984 World Series (Chet Lemon)	.05
22	Dale Murphy	.25
23	Steve Bedrosian	.05
24	Bob Horner	.05
25	Claudell Washington	.05
26	Rick Mahler	.05
27	Rafael Ramirez	.05
28	Craig McMurtry	.05
29	Chris Chambliss	.05
30	Alex Trevino	.05
31	Bruce Benedict	.05
32	Ken Oberkfell	.05
33	Glenn Hubbard	.05
34	Ryne Sandberg	.40
35	Rick Sutcliffe	.05
36	Leon Durham	.05
37	Jody Davis	.05
38	Bob Dernier	.05
39	Keith Moreland	.05
40	Scott Sanderson	.05
41	Lee Smith	.05
42	Ron Cey	.05
43	Steve Trout	.05
44	Gary Matthews	.05
45	Larry Bowa	.05
46	Mario Soto	.05
47	Dave Parker	.05
48	Dave Concepcion	.05
49	Gary Redus	.05
50	Ted Power	.05
51	Nick Esasky	.05
52	Duane Walker	.05
53	Eddie Milner	.05
54	Ron Oester	.05
55	Cesar Cedeno	.05
56	Joe Price	.05
57	Pete Rose	.65
58	Nolan Ryan	.75
59	Jose Cruz	.05
60	Jerry Mumphrey	.05
61	Enos Cabell	.05
62	Bob Knepper	.05
63	Dickie Thon	.05
64	Phil Garner	.05
65	Craig Reynolds	.05
66	Frank DiPino	.05
67	Terry Puhl	.05
68	Bill Doran	.05
69	Joe Niekro	.05
70	Pedro Guerrero	.05
71	Fernando Valenzuela	.05
72	Mike Marshall	.05
73	Alejandro Pena	.05
74	Orel Hershiser	.10
75	Ken Landreaux	.05
76	Bill Russell	.05
77	Steve Sax	.05
78	Rick Honeycutt	.05
79	Mike Scioscia	.05
80	Tom Niedenfuer	.05
81	Candy Maldonado	.05
82	Tim Raines	.05
83	Gary Carter	.30
84	Charlie Lea	.05
85	Jeff Reardon	.05
86	Andre Dawson	.15
87	Tim Wallach	.05
88	Terry Francona	.05
89	Steve Rogers	.05
90	Bryn Smith	.05
91	Bill Gullickson	.05
92	Dan Driessen	.05
93	Doug Flynn	.05
94	Mike Schmidt	.50
95	Tony Armas	.05
96	Dale Murphy	.15
97	Rick Sutcliffe	.05
98	Keith Hernandez	.05
99	George Foster	.05
100	Darryl Strawberry	.05
101	Jesse Orosco	.05
102	Mookie Wilson	.05
103	Doug Sisk	.05
104	Hubie Brooks	.05
105	Ron Darling	.05
106	Wally Backman	.05
107	Dwight Gooden	.05
108	Mike Fitzgerald	.05
109	Walt Terrell	.05
110	Ozzie Virgil	.05
111	Mike Schmidt	.50
112	Steve Carlton	.30
113	Al Holland	.05
114	Juan Samuel	.05
115	Von Hayes	.05
116	Jeff Stone	.05
117	Jerry Koosman	.05
118	Al Oliver	.05
119	John Denny	.05
120	Charles Hudson	.05
121	Garry Maddox	.05
122	Bill Madlock	.05
123	John Candelaria	.05
124	Tony Pena	.05
125	Jason Thompson	.05
126	Lee Lacy	.05
127	Rick Rhoden	.05
128	Doug Frobel	.05
129	Kent Tekulve	.05
130	Johnny Ray	.05
131	Marvell Wynne	.05
132	Larry McWilliams	.05
133	Dale Berra	.05
134	George Hendrick	.05
135	Bruce Sutter	.20
136	Joaquin Andujar	.05
137	Ozzie Smith	.50
138	Andy Van Slyke	.05
139	Lonnie Smith	.05
140	Darrell Porter	.05
141	Willie McGee	.05
142	Tom Herr	.05
143	Dave LaPoint	.05
144	Neil Allen	.05
145	David Green	.05
146	Tony Gwynn	.50
147	Rich Gossage	.05
148	Terry Kennedy	.05
149	Steve Garvey	.15
150	Alan Wiggins	.05
151	Garry Templeton	.05
152	Ed Whitson	.05
153	Tim Lollar	.05
154	Dave Dravecky	.05
155	Graig Nettles	.05
156	Eric Show	.05
157	Carmelo Martinez	.05
158	Bob Brenly	.05
159	Gary Lavelle	.05
160	Jack Clark	.05
161	Jeff Leonard	.05
162	Chili Davis	.05
163	Mike Krukow	.05
164	Johnnie LeMaster	.05
165	Atlee Hammaker	.05
166	Dan Gladden	.05
167	Greg Minton	.05
168	Joel Youngblood	.05
169	Frank Williams	.05
170	Tony Gwynn	.50
171	Don Mattingly	.60
172	Bruce Sutter	.20
173	Dan Quisenberry	.05
174	Tony Gwynn	.50
175	Ryne Sandberg	.40
176	Steve Garvey	.15
177	Dale Murphy	.15
178	Mike Schmidt	.50
179	Darryl Strawberry	.05
180	Gary Carter	.30
181	Ozzie Smith	.50
182	Charlie Lea	.05
183	Lou Whitaker	.05
184	Rod Carew	.30
185	Cal Ripken, Jr.	.75
186	Dave Winfield	.40
187	Reggie Jackson	.40
188	George Brett	.50
189	Lance Parrish	.05
190	Chet Lemon	.05
191	Dave Stieb	.05
192	Gary Carter	.30
193	Mike Schmidt	.50
194	Tony Armas	.05
195	Mike Witt	.05
196	Eddie Murray	.25
197	Cal Ripken, Jr.	.75
198	Scott McGregor	.05
199	Rick Dempsey	.05
200	Tippy Martinez	.05
201	Ken Singleton	.05
202	Mike Boddicker	.05
203	Rich Dauer	.05
204	John Shelby	.05
205	Al Bumbry	.05
206	John Lowenstein	.05
207	Mike Flanagan	.05
208	Jim Rice	.10
209	Tony Armas	.05
210	Wade Boggs	.40
211	Bruce Hurst	.05
212	Dwight Evans	.05
213	Mike Easler	.05
214	Bill Buckner	.05
215	Bob Stanley	.05
216	Jackie Gutierrez	.05
217	Rich Gedman	.05
218	Jerry Remy	.05
219	Marty Barrett	.05
220	Reggie Jackson	.40
221	Geoff Zahn	.05
222	Doug DeCinces	.05
223	Rod Carew	.30
224	Brian Downing	.05
225	Fred Lynn	.05
226	Gary Pettis	.05
227	Mike Witt	.05
228	Bob Boone	.05
229	Tommy John	.05
230	Bobby Grich	.05
231	Ron Romanick	.05
232	Ron Kittle	.05
233	Richard Dotson	.05
234	Harold Baines	.05
235	Tom Seaver	.40
236	Greg Walker	.05
237	Roy Smalley	.05
238	Greg Luzinski	.05
239	Julio Cruz	.05
240	Scott Fletcher	.05
241	Rudy Law	.05
242	Vance Law	.05
243	Carlton Fisk	.30
244	Andre Thornton	.05
245	Julio Franco	.05
246	Brett Butler	.05
247	Bert Blyleven	.05
248	Mike Hargrove	.05
249	George Vukovich	.05
250	Pat Tabler	.05
251	Brook Jacoby	.05
252	Tony Bernazard	.05
253	Ernie Camacho	.05
254	Mel Hall	.05
255	Carmen Castillo	.05
256	Jack Morris	.05
257	Willie Hernandez	.05
258	Alan Trammell	.05
259	Lance Parrish	.05
260	Chet Lemon	.05
261	Lou Whitaker	.05
262	Howard Johnson	.05
263	Barbaro Garbey	.05
264	Dan Petry	.05
265	Aurelio Lopez	.05
266	Larry Herndon	.05
267	Kirk Gibson	.05
268	George Brett	.50
269	Dan Quisenberry	.05
270	Hal McRae	.05
271	Steve Balboni	.05
272	Pat Sheridan	.05
273	Jorge Orta	.05
274	Frank White	.05
275	Bud Black	.05
276	Darryl Motley	.05
277	Willie Wilson	.05
278	Larry Gura	.05
279	Don Slaught	.05
280	Dwight Gooden	.05
281	Mark Langston	.05
282	Tim Raines	.05
283	Rickey Henderson	.30
284	Robin Yount	.30
285	Rollie Fingers	.30
286	Jim Sundberg	.05
287	Cecil Cooper	.05
288	Jaime Cocanower	.05
289	Mike Caldwell	.05
290	Don Sutton	.30
291	Rick Manning	.05
292	Ben Oglivie	.05
293	Moose Haas	.05
294	Ted Simmons	.05
295	Jim Gantner	.05
296	Kent Hrbek	.05
297	Ron Davis	.05
298	Dave Engle	.05
299	Tom Brunansky	.05
300	Frank Viola	.05
301	Mike Smithson	.05
302	Gary Gaetti	.05
303	Tim Teufel	.05
304	Mickey Hatcher	.05
305	John Butcher	.05
306	Darrell Brown	.05
307	Kirby Puckett	.50
308	Dave Winfield	.40
309	Phil Niekro	.30
310	Don Mattingly	.60
311	Don Baylor	.05
312	Willie Randolph	.05
313	Ron Guidry	.05
314	Dave Righetti	.05
315	Bobby Meacham	.05
316	Butch Wynegar	.05
317	Mike Pagliarulo	.05
318	Joe Cowley	.05
319	John Montefusco	.05
320	Dave Kingman	.05
321	Rickey Henderson	.30
322	Bill Caudill	.05
323	Dwayne Murphy	.05
324	Steve McCatty	.05
325	Joe Morgan	.30
326	Mike Heath	.05
327	Chris Codiroli	.05
328	Ray Burris	.05
329	Tony Phillips	.05
330	Carney Lansford	.05
331	Bruce Bochte	.05
332	Alvin Davis	.05
333	Al Cowens	.05
334	Jim Beattie	.05
335	Bob Kearney	.05
336	Ed Vande Berg	.05
337	Mark Langston	.05
338	Dave Henderson	.05
339	Spike Owen	.05
340	Matt Young	.05
341	Jack Perconte	.05
342	Barry Bonnell	.05
343	Mike Stanton	.05
344	Pete O'Brien	.05
345	Charlie Hough	.05
346	Larry Parrish	.05
347	Buddy Bell	.05
348	Frank Tanana	.05
349	Curt Wilkerson	.05
350	Jeff Kunkel	.05
351	Billy Sample	.05
352	Danny Darwin	.05
353	Gary Ward	.05
354	Mike Mason	.05
355	Mickey Rivers	.05
356	Dave Stieb	.05
357	Damaso Garcia	.05
358	Willie Upshaw	.05
359	Lloyd Moseby	.05
360	George Bell	.05
361	Luis Leal	.05
362	Jesse Barfield	.05
363	Dave Collins	.05
364	Roy Lee Jackson	.05
365	Doyle Alexander	.05
366	Alfredo Griffin	.05
367	Cliff Johnson	.05
368	Alvin Davis	.05
369	Juan Samuel	.05
370	Brook Jacoby	.05
371	Dwight Gooden, Mark Langston	.05
372	Mike Fitzgerald	.05
373	Jackie Gutierrez	.05
374	Dan Gladden	.05
375	Carmelo Martinez	.05
376	Kirby Puckett	.50

Super

Still trying to sell collectors on the idea of jumbo-sized cards, Topps returned for a second year with its 4-7/8" x 6-7/8" "Super" set. In fact, the set size was doubled from the previous year, to 60 cards. The Supers are identical to the regular-issue 1985 cards of the same players,

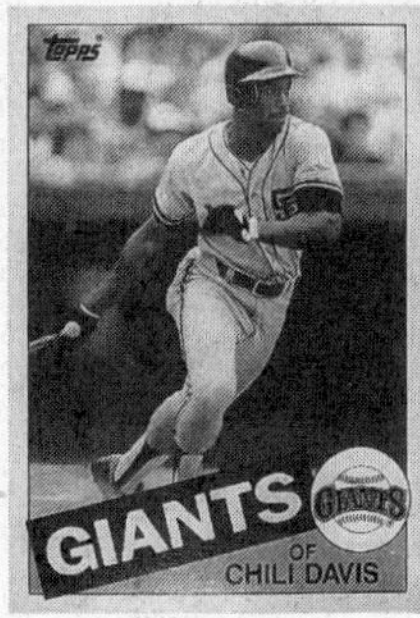

only the card numbers on back were changed. The cards were sold three per pack for 50 cents.

		NM/M
Complete Set (60):		12.00
Common Player:		.25
Wax Pack (1):		.25
Wax Box (24):		6.00
1	Ryne Sandberg	1.00
2	Willie Hernandez	.25
3	Rick Sutcliffe	.25
4	Don Mattingly	1.50
5	Tony Gwynn	1.00
6	Alvin Davis	.25
7	Dwight Gooden	.50
8	Dan Quisenberry	.25
9	Bruce Sutter	.65
10	Tony Armas	.25
11	Dale Murphy	.50
12	Mike Schmidt	1.50
13	Gary Carter	.75
14	Rickey Henderson	.75
15	Tim Raines	.25
16	Mike Boddicker	.25
17	Alejandro Pena	.25
18	Eddie Murray	.75
19	Gary Matthews	.25
20	Mark Langston	.25
21	Mario Soto	.25
22	Dave Stieb	.25
23	Nolan Ryan	3.00
24	Steve Carlton	.75
25	Alan Trammell	.25
26	Steve Garvey	.40
27	Kirk Gibson	.25
28	Juan Samuel	.25
29	Reggie Jackson	1.00
30	Darryl Strawberry	.25
31	Tom Seaver	.75
32	Pete Rose	2.00
33	Dwight Evans	.25
34	Jose Cruz	.25
35	Bert Blyleven	.25
36	Keith Hernandez	.25
37	Robin Yount	.75
38	Joaquin Andujar	.25
39	Lloyd Moseby	.25
40	Chili Davis	.25
41	Kent Hrbek	.25
42	Dave Parker	.25
43	Jack Morris	.25
44	Pedro Guerrero	.25
45	Mike Witt	.25
46	George Brett	1.50
47	Ozzie Smith	1.00
48	Cal Ripken, Jr.	3.00
49	Rich Gossage	.25
50	Jim Rice	.35
51	Harold Baines	.25
52	Fernando Valenzuela	.25
53	Buddy Bell	.25
54	Jesse Orosco	.25
55	Lance Parrish	.25
56	Jason Thompson	.25
57	Tom Brunansky	.25
58	Dave Righetti	.25
59	Dave Kingman	.25
60	Dave Winfield	.75

3-D

These 4-1/4" x 6" cards were something new. Printed on plastic, rather than paper, the player picture on the card is actually raised above the surface much like might be found on a relief map; a true 3-D baseball card. The plastic cards include the player's name, a Topps logo and card number across the top, and a team logo on the side. The backs are blank but have two peel-off adhesive strips so that the card may be attached to a flat surface. There are 30 cards in the set, mostly stars. Cards were sold one per pack for 50 cents.

		NM/M
Complete Set (30):		12.00
Common Player:		.25
Wax Pack (1):		.50
Wax Box (24):		12.50
1	Mike Schmidt	2.00
2	Eddie Murray	.75
3	Dale Murphy	.50
4	George Brett	2.00
5	Pete Rose	2.50
6	Jim Rice	.35
7	Ryne Sandberg	1.50
8	Don Mattingly	2.00
9	Darryl Strawberry	.25
10	Rickey Henderson	.75
11	Keith Hernandez	.25
12	Dave Kingman	.25
13	Tony Gwynn	1.50
14	Reggie Jackson	1.50
15	Gary Carter	.75
16	Cal Ripken, Jr.	3.00
17	Tim Raines	.25
18	Dave Winfield	.75
19	Dwight Gooden	.35
20	Dave Stieb	.25
21	Fernando Valenzuela	.25
22	Mark Langston	.25
23	Bruce Sutter	.65
24	Dan Quisenberry	.25
25	Steve Carlton	.75
26	Mike Boddicker	.25
27	Goose Gossage	.25
28	Jack Morris	.25
29	Rick Sutcliffe	.25
30	Tom Seaver	.75

1986 Topps

The 1986 Topps set consists of 792 cards. Fronts of the 2-1/2" x 3-1/2" cards feature color photos with the Topps logo in the upper right-hand corner while the player's position is in the lower left-hand corner. Above the picture is the team name, while below it is the player's name. The borders are a departure from previous practice, as the top 7/8" is black, while the remainder is white. Once again, a 5,000-set glossy-finish "Tiffany" edition was produced.

		NM/M
Unopened Fact. Set, Retail (792):		65.00
Unopened Fact. Set, Hobby (792):		30.00
Complete Set (792):		25.00
Common Player:		.05
Wax Pack (15):		.75
Wax Box (36):		20.00
Cello Pack (28):		1.00
Cello Box (24):		20.00
Rack Pack (51):		1.25
Rack Box (24):		25.00
Vending Box (500):		10.00
1	Pete Rose	1.50
2	Pete Rose (Special 1963-66)	.50
3	Pete Rose (Special 1967-70)	.50
4	Pete Rose (Special 1971-74)	.50
5	Pete Rose (Special 1975-78)	.50
6	Pete Rose (Special 1972-82)	.50
7	Pete Rose (Special 1983-85)	.50
8	Dwayne Murphy	.05
9	Roy Smith	.05
10	Tony Gwynn	.75
11	Bob Ojeda	.05
12	Jose Uribe **RC**	.05
13	Bob Kearney	.05
14	Julio Cruz	.05
15	Eddie Whitson	.05
16	Rick Schu **RC**	.05
17	Mike Stenhouse	.05
18	Brent Gaff	.05
19	Rich Hebner	.05
20	Lou Whitaker	.05
21	George Bamberger	.05
22	Duane Walker	.05
23	Manny Lee **RC**	.05
24	Len Barker	.05
25	Willie Wilson	.05
26	Frank DiPino	.05
27	Ray Knight	.05
28	Eric Davis	.05
29	Tony Phillips	.05
30	Eddie Murray	.50
31	Jamie Easterly	.05
32	Steve Yeager	.05
33	Jeff Lahti	.05
34	Ken Phelps **RC**	.05
35	Jeff Reardon	.05
36	Tigers Leaders (Lance Parrish)	.05
37	Mark Thurmond	.05
38	Glenn Hoffman	.05
39	Dave Rucker	.05
40	Ken Griffey	.05
41	Brad Wellman	.05
42	Geoff Zahn	.05
43	Dave Engle	.05
44	Lance McCullers **RC**	.05
45	Damaso Garcia	.05
46	Billy Hatcher **RC**	.05
47	Juan Berenguer	.05
48	Bill Almon	.05
49	Rick Manning	.05
50	Dan Quisenberry	.05
52	Chris Welsh	.05
53	Len Dykstra **RC**	.50
54	John Franco	.05
55	Fred Lynn	.05
56	Tom Niedenfuer	.05
57a	Bill Doran	.05
57b	Bobby Wine (Supposed to be #51.)	.05
58	Bill Krueger	.05
59	Andre Thornton	.05
60	Dwight Evans	.05
61	Karl Best	.05
62	Bob Boone	.05
63	Ron Roenicke	.05
64	Floyd Bannister	.05
65	Dan Driessen	.05
66	Cardinals Leaders (Bob Forsch)	.05
67	Carmelo Martinez	.05
68	Ed Lynch	.05
69	Luis Aguayo	.05
70	Dave Winfield	.50
71	Ken Schrom	.05
72	Shawon Dunston	.05
73	Randy O'Neal **RC**	.05
74	Rance Mulliniks	.05
75	Jose DeLeon	.05
76	Dion James	.05
77	Charlie Leibrandt	.05
78	Bruce Benedict	.05
79	Dave Schmidt	.05
80	Darryl Strawberry	.05
81	Gene Mauch	.05
82	Tippy Martinez	.05
83	Phil Garner	.05
84	Curt Young	.05
85	Tony Perez	.40
86	Tom Waddell	.05
87	Candy Maldonado	.05
88	Tom Nieto	.05
89	Randy St. Claire **RC**	.05
90	Garry Templeton	.05
91	Steve Crawford	.05
92	Al Cowens	.05
93	Scot Thompson	.05
94	Rich Bordi	.05
95	Ozzie Virgil	.05
96	Blue Jay Leaders (Jim Clancy)	.05
97	Gary Gaetti	.05
98	Dick Ruthven	.05
99	Buddy Biancalana	.05
100	Nolan Ryan	2.00
101	Dave Bergman	.05
102	Joe Orsulak **RC**	.15
103	Luis Salazar	.05
104	Sid Fernandez	.05
105	Gary Ward	.05
106	Ray Burris	.05
107	Rafael Ramirez	.05
108	Ted Power	.05
109	Len Matuszek	.05
110	Scott McGregor	.05
111	Roger Craig	.05
112	Bill Campbell	.05
113	U.L. Washington	.05
114	Mike Brown	.05
115	Jay Howell	.05
116	Brook Jacoby	.05
117	Bruce Kison	.05
118	Jerry Royster	.05
119	Barry Bonnell	.05
120	Steve Carlton	.50
121	Nelson Simmons	.05
122	Pete Filson	.05
123	Greg Walker	.05
124	Luis Sanchez	.05
125	Dave Lopes	.05
126	Mets Leaders (Mookie Wilson)	.05
127	Jack Howell **RC**	.05
128	John Wathan	.05
129	Jeff Dedmon **RC**	.05
130	Alan Trammell	.05
131	Checklist 1-132	.05
132	Razor Shines	.05
133	Andy McGaffigan	.05
134	Carney Lansford	.05
135	Joe Niekro	.05
136	Mike Hargrove	.05
137	Charlie Moore	.05
138	Mark Davis	.05
139	Daryl Boston	.05
140	John Candelaria	.05
141a	Chuck Cottier	.05
141b	Bob Rodgers (Supposed to be #171.)	.05
142	Bob Jones	.05
143	Dave Van Gorder	.05
144	Doug Sisk	.05
145	Pedro Guerrero	.05
146	Jack Perconte	.05
147	Larry Sheets	.05
148	Mike Heath	.05
149	Brett Butler	.05
150	Joaquin Andujar	.05
151	Dave Stapleton	.05
152	Mike Morgan	.05
153	Ricky Adams	.05
154	Bert Roberge	.05
155	Bob Grich	.05
156	White Sox Leaders (Richard Dotson)	.05
157	Ron Hassey	.05
158	Derrel Thomas	.05
159	Orel Hershiser	.05
160	Chet Lemon	.05
161	Lee Tunnell	.05
162	Greg Gagne	.05
163	Pete Ladd	.05
164	Steve Balboni	.05
165	Mike Davis	.05
166	Dickie Thon	.05
167	Zane Smith **RC**	.05
168	Jeff Burroughs	.05
169	George Wright	.05
170	Gary Carter	.50
172	Jerry Reed	.05
173	Wayne Gross	.05
174	Brian Snyder	.05
175	Steve Sax	.05
176	Jay Tibbs	.05
177	Joel Youngblood	.05
178	Ivan DeJesus	.05
179	Stu Cliburn **RC**	.05
180	Don Mattingly	1.00
181	Al Nipper	.05
182	Bobby Brown	.05
183	Larry Andersen	.05
184	Tim Laudner	.05
185	Rollie Fingers	.40
186	Astros Leaders (Jose Cruz)	.05
187	Scott Fletcher	.05
188	Bob Dernier	.05
189	Mike Mason	.05
190	George Hendrick	.05
191	Wally Backman	.05
192	Milt Wilcox	.05
193	Daryl Sconiers	.05
194	Craig McMurtry	.05
195	Dave Concepcion	.05
196	Doyle Alexander	.05
197	Enos Cabell	.05
198	Ken Dixon	.05
199	Dick Howser	.05
200	Mike Schmidt	1.00
201	Vince Coleman (Record Breaker)	.05
202	Dwight Gooden (Record Breaker)	.05
203	Keith Hernandez (Record Breaker)	.05
204	Phil Niekro (Record Breaker)	.05
205	Tony Perez (Record Breaker)	.05
206	Pete Rose (Record Breaker)	.25
207	Fernando Valenzuela (Record Breaker)	.05
208	Ramon Romero	.05
209	Randy Ready	.05
210	Calvin Schiraldi **RC**	.05
211	Ed Wojna	.05
212	Chris Speier	.05
213	Bob Shirley	.05
214	Randy Bush	.05
215	Frank White	.05
216	A's Leaders (Dwayne Murphy)	.05
217	Bill Scherrer	.05
218	Randy Hunt	.05
219	Dennis Lamp	.05
220	Bob Horner	.05
221	Dave Henderson	.05
222	Craig Gerber	.05
223	Atlee Hammaker	.05
224	Cesar Cedeno	.05
225	Ron Darling	.05
226	Lee Lacy	.05
227	Al Jones	.05
228	Tom Lawless	.05
229	Bill Gullickson	.05
230	Terry Kennedy	.05
231	Jim Frey	.05
232	Rick Rhoden	.05
233	Steve Lyons **RC**	.05
234	Doug Corbett	.05
235	Butch Wynegar	.05
236	Frank Eufemia	.05
237	Ted Simmons	.05
238	Larry Parrish	.05
239	Joel Skinner	.05
240	Tommy John	.10
241	Tony Fernandez	.05
242	Rich Thompson	.05
243	Johnny Grubb	.05
244	Craig Lefferts	.05
245	Jim Sundberg	.05
246	Phillies Leaders (Steve Carlton)	.10
247	Terry Harper	.05
248	Spike Owen	.05
249	Rob Deer **RC**	.05
250	Dwight Gooden	.05
251	Rich Dauer	.05
252	Bobby Castillo	.05
253	Dann Bilardello	.05
254	Ozzie Guillen **RC**	.30
255	Tony Armas	.05
256	Kurt Kepshire	.05
257	Doug DeCinces	.05
258	Tim Burke **RC**	.05
259	Dan Pasqua **RC**	.05
260	Tony Pena	.05
261	Bobby Valentine	.05
262	Mario Ramirez	.05
263	Checklist 133-264	.05
264	Darren Daulton	.05
265	Ron Davis	.05
266	Keith Moreland	.05
267	Paul Molitor	.50
268	Mike Scott	.05
269	Dane Iorg	.05
270	Jack Morris	.05
271	Dave Collins	.05
272	Tim Tolman	.05
273	Jerry Willard	.05
274	Ron Gardenhire	.05
275	Charlie Hough	.05
276	Yankees Leaders (Willie Randolph)	.05
277	Jaime Cocanower	.05
278	Sixto Lezcano	.05
279	Al Pardo	.05
280	Tim Raines	.05
281	Steve Mura	.05
282	Jerry Mumphrey	.05
283	Mike Fischlin	.05
284	Brian Dayett	.05
285	Buddy Bell	.05
286	Luis DeLeon	.05
287	John Christensen **RC**	.05
288	Don Aase	.05
289	Johnnie LeMaster	.05
290	Carlton Fisk	.50
291	Tom Lasorda	.10
292	Chuck Porter	.05
293	Chris Chambliss	.05
294	Danny Cox	.05
295	Kirk Gibson	.05
296	Geno Petralli **RC**	.05
297	Tim Lollar	.05
298	Craig Reynolds	.05
299	Bryn Smith	.05
300	George Brett	1.00
301	Dennis Rasmussen	.05
302	Greg Gross	.05
303	Curt Wardle	.05
304	Mike Gallego **RC**	.10
305	Phil Bradley	.05
306	Padres Leaders (Terry Kennedy)	.05
307	Dave Sax	.05
308	Ray Fontenot	.05
309	John Shelby	.05
310	Greg Minton	.05
311	Dick Schofield	.05
312	Tom Filer	.05
313	Joe DeSa	.05
314	Frank Pastore	.05
315	Mookie Wilson	.05
316	Sammy Khalifa	.05
317	Ed Romero	.05
318	Terry Whitfield	.05
319	Rick Camp	.05
320	Jim Rice	.15
321	Earl Weaver	.10
322	Bob Forsch	.05
323	Jerry Davis	.05
324	Dan Schatzeder	.05
325	Juan Beniquez	.05
326	Kent Tekulve	.05
327	Mike Pagliarulo	.05
328	Pete O'Brien	.05
329	Kirby Puckett	.75
330	Rick Sutcliffe	.05
331	Alan Ashby	.05
332	Darryl Motley	.05
333	Tom Henke **RC**	.05
334	Ken Oberkfell	.05
335	Don Sutton	.40
336	Indians Leaders (Andre Thornton)	.05
337	Darnell Coles	.05
338	Jorge Bell	.05
339	Bruce Berenyi	.05
340	Cal Ripken, Jr.	2.00
341	Frank Williams	.05
342	Gary Redus	.05
343	Carlos Diaz	.05
344	Jim Wohlford	.05
345	Donnie Moore	.05
346	Bryan Little	.05
347	Teddy Higuera **RC**	.10
348	Cliff Johnson	.05
349	Mark Clear	.05
350	Jack Clark	.05
351	Chuck Tanner	.05
352	Harry Spilman	.05
353	Keith Atherton	.05
354	Tony Bernazard	.05
355	Lee Smith	.05
356	Mickey Hatcher	.05
357	Ed Vande Berg	.05
358	Rick Dempsey	.05
359	Mike LaCoss	.05
360	Lloyd Moseby	.05
361	Shane Rawley	.05
362	Tom Paciorek	.05
363	Terry Forster	.05
364	Reid Nichols	.05
365	Mike Flanagan	.05
366	Reds Leaders (Dave Concepcion)	.05
367	Aurelio Lopez	.05
368	Greg Brock	.05
369	Al Holland	.05
370	Vince Coleman **RC**	.35
371	Bill Stein	.05
372	Ben Oglivie	.05
373	Urbano Lugo **RC**	.05
374	Terry Francona	.05
375	Rich Gedman	.05
376	Bill Dawley	.05
377	Joe Carter	.05
378	Bruce Bochte	.05
379	Bobby Meacham	.05
380	LaMarr Hoyt	.05
381	Ray Miller	.05
382	Ivan Calderon **RC**	.05
383	Chris Brown **RC**	.05
384	Steve Trout	.05
385	Cecil Cooper	.05
386	Cecil Fielder **RC**	.75
387	Steve Kemp	.05
388	Dickie Noles	.05
389	Glenn Davis **RC**	.05
390	Tom Seaver	.60
391	Julio Franco	.05
392	John Russell **RC**	.05
393	Chris Pittaro	.05
394	Checklist 265-396	.05
395	Scott Garrelts	.05
396	Red Sox Leaders (Dwight Evans)	.05
397	Steve Buechele **RC**	.10
398	Earnie Riles **RC**	.05
399	Bill Swift	.05
400	Rod Carew	.50
401	Fernando Valenzuela (Turn Back the Clock)	.05
402	Tom Seaver (Turn Back the Clock)	.25
403	Willie Mays (Turn Back the Clock)	.35
404	Frank Robinson (Turn Back the Clock)	.10
405	Roger Maris (Turn Back the Clock)	.30
406	Scott Sanderson	.05
407	Sal Butera	.05
408	Dave Smith	.05
409	Paul Runge **RC**	.05
410	Dave Kingman	.05
411	Sparky Anderson	.10
412	Jim Clancy	.05
413	Tim Flannery	.05
414	Tom Gorman	.05
415	Hal McRae	.05
416	Denny Martinez	.05
417	R.J. Reynolds	.05
418	Alan Knicely	.05
419	Frank Wills	.05
420	Von Hayes	.05
421	Dave Palmer	.05
422	Mike Jorgensen	.05
423	Dan Spillner	.05
424	Rick Miller	.05
425	Larry McWilliams	.05
426	Brewers Leaders (Charlie Moore)	.05
427	Joe Cowley	.05
428	Max Venable	.05
429	Greg Booker	.05
430	Kent Hrbek	.05
431	George Frazier	.05
432	Mark Bailey	.05
433	Chris Codiroli	.05
434	Curt Wilkerson	.05
435	Bill Caudill	.05
436	Doug Flynn	.05
437	Rick Mahler	.05
438	Clint Hurdle	.05
439	Rick Honeycutt	.05
440	Alvin Davis	.05
441	Whitey Herzog	.05
442	Ron Robinson **RC**	.05
443	Bill Buckner	.05
444	Alex Trevino	.05
445	Bert Blyleven	.05
446	Lenn Sakata	.05
447	Jerry Don Gleaton	.05
448	Herm Winningham **RC**	.05
449	Rod Scurry	.05
450	Graig Nettles	.05
451	Mark Brown	.05
452	Bob Clark	.05
453	Steve Jeltz	.05
454	Burt Hooton	.05
455	Willie Randolph	.05
456	Braves Leaders (Dale Murphy)	.10
457	Mickey Tettleton	.05
458	Kevin Bass	.05
459	Luis Leal	.05
460	Leon Durham	.05
461	Walt Terrell	.05
462	Domingo Ramos	.05
463	Jim Gott	.05
464	Ruppert Jones	.05
465	Jesse Orosco	.05
466	Tom Foley	.05
467	Bob James	.05
468	Mike Scioscia	.05
469	Storm Davis	.05
470	Bill Madlock	.05
471	Bobby Cox	.05
472	Joe Hesketh	.05
473	Mark Brouhard	.05
474	John Tudor	.05
475	Juan Samuel	.05
476	Ron Mathis	.05
477	Mike Easler	.05
478	Andy Hawkins	.05
479	Bob Melvin **RC**	.05
480	Oddibe McDowell **RC**	.05
481	Scott Bradley **RC**	.05
482	Rick Lysander	.05
483	George Vukovich	.05
484	Donnie Hill	.05
485	Gary Matthews	.05
486	Angels Leaders (Bob Grich)	.05
487	Bret Saberhagen	.05
488	Lou Thornton	.05
489	Jim Winn	.05
490	Jeff Leonard	.05
491	Pascual Perez	.05
492	Kelvin Chapman	.05
493	Gene Nelson	.05
494	Gary Roenicke	.05
495	Mark Langston	.05
496	Jay Johnstone	.05
497	John Stuper	.05
498	Tito Landrum	.05
499	Bob L. Gibson	.05
500	Rickey Henderson	.50
501	Dave Johnson	.05
502	Glen Cook	.05
503	Mike Fitzgerald	.05
504	Denny Walling	.05
505	Jerry Koosman	.05
506	Bill Russell	.05
507	Steve Ontiveros **RC**	.05
508	Alan Wiggins	.05
509	Ernie Camacho	.05
510	Wade Boggs	.75
511	Ed Nunez	.05
512	Thad Bosley	.05
513	Ron Washington	.05
514	Mike Jones	.05
515	Darrell Evans	.05
516	Giants Leaders (Greg Minton)	.05
517	Milt Thompson **RC**	.05
518	Buck Martinez	.05
519	Danny Darwin	.05
520	Keith Hernandez	.05
521	Nate Snell	.05
522	Bob Bailor	.05
523	Joe Price	.05
524	Darrell Miller **RC**	.05
525	Marvell Wynne	.05
526	Charlie Lea	.05
527	Checklist 397-528	.05
528	Terry Pendleton	.05
529	Marc Sullivan	.05
530	Rich Gossage	.05
531	Tony LaRussa	.05
532	Don Carman **RC**	.05
533	Billy Sample	.05
534	Jeff Calhoun	.05
535	Toby Harrah	.05
536	Jose Rijo	.05
537	Mark Salas	.05
538	Dennis Eckersley	.40
539	Glenn Hubbard	.05
540	Dan Petry	.05
541	Jorge Orta	.05
542	Don Schulze	.05
543	Jerry Narron	.05
544	Eddie Milner	.05
545	Jimmy Key	.05
546	Mariners Leaders (Dave Henderson)	.05
547	Roger McDowell	.05
548	Mike Young	.05
549	Bob Welch	.05
550	Tom Herr	.05
551	Dave LaPoint	.05
552	Marc Hill	.05
553	Jim Morrison	.05
554	Paul Householder	.05
555	Hubie Brooks	.05
556	John Denny	.05
557	Gerald Perry	.05
558	Tim Stoddard	.05
559	Tommy Dunbar	.05
560	Dave Righetti	.05
561	Bob Lillis	.05
562	Joe Beckwith	.05
563	Alejandro Sanchez	.05

564	Warren Brusstar	.05
565	Tom Brunansky	.05
566	Alfredo Griffin	.05
567	Jeff Barkley	.05
568	Donnie Scott	.05
569	Jim Acker	.05
570	Rusty Staub	.10
571	Mike Jeffcoat	.05
572	Paul Zuvella	.05
573	Tom Hume	.05
574	Ron Kittle	.05
575	Mike Boddicker	.05
576	Expos Leaders (Andre Dawson)	.05
577	Jerry Reuss	.05
578	Lee Mazzilli	.05
579	Jim Slaton	.05
580	Willie McGee	.05
581	Bruce Hurst	.05
582	Jim Gantner	.05
583	Al Bumbry	.05
584	Brian Fisher **RC**	.05
585	Garry Maddox	.05
586	Greg Harris	.05
587	Rafael Santana	.05
588	Steve Lake	.05
589	Sid Bream	.05
590	Bob Knepper	.05
591	Jackie Moore	.05
592	Frank Tanana	.05
593	Jesse Barfield	.05
594	Chris Bando	.05
595	Dave Parker	.05
596	Onix Concepcion	.05
597	Sammy Stewart	.05
598	Jim Presley	.05
599	Rick Aguilera **RC**	.25
600	Dale Murphy	.25
601	Gary Lucas	.05
602	Mariano Duncan	.05
603	Bill Laskey	.05
604	Gary Pettis	.05
605	Dennis Boyd	.05
606	Royals Leaders (Hal McRae)	.05
607	Ken Dayley	.05
608	Bruce Bochy	.05
609	Barbaro Garbey	.05
610	Ron Guidry	.05
611	Gary Woods	.05
612	Richard Dotson	.05
613	Roy Smalley	.05
614	Rick Waits	.05
615	Johnny Ray	.05
616	Glenn Brummer	.05
617	Lonnie Smith	.05
618	Jim Pankovits	.05
619	Danny Heep	.05
620	Bruce Sutter	.40
621	John Felske	.05
622	Gary Lavelle	.05
623	Floyd Rayford	.05
624	Steve McCatty	.05
625	Bob Brenly	.05
626	Roy Thomas	.05
627	Ron Oester	.05
628	Kirk McCaskill **RC**	.15
629	Mitch Webster **RC**	.05
630	Fernando Valenzuela	.05
631	Steve Braun	.05
632	Dave Von Ohlen	.05
633	Jackie Gutierrez	.05
634	Roy Lee Jackson	.05
635	Jason Thompson	.05
636	Cubs Leaders (Lee Smith)	.05
637	Rudy Law	.05
638	John Butcher	.05
639	Bo Diaz	.05
640	Jose Cruz	.05
641	Wayne Tolleson	.05
642	Ray Searage	.05
643	Tom Brookens	.05
644	Mark Gubicza	.05
645	Dusty Baker	.05
646	Mike Moore	.05
647	Mel Hall	.05
648	Steve Bedrosian	.05
649	Ronn Reynolds	.05
650	Dave Stieb	.05
651	Billy Martin	.10
652	Tom Browning	.05
653	Jim Dwyer	.05
654	Ken Howell	.05
655	Manny Trillo	.05
656	Brian Harper	.05
657	Juan Agosto	.05
658	Rob Wilfong	.05
659	Checklist 529-660	.05
660	Steve Garvey	.20
661	Roger Clemens	3.00
661	Roger Clemens (Blue streak upper-right.)	7.50
662	Bill Schroeder	.05
663	Neil Allen	.05
664	Tim Corcoran	.05
665	Alejandro Pena	.05
666	Rangers Leaders (Charlie Hough)	.05
667	Tim Teufel	.05
668	Cecilio Guante	.05
669	Ron Cey	.05
670	Willie Hernandez	.05
671	Lynn Jones	.05
672	Rob Picciolo	.05
673	Ernie Whitt	.05
674	Pat Tabler	.05
675	Claudell Washington	.05
676	Matt Young	.05
677	Nick Esasky	.05
678	Dan Gladden	.05
679	Britt Burns	.05
680	George Foster	.05
681	Dick Williams	.05
682	Junior Ortiz	.05
683	Andy Van Slyke	.05
684	Bob McClure	.05
685	Tim Wallach	.05
686	Jeff Stone	.05
687	Mike Trujillo	.05
688	Larry Herndon	.05
689	Dave Stewart	.05
690	Ryne Sandberg	.75
691	Mike Madden	.05
692	Dale Berra	.05
693	Tom Tellmann	.05
694	Garth Iorg	.05
695	Mike Smithson	.05
696	Dodgers Leaders (Bill Russell)	.05
697	Bud Black	.05
698	Brad Komminsk	.05
699	Pat Corrales	.05
700	Reggie Jackson	.75
701	Keith Hernandez/AS	.05
702	Tom Herr/AS	.05
703	Tim Wallach/AS	.05
704	Ozzie Smith/AS	.35
705	Dale Murphy/AS	.10
706	Pedro Guerrero/AS	.05
707	Willie McGee/AS	.05
708	Gary Carter/AS	.25
709	Dwight Gooden/AS	.05
710	John Tudor/AS	.05
711	Jeff Reardon/AS	.05
712	Don Mattingly/AS	.50
713	Damaso Garcia/AS	.05
714	George Brett/AS	.45
715	Cal Ripken, Jr./AS	1.00
716	Rickey Henderson/AS	.25
717	Dave Winfield/AS	.25
718	George Bell/AS	.05
719	Carlton Fisk/AS	.20
720	Bret Saberhagen/AS	.05
721	Ron Guidry/AS	.05
722	Dan Quisenberry/AS	.05
723	Marty Bystrom	.05
724	Tim Hulett	.05
725	Mario Soto	.05
726	Orioles Leaders (Rick Dempsey)	.05
727	David Green	.05
728	Mike Marshall	.05
729	Jim Beattie	.05
730	Ozzie Smith	.75
731	Don Robinson	.05
732	Floyd Youmans **RC**	.05
733	Ron Romanick	.05
734	Marty Barrett	.05
735	Dave Dravecky	.05
736	Glenn Wilson	.05
737	Pete Vuckovich	.05
738	Andre Robertson	.05
739	Dave Rozema	.05
740	Lance Parrish	.05
741	Pete Rose	1.00
742	Frank Viola	.05
743	Pat Sheridan	.05
744	Lary Sorensen	.05
745	Willie Upshaw	.05
746	Denny Gonzalez	.05
747	Rick Cerone	.05
748	Steve Henderson	.05
749	Ed Jurak	.05
750	Gorman Thomas	.05
751	Howard Johnson	.05
752	Mike Krukow	.05
753	Dan Ford	.05
754	Pat Clements **RC**	.05
755	Harold Baines	.05
756	Pirates Leaders (Rick Rhoden)	.05
757	Darrell Porter	.05
758	Dave Anderson	.05
759	Moose Haas	.05
760	Andre Dawson	.30
761	Don Slaught	.05
762	Eric Show	.05
763	Terry Puhl	.05
764	Kevin Gross	.05
765	Don Baylor	.05
766	Rick Langford	.05
767	Jody Davis	.05
768	Vern Ruhle	.05
769	Harold Reynolds **RC**	.25
770	Vida Blue	.05
771	John McNamara	.05
772	Brian Downing	.05
773	Greg Pryor	.05
774	Terry Leach	.05
775	Al Oliver	.05
776	Gene Garber	.05
777	Wayne Krenchicki	.05
778	Jerry Hairston Sr.	.05
779	Rick Reuschel	.05
780	Robin Yount	.50
781	Joe Nolan	.05
782	Ken Landreaux	.05
783	Ricky Horton	.05
784	Alan Bannister	.05
785	Bob Stanley	.05
786	Twins Leaders (Mickey Hatcher)	.05
787	Vance Law	.05
788	Marty Castillo	.05
789	Kurt Bevacqua	.05
790	Phil Niekro	.40
791	Checklist 661-792	.05
792	Charles Hudson	.05

Tiffany

A total of only 5,000 of these specially boxed collectors' edition sets was reported produced. Sold only through hobby dealers' the cards differ from the regular-issue 1986 Topps cards only in the use of white cardboard stock and the application of a high-gloss finish on the cards' fronts.

	NM/M
Unopened Set (792):	100.00
Complete Set (792):	45.00
Common Player:	.25

Traded

This 132-card set of 2-1/2" x 3-1/2" cards was, at issue, one of the most popular sets of recent times. As always, the set features traded veterans, and a better than usual crop of rookies. As in the previous two years, a glossy-finish "Tiffany" edition of 5,000 Traded sets was produced.

		NM/M
Unopened Set (132):		30.00
Complete Set (132):		25.00
Common Player:		.05
1T	Andy Allanson **RC**	.05
2T	Neil Allen	.05
3T	Joaquin Andujar	.05
4T	Paul Assenmacher **RC**	.05
5T	Scott Bailes **RC**	.05
6T	Don Baylor	.15
7T	Steve Bedrosian	.05
8T	Juan Beniquez	.05
9T	Juan Berenguer	.05
10T	Mike Bielecki **RC**	.05
11T	Barry Bonds **RC**	20.00
12T	Bobby Bonilla **RC**	.50
13T	Juan Bonilla	.05
14T	Rich Bordi	.05
15T	Steve Boros	.05
16T	Rick Burleson	.05
17T	Bill Campbell	.05
18T	Tom Candiotti	.05
19T	John Cangelosi **RC**	.05
20T	Jose Canseco **RC**	4.00
21T	Carmen Castillo	.05
22T	Rick Cerone	.05
23T	John Cerutti **RC**	.05
24T	Will Clark **RC**	1.50
25T	Mark Clear	.05
26T	Darnell Coles	.05
27T	Dave Collins	.05
28T	Tim Conroy	.05
29T	Joe Cowley	.05
30T	Joel Davis **RC**	.05
31T	Rob Deer	.05
32T	John Denny	.05
33T	Mike Easler	.05
34T	Mark Eichhorn **RC**	.05
35T	Steve Farr	.05
36T	Scott Fletcher	.05
37T	Terry Forster	.05
38T	Terry Francona	.05
39T	Jim Fregosi	.05
40T	Andres Galarraga **RC**	.35
41T	Ken Griffey	.05
42T	Bill Gullickson	.05
43T	Jose Guzman **RC**	.05
44T	Moose Haas	.05
45T	Billy Hatcher	.05
46T	Mike Heath	.05
47T	Tom Hume	.05
48T	Pete Incaviglia **RC**	.20
49T	Dane Iorg	.05
50T	Bo Jackson **RC**	3.00
51T	Wally Joyner **RC**	.40
52T	Charlie Kerfeld **RC**	.05
53T	Eric King **RC**	.05
54T	Bob Kipper **RC**	.05
55T	Wayne Krenchicki	.05
56T	John Kruk **RC**	.35
57T	Mike LaCoss	.05
58T	Pete Ladd	.05
59T	Mike Laga	.05
60T	Hal Lanier	.05
61T	Dave LaPoint	.05
62T	Rudy Law	.05
63T	Rick Leach	.05
64T	Tim Leary	.05
65T	Dennis Leonard	.05
66T	Jim Leyland	.05
67T	Steve Lyons	.05
68T	Mickey Mahler	.05
69T	Candy Maldonado	.05
70T	Roger Mason **RC**	.05
71T	Bob McClure	.05
72T	Andy McGaffigan	.05
73T	Gene Michael	.05
74T	Kevin Mitchell **RC**	.25
75T	Omar Moreno	.05
76T	Jerry Mumphrey	.05
77T	Phil Niekro	.25
78T	Randy Niemann	.05
79T	Juan Nieves **RC**	.05
80T	Otis Nixon **RC**	.05
81T	Bob Ojeda	.05
82T	Jose Oquendo	.05
83T	Tom Paciorek	.05
84T	Dave Palmer	.05
85T	Frank Pastore	.05
86T	Lou Piniella	.05
87T	Dan Plesac **RC**	.05
88T	Darrell Porter	.05
89T	Rey Quinones **RC**	.05
90T	Gary Redus	.05
91T	Bip Roberts	.05
92T	Billy Jo Robidoux **RC**	.05
93T	Jeff Robinson	.05
94T	Gary Roenicke	.05
95T	Ed Romero	.05
96T	Argenis Salazar	.05
97T	Joe Sambito	.05
98T	Billy Sample	.05
99T	Dave Schmidt	.05
100T	Ken Schrom	.05
101T	Tom Seaver	.50
102T	Ted Simmons	.05
103T	Sammy Stewart	.05
104T	Kurt Stillwell **RC**	.05
105T	Franklin Stubbs	.05
106T	Dale Sveum **RC**	.05
107T	Chuck Tanner	.05
108T	Danny Tartabull **RC**	.05
109T	Tim Teufel	.05
110T	Bob Tewksbury **RC**	.05
111T	Andres Thomas **RC**	.05
112T	Milt Thompson	.05
113T	Robby Thompson **RC**	.05
114T	Jay Tibbs	.05
115T	Wayne Tolleson	.05
116T	Alex Trevino	.05
117T	Manny Trillo	.05
118T	Ed Vande Berg	.05
119T	Ozzie Virgil	.05
120T	Bob Walk	.05
121T	Gene Walter **RC**	.05
122T	Claudell Washington	.05
123T	Bill Wegman **RC**	.05
124T	Dick Williams	.05
125T	Mitch Williams **RC**	.05
126T	Bobby Witt **RC**	.05
127T	Todd Worrell **RC**	.05
128T	George Wright	.05
129T	Ricky Wright	.05
130T	Steve Yeager	.05
131T	Paul Zuvella	.05
132T	Checklist	.05

Traded Tiffany

This collectors' edition differs from the regular 1986 Topps Traded set only in the use of a high-gloss front finish. The set was sold only through hobby channels in a specially design box.

		NM/M
Unopened Set (132):		700.00
Complete Set (132):		450.00
Common Player:		.25
11T	Barry Bonds	200.00

Traded Mickey Mantle Bronze

This 1/4-size metal replica of Mantle's first-ever Topps card was issued to dealers who purchased cases of 1986 Topps Traded sets. Each detail of the 1952 Topps Mantle card is reproduced on the 1-1/4" x 1-3/4" bronze metal mini-card, right down to the stats.

		NM/M
311	Mickey Mantle	9.00

Box Panels

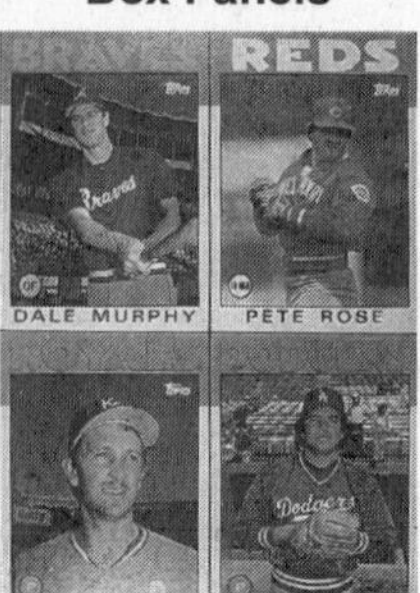

Following the lead of Donruss, which introduced the concept in 1985, Topps produced special cards on the bottom panels of wax boxes. Individual cards measure 2-1/2" x 3-1/2", the same as regular cards. Design of the cards is virtually identical with regular '86 Topps, though the top border is in red, rather than black. The cards are lettered "A" through "P," rather than numbered on the back.

		NM/M
Complete Panel Set:		7.00
Complete Singles Set:		6.00
Common Panel:		1.00
Common Single Player:		.10
Panel		2.00
A	Jorge Bell	.10
B	Wade Boggs	.75
C	George Brett	1.00
D	Vince Coleman	.25
Panel		1.00
E	Carlton Fisk	.50
F	Dwight Gooden	.10
G	Pedro Guerrero	.10
H	Ron Guidry	.10
Panel		2.00
I	Reggie Jackson	.75
J	Don Mattingly	1.00
K	Oddibe McDowell	.10
L	Willie McGee	.10
Panel		2.50
M	Dale Murphy	.35
N	Pete Rose	1.50
O	Bret Saberhagen	.10
P	Fernando Valenzuela	.10

All-Star Glossy Set of 22

As in previous years, Topps continued to make the popular glossy-surfaced cards as an insert in rack packs. The All-Star Glossy set of 2-1/2" x 3-1/2" cards shows little design change from previous years. Cards feature a front color photo and All-Star banner at the top. The bottom has the player's name and position. The set includes the All-Star starting teams as well as the managers and honorary captains.

		NM/M
Complete Set (22):		2.50
Common Player:		.05
1	Sparky Anderson	.05
2	Eddie Murray	.35
3	Lou Whitaker	.05
4	George Brett	.50
5	Cal Ripken, Jr.	.65
6	Jim Rice	.25
7	Rickey Henderson	.35
8	Dave Winfield	.35
9	Carlton Fisk	.35
10	Jack Morris	.05
11	A.L. All-Star Team	.05
12	Dick Williams	.05
13	Steve Garvey	.15
14	Tom Herr	.05
15	Graig Nettles	.05
16	Ozzie Smith	.45
17	Tony Gwynn	.45
18	Dale Murphy	.25
19	Darryl Strawberry	.05
20	Terry Kennedy	.05
21	LaMarr Hoyt	.05
22	N.L. All-Star Team	.05

All-Star Glossy Set of 60

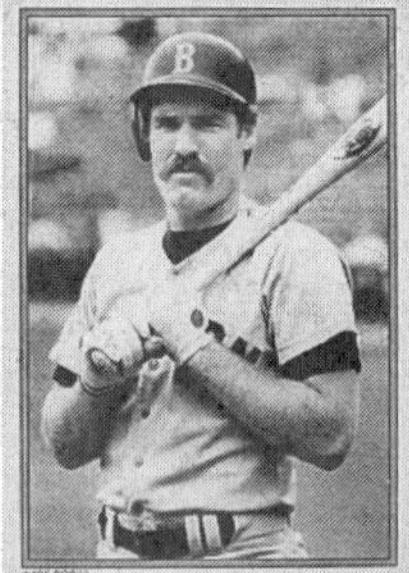

The Topps All-Star & Hot Prospects glossy set of 60 cards represents an expansion of a good idea. The 2-1/2" x 3-1/2" cards had a good following when they were limited to stars, but Topps realized that the addition of top young players would spice up the set even further, so in 1986 it was expanded from 40 to 60 cards. The cards themselves are basically all color glossy pictures with the player's name in very small print in the lower left-hand corner. To obtain the set, it was necessary to send $1 plus six special offer cards from wax packs to Topps for each series. At 60 cards, that meant the process had to be repeated six times as there were 10 cards in each series, making the set quite expensive from the outset.

		NM/M
Complete Set (60):		8.00
Common Player:		.10
1	Oddibe McDowell	.10
2	Reggie Jackson	.50
3	Fernando Valenzuela	.10
4	Jack Clark	.10
5	Rickey Henderson	.40
6	Steve Balboni	.10
7	Keith Hernandez	.10
8	Lance Parrish	.10
9	Willie McGee	.10
10	Chris Brown	.10
11	Darryl Strawberry	.10
12	Ron Guidry	.10
13	Dave Parker	.10
14	Cal Ripken	1.00
15	Tim Raines	.10
16	Rod Carew	.40
17	Mike Schmidt	.75
18	George Brett	.75
19	Joe Hesketh	.10
20	Dan Pasqua	.10
21	Vince Coleman	.10
22	Tom Seaver	.40
23	Gary Carter	.40
24	Orel Hershiser	.10
25	Pedro Guerrero	.10
26	Wade Boggs	.50
27	Bret Saberhagen	.10
28	Carlton Fisk	.40
29	Kirk Gibson	.10
30	Brian Fisher	.10
31	Don Mattingly	.75
32	Tom Herr	.10
33	Eddie Murray	.40
34	Ryne Sandberg	.50
35	Dan Quisenberry	.10
36	Jim Rice	.30
37	Dale Murphy	.30
38	Steve Garvey	.25

39 Roger McDowell .10
40 Earnie Riles .10
41 Dwight Gooden .10
42 Dave Winfield .40
43 Dave Stieb .10
44 Bob Horner .10
45 Nolan Ryan 1.00
46 Ozzie Smith .50
47 Jorge Bell .10
48 Gorman Thomas .10
49 Tom Browning .10
50 Larry Sheets .10
51 Pete Rose .90
52 Brett Butler .10
53 John Tudor .10
54 Phil Bradley .10
55 Jeff Reardon .10
56 Rich Gossage .10
57 Tony Gwynn .50
58 Ozzie Guillen .10
59 Glenn Davis .10
60 Darrell Evans .10

Gallery of Champions

For the third consecutive year Topps issued 12 metal "mini cards," adding an aluminum version to the bronze and silver. The metal replicas were minted 1/4-size (approximately 1-1/4" x 1-3/4") of the regular cards. The bronze and silver sets were issued in leather-like velvet-lined display cases, the alumnium in individual cello packs. A pewter Don Mattingly was issued as a premium to those ordering the sets.

NM/M
Complete Aluminum Set: 15.00
Complete Bronze Set: 50.00
Complete Silver Set: 200.00
(1a) Wade Boggs/Aluminum 2.00
(1b) Wade Boggs/Bronze 15.00
(1s) Wade Boggs/Silver 35.00
(2a) Vince Coleman/Aluminum 1.50
(2b) Vince Coleman/Bronze 4.00
(2s) Vince Coleman/Silver 12.00
(3a) Darrell Evans/Aluminum 1.00
(3b) Darrell Evans/Bronze 4.00
(3s) Darrell Evans/Silver 12.00
(4a) Dwight Gooden/Aluminum 1.00
(4b) Dwight Gooden/Bronze 4.00
(4s) Dwight Gooden/Silver 12.00
(5a) Ozzie Guillen/Aluminum 1.00
(5b) Ozzie Guillen/Bronze 4.00
(5s) Ozzie Guillen/Silver 12.00
(6a) Don Mattingly/Aluminum 4.00
(6b) Don Mattingly/Bronze 20.00
(6s) Don Mattingly/Silver 75.00
(6p) Don Mattingly/Pewter 45.00
(7a) Willie McGee/Aluminum 1.00
(7b) Willie McGee/Bronze 4.00
(7s) Willie McGee/Silver 12.00
(8a) Dale Murphy/Aluminum 1.50
(8b) Dale Murphy/Bronze 7.50
(8s) Dale Murphy/Silver 30.00
(9a) Dan Quisenberry/Aluminum 1.00
(9b) Dan Quisenberry/Bronze 4.00
(9s) Dan Quisenberry/Silver 12.00
(10a) Jeff Reardon/Aluminum 1.00
(10b) Jeff Reardon/Bronze 4.00
(10s) Jeff Reardon/Silver 12.00
(11a) Pete Rose/Aluminum 5.00
(11b) Pete Rose/Bronze 25.00
(11s) Pete Rose/Silver 90.00
(12a) Bret Saberhagen/Aluminum 1.00
(12b) Bret Saberhagen/Bronze 4.00
(12s) Bret Saberhagen/Silver 12.00

Mini League Leaders

Topps had long experimented with bigger cards, but in 1986, they also decided to try smaller ones. These 2-1/8" x 2-15/16" cards feature top players in a number of categories. Sold in plastic packs as a regular Topps issue, the 66-card set is attractive as well as innovative. The cards feature color photos and a minimum of added information on the fronts where only the player's name and Topps logo appear. Backs limited information as well, but do feature enough to justify the player's inclusion in a set of league leaders.

NM/M
Complete Set (66): 5.00
Common Player: .05
Wax Pack (6): .50
Wax Box (36): 10.00
Vend Box (500): 15.00
1 Eddie Murray .35
2 Cal Ripken, Jr. 1.00
3 Wade Boggs .45
4 Dennis Boyd .05
5 Dwight Evans .05
6 Bruce Hurst .05
7 Gary Pettis .05
8 Harold Baines .05
9 Floyd Bannister .05
10 Britt Burns .05
11 Carlton Fisk .35
12 Brett Butler .05
13 Darrell Evans .05
14 Jack Morris .05
15 Lance Parrish .05
16 Walt Terrell .05
17 Steve Balboni .05
18 George Brett .75
19 Charlie Leibrandt .05
20 Bret Saberhagen .05
21 Lonnie Smith .05
22 Willie Wilson .05
23 Bert Blyleven .05
24 Mike Smithson .05
25 Frank Viola .05
26 Ron Guidry .05
27 Rickey Henderson .35
28 Don Mattingly .75
29 Dave Winfield .35
30 Mike Moore .05
31 Gorman Thomas .05
32 Toby Harrah .05
33 Charlie Hough .05
34 Doyle Alexander .05
35 Jimmy Key .05
36 Dave Stieb .05
37 Dale Murphy .20
38 Keith Moreland .05
39 Ryne Sandberg .45
40 Tom Browning .05
41 Dave Parker .05
42 Mario Soto .05
43 Nolan Ryan 1.00
44 Pedro Guerrero .05
45 Orel Hershiser .05
46 Mike Scioscia .05
47 Fernando Valenzuela .05
48 Bob Welch .05
49 Tim Raines .05
50 Gary Carter .35
51 Sid Fernandez .05
52 Dwight Gooden .05
53 Keith Hernandez .05
54 Juan Samuel .05
55 Mike Schmidt .75
56 Glenn Wilson .05
57 Rick Reuschel .05
58 Joaquin Andujar .05
59 Jack Clark .05
60 Vince Coleman .05
61 Danny Cox .05
62 Tom Herr .05
63 Willie McGee .05
64 John Tudor .05
65 Tony Gwynn .45
66 Checklist .05

Stickers

The 1986 Topps stickers are 2-1/8" x 3". The 200-piece set features 316 different subjects, with some stickers including two or three players. Numbers run only to 315, however. The set includes some specialty stickers such as League Championships and World Series themes. Stickers are numbered both front and back and included a chance to win a trip to spring training as well as an offer to buy a complete 1986 Topps regular set. An album for the stickers was available in stores. It feautres Pete Rose in action on the front cover and reproductions of his Topps cards on back.

NM/M
Complete Set (315): 6.00
Common Player: .05
Sticker Album: 1.50
Wax Pack (5): .30
Wax Box (100): 11.00
1 Pete Rose .60
2 Pete Rose .60
3 George Brett .50
4 Rod Carew .40
5 Vince Coleman .05
6 Dwight Gooden .05
7 Phil Niekro .20
8 Tony Perez .30
9 Nolan Ryan .75
10 Tom Seaver .40
11 N.L. Championship Series (Ozzie Smith) .10
12 N.L. Championship Series (Bill Madlock) .05
13 N.L. Championship Series (Cardinals Celebrate) .05
14 A.L. Championship Series (Al Oliver) .05
15 A.L. Championship Series (Jim Sundberg) .05
16 A.L. Championship Series (George Brett) .10
17 World Series (Bret Saberhagen) .05
18 World Series (Dane Iorg) .05
19 World Series (Tito Landrum) .05
20 World Series (John Tudor) .05
21 World Series (Buddy Biancalana) .05
22 World Series (Darryl Motley, Darrell Porter) .05
23 World Series (George Brett, Frank White) .05
24 Nolan Ryan .75
25 Bill Doran .05
26 Jose Cruz .05
27 Mike Scott .05
28 Kevin Bass .05
29 Glenn Davis .05
30 Mark Bailey .05
31 Dave Smith .05
32 Phil Garner .05
33 Dickie Thon .05
34 Bob Horner .05
35 Dale Murphy .25
36 Glenn Hubbard .05
37 Bruce Sutter .20
38 Ken Oberkfell .05
39 Claudell Washington .05
40 Steve Bedrosian .05
41 Terry Harper .05
42 Rafael Ramirez .05
43 Rick Mahler .05
44 Joaquin Andujar .05
45 Willie McGee .05
46 Ozzie Smith .50
47 Vince Coleman .05
48 Danny Cox .05
49 Tom Herr .05
50 Jack Clark .05
51 Andy Van Slyke .05
52 John Tudor .05
53 Terry Pendleton .05
54 Keith Moreland .05
55 Ryne Sandberg .40
56 Lee Smith .05
57 Steve Trout .05
58 Jody Davis .05
59 Gary Matthews .05
60 Leon Durham .05
61 Rick Sutcliffe .05
62 Dennis Eckersley .30
63 Bob Dernier .05
64 Fernando Valenzuela .05
65 Pedro Guerrero .05
66 Jerry Reuss .05
67 Greg Brock .05
68 Mike Scioscia .05
69 Ken Howell .05
70 Bill Madlock .05
71 Mike Marshall .05
72 Steve Sax .05
73 Orel Hershiser .05
74 Andre Dawson .25
75 Tim Raines .05
76 Jeff Reardon .05
77 Hubie Brooks .05
78 Bill Gullickson .05
79 Bryn Smith .05
80 Terry Francona .05
81 Vance Law .05
82 Tim Wallach .05
83 Herm Winningham .05
84 Jeff Leonard .05
85 Chris Brown .05
86 Scott Garrelts .05
87 Jose Uribe .05
88 Manny Trillo .05
89 Dan Driessen .05
90 Dan Gladden .05
91 Mark Davis .05
92 Bob Brenly .05
93 Mike Krukow .05
94 Dwight Gooden .05
95 Darryl Strawberry .05
96 Gary Carter .40
97 Wally Backman .05
98 Ron Darling .05
99 Keith Hernandez .05
100 George Foster .05
101 Howard Johnson .05
102 Rafael Santana .05
103 Roger McDowell .05
104 Steve Garvey .15
105 Tony Gwynn .50
106 Graig Nettles .05
107 Rich Gossage .05
108 Andy Hawkins .05
109 Carmelo Martinez .05
110 Garry Templeton .05
111 Terry Kennedy .05
112 Tim Flannery .05
113 LaMarr Hoyt .05
114 Mike Schmidt .50
115 Ozzie Virgil .05
116 Steve Carlton .40
117 Garry Maddox .05
118 Glenn Wilson .05
119 Kevin Gross .05
120 Von Hayes .05
121 Juan Samuel .05
122 Rick Schu .05
123 Shane Rawley .05
124 Johnny Ray .05
125 Tony Pena .05
126 Rick Reuschel .05
127 Sammy Khalifa .05
128 Marvell Wynne .05
129 Jason Thompson .05
130 Rick Rhoden .05
131 Bill Almon .05
132 Joe Orsulak .05
133 Jim Morrison .05
134 Pete Rose .60
135 Dave Parker .05
136 Mario Soto .05
137 Dave Concepcion .05
138 Ron Oester .05
139 Buddy Bell .05
140 Ted Power .05
141 Tom Browning .05
142 John Franco .05
143 Tony Perez .30
144 Willie McGee .05
145 Dale Murphy .25
146 Tony Gwynn .50
147 Tom Herr .05
148 Steve Garvey .15
149 Dale Murphy .25
150 Darryl Strawberry .05
151 Graig Nettles .05
152 Terry Kennedy .05
153 Ozzie Smith .50
154 LaMarr Hoyt .05
155 Rickey Henderson .40
156 Lou Whitaker .05
157 George Brett .50
158 Eddie Murray .40
159 Cal Ripken, Jr. .75
160 Dave Winfield .40
161 Jim Rice .15
162 Carlton Fisk .40
163 Jack Morris .05
164 Wade Boggs .40
165 Darrell Evans .05
166 Mike Davis .05
167 Dave Kingman .05
168 Alfredo Griffin .05
169 Carney Lansford .05
170 Bruce Bochte .05
171 Dwayne Murphy .05
172 Dave Collins .05
173 Chris Codiroli .05
174 Mike Heath .05
175 Jay Howell .05
176 Rod Carew .40
177 Reggie Jackson .50
178 Doug DeCinces .05
179 Bob Boone .05
180 Ron Romanick .05
181 Bob Grich .05
182 Donnie Moore .05
183 Brian Downing .05
184 Ruppert Jones .05
185 Juan Beniquez .05
186 Dave Stieb .05
187 Jorge Bell .05
188 Willie Upshaw .05
189 Tom Henke .05
190 Damaso Garcia .05
191 Jimmy Key .05
192 Jesse Barfield .05
193 Dennis Lamp .05
194 Tony Fernandez .05
195 Lloyd Moseby .05
196 Cecil Cooper .05
197 Robin Yount .40
198 Rollie Fingers .20
199 Ted Simmons .05
200 Ben Oglivie .05
201 Moose Haas .05
202 Jim Gantner .05
203 Paul Molitor .40
204 Charlie Moore .05
205 Danny Darwin .05
206 Brett Butler .05
207 Brook Jacoby .05
208 Andre Thornton .05
209 Tom Waddell .05
210 Tony Bernazard .05
211 Julio Franco .05
212 Pat Tabler .05
213 Joe Carter .05
214 George Vukovich .05
215 Rich Thompson .05
216 Gorman Thomas .05
217 Phil Bradley .05
218 Alvin Davis .05
219 Jim Presley .05
220 Matt Young .05
221 Mike Moore .05
222 Dave Henderson .05
223 Ed Nunez .05
224 Spike Owen .05
225 Mark Langston .05
226 Cal Ripken, Jr. .75
227 Eddie Murray .40
228 Fred Lynn .05
229 Lee Lacy .05
230 Scott McGregor .05
231 Storm Davis .05
232 Rick Dempsey .05
233 Mike Boddicker .05
234 Mike Young .05
235 Sammy Stewart .05
236 Pete O'Brien .05
237 Oddibe McDowell .05
238 Toby Harrah .05
239 Gary Ward .05
240 Larry Parrish .05
241 Charlie Hough .05
242 Burt Hooton .05
243 Don Slaught .05
244 Curt Wilkerson .05
245 Greg Harris .05
246 Jim Rice .15
247 Wade Boggs .40
248 Rich Gedman .05
249 Dennis Boyd .05
250 Marty Barrett .05
251 Dwight Evans .05
252 Bill Buckner .05
253 Bob Stanley .05
254 Tony Armas .05
255 Mike Easler .05
256 George Brett .50
257 Dan Quisenberry .05
258 Willie Wilson .05
259 Jim Sundberg .05
260 Bret Saberhagen .05
261 Bud Black .05
262 Charlie Leibrandt .05
263 Frank White .05
264 Lonnie Smith .05
265 Steve Balboni .05
266 Kirk Gibson .05
267 Alan Trammell .05
268 Jack Morris .05
269 Darrell Evans .05
270 Dan Petry .05
271 Larry Herndon .05
272 Lou Whitaker .05
273 Lance Parrish .05
274 Chet Lemon .05
275 Willie Hernandez .05
276 Tom Brunansky .05
277 Kent Hrbek .05
278 Mark Salas .05
279 Bert Blyleven .05
280 Tim Teufel .05
281 Ron Davis .05
282 Mike Smithson .05
283 Gary Gaetti .05
284 Frank Viola .05
285 Kirby Puckett .50
286 Carlton Fisk .40
287 Tom Seaver .40
288 Harold Baines .05
289 Ron Kittle .05
290 Bob James .05
291 Rudy Law .05
292 Britt Burns .05
293 Greg Walker .05
294 Ozzie Guillen .05
295 Tim Hulett .05
296 Don Mattingly .50
297 Rickey Henderson .40
298 Dave Winfield .40
299 Butch Wynegar .05
300 Don Baylor .05
301 Eddie Whitson .05
302 Ron Guidry .05
303 Dave Righetti .05
304 Bobby Meacham .05
305 Willie Randolph .05
306 Vince Coleman .05
307 Oddibe McDowell .05
308 Larry Sheets .05
309 Ozzie Guillen .05
310 Earnie Riles .05
311 Chris Brown .05
312 Brian Fisher, Roger McDowell .05
313 Tom Browning .05
314 Glenn Davis .05
315 Mark Salas .05

Super Sample

To preview its oversize Super set for 1986, Topps issued a sample card of Eddie Murray. Front of the 4-7/8" x 6-7/8" card is the same as the issued version. On back, however, is this message: "topps / SPECIAL / COLLECTOR / SAMPLE / ACTUAL PRODUCT TO HAVE / STATISTICS PRINTED ON / WHITE-BOARD CARD BACK."

NM/M
Eddie Murray 6.00

Super

A third year of oversize (4-7/8" x 6-7/8") versions of Topps' regular issue cards saw the set once again hit the 60-card mark. Besides being four times the size of a normal card, the Supers differ only in the number on the back of the card.

NM/M
Complete Set (60): 9.00
Common Player: .25
1 Don Mattingly 1.00
2 Willie McGee .25
3 Bret Saberhagen .25
4 Dwight Gooden .25
5 Dan Quisenberry .25
6 Jeff Reardon .25
7 Ozzie Guillen .25
8 Vince Coleman .25
9 Harold Baines .25
10 Jorge Bell .25
11 Bert Blyleven .25
12 Wade Boggs .60
13 Phil Bradley .25
14 George Brett 1.00
15 Hubie Brooks .25
16 Tom Browning .25
17 Bill Buckner .25
18 Brett Butler .25
19 Gary Carter .45
20 Cecil Cooper .25

21 Darrell Evans .25
22 Dwight Evans .25
23 Carlton Fisk .45
24 Steve Garvey .35
25 Kirk Gibson .25
26 Rich Gossage .25
27 Pedro Guerrero .25
28 Ron Guidry .25
29 Tony Gwynn .60
30 Rickey Henderson .45
31 Keith Hernandez .25
32 Tom Herr .25
33 Orel Hershiser .25
34 Jay Howell .25
35 Reggie Jackson .75
36 Bob James .25
37 Charlie Leibrandt .25
38 Jack Morris .25
39 Dale Murphy .35
40 Eddie Murray .45
41 Dave Parker .25
42 Tim Raines .25
43 Jim Rice .35
44 Dave Righetti .25
45 Cal Ripken, Jr. 2.00
46 Pete Rose 1.50
47 Nolan Ryan 2.00
48 Ryne Sandberg .60
49 Mike Schmidt 1.00
50 Tom Seaver .45
51 Bryn Smith .25
52 Lee Smith .25
53 Ozzie Smith .60
54 Dave Stieb .25
55 Darryl Strawberry .25
56 Gorman Thomas .25
57 John Tudor .25
58 Fernando Valenzuela .25
59 Willie Wilson .25
60 Dave Winfield .45

Super Star

(See 1986 Woolworth.)

Tattoos

Topps returned to tattoos in 1986, marketing a set of 24 different tattoo sheets. Each sheet of tattoos measures 3-7/16" x 14" and includes both player and smaller action tattoos. As the action tattoos were uniform and not of any particular player, they add little value to the sheet. The player tattoos measure 1-1/2" x 2-1/2". With 24 sheets, eight players per sheet, there are 192 players represented in the set. The sheets are numbered.

	NM/M
Complete Set (24):	9.00
Common Sheet:	.40
Pack (1):	.60
Wax Box (36):	13.50

1 Julio Franco, Rich Gossage, Keith Hernandez, Charlie Leibrandt, Jack Perconte, Lee Smith, Dickie Thon, Dave Winfield .60
2 Jesse Barfield, Shawon Dunston, Dennis Eckersley, Brian Fisher, Moose Haas, Mike Moore, Dale Murphy, Bret Saberhagen .50
3 George Bell, Bob Brenly, Steve Carlton, Jose DeLeon, Bob Horner, Bob James, Dan Quisenberry, Andre Thornton .60
4 Mike Davis, Leon Durham, Darrell Evans, Glenn Hubbard, Johnny Ray, Cal Ripken, Ted Simmons 1.50
5 John Candelaria, Rick Dempsey, Steve Garvey, Ozzie Guillen, Gary Matthews, Jesse Orosco, Tony Pena .45
6 Bruce Bochte, George Brett, Cecil Cooper, Sammy Khalifa, Ron Kittle, Scott McGregor, Pete Rose, Mookie Wilson 1.25
7 John Franco, Carney Lansford, Don Mattingly, Graig Nettles, Rick Reuschel, Mike Schmidt, Larry Sheets, Don Sutton 1.50
8 Cecilio Guante, Willie Hernandez, Mike Krukow, Fred Lynn, Phil Niekro, Ed Nunez, Ryne Sandberg, Pat Tabler .75
9 Brett Butler, Chris Codiroli, Jim Gantner, Charlie Hough, Dave Parker, Rick Rhoden, Glenn Wilson, Robin Yount .50
10 Tom Browning, Ron Darling, Von Hayes, Chet Lemon, Tom Seaver, Mike Smithson, Bruce Sutter, Alan Trammell .60
11 Tony Armas, Jose Cruz, Jay Howell, Rick Mahler, Jack Morris, Rafael Ramirez, Dave Righetti, Mike Young .40
12 Alvin Davis, Doug DeCinces, Andy Hawkins, Dennis Lamp, Keith Moreland, Jim Presley, Mario Soto, John Tudor .40
13 Hubie Brooks, Jody Davis, Dwight Evans, Ron Hassey, Charles Hudson, Kirby Puckett, Jose Uribe 1.00
14 Tony Bernazard, Phil Bradley, Bill Buckner, Brian Downing, Dan Driessen, Ron Guidry, LaMarr Hoyt, Garry Maddox .40
15 Buddy Bell, Joe Carter, Tony Fernandez, Tito Landrum, Jeff Leonard, Hal McRae, Willie Randolph, Juan Samuel .40
16 Dennis Boyd, Vince Coleman, Scott Garrelts, Alfredo Griffin, Donnie Moore, Tony Perez, Ozzie Smith, Frank White 1.00
17 Rich Gedman, Kent Hrbek, Reggie Jackson, Mike Marshall, Terry Pendleton, Tim Raines, Mark Salas, Claudell Washington 1.00
18 Chris Brown, Tom Brunansky, Glenn Davis, Ron Davis, Burt Hooton, Darryl Strawberry, Frank Viola, Tim Wallach .40
19 Jack Clark, Bill Doran, Toby Harrah, Bill Madlock, Pete O'Brien, Larry Parrish, Mike Scioscia, Garry Templeton .40
20 Gary Carter, Andre Dawson, Dwight Gooden, Orel Hershiser, Oddibe McDowell, Roger McDowell, Dwayne Murphy, Jim Rice .60
21 Steve Balboni, Mike Easler, Charlie Lea, Lloyd Moseby, Steve Sax, Rick Sutcliffe, Gary Ward, Willie Wilson .40
22 Wade Boggs, Dave Concepcion, Kirk Gibson, Tom Herr, Lance Parrish, Jeff Reardon, Bryn Smith, Gorman Thomas .75
23 Carlton Fisk, Bob Grich, Pedro Guerrero, Willie McGee, Paul Molitor, Mike Scott, Dave Stieb, Lou Whitaker .60
24 Bert Blyleven, Damaso Garcia, Phil Garner, Tony Gwynn, Rickey Henderson, Ben Oglivie, Nolan Ryan, Fernando Valenzuela 1.50

3-D

This set is a second effort in the production of over-size (4-1/2" x 6") plastic cards on which the player figure is embossed. Cards were sold one per pack for 50¢. The 30 players in the set are among the game's top stars. The embossed color photo is bordered at bottom by a strip of contrasting color on which the player name appears. At the top, a row of white baseballs each contain a letter of the team nickname. Backs have no printing, and contain two self-adhesive strips with which the cards can be attached to a hard surface.

	NM/M
Complete Set (30):	9.00
Common Player:	.25
Wax Pack (1):	1.00
Wax Box (24):	15.00

1 Bert Blyleven .25
2 Gary Carter .60
3 Wade Boggs .75
4 Dwight Gooden .25
5 George Brett 1.50
6 Rich Gossage .25
7 Darrell Evans .25
8 Pedro Guerrero .25
9 Ron Guidry .25
10 Keith Hernandez .25
11 Rickey Henderson .60
12 Orel Hershiser .25
13 Reggie Jackson 1.00
14 Willie McGee .25
15 Don Mattingly 1.50
16 Dale Murphy .45
17 Jack Morris .25
18 Dave Parker .25
19 Eddie Murray .60
20 Jeff Reardon .25
21 Dan Quisenberry .25
22 Pete Rose 2.00
23 Jim Rice .45
24 Mike Schmidt 1.50
25 Bret Saberhagen .25
26 Darryl Strawberry .25
27 Dave Stieb .25
28 John Tudor .25
29 Dave Winfield .60
30 Fernando Valenzuela .25

1987 Topps

The design of Topps' set of 792 2-1/2" x 3-1/2" cards is closely akin to the 1962 set in that the player photo is set against a woodgrain border. Instead of a rolling corner, as in 1962, the player photos in '87 feature a couple of clipped corners at top left and bottom right, where the team logo and player name appear. The player's position is not given on the front of the card. For the first time in several years, the trophy which designates members of Topps All-Star Rookie Team returned to the card design. As in the previous three years, Topps issued a glossy-finish "Tiffany" edition of their 792-card set. However, it was speculated that as many as 30,000 sets were produced as opposed to the 5,000 sets printed in 1985 and 1986.

	NM/M
Unopened Factory Set, Retail (792):	30.00
Unopened Factory Set, Hobby (792):	25.00
Complete Set (792):	20.00
Uncut Sheet Set (6):	45.00
Common Player:	.05
Wax Pack (15):	.75
Wax Box (36):	20.00
Cello Pack (31):	1.00
Cello Box (24):	20.00
Rack Pack (49):	1.50
Rack Box (24):	25.00
Vending Box (500):	12.00

1 Roger Clemens (Record Breaker) .45
2 Jim Deshaies (Record Breaker) .05
3 Dwight Evans (Record Breaker) .05
4 Dave Lopes (Record Breaker) .05
5 Dave Righetti (Record Breaker) .05
6 Ruben Sierra (Record Breaker) .05
7 Todd Worrell (Record Breaker) .05
8 Terry Pendleton .05
9 Jay Tibbs .05
10 Cecil Cooper .05
11 Indians Leaders (Jack Aker, Chris Bando, Phil Niekro) .05
12 Jeff Sellers **RC** .05
13 Nick Esasky .05
14 Dave Stewart .05
15 Claudell Washington .05
16 Pat Clements .05
17 Pete O'Brien .05
18 Dick Howser .05
19 Matt Young .05
20 Gary Carter .40
21 Mark Davis .05
22 Doug DeCinces .05
23 Lee Smith .05
24 Tony Walker .05
25 Bert Blyleven .05
26 Greg Brock .05
27 Joe Cowley .05
28 Rick Dempsey .05
29 Jimmy Key .05
30 Tim Raines .05
31 Braves Leaders (Glenn Hubbard, Rafael Ramirez) .05
32 Tim Leary .05
33 Andy Van Slyke .05
34 Jose Rijo .05
35 Sid Bream .05
36 Eric King **RC** .05
37 Marvell Wynne .05
38 Dennis Leonard .05
39 Marty Barrett .05
40 Dave Righetti .05
41 Bo Diaz .05
42 Gary Redus .05
43 Gene Michael .05
44 Greg Harris .05
45 Jim Presley .05
46 Danny Gladden .05
47 Dennis Powell .05
48 Wally Backman .05
49 Terry Harper .05
50 Dave Smith .05
51 Mel Hall .05
52 Keith Atherton .05
53 Ruppert Jones .05
54 Bill Dawley .05
55 Tim Wallach .05
56 Brewers Leaders (Jamie Cocanower, Paul Molitor, Charlie Moore, Herm Starrette) .10
57 Scott Nielsen **RC** .05
58 Thad Bosley .05
59 Ken Dayley .05
60 Tony Pena .05
61 Bobby Thigpen **RC** .05
62 Bobby Meacham .05
63 Fred Toliver **RC** .05
64 Harry Spilman .05
65 Tom Browning .05
66 Marc Sullivan .05
67 Bill Swift .05
68 Tony LaRussa .05
69 Lonnie Smith .05
70 Charlie Hough .05
71 Mike Aldrete **RC** .05
72 Walt Terrell .05
73 Dave Anderson .05
74 Dan Pasqua .05
75 Ron Darling .05
76 Rafael Ramirez .05
77 Bryan Oelkers .05
78 Tom Foley .05
79 Juan Nieves .05
80 Wally Joyner **RC** .35
81 Padres Leaders (Andy Hawkins, Terry Kennedy) .05
82 Rob Murphy **RC** .05
83 Mike Davis .05
84 Steve Lake .05
85 Kevin Bass .05
86 Nate Snell .05
87 Mark Salas .05
88 Ed Wojna .05
89 Ozzie Guillen .05
90 Dave Stieb .05
91 Harold Reynolds .05
92a Urbano Lugo (No trademark on front.) .10
92b Urbano Lugo (Trademark on front.) .05
93 Jim Leyland .05
94 Calvin Schiraldi .05
95 Oddibe McDowell .05
96 Frank Williams .05
97 Glenn Wilson .05
98 Bill Scherrer .05
99 Darryl Motley .05
100 Steve Garvey .15
101 Carl Willis **RC** .05
102 Paul Zuvella .05
103 Rick Aguilera .05
104 Billy Sample .05
105 Floyd Youmans .05
106 Blue Jays Leaders (George Bell, Willie Upshaw) .05
107 John Butcher .05
108 Jim Gantner (Photo reversed.) .05
109 R.J. Reynolds .05
110 John Tudor .05
111 Alfredo Griffin .05
112 Alan Ashby .05
113 Neil Allen .05
114 Billy Beane .05
115 Donnie Moore .05
116 Mike Stanley **RC** .05
117 Jim Beattie .05
118 Bobby Valentine .05
119 Ron Robinson .05
120 Eddie Murray .40
121 Kevin Romine **RC** .05
122 Jim Clancy .05
123 John Kruk .05
124 Ray Fontenot .05
125 Bob Brenly .05
126 Mike Loynd **RC** .05
127 Vance Law .05
128 Checklist 1-132 .05
129 Rick Cerone .05
130 Dwight Gooden .05
131 Pirates Leaders (Sid Bream, Tony Pena) .05
132 Paul Assenmacher **RC** .05
133 Jose Oquendo .05
134 Rich Yett **RC** .05
135 Mike Easler .05
136 Ron Romanick .05
137 Jerry Willard .05
138 Roy Lee Jackson .05
139 Devon White **RC** .40
140 Bret Saberhagen .05
141 Herm Winningham .05
142 Rick Sutcliffe .05
143 Steve Boros .05
144 Mike Scioscia .05
145 Charlie Kerfeld .05
146 Tracy Jones **RC** .05
147 Randy Niemann .05
148 Dave Collins .05
149 Ray Searage .05
150 Wade Boggs .45
151 Mike LaCoss .05
152 Toby Harrah .05
153 Duane Ward **RC** .05
154 Tom O'Malley .05
155 Eddie Whitson .05
156 Mariners Leaders (Bob Kearney, Phil Regan, Matt Young) .05
157 Danny Darwin .05
158 Tim Teufel .05
159 Ed Olwine .05
160 Julio Franco .05
161 Steve Ontiveros .05
162 Mike LaValliere **RC** .10
163 Kevin Gross .05
164 Sammy Khalifa .05
165 Jeff Reardon .05
166 Bob Boone .05
167 Jim Deshaies **RC** .10
168 Lou Piniella .05
169 Ron Washington .05
170 Bo Jackson (Future Stars) 1.50
171 Chuck Cary **RC** .05
172 Ron Oester .05
173 Alex Trevino .05
174 Henry Cotto .05
175 Bob Stanley .05
176 Steve Buechele .05
177 Keith Moreland .05
178 Cecil Fielder .05
179 Bill Wegman .05
180 Chris Brown .05
181 Cardinals Leaders (Mike LaValliere, Ozzie Smith, Ray Soff) .10
182 Lee Lacy .05
183 Andy Hawkins .05
184 Bobby Bonilla .05
185 Roger McDowell .05
186 Bruce Benedict .05
187 Mark Huismann .05
188 Tony Phillips .05
189 Joe Hesketh .05
190 Jim Sundberg .05
191 Charles Hudson .05
192 Cory Snyder **RC** .05
193 Roger Craig .05
194 Kirk McCaskill .05
195 Mike Pagliarulo .05
196 Randy O'Neal .05
197 Mark Bailey .05
198 Lee Mazzilli .05
199 Mariano Duncan .05
200 Pete Rose .75
201 John Cangelosi **RC** .05
202 Ricky Wright .05
203 Mike Kingery **RC** .05
204 Sammy Stewart .05
205 Graig Nettles .05
206 Twins Leaders (Tim Laudner, Frank Viola) .05
207 George Frazier .05
208 John Shelby .05
209 Rick Schu .05
210 Lloyd Moseby .05
211 John Morris **RC** .05
212 Mike Fitzgerald .05
213 Randy Myers **RC** .20
214 Omar Moreno .05
215 Mark Langston .05
216 B.J. Surhoff **RC** (Future Stars) .20
217 Chris Codiroli .05
218 Sparky Anderson .10
219 Cecilio Guante .05
220 Joe Carter .05
221 Vern Ruhle .05
222 Denny Walling .05
223 Charlie Leibrandt .05
224 Wayne Tolleson .05
225 Mike Smithson .05
226 Max Venable .05
227 Jamie Moyer **RC** .05
228 Curt Wilkerson .05
229 Mike Birkbeck **RC** .05
230 Don Baylor .05
231 Giants Leaders (Bob Brenly, Mike Krukow) .05
232 Reggie Williams **RC** .05
233 Russ Morman **RC** .05
234 Pat Sheridan .05
235 Alvin Davis .05
236 Tommy John .10
237 Jim Morrison .05
238 Bill Krueger .05
239 Juan Espino .05
240 Steve Balboni .05
241 Danny Heep .05
242 Rick Mahler .05
243 Whitey Herzog .05
244 Dickie Noles .05
245 Willie Upshaw .05
246 Jim Dwyer .05
247 Jeff Reed **RC** .05
248 Gene Walter .05

249 Jim Pankovits .05
250 Teddy Higuera .05
251 Rob Wilfong .05
252 Denny Martinez .05
253 Eddie Milner .05
254 Bob Tewksbury **RC** .20
255 Juan Samuel .05
256 Royals Leaders (George Brett, Frank White) .15
257 Bob Forsch .05
258 Steve Yeager .05
259 Mike Greenwell **RC** .25
260 Vida Blue .05
261 Ruben Sierra .05
262 Jim Winn .05
263 Stan Javier **RC** .05
264 Checklist 133-264 .05
265 Darrell Evans .05
266 Jeff Hamilton **RC** .05
267 Howard Johnson .05
268 Pat Corrales .05
269 Cliff Speck .05
270 Jody Davis .05
271 Mike Brown .05
272 Andres Galarraga .05
273 Gene Nelson .05
274 Jeff Hearron **RC** .05
275 LaMarr Hoyt .05
276 Jackie Gutierrez .05
277 Juan Agosto .05
278 Gary Pettis .05
279 Dan Plesac **RC** .05
280 Jeffrey Leonard .05
281 Reds Leaders (Bo Diaz, Bill Gullickson, Pete Rose) .10
282 Jeff Calhoun .05
283 Doug Drabek **RC** .25
284 John Moses .05
285 Dennis Boyd .05
286 Mike Woodard **RC** .05
287 Dave Von Ohlen .05
288 Tito Landrum .05
289 Bob Kipper .05
290 Leon Durham .05
291 Mitch Williams .05
292 Franklin Stubbs .05
293 Bob Rodgers .05
294 Steve Jeltz .05
295 Len Dykstra .05
296 Andres Thomas **RC** .05
297 Don Schulze .05
298 Larry Herndon .05
299 Joel Davis .05
300 Reggie Jackson .50
301 Luis Aquino **RC** .05
302 Bill Schroeder .05
303 Juan Berenguer .05
304 Phil Garner .05
305 John Franco .05
306 Red Sox Leaders (Rich Gedman, John McNamara, Tom Seaver) .10
307 Lee Guetterman **RC** .05
308 Don Slaught .05
309 Mike Young .05
310 Frank Viola .05
311 Rickey Henderson (Turn Back the Clock) .10
312 Reggie Jackson (Turn Back the Clock) .10
313 Roberto Clemente (Turn Back the Clock) .50
314 Carl Yastrzemski (Turn Back the Clock) .10
315 Maury Wills (Turn Back the Clock) .05
316 Brian Fisher .05
317 Clint Hurdle .05
318 Jim Fregosi .05
319 Greg Swindell **RC** .10
320 Barry Bonds 8.00
321 Mike Laga .05
322 Chris Bando .05
323 Al Newman **RC** .05
324 Dave Palmer .05
325 Garry Templeton .05
326 Mark Gubicza .05
327 Dale Sveum **RC** .05
328 Bob Welch .05
329 Ron Roenicke .05
330 Mike Scott .05
331 Mets Leaders (Gary Carter, Keith Hernandez, Dave Johnson, Darryl Strawberry) .10
332 Joe Price .05
333 Ken Phelps .05
334 Ed Correa **RC** .05
335 Candy Maldonado .05
336 Allan Anderson **RC** .05
337 Darrell Miller .05
338 Tim Conroy .05
339 Donnie Hill .05
340 Roger Clemens .65
341 Mike Brown .05
342 Bob James .05
343 Hal Lanier .05
344a Joe Niekro (Copyright outside yellow on back.) .25
344b Joe Niekro (Copyright inside yellow on back.) .05
345 Andre Dawson .25
346 Shawon Dunston .05
347 Mickey Brantley **RC** .05
348 Carmelo Martinez .05
349 Storm Davis .05
350 Keith Hernandez .05
351 Gene Garber .05
352 Mike Felder **RC** .05
353 Ernie Camacho .05
354 Jamie Quirk .05
355 Don Carman .05
356 White Sox Leaders (Ed Brinkman, Julio Cruz) .05
357 Steve Fireovid **RC** .05
358 Sal Butera .05
359 Doug Corbett .05
360 Pedro Guerrero .05
361 Mark Thurmond .05
362 Luis Quinones **RC** .05
363 Jose Guzman .05
364 Randy Bush .05
365 Rick Rhoden .05
366 Mark McGwire 3.00
367 Jeff Lahti .05
368 John McNamara .05
369 Brian Dayett .05
370 Fred Lynn .05
371 Mark Eichhorn **RC** .05
372 Jerry Mumphrey .05
373 Jeff Dedmon .05
374 Glenn Hoffman .05
375 Ron Guidry .10
376 Scott Bradley .05
377 John Henry Johnson .05
378 Rafael Santana .05
379 John Russell .05
380 Rich Gossage .05
381 Expos Leaders (Mike Fitzgerald, Bob Rodgers) .05
382 Rudy Law .05
383 Ron Davis .05
384 Johnny Grubb .05
385 Orel Hershiser .05
386 Dickie Thon .05
387 T.R. Bryden **RC** .05
388 Geno Petralli .05
389 Jeff Robinson .05
390 Gary Matthews .05
391 Jay Howell .05
392 Checklist 265-396 .05
393 Pete Rose .60
394 Mike Bielecki .05
395 Damaso Garcia .05
396 Tim Lollar .05
397 Greg Walker .05
398 Brad Havens .05
399 Curt Ford **RC** .05
400 George Brett .50
401 Billy Jo Robidoux .05
402 Mike Trujillo .05
403 Jerry Royster .05
404 Doug Sisk .05
405 Brook Jacoby .05
406 Yankees Leaders (Rickey Henderson, Don Mattingly) .25
407 Jim Acker .05
408 John Mizerock .05
409 Milt Thompson .05
410 Fernando Valenzuela .25
411 Darnell Coles .05
412 Eric Davis .05
413 Moose Haas .05
414 Joe Orsulak .05
415 Bobby Witt **RC** .05
416 Tom Nieto .05
417 Pat Perry **RC** .05
418 Dick Williams .05
419 Mark Portugal **RC** .10
420 Will Clark .40
421 Jose DeLeon .05
422 Jack Howell .05
423 Jaime Cocanower .05
424 Chris Speier .05
425 Tom Seaver .40
426 Floyd Rayford .05
427 Ed Nunez .05
428 Bruce Bochy .05
429 Tim Pyznarski **RC** (Future Stars) .05
430 Mike Schmidt .50
431 Dodgers Leaders (Tom Niedenfuer, Ron Perranoski, Alex Trevino) .05
432 Jim Slaton .05
433 Ed Hearn **RC** .05
434 Mike Fischlin .05
435 Bruce Sutter .35
436 Andy Allanson **RC** .05
437 Ted Power .05
438 Kelly Downs **RC** .05
439 Karl Best .05
440 Willie McGee .05
441 Dave Leiper **RC** .05
442 Mitch Webster .05
443 John Felske .05
444 Jeff Russell .05
445 Dave Lopes .05
446 Chuck Finley **RC** .25
447 Bill Almon .05
448 Chris Bosio **RC** .10
449 Pat Dodson **RC** (Future Stars) .05
450 Kirby Puckett .45
451 Joe Sambito .05
452 Dave Henderson .05
453 Scott Terry **RC** .05
454 Luis Salazar .05
455 Mike Boddicker .05
456 A's Leaders (Carney Lansford, Tony LaRussa, Mickey Tettleton, Dave Von Ohlen) .05
457 Len Matuszek .05
458 Kelly Gruber **RC** .05
459 Dennis Eckersley .35
460 Darryl Strawberry .05
461 Craig McMurtry .05
462 Scott Fletcher .05
463 Tom Candiotti .05
464 Butch Wynegar .05
465 Todd Worrell .05
466 Kal Daniels **RC** .05
467 Randy St. Claire .05
468 George Bamberger .05
469 Mike Diaz **RC** .05
470 Dave Dravecky .05
471 Ronn Reynolds .05
472 Bill Doran .05
473 Steve Farr .05
474 Jerry Narron .05
475 Scott Garrelts .05
476 Danny Tartabull .05
477 Ken Howell .05
478 Tim Laudner .05
479 Bob Sebra **RC** .05
480 Jim Rice .15
481 Phillies Leaders (Von Hayes, Juan Samuel, Glenn Wilson) .05
482 Daryl Boston .05
483 Dwight Lowry .05
484 Jim Traber **RC** .05
485 Tony Fernandez .05
486 Otis Nixon .05
487 Dave Gumpert .05
488 Ray Knight .05
489 Bill Gullickson .05
490 Dale Murphy .20
491 Ron Karkovice **RC** .05
492 Mike Heath .05
493 Tom Lasorda .10
494 Barry Jones **RC** .05
495 Gorman Thomas .05
496 Bruce Bochte .05
497 Dale Mohorcic **RC** .05
498 Bob Kearney .05
499 Bruce Ruffin **RC** .05
500 Don Mattingly .65
501 Craig Lefferts .05
502 Dick Schofield .05
503 Larry Andersen .05
504 Mickey Hatcher .05
505 Bryn Smith .05
506 Orioles Leaders (Rich Bordi, Rick Dempsey, Earl Weaver) .05
507 Dave Stapleton .05
508 Scott Bankhead **RC** .05
509 Enos Cabell .05
510 Tom Henke .05
511 Steve Lyons .05
512 Dave Magadan **RC** (Future Stars) .20
513 Carmen Castillo .05
514 Orlando Mercado .05
515 Willie Hernandez .05
516 Ted Simmons .05
517 Mario Soto .05
518 Gene Mauch .05
519 Curt Young .05
520 Jack Clark .05
521 Rick Reuschel .05
522 Checklist 397-528 .05
523 Earnie Riles .05
524 Bob Shirley .05
525 Phil Bradley .05
526 Roger Mason .05
527 Jim Wohlford .05
528 Ken Dixon .05
529 Alvaro Espinoza **RC** .05
530 Tony Gwynn .45
531 Astros Leaders (Yogi Berra, Hal Lanier, Denis Menke, Gene Tenace) .05
532 Jeff Stone .05
533 Argenis Salazar .05
534 Scott Sanderson .05
535 Tony Armas .05
536 Terry Mulholland **RC** .15
537 Rance Mulliniks .05
538 Tom Niedenfuer .05
539 Reid Nichols .05
540 Terry Kennedy .05
541 Rafael Belliard **RC** .05
542 Ricky Horton .05
543 Dave Johnson .05
544 Zane Smith .05
545 Buddy Bell .05
546 Mike Morgan .05
547 Rob Deer .05
548 Bill Mooneyham **RC** .05
549 Bob Melvin .05
550 Pete Incaviglia .05
551 Frank Wills .05
552 Larry Sheets .05
553 Mike Maddux **RC** .05
554 Buddy Biancalana .05
555 Dennis Rasmussen .05
556 Angels Leaders (Bob Boone, Marcel Lachemann, Mike Witt) .05
557 John Cerutti **RC** .05
558 Greg Gagne .05
559 Lance McCullers .05
560 Glenn Davis .05
561 Rey Quinones **RC** .05
562 Bryan Clutterbuck **RC** .05
563 John Stefero .05
564 Larry McWilliams .05
565 Dusty Baker .05
566 Tim Hulett .05
567 Greg Mathews **RC** .05
568 Earl Weaver .10
569 Wade Rowdon **RC** .05
570 Sid Fernandez .05
571 Ozzie Virgil .05
572 Pete Ladd .05
573 Hal McRae .05
574 Manny Lee .05
575 Pat Tabler .05
576 Frank Pastore .05
577 Dann Bilardello .05
578 Billy Hatcher .05
579 Rick Burleson .05
580 Mike Krukow .05
581 Cubs Leaders (Ron Cey, Steve Trout) .05
582 Bruce Berenyi .05
583 Junior Ortiz .05
584 Ron Kittle .05
585 Scott Bailes **RC** .05
586 Ben Oglivie .05
587 Eric Plunk **RC** .05
588 Wallace Johnson .05
589 Steve Crawford .05
590 Vince Coleman .05
591 Spike Owen .05
592 Chris Welsh .05
593 Chuck Tanner .05
594 Rick Anderson .05
595 Keith Hernandez/AS .05
596 Steve Sax/AS .05
597 Mike Schmidt/AS .35
598 Ozzie Smith/AS .30
599 Tony Gwynn/AS .30
600 Dave Parker/AS .05
601 Darryl Strawberry/AS .05
602 Gary Carter/AS .25
603a Dwight Gooden/AS (No trademark on front) .25
603b Dwight Gooden/AS (Trademark on front) .05
604 Fernando Valenzuela/AS .05
605 Todd Worrell/AS .05
606a Don Mattingly/AS (No trademark on front) .75
606b Don Mattingly/AS (Trademark on front) .35
607 Tony Bernazard/AS .05
608 Wade Boggs/AS .30
609 Cal Ripken, Jr./AS .45
610 Jim Rice/AS .05
611 Kirby Puckett/AS .30
612 George Bell/AS .05
613 Lance Parrish/AS .05
614 Roger Clemens/AS .35
615 Teddy Higuera/AS .05
616 Dave Righetti/AS .05
617 Al Nipper .05
618 Tom Kelly .05
619 Jerry Reed .05
620 Jose Canseco .60
621 Danny Cox .05
622 Glenn Braggs **RC** .05
623 Kurt Stillwell **RC** .05
624 Tim Burke .05
625 Mookie Wilson .05
626 Joel Skinner .05
627 Ken Oberkfell .05
628 Bob Walk .05
629 Larry Parrish .05
630 John Candelaria .05
631 Tigers Leaders (Sparky Anderson, Mike Heath, Willie Hernandez) .05
632 Rob Woodward **RC** .05
633 Jose Uribe .05
634 Rafael Palmeiro **RC** 2.00
635 Ken Schrom .05
636 Darren Daulton .05
637 Bip Roberts **RC** .10
638 Rich Bordi .05
639 Gerald Perry .05
640 Mark Clear .05
641 Domingo Ramos .05
642 Al Pulido .05
643 Ron Shepherd .05
644 John Denny .05
645 Dwight Evans .05
646 Mike Mason .05
647 Tom Lawless .05
648 Barry Larkin **RC** .60
649 Mickey Tettleton .05
650 Hubie Brooks .05
651 Benny Distefano .05
652 Terry Forster .05
653 Kevin Mitchell .05
654 Checklist 529-660 .05
655 Jesse Barfield .05
656 Rangers Leaders (Bobby Valentine, Rickey Wright) .05
657 Tom Waddell .05
658 Robby Thompson **RC** .05
659 Aurelio Lopez .05
660 Bob Horner .05
661 Lou Whitaker .05
662 Frank DiPino .05
663 Cliff Johnson .05
664 Mike Marshall .05
665 Rod Scurry .05
666 Von Hayes .05
667 Ron Hassey .05
668 Juan Bonilla .05
669 Bud Black .05
670 Jose Cruz .05
671a Ray Soff (No "D*" before copyright line.) .20
671b Ray Soff ("D*" before copyright line.) .05
672 Chili Davis .05
673 Don Sutton .35
674 Bill Campbell .05
675 Ed Romero .05
676 Charlie Moore .05
677 Bob Grich .05
678 Carney Lansford .05
679 Kent Hrbek .05
680 Ryne Sandberg .45
681 George Bell .05
682 Jerry Reuss .05
683 Gary Roenicke .05
684 Kent Tekulve .05
685 Jerry Hairston Sr. .05
686 Doyle Alexander .05
687 Alan Trammell .05
688 Juan Beniquez .05
689 Darrell Porter .05
690 Dane Iorg .05
691 Dave Parker .05
692 Frank White .05
693 Terry Puhl .05
694 Phil Niekro .35
695 Chico Walker .05
696 Gary Lucas .05
697 Ed Lynch .05
698 Ernie Whitt .05
699 Ken Landreaux .05
700 Dave Bergman .05
701 Willie Randolph .05
702 Greg Gross .05
703 Dave Schmidt .05
704 Jesse Orosco .05
705 Bruce Hurst .05
706 Rick Manning .05
707 Bob McClure .05
708 Scott McGregor .05
709 Dave Kingman .05
710 Gary Gaetti .05
711 Ken Griffey .05
712 Don Robinson .05
713 Tom Brookens .05
714 Dan Quisenberry .05
715 Bob Dernier .05
716 Rick Leach .05
717 Ed Vande Berg .05
718 Steve Carlton .40
719 Tom Hume .05
720 Richard Dotson .05
721 Tom Herr .05
722 Bob Knepper .05
723 Brett Butler .05
724 Greg Minton .05
725 George Hendrick .05
726 Frank Tanana .05
727 Mike Moore .05
728 Tippy Martinez .05
729 Tom Paciorek .05
730 Eric Show .05
731 Dave Concepcion .05
732 Manny Trillo .05
733 Bill Caudill .05
734 Bill Madlock .05
735 Rickey Henderson .40
736 Steve Bedrosian .05
737 Floyd Bannister .05
738 Jorge Orta .05
739 Chet Lemon .05
740 Rich Gedman .05
741 Paul Molitor .40
742 Andy McGaffigan .05
743 Dwayne Murphy .05
744 Roy Smalley .05
745 Glenn Hubbard .05
746 Bob Ojeda .05
747 Johnny Ray .05
748 Mike Flanagan .05
749 Ozzie Smith .45
750 Steve Trout .05
751 Garth Iorg .05
752 Dan Petry .05
753 Rick Honeycutt .05
754 Dave LaPoint .05
755 Luis Aguayo .05
756 Carlton Fisk .40
757 Nolan Ryan .75
758 Tony Bernazard .05
759 Joel Youngblood .05
760 Mike Witt .05
761 Greg Pryor .05
762 Gary Ward .05
763 Tim Flannery .05
764 Bill Buckner .05
765 Kirk Gibson .05
766 Don Aase .05
767 Ron Cey .05
768 Dennis Lamp .05
769 Steve Sax .05
770 Dave Winfield .40
771 Shane Rawley .05
772 Harold Baines .05
773 Robin Yount .40
774 Wayne Krenchicki .05
775 Joaquin Andujar .05
776 Tom Brunansky .05
777 Chris Chambliss .05
778 Jack Morris .05
779 Craig Reynolds .05
780 Andre Thornton .05
781 Atlee Hammaker .05
782 Brian Downing .05
783 Willie Wilson .05
784 Cal Ripken, Jr. .75
785 Terry Francona .05
786 Jimy Williams .05
787 Alejandro Pena .05
788 Tim Stoddard .05
789 Dan Schatzeder .05
790 Julio Cruz .05
791 Lance Parrish .05
792 Checklist 661-792 .05

Tiffany

Produced in much greater quantity (reportedly 30,000 sets) than the previous years' sets, this specially boxed collectors' edition differs from the regular 1987 Topps cards only in its use of white cardboard stock and a high-gloss finish on the cards' fronts.

NM/M

Unopened Set (792): 90.00
Complete Set (792): 50.00
Common Player: .15
320 Barry Bonds 35.00

Traded

The Topps Traded set consists of 132 cards as did all Traded sets issued by Topps since 1981. Cards measure the standard 2-1/2" x 3-1/2" and are identical in design to the regular edition set. The purpose of the set is to update player trades and feature rookies not included in the regular issue. As they had done the previous three years, Topps produced a glossy-coated "Tiffany" edition of the Traded set. Cards are numbered with a "T" suffix.

NM/M

Complete Set (132): 4.00
Common Player: .05
1 Bill Almon .05
2 Scott Bankhead .05
3 Eric Bell **RC** .05
4 Juan Beniquez .05
5 Juan Berenguer .05
6 Greg Booker .05
7 Thad Bosley .05
8 Larry Bowa .05
9 Greg Brock .05
10 Bob Brower **RC** .05
11 Jerry Browne **RC** .05
12 Ralph Bryant **RC** .05
13 DeWayne Buice **RC** .05
14 Ellis Burks **RC** .50
15 Ivan Calderon .05
16 Jeff Calhoun .05
17 Casey Candaele **RC** .05
18 John Cangelosi .05
19 Steve Carlton .25
20 Juan Castillo **RC** .05
21 Rick Cerone .05
22 Ron Cey .05
23 John Christensen .05
24 Dave Cone **RC** .15
25 Chuck Crim **RC** .05
26 Storm Davis .05
27 Andre Dawson .25
28 Rick Dempsey .05
29 Doug Drabek .05
30 Mike Dunne .05
31 Dennis Eckersley .25
32 Lee Elia .05
33 Brian Fisher .05
34 Terry Francona .05
35 Willie Fraser **RC** .05
36 Billy Gardner .05
37 Ken Gerhart **RC** .05
38 Danny Gladden .05
39 Jim Gott .05
40 Cecilio Guante .05
41 Albert Hall .05
42 Terry Harper .05
43 Mickey Hatcher .05
44 Brad Havens .05

45	Neal Heaton	.05
46	Mike Henneman **RC**	.20
47	Donnie Hill	.05
48	Guy Hoffman	.05
49	Brian Holton **RC**	.05
50	Charles Hudson	.05
51	Danny Jackson **RC**	.05
52	Reggie Jackson	.40
53	Chris James **RC**	.05
54	Dion James	.05
55	Stan Jefferson **RC**	.05
56	Joe Johnson **RC**	.05
57	Terry Kennedy	.05
58	Mike Kingery	.05
59	Ray Knight	.05
60	Gene Larkin **RC**	.05
61	Mike LaValliere	.05
62	Jack Lazorko	.05
63	Terry Leach	.05
64	Tim Leary	.05
65	Jim Lindeman **RC**	.05
66	Steve Lombardozzi **RC**	.05
67	Bill Long **RC**	.05
68	Barry Lyons **RC**	.05
69	Shane Mack **RC**	.05
70	Greg Maddux **RC**	3.00
71	Bill Madlock	.05
72	Joe Magrane **RC**	.05
73	Dave Martinez **RC**	.05
74	Fred McGriff **RC**	.25
75	Mark McLemore **RC**	.05
76	Kevin McReynolds **RC**	.05
77	Dave Meads **RC**	.05
78	Eddie Milner	.05
79	Greg Minton	.05
80	John Mitchell **RC**	.05
81	Kevin Mitchell	.05
82	Charlie Moore	.05
83	Jeff Musselman **RC**	.05
84	Gene Nelson	.05
85	Graig Nettles	.05
86	Al Newman	.05
87	Reid Nichols	.05
88	Tom Niedenfuer	.05
89	Joe Niekro	.05
90	Tom Nieto	.05
91	Matt Nokes **RC**	.10
92	Dickie Noles	.05
93	Pat Pacillo	.05
94	Lance Parrish	.05
95	Tony Pena	.05
96	Luis Polonia **RC**	.05
97	Randy Ready	.05
98	Jeff Reardon	.05
99	Gary Redus	.05
100	Jeff Reed	.05
101	Rick Rhoden	.05
102	Cal Ripken, Sr.	.05
103	Wally Ritchie **RC**	.05
104	Jeff Robinson **RC**	.05
105	Gary Roenicke	.05
106	Jerry Royster	.05
107	Mark Salas	.05
108	Luis Salazar	.05
109	Benny Santiago **RC**	.15
110	Dave Schmidt	.05
111	Kevin Seitzer **RC**	.05
112	John Shelby	.05
113	Steve Shields **RC**	.05
114	John Smiley **RC**	.20
115	Chris Speier	.05
116	Mike Stanley **RC**	.05
117	Terry Steinbach **RC**	.15
118	Les Straker **RC**	.05
119	Jim Sundberg	.05
120	Danny Tartabull	.05
121	Tom Trebelhorn	.05
122	Dave Valle **RC**	.05
123	Ed Vande Berg	.05
124	Andy Van Slyke	.05
125	Gary Ward	.05
126	Alan Wiggins	.05
127	Bill Wilkinson **RC**	.05
128	Frank Williams	.05
129	Matt Williams **RC**	.75
130	Jim Winn	.05
131	Matt Young	.05
132	Checklist 1T-132T	.05

Traded Tiffany

The cards in this specially boxed limited edition version of the Traded set differ from the regular-issue cards only in the application of a high-gloss finish to the cards' fronts. Production was reported as 30,000 sets.

	NM/M
Complete Set (132):	30.00
Common Player:	.15

Traded Willie Mays Bronze

This 1/4-size metal replica was issued to dealers who purchased cases of 1987 Topps Traded sets. Each detail of the 1953 Topps Mays card is reproduced on the 1-1/4" x 1-3/4" bronze metal mini-card, right down to the stats.

		NM/M
244	Willie Mays	10.00

Box Panels

Offering baseball cards on retail boxes for a second straight year, Topps reduced the size of the cards to 2-1/8" x 3". Four different wax pack boxes were available, each featuring two cards that were placed on the sides of the boxes. The card fronts are identical in design to the regular issue cards. The backs are printed in blue and yellow and carry a commentary imitating a newspaper format. The cards are numbered A through H.

		NM/M
Complete Singles Set (8):		2.00
Complete Panel Set (4):		2.50
Common Panel:		.50
Common Single Player:		.15
Panel		.50
A	Don Baylor	.15
B	Steve Carlton	.30
Panel		.50
C	Ron Cey	.15
D	Cecil Cooper	.15
Panel		.75
E	Rickey Henderson	.40
F	Jim Rice	.20
Panel		.75
G	Don Sutton	.25
H	Dave Winfield	.40

All-Star Glossy Set of 22

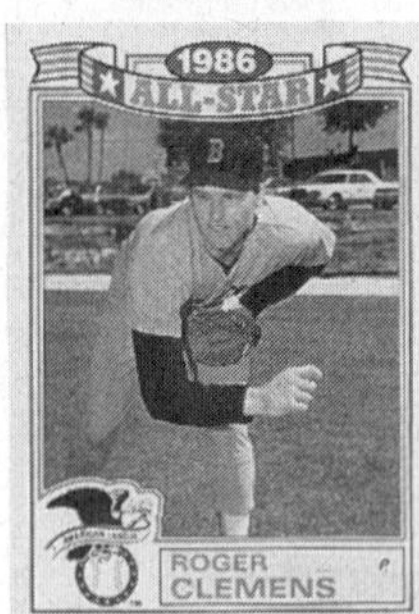

For the fourth consecutive year, Topps produced an All-Star Game commemorative set of 22 cards. The glossy cards, 2-1/2" x 3-1/2", were included in rack packs. Using the same basic design as in previous efforts with a few minor changes, the 1987 edition features American and National League logos on the card fronts. Cards #1-12 feature representatives from the American League, while #13-22 are National Leaguers.

		NM/M
Complete Set (22):		2.50
Common Player:		.05
1	Whitey Herzog	.05
2	Keith Hernandez	.05
3	Ryne Sandberg	.35
4	Mike Schmidt	.50
5	Ozzie Smith	.35
6	Tony Gwynn	.35
7	Dale Murphy	.20
8	Darryl Strawberry	.05
9	Gary Carter	.30
10	Dwight Gooden	.05
11	Fernando Valenzuela	.05
12	Dick Howser	.05
13	Wally Joyner	.05
14	Lou Whitaker	.05
15	Wade Boggs	.35
16	Cal Ripken, Jr.	.60
17	Dave Winfield	.30
18	Rickey Henderson	.30
19	Kirby Puckett	.35
20	Lance Parrish	.05
21	Roger Clemens	.40
22	Teddy Higuera	.05

All-Star Glossy Set of 60

Using the same design as the previous year, the 1987 Topps All-Star glossy set includes 48 All-Star performers plus 12 potential superstars branded as "Hot Prospects." The card fronts are uncluttered, save the player's name found in very small print at the bottom. The set was available via a mail-in offer. Six subsets make up the 60-card set, with each subset being available for $1.00 plus six special offer cards that were found in wax packs.

		NM/M
Complete Set (60):		15.00
Common Player:		.10
1	Don Mattingly	.75
2	Tony Gwynn	.50
3	Gary Gaetti	.10
4	Glenn Davis	.10
5	Roger Clemens	.65
6	Dale Murphy	.25
7	Lou Whitaker	.10
8	Roger McDowell	.10
9	Cory Snyder	.10
10	Todd Worrell	.10
11	Gary Carter	.40
12	Eddie Murray	.40
13	Bob Knepper	.10
14	Harold Baines	.10
15	Jeff Reardon	.10
16	Joe Carter	.10
17	Dave Parker	.10
18	Wade Boggs	.50
19	Danny Tartabull	.10
20	Jim Deshaies	.10
21	Rickey Henderson	.40
22	Rob Deer	.10
23	Ozzie Smith	.50
24	Dave Righetti	.10
25	Kent Hrbek	.10
26	Keith Hernandez	.10
27	Don Baylor	.10
28	Mike Schmidt	.85
29	Pete Incaviglia	.10
30	Barry Bonds	9.00
31	George Brett	.85
32	Darryl Strawberry	.10
33	Mike Witt	.10
34	Kevin Bass	.10
35	Jesse Barfield	.10
36	Bob Ojeda	.10
37	Cal Ripken, Jr.	2.00
38	Vince Coleman	.10
39	Wally Joyner	.10
40	Robby Thompson	.10
41	Pete Rose	1.00
42	Jim Rice	.25
43	Tony Bernazard	.10
44	Eric Davis	.10
45	George Bell	.10
46	Hubie Brooks	.10
47	Jack Morris	.10
48	Tim Raines	.10
49	Mark Eichhorn	.10
50	Kevin Mitchell	.10
51	Dwight Gooden	.10
52	Doug DeCinces	.10
53	Fernando Valenzuela	.10
54	Reggie Jackson	.50
55	Johnny Ray	.10
56	Mike Pagliarulo	.10
57	Kirby Puckett	.50
58	Lance Parrish	.10
59	Jose Canseco	.50
60	Greg Mathews	.10

Baseball Highlights

The "Baseball Highlights" boxed set of 33 cards was prepared by Topps for distribution at stores in the Woolworth's chain, although the retailer's name does not appear on the cards. Each card measures 2-1/2" x 3-1/2" in size and features a memorable baseball event that occurred during the 1986 season. The glossy set sold for $1.99.

Coins

For the first time since 1971, Topps issued a set of baseball "coins." Similar in design to the 1964 edition, the metal discs measure 1-1/2" in diameter. The aluminum coins were sold on a limited basis in retail outlets. Three coins and three sticks of gum were found in a pack. The coin fronts feature a full-color photo along with the player's name, team and position in a white band at the bottom. Gold-colored rims are found for American League players; National League players have silver-colored rims. Backs are silvered and carry the coin number, player's name and personal and statistical information.

		NM/M
Complete Set (48):		7.50
Common Player:		.10
Wax Pack (3):		1.00
Wax Box (24):		15.00
1	Harold Baines	.10
2	Jesse Barfield	.10
3	George Bell	.10
4	Wade Boggs	.45
5	George Brett	1.00
6	Jose Canseco	.25
7	Joe Carter	.10
8	Roger Clemens	.60
9	Alvin Davis	.10
10	Rob Deer	.10
11	Kirk Gibson	.10
12	Rickey Henderson	.35
13	Kent Hrbek	.10
14	Pete Incaviglia	.10
15	Reggie Jackson	.60
16	Wally Joyner	.10
17	Don Mattingly	.75
18	Jack Morris	.10
19	Eddie Murray	.35
20	Kirby Puckett	.45
21	Jim Rice	.15
22	Dave Righetti	.10
23	Cal Ripken, Jr.	1.50
24	Cory Snyder	.10
25	Danny Tartabull	.10
26	Dave Winfield	.35
27	Hubie Brooks	.10
28	Gary Carter	.35
29	Vince Coleman	.10
30	Eric Davis	.10
31	Glenn Davis	.10
32	Steve Garvey	.15
33	Dwight Gooden	.10
34	Tony Gwynn	.45
35	Von Hayes	.10
36	Keith Hernandez	.10
37	Dale Murphy	.20
38	Dave Parker	.10
39	Tony Pena	.10
40	Nolan Ryan	1.50
41	Ryne Sandberg	.45
42	Steve Sax	.10
43	Mike Schmidt	1.00
44	Mike Scott	.10
45	Ozzie Smith	.45
46	Darryl Strawberry	.10
47	Fernando Valenzuela	.10
48	Todd Worrell	.10

Gallery of Champions

Designed as a tribute to 1986's winners of baseball's most prestigious awards, the Gallery of Champions are metal "cards" that are one-quarter size replicas of the regular issue Topps cards. The bronze and silver sets were issued in leather-like velvet-lined display cases; the aluminum sets came cello-wrapped. Hobby dealers who purchased one bronze set or a 16-set case of aluminum "cards" received one free Jose Canseco pewter metal mini-card. The purchase of a silver set included five Canseco pewters.

		NM/M
Complete Aluminum Set (12):		17.50
Complete Bronze Set (12):		75.00
Complete Silver Set (12):		250.00
(1a)	Jesse Barfield/ Aluminum	2.00
(1b)	Jesse Barfield/Bronze	6.00
(1s)	Jesse Barfield/Silver	15.00
(2a)	Wade Boggs/ Aluminum	4.50
(2b)	Wade Boggs/Bronze	15.00
(2s)	Wade Boggs/Silver	30.00
(3a)	Jose Canseco/ Aluminum	3.50
(3b)	Jose Canseco/Bronze	10.00
(3s)	Jose Canseco/Silver	25.00
(3p)	Jose Canseco/Pewter	12.50
(4a)	Joe Carter/Aluminum	2.00
(4b)	Joe Carter/Bronze	6.00
(4s)	Joe Carter/Silver	15.00
(5a)	Roger Clemens/ Aluminum	5.00
(5b)	Roger Clemens/ Bronze	16.00
(5s)	Roger Clemens/Silver	40.00
(6a)	Tony Gwynn/ Aluminum	4.50
(6b)	Tony Gwynn/Bronze	15.00
(6s)	Tony Gwynn/Silver	30.00
(7a)	Don Mattingly/ Aluminum	5.00
(7b)	Don Mattingly/Bronze	17.50
(7s)	Don Mattingly/Silver	45.00
(8a)	Tim Raines/Aluminum	2.00
(8b)	Tim Raines/Bronze	6.00
(8s)	Tim Raines/Silver	15.00
(9a)	Dave Righetti/ Aluminum	2.00
(9b)	Dave Righetti/Bronze	6.00
(9s)	Dave Righetti/Silver	15.00
(10a)	Mike Schmidt/ Aluminum	6.00
(10b)	Mike Schmidt/Bronze	20.00
(10s)	Mike Schmidt/Silver	50.00
(11a)	Mike Scott/Aluminum	2.00
(11b)	Mike Scott/Bronze	6.00
(11s)	Mike Scott/Silver	15.00
(12a)	Todd Worrell/ Aluminum	2.00
(12b)	Todd Worrell/Bronze	6.00
(12s)	Todd Worrell/Silver	15.00

Glossy Rookies

The 1987 Topps Glossy Rookies set of 22 cards was introduced with Topps' new 100-card "Jumbo Packs." Intended for sale in supermarkets, the jumbo packs contained one glossy card. Measuring the standard 2-1/2" x 3-1/2" size, the special insert cards feature the top rookies from the previous season.

		NM/M
Complete Set (22):		3.00
Common Player:		.05
1	Andy Allanson	.05
2	John Cangelosi	.05
3	Jose Canseco	1.00
4	Will Clark	.25
5	Mark Eichhorn	.05
6	Pete Incaviglia	.05
7	Wally Joyner	.05
8	Eric King	.05
9	Dave Magadan	.05
10	John Morris	.05
11	Juan Nieves	.05
12	Rafael Palmeiro	2.50
13	Billy Jo Robidoux	.05
14	Bruce Ruffin	.05
15	Ruben Sierra	.05
16	Cory Snyder	.05
17	Kurt Stillwell	.05
18	Dale Sveum	.05
19	Danny Tartabull	.05
20	Andres Thomas	.05
21	Robby Thompson	.05
22	Todd Worrell	.05

Bobby Grich Night Sheet

In conjunction with a Bobby Grich Night sponsored by the California Angels on May 1, 1987, Sheraton Hotels of Los Angeles and radio station KLAC issued this sheet bearing reproductions of each of Grich's regular issue Topps cards from 1971-1987. The sheet measures 10" x 17-1/2", while the perforated cards, if removed from the sheet, measure the standard 2-1/2" x 3-1/2".

		NM/M
Complete Sheet:		10.00
Common Card:		.75
1971	Bob Grich #193	1.50
1972	Bob Grich #338	.75
1973	Bob Grich #418	.75
1974	Bob Grich #109	.75
1975	Bob Grich #225	.75
1976	Bob Grich #335	.75
1977	Bob Grich #521	.75
1978	Bob Grich #18	.75
1979	Bob Grich #477	.75
1980	Bob Grich #621	.75
1981	Bob Grich #182	.75
1982	Bob Grich #284	.75
1983	Bob Grich #790	.75
1984	Bob Grich #315	.75
1985	Bob Grich #465	.75
1986	Bob Grich #155	.75
1987	Bob Grich #677	.75

Mini League Leaders

Returning for 1987, the Topps "Major League Leaders" set was increased in size from 66 to 76 cards. The 2-1/8" x 3" cards feature woodgrain borders that encompass a white-bordered color photo. Backs are printed in yellow, orange and brown and list the player's official ranking based on his 1986 American or National League statistics. The players

featured are those who finished the top five in their leagues' various batting and pitching categories. The cards were sold in plastic-wrapped packs, seven cards plus a game card per pack.

		NM/M
Complete Set (77):		4.00
Common Player:		.05
Wax Pack (7):		.50
Wax Box (36):		10.00
1	Bob Horner	.05
2	Dale Murphy	.15
3	Lee Smith	.05
4	Eric Davis	.05
5	John Franco	.05
6	Dave Parker	.05
7	Kevin Bass	.05
8	Glenn Davis	.05
9	Bill Doran	.05
10	Bob Knepper	.05
11	Mike Scott	.05
12	Dave Smith	.05
13	Mariano Duncan	.05
14	Orel Hershiser	.05
15	Steve Sax	.05
16	Fernando Valenzuela	.05
17	Tim Raines	.05
18	Jeff Reardon	.05
19	Floyd Youmans	.05
20	Gary Carter	.25
21	Ron Darling	.05
22	Sid Fernandez	.05
23	Dwight Gooden	.05
24	Keith Hernandez	.05
25	Bob Ojeda	.05
26	Darryl Strawberry	.05
27	Steve Bedrosian	.05
28	Von Hayes	.05
29	Juan Samuel	.05
30	Mike Schmidt	.75
31	Rick Rhoden	.05
32	Vince Coleman	.05
33	Danny Cox	.05
34	Todd Worrell	.05
35	Tony Gwynn	.35
36	Mike Krukow	.05
37	Candy Maldonado	.05
38	Don Aase	.05
39	Eddie Murray	.25
40	Cal Ripken, Jr.	1.00
41	Wade Boggs	.35
42	Roger Clemens	.40
43	Bruce Hurst	.05
44	Jim Rice	.15
45	Wally Joyner	.05
46	Donnie Moore	.05
47	Gary Pettis	.05
48	Mike Witt	.05
49	John Cangelosi	.05
50	Tom Candiotti	.05
51	Joe Carter	.05
52	Pat Tabler	.05
53	Kirk Gibson	.05
54	Willie Hernandez	.05
55	Jack Morris	.05
56	Alan Trammell	.05
57	George Brett	.75
58	Willie Wilson	.05
59	Rob Deer	.05
60	Teddy Higuera	.05
61	Bert Blyleven	.05
62	Gary Gaetti	.05
63	Kirby Puckett	.35
64	Rickey Henderson	.25
65	Don Mattingly	.50
66	Dennis Rasmussen	.05
67	Dave Righetti	.05
68	Jose Canseco	.20
69	Dave Kingman	.05
70	Phil Bradley	.05
71	Mark Langston	.05
72	Pete O'Brien	.05
73	Jesse Barfield	.05
74	George Bell	.05
75	Tony Fernandez	.05
76	Tom Henke	.05
77	Checklist	.05

Stickers - Hardback Test

In addition to its regular issue of Panini-produced paper-backed stickers, Topps in 1987 produced a very limited version of the same issue with a hard cardboard back. The Topps hard-back version is virtually identical to the more common Panini version except for the copyright line printed on back. Production of the hard-back version was reported to be 1/10 of 1% of the Panini version.

	NM/M
Complete Set (313):	75.00
Common Player:	.50
Wax Pack (5):	1.00
Wax Box (48):	25.00

Stickers - Panini

For the seventh consecutive year, Topps issued stickers produced by Panini in Italy for use in a special album or yearbook. The 2-1/8" x 3" stickers offer a full-color front with a peel-off paper back. Fronts feature either one full-size player picture or two half-size individual stickers. The yearbook contains 36 glossy, magazine-style pages, all printed in full color. Mike Schmidt, 1986 N.L. MVP, is featured on the covers. The yearbook sold in retail outlets for $.35, while stickers were sold five in a pack for $.25. The number in parentheses in this checklist is the sticker number the player shares the sticker with. Besides the common soft-back sticker made for Topps by Panini, there was a test issue of hard-back stickercards.

		NM/M
Complete Set (313):		15.00
Common Player:		.05
Sticker Album:		1.50
Wax Pack (5):		.25
Wax Box (100):		15.00
1	1986 Highlights (Jim Deshaies/172)	.05
2	1986 Highlights (Roger Clemens/175)	.25
3	1986 Highlights (Roger Clemens/176)	.25
4	1986 Highlights (Dwight Evans/177)	.05
5	1986 Highlights (Dwight Gooden/178)	.05
6	1986 Highlights (Dwight Gooden/180)	.05
7	1986 Highlights (Dave Lopes/181)	.05
8	1986 Highlights (Dave Righetti/182)	.05
9	1986 Highlights (Dave Righetti/183)	.05
10	1986 Highlights (Ruben Sierra/185)	.05
11	1986 Highlights (Todd Worrell/186)	.05
12	1986 Highlights (Todd Worrell/187)	.05
13	N.L. Championship Series (Lenny Dykstra)	.05
14	N.L. Championship Series (Gary Carter)	.15
15	N.L. Championship Series (Mike Scott)	.05
16	A.L. Championship Series (Gary Pettis)	.05
17	A.L. Championship Series (Jim Rice)	.05
18	A.L. Championship Series (Bruce Hurst)	.05
19	1986 World Series (Bruce Hurst)	.05
20	1986 World Series (Wade Boggs)	.15
21	1986 World Series (Lenny Dykstra)	.05
22	1986 World Series (Gary Carter)	.15
23	1986 World Series (Dave Henderson)	.05
24	1986 World Series (Howard Johnson)	.05
25	1986 World Series (Mets Celebrate)	.05
26	Glenn Davis	.05
27	Nolan Ryan/188	.60
28	Charlie Kerfeld/189	.05
29	Jose Cruz/190	.05
30	Phil Garner/191	.05
31	Bill Doran/192	.05
32	Bob Knepper/195	.05
33	Denny Walling/196	.05
34	Kevin Bass/197	.05
35	Mike Scott	.05
36	Dale Murphy	.20
37	Paul Assenmacher/198	.05
38	Ken Oberkfell/200	.05
39	Andres Thomas/201	.05
40	Gene Garber/202	.05
41	Bob Horner	.05
42	Rafael Ramirez/203	.05
43	Rick Mahler/204	.05
44	Omar Moreno/205	.05
45	Dave Palmer/206	.05
46	Ozzie Smith	.35
47	Bob Forsch/207	.05
48	Willie McGee/209	.05
49	Tom Herr/210	.05
50	Vince Coleman/211	.05
51	Andy Van Slyke/212	.05
52	Jack Clark/215	.05
53	John Tudor/216	.05
54	Terry Pendleton/217	.05
55	Todd Worrell	.05
56	Lee Smith	.05
57	Leon Durham/218	.05
58	Jerry Mumphrey/219	.05
59	Shawon Dunston/220	.05
60	Scott Sanderson/221	.05
61	Ryne Sandberg	.35
62	Gary Matthews/222	.05
63	Dennis Eckersley/225	.25
64	Jody Davis/226	.05
65	Keith Moreland/227	.05
66	Mike Marshall/228	.05
67	Bill Madlock/229	.05
68	Greg Brock/230	.05
69	Pedro Guerrero/231	.05
70	Steve Sax	.05
71	Rick Honeycutt/232	.05
72	Franklin Stubbs/235	.05
73	Mike Scioscia/236	.05
74	Mariano Duncan/237	.05
75	Fernando Valenzuela	.05
76	Hubie Brooks	.05
77	Andre Dawson/238	.20
78	Tim Burke/240	.05
79	Floyd Youmans/241	.05
80	Tim Wallach/242	.05
81	Jeff Reardon/243	.05
82	Mitch Webster/244	.05
83	Bryn Smith/245	.05
84	Andres Galarraga/246	.05
85	Tim Raines	.05
86	Chris Brown	.05
87	Bob Brenly/247	.05
88	Will Clark/249	.10
89	Scott Garrelts/250	.05
90	Jeffrey Leonard/251	.05
91	Robby Thompson/252	.05
92	Mike Krukow/255	.05
93	Danny Gladden/256	.05
94	Candy Maldonado/257	.05
95	Chili Davis	.05
96	Dwight Gooden	.05
97	Sid Fernandez/258	.05
98	Len Dykstra/259	.05
99	Bob Ojeda/260	.05
100	Wally Backman/261	.05
101	Gary Carter	.30
102	Keith Hernandez/262	.05
103	Darryl Strawberry/265	.05
104	Roger McDowell/266	.05
105	Ron Darling/267	.05
106	Tony Gwynn	.35
107	Dave Dravecky/268	.05
108	Terry Kennedy/269	.05
109	Rich Gossage/270	.05
110	Garry Templeton/271	.05
111	Lance McCullers/272	.05
112	Eric Show/275	.05
113	John Kruk/276	.05
114	Tim Flannery/277	.05
115	Steve Garvey	.15
116	Mike Schmidt	.45
117	Glenn Wilson/278	.05
118	Kent Tekulve/280	.05
119	Gary Redus/281	.05
120	Shane Rawley/282	.05
121	Von Hayes	.05
122	Don Carman/283	.05
123	Bruce Ruffin/285	.05
124	Steve Bedrosian/286	.05
125	Juan Samuel/287	.05
126	Sid Bream/288	.05
127	Cecilio Guante/289	.05
128	Rick Reuschel/290	.05
129	Tony Pena/291	.05
130	Rick Rhoden	.05
131	Barry Bonds/292	5.00
132	Joe Orsulak/295	.05
133	Jim Morrison/296	.05
134	R.J. Reynolds/297	.05
135	Johnny Ray	.05
136	Eric Davis	.05
137	Tom Browning/298	.05
138	John Franco/300	.05
139	Pete Rose/301	.35
140	Bill Gullickson/302	.05
141	Ron Oester/303	.05
142	Bo Diaz/304	.05
143	Buddy Bell/305	.05
144	Eddie Milner/306	.05
145	Dave Parker	.05
146	Kirby Puckett	.35
147	Rickey Henderson	.30
148	Wade Boggs	.35
149	Lance Parrish	.05
150	Wally Joyner	.05
151	Cal Ripken, Jr.	.75
152	Dave Winfield	.30
153	Lou Whitaker	.05
154	Roger Clemens	.40
155	Tony Gwynn	.35
156	Ryne Sandberg	.35
157	Keith Hernandez	.05
158	Gary Carter	.30
159	Darryl Strawberry	.05
160	Mike Schmidt	.45
161	Dale Murphy	.15
162	Ozzie Smith	.35
163	Dwight Gooden	.05
164	Jose Canseco	.25
165	Curt Young/307	.05
166	Alfredo Griffin/308	.05
167	Dave Stewart/309	.05
168	Mike Davis/310	.05
169	Bruce Bochte/311	.05
170	Dwayne Murphy/312	.05
171	Carney Lansford/313	.05
172	Joaquin Andujar/1	.05
173	Dave Kingman	.05
174	Wally Joyner	.05
175	Gary Pettis/2	.05
176	Dick Schofield/3	.05
177	Donnie Moore/4	.05
178	Brian Downing/5	.05
179	Mike Witt	.05
180	Bob Boone/6	.05
181	Kirk McCaskill/7	.05
182	Doug DeCinces/8	.05
183	Don Sutton/9	.25
184	Jessie Barfield	.05
185	Tom Henke/10	.05
186	Willie Upshaw/11	.05
187	Mark Eichhorn/12	.05
188	Damaso Garcia/27	.05
189	Jim Clancy/28	.05
190	Lloyd Moseby/29	.05
191	Tony Fernandez/30	.05
192	Jimmy Key/31	.05
193	George Bell	.05
194	Rob Deer	.05
195	Mark Clear/32	.05
196	Robin Yount/33	.20
197	Jim Gantner/34	.05
198	Cecil Cooper/37	.05
199	Teddy Higuera	.05
200	Paul Molitor/38	.25
201	Dan Plesac/39	.05
202	Billy Jo Robidoux/40	.05
203	Earnie Riles/42	.05
204	Ken Schrom/43	.05
205	Pat Tabler/44	.05
206	Mel Hall/45	.05
207	Tony Bernazard/47	.05
208	Joe Carter	.05
209	Ernie Camacho/48	.05
210	Julio Franco/49	.05
211	Tom Candiotti/50	.05
212	Brook Jacoby/51	.05
213	Cory Snyder	.05
214	Jim Presley	.05
215	Mike Moore/52	.05
216	Harold Reynolds/53	.05
217	Scott Bradley/54	.05
218	Matt Young/57	.05
219	Mark Langston/58	.05
220	Alvin Davis/59	.05
221	Phil Bradley/60	.05
222	Ken Phelps/62	.05
223	Danny Tartabull	.05
224	Eddie Murray	.30
225	Rick Dempsey/63	.05
226	Fred Lynn/64	.05
227	Mike Boddicker/65	.05
228	Don Aase/66	.05
229	Larry Sheets/67	.05
230	Storm Davis/68	.05
231	Lee Lacy/69	.05
232	Jim Traber/71	.05
233	Cal Ripken, Jr.	.75
234	Larry Parrish	.05
235	Gary Ward/72	.05
236	Pete Incaviglia/73	.05
237	Scott Fletcher/74	.05
238	Greg Harris/77	.05
239	Pete O'Brien	.05
240	Charlie Hough/78	.05
241	Don Slaught/79	.05
242	Steve Buechele/80	.05
243	Oddibe McDowell/81	.05
244	Roger Clemens/82	.30
245	Bob Stanley/83	.05
246	Tom Seaver/84	.20
247	Rich Gedman/87	.05
248	Jim Rice	.15
249	Dennis Boyd/88	.05
250	Bill Buckner/89	.05
251	Dwight Evans/90	.05
252	Don Baylor/91	.05
253	Wade Boggs	.35
254	George Brett	.45
255	Steve Farr/92	.05
256	Jim Sundberg/93	.05
257	Dan Quisenberry/94	.05
258	Charlie Leibrandt/97	.05
259	Argenis Salazar/98	.05
260	Frank White/99	.05
261	Willie Wilson/100	.05
262	Lonnie Smith/102	.05
263	Steve Balboni	.05
264	Darrell Evans	.05
265	Johnny Grubb/103	.05
266	Jack Morris/104	.05
267	Lou Whitaker/105	.05
268	Chet Lemon/107	.05
269	Lance Parrish/108	.05
270	Alan Trammell/109	.05
271	Darnell Coles/110	.05
272	Willie Hernandez/111	.05
273	Kirk Gibson	.05
274	Kirby Puckett	.35
275	Mike Smithson/112	.05
276	Mickey Hatcher/113	.05
277	Frank Viola/114	.05
278	Bert Blyleven/117	.05
279	Gary Gaetti	.05
280	Tom Brunansky/118	.05
281	Kent Hrbek/119	.05
282	Roy Smalley/120	.05
283	Greg Gagne/122	.05
284	Harold Baines	.05
285	Ron Hassey/123	.05
286	Floyd Bannister/124	.05
287	Ozzie Guillen/125	.05
288	Carlton Fisk/126	.25
289	Tim Hulett/127	.05
290	Joe Cowley/128	.05
291	Greg Walker/129	.05
292	Neil Allen/131	.05
293	John Cangelosi	.05
294	Don Mattingly	.45
295	Mike Easler/132	.05
296	Rickey Henderson/133	.20
297	Dan Pasqua/134	.05
298	Dave Winfield/137	.20
299	Dave Righetti	.05
300	Mike Pagliarulo/138	.05
301	Ron Guidry/139	.05
302	Willie Randolph/140	.05
303	Dennis Rasmussen/141	.05
304	Jose Canseco/142	.20
305	Andres Thomas/143	.05
306	Danny Tartabull/144	.05
307	Robby Thompson/165	.05
308	Pete Incaviglia, Cory Snyder/166	.05
309	Dale Sveum/167	.05
310	Todd Worrell/168	.05
311	Andy Allanson/169	.05
312	Bruce Ruffin/170	.05
313	Wally Joyner/171	.05

1988 Topps

The 1988 Topps set features a clean, attractive design of a player photo surrounded by a thin colored frame which is encompassed by a white border. The player's name appears in the lower-right corner in a diagonal colored strip. The team nickname is in large letters at the top of the card. Backs feature black print on orange and gray stock and include the usual player personal and career statistics. Many of the cards contain a new feature titled "This Way To The Clubhouse," which explains how the player joined his current team. The 792-card set includes a number of special subsets including "Future Stars," "Turn Back The Clock," All-Star teams, All-Star rookie selections, and Record Breakers.

		NM/M
Unopened Factory Set, Retail (792):		15.00
Unopened Factory Set, Hobby (792):		15.00
Complete Set (792):		12.00
Common Player:		.05
Wax Pack (15):		.40
Wax Box (36):		15.00
Cello Pack (28):		.70
Cello Box (24):		13.50
Rack Pack (43):		.75
Rack Box (24):		15.00
Vending Box (500):		7.50
1	Vince Coleman (Record Breakers)	.05
2	Don Mattingly (Record Breakers)	.25
3a	Mark McGwire (Record Breakers, white triangle by left foot.)	1.00
3b	Mark McGwire (Record Breakers, no white triangle.)	.40
4a	Eddie Murray (Record Breakers, no mention of record on front.)	.25
4b	Eddie Murray (Record Breakers, record in box on front.)	.20
5	Joe Niekro, Phil Niekro (Record Breakers)	.05
6	Nolan Ryan (Record Breakers)	.40
7	Benito Santiago (Record Breakers)	.05
8	Kevin Elster **RC** (Future Stars)	.05
9	Andy Hawkins	.05
10	Ryne Sandberg	.50
11	Mike Young	.05
12	Bill Schroeder	.05
13	Andres Thomas	.05
14	Sparky Anderson	.10
15	Chili Davis	.05
16	Kirk McCaskill	.05
17	Ron Oester	.05
18a	Al Leiter **RC** (Future Stars, no "NY" on shirt, photo actually Steve George.)	.40
18b	Al Leiter **RC** (Future Stars, "NY" on shirt, correct photo.)	.20
19	Mark Davidson **RC**	.05
20	Kevin Gross	.05
21	Red Sox Leaders (Wade Boggs, Spike Owen)	.10
22	Greg Swindell	.05
23	Ken Landreaux	.05
24	Jim Deshaies	.05
25	Andres Galarraga	.05
26	Mitch Williams	.05
27	R.J. Reynolds	.05
28	Jose Nunez **RC**	.05
29	Argenis Salazar	.05
30	Sid Fernandez	.05
31	Bruce Bochy	.05
32	Mike Morgan	.05
33	Rob Deer	.05
34	Ricky Horton	.05
35	Harold Baines	.05
36	Jamie Moyer	.05
37	Ed Romero	.05
38	Jeff Calhoun	.05
39	Gerald Perry	.05
40	Orel Hershiser	.05
41	Bob Melvin	.05
42	Bill Landrum **RC**	.05
43	Dick Schofield	.05
44	Lou Piniella	.05
45	Kent Hrbek	.05
46	Darnell Coles	.05
47	Joaquin Andujar	.05
48	Alan Ashby	.05
49	Dave Clark **RC**	.05
50	Hubie Brooks	.05
51	Orioles Leaders (Eddie Murray, Cal Ripken, Jr.)	.25
52	Don Robinson	.05
53	Curt Wilkerson	.05
54	Jim Clancy	.05
55	Phil Bradley	.05
56	Ed Hearn	.05
57	Tim Crews **RC**	.05
58	Dave Magadan	.05
59	Danny Cox	.05
60	Rickey Henderson	.40
61	Mark Knudson **RC**	.05
62	Jeff Hamilton	.05
63	Jimmy Jones **RC**	.05
64	Ken Caminiti **RC**	.25
65	Leon Durham	.05

66 Shane Rawley .05
67 Ken Oberkfell .05
68 Dave Dravecky .05
69 Mike Hart **RC** .05
70 Roger Clemens .60
71 Gary Pettis .05
72 Dennis Eckersley .30
73 Randy Bush .05
74 Tom Lasorda .05
75 Joe Carter .05
76 Denny Martinez .05
77 Tom O'Malley .05
78 Dan Petry .05
79 Ernie Whitt .05
80 Mark Langston .05
81 Reds Leaders (John Franco, Ron Robinson) .05
82 Darrel Akerfelds **RC** .05
83 Jose Oquendo .05
84 Cecilio Guante .05
85 Howard Johnson .05
86 Ron Karkovice .05
87 Mike Mason .05
88 Earnie Riles .05
89 Gary Thurman **RC** .05
90 Dale Murphy .20
91 Joey Cora **RC** .10
92 Len Matuszek .05
93 Bob Sebra .05
94 Chuck Jackson **RC** .05
95 Lance Parrish .05
96 Todd Benzinger **RC** .05
97 Scott Garrelts .05
98 Rene Gonzales **RC** .05
99 Chuck Finley .05
100 Jack Clark .05
101 Allan Anderson .05
102 Barry Larkin .05
103 Curt Young .05
104 Dick Williams .05
105 Jesse Orosco .05
106 Jim Walewander **RC** .05
107 Scott Bailes .05
108 Steve Lyons .05
109 Joel Skinner .05
110 Teddy Higuera .05
111 Expos Leaders (Hubie Brooks, Vance Law) .05
112 Les Lancaster **RC** .05
113 Kelly Gruber .05
114 Jeff Russell .05
115 Johnny Ray .05
116 Jerry Don Gleaton .05
117 James Steels **RC** .05
118 Bob Welch .05
119 Robbie Wine **RC** .05
120 Kirby Puckett .50
121 Checklist 1-132 .05
122 Tony Bernazard .05
123 Tom Candiotti .05
124 Ray Knight .05
125 Bruce Hurst .05
126 Steve Jeltz .05
127 Jim Gott .05
128 Johnny Grubb .05
129 Greg Minton .05
130 Buddy Bell .05
131 Don Schulze .05
132 Donnie Hill .05
133 Greg Mathews .05
134 Chuck Tanner .05
135 Dennis Rasmussen .05
136 Brian Dayett .05
137 Chris Bosio .05
138 Mitch Webster .05
139 Jerry Browne .05
140 Jesse Barfield .05
141 Royals Leaders (George Brett, Bret Saberhagen) .20
142 Andy Van Slyke .05
143 Mickey Tettleton .05
144 Don Gordon **RC** .05
145 Bill Madlock .05
146 Donell Nixon **RC** .05
147 Bill Buckner .05
148 Carmelo Martinez .05
149 Ken Howell .05
150 Eric Davis .05
151 Bob Knepper .05
152 Jody Reed **RC** .10
153 John Habyan .05
154 Jeff Stone .05
155 Bruce Sutter .30
156 Gary Matthews .05
157 Atlee Hammaker .05
158 Tim Hulett .05
159 Brad Arnsberg **RC** .05
160 Willie McGee .05
161 Bryn Smith .05
162 Mark McLemore .05
163 Dale Mohorcic .05
164 Dave Johnson .05
165 Robin Yount .40
166 Rick Rodriguez **RC** .05
167 Rance Mulliniks .05
168 Barry Jones .05
169 Ross Jones **RC** .05
170 Rich Gossage .05
171 Cubs Leaders (Shawon Dunston, Manny Trillo) .05
172 Lloyd McClendon **RC** .05
173 Eric Plunk .05
174 Phil Garner .05
175 Kevin Bass .05
176 Jeff Reed .05
177 Frank Tanana .05
178 Dwayne Henry **RC** .05
179 Charlie Puleo .05
180 Terry Kennedy .05
181 Dave Cone .05
182 Ken Phelps .05
183 Tom Lawless .05
184 Ivan Calderon .05
185 Rick Rhoden .05
186 Rafael Palmeiro .35
187 Steve Kiefer **RC** .05
188 John Russell .05
189 Wes Gardner **RC** .05
190 Candy Maldonado .05
191 John Cerutti .05
192 Devon White .05
193 Brian Fisher .05
194 Tom Kelly .05
195 Dan Quisenberry .05
196 Dave Engle .05
197 Lance McCullers .05
198 Franklin Stubbs .05
199 Dave Meads **RC** .05
200 Wade Boggs .50
201 Rangers Leaders (Steve Buechele, Pete Incaviglia, Pete O'Brien, Bobby Valentine) .05
202 Glenn Hoffman .05
203 Fred Toliver .05
204 Paul O'Neill **RC** .05
205 Nelson Liriano **RC** .05
206 Domingo Ramos .05
207 John Mitchell **RC** .05
208 Steve Lake .05
209 Richard Dotson .05
210 Willie Randolph .05
211 Frank DiPino .05
212 Greg Brock .05
213 Albert Hall .05
214 Dave Schmidt .05
215 Von Hayes .05
216 Jerry Reuss .05
217 Harry Spilman .05
218 Dan Schatzeder .05
219 Mike Stanley .05
220 Tom Henke .05
221 Rafael Belliard .05
222 Steve Farr .05
223 Stan Jefferson .05
224 Tom Trebelhorn .05
225 Mike Scioscia .05
226 Dave Lopes .05
227 Ed Correa .05
228 Wallace Johnson .05
229 Jeff Musselman .05
230 Pat Tabler .05
231 Pirates Leaders (Barry Bonds, Bobby Bonilla) .50
232 Bob James .05
233 Rafael Santana .05
234 Ken Dayley .05
235 Gary Ward .05
236 Ted Power .05
237 Mike Heath .05
238 Luis Polonia **RC** .10
239 Roy Smalley .05
240 Lee Smith .05
241 Damaso Garcia .05
242 Tom Niedenfuer .05
243 Mark Ryal **RC** .05
244 Jeff Robinson .05
245 Rich Gedman .05
246 Mike Campbell **RC** (Future Stars) .05
247 Thad Bosley .05
248 Storm Davis .05
249 Mike Marshall .05
250 Nolan Ryan .75
251 Tom Foley .05
252 Bob Brower .05
253 Checklist 133-264 .05
254 Lee Elia .05
255 Mookie Wilson .05
256 Ken Schrom .05
257 Jerry Royster .05
258 Ed Nunez .05
259 Ron Kittle .05
260 Vince Coleman .05
261 Giants Leaders (Will Clark, Candy Maldonado, Kevin Mitchell, Robby Thompson, Jose Uribe) .05
262 Drew Hall **RC** .05
263 Glenn Braggs .05
264 Les Straker **RC** .05
265 Bo Diaz .05
266 Paul Assenmacher .05
267 Billy Bean **RC** .05
268 Bruce Ruffin .05
269 Ellis Burks .05
270 Mike Witt .05
271 Ken Gerhart .05
272 Steve Ontiveros .05
273 Garth Iorg .05
274 Junior Ortiz .05
275 Kevin Seitzer .05
276 Luis Salazar .05
277 Alejandro Pena .05
278 Jose Cruz .05
279 Randy St. Claire .05
280 Pete Incaviglia .05
281 Jerry Hairston Sr. .05
282 Pat Perry .05
283 Phil Lombardi **RC** .05
284 Larry Bowa .05
285 Jim Presley .05
286 Chuck Crim **RC** .05
287 Manny Trillo .05
288 Pat Pacillo **RC** .05
289 Dave Bergman .05
290 Tony Fernandez .05
291 Astros Leaders (Kevin Bass, Billy Hatcher) .05
292 Carney Lansford .05
293 Doug Jones **RC** .05
294 Al Pedrique **RC** .05
295 Bert Blyleven .05
296 Floyd Rayford .05
297 Zane Smith .05
298 Milt Thompson .05
299 Steve Crawford .05
300 Don Mattingly .60
301 Bud Black .05
302 Jose Uribe .05
303 Eric Show .05
304 George Hendrick .05
305 Steve Sax .05
306 Billy Hatcher .05
307 Mike Trujillo .05
308 Lee Mazzilli .05
309 Bill Long **RC** .05
310 Tom Herr .05
311 Scott Sanderson .05
312 Joey Meyer **RC** (Future Stars) .05
313 Bob McClure .05
314 Jimy Williams .05
315 Dave Parker .05
316 Jose Rijo .05
317 Tom Nieto .05
318 Mel Hall .05
319 Mike Loynd .05
320 Alan Trammell .05
321 White Sox Leaders (Harold Baines, Carlton Fisk) .05
322 Vicente Palacios **RC** .05
323 Rick Leach .05
324 Danny Jackson .05
325 Glenn Hubbard .05
326 Al Nipper .05
327 Larry Sheets .05
328 Greg Cadaret **RC** .05
329 Chris Speier .05
330 Eddie Whitson .05
331 Brian Downing .05
332 Jerry Reed .05
333 Wally Backman .05
334 Dave LaPoint .05
335 Claudell Washington .05
336 Ed Lynch .05
337 Jim Gantner .05
338 Brian Holton .05
339 Kurt Stillwell .05
340 Jack Morris .05
341 Carmen Castillo .05
342 Larry Andersen .05
343 Greg Gagne .05
344 Tony LaRussa .05
345 Scott Fletcher .05
346 Vance Law .05
347 Joe Johnson .05
348 Jim Eisenreich .05
349 Bob Walk .05
350 Will Clark .05
351 Cardinals Leaders (Tony Pena, Red Schoendienst) .05
352 Billy Ripken **RC** .05
353 Ed Olwine .05
354 Marc Sullivan .05
355 Roger McDowell .05
356 Luis Aguayo .05
357 Floyd Bannister .05
358 Rey Quinones .05
359 Tim Stoddard .05
360 Tony Gwynn .50
361 Greg Maddux .50
362 Juan Castillo .05
363 Willie Fraser .05
364 Nick Esasky .05
365 Floyd Youmans .05
366 Chet Lemon .05
367 Tim Leary .05
368 Gerald Young **RC** .05
369 Greg Harris .05
370 Jose Canseco .25
371 Joe Hesketh .05
372 Matt Williams .05
373 Checklist 265-396 .05
374 Doc Edwards .05
375 Tom Brunansky .05
376 Bill Wilkinson **RC** .05
377 Sam Horn **RC** .05
378 Todd Frohwirth **RC** .05
379 Rafael Ramirez .05
380 Joe Magrane **RC** .05
381 Angels Leaders (Jack Howell, Wally Joyner) .05
382 Keith Miller **RC** .05
383 Eric Bell .05
384 Neil Allen .05
385 Carlton Fisk .40
386 Don Mattingly/AS .30
387 Willie Randolph/AS .05
388 Wade Boggs/AS .20
389 Alan Trammell/AS .05
390 George Bell/AS .05
391 Kirby Puckett/AS .25
392 Dave Winfield/AS .20
393 Matt Nokes/AS .15
394 Roger Clemens/AS .35
395 Jimmy Key/AS .05
396 Tom Henke/AS .05
397 Jack Clark/AS .05
398 Juan Samuel/AS .05
399 Tim Wallach/AS .05
400 Ozzie Smith/AS .25
401 Andre Dawson/AS .15
402 Tony Gwynn/AS .25
403 Tim Raines/AS .05
404 Benny Santiago/AS .05
405 Dwight Gooden/AS .05
406 Shane Rawley/AS .05
407 Steve Bedrosian/AS .05
408 Dion James .05
409 Joel McKeon **RC** .05
410 Tony Pena .05
411 Wayne Tolleson .05
412 Randy Myers .05
413 John Christensen .05
414 John McNamara .05
415 Don Carman .05
416 Keith Moreland .05
417 Mark Ciardi **RC** .05
418 Joel Youngblood .05
419 Scott McGregor .05
420 Wally Joyner .05
421 Ed Vande Berg .05
422 Dave Concepcion .05
423 John Smiley .05
424 Dwayne Murphy .05
425 Jeff Reardon .05
426 Randy Ready .05
427 Paul Kilgus **RC** .05
428 John Shelby .05
429 Tigers Leaders (Kirk Gibson, Alan Trammell) .05
430 Glenn Davis .05
431 Casey Candaele .05
432 Mike Moore .05
433 Bill Pecota **RC** .05
434 Rick Aguilera .05
435 Mike Pagliarulo .05
436 Mike Bielecki .05
437 Fred Manrique **RC** .05
438 Rob Ducey **RC** .05
439 Dave Martinez .05
440 Steve Bedrosian .05
441 Rick Manning .05
442 Tom Bolton **RC** .05
443 Ken Griffey .05
444 Cal Ripken, Sr. .05
445 Mike Krukow .05
446 Doug DeCinces .05
447 Jeff Montgomery **RC** .20
448 Mike Davis .05
449 Jeff Robinson **RC** .05
450 Barry Bonds .75
451 Keith Atherton .05
452 Willie Wilson .05
453 Dennis Powell .05
454 Marvell Wynne .05
455 Shawn Hillegas **RC** .05
456 Dave Anderson .05
457 Terry Leach .05
458 Ron Hassey .05
459 Yankees Leaders (Willie Randolph, Dave Winfield) .05
460 Ozzie Smith .50
461 Danny Darwin .05
462 Don Slaught .05
463 Fred McGriff .05
464 Jay Tibbs .05
465 Paul Molitor .40
466 Jerry Mumphrey .05
467 Don Aase .05
468 Darren Daulton .05
469 Jeff Dedmon .05
470 Dwight Evans .05
471 Donnie Moore .05
472 Robby Thompson .05
473 Joe Niekro .05
474 Tom Brookens .05
475 Pete Rose .65
476 Dave Stewart .05
477 Jamie Quirk .05
478 Sid Bream .05
479 Brett Butler .05
480 Dwight Gooden .05
481 Mariano Duncan .05
482 Mark Davis .05
483 Rod Booker **RC** .05
484 Pat Clements .05
485 Harold Reynolds .05
486 Pat Keedy **RC** .05
487 Jim Pankovits .05
488 Andy McGaffigan .05
489 Dodgers Leaders (Pedro Guerrero, Fernando Valenzuela) .05
490 Larry Parrish .05
491 B.J. Surhoff .05
492 Doyle Alexander .05
493 Mike Greenwell .05
494 Wally Ritchie **RC** .05
495 Eddie Murray .40
496 Guy Hoffman .05
497 Kevin Mitchell .05
498 Bob Boone .05
499 Eric King .05
500 Andre Dawson .25
501 Tim Birtsas **RC** .05
502 Danny Gladden .05
503 Junior Noboa **RC** .05
504 Bob Rodgers .05
505 Willie Upshaw .05
506 John Cangelosi .05
507 Mark Gubicza .05
508 Tim Teufel .05
509 Bill Dawley .05
510 Dave Winfield .40
511 Joel Davis .05
512 Alex Trevino .05
513 Tim Flannery .05
514 Pat Sheridan .05
515 Juan Nieves .05
516 Jim Sundberg .05
517 Ron Robinson .05
518 Greg Gross .05
519 Mariners Leaders (Phil Bradley, Harold Reynolds) .05
520 Dave Smith .05
521 Jim Dwyer .05
522 Bob Patterson **RC** .05
523 Gary Roenicke .05
524 Gary Lucas .05
525 Marty Barrett .05
526 Juan Berenguer .05
527 Steve Henderson .05
528a Checklist 397-528 (#455 is Steve Carlton) .05
528b Checklist 397-528 (#455 is Shawn Hillegas) .05
529 Tim Burke .05
530 Gary Carter .40
531 Rich Yett .05
532 Mike Kingery .05
533 John Farrell **RC** .05
534 John Wathan .05
535 Ron Guidry .05
536 John Morris .05
537 Steve Buechele .05
538 Bill Wegman .05
539 Mike LaValliere .05
540 Bret Saberhagen .05
541 Juan Beniquez .05
542 Paul Noce **RC** .05
543 Kent Tekulve .05
544 Jim Traber .05
545 Don Baylor .05
546 John Candelaria .05
547 Felix Fermin **RC** .05
548 Shane Mack .05
549 Braves Leaders (Ken Griffey, Dion James, Dale Murphy, Gerald Perry) .05
550 Pedro Guerrero .05
551 Terry Steinbach .05
552 Mark Thurmond .05
553 Tracy Jones .05
554 Mike Smithson .05
555 Brook Jacoby .05
556 Stan Clarke **RC** .05
557 Craig Reynolds .05
558 Bob Ojeda .05
559 Ken Williams **RC** .05
560 Tim Wallach .05
561 Rick Cerone .05
562 Jim Lindeman .05
563 Jose Guzman .05
564 Frank Lucchesi .05
565 Lloyd Moseby .05
566 Charlie O'Brien **RC** .05
567 Mike Diaz .05
568 Chris Brown .05
569 Charlie Leibrandt .05
570 Jeffrey Leonard .05
571 Mark Williamson **RC** .05
572 Chris James .05
573 Bob Stanley .05
574 Graig Nettles .05
575 Don Sutton .30
576 Tommy Hinzo **RC** .05
577 Tom Browning .05
578 Gary Gaetti .05
579 Mets Leaders (Gary Carter, Kevin McReynolds) .05
580 Mark McGwire .65
581 Tito Landrum .05
582 Mike Henneman .05
583 Dave Valle **RC** .05
584 Steve Trout .05
585 Ozzie Guillen .05
586 Bob Forsch .05
587 Terry Puhl .05
588 Jeff Parrett **RC** .05
589 Geno Petralli .05
590 George Bell .05
591 Doug Drabek .05
592 Dale Sveum .05
593 Bob Tewksbury .05
594 Bobby Valentine .05
595 Frank White .05
596 John Kruk .05
597 Gene Garber .05
598 Lee Lacy .05
599 Calvin Schiraldi .05
600 Mike Schmidt .60
601 Jack Lazorko .05
602 Mike Aldrete .05
603 Rob Murphy .05
604 Chris Bando .05
605 Kirk Gibson .05
606 Moose Haas .05
607 Mickey Hatcher .05
608 Charlie Kerfeld .05
609 Twins Leaders (Gary Gaetti, Kent Hrbek) .05
610 Keith Hernandez .05
611 Tommy John .05
612 Curt Ford .05
613 Bobby Thigpen .05
614 Herm Winningham .05
615 Jody Davis .05
616 Jay Aldrich **RC** .05
617 Oddibe McDowell .05
618 Cecil Fielder .05
619 Mike Dunne **RC** .05
620 Cory Snyder .05
621 Gene Nelson .05
622 Kal Daniels .05
623 Mike Flanagan .05
624 Jim Leyland .05
625 Frank Viola .05
626 Glenn Wilson .05
627 Joe Boever **RC** .05
628 Dave Henderson .05
629 Kelly Downs .05
630 Darrell Evans .05
631 Jack Howell .05
632 Steve Shields **RC** .05
633 Barry Lyons **RC** .05
634 Jose DeLeon .05
635 Terry Pendleton .05
636 Charles Hudson .05
637 Jay Bell **RC** .25
638 Steve Balboni .05
639 Brewers Leaders (Glenn Braggs, Tony Muser) .05
640 Garry Templeton .05
641 Rick Honeycutt .05
642 Bob Dernier .05
643 Rocky Childress **RC** .05
644 Terry McGriff **RC** .05
645 Matt Nokes .05
646 Checklist 529-660 .05
647 Pascual Perez .05
648 Al Newman .05
649 DeWayne Buice **RC** .05
650 Cal Ripken, Jr. .75
651 Mike Jackson **RC** .05
652 Bruce Benedict .05
653 Jeff Sellers .05
654 Roger Craig .05
655 Len Dykstra .05
656 Lee Guetterman .05
657 Gary Redus .05
658 Tim Conroy .05
659 Bobby Meacham .05
660 Rick Reuschel .05
661 Nolan Ryan (Turn Back the Clock) .35
662 Jim Rice (Turn Back the Clock) .05
663 Ron Blomberg (Turn Back the Clock) .05
664 Bob Gibson (Turn Back the Clock) .10
665 Stan Musial (Turn Back the Clock) .20
666 Mario Soto .05
667 Luis Quinones .05
668 Walt Terrell .05
669 Phillies Leaders (Lance Parrish, Mike Ryan) .05
670 Dan Plesac .05
671 Tim Laudner .05
672 John Davis **RC** .05
673 Tony Phillips .05
674 Mike Fitzgerald .05
675 Jim Rice .20
676 Ken Dixon .05
677 Eddie Milner .05
678 Jim Acker .05
679 Darrell Miller .05
680 Charlie Hough .05
681 Bobby Bonilla .05
682 Jimmy Key .05
683 Julio Franco .05
684 Hal Lanier .05
685 Ron Darling .05
686 Terry Francona .05
687 Mickey Brantley .05
688 Jim Winn .05
689 Tom Pagnozzi **RC** .05
690 Jay Howell .05
691 Dan Pasqua .05
692 Mike Birkbeck .05
693 Benny Santiago .05
694 Eric Nolte **RC** .05
695 Shawon Dunston .05
696 Duane Ward .05
697 Steve Lombardozzi .05
698 Brad Havens .05
699 Padres Leaders (Tony Gwynn, Benny Santiago) .15
700 George Brett .60
701 Sammy Stewart .05
702 Mike Gallego .05
703 Bob Brenly .05
704 Dennis Boyd .05
705 Juan Samuel .05
706 Rick Mahler .05
707 Fred Lynn .05
708 Gus Polidor **RC** .05
709 George Frazier .05
710 Darryl Strawberry .05
711 Bill Gullickson .05
712 John Moses .05
713 Willie Hernandez .05
714 Jim Fregosi .05
715 Todd Worrell .05
716 Lenn Sakata .05
717 Jay Baller **RC** .05
718 Mike Felder .05

719 Denny Walling .05
720 Tim Raines .05
721 Pete O'Brien .05
722 Manny Lee .05
723 Bob Kipper .05
724 Danny Tartabull .05
725 Mike Boddicker .05
726 Alfredo Griffin .05
727 Greg Booker .05
728 Andy Allanson .05
729 Blue Jays Leaders (George Bell, Fred McGriff) .05
730 John Franco .05
731 Rick Schu .05
732 Dave Palmer .05
733 Spike Owen .05
734 Craig Lefferts .05
735 Kevin McReynolds .05
736 Matt Young .05
737 Butch Wynegar .05
738 Scott Bankhead .05
739 Daryl Boston .05
740 Rick Sutcliffe .05
741 Mike Easler .05
742 Mark Clear .05
743 Larry Herndon .05
744 Whitey Herzog .05
745 Bill Doran .05
746 Gene Larkin **RC** .05
747 Bobby Witt .05
748 Reid Nichols .05
749 Mark Eichhorn .05
750 Bo Jackson .10
751 Jim Morrison .05
752 Mark Grant .05
753 Danny Heep .05
754 Mike LaCoss .05
755 Ozzie Virgil .05
756 Mike Maddux .05
757 John Marzano **RC** .05
758 Eddie Williams **RC** .05
759 A's Leaders (Jose Canseco, Mark McGwire) .35
760 Mike Scott .05
761 Tony Armas .05
762 Scott Bradley .05
763 Doug Sisk .05
764 Greg Walker .05
765 Neal Heaton .05
766 Henry Cotto .05
767 Jose Lind **RC** (Future Stars) .10
768 Dickie Noles .05
769 Cecil Cooper .05
770 Lou Whitaker .05
771 Ruben Sierra .05
772 Sal Butera .05
773 Frank Williams .05
774 Gene Mauch .05
775 Dave Stieb .05
776 Checklist 661-792 .05
777 Lonnie Smith .05
778a Keith Comstock **RC** (White team letters.) .40
778b Keith Comstock **RC** (Blue team letters, white name.) .10
778c Keith Comstock **RC** (Blue team letters, yellow name.) 2.00
779 Tom Glavine **RC** 1.50
780 Fernando Valenzuela .05
781 Keith Hughes **RC** .05
782 Jeff Ballard **RC** .05
783 Ron Roenicke .05
784 Joe Sambito .05
785 Alvin Davis .05
786 Joe Price .05
787 Bill Almon .05
788 Ray Searage .05
789 Indians Leaders (Joe Carter, Cory Snyder) .05
790 Dave Righetti .05
791 Ted Simmons .05
792 John Tudor .05

Tiffany

Sharing a checklist with the regular issue 1988 Topps baseball set, this specially boxed, limited-edition (25,000 sets) features cards printed on white cardboard stock with high-gloss front finish. Topps offered the sets directly to the public in ads in USA Today and Sporting News at a price of $99.

	NM/M
Complete Set (792):	40.00
Common Player:	.15

Traded

In addition to new players and traded veterans, 21 members of the U.S.A. Olympic Baseball team are showcased in this 132-card set, numbered 1T-132T. The 2-1/2" x 3-1/2" cards follow the same design as the basic Topps issue - white borders, large full-color photos, team name (or U.S.A.) in large bold letters at the top of the card face, player name on a diagonal stripe across the lower-right corner. Topps had issued its traded series each year since 1981 in boxed complete sets available only through hobby dealers.

	NM/M
Complete Set (132):	5.00
Common Player:	.05

1 Jim Abbott **RC** (USA) .25
2 Juan Agosto .05
3 Luis Alicea **RC** .05
4 Roberto Alomar **RC** 1.50
5 Brady Anderson **RC** .25
6 Jack Armstrong .05
7 Don August .05
8 Floyd Bannister .05
9 Bret Barberie (USA) .05
10 Jose Bautista **RC** .05
11 Don Baylor .05
12 Tim Belcher .05
13 Buddy Bell .05
14 Andy Benes **RC** (USA) .25
15 Damon Berryhill .05
16 Bud Black .05
17 Pat Borders .05
18 Phil Bradley .05
19 Jeff Branson **RC** (USA) .05
20 Tom Brunansky .05
21 Jay Buhner **RC** .75
22 Brett Butler .05
23 Jim Campanis **RC** (USA) .05
24 Sil Campusano **RC** .05
25 John Candelaria .05
26 Jose Cecena **RC** .05
27 Rick Cerone .05
28 Jack Clark .05
29 Kevin Coffman **RC** .05
30 Pat Combs (USA) .05
31 Henry Cotto .05
32 Chili Davis .05
33 Mike Davis .05
34 Jose DeLeon .05
35 Richard Dotson .05
36 Cecil Espy .05
37 Tom Filer .05
38 Mike Fiore **RC** (USA) .05
39 Ron Gant **RC** .25
40 Kirk Gibson .05
41 Rich Gossage .05
42 Mark Grace **RC** 1.00
43 Alfredo Griffin .05
44 Ty Griffin **RC** (USA) .05
45 Bryan Harvey .05
46 Ron Hassey .05
47 Ray Hayward **RC** .05
48 Dave Henderson .05
49 Tom Herr .05
50 Bob Horner .05
51 Ricky Horton .05
52 Jay Howell .05
53 Glenn Hubbard .05
54 Jeff Innis **RC** .05
55 Danny Jackson .05
56 Darrin Jackson .05
57 Roberto Kelly .05
58 Ron Kittle .05
59 Ray Knight .05
60 Vance Law .05
61 Jeffrey Leonard .05
62 Mike Macfarlane **RC** .05
63 Scotti Madison **RC** .05
64 Kirt Manwaring **RC** .05
65 Mark Marquess (USA) .05
66 Tino Martinez **RC** (USA) .75
67 Billy Masse **RC** (USA) .05
68 Jack McDowell **RC** .25
69 Jack McKeon .05
70 Larry McWilliams .05
71 Mickey Morandini (USA) .05
72 Keith Moreland .05
73 Mike Morgan .05
74 Charles Nagy (USA) .10
75 Al Nipper .05
76 Russ Nixon .05
77 Jesse Orosco .05
78 Joe Orsulak .05
79 Dave Palmer .05
80 Mark Parent **RC** .05
81 Dave Parker .05
82 Dan Pasqua .05
83 Melido Perez .05
84 Steve Peters **RC** .05
85 Dan Petry .05
86 Gary Pettis .05
87 Jeff Pico **RC** .05
88 Jim Poole (USA) .05
89 Ted Power .05
90 Rafael Ramirez .05
91 Dennis Rasmussen .05
92 Jose Rijo .05
93 Earnie Riles .05
94 Luis Rivera **RC** .05
95 Doug Robbins **RC** (USA) .05
96 Frank Robinson .15
97 Cookie Rojas .05
98 Chris Sabo **RC** .10
99 Mark Salas .05
100 Luis Salazar .05
101 Rafael Santana .05
102 Nelson Santovenia **RC** .05
103 Mackey Sasser **RC** .05
104 Calvin Schiraldi .05
105 Mike Schooler **RC** .05
106 Scott Servais **RC** (USA) .05
107 Dave Silvestri (USA) .05
108 Don Slaught .05
109 Joe Slusarski **RC** (USA) .05
110 Lee Smith .05
111 Pete Smith **RC** .05
112 Jim Snyder .05
113 Ed Sprague **RC** (USA) .05
114 Pete Stanicek **RC** .05
115 Kurt Stillwell .05
116 Todd Stottlemyre .05
117 Bill Swift .05
118 Pat Tabler .05
119 Scott Terry **RC** .05
120 Mickey Tettleton .05
121 Dickie Thon .05
122 Jeff Treadway .05
123 Willie Upshaw .05
124 Robin Ventura **RC** .25
125 Ron Washington .05
126 Walt Weiss **RC** .05
127 Bob Welch .05
128 David Wells **RC** .25
129 Glenn Wilson .05
130 Ted Wood **RC** (USA) .05
131 Don Zimmer .05
132 Checklist 1T-132T .05

Traded Tiffany

The high-gloss front surface is all that distinguishes this limited-edition, hobby-only collectors version from the regular Topps Traded boxed set.

	NM/M
Complete Set (132):	25.00
Common Player:	.15

Traded Duke Snider Bronze

This 1/4-size metal replica was issued to dealers who purchased cases of 1988 Topps Traded sets. Each detail of the 1955 Topps Snider card is reproduced on the 1-3/4" x 1-1/4" bronze metal minicard, right down to the stats.

		NM/M
210	Duke Snider	7.50

Box Panels

After a one-year hiatus during which they appeared on the sides of Topps wax pack display boxes, Topps retail box cards returned to box bottoms in 1988. The series includes 16 standard-size baseball cards, four cards per each of four different display boxes. Card fronts follow the same design as the 1988 Topps basic issue; full-color player photos, framed in yellow, surrounded by a white border; diagonal player name lower-right; team name in large letters at the top. Card backs are "numbered" A through P and are printed in black and orange.

		NM/M
Complete Panel Set (4):		3.00
Complete Singles Set (16):		3.00
Common Panel:		.50
Common Single Player:		.10
	Panel	.50
A	Don Baylor	.10
B	Steve Bedrosian	.10
C	Juan Beniquez	.10
D	Bob Boone	.10
	Panel	.75
E	Darrell Evans	.10
F	Tony Gwynn	.50
G	John Kruk	.10
H	Marvell Wynne	.10
	Panel	.60
I	Joe Carter	.10
J	Eric Davis	.10
K	Howard Johnson	.10
L	Darryl Strawberry	.10
	Panel	2.00
M	Rickey Henderson	.40
N	Nolan Ryan	1.00
O	Mike Schmidt	.75
P	Kent Tekulve	.10

All-Star Glossy Set of 22

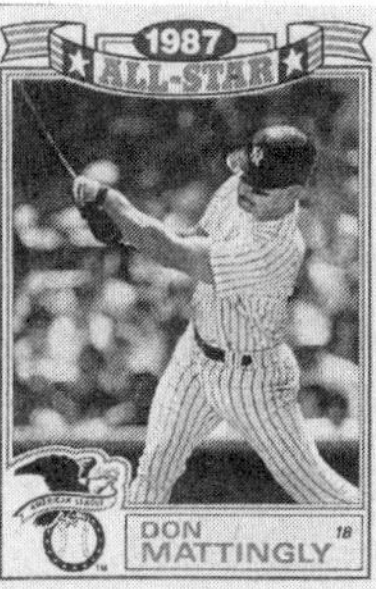

The fifth edition of Topps' special All-Star inserts was included in the company's 1988 rack packs. The 1987 American and National League All-Star lineup, plus honorary captains Jim Hunter and Billy Williams, are featured on the 2-1/2" x 3-1/2" cards. The glossy full-color fronts contain player photos centered between a red and yellow "1987 All-Star" logo at top and the player name (also red and yellow) which is printed in the bottom margin. A league logo is in the lower-left corner. Card backs are printed in red and blue on a white background, with the title and All-Star logo emblem printed above the player name and card number.

		NM/M
Complete Set (22):		3.00
Common Player:		.05
1	John McNamara	.05
2	Don Mattingly	.75
3	Willie Randolph	.05
4	Wade Boggs	.65
5	Cal Ripken, Jr.	1.00
6	George Bell	.05
7	Rickey Henderson	.50
8	Dave Winfield	.50
9	Terry Kennedy	.05
10	Bret Saberhagen	.05
11	Catfish Hunter	.05
12	Davey Johnson	.05
13	Jack Clark	.05
14	Ryne Sandberg	.65
15	Mike Schmidt	.75
16	Ozzie Smith	.65
17	Eric Davis	.05
18	Andre Dawson	.20
19	Darryl Strawberry	.05
20	Gary Carter	.50
21	Mike Scott	.05
22	Billy Williams	.05

All-Star Glossy Set of 60

This collectors' set includes 60 full-color glossy cards featuring All-Stars and Prospects in six separate 10-card sets. Card fronts have a white border and a thin red line framing the player photo, with the player's name in the lower-left corner. Backs, in red and blue, include basic player identification along with the set logo and card number. Sets were marketed via a special offer printed on a card packaged in all Topps wax packs. For six special offer cards and $1.25, collectors received one of the six 10-card sets; 18 special offer cards and $7.50 earned the entire 60-card collection.

		NM/M
Complete Set (60):		4.00
Common Player:		.10
1	Andre Dawson	.20
2	Jesse Barfield	.10
3	Mike Schmidt	.75
4	Ruben Sierra	.10
5	Mike Scott	.10
6	Cal Ripken, Jr.	1.00
7	Gary Carter	.50
8	Kent Hrbek	.10
9	Kevin Seitzer	.10
10	Mike Henneman	.10
11	Don Mattingly	.65
12	Tim Raines	.10
13	Roger Clemens	.65
14	Ryne Sandberg	.60
15	Tony Fernandez	.10
16	Eric Davis	.10
17	Jack Morris	.10
18	Tim Wallach	.10
19	Mike Dunne	.10
20	Mike Greenwell	.10
21	Dwight Evans	.10
22	Darryl Strawberry	.10
23	Cory Snyder	.10
24	Pedro Guerrero	.10
25	Rickey Henderson	.50
26	Dale Murphy	.20
27	Kirby Puckett	.60
28	Steve Bedrosian	.10
29	Devon White	.10
30	Benny Santiago	.10
31	George Bell	.10
32	Keith Hernandez	.10
33	Dave Stewart	.10
34	Dave Parker	.10
35	Tom Henke	.10
36	Willie McGee	.10
37	Alan Trammell	.10
38	Tony Gwynn	.60
39	Mark McGwire	.85
40	Joe Magrane	.10
41	Jack Clark	.10
42	Willie Randolph	.10
43	Juan Samuel	.10
44	Joe Carter	.10
45	Shane Rawley	.10
46	Dave Winfield	.50
47	Ozzie Smith	.60
48	Wally Joyner	.10
49	B.J. Surhoff	.10
50	Ellis Burks	.10
51	Wade Boggs	.60
52	Howard Johnson	.10
53	George Brett	.75
54	Dwight Gooden	.10
55	Jose Canseco	.35
56	Lee Smith	.10
57	Paul Molitor	.50
58	Andres Galarraga	.10
59	Matt Nokes	.10
60	Casey Candaele	.10

American Baseball

This set, ostensibly issued for sale in the United Kingdom, was also made available for

distribution by U.S. hobby dealers. Cards were packaged in checklist-backed boxes with an American flag on the top flap. The 2-1/4" x 3" cards feature full-color photos printed on white stock. The team name, printed in team colors, intersects the red frame at the top of the card. A yellow name banner appears below the photo. Backs have blue borders and cartoon-style horizontal layouts which include a team logo, stats, caricature of the player and a one-line caption. Below the cartoon, a short "Talkin' Baseball" paragraph provides elementary information, designed to acquaint soccer-playing European collectors with baseball rules and terminology. Uncut sheets of all 88 cards are not uncommon.

		NM/M
Complete Set (88):		6.00
Common Player:		.05
Uncut Sheet:		12.00
Wax Box (48):		7.50
1	Harold Baines	.05
2	Steve Bedrosian	.05
3	George Bell	.05
4	Wade Boggs	.60
5	Barry Bonds	1.00
6	Bob Boone	.05
7	George Brett	.75
8	Hubie Brooks	.05
9	Ivan Calderon	.05
10	Jose Canseco	.35
11	Gary Carter	.50
12	Joe Carter	.05
13	Jack Clark	.05
14	Will Clark	.05
15	Roger Clemens	.75
16	Vince Coleman	.05
17	Alvin Davis	.05
18	Eric Davis	.05
19	Glenn Davis	.05
20	Andre Dawson	.20
21	Mike Dunne	.05
22	Dwight Evans	.05
23	Tony Fernandez	.05
24	John Franco	.05
25	Gary Gaetti	.05
26	Kirk Gibson	.05
27	Dwight Gooden	.05
28	Pedro Guerrero	.05
29	Tony Gwynn	.60
30	Billy Hatcher	.05
31	Rickey Henderson	.50
32	Tom Henke	.05
33	Keith Hernandez	.05
34	Orel Hershiser	.05
35	Teddy Higuera	.05
36	Charlie Hough	.05
37	Kent Hrbek	.05
38	Brook Jacoby	.05
39	Dion James	.05
40	Wally Joyner	.05
41	John Kruk	.05
42	Mark Langston	.05
43	Jeffrey Leonard	.05
44	Candy Maldonaldo	.05
45	Don Mattingly	.75
46	Willie McGee	.05
47	Mark McGwire	.85
48	Kevin Mitchell	.05
49	Paul Molitor	.50
50	Jack Morris	.05
51	Lloyd Moseby	.05
52	Dale Murphy	.20
53	Eddie Murray	.50
54	Matt Nokes	.05
55	Dave Parker	.05
56	Larry Parrish	.05
57	Kirby Puckett	.60
58	Tim Raines	.05
59	Willie Randolph	.05
60	Harold Reynolds	.05
61	Cal Ripken, Jr.	1.00
62	Nolan Ryan	1.00
63	Bret Saberhagen	.05
64	Juan Samuel	.05

65 Ryne Sandberg .60
66 Benny Santiago .75
67 Mike Schmidt .75
68 Mike Scott .05
69 Kevin Seitzer .05
70 Larry Sheets .05
71 Ruben Sierra .05
72 Ozzie Smith .60
73 Zane Smith .05
74 Cory Snyder .05
75 Dave Stewart .05
76 Darryl Strawberry .05
77 Rick Sutcliffe .05
78 Danny Tartabull .05
79 Alan Trammell .05
80 Fernando Valenzuela .05
81 Andy Van Slyke .05
82 Frank Viola .05
83 Greg Walker .05
84 Tim Wallach .05
85 Dave Winfield .50
86 Mike Witt .05
87 Robin Yount .50
88 Checklist .05

American Baseball Tiffany

This glossy "Tiffany" edition of the Topps American Baseball set is a complete parallel of the regular-issue.

NM/M
Complete Set (88): 15.00
Common Player: .40

Big Baseball

Topps Big Baseball cards (2-5/8" x 3-3/4") were issued in three series, 88 cards per series (a total set of 264 cards) sold in seven-card packs. The glossy cards are similar in format, both front and back, to the 1956 Topps set. Each card features a portrait and a game-action photo on the front, framed by a wide white border. A white outline highlights the portrait. The player's name appears at bottom on a splash of color that fades from yellow to orange to red to pink. On the card back, the player's name is printed in large red letters across the top, followed by his team name and position in black. Personal info is printed in a red rectangle beside a Topps baseball logo bearing the card number. A triple cartoon strip, in full-color, illustrates career highlights, performance, personal background, etc. A red, white and blue statistics box (pitching, batting, fielding) is printed across the bottom.

NM/M
Complete Set (264): 9.00
Common Player: .05
Wax Pack (7): .50
Wax Box, Series 1-3 (36): 9.00
1 Paul Molitor .45
2 Milt Thompson .05
3 Billy Hatcher .05
4 Mike Witt .05
5 Vince Coleman .05
6 Dwight Evans .05
7 Tim Wallach .05
8 Alan Trammell .05
9 Will Clark .05
10 Jeff Reardon .05
11 Dwight Gooden .05
12 Benny Santiago .05
13 Jose Canseco .35
14 Dale Murphy .20
15 George Bell .05
16 Ryne Sandberg .60
17 Brook Jacoby .05
18 Fernando Valenzuela .05
19 Scott Fletcher .05
20 Eric Davis .05
21 Willie Wilson .05
22 B.J. Surhoff .05
23 Steve Bedrosian .05
24 Dave Winfield .45
25 Bobby Bonilla .05
26 Larry Sheets .05
27 Ozzie Guillen .05
28 Checklist 1-88 .05
29 Nolan Ryan 1.50
30 Bob Boone .05
31 Tom Herr .05
32 Wade Boggs .60
33 Neal Heaton .05
34 Doyle Alexander .05
35 Candy Maldonado .05
36 Kirby Puckett .60
37 Gary Carter .45
38 Lance McCullers .05
39a Terry Steinbach (Black Topps logo on front.) .10
39b Terry Steinbach (White Topps logo on front.) .10
40 Gerald Perry .05
41 Tom Henke .05
42 Leon Durham .05
43 Cory Snyder .05
44 Dale Sveum .05
45 Lance Parrish .05
46 Steve Sax .05
47 Charlie Hough .05
48 Kal Daniels .05
49 Bo Jackson .10
50 Ron Guidry .05
51 Bill Doran .05
52 Wally Joyner .05
53 Terry Pendleton .05
54 Marty Barrett .05
55 Andres Galarraga .05
56 Larry Herndon .05
57 Kevin Mitchell .05
58 Greg Gagne .05
59 Keith Hernandez .05
60 John Kruk .05
61 Mike LaValliere .05
62 Cal Ripken, Jr. 1.50
63 Ivan Calderon .05
64 Alvin Davis .05
65 Luis Polonia .05
66 Robin Yount .45
67 Juan Samuel .05
68 Andres Thomas .05
69 Jeff Musselman .05
70 Jerry Mumphrey .05
71 Joe Carter .05
72 Mike Scioscia .05
73 Pete Incaviglia .05
74 Darry Larkin .05
75 Frank White .05
76 Willie Randolph .05
77 Kevin Bass .05
78 Brian Downing .05
79 Willie McGee .05
80 Ellis Burks .05
81 Hubie Brooks .05
82 Darrell Evans .05
83 Robby Thompson .05
84 Kent Hrbek .05
85 Ron Darling .05
86 Stan Jefferson .05
87 Teddy Higuera .05
88 Mike Schmidt .75
89 Barry Bonds 1.50
90 Jim Presley .05
91 Orel Hershiser .05
92 Jesse Barfield .05
93 Tom Candiotti .05
94 Bret Saberhagen .05
95 Jose Uribe .05
96 Tom Browning .05
97 Johnny Ray .05
98 Mike Morgan .05
100 Jim Sundberg .05
101 Roger McDowell .05
102 Randy Ready .05
103 Mike Gallego .05
104 Steve Buechele .05
105 Greg Walker .05
106 Jose Lind .05
107 Steve Trout .05
108 Rick Rhoden .05
109 Jim Pankovits .05
110 Ken Griffey .05
111 Danny Cox .05
112 Franklin Stubbs .05
113 Lloyd Moseby .05
114 Mel Hall .05
115 Kevin Seitzer .05
116 Tim Raines .05
117 Juan Castillo .05
118 Roger Clemens .75
119 Mike Aldrete .05
120 Mario Soto .05
121 Jack Howell .05
122 Rick Schu .05
123 Jeff Robinson .05
124 Doug Drabek .05
125 Henry Cotto .05
126 Checklist 89-176 .05
127 Gary Gaetti .05
128 Rick Sutcliffe .05
129 Howard Johnson .05
130 Chris Brown .05
131 Dave Henderson .05
132 Curt Wilkerson .05
133 Mike Marshall .05
134 Kelly Gruber .05
135 Julio Franco .05
136 Kurt Stillwell .05
137 Donnie Hill .05
138 Mike Pagliarulo .05
139 Von Hayes .05
140 Mike Scott .05
141 Bob Kipper .05
142 Harold Reynolds .05
143 Bob Brenly .05
144 Dave Concepcion .05
145 Devon White .05
146 Jeff Stone .05
147 Chet Lemon .05
148 Ozzie Virgil .05
149 Todd Worrell .05
150 Mitch Webster .05
151 Rob Deer .05
152 Rich Gedman .05
153 Andre Dawson .20
154 Mike Davis .05
155 Nelson Liriano .05
156 Greg Swindell .05
157 George Brett .75
158 Kevin McReynolds .05
159 Brian Fisher .05
160 Mike Kingery .05
161 Tony Gwynn .60
162 Don Baylor .05
163 Jerry Browne .05
164 Dan Pasqua .05
165 Rickey Henderson .45
166 Brett Butler .05
167 Nick Esasky .05
168 Kirk McCaskill .05
169 Fred Lynn .05
170 Jack Morris .05
171 Pedro Guerrero .05
172 Dave Stieb .05
173 Pat Tabler .05
174 Floyd Bannister .05
175 Rafael Belliard .05
176 Mark Langston .05
177 Greg Mathews .05
178 Claudell Washington .05
179 Mark McGwire 1.00
180 Bert Blyleven .05
181 Jim Rice .15
182 Mookie Wilson .05
183 Willie Fraser .05
184 Andy Van Slyke .05
185 Matt Nokes .05
186 Eddie Whitson .05
187 Tony Fernandez .05
188 Rick Reuschel .05
189 Ken Phelps .05
190 Juan Nieves .05
191 Kirk Gibson .05
192 Glenn Davis .05
193 Zane Smith .05
194 Jose DeLeon .05
195 Gary Ward .05
196 Pascual Perez .05
197 Carlton Fisk .45
198 Oddibe McDowell .05
199 Mark Gubicza .05
200 Glenn Hubbard .05
201 Frank Viola .05
202 Jody Reed .05
203 Len Dykstra .05
204 Dick Schofield .05
205 Sid Bream .05
206 Guillermo Hernandez .05
207 Keith Moreland .05
208 Mark Eichhorn .05
209 Rene Gonzales .05
210 Dave Valle .05
211 Tom Brunansky .05
212 Charles Hudson .05
213 John Farrell .05
214 Jeff Treadway .05
215 Eddie Murray .45
216 Checklist 177-264 .05
217 Greg Brock .05
218 John Shelby .05
219 Craig Reynolds .05
220 Dion James .05
221 Carney Lansford .05
222 Juan Berenguer .05
223 Luis Rivera .05
224 Harold Baines .05
225 Shawon Dunston .05
226 Luis Aguayo .05
227 Pete O'Brien .05
228 Ozzie Smith .60
229 Don Mattingly .75
230 Danny Tartabull .05
231 Andy Allanson .05
232 John Franco .05
233 Mike Greenwell .05
234 Bob Ojeda .05
235 Chili Davis .05
236 Mike Dunne .05
237 Jim Morrison .05
238 Carmelo Martinez .05
239 Ernie Whitt .05
240 Scott Garrelts .05
241 Mike Moore .05
242 Dave Parker .05
243 Tim Laudner .05
244 Bill Wegman .05
245 Bob Horner .05
246 Rafael Santana .05
247 Alfredo Griffin .05
248 Mark Bailey .05
249 Ron Gant .05
250 Bryn Smith .05
251 Lance Johnson .05
252 Sam Horn .05
253 Darryl Strawberry .05
254 Chuck Finley .05
255 Darnell Coles .05
256 Mike Henneman .05
257 Andy Hawkins .05
258 Jim Clancy .05
259 Atlee Hammaker .05
260 Glenn Wilson .05
261 Larry McWilliams .05
262 Jack Clark .05
263 Walt Weiss .05
264 Gene Larkin .05

Cloth Experimental

This is a true experimental issue from Topps: Baseball cards printed on heavy textured paper, much like high-quality paper towels. The cloth cards are the standard 2-1/2" x 3-1/2" in size and feature the fronts as used on Topps' regular '88 baseball card issue. Overprinted across the fronts of some cards are parts of the legend, "SAMPLE ONLY NOT FOR SALE." Backs are blank, and unlike earlier Topps cloth issues, are not gummed for use as stickers. The checklist is presented here in alphabetical order.

NM/M
Complete Set (121): 600.00
Uncut Sheet (121): 500.00
Common Player: 8.00
(1) A's Team Leaders (Jose Canseco, Mark McGwire) 30.00
(2) Rick Aguilera 8.00
(3) Andy Allanson 8.00
(4) Tony Armas 8.00
(5) Keith Atherton 8.00
(6) Steve Balboni 8.00
(7) Billy Bean 8.00
(8) Steve Bedrosian/AS 8.00
(9) George Bell/AS 8.00
(10) Bruce Benedict 8.00
(11) Dave Bergman 8.00
(12) Mike Bielecki 8.00
(13) Tim Birtsas 8.00
(14) Bruce Bochy 8.00
(15) Wade Boggs/AS 40.00
(16) Rod Booker 8.00
(17) Dennis Boyd 8.00
(18) Braves Leaders (Ken Griffey, Dion James, Dale Murphy, Gerald Perry) 15.00
(19) Tom Browning 8.00
(20) Carmen Castillo 8.00
(21) Rick Cerone 8.00
(22) Jack Clark/AS 8.00
(23) Mark Clear 8.00
(24) Roger Clemens/AS 75.00
(25) Pat Clements 8.00
(26) Keith Comstock 8.00
(27) Cecil Cooper 8.00
(28) Joey Cora 8.00
(29) Ed Correa 8.00
(30) Mark Davidson 8.00
(31) Mark Davis 8.00
(32) Jeff Dedmon 8.00
(33) Jim Dwyer 8.00
(34) Doc Edwards 8.00
(35) John Farrell 8.00
(36) Mike Felder 8.00
(37) Curt Ford 8.00
(38) Bob Forsch 8.00
(39) Damaso Garcia 8.00
(40) Tom Glavine 45.00
(41) Mark Grant 8.00
(42) Tony Gwynn (AS) 40.00
(43) Drew Hall 8.00
(44) Jeff Hamilton 8.00
(45) Mike Hart 8.00
(46) Andy Hawkins 8.00
(47) Ed Hearn 8.00
(48) Tom Henke (AS) 8.00
(49) Whitey Herzog 8.00
(50) Shawn Hillegas 8.00
(51) Charles Hudson 8.00
(52) Dave Johnson 8.00
(53) Ron Karkovice 8.00
(54) Pat Keedy 8.00
(55) Jimmy Key (AS) 8.00
(56) Mark Kiefer 8.00
(57) Bob Kipper 8.00
(58) Les Lancaster 8.00
(59) Ken Landreaux 8.00
(60) Craig Lefferts 8.00
(61) Jim Leyland 8.00
(62) Jose Lind 8.00
(63) Gary Lucas 8.00
(64) Frank Lucchesi 8.00
(65) Barry Lyons 8.00
(66) John Marzano 8.00
(67) Greg Mathews 8.00
(68) Don Mattingly/AS 75.00
(69) Len Matuszek 8.00
(70) Kirk McCaskill 8.00
(71) Terry McGriff 8.00
(72) Joey Meyer 8.00
(73) John Mitchell 8.00
(74) Jeff Montgomery 8.00
(75) John Morris 8.00
(76) John Moses 8.00
(77) Tom Nieto 8.00
(78) Matt Nokes/AS 8.00
(79) Charlie O'Brien 8.00
(80) Ed Olwine 8.00
(81) Paul O'Neill 8.00
(82) Steve Ontiveros 8.00
(83) Pat Pacillo 8.00
(84) Tom Pagnozzi 8.00
(85) Jim Pankovitz 8.00
(86) Bill Pecota 8.00
(87) Geno Petralli 8.00
(88) Eric Plunk 8.00
(89) Gus Polidor 8.00
(90) Dennis Powell 8.00
(91) Terry Puhl 8.00
(92) Charlie Puleo 8.00
(93) Shane Rawley/AS 8.00
(94) Rick Rodriguez 8.00
(95) Ron Roenicke 8.00
(96) Pete Rose 200.00
(97) Lenn Sakata 8.00
(98) Joe Sambito 8.00
(99) Juan Samuel/AS 8.00
(100) Rafael Santana 8.00
(101) Dan Schatzeder 8.00
(102) Pat Sheridan 8.00
(103) Steve Shields 8.00
(104) Ted Simmons 8.00
(105) Doug Sisk 8.00
(106) Joel Skinner 8.00
(107) Ozzie Smith/AS 40.00
(108) Chris Speier 8.00
(109) Jim Sundberg 8.00
(110) Don Sutton 15.00
(111) Chuck Tanner 8.00
(112) Mickey Tettleton 8.00
(113) Tim Teufel 8.00
(114) Gary Thurman 8.00
(115) Alex Trevino 8.00
(116) Mike Trujillo 8.00
(117) Twins Leaders (Gary Gaetti, Kent Hrbek) 20.00
(118) Tim Wallach/AS 8.00
(119) Frank Williams 8.00
(120) Dave Winfield/AS 25.00
(121) Butch Wynegar 8.00

Coins

This edition of 60 lightweight metal coins is similar in design to Topps' 1964 set. The 1988 coins are 1-1/2" in diameter and feature full-color player portraits under crimped edges in silver, gold and pink. Curved under the photo is a red and white player name banner pinned by two gold stars. Coin backs list the coin number, player name, personal information and career summary in black letters on a silver background.

NM/M
Factory Boxed Set (60): 20.00
Complete Set (60): 10.00
Common Player: .15
Wax Pack (3): .45
Wax Box (36): 10.00
1 George Bell .15
2 Roger Clemens 1.00
3 Mark McGwire 1.25
4 Wade Boggs .75
5 Harold Baines .15
6 Ivan Calderon .15
7 Jose Canseco .45
8 Joe Carter .15
9 Jack Clark .15
10 Alvin Davis .15
11 Dwight Evans .15
12 Tony Fernandez .15
13 Gary Gaetti .15
14 Mike Greenwell .15
15 Charlie Hough .15
16 Wally Joyner .15
17 Jimmy Key .15
18 Mark Langston .15
19 Don Mattingly 1.00
20 Paul Molitor .60
21 Jack Morris .15
22 Eddie Murray .60
23 Kirby Puckett .75
24 Cal Ripken, Jr. 1.50
25 Bret Saberhagen .15
26 Ruben Sierra .15
27 Cory Snyder .15
28 Terry Steinbach .15
29 Danny Tartabull .15
30 Alan Trammell .15
31 Devon White .15
32 Robin Yount .60
33 Andre Dawson .30
34 Steve Bedrosian .15
35 Benny Santiago .15
36 Tony Gwynn .75
37 Bobby Bonilla .15
38 Will Clark .15
39 Eric Davis .15
40 Mike Dunne .15
41 John Franco .15
42 Dwight Gooden .15
43 Pedro Guerrero .15
44 Dion James .15
45 John Kruk .15
46 Jeffrey Leonard .15
47 Carmelo Martinez .15
48 Dale Murphy .30
49 Tim Raines .15
50 Nolan Ryan 1.50
51 Juan Samuel .15
52 Ryne Sandberg .75
53 Mike Schmidt 1.00
54 Mike Scott .15
55 Ozzie Smith .75
56 Darryl Strawberry .15
57 Rick Sutcliffe .15
58 Fernando Valenzuela .15
59 Tim Wallach .15
60 Todd Worrell .15

Gallery of Champions

These metal replicas are exact reproductions at one-quarter scale of Topps 1988 cards, both front and back. The set includes 12 three-dimensional raised metal cards packaged in a velvet-lined case that bears the title of the set in gold embossed letters. A deluxe limited edition of the set (1,000) was produced in in sterling silver and an economy version in aluminum. A Mark McGwire pewter replica was given as a premium to dealers ordering the aluminum, bronze and silver sets. The special pewter card is distinguished from the regular issue by a diagonal name banner in the lower-right corner; regular replicas have a rectangular name banner parallel to the lower edge of the card.

NM/M
Complete Aluminum Set (12): 10.00
Complete Bronze Set (12): 60.00
Complete Silver Set (12): 140.00
(1a) Steve Bedrosian/Aluminum .50
(1b) Steve Bedrosian/Bronze 1.50
(1s) Steve Bedrosian/Silver 6.00
(2a) George Bell/Aluminum .50
(2b) George Bell/Bronze 1.50
(2s) George Bell/Silver 6.00
(3a) Wade Boggs/Aluminum 1.50
(3b) Wade Boggs/Bronze 6.00
(3s) Wade Boggs/Silver 20.00
(4a) Jack Clark/Aluminum .50
(4b) Jack Clark/Bronze 1.50
(4s) Jack Clark/Silver 6.00
(5a) Roger Clemens/Aluminum 2.00

(5b)	Roger Clemens/Bronze	10.00
(5s)	Roger Clemens/Silver	25.00
(6a)	Andre Dawson/Aluminum	1.00
(6b)	Andre Dawson/Bronze	2.50
(6s)	Andre Dawson/Silver	9.00
(7a)	Tony Gwynn/Aluminum	1.50
(7b)	Tony Gwynn/Bronze	6.00
(7s)	Tony Gwynn/Silver	20.00
(8a)	Mark Langston/Aluminum	.50
(8b)	Mark Langston/Bronze	1.50
(8s)	Mark Langston/Silver	6.00
(9a)	Mark McGwire/Aluminum	2.50
(9b)	Mark McGwire/Bronze	12.50
(9s)	Mark McGwire/Silver	25.00
(9p)	Mark McGwire/Pewter	13.50
(10a)	Dave Righetti/Aluminum	.50
(10b)	Dave Righetti/Bronze	1.50
(10s)	Dave Righetti/Silver	6.00
(11a)	Nolan Ryan/Aluminum	3.00
(11b)	Nolan Ryan/Bronze	15.00
(11s)	Nolan Ryan/Silver	30.00
(12a)	Benny Santiago/Aluminum	.50
(12b)	Benny Santiago/Bronze	1.50
(12s)	Benny Santiago/Silver	6.00

Glossy Rookies

The Topps 1988 Rookies special insert cards follow the same basic design as the All-Star inserts. The set consists of 22 standard-size cards found one per pack in 100-card jumbo cellos. Large, glossy color player photos are printed on a white background below a red, yellow and blue "1987 Rookies" banner. A red and yellow player name appears beneath the photo. Red, white and blue card backs bear the title of the special insert set, the Rookies logo emblem, player name and card number.

		NM/M
Complete Set (22):		3.00
Common Player:		.05
1	Billy Ripken	.05
2	Ellis Burks	.05
3	Mike Greenwell	.05
4	DeWayne Buice	.05
5	Devon White	.05
6	Fred Manrique	.05
7	Mike Henneman	.05
8	Matt Nokes	.05
9	Kevin Seitzer	.05
10	B.J. Surhoff	.05
11	Casey Candaele	.05
12	Randy Myers	.05
13	Mark McGwire	2.50
14	Luis Polonia	.05
15	Terry Steinbach	.05
16	Mike Dunne	.05
17	Al Pedrique	.05
18	Benny Santiago	.05
19	Kelly Downs	.05
20	Joe Magrane	.05
21	Jerry Browne	.05
22	Jeff Musselman	.05

Mini League Leaders

The third consecutive issue of Topps mini-cards (2-1/8" x 3") includes 77 cards spotlighting the top five ranked pitchers and batters. This set is unique in that it was the first time Topps included full-color player photos on both the front and back. Glossy action shots on the card fronts fade into a white border

with a Topps logo in an upper corner. The player's name is printed in bold black letters beneath the photo. Horizontal reverses feature circular player photos on a blue and white background with the card number, player name, personal information, 1987 ranking and lifetime/1987 stats printed in red, black and yellow lettering.

		NM/M
Complete Set (77):		3.00
Common Player:		.05
Wax Pack (7):		.30
Wax Box (36):		6.00
1	Wade Boggs	.60
2	Roger Clemens	.65
3	Dwight Evans	.05
4	DeWayne Buice	.05
5	Brian Downing	.05
6	Wally Joyner	.05
7	Ivan Calderon	.05
8	Carlton Fisk	.50
9	Gary Redus	.05
10	Darrell Evans	.05
11	Jack Morris	.05
12	Alan Trammell	.05
13	Lou Whitaker	.05
14	Bret Saberhagen	.05
15	Kevin Seitzer	.05
16	Danny Tartabull	.05
17	Willie Wilson	.05
18	Teddy Higuera	.05
19	Paul Molitor	.50
20	Dan Plesac	.05
21	Robin Yount	.50
22	Kent Hrbek	.05
23	Kirby Puckett	.60
24	Jeff Reardon	.05
25	Frank Viola	.05
26	Rickey Henderson	.50
27	Don Mattingly	.65
28	Willie Randolph	.05
29	Dave Righetti	.05
30	Jose Canseco	.35
31	Mark McGwire	.75
32	Dave Stewart	.05
33	Phil Bradley	.05
34	Mark Langston	.05
35	Harold Reynolds	.05
36	Charlie Hough	.05
37	George Bell	.05
38	Tom Henke	.05
39	Jimmy Key	.05
40	Dion James	.05
41	Dale Murphy	.20
42	Zane Smith	.05
43	Andre Dawson	.20
44	Lee Smith	.05
45	Rick Sutcliffe	.05
46	Eric Davis	.05
47	John Franco	.05
48	Dave Parker	.05
49	Billy Hatcher	.05
50	Nolan Ryan	1.00
51	Mike Scott	.05
52	Pedro Guerrero	.05
53	Orel Hershiser	.05
54	Fernando Valenzuela	.05
55	Bob Welch	.05
56	Andres Galarraga	.05
57	Tim Raines	.05
58	Tim Wallach	.05
59	Len Dykstra	.05
60	Dwight Gooden	.05
61	Howard Johnson	.05
62	Roger McDowell	.05
63	Darryl Strawberry	.05
64	Steve Bedrosian	.05
65	Shane Rawley	.05
66	Juan Samuel	.05
67	Mike Schmidt	.65
68	Mike Dunne	.05
69	Jack Clark	.05
70	Vince Coleman	.05
71	Willie McGee	.05
72	Ozzie Smith	.50
73	Todd Worrell	.05
74	Tony Gwynn	.60
75	John Kruk	.05
76	Rick Rueschel	.05
77	Checklist	.05

Stickercards

Actually a part of the 1988 Topps Stickers issue, this set consists of 67 cards. The cards are the backs of the peel-off stickers and measure 2-1/8" x 3". To determine total value, combine the prices of the stickers (found in the 1988 Topps Stickers checklist) on the stickercard front with the value assigned to the sticker-card in the following checklist.

		NM/M
Complete Set (67):		3.00
Common Player:		.05
1	Jack Clark	.05
2	Andres Galarraga	.05
3	Keith Hernandez	.05
4	Tom Herr	.05
5	Juan Samuel	.05
6	Ryne Sandberg	.50
7	Terry Pendleton	.05
8	Mike Schmidt	.60
9	Tim Wallach	.05
10	Hubie Brooks	.05
11	Shawon Dunston	.05
12	Ozzie Smith	.50
13	Andre Dawson	.20
14	Eric Davis	.05
15	Pedro Guerrero	.05
16	Tony Gwynn	.50
17	Jeffrey Leonard	.05
18	Dale Murphy	.20
19	Dave Parker	.05
20	Tim Raines	.05
21	Darryl Strawberry	.05
22	Gary Carter	.40
23	Jody Davis	.05
24	Ozzie Virgil	.05
25	Dwight Gooden	.05
26	Mike Scott	.05
27	Rick Sutcliffe	.05
28	Sid Fernandez	.05
29	Neal Heaton	.05
30	Fernando Valenzuela	.05
31	Steve Bedrosian	.05
32	John Franco	.05
33	Lee Smith	.05
34	Wally Joyner	.05
35	Don Mattingly	.60
36	Mark McGwire	.65
37	Willie Randolph	.05
38	Lou Whitaker	.05
39	Frank White	.05
40	Wade Boggs	.50
41	George Brett	.60
42	Paul Molitor	.40
43	Tony Fernandez	.05
44	Cal Ripken, Jr.	.75
45	Alan Trammell	.05
46	Jesse Barfield	.05
47	George Bell	.05
48	Jose Canseco	.35
49	Joe Carter	.05
50	Dwight Evans	.05
51	Rickey Henderson	.40
52	Kirby Puckett	.50
53	Cory Snyder	.05
54	Dave Winfield	.40
55	Terry Kennedy	.05
56	Matt Nokes	.05
57	B.J. Surhoff	.05
58	Roger Clemens	.60
59	Jack Morris	.05
60	Bret Saberhagen	.05
61	Ron Guidry	.05
62	Bruce Hurst	.05
63	Mark Langston	.05
64	Tom Henke	.05
65	Dan Plesac	.05
66	Dave Righetti	.05
67	Checklist	.05

Stickers

This set of 313 stickers (on 198 cards) offers an addition for 1988 - 66 different players are pictured on the backs of the sticker cards. The stickers come in two sizes (2-1/8" x 3" or 1-1/2" x 2-1/8"). Larger stickers fill an entire

card, smaller ones are attached in pairs. A 36-page sticker yearbook with Mark McGwire on the cover has a designated space inside for each sticker, with one page per team and special pages of 1987 Highlights, World Series, All-Stars and Future Stars. No printing appears on the full-color action shot stickers except for a small black number in the lower left corner. Stickers were sold in packs of five (with gum) for 25 cents per pack. Unlike the 1987 Topps Stickers set, different pairings can be found, rather than the same two players/numbers always sharing the same sticker. To determine total value, combine the value of the stickercard (found in the 1988 Topps Stickercard checklist) with the values assigned the stickers in the following checklist.

		NM/M
Complete Set (313):		10.00
Common Player:		.05
Sticker Album:		1.50
Wax Pack (5):		.25
Wax Box (48):		7.00
1-263	1987 Highlights (Mark McGwire, Willie Wilson)	.25
2-304	1987 Highlights (Benny Santiago, Al Pedrique (Future Star))	.05
3-187	1987 Highlights (Don Mattingly, Ernie Whitt)	.20
4-223	1987 Highlights (Vince Coleman, Gary Matthews)	.05
5-272	1987 Highlights (Bob Boone, Jim Morrison)	.05
6-278	1987 Highlights (Steve Bedrosian, Tim Laudner)	.05
7-276	1987 Highlights (Nolan Ryan, Bert Blyleven)	.30
8-306	1987 Highlights (Darrell Evans, Kevin Seitzer (Future Star))	.05
9-255	1987 Highlights (Mike Schmidt, Frank White)	.15
10-256	1987 Highlights (Don Baylor, Dan Quisenberry)	.05
11-145	1987 Highlights (Eddie Murray, Dennis Rasmussen)	.10
12-237	1987 Highlights (Juan Beniquez, Oddibe McDowell)	.05
13	1987 Championship Series (John Tudor)	.05
14	1987 Championship Series (Jeff Reardon)	.05
15	1987 Championship Series (Tom Brunansky)	.05
16	1987 Championship Series (Jeffrey Leonard)	.05
17	1987 Championship Series (Gary Gaetti)	.05
18	1987 Championship Series (Cardinals Celebrate)	.05
19	1987 World Series (Danny Gladden)	.05
20	1987 World Series (Bert Blyleven)	.05
21	1987 World Series (John Tudor)	.05
22	1987 World Series (Tom Lawless)	.05
23	1987 World Series (Curt Ford)	.05
24	1987 World Series (Kent Hrbek)	.05
25	1987 World Series (Frank Viola)	.05
26-216	Dave Smith, Edwin Nunez	.05
27-240	Jim Deshaies, Pete O'Brien	.05
28-171	Billy Hatcher, Mike Davis	.05
29-196	Kevin Bass, Teddy Higuera	.05
30	Mike Scott	.05
31-224	Danny Walling, Eric Bell	.05
32-185	Alan Ashby, Willie Upshaw	.05
33-292	Ken Caminiti, Greg Walker	.05
34-245	Bill Doran, Dwight Evans	.05
35	Glenn Davis	.05
36	Ozzie Virgil	.05
37-260	Ken Oberkfell, Charlie Leibrandt	.05
38-183	Ken Griffey, Devon White	.05
39-287	Albert Hall, Ken Williams	.05
40-310	Zane Smith, Ellis Burks (Future Star)	.05
41-207	Andres Thomas, Julio Franco	.05
42-178	Dion James, Gary Pettis	.05
43-249	Jim Acker, Mike Greenwell	.05
44-226	Tom Glavine, Dave Schmidt	.20
45	Dale Murphy	.20
46	Jack Clark	.05
47-269	Vince Coleman, Matt Nokes	.05
48-221	Ricky Horton, Harold Reynolds	.05
49-303	Terry Pendleton, Gary Ward	.05
50-271	Tom Herr, Eric King	.05
51-265	Joe Magrane, Darrell Evans	.05
52-211	Tony Pena, Brook Jacoby	.05
53-298	Ozzie Smith, Rick Rhoden	.40
54-169	Todd Worrell, Alfredo Griffin	.05
55	Willie McGee	.05
56	Andre Dawson	.25
57-225	Ryne Sandberg, Terry Kennedy	.35
58-291	Keith Moreland, Richard Dotson	.05
59-198	Greg Maddux, Rob Deer	.40
60-290	Jody Davis, Carlton Fisk	.25
61	Rick Sutcliffe	.05
62-295	Jamie Moyer, Mike Pagliarulo	.05
63-172	Leon Durham, Luis Polonia	.05
64-313	Lee Smith, Devon White (Future Star)	.05
65-250	Shawon Dunston, Ellis Burks	.05
66-257	Franklin Stubbs, Danny Tartabull	.05
67-235	Mike Scioscia, Steve Buechele	.05
68-177	Orel Hershiser, Dick Schofield	.05
69-289	Mike Marshall, Bob James	.05
70	Fernando Valenzuela	.05
71-281	Mickey Hatcher, Danny Gladden	.05
72-166	Matt Young, Jay Howell	.05
73-236	Bob Welch, Charlie Hough	.05
74-170	Steve Sax, Dennis Eckersley	.25
75	Pedro Guerrero	.05
76	Tim Raines	.05
77-252	Casey Candaele, Rich Gedman	.05
78-248	Mike Fitzgerald, Marty Barrett	.05
79-301	Andres Galarraga, Claudell Washington	.05
80-212	Neal Heaton, Brett Butler	.05
81-296	Hubie Brooks, Ron Guidry	.05
82-258	Floyd Youmans, Bo Jackson	.10
83-201	Herm Winningham, Robin Yount	.25
84-307	Denny Martinez, Mike Dunne (Future Star)	.05
85	Tim Wallach	.05
86	Jeffrey Leonard	.05
87-251	Will Clark, Roger Clemens	.45
88-288	Kevin Mitchell, Jim Winn	.05
89-267	Mike Aldrete, Kirk Gibson	.05
90-191	Scott Garrelts, Dave Steib	.05
91-231	Jose Uribe, Mike Boddicker	.05
92-246	Bob Brenly, Sam Horn	.05
93-189	Robby Thompson, Lloyd Moseby	.05
94-217	Don Robinson, Jim Presley	.05
95	Candy Maldonado	.05
96	Darryl Strawberry	.05
97-192	Keith Hernandez, Jesse Barfield	.05
98-220	Ron Darling, Dave Valle	.05
99-218	Howard Johnson, Phil Bradley	.05
100-190	Roger McDowell, Jimmy Key	.05
101	Dwight Gooden	.05
102-165	Kevin McReynolds, Tony Phillips	.05
103-275	Sid Fernandez, Tom Brunansky	.05
104-241	Dave Magadan, Scott Fletcher	.05
105-167	Gary Carter, Carney Lansford	.25
106-302	Carmelo Martinez, Dave Winfield	.25
107-205	Eddie Whitson, Mel Hall	.05
108-180	Tim Flannery, DeWayne Buice	.05
109-266	Stan Jefferson, Bill Madlock	.05
110	John Kruk	.05
111-168	Chris Brown, Dave Stewart	.05
112-215	Benny Santiago, Rey Quinones	.05
113-270	Garry Templeton, Lou Whitaker	.05
114-186	Lance McCullers, Tom Henke	.05
115	Tony Gwynn	.50
116	Steve Bedrosian	.05
117-247	Von Hayes, Jim Rice	.10
118-279	Kevin Gross, Gene Larkin	.05
119-238	Bruce Ruffin, Mike Stanley	.05
120-184	Juan Samuel, Jim Clancy	.05
121-182	Shane Rawley, Bob Boone	.05
122-222	Chris James, Scott Bradley	.05
123-199	Lance Parrish, Dale Sveum	.05
124-181	Glenn Wilson, Brian Downing	.05
125	Mike Schmidt	.60
126	Andy Van Slyke	.05
127-297	Jose Lind, Rickey Henderson	.05
128-176	Al Pedrique, Greg Minton	.05
129-277	Bobby Bonilla, Gary Gaetti	.05
130-175	Sid Bream, Jack Howell	.05
131-230	Mike LaValliere, Larry Sheets	.05
132-197	Mike Dunne, Glenn Braggs	.05
133-232	Jeff Robinson, Tom Niedenfuer	.05
134-195	Doug Drabek, Jim Gantner	.05
135	Barry Bonds	.75
136	Dave Parker	.05
137-208	Nick Esasky, Cory Snyder	.05
138-280	Buddy Bell, Jeff Reardon	.05
139-239	Kal Daniels, Pete Incaviglia	.05
140-285	Barry Larkin, Ivan Calderon	.05
141	Eric Davis	.05
142-227	John Franco, Billy Ripken	.05
143-229	Bo Diaz, Ray Knight	.05
144-261	Ron Oester, Kevin Seitzer	.05
146	Eric Davis/AS	.05
147	Ryne Sandberg/AS	.30
148	Andre Dawson/AS	.15
149	Mike Schmidt/AS	.40
150	Jack Clark/AS	.05
151	Darryl Strawberry/AS	.05
152	Gary Carter/AS	.35
153	Ozzie Smith/AS	.35
154	Mike Scott/AS	.05
155	Rickey Henderson/AS	.35
156	Don Mattingly/AS	.40
157	Wade Boggs/AS	.30
158	George Bell/AS	.05
159	Dave Winfield/AS	.35
160	Cal Ripken, Jr./AS	.50

161	Terry Kennedy/AS	.05
162	Willie Randolph/AS	.05
163	Bret Saberhagen/AS	.05
164	Mark McGwire	.65
173	Jose Canseco	.35
174	Mike Witt	.05
179	Wally Joyner	.05
188	George Bell	.05
193	Tony Fernandez	.05
194	Paul Molitor	.40
200-308	Bill Wegman, Jeff Musselman (Future Star)	.05
202-309	B.J. Surhoff, Mark McGwire (Future Star)	.50
203	Dan Plesac	.05
204	Pat Tabler	.05
206-305	Scott Bailes, Casey Candaele (Future Star)	.05
209-312	Chris Bando, Mike Greenwell (Future Star)	.05
210-311	Greg Swindell, Matt Nokes (Future Star)	.05
213	Joe Carter	.05
214	Mark Langston	.05
219	Alvin Davis	.05
228	Cal Ripken, Jr.	.75
233	Eddie Murray	.40
234	Ruben Sierra	.05
242-300	Dale Mohorcic, Dave Righetti	.05
243	Larry Parrish	.05
244	Wade Boggs	.40
253	Bruce Hurst	.05
254	Bret Saberhagen	.05
259	George Brett	.50
262-282	Mark Gubicza, Frank Viola	.05
264-286	Frank Tanana, Donnie Hill	.05
268	Jack Morris	.05
273	Alan Trammell	.05
274	Kent Hrbek	.05
283	Kirby Puckett	.50
284	Ozzie Guillen	.05
293	Harold Baines	.05
294	Willie Randolph	.05
299	Don Mattingly	.50

Campbell's Richie Ashburn Tribute Sheet

Longtime Phillies star, Hall of Famer and broadcaster Richie Ashburn was honored for his 40 years in baseball by the issue of a commemorative card set in the form of a 10" x 14" poster given away as a stadium promotion. A 5" x 7" card picturing the 61-year old Ashburn was at center, with his complete major league stats on back. Surrounding the center card and separated by perforations are reproductions of 12 of Ashburn's baseball cards. The cards are reduced to about 75 percent of actual size and shown on an American flag background. The back of each card is also reproduced, with a cartoon figure of the Campbell's Kid baseball player included on front and back.

	NM/M
Complete Set (Sheet):	25.00
Complete Set, Singles (13):	20.00
Common Card:	2.00
1952 Bowman	2.00
1952 Topps	2.00
1954 Topps	2.00
1956 Topps	2.00
1957 Topps	2.00
1958 Topps	2.00
1959 Topps	2.00
1959 Topps (N.L. Hitting Kings)	2.00
1960 Topps	2.00
1961 Topps	2.00
1962 Topps	2.00
1963 Topps	2.00
Richie Ashburn (1988 Portrait)	2.00

Sports Shots Portfolios

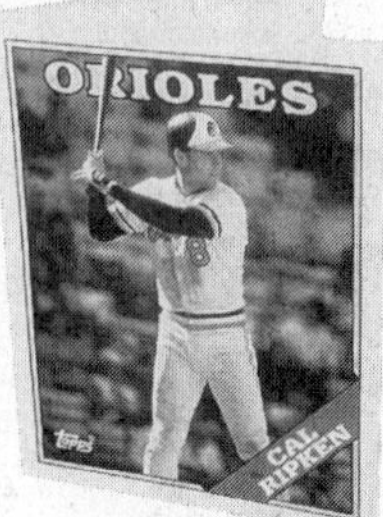

One hundred and thirty of the biggest names from Topps' 1988 baseball card set were reproduced in the form of 9-1/2" x 11-3/4" cardboard folders. The folders reproduce both front and back of the '88 Topps cards and open to offer two pockets for storage. Various manufacturer and licensor logos are the only printing inside. The folders carried a suggested retail price of $1 apiece and were distributed in either team packs or all-star assortments of 50 pieces each. By 1992, the folders were being wholesaled within the hobby at less than 30 cents apiece.

		NM/M
Complete Set (130):		60.00
Common Player:		.50
10	Ryne Sandberg	2.50
15	Chili Davis	.50
25	Andres Galarraga	.50
35	Harold Baines	.50
39	Gerald Perry	.50
40	Orel Hershiser	.50
45	Kent Hrbek	.50
50	Hubie Brooks	.50
55	Phil Bradley	.50
60	Rickey Henderson	2.00
70	Roger Clemens	3.00
75	Joe Carter	.50
80	Mark Langston	.50
90	Dale Murphy	1.00
95	Lance Parrish	.50
100	Jack Clark	.50
102	Barry Larkin	.50
110	Teddy Higuera	.50
118	Bob Welch	.50
120	Kirby Puckett	2.50
130	Buddy Bell	.50
138	Mitch Webster	.50
140	Jesse Barfield	.50
142	Andy Van Slyke	.50
150	Eric Davis	.50
165	Robin Yount	2.00
170	Goose Gossage	.50
180	Terry Kennedy	.50
184	Ivan Calderon	.50
192	Devon White	.50
193	Brian Fisher	.50
195	Dan Quisenberry	.50
197	Lance McCullers	.50
200	Wade Boggs	2.50
210	Willie Randolph	.50
215	Von Hayes	.50
230	Pat Tabler	.50
238	Luis Polonia	.50
240	Lee Smith	.50
250	Nolan Ryan	4.00
260	Vince Coleman	.50
265	Bo Diaz	.50
270	Mike Witt	.50
280	Pete Incaviglia	.50
285	Jim Presley	.50
297	Zane Smith	.50
300	Don Mattingly	3.00
305	Steve Sax	.50
306	Billy Hatcher	.50
320	Alan Trammell	.50
327	Larry Sheets	.50
331	Brian Downing	.50
340	Jack Morris	.50
343	Greg Gagne	.50
350	Will Clark	.50
360	Tony Gwynn	2.50
370	Jose Canseco	1.00
385	Carlton Fisk	2.00
408	Dion James	.50
410	Tony Pena	.50
420	Wally Joyner	.50
424	Dwayne Murphy	.50
430	Glenn Davis	.50
440	Steve Bedrosian	.50
450	Barry Bonds	4.00
452	Willie Wilson	.50
460	Ozzie Smith	2.50
465	Paul Molitor	2.00
470	Dwight Evans	.50
476	Dave Stewart	.50
479	Brett Butler	.50
480	Dwight Gooden	.50
485	Harold Reynolds	.50
490	Larry Parrish	.50
491	B.J. Surhoff	.50
495	Eddie Murray	2.00
497	Kevin Mitchell	.50
500	Andre Dawson	1.00
510	Dave Winfield	2.00
525	Marty Barrett	.50
530	Gary Carter	2.00
540	Bret Saberhagen	.50
550	Pedro Guerrero	.50
555	Brook Jacoby	.50
560	Tim Wallach	.50
565	Lloyd Moseby	.50
570	Jeffrey Leonard	.50
578	Gary Gaetti	.50
580	Mark McGwire	3.50
590	George Bell	.50
596	John Kruk	.50
600	Mike Schmidt	3.00
605	Kirk Gibson	.50
610	Keith Hernandez	.50
613	Bobby Thigpen	.50
615	Jody Davis	.50
619	Mike Dunne	.50
620	Cory Snyder	.50
625	Frank Viola	.50
645	Matt Nokes	.50
649	De Wayne Buice	.50
650	Cal Ripken Jr.	4.00
660	Rick Reuschel	.50
670	Dan Plesac	.50
675	Jim Rice	1.00
680	Charlie Hough	.50
681	Bobby Bonilla	.50
682	Jimmy Key	.50
685	Ron Darling	.50
693	Benito Santiago	.50
700	George Brett	3.00
705	Juan Samuel	.50
710	Darryl Strawberry	.50
715	Todd Worrell	.50
720	Tim Raines	.50
721	Pete O'Brien	.50
725	Mike Boddicker	.50
730	John Franco	.50
740	Rick Sutcliffe	.50
745	Bill Doran	.50
750	Bo Jackson	1.00
755	Ozzie Virgil	.50
760	Mike Scott	.50
764	Greg Walker	.50
770	Lou Whitaker	.50
771	Ruben Sierra	.50
775	Dave Steib	.50
780	Fernando Valenzuela	.50
785	Alvin Davis	.50
790	Dave Righetti	.50

1989 Topps

Ten top young players from the June 1988 draft are featured on "#1 Draft Pick" cards in this full-color basic set of 792 standard-size baseball cards. An additional five cards salute 1989 Future Stars, 22 cards highlight All-Stars, seven contain Record Breakers, five are designated Turn Back The Clock, and six contain checklists. This set features the familiar white borders, but upper-left and lower-right photo corners have been rounded off. A curved name banner in bright red or blue is beneath the team name in large script in the lower-right corner. The card backs are printed in black on a red background and include personal information and complete minor and major league stats. Another new addition in this set is the special Monthly Scoreboard chart that lists monthly stats (April through September) in two of several categories (hits, run, home runs, stolen bases, RBIs, wins, strikeouts, games or saves).

		NM/M
Unopened Factory Set, Retail (792):		25.00
Unopened Factory Set, Hobby (792):		25.00
Complete Set (792):		15.00
Common Player:		.05
Wax Pack (15):		.75
Wax Box (36):		12.00
Cello Pack (29):		1.00
Cello Box (24):		18.00
Rack Pack (43):		.75
Rack Box (24):		15.00
Vending Box (500):		6.00
1	George Bell (Record Breaker)	.05
2	Wade Boggs (Record Breaker)	.25
3	Gary Carter (Record Breaker)	.20
4	Andre Dawson (Record Breaker)	.10
5	Orel Hershiser (Record Breaker)	.05
6	Doug Jones (Record Breaker)	.05
7	Kevin McReynolds (Record Breaker)	.05
8	Dave Eiland **RC**	.05
9	Tim Teufel	.05
10	Andre Dawson	.25
11	Bruce Sutter	.35
12	Dale Sveum	.05
13	Doug Sisk	.05
14	Tom Kelly	.05
15	Robby Thompson	.05
16	Ron Robinson	.05
17	Brian Downing	.05
18	Rick Rhoden	.05
19	Greg Gagne	.05
20	Steve Bedrosian	.05
21	White Sox Leaders (Greg Walker)	.05
22	Tim Crews	.05
23	Mike Fitzgerald	.05
24	Larry Andersen	.05
25	Frank White	.05
26	Dale Mohorcic	.05
27	Orestes Destrade **RC**	.05
28	Mike Moore	.05
29	Kelly Gruber	.05
30	Dwight Gooden	.05
31	Terry Francona	.05
32	Dennis Rasmussen	.05
33	B.J. Surhoff	.05
34	Ken Williams	.05
35	John Tudor	.05
36	Mitch Webster	.05
37	Bob Stanley	.05
38	Paul Runge	.05
39	Mike Maddux	.05
40	Steve Sax	.05
41	Terry Mulholland	.05
42	Jim Eppard **RC**	.05
43	Guillermo Hernandez	.05
44	Jim Snyder	.05
45	Kal Daniels	.05
46	Mark Portugal	.05
47	Carney Lansford	.05
48	Tim Burke	.05
49	Craig Biggio	.05
50	George Bell	.05
51	Angels Leaders (Mark McLemore)	.05
52	Bob Brenly	.05
53	Ruben Sierra	.05
54	Steve Trout	.05
55	Julio Franco	.05
56	Pat Tabler	.05
57	Alejandro Pena	.05
58	Lee Mazzilli	.05
59	Mark Davis	.05
60	Tom Brunansky	.05
61	Neil Allen	.05
62	Alfredo Griffin	.05
63	Mark Clear	.05
64	Alex Trevino	.05
65	Rick Reuschel	.05
66	Manny Trillo	.05
67	Dave Palmer	.05
68	Darrell Miller	.05
69	Jeff Ballard	.05
70	Mark McGwire	.65
71	Mike Boddicker	.05
72	John Moses	.05
73	Pascual Perez	.05
74	Nick Leyva	.05
75	Tom Henke	.05
76	Terry Blocker **RC**	.05
77	Doyle Alexander	.05
78	Jim Sundberg	.05
79	Scott Bankhead	.05
80	Cory Snyder	.05
81	Expos Leaders (Tim Raines)	.05
82	Dave Leiper	.05
83	Jeff Blauser **RC**	.05
84	Bill Bene **RC** (#1 Draft Pick)	.05
85	Kevin McReynolds	.05
86	Al Nipper	.05
87	Larry Owen	.05
88	Darryl Hamilton **RC**	.05
89	Dave LaPoint	.05
90	Vince Coleman	.05
91	Floyd Youmans	.05
92	Jeff Kunkel	.05
93	Ken Howell	.05
94	Chris Speier	.05
95	Gerald Young	.05
96	Rick Cerone	.05
97	Greg Mathews	.05
98	Larry Sheets	.05
99	Sherman Corbett **RC**	.05
100	Mike Schmidt	.50
101	Les Straker	.05
102	Mike Gallego	.05
103	Tim Birtsas	.05
104	Dallas Green	.05
105	Ron Darling	.05
106	Willie Upshaw	.05
107	Jose DeLeon	.05
108	Fred Manrique	.05
109	Hipolito Pena **RC**	.05
110	Paul Molitor	.40
111	Reds Leaders (Eric Davis)	.05
112	Jim Presley	.05
113	Lloyd Moseby	.05
114	Bob Kipper	.05
115	Jody Davis	.05
116	Jeff Montgomery	.05
117	Dave Anderson	.05
118	Checklist 1-132	.05
119	Terry Puhl	.05
120	Frank Viola	.05
121	Garry Templeton	.05
122	Lance Johnson **RC**	.05
123	Spike Owen	.05
124	Jim Traber	.05
125	Mike Krukow	.05
126	Sid Bream	.05
127	Walt Terrell	.05
128	Milt Thompson	.05
129	Terry Clark **RC**	.05
130	Gerald Perry	.05
131	Dave Otto **RC**	.05
132	Curt Ford	.05
133	Bill Long	.05
134	Don Zimmer	.05
135	Jose Rijo	.05
136	Joey Meyer	.05
137	Geno Petralli	.05
138	Wallace Johnson	.05
139	Mike Flanagan	.05
140	Shawon Dunston	.05
141	Indians Leaders (Brook Jacoby)	.05
142	Mike Diaz	.05
143	Mike Campbell	.05
144	Jay Bell	.05
145	Dave Stewart	.05
146	Gary Pettis	.05
147	DeWayne Buice	.05
148	Bill Pecota	.05
149	Doug Dascenzo **RC**	.05
150	Fernando Valenzuela	.05
151	Terry McGriff	.05
152	Mark Thurmond	.05
153	Jim Pankovits	.05
154	Don Carman	.05
155	Marty Barrett	.05
156	Dave Gallagher **RC**	.05
157	Tom Glavine	.25
158	Mike Aldrete	.05
159	Pat Clements	.05
160	Jeffrey Leonard	.05
161	Gregg Olson **RC** (#1 Draft Pick)	.05
162	John Davis	.05
163	Bob Forsch	.05
164	Hal Lanier	.05
165	Mike Dunne	.05
166	Doug Jennings **RC**	.05
167	Steve Searcy **RC** (Future Star)	.05
168	Willie Wilson	.05
169	Mike Jackson	.05
170	Tony Fernandez	.05
171	Braves Leaders (Andres Thomas)	.05
172	Frank Williams	.05
173	Mel Hall	.05
174	Todd Burns **RC**	.05
175	John Shelby	.05
176	Jeff Parrett	.05
177	Monty Fariss **RC** (#1 Draft Pick)	.05
178	Mark Grant	.05
179	Ozzie Virgil	.05
180	Mike Scott	.05
181	Craig Worthington **RC**	.05
182	Bob McClure	.05
183	Oddibe McDowell	.05
184	John Costello **RC**	.05
185	Claudell Washington	.05
186	Pat Perry	.05
187	Darren Daulton	.05
188	Dennis Lamp	.05
189	Kevin Mitchell	.05
190	Mike Witt	.05
191	Sil Campusano **RC**	.05
192	Paul Mirabella	.05
193	Sparky Anderson	.10
194	Greg Harris **RC**	.05
195	Ozzie Guillen	.05
196	Denny Walling	.05
197	Neal Heaton	.05
198	Danny Heep	.05
199	Mike Schooler **RC**	.05
200	George Brett	.50
201	Blue Jays Leaders (Kelly Gruber)	.05
202	Brad Moore **RC**	.05
203	Rob Ducey	.05
204	Brad Havens	.05
205	Dwight Evans	.05
206	Roberto Alomar	.35
207	Terry Leach	.05
208	Tom Pagnozzi	.05
209	Jeff Bittiger **RC**	.05
210	Dale Murphy	.15
211	Mike Pagliarulo	.05
212	Scott Sanderson	.05
213	Rene Gonzales	.05
214	Charlie O'Brien	.05
215	Kevin Gross	.05
216	Jack Howell	.05
217	Joe Price	.05
218	Mike LaValliere	.05
219	Jim Clancy	.05
220	Gary Gaetti	.05
221	Cecil Espy	.05
222	Mark Lewis **RC** (#1 Draft Pick)	.05
223	Jay Buhner	.05
224	Tony LaRussa	.05
225	Ramon Martinez **RC**	.25
226	Bill Doran	.05
227	John Farrell	.05
228	Nelson Santovenia **RC**	.05
229	Jimmy Key	.05
230	Ozzie Smith	.45
231	Padres Leaders (Roberto Alomar)	.05
232	Ricky Horton	.05
233	Gregg Jefferies (Future Star)	.20
234	Tom Browning	.05
235	John Kruk	.05
236	Charles Hudson	.05
237	Glenn Hubbard	.05
238	Eric King	.05
239	Tim Laudner	.05
240	Greg Maddux	.45
241	Brett Butler	.05
242	Ed Vande Berg	.05
243	Bob Boone	.05
244	Jim Acker	.05
245	Jim Rice	.15
246	Rey Quinones	.05
247	Shawn Hillegas	.05
248	Tony Phillips	.05
249	Tim Leary	.05
250	Cal Ripken, Jr.	.75
251	John Dopson **RC**	.05
252	Billy Hatcher	.05
253	Jose Alvarez **RC**	.05
254	Tom LaSorda	.05
255	Ron Guidry	.10
256	Benny Santiago	.05
257	Rick Aguilera	.05
258	Checklist 133-264	.05
259	Larry McWilliams	.05
260	Dave Winfield	.40
261	Cardinals Leaders (Tom Brunansky)	.05
262	Jeff Pico **RC**	.05
263	Mike Felder	.05
264	Rob Dibble **RC**	.10
265	Kent Hrbek	.05
266	Luis Aquino	.05
267	Jeff Robinson	.05
268	Keith Miller	.05
269	Tom Bolton	.05
270	Wally Joyner	.05
271	Jay Tibbs	.05
272	Ron Hassey	.05
273	Jose Lind	.05
274	Mark Eichhorn	.05
275	Danny Tartabull	.05
276	Paul Kilgus	.05
277	Mike Davis	.05
278	Andy McGaffigan	.05
279	Scott Bradley	.05
280	Bob Knepper	.05
281	Gary Redus	.05
282	Cris Carpenter **RC**	.05
283	Andy Allanson	.05
284	Jim Leyland	.05
285	John Candelaria	.05
286	Darrin Jackson	.05
287	Juan Nieves	.05
288	Pat Sheridan	.05
289	Ernie Whitt	.05
290	John Franco	.05
291	Mets Leaders (Darryl Strawberry)	.05
292	Jim Corsi **RC**	.05
293	Glenn Wilson	.05
294	Juan Berenguer	.05
295	Scott Fletcher	.05
296	Ron Gant	.05
297	Oswald Peraza **RC**	.05
298	Chris James	.05
299	Steve Ellsworth **RC**	.05
300	Darryl Strawberry	.05
301	Charlie Leibrandt	.05
302	Gary Ward	.05
303	Felix Fermin	.05
304	Joel Youngblood	.05
305	Dave Smith	.05
306	Tracy Woodson **RC**	.05
307	Lance McCullers	.05
308	Ron Karkovice	.05

309 Mario Diaz **RC** .05
310 Rafael Palmeiro .35
311 Chris Bosio .05
312 Tom Lawless .05
313 Denny Martinez .05
314 Bobby Valentine .05
315 Greg Swindell .05
316 Walt Weiss .05
317 Jack Armstrong **RC** .05
318 Gene Larkin .05
319 Greg Booker .05
320 Lou Whitaker .05
321 Red Sox Leaders (Jody Reed) .05
322 John Smiley .05
323 Gary Thurman .05
324 Bob Milacki **RC** .05
325 Jesse Barfield .05
326 Dennis Boyd .05
327 Mark Lemke **RC** .05
328 Rick Honeycutt .05
329 Bob Melvin .05
330 Eric Davis .05
331 Curt Wilkerson .05
332 Tony Armas .05
333 Bob Ojeda .05
334 Steve Lyons .05
335 Dave Righetti .05
336 Steve Balboni .05
337 Calvin Schiraldi .05
338 Jim Adduci **RC** .05
339 Scott Bailes .05
340 Kirk Gibson .05
341 Jim Deshaies .05
342 Tom Brookens .05
343 Gary Sheffield **RC** (Future Star) 1.50
344 Tom Trebelhorn .05
345 Charlie Hough .05
346 Rex Hudler **RC** .05
347 John Cerutti .05
348 Ed Hearn .05
349 Ron Jones **RC** .05
350 Andy Van Slyke .05
351 Giants Leaders (Bob Melvin) .05
352 Rick Schu .05
353 Marvell Wynne .05
354 Larry Parrish .05
355 Mark Langston .05
356 Kevin Elster .05
357 Jerry Reuss .05
358 Ricky Jordan **RC** .05
359 Tommy John .10
360 Ryne Sandberg .45
361 Kelly Downs .05
362 Jack Lazorko .05
363 Rich Yett .05
364 Rob Deer .05
365 Mike Henneman .05
366 Herm Winningham .05
367 Johnny Paredes **RC** .05
368 Brian Holton .05
369 Ken Caminiti .05
370 Dennis Eckersley .35
371 Manny Lee .05
372 Craig Lefferts .05
373 Tracy Jones .05
374 John Wathan .05
375 Terry Pendleton .05
376 Steve Lombardozzi .05
377 Mike Smithson .05
378 Checklist 265-396 .05
379 Tim Flannery .05
380 Rickey Henderson .40
381 Orioles Leaders (Larry Sheets) .05
382 John Smoltz .50
383 Howard Johnson .05
384 Mark Salas .05
385 Von Hayes .05
386 Andres Galarraga/AS .05
387 Ryne Sandberg/AS .20
388 Bobby Bonilla/AS .05
389 Ozzie Smith/AS .25
390 Darryl Strawberry/AS .05
391 Andre Dawson/AS .05
392 Andy Van Slyke/AS .05
393 Gary Carter/AS .05
394 Orel Hershiser/AS .05
395 Danny Jackson/AS .05
396 Kirk Gibson/AS .05
397 Don Mattingly/AS .30
398 Julio Franco/AS .05
399 Wade Boggs/AS .20
400 Alan Trammell/AS .05
401 Jose Canseco/AS .15
402 Mike Greenwell/AS .05
403 Kirby Puckett/AS .25
404 Bob Boone/AS .05
405 Roger Clemens/AS .30
406 Frank Viola/AS .05
407 Dave Winfield/AS .20
408 Greg Walker .05
409 Ken Dayley .05
410 Jack Clark .05
411 Mitch Williams .05
412 Barry Lyons .05
413 Mike Kingery .05
414 Jim Fregosi .05
415 Rich Gossage .05
416 Fred Lynn .05
417 Mike LaCoss .05
418 Bob Dernier .05
419 Tom Filer .05
420 Joe Carter .05
421 Kirk McCaskill .05
422 Bo Diaz .05
423 Brian Fisher .05
424 Luis Polonia .05
425 Jay Howell .05
426 Danny Gladden .05
427 Eric Show .05
428 Craig Reynolds .05
429 Twins Leaders (Greg Gagne) .05
430 Mark Gubicza .05
431 Luis Rivera .05
432 Chad Kreuter **RC** .10
433 Albert Hall .05
434 Ken Patterson **RC** .05
435 Len Dykstra .05
436 Bobby Meacham .05
437 Andy Benes (#1 Draft Pick) .05
438 Greg Gross .05
439 Frank DiPino .05
440 Bobby Bonilla .05
441 Jerry Reed .05
442 Jose Oquendo .05
443 Rod Nichols **RC** .05
444 Moose Stubing .05
445 Matt Nokes .05
446 Rob Murphy .05
447 Donell Nixon .05
448 Eric Plunk .05
449 Carmelo Martinez .05
450 Roger Clemens .50
451 Mark Davidson .05
452 Israel Sanchez **RC** .05
453 Tom Prince **RC** .05
454 Paul Assenmacher .05
455 Johnny Ray .05
456 Tim Belcher .05
457 Mackey Sasser .05
458 Donn Pall **RC** .05
459 Mariners Leaders (Dave Valle) .05
460 Dave Stieb .05
461 Buddy Bell .05
462 Jose Guzman .05
463 Steve Lake .05
464 Bryn Smith .05
465 Mark Grace .05
466 Chuck Crim .05
467 Jim Walewander .05
468 Henry Cotto .05
469 Jose Bautista **RC** .05
470 Lance Parrish .05
471 Steve Curry **RC** .05
472 Brian Harper .05
473 Don Robinson .05
474 Bob Rodgers .05
475 Dave Parker .05
476 Jon Perlman **RC** .05
477 Dick Schofield .05
478 Doug Drabek .05
479 Mike Macfarlane .05
480 Keith Hernandez .05
481 Chris Brown .05
482 Steve Peters **RC** .05
483 Mickey Hatcher .05
484 Steve Shields .05
485 Hubie Brooks .05
486 Jack McDowell .05
487 Scott Lusader **RC** .05
488 Kevin Coffman .05
489 Phillies Leaders (Mike Schmidt) .15
490 Chris Sabo .05
491 Mike Birkbeck .05
492 Alan Ashby .05
493 Todd Benzinger .05
494 Shane Rawley .05
495 Candy Maldonado .05
496 Dwayne Henry .05
497 Pete Stanicek .05
498 Dave Valle .05
499 Don Heinkel **RC** .05
500 Jose Canseco .35
501 Vance Law .05
502 Duane Ward .05
503 Al Newman .05
504 Bob Walk .05
505 Pete Rose .75
506 Kirt Manwaring .05
507 Steve Farr .05
508 Wally Backman .05
509 Bud Black .05
510 Bob Horner .05
511 Richard Dotson .05
512 Donnie Hill .05
513 Jesse Orosco .05
514 Chet Lemon .05
515 Barry Larkin .05
516 Eddie Whitson .05
517 Greg Brock .05
518 Bruce Ruffin .05
519 Yankees Leaders (Willie Randolph) .05
520 Rick Sutcliffe .05
521 Mickey Tettleton .05
522 Randy Kramer **RC** .05
523 Andres Thomas .05
524 Checklist 397-528 .05
525 Chili Davis .05
526 Wes Gardner .05
527 Dave Henderson .05
528 Luis Medina **RC** .05
529 Tom Foley .05
530 Nolan Ryan .75
531 Dave Hengel **RC** .05
532 Jerry Browne .05
533 Andy Hawkins .05
534 Doc Edwards .05
535 Todd Worrell .05
536 Joel Skinner .05
537 Pete Smith .05
538 Juan Castillo .05
539 Barry Jones .05
540 Bo Jackson .10
541 Cecil Fielder .05
542 Todd Frohwirth .05
543 Damon Berryhill .05
544 Jeff Sellers .05
545 Mookie Wilson .05
546 Mark Williamson .05
547 Mark McLemore .05
548 Bobby Witt .05
549 Cubs Leaders (Jamie Moyer) .05
550 Orel Hershiser .05
551 Randy Ready .05
552 Greg Cadaret .05
553 Luis Salazar .05
554 Nick Esasky .05
555 Bert Blyleven .05
556 Bruce Fields **RC** .05
557 Keith Miller **RC** .05
558 Dan Pasqua .05
559 Juan Agosto .05
560 Tim Raines .05
561 Luis Aguayo .05
562 Danny Cox .05
563 Bill Schroeder .05
564 Russ Nixon .05
565 Jeff Russell .05
566 Al Pedrique .05
567 David Wells .05
568 Mickey Brantley .05
569 German Jimenez **RC** .05
570 Tony Gwynn .45
571 Billy Ripken .05
572 Atlee Hammaker .05
573 Jim Abbott (#1 Draft Pick) .10
574 Dave Clark .05
575 Juan Samuel .05
576 Greg Minton .05
577 Randy Bush .05
578 John Morris .05
579 Astros Leaders (Glenn Davis) .05
580 Harold Reynolds .05
581 Gene Nelson .05
582 Mike Marshall .05
583 Paul Gibson **RC** .05
584 Randy Velarde **RC** .05
585 Harold Baines .05
586 Joe Boever .05
587 Mike Stanley .05
588 Luis Alicea **RC** .05
589 Dave Meads .05
590 Andres Galarraga .05
591 Jeff Musselman .05
592 John Cangelosi .05
593 Drew Hall .05
594 Jimy Williams .05
595 Teddy Higuera .05
596 Kurt Stillwell .05
597 Terry Taylor **RC** .05
598 Ken Gerhart .05
599 Tom Candiotti .05
600 Wade Boggs .45
601 Dave Dravecky .05
602 Devon White .05
603 Frank Tanana .05
604 Paul O'Neill .05
605a Bob Welch (Missing Complete Major League Pitching Record line.) 3.00
605b Bob Welch (Contains Complete Major League Pitching Record line.) .05
606 Rick Dempsey .05
607 Willie Ansley **RC** (#1 Draft Pick) .05
608 Phil Bradley .05
609 Tigers Leaders (Frank Tanana) .05
610 Randy Myers .05
611 Don Slaught .05
612 Dan Quisenberry .05
613 Gary Varsho **RC** .05
614 Joe Hesketh .05
615 Robin Yount .40
616 Steve Rosenberg **RC** .05
617 Mark Parent **RC** .05
618 Rance Mulliniks .05
619 Checklist 529-660 .05
620 Barry Bonds .75
621 Rick Mahler .05
622 Stan Javier .05
623 Fred Toliver .05
624 Jack McKeon .05
625 Eddie Murray .40
626 Jeff Reed .05
627 Greg Harris .05
628 Matt Williams .05
629 Pete O'Brien .05
630 Mike Greenwell .05
631 Dave Bergman .05
632 Bryan Harvey **RC** .10
633 Daryl Boston .05
634 Marvin Freeman **RC** .05
635 Willie Randolph .05
636 Bill Wilkinson .05
637 Carmen Castillo .05
638 Floyd Bannister .05
639 Athletics Leaders (Walt Weiss) .05
640 Willie McGee .05
641 Curt Young .05
642 Argenis Salazar .05
643 Louie Meadows **RC** .05
644 Lloyd McClendon .05
645 Jack Morris .05
646 Kevin Bass .05
647 Randy Johnson **RC** 3.00
648 Sandy Alomar **RC** (Future Star) .25
649 Stewart Cliburn .05
650 Kirby Puckett .45
651 Tom Niedenfuer .05
652 Rich Gedman .05
653 Tommy Barrett **RC** .05
654 Whitey Herzog .05
655 Dave Magadan .05
656 Ivan Calderon .05
657 Joe Magrane .05
658 R.J. Reynolds .05
659 Al Leiter .05
660 Will Clark .05
661 Dwight Gooden (Turn Back the Clock) .05
662 Lou Brock (Turn Back the Clock) .05
663 Hank Aaron (Turn Back the Clock) .15
664 Gil Hodges (Turn Back the Clock) .05
665a Tony Oliva (No copyright line.) 12.50
665b Tony Oliva (With copyright line.) .05
666 Randy St. Claire .05
667 Dwayne Murphy .05
668 Mike Bielecki .05
669 Dodgers Leaders (Orel Hershiser) .05
670 Kevin Seitzer .05
671 Jim Gantner .05
672 Allan Anderson .05
673 Don Baylor .05
674 Otis Nixon .05
675 Bruce Hurst .05
676 Ernie Riles .05
677 Dave Schmidt .05
678 Dion James .05
679 Willie Fraser .05
680 Gary Carter .40
681 Jeff Robinson .05
682 Rick Leach .05
683 Jose Cecena **RC** .05
684 Dave Johnson .05
685 Jeff Treadway .05
686 Scott Terry .05
687 Alvin Davis .05
688 Zane Smith .05
689a Stan Jefferson (Pink triangle at bottom-left photo.) .05
689b Stan Jefferson (Pink/purple triangle.) .05
689c Stan Jefferson (Purple triangle.) .05
690 Doug Jones .05
691 Roberto Kelly .05
692 Steve Ontiveros .05
693 Pat Borders **RC** .05
694 Les Lancaster .05
695 Carlton Fisk .40
696 Don August .05
697 Franklin Stubbs .05
698 Keith Atherton .05
699 Pirates Leaders (Al Pedrique) .05
700 Don Mattingly .50
701 Storm Davis .05
702 Jamie Quirk .05
703 Scott Garrelts .05
704 Carlos Quintana **RC** .05
705 Terry Kennedy .05
706 Pete Incaviglia .05
707 Steve Jeltz .05
708 Chuck Finley .05
709 Tom Herr .05
710 Dave Cone .05
711 Candy Sierra **RC** .05
712 Bill Swift .05
713 Ty Griffin **RC** (#1 Draft Pick) .05
714 Joe M. Morgan .05
715 Tony Pena .05
716 Wayne Tolleson .05
717 Jamie Moyer .05
718 Glenn Braggs .05
719 Danny Darwin .05
720 Tim Wallach .05
721 Ron Tingley **RC** .05
722 Todd Stottlemyre .05
723 Rafael Belliard .05
724 Jerry Don Gleaton .05
725 Terry Steinbach .05
726 Dickie Thon .05
727 Joe Orsulak .05
728 Charlie Puleo .05
729 Rangers Leaders (Steve Buechele) .05
730 Danny Jackson .05
731 Mike Young .05
732 Steve Buechele .05
733 Randy Bockus **RC** .05
734 Jody Reed .05
735 Roger McDowell .05
736 Jeff Hamilton .05
737 Norm Charlton **RC** .05
738 Darnell Coles .05
739 Brook Jacoby .05
740 Dan Plesac .05
741 Ken Phelps .05
742 Mike Harkey **RC** (Future Star) .05
743 Mike Heath .05
744 Roger Craig .05
745 Fred McGriff .05
746 German Gonzalez **RC** .05
747 Wil Tejada **RC** .05
748 Jimmy Jones .05
749 Rafael Ramirez .05
750 Bret Saberhagen .05
751 Ken Oberkfell .05
752 Jim Gott .05
753 Jose Uribe .05
754 Bob Brower .05
755 Mike Scioscia .05
756 Scott Medvin **RC** .05
757 Brady Anderson .05
758 Gene Walter .05
759 Brewers Leaders (Rob Deer) .05
760 Lee Smith .05
761 Dante Bichette **RC** .25
762 Bobby Thigpen .05
763 Dave Martinez .05
764 Robin Ventura (#1 Draft Pick) .25
765 Glenn Davis .05
766 Cecilio Guante .05
767 Mike Capel **RC** .05
768 Bill Wegman .05
769 Junior Ortiz .05
770 Alan Trammell .05
771 Ron Kittle .05
772 Ron Oester .05
773 Keith Moreland .05
774 Frank Robinson .15
775 Jeff Reardon .05
776 Nelson Liriano .05
777 Ted Power .05
778 Bruce Benedict .05
779 Craig McMurtry .05
780 Pedro Guerrero .05
781 Greg Briley **RC** .05
782 Checklist 661-792 .05
783 Trevor Wilson **RC** .05
784 Steve Avery **RC** (#1 Draft Pick) .15
785 Ellis Burks .05
786 Melido Perez .05
787 Dave West **RC** .05
788 Mike Morgan .05
789 Royals Leaders (Bo Jackson) .05
790 Sid Fernandez .05
791 Jim Lindeman .05
792 Rafael Santana .05

Tiffany

This special hobby-only edition shares the checklist with the regular 1989 Topps set. Cards are identical except for the use of white cardboard stock and the high-gloss front coating. Production has been reported as 25,000 sets.

	NM/M
Unopened Set (792):	75.00
Complete Set (792):	40.00
Common Player:	.10

Traded

For the ninth straight year, Topps issued its annual 132-card "Traded" set at the end of the 1989 baseball season. The set, which was packaged in a special box and sold by hobby dealers, includes traded players and rookies who were not in the regular 1989 Topps set.

	NM/M
Unopened Set, Retail (132):	12.50
Unopened Set, Hobby (132):	10.00
Complete Set (132):	7.50
Common Player:	.05

1T Don Aase .05
2T Jim Abbott .05
3T Kent Anderson **RC** .05
4T Keith Atherton .05
5T Wally Backman .05
6T Steve Balboni .05
7T Jesse Barfield .05
8T Steve Bedrosian .05
9T Todd Benzinger .05
10T Geronimo Berroa .05
11T Bert Blyleven .05
12T Bob Boone .05
13T Phil Bradley .05
14T Jeff Brantley **RC** .05
15T Kevin Brown **RC** .05
16T Jerry Browne .05
17T Chuck Cary .05
18T Carmen Castillo .05
19T Jim Clancy .05
20T Jack Clark .05
21T Bryan Clutterbuck .05
22T Jody Davis .05
23T Mike Devereaux .05
24T Frank DiPino .05
25T Benny Distefano .05
26T John Dopson .05
27T Len Dykstra .05
28T Jim Eisenreich .05
29T Nick Esasky .05
30T Alvaro Espinoza .05
31T Darrell Evans .05
32T Junior Felix .05
33T Felix Fermin .05
34T Julio Franco .05
35T Terry Francona .05
36T Cito Gaston .05
37T Bob Geren **RC** (Photo actually Mike Fennell.) .05
38T Tom Gordon **RC** .10
39T Tommy Gregg **RC** .05
40T Ken Griffey .05
41T Ken Griffey Jr. **RC** 6.00
42T Kevin Gross .05
43T Lee Guetterman .05
44T Mel Hall .05
45T Erik Hanson **RC** .05
46T Gene Harris **RC** .05
47T Andy Hawkins .05
48T Rickey Henderson .40
49T Tom Herr .05
50T Ken Hill **RC** .05
51T Brian Holman **RC** .05
52T Brian Holton .05
53T Art Howe .05
54T Ken Howell .05
55T Bruce Hurst .05
56T Chris James .05
57T Randy Johnson 1.50
58T Jimmy Jones .05
59T Terry Kennedy .05
60T Paul Kilgus .05
61T Eric King .05
62T Ron Kittle .05
63T John Kruk .05
64T Randy Kutcher **RC** .05
65T Steve Lake .05
66T Mark Langston .05
67T Dave LaPoint .05
68T Rick Leach .05
69T Terry Leach .05
70T Jim Levebvre .05
71T Al Leiter .05
72T Jeffrey Leonard .05
73T Derek Lilliquist **RC** .05
74T Rick Mahler .05
75T Tom McCarthy **RC** .05
76T Lloyd McClendon .05
77T Lance McCullers .05
78T Oddibe McDowell .05
79T Roger McDowell .05
80T Larry McWilliams .05
81T Randy Milligan .05
82T Mike Moore .05
83T Keith Moreland .05
84T Mike Morgan .05
85T Jamie Moyer .05
86T Rob Murphy .05
87T Eddie Murray .40
88T Pete O'Brien .05
89T Gregg Olson .05
90T Steve Ontiveros .05
91T Jesse Orosco .05
92T Spike Owen .05
93T Rafael Palmeiro .35
94T Clay Parker **RC** .05
95T Jeff Parrett .05
96T Lance Parrish .05
97T Dennis Powell .05
98T Rey Quinones .05
99T Doug Rader .05
100T Willie Randolph .05
101T Shane Rawley .05
102T Randy Ready .05
103T Bip Roberts .05
104T Kenny Rogers **RC** .10
105T Ed Romero .05
106T Nolan Ryan 1.00
107T Luis Salazar .05
108T Juan Samuel .05
109T Alex Sanchez **RC** .05
110T Deion Sanders **RC** .50
111T Steve Sax .05
112T Rick Schu .05
113T Dwight Smith **RC** .05
114T Lonnie Smith .05
115T Billy Spiers **RC** .05
116T Kent Tekulve .05
117T Walt Terrell .05
118T Milt Thompson .05
119T Dickie Thon .05
120T Jeff Torborg .05
121T Jeff Treadway .05
122T Omar Vizquel **RC** .50
123T Jerome Walton **RC** .05

124T	Gary Ward	.05
125T	Claudell Washington	.05
126T	Curt Wilkerson	.05
127T	Eddie Williams	.05
128T	Frank Williams	.05
129T	Ken Williams	.05
130T	Mitch Williams	.05
131T	Steve Wilson **RC**	.05
---	Topps Magazine Subscription Offer Card	.05

Traded Tiffany

The Topps Traded set was issued in a specially boxed, hobby-only edition. Cards are identical to the regular-issue Topps Traded cards except for the application of a high-gloss to the fronts. Production has been reported as 15,000 sets.

	NM/M
Unopened Set (132):	85.00
Complete Set (132):	50.00
Common Player:	.10

Traded Jackie Robinson Bronze

This 1/4-size metal replica of Robinson's first-ever Topps card was issued to dealers who purchased cases of 1989 Topps Traded sets. Each detail of the 1952 Topps Robinson card is reproduced on the 1-1/4" x 1-3/4" bronze metal mini-card, right down to the stats.

		NM/M
312	Jackie Robinson	10.00

Box Panels

Continuing its practice of printing baseball cards on the bottom panels of its wax pack boxes, Topps in 1989 issued a special 16-card set, printing four cards on each of four different box-bottom panels. The cards are identical in design to the regular 1989 Topps cards. They are designated by letter (from A through P) rather than by number.

		NM/M
Complete Panel Set (4):		7.50
Complete Singles Set: (16):		7.50
Common Panel:		1.50
Common Single Player:		.10
	PANEL	1.50
A	George Bell	.10
B	Bill Buckner	.10
C	Darrell Evans	.10
D	Goose Gossage	.10
	PANEL	1.50
E	Greg Gross	.10
F	Rickey Henderson	.60
G	Keith Hernandez	.10
H	Tommy Lasorda	.10
	PANEL	7.50
I	Jim Rice	.20
J	Cal Ripken Jr.	2.00
K	Nolan Ryan	2.00
L	Mike Schmidt	.75
	PANEL	2.00
M	Bruce Sutter	.30
N	Don Sutton	.30
O	Kent Tekulve	.10
P	Dave Winfield	.60

All-Star Glossy Set of 22

The glossy All-Stars were included in the Topps 1989 rack packs. Format was very similar to the sets produced since 1984. Besides the starting lineups of the 1988 All-Star Game, the set included the managers and honorary team captains, Bobby Doerr and Willie Stargell.

		NM/M
Complete Set (22):		3.00
Common Player:		.05
1	Tom Kelly	.05
2	Mark McGwire	.75
3	Paul Molitor	.40
4	Wade Boggs	.50
5	Cal Ripken, Jr.	1.00
6	Jose Canseco	.30
7	Rickey Henderson	.40
8	Dave Winfield	.40
9	Terry Steinbach	.05
10	Frank Viola	.05
11	Bobby Doerr	.05
12	Whitey Herzog	.05
13	Will Clark	.05
14	Ryne Sandberg	.50
15	Bobby Bonilla	.05
16	Ozzie Smith	.50
17	Vince Coleman	.05
18	Andre Dawson	.25
19	Darryl Strawberry	.05
20	Gary Carter	.40
21	Dwight Gooden	.05
22	Willie Stargell	.10

All-Star Glossy Set of 60

For the seventh straight year Topps issued this "send-away" glossy set. Divided into six 10-card sets, it was available only by sending in special offer cards from wax packs. The 2-1/2" x 3-1/2" cards feature full-color photos bordered in white with a thin yellow frame. The player's name appears in small print in the lower-right corner. Red-and-blue-printed flip sides provide basic information. Any of the six 10-card sets were available for $1.25 and six special offer cards. The set was also made available in its complete 60-card set form for $7.50 and 18 special offer cards.

		NM/M
Complete Set (60):		6.00
Common Player:		.05
1	Kirby Puckett	.60
2	Eric Davis	.05
3	Joe Carter	.05
4	Andy Van Slyke	.05
5	Wade Boggs	.60
6	Dave Cone	.05
7	Kent Hrbek	.05
8	Darryl Strawberry	.05
9	Jay Buhner	.05
10	Ron Gant	.05
11	Will Clark	.05
12	Jose Canseco	.35
13	Juan Samuel	.05
14	George Brett	.75
15	Benny Santiago	.05
16	Dennis Eckersley	.40
17	Gary Carter	.50
18	Frank Viola	.05
19	Roberto Alomar	.15
20	Paul Gibson	.05
21	Dave Winfield	.50
22	Howard Johnson	.05
23	Roger Clemens	.65
24	Bobby Bonilla	.05
25	Alan Trammell	.05
26	Kevin McReynolds	.05
27	George Bell	.05
28	Bruce Hurst	.05
29	Mark Grace	.05
30	Tim Belcher	.05
31	Mike Greenwell	.05
32	Glenn Davis	.05
33	Gary Gaetti	.05
34	Ryne Sandberg	.60
35	Rickey Henderson	.50
36	Dwight Evans	.05
37	Doc Gooden	.05
38	Robin Yount	.50
39	Damon Berryhill	.05
40	Chris Sabo	.05
41	Mark McGwire	1.00
42	Ozzie Smith	.60
43	Paul Molitor	.50
44	Andres Galarraga	.05
45	Dave Stewart	.05
46	Tom Browning	.05
47	Cal Ripken, Jr.	1.50
48	Orel Hershiser	.05
49	Dave Gallagher	.05
50	Walt Weiss	.05
51	Don Mattingly	.65
52	Tony Fernandez	.05
53	Tim Raines	.05
54	Jeff Reardon	.05
55	Kirk Gibson	.05
56	Jack Clark	.05
57	Danny Jackson	.05
58	Tony Gwynn	.60
59	Cecil Espy	.05
60	Jody Reed	.05

American Baseball

For the second consecutive year Topps released an 88-card set of baseball cards available in both the United States and the United Kingdom. The mini-sized cards (2-1/4" x 3") are printed on white stock with a low-gloss finish. The game-action color player photo is outlined in red, white and blue and framed in white. Backs are horizontal and include a characterization cartoon along with biographical information and statistics. The cards were sold in packs of five with a stick of bubble gum for 12 pence.

		NM/M
Complete Set (88):		6.00
Common Player:		.05
Wax Pack (5):		.50
Wax Box (48):		8.00
1	Brady Anderson	.05
2	Harold Baines	.05
3	George Bell	.05
4	Wade Boggs	.60
5	Barry Bonds	1.50
6	Bobby Bonilla	.05
7	George Brett	.75
8	Hubie Brooks	.05
9	Tom Brunansky	.05
10	Jay Buhner	.05
11	Brett Butler	.05
12	Jose Canseco	.30
13	Joe Carter	.05
14	Jack Clark	.05
15	Will Clark	.05
16	Roger Clemens	.65
17	Dave Cone	.05
18	Alvin Davis	.05
19	Eric Davis	.05
20	Glenn Davis	.05
21	Andre Dawson	.25
22	Bill Doran	.05
23	Dennis Eckersley	.35
24	Dwight Evans	.05
25	Tony Fernandez	.05
26	Carlton Fisk	.45
27	John Franco	.05
28	Andres Galarraga	.05
29	Ron Gant	.05
30	Kirk Gibson	.05
31	Dwight Gooden	.05
32	Mike Greenwell	.05
33	Mark Gubicza	.05
34	Pedro Gurrero	.05
35	Ozzie Guillen	.05
36	Tony Gwynn	.60
37	Rickey Henderson	.45
38	Orel Hershiser	.05
39	Teddy Higuera	.05
40	Charlie Hough	.05
41	Kent Hrbek	.05
42	Bruce Hurst	.05
43	Bo Jackson	.10
44	Gregg Jefferies	.05
45	Ricky Jordan	.05
46	Wally Joyner	.05
47	Mark Langston	.05
48	Mike Marshall	.05
49	Don Mattingly	.75
50	Fred McGriff	.05
51	Mark McGwire	1.00
52	Kevin McReynolds	.05
53	Paul Molitor	.45
54	Jack Morris	.05
55	Dale Murphy	.20
56	Eddie Murray	.45
57	Pete O'Brien	.05
58	Rafael Palmeiro	.35
59	Gerald Perry	.05
60	Kirby Puckett	.60
61	Tim Raines	.05
62	Johnny Ray	.05
63	Rick Reuschel	.05
64	Cal Ripken	1.50
65	Chris Sabo	.05
66	Juan Samuel	.05
67	Ryne Sandberg	.60
68	Benny Santiago	.05
69	Steve Sax	.05
70	Mike Schmidt	.75
71	Ruben Sierra	.05
72	Ozzie Smith	.60
73	Cory Snyder	.05
74	Dave Stewart	.05
75	Darryl Strawberry	.05
76	Greg Swindell	.05
77	Alan Trammell	.05
78	Fernando Valenzuela	.05
79	Andy Van Slyke	.05
80	Frank Viola	.05
81	Claudell Washington	.05
82	Walt Weiss	.05
83	Lou Whitaker	.05
84	Dave Winfield	.45
85	Mike Witt	.05
86	Gerald Young	.05
87	Robin Yount	.45
88	Checklist	.05

Batting Leaders

The active career batting leaders are showcased in this 22-card set. The 2-1/2" x 3-1/2" cards are printed on super glossy stock with full-color photos and bright red borders. A "Top Active Career Batting Leaders" cup is displayed in a lower corner. The player's name appears above the photo. This set is specially numbered in accordance to career batting average. Wade Boggs is featured on card #1 as the top active career batting leader. The flip sides present batting statistics. One batting leader card was included in each K-Mart blister pack, which also includes 100 cards from the 1989 regular Topps set.

		NM/M
Complete Set (22):		90.00
Common Player:		1.50
1	Wade Boggs	12.00
2	Tony Gwynn	12.00
3	Don Mattingly	16.00
4	Kirby Puckett	12.00
5	George Brett	16.00
6	Pedro Guerrero	1.50
7	Tim Raines	1.50
8	Keith Hernandez	1.50
9	Jim Rice	3.00
10	Paul Molitor	8.00
11	Eddie Murray	8.00
12	Willie McGee	1.50
13	Dave Parker	1.50
14	Julio Franco	1.50
15	Rickey Henderson	8.00
16	Kent Hrbek	1.50
17	Willie Wilson	1.50
18	Johnny Ray	1.50
19	Pat Tabler	1.50
20	Carney Lansford	1.50
21	Robin Yount	8.00
22	Alan Trammell	1.50

Big Baseball

Known by collectors as Topps "Big Baseball," the cards in this 330 card set measure 2-5/8" x 3-3/4" and are patterned after the 1956 Topps cards. The glossy card fronts are horizontally-designed and include two photos of each player, a portrait alongside an action photo. The backs include 1988 and career stats, but are dominated by a color cartoon featuring the player. Members of the 1988 Team U.S.A. Olympic baseball team are included in the set, which was issued in three series of 110 cards each.

		NM/M
Complete Set (330):		9.00
Common Player:		.05
Wax Pack:		.40
Wax Box (36):		7.50
1	Orel Hershiser	.05
2	Harold Reynolds	.05
3	Jody Davis	.05
4	Greg Walker	.05
5	Barry Bonds	1.00
6	Bret Saberhagen	.05
7	Johnny Ray	.05
8	Mike Fiore	.05
9	Juan Castillo	.05
10	Todd Burns	.05
11	Carmelo Martinez	.05
12	Geno Petralli	.05
13	Mel Hall	.05
14	Tom Browning	.05
15	Fred McGriff	.05
16	Kevin Elster	.05
17	Tim Leary	.05
18	Jim Rice	.20
19	Bret Barberie	.05
20	Jay Buhner	.05
21	Atlee Hammaker	.05
22	Lou Whitaker	.05
23	Paul Runge	.05
24	Carlton Fisk	.40
25	Jose Lind	.05
26	Mark Gubicza	.05
27	Billy Ripken	.05
28	Mike Pagliarulo	.05
29	Jim Deshaies	.05
30	Mark McLemore	.05
31	Scott Terry	.05
32	Franklin Stubbs	.05
33	Don August	.05
34	Mark McGwire	.75
35	Eric Show	.05
36	Cecil Espy	.05
37	Ron Tingley	.05
38	Mickey Brantley	.05
39	Paul O'Neill	.05
40	Ed Sprague	.05
41	Len Dykstra	.05
42	Roger Clemens	.60
43	Ron Gant	.05
44	Dan Pasqua	.05
45	Jeff Robinson	.05
46	George Brett	.65
47	Bryn Smith	.05
48	Mike Marshall	.05
49	Doug Robbins	.05
50	Don Mattingly	.65
51	Mike Scott	.05
52	Steve Jeltz	.05
53	Dick Schofield	.05
54	Tom Brunansky	.05
55	Gary Sheffield	.45
56	Dave Valle	.05
57	Carney Lansford	.05
58	Tony Gwynn	.50
59	Checklist	.05
60	Damon Berryhill	.05
61	Jack Morris	.05
62	Brett Butler	.05
63	Mickey Hatcher	.05
64	Bruce Sutter	.35
65	Robin Ventura	.05
66	Junior Oritiz	.05
67	Pat Tabler	.05
68	Greg Swindell	.05
69	Jeff Branson	.05
70	Manny Lee	.05
71	Dave Magadan	.05
72	Rich Gedman	.05
73	Tim Raines	.05
74	Mike Maddux	.05
75	Jim Presley	.05
76	Chuck Finley	.05
77	Jose Oquendo	.05
78	Rob Deer	.05
79	Jay Howell	.05
80	Terry Steinbach	.05
81	Eddie Whitson	.05
82	Ruben Sierra	.05
83	Bruce Benedict	.05
84	Fred Manrique	.05
85	John Smiley	.05
86	Mike Macfarlane	.05
87	Rene Gonzales	.05
88	Charles Hudson	.05
90	Les Straker	.05
91	Carmen Castillo	.05
92	Tracy Woodson	.05
93	Tino Martinez	.15
94	Herm Winningham	.05
95	Kelly Gruber	.05
96	Terry Leach	.05
97	Jody Reed	.05
98	Nelson Santovenia	.05
99	Tony Armas	.05
100	Greg Brock	.05
101	Dave Stewart	.05
102	Roberto Alomar	.20
103	Jim Sundberg	.05
104	Albert Hall	.05
105	Steve Lyons	.05
106	Sid Bream	.05
107	Danny Tartabull	.05
108	Rick Dempsey	.05
109	Rich Renteria	.05
110	Ozzie Smith	.50
111	Steve Sax	.05
112	Kelly Downs	.05
113	Larry Sheets	.05
114	Andy Benes	.05
115	Pete O'Brien	.05
116	Kevin McReynolds	.05
117	Juan Berenguer	.05
118	Billy Hatcher	.05
119	Rick Cerone	.05
120	Andre Dawson	.15
121	Storm Davis	.05
122	Devon White	.05
123	Alan Trammell	.05
124	Vince Coleman	.05
125	Al Leiter	.05
126	Dale Sveum	.05
127	Pete Incaviglia	.05
128	Dave Stieb	.05
129	Kevin Mitchell	.05
130	Dave Schmidt	.05
131	Gary Redus	.05
132	Ron Robinson	.05
133	Darnell Coles	.05
134	Benny Santiago	.05
135	John Farrell	.05
136	Willie Wilson	.05
137	Steve Bedrosian	.05
138	Don Slaught	.05
139	Darryl Strawberry	.05
140	Frank Viola	.05
141	Dave Silvestri	.05
142	Carlos Quintana	.05
143	Vance Law	.05
144	Dave Parker	.05
145	Tim Belcher	.05
146	Will Clark	.05
147	Mark Williamson	.05
148	Ozzie Guillen	.05
149	Kirk McCaskill	.05
150	Pat Sheridan	.05
151	Terry Pendleton	.05
152	Roberto Kelly	.05
153	Joey Meyer	.05
154	Mark Grant	.05
155	Joe Carter	.05
156	Steve Buechele	.05
157	Tony Fernandez	.05
158	Jeff Reed	.05
159	Bobby Bonilla	.05
160	Henry Cotto	.05
161	Kurt Stillwell	.05
162	Mickey Morandini	.05
163	Robby Thompson	.05

164 Rick Schu .05
165 Stan Jefferson .05
166 Ron Darling .05
167 Kirby Puckett .50
168 Bill Doran .05
169 Dennis Lamp .05
170 Ty Griffin .05
171 Ron Hassey .05
172 Dale Murphy .15
173 Andres Galarraga .05
174 Tim Flannery .05
175 Cory Snyder .05
176 Checklist .05
177 Tommy Barrett .05
178 Dan Petry .05
179 Billy Masse .05
180 Terry Kennedy .05
181 Joe Orsulak .05
182 Doyle Alexander .05
183 Willie McGee .05
184 Jim Gantner .05
185 Keith Hernandez .05
186 Greg Gagne .05
187 Kevin Bass .05
188 Mark Eichhorn .05
189 Mark Grace .15
190 Jose Canseco .35
191 Bobby Witt .05
192 Rafael Santana .05
193 Dwight Evans .05
194 Greg Booker .05
195 Brook Jacoby .05
196 Rafael Belliard .05
197 Candy Maldonado .05
198 Mickey Tettleton .05
199 Barry Larkin .05
200 Frank White .05
201 Wally Joyner .05
202 Chet Lemon .05
203 Joe Magrane .05
204 Glenn Braggs .05
205 Scott Fletcher .05
206 Gary Ward .05
207 Nelson Liriano .05
208 Howard Johnson .05
209 Kent Hrbek .05
210 Ken Caminiti .05
211 Mike Greenwell .05
212 Ryne Sandberg .50
213 Joe Slusarski .05
214 Donnell Nixon .05
215 Tim Wallach .05
216 John Kruk .05
217 Charles Nagy .05
218 Alvin Davis .05
219 Oswald Peraza .05
220 Mike Schmidt .65
221 Spike Owen .05
222 Mike Smithson .05
223 Dion James .05
224 Ernie Whitt .05
225 Mike Davis .05
226 Gene Larkin .05
227 Pat Combs .05
228 Jack Howell .05
229 Ron Oester .05
230 Paul Gibson .05
231 Mookie Wilson .05
232 Glenn Hubbard .05
233 Shawon Dunston .05
234 Otis Nixon .05
235 Melido Perez .05
236 Jerry Browne .05
237 Rick Rhoden .05
238 Bo Jackson .10
239 Randy Velarde .05
240 Jack Clark .05
241 Wade Boggs .50
242 Lonnie Smith .05
243 Mike Flanagan .05
244 Willie Randolph .05
245 Oddibe McDowell .05
246 Ricky Jordan .05
247 Greg Briley .05
248 Rex Hudler .05
249 Robin Yount .40
250 Lance Parrish .05
251 Chris Sabo .05
252 Mike Henneman .05
253 Gregg Jefferies .05
254 Curt Young .05
255 Andy Van Slyke .05
256 Rod Booker .05
257 Rafael Palmeiro .35
258 Jose Uribe .05
259 Ellis Burks .05
260 John Smoltz .05
261 Tom Foley .05
262 Lloyd Moseby .05
263 Jim Poole .05
264 Gary Gaetti .05
265 Bob Dernier .05
266 Harold Baines .05
267 Tom Candiotti .05
268 Rafael Ramirez .05
269 Bob Boone .05
270 Buddy Bell .05
271 Rickey Henderson .40
272 Willie Fraser .05
273 Eric Davis .05
274 Jeff Robinson .05
275 Damaso Garcia .05
276 Sid Fernandez .05
277 Stan Javier .05
278 Marty Barrett .05
279 Gerald Perry .05
280 Rob Ducey .05
281 Mike Scioscia .05
282 Randy Bush .05
283 Tom Herr .05
284 Glenn Wilson .05
285 Pedro Guerrero .05
286 Cal Ripken, Jr. 1.00
287 Randy Johnson .50
288 Julio Franco .05
289 Ivan Calderon .05
290 Rich Yett .05
291 Scott Servais .05
292 Bill Pecota .05
293 Ken Phelps .05
294 Chili Davis .05
295 Manny Trillo .05
296 Mike Boddicker .05
297 Geronimo Berroa .05
298 Todd Stottlemyre .05
299 Kirk Gibson .05
300 Wally Backman .05
301 Hubie Brooks .05
302 Von Hayes .05
303 Matt Nokes .05
304 Dwight Gooden .05
305 Walt Weiss .05
306 Mike LaValliere .05
307 Cris Carpenter .05
308 Ted Wood .05
309 Jeff Russell .05
310 Dave Gallagher .05
311 Andy Allanson .05
312 Craig Reynolds .05
313 Kevin Seitzer .05
314 Dave Winfield .40
315 Andy McGaffigan .05
316 Nick Esasky .05
317 Jeff Blauser .05
318 George Bell .05
319 Eddie Murray .40
320 Mark Davidson .05
321 Juan Samuel .05
322 Jim Abbott .05
323 Kal Daniels .05
324 Mike Brumley .05
325 Gary Carter .40
326 Dave Henderson .05
327 Checklist .05
328 Garry Templeton .05
329 Pat Perry .05
330 Paul Molitor .40

Coins

Similar in format to previous Topps coins, this 60-piece set features 1-1/2" diameter coins with rolled colored edges. A shooting star device printed over the player photo gives his name, team and position. Backs have a few biographical details and a summary of the player's previous season performance printed in black on silver. The coins were sold three per pack, with each pack including an offer card for an album to house the pieces.

NM/M
Factory Boxed Set (60): 15.00
Complete Set (60): 7.50
Common Player: .10
Wax Pack (3): .50
Wax Box (36): 8.00
1 Kirk Gibson .10
2 Orel Herhiser .10
3 Chris Sabo .10
4 Tony Gwynn .50
5 Brett Butler .10
6 Bobby Bonilla .10
7 Jack Clark .10
8 Will Clark .10
9 Eric Davis .10
10 Glenn Davis .10
11 Andre Dawson .15
12 John Franco .10
13 Andres Galarraga .10
14 Dwight Gooden .10
15 Mark Grace .10
16 Pedro Guerrero .10
17 Ricky Jordan .10
18 Mike Marshall .10
19 Dale Murphy .15
20 Eddie Murray .40
21 Gerald Perry .10
22 Tim Raines .10
23 Juan Samuel .10
24 Benito Santiago .10
25 Ozzie Smith .50
26 Darryl Strawberry .10
27 Andy Van Slyke .10
28 Gerald Young .10
29 Jose Canseco .35
30 Frank Viola .10
31 Walt Weiss .10
32 Wade Boggs .50
33 Harold Baines .10
34 George Brett .75
35 Jay Buhner .10
36 Joe Carter .10
37 Roger Clemens .60
38 Alvin Davis .10
39 Tony Fernandez .10
40 Carlton Fisk .40
41 Mike Greenwell .10
42 Kent Hrbek .10
43 Don Mattingly .75
44 Fred McGriff .10
45 Mark McGwire 1.00
46 Paul Molitor .40
47 Rafael Palmeiro .35
48 Kirby Puckett .50
49 Johnny Ray .10
50 Cal Ripken, Jr. 1.50
51 Ruben Sierra .10
52 Pete Stanicek .10
53 Dave Stewart .10
54 Greg Swindell .10
55 Danny Tartabull .10
56 Alan Trammell .10
57 Lou Whitaker .10
58 Dave Winfield .40
59 Mike Witt .10
60 Robin Yount .40

Double Headers All-Stars

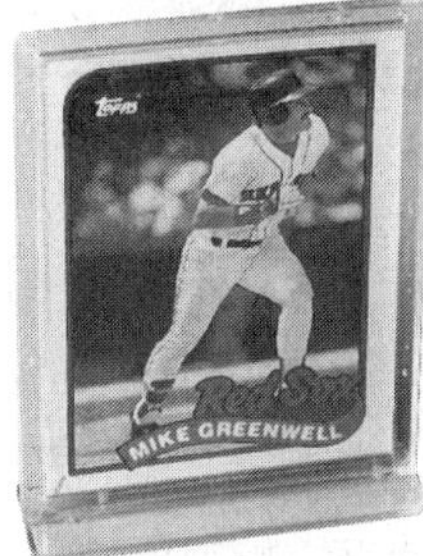

This scarce test issue was produced in two versions, an All-Stars set and a set of exclusively Mets and Yankees players. The "cards" are two-sided miniature (1-5/8" x 2-1/4") reproductions of the player's 1989 Topps card and his Topps rookie card, encased in a clear plastic stand.

NM/M
Complete Set (24): 9.00
Common Player: .50
Wax Pack (1): .50
Wax Box (24): 9.00
(1) Alan Ashby .50
(2) Wade Boggs 1.00
(3) Bobby Bonilla .50
(4) Jose Canseco .65
(5) Will Clark .50
(6) Roger Clemens 1.25
(7) Andre Dawson .60
(8) Dennis Eckersley .65
(9) Carlton Fisk .75
(10) John Franco .50
(11) Julio Franco .50
(12) Kirk Gibson .50
(13) Mike Greenwell .50
(14) Orel Hershiser .50
(15) Danny Jackson .50
(16) Don Mattingly 1.25
(17) Mark McGwire 2.00
(18) Kirby Puckett 1.00
(19) Ryne Sandberg 1.00
(20) Ozzie Smith 1.00
(21) Darryl Strawberry .50
(22) Alan Trammell .50
(23) Andy Van Slyke .50
(24) Frank Viola .50

Double Headers Mets/Yankees Proofs

In advance of its special Mets/Yankees Double Headers novelty issue, Topps prepared a series of proof versions featuring four players from each of the New York teams. Like the later issues, these Double Headers feature miniature versions of the players' Topps rookie cards in a small plastic stand-up frame. However, the proof versions have the rookie cards back-to-back with the players' 1988 Topps cards, rather than 1989 as on the regularly issued pieces. Two different types of wrappers are found for the proofs, an opaque paper envelope picturing Gary Carter's piece and a cellophane wrapper with the proof issue's checklist.

NM/M
Complete Set (8): 425.00
Common Player: 50.00
(1) Gary Carter 125.00
(2) Ron Darling 50.00
(3) Dwight Gooden 50.00
(4) Darryl Strawberry 50.00
(1) Rickey Henderson 125.00
(2) Don Mattingly 200.00
(3) Dave Righetti 50.00
(4) Dave Winfield 125.00

Double Headers Mets/Yankees

This was a regionally issued test for the concept of two "mini" baseball cards of a player encapsulated in clear plastic. Only New York players are represented in the set. Each double header plastic frame holds miniature (1-5/8" x 2-1/4") versions of the player's 1989 Topps card, and his first Topps card, printed on thin paper. The Double Headers of players who also appeared in the All-Star issue are indistinguishable in this version. The stand-ups were sold in boxes of 24 paper-wrapped pieces. It is reported that each box contains a full set. The unnumbered pieces are checklisted here in alphabetical order by team.

NM/M
Complete Set (24): 150.00
Common Player: 10.00
New York Mets Team Set: 85.00
(1) Gary Carter 25.00
(2) David Cone 10.00
(3) Ron Darling 10.00
(4) Len Dykstra 10.00
(5) Doc Gooden 10.00
(6) Keith Hernandez 10.00
(7) Gregg Jefferies 10.00
(8) Howard Johnson 10.00
(9) Kevin McReynolds 10.00
(10) Randy Myers 10.00
(11) Darryl Strawberry .50
(12) Tim Teufel 10.00
(13) Mookie Wilson 10.00
New York Yankees Team Set: 65.00
(14) Richard Dotson 10.00
(15) Rickey Henderson 25.00
(16) Don Mattingly 3.00
(17) Mike Pagliarulo 10.00
(18) Ken Phelps 10.00
(19) Rick Rhoden 10.00
(20) Dave Righetti 10.00
(21) Rafael Santana 10.00
(22) Steve Sax 10.00
(23) Claudell Washington 10.00
(24) Dave Winfield 25.00

Gallery of Champions

Topps continued its issue of 1/4-size metallic ingot reproductions of current-year baseball cards with aluminum, bronze and sterling silver sets in 1989. Again the players represented major award winners from the previous season. The metal mini-cards were sold only as complete sets. Dealers who ordered bronze and silver sets could receive as a bonus a pewter version of the Jose Canseco ingot.

NM/M
Complete Aluminum Set (12): 12.50
Complete Bronze Set (12): 50.00
Complete Silver Set (12): 120.00
(1a) Wade Boggs/Aluminum 3.50
(1b) Wade Boggs/Bronze 10.00
(1s) Wade Boggs/Silver 25.00
(2a) Jose Canseco/Aluminum 2.00
(2b) Jose Canseco/Bronze 5.00
(2s) Jose Canseco/Silver 15.00
(2p) Jose Canseco/Pewter 7.50
(3a) Will Clark/Aluminum 1.00
(3b) Will Clark/Bronze 3.50
(3s) Will Clark/Silver 7.50
(4a) Dennis Eckersley/Aluminum 1.50
(4b) Dennis Eckersley/Bronze 5.00
(4s) Dennis Eckersley/Silver 10.00
(5a) John Franco/Aluminum 1.00
(5b) John Franco/Bronze 3.50
(5s) John Franco/Silver 7.50
(6a) Kirk Gibson/Aluminum 1.00
(6b) Kirk Gibson/Bronze 3.50
(6s) Kirk Gibson/Silver 7.50
(7a) Tony Gwynn/Aluminum 3.50
(7b) Tony Gwynn/Bronze 10.00
(7s) Tony Gwynn/Silver 25.00
(8a) Orel Hershiser/Aluminum 1.00
(8b) Orel Hershiser/Bronze 3.50
(8s) Orel Hershiser/Silver 7.50
(9a) Chris Sabo/Aluminum 1.00
(9b) Chris Sabo/Bronze 3.50
(9s) Chris Sabo/Silver 7.50
(10a) Darryl Strawberry/Aluminum 1.00
(10b) Darryl Strawberry/Bronze 3.50
(10s) Darryl Strawberry/Silver 7.50
(11a) Frank Viola/Aluminum 1.00
(11b) Frank Viola/Bronze 3.50
(11s) Frank Viola/Silver 7.50
(12a) Walt Weiss/Aluminum 1.00
(12b) Walt Weiss/Bronze 3.50
(12s) Walt Weiss/Silver 7.50

Glossy Rookies Set of 22

Bearing the same design and style of the past two years, Topps featured the top first-year players from the 1988 season in this glossy set. The full-color player photo appears beneath the "1988 Rookies" banner. The player's name is displayed beneath the photo. The flip side features the "1988 Rookies Commemorative Set" logo followed by the player ID and card number. Glossy rookies were found only in 100-card jumbo cello packs.

NM/M
Complete Set (22): 5.00
Common Player: .15
1 Roberto Alomar .50
2 Brady Anderson .15
3 Tim Belcher .15
4 Damon Berryhill .15
5 Jay Buhner .25
6 Kevin Elster .15
7 Cecil Espy .15
8 Dave Gallagher .15
9 Ron Gant .25
10 Paul Gibson .15
11 Mark Grace .50
12 Darrin Jackson .15
13 Gregg Jefferies .25
14 Ricky Jordan .15
15 Al Leiter .15
16 Melido Perez .15
17 Chris Sabo .15
18 Nelson Santovenia .15
19 Mackey Sasser .15
20 Gary Sheffield 2.00
21 Walt Weiss .15
22 David Wells .15

Heads Up! Test Issue

Much rarer than the 1990 issue, this 24-card test set debuted the bizarre "shrunken head" format of a die-cut player's head and cap printed on heavy cardboard, approximately 4-1/2" x 6-1/2" in size and sold one per pack. Backs feature both a small plastic suction cup and an adhesive strip for hanging the card. The player's name and team are printed in black on the back. Except for the copyright date on back, the cards of players from the 1989 test set which were repeated in the 1990 regular issue are virtually identical and often sell for much less than those players who were unique to the 1989 set.

NM/M
Complete Set (24): 600.00
Common Player: 12.00
1 Tony Gwynn 65.00
2 Will Clark 17.50
3 Dwight Gooden 12.00
4 Ricky Jordan 12.00
5 Ken Griffey Jr. 150.00
6 Darryl Strawberry 17.50
7 Frank Viola 17.50
8 Bo Jackson 15.00
9 Ryne Sandberg 65.00
10 Gregg Jefferies 17.50
11 Wade Boggs 65.00
12 Ellis Burks 17.50
13 Gary Sheffield 25.00
14 Mark McGwire 150.00
15 Mark Grace 17.50
16 Jim Abbott 12.00
17 Ozzie Smith 65.00
18 Jose Canseco 25.00
19 Don Mattingly 75.00
20 Kirby Puckett 65.00
21 Eric Davis 17.50
22 Mike Greenwell 17.50
23 Dale Murphy 30.00
24 Mike Schmidt 125.00

Mini League Leaders

This 77-card set features baseball's statistical leaders from the 1988 season. It is referred to as a "mini" set because of the cards' small (2-1/8" x 3") size. The glossy cards feature action photos that have a soft focus on all edges. The player's team and name appear along the bottom of the card. The back features a head- shot of the player along with his 1988 season ranking and stats.

NM/M
Complete Set (77): 3.00
Common Player: .05

Wax Pack (7):		.25
Wax Box (36):		6.00
1	Dale Murphy	.20
2	Gerald Perry	.05
3	Andre Dawson	.25
4	Greg Maddux	.65
5	Rafael Palmeiro	.45
6	Tom Browning	.05
7	Kal Daniels	.05
8	Eric Davis	.05
9	John Franco	.05
10	Danny Jackson	.05
11	Barry Larkin	.05
12	Jose Rijo	.05
13	Chris Sabo	.05
14	Nolan Ryan	1.00
15	Mike Scott	.05
16	Gerald Young	.05
17	Kirk Gibson	.05
18	Orel Hershiser	.05
19	Steve Sax	.05
20	John Tudor	.05
21	Hubie Brooks	.05
22	Andres Galarraga	.05
23	Otis Nixon	.05
24	Dave Cone	.05
25	Sid Fernandez	.05
26	Dwight Gooden	.05
27	Kevin McReynolds	.05
28	Darryl Strawberry	.05
29	Juan Samuel	.05
30	Bobby Bonilla	.05
31	Sid Bream	.05
32	Jim Gott	.05
33	Andy Van Slyke	.05
34	Vince Coleman	.05
35	Jose DeLeon	.05
36	Joe Magrane	.05
37	Ozzie Smith	.65
38	Todd Worrell	.05
39	Tony Gwynn	.65
40	Brett Butler	.05
41	Will Clark	.05
42	Rick Reuschel	.05
43	Checklist	.05
44	Eddie Murray	.50
45	Wade Boggs	.65
46	Roger Clemens	.70
47	Dwight Evans	.05
48	Mike Greenwell	.05
49	Bruce Hurst	.05
50	Johnny Ray	.05
51	Doug Jones	.05
52	Greg Swindell	.05
53	Gary Pettis	.05
54	George Brett	.70
55	Mark Gubicza	.05
56	Willie Wilson	.05
57	Teddy Higuera	.05
58	Paul Molitor	.50
59	Robin Yount	.50
60	Allan Anderson	.05
61	Gary Gaetti	.05
62	Kirby Puckett	.65
63	Jeff Reardon	.05
64	Frank Viola	.05
65	Jack Clark	.05
66	Rickey Henderson	.50
67	Dave Winfield	.50
68	Jose Canseco	.35
69	Dennis Eckersley	.45
70	Mark McGwire	.75
71	Dave Stewart	.05
72	Alvin Davis	.05
73	Mark Langston	.05
74	Harold Reynolds	.05
75	George Bell	.05
76	Tony Fernandez	.05
77	Fred McGriff	.05

Stickercards

Once again in 1989 Topps used a stickercard as cardboard backing for its paper sticker issue. Measuring 2-1/8" x 3", the cards are found with either one or two player stickers on back. The stickercards have a player photo on a background of graduated color. Minimal stats and biographic data are presented at the bottom. Values shown are for complete stickercard/sticker(s), without regard to which stickers are on back.

		NM/M
Complete Set (66):		5.00
Common Player:		.05
Wax Pack (5):		.25
Wax Box (48):		6.00
1	George Brett	.65
2	Don Mattingly	.65
3	Mark McGwire	.75
4	Julio Franco	.05
5	Harold Reynolds	.05
6	Lou Whitaker	.05
7	Wade Boggs	.50
8	Gary Gaetti	.05
9	Paul Molitor	.45
10	Tony Fernandez	.05
11	Cal Ripken Jr.	1.00
12	Alan Trammell	.05
13	Jose Canseco	.30
14	Joe Carter	.05
15	Dwight Evans	.05
16	Mike Greenwell	.05
17	Dave Henderson	.05
18	Rickey Henderson	.45
19	Kirby Puckett	.50
20	Dave Winfield	.45
21	Robin Yount	.45
22	Bob Boone	.05
23	Carlton Fisk	.45
24	Geno Petralli	.05
25	Roger Clemens	.65
26	Mark Gubicza	.05
27	Dave Stewart	.05
28	Teddy Higuera	.05
29	Bruce Hurst	.05
30	Frank Viola	.05
31	Dennis Eckersley	.40
32	Doug Jones	.05
33	Jeff Reardon	.05
34	Will Clark	.05
35	Glenn Davis	.05
36	Andres Galarraga	.05
37	Juan Samuel	.05
38	Ryne Sandberg	.50
39	Steve Sax	.05
40	Bobby Bonilla	.05
41	Howard Johnson	.05
42	Vance Law	.05
43	Shawon Dunston	.05
44	Barry Larkin	.05
45	Ozzie Smith	.50
46	Barry Bonds	1.00
47	Eric Davis	.05
48	Andre Dawson	.25
49	Kirk Gibson	.05
50	Tony Gwynn	.50
51	Kevin McReynolds	.05
52	Rafael Palmeiro	.40
53	Darryl Strawberry	.05
54	Andy Van Slyke	.05
55	Gary Carter	.45
56	Mike LaValliere	.05
57	Benito Santiago	.05
58	David Cone	.05
59	Dwight Gooden	.05
60	Orel Hershiser	.05
61	Tom Browning	.05
62	Danny Jackson	.05
63	Bob Knepper	.05
64	Mark Davis	.05
65	John Franco	.05
66	Randy Myers	.05

Stickers

Topps' 1989 stickers were produced in two formats. Some measure 2-1/8" x 3" while there are 128 pairs of half-size (1-1/2" x 2-1/8") stickers. All stickers are attached to Super Star stickercards from which they can be peeled and affixed in a special Yearbook which was sold separately for 50 cents. Stickers have large center photos with white borders. Above and below are zipping fastball graphics trailing graduated color bars (blues for N.L., reds for A.L.). A tiny black sticker number is in the lower-right corner. There is no player name on the stickers; the albums have a box under each space with player data. The half-size stickers are printed in pairs and are checklisted in that fashion. Values given are for complete sticker(s)/stickercard combinations, but without regard for which stickercard is on back.

		NM/M
Complete Set (326):		11.00
Common Player/Pair:		.05
Album:		2.00
1-230	George Bell, Jeff Ballard	.05
2-272	Gary Carter, Steve Farr	.25
3-324	Doug Jones, Mark Grace	.05
4-320	John Franco, Cecil Espy	.05
5-322	Andre Dawson, Ron Gant	.15
6-326	Pat Tabler, Walt Weiss	.05
7-317	Tom Browning, Tim Belcher	.05
8-239	Jeff Reardon, Larry Sheets	.05
9-325	Wade Boggs, Chris Sabo	.30
10-319	Kevin McReynolds, Jay Buhner	.05
11-323	Jose Canseco, Paul Gibson	.20
12-318	Orel Hershiser, Damon Berryhill	.05
13-231	Dave Smith, Mickey Tettleton	.05
14-302	Kevin Bass, Jack McDowell	.05
15-232	Mike Scott, Pete Stanicek	.05
16-256	Bill Doran, Jim Rice	.10
17-207	Rafael Ramirez, Andy Allanson	.05
18-181	Buddy Bell, Jack Howell	.05
19-214	Billy Hatcher, John Farrell	.05
20-275	Nolan Ryan, Frank Tanana	.50
21	Glenn Davis	.05
22	Bob Knepper	.05
23-211	Gerald Young, Tom Candiotti	.05
24-208	Dion James, Julio Franco	.05
25-243	Bruce Sutter, Jeff Russell	.20
26-310	Andres Thomas, Tommy John	.05
27-200	Zane Smith, B.J. Surhoff	.05
28-198	Ozzie Virgil, Teddy Higuera	.05
29-269	Rick Mahler, Floyd Bannister	.05
30-219	Albert Hall, Mickey Brantley	.05
31-203	Pete Smith, Jim Gantner	.05
32	Dale Murphy	.20
33	Gerald Perry	.05
34-177	Ron Gant, Chili Davis	.05
35-244	Bob Horner, Mike Stanley	.05
36-313	Willie McGee, Rafael Santana	.05
37-288	Luis Alicea, Greg Gagne	.05
38-279	Tony Pena, Gary Pettis	.05
39-184	Todd Worrell, Kirk McCaskill	.05
40-228	Pedro Guerrero, Bill Swift	.05
41-174	Tom Brunansky, Dick Schofield	.05
42-262	Terry Pendleton, Frank White	.05
43	Vince Coleman	.05
44	Ozzie Smith	.60
45-240	Jose Oquendo, Cecil Espy	.05
46-191	Vance Law, Pat Borders	.05
47-258	Rafael Palmeiro, Bob Stanley	.25
48-213	Greg Maddux, Greg Swindell	.30
49-229	Shawon Dunston, Jose Bautista	.05
50-210	Mark Grace, Cory Snyder	.05
51-187	Damon Berryhill, Kelly Gruber	.05
52-192	Rick Sutcliffe, Rance Mulliniks	.05
53-291	Jamie Moyer, Juan Berenguer	.05
54	Andre Dawson	.25
55	Ryne Sandberg	.60
56-284	Calvin Schiraldi, Jeff Reardon	.05
57-308	Steve Sax, Jack Clark	.05
58-263	Mike Scioscia, Bret Saberhagen	.05
59-298	Alfredo Griffin, Steve Lyons	.05
60-202	Fernando Valenzuela, Rob Deer	.05
61-286	Jay Howell, Dan Gladden	.05
62-305	Tim Leary, Bobby Thigpen	.05
63-212	John Shelby, Brook Jacoby	.05
64-306	John Tudor, John Candelaria	.05
65	Orel Hershiser	.05
66	Kirk Gibson	.05
67-223	Mike Marshall, Jim Presley	.05
68-206	Luis Rivera, Dale Sveum	.05
69-311	Tim Burke, Mike Pagliarulo	.05
70-253	Tim Wallach, Rich Gedman	.05
71-265	Pascual Perez, Bo Jackson	.05
72-185	Hubie Brooks, Fred McGriff	.05
73-250	Jeff Parrett, Steve Buechele	.05
74-316	Dennis Martinez, Rich Dotson	.05
75-285	Andy McGaffigan, Bert Blyleven	.05
76	Andres Galarraga	.05
77	Rock Raines	.05
78-287	Nelson Santovenia, Kent Hrbek	.05
79-261	Rick Reuschel, Mike Boddicker	.05
80-276	Mike Aldrete, Luis Salazar	.05
81-247	Kelly Downs, Mitch Williams	.05
82-283	Jose Uribe, Chet Lemon	.05
83-190	Mike Krukow, Mike Flanagan	.05
84-179	Kevin Mitchell, Devon White	.05
85-195	Brett Butler, Tom Henke	.05
86-252	Don Robinson, Dwight Evans	.05
87	Robby Thompson	.05
88	Will Clark	.05
89-188	Candy Maldonado, Lloyd Moseby	.05
90-180	Len Dykstra, Bryan Harvey	.05
91-234	Howard Johnson, Rene Gonzalez	.05
92-266	Roger McDowell, Kurt Stillwell	.05
93-222	Keith Hernandez, Steve Balboni	.05
94-178	Gary Carter, Brian Downing	.05
95-277	Kevin McReynolds, Jack Morris	.05
96-307	David Cone, Dave Righetti	.05
97-175	Randy Myers, Bob Boone	.05
98	Darryl Strawberry	.05
99	Doc Gooden	.05
100-257	Ron Darling, Marty Barrett	.05
101-201	Benny Santiago, Greg Brock	.05
102-273	John Kruk, Mike Henneman	.05
103-242	Chris Brown, Ruben Sierra	.05
104-255	Roberto Alomar, Mike Greenwell	.10
105-290	Keith Moreland, Tim Laudner	.05
106-217	Randy Ready, Scott Bailes	.05
107-267	Marvell Wynne, Danny Tartabull	.05
108-176	Lance McCullers, Mike Witt	.05
109	Tony Gwynn	.60
110	Mark Davis	.05
111-236	Andy Hawkins, Tom Niedenfeur	.05
112-233	Steve Bedrosian, Jim Traber	.05
113-196	Phil Bradley, Glenn Braggs	.05
114-189	Steve Jeltz, Tony Fernandez	.05
115-209	Von Hayes, Bud Black	.05
116-245	Kevin Gross, Charlie Hough	.05
117-218	Juan Samuel, Henry Cotto	.05
118-274	Shane Rawley, Doyle Alexander	.05
119-186	Chris James, Jimmy Key	.05
120	Mike Schmidt	.65
121	Don Carman	.05
122-280	Bruce Ruffin, Matt Nokes	.05
123-246	Bob Walk, Scott Fletcher	.05
124-278	John Smiley, Tom Brookens	.05
125-301	Sid Bream, Dan Pasqua	.05
126-251	Jose Lind, Lee Smith	.05
127-309	Barry Bonds, Willie Randolph	.40
128-294	Mike LaValliere, Gene Larkin	.05
129-225	Jeff D. Robinson, Scott Bradley	.05
130-295	Mike Dunne, Dave Gallagher	.05
131	Bobby Bonilla	.05
132	Andy Van Slyke	.05
133-241	Rafael Belliard, Jose Guzman	.05
134-197	Nick Esasky, Dan Plesac	.05
135-300	Bo Diaz, Fred Manrique	.05
136-221	John Franco, Mark Langston	.05
137-312	Barry Larkin, Rickey Henderson	.25
138-173	Eric Davis, Ron Hassey	.05
139-299	Jeff Treadway, Carlton Fisk	.05
140-254	Jose Rijo, Ellis Burks	.05
141-220	Tom Browning, Mike Moore	.05
142	Chris Sabo	.05
143	Danny Jackson	.05
144-199	Kal Daniels, Jeffrey Leonard	.05
145	Rickey Henderson/AS	.50
146	Paul Molitor/AS	.25
147	Wade Boggs/AS	.35
148	Jose Canseco/AS	.20
149	Dave Winfield/AS	.30
150	Cal Ripken Jr./AS	.50
151	Mark McGwire/AS	.40
152	Terry Steinbach/AS	.05
153	Frank Viola/AS	.05
154	Vince Coleman/AS	.05
155	Ryne Sandberg/AS	.35
156	Andre Dawson/AS	.15
157	Darryl Strawberry/AS	.05
158	Bobby Bonilla/AS	.05
159	Will Clark/AS	.05
160	Gary Carter/AS	.05
161	Ozzie Smith/AS	.35
162	Doc Gooden/AS	.05
163-268	Dave Stewart, Willie Wilson	.05
164-297	Dave Henderson, Ivan Calderon	.05
165-321	Terry Steinbach, Dave Gallagher	.05
166-264	Bob Welch, Kevin Seitzer	.05
167-224	Dennis Eckersley, Rey Quinones	.30
168-235	Walt Weiss, Terry Kennedy	.05
169-296	Dave Parker, Melido Perez	.05
170-289	Carney Lansford, Gary Gaetti	.05
171	Jose Canseco	.35
172	Mark McGwire	.75
182	Johnny Ray	.05
183	Wally Joyner	.05
193	George Bell	.05
194	Dave Steib	.05
204	Paul Molitor	.50
205	Robin Yount	.50
215	Doug Jones	.05
216	Joe Carter	.05
226	Harold Reynolds	.05
227	Alvin Davis	.05
237	Cal Ripken Jr.	1.00
238	Eddie Murray	.50
248	Pete O'Brien	.05
249	Pete Incaviglia	.05
259	Roger Clemens	.65
260	Wade Boggs	.60
270	George Brett	.65
271	Mark Gubicza	.05
281	Alan Trammell	.05
282	Lou Whitaker	.05
292	Frank Viola	.05
293	Kirby Puckett	.60
303	Ozzie Guillen	.05
304	Harold Baines	.05
314	Don Mattingly	.65
315	Dave Winfield	.50

LJN Baseball Talk

Another generation of "talking baseball cards" was produced by Topps and the LJN Toy Co. in 1989. After purchasing a hand-held player, collectors could buy sets of four "Baseball Talk Collection" cards for about $4. The 3-1/4" x 5-1/4" cards have a plastic sheet laminated on their backs containing information about the player which could be heard by inserting the card into the player. Fronts of the cards of players active in 1989 reproduce their 1989 Topps cards. The cards of earlier stars reproduce various older Topps cards of those players. Narrators on the cards were Don Drysdale, Joe Torre and Mel Allen.

		NM/M
Complete Set (164):		125.00
Common Player:		1.00
Record Player:		30.00
1	1975 World Series Game 6	1.00
2	1986 World Series Game 6	1.00
3	1986 ALCS Game 6	1.00
4	1956 World Series Game 5	1.00
5	1986 NLCS Game 6	1.00
6	1969 World Series Game 5	1.00
7	1984 World Series Game 5	1.00
8	1988 World Series Game 1	1.00
9	Reggie Jackson	4.00
10	Brooks Robinson	1.50
11	Billy Williams	1.50
12	Bobby Thomson	1.00
13	Harmon Killebrew	1.50
14	Johnny Bench	2.00
15	Tom Seaver	2.00
16	Willie Stargell	1.50
17	Ernie Banks	4.00
18	Gaylord Perry	1.50
19	Bill Mazeroski	1.50
20	Babe Ruth	7.50
21	Lou Gehrig	6.00
22	Ty Cobb	5.00
23	Bob Gibson	1.50
24	Al Kaline	1.50
25	Rod Carew	1.50
26	Lou Brock	1.50
27	Stan Musial	4.00
28	Joe Morgan	1.50
29	Willie McCovey	1.50
30	Duke Snider	4.00
31	Whitey Ford	4.00
32	Eddie Mathews	1.50
33	Carl Yastrzemski	2.00
34	Pete Rose	7.50
35	Hank Aaron/1976	6.00
36	Ralph Kiner	1.50
37	Steve Carlton	1.50
38	Roberto Clemente	7.50
39	Don Drysdale	1.50
40	Robin Roberts	1.50
41	Hank Aaron/1954	6.00
42	Dave Winfield	2.00
43	Alan Trammell	1.00
44	Darryl Strawberry	1.00
45	Ozzie Smith	3.00
46	Kirby Puckett	3.00
47	Will Clark	1.00
48	Keith Hernandez	1.00
49	Wally Joyner	1.00
50	Mike Scott	1.00
51	Eric Davis	1.00
52	George Brett	4.00
53	George Bell	1.00
54	Tommy Lasorda	1.00
55	Rickey Henderson	2.00
56	Robin Yount	2.00
57	Wade Boggs	3.00

58 Roger Clemens 4.00
59 Vince Coleman 1.00
60 Jose Canseco 1.50
61 Fernando Valenzuela 1.00
62 Tony Gwynn 3.00
63 Dwight Gooden 1.00
64 Mark McGwire 6.00
65 Jack Clark 1.00
66 Dale Murphy 1.25
67 Kirk Gibson 1.00
68 Jack Morris 1.00
69 Ryne Sandberg 3.00
70 Nolan Ryan 9.00
71 John Tudor 1.00
72 Mike Schmidt 4.00
73 Dave Righetti 1.00
74 Pedro Guerrero 1.00
75 Rick Sutcliffe 1.00
76 Gary Carter 2.00
77 Cal Ripken Jr. 9.00
78 Andre Dawson 1.25
79 Andy Van Slyke 1.00
80 Tim Raines 1.00
81 Frank Viola 1.00
82 Don Mattingly 4.00
83 Rick Reuschel 1.00
84 Willie McGee 1.00
85 Mark Langston 1.00
86 Ron Darling 1.00
87 Gregg Jefferies 1.00
88 Harold Baines 1.00
89 Eddie Murray 2.00
90 Barry Larkin 1.00
91 Gary Gaetti 1.00
92 Bret Saberhagen 1.00
93 Roger McDowell 1.00
94 Joe Magrane 1.00
95 Juan Samuel 1.00
96 Bert Blyleven 1.00
97 Kal Daniels 1.00
98 Kevin Bass 1.00
99 Glenn Davis 1.00
100 Steve Sax 1.00
101 Rich Gossage 1.00
102 Roger Craig 1.00
103 Carney Lansford 1.00
104 Joe Carter 1.00
105 Bruce Sutter 2.00
106 Barry Bonds 9.00
107 Danny Jackson 1.00
108 Mike Flanagan 1.00
109 Dwight Evans 1.00
110 Ron Guidry 1.00
111 Bruce Hurst 1.00
112 Jim Rice 1.25
113 Oddibe McDowell 1.00
114 Bobby Bonilla 1.00
115 Bob Welch 1.00
116 Dave Parker 1.00
117 Tim Wallach 1.00
118 Tom Henke 1.00
119 Mike Greenwell 1.00
120 Kevin Seitzer 1.00
121 Randy Myers 1.00
122 Andres Galarraga 1.00
123 Orel Hershiser 1.00
124 Cory Snyder 1.00
125 Mike Witt 1.00
126 Mike LaValliere 1.00
127 Pete Incaviglia 1.00
128 Dennis Eckersley 2.00
129 Jimmy Key 1.00
130 John Franco 1.00
131 Dan Plesac 1.00
132 Tony LaRussa 1.00
133 Hubie Brooks 1.00
134 Chili Davis 1.00
135 Bob Boone 1.00
136 Jeff Reardon 1.00
137 Candy Maldonado 1.00
138 Mike Marshall 1.00
139 Tommy John 1.00
140 Chris Sabo 1.00
141 Alvin Davis 1.00
142 Frank White 1.00
143 Harold Reynolds 1.00
144 Lee Smith 1.00
145 John Kruk 1.00
146 Tony Fernandez 1.00
147 Steve Bedrosian 1.00
148 Benito Santiago 1.00
149 Ozzie Guillen 1.00
150 Gerald Perry 1.00
151 Carlton Fisk 2.00
152 Tom Brunansky 1.00
153 Paul Molitor 2.00
154 Todd Worrell 1.00
155 Brett Butler 1.00
156 Sparky Anderson 1.00
157 Kent Hrbek 1.00
158 Frank Tanana 1.00
159 Kevin Mitchell 1.00
160 Charlie Hough 1.00
161 Doug Jones 1.00
162 Lou Whitaker 1.00
163 Fred Lynn 1.00
--- Checklist .50

Sport Shots Portfolios

In its second year, the number of baseball card folders produced by Shaeffer Eaton reproducing current Topps baseball cards was drastically reduced, from 130 to 39. The format remains the same, a 9-1/2" x 11-3/4" cardboard two-pocket folder. The 1989 portfolios are considerably scarcer than the 1988s.

NM/M
Complete Set (39): 40.00
Common Player: 1.00
10 Andre Dawson 1.25
30 Doc Gooden 1.00
70 Mark McGwire 4.00
85 Kevin McReynolds 1.00
110 Paul Molitor 1.50
120 Frank Viola 1.00
145 Dave Stewart 1.00
180 Mike Scott 1.00
200 George Brett 2.50
205 Dwight Evans 1.00
230 Ozzie Smith 2.00
233 Gregg Jefferies 1.00
260 Dave Winfield 1.50
300 Darryl Strawberry 1.00
330 Eric Davis 1.00
335 Dave Righetti 1.00
340 Kirk Gibson 1.00
370 Dennis Eckersley 1.25
380 Rickey Henderson 1.50
425 Jay Howell 1.00
450 Roger Clemens 2.50
480 Keith Hernandez 1.00
500 Jose Canseco 1.25
527 Dave Henderson 1.00
550 Orel Hershiser 1.00
570 Tony Gwynn 2.00
582 Mike A. Marshall 1.00
590 Andres Galarraga 1.00
600 Wade Boggs 2.00
630 Mike Greenwell 1.00
650 Kirby Puckett 2.00
660 Will Clark 1.00
700 Don Mattingly 2.50
710 David Cone 1.00
725 Terry Steinbach 1.00
730 Danny Jackson 1.00
755 Mike Scioscia 1.00
770 Alan Trammell 1.00
785 Ellis Burks 1.00

1990 Topps

The 1990 Topps set again included 792 cards, and sported a newly-designed front that featured six different color schemes. The set led off with a special four-card salute to Nolan Ryan, and features other specials including All-Stars, Number 1 Draft Picks, Record Breakers, managers, rookies, and "Turn Back the Clock" cards. The set also includes a special card commemorating A. Bartlett Giamatti, the late baseball commissioner. Backs are printed in black on a chartreuse background. The set features 725 different individual player cards, the most ever, including 138 players' first appearance in a regular Topps set.

NM/M
Unopened Factory Set, Retail (792): 25.00
Unopened Factory Set, Hobby (792): 20.00
Complete Set (792): 15.00
Common Player: .05
Wax Pack (16): .60
Wax Box (36): 12.00
Cello Pack (31): 1.00
Cello Box (24): 15.00
Rack Pack (45): 1.00
Rack Box (24): 16.00
Vending Box (500): 7.50
1 Nolan Ryan .75
2 Nolan Ryan (Mets) .35
3 Nolan Ryan (Angels) .25
4 Nolan Ryan (Astros) .25
5 Nolan Ryan (Rangers) .25
6 Vince Coleman (Record Breaker) .05
7 Rickey Henderson (Record Breaker) .20
8 Cal Ripken, Jr. (Record Breaker) .40
9 Eric Plunk .05
10 Barry Larkin .05
11 Paul Gibson .05
12 Joe Girardi **RC** .05
13 Mark Williamson .05
14 Mike Fetters **RC** .05
15 Teddy Higuera .05
16 Kent Anderson **RC** .05
17 Kelly Downs .05
18 Carlos Quintana .05
19 Al Newman .05
20 Mark Gubicza .05
21 Jeff Torborg .05
22 Bruce Ruffin .05
23 Randy Velarde .05
24 Joe Hesketh .05
25 Willie Randolph .05
26 Don Slaught .05
27 Rick Leach .05
28 Duane Ward .05
29 John Cangelosi .05
30 David Cone .05
31 Henry Cotto .05
32 John Farrell .05
33 Greg Walker .05
34 Tony Fossas **RC** .05
35 Benito Santiago .05
36 John Costello .05
37 Domingo Ramos .05
38 Wes Gardner .05
39 Curt Ford .05
40 Jay Howell .05
41 Matt Williams .05
42 Jeff Robinson .05
43 Dante Bichette .05
44 Roger Salkeld **RC** (#1 Draft Pick) .10
45 Dave Parker .05
46 Rob Dibble .05
47 Brian Harper .05
48 Zane Smith .05
49 Tom Lawless .05
50 Glenn Davis .05
51 Doug Rader .05
52 Jack Daugherty **RC** .05
53 Mike LaCoss .05
54 Joel Skinner .05
55 Darrell Evans .05
56 Franklin Stubbs .05
57 Greg Vaughn .05
58 Keith Miller .05
59 Ted Power .05
60 George Brett .50
61 Deion Sanders .10
62 Ramon Martinez .05
63 Mike Pagliarulo .05
64 Danny Darwin .05
65 Devon White .05
66 Greg Litton **RC** .05
67 Scott Sanderson .05
68 Dave Henderson .05
69 Todd Frohwirth .05
70 Mike Greenwell .05
71 Allan Anderson .05
72 Jeff Huson **RC** .05
73 Bob Milacki .05
74 Jeff Jackson **RC** (#1 Draft Pick) .05
75 Doug Jones .05
76 Dave Valle .05
77 Dave Bergman .05
78 Mike Flanagan .05
79 Ron Kittle .05
80 Jeff Russell .05
81 Bob Rodgers .05
82 Scott Terry .05
83 Hensley Meulens .05
84 Ray Searage .05
85 Juan Samuel .05
86 Paul Kilgus .05
87 Rick Luecken **RC** .05
88 Glenn Braggs .05
89 Clint Zavaras **RC** .05
90 Jack Clark .05
91 Steve Frey **RC** .05
92 Mike Stanley .05
93 Shawn Hillegas .05
94 Herm Winningham .05
95 Todd Worrell .05
96 Jody Reed .05
97 Curt Schilling .25
98 Jose Gonzalez **RC** .05
99 Rich Monteleone **RC** .05
100 Will Clark .05
101 Shane Rawley .05
102 Stan Javier .05
103 Marvin Freeman .05
104 Bob Knepper .05
105 Randy Myers .05
106 Charlie O'Brien .05
107 Fred Lynn .05
108 Rod Nichols .05
109 Roberto Kelly .05
110 Tommy Helms .05
111 Ed Whited .05
112 Glenn Wilson .05
113 Manny Lee .05
114 Mike Bielecki .05
115 Tony Pena .05
116 Floyd Bannister .05
117 Mike Sharperson **RC** .05
118 Erik Hanson .05
119 Billy Hatcher .05
120 John Franco .05
121 Robin Ventura .05
122 Shawn Abner .05
123 Rich Gedman .05
124 Dave Dravecky .05
125 Kent Hrbek .05
126 Randy Kramer .05
127 Mike Devereaux .05
128 Checklist 1-132 .05
129 Ron Jones .05
130 Bert Blyleven .05
131 Matt Nokes .05
132 Lance Blankenship **RC** .05
133 Ricky Horton .05
134 Earl Cunningham **RC** (#1 Draft Pick) .05
135 Dave Magadan .05
136 Kevin Brown .05
137 Marty Pevey **RC** .05
138 Al Leiter .05
139 Greg Brock .05
140 Andre Dawson .25
141 John Hart .05
142 Jeff Wetherby **RC** .05
143 Rafael Belliard .05
144 Bud Black .05
145 Terry Steinbach .05
146 Rob Richie **RC** .05
147 Chuck Finley .05
148 Edgar Martinez **RC** .05
149 Steve Farr .05
150 Kirk Gibson .05
151 Rick Mahler .05
152 Lonnie Smith .05
153 Randy Milligan .05
154 Mike Maddux .05
155 Ellis Burks .05
156 Ken Patterson .05
157 Craig Biggio .05
158 Craig Lefferts .05
159 Mike Felder .05
160 Dave Righetti .05
161 Harold Reynolds .05
162 Todd Zeile **RC** .20
163 Phil Bradley .05
164 Jeff Juden **RC** (#1 Draft Pick) .05
165 Walt Weiss .05
166 Bobby Witt .05
167 Kevin Appier **RC** .05
168 Jose Lind .05
169 Richard Dotson .05
170 George Bell .05
171 Russ Nixon .05
172 Tom Lampkin **RC** .05
173 Tim Belcher .05
174 Jeff Kunkel .05
175 Mike Moore .05
176 Luis Quinones .05
177 Mike Henneman .05
178 Chris James .05
179 Brian Holton .05
180 Rock Raines .05
181 Juan Agosto .05
182 Mookie Wilson .05
183 Steve Lake .05
184 Danny Cox .05
185 Ruben Sierra .05
186 Dave LaPoint .05
187 Rick Wrona **RC** .05
188 Mike Smithson .05
189 Dick Schofield .05
190 Rick Reuschel .05
191 Pat Borders .05
192 Don August .05
193 Andy Benes .05
194 Glenallen Hill **RC** .05
195 Tim Burke .05
196 Gerald Young .05
197 Doug Drabek .05
198 Mike Marshall .05
199 Sergio Valdez **RC** .05
200 Don Mattingly .50
201 Cito Gaston .05
202 Mike Macfarlane .05
203 Mike Roesler **RC** .05
204 Bob Dernier .05
205 Mark Davis .05
206 Nick Esasky .05
207 Bob Ojeda .05
208 Brook Jacoby .05
209 Greg Mathews .05
210 Ryne Sandberg .45
211 John Cerutti .05
212 Joe Orsulak .05
213 Scott Bankhead .05
214 Terry Francona .05
215 Kirk McCaskill .05
216 Ricky Jordan .05
217 Don Robinson .05
218 Wally Backman .05
219 Donn Pall .05
220 Barry Bonds .75
221 Gary Mielke **RC** .05
222 Kurt Stillwell .05
223 Tommy Gregg .05
224 Delino DeShields **RC** .15
225 Jim Deshaies .05
226 Mickey Hatcher .05
227 Kevin Tapani **RC** .15
228 Dave Martinez .05
229 David Wells .05
230 Keith Hernandez .05
231 Jack McKeon .05
232 Darnell Coles .05
233 Ken Hill **RC** .05
234 Mariano Duncan .05
235 Jeff Reardon .05
236 Hal Morris **RC** .05
237 Kevin Ritz **RC** .05
238 Felix Jose **RC** .05
239 Eric Show .05
240 Mark Grace .05
241 Mike Krukow .05
242 Fred Manrique .05
243 Barry Jones .05
244 Bill Schroeder .05
245 Roger Clemens .50
246 Jim Eisenreich .05
247 Jerry Reed .05
248 Dave Anderson .05
249 Mike Smith **RC** .05
250 Jose Canseco .25
251 Jeff Blauser .05
252 Otis Nixon .05
253 Mark Portugal .05
254 Francisco Cabrera .05
255 Bobby Thigpen .05
256 Marvell Wynne .05
257 Jose DeLeon .05
258 Barry Lyons .05
259 Lance McCullers .05
260 Eric Davis .05
261 Whitey Herzog .05
262 Checklist 133-264 .05
263 Mel Stottlemyre, Jr. **RC** .10
264 Bryan Clutterbuck .05
265 Pete O'Brien .05
266 German Gonzalez .05
267 Mark Davidson .05
268 Rob Murphy .05
269 Dickie Thon .05
270 Dave Stewart .05
271 Chet Lemon .05
272 Bryan Harvey .05
273 Bobby Bonilla .05
274 Goose Gozzo **RC** .05
275 Mickey Tettleton .05
276 Gary Thurman .05
277 Lenny Harris **RC** .05
278 Pascual Perez .05
279 Steve Buechele .05
280 Lou Whitaker .05
281 Kevin Bass .05
282 Derek Lilliquist .05
283 Albert Belle .15
284 Mark Gardner **RC** .05
285 Willie McGee .05
286 Lee Guetterman .05
287 Vance Law .05
288 Greg Briley .05
289 Norm Charlton .05
290 Robin Yount .35
291 Dave Johnson .05
292 Jim Gott .05
293 Mike Gallego .05
294 Craig McMurtry .05
295 Fred McGriff .05
296 Jeff Ballard .05
297 Tom Herr .05
298 Danny Gladden .05
299 Adam Peterson **RC** .05
300 Bo Jackson .10
301 Don Aase .05
302 Marcus Lawton **RC** .05
303 Rick Cerone .05
304 Marty Clary **RC** .05
305 Eddie Murray .35
306 Tom Niedenfuer .05
307 Bip Roberts .05
308 Jose Guzman .05
309 Eric Yelding **RC** .05
310 Steve Bedrosian .05
311 Dwight Smith .05
312 Dan Quisenberry .05
313 Gus Polidor .05
314 Donald Harris **RC** (#1 Draft Pick) .05
315 Bruce Hurst .05
316 Carney Lansford .05
317 Mark Guthrie **RC** .05
318 Wallace Johnson .05
319 Dion James .05
320 Dave Steib .05
321 Joe M. Morgan .05
322 Junior Ortiz .05
323 Willie Wilson .05
324 Pete Harnisch **RC** .05
325 Robby Thompson .05
326 Tom McCarthy **RC** .05
327 Ken Williams .05
328 Curt Young .05
329 Oddibe McDowell .05
330 Ron Darling .05
331 Juan Gonzalez **RC** 1.50
332 Paul O'Neill .05
333 Bill Wegman .05
334 Johnny Ray .05
335 Andy Hawkins .05
336 Ken Griffey Jr. .75
337 Lloyd McClendon .05
338 Dennis Lamp .05
339 Dave Clark .05
340 Fernando Valenzuela .05
341 Tom Foley .05
342 Alex Trevino .05
343 Frank Tanana .05
344 George Canale **RC** .05
345 Harold Baines .05
346 Jim Presley .05
347 Junior Felix **RC** .05
348 Gary Wayne **RC** .05
349 Steve Finley **RC** .15
350 Bret Saberhagen .05
351 Roger Craig .05
352 Bryn Smith .05
353 Sandy Alomar .05
354 Stan Belinda **RC** .05
355 Marty Barrett .05
356 Randy Ready .05
357 Dave West .05
358 Andres Thomas .05
359 Jimmy Jones .05
360 Paul Molitor .35
361 Randy McCament **RC** .05
362 Damon Berryhill .05
363 Dan Petry .05
364 Rolando Roomes **RC** .05
365 Ozzie Guillen .05
366 Mike Heath .05
367 Mike Morgan .05
368 Bill Doran .05
369 Todd Burns .05
370 Tim Wallach .05
371 Jimmy Key .05
372 Terry Kennedy .05
373 Alvin Davis .05
374 Steve Cummings **RC** .05
375 Dwight Evans .05
376 Checklist 265-396 .05
377 Mickey Weston **RC** .05
378 Luis Salazar .05
379 Steve Rosenberg .05
380 Dave Winfield .35
381 Frank Robinson .10
382 Jeff Musselman .05
383 John Morris .05
384 Pat Combs **RC** .05
385 Fred McGriff/AS .05
386 Julio Franco/AS .05
387 Wade Boggs/AS .20
388 Cal Ripken, Jr./AS .40
389 Robin Yount/AS .20
390 Ruben Sierra/AS .05
391 Kirby Puckett/AS .25
392 Carlton Fisk/AS .20
393 Bret Saberhagen/AS .05
394 Jeff Ballard/AS .05
395 Jeff Russell/AS .05
396 A. Bartlett Giamatti .20
397 Will Clark/AS .05
398 Ryne Sandberg/AS .20
399 Howard Johnson/AS .05
400 Ozzie Smith/AS .20
401 Kevin Mitchell/AS .05
402 Eric Davis/AS .05
403 Tony Gwynn/AS .25
404 Craig Biggio/AS .05
405 Mike Scott/AS .05
406 Joe Magrane/AS .05
407 Mark Davis/AS .05
408 Trevor Wilson .05
409 Tom Brunansky .05
410 Joe Boever .05
411 Ken Phelps .05
412 Jamie Moyer .05
413 Brian DuBois **RC** .05
414a Frank Thomas No Name **RC** (No name on front.) 500.00
414b Frank Thomas **RC** (Name on front.) 3.00
415 Shawon Dunston .05
416 Dave Johnson **RC** .05
417 Jim Gantner .05
418 Tom Browning .05
419 Beau Allred **RC** .05
420 Carlton Fisk .35
421 Greg Minton .05
422 Pat Sheridan .05
423 Fred Toliver .05
424 Jerry Reuss .05
425 Bill Landrum .05
426 Jeff Hamilton .05
427 Carmem Castillo .05
428 Steve Davis **RC** .05
429 Tom Kelly .05
430 Pete Incaviglia .05
431 Randy Johnson .35
432 Damaso Garcia .05
433 Steve Olin **RC** .05
434 Mark Carreon **RC** .05
435 Kevin Seitzer .05
436 Mel Hall .05
437 Les Lancaster .05
438 Greg Myers **RC** .05
439 Jeff Parrett .05
440 Alan Trammell .05
441 Bob Kipper .05
442 Jerry Browne .05
443 Cris Carpenter .05
444 Kyle Abbott **RC** (FDP) .10
445 Danny Jackson .05
446 Dan Pasqua .05
447 Atlee Hammaker .05
448 Greg Gagne .05
449 Dennis Rasmussen .05
450 Rickey Henderson .35
451 Mark Lemke .05
452 Luis de los Santos **RC** .05
453 Jody Davis .05
454a Jeff King **RC** (No white on back.) 100.00
454b Jeff King (Correct use of white.) .05
455 Jeffrey Leonard .05
456 Chris Gwynn **RC** .05
457 Gregg Jefferies .05
458 Bob McClure .05
459 Jim Lefebvre .05
460 Mike Scott .05
461 Carlos Martinez **RC** .05
462 Denny Walling .05
463 Drew Hall .05
464 Jerome Walton **RC** .05

465 Kevin Gross .05
466 Rance Mulliniks .05
467 Juan Nieves .05
468 Billy Ripken .05
469 John Kruk .05
470 Frank Viola .05
471 Mike Brumley .05
472 Jose Uribe .05
473 Joe Price .05
474 Rich Thompson .05
475 Bob Welch .05
476 Brad Komminsk .05
477 Willie Fraser .05
478 Mike LaValliere .05
479 Frank White .05
480 Sid Fernandez .05
481 Garry Templeton .05
482 Steve Carter **RC** .05
483 Alejandro Pena .05
484 Mike Fitzgerald .05
485 John Candelaria .05
486 Jeff Treadway .05
487 Steve Searcy .05
488 Ken Oberkfell .05
489 Nick Leyva .05
490 Dan Plesac .05
491 Dave Cochrane **RC** .05
492 Ron Oester .05
493 Jason Grimsley **RC** .05
494 Terry Puhl .05
495 Lee Smith .05
496 Cecil Espy .05
497 Dave Schmidt .05
498 Rick Schu .05
499 Bill Long .05
500 Kevin Mitchell .05
501 Matt Young .05
502 Mitch Webster .05
503 Randy St. Claire .05
504 Tom O'Malley .05
505 Kelly Gruber .05
506 Tom Glavine .25
507 Gary Redus .05
508 Terry Leach .05
509 Tom Pagnozzi .05
510 Dwight Gooden .05
511 Clay Parker .05
512 Gary Pettis .05
513 Mark Eichhorn .05
514 Andy Allanson .05
515 Len Dykstra .05
516 Tim Leary .05
517 Roberto Alomar .15
518 Bill Krueger .05
519 Bucky Dent .05
520 Mitch Williams .05
521 Craig Worthington .05
522 Mike Dunne .05
523 Jay Bell .05
524 Daryl Boston .05
525 Wally Joyner .05
526 Checklist 397-528 .05
527 Ron Hassey .05
528 Kevin Wickander **RC** .05
529 Greg Harris .05
530 Mark Langston .05
531 Ken Caminiti .05
532 Cecilio Guante .05
533 Tim Jones **RC** .05
534 Louie Meadows .05
535 John Smoltz .05
536 Bob Geren **RC** .05
537 Mark Grant .05
538 Billy Spiers **RC** .05
539 Neal Heaton .05
540 Danny Tartabull .05
541 Pat Perry .05
542 Darren Daulton .05
543 Nelson Liriano .05
544 Dennis Boyd .05
545 Kevin McReynolds .05
546 Kevin Hickey .05
547 Jack Howell .05
548 Pat Clements .05
549 Don Zimmer .05
550 Julio Franco .05
551 Tim Crews .05
552 Mike Smith **RC** .05
553 Scott Scudder **RC** .05
554 Jay Buhner .05
555 Jack Morris .05
556 Gene Larkin .05
557 Jeff Innis **RC** .05
558 Rafael Ramirez .05
559 Andy McGaffigan .05
560 Steve Sax .05
561 Ken Dayley .05
562 Chad Kreuter .05
563 Alex Sanchez .05
564 Tyler Houston **RC** (#1 Draft Pick) .10
565 Scott Fletcher .05
566 Mark Knudson .05
567 Ron Gant .05
568 John Smiley .05
569 Ivan Calderon .05
570 Cal Ripken, Jr. .75
571 Brett Butler .05
572 Greg Harris .05
573 Danny Heep .05
574 Bill Swift .05
575 Lance Parrish .05
576 Mike Dyer **RC** .05
577 Charlie Hayes **RC** .05
578 Joe Magrane .05
579 Art Howe .05
580 Joe Carter .05
581 Ken Griffey .05
582 Rick Honeycutt .05
583 Bruce Benedict .05
584 Phil Stephenson **RC** .05
585 Kal Daniels .05
586 Ed Nunez .05
587 Lance Johnson .05
588 Rick Rhoden .05
589 Mike Aldrete .05
590 Ozzie Smith .45
591 Todd Stottlemyre .05
592 R.J. Reynolds .05
593 Scott Bradley .05
594 Luis Sojo **RC** .05
595 Greg Swindell .05
596 Jose DeJesus **RC** .05
597 Chris Bosio .05
598 Brady Anderson .05
599 Frank Williams .05
600 Darryl Strawberry .05
601 Luis Rivera .05
602 Scott Garrelts .05
603 Tony Armas .05
604 Ron Robinson .05
605 Mike Scioscia .05
606 Storm Davis .05
607 Steve Jeltz .05
608 Eric Anthony **RC** .10
609 Sparky Anderson .10
610 Pedro Guerrero .05
611 Walt Terrell .05
612 Dave Gallagher .05
613 Jeff Pico .05
614 Nelson Santovenia .05
615 Rob Deer .05
616 Brian Holman .05
617 Geronimo Berroa .05
618 Eddie Whitson .05
619 Rob Ducey .05
620 Tony Castillo **RC** .05
621 Melido Perez .05
622 Sid Bream .05
623 Jim Corsi .05
624 Darrin Jackson .05
625 Roger McDowell .05
626 Bob Melvin .05
627 Jose Rijo .05
628 Candy Maldonado .05
629 Eric Hetzel **RC** .05
630 Gary Gaetti .05
631 John Wetteland **RC** .15
632 Scott Lusader .05
633 Dennis Cook **RC** .05
634 Luis Polonia .05
635 Brian Downing .05
636 Jesse Orosco .05
637 Craig Reynolds .05
638 Jeff Montgomery .05
639 Tony LaRussa .05
640 Rick Sutcliffe .05
641 Doug Strange **RC** .05
642 Jack Armstrong .05
643 Alfredo Griffin .05
644 Paul Assenmacher .05
645 Jose Oquendo .05
646 Checklist 529-660 .05
647 Rex Hudler .05
648 Jim Clancy .05
649 Dan Murphy **RC** .05
650 Mike Witt .05
651 Rafael Santana .05
652 Mike Boddicker .05
653 John Moses .05
654 Paul Coleman **RC** (#1 Draft Pick) .05
655 Gregg Olson .05
656 Mackey Sasser .05
657 Terry Mulholland .05
658 Donell Nixon .05
659 Greg Cadaret .05
660 Vince Coleman .05
661 Dick Howser (Turn Back the Clock) .05
662 Mike Schmidt (Turn Back the Clock) .10
663 Fred Lynn (Turn Back the Clock) .05
664 Johnny Bench (Turn Back the Clock) .05
665 Sandy Koufax (Turn Back the Clock) .15
666 Brian Fisher .05
667 Curt Wilkerson .05
668 Joe Oliver **RC** .05
669 Tom Lasorda .05
670 Dennis Eckersley .30
671 Bob Boone .05
672 Roy Smith .05
673 Joey Meyer .05
674 Spike Owen .05
675 Jim Abbott .05
676 Randy Kutcher **RC** .05
677 Jay Tibbs .05
678 Kirt Manwaring .05
679 Gary Ward .05
680 Howard Johnson .05
681 Mike Schooler .05
682 Dann Bilardello .05
683 Kenny Rogers .05
684 Julio Machado **RC** .05
685 Tony Fernandez .05
686 Carmelo Martinez .05
687 Tim Birtsas .05
688 Milt Thompson .05
689 Rich Yett .05
690 Mark McGwire .65
691 Chuck Cary .05
692 Sammy Sosa **RC** 4.00
693 Calvin Schiraldi .05
694 Mike Stanton **RC** .05
695 Tom Henke .05
696 B.J. Surhoff .05
697 Mike Davis .05
698 Omar Vizquel .05
699 Jim Leyland .05
700 Kirby Puckett .45
701 Bernie Williams **RC** 1.00
702 Tony Phillips .05
703 Jeff Brantley .05
704 Chip Hale **RC** .05
705 Claudell Washington .05
706 Geno Petralli .05
707 Luis Aquino .05
708 Larry Sheets .05
709 Juan Berneguer .05
710 Von Hayes .05
711 Rick Aguilera .05
712 Todd Benzinger .05
713 Tim Drummond **RC** .05
714 Marquis Grissom **RC** .25
715 Greg Maddux .45
716 Steve Balboni .05
717 Ron Kakovice .05
718 Gary Sheffield .30
719 Wally Whitehurst **RC** .05
720 Andres Galarraga .05
721 Lee Mazzilli .05
722 Felix Fermin .05
723 Jeff Robinson .05
724 Juan Bell **RC** .05
725 Terry Pendleton .05
726 Gene Nelson .05
727 Pat Tabler .05
728 Jim Acker .05
729 Bobby Valentine .05
730 Tony Gwynn .45
731 Don Carman .05
732 Ernie Riles .05
733 John Dopson .05
734 Kevin Elster .05
735 Charlie Hough .05
736 Rick Dempsey .05
737 Chris Sabo .05
738 Gene Harris **RC** .05
739 Dale Sveum .05
740 Jesse Barfield .05
741 Steve Wilson .05
742 Ernie Whitt .05
743 Tom Candiotti .05
744 Kelly Mann **RC** .05
745 Hubie Brooks .05
746 Dave Smith .05
747 Randy Bush .05
748 Doyle Alexander .05
749 Mark Parent .05
750 Dale Murphy .15
751 Steve Lyons .05
752 Tom Gordon .05
753 Chris Speier .05
754 Bob Walk .05
755 Rafael Palmeiro .30
756 Ken Howell .05
757 Larry Walker **RC** .75
758 Mark Thurmond .05
759 Tom Trebelhorn .05
760 Wade Boggs .45
761 Mike Jackson .05
762 Doug Dascenzo .05
763 Denny Martinez .05
764 Tim Teufel .05
765 Chili Davis .05
766 Brian Meyer **RC** .05
767 Tracy Jones .05
768 Chuck Crim .05
769 Greg Hibbard **RC** .05
770 Cory Snyder .05
771 Pete Smith .05
772 Jeff Reed .05
773 Dave Leiper .05
774 Ben McDonald **RC** .20
775 Andy Van Slyke .05
776 Charlie Leibrandt .05
777 Tim Laudner .05
778 Mike Jeffcoat .05
779 Lloyd Moseby .05
780 Orel Hershiser .05
781 Mario Diaz .05
782 Jose Alvarez .05
783 Checklist 661-792 .05
784 Scott Bailes .05
785 Jim Rice .15
786 Eric King .05
787 Rene Gonzales .05
788 Frank DiPino .05
789 John Wathan .05
790 Gary Carter .35
791 Alvaro Espinoza .05
792 Gerald Perry .05

Tiffany

This specially boxed version of Topps' 1990 baseball card set was sold through hobby channels only. The checklist is identical to the regular-issue Topps set and the cards are nearly so. The Tiffany version features white cardboard stock and a high-gloss finish on the fronts.

	NM/M
Unopened Set (792):	115.00
Complete Set (792):	90.00
Common Player:	.10

Traded

For the first time, Topps "Traded" series cards were made available nationwide in retail wax packs. The 132-card set was also sold in complete boxed form as it has been in recent years. The wax pack traded cards feature gray backs, while the boxed set cards feature white backs. Each of the gray-back wax-pack cards can be found with copyright lines preceded by one or two asterisks. The cards are numbered 1T-132T and showcase rookies, players who changed teams and new managers.

	NM/M
Complete Set, Retail (132):	6.00
Complete Set, Hobby (132):	4.00
Common Player:	.05
Wax Pack (7):	.75
Wax Box (36):	9.00

1 Darrel Akerfelds .05
2 Sandy Alomar, Jr. .05
3 Brad Arnsberg .05
4 Steve Avery .05
5 Wally Backman .05
6 Carlos Baerga **RC** .10
7 Kevin Bass .05
8 Willie Blair **RC** .05
9 Mike Blowers **RC** .05
10 Shawn Boskie **RC** .05
11 Daryl Boston .05
12 Dennis Boyd .05
13 Glenn Braggs .05
14 Hubie Brooks .05
15 Tom Brunansky .05
16 John Burkett **RC** .05
17 Casey Candaele .05
18 John Candelaria .05
19 Gary Carter .75
20 Joe Carter .05
21 Rick Cerone .05
22 Scott Coolbaugh **RC** .05
23 Bobby Cox .05
24 Mark Davis .05
25 Storm Davis .05
26 Edgar Diaz **RC** .05
27 Wayne Edwards **RC** .05
28 Mark Eichhorn .05
29 Scott Erickson **RC** .05
30 Nick Esasky .05
31 Cecil Fielder .05
32 John Franco .05
33 Travis Fryman **RC** .25
34 Bill Gullickson .05
35 Darryl Hamilton .05
36 Mike Harkey .05
37 Bud Harrelson .05
38 Billy Hatcher .05
39 Keith Hernandez .05
40 Joe Hesketh .05
41 Dave Hollins **RC** .05
42 Sam Horn .05
43 Steve Howard **RC** .05
44 Todd Hundley **RC** .15
45 Jeff Huson .05
46 Chris James .05
47 Stan Javier .05
48 Dave Justice **RC** .75
49 Jeff Kaiser **RC** .05
50 Dana Kiecker **RC** .05
51 Joe Klink **RC** .05
52 Brent Knackert **RC** .05
53 Brad Komminsk .05
54 Mark Langston .05
55 Tim Layana **RC** .05
56 Rick Leach .05
57 Terry Leach .05
58 Tim Leary .05
59 Craig Lefferts .05
60 Charlie Leibrandt .05
61 Jim Leyritz **RC** .05
62 Fred Lynn .05
63 Kevin Maas **RC** .05
64 Shane Mack .05
65 Candy Maldonado .05
66 Fred Manrique .05
67 Mike Marshall .05
68 Carmelo Martinez .05
69 John Marzano .05
70 Ben McDonald .05
71 Jack McDowell .05
72 John McNamara .05
73 Orlando Mercado .05
74 Stump Merrill .05
75 Alan Mills **RC** .05
76 Hal Morris .05
77 Lloyd Moseby .05
78 Randy Myers .05
79 Tim Naehring **RC** .05
80 Junior Noboa .05
81 Matt Nokes .05
82 Pete O'Brien .05
83 John Olerud **RC** .75
84 Greg Olson **RC** .05
85 Junior Ortiz .05
86 Dave Parker .05
87 Rick Parker **RC** .05
88 Bob Patterson .05
89 Alejandro Pena .05
90 Tony Pena .05
91 Pascual Perez .05
92 Gerald Perry .05
93 Dan Petry .05
94 Gary Pettis .05
95 Tony Phillips .05
96 Lou Pinella .05
97 Luis Polonia .05
98 Jim Presley .05
99 Scott Radinsky **RC** .05
100 Willie Randolph .05
101 Jeff Reardon .05
102 Greg Riddoch .05
103 Jeff Robinson .05
104 Ron Robinson .05
105 Kevin Romine .05
106 Scott Ruskin **RC** .05
107 John Russell .05
108 Bill Sampen **RC** .05
109 Juan Samuel .05
110 Scott Sanderson .05
111 Jack Savage **RC** .05
112 Dave Schmidt .05
113 Red Schoendienst .10
114 Terry Shumpert **RC** .05
115 Matt Sinatro .05
116 Don Slaught .05
117 Bryn Smith .05
118 Lee Smith .05
119 Paul Sorrento **RC** .05
120 Franklin Stubbs .05
121 Russ Swan **RC** .05
122 Bob Tewksbury .05
123 Wayne Tolleson .05
124 John Tudor .05
125 Randy Veres **RC** .05
126 Hector Villanueva **RC** .05
127 Mitch Webster .05
128 Ernie Whitt .05
129 Frank Wills .05
130 Dave Winfield .75
131 Matt Young .05
132 Checklist .05

Traded Tiffany

Identical to the regular Topps Traded issue except for the glossy front surface, this special hobby-only boxed set shares the same checklist.

	NM/M
Complete Set (132):	25.00
Common Player:	.15

Traded Hank Aaron Bronze

This 1/4-size metal replica of Aaron's first-ever Topps card was issued to dealers who purchased cases of 1990 Topps Traded sets. Each detail of the 1954 Topps Aaron card is reproduced on the 1-1/4" x 1-3/4" bronze metal mini-card, right down to the stats.

	NM/M
128 Hank Aaron	15.00

Box Panels

This special 16-card set features four cards on four different box-bottom panels. The cards are identical in de-

sign to the regular 1990 Topps cards. The cards are designated by letter.

	NM/M
Complete Panel Set (4):	7.00
Complete Singles Set (16):	6.00
Common Panel:	1.00
Common Player:	.10

Panel 2.00
A Wade Boggs .60
B George Brett .75
C Andre Dawson .15
D Darrell Evans .10
Panel 1.00
E Dwight Gooden .10
F Rickey Henderson .45
G Tom Lasorda .10
H Fred Lynn .10
Panel 1.50
I Mark McGwire 1.00
J Dave Parker .10
K Jeff Reardon .10
L Rick Reuschel .10
Panel 4.00
M Jim Rice .20
N Cal Ripken, Jr. 1.50
O Nolan Ryan 1.50
P Ryne Sandberg .60

All-Star Glossy Set of 22

One glossy All-Star card was included in each 1990 Topps rack pack. The cards measure 2-1/2" x 3-1/2" and feature a similar style to past glossy All-Star cards. Special cards of All-Star team captains Carl Yastrzemski and Don Drysdale are included in the set.

	NM/M
Complete Set (22):	4.00
Common Player:	.05

1 Tom Lasorda .05
2 Will Clark .05
3 Ryne Sandberg .50
4 Howard Johnson .05
5 Ozzie Smith .40
6 Kevin Mitchell .05
7 Eric Davis .05
8 Tony Gwynn .50
9 Benny Santiago .05
10 Rick Rueschel .05
11 Don Drysdale .10
12 Tony LaRussa .05
13 Mark McGwire .75
14 Julio Franco .05
15 Wade Boggs .50
16 Cal Ripken, Jr. 1.00
17 Bo Jackson .10
18 Kirby Puckett .50
19 Ruben Sierra .05
20 Terry Steinbach .05
21 Dave Stewart .05
22 Carl Yastrzemski .10

All-Star Glossy Set of 60

Sharp color photographs and a clutter-free design are features of the cards in this 60-card send away set. Topps ini-

tiated the redemption series in 1983. Six special offer cards, included in Topps baseball wax packs, were necessary to obtain each of the six 10-card sets in the series.

		NM/M
Complete Set (60):		9.00
Common Player:		.10
1	Ryne Sandberg	.75
2	Nolan Ryan	2.00
3	Glenn Davis	.10
4	Dave Stewart	.10
5	Barry Larkin	.10
6	Carney Lansford	.10
7	Darryl Strawberry	.10
8	Steve Sax	.10
9	Carlos Martinez	.10
10	Gary Sheffield	.50
11	Don Mattingly	1.00
12	Mark Grace	.10
13	Bret Saberhagen	.10
14	Mike Scott	.10
15	Robin Yount	.60
16	Ozzie Smith	.75
17	Jeff Ballard	.10
18	Rick Reuschel	.10
19	Greg Briley	.10
20	Ken Griffey Jr.	1.25
21	Kevin Mitchell	.10
22	Wade Boggs	.75
23	Dwight Gooden	.10
24	George Bell	.10
25	Eric Davis	.10
26	Ruben Sierra	.10
27	Roberto Alomar	.20
28	Gary Gaetti	.10
29	Gregg Olson	.10
30	Tom Gordon	.10
31	Jose Canseco	.45
32	Pedro Guerrero	.10
33	Joe Carter	.10
34	Mike Scioscia	.10
35	Julio Franco	.10
36	Joe Magrane	.10
37	Rickey Henderson	.60
38	Tim Raines	.10
39	Jerome Walton	.10
40	Bob Geren	.10
41	Andre Dawson	.10
42	Mark McGwire	1.50
43	Howard Johnson	.10
44	Bo Jackson	.20
45	Shawon Dunston	.10
46	Carlton Fisk	.60
47	Mitch Williams	.10
48	Kirby Puckett	.75
49	Craig Worthington	.10
50	Jim Abbott	.10
51	Cal Ripken, Jr.	2.00
52	Will Clark	.10
53	Dennis Eckersley	.55
54	Craig Biggio	.10
55	Fred McGriff	.10
56	Tony Gwynn	.75
57	Mickey Tettleton	.10
58	Mark Davis	.10
59	Omar Vizquel	.10
60	Gregg Jefferies	.10

Glossy Rookies

While the size of the annual glossy rookies set increased to 33 cards from previous years' issues of 22, the format remained identical in 1990. Above the player photo is a colored banner with "1989 Rookies." The player's name appears in red in a yellow bar beneath the photo. Backs are printed in red and blue and contain a shield design with the notation, "1989 Rookies Commemorative Set." The player's name, position and team are listed below, along with a card number. Cards are numbered alphabetically in the set. The glossy rookies were found one per pack in jumbo (100-card) cello packs.

		NM/M
Complete Set (33):		6.00
Common Player:		.10
1	Jim Abbott	.10
2	Joey Belle	.50
3	Andy Benes	.10
4	Greg Briley	.10
5	Kevin Brown	.10
6	Mark Carreon	.10
7	Mike Devereaux	.10
8	Junior Felix	.10
9	Bob Geren	.10
10	Tom Gordon	.10
11	Ken Griffey Jr.	5.00
12	Pete Harnisch	.10
13	Greg W. Harris	.10
14	Greg Hibbard	.10
15	Ken Hill	.10
16	Gregg Jefferies	.10
17	Jeff King	.10
18	Derek Lilliquist	.10
19	Carlos Martinez	.10
20	Ramon Martinez	.10
21	Bob Milacki	.10
22	Gregg Olson	.10
23	Donn Pall	.10
24	Kenny Rogers	.10
25	Gary Sheffield	1.50
26	Dwight Smith	.10
27	Billy Spiers	.10
28	Omar Vizquel	.10
29	Jerome Walton	.10
30	Dave West	.10
31	John Wetteland	.10
32	Steve Wilson	.10
33	Craig Worthington	.10

Glossy Rookies Foil-test Cards

To test the use of metallic-foil highlights which it would debut on its 1991 Stadium Club and Desert Shield cards, Topps made a test run using as base cards the 33-piece "1989 Rookies Commemorative Set." The test consists of a 2-1/4" x 1/4" metallic strip with a "topps" logotype punched out of the center. Cards can be found with the strip in many different locations horizontally on the cards' fronts, and in many colors including silver, gold, red, green, blue and purple. Color of foil does not affect values, though a complete set in matching color might command a premium.

		NM/M
Complete Set (33):		40.00
Common Player:		1.00
1	Jim Abbott	1.00
2	Joey Belle	2.00
3	Andy Benes	1.00
4	Greg Briley	1.00
5	Kevin Brown	1.00
6	Mark Carreon	1.00
7	Mike Devereaux	1.00
8	Junior Felix	1.00
9	Bob Geren	1.00
10	Tom Gordon	1.00
11	Ken Griffey Jr.	20.00
12	Pete Harnisch	1.00
13	Greg W. Harris	1.00
14	Greg Hibbard	1.00
15	Ken Hill	1.00
16	Gregg Jefferies	1.00
17	Jeff King	1.00
18	Derek Lilliquist	1.00
19	Carlos Martinez	1.00
20	Ramon Martinez	1.00
21	Bob Milacki	1.00
22	Gregg Olson	1.00
23	Donn Pall	1.00
24	Kenny Rogers	1.00
25	Gary Sheffield	5.00
26	Dwight Smith	1.00
27	Billy Spiers	1.00
28	Omar Vizquel	1.00
29	Jerome Walton	1.00
30	Dave West	1.00
31	John Wetteland	1.00
32	Steve Wilson	1.00
33	Craig Worthington	1.00

Award Winners Commemorative Sheet

Six of 1989's top award winners are pictured in the style of 1990 Topps baseball cards on this sheet issued with blister packed sets of Topps baseball stickers. The cards are blank-backed and use photos which are different from those found on the same players' regular 1990 cards. Each player's award is noted in the panel beneath his name. The sheet measures 8-3/4" x 8-1/8" with individual cards measuring the standard 2-1/2" x 3-1/2".

		NM/M
Complete Set, Sheet:		3.00
Complete Set, Singles (6):		2.00
Common Player:		.10
(1)	Mark Davis (N.L. Cy Young)	.10
(2)	Kevin Mitchell (N.L. MVP)	.10
(3)	Gregg Olson (A.L. R.O.Y.)	.10
(4)	Bret Saberhagen (A.L. Cy Young)	.10
(5)	Jerome Walton (N.L. R.O.Y.)	.10
(6)	Robin Yount (A.L. MVP)	1.50

Batting Leaders

Once again produced as an exclusive insert in jumbo blister packs for K-Mart stores, the 1990 career batting leaders cards are similar in concept and design to the previous year's issue; in fact, some of the same player photos were used. The 22 cards in the set are arranged roughly in order of the players' standings in lifetime batting average. Cards fronts are bordered in bright green; backs are printed in red, white and dark green.

		NM/M
Complete Set (22):		110.00
Common Player:		1.50
1	Wade Boggs	12.50
2	Tony Gwynn	15.00
3	Kirby Puckett	15.00
4	Don Mattingly	20.00
5	George Brett	20.00
6	Pedro Guerrero	1.50
7	Tim Raines	1.50
8	Paul Molitor	12.50
9	Jim Rice	3.00
10	Keith Hernandez	1.50
11	Julio Franco	1.50
12	Carney Lansford	1.50
13	Dave Parker	1.50
14	Willie McGee	1.50
15	Robin Yount	12.50
16	Tony Fernandez	1.50
17	Eddie Murray	12.50
18	Johnny Ray	1.50
19	Lonnie Smith	1.50
20	Phil Bradley	1.50
21	Rickey Henderson	12.50
22	Kent Hrbek	1.50

Big Baseball

For the third consecutive year, Topps issued a 330-card set of oversized cards (2-5/8" x 3-3/4") in three 110-card series. The cards are reminiscent of Topps cards from the mid-1950s, featuring players in portrait and action shots. As in previous years, the cards are printed on white stock with a glossy front finish. Backs include 1989 and career hitting, fielding and pitching stats and a player cartoon. Series 3 cards (#221-330) are believed to have been somewhat scarcer than the first two series.

		NM/M
Complete Set (330):		15.00
Common Player:		.05
Wax Pack (8):		.50
Wax Box, Series 1-2 (36):		7.50
Wax Box, Series 3 (36):		20.00
1	Dwight Evans	.05
2	Kirby Puckett	.60
3	Kevin Gross	.05
4	Ron Hassey	.05
5	Lloyd McClendon	.05
6	Bo Jackson	.10
7	Lonnie Smith	.05
8	Alvaro Espinoza	.05
9	Roberto Alomar	.15
10	Glenn Braggs	.05
11	David Cone	.05
12	Claudell Washington	.05
13	Pedro Guerrero	.05
14	Todd Benzinger	.05
15	Jeff Russell	.05
16	Terry Kennedy	.05
17	Kelly Gruber	.05
18	Alfredo Griffin	.05
19	Mark Grace	.05
20	Dave Winfield	.50
21	Bret Saberhagen	.05
22	Roger Clemens	.65
23	Bob Walk	.05
24	Dave Magadan	.05
25	Spike Owen	.05
26	Jody Davis	.05
27	Kent Hrbek	.05
28	Mark McGwire	1.00
29	Eddie Murray	.50
30	Paul O'Neill	.05
31	Jose DeLeon	.05
32	Steve Lyons	.05
33	Dan Plesac	.05
34	Jack Howell	.05
35	Greg Briley	.05
36	Andy Hawkins	.05
37	Cecil Espy	.05
38	Rick Sutcliffe	.05
39	Jack Clark	.05
40	Dale Murphy	.15
41	Mike Henneman	.05
42	Rick Honeycutt	.05
43	Willie Randolph	.05
44	Marty Barrett	.05
45	Willie Wilson	.05
46	Wallace Johnson	.05
47	Greg Brock	.05
48	Tom Browning	.05
49	Gerald Young	.05
50	Dennis Eckersley	.40
51	Scott Garrelts	.05
52	Gary Redus	.05
53	Al Newman	.05
54	Darryl Boston	.05
55	Ron Oester	.05
56	Danny Tartabull	.05
57	Gregg Jefferies	.05
58	Tom Foley	.05
59	Robin Yount	.50
60	Pat Borders	.05
61	Mike Greenwell	.05
62	Shawon Dunston	.05
63	Steve Buechele	.05
64	Dave Stewart	.05
65	Jose Oquendo	.05
66	Ron Gant	.05
67	Mike Scioscia	.05
68	Randy Velarde	.05
69	Charlie Hayes	.05
70	Tim Wallach	.05
71	Eric Show	.05
72	Eric Davis	.05
73	Mike Gallego	.05
74	Rob Deer	.05
75	Ryne Sandberg	.60
76	Kevin Seitzer	.05
77	Wade Boggs	.60
78	Greg Gagne	.05
79	John Smiley	.05
80	Ivan Calderon	.05
81	Pete Incaviglia	.05
82	Orel Hershiser	.05
83	Carney Lansford	.05
84	Mike Fitzgerald	.05
85	Don Mattingly	.65
86	Chet Lemon	.05
87	Rolando Roomes	.05
88	Bill Spiers	.05
89	Pat Tabler	.05
90	Danny Heep	.05
91	Andre Dawson	.25
92	Randy Bush	.05
93	Tony Gwynn	.60
94	Tom Brunansky	.05
95	Johnny Ray	.05
96	Matt Williams	.05
97	Barry Lyons	.05
98	Jeff Hamilton	.05
99	Tom Glavine	.20
100	Ken Griffey Sr.	.05
101	Tom Henke	.05
102	Dave Righetti	.05
103	Paul Molitor	.50
104	Mike LaValliere	.05
105	Frank White	.05
106	Bob Welch	.05
107	Ellis Burks	.05
108	Andres Galarraga	.05
109	Mitch Williams	.05
110	Checklist	.05
111	Craig Biggio	.05
112	Dave Steib	.05
113	Ron Darling	.05
114	Bert Blyleven	.05
115	Dickie Thon	.05
116	Carlos Martinez	.05
117	Jeff King	.05
118	Terry Steinbach	.05
119	Frank Tanana	.05
120	Mark Lemke	.05
121	Chris Sabo	.05
122	Glenn Davis	.05
123	Mel Hall	.05
124	Jim Gantner	.05
125	Benito Santiago	.05
126	Milt Thompson	.05
127	Rafael Palmeiro	.40
128	Barry Bonds	1.50
129	Mike Bielecki	.05
130	Lou Whitaker	.05
131	Bob Ojeda	.05
132	Dion James	.05
133	Denny Martinez	.05
134	Fred McGriff	.05
135	Terry Pendleton	.05
136	Pat Combs	.05
137	Kevin Mitchell	.05
138	Marquis Grissom	.05
139	Chris Bosio	.05
140	Omar Vizquel	.05
141	Steve Sax	.05
142	Nelson Liriano	.05
143	Kevin Elster	.05
144	Dan Pasqua	.05
145	Dave Smith	.05
146	Craig Worthington	.05
147	Dan Gladden	.05
148	Oddibe McDowell	.05
149	Bip Roberts	.05
150	Randy Ready	.05
151	Dwight Smith	.05
152	Ed Whitson	.05
153	George Bell	.05
154	Tim Raines	.05
155	Sid Fernandez	.05
156	Henry Cotto	.05
157	Harold Baines	.05
158	Willie McGee	.05
159	Bill Doran	.05
160	Steve Balboni	.05
161	Pete Smith	.05
162	Frank Viola	.05
163	Gary Sheffield	.35
164	Bill Landrum	.05
165	Tony Fernandez	.05
166	Mike Heath	.05
167	Jody Reed	.05
168	Wally Joyner	.05
169	Robby Thompson	.05
170	Ken Caminiti	.05
171	Nolan Ryan	1.50
172	Ricky Jordan	.05
173	Lance Blankenship	.05
174	Dwight Gooden	.05
175	Ruben Sierra	.05
176	Carlton Fisk	.50
177	Garry Templeton	.05
178	Mike Devereaux	.05
179	Mookie Wilson	.05
180	Jeff Blauser	.05
181	Scott Bradley	.05
182	Luis Salazar	.05
183	Rafael Ramirez	.05
184	Vince Coleman	.05
185	Doug Drabek	.05
186	Darryl Strawberry	.05
187	Tim Burke	.05
188	Jesse Barfield	.05
189	Barry Larkin	.05
190	Alan Trammell	.05
191	Steve Lake	.05
192	Derek Lilliquist	.05
193	Don Robinson	.05
194	Kevin McReynolds	.05
195	Melido Perez	.05
196	Jose Lind	.05
197	Eric Anthony	.05
198	B.J. Surhoff	.05
199	John Olerud	.05
200	Mike Moore	.05
201	Mark Gubicza	.05
202	Phil Bradley	.05
203	Ozzie Smith	.60
204	Greg Maddux	.60
205	Julio Franco	.05
206	Tom Herr	.05
207	Scott Fletcher	.05
208	Bobby Bonilla	.05
209	Bob Geren	.05
210	Junior Felix	.05
211	Dick Schofield	.05
212	Jim Deshaies	.05
213	Jose Uribe	.05
214	John Kruk	.05
215	Ozzie Guillen	.05
216	Howard Johnson	.05
217	Andy Van Slyke	.05
218	Tim Laudner	.05
219	Manny Lee	.05
220	Checklist	.05
221	Cory Snyder	.05
222	Billy Hatcher	.05
223	Bud Black	.05
224	Will Clark	.05
225	Kevin Tapani	.05
226	Mike Pagliarulo	.05
227	Dave Parker	.05
228	Ben McDonald	.05
229	Carlos Baerga	.05
230	Roger McDowell	.05
231	Delino DeShields	.05
232	Mark Langston	.05
233	Wally Backman	.05
234	Jim Eisenreich	.05
235	Mike Schooler	.05
236	Kevin Bass	.05
237	John Farrell	.05
238	Kal Daniels	.05
239	Tony Phillips	.05
240	Todd Stottlemyre	.05
241	Greg Olson	.05
242	Charlie Hough	.05
243	Mariano Duncan	.05
244	Billy Ripken	.05
245	Joe Carter	.05
246	Tim Belcher	.05
247	Roberto Kelly	.05
248	Candy Maldonado	.05
249	Mike Scott	.05
250	Ken Griffey Jr.	.75
251	Nick Esasky	.05
252	Tom Gordon	.05
253	John Tudor	.05
254	Gary Gaetti	.05
255	Neal Heaton	.05
256	Jerry Browne	.05
257	Jose Rijo	.05
258	Mike Boddicker	.05
259	Brett Butler	.05
260	Andy Benes	.05
261	Kevin Brown	.05
262	Hubie Brooks	.05
263	Randy Milligan	.05
264	John Franco	.05
265	Sandy Alomar	.05
266	Dave Valle	.05
267	Jerome Walton	.05
268	Bob Boone	.05
269	Ken Howell	.05
270	Jose Canseco	.30
271	Joe Magrane	.05
272	Brian DuBois	.05
273	Carlos Quintana	.05
274	Lance Johnson	.05
275	Steve Bedrosian	.05
276	Brook Jacoby	.05
277	Fred Lynn	.05
278	Jeff Ballard	.05
279	Otis Nixon	.05
280	Chili Davis	.05
281	Joe Oliver	.05
282	Brian Holman	.05
283	Juan Samuel	.05
284	Rick Aguilera	.05
285	Jeff Reardon	.05
286	Sammy Sosa	3.00
287	Carmelo Martinez	.05
288	Greg Swindell	.05
289	Erik Hanson	.05
290	Tony Pena	.05
291	Pascual Perez	.05
292	Rickey Henderson	.50

293	Kurt Stillwell	.05
294	Todd Zeile	.05
295	Bobby Thigpen	.05
296	Larry Walker	.05
297	Rob Murphy	.05
298	Mitch Webster	.05
299	Devon White	.05
300	Len Dykstra	.05
301	Keith Hernandez	.05
302	Gene Larkin	.05
303	Jeffrey Leonard	.05
304	Jim Presley	.05
305	Lloyd Moseby	.05
306	John Smoltz	.05
307	Sam Horn	.05
308	Greg Litton	.05
309	Dave Henderson	.05
310	Mark McLemore	.05
311	Gary Pettis	.05
312	Mark Davis	.05
313	Cecil Fielder	.05
314	Jack Armstrong	.05
315	Alvin Davis	.05
316	Doug Jones	.05
317	Eric Yelding	.05
318	Joe Orsulak	.05
319	Chuck Finley	.05
320	Glenn Wilson	.05
321	Harold Reynolds	.05
322	Teddy Higuera	.05
323	Lance Parrish	.05
324	Bruce Hurst	.05
325	Dave West	.05
326	Kirk Gibson	.05
327	Cal Ripken, Jr.	1.50
328	Rick Reuschel	.05
329	Jim Abbott	.05
330	Checklist	.05

George Bush

As a favor to President George Bush, Topps produced a special run of 100 cards in its 1990 design featuring a photo of the president in his Yale University baseball uniform. At least a few of the cards reportedly were inadvertently included in regular Topps packages and made their way into the hobby.

		NM/M
USA1	George Bush (7/05 Auction)	2,000

Coins

Sixty top stars and promising rookies are featured in this fourth annual coin set. Fronts of the 1-1/2" diameter coins feature a portrait photo with a symbolic infield. Player name and team appear below. Most coins feature natural aluminum coloring on the rolled edges and on the back. Special coins of major award winners have different colors in the background and edges. Backs feature a coin number, minimal biographical data and a previous season career summary. Coins were sold three per pack which included an offer card for a coin holder and Topps magazine subscription offer.

		NM/M
Factory Set (60):		15.00
Complete Set (60):		7.50
Common Player:		.15
Wax Pack (3):		.75
Wax Box (36):		9.00
1	Robin Yount	.50
2	Bret Saberhagen	.15
3	Gregg Olson	.15
4	Kirby Puckett	.65
5	George Bell	.15
6	Wade Boggs	.65
7	Jerry Browne	.15
8	Ellis Burks	.15
9	Ivan Calderon	.15
10	Tom Candiotti	.15
11	Alvin Davis	.15
12	Chili Davis	.15
13	Chuck Finley	.15
14	Gary Gaetti	.15
15	Tom Gordon	.15
16	Ken Griffey Jr.	.75
17	Rickey Henderson	.50
18	Kent Hrbek	.15
19	Bo Jackson	.20
20	Carlos Martinez	.15
21	Don Mattingly	.75
22	Fred McGriff	.15
23	Paul Molitor	.50
24	Cal Ripken, Jr.	1.00
25	Nolan Ryan	1.00
26	Steve Sax	.15
27	Gary Sheffield	.30
28	Ruben Sierra	.15
29	Dave Stewart	.15
30	Mickey Tettleton	.15
31	Alan Trammell	.15
32	Lou Whitaker	.15
33	Kevin Mitchell	.15
34	Mark Davis	.15
35	Jerome Walton	.15
36	Tony Gwynn	.65
37	Roberto Alomar	.25
38	Tim Belcher	.15
39	Craig Biggio	.15
40	Barry Bonds	1.00
41	Bobby Bonilla	.15
42	Joe Carter	.15
43	Will Clark	.15
44	Eric Davis	.15
45	Glenn Davis	.15
46	Sid Fernandez	.15
47	Pedro Guerrero	.15
48	Von Hayes	.15
49	Tom Herr	.15
50	Howard Johnson	.15
51	Barry Larkin	.15
52	Joe Magrane	.15
53	Dale Murphy	.25
54	Tim Raines	.15
55	Willie Randolph	.15
56	Ryne Sandberg	.65
57	Dwight Smith	.15
58	Lonnie Smith	.15
59	Robby Thompson	.15
60	Tim Wallach	.15

Double Headers

For a second (and final) year, Topps produced an issue of mini cards encased in plastic stands and marketed as Double Headers. Each piece features a 1-5/8" x 2-1/4" reproduction of the player's Topps rookie card, backed by a reproduction of his card from the regular 1990 Topps set. The size of the DH set was increased from 24 in 1989 to 72 for 1990. The novelties were sold for 50 cents apiece. The unnumbered cards are checklisted here alphabetically.

		NM/M
Complete Set (72):		25.00
Common Player:		.25
Wax Pack (1):		.50
Wax Box (36):		15.00
(1)	Jim Abbott	.25
(2)	Jeff Ballard	.25
(3)	George Bell	.25
(4)	Wade Boggs	1.00
(5)	Barry Bonds	2.50
(6)	Bobby Bonilla	.25
(7)	Ellis Burks	.25
(8)	Jose Canseco	.50
(9)	Joe Carter	.25
(10)	Will Clark	.25
(11)	Roger Clemens	1.25
(12)	Vince Coleman	.25
(13)	Alvin Davis	.25
(14)	Eric Davis	.25
(15)	Glenn Davis	.25
(16)	Mark Davis	.25
(17)	Andre Dawson	.40
(18)	Shawon Dunston	.25
(19)	Dennis Eckersley	.60
(20)	Sid Fernandez	.25
(21)	Tony Fernandez	.25
(22)	Chuck Finley	.25
(23)	Carlton Fisk	.75
(24)	Julio Franco	.25
(25)	Gary Gaetti	.25
(26)	Dwight Gooden	.25
(27)	Mark Grace	.25
(28)	Mike Greenwell	.25
(29)	Ken Griffey Jr.	1.50
(30)	Pedro Guerrero	.25
(31)	Tony Gwynn	1.00
(32)	Von Hayes	.25
(33)	Rickey Henderson	.75
(34)	Orel Hershiser	.25
(35)	Bo Jackson	.35
(36)	Gregg Jefferies	.25
(37)	Howard Johnson	.25
(38)	Ricky Jordan	.25
(39)	Carney Lansford	.25
(40)	Barry Larkin	.25
(41)	Greg Maddux	1.00
(42)	Joe Magrane	.25
(43)	Don Mattingly	1.25
(44)	Fred McGriff	.25
(45)	Mark McGwire	2.00
(46)	Kevin McReynolds	.25
(47)	Kevin Mitchell	.25
(48)	Gregg Olson	.25
(49)	Kirby Puckett	1.00
(50)	Tim Raines	.25
(51)	Harold Reynolds	.25
(52)	Cal Ripken, Jr.	2.50
(53)	Nolan Ryan	2.50
(54)	Bret Saberhagen	.25
(55)	Ryne Sandberg	1.00
(56)	Benito Santiago	.25
(57)	Steve Sax	.25
(58)	Mike Scioscia	.25
(59)	Mike Scott	.25
(60)	Ruben Sierra	.25
(61)	Lonnie Smith	.25
(62)	Ozzie Smith	1.00
(63)	Dave Stewart	.25
(64)	Darryl Strawberry	.25
(65)	Greg Swindell	.25
(66)	Alan Trammell	.25
(67)	Frank Viola	.25
(68)	Tim Wallach	.25
(69)	Jerome Walton	.25
(70)	Lou Whitaker	.25
(71)	Mitch Williams	.25
(72)	Robin Yount	.75

Experimental Mylar Stickers

Testing the concept of refractive printing, with stars in the background of these stickers, Topps produced a trial run of Mylar stickers using fronts from its 1990 Traded card set. Fronts of the 2-1/2" x 3-1/2" stickers are printed on metallic foil. Backs are blank.

		NM/M
Complete Set (6):		400.00
Common Player:		60.00
(1)	Joe Carter	60.00
(2)	Shane Mack	60.00
(3)	Alan Mills	60.00
(4)	Alejandro Pena	60.00
(5)	Gerald Perry	60.00
(6)	Dave Winfield	175.00

Gallery of Champions

The 1990 Topps 1/4-size metal baseball mini-cards were issued only as complete sets in a special display case. As with earlier editions, the 1-1/4" x 1-3/4" ingots do a

creditable job of reproducing the players' 1990 Topps cards, right down to the tiny stats on the back. Players in the set represent the winners of major awards and statistical leaders from the previous season. A pewter Nolan Ryan 1/4-size card was issued as a sales incentive for dealers purchasing the Gallery of Champions sets.

		NM/M
Complete Aluminum Set (12):		15.00
Complete Bronze Set (12):		50.00
Complete Silver Set (12):		100.00
(1a)	Mark Davis/Aluminum	1.00
(1b)	Mark Davis/Bronze	2.50
(1s)	Mark Davis/Silver	5.00
(2a)	Jose DeLeon/ Aluminum	1.00
(2b)	Jose DeLeon/Bronze	2.50
(2s)	Jose DeLeon/Silver	5.00
(3a)	Tony Gwynn/ Aluminum	3.00
(3b)	Tony Gwynn/Bronze	7.50
(3s)	Tony Gwynn/Silver	20.00
(4a)	Fred McGriff/ Aluminum	1.00
(4b)	Fred McGriff/Bronze	2.50
(4s)	Fred McGriff/Silver	5.00
(5a)	Kevin Mitchell/ Aluminum	1.00
(5b)	Kevin Mitchell/Bronze	2.50
(5s)	Kevin Mitchell/Silver	5.00
(6a)	Gregg Olson/ Aluminum	1.00
(6b)	Gregg Olson/Bronze	2.50
(6s)	Gregg Olson/Silver	5.00
(7a)	Kirby Puckett/ Aluminum	3.00
(7b)	Kirby Puckett/Bronze	7.50
(7s)	Kirby Puckett/Silver	20.00
(8a)	Jeff Russell/Aluminum	1.00
(8b)	Jeff Russell/Bronze	2.50
(8s)	Jeff Russell/Silver	5.00
(9a)	Nolan Ryan/ Aluminum	10.00
(9b)	Nolan Ryan/Bronze	20.00
(9s)	Nolan Ryan/Silver	40.00
(9p)	Nolan Ryan/Pewter	35.00
(10a)	Bret Saberhagen/ Aluminum	1.00
(10b)	Bret Saberhagen/ Bronze	2.50
(10s)	Bret Saberhagen/Silver	5.00
(11a)	Jerome Walton/ Aluminum	1.00
(11b)	Jerome Walton/Bronze	2.50
(11s)	Jerome Walton/Silver	5.00
(12a)	Robin Yount/ Aluminum	2.00
(12b)	Robin Yount/Bronze	5.00
(12s)	Robin Yount/Silver	15.00

Golden Spikes Award

This one-card "set" was given out at the United States Baseball Federation awards luncheon in New York City on Nov. 14, 1990, honoring Alex Fernandez as the outstanding amateur baseball player of the year and winner of the Golden Spikes Award. The rough borders found on many of these cards indicates they were cut from the press sheet by hand. Production was reported as 600 cards.

	NM/M
Alex Fernandez	85.00

Heads Up!

Following up a much rarer test issue of the previous year, the Heads Up! Baseball Stars of 1990 was a 24-piece set which received much wider distribution, but proved unpopular with collectors. On heavy cardboard, die-cut to approximately 5" x 6", these novelties featured only a head-and-cap photo of the player. Backs have the player's name and team, along with an adhesive strip and plastic suction cup which could be used to "hang" the player.

		NM/M
Complete Set (24):		10.00
Common Player:		.50
Wax Pack (1):		.75
Wax Box (24):		10.00
1	Tony Gwynn	2.00
2	Will Clark	.50
3	Dwight Gooden	.50
4	Dennis Eckersley	1.25
5	Ken Griffey Jr.	3.00
6	Craig Biggio	.50
7	Bret Saberhagen	.50
8	Bo Jackson	.75
9	Ryne Sandberg	2.00
10	Gregg Olson	.50
11	John Franco	.50
12	Rafael Palmeiro	1.25
13	Gary Sheffield	1.00
14	Mark McGwire	4.00
15	Kevin Mitchell	.50
16	Jim Abbott	.50
17	Harold Reynolds	.50
18	Jose Canseco	1.00
19	Don Mattingly	2.50
20	Kirby Puckett	2.00
21	Tom Gordon	.50
22	Craig Worthington	.50
23	Dwight Smith	.50
24	Jerome Walton	.50

Magazine

Beginning with its debut issue dated Winter, 1990, Topps Magazine included sportscards in each quarterly issue. Generally printed on perforated panels which could be easily separated from the magazine and the other cards, six to eight cards were included in most issues. Most of the cards were original designs, but some depicted then-current players on Topps designs from previous years. For the duration of their issue, the cards were numbered consecutively with a "TM" prefix.

		NM/M
Complete Set (112):		50.00
Common Player:		.25
1	Dave Staton	.25
2	Dan Peltier	.25
3	Ken Griffey Jr.	2.00
4	Ruben Sierra	.25
5	Bret Saberhagen	.25
6	Jerome Walton	.25
7	Kevin Mitchell	.25
8	Mike Scott	.25
9	Bo Jackson	.30
10	Nolan Ryan	3.00
11	Will Clark	.25
12	Robin Yount	.75
13	Joe Morgan	.75
14	Jim Palmer	.75
15	Ben McDonald	.25
16	John Olerud	.25
17	Don Mattingly	1.50
18	Eric Davis, Barry Larkin, Chris Sabo	.25
19	Jim Abbott	.25
20	Sandy Alomar Jr.	.25
21	Jose Canseco	.50
22	Delino DeShields	.25
23	Wade Boggs	1.00
24	Kirby Puckett	1.00
25	Ryne Sandberg	1.00
26	Roger Clemens	1.25
27	Ken Griffey Jr., Ken Griffey Sr.	1.00
28	Cecil Fielder	.25
29	Steve Avery	.25
30	Rickey Henderson	.75
31	Kevin Maas	.25
32	Len Dykstra	.25
33	Darryl Strawberry	.25
34	Mark McGwire	2.25
35	Matt Williams	.25
36	David Justice	.25
37	Cincinnati Reds	.25
38	Todd Van Poppel	.25
39	Jose Offerman	.25
40	Alex Fernandez	.25
41	Carlton Fisk	.75
42	Barry Bonds	3.00
43	Bobby Bonilla	.25
44	Bob Welch	.25
45	Mo Vaughn	.25
46	Tino Martinez	.25
47	D.J. Dozier	.25
48	Frank Thomas	.75
49	Cal Ripken Jr. ('75 Topps Style)	3.00
50	Dave Winfield ('75 Topps Style)	.75
51	Dwight Gooden ('75 Topps Style)	.25
52	Bo Jackson ('75 Topps Style)	.30
53	Kirk Dressendorfer	.25
54	Gary Scott	.25
55	Steve Decker	.25
56	Ray Lankford	.25
57	Ozzie Smith ('86 Topps Style)	1.00
58	Joe Carter ('86 Topps Style)	.25
59	Dave Henderson ('86 Topps Style)	.25
60	Tony Gwynn ('86 Topps Style)	1.00
61	Jeff Bagwell	.75
62	Scott Erickson	.25
63	Pat Kelly	.25
64	Orlando Merced	.25
65	Andre Dawson	.40
66	Reggie Sanders	.25
67	Phil Plantier	.25
68	Paul Molitor	.75
69	Terry Pendleton	.25
70	Julio Franco	.25
71	Lee Smith	.25
72	'91 Minnesota Twins	.25
73	Royce Clayton	.25
74	Tom Glavine	.45
75	Roger Salkeld	.25
76	Robin Ventura	.25
77	John Goodman (As Babe Ruth.)	.25
78	Jack Morris	.25
79	Brien Taylor	.25
80	Howard Johnson	.25
81	Barry Larkin	.25
82	Deion Sanders	.30
83	Mike Mussina	.60
84	Juan Gonzalez	.50
85	Roberto Alomar	.50
86	Fred McGriff	.25
87	Doug Drabek	.25
88	George Brett	1.25
89	Otis Nixon	.25
90	Brady Anderson	.25
91	Gary Sheffield	.50
92	Dave Fleming	.25
93	Jeff Reardon	.25
94	Mark McGwire	2.25
95	Larry Walker	.25
96	John Kruk	.25
97	Carlos Baerga	.25

98	Pat Listach	.25
99	'92 Toronto Blue Jays	.25
100	Eric Karros	.25
101	Bret Boone	.25
102	Al Martin	.25
103	Wil Cordero	.25
104	Tim Salmon	.25
105	Danny Tartabull	.25
106	J.T. Snow	.25
107	Mike Piazza	1.50
108	Frank Viola	.25
109	Nolan Ryan (Mets)	2.25
110	Nolan Ryan (Angels)	2.25
111	Nolan Ryan (Astros)	2.25
112	Nolan Ryan (Rangers)	2.25

Mini League Leaders

The last in a five-year string of mini cards, the 1990 league leaders' set offers players who were in the top five in major batting and pitching stats during the 1989 season. Fronts of the 2-1/8" x 3" cards mimic the regular Topps' design for 1990; featuring an action photo with multi-colored borders. Backs offer a round player portrait photo and information about the statistical achievement, all printed in full color. Cards are numbered alphabetically within teams. The 1990 minis are considerably scarcer than the previous years' offerings.

		NM/M
Complete Set (88):		5.00
Common Player:		.05
1	Jeff Ballard	.05
2	Phil Bradley	.05
3	Wade Boggs	.65
4	Roger Clemens	.75
5	Nick Esasky	.05
6	Jody Reed	.05
7	Bert Blyleven	.05
8	Chuck Finley	.05
9	Kirk McCaskill	.05
10	Devon White	.05
11	Ivan Calderon	.05
12	Bobby Thigpen	.05
13	Joe Carter	.05
14	Gary Pettis	.05
15	Tom Gordon	.05
16	Bo Jackson	.10
17	Bret Saberhagen	.05
18	Kevin Seitzer	.05
19	Chris Bosio	.05
20	Paul Molitor	.50
21	Dan Plesac	.05
22	Robin Yount	.50
23	Kirby Puckett	.65
24	Don Mattingly	.75
25	Steve Sax	.05
26	Storm Davis	.05
27	Dennis Eckersley	.40
28	Rickey Henderson	.50
29	Carney Lansford	.05
30	Mark McGwire	1.00
31	Mike Moore	.05
32	Dave Stewart	.05
33	Alvin Davis	.05
34	Harold Reynolds	.05
35	Mike Schooler	.05
36	Cecil Espy	.05
37	Julio Franco	.05
38	Jeff Russell	.05
39	Nolan Ryan	1.50
40	Ruben Sierra	.05
41	George Bell	.05
42	Tony Fernandez	.05
43	Fred McGriff	.05
44	Dave Steib	.05
45	Checklist	.05
46	Lonnie Smith	.05
47	John Smoltz	.05
48	Mike Bielecki	.05
49	Mark Grace	.05
50	Greg Maddux	.65
51	Ryne Sandberg	.65
52	Mitch Williams	.05
53	Eric Davis	.05
54	John Franco	.05
55	Glenn Davis	.05
56	Mike Scott	.05
57	Tim Belcher	.05
58	Orel Hershiser	.05
59	Jay Howell	.05
60	Eddie Murray	.50
61	Tim Burke	.05
62	Mark Langston	.05
63	Tim Raines	.05
64	Tim Wallach	.05
65	David Cone	.05
66	Sid Fernandez	.05
67	Howard Johnson	.05
68	Juan Samuel	.05
69	Von Hayes	.05
70	Barry Bonds	1.50
71	Bobby Bonilla	.05
72	Andy Van Slyke	.05
73	Vince Coleman	.05
74	Jose DeLeon	.05
75	Pedro Guerrero	.05
76	Joe Magrane	.05
77	Roberto Alomar	.20
78	Jack Clark	.05
79	Mark Davis	.05
80	Tony Gwynn	.65
81	Bruce Hurst	.05
82	Eddie Whitson	.05
83	Brett Butler	.05
84	Will Clark	.05
85	Scott Garrelts	.05
86	Kevin Mitchell	.05
87	Rick Reuschel	.05
88	Robby Thompson	.05

Nolan Ryan Bronze

This full-size bronze reproduction of Ryan's 1990 Topps card was given to dealers who made early orders for Topps' 1991 "Tiffany" sets. A 2,500 piece limit was announced.

	NM/M
Nolan Ryan	50.00

Senior League

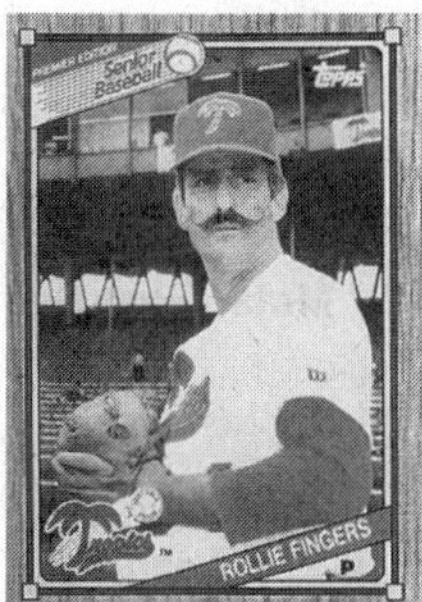

Topps was among several companies to produce a Senior League set in 1990. The set includes 132 cards and was sold as a boxed set. The card fronts have the Senior Baseball and Topps logo on top and the player's name and team logo on the bottom, with a woodgrain-like border surrounding the front photo. The backs of the card include traditional biographical information, plus career major league statistics, career ML bests and stats from any Senior League experience.

		NM/M
Complete Set (132):		5.00
Common Player:		.05
1	George Foster	.15
2	Dwight Lowry	.05
3	Bob Jones	.05
4	Clete Boyer	.05
5	Rafael Landestoy	.05
6	Bob Shirley	.05
7	Ivan Murrell	.05
8	Jerry White	.05
9	Steve Henderson	.05
10	Marty Castillo	.05
11	Bruce Kison	.05
12	George Hendrick	.05
13	Bernie Carbo	.05
14	Jerry Martin	.05
15	Al Hrabosky	.05
16	Luis Gomez	.05
17	Dick Drago	.05
18	Bobby Ramos	.05
19	Joe Pittman	.05
20	Ike Blessitt	.05
21	Bill Travers	.05
22	Dick Williams	.05
23	Randy Lerch	.05
24	Tom Spencer	.05
25	Graig Nettles	.05
26	Jim Gideon	.05
27	Al Bumbry	.05
28	Tom Murphy	.05
29	Rodney Scott	.05
30	Alan Bannister	.05
31	John D'Acquisto	.05
32	Bert Campaneris	.05
33	Bill Lee	.05
34	Jerry Grote	.05
35	Ken Reitz	.05
36	Al Oliver	.15
37	Tim Stoddard	.05
38	Lenny Randle	.05
39	Rick Manning	.05
40	Bobby Bonds	.15
41	Rick Wise	.05
42	Sal Butera	.05
43	Ed Figueroa	.05
44	Ron Washington	.05
45	Elias Sosa	.05
46	Dan Driessen	.05
47	Wayne Nordhagen	.05
48	Vida Blue	.15
49	Butch Hobson	.05
50	Randy Bass	.05
51	Paul Mirabella	.05
52	Steve Kemp	.05
53	Kim Allen	.05
54	Stan Cliburn	.05
55	Derrel Thomas	.05
56	Pete Falcone	.05
57	Willie Aikens	.05
58	Toby Harrah	.05
59	Bob Tolan	.05
60	Rick Waits	.05
61	Jim Morrison	.05
62	Stan Bahnsen	.05
63	Gene Richards	.05
64	Dave Cash	.05
65	Rollie Fingers	.50
66	Butch Benton	.05
67	Tim Ireland	.05
68	Rick Lysander	.05
69	Cesar Cedeno	.05
70	Jim Willoughby	.05
71	Bill Madlock	.15
72	Lee Lacy	.05
73	Milt Wilcox	.05
74	Ron Pruitt	.05
75	Wayne Krenchicki	.05
76	Earl Weaver	.25
77	Pedro Borbon	.05
78	Jose Cruz	.05
79	Steve Ontiveros	.05
80	Mike Easler	.05
81	Amos Otis	.05
82	Mickey Mahler	.05
83	Orlando Gonzalez	.05
84	Doug Simunic	.05
85	Felix Millan	.05
86	Garth Iorg	.05
87	Pete Broberg	.05
88	Roy Howell	.05
89	Dave LaRoche	.05
90	Jerry Manuel	.05
91	Tony Scott	.05
92	Larvell Blanks	.05
93	Joaquin Andujar	.05
94	Tito Landrum	.05
95	Joe Sambito	.05
96	Pat Dobson	.05
97	Dan Meyer	.05
98	Clint Hurdle	.05
99	Pete LaCock	.05
100	Bob Galasso	.05
101	Dave Kingman	.15
102	Jon Matlack	.05
103	Larry Harlow	.05
104	Rick Peterson	.05
105	Joe Hicks	.05
106	Bill Campbell	.05
107	Tom Paciorek	.05
108	Ray Burris	.05
109	Ken Landreaux	.05
110	Steve McCatty	.05
111	Ron LeFlore	.05
112	Joe Decker	.05
113	Leon Roberts	.05
114	Doug Corbett	.05
115	Mickey Rivers	.05
116	Dock Ellis	.05
117	Ron Jackson	.05
118	Bob Molinaro	.05
119	Fergie Jenkins	.50
120	U.L. Washington	.05
121	Roy Thomas	.05
122	Hal McRae	.15
123	Juan Eichelberger	.05
124	Gary Rajsich	.05
125	Dennis Leonard	.05
126	Walt Williams	.05
127	Rennie Stennett	.05
128	Jim Bibby	.05
129	Dyar Miller	.05
130	Luis Pujols	.05
131	Juan Beniquez	.05
132	Checklist	.05

Stickercards

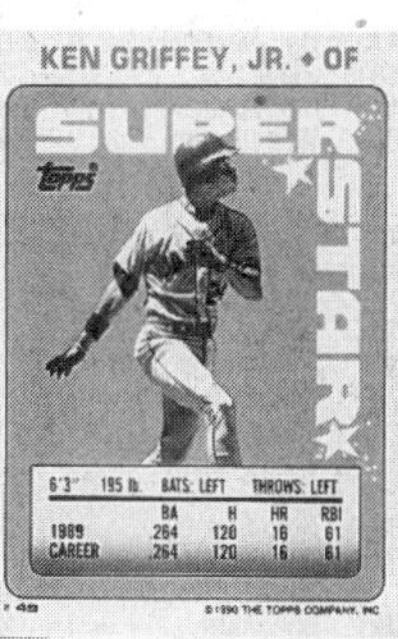

Providing a cardboard backing for its annual series of player stickers, the stickercards are a collectible in themselves. Each 2-1/8" x 3" card is backed by one or two player stickers which could be removed and placed into a special album. The card portion features a player photo set against a solid-color background. A few vitae plus 1989 and career stats are presented in a graduated-color box toward the bottom. The stickercards are sequenced by position within league.

		NM/M
Complete Set (67):		5.00
Common Player:		.05
Wax Pack (5):		.25
Wax Box (48):		10.00
1	Will Clark	.05
2	Glenn Davis	.05
3	Pedro Guerrero	.05
4	Roberto Alomar	.15
5	Gregg Jefferies	.05
6	Ryne Sandberg	.60
7	Bobby Bonilla	.05
8	Howard Johnson	.05
9	Tim Wallach	.05
10	Shawon Dunston	.05
11	Barry Larkin	.05
12	Ozzie Smith	.60
13	Eric Davis	.05
14	Andre Dawson	.25
15	Tony Gwynn	.60
16	Von Hayes	.05
17	Kevin Mitchell	.05
18	Rock Raines	.05
19	Lonnie Smith	.05
20	Darryl Strawberry	.05
21	Jerome Walton	.05
22	Craig Biggio	.05
23	Benito Santiago	.05
24	Mike Scioscia	.05
25	Doc Gooden	.05
26	Rick Reuschel	.05
27	Mike Scott	.05
28	Sid Fernandez	.05
29	Mark Langston	.05
30	Joe Magrane	.05
31	Mark Davis	.05
32	Jay Howell	.05
33	Mitch Williams	.05
34	Don Mattingly	.65
35	Fred McGriff	.05
36	Mark McGwire	.85
37	Julio Franco	.05
38	Steve Sax	.05
39	Lou Whitaker	.05
40	Wade Boggs	.60
41	Gary Gaetti	.05
42	Carney Lansford	.05
43	Tony Fernandez	.05
44	Cal Ripken Jr.	1.00
45	Alan Trammell	.05
46	George Bell	.05
47	Jose Canseco	.35
48	Joe Carter	.05
49	Ken Griffey Jr.	.75
50	Rickey Henderson	.45
51	Bo Jackson	.10
52	Kirby Puckett	.60
53	Ruben Sierra	.05
54	Robin Yount	.45
55	Carlton Fisk	.45
56	Terry Steinbach	.05
57	Mickey Tettleton	.05
58	Nolan Ryan	1.00
59	Bret Saberhagen	.05
60	Dave Stewart	.05
61	Jeff Ballard	.05
62	Chuck Finley	.05
63	Greg Swindell	.05
64	Dennis Eckersley	.40
65	Gregg Olson	.05
66	Jeff Russell	.05
67	Checklist	.05

OPC Stickers

Topps' 1990 stickers were produced in two formats. Some measure 2-1/8" x 3" while there are many pairs of half-size (1-1/2" x 2-1/8") stickers. All stickers are attached to Super Star stickercards from which they can be peeled and affixed in a special yearbook. Stickers have large center photos with a shadow-box effect in the borders, (blues for N.L., reds for A.L.). A tiny black sticker number is in the lower-right corner. There is no player name on the stickers; the albums have a box under each space with player data. The half-size stickers are printed in pairs and are checklisted in that fashion. Values given are for complete sticker(s)/stickercard combinations, but without regard for which stickercard is on back. The checklist and values for the O-Pee-Chee version of this set are identical to those for the Topps brand. Packs of five stickers sold for a quarter; the album with Don Mattingly on the cover retailed for 50 cents. Numbers in parentheses in this checklist indicate with which other sticker the named sticker is paired in the smaller format.

		NM/M
Complete Set (328):		7.50
Common Sticker:		.05
Album:		2.00
1	Rick Cerone/321 (Highlight)	.05
2	Kevin Elster/322 (Highlight)	.05
3	Nolan Ryan/323 (Highlight)	.45
4	Vince Coleman/319 (Highlight)	.05
5	Cal Ripken Jr./240 (Highlight)	.45
6	Jeff Reardon/328 (Highlight)	.05
7	Rickey Henderson/320 (Highlight)	.15
8	Wade Boggs/324 (Highlight)	.30
9	Barry Bonds/325 (Highlight)	.45
10	Gregg Olson/236 (Highlight)	.05
11	Tony Fernandez/327 (Highlight)	.05
12	Ryne Sandberg/326 (Highlight)	.30
13	Glenn Davis	.05
14	Danny Darwin/316	.05
15	Bill Doran/298	.05
16	Dave Smith/225	.05
17	Kevin Bass/278	.05
18	Rafael Ramirez/177	.05
19	Mike Scott	.05
20	Ken Caminiti/235	.05
21	Jim Deshaies/272	.05
22	Gerald Young/314	.05
23	Craig Biggio/186	.05
24	Lonnie Smith	.05
25	Dale Murphy/210	.10
26	Tom Glavine	.15
27	Gerald Perry/313	.05
28	Jeff Blauser/269	.05
29	Jeff Treadway/252	.05
30	John Smoltz/299	.05
31	Darrell Evans/295	.05
32	Oddibe McDowell/265	.05
33	Andres Thomas/304	.05
34	Joe Boever/191	.05
35	Pedro Guerrero	.05
36	Ken Dayley/226	.05
37	Milt Thompson/188	.05
38	Jose DeLeon/180	.05
39	Vince Coleman/293	.05
40	Terry Pendleton/225	.05
41	Joe Magrane	.05
42	Ozzie Smith/179	.30
43	Todd Worrell/195	.05
44	Jose Oquendo/138	.05
45	Tom Brunansky/187	.05
46	Ryne Sandberg	.60
47	Andre Dawson/268	.15
48	Mitch Williams	.05
49	Damon Berryhill/204	.05
50	Jerome Walton/274	.05
51	Greg Maddux/315	.30
52	Dwight Smith/248	.05
53	Shawon Dunston/194	.05
54	Mike Bielecki/239	.05
55	Rick Sutcliffe/305	.05
56	Mark Grace/228	.05
57	Eddie Murray	.40
58	Alfredo Griffin/197	.05
59	Fernando Valenzuela/277	.05
60	Kirk Gibson/201	.05
61	Ramon Martinez/190	.05
62	Mike Marshall/309	.05
63	Orel Hershiser	.05
64	Mike Scioscia/271	.05
65	Jay Howell/279	.05
66	Willie Randolph/283	.05
67	Jeff Hamilton/280	.05
68	Denny Martinez	.05
69	Tim Raines/184	.05
70	Mark Langston	.05
71	Dave Martinez/301	.05
72	Tim Burke/258	.05
73	Spike Owen/232	.05
74	Tim Wallach/254	.05
75	Andres Galarraga/208	.05
76	Kevin Gross/234	.05
77	Hubie Brooks/263	.05
78	Bryn Smith/207	.05
79	Kevin Mitchell	.05
80	Craig Lefferts/256	.05
81	Ernest Riles/247	.05
82	Scott Garrelts/185	.05
83	Robby Thompson/251	.05
84	Don Robinson/282	.05
85	Will Clark	.05
86	Steve Bedrosian/183	.05
87	Brett Butler/284	.05
88	Matt Williams/227	.05
89	Rick Reuschel/291	.05
90	Howard Johnson	.05
91	Darryl Strawberry/246	.05
92	Sid Fernandez	.05
93	David Cone/189	.05
94	Kevin McReynolds/311	.05
95	Frank Viola/229	.05
96	Dwight Gooden/206	.05
97	Kevin Elster/167	.05
98	Ron Darling/289	.05
99	Dave Magadan/257	.05
100	Randy Myers/192	.05
101	Tony Gwynn	.60
102	Mark Davis/312	.05
103	Bip Roberts/212	.05
104	Jack Clark/205	.05
105	Chris James/211	.05
106	Mike Pagliarulo/199	.05
107	Ed Whitson	.05
108	Bruce Hurst/245	.05
109	Roberto Alomar/202	.15
110	Benito Santiago/224	.05
111	Eric Show/307	.05
112	Ricky Jordan	.05
113	Steve Jeltz/203	.05
114	Von Hayes	.05
115	Dickie Thon/182	.05
116	Ken Howell/213	.05
117	John Kruk/306	.05
118	Lenny Dykstra/302	.05
119	Jeff Parrett/300	.05
120	Randy Ready/230	.05
121	Roger McDowell/262	.05
122	Tom Herr/250	.05
123	Barry Bonds	.90
124	Andy Van Slyke/219	.05
125	Bob Walk/216	.05
126	R.J. Reynolds/243	.05
127	Gary Redus/249	.05
128	Bill Landrum/276	.05
129	Bobby Bonilla	.05
130	Doug Drabek/218	.05
131	Jose Lind/221	.05
132	John Smiley/241	.05
133	Mike LaValliere/214	.05
134	Eric Davis	.05
135	Tom Browning/270	.05
136	Barry Larkin	.05
137	Jose Rijo/318	.05
138	Todd Benzinger/292	.05
139	Rick Mahler/217	.05
140	Chris Sabo/196	.05
141	Paul O'Neill/175	.05
142	Danny Jackson/273	.05
143	Rolando Roomes/261	.05
144	John Franco/233	.05
145	Ozzie Smith/AS	.30
146	Tony Gwynn/AS	.30
147	Will Clark/AS	.05
148	Kevin Mitchell/AS	.05
149	Eric Davis/AS	.05
150	Howard Johnson/AS	.05
151	Pedro Guerrero/AS	.05
152	Ryne Sandberg/AS	.35
153	Benito Santiago/AS	.05
154	Rick Reuschel/AS	.05
155	Bo Jackson/AS	.05
156	Wade Boggs/AS	.35
157	Kirby Puckett/AS	.30
158	Harold Baines/AS	.05
159	Julio Franco/AS	.05
160	Cal Ripken Jr./AS	.45
161	Ruben Sierra/AS	.05
162	Mark McGwire/AS	.40
163	Terry Steinbach/AS	.05
164	Dave Stewart/AS	.05

No.	Player	Price
165	Bert Blyleven	.05
166	Wally Joyner/285	.05
167	Kirk McCaskill/290	.05
168	Devon White/223	.05
169	Brian Downing/294	.05
170	Lance Parrish/296	.05
171	Chuck Finley	.05
172	Jim Abbott/317	.05
173	Chili Davis/181	.05
174	Johnny Ray/260	.05
175	Bryan Harvey/141	.05
176	Mark McGwire	.75
177	Jose Canseco/18	.15
178	Mike Moore	.05
179	Dave Parker/42	.05
180	Bob Welch/38	.05
181	Rickey Henderson/173	.25
182	Dennis Eckersley/115	.20
183	Carney Lansford/86	.05
184	Dave Henderson/69	.05
185	Dave Stewart/82	.05
186	Terry Steinbach/23	.05
187	Fred McGriff	.05
188	Junior Felix/37	.05
189	Ernie Whitt/93	.05
190	Dave Smith/61	.05
191	Jimmy Key/34	.05
192	George Bell/100	.05
193	Kelly Gruber	.05
194	Tony Fernandez/53	.05
195	John Cerutti/43	.05
196	Tom Henke/140	.05
197	Nelson Liriano/58	.05
198	Robin Yount	.40
199	Paul Molitor/106	.25
200	Dan Plesac	.05
201	Teddy Higuera/60	.05
202	Gary Sheffield/109	.15
203	B.J. Surhoff/113	.05
204	Rob Deer/49	.05
205	Chris Bosio/104	.05
206	Glenn Braggs/96	.05
207	Jim Gantner/78	.05
208	Greg Brock/75	.05
209	Joe Carter	.05
210	Jerry Browne/25	.05
211	Cory Snyder/105	.05
212	Joey Belle/103	.10
213	Bud Black/116	.05
214	Greg Swindell/133	.05
215	Doug Jones	.05
216	Tom Candiotti/125	.05
217	John Farrell/139	.05
218	Pete O'Brien/130	.05
219	Brook Jacoby/124	.05
220	Alvin Davis	.05
221	Harold Reynolds/131	.05
222	Scott Bankhead	.05
223	Jeffrey Leonard/168	.05
224	Jim Presley/110	.05
225	Ken Griffey Jr./40	.40
226	Greg Briley/36	.05
227	Darnell Coles/88	.05
228	Mike Schooler/56	.05
229	Scott Bradley/95	.05
230	Randy Johnson/120	.25
231	Cal Ripken Jr.	.90
232	Jeff Ballard/73	.05
233	Randy Milligan/144	.05
234	Joe Orsulak/76	.05
235	Billy Ripken/20	.05
236	Mark Williamson/10	.05
237	Mickey Tettleton	.05
238	Gregg Olson/44	.05
239	Craig Worthington/54	.05
240	Bob Milacki/5	.05
241	Phil Bradley/132	.05
242	Nolan Ryan	.90
243	Julio Franco/126	.05
244	Ruben Sierra	.05
245	Harold Baines/128	.05
246	Jeff Kunkel/91	.05
247	Pete Incaviglia/81	.05
248	Kevin Brown/52	.05
249	Cecil Espy/127	.05
250	Rafael Palmeiro/122	.20
251	Steve Buechele/83	.05
252	Jeff Russell/29	.05
253	Wade Boggs	.60
254	Mike Greenwell/74	.05
255	Roger Clemens/16	.35
256	Marty Barrett/80	.05
257	Dwight Evans/99	.05
258	Mike Boddicker/72	.05
259	Ellis Burks	.05
260	John Dopson/174	.05
261	Rob Murphy/143	.05
262	Lee Smith/121	.05
263	Nick Esasky/77	.05
264	Bo Jackson	.10
265	George Brett/32	.35
266	Bret Saberhagen	.05
267	Kevin Seitzer/97	.05
268	Tom Gordon/47	.05
269	Kurt Stillwell/28	.05
270	Steve Farr/135	.05
271	Jim Eisenreich/64	.05
272	Mark Gubicza/21	.05
273	Jeff Montgomery/142	.05
274	Danny Tartabull/50	.05
275	Lou Whitaker	.05
276	Jack Morris/128	.05
277	Frank Tanana/59	.05
278	Chet Lemon/17	.05
279	Fred Lynn/65	.05
280	Mike Heat/67	.05
281	Alan Trammell	.05
282	Mike Henneman/84	.05
283	Gary Pettis/56	.05
284	Jeff Robinson/87	.05
285	Dave Bergman/166	.05
286	Kirby Puckett	.60
287	Kent Hrbek/45	.05
288	Gary Gaetti	.05
289	Jeff Reardon/98	.05
290	Brian Harper/167	.05
291	Gene Larkin/89	.05
292	Dan Gladden/138	.05
293	Al Newman/39	.05
294	Randy Bush/169	.05
295	Greg Gagne/31	.05
296	Allan Anderson/170	.05
297	Bobby Thigpen	.05
298	Ozzie Guillen/15	.05
299	Ivan Calderon/30	.05
300	Carlos Martinez/119	.05
301	Steve Lyons/71	.05
302	Ron Kittle/118	.05
303	Carlton Fisk	.40
304	Melido Perez/33	.05
305	Dave Gallagher/55	.05
306	Dan Pasqua/117	.05
307	Scott Fletcher/111	.05
308	Don Mattingly	.65
309	Dave Righetti/62	.05
310	Steve Sax	.05
311	Alvaro Espinoza/94	.05
312	Roberto Kelly/102	.05
313	Mel Hall/27	.05
314	Jesse Barfield/22	.05
315	Chuck Cary/51	.05
316	Bob Geren/14	.05
317	Andy Hawkins/172	.05
318	Don Slaught/137	.05
319	Jim Abbott/4 (Future Star)	.05
320	Greg Briley/7 (Future Star)	.05
321	Bob Geren/1 (Future Star)	.05
322	Tom Gordon/2 (Future Star)	.05
323	Ken Griffey Jr. (Future Star)	.30
324	Gregg Jefferies/8 (Future Star)	.10
325	Carlos Martinez/9 (Future Star)	.05
326	Gary Sheffield/12 (Future Star)	.15
327	Jerome Walton/11 (Future Star)	.05
328	Craig Worthington/6 (Future Star)	.05

TV All-Stars

This 66-card boxed set was sold only through a television offer in limited markets. Consequently, production numbers are relatively low and single cards are seldom offered in the hobby market. Most of the game's top stars are included in the issue. Fronts feature a high-gloss surface. On the red-bordered backs there are several lines of biographical data plus each player's "Career Bests" in various statistical categories, set against a pastel background shield. Issue price was $22.90.

		NM/M
Complete Set (66):		45.00
Common Player:		.25
1	Mark McGwire	6.50
2	Julio Franco	.25
3	Ozzie Guillen	.25
4	Carney Lansford	.25
5	Bo Jackson	.75
6	Kirby Puckett	3.50
7	Ruben Sierra	.25
8	Carlton Fisk	3.00
9	Nolan Ryan	9.00
10	Rickey Henderson	3.00
11	Jose Canseco	1.50
12	Mark Davis	.25
13	Dennis Eckersley	2.25
14	Chuck Finley	.25
15	Bret Saberhagen	.25
16	Dave Stewart	.25
17	Don Mattingly	5.00
18	Steve Sax	.25
19	Cal Ripken, Jr.	9.00
20	Wade Boggs	3.50
21	George Bell	.25
22	Mike Greenwell	.25
23	Robin Yount	3.00
24	Mickey Tettleton	.25
25	Roger Clemens	5.00
26	Fred McGriff	.25
27	Jeff Ballard	.25
28	Dwight Evans	.25
29	Paul Molitor	3.00
30	Gregg Olson	.25
31	Dan Plesac	.25
32	Greg Swindell	.25
33	Cito Gaston, Tony LaRussa	.25
34	Will Clark	.25
35	Roberto Alomar	.75
36	Barry Larkin	.25
37	Ken Caminiti	.25
38	Eric Davis	.25
39	Tony Gwynn	3.50
40	Kevin Mitchell	.25
41	Craig Biggio	.25
42	Mike Scott	.25
43	Joe Carter	.25
44	Jack Clark	.25
45	Glenn Davis	.25
46	Orel Hershiser	.25
47	Jay Howell	.25
48	Bruce Hurst	.25
49	Dave Smith	.25
50	Pedro Guerrero	.25
51	Ryne Sandberg	3.50
52	Ozzie Smith	3.50
53	Howard Johnson	.25
54	Von Hayes	.25
55	Tim Raines	.25
56	Darryl Strawberry	.25
57	Mike LaValliere	.25
58	Dwight Gooden	.25
59	Bobby Bonilla	.25
60	Tim Burke	.25
61	Sid Fernandez	.25
62	Andres Galarraga	.25
63	Mark Grace	.25
64	Joe Magrane	.25
65	Mitch Williams	.25
66	Roger Craig, Don Zimmer	.25

TV Cardinals Team Set

Available only as a boxed set via a limited television offer, this team set includes cards of all players on the opening day roster plus the manager, selected coaches and many of the organization's top prospects. In many cases this is the first card of a player in major league uniform, and in some cases represents the only card which will ever be issued of the player as a major leaguer. Cards feature a high-gloss front surface. Backs have a red border and feature a "ghost image" of the photo on the front as a background to the statistical and biographical data. Because of the relatively limited production and the fact it was sold as a boxed set only, single cards are seldom available.

		NM/M
Complete Set (66):		20.00
Common Player:		.25
1	Whitey Herzog	.25
2	Steve Braun	.25
3	Rich Hacker	.25
4	Dave Ricketts	.25
5	Jim Riggleman	.25
6	Mike Roarke	.25
7	Cris Carpenter	.25
8	John Costello	.25
9	Danny Cox	.25
10	Ken Dayley	.25
11	Jose DeLeon	.25
12	Frank DiPino	.25
13	Ken Hill	.25
14	Howard Hilton	.25
15	Ricky Horton	.25
16	Joe Magrane	.25
17	Greg Mathews	.25
18	Bryn Smith	.25
19	Scott Terry	.25
20	Bob Tewksbury	.25
21	John Tudor	.25
22	Todd Worrell	.25
23	Tom Pagnozzi	.25
24	Todd Zeile	.50
25	Pedro Guerrero	.25
26	Tim Jones	.25
27	Jose Oquendo	.25
28	Terry Pendleton	.50
29	Ozzie Smith	15.00
30	Denny Walling	.25
31	Tom Brunansky	.25
32	Vince Coleman	.50
33	Dave Collins	.25
34	Willie McGee	.50
35	John Morris	.25
36	Milt Thompson	.25
37	Gibson Alba	.25
38	Scott Arnold	.25
39	Rod Brewer	.25
40	Greg Carmona	.25
41	Mark Clark	.25
42	Stan Clarke	.25
43	Paul Coleman	.25
44	Todd Crosby	.25
45	Brad DuVall	.25
46	John Ericks	.25
47	Bien Figueroa	.25
48	Terry Francona	.25
49	Ed Fulton	.25
50	Bernard Gilkey	1.00
51	Ernie Camacho	.25
52	Mike Hinkle	.25
53	Ray Lankford	1.00
54	Julian Martinez	.25
55	Jesus Mendez	.25
56	Mike Milchin	.25
57	Mauricio Nunez	.25
58	Omar Olivares	.25
59	Geronimo Pena	.25
60	Mike Perez	.25
61	Gaylen Pitts	.25
62	Mark Riggins	.25
63	Tim Sherrill	.25
64	Roy Silver	.25
65	Ray Stephens	.25
66	Craig Wilson	.25

TV Cubs Team Set

Sold only in boxed set form via a limited television offer, this 66-card issue includes all players on the team's 1990 opening day roster as well as the manager, selected coaches and some of the organization's top minor league prospects. For the latter group, this sets offers the first - and in many cases the only - card of the player in a major league uniform. The cards have a high-gloss front surface. Card backs feature a "ghost image" of the color photo used on the front as a background to the stats and biographical information. A red border completes the back design. Because the set was sold only in boxed form, and production was relatively low, single cards are seldom seen in the market.

		NM/M
Complete Set (66):		45.00
Common Player:		.35
1	Don Zimmer	.35
2	Joe Altobelli	.35
3	Chuck Cottier	.35
4	Jose Martinez	.35
5	Dick Pole	.35
6	Phil Roof	.35
7	Paul Assenmacher	.35
8	Mike Bielecki	.35
9	Mike Harkey	.35
10	Joe Kraemer	.35
11	Les Lancaster	.35
12	Greg Maddux	20.00
13	Jose Nunez	.35
14	Jeff Pico	.35
15	Rick Sutcliffe	.75
16	Dean Wilkins	.35
17	Mitch Williams	.35
18	Steve Wilson	.35
19	Damon Berryhill	.35
20	Joe Girardi	.35
21	Rick Wrona	.35
22	Shawon Dunston	.50
23	Mark Grace	5.00
24	Domingo Ramos	.35
25	Luis Salazar	.35
26	Ryne Sandberg	20.00
27	Greg Smith	.35
28	Curtis Wilkerson	.35
29	Dave Clark	.35
30	Doug Dascenzo	.35
31	Andre Dawson	7.50
32	Lloyd McClendon	.35
33	Dwight Smith	.35
34	Jerome Walton	.35
35	Marvell Wynne	.35
36	Alex Arias	.35
37	Bob Bafia	.35
38	Brad Bierley	.35
39	Shawn Boskie	.35
40	Danny Clay	.35
41	Rusty Crockett	.35
42	Earl Cunningham	.35
43	Len Damian	.35
44	Darrin Duffy	.35
45	Ty Griffin	.35
46	Brian Guinn	.35
47	Phil Hannon	.35
48	Phil Harrison	.35
49	Jeff Hearron	.35
50	Greg Kallevig	.35
51	Cedric Landrum	.35
52	Bill Long	.35
53	Derrick May	.35
54	Ray Mullino	.35
55	Erik Pappas	.35
56	Steve Parker	.35
57	Dave Pavlas	.35
58	Laddie Renfroe	.35
59	Jeff Small	.35
60	Doug Strange	.35
61	Gary Varsho	.35
62	Hector Villanueva	.35
63	Rick Wilkins	.35
64	Dana Williams	.35
65	Bill Wrona	.35
66	Fernando Zarranz	.35

TV Mets Team Set

This late-season issue, sold only as a boxed set via a television offer in limited areas, features all of the players on the 1990 opening day roster, plus the manager, selected coaches and many of the organization's top minor league prospects. For many of the prospects, this is the first, if not the only, card on which they appear in major league uniform. A highlight of the back design is a "ghost image" full-color reproduction of the front photo, used as a background to the statistical and biographical information. A red border dominates the remainder of the back design. Because it was sold only as a boxed set, and production was relatively limited, single cards are seldom available.

		NM/M
Complete Set (66):		10.00
Common Player:		.35
1	Dave Johnson	.35
2	Mike Cubbage	.35
3	Doc Edwards	.35
4	Bud Harrelson	.35
5	Greg Pavlick	.35
6	Mel Stottlemyre, Sr.	.35
7	Blaine Beatty	.35
8	David Cone	1.00
9	Ron Darling	.35
10	Sid Fernandez	.35
11	John Franco	.50
12	Dwight Gooden	.50
13	Jeff Innis	.35
14	Julio Machado	.35
15	Jeff Musselman	.35
16	Bob Ojeda	.35
17	Alejandro Pena	.35
18	Frank Viola	.35
19	Wally Whitehurst	.35
20	Barry Lyons	.35
21	Orlando Mercado	.35
22	Mackey Sasser	.35
23	Kevin Elster	.35
24	Gregg Jefferies	.50
25	Howard Johnson	.35
26	Dave Magadan	.35
27	Mike Marshall	.35
28	Tom O'Malley	.35
29	Tim Teufel	.35
30	Mark Carreon	.35
31	Kevin McReynolds	.35
32	Keith Miller	.35
33	Darryl Strawberry	.50
34	Lou Thornton	.35
35	Shawn Barton	.35
36	Tim Bogar	.35
37	Terry Bross	.35
38	Kevin Brown	.35
39	Mike DeButch	.35
40	Alex Diaz	.35
41	Chris Donnels	.35
42	Jeff Gardner	.35
43	Denny Gonzalez	.35
44	Kenny Graves	.35
45	Manny Hernandez	.35
46	Keith Hughes	.35
47	Todd Hundley	.50
48	Chris Jelic	.35
49	Dave Liddell	.35
50	Terry McDaniel	.35
51	Cesar Mejia	.35
52	Scott Nielsen	.35
53	Dale Plummer	.35
54	Darren Reed	.35
55	Gil Roca	.35
56	Jaime Roseboro	.35
57	Roger Samuels	.35
58	Zoilo Sanchez	.35
59	Pete Schourek	.35
60	Craig Shipley	.35
61	Ray Soff	.35
62	Steve Swisher	.35
63	Kelvin Torve	.35
64	Dave Trautwein	.35
65	Julio Valera	.35
66	Alan Zinter	.35

TV Red Sox Team Set

This 66-card set was available only via a television offer in certain limited areas. Production was relatively low and single cards are hard to find. Player selection includes all those on the team's opening day roster in 1990, plus the manager, selected coaches and the team's top minor league prospects. In many cases this represents the first, or even the only, appearance of these prospects on major league baseball cards. Fronts have a high-gloss surface. Card backs, bordered in red, feature a "ghost image" reproduction of the front photo as a background to the statistics and biographical data.

		NM/M
Complete Set (66):		40.00
Common Player:		.35
1	Joe Morgan	.35
2	Dick Berardino	.35
3	Al Bumbry	.35
4	Bill Fischer	.35
5	Richie Hebner	.35

6	Rac Slider	.35
7	Mike Boddicker	.35
8	Roger Clemens	25.00
9	John Dopson	.35
10	Wes Gardner	.35
11	Greg Harris	.35
12	Dana Kiecker	.35
13	Dennis Lamp	.35
14	Rob Murphy	.35
15	Jeff Reardon	.35
16	Mike Rochford	.35
17	Lee Smith	.50
18	Rich Gedman	.35
19	John Marzano	.35
20	Tony Pena	.35
21	Marty Barrett	.35
22	Wade Boggs	15.00
23	Bill Buckner	.50
24	Danny Heep	.35
25	Jody Reed	.35
26	Luis Rivera	.35
27	Billy Jo Robidoux	.35
28	Ellis Burks	.35
29	Dwight Evans	.35
30	Mike Greenwell	.35
31	Randy Kutcher	.35
32	Carlos Quintana	.35
33	Kevin Romine	.35
34	Ed Nottle	.35
35	Mark Meleski	.35
36	Steve Bast	.35
37	Greg Blosser	.35
38	Tom Bolton	.35
39	Scott Cooper	.35
40	Zach Crouch	.35
41	Steve Curry	.35
42	Mike Dalton	.35
43	John Flaherty	.35
44	Angel Gonzalez	.35
45	Eric Hetzel	.35
46	Daryl Irvine	.35
47	Joe Johnson	.35
48	Rick Lancellotti	.35
49	John Leister	.35
50	Derek Livernois	.35
51	Josias Manzanillo	.35
52	Kevin Morton	.35
53	Julius McDougal	.35
54	Tim Naehring	.35
55	Jim Pankovits	.35
56	Mickey Pina	.35
57	Phil Plantier	.35
58	Jerry Reed	.35
59	Larry Shikles	.35
60	Tito Stewart	.35
61	Jeff Stone	.35
62	John Trautwein	.35
63	Gary Tremblay	.35
64	Mo Vaughn	2.50
65	Scott Wade	.35
66	Eric Wedge	.35

TV Yankees Team Set

The first - and in many cases the only - baseball card appearance of top minor league prospects occurs in this special 66-card boxed set which was sold only via a special television offer in limited markets. The set also includes all players on the team's opening day roster, plus the manager and selected coaches. Card fronts have a high-gloss surface. On back, framed by a red border, the design features a "ghost image" of the color front photo, used as a background to the statistical and biographical information. Because the cards were sold only as a complete set, single cards are seldom available.

		NM/M
Complete Set (66):		60.00
Common Player:		.35
1	Bucky Dent	.35
2	Mark Connor	.35
3	Billy Connors	.35
4	Mike Ferraro	.35
5	Joe Sparks	.35
6	Champ Summers	.35
7	Greg Cadaret	.35
8	Chuck Cary	.35
9	Lee Guetterman	.35
10	Andy Hawkins	.35
11	Dave LaPoint	.35
12	Tim Leary	.35
13	Lance McCullers	.35
14	Alan Mills	.35
15	Clay Parker	.35
16	Pascual Perez	.35
17	Eric Plunk	.35
18	Dave Righetti	.35
19	Jeff Robinson	.35
20	Rick Cerone	.35
21	Bob Geren	.35
22	Steve Balboni	.35
23	Mike Blowers	.35
24	Alvaro Espinoza	.35
25	Don Mattingly	40.00
26	Steve Sax	.35
27	Wayne Tolleson	.35
28	Randy Velarde	.35
29	Jesse Barfield	.35
30	Mel Hall	.35
31	Roberto Kelly	.35
32	Luis Polonia	.35
33	Deion Sanders	1.00
34	Dave Winfield	15.00
35	Steve Adkins	.35
36	Oscar Azocar	.35
37	Bob Brower	.35
38	Britt Burns	.35
39	Bob Davidson	.35
40	Brian Dorsett	.35
41	Dave Eiland	.35
42	John Fishel	.35
43	Andy Fox	.35
44	John Habyan	.35
45	Cullen Hartzog	.35
46	Sterling Hitchcock	.35
47	Brian Johnson	.35
48	Jimmy Jones	.35
49	Scott Kamieniecki	.35
50	Mark Leiter	.35
51	Jim Leyritz	.35
52	Jason Maas	.35
53	Kevin Maas	.35
54	Hensley Meulens	.35
55	Kevin Mmahat	.35
56	Rich Monteleone	.35
57	Vince Phillips	.35
58	Carlos Rodriguez	.35
59	Dave Sax	.35
60	Willie Smith	.35
61	Van Snider	.35
62	Andy Stankiewicz	.35
63	Wade Taylor	.35
64	Ricky Torres	.35
65	Jim Walewander	.35
66	Bernie Williams	4.00

1989 Major League Debut

This 150-card set chronicles the debut date of all 1989 Major League rookies. Two checklist cards are also included in this boxed set, listing the players in order of debut date, though the cards are numbered alphabetically. The card fronts resemble the 1990 Topps cards in style. A debut banner appears in an upper corner. The flip sides are horizontal and are printed in black on yellow stock, providing an overview of the player's first game. The set is packaged in a special collectors box and was only available through hobby dealers.

		NM/M
Complete Set (150):		10.00
Common Player:		.05
1	Jim Abbott	.05
2	Beau Allred	.05
3	Wilson Alvarez	.05
4	Kent Anderson	.05
5	Eric Anthony	.05
6	Kevin Appier	.05
7	Larry Arndt	.05
8	John Barfield	.05
9	Billy Bates	.05
10	Kevin Batiste	.05
11	Blaine Beatty	.05
12	Stan Belinda	.05
13	Juan Bell	.05
14	Joey Belle	.25
15	Andy Benes	.05
16	Mike Benjamin	.05
17	Geronimo Berroa	.05
18	Mike Blowers	.05
19	Brian Brady	.05
20	Francisco Cabrera	.05
21	George Canale	.05
22	Jose Cano	.05
23	Steve Carter	.05
24	Pat Combs	.05
25	Scott Coolbaugh	.05
26	Steve Cummings	.05
27	Pete Dalena	.05
28	Jeff Datz	.05
29	Bobby Davidson	.05
30	Drew Denson	.05
31	Gary DiSarcina	.05
32	Brian DuBois	.05
33	Mike Dyer	.05
34	Wayne Edwards	.05
35	Junior Felix	.05
36	Mike Fetters	.05
37	Steve Finley	.05
38	Darren Fletcher	.05
39	LaVel Freeman	.05
40	Steve Frey	.05
41	Mark Gardner	.05
42	Joe Girardi	.05
43	Juan Gonzalez	.50
44	Goose Gozzo	.05
45	Tommy Greene	.05
46	Ken Griffey Jr.	3.00
47	Jason Grimsley	.05
48	Marquis Grissom	.05
49	Mark Guthrie	.05
50	Chip Hale	.05
51	John Hardy	.05
52	Gene Harris	.05
53	Mike Hartley	.05
54	Scott Hemond	.05
55	Xavier Hernandez	.05
56	Eric Hetzel	.05
57	Greg Hibbard	.05
58	Mark Higgins	.05
59	Glenallen Hill	.05
60	Chris Hoiles	.05
61	Shawn Holman	.05
62	Dann Howitt	.05
63	Mike Huff	.05
64	Terry Jorgenson	.05
65	Dave Justice	.25
66	Jeff King	.05
67	Matt Kinzer	.05
68	Joe Kraemer	.05
69	Marcus Lawton	.05
70	Derek Lilliquist	.05
71	Scott Little	.05
72	Greg Litton	.05
73	Rick Lueken	.05
74	Julio Machado	.05
75	Tom Magrann	.05
76	Kelly Mann	.05
77	Randy McCament	.05
78	Ben McDonald	.05
79	Chuck McElroy	.05
80	Jeff McKnight	.05
81	Kent Mercker	.05
82	Matt Merullo	.05
83	Hensley Meulens	.05
84	Kevin Mmahat	.05
85	Mike Munoz	.05
86	Dan Murphy	.05
87	Jaime Navarro	.05
88	Randy Nosek	.05
89	John Olerud	.15
90	Steve Olin	.05
91	Joe Oliver	.05
92	Francisco Oliveras	.05
93	Greg Olson	.05
94	John Orton	.05
95	Dean Palmer	.05
96	Ramon Pena	.05
97	Jeff Peterek	.05
98	Marty Pevey	.05
99	Rusty Richards	.05
100	Jeff Richardson	.05
101	Rob Richie	.05
102	Kevin Ritz	.05
103	Rosario Rodriguez	.05
104	Mike Roesler	.05
105	Kenny Rogers	.05
106	Bobby Rose	.05
107	Alex Sanchez	.05
108	Deion Sanders	.25
109	Jeff Schaefer	.05
110	Jeff Schulz	.05
111	Mike Schwabe	.05
112	Dick Scott	.05
113	Scott Scudder	.05
114	Rudy Seanez	.05
115	Joe Skalski	.05
116	Dwight Smith	.05
117	Greg Smith	.05
118	Mike Smith	.05
119	Paul Sorrento	.05
120	Sammy Sosa	3.00
121	Billy Spiers	.05
122	Mike Stanton	.05
123	Phil Stephenson	.05
124	Doug Strange	.05
125	Russ Swan	.05
126	Kevin Tapani	.05
127	Stu Tate	.05
128	Greg Vaughn	.05
129	Robin Ventura	.15
130	Randy Veres	.05
131	Jose Vizcaino	.05
132	Omar Vizquel	.05
133	Larry Walker	.25
134	Jerome Walton	.05
135	Gary Wayne	.05
136	Lenny Webster	.05
137	Mickey Weston	.05
138	Jeff Wetherby	.05
139	John Wetteland	.05
140	Ed Whited	.05
141	Wally Whitehurst	.05
142	Kevin Wickander	.05
143	Dean Wilkins	.05
144	Dana Williams	.05
145	Paul Wilmet	.05
146	Craig Wilson	.05
147	Matt Winters	.05
148	Eric Yelding	.05
149	Clint Zavaras	.05
150	Todd Zeile	.05
----	Checklist (1 of 2)	.05
----	Checklist (2 of 2)	.05

1991 Topps Pre-Production Sample Sheet

To preview its 40th anniversary set, Topps distributed this 7-1/2" x 10-1/2" uncut sheet. Fronts are idential to the issued versions of each player's card while backs are printed in blue with a large anniversary logo, the player's name, a copyright line and "1991 PRE-PRODUCTION / SAMPLE."

		NM/M
Uncut Sheet:		15.00
Complete Set (9):		15.00
Common Player:		1.00
(1)	Wade Boggs	3.00
(2)	Jose Canseco	2.00
(3)	Roger Clemens	6.00
(4)	Rickey Henderson	2.50
(5)	Bo Jackson	1.50
(6)	Kirt Manwaring	1.00
(7)	Willie Randolph	1.00
(8)	Benny Santiago	1.00
(9)	Walt Weiss	1.00

1991 Topps

Topps celebrated its 40th anniversary in 1991 with the biggest promotional campaign in baseball card history. More than 300,000 vintage Topps cards (or certificates redeemable for valuable older cards) produced from 1952 to 1990 were randomly inserted in packs. Also a grand prize winner received a complete set from each year, and others received a single set from 1952-1990. The 1991 Topps card fronts feature the "Topps 40 Years of Baseball" logo in the upper-left corner. Colored borders frame the player photos. All players of the same team have cards with the same frame/border colors. Both action and posed shots appear in full-color on the card fronts. The flip sides are printed horizontally and feature complete statistics. Record Breakers and other special cards were once again included in the set. The cards measure 2-1/2" x 3-1/2". Many cards can be found with variations in the sheet-letter (A-F) designations in the copyright line on back.

		NM/M
Unopened Factory Set, Retail (792):		30.00
Unopened Factory Set, Hobby (792):		25.00
Complete Set (792):		20.00
Common Player:		.05
Wax Pack (15):		.50
Wax Box (36):		12.50
Cello Pack (34):		1.00
Cello Box (24):		15.00
Rack Pack (45):		1.00
Rack Box (24):		15.00
Vending Box (500):		7.50
1	Nolan Ryan	.75
2	George Brett (Record Breaker)	.25
3	Carlton Fisk (Record Breaker)	.20
4	Kevin Maas (Record Breaker)	.05
5	Cal Ripken, Jr. (Record Breaker)	.40
6	Nolan Ryan (Record Breaker)	.40
7	Ryne Sandberg (Record Breaker)	.30
8	Bobby Thigpen (Record Breaker)	.05
9	Darrin Fletcher **RC**	.05
10	Gregg Olson	.05
11	Roberto Kelly	.05
12	Paul Assenmacher	.05
13	Mariano Duncan	.05
14	Dennis Lamp	.05
15	Von Hayes	.05
16	Mike Heath	.05
17	Jeff Brantley	.05
18	Nelson Liriano	.05
19	Jeff Robinson	.05
20	Pedro Guerrero	.05
21	Joe M. Morgan	.05
22	Storm Davis	.05
23	Jim Gantner	.05
24	Dave Martinez	.05
25	Tim Belcher	.05
26	Luis Sojo	.05
27	Bobby Witt	.05
28	Alvaro Espinoza	.05
29	Bob Walk	.05
30	Gregg Jefferies	.05
31	Colby Ward **RC**	.05
32	Mike Simms **RC**	.05
33	Barry Jones	.05
34	Atlee Hammaker	.05
35	Greg Maddux	.50
36	Donnie Hill	.05
37	Tom Bolton	.05
38	Scott Bradley	.05
39	Jim Neidlinger **RC**	.05
40	Kevin Mitchell	.05
41	Ken Dayley	.05
42a	Chris Hoiles **RC** (White inner photo frame.)	.20
42b	Chris Hoiles **RC** (Gray inner photo frame.)	.10
43	Roger McDowell	.05
44	Mike Felder	.05
45	Chris Sabo	.05
46	Tim Drummond	.05
47	Brook Jacoby	.05
48	Dennis Boyd	.05
49a	Pat Borders (40 stolen bases in Kinston 1986)	.20
49b	Pat Borders (0 stolen bases in Kinston 1986)	.10
50	Bob Welch	.05
51	Art Howe	.05
52	Francisco Oliveras **RC**	.05
53	Mike Sharperson	.05
54	Gary Mielke	.05
55	Jeffrey Leonard	.05
56	Jeff Parrett	.05
57	Jack Howell	.05
58	Mel Stottlemyre	.05
59	Eric Yelding	.05
60	Frank Viola	.05
61	Stan Javier	.05
62	Lee Guetterman	.05
63	Milt Thompson	.05
64	Tom Herr	.05
65	Bruce Hurst	.05
66	Terry Kennedy	.05
67	Rick Honeycutt	.05
68	Gary Sheffield	.25
69	Steve Wilson	.05
70	Ellis Burks	.05
71	Jim Acker	.05
72	Junior Ortiz	.05
73	Craig Worthington	.05
74	Shane Andrews **RC** (#1 Draft Pick)	.10
75	Jack Morris	.05
76	Jerry Browne	.05
77	Drew Hall	.05
78	Geno Petralli	.05
79	Frank Thomas	.35
80a	Fernando Valenzuela (No diamond after 104 ER in 1990.)	.25
80b	Fernando Valenzuela (Diamond after 104 ER in 1990.)	.05
81	Cito Gaston	.05
82	Tom Glavine	.20
83	Daryl Boston	.05
84	Bob McClure	.05
85	Jesse Barfield	.05
86	Les Lancaster	.05
87	Tracy Jones	.05
88	Bob Tewksbury	.05
89	Darren Daulton	.05
90	Danny Tartabull	.05
91	Greg Colbrunn **RC** (Future Star)	.05
92	Danny Jackson	.05
93	Ivan Calderon	.05
94	John Dopson	.05
95	Paul Molitor	.35
96	Trevor Wilson	.05
97a	Brady Anderson (3H, 2RBI in Sept. scoreboard)	.25
97b	Brady Anderson (14H, 3 RBI in Sept. scoreboard)	.05
98	Sergio Valdez	.05
99	Chris Gwynn	.05
100a	Don Mattingly (10 hits 1990)	.50
100b	Don Mattingly (101 hits in 1990)	.50
101	Rob Ducey	.05
102	Gene Larkin	.05
103	Tim Costo **RC** (#1 Draft Pick)	.05
104	Don Robinson	.05
105	Kevin McReynolds	.05
106	Ed Nunez	.05
107	Luis Polonia	.05
108	Matt Young	.05
109	Greg Riddoch	.05
110	Tom Henke	.05
111	Andres Thomas	.05
112	Frank DiPino	.05
113	Carl Everett **RC** (#1 Draft Pick)	.50
114	Lance Dickson **RC** (Future Star)	.05
115	Hubie Brooks	.05
116	Mark Davis	.05
117	Dion James	.05
118	Tom Edens **RC**	.05
119	Carl Nichols **RC**	.05
120	Joe Carter	.05
121	Eric King	.05
122	Paul O'Neill	.05
123	Greg Harris	.05
124	Randy Bush	.05
125	Steve Bedrosian	.05
126	Bernard Gilkey **RC**	.10
127	Joe Price	.05
128	Travis Fryman	.05
129	Mark Eichhorn	.05
130	Ozzie Smith	.50
131a	Checklist 1 (Phil Bradley #727.)	.05
131b	Checklist 1 (Phil Bradley #717.)	.05
132	Jamie Quirk	.05
133	Greg Briley	.05
134	Kevin Elster	.05
135	Jerome Walton	.05
136	Dave Schmidt	.05
137	Randy Ready	.05
138	Jamie Moyer	.05
139	Jeff Treadway	.05
140	Fred McGriff	.05
141	Nick Leyva	.05
142	Curtis Wilkerson	.05
143	John Smiley	.05
144	Dave Henderson	.05
145	Lou Whitaker	.05
146	Dan Plesac	.05
147	Carlos Baerga	.05
148	Rey Palacios	.05
149	Al Osuna **RC**	.05
150	Cal Ripken, Jr.	.75
151	Tom Browning	.05
152	Mickey Hatcher	.05
153	Bryan Harvey	.05
154	Jay Buhner	.05
155a	Dwight Evans (Diamond after 162 G 1982.)	.10
155b	Dwight Evans (No diamond after 162 G 1982.)	.05
156	Carlos Martinez	.05
157	John Smoltz	.05
158	Jose Uribe	.05
159	Joe Boever	.05
160	Vince Coleman	.05
161	Tim Leary	.05
162	Ozzie Canseco **RC**	.10
163	Dave Johnson	.05
164	Edgar Diaz	.05
165	Sandy Alomar	.05
166	Harold Baines	.05

167a Randy Tomlin **RC** ("Harriburg" 1989-90.) .10
167b Randy Tomlin **RC** ("Harrisburg" 1989-90.) .05
168 John Olerud .05
169 Luis Aquino .05
170 Carlton Fisk .35
171 Tony LaRussa .05
172 Pete Incaviglia .05
173 Jason Grimsley .05
174 Ken Caminiti .05
175 Jack Armstrong .05
176 John Orton **RC** .05
177 Reggie Harris **RC** .05
178 Dave Valle .05
179 Pete Harnisch .05
180 Tony Gwynn .50
181 Duane Ward .05
182 Junior Noboa .05
183 Clay Parker .05
184 Gary Green .05
185 Joe Magrane .05
186 Rod Booker .05
187 Greg Cadaret .05
188 Damon Berryhill .05
189 Daryl Irvine **RC** .05
190 Matt Williams .05
191 Willie Blair **RC** .05
192 Rob Deer .05
193 Felix Fermin .05
194 Xavier Hernandez **RC** .05
195 Wally Joyner .05
196 Jim Vatcher **RC** .05
197 Chris Nabholz **RC** .05
198 R.J. Reynolds .05
199 Mike Hartley **RC** .05
200 Darryl Strawberry .05
201 Tom Kelly .05
202 Jim Leyritz **RC** .20
203 Gene Harris .05
204 Herm Winningham .05
205 Mike Perez **RC** .05
206 Carlos Quintana .05
207 Gary Wayne .05
208 Willie Wilson .05
209 Ken Howell .05
210 Lance Parrish .05
211 Brian Barnes **RC** (Future Star) .05
212 Steve Finley .05
213 Frank Wills .05
214 Joe Girardi .05
215 Dave Smith .05
216 Greg Gagne .05
217 Chris Bosio .05
218 Rick Parker **RC** .05
219 Jack McDowell .05
220 Tim Wallach .05
221 Don Slaught .05
222 Brian McRae **RC** .10
223 Allan Anderson .05
224 Juan Gonzalez .20
225 Randy Johnson .35
226 Alfredo Griffin .05
227 Steve Avery .05
228 Rex Hudler .05
229 Rance Mulliniks .05
230 Sid Fernandez .05
231 Doug Rader .05
232 Jose DeJesus .05
233 Al Leiter .05
234 Scott Erickson **RC** .10
235 Dave Parker .05
236a Frank Tanana (No diamond after 269 SO 1975.) .10
236b Frank Tanana (Diamond after 269 SO 1975.) .05
237 Rick Cerone .05
238 Mike Dunne .05
239 Darren Lewis **RC** .05
240 Mike Scott .05
241 Dave Clark .05
242 Mike LaCoss .05
243 Lance Johnson .05
244 Mike Jeffcoat .05
245 Kal Daniels .05
246 Kevin Wickander .05
247 Jody Reed .05
248 Tom Gordon .05
249 Bob Melvin .05
250 Dennis Eckersley .30
251 Mark Lemke .05
252 Mel Rojas **RC** .05
253 Garry Templeton .05
254 Shawn Boskie **RC** .05
255 Brian Downing .05
256 Greg Hibbard .05
257 Tom O'Malley .05
258 Chris Hammond **RC** .05
259 Hensley Meulens .05
260 Harold Reynolds .05
261 Bud Harrelson .05
262 Tim Jones .05
263 Checklist 2 .05
264 Dave Hollins **RC** .05
265 Mark Gubicza .05
266 Carmen Castillo .05
267 Mark Knudson .05
268 Tom Brookens .05
269 Joe Hesketh .05
270a Mark McGwire (1987 SLG .618) .75
270b Mark McGwire (1987 SLG 618) .75
271 Omar Olivares **RC** .05
272 Jeff King .05
273 Johnny Ray .05
274 Ken Williams .05
275 Alan Trammell .05
276 Bill Swift .05
277 Scott Coolbaugh .05
278 Alex Fernandez **RC** (#1 Draft Pick) .10
279a Jose Gonzalez (Photo of Billy Bean, left-handed batter.) .75
279b Jose Gonzalez (Correct photo, right-handed batter.) .05
280 Bret Saberhagen .05
281 Larry Sheets .05
282 Don Carman .05
283 Marquis Grissom .05
284 Bill Spiers .05
285 Jim Abbott .05
286 Ken Oberkfell .05
287 Mark Grant .05
288 Derrick May **RC** .05
289 Tim Birtsas .05
290 Steve Sax .05
291 John Wathan .05
292 Bud Black .05
293 Jay Bell .05
294 Mike Moore .05
295 Rafael Palmeiro .30
296 Mark Williamson .05
297 Manny Lee .05
298 Omar Vizquel .05
299 Scott Radinsky **RC** .05
300 Kirby Puckett .50
301 Steve Farr .05
302 Tim Teufel .05
303 Mike Boddicker .05
304 Kevin Reimer **RC** .05
305 Mike Scioscia .05
306a Lonnie Smith (136 G 1990) .10
306b Lonnie Smith (135 G 1990) .05
307 Andy Benes .05
308 Tom Pagnozzi .05
309 Norm Charlton .05
310 Gary Carter .35
311 Jeff Pico .05
312 Charlie Hayes .05
313 Ron Robinson .05
314 Gary Pettis .05
315 Roberto Alomar .15
316 Gene Nelson .05
317 Mike Fitzgerald .05
318 Rick Aguilera .05
319 Jeff McKnight **RC** .05
320 Tony Fernandez .05
321 Bob Rodgers .05
322 Terry Shumpert **RC** .05
323 Cory Snyder .05
324a Ron Kittle ("6 Home Runs" in career summary) .10
324b Ron Kittle ("7 Home Runs" in career summary) .05
325 Brett Butler .05
326 Ken Patterson .05
327 Ron Hassey .05
328 Walt Terrell .05
329 Dave Justice .05
330 Dwight Gooden .05
331 Eric Anthony .05
332 Kenny Rogers .05
333 Chipper Jones **RC** (#1 Draft Pick) 2.00
334 Todd Benzinger .05
335 Mitch Williams .05
336 Matt Nokes .05
337a Keith Comstock (Mariners logo.) .05
337b Keith Comstock (Cubs logo.) 1.50
338 Luis Rivera .05
339 Larry Walker .05
340 Ramon Martinez .05
341 John Moses .05
342 Mickey Morandini **RC** .10
343 Jose Oquendo .05
344 Jeff Russell .05
345 Len Dykstra .05
346 Jesse Orosco .05
347 Greg Vaughn .05
348 Todd Stottlemyre .05
349 Dave Gallagher .05
350 Glenn Davis .05
351 Joe Torre .05
352 Frank White .05
353 Tony Castillo .05
354 Sid Bream .05
355 Chili Davis .05
356 Mike Marshall .05
357 Jack Savage .05
358 Mark Parent .05
359 Chuck Cary .05
360 Tim Raines .05
361 Scott Garrelts .05
362 Hector Villanueva **RC** .05
363 Rick Mahler .05
364 Dan Pasqua .05
365 Mike Schooler .05
366a Checklist 3 (Carl Nichols #19.) .05
366b Checklist 3 (Carl Nichols #119.) .05
367 Dave Walsh **RC** .05
368 Felix Jose .05
369 Steve Searcy .05
370 Kelly Gruber .05
371 Jeff Montgomery .05
372 Spike Owen .05
373 Darrin Jackson .05
374 Larry Casian **RC** .05
375 Tony Pena .05
376 Mike Harkey .05
377 Rene Gonzales .05
378a Wilson Alvarez **RC** (No 1989 Port Charlotte stats.) .50
378b Wilson Alvarez **RC** (1989 Port Charlotte stats) .20
379 Randy Velarde .05
380 Willie McGee .05
381 Jim Leyland .05
382 Mackey Sasser .05
383 Pete Smith .05
384 Gerald Perry .05
385 Mickey Tettleton .05
386 Cecil Fielder/AS .05
387 Julio Franco/AS .05
388 Kelly Gruber/AS .05
389 Alan Trammell/AS .05
390 Jose Canseco/AS .15
391 Rickey Henderson/AS .20
392 Ken Griffey Jr./AS .35
393 Carlton Fisk/AS .20
394 Bob Welch/AS .05
395 Chuck Finley/AS .05
396 Bobby Thigpen/AS .05
397 Eddie Murray/AS .20
398 Ryne Sandberg/AS .30
399 Matt Williams/AS .05
400 Barry Larkin/AS .05
401 Barry Bonds/AS .40
402 Darryl Strawberry/AS .05
403 Bobby Bonilla/AS .05
404 Mike Scoscia/AS .05
405 Doug Drabek/AS .05
406 Frank Viola/AS .05
407 John Franco/AS .05
408 Ernie Riles .05
409 Mike Stanley .05
410 Dave Righetti .05
411 Lance Blankenship .05
412 Dave Bergman .05
413 Terry Mulholland .05
414 Sammy Sosa .60
415 Rick Sutcliffe .05
416 Randy Milligan .05
417 Bill Krueger .05
418 Nick Esasky .05
419 Jeff Reed .05
420 Bobby Thigpen .05
421 Alex Cole **RC** .05
422 Rick Rueschel .05
423 Rafael Ramirez .05
424 Calvin Schiraldi .05
425 Andy Van Slyke .05
426 Joe Grahe **RC** .05
427 Rick Dempsey .05
428 John Barfield **RC** .05
429 Stump Merrill .05
430 Gary Gaetti .05
431 Paul Gibson .05
432 Delino DeShields .05
433 Pat Tabler .05
434 Julio Machado **RC** .05
435 Kevin Maas .05
436 Scott Bankhead .05
437 Doug Dascenzo .05
438 Vicente Palacios .05
439 Dickie Thon .05
440 George Bell .05
441 Zane Smith .05
442 Charlie O'Brien .05
443 Jeff Innis .05
444 Glenn Braggs .05
445 Greg Swindell .05
446 Craig Grebeck **RC** .05
447 John Burkett .05
448 Craig Lefferts .05
449 Juan Berenguer .05
450 Wade Boggs .50
451 Neal Heaton .05
452 Bill Schroeder .05
453 Lenny Harris .05
454a Kevin Appier (No 1990 Omaha stats.) .15
454b Kevin Appier (1990 Omaha stats) .05
455 Walt Weiss .05
456 Charlie Leibrandt .05
457 Todd Hundley .05
458 Brian Holman .05
459 Tom Trebelhorn .05
460 Dave Steib .05
461a Robin Ventura (Gray inner photo frame at left.) .15
461b Robin Ventura (Red inner photo frame at left.) .05
462 Steve Frey .05
463 Dwight Smith .05
464 Steve Buechele .05
465 Ken Griffey .05
466 Charles Nagy **RC** .05
467 Dennis Cook .05
468 Tim Hulett .05
469 Chet Lemon .05
470 Howard Johnson .05
471 Mike Lieberthal **RC** (#1 Draft Pick) .50
472 Kirt Manwaring .05
473 Curt Young .05
474 Phil Plantier **RC** .10
475 Teddy Higuera .05
476 Glenn Wilson .05
477 Mike Fetters .05
478 Kurt Stillwell .05
479 Bob Patterson .05
480 Dave Magadan .05
481 Eddie Whitson .05
482 Tino Martinez .05
483 Mike Aldrete .05
484 Dave LaPoint .05
485 Terry Pendleton .05
486 Tommy Greene **RC** .05
487 Rafael Belliard .05
488 Jeff Manto **RC** .05
489 Bobby Valentine .05
490 Kirk Gibson .05
491 Kurt Miller **RC** (#1 Draft Pick) .05
492 Ernie Whitt .05
493 Jose Rijo .05
494 Chris James .05
495 Charlie Hough .05
496 Marty Barrett .05
497 Ben McDonald .05
498 Mark Salas .05
499 Melido Perez .05
500 Will Clark .05
501 Mike Bielecki .05
502 Carney Lansford .05
503 Roy Smith .05
504 Julio Valera **RC** .05
505 Chuck Finley .05
506 Darnell Coles .05
507 Steve Jeltz .05
508 Mike York **RC** .05
509 Glenallen Hill .05
510 John Franco .05
511 Steve Balboni .05
512 Jose Mesa **RC** .05
513 Jerald Clark .05
514 Mike Stanton .05
515 Alvin Davis .05
516 Karl Rhodes **RC** .05
517 Joe Oliver .05
518 Cris Carpenter .05
519 Sparky Anderson .10
520 Mark Grace .05
521 Joe Orsulak .05
522 Stan Belinda .05
523 Rodney McCray **RC** .05
524 Darrel Akerfelds .05
525 Willie Randolph .05
526a Moises Alou (37 R 1990 Pirates) .20
526b Moises Alou (0 R 1990 Pirates) .15
527a Checklist 4 (Kevin McReynolds #719) .05
527b Checklist 4 (Kevin McReynolds #105) .05
528 Denny Martinez .05
529 Mark Newfield **RC** (#1 Draft Pick) .05
530 Roger Clemens .60
531 Dave Rhode **RC** .05
532 Kirk McCaskill .05
533 Oddibe McDowell .05
534 Mike Jackson .05
535 Ruben Sierra .05
536 Mike Witt .05
537 Jose Lind .05
538 Bip Roberts .05
539 Scott Terry .05
540 George Brett .60
541 Domingo Ramos .05
542 Rob Murphy .05
543 Junior Felix .05
544 Alejandro Pena .05
545 Dale Murphy .15
546 Jeff Ballard .05
547 Mike Pagliarulo .05
548 Jaime Navarro .05
549 John McNamara .05
550 Eric Davis .05
551 Bob Kipper .05
552 Jeff Hamilton .05
553 Joe Klink **RC** .05
554 Brian Harper .05
555 Turner Ward **RC** .05
556 Gary Ward .05
557 Wally Whitehurst .05
558 Otis Nixon .05
559 Adam Peterson .05
560 Greg Smith **RC** .05
561 Tim McIntosh **RC** (Future Star) .05
562 Jeff Kunkel .05
563 Brent Knackert **RC** .05
564 Dante Bichette .05
565 Craig Biggio .05
566 Craig Wilson **RC** .05
567 Dwayne Henry .05
568 Ron Karkovice .05
569 Curt Schilling .05
570 Barry Bonds .75
571 Pat Combs .05
572 Dave Anderson .05
573 Rich Rodriguez **RC** .05
574 John Marzano .05
575 Robin Yount .35
576 Jeff Kaiser **RC** .05
577 Bill Doran .05
578 Dave West .05
579 Roger Craig .05
580 Dave Stewart .05
581 Luis Quinones .05
582 Marty Clary .05
583 Tony Phillips .05
584 Kevin Brown .05
585 Pete O'Brien .05
586 Fred Lynn .05
587 Jose Offerman **RC** (Future Star) .05
588a Mark Whiten **RC** (Hand inside left border.) .05
588b Mark Whiten **RC** (Hand over left border.) .20
589 Scott Ruskin **RC** .05
590 Eddie Murray .35
591 Ken Hill .05
592 B.J. Surhoff .05
593a Mike Walker **RC** (No 1990 Canton-Akron stats.) .15
593b Mike Walker **RC** (1990 Canton-Akron stats) .05
594 Rich Garces **RC** (Future Star) .05
595 Bill Landrum .05
596 Ronnie Walden **RC** (#1 Draft Pick) .05
597 Jerry Don Gleaton .05
598 Sam Horn .05
599a Greg Myers (No 1990 Syracuse stats.) .10
599b Greg Myers (1990 Syracuse stats) .05
600 Bo Jackson .10
601 Bob Ojeda .05
602 Casey Candaele .05
603a Wes Chamberlain **RC** (Photo of Louie Meadows, no bat.) .75
603b Wes Chamberlain **RC** (Correct photo, holding bat.) .05
604 Billy Hatcher .05
605 Jeff Reardon .05
606 Jim Gott .05
607 Edgar Martinez .05
608 Todd Burns .05
609 Jeff Torborg .05
610 Andres Galarraga .05
611 Dave Eiland .05
612 Steve Lyons .05
613 Eric Show .05
614 Luis Salazar .05
615 Bert Blyleven .05
616 Todd Zeile .05
617 Bill Wegman .05
618 Sil Campusano .05
619 David Wells .05
620 Ozzie Guillen .05
621 Ted Power .05
622 Jack Daugherty .05
623 Jeff Blauser .05
624 Tom Candiotti .05
625 Terry Steinbach .05
626 Gerald Young .05
627 Tim Layana **RC** .05
628 Greg Litton .05
629 Wes Gardner .05
630 Dave Winfield .35
631 Mike Morgan .05
632 Lloyd Moseby .05
633 Kevin Tapani .05
634 Henry Cotto .05
635 Andy Hawkins .05
636 Geronimo Pena **RC** .05
637 Bruce Ruffin .05
638 Mike Macfarlane .05
639 Frank Robinson .05
640 Andre Dawson .20
641 Mike Henneman .05
642 Hal Morris .05
643 Jim Presley .05
644 Chuck Crim .05
645 Juan Samuel .05
646 Andujar Cedeno **RC** .05
647 Mark Portugal .05
648 Lee Stevens **RC** .05
649 Bill Sampen **RC** .05
650 Jack Clark .05
651 Alan Mills **RC** .05
652 Kevin Romine .05
653 Anthony Telford **RC** .05
654 Paul Sorrento **RC** .05
655 Erik Hanson .05
656a Checklist 5 (Vincente Palacios #348.) .05
656b Checklist 5 (Palacios #433.) .05
656c Checklist 5 (Palacios #438.) .05
657 Mike Kingery .05
658 Scott Aldred **RC** .05
659 Oscar Azocar **RC** .05
660 Lee Smith .05
661 Steve Lake .05
662 Rob Dibble .05
663 Greg Brock .05
664 John Farrell .05
665 Mike LaValliere .05
666 Danny Darwin .05
667 Kent Anderson .05
668 Bill Long .05
669 Lou Pinella .05
670 Rickey Henderson .35
671 Andy McGaffigan .05
672 Shane Mack .05
673 Greg Olson **RC** .05
674a Kevin Gross (No diamond after 89 BB 1988.) .10
674b Kevin Gross (Diamond after 89 BB 1988.) .05
675 Tom Brunansky .05
676 Scott Chiamparino **RC** .05
677 Billy Ripken .05
678 Mark Davidson .05
679 Bill Bathe **RC** .05
680 David Cone .05
681 Jeff Schaefer **RC** .05
682 Ray Lankford **RC** .15
683 Derek Lilliquist .05
684 Milt Cuyler **RC** .05
685 Doug Drabek .05
686 Mike Gallego .05
687a John Cerutti (4.46 ERA 1990) .05
687b John Cerutti (4.76 ERA 1990) .05
688 Rosario Rodriguez **RC** .05
689 John Kruk .05
690 Orel Hershiser .05
691 Mike Blowers .05
692a Efrain Valdez **RC** (No text below stats.) .15
692b Efrain Valdez **RC** (Two lines of text below stats.) .05
693 Francisco Cabrera .05
694 Randy Veres .05
695 Kevin Seitzer .05
696 Steve Olin .05
697 Shawn Abner .05
698 Mark Guthrie .05
699 Jim Lefebvre .05
700 Jose Canseco .25
701 Pascual Perez .05
702 Tim Naehring **RC** .05
703 Juan Agosto .05
704 Devon White .05
705 Robby Thompson .05
706a Brad Arnsberg (68.2 IP Rangers 1990) .05
706b Brad Arnsberg (62.2 IP Rangers 1990) .05
707 Jim Eisenreich .05
708 John Mitchell **RC** .05
709 Matt Sinatro .05
710 Kent Hrbek .05
711 Jose DeLeon .05
712 Ricky Jordan .05
713 Scott Scudder .05
714 Marvell Wynne .05
715 Tim Burke .05
716 Bob Geren .05
717 Phil Bradley .05
718 Steve Crawford .05
719 Keith Miller .05
720 Cecil Fielder .05
721 Mark Lee **RC** .05
722 Wally Backman .05
723 Candy Maldonado .05
724 David Segui **RC** .10
725 Ron Gant .05
726 Phil Stephenson .05
727 Mookie Wilson .05
728 Scott Sanderson .05
729 Don Zimmer .05
730 Barry Larkin .05
731 Jeff Gray **RC** .05
732 Franklin Stubbs .05
733 Kelly Downs .05
734 John Russell .05
735 Ron Darling .05
736 Dick Schofield .05
737 Tim Crews .05
738 Mel Hall .05
739 Russ Swan **RC** .05
740 Ryne Sandberg .50
741 Jimmy Key .05
742 Tommy Gregg .05
743 Bryn Smith .05
744 Nelson Santovenia .05
745 Doug Jones .05
746 John Shelby .05
747 Tony Fossas .05
748 Al Newman .05
749 Greg Harris .05
750 Bobby Bonilla .05
751 Wayne Edwards **RC** .05
752 Kevin Bass .05
753 Paul Marak **RC** .05
754 Bill Pecota .05
755 Mark Langston .05
756 Jeff Huson .05
757 Mark Gardner .05
758 Mike Devereaux .05
759 Bobby Cox .05
760 Benny Santiago .05
761 Larry Andersen .05
762 Mitch Webster .05
763 Dana Kiecker **RC** .05
764 Mark Carreon .05
765 Shawon Dunston .05
766 Jeff Robinson .05
767 Dan Wilson **RC** (#1 Draft Pick) .10
768 Donn Pall .05
769 Tim Sherrill **RC** .05
770 Jay Howell .05
771 Gary Redus .05
772 Kent Mercker **RC** .05
773 Tom Foley .05
774 Dennis Rasmussen .05
775 Julio Franco .05
776 Brent Mayne **RC** .05
777 John Candelaria .05
778 Danny Gladden .05
779 Carmelo Martinez .05
780a Randy Myers (Career losses 15.) .10
780b Randy Myers (Career losses 19.) .05
781 Darryl Hamilton .05
782 Jim Deshaies .05
783 Joel Skinner .05
784 Willie Fraser .05
785 Scott Fletcher .05
786 Eric Plunk .05

787 Checklist 6 .05
788 Bob Milacki .05
789 Tom Lasorda .05
790 Ken Griffey Jr. .60
791 Mike Benjamin **RC** .05
792 Mike Greenwell .05

Tiffany

Topps ended its annual run of special collectors' edition boxed sets in 1991, producing the glossy sets inconsiderably more limited quantity than in previous years. Cards are identical to the regular 1991 Topps set except for the use of white cardboard stock and a high-gloss front finish.

NM/M
Unopened Set (792): 135.00
Complete Set (792): 85.00
Common Player: .10

Desert Shield

As a special treat for U.S. armed services personnel serving in the Persian Gulf prior to and during the war with Iraq, Topps produced a special edition featuring a gold-foil overprint honoring the military effort. Enough cards were produced to equal approximately 6,800 sets. While some cards actually reached the troops in the Middle East, many were short-stopped by military supply personnel stateside and sold into the hobby. Many of the cards sent to Saudi Arabia never returned to the U.S., however, making the supply of available cards somewhat scarce. The checklist cards in the set were not overprinted. At least two types of counterfeit overprint have been seen on genuine Topps cards in an attempt to cash in on the scarcity of these war "veterans."

NM/M
Complete Set (792): 1,200
Common Player: 1.00
Wax Pack: 60.00

Traded

"Team USA" players are featured in the 1991 Topps Traded set. The cards feature the same style as the regular 1991 issue, including the 40th anniversary logo. The set includes 132 cards and showcases rookies and traded players along with "Team USA." The cards are numbered with a "T" designation in alphabetical order. Wax-pack versions have a gray cardboard stock (unlike the box-set's white stock). Each of the wax-pack cards can be found with one or two asterisks preceding the copyright line on back.

NM/M
Unopened Retail or Hobby Set (132): 12.00
Complete Set (132): 10.00
Common Player: .05
Wax Pack (7): .65
Wax Box (36): 15.00
1 Juan Agosto .05
2 Roberto Alomar .15
3 Wally Backman .05
4 Jeff Bagwell **RC** 3.00
5 Skeeter Barnes **RC** .05
6 Steve Bedrosian .05
7 Derek Bell **RC** .05
8 George Bell .05
9 Rafael Belliard .05
10 Dante Bichette .05
11 Bud Black .05
12 Mike Boddicker .05
13 Sid Bream .05
14 Hubie Brooks .05
15 Brett Butler .05
16 Ivan Calderon .05
17 John Candelaria .05
18 Tom Candiotti .05
19 Gary Carter .50
20 Joe Carter .05
21 Rick Cerone .05
22 Jack Clark .05
23 Vince Coleman .05
24 Scott Coolbaugh .05
25 Danny Cox .05
26 Danny Darwin .05
27 Chili Davis .05
28 Glenn Davis .05
29 Steve Decker **RC** .05
30 Rob Deer .05
31 Rich DeLucia **RC** .05
32 John Dettmer **RC** (USA) .05
33 Brian Downing .05
34 Darren Dreifort **RC** (USA) .25
35 Kirk Dressendorfer .05
36 Jim Essian .05
37 Dwight Evans .05
38 Steve Farr .05
39 Jeff Fassero **RC** .05
40 Junior Felix .05
41 Tony Fernandez .05
42 Steve Finley .05
43 Jim Fregosi .05
44 Gary Gaetti .05
45 Jason Giambi **RC** (USA) 4.00
46 Kirk Gibson .05
47 Leo Gomez **RC** .05
48 Luis Gonzalez **RC** 1.00
49 Jeff Granger **RC** (USA) .10
50 Todd Greene **RC** (USA) .15
51 Jeffrey Hammonds **RC** (USA) .15
52 Mike Hargrove .05
53 Pete Harnisch .05
54 Rick Helling **RC** (USA) .10
55 Glenallen Hill .05
56 Charlie Hough .05
57 Pete Incaviglia .05
58 Bo Jackson .10
59 Danny Jackson .05
60 Reggie Jefferson **RC** .05
61 Charles Johnson **RC** (USA) .15
62 Jeff Johnson **RC** .05
63 Todd Johnson **RC** (USA) .05
64 Barry Jones .05
65 Chris Jones .05
66 Scott Kamieniecki .05
67 Pat Kelly **RC** .05
68 Darryl Kile **RC** .05
69 Chuck Knoblauch **RC** .05
70 Bill Krueger .05
71 Scott Leius **RC** .05
72 Donnie Leshnock **RC** (USA) .05
73 Mark Lewis .05
74 Candy Maldonado .05
75 Jason McDonald **RC** (USA) .05
76 Willie McGee .05
77 Fred McGriff .05
78 Billy McMillon **RC** (USA) .05
79 Hal McRae .05
80 Dan Melendez **RC** (USA) .05
81 Orlando Merced **RC** .05
82 Jack Morris .05
83 Phil Nevin **RC** (USA) .50
84 Otis Nixon .05
85 Johnny Oates .05
86 Bob Ojeda .05
87 Mike Pagliarulo .05
88 Dean Palmer **RC** .05
89 Dave Parker .05
90 Terry Pendleton .05
91 Tony Phillips **RC** (USA) .10
92 Doug Piatt **RC** .05
93 Ron Polk (U.S.A.) .05
94 Tim Raines .05
95 Willie Randolph .05
96 Dave Righetti .05
97 Ernie Riles .05
98 Chris Roberts **RC** (USA) .05
99 Jeff Robinson (Angels) .05
100 Jeff Robinson (Orioles) .05
101 Ivan Rodriguez **RC** 3.00
102 Steve Rodriguez **RC** (USA) .05
103 Tom Runnells .05
104 Scott Sanderson .05
105 Bob Scanlan **RC** .05
106 Pete Schourek **RC** .10
107 Gary Scott **RC** .05
108 Paul Shuey **RC** (USA) .10
109 Doug Simons **RC** .05
110 Dave Smith .05
111 Cory Snyder .05
112 Luis Sojo .05
113 Kennie Steenstra **RC** (USA) .05
114 Darryl Strawberry .05
115 Franklin Stubbs .05
116 Todd Taylor **RC** (USA) .05
117 Wade Taylor **RC** .05
118 Garry Templeton .05
119 Mickey Tettleton .05
120 Tim Teufel .05
121 Mike Timlin .05
122 David Tuttle **RC** (USA) .05
123 Mo Vaughn **RC** .25
124 Jeff Ware **RC** (USA) .05
125 Devon White .05
126 Mark Whiten .05
127 Mitch Williams .05
128 Craig Wilson **RC** (USA) .05
129 Willie Wilson .05
130 Chris Wimmer **RC** (USA) .05
131 Ivan Zweig **RC** (USA) .05
132 Checklist .05

Traded Tiffany

The final year of production for Topps "Tiffany" parallel boxed sets saw production levels slashed for the 132-card Traded version. Value of the sets has risen dramatically with the hobby's perception of the set's scarcity and the development of key rookies such as Bagwell, Giambi and I-Rod. Like the regular Traded set, cards are numbered in alphabetical order with a "T" suffix.

NM/M
Unopened Set (132): 165.00
Complete Set (132): 90.00
Common Player: .25
Stars and Rookies: 4X

Traded Brooks Robinson Bronze

This 1/4-size metal replica of Robinson's first-ever Topps card was issued to dealers who purchased cases of 1991 Topps Traded sets. Each detail of the 1957 Topps Robinson card is reproduced on the 1-1/4" x 1-3/4" bronze metal mini-card, right down to the stats.

NM/M
328 Brooks Robinson 15.00

Box Panel Cards

Styled like the standard 1991 Topps cards, this 16-card set honors milestones of the featured players. The cards were found on the bottom of wax pack boxes. The cards are designated in alphabetical order by (A-P) and are not numbered.

NM/M
Complete Set (16): 6.00

Common Player: .15
A Bert Blyleven .15
B George Brett 1.25
C Brett Butler .15
D Andre Dawson .50
E Dwight Evans .15
F Carlton Fisk .75
G Alfredo Griffin .15
H Rickey Henderson .75
I Willie McGee .15
J Dale Murphy .50
K Eddie Murray .75
L Dave Parker .15
M Jeff Reardon .15
N Nolan Ryan 2.25
O Juan Samuel .15
P Robin Yount .75

All-Star Glossy Set of 22

Continuing the same basic format used since 1984, these glossy-front rack-pack inserts honor the players, manager and honorary captains of the previous year's All-Star Game. Fronts have a league logo in the lower-left corner, a 1990 All-Star banner above the photo and a Topps 40th anniversary logo superimposed over the photo. Backs have a shield and star design and the legend "1990 All-Star Commemorative Set" above the player's name, position and card number. Backs are printed in red and blue.

NM/M
Complete Set (22): 3.00
Common Player: .05
1 Tony LaRussa .05
2 Mark McGwire .85
3 Steve Sax .05
4 Wade Boggs .50
5 Cal Ripken, Jr. 1.00
6 Rickey Henderson .40
7 Ken Griffey Jr. .75
8 Jose Canseco .30
9 Sandy Alomar, Jr. .05
10 Bob Welch .05
11 Al Lopez .05
12 Roger Craig .05
13 Will Clark .05
14 Ryne Sandberg .50
15 Chris Sabo .05
16 Ozzie Smith .50
17 Kevin Mitchell .05
18 Len Dykstra .05
19 Andre Dawson .15
20 Mike Scioscia .05
21 Jack Armstrong .05
22 Juan Marichal .05

Glossy Rookies

Similar in format to previous years' glossy rookies sets, this 33-card issue was available one per pack in 100-card jumbo cello packs. Card fronts have a colored "1990 Rookies" banner above the player photo,

with the player's name in red in a yellow bar beneath. The Topps 40th anniversary logo appears in one of the upper corners of the photo. Backs are printed in red and blue and feature a "1990 Rookies Commemorative Set" shield logo. The player's name, position, team and card number are printed beneath. Cards are numbered alphabetically.

NM/M
Complete Set (33): 2.00
Common Player: .10
1 Sandy Alomar, Jr. .10
2 Kevin Appier .10
3 Steve Avery .10
4 Carlos Baerga .10
5 John Burkett .10
6 Alex Cole .10
7 Pat Combs .10
8 Delino DeShields .10
9 Travis Fryman .10
10 Marquis Grissom .10
11 Mike Harkey .10
12 Glenallen Hill .10
13 Jeff Huson .10
14 Felix Jose .10
15 Dave Justice .25
16 Jim Leyritz .10
17 Kevin Maas .10
18 Ben McDonald .10
19 Kent Mercker .10
20 Hal Morris .10
21 Chris Nabholz .10
22 Tim Naehring .10
23 Jose Offerman .10
24 John Olerud .25
25 Scott Radinsky .10
26 Scott Ruskin .10
27 Kevin Tapani .10
28 Frank Thomas 1.50
29 Randy Tomlin .10
30 Greg Vaughn .10
31 Robin Ventura .25
32 Larry Walker .10
33 Todd Zeile .10

East Coast National Reprints

Produced in Topps' 40th anniversary year, this four-card set was issued at the 1991 East Coast National card show, the first card show in which Topps had ever participated. A total of 40,000 sets were reportedly issued in the now-standard 2-1/2" x 3-1/2" format. Fronts reproduce first Topps cards of four baseball greats while backs, printed in blue, carry a reprint notice, ad for the card show and Topps copyright.

NM/M
Complete Set (4): 7.50
Common Card: 1.50
(1) Mickey Mantle/1952 5.00
(2) Hank Aaron/1954 3.00
(3) Frank Robinson/1957 1.50
(4) Stan Musial/1958 1.50

Gallery of Champions

Topps final issue of metallic mini-cards continued the theme of honoring the previous year's winners of major awards. The 1/4-size (1-1/4" x 1-3/4") ingots were issued in complete boxed sets of aluminum, bronze and silver in special display cases. To promote quantity sales, Topps offered a special pewter version of the Rickey Henderson ingot.

NM/M
Complete Aluminum Set (12): 22.50
Complete Bronze Set (12): 45.00
Complete Silver Set (12): 180.00
(1a) Sandy Alomar Jr./Aluminum 1.00
(1b) Sandy Alomar Jr./Bronze 2.50
(1s) Sandy Alomar Jr./Silver 6.00
(2a) Barry Bonds/Aluminum 10.00
(2b) Barry Bonds/Bronze 15.00
(2s) Barry Bonds/Silver 65.00
(3a) George Brett/Aluminum 7.50
(3b) George Brett/Bronze 10.00
(3s) George Brett/Silver 50.00
(4a) Doug Drabek/Aluminum 1.00
(4b) Doug Drabek/Bronze 2.50
(4s) Doug Drabek/Silver 6.00
(5a) Cecil Fielder/Aluminum 1.00
(5b) Cecil Fielder/Bronze 2.50
(5s) Cecil Fielder/Silver 6.00
(6a) John Franco/Aluminum 1.00
(6b) John Franco/Bronze 2.50
(6s) John Franco/Silver 6.00
(7a) Rickey Henderson/Aluminum 3.00
(7b) Rickey Henderson/Bronze 6.00
(7s) Rickey Henderson/Silver 35.00
(7p) Rickey Henderson/Pewter 15.00
(8a) Dave Justice/Aluminum 1.25
(8b) Dave Justice/Bronze 3.00
(8s) Dave Justice/Silver 9.00
(9a) Willie McGee/Aluminum 1.00
(9b) Willie McGee/Bronze 2.50
(9s) Willie McGee/Silver 6.00
(10a) Ryne Sandberg/Aluminum 6.00
(10b) Ryne Sandberg/Bronze 7.50
(10s) Ryne Sandberg/Silver 40.00
(11a) Bobby Thigpen/Aluminum 1.00
(11b) Bobby Thigpen/Bronze 2.50
(11s) Bobby Thigpen/Silver 6.00
(12a) Bob Welch/Aluminum 1.00
(12b) Bob Welch/Bronze 2.50
(12s) Bob Welch/Silver 6.00

Golden Spikes Award

Each year the United States Baseball Federation honors the outstanding amateur player with the Golden Spikes Award. This card was handed out at the Nov. 20, 1991 awards banquet honoring Arizona State star Mike Kelly. Production was reported as 600 cards.

NM/M
Mike Kelly 85.00

Joe Garagiola

Virtually identical to the personal business card which Topps produced for long-time NBC announcer and former major leaguer Joe Garagiola in 1976, this 1991 version makes mention of the Today Show on both front and back. The front is in the format of a 1973 Topps card and has a color portrait. The back resembles the 1976 Topps card, is in black-and-white and provides contact information.

		NM/M
1	Joe Garagiola	8.00

Micro

	NM/M
Complete Set (792):	9.00
Common Player:	.05
Stars/Rookies:	1-1.5X

Babe Ruth

This 11-card set by Topps was released in honor of the NBC movie about Babe Ruth. The cards were released on a limited basis. The card fronts feature full-color photos from the movie, while the flip sides are printed horizontally and describe the front photo. The cards are numbered on the back.

		NM/M
Complete Set (11):		12.50
Common Player:		1.00
1	Sunday Oct. 6, NBC	1.00
2	Stephen Lang as Babe Ruth	1.00
3	Bruce Weitz as Miller Huggins	1.00
4	Lisa Zane as Claire Ruth	1.00
5	Donald Moffat as Jacob Ruppert	1.00
6	Neil McDonough as Lou Gehrig	1.00
7	Pete Rose as Ty Cobb	5.00
8	Baseball Consultant (Rod Carew)	2.50
9	Miller Huggins, Babe Ruth	1.00
10	Ruth In Action	1.00
11	Babe Calls His Shot	1.00

Superstar Stand-Ups

Another of Topps' efforts over the years to market candy containers with a baseball player theme, the 1991 Superstar Stand-Ups were a test issue. Sold in a color-printed paper

envelope, Stand-Ups are a hard plastic container filled with candy tablets. In bright see-through colors, the containers measure 2-1/16" x 2-9/16" and are vaguely shaped like a head and shoulders. A paper label attached to the front of the plastic has a player portrait with his team in a banner above and his name in a strip at bottom. Backs have a baseball design on the label with the Topps 40th anniversary logo at top. The player's name, team and position are in color bars at the bottom, with the item number at left. At center are the player's height, weight, birth date, batting and throwing preference and the year and number of his Topps rookie card. Clear (non-colored) plastic containers are also known for each player, though their relative scarcity to the colored pieces is currently undetermined.

		NM/M
Complete Set (36):		45.00
Common Player:		1.00
Wax Pack (1):		1.50
Wax Box (36):		30.00
1	Jim Abbott	1.00
2	Sandy Alomar	1.00
3	Wade Boggs	2.50
4	Barry Bonds	5.00
5	Bobby Bonilla	1.00
6	George Brett	3.00
7	Jose Canseco	1.50
8	Will Clark	1.00
9	Roger Clemens	3.00
10	Eric Davis	1.00
11	Andre Dawson	1.50
12	Len Dykstra	1.00
13	Cecil Fielder	1.00
14	Carlton Fisk	2.00
15	Dwight Gooden	1.00
16	Mark Grace	1.00
17	Ken Griffey Jr.	3.50
18	Tony Gwynn	2.50
19	Rickey Henderson	2.00
20	Bo Jackson	1.50
21	Dave Justice	1.00
22	Kevin Maas	1.00
23	Ramon Martinez	1.00
24	Don Mattingly	3.00
25	Ben McDonald	1.00
26	Mark McGwire	4.00
27	Kevin Mitchell	1.00
28	Cal Ripken, Jr.	5.00
29	Nolan Ryan	5.00
30	Ryne Sandberg	2.50
31	Ozzie Smith	2.50
32	Dave Stewart	1.00
33	Darryl Strawberry	1.00
34	Frank Viola	1.00
35	Matt Williams	1.00
36	Robin Yount	2.00

"1953" Topps Archives Promos

This nine-card set was issued to promote Topps' 1953 Archives set. Besides seven of the cards being reprinted from the '53 set, the promo set included two of the "new" 1953-style cards which were included in the Archives issue - cards of Hank Aaron and Eleanor Engle, the first woman to sign a minor league contract in modern times. Card fronts are identical to the issued Archives cards, while the backs are white with red Archives logo and "Pre-production Sample" notation.

		NM/M
Complete Set (9):		75.00
Common Player:		7.50
(1)	Hank Aaron	12.00
(2)	Roy Campanella	7.50
(3)	Eleanor Engle	7.50
(4)	Bob Feller	7.50
(5)	Whitey Ford	7.50
(6)	Mickey Mantle	20.00
(7)	Willie Mays	12.00
(8)	Jackie Robinson	10.00
(9)	Satchell Paige	10.00

"1953" Topps Archives

Billed as "The Ultimate 1953 Set," this issue reproduced 273 of the original 274-card 1953 Topps set. (Card #174, Billy Loes, was not reproduced due to lack of permission from the former Dodgers pitcher, though cards with #174 are known with a Loes back and another player on the front.) The Archives issue downsized the cards from their original 2-5/8" x 3-3/4" size to the now-standard 2-1/2" x 3-1/2" format. More than 50 cards of players who were not included in the 1953 Topps set were created as part of the Archives issue. Because Topps chose to use black-and-white photos and colorized backgrounds for most of the "extended" cards, rather than paintings as on the original cards, collector interest in the Archives issue was diminished. Only 18,000 cases were reportedly produced.

		NM/M
Complete Set (337):		45.00
Common Player:		.10
Wax Pack (12):		1.50
Wax Box (36):		35.00
1	Jackie Robinson	7.50
2	Luke Easter	.10
3	George Crowe	.10
4	Ben Wade	.10
5	Joe Dobson	.10
6	Sam Jones	.10
7	Bob Borkowski	.10
8	Clem Koshorek	.10
9	Joe Collins	.10
10	Smoky Burgess	.10
11	Sal Yvars	.10
12	Howie Judson	.10
13	Conrado Marrero	.10
14	Clem Labine	.10
15	Bobo Newsom	.10
16	Peanuts Lowrey	.10
17	Billy Hitchcock	.10
18	Ted Lepcio	.10
19	Mel Parnell	.10
20	Hank Thompson	.10
21	Billy Johnson	.10
22	Howie Fox	.10
23	Toby Atwell	.10
24	Ferris Fain	.10
25	Ray Boone	.10
26	Dale Mitchell	.10
27	Roy Campanella	1.50
28	Eddie Pellagrini	.10
29	Hal Jeffcoat	.10
30	Willard Nixon	.10
31	Ewell Blackwell	.10
32	Clyde Vollmer	.10
33	Bob Kennedy	.10
34	George Shuba	.10
35	Irv Noren	.10
36	Johnny Groth	.10
37	Eddie Mathews	1.00
38	Jim Hearn	.10
39	Eddie Miksis	.10
40	John Lipon	.10
41	Enos Slaughter	.50
42	Gus Zernial	.10
43	Gil McDougald	.30
44	Ellis Kinder	.10
45	Grady Hatton	.10
46	Johnny Klippstein	.10
47	Bubba Church	.10
48	Bob Del Greco	.10
49	Faye Throneberry	.10
50	Chuck Dressen	.10
51	Frank Campos	.10
52	Ted Gray	.10
53	Sherman Lollar	.10
54	Bob Feller	1.00
55	Maurice McDermott	.10
56	Gerald Staley	.10
57	Carl Scheib	.10
58	George Metkovich	.10
59	Karl Drews	.10
60	Cloyd Boyer	.10
61	Early Wynn	.50
62	Monte Irvin	.50
63	Gus Niarhos	.10
64	Dave Philley	.10
65	Earl Harrist	.10
66	Orestes Minoso	.25
67	Roy Sievers	.10
68	Del Rice	.10
69	Dick Brodowski	.10
70	Ed Yuhas	.10
71	Tony Bartirome	.10
72	Fred Hutchinson	.10
73	Eddie Robinson	.10
74	Joe Rossi	.10
75	Mike Garcia	.10
76	Pee Wee Reese	1.00
77	John Mize	.75
78	Al Schoendienst	.50
79	Johnny Wyrostek	.10
80	Jim Hegan	.10
81	Joe Black	.10
82	Mickey Mantle	12.50
83	Howie Pollet	.10
84	Bob Hooper	.10
85	Bobby Morgan	.10
86	Billy Martin	.35
87	Ed Lopat	.20
88	Willie Jones	.10
89	Chuck Stobbs	.10
90	Hank Edwards	.10
91	Ebba St. Claire	.10
92	Paul Minner	.10
93	Hal Rice	.10
94	William Kennedy	.10
95	Willard Marshall	.10
96	Virgil Trucks	.10
97	Don Kolloway	.10
98	Cal Abrams	.10
99	Dave Madison	.10
100	Bill Miller	.10
101	Ted Wilks	.10
102	Connie Ryan	.10
103	Joe Astroth	.10
104	Yogi Berra	1.50
105	Joe Nuxhall	.10
106	John Antonelli	.10
107	Danny O'Connell	.10
108	Bob Porterfield	.10
109	Alvin Dark	.10
110	Herman Wehmeier	.10
111	Hank Sauer	.10
112	Ned Garver	.10
113	Jerry Priddy	.10
114	Phil Rizzuto	1.00
115	George Spencer	.10
116	Frank Smith	.10
117	Sid Gordon	.10
118	Gus Bell	.10
119	John Sain	.25
120	Davey Williams	.10
121	Walt Dropo	.10
122	Elmer Valo	.10
123	Tommy Byrne	.10
124	Sibby Sisti	.10
125	Dick Williams	.20
126	Bill Connelly	.10
127	Clint Courtney	.10
128	Wilmer Mizell	.10
129	Keith Thomas	.10
130	Turk Lown	.10
131	Harry Byrd	.10
132	Tom Morgan	.10
133	Gil Coan	.10
134	Rube Walker	.10
135	Al Rosen	.25
136	Ken Heintzelman	.10
137	John Rutherford	.10
138	George Kell	.50
139	Sammy White	.10
140	Tommy Glaviano	.10
141	Allie Reynolds	.25
142	Vic Wertz	.10
143	Billy Pierce	.20
144	Bob Schultz	.10
145	Harry Dorish	.10
146	Granville Hamner	.10
147	Warren Spahn	1.00
148	Mickey Grasso	.10
149	Dom DiMaggio	.25
150	Harry Simpson	.10
151	Hoyt Wilhelm	.50
152	Bob Adams	.10
153	Andy Seminick	.10
154	Dick Groat	.20
155	Dutch Leonard	.10
156	Jim Rivera	.10
157	Bob Addis	.10
158	John Logan	.10
159	Wayne Terwilliger	.10
160	Bob Young	.10
161	Vern Bickford	.10
162	Ted Kluszewski	.35
163	Fred Hatfield	.10
164	Frank Shea	.10
165	Billy Hoeft	.10
166	Bill Hunter	.10
167	Art Schult	.10
168	Willard Schmidt	.10
169	Dizzy Trout	.10
170	Bill Werle	.10
171	Bill Glynn	.10
172	Rip Repulski	.10
173	Preston Ward	.10
175	Ron Kline	.10
176	Don Hoak	.10
177	Jim Dyck	.10
178	Jim Waugh	.10
179	Gene Hermanski	.10
180	Virgil Stallcup	.10
181	Al Zarilla	.10
182	Bob Hofman	.10
183	Stu Miller	.10
184	Hal Brown	.10
185	Jim Pendleton	.10
186	Charlie Bishop	.10
187	Jim Fridley	.10
188	Andy Carey	.10
189	Ray Jablonski	.10
190	Dixie Walker	.10
191	Ralph Kiner	.50
192	Wally Westlake	.10
193	Mike Clark	.10
194	Eddie Kazak	.10
195	Ed McGhee	.10
196	Bob Keegan	.10
197	Del Crandall	.10
198	Forrest Main	.10
199	Marion Fricano	.10
200	Gordon Goldsberry	.10
201	Paul La Palme	.10
202	Carl Sawatski	.10
203	Cliff Fannin	.10
204	Dick Bokelmann	.10
205	Vern Benson	.10
206	Ed Bailey	.10
207	Whitey Ford	1.00
208	Jim Wilson	.10
209	Jim Greengrass	.10
210	Bob Cerv	.10
211	J.W. Porter	.10
212	Jack Dittmer	.10
213	Ray Scarborough	.10
214	Bill Bruton	.10
215	Gene Conley	.10
216	Jim Hughes	.10
217	Murray Wall	.10
218	Les Fusselman	.10
219	Pete Runnels	.10
220	Satchell Paige	4.00
221	Bob Milliken	.10
222	Vic Janowicz	.10
223	John O'Brien	.10
224	Lou Sleater	.10
225	Bobby Shantz	.20
226	Ed Erautt	.10
227	Morris Martin	.10
228	Hal Newhouser	.10
229	Rocky Krshnich	.10
230	Johnny Lindell	.10
231	Solly Hemus	.10
232	Dick Kokos	.10
233	Al Aber	.10
234	Ray Murray	.10
235	John Hetki	.10
236	Harry Perkowski	.10
237	Clarence Podbielan	.10
238	Cal Hogue	.10
239	Jim Delsing	.10
240	Freddie Marsh	.10
241	Al Sima	.10
242	Charlie Silvera	.10
243	Carlos Bernier	.10
244	Willie Mays	7.50
245	Bill Norman	.10
246	Roy Face	.10
247	Mike Sandlock	.10
248	Gene Stephens	.10
249	Ed O'Brien	.10
250	Bob Wilson	.10
251	Sid Hudson	.10
252	Henry Foiles	.10
254	Preacher Roe	.10
255	Dixie Howell	.10
256	Les Peden	.10
257	Bob Boyd	.10
258	Jim Gilliam	.35
259	Roy McMillan	.10
260	Sam Calderone	.10
262	Bob Oldis	.10
263	John Podres	.35
264	Gene Woodling	.35
265	Jackie Jensen	.35
266	Bob Cain	.10
269	Duane Pillette	.10
270	Vern Stephens	.10
272	Bill Antonello	.10
273	Harvey Haddix	.10
274	John Riddle	.10
276	Ken Raffensberger	.10
277	Don Lund	.10
278	Willie Miranda	.10
279	Joe Coleman	.10
280	Milt Bolling	.10
281	Jimmie Dykes	.10
282	Ralph Houk	.35
283	Frank Thomas	.10
284	Bob Lemon	.50
285	Joe Adcock	.10
286	Jimmy Piersall	.10
287	Mickey Vernon	.10
288	Robin Roberts	.50
289	Rogers Hornsby	.50
290	Hank Bauer	.10
291	Hoot Evers	.10
292	Whitey Lockman	.10
293	Ralph Branca	.25
294	Wally Post	.10
295	Phil Cavarretta	.10
296	Gil Hodges	.35
297	Roy Smalley	.10
298	Bob Friend	.10
299	Dusty Rhodes	.25
300	Eddie Stanky	.10
301	Harvey Kuenn	.25
302	Marty Marion	.10
303	Sal Maglie	.10
304	Lou Boudreau	.50
305	Carl Furillo	.35
306	Bobo Holloman	.10
307	Steve O'Neill	.10
308	Carl Erskine	.25
309	Leo Durocher	.25
310	Lew Burdette	.10
311	Richie Ashburn	.50
312	Hoyt Wilhelm	.50
313	Bucky Harris	.50
314	Joe Garagiola	.50
315	Johnny Pesky	.10
316	Fred Haney	.10
317	Hank Aaron	7.50
318	Curt Simmons	.10
319	Ted Williams	7.50
320	Don Newcombe	.35
321	Charlie Grimm	.10
322	Paul Richards	.10
323	Wes Westrum	.10
324	Vern Law	.10
325	Casey Stengel	1.00
326	Hall of Fame Inductees (Dizzy Dean, Al Simmons)	1.00
327	Duke Snider	1.00
328	Bill Rigney	.10
329	Al Lopez	.50
330	Bobby Thomson	.35
331	Nellie Fox	.50
332	Eleanor Engle	.10
333	Larry Doby	.50
334	Billy Goodman	.10
335	Checklist 1-140	.10
336	Checklist 141-280	.10
337	Checklist 281-337	.10

1990 Major League Debut

This 171-card set features the players who made their Major League debut in 1990. The cards are styled like the 1991 Topps cards and are numbered in alphabetical order. The card backs are printed horizontally and feature information about the player's debut and statistics. The issue was sold only as a boxed set through hobby channels.

		NM/M
Complete Set (171):		5.00
Common Player:		.05
1	Paul Abbott	.05
2	Steve Adkins	.05
3	Scott Aldred	.05
4	Gerald Alexander	.05

5	Moises Alou	.25
6	Steve Avery	.05
7	Oscar Azocar	.05
8	Carlos Baerga	.05
9	Kevin Baez	.05
10	Jeff Baldwin	.05
11	Brian Barnes	.05
12	Kevin Bearse	.05
13	Kevin Belcher	.05
14	Mike Bell	.05
15	Sean Berry	.05
16	Joe Bitker	.05
17	Willie Blair	.05
18	Brian Bohanon	.05
19	Mike Bordick	.05
20	Shawn Boskie	.05
21	Rod Brewer	.05
22	Kevin Brown	.10
23	Dave Burba	.05
24	Jim Campbell	.05
25	Ozzie Canseco	.05
26	Chuck Carr	.05
27	Larry Casian	.05
28	Andujar Cedeno	.05
29	Wes Chamberlain	.05
30	Scott Chiamparino	.05
31	Steve Chitren	.05
32	Pete Coachman	.05
33	Alex Cole	.05
34	Jeff Conine	.10
35	Scott Cooper	.05
36	Milt Cuyler	.05
37	Steve Decker	.05
38	Rich DeLucia	.05
39	Delino DeShields	.05
40	Mark Dewey	.05
41	Carlos Diaz	.05
42	Lance Dickson	.05
43	Narciso Elvira	.05
44	Luis Encarnacion	.05
45	Scott Erickson	.05
46	Paul Faries	.05
47	Howard Farmer	.05
48	Alex Fernandez	.05
49	Travis Fryman	.05
50	Rich Garces	.05
51	Carlos Garcia	.05
52	Mike Gardiner	.05
53	Bernard Gilkey	.05
54	Tom Gilles	.05
55	Jerry Goff	.05
56	Leo Gomez	.05
57	Luis Gonzalez	.75
58	Joe Grahe	.05
59	Craig Grebeck	.05
60	Kip Gross	.05
61	Eric Gunderson	.05
62	Chris Hammond	.05
63	Dave Hansen	.05
64	Reggie Harris	.05
65	Bill Haselman	.05
66	Randy Hennis	.05
67	Carlos Hernandez	.05
68	Howard Hilton	.05
69	Dave Hollins	.05
70	Darren Holmes	.05
71	John Hoover	.05
72	Steve Howard	.05
73	Thomas Howard	.05
74	Todd Hundley	.05
75	Daryl Irvine	.05
76	Chris Jelic	.05
77	Dana Kiecker	.05
78	Brent Knackert	.05
79	Jimmy Kremers	.05
80	Jerry Kutzler	.05
81	Ray Lankford	.05
82	Tim Layana	.05
83	Terry Lee	.05
84	Mark Leiter	.05
85	Scott Leius	.05
86	Mark Leonard	.05
87	Darren Lewis	.05
88	Scott Lewis	.05
89	Jim Leyritz	.05
90	Dave Liddell	.05
91	Luis Lopez	.05
92	Kevin Maas	.05
93	Bob MacDonald	.05
94	Carlos Maldonado	.05
95	Chuck Malone	.05
96	Ramon Manon	.05
97	Jeff Manto	.05
98	Paul Marak	.05
99	Tino Martinez	.25
100	Derrick May	.05
101	Brent Mayne	.05
102	Paul McClellan	.05
103	Rodney McCray	.05
104	Tim McIntosh	.05
105	Brian McRae	.05
106	Jose Melendez	.05
107	Orlando Merced	.05
108	Alan Mills	.05
109	Gino Minutelli	.05
110	Mickey Morandini	.05
111	Pedro Munoz	.05
112	Chris Nabholz	.05
113	Tim Naehring	.05
114	Charles Nagy	.05
115	Jim Neidlinger	.05
116	Rafael Novoa	.05
117	Jose Offerman	.05
118	Omar Olivares	.05
119	Javier Ortiz	.05
120	Al Osuna	.05
121	Rick Parker	.05
122	Dave Pavlas	.05
123	Geronimo Pena	.05
124	Mike Perez	.05
125	Phil Plantier	.05
126	Jim Poole	.05
127	Tom Quinlan	.05
128	Scott Radinsky	.05
129	Darren Reed	.05
130	Karl Rhodes	.05
131	Jeff Richardson	.05
132	Rich Rodriguez	.05
133	Dave Rohde	.05
134	Mel Rojas	.05
135	Vic Rosario	.05
136	Rich Rowland	.05
137	Scott Ruskin	.05
138	Bill Sampen	.05
139	Andres Santana	.05
140	David Segui	.05
141	Jeff Shaw	.05
142	Tim Sherrill	.05
143	Terry Shumpert	.05
144	Mike Simms	.05
145	Daryl Smith	.05
146	Luis Sojo	.05
147	Steve Springer	.05
148	Ray Stephens	.05
149	Lee Stevens	.05
150	Mel Stottlemyre, Jr.	.05
151	Glenn Sutko	.05
152	Anthony Telford	.05
153	Frank Thomas	3.00
154	Randy Tomlin	.05
155	Brian Traxler	.05
156	Efrain Valdez	.05
157	Rafael Valdez	.05
158	Julio Valera	.05
159	Jim Vatcher	.05
160	Hector Villanueva	.05
161	Hector Wagner	.05
162	Dave Walsh	.05
163	Steve Wapnick	.05
164	Colby Ward	.05
165	Turner Ward	.05
166	Terry Wells	.05
167	Mark Whiten	.05
168	Mike York	.05
169	Cliff Young	.05
170	Checklist	.05
171	Checklist	.05

1992 Topps Pre-Production

To preview its 1992 card set for dealers, Topps distributed a nine-card sheet in the basic format of its 1992 issue. The 8" x 10" sheets are often found cut into standard 2-1/2" x 3-1/2" singles. Card numbers on the backs of these promo cards do not correspond to the same cards in the regular set, and the stats for 1991 are not included. The preview cards have an orange oval on back, with the words, "1992 Pre-Production Sample."

		NM/M
Uncut Sheet:		6.00
Complete Set (9):		6.00
Common Player:		1.00
3	Shawon Dunston	1.00
16	Mike Heath	1.00
18	Todd Frowirth	1.00
20	Bip Roberts	1.00
131	Rob Dibble	1.00
174	Otis Nixon	1.00
273	Dennis Martinez	1.00
325	Brett Butler	1.00
798	Tom Lasorda	1.00

1992 Topps

This 792-card set features white stock much like the 1991 issue. The card fronts feature full-color action and posed photos with a gray inner frame and the player name and position at bottom. Backs feature biographical information, statistics and stadium photos on player cards where space is available. All-Star cards and #1 Draft Pick cards are once again included. Topps brought back four-player rookie cards in 1992. Nine Top Prospect cards of this nature can be found within the set. "Match the Stats" game cards were inserted into packs of 1992 Topps cards. Special bonus cards were given away to winners of this insert game. This was the first Topps regular-issue baseball card set since 1951 which was sold without bubblegum.

		NM/M
Unopened Fact. Set (802):		30.00
Complete Set (792):		20.00
Common Player:		.05
Golds:		4X
Wax Pack (14):		.50
Wax Box (36):		12.50
Cello Pack (34):		1.00
Cello Box (24):		16.00
Vending Box (500):		6.00
1	Nolan Ryan	.75
2	Rickey Henderson (Record Breaker)	.20
3	Jeff Reardon (Record Breaker)	.05
4	Nolan Ryan (Record Breaker)	.40
5	Dave Winfield (Record Breaker)	.20
6	Brien Taylor **RC** (Draft Pick)	.05
7	Jim Olander **RC**	.05
8	Bryan Hickerson **RC**	.05
9	John Farrell (Draft Pick)	.05
10	Wade Boggs	.45
11	Jack McDowell	.05
12	Luis Gonzalez	.05
13	Mike Scioscia	.05
14	Wes Chamberlain	.05
15	Denny Martinez	.05
16	Jeff Montgomery	.05
17	Randy Milligan	.05
18	Greg Cadaret	.05
19	Jamie Quirk	.05
20	Bip Roberts	.05
21	Buck Rodgers	.05
22	Bill Wegman	.05
23	Chuck Knoblauch	.05
24	Randy Myers	.05
25	Ron Gant	.05
26	Mike Bielecki	.05
27	Juan Gonzalez	.20
28	Mike Schooler	.05
29	Mickey Tettleton	.05
30	John Kruk	.05
31	Bryn Smith	.05
32	Chris Nabholz	.05
33	Carlos Baerga	.05
34	Jeff Juden	.05
35	Dave Righetti	.05
36	Scott Ruffcorn **RC** (Draft Pick)	.05
37	Luis Polonia	.05
38	Tom Candiotti	.05
39	Greg Olson	.05
40	Cal Ripken, Jr.	.75
41	Craig Lefferts	.05
42	Mike Macfarlane	.05
43	Jose Lind	.05
44	Rick Aguilera	.05
45	Gary Carter	.35
46	Steve Farr	.05
47	Rex Hudler	.05
48	Scott Scudder	.05
49	Damon Berryhill	.05
50	Ken Griffey Jr.	.55
51	Tom Runnells	.05
52	Juan Bell	.05
53	Tommy Gregg	.05
54	David Wells	.05
55	Rafael Palmeiro	.30
56	Charlie O'Brien	.05
57	Donn Pall	.05
58	Top Prospects-Catchers (Brad Ausmus **RC**, Jim Campanis **RC**, Dave Nilsson **RC**, Doug Robbins **RC**)	.15
59	Mo Vaughn	.05
60	Tony Fernandez	.05
61	Paul O'Neill	.05
62	Gene Nelson	.05
63	Randy Ready	.05
64	Bob Kipper	.05
65	Willie McGee	.05
66	Scott Stahoviak **RC** (Draft Pick)	.05
67	Luis Salazar	.05
68	Marvin Freeman	.05
69	Kenny Lofton	.05
70	Gary Gaetti	.05
71	Erik Hanson	.05
72	Eddie Zosky **RC**	.05
73	Brian Barnes	.05
74	Scott Leius	.05
75	Bret Saberhagen	.05
76	Mike Gallego	.05
77	Jack Armstrong	.05
78	Ivan Rodriguez	.35
79	Jesse Orosco	.05
80	Dave Justice	.05
81	Ced Landrum **RC**	.05
82	Doug Simons **RC**	.05
83	Tommy Greene	.05
84	Leo Gomez	.05
85	Jose DeLeon	.05
86	Steve Finley	.05
87	Bob MacDonald **RC**	.05
88	Darrin Jackson	.05
89	Neal Heaton	.05
90	Robin Yount	.35
91	Jeff Reed	.05
92	Lenny Harris	.05
93	Reggie Jefferson	.05
94	Sammy Sosa	.45
95	Scott Bailes	.05
96	Tom McKinnon **RC** (Draft Pick)	.05
97	Luis Rivera	.05
98	Mike Harkey	.05
99	Jeff Treadway	.05
100	Jose Canseco	.25
101	Omar Vizquel	.05
102	Scott Kamieniecki **RC**	.05
103	Ricky Jordan	.05
104	Jeff Ballard	.05
105	Felix Jose	.05
106	Mike Boddicker	.05
107	Dan Pasqua	.05
108	Mike Timlin **RC**	.10
109	Roger Craig	.05
110	Ryne Sandberg	.45
111	Mark Carreon	.05
112	Oscar Azocar	.05
113	Mike Greenwell	.05
114	Mark Portugal	.05
115	Terry Pendleton	.05
116	Willie Randolph	.05
117	Scott Terry	.05
118	Chili Davis	.05
119	Mark Gardner	.05
120	Alan Trammell	.05
121	Derek Bell	.05
122	Gary Varsho	.05
123	Bob Ojeda	.05
124	Shawn Livsey **RC** (Draft Pick)	.05
125	Chris Hoiles	.05
126	Top Prospects-1st Baseman (Rico Brogna, John Jaha, Ryan Klesko, Dave Staton)	.05
127	Carlos Quintana	.05
128	Kurt Stillwell	.05
129	Melido Perez	.05
130	Alvin Davis	.05
131	Checklist 1	.05
132	Eric Show	.05
133	Rance Mulliniks	.05
134	Darryl Kile	.05
135	Von Hayes	.05
136	Bill Doran	.05
137	Jeff Robinson	.05
138	Monty Fariss	.05
139	Jeff Innis	.05
140	Mark Grace	.05
141	Jim Leyritz	.05
142	Todd Van Poppel	.05
143	Paul Gibson	.05
144	Bill Swift	.05
145	Danny Tartabull	.05
146	Al Newman	.05
147	Cris Carpenter	.05
148	Anthony Young **RC**	.05
149	Brian Bohanon **RC**	.05
150	Roger Clemens	.50
151	Jeff Hamilton	.05
152	Charlie Leibrandt	.05
153	Ron Karkovice	.05
154	Hensley Meulens	.05
155	Scott Bankhead	.05
156	Manny Ramirez **RC** (Draft Pick)	3.00
157	Keith Miller	.05
158	Todd Frohwirth	.05
159	Darrin Fletcher	.05
160	Bobby Bonilla	.05
161	Casey Candaele	.05
162	Paul Faries **RC**	.05
163	Dana Kiecker	.05
164	Shane Mack	.05
165	Mark Langston	.05
166	Geronimo Pena	.05
167	Andy Allanson	.05
168	Dwight Smith	.05
169	Chuck Crim	.05
170	Alex Cole	.05
171	Bill Plummer	.05
172	Juan Berenguer	.05
173	Brian Downing	.05
174	Steve Frey	.05
175	Orel Hershiser	.05
176	Ramon Garcia **RC**	.05
177	Danny Gladden	.05
178	Jim Acker	.05
179	Top Prospects-2nd Baseman (Cesar Bernhardt **RC**, Bobby DeJardin **RC**, Armando Moreno **RC**, Andy Stankiewicz **RC**)	.05
180	Kevin Mitchell	.05
181	Hector Villanueva	.05
182	Jeff Reardon	.05
183	Brent Mayne	.05
184	Jimmy Jones	.05
185	Benny Santiago	.05
186	Cliff Floyd **RC** (Draft Pick)	.50
187	Ernie Riles	.05
188	Jose Guzman	.05
189	Junior Felix	.05
190	Glenn Davis	.05
191	Charlie Hough	.05
192	Dave Fleming **RC**	.05
193	Omar Oliveras **RC**	.05
194	Eric Karros	.05
195	David Cone	.05
196	Frank Castillo **RC**	.05
197	Glenn Braggs	.05
198	Scott Aldred	.05
199	Jeff Blauser	.05
200	Len Dykstra	.05
201	Buck Showalter	.05
202	Rick Honeycutt	.05
203	Greg Myers	.05
204	Trevor Wilson	.05
205	Jay Howell	.05
206	Luis Sojo	.05
207	Jack Clark	.05
208	Julio Machado	.05
209	Lloyd McClendon	.05
210	Ozzie Guillen	.05
211	Jeremy Hernandez **RC**	.05
212	Randy Velarde	.05
213	Les Lancaster	.05
214	Andy Mota **RC**	.05
215	Rich Gossage	.05
216	Brent Gates **RC** (Draft Pick)	.05
217	Brian Harper	.05
218	Mike Flanagan	.05
219	Jerry Browne	.05
220	Jose Rijo	.05
221	Skeeter Barnes	.05
222	Jaime Navarro	.05
223	Mel Hall	.05
224	Brett Barberie **RC**	.05
225	Roberto Alomar	.15
226	Pete Smith	.05
227	Daryl Boston	.05
228	Eddie Whitson	.05
229	Shawn Boskie	.05
230	Dick Schofield	.05
231	Brian Drahman **RC**	.05
232	John Smiley	.05
233	Mitch Webster	.05
234	Terry Steinbach	.05
235	Jack Morris	.05
236	Bill Pecota	.05
237	Jose Hernandez **RC**	.05
238	Greg Litton	.05
239	Brian Holman	.05
240	Andres Galarraga	.05
241	Gerald Young	.05
242	Mike Mussina	.30
243	Alvaro Espinoza	.05
244	Darren Daulton	.05
245	John Smoltz	.05
246	Jason Pruitt **RC** (Draft Pick)	.05
247	Chuck Finley	.05
248	Jim Gantner	.05
249	Tony Fossas	.05
250	Ken Griffey	.05
251	Kevin Elster	.05
252	Dennis Rasmussen	.05
253	Terry Kennedy	.05
254	Ryan Bowen **RC**	.05
255	Robin Ventura	.05
256	Mike Aldrete	.05
257	Jeff Russell	.05
258	Jim Lindeman	.05
259	Ron Darling	.05
260	Devon White	.05
261	Tom Lasorda	.05
262	Terry Lee **RC**	.05
263	Bob Patterson	.05
264	Checklist 2	.05
265	Teddy Higuera	.05
266	Roberto Kelly	.05
267	Steve Bedrosian	.05
268	Brady Anderson	.05
269	Ruben Amaro **RC**	.05
270	Tony Gwynn	.45
271	Tracy Jones	.05
272	Jerry Don Gleaton	.05
273	Craig Grebeck	.05
274	Bob Scanlan **RC**	.05
275	Todd Zeile	.05
276	Shawn Green **RC** (Draft Pick)	1.50
277	Scott Chiamparino	.05
278	Darryl Hamilton	.05
279	Jim Clancy	.05
280	Carlos Martinez	.05
281	Kevin Appier	.05
282	John Wehner **RC**	.05
283	Reggie Sanders	.05
284	Gene Larkin	.05
285	Bob Welch	.05
286	Gilberto Reyes **RC**	.05
287	Pete Schourek	.05
288	Andujar Cedeno	.05
289	Mike Morgan	.05
290	Bo Jackson	.10
291	Phil Garner	.05
292	Ray Lankford	.05
293	Mike Henneman	.05
294	Dave Valle	.05
295	Alonzo Powell **RC**	.05
296	Tom Brunansky	.05
297	Kevin Brown	.05
298	Kelly Gruber	.05
299	Charles Nagy	.05
300	Don Mattingly	.50
301	Kirk McCaskill	.05
302	Joey Cora	.05
303	Dan Plesac	.05
304	Joe Oliver	.05
305	Tom Glavine	.25
306	Al Shirley **RC** (Draft Pick)	.05
307	Bruce Ruffin	.05
308	Craig Shipley **RC**	.05
309	Dave Martinez	.05
310	Jose Mesa	.05
311	Henry Cotto	.05
312	Mike LaValliere	.05
313	Kevin Tapani	.05
314	Jeff Huson	.05
315	Juan Samuel	.05
316	Curt Schilling	.25
317	Mike Bordick **RC**	.05
318	Steve Howe	.05
319	Tony Phillips	.05
320	George Bell	.05
321	Lou Pinella	.05
322	Tim Burke	.05
323	Milt Thompson	.05
324	Danny Darwin	.05
325	Joe Orsulak	.05
326	Eric King	.05
327	Jay Buhner	.05
328	Joel Johnston **RC**	.05
329	Franklin Stubbs	.05
330	Will Clark	.05
331	Steve Lake	.05
332	Chris Jones **RC**	.05
333	Pat Tabler	.05
334	Kevin Gross	.05
335	Dave Henderson	.05
336	Greg Anthony **RC** (Draft Pick)	.05
337	Alejandro Pena	.05
338	Shawn Abner	.05
339	Tom Browning	.05
340	Otis Nixon	.05
341	Bob Geren	.05
342	Tim Spehr **RC**	.05
343	Jon Vander Wal **RC**	.20
344	Jack Daugherty	.05
345	Zane Smith	.05
346	Rheal Cormier **RC**	.05
347	Kent Hrbek	.05
348	Rick Wilkins **RC**	.10
349	Steve Lyons	.05
350	Gregg Olson	.05
351	Greg Riddoch	.05
352	Ed Nunez	.05
353	Braulio Castillo **RC**	.05
354	Dave Bergman	.05
355	Warren Newson **RC**	.05
356	Luis Quinones	.05
357	Mike Witt	.05
358	Ted Wood **RC**	.05
359	Mike Moore	.05
360	Lance Parrish	.05
361	Barry Jones	.05
362	Javier Ortiz **RC**	.05
363	John Candelaria	.05
364	Glenallen Hill	.05
365	Duane Ward	.05
366	Checklist 3	.05
367	Rafael Belliard	.05
368	Bill Krueger	.05
369	Steve Whitaker **RC** (Draft Pick)	.05
370	Shawon Dunston	.05
371	Dante Bichette	.05
372	Kip Gross **RC**	.05
373	Don Robinson	.05
374	Bernie Williams	.05
375	Bert Blyleven	.05
376	Chris Donnels **RC**	.05
377	Bob Zupcic **RC**	.05
378	Joel Skinner	.05
379	Steve Chitren	.05
380	Barry Bonds	.75
381	Sparky Anderson	.10
382	Sid Fernandez	.05
383	Dave Hollins	.05
384	Mark Lee	.05
385	Tim Wallach	.05
386	Will Clark/AS	.05
387	Ryne Sandberg/AS	.20
388	Howard Johnson/AS	.05
389	Barry Larkin/AS	.05
390	Barry Bonds/AS	.40
391	Ron Gant/AS	.05
392	Bobby Bonilla/AS	.05
393	Craig Biggio/AS	.05

394 Denny Martinez/AS .05
395 Tom Glavine/AS .05
396 Lee Smith/AS .05
397 Cecil Fielder/AS .05
398 Julio Franco/AS .05
399 Wade Boggs/AS .20
400 Cal Ripken, Jr./AS .40
401 Jose Canseco/AS .15
402 Joe Carter/AS .05
403 Ruben Sierra/AS .05
404 Matt Nokes/AS .05
405 Roger Clemens/AS .25
406 Jim Abbott/AS .05
407 Bryan Harvey/AS .05
408 Bob Milacki .05
409 Geno Petralli .05
410 Dave Stewart .05
411 Mike Jackson .05
412 Luis Aquino .05
413 Tim Teufel .05
414 Jeff Ware (Draft Pick) .05
415 Jim Deshaies .05
416 Ellis Burks .05
417 Allan Anderson .05
418 Alfredo Griffin .05
419 Wally Whitehurst .05
420 Sandy Alomar .05
421 Juan Agosto .05
422 Sam Horn .05
423 Jeff Fassero **RC** .05
424 Paul McClellan **RC** .05
425 Cecil Fielder .05
426 Tim Raines .05
427 Eddie Taubensee **RC** .05
428 Dennis Boyd .05
429 Tony LaRussa .05
430 Steve Sax .05
431 Tom Gordon .05
432 Billy Hatcher .05
433 Cal Eldred .05
434 Wally Backman .05
435 Mark Eichhorn .05
436 Mookie Wilson .05
437 Scott Servais **RC** .10
438 Mike Maddux .05
439 Chico Walker **RC** .05
440 Doug Drabek .05
441 Rob Deer .05
442 Dave West .05
443 Spike Owen .05
444 Tyrone Hill **RC** (Draft Pick) .05
445 Matt Williams .05
446 Mark Lewis .05
447 David Segui .05
448 Tom Pagnozzi .05
449 Jeff Johnson **RC** .05
450 Mark McGwire .65
451 Tom Henke .05
452 Wilson Alvarez .05
453 Gary Redus .05
454 Darren Holmes .05
455 Pete O'Brien .05
456 Pat Combs .05
457 Hubie Brooks .05
458 Frank Tanana .05
459 Tom Kelly .05
460 Andre Dawson .25
461 Doug Jones .05
462 Rich Rodriguez .05
463 Mike Simms **RC** .05
464 Mike Jeffcoat .05
465 Barry Larkin .05
466 Stan Belinda .05
467 Lonnie Smith .05
468 Greg Harris .05
469 Jim Eisenreich .05
470 Pedro Guerrero .05
471 Jose DeJesus .05
472 Rich Rowland **RC** .05
473 Top Prospects-3rd Baseman (Frank Bolick **RC**, Craig Paquette **RC**, Tom Redington **RC**, Paul Russo **RC**) .05
474 Mike Rossiter **RC** (Draft Pick) .05
475 Robby Thompson .05
476 Randy Bush .05
477 Greg Hibbard .05
478 Dale Sveum .05
479 Chito Martinez **RC** .05
480 Scott Sanderson .05
481 Tino Martinez .05
482 Jimmy Key .05
483 Terry Shumpert .05
484 Mike Hartley .05
485 Chris Sabo .05
486 Bob Walk .05
487 John Cerutti .05
488 Scott Cooper **RC** .05
489 Bobby Cox .05
490 Julio Franco .05
491 Jeff Brantley .05
492 Mike Devereaux .05
493 Jose Offerman .05
494 Gary Thurman .05
495 Carney Lansford .05
496 Joe Grahe .05
497 Andy Ashby **RC** .10
498 Gerald Perry .05
499 Dave Otto .05
500 Vince Coleman .05
501 Rob Mallicoat **RC** .05
502 Greg Briley .05
503 Pascual Perez .05
504 Aaron Sele **RC** (Draft Pick) .25
505 Bobby Thigpen .05
506 Todd Benzinger .05
507 Candy Maldonado .05
508 Bill Gullickson .05
509 Doug Dascenzo .05
510 Frank Viola .05
511 Kenny Rogers .05
512 Mike Heath .05
513 Kevin Bass .05
514 Kim Batiste **RC** .05
515 Delino DeShields .05
516 Ed Sprague **RC** .05
517 Jim Gott .05
518 Jose Melendez **RC** .05
519 Hal McRae .05
520 Jeff Bagwell .35
521 Joe Hesketh .05
522 Milt Cuyler .05
523 Shawn Hillegas .05
524 Don Slaught .05
525 Randy Johnson .35
526 Doug Piatt **RC** .05
527 Checklist 4 .05
528 Steve Foster **RC** .05
529 Joe Girardi .05
530 Jim Abbott .05
531 Larry Walker .05
532 Mike Huff .05
533 Mackey Sasser .05
534 Benji Gil **RC** (Draft Pick) .05
535 Dave Stieb .05
536 Willie Wilson .05
537 Mark Leiter **RC** .05
538 Jose Uribe .05
539 Thomas Howard .05
540 Ben McDonald .05
541 Jose Tolentino **RC** .05
542 Keith Mitchell **RC** .05
543 Jerome Walton .05
544 Cliff Brantley **RC** .05
545 Andy Van Slyke .05
546 Paul Sorrento .05
547 Herm Winningham .05
548 Mark Guthrie .05
549 Joe Torre .05
550 Darryl Strawberry .05
551 Top Prospects-Shortstops (Manny Alexander, Alex Arias, Wil Cordero, Chipper Jones) .25
552 Dave Gallagher .05
553 Edgar Martinez .05
554 Donald Harris .05
555 Frank Thomas .35
556 Storm Davis .05
557 Dickie Thon .05
558 Scott Garrelts .05
559 Steve Olin .05
560 Rickey Henderson .35
561 Jose Vizcaino .05
562 Wade Taylor **RC** .05
563 Pat Borders .05
564 Jimmy Gonzalez **RC** (Draft Pick) .05
565 Lee Smith .05
566 Bill Sampen .05
567 Dean Palmer .05
568 Bryan Harvey .05
569 Tony Pena .05
570 Lou Whitaker .05
571 Randy Tomlin .05
572 Greg Vaughn .05
573 Kelly Downs .05
574 Steve Avery .05
575 Kirby Puckett .45
576 Heathcliff Slocumb **RC** .05
577 Kevin Seitzer .05
578 Lee Guetterman .05
579 Johnny Oates .05
580 Greg Maddux .45
581 Stan Javier .05
582 Vicente Palacios .05
583 Mel Rojas .05
584 Wayne Rosenthal **RC** .05
585 Lenny Webster **RC** .05
586 Rod Nichols .05
587 Mickey Morandini .05
588 Russ Swan .05
589 Mariano Duncan .05
590 Howard Johnson .05
591 Top Prospects-Outfielders (Jacob Brumfield **RC**, Jeromy Burnitz **RC**, Alan Cockrell **RC**, D.J. Dozier **RC**) .25
592 Denny Neagle **RC** .10
593 Steve Decker .05
594 Brian Barber **RC** (Draft Pick) .05
595 Bruce Hurst .05
596 Kent Mercker .05
597 Mike Magnante **RC** .05
598 Jody Reed .05
599 Steve Searcy .05
600 Paul Molitor .35
601 Dave Smith .05
602 Mike Fetters .05
603 Luis Mercedes **RC** .05
604 Chris Gwynn .05
605 Scott Erickson .05
606 Brook Jacoby .05
607 Todd Stottlemyre .05
608 Scott Bradley .05
609 Mike Hargrove .05
610 Eric Davis .05
611 Brian Hunter **RC** .05
612 Pat Kelly .05
613 Pedro Munoz **RC** .05
614 Al Osuna .05
615 Matt Merullo .05
616 Larry Andersen .05
617 Junior Ortiz .05
618 Top Prospects-Outfielders (Cesar Hernandez **RC**, Steve Hosey **RC**, Dan Peltier **RC**, Jeff McNeely **RC**) .10
619 Danny Jackson .05
620 George Brett .50
621 Dan Gakeler **RC** .05
622 Steve Buechele .05
623 Bob Tewksbury .05
624 Shawn Estes **RC** (Draft Pick) .25
625 Kevin McReynolds .05
626 Chris Haney **RC** .05
627 Mike Sharperson .05
628 Mark Williamson .05
629 Wally Joyner .05
630 Carlton Fisk .35
631 Armando Reynoso **RC** .05
632 Felix Fermin .05
633 Mitch Williams .05
634 Manuel Lee .05
635 Harold Baines .05
636 Greg Harris .05
637 Orlando Merced .05
638 Chris Bosio .05
639 Wayne Housie **RC** .05
640 Xavier Hernandez .05
641 David Howard **RC** .05
642 Tim Crews .05
643 Rick Cerone .05
644 Terry Leach .05
645 Deion Sanders .10
646 Craig Wilson .05
647 Marquis Grissom .05
648 Scott Fletcher .05
649 Norm Charlton .05
650 Jesse Barfield .05
651 Joe Slusarski **RC** .05
652 Bobby Rose .05
653 Dennis Lamp .05
654 Allen Watson **RC** (Draft Pick) .05
655 Brett Butler .05
656 Top Prospects-Outfielders (Rudy Pemberton **RC**, Henry Rodriguez **RC**, Lee Tinsley **RC**, Gerald Williams **RC**) .10
657 Dave Johnson .05
658 Checklist 5 .05
659 Brian McRae .05
660 Fred McGriff .05
661 Bill Landrum .05
662 Juan Guzman .05
663 Greg Gagne .05
664 Ken Hill .05
665 Dave Haas **RC** .05
666 Tom Foley .05
667 Roberto Hernandez **RC** .10
668 Dwayne Henry .05
669 Jim Fregosi .05
670 Harold Reynolds .05
671 Mark Whiten .05
672 Eric Plunk .05
673 Todd Hundley .05
674 Mo Sanford **RC** .05
675 Bobby Witt .05
676 Top Prospects-Pitchers (Pat Mahomes **RC**, Sam Militello **RC**, Roger Salkeld, Turk Wendell **RC**) .15
677 John Marzano .05
678 Joe Klink .05
679 Pete Incaviglia .05
680 Dale Murphy .15
681 Rene Gonzales .05
682 Andy Benes .05
683 Jim Poole **RC** .05
684 Trever Miller **RC** (Draft Pick) .10
685 Scott Livingstone **RC** .05
686 Rich DeLucia .05
687 Harvey Pulliam **RC** .05
688 Tim Belcher .05
689 Mark Lemke .05
690 John Franco .05
691 Walt Weiss .05
692 Scott Ruskin .05
693 Jeff King .05
694 Mike Gardiner **RC** .05
695 Gary Sheffield .30
696 Joe Boever .05
697 Mike Felder .05
698 John Habyan .05
699 Cito Gaston .05
700 Ruben Sierra .05
701 Scott Radinsky .05
702 Lee Stevens .05
703 Mark Wohlers **RC** .05
704 Curt Young .05
705 Dwight Evans .05
706 Rob Murphy .05
707 Gregg Jefferies .05
708 Tom Bolton .05
709 Chris James .05
710 Kevin Maas .05
711 Ricky Bones **RC** .05
712 Curt Wilkerson .05
713 Roger McDowell .05
714 Calvin Reese **RC** (Draft Pick) .10
715 Craig Biggio .05
716 Kirk Dressendorfer **RC** .05
717 Ken Dayley .05
718 B.J. Surhoff .05
719 Terry Mulholland .05
720 Kirk Gibson .05
721 Mike Pagliarulo .05
722 Walt Terrell .05
723 Jose Oquendo .05
724 Kevin Morton **RC** .05
725 Dwight Gooden .05
726 Kirt Manwaring .05
727 Chuck McElroy .05
728 Dave Burba **RC** .05
729 Art Howe .05
730 Ramon Martinez .05
731 Donnie Hill .05
732 Nelson Santovenia .05
733 Bob Melvin .05
734 Scott Hatteberg **RC** (Draft Pick) .10
735 Greg Swindell .05
736 Lance Johnson .05
737 Kevin Reimer .05
738 Dennis Eckersley .35
739 Rob Ducey .05
740 Ken Caminiti .05
741 Mark Gubicza .05
742 Billy Spiers .05
743 Darren Lewis .05
744 Chris Hammond .05
745 Dave Magadan .05
746 Bernard Gilkey .05
747 Willie Banks **RC** .05
748 Matt Nokes .05
749 Jerald Clark .05
750 Travis Fryman .05
751 Steve Wilson .05
752 Billy Ripken .05
753 Paul Assenmacher .05
754 Charlie Hayes .05
755 Alex Fernandez .05
756 Gary Pettis .05
757 Rob Dibble .05
758 Tim Naehring .05
759 Jeff Torborg .05
760 Ozzie Smith .45
761 Mike Fitzgerald .05
762 John Burkett .05
763 Kyle Abbott .05
704 Tyler Green **RC** (Draft Pick) .05
765 Pete Harnisch .05
766 Mark Davis .05
767 Kal Daniels .05
768 Jim Thome .35
769 Jack Howell .05
770 Sid Bream .05
771 Arthur Rhodes **RC** .10
772 Garry Templeton .05
773 Hal Morris .05
774 Bud Black .05
775 Ivan Calderon .05
776 Doug Henry **RC** .05
777 John Olerud .05
778 Tim Leary .05
779 Jay Bell .05
780 Eddie Murray .35
781 Paul Abbott **RC** .05
782 Phil Plantier .05
783 Joe Magrane .05
784 Ken Patterson .05
785 Albert Belle .05
786 Royce Clayton .05
787 Checklist 6 .05
788 Mike Stanton .05
789 Bobby Valentine .05
790 Joe Carter .05
791 Danny Cox .05
792 Dave Winfield .35

Gold Promo Sheet

Similar in form and function to the nine-card promo sheet issued for the regular 1992 Topps set, this 8" x 11" sheet previewed the Topps Gold cards for dealers. Fronts are identical to the regular-issue '92 Topps cards. Backs differ in that actual 1991 stats are not printed, and there is a diamond over the stat box which reads, "1992 Pre-Production Sample." Card numbers on the gold preview cards correspond to the regular Topps cards. Single cards in the standard 2-1/2" x 3-1/2" size are frequently offered cut from these sheets.

		NM/M
Complete Set (Sheet):		8.00
Complete Set (9):		8.00
Common Player:		1.00
1	Nolan Ryan	4.00
15	Dennis Martinez	1.00
20	Bip Roberts	1.00
40	Cal Ripken, Jr.	4.00
261	Tom Lasorda	1.00
370	Shawon Dunston	1.00
512	Mike Heath	1.00
655	Brett Butler	1.00
757	Rob Dibble	1.00

Gold

Topps Gold cards share a checklist and format with the regular-issue 1992 Topps baseball issue except the color bars with the player's name and team printed beneath the photo have been replaced with gold foil. On back the light blue Topps logo printed beneath the stats has been replaced with a gold "ToppsGold" logo. Topps Gold cards were random inserts in all forms of packs. Additionally, factory sets of Gold cards were sold which included an autographed card of Yankees #1 draft pick Brien Taylor, and which had the checklist cards replaced with player cards. Several errors connected with the gold name/team strips are noted; no corrected versions were issued.

		NM/M
Unopened Fact. Set (793):		75.00
Complete Set (792):		35.00
Common Player:		.20
86	Steve Finley (Incorrect name, Mark Davidson, on gold strip.)	.20
131	Terry Mathews	.20
264	Rod Beck	1.00
288	Andujar Cedeno (Incorrect team, Yankees, listed on gold strip.)	.60
366	Tony Perezchica	.20
465	Barry Larkin (Incorrect team, Astros, listed on gold strip.)	2.50
527	Terry McDaniel	.20
532	Mike Huff (Incorrect team, Red Sox, listed on gold strip.)	.20
658	John Ramos	.20
787	Brian Williams	.20
793	Brien Taylor (Autographed edition of 12,000; factory sets only.)	7.50

Gold Winners

A second gold-foil enhanced parallel version of the regular 1992 Topps issue was the Gold Winner cards awarded as prizes in a scratch-off contest found in each pack. Winner cards are identical to the Topps Gold cards except for the addition of a gold-foil "Winner" and star added above the team name. Due to a flaw in the design of the scratch-off game cards, it was easy to win every time and the Winner cards had to be produced in quantities far greater than originally planned, making them rather common. Six checklist cards from the regular issue were replaced with player cards in the Winners edition. Cards were sent to winners in 10-card cello packs.

		NM/M
Complete Set (792):		30.00
Common Player:		.10
Cello Pack (10):		.75
131	Terry Mathews	.15
264	Rod Beck	.25
366	Tony Perezchica	.15
465a	Barry Larkin (team name incorrect, Astros)	2.00
465b	Barry Larkin (team name correct, Reds)	.75
527	Terry McDaniel	.15
658	John Ramos	.15
787	Brian Williams	.15

Traded

Members of the United States baseball team are featured in this 132-card boxed set released by Topps. The cards are styled after the regular 1992 Topps cards and are numbered alphabetically. Several United States baseball players featured in this set were also featured in the 1991 Topps Traded set.

		NM/M
Complete Set (132):		50.00
Common Player:		.05
Golds:		2-4X
1	Willie Adams **RC** (USA)	.05
2	Jeff Alkire (USA)	.05
3	Felipe Alou	.05
4	Moises Alou	.10
5	Ruben Amaro **RC**	.05
6	Jack Armstrong	.05
7	Scott Bankhead	.05
8	Tim Belcher	.05
9	George Bell	.05
10	Freddie Benavides **RC**	.05
11	Todd Benzinger	.05
12	Joe Boever	.05
13	Ricky Bones	.05
14	Bobby Bonilla	.05
15	Hubie Brooks	.05
16	Jerry Browne	.05
17	Jim Bullinger	.05
18	Dave Burba	.05
19	Kevin Campbell **RC**	.05
20	Tom Candiotti	.05
21	Mark Carreon	.05
22	Gary Carter	.75
23	Archi Cianfrocco	.05
24	Phil Clark	.05
25	Chad Curtis **RC**	.50
26	Eric Davis	.05
27	Tim Davis (USA)	.05
28	Gary DiSarcina	.05
29	Darren Dreifort (USA)	.05
30	Mariano Duncan	.05
31	Mike Fitzgerald	.05
32	John Flaherty **RC**	.05
33	Darrin Fletcher	.05
34	Scott Fletcher	.05
35	Ron Fraser (USA)	.05
36	Andres Galarraga	.05
37	Dave Gallagher	.05
38	Mike Gallego	.05

39 Nomar Garciaparra **RC** (USA) 30.00
40 Jason Giambi (USA) 1.00
41 Danny Gladden .05
42 Rene Gonzales .05
43 Jeff Granger (USA) .05
44 Rick Greene (USA) .05
45 Jeffrey Hammonds (USA) .05
46 Charlie Hayes .05
47 Von Hayes .05
48 Rick Helling (USA) .05
49 Butch Henry **RC** .05
50 Carlos Hernandez **RC** .05
51 Ken Hill .05
52 Butch Hobson .05
53 Vince Horsman **RC** .05
54 Pete Incaviglia .05
55 Gregg Jefferies .05
56 Charles Johnson (USA) .05
57 Doug Jones .05
58 Brian Jordan **RC** 2.00
59 Wally Joyner .05
60 Daron Kirkreit **RC** (USA) .20
61 Bill Krueger .05
62 Gene Lamont .05
63 Jim Lefebvre .05
64 Danny Leon **RC** .05
65 Pat Listach .05
66 Kenny Lofton .05
67 Dave Martinez .05
68 Derrick May .05
69 Kirk McCaskill .05
70 Chad McConnell **RC** (USA) .05
71 Kevin McReynolds .05
72 Rusty Meacham **RC** .05
73 Keith Miller .05
74 Kevin Mitchell .05
75 Jason Moler **RC** (USA) .05
76 Mike Morgan .05
77 Jack Morris .05
78 Calvin Murray **RC** (USA) .05
79 Eddie Murray .75
80 Randy Myers .05
81 Denny Neagle **RC** .05
82 Phil Nevin (USA) .10
83 Dave Nilsson .05
84 Junior Ortiz .05
85 Donovan Osborne .05
86 Bill Pecota .05
87 Melido Perez .05
88 Mike Perez **RC** .05
89 Hipolito Pena **RC** .05
90 Willie Randolph .05
91 Darren Reed **RC** .05
92 Bip Roberts .05
93 Chris Roberts (USA) .05
94 Steve Rodriguez (USA) .05
95 Bruce Ruffin .05
96 Scott Ruskin .05
97 Bret Saberhagen .05
98 Rey Sanchez **RC** .05
99 Steve Sax .05
100 Curt Schilling .25
101 Dick Schofield .05
102 Gary Scott .05
103 Kevin Seitzer .05
104 Frank Seminara **RC** .05
105 Gary Sheffield .35
106 John Smiley .05
107 Cory Snyder .05
108 Paul Sorrento .05
109 Sammy Sosa 1.50
110 Matt Stairs **RC** .25
111 Andy Stankiewicz .05
112 Kurt Stillwell .05
113 Rick Sutcliffe .05
114 Bill Swift .05
115 Jeff Tackett **RC** .05
116 Danny Tartabull .05
117 Eddie Taubensee **RC** .05
118 Dickie Thon .05
119 Michael Tucker **RC** (USA) .25
120 Scooter Tucker **RC** .05
121 Marc Valdes **RC** (USA) .05
122 Julio Valera **RC** .05
123 Jason Varitek **RC** (USA) 15.00
124 Ron Villone **RC** (USA) .05
125 Frank Viola .05
126 B.J. Wallace **RC** (USA) .05
127 Dan Walters **RC** .05
128 Craig Wilson (USA) .05
129 Chris Wimmer (USA) .05
130 Dave Winfield .75
131 Herm Winningham .05
132 Checklist .05

Traded Gold

A reported 6,000 sets of 1992 Topps Traded were produced in a gold edition, with gold-foil strips on front bearing the player and team names. The cards are in all other respects identical to the regular boxed Traded issue.

NM/M
Complete Unopened Set (132): 75.00
Complete Set (132): 65.00

Common Player: .25
Stars/Rookies: 4X

Golden Spikes Award

At a Nov. 17, 1992 awards ceremony, Phil Nevin was presented with the U.S. Baseball Federation's Golden Spikes Award, emblematic of his selection as the outstanding amatuer player in the nation. Topps created and handed out at the affair a reported 600 of these cards.

NM/M
Phil Nevin 45.00

Kids

In a market which had increasingly become the province of adult collectors, Topps in 1992 offered an issue unashamedly aimed at the youngster. Called "Topps Kids," the 132-card set features bright colors, garish graphics and the game's top stars. Sold at 35 cents per pack (with bubble gum), the issue was even priced for the young collector. Unfortunately, the concept was a flop and was not repeated in subsequent years. Card fronts feature player photos, sometimes only the player's head on a cartoon body, against a background of wild designs or cartoon ballpark action. Player names at bottom were rendered in superhero comic-book style. Backs feature a few 1991 and career stats, and/or a cartoon or two about the player or baseball trivia.

NM/M
Complete Set (132): 7.50
Common Player: .05
Wax Pack (7): .40
Wax Box (36): 6.00
1 Ryne Sandberg .45
2 Andre Dawson .25
3 George Bell .05
4 Mark Grace .05
5 Shawon Dunston .05
6 Tim Wallach .05
7 Ivan Calderon .05
8 Marquis Grissom .05
9 Delino DeShields .05
10 Denny Martinez .05
11 Dwight Gooden .05
12 Howard Johnson .05
13 John Franco .05
14 Gregg Jefferies .05
15 Kevin McReynolds .05
16 David Cone .05
17 Len Dykstra .05
18 John Kruk .05
19 Von Hayes .05
20 Mitch Williams .05
21 Barry Bonds .75
22 Bobby Bonilla .05
23 Andy Van Slyke .05
24 Doug Drabek .05
25 Ozzie Smith .45
26 Pedro Guerrero .05
27 Todd Zelle .05
28 Lee Smith .05
29 Felix Jose .05
30 Jose DeLeon .05
31 David Justice .05
32 Ron Gant .05
33 Terry Pendleton .05
34 Tom Glavine .25
35 Otis Nixon .05
36 Steve Avery .05
37 Barry Larkin .05
38 Eric Davis .05
39 Chris Sabo .05
40 Rob Dibble .05
41 Paul O'Neill .05
42 Jose Rijo .05
43 Craig Biggio .05
44 Jeff Bagwell .35
45 Ken Caminiti .05
46 Steve Finley .05
47 Darryl Strawberry .05
48 Ramon Martinez .05
49 Brett Butler .05
50 Eddie Murray .35
51 Kal Daniels .05
52 Orel Hershiser .05
53 Tony Gwynn .45
54 Benny Santiago .05
55 Fred McGriff .05
56 Bip Roberts .05
57 Tony Fernandez .05
58 Will Clark .05
59 Kevin Mitchell .05
60 Matt Williams .05
61 Willie McGee .05
62 Dave Righetti .05
63 Cal Ripken, Jr. .75
64 Ben McDonald .05
65 Glenn Davis .05
66 Gregg Olson .05
67 Roger Clemens .50
68 Wade Boggs .45
69 Mike Greenwell .05
70 Ellis Burks .05
71 Sandy Alomar .05
72 Greg Swindell .05
73 Albert Belle .05
74 Mark Whiten .05
75 Alan Trammell .05
76 Cecil Fielder .05
77 Lou Whitaker .05
78 Travis Fryman .05
79 Tony Phillips .05
80 Robin Yount .35
81 Paul Molitor .35
82 B.J. Surhoff .05
83 Greg Vaughn .05
84 Don Mattingly .50
85 Steve Sax .05
86 Kevin Maas .05
87 Mel Hall .05
88 Roberto Kelly .05
89 Joe Carter .05
90 Roberto Alomar .15
91 Dave Stieb .05
92 Kelly Gruber .05
93 Tom Henke .05
94 Chuck Finley .05
95 Wally Joyner .05
96 Dave Winfield .35
97 Jim Abbott .05
98 Mark Langston .05
99 Frank Thomas .35
100 Ozzie Guillen .05
101 Bobby Thigpen .05
102 Robin Ventura .05
103 Bo Jackson .10
104 Tim Raines .05
105 George Brett .50
106 Danny Tartabull .05
107 Bret Saberhagen .05
108 Brian McRae .05
109 Kirby Puckett .45
110 Scott Erickson .05
111 Kent Hrbek .05
112 Chuck Knoblauch .05
113 Chili Davis .05
114 Rick Aguilera .05
115 Jose Canseco .25
116 Dave Henderson .05
117 Dave Stewart .05
118 Rickey Henderson .35
119 Dennis Eckersley .30
120 Harold Baines .05
121 Mark McGwire .60
122 Ken Griffey Jr. .60
123 Harold Reynolds .05
124 Erik Hanson .05
125 Edgar Martinez .05
126 Randy Johnson .35
127 Nolan Ryan .75
128 Ruben Sierra .05
129 Julio Franco .05
130 Rafael Palmeiro .30
131 Juan Gonzalez .20
132 Checklist .05

Micro

Topps returned for a second year with a micro parallel of its regular-issue baseball set, in a format about 40% the size of the standard cards. Sold only in complete-set form, the 1" x 1-3/8" cards also included a dozen gold-enhanced star cards. Stars and rookies among the micros are valued at a percentage of the corresponding regular card.

NM/M
Complete Set (804): 9.00
Common Player: .05
Stars/Rookies: 50-100 Percent
1 Nolan Ryan (Record Breaker) 2.00
2 Rickey Henderson (Record Breaker) .65
10 Wade Boggs .75
50 Ken Griffey Jr. 1.00
100 Jose Canseco .60
270 Tony Gwynn .75
300 Don Mattingly .90
380 Barry Bonds 2.00
397 Cecil Fielder/AS .50
403 Ruben Sierra/AS .50
460 Andre Dawson .55
725 Dwight Gooden .50

Triple Header Photo Balls

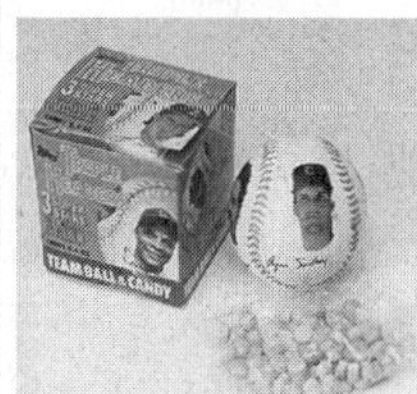

Picture a slightly oversize ping pong ball painted like a baseball with the heads and facsimile autographs of three different players on it and you've got the idea behind the Triple Headers test issue. Very limited in distribution, the team balls were sold in a small box with a package of candy.

NM/M
Complete Set (26): 100.00
Common Ball: 3.50
(1) California Angels (Chuck Finley, Dave Winfield, Wally Joyner) 4.00
(2) Houston Astros (Jeff Bagwell, Craig Biggio, Ken Caminiti) 4.50
(3) Oakland Athletics (Dave Henderson, Jose Canseco, Rickey Henderson) 4.50
(4) Toronto Blue Jays (Roberto Alomar, Kelly Gruber, Joe Carter) 4.00
(5) Atlanta Braves (Ron Gant, Tom Glavine, Dave Justice) 4.00
(6) Milwaukee Brewers (Greg Vaughn, Paul Molitor, Robin Yount) 4.50
(7) St. Louis Cardinals (Todd Zeile, Pedro Guerrero, Ozzie Smith) 4.50
(8) Chicago Cubs (Ryne Sandberg, George Bell, Mark Grace) 4.50
(9) Los Angeles Dodgers (Ramon Martinez, Eddie Murray, Darryl Strawberry) 4.50
(10) Montreal Expos (Delino DeShields, Dennis Martinez, Ivan Calderon) 3.50
(11) San Francisco Giants (Will Clark, Kevin Mitchell, Matt Williams) 3.50
(12) Cleveland Indians (Sandy Alomar Jr., Alex Cole, Mark Lewis) 3.50
(13) Seattle Mariners (Ken Griffey Jr., Harold Reynolds, Ken Griffey Sr.) 10.00
(14) New York Mets (Vince Coleman, Dwight Gooden, Howard Johnson) 3.50
(15) Baltimore Orioles (Ben McDonald, Cal Ripken Jr., Gregg Olson) 12.50
(16) San Diego Padres (Benito Santiago, Fred McGriff, Tony Gwynn) 5.00
(17) Philadelphia Phillies (Len Dykstra, John Kruk, Dale Murphy) 3.50
(18) Pittsburgh Pirates (Andy Van Slyke, Barry Bonds, Bobby Bonilla) 12.50
(19) Cincinnati Reds (Chris Sabo, Eric Davis, Barry Larkin) 3.50
(20) Boston Red Sox (Wade Boggs, Mike Greenwell, Roger Clemens) 6.00
(21) Kansas City Royals (George Brett, Danny Tartabull, Bret Saberhagen) 6.00
(22) Texas Rangers (Julio Franco, Nolan Ryan, Juan Gonzalez) 12.50
(23) Minnesota Twins (Scott Erickson, Kirby Puckett, Kent Hrbek) 5.00
(24) Detroit Tigers (Cecil Fielder, Tony Phillips, Alan Trammell) 3.50
(25) Chicago White Sox (Carlton Fisk, Robin Ventura, Frank Thomas) 5.00
(26) New York Yankees (Don Mattingly, Steve Sax, Willie Randolph) 6.00

1991 Major League Debut

This 194-card set highlights the debut date of 1991 Major League rookies. Two checklist cards are also included in this boxed set. The card fronts resemble the 1992 Topps cards. A debut banner appears in the lower-right corner of the card front. The set is packaged in an attractive collector box and the cards are numbered alphabetically. This set was available only through hobby dealers.

NM/M
Complete Set (194): 12.50
Common Player: .05
1 Kyle Abbott .05
2 Dana Allison .05
3 Rich Amaral .05
4 Ruben Amaro .05
5 Andy Ashby .05
6 Jim Austin .05
7 Jeff Bagwell 4.00
8 Jeff Banister .05
9 Willie Banks .05
10 Bret Barberie .05
11 Kim Batiste .05
12 Chris Beasley .05
13 Rod Beck .05
14 Derek Bell .05
15 Esteban Beltre .05
16 Freddie Benavides .05
17 Rickey Bones .05
18 Denis Boucher .05
19 Ryan Bowen .05
20 Cliff Brantley .05
21 John Briscoe .05
22 Scott Brosius .05
23 Terry Bross .05
24 Jarvis Brown .05
25 Scott Bullett .05
26 Kevin Campbell .05
27 Amalio Carreno .05
28 Matias Carrillo .05
29 Jeff Carter .05
30 Vinny Castilla .05
31 Braulio Castillo .05
32 Frank Castillo .05
33 Darrin Chapin .05
34 Mike Christopher .05
35 Mark Clark .05
36 Royce Clayton .05
37 Stu Cole .05
38 Gary Cooper .05
39 Archie Corbin .05
40 Rheal Cormier .05
41 Chris Cron .05
42 Mike Dalton .05
43 Mark Davis .05
44 Francisco de la Rosa .05
45 Chris Donnels .05
46 Brian Drahman .05
47 Tom Drees .05
48 Kirk Dressendorfer .05
49 Bruce Egloff .05
50 Cal Eldred .05
51 Jose Escobar .05
52 Tony Eusebio .05
53 Hector Fajardo .05
54 Monty Farriss .05
55 Jeff Fassero .05
56 Dave Fleming .05
57 Kevin Flora .05
58 Steve Foster .05
59 Dan Gakeler .05
60 Ramon Garcia .05
61 Chris Gardner .05
62 Jeff Gardner .05
63 Chris George .05
64 Ray Giannelli .05
65 Tom Goodwin .05
66 Mark Grater .05
67 Johnny Guzman .05
68 Juan Guzman .05
69 Dave Haas .05
70 Chris Haney .05
71 Shawn Hare .05
72 Donald Harris .05
73 Doug Henry .05
74 Pat Hentgen .05
75 Gil Heredia .05
76 Jeremy Hernandez .05
77 Jose Hernandez .05
78 Roberto Hernandez .05
79 Bryan Hickerson .05
80 Milt Hill .05
81 Vince Horsman .05
82 Wayne Housie .05
83 Chris Howard .05
84 David Howard .05
85 Mike Humphreys .05
86 Brian Hunter .05
87 Jim Hunter .05
88 Mike Ignasiak .05
89 Reggie Jefferson .05
90 Jeff Johnson .05
91 Joel Johnson .05
92 Calvin Jones .05
93 Chris Jones .05
94 Stacy Jones .05
95 Jeff Juden .05
96 Scott Kamieniecki .05
97 Eric Karros .05
98 Pat Kelly .05
99 John Kiely .05
100 Darryl Kile .05
101 Wayne Kirby .05
102 Garland Kiser .05
103 Chuck Knoblauch .05
104 Randy Knorr .05
105 Tom Kramer .05
106 Ced Landrum .05
107 Patrick Lennon .05
108 Jim Lewis .05

109	Mark Lewis	.05
110	Doug Lindsey	.05
111	Scott Livingstone	.05
112	Kenny Lofton	.10
113	Ever Magallanes	.05
114	Mike Magnante	.05
115	Barry Manuel	.05
116	Josias Manzanillo	.05
117	Chito Martinez	.05
118	Terry Mathews	.05
119	Rob Mauer	.05
120	Tim Mauser	.05
121	Terry McDaniel	.05
122	Rusty Meacham	.05
123	Luis Mercedes	.05
124	Paul Miller	.05
125	Keith Mitchell	.05
126	Bobby Moore	.05
127	Kevin Morton	.05
128	Andy Mota	.05
129	Jose Mota	.05
130	Mike Mussina	2.00
131	Jeff Mutis	.05
132	Denny Neagle	.05
133	Warren Newson	.05
134	Jim Olander	.05
135	Erik Pappas	.05
136	Jorge Pedre	.05
137	Yorkis Perez	.05
138	Mark Petkovsek	.05
139	Doug Piatt	.05
140	Jeff Plympton	.05
141	Harvey Pulliam	.05
142	John Ramos	.05
143	Mike Remlinger	.05
144	Laddie Renfroe	.05
145	Armando Reynoso	.05
146	Arthur Rhodes	.05
147	Pat Rice	.05
148	Nikco Riesgo	.05
149	Carlos Rodriguez	.05
150	Ivan Rodriguez	3.00
151	Wayne Rosenthal	.05
152	Rico Rossy	.05
153	Stan Royer	.05
154	Rey Sanchez	.05
155	Reggie Sanders	.05
156	Mo Sanford	.05
157	Bob Scanlan	.05
158	Pete Schourek	.05
159	Gary Scott	.05
160	Tim Scott	.05
161	Tony Scruggs	.05
162	Scott Servais	.05
163	Doug Simons	.05
164	Heathcliff Slocumb	.05
165	Joe Slusarski	.05
166	Tim Spehr	.05
167	Ed Sprague	.05
168	Jeff Tackett	.05
169	Eddie Taubensee	.05
170	Wade Taylor	.05
171	Jim Thome	2.50
172	Mike Timlin	.05
173	Jose Tolentino	.05
174	John Vander Wal	.05
175	Todd Van Poppel	.05
176	Mo Vaughn	.50
177	Dave Wainhouse	.05
178	Don Wakamatsu	.05
179	Bruce Walton	.05
180	Kevin Ward	.05
181	Dave Weathers	.05
182	Eric Wedge	.05
183	John Wehner	.05
184	Rick Wilkins	.05
185	Bernie Williams	.50
186	Brian Williams	.05
187	Ron Witmeyer	.05
188	Mark Wohlers	.05
189	Ted Wood	.05
190	Anthony Young	.05
191	Eddie Zosky	.05
192	Bob Zupcic	.05
193	Checklist	.05
194	Checklist	.05

1993 Topps Pre-Production

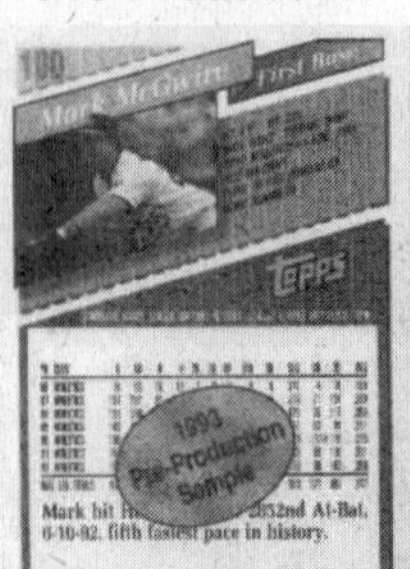

Specially marked 1992 Topps factory sets included this nine-card preview of the coming year's issue. The preview cards are identical to the regular-issue versions except the backs have a gray oval over the stats box with the notation, "1993 Pre-Production Sample."

		NM/M
Complete Set (9):		7.50
Common Player:		.35
1	Robin Yount	.75
2	Barry Bonds	3.00
11	Eric Karros	.50
32	Don Mattingly	1.00
100	Mark McGwire	2.00
150	Frank Thomas	.75
179	Ken Griffey Jr.	1.50
230	Carlton Fisk	.75
250	Chuck Knoblauch	.50

1993 Topps Pre-Production Sheet

Originally produced as an 8" x 11" nine-card sheet, these pre-production sample cards are rarely found as singles. Cards are in the same basic format as the regular-issue 1993 Topps cards. Backs differ in that all cards are numbered "000" with all zeroes for 1992 stats and bogus career highlights. A large gray circle over the stats box reads "1993 Pre-Production Sample For General Look Only."

		NM/M
Uncut Sheet:		6.00
Complete Set (9):		6.00
Common Player:		.50
(1)	Roberto Alomar	.60
(2)	Bobby Bonilla	.50
(3)	Gary Carter	1.00
(4)	Andre Dawson	.75
(5)	Dave Fleming	.50
(6)	Ken Griffey Jr.	3.00
(7)	Pete Incaviglia	.50
(8)	Spike Owen	.50
(9)	Larry Walker	.50

1993 Topps

Topps issued in a two-series format in 1993. Series I includes cards #1-396; Series II comprises #397-825. The card fronts feature full-color photos enclosed by a white border. The player's name and team appear at the bottom. The backs feature an additional player photo and biographical information at the top. The bottom box includes statistics and player information. The cards are numbered in red in a yellow flag on the back. The factory set includes the regular 825 cards plus 10 gold parallels, three Black Gold inserts and nine 1994 preview cards.

		NM/M
Unopened Fact. Set (847):		40.00
Complete Set (825):		30.00
Common Player:		.05
Golds:		3X
Series 1 Wax Pack (15):		1.00
Series 1 Wax Box (36):		25.00
Series 2 Wax Pack (15):		.75
Series 2 Wax Box (36):		15.00
Series 1 Jumbo Pack (41):		2.00
Series 1 Jumbo Box (24):		30.00
Series 2 Jumbo Pack (41):		1.50
Series 2 Jumbo Box (24):		20.00
1	Robin Yount	.50
2	Barry Bonds	1.00
3	Ryne Sandberg	.60
4	Roger Clemens	.65
5	Tony Gwynn	.60
6	Jeff Tackett **RC**	.05
7	Pete Incaviglia	.05
8	Mark Wohlers	.05
9	Kent Hrbek	.05
10	Will Clark	.05
11	Eric Karros	.05
12	Lee Smith	.05
13	Esteban Beltre	.05
14	Greg Briley	.05
15	Marquis Grissom	.05
16	Dan Plesac	.05
17	Dave Hollins	.05
18	Terry Steinbach	.05
19	Ed Nunez	.05
20	Tim Salmon	.05
21	Luis Salazar	.05
22	Jim Eisenreich	.05
23	Todd Stottlemyre	.05
24	Tim Naehring	.05
25	John Franco	.05
26	Skeeter Barnes	.05
27	Carlos Garcia **RC**	.05
28	Joe Orsulak	.05
29	Dwayne Henry	.05
30	Fred McGriff	.05
31	Derek Lilliquist	.05
32	Don Mattingly	.65
33	B.J. Wallace (1992 Draft Pick)	.05
34	Juan Gonzalez	.25
35	John Smoltz	.05
36	Scott Servais	.05
37	Lenny Webster	.05
38	Chris James	.05
39	Roger McDowell	.05
40	Ozzie Smith	.60
41	Alex Fernandez	.05
42	Spike Owen	.05
43	Ruben Amaro	.05
44	Kevin Seitzer	.05
45	Dave Fleming	.05
46	Eric Fox **RC**	.05
47	Bob Scanlan	.05
48	Bert Blyleven	.05
49	Brian McRae	.05
50	Roberto Alomar	.20
51	Mo Vaughn	.05
52	Bobby Bonilla	.05
53	Frank Tanana	.05
54	Mike LaValliere	.05
55	Mark McLemore	.05
56	Chad Mottola **RC** (1992 Draft Pick)	.10
57	Norm Charlton	.05
58	Jose Melendez	.05
59	Carlos Martinez	.05
60	Roberto Kelly	.05
61	Gene Larkin	.05
62	Rafael Belliard	.05
63	Al Osuna	.05
64	Scott Chiamparino	.05
65	Brett Butler	.05
66	John Burkett	.05
67	Felix Jose	.05
68	Omar Vizquel	.05
69	John Vander Wal	.05
70	Roberto Hernandez	.05
71	Ricky Bones	.05
72	Jeff Grotewold **RC**	.05
73	Mike Moore	.05
74	Steve Buechele	.05
75	Juan Guzman	.05
76	Kevin Appier	.05
77	Junior Felix	.05
78	Greg Harris	.05
79	Dick Schofield	.05
80	Cecil Fielder	.05
81	Lloyd McClendon	.05
82	David Segui	.05
83	Reggie Sanders	.05
84	Kurt Stillwell	.05
85	Sandy Alomar	.05
86	John Habyan	.05
87	Kevin Reimer	.05
88	Mike Stanton	.05
89	Eric Anthony	.05
90	Scott Erickson	.05
91	Craig Colbert	.05
92	Tom Pagnozzi	.05
93	Pedro Astacio **RC**	.10
94	Lance Johnson	.05
95	Larry Walker	.05
96	Russ Swan	.05
97	Scott Fletcher	.05
98	Derek Jeter **RC** (1992 Draft Pick)	10.00
99	Mike Williams **RC**	.05
100	Mark McGwire	.85
101	Jim Bullinger **RC**	.05
102	Brian Hunter	.05
103	Jody Reed	.05
104	Mike Butcher **RC**	.05
105	Gregg Jefferies	.05
106	Howard Johnson	.05
107	John Kiely **RC**	.05
108	Jose Lind	.05
109	Sam Horn	.05
110	Barry Larkin	.05
111	Bruce Hurst	.05
112	Brian Barnes	.05
113	Thomas Howard	.05
114	Mel Hall	.05
115	Robby Thompson	.05
116	Mark Lemke	.05
117	Eddie Taubensee	.05
118	David Hulse	.05
119	Pedro Munoz	.05
120	Ramon Martinez	.05
121	Todd Worrell	.05
122	Joey Cora	.05
123	Moises Alou	.05
124	Franklin Stubbs	.05
125	Pete O'Brien	.05
126	Bob Ayrault **RC**	.05
127	Carney Lansford	.05
128	Kal Daniels	.05
129	Joe Grahe	.05
130	Jeff Montgomery	.05
131	Dave Winfield	.50
132	Preston Wilson **RC** (1992 Draft Pick)	.75
133	Steve Wilson	.05
134	Lee Guetterman	.05
135	Mickey Tettleton	.05
136	Jeff King	.05
137	Alan Mills	.05
138	Joe Oliver	.05
139	Gary Gaetti	.05
140	Gary Sheffield	.30
141	Dennis Cook	.05
142	Charlie Hayes	.05
143	Jeff Huson	.05
144	Kent Mercker	.05
145	Eric Young **RC**	.10
146	Scott Leius	.05
147	Bryan Hickerson	.05
148	Steve Finley	.05
149	Rheal Cormier	.05
150	Frank Thomas	.50
151	Archi Cianfrocco **RC**	.05
152	Rich DeLucia	.05
153	Greg Vaughn	.05
154	Wes Chamberlain	.05
155	Dennis Eckersley	.40
156	Sammy Sosa	.60
157	Gary DiSarcina	.05
158	Kevin Koslofski **RC**	.05
159	Doug Linton **RC**	.05
160	Lou Whitaker	.05
161	Chad McDonnell (1992 Draft Pick)	.05
162	Joe Hesketh	.05
163	Tim Wakefield **RC**	.10
164	Leo Gomez	.05
165	Jose Rijo	.05
166	Tim Scott **RC**	.05
167	Steve Olin	.05
168	Kevin Maas	.05
169	Kenny Rogers	.05
170	Dave Justice	.05
171	Doug Jones	.05
172	Jeff Reboulet **RC**	.05
173	Andres Galarraga	.05
174	Randy Velarde	.05
175	Kirk McCaskill	.05
176	Darren Lewis	.05
177	Lenny Harris	.05
178	Jeff Fassero	.05
179	Ken Griffey Jr.	.75
180	Darren Daulton	.05
181	John Jaha	.05
182	Ron Darling	.05
183	Greg Maddux	.60
184	Damion Easley **RC**	.10
185	Jack Morris	.05
186	Mike Magnante	.05
187	John Dopson	.05
188	Sid Fernandez	.05
189	Tony Phillips	.05
190	Doug Drabek	.05
191	Sean Lowe **RC** (1992 Draft Pick)	.05
192	Bob Milacki	.05
193	Steve Foster **RC**	.05
194	Jerald Clark	.05
195	Pete Harnisch	.05
196	Pat Kelly	.05
197	Jeff Frye	.05
198	Alejandro Pena	.05
199	Junior Ortiz	.05
200	Kirby Puckett	.60
201	Jose Uribe	.05
202	Mike Scioscia	.05
203	Bernard Gilkey	.05
204	Dan Pasqua	.05
205	Gary Carter	.50
206	Henry Cotto	.05
207	Paul Molitor	.50
208	Mike Hartley	.05
209	Jeff Parrett	.05
210	Mark Langston	.05
211	Doug Dascenzo	.05
212	Rick Reed	.05
213	Candy Maldonado	.05
214	Danny Darwin	.05
215	Pat Howell **RC**	.05
216	Mark Leiter	.05
217	Kevin Mitchell	.05
218	Ben McDonald	.05
219	Bip Roberts	.05
220	Benny Santiago	.05
221	Carlos Baerga	.05
222	Bernie Williams	.05
223	Roger Pavlik **RC**	.05
224	Sid Bream	.05
225	Matt Williams	.05
226	Willie Banks	.05
227	Jeff Bagwell	.50
228	Tom Goodwin	.05
229	Mike Perez	.05
230	Carlton Fisk	.50
231	John Wetteland	.05
232	Tino Martinez	.05
233	Rick Greene **RC** (1992 Draft Pick)	.05
234	Tim McIntosh	.05
235	Mitch Williams	.05
236	Kevin Campbell **RC**	.05
237	Jose Vizcaino	.05
238	Chris Donnels	.05
239	Mike Boddicker	.05
240	John Olerud	.05
241	Mike Gardiner	.05
242	Charlie O'Brien	.05
243	Rob Deer	.05
244	Denny Neagle	.05
245	Chris Sabo	.05
246	Gregg Olson	.05
247	Frank Seminara	.05
248	Scott Scudder	.05
249	Tim Burke	.05
250	Chuck Knoblauch	.05
251	Mike Bielecki	.05
252	Xavier Hernandez	.05
253	Jose Guzman	.05
254	Cory Snyder	.05
255	Orel Hershiser	.05
256	Wil Cordero	.05
257	Luis Alicea	.05
258	Mike Schooler	.05
259	Craig Grebeck	.05
260	Duane Ward	.05
261	Bill Wegman	.05
262	Mickey Morandini	.05
263	Vince Horsman **RC**	.05
264	Paul Sorrento	.05
265	Andre Dawson	.25
266	Rene Gonzales	.05
267	Keith Miller	.05
268	Derek Bell	.05
269	Todd Steverson **RC** (1992 Draft Pick)	.05
270	Frank Viola	.05
271	Wally Whitehurst	.05
272	Kurt Knudsen **RC**	.05
273	Dan Walters **RC**	.05
274	Rick Sutcliffe	.05
275	Andy Van Slyke	.05
276	Paul O'Neill	.05
277	Mark Whiten	.05
278	Chris Nabholz	.05
279	Todd Burns	.05
280	Tom Glavine	.25
281	Butch Henry **RC**	.05
282	Shane Mack	.05
283	Mike Jackson	.05
284	Henry Rodriguez	.05
285	Bob Tewksbury	.05
286	Ron Karkovice	.05
287	Mike Gallego	.05
288	Dave Cochrane	.05
289	Jesse Orosco	.05
290	Dave Stewart	.05
291	Tommy Greene	.05
292	Rey Sanchez	.05
293	Rob Ducey	.05
294	Brent Mayne	.05
295	Dave Stieb	.05
296	Luis Rivera	.05
297	Jeff Innis	.05
298	Scott Livingstone	.05
299	Bob Patterson	.05
300	Cal Ripken, Jr.	1.00
301	Cesar Hernandez	.05
302	Randy Myers	.05
303	Brook Jacoby	.05
304	Melido Perez	.05
305	Rafael Palmeiro	.40
306	Damon Berryhill	.05
307	Dan Serafini **RC** (1992 Draft Pick)	.05
308	Darryl Kile	.05
309	J.T. Bruett **RC**	.05
310	Dave Righetti	.05
311	Jay Howell	.05
312	Geronimo Pena	.05
313	Greg Hibbard	.05
314	Mark Gardner	.05
315	Edgar Martinez	.05
316	Dave Nilsson	.05
317	Kyle Abbott	.05
318	Willie Wilson	.05
319	Paul Assenmacher	.05
320	Tim Fortugno **RC**	.05
321	Rusty Meacham	.05
322	Pat Borders	.05
323	Mike Greenwell	.05
324	Willie Randolph	.05
325	Bill Gullickson	.05
326	Gary Varsho	.05
327	Tim Hulett	.05
328	Scott Ruskin	.05
329	Mike Maddux	.05
330	Danny Tartabull	.05
331	Kenny Lofton	.05
332	Geno Petralli	.05
333	Otis Nixon	.05
334	Jason Kendall **RC** (1992 Draft Pick)	.50
335	Mark Portugal	.05
336	Mike Pagliarulo	.05
337	Kirt Manwaring	.05
338	Bob Ojeda	.05
339	Mark Clark **RC**	.05
340	John Kruk	.05
341	Mel Rojas	.05
342	Erik Hanson	.05
343	Doug Henry	.05
344	Jack McDowell	.05
345	Harold Baines	.05
346	Chuck McElroy	.05
347	Luis Sojo	.05
348	Andy Stankiewicz	.05
349	Hipolito Pichardo **RC**	.05
350	Joe Carter	.05
351	Ellis Burks	.05
352	Pete Schourek	.05
353	Buddy Groom **RC**	.05
354	Jay Bell	.05
355	Brady Anderson	.05
356	Freddie Benavides	.05
357	Phil Stephenson	.05
358	Kevin Wickander	.05
359	Mike Stanley	.05
360	Ivan Rodriguez	.40
361	Scott Bankhead	.05
362	Luis Gonzalez	.05
363	John Smiley	.05
364	Trevor Wilson	.05
365	Tom Candiotti	.05
366	Craig Wilson	.05
367	Steve Sax	.05
368	Delino Deshields	.05
369	Jaime Navarro	.05
370	Dave Valle	.05
371	Mariano Duncan	.05
372	Rod Nichols	.05
373	Mike Morgan	.05
374	Julio Valera	.05
375	Wally Joyner	.05
376	Tom Henke	.05
377	Herm Winningham	.05
378	Orlando Merced	.05
379	Mike Munoz	.05
380	Todd Hundley	.05
381	Mike Flanagan	.05
382	Tim Belcher	.05
383	Jerry Browne	.05
384	Mike Benjamin	.05
385	Jim Leyritz	.05
386	Ray Lankford	.05
387	Devon White	.05
388	Jeremy Hernandez	.05
389	Brian Harper	.05
390	Wade Boggs	.60
391	Derrick May	.05
392	Travis Fryman	.05
393	Ron Gant	.05
394	Checklist 1-132	.05
395	Checklist 133-264	.05
396	Checklist 265-396	.05
397	George Brett	.65
398	Bobby Witt	.05
399	Daryl Boston	.05
400	Bo Jackson	.10
401	Fred McGriff, Frank Thomas/AS	.20
402	Ryne Sandberg, Carlos Baerga/AS	.30
403	Gary Sheffield, Edgar Martinez/AS	.05
404	Barry Larkin, Travis Fryman/AS	.05
405	Andy Van Slyke, Ken Griffey Jr./AS	.40
406	Larry Walker, Kirby Puckett/AS	.20
407	Barry Bonds, Joe Carter/AS	.50
408	Darren Daulton, Brian Harper/AS	.05
409	Greg Maddux, Roger Clemens/AS	.25
410	Tom Glavine, Dave Fleming/AS	.05
411	Lee Smith, Dennis Eckersley/AS	.15
412	Jamie McAndrew	.05
413	Pete Smith	.05
414	Juan Guerrero	.05
415	Todd Frohwirth	.05
416	Randy Tomlin	.05
417	B.J. Surhoff	.05
418	Jim Gott	.05
419	Mark Thompson (1992 Draft Pick)	.05
420	Kevin Tapani	.05
421	Curt Schilling	.25
422	J.T. Snow **RC**	.40
423	Top Prospects 1B (Ryan Klesko, Ivan Cruz, Bubba Smith, Larry Sutton)	.05
424	John Valentin	.05
425	Joe Girardi	.05
426	Nigel Wilson **RC**	.05
427	Bob MacDonald	.05
428	Todd Zeile	.05
429	Milt Cuyler	.05
430	Eddie Murray	.50
431	Rich Amaral	.05
432	Pete Young	.05
433	Rockies Future Stars (Roger Bailey, Tom Schmidt)	.05
434	Jack Armstrong	.05
435	Willie McGee	.05

436 Greg Harris .05
437 Chris Hammond .05
438 Ritchie Moody **RC** (1992 Draft Pick) .05
439 Bryan Harvey .05
440 Ruben Sierra .05
441 Marlins Future Stars (Don Lemon, Todd Pridy) .05
442 Kevin McReynolds .05
443 Terry Leach .05
444 David Nied .05
445 Dale Murphy .15
446 Luis Mercedes .05
447 Keith Shepherd **RC** .05
448 Ken Caminiti .05
449 James Austin .05
450 Darryl Strawberry .05
451 Top Prospects 2B (Ramon Caraballo, Jon Shave, Brent Gates, Quinton McCracken **RC**) .10
452 Bob Wickman .05
453 Victor Cole .05
454 John Johnstone **RC** .05
455 Chili Davis .05
456 Scott Taylor .05
457 Tracy Woodson .05
458 David Wells .05
459 Derek Wallace **RC** (1992 Draft Pick) .05
460 Randy Johnson .50
461 Steve Reed **RC** .05
462 Felix Fermin .05
463 Scott Aldred .05
464 Greg Colbrunn .05
465 Tony Fernandez .05
466 Mike Felder .05
467 Lee Stevens .05
468 Matt Whiteside .05
469 Dave Hansen .05
470 Rob Dibble .05
471 Dave Gallagher .05
472 Chris Gwynn .05
473 Dave Henderson .05
474 Ozzie Guillen .05
475 Jeff Reardon .05
476 Rockies Future Stars (Mark Voisard, Will Scalzitti) .05
477 Jimmy Jones .05
478 Greg Cadaret .05
479 Todd Pratt .05
480 Pat Listach .05
481 Ryan Luzinski **RC** (1992 Draft Pick) .05
482 Darren Reed .05
483 Brian Griffiths **RC** .05
484 John Wehner .05
485 Glenn Davis .05
486 Eric Wedge **RC** .05
487 Jesse Hollins .05
488 Manuel Lee .05
489 Scott Fredrickson **RC** .05
490 Omar Olivares .05
491 Shawn Hare .05
492 Tom Lampkin .05
493 Jeff Nelson .05
494 Top Prospects 3B (Kevin Young, Adell Davenport, Eduardo Perez, Lou Lucca) .05
495 Ken Hill .05
496 Reggie Jefferson .05
497 Marlins Future Stars (Matt Petersen, Willie Brown) .05
498 Bud Black .05
499 Chuck Crim .05
500 Jose Canseco .30
501 Major League Managers (Johnny Oates, Bobby Cox) .05
502 Major League Managers (Butch Hobson, Jim Lefebvre) .05
503 Major League Managers (Buck Rodgers, Tony Perez) .05
504 Major League Managers (Gene Lamont, Don Baylor) .05
505 Major League Managers (Mike Hargrove, Rene Lachemann) .05
506 Major League Managers (Sparky Anderson, Art Howe) .10
507 Major League Managers (Hal McRae, Tommy Lasorda) .05
508 Major League Manager (Phil Garner, Felipe Alou) .05
509 Major League Managers (Tom Kelly, Jeff Torborg) .05
510 Major League Managers (Buck Showalter, Jim Fregosi) .05
511 Major League Managers (Tony LaRussa, Jim Leyland) .10
512 Major League Managers (Lou Piniella, Joe Torre) .10
513 Major League Managers (Toby Harrah, Jim Riggleman) .05
514 Major League Managers (Cito Gaston, Dusty Baker) .05
515 Greg Swindell .05
516 Alex Arias .05
517 Bill Pecota .05
518 Benji Grigsby **RC** (1992 Draft Pick) .05
519 David Howard .05
520 Charlie Hough .05
521 Kevin Flora .05
522 Shane Reynolds .05
523 Doug Bochtler **RC** .05
524 Chris Hoiles .05
525 Scott Sanderson .05
526 Mike Sharperson .05
527 Mike Fetters .05
528 Paul Quantrill .05
529 Top Propsects SS (Dave Silvestri, Chipper Jones, Benji Gil, Jeff Patzke) .25
530 Sterling Hitchcock .05
531 Joe Millette .05
532 Tom Brunansky .05
533 Frank Castillo .05
534 Randy Knorr .05
535 Jose Oquendo .05
536 Dave Haas .05
537 Rockies Future Stars (Jason Hutchins, Ryan Turner) .05
538 Jimmy Baron (1992 Draft Pick) .05
539 Kerry Woodson .05
540 Ivan Calderon .05
541 Denis Boucher .05
542 Royce Clayton .05
543 Reggie Williams .05
544 Steve Decker .05
545 Dean Palmer .05
546 Hal Morris .05
547 Ryan Thompson **RC** .05
548 Lance Blankenship .05
549 Hensley Meulens .05
550 Scott Radinsky .05
551 Eric Young **RC** .10
552 Jeff Blauser .05
553 Andujar Cedeno .05
554 Arthur Rhodes .05
555 Terry Mulholland .05
556 Darryl Hamilton .05
557 Pedro Martinez .50
558 Marlins Future Stars (Ryan Whitman, Mark Skeels) .05
559 Jamie Arnold **RC** (1992 Draft Pick) .05
560 Zane Smith .05
561 Matt Nokes .05
562 Bob Zupcic .05
563 Shawn Boskie .05
564 Mike Timlin .05
565 Jerald Clark .05
566 Rod Brewer .05
567 Mark Carreon .05
568 Andy Benes .05
569 Shawn Barton .05
570 Tim Wallach .05
571 Dave Mlicki .05
572 Trevor Hoffman .05
573 John Patterson .05
574 DeShawn Warren (1992 Draft Pick) .05
575 Monty Fariss .05
576 Top Prospects OF (Darrell Sherman, Damon Buford, Cliff Floyd, Michael Moore) .05
577 Tim Costo .05
578 Dave Magadan .05
579 Rockies Future Stars (Neil Garret, Jason Bates) .05
580 Walt Weiss .05
581 Chris Haney .05
582 Shawn Abner .05
583 Marvin Freeman .05
584 Casey Candaele .05
585 Ricky Jordan .05
586 Jeff Tabaka .05
587 Manny Alexander .05
588 Mike Trombley .05
589 Carlos Hernandez .05
590 Cal Eldred .05
591 Alex Cole .05
592 Phil Plantier .05
593 Brett Merriman .05
594 Jerry Nielsen .05
595 Shawon Dunston .05
596 Jimmy Key .05
597 Gerald Perry .05
598 Rico Brogna .05
599 Marlins Future Stars (Clemente Nunez, Dan Robinson) .05
600 Bret Saberhagen .05
601 Craig Shipley .05
602 Henry Mercedes .05
603 Jim Thome .40
604 Rod Beck .05
605 Chuck Finley .05
606 J. Owens .05
607 Dan Smith .05
608 Bill Doran .05
609 Lance Parrish .05
610 Denny Martinez .05
611 Tom Gordon .05
612 Byron Mathews (1992 Draft Pick) .05
613 Joel Adamson .05
614 Brian Williams .05
615 Steve Avery .05
616 Top Prospects OF (Matt Mieske, Tracy Sanders, Midre Cummings, Ryan Freeburg) .05
617 Craig Lefferts .05
618 Tony Pena .05
619 Billy Spiers .05
620 Todd Benzinger .05
621 Rockies Future Stars (Mike Kotarski, Greg Boyd) .05
622 Ben Rivera .05
623 Al Martin **RC** .05
624 Sam Militello .05
625 Rick Aguilera .05
626 Danny Gladden .05
627 Andres Berumen .05
628 Kelly Gruber .05
629 Cris Carpenter .05
630 Mark Grace .05
631 Jeff Brantley .05
632 Chris Widger (1992 Draft Pick) .05
633 Russian Angels (Rodolf Razjigaev, Evgenyi Puchkov, Ilya Bogatyrev) .10
634 Mo Sanford .05
635 Albert Belle .05
636 Tim Teufel .05
637 Greg Myers .05
638 Brian Bohanon .05
639 Mike Bordick .05
640 Dwight Gooden .05
641 Marlins Future Stars (Pat Leahy, Gavin Baugh) .05
642 Milt Hill .05
643 Luis Aquino .05
644 Dante Bichette .05
645 Bobby Thigpen .05
646 Rich Scheid .05
647 Brian Sackinsky (1992 Draft Pick) .05
648 Ryan Hawblitzel .05
649 Tom Marsh .05
650 Terry Pendleton .05
651 Rafael Bournigal **RC** .05
652 Dave West .05
653 Steve Hosey .05
654 Gerald Williams .05
655 Scott Cooper .05
656 Gary Scott .05
657 Mike Harkey .05
658 Top Prospects OF (Jeromy Burnitz, Melvin Nieves, Rich Becker, Shon Walker) .05
659 Ed Sprague .05
660 Alan Trammell .05
661 Rockies Future Stars (Garvin Alston, Mike Case) .05
662 Donovan Osborne .05
663 Jeff Gardner .05
664 Calvin Jones .05
665 Darrin Fletcher .05
666 Glenallen Hill .05
667 Jim Rosenbohm (1992 Draft Pick) .05
668 Scott Lewis .05
669 Kip Yaughn .05
670 Julio Franco .05
671 Dave Martinez .05
672 Kevin Bass .05
673 Todd Van Poppel .05
674 Mark Gubicza .05
675 Tim Raines .05
676 Rudy Seanez .05
677 Charlie Leibrandt .05
678 Randy Milligan .05
679 Kim Batiste .05
680 Craig Biggio .05
681 Darren Holmes .05
682 John Candelaria .05
683 Marlins Future Stars (Jerry Stafford, Eddie Christian) .05
684 Pat Mahomes .05
685 Bob Walk .05
686 Russ Springer .05
687 Tony Sheffield (1992 Draft Picks) .05
688 Dwight Smith .05
689 Eddie Zosky .05
690 Bien Figueroa .05
691 Jim Tatum .05
692 Chad Kreuter .05
693 Rich Rodriguez .05
694 Shane Turner .05
695 Kent Bottenfield .05
696 Jose Mesa .05
697 Darrell Whitmore **RC** .05
698 Ted Wood .05
699 Chad Curtis .05
700 Nolan Ryan 1.00
701 Top Prospects C (Mike Piazza, Carlos Delgado, Brook Fordyce, Donnie Leshnock) .85
702 Tim Pugh **RC** .05
703 Jeff Kent .05
704 Rockies Future Stars (Jon Goodrich, Danny Figueroa) .05
705 Bob Welch .05
706 Sherard Clinkscales (1992 Draft Pick) .05
707 Donn Pall .05
708 Greg Olson .05
709 Jeff Juden .05
710 Mike Mussina .30
711 Scott Chiamparino .05
712 Stan Javier .05
713 John Doherty .05
714 Kevin Gross .05
715 Greg Gagne .05
716 Steve Cooke .05
717 Steve Farr .05
718 Jay Buhner .05
719 Butch Henry .05
720 David Cone .05
721 Rick Wilkins .05
722 Chuck Carr .05
723 Kenny Felder **RC** (1992 Draft Pick) .05
724 Guillermo Velasquez .05
725 Billy Hatcher .05
726 Marlins Future Stars (Mike Veneziale, Ken Kendrena) .05
727 Jonathan Hurst .05
728 Steve Frey .05
729 Mark Leonard .05
730 Charles Nagy .05
731 Donald Harris .05
732 Travis Buckley .05
733 Tom Browning .05
734 Anthony Young .05
735 Steve Shifflett .05
736 Jeff Russell .05
737 Wilson Alvarez .05
738 Lance Painter .05
739 Dave Weathers .05
740 Len Dykstra .05
741 Mike Devereaux .05
742 Top Prospects SP (Rene Arocha, Alan Embree, Tim Crabtree **RC**, Brien Taylor) .05
743 Dave Landaker (1992 Draft Pick) .05
744 Chris George .05
745 Eric Davis .05
746 Rockies Future Stars (Mark Strittmatter **RC**, LaMarr Rogers) .05
747 Carl Willis .05
748 Stan Belinda .05
749 Scott Kamieniecki .05
750 Rickey Henderson .50
751 Eric Hillman .05
752 Pat Hentgen .05
753 Jim Corsi .05
754 Brian Jordan .05
755 Bill Swift .05
756 Mike Henneman .05
757 Harold Reynolds .05
758 Sean Berry .05
759 Charlie Hayes .05
760 Luis Polonia .05
761 Darrin Jackson .05
762 Mark Lewis .05
763 Rob Maurer .05
764 Willie Greene .05
765 Vince Coleman .05
766 Todd Revenig .05
767 Rich Ireland (1992 Draft Pick) .05
768 Mike MacFarlane .05
769 Francisco Cabrera .05
770 Robin Ventura .05
771 Kevin Ritz .05
772 Chito Martinez .05
773 Cliff Brantley .05
774 Curtis Leskanic .05
775 Chris Bosio .05
776 Jose Offerman .05
777 Mark Guthrie .05
778 Don Slaught .05
779 Rich Monteleone .05
780 Jim Abbott .05
781 Jack Clark .05
782 Marlins Future Stars (Rafael Mendoza, Dan Roman) .05
783 Heathcliff Slocumb .05
784 Jeff Branson .05
785 Kevin Brown .05
786 Top Prospects RP (Mike Christopher, Ken Ryan, Aaron Taylor, Gus Gandarillas) .05
787 Mike Matthews (1992 Draft Pick) .05
788 Mackey Sasser .05
789 Jeff Conine .05
790 George Bell .05
791 Pat Rapp .05
792 Joe Boever .05
793 Jim Poole .05
794 Andy Ashby .05
795 Deion Sanders .10
796 Scott Brosius .05
797 Brad Pennington (Coming Attraction) .05
798 Greg Blosser (Coming Attraction) .05
799 Jim Edmonds **RC** (Coming Attraction) 1.00
800 Shawn Jeter (Coming Attraction) .05
801 Jesse Levis (Coming Attraction) .05
802 Phil Clark (Coming Attraction) .05
803 Ed Pierce (Coming Attraction) .05
804 Jose Valentin **RC** (Coming Attraction) .05
805 Terry Jorgensen (Coming Attraction) .05
806 Mark Hutton (Coming Attraction) .05
807 Troy Neel (Coming Attraction) .05
808 Bret Boone (Coming Attraction) .05
809 Chris Colon (Coming Attraction) .05
810 Domingo Martinez **RC** (Coming Attraction) .05
811 Javier Lopez (Coming Attraction) .05
812 Matt Walbeck (Coming Attraction) .05
813 Dan Wilson (Coming Attraction) .05
814 Scooter Tucker (Coming Attraction) .05
815 Billy Ashley **RC** (Coming Attraction) .05
816 Tim Laker **RC** (Coming Attraction) .05
817 Bobby Jones (Coming Attraction) .05
818 Brad Brink (Coming Attraction) .05
819 William Pennyfeather (Coming Attraction) .05
820 Stan Royer (Coming Attraction) .05
821 Doug Brocail (Coming Attraction) .05
822 Kevin Rogers (Coming Attraction) .05
823 Checklist 397-528 .05
824 Checklist 541-691 .05
825 Checklist 692-825 .05

Gold

Expanding on the concept begun in 1992, Topps issued a "gold" version of each of its regular 1993 cards as a package insert. One Gold card was found in each wax pack; three per rack-pack and five per jumbo cello pack. Ten Gold cards were included in each factory set. Identical in format to the regular-issue 1993 Topps cards, the Gold version replaces the black or white Topps logo on front with a "ToppsGold" logo in gold-foil. The color bars and angled strips beneath the player photo which carry the player and team ID on regular cards are replaced with a gold-foil version on the insert cards. Backs are identical to the regular cards. The six checklist cards in the regular issue were replaced in the Gold version with cards of players who do not appear in the 1993 Topps set.

		NM/M
Complete Set (825):		40.00
Common Player:		.15
394	Bernardo Brito	.25
395	Jim McNamara	.25
396	Rich Sauveur	.25
823	Keith Brown	.25
824	Russ McGinnis	.25
825	Mike Walker	.25

Black Gold

Randomly inserted in regular 1993 Topps packs, as well as 10 per factory set, Black Gold cards are found in both single-player versions and "Winner" cards. The single-player cards feature an action photo set against a black background and highlighted at top and bottom with gold foil. Backs have another player photo at left, again on a black background. A career summary is printed in a blue box

at right. A "Topps Black Gold" logo appears at top-left, and the player's name is printed in gold foil in an art deco device at top-right. The Winner cards picture tiny versions of the Black Gold player cards for which they could be redeemed by mail. Some, perhaps all, of the mail-in cards can also be found on which the miniature card pictures on front do not correspond to the players named on back. In addition, with each mail-in redemption set, a non-redeemable version of the Winner card was also sent.

		NM/M
Complete Set (44):		7.50
Common Player:		.10
Winner A (1-11):		1.00
Winner B (12-22):		1.00
Winner C (23-33):		1.00
Winner D (34-44):		1.00
Winner AB (1-22):		3.00
Winner CD (23-44):		3.00
Winner ABCD (1-44):		5.00
1	Barry Bonds	1.50
2	Will Clark	.10
3	Darren Daulton	.10
4	Andre Dawson	.25
5	Delino DeShields	.10
6	Tom Glavine	.20
7	Marquis Grissom	.10
8	Tony Gwynn	.75
9	Eric Karros	.10
10	Ray Lankford	.10
11	Barry Larkin	.10
12	Greg Maddux	.75
13	Fred McGriff	.10
14	Joe Oliver	.10
15	Terry Pendleton	.10
16	Bip Roberts	.10
17	Ryne Sandberg	.75
18	Gary Sheffield	.40
19	Lee Smith	.10
20	Ozzie Smith	.75
21	Andy Van Slyke	.10
22	Larry Walker	.10
23	Roberto Alomar	.20
24	Brady Anderson	.10
25	Carlos Baerga	.10
26	Joe Carter	.10
27	Roger Clemens	.85
28	Mike Devereaux	.10
29	Dennis Eckersley	.60
30	Cecil Fielder	.10
31	Travis Fryman	.10
32	Juan Gonzalez	.35
33	Ken Griffey Jr.	1.00
34	Brian Harper	.10
35	Pat Listach	.10
36	Kenny Lofton	.10
37	Edgar Martinez	.10
38	Jack McDowell	.10
39	Mark McGwire	1.00
40	Kirby Puckett	.75
41	Mickey Tettleton	.10
42	Frank Thomas	.65
43	Robin Ventura	.10
44	Dave Winfield	.65

Colorado Rockies Inaugural Year

To mark the team's inaugural year in the Major Leagues, Topps produced a special run of 10,000 of its 1993 factory sets in which each card was embossed with a special gold seal incorporating the Rockies logo. Sets sold for $100 at the team's normal souvenir outlets. The factory sets were sealed with a sticker featuring the inaugural year logo.

	NM/M
Complete Set (825):	80.00
Common Player:	.50

Florida Marlins Inaugural Year

To commemorate the team's inaugural year in the Major Leagues, Topps produced a special edition of 6,000 of its 1993 factory sets in which every card was embossed with a special gold seal incorporating the Marlins logo. The sets were sold for $100 at the team's normal souvenir outlets. Factory sets are sealed with a sticker incorporating the inaugural year logo.

	NM/M
Complete Set (825):	100.00
Common Player:	.50

Traded

The 1993 Topps Traded baseball set features many players in their new uniforms as a result of trades, free agent signings and rookie call-ups. The set also features 35 expansion players from the Colorado Rockies and Florida Marlins, as well as 22 Team USA members exclusive to Topps. The 132-card set is packed in a color deluxe printed box.

		NM/M
Complete Set (132):		20.00
Common Player:		.05
1	Barry Bonds	2.00
2	Rich Renteria	.05
3	Aaron Sele	.05
4	Carlton Loewer **RC** (USA)	.10
5	Erik Pappas	.05
6	Greg McMichael **RC**	.05
7	Freddie Benavides	.05
8	Kirk Gibson	.05
9	Tony Fernandez	.05
10	Jay Gainer **RC** (USA)	.05
11	Orestes Destrade	.05
12	A.J. Hinch **RC** (USA)	.40
13	Bobby Munoz	.05
14	Tom Henke	.05
15	Rob Butler	.05
16	Gary Wayne	.05
17	David McCarty	.05
18	Walt Weiss	.05
19	Todd Helton **RC** (USA)	15.00
20	Mark Whiten	.05
21	Ricky Gutierrez	.05
22	Dustin Hermanson **RC** (USA)	.40
23	Sherman Obando **RC**	.05
24	Mike Piazza	2.00
25	Jeff Russell	.05
26	Jason Bere	.05
27	Jack Voight **RC**	.05
28	Chris Bosio	.05
29	Phil Hiatt	.05
30	Matt Beaumont **RC** (USA)	.05
31	Andres Galarraga	.05
32	Greg Swindell	.05
33	Vinny Castilla	.05
34	Pat Clougherty **RC** (USA)	.05
35	Greg Briley	.05
36	Dallas Green, Davey Johnson	.05
37	Tyler Green	.05
38	Craig Paquette	.05
39	Danny Sheaffer	.05
40	Jim Converse	.05
41	Terry Harvey	.05
42	Phil Plantier	.05
43	Doug Saunders **RC**	.05
44	Benny Santiago	.05
45	Dante Powell **RC** (USA)	.10
46	Jeff Parrett	.05
47	Wade Boggs	.85
48	Paul Molitor	.75
49	Turk Wendell	.05
50	David Wells	.05
51	Gary Sheffield	.35
52	Kevin Young	.05
53	Nelson Liriano	.05
54	Greg Maddux	.85
55	Derek Bell	.05
56	Matt Turner **RC**	.05
57	Charlie Nelson **RC** (USA)	.05
58	Mike Hampton	.05
59	Troy O'Leary **RC**	.10
60	Benji Gil	.05
61	Mitch Lyden **RC**	.05
62	J.T. Snow	.05
63	Damon Buford	.05
64	Gene Harris	.05
65	Randy Myers	.05
66	Felix Jose	.05
67	Todd Dunn **RC** (USA)	.05
68	Jimmy Key	.05
69	Pedro Castellano	.05
70	Mark Merila **RC** (USA)	.05
71	Rich Rodriguez	.05
72	Matt Mieske	.05
73	Pete Incaviglia	.05
74	Carl Everett	.05
75	Jim Abbott	.05
76	Luis Aquino	.05
77	Rene Arocha **RC**	.05
78	Jon Shave **RC**	.05
79	Todd Walker **RC** (USA)	1.00
80	Jack Armstrong	.05
81	Jeff Richardson	.05
82	Blas Minor	.05
83	Dave Winfield	.75
84	Paul O'Neill	.05
85	Steve Reich **RC** (USA)	.10
86	Chris Hammond	.05
87	Hilly Hathaway **RC**	.05
88	Fred McGriff	.05
89	Dave Telgheder **RC**	.05
90	Richie Lewis **RC**	.05
91	Brent Gates	.05
92	Andre Dawson	.15
93	Andy Barkett **RC** (USA)	.05
94	Doug Drabek	.05
95	Joe Klink	.05
96	Willie Blair	.05
97	Danny Graves **RC** (USA)	.05
98	Pat Meares	.05
99	Mike Lansing	.05
100	Marcos Armas **RC**	.05
101	Darren Grass **RC** (USA)	.05
102	Chris Jones	.05
103	Ken Ryan **RC**	.05
104	Ellis Burks	.05
105	Bobby Kelly	.05
106	Dave Magadan	.05
107	Paul Wilson **RC** (USA)	.25
108	Rob Natal	.05
109	Paul Wagner	.05
110	Jeromy Burnitz	.05
111	Monty Fariss	.05
112	Kevin Mitchell	.05
113	Scott Pose **RC**	.05
114	Dave Stewart	.05
115	Russ Johnson **RC** (USA)	.10
116	Armando Reynoso	.05
117	Geronimo Berroa	.05
118	Woody Williams **RC**	.15
119	Tim Bogar **RC**	.05
120	Bob Scafa **RC** (USA)	.05
121	Henry Cotto	.05
122	Gregg Jefferies	.05
123	Norm Charlton	.05
124	Bret Wagner **RC** (USA)	.05
125	David Cone	.05
126	Daryl Boston	.05
127	Tim Wallach	.05
128	Mike Martin **RC** (USA)	.05
129	John Cummings **RC**	.05
130	Ryan Bowen	.05
131	John Powell **RC** (USA)	.05
132	Checklist	.05

Full Shot Super

Just as rivals Upper Deck and Donruss did, Topps issued a set of 21 oversized cards (3-1/2" x 5") that was available in retail outlets in packages that contained one of the large cards and two packs of regular issue Topps cards from the same year. The Topps Full Shot cards feature many of the top players in the game, and unlike the Upper Deck oversized cards, the Topps cards were not enlarged versions of existing cards but rather photos and a design that appeared only in this format.

		NM/M
Complete Set (21):		65.00
Common Player:		2.00
1	Frank Thomas	4.00
2	Ken Griffey Jr.	8.00
3	Barry Bonds	9.00
4	Juan Gonzalez	2.50
5	Roberto Alomar	2.50
6	Mike Piazza	6.50
7	Tony Gwynn	4.50
8	Jeff Bagwell	3.50
9	Tim Salmon	2.00
10	John Olerud	2.00
11	Cal Ripken, Jr.	9.00
12	David McCarty	2.00
13	Darren Daulton	2.00
14	Carlos Baerga	2.00
15	Roger Clemens	5.00
16	John Kruk	2.00
17	Barry Larkin	2.00
18	Gary Sheffield	2.50
19	Tom Glavine	2.50
20	Andres Galarraga	2.00
21	Fred McGriff	2.00

Golden Spikes Award

Darren Dreifort was the 1993 recipient of the U.S. Baseball Federation's Golden Spikes Award, emblematic of his selection as the outstanding amatuer player in the nation. Topps created and handed out at the awards ceremony this special card.

	NM/M
Darren Dreifort	125.00

Magazine Jumbo Rookies

The final four issues of Topps' Magazine in 1993 substituted a 5-1/2" x 8" enlargement of a player's Topps rookie card in place of four of the standard-size inserts found previously. The jumbo rookie cards are identical, front and back, to the original rookie cards but carry a reprint notice on front. In an attempt to increase sales to subscribers and at the newsstands, the stars pictured autographed 100 of their cards to be randomly bound into the magazine and given away in prize drawings.

		NM/M
Complete Set (4):		7.50
Common Player:		1.00
(1)	Dennis Eckersley (1976 Topps)	1.00
(2)	Dave Winfield (1974 Topps)	1.00
(3)	George Brett (1975 Topps)	2.00
(4)	Jerry Koosman, Nolan Ryan (1968 Topps)	4.00

Micro

Topps returned for a final year with a micro parallel of its regular-issue baseball set, in a format about 40 percent the size of the standard cards. Sold only in complete-set form, the 1" x 1-3/8" cards also included a dozen prismatic-foil bordered star cards. Stars and rookies among the micros are valued at a percentage of the corresponding regular card.

		NM/M
Complete Set (837):		11.00
Common Player:		.05
Stars/Rookies:		1-1.5X
1	Robin Yount	.75
20	Tim Salmon	.50
32	Don Mattingly	1.25
50	Roberto Alomar	.60
150	Frank Thomas	.75
155	Dennis Eckersley	.65
179	Ken Griffey Jr.	1.50
200	Kirby Puckett	1.00
397	George Brett	1.25
426	Nigel Wilson	.50
444	David Nied	.50
700	Nolan Ryan	2.00

1994 Topps Preview

Two different versions of this nine-card set exist. A cello-wrapped version, designated (a) in the checklist, was given away to dealers and the hobby press. A second version, designated (b), was included in 1993 Topps factory sets. It is currently unknown which version, if either, will

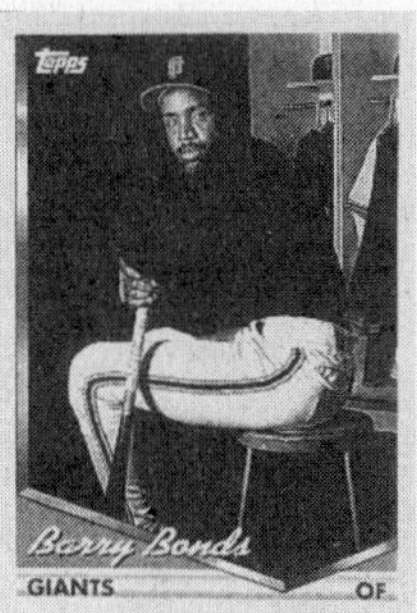

become more valuable due to demand and perceived scarcity. Both versions are similar to the regular-issue '94 Topps cards, except for the sample notation on back.

		NM/M
Complete Set (a)(9):		10.00
Complete Set (b)(9):		10.00
Common Player (a):		.30
Common Player (b):		.30
2a	Barry Bonds (Vertical format.)	4.00
2b	Barry Bonds (Horizontal)	4.00
6a	Jeff Tackett (Full bat label visible.)	.30
6b	Jeff Tackett (Partial bat label.)	.30
34a	Juan Gonzalez (Green triangle behind "Juan.")	.75
34b	Juan Gonzalez (Brown triangle.)	.75
225a	Matt Williams (Green triangle behind "Matt.")	.30
225b	Matt Williams (Blue triangle.)	.30
294a	Carlos Quintana (Team/position yellow.)	.30
294b	Carlos Quintana (Team/position black.)	.30
331a	Ken Lofton (Team/position white.)	.30
331b	Ken Lofton (Team/position black.)	.30
390a	Wade Boggs (Team/position yellow.)	2.00
390b	Wade Boggs (Team/position black.)	2.00
397a	George Brett (Vertical format.)	3.00
397b	George Brett (Horizontal)	3.00
700a	Nolan Ryan (Vertical format.)	4.00
700b	Nolan Ryan (Horizontal)	4.00

1994 Topps

Once again released in two 396-card series, Topps' basic issue for 1994 offers a standard mix of regular player cards, Future Stars, multi-player rookie cards and double-header All-Star cards. On most cards the player photo on front is framed in a home-plate shaped design. The player's name appears in script beneath the photo and a team color-coded strip at bottom carries the team name and position designation. On back is a player photo, a red box at top with biographical details and a marbled panel which carries the stats and a career highlight. Cards are UV coated on each side. Inserts include a gold-foil enhanced parallel card in every pack, plus random Black Gold cards. Factory hobby sets include the 792 base cards plus 10 gold parallels, three Black Gold inserts and three Finest pre-production cards. Factory retails sets have the 792 base cards, 10 Gold, three Black Gold, 10 1995 Topps pre-production cards and three Superstar Sampler cards.

		NM/M
Unopened Retail Set (818):		60.00
Unopened Hobby Set (808)		50.00
Complete Set (792):		35.00
Common Player:		.05
Golds:		2X
Series 1 or 2 Pack (12):		.50
Series 1 or 2 Wax Box (36):		15.00
1	Mike Piazza (All-Star Rookie)	.85
2	Bernie Williams	.05
3	Kevin Rogers	.05
4	Paul Carey (Future Star)	.05
5	Ozzie Guillen	.05
6	Derrick May	.05
7	Jose Mesa	.05
8	Todd Hundley	.05
9	Chris Haney	.05
10	John Olerud	.05
11	Andujar Cedeno	.05
12	John Smiley	.05
13	Phil Plantier	.05
14	Willie Banks	.05
15	Jay Bell	.05
16	Doug Henry	.05
17	Lance Blankenship	.05
18	Greg Harris	.05
19	Scott Livingstone	.05
20	Bryan Harvey	.05
21	Wil Cordero (All-Star Rookie)	.05
22	Roger Pavlik	.05
23	Mark Lemke	.05
24	Jeff Nelson	.05
25	Todd Zeile	.05
26	Billy Hatcher	.05
27	Joe Magrane	.05
28	Tony Longmire (Future Star)	.05
29	Omar Daal	.05
30	Kirt Manwaring	.05
31	Melido Perez	.05
32	Tim Hulett	.05
33	Jeff Schwarz	.05
34	Nolan Ryan	1.00
35	Jose Guzman	.05
36	Felix Fermin	.05
37	Jeff Innis	.05
38	Brent Mayne	.05
39	Huck Flener **RC**	.05
40	Jeff Bagwell	.50
41	Kevin Wickander	.05
42	Ricky Gutierrez	.05
43	Pat Mahomes	.05
44	Jeff King	.05
45	Cal Eldred	.05
46	Craig Paquette	.05
47	Richie Lewis	.05
48	Tony Phillips	.05
49	Armando Reynoso	.05
50	Moises Alou	.05
51	Manuel Lee	.05
52	Otis Nixon	.05
53	Billy Ashley (Future Star)	.05
54	Mark Whiten	.05
55	Jeff Russell	.05
56	Chad Curtis	.05
57	Kevin Stocker	.05
58	Mike Jackson	.05
59	Matt Nokes	.05
60	Chris Bosio	.05
61	Damon Buford	.05
62	Tim Belcher	.05
63	Glenallen Hill	.05
64	Bill Wertz	.05
65	Eddie Murray	.50
66	Tom Gordon	.05
67	Alex Gonzalez (Future Star)	.05
68	Eddie Taubensee	.05
69	Jacob Brumfield	.05
70	Andy Benes	.05
71	Rich Becker (Future Star)	.05
72	Steve Cooke (All-Star Rookie)	.05
73	Billy Spiers	.05
74	Scott Brosius	.05
75	Alan Trammell	.05
76	Luis Aquino	.05
77	Jerald Clark	.05
78	Mel Rojas	.05
79	OF Prospects (Billy Masse, Stanton Cameron, Tim Clark, Craig McClure)	.05
80	Jose Canseco	.30
81	Greg McMichael (All-Star Rookie)	.05
82	Brian Turang	.05
83	Tom Urban	.05

No.	Card	Value
84	Garret Anderson (Future Star)	.05
85	Tony Pena	.05
86	Ricky Jordan	.05
87	Jim Gott	.05
88	Pat Kelly	.05
89	Bud Black	.05
90	Robin Ventura	.05
91	Rick Sutcliffe	.05
92	Jose Bautista	.05
93	Bob Ojeda	.05
94	Phil Hiatt	.05
95	Tim Pugh	.05
96	Randy Knorr	.05
97	Todd Jones (Future Star)	.05
98	Ryan Thompson	.05
99	Tim Mauser	.05
100	Kirby Puckett	.60
101	Mark Dewey	.05
102	B.J. Surhoff	.05
103	Sterling Hitchcock	.05
104	Alex Arias	.05
105	David Wells	.05
106	Daryl Boston	.05
107	Mike Stanton	.05
108	Gary Redus	.05
109a	Delino DeShields (Red "Expos, 2B.")	2.00
109b	Delino DeShields (Yellow "Expos, 2B.")	.05
110	Lee Smith	.05
111	Greg Litton	.05
112	Frank Rodriguez (Future Star)	.05
113	Russ Springer	.05
114	Mitch Williams	.05
115	Eric Karros	.05
116	Jeff Brantley	.05
117	Jack Voight	.05
118	Jason Bere	.05
119	Kevin Roberson	.05
120	Jimmy Key	.05
121	Reggie Jefferson	.05
122	Jeromy Burnitz	.05
123	Billy Brewer (Future Star)	.05
124	Willie Canate	.05
125	Greg Swindell	.05
126	Hal Morris	.05
127	Brad Ausmus	.05
128	George Tsamis	.05
129	Denny Neagle	.05
130	Pat Listach	.05
131	Steve Karsay	.05
132	Bret Barberie	.05
133	Mark Leiter	.05
134	Greg Colbrunn	.05
135	David Nied	.05
136	Dean Palmer	.05
137	Steve Avery	.05
138	Bill Haselman	.05
139	Tripp Cromer (Future Star)	.05
140	Frank Viola	.05
141	Rene Gonzales	.05
142	Curt Schilling	.25
143	Tim Wallach	.05
144	Bobby Munoz	.05
145	Brady Anderson	.05
146	Rod Beck	.05
147	Mike LaValliere	.05
148	Greg Hibbard	.05
149	Kenny Lofton	.05
150	Dwight Gooden	.05
151	Greg Gagne	.05
152	Ray McDavid (Future Star)	.05
153	Chris Donnels	.05
154	Dan Wilson	.05
155	Todd Stottlemyre	.05
156	David McCarty	.05
157	Paul Wagner	.05
158	SS Prospects (Orlando Miller, Brandon Wilson, Derek Jeter, Mike Neal)	1.00
159	Mike Fetters	.05
160	Scott Lydy	.05
161	Darrell Whitmore	.05
162	Bob MacDonald	.05
163	Vinny Castilla	.05
164	Denis Boucher	.05
165	Ivan Rodriguez	.40
166	Ron Gant	.05
167	Tim Davis	.05
168	Steve Dixon	.05
169	Scott Fletcher	.05
170	Terry Mulholland	.05
171	Greg Myers	.05
172	Brett Butler	.05
173	Bob Wickman	.05
174	Dave Martinez	.05
175	Fernando Valenzuela	.05
176	Craig Grebeck	.05
177	Shawn Boskie	.05
178	Albie Lopez	.05
179	Butch Huskey (Future Star)	.05
180	George Brett	.65
181	Juan Guzman	.05
182	Eric Anthony	.05
183	Bob Dibble	.05
184	Craig Shipley	.05
185	Kevin Tapani	.05
186	Marcus Moore	.05
187	Graeme Lloyd	.05
188	Mike Bordick	.05
189	Chris Hammond	.05
190	Cecil Fielder	.05
191	Curtis Leskanic	.05
192	Lou Frazier	.05
193	Steve Dreyer	.05
194	Javier Lopez (Future Star)	.05
195	Edgar Martinez	.05
196	Allen Watson	.05
197	John Flaherty	.05
198	Kurt Stillwell	.05
199	Danny Jackson	.05
200	Cal Ripken, Jr.	1.00
201	Mike Bell (Draft Pick)	.05
202	Alan Benes **RC** (Draft Pick)	.10
203	Matt Farner (Draft Pick)	.05
204	Jeff Granger **RC** (Draft Pick)	.05
205	Brooks Kieschnick **RC** (Draft Pick)	.05
206	Jeremy Lee (Draft Pick)	.05
207	Charles Peterson **RC** (Draft Pick)	.05
208	Andy Rice (Draft Pick)	.05
209	Billy Wagner **RC** (Draft Pick)	.25
210	Kelly Wunsch (Draft Pick)	.05
211	Tom Candiotti	.05
212	Domingo Jean (Draft Pick)	.05
213	John Burkett	.05
214	George Bell	.05
215	Dan Plesac	.05
216	Manny Ramirez (Future Star)	.60
217	Mike Maddux	.05
218	Kevin McReynolds	.05
219	Pat Borders	.05
220	Doug Drabek	.05
221	Larry Luebbers	.05
222	Trevor Hoffman	.05
223	Pat Meares	.05
224	Danny Miceli (Future Star)	.05
225	Greg Vaughn	.05
226	Scott Hemond	.05
227	Pat Rapp	.05
228	Kirk Gibson	.05
229	Lance Painter	.05
230	Larry Walker	.05
231	Benji Gil (Future Star)	.05
232	Mark Wohlers	.05
233	Rich Amaral	.05
234	Erik Pappas	.05
235	Scott Cooper	.05
236	Mike Butcher	.05
237	OF Prospects (Curtis Pride **RC**, Shawn Green, Mark Sweeney, Eddie Davis)	.35
238	Kim Batiste	.05
239	Paul Assenmacher	.05
240	Will Clark	.05
241	Jose Offerman	.05
242	Todd Frohwirth	.05
243	Tim Raines	.05
244	Rick Wilkins	.05
245	Bret Saberhagen	.05
246	Thomas Howard	.05
247	Stan Belinda	.05
248	Rickey Henderson	.50
249	Brian Williams	.05
250	Barry Larkin	.05
251	Jose Valentin (Future Star)	.05
252	Lenny Webster	.05
253	Blas Minor	.05
254	Tim Teufel	.05
255	Bobby Witt	.05
256	Walt Weiss	.05
257	Chad Kreuter	.05
258	Roberto Mejia	.05
259	Cliff Floyd (Future Star)	.05
260	Julio Franco	.05
261	Rafael Belliard	.05
262	Marc Newfield	.05
263	Gerald Perry	.05
264	Ken Ryan	.05
265	Chili Davis	.05
266	Dave West	.05
267	Royce Clayton	.05
268	Pedro Martinez	.50
269	Mark Hutton	.05
270	Frank Thomas	.50
271	Brad Pennington	.05
272	Mike Harkey	.05
273	Sandy Alomar	.05
274	Dave Gallagher	.05
275	Wally Joyner	.05
276	Ricky Trlicek	.05
277	Al Osuna	.05
278	Calvin Reese (Future Star)	.05
279	Kevin Higgins	.05
280	Rick Aguilera	.05
281	Orlando Merced	.05
282	Mike Mohler	.05
283	John Jaha	.05
284	Robb Nen	.05
285	Travis Fryman	.05
286	Mark Thompson (Future Star)	.05
287	Mike Lansing (All-Star Rookie)	.05
288	Craig Lefferts	.05
289	Damon Berryhill	.05
290	Randy Johnson	.50
291	Jeff Reed	.05
292	Danny Darwin	.05
293	J.T. Snow (All-Star Rookie)	.05
294	Tyler Green	.05
295	Chris Hoiles	.05
296	Roger McDowell	.05
297	Spike Owen	.05
298	Salomon Torres (Future Star)	.05
299	Wilson Alvarez	.05
300	Ryne Sandberg	.60
301	Derek Lilliquist	.05
302	Howard Johnson	.05
303	Greg Cadaret	.05
304	Pat Hentgen	.05
305	Craig Biggio	.05
306	Scott Service	.05
307	Melvin Nieves	.05
308	Mike Trombley	.05
309	Carlos Garcia (All-Star Rookie)	.05
310	Robin Yount	.50
311	Marcos Armas	.05
312	Rich Rodriguez	.05
313	Justin Thompson (Future Star)	.05
314	Danny Sheaffer	.05
315	Ken Hill	.05
316	P Propsects (Chad Ogea **RC**, Duff Brumley **RC**, Terrell Wade **RC**, Chris Michalak **RC**)	.10
317	Cris Carpenter	.05
318	Jeff Blauser	.05
319	Ted Power	.05
320	Ozzie Smith	.60
321	John Dopson	.05
322	Chris Turner	.05
323	Pete Incaviglia	.05
324	Alan Mills	.05
325	Jody Reed	.05
326	Rich Monteleone	.05
327	Mark Carreon	.05
328	Donn Pall	.05
329	Matt Walbeck (Future Star)	.05
330	Charles Nagy	.05
331	Jeff McKnight	.05
332	Jose Lind	.05
333	Mike Timlin	.05
334	Doug Jones	.05
335	Kevin Mitchell	.05
336	Luis Lopez	.05
337	Shane Mack	.05
338	Randy Tomlin	.05
339	Matt Mieske	.05
340	Mark McGwire	.85
341	Nigel Wilson (Future Star)	.05
342	Danny Gladden	.05
343	Mo Sanford	.05
344	Sean Berry	.05
345	Kevin Brown	.05
346	Greg Olson	.05
347	Dave Magadan	.05
348	Rene Arocha	.05
349	Carlos Quintana	.05
350	Jim Abbott	.05
351	Gary DiSarcina	.05
352	Ben Rivera	.05
353	Carlos Hernandez	.05
354	Darren Lewis	.05
355	Harold Reynolds	.05
356	Scott Ruffcorn (Future Star)	.05
357	Mark Gubicza	.05
358	Paul Sorrento	.05
359	Anthony Young	.05
360	Mark Grace	.05
361	Rob Butler	.05
362	Kevin Bass	.05
363	Eric Helfand (Future Star)	.05
364	Derek Bell	.05
365	Scott Erickson	.05
366	Al Martin	.05
367	Ricky Bones	.05
368	Jeff Branson	.05
369	3B Prospects (Luis Ortiz, David Bell, Jason Giambi, George Arias **RC**)	.30
370a	Benny Santiago	.05
370b	Mark McLemore (Originally checklisted as #379.)	.05
371	John Doherty	.05
372	Joe Girardi	.05
373	Tim Scott	.05
374	Marvin Freeman	.05
375	Deion Sanders	.10
376	Roger Salkeld	.05
377	Bernard Gilkey	.05
378	Tony Fossas	.05
380	Darren Daulton	.05
381	Chuck Finley	.05
382	Mitch Webster	.05
383	Gerald Williams	.05
384	Frank Thomas, Fred McGriff/AS	.30
385	Roberto Alomar, Robby Thompson/AS	.05
386	Wade Boggs, Matt Williams/AS	.35
387	Cal Ripken, Jr., Jeff Blauser/AS	.50
388	Ken Griffey Jr., Len Dykstra/AS	.40
389	Juan Gonzalez, Dave Justice/AS	.10
390	Albert Belle, Barry Bonds/AS	.45
391	Mike Stanley, Mike Piazza/AS	.45
392	Jack McDowell, Greg Maddux/AS	.35
393	Jimmy Key, Tom Glavine/AS	.05
394	Jeff Montgomery, Randy Myers/AS	.05
395	Checklist 1	.05
396	Checklist 2	.05
397	Tim Salmon (All-Star Rookie)	.10
398	Todd Benzinger	.05
399	Frank Castillo	.05
400	Ken Griffey Jr.	.75
401	John Kruk	.05
402	Dave Telgheder	.05
403	Gary Gaetti	.05
404	Jim Edmonds	.05
405	Don Slaught	.05
406	Jose Oquendo	.05
407	Bruce Ruffin	.05
408	Phil Clark	.05
409	Joe Klink	.05
410	Lou Whitaker	.05
411	Kevin Seitzer	.05
412	Darrin Fletcher	.05
413	Kenny Rogers	.05
414	Bill Pecota	.05
415	Dave Fleming	.05
416	Luis Alicea	.05
417	Paul Quantrill	.05
418	Damion Easley	.05
419	Wes Chamberlain	.05
420	Harold Baines	.05
421	Scott Radinsky	.05
422	Rey Sanchez	.05
423	Junior Ortiz	.05
424	Jeff Kent	.05
425	Brian McRae	.05
426	Ed Sprague	.05
427	Tom Edens	.05
428	Willie Greene	.05
429	Bryan Hickerson	.05
430	Dave Winfield	.50
431	Pedro Astacio	.05
432	Mike Gallego	.05
433	Dave Burba	.05
434	Bob Walk	.05
435	Darryl Hamilton	.05
436	Vince Horsman	.05
437	Bob Natal	.05
438	Mike Henneman	.05
439	Willie Blair	.05
440	Denny Martinez	.05
441	Dan Peltier	.05
442	Tony Tarasco	.05
443	John Cummings	.05
444	Geronimo Pena	.05
445	Aaron Sele	.05
446	Stan Javier	.05
447	Mike Williams	.05
448	1B Prospects (Greg Pirkl, Roberto Petagine, D.J. Boston, Shawn Wooten)	.05
449	Jim Poole	.05
450	Carlos Baerga	.05
451	Bob Scanlan	.05
452	Lance Johnson	.05
453	Eric Hillman	.05
454	Keith Miller	.05
455	Dave Stewart	.05
456	Pete Harnisch	.05
457	Roberto Kelly	.05
458	Tim Worrell	.05
459	Pedro Munoz	.05
460	Orel Hershiser	.05
461	Randy Velarde	.05
462	Trevor Wilson	.05
463	Jerry Goff	.05
464	Bill Wegman	.05
465	Dennis Eckersley	.40
466	Jeff Conine (All-Star Rookie)	.05
467	Joe Boever	.05
468	Dante Bichette	.05
469	Jeff Shaw	.05
470	Rafael Palmeiro	.40
471	Phil Leftwich **RC**	.05
472	Jay Buhner	.05
473	Bob Tewksbury	.05
474	Tim Naehring	.05
475	Tom Glavine	.25
476	Dave Hollins	.05
477	Arthur Rhodes	.05
478	Joey Cora	.05
479	Mike Morgan	.05
480	Albert Belle	.05
481	John Franco	.05
482	Hipolito Pichardo	.05
483	Duane Ward	.05
484	Luis Gonzalez	.05
485	Joe Oliver	.05
486	Wally Whitehurst	.05
487	Mike Benjamin	.05
488	Eric Davis	.05
489	Scott Kamieniecki	.05
490	Kent Hrbek	.05
491	John Hope **RC**	.05
492	Jesse Orosco	.05
493	Troy Neel	.05
494	Ryan Bowen	.05
495	Mickey Tettleton	.05
496	Chris Jones	.05
497	John Wetteland	.05
498	David Hulse	.05
499	Greg Maddux	.60
500	Bo Jackson	.10
501	Donovan Osborne	.05
502	Mike Greenwell	.05
503	Steve Frey	.05
504	Jim Eisenreich	.05
505	Robby Thompson	.05
506	Leo Gomez	.05
507	Dave Staton	.05
508	Wayne Kirby (All-Star Rookie)	.05
509	Tim Bogar	.05
510	David Cone	.05
511	Devon White	.05
512	Xavier Hernandez	.05
513	Tim Costo	.05
514	Gene Harris	.05
515	Jack McDowell	.05
516	Kevin Gross	.05
517	Scott Leius	.05
518	Lloyd McClendon	.05
519	Alex Diaz **RC**	.05
520	Wade Boggs	.60
521	Bob Welch	.05
522	Henry Cotto	.05
523	Mike Moore	.05
524	Tim Laker	.05
525	Andres Galarraga	.05
526	Jamie Moyer	.05
527	2B Prospects (Norberto Martin, Ruben Santana, Jason Hardtke, Chris Sexton)	.05
528	Sid Bream	.05
529	Erik Hanson	.05
530	Ray Lankford	.05
531	Rob Deer	.05
532	Rod Correia	.05
533	Roger Mason	.05
534	Mike Devereaux	.05
535	Jeff Montgomery	.05
536	Dwight Smith	.05
537	Jeremy Hernandez	.05
538	Ellis Burks	.05
539	Bobby Jones	.05
540	Paul Molitor	.50
541	Jeff Juden	.05
542	Chris Sabo	.05
543	Larry Casian	.05
544	Jeff Gardner	.05
545	Ramon Martinez	.05
546	Paul O'Neill	.05
547	Steve Hosey	.05
548	Dave Nilsson	.05
549	Ron Darling	.05
550	Matt Williams	.05
551	Jack Armstrong	.05
552	Bill Krueger	.05
553	Freddie Benavides	.05
554	Jeff Fassero	.05
555	Chuck Knoblauch	.05
556	Guillermo Velasquez	.05
557	Joel Johnston	.05
558	Tom Lampkin	.05
559	Todd Van Poppel	.05
560	Gary Sheffield	.30
561	Skeeter Barnes	.05
562	Darren Holmes	.05
563	John Vander Wal	.05
564	Mike Ignasiak	.05
565	Fred McGriff	.05
566	Luis Polonia	.05
567	Mike Perez	.05
568	John Valentin	.05
569	Mike Felder	.05
570	Tommy Greene	.05
571	David Segui	.05
572	Roberto Hernandez	.05
573	Steve Wilson	.05
574	Willie McGee	.05
575	Randy Myers	.05
576	Darrin Jackson	.05
577	Eric Plunk	.05
578	Mike MacFarlane	.05
579	Doug Brocail	.05
580	Steve Finley	.05
581	John Roper	.05
582	Danny Cox	.05
583	Chip Hale	.05
584	Scott Bullett	.05
585	Kevin Reimer	.05
586	Brent Gates	.05
587	Matt Turner	.05
588	Rich Rowland	.05
589	Kent Bottenfield	.05
590	Marquis Grissom	.05
591	Doug Strange	.05
592	Jay Howell	.05
593	Omar Vizquel	.05
594	Rheal Cormier	.05
595	Andre Dawson	.25
596	Hilly Hathaway	.05
597	Todd Pratt	.05
598	Mike Mussina	.30
599	Alex Fernandez	.05
600	Don Mattingly	.65
601	Frank Thomas (Measures of Greatness)	.25
602	Ryne Sandberg (Measures of Greatness)	.30
603	Wade Boggs (Measures of Greatness)	.30
604	Cal Ripken, Jr. (Measures of Greatness)	.50
605	Barry Bonds (Measures of Greatness)	.50
606	Ken Griffey Jr. (Measures of Greatness)	.40
607	Kirby Puckett (Measures of Greatness)	.35
608	Darren Daulton (Measures of Greatness)	.05
609	Paul Molitor (Measures of Greatness)	.25
610	Terry Steinbach	.05
611	Todd Worrell	.05
612	Jim Thome	.40
613	Chuck McElroy	.05
614	John Habyan	.05
615	Sid Fernandez	.05
616	OF Prospects (Eddie Zambrano, Glenn Murray, Chad Mottola, Jermaine Allensworth **RC**)	.05
617	Steve Bedrosian	.05
618	Rob Ducey	.05
619	Tom Browning	.05
620	Tony Gwynn	.60
621	Carl Willis	.05
622	Kevin Young	.05
623	Rafael Novoa	.05
624	Jerry Browne	.05
625	Charlie Hough	.05
626	Chris Gomez	.05
627	Steve Reed	.05
628	Kirk Rueter	.05
629	Matt Whiteside	.05
630	Dave Justice	.05
631	Brad Holman	.05
632	Brian Jordan	.05
633	Scott Bankhead	.05
634	Torey Lovullo	.05
635	Len Dykstra	.05
636	Ben McDonald	.05
637	Steve Howe	.05
638	Jose Vizcaino	.05
639	Bill Swift	.05
640	Darryl Strawberry	.05
641	Steve Farr	.05
642	Tom Kramer	.05
643	Joe Orsulak	.05
644	Tom Henke	.05
645	Joe Carter	.05
646	Ken Caminiti	.05
647	Reggie Sanders	.05
648	Andy Ashby	.05
649	Derek Parks	.05
650	Andy Van Slyke	.05
651	Juan Bell	.05
652	Roger Smithberg	.05
653	Chuck Carr	.05
654	Bill Gullickson	.05
655	Charlie Hayes	.05
656	Chris Nabholz	.05
657	Karl Rhodes	.05
658	Pete Smith	.05
659	Bret Boone	.05
660	Gregg Jefferies	.05
661	Bob Zupcic	.05
662	Steve Sax	.05
663	Mariano Duncan	.05
664	Jeff Tackett	.05
665	Mark Langston	.05
666	Steve Buechele	.05
667	Candy Maldonado	.05
668	Woody Williams	.05
669	Tim Wakefield	.05
670	Danny Tartabull	.05
671	Charlie O'Brien	.05
672	Felix Jose	.05
673	Bobby Ayala	.05
674	Scott Servais	.05
675	Roberto Alomar	.15
676	Pedro Martinez	.05
677	Eddie Guardado	.05
678	Mark Lewis	.05
679	Jaime Navarro	.05
680	Ruben Sierra	.05
681	Rick Renteria	.05
682	Storm Davis	.05
683	Cory Snyder	.05
684	Ron Karkovice	.05
685	Juan Gonzalez	.25
686	C Prospects (Chris Howard, Carlos Delgado, Jason Kendall, Paul Bako)	.40
687	John Smoltz	.05
688	Brian Dorsett	.05
689	Omar Olivares	.05
690	Mo Vaughn	.05
691	Joe Grahe	.05
692	Mickey Morandini	.05
693	Tino Martinez	.05
694	Brian Barnes	.05
695	Mike Stanley	.05
696	Mark Clark	.05
697	Dave Hansen	.05
698	Willie Wilson	.05
699	Pete Schourek	.05
700	Barry Bonds	1.00
701	Kevin Appier	.05
702	Tony Fernandez	.05
703	Darryl Kile	.05
704	Archi Cianfrocco	.05
705	Jose Rijo	.05
706	Brian Harper	.05

707 Zane Smith .05
708 Dave Henderson .05
709 Angel Miranda .05
710 Orestes Destrade .05
711 Greg Gohr .05
712 Eric Young .05
713 P Prospects (Todd Williams, Ron Watson, Kirk Bullinger, Mike Welch) .05
714 Tim Spehr .05
715 Hank Aaron (20th Anniversary #715) .50
716 Nate Minchey .05
717 Mike Blowers .05
718 Kent Mercker .05
719 Tom Pagnozzi .05
720 Roger Clemens .65
721 Eduardo Perez .05
722 Milt Thompson .05
723 Gregg Olson .05
724 Kirk McCaskill .05
725 Sammy Sosa .60
726 Alvaro Espinoza .05
727 Henry Rodriguez .05
728 Jim Leyritz .05
729 Steve Scarsone .05
730 Bobby Bonilla .05
731 Chris Gwynn .05
732 Al Leiter .05
733 Bip Roberts .05
734 Mark Portugal .05
735 Terry Pendleton .05
736 Dave Valle .05
737 Paul Kilgus .05
738 Greg Harris .05
739 Jon Ratliff **RC** (Draft Pick) .05
740 Kirk Presley **RC** (Draft Pick) .05
741 Josue Estrada **RC** (Draft Pick) .05
742 Wayne Gomes **RC** (Draft Pick) .10
743 Pat Watkins **RC** (Draft Pick) .05
744 Jamey Wright **RC** (Draft Pick) .05
745 Jay Powell **RC** (Draft Pick) .05
746 Ryan McGuire **RC** (Draft Pick) .05
747 Marc Barcelo **RC** (Draft Pick) .05
748 Sloan Smith **RC** (Draft Pick) .05
749 John Wasdin **RC** (Draft Pick) .05
750 Marc Valdes (Draft Pick) .05
751 Dan Ehler **RC** (Draft Pick) .05
752 Andre King **RC** (Draft Pick) .05
753 Greg Keagle **RC** (Draft Pick) .05
754 Jason Myers **RC** (Draft Pick) .05
755 Dax Winslett **RC** (Draft Pick) .05
756 Casey Whitten **RC** (Draft Pick) .05
757 Tony Fuduric **RC** (Draft Pick) .05
758 Greg Norton **RC** (Draft Pick) .05
759 Jeff D'Amico **RC** (Draft Pick) .05
760 Ryan Hancock **RC** (Draft Pick) .05
761 David Cooper **RC** (Draft Pick) .05
762 Kevin Orie **RC** (Draft Pick) .05
763 John O'Donoghue, Mike Oquist (Coming Attractions) .05
764 Cory Bailey, Scott Hatteberg (Coming Attractions) .05
765 Mark Holzemer, Paul Swingle (Coming Attractions) .05
766 James Baldwin, Rod Bolton (Coming Attractions) .05
767 Jerry DiPoto **RC**, Julian Tavarez **RC** (Coming Attractions) .10
768 Danny Bautista, Sean Bergman (Coming Attractions) .05
769 Bob Hamelin, Joe Vitiello (Coming Attractions) .05
770 Mark Kiefer, Troy O'Leary (Coming Attractions) .05
771 Denny Hocking, Oscar Munoz (Coming Attractions) .05
772 Russ Davis, Brien Taylor (Coming Attractions) .05
773 Kurt Abbott, Miguel Jimenez (Coming Attractions) .05
774 Kevin King, Eric Plantenberg (Coming Attractions) .05
775 Jon Shave, Desi Wilson (Coming Attractions) .05
776 Domingo Cedeno, Paul Spoljaric (Coming Attractions) .05
777 Chipper Jones, Ryan Klesko (Coming Attractions) .60
778 Steve Trachsel, Turk Wendell (Coming Attractions) .05
779 Johnny Ruffin, Jerry Spradlin (Coming Attractions) .05
780 Jason Bates, John Burke (Coming Attractions) .05
781 Carl Everett, Dave Weathers (Coming Attractions) .05
782 Gary Mota, James Mouton (Coming Attractions) .05
783 Raul Mondesi, Ben Van Ryn (Coming Attractions) .05
784 Gabe White, Rondell White (Coming Attractions) .05
785 Brook Fordyce, Bill Pulsipher (Coming Attractions) .05
786 Kevin Foster, Gene Schall (Coming Attractions) .05
787 Rich Aude, Midre Cummings (Coming Attractions) .05
788 Brian Barber, Richard Batchelor (Coming Attractions) .05
789 Brian Johnson **RC**, Scott Sanders (Coming Attractions) .05
790 Rikkert Faneyte, J.R. Phillips (Coming Attractions) .05
791 Checklist 3 .05
792 Checklist 4 .05

Gold

This premium parallel set was issued as inserts in virtually all forms of Topps packaging. Identical in all other ways to the regular Topps cards, the Gold version replaces the white or black Topps logo on front with a gold-foil "Topps Gold" logo, and prints either the player name or card title in gold foil. The four checklist cards from the regular issue are replaced with cards of players not found in the regular Topps set.

	NM/M
Complete Set (792):	50.00
Common Player:	.15

Black Gold

Black Gold inserts returned for 1994 randomly included in all types of Topps packaging. Single cards, as well as cards redeemable by mail for 11, 22 or 44 Black Gold cards, were produced. The basic single-player card features an action photo, the background of which has been almost completely blacked out. At top is the team name in black letters against a gold prismatic foil background. The player name at bottom is in the same gold foil. On back, bordered in white, is a background which fades from black at top to gray at the bottom and is gridded with white lines. At left is another player action photo. The Topps Black Gold logo and player name appear in gold foil; the latter printed on a simulated wooden board "hanging" from the top of the card. A second hanging plank has player stats and rankings from the 1993 season. The multi-card redemption cards come in two versions. The type found in packs has all 11, 22 or 44 of the cards pictured on front in miniature and redemption details printed on back. A second version, returned with the single cards won, has on back a checklist and non-redemption notice. Stated odds of winning Black Gold cards were one in 72 packs for single cards; one in 180 packs for 11-card winners and one in 720 packs (one per foil-pack case) for a 22-card winner.

		NM/M
Complete Set (44):		10.00
Complete Series 1 (22):		6.00
Complete Series 2 (22):		4.00
Common Player:		.10
1	Roberto Alomar	.20
2	Carlos Baerga	.10
3	Albert Belle	.10
4	Joe Carter	.10
5	Cecil Fielder	.10
6	Travis Fryman	.10
7	Juan Gonzalez	.25
8	Ken Griffey Jr.	.75
9	Chris Hoiles	.10
10	Randy Johnson	.45
11	Kenny Lofton	.10
12	Jack McDowell	.10
13	Paul Molitor	.45
14	Jeff Montgomery	.10
15	John Olerud	.10
16	Rafael Palmeiro	.45
17	Kirby Puckett	.60
18	Cal Ripken, Jr.	1.50
19	Tim Salmon	.10
20	Mike Stanley	.10
21	Frank Thomas	.50
22	Robin Ventura	.10
23	Jeff Bagwell	.45
24	Jay Bell	.10
25	Craig Biggio	.10
26	Jeff Blauser	.10
27	Barry Bonds	1.50
28	Darren Daulton	.10
29	Len Dykstra	.10
30	Andres Galarraga	.10
31	Ron Gant	.10
32	Tom Glavine	.10
33	Mark Grace	.10
34	Marquis Grissom	.10
35	Gregg Jefferies	.10
36	Dave Justice	.10
37	John Kruk	.10
38	Greg Maddux	.60
39	Fred McGriff	.10
40	Randy Myers	.10
41	Mike Piazza	1.00
42	Sammy Sosa	.60
43	Robby Thompson	.10
44	Matt Williams	.10
---	Winner A	.50
---	Winner B	.50
---	Winner C	.50
---	Winner D	.50
---	Winner A/B	.60
---	Winner C/D	.60
---	Winner A/B/C/D	.75

Traded

Topps Traded features top prospects and rookies as well as traded veterans. Also included in the boxed set is an eight-card Topps Finest subset of six MVPs and two Rookie of the Year cards. Regular cards have the same design as the previously released '94 Topps set. "Anatomy of a

Trade" is a two-card subset that includes Roberto Kelly/Deion Sanders and Pedro Martinez/Delino DeShields on a split, puzzle-like front. There is also a Prospect card, showcasing a top prospect from AAA, AA and A, as well as a top-rated draft pick. In addition, there are 12 Draft Pick cards included in the Traded set. Finally, two cards pay tribute to Ryne Sandberg, one in a Phillies uniform, one with the Cubs.

		NM/M
Complete Set (140):		30.00
Common Player:		.05
1	Paul Wilson (Draft Pick)	.05
2	Bill Taylor	.05
3	Dan Wilson	.05
4	Mark Smith	.05
5	Toby Borland	.05
6	Dave Clark	.05
7	Denny Martinez	.05
8	Dave Gallagher	.05
9	Josias Manzanillo	.05
10	Brian Anderson	.05
11	Damon Berryhill	.05
12	Alex Cole	.05
13	Jacob Shumate (Draft Pick)	.05
14	Oddibe McDowell	.05
15	Willie Banks	.05
16	Jerry Browne	.05
17	Donnie Elliott	.05
18	Ellis Burks	.05
19	Chuck McElroy	.05
20	Luis Polonia	.05
21	Brian Harper	.05
22	Mark Portugal	.05
23	Dave Henderson	.05
24	Mark Acre	.05
25	Julio Franco	.05
26	Darren Hall	.05
27	Eric Anthony	.05
28	Sid Fernandez	.05
29	Rusty Greer **RC**	.25
30	Riccardo Ingram	.05
31	Gabe White	.05
32	Tim Belcher	.05
33	Terrence Long **RC** (Draft Pick)	1.00
34	Mark Dalesandro **RC**	.05
35	Mike Kelly	.05
36	Jack Morris	.05
37	Jeff Brantley	.05
38	Larry Barnes **RC** (Draft Pick)	.05
39	Brian Hunter	.05
40	Otis Nixon	.05
41	Bret Wagner (Draft Pick)	.05
42	Anatomy of a Trade (Pedro Martinez, Delino DeShields)	.25
43	Heathcliff Slocumb	.05
44	Ben Grieve **RC** (Draft Pick)	.35
45	John Hudek	.05
46	Shawon Dunston	.05
47	Greg Colbrunn	.05
48	Joey Hamilton	.05
49	Marvin Freeman	.05
50	Terry Mulholland	.05
51	Keith Mitchell	.05
52	Dwight Smith	.05
53	Shawn Boskie	.05
54	Kevin Witt **RC** (Draft Pick)	.05
55	Ron Gant	.05
56	1994 Prospects (Trenidad Hubbard, Jason Schmidt **RC**, Larry Sutton, Stephen Larkin)	10.00
57	Jody Reed	.05
58	Rick Helling	.05
59	John Powell (Draft Pick)	.05
60	Eddie Murray	.60
61	Joe Hall	.05
62	Jorge Fabregas	.05
63	Mike Mordecai	.05
64	Ed Vosberg	.05
65	Rickey Henderson	.60
66	Tim Grieve (Draft pick)	.05
67	Jon Lieber	.05
68	Chris Howard	.05
69	Matt Walbeck	.05
70	Chan Ho Park	.15
71	Bryan Eversgerd	.05
72	John Dettmer	.05
73	Erik Hanson	.05
74	Mike Thurman (Draft Pick)	.05
75	Bobby Ayala	.05
76	Rafael Palmeiro	.50
77	Bret Boone	.05
78	Paul Shuey (Future Star)	.05
79	Kevin Foster	.05
80	Dave Magadan	.05
81	Bip Roberts	.05
82	Howard Johnson	.05
83	Xavier Hernandez	.05
84	Ross Powell	.05
85	Doug Million **RC** (Draft Pick)	.05
86	Geronimo Berroa	.05
87	Mark Farris **RC** (Draft Pick)	.05
88	Butch Henry	.05
89	Junior Felix	.05
90	Bo Jackson	.10
91	Hector Carrasco	.05
92	Charlie O'Brien	.05
93	Omar Vizquel	.05
94	David Segui	.05
95	Dustin Hermanson (Draft Pick)	.05
96	Gar Finnvold	.05
97	Dave Stevens	.05
98	Corey Pointer (Draft Pick)	.05
99	Felix Fermin	.05
100	Lee Smith	.05
101	Reid Ryan (Draft Pick)	.15
102	Bobby Munoz	.05
103	Anatomy of a Trade (Deion Sanders, Roberto Kelly)	.05
104	Turner Ward	.05
105	William Van Landingham	.05
106	Vince Coleman	.05
107	Stan Javier	.05
108	Darrin Jackson	.05
109	C.J. Nitkowski (Draft Pick)	.05
110	Anthony Young	.05
111	Kurt Miller	.05
112	Paul Konerko **RC** (Draft Pick)	15.00
113	Walt Weiss	.05
114	Daryl Boston	.05
115	Will Clark	.05
116	Matt Smith **RC** (Draft Pick)	.05
117	Mark Leiter	.05
118	Gregg Olson	.05
119	Tony Pena	.05
120	Jose Vizcaino	.05
121	Rick White	.05
122	Rich Rowland	.05
123	Jeff Reboulet	.05
124	Greg Hibbard	.05
125	Chris Sabo	.05
126	Doug Jones	.05
127	Tony Fernandez	.05
128	Carlos Reyes	.05
129	Kevin Brown (Draft Pick)	.05
130	Commemorative (Ryne Sandberg)	1.00
131	Commemorative (Ryne Sandberg)	1.00
132	Checklist 1-132	.05

Traded Finest Inserts

Eight Finest cards were included in the 1994 Topps Traded set. Cards picture the player on a blue and gold background. Either Rookie of the Year or MVP is printed across the bottom opposite the player's name, indicating the player's candidacy for such an award in 1994. Backs offer a portrait photo, stats through the All-Star break and comments on the player's season to that point.

		NM/M
Complete Set (8):		6.00
Common Player:		.25
1	Greg Maddux	1.50
2	Mike Piazza	2.00
3	Matt Williams	.25
4	Raul Mondesi	.25
5	Ken Griffey Jr.	2.00
6	Kenny Lofton	.25
7	Frank Thomas	1.25
8	Manny Ramirez	1.00

Bilingual

Produced in a limited edition said to be 5,000 sets, this issue is a close parallel to the regular 1994 Topps baseball card issue. Each card is virtually identical to the regular Topps card except that backs are printed in English and Spanish. The set was test marketed in areas with a high percentage of Hispanic population and was also sold through Topps' Stadium Club. The bilingual edition was sold only in factory set form. A special feature of the set was the inclusion of 10 "Topps Leyendas/Legends" cards of former Latin stars.

		NM/M
Factory Set (792+10):		225.00
Common Player:		.50
1	Felipe Alou	3.00
2	Ruben Amaro	1.00
3	Luis Aparicio	7.50
4	Rod Carew	7.50
5	Chico Carrasquel	1.50
6	Orlando Cepeda	7.50
7	Juan Marichal	7.50
8	Minnie Minoso	6.00
9	Cookie Rojas	1.00
10	Luis Tiant	2.00

"1954" Archives

Marketed as "The Ultimate 1954 Series," the Archives set was a virtual reproduction of the popular 1954 Topps issue. Of the 250 cards in the original set, 248 were included in the Archives release. Ted Williams, who was on cards #1 and 250 in the '54 set, was contractually prohibited by Upper Deck from appearing in the Archives issue. Eight "1954 Prospect" cards featuring future Hall of Famers and star players were appended to the reproduction cards to create a 256-card Archives issue. Cards were sold in 12-card packs, with one Gold card in each pack. There were 1,954 personally autographed cards of Henry Aaron inserted at random, along with cards that could be redeemed for genuine 1954 Topps cards and complete sets of Gold Archives cards. The Archives cards were produced in the now-standard 2-1/2" x 3-1/2" size, instead of the original 1954 dimensions of 2-5/8" x 3-3/4". That format allowed the Archives cards to have a white border at top which the originals lack. While the card backs identify the Archives issue, they do not specify a 1994 production date anywhere.

		NM/M
Complete Set (256):		90.00
Common Player:		.25
Wax Pack (12):		4.00
Wax Box (24):		65.00
2	Gus Zernial	.25
3	Monte Irvin	.75
4	Hank Sauer	.25
5	Ed Lopat	.40
6	Pete Runnels	.25
7	Ted Kluszewski	.60
8	Bobby Young	.25
9	Harvey Haddix	.25
10	Jackie Robinson	4.50
11	Paul Smith	.25
12	Del Crandall	.25
13	Billy Martin	.60
14	Preacher Roe	.40
15	Al Rosen	.25
16	Vic Janowicz	.25
17	Phil Rizzuto	1.00
18	Walt Dropo	.25
19	Johnny Lipon	.25
20	Warren Spahn	.75
21	Bobby Shantz	.25
22	Jim Greengrass	.25
23	Luke Easter	.25
24	Granny Hamner	.25
25	Harvey Kuenn	.25
26	Ray Jablonski	.25
27	Ferris Fain	.25
28	Paul Minner	.25
29	Jim Hegan	.25
30	Eddie Mathews	.75
31	Johnny Klippstein	.25
32	Duke Snider	1.50
33	Johnny Schmitz	.25
34	Jim Rivera	.25
35	Junior Gilliam	.40
36	Hoyt Wilhelm	.75
37	Whitey Ford	1.25
38	Eddie Stanky	.25
39	Sherman Lollar	.25
40	Mel Parnell	.25
41	Willie Jones	.25
42	Don Mueller	.25
43	Dick Groat	.25
44	Ned Garver	.25
45	Richie Ashburn	.75
46	Ken Raffensberger	.25
47	Ellis Kinder	.25
48	Billy Hunter	.25
49	Ray Murray	.25
50	Yogi Berra	1.50
51	Johnny Lindell	.25
52	Vic Power	.25
53	Jack Dittmer	.25
54	Vern Stephens	.25
55	Phil Cavarretta	.25
56	Willie Miranda	.40
57	Luis Aloma	.25
58	Bob Wilson	.25
59	Gene Conley	.25
60	Frank Baumholtz	.25
61	Bob Cain	.25
62	Eddie Robinson	.40
63	Johnny Pesky	.25
64	Hank Thompson	.25
65	Bob Swift	.25
66	Ted Lepcio	.25
67	Jim Willis	.25
68	Sam Calderone	.25
69	Bud Podbielan	.25
70	Larry Doby	.75
71	Frank Smith	.25
72	Preston Ward	.25
73	Wayne Terwilliger	.25
74	Bill Taylor	.25
75	Fred Haney	.25
76	Bob Scheffing	.25
77	Ray Boone	.25
78	Ted Kazanski	.25
79	Andy Pafko	.25
80	Jackie Jensen	.25
81	Dave Hoskins	.25
82	Milt Bolling	.25
83	Joe Collins	.40
84	Dick Cole	.25
85	Bob Turley	.75
86	Billy Herman	.40
87	Roy Face	.25
88	Matt Batts	.25
89	Howie Pollet	.25
90	Willie Mays	4.50
91	Bob Oldis	.25
92	Wally Westlake	.25
93	Sid Hudson	.25
94	Ernie Banks	4.50
95	Hal Rice	.25
96	Charlie Silvera	.40
97	Jerry Lane	.25
98	Joe Black	.25
99	Bob Hofman	.25
100	Bob Keegan	.25
101	Gene Woodling	.40
102	Gil Hodges	1.25
103	Jim Lemon	.25
104	Mike Sandlock	.25
105	Andy Carey	.40
106	Dick Kokos	.25
107	Duane Pillette	.25
108	Thornton Kipper	.25
109	Bill Bruton	.25
110	Harry Dorish	.25
111	Jim Delsing	.25
112	Bill Renna	.25
113	Bob Boyd	.25
114	Dean Stone	.25
115	"Rip" Repulski	.25
116	Steve Bilko	.25
117	Solly Hemus	.25
118	Carl Scheib	.25
119	Johnny Antonelli	.25
120	Roy McMillan	.25
121	Clem Labine	.40
122	Johnny Logan	.25
123	Bobby Adams	.25
124	Marion Fricano	.25
125	Harry Perkowski	.25
126	Ben Wade	.25
127	Steve O'Neill	.25
128	Hank Aaron	7.50
129	Forrest Jacobs	.25
130	Hank Bauer	.75
131	Reno Bertoia	.25
132	Tom Lasorda	3.00
133	Del Baker	.25
134	Cal Hogue	.25
135	Joe Presko	.25
136	Connie Ryan	.25
137	Wally Moon	.25
138	Bob Borkowski	.25
139	Ed & Johnny O'Brien	.60
140	Tom Wright	.25
141	Joe Jay	.25
142	Tom Poholsky	.25
143	Rollie Hemsley	.25
144	Bill Werle	.25
145	Elmer Valo	.25
146	Don Johnson	.25
147	John Riddle	.25
148	Bob Trice	.25
149	Jim Robertson	.25
150	Dick Kryhoski	.25
151	Alex Grammas	.25
152	Mike Blyzka	.25
153	Rube Walker	.25
154	Mike Fornieles	.25
155	Bob Kennedy	.25
156	Joe Coleman	.25
157	Don Lenhardt	.25
158	Peanuts Lowrey	.25
159	Dave Philley	.25
160	Red Kress	.25
161	John Hetki	.25
162	Herman Wehmeier	.25
163	Frank House	.25
164	Stu Miller	.25
165	Jim Pendleton	.25
166	Johnny Podres	.40
167	Don Lund	.25
168	Morrie Martin	.25
169	Jim Hughes	.25
170	Dusty Rhodes	.25
171	Leo Kiely	.25
172	Hal Brown	.25
173	Jack Harshman	.25
174	Tom Qualters	.25
175	Frank Leja	.40
176	Bob Keely	.25
177	Bob Milliken	.25
178	Bill Glynn	.25
179	Gair Allie	.25
180	Wes Westrum	.25
181	Mel Roach	.25
182	Chuck Harmon	.25
183	Earle Combs	.25
184	Ed Bailey	.25
185	Chuck Stobbs	.25
186	Karl Olson	.25
187	Heinie Manush	.25
188	Dave Jolly	.25
189	Bob Ross	.25
190	Ray Herbert	.25
191	Dick Schofield	.25
192	Cot Deal	.25
193	Johnny Hopp	.25
194	Bill Sarni	.25
195	Bill Consolo	.25
196	Stan Jok	.25
197	Schoolboy Rowe	.25
198	Carl Sawatski	.25
199	Rocky Nelson	.25
200	Larry Jansen	.25
201	Al Kaline	4.50
202	Bob Purkey	.25
203	Harry Brecheen	.25
204	Angel Scull	.25
205	Johnny Sain	.40
206	Ray Crone	.25
207	Tom Oliver	.25
208	Grady Hatton	.25
209	Charlie Thompson	.25
210	Bob Buhl	.25
211	Don Hoak	.40
212	Mickey Micelotta	.25
213	John Fitzpatrick	.25
214	Arnold Portocarrero	.25
215	Ed McGhee	.25
216	Al Sima	.25
217	Paul Schreiber	.25
218	Fred Marsh	.25
219	Charlie Kress	.25
220	Ruben Gomez	.25
221	Dick Brodowski	.25
222	Bill Wilson	.25
223	Joe Haynes	.25
224	Dick Weik	.25
225	Don Liddle	.25
226	Jehosie Heard	.25
227	Buster Mills	.25
228	Gene Hermanski	.25
229	Bob Talbot	.25
230	Bob Kuzava	.40
231	Roy Smalley	.25
232	Lou Limmer	.25
233	Augie Galan	.25
234	Jerry Lynch	.25
235	Vern Law	.25
236	Paul Penson	.25
237	Mike Ryba	.25
238	Al Aber	.25
239	Bill Skowron	.75
240	Sam Mele	.25
241	Bob Miller	.25
242	Curt Roberts	.25
243	Ray Blades	.25
244	Leroy Wheat	.25
245	Roy Sievers	.25
246	Howie Fox	.25
247	Eddie Mayo	.25
248	Al Smith	.25
249	Wilmer Mizell	.25
251	Roberto Clemente	7.50
252	Bob Grim	.40
253	Elston Howard	.75
254	Harmon Killebrew	1.25
255	Camilo Pascual	.25
256	Herb Score	.25
257	Bill Virdon	.25
258	Don Zimmer	.50

"1954" Archives Gold

Issued as a premium insert at the rate of one per foil pack, gold versions of each of the cards in the 1954 Archives set differ from the regular cards only in that the team logo at top and player facsimile autograph on bottom are printed in gold foil. Redemption cards for complete Archives gold sets were also randomly inserted into Archives packs.

		NM/M
Complete Set (256):		150.00
Common Player:		.45
128	Hank Aaron/Auto.	125.00

1995 Topps Pre-production

The "Baker's Dozen" version of Topps' 1994 factory baseball card set includes a 10-card pre-production sample of the company's 1995 issue. The sample features nine regular-issue cards and one of them in its Spectralite foil-printed version, as used on the Cyberstats insert cards. Cards are virtually identical to the regular '95 Topps except the backs have a "PP" prefix to the card number and "PRE-PRODUCTION SAMPLE" instead of 1994 season stats.

		NM/M
Complete Set (9):		6.00
Complete Set, Cyberstats (9):		20.00
1	Larry Walker	.50
1	Larry Walker (Spectralite)	1.50
2	Mike Piazza	2.50
2	Mike Piazza (Spectralite)	7.50
3	Greg Vaughn	.50
3	Greg Vaughn (Spectralite)	1.50
4	Sandy Alomar Jr.	.50
4	Sandy Alomar Jr. (Spectralite)	1.50
5	Travis Fryman	.50
5	Travis Fryman (Spectralite)	1.50
6	Ken Griffey Jr.	2.50
6	Ken Griffey Jr. (Spectralite)	7.50
7	Mike Devereaux	.50
7	Mike Devereaux (Spectralite)	1.50
8	Roberto Hernandez	.50
8	Roberto Hernandez (Spectralite)	1.50
9	Alex Fernandez	.50
9	Alex Fernandez (Spectralite)	1.50

1995 Topps

Topps 1995 baseball arrived offering Cyberstats, which projected full-season statistics for the strike shortened year, as well as League Leaders and Stadium Club First Day Issue preproduction inserts. Series 1 comprises 396 cards, including subsets of Draft Picks, Star Tracks, a Babe Ruth commemorative card and the Topps All-Stars, featuring two players per card at each position. Regular cards have a ragged white border around the player photo, with his name in gold foil under the picture. Series 2 concluded the Cyberstats inserts and added 264 cards to the regular set. Subsets in Series 2 include a continuation of the Draft Picks as well as two-player On Deck cards and four-player Prospects cards, arranged by position. Besides the 660 base cards, hobby-version factory sets include 10 Stadium Club 1st Day previews and seven Cyberstat Season in Review cards. Two versions of the retail factory sets were made. One has 660 regular cards, 20 Cyberstats parallels and four League Leader inserts. The other has the base set of 660 plus 10 Opening Day cards and seven Cyberstat Season in Review.

		NM/M
Unopened Hobby Set (677):		100.00
Unopened Retail Set (684):		75.00
Unopened Retail Set (677):		85.00
Complete Set (660):		45.00
Common Player:		.05
Series 1 or 2 Pack (15):		1.25
Series 1 or 2 Wax Box (36):		25.00
1	Frank Thomas	.75
2	Mickey Morandini	.05
3a	Babe Ruth (100th Birthday, no gold "Topps" logo)	2.00
3b	Babe Ruth (100th Birthday, gold "Topps" logo)	2.00
4	Scott Cooper	.05
5	David Cone	.05
6	Jacob Shumate (Draft Pick)	.05
7	Trevor Hoffman	.05
8	Shane Mack	.05
9	Delino DeShields	.05
10	Matt Williams	.05
11	Sammy Sosa	1.00
12	Gary DiSarcina	.05
13	Kenny Rogers	.05
14	Jose Vizcaino	.05
15	Lou Whitaker	.05
16	Ron Darling	.05
17	Dave Nilsson	.05
18	Chris Hammond	.05
19	Sid Bream	.05
20	Denny Martinez	.05
21	Orlando Merced	.05
22	John Wetteland	.05
23	Mike Devereaux	.05
24	Rene Arocha	.05
25	Jay Buhner	.05
26	Darren Holmes	.05
27	Hal Morris	.05
28	Brian Buchanan **RC** (Draft Pick)	.10
29	Keith Miller	.05
30	Paul Molitor	.75
31	Dave West	.05
32	Tony Tarasco	.05
33	Scott Sanders	.05
34	Eddie Zambrano	.05
35	Ricky Bones	.05
36	John Valentin	.05
37	Kevin Tapani	.05
38	Tim Wallach	.05
39	Darren Lewis	.05
40	Travis Fryman	.05
41	Mark Leiter	.05
42	Jose Bautista	.05
43	Pete Smith	.05
44	Bret Barberie	.05
45	Dennis Eckersley	.65
46	Ken Hill	.05
47	Chad Ogea (Star Track)	.05
48	Pete Harnisch	.05
49	James Baldwin (Future Star)	.05
50	Mike Mussina	.45
51	Al Martin	.05
52	Mark Thompson (Star Track)	.05
53	Matt Smith (Draft Pick)	.05
54	Joey Hamilton (All Star Rookie)	.05
55	Edgar Martinez	.05
56	John Smiley	.05
57	Rey Sanchez	.05
58	Mike Timlin	.05
59	Ricky Bottalico (Star Track)	.05
60	Jim Abbott	.05
61	Mike Kelly	.05
62	Brian Jordan	.05
63	Ken Ryan	.05
64	Matt Mieske	.05
65	Rick Aguilera	.05
66	Ismael Valdes	.05
67	Royce Clayton	.05
68	Junior Felix	.05
69	Harold Reynolds	.05
70	Juan Gonzalez	.35
71	Kelly Stinnett	.05
72	Carlos Reyes	.05
73	Dave Weathers	.05
74	Mel Rojas	.05
75	Doug Drabek	.05
76	Charles Nagy	.05
77	Tim Raines	.05
78	Midre Cummings	.05
79	1B Prospects (Gene Schall, Scott Talanoa **RC**, Harold Williams **RC**, Ray Brown **RC**)	.05
80	Rafael Palmeiro	.65
81	Charlie Hayes	.05
82	Ray Lankford	.05
83	Tim Davis	.05
84	C.J. Nitkowski **RC** (Draft Pick)	.05
85	Andy Ashby	.05
86	Gerald Williams	.05
87	Terry Shumpert	.05
88	Heathcliff Slocumb	.05
89	Domingo Cedeno	.05
90	Mark Grace	.05
91	Brad Woodall **RC** (Star Track)	.10
92	Gar Finnvold	.05
93	Jaime Navarro	.05
94	Carlos Hernandez	.05
95	Mark Langston	.05
96	Chuck Carr	.05
97	Mike Gardiner	.05
98	David McCarty	.05
99	Cris Carpenter	.05
100	Barry Bonds	2.00
101	David Segui	.05
102	Scott Brosius	.05
103	Mariano Duncan	.05
104	Kenny Lofton	.05
105	Ken Caminiti	.05
106	Darrin Jackson	.05
107	Jim Poole	.05
108	Wil Cordero	.05
109	Danny Miceli	.05
110	Walt Weiss	.05
111	Tom Pagnozzi	.05
112	Terrence Long (Draft Pick)	.05
113	Bret Boone	.05
114	Daryl Boston	.05
115	Wally Joyner	.05
116	Rob Butler	.05
117	Rafael Belliard	.05
118	Luis Lopez	.05
119	Tony Fossas	.05
120	Len Dykstra	.05
121	Mike Morgan	.05
122	Denny Hocking	.05
123	Kevin Gross	.05
124	Todd Benzinger	.05
125	John Doherty	.05
126	Eduardo Perez	.05
127	Dan Smith	.05
128	Joe Orsulak	.05
129	Brent Gates	.05
130	Jeff Conine	.05
131	Doug Henry	.05
132	Paul Sorrento	.05
133	Mike Hampton	.05
134	Tim Spehr	.05
135	Julio Franco	.05
136	Mike Dyer	.05
137	Chris Sabo	.05
138	Rheal Cormier	.05
139	Paul Konerko (Draft Pick)	.25
140	Dante Bichette	.05
141	Chuck McElroy	.05
142	Mike Stanley	.05
143	Bob Hamelin (All Star Rookie)	.05
144	Tommy Greene	.05
145	John Smoltz	.05
146	Ed Sprague	.05
147	Ray McDavid (Star Track)	.05
148	Otis Nixon	.05
149	Turk Wendell	.05
150	Chris James	.05
151	Derek Parks	.05
152	Jose Offerman	.05
153	Tony Clark (Future Star)	.05
154	Chad Curtis	.05
155	Mark Portugal	.05
156	Bill Pulsipher (Future Star)	.05
157	Troy Neel	.05
158	Dave Winfield	.75
159	Bill Wegman	.05
160	Benny Santiago	.05
161	Jose Mesa	.05
162	Luis Gonzalez	.05
163	Alex Fernandez	.05
164	Freddie Benavides	.05
165	Ben McDonald	.05
166	Blas Minor	.05
167	Bret Wagner (Draft Pick)	.05
168	Mac Suzuki (Future Star)	.05
169	Roberto Mejia	.05
170	Wade Boggs	1.00
171	Calvin Reese (Future Star)	.05
172	Hipolito Pichardo	.05
173	Kim Batiste	.05
174	Darren Hall	.05
175	Tom Glavine	.25
176	Phil Plantier	.05
177	Chris Howard	.05
178	Karl Rhodes	.05
179	LaTroy Hawkins (Future Star)	.05
180	Raul Mondesi (All Star Rookie)	.05
181	Jeff Reed	.05
182	Milt Cuyler	.05
183	Jim Edmonds	.05
184	Hector Fajardo	.05
185	Jeff Kent	.05
186	Wilson Alvarez	.05
187	Geronimo Berroa	.05
188	Billy Spiers	.05
189	Derek Lilliquist	.05
190	Craig Biggio	.05
191	Roberto Hernandez	.05
192	Bob Natal	.05
193	Bobby Ayala	.05
194	Travis Miller **RC** (Draft Pick)	.10
195	Bob Tewksbury	.05
196	Rondell White	.05
197	Steve Cooke	.05
198	Jeff Branson	.05
199	Derek Jeter (Future Star)	2.00
200	Tim Salmon	.05
201	Steve Frey	.05
202	Kent Mercker	.05
203	Randy Johnson	.75
204	Todd Worrell	.05

205 Mo Vaughn .05
206 Howard Johnson .05
207 John Wasdin (Future Star) .05
208 Eddie Williams .05
209 Tim Belcher .05
210 Jeff Montgomery .05
211 Kirt Manwaring .05
212 Ben Grieve (Draft Pick) .05
213 Pat Hentgen .05
214 Shawon Dunston .05
215 Mike Greenwell .05
216 Alex Diaz .05
217 Pat Mahomes .05
218 Dave Hanson .05
219 Kevin Rogers .05
220 Cecil Fielder .05
221 Andrew Lorraine (Star Track) .05
222 Jack Armstrong .05
223 Todd Hundley .05
224 Mark Acre .05
225 Darrell Whitmore .05
226 Randy Milligan .05
227 Wayne Kirby .05
228 Darryl Kile .05
229 Bob Zupcic .05
230 Jay Bell .05
231 Dustin Hermanson (Draft Pick) .05
232 Harold Baines .05
233 Alan Benes (Future Star) .05
234 Felix Fermin .05
235 Ellis Burks .05
236 Jeff Brantley .05
237 OF Prospects (Brian Hunter, Jose Malave, Shane Pullen, Karim Garcia **RC**) .40
238 Matt Nokes .05
239 Ben Rivera .05
240 Joe Carter .05
241 Jeff Granger (Star Track) .05
242 Terry Pendleton .05
243 Melvin Nieves .05
244 Frank Rodriguez (Future Star) .05
245 Darryl Hamilton .05
246 Brooks Kieschnick (Future Star) .05
247 Todd Hollandsworth (Future Star) .05
248 Joe Rosselli (Future Star) .05
249 Bill Gullickson .05
250 Chuck Knoblauch .05
251 Kurt Miller (Star Track) .05
252 Bobby Jones .05
253 Lance Blankenship .05
254 Matt Whiteside .05
255 Darrin Fletcher .05
256 Eric Plunk .05
257 Shane Reynolds .05
258 Norberto Martin .05
259 Mike Thurman (Draft Pick) .05
260 Andy Van Slyke .05
261 Dwight Smith .05
262 Allen Watson .05
263 Dan Wilson .05
264 Brent Mayne .05
265 Bip Roberts .05
266 Sterling Hitchcock .05
267 Alex Gonzalez (Star Track) .05
268 Greg Harris .05
269 Ricky Jordan .05
270 Johnny Ruffin .05
271 Mike Stanton .05
272 Rich Rowland .05
273 Steve Trachsel .05
274 Pedro Munoz .05
275 Ramon Martinez .05
276 Dave Henderson .05
277 Chris Gomez (All Star Rookie) .05
278 Joe Grahe .05
279 Rusty Greer .05
280 John Franco .05
281 Mike Bordick .05
282 Jeff D'Amico (Future Star) .05
283 Dave Magadan .05
284 Tony Pena .05
285 Greg Swindell .05
286 Doug Million (Draft Pick) .05
287 Gabe White (Star Track) .05
288 Trey Beamon (Future Star) .05
289 Arthur Rhodes .05
290 Juan Guzman .05
291 Jose Oquendo .05
292 Willie Blair .05
293 Eddie Taubensee .05
294 Steve Howe .05
295 Greg Maddux 1.00
296 Mike MacFarlane .05
297 Curt Schilling .25
298 Phil Clark .05
299 Woody Williams .05
300 Jose Canseco .40
301 Aaron Sele .05
302 Carl Willis .05
303 Steve Buechele .05
304 Dave Burba .05
305 Orel Hershiser .05
306 Damion Easley .05
307 Mike Henneman .05
308 Josias Manzanillo .05
309 Kevin Seitzer .05
310 Ruben Sierra .05
311 Bryan Harvey .05
312 Jim Thome .45
313 Ramon Castro **RC** (Draft Pick) .05
314 Lance Johnson .05
315 Marquis Grissom .05
316 SP Prospects (Terrell Wade, Juan Acevedo, Matt Arrandale, Eddie Priest **RC**) .05
317 Paul Wagner .05
318 Jamie Moyer .05
319 Todd Zeile .05
320 Chris Bosio .05
321 Steve Reed .05
322 Erik Hanson .05
323 Luis Polonia .05
324 Ryan Klesko .05
325 Kevin Appier .05
326 Jim Eisenreich .05
327 Randy Knorr .05
328 Craig Shipley .05
329 Tim Naehring .05
330 Randy Myers .05
331 Alex Cole .05
332 Jim Gott .05
333 Mike Jackson .05
334 John Flaherty .05
335 Chili Davis .05
336 Benji Gil (Star Track) .05
337a Jason Jacome (No Diamond Vision logo on back photo.) .25
337b Jason Jacome (Diamond Vision logo on back photo.) .05
338 Stan Javier .05
339 Mike Fetters .05
340 Rick Renteria .05
341 Kevin Witt (Draft Pick) .05
342 Scott Servais .05
343 Craig Grebeck .05
344 Kirk Rueter .05
345 Don Slaught .05
346 Armando Benitez **RC** (Star Track) .15
347 Ozzie Smith 1.00
348 Mike Blowers .05
349 Armando Reynoso .05
350 Barry Larkin .05
351 Mike Williams .05
352 Scott Kamieniecki .05
353 Gary Gaetti .05
354 Todd Stottlemyre .05
355 Fred McGriff .05
356 Tim Mauser .05
357 Chris Gwynn .05
358 Frank Castillo .05
359 Jeff Reboulet .05
360 Roger Clemens 1.00
361 Mark Carreon .05
362 Chad Kreuter .05
363 Mark Farris (Draft Pick) .05
364 Bob Welch .05
365 Dean Palmer .05
366 Jeromy Burnitz .05
367 B.J. Surhoff .05
368 Mike Butcher .05
369 RP Prospects (Brad Clontz, Steve Phoenix, Scott Gentile, Bucky Buckles) .05
370 Eddie Murray .75
371 Orlando Miller (Star Track) .05
372 Ron Karkovice .05
373 Richie Lewis .05
374 Lenny Webster .05
375 Jeff Tackett .05
376 Tom Urbani .05
377 Tino Martinez .05
378 Mark Dewey .05
379 Charlie O'Brien .05
380 Terry Mulholland .05
381 Thomas Howard .05
382 Chris Haney .05
383 Billy Hatcher .05
384 Jeff Bagwell, Frank Thomas/AS .45
385 Bret Boone, Carlos Baerga/AS .05
386 Matt Williams, Wade Boggs/AS .30
387 Wil Cordero, Cal Ripken Jr./AS 1.00
388 Barry Bonds, Ken Griffey Jr./AS 1.00
389 Tony Gwynn, Albert Belle/AS .50
390 Dante Bichette, Kirby Puckett/AS .50
391 Mike Piazza, Mike Stanley/AS .75
392 Greg Maddux, David Cone/AS .50
393 Danny Jackson, Jimmy Key/AS .05
394 John Franco, Lee Smith/AS .05
395 Checklist 1-198 .05
396 Checklist 199-396 .05
397 Ken Griffey Jr. 1.25
398 Rick Heiserman **RC** (Draft Pick) .05
399 Don Mattingly 1.00
400 Henry Rodriguez .05
401 Lenny Harris .05
402 Ryan Thompson .05
403 Darren Oliver .05
404 Omar Vizquel .05
405 Jeff Bagwell .75
406 Doug Webb **RC** (Draft Pick) .05
407 Todd Van Poppel .05
408 Leo Gomez .05
409 Mark Whiten .05
410 Pedro Martinez .05
411 Reggie Sanders .05
412 Kevin Foster .05
413 Danny Tartabull .05
414 Jeff Blauser .05
415 Mike Magnante .05
416 Tom Candiotti .05
417 Rod Beck .05
418 Jody Reed .05
419 Vince Coleman .05
420 Danny Jackson .05
421 Ryan Nye **RC** (Draft Pick) .05
422 Larry Walker .05
423 Russ Johnson (Draft Pick) .05
424 Pat Borders .05
425 Lee Smith .05
426 Paul O'Neill .05
427 Devon White .05
428 Jim Bullinger .05
429 SP Prospects (Greg Hansell, Brian Sackinsky, Carey Paige, Rob Welch) .05
430 Steve Avery .05
431 Tony Gwynn 1.00
432 Pat Meares .05
433 Bill Swift .05
434 David Wells .05
435 John Briscoe .05
436 Roger Pavlik .05
437 Jayson Peterson **RC** (Draft Pick) .05
438 Roberto Alomar .15
439 Billy Brewer .05
440 Gary Sheffield .40
441 Lou Frazier .05
442 Terry Steinbach .05
443 Jay Payton **RC** (Draft Pick) .25
444 Jason Bere .05
445 Denny Neagle .05
446 Andres Galarraga .05
447 Hector Carrasco .05
448 Bill Risley .05
449 Andy Benes .05
450 Jim Leyritz .05
451 Jose Oliva .05
452 Greg Vaughn .05
453 Rich Monteleone .05
454 Tony Eusebio .05
455 Chuck Finley .05
456 Kevin Brown .05
457 Joe Boever .05
458 Bobby Munoz .05
459 Bret Saberhagen .05
460 Kurt Abbott .05
461 Bobby Witt .05
462 Cliff Floyd .05
463 Mark Clark .05
464 Andujar Cedeno .05
465 Marvin Freeman .05
466 Mike Piazza 1.25
467 Willie Greene .05
468 Pat Kelly .05
469 Carlos Delgado .40
470 Willie Banks .05
471 Matt Walbeck .05
472 Mark McGwire 1.50
473 McKay Christensen (Draft Pick) .05
474 Alan Trammell .05
475 Tom Gordon .05
476 Greg Colbrunn .05
477 Darren Daulton .05
478 Albie Lopez .05
479 Robin Ventura .05
480 C Prospects (Eddie Perez **RC**, Jason Kendall, Einar Diaz **RC**, Bret Hemphill) .20
481 Bryan Eversgerd .05
482 Dave Fleming .05
483 Scott Livingstone .05
484 Pete Schourek .05
485 Bernie Williams .05
486 Mark Lemke .05
487 Eric Karros .05
488 Scott Ruffcorn .05
489 Billy Ashley .05
490 Rico Brogna .05
491 John Burkett .05
492 Cade Gaspar **RC** (Draft Pick) .05
493 Jorge Fabregas .05
494 Greg Gagne .05
495 Doug Jones .05
496 Troy O'Leary .05
497 Pat Rapp .05
498 Butch Henry .05
499 John Olerud .05
500 John Hudek .05
501 Jeff King .05
502 Bobby Bonilla .05
503 Albert Belle .05
504 Rick Wilkins .05
505 John Jaha .05
506 Nigel Wilson .05
507 Sid Fernandez .05
508 Deion Sanders .05
509 Gil Heredia .05
510 Scott Elarton **RC** (Draft Pick) .10
511 Melido Perez .05
512 Greg McMichael .05
513 Rusty Meacham .05
514 Shawn Green .35
515 Carlos Garcia .05
516 Dave Stevens .05
517 Eric Young .05
518 Omar Daal .05
519 Kirk Gibson .05
520 Spike Owen .05
521 Jacob Cruz **RC** (Draft Pick) .05
522 Sandy Alomar .05
523 Steve Bedrosian .05
524 Ricky Gutierrez .05
525 Dave Veres .05
526 Gregg Jefferies .05
527 Jose Valentin .05
528 Robb Nen .05
529 Jose Rijo .05
530 Sean Berry .05
531 Mike Gallego .05
532 Roberto Kelly .05
533 Kevin Stocker .05
534 Kirby Puckett 1.00
535 Chipper Jones 1.00
536 Russ Davis .05
537 Jon Lieber .05
538 Trey Moore **RC** (Draft Pick) .05
539 Joe Girardi .05
540 2B Prospects (Quilvio Veras, Arquimedez Pozo, Miguel Cairo, Jason Camilli) .05
541 Tony Phillips .05
542 Brian Anderson .05
543 Ivan Rodriguez .65
544 Jeff Cirillo .05
545 Joey Cora .05
546 Chris Hoiles .05
547 Bernard Gilkey .05
548 Mike Lansing .05
549 Jimmy Key .05
550 Mark Wohlers .05
551 Chris Clemons **RC** (Draft Pick) .05
552 Vinny Castilla .05
553 Mark Guthrie .05
554 Mike Lieberthal .05
555 Tommy Davis **RC** (Draft Pick) .05
556 Robby Thompson .05
557 Danny Bautista .05
558 Will Clark .05
559 Rickey Henderson .75
560 Todd Jones .05
561 Jack McDowell .05
562 Carlos Rodriguez .05
563 Mark Eichhorn .05
564 Jeff Nelson .05
565 Eric Anthony .05
566 Randy Velarde .05
567 Javy Lopez .05
568 Kevin Mitchell .05
569 Steve Karsay .05
570 Brian Meadows **RC** (Draft Pick) .10
571 SS Prospects (Rey Ordonez **RC**, Mike Metcalfe, Ray Holbert, Kevin Orie) .40
572 John Kruk .05
573 Scott Leius .05
574 John Patterson .05
575 Kevin Brown .05
576 Mike Moore .05
577 Manny Ramirez .75
578 Jose Lind .05
579 Derrick May .05
580 Cal Eldred .05
581 3B Prospects (David Bell, Joel Chelmis, Lino Diaz, Aaron Boone **RC**) .15
582 J.T. Snow .05
583 Luis Sojo .05
584 Moises Alou .05
585 Dave Clark .05
586 Dave Hollins .05
587 Nomar Garciaparra (Draft Pick) 2.00
588 Cal Ripken Jr. 2.00
589 Pedro Astacio .05
590 J.R. Phillips .05
591 Jeff Frye .05
592 Bo Jackson .10
593 Steve Ontiveros .05
594 David Nied .05
595 Brad Ausmus .05
596 Carlos Baerga .05
597 James Mouton .05
598 Ozzie Guillen .05
599 OF Prospects (Ozzie Timmons, Curtis Goodwin, Johnny Damon, Jeff Abbott **RC**) .25
600 Yorkis Perez .05
601 Rich Rodriguez .05
602 Mark McLemore .05
603 Jeff Fassero .05
604 John Roper .05
605 Mark Johnson **RC** (Draft Pick) .10
606 Wes Chamberlain .05
607 Felix Jose .05
608 Tony Longmire .05
609 Duane Ward .05
610 Brett Butler .05
611 William Van Landingham .05
612 Mickey Tettleton .05
613 Brady Anderson .05
614 Reggie Jefferson .05
615 Mike Kingery .05
616 Derek Bell .05
617 Scott Erickson .05
618 Bob Wickman .05
619 Phil Leftwich .05
620 Dave Justice .05
621 Paul Wilson (Draft Pick) .05
622 Pedro Martinez .75
623 Terry Mathews .05
624 Brian McRae .05
625 Bruce Ruffin .05
626 Steve Finley .05
627 Ron Gant .05
628 Rafael Bournigal .05
629 Darryl Strawberry .05
630 Luis Alicea .05
631 Mark Smith, Scott Klingenbeck (On Deck) .05
632 Cory Bailey, Scott Hatteberg (On Deck) .05
633 Todd Greene, Troy Percival (On Deck) .05
634 Rod Bolton, Olmedo Saenz (On Deck) .05
635 Herb Perry, Steve Kline (On Deck) .05
636 Sean Bergman, Shannon Penn (On Deck) .05
637 Joe Vitiello, Joe Randa (On Deck) .05
638 Jose Mercedes, Duane Singleton (On Deck) .05
639 Marty Cordova, Marc Barcelo (On Deck) .10
640 Ruben Rivera, Andy Pettitte (On Deck) .10
641 Willie Adams, Scott Spiezio (On Deck) .05
642 Eddie Diaz, Desi Relaford (On Deck) .05
643 Jon Shave, Terrell Lowery (On Deck) .05
644 Paul Spoljaric, Angel Martinez (On Deck) .05
645 Damon Hollins, Tony Graffanino (On Deck) .05
646 Darron Cox, Doug Glanville (On Deck) .05
647 Tim Belk, Pat Watkins (On Deck) .05
648 Rod Pedraza, Phil Schneider (On Deck) .05
649 Marc Valdes, Vic Darensbourg (On Deck) .05
650 Rick Huisman, Roberto Petagine (On Deck) .05
651 Ron Coomer, Roger Cedeno (On Deck) .05
652 Carlos Perez **RC**, Shane Andrews (On Deck) .10
653 Jason Isringhausen, Chris Roberts (On Deck) .05
654 Kevin Jordan, Wayne Gomes (On Deck) .05
655 Esteban Loaiza, Steve Pegues (On Deck) .05
656 John Frascatore, Terry Bradshaw (On Deck) .05
657 Bryce Florie, Andres Berumen (On Deck) .05
658 Keith Williams, Dan Carlson (On Deck) .05
659 Checklist .05
660 Checklist .05

Cyberstats

Inserted into all types of Topps packaging at the rate of about one per 15 cards, this special series attempted to "complete" the statistics from the strike-shortened 1994 baseball season for nearly 400 players. Topps used computer modeling to predict how each player would have ended the season. Fronts of the cards are the same as found in the regular Topps set, except they have been printed on metallic foil. Backs have a black background.

NM/M
Complete Set (396): 25.00
Common Player: .10
1 Frank Thomas .75
2 Mickey Morandini .10
3 Todd Worrell .10
4 David Cone .10
5 Trevor Hoffman .10
6 Shane Mack .10
7 Delino DeShields .10
8 Matt Williams .10
9 Sammy Sosa 1.00
10 Gary DiSarcina .10
11 Kenny Rogers .10
12 Jose Vizcaino .10
13 Lou Whitaker .10
14 Ron Darling .10
15 Dave Nilsson .10
16 Dennis Martinez .10
17 Orlando Merced .10
18 John Wetteland .10
19 Mike Devereaux .10
20 Rene Arocha .10
21 Jay Buhner .10
22 Hal Morris .10
23 Paul Molitor .75
24 Dave West .10
25 Scott Sanders .10
26 Eddie Zambrano .10
27 Ricky Bones .10
28 John Valentin .10
29 Kevin Tapani .10
30 Tim Wallach .10
31 Darren Lewis .10
32 Travis Fryman .10
33 Bret Barberie .10
34 Dennis Eckersley .65
35 Ken Hill .10
36 Pete Harnisch .10
37 Mike Mussina .50
38 Dave Winfield .75
39 Joey Hamilton .10
40 Edgar Martinez .10
41 John Smiley .10
42 Jim Abbott .10
43 Mike Kelly .10
44 Brian Jordan .10
45 Ken Ryan .10
46 Matt Mieske .10
47 Rick Aguilera .10
48 Ismael Valdes .10
49 Royce Clayton .10
50 Juan Gonzalez .35
51 Mel Rojas .10
52 Doug Drabek .10
53 Charles Nagy .10
54 Tim Raines .10
55 Midre Cummings .10
56 Rafael Palmeiro .65
57 Charlie Hayes .10
58 Ray Lankford .10
59 Tim Davis .10
60 Andy Ashby .10
61 Mark Grace .10
62 Mark Langston .10
63 Chuck Carr .10
64 Barry Bonds 2.00
65 David Segui .10
66 Mariano Duncan .10
67 Kenny Lofton .10
68 Ken Caminiti .10
69 Darrin Jackson .10
70 Wil Cordero .10
71 Walt Weiss .10
72 Tom Pagnozzi .10
73 Bret Boone .10
74 Wally Joyner .10
75 Luis Lopez .10

No.	Player	Price
76	Len Dykstra	.10
77	Pedro Munoz	.10
78	Kevin Gross	.10
79	Eduardo Perez	.10
80	Brent Gates	.10
81	Jeff Conine	.10
82	Paul Sorrento	.10
83	Julio Franco	.10
84	Chris Sabo	.10
85	Dante Bichette	.10
86	Mike Stanley	.10
87	Bob Hamelin	.10
88	Tommy Greene	.10
89	Jeff Brantley	.10
90	Ed Sprague	.10
91	Otis Nixon	.10
92	Chad Curtis	.10
93	Chuck McElroy	.10
94	Troy Neel	.10
95	Benito Santiago	.10
96	Jose Mesa	.10
97	Luis Gonzalez	.10
98	Alex Fernandez	.10
99	Ben McDonald	.10
100	Wade Boggs	1.00
101	Tom Glavine	.35
102	Phil Plantier	.10
103	Raul Mondesi	.10
104	Jim Edmonds	.10
105	Jeff Kent	.10
106	Wilson Alvarez	.10
107	Geronimo Berroa	.10
108	Craig Biggio	.10
109	Roberto Hernandez	.10
110	Bobby Ayala	.10
111	Bob Tewksbury	.10
112	Rondell White	.10
113	Steve Cooke	.10
114	Tim Salmon	.10
115	Kent Mercker	.10
116	Randy Johnson	.75
117	Mo Vaughn	.10
118	Eddie Williams	.10
119	Jeff Montgomery	.10
120	Kirt Manwaring	.10
121	Pat Hentgen	.10
122	Shawon Dunston	.10
123	Tim Belcher	.10
124	Cecil Fielder	.10
125	Todd Hundley	.10
126	Mark Acre	.10
127	Darrell Whitmore	.10
128	Darryl Kile	.10
129	Jay Bell	.10
130	Harold Baines	.10
131	Felix Fermin	.10
132	Ellis Burks	.10
133	Joe Carter	.10
134	Terry Pendleton	.10
135	Junior Felix	.10
136	Bill Gullickson	.10
137	Melvin Nieves	.10
138	Chuck Knoblauch	.10
139	Bobby Jones	.10
140	Darrin Fletcher	.10
141	Andy Van Slyke	.10
142	Allen Watson	.10
143	Dan Wilson	.10
144	Bip Roberts	.10
145	Sterling Hitchcock	.10
146	Johnny Ruffin	.10
147	Steve Trachsel	.10
148	Ramon Martinez	.10
149	Dave Henderson	.10
150	Chris Gomez	.10
151	Rusty Greer	.10
152	John Franco	.10
153	Mike Bordick	.10
154	Dave Magadan	.10
155	Greg Swindell	.10
156	Arthur Rhodes	.10
157	Juan Guzman	.10
158	Greg Maddux	1.00
159	Mike Macfarlane	.10
160	Curt Schilling	.35
161	Jose Canseco	.40
162	Aaron Sele	.10
163	Steve Buechele	.10
164	Orel Hershiser	.10
165	Mike Henneman	.10
166	Kevin Seitzer	.10
167	Ruben Sierra	.10
168	Alex Cole	.10
169	Jim Thome	.65
170	Lance Johnson	.10
171	Marquis Grissom	.10
172	Jamie Moyer	.10
173	Todd Zeile	.10
174	Chris Bosio	.10
175	Steve Howe	.10
176	Luis Polonia	.10
177	Ryan Klesko	.10
178	Kevin Appier	.10
179	Tim Naehring	.10
180	Randy Myers	.10
181	Mike Jackson	.10
182	Chili Davis	.10
183	Jason Jacome	.10
184	Stan Javier	.10
185	Scott Servais	.10
186	Kirk Rueter	.10
187	Don Slaught	.10
188	Ozzie Smith	1.00
189	Barry Larkin	.10
190	Gary Gaetti	.10
191	Fred McGriff	.10
192	Roger Clemens	1.00
193	Dean Palmer	.10
194	Jeromy Burnitz	.10
195	Scott Kamieniecki	.10
196	Eddie Murray	.75
197	Ron Karkovice	.10
198	Tino Martinez	.10
199	Ken Griffey Jr.	1.25
200	Don Mattingly	1.00
201	Henry Rodriguez	.10
202	Lenny Harris	.10
203	Ryan Thompson	.10
204	Darren Oliver	.10
205	Omar Vizquel	.10
206	Jeff Bagwell	.75
207	Todd Van Poppel	.10
208	Leo Gomez	.10
209	Mark Whiten	.10
210	Pedro Martinez	.10
211	Reggie Sanders	.10
212	Kevin Foster	.10
213	Danny Tartabull	.10
214	Jeff Blauser	.10
215	Mike Magnante	.10
216	Tom Candiotti	.10
217	Rod Beck	.10
218	Jody Reed	.10
219	Vince Coleman	.10
220	Danny Jackson	.10
221	Larry Walker	.10
222	Pat Borders	.10
223	Lee Smith	.10
224	Paul O'Neill	.10
225	Devon White	.10
226	Jim Bullinger	.10
227	Steve Avery	.10
228	Tony Gwynn	1.00
229	Pat Meares	.10
230	Bill Swift	.10
231	David Wells	.10
232	John Briscoe	.10
233	Roger Pavlik	.10
234	Roberto Alomar	.30
235	Billy Brewer	.10
236	Gary Sheffield	.40
237	Lou Frazier	.10
238	Terry Steinbach	.10
239	Omar Daal	.10
240	Jason Bere	.10
241	Denny Neagle	.10
242	Danny Bautista	.10
243	Hector Carrasco	.10
244	Bill Risley	.10
245	Andy Benes	.10
246	Jim Leyritz	.10
247	Jose Oliva	.10
248	Greg Vaughn	.10
249	Rich Monteleone	.10
250	Tony Eusebio	.10
251	Chuck Finley	.10
252	Joe Boever	.10
253	Bobby Munoz	.10
254	Bret Saberhagen	.10
255	Kurt Abbott	.10
256	Bobby Witt	.10
257	Cliff Floyd	.10
258	Mark Clark	.10
259	Andujar Cedeno	.10
260	Marvin Freeman	.10
261	Mike Piazza	1.25
262	Pat Kelly	.10
263	Carlos Delgado	.45
264	Willie Banks	.10
265	Matt Walbeck	.10
266	Mark McGwire	1.50
267	Alan Trammell	.10
268	Tom Gordon	.10
269	Greg Colbrunn	.10
270	Darren Daulton	.10
271	Albie Lopez	.10
272	Robin Ventura	.10
273	Bryan Eversgerd	.10
274	Dave Fleming	.10
275	Scott Livingstone	.10
276	Pete Schourek	.10
277	Bernie Williams	.10
278	Mark Lemke	.10
279	Eric Karros	.10
280	Billy Ashley	.10
281	Rico Brogna	.10
282	John Burkett	.10
283	Jorge Fabregas	.10
284	Greg Gagne	.10
285	Doug Jones	.10
286	Troy O'Leary	.10
287	Pat Rapp	.10
288	Butch Henry	.10
289	John Olerud	.10
290	John Hudek	.10
291	Jeff King	.10
292	Bobby Bonilla	.10
293	Albert Belle	.10
294	Rick Wilkins	.10
295	John Jaha	.10
296	Sid Fernandez	.10
297	Deion Sanders	.10
298	Gil Heredia	.10
299	Melido Perez	.10
300	Greg McMichael	.10
301	Rusty Meacham	.10
302	Shawn Green	.35
303	Carlos Garcia	.10
304	Dave Stevens	.10
305	Eric Young	.10
306	Kirk Gibson	.10
307	Spike Owen	.10
308	Sandy Alomar	.10
309	Ricky Gutierrez	.10
310	Dave Veres	.10
311	Gregg Jefferies	.10
312	Jose Valentin	.10
313	Robb Nen	.10
314	Jose Rijo	.10
315	Sean Berry	.10
316	Mike Gallego	.10
317	Roberto Kelly	.10
318	Kevin Stocker	.10
319	Kirby Puckett	1.00
320	Jon Lieber	.10
321	Joe Girardi	.10
322	Tony Phillips	.10
323	Brian Anderson	.10
324	Ivan Rodriguez	.65
325	Jeff Cirillo	.10
326	Joey Cora	.10
327	Chris Hoiles	.10
328	Bernard Gilkey	.10
329	Mike Lansing	.10
330	Jimmy Key	.10
331	Vinny Castilla	.10
332	Mark Guthrie	.10
333	Mike Lieberthal	.10
334	Will Clark	.10
335	Rickey Henderson	.75
336	Todd Jones	.10
337	Jack McDowell	.10
338	Carlos Rodriguez	.10
339	Mark Eichhorn	.10
340	Jeff Nelson	.10
341	Eric Anthony	.10
342	Randy Velarde	.10
343	Javier Lopez	.10
344	Kevin Mitchell	.10
345	Steve Bedrosian	.10
346	John Kruk	.10
347	Scott Leius	.10
348	John Patterson	.10
349	Kevin Brown	.10
350	Mike Moore	.10
351	Manny Ramirez	.75
352	Jose LInd	.10
353	Derrick May	.10
354	Cal Eldred	.10
355	J.T. Snow	.10
356	Luis Sojo	.10
357	Moises Alou	.10
358	Dave Clark	.10
359	Dave Hollins	.10
360	Cal Ripken Jr.	2.00
361	Pedro Astacio	.10
362	Tony Longmire	.10
363	Jeff Frye	.10
364	Bo Jackson	.20
365	Steve Ontiveros	.10
366	David Nied	.10
367	Brad Ausmus	.10
368	Carlos Baerga	.10
369	James Mouton	.10
370	Ozzie Guillen	.10
371	Yorkis Perez	.10
372	Rich Rodriguez	.10
373	Mark McLemore	.10
374	Jeff Fassero	.10
375	John Roper	.10
376	Wes Chamberlain	.10
377	Felix Jose	.10
378	Brett Butler	.10
379	William Van Landingham	.10
380	Mickey Tettleton	.10
381	Brady Anderson	.10
382	Reggie Jefferson	.10
383	Mike Kingery	.10
384	Derek Bell	.10
385	Scott Erickson	.10
386	Bob Wickman	.10
387	Phil Leftwich	.10
388	Dave Justice	.10
389	Pedro Martinez	.75
390	Terry Mathews	.10
391	Brian McRae	.10
392	Bruce Ruffin	.10
393	Steve Finley	.10
394	Rafael Bournigal	.10
395	Darryl Strawberry	.10
396	Luis Alicea	.10

Cyberstat Season in Review

This special edition of Cyberstat cards was available only in Topps factory sets. Carrying forward the idea of computerized projections to complete the strike-shortened 1994 season, the Season in Review cards speculate on career milestones and the playoffs that never happened. The Season in Review cards have player action photos printed on a foil background resembling the U.S. flag. Names are in gold foil. Backs have a black background and a recap of the computer simulation.

		NM/M
Complete Set (7):		10.00
Common Player:		1.00
1	Barry Bonds (61 Home Runs)	6.00
2	Jose Canseco (AL West One-Game Playoff)	2.00
3	Juan Gonzalez (AL Divisional Playoffs)	1.50
4	Fred McGriff (NL Divisional Playoffs)	1.00
5	Carlos Baerga (ALCS MVP)	1.00
6	Ryan Klesko (NLCS MVP)	1.00
7	Kenny Lofton (World Series MVP)	1.00

League Leaders

League Leaders is a 50-card insert set found in one of every six retail packs only of both Series I and II. The set includes the top five players in each league across 10 statistical categories. Cards featured the statistical category running up the right side, with the player's name across the bottom. Photo backgrounds have been darkened and posterized to make the player action stand out. Backs have the player's stat rankings within his division and league, and a bar graph at bottom gives his performance in that statistical category for the previous five seasons.

		NM/M
Complete Set (50):		20.00
Common Player:		.15
1	Albert Belle	.15
2	Kevin Mitchell	.15
3	Wade Boggs	1.50
4	Tony Gwynn	1.50
5	Moises Alou	.15
6	Andres Galarraga	.15
7	Matt Williams	.15
8	Barry Bonds	4.00
9	Frank Thomas	.75
10	Jose Canseco	.50
11	Jeff Bagwell	.75
12	Kirby Puckett	1.50
13	Julio Franco	.15
14	Albert Belle	.15
15	Fred McGriff	.15
16	Kenny Lofton	.15
17	Otis Nixon	.15
18	Brady Anderson	.15
19	Deion Sanders	.15
20	Chuck Carr	.15
21	Pat Hentgen	.15
22	Andy Benes	.15
23	Roger Clemens	1.75
24	Greg Maddux	1.50
25	Pedro Martinez	.75
26	Paul O'Neill	.15
27	Jeff Bagwell	.75
28	Frank Thomas	.75
29	Hal Morris	.15
30	Kenny Lofton	.15
31	Ken Griffey Jr.	2.00
32	Jeff Bagwell	.75
33	Albert Belle	.15
34	Fred McGriff	.15
35	Cecil Fielder	.15
36	Matt Williams	.15
37	Joe Carter	.15
38	Dante Bichette	.15
39	Frank Thomas	.75
40	Mike Piazza	2.00
41	Craig Biggio	.15
42	Vince Coleman	.15
43	Marquis Grissom	.15
44	Chuck Knoblauch	.15
45	Darren Lewis	.15
46	Randy Johnson	.75
47	Jose Rijo	.15
48	Chuck Finley	.15
49	Bret Saberhagen	.15
50	Kevin Appier	.15

Total Bases Finest

Printed in Topps Finest technology, including a peel-off plastic protector coating on the front, these cards honor the 1994 statistical leaders in total bases. The cards have a silver waffle-texture background on front as a background to the color action photo. At bottom is a team logo and team-color bar with the player's name. Backs feature a portrait photo and the player's total base stats. These inserts are found in Series II Topps packs at an average rate of one per 36 packs (one box).

		NM/M
Complete Set (15):		12.00
Common Player:		.50
1	Jeff Bagwell	1.25
2	Albert Belle	.50
3	Ken Griffey Jr.	2.00
4	Frank Thomas	1.25
5	Matt Williams	.50
6	Dante Bichette	.50
7	Barry Bonds	2.50
8	Moises Alou	.50
9	Andres Galarraga	.50
10	Kenny Lofton	.50
11	Rafael Palmeiro	1.00
12	Tony Gwynn	1.50
13	Kirby Puckett	1.50
14	Jose Canseco	.75
15	Jeff Conine	.50

Traded and Rookies

Traded players, free agents signed by new teams and all the up-and-coming rookies are the meat of the 1995 Topps Traded and Rookies set, sold for the first time exclusively in foil-pack form. Maintaining the same format used in Series 1 and 2 Topps, the updates also reused the Future Star, Draft Pick and Star Track subsets, along with four-player Prospects cards. New subsets included Rookie of the Year Candidates, All-Stars, On Deck and "At the Break," 10 cards chronicling star players' performances through the first half of the 1995 season. A double-thick, foil-printed version of the "At the Break" cards called "Power Boosters" were the only inserts in the Traded/Rookies set.

		NM/M
Complete Set (165):		30.00
Common Player:		.05
Pack (11):		2.50
Wax Box (36):		60.00
1	Frank Thomas (At The Break)	.50
2	Ken Griffey Jr. (At The Break)	.65
3	Barry Bonds (At The Break)	1.00
4	Albert Belle (At The Break)	.05
5	Cal Ripken Jr. (At The Break)	1.00
6	Mike Piazza (At The Break)	.75
7	Tony Gwynn (At The Break)	.60
8	Jeff Bagwell (At The Break)	.45
9	Mo Vaughn (At The Break)	.05
10	Matt Williams (At The Break)	.05
11	Ray Durham	.05
12	Juan LeBron (Photo Carlos Beltran.) **RC** (Draft Pick)	5.00
13	Shawn Green (Rookie of the Year Candidate)	.50
14	Kevin Gross	.05
15	Jon Nunnally	.05
16	Brian Maxcy **RC**	.05
17	Mark Kiefer	.05
18	Carlos Beltran **RC** (Draft Pick)(Photo actually Juan Beltran.)	15.00
19	Mike Mimbs **RC**	.05
20	Larry Walker	.05
21	Chad Curtis	.05
22	Jeff Barry	.05
23	Joe Oliver	.05
24	Tomas Perez **RC**	.05
25	Michael Barrett **RC** (Draft Pick)	1.50
26	Brian McRae	.05
27	Derek Bell	.05
28	Ray Durham (Rookie of the Year Candidate)	.05
29	Todd Williams	.05
30	Ryan Jaroncyk **RC** (Draft Pick)	.05
31	Todd Steverson	.05
32	Mike Devereaux	.05
33	Rheal Cormier	.05
34	Benny Santiago	.05
35	Bobby Higginson **RC**	.50
36	Jack McDowell	.05
37	Mike Macfarlane	.05
38	Tony McKnight **RC** (Draft Pick)	.05
39	Brian Hunter (Rookie of the Year Candidate)	.05
40	Hideo Nomo **RC** (Star Track)	2.00
41	Brett Butler	.05
42	Donovan Osborne	.05
43	Scott Karl	.05
44	Tony Phillips	.05
45	Marty Cordova (Rookie of the Year Candidate)	.20
46	Dave Mlicki	.05
47	Bronson Arroyo **RC** (Draft Pick)	4.00
48	John Burkett	.05
49	J.D. Smart **RC** (Draft Pick)	.05
50	Mickey Tettleton	.05
51	Todd Stottlemyre	.05
52	Mike Perez	.05
53	Terry Mulholland	.05
54	Edgardo Alfonzo	.05
55	Zane Smith	.05
56	Jacob Brumfield	.05
57	Andujar Cedeno	.05
58	Jose Parra	.05
59	Manny Alexander	.05
60	Tony Tarasco	.05
61	Orel Hershiser	.05
62	Tim Scott	.05
63	Felix Rodriguez **RC**	.05
64	Ken Hill	.05
65	Marquis Grissom	.05
66	Lee Smith	.05
67	Jason Bates (Rookie of the Year Candidate)	.05
68	Felipe Lira	.05
69	Alex Hernandez **RC** (Draft Pick)	.10
70	Tony Fernandez	.05
71	Scott Radinsky	.05
72	Jose Canseco	.50
73	Mark Grudzielanek **RC**	.50
74	Ben Davis **RC** (Draft Pick)	.25
75	Jim Abbott	.05
76	Roger Bailey	.05
77	Gregg Jefferies	.05
78	Erik Hanson	.05
79	Brad Radke **RC**	1.50
80	Jaime Navarro	.05

#	Player	NM/M
81	John Wetteland	.05
82	Chad Fonville **RC**	.10
83	John Mabry	.05
84	Glenallen Hill	.05
85	Ken Caminiti	.05
86	Tom Goodwin	.05
87	Darren Bragg	.05
88	1995 Prospects (Pitchers) (Pat Ahearne **RC**, Gary Rath **RC**, Larry Wimberly **RC**, Robbie Bell **RC**)	.10
89	Jeff Russell	.05
90	Dave Gallagher	.05
91	Steve Finley	.05
92	Vaughn Eshelman	.05
93	Kevin Jarvis	.05
94	Mark Gubicza	.05
95	Tim Wakefield	.05
96	Bob Tewksbury	.05
97	Sid Roberson **RC**	.05
98	Tom Henke	.05
99	Michael Tucker (Future Star)	.05
100	Jason Bates	.05
101	Otis Nixon	.05
102	Mark Whiten	.05
103	Dilson Torres	.05
104	Melvin Bunch **RC**	.05
105	Terry Pendleton	.05
106	Corey Jenkins **RC** (Draft Pick)	.05
107	On Deck (Glenn Dishman **RC**, Rob Grable **RC**)	.05
108	Reggie Taylor **RC** (Draft Pick)	.05
109	Curtis Goodwin (Rookie of the Year Candidate)	.05
110	David Cone	.05
111	Antonio Osuna	.05
112	Paul Shuey	.05
113	Doug Jones	.05
114	Mark McLemore	.05
115	Kevin Ritz	.05
116	John Kruk	.05
117	Trevor Wilson	.05
118	Jerald Clark	.05
119	Julian Tavarez	.05
120	Tim Pugh	.05
121	Todd Zeile	.05
122	1995 Prospects (Fielders) (Mark Sweeney **RC**, George Arias, Richie Sexson **RC**, Brian Schneider **RC**)	4.00
123	Bobby Witt	.05
124	Hideo Nomo (Rookie of the Year Candidate)	1.00
125	Joey Cora	.05
126	Jim Scharrer **RC** (Draft Pick)	.05
127	Paul Quantrill	.05
128	Chipper Jones (Rookie of the Year Candidate)	.75
129	Kenny James **RC** (Draft Pick)	.05
130	On Deck (Lyle Mouton, Mariano Rivera)	.15
131	Tyler Green (Rookie of the Year Candidate)	.05
132	Brad Clontz	.05
133	Jon Nunnally (Rookie of the Year Candidate)	.05
134	Dave Magadan	.05
135	Al Leiter	.05
136	Bret Barberie	.05
137	Bill Swift	.05
138	Scott Cooper	.05
139	Roberto Kelly	.05
140	Charlie Hayes	.05
141	Pete Harnisch	.05
142	Rich Amaral	.05
143	Rudy Seanez	.05
144	Pat Listach	.05
145	Quilvio Veras (Rookie of the Year Candidate)	.05
146	Jose Olmeda **RC** (Draft Pick)	.05
147	Roberto Petagine	.05
148	Kevin Brown	.05
149	Phil Plantier	.05
150	Carlos Perez **RC** (Rookie of the Year Candidate)	.05
151	Pat Borders	.05
152	Tyler Green	.05
153	Stan Belinda	.05
154	Dave Stewart	.05
155	Andre Dawson	.25
156	Frank Thomas, Fred McGriff/AS	.30
157	Carlos Baerga, Craig Biggio/AS	.05
158	Wade Boggs, Matt Williams/AS	.35
159	Cal Ripken Jr., Ozzie Smith/AS	.75
160	Ken Griffey Jr., Tony Gwynn/AS	.40
161	Albert Belle, Barry Bonds/AS	.75
162	Kirby Puckett, Len Dykstra/AS	.35
163	Ivan Rodriguez, Mike Piazza/AS	.40
164	Randy Johnson, Hideo Nomo/AS	.25
165	Checklist	.05

Traded and Rookies Power Boosters

Virtually identical to the first 10 cards of the 1995 Topps Traded and Rookies issue, the "At the Break" subset is the only insert found in Traded packs. Cards are printed on double-thick cardboard stock on metallized foil. The chase cards are found at an average rate of one per 36 packs.

		NM/M
Complete Set (10):		20.00
Common Player:		.75
1	Frank Thomas	1.50
2	Ken Griffey Jr.	3.00
3	Barry Bonds	5.00
4	Albert Belle	.75
5	Cal Ripken Jr.	5.00
6	Mike Piazza	3.00
7	Tony Gwynn	2.50
8	Jeff Bagwell	1.50
9	Mo Vaughn	.75
10	Matt Williams	.75

Opening Day

This 10-card set featuring top performers on the belated opening day of the 1995 season was available exclusively in retail factory sets. Card fronts feature color action photos printed on textured foil in a U.S. flag-like design. A large colorful Opening Day logo appears in an upper corner while the player's key stats from that game appear in a foil box at lower-right. Backs have a portrait photo along with complete details and a stats line of the opening day performance.

		NM/M
Complete Set (10):		7.50
Common Player:		.75
1	Kevin Appier	.75
2	Dante Bichette	.75
3	Ken Griffey Jr.	3.50
4	Todd Hundley	.75
5	John Jaha	.75
6	Fred McGriff	.75
7	Raul Mondesi	.75
8	Manny Ramirez	2.50
9	Danny Tartabull	.75
10	Devon White	.75

Archives Brooklyn Dodgers

In a departure from its program of complete set reissues, Topps' Archives baseball series for 1995 was a tribute to the 40th anniversary of the Brooklyn Dodgers' 1955 World's Series victory over the archrival Yankees. Besides

reprinting all of the Dodgers' cards from the 1952-56 Topps sets and the 1955 Bowman issue, the Archives release included some 30 "cards that never were," done in the styles of the 1952-55 Topps issues. Those cards are designated with an "N" suffix in parentheses. The old larger format of the vintage cards has been reduced to the standard 2-1/2" x 3-1/2" format for the Archives versions. Cards are UV coated on each side. Each card carries its original or an "extended" card number in the normal location, plus a tiny Archives series card number at the bottom in the fine print. The numbers on cards #97-109 do not coincide with those listed on the checklist card. The only chase cards in the issue were autographed versions of Sandy Koufax's 1956 Archives card. Cards #111-165 are short-printed in relation to cards #1-110.

		NM/M
Complete Set (165):		75.00
Common Player:		.10
Wax Pack (10):		5.00
Wax Box (24):		110.00
1	Andy Pafko (52T)	.25
2	Wayne Terwilliger (52T)	.10
3	Billy Loes (52T)	.25
4	Gil Hodges (52T)	.50
5	Duke Snider (52T)	.75
6	Jim Russell (52T)	.10
7	Chris Van Cuyk (52T)	.10
8	Preacher Roe (52T)	.10
9	Johnny Schmitz (52T)	.10
10	Bud Podbielan (52T)	.10
11	Phil Haugstad (52T)	.10
12	Clyde King (52T)	.10
13	Billy Cox (52T)	.10
14	Rocky Bridges (52T)	.10
15	Carl Erskine (52T)	.10
16	Erv Palica (52T)	.10
17	Ralph Branca (52T)	.10
18	Jackie Robinson (52T)	2.00
19	Roy Campanella (52T)	.75
20	Rube Walker (52T)	.10
21	Johnny Rutherford (52T)	.10
22	Joe Black (52T)	.25
23	George Shuba (52T)	.10
24	Pee Wee Reese (52T)	.75
25	Clem Labine (52T)	.10
26	Bobby Morgan (52T)	.10
27	Cookie Lavagetto (52T)	.10
28	Chuck Dressen (52T)	.10
29	Ben Wade (52T)	.10
30	Rocky Nelson (52T)	.10
31	Billy Herman (52T)	.10
32	Jake Pitler (52T)	.10
33	Dick Williams (52T)	.10
34	Cal Abrams (52N)	.25
35	Carl Furillo (52N)	.25
36	Don Newcombe (52N)	.25
37	Jackie Robinson (53T)	2.00
38	Ben Wade (53T)	.10
39	Clem Labine (53T)	.10
40	Roy Campanella (53T)	.75
41	George Shuba (53T)	.10
42	Chuck Dressen (53T)	.10
43	Pee Wee Reese (53T)	.75
44	Joe Black (53T)	.25
45	Bobby Morgan (53T)	.10
46	Dick Williams (53T)	.10
47	Rube Walker (53T)	.10
48	Johnny Rutherford (53T)	.10
49	Billy Loes (53T)	.15
50	Don Hoak (53T)	.10
51	Jim Hughes (53T)	.10
52	Bob Milliken (53T)	.10
53	Preacher Roe (53T)	.10
54	Dixie Howell (53T)	.10
55	Junior Gilliam (53T)	.25
56	Johnny Podres (53T)	.25
57	Bill Antonello (53T)	.10
58	Ralph Branca (53N)	.25
59	Gil Hodges (53N)	.60
60	Carl Furillo (53N)	.45
61	Carl Erskine (53N)	.25
62	Don Newcombe (53N)	.35
63	Duke Snider (53N)	.75
64	Billy Cox (53N)	.25
65	Russ Meyer (53N)	.25
66	Jackie Robinson (54T)	2.00
67	Preacher Roe (54T)	.10
68	Duke Snider (54T)	.75
69	Junior Gilliam (54T)	.10
70	Billy Herman (54T)	.10
71	Joe Black (54T)	.15
72	Gil Hodges (54T)	.50
73	Clem Labine (54T)	.10
74	Ben Wade (54T)	.10
75	Tommy Lasorda (54T)	1.00
76	Rube Walker (54T)	.10
77	Johnny Podres (54T)	.10
78	Jim Hughes (54T)	.10
79	Bob Milliken (54T)	.10
80	Charlie Thompson (54T)	.10
81	Don Hoak (54T)	.10
82	Roberto Clemente (54N)	1.00
83	Don Zimmer (54N)	.25
84	Roy Campanella (54N)	1.00
85	Billy Cox (54N)	.45
86	Carl Erskine (54N)	.45
87	Carl Furillo (54N)	.45
88	Don Newcombe (54N)	.45
89	Pee Wee Reese (54N)	1.00
90	George Shuba (54N)	.25
91	Junior Gilliam (55T)	.10
92	Billy Herman (55T)	.10
93	Johnny Podres (55T)	.10
94	Don Hoak (55T)	.10
95	Jackie Robinson (55T)	2.00
96	Jim Hughes (55T)	.10
97	Bob Borkowski (55N)	.10
98	Sandy Amoros (55T)	.10
99	Karl Spooner (55T)	.10
100	Don Zimmer (55T)	.10
101	Rube Walker (55T)	.10
102	Bob Milliken (55T)	.10
103	Sandy Koufax (55T)	2.00
104	Joe Black (55T)	.20
105	Clem Labine (55T)	.10
106	Gil Hodges (55T)	.50
107	Ed Roebuck (55T)	.10
108	Bert Hamric (55T)	.10
109	Duke Snider (55T)	.75
110	Walter Alston (55N)	.25
111	Roger Craig (55N)	.75
112	Don Drysdale (55N)	3.00
113	Dixie Howell (55N)	.50
114	Frank Kellert (55N)	.50
115	Tommy Lasorda (55N)	2.50
116	Chuck Templeton (55N)	.50
117	World Series Game 3, Dodgers Stay Alive (Jackie Robinson (55N))	1.00
118	World Series Game 4, Series Knotted (Gil Hodges (55N))	1.00
119	World Series Game 5, Dodgers Lead (Duke Snider (55N))	1.00
120	World Series Game 7, Dodgers Reign (Johnny Podres (55N))	1.00
121	Don Hoak (55B)	.35
122	Roy Campanella (55B)	2.00
123	Pee Wee Reese (55B)	2.00
124	Bob Darnell (55B)	.50
125	Don Zimmer (55B)	.50
126	George Shuba (55B)	.50
127	Johnny Podres (55B)	.50
128	Junior Gilliam (55B)	.65
129	Don Newcombe (55B)	.65
130	Jim Hughes (55B)	.50
131	Gil Hodges (55B)	2.00
132	Carl Furillo (55B)	1.00
133	Carl Erskine (55B)	.50
134	Erv Palica (55B)	.50
135	Russ Meyer (55B)	.50
136	Billy Loes (55B)	.50
137	Walt Moryn (55B)	.50
138	Chico Fernandez (55B)	.50
139	Charley Neal (55B)	.50
140	Ken Lehman (55B)	.50
141	Walter Alston (56T)	1.00
142	Jackie Robinson (56T)	6.00
143	Sandy Amoros (56T)	.50
144	Ed Roebuck (56T)	.50
145	Roger Craig (56T)	.50
146	Sandy Koufax (56T)	5.00
146a	Sandy Koufax (56T, autographed)	650.00
147	Karl Spooner (56T)	.50
148	Don Zimmer (56T)	.50
149	Roy Campanella (56T)	3.00
150	Gil Hodges (56T)	2.50
151	Duke Snider (56T)	4.50
152	Team photo (56T)	5.00
153	Johnny Podres (56T)	.50
154	Don Bessent (56T)	.50
155	Carl Furillo (56T)	.75
156	Randy Jackson (56T)	.50
157	Carl Erskine (56T)	.50
158	Don Newcombe (56T)	.65
159	Pee Wee Reese (56T)	2.50
160	Billy Loes (56T)	.50
161	Junior Gilliam (56T)	.65
162	Clem Labine (56T)	.50
163	Charley Neal (56T)	.50
164	Rube Walker (56T)	.50
165	Checklist	.05

DIII

Describing its cards as featuring "infinite depth perspectives" with game-action photos, Topps entered the 3-D card market with its Dimension III product. Utilizing "super thick laminated construction" to provide the illusion of depth, the cards feature borderless action photos on front. Backs are conventionally printed with a color portrait photo and several sets of stats that go beyond the usual to the provide a more in-depth look at the player's performance.

		NM/M
Complete Set (59):		10.00
Common Player:		.15
Retail Pack (3):		.50
Retail Wax Box (24):		9.00
Hobby Pack (5):		.65
Hobby Wax Box (24):		12.50
1	Dave Justice	.15
2	Cal Ripken Jr.	2.50
3	Ruben Sierra	.15
4	Roberto Alomar	.25
5	Dennis Martinez	.15
6	Todd Zeile	.15
7	Albert Belle	.15
8	Chuck Knoblauch	.15
9	Roger Clemens	1.25
10	Cal Eldred	.15
11	Dennis Eckersley	.75
12	Andy Benes	.15
13	Moises Alou	.15
14	Andres Galarraga	.15
15	Jim Thome	.65
16	Tim Salmon	.15
17	Carlos Garcia	.15
18	Scott Leius	.15
19	Jeff Montgomery	.15
20	Brian Anderson	.15
21	Will Clark	.15
22	Bobby Bonilla	.15
23	Mike Stanley	.15
24	Barry Bonds	2.50
25	Jeff Conine	.15
26	Paul O'Neill	.15
27	Mike Piazza	1.50
28	Tom Glavine	.35
29	Jim Edmonds	.15
30	Lou Whitaker	.15
31	Jeff Frye	.15
32	Ivan Rodriguez	.75
33	Bret Boone	.15
34	Mike Greenwell	.15
35	Mark Grace	.15
36	Darren Lewis	.15
37	Don Mattingly	1.25
38	Jose Rijo	.15
39	Robin Ventura	.15
40	Bob Hamelin	.15
41	Tim Wallach	.15
42	Tony Gwynn	1.00
43	Ken Griffey Jr.	1.50
44	Doug Drabek	.15
45	Rafael Palmeiro	.75
46	Dean Palmer	.15
47	Bip Roberts	.15
48	Barry Larkin	.15
49	Dave Nilsson	.15
50	Wil Cordero	.15
51	Travis Fryman	.15
52	Chuck Carr	.15
53	Rey Sanchez	.15
54	Walt Weiss	.15
55	Joe Carter	.15
56	Len Dykstra	.15
57	Orlando Merced	.15
58	Ozzie Smith	1.00
59	Chris Gomez	.15

DIII Zone

A barrage of baseballs in the background, behind a player action photo, are fea-

tured on the front of this DIII chase set. Backs have a blazing baseball across the top and a description and stats of the pictured player's hot streaks of the previous season -- those times when athletes are said to be "in the zone." The inserts are found on average of one per six packs.

		NM/M
Complete Set (6):		4.00
Common Player:		.50
1	Frank Thomas	1.00
2	Kirby Puckett	1.50
3	Jeff Bagwell	1.00
4	Fred McGriff	.50
5	Raul Mondesi	.50
6	Kenny Lofton	.50

Embossed

Taking the embossed sportscard idea which Action Packed developed years earlier to a new level, Topps Embossed baseball features the tactile image on both sides of the card. Fronts have a lightly textured border while the central player photo is deeply embossed. The player name is embossed in gold-foil letters at bottom. Backs have another embossed player photo and various levels of embossing around the borders and boxes which contain stats and trivia.

		NM/M
Complete Set (140):		7.50
Common Player:		.10
Embossed Golds:		2X
Wax Pack (6+1):		1.50
Wax Box (24):		22.50
1	Kenny Lofton	.10
2	Gary Sheffield	.35
3	Hal Morris	.10
4	Cliff Floyd	.10
5	Pat Hentgen	.10
6	Tony Gwynn	.75
7	Jose Valentin	.10
8	Jason Bere	.10
9	Jeff Kent	.10
10	John Valentin	.10
11	Brian Anderson	.10
12	Deion Sanders	.10
13	Ryan Thompson	.10
14	Ruben Sierra	.10
15	Jay Bell	.10
16	Chuck Carr	.10
17	Brent Gates	.10
18	Bret Boone	.10
19	Paul Molitor	.60
20	Chili Davis	.10
21	Ryan Klesko	.10
22	Will Clark	.10
23	Greg Vaughn	.10
24	Moises Alou	.10
25	Ray Lankford	.10
26	Jose Rijo	.10
27	Bobby Jones	.10
28	Rick Wilkins	.10
29	Cal Eldred	.10

30 Juan Gonzalez .30
31 Royce Clayton .10
32 Bryan Harvey .10
33 Dave Nilsson .10
34 Chris Hoiles .10
35 David Nied .10
36 Javy Lopez .10
37 Tim Wallach .10
38 Bobby Bonilla .10
39 Danny Tartabull .10
40 Andy Benes .10
41 Dean Palmer .10
42 Chris Gomez .10
43 Kevin Appier .10
44 Brady Anderson .10
45 Alex Fernandez .10
46 Roberto Kelly .10
47 Dave Hollins .10
48 Chuck Finley .10
49 Wade Boggs .75
50 Travis Fryman .10
51 Ken Griffey Jr. 1.00
52 John Olerud .10
53 Delino DeShields .10
54 Ivan Rodriguez .50
55 Tommy Greene .10
56 Tom Pagnozzi .10
57 Bip Roberts .10
58 Luis Gonzalez .10
59 Rey Sanchez .10
60 Ken Ryan .10
61 Darren Daulton .10
62 Rick Aguilera .10
63 Wally Joyner .10
64 Mike Greenwell .10
65 Jay Buhner .10
66 Craig Biggio .10
67 Charles Nagy .10
68 Devon White .10
69 Randy Johnson .60
70 Shawon Dunston .10
71 Kirby Puckett .75
72 Paul O'Neill .10
73 Tino Martinez .10
74 Carlos Garcia .10
75 Ozzie Smith .75
76 Cecil Fielder .10
77 Mike Stanley .10
78 Lance Johnson .10
79 Tony Phillips .10
80 Bobby Munoz .10
81 Kevin Tapani .10
82 William Van Landingham .10
83 Dante Bichette .10
84 Tom Candiotti .10
85 Wil Cordero .10
86 Jeff Conine .10
87 Joey Hamilton .10
88 Mark Whiten .10
89 Jeff Montgomery .10
90 Andres Galarraga .10
91 Roberto Alomar .20
92 Orlando Merced .10
93 Mike Mussina .35
94 Pedro Martinez .60
95 Carlos Baerga .10
96 Steve Trachsel .10
97 Lou Whitaker .10
98 David Cone .10
99 Chuck Knoblauch .10
100 Frank Thomas .60
101 Dave Justice .10
102 Raul Mondesi .10
103 Rickey Henderson .60
104 Doug Drabek .10
105 Sandy Alomar .10
106 Roger Clemens .85
107 Mark McGwire 1.20
108 Tim Salmon .10
109 Greg Maddux .75
110 Mike Piazza 1.00
111 Tom Glavine .30
112 Walt Weiss .10
113 Cal Ripken Jr. 1.50
114 Eddie Murray .60
115 Don Mattingly .85
116 Ozzie Guillen .10
117 Bob Hamelin .10
118 Jeff Bagwell .60
119 Eric Karros .10
120 Barry Bonds 1.50
121 Mickey Tettleton .10
122 Mark Langston .10
123 Robin Ventura .10
124 Bret Saberhagen .10
125 Albert Belle .10
126 Rafael Palmeiro .50
127 Fred McGriff .10
128 Jimmy Key .10
129 Barry Larkin .10
130 Tim Raines .10
131 Len Dykstra .10
132 Todd Zeile .10
133 Joe Carter .10
134 Matt Williams .10
135 Terry Steinbach .10
136 Manny Ramirez .60
137 John Wetteland .10
138 Rod Beck .10
139 Mo Vaughn .10
140 Darren Lewis .10

Embossed Golden Idols

The only insert in the Topps Embossed baseball set was a parallel set of the 140 cards rendered in gold tones

on front and inserted at the rate of one per pack. Backs are identical to the regular version.

	NM/M
Complete Set (140):	25.00
Common Player:	.25

Legends of the '60s

Twelve of the true superstars of the 1960s are featured on one of their best Topps card designs in this collection of 6-oz. bronze metal cards. In 2-1/2" x 3-1/2" size, the ingots' fronts reproduce one of the player's 1960s Topps cards. Backs have been modified to present entire career stats. The set was sold in a mail-order subscription plan and included a custom wood box to house the collection.

	NM/M
Complete Set (12):	100.00
Common Player:	7.50
(1) Hank Aaron/1965	10.00
(2) Roberto Clemente/1965	10.00
(3) Don Drysdale/1965	7.50
(4) Bob Gibson/1964	7.50
(5) Harmon Killebrew/1968	7.50
(6) Juan Marichal/1966	7.50
(7) Willie Mays/1964	10.00
(8) Willie McCovey/1961	7.50
(9) Brooks Robinson/1969	7.50
(10) Frank Robinson/1962	7.50
(11) Billy Williams/1967	7.50
(12) Carl Yastrzemski/1966	7.50

Own the Game Instant Winner

Randomly packaged at a rate between 1:60 and 1:120, depending on type of packaging, Instant Winner cards were available in 1995 Topps baseball. The grand prize was a $40,000 "Baseball Passport" good for games, flights, hotels, etc., for 60 days during the 1996 season. Other prizes included personalized Topps baseball cards picturing the winner and Topps Spectra Light cards in team sets, league sets or a complete set. Prize cards had to be redeemed by Jan. 31, 1996.

Ted Williams Tunnel Opening Commemorative

This card was produced as the header for a 13-card set distributed at a luncheon in conjunction with Dec. 15, 1995 opening day ceremonies for the Ted Williams Tunnel, connecting South Boston with the city's airport, running beneath Boston Harbor. Just 3,000 sets were reported produced. This card is in the style of Topps' regular 1996 baseball card set and features gold-foil highlights on front. A career summary is on back. The card was later offered free with a $75 purchase from Topps Stadium Club. (See also 1995 Choice Marketing Ted Williams Tunnel Opening Day Set.)

	NM/M
9 Ted Williams	35.00

"1952" Gold Mickey Mantle

This down-sized (2-1/2" x 3-1/2") version of Topps' first Mickey Mantle card was produced with embossed 22K gold-foil design on front and back and individually serial numbered within an edition of 50,000.

	NM/M
311 Mickey Mantle	10.00

1996 Topps Pre-Production

This set of promo cards was reportedly included in some 1995 Topps factory Hobby sets as an unadvertised insert. Cards are in the format of the forthcoming 1996 issue but do not have 1995 stats or career updates, and are numbered with a "PP" prefix.

	NM/M
Complete Set (9):	25.00
Common Player:	2.00
PP1 Cal Ripken Jr.	10.00
PP2 Thomas Howard	2.00

PP3 Rafael Bournigal	2.00
PP4 Ron Gant	2.00
PP5 Chipper Jones	7.50
PP6 Frank Thomas	6.00
PP7 Barry Bonds	10.00
PP8 Fred McGriff	2.00
PP9 Hideo Nomo	6.00

1996 Topps

At 440 cards, the basic Topps set for 1996 was the smallest regular-issue from the company since it adopted the 2-1/2" x 3-1/2" format in 1957. Honoring the late Mickey Mantle on card No. 7, Topps announced it would hereafter retire that card number. Subsets in the 220-card Series 1 are Star Power, Commemoratives, Draft Picks, Tribute, AAA Stars and Future Stars. Series 2 subsets repeat Star Power and Draft Picks and add Prospects, Now Appearing and Rookie All-Stars. Three different factory sets were available with each including the 440-card base set and various inserts. The "Cereal Box" set, so named because of the resemblance of its four component boxes to single-serving cereal boxes, has four of the Mantle inserts. The Retail and Hobby sets each include seven randomly packed chase cards, a plastic-cased #7 Mantle card labeled "Last Day Production" and a Mantle Foundation card. In addition the Retail version has one of the 19 Mantle reprints.

	NM/M
Unopened Hobby Set (449):	40.00
Unopened Retail Set (450):	40.00
Unopened Cereal Box Set (444):	35.00
Complete Set (440):	25.00
Common Player:	.05
Wax Pack (12):	1.50
Wax Box (36):	35.00
Cello Pack (17):	2.50
Cello Box (24):	40.00
Vending Box (500):	12.50

1 Tony Gwynn (Star Power) .50
2 Mike Piazza (Star Power) .75
3 Greg Maddux (Star Power) .50
4 Jeff Bagwell (Star Power) .40
5 Larry Walker (Star Power) .05
6 Barry Larkin (Star Power) .05
7 Mickey Mantle (Commemorative) 4.00
8 Tom Glavine (Star Power) .05
9 Craig Biggio (Star Power) .05
10 Barry Bonds (Star Power) 1.00
11 Heathcliff Slocumb (Star Power) .05
12 Matt Williams (Star Power) .05
13 Todd Helton (Draft Pick) .75
14 Mark Redman (Draft Pick) .05
15 Michael Barrett (Draft Pick) .05
16 Ben Davis (Draft Pick) .05
17 Juan LeBron (Draft Pick) .05
18 Tony McKnight (Draft Pick) .05
19 Ryan Jaroncyk (Draft Pick) .05
20 Corey Jenkins (Draft Pick) .05
21 Jim Scharrer (Draft Pick) .05
22 Mark Bellhorn **RC** (Draft Pick) .10
23 Jarrod Washburn **RC** (Draft Pick) .50
24 Geoff Jenkins **RC** (Draft Pick) 1.00
25 Sean Casey **RC** (Draft Pick) 3.00
26 Brett Tomko **RC** (Draft Pick) .10
27 Tony Fernandez .05
28 Rich Becker .05
29 Andujar Cedeno .05
30 Paul Molitor .75
31 Brent Gates .05
32 Glenallen Hill .05
33 Mike MacFarlane .05
34 Manny Alexander .05
35 Todd Zeile .05
36 Joe Girardi .05
37 Tony Tarasco .05
38 Tim Belcher .05
39 Tom Goodwin .05
40 Orel Hershiser .05
41 Tripp Cromer .05
42 Sean Bergman .05
43 Troy Percival .05
44 Kevin Stocker .05
45 Albert Belle .05
46 Tony Eusebio .05
47 Sid Roberson .05
48 Todd Hollandsworth .05
49 Mark Wohlers .05
50 Kirby Puckett 1.00
51 Darren Holmes .05
52 Ron Karkovice .05
53 Al Martin .05
54 Pat Rapp .05
55 Mark Grace .05
56 Greg Gagne .05
57 Stan Javier .05
58 Scott Sanders .05
59 J.T. Snow .05
60 David Justice .05
61 Royce Clayton .05
62 Kevin Foster .05
63 Tim Naehring .05
64 Orlando Miller .05
65 Mike Mussina .35
66 Jim Eisenreich .05
67 Felix Fermin .05
68 Bernie Williams .05
69 Robb Nen .05
70 Ron Gant .05
71 Felipe Lira .05
72 Jacob Brumfield .05
73 John Mabry .05
74 Mark Carreon .05
75 Carlos Baerga .05
76 Jim Dougherty .05
77 Ryan Thompson .05
78 Scott Leius .05
79 Roger Pavlik .05
80 Gary Sheffield .45
81 Julian Tavarez .05
82 Andy Ashby .05
83 Mark Lemke .05
84 Omar Vizquel .05
85 Darren Daulton .05
86 Mike Lansing .05
87 Rusty Greer .05
88 Dave Stevens .05
89 Jose Offerman .05
90 Tom Henke .05
91 Troy O'Leary .05
92 Michael Tucker .05
93 Marvin Freeman .05
94 Alex Diaz .05
95 John Wetteland .05
96 Cal Ripken Jr. (Tribute Card) 1.00
97 Mike Mimbs .05
98 Bobby Higginson .05
99 Edgardo Alfonzo .05
100 Frank Thomas .75
101 Steve Gibraltar, Bob Abreu (AAA Stars) .05
102 Brian Givens, T.J. Mathews (AAA Stars) .05
103 Chris Pritchett, Trenidad Hubbard (AAA Stars) .05
104 Eric Owens, Butch Huskey (AAA Stars) .05
105 Doug Drabek .05
106 Tomas Perez .05
107 Mark Leiter .05
108 Joe Oliver .05
109 Tony Castillo .05
110 Checklist .05
111 Kevin Seitzer .05
112 Pete Schourek .05
113 Sean Berry .05
114 Todd Stottlemyre .05
115 Joe Carter .05
116 Jeff King .05
117 Dan Wilson .05
118 Kurt Abbott .05
119 Lyle Mouton .05
120 Jose Rijo .05
121 Curtis Goodwin .05
122 Jose Valentin **RC** .05
123 Ellis Burks .05
124 David Cone .05
125 Eddie Murray .75
126 Brian Jordan .05
127 Darrin Fletcher .05
128 Curt Schilling .25
129 Ozzie Guillen .05
130 Kenny Rogers .05
131 Tom Pagnozzi .05
132 Garret Anderson .05
133 Bobby Jones .05
134 Chris Gomez .05
135 Mike Stanley .05
136 Hideo Nomo .35
137 Jon Nunnally .05
138 Tim Wakefield .05
139 Steve Finley .05
140 Ivan Rodriguez .65
141 Quilvio Veras .05
142 Mike Fetters .05
143 Mike Greenwell .05
144 Bill Pulsipher .05
145 Mark McGwire 1.50
146 Frank Castillo .05
147 Greg Vaughn .05
148 Pat Hentgen .05
149 Walt Weiss .05
150 Randy Johnson .75
151 David Segui .05
152 Benji Gil .05
153 Tom Candiotti .05
154 Geronimo Berroa .05
155 John Franco .05
156 Jay Bell .05
157 Mark Gubicza .05
158 Hal Morris .05
159 Wilson Alvarez .05
160 Derek Bell .05
161 Ricky Bottalico .05
162 Bret Boone .05
163 Brad Radke .05
164 John Valentin .05
165 Steve Avery .05
166 Mark McLemore .05
167 Danny Jackson .05
168 Tino Martinez .05
169 Shane Reynolds .05
170 Terry Pendleton .05
171 Jim Edmonds .05
172 Esteban Loaiza .05
173 Ray Durham .05
174 Carlos Perez .05
175 Raul Mondesi .05
176 Steve Ontiveros .05
177 Chipper Jones 1.00
178 Otis Nixon .05
179 John Burkett .05
180 Gregg Jefferies .05
181 Denny Martinez .05
182 Ken Caminiti .05
183 Doug Jones .05
184 Brian McRae .05
185 Don Mattingly 1.00
186 Mel Rojas .05
187 Marty Cordova .05
188 Vinny Castilla .05
189 John Smoltz .05
190 Travis Fryman .05
191 Chris Hoiles .05
192 Chuck Finley .05
193 Ryan Klesko .05
194 Alex Fernandez .05
195 Dante Bichette .05
196 Eric Karros .05
197 Roger Clemens 1.00
198 Randy Myers .05
199 Tony Phillips .05
200 Cal Ripken Jr. 2.00
201 Rod Beck .05
202 Chad Curtis .05
203 Jack McDowell .05
204 Gary Gaetti .05
205 Ken Griffey Jr. 1.25
206 Ramon Martinez .05
207 Jeff Kent .05
208 Brad Ausmus .05
209 Devon White .05
210 Jason Giambi (Future Star) .45
211 Nomar Garciaparra (Future Star) 1.00
212 Billy Wagner (Future Star) .05
213 Todd Greene (Future Star) .05
214 Paul Wilson (Future Star) .05
215 Johnny Damon (Future Star) .25
216 Alan Benes (Future Star) .05

217	Karim Garcia (Future Star)	.10
218	Dustin Hermanson (Future Star)	.05
219	Derek Jeter (Future Star)	2.00
220	Checklist	.05
221	Kirby Puckett (Star Power)	.50
222	Cal Ripken Jr. (Star Power)	1.00
223	Albert Belle (Star Power)	.05
224	Randy Johnson (Star Power)	.40
225	Wade Boggs (Star Power)	.50
226	Carlos Baerga (Star Power)	.05
227	Ivan Rodriguez (Star Power)	.30
228	Mike Mussina (Star Power)	.25
229	Frank Thomas (Star Power)	.40
230	Ken Griffey Jr. (Star Power)	.75
231	Jose Mesa (Star Power)	.05
232	Matt Morris **RC** (Draft Pick)	1.00
233	Craig Wilson **RC** (Draft Pick)	.50
234	Alvie Shepherd **RC** (Draft Pick)	.05
235	Randy Winn **RC** (Draft Pick)	.05
236	David Yocum **RC** (Draft Pick)	.05
237	Jason Brester **RC** (Draft Pick)	.05
238	Shane Monahan **RC** (Draft Pick)	.05
239	Brian McNichol **RC** (Draft Pick)	.05
240	Reggie Taylor (Draft Pick)	.05
241	Garrett Long (Draft Pick)	.05
242	Jonathan Johnson **RC** (Draft Pick)	.05
243	Jeff Liefer **RC** (Draft Pick)	.05
244	Brian Powell **RC** (Draft Pick)	.05
245	Brian Buchanan (Draft Pick)	.05
246	Mike Piazza	1.25
247	Edgar Martinez	.05
248	Chuck Knoblauch	.05
249	Andres Galarraga	.05
250	Tony Gwynn	1.00
251	Lee Smith	.05
252	Sammy Sosa	1.00
253	Jim Thome	.45
254	Frank Rodriguez	.05
255	Charlie Hayes	.05
256	Bernard Gilkey	.05
257	John Smiley	.05
258	Brady Anderson	.05
259	Rico Brogna	.05
260	Kirt Manwaring	.05
261	Len Dykstra	.05
262	Tom Glavine	.25
263	Vince Coleman	.05
264	John Olerud	.05
265	Orlando Merced	.05
266	Kent Mercker	.05
267	Terry Steinbach	.05
268	Brian Hunter	.05
269	Jeff Fassero	.05
270	Jay Buhner	.05
271	Jeff Brantley	.05
272	Tim Raines	.05
273	Jimmy Key	.05
274	Mo Vaughn	.05
275	Andre Dawson	.25
276	Jose Mesa	.05
277	Brett Butler	.05
278	Luis Gonzalez	.05
279	Steve Sparks	.05
280	Chili Davis	.05
281	Carl Everett	.05
282	Jeff Cirillo	.05
283	Thomas Howard	.05
284	Paul O'Neill	.05
285	Pat Meares	.05
286	Mickey Tettleton	.05
287	Rey Sanchez	.05
288	Bip Roberts	.05
289	Roberto Alomar	.15
290	Ruben Sierra	.05
291	John Flaherty	.05
292	Bret Saberhagen	.05
293	Barry Larkin	.05
294	Sandy Alomar	.05
295	Ed Sprague	.05
296	Gary DiSarcina	.05
297	Marquis Grissom	.05
298	John Frascatore	.05
299	Will Clark	.05
300	Barry Bonds	2.00
301	Ozzie Smith	1.00
302	Dave Nilsson	.05
303	Pedro Martinez	.75
304	Joey Cora	.05
305	Rick Aguilera	.05
306	Craig Biggio	.05
307	Jose Vizcaino	.05
308	Jeff Montgomery	.05
309	Moises Alou	.05
310	Robin Ventura	.05
311	David Wells	.05
312	Delino DeShields	.05
313	Trevor Hoffman	.05
314	Andy Benes	.05
315	Deion Sanders	.05
316	Jim Bullinger	.05
317	John Jaha	.05
318	Greg Maddux	1.00
319	Tim Salmon	.05
320	Ben McDonald	.05
321	Sandy Martinez **RC**	.05
322	Dan Miceli	.05
323	Wade Boggs	1.00
324	Ismael Valdes	.05
325	Juan Gonzalez	.35
326	Charles Nagy	.05
327	Ray Lankford	.05
328	Mark Portugal	.05
329	Bobby Bonilla	.05
330	Reggie Sanders	.05
331	Jamie Brewington	.05
332	Aaron Sele	.05
333	Pete Harnisch	.05
334	Cliff Floyd	.05
335	Cal Eldred	.05
336	Jason Bates (Now Appearing)	.05
337	Tony Clark (Now Appearing)	.05
338	Jose Herrera (Now Appearing)	.05
339	Alex Ochoa (Now Appearing)	.05
340	Mark Loretta (Now Appearing)	.05
341	Donne Wall **RC** (Now Appearing)	.05
342	Jason Kendall (Now Appearing)	.05
343	Shannon Stewart (Now Appearing)	.05
344	Brooks Kieschnick (Now Appearing)	.05
345	Chris Snopek (Now Appearing)	.05
346	Ruben Rivera (Now Appearing)	.05
347	Jeff Suppan (Now Appearing)	.05
348	Phil Nevin (Now Appearing)	.05
349	John Wasdin (Now Appearing)	.05
350	Jay Payton (Now Appearing)	.05
351	Tim Crabtree (Now Appearing)	.05
352	Rick Krivda (Now Appearing)	.05
353	Bob Wolcott (Now Appearing)	.05
354	Jimmy Haynes (Now Appearing)	.05
355	Herb Perry	.05
356	Ryne Sandberg	1.00
357	Harold Baines	.05
358	Chad Ogea	.05
359	Lee Tinsley	.05
360	Matt Williams	.05
361	Randy Velarde	.05
362	Jose Canseco	.40
363	Larry Walker	.05
364	Kevin Appier	.05
365	Darryl Hamilton	.05
366	Jose Lima	.05
367	Javy Lopez	.05
368	Dennis Eckersley	.65
369	Jason Isringhausen	.05
370	Mickey Morandini	.05
371	Scott Cooper	.05
372	Jim Abbott	.05
373	Paul Sorrento	.05
374	Chris Hammond	.05
375	Lance Johnson	.05
376	Kevin Brown	.05
377	Luis Alicea	.05
378	Andy Pettitte	.25
379	Dean Palmer	.05
380	Jeff Bagwell	.75
381	Jaime Navarro	.05
382	Rondell White	.05
383	Erik Hanson	.05
384	Pedro Munoz	.05
385	Heathcliff Slocumb	.05
386	Wally Joyner	.05
387	Bob Tewksbury	.05
388	David Bell	.05
389	Fred McGriff	.05
390	Mike Henneman	.05
391	Robby Thompson	.05
392	Norm Charlton	.05
393	Cecil Fielder	.05
394	Benito Santiago	.05
395	Rafael Palmeiro	.65
396	Ricky Bones	.05
397	Rickey Henderson	.75
398	C.J. Nitkowski	.05
399	Shawon Dunston	.05
400	Manny Ramirez	.75
401	Bill Swift	.05
402	Chad Fonville	.05
403	Joey Hamilton	.05
404	Alex Gonzalez	.05
405	Roberto Hernandez	.05
406	Jeff Blauser	.05
407	LaTroy Hawkins	.05
408	Greg Colbrunn	.05
409	Todd Hundley	.05
410	Glenn Dishman	.05
411	Joe Vitiello	.05
412	Todd Worrell	.05
413	Wil Cordero	.05
414	Ken Hill	.05
415	Carlos Garcia	.05
416	Bryan Rekar	.05
417	Shawn Green (Topps Rookie All-Star)	.40
418	Tyler Green	.05
419	Mike Blowers	.05
420	Kenny Lofton	.05
421	Denny Neagle	.05
422	Jeff Conine	.05
423	Mark Langston	.05
424	Steve Cox, Jesse Ibarra **RC**, Derrek Lee, Ron Wright **RC** (Prospects)	.10
425	Jim Bonnici **RC**, Billy Owens, Richie Sexson, Daryle Ward **RC** (Prospects)	.10
426	Kevin Jordan, Bobby Morris **RC**, Desi Relaford, Adam Riggs **RC** (Prospects)	.10
427	Tim Harkrider, Rey Ordonez, Neifi Perez, Enrique Wilson (Prospects)	.05
428	Bartolo Colon, Doug Million, Rafael Orellano, Ray Ricken **RC** (Prospects)	.05
429	Jeff D'Amico, Marty Janzen **RC**, Gary Rath, Clint Sodowsky (Prospects)	.05
430	Matt Drews, Rich Hunter **RC**, Matt Ruebel **RC**, Bret Wagner (Prospects)	.05
431	Jaime Bluma, Dave Coggin **RC**, Steve Montgomery, Brandon Reed (Prospects)	.05
432	Mike Figga, Raul Ibanez **RC**, Paul Konerko, Julio Mosquera (Prospects)	.25
433	Brian Barber, Marc Kroon, Marc Valdes, Don Wengert (Prospects)	.05
434	George Arias, Chris Haas **RC**, Scott Rolen, Scott Spiezio (Prospects)	.50
435	Brian Banks **RC**, Vladimir Guerrero, Andruw Jones, Billy McMillon (Prospects)	.50
436	Roger Cedeno, Derrick Gibson, Ben Grieve, Shane Spencer **RC** (Prospects)	.50
437	Anton French, Demond Smith, Darond Stovall **RC**, Keith Williams (Prospects)	.05
438	Michael Coleman **RC**, Jacob Cruz, Richard Hidalgo, Charles Peterson (Prospects)	.10
439	Trey Beamon, Yamil Benitez, Jermaine Dye, Angel Echevarria (Prospects)	.05
440	Checklist	.05

Classic Confrontations

Head-to-head stats among baseball's top pitchers and hitters are featured in this insert set. The cards were seeded one per pack in the special 50-cent packs sold exclusively at Wal-Mart during the T206 Honus Wagner card giveaway promotion. Fronts have player action poses against a granite background and are highlighted in gold foil. Backs have a portrait photo and stats.

		NM/M
Complete Set (15):		3.50
Common Player:		.06
1	Ken Griffey Jr.	.65
2	Cal Ripken Jr.	1.00
3	Edgar Martinez	.05
4	Kirby Puckett	.45
5	Frank Thomas	.35
6	Barry Bonds	1.00
7	Reggie Sanders	.05
8	Andres Galarraga	.05
9	Tony Gwynn	.45
10	Mike Piazza	.65
11	Randy Johnson	.35
12	Mike Mussina	.25
13	Roger Clemens	.50
14	Tom Glavine	.25
15	Greg Maddux	.45

Mickey Mantle Commemorative Last Day

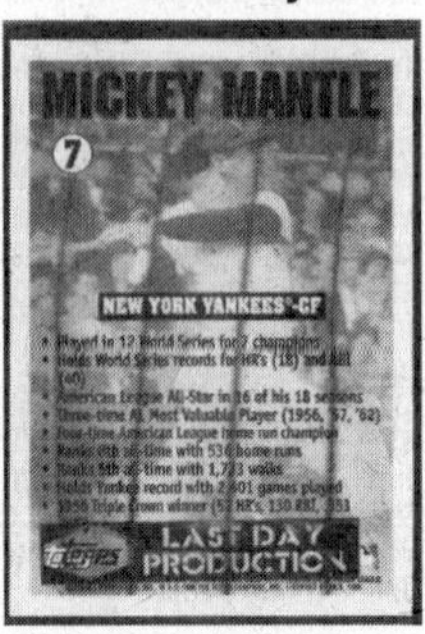

To mark the last day on which Topps would produce a #7 baseball card, the Mantle card from its 1996 set was issued in this sealed plastic case with a gold-foil logo on back.

		NM/M
7	Mickey Mantle	5.00

Mickey Mantle Reprints

One of Mickey Mantle's regular-issue Bowman or Topps cards from each year 1951-1969 was reproduced in 2-1/2" x 3-1/2" format as a Series 1 insert. Each card carries a gold-foil commemorative seal in one corner of the front. The reprints are found one per six retail packs and, in hobby, once per nine packs. The 1965-69 reprints were somewhat short-printed (four 1965-69 cards for each five 1951-1964) and are 20 percent scarcer.

		NM/M
Complete Set (19):		90.00
Common Mantle:		5.00
Common SP Mantle (15-19):		8.00
1	1951 Bowman #253	15.00
2	1952 Topps #311	15.00
3	1953 Topps #82	5.00
4	1954 Bowman #65	5.00
5	1955 Bowman #202	5.00
6	1956 Topps #135	5.00
7	1957 Topps #95	5.00
8	1958 Topps #150	5.00
9	1959 Topps #10	5.00
10	1960 Topps #350	5.00
11	1961 Topps #300	5.00
12	1962 Topps #200	5.00
13	1963 Topps #200	5.00
14	1964 Topps #50	5.00
15	1965 Topps #350	8.00
16	1966 Topps #50	8.00
17	1967 Topps #150	8.00
18	1968 Topps #280	8.00
19	1969 Topps #500	8.00

Mickey Mantle Finest Reprints

Nineteen of Mickey Mantle's regular-issue Bowman and Topps cards from 1951-1969 were printed in Finest technology for this Series 2 insert set. Each card's chrome front is protected with a peel-off plastic layer. Average insertion rate for the Mantle Finest reprints is one per 18 packs. The 1965-69 reprints were printed in a ratio of four for every five 1951-64 reprints, making them 20 percent scarcer. Unmarked Refractor versions of each card were inserted at an average rate of 1:144 packs.

		NM/M
Complete Set (19):		90.00
Common Card (1-14):		6.00
Common Shortprint (15-19):		8.00
Refractors:		3X
Inserted 1:144		
1	1951 Bowman #253	15.00
2	1952 Topps #311	15.00
3	1953 Topps #82	6.00
4	1954 Bowman #65	6.00
5	1955 Bowman #202	6.00
6	1956 Topps #135	6.00
7	1957 Topps #95	6.00
8	1958 Topps #150	6.00
9	1959 Topps #10	6.00
10	1960 Topps #350	6.00
11	1961 Topps #300	6.00
12	1962 Topps #200	6.00
13	1963 Topps #200	6.00
14	1964 Topps #50	6.00
15	1965 Topps #350	8.00
16	1966 Topps #50	8.00
17	1967 Topps #150	8.00
18	1968 Topps #280	8.00
19	1969 Topps #500	8.00

Mickey Mantle Case Inserts

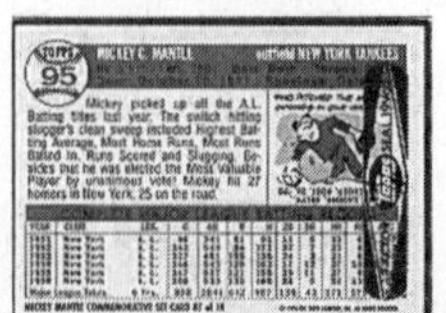

Inserted one per case of Series 2 Topps, these special versions of the 19 Mickey Mantle reprint cards come sealed in a soft plastic holder. The plastic sleeve has a gold-foil stamp at bottom-back which reads "FACTORY TOPPS SEAL 1996." Like the other Mantle reprints, the 1965-69 cards are somewhat scarcer due to short-printing.

		NM/M
Complete Set (19):		375.00
Common Mantle:		20.00
Common SP Mantle (15-19):		30.00
1	1951 Bowman #253	60.00
2	1952 Topps #311	60.00
3	1953 Topps #82	30.00
4	1954 Bowman #65	20.00
5	1955 Bowman #202	20.00
6	1956 Topps #135	20.00
7	1957 Topps #95	20.00
8	1958 Topps #150	20.00
9	1959 Topps #10	20.00
10	1960 Topps #350	20.00
11	1961 Topps #300	20.00
12	1962 Topps #200	20.00
13	1963 Topps #200	20.00
14	1964 Topps #50	20.00
15	1965 Topps #350	30.00
16	1966 Topps #50	30.00
17	1967 Topps #150	30.00
18	1968 Topps #280	30.00
19	1969 Topps #500	30.00

Mickey Mantle Redemption

Each of the 19 Mantle reprint cards, minus the commemorative gold-foil stamp on front, was also issued in a sweepstakes set. Seeded one per 108 packs, these cards could be sent in for a chance to win the authentic Mantle card pictured on front. Between one and 10 genuine Mantles were awarded for each of the 19 years. Cards entered in the sweepstakes were not returned when the contest ended Oct. 15, 1996. The sweepstakes cards are a Series 2 exclusive insert.

		NM/M
Complete Set (19):		200.00
Common Mantle:		10.00
Inserted 1:108 Series 2 Retail		
1	1951 Bowman #253	35.00
2	1952 Topps #311	35.00
3	1953 Topps #82	15.00
4	1954 Bowman #65	10.00
5	1955 Bowman #202	10.00
6	1956 Topps #135	10.00
7	1957 Topps #95	10.00
8	1958 Topps #150	10.00
9	1959 Topps #10	10.00
10	1960 Topps #350	10.00
11	1961 Topps #300	10.00
12	1962 Topps #200	10.00
13	1963 Topps #200	10.00
14	1964 Topps #50	10.00
15	1965 Topps #350	10.00
16	1966 Topps #50	10.00
17	1967 Topps #150	10.00
18	1968 Topps #280	10.00
19	1969 Topps #500	10.00

Mickey Mantle Commemorative Card Sheet

In conjunction with its program of reprinting most of the Mick's Topps and Bowman cards of the 1950s-1960s, Topps created this limited edition (numbered to 10,000) framed sheet depicting 20 cards surrounding an enlarged portrait from his famed 1952 Topps card. The sheet is embossed with a gold-foil #7 seal and was sold with a certificate of authenticity from Topps' president. The framed sheet measures about 19-1/2" x 25."

	NM/M
Framed Sheet:	80.00

Mickey Mantle Foundation

This black-and-white card was an insert exclusive to specially marked 1996 Topps factory sets. In standard 2-1/2" x 3-1/2" format, the card offers on its back information about the foundation and its work in health care and organ donation causes.

	NM/M
Mickey Mantle	4.00

Masters of the Game

Appearing at a one per 18 pack rate, these inserts are exclusive to Series 1 hobby packs.

		NM/M
Complete Set (20):		20.00
Common Player:		.35
1	Dennis Eckersley	.75
2	Denny Martinez	.35
3	Eddie Murray	1.00
4	Paul Molitor	1.00
5	Ozzie Smith	1.50
6	Rickey Henderson	1.00
7	Tim Raines	.35
8	Lee Smith	.35
9	Cal Ripken Jr.	4.00
10	Chili Davis	.35
11	Wade Boggs	1.50
12	Tony Gwynn	1.50
13	Don Mattingly	2.00
14	Bret Saberhagen	.35
15	Kirby Puckett	1.50
16	Joe Carter	.35
17	Roger Clemens	2.00
18	Barry Bonds	4.00
19	Greg Maddux	1.50
20	Frank Thomas	1.00

Mystery Finest

Each Mystery Finest insert has an opaque black film over the card front, concealing the identity of the player until removed. The inserts are seeded at the rate of one per 36 packs.

		NM/M
Complete Set (21)		25.00
Common Player:		.50
Refractors:		1.5X
M1	Hideo Nomo	1.00
M2	Greg Maddux	2.00
M3	Randy Johnson	1.50
M4	Chipper Jones	2.00
M5	Marty Cordova	.50
M6	Garret Anderson	.50
M7	Cal Ripken Jr.	4.00
M8	Kirby Puckett	2.00
M9	Tony Gwynn	2.00
M10	Manny Ramirez	1.50
M11	Jim Edmonds	.50
M12	Mike Piazza	2.50
M13	Barry Bonds	4.00
M14	Raul Mondesi	.50
M15	Sammy Sosa	2.00
M16	Ken Griffey Jr.	2.50
M17	Albert Belle	.50
M18	Dante Bichette	.50
M19	Mo Vaughn	.50
M20	Jeff Bagwell	1.50
M21	Frank Thomas	1.50

5-Star Mystery Finest

The 5-Star Mystery Finest inserts have an opaque black film over the card front, like the regular Mystery Finest, but has the words "5-Star" in large letters across the background. They are inserted at the average rate of one per 36 packs.

		NM/M
Complete Set (5):		12.50
Common Player:		2.00
Refractors:		2X
M22	Hideo Nomo	2.00
M23	Cal Ripken Jr.	5.00
M24	Mike Piazza	3.00
M25	Ken Griffey Jr.	3.00
M26	Frank Thomas	2.50

Power Boosters

This insert set is printed in Topps' "Power Matrix" technology, replacing two regular cards when found on the average of once per 36 packs. The Power Boosters reproduce the Star Power and Draft Picks subsets on a double-thick card.

		NM/M
Complete Set (26):		30.00
Common Player:		1.00
1	Tony Gwynn (Star Power)	2.00
2	Mike Piazza (Star Power)	3.00
3	Greg Maddux (Star Power)	2.00
4	Jeff Bagwell (Star Power)	1.50
5	Larry Walker (Star Power)	1.00
6	Barry Larkin (Star Power)	1.00
8	Tom Glavine (Star Power)	1.25
9	Craig Biggio (Star Power)	1.00
10	Barry Bonds (Star Power)	4.00
11	Heathcliff Slocumb (Star Power)	1.00
12	Matt Williams (Star Power)	1.00
13	Todd Helton (Draft Pick)	4.00
14	Mark Redman (Draft Pick)	1.00
15	Michael Barrett (Draft Pick)	1.00
16	Ben Davis (Draft Pick)	1.00
17	Juan LeBron (Draft Pick)	1.00
18	Tony McKnight (Draft Pick)	1.00
19	Ryan Jaroncyk (Draft Pick)	1.00
20	Corey Jenkins (Draft Pick)	1.00
21	Jim Scharrer (Draft Pick)	1.00
22	Mark Bellhorn (Draft Pick)	1.00
23	Jarrod Washburn (Draft Pick)	1.00
24	Geoff Jenkins (Draft Pick)	1.00
25	Sean Casey (Draft Pick)	2.00
26	Brett Tomko (Draft Pick)	1.00

Profiles-AL

Ten cards from this insert issue can be found in each of Topps Series 1 and 2. Analyzing an up-and-coming star, the cards are found every 12th pack, on average.

		NM/M
Complete Set (20):		8.00
Common Player:		.25
1	Roberto Alomar	.30
2	Carlos Baerga	.25
3	Albert Belle	.25
4	Cecil Fielder	.25
5	Ken Griffey Jr.	1.00
6	Randy Johnson	.60
7	Paul O'Neill	.25
8	Cal Ripken Jr.	1.50
9	Frank Thomas	.60
10	Mo Vaughn	.25
11	Jay Buhner	.25
12	Marty Cordova	.25
13	Jim Edmonds	.25
14	Juan Gonzalez	.35
15	Kenny Lofton	.25
16	Edgar Martinez	.25
17	Don Mattingly	.75
18	Mark McGwire	1.25
19	Rafael Palmeiro	.50
20	Tim Salmon	.25

Profiles-NL

Projected future stars of the National League are featured in this insert set. Ten players each are found in Series 1 and 2 packs at the rate of one per 12, on average.

		NM/M
Complete Set (20):		7.00
Common Player:		.25
1	Jeff Bagwell	.60
2	Derek Bell	.25
3	Barry Bonds	1.50
4	Greg Maddux	.75
5	Fred McGriff	.25
6	Raul Mondesi	.25
7	Mike Piazza	1.00
8	Reggie Sanders	.25
9	Sammy Sosa	.75
10	Larry Walker	.25
11	Dante Bichette	.25
12	Andres Galarraga	.25
13	Ron Gant	.25
14	Tom Glavine	.35
15	Chipper Jones	.75
16	David Justice	.25
17	Barry Larkin	.25
18	Hideo Nomo	.40
19	Gary Sheffield	.40
20	Matt Williams	.25

Road Warriors

These inserts feature top hitters and were only found in Series 2 packs sold at Wal-Mart stores. Cards have an RW prefix to their number. Fronts have action photos and gold foil highlights. Backs feature a portrait photo and hitting stats from the player's favorite out-of-town ballparks.

		NM/M
Complete Set (20):		9.00
Common Player:		.25
1	Derek Bell	.25
2	Albert Belle	.25
3	Craig Biggio	.25
4	Barry Bonds	2.50
5	Jay Buhner	.25
6	Jim Edmonds	.25
7	Gary Gaetti	.25
8	Ron Gant	.25
9	Edgar Martinez	.25
10	Tino Martinez	.25
11	Mark McGwire	1.50
12	Mike Piazza	1.25
13	Manny Ramirez	1.00
14	Tim Salmon	.25
15	Reggie Sanders	.25
16	Frank Thomas	1.00
17	John Valentin	.25
18	Mo Vaughn	.25
19	Robin Ventura	.25
20	Matt Williams	.25

Wrecking Crew

Printed on foilboard stock, cards of 15 players known for their hitting prowess are featured in this insert set. Found only in Series 2 hobby packs, the inserts are a one per 72 packs find, on average. Cards are numbered with a "WC" prefix.

		NM/M
Complete Set (15):		20.00
Common Player:		.50
1	Jeff Bagwell	1.50
2	Albert Belle	.50
3	Barry Bonds	5.00
4	Jose Canseco	.75
5	Joe Carter	.50
6	Cecil Fielder	.50
7	Ron Gant	.50
8	Juan Gonzalez	.75
9	Ken Griffey Jr.	3.00
10	Fred McGriff	.50
11	Mark McGwire	4.00
12	Mike Piazza	3.00
13	Frank Thomas	1.50
14	Mo Vaughn	.50
15	Matt Williams	.50

Team Topps

Some of baseball's most popular players and their teammates are featured on specially marked cards sold in blister packed team sets along with a jumbo "Big Topps" version of the team superstar's card. The team sets were a Wal-Mart exclusive, selling for around $5. Most of the Team Topps cards are identical to the regular-issue versions except for the addition of a gold-foil Team Topps logo on the card front. Several cards in this special issue have had their regular and Star Power backs transposed.

		NM/M
Complete Set (84):		25.00
Common Player:		.10
Orioles Team Set (19):		8.00
	Cal Ripken, Jr. Big Topps:	4.00
34	Manny Alexander	.10
65	Mike Mussina (Star Power front, regular back)	.50
96	Cal Ripken Jr. (2,131)	1.25
121	Curtis Goodwin	.10
183	Doug Jones	.10
191	Chris Hoiles	.10
200	Cal Ripken Jr.	2.50
222	Cal Ripken Jr. (Star Power)	1.25
228	Mike Mussina (Regular-card front, Star Power back)	.50
234	Alvie Shepherd (Draft Pick)	.10
258	Brady Anderson	.10
320	Ben McDonald	.10
329	Bobby Bonilla	.10
352	Rick Krivda (Now Appearing)	.10
354	Jimmy Haynes (Now Appearing)	.10
357	Harold Baines	.10
376	Kevin Brown	.10
395	Rafael Palmeiro	.65
Cubs Team Set (16):		5.00
	Ryne Sandberg Big Topps:	3.00
35	Todd Zeile	.10
55	Mark Grace	.10
62	Kevin Foster	.10
146	Frank Castillo	.10
184	Brian McRae	.10
198	Randy Myers	.10
239	Brian McNichol (Draft Pick)	.10
252	Sammy Sosa	1.00
278	Luis Gonzalez	.10
287	Rey Sanchez	.10
316	Jim Bullinger	.10
344	Brooks Kieshnick (Now Appearing)	.10
356	Ryne Sandberg	1.00
381	Jaime Navarro	.10
399	Shawon Dunston	.10
White Sox Team Set (15):		5.00
	Frank Thomas Big Topps:	2.50
52	Ron Karkovice	.10
100	Frank Thomas	.75
119	Lyle Mouton	.10
129	Ozzie Guillen	.10
159	Wilson Alvarez	.10
173	Ray Durham (All-Star Rookie)	.10
194	Alex Fernandez	.10
229	Frank Thomas (Star Power)	.40
243	Jeff Liefer (Draft Pick)	.10
272	Tim Raines	.10
310	Robin Ventura	.10
345	Chris Snopek (Now Appearing)	.10
375	Lance Johnson	.10
405	Roberto Hernandez	.10
Yankees Team Set (19):		8.00
	Derek Jeter Big Topps:	4.00
7	Mickey Mantle	3.00
27	Tony Fernandez	.10
68	Bernie Williams	.10
95	John Wetteland	.10
124	David Cone	.10
135	Mike Stanley	.10
185	Don Mattingly	1.25
203	Jack McDowell	.10
219	Derek Jeter (Future Star)	2.50
225	Wade Boggs (Star Power)	.50
245	Brian Buchanan (Draft Pick)	.10
273	Jimmy Key	.10
284	Paul O'Neill	.10
290	Ruben Sierra	.10
323	Wade Boggs	1.00
346	Ruben Rivera (Now Appearing)	.10
361	Randy Velarde	.10
378	Andy Pettitte	.35
Rangers team set (15):		5.00
	Juan Gonzalez Big Topps:	2.00
79	Roger Pavlik	.10
87	Rusty Greer	.10
130	Kenny Rogers	.10
140	Ivan Rodriguez	.65
152	Benji Gil	.10
166	Mark McLemore	.10
178	Otis Nixon	.10
227	Ivan Rodriguez (Star Power)	.35
242	Jonathan Johnson (Draft Pick)	.10
286	Mickey Tettleton	.10
299	Will Clark	.10
325	Juan Gonzalez	.35
387	Bob Tewksbury	.10
379	Dean Palmer	.10

American League Champion Cleveland Indians

Sold in a blister pack at Wal-Mart stores, this team set features specially overprinted versions of the Indians' regular '96 Topps cards, along with a super-size "Big Topps" card of Albert Belle. Each card carries a color logo recognizing the Tribe's A.L. Championship season of 1995. Sets sold for around $5.

		NM/M
Complete Set (21):		4.00
Common Player:		.10
Albert Belle Big Topps:		2.00
25	Sean Casey	1.50
40	Orel Hershiser	.10
45	Albert Belle	.10
75	Carlos Baerga	.10
81	Julian Tavarez	.10
84	Omar Vizquel	.10
125	Eddie Murray	.75
181	Denny Martinez	.10
223	Albert Belle (Star Power)	.10
226	Carlos Baerga (Star Power)	.10
231	Jose Mesa (Star Power)	.10
253	Jim Thome	.65
276	Jose Mesa	.10
294	Sandy Alomar	.10
326	Charles Nagy	.10
355	Herb Perry	.10
358	Chad Ogea	.10
373	Paul Sorrento	.10
400	Manny Ramirez	.75
414	Ken Hill	.10
420	Kenny Lofton	.10

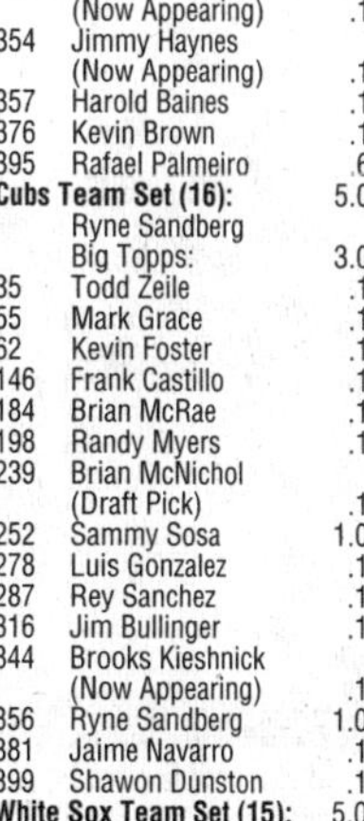

A.L. West Champion Seattle Mariners

These specially marked versions of Topps' regular '96 cards were sold for around $5 in a blister pack with a Ken Griffey, Jr. "Big Topps" card. The team sets were a Wal-Mart exclusive. Each of the Mariners' cards is overprinted with a color A.L. West Champions logo. Cards are otherwise identical to the regular issue.

		NM/M
Complete Set (18):		3.50
Common Player:		.10
Ken Griffey, Jr. Big Topps:		3.50
38	Tim Belcher	.10
67	Felix Fermin	.10
94	Alex Diaz	.10
117	Dan Wilson	.10
150	Randy Johnson	.75
168	Tino Martinez	.10
205	Ken Griffey Jr.	1.50
224	Randy Johnson (Star Power)	.40
230	Ken Griffey Jr. (Star Power)	.75
238	Shane Monahan (Draft Pick)	.10
247	Edgar Martinez	.10
263	Vince Coleman	.10
270	Jay Buhner	.10
304	Joey Cora	.10
314	Andy Benes	.10
353	Bob Wolcott (Now Appearing)	.10
392	Norm Charlton	.10
419	Mike Blowers	.10

Dodger Stadium 35th Anniversary L.A. Dodgers

Celebrating 35 seasons of play in Chavez Ravine, this team set of specially marked cards was issued in a blister pack with a jumbo Hideo Nomo "Big Topps" card. Selling for about $5, the team set was a Wal-Mart exclusive. Otherwise identical to the regular '96 Topps cards, these are overprinted with a colorful 35 Seasons logo. The backs of the two Mike Piazza cards in the set were switched. His regular card has the Star Power back (#2) while his Star Power card (#246) has the regular-issue back.

		NM/M
Complete Set (16):		5.00
Common Player:		.10
Hideo Nomo Big Topps:		2.00
2	Mike Piazza (Star Power back)	2.50
48	Todd Hollandsworth	.10
89	Jose Offerman	.10
136	Hideo Nomo (All-Star Rookie)	1.00
153	Tom Candiotti	.10
175	Raul Mondesi	.10
196	Eric Karros	.10
206	Ramon Martinez	.10
217	Karim Garcia (Future Star)	.25
236	David Yocum (Draft Pick)	.10
246	Mike Piazza (Star Power front)	2.50
277	Brett Butler	.10
312	Delino DeShields	.10
324	Ismael Valdes	.10
402	Chad Fonville	.10
412	Todd Worrell	.10

World Champions Atlanta Braves

These specially marked versions of Topps regular 1996 cards feature a color World Champions logo overprinted on the front of each card. They were sold as a team set along with a 3-1/2" x 5" "Big Topps" card at Wal-Mart stores for around $5.

		NM/M
Complete Set (17):		4.00
Common Player:		.10
Greg Maddux Big Topps:		3.00
3	Greg Maddux (Star Power)	.50
8	Tom Glavine (Star Power)	.15
12	Jim Scharrer (Draft Pick)	.10
49	Mark Wohlers	.10
60	David Justice	.10
83	Mark Lemke	.10
165	Steve Avery	.10
177	Chipper Jones (All-Star Rookie)	2.00
189	John Smoltz	.10
193	Ryan Klesko	.10
262	Tom Glavine	.30
266	Kent Mercker	.10
297	Marquis Grissom	.10
318	Greg Maddux	1.00
367	Javy Lopez	.10
389	Fred McGriff	.10
406	Jeff Blauser	.10

Big Topps

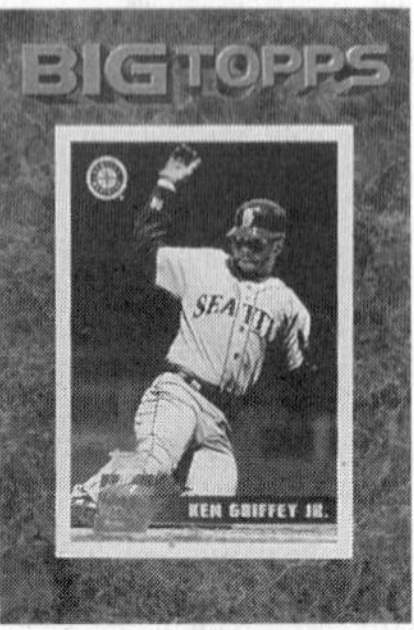

These double-size (3-1/2" x 5") cards are found exclusively in team-set blister packs prepared by Treat Entertainments for sale at Wal-Mart stores. Suggested retail price was just under $5. The Big Topps cards feature the fronts of the players' regular 1996 Topps card set against a marbled green background. Backs are in black-and-white with copyright data and licensors' logos. The unnumbered cards are checklisted here alphabetically.

		NM/M
Complete Set (9):		20.00
Common Player:		2.00
(1)	Albert Belle	2.00
(2)	Juan Gonzalez	2.00
(3)	Ken Griffey Jr.	3.50
(4)	Derek Jeter	4.00
(5)	Greg Maddux	3.00
(6)	Hideo Nomo	2.00
(7)	Cal Ripken Jr.	4.00
(8)	Ryne Sandberg	3.00
(9)	Frank Thomas	2.50

1996 Topps Chrome Promo Sheet

This promotional sheet was issued to promote the first annual issue of Topps Chrome baseball cards. The 8" x 5" sheet reproduces three of the card fronts from the forthcoming set in Topps' "Brilliant Chromium" technology. Back of the sheet is conventionally printed and advertises the set and its chase cards.

	NM/M
Sheet:	5.00

1996 Topps Chrome

In conjunction with baseball's postseason, Topps introduced the premiere edition of Chrome Baseball. The set has 165 of the elite players from 1996 Topps Series 1 and 2. Card #7 is a Mickey Mantle tribute card. There are two insert sets: Masters of the Game and Wrecking Crew, and scarcer Refractor versions for each.

		NM/M
Complete Set (165):		40.00
Common Player:		.10
Refractors:		3X
Pack (4):		2.00
Wax Box (24):		30.00
1	Tony Gwynn (Star Power)	1.00
2	Mike Piazza (Star Power)	1.25
3	Greg Maddux (Star Power)	1.00
4	Jeff Bagwell (Star Power)	.75
5	Larry Walker (Star Power)	.10
6	Barry Larkin (Star Power)	.10
7	Mickey Mantle (Commemorative)	9.00
8	Tom Glavine (Star Power)	.10
9	Craig Biggio (Star Power)	.10
10	Barry Bonds (Star Power)	2.00
11	Heathcliff Slocumb (Star Power)	.10
12	Matt Williams (Star Power)	.10
13	Todd Helton (Draft Pick)	2.00
14	Paul Molitor	1.50
15	Glenallen Hill	.10
16	Troy Percival	.10
17	Albert Belle	.10
18	Mark Wohlers	.10
19	Kirby Puckett	2.00
20	Mark Grace	.10
21	J.T. Snow	.10
22	David Justice	.10
23	Mike Mussina	.75
24	Bernie Williams	.10
25	Ron Gant	.10
26	Carlos Baerga	.10
27	Gary Sheffield	.65
28	Cal Ripken Jr. (Tribute Card)	2.00
29	Frank Thomas	1.50
30	Kevin Seitzer	.10
31	Joe Carter	.10
32	Jeff King	.10
33	David Cone	.10
34	Eddie Murray	1.50
35	Brian Jordan	.10
36	Garret Anderson	.10
37	Hideo Nomo	.75
38	Steve Finley	.10
39	Ivan Rodriguez	1.25
40	Quilvio Veras	.10
41	Mark McGwire	3.00
42	Greg Vaughn	.10
43	Randy Johnson	1.50
44	David Segui	.10
45	Derek Bell	.10
46	John Valentin	.10
47	Steve Avery	.10
48	Tino Martinez	.10
49	Shane Reynolds	.10
50	Jim Edmonds	.10
51	Raul Mondesi	.10
52	Chipper Jones	2.00
53	Gregg Jefferies	.10
54	Ken Caminiti	.10
55	Brian McRae	.10
56	Don Mattingly	2.25
57	Marty Cordova	.10
58	Vinny Castilla	.10
59	John Smoltz	.10
60	Travis Fryman	.10
61	Ryan Klesko	.10
62	Alex Fernandez	.10
63	Dante Bichette	.10
64	Eric Karros	.10
65	Roger Clemens	2.25
66	Randy Myers	.10
67	Cal Ripken Jr.	4.00
68	Rod Beck	.10
69	Jack McDowell	.10
70	Ken Griffey Jr.	2.50
71	Ramon Martinez	.10
72	Jason Giambi (Future Star)	.75
73	Nomar Garciaparra (Future Star)	2.00
74	Billy Wagner (Future Star)	.10
75	Todd Greene (Future Star)	.10
76	Paul Wilson (Future Star)	.10
77	Johnny Damon (Future Star)	.35
78	Alan Benes (Future Star)	.10
79	Karim Garcia (Future Star)	.25
80	Derek Jeter (Future Star)	4.00
81	Kirby Puckett (Star Power)	1.00
82	Cal Ripken Jr. (Star Power)	2.00
83	Albert Belle (Star Power)	.10
84	Randy Johnson (Star Power)	.40
85	Wade Boggs (Star Power)	1.00
86	Carlos Baerga (Star Power)	.10
87	Ivan Rodriguez (Star Power)	.35
88	Mike Mussina (Star Power)	.30
89	Frank Thomas (Star Power)	.75
90	Ken Griffey Jr. (Star Power)	1.25
91	Jose Mesa (Star Power)	.10
92	Matt Morris **RC** (Draft Pick)	1.00
93	Mike Piazza	2.50
94	Edgar Martinez	.10
95	Chuck Knoblauch	.10
96	Andres Galarraga	.10
97	Tony Gwynn	2.00
98	Lee Smith	.10
99	Sammy Sosa	2.00
100	Jim Thome	1.25
101	Bernard Gilkey	.10
102	Brady Anderson	.10
103	Rico Brogna	.10
104	Lenny Dykstra	.10
105	Tom Glavine	.35
106	John Olerud	.10
107	Terry Steinbach	.10
108	Brian Hunter	.10
109	Jay Buhner	.10
110	Mo Vaughn	.10
111	Jose Mesa	.10
112	Brett Butler	.10
113	Chili Davis	.10
114	Paul O'Neill	.10
115	Roberto Alomar	.35
116	Barry Larkin	.10
117	Marquis Grissom	.10
118	Will Clark	.10
119	Barry Bonds	4.00
120	Ozzie Smith	2.00
121	Pedro Martinez	1.50
122	Craig Biggio	.10
123	Moises Alou	.10
124	Robin Ventura	.10
125	Greg Maddux	2.00
126	Tim Salmon	.10
127	Wade Boggs	2.00
128	Ismael Valdes	.10
129	Juan Gonzalez	.75
130	Ray Lankford	.10
131	Bobby Bonilla	.10
132	Reggie Sanders	.10
133	Alex Ochoa (Now Appearing)	.10
134	Mark Loretta (Now Appearing)	.10
135	Jason Kendall (Now Appearing)	.10
136	Brooks Kieschnick (Now Appearing)	.10
137	Chris Snopek (Now Appearing)	.10
138	Ruben Rivera (Now Appearing)	.10
139	Jeff Suppan (Now Appearing)	.10
140	John Wasdin (Now Appearing)	.10
141	Jay Payton (Now Appearing)	.10
142	Rick Krivda (Now Appearing)	.10
143	Jimmy Haynes (Now Appearing)	.10
144	Ryne Sandberg	2.00
145	Matt Williams	.10
146	Jose Canseco	.65
147	Larry Walker	.10
148	Kevin Appier	.10
149	Javy Lopez	.10
150	Dennis Eckersley	1.25
151	Jason Isringhausen	.10
152	Dean Palmer	.10
153	Jeff Bagwell	1.50
154	Rondell White	.10
155	Wally Joyner	.10
156	Fred McGriff	.10
157	Cecil Fielder	.10
158	Rafael Palmeiro	1.25
159	Rickey Henderson	1.50
160	Shawon Dunston	.10
161	Manny Ramirez	1.50
162	Alex Gonzalez	.10
163	Shawn Green	.45
164	Kenny Lofton	.10
165	Jeff Conine	.10

Masters of the Game

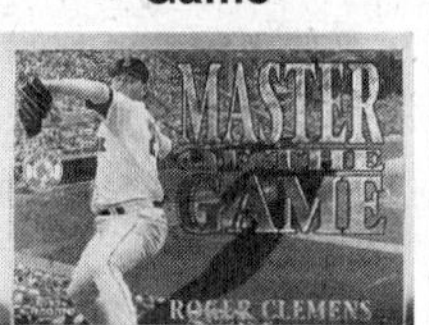

These 1996 Topps Chrome inserts were seeded one per every 12 packs. Each of the cards is also reprinted in a Refractor version; these cards are seeded one per every 36 packs.

		NM/M
Complete Set (20):		35.00
Common Player:		1.00
Refractors:		1.5X
1	Dennis Eckersley	2.00
2	Denny Martinez	1.00
3	Eddie Murray	2.50
4	Paul Molitor	2.50
5	Ozzie Smith	3.50
6	Rickey Henderson	2.50
7	Tim Raines	1.00
8	Lee Smith	1.00
9	Cal Ripken Jr.	6.00
10	Chili Davis	1.00
11	Wade Boggs	3.50
12	Tony Gwynn	3.50
13	Don Mattingly	4.00
14	Bret Saberhagen	1.00
15	Kirby Puckett	3.50
16	Joe Carter	1.00
17	Roger Clemens	4.00
18	Barry Bonds	6.00
19	Greg Maddux	3.50
20	Frank Thomas	2.50

Wrecking Crew

Wrecking Crew insert cards were inserted one per every 24 packs of 1996 Topps Chrome Baseball. Refractor versions were also made for these cards;

they are seeded one per every 72 packs. Cards are numbered with a "WC" prefix.

		NM/M
Complete Set (15):		25.00
Common Player:		1.00
Refractors:		1.5X
1	Jeff Bagwell	2.50
2	Albert Belle	1.00
3	Barry Bonds	5.00
4	Jose Canseco	1.50
5	Joe Carter	1.00
6	Cecil Fielder	1.00
7	Ron Gant	1.00
8	Juan Gonzalez	1.25
9	Ken Griffey Jr.	3.50
10	Fred McGriff	1.00
11	Mark McGwire	4.00
12	Mike Piazza	4.00
13	Frank Thomas	2.50
14	Mo Vaughn	1.00
15	Matt Williams	1.00

1996 Topps Gallery

This 180-card set is printed on 24-point stock utilizing metallic inks and a high-definition printing process. Then a high-gloss film is applied to each card, followed by foil stamping. The regular set is broken down into five subsets - The Classics, The Modernists, The Futurists, The Masters and New Editions. Each theme has a different design. Gallery also has four insert sets. Player's Private Issue cards are a parallel set to the main issue; these cards are seeded one per every 12 packs. The backs are sequentially numbered from 0-999, with the first 100 cards sent to the players; the rest are inserted into packs. The backs are UV coated on the photo only, to allow for autographing. The other insert sets are Expressionists, Photo Gallery and a Mickey Mantle Masterpiece card.

		NM/M
Complete Set (180):		20.00
Common Player:		.10
Private Issue:		8X
Pack (8):		1.50
Wax Box (24):		27.50
1	Tom Glavine	.35
2	Carlos Baerga	.10
3	Dante Bichette	.10
4	Mark Langston	.10
5	Ray Lankford	.10
6	Moises Alou	.10
7	Marquis Grissom	.10
8	Ramon Martinez	.10
8p	Ramon Martinez (Unmarked promo, "Pitcher" spelled out under photo on back.)	2.50
9	Steve Finley	.10

#	Player	NM/M
10	Todd Hundley	.10
11	Brady Anderson	.10
12	John Valentin	.10
13	Heathcliff Slocumb	.10
14	Ruben Sierra	.10
15	Jeff Conine	.10
16	Jay Buhner	.10
16p	Jay Buhner (Unmarked promo; height, weight and "Bats" on same line.)	2.50
17	Sammy Sosa	1.00
18	Doug Drabek	.10
19	Jose Mesa	.10
20	Jeff King	.10
21	Mickey Tettleton	.10
22	Jeff Montgomery	.10
23	Alex Fernandez	.10
24	Greg Vaughn	.10
25	Chuck Finley	.10
26	Terry Steinbach	.10
27	Rod Beck	.10
28	Jack McDowell	.10
29	Mark Wohlers	.10
30	Lenny Dykstra	.10
31	Bernie Williams	.10
32	Travis Fryman	.10
33	Jose Canseco	.45
34	Ken Caminiti	.10
35	Devon White	.10
36	Bobby Bonilla	.10
37	Paul Sorrento	.10
38	Ryne Sandberg	1.00
39	Derek Bell	.10
40	Bobby Jones	.10
41	J.T. Snow	.10
42	Denny Neagle	.10
43	Tim Wakefield	.10
44	Andres Galarraga	.10
45	David Segui	.10
46	Lee Smith	.10
47	Mel Rojas	.10
48	John Franco	.10
49	Pete Schourek	.10
50	John Wetteland	.10
51	Paul Molitor	.75
52	Ivan Rodriguez	.65
53	Chris Hoiles	.10
54	Mike Greenwell	.10
55	Orel Hershiser	.10
56	Brian McRae	.10
57	Geronimo Berroa	.10
58	Craig Biggio	.10
59	David Justice	.10
59p	David Justice (Unmarked promo; height,weight and "Bats"on same line.)	2.50
60	Lance Johnson	.10
61	Andy Ashby	.10
62	Randy Myers	.10
63	Gregg Jefferies	.10
64	Kevin Appier	.10
65	Rick Aguilera	.10
66	Shane Reynolds	.10
67	John Smoltz	.10
68	Ron Gant	.10
69	Eric Karros	.10
70	Jim Thome	.65
71	Terry Pendleton	.10
72	Kenny Rogers	.10
73	Robin Ventura	.10
74	Dave Nilsson	.10
75	Brian Jordan	.10
76	Glenallen Hill	.10
77	Greg Colbrunn	.10
78	Roberto Alomar	.25
79	Rickey Henderson	.75
80	Carlos Garcia	.10
81	Dean Palmer	.10
82	Mike Stanley	.10
83	Hal Morris	.10
84	Wade Boggs	1.00
85	Chad Curtis	.10
86	Roberto Hernandez	.10
87	John Olerud	.10
88	Frank Castillo	.10
89	Rafael Palmeiro	.65
90	Trevor Hoffman	.10
91	Marty Cordova	.10
92	Hideo Nomo	.35
93	Johnny Damon	.30
94	Bill Pulsipher	.10
95	Garret Anderson	.10
96	Ray Durham	.10
97	Ricky Bottalico	.10
98	Carlos Perez	.10
99	Troy Percival	.10
100	Chipper Jones	1.00
101	Esteban Loaiza	.10
102	John Mabry	.10
103	Jon Nunnally	.10
104	Andy Pettitte	.35
105	Lyle Mouton	.10
106	Jason Isringhausen	.10
107	Brian Hunter	.10
108	Quilvio Veras	.10
109	Jim Edmonds	.10
110	Ryan Klesko	.10
111	Pedro Martinez	.75
112	Joey Hamilton	.10
113	Vinny Castilla	.10
114	Alex Gonzalez	.10
115	Raul Mondesi	.10
116	Rondell White	.10
117	Dan Miceli	.10
118	Tom Goodwin	.10
119	Bret Boone	.10
120	Shawn Green	.35
121	Jeff Cirillo	.10
122	Rico Brogna	.10
123	Chris Gomez	.10
124	Ismael Valdes	.10
125	Javy Lopez	.10
126	Manny Ramirez	.75
127	Paul Wilson	.10
128	Billy Wagner	.10
129	Eric Owens	.10
130	Todd Greene	.10
131	Karim Garcia	.10
132	Jimmy Haynes	.10
133	Michael Tucker	.10
134	John Wasdin	.10
135	Brooks Kieschnick	.10
136	Alex Ochoa	.10
137	Ariel Prieto	.10
138	Tony Clark	.10
139	Mark Loretta	.10
140	Rey Ordonez	.10
141	Chris Snopek	.10
142	Roger Cedeno	.10
143	Derek Jeter	2.00
144	Jeff Suppan	.10
145	Greg Maddux	1.00
146	Ken Griffey Jr.	1.25
147	Tony Gwynn	1.00
148	Darren Daulton	.10
149	Will Clark	.10
150	Mo Vaughn	.10
151	Reggie Sanders	.10
152	Kirby Puckett	1.00
153	Paul O'Neill	.10
154	Tim Salmon	.10
155	Mark McGwire	1.50
156	Barry Bonds	2.00
157	Albert Belle	.10
158	Edgar Martinez	.10
159	Mike Mussina	.35
160	Cecil Fielder	.10
161	Kenny Lofton	.10
162	Randy Johnson	.75
163	Juan Gonzalez	.35
164	Jeff Bagwell	.75
165	Joe Carter	.10
166	Mike Piazza	1.25
167	Eddie Murray	.75
168	Cal Ripken Jr.	2.00
169	Barry Larkin	.10
170	Chuck Knoblauch	.10
171	Chili Davis	.10
172	Fred McGriff	.10
173	Matt Williams	.10
174	Roger Clemens	1.00
175	Frank Thomas	.75
176	Dennis Eckersley	.10
177	Gary Sheffield	.40
178	David Cone	.10
179	Larry Walker	.10
180	Mark Grace	.10

Players Private Issue

The first 999 examples of each of the base cards in the Gallery issue are designated on the front with a gold-foil stamp as "Players Private Issue." The first 100 of those cards were given to the depicted player, the others are randomly packed. Besides the logo on front, the PPI cards are identified on back with an individual serial number.

	NM/M
Complete Set (180):	200.00
Common Player:	1.00
Stars:	8X

Expressionists

These 1996 Topps Gallery inserts feature 20 team leaders printed on triple foil-stamped and texture-embossed cards. Cards are seeded one per every 24 packs.

#	Player	NM/M
	Complete Set (20):	20.00
	Common Player:	.35
1	Mike Piazza	3.00
2	J.T. Snow	.35
3	Ken Griffey Jr.	3.00
4	Kirby Puckett	2.00
5	Carlos Baerga	.35
6	Chipper Jones	2.00
7	Hideo Nomo	.75
8	Mark McGwire	4.00
9	Gary Sheffield	.75
10	Randy Johnson	1.25
11	Ray Lankford	.35
12	Sammy Sosa	2.00
13	Denny Martinez	.35
14	Jose Canseco	.75
15	Tony Gwynn	2.00
16	Edgar Martinez	.35
17	Reggie Sanders	.35
18	Andres Galarraga	.35
19	Albert Belle	.35
20	Barry Larkin	.35

Masterpiece

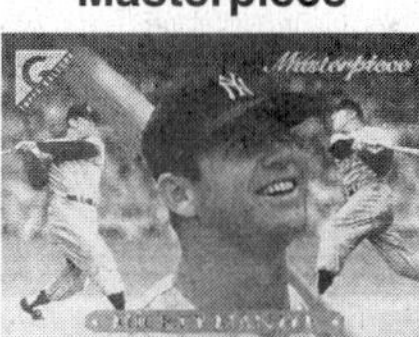

Topps continues its tribute to Mickey Mantle with this 1996 Topps Gallery insert card. The card, seeded one per every 48 packs, has three photos of Mantle on the front, with his comprehensive career statistics on the back.

#	Player	NM/M
MP1	Mickey Mantle	6.00

Photo Gallery

Photo Gallery is a collection of 15 cards featuring photography of baseball's biggest stars and greatest moments from the last season. The text on the card includes details of the card's front and back photos. The cards are seeded one per every 30 packs. Cards are numbered with a "PG" prefix.

#	Player	NM/M
	Complete Set (15):	20.00
	Common Player:	.75
1	Eddie Murray	2.00
2	Randy Johnson	2.00
3	Cal Ripken Jr.	5.00
4	Bret Boone	.75
5	Frank Thomas	2.00
6	Jeff Conine	.75
7	Johnny Damon	.85
8	Roger Clemens	3.00
9	Albert Belle	.75
10	Ken Griffey Jr.	4.00
11	Kirby Puckett	2.50
12	David Justice	.75
13	Bobby Bonilla	.75
14	Larry Walker, Andres Galarraga, Vinny Castilla, Dante Bichette	1.00
15	Mark Wohlers, Javier Lopez	.75

Derek Jeter Panel

The method of issue for this triple-size (about 7-1/2" x 3-1/2") panel is uncertain. It has been reported that the piece was inserted into some 1995 Topps Hobby factory sets as an unadvertised bonus. The front has an action sequence showing the Yankees shortstop turning a double play. On back is personal data, minor and major league stats, a repeat of the center photo and a few sentences about the budding superstar.

	NM/M
Derek Jeter	7.50

Landmark Medallions

Milestones of the 1995 season are recalled in this set of limited edition (2,000) medallions. Each of the 2-1/2" x 3-1/2" pieces features a Topps Finest technology card bonded to a 1/8" thick, 4-oz. burnished bronze ingot, then clear-coated. Backs have career stats and a description of the milestone minted into the bronze. The issue was sold only as complete sets through Topps Stadium Club; issue price was $100.

#	Player	NM/M
	Complete Set (4):	75.00
	Common Player:	10.00
1	Greg Maddux (4th straight Cy Young)	20.00
2	Albert Belle (First 50 HR/50 2B season)	10.00
3	Cal Ripken, Jr. (2,131 consecutive games)	35.00
4	Eddie Murray (3,000 hits)	15.00

1996 Topps Laser

Topps' 1996 Laser Baseball was the first set to use laser-cut technology on every card, creating surgically-precise latticework across the entire card. Every card in the 128-card regular issue set features one of four designs laser-cut into 20-point stock. One card from each of the four different designs is found in each four-card pack. Three different laser-cut insert sets were also produced: Bright Spots, Power Cuts and Stadium Stars. Cards 1-8 from each insert set were in Series 1 packs; cards 9-16 were seeded in Series 2 packs. A slightly oversize (1-5/8" x 3-5/8") checklist card in each pack helped protect the delicate die-cut details from damage.

#	Player	NM/M
	Complete Set (128):	27.50
	Common Player:	.10
	Series 1 or 2 Pack (4):	1.50
	Series 1 or 2 Wax Box (24):	22.50
1	Moises Alou	.10
2	Derek Bell	.10
3	Joe Carter	.10
4	Jeff Conine	.10
5	Darren Daulton	.10
6	Jim Edmonds	.10
7	Ron Gant	.10
8	Juan Gonzalez	.50
9	Brian Jordan	.10
10	Ryan Klesko	.10
11	Paul Molitor	1.00
12	Tony Phillips	.10
13	Manny Ramirez	1.00
14	Sammy Sosa	1.50
15	Devon White	.10
16	Bernie Williams	.10
17	Garret Anderson	.10
18	Jay Bell	.10
19	Craig Biggio	.10
20	Bobby Bonilla	.10
21	Ken Caminiti	.10
22	Shawon Dunston	.10
23	Mark Grace	.10
23p	Mark Grace (Unmarked promo, plain, rather than brushed, gold foil.)	2.00
24	Gregg Jefferies	.10
25	Jeff King	.10
26	Javy Lopez	.10
27	Edgar Martinez	.10
28	Dean Palmer	.10
29	J.T. Snow	.10
30	Mike Stanley	.10
30p	Mike Stanley (Unmarked promo; plain, rather than brushed, gold foil.)	1.00
31	Terry Steinbach	.10
32	Robin Ventura	.10
33	Roberto Alomar	.20
34	Jeff Bagwell	1.00
35	Dante Bichette	.10
36	Wade Boggs	1.50
37	Barry Bonds	3.00
38	Jose Canseco	.50
39	Vinny Castilla	.10
40	Will Clark	.10
41	Marty Cordova	.10
42	Ken Griffey Jr.	2.00
43	Tony Gwynn	1.50
44	Rickey Henderson	1.00
45	Chipper Jones	1.50
46	Mark McGwire	2.50
47	Brian McRae	.10
48	Ryne Sandberg	1.50
49	Andy Ashby	.10
50	Alan Benes	.10
51	Andy Benes	.10
52	Roger Clemens	1.75
53	Doug Drabek	.10
54	Dennis Eckersley	.75
55	Tom Glavine	.35
56	Randy Johnson	1.00
57	Mark Langston	.10
58	Denny Martinez	.10
59	Jack McDowell	.10
60	Hideo Nomo	.50
61	Shane Reynolds	.10
62	John Smoltz	.10
63	Paul Wilson	.10
64	Mark Wohlers	.10
65	Shawn Green	.35
66	Marquis Grissom	.10
67	Dave Hollins	.10
68	Todd Hundley	.10
69	David Justice	.10
70	Eric Karros	.10
71	Ray Lankford	.10
72	Fred McGriff	.10
73	Hal Morris	.10
74	Eddie Murray	1.00
75	Paul O'Neill	.10
76	Rey Ordonez	.10
77	Reggie Sanders	.10
78	Gary Sheffield	.45
79	Jim Thome	.75
80	Rondell White	.10
81	Travis Fryman	.10
82	Derek Jeter	3.00
83	Chuck Knoblauch	.10
84	Barry Larkin	.10
85	Tino Martinez	.10
86	Raul Mondesi	.10
87	John Olerud	.10
88	Rafael Palmeiro	.75
89	Mike Piazza	2.00
90	Cal Ripken Jr.	3.00
91	Ivan Rodriguez	.75
92	Frank Thomas	1.00
93	John Valentin	.10
94	Mo Vaughn	.10
95	Quilvio Veras	.10
96	Matt Williams	.10
97	Brady Anderson	.10
98	Carlos Baerga	.10
99	Albert Belle	.10
100	Jay Buhner	.10
101	Johnny Damon	.35
102	Chili Davis	.10
103	Ray Durham	.10
104	Lenny Dykstra	.10
105	Cecil Fielder	.10
106	Andres Galarraga	.10
107	Brian Hunter	.10
108	Kenny Lofton	.10
109	Kirby Puckett	1.50
110	Tim Salmon	.10
111	Greg Vaughn	.10
112	Larry Walker	.10
113	Rick Aguilera	.10
114	Kevin Appier	.10
115	Kevin Brown	.10
116	David Cone	.10
117	Alex Fernandez	.10
118	Chuck Finley	.10
119	Joey Hamilton	.10
120	Jason Isringhausen	.10
121	Greg Maddux	1.50
122	Pedro Martinez	1.00
123	Jose Mesa	.10
124	Jeff Montgomery	.10
125	Mike Mussina	.50
126	Randy Myers	.10
127	Kenny Rogers	.10
128	Ismael Valdes	.10
	Series 1 Checklist	.05
	Series 2 Checklist	.05

Bright Spots

Top young stars are featured on these insert cards, which use etched silver and gold diffraction foil. The cards are seeded one per 20 packs. Numbers 1-8 are in Series 1 packs; cards 9-16 are in Series 2 packs.

#	Player	NM/M
	Complete Set (16):	17.50
	Common Player:	.50
1	Brian Hunter	.50
2	Derek Jeter	4.50
3	Jason Kendall	.50
4	Brooks Kieschnick	.50
5	Rey Ordonez	.50
6	Jason Schmidt	.50
7	Chris Snopek	.50
8	Bob Wolcott	.50
9	Alan Benes	.50
10	Marty Cordova	.50
11	Jimmy Haynes	.50
12	Todd Hollandsworth	.50
13	Derek Jeter	4.50
14	Chipper Jones	3.00
15	Hideo Nomo	1.00
16	Paul Wilson	.50

Power Cuts

This insert set spotlights 16 of the game's top power hitters on etched foil and gold diffraction foil cards. These cards were seeded one per 40

packs; numbers 1-8 were in Series 1 packs; cards 9-16 were in Series 2 packs.

		NM/M
Complete Set (16):		20.00
Common Player:		.75
1	Albert Belle	.75
2	Jay Buhner	.75
3	Fred McGriff	.75
4	Mike Piazza	3.00
5	Tim Salmon	.75
6	Frank Thomas	2.00
7	Mo Vaughn	.75
8	Matt Williams	.75
9	Jeff Bagwell	2.00
10	Barry Bonds	5.00
11	Jose Canseco	1.00
12	Cecil Fielder	.75
13	Juan Gonzalez	1.00
14	Ken Griffey Jr.	3.00
15	Sammy Sosa	2.50
16	Larry Walker	.75

Stadium Stars

These 1996 Topps Laser cards are the most difficult to find; they are seeded one per every 60 packs. The 16 cards feature a laser-sculpted cover that folds back to reveal striated silver and gold etched diffraction foil on each card front. Cards 1-8 were in Series I packs; numbers 9-16 were Series II inserts.

		NM/M
Complete Set (16):		45.00
Common Player:		1.50
1	Carlos Baerga	1.50
2	Barry Bonds	10.00
3	Andres Galarraga	1.50
4	Ken Griffey Jr.	7.50
5	Barry Larkin	1.50
6	Raul Mondesi	1.50
7	Kirby Puckett	5.00
8	Cal Ripken Jr.	10.00
9	Will Clark	1.50
10	Roger Clemens	6.00
11	Tony Gwynn	5.00
12	Randy Johnson	4.00
13	Kenny Lofton	1.50
14	Edgar Martinez	1.50
15	Ryne Sandberg	5.00
16	Frank Thomas	4.00

League Leaders Finest Bronze

Specially designed Topps Finest cards are bedded to a slab of bronze and clear-coated in this set honoring major award winners from the 1995 season. A "League Leaders" logo at top has the player's award inscribed. Backs of the 2-3/4" x 3-3/4" ingots are silk-screened with season and career stats. The issue was sold only in complete sets (2,000 limit) through Topps Stadium Club for $80.

		NM/M
Complete Set (6):		75.00
Common Player:		10.00
(1)	Mo Vaughn (A.L. MVP)	10.00
(2)	Barry Larkin (N.L. MVP)	10.00
(3)	Randy Johnson (A.L. CY)	15.00
(4)	Greg Maddux (N.L. CY)	30.00
(5)	Marty Cordova (A.L. ROY)	10.00
(6)	Hideo Nomo (N.L. ROY)	15.00

Legends of the '50s

A dozen of the greatest players of the 1950s ever to grace a Topps card are featured in this set of bronze replicas. Each player's card is reproduced in a 4-oz. bronze version in 2-1/2" x 3-1/2" format. The card fronts are faithfully reproduced on each ingot, while the backs have been modified to present the player's lifetime stats. The ingots were sold through Topps' Stadium Club for about $45 apiece through a monthly subscription plan. The complete set was housed in a special wooden display case. The ingots are checklisted here alphabetically, with the year of Topps card reproduced noted parenthetically.

		NM/M
Complete Set (12):		275.00
Common Player:		20.00
(1)	Ernie Banks/1954	20.00
(2)	Yogi Berra/1952	20.00
(3)	Roy Campanella/1952	20.00
(4)	Whitey Ford/1953	20.00
(5)	Mickey Mantle/1952	35.00
(6)	Eddie Mathews/1952	20.00
(7)	Willie Mays/1953	25.00
(8)	Stan Musial/1959	20.00
(9)	Jackie Robinson/1952	20.00
(10)	Duke Snider/1955	20.00
(11)	Warren Spahn/1952	20.00
(12)	Ted Williams/1954 (#250)	30.00

"1952" Gold Willie Mays

This reproduction of Topps' 1952 card #261 is embossed and covered in 22 karat gold foil. Each full-size replica card is serially numbered within an edition of 50,000.

		NM/M
261	Willie Mays	12.00

"1954" Ted Williams Gold

This reproduction of Topps' 1954 card #1, Ted Williams, is embossed and covered in 22 karat gold foil. Each full-size replica card is serially numbered within an edition of 50,000.

		NM/M
1	Ted Williams	12.00

"1959" Stan Musial Gold

Topps' first regular-issue card of Stan Musial was reproduced in a full-size (2-1/2" x 3-1/2") 22-karat gold foil edition sold through Topps' Stadium Club. Each of the gold replicas bears a unique serial number. Issue price of the card was about $30.

		NM/M
150	Stan Musial	10.00

1997 Topps

Topps' 1997 set includes the first-ever player cards of the expansion Diamondbacks and Devil Rays; 16 Mickey Mantle reprints; a special Jackie Robinson tribute card; 27 Willie Mays Topps and Bowman reprints; randomly-inserted Willie Mays autographed reprint cards; and Inter-League Finest and Finest Refractors cards. The base set has 275 cards in Series 1 and 220 cards in Series 2. Each

card front has a glossy coating on the photo and a spot matte finish on the border, with gold-foil graphics. Card backs have informative text, complete player stats and biographies, and a second photo. Mantle reprints, seeded one per 12 packs, feature the 16 remaining Mantle cards which were not reprinted in 1996, stamped with a gold foil logo, and numbered from #21 to #36. Willie Mays has 27 of his cards reprinted and seeded one per eight packs. Each card also has a gold foil stamp. As a special hobby-exclusive bonus, 1,000 Mays reprints were autographed and randomly inserted in packs. Five other insert sets were made: All-Stars, Inter-League Finest and Inter-League Finest Refractors, Sweet Strokes and Hobby Masters. Two factory sets, comprising the 495 base cards and either seven or eight random inserts were produced and currently enjoy a significant premium over hand-collated sets.

		NM/M
Unopened Fact. Set (504):		110.00
Unopened Fact. Set (503):		145.00
Complete Set (495):		65.00
Common Player:		.05
Ser. 1 or 2 Pack (11):		1.00
Ser. 1 or 2 Wax Box (36):		20.00
Ser. 1 or 2 Vending Box (500):		12.00
1	Barry Bonds	2.00
2	Tom Pagnozzi	.05
3	Terrell Wade	.05
4	Jose Valentin	.05
5	Mark Clark	.05
6	Brady Anderson	.05
8	Wade Boggs	1.00
9	Scott Stahoviak	.05
10	Andres Galarraga	.05
11	Steve Avery	.05
12	Rusty Greer	.05
13	Derek Jeter	2.00
14	Ricky Bottalico	.05
15	Andy Ashby	.05
16	Paul Shuey	.05
17	F.P. Santangelo	.05
18	Royce Clayton	.05
19	Mike Mohler	.05
20	Mike Piazza	1.50
21	Jaime Navarro	.05
22	Billy Wagner	.05
23	Mike Timlin	.05
24	Garret Anderson	.05
25	Ben McDonald	.05
26	Mel Rojas	.05
27	John Burkett	.05
28	Jeff King	.05
29	Reggie Jefferson	.05
30	Kevin Appier	.05
31	Felipe Lira	.05
32	Kevin Tapani	.05
33	Mark Portugal	.05
34	Carlos Garcia	.05
35	Joey Cora	.05
36	David Segui	.05
37	Mark Grace	.05
38	Erik Hanson	.05
39	Jeff D'Amico	.05
40	Jay Buhner	.05
41	B.J. Surhoff	.05
42	Jackie Robinson	1.50
43	Roger Pavlik	.05
44	Hal Morris	.05
45	Mariano Duncan	.05
46	Harold Baines	.05
47	Jorge Fabregas	.05
48	Jose Herrera	.05
49	Jeff Cirillo	.05
50	Tom Glavine	.25
51	Pedro Astacio	.05
52	Mark Gardner	.05
53	Arthur Rhodes	.05
54	Troy O'Leary	.05
55	Bip Roberts	.05
56	Mike Lieberthal	.05
57	Shane Andrews	.05
58	Scott Karl	.05
59	Gary DiSarcina	.05
60	Andy Pettitte	.25
61a	Kevin Elster	.05
61b	Mike Fetters (Should be #84.)	.05
62	Mark McGwire	1.75
63	Dan Wilson	.05
64	Mickey Morandini	.05
65	Chuck Knoblauch	.05
66	Tim Wakefield	.05
67	Raul Mondesi	.05
68	Todd Jones	.05
69	Albert Belle	.05
70	Trevor Hoffman	.05
71	Eric Young	.05
72	Robert Perez	.05
73	Butch Huskey	.05
74	Brian McRae	.05
75	Jim Edmonds	.05
76	Mike Henneman	.05
77	Frank Rodriguez	.05
78	Danny Tartabull	.05
79	Robby Nen	.05
80	Reggie Sanders	.05
81	Ron Karkovice	.05
82	Benny Santiago	.05
83	Mike Lansing	.05
85	Craig Biggio	.05
86	Mike Bordick	.05
87	Ray Lankford	.05
88	Charles Nagy	.05
89	Paul Wilson	.05
90	John Wetteland	.05
91	Tom Candiotti	.05
92	Carlos Delgado	.45
93	Derek Bell	.05
94	Mark Lemke	.05
95	Edgar Martinez	.05
96	Rickey Henderson	.75
97	Greg Myers	.05
98	Jim Leyritz	.05
99	Mark Johnson	.05
100	Dwight Gooden (Season Highlights)	.05
101	Al Leiter (Season Highlights)	.05
102a	John Mabry (Season Highlights) (Last line on back ends "... Mabry".)	.05
102b	John Mabry (Season Highlights) (Last line on back ends "...walked.")	.05
103	Alex Ochoa (Season Highlights)	.05
104	Mike Piazza (Season Highlights)	.75
105	Jim Thome	.65
106	Ricky Otero	.05
107	Jamey Wright	.05
108	Frank Thomas	.75
109	Jody Reed	.05
110	Orel Hershiser	.05
111	Terry Steinbach	.05
112	Mark Loretta	.05
113	Turk Wendell	.05
114	Marvin Benard	.05
115	Kevin Brown	.05
116	Robert Person	.05
117	Joey Hamilton	.05
118	Francisco Cordova	.05
119	John Smiley	.05
120	Travis Fryman	.05
121	Jimmy Key	.05
122	Tom Goodwin	.05
123	Mike Greenwell	.05
124	Juan Gonzalez	.35
125	Pete Harnisch	.05
126	Roger Cedeno	.05
127	Ron Gant	.05
128	Mark Langston	.05
129	Tim Crabtree	.05
130	Greg Maddux	1.00
131	William Van Landingham	.05
132	Wally Joyner	.05
133	Randy Myers	.05
134	John Valentin	.05
135	Bret Boone	.05
136	Bruce Ruffin	.05
137	Chris Snopek	.05
138	Paul Molitor	.75
139	Mark McLemore	.05
140	Rafael Palmeiro	.65
141	Herb Perry	.05
142	Luis Gonzalez	.05
143	Doug Drabek	.05
144	Ken Ryan	.05
145	Todd Hundley	.05
146	Ellis Burks	.05
147	Ozzie Guillen	.05
148	Rich Becker	.05
149	Sterling Hitchcock	.05
150	Bernie Williams	.05
151	Mike Stanley	.05
152	Roberto Alomar	.25
153	Jose Mesa	.05
154	Steve Trachsel	.05
155	Alex Gonzalez	.05
156	Troy Percival	.05
157	John Smoltz	.05
158	Pedro Martinez	.75
159	Jeff Conine	.05
160	Bernard Gilkey	.05
161	Jim Eisenreich	.05
162	Mickey Tettleton	.05
163	Justin Thompson	.05
164	Jose Offerman	.05
165	Tony Phillips	.05
166	Ismael Valdes	.05
167	Ryne Sandberg	1.00
168	Matt Mieske	.05
169	Geronimo Berroa	.05
170	Otis Nixon	.05
171	John Mabry	.05
172	Shawon Dunston	.05
173	Omar Vizquel	.05
174	Chris Holles	.05
175	Doc Gooden	.05
176	Wilson Alvarez	.05
177	Todd Hollandsworth	.05
178	Roger Salkeld	.05
179	Rey Sanchez	.05
180	Rey Ordonez	.05
181	Denny Martinez	.05
182	Ramon Martinez	.05
183	Dave Nilsson	.05
184	Marquis Grissom	.05
185	Randy Velarde	.05
186	Ron Coomer	.05
187	Tino Martinez	.05
188	Jeff Brantley	.05
189	Steve Finley	.05
190	Andy Benes	.05
191	Terry Adams	.05
192	Mike Blowers	.05
193	Russ Davis	.05
194	Darryl Hamilton	.05
195	Jason Kendall	.05
196	Johnny Damon	.25
197	Dave Martinez	.05
198	Mike Macfarlane	.05
199	Norm Charlton	.05
200	Doug Million, Damian Moss, Bobby Rodgers (Prospect)	.05
201	Geoff Jenkins, Raul Ibanez, Mike Cameron (Prospect)	.05
202	Sean Casey, Jim Bonnici, Dmitri Young (Prospect)	.15
203	Jed Hansen, Homer Bush, Felipe Crespo (Prospect)	.05
204	Kevin Orie, Gabe Alvarez, Aaron Boone (Prospect)	.05
205	Ben Davis, Kevin Brown, Bobby Estalella (Prospect)	.05
206	Billy McMillon, Bubba Trammell **RC**, Dante Powell (Prospect)	.25
207	Jarrod Washburn, Marc Wilkins **RC**, Glendon Rusch (Prospect)	.05
208	Brian Hunter	.05
209	Jason Giambi	.45
210	Henry Rodriguez	.05
211	Edgar Renteria	.05
212	Edgardo Alfonzo	.05
213	Fernando Vina	.05
214	Shawn Green	.40
215	Ray Durham	.05
216	Joe Randa	.05
217	Armando Reynoso	.05
218	Eric Davis	.05
219	Bob Tewksbury	.05
220	Jacob Cruz	.05
221	Glenallen Hill	.05
222	Gary Gaetti	.05
223	Donne Wall	.05
224	Brad Clontz	.05
225	Marty Janzen	.05
226	Todd Worrell	.05
227	John Franco	.05
228	David Wells	.05
229	Gregg Jefferies	.05
230	Tim Naehring	.05
231	Thomas Howard	.05
232	Roberto Hernandez	.05
233	Kevin Ritz	.05
234	Julian Tavarez	.05
235	Ken Hill	.05
236	Greg Gagne	.05
237	Bobby Chouinard	.05
238	Joe Carter	.05
239	Jermaine Dye	.05
240	Antonio Osuna	.05
241	Julio Franco	.05
242	Mike Grace	.05
243	Aaron Sele	.05
244	David Justice	.05
245	Sandy Alomar	.05
246	Jose Canseco	.45
247	Paul O'Neill	.05
248	Sean Berry	.05
249	Nick Bierbrodt **RC**, Kevin Sweeney **RC** (Diamond Backs)	.05
250	Larry Rodriguez **RC**, Vladimir Nunez **RC** (Diamond Backs)	.10
251	Ron Hartman, David Hayman (Diamond Backs)	.05
252	Alex Sanchez, Matt Quatraro (Devil Rays)	.05
253	Ronni Seberino, Pablo Ortega **RC** (Devil Rays)	.05
254	Rex Hudler	.05
255	Orlando Miller	.05
256	Mariano Rivera	.10
257	Brad Radke	.05
258	Bobby Higginson	.05
259	Jay Bell	.05
260	Mark Grudzielanek	.05
261	Lance Johnson	.05
262	Ken Caminiti	.05
263	J.T. Snow	.05
264	Gary Sheffield	.45
265	Darrin Fletcher	.05
266	Eric Owens	.05
267	Luis Castillo	.05
268	Scott Rolen	.65
269	Todd Noel **RC**, John Oliver (Draft Pick)	.05
270	Robert Stratton **RC**, Corey Lee **RC** (Draft Pick)	.05
271	Gil Meche **RC**, Matt Halloran **RC** (Draft Pick)	.50
272	Eric Milton **RC**, Dermal Brown (Draft Pick)	.25
273	Josh Garrett **RC**, Chris Reitsma **RC** (Draft Pick)	.10
274	A.J. Zapp **RC**, Jason Marquis **RC** (Draft Pick)	.50
275	Checklist	.05
276a	Checklist	.05
276b	Chipper Jones (Should be #277.)	1.00
278	Orlando Merced	.05
279	Ariel Prieto	.05
280	Al Leiter	.05
281	Pat Meares	.05
282	Darryl Strawberry	.05
283	Jamie Moyer	.05
284	Scott Servais	.05
285	Delino DeShields	.05
286	Danny Graves	.05
287	Gerald Williams	.05
288	Todd Greene	.05
289	Rico Brogna	.05
290	Derrick Gibson	.05
291	Joe Girardi	.05
292	Darren Lewis	.05
293	Nomar Garciaparra	1.00
294	Greg Colbrunn	.05
295	Jeff Bagwell	.75
296	Brent Gates	.05
297	Jose Vizcaino	.05
298	Alex Ochoa	.05
299	Sid Fernandez	.05
300	Ken Griffey Jr.	1.50
301	Chris Gomez	.05
302	Wendell Magee	.05
303	Darren Oliver	.05
304	Mel Nieves	.05
305	Sammy Sosa	1.00
306	George Arias	.05
307	Jack McDowell	.05
308	Stan Javier	.05
309	Kimera Bartee	.05
310	James Baldwin	.05
311	Rocky Coppinger	.05
312	Keith Lockhart	.05
313	C.J. Nitkowski	.05
314	Allen Watson	.05
315	Darryl Kile	.05
316	Amaury Telemaco	.05
317	Jason Isringhausen	.05
318	Manny Ramirez	.75
319	Terry Pendleton	.05
320	Tim Salmon	.05
321	Eric Karros	.05
322	Mark Whiten	.05
323	Rick Krivda	.05
324	Brett Butler	.05
325	Randy Johnson	.75
326	Eddie Taubensee	.05
327	Mark Leiter	.05
328	Kevin Gross	.05
329	Ernie Young	.05
330	Pat Hentgen	.05
331	Rondell White	.05
332	Bobby Witt	.05
333	Eddie Murray	.75
334	Tim Raines	.05
335	Jeff Fassero	.05
336	Chuck Finley	.05
337	Willie Adams	.05
338	Chan Ho Park	.05
339	Jay Powell	.05
340	Ivan Rodriguez	.65
341	Jermaine Allensworth	.05
342	Jay Payton	.05
343	T.J. Mathews	.05
344	Tony Batista	.05
345	Ed Sprague	.05
346	Jeff Kent	.05
347	Scott Erickson	.05
348	Jeff Suppan	.05
349	Pete Schourek	.05
350	Kenny Lofton	.05
351	Alan Benes	.05
352	Fred McGriff	.05
353	Charlie O'Brien	.05

354	Darren Bragg	.05
355	Alex Fernandez	.05
356	Al Martin	.05
357	Bob Wells	.05
358	Chad Mottola	.05
359	Devon White	.05
360	David Cone	.05
361	Bobby Jones	.05
362	Scott Sanders	.05
363	Karim Garcia	.15
364	Kirt Manwaring	.05
365	Chili Davis	.05
366	Mike Hampton	.05
367	Chad Ogea	.05
368	Curt Schilling	.25
369	Phil Nevin	.05
370	Roger Clemens	1.25
371	Willie Greene	.05
372	Kenny Rogers	.05
373	Jose Rijo	.05
374	Bobby Bonilla	.05
375	Mike Mussina	.35
376	Curtis Pride	.05
377	Todd Walker	.05
378	Jason Bere	.05
379	Heathcliff Slocumb	.05
380	Dante Bichette	.05
381	Carlos Baerga	.05
382	Livan Hernandez	.05
383	Jason Schmidt	.05
384	Kevin Stocker	.05
385	Matt Williams	.05
386	Bartolo Colon	.05
387	Will Clark	.05
388	Dennis Eckersley	.65
389	Brooks Kieschnick	.05
390	Ryan Klesko	.05
391	Mark Carreon	.05
392	Tim Worrell	.05
393	Dean Palmer	.05
394	Wil Cordero	.05
395	Javy Lopez	.05
396	Rich Aurilia	.05
397	Greg Vaughn	.05
398	Vinny Castilla	.05
399	Jeff Montgomery	.05
400	Cal Ripken Jr.	2.00
401	Walt Weiss	.05
402	Brad Ausmus	.05
403	Ruben Rivera	.05
404	Mark Wohlers	.05
405	Rick Aguilera	.05
406	Tony Clark	.05
407	Lyle Mouton	.05
408	Bill Pulsipher	.05
409	Jose Rosado	.05
410	Tony Gwynn	1.00
411	Cecil Fielder	.05
412	John Flaherty	.05
413	Lenny Dykstra	.05
414	Ugueth Urbina	.05
415	Brian Jordan	.05
416	Bob Abreu	.05
417	Craig Paquette	.05
418	Sandy Martinez	.05
419	Jeff Blauser	.05
420	Barry Larkin	.05
421	Kevin Seitzer	.05
422	Tim Belcher	.05
423	Paul Sorrento	.05
424	Cal Eldred	.05
425	Robin Ventura	.05
426	John Olerud	.05
427	Bob Wolcott	.05
428	Matt Lawton	.05
429	Rod Beck	.05
430	Shane Reynolds	.05
431	Mike James	.05
432	Steve Wojciechowski	.05
433	Vladimir Guerrero	.75
434	Dustin Hermanson	.05
435	Marty Cordova	.05
436	Marc Newfield	.05
437	Todd Stottlemyre	.05
438	Jeffrey Hammonds	.05
439	Dave Stevens	.05
440	Hideo Nomo	.35
441	Mark Thompson	.05
442	Mark Lewis	.05
443	Quinton McCracken	.05
444	Cliff Floyd	.05
445	Denny Neagle	.05
446	John Jaha	.05
447	Mike Sweeney	.05
448	John Wasdin	.05
449	Chad Curtis	.05
450	Mo Vaughn	.05
451	Donovan Osborne	.05
452	Ruben Sierra	.05
453	Michael Tucker	.05
454	Kurt Abbott	.05
455	Andruw Jones	.75
456	Shannon Stewart	.05
457	Scott Brosius	.05
458	Juan Guzman	.05
459	Ron Villone	.05
460	Moises Alou	.05
461	Larry Walker	.05
462	Eddie Murray (Season Highlights)	.40
463	Paul Molitor (Season Highlights)	.40
464	Hideo Nomo (Season Highlights)	.20
465	Barry Bonds (Season Highlights)	1.00
466	Todd Hundley (Season Highlights)	.05
467	Rheal Cormier	.05
468	Jason Conti **RC**	.05
469	Rod Barajas **RC**	.05
470	Jared Sandberg, Cedric Bowers **RC**	.05
471	Paul Wilders, Chie Gunner **RC**	.05
472	Mike Decelle, Marcus McCain **RC**	.05
473	Todd Zeile	.05
474	Neifi Perez	.05
475	Jeromy Burnitz	.05
476	Trey Beamon	.05
477	John Patterson, Braden Looper **RC** (Draft Picks)	.15
478	Danny Peoples **RC**, Jake Westbrook **RC** (Draft Picks)	.25
479	Eric Chavez **RC**, Adam Eaton (Draft Picks)	.75
480	Joe Lawrence **RC**, Pete Tucci (Draft Picks)	.05
481	Kris Benson, Billy Koch **RC** (Draft Picks)	.25
482	John Nicholson, Andy Prater (Draft Picks)	.05
483	Mark Kotsay **RC**, Mark Johnson (Draft Picks)	.25
484	Armando Benitez	.05
485	Mike Matheny	.05
486	Jeff Reed	.05
487	Mark Bellhorn, Russ Johnson, Enrique Wilson (Prospects)	.05
488	Ben Grieve, Richard Hidalgo, Scott Morgan **RC** (Prospects)	.05
489	Paul Konerko, Derrek Lee, Ron Wright (Prospects)	.50
490	Wes Helms, Bill Mueller **RC**, Brad Seitzer (Prospects)	.50
491	Jeff Abbott, Shane Monahan, Edgard Velazquez (Prospects)	.05
492	Jimmy Anderson **RC**, Ron Blazier, Gerald Witasick Jr. (Prospects)	.05
493	Darin Blood, Heath Murray, Carl Pavano (Prospects)	.05
494	Mark Redman, Mike Villano **RC**, Nelson Figueroa (Prospects)	.05
495	Checklist	.05
496	Checklist	.05

All-Stars

Topps' 1997 All-Stars insert cards, printed on a dazzling rainbow foilboard, feature the top players from each position. There are 22 cards, 11 from each league, which showcase the top three players from each position as voted by Topps' sports department. On the front of each card is a photo of a "first team" all-star player; the back has a different photo of that player, who appears alongside the "second team" and "third team" selections. These cards are seeded one per every 18 1997 Topps Series I packs. Cards are numbered with an "AS" prefix.

		NM/M
Complete Set (22):		12.00
Common Player:		.25
1	Ivan Rodriguez	.75
2	Todd Hundley	.25
3	Frank Thomas	1.00
4	Andres Galarraga	.25
5	Chuck Knoblauch	.25
6	Eric Young	.25
7	Jim Thome	.75
8	Chipper Jones	1.50
9	Cal Ripken Jr.	3.00
10	Barry Larkin	.25
11	Albert Belle	.25
12	Barry Bonds	3.00
13	Ken Griffey Jr.	2.00
14	Ellis Burks	.25
15	Juan Gonzalez	.60
16	Gary Sheffield	.50
17	Andy Pettitte	.35
18	Tom Glavine	.35
19	Pat Hentgen	.25
20	John Smoltz	.25
21	Roberto Hernandez	.25
22	Mark Wohlers	.25

Awesome Impact

This flashy insert exclusive to Series 2 retail packaging features young players who have quickly made their mark in the big leagues. Fronts have player action photos against a background of silver primatic geometric shapes. Backs are horizontal with a player portrait photo, recent stats and a few words about the player's current and projected impact. Stated odds of finding this insert are one per 18 packs. Cards are numbered with an "AI" prefix.

		NM/M
Complete Set (20):		20.00
Common Player:		.40
1	Jaime Bluma	.40
2	Tony Clark	.40
3	Jermaine Dye	.40
4	Nomar Garciaparra	4.50
5	Vladimir Guerrero	3.00
6	Todd Hollandsworth	.40
7	Derek Jeter	6.00
8	Andruw Jones	3.00
9	Chipper Jones	4.50
10	Jason Kendall	.40
11	Brooks Kieschnick	.40
12	Alex Ochoa	.40
13	Rey Ordonez	.40
14	Neifi Perez	.40
15	Edgar Renteria	.40
16	Mariano Rivera	.50
17	Ruben Rivera	.40
18	Scott Rolen	2.25
19	Billy Wagner	.40
20	Todd Walker	.40

Inter-League Match Ups

The double-sided Inter-League Finest and Inter-League Finest Refractors (seeded one in 36 and one in 216 Topps Series 1 packs respectively) feature top individual matchups from inter-league rivalries. One player from each major league team is represented, for a total of 28 players on 14 different cards. Each card is covered with a Finest clear protector. Cards are numbered with an "ILM" prefix.

		NM/M
Complete Set (14):		16.00
Common Card:		.50
Refractors:		1.5X
1	Mark McGwire, Barry Bonds	3.00
2	Tim Salmon, Mike Piazza	2.00
3	Ken Griffey Jr., Dante Bichette	2.00
4	Juan Gonzalez, Tony Gwynn	1.50
5	Frank Thomas, Sammy Sosa	1.50
6	Albert Belle, Barry Larkin	.50
7	Johnny Damon, Brian Jordan	.75
8	Paul Molitor, Jeff King	1.00
9	John Jaha, Jeff Bagwell	1.00
10	Bernie Williams, Todd Hundley	.50
11	Joe Carter, Henry Rodriguez	.50
12	Cal Ripken Jr., Gregg Jefferies	3.00
13	Mo Vaughn, Chipper Jones	1.50
14	Travis Fryman, Gary Sheffield	.75

Derek Jeter Autograph

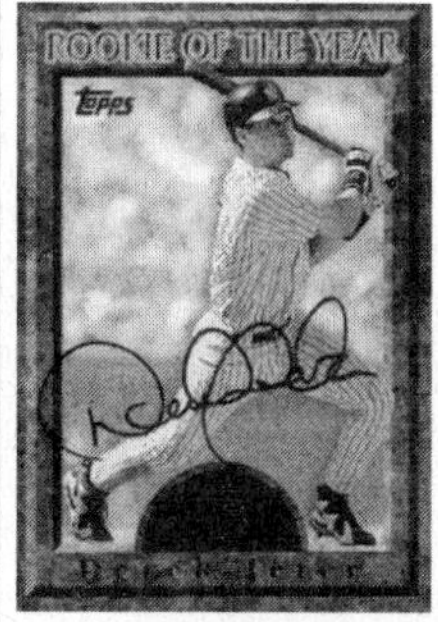

An authentically autographed card honoring Derek Jeter as Rookie of the Year was a random insert found on average of one per 576 packs of Topps Series 2.

	NM/M
Derek Jeter	130.00

Hobby Masters

These 20 cards lead the way as dealers' top selections. The cards, printed on 28-point diffraction foilboard, replace two regular cards in every 36th pack of 1997 Topps Series 1 product. Cards are numbered with a "HM" prefix.

		NM/M
Complete Set (20):		30.00
Common Player:		.75
1	Ken Griffey Jr.	3.00
2	Cal Ripken Jr.	4.50
3	Greg Maddux	2.25
4	Albert Belle	.75
5	Tony Gwynn	2.25
6	Jeff Bagwell	1.50
7	Randy Johnson	1.50
8	Raul Mondesi	.75
9	Juan Gonzalez	1.00
10	Kenny Lofton	.75
11	Frank Thomas	1.50
12	Mike Piazza	3.00
13	Chipper Jones	2.25
14	Brady Anderson	.75
15	Ken Caminiti	.75
16	Barry Bonds	4.50
17	Mo Vaughn	.75
18	Derek Jeter	4.50
19	Sammy Sosa	2.25
20	Andres Galarraga	.75

Mickey Mantle Reprints

All 16 remaining Mickey Mantle cards that were not reprinted in 1996 Topps Baseball are found in this insert, seeded every 12 packs of Series I Topps. The set starts off with No. 21 and runs through No. 36 since the '96 reprints were numbered 1-20.

		NM/M
Complete Set (16):		60.00
Common Card:		5.00
Inserted 1:12 Series 1		
21	1953 Bowman #44	5.00
22	1953 Bowman #59	5.00
23	1957 Topps #407	5.00
24	1958 Topps #418	5.00
25	1958 Topps #487	5.00
26	1959 Topps #461	5.00
27	1959 Topps #564	5.00
28	1960 Topps #160	5.00
29	1960 Topps #563	5.00
30	1961 Topps #406	5.00
31	1961 Topps #475	5.00
32	1961 Topps #578	5.00
33	1962 Topps #18	5.00
34	1962 Topps #318	5.00
35	1962 Topps #471	5.00
36	1964 Topps #331	5.00

Mickey Mantle Finest

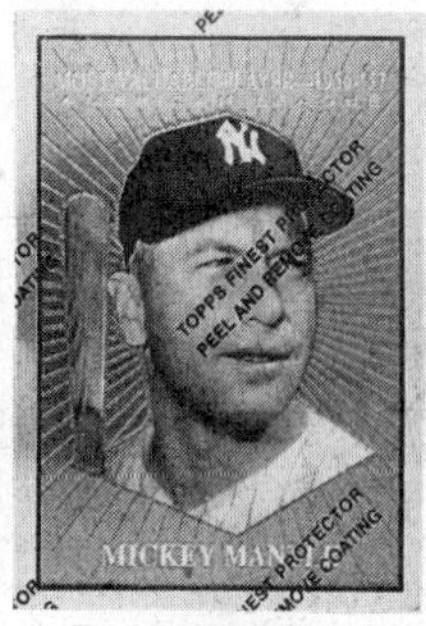

The Mickey Mantle reprint inserts found in Series 1 were re-issued in Series 2 in Finest technology, found on average of every 24 packs. Refractor versions of each Finest reprint were inserted at a 1:216 rate.

		NM/M
Complete Set (16):		70.00
Common Card:		5.00
Inserted 1:24 Series 2		
Refractor:		4X
Inserted 1:216		
21	1953 Bowman #44	5.00
22	1953 Bowman #59	7.50
23	1957 Topps #407	5.00
24	1958 Topps #418	5.00
25	1958 Topps #487	5.00
26	1959 Topps #461	5.00
27	1959 Topps #564	5.00
28	1960 Topps #160	5.00
29	1960 Topps #563	5.00
30	1961 Topps #406	5.00
31	1961 Topps #475	5.00
32	1961 Topps #578	5.00
33	1962 Topps #18	5.00
34	1962 Topps #318	5.00
35	1962 Topps #471	5.00
36	1964 Topps #331	5.00

Mickey Mantle Case Inserts

Inserted one per case of Series 1 Topps, these reprints of 16 Mickey Mantle special cards of the 1950s-1960s come sealed in a soft plastic holder. The plastic sleeve has a gold-foil stamp at bottom-back which reads "FACTORY TOPPS SEAL 1997."

		NM/M
Complete Set (16):		160.00
Common Card:		12.50
21	1953 Bowman #44	12.50
22	1953 Bowman #59	18.00
23	1957 Topps #407	12.50
24	1958 Topps #418	12.50
25	1958 Topps #487	12.50
26	1959 Topps #461	12.50
27	1959 Topps #564	12.50
28	1960 Topps #160	12.50
29	1960 Topps #563	12.50
30	1961 Topps #406	12.50
31	1961 Topps #475	12.50
32	1961 Topps #578	12.50
33	1962 Topps #18	12.50
34	1962 Topps #318	12.50
35	1962 Topps #471	12.50
36	1964 Topps #331	12.50

Willie Mays Reprints

There are 27 different Willie Mays cards reprinted in Series 1 and seeded every eight packs. The inserts form a collection of Topps and Bowman cards from throughout Mays' career and each is highlighted by a special commemorative gold foil stamp. Many of the Mays reprints can also be found in an autographed edition, bearing a special "Certified Autograph Issue" gold-foil logo.

		NM/M
Complete Set (27):		50.00
Common Card:		3.00
Autographed Card:		120.00
1	1951 Bowman #305	6.00
2	1952 Topps #261	4.00
3	1953 Topps #244	3.00
4	1954 Bowman #89	3.00
5	1954 Topps #90	3.00
6	1955 Bowman #184	3.00
7	1955 Topps #194	3.00
8	1956 Topps #130	3.00
9	1957 Topps #10	3.00
10	1958 Topps #5	3.00
11	1959 Topps #50	3.00
12	1960 Topps #200	3.00
13	1960 Topps #564	3.00
14	1961 Topps #150	3.00
15	1961 Topps #579	3.00
16	1962 Topps #300	3.00
17	1963 Topps #300	3.00
18	1964 Topps #150	3.00
19	1965 Topps #250	3.00
20	1966 Topps #1	3.00
21	1967 Topps #200	3.00
22	1968 Topps #50	3.00

23	1969 Topps #190	3.00
24	1970 Topps #600	3.00
25	1971 Topps #600	3.00
26	1972 Topps #49	3.00
27	1973 Topps #305	3.00

Willie Mays Reprint Autographs

According to Topps, only 19 of the 27 different Willie Mays cards reprinted in Series 1 exist in authentically autographed form, bearing a special "Certified Autograph Issue" gold-foil logo.

		NM/M
Common Card:		120.00
1	1951 Bowman #305	150.00
2	1952 Topps #261	120.00
3	1953 Topps #244	120.00
6	1955 Bowman #184	120.00
7	1955 Topps #194	120.00
9	1957 Topps #10	120.00
10	1958 Topps #5	120.00
12	1960 Topps #200	120.00
13	1960 Topps #564	120.00
14	1961 Topps #150	120.00
15	1961 Topps #579	120.00
17	1963 Topps #300	120.00
18	1964 Topps #150	120.00
19	1965 Topps #250	120.00
20	1966 Topps #1	120.00
23	1969 Topps #190	120.00
24	1970 Topps #600	120.00
26	1972 Topps #49	120.00
27	1973 Topps #305	120.00

Willie Mays Finest

Series 2 offered collectors a chance to find Finest technology versions of each of the 27 commemorative reprint Topps and Bowman cards from throughout Mays' career. The Finest reprints are found one in every 30 packs, on average, with Refractor versions seeded 1:180.

		NM/M
Complete Set (27):		60.00
Common Card:		3.00
Refractor:		3X
Inserted 1:180		
1	1951 Bowman #305	6.00
2	1952 Topps #261	4.00
3	1953 Topps #244	3.00
4	1954 Bowman #89	3.00
5	1954 Topps #90	3.00
6	1955 Bowman #184	3.00
7	1955 Topps #194	3.00
8	1956 Topps #130	3.00
9	1957 Topps #10	3.00
10	1958 Topps #5	3.00
11	1959 Topps #50	3.00
12	1960 Topps #200	3.00
13	1960 Topps #564	3.00
14	1961 Topps #150	3.00
15	1961 Topps #579	3.00
16	1962 Topps #300	3.00
17	1963 Topps #300	3.00
18	1964 Topps #150	3.00
19	1965 Topps #250	3.00
20	1966 Topps #1	3.00
21	1967 Topps #200	3.00
22	1968 Topps #50	3.00
23	1969 Topps #190	3.00
24	1970 Topps #600	3.00
25	1971 Topps #600	3.00
26	1972 Topps #49	3.00
27	1973 Topps #305	3.00

Willie Mays Commemorative Super

This oversize (4-1/4" x 5-3/4") version of card #2 (1952 Topps) in the Willie Mays Commemorative Reprint series was available exclusively

in a special retail packaging of 10 1997 Topps Series 1 foil packs. Like the regular-size reprints, it has a gold-foil commemorative stamp on front.

		NM/M
2	Willie Mays (1952 Topps)	5.00

Season's Best

Season's Best features 25 players on prismatic illusion foilboard, and can be found every six packs. The set has the top five players from five statistical categories: home runs, RBIs, batting average, steals, and wins. Season's Best were found in packs of Topps Series II, and later reprinted on chromium stock as part of Topps Chrome.

		NM/M
Complete Set (25):		12.00
Common Player:		.25
1	Tony Gwynn	1.50
2	Frank Thomas	1.25
3	Ellis Burks	.25
4	Paul Molitor	1.25
5	Chuck Knoblauch	.25
6	Mark McGwire	3.00
7	Brady Anderson	.25
8	Ken Griffey Jr.	2.00
9	Albert Belle	.25
10	Andres Galarraga	.25
11	Andres Galarraga	.25
12	Albert Belle	.25
13	Juan Gonzalez	.75
14	Mo Vaughn	.25
15	Rafael Palmeiro	1.00
16	John Smoltz	.25
17	Andy Pettitte	.50
18	Pat Hentgen	.25
19	Mike Mussina	.50
20	Andy Benes	.25
21	Kenny Lofton	.25
22	Tom Goodwin	.25
23	Otis Nixon	.25
24	Eric Young	.25
25	Lance Johnson	.25

Series 2 Supers

At 3-3/4" x 5-1/4", these premium cards are nearly identical to the regular-issue versions except for size. Also, whereas the regular cards have a front format which combines a high-gloss central area with a matte finish near the borders, the supers have just one finish on the front which is a semi-gloss. The supers also have different card numbers on back. One of the supers was included in each boxed lot of 15 Series II foil packs sold at large retail outlets with a price tag of about $15.

		NM/M
Complete Set (3):		10.00
1	Chipper Jones	3.00
2	Ken Griffey Jr.	4.00
3	Cal Ripken Jr.	5.00

Sweet Strokes

These retail-exclusive Sweet Strokes insert cards consist of 15 Power Matrix foil cards of the top hitters in the game. These players have the swings to produce game winning-hits. The cards were seeded one per every 12 1997 Topps Series I retail packs. Cards are numbered with a "SS" prefix.

		NM/M
Complete Set (15):		15.00
Common Player:		.35
1	Roberto Alomar	.50
2	Jeff Bagwell	1.25
3	Albert Belle	.35
4	Barry Bonds	3.00
5	Mark Grace	.35
6	Ken Griffey Jr.	2.00
7	Tony Gwynn	1.50
8	Chipper Jones	1.50
9	Edgar Martinez	.35
10	Mark McGwire	2.50
11	Rafael Palmeiro	1.00
12	Mike Piazza	2.00
13	Gary Sheffield	.75
14	Frank Thomas	1.25
15	Mo Vaughn	.35

Team Timber

Team Timber was a 16-card insert that was exclusive to retail packs and inserted one per 36. The set displays the game's top sluggers on laminated litho wood cards. Cards are numbered with a "TT" prefix.

		NM/M
Complete Set (16):		24.00
Common Player:		.50
1	Ken Griffey Jr.	3.00
2	Ken Caminiti	.50
3	Bernie Williams	.50
4	Jeff Bagwell	1.50
5	Frank Thomas	1.50
6	Andres Galarraga	.50
7	Barry Bonds	5.00
8	Rafael Palmeiro	1.25
9	Brady Anderson	.50
10	Juan Gonzalez	.75
11	Mo Vaughn	.50
12	Mark McGwire	4.00
13	Gary Sheffield	.90
14	Albert Belle	.50
15	Chipper Jones	2.50
16	Mike Piazza	3.00

1997 Topps Chrome

Chrome Baseball reprinted the top 165 cards from Topps Series I and II baseball on a chromium, metallized stock. Chrome sold in four-card packs and included three insert sets: Diamond Duos, which was created exclusively for this product, Season's Best and Topps All-Stars, which were both reprinted from Topps products. Refractor versions of each card were found every 12 packs.

		NM/M
Complete Set (165):		35.00
Common Player:		.10
Refractors:		2X
Pack (4):		1.50
Wax Box (24):		25.00
1	Barry Bonds	3.00
2	Jose Valentin	.10
3	Brady Anderson	.10
4	Wade Boggs	1.50
5	Andres Galarraga	.10
6	Rusty Greer	.10
7	Derek Jeter	3.00
8	Ricky Bottalico	.10
9	Mike Piazza	2.00
10	Garret Anderson	.10
11	Jeff King	.10
12	Kevin Appier	.10
13	Mark Grace	.10
14	Jeff D'Amico	.10
15	Jay Buhner	.10
16	Hal Morris	.10
17	Harold Baines	.10
18	Jeff Cirillo	.10
19	Tom Glavine	.35
20	Andy Pettitte	.35
21	Mark McGwire	2.50
22	Chuck Knoblauch	.10
23	Raul Mondesi	.10
24	Albert Belle	.10
25	Trevor Hoffman	.10
26	Eric Young	.10
27	Brian McRae	.10
28	Jim Edmonds	.10
29	Robb Nen	.10
30	Reggie Sanders	.10
31	Mike Lansing	.10
32	Craig Biggio	.10
33	Ray Lankford	.10
34	Charles Nagy	.10
35	Paul Wilson	.10
36	John Wetteland	.10
37	Derek Bell	.10
38	Edgar Martinez	.10
39	Rickey Henderson	1.00
40	Jim Thome	.75
41	Frank Thomas	1.00
42	Jackie Robinson (Tribute)	2.00
43	Terry Steinbach	.10
44	Kevin Brown	.10
45	Joey Hamilton	.10
46	Travis Fryman	.10
47	Juan Gonzalez	.50
48	Ron Gant	.10
49	Greg Maddux	1.50
50	Wally Joyner	.10
51	John Valentin	.10
52	Bret Boone	.10
53	Paul Molitor	1.00
54	Rafael Palmeiro	.75
55	Todd Hundley	.10
56	Ellis Burks	.10
57	Bernie Williams	.10
58	Roberto Alomar	.25
59	Jose Mesa	.10
60	Troy Percival	.10
61	John Smoltz	.10
62	Jeff Conine	.10
63	Bernard Gilkey	.10
64	Mickey Tettleton	.10
65	Justin Thompson	.10
66	Tony Phillips	.10
67	Ryne Sandberg	1.50
68	Geronimo Berroa	.10
69	Todd Hollandsworth	.10
70	Rey Ordonez	.10
71	Marquis Grissom	.10
72	Tino Martinez	.10
73	Steve Finley	.10
74	Andy Benes	.10
75	Jason Kendall	.10
76	Johnny Damon	.35
77	Jason Giambi	.50
78	Henry Rodriguez	.10
79	Edgar Renteria	.10
80	Ray Durham	.10
81	Gregg Jefferies	.10
82	Roberto Hernandez	.10
83	Joe Carter	.10
84	Jermaine Dye	.10
85	Julio Franco	.10
86	David Justice	.10
87	Jose Canseco	.50
88	Paul O'Neill	.10
89	Mariano Rivera	.15
90	Bobby Higginson	.10
91	Mark Grudzielanek	.10
92	Lance Johnson	.10
93	Ken Caminiti	.10
94	Gary Sheffield	.50
95	Luis Castillo	.10
96	Scott Rolen	.75
97	Chipper Jones	1.50
98	Darryl Strawberry	.10
99	Nomar Garciaparra	1.50
100	Jeff Bagwell	1.00
101	Ken Griffey Jr.	2.00
102	Sammy Sosa	1.50
103	Jack McDowell	.10
104	James Baldwin	.10
105	Rocky Coppinger	.10
106	Manny Ramirez	1.00
107	Tim Salmon	.10
108	Eric Karros	.10
109	Brett Butler	.10
110	Randy Johnson	1.00
111	Pat Hentgen	.10
112	Rondell White	.10
113	Eddie Murray	1.00
114	Ivan Rodriguez	.75
115	Jermaine Allensworth	.10
116	Ed Sprague	.10
117	Kenny Lofton	.10
118	Alan Benes	.10
119	Fred McGriff	.10
120	Alex Fernandez	.10
121	Al Martin	.10
122	Devon White	.10
123	David Cone	.10
124	Karim Garcia	.25
125	Chili Davis	.10
126	Roger Clemens	1.75
127	Bobby Bonilla	.10
128	Mike Mussina	.50
129	Todd Walker	.10
130	Dante Bichette	.10
131	Carlos Baerga	.10
132	Matt Williams	.10
133	Will Clark	.10
134	Dennis Eckersley	.75
135	Ryan Klesko	.10
136	Dean Palmer	.10
137	Javy Lopez	.10
138	Greg Vaughn	.10
139	Vinny Castilla	.10
140	Cal Ripken Jr.	3.00
141	Ruben Rivera	.10
142	Mark Wohlers	.10
143	Tony Clark	.10
144	Jose Rosado	.10
145	Tony Gwynn	1.50
146	Cecil Fielder	.10
147	Brian Jordan	.10
148	Bob Abreu	.10
149	Barry Larkin	.10
150	Robin Ventura	.10
151	John Olerud	.10
152	Rod Beck	.10
153	Vladimir Guerrero	1.00
154	Marty Cordova	.10
155	Todd Stottlemyre	.10
156	Hideo Nomo	.50
157	Denny Neagle	.10
158	John Jaha	.10
159	Mo Vaughn	.10
160	Andruw Jones	1.00
161	Moises Alou	.10
162	Larry Walker	.10
163	Eddie Murray (Season Highlights)	.75
164	Paul Molitor (Season Highlights)	.75
165	Checklist	.10

All-Stars

Topps Chrome All-Stars display the same 22 cards found in Topps Series I, however these are reprinted on a Chrome stock. Regular versions are seeded every 24 packs, while Refractor versions arrive every 72 packs. Cards are numbered with an "AS" prefix.

		NM/M
Complete Set (22):		25.00
Common Player:		.75
Refractors:		1.5X
1	Ivan Rodriguez	1.50
2	Todd Hundley	.75
3	Frank Thomas	2.00
4	Andres Galarraga	.75
5	Chuck Knoblauch	.75
6	Eric Young	.75
7	Jim Thome	1.50
8	Chipper Jones	3.00
9	Cal Ripken Jr.	6.00
10	Barry Larkin	.75
11	Albert Belle	.75
12	Barry Bonds	6.00
13	Ken Griffey Jr.	4.00
14	Ellis Burks	.75
15	Juan Gonzalez	1.00
16	Gary Sheffield	1.25
17	Andy Pettitte	1.00
18	Tom Glavine	1.00
19	Pat Hentgen	.75
20	John Smoltz	.75
21	Roberto Hernandez	.75
22	Mark Wohlers	.75

Diamond Duos

Diamond Duos is the only one of the three insert sets in Chrome Baseball that was developed exclusively for this product. The set has 10 cards featuring two superstar teammates on double-sided chromium cards. Diamond Duos are found every 36 packs, while Refractor versions are found every 108 packs. Cards are numbered with a "DD" prefix.

		NM/M
Complete Set (10):		17.50
Common Player:		.50
Refractors:		1.5X
1	Chipper Jones, Andruw Jones	2.00
2	Derek Jeter, Bernie Williams	4.00
3	Ken Griffey Jr., Jay Buhner	2.50
4	Kenny Lofton, Manny Ramirez	1.50
5	Jeff Bagwell, Craig Biggio	1.50
6	Juan Gonzalez, Ivan Rodriguez	1.25
7	Cal Ripken Jr., Brady Anderson	4.00
8	Mike Piazza, Hideo Nomo	2.50
9	Andres Galarraga, Dante Bichette	.50
10	Frank Thomas, Albert Belle	1.50

Season's Best

Season's Best includes the 25 players found in Topps Series II, but in a chromium version. The top five players from five statistical categories, including Leading Looters, Bleacher Reachers and Kings of Swing. Regular versions are seeded every 18 packs, with Refractors every 54 packs.

		NM/M
Complete Set (25):		17.50
Common Player:		.50
Refractors:		1.5X
1	Tony Gwynn	2.00
2	Frank Thomas	1.50
3	Ellis Burks	.50
4	Paul Molitor	1.50
5	Chuck Knoblauch	.50
6	Mark McGwire	4.00
7	Brady Anderson	.50
8	Ken Griffey Jr.	3.00
9	Albert Belle	.50
10	Andres Galarraga	.50
11	Andres Galarraga	.50
12	Albert Belle	.50
13	Juan Gonzalez	.75
14	Mo Vaughn	.50
15	Rafael Palmeiro	1.25
16	John Smoltz	.50
17	Andy Pettitte	.75
18	Pat Hentgen	.50
19	Mike Mussina	.75
20	Andy Benes	.50
21	Kenny Lofton	.50
22	Tom Goodwin	.50
23	Otis Nixon	.50
24	Eric Young	.50
25	Lance Johnson	.50

Jumbos

These large-format (3-3/4" x 5-1/4") Topps Chrome cards were produced for sale in special retail packaging offering one jumbo card and five packs of Topps Chrome for about $15. The jumbos are identical in design to the regular-issue Chrome cards of the same players. Because they were offered in a windowed retail package, it was easy for collectors to pick the card they wanted.

		NM/M
Complete Set (6):		10.00
Common Player:		.75
9	Mike Piazza	2.00
94	Gary Sheffield	.75
97	Chipper Jones	1.50
101	Ken Griffey Jr.	2.00
102	Sammy Sosa	1.50
140	Cal Ripken Jr.	3.00

1997 Topps Gallery Pre-production

In its second year Topps Gallery was produced in a greatly improved combination of card stock, graphic highlights and inserts. To reintroduce the hobby to the issue, Topps distributed these promotional samples to dealers and the press. Except for the "PP" prefix to the card number on front, the samples are virtually identical to the issued versions.

		NM/M
Complete Set (4):		25.00
Common Player:		3.00
1	Andruw Jones	5.00
2	Derek Jeter	9.00
3	Mike Piazza	10.00
4	Craig Biggio	3.00

1997 Topps Gallery

The second year of Gallery features 180 cards printed on extra-thick 24-point stock. Card fronts feature a player photo surrounded by an embossed foil "frame" to give each card the look of a piece of artwork. Backs contain career stats and biographical information on each player. Inserts include Peter Max Serigraphs, Signature Series Serigraphs, Player's Private Issue (parallel set), Photo Gallery and Gallery of Heroes. Cards were sold exclusively in hobby shops in eight-card packs for $4 each.

		NM/M
Complete Set (180):		20.00
Common Player:		.10
Pack (8):		1.50
Wax Box (24):		25.00
1	Paul Molitor	.75
2	Devon White	.10
3	Andres Galarraga	.10
4	Cal Ripken Jr.	3.00
5	Tony Gwynn	1.50
6	Mike Stanley	.10
7	Orel Hershiser	.10
8	Jose Canseco	.50
9	Chili Davis	.10
10	Harold Baines	.10
11	Rickey Henderson	.75
12	Darryl Strawberry	.10
13	Todd Worrell	.10
14	Cecil Fielder	.10
15	Gary Gaetti	.10
16	Bobby Bonilla	.10
17	Will Clark	.10
18	Kevin Brown	.10
19	Tom Glavine	.35
20	Wade Boggs	1.50
21	Edgar Martinez	.10
22	Lance Johnson	.10
23	Gregg Jefferies	.10
24	Bip Roberts	.10
25	Tony Phillips	.10
26	Greg Maddux	1.50
27	Mickey Tettleton	.10
28	Terry Steinbach	.10
29	Ryne Sandberg	1.50
30	Wally Joyner	.10
31	Joe Carter	.10
32	Ellis Burks	.10
33	Fred McGriff	.10
34	Barry Larkin	.10
35	John Franco	.10
36	Rafael Palmeiro	.65
37	Mark McGwire	2.50
38	Ken Caminiti	.10
39	David Cone	.10
40	Julio Franco	.10
41	Roger Clemens	1.75
42	Barry Bonds	3.00
43	Dennis Eckersley	.65
44	Eddie Murray	.75
45	Paul O'Neill	.10
46	Craig Biggio	.10
47	Roberto Alomar	.20
48	Mark Grace	.10
49	Matt Williams	.10
50	Jay Buhner	.10
51	John Smoltz	.10
52	Randy Johnson	.75
53	Ramon Martinez	.10
54	Curt Schilling	.35
55	Gary Sheffield	.50
56	Jack McDowell	.10
57	Brady Anderson	.10
58	Dante Bichette	.10
59	Ron Gant	.10
60	Alex Fernandez	.10
61	Moises Alou	.10
62	Travis Fryman	.10
63	Dean Palmer	.10
64	Todd Hundley	.10
65	Jeff Brantley	.10
66	Bernard Gilkey	.10
67	Geronimo Berroa	.10
68	John Wetteland	.10
69	Robin Ventura	.10
70	Ray Lankford	.10
71	Kevin Appier	.10
72	Larry Walker	.10
73	Juan Gonzalez	.40
74	Jeff King	.10
75	Greg Vaughn	.10
76	Steve Finley	.10
77	Brian McRae	.10
78	Paul Sorrento	.10
79	Ken Griffey Jr.	2.00
80	Omar Vizquel	.10
81	Jose Mesa	.10
82	Albert Belle	.10
83	Glenallen Hill	.10
84	Sammy Sosa	1.50
85	Andy Benes	.10
86	David Justice	.10
87	Marquis Grissom	.10
88	John Olerud	.10
89	Tino Martinez	.10
90	Frank Thomas	.75
91	Raul Mondesi	.10
92	Steve Trachsel	.10
93	Jim Edmonds	.10
94	Rusty Greer	.10
95	Joey Hamilton	.10
96	Ismael Valdes	.10
97	Dave Nilsson	.10
98	John Jaha	.10
99	Alex Gonzalez	.10
100	Javy Lopez	.10
101	Ryan Klesko	.10
102	Tim Salmon	.10
103	Bernie Williams	.10
104	Roberto Hernandez	.10
105	Chuck Knoblauch	.10
106	Mike Lansing	.10
107	Vinny Castilla	.10
108	Reggie Sanders	.10
109	Mo Vaughn	.10
110	Rondell White	.10
111	Ivan Rodriguez	.65
112	Mike Mussina	.40
113	Carlos Baerga	.10
114	Jeff Conine	.10
115	Jim Thome	.65
116	Manny Ramirez	.75
117	Kenny Lofton	.10
118	Wilson Alvarez	.10
119	Eric Karros	.10
120	Robb Nen	.10
121	Mark Wohlers	.10
122	Ed Sprague	.10
123	Pat Hentgen	.10
124	Juan Guzman	.10
125	Derek Bell	.10
126	Jeff Bagwell	.75
127	Eric Young	.10
128	John Valentin	.10
129	Al Martin (Photo actually Javy Lopez.)	.10
130	Trevor Hoffman	.10
131	Henry Rodriguez	.10
132	Pedro Martinez	.75
133	Mike Piazza	2.00
134	Brian Jordan	.10
135	Jose Valentin	.10
136	Jeff Cirillo	.10
137	Chipper Jones	1.50
138	Ricky Bottalico	.10
139	Hideo Nomo	.40
140	Troy Percival	.10
141	Rey Ordonez	.10
142	Edgar Renteria	.10
143	Luis Castillo	.10
144	Vladimir Guerrero	.75
145	Jeff D'Amico	.10
146	Andruw Jones	.75
147	Darin Erstad	.25
148	Bob Abreu	.10
149	Carlos Delgado	.45
150	Jamey Wright	.10
151	Nomar Garciaparra	1.50
152	Jason Kendall	.10
153	Jermaine Allensworth	.10
154	Scott Rolen	.65
155	Rocky Coppinger	.10
156	Paul Wilson	.10
157	Garret Anderson	.10
158	Mariano Rivera	.15
159	Ruben Rivera	.10
160	Andy Pettitte	.35
161	Derek Jeter	3.00
162	Neifi Perez	.10
163	Ray Durham	.10
164	James Baldwin	.10
165	Marty Cordova	.10
166	Tony Clark	.10
167	Michael Tucker	.10
168	Mike Sweeney	.10
169	Johnny Damon	.25
170	Jermaine Dye	.10
171	Alex Ochoa	.10
172	Jason Isringhausen	.10
173	Mark Grudzielanek	.10
174	Jose Rosado	.10
175	Todd Hollandsworth	.10
176	Alan Benes	.10
177	Jason Giambi	.45
178	Billy Wagner	.10
179	Justin Thompson	.10
180	Todd Walker	.10

Players Private Issue

A parallel version of the Gallery issue called Players Private Issue was produced as a 1:12 pack insert. The PPI cards differ from the regular version in the use of a "PPI-" prefix to the card number on front and the application of a small silver PPI seal in a lower corner. On back, the line "One of 250 Issued" has been added.

	NM/M
Common Player:	1.00
Stars:	5X

Gallery of Heroes

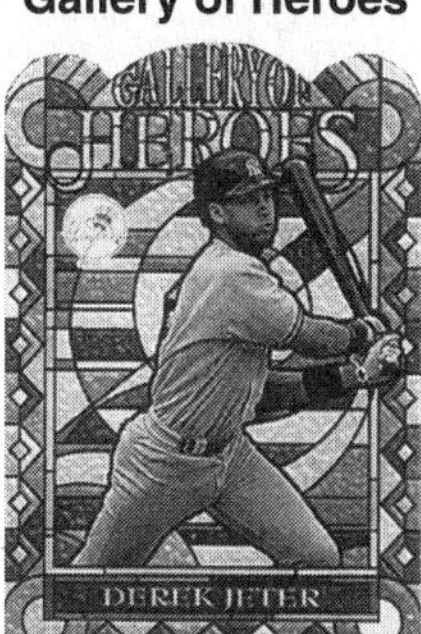

This 10-card die-cut insert features a design resembling stained glass. Cards were inserted 1:36 packs. Cards are numbered with a "GH" prefix.

		NM/M
Complete Set (10):		30.00
Common Player:		1.50
1	Derek Jeter	6.00
2	Chipper Jones	3.00
3	Frank Thomas	2.50
4	Ken Griffey Jr.	4.00
5	Cal Ripken Jr.	6.00
6	Mark McGwire	5.00
7	Mike Piazza	4.00
8	Jeff Bagwell	2.50
9	Tony Gwynn	3.00
10	Mo Vaughn	1.50

Peter Max

Noted artist Peter Max has painted renditions of 10 superstar players and offered his commentary about those players on the backs. Cards were inserted 1:24 packs. In addition, Max-autographed cards signed and numbered from an edition of 40 are inserted 1:1,200 packs.

		NM/M
Complete Set (10):		60.00
Common Player:		3.00
Peter Max Autographed:		100.00
1	Derek Jeter	10.00
2	Albert Belle	3.00
3	Ken Caminiti	3.00
4	Chipper Jones	6.00
5	Ken Griffey Jr.	7.50
6	Frank Thomas	5.00
7	Cal Ripken Jr.	10.00
8	Mark McGwire	9.00
9	Barry Bonds	10.00
10	Mike Piazza	7.50

Photo Gallery

This 21-card set features full-bleed, high-gloss action photos of some of the game's top stars. Cards were inserted 1:24 packs. They are numbered with a "PG" prefix.

		NM/M
Complete Set (16):		15.00
Common Player:		.50
1	World Series	.50
2	Paul Molitor	1.00
3	Eddie Murray	1.00
4	Ken Griffey Jr.	2.50
5	Chipper Jones	1.50
6	Derek Jeter	3.50
7	Frank Thomas	1.00
8	Mark McGwire	3.00
9	Kenny Lofton	.50
10	Gary Sheffield	.65
11	Mike Piazza	2.50
12	Vinny Castilla	.50
13	Andres Galarraga	.50
14	Andy Pettitte	.50
15	Robin Ventura	.50
16	Barry Larkin	.50

Screenplays

Twenty of the game's top stars were featured in this multi-part collectible. The packaging is a 5-1/8" diameter lithographed steel can. The can was shrink-wrapped at the factory with a round checklist disc covering the color player photo on top of the can. The top has a woodgrain border around the photo and a gold facsimile autograph. The back of the topper disc has a career summary of the player. Inside the tin is a 2-1/2" x 3-1/2" plastic motion card with several seconds of game action shown as the angle of view changes. The card is covered by a peel-off protective layer on front and back. Foam pieces in the package allow both the can and card to be displayed upright. Issue price was about $10 per can. The unnumbered cans are checklisted here alphabetically. Values shown are for can/card combinations.

		NM/M
Complete Set (20):		25.00
Common Player:		1.00
Pack (1):		2.50
Wax Box (21):		30.00
(1)	Jeff Bagwell	2.00
(2)	Albert Belle	1.00
(3)	Barry Bonds	5.00
(4)	Andres Galarraga	1.00
(5)	Nomar Garciaparra	2.50
(6)	Juan Gonzalez	1.25
(7)	Ken Griffey Jr.	3.00
(8)	Tony Gwynn	2.50
(9)	Derek Jeter	5.00
(10)	Randy Johnson	2.00
(11)	Andruw Jones	2.00
(12)	Chipper Jones	2.50
(13)	Kenny Lofton	1.00
(14)	Mark McGwire	4.00
(15)	Paul Molitor	2.00
(16)	Hideo Nomo	1.25
(17)	Cal Ripken Jr.	5.00
(18)	Sammy Sosa	2.50
(19)	Frank Thomas	2.00
(20)	Jim Thome	1.50

Screenplays Inserts

		NM/M
Complete Set (6):		35.00
Common Player:		2.00
1	Larry Walker	2.00
2	Cal Ripken Jr.	12.50
3	Chipper Jones	6.00
4	Frank Thomas	5.00
5	Mike Piazza	7.50
6	Ken Griffey Jr.	7.50

1997 Topps Stars Promos

These promo cards introduced Topps' new line of premium cards. They are in the same basic format as the regular issue, but are marked "PRE-PRODUCTION / SAMPLE" in the stats box on back.

		NM/M
Complete Set (3):		5.00
Common Player:		1.00
PP1	Larry Walker	1.00
PP2	Roger Clemens	3.00
PP3	Frank Thomas	2.00

1997 Topps Stars

The premiere version of this product was sold only to hobby shops that were members of the Topps Home Team Advantage program. Each of the 125 regular cards in the set is printed on 20-point stock. Card fronts feature spot UV coating with a textured star pattern running down one side of the card. Inserts include the parallel Always Mint set, as well as '97 All-Stars, Future All-Stars, All-Star memories, and Autographed Rookie Reprints. Cards were sold in seven-card packs for $3 each.

		NM/M
Complete Set (125):		30.00
Common Player:		.10
Always Mint Stars, RC's:		8X
Pack (7):		3.00
Wax Box (24):		65.00
1	Larry Walker	.10
2	Tino Martinez	.10
3	Cal Ripken Jr.	3.00
4	Ken Griffey Jr.	2.00
5	Chipper Jones	1.50
6	David Justice	.10
7	Mike Piazza	2.00
8	Jeff Bagwell	1.00
9	Ron Gant	.10
10	Sammy Sosa	2.00
11	Tony Gwynn	1.50
12	Carlos Baerga	.10
13	Frank Thomas	1.00
14	Moises Alou	.10
15	Barry Larkin	.10
16	Ivan Rodriguez	.75
17	Greg Maddux	1.50
18	Jim Edmonds	.10
19	Jose Canseco	.50

20	Rafael Palmeiro	.75
21	Paul Molitor	1.00
22	Kevin Appier	.10
23	Raul Mondesi	.10
24	Lance Johnson	.10
25	Edgar Martinez	.10
26	Andres Galarraga	.10
27	Mo Vaughn	.10
28	Ken Caminiti	.10
29	Cecil Fielder	.10
30	Harold Baines	.10
31	Roberto Alomar	.25
32	Shawn Estes	.10
33	Tom Glavine	.35
34	Dennis Eckersley	.75
35	Manny Ramirez	1.00
36	John Olerud	.10
37	Juan Gonzalez	.50
38	Chuck Knoblauch	.10
39	Albert Belle	.10
40	Vinny Castilla	.10
41	John Smoltz	.10
42	Barry Bonds	3.00
43	Randy Johnson	1.00
44	Brady Anderson	.10
45	Jeff Blauser	.10
46	Craig Biggio	.10
47	Jeff Conine	.10
48	Marquis Grissom	.10
49	Mark Grace	.10
50	Roger Clemens	1.75
51	Mark McGwire	2.50
52	Fred McGriff	.10
53	Gary Sheffield	.50
54	Bobby Jones	.10
55	Eric Young	.10
56	Robin Ventura	.10
57	Wade Boggs	1.50
58	Joe Carter	.10
59	Ryne Sandberg	1.50
60	Matt Williams	.10
61	Todd Hundley	.10
62	Dante Bichette	.10
63	Chili Davis	.10
64	Kenny Lofton	.10
65	Jay Buhner	.10
66	Will Clark	.10
67	Travis Fryman	.10
68	Pat Hentgen	.10
69	Ellis Burks	.10
70	Mike Mussina	.40
71	Hideo Nomo	.50
72	Sandy Alomar	.10
73	Bobby Bonilla	.10
74	Rickey Henderson	1.00
75	David Cone	.10
76	Terry Steinbach	.10
77	Pedro Martinez	1.00
78	Jim Thome	.75
79	Rod Beck	.10
80	Randy Myers	.10
81	Charles Nagy	.10
82	Mark Wohlers	.10
83	Paul O'Neill	.10
84	Curt Schilling	.35
85	Joey Cora	.10
86	John Franco	.10
87	Kevin Brown	.10
88	Benito Santiago	.10
89	Ray Lankford	.10
90	Bernie Williams	.10
91	Jason Dickson	.10
92	Jeff Cirillo	.10
93	Nomar Garciaparra	2.00
94	Mariano Rivera	.15
95	Javy Lopez	.10
96	Tony Womack **RC**	.25
97	Jose Rosado	.10
98	Denny Neagle	.10
99	Darryl Kile	.10
100	Justin Thompson	.10
101	Juan Encarnacion	.10
102	Brad Fullmer	.10
103	Kris Benson **RC**	.75
104	Todd Helton	1.00
105	Paul Konerko	.10
106	Travis Lee **RC**	1.00
107	Todd Greene	.10
108	Mark Kotsay **RC**	.50
109	Carl Pavano	.10
110	Kerry Wood **RC**	4.00
111	Jason Romano **RC**	.10
112	Geoff Goetz **RC**	.10
113	Scott Hodges **RC**	.10
114	Aaron Akin **RC**	.10
115	Vernon Wells **RC**	6.00
116	Chris Stowe **RC**	.10
117	Brett Caradonna **RC**	.10
118	Adam Kennedy **RC**	1.00
119	Jayson Werth **RC**	.10
120	Glenn Davis **RC**	.10
121	Troy Cameron **RC**	.10
122	J.J. Davis **RC**	.10
123	Jason Dellaero **RC**	.10
124	Jason Standridge **RC**	.10
125	Lance Berkman **RC**	2.00

Always Mint

This set parallels the regular Topps Stars issue and was inserted at the announced rate of one card per 12 packs. Identical in design to the regular version, the Always Mint cards have metallic foil background on the player portion of the front

photos. Backs of the Always Mint parallels have a shiny metallic silver background.

	NM/M
Complete Set (125):	250.00
Common Player:	.50
Stars/Rookies:	8X

All-Star Memories

This 10-card insert features stars who have had memorable performances in previous All-Star Games. Cards feature a laser-cut cascade of stars on a foilboard stock. Backs have another photo and a description of the All-Star memory. The cards were inserted 1:24 packs. Cards are numbered with an "ASM" prefix.

		NM/M
Complete Set (10):		20.00
Common Player:		1.00
1	Cal Ripken Jr.	6.00
2	Jeff Conine	1.00
3	Mike Piazza	4.00
4	Randy Johnson	2.00
5	Ken Griffey Jr.	4.00
6	Fred McGriff	1.00
7	Moises Alou	1.00
8	Hideo Nomo	1.25
9	Larry Walker	1.00
10	Sandy Alomar	1.00

Future All-Stars

This 15-card set showcases the top candidates to make their All-Star Game debut in 1998. Cards feature a prismatic rainbow foil background and were inserted 1:12 packs. Cards are numbered with a "FAS" prefix.

		NM/M
Complete Set (15):		17.50
Common Player:		.75
1	Derek Jeter	4.00
2	Andruw Jones	2.50
3	Vladimir Guerrero	3.00
4	Scott Rolen	2.50
5	Jose Guillen	.75
6	Jose Cruz, Jr.	.75
7	Darin Erstad	2.50
8	Tony Clark	.75
9	Scott Spiezio	.75
10	Kevin Orie	.75
11	Calvin Reese	.75
12	Billy Wagner	.75
13	Matt Morris	.75
14	Jeremi Gonzalez	.75
15	Hideki Irabu	.75

Rookie Reprints

Fifteen Topps rookie cards of Hall of Famers were reprinted as a one-per-six-packs insert. Regardless of original size, all reprints are 2-1/2" x 3-1/2" with a reprint notice on back.

		NM/M
Complete Set (15):		25.00
Common Player:		2.00
(1)	Luis Aparicio	2.00
(2)	Richie Ashburn	2.00
(3)	Jim Bunning	2.00
(4)	Bob Feller	2.00
(5)	Rollie Fingers	2.00
(6)	Monte Irvin	2.00
(7)	Al Kaline	3.00
(8)	Ralph Kiner	2.00
(9)	Eddie Mathews	3.00
(10)	Hal Newhouser	2.00
(11)	Gaylord Perry	2.00
(12)	Robin Roberts	2.00
(13)	Brooks Robinson	3.00
(14)	Enos Slaughter	2.00
(15)	Earl Weaver	2.00

Autographed Rookie Reprints

Fourteen different Hall of Famers autographed reprinted versions of their Topps rookie cards as a one-per-30-pack insert. Each card features a special certified stamp. Richie Ashburn was to have been card #2, but he died before he could autograph them.

		NM/M
Common Player:		15.00
(1)	Luis Aparicio	20.00
(3)	Jim Bunning	30.00
(4)	Bob Feller	35.00
(5)	Rollie Fingers	15.00
(6)	Monte Irvin	15.00
(7)	Al Kaline	30.00
(8)	Ralph Kiner	25.00
(9)	Eddie Mathews	75.00
(10)	Hal Newhouser	40.00
(11)	Gaylord Perry	15.00
(12)	Robin Roberts	30.00
(13)	Brooks Robinson	40.00
(14)	Enos Slaughter	30.00
(15)	Earl Weaver	20.00

1997 All-Stars

This 20-card insert honors participants of the 1997 All-Star Game in Cleveland. Cards were inserted 1:24 packs. Fronts are printed on prismatic foil with hundreds of

stars in the background. On back is another player photo and his All-Star Game 1997 and career stats. Cards are numbered with an "AS" prefix.

		NM/M
Complete Set (20):		60.00
Common Player:		1.50
1	Greg Maddux	6.00
2	Randy Johnson	4.50
3	Tino Martinez	1.50
4	Jeff Bagwell	4.50
5	Ivan Rodriguez	3.50
6	Mike Piazza	7.50
7	Cal Ripken Jr.	12.00
8	Ken Caminiti	1.50
9	Tony Gwynn	6.00
10	Edgar Martinez	1.50
11	Craig Biggio	1.50
12	Roberto Alomar	2.00
13	Larry Walker	1.50
14	Brady Anderson	1.50
15	Barry Bonds	12.00
16	Ken Griffey Jr.	7.50
17	Ray Lankford	1.50
18	Paul O'Neill	1.50
19	Jeff Blauser	1.50
20	Sandy Alomar	1.50

Dodger Rookie of the Year Collection

Available only through Topps Stadium Club and at Dodger Stadium, this set of special cards honors the five consecutive (1992-96) N.L. Rookies of the Year - all L.A. Dodgers - as well as the first-ever Rookie of the Year, Jackie Robinson. The cards feature reproductions of the players' rookie cards printed on front in metallic foil and with an N.L. Rookie of the Year logo and year banner. Backs are virtually identical to the regular-issue cards, but include a reprint line in the fine print. Raul Mondesi's card is a different version of the '94 Topps Coming Attractions subset card which he shared with Ben Van Ryn. Production was reported at 4,000 sets.

		NM/M
Complete Set (6):		35.00
Common Player:		3.00
1	Jackie Robinson (1952 Topps)	20.00
2	Mike Piazza (1992 Bowman)	10.00
3	Eric Karros (1993 Topps)	3.00
4	Raul Mondesi (1994 Topps)	3.00
5	Hideo Nomo (1995 Topps Traded)	7.50
6	Todd Hollandsworth (1996 Topps)	3.00

"Pro Shooters" Photo Marbles

This limited distribution test issue was another attempt to market marbles with baseball player photos. The hard plastic 1" diameter marbles have a black composite band around the circumference. On one side is a player portrait, on the other is a team logo at center with the player name in a strip below and a number "... of 60" in a strip above. The Topps name does not appear. They were sold two per pack.

		NM/M
Complete Set (60):		1,000
Common Player:		10.00
1	Roberto Alomar	15.00
2	Brady Anderson	10.00
3	Carlos Baerga	10.00
4	Jeff Bagwell	30.00
5	Albert Belle	10.00
6	Dante Bichette	10.00
7	Craig Biggio	10.00
8	Wade Boggs	40.00
9	Barry Bonds	60.00
10	Jay Buhner	10.00
11	Ken Caminiti	10.00
12	Jose Canseco	15.00
13	Roger Clemens	42.50
14	David Cone	10.00
15	Cecil Fielder	10.00
16	Travis Fryman	10.00
17	Andres Galarraga	10.00
18	Ron Gant	10.00
19	Bernard Gilkey	10.00
20	Tom Glavine	12.50
21	Juan Gonzalez	15.00
22	Mark Grace	10.00
23	Ken Griffey Jr.	45.00
24	Tony Gwynn	40.00
25	Todd Hundley	10.00
26	John Jaha	10.00
27	Derek Jeter	60.00
28	Lance Johnson	10.00
29	Randy Johnson	30.00
30	Andruw Jones	30.00
31	Chipper Jones	40.00
32	Brian Jordan	10.00
33	Jason Kendall	10.00
34	Chuck Knoblauch	10.00
35	Ray Lankford	10.00
36	Barry Larkin	10.00
37	Kenny Lofton	10.00
38	Greg Maddux	40.00
39	Edgar Martinez	10.00
40	Fred McGriff	10.00
41	Mark McGwire	50.00
42	Paul Molitor	30.00
43	Raul Mondesi	10.00
44	Eddie Murray	30.00
45	Mike Mussina	15.00
46	Hideo Nomo	15.00
47	Rafael Palmeiro	25.00
48	Andy Pettitte	15.00
49	Mike Piazza	45.00
50	Cal Ripken Jr.	60.00
51	Ivan Rodriguez	25.00
52	Tim Salmon	10.00
53	Ryne Sandberg	40.00
54	Gary Sheffield	15.00
55	John Smoltz	10.00
56	Sammy Sosa	40.00
57	Frank Thomas	30.00
58	Mo Vaughn	10.00
59	Bernie Williams	10.00
60	Matt Williams	10.00
1 of 2	Checklist Card 1-30	30.00
2 of 2	Checklist Card 31-60	30.00

22k Gold

These 22-karat gold-foil cards were created for direct sale by Topps. They reproduce, front and back, Griffey's and Ripken's regular-issue 1997 Topps cards, and feature a 1997-style card of Irabu, who did not appear on a regular Topps card that year. The 2-1/2" x 3-1/2" cards are individually serial numbered and were sold in a protective display holder. Initially priced at $30 apiece, they were discounted in a later offer to $19.95.

		NM/M
Complete Set (3):		60.00
Common Player:		20.00
300	Ken Griffey Jr.	15.00
400	Cal Ripken Jr.	20.00
----	Hideki Irabu	15.00

1998 Topps Pre-Production

To give potential customers a feel for its 1998 baseball cards, Topps issued this series of pre-production samples. Cards are identical in format to the issued versions except they are numbered with a "PP" prefix and the 1997 stats line reads "PRE-PRODUCTION SAMPLE."

		NM/M
Complete Set (6):		4.00
Common Player:		.25
PP1	Carlos Baerga	.25
PP2	Jeff Bagwell	.75
PP3	Marquis Grissom	.25
PP4	Derek Jeter	1.50
PP5	Randy Johnson	.75
PP6	Mike Piazza	1.00

1998 Topps

Topps issued two series in 1998, a total of 503 base cards; 282 in Series 1 and 221 in Series 2. Cards feature a gold border instead of the traditional white of past years. The product features Roberto Clemente inserts and a tribute card No. 21 in the base set. Series 1 subsets Series Highlights, Expansion Team Prospects, Interleague Highlights, Season Highlights, Prospects and Draft Picks. Subsets in Series II included: Expansion Teams, InterLeague Preview, Season Highlights, Prospects and Draft Picks. Every card in the set is paralleled in a Minted in Cooperstown insert that was stamped on-site at the Baseball Hall of Fame in Cooperstown. Inserts in Series 1 include: Roberto Clemente Reprints, Clemente Finest, Clemente Tribute, Memorabilila Madness, Etch a Sketch, Mystery Finest, Flashback and Baby Boomers. Inserts in Series 2 included: Clemente Reprints, Clemente Finest, 1998 Rookie Class, Mystery Finest, Milestones, Focal Points, and Clout 9. A factory set includes the 503 base cards, eight randomly selected inserts and one Clemente card sealed in a gold-foil stamped soft plastic case.

NM/M
Unopened Fact. Set (511): 85.00
Complete Set (503): 40.00
Common Player: .05
Minted: 6X
Inserted 1:8
Series 1 or 2 Pack (11): 1.00
Series 1 or 2 Wax Box (36): 25.00
1 Tony Gwynn 1.00
2 Larry Walker .05
3 Billy Wagner .05
4 Denny Neagle .05
5 Vladimir Guerrero .75
6 Kevin Brown .05
8 Mariano Rivera .10
9 Tony Clark .05
10 Deion Sanders .05
11 Francisco Cordova .05
12 Matt Williams .05
13 Carlos Baerga .05
14 Mo Vaughn .05
15 Bobby Witt .05
16 Matt Stairs .05
17 Chan Ho Park .05
18 Mike Bordick .05
19 Michael Tucker .05
20 Frank Thomas .75
21 Roberto Clemente 1.50
22 Dmitri Young .05
23 Steve Trachsel .05
24 Jeff Kent .05
25 Scott Rolen .50
26 John Thomson .05
27 Joe Vitiello .05
28 Eddie Guardado .05
29 Charlie Hayes .05
30 Juan Gonzalez .40
31 Garret Anderson .05
32 John Jaha .05
33 Omar Vizquel .05
34 Brian Hunter .05
35 Jeff Bagwell .75
36 Mark Lemke .05
37 Doug Glanville .05
38 Dan Wilson .05
39 Steve Cooke .05
40 Chili Davis .05
41 Mike Cameron .05
42 F.P. Santangelo .05
43 Brad Ausmus .05
44 Gary DiSarcina .05
45 Pat Hentgen .05
46 Wilton Guerrero .05
47 Devon White .05
48 Danny Patterson .05
49 Pat Meares .05
50 Rafael Palmeiro .65
51 Mark Gardner .05
52 Jeff Blauser .05
53 Dave Hollins .05
54 Carlos Garcia .05
55 Ben McDonald .05
56 John Mabry .05
57 Trevor Hoffman .05
58 Tony Fernandez .05
59 Rich Loiselle .05
60 Mark Leiter .05
61 Pat Kelly .05
62 John Flaherty .05
63 Roger Bailey .05
64 Tom Gordon .05
65 Ryan Klesko .05
66 Darryl Hamilton .05
67 Jim Eisenreich .05
68 Butch Huskey .05
69 Mark Grudzielanek .05
70 Marquis Grissom .05
71 Mark McLemore .05
72 Gary Gaetti .05
73 Greg Gagne .05
74 Lyle Mouton .05
75 Jim Edmonds .05
76 Shawn Green .25
77 Greg Vaughn .05
78 Terry Adams .05
79 Kevin Polcovich **RC** .05
80 Troy O'Leary .05
81 Jeff Shaw .05
82 Rich Becker .05
83 David Wells .05
84 Steve Karsay .05
85 Charles Nagy .05
86 B.J. Surhoff .05
87 Jamey Wright .05
88 James Baldwin .05
89 Edgardo Alfonzo .05
90 Jay Buhner .05
91 Brady Anderson .05
92 Scott Servais .05
93 Edgar Renteria .05
94 Mike Lieberthal .05
95 Rick Aguilera .05
96 Walt Weiss .05
97 Deivi Cruz .05
98 Kurt Abbott .05
99 Henry Rodriguez .05
100 Mike Piazza 1.25
101 Bill Taylor .05
102 Todd Zeile .05
103 Rey Ordonez .05
104 Willie Greene .05
105 Tony Womack .05
106 Mike Sweeney .05
107 Jeffrey Hammonds .05
108 Kevin Orie .05
109 Alex Gonzalez .05
110 Jose Canseco .50
111 Paul Sorrento .05
112 Joey Hamilton .05
113 Brad Radke .05
114 Steve Avery .05
115 Esteban Loaiza .05
116 Stan Javier .05
117 Chris Gomez .05
118 Royce Clayton .05
119 Orlando Merced .05
120 Kevin Appier .05
121 Mel Nieves .05
122 Joe Girardi .05
123 Rico Brogna .05
124 Kent Mercker .05
125 Manny Ramirez .75
126 Jeromy Burnitz .05
127 Kevin Foster .05
128 Matt Morris .05
129 Jason Dickson .05
130 Tom Glavine .25
131 Wally Joyner .05
132 Rick Reed .05
133 Todd Jones .05
134 Dave Martinez .05
135 Sandy Alomar .05
136 Mike Lansing .05
137 Sean Berry .05
138 Doug Jones .05
139 Todd Stottlemyre .05
140 Jay Bell .05
141 Jaime Navarro .05
142 Chris Hoiles .05
143 Joey Cora .05
144 Scott Spiezio .05
145 Joe Carter .05
146 Jose Guillen .05
147 Damion Easley .05
148 Lee Stevens .05
149 Alex Fernandez .05
150 Randy Johnson .75
151 J.T. Snow .05
152 Chuck Finley .05
153 Bernard Gilkey .05
154 David Segui .05
155 Dante Bichette .05
156 Kevin Stocker .05
157 Carl Everett .05
158 Jose Valentin .05
159 Pokey Reese .05
160 Derek Jeter 2.00
161 Roger Pavlik .05
162 Mark Wohlers .05
163 Ricky Bottalico .05
164 Ozzie Guillen .05
165 Mike Mussina .50
166 Gary Sheffield .50
167 Hideo Nomo .40
168 Mark Grace .05
169 Aaron Sele .05
170 Darryl Kile .05
171 Shawn Estes .05
172 Vinny Castilla .05
173 Ron Coomer .05
174 Jose Rosado .05
175 Kenny Lofton .05
176 Jason Giambi .50
177 Hal Morris .05
178 Darren Bragg .05
179 Orel Hershiser .05
180 Ray Lankford .05
181 Hideki Irabu .05
182 Kevin Young .05
183 Javy Lopez .05
184 Jeff Montgomery .05
185 Mike Holtz .05
186 George Williams .05
187 Cal Eldred .05
188 Tom Candiotti .05
189 Glenallen Hill .05
190 Brian Giles .05
191 Dave Mlicki .05
192 Garrett Stephenson .05
193 Jeff Frye .05
194 Joe Oliver .05
195 Bob Hamelin .05
196 Luis Sojo .05
197 LaTroy Hawkins .05
198 Kevin Elster .05
199 Jeff Reed .05
200 Dennis Eckersley .65
201 Bill Mueller .05
202 Russ Davis .05
203 Armando Benitez .05
204 Quilvio Veras .05
205 Tim Naehring .05
206 Quinton McCracken .05
207 Raul Casanova .05
208 Matt Lawton .05
209 Luis Alicea .05
210 Luis Gonzalez .05
211 Allen Watson .05
212 Gerald Williams .05
213 David Bell .05
214 Todd Hollandsworth .05
215 Wade Boggs 1.00
216 Jose Mesa .05
217 Jamie Moyer .05
218 Darren Daulton .05
219 Mickey Morandini .05
220 Rusty Greer .05
221 Jim Bullinger .05
222 Jose Offerman .05
223 Matt Karchner .05
224 Woody Williams .05
225 Mark Loretta .05
226 Mike Hampton .05
227 Willie Adams .05
228 Scott Hatteberg .05
229 Rich Amaral .05
230 Terry Steinbach .05
231 Glendon Rusch .05
232 Bret Boone .05
233 Robert Person .05
234 Jose Hernandez .05
235 Doug Drabek .05
236 Jason McDonald .05
237 Chris Widger .05
238 Tom Martin **RC** .05
239 Dave Burba .05
240 Pete Rose II .05
241 Bobby Ayala .05
242 Tim Wakefield .05
243 Dennis Springer .05
244 Tim Belcher .05
245 Jon Garland, Geoff Goetz (Draft Pick) .05
246 Glenn Davis, Lance Berkman (Draft Pick) .05
247 Vernon Wells, Aaron Akin (Draft Pick) .10
248 Adam Kennedy, Jason Romano (Draft Pick) .10
249 Jason Dellaero, Troy Cameron (Draft Pick) .05
250 Alex Sanchez, Jared Sandberg **RC** (Expansion Team Prospects) .10
251 Pablo Ortega, Jim Manias (Expansion Team Prospects) .05
252 Jason Conti, Mike Stoner **RC** (Expansion Team Prospects) .10
253 John Patterson, Larry Rodriguez (Expansion Team Prospects) .05
254 Adrian Beltre, Ryan Minor **RC**, Aaron Boone (Prospect) .15
255 Ben Grieve, Brian Buchanan, Dermal Brown (Prospect) .05
256 Carl Pavano, Kerry Wood, Gil Meche (Prospect) .15
257 David Ortiz, Daryle Ward, Richie Sexson (Prospect) .50
258 Randy Winn, Juan Encarnacion, Andrew Vessel (Prospect) .10
259 Kris Benson, Travis Smith, Courtney Duncan (Prospect) .05
260 Chad Hermansen, Brent Butler, Warren Morris **RC** (Prospect) .10
261 Ben Davis, Elieser Marrero, Ramon Hernandez (Prospect) .05
262 Eric Chavez, Russell Branyan, Russ Johnson (Prospect) .20
263 Todd Dunwoody, John Barnes, Ryan Jackson **RC** (Prospect) .10
264 Matt Clement, Roy Halladay, Brian Fuentes **RC** (Prospect) .05
265 Randy Johnson (Season Highlight) .15
266 Kevin Brown (Season Highlight) .05
267 Ricardo Rincon, Francisco Cordova (Season Highlight) .05
268 Nomar Garciaparra (Season Highlight) .50
269 Tino Martinez (Season Highlight) .05
270 Chuck Knoblauch (Interleague) .05
271 Pedro Martinez (Interleague) .40
272 Denny Neagle (Interleague) .05
273 Juan Gonzalez (Interleague) .20
274 Andres Galarraga (Interleague) .05
275 Checklist .05
276 Checklist .05
277 Moises Alou (World Series) .05
278 Sandy Alomar (World Series) .05
279 Gary Sheffield (World Series) .05
280 Matt Williams (World Series) .05
281 Livan Hernandez (World Series) .05
282 Chad Ogea (World Series) .05
283 Marlins Win (World Series) .05
284 Tino Martinez .05
285 Roberto Alomar .20
286 Jeff King .05
287 Brian Jordan .05
288 Darin Erstad .15
289 Ken Caminiti .05
290 Jim Thome .60
291 Paul Molitor .75
292 Ivan Rodriguez .65
293 Bernie Williams .05
294 Todd Hundley .05
295 Andres Galarraga .05
296 Greg Maddux 1.00
297 Edgar Martinez .05
298 Ron Gant .05
299 Derek Bell .05
300 Roger Clemens 1.00
301 Rondell White .05
302 Barry Larkin .05
303 Robin Ventura .05
304 Jason Kendall .05
305 Chipper Jones 1.00
306 John Franco .05
307 Sammy Sosa 1.00
308 Troy Percival .05
309 Chuck Knoblauch .05
310 Ellis Burks .05
311 Al Martin .05
312 Tim Salmon .05
313 Moises Alou .05
314 Lance Johnson .05
315 Justin Thompson .05
316 Will Clark .05
317 Barry Bonds 2.00
318 Craig Biggio .05
319 John Smoltz .05
320 Cal Ripken Jr. 2.00
321 Ken Griffey Jr. 1.25
322 Paul O'Neill .05
323 Todd Helton .65
324 John Olerud .05
325 Mark McGwire 1.50
326 Jose Cruz Jr. .05
327 Jeff Cirillo .05
328 Dean Palmer .05
329 John Wetteland .05
330 Steve Finley .05
331 Albert Belle .05
332 Curt Schilling .25
333 Raul Mondesi .05
334 Andruw Jones .75
335 Nomar Garciaparra 1.00
336 David Justice .05
337 Andy Pettitte .25
338 Pedro Martinez .75
339 Travis Miller .05
340 Chris Stynes .05
341 Gregg Jefferies .05
342 Jeff Fassero .05
343 Craig Counsell .05
344 Wilson Alvarez .05
345 Bip Roberts .05
346 Kelvim Escobar .05
347 Mark Bellhorn .05
348 Cory Lidle **RC** .05
349 Fred McGriff .05
350 Chuck Carr .05
351 Bob Abreu .05
352 Juan Guzman .05
353 Fernando Vina .05
354 Andy Benes .05
355 Dave Nilsson .05
356 Bobby Bonilla .05
357 Ismael Valdes .05
358 Carlos Perez .05
359 Kirk Rueter .05
360 Bartolo Colon .05
361 Mel Rojas .05
362 Johnny Damon .25
363 Geronimo Berroa .05
364 Reggie Sanders .05
365 Jermaine Allensworth .05
366 Orlando Cabrera .05
367 Jorge Fabregas .05
368 Scott Stahoviak .05
369 Ken Cloude .05
370 Donovan Osborne .05
371 Roger Cedeno .05
372 Neifi Perez .05
373 Chris Holt .05
374 Cecil Fielder .05
375 Marty Cordova .05
376 Tom Goodwin .05
377 Jeff Suppan .05
378 Jeff Brantley .05
379 Mark Langston .05
380 Shane Reynolds .05
381 Mike Fetters .05
382 Todd Greene .05
383 Ray Durham .05
384 Carlos Delgado .30
385 Jeff D'Amico .05
386 Brian McRae .05
387 Alan Benes .05
388 Heathcliff Slocumb .05
389 Eric Young .05
390 Travis Fryman .05
391 David Cone .05
392 Otis Nixon .05
393 Jeremi Gonzalez .05
394 Jeff Juden .05
395 Jose Vizcaino .05
396 Ugueth Urbina .05
397 Ramon Martinez .05
398 Robb Nen .05
399 Harold Baines .05
400 Delino DeShields .05
401 John Burkett .05
402 Sterling Hitchcock .05
403 Mark Clark .05
404 Terrell Wade .05
405 Scott Brosius .05
406 Chad Curtis .05
407 Brian Johnson .05
408 Roberto Kelly .05
409 Dave Dellucci **RC** .15
410 Michael Tucker .05
411 Mark Kotsay .05
412 Mark Lewis .05
413 Ryan McGuire .05
414 Shawon Dunston .05
415 Brad Rigby .05
416 Scott Erickson .05
417 Bobby Jones .05
418 Darren Oliver .05
419 John Smiley .05
420 T.J. Mathews .05
421 Dustin Hermanson .05
422 Mike Timlin .05
423 Willie Blair .05
424 Manny Alexander .05
425 Bob Tewksbury .05
426 Pete Schourek .05
427 Reggie Jefferson .05
428 Ed Sprague .05
429 Jeff Conine .05
430 Roberto Hernandez .05
431 Tom Pagnozzi .05
432 Jaret Wright .05
433 Livan Hernandez .05
434 Andy Ashby .05
435 Todd Dunn .05
436 Bobby Higginson .05
437 Rod Beck .05
438 Jim Leyritz .05
439 Matt Williams .05
440 Brett Tomko .05
441 Joe Randa .05
442 Chris Carpenter .05
443 Dennis Reyes .05
444 Al Leiter .05
445 Jason Schmidt .05
446 Ken Hill .05
447 Shannon Stewart .05
448 Enrique Wilson .05
449 Fernando Tatis .05
450 Jimmy Key .05
451 Darrin Fletcher .05
452 John Valentin .05
453 Kevin Tapani .05
454 Eric Karros .05
455 Jay Bell .05
456 Walt Weiss .05
457 Devon White .05
458 Carl Pavano .05
459 Mike Lansing .05
460 John Flaherty .05
461 Richard Hidalgo .05
462 Quinton McCracken .05
463 Karim Garcia .15
464 Miguel Cairo .05
465 Edwin Diaz .05
466 Bobby Smith .05
467 Yamil Benitez .05
468 Rich Butler **RC** .05
469 Ben Ford **RC** .05
470 Bubba Trammell .05
471 Brent Brede .05
472 Brooks Kieschnick .05
473 Carlos Castillo .05
474 Brad Radke (Season Highlight) .05
475 Roger Clemens (Season Highlight) .50
476 Curt Schilling (Season Highlight) .05
477 John Olerud (Season Highlight) .05
478 Mark McGwire (Season Highlight) .75
479 Mike Piazza, Ken Griffey Jr. (Interleague) .75
480 Jeff Bagwell, Frank Thomas (Interleague) .50
481 Chipper Jones, Nomar Garciaparra (Interleague) .65
482 Larry Walker, Juan Gonzalez (Interleague) .30
483 Gary Sheffield, Tino Martinez (Interleague) .05
484 Derrick Gibson, Michael Coleman, Norm Hutchins (Prospect) .05
485 Braden Looper, Cliff Politte, Brian Rose (Prospect) .05
486 Eric Milton, Jason Marquis, Corey Lee (Prospect) .05
487 A.J. Hinch, Mark Osborne, Robert Fick **RC** (Prospect) .10
488 Aramis Ramirez, Alex Gonzalez, Sean Casey (Prospect) .15
489 Donnie Bridges **RC**, Tim Drew **RC** (Draft Pick) .10
490 Ntema Ndungidi **RC**, Darnell McDonald **RC** (Draft Pick) .10
491 Ryan Anderson **RC**, Mark Mangum (Draft Pick) .25
492 J.J. Davis, Troy Glaus **RC** (Draft Pick) 2.00
493 Jayson Werth, Dan Reichert **RC** (Draft Pick) .10
494 John Curtice **RC**, Mike Cuddyer **RC** (Draft Pick) .25
495 Jack Cust **RC**, Jason Standridge (Draft Pick) 1.00
496 Brian Anderson (Expansion Team Prospect) .05
497 Tony Saunders (Expansion Team Prospect) .05
498 Vladimir Nunez, Jhensy Sandoval **RC** (Expansion Team Prospect) .10
499 Brad Penny, Nick Bierbrodt (Expansion Team Prospect) .05
500 Dustin Carr **RC**, Luis Cruz **RC** (Expansion Team Prospect) .05
501 Marcus McCain **RC**, Cedrick Bowers **RC** (Expansion Team Prospect) .05
502 Checklist .05
503 Checklist .05
504 Alex Rodriguez 1.50

Minted in Cooperstown

As part of an effort to promote interest in the various major sports' halls of fame, Topps produced this parallel version of its Series 1 baseball set. A special embossing machine was set up at the National Baseball Hall of Fame in Cooperstown to apply a bronze-foil "MINTED IN COOPERSTOWN" logo to cards. Twenty-card sheets of the logoed cards were sold on the premises and single cards were inserted into foil packs.

NM/M
Common Card: .50
Stars/Rookies: 6X

Arizona Diamondbacks Inaugural Season

To mark the team's inaugural year in the Major Leagues, Topps produced a special run of 5,000 factory sets in which each card was embossed with a special gold seal incorporating the D-Backs logo. Sets were sold only at the team's normal souvenir outlets.

NM/M
Complete Set (503): 80.00
Common Player: .50
Stars/Rookies: 6X

Tampa Bay Devil Rays Inaugural Season

To mark the team's inaugural year in the Major Leagues, Topps produced a special run of 5,000 factory sets in which each card was embossed with a special gold seal incorporating the D-Rays logo. Sets were sold only at the team's normal souvenir outlets.

	NM/M
Complete Set (503):	100.00
Common Player:	.50
Stars/Rookies:	6X

Baby Boomers

This 15-card retail exclusive insert was seeded one per 36 packs of Series 1. It featured some of the top young players in the game and was numbered with a "BB" prefix.

		NM/M
Complete Set (15):		15.00
Common Player:		.75
Inserted 1:36 Retail		
1	Derek Jeter	6.00
2	Scott Rolen	1.00
3	Nomar Garciaparra	3.50
4	Jose Cruz Jr.	.75
5	Darin Erstad	.85
6	Todd Helton	1.50
7	Tony Clark	.75
8	Jose Guillen	.75
9	Andruw Jones	1.00
10	Vladimir Guerrero	1.50
11	Mark Kotsay	.75
12	Todd Greene	.75
13	Andy Pettitte	.85
14	Justin Thompson	.75
15	Alan Benes	.75

Roberto Clemente Reprints

Nineteen different Topps Clemente cards were reprinted with a gold foil stamp and included 1998 Topps. Odd numbers were included in Series I, while even numbers were inserted into Series II, both at a rate of one per 18 packs. The insert was created to honor the memory of the 25th anniversary of Clemente's death.

		NM/M
Complete Set (19):		50.00
Common Card:		2.50
Inserted 1:18		
1	1955	4.00
2	1956	2.50
3	1957	2.50
4	1958	2.50
5	1959	2.50
6	1960	2.50
7	1961	2.50
8	1962	2.50
9	1963	2.50
10	1964	2.50
11	1965	2.50
12	1966	2.50
13	1967	2.50
14	1968	2.50
15	1969	2.50
16	1970	2.50
17	1971	2.50
18	1972	2.50
19	1973	2.50

Roberto Clemente Finest

Clemente Finest inserts were included in both Series I and II at a rate of one per 72 packs. There were a total of 19 different, with odd numbers in Series I and even numbers in Series II. The insert helped honor the memory of the 25th anniversary of his death.

		NM/M
Complete Set (19):		60.00
Common Card:		4.00
Inserted 1:72		
Refractors:		2X
Inserted 1:288		
1	1955	6.00
2	1956	4.00
3	1957	4.00
4	1958	4.00
5	1959	4.00
6	1960	4.00
7	1961	4.00
8	1962	4.00
9	1963	4.00
10	1964	4.00
11	1965	4.00
12	1966	4.00
13	1967	4.00
14	1968	4.00
15	1969	4.00
16	1970	4.00
17	1971	4.00
18	1972	4.00
19	1973	4.00

Roberto Clemente "Tin" Reprints

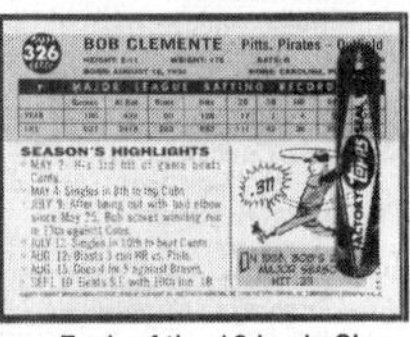

Each of the 19 basic Clemente reprint cards can also be found in a factory-sealed, gold-foil stamped soft plastic case. These were inserted in special retail-only tin boxes and one per factory set of 1998 Topps.

		NM/M
Complete Set (19):		60.00
Common Card:		4.00
1	1955	8.00
2	1956	4.00
3	1957	4.00
4	1958	4.00
5	1959	4.00
6	1960	4.00
7	1961	4.00
8	1962	4.00
9	1963	4.00
10	1964	4.00
11	1965	4.00
12	1966	4.00
13	1967	4.00
14	1968	4.00
15	1969	4.00
16	1970	4.00
17	1971	4.00
18	1972	4.00
19	1973	4.00

Roberto Clemente Commemorative Tins

This series of commemorative tin card "packs" reproduces in an enlarged (about 3" x 4-5/8" x 3/4") format the front and back of four of Roberto Clemente's Topps cards. Each tin, originally retailing for about $5, contains a plastic-sealed Clemente reprint card.

	NM/M
Complete Set (4):	10.00
Roberto Clemente/1955	3.50
Roberto Clemente/1956	2.50
Roberto Clemente/1965	2.50
Roberto Clemente/1971	2.50

Roberto Clemente Tribute

Five Clemente Tribute cards were produced for Series I and inserted in one per 12 packs. The set features some classic photos of Clemente and honor his memory in the 25th anniversary of his death. Clemente Tribute cards are numbered with a "RC" prefix.

		NM/M
Complete Set (5):		3.00
Common Clemente:		.75
Inserted 1:12		
1-5	Roberto Clemente	.75

Clout 9

Clout 9 captured nine players known for their statistical supremacy. Cards were numbered with a "C" prefix and inserted one per 72 packs of Series 2.

		NM/M
Complete Set (9):		17.50
Common Player:		1.00
Inserted 1:72		
1	Edgar Martinez	1.00
2	Mike Piazza	5.00
3	Frank Thomas	2.00
4	Craig Biggio	1.00
5	Vinny Castilla	1.00
6	Jeff Blauser	1.00
7	Barry Bonds	7.50
8	Ken Griffey Jr.	5.00
9	Larry Walker	1.00

Etch-A-Sketch

Etch-a-Sketch featured nine different players depicted by nationally acclaimed artist George Vlosich III. Known as "The Etch-a-Sketch Kid," Vlosich created each one of these Series I inserts, which were inserted at a rate of one per 36 packs. Cards are numbered with an "ES" prefix.

		NM/M
Complete Set (9):		20.00
Common Player:		1.00
Inserted 1:36		
1	Albert Belle	1.00
2	Barry Bonds	6.00
3	Ken Griffey Jr.	4.00
4	Greg Maddux	3.00
5	Hideo Nomo	1.50
6	Mike Piazza	4.00
7	Cal Ripken Jr.	6.00
8	Frank Thomas	2.00
9	Mo Vaughn	1.00

Flashback

This double-sided insert offers "then and now" photos of 10 top major leaguers. One side pictures the player circa 1998, while the other side shows him at the beginning of his major league career. Flashback inserts were seeded one per 72 packs and numbered with a "FB" prefix.

		NM/M
Complete Set (10):		22.50
Common Player:		1.00
Inserted 1:72		
1	Barry Bonds	7.50
2	Ken Griffey Jr.	5.00
3	Paul Molitor	2.00
4	Randy Johnson	2.00
5	Cal Ripken Jr.	7.50
6	Tony Gwynn	3.00
7	Kenny Lofton	1.00
8	Gary Sheffield	1.50
9	Deion Sanders	1.00
10	Brady Anderson	1.00

Focal Point

This hobby exclusive insert focuses on the skills that have made the players great. Focal Point inserts were available in Series 2 packs, seeded one per 36, and are numbered with a "FP" prefix.

		NM/M
Complete Set (15):		25.00
Common Player:		.75
Inserted 1:36		
1	Juan Gonzalez	.85
2	Nomar Garciaparra	2.50
3	Jose Cruz Jr.	.75
4	Cal Ripken Jr.	5.00
5	Ken Griffey Jr.	3.50
6	Ivan Rodriguez	1.00
7	Larry Walker	.75
8	Barry Bonds	5.00
9	Roger Clemens	3.00
10	Frank Thomas	1.50
11	Chuck Knoblauch	.75
12	Mike Piazza	3.50
13	Greg Maddux	2.50
14	Vladimir Guerrero	1.50
15	Andruw Jones	1.50

Hallbound

Hall Bound features players who were considered locks to be inducted into the Hall of Fame when their career was over. This insert was exclusive to Series 1 hobby packs and seeded one per 36. Cards are numbered with a "HB" prefix.

		NM/M
Complete Set (15):		45.00
Common Player:		1.50
1	Paul Molitor	2.50
2	Tony Gwynn	3.50
3	Wade Boggs	3.50
4	Roger Clemens	4.00
5	Dennis Eckersley	2.00
6	Cal Ripken Jr.	7.50
7	Greg Maddux	3.50
8	Rickey Henderson	2.50
9	Ken Griffey Jr.	5.00
10	Frank Thomas	2.50
11	Mark McGwire	6.00
12	Barry Bonds	7.50
13	Mike Piazza	5.00
14	Juan Gonzalez	1.50
15	Randy Johnson	2.50

Inter-League Mystery Finest

Five of the 1997 season's most intriguing inter-league matchups are showcased with four cards each in Inter-League Mystery Finest. Regular versions of this Series 1 insert are seeded one per 36 packs, while Refractor versions are seeded one per 144 packs. Cards are numbered with an "ILM" prefix.

		NM/M
Complete Set (20):		35.00
Common Player:		.75
Inserted 1:36		
Refractors:		1.5X
Inserted 1:144		
1	Chipper Jones	3.00
2	Cal Ripken Jr.	6.50
3	Greg Maddux	3.00
4	Rafael Palmeiro	1.50
5	Todd Hundley	.75
6	Derek Jeter	6.50
7	John Olerud	.75
8	Tino Martinez	.75
9	Larry Walker	.75
10	Ken Griffey Jr.	4.00
11	Andres Galarraga	.75
12	Randy Johnson	2.00
13	Mike Piazza	4.00
14	Jim Edmonds	.75
15	Eric Karros	.75
16	Tim Salmon	.75
17	Sammy Sosa	3.00
18	Frank Thomas	2.00
19	Mark Grace	.75
20	Albert Belle	.75

Milestones

Milestones features 10 records that could be broken during the 1998 season and the players who have the best shot at breaking them. This retail exclusive insert is seeded one per 36 packs and is numbered with a "MS" prefix.

		NM/M
Complete Set (10):		17.50
Common Player:		.75
MS1	Barry Bonds	5.00
MS2	Roger Clemens	2.50
MS3	Dennis Eckersley	1.00
MS4	Juan Gonzalez	.75
MS5	Ken Griffey Jr.	3.00
MS6	Tony Gwynn	2.00
MS7	Greg Maddux	2.00
MS8	Mark McGwire	4.00
MS9	Cal Ripken Jr.	5.00
MS10	Frank Thomas	1.25

Mystery Finest

This 20-card insert set features top players on bordered and borderless designs, with Refractor versions of each. Exclusive to Series 2 packs, bordered cards are seeded 1:36 packs, borderless are seeded 1:72 packs, bordered Refractors are 1:108 and borderless Refractors are seeded 1:288 packs. Mystery Finest inserts are numbered with a "M" prefix.

	NM/M
Complete Set (20):	25.00
Common Player:	.50
Inserted 1:36	

Borderless 1:72: 1.5X
Bordered Refractors 1:108: 1.5X
Borderless Refractors 1:288: 2X
1 Nomar Garciaparra 1.50
2 Chipper Jones 1.50
3 Scott Rolen .75
4 Albert Belle .50
5 Mo Vaughn .50
6 Jose Cruz Jr. .50
7 Mark McGwire 3.00
8 Derek Jeter 3.50
9 Tony Gwynn 1.50
10 Frank Thomas 1.00
11 Tino Martinez .50
12 Greg Maddux 1.50
13 Juan Gonzalez .75
14 Larry Walker .50
15 Mike Piazza 2.50
16 Cal Ripken Jr. 3.50
17 Jeff Bagwell 1.00
18 Andruw Jones 1.00
19 Barry Bonds 3.50
20 Ken Griffey Jr. 2.50

Rookie Class

Rookie Class features 10 young stars from 1998 and was exclusive to Series II packs. The cards were inserted one per 12 packs and numbered with a "R" prefix.

NM/M
Complete Set (10): 4.00
Common Player: .25
Inserted 1:12
1 Travis Lee .50
2 Richard Hidalgo .25
3 Todd Helton 2.00
4 Paul Konerko .75
5 Mark Kotsay .25
6 Derrek Lee 1.50
7 Eli Marrero .25
8 Fernando Tatis .25
9 Juan Encarnacion .25
10 Ben Grieve .25

1998 Topps Chrome

All 502 1998 Topps cards were reprinted in chromium versions for Topps Chrome. Chrome was released in two series; Series 1 containing 282 cards and Series 2 including 220 cards. Four-card packs had a suggested retail price of $3. Card fronts include a Topps Chrome logo. The issue offers a sampling of the inserts from Topps, along with Refractor versions of every card and insert. Series 1 inserts included: Flashbacks, Baby Boomers and Hallbound. Series 2 inserts included: Milestones, '98 Rookie Class and Clout 9.

NM/M
Complete Set (502): 100.00
Common Player: .10
Refractors: 5X
Inserted 1:12
Foil Pack (4): 1.50
Foil Box (24): 25.00
1 Tony Gwynn 2.00
2 Larry Walker .10
3 Billy Wagner .10
4 Denny Neagle .10
5 Vladimir Guerrero 1.50
6 Kevin Brown .10
8 Mariano Rivera .10
9 Tony Clark .10
10 Deion Sanders .10
11 Francisco Cordova .10
12 Matt Williams .10
13 Carlos Baerga .10
14 Mo Vaughn .10
15 Bobby Witt .10
16 Matt Stairs .10
17 Chan Ho Park .10
18 Mike Bordick .10
19 Michael Tucker .10
20 Frank Thomas 1.50
21 Roberto Clemente (Tribute) 2.50
22 Dmitri Young .10
23 Steve Trachsel .10
24 Jeff Kent .10
25 Scott Rolen .75
26 John Thomson .10
27 Joe Vitiello .10
28 Eddie Guardado .10
29 Charlie Hayes .10
30 Juan Gonzalez .75
31 Garret Anderson .10
32 John Jaha .10
33 Omar Vizquel .10
34 Brian Hunter .10
35 Jeff Bagwell 1.50
36 Mark Lemke .10
37 Doug Glanville .10
38 Dan Wilson .10
39 Steve Cooke .10
40 Chili Davis .10
41 Mike Cameron .10
42 F.P. Santangelo .10
43 Brad Ausmus .10
44 Gary DiSarcina .10
45 Pat Hentgen .10
46 Wilton Guerrero .10
47 Devon White .10
48 Danny Patterson .10
49 Pat Meares .10
50 Rafael Palmeiro 1.00
51 Mark Gardner .10
52 Jeff Blauser .10
53 Dave Hollins .10
54 Carlos Garcia .10
55 Ben McDonald .10
56 John Mabry .10
57 Trevor Hoffman .10
58 Tony Fernandez .10
59 Rich Loiselle .10
60 Mark Leiter .10
61 Pat Kelly .10
62 John Flaherty .10
63 Roger Bailey .10
64 Tom Gordon .10
65 Ryan Klesko .10
66 Darryl Hamilton .10
67 Jim Eisenreich .10
68 Butch Huskey .10
69 Mark Grudzielanek .10
70 Marquis Grissom .10
71 Mark McLemore .10
72 Gary Gaetti .10
73 Greg Gagne .10
74 Lyle Mouton .10
75 Jim Edmonds .10
76 Shawn Green .35
77 Terry Vaughn .10
78 Terry Adams .10
79 Kevin Polcovich **RC** .10
80 Troy O'Leary .10
81 Jeff Shaw .10
82 Rich Becker .10
83 David Wells .10
84 Steve Karsay .10
85 Charles Nagy .10
86 B.J. Surhoff .10
87 Jamey Wright .10
88 James Baldwin .10
89 Edgardo Alfonzo .10
90 Jay Buhner .10
91 Brady Anderson .10
92 Scott Servais .10
93 Edgar Renteria .10
94 Mike Lieberthal .10
95 Rick Aguilera .10
96 Walt Weiss .10
97 Deivi Cruz .10
98 Kurt Abbott .10
99 Henry Rodriguez .10
100 Mike Piazza 2.25
101 Bill Taylor .10
102 Todd Zeile .10
103 Rey Ordonez .10
104 Willie Greene .10
105 Tony Womack .10
106 Mike Sweeney .10
107 Jeffrey Hammonds .10
108 Kevin Orie .10
109 Alex Gonzalez .10
110 Jose Canseco .60
111 Paul Sorrento .10
112 Joey Hamilton .10
113 Brad Radke .10
114 Steve Avery .10
115 Esteban Loaiza .10
116 Stan Javier .10
117 Chris Gomez .10
118 Royce Clayton .10
119 Orlando Merced .10
120 Kevin Appier .10
121 Mel Nieves .10
122 Joe Girardi .10
123 Rico Brogna .10
124 Kent Mercker .10
125 Manny Ramirez 1.50
126 Jeromy Burnitz .10
127 Kevin Foster .10
128 Matt Morris .10
129 Jason Dickson .10
130 Tom Glavine .35
131 Wally Joyner .10
132 Rick Reed .10
133 Todd Jones .10
134 Dave Martinez .10
135 Sandy Alomar .10
136 Mike Lansing .10
137 Sean Berry .10
138 Doug Jones .10
139 Todd Stottlemyre .10
140 Jay Bell .10
141 Jaime Navarro .10
142 Chris Hoiles .10
143 Joey Cora .10
144 Scott Spiezio .10
145 Joe Carter .10
146 Jose Guillen .10
147 Damion Easley .10
148 Lee Stevens .10
149 Alex Fernandez .10
150 Randy Johnson 1.50
151 J.T. Snow .10
152 Chuck Finley .10
153 Bernard Gilkey .10
154 David Segui .10
155 Dante Bichette .10
156 Kevin Stocker .10
157 Carl Everett .10
158 Jose Valentin .10
159 Pokey Reese .10
160 Derek Jeter 3.00
161 Roger Pavlik .10
162 Mark Wohlers .10
163 Ricky Bottalico .10
164 Ozzie Guillen .10
165 Mike Mussina .60
166 Gary Sheffield .50
167 Hideo Nomo .75
168 Mark Grace .50
169 Aaron Sele .10
170 Darryl Kile .10
171 Shawn Estes .10
172 Vinny Castilla .10
173 Ron Coomer .10
174 Jose Rosado .10
175 Kenny Lofton .10
176 Jason Giambi .65
177 Hal Morris .10
178 Darren Bragg .10
179 Orel Hershiser .10
180 Ray Lankford .10
181 Hideki Irabu .10
182 Kevin Young .10
183 Javy Lopez .10
184 Jeff Montgomery .10
185 Mike Holtz .10
186 George Williams .10
187 Cal Eldred .10
188 Tom Candiotti .10
189 Glenallen Hill .10
190 Brian Giles .10
191 Dave Mlicki .10
192 Garrett Stephenson .10
193 Jeff Frye .10
194 Joe Oliver .10
195 Bob Hamelin .10
196 Luis Sojo .10
197 LaTroy Hawkins .10
198 Kevin Elster .10
199 Jeff Reed .10
200 Dennis Eckersley 1.00
201 Bill Mueller .10
202 Russ Davis .10
203 Armando Benitez .10
204 Quilvio Veras .10
205 Tim Naehring .10
206 Quinton McCracken .10
207 Raul Casanova .10
208 Matt Lawton .10
209 Luis Alicea .10
210 Luis Gonzalez .10
211 Allen Watson .10
212 Gerald Williams .10
213 David Bell .10
214 Todd Hollandsworth .10
215 Wade Boggs 2.00
216 Jose Mesa .10
217 Jamie Moyer .10
218 Darren Daulton .10
219 Mickey Morandini .10
220 Rusty Greer .10
221 Jim Bullinger .10
222 Jose Offerman .10
223 Matt Karchner .10
224 Woody Williams .10
225 Mark Loretta .10
226 Mike Hampton .10
227 Willie Adams .10
228 Scott Hatteberg .10
229 Rich Amaral .10
230 Terry Steinbach .10
231 Glendon Rusch .10
232 Bret Boone .10
233 Robert Person .10
234 Jose Hernandez .10
235 Doug Drabek .10
236 Jason McDonald .10
237 Chris Widger .10
238 Tom Martin **RC** .10
239 Dave Burba .10
240 Pete Rose .10
241 Bobby Ayala .10
242 Tim Wakefield .10
243 Dennis Springer .10
244 Tim Belcher .10
245 Jon Garland, Geoff Goetz (Draft Pick) .10
246 Glenn Davis, Lance Berkman (Draft Pick) .25
247 Vernon Wells, Aaron Akin (Draft Pick) .15
248 Adam Kennedy, Jason Romano (Draft Pick) .25
249 Jason Dellaero, Troy Cameron (Draft Pick) .10
250 Alex Sanchez, Jared Sandberg **RC** (Expansion) .25
251 Pablo Ortega, James Manias **RC** (Expansion) .10
252 Jason Conti, Mike Stoner **RC** (Expansion) .10
253 John Patterson, Larry Rodriguez (Expansion) .10
254 Adrian Beltre, Ryan Minor **RC**, Aaron Boone (Prospect) .25
255 Ben Grieve, Brian Buchanan, Dermal Brown (Prospect) .10
256 Carl Pavano, Kerry Wood, Gil Meche (Prospect) .75
257 David Ortiz, Daryle Ward, Richie Sexson (Prospect) .65
258 Randy Winn, Juan Encarnacion, Andrew Vessel (Prospect) .10
259 Kris Benson, Travis Smith, Courtney Duncan (Prospect) .15
260 Chad Hermansen, Brent Butler, Warren Morris **RC** (Prospect) .15
261 Ben Davis, Elieser Marrero, Ramon Hernandez (Prospect) .10
262 Eric Chavez, Russell Branyan, Russ Johnson (Prospect) .25
263 Todd Dunwoody, John Barnes, Ryan Jackson **RC** (Prospect) .15
264 Matt Clement, Roy Halladay, Brian Fuentes (Prospect) .20
265 Randy Johnson (Season Highlight) .50
266 Kevin Brown (Season Highlight) .10
267 Francisco Cordova, Ricardo Rincon (Season Highlight) .10
268 Nomar Garciaparra (Season Highlight) .75
269 Tino Martinez (Season Highlight) .10
270 Chuck Knoblauch (Inter-League) .10
271 Pedro Martinez (Inter-League) .40
272 Denny Neagle (Inter-League) .10
273 Juan Gonzalez (Inter-League) .20
274 Andres Galarraga (Inter-League) .10
275 Checklist .10
276 Checklist .10
277 Moises Alou (World Series) .10
278 Sandy Alomar (World Series) .10
279 Gary Sheffield (World Series) .10
280 Matt Williams (World Series) .10
281 Livan Hernandez (World Series) .10
282 Chad Ogea (World Series) .10
283 Marlins Win (World Series) .10
284 Tino Martinez .10
285 Roberto Alomar .35
286 Jeff King .10
287 Brian Jordan .10
288 Darin Erstad .30
289 Ken Caminiti .10
290 Jim Thome .90
291 Paul Molitor 1.50
292 Ivan Rodriguez 1.00
293 Bernie Williams .10
294 Todd Hundley .10
295 Andres Galarraga .10
296 Greg Maddux 2.00
297 Edgar Martinez .10
298 Ron Gant .10
299 Derek Bell .10
300 Roger Clemens 2.00
301 Rondell White .10
302 Barry Larkin .10
303 Robin Ventura .10
304 Jason Kendall .10
305 Chipper Jones 2.00
306 John Franco .10
307 Sammy Sosa 2.00
308 Troy Percival .10
309 Chuck Knoblauch .10
310 Ellis Burks .10
311 Al Martin .10
312 Tim Salmon .10
313 Moises Alou .10
314 Lance Johnson .10
315 Justin Thompson .10
316 Will Clark .10
317 Barry Bonds 3.00
318 Craig Biggio .10
319 John Smoltz .10
320 Cal Ripken Jr. 3.00
321 Ken Griffey Jr. 2.25
322 Paul O'Neill .10
323 Todd Helton 1.50
324 John Olerud .10
325 Mark McGwire 2.50
326 Jose Cruz Jr. .10
327 Jeff Cirillo .10
328 Dean Palmer .10
329 John Wetteland .10
330 Steve Finley .10
331 Albert Belle .10
332 Curt Schilling .35
333 Raul Mondesi .10
334 Andruw Jones 1.50
335 Nomar Garciaparra 2.00
336 David Justice .10
337 Andy Pettitte .30
338 Pedro Martinez 1.50
339 Travis Miller .10
340 Chris Stynes .10
341 Gregg Jefferies .10
342 Jeff Fassero .10
343 Craig Counsell .10
344 Wilson Alvarez .10
345 Bip Roberts .10
346 Kelvim Escobar .10
347 Mark Bellhorn .10
348 Cory Lidle .10
349 Fred McGriff .10
350 Chuck Carr .10
351 Bob Abreu .10
352 Juan Guzman .10
353 Fernando Vina .10
354 Andy Benes .10
355 Dave Nilsson .10
356 Bobby Bonilla .10
357 Ismael Valdes .10
358 Carlos Perez .10
359 Kirk Rueter .10
360 Bartolo Colon .10
361 Mel Rojas .10
362 Johnny Damon .35
363 Geronimo Berroa .10
364 Reggie Sanders .10
365 Jermaine Allensworth .10
366 Orlando Cabrera .10
367 Jorge Fabregas .10
368 Scott Stahoviak .10
369 Ken Cloude .10
370 Donovan Osborne .10
371 Roger Cedeno .10
372 Neifi Perez .10
373 Chris Holt .10
374 Cecil Fielder .10
375 Marty Cordova .10
376 Tom Goodwin .10
377 Jeff Suppan .10
378 Jeff Brantley .10
379 Mark Langston .10
380 Shane Reynolds .10
381 Mike Fetters .10
382 Todd Greene .10
383 Ray Durham .10
384 Carlos Delgado .35
385 Jeff D'Amico .10
386 Brian McRae .10
387 Alan Benes .10
388 Heathcliff Slocumb .10
389 Eric Young .10
390 Travis Fryman .10
391 David Cone .10
392 Otis Nixon .10
393 Jeremi Gonzalez .10
394 Jeff Juden .10
395 Jose Vizcaino .10
396 Ugueth Urbina .10
397 Ramon Martinez .10
398 Robb Nen .10
399 Harold Baines .10
400 Delino DeShields .10
401 John Burkett .10
402 Sterling Hitchcock .10
403 Mark Clark .10
404 Terrell Wade .10
405 Scott Brosius .10
406 Chad Curtis .10
407 Brian Johnson .10
408 Roberto Kelly .10
409 Dave Dellucci **RC** .25
410 Michael Tucker .10
411 Mark Kotsay .10
412 Mark Lewis .10
413 Ryan McGuire .10
414 Shawon Dunston .10
415 Brad Rigby .10
416 Scott Erickson .10
417 Bobby Jones .10
418 Darren Oliver .10
419 John Smiley .10
420 T.J. Mathews .10
421 Dustin Hermanson .10
422 Mike Timlin .10
423 Willie Blair .10
424 Manny Alexander .10
425 Bob Tewksbury .10
426 Pete Schourek .10
427 Reggie Jefferson .10
428 Ed Sprague .10
429 Jeff Conine .10
430 Roberto Hernandez .10
431 Tom Pagnozzi .10
432 Jaret Wright .10
433 Livan Hernandez .10
434 Andy Ashby .10
435 Todd Dunn .10
436 Bobby Higginson .10
437 Rod Beck .10
438 Jim Leyritz .10
439 Matt Williams .10
440 Brett Tomko .10
441 Joe Randa .10
442 Chris Carpenter .10
443 Dennis Reyes .10
444 Al Leiter .10
445 Jason Schmidt .10
446 Ken Hill .10
447 Shannon Stewart .10
448 Enrique Wilson .10
449 Fernando Tatis .10
450 Jimmy Key .10
451 Darrin Fletcher .10
452 John Valentin .10
453 Kevin Tapani .10
454 Eric Karros .10
455 Jay Bell .10
456 Walt Weiss .10
457 Devon White .10
458 Carl Pavano .10
459 Mike Lansing .10
460 John Flaherty .10
461 Richard Hidalgo .10
462 Quinton McCracken .10
463 Karim Garcia .20
464 Miguel Cairo .10
465 Edwin Diaz .10
466 Bobby Smith .10
467 Yamil Benitez .10
468 Rich Butler **RC** .10
469 Ben Ford **RC** .10
470 Bubba Trammell .10
471 Brent Brede .10
472 Brooks Kieschnick .10
473 Carlos Castillo .10
474 Brad Radke (Season Highlight) .10
475 Roger Clemens (Season Highlight) 1.00
476 Curt Schilling (Season Highlight) .15
477 John Olerud (Season Highlight) .10
478 Mark McGwire (Season Highlight) 1.25
479 Mike Piazza, Ken Griffey Jr. (Interleague) 1.25
480 Jeff Bagwell, Frank Thomas (Interleague) 1.00
481 Chipper Jones, Nomar Garciaparra (Interleague) 1.00
482 Larry Walker, Juan Gonzalez (Interleague) .20
483 Gary Sheffield, Tino Martinez (Interleague) .10
484 Derrick Gibson, Michael Coleman, Norm Hutchins (Prospect) .10
485 Braden Looper, Cliff Politte, Brian Rose (Prospect) .15
486 Eric Milton, Jason Marquis, Corey Lee (Prospect) .25
487 A.J. Hinch, Mark Osborne, Robert Fick **RC** (Prospect) .25
488 Aramis Ramirez, Alex Gonzalez, Sean Casey (Prospect) .25
489 Donnie Bridges **RC**, Tim Drew **RC** (Draft Pick) .20
490 Ntema Ndungidi **RC**, Darnell McDonald **RC** (Draft Pick) .10
491 Ryan Anderson **RC**, Mark Mangum (Draft Pick) .50
492 J.J. Davis, Troy Glaus **RC** (Draft Pick) 3.00
493 Jayson Werth, Dan Reichert (Draft Pick) .10

494	John Curtice **RC**, Mike Cuddyer **RC** (Draft Pick)	.50
495	Jack Cust **RC**, Jason Standridge (Draft Pick)	4.00
496	Brian Anderson (Expansion Team Prospect)	.10
497	Tony Saunders (Expansion Team Prospect)	.10
498	Vladimir Nunez, Jhensy Sandoval **RC** (Expansion Team Prospect)	.10
499	Brad Penny, Nick Bierbrodt (Expansion Team Prospect)	.10
500	Dustin Carr **RC**, Luis Cruz **RC** (Expansion Team Prospect)	.10
501	Marcus McCain **RC**, Cedrick Bowers **RC** (Expansion Team Prospect)	.10
502	Checklist	.10
503	Checklist	.10
504	Alex Rodriguez	2.50
		.10

Refractors

Each card in the regular Topps Series 1 and Series 2 Chrome issue could also be found in a refractor version seeded approximately one per 12 packs. Refractor versions are so designated above the card number on back.

	NM/M
Common Player:	.50
Stars/Rookies:	5X

Baby Boomers

This 15-card insert featured players with less than three years of experience. Cards were inserted one per 24 packs, with Refractor versions found every 72 packs of Series I. Cards were numbered with a "BB" prefix.

		NM/M
Complete Set (15):		16.00
Common Player:		.75
Inserted 1:24		
Refractors:		1.5X
Inserted 1:72		
1	Derek Jeter	6.00
2	Scott Rolen	.90
3	Nomar Garciaparra	3.50
4	Jose Cruz Jr.	.75
5	Darin Erstad	.90
6	Todd Helton	1.50
7	Tony Clark	.75
8	Jose Guillen	.75
9	Andruw Jones	1.50
10	Vladimir Guerrero	1.50
11	Mark Kotsay	.75
12	Todd Greene	.75
13	Andy Pettitte	.90
14	Justin Thompson	.75
15	Alan Benes	.75

Clout 9

This nine-card insert included players for their statistical supremacy. Clout 9 cards were found in Series II packs at a rate of one per 24 packs, with Refractor versions every 72 packs. Cards are numbered with a "C" prefix.

		NM/M
Complete Set (9):		15.00
Common Player:		.75
Inserted 1:24		
Refractors:		1.5X
Inserted 1:72		
1	Edgar Martinez	.75
2	Mike Piazza	3.50
3	Frank Thomas	1.50
4	Craig Biggio	.75
5	Vinny Castilla	.75
6	Jeff Blauser	.75
7	Barry Bonds	6.00
8	Ken Griffey Jr.	3.50
9	Larry Walker	.75

Flashback

This 10-card double-sided insert features top players as they looked in 1998 on one side, and how they looked when they first appeared in the majors on the other side. Flashback inserts were seeded one per 24 packs of Series I, with Refractors every 72 packs. This insert was numbered with a "FB" prefix.

		NM/M
Complete Set (10):		16.00
Common Player:		.75
Inserted 1:24		
Refractors:		1.5X
Inserted 1:72		
1	Barry Bonds	6.00
2	Ken Griffey Jr.	3.50
3	Paul Molitor	1.50
4	Randy Johnson	1.50
5	Cal Ripken Jr.	6.00
6	Tony Gwynn	2.50
7	Kenny Lofton	.75
8	Gary Sheffield	.85
9	Deion Sanders	.75
10	Brady Anderson	.75

Hallbound

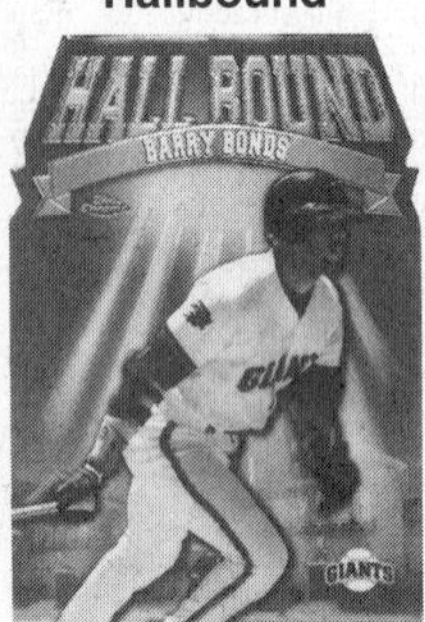

Hallbound highlighted 15 players destined for the Hall of Fame on die-cut cards. Inserted at a rate of one per 24 packs of Series I, with Refractors every 72 packs, these were numbered with a "HB" prefix.

		NM/M
Complete Set (15):		35.00
Common Player:		1.50
Inserted 1:24		
Refractors:		1.5X
Inserted 1:72		
1	Paul Molitor	2.00
2	Tony Gwynn	2.50
3	Wade Boggs	2.50
4	Roger Clemens	3.00
5	Dennis Eckersley	1.50
6	Cal Ripken Jr.	6.00
7	Greg Maddux	2.50
8	Rickey Henderson	2.00
9	Ken Griffey Jr.	3.50
10	Frank Thomas	2.00
11	Mark McGwire	4.50
12	Barry Bonds	6.00
13	Mike Piazza	3.50
14	Juan Gonzalez	1.50
15	Randy Johnson	2.00

Milestones

Ten superstars who were within reach of major records for the 1998 season are featured in Milestones. This Series II insert was seeded one per 24 packs, with Refractor versions seeded one per 72 packs. Milestones were numbered with a "MS" prefix.

		NM/M
Complete Set (10):		25.00
Common Player:		1.00
Inserted 1:24		
Refractors:		1.5X
Inserted 1:72		
1	Barry Bonds	6.00
2	Roger Clemens	3.00
3	Dennis Eckersley	1.00
4	Juan Gonzalez	1.00
5	Ken Griffey Jr.	3.50
6	Tony Gwynn	2.50
7	Greg Maddux	2.50
8	Mark McGwire	4.50
9	Cal Ripken Jr.	6.00
10	Frank Thomas	1.50

Rookie Class

This insert featured 10 players with less than one year of major league experience. Inserted in Series II packs at a rate of one per 12 packs, with Refractors every 24 packs, '98 Rookie Class inserts were numbered with a "R" prefix.

		NM/M
Complete Set (10):		10.00
Common Player:		.75
Inserted 1:12		
Refractors:		1.5X
Inserted 1:24		
1	Travis Lee	1.00
2	Richard Hidalgo	.75
3	Todd Helton	4.50
4	Paul Konerko	1.50
5	Mark Kotsay	.75
6	Derrek Lee	3.00
7	Eli Marrero	.75
8	Fernando Tatis	.75
9	Juan Encarnacion	.75
10	Ben Grieve	.75

Super Chrome

This 36-card oversized set featured some of the top players from Chrome on 4-1/8" x 5-3/4" cards. The product sold in three-card packs and featured the same photography as Topps and Topps Chrome before it, but added a Super Chrome logo. Refractor versions of each card were also available, inserted one per 12 packs.

		NM/M
Complete Set (36):		20.00
Common Player:		.25
Refractors:		1.5X
Inserted 1:12		
Pack (3):		2.50
Wax Box (12):		25.00
1	Tony Gwynn	1.00
2	Larry Walker	.25
3	Vladimir Guerrero	.75
4	Mo Vaughn	.25
5	Frank Thomas	.75
6	Barry Larkin	.25
7	Scott Rolen	.65
8	Juan Gonzalez	.75
9	Jeff Bagwell	.75
10	Ryan Klesko	.25
11	Mike Piazza	1.50
12	Randy Johnson	.75
13	Derek Jeter	3.00
14	Gary Sheffield	.50
15	Hideo Nomo	.50
16	Tino Martinez	.25
17	Ivan Rodriguez	.65
18	Bernie Williams	.25
19	Greg Maddux	1.00
20	Roger Clemens	1.25
21	Roberto Clemente	2.00
22	Chipper Jones	1.00
23	Sammy Sosa	1.00
24	Tony Clark	.25
25	Barry Bonds	3.00
26	Craig Biggio	.25
27	Cal Ripken Jr.	3.00
28	Ken Griffey Jr.	1.50
29	Todd Helton	.65
30	Mark McGwire	2.00
31	Jose Cruz	.25
32	Albert Belle	.25
33	Andruw Jones	.75
34	Nomar Garciaparra	1.00
35	Andy Pettitte	.45
36	Alex Rodriguez	2.00

1998 Topps Gallery Pre-Production Samples

To introduce its premium Gallery line for 1998, Topps issued this set of pre-production samples showcasing several of the different technologies to be found in the issue. The samples are virtually identical to the issued versions except for the use of a "PP" prefix to the card number.

		NM/M
Complete Set (5):		7.50
Common Player:		1.50
PP1	Andruw Jones/ Portraits	1.50
PP2	Juan Gonzalez (Permanent Collection)	1.00
PP3	Barry Bonds (Expressionists)	3.00
PP4	Derek Jeter (Exhibitions)	3.00
PP5	Nomar Garciaparra (Impressions)	2.00

1998 Topps Gallery

Gallery returned in 1998 with a 150-card set broken up into five different subsets - Exhibitions, Impressions, Expressionists, Portraits and Permanent Collection. The set was paralleled twice - first in a Player's Private Issue set and, second in Gallery Proofs. Gallery cards were made to look like works of art instead of simply a photo of the player on cardboard, and were sold in six-card packs. Inserts in this single-series product include: Photo Gallery, Gallery of Heroes and Awards Gallery.

		NM/M
Complete Set (150):		15.00
Common Player:		.10
Pack (6):		1.50
Wax Box (24):		25.00
1	Andruw Jones	1.00
2	Fred McGriff	.10
3	Wade Boggs	1.50
4	Pedro Martinez	1.00
5	Matt Williams	.10
6	Wilson Alvarez	.10
7	Henry Rodriguez	.10
8	Jay Bell	.10
9	Marquis Grissom	.10
10	Darryl Kile	.10
11	Chuck Knoblauch	.10
12	Kenny Lofton	.10
13	Quinton McCracken	.10
14	Andres Galarraga	.10
15	Brian Jordan	.10
16	Mike Lansing	.10
17	Travis Fryman	.10
18	Tony Saunders	.10
19	Moises Alou	.10
20	Travis Lee	.10
21	Garret Anderson	.10
22	Ken Caminiti	.10
23	Pedro Astacio	.10
24	Ellis Burks	.10
25	Albert Belle	.10
26	Alan Benes	.10
27	Jay Buhner	.10
28	Derek Bell	.10
29	Jeromy Burnitz	.10
30	Kevin Appier	.10
31	Jeff Cirillo	.10
32	Bernard Gilkey	.10
33	David Cone	.10
34	Jason Dickson	.10
35	Jose Cruz Jr.	.10
36	Marty Cordova	.10
37	Ray Durham	.10
38	Jaret Wright	.10
39	Billy Wagner	.10
40	Roger Clemens	1.75
41	Juan Gonzalez	.50
42	Jeremi Gonzalez	.10
43	Mark Grudzielanek	.10
44	Tom Glavine	.35
45	Barry Larkin	.10
46	Lance Johnson	.10
47	Bobby Higginson	.10
48	Mike Mussina	.50
49	Al Martin	.10
50	Mark McGwire	2.50
51	Todd Hundley	.10
52	Ray Lankford	.10
53	Jason Kendall	.10
54	Javy Lopez	.10
55	Ben Grieve	.10
56	Randy Johnson	1.00
57	Jeff King	.10
58	Mark Grace	.10
59	Rusty Greer	.10
60	Greg Maddux	1.50
61	Jeff Kent	.10
62	Rey Ordonez	.10
63	Hideo Nomo	.50
64	Charles Nagy	.10
65	Rondell White	.10
66	Todd Helton	.75
67	Jim Thome	.75
68	Denny Neagle	.10
69	Ivan Rodriguez	.75
70	Vladimir Guerrero	1.00
71	Jorge Posada	.10
72	J.T. Snow Jr.	.10
73	Reggie Sanders	.10
74	Scott Rolen	.75
75	Robin Ventura	.10
76	Mariano Rivera	.15
77	Cal Ripken Jr.	3.00
78	Justin Thompson	.10
79	Mike Piazza	2.00
80	Kevin Brown	.10
81	Sandy Alomar	.10
82	Craig Biggio	.10
83	Vinny Castilla	.10
84	Eric Young	.10
85	Bernie Williams	.10
86	Brady Anderson	.10
87	Bobby Bonilla	.10
88	Tony Clark	.10
89	Dan Wilson	.10
90	John Wetteland	.10
91	Barry Bonds	3.00
92	Chan Ho Park	.10
93	Carlos Delgado	.35
94	David Justice	.10
95	Chipper Jones	1.50
96	Shawn Estes	.10
97	Jason Giambi	.60
98	Ron Gant	.10
99	John Olerud	.10
100	Frank Thomas	1.00
101	Jose Guillen	.10
102	Brad Radke	.10
103	Troy Percival	.10
104	John Smoltz	.10
105	Edgardo Alfonzo	.10
106	Dante Bichette	.10
107	Larry Walker	.10
108	John Valentin	.10
109	Roberto Alomar	.30
110	Mike Cameron	.10
111	Eric Davis	.10
112	Johnny Damon	.35
113	Darin Erstad	.30
114	Omar Vizquel	.10
115	Derek Jeter	3.00
116	Tony Womack	.10
117	Edgar Renteria	.10
118	Raul Mondesi	.10
119	Tony Gwynn	1.50
120	Ken Griffey Jr.	2.00
121	Jim Edmonds	.10
122	Brian Hunter	.10
123	Neifi Perez	.10
124	Dean Palmer	.10
125	Alex Rodriguez	2.50
126	Tim Salmon	.10
127	Curt Schilling	.35
128	Kevin Orie	.10
129	Andy Pettitte	.30
130	Gary Sheffield	.50
131	Jose Rosado	.10
132	Manny Ramirez	1.00
133	Rafael Palmeiro	.75
134	Sammy Sosa	1.50
135	Jeff Bagwell	1.00
136	Delino DeShields	.10
137	Ryan Klesko	.10
138	Mo Vaughn	.10
139	Steve Finley	.10
140	Nomar Garciaparra	1.50
141	Paul Molitor	1.00
142	Pat Hentgen	.10
143	Eric Karros	.10
144	Bobby Jones	.10
145	Tino Martinez	.10
146	Matt Morris	.10
147	Livan Hernandez	.10
148	Edgar Martinez	.10
149	Paul O'Neill	.10
150	Checklist	.10

Player's Private Issue

Player's Private Issue inserts parallel the 150-card base set with a distinct design and embossing. The average insertion rate is one per 12 packs.

	NM/M
Common Player:	1.00
Stars/Rookies:	4X
Production 250 Sets	

Player's Private Issue Auction Cards

These special auction points cards were seeded one per pack of Gallery. Fronts are identical to the much scarcer PPI cards. Backs, however, differ greatly. Where regular PPI cards have a player photo, serial number, etc., these auction points cards have details of the procedure by which points could be accumulated and used to bid for original photos and printing plates. The redemption period ended Oct. 16, 1998.

	NM/M
Complete Set (150):	60.00

Common Player: .25
Stars/Rookies: 1.5X

Gallery Proofs

This hobby-only parallel set included all 150 cards in the base set. Gallery Proofs were sequentially numbered to 125 sets.

NM/M
Common Player: 1.50
Stars/Rookies: 4X
Production 125 Sets

Awards Gallery

Awards Gallery featured 10 players who earned the highest honors in the game on a horizontal design. Fronts featured a shot of the player and the award he won on silver foilboard. These were inserted every 24 packs and numbered with an "AG" prefix.

NM/M
Complete Set (10): 18.00
Common Player: 1.00
Inserted 1:24
1 Ken Griffey Jr. 4.00
2 Larry Walker 1.00
3 Roger Clemens 2.50
4 Pedro Martinez 1.50
5 Nomar Garciaparra 2.00
6 Scott Rolen 1.00
7 Frank Thomas 1.50
8 Tony Gwynn 2.00
9 Mark McGwire 5.00
10 Livan Hernandez 1.00

Gallery of Heroes

Gallery of Heroes is a 15-card insert printed on colored, die-cut plastic that resembles a stained glass window. Cards were inserted one per 24 packs and numbered with a "GH" prefix. More is less in the case in the jumbo (3-1/4" x 4-1/2") version of the cards which were inserted one per hobby box. Cards are numbered with a "GH" prefix.

NM/M
Complete Set (15): 80.00
Common Player: 1.25
Inserted 1:24
Jumbo Version (1:24): 75 Percent
1 Ken Griffey Jr. 8.00
2 Derek Jeter 15.00
3 Barry Bonds 15.00
4 Alex Rodriguez 12.00
5 Frank Thomas 4.00
6 Nomar Garciaparra 6.00
7 Mark McGwire 12.00
8 Mike Piazza 8.00
9 Cal Ripken Jr. 15.00
10 Jose Cruz Jr. 1.25
11 Jeff Bagwell 4.00
12 Chipper Jones 6.00
13 Juan Gonzalez 2.00
14 Hideo Nomo 2.00
15 Greg Maddux 6.00

Photo Gallery

This 10-card insert captured unique shots of players on a silver foilboard design.

Photo Gallery inserts were seeded one per 24 packs and numbered with a "PG" prefix.

NM/M
Complete Set (10): 25.00
Common Player: 1.00
Inserted 1:24
1 Alex Rodriguez 3.00
2 Frank Thomas 2.00
3 Derek Jeter 4.00
4 Cal Ripken Jr. 4.00
5 Ken Griffey Jr. 2.50
6 Mike Piazza 2.50
7 Nomar Garciaparra 2.25
8 Tim Salmon 1.00
9 Jeff Bagwell 2.00
10 Barry Bonds 4.00

Printing Plates

The aluminum press plates used to print the Gallery cards were issued as random pack inserts. Each card's front and back can be found in four different color variations. Because of the unique nature of each plate, assignment of catalog values is not feasible.

NM/M
Common Player, Front: 50.00
Common Player, Back: 35.00

Gold Label Class 1 (Fielding, Follow-thru)

Topps debuted its Gold Label brand with 100 cards printed on 30-point "spectral-reflective stock" with gold foil stamping and two shots of the player on each card front. Cards arrived in Gold Label, Black Label and Red Label versions, each with varying levels of scarcity. The rarity of the cards was determined by the photo and foil stamping on the cards. In the foreground of each card front, the photograph is the same, but in the background one of three shots is featured. Class 1, fielding, are considered base cards; Class 2: running (inserted 1:4 packs) and Class 3, hitting (inserted 1:8 packs) are seeded levels. For pitching the levels are: Class 1, set position (base); Class 2, throwing (inserted 1:4 packs) and Class 3, follow-through (inserted 1:8 packs). Black Label cards are scarcer, while Red Label cards are scarcer yet. In addition, 1 of 1 cards exist for each Class and version. Class 1 cards have matte gold-foil graphic highlights on front. Black Label Class 1 cards were inserted one per eight packs. Red Label Class 1 cards are a 1:99 insert and are serially numbered to 100.

NM/M
Complete Set (100): 12.00
Gold Label Common Player: .10
Black Label Common Player: .35
Black Label Stars/RC's: 4X
Red Label Common Player: 1.50
Red Label Stars/RC's: 12X
Pack (5): 2.00
Wax Box (24): 40.00
1 Kevin Brown .10
2 Greg Maddux 1.25
3 Albert Belle .10
4 Andres Galarraga .10
5 Craig Biggio .10
6 Matt Williams .10
7 Derek Jeter 3.00
8 Randy Johnson 1.00
9 Jay Bell .10
10 Jim Thome .75
11 Roberto Alomar .30
12 Tom Glavine .35
13 Reggie Sanders .10
14 Tony Gwynn 1.25
15 Mark McGwire 2.00
16 Jeromy Burnitz .10
17 Andruw Jones 1.00
18 Jay Buhner .10
19 Robin Ventura .10
20 Jeff Bagwell 1.00
21 Roger Clemens 1.25
22 Masato Yoshii **RC** .25
23 Travis Fryman .10
24 Rafael Palmeiro .75
25 Alex Rodriguez 2.00
26 Sandy Alomar .10
27 Chipper Jones 1.25
28 Rusty Greer .10
29 Cal Ripken Jr. 3.00
30 Tony Clark .10
31 Derek Bell .10
32 Fred McGriff .10
33 Paul O'Neill .10
34 Moises Alou .10
35 Henry Rodriguez .10
36 Steve Finley .10
37 Marquis Grissom .10
38 Jason Giambi .60
39 Javy Lopez .10
40 Damion Easley .10
41 Mariano Rivera .15
42 Mo Vaughn .10
43 Mike Mussina .40
44 Jason Kendall .10
45 Pedro Martinez 1.00
46 Frank Thomas 1.00
47 Jim Edmonds .10
48 Hideki Irabu .10
49 Eric Karros .10
50 Juan Gonzalez .50
51 Ellis Burks .10
52 Dean Palmer .10
53 Scott Rolen .60
54 Raul Mondesi .10
55 Quinton McCraken .10
56 John Olerud .10
57 Ken Caminiti .10
58 Brian Jordan .10
59 Wade Boggs 1.25
60 Mike Piazza 1.50
61 Darin Erstad .30
62 Curt Schilling .35
63 David Justice .10
64 Kenny Lofton .10
65 Barry Bonds 3.00
66 Ray Lankford .10
67 Brian Hunter .10
68 Chuck Knoblauch .10
69 Vinny Castilla .10
70 Vladimir Guerrero 1.00
71 Tim Salmon .10
72 Larry Walker .10
73 Paul Molitor 1.00
74 Barry Larkin .10
75 Edgar Martinez .10
76 Bernie Williams .10
77 Dante Bichette .10
78 Nomar Garciaparra 1.25
79 Ben Grieve .10
80 Ivan Rodriguez .75
81 Todd Helton .75
82 Ryan Klesko .10
83 Sammy Sosa 1.25
84 Travis Lee .10
85 Jose Cruz .10
86 Mark Kotsay .10
87 Richard Hidalgo .10
88 Rondell White .10
89 Greg Vaughn .10
90 Gary Sheffield .50
91 Paul Konerko .25
92 Mark Grace .10
93 Kevin Millwood **RC** 1.00
94 Manny Ramirez 1.00
95 Tino Martinez .10
96 Brad Fullmer .10
97 Todd Walker .10
98 Carlos Delgado .45
99 Kerry Wood .60
100 Ken Griffey Jr. 1.50

Gold Label Class 2 (Running, Set Position)

Class 2 Gold Label and parallels feature background photos on front of position players running and pitchers in the set position. Class 2 cards have sparkling silver-foil graphic highlights on front and were inserted one per two packs. Black Label Class 2 cards were inserted one per 16 packs. Red Label Class 2 cards are a 1:198 insert and are serially numbered to 50.

NM/M
Complete Set (100): 50.00
Gold Label Common Player: .35
Gold Label Stars/RC's: 2X
Black Label Common Player: 1.00
Black Label Stars/RC's: 4X
Red Label Common Player: 4.00
Red Label Stars/RC's: 25X

Gold Label Class 3 (Hitting, Throwing)

Class 3 Gold Label and parallels feature background photos on front of position players hitting and pitchers throwing. Class 3 cards have sparkling gold-foil graphic highlights on front and were inserted one per four packs. Black Label Class 3 cards were inserted one per 32 packs. Red Label Class 2 cards are a 1:396 insert and are serially numbered to 25.

NM/M
Complete Set (100): 120.00
Common Player: .75
Gold Label Stars/RC's: 2.5X
Black Label Common Player: 2.00
Black Label Stars/RC's 6X
Red Label Common Player: 6.00
Red Label Stars/RC's: 35X

Gold Label 1 of 1

Each of the Classes and color versions of Topps Gold Label cards was paralleled in a 1 of 1 insert which was to be found on average of one per 1,085 packs. Each player, thus, can be found on nine different 1 of 1 cards in the issue.

Gold Label Home Run Race

Home Run Race of '98 was a four-card insert set. Each of the current players' cards features a background photo of Roger Maris, while the fourth card features two shots of Maris. Gold, Black and Red Label versions are identified by the different foil-stamp logos. Gold cards were inserted 1:12 packs, Black Label cards were inserted 1:48 packs and Red Label cards were sequentially numbered to 61 and inserted 1:4,055 packs. The Home Run Race inserts are exclusive to Topps Home Team Advantage boxes.

NM/M
Complete Set (4): 7.50
Common Player: 2.00
Black Label: 2X
Red Label: 4X
HR1 Roger Maris 3.00
HR2 Mark McGwire 3.00
HR3 Ken Griffey Jr. 2.50
HR4 Sammy Sosa 2.00

Opening Day

Topps Opening Day was a retail exclusive product comprising 165 cards, with 110 from Series 1 and 55 from Series 2. The cards from Series 2 were available in this product prior to the regular-issue cards being released. Opening Day cards feature a silver border vs. the gold border in the regular set, and include a silver-foil Opening Day stamp.

NM/M
Complete Set (165): 10.00
Common Player: .05
Wax Pack (7): .65
Wax Box (22): 10.00
1 Tony Gwynn .65
2 Larry Walker .05
3 Billy Wagner .05
4 Denny Neagle .05
5 Vladimir Guerrero .50
6 Kevin Brown .05
7 Mariano Rivera .15
8 Tony Clark .05
9 Deion Sanders .05
10 Matt Williams .05
11 Carlos Baerga .05
12 Mo Vaughn .05
13 Chan Ho Park .05
14 Frank Thomas .50
15 John Jaha .05
16 Steve Trachsel .05
17 Jeff Kent .05
18 Scott Rolen .40
19 Juan Gonzalez .25
20 Garret Anderson .05
21 Roberto Clemente 1.00
22 Omar Vizquel .05
23 Brian Hunter .05
24 Jeff Bagwell .50
25 Chili Davis .05
26 Mike Cameron .05
27 Pat Hentgen .05
28 Wilton Guerrero .05
29 Devon White .05
30 Rafael Palmeiro .40
31 Jeff Blauser .05
32 Dave Hollins .05
33 Trevor Hoffman .05
34 Ryan Klesko .05
35 Butch Huskey .05
36 Mark Grudzielanek .05
37 Marquis Grissom .05
38 Jim Edmonds .05
39 Greg Vaughn .05
40 David Wells .05
41 Charles Nagy .05
42 B.J. Surhoff .05
43 Edgardo Alfonzo .05
44 Jay Buhner .05
45 Brady Anderson .05
46 Edgar Renteria .05
47 Rick Aguilera .05
48 Henry Rodriguez .05
49 Mike Piazza .75
50 Todd Zeile .05
51 Rey Ordonez .05
52 Tony Womack .05
53 Mike Sweeney .05
54 Jeffrey Hammonds .05
55 Kevin Orie .05
56 Alex Gonzalez .05
57 Jose Canseco .35
58 Joey Hamilton .05
59 Brad Radke .05
60 Kevin Appier .05
61 Manny Ramirez .50
62 Jeromy Burnitz .05
63 Matt Morris .05
64 Jason Dickson .05
65 Tom Glavine .25
66 Wally Joyner .05
67 Todd Jones .05
68 Sandy Alomar .05
69 Mike Lansing .05
70 Todd Stottlemyre .05
71 Jay Bell .05
72 Joey Cora .05
73 Scott Spiezio .05
74 Joe Carter .05
75 Jose Guillen .05
76 Damion Easley .05
77 Alex Fernandez .05
78 Randy Johnson .50
79 J.T. Snow .05
80 Bernard Gilkey .05
81 David Segui .05
82 Dante Bichette .05
83 Derek Jeter 1.50
84 Mark Wohlers .05
85 Ricky Bottalico .05
86 Mike Mussina .35
87 Gary Sheffield .35
88 Hideo Nomo .25
89 Mark Grace .05
90 Darryl Kile .05
91 Shawn Estes .05
92 Vinny Castilla .05
93 Jose Rosado .05
94 Kenny Lofton .05
95 Jason Giambi .35
96 Ray Lankford .05
97 Hideki Irabu .05
98 Javy Lopez .05
99 Jeff Montgomery .05
100 Dennis Eckersley .40
101 Armando Benitez .05
102 Tim Naehring .05
103 Luis Gonzalez .05
104 Todd Hollandsworth .05
105 Wade Boggs .65
106 Mickey Morandini .05
107 Rusty Greer .05
108 Terry Steinbach .05
109 Pete Rose II .05
110 Checklist .05
111 Tino Martinez .05
112 Roberto Alomar .20
113 Jeff King .05
114 Brian Jordan .05
115 Darin Erstad .25

116	Ken Caminiti	.05
117	Jim Thome	.60
118	Paul Molitor	.50
119	Ivan Rodriguez	.40
120	Bernie Williams	.05
121	Todd Hundley	.05
122	Andres Galarraga	.05
123	Greg Maddux	.65
124	Edgar Martinez	.05
125	Ron Gant	.05
126	Derek Bell	.05
127	Roger Clemens	.70
128	Rondell White	.05
129	Barry Larkin	.05
130	Robin Ventura	.05
131	Jason Kendall	.05
132	Chipper Jones	.65
133	John Franco	.05
134	Sammy Sosa	.65
135	Chuck Knoblauch	.05
136	Ellis Burks	.05
137	Al Martin	.05
138	Tim Salmon	.05
139	Moises Alou	.05
140	Lance Johnson	.05
141	Justin Thompson	.05
142	Will Clark	.05
143	Barry Bonds	1.50
144	Craig Biggio	.05
145	John Smoltz	.05
146	Cal Ripken Jr.	1.50
147	Ken Griffey Jr.	.75
148	Paul O'Neill	.05
149	Todd Helton	.40
150	John Olerud	.05
151	Mark McGwire	1.00
152	Jose Cruz Jr.	.05
153	Jeff Cirillo	.05
154	Dean Palmer	.05
155	John Wetteland	.05
156	Eric Karros	.05
157	Steve Finley	.05
158	Albert Belle	.05
159	Curt Schilling	.25
160	Raul Mondesi	.05
161	Andruw Jones	.50
162	Nomar Garciaparra	.65
163	David Justice	.05
164	Andy Pettitte	.20
165	Pedro Martinez	.50

SportzCubz Prototypes

This rare "Product Prototype" (says so right on the back) was designed to allow collectors to get creative in making 3-D structures featuring their favorite ballplayers. About 3" square, the plastic pieces have slots and tabs which would allow them to be connected in a variety of ways. Fronts have action photos on a large team logo. Backs have a portrait photo, personal data, recent stats, a career highlight or two and essential licensing data. The product was never rolled out for public consumption and it is unknown to what extent the prototypes were produced or have found their way into collectors' hands. Therefore, no pricing is provided.

Complete Set (25):

1998 Topps Stars Pre-Production

These promotional cards introduced the new Stars brand from Topps to dealers and the hobby press. The cards are virtually identical to the regularly-issued version except for the numbering on back, which has a "PP" prefix and serial numbers "000/000."

		NM/M
Complete Set (6):		5.00
Common Player:		.50
PP1	Mike Piazza	3.00
PP2	Darin Erstad	.60
PP3	Vinny Castilla	.50
PP4	Craig Biggio	.50
PP5	Ivan Rodriguez	.75
PP6	Pedro Martinez	1.00

1998 Topps Stars

Topps Stars adopted an all-sequential numbering format in 1998 with a 150-card set. Every card was available in a bronze (numbered to 9,799), red (9,799), silver (4,399), gold (2,299) and gold rainbow format (99) with different color foil to distinguish the groups. Players were each judged in five categories: arm strength, hit for average, power, defense and speed. Inserts in the product include: Galaxy, Luminaries, Supernovas, Rookie Reprints and Rookie Reprint Autographs. All regular-issue cards and inserts were individually numbered except the Rookie Reprints.

		NM/M
Complete Set, Red or Bronze (150):		24.00
Common Player, Red or Bronze:		.10
Production 9,799 sets each.		
Pack (6):		1.25
Wax Box (24):		25.00
1	Greg Maddux	1.50
2	Darryl Kile	.10
3	Rod Beck	.10
4	Ellis Burks	.10
5	Gary Sheffield	.40
6	David Ortiz	.10
7	Marquis Grissom	.10
8	Tony Womack	.10
9	Mike Mussina	.60
10	Bernie Williams	.10
11	Andy Benes	.10
12	Rusty Greer	.10
13	Carlos Delgado	.35
14	Jim Edmonds	.10
15	Raul Mondesi	.10
16	Andres Galarraga	.10
17	Wade Boggs	1.50
18	Paul O'Neill	.10
19	Edgar Renteria	.10
20	Tony Clark	.10
21	Vladimir Guerrero	1.00
22	Moises Alou	.10
23	Bernard Gilkey	.10
24	Lance Johnson	.10
25	Ben Grieve	.10
26	Sandy Alomar	.10
27	Ray Durham	.10
28	Shawn Estes	.10
29	David Segui	.10
30	Javy Lopez	.10
31	Steve Finley	.10
32	Rey Ordonez	.10
33	Derek Jeter	3.00
34	Henry Rodriguez	.10
35	Mo Vaughn	.10
36	Richard Hidalgo	.10
37	Omar Vizquel	.10
38	Johnny Damon	.35
39	Brian Hunter	.10
40	Matt Williams	.10
41	Chuck Finley	.10
42	Jeromy Burnitz	.10
43	Livan Hernandez	.10
44	Delino DeShields	.10
45	Charles Nagy	.10
46	Scott Rolen	.75
47	Neifi Perez	.10
48	John Wetteland	.10
49	Eric Milton	.10
50	Mike Piazza	2.00
51	Cal Ripken Jr.	3.00
52	Mariano Rivera	.25
53	Butch Huskey	.10
54	Quinton McCracken	.10
55	Jose Cruz Jr.	.10
56	Brian Jordan	.10
57	Hideo Nomo	.50
58	Masato Yoshii	.10
59	Cliff Floyd	.10
60	Jose Guillen	.10
61	Jeff Shaw	.10
62	Edgar Martinez	.10
63	Rondell White	.10
64	Hal Morris	.10
65	Barry Larkin	.10
66	Eric Young	.10
67	Ray Lankford	.10
68	Derek Bell	.10
69	Charles Johnson	.10
70	Robin Ventura	.10
71	Chuck Knoblauch	.10
72	Kevin Brown	.10
73	Jose Valentin	.10
74	Jay Buhner	.10
75	Tony Gwynn	1.50
76	Andy Pettitte	.30
77	Edgardo Alfonzo	.10
78	Kerry Wood	.40
79	Darin Erstad	.30
80	Paul Konerko	.15
81	Jason Kendall	.10
82	Tino Martinez	.10
83	Brad Radke	.10
84	Jeff King	.10
85	Travis Lee	.10
86	Jeff Kent	.10
87	Trevor Hoffman	.10
88	David Cone	.10
89	Jose Canseco	.40
90	Juan Gonzalez	.50
91	Todd Hundley	.10
92	John Valentin	.10
93	Sammy Sosa	1.50
94	Jason Giambi	.40
95	Chipper Jones	1.50
96	Jeff Blauser	.10
97	Brad Fullmer	.10
98	Derrek Lee	.60
99	Denny Neagle	.10
100	Ken Griffey Jr.	2.00
101	David Justice	.10
102	Tim Salmon	.10
103	J.T. Snow	.10
104	Fred McGriff	.10
105	Brady Anderson	.10
106	Larry Walker	.10
107	Jeff Cirillo	.10
108	Andruw Jones	1.00
109	Manny Ramirez	1.00
110	Justin Thompson	.10
111	Vinny Castilla	.10
112	Chan Ho Park	.10
113	Mark Grudzielanek	.10
114	Mark Grace	.10
115	Ken Caminiti	.10
116	Ryan Klesko	.10
117	Rafael Palmeiro	.75
118	Pat Hentgen	.10
119	Eric Karros	.10
120	Randy Johnson	1.00
121	Roberto Alomar	.25
122	John Olerud	.10
123	Paul Molitor	1.00
124	Dean Palmer	.10
125	Nomar Garciaparra	1.50
126	Curt Schilling	.30
127	Jay Bell	.10
128	Craig Biggio	.10
129	Marty Cordova	.10
130	Ivan Rodriguez	.75
131	Todd Helton	.75
132	Jim Thome	.65
133	Albert Belle	.10
134	Mike Lansing	.10
135	Mark McGwire	2.50
136	Roger Clemens	1.75
137	Tom Glavine	.30
138	Ron Gant	.10
139	Alex Rodriguez	2.50
140	Jeff Bagwell	1.00
141	John Smoltz	.10
142	Kenny Lofton	.10
143	Dante Bichette	.10
144	Pedro Martinez	1.00
145	Barry Bonds	3.00
146	Travis Fryman	.10
147	Bobby Jones	.10
148	Bobby Higginson	.10
149	Reggie Sanders	.10
150	Frank Thomas	1.00
	Checklist	.05

Silver

	NM/M
Common Silver:	.50
Silver Stars:	1.5X
Production 4,399 Sets	

Gold

	NM/M
Common Gold:	1.00
Gold Stars:	2X
Production 2,299 Sets	

Gold Rainbow

Each card in Topps Stars was available in a Gold Rainbow version. This was the most limited of the five parallels and was numbered to 99. Cards featured gold prismatic foil on the front and were seeded every 46 packs.

	NM/M
Common Gold Rainbow:	4.00
Gold Rainbow Stars:	8X
Production 99 Sets	

Galaxy

Galaxy featured 10 players who possess all five skills featured in Topps Stars Baseball. Four versions were available and sequentially numbered, including: Bronze (numbered to 100, inserted 1:682 packs), Silver (numbered to 75, inserted 1:910), Gold (numbered to 50, inserted 1:1,364) and Gold Rainbow (numbered to 5, inserted 1:13,643).

		NM/M
Complete Set (10):		150.00
Common Player:		7.50
Production 100 Sets		
Silvers:		1.5X
Production 75 Sets		
Golds:		2X
Production 50 Sets		
Gold Rainbows: Values Undetermined		
Production Five Sets		
G1	Barry Bonds	40.00
G2	Jeff Bagwell	15.00
G3	Nomar Garciaparra	20.00
G4	Chipper Jones	20.00
G5	Ken Griffey Jr.	25.00
G6	Sammy Sosa	20.00
G7	Larry Walker	7.50
G8	Alex Rodriguez	35.00
G9	Craig Biggio	7.50
G10	Raul Mondesi	7.50

Luminaries

Luminaries feature three top players in each "tool" group. The 15-card insert has four parallel sequentially numbered versions inserted as follows: bronze (numbered to 100, inserted 1:455), silver (numbered to 75, inserted 1:606), gold (numbered to 50, inserted 1:910) and gold rainbow (numbered to 5, inserted 1:9,095).

		NM/M
Complete Set (15):		140.00
Common Player:		4.00
Production 100 Sets		
Silver (75 Sets):		1.5X
Gold (50 Sets):		1.5X
Gold Rainbow (Five Sets): Values Undetermined		
L1	Ken Griffey Jr.	15.00
L2	Mark McGwire	20.00
L3	Juan Gonzalez	5.00
L4	Tony Gwynn	12.50
L5	Frank Thomas	10.00
L6	Mike Piazza	15.00
L7	Chuck Knoblauch	4.00
L8	Kenny Lofton	4.00
L9	Barry Bonds	25.00
L10	Matt Williams	4.00
L11	Raul Mondesi	4.00
L12	Ivan Rodriguez	7.50
L13	Alex Rodriguez	20.00
L14	Nomar Garciaparra	12.50
L15	Ken Caminiti	4.00

Supernovas

Supernovas was a 10-card insert in Topps Stars and included rookies and prospects who either have all five tools focused on in the product, or excel dramatically in one of the five. Four sequentially numbered levels were available, with insert rates as follows: bronze (numbered to 100, inserted 1:682), silver (numbered to 75, inserted 1:910), gold (numbered to 50, inserted 1:1,364) and gold rainbow (numbered to 5, inserted 1:13,643).

		NM/M
Complete Set (10):		35.00
Common Player:		2.00
Production 100 Sets		
Silver:		1.5X
Production 75 Sets		
Gold:		1.5X
Production 50 Sets		
Gold Rainbow: Values Undetermined		
Production Five Sets		
S1	Ben Grieve	2.00
S2	Travis Lee	2.00
S3	Todd Helton	10.00
S4	Adrian Beltre	2.50
S5	Derrek Lee	6.00
S6	David Ortiz	6.00
S7	Brad Fullmer	2.00
S8	Mark Kotsay	2.00
S9	Paul Konerko	2.50
S10	Kerry Wood	6.00

Rookie Reprints

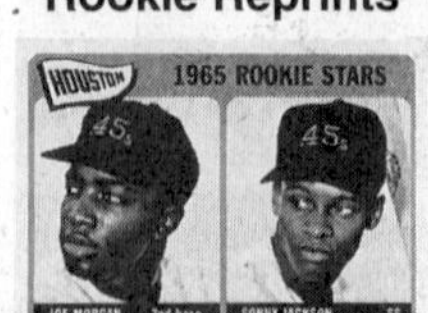

Topps reprinted the rookie cards of five Hall of Famers in Rookie Reprints. The cards are inserted one per 24 packs and have UV coating.

		NM/M
Complete Set (5):		7.00
Common Player:		1.50
1968	Johnny Bench	1.50
1953	Whitey Ford	1.50
1965	Joe Morgan	1.50
1973	Mike Schmidt	1.50
1960	Carl Yastrzemski	2.00

Rookie Reprints Autographs

Autographed versions of all five Rookie Reprint inserts were available and seeded one per 273 packs. Each card arrive with a Topps "Certified Autograph Issue" stamp to ensure its authenticity.

		NM/M
Complete Set (5):		175.00
Common Player:		25.00
1968	Johnny Bench	75.00
1953	Whitey Ford	50.00
1965	Joe Morgan	25.00
1973	Mike Schmidt	90.00
1960	Carl Yastrzemski	90.00

'N Steel

Stars 'N Steel was a 44-card set printed on four-colored textured film laminate bonded to a sheet of 25-gauge metal. Regular cards featured a silver colored border while gold versions were also available and seeded one per 12 packs. Stars 'N Steel was available only to Home Team Advantage members and was packaged in three-card packs that arrived in a sturdy, tri-fold stand-up display unit. A second parallel version was also available featuring gold holographic technology and was seeded one per 40 packs.

		NM/M
Complete Set (44):		40.00
Common Player:		.25
Golds:		2X
Holographics:		7X
Pack (3):		3.50
Wax Box (12):		30.00
1	Roberto Alomar	.50
2	Jeff Bagwell	1.25
3	Albert Belle	.25
4	Dante Bichette	.25
5	Barry Bonds	4.00
6	Jay Buhner	.25
7	Ken Caminiti	.25
8	Vinny Castilla	.25
9	Roger Clemens	2.25
10	Jose Cruz Jr.	.25
11	Andres Galarraga	.25
12	Nomar Garciaparra	2.00
13	Juan Gonzalez	.65
14	Mark Grace	.25
15	Ken Griffey Jr.	2.50
16	Tony Gwynn	2.00
17	Todd Hundley	.25
18	Derek Jeter	4.00
19	Randy Johnson	1.25
20	Andruw Jones	1.25
21	Chipper Jones	2.00
22	David Justice	.25
23	Ray Lankford	.25
24	Barry Larkin	.25
25	Kenny Lofton	.25
26	Greg Maddux	2.00
27	Edgar Martinez	.25
28	Tino Martinez	.25
29	Mark McGwire	3.00
30	Paul Molitor	1.25
31	Rafael Palmeiro	1.00
32	Mike Piazza	2.50
33	Manny Ramirez	1.25
34	Cal Ripken Jr.	4.00

35 Ivan Rodriguez 1.00
36 Scott Rolen .75
37 Tim Salmon .25
38 Gary Sheffield .50
39 Sammy Sosa 2.00
40 Frank Thomas 1.25
41 Jim Thome 1.00
42 Mo Vaughn .25
43 Larry Walker .25
44 Bernie Williams .25

1998 Topps TEK Pre-Production

Each of three players' Tek cards can also be found in two versions marked diagonally across the card number on back "Pre-production." The gold-foil version is much scarcer than the silver.

NM/M
Complete Set, Silver (3): 10.00
Complete Set, Gold (3): 45.00
23 Mark McGwire/Silver 6.00
23 Mark McGwire/Gold 30.00
45 Roger Clemens/Silver 5.00
45 Roger Clemens/Gold 20.00
? Raul Mondesi/Silver .50
? Raul Mondesi/Gold 2.50

1998 Topps TEK

A myriad of collecting methods was created with this innovative product which features 90 different players each printed on an acetate stock with 90 different background patterns. A parallel series utilizing Diffraction technology was inserted at the rate of one per six packs. Each of the 8,100 different cards was created in the same quantity, so there is no differentiation in value among patterns.

NM/M
Complete Set (90): 75.00
Common Player: .25
Pack (4): 4.00
Wax Box (20): 80.00
1 Ben Grieve .25
2 Kerry Wood 1.50
3 Barry Bonds 8.00
4 John Olerud .25
5 Ivan Rodriguez 2.00
6 Frank Thomas 2.50
7 Bernie Williams .25
8 Dante Bichette .25
9 Alex Rodriguez 6.00
10 Tom Glavine .50
11 Eric Karros .25
12 Craig Biggio .25
13 Mark McGwire 6.00
14 Derek Jeter 8.00
15 Nomar Garciaparra 4.00
16 Brady Anderson .25
17 Vladimir Guerrero 2.50
18 David Justice .25
19 Chipper Jones 4.00
20 Jim Edmonds .25
21 Roger Clemens 4.50
22 Mark Kotsay .25
23 Tony Gwynn 4.00
24 Todd Walker .25
25 Tino Martinez .25
26 Andruw Jones 2.50
27 Sandy Alomar .25
28 Sammy Sosa 4.00
29 Gary Sheffield 1.50
30 Ken Griffey Jr. 5.00
31 Aramis Ramirez .25
32 Curt Schilling .50
33 Robin Ventura .25
34 Larry Walker .25
35 Darin Erstad 1.25
36 Todd Dunwoody .25
37 Paul O'Neill .25
38 Vinny Castilla .25
39 Randy Johnson 2.50
40 Rafael Palmeiro 2.00
41 Pedro Martinez 2.50
42 Derek Bell .25
43 Carlos Delgado .50
44 Matt Williams .25
45 Kenny Lofton .25
46 Edgar Renteria .25
47 Albert Belle .25
48 Jeromy Burnitz .25
49 Adrian Beltre .40
50 Greg Maddux 4.00
51 Cal Ripken Jr. 8.00
52 Jason Kendall .25
53 Ellis Burks .25
54 Paul Molitor 2.50
55 Moises Alou .25
56 Raul Mondesi .25
57 Barry Larkin .25
58 Tony Clark .25
59 Travis Lee .25
60 Juan Gonzalez 1.25
61 Troy Glaus **RC** 3.00
62 Jose Cruz Jr. .25
63 Paul Konerko .40
64 Edgar Martinez .25
65 Javy Lopez .25
66 Manny Ramirez 2.50
67 Roberto Alomar .75
68 Ken Caminiti .25
69 Todd Helton 1.50
70 Chuck Knoblauch .25
71 Kevin Brown .25
72 Tim Salmon .25
73 Orlando Hernandez **RC** 1.00
74 Jeff Bagwell 2.50
75 Brian Jordan .25
76 Derrek Lee 1.50
77 Brad Fullmer .25
78 Mark Grace .25
79 Jeff King .25
80 Mike Mussina 1.50
81 Jay Buhner .25
82 Quinton McCracken .25
83 A.J. Hinch .25
84 Richard Hidalgo .25
85 Andres Galarraga .25
86 Mike Piazza 5.00
87 Mo Vaughn .25
88 Scott Rolen 1.50
89 Jim Thome 2.00
90 Ray Lankford .25

Diffraction

Not only can each of the 90 cards in Topps TEK be found in 90 different background patterns, but each can be found in a parallel edition printed with diffraction foil. The parallels are inserted on an average of one per six packs. Like the regular issue TEKs, all patterns were produced equally and there is no value differentiation among them.

NM/M
Complete Set (90): 400.00
Common Player: 4.00
Stars/RC's: 4X

1999 Topps Pre-Production

To give potential customers a feel for its 1999 baseball cards, Topps issued this se-

ries of pre-production samples. Cards are identical in format to the issued versions except they are numbered with a "PP" prefix and the 1998 stats line reads "PRE-PRODUCTION SAMPLE."

NM/M
Complete Set (6): 7.00
Common Player: .50
PP1 Roger Clemens 2.00
PP2 Sammy Sosa 2.00
PP3 Derek Jeter 2.50
PP4 Walt Weiss .50
PP5 Darin Erstad .75
PP6 Jason Kendall .50

1999 Topps

Released in two series, the 462-card set includes two home run record subsets, featuring McGwire and Sosa. McGwire's subset card #220 has 70 different versions, commemorating each of his home runs, including where it was hit, the pitcher, date and estimated distance. Sosa's subset card #461 has 66 different versions. Other subsets include World Series Highlights, Prospects, Draft Picks and Season Highlights. Each pack contains 11 cards with an SRP of $1.29. MVPs are the only parallel. They feature a special Topps MVP logo; 100 cards of each player exist. If the player on the card was named a weekly Topps MVP, collectors won a special set of redemption cards.

NM/M
Unop. Hobby Set (462): 40.00
Unop. Retail Set (463): 50.00
Complete Set (462): 35.00
Common Player: .05
MVP Stars/Rookies: 20X
Ser. 1 or 2 Hobby Pack (11): 1.25
Ser. 1 or 2 Hobby Box (36): 40.00
Ser. 1 or 2 Retail Pack (8): 1.00
Ser. 1 or 2 Retail Box (22): 20.00
Ser. 1 or 2 Jumbo Pack (40): 3.50
Ser. 1 or 2 Jumbo Box (12): 30.00
1 Roger Clemens 1.00
2 Andres Galarraga .05
3 Scott Brosius .05
4 John Flaherty .05
5 Jim Leyritz .05
6 Ray Durham .05
7 Joe Vizcaino .05
8 Will Clark .05
10 David Wells .05
11 Jose Guillen .05
12 Scott Hatteberg .05
13 Edgardo Alfonzo .05
14 Mike Bordick .05
15 Manny Ramirez .75
16 Greg Maddux 1.00
17 David Segui .05
18 Darryl Strawberry .05
19 Brad Radke .05
20 Kerry Wood .40
21 Matt Anderson .05
22 Derrek Lee .60
23 Mickey Morandini .05
24 Paul Konerko .15
25 Travis Lee .15
26 Ken Hill .05
27 Kenny Rogers .05
28 Paul Sorrento .05
29 Quilvio Veras .05
30 Todd Walker .05
31 Ryan Jackson .05
32 John Olerud .05
33 Doug Glanville .05
34 Nolan Ryan 2.00
35 Ray Lankford .05
36 Mark Loretta .05
37 Jason Dickson .05
38 Sean Bergman .05
39 Quinton McCracken .05
40 Bartolo Colon .05
41 Brady Anderson .05
42 Chris Stynes .05
43 Jorge Posada .05
44 Justin Thompson .05
45 Johnny Damon .30
46 Armando Benitez .05
47 Brant Brown .05
48 Charlie Hayes .05
49 Darren Dreifort .05
50 Juan Gonzalez .40
51 Chuck Knoblauch .05
52 Todd Helton (Rookie All-Star) .75
53 Rick Reed .05
54 Chris Gomez .05
55 Gary Sheffield .45
56 Rod Beck .05
57 Rey Sanchez .05
58 Garret Anderson .05
59 Jimmy Haynes .05
60 Steve Woodard .05
61 Rondell White .05
62 Vladimir Guerrero .75
63 Eric Karros .05
64 Russ Davis .05
65 Mo Vaughn .05
66 Sammy Sosa 1.00
67 Troy Percival .05
68 Kenny Lofton .05
69 Bill Taylor .05
70 Mark McGwire 1.50
71 Roger Cedeno .05
72 Javy Lopez .05
73 Damion Easley .05
74 Andy Pettitte .25
75 Tony Gwynn 1.00
76 Ricardo Rincon .05
77 F.P. Santangelo .05
78 Jay Bell .05
79 Scott Servais .05
80 Jose Canseco .40
81 Roberto Hernandez .05
82 Todd Dunwoody .05
83 John Wetteland .05
84 Mike Caruso (Rookie All-Star) .05
85 Derek Jeter 2.00
86 Aaron Sele .05
87 Jose Lima .05
88 Ryan Christenson .05
89 Jeff Cirillo .05
90 Jose Hernandez .05
91 Mark Kotsay (Rookie All-Star) .05
92 Darren Bragg .05
93 Albert Belle .05
94 Matt Lawton .05
95 Pedro Martinez .75
96 Greg Vaughn .05
97 Neifi Perez .05
98 Gerald Williams .05
99 Derek Bell .05
100 Ken Griffey Jr. 1.25
101 David Cone .05
102 Brian Johnson .05
103 Dean Palmer .05
104 Javier Valentin .05
105 Trevor Hoffman .05
106 Butch Huskey .05
107 Dave Martinez .05
108 Billy Wagner .05
109 Shawn Green .30
110 Ben Grieve (Rookie All-Star) .05
111 Tom Goodwin .05
112 Jaret Wright .05
113 Aramis Ramirez .05
114 Dmitri Young .05
115 Hideki Irabu .05
116 Roberto Kelly .05
117 Jeff Fassero .05
118 Mark Clark .05
119 Jason McDonald .05
120 Matt Williams .05
121 Dave Burba .05
122 Bret Saberhagen .05
123 Deivi Cruz .05
124 Chad Curtis .05
125 Scott Rolen .65
126 Lee Stevens .05
127 J.T. Snow Jr. .05
128 Rusty Greer .05
129 Brian Meadows .05
130 Jim Edmonds .05
131 Ron Gant .05
132 A.J. Hinch (Rookie All-Star) .05
133 Shannon Stewart .05
134 Brad Fullmer .05
135 Cal Eldred .05
136 Matt Walbeck .05
137 Carl Everett .05
138 Walt Weiss .05
139 Fred McGriff .05
140 Darin Erstad .25
141 Dave Nilsson .05
142 Eric Young .05
143 Dan Wilson .05
144 Jeff Reed .05
145 Brett Tomko .05
146 Terry Steinbach .05
147 Seth Greisinger .05
148 Pat Meares .05
149 Livan Hernandez .05
150 Jeff Bagwell .75
151 Bob Wickman .05
152 Omar Vizquel .05
153 Eric Davis .05
154 Larry Sutton .05
155 Magglio Ordonez (Rookie All-Star) .40
156 Eric Milton .05
157 Darren Lewis .05
158 Rick Aguilera .05
159 Mike Lieberthal .05
160 Robb Nen .05
161 Brian Giles .05
162 Jeff Brantley .05
163 Gary DiSarcina .05
164 John Valentin .05
165 David Dellucci .05
166 Chan Ho Park .05
167 Masato Yoshii .05
168 Jason Schmidt .05
169 LaTroy Hawkins .05
170 Bret Boone .05
171 Jerry DiPoto .05
172 Mariano Rivera .10
173 Mike Cameron .05
174 Scott Erickson .05
175 Charles Johnson .05
176 Bobby Jones .05
177 Francisco Cordova .05
178 Todd Jones .05
179 Jeff Montgomery .05
180 Mike Mussina .40
181 Bob Abreu .05
182 Ismael Valdes .05
183 Andy Fox .05
184 Woody Williams .05
185 Denny Neagle .05
186 Jose Valentin .05
187 Darrin Fletcher .05
188 Gabe Alvarez .05
189 Eddie Taubensee .05
190 Edgar Martinez .05
191 Jason Kendall .05
192 Darryl Kile .05
193 Jeff King .05
194 Rey Ordonez .05
195 Andruw Jones .75
196 Tony Fernandez .05
197 Jamey Wright .05
198 B.J. Surhoff .05
199 Vinny Castilla .05
200 David Wells (Season Highlight) .05
201 Mark McGwire (Season Highlight) .75
202 Sammy Sosa (Season Highlight) .50
203 Roger Clemens (Season Highlight) .50
204 Kerry Wood (Season Highlight) .15
205 Lance Berkman, Mike Frank, Gabe Kapler (Prospects) .15
206 Alex Escobar **RC**, Ricky Ledee, Mike Stoner (Prospects) .25
207 Peter Bergeron **RC**, Jeremy Giambi, George Lombard (Prospects) .30
208 Michael Barrett, Ben Davis, Robert Fick (Prospects) .05
209 Pat Cline, Ramon Hernandez, Jayson Werth (Prospects) .05
210 Bruce Chen, Chris Enochs, Ryan Anderson (Prospects) .05
211 Mike Lincoln, Octavio Dotel, Brad Penny (Prospects) .05
212 Chuck Abbott, Brent Butler, Danny Klassen (Prospects) .05
213 Chris Jones, Jeff Urban **RC** (Draft Pick) .05
214 Arturo McDowell **RC**, Tony Torcato **RC** (Draft Pick) .25
215 Josh McKinley **RC**, Jason Tyner **RC** (Draft Pick) .25
216 Matt Burch **RC**, Seth Etherton **RC** (Draft Pick) .25
217 Mamon Tucker **RC**, Rick Elder **RC** (Draft Pick) .10
218 J.M. Gold **RC**, Ryan Mills **RC** (Draft Pick) .10
219 Adam Brown **RC**, Choo Freeman **RC** (Draft Pick) .25
220 Home Run Record #1 (M. McGwire) 20.00
220 HR Record #2-60 (M. McGwire) 6.00
220 HR Record #61-62 (M. McGwire) 10.00
220 HR Record #63-69 (M. McGwire) 15.00
220 HR Record #70 (Mark McGwire) 40.00
221 Larry Walker (League Leader) .05
222 Bernie Williams (League Leader) .05
223 Mark McGwire (League Leader) .75
224 Ken Griffey Jr. (League Leader) .65
225 Sammy Sosa (League Leader) .50
226 Juan Gonzalez (League Leader) .20
227 Dante Bichette (League Leader) .05
228 Alex Rodriguez (League Leader) .75
229 Sammy Sosa (League Leader) .50
230 Derek Jeter (League Leader) 1.00
231 Greg Maddux (League Leader) .50
232 Roger Clemens (League Leader) .50
233 Ricky Ledee (World Series) .05
234 Chuck Knoblauch (World Series) .05
235 Bernie Williams (World Series) .05
236 Tino Martinez (World Series) .05
237 Orlando Hernandez (World Series) .05
238 Scott Brosius (World Series) .05
239 Andy Pettitte (World Series) .05
240 Mariano Rivera (World Series) .05
241 Checklist .05
242 Checklist .05
243 Tom Glavine .25
244 Andy Benes .05
245 Sandy Alomar .05
246 Wilton Guerrero .05
247 Alex Gonzalez .05
248 Roberto Alomar .30
249 Ruben Rivera .05
250 Eric Chavez .15
251 Ellis Burks .05
252 Richie Sexson .05
253 Steve Finley .05
254 Dwight Gooden .05
255 Dustin Hermanson .05
256 Kirk Rueter .05
257 Steve Trachsel .05
258 Gregg Jefferies .05
259 Matt Stairs .05
260 Shane Reynolds .05
261 Gregg Olson .05
262 Kevin Tapani .05
263 Matt Morris .05
264 Carl Pavano .05
265 Nomar Garciaparra 1.00
266 Kevin Young .05
267 Rick Helling .05
268 Mark Leiter .05
269 Brian McRae .05
270 Cal Ripken Jr. 2.00
271 Jeff Abbott .05
272 Tony Batista .05
273 Bill Simas .05
274 Brian Hunter .05
275 John Franco .05
276 Devon White .05
277 Rickey Henderson .75
278 Chuck Finley .05
279 Mike Blowers .05
280 Mark Grace .05
281 Randy Winn .05
282 Bobby Bonilla .05
283 David Justice .05
284 Shane Monahan .05
285 Kevin Brown .05
286 Todd Zeile .05
287 Al Martin .05
288 Troy O'Leary .05
289 Darryl Hamilton .05
290 Tino Martinez .05
291 David Ortiz .45
292 Tony Clark .05
293 Ryan Minor .05
294 Reggie Sanders .05
295 Wally Joyner .05
296 Cliff Floyd .05
297 Shawn Estes .05
298 Pat Hentgen .05
299 Scott Elarton .05
300 Alex Rodriguez 1.50
301 Ozzie Guillen .05
302 Manny Martinez .05

303 Ryan McGuire .05
304 Brad Ausmus .05
305 Alex Gonzalez .05
306 Brian Jordan .05
307 John Jaha .05
308 Mark Grudzielanek .05
309 Juan Guzman .05
310 Tony Womack .05
311 Dennis Reyes .05
312 Marty Cordova .05
313 Ramiro Mendoza .05
314 Robin Ventura .05
315 Rafael Palmeiro .60
316 Ramon Martinez .05
317 John Mabry .05
318 Dave Hollins .05
319 Tom Candiotti .05
320 Al Leiter .05
321 Rico Brogna .05
322 Jimmy Key .05
323 Bernard Gilkey .05
324 Jason Giambi .45
325 Craig Biggio .05
326 Troy Glaus .65
327 Delino DeShields .05
328 Fernando Vina .05
329 John Smoltz .05
330 Jeff Kent .05
331 Roy Halladay .05
332 Andy Ashby .05
333 Tim Wakefield .05
334 Tim Belcher .05
335 Bernie Williams .05
336 Desi Relaford .05
337 John Burkett .05
338 Mike Hampton .05
339 Royce Clayton .05
340 Mike Piazza 1.25
341 Jeremi Gonzalez .05
342 Mike Lansing .05
343 Jamie Moyer .05
344 Ron Coomer .05
345 Barry Larkin .05
346 Fernando Tatis .05
347 Chili Davis .05
348 Bobby Higginson .05
349 Hal Morris .05
350 Larry Walker .05
351 Carlos Guillen .05
352 Miguel Tejada .05
353 Travis Fryman .05
354 Jarrod Washburn .05
355 Chipper Jones 1.00
356 Todd Stottlemyre .05
357 Henry Rodriguez .05
358 Eli Marrero .05
359 Alan Benes .05
360 Tim Salmon .05
361 Luis Gonzalez .05
362 Scott Spiezio .05
363 Chris Carpenter .05
364 Bobby Howry .05
365 Raul Mondesi .05
366 Ugueth Urbina .05
367 Tom Evans .05
368 Kerry Ligtenberg **RC** .15
369 Adrian Beltre .15
370 Ryan Klesko .05
371 Wilson Alvarez .05
372 John Thomson .05
373 Tony Saunders .05
374 Mike Stanley .05
375 Ken Caminiti .05
376 Jay Buhner .05
377 Bill Mueller .05
378 Jeff Blauser .05
379 Edgar Renteria .05
380 Jim Thome .60
381 Joey Hamilton .05
382 Calvin Pickering .05
383 Marquis Grissom .05
384 Omar Daal .05
385 Curt Schilling .25
386 Jose Cruz Jr. .05
387 Chris Widger .05
388 Pete Harnisch .05
389 Charles Nagy .05
390 Tom Gordon .05
391 Bobby Smith .05
392 Derrick Gibson .05
393 Jeff Conine .05
394 Carlos Perez .05
395 Barry Bonds 2.00
396 Mark McLemore .05
397 Juan Encarnacion .05
398 Wade Boggs 1.00
399 Ivan Rodriguez .65
400 Moises Alou .05
401 Jeromy Burnitz .05
402 Sean Casey .10
403 Jose Offerman .05
404 Joe Fontenot .05
405 Kevin Millwood .05
406 Lance Johnson .05
407 Richard Hidalgo .05
408 Mike Jackson .05
409 Brian Anderson .05
410 Jeff Shaw .05
411 Preston Wilson .05
412 Todd Hundley .05
413 Jim Parque .05
414 Justin Baughman .05
415 Dante Bichette .05
416 Paul O'Neill .05
417 Miguel Cairo .05
418 Randy Johnson .75
419 Jesus Sanchez .05
420 Carlos Delgado .30
421 Ricky Ledee .05
422 Orlando Hernandez .05
423 Frank Thomas .75
424 Pokey Reese .05
425 Carlos Lee, Mike Lowell, Kit Pellow **RC** (Prospect) .25
426 Michael Cuddyer, Mark DeRosa, Jerry Hairston Jr. (Prospect) .05
427 Marlon Anderson, Ron Belliard, Orlando Cabrera (Prospect) .10
428 Micah Bowie **RC**, Phil Norton **RC**, Randy Wolf (Prospect) .10
429 Jack Cressend, Jason Rakers, John Rocker (Prospect) .10
430 Ruben Mateo, Scott Morgan, Mike Zywica **RC** (Prospect) .10
431 Jason LaRue, Matt LeCroy **RC**, Mitch Meluskey (Prospect) .10
432 Gabe Kapler, Armando Rios, Fernando Seguignol (Prospect) .05
433 Adam Kennedy, Mickey Lopez **RC**, Jackie Rexrode (Prospect) .10
434 Jose Fernandez **RC**, Jeff Liefer, Chris Truby (Prospect) .10
435 Corey Koskie, Doug Mientkiewicz, Damon Minor (Prospect) .10
436 Roosevelt Brown **RC**, Dernell Stenson, Vernon Wells (Prospect) .10
437 A.J. Burnett **RC**, John Nicholson, Billy Koch (Prospect) .25
438 Matt Belisle **RC**, Matt Roney **RC** (Draft Pick) .10
439 Austin Kearns **RC**, Chris George **RC** (Draft Pick) 2.50
440 Nate Bump **RC**, Nate Cornejo **RC** (Draft Pick) .40
441 Brad Lidge **RC**, Mike Nannini **RC** (Draft Pick) .25
442 Matt Holiday **RC**, Jeff Winchester **RC** (Draft Pick) .25
443 Adam Everett **RC**, Chip Ambres **RC** (Draft Pick) .25
444 Pat Burrell **RC**, Eric Valent **RC** (Draft Pick) 1.50
445 Roger Clemens (Strikeout Kings) .50
446 Kerry Wood (Strikeout Kings) .15
447 Curt Schilling (Strikeout Kings) .05
448 Randy Johnson (Strikeout Kings) .40
449 Pedro Martinez (Strikeout Kings) .40
450 Jeff Bagwell, Andres Galarraga, Mark McGwire (All-Topps) .50
451 John Olerud, Jim Thome, Tino Martinez (All-Topps) .30
452 Alex Rodriguez, Nomar Garciaparra, Derek Jeter (All-Topps) .60
453 Vinny Castilla, Chipper Jones, Scott Rolen (All-Topps) .40
454 Sammy Sosa, Ken Griffey Jr., Juan Gonzalez (All-Topps) .50
455 Barry Bonds, Manny Ramirez, Larry Walker (All-Topps) .60
456 Frank Thomas, Tim Salmon, David Justice (All-Topps) .30
457 Travis Lee, Todd Helton, Ben Grieve (All-Topps) .30
458 Vladimir Guerrero, Greg Vaughn, Bernie Williams (All-Topps) .25
459 Mike Piazza, Ivan Rodriguez, Jason Kendall (All-Topps) .50
460 Roger Clemens, Kerry Wood, Greg Maddux (All-Topps) .45
461 Home Run Parade #1 (Sammy Sosa) 10.00
461 HR Parade #2-60 (Sammy Sosa) 4.00
461 HR Parade #61-62 (Sammy Sosa) 10.00
461 HR Parade #63-65 (Sammy Sosa) 6.00
461 HR Parade #66 (Sammy Sosa) 20.00
462 Checklist .05
463 Checklist .05

MVP Promotion

Each of the 198 regular-issue players' cards in Series 1 and cards #243-444 in Series 2 were issued in a parallel version of 100 each for use in an MVP of the Week sweepstakes. Overprinted with a large gold-foil seal on front, the MVP cards have contest rules on back. The MVP cards were inserted at ratios of between 1:142 (HTA) and 1:515 (Hobby) packs. Cards of players who won MVP of the Week during the 1999 season could be redeemed for a special set of MVP cards prior to the Dec. 31, 1999 deadline. Winning players' cards are checklisted here according to their regular-issue card number. Because they were not returned when redeemed, they are in shorter supply than non-winning cards, though market value is not significantly affected.

NM/M
Common Player: 3.00
Stars/Rookies: 20X

MVP Redemption

Person redeeming winning MVP contest cards prior to Dec. 31, 1999, received this set of 25 cards corresponding to the weekly winners. Cards have an MVP prefix.

NM/M
Complete Set (25): 30.00
Common Player: .50
1 Raul Mondesi .50
2 Tim Salmon .50
3 Fernando Tatis .50
4 Larry Walker .50
5 Fred McGriff .50
6 Nomar Garciaparra 3.00
7 Rafael Palmeiro 1.50
8 Randy Johnson 2.00
9 Mike Lieberthal .50
10 B.J. Surhoff .50
11 Todd Helton 2.00
12 Tino Martinez .50
13 Scott Rolen 1.50
14 Mike Piazza 4.00
15 David Cone .50
16 Tony Clark .50
17 Roberto Alomar .60
18 Miguel Tejada .75
19 Alex Rodriguez 5.00
20 J.T. Snow .50
21 Ray Lankford .50
22 Mo Vaughn .50
23 Paul O'Neill .50
24 Chipper Jones 3.00
25 Mark McGwire 5.00

All-Matrix

This 30-card set features holo-foil card fronts and features the top stars in the game.

Each card is numbered with a "AM" prefix on card backs and are seeded 1:18 packs.

NM/M
Complete Set (30): 45.00
Common Player: .75
Inserted 1:18
AM1 Mark McGwire 6.00
AM2 Sammy Sosa 3.50
AM3 Ken Griffey Jr. 4.50
AM4 Greg Vaughn .75
AM5 Albert Belle .75
AM6 Vinny Castilla .75
AM7 Jose Canseco 1.25
AM8 Juan Gonzalez 1.25
AM9 Manny Ramirez 2.50
AM10 Andres Galarraga .75
AM11 Rafael Palmeiro 2.00
AM12 Alex Rodriguez 6.00
AM13 Mo Vaughn .75
AM14 Eric Chavez 1.25
AM15 Gabe Kapler .75
AM16 Calvin Pickering .75
AM17 Ruben Mateo .75
AM18 Roy Halladay 1.25
AM19 Jeremy Giambi .75
AM20 Alex Gonzalez .75
AM21 Ron Belliard .75
AM22 Marlon Anderson .75
AM23 Carlos Lee .75
AM24 Kerry Wood 1.25
AM25 Roger Clemens 3.50
AM26 Curt Schilling 1.25
AM27 Kevin Brown .75
AM28 Randy Johnson 2.50
AM29 Pedro Martinez 2.50
AM30 Orlando Hernandez .75

All-Topps Mystery Finest

This 33-card set features a black opaque covering that collectors peel off to reveal the player. Each card is numbered with a "M" prefix and inserted 1:36 packs. A parallel Refractor version is also randomly seeded and inserted 1:144 packs.

NM/M
Complete Set (33): 100.00
Common Player: 1.00
Inserted 1:36
Refractors: 1.5X
Inserted 1:144
M1 Jeff Bagwell 4.25
M2 Andres Galarraga 1.00
M3 Mark McGwire 9.00
M4 John Olerud 1.00
M5 Jim Thome 2.50
M6 Tino Martinez 1.00
M7 Alex Rodriguez 9.00
M8 Nomar Garciaparra 5.00
M9 Derek Jeter 12.50
M10 Vinny Castilla 1.00
M11 Chipper Jones 5.00
M12 Scott Rolen 3.00
M13 Sammy Sosa 5.00
M14 Ken Griffey Jr. 7.50
M15 Juan Gonzalez 2.00
M16 Barry Bonds 12.50
M17 Manny Ramirez 4.50
M18 Larry Walker 1.00
M19 Frank Thomas 4.50
M20 Tim Salmon 1.00
M21 David Justice 1.00
M22 Travis Lee 1.50
M23 Todd Helton 4.50
M24 Ben Grieve 1.00
M25 Vladimir Guerrero 4.50
M26 Greg Vaughn 1.00
M27 Bernie Williams 1.00
M28 Mike Piazza 7.50
M29 Ivan Rodriguez 3.50
M30 Jason Kendall 1.00
M31 Roger Clemens 6.00
M32 Kerry Wood 2.00
M33 Greg Maddux 5.00

Autographs

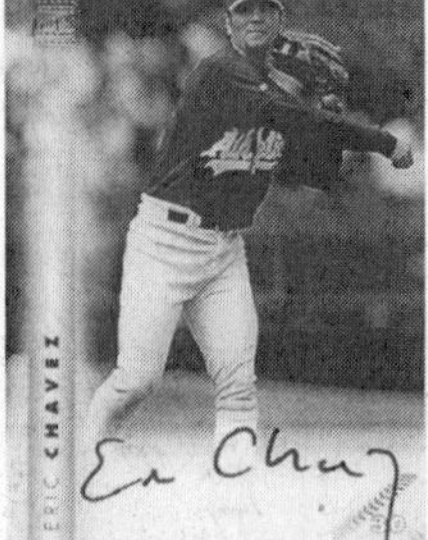

Autographs were inserted exclusively in hobby packs in both Topps series 1 and 2. Each series had eight cards with each one carrying the Topps Certified Autograph Issue stamp. Series 1 Autographs were seeded 1:532 packs while Series 2 were found 1:501 packs.

NM/M
Common Player: 8.00
Series 1 Inserted 1:532 H
Series 2 Inserted 1:501 H
A1 Roger Clemens 100.00
A2 Chipper Jones 40.00
A3 Scott Rolen 25.00
A4 Alex Rodriguez 100.00
A5 Andres Galarraga 8.00
A6 Rondell White 8.00
A7 Ben Grieve 8.00
A8 Troy Glaus 20.00
A9 Moises Alou 15.00
A10 Barry Bonds 180.00
A11 Vladimir Guerrero 35.00
A12 Andruw Jones 20.00
A13 Darin Erstad 12.00
A14 Shawn Green 16.00
A15 Eric Chavez 20.00
A16 Pat Burrell 25.00

Hall of Fame

Found exclusively in hobby packs, Hall of Fame Collection is a 10-card set featured on cards that silhouette their images against their respective Hall of Fame plaques. These were seeded 1:12 packs.

NM/M
Complete Set (10): 8.00
Common Player: .50
Inserted 1:12 H
HOF1 Mike Schmidt 1.50
HOF2 Brooks Robinson .75
HOF3 Stan Musial 1.50
HOF4 Willie McCovey .50
HOF5 Eddie Mathews .75
HOF6 Reggie Jackson 1.50
HOF7 Ernie Banks 1.00
HOF8 Whitey Ford .75
HOF9 Bob Feller .50
HOF10 Yogi Berra 1.00

Lords of the Diamond

Inserted in every 18 packs this 15-card set features the top players in the game includ-

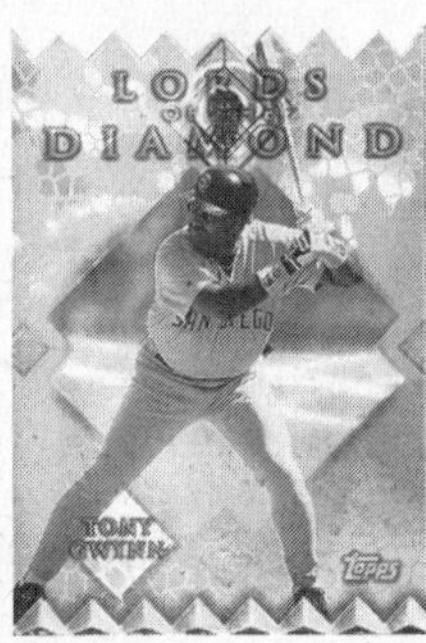

ing Barry Bonds and Ken Griffey Jr. Card fronts include a holographic look with die-cutting across the top of the card on a silver background.

NM/M
Complete Set (15): 13.00
Common Player: .25
Inserted 1:18
LD1 Ken Griffey Jr. 1.25
LD2 Chipper Jones 1.00
LD3 Sammy Sosa 1.00
LD4 Frank Thomas .75
LD5 Mark McGwire 1.50
LD6 Jeff Bagwell .75
LD7 Alex Rodriguez 1.50
LD8 Juan Gonzalez .40
LD9 Barry Bonds 2.00
LD10 Nomar Garciaparra 1.00
LD11 Darin Erstad .35
LD12 Tony Gwynn 1.00
LD13 Andres Galarraga .25
LD14 Mike Piazza 1.25
LD15 Greg Maddux 1.00

New Breed

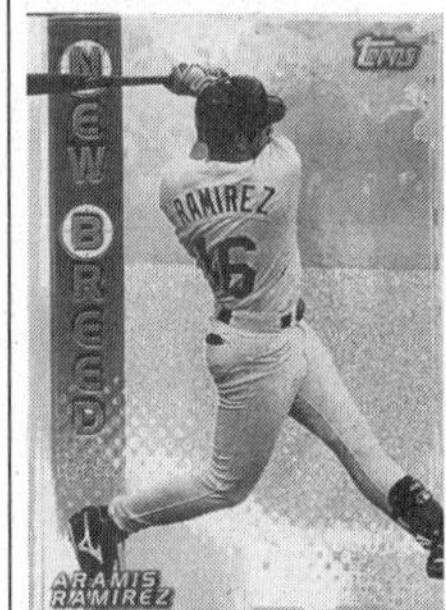

The next generation of stars are featured in this 15-card set that showcases the young talent on a silver foil card. These are seeded 1:18 packs.

NM/M
Complete Set (15): 9.00
Common Player: .25
Inserted 1:18
NB1 Darin Erstad .50
NB2 Brad Fullmer .25
NB3 Kerry Wood .50
NB4 Nomar Garciaparra 1.50
NB5 Travis Lee .35
NB6 Scott Rolen .75
NB7 Todd Helton .75
NB8 Vladimir Guerrero 1.00
NB9 Derek Jeter 3.00
NB10 Alex Rodriguez 2.00
NB11 Ben Grieve .25
NB12 Andruw Jones 1.00
NB13 Paul Konerko .40
NB14 Aramis Ramirez .25
NB15 Adrian Beltre .35

Picture Perfect

This 10-card set features a full bleed photo of baseball's biggest stars, including Derek Jeter and Ken Griffey Jr. These are found one per eight packs.

		NM/M
Complete Set (10):		5.00
Common Player:		.25
Inserted 1:8		
P1	Ken Griffey Jr.	.75
P2	Kerry Wood	.30
P3	Pedro Martinez	.45
P4	Mark McGwire	.90
P5	Greg Maddux	.60
P6	Sammy Sosa	.60
P7	Greg Vaughn	.25
P8	Juan Gonzalez	.30
P9	Jeff Bagwell	.45
P10	Derek Jeter	1.50

Power Brokers

This 20-card set features baseball's biggest superstars including McGwire, Sosa and Chipper Jones. The cards are die-cut at the top and printed on Finest technology. Power Brokers are inserted in every 36 packs. A Refractor parallel version also exists, which are seeded 1:144 packs.

		NM/M
Complete Set (20):		20.00
Common Player:		.25
Inserted 1:36		
Refractors:		1.5X
Inserted 1:144		
PB1	Mark McGwire	3.00
PB2	Andres Galarraga	.25
PB3	Ken Griffey Jr.	2.00
PB4	Sammy Sosa	1.50
PB5	Juan Gonzalez	.50
PB6	Alex Rodriguez	3.00
PB7	Frank Thomas	1.00
PB8	Jeff Bagwell	1.00
PB9	Vinny Castilla	.25
PB10	Mike Piazza	2.00
PB11	Greg Vaughn	.25
PB12	Barry Bonds	4.00
PB13	Mo Vaughn	.25
PB14	Jim Thome	.65
PB15	Larry Walker	.25
PB16	Chipper Jones	1.50
PB17	Nomar Garciaparra	1.50
PB18	Manny Ramirez	1.00
PB19	Roger Clemens	1.75
PB20	Kerry Wood	.65

Record Numbers

This 10-card set highlights achievements from the game's current stars, including Nomar Garciaparra's 30 game hitting streak, the longest by a rookie in major league history. These inserts are randomly seeded 1:8 packs, each card is numbered on the back with a "RN" prefix.

		NM/M
Complete Set (10):		8.00
Common Player:		.50
Inserted 1:8		
RN1	Mark McGwire	1.50
RN2	Mike Piazza	1.00
RN3	Curt Schilling	.75
RN4	Ken Griffey Jr.	1.50
RN5	Sammy Sosa	.75
RN6	Nomar Garciaparra	.75
RN7	Kerry Wood	.50
RN8	Roger Clemens	1.50
RN9	Cal Ripken Jr.	2.00
RN10	Mark McGwire	1.50

Record Numbers Gold

This is a parallel of the Record Numbers insert set, each card features the appropriate sequential numbering based on the featured players' highlighted record. Each card is numbered with a "RN" prefix on the back.

		NM/M
Common Player:		8.00
RN1	Mark McGwire/70	40.00
RN2	Mike Piazza/362	15.00
RN3	Curt Schilling/319	8.00
RN4	Ken Griffey Jr./350	20.00
RN5	Sammy Sosa/20	20.00
RN6	Nomar Garciaparra/30	20.00
RN7	Kerry Wood/20	15.00
RN8	Roger Clemens/20	40.00
RN9	Cal Ripken Jr./2,632	15.00
RN10	Mark McGwire/162	20.00

Nolan Ryan Reprints

Topps reprinted all 27 of Nolan Ryan's basic Topps cards, with 14 odd numbers appearing in Series 1 and the remaining 13 even cards inserted into Series 2 packs. Each card is stamped with a gold Topps commemorative stamp on the front for identification. Reprints were seeded in every 18 packs. Ryan also autographed a number of the reprints for both series. Series 1 Ryan autographs are seeded 1:4,260, with Series 2 autographs found 1:5,007 packs. Ryan autographs were inserted exclusively in hobby packs.

		NM/M
Complete Set (27):		40.00
Common Ryan:		3.00
Inserted 1:18		
Nolan Ryan Autograph:		150.00
1	Nolan Ryan/1968	7.50
2	Nolan Ryan/1969	4.50
3	Nolan Ryan/1970	3.00
4	Nolan Ryan/1971	3.00
5	Nolan Ryan/1972	3.00
6	Nolan Ryan/1973	3.00
7	Nolan Ryan/1974	3.00
8	Nolan Ryan/1975	3.00
9	Nolan Ryan/1976	3.00
10	Nolan Ryan/1977	3.00
11	Nolan Ryan/1978	3.00
12	Nolan Ryan/1979	3.00
13	Nolan Ryan/1980	3.00
14	Nolan Ryan/1981	3.00
15	Nolan Ryan/1982	3.00
16	Nolan Ryan/1983	3.00
17	Nolan Ryan/1984	3.00
18	Nolan Ryan/1985	3.00
19	Nolan Ryan/1986	3.00
20	Nolan Ryan/1987	3.00
21	Nolan Ryan/1988	3.00
22	Nolan Ryan/1989	3.00
23	Nolan Ryan/1990	3.00
24	Nolan Ryan/1991	3.00
25	Nolan Ryan/1992	3.00
26	Nolan Ryan/1993	3.00
27	Nolan Ryan/1994	3.00

Nolan Ryan Reprint Autographs

Topps reprinted all 27 of Nolan Ryan's basic Topps cards, with 14 odd numbers appearing in Series 1 and the remaining 13 even cards inserted into Series 2 packs. Each card is stamped with a gold Topps commemorative stamp on the front for identification. Ryan-autographed reprints, found exclusively in hobby packs, are seeded 1:4,260 in Series 1, with Series 2 autographs found 1:5,007 packs.

		NM/M
Common Card:		150.00
1	Nolan Ryan/1968	200.00
2	Nolan Ryan/1969	150.00
3	Nolan Ryan/1970	150.00
4	Nolan Ryan/1971	150.00
5	Nolan Ryan/1972	150.00
6	Nolan Ryan/1973	150.00
7	Nolan Ryan/1974	150.00
8	Nolan Ryan/1975	150.00
9	Nolan Ryan/1976	150.00
10	Nolan Ryan/1977	150.00
11	Nolan Ryan/1978	150.00
12	Nolan Ryan/1979	150.00
13	Nolan Ryan/1980	150.00
14	Nolan Ryan/1981	150.00
15	Nolan Ryan/1982	150.00
16	Nolan Ryan/1983	150.00
17	Nolan Ryan/1984	150.00
18	Nolan Ryan/1985	150.00
19	Nolan Ryan/1986	150.00
20	Nolan Ryan/1987	150.00
21	Nolan Ryan/1988	150.00
22	Nolan Ryan/1989	150.00
23	Nolan Ryan/1990	150.00
24	Nolan Ryan/1991	150.00
25	Nolan Ryan/1992	150.00
26	Nolan Ryan/1993	150.00
27	Nolan Ryan/1994	150.00

Nolan Ryan Finest Reprints

This 27-card set reprinted all 27 of Ryan's basic Topps cards. Odd numbers were distributed in Series 1 packs, with even numbers distributed in Series 2 packs. These are seeded 1:72 packs in both series 1 and 2 packs. A Refractor parallel version is inserted 1:288 packs.

		NM/M
Complete Set (27):		125.00
Common Card:		5.00
Inserted 1:72		
Refractors:		2X
Inserted 1:288		
1	1968	12.50
2	1969	7.50
3	1970	5.00
4	1971	5.00
5	1972	5.00
6	1973	5.00
7	1974	5.00
8	1975	5.00
9	1976	5.00
10	1977	5.00
11	1978	5.00
12	1979	5.00
13	1980	5.00
14	1981	5.00
15	1982	5.00
16	1983	5.00
17	1984	5.00
18	1985	5.00
19	1986	5.00
20	1987	5.00
21	1988	5.00
22	1989	5.00
23	1990	5.00
24	1991	5.00
25	1992	5.00
26	1992	5.00
27	1992	5.00

Traded and Rookies

Identical in design to the base 1999 Topps cards the 121-card set includes players involved in pre and mid-season transactions as well as top prospects and 1999 Draft Picks. Released in a boxed set, each set also includes one autographed card from the 75 rookie/draft pick cards in the set.

		NM/M
Unopened Set (122):		30.00
Complete Set, No Autograph (121):		10.00
Common Player:		.10
1	Seth Etherton	.10
2	Mark Harriger **RC**	.10
3	Matt Wise **RC**	.25
4	Carlos Hernandez **RC**	.15
5	Julio Lugo **RC**	.25
6	Mike Nannini	.10
7	Justin Bowles **RC**	.10
8	Mark Mulder **RC**	.75
9	Roberto Vaz **RC**	.10
10	Felipe Lopez **RC**	.75
11	Matt Belisle	.10
12	Micah Bowie	.10
13	Ruben Quevedo **RC**	.10
14	Jose Garcia **RC**	.10
15	David Kelton **RC**	.25
16	Phillip Norton	.10
17	Corey Patterson **RC**	.75
18	Ron Walker **RC**	.10
19	Paul Hoover **RC**	.10
20	Ryan Rupe **RC**	.15
21	J.D. Closser **RC**	.10
22	Rob Ryan **RC**	.10
23	Steve Colyer **RC**	.10
24	Bubba Crosby **RC**	.50
25	Luke Prokopec **RC**	.10
26	Matt Blank **RC**	.10
27	Josh McKinley	.10
28	Nate Bump	.10
29	Giuseppe Chiaramonte **RC**	.10
30	Arturo McDowell	.10
31	Tony Torcato	.10
32	Dave Roberts	.10
33	C.C. Sabathia **RC**	1.50
34	Sean Spencer **RC**	.10
35	Chip Ambres	.10
36	A.J. Burnett	.15
37	Mo Bruce **RC**	.10
38	Jason Tyner	.10
39	Mamon Tucker	.10
40	Sean Burroughs **RC**	.25
41	Kevin Eberwein **RC**	.10
42	Junior Herndon **RC**	.10
43	Bryan Wolff **RC**	.10
44	Pat Burrell	.50
45	Eric Valent	.10
46	Carlos Pena **RC**	1.00
47	Mike Zywica	.10
48	Adam Everett	.10
49	Juan Pena **RC**	.50
50	Adam Dunn **RC**	3.00
51	Austin Kearns	.75
52	Jacobo Sequea **RC**	.10
53	Choo Freeman	.10
54	Jeff Winchester	.10
55	Matt Burch	.10
56	Chris George	.10
57	Scott Mullen **RC**	.10
58	Kit Pellow	.10
59	Mark Quinn **RC**	.15
60	Nate Cornejo	.10
61	Ryan Mills **RC**	.25
62	Kevin Beirne **RC**	.10
63	Kip Wells **RC**	.50
64	Juan Rivera **RC**	.25
65	Alfonso Soriano **RC**	4.00
66	Josh Hamilton **RC**	4.00
67	Josh Girdley **RC**	.10
68	Kyle Snyder **RC**	.15
69	Mike Paradis **RC**	.10
70	Jason Jennings **RC**	.25
71	David Walling **RC**	.10
72	Omar Ortiz **RC**	.10
73	Jay Gehrke **RC**	.10
74	Casey Burns **RC**	.10
75	Carl Crawford **RC**	2.00
76	Reggie Sanders	.10
77	Will Clark	.10
78	David Wells	.10
79	Paul Konerko	.20
80	Armando Benitez	.10
81	Brant Brown	.10
82	Mo Vaughn	.10
83	Jose Canseco	.25
84	Albert Belle	.10
85	Dean Palmer	.10
86	Greg Vaughn	.10
87	Mark Clark	.10
88	Pat Meares	.10
89	Eric Davis	.10
90	Brian Giles	.10
91	Jeff Brantley	.10
92	Bret Boone	.10
93	Ron Gant	.10
94	Mike Cameron	.10
95	Charles Johnson	.10
96	Denny Neagle	.10
97	Brian Hunter	.10
98	Jose Hernandez	.10
99	Rick Aguilera	.10
100	Tony Batista	.10
101	Roger Cedeno	.10
102	Creighton Gubanich	.10
103	Tim Belcher	.10
104	Bruce Aven	.10
105	Brian Daubach **RC**	.25
106	Ed Sprague	.10
107	Michael Tucker	.10
108	Homer Bush	.10
109	Armando Reynoso	.10
110	Brook Fordyce	.10
111	Matt Mantei	.10
112	Jose Guillen	.10
113	Kenny Rogers	.10
114	Livan Hernandez	.10
115	Butch Huskey	.10
116	David Segui	.10
117	Darryl Hamilton	.10
118	Jim Leyritz	.10
119	Randy Velarde	.10
120	Bill Taylor	.10
121	Kevin Appier	.10

Traded and Rookies Autographs

These autographs have identical photos and design from the Traded and Rookies set. Seeded one per boxed set, each card has a "Topps Certified Autograph Issue" stamp ensuring its authenticity. Cards of the first 75 rookies/draft picks included in the 121-card boxed set can be found in this autographed version.

		NM/M
Common Player:		3.00
Inserted 1:Set		
1	Seth Etherton	3.00
2	Mark Harriger	3.00
3	Matt Wise	5.00
4	Carlos Hernandez	5.00
5	Julio Lugo	20.00
6	Mike Nannini	3.00
7	Justin Bowles	3.00
8	Mark Mulder	20.00
9	Roberto Vaz	3.00
10	Felipe Lopez	20.00
11	Matt Belisle	3.00
12	Micah Bowie	3.00
13	Ruben Quevedo	5.00
14	Jose Garcia	5.00
15	David Kelton	10.00
16	Phillip Norton	5.00
17	Corey Patterson	25.00
18	Ron Walker	3.00
19	Paul Hoover	3.00
20	Ryan Rupe	4.00
21	J.D. Closser	8.00
22	Rob Ryan	3.00
23	Steve Colyer	5.00
24	Bubba Crosby	15.00
25	Luke Prokopec	3.00
26	Matt Blank	3.00
27	Josh McKinley	5.00
28	Nate Bump	5.00
29	Giuseppe Chiaramonte	3.00
30	Arturo McDowell	3.00
31	Tony Torcato	5.00
32	Dave Roberts	10.00
33	C.C. Sabathia	75.00
34	Sean Spencer	3.00
35	Chip Ambres	3.00
36	A.J. Burnett	25.00
37	Mo Bruce	3.00
38	Jason Tyner	3.00
39	Mamon Tucker	3.00
40	Sean Burroughs	10.00
41	Kevin Eberwein	3.00
42	Junior Herndon	3.00
43	Bryan Wolff	3.00
44	Pat Burrell	25.00
45	Eric Valent	8.00
46	Carlos Pena	30.00
47	Mike Zywica	3.00
48	Adam Everett	15.00
49	Juan Pena	5.00
50	Adam Dunn	100.00
51	Austin Kearns	25.00
52	Jacobo Sequea	3.00
53	Choo Freeman	8.00
54	Jeff Winchester	3.00
55	Matt Burch	3.00
56	Chris George	4.00
57	Scott Mullen	3.00
58	Kit Pellow	3.00
59	Mark Quinn	3.00
60	Nate Cornejo	8.00
61	Ryan Mills	3.00
62	Kevin Beirne	4.00
63	Kip Wells	8.00
64	Juan Rivera	10.00
65	Alfonso Soriano	160.00
66	Josh Hamilton	100.00
67	Josh Girdley	3.00
68	Kyle Snyder	5.00
69	Mike Paradis	3.00
70	Jason Jennings	10.00
71	David Walling	3.00
72	Omar Ortiz	3.00
73	Jay Gehrke	5.00
74	Casey Burns	3.00
75	Carl Crawford	100.00

Supers

These oversize (3-1/2" x 5") versions of Topps cards were issued one per box in hobby and Home Team Advantage boxes. Eight cards were issued in each of Series 1 and 2. Other than their size and the card numbers on back, the supers are identical to the regular versions.

		NM/M
Complete Set (16):		17.50
Common Player:		.50
1	Roger Clemens	1.25
2	Greg Maddux	1.25
3	Kerry Wood	.75
4	Juan Gonzalez	.75
5	Sammy Sosa	1.25
6	Mark McGwire	2.50
7	Ken Griffey Jr.	2.00
8	Ben Grieve	.50
1	Nomar Garciaparra	1.25
2	Cal Ripken Jr.	3.00
3	Alex Rodriguez	2.00
4	Mike Piazza	1.50
5	Larry Walker	.50
6	Chipper Jones	1.25
7	Barry Bonds	3.00
8	Frank Thomas	1.00

Action Flats

"Dynamic action poses . . . painstakingly capturing one of their signature plays" are featured in this issue of plastic player figures. The figures are about 3" tall by 2-1/2" wide and stand on a plastic base. In the manner of early 20th Century tin soldiers, there is little depth to the figures. Each handpainted figure is sold in a plastic-windowed box which includes a

special foil-stamped version of the player's 1999 Topps card inside. Each figure was also produced in a short-printed "away" jersey version, with 10 of the players seeded at the rate of one per 12 figures, Sosa at a 1:24 rate and McGwire at a 1:36 rate. Suggested retail price at issue was $2.99. Values shown are for unopened packages.

		NM/M
Complete Set, "Home" (12):		6.00
Complete Set, "Away" (12):		12.00
Common Player, "Home":		.50
Common Player, "Away":		.75
1	Chipper Jones	.50
2	Greg Maddux	.50
3	Mark McGwire	1.00
4	Sammy Sosa	.50
5	Kerry Wood	.50
6	Barry Bonds	1.50
7	Alex Rodriguez	1.00
8	Ken Griffey Jr.	.75
9	Cal Ripken Jr.	1.50
10	Juan Gonzalez	.50
11	Nomar Garciaparra	.50
12	Derek Jeter	1.50
1	Chipper Jones	.75
2	Greg Maddux	.75
3	Mark McGwire	1.50
4	Sammy Sosa	.75
5	Kerry Wood	.75
6	Barry Bonds	2.00
7	Alex Rodriguez	1.50
8	Ken Griffey Jr.	1.00
9	Cal Ripken Jr.	2.00
10	Juan Gonzalez	.75
11	Nomar Garciaparra	.75
12	Derek Jeter	2.00

1999 Topps Chrome

The 462-card base set is a chromium parallel version of Topps baseball. Included are the Mark McGwire #220 and Sammy Sosa #461 home run subset cards, which commemorate each of their home runs. Each pack contains four cards with a S.R.P. of $3.00 per pack.

		NM/M
Complete Set (461):		75.00
Common Player:		.15
Refractors:		4X
Inserted 1:12		
Ser. 1 or 2 Pack (4):		1.50
Ser. 1 or 2 Box (24):		30.00
1	Roger Clemens	1.75
2	Andres Galarraga	.15
3	Scott Brosius	.15
4	John Flaherty	.15
5	Jim Leyritz	.15
6	Ray Durham	.15
8	Joe Vizcaino	.15
9	Will Clark	.15
10	David Wells	.15
11	Jose Guillen	.15
12	Scott Hatteberg	.15
13	Edgardo Alfonzo	.15
14	Mike Bordick	.15
15	Manny Ramirez	1.00
16	Greg Maddux	1.50
17	David Segui	.15
18	Darryl Strawberry	.15
19	Brad Radke	.15
20	Kerry Wood	.40
21	Matt Anderson	.15
22	Derrek Lee	.60
23	Mickey Morandini	.15
24	Paul Konerko	.30
25	Travis Lee	.15
26	Ken Hill	.15
27	Kenny Rogers	.15
28	Paul Sorrento	.15
29	Quilvio Veras	.15
30	Todd Walker	.15
31	Ryan Jackson	.15
32	John Olerud	.15
33	Doug Glanville	.15
34	Nolan Ryan	3.00
35	Ray Lankford	.15
36	Mark Loretta	.15
37	Jason Dickson	.15
38	Sean Bergman	.15
39	Quinton McCracken	.15
40	Bartolo Colon	.15
41	Brady Anderson	.15
42	Chris Stynes	.15
43	Jorge Posada	.15
44	Justin Thompson	.15
45	Johnny Damon	.40
46	Armando Benitez	.15
47	Brant Brown	.15
48	Charlie Hayes	.15
49	Darren Dreifort	.15
50	Juan Gonzalez	.50
51	Chuck Knoblauch	.15
52	Todd Helton (Rookie All-Star)	1.00
53	Rick Reed	.15
54	Chris Gomez	.15
55	Gary Sheffield	.50
56	Rod Beck	.15
57	Rey Sanchez	.15
58	Garret Anderson	.15
59	Jimmy Haynes	.15
60	Steve Woodard	.15
61	Rondell White	.15
62	Vladimir Guerrero	1.00
63	Eric Karros	.15
64	Russ Davis	.15
65	Mo Vaughn	.15
66	Sammy Sosa	1.50
67	Troy Percival	.15
68	Kenny Lofton	.15
69	Bill Taylor	.15
70	Mark McGwire	2.50
71	Roger Cedeno	.15
72	Javy Lopez	.15
73	Damion Easley	.15
74	Andy Pettitte	.35
75	Tony Gwynn	1.50
76	Ricardo Rincon	.15
77	F.P. Santangelo	.15
78	Jay Bell	.15
79	Scott Servais	.15
80	Jose Canseco	.50
81	Roberto Hernandez	.15
82	Todd Dunwoody	.15
83	John Wetteland	.15
84	Mike Caruso (Rookie All-Star)	.15
85	Derek Jeter	3.00
86	Aaron Sele	.15
87	Jose Lima	.15
88	Ryan Christenson	.15
89	Jeff Cirillo	.15
90	Jose Hernandez	.15
91	Mark Kotsay (Rookie All-Star)	.15
92	Darren Bragg	.15
93	Albert Belle	.15
94	Matt Lawton	.15
95	Pedro Martinez	1.00
96	Greg Vaughn	.15
97	Neifi Perez	.15
98	Gerald Williams	.15
99	Derek Bell	.15
100	Ken Griffey Jr.	2.00
101	David Cone	.15
102	Brian Johnson	.15
103	Dean Palmer	.15
104	Javier Valentin	.15
105	Trevor Hoffman	.15
106	Butch Huskey	.15
107	Dave Martinez	.15
108	Billy Wagner	.15
109	Shawn Green	.35
110	Ben Grieve (Rookie All-Star)	.15
111	Tom Goodwin	.15
112	Jaret Wright	.15
113	Aramis Ramirez	.15
114	Dmitri Young	.15
115	Hideki Irabu	.15
116	Roberto Kelly	.15
117	Jeff Fassero	.15
118	Mark Clark	.15
119	Jason McDonald	.15
120	Matt Williams	.15
121	Dave Burba	.15
122	Bret Saberhagen	.15
123	Deivi Cruz	.15
124	Chad Curtis	.15
125	Scott Rolen	.75
126	Lee Stevens	.15
127	J.T. Snow Jr.	.15
128	Rusty Greer	.15
129	Brian Meadows	.15
130	Jim Edmonds	.15
131	Ron Gant	.15
132	A.J. Hinch (Rookie All-Star)	.15
133	Shannon Stewart	.15
134	Brad Fullmer	.15
135	Cal Eldred	.15
136	Matt Walbeck	.15
137	Carl Everett	.15
138	Walt Weiss	.15
139	Fred McGriff	.15
140	Darin Erstad	.40
141	Dave Nilsson	.15
142	Eric Young	.15
143	Dan Wilson	.15
144	Jeff Reed	.15
145	Brett Tomko	.15
146	Terry Steinbach	.15
147	Seth Greisinger	.15
148	Pat Meares	.15
149	Livan Hernandez	.15
150	Jeff Bagwell	1.00
151	Bob Wickman	.15
152	Omar Vizquel	.15
153	Eric Davis	.15
154	Larry Sutton	.15
155	Maggio Ordonez (Rookie All-Star)	.45
156	Eric Milton	.15
157	Darren Lewis	.15
158	Rick Aguilera	.15
159	Mike Lieberthal	.15
160	Robb Nen	.15
161	Brian Giles	.15
162	Jeff Brantley	.15
163	Gary DiSarcina	.15
164	John Valentin	.15
165	David Dellucci	.15
166	Chan Ho Park	.15
167	Masato Yoshii	.15
168	Jason Schmidt	.15
169	LaTroy Hawkins	.15
170	Bret Boone	.15
171	Jerry DiPoto	.15
172	Mariano Rivera	.25
173	Mike Cameron	.15
174	Scott Erickson	.15
175	Charles Johnson	.15
176	Bobby Jones	.15
177	Francisco Cordova	.15
178	Todd Jones	.15
179	Jeff Montgomery	.15
180	Mike Mussina	.50
181	Bob Abreu	.15
182	Ismael Valdes	.15
183	Andy Fox	.15
184	Woody Williams	.15
185	Denny Neagle	.15
186	Jose Valentin	.15
187	Darrin Fletcher	.15
188	Gabe Alvarez	.15
189	Eddie Taubensee	.15
190	Edgar Martinez	.15
191	Jason Kendall	.15
192	Darryl Kile	.15
193	Jeff King	.15
194	Rey Ordonez	.15
195	Andruw Jones	1.00
196	Tony Fernandez	.15
197	Jamey Wright	.15
198	B.J. Surhoff	.15
199	Vinny Castilla	.15
200	David Wells (Season Highlight)	.15
201	Mark McGwire (Season Highlight)	1.25
202	Sammy Sosa (Season Highlight)	.75
203	Roger Clemens (Season Highlight)	.85
204	Kerry Wood (Season Highlight)	.20
205	Lance Berkman, Mike Frank, Gabe Kapler (Prospects)	.15
206	Alex Escobar **RC**, Ricky Ledee, Mike Stoner (Prospects)	.50
207	Peter Bergeron **RC**, Jeremy Giambi, George Lombard (Prospects)	.50
208	Michael Barrett, Ben Davis, Robert Fick (Prospects)	.15
209	Pat Cline, Ramon Hernandez, Jayson Werth (Prospects)	.20
210	Bruce Chen, Chris Enochs, Ryan Anderson (Prospects)	.15
211	Mike Lincoln, Octavio Dotel, Brad Penny (Prospects)	.15
212	Chuck Abbott, Brent Butler, Danny Klassen (Prospects)	.15
213	Chris Jones, Jeff Urban **RC** (Draft Pick)	.15
214	Arturo McDowell **RC**, Tony Torcato **RC** (Draft Pick)	.25
215	Josh McKinley **RC**, Jason Tyner **RC** (Draft Pick)	.30
216	Matt Burch **RC**, Seth Etherton **RC** (Draft Pick)	.15
217	Mamon Tucker **RC**, Rick Elder **RC** (Draft Pick)	.20
218	J.M. Gold **RC**, Ryan Mills **RC** (Draft Pick)	.15
219	Adam Brown **RC**, Choo Freeman **RC** (Draft Pick)	.20
220	Mark McGwire HR #1 (Record Breaker)	15.00
220	Mark McGwire HR #2-60	10.00
220	McGwire HR #61-62	15.00
220	McGwire HR #63-69	12.50
220	McGwire HR #70	40.00
221	Larry Walker (League Leader)	.15
222	Bernie Williams (League Leader)	.15
223	Mark McGwire (League Leader)	1.25
224	Ken Griffey Jr. (League Leader)	1.00
225	Sammy Sosa (League Leader)	.75
226	Juan Gonzalez (League Leader)	.35
227	Dante Bichette (League Leader)	.15
228	Alex Rodriguez (League Leader)	1.25
229	Sammy Sosa (League Leader)	.75
230	Derek Jeter (League Leader)	1.50
231	Greg Maddux (League Leader)	.75
232	Roger Clemens (League Leader)	.75
233	Ricky Ledee (World Series)	.15
234	Chuck Knoblauch (World Series)	.15
235	Bernie Williams (World Series)	.15
236	Tino Martinez (World Series)	.15
237	Orlando Hernandez (World Series)	.15
238	Scott Brosius (World Series)	.15
239	Andy Pettitte (World Series)	.15
240	Mariano Rivera (World Series)	.15
241	Checklist	.15
242	Checklist	.15
243	Tom Glavine	.35
244	Andy Benes	.15
245	Sandy Alomar	.15
246	Wilton Guerrero	.15
247	Alex Gonzalez	.15
248	Roberto Alomar	.30
249	Ruben Rivera	.15
250	Eric Chavez	.15
251	Ellis Burks	.15
252	Richie Sexson	.15
253	Steve Finley	.15
254	Dwight Gooden	.15
255	Dustin Hermanson	.15
256	Kirk Rueter	.15
257	Steve Trachsel	.15
258	Gregg Jefferies	.15
259	Matt Stairs	.15
260	Shane Reynolds	.15
261	Gregg Olson	.15
262	Kevin Tapani	.15
263	Matt Morris	.15
264	Carl Pavano	.15
265	Nomar Garciaparra	1.50
266	Kevin Young	.15
267	Rick Helling	.15
268	Matt Franco	.15
269	Brian McRae	.15
270	Cal Ripken Jr.	3.00
271	Jeff Abbott	.15
272	Tony Batista	.15
273	Bill Simas	.15
274	Brian Hunter	.15
275	John Franco	.15
276	Devon White	.15
277	Rickey Henderson	1.00
278	Chuck Finley	.15
279	Mike Blowers	.15
280	Mark Grace	.15
281	Randy Winn	.15
282	Bobby Bonilla	.15
283	David Justice	.15
284	Shane Monahan	.15
285	Kevin Brown	.15
286	Todd Zeile	.15
287	Al Martin	.15
288	Troy O'Leary	.15
289	Darryl Hamilton	.15
290	Tino Martinez	.15
291	David Ortiz	.50
292	Tony Clark	.15
293	Ryan Minor	.15
294	Reggie Sanders	.15
295	Wally Joyner	.15
296	Cliff Floyd	.15
297	Shawn Estes	.15
298	Pat Hentgen	.15
299	Scott Elarton	.15
300	Alex Rodriguez	2.50
301	Ozzie Guillen	.15
302	Hideo Martinez	.15
303	Ryan McGuire	.15
304	Brad Ausmus	.15
305	Alex Gonzalez	.15
306	Brian Jordan	.15
307	John Jaha	.15
308	Mark Grudzielanek	.15
309	Juan Guzman	.15
310	Tony Womack	.15
311	Dennis Reyes	.15
312	Marty Cordova	.15
313	Ramiro Mendoza	.15
314	Robin Ventura	.15
315	Rafael Palmeiro	.65
316	Ramon Martinez	.15
317	Pedro Astacio	.15
318	Dave Hollins	.15
319	Tom Candiotti	.15
320	Al Leiter	.15
321	Rico Brogna	.15
322	Reggie Jefferson	.15
323	Bernard Gilkey	.15
324	Jason Giambi	.40
325	Craig Biggio	.15
326	Troy Glaus	.75
327	Delino DeShields	.15
328	Fernando Vina	.15
329	John Smoltz	.15
330	Jeff Kent	.15
331	Roy Halladay	.15
332	Andy Ashby	.15
333	Tim Wakefield	.15
334	Roger Clemens	1.75
335	Bernie Williams	.15
336	Desi Relaford	.15
337	John Burkett	.15
338	Mike Hampton	.15
339	Royce Clayton	.15
340	Mike Piazza	2.00
341	Jeremi Gonzalez	.15
342	Mike Lansing	.15
343	Jamie Moyer	.15
344	Ron Coomer	.15
345	Barry Larkin	.15
346	Fernando Tatis	.15
347	Chili Davis	.15
348	Bobby Higginson	.15
349	Hal Morris	.15
350	Larry Walker	.15
351	Carlos Guillen	.15
352	Miguel Tejada	.30
353	Travis Fryman	.15
354	Jarrod Washburn	.15
355	Chipper Jones	1.50
356	Todd Stottlemyre	.15
357	Henry Rodriguez	.15
358	Eli Marrero	.15
359	Alan Benes	.15
360	Tim Salmon	.15
361	Luis Gonzalez	.15
362	Scott Spiezio	.15
363	Chris Carpenter	.15
364	Bobby Howry	.15
365	Raul Mondesi	.15
366	Ugueth Urbina	.15
367	Tom Evans	.15
368	Kerry Ligtenberg **RC**	.40
369	Adrian Beltre	.35
370	Ryan Klesko	.15
371	Wilson Alvarez	.15
372	John Thomson	.15
373	Tony Saunders	.15
374	Mike Stanley	.15
375	Ken Caminiti	.15
376	Jay Buhner	.15
377	Bill Mueller	.15
378	Jeff Blauser	.15
379	Edgar Renteria	.15
380	Jim Thome	.60
381	Joey Hamilton	.15
382	Calvin Pickering	.15
383	Marquis Grissom	.15
384	Omar Daal	.15
385	Curt Schilling	.35
386	Jose Cruz Jr.	.15
387	Chris Widger	.15
388	Pete Harnisch	.15
389	Charles Nagy	.15
390	Tom Gordon	.15
391	Bobby Smith	.15
392	Derrick Gibson	.15
393	Jeff Conine	.15
394	Carlos Perez	.15
395	Barry Bonds	3.00
396	Mark McLemore	.15
397	Juan Encarnacion	.15
398	Wade Boggs	1.50
399	Ivan Rodriguez	.75
400	Moises Alou	.15
401	Jeromy Burnitz	.15
402	Sean Casey	.25
403	Jose Offerman	.15
404	Joe Fontenot	.15
405	Kevin Millwood	.15
406	Lance Johnson	.15
407	Richard Hidalgo	.15
408	Mike Jackson	.15
409	Brian Anderson	.15
410	Jeff Shaw	.15
411	Preston Wilson	.15
412	Todd Hundley	.15
413	Jim Parque	.15
414	Justin Baughman	.15
415	Dante Bichette	.15
416	Paul O'Neill	.15
417	Miguel Cairo	.15
418	Randy Johnson	1.00
419	Jesus Sanchez	.15
420	Carlos Delgado	.35
421	Ricky Ledee	.15
422	Orlando Hernandez	.15
423	Frank Thomas	1.00
424	Pokey Reese	.15
425	Carlos Lee, Mike Lowell, Kit Pellow **RC** (Prospect)	.30
426	Michael Cuddyer, Mark DeRosa, Jerry Hairston Jr. **RC** (Prospect)	.60
427	Marlon Anderson, Ron Belliard, Orlando Cabrera (Prospect)	.45
428	Micah Bowie **RC**, Phil Norton **RC**, Randy Wolf (Prospect)	.35
429	Jack Cressend, Jason Rakers, John Rocker (Prospect)	.25
430	Ruben Mateo, Scott Morgan, Mike Zywica **RC** (Prospect)	.25
431	Jason LaRue, Matt LeCroy **RC**, Mitch Meluskey **RC** (Prospect)	.25
432	Gabe Kapler, Armando Rios **RC**, Fernando Seguignol (Prospect)	.25
433	Adam Kennedy, Mickey Lopez **RC**, Jackie Rexrode (Prospect)	.25
434	Jose Fernandez **RC**, Jeff Liefer, Chris Truby (Prospect)	.25
435	Corey Koskie, Doug Mientkiewicz **RC**, Damon Minor (Prospect)	.60
436	Roosevelt Brown **RC**, Dernell Stenson, Vernon Wells (Prospect)	.25
437	A.J. Burnett **RC**, John Nicholson, Billy Koch (Prospect)	.75
438	Matt Belisle **RC**, Matt Roney **RC** (Draft Pick)	.30
439	Austin Kearns **RC**, Chris George **RC** (Draft Pick)	3.00
440	Nate Bump **RC**, Nate Cornejo **RC** (Draft Pick)	.40
441	Brad Lidge **RC**, Mike Nannini **RC** (Draft Pick)	.60
442	Matt Holliday **RC**, Jeff Winchester **RC** (Draft Pick)	8.00
443	Adam Everett **RC**, Chip Ambres **RC** (Draft Pick)	.30
444	Pat Burrell **RC**, Eric Valent **RC** (Draft Pick)	3.00
445	Roger Clemens (Strikeout Kings)	.85
446	Kerry Wood (Strikeout Kings)	.20
447	Curt Schilling (Strikeout Kings)	.15
448	Randy Johnson (Strikeout Kings)	.50
449	Pedro Martinez (Strikeout Kings)	.50
450	Jeff Bagwell, Andres Galarraga, Mark McGwire (All-Topps)	1.25
451	John Olerud, Jim Thome, Tino Martinez (All-Topps)	.40
452	Alex Rodriguez, Nomar Garciaparra, Derek Jeter (All-Topps)	1.50
453	Vinny Castilla, Chipper Jones, Scott Rolen (All-Topps)	.75
454	Sammy Sosa, Ken Griffey Jr., Juan Gonzalez (All-Topps)	1.00
455	Barry Bonds, Manny Ramirez, Larry Walker (All-Topps)	1.50
456	Frank Thomas, Tim Salmon, David Justice (All-Topps)	.60
457	Travis Lee, Todd Helton, Ben Grieve (All-Topps)	.50
458	Vladimir Guerrero, Greg Vaughn, Bernie Williams (All-Topps)	.50
459	Mike Piazza, Ivan Rodriguez, Jason Kendall (All-Topps)	1.00

460	Roger Clemens, Kerry Wood, Greg Maddux (All-Topps)	1.00
461	Sammy Sosa #1 (Home Run Parade)	10.00
461	Sammy Sosa HR #2-60	6.00
461	S. Sosa HR #61-62	10.00
461	S. Sosa HR #63-65	7.50
461	S. Sosa HR #66	20.00
---	Checklist 1-100	.15
---	Checklist - inserts	.15

All-Etch

Inserted in Series 2 packs, All-Etch has three different styles of inserts. '99 Rookie Rush features rookies who have the best shot of winning '99 Rookie of the Year. Club 40 features 13 players who hit 40 homers or more in 1998, and Club K features seven pitchers known for their strikeout abilities. Each is inserted 1:6 packs, while Refractor versions are seeded 1:24 packs.

		NM/M
Complete Set (30):		15.00
Common Player:		.35
Inserted 1:6		
Refractors:		1.5X
Inserted 1:24		
1	Mark McGwire	3.00
2	Sammy Sosa	1.50
3	Ken Griffey Jr.	2.00
4	Greg Vaughn	.25
5	Albert Belle	.25
6	Vinny Castilla	.25
7	Jose Canseco	.50
8	Juan Gonzalez	.50
9	Manny Ramirez	1.00
10	Andres Galarraga	.25
11	Rafael Palmeiro	.75
12	Alex Rodriguez	3.00
13	Mo Vaughn	.25
14	Eric Chavez	.40
15	Gabe Kapler	.25
16	Calvin Pickering	.25
17	Ruben Mateo	.25
18	Roy Halladay	.40
19	Jeremy Giambi	.25
20	Alex Gonzalez	.25
21	Ron Belliard	.25
22	Marlon Anderson	.25
23	Carlos Lee	.25
24	Kerry Wood	.50
25	Roger Clemens	1.50
26	Curt Schilling	.50
27	Kevin Brown	.25
28	Randy Johnson	1.00
29	Pedro Martinez	1.00
30	Orlando Hernandez	.25

Early Road to the Hall

This insert set spotlights players with less than 10 years in the Majors but who are gunning towards their respective spots in Cooperstown. The cards feature chromium technology, with an insert rate of 1:12 packs. A Refractor parallel edition, numbered to 100 each, was a 1:944 hobby-only insert.

		NM/M
Complete Set (10):		12.00
Common Player:		.50
Inserted 1:12		
Refractors (#'d to 100):		6X
ER1	Nomar Garciaparra	1.50
ER2	Derek Jeter	3.00
ER3	Alex Rodriguez	2.50
ER4	Juan Gonzalez	.50
ER5	Ken Griffey Jr.	2.00
ER6	Chipper Jones	1.50
ER7	Vladimir Guerrero	1.00
ER8	Jeff Bagwell	1.00
ER9	Ivan Rodriguez	.75
ER10	Frank Thomas	1.00

Fortune 15

Fortune 15 showcases the baseball's best players and hot rookies. They are inserted in Series 2 packs at a rate of 1:12. A Refractor version also exists found exclusively in hobby packs at a rate of 1:627 packs. Refractors are sequentially numbered to 100.

		NM/M
Complete Set (15):		17.50
Common Player:		.50
Inserted 1:12		
Refractors (#'d to 100):		4X
1	Alex Rodriguez	2.25
2	Nomar Garciaparra	1.25
3	Derek Jeter	3.00
4	Troy Glaus	.75
5	Ken Griffey Jr.	1.50
6	Vladimir Guerrero	1.00
7	Kerry Wood	.65
8	Eric Chavez	.65
9	Greg Maddux	1.25
10	Mike Piazza	1.50
11	Sammy Sosa	1.25
12	Mark McGwire	2.25
13	Ben Grieve	.50
14	Chipper Jones	1.25
15	Manny Ramirez	1.00

Home Run Heroes

These cards were part of an unannounced multi-manufacturer (Fleer, Upper Deck, Topps, Pacific) insert program exclusive to Wal-Mart. Each company produced cards of Mark McGwire and Sammy Sosa, along with two other premier sluggers. Each company's cards share a "Power Elite" logo at top and "Home Run Heroes" logo vertically at right.

		NM/M
Complete Set (4):		5.00
Common Player:		1.00
9	Mark McGwire	2.00
10	Sammy Sosa	1.50
11	Alex Rodriguez	2.00
12	Vladimir Guerrero	1.00

Lords of the Diamond

Parallel to the Topps version, this insert set features die-cutting across the card top and is seeded 1:8 in Series 1 packs. Refractor versions can be found 1:24 packs.

		NM/M
Complete Set (15):		20.00
Common Player:		.40
Inserted 1:8		
Refractors:		2X
Inserted 1:24		
LD1	Ken Griffey Jr.	2.00
LD2	Chipper Jones	1.50
LD3	Sammy Sosa	1.50
LD4	Frank Thomas	1.25
LD5	Mark McGwire	2.50
LD6	Jeff Bagwell	1.25
LD7	Alex Rodriguez	2.25
LD8	Juan Gonzalez	.65
LD9	Barry Bonds	3.00
LD10	Nomar Garciaparra	1.50
LD11	Darin Erstad	.50
LD12	Tony Gwynn	1.50
LD13	Andres Galarraga	.40
LD14	Mike Piazza	2.00
LD15	Greg Maddux	1.50

New Breed

A parallel version utilizing chromium technology, this insert set features the top young stars in the game and is seeded 1:24 packs. A Refractor version also exists, found 1:72 packs.

		NM/M
Complete Set (15):		30.00
Common Player:		.50
Inserted 1:24		
Refractors:		1.5X
Inserted 1:72		
NB1	Darin Erstad	.75
NB2	Brad Fullmer	.50
NB3	Kerry Wood	.75
NB4	Nomar Garciaparra	5.00
NB5	Travis Lee	.65
NB6	Scott Rolen	2.00
NB7	Todd Helton	3.00
NB8	Vladimir Guerrero	3.00
NB9	Derek Jeter	7.50
NB10	Alex Rodriguez	6.00
NB11	Ben Grieve	.50
NB12	Andruw Jones	3.00
NB13	Paul Konerko	.75
NB14	Aramis Ramirez	.50
NB15	Adrian Beltre	.75

Record Numbers

This insert set salutes nine record-setters who have earned a mark of distinction, including Cal Ripken Jr. for his record setting consecutive game streak. Inserted randomly in Series 2 packs at a rate of 1:36 packs. Refractor parallel versions are seeded 1:144 packs.

		NM/M
Complete Set (10):		20.00
Common Player:		.50
Inserted 1:36		
Refractors:		1.5X
Inserted 1:144		
1	Mark McGwire	3.00
2	Craig Biggio	.50
3	Barry Bonds	4.00
4	Ken Griffey Jr.	2.50
5	Sammy Sosa	2.00
6	Alex Rodriguez	3.00
7	Kerry Wood	1.00
8	Roger Clemens	2.00
9	Cal Ripken Jr.	4.00
10	Mark McGwire	3.00

Traded and Rookies

Actually issued in 2000, this parallel of the Topps Traded set utilizing Chromium technology was issued only in complete set form.

		NM/M
Complete Set (121):		60.00
Common Player:		.15
1	Seth Etherton	.15
2	Mark Harriger **RC**	.25
3	Matt Wise **RC**	.50
4	Carlos Hernandez **RC**	.50
5	Julio Lugo **RC**	1.50
6	Mike Nannini	.15
7	Justin Bowles **RC**	.25
8	Mark Mulder **RC**	3.00
9	Roberto Vaz **RC**	.15
10	Felipe Lopez **RC**	3.00
11	Matt Belisle	.15
12	Micah Bowie	.15
13	Ruben Quevedo **RC**	.25
14	Jose Garcia **RC**	.15
15	David Kelton **RC**	1.00
16	Phillip Norton	.15
17	Corey Patterson **RC**	2.50
18	Ron Walker **RC**	.15
19	Paul Hoover **RC**	.15
20	Ryan Rupe **RC**	.25
21	J.D. Closser **RC**	.15
22	Rob Ryan **RC**	.15
23	Steve Colyer **RC**	.15
24	Bubba Crosby **RC**	1.00
25	Luke Prokopec **RC**	.15
26	Matt Blank **RC**	.15
27	Josh McKinley	.15
28	Nate Bump	.15
29	Giuseppe Chiaramonte **RC**	.15
30	Arturo McDowell	.15
31	Tony Torcato	.15
32	Dave Roberts	.15
33	C.C. Sabathia **RC**	4.00
34	Sean Spencer **RC**	.15
35	Chip Ambres	.15
36	A.J. Burnett	.50
37	Mo Bruce **RC**	.15
38	Jason Tyner	.15
39	Mamon Tucker	.15
40	Sean Burroughs **RC**	.75
41	Kevin Eberwein **RC**	.15
42	Junior Herndon **RC**	.25
43	Bryan Wolff **RC**	.15
44	Pat Burrell	1.00
45	Eric Valent	.15
46	Carlos Pena **RC**	3.00
47	Mike Zywica	.15
48	Adam Everett	.15
49	Juan Pena **RC**	.75
50	Adam Dunn **RC**	10.00
51	Austin Kearns	2.00
52	Jacobo Sequea **RC**	.15
53	Choo Freeman	.50
54	Jeff Winchester	.15
55	Matt Burch	.15
56	Chris George	.25
57	Scott Mullen **RC**	.15
58	Kit Pellow	.15
59	Mark Quinn **RC**	.75
60	Nate Cornejo	.15
61	Ryan Mills **RC**	.15
62	Kevin Beirne **RC**	.15
63	Kip Wells **RC**	.75
64	Juan Rivera **RC**	1.00
65	Alfonso Soriano **RC**	10.00
66	Josh Hamilton **RC**	12.00
67	Josh Girdley **RC**	.15
68	Kyle Snyder **RC**	.25
69	Mike Paradis **RC**	.25
70	Jason Jennings **RC**	.25
71	David Walling **RC**	.25
72	Omar Ortiz **RC**	.15
73	Jay Gehrke **RC**	.15
74	Casey Burns **RC**	.15
75	Carl Crawford **RC**	8.00
76	Reggie Sanders	.15
77	Will Clark	.15
78	David Wells	.15
79	Paul Konerko	.30
80	Armando Benitez	.15
81	Brant Brown	.15
82	Mo Vaughn	.15
83	Jose Canseco	.75
84	Albert Belle	.15
85	Dean Palmer	.15
86	Greg Vaughn	.15
87	Mark Clark	.15
88	Pat Meares	.15
89	Eric Davis	.15
90	Brian Giles	.15
91	Jeff Brantley	.15
92	Bret Boone	.15
93	Ron Gant	.15
94	Mike Cameron	.15
95	Charles Johnson	.15
96	Denny Neagle	.15
97	Brian Hunter	.15
98	Jose Hernandez	.15
99	Rick Aguilera	.15
100	Tony Batista	.15
101	Roger Cedeno	.15
102	Creighton Gubanich	.15
103	Tim Belcher	.15
104	Bruce Aven	.15
105	Brian Daubach **RC**	.75
106	Ed Sprague	.15
107	Michael Tucker	.15
108	Homer Bush	.15
109	Armando Reynoso	.15
110	Brook Fordyce	.15
111	Matt Mantei	.15
112	Jose Guillen	.15
113	Kenny Rogers	.15
114	Livan Hernandez	.15
115	Butch Huskey	.15
116	David Segui	.15
117	Darryl Hamilton	.15
118	Jim Leyritz	.15
119	Randy Velarde	.15
120	Bill Taylor	.15
121	Kevin Appier	.15

Super Chrome

Using identical photos from Topps Chrome Baseball, Topps supersized 36 players to 4-1/8" x 5-3/4" card size. The cards are done on standard chromium technology. Each pack contains three oversized cards and sells for S.R.P. of $4.99. There also is a Refractor parallel set, which are seeded 1:12 packs.

		NM/M
Complete Set (36):		45.00
Common Player:		.50
Refractors:		2X
Inserted 1:12		
Pack (3):		4.50
Wax Box (12):		48.00
1	Roger Clemens	2.25
2	Andres Galarraga	.50
3	Manny Ramirez	1.50
4	Greg Maddux	2.00
5	Kerry Wood	.75
6	Travis Lee	.75
7	Nolan Ryan	4.50
8	Juan Gonzalez	.75
9	Vladimir Guerrero	1.50
10	Sammy Sosa	2.00
11	Mark McGwire	3.00
12	Javy Lopez	.50
13	Tony Gwynn	2.00
14	Derek Jeter	4.50
15	Albert Belle	.50
16	Pedro Martinez	1.50
17	Greg Vaughn	.50
18	Ken Griffey Jr.	2.50
19	Ben Grieve	.50
20	Vinny Castilla	.50
21	Moises Alou	.50
22	Barry Bonds	4.50
23	Nomar Garciaparra	2.00
24	Chipper Jones	2.00
25	Mike Piazza	2.50
26	Alex Rodriguez	3.00
27	Ivan Rodriguez	1.25
28	Frank Thomas	1.50
29	Larry Walker	.50
30	Troy Glaus	1.00
31	David Wells (Season Highlight)	.50
32	Roger Clemens (Season Highlight)	1.00
33	Kerry Wood (Season Highlight)	.50
34	Mark McGwire (Home Run Record)	3.00
35	Sammy Sosa (Home Run Parade)	2.00
36	World Series	.50

1999 Topps Gallery Pre-Production

Topps debuted its 1999 Gallery set with this trio of sample cards. Format is virtually identical to issued cards except for the use of a "PP" prefix to the card numbers on back.

		NM/M
Complete Set (3):		5.00
Common Player:		2.00
PP1	Scott Rolen	2.00
PP2	Andres Galarraga (Masters)	2.00
PP3	Brad Fullmer (Artisans)	2.00

1999 Topps Gallery

This 150-card base set features a white textured border surrounding the player image with the player's name, team name and Topps Gallery logo stamped in gold foil. The first 100 cards in the set portray veteran players while the final 50 cards are short-printed in three subsets: Masters, Artisans and Apprentices. Card backs have a monthly batting or pitching record from the '98 season, a player photo and vital information.

		NM/M
Complete Set (150):		60.00
Common Player (1-100):		.10
Common Player (101-150):		.25
Player's Private Issue:		5X
PPI SP's:		3X
Production 250 Sets		
Pack (6):		3.00
Wax Box (24):		45.00
1	Mark McGwire	1.50
2	Jim Thome	.35
3	Bernie Williams	.10
4	Larry Walker	.10
5	Juan Gonzalez	.30
6	Ken Griffey Jr.	1.00
7	Raul Mondesi	.10
8	Sammy Sosa	.75
9	Greg Maddux	.75
10	Jeff Bagwell	.60
11	Vladimir Guerrero	.60
12	Scott Rolen	.50
13	Nomar Garciaparra	.75
14	Mike Piazza	1.00
15	Travis Lee	.15
16	Carlos Delgado	.35
17	Darin Erstad	.25
18	David Justice	.10
19	Cal Ripken Jr.	2.00
20	Derek Jeter	2.00
21	Tony Clark	.10
22	Barry Larkin	.10
23	Greg Vaughn	.10
24	Jeff Kent	.10
25	Wade Boggs	.75
26	Andres Galarraga	.10
27	Ken Caminiti	.10
28	Jason Kendall	.10
29	Todd Helton	.60
30	Chuck Knoblauch	.10
31	Roger Clemens	.85
32	Jeromy Burnitz	.10
33	Javy Lopez	.10
34	Roberto Alomar	.25
35	Eric Karros	.10
36	Ben Grieve	.10
37	Eric Davis	.10
38	Rondell White	.10
39	Dmitri Young	.10
40	Ivan Rodriguez	.50
41	Paul O'Neill	.10
42	Jeff Cirillo	.10
43	Kerry Wood	.30
44	Albert Belle	.10
45	Frank Thomas	.60
46	Manny Ramirez	.60
47	Tom Glavine	.25
48	Mo Vaughn	.10
49	Jose Cruz Jr.	.10
50	Sandy Alomar	.10
51	Edgar Martinez	.10
52	John Olerud	.10
53	Todd Walker	.10
54	Tim Salmon	.10
55	Derek Bell	.10
56	Matt Williams	.10
57	Alex Rodriguez	1.50
58	Rusty Greer	.10
59	Vinny Castilla	.10
60	Jason Giambi	.30
61	Mark Grace	.10
62	Jose Canseco	.40
63	Gary Sheffield	.40
64	Brad Fullmer	.10
65	Trevor Hoffman	.10
66	Mark Kotsay	.10
67	Mike Mussina	.25
68	Johnny Damon	.30
69	Tino Martinez	.10
70	Curt Schilling	.25
71	Jay Buhner	.10
72	Kenny Lofton	.10
73	Randy Johnson	.60
74	Kevin Brown	.10
75	Brian Jordan	.10
76	Craig Biggio	.10
77	Barry Bonds	2.00
78	Tony Gwynn	.75
79	Jim Edmonds	.10
80	Shawn Green	.35
81	Todd Hundley	.10
82	Cliff Floyd	.10
83	Jose Guillen	.10
84	Dante Bichette	.10
85	Moises Alou	.10
86	Chipper Jones	.75
87	Ray Lankford	.10
88	Fred McGriff	.10
89	Rod Beck	.10
90	Dean Palmer	.10
91	Pedro Martinez	.60
92	Andruw Jones	.60
93	Robin Ventura	.10
94	Ugueth Urbina	.10
95	Orlando Hernandez	.10
96	Sean Casey	.15
97	Denny Neagle	.10
98	Troy Glaus	.60
99	John Smoltz	.10
100	Al Leiter	.10
101	Ken Griffey Jr.	1.50
102	Frank Thomas	.75
103	Mark McGwire	2.00
104	Sammy Sosa	1.00
105	Chipper Jones	1.00
106	Alex Rodriguez	2.00
107	Nomar Garciaparra	1.00
108	Juan Gonzalez	.40
109	Derek Jeter	3.00
110	Mike Piazza	1.50
111	Barry Bonds	3.00
112	Tony Gwynn	1.00
113	Cal Ripken Jr.	3.00
114	Greg Maddux	1.00
115	Roger Clemens	1.25
116	Brad Fullmer	.25
117	Kerry Wood	.50
118	Ben Grieve	.25
119	Todd Helton	.65
120	Kevin Millwood	.25
121	Sean Casey	.35
122	Vladimir Guerrero	.75
123	Travis Lee	.25
124	Troy Glaus	.65
125	Bartolo Colon	.25
126	Andruw Jones	.75
127	Scott Rolen	.60
128	Alfonso Soriano **RC**	4.00
129	Nick Johnson **RC**	1.00
130	Matt Belisle **RC**	.25
131	Jorge Toca **RC**	.25
132	Masao Kida **RC**	.25
133	Carlos Pena **RC**	1.50
134	Adrian Beltre	.40
135	Eric Chavez	.40
136	Carlos Beltran	.65
137	Alex Gonzalez	.25
138	Ryan Anderson	.25
139	Ruben Mateo	.25
140	Bruce Chen	.25
141	Pat Burrell **RC**	3.00
142	Michael Barrett	.25
143	Carlos Lee	.25
144	Mark Mulder **RC**	1.00
145	Choo Freeman **RC**	.50
146	Gabe Kapler	.25
147	Juan Encarnacion	.25
148	Jeremy Giambi	.25
149	Jason Tyner **RC**	.35
150	George Lombard	.25
		.10
	Checklist Folder 1 (1:3 Packs)	.10
	Checklist Folder 2 (1:3)	.10
	Checklist Folder 3 (1:3)	.10
	Checklist Folder 4 (1:12)	.25
	Checklist Folder 5 (1:240)	1.50
	Checklist Folder 6 (1:640)	3.00

Player's Private Issue

This parallel to the 150 regular cards in 1999 Gallery is limited to 250 serially numbered cards of each. Stated odds of insertion were one per 17 packs.

	NM/M
Common Player:	1.00
Stars:	5X
SP's:	3X
Production 250 Sets	

Autograph Cards

Three of baseball's top young third basemen are featured in this autographed set. The insertion odds are 1:209.

		NM/M
Common Player:		10.00
Inserted 1:209		
GA1	Troy Glaus	15.00
GA2	Adrian Beltre	10.00
GA3	Eric Chavez	10.00

Awards Gallery

This 10-card set features players who have earned the highest honors in baseball. Each insert commemorates the player's award by stamping his achievement on the bottom of the card front. Card fronts have silver borders surrounding the player's image. These are seeded 1:12 and card numbers have a "AG" prefix.

		NM/M
Complete Set (10):		12.50
Common Player:		.50
Inserted 1:12		
AG1	Kerry Wood	.75
AG2	Ben Grieve	.50
AG3	Roger Clemens	2.50
AG4	Tom Glavine	.75
AG5	Juan Gonzalez	.75
AG6	Sammy Sosa	3.00
AG7	Ken Griffey Jr.	3.00
AG8	Mark McGwire	4.00
AG9	Bernie Williams	.50
AG10	Larry Walker	.50

Exhibitions

This 20-card set is done on textured 24-point stock and features baseball's top stars. Exhibitions are seeded 1:48 packs.

		NM/M
Complete Set (20):		75.00
Common Player:		2.00
Inserted 1:48		
E1	Sammy Sosa	4.50
E2	Mark McGwire	7.50
E3	Greg Maddux	4.50
E4	Roger Clemens	5.00
E5	Ben Grieve	2.00
E6	Kerry Wood	2.25
E7	Ken Griffey Jr.	6.00
E8	Tony Gwynn	4.50
E9	Cal Ripken Jr.	10.00
E10	Frank Thomas	4.00
E11	Jeff Bagwell	4.00
E12	Derek Jeter	10.00
E13	Alex Rodriguez	7.50
E14	Nomar Garciaparra	4.50
E15	Manny Ramirez	4.00
E16	Vladimir Guerrero	4.00
E17	Darin Erstad	2.25
E18	Scott Rolen	3.00
E19	Mike Piazza	6.00
E20	Andres Galarraga	2.00

Gallery of Heroes

This 10-card set is done on card stock that simulates medieval stained glass. Gallery of Heroes are found 1:24 packs.

		NM/M
Complete Set (10):		30.00
Common Player:		.75
Inserted 1:24		
GH1	Mark McGwire	6.00
GH2	Sammy Sosa	3.50
GH3	Ken Griffey Jr.	4.50
GH4	Mike Piazza	4.50
GH5	Derek Jeter	7.50
GH6	Nomar Garciaparra	4.50
GH7	Kerry Wood	1.50
GH8	Ben Grieve	.75
GH9	Chipper Jones	3.50
GH10	Alex Rodriguez	6.00

Heritage

Nineteen contemporary legends and Hall-of-Famer Hank Aaron are artistically depicted using the 1953 Topps design as a template. For a chance to bid on the original art used in the development of this insert set, collectors were able to enter the Topps Gallery Auction. Collectors could accumulate auction points found in Topps Gallery packs. Heritages are seeded 1:12 packs. A parallel called Heritage Proofs are also randomly inserted 1:48 packs and have a chrome styrene finish.

		NM/M
Complete Set (20):		100.00
Common Player:		2.50
Inserted 1:12		
Heritage Proofs:		1.5X
Inserted 1:48		
TH1	Hank Aaron	10.00
TH2	Ben Grieve	2.50
TH3	Nomar Garciaparra	7.50
TH4	Roger Clemens	8.50
TH5	Travis Lee	2.50
TH6	Tony Gwynn	7.50
TH7	Alex Rodriguez	12.50
TH8	Ken Griffey Jr.	10.00
TH9	Derek Jeter	15.00
TH10	Sammy Sosa	7.50
TH11	Scott Rolen	2.50
TH12	Chipper Jones	7.50
TH13	Cal Ripken Jr.	15.00
TH14	Kerry Wood	3.00
TH15	Barry Bonds	15.00
TH16	Juan Gonzalez	3.00
TH17	Mike Piazza	10.00
TH18	Greg Maddux	7.50
TH19	Frank Thomas	6.00
TH20	Mark McGwire	12.50

Heritage Proofs

Heritage Proofs are a parallel to the 1953-style inserts. Printed on chrome styrene, the proofs have a silver metallic background on front and the notation on bottom-back, "1953 TOPPS HERITAGE PROOF." The proof versions are found on average of one per 48 packs.

		NM/M
Complete Set (20):		175.00
Common Player:		3.00
TH1	Hank Aaron	15.00
TH2	Ben Grieve	3.00
TH3	Nomar Garciaparra	10.00
TH4	Roger Clemens	11.50
TH5	Travis Lee	3.00
TH6	Tony Gwynn	10.00
TH7	Alex Rodriguez	15.00
TH8	Ken Griffey Jr.	12.50
TH9	Derek Jeter	20.00
TH10	Sammy Sosa	12.50
TH11	Scott Rolen	5.00
TH12	Chipper Jones	10.00
TH13	Cal Ripken Jr.	20.00
TH14	Kerry Wood	4.00
TH15	Barry Bonds	20.00
TH16	Juan Gonzalez	7.50
TH17	Mike Piazza	12.50
TH18	Greg Maddux	10.00
TH19	Frank Thomas	7.50
TH20	Mark McGwire	15.00

Heritage Lithographs

Eight of the paintings used to create the Heritage inserts for 1999 Topps Gallery were reproduced as enlarged limited-edition offset lithographs. The paintings of Bill Purdom and James Fiorentino were reproduced in an 18" x 25" serially-numbered, artist-signed edition of 600 pieces each. The lithos were offered through Bill Goff Inc / Good Sports at $60 each unframed.

		NM/M
Complete Set (8):		400.00
Single Player:		60.00
(1)	Roger Clemens	60.00
(2)	Nomar Garciaparra	60.00
(3)	Ken Griffey Jr.	60.00
(4)	Derek Jeter	60.00
(5)	Mark McGwire	60.00
(6)	Mike Piazza	60.00
(7)	Cal Ripken Jr.	60.00
(8)	Sammy Sosa	60.00

Heritage Super Promos

Actually issued as a Topps handout at the 2000 National Sports Collectors Convention Corporate Block Party, this set depicts eight of the 1953 Topps-style cards which had been created for the Gallery Heritage insert series in 1999. The super-size (3-3/4" x 5-1/8") promos are printed on thin, glossy stock. Fronts have card-style artwork by Bill Goff or Bill Purdom. Backs are in black-and-white with player information and advertising by the artists, along with MLB and MLBPA licensor logos. The unnumbered cards are checklisted here alphabetically.

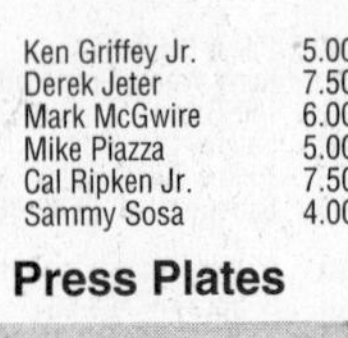

		NM/M
Complete Set (8):		40.00
Common Player:		4.00
(1)	Roger Clemens	4.50
(2)	Nomar Garciaparra	4.00
(3)	Ken Griffey Jr.	5.00
(4)	Derek Jeter	7.50
(5)	Mark McGwire	6.00
(6)	Mike Piazza	5.00
(7)	Cal Ripken Jr.	7.50
(8)	Sammy Sosa	4.00

Press Plates

The aluminum press plates used to print the Gallery cards were inserted at a rate of one per 985 packs. Each card's front and back can be found in four different color variations. Because of the unique nature of each plate, assignment of catalog values is not feasible.

	NM/M
Common Player:	25.00

1999 Topps Gold Label Pre-Production

This trio of pre-production samples previews Topps' 1999 version of its high-end Gold Label brand. Cards are nearly identical in format to the issued version except for the "PP" prefix to card numbers on back

		NM/M
Complete Set (3):		3.00
Common Player:		1.00
PP1	Tom Glavine	1.00
PP2	Tino Martinez	1.00
PP3	Jim Thome	2.00

1999 Topps Gold Label Class 1

This set consists of 100 cards on 35-point spectral-reflective rainbow stock with gold foil stamping. All cards are available in three versions each with the same foreground photo, but with different background photos that vary by category: Class 1

(fielding), Class 2 (running, 1:2), Class 3 (hitting, 1:4). In addition each variation has a different version of the player's team logo in the background. Variations for pitchers are Class 1, set position; Class 2, wind-up, and Class 3, throwing. Black Label parallels were inserted at the rate of between 1:8 and 1:12, depending on packaging. Red Label parallels, serially numbered to 100 each were inserted at rates from 1:118 to 1:148. A One to One parallel version also exists and is limited to one numbered card for each variation and color (Gold, Black and Red), for a total of 900 cards inserted about one per 1,500 packs.

		NM/M
Complete Set (100):		30.00
Common Gold Label:		.10
Common Black Label:		.50
Black Label Stars:		3X
Common Red Label:		2.00
Red Label Stars:		12X
Pack (5):		3.00
Wax Box (24):		50.00
1	Mike Piazza	2.00
2	Andres Galarraga	.10
3	Mark Grace	.10
4	Tony Clark	.10
5	Jim Thome	.60
6	Tony Gwynn	1.50
7	Kelly Dransfeldt **RC**	.15
8	Eric Chavez	.25
9	Brian Jordan	.10
10	Todd Hundley	.10
11	Rondell White	.10
12	Dmitri Young	.10
13	Jeff Kent	.10
14	Derek Bell	.10
15	Todd Helton	.75
16	Chipper Jones	1.50
17	Albert Belle	.10
18	Barry Larkin	.10
19	Dante Bichette	.10
20	Gary Sheffield	.50
21	Cliff Floyd	.10
22	Derek Jeter	3.00
23	Jason Giambi	.50
24	Ray Lankford	.10
25	Alex Rodriguez	2.50
26	Ruben Mateo	.10
27	Wade Boggs	1.50
28	Carlos Delgado	.45
29	Tim Salmon	.10
30	Alfonso Soriano **RC**	5.00
31	Javy Lopez	.10
32	Jason Kendall	.10
33	Nick Johnson **RC**	1.00
34	A.J. Burnett **RC**	1.00
35	Troy Glaus	.75
36	Pat Burrell **RC**	3.00
37	Jeff Cirillo	.10
38	David Justice	.10
39	Ivan Rodriguez	.75
40	Bernie Williams	.10
41	Jay Buhner	.10
42	Mo Vaughn	.10
43	Randy Johnson	1.00
44	Pedro Martinez	1.00
45	Larry Walker	.10
46	Todd Walker	.10
47	Roberto Alomar	.25
48	Kevin Brown	.10
49	Mike Mussina	.40
50	Tom Glavine	.25
51	Curt Schilling	.25
52	Ken Caminiti	.10
53	Brad Fullmer	.10
54	Bobby Seay **RC**	.10
55	Orlando Hernandez	.10
56	Sean Casey	.10
57	Al Leiter	.10
58	Sandy Alomar	.10
59	Mark Kotsay	.10
60	Matt Williams	.10
61	Raul Mondesi	.10
62	Joe Crede **RC**	5.00
63	Jim Edmonds	.10
64	Jose Cruz Jr.	.10
65	Juan Gonzalez	.50
66	Sammy Sosa	1.50
67	Cal Ripken Jr.	3.00
68	Vinny Castilla	.10
69	Craig Biggio	.10
70	Mark McGwire	2.50
71	Greg Vaughn	.10
72	Greg Maddux	1.50
73	Paul O'Neill	.10
74	Scott Rolen	.65
75	Ben Grieve	.10
76	Vladimir Guerrero	1.00
77	John Olerud	.10
78	Eric Karros	.10
79	Jeromy Burnitz	.10
80	Jeff Bagwell	1.00
81	Kenny Lofton	.10
82	Manny Ramirez	1.00
83	Andruw Jones	1.00
84	Travis Lee	.15
85	Darin Erstad	.25
86	Nomar Garciaparra	1.50
87	Frank Thomas	1.00
88	Moises Alou	.10
89	Tino Martinez	.10
90	Carlos Pena **RC**	1.50
91	Shawn Green	.40
92	Rusty Greer	.10
93	Matt Belisle **RC**	.25
94	Adrian Beltre	.25
95	Roger Clemens	1.75
96	John Smoltz	.10
97	Mark Mulder **RC**	1.00
98	Kerry Wood	.50
99	Barry Bonds	3.00
100	Ken Griffey Jr.	2.00
	Checklist folder	.05

Class 2

Background photos for Class 2 Gold Label and color parallels show position players running and pitchers in their windup. Class 2 Gold Label cards are inserted at the rate of one in two Home Team Advantage packs, and one in four retail packs. Black Label versions are inserted 1:16 HTA and 1:24 R. Red Labels, numbered to 50 each, are found in HTA at a 1:237 rate, and in retail at 1:296.

	NM/M
Complete Set (100):	75.00
Common Gold Label:	.25
Gold Label Stars:	1.5X
Common Black Label:	2.00
Black Label Stars:	4X
Common Red Label:	6.00
Red Label Stars:	15X

Class 3

Background photos for Class 3 Gold Label and color parallels show position players hitting and pitchers pitching. Class 3 Gold Label cards are inserted at the rate of one in four Home Team Advantage packs, and one in eight retail packs. Black Label versions are inserted 1:32 HTA and 1:48 R. Red Labels, numbered to 25 each, are found in HTA at a 1:473 rate, and in retail at 1:591.

	NM/M
Complete Set (100):	125.00
Common Gold Label:	.50
Gold Label Stars: 2	
Common Black Label:	3.00
Black Label Stars:	6X
Common Red Label:	12.00
Red Label Stars:	35X

One to One

Depending on type of packaging, these rare parallels are found at the rate of only

one per approximately 1,200-1,600 packs. Each of the three Classes in Gold, Red and Black versions can be found as a One to One insert, for a total of nine "unique" cards for each player in the base set and three in the Race to Aaron insert series. Backs of the One to One cards are printed in silver foil with a "1/1" foil serial number.

	NM/M
Common Player, Base Set:	50.00
Common Player, Race to Aaron:	150.00

Race to Aaron

This 10-card set features the best current players who are chasing Hank Aaron's career home run and career RBI records. Each player is pictured in the foreground with Aaron silhouetted in the background on the card front. These are seeded 1:12 packs. Two parallel versions also exist: Black and Red. Blacks have black foil stamping and are seeded 1:48 packs. Reds have red foil stamping and are limited to 44 sequentially numbered sets.

		NM/M
Complete Set (10):		20.00
Common Player:		1.00
Blacks:		2X
Reds:		12X
1	Mark McGwire	4.50
2	Ken Griffey Jr.	3.00
3	Alex Rodriguez	4.50
4	Vladimir Guerrero	1.50
5	Albert Belle	1.00
6	Nomar Garciaparra	2.50
7	Ken Griffey Jr.	3.00
8	Alex Rodriguez	4.50
9	Juan Gonzalez	1.00
10	Barry Bonds	7.50

Name Mismatches

Because of faulty alignment when the gold-foil logo and player name were applied to card fronts, some Gold Label cards are found with the wrong name on front. Because each of these error cards is rare or possibly unique, and the demand is dependent on the combination of photo and name, it is not possible to assign values.

Opening Day

This retail exclusive product is comprised of 165 cards. Base cards have a silver border, and the Opening Day logo stamped with silver foil. Packs are pre-priced at $.99, each pack has seven cards. Hank Aaron autographs are randomly seeded and are stamped with the Topps "Certified Autograph Issue" stamp. The insertion rate for the autograph is 1:29,642 packs.

		NM/M
Complete Set (165):		20.00
Common Player:		.10
Hank Aaron Autograph:		150.00
Pack (7):		1.50
Wax Box (24):		20.00
1	Hank Aaron	3.00
2a	Roger Clemens	1.25
2b	Andres Galarraga (should be #3)	.10
4	Scott Brosius	.10
5	Ray Durham	.10
6	Will Clark	.10
7	David Wells	.10
8	Jose Guillen	.10
9	Edgardo Alfonzo	.10
10	Manny Ramirez	.75
11	Greg Maddux	1.00
12	David Segui	.10
13	Darryl Strawberry	.10
14	Brad Radke	.10
15	Kerry Wood	.35
16	Paul Konerko	.30
17	Travis Lee	.25
18	Kenny Rogers	.10
19	Todd Walker	.10
20	John Olerud	.10
21	Nolan Ryan	2.00
22	Ray Lankford	.10
23	Bartolo Colon	.10
24	Brady Anderson	.10
25	Jorge Posada	.10
26	Justin Thompson	.10
27	Juan Gonzalez	.40
28	Chuck Knoblauch	.10
29	Todd Helton	.65
30	Gary Sheffield	.40
31	Rod Beck	.10
32	Garret Anderson	.10
33	Rondell White	.10
34	Vladimir Guerrero	.75
35	Eric Karros	.10
36	Mo Vaughn	.10
37	Sammy Sosa	1.00
38	Kenny Lofton	.10
39	Mark McGwire	2.00
40	Javy Lopez	.10
41	Damion Easley	.10
42	Andy Pettitte	.30
43	Tony Gwynn	1.00
44	Jay Bell	.10
45	Jose Canseco	.45
46	John Wetteland	.10
47	Mike Caruso	.10
48	Derek Jeter	3.00
49	Aaron Sele	.10
50	Jeff Cirillo	.10
51	Mark Kotsay	.10
52	Albert Belle	.10
53	Matt Lawton	.10
54	Pedro Martinez	.75
55	Greg Vaughn	.10
56	Neifi Perez	.10
57	Derek Bell	.10
58	Ken Griffey Jr.	1.50
59	David Cone	.10
60	Dean Palmer	.10
61	Trevor Hoffman	.10
62	Billy Wagner	.10
63	Shawn Green	.25
64	Ben Grieve	.10
65	Tom Goodwin	.10
66	Jaret Wright	.10
67	Dmitri Young	.10
68	Hideki Irabu	.10
69	Jeff Fassero	.10
70	Matt Williams	.10
71	Bret Saberhagen	.10
72	Chad Curtis	.10
73	Scott Rolen	.60
74	J.T. Snow Jr.	.10
75	Rusty Greer	.10
76	Jim Edmonds	.10
77	Ron Gant	.10
78	A.J. Hinch	.10
79	Shannon Stewart	.10
80	Brad Fullmer	.10
81	Walt Weiss	.10
82	Fred McGriff	.10
83	Darin Erstad	.25
84	Eric Young	.10
85	Livan Hernandez	.10
86	Jeff Bagwell	.75
87	Omar Vizquel	.10
88	Eric Davis	.10
89	Magglio Ordonez	.25
90	John Valentin	.10
91	Dave Dellucci	.10
92	Chan Ho Park	.10
93	Masato Yoshii	.10
94	Bret Boone	.10
95	Mariano Rivera	.20
96	Bobby Jones	.10
97	Francisco Cordova	.10
98	Mike Mussina	.40
99	Denny Neagle	.10
100	Edgar Martinez	.10
101	Jason Kendall	.10
102	Jeff King	.10
103	Rey Ordonez	.10
104	Andruw Jones	.75
105	Vinny Castilla	.10
106	Troy Glaus	.65
107	Tom Glavine	.40
108	Moises Alou	.10
109	Carlos Delgado	.40
110	Raul Mondesi	.10
111	Shane Reynolds	.10
112	Jason Giambi	.60
113	Jose Cruz Jr.	.10
114	Craig Biggio	.10
115	Tim Salmon	.10
116	Chipper Jones	1.00
117	Andy Benes	.10
118	John Smoltz	.10
119	Jeromy Burnitz	.10
120	Randy Johnson	.75
121	Mark Grace	.10
122	Henry Rodriguez	.10
123	Ryan Klesko	.10
124	Kevin Millwood	.10
125	Sean Casey	.20
126	Brian Jordan	.10
127	Kevin Brown	.10
128	Orlando Hernandez	.10
129	Barry Bonds	3.00
130	David Justice	.10
131	Carlos Perez	.10
132	Andy Ashby	.10
133	Paul O'Neill	.10
134	Curt Schilling	.40
135	Alex Rodriguez	2.00
136	Cliff Floyd	.10
137	Rafael Palmeiro	.60
138	Nomar Garciaparra	1.00
139	Mike Piazza	1.50
140	Roberto Alomar	.30
141	Todd Hundley	.10
142	Jeff Kent	.10
143	Barry Larkin	.10
144	Cal Ripken Jr.	3.00
145	Jay Buhner	.10
146	Kevin Young	.10
147	Ivan Rodriguez	.65
148	Al Leiter	.10
149	Sandy Alomar	.10
150	Bernie Williams	.10
151	Ellis Burks	.10
152	Wally Joyner	.10
153	Bobby Higginson	.10
154	Tony Clark	.10
155	Larry Walker	.10
156	Frank Thomas	.75
157	Tino Martinez	.10
158	Jim Thome	.60
159	Dante Bichette	.10
160	David Wells (Season Highlights)	.10
161	Roger Clemens (Season Highlights)	.50
162	Kerry Wood (Season Highlights)	.15
163	Mark McGwire (HR Record #70)	4.00
164	Sammy Sosa (HR Record #66)	1.50
165	Checklist	.10

1999 Topps Stars Pre-Production

Five-card cello packs of pre-production samples were distributed to introduce Topps'

new concept for its Stars brand. The samples follow the format of the issued versions except for the use of a "PP" prefix to the card number on back.

		NM/M
Complete Set (5):		5.00
Common Player:		.75
PP1	Paul O'Neill (Base card.)	.75
PP2	Vinny Castilla (One-star.)	.75
PP3	Darin Erstad (Two-star.)	1.00
PP4	Kerry Wood (Three-star.)	1.50
PP5	Chipper Jones (Four-star.)	3.00

1999 Topps Stars

Topps Stars consists of 180 cards on 20-point stock with foil stamping and metallic inks. The set is comprised of 150 base cards and 30 subset cards: Luminaries and Supernovas. Packs contain six cards; three base cards, two One-Star cards and one Two-Star card on the average.

		NM/M
Complete Set (180):		20.00
Common Player:		.05
Pack (6):		1.50
Wax Box (24):		25.00
1	Ken Griffey Jr.	.75
2	Chipper Jones	.50
3	Mike Piazza	.75
4	Nomar Garciaparra	.50
5	Derek Jeter	1.50
6	Frank Thomas	.40
7	Ben Grieve	.05
8	Mark McGwire	1.00
9	Sammy Sosa	.50
10	Alex Rodriguez	1.00
11	Troy Glaus	.35
12	Eric Chavez	.25
13	Kerry Wood	.30
14	Barry Bonds	1.50
15	Vladimir Guerrero	.40
16	Albert Belle	.05
17	Juan Gonzalez	.20
18	Roger Clemens	.60
19	Ruben Mateo	.05
20	Cal Ripken Jr.	1.50
21	Darin Erstad	.25
22	Jeff Bagwell	.40
23	Roy Halladay	.10
24	Todd Helton	.35
25	Michael Barrett	.05
26	Manny Ramirez	.40
27	Fernando Seguignol	.05
28	Pat Burrell **RC**	2.00
29	Andruw Jones	.40
30	Randy Johnson	.40
31	Jose Canseco	.30
32	Brad Fullmer	.05
33	Alex Escobar **RC**	.10
34	Alfonso Soriano **RC**	3.00
35	Larry Walker	.05
36	Matt Clement	.05
37	Mo Vaughn	.05
38	Bruce Chen	.05
39	Travis Lee	.20

40	Adrian Beltre	.10
41	Alex Gonzalez	.05
42	Jason Tyner **RC**	.10
43	George Lombard	.05
44	Scott Rolen	.25
45	Mark Mulder **RC**	.50
46	Gabe Kapler	.05
47	Choo Freeman **RC**	.10
48	Tony Gwynn	.50
49	A.J. Burnett **RC**	.25
50	Matt Belisle **RC**	.10
51	Greg Maddux	.50
52	John Smoltz	.05
53	Mark Grace	.05
54	Wade Boggs	.50
55	Bernie Williams	.05
56	Pedro Martinez	.40
57	Barry Larkin	.05
58	Orlando Hernandez	.05
59	Jason Kendall	.05
60	Mark Kotsay	.05
61	Jim Thome	.35
62	Gary Sheffield	.30
63	Preston Wilson	.05
64	Rafael Palmeiro	.35
65	David Wells	.05
66	Shawn Green	.30
67	Tom Glavine	.25
68	Jeromy Burnitz	.05
69	Kevin Brown	.05
70	Rondell White	.05
71	Roberto Alomar	.25
72	Cliff Floyd	.05
73	Craig Biggio	.05
74	Greg Vaughn	.05
75	Ivan Rodriguez	.35
76	Vinny Castilla	.05
77	Todd Walker	.05
78	Paul Konerko	.15
79	Andy Brown **RC**	.05
80	Todd Hundley	.05
81	Dmitri Young	.05
82	Tony Clark	.05
83	Nick Johnson **RC**	.50
84	Mike Caruso	.05
85	David Ortiz	.35
86	Matt Williams	.05
87	Raul Mondesi	.05
88	Kenny Lofton	.05
89	Miguel Tejada	.10
90	Dante Bichette	.05
91	Jorge Posada	.05
92	Carlos Beltran	.25
93	Carlos Delgado	.30
94	Javy Lopez	.05
95	Aramis Ramirez	.05
96	Neifi Perez	.05
97	Marlon Anderson	.05
98	David Cone	.05
99	Moises Alou	.05
100	John Olerud	.05
101	Tim Salmon	.05
102	Jason Giambi	.30
103	Sandy Alomar	.05
104	Curt Schilling	.25
105	Andres Galarraga	.05
106	Rusty Greer	.05
107	Bobby Seay **RC**	.05
108	Eric Young	.05
109	Brian Jordan	.05
110	Eric Davis	.05
111	Will Clark	.05
112	Andy Ashby	.05
113	Edgardo Alfonzo	.05
114	Paul O'Neill	.05
115	Denny Neagle	.05
116	Eric Karros	.05
117	Ken Caminiti	.05
118	Garret Anderson	.05
119	Todd Stottlemyre	.05
120	David Justice	.05
121	Francisco Cordova	.05
122	Robin Ventura	.05
123	Mike Mussina	.25
124	Hideki Irabu	.05
125	Justin Thompson	.05
126	Mariano Rivera	.15
127	Delino DeShields	.05
128	Steve Finley	.05
129	Jose Cruz Jr.	.05
130	Ray Lankford	.05
131	Jim Edmonds	.05
132	Charles Johnson	.05
133	Al Leiter	.05
134	Jose Offerman	.05
135	Eric Milton	.05
136	Dean Palmer	.05
137	Johnny Damon	.25
138	Andy Pettitte	.20
139	Ray Durham	.05
140	Ugueth Urbina	.05
141	Marquis Grissom	.05
142	Ryan Klesko	.05
143	Brady Anderson	.05
144	Bobby Higginson	.05
145	Chuck Knoblauch	.05
146	Rickey Henderson	.40
147	Kevin Millwood	.05
148	Fred McGriff	.05
149	Damion Easley	.05
150	Tino Martinez	.05
151	Greg Maddux (Luminaries)	.30
152	Scott Rolen (Luminaries)	.20
153	Pat Burrell (Luminaries)	.75
154	Roger Clemens (Luminaries)	.35
155	Albert Belle (Luminaries)	.05
156	Troy Glaus (Luminaries)	.25
157	Cal Ripken Jr. (Luminaries)	.75
158	Alfonso Soriano (Luminaries)	.75
159	Manny Ramirez (Luminaries)	.25
160	Eric Chavez (Luminaries)	.10
161	Kerry Wood (Luminaries)	.20
162	Tony Gwynn (Luminaries)	.30
163	Barry Bonds (Luminaries)	.75
164	Ruben Mateo (Luminaries)	.05
165	Todd Helton (Luminaries)	.20
166	Darin Erstad (Luminaries)	.05
167	Jeff Bagwell (Luminaries)	.25
168	Juan Gonzalez (Luminaries)	.15
169	Mo Vaughn (Luminaries)	.05
170	Vladimir Guerrero (Luminaries)	.25
171	Nomar Garciaparra (Supernovas)	.35
172	Derek Jeter (Supernovas)	.75
173	Alex Rodriguez (Supernovas)	.50
174	Ben Grieve (Supernovas)	.05
175	Mike Piazza (Supernovas)	.40
176	Chipper Jones (Supernovas)	.35
177	Frank Thomas (Supernovas)	.25
178	Ken Griffey Jr. (Supernovas)	.40
179	Sammy Sosa (Supernovas)	.35
180	Mark McGwire (Supernovas)	.50
	Checklist 1 (1-45)	.05
	Checklist 2 (46-136)	.05
	Checklist 3 (137-150, inserts)	.05

Foil

Metallic foil in the background and a serial number on back from within a specific edition identifies this parallel. Stated odds of insertion were one in 15 packs for parallels of the 180 base cards, numbered to 299 each. One-Star foil parallels are numbered to 249 and inserted 1:33. The Two-Star Foils are numbered to 199 each and found on average of one per 82 packs. With insertion odds of 1:410, the Three-Star Foil parallels are numbered within an edition of 99. At the top of the scarcity scale, the Foil Four-Star parallels are sequentially numbered to 49 and are a one per 650-pack find.

	NM/M
Complete Base Set (180):	90.00
Common Foil Player:	.15
Foil Stars:	3X

One-Star

One-Star inserts include card numbers 1-100 from the base set and have silver foil stamping with one star on the bottom left portion of the card front. These are seeded two per pack. A foil One-Star par-

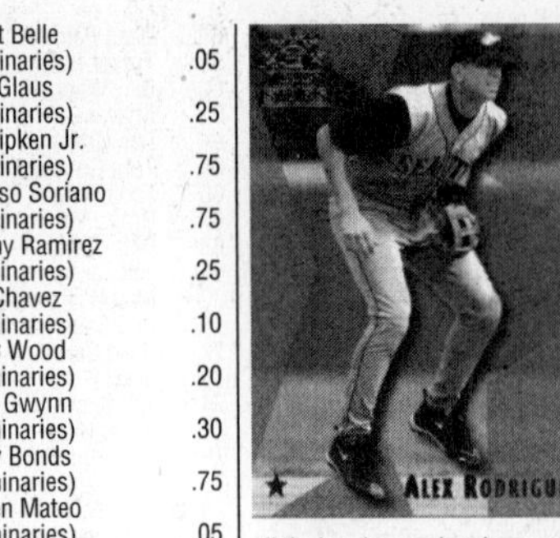

allel also is randomly seeded and sequentially numbered to 249 sets. These are a 1:33 pack insert.

		NM/M
Complete Set (100):		25.00
Common Player:		.10
Foils (249 each):		2X
1	Ken Griffey Jr.	1.25
2	Chipper Jones	1.00
3	Mike Piazza	1.25
4	Nomar Garciaparra	1.00
5	Derek Jeter	2.00
6	Frank Thomas	.75
7	Ben Grieve	.10
8	Mark McGwire	1.50
9	Sammy Sosa	1.00
10	Alex Rodriguez	1.50
11	Troy Glaus	.65
12	Eric Chavez	.25
13	Kerry Wood	.35
14	Barry Bonds	2.00
15	Vladimir Guerrero	.75
16	Albert Belle	.10
17	Juan Gonzalez	.40
18	Roger Clemens	1.00
19	Ruben Mateo	.10
20	Cal Ripken Jr.	2.00
21	Darin Erstad	.30
22	Jeff Bagwell	.75
23	Roy Halladay	.20
24	Todd Helton	.65
25	Michael Barrett	.10
26	Manny Ramirez	.75
27	Fernando Seguignol	.10
28	Pat Burrell	1.00
29	Andruw Jones	.75
30	Randy Johnson	.75
31	Jose Canseco	.40
32	Brad Fullmer	.10
33	Alex Escobar	.10
34	Alfonso Soriano	1.00
35	Larry Walker	.10
36	Matt Clement	.25
37	Mo Vaughn	.10
38	Bruce Chen	.10
39	Travis Lee	.15
40	Adrian Beltre	.20
41	Alex Gonzalez	.10
42	Jason Tyner	.10
43	George Lombard	.10
44	Scott Rolen	.50
45	Mark Mulder	.50
46	Gabe Kapler	.10
47	Choo Freeman	.10
48	Tony Gwynn	1.00
49	A.J. Burnett	.15
50	Matt Belisle	.10
51	Greg Maddux	1.00
52	John Smoltz	.10
53	Mark Grace	.10
54	Wade Boggs	1.00
55	Bernie Williams	.10
56	Pedro Martinez	.75
57	Barry Larkin	.10
58	Orlando Hernandez	.10
59	Jason Kendall	.10
60	Mark Kotsay	.10
61	Jim Thome	.45
62	Gary Sheffield	.40
63	Preston Wilson	.10
64	Rafael Palmeiro	.60
65	David Wells	.10
66	Shawn Green	.30
67	Tom Glavine	.30
68	Jeromy Burnitz	.10
69	Kevin Brown	.10
70	Rondell White	.10
71	Roberto Alomar	.25
72	Cliff Floyd	.10
73	Craig Biggio	.10
74	Greg Vaughn	.10
75	Ivan Rodriguez	.60
76	Vinny Castilla	.10
77	Todd Walker	.10
78	Paul Konerko	.20
79	Andy Brown	.10
80	Todd Hundley	.10
81	Dmitri Young	.10
82	Tony Clark	.10
83	Nick Johnson	.50
84	Mike Caruso	.10
85	David Ortiz	.40
86	Matt Williams	.10
87	Raul Mondesi	.10
88	Kenny Lofton	.10
89	Miguel Tejada	.20
90	Dante Bichette	.10
91	Jorge Posada	.10
92	Carlos Beltran	.20
93	Carlos Delgado	.25
94	Javy Lopez	.10
95	Aramis Ramirez	.10
96	Neifi Perez	.10
97	Marlon Anderson	.10
98	David Cone	.10
99	Moises Alou	.10
100	John Olerud	.10

Two-Star

Two-Stars are inserted one per pack and feature light gold metallic inks and foil stamping. Two-Stars include card numbers 1-50 from the base set. A Two-Star foil parallel is also randomly seeded and limited to 199 sequentially numbered sets.

		NM/M
Complete Set (50):		50.00
Common Player:		.25
Foils:		3X
1	Ken Griffey Jr.	2.00
2	Chipper Jones	1.50
3	Mike Piazza	2.00
4	Nomar Garciaparra	1.50
5	Derek Jeter	3.00
6	Frank Thomas	1.00
7	Ben Grieve	.25
8	Mark McGwire	2.50
9	Sammy Sosa	1.50
10	Alex Rodriguez	2.50
11	Troy Glaus	.75
12	Eric Chavez	.30
13	Kerry Wood	.40
14	Barry Bonds	3.00
15	Vladimir Guerrero	1.00
16	Albert Belle	.25
17	Juan Gonzalez	.50
18	Roger Clemens	1.75
19	Ruben Mateo	.25
20	Cal Ripken Jr.	3.00
21	Darin Erstad	.75
22	Jeff Bagwell	1.00
23	Roy Halladay	.40
24	Todd Helton	.75
25	Michael Barrett	.25
26	Manny Ramirez	1.00
27	Fernando Seguignol	.25
28	Pat Burrell	1.50
29	Andruw Jones	1.00
30	Randy Johnson	1.00
31	Jose Canseco	.50
32	Brad Fullmer	.25
33	Alex Escobar	.25
34	Alfonso Soriano	1.50
35	Larry Walker	.25
36	Matt Clement	.30
37	Mo Vaughn	.25
38	Bruce Chen	.25
39	Travis Lee	.30
40	Adrian Beltre	.30
41	Alex Gonzalez	.25
42	Jason Tyner	.25
43	George Lombard	.25
44	Scott Rolen	.65
45	Mark Mulder	.45
46	Gabe Kapler	.25
47	Choo Freeman	.25
48	Tony Gwynn	1.50
49	A.J. Burnett	.30
50	Matt Belisle	.25

Three-Star

Three-Star inserts are a partial parallel from the base set including cards 1-20. Inserted 1:5 packs, these cards feature refractive silver foil stamping along with gold metallic inks. A Three-Star parallel also is randomly inserted featuring gold stamping and limited to 99 serial numbered sets, inserted one per 410 packs.

		NM/M
Complete Set (20):		30.00
Common Player:		.50
Foils:		4X
1	Ken Griffey Jr.	2.50
2	Chipper Jones	2.00
3	Mike Piazza	2.50
4	Nomar Garciaparra	2.00
5	Derek Jeter	4.00
6	Frank Thomas	1.50
7	Ben Grieve	.50
8	Mark McGwire	3.00
9	Sammy Sosa	2.00
10	Alex Rodriguez	3.00
11	Troy Glaus	1.25
12	Eric Chavez	.60
13	Kerry Wood	.75
14	Barry Bonds	4.00
15	Vladimir Guerrero	1.50
16	Albert Belle	.50
17	Juan Gonzalez	.75
18	Roger Clemens	2.25
19	Ruben Mateo	.50
20	Cal Ripken Jr.	4.00

Four-Star

Four-Star inserts include cards numbered 1-10 from the base set and are seeded 1:10 packs. The cards feature dark metallic inks and refractive foil stamping on front. A Four-Star parallel is also randomly seeded and has gold metallic inks. Sequentially numbered to 49, it is inserted at the rate of one per 650 packs.

		NM/M
Complete Set (10):		30.00
Common Player:		1.00
Foils:		2X
1	Ken Griffey Jr.	4.00
2	Chipper Jones	3.00
3	Mike Piazza	4.00
4	Nomar Garciaparra	3.00
5	Derek Jeter	6.00
6	Frank Thomas	2.50
7	Ben Grieve	1.00
8	Mark McGwire	5.00
9	Sammy Sosa	3.00
10	Alex Rodriguez	5.00

Bright Futures

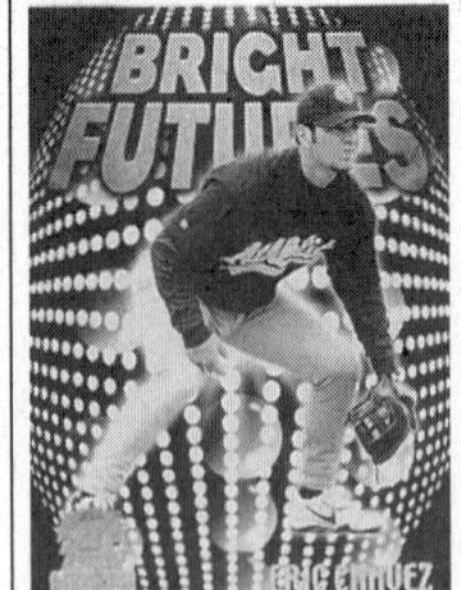

This 10-card set features top prospects with a brilliant future ahead of them. Each card features foil stamping and is sequentially numbered to 1,999. Cards have a "BF" prefix to the number. A metallized foil parallel version is also randomly seeded (1:2,702) and limited to 30 numbered sets.

		NM/M
Complete Set (10):		20.00
Common Player:		1.50
Production 1,999 Sets		
Foil (30 Each):		8X
1	Troy Glaus	3.00
2	Eric Chavez	2.00
3	Adrian Beltre	2.00
4	Michael Barrett	1.50
5	Fernando Seguignol	1.50
6	Alex Gonzalez	1.50
7	Matt Clement	1.50
8	Pat Burrell	6.00
9	Ruben Mateo	1.50
10	Alfonso Soriano	6.00

Galaxy

This 10-card set highlights the top players in baseball with foil stamping and limited to 1,999 numbered sets, inserted at the rate of one per 41 packs. Each card is numbered on the back with a "G" prefix. A Galaxy foil parallel version is randomly seeded (1:2,702) and sequentially numbered to 30 sets.

		NM/M
Complete Set (10):		25.00
Common Player:		1.00
Production 1,999 Sets		
Foil (30 Each):		8X
1	Mark McGwire	5.00
2	Roger Clemens	3.00
3	Nomar Garciaparra	4.00
4	Alex Rodriguez	5.00
5	Kerry Wood	1.50
6	Ben Grieve	1.00
7	Derek Jeter	6.00
8	Vladimir Guerrero	2.50
9	Ken Griffey Jr.	4.00
10	Sammy Sosa	3.00

Rookie Reprints

Topps reprinted five Hall of Famers' rookie cards. The rookie reprints are inserted 1:65 packs and limited to 2,500 numbered sets.

		NM/M
Complete Set (5):		10.00
Common Player:		2.00
Production 2,500 Sets		
1	Frank Robinson	2.00
2	Ernie Banks	3.00
3	Yogi Berra	3.00
4	Bob Gibson	2.00
5	Tom Seaver	3.00

Rookie Reprints Autographs

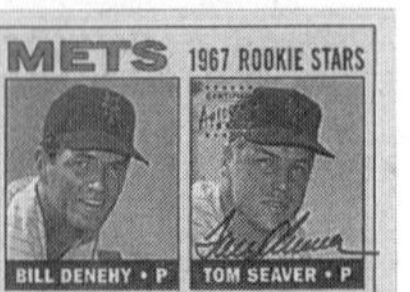

These foil stamped inserts feature the "Topps Certified Autograph Issue" stamp and are inserted 1:406 packs. The Ernie Banks autograph is inserted 1:812 packs.

		NM/M
Complete Set (5):		150.00
Common Player:		20.00
Inserted 1:406		
Banks Inserted 1:812		
1	Frank Robinson	25.00
2	Ernie Banks	70.00
3	Yogi Berra	35.00
4	Bob Gibson	20.00
5	Tom Seaver	65.00

'N Steel

Using Serilusion technology, each borderless card features a four-colored textured film laminate bonded to a sheet of strong 25-gauge metal. Each pack contains three cards, packaged in a stand-up tri-fold display unit, at an S.R.P. of $9.99. There are two parallels to the 44-card set, Gold and Domed Holographics. Golds are seeded 1:12 packs, Holographics are found every 24 packs.

		NM/M
Complete Set (44):		65.00
Common Player:		.50
Gold:		4X
Inserted 1:12		
Holographic Dome:		6X
Inserted 1:24		
Pack (3):		4.00
Wax Box (12):		40.00
1	Kerry Wood	1.00
2	Ben Grieve	.50
3	Chipper Jones	3.00
4	Alex Rodriguez	5.00
5	Mo Vaughn	.50
6	Bernie Williams	.50
7	Juan Gonzalez	1.00
8	Vinny Castilla	.50
9	Tony Gwynn	3.00
10	Manny Ramirez	2.00
11	Raul Mondesi	.50
12	Roger Clemens	3.50
13	Darin Erstad	.75
14	Barry Bonds	6.00
15	Cal Ripken Jr.	6.00
16	Barry Larkin	.50
17	Scott Rolen	1.00
18	Albert Belle	.50
19	Craig Biggio	.50
20	Tony Clark	.50
21	Mark McGwire	5.00
22	Andres Galarraga	.50
23	Kenny Lofton	.50
24	Pedro Martinez	2.00
25	Paul O'Neill	.50
26	Ken Griffey Jr.	4.00
27	Travis Lee	75.00
28	Tim Salmon	.50
29	Frank Thomas	2.00
30	Larry Walker	.50
31	Moises Alou	.50
32	Vladimir Guerrero	2.00
33	Ivan Rodriguez	1.50
34	Derek Jeter	6.00
35	Greg Vaughn	.50
36	Gary Sheffield	1.00
37	Carlos Delgado	1.00
38	Greg Maddux	3.00
39	Sammy Sosa	3.00
40	Mike Piazza	4.00
41	Nomar Garciaparra	3.00
42	Dante Bichette	.50
43	Jeff Bagwell	2.00
44	Jim Thome	1.50

'N Steel Gold Domed Holographics

This parallel edition was inserted at a rate of one per box. Cards are basically the same as the regular-issue, except for the use of holographic foil highlights on front and the presence of a thick plastic dome which covers the front.

	NM/M
Complete Set (44):	600.00
Common Player:	6.00
Stars:	8X

1999 Topps TEK Pre-Production

The second edition of Topps TEK was introduced with this trio of star cards. The preview cards are virtually identical in format to the issued version, except for the use of "PP" prefixes to card numbers on back.

		NM/M
Complete Set (3):		5.00
Common Player:		1.00
PP1A	Derek Jeter	4.00
PP2A	Moises Alou	1.00
PP3A	Tony Clark	1.00

1999 Topps TEK

Topps TEK baseball contains 45 players, with all cards printed on a transparent, 27-point stock. Each player is featured in two different versions (A & B), which are noted on the card back. The versions are differentiated by type of player uniform (home is version A and away uniforms are version B). Each version also has 30 different baseball focused background patterns; as a result every player in the 45-card set has 60 total cards. There also is a Gold parallel set that has a gold design and all versions are paralleled. Each gold card is numbered to 10, with an insertion rate of 1:15 packs.

		NM/M
Complete Set (45):		30.00
Common Player:		.25
Common Gold (10 Each Variation):		2.00
Gold Stars:		10X
Pack (4):		3.00
Wax Box (20):		45.00
1	Ben Grieve	.25
2	Andres Galarraga	.25
3	Travis Lee	.35
4	Larry Walker	.25
5	Ken Griffey Jr.	2.50
6	Sammy Sosa	2.00
7	Mark McGwire	3.00
8	Roberto Alomar	.40
9	Wade Boggs	2.00
10	Troy Glaus	.75
11	Craig Biggio	.25
12	Kerry Wood	.50
13	Vladimir Guerrero	1.00
14	Albert Belle	.25
15	Mike Piazza	2.50
16	Chipper Jones	2.00
17	Randy Johnson	1.00
18	Adrian Beltre	.45
19	Barry Bonds	4.00
20	Jim Thome	.65
21	Greg Vaughn	.25
22	Scott Rolen	.65
23	Ivan Rodriguez	.75
24	Derek Jeter	4.00
25	Cal Ripken Jr.	4.00
26	Mark Grace	.25
27	Bernie Williams	.25
28	Darin Erstad	.75
29	Eric Chavez	.35
30	Tom Glavine	.50
31	Jeff Bagwell	1.00
32	Manny Ramirez	1.00
33	Tino Martinez	.25
34	Todd Helton	.75
35	Jason Kendall	.25
36	Pat Burrell **RC**	2.50
37	Tony Gwynn	2.00
38	Nomar Garciaparra	2.00
39	Frank Thomas	1.00
40	Orlando Hernandez	.25
41	Juan Gonzalez	.50
42	Alex Rodriguez	3.00
43	Greg Maddux	2.00
44	Mo Vaughn	.25
45	Roger Clemens	2.25
	Version A Checklist Folder (Orange)	.05
	Version B Checklist Folder (Green)	.05

Gold

Each of the two player versions on each of the 30 background patterns was paralleled in a gold insert version. Cards share the same front and back designs and photos but feature gold graphics. Each card is serially numbered within an edition of just 10. Insertion rate is one per 15 packs.

	NM/M
Common Gold:	2.00
Gold Stars:	10X

Fantastek Phenoms

This 10-card set highlights top young prospects on a transparent plastic stock with silver and blue highlighting. These are inserted 1:18 packs.

		NM/M
Complete Set (10):		15.00
Common Player:		.75
Inserted 1:18		
F1	Eric Chavez	1.50
F2	Troy Glaus	4.00
F3	Pat Burrell	4.00
F4	Alex Gonzalez	.75
F5	Carlos Lee	1.00
F6	Ruben Mateo	.75
F7	Carlos Beltran	2.00
F8	Adrian Beltre	1.50
F9	Bruce Chen	.75
F10	Ryan Anderson	.75

Teknicians

This 10-card set focuses on baseball's top stars on a clear, plastic stock utilizing metallic blue, silver and red inks. These are inserted 1:18 packs.

		NM/M
Complete Set (10):		24.00
Common Player:		1.00
Inserted 1:18		
T1	Ken Griffey Jr.	3.00
T2	Mark McGwire	4.00
T3	Kerry Wood	1.00
T4	Ben Grieve	1.00
T5	Sammy Sosa	2.50
T6	Derek Jeter	6.00
T7	Alex Rodriguez	4.00
T8	Roger Clemens	2.50
T9	Nomar Garciaparra	2.50
T10	Vladimir Guerrero	1.50

2000 Topps Pre-Production

Though carrying a "PP" prefix as previous years' pre-production samples, this three-card issue was not distributed until July-August at the National and SportsFest conventions. The three-card cello packs contain cards which differ from the regular issued versions only in their numbers and the fact that they have white borders, rather than the pewter borders found on regular-issue cards.

		NM/M
Complete Set (3):		5.00
Common Player:		2.00
PP1	Brady Anderson	2.00
PP2	Jason Kendall	2.00
PP3	Ryan Klesko	2.00

2000 Topps

Released in two series the card fronts have a silver border with the Topps logo, player name and position stamped with gold foil. Card backs have complete year-by-year statistics along with a small photo in the upper right portion and the player's vital information. Subsets within the first series 239-card set include Draft Picks, Prospects, Magic Moments, Season Highlights and 20th Century's Best. The Topps MVP promotion is a parallel of 200 of the base cards, excluding subsets, with a special Topps MVP logo. 100 cards of each player was produced and if the featured player is named MVP for a week, collectors win a prize.

		NM/M
Complete Set (478):		50.00
Complete Series I Set (239):		25.00
Complete Series II Set (239):		25.00
Common Player:		.10
MVP Stars:		20-40X
Yng Stars & RC's:		10-20X
Production 100 Sets		
5 Versions for 236-240, 475-479		
Pack (11):		1.00
Wax Box (36):		30.00
1	Mark McGwire	1.00
2	Tony Gwynn	.75
3	Wade Boggs	.75
4	Cal Ripken Jr.	1.50
5	Matt Williams	.10
6	Jay Buhner	.10
8	Jeff Conine	.10
9	Todd Greene	.10
10	Mike Lieberthal	.10
11	Steve Avery	.10
12	Bret Saberhagen	.10
13	Magglio Ordonez	.20
14	Brad Radke	.10
15	Derek Jeter	1.50
16	Javy Lopez	.10
17	Russ David	.10
18	Armando Benitez	.10
19	B.J. Surhoff	.10
20	Darryl Kile	.10
21	Mark Lewis	.10
22	Mike Williams	.10
23	Mark McLemore	.10
24	Sterling Hitchcock	.10
25	Darin Erstad	.20
26	Ricky Gutierrez	.10
27	John Jaha	.10
28	Homer Bush	.10
29	Darrin Fletcher	.10
30	Mark Grace	.10
31	Fred McGriff	.10
32	Omar Daal	.10
33	Eric Karros	.10
34	Orlando Cabrera	.15
35	J.T. Snow Jr.	.10
36	Luis Castillo	.10
37	Rey Ordonez	.10
38	Bob Abreu	.20
39	Warren Morris	.10
40	Juan Gonzalez	.20
41	Mike Lansing	.10
42	Chili Davis	.10
43	Dean Palmer	.10
44	Hank Aaron	1.00
45	Jeff Bagwell	.60
46	Jose Valentin	.10
47	Shannon Stewart	.10
48	Kent Bottenfield	.10
49	Jeff Shaw	.10
50	Sammy Sosa	.75
51	Randy Johnson	.60
52	Benny Agbayani	.10
53	Dante Bichette	.10
54	Pete Harnisch	.10
55	Frank Thomas	.60
56	Jorge Posada	.10
57	Todd Walker	.10
58	Juan Encarnacion	.15
59	Mike Sweeney	.10
60	Pedro Martinez	.60
61	Lee Stevens	.10
62	Brian Giles	.10
63	Chad Ogea	.10
64	Ivan Rodriguez	.50
65	Roger Cedeno	.10
66	David Justice	.10
67	Steve Trachsel	.10
68	Eli Marrero	.10
69	Dave Nilsson	.10
70	Ken Caminiti	.10
71	Tim Raines	.10
72	Brian Jordan	.10
73	Jeff Blauser	.10
74	Bernard Gilkey	.10
75	John Flaherty	.10
76	Brent Mayne	.10
77	Jose Vidro	.10
78	Jeff Fassero	.10
79	Bruce Aven	.10
80	John Olerud	.10
81	Pokey Reese	.10
82	Woody Williams	.10
83	Ed Sprague	.10
84	Joe Girardi	.10
85	Barry Larkin	.10
86	Mike Caruso	.10
87	Bobby Higginson	.10
88	Roberto Kelly	.10
89	Edgar Martinez	.10
90	Mark Kotsay	.10
91	Paul Sorrento	.10
92	Eric Young	.10
93	Carlos Delgado	.40
94	Troy Glaus	.50
95	Ben Grieve	.10
96	Jose Lima	.10
97	Garret Anderson	.10
98	Luis Gonzalez	.10
99	Carl Pavano	.10
100	Alex Rodriguez	1.25
101	Preston Wilson	.10
102	Ron Gant	.10
103	Harold Baines	.10
104	Rickey Henderson	.60
105	Gary Sheffield	.40
106	Mickey Morandini	.10
107	Jim Edmonds	.10
108	Kris Benson	.10
109	Adrian Beltre	.20
110	Alex Fernandez	.10
111	Dan Wilson	.10
112	Mark Clark	.10
113	Greg Vaughn	.10
114	Neifi Perez	.10
115	Paul O'Neill	.10
116	Jermaine Dye	.10
117	Todd Jones	.10
118	Terry Steinbach	.10
119	Greg Norton	.10
120	Curt Schilling	.25
121	Todd Zeile	.10
122	Edgardo Alfonzo	.10
123	Ryan McGuire	.10
124	Stan Javier	.10
125	John Smoltz	.10
126	Bob Wickman	.10
127	Richard Hidalgo	.10
128	Chuck Finley	.10
129	Billy Wagner	.10
130	Todd Hundley	.10
131	Dwight Gooden	.10
132	Russ Ortiz	.10
133	Mike Lowell	.10
134	Reggie Sanders	.10
135	John Valentin	.10
136	Brad Ausmus	.10
137	Chad Kreuter	.10
138	David Cone	.10
139	Brook Fordyce	.10
140	Roberto Alomar	.25
141	Charles Nagy	.10
142	Brian Hunter	.10
143	Mike Mussina	.30
144	Robin Ventura	.10
145	Kevin Brown	.10
146	Pat Hentgen	.10
147	Ryan Klesko	.10
148	Derek Bell	.10
149	Andy Sheets	.10
150	Larry Walker	.10
151	Scott Williamson	.10
152	Jose Offerman	.10
153	Doug Mientkiewicz	.10
154	John Snyder **RC**	.10
155	Sandy Alomar	.10
156	Joe Nathan	.10
157	Lance Johnson	.10
158	Odalis Perez	.10
159	Hideo Nomo	.25
160	Steve Finley	.10
161	Dave Martinez	.10
162	Matt Walbeck	.10
163	Bill Spiers	.10
164	Fernando Tatis	.10
165	Kenny Lofton	.10
166	Paul Byrd	.10
167	Aaron Sele	.10
168	Eddie Taubensee	.10
169	Reggie Jefferson	.10
170	Roger Clemens	.85
171	Francisco Cordova	.10
172	Mike Bordick	.10
173	Wally Joyner	.10
174	Marvin Benard	.10
175	Jason Kendall	.10
176	Mike Stanley	.10
177	Chad Allen	.10
178	Carlos Beltran	.25
179	Deivi Cruz	.10
180	Chipper Jones	.75
181	Vladimir Guerrero	.60
182	Dave Burba	.10
183	Tom Goodwin	.10
184	Brian Daubach	.10
185	Jay Bell	.10
186	Roy Halladay	.25
187	Miguel Tejada	.25
188	Armando Rios	.10
189	Fernando Vina	.10
190	Eric Davis	.10
191	Henry Rodriguez	.10
192	Joe McEwing	.10
193	Jeff Kent	.10
194	Mike Jackson	.10
195	Mike Morgan	.10
196	Jeff Montgomery	.10
197	Jeff Zimmerman	.10
198	Tony Fernandez	.10
199	Jason Giambi	.40
200	Jose Canseco	.40
201	Alex Gonzalez	.10
202	Jack Cust, Mike Colangelo, Dee Brown	.10
203	Felipe Lopez, Alfonso Soriano, Pablo Ozuna	.75
204	Erubiel Durazo, Pat Burrell, Nick Johnson	.25
205	John Sneed **RC**, Kip Wells, Matt Blank	.10
206	Josh Kalinowski **RC**, Michael Tejera **RC**, Chris Mears	.10
207	Roosevelt Brown, Corey Patterson, Lance Berkman	.25
208	Kit Pellow, Kevin Barker, Russ Branyan	.10
209	B.J. Garbe **RC**, Larry Bigbie **RC**	1.00

210 Eric Munson, Bobby Bradley **RC** .25
211 Josh Girdley, Kyle Snyder .10
212 Chance Caple **RC**, Jason Jennings .25
213 Ryan Christiansen **RC**, Brett Myers **RC** 1.50
214 Jason Stumm **RC**, Rob Purvis **RC** .25
215 David Walling, Mike Paradis .10
216 Omar Ortiz, Jay Gehrke .10
217 David Cone (Season Highlights) .10
218 Jose Jimenez (Season Highlights) .10
219 Chris Singleton (Season Highlights) .10
220 Fernando Tatis (Season Highlights) .10
221 Todd Helton (Season Highlights) .20
222 Kevin Millwood (Post-Season Highlights) .15
223 Todd Pratt (Post-Season Highlights) .10
224 Orlando Hernandez (Post-Season Highlights) .20
225 (Post-Season Highlights) .10
226 (Post-Season Highlights) .10
227 Bernie Williams (Post-Season Highlights) .25
228 Mariano Rivera (Post-Season Highlights) .20
229 Tony Gwynn (20th Century's Best) .50
230 Wade Boggs (20th Century's Best) .25
231 Tim Raines (20th Century's Best) .10
232 Mark McGwire (20th Century's Best) 2.00
233 Rickey Henderson (20th Century's Best) .25
234 Rickey Henderson (20th Century's Best) .25
235 Roger Clemens (20th Century's Best) 1.50
236 Mark McGwire (Magic Moments) 2.00
237 Hank Aaron (Magic Moments) 2.00
238 Cal Ripken Jr. (Magic Moments) 3.00
239 Wade Boggs (Magic Moments) .75
240 Tony Gwynn (Magic Moments) 1.00
Series 1 checklist (1-201) .05
Series 1 checklist (202-240, inserts) .05
241 Tom Glavine .25
242 David Wells .10
243 Kevin Appier .10
244 Troy Percival .10
245 Ray Lankford .10
246 Marquis Grissom .10
247 Randy Winn .10
248 Miguel Batista .10
249 Darren Dreifort .10
250 Barry Bonds 1.50
251 Harold Baines .10
252 Cliff Floyd .10
253 Freddy Garcia .10
254 Kenny Rogers .10
255 Ben Davis .10
256 Charles Johnson .10
257 John Burkett .10
258 Desi Relaford .10
259 Al Martin .10
260 Andy Pettitte .20
261 Carlos Lee .10
262 Matt Lawton .10
263 Andy Fox .10
264 Chan Ho Park .10
265 Billy Koch .10
266 Dave Roberts .10
267 Carl Everett .10
268 Orel Hershiser .10
269 Trot Nixon .10
270 Rusty Greer .10
271 Will Clark .10
272 Quilvio Veras .10
273 Rico Brogna .10
274 Devon White .10
275 Tim Hudson .25
276 Mike Hampton .10
277 Miguel Cairo .10
278 Darren Oliver .10
279 Jeff Cirillo .10
280 Al Leiter .10
281 Brant Brown .10
282 Carlos Febles .10
283 Pedro Astacio .10
284 Juan Guzman .10
285 Orlando Hernandez .20
286 Paul Konerko .15
287 Tony Clark .10
288 Aaron Boone .10
289 Ismael Valdes .10
290 Moises Alou .10
291 Kevin Tapani .10
292 John Franco .10
293 Todd Zeile .10
294 Jason Schmidt .15
295 Johnny Damon .25
296 Scott Brosius .10
297 Travis Fryman .10
298 Jose Vizcaino .10
299 Eric Chavez .20
300 Mike Piazza 1.00
301 Matt Clement .10
302 Cristian Guzman .10
303 Darryl Strawberry .10
304 Jeff Abbott .10
305 Brett Tomko .10
306 Mike Lansing .10
307 Eric Owens .10
308 Livan Hernandez .10
309 Rondell White .10
310 Todd Stottlemyre .10
311 Chris Carpenter .10
312 Ken Hill .10
313 Mark Loretta .10
314 John Rocker .10
315 Richie Sexson .25
316 Ruben Mateo .10
317 Joe Randa .10
318 Mike Sirotka .10
319 Jose Rosado .10
320 Matt Mantei .10
321 Kevin Millwood .10
322 Gary DiSarcina .10
323 Dustin Hermanson .10
324 Mike Stanton .10
325 Kirk Rueter .10
326 Damian Miller .10
327 Doug Glanville .10
328 Scott Rolen .50
329 Ray Durham .10
330 Butch Huskey .10
331 Mariano Rivera .20
332 Darren Lewis .10
333 Ramiro Mendoza .10
334 Mark Grudzielanek .10
335 Mike Cameron .10
336 Kelvim Escobar .10
337 Bret Boone .10
338 Mo Vaughn .10
339 Craig Biggio .10
340 Michael Barrett .10
341 Marlon Anderson .10
342 Bobby Jones .10
343 John Halama .10
344 Todd Ritchie .10
345 Chuck Knoblauch .10
346 Rick Reed .10
347 Kelly Stinnett .10
348 Tim Salmon .10
349 A.J. Hinch .10
350 Jose Cruz Jr. .10
351 Roberto Hernandez .10
352 Edgar Renteria .10
353 Jose Hernandez .10
354 Brad Fullmer .10
355 Trevor Hoffman .10
356 Troy O'Leary .10
357 Justin Thompson .10
358 Kevin Young .10
359 Hideki Irabu .10
360 Jim Thome .50
361 Todd Dunwoody .10
362 Octavio Dotel .10
363 Omar Vizquel .10
364 Raul Mondesi .10
365 Shane Reynolds .10
366 Bartolo Colon .10
367 Chris Widger .10
368 Gabe Kapler .10
369 Bill Simas .10
370 Tino Martinez .10
371 John Thomson .10
372 Delino DeShields .10
373 Carlos Perez .10
374 Eddie Perez .10
375 Jeromy Burnitz .10
376 Jimmy Haynes .10
377 Travis Lee .10
378 Darryl Hamilton .10
379 Jamie Moyer .10
380 Alex Gonzalez .10
381 John Wetteland .10
382 Vinny Castilla .10
383 Jeff Suppan .10
384 Chad Curtis .10
385 Robb Nen .10
386 Wilson Alvarez .10
387 Andres Galarraga .10
388 Mike Remlinger .10
389 Geoff Jenkins .10
390 Matt Stairs .10
391 Bill Mueller .10
392 Mike Lowell .10
393 Andy Ashby .10
394 Ruben Rivera .10
395 Todd Helton .50
396 Bernie Williams .10
397 Royce Clayton .10
398 Manny Ramirez .60
399 Kerry Wood .20
400 Ken Griffey Jr. .75
401 Enrique Wilson .10
402 Joey Hamilton .10
403 Shawn Estes .10
404 Ugueth Urbina .10
405 Albert Belle .10
406 Rick Helling .10
407 Steve Parris .10
408 Eric Milton .10
409 Dave Mlicki .10
410 Shawn Green .25
411 Jaret Wright .10
412 Tony Womack .10
413 Vernon Wells .15
414 Ron Belliard .10
415 Ellis Burks .10
416 Scott Erickson .10
417 Rafael Palmeiro .35
418 Damion Easley .10
419 Jamey Wright .10
420 Corey Koskie .10
421 Bobby Howry .10
422 Ricky Ledee .10
423 Dmitri Young .10
424 Sidney Ponson .10
425 Greg Maddux .75
426 Jose Guillen .10
427 Jon Lieber .10
428 Andy Benes .10
429 Randy Velarde .10
430 Sean Casey .20
431 Torii Hunter .20
432 Ryan Rupe .10
433 David Segui .10
434 Rich Aurilia .10
435 Nomar Garciaparra .75
436 Denny Neagle .10
437 Ron Coomer .10
438 Chris Singleton .10
439 Tony Batista .10
440 Andruw Jones .60
441 Adam Piatt, Aubrey Huff, Sean Burroughs (Prospects) .20
442 Rafael Furcal, Jason Dallero, Travis Dawkins (Prospects) .20
443 Wilton Veras, Joe Crede, Mike Lamb **RC** (Prospects) .10
444 Julio Zuleta **RC**, Dernell Stenson, Jorge Toca (Prospects) .20
445 Tim Raines Jr., Gary Mathews Jr., Garry Maddox Jr. **RC** (Prospects) .20
446 Matt Riley, Mark Mulder, C.C. Sabathia (Prospects) .10
447 Scott Downs **RC**, Chris George, Matt Belisle (Prospects) .10
448 Doug Mirabelli, Ben Petrick, Jayson Werth (Prospects) .10
449 Josh Hamilton, Corey Myers **RC** (Draft Picks) .25
450 Ben Christensen **RC**, Brett Myers (Draft Picks) .20
451 Barry Zito **RC**, Ben Sheets **RC** (Draft Picks) 2.00
452 Ty Howington **RC**, Kurt Ainsworth **RC** (Draft Picks) .25
453 Rick Asadoorian **RC**, Vince Faison **RC** (Draft Picks) .10
454 Keith Reed **RC**, Jeff Heaverlo **RC** (Draft Picks) .20
455 Mike MacDougal **RC**, Jay Gehrke (Draft Picks) .25
466 Mark McGwire (Season Highlights) .75
457 Cal Ripken Jr. (Season Highlights) 1.00
458 Wade Boggs (Season Highlights) .25
459 Tony Gwynn (Season Highlights) .50
460 Jesse Orosco (Season Highlights) .10
461 Nomar Garciaparra, Larry Walker (League Leaders) .50
462 Mark McGwire, Ken Griffey Jr. (League Leaders) .50
463 Mark McGwire, Manny Ramirez (League Leaders) .50
464 Randy Johnson, Pedro Martinez (League Leaders) .25
465 Randy Johnson, Pedro Martinez (League Leaders) .25
466 Luis Gonzalez, Derek Jeter (League Leaders) .50
467 Manny Ramirez, Larry Walker (League Leaders) .25
468 Tony Gwynn (20th Century's Best) .75
469 Mark McGwire (20th Century's Best) 2.00
470 Frank Thomas (20th Century's Best) .50
471 Harold Baines (20th Century's Best) .10
472 Roger Clemens (20th Century's Best) .75
473 John Franco (20th Century's Best) .10
474 John Franco (20th Century's Best) .10
475 Ken Griffey Jr. (Magic Moments) 1.50
476 Barry Bonds (Magic Moments) 2.00
477 Sammy Sosa (Magic Moments) 1.25
478 Derek Jeter (Magic Moments) 2.50
479 Alex Rodriguez (Magic Moments) 2.00

Hank Aaron Reprints

This 23-card set reprints all of Aaron's 23-regular issued Topps cards and are seeded 1:18 packs.

	NM/M
Complete Set (23):	60.00
Common Aaron:	3.00
Inserted 1:18	
Autographed:	300.00
"Limited Edition" 4,000 Sets:	1X
1 Hank Aaron - 1954	8.00
2 Hank Aaron - 1955	3.00
3 Hank Aaron - 1956	3.00
4 Hank Aaron - 1957	3.00
5 Hank Aaron - 1958	3.00
6 Hank Aaron - 1959	3.00
7 Hank Aaron - 1960	3.00
8 Hank Aaron - 1961	3.00
9 Hank Aaron - 1962	3.00
10 Hank Aaron - 1963	3.00
11 Hank Aaron - 1964	3.00
12 Hank Aaron - 1965	3.00
13 Hank Aaron - 1966	3.00
14 Hank Aaron - 1967	3.00
15 Hank Aaron - 1968	3.00
16 Hank Aaron - 1969	3.00
17 Hank Aaron - 1970	3.00
18 Hank Aaron - 1971	3.00
19 Hank Aaron - 1972	3.00
20 Hank Aaron - 1973	3.00
21 Hank Aaron - 1974	3.00
22 Hank Aaron - 1975	3.00
23 Hank Aaron - 1976	3.00

Hank Aaron Chrome Reprints

This 23-card set reprints Aaron's regular issued Topps cards utilizing Chromium technology. Each card has a commemorative logo and are seeded 1:72 packs. A Refractor parallel version is also randomly inserted 1:288 packs and have Refractor printed underneath the number on the card back.

	NM/M
Complete Set (23):	90.00
Common Aaron:	5.00
Inserted 1:72	
Refractors:	3X
Inserted 1:288	
1 Hank Aaron - 1954	10.00
2 Hank Aaron - 1955	5.00
3 Hank Aaron - 1956	5.00
4 Hank Aaron - 1957	5.00
5 Hank Aaron - 1958	5.00
6 Hank Aaron - 1959	5.00
7 Hank Aaron - 1960	5.00
8 Hank Aaron - 1961	5.00
9 Hank Aaron - 1962	5.00
10 Hank Aaron - 1963	5.00
11 Hank Aaron - 1964	5.00
12 Hank Aaron - 1965	5.00
13 Hank Aaron - 1966	5.00
14 Hank Aaron - 1967	5.00
15 Hank Aaron - 1968	5.00
16 Hank Aaron - 1969	5.00
17 Hank Aaron - 1970	5.00
18 Hank Aaron - 1971	5.00
19 Hank Aaron - 1972	5.00
20 Hank Aaron - 1973	5.00
21 Hank Aaron - 1974	5.00
22 Hank Aaron - 1975	5.00
23 Hank Aaron - 1976	5.00

All-Star Rookie Team

	NM/M
Complete Set (10):	10.00
Common Player:	.25
Inserted 1:36	
"Limited Edition" 4,000 Sets:	1X
1 Mark McGwire	3.00
2 Chuck Knoblauch	.25
3 Chipper Jones	2.00
4 Cal Ripken Jr.	4.00
5 Manny Ramirez	1.00
6 Jose Canseco	.75
7 Ken Griffey Jr.	2.00
8 Mike Piazza	2.00
9 Dwight Gooden	.25
10 Billy Wagner	.25

All-Topps Team

This insert set spotlights 10 National League (Series 1) and 10 A.L. (Series 2) players who are deemed the best at their respective position. On front, a Hall of Fame style plaque design features gold-foil highlights. Backs offer stat comparisons to contemporary players and Hall of Fame greats at their position. These were seeded 1:12 packs. Cards are numbered with an "AT" prefix.

	NM/M
Complete Set (20):	15.00
Common Player:	.25
Inserted 1:12	
"Limited Edition" 4,000 Sets:	1X
1 Greg Maddux	1.50
2 Mike Piazza	1.50
3 Mark McGwire	2.50
4 Craig Biggio	.40
5 Chipper Jones	1.50
6 Barry Larkin	.40
7 Barry Bonds	2.50
8 Andruw Jones	.75
9 Sammy Sosa	1.50
10 Larry Walker	.40
11 Pedro Martinez	1.00
12 Ivan Rodriguez	.50
13 Rafael Palmeiro	.50
14 Roberto Alomar	.50
15 Cal Ripken Jr.	3.00
16 Derek Jeter	3.00
17 Albert Belle	.25
18 Ken Griffey Jr.	1.50
19 Manny Ramirez	.75
20 Jose Canseco	.50

Autographs

Inserted exclusively in Series 1 and 2 hobby packs, each card features the "Topps Certified Autograph Issue" stamp and is autographed on the card front.

	NM/M
Common Player:	8.00
Group A 1:7,589	
Group B 1:4,553	
Group C 1:518	
Group D 1:911	
Group E 1:1,138	
1 Alex Rodriguez/A	100.00
2 Tony Gwynn/A	50.00
3 Vinny Castilla/B	15.00
4 Sean Casey/B	15.00
5 Shawn Green/C	25.00
6 Rey Ordonez/C	8.00
7 Matt Lawton/C	15.00
8 Tony Womack/C	8.00
9 Gabe Kapler/D	10.00
10 Pat Burrell/D	20.00
11 Preston Wilson/D	15.00
12 Troy Glaus/D	30.00
13 Carlos Beltran/D	40.00
14 Josh Girdley/E	8.00
15 B.J. Garbe/E	8.00
16 Derek Jeter/A	125.00
17 Cal Ripken Jr./A	150.00
18 Ivan Rodriguez/B	40.00
19 Rafael Palmeiro/B	40.00
20 Vladimir Guerrero/E	45.00
21 Raul Mondesi/C	15.00
22 Scott Rolen/C	40.00
23 Billy Wagner/C	10.00
24 Fernando Tatis/C	8.00
25 Ruben Mateo/D	8.00
26 Carlos Febles/D	8.00
27 Mike Sweeney/E	10.00
28 Alex Gonzalez/D	10.00
29 Miguel Tejada/D	40.00
30 Josh Hamilton/E	30.00

Century Best

	NM/M
Common Player:	2.00
Ser. 1 1:869 H	
Ser. 2 1:362	
CB1 Tony Gwynn/339	8.00
CB2 Wade Boggs/578	4.00
CB3 Lance Johnson/117	2.00
CB4 Mark McGwire/522	20.00
CB5 Rickey Henderson/1,334	4.00
CB6 Rickey Henderson/2,103	4.00
CB7 Roger Clemens/247	12.00
CB8 Tony Gwynn/3,067	6.00
CB9 Mark McGwire/587	20.00
CB10 Frank Thomas/440	6.00
CB11 Harold Baines/1,583	2.00
CB12 Roger Clemens/3,316	8.00
CB13 John Franco/264	2.00
CB14 John Franco/416	2.00

Combos

	NM/M
Complete Set (10):	15.00
Common Card:	1.00

Inserted 1:18
"Limited Edition" 4,000 Sets: 1X
1 Roberto Alomar, Manny Ramirez, Kenny Lofton, Jim Thome 1.00
2 Tom Glavine, Greg Maddux, John Smoltz 1.50
3 Derek Jeter, Bernie Williams, Tino Martinez 3.00
4 Ivan Rodriguez, Mike Piazza 1.50
5 Nomar Garciaparra, Alex Rodriguez, Derek Jeter 3.00
6 Sammy Sosa, Mark McGwire 3.00
7 Pedro Martinez, Randy Johnson 1.00
8 Barry Bonds, Ken Griffey Jr. 2.50
9 Chipper Jones, Ivan Rodriguez 1.50
10 Cal Ripken Jr., Tony Gwynn, Wade Boggs 3.00

Hands of Gold

This seven-card insert set highlights players who have won at least five gold gloves. Each card is foil stamped and die-cut and is seeded 1:18 packs.

NM/M
Complete Set (7): 5.00
Common Player: .25
Inserted 1:18
"Limited Edition" 4,000 Sets: 1X
1 Barry Bonds 2.50
2 Ivan Rodriguez .75
3 Ken Griffey Jr. 1.50
4 Roberto Alomar .75
5 Tony Gwynn 1.00
6 Omar Vizquel .25
7 Greg Maddux 1.50

Mark McGwire 1985 Rookie Reprint

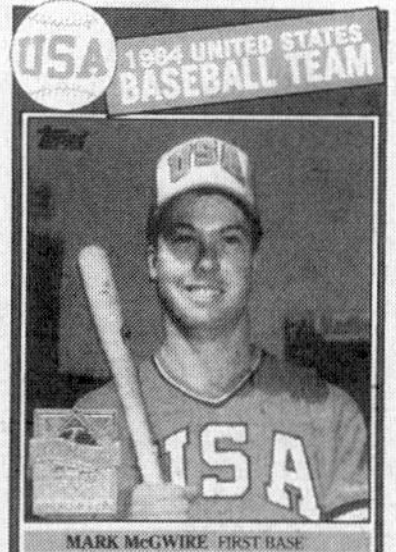

This insert pays tribute to baseball's reigning single season home run record holder by reprinting his '85 Topps Rookie card. Card fronts have a commemorative gold stamp and is seeded 1:36 packs.

NM/M
Complete Set (1): 6.00
Mark McGwire 6.00

Own the Game

NM/M
Complete Set (30): 15.00
Common Player: .15
Inserted 1:12
"Limited Edition" 4,000 Sets: 1X
1 Derek Jeter 2.00
2 B.J. Surhoff .15
3 Luis Gonzalez .25
4 Manny Ramirez .50
5 Rafael Palmeiro .40
6 Mark McGwire 1.50
7 Mark McGwire 1.50
8 Sammy Sosa 1.00
9 Ken Griffey Jr. 1.00
10 Larry Walker .25
11 Nomar Garciaparra 1.50
12 Derek Jeter 2.00
13 Larry Walker .25
14 Mark McGwire 1.50
15 Manny Ramirez .50
16 Pedro Martinez .75
17 Randy Johnson .75
18 Kevin Millwood .25
19 Pedro Martinez .75
20 Randy Johnson .75
21 Kevin Brown .25
22 Chipper Jones 1.00
23 Ivan Rodriguez .50
24 Mariano Rivera .25
25 Scott Williamson .15
26 Carlos Beltran .25
27 Randy Johnson .75
28 Pedro Martinez .75
29 Sammy Sosa 1.00
30 Manny Ramirez .50

Perennial All-Stars

This 10-card set highlights 10 superstars who have consistently achieved All-Star recognition. Card fronts feature a silver holographic foil throughout, while card backs have the featured player's career All-Star statistics. These were seeded 1:18 packs. Cards are numbered with a "PA" prefix.

NM/M
Complete Set (10): 10.00
Common Player: .50
Inserted 1:18
"Limited Edition" 4,000 Sets: 1X
1 Ken Griffey Jr. 1.00
2 Derek Jeter 2.00
3 Sammy Sosa 1.00
4 Cal Ripken Jr. 2.00
5 Mike Piazza 1.00
6 Nomar Garciaparra 1.50
7 Jeff Bagwell .50
8 Barry Bonds 1.50
9 Alex Rodriguez 1.50
10 Mark McGwire 1.50

Power Players

This 20-card set highlights the top power hitters in the game and are printed on a holographic silver foil front. They are numbered with a "P" prefix and are seeded 1:8 packs.

NM/M
Complete Set (20): 10.00
Common Player: .25
Inserted 1:8
"Limited Edition" 4,000 Sets: 1X
1 Juan Gonzalez .50
2 Ken Griffey Jr. 1.00
3 Mark McGwire 1.50
4 Nomar Garciaparra 1.50
5 Barry Bonds 1.50
6 Mo Vaughn .25
7 Larry Walker .25
8 Alex Rodriguez 1.50
9 Jose Canseco .25
10 Jeff Bagwell .50
11 Manny Ramirez .50
12 Albert Belle .25
13 Frank Thomas .50
14 Mike Piazza 1.00
15 Chipper Jones 1.00
16 Sammy Sosa 1.00
17 Vladimir Guerrero .50
18 Scott Rolen .50
19 Raul Mondesi .25
20 Derek Jeter 2.00

Stadium Relics

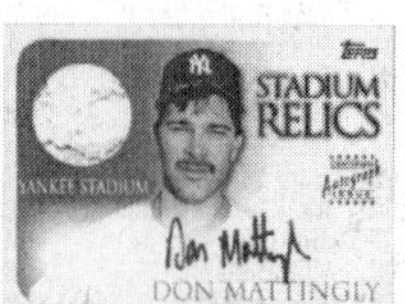

Inserted exclusively in Home-Team Advantage packs, this five-card set features historical baseball stadiums and the autograph of the players who made them sacred. Besides the player autograph, the cards also have a piece of base from the featured stadium embedded into each card. These were seeded 1:165 HTA packs and are numbered with a "SR" prefix.

NM/M
Common Player: 40.00
Inserted 1:165 HTA
1 Don Mattingly 150.00
2 Carl Yastrzemski 100.00
3 Ernie Banks 75.00
4 Johnny Bench 75.00
5 Willie Mays 150.00
6 Mike Schmidt 100.00
7 Lou Brock 50.00
8 Al Kaline 75.00
9 Paul Molitor 60.00
10 Eddie Matthews 75.00

Supers

Each box of Topps foil packs includes one upwrapped box-topper card in an oversize (3-1/2" x 5") format. Except for its size, the super version differs from the same players' issued cards only in the numbering on back which designates each card "x of 8."

NM/M
Complete Set (16): 35.00
Common Player: 1.00
Inserted 1:Box
1 Mark McGwire 5.00

2 Hank Aaron 5.00
3 Derek Jeter 3.00
4 Sammy Sosa 3.00
5 Alex Rodriguez 3.00
6 Chipper Jones 4.00
7 Cal Ripken Jr. 4.00
8 Pedro Martinez 2.00
1 Barry Bonds 1.50
2 Orlando Hernandez 1.00
3 Mike Piazza 3.00
4 Manny Ramirez 1.50
5 Ken Griffey Jr. 4.00
6 Rafael Palmeiro 1.00
7 Greg Maddux 2.50
8 Nomar Garciaparra 3.00

21st Century Topps

Printed on a silver holographic foil front, this 10-card set highlights young players who are poised to thrive into the next millenium. These are seeded 1:18 packs are numbered on the card backs with a "C" prefix.

NM/M
Complete Set (10): 5.00
Common Player: .25
Inserted 1:18
"Limited Edition" 4,000 Sets: 1X
1 Ben Grieve .25
2 Alex Gonzalez .25
3 Derek Jeter 2.00
4 Sean Casey .25
5 Nomar Garciaparra 1.50
6 Alex Rodriguez 1.50
7 Scott Rolen .50
8 Andruw Jones .50
9 Vladimir Guerrero .50
10 Todd Helton .50

2000 Topps Traded and Rookies

NM/M
Complete Set (135): 25.00
Common Player: .10
Unopened Set (136): 50.00
1 Mike MacDougal **RC** .20
2 Andy Tracy **RC** .20
3 Brandon Phillips **RC** .75
4 Brandon Inge **RC** .75
5 Robbie Morrison **RC** .25
6 Josh Pressley **RC** .20
7 Todd Moser **RC** .25
8 Rob Purvis **RC** .25
9 Chance Caple **RC** .25
10 Ben Sheets .75
11 Russ Jacobson **RC** .10
12 Brian Cole **RC** .10
13 Brad Baker **RC** .25
14 Alex Cintron **RC** .40
15 Lyle Overbay **RC** 1.00
16 Mike Edwards **RC** .20
17 Sean McGowan **RC** .25
18 Jose Molina **RC** .25
19 Marcos Castillo **RC** .20
20 Josue Espada **RC** .20
21 Alex Gordon **RC** .10
22 Rob Pugmire **RC** .10
23 Jason Stumm **RC** .25
24 Ty Howington **RC** .40
25 Brett Myers .50
26 Maicer Izturis **RC** .10
27 John McDonald **RC** .10
28 Wilfredo Rodriguez **RC** .25
29 Carlos Zambrano **RC** 3.00
30 Alejandro Diaz **RC** .20
31 Geraldo Guzman **RC** .20
32 J.R. House **RC** .50
33 Elvin Nina **RC** .10
34 Juan Pierre **RC** .50
35 Ben Johnson **RC** .50
36 Jeff Bailey **RC** .20
37 Miguel Olivo **RC** .10
38 Francisco Rodriguez **RC** 2.00
39 Tony Pena Jr. **RC** .25
40 Miguel Cabrera **RC** 15.00
41 Asdrubal Oropeza **RC** .10
42 Junior Zamora **RC** .10
43 Jovanny Cedeno **RC** .25
44 John Sneed **RC** .10
45 Josh Kalinowski **RC** .10
46 Mike Young **RC** 3.00
47 Rico Washington **RC** .10
48 Chad Durbin **RC** .40
49 Junior Brignac **RC** .25
50 Carlos Hernandez **RC** .40
51 Cesar Izturis **RC** .50
52 Oscar Salazar **RC** .25
53 Pat Strange **RC** .25
54 Rick Asadoorian .15
55 Keith Reed **RC** .25
56 Leo Estrella **RC** .10
57 Wascar Serrano **RC** .10
58 Richard Gomez **RC** .25
59 Ramon Santiago **RC** .25
60 Jovanny Sosa **RC** .25
61 Aaron Rowand **RC** .50
62 Junior Guerrero **RC** .25
63 Luis Terrero **RC** .25
64 Brian Sanches **RC** .10
65 Scott Sobkowiak **RC** .25
66 Gary Majewski **RC** .10
67 Barry Zito 1.00
68 Ryan Christianson **RC** .40
69 Cristian Guerrero **RC** .40
70 Tomas de la Rosa **RC** .10
71 Andrew Beinbrink **RC** .25
72 Ryan Knox **RC** .10
73 Alex Graman **RC** .25
74 Juan Guzman **RC** .10
75 Ruben Salazar **RC** .40
76 Luis Matos **RC** .40
77 Tony Mota **RC** .10
78 Doug Davis **RC** .50
79 Ben Christensen **RC** .25
80 Mike Lamb .10
81 Adrian Gonzalez **RC** (Draft Picks) 1.50
82 Mike Stodolka **RC** (Draft Picks) .25
83 Adam Johnson **RC** (Draft Picks) .25
84 Matt Wheatland **RC** (Draft Picks) .25
85 Corey Smith **RC** (Draft Picks) .50
86 Rocco Baldelli **RC** (Draft Picks) 1.50
87 Keith Bucktrot **RC** (Draft Picks) .25
88 Adam Wainwright **RC** (Draft Picks) 1.50
89 Scott Thorman **RC** (Draft Picks) 1.50
90 Tripper Johnson **RC** (Draft Picks) .50
91 Jim Edmonds .25
92 Masato Yoshii .10
93 Adam Kennedy .10
94 Darryl Kile .10
95 Mark McLemore .10
96 Ricky Gutierrez .10
97 Juan Gonzalez .40
98 Melvin Mora .10
99 Dante Bichette .10
100 Lee Stevens .10
101 Roger Cedeno .10
102 John Olerud .25
103 Eric Young .10
104 Mickey Morandini .10
105 Travis Lee .10
106 Greg Vaughn .10
107 Todd Zeile .10
108 Chuck Finley .10
109 Ismael Valdes .10
110 Ron Henika .10
111 Pat Hentgen .10
112 Ryan Klesko .10
113 Derek Bell .10
114 Hideo Nomo .40
115 Aaron Sele .10
116 Fernando Vina .10
117 Wally Joyner .10
118 Brian Hunter .10
119 Joe Girardi .10
120 Omar Daal .10
121 Brook Fordyce .10
122 Jose Valentin .10
123 Curt Schilling .40
124 B.J. Surhoff .10
125 Henry Rodriguez .10
126 Mike Bordick .10
127 David Justice .25
128 Charles Johnson .10
129 Will Clark .25
130 Dwight Gooden .10
131 David Segui .10
132 Denny Neagle .10
133 Andy Ashby .10
134 Bruce Chen .10
135 Jason Bere .10

Autographs

NM/M
Common Player: 4.00
Inserted 1:Set
1 Mike MacDougal 8.00
2 Andy Tracy 8.00
3 Brandon Phillips 50.00
4 Brandon Inge 25.00
5 Robbie Morrison 4.00
6 Josh Pressley 4.00
7 Todd Moser 4.00
8 Rob Purvis 4.00
9 Chance Caple 4.00
10 Ben Sheets 40.00
11 Russ Jacobson 4.00
12 Brian Cole 4.00
13 Brad Baker 4.00
14 Alex Cintron 10.00
15 Lyle Overbay 30.00
16 Mike Edwards 4.00
17 Sean McGowan 4.00
18 Jose Molina 4.00
19 Marcos Castillo 4.00
20 Josue Espada 4.00
21 Alex Gordon 4.00
22 Rob Pugmire 4.00
23 Jason Stumm 4.00
24 Ty Howington 8.00
25 Brett Myers 25.00
26 Maicer Izturis 8.00
27 John McDonald 4.00
28 Wilfredo Rodriguez 4.00
29 Carlos Zambrano 140.00
30 Alejandro Diaz 4.00
31 Geraldo Guzman 4.00
32 J.R. House 8.00
33 Elvin Nina 4.00
34 Juan Pierre 25.00
35 Ben Johnson 10.00
36 Jeff Bailey 4.00
37 Miguel Olivo 10.00
38 Francisco Rodriguez 50.00
39 Tony Pena Jr. 4.00
40 Miguel Cabrera 500.00
41 Asdrubal Oropeza 4.00
42 Junior Zamora 4.00
43 Jovanny Cedeno 4.00
44 John Sneed 4.00
45 Josh Kalinowski 8.00
46 Mike Young 100.00
47 Rico Washington 4.00
48 Chad Durbin 4.00
49 Junior Brignac 4.00
50 Carlos Hernandez 8.00
51 Cesar Izturis 10.00
52 Oscar Salazar 4.00
53 Pat Strange 4.00
54 Rick Asadoorian 4.00
55 Keith Reed 4.00
56 Leo Estrella 4.00
57 Wascar Serrano 4.00
58 Richard Gomez 4.00
59 Ramon Santiago 4.00
60 Jovanny Sosa 4.00
61 Aaron Rowand 30.00
62 Junior Guerrero 4.00
63 Luis Terrero 10.00
64 Brian Sanches 4.00
65 Scott Sobkowiak 4.00
66 Gary Majewski 8.00
67 Barry Zito 30.00
68 Ryan Christianson 8.00
69 Cristian Guerrero 8.00
70 Tomas de la Rosa 4.00
71 Andrew Beinbrink 4.00
72 Ryan Knox 4.00

73	Alex Graman	4.00
74	Juan Guzman	4.00
75	Ruben Salazar	4.00
76	Luis Matos	10.00
77	Tony Mota	4.00
78	Doug Davis	15.00
79	Ben Christensen	4.00
80	Mike Lamb	10.00

2000 Topps Opening Day

Essentially identical in design to 2000 Topps regular cards, Opening Day has a silver border with "2000 Opening Day" stamped in silver foil on the card front. The checklist is made up of cards from Series 1 and 2 from Topps base set with identical photos. The rookie reprint card of Hank Aaron was intended to carry card #110, but it does not appear, only the original '54 Topps card #128.

		NM/M
Complete Set (165):		30.00
Common Player:		.15
Pack (8):		1.00
Wax Box (36):		25.00
1	Mark McGwire	2.00
2	Tony Gwynn	1.00
3	Wade Boggs	.40
4	Cal Ripken Jr.	2.50
5	Matt Williams	.20
6	Jay Buhner	.15
7	Mike Lieberthal	.15
8	Magglio Ordonez	.25
9	Derek Jeter	2.00
10	Javy Lopez	.25
11	Armando Benitez	.15
12	Darin Erstad	.25
13	Mark Grace	.25
14	Eric Karros	.15
15	J.T. Snow Jr.	.15
16	Luis Castillo	.15
17	Rey Ordonez	.15
18	Bob Abreu	.15
19	Warren Morris	.15
20	Juan Gonzalez	.75
21	Dean Palmer	.15
22	Hank Aaron	2.00
23	Jeff Bagwell	.75
24	Sammy Sosa	1.50
25	Randy Johnson	.75
26	Dante Bichette	.15
27	Frank Thomas	.75
28	Pedro Martinez	.75
29	Brian Giles	.20
30	Ivan Rodriguez	.50
31	Roger Cedeno	.15
32	David Justice	.25
33	Ken Caminiti	.15
34	Brian Jordan	.15
35	John Olerud	.25
36	Pokey Reese	.15
37	Barry Larkin	.25
38	Edgar Martinez	.15
39	Carlos Delgado	.50
40	Troy Glaus	.40
41	Ben Grieve	.15
42	Jose Lima	.15
43	Luis Gonzalez	.15
44	Alex Rodriguez	2.00
45	Preston Wilson	.20
46	Rickey Henderson	.40
47	Gary Sheffield	.25
48	Jim Edmonds	.25
49	Greg Vaughn	.15
50	Neifi Perez	.15
51	Paul O'Neill	.25
52	Jermaine Dye	.15
53	Curt Schilling	.25
54	Edgardo Alfonzo	.15
55	John Smoltz	.20
56	Chuck Finley	.15
57	Billy Wagner	.15
58	David Cone	.25
59	Roberto Alomar	.50
60	Charles Nagy	.15
61	Mike Mussina	.50
62	Robin Ventura	.25
63	Kevin Brown	.15
64	Pat Hentgen	.15
65	Ryan Klesko	.15
66	Derek Bell	.15
67	Larry Walker	.25
68	Scott Williamson	.15
69	Jose Offerman	.15
70	Doug Mientkiewicz	.15
71	John Snyder	.15
72	Sandy Alomar	.15
73	Joe Nathan	.15
74	Steve Finley	.15
75	Dave Martinez	.15
76	Fernando Tatis	.15
77	Kenny Lofton	.20
78	Paul Byrd	.15
79	Aaron Sele	.15
80	Roger Clemens	1.50
81	Francisco Cordova	.15
82	Wally Joyner	.15
83	Jason Kendall	.25
84	Carlos Beltran	.15
85	Chipper Jones	1.50
86	Vladimir Guerrero	.75
87	Tom Goodwin	.15
88	Brian Daubach	.15
89	Jay Bell	.15
90	Roy Halladay	.25
91	Miguel Tejada	.40
92	Eric Davis	.15
93	Henry Rodriguez	.15
94	Joe McEwing	.15
95	Jeff Kent	.25
96	Jeff Zimmerman	.15
97	Tony Fernandez	.15
98	Jason Giambi	.75
99	Jose Canseco	.40
100	Alex Gonzalez	.15
101	Erubiel Durazo, Pat Burrell, Nick Johnson (Prospects)	.40
102	Corey Patterson, Roosevelt Brown, Lance Berkman (Prospects)	.25
103	Eric Munson, Bobby Bradley **RC** (Draft Picks)	.25
104	Josh Hamilton, Corey Myers **RC** (Draft Picks)	.25
105	Mark McGwire (Magic Moments)	2.00
106	Hank Aaron (Magic Moments)	2.00
107	Cal Ripken Jr. (Magic Moments)	2.50
108	Wade Boggs (Magic Moments)	.40
109	Tony Gwynn (Magic Moments)	1.00
(110)	Hank Aaron (Rookie Reprint)	2.00
111	Tom Glavine	.40
112	Mo Vaughn	.20
113	Tino Martinez	.25
114	Craig Biggio	.25
115	Tim Hudson	.25
116	John Wetteland	.15
117	Ellis Burks	.15
118	David Wells	.15
119	Rico Brogna	.15
120	Greg Maddux	1.50
121	Jeromy Burnitz	.15
122	Raul Mondesi	.25
123	Rondell White	.25
124	Barry Bonds	2.00
125	Orlando Hernandez	.25
126	Bartolo Colon	.15
127	Tim Salmon	.25
128	Kevin Young	.15
129	Troy O'Leary	.15
130	Jim Thome	.50
131	Ray Durham	.15
132	Tony Clark	.15
133	Mariano Rivera	.25
134	Omar Vizquel	.15
135	Ken Griffey Jr.	1.50
136	Shawn Green	.40
137	Cliff Floyd	.15
138	Al Leiter	.15
139	Mike Hampton	.15
140	Mike Piazza	1.50
141	Andy Pettitte	.25
142	Albert Belle	.20
143	Scott Rolen	.75
144	Rusty Greer	.15
145	Kevin Millwood	.25
146	Ivan Rodriguez	.75
147	Nomar Garciaparra	1.50
148	Denny Neagle	.15
149	Manny Ramirez	.75
150	Vinny Castilla	.15
151	Andruw Jones	.50
152	Johnny Damon	.15
153	Eric Milton	.15
154	Todd Helton	.50
155	Rafael Palmeiro	.50
156	Damion Easley	.15
157	Carlos Febles	.15
158	Paul Konerko	.15
159	Bernie Williams	.50
160	Ken Griffey Jr. (Magic Moments)	1.50
161	Barry Bonds (Magic Moments)	2.00
162	Sammy Sosa (Magic Moments)	2.00
163	Derek Jeter (Magic Moments)	2.00
164	Alex Rodriguez (Magic Moments)	2.00
165	Checklist (Magic Moments)	.15

Autographs

		NM/M
Common Player:		25.00
1	Edgardo Alfonzo	25.00
2	Wade Boggs	60.00
3	Robin Ventura	25.00
4	Josh Hamilton	25.00
5	Vernon Wells	30.00

2000 Topps Chrome

The base set consists of 478 cards utilizing Topps Chromium technology and features the same photos and basic design as the 2000 Topps base set. Subsets include Prospects, 20th Century's Best, Magic Moments and Post Season Highlights. A parallel Refractor version is also available 1:12 packs.

		NM/M
Complete Set (478):		100.00
Complete Series I Set (239):		50.00
Complete Series II Set (239):		50.00
Common Player:		.25
Pack (4):		1.50
Wax Box (24):		30.00
1	Mark McGwire	3.00
2	Tony Gwynn	1.50
3	Wade Boggs	.75
4	Cal Ripken Jr.	4.00
5	Matt Williams	.40
6	Jay Buhner	.40
8	Jeff Conine	.25
9	Todd Greene	.25
10	Mike Lieberthal	.25
11	Steve Avery	.25
12	Bret Saberhagen	.25
13	Magglio Ordonez	.50
14	Brad Radke	.25
15	Derek Jeter	4.00
16	Javy Lopez	.50
17	Russ David	.25
18	Armando Benitez	.25
19	B.J. Surhoff	.25
20	Darryl Kile	.25
21	Mark Lewis	.25
22	Mike Williams	.25
23	Mark McLemore	.25
24	Sterling Hitchcock	.25
25	Darin Erstad	.50
26	Ricky Gutierrez	.25
27	John Jaha	.25
28	Homer Bush	.25
29	Darrin Fletcher	.25
30	Mark Grace	.75
31	Fred McGriff	.50
32	Omar Daal	.25
33	Eric Karros	.40
34	Orlando Cabrera	.40
35	J.T. Snow Jr.	.25
36	Luis Castillo	.25
37	Rey Ordonez	.25
38	Bob Abreu	.40
39	Warren Morris	.25
40	Juan Gonzalez	1.00
41	Mike Lansing	.25
42	Chili Davis	.25
43	Dean Palmer	.25
44	Hank Aaron	3.00
45	Jeff Bagwell	1.00
46	Jose Valentin	.25
47	Shannon Stewart	.25
48	Kent Bottenfield	.25
49	Jeff Shaw	.25
50	Sammy Sosa	2.00
51	Randy Johnson	1.50
52	Benny Agbayani	.25
53	Dante Bichette	.25
54	Pete Harnisch	.25
55	Frank Thomas	1.00
56	Jorge Posada	.75
57	Todd Walker	.25
58	Juan Encarnacion	.40
59	Mike Sweeney	.25
60	Pedro Martinez	1.50
61	Lee Stevens	.25
62	Brian Giles	.50
63	Chad Ogea	.25
64	Ivan Rodriguez	1.00
65	Roger Cedeno	.25
66	David Justice	.50
67	Steve Trachsel	.25
68	Eli Marrero	.25
69	Dave Nilsson	.25
70	Ken Caminiti	.25
71	Tim Raines	.25
72	Brian Jordan	.25
73	Jeff Blauser	.25
74	Bernard Gilkey	.25
75	John Flaherty	.25
76	Brent Mayne	.25
77	Jose Vidro	.25
78	Jeff Fassero	.25
79	Bruce Aven	.25
80	John Olerud	.50
81	Juan Guzman	.25
82	Woody Williams	.25
83	Ed Sprague	.25
84	Joe Girardi	.25
85	Barry Larkin	.50
86	Mike Caruso	.25
87	Bobby Higginson	.25
88	Roberto Kelly	.25
89	Edgar Martinez	.40
90	Mark Kotsay	.25
91	Paul Sorrento	.25
92	Eric Young	.25
93	Carlos Delgado	1.00
94	Troy Glaus	1.00
95	Ben Grieve	.25
96	Jose Lima	.25
97	Garret Anderson	.50
98	Luis Gonzalez	.50
99	Carl Pavano	.25
100	Alex Rodriguez	3.00
101	Preston Wilson	.40
102	Ron Gant	.40
103	Harold Baines	.25
104	Rickey Henderson	.50
105	Gary Sheffield	.75
106	Mickey Morandini	.25
107	Jim Edmonds	.50
108	Kris Benson	.25
109	Adrian Beltre	.25
110	Alex Fernandez	.25
111	Dan Wilson	.25
112	Mark Clark	.25
113	Greg Vaughn	.25
114	Neifi Perez	.25
115	Paul O'Neill	.50
116	Jermaine Dye	.25
117	Todd Jones	.25
118	Terry Steinbach	.25
119	Greg Norton	.25
120	Curt Schilling	.75
121	Todd Zeile	.25
122	Edgardo Alfonzo	.25
123	Ryan McGuire	.25
124	Stan Javier	.25
125	John Smoltz	.40
126	Bob Wickman	.25
127	Richard Hidalgo	.25
128	Chuck Finley	.25
129	Billy Wagner	.25
130	Todd Hundley	.25
131	Dwight Gooden	.40
132	Russ Ortiz	.25
133	Mike Lowell	.25
134	Reggie Sanders	.25
135	John Valentin	.25
136	Brad Ausmus	.25
137	Chad Kreuter	.25
138	David Cone	.40
139	Brook Fordyce	.25
140	Roberto Alomar	.75
141	Charles Nagy	.25
142	Brian Hunter	.25
143	Mike Mussina	.75
144	Robin Ventura	.40
145	Kevin Brown	.40
146	Pat Hentgen	.25
147	Ryan Klesko	.40
148	Derek Bell	.25
149	Andy Sheets	.25
150	Larry Walker	.50
151	Scott Williamson	.25
152	Jose Offerman	.25
153	Doug Mientkiewicz	.25
154	John Snyder **RC**	.40
155	Sandy Alomar	.25
156	Joe Nathan	.25
157	Lance Johnson	.25
158	Odalis Perez	.25
159	Hideo Nomo	.75
160	Steve Finley	.25
161	Dave Martinez	.25
162	Matt Walbeck	.25
163	Bill Spiers	.25
164	Fernando Tatis	.25
165	Kenny Lofton	.40
166	Paul Byrd	.25
167	Aaron Sele	.25
168	Eddie Taubensee	.25
169	Reggie Jefferson	.25
170	Roger Clemens	2.50
171	Francisco Cordova	.25
172	Mike Bordick	.25
173	Wally Joyner	.25
174	Marvin Benard	.25
175	Jason Kendall	.40
176	Mike Stanley	.25
177	Chad Allen	.25
178	Carlos Beltran	.50
179	Deivi Cruz	.25
180	Chipper Jones	2.00
181	Vladimir Guerrero	1.50
182	Dave Burba	.25
183	Tom Goodwin	.25
184	Brian Daubach	.25
185	Jay Bell	.25
186	Roy Halladay	.50
187	Miguel Tejada	.50
188	Armando Rios	.25
189	Fernando Vina	.25
190	Eric Davis	.40
191	Henry Rodriguez	.25
192	Joe McEwing	.25
193	Jeff Kent	.50
194	Mike Jackson	.25
195	Mike Morgan	.25
196	Jeff Montgomery	.25
197	Jeff Zimmerman	.25
198	Tony Fernandez	.25
199	Jason Giambi	1.00
200	Jose Canseco	.75
201	Alex Gonzalez	.25
202	Jack Cust, Mike Colangelo, Dee Brown	.50
203	Felipe Lopez, Alfonso Soriano, Pablo Ozuna	3.00
204	Erubiel Durazo, Pat Burrell, Nick Johnson	.75
205	John Sneed **RC**, Kip Wells, Matt Blank	.50
206	Josh Kalinowski **RC**, Michael Tejera **RC**, Chris Mears	.50
207	Roosevelt Brown, Corey Patterson, Lance Berkman	.50
208	Kit Pellow, Kevin Barker, Russ Branyan	.40
209	B.J. Garbe **RC**, Larry Bigbie **RC**	3.00
210	Eric Munson, Bobby Bradley **RC**	.75
211	Josh Girdley, Kyle Snyder	.50
212	Chance Caple **RC**, Jason Jennings	.50
213	Ryan Christiansen **RC**, Brett Myers **RC**	6.00
214	Jason Stumm **RC**, Rob Purvis **RC**	.75
215	David Walling, Mike Paradis	.40
216	Omar Ortiz, Jay Gehrke	.40
217	David Cone (Season Highlights)	.40
218	Jose Jimenez (Season Highlights)	.25
219	Chris Singleton (Season Highlights)	.25
220	Fernando Tatis (Season Highlights)	.25
221	Todd Helton (Season Highlights)	1.00
222	Kevin Millwood (Post-Season Highlights)	.50
223	Todd Pratt (Post-Season Highlights)	.25
224	Orlando Hernandez (Post-Season Highlights)	.25
225	Post-Season Highlights	.25
226	Post-Season Highlights	.25
227	Bernie Williams (Post-Season Highlights)	.75
228	Mariano Rivera (Post-Season Highlights)	.50
229	Tony Gwynn (20th Century's Best)	1.50
230	Wade Boggs (20th Century's Best)	.50
231	Tim Raines (20th Century's Best)	.25
232	Mark McGwire (20th Century's Best)	3.00
233	Rickey Henderson (20th Century's Best)	.75
234	Rickey Henderson (20th Century's Best)	.75
235	Roger Clemens (20th Century's Best)	2.00
236	Mark McGwire (Magic Moments)	5.00
237	Hank Aaron (Magic Moments)	5.00
238	Cal Ripken Jr. (Magic Moments)	6.00
239	Wade Boggs (Magic Moments)	1.00
240	Tony Gwynn (Magic Moments)	3.00
	Series 1 checklist (1-201)	.05
	Series 1 checklist (202-240, inserts)	.05
241	Tom Glavine	.50
242	David Wells	.25
243	Kevin Appier	.25
244	Troy Percival	.25
245	Ray Lankford	.25
246	Marquis Grissom	.25
247	Randy Winn	.25
248	Miguel Batista	.25
249	Darren Dreifort	.25
250	Barry Bonds	3.00
251	Harold Baines	.25
252	Cliff Floyd	.25
253	Freddy Garcia	.40
254	Kenny Rogers	.25
255	Ben Davis	.25
256	Charles Johnson	.25
257	John Burkett	.25
258	Desi Relaford	.25
259	Al Martin	.25
260	Andy Pettitte	.50
261	Carlos Lee	.25
262	Matt Lawton	.25
263	Andy Fox	.25
264	Chan Ho Park	.25
265	Billy Koch	.25
266	Dave Roberts	.25
267	Carl Everett	.25
268	Orel Hershiser	.25
269	Trot Nixon	.25
270	Rusty Greer	.25
271	Will Clark	.75
272	Quilvio Veras	.25
273	Rico Brogna	.25
274	Devon White	.25
275	Tim Hudson	.50
276	Mike Hampton	.25
277	Miguel Cairo	.25
278	Darren Oliver	.25
279	Jeff Cirillo	.25
280	Al Leiter	.25
281	Brant Brown	.25
282	Carlos Febles	.25
283	Pedro Astacio	.25
284	Juan Guzman	.25
285	Orlando Hernandez	.25
286	Paul Konerko	.25
287	Tony Clark	.25
288	Aaron Boone	.50
289	Ismael Valdes	.25
290	Moises Alou	.50
291	Kevin Tapani	.25
292	John Franco	.25
293	Todd Zeile	.25
294	Jason Schmidt	.25
295	Johnny Damon	.40
296	Scott Brosius	.25
297	Travis Fryman	.40
298	Jose Vizcaino	.25
299	Eric Chavez	.50
300	Mike Piazza	2.00
301	Matt Clement	.25
302	Cristian Guzman	.25
303	Darryl Strawberry	.40
304	Jeff Abbott	.25
305	Brett Tomko	.25
306	Mike Lansing	.25
307	Eric Owens	.25
308	Livan Hernandez	.25
309	Rondell White	.40
310	Todd Stottlemyre	.25
311	Chris Carpenter	.25
312	Ken Hill	.25
313	Mark Loretta	.25
314	John Rocker	.25
315	Richie Sexson	.75
316	Ruben Mateo	.25
317	Ramon Martinez	.25
318	Mike Sirotka	.25
319	Jose Rosado	.25
320	Matt Mantei	.25
321	Kevin Millwood	.50
322	Gary DiSarcina	.25
323	Dustin Hermanson	.25
324	Mike Stanton	.25
325	Kirk Rueter	.25
326	Damian Miller	.25
327	Doug Glanville	.25
328	Scott Rolen	1.00
329	Ray Durham	.25
330	Butch Huskey	.25
331	Mariano Rivera	.50
332	Darren Lewis	.25
333	Ramiro Mendoza	.25
334	Mark Grudzielanek	.25
335	Mike Cameron	.25
336	Kelvim Escobar	.25
337	Bret Boone	.40
338	Mo Vaughn	.40
339	Craig Biggio	.40
340	Michael Barrett	.25
341	Marlon Anderson	.25
342	Bobby Jones	.25
343	John Halama	.25
344	Todd Ritchie	.25
345	Chuck Knoblauch	.25
346	Rick Reed	.25
347	Kelly Stinnett	.25
348	Tim Salmon	.50
349	A.J. Hinch	.25
350	Jose Cruz Jr.	.25

351 Roberto Hernandez .25
352 Edgar Renteria .25
353 Jose Hernandez .25
354 Brad Fullmer .25
355 Trevor Hoffman .25
356 Troy O'Leary .25
357 Justin Thompson .25
358 Kevin Young .25
359 Hideki Irabu .25
360 Jim Thome 1.00
361 Todd Dunwoody .25
362 Octavio Dotel .25
363 Omar Vizquel .40
364 Raul Mondesi .40
365 Shane Reynolds .25
366 Bartolo Colon .25
367 Chris Widger .25
368 Gabe Kapler .25
369 Bill Simas .25
370 Tino Martinez .50
371 John Thomson .25
372 Delino DeShields .25
373 Carlos Perez .25
374 Eddie Perez .25
375 Jeromy Burnitz .25
376 Jimmy Haynes .25
377 Travis Lee .25
378 Darryl Hamilton .25
379 Jamie Moyer .25
380 Alex Gonzalez .25
381 John Wetteland .25
382 Vinny Castilla .40
383 Jeff Suppan .25
384 Chad Curtis .25
385 Robb Nen .25
386 Wilson Alvarez .25
387 Andres Galarraga .50
388 Mike Remlinger .25
389 Geoff Jenkins .40
390 Matt Stairs .25
391 Bill Mueller .25
392 Mike Lowell .25
393 Andy Ashby .25
394 Ruben Rivera .25
395 Todd Helton 1.00
396 Bernie Williams .75
397 Royce Clayton .25
398 Manny Ramirez 1.00
399 Kerry Wood .75
400 Ken Griffey Jr. 2.00
401 Enrique Wilson .25
402 Joey Hamilton .25
403 Shawn Estes .25
404 Ugueth Urbina .25
405 Albert Belle .30
406 Rick Helling .25
407 Steve Parris .25
408 Eric Milton .25
409 Dave Mlicki .25
410 Shawn Green .50
411 Jaret Wright .25
412 Tony Womack .25
413 Vernon Wells .50
414 Ron Belliard .25
415 Ellis Burks .25
416 Scott Erickson .25
417 Rafael Palmeiro .75
418 Damion Easley .25
419 Jamey Wright .25
420 Corey Koskie .25
421 Bobby Howry .25
422 Ricky Ledee .25
423 Dmitri Young .25
424 Sidney Ponson .25
425 Greg Maddux 2.00
426 Jose Guillen .25
427 Jon Lieber .25
428 Andy Benes .25
429 Randy Velarde .25
430 Sean Casey .40
431 Torii Hunter .50
432 Ryan Rupe .25
433 David Segui .25
434 Rich Aurilia .25
435 Nomar Garciaparra 3.00
436 Denny Neagle .25
437 Ron Coomer .25
438 Chris Singleton .25
439 Tony Batista .25
440 Andruw Jones 1.00
441 Adam Piatt, Aubrey Huff, Sean Burroughs (Prospects) .50
442 Rafael Furcal, Jason Dallero, Travis Dawkins (Prospects) .50
443 Wilton Veras, Joe Crede, Mike Lamb **RC** (Prospects) .25
444 Julio Zuleta **RC**, Dernell Stenson, Jorge Toca (Prospects) .25
445 Tim Raines Jr., Gary Mathews Jr., Garry Maddox Jr. **RC** (Prospects) .50
446 Matt Riley, Mark Mulder, C.C. Sabathia (Prospects) .25
447 Scott Downs **RC**, Chris George, Matt Belisle (Prospects) .50
448 Doug Mirabelli, Ben Petrick, Jayson Werth (Prospects) .25
449 Josh Hamilton, Corey Myers **RC** (Draft Picks) .50
450 Ben Christensen **RC**, Brett Myers (Draft Picks) .50
451 Barry Zito **RC**, Ben Sheets **RC** (Draft Picks) 10.00
452 Ty Howington **RC**, Kurt Ainsworth **RC** (Draft Picks) 2.00
453 Rick Asadoorian **RC**, Vince Faison **RC** (Draft Picks) .50
454 Keith Reed **RC**, Jeff Heaverlo **RC** (Draft Picks) .50
455 Mike MacDougal **RC**, Jay Gehrke (Draft Picks) 1.50
456 Mark McGwire (Season Highlights) 3.00
457 Cal Ripken Jr. (Season Highlights) 4.00
458 Wade Boggs (Season Highlights) .75
459 Tony Gwynn (Season Highlights) 1.50
460 Jesse Orosco (Season Highlights) .25
461 Nomar Garciaparra, Larry Walker (League Leaders) 1.50
462 Mark McGwire, Ken Griffey Jr. (League Leaders) 1.50
463 Mark McGwire, Manny Ramirez (League Leaders) 1.50
464 Randy Johnson, Pedro Martinez (League Leaders) 1.00
465 Randy Johnson, Pedro Martinez (League Leaders) 1.00
466 Luis Gonzalez, Derek Jeter (League Leaders) 2.00
467 Manny Ramirez, Larry Walker (League Leaders) .75
468 Tony Gwynn (20th Century's Best) 1.50
469 Mark McGwire (20th Century's Best) 3.00
470 Frank Thomas (20th Century's Best) .75
471 Harold Baines (20th Century's Best) .25
472 Roger Clemens (20th Century's Best) 1.50
473 John Franco (20th Century's Best) .25
474 John Franco (20th Century's Best) .25
475 Ken Griffey Jr. (Magic Moments) 3.00
476 Barry Bonds (Magic Moments) 5.00
477 Sammy Sosa (Magic Moments) 4.00
478 Derek Jeter (Magic Moments) 6.00
479 Alex Rodriguez (Magic Moments) 5.00

Refractors

A parallel to the base set, Refractors have a reflective sheen to them when held up to light. They are seeded 1:12 packs and have "Refractor" written underneath the card number on the back.

Stars: 3-5X
Young Stars/RC's: 1-2X
Inserted 1:12

All-Star Rookie Team

This 10-card set highlights players who lived up to the high expectations placed on them during their rookie

season. These are seeded 1:16 packs and are numbered with an "RT" prefix on the card back. A Refractor parallel is also randomly inserted, seeded 1:80 packs. "Refractor" is printed under the card number on the back.

		NM/M
Complete Set (10):		10.00
Common Player:		.50
Inserted 1:16		
Refractors:		2-3X
Inserted 1:80		
1	Mark McGwire	3.00
2	Chuck Knoblauch	.50
3	Chipper Jones	2.00
4	Cal Ripken Jr.	4.00
5	Manny Ramirez	1.00
6	Jose Canseco	.75
7	Ken Griffey Jr.	2.00
8	Mike Piazza	2.00
9	Dwight Gooden	.50
10	Billy Wagner	.50

All-Topps Team

These feature top National League players and picks a top player for each position. They have a brown border utilizing Topps Chromium technology. Card backs have a small photo along with statistical comparisons made to current and former greats for their respective position. Backs are numbered with a "AT" prefix and are seeded 1:32 packs. A Refractor parallel is inserted 1:160 packs.

		NM/M
Complete Set (20):		40.00
Complete Series I Set (10):		20.00
Complete Series II Set (10):		20.00
Common Player:		.50
Inserted 1:32		
Refractors:		2-3X
Inserted 1:160		
1	Greg Maddux	3.00
2	Mike Piazza	3.00
3	Mark McGwire	5.00
4	Craig Biggio	1.00
5	Chipper Jones	3.00
6	Barry Larkin	1.00
7	Barry Bonds	5.00
8	Andruw Jones	1.50
9	Sammy Sosa	3.00
10	Larry Walker	1.00
11	Pedro Martinez	2.00
12	Ivan Rodriguez	1.00
13	Rafael Palmeiro	1.00
14	Roberto Alomar	1.00
15	Cal Ripken Jr.	6.00
16	Derek Jeter	6.00
17	Albert Belle	.50
18	Ken Griffey Jr.	3.00
19	Manny Ramirez	1.50
20	Jose Canseco	1.00

Allegiance

Allegiance features 20 stars who have spent their entire career with one team. They

are seeded 1:16 and are numbered with a "TA" prefix. There is also a hobby-exclusive Refractor parallel version, sequentially numbered to 100 and inserted 1:424 packs.

		NM/M
Complete Set (20):		30.00
Common Player:		.75
Inserted 1:16		
Refractors:		5X
Inserted 1:424		
1	Derek Jeter	6.00
2	Ivan Rodriguez	1.00
3	Alex Rodriguez	5.00
4	Cal Ripken Jr.	6.00
5	Mark Grace	1.00
6	Tony Gwynn	2.00
7	Juan Gonzalez	1.50
8	Frank Thomas	1.50
9	Manny Ramirez	1.50
10	Barry Larkin	.75
11	Bernie Williams	1.50
12	Raul Mondesi	.75
13	Vladimir Guerrero	1.50
14	Craig Biggio	.75
15	Nomar Garciaparra	4.00
16	Andruw Jones	1.50
17	Jim Thome	1.50
18	Scott Rolen	1.50
19	Chipper Jones	3.00
20	Ken Griffey Jr.	3.00

Combos

Ten player combinations linked by a common element are featured in this set. Combos are found 1:16 packs and are numbered with a "TC" prefix on the card back. A Refractor parallel is randomly seeded 1:80 packs and have "Refractor" printed under the card number on the back.

		NM/M
Complete Set (10):		20.00
Common Player:		1.00
Inserted 1:16		
Refractors:		2-3X
Inserted 1:80		
1	Roberto Alomar, Manny Ramirez, Kenny Lofton, Jim Thome	1.00
2	Tom Glavine, Greg Maddux, John Smoltz	2.00
3	Derek Jeter, Bernie Williams, Tino Martinez	4.00
4	Ivan Rodriguez, Mike Piazza	2.00
5	Nomar Garciaparra, Alex Rodriguez, Derek Jeter	4.00
6	Sammy Sosa, Mark McGwire	4.00
7	Pedro Martinez, Randy Johnson	1.50
8	Barry Bonds, Ken Griffey Jr.	3.00
9	Chipper Jones, Ivan Rodriguez	2.00
10	Cal Ripken Jr., Tony Gwynn, Wade Boggs	4.00

Kings

This 10-card set spotlights hitters who have averaged 30 or more homeruns per season for their career. Kings are seeded 1:32 packs and are numbered with an "CK" prefix on the card back. A Refractor parallel is also randomly inserted and are serially numbered to the featured player's career homerun total.

		NM/M
Complete Set (10):		25.00
Common Player:		1.50
Inserted 1:32		
1	Mark McGwire	5.00
2	Sammy Sosa	3.00
3	Ken Griffey Jr.	3.00
4	Mike Piazza	3.00
5	Alex Rodriguez	5.00
6	Manny Ramirez	1.50
7	Barry Bonds	6.00
8	Nomar Garciaparra	4.00
9	Chipper Jones	3.00
10	Vladimir Guerrero	1.50

Mark McGwire 1985 Rookie Reprint

This insert is a chromium reprinted version of McGwire's 1985 Topps rookie card. Each card features a commemorative gold-foil stamp. The insertion rate is 1:32 packs. A hobby-exclusive Refractor version is also inserted, limited to 70 sequentially numbered sets and seeded 1:12,116 packs.

	NM/M
Complete Set (1):	5.00
Inserted 1:32	
Refractor:	50.00
Production 70 cards.	
Mark McGwire	5.00

Millennium Stars

This 10-card set features stars who had less than three years major league experience in 2000. Millennium Stars are seeded 1:32 packs and are numbered with an "NMS" prefix. A Refractor parallel is randomly inserted in 1:160 packs and has "Refractor" printed under the card number on the back.

		NM/M
Complete Set (10):		10.00
Common Player:		.50
Inserted 1:32		
Refractors:		2-3X
Inserted 1:160		
1	Nomar Garciaparra	4.00
2	Vladimir Guerrero	1.50
3	Sean Casey	.75
4	Richie Sexson	1.00
5	Todd Helton	1.50
6	Carlos Beltran	.75
7	Kevin Millwood	.75
8	Ruben Mateo	.50
9	Pat Burrell	1.00
10	Alfonso Soriano	2.00

Own the Game

This 30-card set spotlights statistical stars and 1999 Major League Baseball award winners. These were seeded 1:11 packs and are numbered with an "OTG" prefix on the card back. A Refractor parallel is randomly inserted 1:55 packs and has "Refractor" written under the card number on the back.

		NM/M
Complete Set (30):		30.00
Common Player:		.25
Inserted 1:12		
Refractors:		2-3X
Inserted 1:55		
1	Derek Jeter	4.00
2	B.J. Surhoff	.25
3	Luis Gonzalez	.50
4	Manny Ramirez	1.00
5	Rafael Palmeiro	1.00
6	Mark McGwire	3.00
7	Mark McGwire	3.00
8	Sammy Sosa	2.00
9	Ken Griffey Jr.	2.00
10	Larry Walker	.50
11	Nomar Garciaparra	3.00
12	Derek Jeter	4.00
13	Larry Walker	.50
14	Mark McGwire	3.00
15	Manny Ramirez	1.00
16	Pedro Martinez	1.50
17	Randy Johnson	1.50
18	Kevin Millwood	.50
19	Pedro Martinez	1.50
20	Randy Johnson	1.50
21	Kevin Brown	.50
22	Chipper Jones	2.00
23	Ivan Rodriguez	1.00
24	Mariano Rivera	.50
25	Scott Williamson	.25
26	Carlos Beltran	.50
27	Randy Johnson	1.50
28	Pedro Martinez	1.50
29	Sammy Sosa	2.00
30	Manny Ramirez	1.00

Power Players

Twenty of the leading power hitters are featured on a colorful design. They are seeded 1:8 packs and are numbered with a "P" prefix. A Refractor parallel is also randomly seeded 1:40 packs.

		NM/M
Complete Set (20):		25.00
Common Player:		.25
Inserted 1:8		
Refractors:		2-3X
Inserted 1:40		
1	Juan Gonzalez	1.00
2	Ken Griffey Jr.	2.00
3	Mark McGwire	3.00
4	Nomar Garciaparra	3.00

5 Barry Bonds 3.00
6 Mo Vaughn .40
7 Larry Walker .50
8 Alex Rodriguez 3.00
9 Jose Canseco .75
10 Jeff Bagwell 1.00
11 Manny Ramirez 1.00
12 Albert Belle .25
13 Frank Thomas 1.00
14 Mike Piazza 2.00
15 Chipper Jones 2.00
16 Sammy Sosa 2.00
17 Vladimir Guerrero 1.00
18 Scott Rolen 1.00
19 Raul Mondesi .40
20 Derek Jeter 4.00

21st Century Topps

This 10-card set focuses on the top young stars in baseball heading into the next century. These were seeded 1:16 packs and are numbered with a "C" prefix on the card back. A Refractor parallel version is also seeded 1:80 packs.

NM/M
Complete Set (10): 10.00
Common Player: .25
Inserted 1:16
Refractors: 2-3X
Inserted 1:80
1 Ben Grieve .25
2 Alex Gonzalez .25
3 Derek Jeter 4.00
4 Sean Casey .50
5 Nomar Garciaparra 3.00
6 Alex Rodriguez 3.00
7 Scott Rolen 1.00
8 Andruw Jones 1.00
9 Vladimir Guerrero 1.00
10 Todd Helton 1.00

Traded and Rookies

NM/M
Complete Set (135): 60.00
Common Player: .25
1 Mike MacDougal RC 1.00
2 Andy Tracy RC .50
3 Brandon Phillips RC 3.00
4 Brandon Inge RC 1.50
5 Robbie Morrison RC .50
6 Josh Pressley RC .50
7 Todd Moser RC .50
8 Rob Purvis RC .50
9 Chance Caple RC .50
10 Ben Sheets 2.00
11 Russ Jacobson RC .50
12 Brian Cole RC .50
13 Brad Baker RC .50
14 Alex Cintron RC .75
15 Lyle Overbay RC 2.00
16 Mike Edwards RC .50
17 Sean McGowan RC .50
18 Jose Molina RC .50
19 Marcos Castillo RC .50
20 Josue Espada RC .50
21 Alex Gordon RC .50
22 Rob Pugmire RC .50
23 Jason Stumm RC .50
24 Ty Howington RC 1.00
25 Brett Myers 1.00
26 Maicer Izturis RC .50
27 John McDonald RC .50
28 Wilfredo Rodriguez RC .50
29 Carlos Zambrano RC 6.00
30 Alejandro Diaz RC .50
31 Geraldo Guzman RC .50
32 J.R. House RC .75
33 Elvin Nina RC .50
34 Juan Pierre RC 2.00
35 Ben Johnson RC 1.00
36 Jeff Bailey RC .50
37 Miguel Olivo RC .50
38 Francisco Rodriguez RC 4.00
39 Tony Pena Jr. RC .50
40 Miguel Cabrera RC 50.00
41 Asdrubal Oropeza RC .50
42 Junior Zamora RC .50
43 Jovanny Cedeno RC .50
44 John Sneed RC .50
45 Josh Kalinowski RC .50
46 Mike Young RC 8.00
47 Rico Washington RC .50
48 Chad Durbin RC .50
49 Junior Brignac RC .50
50 Carlos Hernandez RC .50
51 Cesar Izturis RC 1.00
52 Oscar Salazar RC .50
53 Pat Strange RC .50
54 Rick Asadoorian .50
55 Keith Reed RC .50
56 Leo Estrella RC .50
57 Wascar Serrano RC .50
58 Richard Gomez RC .50
59 Ramon Santiago RC .50
60 Jovanny Sosa RC .50
61 Aaron Rowand RC 3.00
62 Junior Guerrero RC .50
63 Luis Terrero RC .75
64 Brian Sanches RC .50
65 Scott Sobkowiak RC .50
66 Gary Majewski RC .50
67 Barry Zito 2.00
68 Ryan Christianson RC .50
69 Cristian Guerrero RC .50
70 Tomas de la Rosa RC .50
71 Andrew Beinbrink RC .50
72 Ryan Knox RC .50
73 Alex Graman RC .50
74 Juan Guzman RC .50
75 Ruben Salazar RC .50
76 Luis Matos RC .75
77 Tony Mota RC .50
78 Doug Davis RC .75
79 Ben Christensen RC .50
80 Mike Lamb .50
81 Adrian Gonzalez RC (Draft Picks) 5.00
82 Mike Stodolka RC (Draft Picks) .50
83 Adam Johnson RC (Draft Picks) .50
84 Matt Wheatland RC (Draft Picks) .50
85 Corey Smith RC (Draft Picks) .75
86 Rocco Baldelli RC (Draft Picks) 4.00
87 Keith Bucktrot RC (Draft Picks) .50
88 Adam Wainwright RC (Draft Picks) 5.00
89 Scott Thorman RC (Draft Picks) 2.00
90 Tripper Johnson RC (Draft Picks) .75
91 Jim Edmonds .50
92 Masato Yoshii .25
93 Adam Kennedy .25
94 Darryl Kile .25
95 Mark McLemore .25
96 Ricky Gutierrez .25
97 Juan Gonzalez .50
98 Melvin Mora .25
99 Dante Bichette .25
100 Lee Stevens .25
101 Roger Cedeno .25
102 John Olerud .40
103 Eric Young .25
104 Mickey Morandini .25
105 Travis Lee .25
106 Greg Vaughn .25
107 Todd Zeile .25
108 Chuck Finley .25
109 Ismael Valdes .25
110 Ron Henika .25
111 Pat Hentgen .25
112 Ryan Klesko .40
113 Derek Bell .25
114 Hideo Nomo 1.00
115 Aaron Sele .25
116 Fernando Vina .25
117 Wally Joyner .25
118 Brian Hunter .25
119 Joe Girardi .25
120 Omar Daal .25
121 Brook Fordyce .25
122 Jose Valentin .25
123 Curt Schilling .75
124 B.J. Surhoff .25
125 Henry Rodriguez .25
126 Mike Bordick .25
127 David Justice .50
128 Charles Johnson .25
129 Will Clark .75
130 Dwight Gooden .25
131 David Segui .25
132 Denny Neagle .25
133 Andy Ashby .25
134 Bruce Chen .25
135 Jason Bere .25

FanFest Honus Wagner T206 Reprint

In conjunction with the forthcoming sale of the finest-known T206 Honus Wagner card in July, 2000, Topps produced this reprint as a promotional device for the seller (Robert Edwards Auction) and principal venue (eBay). The card was distributed at the All-Star FanFest in Atlanta. Front of the 1-1/2" x 2-5/8" card reproduces the 1909 Wagner card. The black-and-white back details the history of the card and makes note of the upcoming sale.

NM/M
Honus Wagner 5.00

2000 Topps Gallery

The base set consists of 150 cards. Cards 101-150 are broken down into two subsets Masters of the Game (20 cards) and Students of the Game (30 cards). The subset cards are found one per pack. Card fronts have a tan textured border around the player photo with the player name, team and Gallery logo stamped in gold foil. Card backs have a small photo, brief career note and the featured player's '99 statistics. Gallery was a hobby exclusive product. Five-card packs carried a $3 SRP.

NM/M
Complete Set (150): 40.00
Common Player: .15
Common (101-150): .50
Inserted 1:1
Pack (6): 2.00
Wax Box (24): 40.00
1 Nomar Garciaparra 1.50
2 Kevin Millwood .25
3 Jay Bell .15
4 Rusty Greer .15
5 Bernie Williams .50
6 Barry Larkin .25
7 Carlos Beltran .25
8 Damion Easley .15
9 Maggio Ordonez .25
10 Matt Williams .20
11 Shannon Stewart .15
12 Ray Lankford .15
13 Vinny Castilla .20
14 Miguel Tejada .25
15 Craig Biggio .25
16 Chipper Jones 1.00
17 Albert Belle .20
18 Doug Glanville .15
19 Brian Giles .25
20 Shawn Green .25
21 J.T. Snow Jr. .15
22 Luis Gonzalez .25
23 Carlos Delgado .50
24 J.D. Drew .25
25 Ivan Rodriguez .50
26 Tino Martinez .25
27 Erubiel Durazo .20
28 Scott Rolen .50
29 Gary Sheffield .40
30 Manny Ramirez .50
31 Luis Castillo .15
32 Fernando Tatis .15
33 Darin Erstad .25
34 Tim Hudson .25
35 Sammy Sosa 1.00
36 Jason Kendall .25
37 Todd Walker .15
38 Orlando Hernandez .25
39 Pokey Reese .15
40 Mike Piazza 1.00
41 B.J. Surhoff .15
42 Tony Gwynn .75
43 Kevin Brown .25
44 Preston Wilson .25
45 Kenny Lofton .25
46 Rondell White .20
47 Frank Thomas .50
48 Neifi Perez .15
49 Edgardo Alfonzo .15
50 Ken Griffey Jr. 1.00
51 Barry Bonds 1.50
52 Brian Jordan .15
53 Raul Mondesi .25
54 Troy Glaus .50
55 Curt Schilling .40
56 Mike Mussina .50
57 Brian Daubach .15
58 Roger Clemens 1.00
59 Carlos Febles .15
60 Todd Helton .50
61 Mark Grace .40
62 Randy Johnson .75
63 Jeff Bagwell .50
64 Tom Glavine .25
65 Adrian Beltre .20
66 Rafael Palmeiro .50
67 Paul O'Neill .25
68 Robin Ventura .25
69 Ray Durham .15
70 Mark McGwire 1.50
71 Greg Vaughn .15
72 Javy Lopez .25
73 Jeromy Burnitz .15
74 Mike Lieberthal .15
75 Cal Ripken Jr. 2.00
76 Juan Gonzalez .50
77 Sean Casey .25
78 Jermaine Dye .15
79 John Olerud .25
80 Jose Canseco .40
81 Eric Karros .20
82 Roberto Alomar .40
83 Ben Grieve .15
84 Greg Maddux 1.00
85 Pedro Martinez .75
86 Tony Clark .15
87 Richie Sexson .25
88 Cliff Floyd .15
89 Eric Chavez .25
90 Andruw Jones .50
91 Vladimir Guerrero .50
92 Alex Gonzalez .15
93 Jim Thome .50
94 Bob Abreu .25
95 Derek Jeter 2.00
96 Larry Walker .25
97 John Smoltz .25
98 Mo Vaughn .20
99 Jason Giambi .50
100 Alex Rodriguez 1.50
101 Mark McGwire (Masters of the Game) 2.50
102 Sammy Sosa (Masters of the Game) 1.50
103 Alex Rodriguez (Masters of the Game) 2.50
104 Derek Jeter (Masters of the Game) 3.00
105 Greg Maddux (Masters of the Game) 1.50
106 Jeff Bagwell (Masters of the Game) .75
107 Nomar Garciaparra (Masters of the Game) 2.00
108 Mike Piazza (Masters of the Game) 1.50
109 Pedro Martinez (Masters of the Game) 1.00
110 Chipper Jones (Masters of the Game) 1.50
111 Randy Johnson (Masters of the Game) 1.00
112 Barry Bonds (Masters of the Game) 2.50
113 Ken Griffey Jr. (Masters of the Game) 1.50
114 Manny Ramirez (Masters of the Game) .75
115 Ivan Rodriguez (Masters of the Game) .75
116 Juan Gonzalez (Masters of the Game) .75
117 Vladimir Guerrero (Masters of the Game) .75
118 Tony Gwynn (Masters of the Game) 1.00
119 Larry Walker (Masters of the Game) .50
120 Cal Ripken Jr. (Masters of the Game) 3.00
121 Josh Hamilton (Students of the Game) .50
122 Corey Patterson (Students of the Game) .50
123 Pat Burrell (Students of the Game) .50
124 Nick Johnson (Students of the Game) .50
125 Adam Piatt (Students of the Game) .50
126 Rick Ankiel (Students of the Game) .50
127 A.J. Burnett (Students of the Game) .50
128 Ben Petrick (Students of the Game) .50
129 Rafael Furcal (Students of the Game) .75
130 Alfonso Soriano (Students of the Game) 2.00
131 Dee Brown (Students of the Game) .50
132 Ruben Mateo (Students of the Game) .50
133 Pablo Ozuna (Students of the Game) .50
134 Sean Burroughs (Students of the Game) .75
135 Mark Mulder (Students of the Game) .75
136 Jason Jennings (Students of the Game) .50
137 Eric Munson (Students of the Game) .50
138 Vernon Wells (Students of the Game) .75
139 Brett Myers RC (Students of the Game) 3.00
140 Ben Christensen RC (Students of the Game) .50
141 Bobby Bradley RC (Students of the Game) .50
142 Ruben Salazar RC (Students of the Game) .50
143 Ryan Christianson RC (Students of the Game) .50
144 Corey Myers RC (Students of the Game) .50
145 Aaron Rowand RC (Students of the Game) 1.00
146 Julio Zuleta RC (Students of the Game) .50
147 Kurt Ainsworth RC (Students of the Game) 1.00
148 Scott Downs RC (Students of the Game) .50
149 Larry Bigbie RC (Students of the Game) 1.50
150 Chance Caple RC (Students of the Game) .50

Players Private Issue

A parallel to the 150-card base set, Players Private Issue differ from the base cards with silver foil stamping on the card front and "Players Private Issue" stamped in silver foil across the card bottom. Card backs are serial numbered in an edition of 250 sets.

Stars (1-100): 4-8X
SPs (101-150): 2-4X
Production 250 Sets

Autographs

This five-card set features top prospects. Each card is stamped with the Topps Certified Autograph Issue logo and the Topps Authentication sticker. Autographs are seeded 1:153 packs.

NM/M
Common Player: 5.00
Inserted 1:153
RA Rick Ankiel 15.00
RM Ruben Mateo 5.00
CP Corey Patterson 15.00
BP Ben Petrick 5.00
VW Vernon Wells 20.00

Gallery Exhibits

This 30-card set traces the history of art from medieval to contemporary. Card fronts have gold foil stamping and the card backs are numbered with a "GE" prefix and are found 1:18 packs.

NM/M
Complete Set (30): 50.00
Common Player: .50
Inserted 1:18
1 Mark McGwire 5.00
2 Jeff Bagwell 1.50
3 Mike Piazza 3.00
4 Alex Rodriguez 5.00
5 Nomar Garciaparra 4.00
6 Ivan Rodriguez 1.50
7 Chipper Jones 3.00
8 Cal Ripken Jr. 6.00
9 Tony Gwynn 2.00
10 Jose Canseco 1.00
11 Albert Belle .50
12 Greg Maddux 3.00
13 Barry Bonds 5.00
14 Ken Griffey Jr. 3.00
15 Juan Gonzalez 1.50
16 Rickey Henderson 1.00
17 Craig Biggio .75
18 Vladimir Guerrero 1.50
19 Rey Ordonez .50
20 Roberto Alomar 1.00
21 Derek Jeter 6.00
22 Manny Ramirez 1.50
23 Shawn Green 1.00
24 Sammy Sosa 3.00
25 Larry Walker 1.00
26 Pedro Martinez 2.00
27 Randy Johnson 2.00
28 Pat Burrell 1.00
29 Josh Hamilton 1.00
30 Corey Patterson 1.00

Gallery of Heroes

This 10-card set is printed on an acetate stock that simulates stained glass. Gallery of Heroes are found on the average of 1:24 packs and are numbered with a "GH" prefix on the card back.

NM/M
Complete Set (10): 20.00
Common Player: 1.00
Inserted 1:24

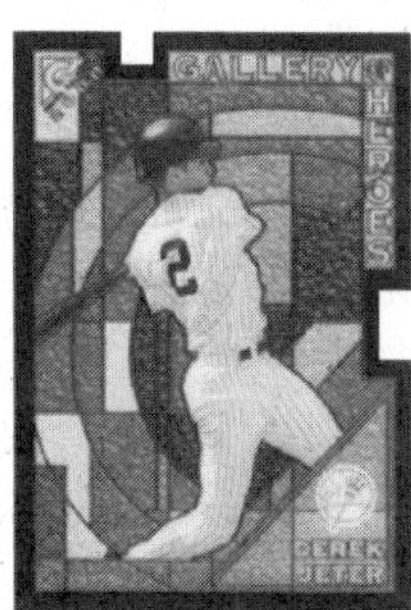

1 Alex Rodriguez 3.00
2 Chipper Jones 2.00
3 Pedro Martinez 1.50
4 Sammy Sosa 2.00
5 Mark McGwire 3.00
6 Nomar Garciaparra 3.00
7 Vladimir Guerrero 1.00
8 Ken Griffey Jr. 2.00
9 Mike Piazza 2.00
10 Derek Jeter 4.00

Press Plates

The aluminum press plates used to print the Gallery cards were inserted at a rate of one per 1,200 packs. Each card's front and back can be found in four different color variations. Because of the unique nature of each plate, assignment of catalog values in not feasible.

NM/M
Common Player: 50.00

Proof Positive

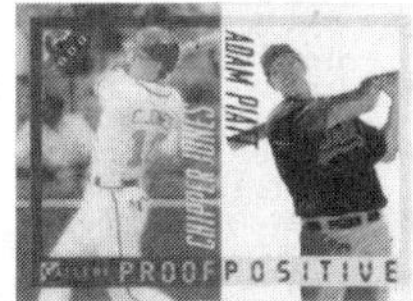

This 10-card set features both positive and negative photography. Done on a horizontal format the inserts pair a current star with a top prospect at the same position. Printed on a clear polycarbonate stock they were inserted 1:48 packs and are numbered with a "P" prefix.

NM/M
Complete Set (10): 40.00
Common Player: 3.00
Inserted 1:48
1 Ken Griffey Jr., Ruben Mateo 4.00
2 Derek Jeter, Alfonso Soriano 6.00
3 Mark McGwire, Pat Burrell 6.00
4 Pedro Martinez, A.J. Burnett 3.00
5 Alex Rodriguez, Rafael Furcal 6.00
6 Sammy Sosa, Corey Patterson 4.00
7 Randy Johnson, Rick Ankiel 3.00
8 Chipper Jones, Adam Piatt 4.00
9 Nomar Garciaparra, Pablo Ozuna 6.00
10 Mike Piazza, Eric Munson 4.00

Topps Heritage

Twenty current players are artistically depicted using the 1954 Topps card design as a template. They are seeded 1:12 packs and are numbered on the card back with a "TGH" prefix. As an added bonus the original artwork used in the development of the set is available through the Topps Gallery Auction. Auction points cards are found in every pack of Gallery.

NM/M
Complete Set (20): 100.00
Common Player: 2.00
Inserted 1:12
Proofs: 1-2X
Inserted 1:27
1 Mark McGwire 12.00
2 Sammy Sosa 8.00
3 Greg Maddux 8.00
4 Mike Piazza 8.00
5 Ivan Rodriguez 4.00
6 Manny Ramirez 4.00
7 Jeff Bagwell 4.00
8 Sean Casey 2.00
9 Orlando Hernandez 2.00
10 Randy Johnson 5.00
11 Pedro Martinez 5.00
12 Vladimir Guerrero 4.00
13 Shawn Green 2.50
14 Ken Griffey Jr. 8.00
15 Alex Rodriguez 12.00
16 Nomar Garciaparra 10.00
17 Derek Jeter 15.00
18 Tony Gwynn 5.00
19 Chipper Jones 8.00
20 Cal Ripken Jr. 15.00

Lithos

Eight cards from the Topps Gallery set were issued in the form of limited edition lithographs by Bill Goff Inc. Measuring 18" x 25", the lithographs were each produced in an edition of 600, with 60 artist's proofs. Issue price on the lithos was $80 for single-player pieces and $100 for the multi-player prints.

NM/M
Complete Set (8): 675.00
Common Player: 80.00
(1) Shawn Green (1954 Topps Style) 80.00
(2) Ken Griffey Jr. (1954 Topps Style) 80.00
(3) Chipper Jones (1954 Topps Style) 80.00
(4) Pedro Martinez (1954 Topps Style) 80.00
(5) Alex Rodriguez (1954 Topps Style) 80.00
(6) Ivan Rodriguez (1954 Topps Style) 80.00
(7) Three of a Kind (Nomar Garciaparra, Alex Rodriguez, Derek Jeter) 100.00
(8) Torre's Terrors (Paul O'Neill, Derek Jeter, Bernie Williams, Tino Martinez) 100.00

2000 Topps Gold Label Pre-Production

A Derek Jeter card in each of the three classes of Gold Label was produced as a promo and distributed in three-card cello packs.

NM/M
Complete Set (3): 7.50
Common Card: 3.00
PP1 Derek Jeter/Btg 3.00
PP2 Derek Jeter/Fldg 3.00
PP3 Derek Jeter/Running 3.00

2000 Topps Gold Label Class 1

Each base card in the 100-card set has three different classes, each noted on the card back below the featured player's team logo. Each base card is also printed on 35-point rainbow styrene stock with gold foil stamping. Besides the notation on the card back, Class 1's can also be identified by the action in the background photo. Hitters are hitting and pitchers are at the start of their wind-up. A Gold die-cut parallel is also randomly seeded and are serially numbered to 100.

NM/M
Complete Set (100): 25.00
Common Player: .25
Gold Parallel: 4-8X
Production 100 Sets
Pack (3): 2.00
Wax Box (24): 30.00
1 Sammy Sosa 1.50
2 Greg Maddux 1.50
3 Dee Brown .25
4 Rondell White .40
5 Fernando Tatis .25
6 Troy Glaus .75
7 Nick Johnson .40
8 Albert Belle .30
9 Scott Rolen .75
10 Rafael Palmeiro .50
11 Tony Gwynn 1.00
12 Kevin Brown .40
13 Roberto Alomar .50
14 John Olerud .40
15 Rick Ankiel .25
16 Chipper Jones 1.50
17 Craig Biggio .40
18 Mark Mulder .40
19 Carlos Delgado .75
20 Alex Gonzalez .25
21 Gabe Kapler .25
22 Derek Jeter 3.00
23 Carlos Beltran .40
24 Todd Helton .75
25 Mark McGwire 2.50
26 Ben Grieve .25
27 Rafael Furcal .40
28 Vernon Wells .40
29 Greg Vaughn .25
30 Vladimir Guerrero .75
31 Mike Piazza 1.50
32 Roger Clemens 2.00
33 Barry Larkin .40
34 Pedro Martinez 1.00
35 Matt Williams .30
36 Mo Vaughn .30
37 Tim Hudson .40
38 Andruw Jones .75
39 Vinny Castilla .25
40 Frank Thomas .75
41 Pokey Reese .25
42 Corey Patterson .40
43 Jeromy Burnitz .25
44 Preston Wilson .40
45 Juan Gonzalez .75
46 Brian Giles .40
47 Todd Walker .25
48 Magglio Ordonez .40
49 Alfonso Soriano 1.00
50 Ken Griffey Jr. 1.50
51 Michael Barrett .25
52 Shawn Green .50
53 Erubiel Durazo .40
54 Adam Piatt .25
55 Pat Burrell .50
56 Mike Mussina .50
57 Bernie Williams .75
58 Sean Casey .40
59 Randy Johnson 1.00
60 Jeff Bagwell .75
61 Eric Chavez .50
62 Josh Hamilton .50
63 A.J. Burnett .25
64 Jim Thome .75
65 Raul Mondesi .40
66 Jason Kendall .40
67 Mike Lieberthal .25
68 Robin Ventura .40
69 Ivan Rodriguez .50
70 Larry Walker .40
71 Eric Munson .25
72 Brian Jordan .25
73 Edgardo Alfonzo .25
74 Curt Schilling .50
75 Nomar Garciaparra 2.00
76 Mark Grace .50
77 Shannon Stewart .25
78 J.D. Drew .40
79 Jack Cust .25
80 Cal Ripken Jr. 3.00
81 Bob Abreu .40
82 Ruben Mateo .25
83 Orlando Hernandez .25
84 Kris Benson .25
85 Barry Bonds 2.50
86 Manny Ramirez .75
87 Jose Canseco .50
88 Sean Burroughs .25
89 Kevin Millwood .40
90 Alex Rodriguez 2.50
91 Brett Myers **RC** 3.00
92 Rick Asadoorian **RC** .40
93 Ben Christensen **RC** .40
94 Bobby Bradley **RC** .50
95 Corey Myers **RC** .50
96 Brad Baisley **RC** .50
97 Aaron McNeal **RC** .50
98 Aaron Rowand **RC** .75
99 Scott Downs **RC** .40
100 Michael Tejera **RC** .40

Class 2

Each base card in the 100-card set has three different classes, each noted on the card back below the featured player's team logo. Each base card is also printed on 35-point rainbow styrene stock with gold foil stamping. Besides the notation on the card back, Class 2's can also be identified by the action in the background photo. Hitters are fielding and pitchers are in a throwing motion. A Gold die-cut parallel is also randomly seeded and are serially numbered to 100.

Same prices as Class 1.
Gold Parallel: 4-8X

Class 3

Each base card in the 100-card set has three different classes, each noted on the card back below the featured player's team logo. Each base card is also printed on 35-point rainbow styrene stock with gold foil stamping. Besides the notation on the card back, Class 3's can also be identified by the action in the background photo. Hitters are running and pitchers are in their follow through. A Gold die-cut parallel is also randomly seeded and are serially numbered to 100.

Same prices as Class 1.
Gold Parallel: 4-8X
Production 100 Sets

Bullion

This 10-card set features three teammates superimposed over their team logo on a gold holo-foiled front with gold foil stamping. They are seeded 1:53 packs and are numbered on the card back with a "B" prefix.

NM/M
Complete Set (10): 125.00
Common Player: 4.00
Inserted 1:53
1 Jim Thome, Manny Ramirez, Roberto Alomar 6.00
2 Derek Jeter, Orlando Hernandez, Bernie Williams 15.00
3 Chipper Jones, Andruw Jones, Greg Maddux 12.00
4 Alex Rodriguez, Jay Buhner, John Olerud 20.00
5 Nomar Garciaparra, Pedro Martinez, Brian Daubach 15.00
6 Mark McGwire, J.D. Drew, Rick Ankiel 20.00
7 Sammy Sosa, Mark Grace, Kerry Wood 15.00
8 Ken Griffey Jr., Sean Casey, Barry Larkin 20.00
9 Mike Piazza, Edgardo Alfonzo, Robin Ventura 15.00
10 Randy Johnson, Matt Williams, Erubiel Durazo 6.00

End of the Rainbow

This 15-card set highlights some of baseball's top prospects on a silver holo foiled card front with gold foil stamping. Card backs are numbered with an "ER" prefix and are seeded 1:11 packs.

NM/M
Complete Set (15): 8.00
Common Player: .50
Inserted 1:11
1 Pat Burrell 1.50
2 Corey Patterson 1.00
3 Josh Hamilton 1.00
4 Eric Munson .50
5 Sean Burroughs .75
6 Jack Cust .50
7 Rafael Furcal .75
8 Ruben Salazar .50
9 Brett Myers 1.00
10 Wes Anderson .50
11 Nick Johnson 1.00
12 Scott Downs .50
13 Choo Freeman .50
14 Brad Baisley .50
15 A.J. Burnett .75

Prospector's Dream

These inserts feature 10 players whose success was projected early in their careers. Card fronts feature gold holo foil with the player name, Gold Label logo and insert name stamped in gold foil. Card backs are numbered with an "PD" prefix. They are inserted 1:26 packs.

NM/M
Complete Set (10): 15.00
Common Player: .50
Inserted 1:26
1 Mark McGwire 3.00
2 Alex Rodriguez 3.00
3 Nomar Garciaparra 3.00
4 Pat Burrell .75
5 Todd Helton 1.00
6 Derek Jeter 4.00
7 Adam Piatt .50
8 Chipper Jones 2.00
9 Shawn Green .75
10 Josh Hamilton 1.00

The Treasury

This 25-card set spotlights 15 veterans and 10 prospects on a silver holo foiled front with gold foil stamping. They have an insertion ratio of 1:21 packs and are numbered on the card back with an "T" prefix.

NM/M
Complete Set (25): 40.00
Common Player: .50
Inserted 1:21
1 Ken Griffey Jr. 3.00
2 Derek Jeter 6.00
3 Chipper Jones 3.00
4 Manny Ramirez 1.50
5 Nomar Garciaparra 4.00
6 Sammy Sosa 3.00
7 Cal Ripken Jr. 6.00
8 Alex Rodriguez 5.00
9 Mike Piazza 3.00
10 Pedro Martinez 2.00
11 Vladimir Guerrero 1.50
12 Jeff Bagwell 1.50
13 Shawn Green 1.00
14 Greg Maddux 3.00
15 Mark McGwire 5.00
16 Josh Hamilton 1.00
17 Corey Patterson 1.00
18 Dee Brown .50
19 Rafael Furcal .75
20 Pat Burrell 1.00
21 Alfonso Soriano 3.00
22 Adam Piatt .50
23 A.J. Burnett .75
24 Mark Mulder .75
25 Ruben Mateo .50

Name Mismatches

Because of faulty alignment when the gold-foil logo and player name were applied to card fronts, some Gold Label cards are found with the wrong name on front. Because each of these error cards is rare or possibly unique, and the demand is dependent on the combination of photo and name, it is not possible to assign values.

2000 Topps HD

This super-premium product consists of 100 regular base cards comprised of 88 veterans and 12 rookies. The base cards feature hyper-color technology and printed on a very thick 50-pt. card stock. Card backs have a small photo, career highlight and complete year-by-year statistics. A Platinum parallel to the base set is also randomly seeded and are sequentially numbered to 99 sets.

		NM/M
Complete Set (100):		30.00
Common Player:		.25
Platinums:		4-8X
Production 99 Sets		
Pack (4):		1.50
Wax Box (20):		30.00
1	Derek Jeter	3.00
2	Andruw Jones	.75
3	Ben Grieve	.25
4	Carlos Beltran	.40
5	Randy Johnson	1.00
6	Javy Lopez	.40
7	Gary Sheffield	.50
8	John Olerud	.40
9	Vinny Castilla	.25
10	Barry Larkin	.40
11	Tony Clark	.25
12	Roberto Alomar	.50
13	Brian Jordan	.25
14	Wade Boggs	.50
15	Carlos Febles	.25
16	Alfonso Soriano	1.50
17	A.J. Burnett	.25
18	Matt Williams	.25
19	Alex Gonzalez	.25
20	Larry Walker	.40
21	Jeff Bagwell	.75
22	Al Leiter	.25
23	Ken Griffey Jr.	1.50
24	Ruben Mateo	.25
25	Mark Grace	.50
26	Carlos Delgado	.75
27	Vladimir Guerrero	.75
28	Kenny Lofton	.40
29	Rusty Greer	.25
30	Pedro Martinez	1.00
31	Todd Helton	.75
32	Ray Lankford	.25
33	Jose Canseco	.50
34	Raul Mondesi	.40
35	Mo Vaughn	.40
36	Eric Chavez	.40
37	Manny Ramirez	.75
38	Jason Kendall	.40
39	Mike Mussina	.50
40	Dante Bichette	.25
41	Troy Glaus	.75
42	Rickey Henderson	.50
43	Pablo Ozuna	.25
44	Michael Barrett	.25
45	Tony Gwynn	1.00
46	John Smoltz	.40
47	Rafael Palmeiro	.50
48	Curt Schilling	.50
49	Todd Walker	.25
50	Greg Vaughn	.25
51	Orlando Hernandez	.25
52	Jim Thome	.75
53	Pat Burrell	.50
54	Tim Salmon	.40
55	Tom Glavine	.40
56	Travis Lee	.25
57	Gabe Kapler	.25
58	Greg Maddux	1.50
59	Scott Rolen	.75
60	Cal Ripken Jr.	3.00
61	Preston Wilson	.40
62	Ivan Rodriguez	.50
63	Johnny Damon	.40
64	Bernie Williams	.50
65	Barry Bonds	2.50
66	Sammy Sosa	1.50
67	Robin Ventura	.40
68	Tony Fernandez	.25
69	Jay Bell	.25
70	Mark McGwire	2.50
71	Jeromy Burnitz	.25
72	Chipper Jones	1.50
73	Josh Hamilton	.25
74	Darin Erstad	.40
75	Alex Rodriguez	2.50
76	Sean Casey	.40
77	Tino Martinez	.40
78	Juan Gonzalez	.75
79	Cliff Floyd	.25
80	Craig Biggio	.40
81	Shawn Green	.50
82	Adrian Beltre	.25
83	Mike Piazza	1.50
84	Nomar Garciaparra	2.00
85	Kevin Brown	.40
86	Roger Clemens	2.00
87	Frank Thomas	.75
88	Albert Belle	.25
89	Erubiel Durazo	.25
90	David Walling	.25
91	John Sneed **RC**	.50
92	Larry Bigbie **RC**	1.50
93	B.J. Garbe **RC**	.50
94	Bobby Bradley **RC**	.75
95	Ryan Christiansen **RC**	.50
96	Jay Gerhke **RC**	.50
97	Jason Stumm **RC**	.50
98	Brett Myers **RC**	4.00
99	Chance Caple **RC**	.50
100	Corey Myers **RC**	.75

Autographs

This two-card set features Cal Ripken Jr. and Derek Jeter. Card fronts include the Topps "Certified Autograph Issue" logo stamp as well as the Topps 3M authentication sticker to verify its authenticity. The insert rate for Jeter is 1:859 and Ripken Jr. 1:4,386.

		NM/M
Jeter 1:859		
Ripken 1:4,386		
1	Derek Jeter	150.00
2	Cal Ripken Jr.	250.00

Ballpark Figures

This 10-card set features a baseball field designed die-cut. These are seeded 1:11 packs and are numbered with a "BF" prefix on the card back.

		NM/M
Complete Set (10):		15.00
Common Player:		.50
Inserted 1:11		
1	Mark McGwire	3.00
2	Ken Griffey Jr.	2.00
3	Nomar Garciaparra	3.00
4	Derek Jeter	4.00
5	Sammy Sosa	2.00
6	Mike Piazza	2.00
7	Juan Gonzalez	1.00
8	Larry Walker	.75
9	Ben Grieve	.50
10	Barry Bonds	3.00

Clearly Refined

This 10-card set focuses on baseball's top young stars heading into the 2000 season. They are printed on high definition card stock and are seeded 1:20 packs. These are numbered with a "CR" prefix on the card back.

		NM/M
Complete Set (10):		8.00
Common Player:		.50
Inserted 1:20		
1	Alfonso Soriano	3.00
2	Ruben Mateo	.50
3	Josh Hamilton	.75
4	Chad Hermansen	.50
5	Ryan Anderson	.50
6	Nick Johnson	1.00
7	Octavio Dotel	.50
8	Peter Bergeron	.50
9	Adam Piatt	.50
10	Pat Burrell	2.00

Image

This 10-card insert set highlights those batters with the best eyes at the plate. These were seeded 1:44 packs and are numbered with a "HD" prefix on the card back.

		NM/M
Complete Set (10):		30.00
Common Player:		1.00
Inserted 1:44		
1	Sammy Sosa	3.00
2	Mark McGwire	5.00
3	Derek Jeter	6.00
4	Albert Belle	1.00
5	Vladimir Guerrero	1.50
6	Ken Griffey Jr.	3.00
7	Mike Piazza	3.00
8	Alex Rodriguez	5.00
9	Barry Bonds	5.00
10	Nomar Garciaparra	4.00

On The Cutting Edge

This 10-card insert set is die-cut down the right hand side of the card highlighting the five-tool stars top five baseball attributes. These are inserted 1:22 packs and are numbered with a "CE" prefix on the card back.

		NM/M
Complete Set (10):		15.00
Common Player:		.50
Inserted 1:22		
1	Andruw Jones	1.00
2	Nomar Garciaparra	3.00
3	Barry Bonds	3.00
4	Larry Walker	.50
5	Vladimir Guerrero	1.00
6	Jeff Bagwell	1.00
7	Derek Jeter	4.00
8	Sammy Sosa	2.00
9	Alex Rodriguez	3.00
10	Ken Griffey Jr.	2.00

Opening Day 2K

As part of a multi-manufacturer promotion, Topps issued eight cards of an "Opening Day 2K" set. Packages containing some of the 32 cards in the issue were distributed by MLB teams early in the season. The cards were also available exclusively as inserts in Topps Opening Day packs sold at KMart stores early in the season. The Topps OD2K cards have gold-foil graphic highlights on front. Backs have portrait photos, stats and are numbered with an "OD" prefix.

		NM/M
Complete Set (8):		6.00
Common Player:		.50
1	Mark McGwire	2.00
2	Barry Bonds	.75
3	Ivan Rodriguez	.75
4	Sean Casey	.65
5	Derek Jeter	1.00
6	Vladimir Guerrero	1.00
7	Preston Wilson	.65
8	Ben Grieve	.50

2000 Topps Stars

The base set consists of 200 cards, including a 50-card Spotlights subset (151-200). Card fronts have a shadow image of the featured player in the background of the player photo. The Topps Stars logo, player name, team logo and position are stamped in silver foil.

		NM/M
Complete Set (200):		35.00
Common Player:		.10
Pack (6):		2.00
Box (24):		40.00
1	Vladimir Guerrero	.75
2	Eric Karros	.10
3	Omar Vizquel	.20
4	Ken Griffey Jr.	1.50
5	Preston Wilson	.20
6	Albert Belle	.20
7	Ryan Klesko	.10
8	Bob Abreu	.20
9	Warren Morris	.10
10	Rafael Palmeiro	.40
11	Nomar Garciaparra	2.00
12	Dante Bichette	.10
13	Jeff Cirillo	.10
14	Carlos Beltran	.10
15	Tony Clark	.10
16	Ray Durham	.10
17	Mark McGwire	2.00
18	Jim Thome	.50
19	Todd Walker	.10
20	Richie Sexson	.40
21	Adrian Beltre	.10
22	Jay Bell	.10
23	Craig Biggio	.25
24	Ben Grieve	.15
25	Greg Maddux	1.50
26	Fernando Tatis	.10
27	Jeromy Burnitz	.10
28	Vinny Castilla	.10
29	Mark Grace	.25
30	Derek Jeter	2.00
31	Larry Walker	.25
32	Ivan Rodriguez	.50
33	Curt Schilling	.40
34	Mike Lamb **RC**	.25
35	Kevin Brown	.20
36	Andruw Jones	.40
37	Chris Mears **RC**	.10
38	Bartolo Colon	.10
39	Edgardo Alfonzo	.15
40	Brady Anderson	.20
41	Andres Galarraga	.25
42	Scott Rolen	.50
43	Manny Ramirez	.75
44	Carlos Delgado	.50
45	David Cone	.10
46	Carl Everett	.10
47	Chipper Jones	1.50
48	Barry Bonds	2.00
49	Dean Palmer	.10
50	Frank Thomas	.75
51	Paul O'Neill	.25
52	Mo Vaughn	.20
53	Todd Helton	.75
54	Jason Giambi	1.00
55	Brian Jordan	.10
56	Luis Gonzalez	.25
57	Alex Rodriguez	2.00
58	J.D. Drew	.10
59	Javy Lopez	.20
60	Tony Gwynn	1.00
61	Jason Kendall	.20
62	Pedro Martinez	.75
63	Matt Williams	.25
64	Gary Sheffield	.40
65	Roberto Alomar	.50
66	Lyle Overbay **RC**	1.00
67	Jeff Bagwell	.75
68	Tim Hudson	.40
69	Sammy Sosa	1.50
70	Keith Reed **RC**	.10
71	Robin Ventura	.20
72	Cal Ripken Jr.	2.50
73	Alex Gonzalez	.10
74	Aaron McNeal **RC**	.10
75	Mike Lieberthal	.10
76	Brian Giles	.25
77	Kevin Millwood	.10
78	Troy O'Leary	.10
79	Raul Mondesi	.20
80	John Olerud	.20
81	David Justice	.25
82	Erubiel Durazo	.10
83	Shawn Green	.40
84	Tino Martinez	.20
85	Greg Vaughn	.15
86	Tom Glavine	.25
87	Jose Canseco	.40
88	Kenny Lofton	.25
89	Brian Daubach	.10
90	Mike Piazza	1.50
91	Randy Johnson	.75
92	Pokey Reese	.10
93	Troy Glaus	.50
94	Kerry Wood	.25
95	Sean Casey	.20
96	Magglio Ordonez	.40
97	Bernie Williams	.50
98	Juan Gonzalez	.75
99	Barry Larkin	.25
100	Orlando Hernandez	.20
101	Roger Clemens	1.50
102	Bob Gibson (Retired Stars)	.40
103	Gary Carter (Retired Stars)	.10
104	Willie Stargell (Retired Stars)	.10
105	Joe Morgan (Retired Stars)	.40
106	Brooks Robinson (Retired Stars)	.50
107	Ozzie Smith (Retired Stars)	.50
108	Carl Yastrzemski (Retired Stars)	.25
109	Al Kaline (Retired Stars)	.40
110	Frank Robinson (Retired Stars)	.50
111	Lance Berkman (Shining Prospects)	.10
112	Adam Piatt (Shining Prospects)	.20
113	Vernon Wells (Shining Prospects)	.25
114	Rafael Furcal (Shining Prospects)	.25
115	Rick Ankiel (Shining Prospects)	.20
116	Corey Patterson (Shining Prospects)	.15
117	Josh Hamilton (Shining Prospects)	.25
118	Jack Cust (Shining Prospects)	.20
119	Josh Girdley (Shining Prospects)	.10
120	Pablo Ozuna (Shining Prospects)	.10
121	Sean Burroughs (Shining Prospects)	.25
122	Pat Burrell (Shining Prospects)	.25
123	Chad Hermansen (Shining Prospects)	.10
124	Ruben Mateo (Shining Prospects)	.10
125	Ben Petrick (Shining Prospects)	.10
126	Dee Brown (Shining Prospects)	.10
127	Eric Munson (Shining Prospects)	.10
128	Ruben Salazar (Shining Prospects)	.10
129	Kip Wells (Shining Prospects)	.10
130	Alfonso Soriano (Shining Prospects)	1.00
131	Mark Mulder (Shining Prospects)	.25
132	Roosevelt Brown (Shining Prospects)	.10
133	Nick Johnson (Shining Prospects)	.40
134	Kyle Snyder (Shining Prospects)	.10
135	David Walling (Shining Prospects)	.10
136	Geraldo Guzman **RC**	.25
137	John Sneed **RC**	.25
138	Ben Christensen **RC**	.40
139	Corey Myers **RC**	.25
140	Jose Ortiz **RC**	3.00
141	Ryan Christianson **RC**	.25
142	Brett Myers **RC**	3.00
143	Bobby Bradley **RC**	.25
144	Rick Asadoorian **RC**	.25
145	Julio Zuleta **RC**	.40
146	Ty Howington **RC**	1.00
147	Josh Kalinowski **RC**	.40
148	B.J. Garbe **RC**	.50
149	Scott Downs **RC**	.40
150	Dan Wright **RC**	.25
151	Jeff Bagwell (Veterans)	.40
152	Vladimir Guerrero (Veterans)	.50
153	Mike Piazza (Veterans)	1.00
154	Juan Gonzalez (Veterans)	.40
155	Ivan Rodriguez (Veterans)	.40
156	Manny Ramirez (Veterans)	.40
157	Sammy Sosa (Veterans)	1.00
158	Chipper Jones (Veterans)	.75
159	Shawn Green (Veterans)	.20
160	Ken Griffey Jr. (Veterans)	.75
161	Cal Ripken Jr. (Veterans)	1.25
162	Nomar Garciaparra (Veterans)	1.00
163	Derek Jeter (Veterans)	1.00
164	Barry Bonds (Veterans)	1.00
165	Greg Maddux (Veterans)	.75
166	Mark McGwire (Veterans)	1.00
167	Roberto Alomar (Veterans)	.25
168	Alex Rodriguez (Veterans)	1.25
169	Randy Johnson (Veterans)	.40
170	Tony Gwynn (Veterans)	.50
171	Pedro Martinez (Veterans)	.40
172	Bob Gibson (Retired Stars)	.25
173	Gary Carter (Retired Stars)	.10
174	Willie Stargell (Retired Stars)	.25
175	Joe Morgan (Retired Stars)	.25
176	Brooks Robinson (Retired Stars)	.40
177	Ozzie Smith (Retired Stars)	.50
178	Carl Yastrzemski (Retired Stars)	.20
179	Al Kaline (Retired Stars)	.25
180	Frank Robinson (Retired Stars)	.40
181	Adam Piatt (Prospects)	.20
182	Alfonso Soriano (Prospects)	.75
183	Corey Patterson (Prospects)	.25
184	Vernon Wells (Prospects)	.40
185	Pat Burrell (Prospects)	.20
186	Mark Mulder (Prospects)	.10
187	Eric Munson (Prospects)	.10
188	Rafael Furcal (Prospects)	.15
189	Rick Ankiel (Prospects)	.20
190	Ruben Mateo (Prospects)	.10
191	Sean Burroughs (Prospects)	.20

192 Josh Hamilton (Prospects) .40
193 Brett Myers 1.00
194 Ben Christensen .20
195 Ty Howington .25
196 Rick Asadoorian .20
197 Josh Kalinowski .20
198 Corey Myers .25
199 Ryan Christianson .25
200 John Sneed .25

Blue

A parallel to the 200-card base set the player shadow has blue tint and the Topps Stars logo, player name, team logo and position are stamped in blue foil. Cards 1-150 are serially numbered on the card back to 299 and cards 151-200 are serially numbered to 99.

Stars (1-150): 3-5X
Production 299 Sets
Stars (151-180): 4-8X
Rookies (181-200): 2-4X
Production 99 Sets

All-Star Authority

This 14-card set features a gold and silver holo foiled front with gold etching. Card backs are numbered with an "AS" prefix. They are found on the the average of 1:13 packs.

NM/M
Complete Set (14): 25.00
Common Player: 1.00
Inserted 1:13
1 Mark McGwire 3.00
2 Sammy Sosa 2.00
3 Ken Griffey Jr. 2.00
4 Cal Ripken Jr. 4.00
5 Tony Gwynn 1.50
6 Barry Bonds 4.00
7 Mike Piazza 2.00
8 Pedro Martinez 1.50
9 Chipper Jones 2.00
10 Manny Ramirez 1.00
11 Alex Rodriguez 3.00
12 Derek Jeter 4.00
13 Nomar Garciaparra 3.00
14 Roberto Alomar 1.00

Autographs

A combination of retired and current players make up this 13-card set. The set is broken down into two levels: A and B. Level A autographs are seeded 1:382 packs and Level B autographs are found 1:1,636 packs. Each card features the Topps "Certified Autograph Issue" stamp and the Topps "Genuine Issue" sticker on the card back. Card backs are numbered with the featured player's initials.

NM/M
Common Player: 10.00
Group A 1:382
Group B 1:1,636
RA Rick Ankiel/A 10.00
GC Gary Carter/B 60.00
RF Rafael Furcal/A 15.00
BG Bob Gibson/A 25.00
DJ Derek Jeter/A 90.00
AK Al Kaline/B 50.00
KM Kevin Millwood/A 15.00
JM Joe Morgan/B 40.00
BR Brooks Robinson/B 40.00
FR Frank Robinson/B 20.00
OS Ozzie Smith/B 35.00
WS Willie Stargell/B 50.00
CY Carl Yastrzemski/B 65.00

Game Gear Bats

A piece of the featured player's game-used bat is embedded into the card front and are seeded 1:175 packs.

NM/M
Common Player: 10.00
Group A 1:2,289
Group B 1:1,153
Group C 1:409
1 Rafael Furcal/C 10.00
2 Sean Burroughs/B 10.00
3 Corey Patterson/B 10.00
4 Chipper Jones/B 40.00
5 Vernon Wells/C 15.00
6 Alfonso Soriano/B 25.00
7 Eric Munson/C 10.00
8 Ben Petrick/B 10.00
9 Dee Brown/A 10.00
10 Lance Berkman/C 15.00

Game Gear Jersey

A piece of the featured player's game-used jersey is embedded into the card front and are seeded 1:382 packs.

NM/M
Common Player: 10.00
Inserted 1:382
1 Kevin Millwood 10.00
2 Brad Penny 10.00
3 J.D. Drew 15.00

Progression

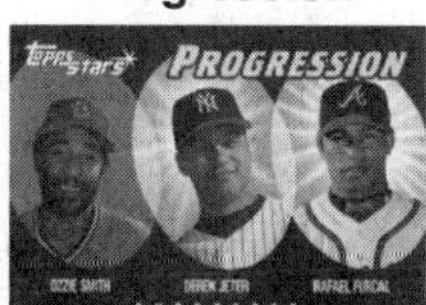

Each of the nine cards features three players on a horizontal format, progressing from past, present and future stars at each of the nine positions. They were seeded 1:13 packs and are numbered on the back with an "P" prefix.

NM/M
Complete Set (9): 15.00
Common Player: 1.00
Inserted 1:13
1 Bob Gibson, Pedro Martinez, Rick Ankiel 1.50
2 Gary Carter, Mike Piazza, Ben Petrick 2.00
3 Willie Stargell, Mark McGwire, Pat Burrell 3.00
4 Joe Morgan, Roberto Alomar, Ruben Salazar 1.00
5 Brooks Robinson, Chipper Jones, Sean Burroughs 2.00
6 Ozzie Smith, Derek Jeter, Rafael Furcal 3.00
7 Carl Yastrzemski, Barry Bonds, Josh Hamilton 4.00
8 Al Kaline, Ken Griffey Jr., Ruben Mateo 2.00
9 Frank Robinson, Manny Ramirez, Corey Patterson 1.50

Walk of Fame

This 15-card set spotlights the top stars on a silver and gold holo foiled card front. Card backs feature comparative commentary with the all-time best at their respective positions and are numbered with an "WF" prefix. They are seeded 1:8 packs.

NM/M
Complete Set (15): 15.00
Common Player: .75
Inserted 1:8
1 Cal Ripken Jr. 3.00
2 Ken Griffey Jr. 1.50
3 Mark McGwire 2.00
4 Sammy Sosa 1.50
5 Alex Rodriguez 2.00
6 Derek Jeter 2.50
7 Nomar Garciaparra 2.00
8 Chipper Jones 1.50
9 Manny Ramirez 1.00
10 Mike Piazza 1.50
11 Vladimir Guerrero 1.00
12 Barry Bonds 3.00
13 Tony Gwynn 1.00
14 Roberto Alomar .75
15 Pedro Martinez 1.00

Subway Series Parade Promos

During the October 30 World Series victory parade in New York, Topps randomly distributed a pair of special cards promoting its forthcoming Subway Series boxed set. Besides regular versions of each card, a foil version was also produced in a hand-numbered edition of 1,000 each, with 500 given to Topps employees. Cards have group photos of the team's celebrating on front, with the title in a black band on top, along with a team logo and the subway station number. Backs are in blue and orange on white and have a team logo printed beneath a short post-season summary. At bottom are ads for Topps' Subway Series commemorative set and information on a sweepstakes for 2001 Yankees or Mets tickets.

NM/M
N.L. Champs 3.00
N.L. Champs (Foil) 6.00
Yankees Win Subway Series 5.00
Yankees Win Subway Series (Foil) 10.00

Subway Series Parade Promos - Mets Win

To cover themselves in the event the Mets had won the 2000 Subway Series against the Yankees, Topps printed up a "Mets Win" card for distribution as a promo for its Subway Series set. When the Yankees won, the Mets Win card was not released. Early in 2002, a quantity (50) of these cards surfaced, reportedly having been given to a Topps employee in 2000. The Mets Win cards are nearly identical to the issued Yankees version, with an on-field celebration group hug on front and information about the Series on back, along with information about the Subway Series card set and other Topps products.

NM/M
Mets Win Subway Series 90.00

Subway Series

NM/M
Complete Fact. Set (101): 70.00
Complete Set (100): 20.00
Common Player: .20
1 Mike Piazza 3.00
2 Jay Payton .20
3 Edgardo Alfonzo .40
4 Todd Pratt .20
5 Todd Zeile .20
6 Mike Bordick .20
7 Robin Ventura .40
8 Benny Agbayani .20
9 Timo Perez .50
10 Kurt Abbott .20
11 Matt Franco .20
12 Bubba Trammell .20
13 Darryl Hamilton .20
14 Lenny Harris .20
15 Joe McEwing .20
16 Mike Hampton .40
17 Al Leiter .40
18 Rick Reed .20
19 Bobby Jones .20
20 Glendon Rusch .20
21 Armando Benitez .20
22 John Franco .20
23 Rick White .20
24 Dennis Cook .20
25 Turk Wendell .20
26 Bobby Valentine .20
27 Derek Jeter 4.00
28 Chuck Knoblauch .40
29 Tino Martinez .30
30 Jorge Posada .40
31 Luis Sojo .20
32 Scott Brosius .20
33 Chris Turner .20
34 Bernie Williams .75
35 David Justice .75
36 Paul O'Neill .40
37 Glenallen Hill .20
38 Jose Vizcaino .20
39 Luis Polonia .20
40 Clay Bellinger .20
41 Orlando Hernandez .40
42 Roger Clemens 1.50
43 Andy Pettitte .50
44 Denny Neagle .20
45 Dwight Gooden .30
46 David Cone .20
47 Mariano Rivera .50
48 Jeff Nelson .20
49 Mike Stanton .20
50 Jason Grimsley .20
51 Jose Canseco .75
52 Joe Torre .50
53 Edgardo Alfonzo .40
54 Darryl Hamilton .20
55 John Franco .20
56 Benny Agbayani .20
57 Bobby Jones .20
58 New York Mets .20
59 Bobby Valentine .20
60 Mike Piazza 3.00
61 Armando Benitez .20
62 Mike Piazza 3.00
63 Mike Piazza 3.00
64 Todd Zeile .20
65 Timo Perez .50
66 Timo Perez .50
67 Mike Hampton .40
68 Andy Pettitte .50
69 Tino Martinez .30
70 Joe Torre .50
71 New York Yankees .40
72 Orlando Hernandez .40
73 Bernie Williams .75
74 Andy Pettitte .50
75 Mariano Rivera .50
76 New York Yankees .40
77 Roger Clemens 1.50
78 Derek Jeter 4.00
79 David Justice .75
80 Mariano Rivera .50
81 Tino Martinez .30
82 New York Yankees .40
83 Jorge Posada .40
84 Chuck Knoblauch .40
85 Jose Vizcaino .20
86 Roger Clemens 1.50
87 Mike Piazza 3.00
88 Clay Bellinger .20
89 Robin Ventura .40
90 Benny Agbayani .20
91 Orlando Hernandez .40
92 Derek Jeter 4.00
93 Mike Piazza 3.00
94 Mariano Rivera .50
95 Derek Jeter 3.00
96 Luis Sojo .20
97 New York Yankees .40
98 Mike Hampton .40
99 David Justice .75
100 Derek Jeter 4.00

Subway Series Fan Fare

NM/M
Common Player: 25.00
Inserted 1:Set
1 Timo Perez 35.00
2 Edgardo Alfonzo 40.00
3 Mike Piazza 120.00
4 Robin Ventura 35.00
5 Todd Zeile 25.00
6 Benny Agbayani 25.00
7 Jay Payton 25.00
8 Mike Bordick 25.00
9 Matt Franco 25.00
10 Mike Hampton 40.00
11 Al Leiter 40.00
12 Rick Reed 25.00
13 Bobby Jones 25.00
14 Glendon Rusch 25.00
15 Darryl Hamilton 25.00
16 Turk Wendell 25.00
17 John Franco 25.00
18 Armando Benitez 25.00
19 Chuck Knoblauch 35.00
20 Derek Jeter 200.00
21 David Justice 40.00
22 Bernie Williams 50.00
23 Jorge Posada 40.00
24 Paul O'Neill 50.00
25 Tino Martinez 35.00
26 Luis Sojo 25.00
27 Scott Brosius 25.00
28 Jose Canseco 50.00
29 Orlando Hernandez 35.00
30 Roger Clemens 100.00
31 Andy Pettitte 40.00
32 Denny Neagle 25.00
33 David Cone 25.00
34 Jeff Nelson 25.00
35 Mike Stanton 25.00
36 Mariano Rivera 60.00

2000 Topps TEK

Forty-five players make up this set including 5 rookies (41-45). Each card is printed on a transparent, polycarbonate stock with patterns 1-15 featuring silver foil metalization. All 45 players are featured on 20 different player focused background patterns. Card backs have two numbers, the first is the player's card number within the set and the second is the pattern number. Patterns 16-20 have color variations and have an insertion rate of 1:10 packs. Each pack contains 4 TEK cards with an SRP of $5.

NM/M
Complete Set (45): 25.00
Common Player: .40
Common Rookie (41-45): .75
2,000 serial numbered rookies
Pack (4): 2.00
Box (20): 30.00
1 Mike Piazza 1.50
2 Chipper Jones 1.50
3 Juan Gonzalez .75
4 Ivan Rodriguez .50
5 Cal Ripken Jr. 3.00
6 A.J. Burnett .40
7 Jim Thome .75
8 Mo Vaughn .40
9 Andruw Jones .75
10 Mark McGwire 2.00
11 Jose Canseco .50
12 Shawn Green .50
13 Barry Bonds 3.00
14 Bernie Williams .50
15 Manny Ramirez .75
16 Greg Maddux 1.50
17 Carlos Beltran .40
18 Pedro Martinez 1.00
19 Jeff Bagwell .75
20 Sammy Sosa 2.00
21 J.D. Drew .40
22 Randy Johnson 1.00
23 Larry Walker .40
24 Frank Thomas .75
25 Orlando Hernandez .40
26 Scott Rolen .75
27 Tony Gwynn 1.00
28 Rick Ankiel .40
29 Roberto Alomar .75
30 Ken Griffey Jr. 1.50
31 Vladimir Guerrero 1.00
32 Derek Jeter 3.00
33 Nomar Garciaparra 2.00
34 Alex Rodriguez 2.50
35 Sean Casey .40
36 Adam Piatt (Prospects) .40
37 Corey Patterson (Prospects) .40
38 Josh Hamilton (Prospects) .40
39 Pat Burrell (Prospects) .50
40 Eric Munson (Prospects) .40
41 Ruben Salazar **RC** (Rookies) .75
42 John Sneed **RC** (Rookies) .75
43 Josh Girdley **RC** (Rookies) .75
44 Brett Myers **RC** (Rookies) 4.00
45 Rick Asadoorian **RC** (Rookies) .75

Color

Color variations make up patterns 16-20 of the base set and instead of metallic silver foil they have a different color background. They are seeded on the average of 1:10 packs.

Patterns 16-20: 1-2X
Inserted 1:10

Gold

This parallel to the base set has a rounded top corner and rounded bottom corner

with a gold background. Each pattern is serially numbered on the card back in an edition of 10 sets.

Stars: 8-15X
Rookies: 4-8X
Production 10 Sets

ArchiTEKs

Printed on a clear, polycarbonate card stock the TEK logo, and player name are stamped in gold foil. Card backs are numbered with an "A" prefix. They are found on the average of 1:5 packs.

NM/M
Complete Set (18): 20.00
Common Player: .50
Inserted 1:5
1 Nomar Garciaparra 2.00
2 Derek Jeter 3.00
3 Chipper Jones 1.50
4 Vladimir Guerrero 1.00
5 Mark McGwire 2.50
6 Ken Griffey Jr. 1.50
7 Mike Piazza 1.50
8 Jeff Bagwell 1.00
9 Larry Walker .50
10 Manny Ramirez 1.00
11 Alex Rodriguez 2.00
12 Sammy Sosa 2.00
13 Shawn Green .50
14 Juan Gonzalez .75
15 Barry Bonds 3.00
16 Pedro Martinez 1.00
17 Cal Ripken Jr. 3.00
18 Ivan Rodriguez .75

DramaTEK Performers

Printed on a clear, polycarbonate stock, the insert name and TEK logo are stamped in blue foil. Card backs are numbered with a "DP" prefix and are seeded 1:10 packs.

NM/M
Complete Set (9): 15.00
Common Player: 1.50
Inserted 1:10
1 Mark McGwire 3.00
2 Sammy Sosa 2.50
3 Ken Griffey Jr. 2.00
4 Nomar Garciaparra 3.00
5 Chipper Jones 2.00
6 Mike Piazza 2.00
7 Alex Rodriguez 3.00
8 Derek Jeter 3.00
9 Vladimir Guerrero 1.50

TEKtonics

This nine-card set features baseball's top hitters on a die-cut design on a clear, polycarbonate stock. Card backs are numbered with a "TT" prefix and are inserted 1:30 packs.

NM/M
Complete Set (9): 35.00
Common Player: 4.00
Inserted 1:30
1 Derek Jeter 6.00
2 Mark McGwire 6.00
3 Ken Griffey Jr. 4.00
4 Mike Piazza 4.00
5 Alex Rodriguez 6.00
6 Chipper Jones 4.00
7 Nomar Garciaparra 6.00
8 Sammy Sosa 5.00
9 Cal Ripken Jr. 8.00

2001 Topps Promo Cards

Since a 50th anniversary only comes around once, Topps made a big deal in promoting its 2001 baseball card issue with an oversize promo pack. Each gold-foil finfold pack contains eight 9" x 12-1/2" glossy promo cards. Fronts reproduce various cards from the base set, subsets and inserts while backs provide further photos and details.

NM/M
Complete Set (8): 25.00
Common Player: 3.00
(1) Hank Aaron (1954 Topps) 7.50
(2) Johnny Bench (Golden Anniversary Great) 4.00
(3) Mark McGwire (base card) 5.00
(4) Nolan Ryan (King of Kings) 15.00
(5) Mike Schmidt (Golden Greats) 4.00
(6) Bob Gibson, Pedro Martinez (Topps Combos) 3.00
(7) Checklist .50
(8) Header .50

2001 Topps

NM/M
Complete Set (790): 70.00
Complete Ser. 1 Set (405): 30.00
Complete Ser. 2 Set (385): 40.00
Common Player: .10
Complete Factory Set, Blue (795): 75.00

Complete Factory Set, Gold (795): 75.00
Ser. 1 Pack (10): 1.50
Ser. 1 Box (36): 45.00
Ser. 2 Pack (10): 1.50
Ser. 2 Box (36): 45.00
1 Cal Ripken Jr. 1.50
2 Chipper Jones 1.00
3 Roger Cedeno .10
4 Garret Anderson .10
5 Robin Ventura .20
6 Daryle Ward .10
7 Not Issued
8 Ron Gant .20
9 Phil Nevin .10
10 Jermaine Dye .10
11 Chris Singleton .10
12 Mike Stanton .10
13 Brian Hunter .10
14 Mike Redmond .10
15 Jim Thome .25
16 Brian Jordan .10
17 Joe Girardi .10
18 Steve Woodard .10
19 Dustin Hermanson .10
20 Shawn Green .30
21 Todd Stottlemyre .10
22 Dan Wilson .10
23 Todd Pratt .10
24 Derek Lowe .10
25 Juan Gonzalez .40
26 Clay Bellinger .10
27 Jeff Fassero .10
28 Pat Meares .10
29 Eddie Taubensee .10
30 Paul O'Neill .25
31 Jeffrey Hammonds .10
32 Pokey Reese .10
33 Mike Mussina .30
34 Rico Brogna .10
35 Jay Buhner .10
36 Steve Cox .10
37 Quilvio Veras .10
38 Marquis Grissom .10
39 Shigetoshi Hasegawa .10
40 Shane Reynolds .10
41 Adam Piatt .10
42 Luis Polonia .10
43 Brook Fordyce .10
44 Preston Wilson .10
45 Ellis Burks .10
46 Armando Rios .10
47 Chuck Finley .10
48 Dan Plesac .10
49 Shannon Stewart .10
50 Mark McGwire 1.00
51 Mark Loretta .10
52 Gerald Williams .10
53 Eric Young .10
54 Peter Bergeron .10
55 Dave Hansen .10
56 Arthur Rhodes .10
57 Bobby Jones .10
58 Matt Clement .10
59 Mike Benjamin .10
60 Pedro Martinez .50
61 Jose Canseco .40
62 Matt Anderson .10
63 Torii Hunter .10
64 Carlos Lee .10
65 David Cone .10
66 Ray Sanchez .10
67 Eric Chavez .20
68 Rick Helling .10
69 Manny Alexander .10
70 John Franco .10
71 Mike Bordick .10
72 Andres Galarraga .25
73 Jose Cruz Jr. .10
74 Mike Matheny .10
75 Randy Johnson .50
76 Richie Sexson .10
77 Vladimir Nunez .10
78 Harold Baines .10
79 Aaron Boone .10
80 Darin Erstad .40
81 Alex Gonzalez .10
82 Gil Heredia .10
83 Shane Andrews .10
84 Todd Hundley .10
85 Bill Mueller .10
86 Mark McLemore .10
87 Scott Spiezio .10
88 Kevin McGlinchy .10
89 Bubba Trammell .10
90 Manny Ramirez .50
91 Mike Lamb .10
92 Scott Karl .10
93 Brian Buchanan .10
94 Chris Turner .10
95 Mike Sweeney .10
96 John Wetteland .10
97 Rob Bell .10
98 Pat Rapp .10
99 John Burkett .10
100 Derek Jeter 1.50
101 J.D. Drew .25
102 Jose Offerman .10
103 Rick Reed .10
104 Will Clark .30
105 Rickey Henderson .25
106 Dave Berg .10
107 Kirk Rueter .10
108 Lee Stevens .10
109 Jay Bell .10
110 Fred McGriff .20
111 Julio Zuleta .10
112 Brian Anderson .10
113 Orlando Cabrera .10
114 Alex Fernandez .10
115 Derek Bell .10
116 Eric Owens .10
117 Brian Bohannon .10
118 Dennys Reyes .10
119 Mike Stanley .10
120 Jorge Posada .20
121 Rich Becker .10
122 Paul Konerko .10
123 Mike Remlinger .10
124 Travis Lee .10
125 Ken Caminiti .10
126 Kevin Barker .10
127 Paul Quantrill .10
128 Ozzie Guillen .10
129 Kevin Tapani .10
130 Mark Johnson .10
131 Randy Wolf .10
132 Michael Tucker .10
133 Darren Lewis .10
134 Joe Randa .10
135 Jeff Cirillo .10
136 David Ortiz .10
137 Herb Perry .10
138 Jeff Nelson .10
139 Chris Stynes .10
140 Johnny Damon .10
141 Desi Relaford .10
142 Jason Schmidt .10
143 Charles Johnson .10
144 Pat Burrell .40
145 Gary Sheffield .25
146 Tom Glavine .25
147 Jason Isringhausen .10
148 Chris Carpenter .10
149 Jeff Suppan .10
150 Ivan Rodriguez .50
151 Luis Sojo .10
152 Ron Villone .10
153 Mike Sirotka .10
154 Chuck Knoblauch .20
155 Jason Kendall .10
156 Dennis Cook .10
157 Bobby Estalella .10
158 Jose Guillen .10
159 Thomas Howard .10
160 Carlos Delgado .50
161 Benji Gil .10
162 Tim Bogar .10
163 Kevin Elster .10
164 Scott Downs .10
165 Andy Benes .10
166 Adrian Beltre .10
167 David Bell .10
168 Turk Wendell .10
169 Pete Harnisch .10
170 Roger Clemens .75
171 Scott Williamson .10
172 Kevin Jordan .10
173 Brad Penny .10
174 John Flaherty .10
175 Troy Glaus .50
176 Kevin Appier .10
177 Walt Weiss .10
178 Tyler Houston .10
179 Michael Barrett .10
180 Mike Hampton .10
181 Francisco Cordova .10
182 Mike Jackson .10
183 David Segui .10
184 Carlos Febles .10
185 Roy Halladay .10
186 Seth Etherton .10
187 Charlie Hayes .10
188 Fernando Tatis .10
189 Steve Trachsel .10
190 Livan Hernandez .10
191 Joe Oliver .10
192 Stan Javier .10
193 B.J. Surhoff .10
194 Rob Ducey .10
195 Barry Larkin .25
196 Danny Patterson .10
197 Bobby Howry .10
198 Dmitri Young .10
199 Brian Hunter .10
200 Alex Rodriguez 1.00
201 Hideo Nomo .25
202 Luis Alicea .10
203 Warren Morris .10
204 Antonio Alfonseca .10
205 Edgardo Alfonzo .20
206 Mark Grudzielanek .10
207 Fernando Vina .10
208 Willie Greene .10
209 Homer Bush .10
210 Jason Giambi .30
211 Mike Morgan .10
212 Steve Karsay .10
213 Matt Lawton .10
214 Wendell Magee Jr. .10
215 Rusty Greer .10
216 Keith Lockhart .10
217 Billy Koch .10
218 Todd Hollandsworth .10
219 Raul Ibanez .10
220 Tony Gwynn .75
221 Carl Everett .20
222 Hector Carrasco .10
223 Jose Valentin .10
224 Deivi Cruz .10
225 Bret Boone .10
226 Kurt Abbott .10
227 Melvin Mora .10
228 Danny Graves .10
229 Jose Jimenez .10
230 James Baldwin .10
231 C.J. Nitkowski .10
232 Jeff Zimmerman .10
233 Mike Lowell .10
234 Hideki Irabu .10
235 Greg Vaughn .20
236 Omar Daal .10
237 Darren Dreifort .10
238 Gil Meche .10
239 Damian Jackson .10
240 Frank Thomas .75
241 Travis Miller .10
242 Jeff Frye .10
243 Dave Magadan .10
244 Luis Castillo .10
245 Bartolo Colon .10
246 Steve Kline .10
247 Shawon Dunston .10
248 Rick Aguilera .10
249 Omar Olivares .10
250 Craig Biggio .20
251 Scott Schoeneweis .10
252 Dave Veres .10
253 Ramon Martinez .10
254 Jose Vidro .10
255 Todd Helton .50
256 Greg Norton .10
257 Jacque Jones .10
258 Jason Grimsley .10
259 Dan Reichert .10
260 Robb Nen .10
261 Mark Clark .10
262 Scott Hatteberg .10
263 Doug Brocail .10
264 Mark Johnson .10
265 Eric Davis .20
266 Terry Shumpert .10
267 Kevin Millar .10
268 Ismael Valdes .10
269 Richard Hidalgo .20
270 Randy Velarde .10
271 Bengie Molina .10
272 Tony Womack .10
273 Enrique Wilson .10
274 Jeff Brantley .10
275 Rick Ankiel .25
276 Terry Mulholland .10
277 Ron Belliard .10
278 Terrence Long .10
279 Alberto Castillo .10
280 Royce Clayton .10
281 Joe McEwing .10
282 Jason McDonald .10
283 Ricky Bottalico .10
284 Keith Foulke .10
285 Brad Radke .10
286 Gabe Kapler .10
287 Pedro Astacio .10
288 Armando Reynoso .10
289 Darryl Kile .10
290 Reggie Sanders .10
291 Esteban Yan .10
292 Joe Nathan .10
293 Jay Payton .10
294 Francisco Cordero .10
295 Gregg Jefferies .10
296 LaTroy Hawkins .10
297 Jeff Tam .10
298 Jacob Cruz .10
299 Chris Holt .10
300 Vladimir Guerrero .75
301 Marvin Benard .10
302 Matt Franco .10
303 Mike Williams .10
304 Sean Bergman .10
305 Juan Encarnacion .10
306 Russ Davis .10
307 Hanley Frias .10
308 Ramon Hernandez .10
309 Matt Walbeck .10
310 Bill Spiers .10
311 Bob Wickman .10
312 Sandy Alomar .10
313 Eddie Guardado .10
314 Shane Halter .10
315 Geoff Jenkins .20
316 Gerald Witasick .10
317 Damian Miller .10
318 Darrin Fletcher .10
319 Rafael Furcal .25
320 Mark Grace .25
321 Mark Mulder .10
322 Joe Torre (Managers) .10
323 Bobby Cox (Managers) .10
324 Mike Scioscia (Managers) .10
325 Mike Hargrove (Managers) .10
326 Jimy Williams (Managers) .10
327 Jerry Manuel (Managers) .10
328 Buck Showalter (Managers) .10
329 Charlie Manuel (Managers) .10
330 Don Baylor (Managers) .10
331 Phil Garner (Managers) .10
332 Jack McKeon (Managers) .10
333 Tony Muser (Managers) .10
334 Buddy Bell (Managers) .10
335 Tom Kelly (Managers) .10
336 John Boles (Managers) .10
337 Art Howe (Managers) .10
338 Larry Dierker (Managers) .10
339 Lou Pinella (Managers) .10
340 Davey Johnson (Managers) .10
341 Larry Rothschild (Managers) .10
342 Davey Lopes (Managers) .10
343 Johnny Oates (Managers) .10
344 Felipe Alou (Managers) .10
345 Jim Fregosi (Managers) .10
346 Bobby Valentine (Managers) .10
347 Terry Francona (Managers) .10
348 Gene Lamont (Managers) .10
349 Tony LaRussa (Managers) .10
350 Bruce Bochy (Managers) .10
351 Dusty Baker (Managers) .10
352 Adrian Gonzalez, Adam Johnson (Draft Picks) .75
353 Matt Wheatland, Brian Digby (Draft Picks) .40
354 Tripper Johnson, Scott Thorman (Draft Picks) .40
355 Phil Dumatrait, Adam Wainwright (Draft Picks) .50
356 Scott Heard, David Parrish **RC** (Draft Picks) .40
357 Rocco Baldelli, Mark Folsom **RC** (Draft Picks) .40
358 Dominic Rich **RC**, Aaron Herr (Draft Picks) .40
359 Mike Stodolka, Sean Burnett (Draft Picks) .25
360 Derek Thompson, Corey Smith (Draft Picks) .40
361 Danny Borrell **RC**, Jason Bourgeois **RC** (Draft Picks) .40
362 Chin-Feng Chen, Corey Patterson, Josh Hamilton (Prospects) .25
363 Ryan Anderson, Barry Zito, C.C. Sabathia (Prospects) .50
364 Scott Sobkowiak, David Walling, Ben Sheets (Prospects) .50
365 Ty Howington, Josh Kalinowski, Josh Girdley (Prospects) .10
366 Hee Seop Choi **RC**, Aaron McNeal, Jason Hart (Prospects) 1.00
367 Bobby Bradley, Kurt Ainsworth, Chin-Hui Tsao (Prospects) .40
368 Mike Glendenning, Kenny Kelly, Juan Silvestri **RC** (Prospects) .25
369 J.R. House, Ramon Castro, Ben Davis (Prospects) .25
370 Chance Caple, Rafael Soriano **RC**, Pasqual Coco (Prospects) .50
371 Travis Hafner **RC**, Eric Munson, Bucky Jacobsen (Prospects) 1.50
372 Jason Conti, Chris Wakeland, Brian Cole (Prospects) .20
373 Scott Seabol, Aubrey Huff, Joe Crede (Prospects) .40
374 Adam Everett, Jose Ortiz, Keith Ginter (Prospects) .25
375 Carlos Hernandez, Geraldo Guzman, Adam Eaton (Prospects) .25

376 Bobby Kielty, Milton Bradley, Juan Rivera (Prospects) .25
377 Mark McGwire (Golden Moments) .75
378 Don Larsen (Golden Moments) .20
379 Bobby Thomson (Golden Moments) .10
380 Bill Mazeroski (Golden Moments) .20
381 Reggie Jackson (Golden Moments) .40
382 Kirk Gibson (Golden Moments) .10
383 Roger Maris (Golden Moments) .40
384 Cal Ripken Jr. (Golden Moments) .75
385 Hank Aaron (Golden Moments) .75
386 Joe Carter (Golden Moments) .10
387 Cal Ripken Jr. (Season Highlights) .75
388 Randy Johnson (Season Highlights) .30
389 Ken Griffey Jr. (Season Highlights) .50
390 Troy Glaus (Season Highlights) .30
391 Kazuhiro Sasaki (Season Highlights) .40
392 Sammy Sosa, Troy Glaus (League Leaders) .50
393 Todd Helton, Edgar Martinez (League Leaders) .25
394 Nomar Garciaparra, Todd Helton (League Leaders) .50
395 Barry Bonds, Jason Giambi (League Leaders) .40
396 Todd Helton, Manny Ramirez (League Leaders) .25
397 Todd Helton, Darin Erstad (League Leaders) .25
398 Kevin Brown, Pedro Martinez (League Leaders) .25
399 Randy Johnson, Pedro Martinez (League Leaders) .25
400 Will Clark (Playoff Highlights) .20
401 NY Mets Divisional Highlight .10
402 NY Yankees Divisional Highlight .10
403 Seattle Mariners Divisional Highlight .10
404 Mike Hampton (Playoff Highlights) .10
405 NY Yankees ALCS Highlight .75
406 World Series Highlight 1.00
407 Jeff Bagwell .50
408 Brant Brown .10
409 Brad Fullmer .10
410 Dean Palmer .10
411 Gregg Zaun .10
412 Jose Vizcaino .10
413 Jeff Abbott .10
414 Travis Fryman .15
415 Mike Cameron .10
416 Matt Mantei .10
417 Alan Benes .10
418 Mickey Morandini .10
419 Troy Percival .10
420 Eddie Perez .10
421 Vernon Wells .10
422 Ricky Gutierrez .10
423 Carlos Hernandez .10
424 Chan Ho Park .15
425 Armando Benitez .10
426 Sidney Ponson .10
427 Adrian Brown .10
428 Ruben Mateo .20
429 Alex Ochoa .10
430 Jose Rosado .10
431 Masato Yoshii .10
432 Corey Koskie .10
433 Andy Pettitte .20
434 Brian Daubach .10
435 Sterling Hitchcock .10
436 Timo Perez .10
437 Shawn Estes .10
438 Tony Armas Jr. .10
439 Danny Bautista .10
440 Randy Winn .10
441 Wilson Alvarez .10
442 Rondell White .15
443 Jeromy Burnitz .10
444 Kelvim Escobar .10
445 Paul Bako .10
446 Javier Vazquez .10
447 Eric Gagne .10
448 Kenny Lofton .20
449 Mark Kotsay .10
450 Jamie Moyer .10
451 Delino DeShields .10
452 Rey Ordonez .10
453 Russ Ortiz .10
454 Dave Burba .10
455 Eric Karros .15
456 Felix Martinez .10
457 Tony Batista .10
458 Bobby Higginson .10
459 Jeff D'Amico .10
460 Shane Spencer .10
461 Brent Mayne .10
462 Glendon Rusch .10
463 Chris Gomez .10
464 Jeff Shaw .10
465 Damon Buford .10
466 Mike DiFelice .10
467 Jimmy Haynes .10
468 Billy Wagner .10
469 A.J. Hinch .10
470 Gary DiSarcina .10
471 Tom Lampkin .10
472 Adam Eaton .10
473 Brian Giles .15
474 John Thomson .10
475 Cal Eldred .10
476 Ramiro Mendoza .10
477 Scott Sullivan .10
478 Scott Rolen .25
479 Todd Ritchie .10
480 Pablo Ozuna .10
481 Carl Pavano .10
482 Matt Morris .10
483 Matt Stairs .10
484 Tim Belcher .10
485 Lance Berkman .15
486 Brian Meadows .10
487 Bobby Abreu .10
488 John Vander Wal .10
489 Donnie Sadler .10
490 Damion Easley .10
491 David Justice .25
492 Ray Durham .10
493 Todd Zeile .10
494 Desi Relaford .10
495 Cliff Floyd .10
496 Scott Downs .10
497 Barry Bonds 1.00
498 Jeff D'Amico .10
499 Octavio Dotel .10
500 Kent Mercker .10
501 Craig Grebeck .10
502 Roberto Hernandez .10
503 Matt Williams .15
504 Bruce Aven .10
505 Brett Tomko .10
506 Kris Benson .10
507 Neifi Perez .10
508 Alfonso Soriano .50
509 Keith Osik .10
510 Matt Franco .10
511 Steve Finley .10
512 Olmedo Saenz .10
513 Esteban Loaiza .10
514 Adam Kennedy .10
515 Scott Elarton .10
516 Moises Alou .15
517 Bryan Rekar .10
518 Darryl Hamilton .10
519 Osvaldo Fernandez .10
520 Kip Wells .10
521 Bernie Williams .40
522 Mike Darr .10
523 Marlon Anderson .10
524 Derrek Lee .10
525 Ugueth Urbina .10
526 Vinny Castilla .10
527 David Wells .10
528 Jason Marquis .10
529 Orlando Palmeiro .10
530 Carlos Perez .10
531 J.T. Snow Jr. .10
532 Al Leiter .15
533 Jimmy Anderson .10
534 Brett Laxton .10
535 Butch Huskey .10
536 Orlando Hernandez .20
537 Magglio Ordonez .15
538 Willie Blair .10
539 Kevin Sefcik .10
540 Chad Curtis .10
541 John Halama .10
542 Andy Fox .10
543 Juan Guzman .10
544 Frank Menechino .10
545 Raul Mondesi .15
546 Tim Salmon .15
547 Ryan Rupe .10
548 Jeff Reed .10
549 Mike Mordecai .10
550 Jeff Kent .15
551 Wiki Gonzalez .10
552 Kenny Rogers .10
553 Kevin Young .10
554 Brian Johnson .10
555 Tom Goodwin .10
556 Tony Clark .10
557 Mac Suzuki .10
558 Brian Moehler .10
559 Jim Parque .10
560 Mariano Rivera .20
561 Trot Nixon .10
562 Mike Mussina .30
563 Nelson Figueroa .10
564 Alex Gonzalez .10
565 Benny Agbayani .10
566 Ed Sprague .10
567 Scott Erickson .10
568 Abraham Nunez .10
569 Jerry DiPoto .10
570 Sean Casey .10
571 Wilton Veras .10
572 Joe Mays .10
573 Bill Simas .10
574 Doug Glanville .10
575 Scott Sauerbeck .10
576 Ben Davis .10
577 Jesus Sanchez .10
578 Ricardo Rincon .10
579 John Olerud .15
580 Curt Schilling .15
581 Alex Cora .10
582 Pat Hentgen .10
583 Javy Lopez .15
584 Ben Grieve .15
585 Frank Castillo .10
586 Kevin Stocker .10
587 Mark Sweeney .10
588 Ray Lankford .10
589 Turner Ward .10
590 Felipe Crespo .10
591 Omar Vizquel .15
592 Mike Lieberthal .10
593 Ken Griffey Jr. 1.00
594 Troy O'Leary .10
595 Dave Mlicki (Front photo actually Brian Moehler.) .10
596 Manny Ramirez .50
597 Mike Lansing .10
598 Rich Aurilia .10
599 Russ Branyan .10
600 Russ Johnson .10
601 Gregg Colbrunn .10
602 Andruw Jones .40
603 Henry Blanco .10
604 Jarrod Washburn .10
605 Tony Eusebio .10
606 Aaron Sele .10
607 Charles Nagy .10
608 Ryan Klesko .10
609 Dante Bichette .10
610 Bill Haselman .10
611 Jerry Spradlin .10
612 Alex Rodriguez 1.00
613 Jose Silva .10
614 Darren Oliver .10
615 Pat Mahomes .10
616 Roberto Alomar .40
617 Edgar Renteria .10
618 Jon Lieber .10
619 John Rocker .10
620 Miguel Tejada .15
621 Mo Vaughn .15
622 Jose Lima .10
623 Kerry Wood .15
624 Mike Timlin .10
625 Wil Cordero .10
626 Albert Belle .15
627 Bobby Jones .10
628 Doug Mirabelli .10
629 Jason Tyner .10
630 Andy Ashby .10
631 Jose Hernandez .10
632 Devon White .10
633 Ruben Rivera .10
634 Steve Parris .10
635 David McCarty .10
636 Jose Canseco .25
637 Todd Walker .10
638 Stan Spencer .10
639 Wayne Gomes .10
640 Freddy Garcia .10
641 Jeremy Giambi .10
642 Luis Lopez .10
643 John Smoltz .10
644 Kelly Stinnett .10
645 Kevin Brown .10
646 Wilton Guerrero .10
647 Al Martin .10
648 Woody Williams .10
649 Brian Rose .10
650 Rafael Palmeiro .30
651 Pete Schourek .10
652 Kevin Jarvis .10
653 Mark Redman .10
654 Ricky Ledee .10
655 Larry Walker .20
656 Paul Byrd .10
657 Jason Bere .10
658 Rick White .10
659 Calvin Murray .10
660 Greg Maddux 1.00
661 Ron Gant .10
662 Eli Marrero .10
663 Graeme Lloyd .10
664 Trevor Hoffman .10
665 Nomar Garciaparra 1.00
666 Glenallen Hill .10
667 Matt LeCroy .10
668 Justin Thompson .10
669 Brady Anderson .10
670 Miguel Batista .10
671 Erubiel Durazo .10
672 Kevin Millwood .10
673 Mitch Meluskey .10
674 Luis Gonzalez .15
675 Edgar Martinez .10
676 Robert Person .10
677 Benito Santiago .10
678 Todd Jones .10
679 Tino Martinez .15
680 Carlos Beltran .10
681 Gabe White .10
682 Bret Saberhagen .10
683 Jeff Conine .10
684 Jaret Wright .10
685 Bernard Gilkey .10
686 Garrett Stephenson .10
687 Jamey Wright .10
688 Sammy Sosa 1.00
689 John Jaha .10
690 Ramon Martinez .10
691 Robert Fick .10
692 Eric Milton .10
693 Denny Neagle .10
694 Ron Coomer .10
695 John Valentin .10
696 Placido Polanco .10
697 Tim Hudson .15
698 Marty Cordova .10
699 Chad Kreuter .10
700 Frank Catalanotto .10
701 Tim Wakefield .10
702 Jim Edmonds .15
703 Michael Tucker .10
704 Cristian Guzman .10
705 Joey Hamilton .10
706 Mike Piazza 1.00
707 Dave Martinez .10
708 Mike Hampton .15
709 Bobby Bonilla .10
710 Juan Pierre .10
711 John Parrish .10
712 Kory DeHaan .10
713 Brian Tollberg .10
714 Chris Truby .10
715 Emil Brown .10
716 Ryan Dempster .10
717 Rich Garces .10
718 Mike Myers .10
719 Luis Ordaz .10
720 Kazuhiro Sasaki .10
721 Mark Quinn .10
722 Ramon Ortiz .10
723 Kerry Ligtenberg .10
724 Rolando Arrojo .10
725 Tsuyoshi Shinjo **RC** 1.00
726 Ichiro Suzuki **RC** 15.00
727 Roy Oswalt, Pat Strange, Jon Rauch (Prospects) .25
728 Phil Wilson **RC**, Jake Peavy **RC**, Darwin Cubillan **RC** (Prospects) .75
729 Steve Smyth **RC**, Mike Bynum, Nathan Haynes (Prospects) .40
730 Michael Cuddyer, Joe Lawrence, Choo Freeman (Prospects) .10
731 Carlos Pena, Larry Barnes, Dewayne Wise (Prospects) .10
732 Gookie Dawkins, Erick Almonte **RC**, Felipe Lopez (Prospects) .40
733 Alex Escobar, Eric Valent, Brad Wilkerson (Prospects) .10
734 Toby Hall, Rod Barajas, Jeff Goldbach **RC** (Prospects) .10
735 Jason Romano, Marcus Giles, Pablo Ozuna (Prospects) .10
736 Dee Brown, Jack Cust, Vernon Wells (Prospects) .10
737 David Espinosa, Luis Montanez **RC** (Draft Picks) .40
738 Anthony Pluta, Justin Wayne **RC** (Draft Picks) .50
739 Josh Axelson **RC**, Carmen Cali **RC** (Draft Picks) .50
740 Shaun Boyd **RC**, Chris Morris **RC** (Draft Picks) .50
741 Tommy Arko **RC**, Dan Moylan **RC** (Draft Picks) .50
742 Luis Cotto **RC**, Luis Escobar (Draft Picks) .40
743 Brandon Mims **RC**, Blake Williams **RC** (Draft Picks) .40
744 Chris Russ **RC**, Bryan Edwards (Draft Picks) .40
745 Joe Torres, Ben Diggins (Draft Picks) .10
746 Mark Dalesandro, Edwin Encarnacion **RC** (Draft Picks) .50
747 Brian Bass **RC**, Odannis Ayala **RC** (Draft Picks) .40
748 Jason Kaanoi **RC**, Michael Mathews **RC** (Draft Picks) .10
749 Stuart McFarland **RC**, Adam Sterrett **RC** (Draft Picks) .40
750 David Krynzel, Grady Sizemore (Draft Picks) .50
751 Keith Bucktrot, Dane Sardinha (Draft Picks) .10
752 Anaheim Angels .10
753 Arizona Diamondbacks .10
754 Atlanta Braves .10
755 Baltimore Orioles .10
756 Boston Red Sox .10
757 Chicago Cubs .10
758 Chicago White Sox .10
759 Cincinnati Reds .10
760 Cleveland Indians .10
761 Colorado Rockies .10
762 Detroit Tigers .10
763 Florida Marlins .10
764 Houston Astros .10
765 Kansas City Royals .10
766 Los Angeles Dodgers .10
767 Milwaukee Brewers .10
768 Minnesota Twins .10
769 Montreal Expos .10
770 New York Mets .10
771 New York Yankees .75
772 Oakland Athletics .10
773 Philadelphia Phillies .10
774 Pittsburgh Pirates .10
775 San Diego Padres .10
776 San Francisco Giants .10
777 Seattle Mariners .10
778 St. Louis Cardinals .10
779 Tampa Bay Devil Rays .10
780 Texas Rangers .10
781 Toronto Blue Jays .10
782 Bucky Dent (Golden Moments) .10
783 Jackie Robinson (Golden Moments) 1.00
784 Roberto Clemente (Golden Moments) 1.00
785 Nolan Ryan (Golden Moments) 1.50
786 Kerry Wood (Golden Moments) .10
787 Rickey Henderson (Golden Moments) .20
788 Lou Brock (Golden Moments) .25
789 David Wells (Golden Moments) .10
790 Andruw Jones (Golden Moments) .25
791 Carlton Fisk (Golden Moments) .10

Gold

Stars: 8-15X
Prospects and RC's: 3-6X
Inserted 1:17

Home Team Advantage

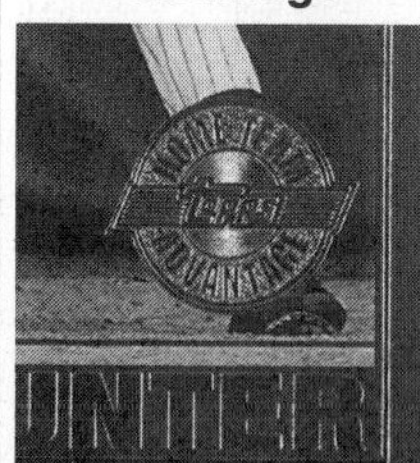

Cards which bear a bright, embossed gold-foil "Topps Home Team Advantage" seal in a lower corner originated in the Topps factory set. Individual cards may command a small premium from single-player specialist collectors.

Common Player:
Star: +25 Percent

A Look Ahead

NM/M
Complete Set (10): 15.00
Common Player: .50
Inserted 1:25
1 Vladimir Guerrero 1.50
2 Derek Jeter 4.00
3 Todd Helton 1.00
4 Alex Rodriguez 3.00
5 Ken Griffey Jr. 2.00
6 Nomar Garciaparra 3.00
7 Chipper Jones 2.00
8 Ivan Rodriguez 1.00
9 Pedro Martinez 1.50
10 Rick Ankiel .50

A Tradition Continued

NM/M
Complete Set (30): 50.00
Common Player: .50
Inserted 1:17
1 Chipper Jones 3.00
2 Cal Ripken Jr. 6.00
3 Mike Piazza 3.00
4 Ken Griffey Jr. 3.00
5 Randy Johnson 1.50
6 Derek Jeter 5.00
7 Scott Rolen 1.50
8 Nomar Garciaparra 4.00
9 Roberto Alomar 1.00
10 Greg Maddux 3.00
11 Ivan Rodriguez 1.50
12 Jeff Bagwell 1.50
13 Ivan Rodriguez 1.50
14 Pedro Martinez 2.00
15 Sammy Sosa 4.00
16 Jim Edmonds 1.00
17 Mo Vaughn .50
18 Barry Bonds 5.00
19 Larry Walker .75
20 Mark McGwire 4.00
21 Vladimir Guerrero 2.00
22 Andruw Jones 1.50
23 Todd Helton 1.50
24 Kevin Brown .75
25 Tony Gwynn 2.00
26 Manny Ramirez 1.50
27 Roger Clemens 4.00
28 Frank Thomas 1.50
29 Shawn Green .75
30 Jim Thome 1.50

Autographs

NM/M
Common Player:
Group A 1:22,866
Group B 1:3,054
Group C 1:1,431
Group D 1:18,339
Group E 1:13,737
Group F 1:11,015
Group G 1:625
HA Hank Aaron 250.00
DA Dick Allen 25.00
RA Rick Ankiel 10.00
RB Rocco Baldelli 30.00
EB Ernie Banks 100.00
YB Yogi Berra 80.00
LB Lou Brock 50.00
PB Pat Burrell 15.00
RC Rod Carew 50.00
MC Mike Cuellar 15.00
WF Whitey Ford 40.00
RF Rafael Furcal 25.00
BG Bob Gibson 40.00
AG Adrian Gonzalez 15.00
SH Scott Heard 15.00

WH Willie Hernandez 10.00
AJ Adam Johnson 10.00
CJ Chipper Jones 80.00
SK Sandy Koufax 500.00
ML Mike Lamb 10.00
VL Vernon Law 15.00
JM Jason Marquis 10.00
WM Willie Mays 250.00
MO Magglio Ordonez 20.00
AP Andy Pafko 30.00
BR Brooks Robinson 80.00
JR Joe Rudi 15.00
MS Mike Schmidt 100.00
MS Mike Stodolka 15.00
RS Ron Swoboda 30.00
GT Garry Templeton 30.00
JV Jose Vidro 20.00
MW Matt Wheatland 20.00
TZ Todd Zeile 20.00

Autographs Series 2

NM/M
Common Player: 10.00
DA Denny Abreu 10.00
TA Tony Alvarez 10.00
RB Rocco Baldelli 30.00
GB George Bell 10.00
JB Johnny Bench 60.00
BB Barry Bonds 100.00
MB Milton Bradley 15.00
GHB George Brett 175.00
MAB Mike Bynum 10.00
EB Eric Byrnes 10.00
JC Jorge Cantu 10.00
CC Chris Clapinski 10.00
WD Willie Davis 40.00
JDD J.D. Drew 30.00
TDLR Tomas de la Rosa 10.00
CD Chad Durbin 10.00
CE Carl Erskine 25.00
BE Brian Esposito 15.00
WF Whitey Ford 40.00
EF Eddy Furniss 15.00
BG Bob Gibson 40.00
MG Mike Glendenning 15.00
AG Adrian Gonzalez 20.00
NG Nick Green 10.00
KG Kevin Gregg 10.00
DG Dick Groat 25.00
GG Geraldo Guzman 10.00
YH Yamid Haad 10.00
TH Todd Helton 40.00
AH Aaron Herr 15.00
KH Ken Holtzman 20.00
RJ Reggie Jackson 100.00
NJ Neil Jenkins 15.00
AJ Adam Johnson 10.00
TJ Tripper Johnson 15.00
BK Bobby Kielty 10.00
JL John Lackey 10.00
ML Matt Lawton 15.00
CL Colby Lewis 10.00
MFL Mike Lockwood 10.00
GM Gary Matthews 20.00
LM Luis Montanez 15.00
EM Eric Munson 15.00
SM Stan Musial 150.00
BO Ben Oglivie 15.00
AO Augie Ojeda 10.00
ER Erasmo Ramirez 15.00
CR Chris Richard 15.00
JR Juan Rincon 10.00
LR Luis Rivas 20.00
SR Scott Rolen 35.00
NR Nolan Ryan 200.00
JS Juan Salas 10.00
TS Tom Seaver 150.00
CS Carlos Silva 10.00
GS Grady Sizemore 125.00
CCS Corey Smith 10.00
MS Mike Stodolka 10.00
MS Mike Sweeney 15.00
KT Kent Tekulve 20.00
DT Derek Thompson 10.00
ST Scott Thorman 10.00
BT Brian Tollberg 15.00
JW Justin Wayne 20.00
MW Michael Wenner 15.00
MJW Matt Wheatland 15.00
WW Wilbur Wood 20.00
CY Carl Yastrzemski 75.00

Base Hit

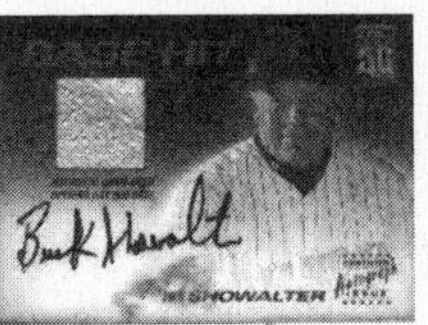

NM/M
Complete Set (28): 450.00
Common Player: 25.00
BH1 Mike Scioscia 35.00
BH2 Larry Dierker 25.00
BH3 Art Howe 25.00
BH4 Jim Fregosi 25.00
BH5 Bobby Cox 35.00
BH6 Davey Lopes 25.00
BH7 Tony LaRussa 30.00
BH8 Don Baylor 35.00
BH9 Larry Rothschild 25.00
BH10 Buck Showalter 30.00
BH11 Davey Johnson 30.00
BH12 Felipe Alou 30.00
BH13 Charlie Manuel 25.00
BH14 Lou Piniella 30.00
BH15 John Boles 25.00
BH16 Bobby Valentine 30.00
BH17 Mike Hargrove 25.00
BH18 Bruce Bochy 25.00
BH19 Terry Francona 25.00
BH20 Gene Lamont 25.00
BH21 Johnny Oates 25.00
BH22 Jimy Williams 25.00
BH23 Jack McKeon 25.00
BH24 Buddy Bell 25.00
BH25 Tony Muser 25.00
BH26 Phil Garner 25.00
BH27 Tom Kelly 25.00
BH28 Jerry Manuel 25.00

Before There Was Topps

NM/M
Complete Set (10): 20.00
Common Player: 1.50
Inserted 1:25
BT1 Lou Gehrig 4.00
BT2 Babe Ruth 5.00
BT3 Cy Young 2.00
BT4 Walter Johnson 2.00
BT5 Ty Cobb 4.00
BT6 Tris Speaker 1.50
BT7 Honus Wagner 2.00
BT8 Christy Mathewson 1.50
BT9 Grover Alexander 1.50
BT0 Joe DiMaggio 4.00

Combos

NM/M
Complete Set (20): 25.00
Common Player: 1.50
Inserted 1:12
1 Yogi Berra, Whitey Ford, Reggie Jackson, Don Mattingly, Derek Jeter 3.00
2 Brooks Robinson, Cal Ripken Jr. 3.00
3 Barry Bonds, Willie Mays 3.00
4 Bob Gibson, Pedro Martinez 1.50
5 Ivan Rodriguez, Johnny Bench 2.00
6 Ernie Banks, Alex Rodriguez 2.50
7 Joe Morgan, Ken Griffey Jr., Barry Larkin, Johnny Bench 2.50
8 Vladimir Guerrero, Roberto Clemente 2.50
9 Ted Williams, Carl Yastrzemski, Nomar Garciaparra 3.00
10 Joe Torre, Casey Stengel 1.50
11 Kevin Brown, Sandy Koufax, Don Drysdale 3.00
12 Mark McGwire, Sammy Sosa, Roger Maris, Babe Ruth 3.00
13 Ted Williams, Carl Yastrzemski, Nomar Garciaparra 3.00
14 Greg Maddux, Roger Clemens, Cy Young 2.00
15 Tony Gwynn, Ted Williams 3.00
16 Cal Ripken Jr., Lou Gehrig 4.00
17 Sandy Koufax, Randy Johnson, Warren Spahn, Steve Carlton 3.00
18 Mike Piazza, Josh Gibson 2.00
19 Barry Bonds, Willie Mays 3.00
20 Jackie Robinson, Larry Doby 2.50

Future Archives Gold Bordered Reprints

NM/M
Complete Set (20): 60.00
Common Player: 2.00
Inserted five per factory set.
1 Barry Bonds/1987 6.00
2 Chipper Jones/1991 8.00
3 Cal Ripken Jr./1982 12.00
4 Shawn Green/1992 2.00
5 Frank Thomas/1990 5.00
6 Derek Jeter/1993 9.00
7 Geoff Jenkins/1996 2.00
8 Jim Edmonds/1993 2.00
9 Bernie Williams/1990 2.00
10 Sammy Sosa/1990 6.00
11 Rickey Henderson/1980 6.00
12 Tony Gwynn/1983 6.00
13 Randy Johnson/1989 3.00
14 Juan Gonzalez/1990 3.00
15 Gary Sheffield/1989 2.00
16 Manny Ramirez/1992 3.00
17 Pokey Reese/1992 2.00
18 Preston Wilson/1993 2.00
19 Jay Payton/1995 2.00
20 Rafael Palmeiro/1987 3.00

Golden Anniversary

NM/M
Complete Set (50): 60.00
Common Player: .50
Inserted 1:10
1 Hank Aaron 3.00
2 Ernie Banks 1.50
3 Mike Schmidt 3.00
4 Willie Mays 4.00
5 Johnny Bench 1.50
6 Tom Seaver 1.00
7 Frank Robinson 1.00
8 Sandy Koufax 3.00
9 Bob Gibson 1.00
10 Ted Williams 4.00
11 Cal Ripken Jr. 5.00
12 Tony Gwynn 1.50
13 Mark McGwire 3.00
14 Ken Griffey Jr. 2.00
15 Greg Maddux 2.00
16 Roger Clemens 3.00
17 Barry Bonds 4.00
18 Rickey Henderson .75
19 Mike Piazza 2.00
20 Jose Canseco 1.00
21 Derek Jeter 4.00
22 Nomar Garciaparra 3.00
23 Alex Rodriguez 3.00
24 Sammy Sosa 2.50
25 Ivan Rodriguez 1.00
26 Vladimir Guerrero 1.50
27 Chipper Jones 2.00
28 Jeff Bagwell 1.00
29 Pedro Martinez 1.50
30 Randy Johnson 1.50
31 Pat Burrell 1.00
32 Josh Hamilton .50
33 Nick Johnson .50
34 Corey Patterson .50
35 Eric Munson .50
36 Sean Burroughs .50
37 Alfonso Soriano 1.50
38 Chin-Feng Chen .50
39 Barry Zito .75
40 Adrian Gonzalez .50
41 Mark McGwire 3.00
42 Nomar Garciaparra 3.00
43 Todd Helton 1.00
44 Matt Williams .50
45 Troy Glaus .75
46 Geoff Jenkins .50
47 Frank Thomas 1.00
48 Mo Vaughn .50
49 Barry Larkin .75
50 J.D. Drew .50

Hit Parade

NM/M
Complete Set (6):
Common Player: 25.00
1:2,600 Retail
HP1 Reggie Jackson 40.00
HP2 Dave Winfield 25.00
HP3 Eddie Murray 25.00
HP4 Rickey Henderson 25.00
HP5 Robin Yount 25.00
HP6 Carl Yastrzemski 65.00

King of Kings

NM/M
Common Card: 25.00
Inserted 1:2,056
1 Hank Aaron 75.00
2 Nolan Ryan 75.00
3 Rickey Henderson 30.00
5 Bob Gibson 25.00
6 Nolan Ryan 75.00

King of Kings Golden Edition

NM/M
Production 50 cards.
KKGE Hank Aaron, Nolan Ryan, Rickey Henderson 250.00

Noteworthy

NM/M
Complete Set (50): 40.00
Common Player: .50
Inserted 1:8
TN1 Mark McGwire 2.00
TN2 Derek Jeter 2.50
TN3 Sammy Sosa 2.00
TN4 Todd Helton 1.00
TN5 Alex Rodriguez 2.00
TN6 Chipper Jones 1.50
TN7 Barry Bonds 3.00
TN8 Ken Griffey Jr. 1.50
TN9 Nomar Garciaparra 2.00
TN10 Frank Thomas 1.00
TN11 Randy Johnson 1.00
TN12 Cal Ripken Jr. 3.00
TN13 Mike Piazza 1.50
TN14 Ivan Rodriguez 1.00
TN15 Jeff Bagwell 1.00
TN16 Vladimir Guerrero 1.00
TN17 Greg Maddux 1.50
TN18 Tony Gwynn 1.00
TN19 Larry Walker .50
TN20 Juan Gonzalez .75
TN21 Scott Rolen 1.00
TN22 Jason Giambi 1.00
TN23 Jeff Kent .50
TN24 Pat Burrell .75
TN25 Pedro Martinez 1.00
TN26 Willie Mays 2.00
TN27 Whitey Ford .75
TN28 Jackie Robinson 2.00
TN29 Ted Williams 2.50
TN30 Babe Ruth 3.00
TN31 Warren Spahn 1.00
TN32 Nolan Ryan 3.00
TN33 Yogi Berra 1.00
TN34 Mike Schmidt 2.00
TN35 Steve Carlton .75
TN36 Brooks Robinson 1.00
TN37 Bob Gibson 1.00
TN38 Reggie Jackson 1.00
TN39 Johnny Bench 1.50
TN40 Ernie Banks 1.00
TN41 Eddie Mathews .50
TN42 Don Mattingly 2.50
TN43 Duke Snider .75
TN44 Hank Aaron 2.00
TN45 Roberto Clemente 2.00
TN46 Harmon Killebrew 1.00
TN47 Frank Robinson 1.00
TN48 Stan Musial 2.00
TN49 Lou Brock .50
TN50 Joe Morgan .50

Originals

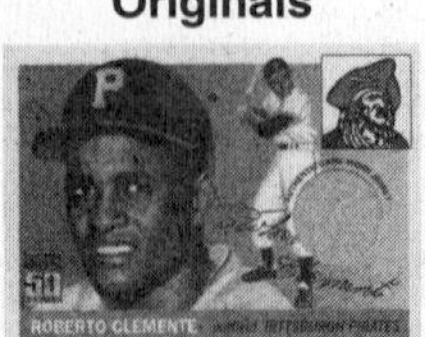

NM/M
Common Player: 10.00
Series 1 1:1,172
Series 2 1:1,023
1 Roberto Clemente/1955 80.00
2 Carl Yastrzemski/1960 30.00
3 Mike Schmidt/1974 30.00
4 Wade Boggs/1983 10.00
5 Chipper Jones/1991 15.00
6 Willie Mays 40.00
7 Lou Brock 15.00
8 Dave Parker 10.00
9 Barry Bonds 40.00
10 Alex Rodriguez 25.00

The Shot Heard Round The World Autograph

NM/M
B. Thomson/R. Branca Ralph Branca, Bobby Thomson 40.00

Through the Years

NM/M
Complete Set (50): 100.00
Common Player: 1.50
Inserted 1:8
1 Yogi Berra 2.00
2 Roy Campanella 2.00
3 Willie Mays 5.00
4 Andy Pafko 1.50
5 Jackie Robinson 4.00
6 Stan Musial 4.00
7 Duke Snider 2.00
8 Warren Spahn 2.50
9 Ted Williams 6.00
10 Eddie Matthews 2.00
11 Willie McCovey 1.50
12 Frank Robinson 2.00
13 Ernie Banks 3.00
14 Hank Aaron 5.00
15 Sandy Koufax 4.00
16 Bob Gibson 2.00
17 Harmon Killebrew 2.00
18 Whitey Ford 2.00
19 Roberto Clemente 5.00
20 Juan Marichal 1.50
21 Johnny Bench 3.00
22 Willie Stargell 1.50
23 Joe Morgan 1.50
24 Carl Yastrzemski 2.00
25 Reggie Jackson 2.00
26 Tom Seaver 2.00
27 Steve Carlton 1.50
28 Jim Palmer 1.50
29 Rod Carew 1.50
30 George Brett 5.00
31 Roger Clemens 4.00
32 Don Mattingly 5.00
33 Ryne Sandberg 3.00
34 Mike Schmidt 4.00
35 Cal Ripken Jr. 6.00
36 Tony Gwynn 2.00
37 Ozzie Smith 3.00
38 Wade Boggs 1.50
39 Nolan Ryan 6.00
40 Robin Yount 2.00
41 Mark McGwire 5.00
42 Ken Griffey Jr. 4.00
43 Sammy Sosa 4.00
44 Alex Rodriguez 4.00
45 Barry Bonds 6.00
46 Mike Piazza 3.00
47 Chipper Jones 3.00
48 Greg Maddux 3.00
49 Nomar Garciaparra 4.00
50 Derek Jeter 5.00

Two of a Kind

NM/M
Inserted 1:30,167
TK Bo Jackson, Deion Sanders 75.00

What Could've Been

NM/M
Complete Set (10): 15.00
Common Player: 1.00
Inserted 1:25
WCB1 Josh Gibson 3.00

WCB2 Leroy "Satchel" Paige 3.00
WCB3 Walter "Buck" Leonard 2.00
WCB4 James "Cool Papa" Bell 2.00
WCB5 Andrew "Rube" Foster 2.00
WCB6 Martin Dihigo 1.00
WCB7 William "Judy" Johnson 1.50
WCB8 Mule Suttles 1.00
WCB9 Ray Dandridge 1.00
WCB10 John Henry "Pop" Lloyd 2.00

2001 Topps Opening Day

NM/M

Complete Set (165): 35.00
Common Player: .15
Pack (7): 1.00
Box (24): 20.00

1 Cal Ripken Jr. 2.50
2 Chipper Jones 1.50
3 Garret Anderson .40
4 Robin Ventura .20
5 Jermaine Dye .15
6 Jim Thome .75
7 Brian Jordan .15
8 Shawn Green .40
9 Juan Gonzalez .75
10 Paul O'Neill .25
11 Pokey Reese .15
12 Mike Mussina .40
13 Jay Buhner .15
14 Shane Reynolds .15
15 Adam Piatt .15
16 Preston Wilson .15
17 Ellis Burks .15
18 Chuck Finley .15
19 Shannon Stewart .15
20 Mark McGwire 2.00
21 Mark Loretta .15
22 Bobby Jones .15
23 Matt Clement .15
24 Pedro J. Martinez 1.00
25 Carlos Lee .15
26 John Franco .15
27 Andres Galarraga .25
28 Jose Cruz Jr. .15
29 Randy Johnson .75
30 Richie Sexson .40
31 Darin Erstad .30
32 Manny Ramirez .75
33 Mike Sweeney .15
34 John Wetteland .15
35 Derek Jeter 2.50
36 J.D. Drew .15
37 Rick Reed .15
38 Jay Bell .15
39 Fred McGriff .25
40 Orlando Cabrera .15
41 Eric Owens .15
42 Jorge Posada .40
43 Jeff Cirillo .15
44 Johnny Damon .25
45 Charles Johnson .15
46 Pat Burrell .40
47 Gary Sheffield .40
48 Tom Glavine .30
49 Ivan Rodriguez .75
50 Chuck Knoblauch .15
51 Jason Kendall .15
52 Carlos Delgado .60
53 Roger Clemens 1.50
54 Brad Penny .15
55 Troy Glaus .75
56 Mike Hampton .15
57 Carlos Febles .15
58 Seth Etherton .15
59 Fernando Tatis .15
60 Livan Hernandez .15
61 Barry Larkin .30
62 Alex Rodriguez 2.00
63 Warren Morris .15
64 Antonio Alfonseca .15
65 Edgardo Alfonzo .15
66 Fernando Vina .15
67 Jason Giambi .75
68 Matt Lawton .15
69 Rusty Greer .15
70 Tony Gwynn 1.00
71 Carl Everett .15
72 Bret Boone .25
73 James Baldwin .15
74 Greg Vaughn .15
75 Darren Dreifort .15
76 Frank Thomas 1.00
77 Luis Castillo .15
78 Bartolo Colon .25
79 Craig Biggio .25
80 Jose Vidro .15
81 Todd Helton .75
82 Jacque Jones .15
83 Robb Nen .15
84 Richard Hidalgo .15
85 Tony Womack .15
86 Rick Ankiel .15
87 Terrence Long .15
88 Brad Radke .15
89 Gabe Kapler .15
90 Pedro Astacio .15
91 Darryl Kile .15
92 Jay Payton .15
93 Vladimir Guerrero 1.00
94 Juan Encarnacion .15
95 Ramon Hernandez .15
96 Sandy Alomar .15
97 Geoff Jenkins .25
98 Rafael Furcal .25
99 Mark Grace .25
100 Mark Mulder .25
101 Jim Edmonds .40
102 Tim Salmon .25
103 Jeff Bagwell .75
104 Jose Canseco .40
105 Ben Grieve .15
106 Ryan Klesko .25
107 Javy Lopez .25
108 Greg Maddux 1.50
109 Andruw Jones .50
110 Jeromy Burnitz .15
111 Ray Lankford .15
112 Sammy Sosa 1.50
113 Raul Mondesi .25
114 Mike Piazza 1.50
115 Todd Zeile .15
116 Eric Karros .15
117 Barry Bonds 2.50
118 J.T. Snow .15
119 Jeff Kent .15
120 David Justice .25
121 Matt Williams .25
122 Brian Giles .25
123 Edgar Martinez .15
124 Ken Griffey Jr. 1.50
125 Al Leiter .25
126 Kevin Brown .25
127 John Olerud .25
128 Roberto Alomar .50
129 Rafael Palmeiro .40
130 Steve Finley .15
131 Tim Hudson .40
132 Scott Rolen .75
133 Nomar Garciaparra 1.50
134 Mo Vaughn .15
135 Larry Walker .30
136 Albert Belle .15
137 Ray Durham .15
138 Andy Pettitte .40
139 Mariano Rivera .25
140 Bernie Williams .50
141 David Wells .15
142 Magglio Ordonez .40
143 Kevin Millwood .15
144 Cliff Floyd .15
145 Rich Aurilia .15
146 Eric Chavez .15
147 Scott Elarton .15
148 Tony Armas Jr. .15
149 Mark Redman .15
150 Javier Vazquez .15
151 Adrian Gonzalez, Adam Johnson .50
152 Mike Stodolka, Sean Burnett .15
153 David Walling, Ben Sheets .50
154 Chin-Feng Chen, Corey Patterson, Josh Hamilton .25
155 Mark McGwire (Golden Moments) 1.00
156 Bobby Thomson (Golden Moments) .15
157 Bill Mazeroski (Golden Moments) .15
158 Cal Ripken Jr. (Golden Moments) 1.00
159 Hank Aaron (Golden Moments) 1.00
160 Bucky Dent (Golden Moments) .15
161 Jackie Robinson (Golden Moments) 1.00
162 Roberto Clemente (Golden Moments) 1.00
163 Nolan Ryan (Golden Moments) 1.00
164 Kerry Wood (Golden Moments) .25
165 Checklist .15

Autographs

NM/M

Common Autograph: 20.00
TH Todd Helton 40.00
CJ Chipper Jones 100.00
MO Magglio Ordonez 25.00
CP Corey Patterson 20.00

Team Logo Stickers

NM/M

Complete Set (30): 6.00
Sticker: .25
Each team represented

2001 Topps American Pie

NM/M

Complete Set (150): 30.00
Common Player: .20
Pack (5): 3.00
Box (24): 50.00

1 Al Kaline .40
2 Al Oliver .20
3 Andre Dawson .20
4 Bert Blyleven .20
5 Bill Buckner .20
6 Bill Mazeroski .20
7 Bob Gibson .50
8 Bill Freeman .20
9 Bobby Grich .20
10 Bobby Murcer .20
11 Bobby Richardson .20
12 Boog Powell .20
13 Brooks Robinson .50
14 Carl Yastrzemski .75
15 Carlton Fisk .40
16 Clete Boyer .20
17 Curt Flood .20
18 Dale Murphy .30
19 Tony Conigliaro .20
20 Dave Parker .20
21 Dave Winfield .50
22 Dick Allen .20
23 Dick Groat .20
24 Don Drysdale .50
25 Don Sutton .20
26 Dwight Evans .20
27 Eddie Mathews .75
28 Elston Howard .20
29 Frank Howard .20
30 Frank Robinson .50
31 Fred Lynn .20
32 Gary Carter .20
33 Gaylord Perry .20
34 Norm Cash .20
35 George Brett 1.50
36 George Foster .20
37 Goose Gossage .20
38 Graig Nettles .20
39 Greg Luzinski .20
41 Harmon Killebrew .75
42 Jack Clark .20
43 Jack Morris .20
44 Jim Wynn .20
45 Jim Kaat .20
46 Jim Palmer .20
47 Joe Pepitone .20
48 Joe Rudi .20
49 Johnny Bench 1.00
50 Juan Marichal .40
51 Keith Hernandez .20
52 Bucky Dent .20
53 Lou Brock .40
54 Ron Cey .20
55 Luis Aparicio .20
56 Luis Tiant .20
57 Mark Fidrych .20
58 Maury Wills .20
59 Mickey Lolich .20
60 Mickey Rivers .20
61 Mike Schmidt 1.00
62 Moose Skowron .20
63 Nolan Ryan 3.00
64 Orlando Cepeda .20
65 Ozzie Smith .75
66 Phil Niekro .20
67 Reggie Jackson .75
68 Reggie Smith .20
69 Rico Carty .20
70 Roberto Clemente 2.00
71 Robin Yount .75
72 Roger Maris 1.50
73 Rollie Fingers .20
74 Ron Guidry .20
75 Ron Santo .20
76 Ron Swoboda .20
77 Sal Bando .20
78 Sam McDowell .20
79 Steve Carlton .40
80 Thurman Munson 1.00
81 Tim McCarver .20
82 Tom Seaver .75
83 Mike Cuellar .20
84 Tony Kubek .20
85 Tommy John .20
86 Tony Perez .20
87 Tug McGraw .20
88 Vida Blue .20
89 Warren Spahn .75
90 Whitey Ford .50
91 Willie Mays 2.00
92 Willie McCovey .20
93 Willie Stargell .50
94 Yogi Berra 1.00
95 Stan Musial 1.00
96 Jim Piersall .20
97 Duke Snider .50
98 Bruce Sutter .30
99 Dave Concepcion .20
100 Darrell Evans .20
101 Dennis Eckersley .40
102 Hoyt Wilhelm .20
103 Minnie Minoso .20
104 Don Newcombe .20
105 Richie Ashburn .20
106 Alan Trammell .20
107 Jim "Catfish" Hunter .20
108 Lou Whitaker .20
109 Johnny Podres .20
110 Denny Martinez .20
111 Willie Horton .20
112 Dean Chance .20
113 Fergie Jenkins .20
114 Cecil Cooper .20
115 Rick Reuschel .20
116 Space Race (Events) .20
117 Man On The Moon (Events) .50
118 Woodstock (Events) .50
119 Peace Movement/Flower Power (Events) .20
120 N.Y. Worlds Fair (Events) .20
121 Vietnam War (Events) .20
122 Vietnam Cease Fire (Events) .20
123 Kennedy Elected President (Events) .50
124 Kennedy Assassination (Events) .20
125 Malcom X (Events) .20
126 Nixon Elected President (Events) .20
127 Watergate (Events) .20
128 Nixon Resigns (Events) .20
129 Cuban Missile Crisis (Events) .20
130 Astrodome (Events) .20
131 Secretariat (Events) .20
132 Lyndon Johnson Signs Civil Rights Bill (Events) .20
133 Atomic Bomb Test Ban Treaty (Events) .20
134 Bi Centennial (Events) .20
135 String Bikini (Events) .20
136 Birth Control Pill (Events) .20
137 Studio 54 (Events) .20
138 Motown (Events) .20
139 Microsoft Started (Events) .20
140 Internet Developed (Events) .20
141 John F. Kennedy (Personalities) 1.50
142 Marilyn Monroe (Personalities) 1.50
143 Elvis Presley (Personalities) 1.50
144 Jimi Hendrix (Personalities) 1.00
145 Arthur Ashe (Personalities) .20
146 Richard Nixon (Personalities) .20
147 James Dean (Personalities) .20
148 Janis Joplin (Personalities) .50
149 Frank Sinatra (Personalities) 1.00
150 Malcom X (Personalities) .50

Autoproofs Baseball Legends

No pricing due to scarcity.
Production 25 Sets

Decade Leaders

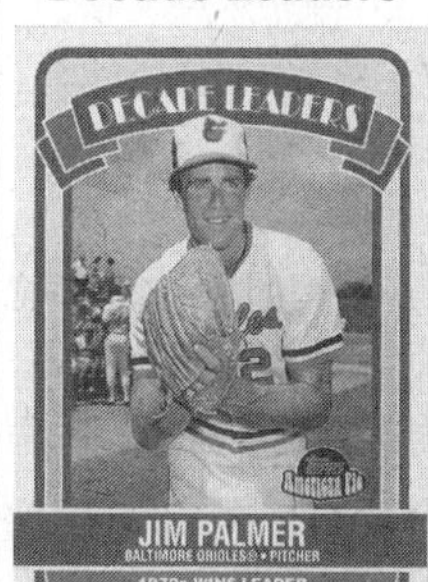

NM/M

Complete Set (10): 15.00
Common Player: 1.00
Inserted 1:12

DL1 Willie Stargell 1.50
DL2 Harmon Killebrew 1.50
DL3 Johnny Bench 2.00
DL4 Hank Aaron 3.00
DL5 Rod Carew 1.00
DL6 Roberto Clemente 3.00
DL7 Nolan Ryan 4.00
DL8 Bob Gibson 1.50
DL9 Jim Palmer 1.00
DL10 Juan Marichal 1.00

Entertainment Stars

NM/M

Production 500 Sets

1 Lou Ferrigno (Incredible Hulk) 50.00
2 Adam West (Batman) 60.00
3 Danny Bonaduce (Partridge Family) 30.00

Legends Autographs

NM/M

Common Player: 10.00
Inserted 1:211

TT1R Willie Mays 100.00
TT14R Johnny Bench 60.00
TT48R Bobby Richardson 20.00
TT8R Carl Yastrzemski 50.00
TT13R Warren Spahn 25.00
TT15R Reggie Jackson 50.00
TT18R Bob Gibson 20.00
TT25R Luis Tiant 10.00
TT29R Moose Skowron 10.00
TT31R Clete Boyer 10.00
TT33R Vida Blue 15.00
TT35R Joe Pepitone 10.00
TT37R Tug McGraw 15.00
TT47R Frank Howard 10.00
TT49R Tony Kubek 40.00
TT50R Mickey Lolich 10.00

Profiles In Courage

NM/M

Complete Set (20): 25.00
Common Player: 1.00
Inserted 1:8

PIC1 Roger Maris 2.00
PIC2 Lou Brock 1.00
PIC3 Brooks Robinson 1.50
PIC4 Carl Yastrzemski 1.50
PIC5 Mike Schmidt 2.50
PIC6 Hank Aaron 3.00
PIC7 Tom Seaver 1.50
PIC8 Willie Mays 3.00
PIC9 Graig Nettles 1.00
PIC10 Frank Robinson 1.50
PIC11 Rollie Fingers 1.00
PIC12 Tony Perez 1.00
PIC13 George Brett 3.00
PIC14 Robin Yount 1.50
PIC15 Nolan Ryan 4.00
PIC16 Warren Spahn 1.50
PIC17 Johnny Bench 2.00
PIC18 Vida Blue 1.00
PIC19 Roberto Clemente 3.00
PIC20 Thurman Munson 2.00

Rookie Reprint Relics

NM/M

Common Player: 10.00
Inserted 1:116

JB Johnny Bench 20.00
GB George Brett 40.00
SC Steve Carlton 15.00
GC Gary Carter 10.00
AD Andre Dawson 10.00
DE Dennis Eckersley 10.00
MF Mark Fidrych 10.00
BG Bobby Grich 10.00
RJ Reggie Jackson 15.00
JK Jim Kaat 10.00
TMC Tim McCarver 10.00
TM Thurman Munson 35.00
BM Bobby Murcer 10.00
AO Al Oliver 10.00
BP Boog Powell 10.00
OS Ozzie Smith 20.00
DS Don Sutton 10.00
DW Dave Winfield 10.00
RY Robin Yount 20.00

Timeless Classics Relics

NM/M

Common Player: 8.00
Inserted 1:80

Sam McDowell 8.00
Frank Howard 8.00
Dick Groat 8.00
Roger Maris 50.00
Orlando Cepeda 10.00
Willie Mays 40.00
Carl Yastrzemski 30.00
Roberto Clemente 60.00
Harmon Killebrew 20.00
Brooks Robinson 20.00
Tony Conigliaro 15.00
Frank Robinson 15.00
Hank Aaron 40.00
Willie McCovey 15.00
Rico Carty 8.00
Johnny Bench 20.00
Willie Stargell 15.00
Steve Carlton 15.00
Norm Cash 8.00
Reggie Jackson 15.00
Mike Schmidt 30.00
Mickey Rivers 8.00
Tom Seaver 20.00
George Brett 40.00
George Foster 8.00
Graig Nettles 8.00
Nolan Ryan 40.00
Dave Parker 10.00
Dick Allen 8.00
Fred Lynn 8.00
Keith Hernandez 8.00
Dave Winfield 15.00

Woodstock Relics

NM/M

Common Player: 8.00
Inserted 1:138

GB George Brett 40.00
BB Bill Buckner 8.00
OC Orlando Cepeda 10.00
DE Dwight Evans 8.00
CF Carlton Fisk 15.00
BF Bill Freehan 8.00
DG Dick Groat 8.00
RJ Reggie Jackson 15.00
TK Ted Kluszewski 8.00
FL Fred Lynn 8.00
WM Willie Mays 45.00
SM Stan Musial 40.00
TP Tony Perez 8.00
JP Jimmy Piersall 8.00
BR Brooks Robinson 15.00
FR Frank Robinson 15.00
JR Joe Rudi 8.00
DS Duke Snider 15.00

WS Willie Stargell 15.00
MW Maury Wills 8.00
DW Dave Winfield 8.00
WS Woodstock 15.00
JW Jim Wynn 8.00
CY Carl Yastrzemski 30.00
RY Robin Yount 20.00

2001 Topps Archives

NM/M
Complete Set (450): 150.00
Complete Series 1 (225): 75.00
Complete Series 2 (225): 75.00
Common Player: .40
Pack (8): 4.50
Box (20): 80.00

1 Johnny Antonelli .40
2 Yogi Berra 2.50
3 Dom DiMaggio .40
4 Carl Erskine .40
5 Joe Garagiola .50
6 Monte Irvin .40
7 Vernon Law .40
8 Eddie Mathews 2.00
9 Willie Mays 5.00
10 Gil McDougald .40
11 Andy Pafko .40
12 Phil Rizzuto .75
13 Preacher Roe .40
14 Hank Sauer .50
15 Bobby Shantz .40
16 Enos Slaughter .50
17 Warren Spahn 2.00
18 Mickey Vernon .40
19 Early Wynn .40
20 Whitey Ford 1.00
21 Johnny Podres .40
22 Ernie Banks 2.00
23 Moose Skowron .40
24 Harmon Killebrew 2.00
25 Ted Williams 6.00
26 Jimmy Piersall .40
27 Frank Thomas .40
28 Bill Mazeroski .50
29 Bobby Richardson .40
30 Frank Robinson 1.50
31 Stan Musial 3.00
32 Johnny Callison .40
33 Bob Gibson 2.00
34 Frank Howard .50
35 Willie McCovey .40
36 Carl Yastrzemski 2.00
37 Jim Maloney .40
38 Ron Santo .40
39 Lou Brock .75
40 Tim McCarver .50
41 Joe Pepitone .40
42 Boog Powell .50
43 Bill Freehan .40
44 Dick Allen .40
45 Willie Horton .40
46 Mickey Lolich .40
47 Wilbur Wood .40
48 Bert Campaneris .40
49 Rod Carew 1.50
50 Tug McGraw .40
51 Tony Perez .75
52 Luis Tiant .40
53 Bobby Murcer .40
54 Don Sutton .75
55 Ken Holtzman .40
56 Reggie Smith .40
57 Hal McRae .40
58 Roy White .40
59 Reggie Jackson 3.00
60 Graig Nettles .40
61 Joe Rudi .40
62 Vida Blue .50
63 Darrell Evans .40
64 David Concepcion .40
65 Bobby Grich .40
66 Greg Luzinski .40
67 Cecil Cooper .40
68 George Hendrick .40
69 Dwight Evans .40
70 Gary Matthews .40
71 Mike Schmidt 3.00
72 Dave Parker .40
73 Dave Winfield 1.00
74 Gary Carter .40
75 Dennis Eckersley .75
76 Kent Tekulve .40
77 Andre Dawson .75
78 Denny Martinez .40
79 Bruce Sutter .75
80 Jack Morris .40
81 Ozzie Smith 1.50
82 Lee Smith .40
83 Don Mattingly 4.00
84 Joe Carter .40
85 Kirby Puckett 3.00
86 Joe Adcock .40
87 Gus Bell .40
88 Roy Campanella 2.00
89 Jackie Jensen .40
90 Johnny Mize .75
91 Allie Reynolds .40
92 Al Rosen .40
93 Hal Newhouser .40
94 Harvey Kuenn .40
95 Nellie Fox .75
96 Elston Howard .40
97 Sal Maglie .40
98 Roger Maris 3.00
99 Norm Cash .40
100 Thurman Munson 2.50
101 Roy Campanella 1.50
102 Joe Garagiola .75
103 Dom DiMaggio .40
104 Johnny Mize .50
105 Allie Reynolds .40
106 Preacher Roe .40
107 Hal Newhouser .40
108 Monte Irvin .40
109 Carl Erskine .40
110 Enos Slaughter .40
111 Gil McDougald .40
112 Andy Pafko .40
113 Sal Maglie .40
114 Johnny Antonelli .40
115 Phil Rizzuto .50
116 Yogi Berra 1.50
117 Early Wynn .40
118 Mickey Vernon .40
119 Gus Bell .40
120 Ted Williams 4.00
121 Frank Thomas .40
122 Bobby Richardson .40
123 Whitey Ford 1.00
124 Vernon Law .40
125 Jimmy Piersall .40
126 Moose Skowron .40
127 Joe Adcock .40
128 Johnny Podres .40
129 Ernie Banks 1.50
130 Jim Maloney .40
131 Johnny Callison .40
132 Eddie Mathews 1.50
133 Joe Pepitone .40
134 Warren Spahn 1.50
135 Bill Mazeroski .40
136 Norm Cash .40
137 Bob Gibson 1.00
138 Harmon Killebrew 1.50
139 Frank Robinson 1.00
140 Ron Santo .40
141 Hank Sauer .40
142 Bobby Shantz .40
143 Nellie Fox .50
144 Elston Howard .40
145 Jackie Jensen .40
146 Al Rosen .40
147 Dick Allen .40
148 Bill Freehan .40
149 Boog Powell .40
150 Lou Brock .75
151 Rod Carew .75
152 Wilbur Wood .40
153 Thurman Munson 1.50
154 Ken Holtzman .40
155 Willie Horton .40
156 Mickey Lolich .40
157 Tim McCarver .40
158 Willie McCovey .40
159 Roy White .40
160 Bobby Murcer .40
161 Joe Rudi .40
162 Reggie Smith .40
163 Luis Tiant .40
164 Bert Campaneris .40
165 Frank Howard .40
166 Harvey Kuenn .50
167 Greg Luzinski .40
168 Tug McGraw .40
169 Willie Mays 3.00
170 Roger Maris 2.00
171 Vida Blue .40
172 Bobby Grich .40
173 Reggie Jackson 2.00
174 Hal McRae .40
175 Carl Yastrzemski 1.00
176 David Concepcion .40
177 Cecil Cooper .40
178 George Hendrick .40
179 Gary Matthews .40
180 Stan Musial 2.00
181 Graig Nettles .40
182 Don Sutton .50
183 Kent Tekulve .40
184 Bruce Sutter .75
185 Darrell Evans .40
186 Mike Schmidt 2.00
187 Dave Parker .40
188 Dwight Evans .40
189 Gary Carter .40
190 Jack Morris .40
191 Tony Perez .50
192 Dave Winfield .75
193 Andre Dawson .50
194 Lee Smith .40
195 Ozzie Smith 1.00
196 Denny Martinez .40
197 Don Mattingly 2.50
198 Joe Carter .40
199 Dennis Eckersley .75
200 Kirby Puckett 2.00
201 Walter Alston .40
202 Casey Stengel .75
203 Sparky Anderson .40
204 Tommy Lasorda .75
205 Whitey Herzog .40
206 Harmon Killebrew, Frank Howard, Reggie Jackson (League Leader) .40
207 Hank Aaron, Early Wynn, Ron Santo, Willie McCovey (League Leader) 2.50
208 Frank Robinson, Harmon Killebrew, Boog Powell (League Leader) 1.50
209 Tony Oliva, Frank Robinson, Frank Howard (League Leader) .75
210 Hank Aaron, Willie McCovey, Willie Mays, Orlando Cepeda (League Leader) 2.50
211 Hank Aaron, Frank Robinson, Willie Mays, Ernie Banks (League Leader) 2.50
212 Carl Yastrzemski, Harmon Killebrew, Frank Howard (League Leaders) 1.50
213 Ernie Banks (Highlight) 1.50
214 Hank Aaron (Highlight) 2.50
215 Willie Mays (Highlight) 2.50
216 Al Kaline (Highlight) .75
217 Stan Musial (Highlight) 2.00
218 Duke Snider (Highlight) .75
219 Frank Robinson, Hank Bauer, Frank Robinson (Highlight) .50
220 Willie Mays, Stan Musial (Highlight) 1.50
221 Whitey Ford (World Series Highlight) .75
222 Jerry Koosman (World Series Highlight) .40
223 Bob Gibson (World Series Highlight) .75
224 Gil Hodges (World Series Highlight) .40
225 Reggie Jackson (World Series Highlight) 1.50
226 Hank Bauer .40
227 Ralph Branca .40
228 Joe Garagiola .75
229 Bob Feller 2.00
230 Dick Groat .40
231 George Kell .40
232 Bob Boone .40
233 Minnie Minoso .40
234 Billy Pierce .40
235 Robin Roberts .50
236 Johnny Sain .40
237 Red Schoendienst .40
238 Curt Simmons .40
239 Duke Snider 2.00
240 Bobby Thomson .40
241 Hoyt Wilhelm .40
242 Elroy Face .40
243 Ralph Kiner .75
244 Hank Aaron 4.00
245 Al Kaline 2.00
246 Don Larsen 1.50
247 Tug McGraw .40
248 Don Newcombe .75
249 Herb Score .40
250 Clete Boyer .40
251 Lindy McDaniel .40
252 Brooks Robinson 2.50
253 Orlando Cepeda .60
254 Larry Bowa .40
255 Mike Cuellar .40
256 Jim Perry .40
257 Dave Parker .40
258 Maury Wills .40
259 Willie Davis .40
260 Juan Marichal .60
261 Jim Bouton .40
262 Dean Chance .40
263 Sam McDowell .40
264 Whitey Ford 3.00
265 Bob Uecker 2.00
266 Willie Stargell 2.00
267 Rico Carty .40
268 Tommy John .40
269 Phil Niekro .60
270 Paul Blair .40
271 Steve Carlton 3.00
272 Jim Lonborg .40
273 Tony Perez .60
274 Ron Swoboda .40
275 Fergie Jenkins .75
276 Jim Palmer 1.50
277 Sal Bando .40
278 Tom Seaver 4.00
279 Johnny Bench 4.00
280 Nolan Ryan 6.00
281 Rollie Fingers .50
282 Sparky Lyle .40
283 Al Oliver .40
284 Bob Watson .40
285 Bill Buckner .40
286 Bert Blyleven .40
287 George Foster .40
288 Al Hrabosky .40
289 Cecil Cooper .40
290 Carlton Fisk 1.00
291 Mickey Rivers .40
292 Goose Gossage .40
293 Rick Reuschel .40
294 Bucky Dent .40
295 Frank Tanana .40
296 George Brett 4.00
297 Keith Hernandez .40
298 Fred Lynn .40
299 Robin Yount 3.00
300 Ron Guidry .40
301 Jack Clark .40
302 Mark Fidrych .40
303 Dale Murphy 1.50
304 Willie Hernandez .40
305 Lou Whitaker .40
306 Kirk Gibson .75
307 Wade Boggs 3.00
308 Ryne Sandberg 4.00
309 Orel Hershiser .40
310 Jimmy Key .40
311 Richie Ashburn .40
312 Smoky Burgess .40
313 Gil Hodges 1.50
314 Ted Kluszewski .40
315 Pee Wee Reese 1.00
316 Jackie Robinson 4.00
317 Harvey Haddix .40
318 Satchel Paige 3.00
319 Roberto Clemente 5.00
320 Carl Furillo .40
321 Don Drysdale 2.00
322 Curt Flood .40
323 Bob Allison .40
324 Tony Conigliaro .40
325 Dan Quisenberry .40
326 Ralph Branca .40
327 Bob Feller 1.00
328 Satchel Paige 3.00
329 George Kell .40
330 Pee Wee Reese 1.00
331 Bobby Thomson .40
332 Carl Furillo .40
333 Hank Bauer .40
334 Herb Score .40
335 Richie Ashburn .40
336 Billy Pierce .40
337 Duke Snider 2.00
338 Harvey Haddix .40
339 Robin Roberts .40
340 Dick Groat .40
341 Curt Simmons .40
342 Bob Uecker 1.00
343 Smoky Burgess .40
344 Jim Bouton .40
345 Elroy Face .40
346 Don Drysdale 1.00
347 Bob Allison .40
348 Clete Boyer .40
349 Dean Chance .40
350 Tony Conigliaro .40
351 Curt Flood .40
352 Hoyt Wilhelm .40
353 Ron Swoboda .40
354 Roberto Clemente 3.00
355 Tug McGraw .40
356 Orlando Cepeda .40
357 Joe Garagiola .40
358 Juan Marichal .50
359 Sam McDowell .40
360 Johnny Sain .40
361 Ted Kluszewski .40
362 Al Kaline 2.00
363 Lindy McDaniel .40
364 Don Newcombe .40
365 Jim Perry .40
366 Hank Aaron 4.00
367 Don Larsen 1.00
368 Mike Cuellar .40
369 Willie Davis .40
370 Ralph Kiner .50
371 Minnie Minoso .40
372 Larry Bowa .40
373 Brooks Robinson 1.00
374 Bob Boone .40
375 Jim Lonborg .40
376 Paul Blair .40
377 Rico Carty .40
378 Sal Bando .40
379 Mark Fidrych .40
380 Al Hrabosky .40
381 Willie Stargell 1.00
382 Johnny Bench 2.50
383 Dave Parker .40
384 Sparky Lyle .40
385 Fergie Jenkins .50
386 Jim Palmer 1.00
387 Whitey Ford 2.00
388 Tony Perez .40
389 Mickey Rivers .40
390 Bob Watson .40
391 Rollie Fingers .40
392 George Foster .40
393 Al Oliver .40
394 Tom Seaver 3.00
395 Maury Wills .40
396 Steve Carlton 1.00
397 Cecil Cooper .40
398 Bill Buckner .40
399 Phil Niekro .40
400 Red Schoendienst .40
401 Ron Guidry .40
402 Willie Hernandez .40
403 Tommy John .40
404 Gil Hodges .40
405 Bucky Dent .40
406 Keith Hernandez .40
407 Dan Quisenberry .40
408 Fred Lynn .40
409 Rick Reuschel .40
410 Jackie Robinson 3.00
411 Goose Gossage .40
412 Bert Blyleven .40
413 Jack Clark .40
414 Carlton Fisk .50
415 Dale Murphy .75
416 Frank Tanana .40
417 George Brett 3.00
418 Robin Yount 2.50
419 Kirk Gibson .50
420 Lou Whitaker .40
421 Ryne Sandberg 2.50
422 Jimmy Key .40
423 Nolan Ryan 5.00
424 Wade Boggs .75
425 Orel Hershiser .40
426 Billy Martin (Managers) .40
427 Ralph Houk (Managers) .40
428 Chuck Tanner (Managers) .40
429 Earl Weaver (Managers) .40
430 Leo Durocher (Managers) .40
431 Tony Conigliaro, Norm Cash, Willie Horton (League Leaders) .40
432 Ernie Banks, Hank Aaron, Eddie Mathews, Clete Boyer (League Leaders) 1.50
433 Norm Cash, Frank Howard, Al Kaline, Jimmy Piersall (League Leaders) .40
434 Goose Gossage, Rollie Fingers (League Leaders) .40
435 Nolan Ryan, Tom Seaver (League Leaders) .40
436 Reggie Jackson, Willie Stargell (League Leaders) .75
437 Johnny Bench, Dick Allen (League Leaders) .75
438 Roger Maris (Decade Highlights) 3.00
439 Carl Yastrzemski (Decade Highlights) 2.00
440 Nolan Ryan (Decade Highlights) 4.00
441 Cincinnati Reds (Decade Highlights) .75
442 Tony Perez (Decade Highlights) .40
443 Steve Carlton (Decade Highlights) .75
444 Wade Boggs (Decade Highlights) .75
445 Andre Dawson (Decade Highlights) .40
446 Whitey Ford (World Series Highlights) 1.50
447 Hank Aaron (World Series Highlights) 4.00
448 Bob Gibson (World Series Highlights) .75
449 Roberto Clemente (World Series Highlights) 4.00
450 Orioles/Jackie Robinson (World Series Highlights) 1.50

Autographs

NM/M
Common Player: 10.00
Inserted 1:box

TAA1 Johnny Antonelli 15.00
TAA2 Hank Bauer 20.00
TAA3 Yogi Berra/50 350.00
TAA4 Ralph Branca 20.00
TAA5 Dom DiMaggio 50.00
TAA6 Joe Garagiola 40.00
TAA7 Carl Erskine 25.00
TAA8 Bob Feller 25.00
TAA10 Dick Groat 50.00
TAA11 Monte Irvin 20.00
TAA12 George Kell 20.00
TAA13 Vernon Law 15.00
TAA14 Bob Boone 10.00
TAA16 Willie Mays/50 500.00
TAA17 Gil McDougald 20.00
TAA18 Minnie Minoso 30.00
TAA19 Andy Pafko 30.00
TAA20 Billy Pierce 10.00
TAA21 Phil Rizzuto/200 100.00
TAA22 Robin Roberts 40.00
TAA23 Preacher Roe 20.00
TAA24 Johnny Sain 20.00
TAA25 Hank Sauer 20.00
TAA26 Red Schoendienst 25.00
TAA27 Bobby Shantz 10.00
TAA28 Curt Simmons 10.00
TAA29 Enos Slaughter 30.00
TAA30 Duke Snider 80.00
TAA31 Warren Spahn 120.00
TAA32 Bobby Thomson 20.00
TAA33 Mickey Vernon 15.00
TAA34 Hoyt Wilhelm 30.00
TAA35 Jim Wynn 10.00
TAA36 Elroy Face 10.00
TAA37 Gaylord Perry 35.00
TAA38 Ralph Kiner 50.00
TAA39 Johnny Podres 10.00
TAA40 Hank Aaron/50 1,400
TAA41 Ernie Banks/50 450.00
TAA42 Al Kaline 150.00
TAA43 Moose Skowron 15.00
TAA44 Don Larsen 180.00
TAA45 Harmon Killebrew 140.00
TAA46 Tug McGraw 30.00
TAA48 Don Newcombe 20.00
TAA49 Jimmy Piersall 15.00
TAA50 Herb Score 15.00
TAA51 Frank Thomas 10.00
TAA52 Clete Boyer 15.00
TAA53 Bill Mazeroski 60.00
TAA54 Lindy McDaniel 10.00
TAA55 Bobby Richardson 15.00
TAA56 Brooks Robinson/SP 200.00
TAA57 Frank Robinson 80.00
TAA58 Orlando Cepeda 75.00
TAA59 Stan Musial/50 300.00
TAA60 Larry Bowa 25.00
TAA61 Johnny Callison 10.00
TAA62 Mike Cuellar 15.00
TAA63 Bob Gibson/SP/50 180.00
TAA64 Jim Perry 10.00
TAA65 Frank Howard 15.00
TAA66 David Palmer 15.00
TAA67 Willie McCovey 80.00
TAA68 Maury Wills 15.00
TAA69 Carl Yastrzemski 200.00
TAA70 Willie Davis 10.00
TAA71 Jim Maloney 10.00
TAA73 Ron Santo 30.00
TAA74 Jim Bouton 25.00
TAA75 Lou Brock/50 180.00
TAA76 Dean Chance 10.00
TAA77 Tim McCarver/200 50.00
TAA78 Sam McDowell 15.00
TAA79 Joe Pepitone 20.00
TAA80 Whitey Ford 120.00
TAA81 Boog Powell 20.00
TAA83 Bill Freehan 10.00
TAA85 Dick Allen 30.00
TAA86 Rico Carty 10.00
TAA87 Willie Horton 10.00
TAA88 Tommy John 15.00
TAA89 Mickey Lolich 10.00
TAA90 Phil Niekro 30.00
TAA91 Wilbur Wood 10.00
TAA92 Paul Blair 10.00
TAA93 Bert Campaneris 10.00
TAA94 Steve Carlton 40.00
TAA96 Jim Lonborg 10.00
TAA97 Luis Aparicio 40.00
TAA98 Tony Perez 40.00
TAA99 Joe Morgan/200 60.00
TAA100 Ron Swoboda 25.00
TAA101 Luis Tiant 15.00
TAA102 Fergie Jenkins 30.00
TAA103 Bobby Murcer 30.00
TAA104 Jim Palmer 75.00
TAA106 Sal Bando 10.00
TAA107 Ken Holtzman 40.00
TAA108 Tom Seaver/50 200.00
TAA110 Johnny Bench 225.00
TAA111 Hal McRae 10.00
TAA112 Nolan Ryan 400.00
TAA113 Roy White 10.00
TAA114 Rollie Fingers 25.00
TAA115 Reggie Jackson/50 200.00
TAA116 Sparky Lyle 15.00
TAA117 Graig Nettles 20.00
TAA118 Al Oliver 10.00
TAA119 Joe Rudi 15.00
TAA120 Bob Watson 10.00
TAA121 Vida Blue 10.00
TAA122 Bill Buckner 10.00
TAA123 Darrell Evans 10.00
TAA124 Bert Blyleven 25.00
TAA125 David Concepcion 15.00
TAA126 George Foster 10.00
TAA127 Bobby Grich 10.00
TAA128 Al Hrabosky 10.00
TAA129 Greg Luzinski 20.00
TAA130 Cecil Cooper 10.00
TAA131 Ron Cey 10.00
TAA132 Carlton Fisk 90.00
TAA133 George Hendrick 10.00
TAA134 Mickey Rivers 10.00
TAA135 Dwight Evans 20.00
TAA136 Goose Gossage 10.00
TAA137 Gary Matthews 10.00
TAA138 Rick Reuschel 10.00
TAA139 Mike Schmidt 300.00

TAA140 Bucky Dent 25.00
TAA141 Jim Kaat 25.00
TAA142 Frank Tanana 10.00
TAA143 Dave Winfield/200 90.00
TAA144 George Brett 300.00
TAA145 Gary Carter/200 60.00
TAA146 Keith Hernandez 25.00
TAA147 Fred Lynn 25.00
TAA148 Robin Yount/ SP/200 150.00
TAA149 Dennis Eckersley/ SP/200 80.00
TAA150 Ron Guidry 25.00
TAA151 Kent Tekulve 15.00
TAA152 Jack Clark 10.00
TAA153 Andre Dawson/ SP/200 60.00
TAA154 Mark Fidrych 20.00
TAA155 Denny Martinez/ SP/200 40.00
TAA156 Dale Murphy 50.00
TAA157 Bruce Sutter 35.00
TAA158 Willie Hernandez 10.00
TAA160 Lou Whitaker 15.00
TAA162 Kirk Gibson 30.00
TAA163 Lee Smith 15.00
TAA164 Wade Boggs 80.00
TAA165 Ryne Sandberg/ SP/200 160.00
TAA166 Don Mattingly 125.00
TAA167 Joe Carter/SP/200 30.00
TAA168 Orel Hershiser 40.00
TAA169 Kirby Puckett 150.00
TAA170 Jimmy Key 30.00

Baseball Bucks

NM/M
Valid to 3/02 for Topps merchandise:
TB1 Willie Mays ($1/15,000) 2.00
TB2 Roberto Clemente ($5/1,000) 4.00
TB3 Jackie Robinson ($10/500) 10.00

Game-Used Bat

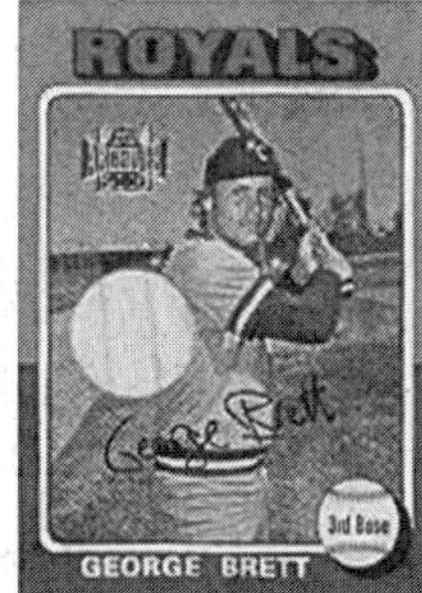

NM/M
Common Player: 15.00
1 Johnny Bench 30.00
2 George Brett 50.00
3 Fred Lynn 15.00
4 Reggie Jackson 25.00
5 Mike Schmidt 50.00
6 Willie Stargell 20.00

Game-Used Bat Autograph

NM/M
Common Player: 120.00
Production 25 Sets
1 Johnny Bench 150.00
2 George Brett 200.00
3 Fred Lynn 75.00

Topps Final Autoproof

NM/M
Common Player: 30.00
Carlton Fisk 60.00
Wade Boggs 40.00
Willie Mays 120.00
Willie McCovey 30.00
Jim Palmer 30.00
Robin Roberts 30.00
Duke Snider 40.00
Warren Spahn 40.00
Hoyt Wilhelm 30.00
Carl Yastrzemski 80.00

Reserve

NM/M
Complete Set (100): 90.00
Common Player: .75
Hobby Pack (5): 8.00
Hobby Box (10 + auto. ball): 125.00
1 Joe Adcock .75
2 Brooks Robinson 3.00
3 Luis Aparicio .75
4 Richie Ashburn .75
5 Hank Bauer .75
6 Johnny Bench 4.00
7 Wade Boggs 2.00
8 Moose Skowron .75
9 George Brett 5.00
10 Lou Brock 2.00
11 Roy Campanella 4.00
12 Willie Hernandez .75
13 Steve Carlton 2.00
14 Gary Carter .75
15 Hoyt Wilhelm .75
16 Orlando Cepeda .75
17 Roberto Clemente 8.00
18 Dale Murphy 1.50
19 Dave Concepcion .75
20 Dom DiMaggio .75
21 Larry Doby .75
22 Don Drysdale 4.00
23 Dennis Eckersley .75
24 Bob Feller 2.00
25 Rollie Fingers .75
26 Carlton Fisk 2.00
27 Nellie Fox 1.50
28 Mickey Rivers .75
29 Tommy John .75
30 Johnny Sain .75
31 Keith Hernandez .75
32 Gil Hodges .75
33 Elston Howard 3.00
34 Frank Howard .75
35 Bob Gibson 5.00
36 Fergie Jenkins .75
37 Jackie Jensen .75
38 Al Kaline 3.00
39 Harmon Killebrew 5.00
40 Ralph Kiner .75
41 Dick Groat .75
42 Don Larsen .75
43 Ralph Branca .75
44 Mickey Lolich .75
45 Juan Marichal 3.00
46 Roger Maris 6.00
47 Bobby Thomson .75
48 Eddie Mathews 4.00
49 Don Mattingly 8.00
50 Willie McCovey 2.00
51 Gil McDougald .75
52 Tug McGraw .75
53 Billy Pierce .75
54 Minnie Minoso .75
55 Johnny Mize 2.00
56 Elroy Face .75
57 Joe Morgan 1.50
58 Thurman Munson 5.00
59 Stan Musial 5.00
60 Phil Niekro .75
61 Paul Blair .75
62 Andy Pafko .75
63 Satchel Paige 5.00
64 Tony Perez .75
65 Sal Bando .75
66 Jimmy Piersall .75
67 Kirby Puckett 5.00
68 Phil Rizzuto 3.00
69 Robin Roberts .75
70 Jackie Robinson 8.00
71 Ryne Sandberg 3.00
72 Mike Schmidt 4.00
73 Red Schoendienst .75
74 Herb Score .75
75 Enos Slaughter .75
76 Ozzie Smith 3.00
77 Warren Spahn 2.00
78 Don Sutton .75
79 Luis Tiant .75
80 Ted Kluszewski .75
81 Whitey Ford 3.00
82 Maury Wills .75
83 Dave Winfield 2.00
84 Early Wynn .75
85 Carl Yastrzemski 3.00
86 Robin Yount 4.00
87 Bob Allison .75
88 Clete Boyer .75
89 Reggie Jackson 3.00
90 Yogi Berra 5.00
91 Willie Mays 8.00
92 Jim Palmer .75
93 Pee Wee Reese 2.00
94 Frank Robinson 2.00
95 Boog Powell .75
96 Willie Stargell 3.00
97 Nolan Ryan 10.00
98 Tom Seaver 4.00
99 Duke Snider 3.00
100 Bill Mazeroski .75

Reserve Autographs

NM/M
Common Autograph: 10.00
Inserted 1:10
1 Willie Mays 160.00
2 Whitey Ford 60.00
3 Nolan Ryan 175.00
4 Carl Yastrzemski 90.00
5 Frank Robinson 40.00
6 Tom Seaver 80.00
7 Warren Spahn 75.00
8 Johnny Bench 100.00
9 Reggie Jackson 80.00
10 Bob Gibson 40.00
11 Bob Feller 20.00
12 Gil McDougald 15.00
13 Luis Tiant 10.00
14 Minnie Minoso 10.00
16 Herb Score 10.00
17 Moose Skowron 15.00
18 Maury Wills 10.00
19 Clete Boyer 15.00
21 Don Larsen 20.00
23 Tug McGraw 20.00
25 Robin Roberts 20.00
26 Frank Howard 20.00
27 Mickey Lolich 10.00
29 Tommy John 10.00
32 Dick Groat 15.00
33 Elroy Face 10.00
34 Paul Blair 10.00

Reserve Autographed Baseball

NM/M
Common Autograph: 15.00
Inserted 1:Box
1 Johnny Bench/100 80.00
2 Paul Blair/1,000 15.00
3 Clete Boyer/1,000 15.00
4 Ralph Branca/400 25.00
5 Elroy Face/1,000 15.00
6 Bob Feller/1,000 25.00
7 Whitey Ford/100 60.00
8 Bob Gibson/1,000 30.00
9 Dick Groat/1,000 15.00
10 Frank Howard/1,000 15.00
11 Reggie Jackson/100 75.00
12 Don Larsen/100 30.00
13 Mickey Lolich/500 15.00
14 Willie Mays/100 150.00
15 Gil McDougald/500 20.00
16 Tug McGraw/1,000 15.00
17 Minnie Minoso/1,000 15.00
18 Andy Pafko/500 25.00
19 Joe Pepitone/1,000 15.00
20 Robin Roberts/1,000 25.00
21 Frank Robinson/100 50.00
22 Nolan Ryan/100 150.00
23 Herb Score/500 20.00
24 Tom Seaver/100 80.00
25 Moose Skowron/ 1,000 15.00
26 Warren Spahn/100 50.00
27 Bobby Thomson/400 20.00
28 Luis Tiant/500 20.00
29 Carl Yastrzemski/ 100 100.00
30 Maury Wills/1,000 20.00

Reserve Bat Relics

NM/M
Common Player: 8.00
Overall Relic Odds 1:10
21 Al Kaline 20.00
22 Carl Yastrzemski 25.00
23 Carlton Fisk 15.00
24 Dale Murphy 15.00
25 Dave Winfield 10.00
26 Dick Groat 8.00
27 Dom DiMaggio 15.00
28 Don Mattingly 40.00
29 Gary Carter 8.00
30 George Kell 15.00
31 Harmon Killebrew 20.00
32 Jackie Jensen 15.00
33 Jackie Robinson 75.00
34 Jimmy Piersall 8.00
35 Joe Adcock 8.00
36 Joe Carter 8.00
37 Johnny Mize 10.00
38 Kirk Gibson 8.00
39 Mickey Vernon 8.00
40 Mike Schmidt 40.00
41 Ryne Sandberg 40.00
42 Ozzie Smith 20.00
43 Ted Kluszewski 10.00
44 Wade Boggs 10.00
45 Willie Mays 60.00
46 Duke Snider 15.00
47 Harvey Kuenn 8.00
48 Robin Yount 20.00
49 Red Schoendienst 8.00
50 Elston Howard 10.00
51 Bob Allison 8.00

Reserve Jersey Relics

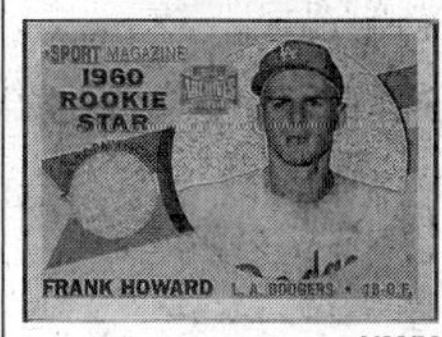

NM/M
Common Player: 8.00
Overall Relic Odds 1:10
1 Brooks Robinson 15.00
2 Tony Conigliaro 15.00
3 Frank Howard 8.00
4 Don Sutton 10.00
5 Ferguson Jenkins 8.00
6 Frank Robinson 15.00
7 Don Mattingly 40.00
8 Willie Stargell 15.00
9 Moose Skowron 15.00
10 Fred Lynn 8.00
11 George Brett 40.00
12 Nolan Ryan 50.00
13 Orlando Cepeda 10.00
14 Reggie Jackson 15.00
15 Steve Carlton 15.00
16 Tom Seaver 20.00
17 Thurman Munson 25.00
18 Yogi Berra 20.00
19 Willie McCovey 15.00
20 Robin Yount 20.00

Chicago Cubs Reprints

This series of reprints of popular Cubs players' cards was part of Topps' 50th Anniversary celebration in 2001. Each card was printed in a serially-numbered edition of 30,000 and given to fans at special promotional dates. About 200 of each player's card were autographed and randomly distributed.

NM/M
Complete Set (10): 75.00
Common Player: 5.00
1952 Andy Pafko 7.50
1952 Andy Pafko/Auto. 25.00
1958 Ernie Banks 20.00
1958 Ernie Banks/Auto. 75.00
1961 Ron Santo 7.50
1961 Ron Santo/Auto. 45.00
1971 Fergie Jenkins 7.50
1971 Fergie Jenkins/Auto. 45.00
1972 Billy Williams 7.50
1972 Billy Williams/Auto. 45.00
1979 Bruce Sutter 7.50
1979 Bruce Sutter/Auto. 45.00
1984 Ryne Sandberg 20.00
1984 Ryne Sandberg/Auto. 75.00
1985 Rick Sutcliffe 5.00
1985 Rick Sutcliffe/Auto. 25.00
1988 Andre Dawson 6.00
1988 Andre Dawson/Auto. 45.00
1998 Sammy Sosa 20.00
1998 Sammy Sosa/Auto. 75.00

2001 Topps Chrome

NM/M
Complete Set (660): 225.00
Complete Series 1 (330): 100.00
Complete Series 2 (330): 125.00
Common Player: .25
Series 1 Pack (4): 2.00
Series 1 Box (24): 40.00
Series 2 Pack (4): 6.00
Series 2 Box (24): 120.00
1 Cal Ripken Jr. 3.00
2 Chipper Jones 1.00
3 Roger Cedeno .25
4 Garret Anderson .50
5 Robin Ventura .40
6 Daryle Ward .25
8 Phil Nevin .25
9 Jermaine Dye .25
10 Chris Singleton .25
11 Mike Redmond .25
12 Jim Thome 1.00
13 Brian Jordan .25
14 Dustin Hermanson .25
15 Shawn Green .50
16 Todd Stottlemyre .25
17 Dan Wilson .25
18 Derek Lowe .25
19 Juan Gonzalez .75
20 Pat Meares .25
21 Paul O'Neill .50
22 Jeffrey Hammonds .25
23 Pokey Reese .25
24 Mike Mussina .75
25 Rico Brogna .25
26 Jay Buhner .25
27 Steve Cox .25
28 Quilvio Veras .25
29 Marquis Grissom .25
30 Shigetoshi Hasegawa .25
31 Shane Reynolds .25
32 Adam Piatt .25
33 Preston Wilson .25
34 Ellis Burks .25
35 Armando Rios .25
36 Chuck Finley .25
37 Shannon Stewart .25
38 Mark McGwire 2.50
39 Gerald Williams .25
40 Eric Young .25
41 Peter Bergeron .25
42 Arthur Rhodes .25
43 Bobby Jones .25
44 Matt Clement .25
45 Pedro Martinez 1.00
46 Jose Canseco .75
47 Matt Anderson .25
48 Torii Hunter .50
49 Carlos Lee .50
50 Eric Chavez .50
51 Rick Helling .25
52 John Franco .25
53 Mike Bordick .25
54 Andres Galarraga .40
55 Jose Cruz Jr. .25
56 Mike Matheny .25
57 Randy Johnson 1.00
58 Richie Sexson .75
59 Vladimir Nunez .25
60 Aaron Boone .25
61 Darin Erstad .50
62 Alex Gonzalez .25
63 Gil Heredia .25
64 Shane Andrews .25
65 Todd Hundley .25
66 Bill Mueller .25
67 Mark McLemore .25
68 Scott Spiezio .25
69 Kevin McGlinchy .25
70 Manny Ramirez 1.00
71 Mike Lamb .25
72 Brian Buchanan .25
73 Mike Sweeney .25
74 John Wetteland .25
75 Rob Bell .25
76 John Burkett .25
77 Derek Jeter 3.00
78 J.D. Drew .50
79 Jose Offerman .25
80 Rick Reed .25
81 Will Clark .75
82 Rickey Henderson .75
83 Kirk Rueter .25
84 Lee Stevens .25
85 Jay Bell .25
86 Fred McGriff .50
87 Julio Zuleta .25
88 Brian Anderson .25
89 Orlando Cabrera .25
90 Alex Fernandez .25
91 Derek Bell .25
92 Eric Owens .25
93 Dennys Reyes .25
94 Mike Stanley .25
95 Jorge Posada .75
96 Paul Konerko .50
97 Mike Remlinger .25
98 Travis Lee .25
99 Ken Caminiti .25
100 Kevin Barker .25
101 Ozzie Guillen .25
102 Randy Wolf .25
103 Michael Tucker .25
104 Darren Lewis .25
105 Joe Randa .25
106 Jeff Cirillo .25
107 David Ortiz 1.00
108 Herb Perry .25
109 Jeff Nelson .25
110 Chris Stynes .25
111 Johnny Damon 1.00
112 Jason Schmidt .50
113 Charles Johnson .25
114 Pat Burrell .50
115 Gary Sheffield .75
116 Tom Glavine .50
117 Jason Isringhausen .25
118 Chris Carpenter .50
119 Jeff Suppan .25
120 Ivan Rodriguez 1.00
121 Luis Sojo .25
122 Ron Villone .25
123 Mike Sirotka .25
124 Chuck Knoblauch .25
125 Jason Kendall .25
126 Bobby Estalella .25
127 Jose Guillen .25
128 Carlos Delgado 1.00
129 Benji Gil .25
130 Einar Diaz .25
131 Andy Benes .25
132 Adrian Beltre .50
133 Roger Clemens 3.00
134 Scott Williamson .25
135 Brad Penny .25
136 Troy Glaus .50
137 Kevin Appier .25
138 Walt Weiss .25
139 Michael Barrett .25
140 Mike Hampton .25
141 Francisco Cordova .25
142 David Segui .25
143 Carlos Febles .25
144 Roy Halladay .50
145 Seth Etherton .25
146 Fernando Tatis .25
147 Livan Hernandez .25
148 B.J. Surhoff .25
149 Barry Larkin .50
150 Bobby Howry .25
151 Dmitri Young .25

152 Brian Hunter .25
153 Alex Rodriguez 3.00
154 Hideo Nomo .75
155 Warren Morris .25
156 Antonio Alfonseca .25
157 Edgardo Alfonzo .25
158 Mark Grudzielanek .25
159 Fernando Vina .25
160 Homer Bush .25
161 Jason Giambi 1.00
162 Steve Karsay .25
163 Matt Lawton .25
164 Rusty Greer .25
165 Billy Koch .25
166 Todd Hollandsworth .25
167 Raul Ibanez .25
168 Tony Gwynn 1.00
169 Carl Everett .25
170 Hector Carrasco .25
171 Jose Valentin .25
172 Deivi Cruz .25
173 Bret Boone .25
174 Melvin Mora .25
175 Danny Graves .25
176 Jose Jimenez .25
177 James Baldwin .25
178 C.J. Nitkowski .25
179 Jeff Zimmerman .25
180 Mike Lowell .25
181 Hideki Irabu .25
182 Greg Vaughn .25
183 Omar Daal .25
184 Darren Dreifort .25
185 Gil Meche .25
186 Damian Jackson .25
187 Frank Thomas 1.00
188 Luis Castillo .25
189 Bartolo Colon .50
190 Craig Biggio .50
191 Scott Schoeneweis .25
192 Dave Veres .25
193 Ramon Martinez .25
194 Jose Vidro .25
195 Todd Helton .75
196 Greg Norton .25
197 Jacque Jones .25
198 Jason Grimsley .25
199 Dan Reichert .25
200 Robb Nen .25
201 Scott Hatteberg .25
202 Terry Shumpert .25
203 Kevin Millar .25
204 Ismael Valdes .25
205 Richard Hidalgo .25
206 Randy Velarde .25
207 Bengie Molina .25
208 Tony Womack .25
209 Enrique Wilson .25
210 Jeff Brantley .25
211 Rick Ankiel .25
212 Terry Mulholland .25
213 Ron Belliard .25
214 Terrence Long .25
215 Alberto Castillo .25
216 Royce Clayton .25
217 Joe McEwing .25
218 Jason McDonald .25
219 Ricky Bottalico .25
220 Keith Foulke .25
221 Brad Radke .25
222 Gabe Kapler .25
223 Pedro Astacio .25
224 Armando Reynoso .25
225 Darryl Kile .25
226 Reggie Sanders .25
227 Esteban Yan .25
228 Joe Nathan .25
229 Jay Payton .25
230 Francisco Cordero .25
231 Gregg Jefferies .25
232 LaTroy Hawkins .25
233 Jacob Cruz .25
234 Chris Holt .25
235 Vladimir Guerrero 1.00
236 Marvin Benard .25
237 Alex Ramirez .25
238 Mike Williams .25
239 Sean Bergman .25
240 Juan Encarnacion .25
241 Russ Davis .25
242 Ramon Hernandez .25
243 Sandy Alomar .25
244 Eddie Guardado .25
245 Shane Halter .25
246 Geoff Jenkins .50
247 Brian Meadows .25
248 Damian Miller .25
249 Darrin Fletcher .25
250 Rafael Furcal .50
251 Mark Grace .75
252 Mark Mulder .50
253 Joe Torre (Managers) .75
254 Bobby Cox (Managers) .25
255 Mike Scioscia (Managers) .25
256 Mike Hargrove (Managers) .25
257 Jimy Williams (Managers) .25
258 Jerry Manuel (Managers) .25
259 Charlie Manuel (Managers) .25
260 Don Baylor (Managers) .25
261 Phil Garner (Managers) .25
262 Tony Muser (Managers) .25
263 Buddy Bell (Managers) .25
264 Tom Kelly (Managers) .25
265 John Boles (Managers) .25
266 Art Howe (Managers) .25
267 Larry Dierker (Managers) .25
268 Lou Pinella (Managers) .25
269 Larry Rothschild (Managers) .25
270 Davey Lopes (Managers) .25
271 Johnny Oates (Managers) .25
272 Felipe Alou (Managers) .25
273 Bobby Valentine (Managers) .25
274 Tony LaRussa (Managers) .25
275 Bruce Bochy (Managers) .25
276 Dusty Baker (Managers) .25
277 Adrian Gonzalez, Adam Johnson (Draft Picks and Prospects) 1.00
278 Matt Wheatland, Brian Digby (Draft Picks and Prospects) .50
279 Tripper Johnson, Scott Thorman (Draft Picks and Prospects) 1.00
280 Phil Dumatrait, Adam Wainwright (Draft Picks and Prospects) 1.00
281 Scott Heard, David Parrish **RC** (Draft Picks and Prospects) .75
282 Rocco Baldelli, Mark Folsom **RC** (Draft Picks and Prospects) 1.00
283 Dominic Rich **RC**, Aaron Herr (Draft Picks and Prospects) .75
284 Mike Stodolka, Sean Burnett (Draft Picks and Prospects) .75
285 Derek Thompson, Corey Smith (Draft Picks and Prospects) .75
286 Danny Borrell **RC**, Jason Bourgeois **RC** (Draft Picks and Prospects) .75
287 Chin Feng Chen, Corey Patterson, Josh Hamilton (Draft Picks and Prospects) .75
288 Ryan Anderson, Barry Zito, C.C. Sabathia (Draft Picks and Prospects) .75
289 Scott Sobkowiak, David Walling, Ben Sheets (Draft Picks and Prospects) .75
290 Ty Howington, Josh Kalinowski, Josh Girdley (Draft Picks and Prospects) .50
291 Hee Seop Choi **RC**, Aaron McNeal, Jason Hart (Draft Picks and Prospects) 1.00
292 Bobby Bradley, Kurt Ainsworth, Chin-Hui Tsao (Draft Picks and Prospects) .75
293 Mike Glendenning, Kenny Kelly, Juan Silvestri (Draft Picks and Prospects) .50
294 J.R. House, Ramon Castro, Ben Davis (Draft Picks and Prospects) .50
295 Chance Caple, Rafael Soriano **RC**, Pascual Coco (Draft Picks and Prospects) 1.00
296 Travis Hafner **RC**, Eric Munson, Bucky Jacobsen (Draft Picks and Prospects) 6.00
297 Jason Conti, Chris Wakeland, Brian Cole (Draft Picks and Prospects) .75
298 Scott Seabol, Aubrey Huff, Joe Crede (Draft Picks and Prospects) .50
299 Adam Everett, Jose Ortiz, Keith Ginter (Draft Picks and Prospects) .50
300 Carlos Hernandez, Geraldo Guzman, Adam Eaton (Draft Picks and Prospects) .75
301 Bobby Kielty, Milton Bradley, Juan Rivera (Draft Picks and Prospects) .50
302 Mark McGwire (Golden Moments) 2.00
303 Don Larsen (Golden Moments) .75
304 Bobby Thomson (Golden Moments) .25
305 Bill Mazeroski (Golden Moments) .25
306 Reggie Jackson (Golden Moments) 1.00
307 Kirk Gibson (Golden Moments) .25
308 Roger Maris (Golden Moments) 1.50
309 Cal Ripken Jr. (Golden Moments) 3.00
310 Hank Aaron (Golden Moments) 3.00
311 Joe Carter (Golden Moments) .25
312 Cal Ripken Jr. (Season Highlights) 3.00
313 Randy Johnson (Season Highlights) 1.00
314 Ken Griffey Jr. (Season Highlights) 2.00
315 Troy Glaus (Season Highlights) .75
316 Kazuhiro Sasaki (Season Highlights) .25
317 Sammy Sosa, Troy Glaus (League Leaders) 1.00
318 Todd Helton, Edgar Martinez (League Leaders) .50
319 Todd Helton, Nomar Garciaparra (League Leaders) 1.00
320 Barry Bonds, Jason Giambi (League Leaders) 1.50
321 Todd Helton, Manny Ramirez (League Leaders) .50
322 Todd Helton, Darin Erstad (League Leaders) .50
323 Kevin Brown, Pedro Martinez (League Leaders) .75
324 Randy Johnson, Pedro Martinez (League Leaders) .75
325 Will Clark (Post Season Highlights) .40
326 New York Mets (Post Season Highlights) .25
327 New York Yankees (Post Season Highlights) 1.00
328 Seattle Mariners (Post Season Highlights) .25
329 Mike Hampton (Post Season Highlights) .25
330 New York Yankees (Post Season Highlights) 1.00
331 World Series (Post Season Highlights) 1.50
332 Jeff Bagwell 1.00
333 Andy Pettitte .75
334 Tony Armas Jr. .25
335 Jeromy Burnitz .25
336 Javier Vazquez .25
337 Eric Karros .25
338 Brian Giles .50
339 Scott Rolen 1.00
340 David Justice .50
341 Ray Durham .25
342 Todd Zeile .25
343 Cliff Floyd .25
344 Barry Bonds 3.00
345 Matt Williams .50
346 Steve Finley .25
347 Scott Elarton .25
348 Bernie Williams .75
349 David Wells .25
350 J.T. Snow .25
351 Al Leiter .40
352 Magglio Ordonez .50
353 Raul Mondesi .25
354 Tim Salmon .50
355 Jeff Kent .40
356 Mariano Rivera .50
357 John Olerud .50
358 Javy Lopez .50
359 Ben Grieve .50
360 Ray Lankford .25
361 Ken Griffey Jr. 2.00
362 Rich Aurilia .25
363 Andruw Jones 1.00
364 Ryan Klesko .50
365 Roberto Alomar .75
366 Miguel Tejada .50
367 Mo Vaughn .50
368 Albert Belle .25
369 Jose Canseco .50
370 Kevin Brown .50
371 Rafael Palmeiro .75
372 Mark Redman .25
373 Larry Walker .50
374 Greg Maddux 2.00
375 Nomar Garciaparra 1.00
376 Kevin Millwood .50
377 Edgar Martinez .50
378 Sammy Sosa 1.50
379 Tim Hudson .50
380 Jim Edmonds .50
381 Mike Piazza 1.50
382 Brant Brown .25
383 Brad Fullmer .25
384 Alan Benes .25
385 Mickey Morandini .25
386 Troy Percival .25
387 Eddie Perez .25
388 Vernon Wells .25
389 Ricky Gutierrez .25
390 Rondell White .25
391 Kevin Escobar .25
392 Tony Batista .25
393 Jimmy Haynes .25
394 Billy Wagner .50
395 A.J. Hinch .25
396 Matt Morris .25
397 Lance Berkman .75
398 Jeff D'Amico .25
399 Octavio Dotel .25
400 Olmedo Saenz .25
401 Esteban Loaiza .25
402 Adam Kennedy .25
403 Moises Alou .50
404 Orlando Palmeiro .25
405 Kevin Young .25
406 Tom Goodwin .25
407 Mac Suzuki .25
408 Pat Hentgen .25
409 Kevin Stocker .25
410 Mark Sweeney .25
411 Tony Eusebio .25
412 Edgar Renteria .25
413 John Rocker .25
414 Jose Lima .25
415 Kerry Wood .50
416 Mike Timlin .25
417 Jose Hernandez .25
418 Jeremy Giambi .25
419 Luis Lopez .25
420 Mitch Meluskey .25
421 Garrett Stephenson .25
422 Jamey Wright .25
423 John Jaha .25
424 Placido Polanco .25
425 Marty Cordova .25
426 Joey Hamilton .25
427 Travis Fryman .25
428 Mike Cameron .25
429 Matt Mantei .25
430 Chan Ho Park .25
431 Shawn Estes .25
432 Danny Bautista .25
433 Wilson Alvarez .25
434 Kenny Lofton .40
435 Russ Ortiz .25
436 Dave Burba .25
437 Felix Martinez .25
438 Jeff Shaw .25
439 Mike Difelice .25
440 Roberto Hernandez .25
441 Bryan Rekar .25
442 Ugueth Urbina .25
443 Vinny Castilla .25
444 Carlos Perez .25
445 Juan Guzman .25
446 Ryan Rupe .25
447 Mike Mordecai .25
448 Ricardo Rincon .25
449 Curt Schilling 1.00
450 Alex Cora .25
451 Turner Ward .25
452 Omar Vizquel .40
453 Russ Branyan .25
454 Russ Johnson .25
455 Gregg Colbrunn .25
456 Charles Nagy .25
457 Wil Cordero .25
458 Jason Tyner .25
459 Devon White .25
460 Kelly Stinnett .25
461 Wilton Guerrero .25
462 Jason Bere .25
463 Calvin Murray .25
464 Miguel Batista .25
465 Erubiel Durazo .25
466 Luis Gonzalez .50
467 Jaret Wright .25
468 Chad Kreuter .25
469 Armando Benitez .25
470 Sidney Ponson .25
471 Adrian Brown .25
472 Sterling Hitchcock .25
473 Timoniel Perez .25
474 Jamie Moyer .25
475 Delino DeShields .25
476 Glendon Rusch .25
477 Chris Gomez .25
478 Adam Eaton .25
479 Pablo Ozuna .25
480 Bob Abreu .50
481 Kris Benson .25
482 Keith Osik .25
483 Darryl Hamilton .25
484 Marlon Anderson .25
485 Jimmy Anderson .25
486 John Halama .25
487 Nelson Figueroa .25
488 Alex Gonzalez .25
489 Benny Agbayani .25
490 Ed Sprague .25
491 Scott Erickson .25
492 Doug Glanville .25
493 Jesus Sanchez .25
494 Mike Lieberthal .25
495 Aaron Sele .25
496 Pat Mahomes .25
497 Ruben Rivera .25
498 Wayne Gomes .25
499 Freddy Garcia .25
500 Al Martin .25
501 Woody Williams .25
502 Paul Byrd .25
503 Rick White .25
504 Trevor Hoffman .25
505 Brady Anderson .25
506 Robert Person .25
507 Jeff Conine .25
508 Chris Truby .25
509 Emil Brown .25
510 Ryan Dempster .25
511 Ruben Mateo .25
512 Alex Ochoa .25
513 Jose Rosado .25
514 Masato Yoshii .25
515 Brian Daubach .25
516 Jeff D'Amico .25
517 Brent Mayne .25
518 John Thomson .25
519 Todd Ritchie .25
520 John Vander Wal .25
521 Neifi Perez .25
522 Chad Curtis .25
523 Kenny Rogers .25
524 Trot Nixon .25
525 Sean Casey .25
526 Wilton Veras .25
527 Troy O'Leary .25
528 Dante Bichette .25
529 Jose Silva .25
530 Darren Oliver .25
531 Steve Parris .25
532 David McCarty .25
533 Todd Walker .25
534 Brian Rose .25
535 Pete Schourek .25
536 Ricky Ledee .25
537 Justin Thompson .25
538 Benito Santiago .25
539 Carlos Beltran .40
540 Gabe White .25
541 Bret Saberhagen .25
542 Ramon Martinez .25
543 John Valentin .25
544 Frank Catalanotto .25
545 Tim Wakefield .25
546 Michael Tucker .25
547 Juan Pierre .25
548 Rich Garces .25
549 Luis Ordaz .25
550 Jerry Spradlin .25
551 Corey Koskie .25
552 Cal Eldred .25
553 Alfonso Soriano 1.00
554 Kip Wells .25
555 Orlando Hernandez .40
556 Bill Simas .25
557 Jim Parque .25
558 Joe Mays .25
559 Tim Belcher .25
560 Shane Spencer .25
561 Glenallen Hill .25
562 Matt LeCroy .25
563 Tino Martinez .25
564 Eric Milton .25
565 Ron Coomer .25
566 Cristian Guzman .25
567 Kazuhiro Sasaki .25
568 Mark Quinn .25
569 Eric Gagne .25
570 Kerry Ligtenberg .25
571 Rolando Arrojo .25
572 Jon Lieber .25
573 Jose Vizcaino .25
574 Jeff Abbott .25
575 Carlos Hernandez .25
576 Scott Sullivan .25
577 Matt Stairs .25
578 Tom Lampkin .25
579 Donnie Sadler .25
580 Desi Relaford .25
581 Scott Downs .25
582 Mike Mussina .75
583 Ramon Ortiz .25
584 Mike Myers .25
585 Frank Castillo .25
586 Manny Ramirez 1.00
587 Alex Rodriguez 3.00
588 Andy Ashby .25
589 Felipe Crespo .25
590 Bobby Bonilla .25
591 Denny Neagle .25
592 Dave Martinez .25
593 Mike Hampton .25
594 Gary DiSarcina .25
595 Tsuyoshi Shinjo **RC** .75
596 Albert Pujols **RC** 80.00
597 Roy Oswalt, Pat Strange, Jon Rauch (Prospects) .75
598 Phil Wilson **RC**, Jake Peavy **RC**, Darwin Cubillan **RC** (Prospects) 10.00
599 Nathan Haynes, Steve Smyth **RC**, Mike Bynum (Prospects) .75
600 Joe Lawrence, Choo Freeman, Michael Cuddyer (Prospects) .50
601 Larry Barnes, Dewayne Wise, Carlos Pena (Prospects) .25
602 Felipe Lopez, Gookie Dawkins, Erick Almonte **RC** (Prospects) 1.00
603 Brad Wilkerson, Alex Escobar, Eric Valent (Prospects) .25
604 Jeff Goldbach **RC**, Toby Hall, Rod Barajas (Prospects) .25
605 Marcus Giles, Pablo Ozuna, Jason Romano (Prospects) .25
606 Vernon Wells, Jack Cust, Dee Brown (Prospects) .25
607 Luis Montanez **RC**, David Espinosa (Draft Picks) 1.00
608 John Lackey, Justin Wayne **RC** (Draft Picks) 1.00
609 Josh Axelson **RC**, Carmen Cali **RC** (Draft Picks) 1.00
610 Shaun Boyd **RC**, Chris Morris **RC** (Draft Picks) 1.00
611 Dan Moylan **RC**, Tommy Arko **RC** (Draft Picks) 1.00
612 Luis Cotto **RC**, Luis Escobar (Draft Picks) 1.00
613 Blake Williams **RC**, Brandon Mims **RC** (Draft Picks) 1.00
614 Chris Russ **RC**, Bryan Edwards (Draft Picks) 1.00
615 Joe Torres, Ben Diggins (Draft Picks) .25
616 Mark Dalesandro, Edwin Encarnacion **RC** (Draft Picks) 5.00
617 Brian Bass **RC**, Odannis Ayala **RC** (Draft Picks) 1.00
618 Jason Kaanoi **RC**, Michael Mathews **RC** (Draft Picks) .50
619 Stuart McFarland **RC**, Adam Sterrett **RC** (Draft Picks) 1.00
620 David Krynzel, Grady Sizemore (Draft Picks) 1.00
621 Keith Bucktrot, Dane Sardinha (Draft Picks) .25
622 Anaheim Angels .25
623 Arizona Diamondbacks .25
624 Atlanta Braves .25
625 Baltimore Orioles .25
626 Boston Red Sox .25
627 Chicago Cubs .25
628 Chicago White Sox .25
629 Cincinnati Reds .25
630 Cleveland Indians .25
631 Colorado Rockies .25
632 Detroit Tigers .25
633 Florida Marlins .25
634 Houston Astros .25
635 Kansas City Royals .25
636 Los Angeles Dodgers .25
637 Milwaukee Brewers .25
638 Minnesota Twins .25
639 Montreal Expos .25
640 New York Mets .25
641 New York Yankees 1.50
642 Oakland Athletics .25
643 Philadelphia Phillies .25
644 Pittsburgh Pirates .25
645 San Diego Padres .25
646 San Francisco Giants .25
647 Seattle Mariners .25
648 St. Louis Cardinals .25
649 Tampa Bay Devil Rays .25
650 Texas Rangers .25
651 Toronto Blue Jays .25
652 Bucky Dent (Golden Moments) .25
653 Jackie Robinson (Golden Moments) 1.50
654 Roberto Clemente (Golden Moments) 1.50
655 Nolan Ryan (Golden Moments) 2.50
656 Kerry Wood (Golden Moments) .50
657 Rickey Henderson (Golden Moments) .75
658 Lou Brock (Golden Moments) .50
659 David Wells (Golden Moments) .25
660 Andruw Jones (Golden Moments) .75
661 Carlton Fisk (Golden Moments) .25

Retrofractors

Stars: 3-5X
Inserted 1:12

Before There Was Topps

		NM/M
Complete Set (10):		40.00
Common Player:		3.00
Inserted 1:20		
Refractors:		2-4X
Inserted 1:200		
BT1	Lou Gehrig	8.00
BT2	Babe Ruth	10.00
BT3	Cy Young	5.00
BT4	Walter Johnson	3.00
BT5	Ty Cobb	8.00
BT6	Rogers Hornsby	3.00
BT7	Honus Wagner	4.00
BT8	Christy Mathewson	3.00
BT9	Grover Alexander	3.00
BT10	Joe DiMaggio	8.00

Combos

		NM/M
Complete Set (20):		80.00
Common Card:		2.00
Inserted 1:12		
Refractors:		2-4X
Inserted 1:120		
1	Derek Jeter, Yogi Berra, Whitey Ford, Don Mattingly, Reggie Jackson	6.00
2	Chipper Jones, Mike Schmidt	6.00
3	Brooks Robinson, Cal Ripken Jr.	8.00
4	Bob Gibson, Pedro Martinez	3.00
5	Ivan Rodriguez, Johnny Bench	4.00
6	Ernie Banks, Alex Rodriguez	6.00
7	Joe Morgan, Ken Griffey Jr., Barry Larkin	5.00
8	Vladimir Guerrero, Roberto Clemente	6.00
9	Ken Griffey Jr., Hank Aaron	6.00
10	Casey Stengel, Joe Torre	2.00
TC11	Kevin Brown, Sandy Koufax, Don Drysdale	5.00
TC12	Mark McGwire, Sammy Sosa, Roger Marris, Babe Ruth	8.00
TC13	Ted Williams, Carl Yastrzemski, Nomar Garciaparra	8.00
TC14	Greg Maddux, Roger Clemens, Cy Young	5.00
TC15	Tony Gwynn, Ted Williams	6.00
TC16	Cal Ripken Jr., Lou Gehrig	10.00
TC17	Sandy Koufax, Randy Johnson, Warren Spahn, Steve Carlton	4.00
TC18	Mike Piazza, Josh Gibson	5.00
TC19	Barry Bonds, Willie Mays	8.00
TC20	Jackie Robinson, Larry Doby	5.00

Golden Anniversary

		NM/M
Complete Set (50):		120.00
Common Player:		1.00
Inserted 1:10		
Refractors:		2-4X
Inserted 1:100		
1	Hank Aaron	6.00
2	Ernie Banks	3.00
3	Mike Schmidt	5.00
4	Willie Mays	6.00
5	Johnny Bench	4.00
6	Tom Seaver	3.00
7	Frank Robinson	2.00
8	Sandy Koufax	5.00
9	Bob Gibson	3.00
10	Ted Williams	8.00
11	Cal Ripken Jr.	8.00
12	Tony Gwynn	3.00
13	Mark McGwire	6.00
14	Ken Griffey Jr.	4.00
15	Greg Maddux	4.00
16	Roger Clemens	6.00
17	Barry Bonds	8.00
18	Rickey Henderson	1.50
19	Mike Piazza	4.00
20	Jose Canseco	2.00
21	Derek Jeter	6.00
22	Nomar Garciaparra	5.00
23	Alex Rodriguez	5.00
24	Sammy Sosa	5.00
25	Ivan Rodriguez	2.00
26	Vladimir Guerrero	3.00
27	Chipper Jones	4.00
28	Jeff Bagwell	2.00
29	Pedro Martinez	3.00
30	Randy Johnson	3.00
31	Pat Burrell	1.50
32	Josh Hamilton	1.00
33	Ryan Anderson	1.00
34	Corey Patterson	1.50
35	Eric Munson	1.00
36	Sean Burroughs	1.00
37	C.C. Sabathia	1.00
38	Chin-Feng Chen	1.00
39	Barry Zito	1.50
40	Adrian Gonzalez	1.00
41	Mark McGwire	6.00
42	Nomar Garciaparra	5.00
43	Todd Helton	2.00
44	Matt Williams	1.00
45	Troy Glaus	1.50
46	Geoff Jenkins	1.00
47	Frank Thomas	2.00
48	Mo Vaughn	1.00
49	Barry Larkin	1.50
50	J.D. Drew	1.00

King of Kings

		NM/M
Common Player:		40.00
Inserted 1:5,175 H		
Inserted 1:5,209 R		
KKR1	Hank Aaron	80.00
KKR2	Nolan Ryan	120.00
KKR3	Rickey Henderson	40.00
KKR5	Bob Gibson	40.00
KKR6	Nolan Ryan	120.00

King of Kings Golden Edition

Inserted 1:59,220 H

Past To Present

		NM/M
Complete Set (10):		20.00
Common Player:		1.50
Inserted 1:18		
Refractors:		1.5-3X
Inserted 1:180		
1	Phil Rizzuto, Derek Jeter	6.00
2	Warren Spahn, Greg Maddux	4.00
3	Yogi Berra, Jorge Posada	3.00
4	Willie Mays, Barry Bonds	6.00
5	Red Schoendienst, Fernando Vina	1.50
6	Duke Snider, Shawn Green	2.00
7	Bob Feller, Bartolo Colon	1.50
8	Johnny Mize, Tino Martinez	1.50
9	Larry Doby, Manny Ramirez	2.00
10	Eddie Mathews, Chipper Jones	3.00

Through The Years

		NM/M
Complete Set (50):		200.00
Common Player:		2.00
Inserted 1:10		
Refractors:		2-4X
Inserted 1:100		
1	Yogi Berra	4.00
2	Roy Campanella	4.00
3	Willie Mays	8.00
4	Andy Pafko	2.00
5	Jackie Robinson	8.00
6	Stan Musial	5.00
7	Duke Snider	4.00
8	Warren Spahn	4.00
9	Ted Williams	10.00
10	Eddie Matthews	4.00
11	Willie McCovey	2.00
12	Frank Robinson	3.00
13	Ernie Banks	5.00
14	Hank Aaron	8.00
15	Sandy Koufax	6.00
16	Bob Gibson	4.00
17	Harmon Killebrew	3.00
18	Whitey Ford	3.00
19	Roberto Clemente	8.00
20	Juan Marichal	2.00
21	Johnny Bench	5.00
22	Willie Stargell	3.00
23	Joe Morgan	2.00
24	Carl Yastrzemski	5.00
25	Reggie Jackson	4.00
26	Tom Seaver	4.00
27	Steve Carlton	3.00
28	Jim Palmer	2.00
29	Rod Carew	3.00
30	George Brett	8.00
31	Roger Clemens	8.00
32	Don Mattingly	8.00
33	Ryne Sandberg	6.00
34	Mike Schmidt	8.00
35	Cal Ripken Jr.	10.00
36	Tony Gwynn	4.00
37	Ozzie Smith	5.00
38	Wade Boggs	3.00
39	Nolan Ryan	10.00
40	Robin Yount	4.00
41	Mark McGwire	8.00
42	Ken Griffey Jr.	5.00
43	Sammy Sosa	6.00
44	Alex Rodriguez	6.00
45	Barry Bonds	8.00
46	Mike Piazza	5.00
47	Chipper Jones	5.00
48	Greg Maddux	5.00
49	Nomar Garciaparra	6.00
50	Derek Jeter	8.00

Topps Originals

		NM/M
Common Player:		15.00
Inserted 1:1,783 H		
Inserted 1:1,788 R		
Refractors 10 sets produced.		
1	Roberto Clemente	180.00
2	Carl Yastrzemski	60.00
3	Mike Schmidt	75.00
4	Wade Boggs	20.00
5	Chipper Jones	40.00
7	Lou Brock	20.00
8	Dave Parker	15.00
9	Barry Bonds	80.00
10	Alex Rodriguez	50.00

What Could've Been

		NM/M
Complete Set (10):		25.00
Common Player:		2.00
Inserted 1:30		
Refractors:		2-4X
Inserted 1:300		
WCB1	Josh Gibson	6.00
WCB2	Satchel Paige	6.00
WCB3	Buck Leonard	3.00
WCB4	James "Cool Pap Bell	4.00
WCB5	Andrew "Rube" Foster	3.00
WCB6	Martin Dihigo	2.00
WCB7	William "Judy" Johnson	3.00
WCB8	Mule Suttles	2.00
WCB9	Ray Dandridge	2.00
WCB10	John Henry Lloyd	2.00

2001 Topps Traded & Rookies

		NM/M
Complete Topps Set (265):		140.00
Common Player:		.10
Chrome cards:		2-3X
Pack (8 + 2 Chrome):		8.00
Box (24):		175.00
T1	Sandy Alomar Jr.	.10
T2	Kevin Appier	.10
T3	Brad Ausmus	.10
T4	Derek Bell	.10
T5	Bret Boone	.20
T6	Rico Brogna	.10
T7	Ellis Burks	.10
T8	Ken Caminiti	.10
T9	Roger Cedeno	.10
T10	Royce Clayton	.10
T11	Enrique Wilson	.10
T12	Rheal Cormier	.10
T13	Eric Davis	.10
T14	Shawon Duston	.10
T15	Andres Galarraga	.20
T16	Tom Gordon	.10
T17	Mark Grace	.50
T18	Jeffrey Hammonds	.10
T19	Dustin Hermanson	.10
T20	Quinton McCracken	.10
T21	Todd Hundley	.10
T22	Charles Johnson	.10
T23	Marquis Grissom	.10
T24	Jose Mesa	.10
T25	Terry Mulholland	.10
T26	John Rocker	.10
T27	Jeff Frye	.10
T28	Reggie Sanders	.10
T29	David Segui	.10
T30	Mike Sirotka	.10
T31	Fernando Tatis	.10
T32	Steve Trachsel	.10
T33	Ismael Valdes	.10
T34	Randy Velarde	.10
T35	Brian Boehringer	.10
T36	Mike Bordick	.10
T37	Ken Bottenfield	.10
T38	Pat Rapp	.10
T39	Jeff Nelson	.10
T40	Ricky Bottalico	.10
T41	Deion Sanders	.20
T42	Hideo Nomo	.50
T43	Bill Mueller	.10
T44	Roberto Kelly	.10
T45	Chris Holt	.10
T46	Mike Jackson	.10
T47	Devon White	.10
T48	Gerald Williams	.10
T49	Eddie Taubensee	.10
T50	Brian Hunter	.10
T51	Nelson Cruz	.10
T52	Jeff Fassero	.10
T53	Bubba Trammell	.10
T54	Bo Porter	.10
T55	Greg Norton	.10
T56	Benito Santiago	.10
T57	Ruben Rivera	.10
T58	Dee Brown	.10
T59	Jose Canseco	.50
T60	Chris Michalak	.10
T61	Tim Worrell	.10
T62	Matt Clement	.10
T63	Bill Pulsipher	.10
T64	Troy Brohawn	.10
T65	Mark Kotsay	.10
T66	Jose Lima	.10
T67	Shea Hillenbrand	.10
T68	Ted Lilly	.10
T69	Jermaine Dye	.10
T70	Jerry Hairston Jr.	.10
T71	John Mabry	.10
T72	Kurt Abbott	.10
T73	Eric Owens	.10
T74	Jeff Brantley	.10
T75	Vinny Castilla	.10
T76	Ron Villone	.10
T77	Ricky Henderson	.40
T78	Jason Grimsley	.10
T79	Christian Parker **RC**	.10
T80	Donnie Wall	.10
T81	Alex Arias	.10
T82	Willis Roberts	.10
T83	Ryan Minor	.10
T84	Jason LaRue	.10
T85	Ruben Sierra	.10
T86	Johnny Damon	.75
T87	Juan Gonzalez	.40
T88	Mac Suzuki	.10
T89	Tony Batista	.10
T90	Jay Witasick	.10
T91	Brent Abernathy	.10
T92	Paul LoDuca	.10
T93	Wes Helms	.10
T94	Milton Bradley	.10
T95	Matt LeCroy	.10
T96	A.J. Hinch	.10
T97	Bud Smith **RC**	.10
T98	Adam Dunn	.50
T99	Albert Pujols, Ichiro Suzuki	15.00
T100	Carlton Fisk	.25
T101	Tim Raines	.25
T102	Juan Marichal	.25
T103	Dave Winfield	.50
T104	Reggie Jackson	1.00
T105	Cal Ripken Jr.	3.00
T106	Ozzie Smith	1.00
T107	Tom Seaver	1.00
T108	Lou Piniella	.25
T109	Dwight Gooden	.25
T110	Bret Saberhagen	.25
T111	Gary Carter	.25
T112	Jack Clark	.25
T113	Rickey Henderson	.75
T114	Barry Bonds	3.00
T115	Bobby Bonilla	.25
T116	Jose Canseco	.75
T117	Will Clark	.50
T118	Andres Galarraga	.25
T119	Bo Jackson	.75
T120	Wally Joyner	.25
T121	Ellis Burks	.25
T122	David Cone	.25
T123	Greg Maddux	1.00
T124	Willie Randolph	.25
T125	Dennis Eckersley	.25
T126	Matt Williams	.40
T127	Joe Morgan	.50
T128	Fred McGriff	.40
T129	Roberto Alomar	.50
T130	Lee Smith	.25
T131	David Wells	.25
T132	Ken Griffey Jr.	2.00
T133	Deion Sanders	.50
T134	Nolan Ryan	2.00
T135	David Justice	.25
T136	Joe Carter	.25
T137	Jack Morris	.10
T138	Mike Piazza	1.50
T139	Barry Bonds	2.00
T140	Terrence Long	.10
T141	Ben Grieve	.10
T142	Richie Sexson	.25
T143	Sean Burroughs	.10
T144	Alfonso Soriano	.50
T145	Bob Boone	.10
T146	Larry Bowa	.10
T147	Bob Brenly	.10
T148	Buck Martinez	.10
T149	Lloyd McClendon	.10
T150	Jim Tracy	.10
T151	Jared Abruzzo **RC**	.50
T152	Kurt Ainsworth	.10
T153	Willie Bloomquist	.10
T154	Ben Broussard	.10
T155	Bobby Bradley	.10
T156	Mike Bynum	.10
T157	Ken Harvey	.10
T158	Ryan Christianson	.10
T159	Ryan Kohlmeier	.10
T160	Joe Crede	.50
T161	Jack Cust	.10
T162	Ben Diggins	.10
T163	Phil Dumatrait	.10
T164	Alex Escobar	.10
T165	Miguel Olivo	.10
T166	Chris George	.10
T167	Marcus Giles	.10
T168	Keith Ginter	.10
T169	Josh Girdley	.10
T170	Tony Alvarez	.10
T171	Scott Seabol	.10
T172	Josh Hamilton	.10
T173	Jason Hart	.10
T174	Israel Alcantara	.10
T175	Jake Peavy	2.50
T176	Stubby Clapp **RC**	.40
T177	D'Angelo Jimenez	.10
T178	Nick Johnson	.10
T179	Ben Johnson	.10
T180	Larry Bigbie	.10
T181	Allen Levrault	.10
T182	Felipe Lopez	.10
T183	Sean Burnett	.10
T184	Nick Neugebauer	.10
T185	Austin Kearns	.25
T186	Corey Patterson	.25
T187	Carlos Pena	.10
T188	Ricardo Rodriguez **RC**	.50
T189	Juan Rivera	.10
T190	Grant Roberts	.10
T191	Adam Pettyjohn **RC**	.25
T192	Jared Sandberg	.10
T193	Xavier Nady	.25
T194	Dane Sardinha	.10
T195	Shawn Sonnier	.10
T196	Rafael Soriano	.25
T197	Brian Specht **RC**	.25
T198	Aaron Myette	.10
T199	Juan Uribe **RC**	.40
T200	Jayson Werth	.10
T201	Brad Wilkerson	.10
T202	Horacio Estrada	.10
T203	Joel Pineiro	.10
T204	Matt LeCroy	.10
T205	Michael Coleman	.10
T206	Ben Sheets	.40
T207	Eric Byrnes	.10
T208	Sean Burroughs	.10
T209	Ken Harvey	.10
T210	Travis Hafner	2.50
T211	Erick Almonte	.10
T212	Jason Belcher **RC**	.50
T213	Wilson Betemit **RC**	.75
T214	Hank Blalock **RC**	2.00
T215	Danny Borrell	.10
T216	John Buck **RC**	.50
T217	Freddie Bynum **RC**	.50
T218	Noel Devarez **RC**	.25
T219	Juan Diaz **RC**	.25
T220	Felix Diaz **RC**	.25
T221	Josh Fogg **RC**	.50
T222	Matt Ford **RC**	.25
T223	Scott Heard	.10
T224	Ben Hendrickson **RC**	.25
T225	Cody Ross **RC**	.50
T226	Adrian Hernandez **RC**	.40
T227	Alfredo Amezaga **RC**	.50
T228	Bob Keppel **RC**	.25
T229	Ryan Madson **RC**	.50
T230	Octavio Martinez **RC**	.25
T231	Hee Seop Choi	.40
T232	Thomas Mitchell	.10
T233	Luis Montanez	.10
T234	Andy Morales **RC**	.40
T235	Justin Morneau **RC**	5.00
T236	Greg "Toe" Nash **RC**	.25
T237	Valentino Pasucci **RC**	.25
T238	Roy Smith **RC**	.40
T239	Antonio Perez **RC**	.40
T240	Chad Petty **RC**	.50
T241	Steve Smyth	.10
T242	Jose Reyes **RC**	20.00
T243	Eric Reynolds **RC**	.40
T244	Dominic Rich	.10
T245	Jason Richardson **RC**	.25
T246	Ed Rogers **RC**	.40
T247	Albert Pujols **RC**	50.00
T248	Esix Snead **RC**	.25
T249	Luis Torres **RC**	.25
T250	Matt White **RC**	.40
T251	Blake Williams	.10
T252	Chris Russ	.10
T253	Joe Kennedy **RC**	.25
T254	Jeff Randazzo **RC**	.25
T255	Beau Hale **RC**	.25
256	Brad Hennessey **RC**	.25
257	Jake Gautreau **RC**	.25
258	Jeff Mathis **RC**	.75
259	Aaron Heilman **RC**	.50
260	Bronson Sardinha **RC**	.50
261	Irvin Guzman **RC**	4.00
262	Gabe Gross **RC**	.50
263	J.D. Martin **RC**	.40
264	Chris Smith **RC**	.25
265	Kenny Baugh **RC**	.40

Autographs

		NM/M
Common Autograph:		15.00
JD	Johnny Damon	30.00
MM	Mike Mussina	25.00

Legends Autographs

		NM/M
Common Player:		
TT51	Ralph Branca	15.00
TTF47	Frank Howard	25.00
TTF50	Mickey Lolich	15.00
TT37	Tug McGraw	15.00
TT48F	Bobby Richardson	20.00
TT36F	Enos Slaughter	25.00
TT13	Warren Spahn	40.00
TT43	Bobby Thomson	20.00

Relics

		NM/M
Common Player:		4.00
Inserted 1:29		
SA	Sandy Alomar Jr.	4.00
DB	Derek Bell	4.00
BB	Bobby Bonilla	4.00
BB	Bret Boone	4.00
RB	Rico Brogna	4.00
KC	Ken Caminiti	4.00
JC	Jose Canseco	8.00
ROC	Roger Cedeno	4.00
RSC	Royce Clayton	4.00
JD	Johnny Damon	10.00
ED	Eric Davis	4.00
JD	Jermaine Dye	4.00
AG	Andres Galarraga	4.00
RG	Ron Gant	4.00
JG	Juan Gonzalez	6.00
MG	Mark Grace	8.00
MG	Marquis Grissom	4.00
JH	Jeffrey Hammonds	4.00
MH	Mike Hampton	4.00
DH	Dustin Hermanson	4.00
TH	Todd Hundley	4.00
CJ	Charles Johnson	4.00
FM	Fred McGriff	5.00
BM	Bill Mueller	4.00
DN	Denny Neagle	4.00
HR	Hideo Nomo	25.00
NP	Neifi Perez	4.00
TR	Tim Raines	4.00
RS	Ruben Sierra	4.00
MS	Matt Stairs	4.00
KS	Kelly Stinnett	4.00
FT	Fernando Tatis	4.00
DW	David Wells	4.00
GW	Gerald Williams	4.00
EW	Enrique Wilson	4.00

Dual-Traded Relics

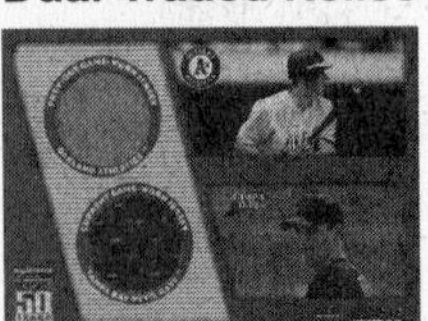

		NM/M
Common Player:		4.00
DB	Derek Bell	4.00
MG	Mark Grace	10.00
BG	Ben Grieve	4.00
DH	Dustin Hermanson	4.00
MR	Manny Ramirez	15.00

Farewell Dual Relic

		NM/M
Inserted 1:4,693		
RG	Cal Ripken, Tony Gwynn	80.00

Hall of Fame Relics

		NM/M
Complete Set (1):		
PW	Kirby Puckett, Dave Winfield	40.00

Rookie Relics

		NM/M
Common Player:		4.00
Inserted 1:91		
AP	Albert Pujols	150.00
TS	Tsuyoshi Shinjo	4.00
AB	Angel Berroa	6.00
BO	Bill Ortega	4.00
HC	Humberto Cota	4.00
JL	Jason Lane	4.00
JS	Jamal Strong	4.00
JV	Jose Valverde	4.00
JY	Jason Young	4.00
NC	Nate Cornejo	4.00
NN	Nick Neugebauer	4.00
PF	Pedro Feliz	4.00
RS	Richard Stahl	4.00
SB	Sean Burroughs	4.00
SS	Jae Weong Seo	6.00
WB	Wilson Betemit	8.00
WR	Wilken Ruan	4.00

Who Would Have Thought

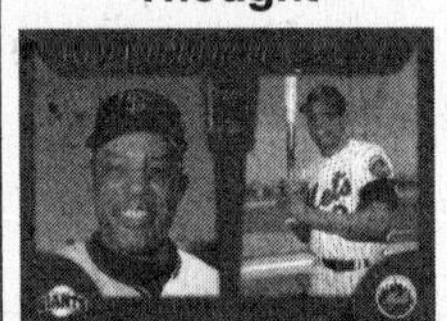

		NM/M
Complete Set (20):		15.00
Common Player:		.75
Inserted 1:8		
WWH1	Nolan Ryan	3.00
WWH2	Ozzie Smith	1.50
WWH3	Tom Seaver	1.50
WWH4	Steve Carlton	.75
WWH5	Reggie Jackson	1.50
WWH6	Frank Robinson	1.00
WWH7	Keith Hernandez	.75
WWH8	Andre Dawson	.75
WWH9	Lou Brock	.75
WWH10	Dennis Eckersley	.75
WWH11	Dave Winfield	1.00
WWH12	Rod Carew	1.00
WWH13	Willie Randolph	.75
WWH14	Doc Gooden	.75
WWH15	Carlton Fisk	1.00
WWH16	Dale Murphy	.75
WWH17	Paul Molitor	1.00
WWH18	Gary Carter	.75
WWH19	Wade Boggs	1.00
WWH20	Willie Mays	3.00

eTopps

Operating along the lines of a stock exchange, with collectors able to buy and sell the cards without ever taking physical possession, eTopps was launched in October and had about 10 "Initial Player Offerings" (new cards) issued per week to a total of 75. Issue price and quantity available were announced at the time of release. If a card was not sold out during its five-day order period, the unsold cards were destroyed. Fronts have portrait and action photos, player identification and an eTopps logo, printed on refractive metalic foil. Backs, labeled, "Inaugural Edition," have a portrait photo, personal data and stats, along with 2000 highlights and a projection for the 2001 season. A circular holographic seal at top-right has a serial number. Each card is issued in a thick plastic holder that is sealed with an eTopps holographic sticker. Cards are skip-numbered between 1-150, as it was originally intended that 150 cards would be issued the first year. Shown in parentheses for each player are the initial offering price and the quantity reported issued by Topps. Values shown are for cards in a virtual portfolio, rather than "in hand." Taking physical possession of a card from an eTopps portfolio requires payment of a delivery fee of $7.

		NM/M
Complete Set (75):		1,350
Common Player:		1.50
1	Nomar Garciaparra ($9.50 / 1,315)	10.00
2	Chipper Jones ($9.50 / 674)	90.00
3	Jeff Bagwell ($6.50 / 485)	35.00
4	Randy Johnson ($6.50 / 1,499)	20.00
7	Adam Dunn ($6.50 / 4,197)	5.00
8	J.D. Drew ($6.50 / 767)	10.00
9	Larry Walker ($6.50 / 420)	25.00
10	Edgardo Alfonzo ($6.50 / 338)	65.00
11	Lance Berkman ($6.50 / 595)	35.00
12	Tony Gwynn ($6.50 / 828)	30.00
13	Andruw Jones ($6.50 / 908)	22.50
15	Troy Glaus ($6.50 / 862)	10.00
17	Sammy Sosa ($9.50 / 2,487)	5.00
21	Darin Erstad ($3.50 / 664)	10.00
22	Barry Bonds ($9.50 / 1,567)	95.00
27	Derek Jeter ($9.50 / 1,041)	50.00
29	Curt Schilling ($6.50 / 2,125)	5.00
30	Roberto Alomar ($6.50 / 448)	20.00
31	Luis Gonzalez ($6.50 / 1,104)	3.00
32	Jimmy Rollins ($3.50 / 1,307)	5.00
34	Joe Crede ($3.50 / 1,050)	10.00
39	Sean Casey ($6.50 / 537)	30.00
46	Alex Rodriguez ($9.50 / 2,212)	35.00
47	Tom Glavine ($6.50 / 437)	35.00
50	Jose Ortiz ($3.50 / 738)	5.00
51	Cal Ripken Jr. ($6.50 / 2,201)	30.00
52	Bobby Abreu ($3.50 / 677)	27.50
55	Alex Escobar ($3.50 / 931)	4.00
56	Ivan Rodriguez ($6.50 / 698)	15.00
59	Jeff Kent ($6.50 / 452)	20.00
62	Rick Ankiel ($6.50 / 752)	6.00
65	Craig Biggio ($6.50 / 410)	40.00
66	Carlos Delgado ($6.50 / 398)	40.00
68	Greg Maddux ($6.50 / 1,031)	15.00
69	Kerry Wood ($3.50 / 1,056)	9.00
71	Todd Helton ($6.50 / 978)	20.00
72	Mariano Rivera ($6.50 / 824)	20.00
73	Jason Kendall ($3.50 / 672)	10.00
75	Scott Rolen ($6.50 / 498)	40.00
76	Kazuhiro Sasaki ($6.50 / 5,000)	2.00
77	Roy Oswalt ($6.50 / 915)	20.00
78	C.C. Sabathia ($6.50 / 1,974)	3.00
83	Brian Giles ($6.50 / 400)	25.00
87	Rafael Furcal ($3.50 / 646)	9.00
88	Mike Mussina ($6.50 / 793)	12.50
89	Gary Sheffield ($6.50 / 359)	50.00
92	Mark McGwire ($9.50 / 2,908)	10.00
94	Tsuyoshi Shinjo ($3.50 / 3,000)	1.50
99	Jose Vidro ($3.50 / 443)	25.00
100	Ichiro Suzuki ($6.50 / 10,000)	12.50
105	Manny Ramirez ($6.50 / 1,074)	15.00
109	Juan Gonzalez ($6.50 / 558)	9.00
112	Ken Griffey Jr. ($9.50 / 2,398)	12.00
114	Tim Hudson ($6.50 / 663)	17.50
115	Nick Johnson ($6.50 / 1,217)	5.00
118	Jason Giambi ($9.50 / 897)	10.00
122	Rafael Palmeiro ($6.50 / 464)	20.00
124	Vladimir Guerrero ($6.50 / 854)	30.00
125	Vernon Wells ($6.50 / 349)	80.00
127	Roger Clemens ($9.50 / 1,462)	30.00
128	Frank Thomas ($6.50 / 834)	15.00
129	Carlos Beltran ($3.50 / 489)	50.00
130	Pat Burrell ($3.50 / 1,253)	15.00
131	Pedro Martinez ($9.50 / 1,038)	15.00
132	Mike Piazza ($9.50 / 1,379)	10.00
135	Luis Montanez ($3.50 / 5,000)	1.50
140	Sean Burroughs ($3.50 / 5,000)	1.50
141	Barry Zito ($6.50 / 843)	22.50
142	Bobby Bradley ($3.50 / 5,000)	1.50
143	Albert Pujols ($6.50 / 5,000)	45.00
143a	Albert Pujols (32 autographed pieces sold by Topps 6/05 for $199 each.)	1,500
144	Ben Sheets ($3.50 / 1,713)	5.00
145	Alfonso Soriano ($6.50 / 1,699)	15.00
146	Josh Hamilton ($3.50 / 5,000)	1.50
147	Eric Munson ($3.50 / 5,000)	1.50
150	Mark Mulder ($3.50 / 4,335)	2.00

2001 Topps Fusion

		NM/M
Complete Set (250):		100.00
Common Player:		.25
Pack (5):		2.50
Box (24):		50.00
1	Albert Belle	.25
2	Albert Belle	.25
3	Albert Belle	.25
4	Nick Bierbrodt	.25
5	Alex Rodriguez	2.50
6	Alex Rodriguez	2.50
7	Alex Rodriguez	2.50
8	Alex Rodriguez	2.50
9	Eric Munson	.25
10	Barry Bonds	3.00
11	Andruw Jones	.75
12	Antonio Alfonseca	.25
13	Andres Galarraga	.40
14	Joe Crede	.25
15	Barry Larkin	.40
16	Barry Bonds	3.00
17	Barry Bonds	3.00
18	Andruw Jones	.75
19	C.C. Sabathia	.25
20	Bobby Higginson	.25
21	Barry Larkin	.40
22	Ben Grieve	.25
23	Barry Bonds	3.00
24	Corey Patterson	.25
25	Carlos Delgado	.75
26	Bernie Williams	.50
27	Brian Giles	.40
28	Barry Larkin	.40
29	Gookie Dawkins	.25
30	Chipper Jones	1.50
31	Brian Giles	.40
32	Carlos Delgado	.75
33	Ben Grieve	.25
34	Geoff Goetz	.25
35	Cristian Guzman	.25
36	Cal Ripken Jr.	3.00
37	Chipper Jones	1.50
38	Bernie Williams	.50
39	Pablo Ozuna	.25
40	Dante Bichette	.25
41	Carlos Delgado	.75
42	Craig Biggio	.25
43	Cal Ripken Jr.	3.00
44	Tim Redding	.25
45	Darin Erstad	.50
46	Chipper Jones	1.50
47	Darin Erstad	.50
48	Carlos Delgado	.75
49	Josh Hamilton	.25
50	Derek Jeter	3.00
51	Darin Erstad	.50
52	Dean Palmer	.25
53	Chipper Jones	1.50
54	Chin-Feng Chen	.25
55	Edgar Martinez	.25
56	Derek Jeter	3.00
57	Derek Jeter	3.00
58	Craig Biggio	.25
59	Keith Ginter	.25
60	Edgardo Alfonzo	.25
61	Edgar Martinez	.25
62	Edgardo Alfonzo	.25
63	David Justice	.50
64	Roy Oswalt	.25
65	Eric Karros	.25
66	Edgardo Alfonzo	.25
67	Frank Thomas	1.00
68	Dean Palmer	.25
69	Alfonso Soriano	1.00
70	Fernando Vina	.25
71	Frank Thomas	1.00
72	Garret Anderson	.40
73	Derek Jeter	3.00
74	Bobby Bradley	.25
75	Frank Thomas	1.00
76	Gary Sheffield	.50
77	Geoff Jenkins	.25
78	Edgar Martinez	.25
79	Nick Johnson	.25
80	Fred McGriff	.40
81	Geoff Jenkins	.25
82	Greg Maddux	1.50
83	Edgardo Alfonzo	.25
84	Hee Seop Choi **RC**	2.00
85	Garret Anderson	.50
86	Greg Maddux	1.50
87	Ivan Rodriguez	.75
88	Eric Karros	.25
89	Scott Seabol	.25
90	Ivan Rodriguez	.75
91	Ivan Rodriguez	.75
92	J.D. Drew	.25
93	Frank Thomas	1.00
94	Ryan Anderson	.25
95	Jason Giambi	.75
96	Jason Giambi	.75
97	Jason Kendall	.25
98	Gary Sheffield	.50
99	Milton Bradley	.25
100	Jason Kendall	.25
101	Jason Kendall	.25
102	Jeff Bagwell	.75
103	Greg Maddux	1.50
104	Sean Burroughs	.25
105	Jay Bell	.25
106	Jeff Bagwell	.75
107	Jeffrey Hammonds	.25
108	Ivan Rodriguez	.75
109	Ben Petrick	.25
110	Jeff Bagwell	.75
111	Jeff Cirillo	.25
112	Jermaine Dye	.25
113	J.T. Snow Jr.	.25
114	Ben Davis	.25
115	Jeff Cirillo	.25
116	Jeff Kent	.25
117	Jeromy Burnitz	.25
118	Jay Bell	.25
119	Jason Hart	.25
120	Jeff Kent	.25
121	Jermaine Dye	.25
122	John Olerud	.25
123	Jeff Bagwell	.75
124	Jeff Segar **RC**	.50
125	Jeromy Burnitz	.25
126	Jeromy Burnitz	.25
127	Johnny Damon	.25
128	Jim Edmonds	.40
129	Tim Christman **RC**	.50
130	Jim Thome	.75
131	Jim Edmonds	.40
132	Jorge Posada	.50
133	Jim Thome	.75
134	Danny Borrell **RC**	.50
135	Johnny Damon	.25
136	Jim Thome	.75
137	Jose Vidro	.25
138	Ken Griffey Jr.	1.50
139	Sean Burnett	.25
140	Larry Walker	.40
141	Jose Vidro	.25
142	Ken Griffey Jr.	1.50
143	Larry Walker	.40
144	Robert Keppell **RC**	1.00
145	Luis Castillo	.25
146	Ken Griffey Jr.	1.50
147	Kevin Brown	.40
148	Manny Ramirez	.75
149	David Parrish **RC**	.25
150	Manny Ramirez	.75
151	Kevin Brown	.40
152	Luis Castillo	.25
153	Mark Grace	.50
154	Mike Jacobs **RC**	.50
155	Mark Grace	.50
156	Larry Walker	.40
157	Magglio Ordonez	.40
158	Mark McGwire	2.00
159	Adam Johnson	.25
160	Mark McGwire	2.00
161	Magglio Ordonez	.50
162	Mark McGwire	2.00
163	Matt Williams	.40
164	Oscar Ramirez **RC**	.50
165	Mike Piazza	1.50
166	Manny Ramirez	.75
167	Mike Piazza	1.50
168	Mike Mussina	.50
169	Odannis Ayala **RC**	.25
170	Mike Sweeney	.25
171	Mark McGwire	2.00
172	Nomar Garciaparra	2.50
173	Mike Piazza	1.50
174	J.R. House	.25
175	Neifi Perez	.25
176	Mike Piazza	1.50
177	Pedro Martinez	1.00
178	Mo Vaughn	.25
179	Shawn Fagan **RC**	.50
180	Nomar Garciaparra	2.50
181	Mo Vaughn	.25
182	Rafael Palmeiro	.50
183	Nomar Garciaparra	2.50
184	Chris Bass **RC**	.75
185	Raul Mondesi	.25
186	Nomar Garciaparra	2.50
187	Randy Johnson	1.00
188	Omar Vizquel	.25
189	Erick Almonte **RC**	1.00
190	Ray Durham	.25
191	Pedro Martinez	1.00
192	Robb Nen	.25
193	Pedro Martinez	1.00
194	Luis Montanez **RC**	1.00
195	Ray Lankford	.25
196	Rafael Palmeiro	.50
197	Roberto Alomar	.75
198	Rafael Palmeiro	.50
199	Chad Petty **RC**	.50
200	Richard Hidalgo	.25
201	Randy Johnson	1.00
202	Robin Ventura	.25
203	Randy Johnson	1.00
204	Derek Thompson	.25
205	Sammy Sosa	2.00
206	Roberto Alomar	.75
207	Sammy Sosa	2.00
208	Raul Mondesi	.25
209	Scott Heard	.25
210	Scott Rolen	.75
211	Sammy Sosa	2.00
212	Scott Rolen	.75
213	Roberto Alomar	.75
214	Dominic Rich **RC**	.50
215	Sean Casey	.25
216	Scott Rolen	.75
217	Sean Casey	.25
218	Robin Ventura	.25
219	William Smith **RC**	.50
220	Tim Salmon	.40
221	Sean Casey	.25
222	Shannon Stewart	.25
223	Sammy Sosa	2.00
224	Joel Pieniero **RC**	.50
225	Tino Martinez	.25
226	Shawn Green	.40
227	Shawn Green	.40
228	Scott Rolen	.50
229	Greg Morrison **RC**	.50
230	Tony Gwynn	1.00
231	Todd Helton	.75
232	Steve Finley	.25
233	Scott Williamson	.25
234	Talmadge Nunnari	.25
235	Tony Womack	.25
236	Tony Batista	.25
237	Tim Salmon	.40
238	Shawn Green	.25
239	Carlos Villalobos **RC**	.50
240	Troy Glaus	.50
241	Troy Glaus	.50
242	Todd Helton	.75
243	Tim Salmon	.40
244	Marco Scutaro **RC**	.50
245	Troy O'Leary	.25
246	Vladimir Guerrero	1.00

247 Vladimir Guerrero 1.00
248 Vladimir Guerrero 1.00
249 Horacio Estrada .25
250 Vladimir Guerrero 1.00

Autographs

NM/M
Common Player: 5.00
Inserted 1:23
1 Rafael Furcal 10.00
2 Mike Lamb 5.00
3 Jason Marquis 5.00
4 Milton Bradley 5.00
5 Barry Zito 20.00
6 Derrek Lee 20.00
7 Corey Patterson 10.00
8 Josh Hamilton 30.00
9 Sean Burroughs 8.00
10 Jason Hart 5.00
11 Luis Montanez 5.00
12 Robert Keppell 5.00
13 Blake Williams 10.00
14 Phil Wilson 5.00
15 Jake Peavy 40.00
16 Alex Rodriguez 70.00
17 Ivan Rodriguez 20.00
18 Don Larsen 20.00
19 Todd Helton 20.00
20 Carlos Delgado 15.00
21 Geoff Jenkins 10.00
22 Willie Stargell 30.00
23 Frank Robinson 30.00
24 Warren Spahn 40.00
25 Harmon Killebrew 30.00
26 Chipper Jones 30.00
27 Chipper Jones 30.00
28 Chipper Jones 30.00
29 Chipper Jones 30.00
30 Chipper Jones 30.00
31 Rocco Baldelli 25.00
32 Keith Ginter 5.00
33 J.R. House 8.00
34 Alex Cabrera 5.00
35 Tony Alvarez 5.00
36 Pablo Ozuna 5.00
37 Juan Salas 5.00

Feature

NM/M
Common Player: 4.00
Inserted 1:51
1 Ivan Rodriguez 8.00
2 Rickey Henderson 15.00
3 John Smoltz 5.00
4 Tom Glavine 8.00
5 Willie Stargell 8.00
6 Frank Thomas 8.00
7 Carlos Delgado 8.00
8 Todd Helton 8.00
9 Adrian Gonzalez 5.00
10 Pat Burrell 8.00
11 Jose Vidro 4.00
12 Roberto Alomar 8.00
13 Chipper Jones 10.00
14 Robin Ventura 5.00
15 J.D. Drew 5.00
16 Matt Lawton 4.00
17 Josh Hamilton 4.00
18 Chin-Feng Chen 25.00
19 Rafael Furcal 8.00
20 Miguel Tejada 8.00
21 Josh Beckett 8.00
22 Ryan Anderson 4.00

Double Feature

NM/M
Common Duo: 10.00
1 Ivan Rodriguez, Rickey Henderson 40.00
2 John Smoltz, Tom Glavine 15.00
3 Willie Stargell, Frank Thomas 20.00
4 Carlos Delgado, Todd Helton 15.00
5 Adrian Gonzalez, Pat Burrell 15.00
6 Jose Vidro, Roberto Alomar 15.00
7 Chipper Jones, Robin Ventura 20.00
8 J.D. Drew, Matt Lawton 10.00
9 Josh Hamilton, Chin-Feng Chen 25.00
10 Rafael Furcal, Miguel Tejada 15.00
11 Josh Beckett, Ryan Anderson 15.00

2001 Topps Gallery

NM/M
Complete Set (152): 120.00
Common Player: .15
Common Rookie: 1.50
Inserted 1:3.5
Common Prospect: .50
Inserted 1:2.5
Common Retired: 1.00
Inserted 1:5
Pack (6): 5.00
Box (24): 100.00
Set price includes one Suzuki rookie.
1 Darin Erstad .40
2 Chipper Jones 1.50
3 Nomar Garciaparra 2.50
4 Fernando Vina .15
5 Bartolo Colon .25
6 Bobby Higginson .15
7 Antonio Alfonseca .15
8 Mike Sweeney .15
9 Kevin Brown .25
10 Jose Vidro .15
11 Derek Jeter 3.00
12 Jason Giambi .75
13 Pat Burrell .50
14 Jeff Kent .25
15 Alex Rodriguez 2.50
16 Rafael Palmeiro .50
17 Garret Anderson .40
18 Brad Fullmer .15
19 Doug Glanville .15
20 Mark Quinn .15
21 Mo Vaughn .25
22 Andruw Jones .75
23 Pedro Martinez 1.00
24 Ken Griffey Jr. 1.50
25 Roberto Alomar .75
26 Dean Palmer .15
27 Jeff Bagwell .75
28 Jermaine Dye .15
29 Chan Ho Park .15
30 Vladimir Guerrero 1.00
31 Bernie Williams .50
32 Ben Grieve .15
33 Jason Kendall .15
34 Barry Bonds 3.00
35 Jim Edmonds .40
36 Ivan Rodriguez .75
37 Javy Lopez .25
38 J.T. Snow .15
39 Erubiel Durazo .15
40 Terrence Long .15
41 Tim Salmon .25
42 Greg Maddux 1.50
43 Sammy Sosa 2.00
44 Sean Casey .25
45 Jeff Cirillo .15
46 Juan Gonzalez .75
47 Richard Hidalgo .25
48 Shawn Green .25
49 Jeromy Burnitz .15
50 Willie Mays 15.00
51 David Justice .25
52 Tim Hudson .40
53 Brian Giles .25
54 Robb Nen .15
55 Fernando Tatis .15
56 Tony Batista .15
57 Pokey Reese .15
58 Ray Durham .15
59 Greg Vaughn .15
60 Kazuhiro Sasaki .15
61 Troy Glaus .50
62 Rafael Furcal .40
63 Magglio Ordonez .40
64 Jim Thome .75
65 Todd Helton .75
66 Preston Wilson .15
67 Moises Alou .25
68 Gary Sheffield .40
69 Geoff Jenkins .25
70 Mike Piazza 1.50
71 Jorge Posada .50
72 Bobby Abreu .25
73 Phil Nevin .15
74 John Olerud .25
75 Mark McGwire 2.00
76 Jose Cruz Jr. .15
77 David Segui .15
78 Neifi Perez .15
79 Omar Vizquel .25
80 Rick Ankiel .15
81 Randy Johnson 1.00
82 Albert Belle .15
83 Frank Thomas .75
84 Manny Ramirez .75
85 Larry Walker .25
86 Luis Castillo .15
87 Johnny Damon .25
88 Adrian Beltre .25
89 Cristian Guzman .15
90 Jay Payton .15
91 Miguel Tejada .40
92 Scott Rolen .75
93 Ryan Klesko .40
94 Edgar Martinez .25
95 Fred McGriff .25
96 Carlos Delgado .75
97 Barry Zito .50
98 Mike Lieberthal .15
99 Trevor Hoffman .15
100 Gabe Kapler .15
101 Edgardo Alfonzo .15
102 Corey Patterson .50
103 Alfonso Soriano 1.00
104 Keith Ginter .50
105 Keith Reed .50
106 Nick Johnson .50
107 Carlos Pena .50
108 Vernon Wells .50
109 Roy Oswalt .75
110 Alex Escobar .50
111 Adam Everett .50
112 Jimmy Rollins .50
113 Marcus Giles .50
114 Jack Cust .50
115 Chin-Feng Chen 1.00
116 Pablo Ozuna .50
117 Ben Sheets .50
118 Adrian Gonzalez .50
119 Ben Davis .50
120 Eric Valent .50
121 Scott Heard .50
122 David Parrish **RC** 1.50
123 Sean Burnett .50
124 Derek Thompson .50
125 Tim Christman **RC** 1.50
126 Mike Jacobs **RC** 1.00
127 Luis Montanez **RC** 1.50
128 Chris Bass **RC** 1.50
129 William Smith **RC** 1.50
130 Justin Wayne **RC** 2.00
131 Shawn Fagan **RC** 1.50
132 Chad Petty **RC** 1.50
133 J.R. House .50
134 Joel Pineiro .50
135 Albert Pujols **RC** 75.00
136 Carmen Cali **RC** 1.50
137 Steve Smyth **RC** 1.50
138 John Lackey .50
139 Bob Keppel **RC** 1.50
140 Dominic Rich **RC** 1.50
141 Josh Hamilton .50
142 Nolan Ryan 5.00
143 Tom Seaver 1.50
144 Reggie Jackson 1.50
145 Johnny Bench 1.50
146 Warren Spahn 1.50
147 Brooks Robinson 1.50
148 Carl Yastrzemski 1.00
149 Al Kaline 1.00
150 Bob Feller 1.00
151a Ichiro Suzuki/ English **RC** 25.00
151b Ichiro Suzuki/ Japanese **RC** 25.00

Autographs

NM/M
Common Autograph: 15.00
Inserted 1:232
RA Rick Ankiel 15.00
BB Barry Bonds 150.00
PB Pat Burrell 20.00
AG Adrian Gonzalez 15.00
AR Alex Rodriguez 100.00
IR Ivan Rodriguez 50.00

Baseball Bucks

NM/M
1:102 insert; used in Gallery Auction:
$5 Johnny Bench 1.50

Heritage

NM/M
Complete Set (10): 30.00
Common Player: 2.00
Inserted 1:12
1 Todd Helton 3.00
2 Greg Maddux 4.00
3 Pedro Martinez 3.00
4 Orlando Cepeda 2.00
5 Willie McCovey 2.00
6 Ken Griffey Jr. 4.00
7 Alex Rodriguez 6.00
8 Derek Jeter 8.00
9 Mark McGwire 6.00
10 Vladimir Guerrero 3.00

Heritage Relic

NM/M
Common Player: 10.00
Inserted 1:133
Orlando Cepeda 10.00
Greg Maddux 25.00
Pedro Martinez 20.00
Willie McCovey 10.00

Heritage Autographed Relic

NM/M
Production 25 Sets
Orlando Cepeda 75.00
Willie McCovey 100.00

Star Gallery

NM/M
Complete Set (10): 15.00
Common Player: 1.00
Inserted 1:8
1 Vladimir Guerrero 1.00
2 Alex Rodriguez 2.50
3 Derek Jeter 3.00
4 Nomar Garciaparra 2.50
5 Ken Griffey Jr. 1.50
6 Mark McGwire 2.00
7 Chipper Jones 1.50
8 Sammy Sosa 2.00
9 Barry Bonds 3.00
10 Mike Piazza 1.50

Originals Relics

NM/M
Common Player: 8.00
Inserted 1:133
RA Roberto Alomar 10.00
JD Jermaine Dye 8.00
DE Darin Erstad 8.00
JG Jason Giambi 10.00
AG Adrian Gonzalez 8.00
SG Shawn Green 10.00
AJ Andruw Jones 10.00
JK Jason Kendall 8.00
JFK Jeff Kent 8.00
RP Rafael Palmeiro 10.00
PR Pokey Reese 8.00
SS Sammy Sosa 20.00
RV Robin Ventura 8.00
BW Bernie Williams 10.00
PW Preston Wilson 8.00

Press Plates

The aluminum press plates used to print the Gallery cards were inserted at a rate of one per 1,200 packs. Each card's front and back can be found in four different color variations. Because of the unique nature of each plate, assignment of catalog values in not feasible.

NM/M
Common Player: 50.00

Team Topps Legends Autographs

NM/M
Common Autograph: 10.00
Inserted 1:286
23R Gil McDougald 10.00
27F Andy Pafko 20.00
10R Frank Robinson 20.00
28F Herb Score 10.00
25R Luis Tiant 10.00

2001 Topps Gold Label

NM/M
Complete Set (115): 80.00
Common Player: .25
Common Rookie: 4.00
Production 999
Golds: 2-3X
Production 999
Gold Rookies: 2-3X
Production 99
Pack (5): 3.00
Box (24): 50.00
1 Adrian Beltre .40
2 Danny Borrell **RC** 4.00
3 Albert Belle .25
4 Alex Cabrera .25
5 Alex Rodriguez 2.50
6 Andruw Jones .75
7 Antonio Alfonseca .25
8 Barry Bonds 3.00
9 Barry Larkin .50
10 Ben Grieve .25
11 Ben Molina .25
12 Bernie Williams .50
13 Bobby Abreu .40
14 Bobby Higginson .25
15 Brad Fullmer .25
16 Brian Giles .40
17 Cal Ripken Jr. 3.00
18 Carlos Delgado .75
19 Chad Petty **RC** 4.00
20 Charles Johnson .25
21 Chipper Jones 1.50
22 Cristian Guzman .25
23 Darin Erstad .40
24 David Justice .40
25 David Segui .25
26 Derek Jeter 2.50
27 Edgar Martinez .40
28 Edgardo Alfonzo .25
29 Fernando Tatis .25
30 Eric Karros .25
31 Eric Munson .25
32 Eric Young .25
33 Frank Thomas .75
34 Fernando Vina .25
35 Garret Anderson .50
36 Gary Sheffield .50
37 Geoff Jenkins .40
38 Greg Maddux 1.50
39 Ivan Rodriguez .75
40 J.D. Drew .40
41 J.R. House .25
42 J.T. Snow Jr. .25
43 Jason Giambi .75
44 Jason Kendall .40
45 Jay Payton .25
46 Jeff Bagwell .75
47 Jeff Cirillo .25
48 Jeff Kent .40
49 Chan Ho Park .25
50 Jermaine Dye .25
51 Jeromy Burnitz .25
52 Jim Edmonds .50
53 Jim Thome .75
54 John Olerud .50
55 Johnny Damon .40
56 Jorge Posada .50
57 Jose Cruz Jr. .25
58 Jose Vidro .25
59 Josh Hamilton .25
60 Juan Gonzalez .75
61 Steve Smyth **RC** 4.00
62 Justin Wayne **RC** 8.00
63 Kazuhiro Sasaki .25
64 Ken Griffey Jr. 1.50
65 Kevin Brown .40
66 Kevin Young .25
67 Larry Walker .40
68 Luis Castillo .25
69 Steve Finley .25
70 Magglio Ordonez .50
71 Manny Ramirez .75
72 Mark McGwire 2.50
73 Mark Quinn .25
74 Miguel Tejada .50
75 Mike Piazza 1.50
76 Mike Sweeney .25
77 Mo Vaughn .25
78 Moises Alou .40
79 Nomar Garciaparra 2.00
80 Pat Burrell .50
81 Paul Konerko .25
82 Pedro Martinez 1.00
83 Phil Nevin .25
84 Preston Wilson .25
85 Rafael Furcal .25
86 Todd Zeile .25
87 Randy Johnson 1.00
88 Travis Lee .25
89 Carl Everett .25

90	Quilvio Veras	.25
91	Rick Ankiel	.25
92	Rick Brosseau **RC**	4.00
93	Robert Keppell **RC**	4.00
94	Roberto Alomar	.50
95	Ryan Klesko	.40
96	Sammy Sosa	2.00
97	Scott Heard	4.00
98	Scott Rolen	.75
99	Sean Casey	.50
100	Shawn Green	.40
101	Terrence Long	.25
102	Tim Salmon	.40
103	Todd Helton	.75
104	Tom Glavine	.50
105	Tony Batista	.25
106	Travis Baptist **RC**	4.00
107	Troy Glaus	.50
108	Victor Hall **RC**	4.00
109	Vladimir Guerrero	1.00
110	Tim Hudson	.40
111	Brian Roberts **RC**	2.00
112	Virgil Chevalier **RC**	4.00
113	Fernando Rodney **RC**	4.00
114	Paul Phillips **RC**	4.00
115	Cesar Bolivar **RC**	4.00

Class 2

Stars:	1-2X
Inserted 1:4	
Rookies:	1-1.5X
Production 699	
Golds:	2-3X
Production 699	
Gold Rookies:	2-3X
Production 69	

Class 3

Stars:	2-3X
Inserted 1:12	
Rookies:	1-2X
Production 299	
Golds:	3-5X
Production 299	
Gold Rookies:	2-4X
Production 29	

Masterpiece

A 1-of-1 "masterpiece" card was created for each card in each of the three Classes of Topps Gold Label. Because of scarcity and widely varying demand, catalog values cannot be given.

	NM/M
Common Player:	50.00

Gold Fixtures

		NM/M
Complete Set (10):		150.00
Common Player:		8.00
Inserted 1:374		
1	Alex Rodriguez	20.00
2	Mark McGwire	20.00
3	Derek Jeter	25.00
4	Nomar Garciaparra	20.00
5	Chipper Jones	15.00
6	Sammy Sosa	20.00
7	Ken Griffey Jr.	15.00
8	Carlos Delgado	8.00
9	Frank Thomas	10.00
10	Barry Bonds	25.00

MLB Awards Ceremony

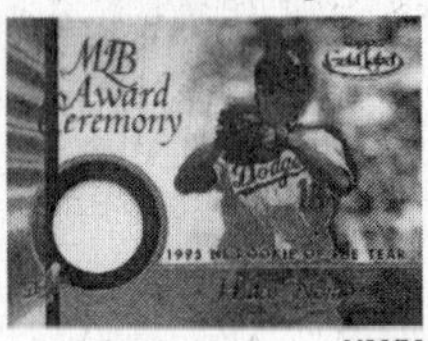

		NM/M
Common Player:		4.00
Inserted 1:24		
SA	Sandy Alomar/Bat	4.00
JB	Jeff Bagwell/Bat	8.00
AB	Albert Belle/Bat	4.00
CB	Carlos Beltran/Bat	4.00
DB	Dante Bichette	4.00
BB	Barry Bonds/Jsy	25.00
BB	Barry Bonds/Bat	25.00
SB	Scott Brosius/Bat	5.00
JC	Jose Canseco//Jsy	6.00
JC	Jose Canseco/Bat	6.00
WC	Will Clark/Bat	6.00
RC	Roger Clemens//Jsy	20.00
MC	Marty Cordova/Bat	4.00
RF	Rafael Furcal/Bat	6.00
AG	Andres Galarraga/Bat	4.00
NG	Nomar Garciaparra/Jsy	20.00
NG	Nomar Garciaparra/Bat	20.00
JG	Jason Giambi/Bat	8.00
TG	Troy Glaus/Bat	8.00
TG	Tom Glavine/Jsy	6.00
JG	Juan Gonzalez/Jsy	8.00
JG	Juan Gonzalez/Bat	8.00
DG	Dwight Gooden/Jsy	4.00
BG	Ben Grieve/Jsy	4.00
KG	Ken Griffey Jr./Jsy	15.00
KG	Ken Griffey Jr./Bat	15.00
TG	Tony Gwynn/Bat	10.00
TH	Todd Helton/Bat	8.00
RH	Rickey Henderson/Jsy	15.00
TH	Todd Hollandsworth/Bat	4.00
DJ	Derek Jeter/Bat	25.00
RJ	Randy Johnson/Jsy	10.00
CJ	Chipper Jones/Jsy	10.00
DJ	David Justice/Jsy	5.00
JK	Jeff Kent/Bat	4.00
CK	Chuck Knoblauch/Bat	4.00
BL	Barry Larkin/Bat	8.00
GM	Greg Maddux/Jsy	15.00
EM	Edgar Martinez/Bat	6.00
PM	Pedro Martinez/Jsy	10.00
FM	Fred McGriff/Bat	5.00
MM	Mark McGwire/Bat	60.00
MM	Mark McGwire/Jsy	60.00
RM	Raul Mondesi/Bat	4.00
HN	Hideo Nomo/Jsy	25.00
JO	John Olerud/Bat	4.00
PO	Paul O'Neill/Bat	5.00
MP	Mike Piazza/Bat	12.00
CR	Cal Ripken Jr./Jsy	35.00
AR	Alex Rodriguez/Bat	15.00
IR	Ivan Rodriguez/Jsy	8.00
SR	Scott Rolen/Jsy	8.00
TS	Tim Salmon/Jsy	4.00
KS	Kazuhiro Sasaki/Jsy	5.00
GS	Gary Sheffield/Bat	6.00
JS	John Smoltz/Jsy	4.00
SS	Sammy Sosa/Bat	15.00
SS	Sammy Sosa/Jsy	15.00
DS	Darryl Strawberry/Jsy	4.00
DS	Darryl Strawberry/Bat	4.00
FT	Frank Thomas/Bat	8.00
FT	Frank Thomas/Jsy	8.00
MV	Mo Vaughn/Jsy	4.00
MV	Mo Vaughn/Bat	4.00
LW	Larry Walker/Bat	5.00
LW	Larry Walker/Jsy	5.00
JW	John Wetteland/Jsy	4.00
BW	Bernie Williams/Bat	8.00
MW	Matt Williams/Bat	5.00

2001 Topps HD

		NM/M
Complete Set (120):		50.00
Common Player:		.25
Common (101-120):		1.00
Inserted 1:6		
Pack (4):		2.50
Box (20):		40.00
1	Derek Jeter	3.00
2	Maggio Ordonez	.50
3	Eric Munson	.25
4	Jermaine Dye	.25
5	Larry Walker	.40
6	Pokey Reese	.25
7	Pedro Martinez	1.00
8	Rafael Palmeiro	.75
9	Jason Kendall	.40
10	Mike Lieberthal	.25
11	Ryan Klesko	.40
12	Cal Ripken Jr.	3.00
13	Mike Piazza	1.50
14	Adam Sterrett **RC**	.75
15	John Olerud	.40
16	Manny Ramirez	.75
17	Chad Petty **RC**	.75
18	Vladimir Guerrero	1.00
19	Kevin Brown	.40
20	Luis Cotto **RC**	.50
21	Josh Hamilton	.25
22	Mark Grace	.50
23	Mark McGwire	2.50
24	Jeromy Burnitz	.25
25	Andruw Jones	.75
26	Raul Mondesi	.40
27	Stuart McFarland **RC**	.50
28	Craig Biggio	.40
29	Troy Glaus	.50
30	Carlos Delgado	.75
31	Rafael Furcal	.40
32	J.D. Drew	.25
33	Corey Patterson	.40
34	Gary Sheffield	.50
35	Jeff Kent	.40
36	Alex Rodriguez	2.50
37	Edgardo Alfonzo	.25
38	Jeff Segar **RC**	.50
39	Bobby Abreu	.40
40	Brian Giles	.40
41	Jason Smith **RC**	.40
42	Mo Vaughn	.25
43	Pat Burrell	.50
44	Barry Larkin	.50
45	Carlos Beltran	.50
46	Eric Mosley **RC**	.50
47	Alfonso Soriano	1.00
48	Tim Salmon	.40
49	Jason Giambi	.75
50	Greg Maddux	1.50
51	Randy Johnson	1.00
52	Jose Vidro	.25
53	Edgar Martinez	.40
54	Albert Belle	.25
55	Ivan Rodriguez	.75
56	Sean Casey	.25
57	Jorge Posada	.50
58	Preston Wilson	.25
59	Paul Konerko	.25
60	Todd Helton	.75
61	Dominic Rich **RC**	.50
62	Tony Gwynn	1.00
63	Bernie Williams	.75
64	Anthony Brewer **RC**	.50
65	Shawn Green	.50
66	Jeff Bagwell	.75
67	Jose Cruz Jr.	.25
68	Darin Erstad	.40
69	Jim Edmonds	.50
70	Frank Thomas	.75
71	Ryan Anderson	.25
72	Scott Rolen	.75
73	Jeff Cirillo	.25
74	Chris Bass **RC**	.50
75	William Smith **RC**	.50
76	Trot Nixon	.25
77	Bobby Bradley	.25
78	Odannis Ayala **RC**	.50
79	Jim Thome	.75
80	Sammy Sosa	2.00
81	Geoff Jenkins	.40
82	Ben Grieve	.25
83	Andres Galarraga	.40
84	Rick Ankiel	.25
85	Barry Bonds	3.00
86	Alex Gonzalez	.25
87	Sean Burroughs	.25
88	Nomar Garciaparra	2.00
89	Ken Griffey Jr.	1.50
90	Tim Hudson	.50
91	Chipper Jones	1.50
92	Matt Williams	.40
93	Roberto Alomar	.75
94	Adrian Gonzalez	.40
95	Juan Gonzalez	.75
96	Brian Bass **RC**	.50
97	Rick Brosseau **RC**	.50
98	Mariano Rivera	.40
99	James Baldwin	.25
100	Dean Palmer	.25
101	Pedro Martinez	2.00
102	Randy Johnson	2.00
103	Greg Maddux	3.00
104	Sammy Sosa	4.00
105	Mark McGwire	5.00
106	Ivan Rodriguez	1.50
107	Mike Piazza	3.00
108	Chipper Jones	3.00
109	Vladimir Guerrero	2.00
110	Alex Rodriguez	5.00
111	Ken Griffey Jr.	3.00
112	Cal Ripken Jr.	6.00
113	Derek Jeter	6.00
114	Barry Bonds	6.00
115	Nomar Garciaparra	4.00
116	Jeff Bagwell	1.50
117	Todd Helton	1.50
118	Darin Erstad	1.00
119	Shawn Green	1.00
120	Roberto Alomar	1.00

Platinum

Stars (1-100):	4-8X
Stars (101-120):	2-4X
Production 199 Sets	

Autographed Cards

		NM/M
Common Player:		10.00
Inserted 1:431		
1	Todd Helton	25.00
2	Rick Ankiel	10.00
3	Mark Quinn	10.00
4	Adrian Gonzalez	10.00

Game Defined

		NM/M
Complete Set (10):		25.00
Common Player:		1.50
Inserted 1:24		
Platinum:		1.5-2X
Inserted 1:72		
1	Ken Griffey Jr.	3.00
2	Derek Jeter	5.00
3	Sammy Sosa	3.00
4	Mark McGwire	4.00
5	Todd Helton	1.50
6	Mike Piazza	3.00
7	Chipper Jones	2.50
8	Vladimir Guerrero	1.50
9	Alex Rodriguez	4.00
10	Nomar Garciaparra	3.00

Game-Worn Jersey

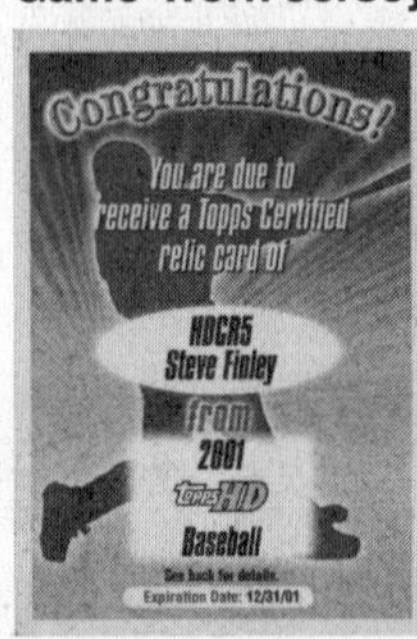

		NM/M
Common Card:		5.00
Inserted 1:108		
Cards 5-8 are redemptions.		
1	Grant Roberts	5.00
2	Vernon Wells	10.00
3	Travis Dawkins	5.00
4	Ramon Ortiz	5.00
5	Steve Finley	5.00
6	Ramon Hernandez	5.00
7	Jay Payton	8.00
8	Jeromy Burnitz	5.00

Images of Excellence

		NM/M
Complete Set (10):		15.00
Common Player:		1.00
Inserted 1:8		
Platinum:		1.5-2X
Inserted 1:24		
1	Willie Mays	2.50
2	Reggie Jackson	1.00
3	Ernie Banks	1.50
4	Hank Aaron	2.50
5	Ted Williams	2.50
6	Mike Schmidt	2.00
7	Tom Seaver	1.00
8	Johnny Bench	1.50
9	George Brett	2.50
10	Nolan Ryan	3.00

20-20

		NM/M
Complete Set (10):		15.00
Common Player:		.50
Inserted 1:12		
Platinum:		1.5-2X
Inserted 1:36		
1	Barry Bonds	4.00
2	Chipper Jones	2.00
3	Ken Griffey Jr.	2.00
4	Alex Rodriguez	3.00
5	Ivan Rodriguez	1.00
6	Sammy Sosa	2.50
7	Roberto Alomar	.75
8	Larry Walker	.50
9	Shawn Green	.75
10	Jeff Bagwell	1.00

2001 Topps Heritage Pre-Production

To introduce its retro-look 2001 Heritage baseball set, Topps issued a cello-packaged, three-card promo set. The cards are in the same format as the regular-issue Heritage series, except that all the stats on back are zeroes and the cards are numbered with a "PP" prefix.

		NM/M
Complete Set (3):		6.00
Common Player:		2.00
PP1	Kevin Brown	2.00
PP2	Andres Galarraga	2.00
PP3	Roger Clemens	4.00

2001 Topps Heritage

		NM/M
Complete Set (407):		275.00
Complete Master Set (487):		320.00
Common Player:		.50
Common SP (311-407):		2.50
Inserted 1:2		
Pack (8):		13.00
Box (24):		275.00
1	Kris Benson	.50
2	Brian Jordan	.50
3	Fernando Vina	.50
4	Mike Sweeney	.50
5	Rafael Palmeiro	2.00
6	Paul O'Neill	1.00
7	Todd Helton	2.50
8	Ramiro Mendoza	.50
9	Kevin Millwood	1.00
10	Chuck Knoblauch	.75
11	Derek Jeter	10.00
12	Alex Rodriguez	8.00
13	Geoff Jenkins	.75
14	David Justice	1.00
15	David Cone	.50
16	Andres Galarraga	1.00
17	Garret Anderson	1.00
18	Roger Cedeno	.50
19	Randy Velarde	.50
20	Carlos Delgado	2.00
21	Quilvio Veras	.50
22	Jose Vidro	.50
23	Corey Patterson	.75
24	Jorge Posada	1.00
25	Eddie Perez	.50
26	Jack Cust	.50
27	Sean Burroughs	.75
28	Randy Wolf	.50
29	Mike Lamb	.50
30	Rafael Furcal	.75
31	Barry Bonds	8.00
32	Tim Hudson	.75
33	Tom Glavine	1.50
34	Javy Lopez	.75
35	Aubrey Huff	.50
36	Wally Joyner	.50
37	Magglio Ordonez	1.00
38	Matt Lawton	.50
39	Mariano Rivera	1.00
40	Andy Ashby	.50
41	Mark Buehrle	3.00
42	Esteban Loaiza	.50
43	Mark Redman	.50
44	Mark Quinn	.50
45	Tino Martinez	.75
46	Joe Mays	.50
47	Walt Weiss	.50
48	Roger Clemens	6.00
49	Greg Maddux	5.00
50	Richard Hidalgo	.75
51	Orlando Hernandez	.75
52	Chipper Jones	5.00
53	Ben Grieve	.50
54	Jimmy Haynes	.50
55	Ken Caminiti	.50
56	Tim Salmon	1.00
57	Andy Pettitte	1.00
58	Darin Erstad	1.00
59	Marquis Grissom	.50
60	Raul Mondesi	.75
61	Bengie Molina	.50
62	Miguel Tejada	1.00
63	Jose Cruz Jr.	.50
64	Billy Koch	.50
65	Troy Glaus	2.00
66	Cliff Floyd	.50
67	Tony Batista	.50
68	Jeff Bagwell	2.50
69	Billy Wagner	.50
70	Eric Chavez	.75
71	Troy Percival	.50
72	Andruw Jones	2.50
73	Shane Reynolds	.50
74	Barry Zito	2.50
75	Roy Halladay	1.00
76	David Wells	.50
77	Jason Giambi	1.50
78	Scott Elarton	.50
79	Moises Alou	.75

80 Adam Piatt .75
81 Wilton Veras .50
82 Darryl Kile .50
83 Johnny Damon .50
84 Tony Armas Jr. .50
85 Ellis Burks .50
86 Jamey Wright .50
87 Jose Vizcaino .50
88 Bartolo Colon .50
89 Carmen Cali **RC** .50
90 Kevin Brown .75
91 Josh Hamilton .50
92 Jay Buhner .50
93 Scott Pratt **RC** .50
94 Alex Cora .50
95 Luis Montanez **RC** 1.00
96 Dmitri Young .50
97 J.T. Snow Jr. .50
98 Damion Easley .50
99 Greg Norton .50
100 Matt Wheatland .50
101 Chin-Feng Chen .50
102 Tony Womack .50
103 Adam Kennedy .50
104 J.D. Drew .50
105 Carlos Febles .50
106 Jim Thome 1.00
107 Danny Graves .50
108 Dave Mlicki .50
109 Ron Coomer .50
110 James Baldwin .50
111 Shaun Boyd **RC** .75
112 Brian Bohannon .50
113 Jacque Jones .50
114 Alfonso Soriano 1.50
115 Tony Clark .50
116 Terrence Long .50
117 Todd Hundley .50
118 Kazuhiro Sasaki .50
119 Brian Sellier **RC** .50
120 John Olerud .75
121 Javier Vazquez .50
122 Sean Burnett .50
123 Matt LeCroy .50
124 Erubiel Durazo .50
125 Juan Encarnacion .50
126 Pablo Ozuna .50
127 Russ Ortiz .50
128 David Segui .50
129 Mark McGwire 3.00
130 Mark Grace 1.00
131 Fred McGriff .75
132 Carl Pavano .50
133 Derek Thompson .50
134 Shawn Green .75
135 B.J. Surhoff .50
136 Michael Tucker .50
137 Jason Isringhausen .50
138 Eric Milton .50
139 Mike Stodolka .50
140 Milton Bradley .50
141 Curt Schilling .75
142 Sandy Alomar .50
143 Brent Mayne .50
144 Todd Jones .50
145 Charles Johnson .50
146 Dean Palmer .50
147 Masato Yoshii .50
148 Edgar Renteria .50
149 Joe Randa .50
150 Adam Johnson .50
151 Greg Vaughn .50
152 Adrian Beltre .75
153 Glenallen Hill .50
154 David Parrish **RC** .75
155 Neifi Perez .50
156 Pete Harnisch .50
157 Paul Konerko .50
158 Dennys Reyes .50
159 Jose Lima .50
160 Eddie Taubensee .50
161 Miguel Cairo .50
162 Jeff Kent .75
163 Dustin Hermanson .50
164 Alex Gonzalez .50
165 Hideo Nomo .75
166 Sammy Sosa 2.00
167 C.J. Nitkowski .50
168 Cal Eldred .50
169 Jeff Abbott .50
170 Jim Edmonds .75
171 Mark Mulder .75
172 Dominic Rich **RC** .50
173 Ray Lankford .50
174 Danny Borrell **RC** .75
175 Rick Aguilera .50
176 Shannon Stewart .50
177 Steve Finley .50
178 Jim Parque .50
179 Kevin Appier .50
180 Adrian Gonzalez .75
181 Tom Goodwin .50
182 Kevin Tapani .50
183 Fernando Tatis .50
184 Mark Grudzielanek .50
185 Ryan Anderson .50
186 Jeffrey Hammonds .50
187 Corey Koskie .50
188 Brad Fullmer .50
189 Rey Sanchez .50
190 Michael Barrett .50
191 Rickey Henderson 1.00
192 Jermaine Dye .50
193 Scott Brosius .50
194 Matt Anderson .50
195 Brian Buchanan .50
196 Derrek Lee .50
197 Larry Walker .75
198 David Krynzel .50
199 Vinny Castilla .50
200 Ken Griffey Jr. 2.00
201 Matt Stairs .50
202 Ty Howington .50
203 Andy Benes .50
204 Luis Gonzalez .75
205 Brian Moehler .50
206 Harold Baines .50
207 Pedro Astacio .50
208 Cristian Guzman .50
209 Kip Wells .50
210 Frank Thomas 1.00
211 Jose Rosado .50
212 Vernon Wells .50
213 Bobby Higginson .50
214 Juan Gonzalez 1.00
215 Omar Vizquel .75
216 Bernie Williams 1.00
217 Aaron Sele .50
218 Shawn Estes .50
219 Roberto Alomar 1.00
220 Rick Ankiel .50
221 Josh Kalinowski .50
222 David Bell .50
223 Keith Foulke .50
224 Craig Biggio .75
225 Shawn Fagan **RC** .50
226 Scott Williamson .50
227 Ron Belliard .50
228 Chris Singleton .50
229 Alex Serrano .50
230 Deivi Cruz .50
231 Eric Munson .50
232 Luis Castillo .50
233 Edgar Martinez .75
234 Jeff Shaw .50
235 Jeromy Burnitz .50
236 Richie Sexson .75
237 Will Clark 1.00
238 Ron Villone .50
239 Kerry Wood 1.00
240 Rich Aurilia .50
241 Mo Vaughn .50
242 Travis Fryman .75
243 Manny Ramirez 1.00
244 Chris Stynes .50
245 Ray Durham .50
246 Juan Uribe **RC** .50
247 Juan Guzman .50
248 Lee Stevens .50
249 Devon White .50
250 Kyle Lohse **RC** 1.50
251 Bryan Wolff .50
252 Rick Brousseau **RC** .50
253 Eric Young .50
254 Freddy Garcia .50
255 Jay Bell .50
256 Steve Cox .50
257 Torii Hunter .75
258 Jose Canseco .75
259 Brad Ausmus .50
260 Jeff Cirillo .50
261 Brad Penny .50
262 Antonio Alfonseca .50
263 Russ Branyan .50
264 Scott Heard .50
265 John Lackey .50
266 Justin Wayne **RC** 1.00
267 Brad Radke .50
268 Todd Stottlemyre .50
269 Mark Loretta .50
270 Matt Williams .50
271 Kenny Lofton .50
272 Jeff D'Amico .50
273 Jamie Moyer .50
274 Darren Dreifort .50
275 Denny Neagle .50
276 Orlando Cabrera .50
277 Chuck Finley .50
278 Miguel Batista .50
279 Carlos Beltran .50
280 Eric Karros .50
281 Mark Kotsay .50
282 Ryan Dempster .50
283 Barry Larkin .75
284 Jeff Suppan .50
285 Gary Sheffield .75
286 Jose Valentin .50
287 Robb Nen .50
288 Chan Ho Park .50
289 John Halama .50
290 Steve Smyth **RC** .50
291 Gerald Williams .50
292 Preston Wilson .50
293 Victor Hall **RC** .75
294 Ben Sheets .50
295 Eric Davis .50
296 Kirk Rueter .50
297 Chad Petty **RC** .75
298 Kevin Millar .50
299 Marvin Benard .50
300 Vladimir Guerrero 1.00
301 Livan Hernandez .50
302 Travis Baptist **RC** .75
303 Bill Mueller .50
304 Mike Cameron .50
305 Randy Johnson 1.50
306 Alan Mahaffey **RC** .50
307 Timo Perez (No facsimile autograph.) .50
308 Pokey Reese .50
309 Ryan Rupe .50
310 Carlos Lee .50
311 Doug Glanville 2.50
312 Jay Payton 2.50
313 Troy O'Leary 2.50
314 Francisco Cordero 2.50
315 Rusty Greer 2.50
316 Cal Ripken Jr. 25.00
317 Ricky Ledee 2.50
318 Brian Daubach 2.50
319 Robin Ventura 3.00
320 Todd Zeile 3.00
321 Francisco Cordova 2.50
322 Henry Rodriguez 2.50
323 Pat Meares 2.50
324 Glendon Rusch 2.50
325 Keith Osik 2.50
326 Robert Keppell **RC** 4.00
327 Bobby Jones 2.50
328 Alex Ramirez 2.50
329 Robert Person 2.50
330 Ruben Mateo 2.50
331 Rob Bell 2.50
332 Carl Everett 2.50
333 Jason Schmidt 3.00
334 Scott Rolen 5.00
335 Jimmy Anderson 2.50
336 Bret Boone 3.00
337 Delino DeShields 2.50
338 Trevor Hoffman 2.50
339 Bob Abreu 3.00
340 Mike Williams 2.50
341 Mike Hampton 3.00
342 John Wetteland 2.50
343 Scott Erickson 2.50
344 Enrique Wilson 2.50
345 Tim Wakefield 2.50
346 Mike Lowell 2.50
347 Todd Pratt 2.50
348 Brook Fordyce 2.50
349 Benny Agbayani 2.50
350 Gabe Kapler 3.00
351 Sean Casey 3.00
352 Darren Oliver 2.50
353 Todd Ritchie 2.50
354 Kenny Rogers 2.50
355 Jason Kendall 3.00
356 John Vander Wal 2.50
357 Ramon Martinez 2.50
358 Edgardo Alfonzo 2.50
359 Phil Nevin 2.50
360 Albert Belle 2.50
361 Ruben Rivera 2.50
362 Pedro Martinez 10.00
363 Derek Lowe 2.50
364 Pat Burrell 5.00
365 Mike Mussina 5.00
366 Brady Anderson 2.50
367 Darren Lewis 2.50
368 Sidney Ponson 2.50
369 Adam Eaton 2.50
370 Eric Owens 2.50
371 Aaron Boone 2.50
372 Matt Clement 2.50
373 Derek Bell 2.50
374 Trot Nixon 2.50
375 Travis Lee 2.50
376 Mike Benjamin 2.50
377 Jeff Zimmerman 2.50
378 Mike Lieberthal 2.50
379 Rick Reed 2.50
380 Nomar Garciaparra 15.00
381 Omar Daal 2.50
382 Ryan Klesko 3.00
383 Rey Ordonez 2.50
384 Kevin Young 2.50
385 Rick Helling 2.50
386 Brian Giles 4.00
387 Tony Gwynn 8.00
388 Ed Sprague 2.50
389 J.R. House 2.50
390 Scott Hatteberg 2.50
391 John Valentin 2.50
392 Melvin Mora 2.50
393 Royce Clayton 2.50
394 Jeff Fassero 2.50
395 Manny Alexander 2.50
396 John Franco 2.50
397 Luis Alicea 2.50
398 Ivan Rodriguez 5.00
399 Kevin Jordan 2.50
400 Jose Offerman 2.50
401 Jeff Conine 2.50
402 Seth Etherton 2.50
403 Mike Bordick 2.50
404 Al Leiter 3.00
405 Mike Piazza 10.00
406 Armando Benitez 2.50
407 Warren Morris 2.50

Chrome

NM/M

Common Player: 3.00
Production 552 Sets
1 Cal Ripken Jr. 40.00
2 Jim Thome 10.00
3 Derek Jeter 40.00
4 Andres Galarraga 4.00
5 Carlos Delgado 8.00
6 Roberto Alomar 8.00
7 Tom Glavine 8.00
8 Gary Sheffield 5.00
9 Mo Vaughn 3.00
10 Preston Wilson 3.00
11 Mike Mussina 8.00
12 Greg Maddux 30.00
13 Ivan Rodriguez 10.00
14 Al Leiter 3.00
15 Seth Etherton 3.00
16 Edgardo Alfonzo 3.00
17 Richie Sexson 3.00
18 Andruw Jones 10.00
19 Bartolo Colon 3.00
20 Darin Erstad 5.00
21 Kevin Brown 4.00
22 Mike Sweeney 3.00
23 Mike Piazza 30.00
24 Rafael Palmeiro 10.00
25 Terrence Long 3.00
26 Kazuhiro Sasaki 3.00
27 John Olerud 5.00
28 Mark McGwire 30.00
29 Fred McGriff 5.00
30 Todd Helton 10.00
31 Curt Schilling 5.00
32 Alex Rodriguez 30.00
33 Jeff Kent 4.00
34 Pat Burrell 8.00
35 Jim Edmonds 6.00
36 Mark Mulder 3.00
37 Troy Glaus 8.00
38 Jay Payton 3.00
39 Jermaine Dye 3.00
40 Larry Walker 5.00
41 Ken Griffey Jr. 30.00
42 Jeff Bagwell 10.00
43 Rick Ankiel 3.00
44 Mark Redman 3.00
45 Edgar Martinez 3.00
46 Mike Hampton 4.00
47 Manny Ramirez 10.00
48 Ray Durham 3.00
49 Rafael Furcal 3.00
50 Sean Casey 4.00
51 Jose Canseco 10.00
52 Barry Bonds 40.00
53 Tim Hudson 5.00
54 Barry Zito 10.00
55 Chuck Finley 3.00
56 Magglio Ordonez 4.00
57 David Wells 3.00
58 Jason Giambi 8.00
59 Tony Gwynn 15.00
60 Vladimir Guerrero 15.00
61 Randy Johnson 15.00
62 Bernie Williams 8.00
63 Craig Biggio 5.00
64 Jason Kendall 3.00
65 Pedro Martinez 15.00
66 Mark Quinn 3.00
67 Frank Thomas 15.00
68 Nomar Garciaparra 30.00
69 Brian Giles 5.00
70 Shawn Green 5.00
71 Roger Clemens 25.00
72 Sammy Sosa 30.00
73 Juan Gonzalez 10.00
74 Orlando Hernandez 4.00
75 Chipper Jones 20.00
76 Josh Hamilton 3.00
77 Adam Johnson 3.00
78 Shaun Boyd 3.00
79 Alfonso Soriano 15.00
80 Derek Thompson 3.00
81 Adrian Gonzalez 3.00
82 Ryan Anderson 3.00
83 Corey Patterson 5.00
84 J.R. House 3.00
85 Sean Burroughs 3.00
86 Scott Heard 3.00
87 John Lackey 3.00
88 Ben Sheets 4.00
89 Wilson Betemit 3.00
90 Robert Keppell 3.00
91 Luis Montanez 3.00
92 Sean Burnett 3.00
93 Justin Wayne 5.00
94 Eric Munson 3.00
95 Steve Smyth 3.00
96 Rick Brousseau 3.00
97 Carmen Cali 3.00
98 Brian Sellier 3.00
99 David Parrish 3.00
100 Danny Borrell 3.00
101 Chad Petty 3.00
102 Dominic Rich 3.00
103 Shawn Fagan 3.00
104 Alex Serrano 3.00
105 Juan Uribe 3.00
106 Travis Baptist 3.00
107 Alan Mahaffey 3.00
108 Kyle Lohse 4.00
109 Victor Hall 3.00
110 Scott Pratt 3.00

Classic Renditions

NM/M

Complete Set (10): 15.00
Common Player: 1.00
Inserted 1:5

1 Mark McGwire 2.50
2 Nomar Garciaparra 2.00
3 Barry Bonds 3.00
4 Sammy Sosa 2.00
5 Chipper Jones 1.50
6 Pat Burrell 1.00
7 Frank Thomas 1.00
8 Manny Ramirez 1.00
9 Derek Jeter 3.00
10 Ken Griffey Jr. 2.00

Classic Renditions Autographs

NM/M

Production 25 sets
BB Barry Bonds 650.00
CJ Chipper Jones 350.00
NG Nomar Garciaparra 450.00

Clubhouse Collection Autographs

NM/M

Common Player:
MM Minnie Monoso/25 120.00
RS Red Schoendienst/ 25 150.00

Clubhouse Collection Game-Used

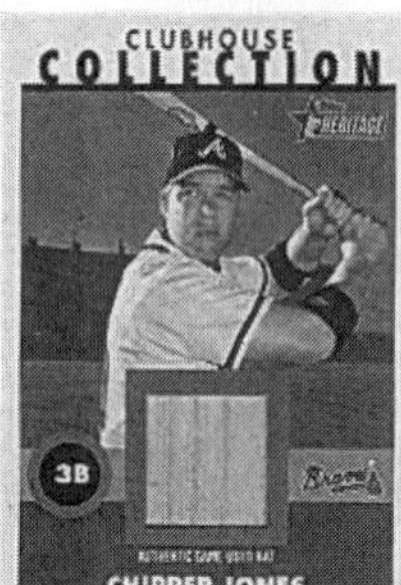

NM/M

Common Player: 25.00
MM Minnie Monoso 25.00
RS Red Schoendienst 30.00
DS Duke Snider 40.00
EM Eddie Mathews 40.00
CJ Chipper Jones 40.00
RA Richie Ashburn 30.00
FT Frank Thomas 40.00
FV Fernando Vina 25.00
SG Shawn Green 30.00
WM Willie Mays 150.00
BB Barry Bonds 80.00
SR Scott Rolen 40.00

Clubhouse Collection Dual Game-Used

NM/M

Common Card: 75.00
Production 52 Sets

MMFT Minnie Monoso, Frank Thomas 100.00
RSFV Red Schoendienst, Fernando Vina 75.00
DSSG Duke Snider, Shawn Green 150.00
RAPB Richie Ashburn, Scott Rolen 100.00
EMCJ Eddie Mathews, Chipper Jones 125.00
WMBB Willie Mays, Barry Bonds 250.00

Grandstand Glory

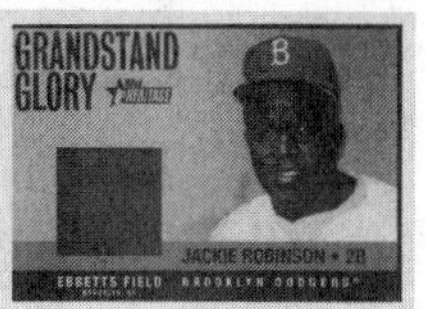

NM/M

Common Player: 20.00
Inserted 1:211
PR Phil Rizzuto 30.00
YB Yogi Berra 30.00
RA Richie Ashburn 20.00
RR Robin Roberts 20.00
WM Willie Mays 60.00
NF Nellie Fox 20.00
JR Jackie Robinson 50.00

New Age Performers

NM/M

Complete Set (15): 20.00
Common Player: 1.00
Inserted 1:8
1 Mike Piazza 1.50
2 Sammy Sosa 2.00
3 Alex Rodriguez 2.50
4 Barry Bonds 3.00
5 Ken Griffey Jr. 1.50
6 Chipper Jones 1.50
7 Randy Johnson 1.00
8 Derek Jeter 3.00
9 Nomar Garciaparra 2.00
10 Mark McGwire 2.50
11 Jeff Bagwell 1.00
12 Pedro Martinez 1.00
13 Todd Helton 1.00
14 Vladimir Guerrero 1.00
15 Greg Maddux 2.00

Real One Autographs

NM/M

Common Player: 30.00
Current MLB Players
200 Blue-Inked Produced
52 Red-Inked Produced
Prices listed for Blue sigs.

RH	Richard Hidalgo	30.00
TL	Terrence Long	30.00
CD	Carlos Delgado	60.00
CJ	Chipper Jones	150.00
TG	Tom Glavine	100.00
GJ	Geoff Jenkins	40.00
JM	Joe Mays	30.00
FV	Fernando Vina	30.00
CP	Corey Patterson	40.00
JV	Jose Vidro	30.00
BB	Barry Bonds	275.00
AR	Alex Rodriguez	200.00
AH	Aubrey Huff	40.00
SPB	Sean Burroughs	30.00
RW	Randy Wolf	30.00
KB	Kris Benson	30.00
ML	Mike Lamb	30.00
TH	Todd Helton	80.00
MQ	Mark Quinn	30.00
MS	Mike Sweeney	30.00
ML	Matt Lawton	35.00
MO	Magglio Ordonez	40.00
MB	Mark Buehrle	50.00
MR	Mark Redman	30.00
CF	Cliff Floyd	30.00
NG	Nomar Garciaparra	150.00
1952 MLB Players		
MV	Mickey Vernon	40.00
HB	Hank Bauer	80.00
DD	Dom DiMaggio	100.00
LD	Larry Doby	90.00
JG	Joe Garagiola	75.00
DG	Dick Groat	60.00
MI	Monte Irvin	75.00
VL	Vernon Law	50.00
EM	Eddie Matthews	200.00
WM	Willie Mays	200.00
GM	Gil McDougald	60.00
MM	Minnie Monoso	80.00
AP	Andy Pafko	75.00
PFR	Phil Rizzuto	120.00
PR	Preacher Roe	100.00
JS	Johnny Sain	60.00
HS	Hank Sauer	60.00
RS	Red Schoendienst	75.00
BS	Bobby Shantz	40.00
CS	Curt Simmons	40.00
ES	Enos Slaughter	100.00
DS	Duke Snider	180.00
WS	Warren Spahn	120.00
BT	Bobby Thomson	85.00
HW	Hoyt Wilhelm	90.00
RR	Robin Roberts	80.00

Then and Now

		NM/M
Complete Set (10):		15.00
Common Player:		1.50
Inserted 1:8		
1	Yogi Berra, Mike Piazza	1.50
2	Duke Snider, Sammy Sosa	2.00
3	Willie Mays, Ken Griffey Jr.	2.00
4	Phil Rizzuto, Derek Jeter	3.00
5	Pee Wee Reese, Nomar Garciaparra	2.00
6	Jackie Robinson, Alex Rodriguez	2.50
7	Johnny Mize, Mark McGwire	2.50
8	Bob Feller, Pedro Martinez	1.50
9	Robin Roberts, Greg Maddux	2.00
10	Warren Spahn, Randy Johnson	1.50

Time Capsule

		NM/M
Common Player:		20.00
Inserted 1:369		
WM	Willie Mays	75.00
TW	Ted Williams	85.00
DN	Don Newcombe	20.00
WF	Whitey Ford	30.00
WMTW	Ted Williams, Willie Mays/52	200.00

2001 Topps Reserve

		NM/M
Complete Set (151):		
Common Player:		.40
Common SP (101-150):		4.00
Production 1,500		
Sealed Hobby Box (10):		150.00
1	Darin Erstad	.50
2	Moises Alou	.50
3	Tony Batista	.40
4	Andruw Jones	.75
5	Edgar Renteria	.40
6	Eric Young	.40
7	Steve Finley	.40
8	Adrian Beltre	.40
9	Vladimir Guerrero	1.00
10	Barry Bonds	3.00
11	Juan Gonzalez	.75
12	Jay Buhner	.40
13	Luis Castillo	.40
14	Cal Ripken Jr.	3.00
15	Bob Abreu	.40
16	Ivan Rodriguez	.75
17	Nomar Garciaparra	2.00
18	Todd Helton	.75
19	Bobby Higginson	.40
20	Jorge Posada	.50
21	Tim Salmon	.50
22	Jason Giambi	.75
23	Jose Cruz Jr.	.40
24	Chipper Jones	1.50
25	Jim Edmonds	.50
26	Gerald Williams	.40
27	Randy Johnson	1.00
28	Gary Sheffield	.50
29	Jeff Kent	.40
30	Jim Thome	.75
31	John Olerud	.50
32	Cliff Floyd	.40
33	Mike Lowell	.40
34	Phil Nevin	.40
35	Scott Rolen	.75
36	Alex Rodriguez	2.50
37	Ken Griffey Jr.	2.00
38	Neifi Perez	.40
39	Christian Guzman	.40
40	Mariano Rivera	.40
41	Troy Glaus	.75
42	Johnny Damon	.40
43	Rafael Furcal	.40
44	Jeromy Burnitz	.40
45	Mark McGwire	2.00
46	Fred McGriff	.40
47	Matt Williams	.40
48	Kevin Brown	.40
49	J.T. Snow	.40
50	Kenny Lofton	.40
51	Al Martin	.40
52	Antonio Alfonseca	.40
53	Edgardo Alfonzo	.40
54	Ryan Klesko	.40
55	Pat Burrell	.50
56	Rafael Palmeiro	.75
57	Sean Casey	.40
58	Jeff Cirillo	.40
59	Ray Durham	.40
60	Derek Jeter	3.00
61	Jeff Bagwell	.75
62	Carlos Delgado	.75
63	Tom Glavine	.50
64	Richie Sexson	.50
65	J.D. Drew	.40
66	Ben Grieve	.40
67	Mark Grace	.50
68	Shawn Green	.40
69	Robb Nen	.40
70	Omar Vizquel	.40
71	Edgar Martinez	.40
72	Preston Wilson	.40
73	Mike Piazza	1.50
74	Tony Gwynn	1.00
75	Jason Kendall	.40
76	Manny Ramirez	.75
77	Pokey Reese	.40
78	Mike Sweeney	.40
79	Magglio Ordonez	.50
80	Bernie Williams	.75
81	Richard Hidalgo	.40
82	Brad Fullmer	.40
83	Greg Maddux	2.00
84	Geoff Jenkins	.40
85	Sammy Sosa	2.00
86	Luis Gonzalez	.50
87	Eric Karros	.40
88	Jose Vidro	.40
89	Rich Aurilia	.40
90	Roberto Alomar	.75
91	Mike Cameron	.40
92	Mike Mussina	.60
93	Albert Belle	.40
94	Mike Lieberthal	.40
95	Brian Giles	.40
96	Pedro Martinez	1.00
97	Barry Larkin	.50
98	Jermaine Dye	.40
99	Frank Thomas	.75
100	David Justice	.50
101	Gary Johnson **RC**	4.00
102	Matt Ford **RC**	4.00
103	Albert Pujols **RC**	140.00
104	Brad Cresse	4.00
105	Valentino Pascucci **RC**	4.00
106	Bob Keppel **RC**	4.00
107	Luis Torres **RC**	4.00
108	Tony Blanco **RC**	6.00
109	Ronnie Corona **RC**	4.00
110	Phil Wilson **RC**	4.00
111	John Buck **RC**	4.00
112	Jim Journell **RC**	4.00
113	Victor Hall **RC**	4.00
114	Jeff Andra **RC**	4.00
115	Greg Nash **RC**	4.00
116	Travis Hafner **RC**	25.00
117	Casey Fossum **RC**	4.00
118	Miguel Olivo	4.00
119	Elpidio Guzman **RC**	4.00
120	Jason Belcher **RC**	4.00
121	Esix Snead **RC**	4.00
122	Joe Thurston **RC**	4.00
123	Rafael Soriano **RC**	6.00
124	Ed Rogers **RC**	4.00
125	Omar Beltre **RC**	4.00
126	Brett Gray **RC**	4.00
127	Deivi Mendez **RC**	4.00
128	Freddie Bynum **RC**	4.00
129	David Krynzel	4.00
130	Blake Williams **RC**	4.00
131	Reggie Abercrombie **RC**	8.00
132	Miguel Villilo **RC**	4.00
133	Ryan Madson **RC**	10.00
134	Matt Thompson **RC**	4.00
135	Mark Burnett **RC**	4.00
136	Andy Beal **RC**	4.00
137	Ryan Ludwick **RC**	6.00
138	Roberto Miniel **RC**	4.00
139	Steve Smyth **RC**	4.00
140	Ben Washburn **RC**	4.00
141	Marvin Seale **RC**	4.00
142	Reggie Griggs **RC**	4.00
143	Seung Song **RC**	4.00
144	Chad Petty **RC**	4.00
145	Noel Devarez **RC**	4.00
146	Matt Butler **RC**	4.00
147	Brett Evert **RC**	4.00
148	Cesar Izturis	4.00
149	Troy Farnsworth **RC**	4.00
150	Brian Schmitt **RC**	4.00
151	Ichiro Suzuki **RC**	50.00

Game-Used Bat

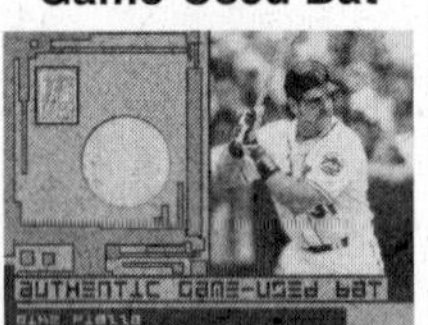

		NM/M
Common Player:		4.00
Inserted 1:Box		
JB	Jeff Bagwell	8.00
BB	Barry Bonds	25.00
CD	Carlos Delgado	6.00
JE	Jim Edmonds	6.00
DE	Darin Erstad	4.00
RF	Rafael Furcal	4.00
NG	Nomar Garciaparra	20.00
VG	Vladimir Guerrero	10.00
TG	Tony Gwynn	10.00
CJ	Chipper Jones	10.00
MP	Mike Piazza	15.00
AR	Alex Rodriguez	15.00
IR	Ivan Rodriguez	8.00
BW	Bernie Williams	8.00

Game-Worn Uniform

		NM/M
Common Player:		4.00
Inserted 1:Box		
RA	Roberto Alomar	8.00
BB	Barry Bonds	25.00
CD	Carlos Delgado	8.00
JE	Jim Edmonds	6.00
NG	Nomar Garciaparra	15.00
JG	Juan Gonzalez	8.00
SG	Shawn Green	5.00
VG	Vladimir Guerrero	8.00
TG	Tony Gwynn	10.00
TH	Todd Helton	8.00
RJ	Randy Johnson	8.00
CJ	Chipper Jones	10.00
DJ	David Justice	4.00
GM	Greg Maddux	15.00
PM	Pedro Martinez	8.00
RP	Rafael Palmeiro	8.00
AR	Alex Rodriguez	15.00
IR	Ivan Rodriguez	8.00
SR	Scott Rolen	8.00
FT	Frank Thomas	8.00

Rookie Autographed Baseballs

	NM/M
Common Player:	10.00
Inserted 1:Box w/holder.	
Reggie Abercrombie	10.00
Jeff Andra	10.00
Andy Beal	10.00
Jason Belcher	10.00
Omar Beltre	10.00
Tony Blanco	15.00
John Buck	15.00
Mark Burnett	10.00
Freddie Bynum	10.00
Ronnie Corona	10.00
Noel Devarez	10.00
Matt Ford	10.00
Casey Fossum	15.00
Brett Gray	10.00
Reggie Griggs	10.00
Elpidio Guzman	10.00
Travis Hafner	60.00
Victor Hall	10.00
Gary Johnson	10.00
Jim Journell	10.00
Bob Keppel	15.00
David Krynzel	15.00
Ryan Ludwick	15.00
Ryan Madson	15.00
Deivi Mendez	10.00
Roberto Miniel	10.00
Greg Nash	10.00
Chad Petty	10.00
Albert Pujols	400.00
Ed Rogers	10.00
Marvin Seale	10.00
Steve Smyth	10.00
Esix Snead	10.00
Seung Song	10.00
Rafael Soriano	15.00
Matt Thompson	10.00
Joe Thurston	10.00
Luis Torres	10.00
Miguel Villilo	10.00
Ben Washburn	10.00

Rookie Graded Autograph

	NM/M
Common Rookie:	10.00
Inserted 1:Box	
Prices for PSA 8	
PSA 9s:	1.5X
Reggie Abercrombie	10.00
Jeff Andra	10.00
Andy Beal	10.00
Jason Belcher	10.00
Omar Beltre	10.00
Tony Blanco	10.00
John Buck	10.00
Mark Burnett	10.00
Freddie Bynum	10.00
Ronnie Corona	10.00
Noel Devarez	10.00
Matt Ford	10.00
Casey Fossum	15.00
Brett Gray	10.00
Reggie Griggs	10.00
Elpidio Guzman	10.00
Travis Hafner	65.00
Victor Hall	10.00
Gary Johnson	10.00
Jim Journell	10.00
David Krynzel	10.00
Ryan Ludwick	20.00
Ryan Madson	10.00
Deivi Mendez	10.00
Roberto Miniel	10.00
Greg Nash	10.00
Miguel Olivo	10.00
Valentino Pascucci	10.00
Chad Petty	10.00
Albert Pujols	375.00
Ed Rogers	10.00
Marvin Seale	10.00
Steve Smyth	10.00
Esix Snead	10.00
Seung Song	10.00
Rafael Soriano	15.00
Matt Thompson	10.00
Joe Thurston	15.00
Luis Torres	10.00
Miguel Villilo	10.00
Ben Washburn	10.00
Blake Williams	10.00
Phil Wilson	10.00

2001 Topps Stars

		NM/M
Complete Set (200):		90.00
Common Player:		.15
Pack (6):		5.00
Box (24):		100.00
1	Darin Erstad	.25
2	Luis Gonzalez	.25
3	Rafael Furcal	.25
4	Dante Bichette	.15
5	Sammy Sosa	1.25
6	Ken Griffey Jr.	1.00
7	Jim Thome	.50
8	Bobby Higginson	.15
9	Cliff Floyd	.15
10	Lance Berkman	.25
11	Eric Karros	.15
12	Jeromy Burnitz	.15
13	Jose Vidro	.15
14	Benny Agbayani	.15
15	Jorge Posada	.40
16	Ramon Hernandez	.15
17	Jason Kendall	.25
18	Jeff Kent	.25
19	John Olerud	.25
20	Al Martin	.15
21	Gerald Williams	.15
22	Gabe Kapler	.15
23	Carlos Delgado	.50
24	Mariano Rivera	.25
25	Javy Lopez	.25
26	Paul Konerko	.15
27	Daryle Ward	.15
28	Mike Lieberthal	.15
29	Tom Goodwin	.15
30	Garret Anderson	.40
31	Steve Finley	.15
32	Brian Jordan	.15
33	Nomar Garciaparra	1.50
34	Ray Durham	.15
35	Sean Casey	.25
36	Kenny Lofton	.25
37	Dean Palmer	.15
38	Jeff Bagwell	.50
39	Mike Sweeney	.15
40	Adrian Beltre	.25
41	Richie Sexson	.40
42	Vladimir Guerrero	.75
43	Derek Jeter	2.00
44	Miguel Tejada	.25
45	Doug Glanville	.15
46	Brian Giles	.25
47	Marvin Benard	.15
48	Edgar Martinez	.25
49	Edgar Renteria	.15
50	Fred McGriff	.25
51	Ivan Rodriguez	.50
52	Brad Fullmer	.15
53	Antonio Alfonseca	.15
54	Tom Glavine	.40
55	Warren Morris	.15
56	Johnny Damon	.25
57	Dmitri Young	.15
58	Mo Vaughn	.15
59	Randy Johnson	.75
60	Greg Maddux	1.00
61	Carl Everett	.15
62	Magglio Ordonez	.25
63	Pokey Reese	.15
64	Todd Helton	.50
65	Preston Wilson	.15
66	Richard Hidalgo	.15
67	Jermaine Dye	.15
68	Gary Sheffield	.40
69	Geoff Jenkins	.25
70	Edgardo Alfonzo	.15
71	Paul O'Neill	.25
72	Terrence Long	.15
73	Bob Abreu	.25
74	Kevin Young	.15
75	J.T. Snow	.15
76	Alex Rodriguez	1.50
77	Jim Edmonds	.25
78	Mark McGwire	1.50
79	Tony Batista	.15
80	Darrin Fletcher	.15
81	Robb Nen	.15
82	Jose Offerman	.15
83	Travis Fryman	.25
84	Joe Randa	.15
85	Omar Vizquel	.25
86	Tim Salmon	.25
87	Andruw Jones	.50
88	Albert Belle	.15
89	Manny Ramirez	.50
90	Frank Thomas	.50
91	Barry Larkin	.40
92	Neifi Perez	.15
93	Luis Castillo	.15
94	Moises Alou	.25
95	Mark Quinn	.15
96	Kevin Brown	.25
97	Cristian Guzman	.15
98	Mike Piazza	1.00
99	Bernie Williams	.40
100	Jason Giambi	.50
101	Scott Rolen	.75
102	Phil Nevin	.15
103	Rich Aurilia	.15
104	Mike Cameron	.15
105	Fernando Vina	.15
106	Greg Vaughn	.15
107	Jose Cruz	.15
108	Raul Mondesi	.15
109	Ben Molina	.15
110	Pedro Martinez	.75
111	Todd Hollandsworth	.15
112	Jacque Jones	.15
113	Rickey Henderson	.25
114	Troy Glaus	.40
115	Chipper Jones	1.00
116	Delino DeShields	.15
117	Eric Young	.15
118	Jose Valentin	.15
119	Roberto Alomar	.40
120	Jeff Cirillo	.15
121	Mike Lowell	.15
122	Julio Lugo	.15
123	Shawn Green	.25
124	Marquis Grissom	.15
125	Matt Lawton	.15
126	Jay Payton	.15
127	David Justice	.25
128	Eric Chavez	.25
129	Pat Burrell	.50
130	Ryan Klesko	.25
131	Barry Bonds	2.00
132	Jay Buhner	.15
133	J.D. Drew	.25
134	Rafael Palmeiro	.50
135	Shannon Stewart	.15
136	Juan Gonzalez	.50
137	Tony Womack	.15
138	Carlos Lee	.15
139	Derrek Lee	.15
140	Ben Grieve	.15
141	Ron Belliard	.15
142	Stan Musial	1.50
143	Ernie Banks	1.00
144	Jim Palmer	.50
145	Tony Perez	.25
146	Duke Snider	.50
147	Rod Carew	.40
148	Warren Spahn	.75
149	Yogi Berra	.75
150	Juan Marichal	.25
151	Eric Munson	.15
152	Carlos Pena	.15
153	Joe Crede	.15
154	Ryan Anderson	.15
155	Milton Bradley	.15
156	Sean Burroughs	.15
157	Corey Patterson	.25
158	C.C. Sabathia	.15
159	Ben Petrick	.15
160	Aubrey Huff	.15
161	Gookie Dawkins	.15
162	Ben Sheets	.25
163	Pablo Ozuna	.15
164	Eric Valent	.15
165	Rod Barajas	.15
166	Chin-Feng Chen	.40
167	Josh Hamilton	.25
168	Keith Ginter	.15
169	Vernon Wells	.25

170	Dernell Stenson	.15
171	Alfonso Soriano	.75
172	Jason Marquis	.15
173	Nick Johnson	.15
174	Adam Everett	.15
175	Jimmy Rollins	.25
176	Ben Diggins	.15
177	John Lackey	.15
178	Scott Heard	.15
179	Brian Hitchcox **RC**	.50
180	Odannis Ayala **RC**	.50
181	Scott Pratt **RC**	.50
182	Greg Runser **RC**	.50
183	Chris Russ **RC**	.50
184	Derek Thompson	.50
185	Jason Jones **RC**	.50
186	Dominic Rich **RC**	.50
187	Chad Petty **RC**	.50
188	Steve Smyth **RC**	.50
189	Bryan Hebson **RC**	.50
190	Danny Borrell **RC**	.50
191	Bob Keppel **RC**	.50
192	Justin Wayne **RC**	1.00
193	Reggie Abercrombie **RC**	1.00
194	Travis Baptist **RC**	.50
195	Shawn Fagan **RC**	.50
196	Jose Reyes **RC**	25.00
197	Chris Bass **RC**	.50
198	Albert Pujols **RC**	75.00
199	Luis Cotto **RC**	.50
200	Jake Peavy **RC**	4.00

Elimination

Stars: 5-10X
Production 100 Sets
Redemp. deadline 10/19/01.

Gold

Stars: 2-5X
Production 499 Sets

Onyx

Stars: 6-12X
Rookies: 4-6X
Production 99 Sets

Autographs

		NM/M
Common Player:		15.00
Inserted 1:353		
EB	Ernie Banks	50.00
YB	Yogi Berra	40.00
RC	Rod Carew	30.00
CD	Carlos Delgado	15.00
TH	Todd Helton	30.00
JM	Juan Marichal	30.00
EM	Eric Munson	10.00
SM	Stan Musial	80.00
JP	Jim Palmer	25.00
TP	Tony Perez	25.00
IR	Ivan Rodriguez	30.00
DS	Duke Snider	35.00
WS	Warren Spahn	40.00

Game Gear Bats

		NM/M
Common Player:		5.00
Inserted 1:187		
AB	Adrian Beltre	5.00
LB	Lance Berkman	6.00
SB	Sean Burroughs	5.00
MC	Michael Cuddyer	5.00
BD	Ben Davis	5.00
JDD	J.D. Drew	5.00
ED	Erubiel Durazo	5.00
JE	Juan Encarnacion	5.00
RF	Rafael Furcal	8.00
AK	Adam Kennedy	5.00
GL	George Lombard	5.00
TL	Terrence Long	5.00
FL	Felipe Lopez	5.00
GM	Gary Mathews	5.00
CP	Corey Patterson	8.00
NP	Neifi Perez	5.00
AP	Adam Piatt	5.00
SR	Scott Rolen	15.00
FS	Fernando Seguignol	5.00
RS	Richie Sexson	10.00

Game Gear Bats Autographs

Inserted 1:12,240
No pricing due to scarcity.

Game Gear Jerseys

		NM/M
Common Player:		4.00
Inserted 1:61		
EA	Edgardo Alfonzo	4.00
RA	Roberto Alomar	8.00
BB	Barry Bonds	25.00
LC	Luis Castillo	4.00
TG	Tony Gwynn	10.00
TH	Todd Helton	8.00
AJ	Andruw Jones	8.00
CJ	Chipper Jones	10.00
EM	Edgar Martinez	8.00
MO	Magglio Ordonez	5.00
MP	Mike Piazza	15.00
SS	Sammy Sosa	25.00
SHS	Shannon Stewart	4.00
FT	Frank Thomas	8.00
JV	Jose Vidro	4.00

Game Gear Jerseys Autographs

Inserted 1:19,288
No pricing due to scarcity.

Progression

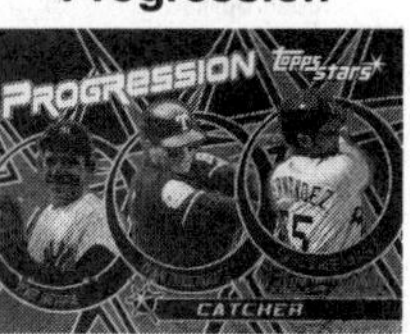

		NM/M
Complete Set (9):		10.00
Common Player:		1.00
Inserted 1:8		
P1	Ernie Banks, Alex Rodriguez, Felipe Lopez	3.00
P2	Yogi Berra, Ivan Rodriguez, Ramon Hernandez	2.00
P3	Tony Perez, Carlos Delgado, Eric Munson	1.00
P4	Rod Carew, Roberto Alomar, Jose Ortiz	1.00
P5	Stan Musial, Darin Erstad, Alex Escobar	2.00
P6	Jim Palmer, Kevin Brown, Kurt Ainsworth	1.00
P7	Duke Snider, Jim Edmonds, Vernon Wells	1.00
P8	Warren Spahn, Randy Johnson, Ryan Anderson	1.50
P9	Juan Marichal, Bartolo Colon, Bobby Bradley	1.00

Players Choice Award Nominees

		NM/M
Complete Set (10):		15.00
Common Player:		1.50
Inserted 1:12		
1	Barry Bonds, Carlos Delgado, Todd Helton	4.00
2	Gary Sheffield, Eric Davis, Turk Wendell	1.50
3	Alex Rodriguez, Carlos Delgado, Frank Thomas	3.00
4	David Wells, Pedro Martinez, Andy Pettitte	2.00
5	Mark Quinn, Terrence Long, Kazuhiro Sasaki	1.50
6	Jay Buhner, Frank Thomas, Bobby Higginson	1.50
7	Barry Bonds, Todd Helton, Jeff Kent	4.00
8	Tom Glavine, Randy Johnson, Greg Maddux	2.50
9	Rick Ankiel, Rafael Furcal, Jay Payton	1.50
10	Moises Alou, Andres Galarraga, Jeff D'Amico	1.50

Player Choice Awards Relics

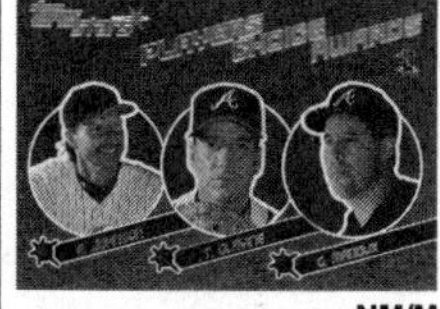

		NM/M
Common Player:		10.00
Inserted 1:1,530		
1	Carlos Delgado	15.00
2	Eric Davis	10.00
3	Carlos Delgado	15.00
4	Pedro Martinez	25.00
5	Terrence Long	10.00
6	Frank Thomas	20.00
7	Todd Helton	15.00
8	Randy Johnson	25.00
9	Rafael Furcal	15.00
10	Andres Galarraga	10.00

2001 Topps Tribute

		NM/M
Complete Set (90):		300.00
Common Player:		2.00
Pack (3):		75.00
Box (6):		425.00
1	Pee Wee Reese	2.00
2	Babe Ruth	15.00
3	Ralph Kiner	2.00
4	Brooks Robinson	5.00
5	Don Sutton	2.00
6	Carl Yastrzemski	8.00
7	Roger Maris	10.00
8	Andre Dawson	2.00
9	Luis Aparicio	2.00
10	Wade Boggs	4.00
11	Johnny Bench	8.00
12	Ernie Banks	6.00
13	Thurman Munson	5.00
14	Harmon Killebrew	5.00
15	Ted Kluszewski	2.00
16	Bob Feller	3.00
17	Mike Schmidt	10.00
18	Warren Spahn	4.00
19	Jim Palmer	3.00
20	Don Mattingly	12.00
21	Willie Mays	10.00
22	Gil Hodges	2.00
23	Juan Marichal	2.00
24	Robin Yount	6.00
25	Nolan Ryan	12.00
26	Dave Winfield	3.00
27	Hank Greenberg	2.00
28	Honus Wagner	8.00
29	Nolan Ryan	12.00
30	Phil Niekro	2.00
31	Robin Roberts	2.00
32	Casey Stengel	3.00
33	Willie McCovey	2.00
34	Roy Campanella	4.00
35	Rollie Fingers	2.00
36	Tom Seaver	5.00
37	Jackie Robinson	10.00
38	Hank Aaron	10.00
39	Bob Gibson	4.00
40	Carlton Fisk	4.00
41	Hank Aaron	10.00
42	George Brett	10.00
43	Orlando Cepeda	2.00
44	Red Schoendienst	2.00
45	Don Drysdale	4.00
46	Mel Ott	4.00
47	Casey Stengel	3.00
48	Al Kaline	4.00
49	Reggie Jackson	5.00
50	Tony Perez	2.00
51	Ozzie Smith	6.00
52	Billy Martin	4.00
53	Bill Dickey	2.00
54	Catfish Hunter	2.00
55	Duke Snider	4.00
56	Dale Murphy	2.00
57	Bobby Doerr	2.00
58	Earl Averill	2.00
59	Carlton Fisk	4.00
60	Tom Lasorda	2.00
61	Lou Gehrig	12.00
62	Enos Slaughter	2.00
63	Jim Bunning	2.00
64	Rollie Fingers	2.00
65	Frank Robinson	4.00
66	Earl Weaver	2.00
67	Eddie Mathews	5.00
68	Kirby Puckett	5.00
69	Phil Rizzuto	4.00
70	Lou Brock	4.00
71	Walt Alston	2.00
72	Bill Pierce	2.00
73	Joe Morgan	2.00
74	Roberto Clemente	12.00
75	Whitey Ford	4.00
76	Richie Ashburn	2.00
77	Elston Howard	2.00
78	Gary Carter	2.00
79	Carl Hubbell	2.00
80	Yogi Berra	6.00
81	Ken Boyer	2.00
82	Nolan Ryan	12.00
83	Bill Mazeroski	2.00
84	Dizzy Dean	4.00
85	Nellie Fox	2.00
86	Stan Musial	10.00
87	Steve Carlton	4.00
88	Willie Stargell	4.00
89	Hal Newhouser	2.00
90	Frank Robinson	4.00

Franchise Figures

		NM/M
Inserted 1:34		
AL	Walt Alston, Tommy Lasorda	50.00
AFF	Luis Aparicio, Nellie Fox, Carlton Fisk	125.00
BPKR	Johnny Bench, Tony Perez, Ted Kluszewski, Frank Robinson, Joe Morgan	150.00
CD	Gary Carter, Andre Dawson	40.00
HDB	Bill Dickey, Elston Howard, Yogi Berra	150.00
FY	Carlton Fisk, Carl Yastrzemski	150.00
HSS	Gil Hodges, Casey Stengel, Tom Seaver	150.00
JM	Reggie Jackson, Billy Martin	125.00
KG	Al Kaline, Hank Greenberg	150.00
MMC	Willie Mays, Willie McCovey, Orlando Cepeda	200.00
MCS	Bill Mazeroski, Roberto Clemente, Willie Stargell	185.00
MM	Thurman Munson, Don Mattingly	200.00
MMA	Dale Murphy, Ed Mathews, Hank Aaron	185.00
PK	Kirby Puckett, Harmon Killebrew	100.00
RSC	Pee Wee Reese, Duke Snider, Roy Campanella	160.00
RR	Brooks Robinson, Frank Robinson	75.00
RG	Babe Ruth, Lou Gehrig	500.00
SAC	Mike Schmidt, Richie Ashburn, Steve Carlton	125.00
SBSM	Ozzie Smith, Lou Brock, Red Schoendienst, Stan Musial	125.00

Game-Used Bat Relics

		NM/M
Common Player:		20.00
Inserted 1:2		
HA	Hank Aaron	50.00
LA	Luis Aparicio	20.00
RA	Richie Ashburn	25.00
KB	Ken Boyer	20.00
GB	George Brett	40.00
LB	Lou Brock	20.00
RC	Roy Campanella	30.00
RCL	Roberto Clemente	80.00
CF	Carlton Fisk	25.00
LG	Lou Gehrig	160.00
HG	Hank Greenberg	50.00
GH	Gil Hodges	25.00
RJ	Reggie Jackson	30.00
AK	Al Kaline	30.00
HK	Harmon Killebrew	30.00
RM	Roger Maris	50.00
BM	Billy Martin	20.00
DM	Don Mattingly	50.00
WM	Willie McCovey	25.00
TM	Thurman Munson	35.00
PWR	Pee Wee Reese	20.00
BRO	Brooks Robinson	30.00
FRR	Frank Robinson	30.00
BR	Babe Ruth	200.00
OS	Ozzie Smith	35.00
CS	Casey Stengel	20.00
HW	Honus Wagner	200.00
CY	Carl Yastrzemski	40.00

Game-Worn Patch And Number Relics

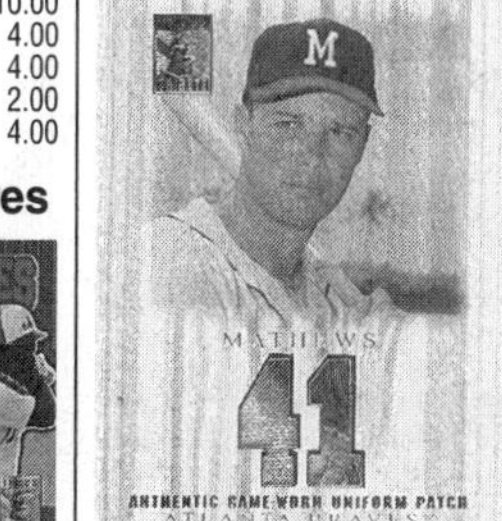

		NM/M
Common Player:		60.00
Inserted 1:61		
WA	Walt Alston	60.00
JB	Johnny Bench	180.00
YB	Yogi Berra	150.00
WB	Wade Boggs	80.00
LB	Lou Brock	60.00
BD	Bill Dickey	150.00
BDO	Bobby Doerr	100.00
HK	Harmon Killebrew	250.00
TL	Tom Lasorda	80.00
JM	Juan Marichal	75.00
EM	Eddie Mathews	150.00
KB	Kirby Puckett	250.00
NR	Nolan Ryan	300.00
MS	Mike Schmidt	250.00
RS	Red Schoendienst	80.00
DW	Dave Winfield	80.00
CY	Carl Yastrzemski	200.00
RY	Robin Yount	100.00

Retired Game-Worn Relics

		NM/M
Common Player:		20.00
Inserted 1:2		
WA	Walt Alston	20.00
EB	Ernie Banks	30.00
EBA	Ernie Banks	30.00
JB	Johnny Bench	30.00
YB	Yogi Berra	30.00
WB	Wade Boggs	20.00
GB	George Brett	50.00
LB	Lou Brock	25.00
SC	Steve Carlton	25.00
DD	Dizzy Dean	40.00
BD	Bill Dickey	20.00
BDO	Bobby Doerr	25.00
NF	Nellie Fox	20.00
HK	Harmon Killebrew	30.00
TL	Tom Lasorda	20.00
JMG	Juan Marichal	30.00
EM	Eddie Mathews	30.00
DM	Don Mattingly	50.00
WMF	Willie Mays	75.00
WMW	Willie Mays	75.00
SM	Stan Musial	75.00
JP	Jim Palmer	20.00
KP	Kirby Puckett	30.00
FR	Frank Robinson	25.00
NRA	Nolan Ryan	80.00
NRH	Nolan Ryan	80.00
NRR	Nolan Ryan	80.00
MSB	Mike Schmidt	50.00
MSW	Mike Schmidt	50.00
RS	Red Schoendienst	20.00
WST	Willie Stargell	20.00
CS	Casey Stengel	20.00
DW	Dave Winfield	20.00
CY	Carl Yastrzemski/White	40.00
CYA	Carl Yastrzemski/Gray	40.00
RY	Robin Yount	30.00

Frank Robinson Dual Relic

		NM/M
Inserted 1:860		
FR-RO	Frank Robinson	90.00

Nolan Ryan Tri-Relic

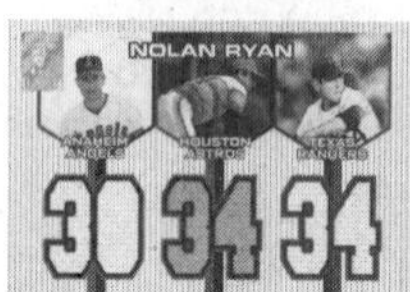

		NM/M
Randomly inserted.		
NR	Nolan Ryan	475.00

Casey Stengel Dual Relic

		NM/M
Inserted 1:860		
CS	Casey Stengel	100.00

Vintage Buy-Back Cards

No pricing due to scarcity.

Post Collector's Series

Baseball cards returned to boxes of Post cereals in 2001 with a special edition of Topps cards. The baseball cards were issued two per cello pack along with an introductory "pass" to the cereal company's web site for kids. The top card in each pack was visible through a window cut in the specially marked cereal boxes. The 2-1/2" x 3-1/2" cards have game-action photos which are borderless at the top and sides. At bottom are color strips with the player's position and name. A team logo in the lower-left corner of the photo and the Topps 50th anniversary logo is at upper-left. Backs have a portrait photo, facsimile autograph, biographical data, recent stats and various league, and sponsor logos.

		NM/M
Complete Set (18):		10.00
Common Player:		.25
1	Alex Rodriguez	1.50
2	Barry Bonds	2.00
3	Bernie Williams	.35
4	Frank Thomas	.75
5	Greg Maddux	1.00
6	Mark McGwire	1.50
7	Manny Ramirez	.75
8	Orlando Hernandez	.25
9	Pedro Martinez	.60
10	Gary Sheffield	.45
11	Jermaine Dye	.25
12	Mike Piazza	1.50
13	Barry Larkin	.25
14	Brad Radke	.25
15	Ivan Rodriguez	.60
16	Moises Alou	.25
17	Tony Gwynn	1.00
18	Todd Helton	.75

Post 500 Home Run Club

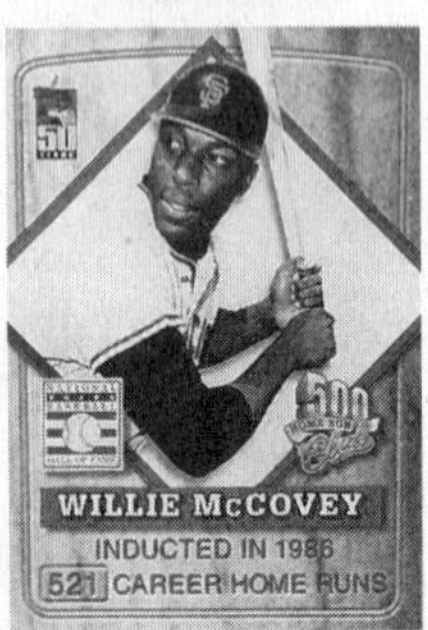

Baseball cards returned to boxes of Post cereals in 2001 with a special edition of Topps cards. The baseball cards were issued two per cello pack. The top card in each pack was visible through a window cut in the specially marked cereal boxes. The 2-1/2" x 3-1/2" cards have player photos in a white diamond on a wood-look background. Player name is in a red strip below. At center-left is a Hall of Fame logo, with a 500 Home Run Club logo opposite. The Topps 50th anniversary logo is at upper-left. Backs have complete major league stats, biographical data and various league and sponsor logos.

		NM/M
Complete Set (8):		7.50
Common Player:		1.00
1	Babe Ruth	2.00
2	Ernie Banks	1.50
3	Jimmie Foxx	1.00
4	Willie McCovey	1.00
5	Frank Robinson	1.00
6	Harmon Killebrew	1.00
7	Mike Schmidt	1.50
8	Reggie Jackson	1.50

2002 Topps Promos

Topps previewed the format of its 2002 base set with a three-card promo issue.

		NM/M
Complete Set (3):		6.00
Common Player:		2.00
P1	Sammy Sosa	3.00
P2	Jason Giambi	2.00
P3	Curt Schilling	2.00

2002 Topps

		NM/M
Complete Set (718):		70.00
Complete Factory Set (723):		80.00
Complete Series 1 (365):		35.00
Complete Series 2 (354):		35.00
Common Player:		.10
Pack (10):		1.50
Box (36):		40.00
1	Pedro Martinez	.50
2	Mike Stanton	.10
3	Brad Penny	.10
4	Mike Matheny	.10
5	Johnny Damon	.20
6	Bret Boone	.20
7	Not Issued (Retired)	.10
8	Chris Truby	.10
9	B.J. Surhoff	.10
10	Mike Hampton	.10
11	Juan Pierre	.10
12	Mark Buehrle	.10
13	Bob Abreu	.20
14	David Cone	.10
15	Aaron Sele	.10
16	Fernando Tatis	.10
17	Bobby Jones	.10
18	Rick Helling	.10
19	Dmitri Young	.10
20	Mike Mussina	.40
21	Mike Sweeney	.10
22	Cristian Guzman	.10
23	Ryan Kohlmeier	.10
24	Adam Kennedy	.10
25	Larry Walker	.25
26	Eric Davis	.10
27	Jason Tyner	.10
28	Eric Young	.10
29	Jason Marquis	.10
30	Luis Gonzalez	.20
31	Kevin Tapani	.10
32	Orlando Cabrera	.10
33	Marty Cordova	.10
34	Brad Ausmus	.10
35	Livan Hernandez	.10
36	Alex Gonzalez	.10
37	Edgar Renteria	.20
38	Bengie Molina	.10
39	Frank Menechino	.10
40	Rafael Palmeiro	.40
41	Brad Fullmer	.10
42	Julio Zuleta	.10
43	Darren Dreifort	.10
44	Trot Nixon	.10
45	Trevor Hoffman	.10
46	Vladimir Nunez	.10
47	Mark Kotsay	.10
48	Kenny Rogers	.10
49	Ben Petrick	.10
50	Jeff Bagwell	.40
51	Juan Encarnacion	.10
52	Ramiro Mendoza	.10
53	Brian Meadows	.10
54	Chad Curtis	.10
55	Aramis Ramirez	.25
56	Mark McLemore	.10
57	Dante Bichette	.10
58	Scott Schoeneweis	.10
59	Jose Cruz Jr.	.10
60	Roger Clemens	1.00
61	Jose Guillen	.10
62	Darren Oliver	.10
63	Chris Reitsma	.10
64	Jeff Abbott	.10
65	Robin Ventura	.10
66	Denny Neagle	.10
67	Al Martin	.10
68	Benito Santiago	.10
69	Roy Oswalt	.20
70	Juan Gonzalez	.40
71	Garret Anderson	.25
72	Bobby Bonilla	.10
73	Danny Bautista	.10
74	J.T. Snow Jr.	.10
75	Derek Jeter	1.50
76	John Olerud	.20
77	Kevin Appier	.10
78	Phil Nevin	.20
79	Sean Casey	.20
80	Troy Glaus	.40
81	Joe Randa	.10
82	Jose Valentin	.10
83	Ricky Bottalico	.10
84	Todd Zeile	.10
85	Barry Larkin	.25
86	Bob Wickman	.10
87	Jeff Shaw	.10
88	Greg Vaughn	.10
89	Fernando Vina	.10
90	Mark Mulder	.25
91	Paul Bako	.10
92	Aaron Boone	.10
93	Esteban Loaiza	.10
94	Richie Sexson	.40
95	Alfonso Soriano	.50
96	Tony Womack	.10
97	Paul Shuey	.10
98	Melvin Mora	.10
99	Tony Gwynn	.50
100	Vladimir Guerrero	.50
101	Keith Osik	.10
102	Randy Velarde	.10
103	Scott Williamson	.10
104	Daryle Ward	.10
105	Doug Mientkiewicz	.10
106	Stan Javier	.10
107	Russ Ortiz	.10
108	Wade Miller	.10
109	Luke Prokopec	.10
110	Andruw Jones	.40
111	Ron Coomer	.10
112	Dan Wilson	.10
113	Luis Castillo	.10
114	Derek Bell	.10
115	Gary Sheffield	.20
116	Ruben Rivera	.10
117	Paul O'Neill	.20
118	Craig Paquette	.10
119	Chris Michalak	.10
120	Brad Radke	.10
121	Jorge Fabregas	.10
122	Randy Winn	.10
123	Tom Goodwin	.10
124	Jaret Wright	.10
125	Manny Ramirez	.40
126	Al Leiter	.20
127	Ben Davis	.10
128	Frank Catalanotto	.10
129	Jose Cabrera	.10
130	Magglio Ordonez	.20
131	Jose Macias	.10
132	Ted Lilly	.10
133	Chris Holt	.10
134	Eric Milton	.10
135	Shannon Stewart	.10
136	Omar Olivares	.10
137	David Segui	.10
138	Jeff Nelson	.10
139	Matt Williams	.25
140	Ellis Burks	.10
141	Jason Bere	.10
142	Jimmy Haynes	.10
143	Ramon Hernandez	.10
144	Craig Counsell (Front photo actually Greg Colbrunn.)	.10
145	John Smoltz	.10
146	Homer Bush	.10
147	Quilvio Veras	.10
148	Esteban Yan	.10
149	Ramon Ortiz	.10
150	Carlos Delgado	.30
151	Lee Stevens	.10
152	Wil Cordero	.10
153	Mike Bordick	.10
154	John Flaherty	.10
155	Omar Daal	.10
156	Todd Ritchie	.10
157	Carl Everett	.10
158	Scott Sullivan	.10
159	Deivi Cruz	.10
160a	Albert Pujols (Back photo is Placido Polanco.) (In cap.)	1.00
160b	Albert Pujols (Back photo corrected)(No cap.)	10.00
161	Royce Clayton	.10
162	Jeff Suppan	.10
163	C.C. Sabathia	.10
164	Jimmy Rollins	.25
165	Rickey Henderson	.25
166	Rey Ordonez	.10
167	Shawn Estes	.10
168	Reggie Sanders	.10
169	Jon Lieber	.10
170	Armando Benitez	.10
171	Mike Remlinger	.10
172	Billy Wagner	.10
173	Troy Percival	.10
174	Devon White	.10
175	Ivan Rodriguez	.40
176	Dustin Hermanson	.10
177	Brian Anderson	.10
178	Graeme Lloyd	.10
179	Russ Branyan	.10
180	Bobby Higginson	.10
181	Alex Gonzalez	.10
182	John Franco	.10
183	Sidney Ponson	.10
184	Jose Mesa	.10
185	Todd Hollandsworth	.10
186	Kevin Young	.10
187	Tim Wakefield	.10
188	Craig Biggio	.20
189	Jason Isringhausen	.10
190	Mark Quinn	.10
191	Glendon Rusch	.10
192	Damian Miller	.10
193	Sandy Alomar	.10
194	Scott Brosius	.10
195	Dave Martinez	.10
196	Danny Graves	.10
197	Shea Hillenbrand	.10
198	Jimmy Anderson	.10
199	Travis Lee	.10
200	Randy Johnson	.50
201	Carlos Beltran	.25
202	Jerry Hairston Jr.	.10
203	Jesus Sanchez	.10
204	Eddie Taubensee	.10
205	David Wells	.10
206	Russ Davis	.10
207	Michael Barrett	.10
208	Marquis Grissom	.10
209	Byung-Hyun Kim	.10
210	Hideo Nomo	.25
211	Ryan Rupe	.10
212	Ricky Gutierrez	.10
213	Darryl Kile	.10
214	Rico Brogna	.10
215	Terrence Long	.10
216	Mike Jackson	.10
217	Jamey Wright	.10
218	Adrian Beltre	.20
219	Benny Agbayani	.10
220	Chuck Knoblauch	.10
221	Randy Wolf	.10
222	Andy Ashby	.10
223	Corey Koskie	.10
224	Roger Cedeno	.10
225	Ichiro Suzuki	1.00
226	Keith Foulke	.10
227	Ryan Minor	.10
228	Shawon Dunston	.10
229	Alex Cora	.10
230	Jeromy Burnitz	.10
231	Mark Grace	.25
232	Aubrey Huff	.10
233	Jeffrey Hammonds	.10
234	Olmedo Saenz	.10
235	Brian Jordan	.10
236	Jeremy Giambi	.10
237	Joe Girardi	.10
238	Eric Gagne	.25
239	Masato Yoshii	.10
240	Greg Maddux	.75
241	Bryan Rekar	.10
242	Ray Durham	.10
243	Torii Hunter	.20
244	Derrek Lee	.20
245	Jim Edmonds	.25
246	Einar Diaz	.10
247	Brian Bohanon	.10
248	Ron Belliard	.10
249	Mike Lowell	.20
250	Sammy Sosa	1.00
251	Richard Hidalgo	.10
252	Bartolo Colon	.10
253	Jorge Posada	.25
254	LaTroy Hawkins	.10
255	Paul LoDuca	.10
256	Carlos Febles	.10
257	Nelson Cruz	.10
258	Edgardo Alfonzo	.10
259	Joey Hamilton	.10
260	Cliff Floyd	.10
261	Wes Helms	.10
262	Jay Bell	.10
263	Mike Cameron	.10
264	Paul Konerko	.10
265	Jeff Kent	.20
266	Robert Fick	.10
267	Allen Levrault	.10
268	Placido Polanco	.10
269	Marlon Anderson	.10
270	Mariano Rivera	.20
271	Chan Ho Park	.10
272	Jose Vizcaino	.10
273	Jeff D'Amico	.10
274	Mark Gardner	.10
275	Travis Fryman	.10
276	Darren Lewis	.10
277	Bruce Bochy	.10
278	Jerry Manuel	.10
279	Bob Brenly	.10
280	Don Baylor	.10
281	Davey Lopes	.10
282	Jerry Narron	.10
283	Tony Muser	.10
284	Hal McRae	.10
285	Bobby Cox	.10
286	Larry Dierker	.10
287	Phil Garner	.10
288	Jimy Williams	.10
289	Bobby Valentine	.10
290	Dusty Baker	.10
291	Lloyd McLendon	.10
292	Mike Scioscia	.10
293	Buck Martinez	.10
294	Larry Bowa	.10
295	Tony LaRussa	.10
296	Jeff Torborg	.10
297	Tom Kelly	.10
298	Mike Hargrove	.10
299	Art Howe	.10
300	Lou Pinella	.10
301	Charlie Manuel	.10
302	Buddy Bell	.10
303	Tony Perez	.10
304	Bob Boone	.10
305	Joe Torre	.25
306	Jim Tracy	.10
307	Jason Lane	.10
308	Chris George	.10
309	Hank Blalock	.25
310	Joe Borchard	.10
311	Marlon Byrd	.10
312	Raymond Cabrera **RC**	.25
313	Freddy Sanchez **RC**	.40
314	Scott Wiggins **RC**	.40
315	Jason Maule **RC**	.30
316	Dionys Cesar **RC**	.40
317	Boof Bonser	.10
318	Juan Tolentino **RC**	.40
319	Earl Snyder **RC**	.25
320	Travis Wade **RC**	.25
321	Napoleon Calzado **RC**	.40
322	Eric Glaser **RC**	.40
323	Craig Kuzmic **RC**	.40
324	Nic Jackson **RC**	.50
325	Mike Rivera	.10
326	Jason Bay **RC**	1.00
327	Chris Smith	.10
328	Jake Gautreau	.10
329	Gabe Gross	.10
330	Kenny Baugh	.10
331	J.D. Martin	.10
332	Barry Bonds	1.00
333	Rickey Henderson	.25
334	Bud Smith	.10
335	Rickey Henderson	.25
336	Barry Bonds	1.00
337	Ichiro Suzuki, Jason Giambi, Roberto Alomar	.50
338	Alex Rodriguez, Ichiro Suzuki, Bret Boone	.50
339	Alex Rodriguez, Jim Thome, Rafael Palmeiro	.40
340	Bret Boone, Juan Gonzalez, Alex Rodriguez	.40
341	Freddy Garcia, Mike Mussina, Joe Mays	.15
342	Hideo Nomo, Mike Mussina, Roger Clemens	.40
343	Larry Walker, Todd Helton, Moises Alou	.25
344	Sammy Sosa, Todd Helton, Barry Bonds	.40
345	Barry Bonds, Sammy Sosa, Luis Gonzalez	.40
346	Sammy Sosa, Todd Helton, Luis Gonzalez	.40
347	Curt Schilling, Randy Johnson, John Burkett	.20
348	Randy Johnson, Curt Schilling, Chan Ho Park	.20
349	Seattle Mariners	.25
350	Oakland A's	.10
351	New York Yankees	.50
352	Cleveland Indians	.10
353	Arizona Diamondbacks	.10
354	Atlanta Braves	.10
355	St. Louis Cardinals	.10
356	Houston Astros	.10
357	D'backs vs. Rockies	.10
358	Mets vs. Pirates	.10
359	Braves vs. Phillies	.10
360	D'backs vs. Phillies	.10
361	Yankees vs. White Sox	.10
362	Cubs vs. Reds	.10
363	Angels vs. Mariners	.10
364	Astros vs. Giants	.10
365	Barry Bonds Race to 70 #1	10.00
365	Barry Bonds HR #2-69	8.00
365	Barry Bonds HR #70	15.00
365	Barry Bonds HR #71	10.00
365	Barry Bonds HR #72	10.00
365	Barry Bonds HR #73	50.00
366	Pat Meares	.10
367	Mike Lieberthal	.10
368	Scott Erickson	.10
369	Ron Gant	.10
370	Moises Alou	.25
371	Chad Kreuter	.10
372	Willis Roberts	.10
373	Toby Hall	.10
374	Miguel Batista	.10
375	John Burkett	.10
376	Cory Lidle	.10
377	Nick Neugebauer	.10
378	Jay Payton	.10
379	Steve Karsay	.10
380	Eric Chavez	.20
381	Kelly Stinnett	.10
382	Jarrod Washburn	.10
383	C.J. Nitkowski	.10
384	Jeff Conine	.10
385	Fred McGriff	.10
386	Marvin Benard	.10
387	Dave Burba	.10
388	Dennis Cook	.10
389	Rick Reed	.10
390	Tom Glavine	.25
391	Rondell White	.15
392	Matt Morris	.20
393	Pat Rapp	.10
394	Robert Person	.10
395	Omar Vizquel	.15
396	Jeff Cirillo	.10
397	Dave Mlicki	.10
398	Jose Ortiz	.10
399	Ryan Dempster	.10
400	Curt Schilling	.25
401	Peter Bergeron	.10
402	Kyle Lohse	.10
403	Craig Wilson	.10
404	David Justice	.20
405	Darin Erstad	.20
406	Jose Mercedes	.10
407	Carl Pavano	.10
408	Albie Lopez	.10
409	Alex Ochoa	.10
410	Chipper Jones	.50
411	Tyler Houston	.10
412	Dean Palmer	.10
413	Damian Jackson	.10
414	Josh Towers	.10
415	Rafael Furcal	.20
416	Ken Caminiti	.10
417	Herb Perry	.10
418	Mike Sirotka	.10
419	Mark Wohlers	.10
420	Nomar Garciaparra	1.00
421	Felipe Lopez	.10
422	Joe McEwing	.10
423	Jacque Jones	.10
424	Julio Franco	.10
425	Frank Thomas	.40
426	So Taguchi **RC**	.50
427	Kazuhisa Ishii **RC**	1.00
428	D'Angelo Jimenez	.10
429	Chris Stynes	.10
430	Kerry Wood	.50
431	Chris Singleton	.10
432	Erubiel Durazo	.10
433	Matt Lawton	.10
434	Bill Mueller	.10
435	Jose Canseco	.25
436	Ben Grieve	.10
437	Terry Mulholland	.10
438	David Bell	.10
439	A.J. Pierzynski	.10
440	Adam Dunn	.40
441	Jon Garland	.10
442	Jeff Fassero	.10
443	Julio Lugo	.10
444	Carlos Guillen	.10
445	Orlando Hernandez	.20
446	Mark Loretta	.10
447	Scott Spiezio	.10
448	Kevin Millwood	.20
449	Jamie Moyer	.10
450	Todd Helton	.40
451	Todd Walker	.10
452	Jose Lima	.10
453	Brook Fordyce	.10
454	Aaron Rowand	.10
455	Barry Zito	.20
456	Eric Owens	.10
457	Charles Nagy	.10
458	Raul Ibanez	.10
459	Joe Mays	.10
460	Jim Thome	.50
461	Adam Eaton	.10
462	Felix Martinez	.10
463	Vernon Wells	.10
464	Donnie Sadler	.10
465	Tony Clark	.10
466	Jose Hernandez	.10
467	Ramon Martinez	.10
468	Rusty Greer	.10
469	Rod Barajas	.10
470	Lance Berkman	.25
471	Brady Anderson	.10
472	Pedro Astacio	.10
473	Shane Halter	.10
474	Bret Prinz	.10
475	Edgar Martinez	.20
476	Steve Trachsel	.10

477 Gary Matthews Jr. .10
478 Ismael Valdes .10
479 Juan Uribe .10
480 Shawn Green .20
481 Kirk Rueter .10
482 Damion Easley .10
483 Chris Carpenter .10
484 Kris Benson .10
485 Antonio Alfonseca .10
486 Kyle Farnsworth .10
487 Brandon Lyon .10
488 Hideki Irabu .10
489 David Ortiz .25
490 Mike Piazza 1.00
491 Derek Lowe .10
492 Chris Gomez .10
493 Mark Johnson .10
494 John Rocker .10
495 Eric Karros .10
496 Bill Haselman .10
497 Dave Veres .10
498 Gil Heredia .10
499 Tomokazu Ohka .10
500 Barry Bonds 1.50
501 David Dellucci .10
502 Ed Sprague .10
503 Tom Gordon .10
504 Javier Vazquez .10
505 Ben Sheets .25
506 Wilton Guerrero .10
507 John Halama .10
508 Mark Redman .10
509 Jack Wilson .10
510 Bernie Williams .40
511 Miguel Cairo .10
512 Denny Hocking .10
513 Tony Batista .10
514 Mark Grudzielanek .10
515 Jose Vidro .10
516 Sterling Hitchcock .10
517 Billy Koch .10
518 Matt Clement .10
519 Bruce Chen .10
520 Roberto Alomar .40
521 Orlando Palmeiro .10
522 Steve Finley .10
523 Danny Patterson .10
524 Terry Adams .10
525 Tino Martinez .10
526 Tony Armas Jr. .10
527 Geoff Jenkins .20
528 Chris Michalak .10
529 Corey Patterson .20
530 Brian Giles .20
531 Jose Jimenez .10
532 Joe Kennedy .10
533 Armando Rios .10
534 Osvaldo Fernandez .10
535 Ruben Sierra .10
536 Octavio Dotel .10
537 Luis Sojo .10
538 Brent Butler .10
539 Pablo Ozuna .10
540 Freddy Garcia .10
541 Chad Durbin .10
542 Orlando Merced .10
543 Michael Tucker .10
544 Roberto Hernandez .10
545 Pat Burrell .25
546 A.J. Burnett .10
547 Bubba Trammell .10
548 Scott Elarton .10
549 Mike Darr .10
550 Ken Griffey Jr. 1.00
551 Ugueth Urbina .10
552 Todd Jones .10
553 Delino DeShields .10
554 Adam Piatt .10
555 Jason Kendall .10
556 Hector Ortiz .10
557 Turk Wendell .10
558 Rob Bell .10
559 Sun-Woo Kim .10
560 Raul Mondesi .10
561 Brent Abernathy .10
562 Seth Etherton .10
563 Shawn Wooten .10
564 Jay Buhner .10
565 Andres Galarraga .10
566 Shane Reynolds .10
567 Rod Beck .10
568 Dee Brown .10
569 Pedro Feliz .10
570 Ryan Klesko .10
571 John Vander Wal .10
572 Nick Bierbrodt .10
573 Joe Nathan .10
574 James Baldwin .10
575 J.D. Drew .20
576 Greg Colbrunn .10
577 Doug Glanville .10
578 Rey Sanchez .10
579 Todd Van Poppel .10
580 Rich Aurilia .10
581 Chuck Finley .10
582 Abraham Nunez .10
583 Kenny Lofton .20
584 Brian Daubach .10
585 Miguel Tejada .25
586 Nate Cornejo .10
587 Kazuhiro Sasaki .10
588 Chris Richard .10
589 Armando Reynoso .10
590 Tim Hudson .20
591 Neifi Perez .10
592 Steve Cox .10
593 Henry Blanco .10
594 Ricky Ledee .10
595 Tim Salmon .20
596 Luis Rivas .10
597 Jeff Zimmerman .10
598 Matt Stairs .10
599 Preston Wilson .10
600 Mark McGwire 1.50
601 Timo Perez .10
602 Matt Anderson .10
603 Todd Hundley .10
604 Rick Ankiel .10
605 Tsuyoshi Shinjo .10
606 Woody Williams .10
607 Jason LaRue .10
608 Carlos Lee .10
609 Russ Johnson .10
610 Scott Rolen .50
611 Brent Mayne .10
612 Darrin Fletcher .10
613 Ray Lankford .10
614 Troy O'Leary .10
615 Javier Lopez .20
616 Randy Velarde .10
617 Vinny Castilla .10
618 Milton Bradley .10
619 Ruben Mateo .10
620 Jason Giambi .40
621 Andy Benes .10
622 Tony Eusebio .10
623 Andy Pettitte .20
624 Jose Offerman .10
625 Mo Vaughn .20
626 Steve Sparks .10
627 Mike Matthews .10
628 Robb Nen .10
629 Kip Wells .10
630 Kevin Brown .20
631 Arthur Rhodes .10
632 Gabe Kapler .10
633 Jermaine Dye .10
634 Josh Beckett .25
635 Pokey Reese .10
636 Benji Gil .10
637 Marcus Giles .10
638 Julian Tavarez .10
639 Jason Schmidt .25
640 Alex Rodriguez 1.25
641 Anaheim Angels .10
642 Arizona Diamondbacks .10
643 Atlanta Braves .10
644 Baltimore Orioles .10
645 Boston Red Sox .10
646 Chicago Cubs .10
647 Chicago White Sox .10
648 Cincinnati Reds .10
649 Cleveland Indians .10
650 Colorado Rockies .10
651 Detroit Tigers .10
652 Florida Marlins .10
653 Houston Astros .10
654 Kansas City Royals .10
655 Los Angeles Dodgers .10
656 Milwaukee Brewers .10
657 Minnesota Twins .10
658 Montreal Expos .10
659 New York Mets .10
660 New York Yankees .10
661 Oakland Athletics .10
662 Philadelphia Phillies .10
663 Pittsburgh Pirates .10
664 San Diego Padres .10
665 San Francisco Giants .10
666 Seattle Mariners .10
667 St. Louis Cardinals .10
668 Tampa Bay Devil Rays .10
669 Texas Rangers .10
670 Toronto Blue Jays .10
671 Juan Cruz .25
672 Kevin Cash **RC** .50
673 Jimmy Gobble **RC** .75
674 Mike Hill **RC** .40
675 Taylor Buchholz **RC** .40
676 Bill Hall .10
677 Brett Roneberg **RC** .40
678 Royce Huffman **RC** .40
679 Chris Tritle **RC** .40
680 Nate Espy **RC** .40
681 Nick Alvarez **RC** .50
682 Jason Botts **RC** .40
683 Ryan Gripp **RC** .40
684 Dan Phillips **RC** .50
685 Pablo Arias **RC** .50
686 John Rodriguez **RC** .40
687 Rich Harden **RC** 3.00
688 Neal Frendling **RC** .50
689 Rich Thompson **RC** .40
690 Greg Montalbano **RC** .40
691 Leonard Dinardo **RC** .40
692 Ryan Raburn **RC** .40
693 Josh Barfield 1.00
694 David Bacani **RC** .40
695 Dan Johnson **RC** .50
696 Mike Mussina (Gold Glove Award Winners) .25
697 Ivan Rodriguez (Gold Glove Award Winners) .25
698 Doug Mientkiewicz (Gold Glove Award Winners) .10
699 Roberto Alomar (Gold Glove Award Winners) .25
700 Eric Chavez (Gold Glove Award Winners) .15
701 Omar Vizquel (Gold Glove Award Winners) .10
702 Mike Cameron (Gold Glove Award Winners) .15
703 Torii Hunter (Gold Glove Award Winners) .10
704 Ichiro Suzuki (Gold Glove Award Winners) .50
705 Greg Maddux (Gold Glove Award Winners) .50
706 Brad Ausmus (Gold Glove Award Winners) .10
707 Todd Helton (Gold Glove Award Winners) .25
708 Fernando Vina (Gold Glove Award Winners) .10
709 Scott Rolen (Gold Glove Award Winners) .40
710 Orlando Cabrera (Gold Glove Award Winners) .10
711 Andruw Jones (Gold Glove Award Winners) .15
712 Jim Edmonds (Gold Glove Award Winners) .10
713 Larry Walker (Gold Glove Award Winners) .15
714 Roger Clemens (Cy Young Award Winners) .50
715 Randy Johnson (Cy Young Award Winners) .25
716 Ichiro Suzuki (MVP Award Winners) .50
717 Barry Bonds (MVP Award Winners) .75
718 Ichiro Suzuki (ROY Award Winners) .50
719 Albert Pujols (ROY Award Winners) .50

Gold

NM/M
Complete Set (659): 700.00
Stars: 5-10X
Production 2,002 Sets

Limited

NM/M
Complete Set (790): 165.00
Includes all 73 B. Bonds #365 HR cards.

Aces

NM/M
Common Player: 10.00
Inserted 1:1,180
MH Mike Hampton 10.00
RJ Randy Johnson 20.00
GM Greg Maddux 30.00
PM Pedro Martinez 20.00
MM Mark Mulder 10.00

All-World Team

NM/M
Complete Set (25): 25.00
Common Player: .50
Inserted 1:12
AW-1 Ichiro Suzuki 3.00
AW-2 Barry Bonds 4.00
AW-3 Pedro Martinez 1.50
AW-4 Juan Gonzalez 1.00
AW-5 Larry Walker .50
AW-6 Sammy Sosa 3.00
AW-7 Mariano Rivera .75
AW-8 Vladimir Guerrero 1.50
AW-9 Alex Rodriguez 3.00
AW-10 Albert Pujols 3.00
AW-11 Luis Gonzalez .50
AW-12 Ken Griffey Jr. 2.50
AW-13 Kazuhiro Sasaki .50
AW-14 Bob Abreu .50
AW-15 Todd Helton 1.00
AW-16 Nomar Garciaparra 2.50
AW-17 Miguel Tejada .75
AW-18 Roger Clemens 3.00
AW-19 Mike Piazza 2.50
AW-20 Carlos Delgado 1.00
AW-21 Derek Jeter 4.00
AW-22 Hideo Nomo .75
AW-23 Randy Johnson 1.50
AW-24 Ivan Rodriguez 1.00
AW-25 Chan Ho Park .50

Autographs

NM/M
Common Player: 5.00
TA1 Carlos Delgado 40.00
TA2 Ivan Rodriguez 50.00
TA3 Miguel Tejada 30.00
TA4 Geoff Jenkins 10.00
TA5 Johnny Damon 40.00
TA6 Tim Hudson 25.00
TA7 Terrence Long 10.00
TA8 Gabe Kapler 10.00
TA9 Magglio Ordonez 20.00
TA10 Barry Bonds 180.00
TA11 Pat Burrell 20.00
TA12 Mike Mussina 40.00
TA13 Eric Valent 5.00
TA14 Xavier Nady 8.00
TA15 Cristian Guerrero 5.00
TA16 Ben Sheets 15.00
TA17 Corey Patterson 15.00
TA18 Carlos Pena 5.00
TA19 Alex Rodriguez 80.00
Series 2
TA-AB Adrian Beltre 25.00
TA-JD Jermaine Dye 15.00
TA-AE Alex Escobar 8.00
TA-CF Cliff Floyd 15.00
TA-RF Rafael Furcal 20.00
TA-BG Brian Giles 20.00
TA-KG Keith Ginter 8.00
TA-TG Troy Glaus 40.00
TA-BGR Ben Grieve 20.00
TA-CG Cristian Guzman 15.00
TA-JH Josh Hamilton 25.00
TA-NJ Nick Johnson 5.00
TA-RK Ryan Klesko 20.00
TA-JO Jose Ortiz 10.00
TA-RO Roy Oswalt 15.00
TA-RP Rafael Palmeiro 50.00
TA-AR Alex Rodriguez 80.00
TA-JR Jimmy Rollins 25.00
TA-RS Richie Sexson 25.00
TA-MS Mike Sweeney 20.00
TA-JW Justin Wayne 10.00
TA-BW Brad Wilkerson 10.00

Battery Mates Relic

NM/M
Inserted 1:4,401
ML Greg Maddux, Javy Lopez 30.00
LP Al Leiter, Mike Piazza 30.00

Coaches Collection Relics

NM/M
Common Card 8.00
Inserted 1:236 Retail
AH Art Howe 8.00
AT Alan Trammell 15.00
BB Bruce Bochy 8.00
BM Buck Martinez 8.00
BV Bobby Valentine 15.00
BW Billy Williams 15.00
BBE Buddy Bell 15.00
BBR Bob Brenly 15.00
DB Dusty Baker 20.00
DL Davey Lopes 15.00
DBA Don Baylor 15.00
EH Elrod Hendricks 8.00
EM Eddie Murray 40.00
FW Frank White 15.00
HM Hal McRae 8.00
JT Joe Torre 10.00
KG Ken Griffey Sr. 8.00
LB Larry Bowa 15.00
LP Lance Parrish 15.00
MH Mike Hargrove 10.00
MS Mike Scioscia 15.00
MW Mookie Wilson 10.00
PG Phil Garner 10.00
PM Paul Molitor 40.00
TP Tony Perez 10.00
WR Willie Randolph 15.00

Draft Picks

NM/M
Complete Set (10): 40.00
1-5 in Green Factory Sets
6-10 in Holiday Factory Sets
1 Scott Moore 6.00
2 Val Majewski 6.00
3 Brian Slocum 4.00
4 Chris Gruler 6.00
5 Mark Schramek 6.00
6 Joe Saunders 4.00
7 Jeff Francis 8.00
8 Royce Ring 6.00
9 Greg Miller 8.00
10 Brandon Weeden 4.00

Deuces Are Wild

NM/M
Common Card: 15.00
Inserted 1:1,962
JG Randy Johnson, Luis Gonzalez 30.00
BK Barry Bonds, Jeff Kent 40.00
TA Jim Thome, Roberto Alomar 30.00
WH Larry Walker, Todd Helton 25.00
BG Bret Boone, Freddy Garcia 15.00

East Meets West

NM/M
Complete Set (8): 6.00
Common Player: 1.00
Inserted 1:24
EW-HN Hideo Nomo, Masanori Murakami 2.00
EW-HI Hideki Irabu, Masanori Murakami 1.00
EW-SH Shigetoshi Hasegawa, Masanori Murakami 1.00
EW-MY Masato Yoshii, Masanori Murakami 1.00
EW-TS Tsuyoshi Shinjo, Masanori Murakami 1.00
EW-KS Kazuhiro Sasaki, Masanori Murakami 1.00
EW-MS Mac Suzuki, Masanori Murakami 1.00
EW-TO Tomo Ohka, Masanori Murakami 1.00

East Meets West Relics

NM/M
Common Player: 15.00
Inserted 1:3,419
HN Hideo Nomo 40.00
KS Kazuhiro Sasaki 15.00
TS Tsuyoshi Shinjo 15.00

Ebbets Field Seat Relics

NM/M
Inserted 1:9,116
JB Joe Black 100.00
RC Roy Campanella 250.00
BC Billy Cox 100.00
CF Carl Furillo 100.00
GH Gil Hodges 250.00
AP Andy Pafko 100.00
PWR Pee Wee Reese 250.00
JR Jackie Robinson 250.00
DS Duke Snider 200.00

Dual Ebbets/ Yankee Seat Relic

Complete Set (1):

Dual Ebbets/ Yankee Autographed Seat Relic

Complete Set (1):

Ebbets Field/ Yankee Stadium Seat Dual Relic

Complete Set (1):

Hall of Fame Vintage BuyBacks AutoProofs

NM/M
Common Autograph: 15.00
BR16 Brooks Robinson 82 KM/200 50.00
EW10 Earl Weaver 87/100 15.00
FJ33 Fergie Jenkins 84/100 15.00
GP26 Gaylord Perry 82/100 15.00
GP29 Gaylord Perry 83/100 15.00
GP30 Gaylord Perry 83 SV/200 15.00
OC1 Orlando Cepeda 82 KM/200 15.00
RF15 Rollie Fingers 81/300 15.00
RF16 Rollie Fingers 81 LL/100 15.00
RF18 Rollie Fingers 82/100 15.00
RF19 Rollie Fingers 82 IA/200 15.00
RF21 Rollie Fingers 82 KM/300 15.00
RF22 Rollie Fingers 83/200 15.00
RF24 Rollie Fingers 84/200 15.00
RF27 Rollie Fingers 85/300 15.00
RF28 Rollie Fingers 86/100 15.00
SC5 Steve Carlton 84 LL/100 25.00
SC6 Steve Carlton 85/200 25.00
SC8 Steve Carlton 87/200 25.00

Heart of the Order Relic

NM/M
Inserted 1:4,247
KBA Jeff Kent, Barry Bonds, Rich Aurilia 75.00
TGA Jim Thome, Juan Gonzalez, Roberto Alomar 50.00
ARB Bob Abreu, Scott Rolen, Pat Burrell 50.00
OWM Paul O'Neill, Bernie Williams, Tino Martinez 50.00

Hit and Run Relic

NM/M
Inserted 1:4,241
JD Johnny Damon 10.00
DE Darin Erstad 10.00
RF Rafael Furcal 10.00

Hobby Masters

NM/M
Complete Set (20): 40.00
Common Player: 1.00
Inserted 1:25
1 Mark McGwire 5.00
2 Derek Jeter 5.00
3 Chipper Jones 2.00
4 Roger Clemens 4.00
5 Vladimir Guerrero 2.00
6 Ichiro Suzuki 3.00
7 Todd Helton 1.50
8 Alex Rodriguez 4.00
9 Albert Pujols 4.00
10 Sammy Sosa 3.00
11 Ken Griffey Jr. 3.00
12 Randy Johnson 2.00
13 Nomar Garciaparra 3.00
14 Ivan Rodriguez 1.50
15 Manny Ramirez 1.50
16 Barry Bonds 5.00
17 Mike Piazza 3.00
18 Pedro Martinez 1.50
19 Jeff Bagwell 1.50
20 Luis Gonzalez 1.00

Jack of All Trades

NM/M
Inserted 1:1,350
RO Roberto Alomar/Bat 20.00
BB Barry Bonds/Jsy 35.00
AJ Andruw Jones/Jsy 10.00
IR Ivan Rodriguez/Jsy 15.00
BW Bernie Williams/Jsy 15.00

Kings of the Clubhouse

NM/M
Common Player: 10.00
Inserted 1:1,449 Ser. 2
TG Tom Glavine/Jsy 15.00
TH Todd Helton/Jsy 15.00
RJ Randy Johnson/Jsy 20.00
EM Edgar Martinez/Jsy 10.00
PO Paul O'Neill/Bat 20.00

Like Father Like Son Relic

NM/M
Common Duo:
Inserted 1:1,304 Retail
AL Roberto Alomar, Sandy Alomar, Sandy Alomar Jr. 40.00
BE Dale Berra, Yogi Berra 50.00
BON Bobby Bonds, Barry Bonds 80.00
BOO Bob Boone, Bret Boone, Aaron Boone 40.00
CR Jose Cruz, Jose Cruz Jr. 40.00

Own The Game

NM/M
Complete Set (30): 25.00
Common Player: .50
Inserted 1:12
OG1 Moises Alou .75
OG2 Roberto Alomar .75
OG3 Luis Gonzalez .50
OG4 Bret Boone .75
OG5 Barry Bonds 4.00
OG6 Jim Thome 1.50
OG7 Jimmy Rollins .75
OG8 Cristian Guzman .50
OG9 Lance Berkman .75
OG10 Mike Sweeney .50
OG11 Rich Aurilia .50
OG12 Ichiro Suzuki 2.50
OG13 Luis Gonzalez .50
OG14 Ichiro Suzuki 2.50
OG15 Jimmy Rollins .75
OG16 Roger Cedeno .50
OG17 Barry Bonds 4.00
OG18 Jim Thome 1.50
OG19 Curt Schilling 1.00
OG20 Roger Clemens 3.00
OG21 Curt Schilling 1.00
OG22 Brad Radke .50
OG23 Greg Maddux 2.00
OG24 Mark Mulder .75
OG25 Jeff Shaw .50
OG26 Mariano Rivera .75
OG27 Randy Johnson 1.50
OG28 Pedro Martinez 1.50
OG29 John Burkett .50
OG30 Tim Hudson .75

Prime Cuts Pine Tar Series

NM/M
Common Player: 15.00
Inserted 1:4,420
BB Barry Bonds 60.00
LG Luis Gonzalez 20.00
TG Tony Gwynn 40.00
TH Todd Helton 25.00
AP Albert Pujols 40.00
Series 2
Inserted 1:1,043
Trademark Series: 1.5-2X
Inserted 1:2,087 Ser. 2
Prime Cuts Barrel: 2-4X
Inserted 1:7,824 Ser. 2
WB Wilson Betemit 15.00
SB Sean Burroughs 15.00
JC Joe Crede 20.00
AD Adam Dunn 30.00
AE Alex Escobar 15.00
MG Marcus Giles 15.00
AG Alexis Gomez 15.00
TH Toby Hall 15.00
JH Josh Hamilton 15.00
NJ Nick Johnson 15.00
XN Xavier Nady 15.00
CP Corey Patterson 20.00
CPE Carlos Pena 15.00
AR Aaron Rowand 25.00
RS Ruben Salazar 15.00

Prime Cuts Autograph Series

No Pricing

Ring Masters

NM/M
Complete Set (10): 15.00
Common Player: .50
Inserted 1:25
1 Derek Jeter 4.00
2 Mark McGwire 4.00
3 Mariano Rivera 1.00
4 Gary Sheffield .75
5 Al Leiter .50
6 Chipper Jones 1.50
7 Roger Clemens 3.00
8 Greg Maddux 2.00
9 Roberto Alomar 1.00
10 Paul O'Neill .50

Team Topps Legends Autographs

NM/M
Common Player: 25.00
TT6R Whitey Ford 60.00
TT8R Bob Gibson 40.00
TT47R Frank Howard 25.00
TT46F Robin Roberts 25.00
TT13F Warren Spahn 40.00
Series 2

Three of a Kind

NM/M
Common Card:
Inserted 1:2,039
SPA Tsuyoshi Shinjo, Mike Piazza, Edgardo Alfonzo 50.00
LOC Carlos Lee, Magglio Ordonez, Jose Canseco 50.00
FBJ Rafael Furcal, Wilson Betemit, Andruw Jones 40.00
PSW Jorge Posada, Alfonso Soriano, Bernie Williams 50.00
BDB A.J. Burnett, Ryan Dempster, Josh Beckett 40.00

Trademark Series

Common Player:

Turn Two Relic

NM/M
Inserted 1:4,401
TW Alan Trammell, Lou Whitaker 40.00
VA Omar Vizquel, Roberto Alomar 40.00

Yankee Stadium Seat Relics

NM/M
Inserted 1:579
HB Hank Bauer 100.00
YB Yogi Berra 250.00
JC Joe Collins 100.00
BM Billy Martin 250.00
GM Gil McDougald 100.00
JM Johnny Mize 100.00
AR Allie Reynolds 100.00
PR Phil Rizzuto 250.00
GW Gene Woodling 100.00

2 Bagger Relic

NM/M
Inserted 1:3,733
TG Tony Gwynn 30.00
TH Todd Helton 20.00
SR Scott Rolen 20.00

1952 Player Autographs

NM/M
Inserted 1:7,524
HBA Hank Bauer 75.00
YBA Yogi Berra 100.00
PRA Preacher Roe 70.00

1952 Reprint Autographs

NM/M
Common Autograph: 25.00
Inserted 1:10,268
JBA Joe Black 90.00
CEA Carl Erskine 50.00
GMA Gil McDougal 40.00
APA Andy Pafko 60.00
PRA Phil Rizzuto 80.00
DSA Duke Snider 100.00

1952 World Series Highlights

NM/M
Complete Set (7): 10.00
Common Player: 2.00
Inserted 1:25
52WS-1 Dodgers' Game 1 Starting Line Up 3.00
52WS-2 Dodgers Celebrate Game 3 Win! 2.00
52WS-3 Carl Erskine Wins Game 5 2.00
Series 2
52WS-2Game 2 2.00
52WS-4Game 4 2.00
52WS-6Game 6 2.00
52WS-7Game 7 2.00

1952 World Series Tribute

NM/M
Complete Set (19): 50.00
Common Player: 3.00
Inserted 1:25
1 Roy Campanella 4.00
2 Duke Snider 4.00
3 Carl Erskine 3.00
4 Andy Pafko 3.00
5 Johnny Mize 3.00
6 Billy Martin 4.00
7 Phil Rizzuto 4.00
8 Gil McDougal 3.00
9 Allie Reynolds 3.00
10 Jackie Robinson 4.00
Series 2
11 Preacher Roe 3.00
12 Gil Hodges 3.00
13 Billy Cox 3.00
14 Yogi Berra 4.00
15 Gene Woodling 3.00
16 Jerry Sain 3.00
17 Ralph Houk 3.00
18 Joe Collins 3.00
19 Hank Bauer 3.00

American Pie American Sluggers

NM/M
Complete Set (25): 25.00
Common Player: .50
Inserted 1:1
Each card issued in blue, gold, silver and red; no value differential.
AD Andre Dawson .50
AK Al Kaline 1.00
BR Brooks Robinson 1.00
CC Cecil Cooper .50
CF Carlton Fisk 1.00
CY Carl Yastrzemski 2.00
DS Duke Snider 1.00
DW Dave Winfield 1.00
EM Eddie Mathews 1.00
FH Frank Howard .50
FL Fred Lynn .50
FR Frank Robinson 1.00
GB George Brett 3.00
GF George Foster .50
HK Harmon Killebrew 1.00
JC Jack Clark .50
JCC Joe Carter .50
KG Kirk Gibson .50
MI Monte Irvin .50
MS Mike Schmidt 3.00
RC Rod Carew 1.00
RJ Reggie Jackson 2.50
RS Ryne Sandberg 2.00
TK Ted Kluszewski 1.00
WM Willie Mays 4.00

American Pie Spirit of America

NM/M
Complete Set (150): 30.00
Common Player: .25
Pack (7): 5.00
Box (24): 100.00
1 Warren Spahn .75
2 Reggie Jackson .75
3 Bill Mazeroski .25
4 Carl Yastrzemski .75
5 Whitey Ford .75
6 Ralph Houk .25
7 Rod Carew .50
8 Kirk Gibson .25
9 Bobby Thomson .25
10 Don Newcombe .25
11 Gaylord Perry .25
12 Bruce Sutter .40
13 Bob Gibson .50
14 Brooks Robinson 1.00
15 Steve Carlton .50
16 Robin Yount 1.00
17 Ernie Banks .75
18 Lou Brock .75
19 Al Kaline .75
20 Carlton Fisk .75
21 Frank Robinson .75
22 Bobby Bonds .25
23 Andre Dawson .25
24 Rich "Goose" Gossage .25
25 Fred Lynn .25
26 Keith Hernandez .25
27 Rollie Fingers .25
28 Juan Marichal .25
29 Maury Wills .25
30 Dave Winfield .25
31 Frank Howard .25
32 Tony Gwynn 1.00
33 Jim Palmer .50
34 Mike Schmidt 1.50
35 Bo Jackson .75
36 Ferguson Jenkins .25
37 Bobby Richardson .25
38 Harmon Killebrew .75
39 Monte Irvin .25
40 Jim Abbott .50
41 Wade Boggs .75
42 Jackie Robinson 2.00
43 Ralph Branca .25
44 Minnie Minoso .25
45 Tug McGraw .25
46 Willie Mays 2.00
47 Nolan Ryan 3.00
48 Duke Snider 1.00
49 Tom Seaver 1.00
50 Casey Stengel .50
51 D-Day .75
52 Gulf War .25
53 Vietnam War .25
54 Korean War .25
55 Secret Service .25
56 Crayons .25
57 Hoover Dam .25
58 Penicillin .25
59 Polio Vaccine .25
60 Empire State Building .25
61 Television .25
62 Free Speech .25
63 Voyager Mission .25
64 Space Shuttle .25
65 Ellis Island .25
66 Statue of Liberty .25
67 Battle of the Bulge .25
68 Battle of Midway .25
69 Iwo Jima .25
70 Panama Canal .25
71 Spirit of St. Louis/Lindbergh .25
72 Civil Rights/We Shall Overcome .25
73 Space Race .25
74 Alaska Pipeline .25
75 Teddy Bear .25
76 Sea Biscuit .25
77 Bazooka Joe .25
78 Mt. Rushmore .25
79 Yellowstone Park .25
80 Niagara Falls .25
81 Grand Canyon .25
82 Hoola Hoop .25
83 George Patton .50
84 Audie Murphy .25
85 Amelia Earhart .25
86 Glen Miller .25
87 Rick Monday .25
88 Buzz Aldrin .25
89 Rosa Parks .25
90 Edward R. Murrow .25
91 Susan B. Anthony .25
92 Bobby Kennedy .25
93 Gloria Steinem .25
94 Hank Greenberg .75
95 Jimmy Doolittle .25
96 Thurgood Marshall .25
97 Ernest Hemingway .75
98 Henry Ford .25
99 Wright Brothers .25
100 Thomas Edison .75
101 Albert Einstein .75
102 Will Rogers .25
103 George Gershwin .25
104 Irving Berlin .25
105 Frank Lloyd Wright .25
106 Howard Hughes .25
107 George M. Cohan .25
108 Jack Kerouac .25
109 Harry Houdini .25
110 Helen Keller .25
111 John McCain .25
112 Andrew Carnegie .25
113 Sandra Day O'Connor .25
114 Brooklyn Bridge .25
115 Douglas MacArthur .25
116 Elvis Presley 1.00
117 George Burns .25
118 Judy Garland .50
119 Buddy Holly .50
120 Don McLean .25
121 Marilyn Monroe 1.00
122 Humphrey Bogart .50
123 Gary Cooper .25
124 The Andrews Sisters .25
125 Jim Thorpe 1.00
126 Joe Louis .75
127 Jesse Owens .50
128 Kate Smith .25
129 W.C. Fields .25
130 Bette Davis .25
131 Jayne Mansfield .25
132 Teddy Roosevelt .50
133 Franklin D. Roosevelt .75
134 Harry Truman .25
135 Dwight Eisenhower .50
136 George H.W. Bush .50
137 George W. Bush .50
138 John F. Kennedy 1.00
139 Lyndon B. Johnson .25
140 William Taft .25
141 Horace Harding .25
142 Woodrow Wilson .25
143 Richard Nixon .25
144 Bill Clinton .25
145 Jimmy Carter .25
146 Herbert Hoover .25
147 Gerald Ford .25
148 Ronald Reagan .25
149 Calvin Coolidge .25
150 William McKinley .25

American Pie Through the Years Relics

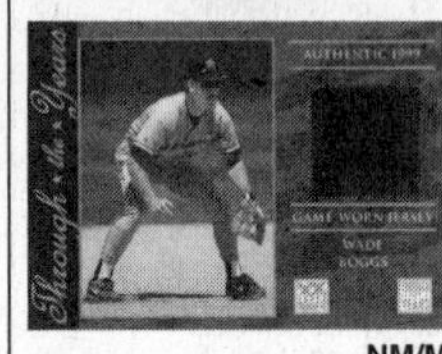

NM/M
Common Player: 8.00
Inserted 1:11
JA Jim Abbott 15.00
DA Dick Allen 8.00
JB Johnny Bench 20.00
WB Wade Boggs 10.00
BB Bill Buckner 8.00
JC Jack Clark 8.00
AD Andre Dawson 10.00
KT Jim Kaat 10.00
EM Eddie Mathews 15.00
DM Don Mattingly 40.00
WM Willie Mays 40.00
MM Minnie Minoso 15.00
RM Rick Monday 10.00
JM Joe Morgan 10.00
TM Thurman Munson 30.00
AL Al Oliver 8.00
DP Dave Parker 10.00
GP Gaylord Perry 10.00
FR Frank Robinson 15.00
JR Joe Rudi 10.00
NR Nolan Ryan 40.00
TS Tom Seaver 20.00
WS Willie Stargell 15.00
DS Darryl Strawberry 15.00
DW Dave Winfield 12.00
CY Carl Yastrzemski 20.00

2002 Topps Archives

NM/M
Complete Set (200): 70.00
Common Player: .40
Pack (8): 3.00
Box (20): 50.00
1 Willie Mays 3.00
2 Dale Murphy .40
3 Dave Winfield .75
4 Roger Maris 2.00
5 Ron Cey .40
6 Lee Smith .40
7 Len Dykstra .40
8 Ray Fosse .40
9 Warren Spahn 1.00
10 Herb Score .40
11 Jim Wynn .40
12 Sam McDowell .40
13 Fred Lynn .40
14 Yogi Berra 1.50
15 Ron Santo .40
16 Alvin Dark .40
17 Bill Buckner .40
18 Rollie Fingers .60
19 Tony Gwynn 1.50
20 Red Schoendienst .40
21 Gaylord Perry .40
22 Jose Cruz .40
23 Dennis Martinez .40
24 Dave McNally .40
25 Norm Cash .40
26 Ted Kluszewski .40
27 Rick Reuschel .40
28 Bruce Sutter .75
29 Don Larsen .40
30 Claudell Washington .40
31 Luis Aparicio .40
32 Clete Boyer .40
33 Rich "Goose" Gossage .40
34 Ray Knight .40
35 Roy Campanella 1.50
36 Tug McGraw .40
37 Bob Lemon .40
38 Willie Stargell 1.00
39 Roberto Clemente 3.00
40 Jim Fregosi .40
41 Reggie Smith .40
42 Dave Parker .40
43 Darrell Evans .40
44 Ryne Sandberg 2.00
45 Manny Mota .40
46 Dennis Eckersley .60
47 Nellie Fox .40
48 Gil Hodges .40
49 Reggie Jackson 1.50
50 Bobby Shantz .40
51 Cecil Cooper .40
52 Jim Kaat .40
53 George Hendrick .40
54 Johnny Podres .40
55 Bob Gibson 1.00
56 Vern Law .40
57 Joe Adcock .40
58 Jack Clark .40
59 Bill Mazeroski .40
60 Carl Yastrzemski 1.50
61 Bobby Murcer .40
62 Davey Johnson .40
63 Jim Palmer .75
64 Roy Face .40
65 Dean Chance .40
66 Bill "Moose" Skowron .40
67 Dwight Evans .40
68 Kirk Gibson .40
69 Sal Bando .40
70 Mike Schmidt 2.00
71 Bo Jackson .75
72 Chris Chambliss .40
73 Fergie Jenkins .75
74 Brooks Robinson 1.50
75 Bobby Richardson .40
76 Duke Snider 1.50
77 Allie Reynolds .40
78 Harmon Killebrew 1.50
79 Steve Carlton 1.00
80 Bert Blyleven .40
81 Phil Niekro .40
82 Lew Burdette .40
83 Hoyt Wilhelm .40
84 Curt Flood .40
85 Guillermo Hernandez .40
86 Robin Yount 1.50
87 Robin Roberts .40
88 Whitey Ford 1.00
89 Tony Oliva .75
90 Don Newcombe .40
91 Al Oliver .40
92 Mike Cuellar .40
93 Mike Scott .40
94 Dick Allen .40
95 Jimmy Piersall .40
96 Bill Freehan .40
97 Willie Horton .40
98 Bob Friend .40
99 Ken Holtzman .40
100 Rico Carty .40
101 Gil McDougald .40
102 Lee May .40
103 Joe Pepitone .40
104 Gene Tenace .40
105 Gary Carter .40
106 Tim McCarver .40
107 Ernie Banks 1.50
108 George Foster .40
109 Lou Brock 1.00
110 Dick Groat .40
111 Graig Nettles .40
112 Boog Powell .40
113 Joe Carter .40
114 Juan Marichal .75
115 Larry Doby .40
116 Fernando Valenzuela .40
117 Luis Tiant .40
118 Early Wynn .40
119 Bill Madlock .40
120 Eddie Mathews 1.50
121 George Brett 3.00
122 Al Kaline 1.50
123 Frank Howard .40
124 Mickey Lolich .40
125 Kirby Puckett 3.00
126 Bob Cerv .40
127 Will Clark 1.00
128 Vida Blue .40
129 Kevin Mitchell .40
130 Bucky Dent .40
131 Tom Seaver 2.00
132 Jerry Koosman .40
133 Orlando Cepeda .40
134 Nolan Ryan 4.00
135 Tony Kubek .40
136 Don Drysdale 1.00
137 Paul Blair .40
138 Elston Howard .40
139 Joe Rudi .40
140 Tommie Agee .40
141 Richie Ashburn .40
142 Jim Bunning .40
143 Hank Sauer .40
144 Greg Luzinski .40
145 Ron Guidry .40
146 Rod Carew 1.00
147 Andre Dawson .75
148 Keith Hernandez .40
149 Carlton Fisk 1.00
150 Cleon Jones .40
151 Don Mattingly 3.00
152 Vada Pinson .40
153 Ozzie Smith 1.50
154 Dave Concepcion .40
155 Al Rosen .40
156 Tommy John .40
157 Bob Ojeda .40
158 Frank Robinson 1.50
159 Darryl Strawberry .40
160 Bobby Bonds .40
161 Bert Campaneris .40
162 Jim "Catfish" Hunter .40
163 Bud Harrelson .40

164 Dwight Gooden .40
165 Wade Boggs 1.00
166 Joe Morgan 1.00
167 Ron Swoboda .40
168 Hank Aaron 4.00
169 Steve Garvey .40
170 Mickey Rivers .40
171 Johnny Bench 3.00
172 Ralph Terry .40
173 Billy Pierce .40
174 Thurman Munson 2.50
175 Don Sutton .40
176 Sparky Anderson .40
177 Gil Hodges .40
178 Davey Johnson .40
179 Frank Robinson 1.50
180 Red Schoendienst .40
181 Roger Maris 2.00
182 Willie Mays 3.00
183 Luis Aparicio .40
184 Nellie Fox .40
185 Ernie Banks 1.50
186 Orlando Cepeda .75
187 Whitey Ford 1.00
188 Bob Gibson 1.00
189 Bill Mazeroski .40
190 Hank Aaron 3.00
191 League Leaders (Elston Howard, Harmon Killebrew, Carl Yastrzemski) .75
192 League Leaders (Orlando Cepeda, Jackie Robinson, Willie Mays) 2.00
193 League Leaders (Hank Aaron, Roberto Clemente, Dick Allen) 2.00
194 League Leaders (Tom Seaver, Phil Niekro, Fergie Jenkins, Juan Marichal) 1.00
195 League Leaders (Jim Palmer, Jim Hunter, Dennis Eckersley) .65
196 Hank Aaron 3.00
197 Brooks Robinson 1.50
198 Tom Seaver 1.50
199 Jim Palmer .75
200 Lou Brock 1.00

Autographs

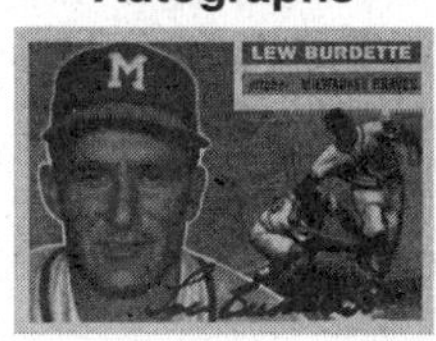

NM/M
Common Autograph: 10.00
Inserted 1:22
HA Hank Aaron 250.00
DA Dick Allen 25.00
SB Sal Bando 20.00
EB Ernie Banks 125.00
BB Bobby Bonds 25.00
GB George Brett 250.00
JBU Jim Bunning 40.00
LB Lew Burdette 20.00
BC Bert Campaneris 10.00
GC Gary Carter 50.00
RCE Ron Cey 15.00
CC Chris Chambliss 15.00
JCR Jose Cruz 15.00
AD Alvin Dark 25.00
BD Bucky Dent 20.00
LD Len Dykstra 20.00
DEV Darrell Evans 15.00
GF George Foster 15.00
JF Jim Fregosi 10.00
SG Steve Garvey 15.00
DG Dwight Gooden 25.00
DGR Dick Groat 15.00
BH Bud Harrelson 15.00
WH Willie Hernandez 10.00
KH Keith Hernandez 40.00
BJ Bo Jackson 80.00
FJ Fergie Jenkins 20.00
TJ Tommy John 15.00
JK Jim Kaat 20.00
AK Al Kaline 125.00
HK Harmon Killebrew 110.00
JKO Jerry Koosman 65.00
GL Greg Luzinski 20.00
FL Fred Lynn 20.00
DM Dave McNally 20.00
KM Kevin Mitchell 20.00
DN Don Newcombe 15.00
TO Tony Oliva 30.00
JP Jim Palmer 50.00
DP Dave Parker 20.00
GP Gaylord Perry 20.00
BP Billy Pierce 10.00
JPI Jimmy Piersall 15.00
JPO Johnny Podres 15.00
BPO Boog Powell 25.00
KP Kirby Puckett 150.00
MR Mickey Rivers 10.00
BRO Brooks Robinson 80.00
JR Joe Rudi 15.00
RS Ron Santo 30.00
MS Mike Schmidt 150.00

LS Lee Smith 20.00
RSM Reggie Smith 15.00
BS Bruce Sutter 35.00
RT Ralph Terry 25.00
HW Hoyt Wilhelm 20.00
DW Dave Winfield 85.00
RY Robin Yount 100.00

AutoProofs

NM/M
Quantity produced listed
1 Gary Carter/80 40.00
2 Jose Cruz/95 25.00
4 Bo Jackson/300 50.00
5 Kevin Mitchell/65 25.00
6 Kirby Puckett/65 75.00
7 Mike Schmidt/147 90.00
8 Ozzie Smith/105 75.00
9 Darryl Strawberry/181 40.00
11 Robin Yount/39 100.00

Game-Used Bat

NM/M
Common Player:
Group A 1:106
Group B 1:282
JB Johnny Bench 20.00
GB George Brett 40.00
GC Gary Carter 10.00
JC Joe Carter 10.00
NC Norm Cash 10.00
AD Andre Dawson 8.00
DE Dwight Evans 8.00
BF Bill Freehan 8.00
WH Willie Horton 10.00
RJ Reggie Jackson 15.00
DM Don Mattingly 50.00
RM Roger Maris 50.00
JM Joe Morgan 10.00
DP Dave Parker 10.00
BR Brooks Robinson 20.00
RS Ron Santo 20.00
WS Willie Stargell 15.00
CY Carl Yastrzemski 40.00
RY Robin Yount 20.00

Game-Worn Uniform

NM/M
Common Player: 8.00
Inserted 1:28
SA Sparky Anderson 10.00
WB Wade Boggs 15.00
BB Bobby Bonds 8.00
GB George Brett 30.00
OC Orlando Cepeda 10.00
WC Will Clark 20.00
DC Dave Concepcion 8.00
DE Dennis Eckersley 10.00
SG Steve Garvey 10.00
FL Fred Lynn 8.00
DM Dale Murphy 20.00
PN Phil Niekro 10.00
GP Gaylord Perry 10.00
KP Kirby Puckett 20.00
FR Frank Robinson 15.00
NR Nolan Ryan 40.00
RS Ryne Sandberg 30.00
OS Ozzie Smith 20.00
DS Don Sutton 10.00
DW Dave Winfield 10.00

Stadium Seat

NM/M
Common Player: 8.00
RA Richie Ashburn 15.00
SA Sparky Anderson 10.00
EB Ernie Banks 25.00
YB Yogi Berra 20.00
JB Jim Bunning 10.00
RC Rod Carew 20.00
JC Joe Carter 10.00
NF Nellie Fox 15.00
RG Ron Guidry 10.00
TK Ted Kluszewski 15.00
BL Bob Lemon 10.00
ML Mickey Lolich 10.00
EM Eddie Mathews 20.00
SM Sam McDowell 8.00
JP Jim Palmer 10.00
DP Dave Parker 10.00
HS Herb Score 10.00
DS Duke Snider 20.00
WS Warren Spahn 15.00

2002 Topps Archives Reserve

NM/M
Complete Set (100): 100.00
Common Player: .75
Box (10 Packs + Auto. Baseball): 125.00

1 Lee Smith .75
2 Gaylord Perry .75
3 Al Oliver .75
4 Rich "Goose" Gossage .75
5 Bill Madlock .75
6 Rod Carew 1.50
7 Fred Lynn .75
8 Frank Robinson 2.00
9 Al Kaline 2.50
10 Len Dykstra .75
11 Carlton Fisk 1.50
12 Nellie Fox 1.00
13 Reggie Jackson 3.00
14 Bob Gibson 2.00
15 Bill Buckner .75
16 Harmon Killebrew 2.00
17 Gary Carter 1.50
18 Dave Winfield 1.50
19 Ozzie Smith 2.50
20 Dwight Evans .75
21 Dave Concepcion .75
22 Joe Morgan 1.00
23 Clete Boyer .75
24 Will Clark 1.50
25 Lee May .75
26 Kevin Mitchell .75
27 Roger Maris 3.00
28 Mickey Lolich .75
29 Luis Aparicio .75
30 George Foster .75
31 Don Mattingly 6.00
32 Fernando Valenzuela .75
33 Bobby Bonds .75
34 Jim Palmer 1.50
35 Dennis Eckersley 1.00
36 Kirby Puckett 3.00
37 Jose Cruz .75
38 Richie Ashburn .75
39 Whitey Ford 2.00
40 Robin Roberts .75
41 Don Newcombe .75
42 Roy Campanella 2.50
43 Dennis Martinez .75
44 Larry Doby 1.00
45 Steve Garvey .75
46 Thurman Munson 3.00
47 Dale Murphy 1.50
48 Bill "Moose" Skowron .75
49 Tom Seaver 3.00
50 Orlando Cepeda .75
51 Graig Nettles .75
52 Willie Stargell 1.50
53 Yogi Berra 2.50
54 Steve Carlton 1.50
55 Don Sutton .75
56 Brooks Robinson 1.50
57 Vida Blue .75
58 Rollie Fingers 1.00
59 Jim Bunning .75
60 Nolan Ryan 8.00
61 Hank Aaron 6.00
62 Fergie Jenkins .75
63 Andre Dawson 1.00
64 Ernie Banks 2.50
65 Early Wynn .75
66 Duke Snider 1.50
67 Red Schoendienst .75
68 Don Drysdale 1.00
69 Jim "Catfish" Hunter 1.00
70 George Brett 6.00
71 Elston Howard 1.00
72 Wade Boggs 1.50
73 Keith Hernandez .75
74 Billy Pierce .75
75 Ted Kluszewski .75
76 Carl Yastrzemski 4.00
77 Bert Blyleven .75
78 Tony Oliva .75
79 Joe Carter .75
80 Johnny Bench 3.00
81 Tony Gwynn 3.00
82 Mike Schmidt 4.00
83 Phil Niekro .75
84 Juan Marichal .75
85 Eddie Mathews 2.50
86 Boog Powell .75
87 Dwight Gooden .75
88 Darryl Strawberry .75
89 Roberto Clemente 6.00
90 Ryne Sandberg 5.00
91 Jack Clark .75
92 Willie Mays 6.00
93 Ron Guidry .75
94 Kirk Gibson .75
95 Lou Brock 1.00
96 Robin Yount 2.50
97 Bill Mazeroski .75
98 Dave Parker .75
99 Hoyt Wilhelm .75
100 Warren Spahn 1.50

Autographed Baseballs

NM/M
Common Auto. Ball: 15.00
Inserted 1:Box
Luis Aparicio/1,600 25.00
Ernie Banks/50 75.00
Yogi Berra/100 85.00
Lou Brock/400 40.00
Jim Bunning/500 35.00
Gary Carter/500 40.00
Rich Gossage/500 20.00
Fergie Jenkins/1,000 20.00
Al Kaline/250 75.00
Harmon Killebrew/250 60.00
Joe Morgan/250 40.00
Graig Nettles/1,600 15.00
Jim Palmer/400 25.00
Gaylord Perry/500 15.00
Brooks Robinson/500 40.00
Mike Schmidt/250 125.00
Duke Snider/100 65.00
Dave Winfield/1650 30.00
Robin Yount/250 90.00

Best Years Autographs

NM/M
Common Autograph: 12.00
Inserted 1:15 Hobby
LA Luis Aparicio 15.00
EB Ernie Banks 70.00
YB Yogi Berra 60.00
LB Lou Brock 25.00
GC Gary Carter 20.00
FJ Fergie Jenkins 12.00
AK Al Kaline 40.00
HK Harmon Killebrew 40.00
WM Willie Mays 120.00
JM Joe Morgan 25.00
GN Graig Nettles 12.00
GP Gaylord Perry 15.00
BR Brooks Robinson 25.00
MS Mike Schmidt 125.00
LS Lee Smith 12.00
DS Duke Snider 60.00
RY Robin Yount 80.00

Best Years Game-Used Bat

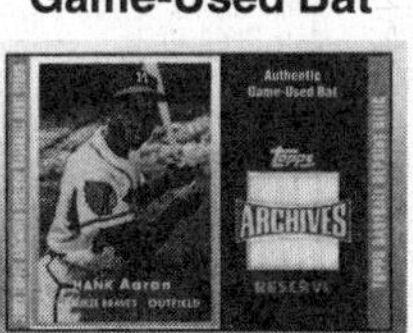

NM/M
Common Player: 10.00
Inserted 1:22
HAB Hank Aaron 40.00
GBB George Brett 25.00
OC Orlando Cepeda 10.00
CF Carlton Fisk 10.00
RM Roger Maris 70.00
EMB Eddie Mathews 20.00
DMB Don Mattingly 30.00
TM Thurman Munson 30.00
DW Dave Winfield 10.00
CYB Carl Yastrzemski 25.00

Best Years Game-Worn Uniforms

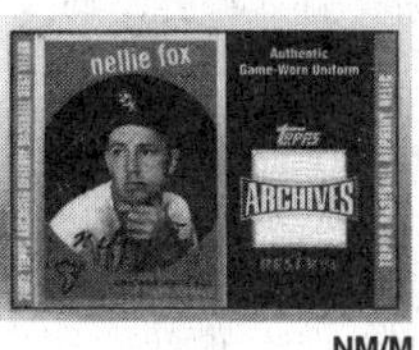

NM/M
Common Player: 10.00
Inserted 1:7 Hobby
EB Ernie Banks 25.00
JBU Johnny Bench 15.00
WBJ Wade Boggs 10.00
GCJ Gary Carter 12.00
WC Will Clark 15.00
NF Nellie Fox 15.00
TG Tony Gwynn 15.00
JM Juan Marichal 12.00
WM Willie Mays 35.00
KPJ Kirby Puckett 15.00
BR Brooks Robinson 12.00
NR Nolan Ryan 30.00
RSJ Red Schoendienst 10.00
WS Willie Stargell 15.00
RYU Robin Yount 12.00

Team Topps Legends Autographs

NM/M
Common Player:
Rich "Goose" Gossage 10.00
Graig Nettles 10.00
Jim Palmer 15.00
Gaylord Perry 15.00

2002 Topps Chrome

NM/M
Complete Set (685): 200.00
Common Player: .25
Pack (4): 2.00
Box (24): 40.00
1 Pedro Martinez 1.25
2 Mike Stanton .25
3 Brad Penny .25
4 Mike Matheny .25
5 Johnny Damon .40
6 Bret Boone .40
7 Retired # not issued
8 Chris Truby .25
9 B.J. Surhoff .25
10 Mike Hampton .40
11 Juan Pierre .25
12 Mark Buehrle .25
13 Bob Abreu .50
14 David Cone .25
15 Aaron Sele .25
16 Fernando Tatis .25
17 Bobby Jones .25
18 Rick Helling .25
19 Dmitri Young .25
20 Mike Mussina 1.00
21 Mike Sweeney .25
22 Cristian Guzman .25
23 Ryan Kohlmeier .25
24 Adam Kennedy .25
25 Larry Walker .50
26 Eric Davis .40
27 Jason Tyner .25
28 Eric Young .25
29 Jason Marquis .25
30 Luis Gonzalez .50
31 Kevin Tapani .25
32 Orlando Cabrera .25
33 Marty Cordova .25
34 Brad Ausmus .25
35 Livan Hernandez .25
36 Alex Gonzalez .25
37 Edgar Renteria .50
38 Bengie Molina .25
39 Frank Menechino .25
40 Rafael Palmeiro 1.00
41 Brad Fullmer .25
42 Julio Zuleta .25
43 Darren Dreifort .25
44 Trot Nixon .50
45 Trevor Hoffman .25
46 Vladimir Nunez .25
47 Mark Kotsay .25
48 Kenny Rogers .25
49 Ben Petrick .25
50 Jeff Bagwell 1.00
51 Juan Encarnacion .25
52 Ramiro Mendoza .25
53 Brian Meadows .25
54 Chad Curtis .25
55 Aramis Ramirez .50
56 Mark McLemore .25
57 Dante Bichette .25
58 Scott Schoeneweis .25
59 Jose Cruz .25
60 Roger Clemens 3.00
61 Jose Guillen .25
62 Darren Oliver .25
63 Chris Reitsma .25
64 Jeff Abbott .25
65 Robin Ventura .25
66 Denny Neagle .25
67 Al Martin .25
68 Benito Santiago .25
69 Roy Oswalt .50
70 Juan Gonzalez 1.00
71 Garret Anderson .75
72 Bobby Bonilla .25
73 Danny Bautista .25
74 J.T. Snow .25
75 Derek Jeter 4.00
76 John Olerud .50
77 Kevin Appier .25
78 Phil Nevin .25
79 Sean Casey .50
80 Troy Glaus .75
81 Joe Randa .25
82 Jose Valentin .25
83 Ricky Bottalico .25
84 Todd Zeile .25
85 Barry Larkin .75
86 Bob Wickman .25
87 Jeff Shaw .25
88 Greg Vaughn .25
89 Fernando Vina .25
90 Mark Mulder .50
91 Paul Bako .25
92 Aaron Boone .25
93 Esteban Loaiza .25
94 Richie Sexson .75
95 Alfonso Soriano 1.00
96 Tony Womack .25
97 Paul Shuey .25
98 Melvin Mora .25
99 Tony Gwynn 1.50
100 Vladimir Guerrero 1.50
101 Keith Osik .25
102 Randy Velarde .25
103 Scott Williamson .25
104 Daryle Ward .25
105 Doug Mientkiewicz .25
106 Stan Javier .25
107 Russ Ortiz .25
108 Wade Miller .25
109 Luke Prokopec .25
110 Andruw Jones 1.00
111 Ron Coomer .25
112 Dan Wilson .25
113 Luis Castillo .25
114 Derek Bell .25
115 Gary Sheffield .75
116 Ruben Rivera .25
117 Paul O'Neill .50
118 Craig Paquette .25
119 Kelvim Escobar .25
120 Brad Radke .25
121 Jorge Fabregas .25
122 Randy Winn .25
123 Tom Goodwin .25
124 Jaret Wright .25
125 Bonds-Race to 73 40.00
126 Al Leiter .50
127 Ben Davis .25
128 Frank Catalanotto .25
129 Jose Cabrera .25
130 Magglio Ordonez .50
131 Jose Macias .25
132 Ted Lilly .25
133 Chris Holt .25
134 Eric Milton .25
135 Shannon Stewart .25
136 Omar Olivares .25
137 David Segui .25
138 Jeff Nelson .25
139 Matt Williams .25
140 Ellis Burks .25
141 Jason Bere .25
142 Jimmy Haynes .25
143 Ramon Hernandez .25

No.	Player	Price
144	Craig Counsell	.25
145	John Smoltz	.50
146	Homer Bush	.25
147	Quilvio Veras	.25
148	Esteban Yan	.25
149	Ramon Ortiz	.25
150	Carlos Delgado	.75
151	Lee Stevens	.25
152	Wil Cordero	.25
153	Mike Bordick	.25
154	John Flaherty	.25
155	Omar Daal	.25
156	Todd Ritchie	.25
157	Carl Everett	.25
158	Scott Sullivan	.25
159	Deivi Cruz	.25
160	Albert Pujols	3.00
161	Royce Clayton	.25
162	Jeff Suppan	.25
163	C.C. Sabathia	.25
164	Jimmy Rollins	.50
165	Rickey Henderson	.50
166	Rey Ordonez	.25
167	Shawn Estes	.25
168	Reggie Sanders	.25
169	Jon Lieber	.25
170	Armando Benitez	.25
171	Mike Remlinger	.25
172	Billy Wagner	.25
173	Troy Percival	.25
174	Devon White	.25
175	Ivan Rodriguez	1.00
176	Dustin Hermanson	.25
177	Brian Anderson	.25
178	Graeme Lloyd	.25
179	Russell Branyan	.25
180	Bobby Higginson	.25
181	Alex Gonzalez	.25
182	John Franco	.25
183	Sidney Ponson	.25
184	Jose Mesa	.25
185	Todd Hollandsworth	.25
186	Kevin Young	.25
187	Tim Wakefield	.25
188	Craig Biggio	.50
189	Jason Isringhausen	.25
190	Mark Quinn	.25
191	Glendon Rusch	.25
192	Damian Miller	.25
193	Sandy Alomar	.25
194	Scott Brosius	.25
195	Dave Martinez	.25
196	Danny Graves	.25
197	Shea Hillenbrand	.25
198	Jimmy Anderson	.25
199	Travis Lee	.25
200	Randy Johnson	1.50
201	Carlos Beltran	.50
202	Jerry Hairston Jr.	.25
203	Jesus Sanchez	.25
204	Eddie Taubensee	.25
205	David Wells	.25
206	Russ Davis	.25
207	Michael Barrett	.25
208	Marquis Grissom	.25
209	Byung-Hyun Kim	.25
210	Hideo Nomo	.75
211	Ryan Rupe	.25
212	Ricky Gutierrez	.25
213	Darryl Kile	.25
214	Rico Brogna	.25
215	Terrence Long	.25
216	Mike Jackson	.25
217	Jamey Wright	.25
218	Adrian Beltre	.50
219	Benny Agbayani	.25
220	Chuck Knoblauch	.25
221	Randy Wolf	.25
222	Andy Ashby	.25
223	Corey Koskie	.25
224	Roger Cedeno	.25
225	Ichiro Suzuki	3.00
226	Keith Foulke	.25
227	Ryan Minor	.25
228	Shawon Dunston	.25
229	Alex Cora	.25
230	Jeromy Burnitz	.25
231	Mark Grace	.75
232	Aubrey Huff	.25
233	Jeffrey Hammonds	.25
234	Olmedo Saenz	.25
235	Brian Jordan	.25
236	Jeremy Giambi	.25
237	Joe Girardi	.25
238	Eric Gagne	.50
239	Masato Yoshii	.25
240	Greg Maddux	2.00
241	Bryan Rekar	.25
242	Ray Durham	.25
243	Torii Hunter	.50
244	Derrek Lee	.50
245	Jim Edmonds	.75
246	Einar Diaz	.25
247	Brian Bohanon	.25
248	Ron Belliard	.25
249	Mike Lowell	.50
250	Sammy Sosa	2.50
251	Richard Hidalgo	.40
252	Bartolo Colon	.25
253	Jorge Posada	.50
254	LaTroy Hawkins	.25
255	Paul LoDuca	.25
256	Carlos Febles	.25
257	Nelson Cruz	.25
258	Edgardo Alfonzo	.25
259	Joey Hamilton	.25
260	Cliff Floyd	.25
261	Wes Helms	.25
262	Jay Bell	.25
263	Mike Cameron	.25
264	Paul Konerko	.25
265	Jeff Kent	.50
266	Robert Fick	.25
267	Allen Levrault	.25
268	Placido Polanco	.25
269	Marlon Anderson	.25
270	Mariano Rivera	.50
271	Chan Ho Park	.25
272	Jose Vizcaino	.25
273	Jeff D'Amico	.25
274	Mark Gardner	.25
275	Travis Fryman	.25
276	Darren Lewis	.25
277	Bruce Bochy	.25
278	Jerry Manuel	.25
279	Bob Brenly	.25
280	Don Baylor	.25
281	Davey Lopes	.25
282	Jerry Narron	.25
283	Tony Muser	.25
284	Hal McRae	.25
285	Bobby Cox	.25
286	Larry Dierker	.25
287	Phil Garner	.25
288	Jimy Williams	.25
289	Bobby Valentine	.25
290	Dusty Baker	.25
291	Lloyd McLendon	.25
292	Mike Scioscia	.25
293	Buck Martinez	.25
294	Larry Bowa	.25
295	Tony LaRussa	.25
296	Jeff Torborg	.25
297	Tom Kelly	.25
298	Mike Hargrove	.25
299	Art Howe	.25
300	Lou Piniella	.25
301	Charlie Manuel	.25
302	Buddy Bell	.25
303	Tony Perez	.25
304	Bob Boone	.25
305	Joe Torre	.25
306	Jim Tracy	.25
307	Jason Lane	1.00
308	Chris George	.25
309	Hank Blalock	2.00
310	Joe Borchard	.25
311	Marlon Byrd	.50
312	Raymond Cabrera **RC**	1.00
313	Freddy Sanchez **RC**	4.00
314	Scott Wiggins **RC**	1.00
315	Jason Maule **RC**	1.00
316	Dionys Cesar **RC**	1.50
317	Boof Bonser	.25
318	Juan Tolentino **RC**	1.50
319	Earl Snyder **RC**	1.50
320	Travis Wade **RC**	1.50
321	Napoleon Calzado **RC**	1.50
322	Eric Glaser **RC**	1.50
323	Craig Kuzmic **RC**	1.50
324	Nic Jackson **RC**	1.50
325	Mike Rivera	.25
326	Jason Bay **RC**	8.00
327	Chris Smith	.25
328	Jake Gautreau	.25
329	Gabe Gross	.25
330	Kenny Baugh	.25
331	J.D. Martin	.25
366	Pat Meares	.25
367	Mike Lieberthal	.25
368	Scott Erickson	.25
369	Ron Gant	.25
370	Moises Alou	.50
371	Chad Kreuter	.25
372	Willis Roberts	.25
373	Toby Hall	.25
374	Miguel Batista	.25
375	John Burkett	.25
376	Cory Lidle	.25
377	Nick Neugebauer	.25
378	Jay Payton	.25
379	Steve Karsay	.25
380	Eric Chavez	.50
381	Kelly Stinnett	.25
382	Jarrod Washburn	.25
383	C.J. Nitkowski	.25
384	Jeff Conine	.25
385	Fred McGriff	.50
386	Marvin Benard	.25
387	Dave Burba	.25
388	Dennis Cook	.25
389	Rick Reed	.25
390	Tom Glavine	.75
391	Rondell White	.25
392	Matt Morris	.50
393	Pat Rapp	.25
394	Robert Person	.25
395	Omar Vizquel	.40
396	Jeff Cirillo	.25
397	Dave Mlicki	.25
398	Jose Ortiz	.25
399	Ryan Dempster	.25
400	Curt Schilling	.75
401	Peter Bergeron	.25
402	Kyle Lohse	.25
403	Craig Wilson	.25
404	David Justice	.75
405	Darin Erstad	.50
406	Jose Mercedes	.25
407	Carl Pavano	.25
408	Albie Lopez	.25
409	Alex Ochoa	.25
410	Chipper Jones	1.50
411	Tyler Houston	.25
412	Dean Palmer	.25
413	Damian Jackson	.25
414	Josh Towers	.25
415	Rafael Furcal	.50
416	Mike Morgan	.25
417	Herb Perry	.25
418	Mike Sirotka	.25
419	Mark Wohlers	.25
420	Nomar Garciaparra	2.50
421	Felipe Lopez	.25
422	Joe McEwing	.25
423	Jacque Jones	.25
424	Julio Franco	.25
425	Frank Thomas	1.00
426	Kent Bottenfield	.25
427	Mac Suzuki	.25
428	D'Angelo Jimenez	.25
429	Chris Stynes	.25
430	Kerry Wood	1.50
431	Chris Singleton	.25
432	Erubiel Durazo	.25
433	Matt Lawton	.25
434	Bill Mueller	.25
435	Jose Canseco	.50
436	Ben Grieve	.25
437	Terry Mulholland	.25
438	David Bell	.25
439	A.J. Pierzynski	.25
440	Adam Dunn	1.00
441	Jon Garland	.25
442	Jeff Fassero	.25
443	Julio Lugo	.25
444	Carlos Guillen	.25
445	Orlando Hernandez	.25
446	Mark Loretta	.25
447	Scott Spiezio	.25
448	Kevin Millwood	.50
449	Jamie Moyer	.25
450	Todd Helton	1.00
451	Todd Walker	.25
452	Jose Lima	.25
453	Brook Fordyce	.25
454	Aaron Rowand	.25
455	Barry Zito	.50
456	Eric Owens	.25
457	Charles Nagy	.25
458	Raul Ibanez	.25
459	Joe Mays	.25
460	Jim Thome	1.50
461	Adam Eaton	.25
462	Felix Martinez	.25
463	Vernon Wells	.25
464	Donnie Sadler	.25
465	Tony Clark	.25
466	Jose Hernandez	.25
467	Ramon Martinez	.25
468	Rusty Greer	.25
469	Rod Barajas	.25
470	Lance Berkman	.75
471	Brady Anderson	.25
472	Pedro Astacio	.25
473	Shane Halter	.25
474	Bret Prinz	.25
475	Edgar Martinez	.50
476	Steve Trachsel	.25
477	Gary Matthews Jr.	.25
478	Ismael Valdes	.25
479	Juan Uribe	.25
480	Shawn Green	.75
481	Kirk Rueter	.25
482	Damion Easley	.25
483	Chris Carpenter	.25
484	Kris Benson	.25
485	Antonio Alfonseca	.25
486	Kyle Farnsworth	.25
487	Brandon Lyon	.25
488	Hideki Irabu	.25
489	David Ortiz	.50
490	Mike Piazza	2.50
491	Derek Lowe	.25
492	Chris Gomez	.25
493	Mark Johnson	.25
494	John Rocker	.25
495	Eric Karros	.25
496	Bill Haselman	.25
497	Dave Veres	.25
498	Gil Heredia	.25
499	Tomokazu Ohka	.25
500	Barry Bonds	4.00
501	David Dellucci	.25
502	Ed Sprague	.25
503	Tom Gordon	.25
504	Javier Vazquez	.25
505	Ben Sheets	.75
506	Wilton Guerrero	.25
507	John Halama	.25
508	Mark Redman	.25
509	Jack Wilson	.25
510	Bernie Williams	.75
511	Miguel Cairo	.25
512	Denny Hocking	.25
513	Tony Batista	.25
514	Mark Grudzielanek	.25
515	Jose Vidro	.25
516	Sterling Hitchcock	.25
517	Billy Koch	.25
518	Matt Clement	.25
519	Bruce Chen	.25
520	Roberto Alomar	1.00
521	Orlando Palmeiro	.25
522	Steve Finley	.25
523	Danny Patterson	.25
524	Terry Adams	.25
525	Tino Martinez	.25
526	Tony Armas Jr.	.25
527	Geoff Jenkins	.50
528	Chris Michalak	.25
529	Corey Patterson	.50
530	Brian Giles	.50
531	Jose Jimenez	.25
532	Joe Kennedy	.25
533	Armando Rios	.25
534	Osvaldo Fernandez	.25
535	Ruben Sierra	.25
536	Octavio Dotel	.25
537	Luis Sojo	.25
538	Brent Butler	.25
539	Pablo Ozuna	.25
540	Freddy Garcia	.25
541	Chad Durbin	.25
542	Orlando Merced	.25
543	Michael Tucker	.25
544	Roberto Hernandez	.25
545	Pat Burrell	.50
546	A.J. Burnett	.25
547	Bubba Trammell	.25
548	Scott Elarton	.25
549	Mike Darr	.25
550	Ken Griffey Jr.	2.00
551	Ugueth Urbina	.25
552	Todd Jones	.25
553	Delino DeShields	.25
554	Adam Piatt	.25
555	Jason Kendall	.25
556	Hector Ortiz	.25
557	Turk Wendell	.25
558	Rob Bell	.25
559	Sun-Woo Kim	.25
560	Raul Mondesi	.50
561	Brent Abernathy	.25
562	Seth Etherton	.25
563	Shawn Wooten	.25
564	Jay Buhner	.25
565	Andres Galarraga	.50
566	Shane Reynolds	.25
567	Rod Beck	.25
568	Dee Brown	.25
569	Pedro Feliz	.25
570	Ryan Klesko	.25
571	John Vander Wal	.25
572	Nick Bierbrodt	.25
573	Joe Nathan	.25
574	James Baldwin	.25
575	J.D. Drew	.75
576	Greg Colbrunn	.25
577	Doug Glanville	.25
578	Rey Sanchez	.25
579	Todd Van Poppel	.25
580	Rich Aurilia	.25
581	Chuck Finley	.25
582	Abraham Nunez	.25
583	Kenny Lofton	.50
584	Brian Daubach	.25
585	Miguel Tejada	.75
586	Nate Cornejo	.25
587	Kazuhiro Sasaki	.50
588	Chris Richard	.25
589	Armando Reynoso	.25
590	Tim Hudson	.75
591	Neifi Perez	.25
592	Steve Cox	.25
593	Henry Blanco	.25
594	Ricky Ledee	.25
595	Tim Salmon	.50
596	Luis Rivas	.25
597	Jeff Zimmerman	.25
598	Matt Stairs	.25
599	Preston Wilson	.25
600	Mark McGwire	4.00
601	Timo Perez	.25
602	Matt Anderson	.25
603	Todd Hundley	.25
604	Rick Ankiel	.25
605	Tsuyoshi Shinjo	.25
606	Woody Williams	.25
607	Jason LaRue	.25
608	Carlos Lee	.25
609	Russ Johnson	.25
610	Scott Rolen	1.50
611	Brent Mayne	.25
612	Darrin Fletcher	.25
613	Ray Lankford	.25
614	Troy O'Leary	.25
615	Javier Lopez	.50
616	Randy Velarde	.25
617	Vinny Castilla	.25
618	Milton Bradley	.25
619	Ruben Mateo	.25
620	Jason Giambi	1.00
621	Andy Benes	.25
622	Joe Mauer **RC**	12.00
623	Andy Pettitte	.75
624	Jose Offerman	.25
625	Mo Vaughn	.50
626	Steve Sparks	.25
627	Mike Matthews	.25
628	Robb Nen	.25
629	Kip Wells	.25
630	Kevin Brown	.50
631	Arthur Rhodes	.25
632	Gabe Kapler	.25
633	Jermaine Dye	.25
634	Josh Beckett	.75
635	Pokey Reese	.25
636	Benji Gil	.25
637	Marcus Giles	.25
638	Julian Tavarez	.25
639	Jason Schmidt	.50
640	Alex Rodriguez	3.00
641	Anaheim Angels	.25
642	Arizona Diamondbacks	.25
643	Atlanta Braves	.25
644	Baltimore Orioles	.25
645	Boston Red Sox	.25
646	Chicago Cubs	.25
647	Chicago White Sox	.25
648	Cincinnati Reds	.25
649	Cleveland Indians	.25
650	Colorado Rockies	.25
651	Detroit Tigers	.25
652	Florida Marlins	.25
653	Houston Astros	.25
654	Kansas City Royals	.25
655	Los Angeles Dodgers	.25
656	Milwaukee Brewers	.25
657	Minnesota Twins	.25
658	Montreal Expos	.25
659	New York Mets	.25
660	New York Yankees	1.00
661	Oakland Athletics	.25
662	Philadelphia Phillies	.25
663	Pittsburgh Pirates	.25
664	San Diego Padres	.25
665	San Francisco Giants	.25
666	Seattle Mariners	.25
667	St. Louis Cardinals	.25
668	Tampa Bay Devil Rays	.25
669	Texas Rangers	.25
670	Toronto Blue Jays	.25
671	Juan Cruz	.25
672	Kevin Cash **RC**	1.00
673	Jimmy Gobble **RC**	3.00
674	Mike Hill **RC**	.75
675	Taylor Buchholz **RC**	.75
676	Bill Hall	.75
677	Brett Roneberg **RC**	.75
678	Royce Huffman **RC**	.75
679	Chris Tritle **RC**	1.00
680	Nate Espy **RC**	.50
681	Nick Alvarez **RC**	1.00
682	Jason Botts **RC**	1.50
683	Ryan Gripp **RC**	.75
684	Dan Phillips **RC**	.50
685	Pablo Arias **RC**	.75
686	John Rodriguez **RC**	.75
687	Rich Harden **RC**	10.00
688	Neal Frendling **RC**	1.00
689	Rich Thompson **RC**	.50
690	Greg Montalbano **RC**	1.00
691	Leonard Dinardo **RC**	.75
692	Ryan Raburn **RC**	.50
693	Josh Barfield	5.00
694	David Bacani **RC**	.75
695	Dan Johnson **RC**	2.00
696	Mike Mussina	.50
697	Ivan Rodriguez	.50
698	Doug Mientkiewicz	.25
699	Roberto Alomar	.50
700	Eric Chavez	.25
701	Omar Vizquel	.25
702	Mike Cameron	.25
703	Torii Hunter	.25
704	Ichiro Suzuki	1.50
705	Greg Maddux	1.00
706	Brad Ausmus	.25
707	Todd Helton	.75
708	Fernando Vina	.25
709	Scott Rolen	.75
710	Orlando Cabrera	.25
711	Andruw Jones	.50
712	Jim Edmonds	.25
713	Larry Walker	.25
714	Roger Clemens	1.50
715	Randy Johnson	.75
716	Ichiro Suzuki	1.50
717	Barry Bonds	2.00
718	Ichiro Suzuki	1.50
719	Albert Pujols	1.50

Black Refractor

Stars: 5-10X
Production 50 Sets

Gold Refractor

Stars: 2-4X
Inserted 1:4

Aces

		NM/M
Common Player:		10.00
KB	Kevin Brown	10.00
TH	Tim Hudson	10.00
AL	Al Leiter	10.00
CS	Curt Schilling	15.00
BZ	Barry Zito	10.00

Batterymates

		NM/M
Inserted 1:349		
GL	Tom Glavine, Javy Lopez	20.00
HP	Mike Hampton, Ben Petrick	10.00

Deuces Are Wild

		NM/M
Common Card:		
Inserted 1:428		
CA	Andruw Jones, Chipper Jones	40.00
BT	Bernie Williams, Tino Martinez	25.00
RC	Ryan Dempster, Cliff Floyd	10.00

Jack of All Trades

		NM/M
Common Player:		10.00
CJ	Chipper Jones	20.00
MO	Magglio Ordonez	10.00
AR	Alex Rodriguez	25.00

Kings of the Clubhouse

		NM/M
Common Player:		15.00
JB	Jeff Bagwell	15.00
TG	Tony Gwynn	20.00
AR	Alex Rodriguez	25.00

Like Father, Like Son Relics

		NM/M
Inserted 1:790		
WI	Preston Wilson, Mookie Wilson	10.00

Three of a Kind

		NM/M
Common Card		
AIR	Alex Rodriguez, Ivan Rodriguez, Rafael Palmeiro	50.00
BEJ	Bret Boone, Edgar Martinez, John Olerud	25.00
JCL	Jeff Bagwell, Craig Biggio, Lance Berkman	40.00

Top Of The Order

		NM/M
Common Player:		8.00
Inserted 1:106		
BA	Benny Agbayani/Jsy	8.00
PB	Peter Bergeron/Jsy	8.00
CB	Craig Biggio/Jsy	15.00
JD	Johnny Damon/Bat	10.00
RF	Rafael Furcal/Bat	10.00
RH	Rickey Henderson/Bat	20.00
JK	Jason Kendall/Bat	10.00
CK	Chuck Knoblauch/Bat	8.00
PL	Paul LoDuca/Bat	10.00
KL	Kenny Lofton/Jsy	10.00
JP	Juan Pierre/Bat	10.00
SS	Shannon Stewart/Jsy	10.00

1952 Player Reprints

		NM/M
Complete Set (19):		50.00
Common Card:		3.00
Inserted 1:8		
Refractors:		2X
Inserted 1:24		
52R-1	Roy Campanella	4.00
52R-2	Duke Snider	4.00
52R-3	Carl Erskine	3.00
52R-4	Andy Pafko	3.00

52R-5	Johnny Mize	3.00
52R-6	Billy Martin	4.00
52R-7	Phil Rizzuto	4.00
52R-8	Gil McDougald	3.00
52R-9	Allie Reynolds	3.00
52R-10	Jackie Robinson	5.00
52R-11	Preacher Roe	3.00
52R-12	Gil Hodges	3.00
52R-13	Billy Cox	3.00
52R-14	Yogi Berra	4.00
52R-15	Gene Woodling	3.00
52R-16	Johnny Sain	3.00
52R-17	Ralph Houk	3.00
52R-18	Joe Collins	3.00
52R-19	Hank Bauer	3.00

2002 Topps eTopps

Topps continued its on-line card program with a second annual eTopps edition in 2002. Initial Player Offerings were again made for only one week with allocations having to be made for some cards in high demand. After the IPO, cards could be bought and sold within portfolios, or physically delivered (for a fee) for more traditional venues. The 2-1/2" x 3-1/2" cards are printed on metallic foil with vertical portrait and action photos on front. Horizontal backs have another portrait photo, a 2001 recap and 2002 "prospectus," and a few biographical bits and stats. The listings here include the initial offering price and the number of cards sold during the open ordering period. Values shown are for cards in a virtual portfolio, rather than "in hand." Taking physical possession of a card from an eTopps portfolio costs about $7.

		NM/M
Complete Set (107):		185.00
Common Player:		1.50
1	Ichiro Suzuki ($9.50 / 9,477)	2.00
2	Jason Giambi ($9.50 / 5,142)	1.50
3	Roberto Alomar ($6.50 / 2,711)	1.50
4	Bret Boone ($4 / 2,000)	6.00
5	Frank Catalanotto ($6.50 / 2,000)	6.00
6	Alex Rodriguez ($9.50 / 6,393)	3.00
7	Jim Thome ($6.50 / 2,927)	2.00
8	Toby Hall ($6.50 / 2,000)	1.50
9	Troy Glaus ($6.50 / 4,323)	1.50
10	Derek Jeter ($9.50 / 8,000)	4.00
11	Alfonso Soriano ($6.50 / 5,000)	1.50
12	Eric Chavez ($6.50 / 4,334)	1.50
13	Preston Wilson ($4 / 2,000)	1.50
14	Bernie Williams ($6.50 / 4,436)	1.50
15	Larry Walker ($6.50 / 2,546)	1.50
16	Todd Helton ($9.50 / 3,430)	1.50
17	Moises Alou ($6.50 / 2,856)	1.50
18	Lance Berkman ($6.50 / 5,000)	1.50
19	Chipper Jones ($6.50 / 4,734)	1.50
20	Andruw Jones ($6.50 / 4,849)	1.50
21	Barry Bonds ($9.50 / 6,658)	7.50
22	Sammy Sosa ($9.50 / 8,000)	1.50
23	Luis Gonzalez ($6.50 / 2,671)	1.50
24	Shawn Green ($6.50 / 4,438)	1.50
25	Jeff Bagwell ($9.50 / 3,359)	1.50
26	Albert Pujols ($6.50 / 5,531)	4.00
27	Rafael Palmeiro ($6.50 / 2,700)	1.50
28	Jimmy Rollins ($4 / 5,000)	1.50
29	Vladimir Guerrero ($6.50 / 6,000)	1.50
30	Jeff Kent ($6.50 / 3,000)	1.50
31	Ken Griffey Jr. ($9.50 / 4,569)	2.00
32	Magglio Ordonez ($6.50 / 4,000)	1.50
33	Mike Piazza ($9.50 / 4,202)	1.50
34	Pedro Martinez ($9.50 / 6,000)	1.50
35	Mark Mulder ($6.50 / 4,000)	1.50
36	Roger Clemens ($9.50 / 4,567)	2.50
37	Freddy Garcia ($6.50 / 4,986)	1.50
38	Tim Hudson ($6.50 / 2,000)	1.50
39	Mike Mussina ($6.50 / 3,708)	1.50
40	Joe Mays ($4 / 3,000)	1.50
41	Barry Zito ($6.50 / 3,590)	1.50
42	Jermaine Dye ($6.50 / 2,693)	1.50
43	Mariano Rivera ($6.50 / 3,709)	1.50
44	Randy Johnson ($9.50 / 6,211)	1.50
45	Curt Schilling ($6.50 / 5,190)	1.50
46	Greg Maddux ($9.50 / 4,008)	1.50
47	Javier Vazquez ($6.50 / 3,000)	1.50
48	Kerry Wood ($6.50 / 3,346)	1.50
49	Wilson Betemit ($6.50 / 2,377)	1.50
50	Adam Dunn ($6.50 / 6,000)	1.50
51	Josh Beckett ($6.50 / 5,000)	2.00
52	Paul LoDuca ($4 / 3,998)	1.50
53	Ben Sheets ($4 / 3,842)	1.50
54	Eric Valent ($4 / 5,000)	1.50
55	Brian Giles ($6.50 / 2,000)	1.50
56	Mo Vaughn ($6.50 / 2,772)	1.50
57	C.C. Sabathia ($6.50 / 2,525)	1.50
58	Nick Johnson ($6.50 / 5,000)	1.50
59	Miguel Tejada ($6.50 / 4,000)	1.50
60	Carlos Delgado ($6.50 / 3,604)	1.50
61	Tsuyoshi Shinjo ($4 / 3,000)	1.50
62	Juan Gonzalez ($6.50 / 2,361)	1.50
63	Mike Sweeney ($6.50 / 3,175)	1.50
64	Ivan Rodriguez ($9.50 / 3,000)	1.50
65	Bud Smith ($4.00 / 3,000)	2.00
66	Brandon Duckworth ($6.50 / 2,000)	4.00
67	Xavier Nady ($4 / 4,000)	1.50
68	D'Angelo Jiminez ($6.50 / 1,725)	1.50
69	Roy Oswalt ($6.50 / 3,523)	1.50
70	J.D. Drew ($9.50 / 3,195)	1.50
71	Cliff Floyd ($6.50 / 3,575)	1.50
72	Kevin Brown ($6.50 / 3,000)	1.50
73	Gary Sheffield ($6.50 / 2,593)	2.00
74	Aramis Ramirez ($6.50 / 3,000)	1.50
75	Nomar Garciaparra ($9.50 / 5,090)	1.50
76	Phil Nevin ($6.50 / 2,348)	1.50
77	Juan Cruz ($4 / 4,000)	1.50
78	Hideo Nomo ($6.50 / 2,857)	1.50
79	Chris George ($4 / 3,000)	1.50
80	Matt Morris ($4 / 3,000)	1.50
81	Corey Patterson ($6.50 / 4,000)	1.50
82	Joel Pineiro ($6.50 / 4,776)	1.50
83	Mark Buehrle ($4 / 3,000)	4.00
84	Shannon Stewart ($4 / 1,992)	1.50
85	Kazuhiro Sasaki ($6.50 / 4,000)	1.50
86	Carlos Pena ($4 / 4,000)	1.50
87	Brad Penny ($6.50 / 3,000)	1.50
88	Rich Aurilia ($6.50 / 2,795)	2.00
89	Wade Miller ($4 / 4,000)	1.50
90	Tim Raines Jr. ($4 / 5,000)	1.50
91	Kazuhisa Ishii ($6.50 / 6,000)	1.50
92	Hank Blalock ($6.50 / 5,000)	3.00
93	So Taguchi ($4 /5,000)	1.50
94	Mark Prior ($9.50 / 5,000)	9.00
95	Rickey Henderson ($9.50 / 4,013)	3.50
96	Austin Kearns ($6.50 / 6,000)	1.50
97	Tom Glavine ($9.50 / 3,000)	1.50
98	Manny Ramirez ($6.50 / 4,905)	1.50
99	Shea Hillenbrand ($6.50 / 4,000)	1.50
100	Junior Spivey ($6.50 / 5,000)	1.50
101	Derek Lowe ($6.50 / 4,911)	1.50
102	Torii Hunter ($6.50 / 4,000)	1.50
103	Juan Rivera ($6.50 / 4,000)	1.50
104	Eric Hinske ($6.50 / 5,000)	1.50
105	Bobby Hill ($6.50 / 3,000)	1.50
106	Rafael Soriano ($6.50 / 4,000)	1.50
107	Jim Edmonds ($6.50 / 3,851)	2.00

Classics

Topps expanded its eTopps line-up in 2002 with the issue of 20 cards of former greats. Like regular eTopps cards, they could only be ordered during a one-week Initial Player Offering period. Cards were issued in a quantity of 4,000 each at $12.50. Fronts have a color or colorized action photo, backs have a picture of one of that player's Topps cards, along with career notes, stats, etc. Values shown are latest auction prices realized on the date cited and represent cards in a virtual portfolio rather than "in hand." The cost to physically move a card from an eTopps portfolio into one's possession is about $7.

		NM/M
Complete Set (20):		90.00
Common Player:		3.50
1	Babe Ruth	15.00
2	Tom Seaver	3.50
3	Honus Wagner	4.00
4	Warren Spahn	3.50
5	Frank Robinson	3.50
6	Whitey Ford	3.50
7	Bob Gibson	3.50
8	Reggie Jackson	5.00
9	Joe Morgan	3.50
10	Harmon Killebrew	3.50
11	Eddie Mathews	3.50
12	Willie Mays	9.00
12a	Willie Mays (2004 autographed edition of 100)	135.00
13	Brooks Robinson	3.50
14	Ty Cobb	5.00
15	Carl Yastrzemski	4.00
16	Jackie Robinson	7.00
17	Mike Schmidt	4.50
18	Nolan Ryan	9.00
19	Duke Snider	3.50
20	Stan Musial	4.50

Events

Special events during the 2002 season were commemorated by Topps with the issue of special eTopps cards. Like the regular-issue eTopps, the cards were only available directly from Topps on-line. Five thousand of each card were issued with an initial order price of $8 each. Only the baseball related Events cards are listed here. Values shown are for cards in a virtual portfolio. Taking physical possession of a card from an eTopps portfolio costs about $7 apiece.

		NM/M
1	Mike Cameron (Four HR)(5,000)	1.00
2	Shawn Green (Four HR, 19 TB)(5,000)	1.00
4	Oakland A's (20 Straight Wins)(5,000)	1.00
5	Greg Maddux (15+ Wins, 15 Years)(3,851)	1.50

2002 Topps Gallery

		NM/M
Complete Set (200):		60.00
Common Player:		.25
Common (151-200):		.75
Inserted 1:1		
Pack (6):		1.50
Box (24):		30.00
1	Jason Giambi	.50
2	Mark Grace	.40
3	Bret Boone	.40
4	Antonio Alfonseca	.25
5	Kevin Brown	.40
6	Cristian Guzman	.25
7	Magglio Ordonez	.40
8	Luis Gonzalez	.40
9	Jorge Posada	.40
10	Roberto Alomar	.50
11	Mike Sweeney	.25
12	Jeff Kent	.40
13	Matt Morris	.40
14	Alfonso Soriano	.75
15	Adam Dunn	.50
16	Neifi Perez	.25
17	Todd Walker	.25
18	J.D. Drew	.40
19	Eric Chavez	.40
20	Alex Rodriguez	1.50
21	Ray Lankford	.25
22	Roger Cedeno	.25
23	Chipper Jones	.75
24	Jose Canseco	.50
25	Mike Piazza	1.50
26	Freddy Garcia	.25
27	Todd Helton	.50
28	Tino Martinez	.40
29	Kazuhiro Sasaki	.25
30	Curt Schilling	.50
31	Mark Buehrle	.25
32	John Olerud	.40
33	Brad Radke	.25
34	Steve Sparks	.25
35	Jason Tyner	.25
36	Jeff Shaw	.25
37	Mariano Rivera	.40
38	Russ Ortiz	.25
39	Richard Hidalgo	.25
40	Barry Bonds	2.00
41	John Burkett	.25
42	Tim Hudson	.40
43	Mike Hampton	.25
44	Orlando Cabrera	.25
45	Barry Zito	.40
46	C.C. Sabathia	.25
47	Chan Ho Park	.25
48	Tom Glavine	.50
49	Aramis Ramirez	.40
50	Lance Berkman	.40
51	Al Leiter	.25
52	Phil Nevin	.25
53	Javier Vazquez	.25
54	Troy Glaus	.40
55	Tsuyoshi Shinjo	.25
56	Albert Pujols	1.50
57	John Smoltz	.40
58	Derek Jeter	2.00
59	Robb Nen	.25
60	Jason Kendall	.25
61	Eric Gagne	.50
62	Vladimir Guerrero	.75
63	Corey Patterson	.40
64	Rickey Henderson	.50
65	Jack Wilson	.25
66	Jason LaRue	.25
67	Sammy Sosa	1.50
68	Ken Griffey Jr.	1.00
69	Randy Johnson	.75
70	Nomar Garciaparra	1.50
71	Ivan Rodriguez	.50
72	J.T. Snow	.25
73	Darryl Kile	.25
74	Andruw Jones	.50
75	Brian Giles	.40
76	Pedro Martinez	.75
77	Jeff Bagwell	.50
78	Rafael Palmeiro	.50
79	Ryan Dempster	.25
80	Jeff Cirillo	.25
81	Geoff Jenkins	.40
82	Brandon Duckworth	.25
83	Roger Clemens	1.50
84	Fred McGriff	.40
85	Hideo Nomo	.50
86	Larry Walker	.40
87	Sean Casey	.40
88	Trevor Hoffman	.25
89	Robert Fick	.25
90	Armando Benitez	.25
91	Jeromy Burnitz	.25
92	Bernie Williams	.50
93	Carlos Delgado	.50
94	Troy Percival	.25
95	Nate Cornejo	.25
96	Derrek Lee	.40
97	Jose Ortiz	.25
98	Brian Jordan	.25
99	Jose Cruz	.25
100	Ichiro Suzuki	1.50
101	Jose Mesa	.25
102	Tim Salmon	.40
103	Bud Smith	.25
104	Paul LoDuca	.25
105	Juan Pierre	.25
106	Ben Grieve	.25
107	Russell Branyan	.25
108	Bobby Abreu	.40
109	Moises Alou	.40
110	Richie Sexson	.50
111	Jerry Hairston Jr.	.25
112	Marlon Anderson	.25
113	Juan Gonzalez	.50
114	Craig Biggio	.40
115	Carlos Beltran	.50
116	Eric Milton	.25
117	Cliff Floyd	.25
118	Rich Aurilia	.25
119	Adrian Beltre	.40
120	Jason Bere	.25
121	Darin Erstad	.40
122	Ben Sheets	.40
123	Johnny Damon	.40
124	Jimmy Rollins	.40
125	Shawn Green	.40
126	Greg Maddux	1.00
127	Mark Mulder	.40
128	Bartolo Colon	.25
129	Shannon Stewart	.25
130	Ramon Ortiz	.25
131	Kerry Wood	.75
132	Ryan Klesko	.25
133	Preston Wilson	.25
134	Roy Oswalt	.40
135	Rafael Furcal	.25
136	Eric Karros	.25
137	Nick Neugebauer	.25
138	Doug Mientkiewicz	.25
139	Paul Konerko	.40
140	Bobby Higginson	.25
141	Garret Anderson	.40
142	Wes Helms	.25
143	Brent Abernathy	.25
144	Scott Rolen	.75
145	Dmitri Young	.25
146	Jim Thome	.75
147	Raul Mondesi	.25
148	Pat Burrell	.40
149	Gary Sheffield	.40
150	Miguel Tejada	.40
151	Brandon Inge	.75
152	Carlos Pena	.75
153	Jason Lane	.75
154	Nathan Haynes	.75
155	Hank Blalock	1.50
156	Juan Cruz	.75
157	Morgan Ensberg	.75
158	Sean Burroughs	.75
159	Ed Rogers	.75
160	Nick Johnson	.75
161	Orlando Hudson	.75
162	Anastacio Martinez **RC**	.75
163	Jeremy Affeldt	.75
164	Brandon Claussen	.75
165	Deivis Santos	.75
166	Mike Rivera	.75
167	Carlos Silva	.75
168	Valentino Pascucci	.75
169	Xavier Nady	.75
170	David Espinosa	.75
171	Dan Phillips **RC**	.75
172	Tony Fontana **RC**	.75
173	Juan Silvestre	.75
174	Henry Pichardo **RC**	.75
175	Pablo Arias **RC**	.75
176	Brett Roneberg **RC**	.75
177	Chad Qualls **RC**	.75
178	Greg Sain **RC**	.75
179	Rene Reyes **RC**	.75
180	So Taguchi **RC**	2.00
181	Dan Johnson **RC**	2.50
182	Justin Backsmeyer **RC**	.75
183	Juan Gonzalez	.75
184	Jason Ellison **RC**	.75
185	Kazuhisa Ishii **RC**	3.00
186	Joe Mauer **RC**	8.00
187	James Shanks **RC**	.75
188	Kevin Cash **RC**	.75
189	J.J. Trujillo **RC**	.75
190	Jorge Padilla **RC**	1.00
191	Nolan Ryan	4.00
192	George Brett	3.00
193	Ryne Sandberg	2.00
194	Robin Yount	1.50
195	Tom Seaver	1.00
196	Mike Schmidt	2.00
197	Frank Robinson	1.00
198	Harmon Killebrew	1.00
199	Kirby Puckett	2.00
200	Don Mattingly	4.00

Autographs

		NM/M
Common Player:		8.00
Inserted 1:192		
LB	Lance Berkman	30.00
BBO	Bret Boone	20.00
JD	J.D. Drew	25.00
LG	Luis Gonzalez	20.00
SG	Shawn Green	25.00
JL	Jason Lane	8.00
MO	Magglio Ordonez	20.00
JP	Jorge Posada	40.00
JS	Juan Silvestre	8.00

Baseball Bucks

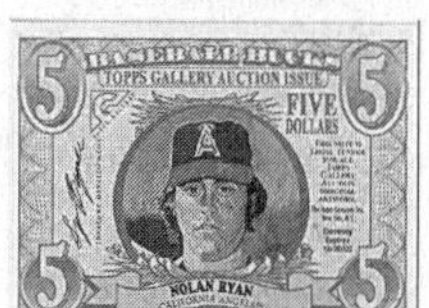

		NM/M
Used for gallery original art auctions:		
$5	Nolan Ryan	2.50

Originals Relics

		NM/M
Common Player:		8.00
Inserted 1:169		
BBO	Bret Boone	8.00
JC	Jose Canseco	10.00
CD	Carlos Delgado	8.00
JG	Juan Gonzalez	10.00
LG	Luis Gonzalez	8.00
TG	Tony Gwynn	15.00
TH	Todd Helton	12.00
AJ	Andruw Jones	8.00
CJ	Chipper Jones	10.00
TM	Tino Martinez	10.00
MP	Mike Piazza	20.00
AP	Albert Pujols	35.00
AR	Alex Rodriguez	15.00
AS	Alfonso Soriano	10.00
BW	Bernie Williams	10.00

Heritage

	NM/M
Complete Set (25):	100.00

Common Player:		2.00
Inserted 1:12		
RA	Roberto Alomar	4.00
BBO	Bret Boone	2.00
RC	Roger Clemens	8.00
JG	Jason Giambi	3.00
LG	Luis Gonzalez	2.00
SG	Shawn Green	3.00
KG	Ken Griffey Jr.	6.00
TG	Tony Gwynn	4.00
RJ	Reggie Jackson	4.00
CJ	Chipper Jones	4.00
AK	Al Kaline	4.00
GM	Greg Maddux	5.00
PM	Pedro Martinez	4.00
MM	Mark McGwire	10.00
SM	Stan Musial	5.00
MP	Mike Piazza	6.00
BR	Brooks Robinson	4.00
AR	Alex Rodriguez	8.00
NR	Nolan Ryan	10.00
MS	Mike Schmidt	6.00
TS	Tom Seaver	4.00
TSH	Tsuyoshi Shinjo	2.00
SS	Sammy Sosa	8.00
CY	Carl Yastrzemski	5.00
RY	Robin Yount	5.00

Heritage Autographs

		NM/M
Inserted 1:240		
BBO	Bret Boone	20.00
LG	Luis Gonzalez	25.00
SG	Shawn Green	25.00

Heritage Relics

		NM/M
Common Player:		8.00
Inserted 1:85		
BBO	Bret Boone	8.00
LG	Luis Gonzalez	8.00
TG	Tony Gwynn	15.00
CJ	Chipper Jones	10.00
GM	Greg Maddux	15.00
PM	Pedro Martinez	15.00
MP	Mike Piazza	15.00
AR	Alex Rodriguez	15.00
TS	Tsuyoshi Shinjo	8.00

Press Plates

The aluminum press plates used to print the Gallery cards were inserted at a rate of one per 1,200 packs. Each card's front and back can be found in four different color variations. Because of the unique nature of each plate, assignment of catalog values in not feasible.

	NM/M
Common Player:	50.00

Team Topps Legends Autographs

	NM/M
Inserted 1:1,019	
Luis Aparicio	15.00
Jim Bunning	20.00
Fergie Jenkins	15.00
Carl Yastrzemski	65.00

2002 Topps Gold Label

		NM/M
Complete Set (200):		60.00
Common Player:		.25
Pack (4):		3.00
Box (18):		40.00
1	Alex Rodriguez	1.50
2	Derek Jeter	2.00
3	Luis Gonzalez	.40
4	Troy Glaus	.40
5	Albert Pujols	1.50
6	Lance Berkman	.40
7	J.D. Drew	.40
8	Chipper Jones	.75
9	Miguel Tejada	.40
10	Randy Johnson	.75
11	Mike Cameron	.25
12	Brian Giles	.40
13	Roger Cedeno	.25
14	Kerry Wood	.75
15	Ken Griffey Jr.	1.00
16	Carlos Lee	.25
17	Todd Helton	.50
18	Gary Sheffield	.40
19	Richie Sexson	.40
20	Vladimir Guerrero	.75
21	Bobby Higginson	.25
22	Roger Clemens	1.50
23	Barry Zito	.40
24	Juan Pierre	.25
25	Pedro Martinez	.75
26	Sean Casey	.40
27	David Segui	.25
28	Jose Garcia	.25
29	Curt Schilling	.50
30	Bernie Williams	.50
31	Ben Grieve	.25
32	Hideo Nomo	.40
33	Aramis Ramirez	.40
34	Cristian Guzman	.25
35	Rich Aurilia	.25
36	Greg Maddux	1.00
37	Eric Chavez	.40
38	Shawn Green	.40
39	Luis Rivas	.25
40	Magglio Ordonez	.40
41	Jose Vidro	.25
42	Mariano Rivera	.40
43	Chris Tritle **RC**	.50
44	C.C. Sabathia	.25
45	Larry Walker	.40
46	Raul Mondesi	.25
47	Kevin Brown	.40
48	Jeff Bagwell	.50
49	Earl Snyder **RC**	.50
50	Jason Giambi	.50
51	Ichiro Suzuki	1.50
52	Andruw Jones	.50
53	Ivan Rodriguez	.50
54	Jim Edmonds	.40
55	Preston Wilson	.25
56	Greg Vaughn	.25
57	Jon Lieber	.25
58	Justin Sherrod **RC**	.50
59	Marcus Giles	.25
60	Roberto Alomar	.40
61	Pat Burrell	.40
62	Doug Mientkiewicz	.25
63	Mark Mulder	.40
64	Mike Hampton	.25
65	Adam Dunn	.50
66	Moises Alou	.40
67	Jose Cruz Jr.	.25
68	Derek Bell	.25
69	Sammy Sosa	1.50
70	Joe Mays	.25
71	Phil Nevin	.25
72	Edgardo Alfonzo	.25
73	Barry Bonds	2.00
74	Edgar Martinez	.40
75	Juan Encarnacion	.25
76	Jason Tyner	.25
77	Edgar Renteria	.40
78	Bret Boone	.40
79	Scott Rolen	.75
80	Nomar Garciaparra	1.50
81	Frank Thomas	.50
82	Roy Oswalt	.40
83	Tsuyoshi Shinjo	.25
84	Ben Sheets	.40
85	Hank Blalock	.40
86	Carlos Delgado	.50
87	Tim Hudson	.40
88	Alfonso Soriano	.75
89	Michael Hill **RC**	.50
90	Jim Thome	.75
91	Craig Biggio	.40
92	Ryan Klesko	.25
93	Geoff Jenkins	.40
94	Matt Morris	.40
95	Jorge Posada	.40
96	Cliff Floyd	.40
97	Jimmy Rollins	.40
98	Mike Sweeney	.25
99	Frank Catalanotto	.25
100	Mike Piazza	1.25
101	Mark Quinn	.25
102	Torii Hunter	.40
103	Lee Stevens	.25
104	Byung-Hyug Kim	.25
105	Freddy Sanchez **RC**	.50
106	David Cone	.25
107	Jerry Hairston Jr.	.25
108	Kyle Farnsworth	.25
109	Rafael Furcal	.25
110	Bartolo Colon	.25
111	Juan Rivera	.25
112	Kevin Young	.25
113	Chris Narveson **RC**	1.00
114	Richard Hidalgo	.25
115	Andy Pettitte	.40
116	Darin Erstad	.40
117	Corey Koskie	.25
118	Rickey Henderson	.50
119	Derrek Lee	.40
120	Sean Burroughs	.25
121	Paul Konerko	.25
122	Ross Peeples **RC**	.50
123	Terrence Long	.25
124	John Smoltz	.40
125	Brandon Duckworth	.25
126	Luis Maza	.25
127	Morgan Ensberg	.25
128	Eric Valent	.25
129	Shannon Stewart	.25
130	D'Angelo Jimenez	.25
131	Jeff Cirillo	.25
132	Jack Cust	.25
133	Dmitri Young	.25
134	Darryl Kile	.25
135	Reggie Sanders	.25
136	Marlon Byrd	.25
137	Napoleon Calzado **RC**	.50
138	Javy Lopez	.40
139	Orlando Cabrera	.25
140	Mike Mussina	.40
141	Josh Beckett	.40
142	Kazuhiro Sasaki	.25
143	Jermaine Dye	.25
144	Carlos Beltran	.40
145	Trevor Hoffman	.25
146	Kazuhisa Ishii **RC**	2.00
147	Alex Gonzalez	.25
148	Marty Cordova	.25
149	Kevin Deaton **RC**	.50
150	Toby Hall	.25
151	Rafael Palmeiro	.50
152	John Olerud	.40
153	David Eckstein	.25
154	Doug Glanville	.25
155	Johnny Damon	.40
156	Javier Vazquez	.25
157	Jason Bay **RC**	2.00
158	Robb Nen	.25
159	Rafael Soriano	.25
160	Placido Polanco	.25
161	Garret Anderson	.40
162	Aaron Boone	.25
163	Mike Lieberthal	.25
164	Joe Mauer **RC**	10.00
165	Matt Lawton	.25
166	Juan Tolentino **RC**	.50
167	Alex Gonzalez	.25
168	Steve Finley	.25
169	Troy Percival	.25
170	Bud Smith	.25
171	Freddie Garcia	.25
172	Ray Lankford	.25
173	Tim Redding	.25
174	Ryan Dempster	.25
175	Travis Lee	.25
176	Jeff Kent	.40
177	Ramon Hernandez	.25
178	Carl Everett	.25
179	Tom Glavine	.40
180	Juan Gonzalez	.50
181	Nick Johnson	.25
182	Mike Lowell	.40
183	Al Leiter	.40
184	Jason Maule **RC**	.50
185	Wilson Betemit	.25
186	Tino Martinez	.25
187	Jason Standridge	.25
188	Mike Peeples **RC**	.50
189	Jason Kendall	.40
190	Fred McGriff	.40
191	John Rodriguez **RC**	.50
192	Brett Roneberg **RC**	.50
193	Marlyn Tisdale **RC**	.50
194	J.T. Snow	.25
195	Craig Kuzmic **RC**	.75
196	Cory Lidle	.25
197	Alex Cintron	.25
198	Fernando Vina	.25
199	Austin Kearns	.50
200	Paul LoDuca	.25

Class One Gold

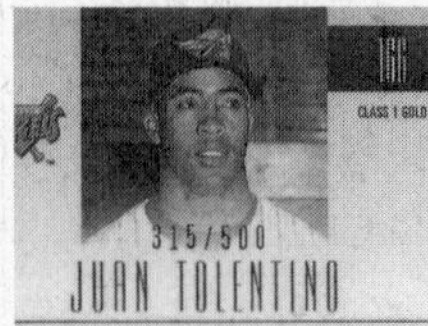

Stars:	2-4X
Production 500 Sets	

Class Two Platinum

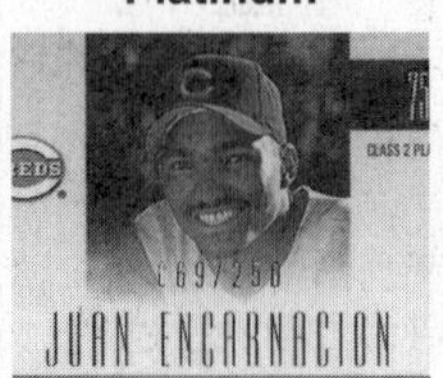

Stars:	4-8X
Production 250 Sets	

Class Three Titanium

Stars:	6-10X
Production 100 Sets	

Platinum Memorabilia

Platinum:	.75-1.5X
Titanium Memorabilia:	1-2X

All-Star MVP Winners

		NM/M
Common Player:		8.00
RA	Roberto Alomar	10.00
SA	Sandy Alomar	8.00
BLB	Bobby Bonds	8.00
DC	Dave Concepcion	8.00
SG2	Steve Garvey	10.00
KG	Ken Griffey Sr.	8.00
BM1	Bill Madlock	8.00
FM	Fred McGriff	10.00
DP3	Dave Parker	8.00
TP	Tony Perez	10.00
MP	Mike Piazza	15.00
KP2	Kirby Puckett	15.00
TR	Tim Raines	8.00

Batting Average

		NM/M
Common Player:		8.00
WB	Wade Boggs	15.00
BB	Bill Buckner	8.00
RC2	Rod Carew	15.00
RAC	Rico Carty	8.00
NC	Norm Cash	15.00
TG1	Tony Gwynn	15.00
TG2	Tony Gwynn	15.00
BM2	Bill Madlock	8.00
DP4	Dave Parker	8.00
KP3	Kirby Puckett	15.00
LW	Larry Walker	8.00
CY2	Carl Yastrzemski	30.00

Cy Young Winners

		NM/M
Common Player:		8.00
RWC	Roger Clemens	15.00
DE	Dennis Eckersley	8.00
RJ	Randy Johnson	12.00
BS	Bret Saberhagen	8.00
JS	John Smoltz	8.00

Home Run Champions

		NM/M
Common Player:		8.00
BB2	Barry Bonds	20.00
GF	George Foster	8.00
TK2	Ted Kluszewski	15.00
KM2	Kevin Mitchell	8.00
DM2	Dale Murphy	40.00
AR	Alex Rodriguez	15.00
DS1	Darryl Strawberry	10.00

League Championship MVP Winners

		NM/M
Common Player:		8.00
GB2	George Brett	40.00
WC	Will Clark	15.00
CC	Craig Counsell	8.00
RH	Rickey Henderson	15.00
JL	Javier Lopez	8.00
AEP	Andy Pettitte	12.00
KP1	Kirby Puckett	15.00
FW	Frank White	8.00
BFW	Bernie Williams	10.00

MLB Moments in Time

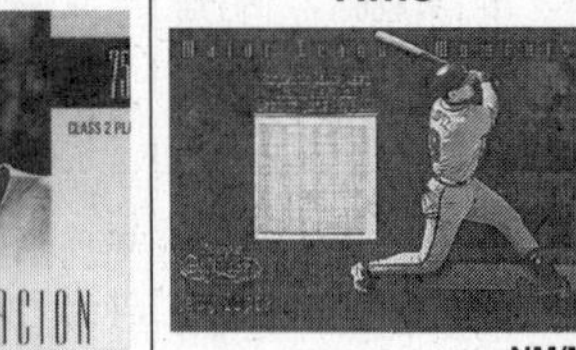

		NM/M
Common Player:		8.00
BLB	Barry Bonds	20.00
BB1	Bret Boone	8.00
BB2	Bret Boone	8.00
CD	Carlos Delgado	8.00
TG	Tony Gwynn	15.00
TH	Toby Hall	8.00
CL	Carlos Lee	8.00
JL	Javy Lopez	8.00
MO	Magglio Ordonez	10.00
RP1	Rafael Palmeiro	10.00
RP2	Rafael Palmeiro	10.00
AR	Alex Rodriguez	15.00

MVP Winners

		NM/M
Common Player:		8.00
EB	Ernie Banks	20.00
DB	Don Baylor	8.00
YB	Yogi Berra	15.00
BB1	Barry Bonds	20.00
GB1	George Brett	40.00
SG1	Steve Garvey	8.00
KHG	Kirk Gibson	8.00
KH	Keith Hernandez	10.00
RJ1	Reggie Jackson	15.00
DM	Don Mattingly	40.00
KM1	Kevin Mitchell	8.00
JM	Joe Morgan	8.00
DM1	Dale Murphy	40.00
DP1	Dave Parker	8.00
BR	Brooks Robinson	15.00
FR	Frank Robinson	12.00
RS	Ryne Sandberg	40.00
HS	Hank Sauer	8.00
WS	Willie Stargell	15.00
JT	Joe Torre	10.00
MW	Maury Wills	8.00
CY1	Carl Yastrzemski	30.00
RY	Robin Yount	20.00

RBI Leaders

		NM/M
Common Player:		8.00
BRB	Bret Boone	8.00
BRB2	Bret Boone	8.00
GC	Gary Carter	8.00
GL	Greg Luzinski	8.00
EM1	Eddie Murray	12.00
AO	Al Oliver	8.00
DP2	Dave Parker	8.00
DW	Dave Winfield	12.00

Rookie of the Year Winners

		NM/M
Common Player:		8.00
DA	Dick Allen	15.00
AB	Al Bumbry	8.00
RC1	Rod Carew	15.00
CF	Carlton Fisk	15.00
MH	Mike Hargrove	8.00
DJ	Dave Justice	10.00
EM2	Eddie Murray	12.00
LP	Lou Piniella	10.00
AP	Albert Pujols	20.00
DS2	Darryl Strawberry	15.00
FV	Fernando Valenzuela	8.00
BW	Billy Williams	10.00

World Series MVP Winners

		NM/M
Common Player:		8.00
JB	Johnny Bench	15.00
RCC	Ron Cey	8.00
RJ2	Reggie Jackson	15.00
PM	Paul Molitor	15.00
MR	Mariano Rivera	10.00

2002 Topps Heritage

		NM/M
Complete Set (440):		325.00
Common Player:		.25
Common (364-446):		3.00
Inserted 1:2		
Pack (8):		4.00
Box (24):		90.00
1	Ichiro Suzuki/SP	10.00
2	Darin Erstad	.50
3	Rod Beck	.25
4	Doug Mientkiewicz	.25
5	Mike Sweeney	.25
6	Roger Clemens	2.50
7	Jason Tyner	.25
8	Alex Gonzalez	.25
9	Eric Young	.25
10	Randy Johnson	1.50
10	Randy Johnson/SP	6.00
11	Aaron Sele	.25
12	Tony Clark	.25
13	C.C. Sabathia	.25
14	Melvin Mora	.25
15	Tim Hudson	.50
16	Ben Petrick	.25
17	Tom Glavine	.75
18	Jason Lane	.25
19	Larry Walker	.50
20	Mark Mulder	.50
21	Steve Finley	.25
22	Bengie Molina	.25
23	Rob Bell	.25
24	Nathan Haynes	.25
25	Rafael Furcal	.50
25	Rafael Furcal/SP	3.00
26	Mike Mussina	1.00
27	Paul LoDuca	.25
28	Torii Hunter	.50
29	Carlos Lee	.25
30	Jimmy Rollins	.50
31	Arthur Rhodes	.25
32	Ivan Rodriguez	1.00
33	Wes Helms	.25
34	Cliff Floyd	.25
35	Julian Tavarez	.25
36	Mark McGwire	4.00
37	Chipper Jones/SP	6.00
38	Denny Neagle	.25
39	Odalis Perez	.25
40	Antonio Alfonseca	.25
41	Edgar Renteria	.50
42	Troy Glaus	.75
43	Scott Brosius	.25
44	Abraham Nunez	.25
45	Jamey Wright	.25
46	Bobby Bonilla	.25
47	Ismael Valdes	.25
48	Chris Reitsma	.25
49	Neifi Perez	.25
50	Juan Cruz	.25
51	Kevin Brown	.50
52	Ben Grieve	.25
53	Alex Rodriguez/SP	10.00
54	Charles Nagy	.25
55	Reggie Sanders	.25
56	Nelson Figueroa	.25
57	Felipe Lopez	.25
58	Bill Ortega	.25
59	Mac Suzuki	.25
60	Johnny Estrada	.25
61	Bob Wickman	.25
62	Doug Glanville	.25
63	Jeff Cirillo	.50
63	Jeff Cirillo/SP	3.00
64	Corey Patterson	.50
65	Aaron Myette	.25
66	Magglio Ordonez	.50
67	Ellis Burks	.25
68	Miguel Tejada	.50
69	John Olerud	.50
69	John Olerud/SP	4.00
70	Greg Vaughn	.25
71	Andy Pettitte	.75
72	Mike Matheny	.25
73	Brandon Duckworth	.25
74	Scott Schoeneweis	.25
75	Mike Lowell	.50
76	Einar Diaz	.25
77	Tino Martinez	.50
78	Matt Williams	.50

79 Jason Young **RC** 1.00
80 Nate Cornejo .25
81 Andres Galarraga .40
82 Bernie Williams/SP 6.00
83 Ryan Klesko .25
84 Dan Wilson .25
85 Henry Pichardo **RC** .50
86 Ray Durham .25
87 Omar Daal .25
88 Derrek Lee .50
89 Al Leiter .50
90 Darrin Fletcher .25
91 Josh Beckett .75
92 Johnny Damon .50
92 Johnny Damon/SP 5.00
93 Abraham Nunez .25
94 Ricky Ledee .25
95 Richie Sexson .75
96 Adam Kennedy .25
97 Raul Mondesi .25
98 John Burkett .25
99 Ben Sheets .50
99 Ben Sheets/SP 4.00
100 Preston Wilson .25
100 Preston Wilson/SP 3.00
101 Boof Bonser .25
102 Shigetoshi Hasegawa .25
103 Carlos Febles .25
104 Jorge Posada/SP 5.00
105 Michael Tucker .25
106 Roberto Hernandez .25
107 John Rodriguez **RC** .75
108 Danny Graves .25
109 Rich Aurilia .25
110 Jon Lieber .25
111 Tim Hummel **RC** .50
112 J.T. Snow .25
113 Kris Benson .25
114 Derek Jeter 4.00
115 John Franco .25
116 Matt Stairs .25
117 Ben Davis .25
118 Darryl Kile .25
119 Mike Peeples **RC** .50
120 Kevin Tapani .25
121 Armando Benitez .25
122 Damian Miller .25
123 Jose Jimenez .25
124 Pedro Astacio .25
125 Marlyn Tisdale **RC** .50
126 Deivi Cruz .25
127 Paul O'Neill .75
128 Jermaine Dye .25
129 Marcus Giles .25
130 Mark Loretta .25
131 Garret Anderson .50
132 Todd Ritchie .25
133 Joe Crede .25
134 Kevin Millwood .50
135 Shane Reynolds .25
136 Mark Grace .75
137 Shannon Stewart .25
138 Nick Neugebauer .25
139 Nic Jackson **RC** .75
140 Robb Nen .25
141 Dmitri Young .25
142 Kevin Appier .25
143 Jack Cust .25
144 Andres Torres .25
145 Frank Thomas 1.00
146 Jason Kendall .25
147 Greg Maddux 2.00
148 David Justice .50
149 Hideo Nomo .75
150 Bret Boone .50
151 Wade Miller .25
152 Jeff Kent .50
153 Scott Williamson .25
154 Julio Lugo .25
155 Bobby Higginson .25
156 Geoff Jenkins .50
157 Darren Dreifort .25
158 Freddy Sanchez **RC** .75
159 Bud Smith .25
160 Phil Nevin .25
161 Cesar Izturis .25
162 Sean Casey .50
163 Jose Ortiz .25
164 Brent Abernathy .25
165 Kevin Young .25
166 Daryle Ward .25
167 Trevor Hoffman .25
168 Rondell White .25
169 Kip Wells .25
170 John Vander Wal .25
171 Jose Lima .25
172 Wilton Guerrero .25
173 Aaron Dean .25
174 Rick Helling .25
175 Juan Pierre .25
176 Jay Bell .25
177 Craig House .25
178 David Bell .25
179 Pat Burrell .50
180 Eric Gagne .75
181 Adam Pettyjohn .25
182 Ugueth Urbina .25
183 Peter Bergeron .25
184 Adrian Gonzalez .25
184 Adrian Gonzalez/SP 4.00
185 Damion Easley .25
186 Gookie Dawkins .25
187 Matt Lawton .25
188 Frank Catalanotto .25
189 David Wells .25
190 Roger Cedeno .25
191 Brian Giles .50
192 Julio Zuleta .25
193 Timo Perez .25
194 Billy Wagner .25
195 Craig Counsell .25
196 Bart Miadich .25
197 Gary Sheffield .75
198 Richard Hidalgo .50
199 Juan Uribe .25
200 Curt Schilling 1.00
201 Javy Lopez .50
202 Jimmy Haynes .25
203 Jim Edmonds .75
204 Pokey Reese .25
204 Pokey Reese/SP 3.00
205 Matt Clement .25
206 Dean Palmer .25
207 Nick Johnson .25
208 Nate Espy **RC** .75
209 Pedro Feliz .25
210 Aaron Rowand .25
211 Masato Yoshii .25
212 Jose Cruz .25
213 Paul Byrd .25
214 Mark Phillips **RC** 1.00
215 Benny Agbayani .25
216 Frank Menechino .25
217 John Flaherty .25
218 Brian Boehringer .25
219 Todd Hollandsworth .25
220 Sammy Sosa/SP 8.00
221 Steve Sparks .25
222 Homer Bush .25
223 Mike Hampton .50
224 Bobby Abreu .50
225 Barry Larkin .75
226 Ryan Rupe .25
227 Bubba Trammell .25
228 Todd Zeile .25
229 Jeff Shaw .25
230 Alex Ochoa .25
231 Orlando Cabrera .25
232 Jeremy Giambi .25
233 Tomo Ohka .25
234 Luis Castillo .25
235 Chris Holt .25
236 Shawn Green .50
237 Sidney Ponson .25
238 Lee Stevens .25
239 Hank Blalock .50
240 Randy Winn .25
241 Pedro Martinez 1.50
242 Vinny Castillo .25
243 Steve Karsay .25
244 Barry Bonds/SP 15.00
245 Jason Bere .25
246 Scott Rolen 1.50
246 Scott Rolen/SP 6.00
247 Ryan Kohlmeier .25
248 Kerry Wood 1.50
249 Aramis Ramirez .50
250 Lance Berkman .75
251 Omar Vizquel .50
252 Juan Encarnacion .25
254 David Segui .25
255 Brian Anderson .25
256 Jay Payton .25
257 Mark Grudzielanek .25
258 Jimmy Anderson .25
259 Eric Valent .25
260 Chad Durbin .25
262 Alex Gonzalez .25
263 Scott Dunn .25
264 Scott Elarton .25
265 Tom Gordon .25
266 Moises Alou .50
269 Mark Buehrle .25
270 Jerry Hairston Jr. .25
272 Luke Prokopec .25
273 Graeme Lloyd .25
274 Bret Prinz .25
276 Chris Carpenter .25
277 Ryan Minor .25
278 Jeff D'Amico .25
279 Raul Ibanez .25
280 Joe Mays .25
281 Livan Hernandez .25
282 Robin Ventura .40
283 Gabe Kapler .40
284 Tony Batista .25
285 Ramon Hernandez .25
286 Craig Paquette .25
287 Mark Kotsay .25
288 Mike Lieberthal .25
289 Joe Borchard .25
290 Cristian Guzman .25
291 Craig Biggio .40
292 Joaquin Benoit .25
293 Ken Caminiti .25
294 Sean Burroughs .50
295 Eric Karros .50
296 Eric Chavez .50
297 LaTroy Hawkins .25
298 Alfonso Soriano 1.00
299 John Smoltz .50
300 Adam Dunn 1.00
301 Ryan Dempster .25
302 Travis Hafner .50
303 Russell Branyan .25
304 Dustin Hermanson .25
305 Jim Thome 1.50
306 Carlos Beltran .75
307 Jason Botts **RC** .75
308 David Cone .25
309 Ivanon Coffie .25
310 Brian Jordan .25
311 Todd Walker .25
312 Jeromy Burnitz .25
313 Tony Armas .25
314 Jeff Conine .25
315 Todd Jones .25
316 Roy Oswalt .50
317 Aubrey Huff .25
318 Josh Fogg .25
319 Jose Vidro .25
320 Jace Brewer .25
321 Mike Redmond .25
322 Noochie Varner **RC** 1.00
323 Russ Ortiz .25
324 Edgardo Alfonzo .25
325 Ruben Sierra .25
326 Calvin Murray .25
327 Marlon Anderson .25
328 Albie Lopez .25
329 Chris Gomez .25
330 Fernando Tatis .25
331 Stubby Clapp .25
332 Rickey Henderson .75
333 Brad Radke .25
334 Brent Mayne .25
335 Cory Lidle .25
336 Edgar Martinez .50
337 Aaron Boone .25
338 Jay Witasick .25
339 Benito Santiago .25
340 Jose Mercedes .25
341 Fernando Vina .25
342 A.J. Pierzynski .25
343 Jeff Bagwell 1.00
344 Brian Bohanon .25
345 Adrian Beltre .50
346 Troy Percival .25
347 Napoleon Calzado **RC** .75
348 Ruben Rivera .25
349 Rafael Soriano .25
350 Damian Jackson .25
351 Joe Randa .25
352 Chan Ho Park .25
353 Dante Bichette .25
354 Bartolo Colon .25
355 Jason Bay **RC** 5.00
356 Shea Hillenbrand .25
357 Matt Morris .50
358 Brad Penny .25
359 Mark Quinn .25
360 Marquis Grissom .25
361 Henry Blanco .25
362 Billy Koch .25
363 Mike Cameron .25
364 Albert Pujols 10.00
365 Paul Konerko 3.00
366 Eric Milton 3.00
367 Nick Bierbrodt 3.00
368 Rafael Palmeiro 5.00
369 Jorge Padilla **RC** 4.00
370 Jason Giambi 4.00
371 Mike Piazza 10.00
372 Alex Cora 3.00
373 Todd Helton 6.00
374 Juan Gonzalez 6.00
375 Mariano Rivera 4.00
376 Jason LaRue 3.00
377 Tony Gwynn 6.00
378 Wilson Betemit 3.00
379 J.J. Trujillo **RC** 3.00
380 Brad Ausmus 3.00
381 Chris George 3.00
382 Jose Canseco 5.00
383 Ramon Ortiz 3.00
384 John Rocker 3.00
385 Rey Ordonez 3.00
386 Ken Griffey Jr. 10.00
387 Juan Pena 3.00
388 Michael Barrett 3.00
389 J.D. Drew 4.00
390 Corey Koskie 3.00
391 Vernon Wells 3.00
392 Juan Tolentino **RC** 3.00
393 Luis Gonzalez 4.00
394 Terrance Long 3.00
395 Travis Lee 3.00
396 Earl Snyder **RC** 3.00
397 Nomar Garciaparra 10.00
398 Jason Schmidt 4.00
399 David Espinosa 3.00
400 Steve Green 3.00
401 Jack Wilson 3.00
402 Chris Tritle **RC** 3.00
403 Angel Berroa 3.00
404 Josh Towers 3.00
405 Andruw Jones 4.00
406 Brent Butler 3.00
407 Craig Kuzmic **RC** 3.00
408 Derek Bell 3.00
409 Eric Glaser **RC** 3.00
410 Joel Pineiro 3.00
411 Alexis Gomez 3.00
412 Mike Rivera 3.00
413 Shawn Estes 3.00
414 Milton Bradley 3.00
415 Carl Everett 3.00
416 Kazuhiro Sasaki 3.00
417 Tony Fontana **RC** 3.00
418 Josh Pearce 3.00
419 Gary Matthews Jr. 3.00
420 Raymond Cabrera **RC** 3.00
421 Joe Kennedy 3.00
422 Jason Maule **RC** 3.00
423 Casey Fossum 3.00
424 Christian Parker 3.00
425 Laynce Nix **RC** 5.00
426 Byung-Hyun Kim 3.00
427 Freddy Garcia 3.00
428 Herbert Perry 3.00
429 Jason Marquis 3.00
430 Sandy Alomar Jr. 3.00
431 Roberto Alomar 5.00
432 Tsuyoshi Shinjo 3.00
433 Tim Wakefield 3.00
434 Robert Fick 3.00
435 Vladimir Guerrero 6.00
436 Jose Mesa 3.00
437 Scott Spiezio 3.00
438 Jose Hernandez 3.00
439 Jose Acevedo 3.00
440 Brian West **RC** 3.00
441 Barry Zito 4.00
442 Luis Maza 3.00
443 Marlon Byrd 4.00
444 A.J. Burnett 3.00
445 Dee Brown 3.00
446 Carlos Delgado 5.00

Chrome

Stars (1-100): 6-10X
RC's: 3-6X
Production 553 Sets

Classic Renditions

NM/M
Complete Set (10): 10.00
Common Player: .50
Inserted 1:12
CR-1 Kerry Wood 2.00
CR-2 Brian Giles 1.00
CR-3 Roger Cedeno .50
CR-4 Jason Giambi 1.50
CR-5 Albert Pujols 4.00
CR-6 Mark Buehrle .50
CR-7 Cristian Guzman .50
CR-8 Jimmy Rollins .50
CR-9 Jim Thome 2.00
CR-10 Shawn Green 1.00

Classic Renditions Autographs

Production 25 Sets

Clubhouse Collection

NM/M
Common Player: 15.00
Jersey 1:332
Bat 1:498
RA Rich Aurilia/Bat 15.00
YB Yogi Berra/Jsy 40.00
BB Barry Bonds/Bat 60.00
AD Alvin Dark/Bat 25.00
NG Nomar Garciaparra/Bat 50.00
GK George Kell/Jsy 25.00
GM Greg Maddux/Jsy 30.00
EM Eddie Mathews/Jsy 35.00
WM Willie Mays/Bat 75.00
CP Corey Patterson/Bat 20.00
JP Jorge Posada/Bat 25.00
HS Hank Sauer/Bat 20.00

Clubhouse Collection Autograph Relics

No Pricing
Production 25 Sets

Clubhouse Collection Dual Relics

NM/M
Production 53 Sets
SM Eddie Mathews, Greg Maddux 150.00
BP Yogi Berra, Jorge Posada 125.00
SP Hank Sauer, Corey Patterson 75.00
KR George Kell, Nomar Garciaparra 100.00
DA Alvin Dark, Rich Aurilia 100.00
MB Willie Mays, Barry Bonds 200.00

Grandstand Glory Stadium Seat

NM/M
Common Player: 10.00
Inserted 1:133
RC Roy Campanella 25.00
BF Bob Feller 20.00
WF Whitey Ford 20.00
TK Ted Kluszewski 20.00
BM Billy Martin 25.00
HN Hal Newhouser 15.00
SP Satchel Paige 40.00
BP Billy Pierce 15.00
HS Hank Sauer 10.00
BS Bobby Shantz 15.00
WS Warren Spahn 20.00
EW Early Wynn 15.00

New Age Performers

NM/M
Complete Set (15): 30.00
Common Player: 1.00
Inserted 1:15
NA-1 Luis Gonzalez 1.00
NA-2 Mark McGwire 5.00
NA-3 Barry Bonds 5.00
NA-4 Ken Griffey Jr. 3.00
NA-5 Ichiro Suzuki 3.00
NA-6 Sammy Sosa 3.00
NA-7 Andruw Jones 1.00
NA-8 Derek Jeter 5.00
NA-9 Todd Helton 1.50
NA-10 Alex Rodriguez 4.00
NA-11 Jason Giambi 1.50
NA-12 Bret Boone 1.00
NA-13 Roberto Alomar 1.00
NA-14 Albert Pujols 4.00
NA-15 Vladimir Guerrero 1.50

Real One Autographs

NM/M
Common Autograph: 20.00
Inserted 1:180
Red Ink: .75-1.5X
Production 53
YB Yogi Berra 100.00
JB Joe Black 50.00
RB Ray Boone 60.00
AC Andy Carey 40.00
RCL Roger Clemens 125.00
AD Alvin Dark 60.00
DD Dom DiMaggio 80.00
JE Jim Edmonds 50.00
RF Roy Face 60.00
BF Bob Feller 60.00
WF Whitey Ford 80.00
CG Brian Giles 25.00
CG Cristian Guzman 20.00
MI Monte Irvin 60.00
GK George Kell 60.00
WM Willie Mays 200.00
GM Gil McDougald 75.00
OM Orestes Minoso 60.00
JP John Podres 60.00
PR Phil Rizzuto 80.00
ARO Alex Rodriguez 140.00
PRO Preacher Roe 60.00
AR Al Rosen 75.00
ASC Al Schoendienst 50.00
BS Bobby Shantz 50.00
ES Enos Slaughter 80.00
WS Warren Spahn 100.00
HW Hoyt Wilhelm 60.00

Real One Autographs Red Ink

Red Ink: .75-1.5X
Production 53 Sets

Team Topps Legends Autographs

NM/M
Inserted 1:613
Vida Blue 20.00
Frank Howard 30.00
Mickey Lolich 25.00
Frank Robinson 40.00
Bobby Thomson 30.00

Then and Now

NM/M
Complete Set (10): 15.00
Common Player: 1.00
Inserted 1:15
TN-1 Ed Mathews, Barry Bonds 4.00
TN-2 Al Rosen, Alex Rodriguez 4.00
TN-3 Carl Furillo, Larry Walker 1.00
TN-4 Mickey Vernon, Ichiro Suzuki 3.00
TN-5 Roy Campanella, Sammy Sosa 3.00
TN-6 Al Rosen, Bret Boone 1.00
TN-7 Warren Spahn, Randy Johnson 2.00
TN-8 Ed Lopat, Freddy Garcia 1.00
TN-9 Robin Roberts, Randy Johnson 2.00
TN-10 Billy Pierce, Hideo Nomo 1.50

2002 Topps Opening Day

NM/M
Complete Set (165): 40.00
Common Player: .10
Pack (7): 1.00
Box (36): 30.00
1 Roy Oswalt .25
2 Derek Jeter 2.00
3 Dmitri Young .10
4 Ramon Hernandez .10
5 Albert Pujols 1.50
6 Sean Casey .25
7 Joe Randa .10
8 Craig Counsell .10
9 John Olerud .25
10 Troy Glaus .40
11 Adam Kennedy .10
12 Carlos Delgado .40
13 Bobby Abreu .20
14 J.T. Snow Jr. .10
15 Ivan Rodriguez .50
16 Mike Lowell .25
17 Juan Pierre .10
18 Magglio Ordonez .30
19 Greg Maddux 1.00
20 Jorge Posada .25
21 Johnny Damon .20
22 Mike Hampton .10
23 Paul LoDuca .10
24 Terrence Long .10
25 Jeff Bagwell .50
26 Shannon Stewart .10
27 Brad Radke .10
28 Brian Jordan .10
29 Lee Stevens .10
30 Cliff Floyd .10
31 Roger Clemens 1.00
32 Mike Matheny .10
33 Alfonso Soriano .50
34 Randy Johnson .75
35 Mike Sweeney .10
36 Jose Cruz Jr. .20
37 Fernando Tatis .10
38 Eric Young .10
39 Ruben Rivera .10
40 Mike Mussina .50
41 Alex Gonzalez .10

42 Edgardo Alfonzo .10
43 Torii Hunter .25
44 Richie Sexson .25
45 Bret Boone .20
46 John Smoltz .20
47 Bengie Molina .10
48 Trot Nixon .10
49 Mike Cameron .10
50 Mariano Rivera .20
51 Ichiro Suzuki 1.50
52 Cristian Guzman .10
53 Andruw Jones .40
54 Jerry Hairston Jr. .10
55 Brad Fullmer .10
56 Luis Gonzalez .25
57 Placido Polanco .10
58 Jason Tyner .10
59 Dan Wilson .10
60 Jim Edmonds .25
61 Larry Walker .25
62 Edgar Renteria .25
63 Orlando Cabrera .10
64 Sammy Sosa 1.50
65 Derrek Lee .20
66 C.C. Sabathia .10
67 Aaron Boone .10
68 Royce Clayton .10
69 Darryl Kile .10
70 Vladimir Guerrero .75
71 Bud Smith .10
72 Adrian Beltre .20
73 Barry Bonds 15.00
74 Ben Petrick .10
75 Derek Bell .10
76 Jeff Kent .20
77 Ricky Gutierrez .10
78 Rafael Palmeiro .50
79 Doug Mientkiewicz .10
80 Fernando Vina .10
81 Mark Mulder .20
82 Carlos Beltran .25
83 Juan Encarnacion .10
84 Jimmy Rollins .20
85 Pedro J. Martinez .50
86 Aramis Ramirez .25
87 Reggie Sanders .10
88 Gary Sheffield .25
89 Bartolo Colon .10
90 Jose Macias .10
91 Bobby Higginson .10
92 Craig Biggio .20
93 Al Leiter .20
94 Juan Gonzalez .50
95 Jose Valentin .10
96 Jon Lieber .10
97 Alex Gonzalez .10
98 Jose Mesa .10
99 Sandy Alomar .10
100 Barry Bonds 2.00
101 Todd Walker .10
102 Kevin Young .10
103 Ken Griffey Jr. 1.00
104 Mark McGwire 2.00
105 Jason Giambi .50
106 Todd Helton .50
107 Mike Piazza 1.00
108 Nomar Garciaparra 1.50
109 Bernie Williams .40
110 Shawn Wooten .10
111 Eric Chavez .20
112 Curt Schilling .40
113 Roberto Alomar .50
114 Chipper Jones .75
115 Edgar Martinez .20
116 Shawn Green .20
117 Ben Grieve .10
118 Jermaine Dye .10
119 Steve Finley .10
120 Adam Dunn .25
121 Preston Wilson .10
122 Lance Berkman .20
123 Ben Sheets .25
124 Ryan Klesko .10
125 Brian Giles .25
126 Marcus Giles .10
127 Craig Wilson .10
128 Miguel Tejada .25
129 Andres Galarraga .20
130 Alex Rodriguez 1.50
131 David Justice .25
132 Barry Zito .25
133 Scott Rolen .75
134 Brent Abernathy .10
135 Raul Mondesi .20
136 Josh Towers .10
137 Rafael Furcal .10
138 Gabe Kapler .10
139 Fred McGriff .25
140 Jeff Conine .10
141 Mike Lieberthal .10
142 Frank Thomas .50
143 Jason Kendall .10
144 Toby Hall .10
145 Pat Burrell .30
146 J.D. Drew .25
147 Javier Lopez .25
148 Carlos Lee .10
149 Doug Glanville .10
150 Ruben Sierra .10
151 Julio Franco .10
152 Tim Hudson .20
153 Rich Aurilia .10
154 Geoff Jenkins .10
155 Tsuyoshi Shinjo .10
156 Moises Alou .20
157 Jim Thome .75
158 Steve Cox .10
159 Kevin Brown .20
160 Barry Bonds .50
161 Rickey Henderson .20
162 Bud Smith .10
163 Rickey Henderson .20
164 Barry Bonds .50
165 Checklist .10

Autographs

NM/M
Common Auto.: 10.00
GJ Geoff Jenkins 15.00
NJ Nick Johnson 10.00
BS Ben Sheets 25.00

2002 Topps Pristine

NM/M
Complete Set (210):
Common Player: .75
Common Uncommon RC: 3.00
Production 1,999
Common Rare RC: 5.00
Production 799
Pack (8): 30.00
Box (5): 125.00
1 Alex Rodriguez 5.00
2 Carlos Delgado 1.50
3 Jimmy Rollins .75
4 Jason Kendall .75
5 John Olerud 1.00
6 Albert Pujols 5.00
7 Curt Schilling 2.00
8 Gary Sheffield 1.00
9 Johnny Damon 1.00
10 Ichiro Suzuki 4.00
11 Pat Burrell 1.00
12 Garret Anderson 1.00
13 Andruw Jones 1.50
14 Kerry Wood 2.00
15 Kenny Lofton 1.00
16 Adam Dunn 1.50
17 Juan Pierre .75
18 Josh Beckett 1.00
19 Roy Oswalt 1.00
20 Derek Jeter 6.00
21 Jose Vidro .75
22 Richie Sexson 1.50
23 Mike Sweeney .75
24 Jeff Kent 1.00
25 Jason Giambi 1.50
26 Bret Boone 1.50
27 J.D. Drew 1.00
28 Shannon Stewart .75
29 Miguel Tejada 1.00
30 Barry Bonds 6.00
31 Randy Johnson 2.00
32 Pedro J. Martinez 2.00
33 Magglio Ordonez 1.00
34 Todd Helton 1.50
35 Craig Biggio 1.00
36 Shawn Green 1.00
37 Vladimir Guerrero 2.00
38 Mo Vaughn 1.00
39 Alfonso Soriano 2.00
40 Barry Zito 1.00
41 Aramis Ramirez 1.00
42 Ryan Klesko 1.00
43 Ruben Sierra .75
44 Tino Martinez .75
45 Toby Hall .75
46 Ivan Rodriguez 1.50
47 Raul Mondesi .75
48 Carlos Pena .75
49 Darin Erstad 1.00
50 Sammy Sosa 4.00
51 Bartolo Colon 1.00
52 Robert Fick .75
53 Cliff Floyd .75
54 Brian Jordan .75
55 Torii Hunter 1.00
56 Roberto Alomar 1.00
57 Roger Clemens 4.00
58 Mark Mulder 1.00
59 Brian Giles 1.00
60 Mike Piazza 4.00
61 Rich Aurilia .75
62 Freddy Garcia .75
63 Jim Edmonds 1.50
64 Eric Hinske .75
65 Jeremy Giambi .75
66 Javier Vazquez .75
67 Cristian Guzman .75
68 Paul LoDuca .75
69 Bobby Abreu 1.00
70 Nomar Garciaparra 4.00
71 Troy Glaus 1.00
72 Chipper Jones 2.00
73 Scott Rolen 2.00
74 Lance Berkman 1.00
75 C.C. Sabathia .75
76 Bernie Williams 1.00
77 Rafael Palmeiro 1.50
78 Phil Nevin .75
79 Kazuhiro Sasaki .75
80 Eric Chavez 1.00
81 Jorge Posada 1.00
82 Edgardo Alfonzo .75
83 Geoff Jenkins 1.00
84 Preston Wilson .75
85 Jim Thome 2.00
86 Frank Thomas 1.50
87 Jeff Bagwell 1.50
88 Greg Maddux 3.00
89 Mark Prior 3.00
90 Larry Walker 1.00
91 Luis Gonzalez 1.00
92 Tim Hudson 1.00
93 Tsuyoshi Shinjo .75
94 Juan Gonzalez 1.50
95 Shea Hillenbrand .75
96 Paul Konerko .75
97 Tom Glavine 1.50
98 Marty Cordova .75
99 Moises Alou 1.00
100 Ken Griffey Jr. 4.00
101 Hank Blalock 1.50
102 Matt Morris 1.00
103 Robb Nen .75
104 Mike Cameron .75
105 Mark Buehrle .75
106 Sean Burroughs .75
107 Orlando Cabrera .75
108 Jeromy Burnitz .75
109 Juan Uribe .75
110 Eric Milton .75
111 Carlos Lee .75
112 Jose Mesa .75
113 Morgan Ensberg .75
114 Mike Rivera .75
115 Juan Cruz .75
116 Mike Lieberthal .75
117 Armando Benitez .75
118 Vinny Castilla .75
119 Russ Ortiz .75
120 Mike Lowell 1.00
121 Corey Patterson 1.00
122 Mike Mussina 1.50
123 Rafael Furcal .75
124 Mark Grace 1.50
125 Ben Sheets 1.00
126 John Smoltz 1.00
127 Fred McGriff 1.00
128 Nick Johnson .75
129 J.T. Snow .75
130 Jeff Cirillo .75
131 Trevor Hoffman .75
132 Kevin Brown 1.00
133 Mariano Rivera 1.50
134 Marlon Anderson .75
135 Al Leiter .75
136 Doug Mientkiewicz .75
137 Eric Karros .75
138 Bobby Higginson .75
139 Sean Casey 1.00
140 Troy Percival .75
141 Willie Mays 5.00
142 Carl Yastrzemski 3.00
143 Stan Musial 4.00
144 Harmon Killebrew 3.00
145 Mike Schmidt 5.00
146 Duke Snider 2.00
147 Brooks Robinson 3.00
148 Frank Robinson 2.00
149 Nolan Ryan 8.00
150 Reggie Jackson 3.00
151 Joe Mauer/C **RC** 20.00
152 Joe Mauer/U **RC** 25.00
153 Joe Mauer/R **RC** 35.00
154 Colt Griffin/C 3.00
155 Colt Griffin/U 5.00
156 Colt Griffin/R 8.00
157 Jason Simontacchi/C **RC** 2.00
158 Jason Simontacchi/U **RC** 3.00
159 Jason Simontacchi/R **RC** 5.00
160 Casey Kotchman/C 5.00
161 Casey Kotchman/U 8.00
162 Casey Kotchman/R 15.00
163 Greg Sain/C **RC** 1.50
164 Greg Sain/U **RC** 3.00
165 Greg Sain/R **RC** 5.00
166 David Wright/C 40.00
167 David Wright/U 50.00
168 David Wright/R 60.00
169 Scott Hairston/C 4.00
170 Scott Hairston/U 6.00
171 Scott Hairston/R 10.00
172 Rolando Viera/C **RC** 1.50
173 Rolando Viera/U **RC** 3.00
174 Rolando Viera/R **RC** 5.00
175 Tyrell Godwin/C 1.50
176 Tyrell Godwin/U 3.00
177 Tyrell Godwin/R 5.00
178 Jesus Cota/C **RC** 1.50
179 Jesus Cota/U **RC** 3.00
180 Jesus Cota/R **RC** 5.00
181 Dan Johnson/C **RC** 5.00
182 Dan Johnson/U **RC** 10.00
183 Dan Johnson/R **RC** 15.00
184 Mario Ramos/C **RC** 1.50
185 Mario Ramos/U 3.00
186 Mario Ramos/R 5.00
187 Jason Dubois/C **RC** 4.00
188 Jason Dubois/U **RC** 6.00
189 Jason Dubois/R **RC** 10.00
190 Jonny Gomes/C **RC** 8.00
191 Jonny Gomes/U **RC** 15.00
192 Jonny Gomes/R **RC** 20.00
193 Chris Snelling/C **RC** 2.00
194 Chris Snelling/U **RC** 4.00
195 Chris Snelling/R **RC** 6.00
196 Hansel Izquierdo/C **RC** 2.00
197 Hansel Izquierdo/U **RC** 4.00
198 Hansel Izquierdo/R **RC** 6.00
199 So Taguchi/C **RC** 3.00
200 So Taguchi/U **RC** 5.00
201 So Taguchi/R **RC** 8.00
202 Kazuhisa Ishii/C **RC** 3.00
203 Kazuhisa Ishii/U **RC** 5.00
204 Kazuhisa Ishii/R **RC** 8.00
205 Jorge Padilla/C **RC** 1.50
206 Jorge Padilla/U **RC** 3.00
207 Jorge Padilla/R **RC** 5.00
208 Earl Snyder/C **RC** 2.00
209 Earl Snyder/U **RC** 4.00
210 Earl Snyder/R **RC** 6.00

Refractors

Stars (1-150): 2-4X
Production 149
Common Rookies: .75-1.5X
Production 1,999
Uncommon Rookies: 1-2X
Production 799
Rare Rookies: 2-3X
Production 149
Gold Refractors (1-150): 3-5X
Gold Common RC's: 4-8X
Gold Uncommon RC's: 2-4X
Gold Rare RC's: 1-2X
Production 70 Sets
All Refractors are uncirculated.

Fall Memories

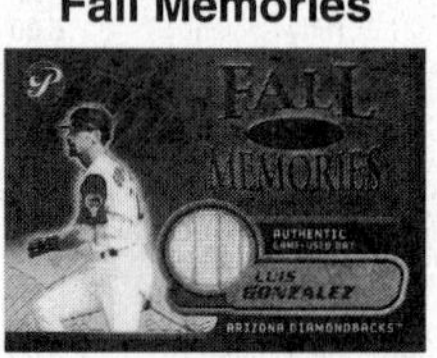

NM/M
Common Player: 5.00
Varying quantities produced
JB Johnny Bench 15.00
BB Barry Bonds 30.00
GB George Brett 25.00
TG Tom Glavine 8.00
LG Luis Gonzalez 5.00
MG Mark Grace 12.00
SG Shawn Green 6.00
TH Todd Helton 8.00
RJ Reggie Jackson 15.00
AJ Andruw Jones 8.00
CP Chipper Jones 10.00
TM Tino Martinez 8.00
WM Willie Mays 40.00
EM Eddie Murray 15.00
JP Jorge Posada 8.00
KP Kirby Puckett 15.00
CS Curt Schilling 8.00
GS Gary Sheffield 5.00
AS Alfonso Soriano 10.00
BW Bernie Williams 8.00

In The Gap

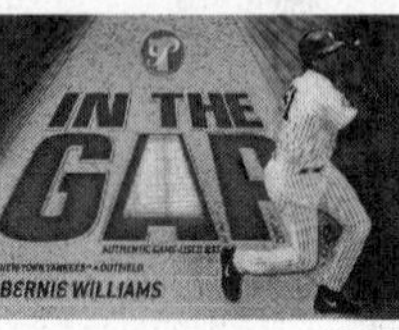

NM/M
Common Player: 5.00
Varying quantities produced
RA Roberto Alomar 10.00
LB Lance Berkman 8.00
WBE Wilson Betemit 5.00
WB Wade Boggs 8.00
BBO Barry Bonds 25.00
BB Bret Boone 6.00
EC Eric Chavez 8.00
CD Carlos Delgado 6.00
AD Adam Dunn 10.00
JE Jim Edmonds 6.00
DE Darin Erstad 5.00
NG Nomar Garciaparra 15.00
TG Tony Gwynn 15.00
TH Todd Helton 8.00
RH Rickey Henderson 10.00
AJ Andruw Jones 10.00
JK Jeff Kent 5.00
RK Ryan Klesko 8.00
PL Paul LoDuca 10.00
RP Rafael Palmeiro 10.00
MP Mike Piazza 15.00
AP Albert Pujols 15.00
ARA Aramis Ramirez 8.00
AR Alex Rodriguez 15.00
IR Ivan Rodriguez 8.00
TS Tsuyoshi Shinjo 5.00
AS Alfonso Soriano 10.00
LW Larry Walker 5.00
BW Bernie Williams 15.00
PW Preston Wilson 5.00

Patches

No Pricing
Production 25 Sets

Personal Endorsements

NM/M
Common Autograph: 8.00
Inserted 1:Box
RA Roberto Alomar 30.00
KB Kenny Baugh 8.00
LB Lance Berkman 30.00
BB Barry Bonds 180.00
DB Dewon Brazelton 15.00
JD Johnny Damon 30.00
GF Gavin Floyd 25.00
CG Cristian Guzman 10.00
IG Irvin Guzman 10.00
OH Orlando Hudson 10.00
KI Kazuhisa Ishii 30.00
CK Casey Kotchman 20.00
JL Jason Lane 8.00
CW Corwin Malone 8.00
NN Nick Neugebauer 8.00
AP Albert Pujols 125.00
JR Jimmy Rollins 20.00
BS Ben Sheets 20.00
JS Juan Silvestre 8.00
ST So Taguchi 15.00
MT Marcus Thames 8.00

Popular Demand

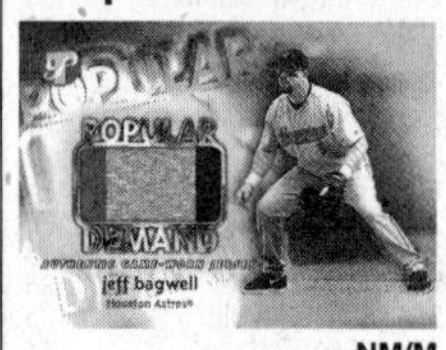

NM/M
Common Player: 5.00
Varying quantities produced
RA Roberto Alomar 10.00
JB Jeff Bagwell 10.00
WB Wade Boggs 8.00
BBO Barry Bonds 25.00
BB Bret Boone 5.00
CD Carlos Delgado 5.00
AD Adam Dunn 8.00
NG Nomar Garciaparra 15.00
SG Shawn Green 5.00
TG Tony Gwynn 12.00
TH Todd Helton 8.00
CJ Chipper Jones 12.00
DM Don Mattingly 35.00
MP Mike Piazza 15.00
AP Albert Pujols 20.00
AR Alex Rodriguez 15.00
IR Ivan Rodriguez 8.00
CS Curt Schilling 8.00
FT Frank Thomas 10.00
LW Larry Walker 5.00

Portions

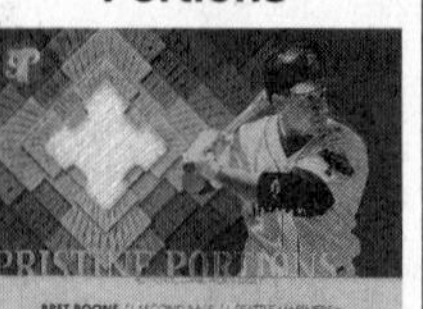

NM/M
Common Player: 5.00
Varying quantities produced
RA Roberto Alomar 10.00
JB Jeff Bagwell 10.00
LB Lance Berkman 10.00
CB Craig Biggio 8.00
BBO Barry Bonds 20.00
BB Bret Boone 5.00
CD Carlos Delgado 5.00
RD Ryan Dempster 5.00
AD Adam Dunn 8.00
CF Cliff Floyd 5.00
RF Rafael Furcal 5.00
NG Nomar Garciaparra 15.00
CG Cristian Guzman 5.00
TH Todd Helton 8.00
NJ Nick Johnson 5.00
LD Paul LoDuca 5.00
GM Greg Maddux 10.00
EM Edgar Martinez 10.00
MM Mike Mussina 10.00
MO Magglio Ordonez 5.00
RP Rafael Palmeiro 8.00
MP Mike Piazza 15.00
JP Jorge Posada 8.00
AP Albert Pujols 15.00
AR Alex Rodriguez 15.00
IR Ivan Rodriguez 8.00
NR Nolan Ryan 30.00
KS Kazuhiro Sasaki 5.00

2002 Topps Reserve

NM/M
Complete Set (150): 120.00
Common Player: .25
Common (136-150): 4.00
Production 999
Silver parallel (1-135): 4-8X
Silver (136-150): .75-1.5X
Production 150
Box:10 Packs & 1 Auto. Helmet: 100.00
1 Alex Rodriguez 2.50
2 Tsuyoshi Shinjo .25
3 Craig Biggio .40
4 Troy Glaus .50
5 Mike Rivera .25
6 Curt Schilling .75
7 Garret Anderson .50
8 Ben Sheets .50
9 Todd Helton .75
10 Paul Konerko .50
11 Sammy Sosa 2.00
12 Bud Smith .25
13 Jeff Bagwell .75
14 Albert Pujols 2.00
15 Jose Vidro .25
16 Carlos Delgado .50
17 Torii Hunter .50
18 Jerry Hairston Jr. .25
19 Troy Percival .25
20 Vladimir Guerrero 1.00
21 Geoff Jenkins .40
22 Carlos Pena .25
23 Juan Gonzalez .75
24 Raul Mondesi .25
25 Jimmy Rollins .40
26 Mariano Rivera .50
27 Jorge Posada .50
28 Magglio Ordonez .50
29 Roberto Alomar .50
30 Randy Johnson 1.00
31 Xavier Nady .25
32 Terrence Long .25
33 Chipper Jones 1.00
34 Rich Aurilia .25
35 Aramis Ramirez .50
36 Jim Thome 1.00
37 Bret Boone .50
38 Angel Berroa .25
39 Jeff Conine .25
40 Cliff Floyd .25
41 Pedro J. Martinez 1.00
42 J.D. Drew .50
43 Kazuhiro Sasaki .25
44 Jon Rauch .25
45 Orlando Hudson .25
46 Scott Rolen 1.00
47 Rafael Furcal .25
48 Brad Penny .25
49 Miguel Tejada .50
50 Orlando Cabrera .25
51 Bobby Abreu .50
52 Darin Erstad .50
53 Edgar Martinez .40
54 Ben Grieve .25
55 Shawn Green .50
56 Ivan Rodriguez .75
57 Josh Beckett .50
58 Ray Durham .25
59 Jason Hart .25
60 Nathan Haynes .25
61 Jason Giambi .75
62 Eric Chavez .50
63 Matt Morris .40
64 Lance Berkman .50
65 Jeff Kent .40
66 Andruw Jones .50

67 Brian Giles .50
68 Morgan Ensberg .25
69 Pat Burrell .50
70 Ken Griffey Jr. 2.00
71 Carlos Beltran .50
72 Ichiro Suzuki 2.00
73 Larry Walker .50
74 J.J. Putz **RC** .50
75 Mike Piazza 2.00
76 Rafael Palmeiro .75
77 Mark Prior 2.00
78 Toby Hall .25
79 Pokey Reese .25
80 Mike Mussina .50
81 Omar Vizquel .25
82 Shannon Stewart .25
83 Jeromy Burnitz .25
84 Bernie Williams .50
85 C.C. Sabathia .25
86 Mike Hampton .25
87 Kevin Brown .50
88 Juan Cruz .25
89 Jeff Weaver .25
90 Jason Lane .25
91 Adam Dunn .75
92 Jose Cruz Jr. .25
93 Marlon Anderson .25
94 Jeff Cirillo .25
95 Mark Buehrle .25
96 Austin Kearns .50
97 Tim Hudson .50
98 Brian Jordan .25
99 Phil Nevin .25
100 Barry Bonds 3.00
101 Derek Jeter 3.00
102 Javier Vazquez .25
103 Jason Kendall .40
104 Jim Edmonds .50
105 Kenny Kelly .25
106 Juan Pena .25
107 Mark Grace .50
108 Roger Clemens 2.00
109 Barry Zito .50
110 Greg Vaughn .25
111 Greg Maddux 1.50
112 Richie Sexson .50
113 Jermaine Dye .25
114 Kerry Wood 1.00
115 Matt Lawton .25
116 Sean Casey .50
117 Gary Sheffield .50
118 Preston Wilson .25
119 Cristian Guzman .25
120 Mike Sweeney .25
121 Neifi Perez .25
122 Paul LoDuca .25
123 Luis Gonzalez .50
124 Ryan Klesko .25
125 Alfonso Soriano 1.00
126 Bobby Higginson .25
127 Juan Pierre .25
128 Moises Alou .50
129 Roy Oswalt .50
130 Nomar Garciaparra 2.00
131 Fred McGriff .40
132 Edgardo Alfonzo .25
133 Johnny Damon .40
134 Dewon Brazelton .25
135 Mark Mulder .50
136 So Taguchi **RC** 8.00
137 Mario Ramos 4.00
138 Dan Johnson **RC** 15.00
139 Hansel Izquierdo **RC** 5.00
140 Kazuhisa Ishii **RC** 10.00
141 Jon Switzer 4.00
142 Chris Tritle **RC** 6.00
143 Chris Snelling **RC** 8.00
144 Chone Figgins **RC** 8.00
145 Dan Phillips **RC** 4.00
146 John Rodriguez **RC** 4.00
147 Colt Griffin 8.00
148 Jonny Gomes **RC** 15.00
149 Josh Barfield 10.00
150 Joe Mauer **RC** 30.00

Silver

Stars (1-135): 4-8X
SP's (136-150): .75-1.5X

Autographed Mini-Helmets

NM/M
Common Helmet: 20.00
1:Box
Gold Ink Autographs: No Pricing
Production 25
Roberto Alomar 45.00
Moises Alou 25.00
Lance Berkman 35.00
Bret Boone 25.00
Eric Chavez 30.00
Adam Dunn 40.00
Cliff Floyd 20.00
Troy Glaus 40.00
Luis Gonzalez 30.00
Todd Helton 50.00
Magglio Ordonez 25.00
Rafael Palmeiro 40.00
Albert Pujols 200.00
Alex Rodriguez 125.00
Scott Rolen 35.00
Jimmy Rollins 30.00
Alfonso Soriano 50.00
Barry Zito 30.00

Game-Used Baseball

NM/M
Inserted 1:1,761
I Ichiro Suzuki 65.00

Game-Used Bat

NM/M
Common Player: 5.00
Inserted 1:12
RA Roberto Alomar 10.00
JB Jeff Bagwell 10.00
BB Barry Bonds 20.00
CD Carlos Delgado 8.00
JG Juan Gonzalez 8.00
LG Luis Gonzalez 5.00
TG Tony Gwynn 12.00
RH Rickey Henderson 10.00
CJ Chipper Jones 10.00
AJ Andruw Jones 8.00
TM Tino Martinez 8.00
RP Rafael Palmeiro 8.00
MB Mike Piazza 15.00
AP Albert Pujols 15.00
AR Alex Rodriguez 12.00
IR Ivan Rodriguez 8.00
TS Tsuyoshi Shinjo 5.00
AS Alfonso Soriano 10.00
FT Frank Thomas 8.00
BW Bernie Williams 8.00

Game-Worn Patch

No Pricing
Production 25 Sets

Game-Worn Uniform

NM/M
Common Player: 5.00
Inserted 1:5
BB Barry Bonds 20.00
BBO Bret Boone 5.00
DE Darin Erstad 5.00
NG Nomar Garciaparra 15.00
LG Luis Gonzalez 5.00
TG Tony Gwynn 10.00
TH Todd Helton 8.00
RJ Randy Johnson 10.00
AJ Andruw Jones 6.00
CJ Chipper Jones 10.00
GM Greg Maddux 12.00
PM Pedro Martinez 10.00
MM Mark Mulder 5.00
MO Magglio Ordonez 5.00
RP Rafael Palmeiro 8.00
MP Mike Piazza 12.00
AP Albert Pujols 15.00
AR Alex Rodriguez 12.00
IR Ivan Rodriguez 8.00
SR Scott Rolen 10.00
KS Kazuhiro Sasaki 5.00
CS Curt Schilling 8.00
FT Frank Thomas 8.00
KW Kerry Wood 10.00

2002 Topps Super Teams

NM/M
Complete Set: 40.00
Common Player: .25
Pack (7): 3.50
Box (20): 60.00
1 Leo Durocher .25
2 Whitey Lockman .25
3 Alvin Dark .25
4 Monte Irvin .50
5 Willie Mays 2.50

6 Wes Westrum .25
7 Johnny Antonelli .25
8 Sal Maglie .25
9 Dusty Rhodes .25
10 Davey Williams .25
11 Hoyt Wilhelm .25
12 Don Mueller .25
13 Dusty Rhodes .25
14 Willie Mays, Monte Irvin, Dusty Rhodes .75
15 Walt Alston .25
16 Gil Hodges .75
17 Jim Gilliam .25
18 Pee Wee Reese .50
19 Jackie Robinson 2.00
20 Duke Snider 1.00
21 Carl Furillo .25
22 Roy Campanella 1.00
23 Don Newcombe .25
24 Don Hoak .25
25 Johnny Podres .25
26 Clem Labine .25
27 Johnny Podres .25
28 Pee Wee Reese, Jackie Robinson, Duke Snider 1.00
29 Fred Haney .25
30 Joe Adcock .25
31 Frank Torre .25
32 Red Schoendienst .25
33 Johnny Logan .25
34 Eddie Mathews 1.00
35 Hank Aaron 3.00
36 Andy Pafko .25
37 Wes Covington .25
38 Lew Burdette .25
39 Warren Spahn 1.00
40 Del Crandall .25
41 Lew Burdette .25
42 Warren Spahn, Eddie Mathews, Hank Aaron 1.50
43 Danny Murtaugh .25
44 Dick Stuart .25
45 Bill Mazeroski .25
46 Dick Groat .25
47 Don Hoak .25
48 Gino Cimoli .25
49 Bill Virdon .25
50 Roberto Clemente 2.50
51 Smoky Burgess .25
52 Bob Friend .25
53 Vernon Law .25
55 Roy Face .25
56 Bill Mazeroski .25
57 Roberto Clemente, Bill Mazeroski, Dick Groat 1.00
58 Ralph Houk .25
59 Bill "Moose" Skowron .50
60 Bobby Richardson .25
61 Tony Kubek .25
62 Clete Boyer .25
63 Yogi Berra 1.50
64 Bob Cerv .25
65 Roger Maris 1.50
66 Elston Howard .25
67 Whitey Ford 1.00
68 Ralph Terry .25
69 Johnny Blanchard .25
70 Whitey Ford 1.00
71 Yogi Berra, Roger Maris, Elston Howard, Bill "Moose" Skowron 1.00
72 Red Schoendienst .25
73 Orlando Cepeda .40
74 Julian Javier .25
75 Dal Maxvill .25
76 Mike Shannon .25
77 Lou Brock .75
78 Roger Maris 1.50
79 Curt Flood .25
80 Tim McCarver .25
81 Steve Carlton .75
82 Bob Gibson 1.00
83 Nelson Briles .25
84 Bobby Tolan .25
85 Bob Gibson 1.00
86 Bob Gibson, Steve Carlton, Orlando Cepeda, Lou Brock .50
87 Gil Hodges .25
88 Ed Kranepool .25
89 Buddy Harrelson .25
90 Wayne Garrett .25
91 Cleon Jones .25
92 Tommie Agee .25
93 Ron Swoboda .25
94 Al Weis .25
95 Jerry Grote .25
96 Tom Seaver 1.00
97 Jerry Koosman .25
98 Tug McGraw .25
99 Nolan Ryan 3.00
100 Donn Clendenon .25
101 Tom Seaver, Jerry Koosman, Tug McGraw, Nolan Ryan 1.00
102 Earl Weaver .25
103 Boog Powell .25
104 Davey Johnson .25
105 Mark Belanger .25
106 Brooks Robinson 1.00
107 Don Buford .25
108 Paul Blair .25
109 Frank Robinson 1.00
110 Dick Hall .25
111 Jim Palmer .75
112 Mike Cuellar .25
113 Dave McNally .25
114 Andy Etchebarren .25
115 Brooks Robinson 1.00
116 Dick Hall, Jim Palmer, Mike Cuellar, Dave McNally .40
117 Alvin Dark .25
118 Gene Tenace .25
119 Dick Green .25
120 Bert Campaneris .25
121 Sal Bando .25
122 Reggie Jackson 1.00
123 Joe Rudi .25
124 Claudell Washington .25
125 Ray Fosse .25
126 Vida Blue .40
127 Rollie Fingers .25
128 Jim "Catfish" Hunter .50
129 Ken Holtzman .25
130 Rollie Fingers .25
131 Jim "Catfish" Hunter, Sal Bando, Reggie Jackson, Rollie Fingers .50
132 Davey Johnson .25
133 Keith Hernandez .25
134 Wally Backman .25
135 Rafael Santana .25
136 Ray Knight .25
137 Len Dykstra .25
138 Darryl Strawberry .25
139 Kevin Mitchell .25
140 Dwight Gooden .25
141 Bob Ojeda .25
142 Sid Fernandez .25
143 Ron Darling .25
144 Gary Carter .25
145 Ray Knight .25
146 Darryl Strawberry, Dwight Gooden, Keith Hernandez .25

Retrofractor

Cards (1-146): 2-4X
#'d to year team won World Series

Autographs

NM/M
Common Autograph: 10.00
Inserted 1:19
YB Yogi Berra 60.00
VB Vida Blue 15.00
CB Clete Boyer 15.00
SC Steve Carlton 25.00
MI Monte Irvin 15.00
RJ Reggie Jackson 50.00
TK Tony Kubek 30.00
TM Tug McGraw 15.00
AP Andy Pafko 20.00
JP Jim Palmer 25.00
JPO Johnny Podres 15.00
BR Bobby Richardson 15.00
BRO Brooks Robinson 30.00
NR Nolan Ryan 150.00
TS Tom Seaver 40.00
MS Bill "Moose" Skowron 20.00
WS Warren Spahn 40.00
HW Hoyt Wilhelm 15.00

A View To a Thrill Seat Relics

NM/M
Common Player: 10.00
Inserted 1:30
HA Hank Aaron 20.00
YB Yogi Berra 15.00
LB Lew Burdette 10.00
RC Roberto Clemente 50.00
WF Whitey Ford 15.00
BG Bob Gibson 15.00
RMB Roger Maris/Cardinals 20.00
RMY Roger Maris/Yankees 40.00
EM Eddie Mathews 15.00
WM Willie Mays 30.00
BM Bill Mazeroski 10.00
JP Jim Palmer 10.00
BP Boog Powell 10.00
BR Brooks Robinson 15.00
FR Frank Robinson 15.00
RS Red Schoendienst 10.00
DS Duke Snider 15.00
WS Warren Spahn 15.00

A View To A Thrill Autograph Relics

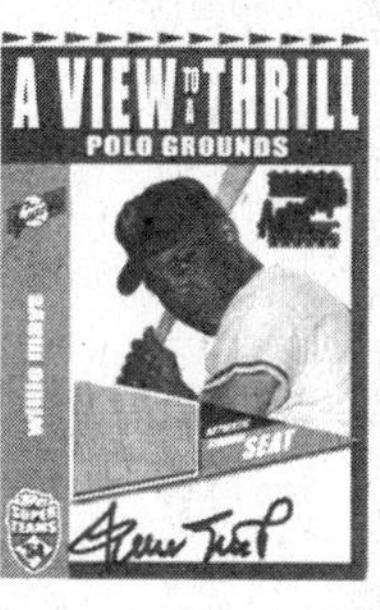

NM/M
Produced listed
WFA Whitey Ford/61 100.00
BGA Bob Gibson/67 60.00
WMA Willie Mays/54 150.00
DSA Duke Snider/55 80.00
WSA Warren Spahn/57 60.00

Classic Combos

NM/M
Common Card: 40.00
Inserted 1:865
AJ Tommie Agee, Cleon Jones 40.00
JR Reggie Jackson, Joe Rudi 40.00
RR Brooks Robinson, Frank Robinson 50.00
SK Tom Seaver, Jerry Koosman 50.00
SRBK "Moose" Skowron, Bobby Richardson, Clete Boyer, Tony Kubek 80.00

Relics

NM/M
Common Player: 10.00
TA Tommie Agee/Bat 20.00
SBB Sal Bando/Bat 10.00
SBJ Sal Bando/Jsy 10.00
MB Mark Belanger/Bat 10.00
PB Paul Blair/Bat 10.00
CB Clete Boyer/Bat 10.00
LB Lew Burdette/Jsy 15.00
SB Smoky Burgess/Bat 10.00
BC Bert Campaneris/Jsy 15.00
GC Gary Carter/Jacket 20.00
GCB Gary Carter/Bat 15.00
GCJ Gary Carter/Jsy 15.00
OC Orlando Cepeda/Bat 15.00
BCE Bob Cerv/Bat 10.00
GCI Gino Cimoli/Bat 10.00
DC Del Crandel/Bat 10.00
MC Mike Cuellar/Jsy 10.00
RD Ron Darling/Jsy 10.00
LD Len Dykstra/Bat 15.00
RF Ray Fosse/Bat 10.00
BF Bob Friend/Jsy 10.00
WG Wayne Garrett/Bat 10.00
DG Dwight Gooden/Jsy 15.00
DH Don Hoak/Bat 10.00
RH Ralph Houk/Jsy 10.00
RJ Reggie Jackson/Bat 35.00
DJ Davey Johnson/Bat 10.00
CJ Cleon Jones/Bat 20.00
RK Ray Knight/Bat 10.00
JK Jerry Koosman/Jsy 10.00
EK Ed Kranepool/Jsy 15.00
TK Tony Kubek/Bat 25.00
TM Tug McGraw/Jsy 15.00
DM Dave McNally/Jsy 10.00
KM Kevin Mitchell/Bat 10.00
AP Andy Pafko/Bat 10.00
BR Bobby Richardson/Bat 25.00
BRO Brooks Robinson/Bat 25.00
FR Frank Robinson/Bat 20.00
JR Joe Rudi/Bat 10.00
NR Nolan Ryan/Bat 75.00
RS Red Schoendienst/Bat 10.00
TS Tom Seaver/Bat 20.00
MS "Moose" Skowron/Bat 20.00
DS Darryl Strawberry/Bat 20.00
CW Claudell Washington/Bat 10.00

Super Teammates

NM/M
Complete Set (5): 10.00
Common Card: 2.00
Inserted 1:10
BG Lou Brock, Bob Gibson 2.00
FB Whitey Ford, Yogi Berra 4.00
MI Willie Mays, Monte Irvin 4.00
RR Brooks Robinson, Frank Robinson 3.00

SRBK Bill "Moose" Skowron, Bobby Richardson, Clete Boyer, Tony Kubek 2.00

Super Teammates Autographs

NM/M
Production 50 Sets
BGA Lou Brock, Bob Gibson 100.00
FBA Whitey Ford, Yogi Berra 150.00
MIA Willie Mays, Monte Irvin 180.00
RRA Brooks Robinson, Frank Robinson 100.00
SRBKA Bill "Moose" Skowron, Bobby Richardson, Clete Boyer, Tony Kubek 200.00

2002 Topps Ten

NM/M
Complete Set (200): 40.00
Common Player: .15
Pack (7): 2.00
Box (24): 40.00
1 Ichiro Suzuki 1.00
2 Rich Aurilia .15
3 Bret Boone .25
4 Juan Pierre .15
5 Shannon Stewart .15
6 Alex Rodriguez 1.00
7 Luis Gonzalez .25
8 Todd Helton .50
9 Garret Anderson .25
10 Albert Pujols 1.00
11 Lance Berkman .25
12 Todd Helton .50
13 Jeff Kent .15
14 Bob Abreu .25
15 Jason Giambi .40
16 Albert Pujols 1.00
17 Mike Sweeney .15
18 Vladimir Guerrero .50
19 Cliff Floyd .15
20 Shannon Stewart .15
21 Cristian Guzman .15
22 Roberto Alomar .40
23 Carlos Beltran .25
24 Jimmy Rollins .25
25 Roger Cedeno .15
26 Juan Pierre .15
27 Juan Uribe .15
28 Luis Castillo .15
29 Ray Durham .15
30 Mark McLemore .15
31 Barry Bonds 1.50
32 Sammy Sosa 1.00
33 Luis Gonzalez .25
34 Alex Rodriguez 1.00
35 Shawn Green .25
36 Todd Helton .50
37 Jim Thome .50
38 Rafael Palmeiro .40
39 Richie Sexson .25
40 Phil Nevin .15
41 Troy Glaus .40
42 Sammy Sosa 1.00
43 Todd Helton .50
44 Luis Gonzalez .25
45 Bret Boone .25
46 Juan Gonzalez .40
47 Barry Bonds 1.50
48 Alex Rodriguez 1.00
49 Jeff Bagwell .50

50 Albert Pujols 1.00
51 Phil Nevin .15
52 Ichiro Suzuki 1.00
53 Larry Walker .25
54 Jason Giambi .40
55 Roberto Alomar .40
56 Todd Helton .50
57 Moises Alou .25
58 Lance Berkman .25
59 Bret Boone .25
60 Frank Catalanotto .15
61 Chipper Jones .50
62 Barry Bonds 1.50
63 Sammy Sosa 1.00
64 Luis Gonzalez .25
65 Todd Helton .50
66 Larry Walker .25
67 Jason Giambi .40
68 Jim Thome .50
69 Alex Rodriguez 1.00
70 Lance Berkman .25
71 Albert Pujols 1.00
72 Ichiro Suzuki 1.00
73 Roger Cedeno .15
74 Juan Pierre .15
75 Jimmy Rollins .25
76 Alfonso Soriano .50
77 Mark McLemore .15
78 Chuck Knoblauch .15
79 Vladimir Guerrero .50
80 Bob Abreu .25
81 Mike Cameron .15
82 Sammy Sosa 1.00
83 Alex Rodriguez 1.00
84 Todd Helton .50
85 Barry Bonds 1.50
86 Luis Gonzalez .25
87 Ichiro Suzuki 1.00
88 Jeff Bagwell .50
89 Cliff Floyd .15
90 Shawn Green .25
91 Craig Biggio .15
92 Juan Pierre .15
93 Fernando Vina .15
94 Paul LoDuca .15
95 Mark Grace .25
96 Eric Young .15
97 Placido Polanco .15
98 Jason Kendall .15
99 Ichiro Suzuki 1.00
100 Orlando Cabrera .15
101 Rey Sanchez .15
102 Ichiro Suzuki 1.00
103 Edgar Martinez .25
104 Bret Boone .25
105 Barry Bonds 1.50
106 Ivan Rodriguez .40
107 Mike Piazza 1.00
108 Sammy Sosa 1.00
109 John Olerud .25
110 Roberto Alomar .40
111 Roberto Alomar .40
112 Mark McGwire 1.50
113 Barry Larkin .25
114 Ken Griffey Jr. 1.00
115 Rickey Henderson .25
116 Barry Bonds 1.50
117 Ivan Rodriguez .40
118 Mike Piazza 1.00
119 Roger Clemens 1.00
120 Randy Johnson .50
121 Albert Pujols 1.00
122 Ichiro Suzuki 1.00
123 Roy Oswalt .25
124 C.C. Sabathia .15
125 Jimmy Rollins .25
126 Alfonso Soriano .50
127 David Eckstein .15
128 Adam Dunn .50
129 Bud Smith .15
130 Tsuyoshi Shinjo .15
131 Matt Morris .15
132 Curt Schilling .25
133 Randy Johnson .50
134 Mark Mulder .25
135 Roger Clemens 1.00
136 Jon Lieber .15
137 Jamie Moyer .15
138 Freddy Garcia .15
139 Tim Hudson .25
140 C.C. Sabathia .15
141 Randy Johnson .50
142 Curt Schilling .25
143 John Burkett .15
144 Freddy Garcia .15
145 Greg Maddux .75
146 Darryl Kile .15
147 Mike Mussina .40
148 Joe Mays .15
149 Matt Morris .25
150 Russ Ortiz .15
151 Randy Johnson .50
152 Curt Schilling .25
153 Hideo Nomo .15
154 Chan Ho Park .15
155 Kerry Wood .50
156 Mike Mussina .40
157 Roger Clemens 1.00
158 Javier Vazquez .15
159 Barry Zito .25
160 Bartolo Colon .15
161 Mariano Rivera .25
162 Robb Nen .15
163 Kazuhiro Sasaki .15
164 Armando Benitez .15
165 Trevor Hoffman .15
166 Jeff Shaw .15
167 Keith Foulke .15
168 Jose Mesa .15
169 Troy Percival .15
170 Billy Wagner .15
171 Pat Burrell .25
172 Raul Mondesi .15
173 Gary Sheffield .25
174 Carlos Beltran .25
175 Vladimir Guerrero .50
176 Torii Hunter .25
177 Jeromy Burnitz .15
178 Tim Salmon .15
179 Jim Edmonds .25
180 Tsuyoshi Shinjo .15
181 Greg Maddux .75
182 Roberto Alomar .40
183 Ken Griffey Jr. 1.00
184 Ivan Rodriguez .40
185 Omar Vizquel .15
186 Barry Bonds 1.50
187 Devon White .15
188 J.T. Snow .15
189 Larry Walker .25
190 Robin Ventura .15
191 Mark Phillips **RC** 3.00
192 Clint Nageotte **RC** 2.00
193 Mauricio Lara **RC** .75
194 Nic Jackson **RC** .75
195 Chris Tritle **RC** .75
196 Ryan Gripp **RC** .75
197 Greg Montalbano **RC** .75
198 Noochie Varner **RC** .75
199 Nick Alvarez **RC** .75
200 Craig Kuzmic **RC** .75

Die-Cut

Stars (1-200): 2-4X
Inserted 1:4

Autographs

NM/M
Common Autograph: 10.00
Inserted 1:67
BB Barry Bonds 180.00
BBO Bret Boone 20.00
RCL Roger Clemens 100.00
JE Jim Edmonds 25.00
CF Cliff Floyd 10.00
LG Luis Gonzalez 15.00
CG Cristian Guzman 10.00
RO Roy Oswalt 15.00
JR Jimmy Rollins 15.00
BZ Barry Zito 20.00

Relics

NM/M
Common Player: 8.00
Bat Relic 1:27
Jersey Relic 1:26
BA Bob Abreu/Bat 12.00
RA Roberto Alomar/Bat 15.00
MA Moises Alou/Bat 8.00
GA Garret Anderson/Bat 10.00
JBA Jeff Bagwell/Jsy 15.00
CB Carlos Beltran/Bat 10.00
AB Armando Benitez/Jsy 8.00
LB Lance Berkman/Bat 15.00
CBI Craig Biggio/Jsy 15.00
BB Barry Bonds/Jsy 25.00
BBO Bret Boone/Bat 10.00
JBU John Burkett/Jsy 8.00
JB Jeromy Burnitz/Jsy 8.00
MC Mike Cameron/Bat 10.00
LC Luis Castillo/Bat 8.00
RC Roger Cedeno/Bat 8.00
BC Bartolo Colon/Jsy 8.00
RD Ray Durham/Bat 8.00
JE Jim Edmonds/Bat 15.00
CF Cliff Floyd/Bat 8.00
FG Freddy Garcia/Jsy 8.00
JGO Juan Gonzalez/Bat 10.00
LG Luis Gonzalez/Bat 10.00
MG Mark Grace/Bat 20.00
SG Shawn Green/Bat 10.00
CG Cristian Guzman/Bat 10.00
TH Todd Helton/Bat 15.00
THO Trevor Hoffman/Jsy 10.00
THU Torii Hunter/Bat 15.00
RJ Randy Johnson/Jsy 20.00
CJ Chipper Jones/Bat 20.00
JK Jason Kendall/Jsy 10.00
JKE Jeff Kent/Jsy 10.00
CK Chuck Knoblauch/Bat 10.00
PL Paul LoDuca/Bat 10.00
GM Greg Maddux/Jsy 20.00
EM Edgar Martinez/Jsy 10.00
MM Mark McLemore/Bat 8.00
PM Raul Mondesi/Bat 8.00
PN Phil Nevin/Bat 8.00
JO John Olerud/Jsy 10.00
RP Rafael Palmeiro/Jsy 12.00
CP Chan Ho Park/Jsy 10.00
MP Mike Piazza/Jsy 20.00
JP Juan Pierre/Jsy 10.00
PP Placido Polanco/Bat 10.00
AP Albert Pujols/Bat 25.00
AR Alex Rodriguez/Jsy 15.00
TS Tim Salmon/Bat 10.00
CS Curt Schilling/Jsy 15.00
RS Richie Sexson/Bat 10.00
GS Gary Sheffield/Jsy 10.00
TSH Tsuyoshi Shinjo/Bat 10.00
JS J.T. Snow/Bat 8.00
AS Alfonso Soriano/Bat 15.00
SS Shannon Stewart/Bat 8.00
MS Mike Sweeney/Bat 15.00
JT Jim Thome/Bat 20.00
RV Robin Ventura/Bat 8.00
FV Fernando Vina/Bat 10.00
OV Omar Vizquel/Bat 10.00
BW Billy Wagner/Jsy 10.00
LW Larry Walker/Bat 10.00
DW Devon White/Bat 8.00
BZ Barry Zito/Jsy 10.00

Team Topps Legends Autographs

NM/M
Common Player:
Carl Yastrzemski 65.00

2002 Topps Total Pre-Production

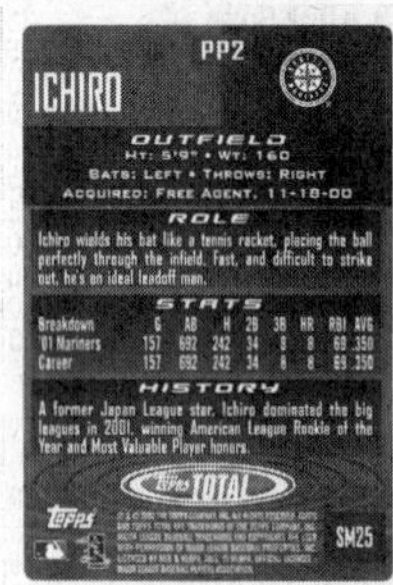

NM/M
Complete Set (3): 6.00
Common Player: 2.00
PP1 Barry Bonds 2.00
PP2 Ichiro 2.00
PP3 Hank Blalock 2.00

2002 Topps Total

NM/M
Complete Set (990): 125.00
Common Player: .10
Pack (10): 1.00
Box (36): 30.00
1 Joe Mauer **RC** 5.00
2 Derek Jeter 2.00
3 Shawn Green .25
4 Vladimir Guerrero .50
5 Mike Piazza 1.50
6 Brandon Duckworth .10
7 Aramis Ramirez .10
8 Josh Barfield 1.00
9 Troy Glaus .40
10 Sammy Sosa 1.00
11 Rod Barajas .10
12 Tsuyoshi Shinjo .25
13 Larry Bigbie .10
14 Tino Martinez .10
15 Craig Biggio .25
16 Anastacio Martinez **RC** .40
17 John McDonald .10
18 Kyle Kane **RC** .30
19 Aubrey Huff .10
20 Juan Cruz .10
21 Doug Creek .10
22 Luther Hackman .10
23 Rafael Furcal .10
24 Andres Torres .10
25 Jason Giambi .50
26 Jose Paniagua .10
27 Jose Offerman .10
28 Alex Arias .10
29 J.M. Gold .10
30 Jeff Bagwell .50
31 Brent Cookson **RC** .20
32 Kelly Wunsch .10
33 Larry Walker .25
34 Luis Gonzalez .25
35 John Franco .10
36 Roy Oswalt .25
37 Tom Glavine .25
38 C.C. Sabathia .10
39 Jay Gibbons .10
40 Wilson Betemit .10
41 Tony Armas .10
42 Mo Vaughn .10
43 Gerard Oakes **RC** .40
44 Dmitri Young .10
45 Tim Salmon .10
46 Barry Zito .10
47 Adrian Gonzalez .10
48 Joe Davenport .10
49 Adrian Hernandez .10
50 Randy Johnson .50
51 Benito Baez .10
52 Adam Pettyjohn .10
53 Alex Escobar .10
54 Stevenson Agosto **RC** .25
55 Omar Daal .10
56 Mike Buddie .10
57 Dave Williams .10
58 Marquis Grissom .10
59 Pat Burrell .25
60 Mark Prior 2.00
61 Mike Bynum .10
62 Mike Hill **RC** .25
63 Brandon Backe **RC** .25
64 Dan Wilson .10
65 Nick Johnson .10
66 Jason Grimsley .10
67 Russ Johnson .10
68 Todd Walker .10
69 Kyle Farnsworth .10
70 Ben Broussard .10
71 Garrett Guzman **RC** .50
72 Terry Mulholland .10
73 Tyler Houston .10
74 Jace Brewer .10
75 Chris Baker **RC** .25
76 Frank Catalanotto .10
77 Mike Redmond .10
78 Matt Wise .10
79 Fernando Vina .10
80 Kevin Brown .10
81 Grant Balfour .10
82 Clint Nageotte **RC** .75
83 Jeff Tam .10
84 Steve Trachsel .10
85 Tomokazu Ohka .10
86 Keith McDonald .10
87 Jose Ortiz .10
88 Rusty Greer .10
89 Jeff Suppan .10
90 Moises Alou .10
91 Juan Encarnacion .10
92 Tyler Yates **RC** .40
93 Scott Strickland .10
94 Brent Butler .10
95 Jon Rauch .10
96 Brian Mallette **RC** .25
97 Joe Randa .10
98 Cesar Crespo .10
99 Felix Rodriguez .10
100 Chipper Jones .75
101 Victor Martinez .10
102 Danny Graves .10
103 Brandon Berger **RC** .10
104 Carlos Garcia .10
105 Alfonso Soriano .75
106 Allan Simpson **RC** .25
107 Brad Thomas .10
108 Devon White .10
109 Scott Chiasson .10
110 Cliff Floyd .10
111 Scott Williamson .10
112 Julio Zuleta .10
113 Terry Adams .10
114 Zach Day .10
115 Ben Grieve .10
116 Mark Ellis .10
117 Bobby Jenks **RC** .75
118 LaTroy Hawkins .10
119 Tim Raines Jr. .10
120 Juan Uribe .10
121 Bob Scanlan .10
122 Brad Nelson **RC** 1.50
123 Adam Johnson .10
124 Raul Casanova .10
125 Jeff D'Amico .10
126 Aaron Cook **RC** .50
127 Alan Benes .10
128 Mark Little .10
129 Randy Wolf .10
130 Phil Nevin .10
131 Guillermo Mota .10
132 Nick Neugebauer .10
133 Pedro Borbon .10
134 Doug Mientkiewicz .10
135 Edgardo Alfonzo .10
136 Dustan Mohr .10
137 Dan Reichert .10
138 Dewon Brazelton .10
139 Orlando Cabrera .10
140 Todd Hollandsworth .10
141 Darren Dreifort .10
142 Jose Valentin .10
143 Josh Kalinowski .10
144 Randy Keisler .10
145 Bret Boone .10
146 Roosevelt Brown .10
147 Brent Abernathy .10
148 Jorge Julio .10
149 Alex Gonzalez .10
150 Juan Pierre .10
151 Roger Cedeno .10
152 Javier Vazquez .10
153 Armando Benitez .10
154 Dave Burba .10
155 Brad Penny .10
156 Ryan Jensen .10
157 Jeromy Burnitz .10
158 Matt Childers **RC** .40
159 Wilmy Caceres .10
160 Roger Clemens .10
161 Michael Tejera .10
162 Jason Christiansen .10
163 Pokey Reese .10
164 Ivanon Coffie .10
165 Joaquin Benoit .10
166 Mike Matheny .10
167 Eric Cammack .10
168 Alex Graman .10
169 Brook Fordyce .10
170 Mike Lieberthal .10
171 Giovanni Carrara .10
172 Antonio Perez .10
173 Fernando Tatis .10
174 Jason Bay **RC** 2.00
175 Jason Botts **RC** .50
176 Danys Baez .10
177 Shea Hillenbrand .10
178 Jack Cust .10
179 Clay Bellinger .10
180 Roberto Alomar .10
181 Graeme Lloyd .10
182 Clint Weibl **RC** .40
183 Royce Clayton .10
184 Ben Davis .10
185 Brian Adams .25
186 Jack Wilson .10
187 David Coggin .10
188 Derrick Turnbow .10
189 Vladimir Nunez .10
190 Mariano Rivera .10
191 Wilson Guzman .10
192 Michael Barrett .10
193 Corey Patterson .10
194 Luis Sojo .10
195 Scott Elarton .10
196 Charles Thomas .25
197 Ricky Bottalico .10
198 Wilfredo Rodriguez .10
199 Ricardo Rincon .10
200 John Smoltz .10
201 Travis Miller .10
202 Ben Weber .10
203 T.J. Tucker .10
204 Terry Shumpert .10
205 Bernie Williams .10
206 Russ Ortiz .10
207 Nate Rolison .10
208 Jose Cruz Jr. .10
209 Bill Ortega .10
210 Carl Everett .10
211 Luis Lopez .10
212 Brian Wolfe **RC** .25
213 Doug Davis .10
214 Troy Mattes .10
215 Al Leiter .10
216 Joe Mays .10
217 Bobby Smith .10
218 J.J. Trujillo **RC** .25
219 Hideo Nomo .25
220 Jimmy Rollins .25
221 Bobby Seay .10
222 Mike Thurman .10
223 Bartolo Colon .10
224 Jesus Sanchez .10
225 Ray Durham .10
226 Juan Diaz .10
227 Lee Stevens .10
228 Ben Howard **RC** .75
229 James Moulton .10
230 Paul Quantrill .10
231 Randy Knorr .10
232 Abraham Nunez .10
233 Mike Fetters .10
234 Mario Encarnacion .10
235 Jeremy Fikac .10
236 Travis Lee .10
237 Bob File .10
238 Pete Harnisch .10
239 Randy Galvez **RC** .25
240 Geoff Goetz .10
241 Gary Glover .10
242 Troy Percival .10
243 Lenny Dinardo **RC** .40
244 Jonny Gomes **RC** 2.00
245 Jesus Medrano **RC** .25
246 Rey Ordonez .10
247 Juan Gonzalez .50
248 Jose Guillen .10
249 Franklin German **RC** .25
250 Mike Mussina .40
251 Ugueth Urbina .10
252 Melvin Mora .10
253 Gerald Williams .10
254 Jared Sandberg .10
255 Darrin Fletcher .10
256 A.J. Pierzynski .10
257 Lenny Harris .10
258 Blaine Neal .10
259 Denny Neagle .10
260 Jason Hart .10
261 Henry Mateo .10
262 Rheal Cormier .10
263 Luis Terrero .10
264 Shigetoshi Hasegawa .10
265 Bill Haselman .10
266 Scott Hatteberg .10
267 Adam Hyzdu .10
268 Mike Williams .10
269 Marlon Anderson .10
270 Bruce Chen .10
271 Eli Marrero .10
272 Jimmy Haynes .10
273 Bronson Arroyo .10
274 Kevin Jordan .10
275 Rick Helling .10
276 Mark Loretta .10
277 Dustin Hermanson .10
278 Pablo Ozuna .10
279 Syketo Anderson **RC** .25
280 Jermaine Dye .10
281 Will Smith .10
282 Brian Daubach .10
283 Eric Hinske .10
284 Joe Jiannetti **RC** .40
285 Chan Ho Park .10
286 Curtis Legendre **RC** .25
287 Jeff Reboulet .10
288 Scott Rolen .50
289 Chris Richard .10
290 Eric Chavez .25
291 Scot Shields .10
292 Donnie Sadler .10
293 Dave Veres .10
294 Craig Counsell .10
295 Armando Reynoso .10
296 Kyle Lohse .10
297 Arthur Rhodes .10
298 Sidney Ponson .10
299 Trevor Hoffman .10
300 Kerry Wood .25
301 Danny Bautista .10
302 Scott Sauerbeck .10
303 Johnny Estrada .10
304 Mike Timlin .10
305 Orlando Hernandez .25
306 Tony Clark .10
307 Tomas Perez .10
308 Marcus Giles .10
309 Mike Bordick .10
310 Jorge Posada .25
311 Jason Conti .10
312 Kevin Millar .10
313 Paul Shuey .10
314 Jake Mauer **RC** .75
315 Luke Hudson .10
316 Angel Berroa .10
317 Fred Bastardo **RC** .25
318 Shawn Estes .10
319 Andy Ashby .10
320 Ryan Klesko .10
321 Kevin Appier .10
322 Juan Pena .10
323 Alex Herrera .10
324 Robb Nen .10
325 Orlando Hudson .10
326 Lyle Overbay .10
327 Ben Sheets .25
328 Mike DiFelice .10
329 Pablo Arias **RC** .25
330 Mike Sweeney .10
331 Rick Ankiel .10
332 Tomas De La Rosa .25
333 Kazuhisa Ishii **RC** 1.00
334 Jose Reyes .10
335 Jeremy Giambi .10
336 Jose Mesa .10
337 Ralph Roberts **RC** .25
338 Jose Nunez .10
339 Curt Schilling .40
340 Sean Casey .20
341 Bob Wells .10
342 Carlos Beltran .10
343 Alexis Gomez .10
344 Brandon Claussen .25
345 Buddy Groom .10
346 Mark Phillips **RC** .50
347 Francisco Cordova .10
348 Joe Oliver .10
349 Danny Patterson .10
350 Joel Pineiro .10
351 J.R. House .10
352 Benny Agbayani .10
353 Jose Vidro .10
354 Reed Johnson **RC** .10
355 Mike Lowell .10
356 Scott Schoeneweis .10
357 Brian Jordan .10
358 Steve Finley .10
359 Randy Choate .10
360 Jose Lima .10
361 Miguel Olivo .10
362 Kenny Rogers .10
363 David Justice .20
364 Brandon Knight .10
365 Joe Kennedy .10
366 Eric Valent .10
367 Nelson Cruz .10
368 Brian Giles .25
369 Charles Gibson Jr. .10
370 Juan Pena .10
371 Mark Redman .10
372 Billy Koch .10
373 Ted Lilly .10
374 Craig Paquette .10
375 Kevin Jarvis .10
376 Scott Erickson .10
377 Josh Paul .10
378 Darwin Cubillan .10
379 Nelson Figueroa .10
380 Darin Erstad .20
381 Jeremy Hill **RC** .25
382 Elvin Nina .10
383 David Wells .25
384 Jay Caligiuri **RC** .40
385 Freddy Garcia .10
386 Damian Miller .10
387 Bobby Higginson .10
388 Alejandro Giron **RC** .25
389 Ivan Rodriguez .40

390	Ed Rogers	.10
391	Andy Benes	.10
392	Matt Blank	.10
393	Ryan Vogelsong	.10
394	Kelly Ramos **RC**	.25
395	Eric Karros	.10
396	Bobby Jones	.10
397	Omar Vizquel	.25
398	Matt Perisho	.10
399	Delino DeShields	.10
400	Carlos Hernandez	.10
401	Derrek Lee	.10
402	Kirk Rueter	.10
403	David Wright	30.00
404	Paul LoDuca	.10
405	Brian Schneider	.10
406	Milton Bradley	.10
407	Daryle Ward	.10
408	Cody Ransom	.10
409	Fernando Rodney	.10
410	John Suomi **RC**	.20
411	Joe Girardi	.10
412	Demetrius Heath **RC**	.25
413	John Foster **RC**	.25
414	Doug Glanville	.10
415	Ryan Kohlmeier	.10
416	Mike Matthews	.10
417	Craig Wilson	.10
418	Jay Witasick	.10
419	Jay Payton	.10
420	Andruw Jones	.40
421	Benji Gil	.10
422	Jeff Liefer	.10
423	Kevin Young	.10
424	Richie Sexson	.25
425	Cory Lidle	.10
426	Shane Halter	.10
427	Jesse Foppert	.40
428	Jose Molina	.10
429	Nick Alvarez **RC**	.40
430	Brian L. Hunter	.10
431	Clifford Bartosh **RC**	.25
432	Junior Spivey	.10
433	Eric Good **RC**	.25
434	Chin-Feng Chen	.10
435	T.J. Mathews	.10
436	Rich Rodriguez	.10
437	Bobby Abreu	.20
438	Joe McEwing	.10
439	Michael Tucker	.10
440	Preston Wilson	.10
441	Mike MacDougal	.10
442	Shannon Stewart	.10
443	Bob Howry	.10
444	Mike Benjamin	.10
445	Erik Hiljus	.10
446	Ryan Gripp **RC**	.25
447	Jose Vizcaino	.10
448	Shawn Wooten	.10
449	Steve Kent **RC**	.25
450	Ramiro Mendoza	.10
451	Jake Westbrook	.10
452	Joe Lawrence	.10
453	Jae Weong Seo	.10
454	Ryan Fry **RC**	.20
455	Darren Lewis	.10
456	Brad Wilkerson	.10
457	Gustavo Chacin **RC**	.25
458	Adrian Brown	.10
459	Mike Cameron	.10
460	Bud Smith	.10
461	Derrick Lewis	.10
462	Derek Lowe	.10
463	Matt Williams	.10
464	Jason Jennings	.10
465	Albie Lopez	.10
466	Felipe Lopez	.10
467	Luke Allen	.10
468	Brian Anderson	.10
469	Matt Riley	.10
470	Ryan Dempster	.10
471	Matt Ginter	.10
472	David Ortiz	.10
473	Cole Barthel	.10
474	Damian Jackson	.10
475	Andy Van Hekken	.10
476	Doug Brocail	.10
477	Denny Hocking	.10
478	Sean Douglass	.10
479	Eric Owens	.10
480	Ryan Ludwick	.10
481	Todd Pratt	.10
482	Aaron Sele	.10
483	Edgar Renteria	.10
484	Raymond Cabrera **RC**	.25
485	Brandon Lyon	.10
486	Chase Utley	.25
487	Robert Fick	.10
488	Wilfredo Cordero	.10
489	Octavio Dotel	.10
490	Paul Abbott	.10
491	Jason Kendall	.10
492	Jarrod Washburn	.10
493	Dane Sardinha	.10
494	Jung Bong	.10
495	J.D. Drew	.10
496	Jason Schmidt	.10
497	Mike Magnante	.10
498	Jorge Padilla **RC**	.50
499	Eric Gagne	.10
500	Todd Helton	.50
501	Jeff Weaver	.10
502	Alex Sanchez	.10
503	Ken Griffey Jr.	.10
504	Abraham Nunez	.10
505	Reggie Sanders	.10
506	Casey Kotchman	2.00
507	Jim Mann	.10

508	Matt LeCroy	.10
509	Frank Castillo	.10
510	Geoff Jenkins	.20
511	Jayson Durocher **RC**	.20
512	Ellis Burks	.10
513	Aaron Fultz	.10
514	Hiram Bocachica	.10
515	Nate Espy **RC**	.10
516	Placido Polanco	.10
517	Kerry Ligtenberg	.10
518	Doug Nickle	.10
519	Ramon Ortiz	.10
520	Greg Swindell	.10
521	J.J. Davis	.10
522	Sandy Alomar	.10
523	Chris Carpenter	.10
524	Vance Wilson	.10
525	Nomar Garciaparra	1.00
526	Jim Mecir	.10
527	Taylor Buchholz **RC**	.25
528	Brent Mayne	.10
529	John Rodriguez **RC**	.25
530	David Segui	.10
531	Nate Cornejo	.10
532	Gil Heredia	.10
533	Esteban Loaiza	.10
534	Pat Mahomes	.10
535	Matt Morris	.20
536	Todd Stottlemyre	.10
537	Brian Lesher	.10
538	Arturo McDowell	.10
539	Felix Diaz	.10
540	Mark Mulder	.10
541	Kevin Frederick **RC**	.25
542	Andy Fox	.10
543	Dionys Cesar **RC**	.10
544	Justin Miller	.10
545	Keith Osik	.10
546	Shane Reynolds	.10
547	Mike Myers	.10
548	Raul Chavez **RC**	.25
549	Joe Nathan	.10
550	Ryan Anderson	.10
551	Jason Marquis	.10
552	Marty Cordova	.10
553	Kevin Tapani	.10
554	Jimmy Anderson	.10
555	Pedro Martinez	.50
556	Rocky Biddle	.10
557	Alex Ochoa	.10
558	D'Angelo Jimenez	.10
559	Wilkin Ruan	.10
560	Terrence Long	.10
561	Mark Lukasiewicz	.10
562	Jose Santiago	.10
563	Brad Fullmer	.10
564	Corky Miller	.10
565	Matt White	.10
566	Mark Grace	.30
567	Raul Ibanez	.10
568	Josh Towers	.10
569	Juan Gonzalez	.40
570	Brian Buchanan	.10
571	Ken Harvey	.10
572	Jeffrey Hammonds	.10
573	Wade Miller	.10
574	Elpidio Guzman	.10
575	Kevin Olsen	.10
576	Austin Kearns	.40
577	Tim Kalita **RC**	.40
578	David Dellucci	.10
579	Alex Gonzalez	.10
580	Joe Orloski **RC**	.20
581	Gary Matthews Jr.	.10
582	Ryan Mills	.10
583	Erick Almonte	.10
584	Jeremy Affeldt	.10
585	Chris Tritle **RC**	1.00
586	Michael Cuddyer	.10
587	Kris Foster	.10
588	Russell Branyan	.10
589	Darren Oliver	.10
590	Freddie Money **RC**	.25
591	Carlos Lee	.10
592	Tim Wakefield	.10
593	Bubba Trammell	.10
594	John Koronka **RC**	3.00
595	Geoff Blum	.10
596	Darryl Kile	.10
597	Neifi Perez	.10
598	Torii Hunter	.10
599	Luis Castillo	.10
600	Mark Buehrle	.10
601	Jeff Zimmerman	.10
602	Mike DeJean	.10
603	Julio Lugo	.10
604	Chad Hermansen	.10
605	Keith Foulke	.10
606	Lance Davis	.10
607	Jeff Austin **RC**	.25
608	Brandon Inge	.10
609	Orlando Merced	.10
610	Johnny Damon	.10
611	Doug Henry	.10
612	Adam Kennedy	.10
613	Wiki Gonzalez	.10
614	Brian West **RC**	.25
615	Andy Pettitte	.10
616	Chone Figgins **RC**	.25
617	Matt Lawton	.10
618	Paul Rigdon	.10
619	Keith Lockhart	.10
620	Tim Redding	.10
621	John Parrish	.10
622	Chad Hutchinson	.10
623	Todd Greene	.10
624	David Eckstein	.10
625	Greg Montalbano **RC**	1.00

626	Joe Beimel	.10
627	Adrian Beltre	.20
628	Charles Nagy	.10
629	Cristian Guzman	.10
630	Toby Hall	.10
631	Jose Hernandez	.10
632	Jose Macias	.10
633	Jaret Wright	.10
634	Steve Parris	.10
635	Gene Kingsdale	.10
636	Tim Worrell	.10
637	Billy Martin	.10
638	Jovanny Cedeno	.10
639	Curt Leskanic	.10
640	Tim Hudson	.20
641	Juan Castro	.10
642	Rafael Soriano	.10
643	Juan Rincon	.10
644	Mark DeRosa	.10
645	Carlos Pena	.10
646	Robin Ventura	.20
647	Odalis Perez	.10
648	Damion Easley	.10
649	Benito Santiago	.10
650	Alex Rodriguez	1.50
651	Aaron Rowand	.10
652	Alex Cora	.10
653	Bobby Kielty	.10
654	Jose Rodriguez	.10
655	Herbert Perry	.10
656	Jeff Urban	.10
657	Paul Bako	.10
658	Shane Spencer	.10
659	Pat Hentgen	.10
660	Jeff Kent	.20
661	Mark McLemore	.10
662	Chuck Knoblauch	.10
663	Blake Stein	.10
664	Brett Roneberg **RC**	.25
665	Josh Phelps	.10
666	Byung-Hyun Kim	.10
667	Dave Martinez	.10
668	Mike Maroth	.10
669	Shawn Chacon	.10
670	Billy Wagner	.10
671	Luis Alicea	.10
672	Sterling Hitchcock	.10
673	Adam Piatt	.10
674	Ryan Franklin	.10
675	Luke Prokopec	.10
676	Alfredo Amezega	.10
677	Gookie Dawkins	.10
678	Eric Byrnes	.10
679	Barry Larkin	.25
680	Albert Pujols	1.00
681	Edwards Guzman	.10
682	Jason Bere	.10
683	Adam Everett	.10
684	Greg Colbrunn	.10
685	Brandon Puffer **RC**	.40
686	Mark Kotsay	.10
687	Willie Bloomquist	.10
688	Hank Blalock	.25
689	Travis Hafner	.10
690	Lance Berkman	.40
691	Joe Crede	.10
692	Chuck Finley	.10
693	John Grabow	.10
694	Randy Winn	.10
695	Mike James	.10
696	Kris Benson	.10
697	Bret Prinz	.10
698	Jeff Williams	.10
699	Eric Munson	.10
700	Mike Hampton	.10
701	Ramon E. Martinez	.10
702	Hansel Izquierdo **RC**	.25
703	Nathan Haynes	.10
704	Eddie Taubensee	.10
705	Esteban German	.10
706	Ross Gload	.10
707	Matthew Merricks **RC**	.20
708	Chris Piersoll **RC**	.25
709	Seth Greisinger	.10
710	Ichiro Suzuki	1.00
711	Cesar Izturis	.10
712	Brad Cresse	.10
713	Carl Pavano	.10
714	Steve Sparks	.10
715	Dennis Tankersley	.10
716	Kelvim Escobar	.10
717	Jason LaRue	.10
718	Corey Koskie	.10
719	Vinny Castilla	.10
720	Tim Drew	.10
721	Chin-Hui Tsao	.10
722	Paul Byrd	.10
723	Alex Cintron	.10
724	Orlando Palmeiro	.10
725	Ramon Hernandez	.10
726	Mark Johnson	.10
727	B.J. Ryan	.10
728	Wendell Magee	.10
729	Michael Coleman	.10
730	Mario Ramos	.50
731	Mike Stanton	.10
732	Dee Brown	.10
733	Brad Ausmus	.10
734	Napoleon Calzado **RC**	.25
735	Woody Williams	.10
736	Paxton Crawford	.10
737	Jason Karnuth	.10
738	Michael Restovich	.10
739	Ramon Castro	.10
740	Maggio Ordonez	.25
741	Tom Gordon	.10
742	Mark Grudzielanek	.10
743	Jamie Moyer	.10

744	Marlyn Tisdale **RC**	.20
745	Steve Kline	.10
746	Adam Eaton	.10
747	Eric Glaser **RC**	.25
748	Sean DePaula	.10
749	Greg Norton	.10
750	Steve Reed	.10
751	Ricardo Aramboles	.10
752	Matt Mantei	.10
753	Gene Stechschulte	.10
754	Chuck McElroy	.10
755	Barry Bonds	1.50
756	Matt Anderson	.10
757	Yorvit Torrealba	.10
758	Jason Standridge	.10
759	Desi Relaford	.10
760	Jolbert Cabrera	.10
761	Chris George	.10
762	Erubiel Durazo	.10
763	Paul Konerko	.25
764	Tike Redman	.10
765	Chad Ricketts **RC**	.20
766	Roberto Hernandez	.10
767	Mark Lewis	.10
768	Livan Hernandez	.10
769	Carlos Brackley **RC**	.25
770	Kazuhiro Sasaki	.10
771	Bill Hall	.10
772	Nelson Castro **RC**	.25
773	Eric Milton	.10
774	Tom Davey	.10
775	Todd Ritchie	.10
776	Seth Etherton	.10
777	Chris Singleton	.10
778	Robert Averette **RC**	.20
779	Robert Person	.10
780	Fred McGriff	.25
781	Richard Hidalgo	.10
782	Kris Wilson	.10
783	John Rocker	.10
784	Justin Kaye	.10
785	Glendon Rusch	.10
786	Greg Vaughn	.10
787	Mike Lamb	.10
788	Greg Myers	.10
789	Nate Field **RC**	.25
790	Jim Edmonds	.25
791	Olmedo Saenz	.10
792	Jason Johnson	.10
793	Mike Lincoln	.10
794	Todd Coffey	.10
795	Jesus Sanchez	.10
796	Aaron Myette	.10
797	Tony Womack	.10
798	Chad Kreuter	.10
799	Brady Clark	.10
800	Adam Dunn	.50
801	Jacque Jones	.10
802	Kevin Millwood	.10
803	Mike Rivera	.10
804	Jim Thome	.40
805	Jeff Conine	.10
806	Elmer Dessens	.10
807	Randy Velarde	.10
808	Carlos Delgado	.30
809	Steve Karsay	.10
810	Casey Fossum	.10
811	J.C. Romero	.10
812	Chris Truby	.10
813	Tony Graffanino	.10
814	Wascar Serrano	.10
815	Delvin James	.10
816	Pedro Feliz	.10
817	Damian Rolls	.10
818	Scott Linebrink	.10
819	Rafael Palmeiro	.40
820	Javy Lopez	.10
821	Larry Barnes	.10
822	Brian Lawrence	.10
823	Scotty Layfield **RC**	.25
824	Jeff Cirillo	.10
825	Willis Roberts	.10
826	Rich Harden **RC**	4.00
827	Chris Snelling **RC**	1.00
828	Gary Sheffield	.25
829	Jeff Heaverlo	.10
830	Matt Clement	.10
831	Rich Garces	.10
832	Rondell White	.10
833	Henry Pichardo **RC**	.25
834	Aaron Boone	.10
835	Ruben Sierra	.10
836	Deivis Santos	.10
837	Tony Batista	.10
838	Rob Bell	.10
839	Frank Thomas	.50
840	Jose Silva	.10
841	Dan Johnson **RC**	.50
842	Steve Cox	.10
843	Jose Acevedo	.10
844	Jay Bell	.10
845	Mike Sirotka	.10
846	Garret Anderson	.10
847	James Shanks **RC**	.25
848	Trot Nixon	.10
849	Keith Ginter	.10
850	Tim Spooneybarger	.10
851	Matt Stairs	.10
852	Chris Stynes	.10
853	Marvin Bernard	.10
854	Raul Mondesi	.20
855	Jeremy Owens	.10
856	Jon Garland	.10
857	Mitch Meluskey	.10
858	Chad Durbin	.10
859	John Burkett	.10
860	Jon Switzer	.10
861	Peter Bergeron	.10

862	Jesus Colome	.10
863	Todd Hundley	.10
864	Ben Petrick	.10
865	So Taguchi **RC**	.75
866	Ryan Drese	.10
867	Mike Trombley	.10
868	Rick Reed	.10
869	Mark Teixeira	.20
870	Corey Thurman **RC**	.10
871	Brian Roberts	.10
872	Mike Timlin	.10
873	Chris Reitsma	.10
874	Jeff Fassero	.10
875	Carlos Valderrama	.10
876	John Lackey	.10
877	Travis Fryman	.10
878	Ismael Valdes	.10
879	Rick White	.10
880	Edgar Martinez	.10
881	Dean Palmer	.10
882	Matt Allegra **RC**	.20
883	Greg Sain **RC**	.25
884	Carlos Silva	.10
885	Jose Valverde **RC**	.25
886	Dernell Stenson	.10
887	Todd Van Poppel	.10
888	Wes Anderson	.10
889	Bill Mueller	.10
890	Morgan Ensberg	.10
891	Marcus Thames	.10
892	Adam Walker **RC**	.10
893	John Halama	.10
894	Frank Menechino	.10
895	Greg Maddux	1.00
896	Gary Bennett	.10
897	Mauricio Lara **RC**	.25
898	Mike Young	.10
899	Travis Phelps	.10
900	Rich Aurilia	.10
901	Henry Blanco	.10
902	Carlos Febles	.10
903	Scott MacRae	.10
904	Lou Merloni	.10
905	Dicky Gonzalez	.10
906	Jeff DaVanon	.10
907	A.J. Burnett	.10
908	Einar Diaz	.10
909	Julio Franco	.10
910	John Olerud	.25
911	Mark Hamilton **RC**	.25
912	David Riske	.10
913	Jason Tyner	.10
914	Britt Reames	.10
915	Vernon Wells	.10
916	Eddie Perez	.10
917	Edwin Almonte **RC**	.25
918	Enrique Wilson	.10
919	Chris Gomez	.10
920	Jayson Werth	.10
921	Jeff Nelson	.10
922	Freddy Sanchez **RC**	.75
923	John Vander Wal	.10
924	Chad Qualls **RC**	.25
925	Gabe White	.10
926	Chad Harville	.10
927	Ricky Gutierrez	.10
928	Carlos Guillen	.10
929	B.J. Surhoff	.10
930	Chris Woodard	.10
931	Ricardo Rodriguez	.10
932	Jimmy Gobble **RC**	1.00
933	Jon Lieber	.10
934	Craig Kuzmic **RC**	.25
935	Eric Young	.10
936	Gregg Zaun	.10
937	Miguel Batista	.10
938	Danny Wright	.10
939	Todd Zeile	.10
940	Chad Zerbe	.10
941	Jason Young **RC**	.50
942	Ronnie Belliard	.10
943	John Ennis **RC**	.10
944	John Flaherty	.10
945	Jerry Hairston Jr.	.10
946	Al Levine	.10
947	Antonio Alfonseca	.10
948	Brian Moehler	.10
949	Calvin Murray	.10
950	Nick Bierbrodt	.10
951	Sun-Woo Kim	.10
952	Noochie Varner **RC**	.50
953	Luis Rivas	.10
954	Donnie Bridges	.10
955	Ramon Vazquez	.10
956	Luis Garcia	.10
957	Mark Quinn	.10
958	Armando Rios	.10
959	Chad Fox	.10
960	Hee Seop Choi	.10
961	Turk Wendell	.10
962	Adam Roller **RC**	.20
963	Grant Roberts	.10
964	Ben Molina	.10
965	Juan Rivera	.10
966	Matt Kinney	.10
967	Rod Beck	.10
968	Xavier Nady	.10
969	Masato Yoshii	.10
970	Miguel Tejada	.25
971	Danny Kolb	.10
972	Mike Remlinger	.10
973	Ray Lankford	.10
974	Ryan Minor	.10
975	J.T. Snow	.10
976	Brad Radke	.10
977	Jason Lane	.10
978	Jamey Wright	.10
979	Tom Goodwin	.10

980	Erik Bedard	.10
981	Gabe Kapler	.10
982	Brian Reith	.10
983	Nic Jackson **RC**	.50
984	Kurt Ainsworth	.10
985	Jason Isringhausen	.10
986	Willie Harris	.10
987	David Cone	.10
988	Bob Wickman	.10
989	Wes Helms	.10
990	Josh Beckett	.25

Award Winners

		NM/M
Complete Set (30):		25.00
Common Player:		.50
Inserted 1:6		
AW1	Ichiro Suzuki	2.00
AW2	Albert Pujols	2.00
AW3	Barry Bonds	3.00
AW4	Ichiro Suzuki	2.00
AW5	Randy Johnson	1.00
AW6	Roger Clemens	2.00
AW7	Jason Giambi	.75
AW8	Bret Boone	.50
AW9	Troy Glaus	.75
AW10	Alex Rodriguez	2.50
AW11	Juan Gonzalez	.75
AW12	Ichiro Suzuki	2.00
AW13	Jorge Posada	.75
AW14	Edgar Martinez	.50
AW15	Todd Helton	.75
AW16	Jeff Kent	.50
AW17	Albert Pujols	2.00
AW18	Rich Aurilia	.50
AW19	Barry Bonds	3.00
AW20	Luis Gonzalez	.50
AW21	Sammy Sosa	2.00
AW22	Mike Piazza	2.00
AW23	Mike Hampton	.50
AW24	Ruben Sierra	.50
AW25	Matt Morris	.50
AW26	Curt Schilling	.75
AW27	Alex Rodriguez	2.50
AW28	Barry Bonds	3.00
AW29	Jim Thome	1.00
AW30	Barry Bonds	3.00

Total Production

		NM/M
Complete Set (10):		15.00
Common Player:		.75
Inserted 1:12		
TP1	Alex Rodriguez	3.00
TP2	Barry Bonds	3.00
TP3	Ichiro Suzuki	2.00
TP4	Edgar Martinez	.75
TP5	Jason Giambi	1.00
TP6	Todd Helton	1.00
TP7	Nomar Garciaparra	2.50
TP8	Vladimir Guerrero	1.00
TP9	Sammy Sosa	2.00
TP10	Chipper Jones	2.00

Total Topps

		NM/M
Complete Set (50):		35.00
Common Player:		.50
Inserted 1:3		
TT1	Roberto Alomar	.75
TT2	Moises Alou	.50
TT3	Jeff Bagwell	1.00
TT4	Lance Berkman	.75
TT5	Barry Bonds	2.00
TT6	Bret Boone	.50
TT7	Kevin Brown	.50

TT8	Eric Chavez	.50
TT9	Roger Clemens	1.50
TT10	Carlos Delgado	.50
TT11	Cliff Floyd	.50
TT12	Nomar Garciaparra	2.50
TT13	Jason Giambi	1.00
TT14	Brian Giles	.75
TT15	Troy Glaus	.75
TT16	Tom Glavine	.50
TT17	Luis Gonzalez	.50
TT18	Juan Gonzalez	.75
TT19	Shawn Green	.50
TT20	Ken Griffey Jr.	2.50
TT21	Vladimir Guerrero	1.00
TT22	Jorge Posada	.50
TT23	Todd Helton	.75
TT24	Tim Hudson	.50
TT25	Derek Jeter	4.00
TT26	Randy Johnson	1.00
TT27	Andruw Jones	.75
TT28	Chipper Jones	2.00
TT29	Jeff Kent	.50
TT30	Greg Maddux	2.00
TT31	Edgar Martinez	.50
TT32	Pedro Martinez	1.00
TT33	Magglio Ordonez	.50
TT34	Rafael Palmeiro	.50
TT35	Mike Piazza	3.00
TT36	Albert Pujols	2.00
TT37	Aramis Ramirez	.50
TT38	Mariano Rivera	.50
TT39	Alex Rodriguez	3.00
TT40	Ivan Rodriguez	.75
TT41	Curt Schilling	.75
TT42	Gary Sheffield	.50
TT43	Sammy Sosa	2.00
TT44	Ichiro Suzuki	4.00
TT45	Miguel Tejada	.50
TT46	Frank Thomas	1.00
TT47	Jim Thome	.75
TT48	Larry Walker	.50
TT49	Bernie Williams	.50
TT50	Kerry Wood	.50

2002 Topps Traded & Rookies

		NM/M
Complete Set (275):		125.00
Common Player:		.15
Common SP (1-110):		.50
Chrome Cards:		2-4X
2:Pack		
Pack (10):		3.00
Box (24):		60.00
T1	Jeff Weaver	.50
T2	Jay Powell	.50
T3	Alex Gonzalez	.50
T4	Jason Isringhausen	.50
T5	Darren Oliver	.50
T6	Hector Ortiz	.50
T7	Chuck Knoblauch	.50
T8	Brian L. Hunter	.50
T9	Dustan Mohr	.50
T10	Eric Hinske	.50
T11	Roger Cedeno	.50
T12	Eddie Perez	.50
T13	Jeromy Burnitz	.50
T14	Bartolo Colon	.50
T15	Rick Helling	.50
T16	Dan Plesac	.50
T17	Scott Strickland	.50
T18	Antonio Alfonseca	.50
T19	Ricky Gutierrez	.50
T20	John Valentin	.50
T21	Raul Mondesi	.50
T22	Ben Davis	.50
T23	Nelson Figueroa	.50
T24	Earl Snyder	.50
T25	Robin Ventura	.50
T26	Jimmy Haynes	.50
T27	Kenny Kelly	.50
T28	Morgan Ensberg	.50
T29	Reggie Sanders	.50
T30	Shigetoshi Hasegawa	.50
T31	Allen Levrault	.50
T32	Russell Branyan	.50
T33	Jose Guillen	.50
T34	Jose Paniagua	.50
T35	Kent Mercker	.50
T36	Jesse Orosco	.50
T37	Gregg Zaun	.50
T38	Reggie Taylor	.50
T39	Andres Galarraga	.50
T40	Chris Truby	.50
T41	Bruce Chen	.50
T42	Darren Lewis	.50
T43	Ryan Kohlmeier	.50
T44	John McDonald	.50
T45	Omar Daal	.50
T46	Matt Clement	.50
T47	Glendon Rusch	.50
T48	Chan Ho Park	.50
T49	Benny Agbayani	.50
T50	Juan Gonzalez	1.50
T51	Carlos Baerga	.50
T52	Tim Raines	.50
T53	Kevin Appier	.50
T54	Marty Cordoua	.50
T55	Jeff D'Amico	.50
T56	Dmitri Young	.50
T57	Roosevelt Brown	.50
T58	Dustin Hermanson	.50
T59	Jose Rijo	.50
T60	Todd Ritchie	.50
T61	Lee Stevens	.50
T62	Shane Heams	.50
T63	Eric Young	.50
T64	Chuck Finley	.50
T65	Dicky Gonzalez	.50
T66	Jose Macias	.50
T67	Gabe Kapler	.50
T68	Sandy Alomar Jr.	.50
T69	Henry Blanco	.50
T70	Julian Tavarez	.50
T71	Paul Bako	.50
T72	Dave Burba	.50
T73	Brian Jordan	.50
T74	Rickey Henderson	1.00
T75	Kevin Mench	.50
T76	Hideo Nomo	1.00
T77	Mark Sweeney	.50
T78	Brad Fullmer	.50
T79	Carl Everett	.50
T80	David Wells	.50
T81	Aaron Sele	.50
T82	Todd Hollandsworth	.50
T83	Vicente Padilla	.50
T84	Chris Latham	.50
T85	Corky Miller	.50
T86	Josh Fogg	.50
T87	Calvin Murray	.50
T88	Craig Paquette	.50
T89	Jay Payton	.50
T90	Carlos Pena	.50
T91	Juan Encarnacion	.50
T92	Rey Sanchez	.50
T93	Ryan Dempster	.50
T94	Mario Encarnacion	.50
T95	Jorge Julio	.50
T96	John Mabry	.50
T97	Todd Zeile	.50
T98	Johnny Damon	.50
T99	Deivi Cruz	.50
T100	Gary Sheffield	1.00
T101	Ted Lilly	.50
T102	Todd Van Poppel	.50
T103	Shawn Estes	.50
T104	Cesar Izturis	.50
T105	Ron Coomer	.50
T106	Grady Little	.50
T107	Jimy Williams	.50
T108	Tony Pena	.50
T109	Frank Robinson	.50
T110	Ron Gardenhire	.50
T111	Dennis Tankersley	.15
T112	Alejandro Cadena **RC**	.25
T113	Justin Reid **RC**	.25
T114	Nate Field **RC**	.25
T115	Rene Reyes **RC**	.25
T116	Nelson Castro **RC**	.25
T117	Miguel Olivo	.15
T118	David Espinosa	.15
T119	Chris Bootcheck **RC**	.40
T120	Rob Henkel **RC**	.25
T121	Steve Bechler **RC**	.25
T122	Mark Outlaw **RC**	.25
T123	Henry Pichardo **RC**	.25
T124	Michael Floyd **RC**	.25
T125	Richard Lane **RC**	.25
T126	Peter Zamora **RC**	.25
T127	Javier Colina	.15
T128	Greg Sain **RC**	.25
T129	Ronnie Merrill	.25
T130	Gavin Floyd	1.50
T131	Josh Bonifay **RC**	.25
T132	Tommy Marx **RC**	.25
T133	Gary Cates Jr. **RC**	.25
T134	Neal Cotts	.50
T135	Angel Berroa	.25
T136	Elio Serrano **RC**	.25
T137	J.J. Putz **RC**	.25
T138	Ruben Gotay **RC**	.25
T139	Eddie Rogers **RC**	.25
T140	Wily Mo Pena	.25
T141	Tyler Yates **RC**	.25
T142	Colin Young **RC**	.25
T143	Chance Caple	.15
T144	Ben Howard **RC**	.25
T145	Ryan Bukvich **RC**	.25
T146	Clifford Bartosh **RC**	.25
T147	Brandon Claussen	.25
T148	Cristian Guerrero	.15
T149	Derrick Lewis	.15
T150	Eric Miller **RC**	.25
T151	Justin Huber **RC**	.75
T152	Adrian Gonzalez	.25
T153	Brian West **RC**	.25
T154	Chris Baker **RC**	.25
T155	Drew Henson	.15
T156	Scott Hairston	.75
T157	Jason Simontacchi **RC**	.75
T158	Jason Arnold	.40
T159	Brandon Phillips	.15
T160	Adam Roller **RC**	.25
T161	Scotty Layfield **RC**	.25
T162	Freddie Money **RC**	.25
T163	Noochie Varner **RC**	.50
T164	Terrance Hill **RC**	.25
T165	Jeremy Hill **RC**	.25
T166	Carlos Cabrera **RC**	.25
T167	Jose Morban **RC**	.25
T168	Kevin Frederick **RC**	.25
T169	Mark Teixeira	.40
T170	Brian Rogers	.15
T171	Anastacio Martinez **RC**	.25
T172	Bobby Jenks **RC**	.75
T173	David Gil **RC**	.25
T174	Andres Torres	.15
T175	James Barrett **RC**	.25
T176	Jimmy Journell	.15
T177	Brett Kay **RC**	.25
T178	Jason Young **RC**	.25
T179	Mark Hamilton **RC**	.25
T180	Jose Bautista **RC**	.50
T181	Blake McGinley **RC**	.25
T182	Ryan Mottl **RC**	.25
T183	Jeff Austin **RC**	.25
T184	Xavier Nady	.15
T185	Kyle Kane **RC**	.25
T186	Travis Foley	.15
T187	Nathan Kaup **RC**	.25
T188	Eric Cyr **RC**	.25
T189	Josh Cisneros **RC**	.25
T190	Brad Nelson **RC**	.75
T191	Clint Weibl **RC**	.25
T192	Ron Calloway **RC**	.25
T193	Jung Bong	.15
T194	Rolando Viera **RC**	.25
T195	Jason Bulger **RC**	.25
T196	Chone Figgins **RC**	.75
T197	Jimmy Alvarez **RC**	.25
T198	Joel Crump **RC**	.25
T199	Ryan Doumit **RC**	1.50
T200	Demetrius Heath **RC**	.25
T201	John Ennis **RC**	.25
T202	Doug Sessions **RC**	.25
T203	Clinton Hosford **RC**	.25
T204	Chris Narveson **RC**	.25
T205	Ross Peeples **RC**	.25
T206	Alexander Requena **RC**	.25
T207	Matt Erickson **RC**	.25
T208	Brian Forystek **RC**	.25
T209	Dewon Brazelton	.15
T210	Nathan Haynes	.15
T211	Jack Cust	.15
T212	Jesse Foppert	.75
T213	Jesus Cota **RC**	.25
T214	Juan Gonzalez	.15
T215	Tim Kalita **RC**	.25
T216	Manny Delcarmen **RC**	2.00
T217	Jim Kavourias	.15
T218	C.J. Wilson **RC**	.25
T219	Edwin Yan **RC**	.25
T220	Andy Van Hekken	.15
T221	Michael Cuddyer	.15
T222	Jeff Verplancke **RC**	.25
T223	Mike Wilson **RC**	.25
T224	Corwin Malone	.15
T225	Chris Snelling **RC**	.50
T226	Joe Rogers **RC**	.25
T227	Jason Bay	.50
T228	Ezequiel Astacio **RC**	.25
T229	Joey Hammond **RC**	.25
T230	Chris Duffy **RC**	.25
T231	Mark Prior	1.00
T232	Hansel Izquierdo **RC**	.25
T233	Franklyn German **RC**	.25
T234	Alexis Gomez	.15
T235	Jorge Padilla **RC**	.25
T236	Ryan Snare **RC**	.25
T237	Deivis Santos	.15
T238	Taggert Bozied **RC**	1.00
T239	Mike Peeples **RC**	.25
T240	Ronald Acuna **RC**	.25
T241	Koyie Hill	.15
T242	Garrett Guzman **RC**	.25
T243	Ryan Church **RC**	1.00
T244	Tony Fontana **RC**	.25
T245	Keto Anderson **RC**	.25
T246	Brad Bouras **RC**	.25
T247	Jason Dubois **RC**	1.00
T248	Angel Guzman **RC**	2.00
T249	Joel Hanrahan **RC**	.50
T250	Joe Jiannetti **RC**	.25
T251	Sean Pierce **RC**	.25
T252	Jake Mauer **RC**	.25
T253	Marshall McDougall **RC**	.50
T254	Edwin Almonte **RC**	.25
T255	Shawn Riggans **RC**	.25
T256	Steven Shell	.15
T257	Kevin Hooper **RC**	.40
T258	Michael Frick **RC**	.25
T259	Travis Chapman **RC**	.40
T260	Tim Hummel **RC**	.25
T261	Adam Morrissey **RC**	.25
T262	Dontrelle Willis **RC**	5.00
T263	Justin Sherrod **RC**	.25
T264	Gerald Smiley **RC**	.25
T265	Tony Miller **RC**	.25
T266	Nolan Ryan	1.50
T267	Reggie Jackson	.50
T268	Steve Garvey	.15
T269	Wade Boggs	.25
T270	Sammy Sosa	1.00
T271	Curt Schilling	.25
T272	Mark Grace	.25
T273	Jason Giambi	.50
T274	Ken Griffey Jr.	.75
T275	Roberto Alomar	.40

Gold

Gold Stars:	2-4X
Production 2,002 Sets	
Chrome Refractors:	3-5X
Inserted 1:12	

Farewell Relics

		NM/M
Randomly inserted.		
JC	Jose Canseco	10.00

Hall of Fame Relics

		NM/M
Randomly inserted.		
HOF-OS	Ozzie Smith	25.00

Signature Moves Autographs

		NM/M
Common Autograph:		8.00
Inserted 1:91		
RA	Roberto Alomar	30.00
MA	Moises Alou	15.00
TBL	Tony Blanco	8.00
BB	Boof Bonser	8.00
AC	Antoine Cameron	10.00
BC	Brandon Claussen	15.00
MC	Matt Cooper	8.00
JD	Johnny Damon	30.00
JDA	Jeff DaVanon	8.00
VD	Victor Diaz	12.00
RH	Ryan Hannaman	8.00
KI	Kazuhisa Ishii	40.00
FJ	Forrest Johnson	8.00
TL	Todd Linden	15.00
CM	Corwin Malone	8.00
JM	Jake Mauer	8.00
AM	Andy Morales	8.00
RM	Ramon Moreta	8.00
JMO	Justin Morneau	30.00
JP	Juan Pena	8.00
JS	Juan Silvestre	8.00
CS	Chris Smith	8.00
DT	Dennis Tankersley	8.00
MT	Marcus Thames	8.00
CU	Chase Utley	70.00
JW	Justin Wayne	8.00

Team Topps Legends Autographs

	NM/M
Common Autograph:	10.00
Inserted 1:1,097	
Johnny Bench	40.00
Vida Blue	10.00
Clete Boyer	12.00
Whitey Ford	30.00
Bob Gibson	25.00
Joe Pepitone	10.00
Bobby Richardson	10.00
Bill "Moose" Skowron	10.00
Enos Slaughter	18.00
Carl Yastrzemski	60.00

Tools of the Trade Relics

		NM/M
Common Player:		5.00
Bat Relics 1:34		
Jersey Relics 1:426		
RAB	Roberto Alomar/Bat	8.00
MA	Moises Alou/Bat	8.00
DB	David Bell/Bat	5.00
JBU	Jeromy Burnitz/Bat	5.00
JC	Jose Canseco/Bat	10.00
VC	Vinny Castilla/Bat	5.00
JCI	Jeff Cirillo/Bat	5.00
TC	Tony Clark/Bat	5.00
JDB	Johnny Damon/Bat	6.00
CE	Carl Everett/Bat	5.00
BF	Brad Fullmer/Bat	5.00
AG	Andres Galarraga/Bat	6.00
JG	Juan Gonzalez/Jsy	8.00
RHB	Rickey Henderson/Bat	10.00
BJ	Brian Jordan/Bat	5.00
DJ	David Justice/Bat	5.00
CK	Chuck Knoblauch/Bat	5.00
MLB	Matt Lawton/Bat	5.00
KL	Kenny Lofton/Bat	5.00
TM	Tino Martinez/Bat	6.00
CP	Carlos Pena/Bat	8.00
JP	Josh Phelps/Jsy	6.00
TR	Tim Raines/Bat	5.00
RS	Reggie Sanders/Bat	5.00
GS	Gary Sheffield/Bat	5.00
TS	Tsuyoshi Shinjo/Bat	5.00
RSI	Ruben Sierra/Bat	5.00
MT	Michael Tucker/Bat	5.00
MV	Mo Vaughn/Jsy	6.00
MVB	Mo Vaughn/Bat	6.00
RV	Robin Ventura/Bat	6.00
RW	Rondell White/Bat	5.00
EY	Eric Young/Bat	5.00

Tools of the Trade Dual Relics

		NM/M
Common Card:		8.00
Inserted 1:539		
MA	Moises Alou	10.00
HN	Hideo Nomo	35.00
CP	Chan Ho Park	8.00

2002 Topps Tribute

		NM/M
Complete Set (90):		120.00
Common Player:		1.50
Pack (5):		35.00
Box (6):		150.00
1	Hank Aaron	6.00
2	Rogers Hornsby	2.50
3	Bobby Thomson	1.50
4	Eddie Collins	1.50
5	Joe Carter	1.50
6	Jim Palmer	1.50
7	Willie Mays	6.00
8	Willie Stargell	2.50
9	Vida Blue	1.50
10	Whitey Ford	3.00
11	Bob Gibson	3.00
12	Nellie Fox	2.00
13	Napoleon Lajoie	2.00
14	Frankie Frisch	1.50
15	Nolan Ryan	10.00
16	Brooks Robinson	2.50
17	Kirby Puckett	5.00
18	Fergie Jenkins	1.50
19	Edd Roush	1.50
20	Honus Wagner	6.00
21	Richie Ashburn	1.50
22	Bob Feller	1.50
23	Joe Morgan	1.50
24	Orlando Cepeda	1.50
25	Steve Garvey	1.50
26	Hank Greenberg	1.50
27	Stan Musial	5.00
28	Sam Crawford	1.50
29	Jim Rice	1.50
30	Hack Wilson	2.50
31	Lou Brock	1.50
32	Mickey Vernon	1.50
33	Chuck Klein	1.50
34	Joe Jackson	6.00
35	Duke Snider	3.00
36	Ryne Sandberg	5.00
37	Johnny Bench	5.00
38	Sam Rice	1.50
39	Lou Gehrig	8.00
40	Robin Yount	3.00
41	Don Sutton	1.50
42	Jim Bottomley	1.50
43	Billy Herman	1.50
44	Zach Wheat	1.50
45	Juan Marichal	1.50
46	Bert Blyleven	1.50
47	Jackie Robinson	6.00
48	Gil Hodges	1.50
49	Mike Schmidt	6.00
50	Dale Murphy	1.50
51	Phil Rizzuto	1.50
52	Ty Cobb	6.00
53	Andre Dawson	1.50
54	Fred Lindstrom	1.50
55	Roy Campanella	3.00
56	Don Larsen	2.00
57	Harry Heilmann	1.50
58	Jim "Catfish" Hunter	1.50
59	Frank Robinson	2.00
60	Bill Mazeroski	1.50
61	Roger Maris	6.00
62	Dave Winfield	2.50
63	Warren Spahn	2.50
64	Babe Ruth	10.00
65	Ernie Banks	4.00
66	Wade Boggs	2.00
67	Carl Yastrzemski	3.00
68	Ron Santo	1.50
69	Dennis Martinez	1.50
70	Yogi Berra	4.00
71	Paul Waner	1.50
72	George Brett	6.00
73	Eddie Mathews	3.00
74	Bill Dickey	1.50
75	Carlton Fisk	2.00
76	Thurman Munson	5.00
77	Reggie Jackson	4.00
78	Phil Niekro	1.50
79	Luis Aparicio	1.50
80	Steve Carlton	1.50
81	Tris Speaker	1.50
82	Johnny Mize	1.50
83	Tom Seaver	4.00
84	Heinie Manush	1.50
85	Tommy John	1.50
86	Joe Cronin	1.50
87	Don Mattingly	8.00
88	Kirk Gibson	1.50
89	Bo Jackson	3.00
90	Mel Ott	1.50

First Impressions

Cards #'d 51-86:	3-5X
Cards #'d 26-50:	4-8X
#'d to last two digits of Rk year	
Lasting Impressions	
Cards #'d 51-96:	3-5X
Cards #'d 26-50:	4-8X
#'d to last two digits of final season	
Production under 25 not priced.	

Marks of Excellence

		NM/M
Inserted 1:61		
LB	Lou Brock	50.00
SC	Steve Carlton	50.00
DL	Don Larsen	50.00
SM	Stan Musial	100.00
MS	Mike Schmidt	85.00
WS	Warren Spahn	65.00

Marks of Excellence Relics

		NM/M
Inserted 1:61		
FJ	Fergie Jenkins	40.00
DM	Don Mattingly	120.00
JP	Jim Palmer	40.00
BR	Brooks Robinson	75.00
DS	Duke Snider	60.00
RY	Robin Yount	70.00

Matching Marks Dual

		NM/M
Common Card:		10.00
Inserted 1:11		
SBA	Ron Santo, Ernie Banks	25.00
YK	Carl Yastrzemski, Chuck Klein	65.00
WY	Dave Winfield, Carl Yastrzemski	25.00
WYO	Dave Winfield, Robin Yount	20.00
SM	Duke Snider, Willie Mays	85.00

RJ	Frank Robinson, Reggie Jackson	50.00
BMA	George Brett, Don Mattingly	90.00
GH	Steve Garvey, Gil Hodges	20.00
AR	Hank Aaron, Babe Ruth	300.00
GA	Hank Greenberg, Richie Ashburn	80.00
PJ	Jim Palmer, Tommy John	20.00
NS	Phil Niekro, Tom Seaver	15.00
SR	Willie Stargell, Jim Rice	15.00
BF	Johnny Bench, Carlton Fisk	50.00
RS	Nolan Ryan, Tom Seaver	125.00
JS	Fergie Jenkins, Tom Seaver	35.00
YP	Robin Yount, Kirby Puckett	60.00
SB	Tris Speaker, George Brett	100.00
BM	Vida Blue, Dennis Martinez	10.00
BB	Wade Boggs, George Brett	40.00
MA	Willie Mays, Hank Aaron	200.00
BS	Bert Blyleven, Don Sutton	15.00

Memorable Materials

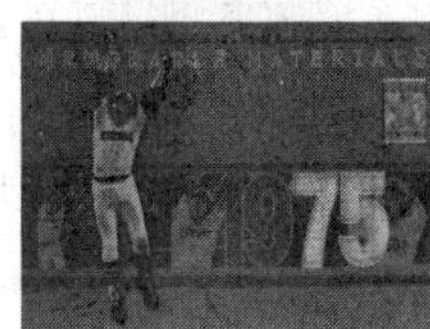

		NM/M
Common Player:		10.00
Season parallel:		1.5-3X
#'d to last two digits yr event occurred		
Jsy Number para.#'d 40-75:		1.5-3X
Under 40 not priced.		
Numbered to jersey #.		
HA	Hank Aaron	40.00
GB	George Brett	35.00
RC	Roy Campanella	30.00
JC	Joe Carter	10.00
CF	Carlton Fisk	20.00
KG	Kirk Gibson	15.00
BJ	Bo Jackson	25.00
RJ	Reggie Jackson	20.00
CK	Chuck Klein	25.00
RM	Roger Maris	75.00
DM	Don Mattingly	40.00
BM	Bill Mazeroski	15.00
JM	Joe Morgan	15.00
TM	Thurman Munson	50.00
KP	Kirby Puckett	30.00
PR	Phil Rizzuto	25.00
JR	Jackie Robinson	50.00
NR	Nolan Ryan	50.00
BT	Bobby Thomson	15.00
HW	Hack Wilson	40.00
CY	Carl Yastrzemski	30.00

Milestone Materials

		NM/M
Common Player:		10.00
Inserted 1:4		
Season parallel #'d 51-95:		1.5-3X
#'d to last two digits milestone season		
Jersey Number par.#'d 51-95:		1.5-3X
Numbered to Jersey Number.		
Under 50 not priced yet.		
LA	Luis Aparicio	15.00
EB	Ernie Banks	30.00
JB	Johnny Bench	20.00
YB	Yogi Berra	25.00
WB	Wade Boggs	15.00
JBO	Jim Bottomley	20.00
OC	Orlando Cepeda	15.00
TC	Ty Cobb	150.00
EC	Eddie Collins	30.00
SC	Sam Crawford	25.00
JC	Joe Cronin	20.00
AD	Andre Dawson	15.00
BD	Bill Dickey	15.00
BF	Bob Feller	15.00
WF	Whitey Ford	25.00
NF	Nellie Fox	30.00
FF	Frankie Frisch	25.00
LG	Lou Gehrig	150.00
BG	Bob Gibson	15.00
HH	Harry Heilmann	20.00
BH	Billy Herman	10.00
RH	Rogers Hornsby	50.00
CH	Jim "Catfish" Hunter	12.00
RJ	Reggie Jackson	20.00
NL	Napoleon Lajoie	60.00
FL	Fred Lindstrom	15.00
HM	Heinie Manush	20.00
JMA	Juan Marichal	15.00
EM	Eddie Mathews	20.00
WH	Willie Mays	45.00
JM	Johnny Mize	15.00
DM	Dale Murphy	20.00
MO	Mel Ott	40.00
JP	Jim Palmer	15.00
SR	Sam Rice	20.00
BRO	Brooks Robinson	20.00
FR	Frank Robinson	20.00
ER	Edd Roush	25.00
BR	Babe Ruth	160.00
NR	Nolan Ryan	50.00
RS	Ryne Sandberg	30.00
TS	Tom Seaver	15.00
DS	Duke Snider	20.00
TSP	Tris Speaker	65.00
WS	Willie Stargell	15.00
MV	Mickey Vernon	15.00
HW	Honus Wagner	140.00
PW	Paul Waner	30.00
ZW	Zach Wheat	40.00
RY	Robin Yount	25.00

Pasttime Patches

		NM/M
Inserted 1:92		
JB	Johnny Bench	125.00
WB	Wade Boggs	90.00
GB	George Brett	200.00
BD	Bill Dickey	100.00
EM	Eddie Mathews	125.00
DM	Don Mattingly	160.00
JP	Jim Palmer	75.00
KP	Kirby Puckett	125.00
NRA	Nolan Ryan	200.00
NRR	Nolan Ryan	200.00
DW	Dave Winfield	100.00
CY	Carl Yastrzemski	180.00
RY	Robin Yount	100.00

Signature Cuts

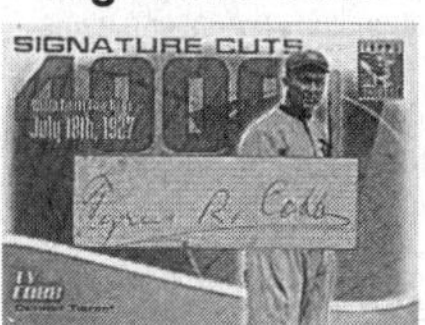

		NM/M
Reported production two each.		
Inserted 1:9936		
SC-TC	Ty Cobb (4/04 Auction)	4,725

"The Catch" Dual

		NM/M
Inserted 1:1,023		
MW	Willie Mays, Vic Wertz	250.00
MW	Willie Mays, Vic Wertz/54	300.00

2002 Topps206

		NM/M
Complete Set (456):		150.00
Common Player:		.20
Common (141-155, 271-285):		1.00
Inserted 1:2		
Series I Pack (8):		6.00
Series I Box (20):		100.00
Series II Pack (8):		4.00
Series II Box (20):		60.00
Series III Pack (8):		6.00
Series III Box (20):		100.00
1	Vladimir Guerrero	.75
2	Sammy Sosa	1.50
3	Garret Anderson	.40
4	Rafael Palmeiro	.50
5	Juan Gonzalez	.50
6	John Smoltz	.40
7	Mark Mulder	.40
8	Jon Lieber	.20
9	Greg Maddux	1.00
10	Moises Alou	.40
11	Joe Randa	.20
12	Bobby Abreu	.40
13	Ryan Kohlmeier	.20
14	Kerry Wood	.75
15	Craig Biggio	.40
16	Curt Schilling	.50
17	Brian Jordan	.20
18	Edgardo Alfonzo	.20
19	Darren Dreifort	.20
20	Todd Helton	.50
21	Ramon Ortiz	.20
22	Ichiro Suzuki	1.50
23	Jimmy Rollins	.50
24	Darin Erstad	.40
25	Shawn Green	.40
26	Tino Martinez	.30
27	Bret Boone	.40
28	Alfonso Soriano	.75
29	Chan Ho Park	.40
30	Roger Clemens	1.50
31	Cliff Floyd	.20
32	Johnny Damon	.40
33	Frank Thomas	.50
34	Barry Bonds	2.00
35	Luis Gonzalez	.40
36	Carlos Lee	.20
37	Roberto Alomar	.50
38	Carlos Delgado	.50
39	Nomar Garciaparra	1.50
40	Jason Kendall	.40
41	Scott Rolen	.75
42	Tom Glavine	.40
43	Ryan Klesko	.20
44	Brian Giles	.40
45	Bud Smith	.20
46	Charles Nagy	.20
47	Tony Gwynn	.75
48	C.C. Sabathia	.20
49	Manny Ramirez	.75
50	Jerry Hairston Jr.	.20
51	Jeromy Burnitz	.20
52	David Justice	.40
53	Bartolo Colon	.20
54	Andres Galarraga	.30
55	Jeff Weaver	.20
56	Terrance Long	.20
57	Tsuyoshi Shinjo	.20
58	Barry Zito	.40
59	Mariano Rivera	.40
60	John Olerud	.20
61	Randy Johnson	.75
62	Kenny Lofton	.40
63	Jermaine Dye	.20
64	Troy Glaus	.50
65	Larry Walker	.40
66	Hideo Nomo	.40
67	Mike Mussina	.50
68	Paul LoDuca	.20
69	Magglio Ordonez	.40
70	Paul O'Neill	.40
71	Sean Casey	.40
72	Lance Berkman	.40
73	Adam Dunn	.50
74	Aramis Ramirez	.40
75	Rafael Furcal	.40
76	Gary Sheffield	.40
77	Todd Hollandsworth	.20
78	Chipper Jones	1.00
79	Bernie Williams	.50
80	Richard Hidalgo	.25
81	Eric Chavez	.40
82	Mike Piazza	1.50
83	J.D. Drew	.40
84	Ken Griffey Jr.	1.00
85	Joe Kennedy	.20
86	Joel Pineiro	.20
87	Josh Towers	.20
88	Andruw Jones	.50
89	Carlos Beltran	.40
90	Mike Cameron	.20
91	Albert Pujols	1.50
92	Alex Rodriguez	1.50
93	Omar Vizquel	.30
94	Juan Encarnacion	.20
95	Jeff Bagwell	.50
96	Jose Canseco	.40
97	Ben Sheets	.40
98	Mark Grace	.40
99	Mike Sweeney	.20
100	Mark McGwire	2.00
101	Ivan Rodriguez	.75
102	Rich Aurilia	.20
103	Cristian Guzman	.20
104	Roy Oswalt	.40
105	Tim Hudson	.40
106	Brent Abernathy	.20
107	Mike Hampton	.20
108	Miguel Tejada	.40
109	Bobby Higginson	.20
110	Edgar Martinez	.40
111	Jorge Posada	.40
112	Jason Giambi	.50
113	Pedro Astacio	.20
114	Kazuhiro Sasaki	.20
115	Preston Wilson	.20
116	Jason Bere	.20
117	Mark Quinn	.20
118	Pokey Reese	.20
119	Derek Jeter	2.00
120	Shannon Stewart	.20
121	Jeff Kent	.40
122	Jeremy Giambi	.20
123	Pat Burrell	.40
124	Jim Edmonds	.40
125	Mark Buehrle	.20
126	Kevin Brown	.40
127	Raul Mondesi	.20
128	Pedro Martinez	.75
129	Jim Thome	.75
130	Russ Ortiz	.20
131	Brandon Duckworth	.20
132	Ryan Jamison **RC**	.50
133	Brandon Inge	.20
134	Felipe Lopez	.20
135	Jason Lane	.20
136	Forrest Johnson **RC**	.50
137	Greg Nash	.20
138	Covelli Crisp	.20
139	Nick Neugebauer	.20
140	Dustan Mohr	.20
141	Freddy Sanchez **RC**	1.00
142	Justin Backsmeyer **RC**	1.00
143	Jorge Julio	1.00
144	Ryan Mottl **RC**	1.00
145	Chris Tritle **RC**	1.00
146	Noochie Varner **RC**	1.00
147	Brian Rogers	1.00
148	Michael Hill **RC**	1.00
149	Luis Pineda	1.00
150	Rich Thompson **RC**	1.00
151	Bill Hall	1.00
152	Jose Dominguez **RC**	1.50
153	Justin Woodrow **RC**	1.00
154	Nic Jackson **RC**	1.00
155	Laynce Nix **RC**	4.00
156	Hank Aaron	3.00
157	Ernie Banks	1.50
158	Johnny Bench	1.50
159	George Brett	4.00
160	Carlton Fisk	.50
161	Bob Gibson	.75
162	Reggie Jackson	1.00
163	Don Mattingly	4.00
164	Kirby Puckett	1.50
165	Frank Robinson	1.00
166	Nolan Ryan	5.00
167	Tom Seaver	1.00
168	Mike Schmidt	2.00
169	Dave Winfield	.50
170	Carl Yastrzemski	1.00
171	Frank Chance	.75
172	Ty Cobb	3.00
173	Sam Crawford	1.00
174	Johnny Evers	.75
175	John McGraw	1.00
176	Eddie Plank	.50
177	Tris Speaker	1.00
178	Joe Tinker	.50
179	Honus Wagner	5.00
180	Cy Young	2.50
181	Javier Vazquez	.20
182	Mark Mulder	.40
183	Roger Clemens	1.50
184	Kazuhisa Ishii **RC**	1.50
185	Roberto Alomar	.50
186	Lance Berkman	.40
187	Adam Dunn	.50
188	Aramis Ramirez	.40
189	Chuck Knoblauch	.20
190	Nomar Garciaparra	1.50
191	Brad Penny	.20
192	Gary Sheffield	.40
193	Alfonso Soriano	.75
194	Andruw Jones	.50
195	Randy Johnson	.75
196	Corey Patterson	.40
197	Milton Bradley	.20
198	Johnny Damon	.40
199	Paul LoDuca	.20
200	Albert Pujols	1.50
201	Scott Rolen	.75
202	J.D. Drew	.40
203	Vladimir Guerrero	.75
204	Jason Giambi	.50
205	Moises Alou	.40
206	Magglio Ordonez	.40
207	Carlos Febles	.20
208	So Taguchi **RC**	.75
209	Rafael Palmeiro	.50
210	David Wells	.50
211	Orlando Cabrera	.20
212	Sammy Sosa	1.50
213	Armando Benitez	.20
214	Wes Helms	.20
215	Mariano Rivera	.40
216	Jimmy Rollins	.50
217	Matt Lawton	.20
218	Shawn Green	.40
219	Bernie Williams	.50
220	Bret Boone	.40
221	Alex Rodriguez	2.00
222	Roger Cedeno	.20
223	Marty Cordova	.20
224	Fred McGriff	.40
225	Chipper Jones	.75
226	Kerry Wood	.75
227	Larry Walker	.40
228	Robin Ventura	.40
229	Robert Fick	.40
230	Tino Martinez	.40
231	Ben Petrick	.20
232	Neifi Perez	.20
233	Pedro Martinez	.75
234	Brian Jordan	.20
235	Freddy Garcia	.20
236	Derek Jeter	2.00
237	Ben Grieve	.20
238	Barry Bonds	2.00
239	Luis Gonzalez	.40
240	Shane Halter	.20
241	Brian Giles	.40
242	Bud Smith	.20
243	Richie Sexson	.40
244	Barry Zito	.40
245	Eric Milton	.20
246	Ivan Rodriguez	.75
247	Toby Hall	.20
248	Mike Piazza	1.50
249	Ruben Sierra	.20
250	Tsuyoshi Shinjo	.20
251	Jermaine Dye	.20
252	Roy Oswalt	.40
253	Todd Helton	.50
254	Adrian Beltre	.40
255	Doug Mientkiewicz	.20
256	Ichiro Suzuki	1.50
257	C.C. Sabathia	.20
258	Paul Konerko	.20
259	Ken Griffey Jr.	1.00
260	Jeromy Burnitz	.20
261	Hank Blalock	.50
262	Mark Prior	1.50
263	Josh Beckett	.50
264	Carlos Pena	.20
265	Sean Burroughs	.20
266	Austin Kearns	.40
267	Chin-Hui Tsao	.20
268	Dewon Brazelton	.20
269	J.D. Martin	.20
270	Marlon Byrd	.20
271	Joe Mauer **RC**	8.00
272	Jason Botts **RC**	1.00
273	Mauricio Lara **RC**	1.00
274	Jonny Gomes **RC**	3.00
275	Gavin Floyd	1.00
276	Alexander Requena **RC**	1.00
277	Jimmy Gobble **RC**	1.00
278	Chris Duffy **RC**	1.00
279	Colt Griffin	1.00
280	Ryan Church **RC**	1.50
281	Beltran Perez	1.00
282	Clint Nageotte **RC**	1.50
283	Justin Schuda **RC**	1.00
284	Scott Hairston	1.50
285	Mario Ramos	1.00
286	Tom Seaver	2.00
287	Hank Aaron	3.00
288	Mike Schmidt	3.00
289	Robin Yount	1.50
290	Joe Morgan	1.00
291	Frank Robinson	1.00
292	Reggie Jackson	2.00
293	Nolan Ryan	4.00
294	Dave Winfield	1.00
295	Willie Mays	3.00
296	Brooks Robinson	1.50
297	Mark McGwire	3.00
298	Honus Wagner	3.00
299	Sherry Magee	1.00
300	Frank Chance	1.00
301	Larry Doyle	1.00
302	John McGraw	2.00
303	Jimmy Collins	1.00
304	Buck Herzog	1.00
305	Sam Crawford	1.00
306	Cy Young	2.50
307	Honus Wagner	3.00
308	Alex Rodriguez	2.00
308	Alex Rodriguez/ SP Blue Jsy	4.00
309	Vernon Wells	.20
310	Barry Bonds	2.00
310	Barry Bonds/ SP Cream Jsy	6.00
311	Vicente Padilla	.20
312	Alfonso Soriano	.75
312	A.Soriano/ SP No Wristband	1.50
313	Mike Piazza	1.50
314	Jacque Jones	.20
315	Shawn Green/SP	1.50
316	Paul Byrd	.20
317	Lance Berkman	.40
318	Larry Walker	.40
319	Ken Griffey Jr./SP	3.00
320	Shea Hillenbrand	.20
321	Jay Gibbons	.20
322	Andruw Jones	.50
323	Luis Gonzalez/SP	1.50
324	Garret Anderson	.40
325	Roy Halladay	.40
326	Randy Winn	.20
327	Matt Morris	.40
328	Robb Nen	.20
329	Trevor Hoffman	.20
330	Kip Wells	.20
331	Orlando Hernandez	.30
332	Rey Ordonez	.20
333	Torii Hunter	.40
334	Geoff Jenkins	.40
335	Eric Karros	.20
336	Mike Lowell	.40
337	Nick Johnson	.20
338	Randall Simon	.20
339	Ellis Burks	.20
340	Sammy Sosa	1.50
340	Sammy Sosa/ SP Blue Jsy	4.00
341	Pedro J. Martinez	.75
342	Junior Spivey	.20
343	Vinny Castilla	.20
344	Randy Johnson/SP	2.00
345	Chipper Jones/SP	1.50
346	Orlando Hudson	.20
347	Albert Pujols/SP	5.00
348	Rondell White	.20
349	Vladimir Guerrero	.75
350	Mark Prior	1.00
350	Mark Prior/ SP Red Background	3.00
351	Eric Gagne	.50
352	Todd Zeile	.20
353	Manny Ramirez/SP	2.00
354	Kevin Millwood	.40
355	Troy Percival	.20
356	Jason Giambi	.50
356	Jason Giambi/ SP White Jsy	1.50
357	Bartolo Colon	.20
358	Jeremy Giambi	.20
359	Jose Cruz Jr.	.20
360	Ichiro Suzuki	1.50
360	Ichiro/ SP Blue Warm-Up	3.00
361	Eddie Guardado	.20
362	Ivan Rodriguez	.50
363	Carl Crawford	.20
364	Jason Simontacchi **RC**	.50
365	Kenny Lofton	.40
366	Raul Mondesi	.20
367	A.J. Pierzynski	.20
368	Ugueth Urbina	.20
369	Rodrigo Lopez	.20
370	Nomar Garciaparra	1.50
370	N. Garciaparra/ SP 1 Bat	3.00
371	Craig Counsell	.20
372	Barry Larkin	.40
373	Carlos Pena	.20
374	Luis Castillo	.20
375	Raul Ibanez	.20
376	Kazuhisa Ishii/SP	1.50
377	Derek Lowe	.20
378	Curt Schilling	.50
379	Jim Thome	.75
380	Derek Jeter	2.00
380	D. Jeter/ SP Blue background	5.00
381	Pat Burrell	.50
382	Jamie Moyer	.20
383	Eric Hinske	.20
384	Scott Rolen	.75
385	Miguel Tejada/SP	1.50
386	Andy Pettitte	.40
387	Mike Lieberthal	.20
388	Al Leiter	.40
389	Todd Helton/SP	2.00
390	Adam Dunn	.50
390	Adam Dunn/ SP with bat	2.00
391	Cliff Floyd	.20
392	Tim Salmon	.40
393	Joe Torre	.50
394	Bobby Cox	.20
395	Tony LaRussa	.20
396	Art Howe	.20
397	Bob Brenly	.20
398	Ron Gardenhire	.20
399	Mike Cuddyer	.20
400	Joe Mauer	2.50
401	Mark Teixeira	.50
402	Hee Seop Choi	.20
403	Angel Berroa	.20
404	Jesse Foppert	.50
405	Bobby Crosby	.50
406	Jose Reyes	.50
407	Casey Kotchman	1.00
408	Aaron Heilman	.20
409	Adrian Gonzalez	.20
410	Delwyn Young **RC**	.75
411	Brett Myers	.20
412	Justin Huber **RC**	1.00
413	Drew Henson	.20
414	Taggert Bozied **RC**	1.00
415	Dontrelle Willis **RC**	6.00
416	Rocco Baldelli	.50
417	Jason Stokes **RC**	2.50
418	Brandon Phillips	.20
419	Jake Blalock/SP **RC**	2.00
420	Micah Schilling/SP **RC**	1.00
421	Denard Span/SP **RC**	1.00
422	James Loney/SP **RC**	4.00
423	Wes Bankston/SP **RC**	1.50
424	Jeremy Hermida/ SP **RC**	6.00
425	Curtis Granderson/ SP **RC**	3.00
426	Jason Pridie/SP **RC**	1.00
427	Larry Broadway/ SP **RC**	1.00
428	Khalil Greene/SP **RC**	5.00
429	Joey Votto/SP **RC**	2.50
430	B.J. Upton/SP **RC**	8.00
431	Sergio Santos/SP **RC**	2.00
432	Brian Dopirak/SP **RC**	2.00
433	Ozzie Smith/SP	2.00
434	Wade Boggs/SP	1.00
435	Yogi Berra/SP	3.00
436	Al Kaline/SP	2.00
437	Robin Roberts/SP	1.00
438	Roberto Clemente/SP	8.00
439	Gary Carter/SP	1.00
440	Fergie Jenkins/SP	1.00
441	Orlando Cepeda/SP	1.00
442	Rod Carew/SP	1.50
443	Harmon Killebrew/SP	2.50
444	Duke Snider/SP	2.00
445	Stan Musial/SP	5.00
446	Hank Greenberg/SP	1.00
447	Lou Brock/SP	1.00
448	Jim Palmer	.50
449	John McGraw	.75
450	Mordecai Brown	.50
451	Christy Mathewson	1.00
452	Sam Crawford	.50

453 Bill O'Hara .50
454 Joe Tinker .50
455 Napoleon Lajoie .75
456 Honus Wagner 3.00

T206 Mini Parallel

Polar Bear: 2-3X
Tolstoi Black: 2-5X
Average 4:Box
Tolstoi Red: 4-8X
Average 2:Box
Cycle: 6-12X
Average 1:Box
Series 2
Polar Bear: 2-3X
Piedmont Black: 3-5X
Piedmond Red: 4-8X
Carolina Brights: 6-12X
Series 3
Polar Bear: 2-3X
Sweet Caporal Red: 3-5X
Sweet Caporal Blue or Black: 4-6X
Uzit: 6-12X
Bazooka Backs: No Pricing
Production 30
Drum Backs: No Pricing
Production 20
Lenox Variations: No Pricing
Production 10
American Beauty Variation: No Pricing
Production 5

Autographs

NM/M
Common Player: 8.00
Inserted 1:41
BB Barry Bonds 200.00
RC Roger Clemens 150.00
JE Jim Edmonds 30.00
BG Brian Giles 15.00
CG Cristian Guzman 15.00
BI Brandon Inge 10.00
RJ Ryan Jamison 8.00
FJ Forrest Johnson 8.00
JJ Jorge Julio 10.00
FL Felipe Lopez 15.00
GN Greg Nash 8.00
MO Magglio Ordonez 20.00
AR Alex Rodriguez 100.00
JR Jimmy Rollins 20.00
BZ Barry Zito 20.00

Autographs Series 2

NM/M
Common Player: 8.00
Inserted 1:55
MA Moises Alou 30.00
LB Lance Berkman 35.00
HB Hank Blalock 30.00
DB Dewon Brazelton 8.00
MB Marlon Byrd 10.00
EC Eric Chavez 30.00
JD Johnny Damon 25.00
GF Gavin Floyd 20.00
LG Luis Gonzalez 20.00
KI Kazuhisa Ishii 40.00
JDM J.D. Martin 8.00
JM Joe Mauer 100.00
MP Mark Prior 40.00
AP Albert Pujols 140.00
SR Scott Rolen 40.00
RS Richie Sexson 15.00
BS Ben Sheets 20.00
BSM Bud Smith 10.00
ST So Taguchi 25.00
CT Chris Tritle 10.00

Autographs Series 3

NM/M
Common Autograph: 8.00
MB Milton Bradley 10.00
JC Jose Cruz Jr. 15.00
DE David Eckstein 8.00
DH Drew Henson 15.00
ML Mike Lamb 8.00
MT Marcus Thames 8.00
JV Jose Vidro 10.00

Relics

NM/M
Common Player: 5.00
Overall Relics 1:11
RA Roberto Alomar/Jsy 10.00
JB Jeff Bagwell/Jsy 10.00
CB Craig Biggio/Jsy 8.00
BB Barry Bonds/Jsy 25.00
BBO Bret Boone/Jsy 8.00
MC Mike Cameron/Jsy 5.00
JC Jose Canseco/Bat 10.00
CD Carlos Delgado/Jsy 8.00
JED Jim Edmonds/Jsy 10.00
CF Cliff Floyd/Jsy 5.00
JGI Jason Giambi/Jsy 8.00
JG Jeremy Giambi/Jsy 5.00
TG Tom Glavine/Jsy 8.00
SG Shawn Green/Jsy 8.00
TGW Tony Gwynn/Jsy 15.00
TH Todd Helton/Jsy 10.00
RJ Randy Johnson/Jsy 15.00
AJ Andruw Jones/Jsy 8.00
CJ Chipper Jones/Jsy 10.00
CL Carlos Lee/Jsy 5.00
KL Kenny Lofton/Jsy 5.00
GM Greg Maddux/Jsy 15.00
EM Edgar Martinez/Jsy 10.00
TM Tino Martinez/Jsy 10.00
JO John Olerud/Jsy 5.00
PO Paul O'Neill/Jsy 8.00
MO Magglio Ordonez/Jsy 6.00
CP Chan Ho Park/Bat 5.00
MP Mike Piazza/Jsy 15.00
AP Albert Pujols/Bat 25.00
IR Ivan Rodriguez/Jsy 10.00
AS Alfonso Soriano/Bat 10.00
SS Shannon Stewart/Bat 8.00
FT Frank Thomas/Jsy 10.00
JT Jim Thome/Jsy 20.00
LW Larry Walker/Jsy 5.00
JW Jeff Weaver/Jsy 5.00
BW Bernie Williams/Jsy 8.00
BZ Barry Zito/Jsy 8.00

Relics Series 2

NM/M
Common Player: 5.00
Jerseys 1:18
Bats 1:40
RA Roberto Alomar/Bat 10.00
JB Jeff Bagwell/Jsy 8.00
BB Barry Bonds/Jsy 20.00
BBO Bret Boone/Jsy 6.00
KB Kevin Brown/Jsy 6.00
AB A.J. Burnett/Jsy 5.00
SB Sean Burroughs/Bat 8.00
EC Eric Chavez/Bat 8.00
TC Ty Cobb/Bat 420.00
JC Jimmy Collins/Bat 45.00
SCR Sam Crawford/Bat 50.00
JD Johnny Damon/Bat 12.00
RD Ryan Dempster/Jsy 5.00
BD Brandon Duckworth/Jsy 5.00
AD Adam Dunn/Bat 10.00
DE Darin Erstad/Jsy 5.00
JEV Johnny Evers/Bat 50.00
CF Cliff Floyd/Jsy 5.00
TGL Tom Glavine/Jsy 8.00
JG Juan Gonzalez/Bat 10.00
MG Mark Grace/Bat 10.00
SG Shawn Green/Jsy 6.00
CG Cristian Guzman/Jsy 5.00
TG Tony Gwynn/Jsy 15.00
TH Toby Hall/Jsy 5.00
JH Josh Hamilton/Bat 10.00
THE Todd Helton/Jsy 8.00
RH Rickey Henderson/Bat 15.00
BH Buck Herzog/Bat 30.00
JJ Jason Jennings/Jsy 5.00
RJ Randy Johnson/Jsy 10.00
AJ Andruw Jones/Jsy 8.00
CJO Chipper Jones/Jsy 10.00
JK Jeff Kent/Jsy 5.00
BL Barry Larkin/Jsy 8.00
TL Travis Lee/Bat 5.00
GM Greg Maddux/Jsy 12.00
EM Edgar Martinez/Jsy 8.00
TM Tino Martinez/Bat 10.00
JM Joe Mays/Jsy 5.00
JMC John McGraw/Bat 60.00
FM Fred McGriff/Bat 8.00
JO John Olerud/Jsy 5.00
RP Rafael Palmeiro/Jsy 8.00
BP Brad Penny/Jsy 5.00
MP Mike Piazza/Jsy 15.00
AP Albert Pujols/Jsy 15.00
ARA Aramis Ramirez/Bat 10.00
AR Alex Rodriguez/Bat 20.00
IR Ivan Rodriguez/Jsy 8.00
CS Curt Schilling/Bat 15.00
GS Gary Sheffield/Bat 8.00
TS Tsuyoshi Shinjo/Bat 5.00
AS Alfonso Soriano/Bat 10.00
MT Miguel Tejada/Bat 8.00
FT Frank Thomas/Jsy 8.00
JTH Jim Thome/Bat 15.00
JT Joe Tinker/Bat 40.00
MV Mo Vaughn/Bat 8.00
RV Robin Ventura/Bat 5.00
HWA Honus Wagner/Bat 400.00
LW Larry Walker/Jsy 5.00
BW Bernie Williams/Jsy 8.00
MW Matt Williams/Jsy 5.00
PW Preston Wilson/Jsy 5.00

Relics Series 3

NM/M
Common Player: 5.00
RA Roberto Alomar/Bat 8.00
JB Jeff Bagwell/Bat 8.00
WB Wilson Betemit/Bat 5.00
PB Pat Burrell/Bat 10.00
EC Eric Chavez/Jsy 8.00
AD Adam Dunn/Bat 10.00
JE Jim Edmonds/Jsy 8.00
NG Nomar Garciaparra/Bat 20.00
LG Luis Gonzalez/Jsy 5.00
TG Tony Gwynn/Jsy 10.00
TH Todd Helton/Jsy 8.00
RH Rickey Henderson/Bat 15.00
NJ Nick Johnson/Bat 5.00
RJ Randy Johnson/Jsy 10.00
AJ Andruw Jones/Jsy 8.00
CJ Chipper Jones/Jsy 10.00
PM Pedro Martinez/Jsy 12.00
DM Doug Mientkiewicz/Jsy 6.00
RP Rafael Palmeiro/Jsy 8.00
CP Corey Patterson/Bat 6.00
MP Mike Piazza/Jsy 15.00
AP Albert Pujols/Bat 20.00
AR Alex Rodriguez/Bat 15.00
IR Ivan Rodriguez/Bat 8.00
SR Scott Rolen/Bat 10.00
CS Curt Schilling/Bat 8.00
GS Gary Sheffield/Bat 8.00
TS Tsuyoshi Chinjo/Bat 5.00
AS Alfonso Soriano/Bat 10.00
MTE Miguel Tejada/Jsy 8.00
FT Frank Thomas/Jsy 8.00
JT Jim Thome/Jsy 10.00
MV Mo Vaughn/Jsy 5.00
BW Bernie Williams/Jsy 8.00
BZ Barry Zito/Jsy 6.00

Reprint Relics

NM/M
Common Player: 75.00
SC Sam Crawford 90.00
JE Johnny Evers 90.00
JM John McGraw 75.00
TS Tris Speaker 140.00
HW Honus Wagner 400.00

Team Topps Legends Autographs

NM/M
Inserted 1:7,093
Nolan Ryan 400.00

Team Topps Legends Autographs Series 2

NM/M
Inserted 1:260
Ralph Branca 25.00
Andy Pafko 20.00
Joe Pepitone 10.00
Tom Seaver 60.00
Warren Spahn 25.00
Luis Tiant 10.00

Team 206

NM/M
Complete Set (20): 10.00
Common Player: .25
Inserted 1:Pack
1 Barry Bonds 2.00
2 Ivan Rodriguez .50
3 Luis Gonzalez .25
4 Jason Giambi .50
5 Pedro Martinez .75
6 Larry Walker .25
7 Bobby Abreu .40
8 Derek Jeter 2.00
9 Bret Boone .40
10 Mike Piazza 1.00
11 Alex Rodriguez 1.50
12 Roger Clemens 1.50
13 Albert Pujols 1.50
14 Randy Johnson .75
15 Sammy Sosa 1.50
16 Cristian Guzman .25
17 Shawn Green .40
18 Curt Schilling .50
19 Ichiro Suzuki 1.00
20 Chipper Jones .75

Team 206 Series 2

NM/M
Complete Set (25): 10.00
Common Player: .25
Inserted 1:1
1 Alex Rodriguez 1.50
2 Sammy Sosa 1.50
3 Jason Giambi .50
4 Nomar Garciaparra 1.25
5 Ichiro Suzuki 1.00
6 Chipper Jones .75
7 Derek Jeter 2.00
8 Barry Bonds 2.00
9 Mike Piazza 1.50
10 Randy Johnson .75
11 Shawn Green .25
12 Todd Helton .50
13 Luis Gonzalez .25
14 Albert Pujols 1.50
15 Curt Schilling .50
16 Scott Rolen .75
17 Ivan Rodriguez .50
18 Roberto Alomar .50
19 Cristian Guzman .25
20 Bret Boone .25
21 Barry Zito .40
22 Larry Walker .25
23 Eric Chavez .25
24 Roger Clemens 1.50
25 Pedro Martinez .75

Team 206 Series 3

NM/M
Complete Set (30): 10.00
Common Player: .25
Inserted 1:1
1 Ichiro Suzuki 1.00
2 Kazuhisa Ishii .25
3 Alex Rodriguez 1.50
4 Mark Prior 1.00
5 Derek Jeter 2.00
6 Sammy Sosa 1.50
7 Nomar Garciaparra 1.25
8 Mike Piazza 1.00
9 Jason Giambi .50
10 Vladimir Guerrero .75
11 Curt Schilling .50
12 Jim Thome .75
13 Adam Dunn .50
14 Albert Pujols 1.50
15 Pat Burrell .50
16 Chipper Jones .75
17 Randy Johnson .75
18 Todd Helton .50
19 Luis Gonzalez .25
20 Alfonso Soriano .75
21 Shawn Green .40
22 Pedro J. Martinez .75
23 Lance Berkman .40
24 Ivan Rodriguez .50
25 Larry Walker .25
26 Andruw Jones .40
27 Ken Griffey Jr. 1.00
28 Eric Hinske .25
29 Mike Sweeney .25
30 Miguel Tejada .50

1982 California Angels Reprints

Commemorating the 20th anniversary of the A.L. West Championship Angels, Fox Sport Net issued this reprint set of the team's stars. Fronts are identical to the originals. Backs also closely reproduce the 1982 versions, but have a shaded box at the right end with a card number and updated copyright information. Fifteen thousand sets, cello-wrapped with a sponsor's header card, were given to fans attending an Anaheim game.

NM/M
Complete Set (10): 10.00
Common Player: .50
1 Don Baylor 1.00
2 Rod Carew 2.00
3 Doug DeCinces .50
4 Brian Downing .50
5 Reggie Jackson 5.00
6 Fred Lynn 1.00
7 Geoff Zahn .50
8 Bob Boone 1.00
9 Bob Grich .75
-- Header Card .05

Chicago Cubs Reprints

For a second year the Cubs contracted with Topps to provide a series of reprint cards for use as give-aways at special games throughout the season. Each reprint features a Wrigley Field logo on front and is sequentially numbered to 20,000 in a strip of gold foil on back. Each card was distributed in a cello wrapper with the date of the promotion and names of the sponsor(s).

NM/M
Complete Set (11): 35.00
Common Player: 2.50
1954 Ernie Banks 12.50
1961 Don Cardwell 2.50
1961 Billy Williams 5.00
1962 Ken Hubbs 3.50
1969 Ken Holtzman 2.50
1972 Milt Pappas 2.50
1979 Dave Kingman 3.00
1980 Bill Buckner 3.00
1984 Lee Smith 3.00
1998 Kerry Wood 4.00
2002 Sammy Sosa 5.00

Milwaukee Brewers Reprints

Topps cards of former Brewers favorites were reprinted and distributed one per month at selected home games. The cards are nearly identical to the originals except for a sponsor's (St. Michael Hospital) logo on front and a reprint notice on back.

NM/M
Complete Set (6): 25.00
Common Player: 4.00
(1) Don Money/1978 4.00
(2) Cecil Cooper/1979 4.00
(3) Ben Oglivie/1980 4.00
(4) Gorman Thomas/1981 4.00
(5) Robin Yount/1982 7.50
(6) Paul Molitor/1992 7.50

Post Collector's Series

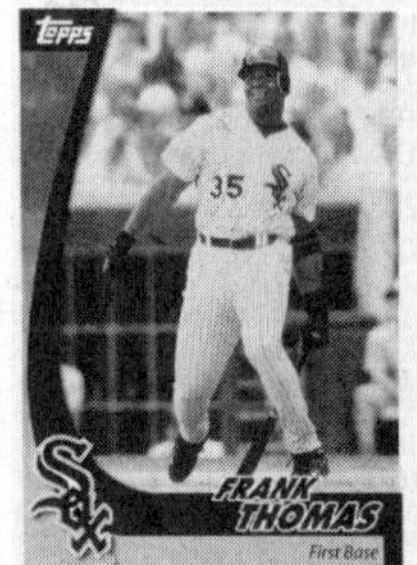

For a second consecutive year in 2002, Post cereals packaged a special edition of Topps cards. The baseball cards were issued two per cello pack. The 2-1/2" x 3-1/2" cards have game-action photos with the background printed in a matte finish. The player portion of the photo and the surrounding team-color coded graphics at the sides and bottom have spot gloss. At bottom-right are the player's position and name. A team logo in the lower-left corner and the Topps logo is at upper-left. Backs have a portrait photo, biographical data, 2001 monthly stats and various league and sponsor logos. An album to house the collection was available by mail for $8.95 and two proofs of purchase.

NM/M
Complete Set (30): 10.00
Common Player: .25
Album: 9.00
1 Alex Rodriguez 1.50
2 Pedro Martinez .50
3 Bernie Williams .35
4 Mike Piazza 1.00
5 Jim Edmonds .25
6 Rich Aurilia .25
7 Sammy Sosa 1.25
8 Sean Casey .25
9 Ichiro 2.00
10 Jason Giambi .40
11 Todd Helton .50
12 Chipper Jones 1.00

13 Frank Thomas .65
14 Scott Rolen .35
15 Carlos Delgado .35
16 Jeff Bagwell .65
17 Jim Thome .25
18 Shawn Green .35
19 Luis Gonzales .50
20 Vladimir Guerrero .65
21 Troy Glaus .50
22 Ryan Klesko .25
23 Jeromy Burnitz .25
24 Bobby Higginson .25
25 Jason Kendall .25
26 Cliff Floyd .25
27 Greg Vaughn .25
28 Brad Radke .25
29 Mike Sweeney .25
30 Jeff Conine .25

2003 Topps

NM/M
Complete Set (720): 70.00
Sealed Factory Set (725): 70.00
Complete Series 1 Set (366): 35.00
Complete Series 2 Set (355): 35.00
Common Player: .10
Series 1 & 2 Pack (10): 1.50
Series 1 & 2 Box (36): 35.00
Series 2 Jumbo Box: 45.00
White Topps "throw-back" logo.
Series 1 (1:8852): Value Undetermined
Series 2 (1:4487): Value Undetermined

1a Alex Rodriguez (Red Topps) 1.00
2 Dan Wilson .10
3 Jimmy Rollins .25
4 Jermaine Dye .10
5 Steve Karsay .10
6 Timoniel Perez .10
8 Jose Vidro .10
9 Eddie Guardado .10
10a Mark Prior (Red Topps) .50
11a Curt Schilling (Red Topps) .40
12 Dennis Cook .10
13 Andruw Jones .40
14 David Segui .10
15 Trot Nixon .10
16 Antonio Alfonseca .10
17 Magglio Ordonez .20
18 Jason LaRue .10
19 Danys Baez .10
20a Todd Helton (Red Topps) .40
21 Denny Neagle .10
22 Dave Mlicki .10
23 Roberto Hernandez .10
24 Odalis Perez .10
25 Nick Neugebauer .10
26 David Ortiz .10
27 Andres Galarraga .15
28 Edgardo Alfonzo .10
29 Chad Bradford .10
30a Jason Giambi (Red Topps) .40
31 Brian Giles .25
32 Deivi Cruz .10
33 Robb Nen .10
34 Jeff Nelson .10
35 Edgar Renteria .10
36 Aubrey Huff .10
37 Brandon Duckworth .10
38 Juan Gonzalez .40
39 Sidney Ponson .10
40 Eric Hinske .10
41 Kevin Appier .10
42 Danny Bautista .10
43 Javier Lopez .10
44 Jeff Conine .10
45 Carlos Baerga .10
46 Ugueth Urbina .10
47 Mark Buehrle .10
48 Aaron Boone .10
49 Chuck Finley .10
50a Sammy Sosa (Red Topps) 1.00
51 Jose Jimenez .10
52 Chris Truby .10
53 Luis Castillo .10
54 Orlando Merced .10
55 Brian Jordan .10
56 Eric Young .10
57 Bobby Kielty .10
58 Luis Rivas .10
59 Brad Wilkerson .10
60 Roberto Alomar .40
61a Roger Clemens (Red Topps) 1.00
62 Scott Hatteberg .10
63 Andy Ashby .10
64 Mike Williams .10
65 Ron Gant .10
66 Benito Santiago .10
67 Bret Boone .10
68 Matt Morris .10
69 Troy Glaus .40
70 Austin Kearns .25
71 Jim Thome .40
72 Rickey Henderson .40
73a Luis Gonzalez (Red Topps) .20
74 Brad Fullmer .10
75 Benny Agbayani .10
76 Randy Wolf .10
77a Miguel Tejada (Red Topps) .25
78 Jimmy Anderson .10
79 Ramon Martinez .10
80a Ivan Rodriguez (Red Topps) .40
81 John Flaherty .10
82 Shannon Stewart .10
83 Orlando Palmeiro .10
84 Rafael Furcal .10
85 Kenny Rogers .10
86 Bud Smith .10
87 Mo Vaughn .15
88 Jose Cruz Jr. .10
89 Mike Matheny .10
90a Alfonso Soriano (Red Topps) .50
91 Orlando Cabrera .10
92 Jeffrey Hammonds .10
93 Hideo Nomo .25
94 Carlos Febles .10
95 Billy Wagner .10
96 Alex Gonzalez .10
97 Todd Zeile .10
98 Omar Vizquel .20
99 Jose Rijo .10
100a Ichiro Suzuki (Red Topps) 1.00
101 Steve Cox .10
102 Hideki Irabu .10
103 Roy Halladay .10
104 David Eckstein .10
105 Greg Maddux .75
106 Chris Richard .10
107 Travis Driskill .10
108 Fred McGriff .15
109 Frank Thomas .50
110 Shawn Green .20
111 Ruben Quevedo .10
112 Jacque Jones .10
113 Tomokazu Ohka .10
114 Joe McEwing .10
115 Ramiro Mendoza .10
116 Mark Mulder .20
117 Mike Lieberthal .10
118 Jack Wilson .10
119 Randall Simon .10
120 Bernie Williams .40
121 Marvin Benard .10
122 Jamie Moyer .10
123 Andy Benes .10
124 Tino Martinez .10
125 Esteban Yan .10
126 Gabe Kapler .10
127 Jason Isringhausen .10
128 Chris Carpenter .10
129 Mike Cameron .10
130a Gary Sheffield (Red Topps) .25
131 Geronimo Gil .10
132 Brian Daubach .10
133 Corey Patterson .10
134 Aaron Rowand .10
135 Chris Reitsma .10
136 Bob Wickman .10
137 Paul Shuey .10
138 Jason Jennings .10
139 Brandon Inge .10
140 Larry Walker .20
141 Ramon Santiago .10
142 Hansel Izquierdo .10
143 Jose Vizcaino .10
144 Mark Quinn .10
145 Michael Tucker .10
146 Darren Dreifort .10
147 Mark Loretta .10
148 Corey Koskie .10
149 Tony Armas Jr. .10
150a Kazuhisa Ishii (Red Topps) .10
151 Al Leiter .10
152 Steve Trachsel .10
153 Mike Stanton .10
154 David Justice .15
155 Marlon Anderson .10
156 Jason Kendall .10
157 Brian Lawrence .10
158 J.T. Snow Jr. .10
159 Edgar Martinez .10
160a Pat Burrell (Red Topps) .25
161 Kerry Robinson .10
162 Greg Vaughn .10
163 Carl Everett .10
164 Vernon Wells .10
165 Jose Mesa .10
166 Troy Percival .10
167 Erubiel Durazo .10
168 Jason Marquis .10
169 Jerry Hairston Jr. .10
170a Vladimir Guerrero (Red Topps) .50
171 Byung-Hyun Kim .10
172 Marcus Giles .10
173 Johnny Damon .10
174 Jon Lieber .10
175 Ray Durham .10
176 Sean Casey .10
177a Adam Dunn (Red Topps) .40
178 Juan Pierre .10
179 Damion Easley .10
180a Barry Zito (Red Topps) .25
181 Abraham Nunez .10
182 Pokey Reese .10
183 Jeff Kent .20
184 Russ Ortiz .10
185 Ruben Sierra .10
186 Brent Abernathy .10
187 Ismael Valdes .10
188 Darrin Fletcher .10
189 Craig Counsell .10
190 David Wells .10
191 Ramon Hernandez .10
192 Adam Kennedy .10
193 Tony Womack .10
194 Wes Helms .10
195 Tony Batista .10
196 Rolando Arrojo .10
197 Matt Clement .10
198 Sandy Alomar .10
199 Scott Sullivan .10
200a Albert Pujols (Red Topps) 1.00
201 Kirk Rueter .10
202 Phil Nevin .10
203 Kip Wells .10
204 Ron Coomer .10
205 Jeromy Burnitz .10
206 Kyle Lohse .10
207 Paul Bako .10
208 Paul LoDuca .10
209 Carlos Beltran .10
210 Roy Oswalt .25
211 Mike Lowell .10
212 Robert Fick .10
213 Todd Jones .10
214 C.C. Sabathia .10
215 Danny Graves .10
216 Todd Hundley .10
217 Tim Wakefield .10
218 Dustin Hermanson .10
219 Kevin Millwood .10
220 Jorge Posada .25
221 Bobby Jones .10
222 Carlos Guillen .10
223 Fernando Vina .10
224 Ryan Rupe .10
225 Kelvim Escobar .10
226 Ramon Ortiz .10
227 Junior Spivey .10
228 Juan Cruz .10
229 Melvin Mora .10
230a Lance Berkman (Red Topps) .25
231 Brent Butler .10
232 Matt Anderson .10
233 Derrek Lee .10
234 Matt Lawton .10
235 Chuck Knoblauch .10
236 Eric Gagne .10
237 Alex Sanchez .10
238 Denny Hocking .10
239 Rick Reed .10
240 Rey Ordonez .10
241 Orlando Hernandez .10
242 Robert Person .10
243 Sean Burroughs .10
244 Jeff Cirillo .10
245 Mike Lamb .10
246 Jose Valentin .10
247 Ellis Burks .10
248 Shawn Chacon .10
249 Josh Beckett .10
250a Nomar Garciaparra (Red Topps) 1.00
251 Craig Biggio .20
252 Joe Randa .10
253 Mark Grudzielanek .10
254 Glendon Rusch .10
255 Michael Barrett .10
256 Tyler Houston .10
257 Ryan Dempster .10
258 Wade Miller .10
259 Adrian Beltre .20
260 Vicente Padilla .10
261 Kazuhiro Sasaki .10
262 Mike Scioscia .10
263 Bobby Cox .10
264 Mike Hargrove .10
265 Grady Little .10
266 Alex Gonzalez .10
267 Jerry Manuel .10
268 Bob Boone .10
269 Joel Skinner .10
270 Clint Hurdle .10
271 Luis Pujols .10
272 Bob Brenly .10
273 Jeff Torborg .10
274 Jimy Williams .10
275 Tony Pena .10
276 Jim Tracy .10
277 Jerry Royster .10
278 Ron Gardenhire .10
279 Frank Robinson .10
280 Bobby Valentine .10
281 Joe Torre .10
282 Art Howe .10
283 Larry Bowa .10
284 Lloyd McClendon .10
285 Bruce Bochy .10
286 Dusty Baker .10
287 Lou Pinella .10
288 Tony LaRussa .10
289 Hal McRae .10
290 Jerry Narron .10
291 Carlos Tosca .10
292 Chris Duncan **RC** 2.00
293 Franklin Gutierrez **RC** 1.00
294 Adam LaRoche .10
295 Manuel Ramirez **RC** .10
296 Il Kim **RC** .10
297 Wayne Lydon **RC** .20
298 Daryl Clark **RC** .25
299 Sean Pierce .10
300a Andy Marte **RC** (Red Topps) 1.00
301 Matt Peterson **RC** .25
302 Gonzalo Lopez **RC** .25
303 Bernie Castro **RC** .10
304 Cliff Lee .10
305 Jason Perry **RC** .50
306 Jaime Bubela **RC** .10
307 Alexis Rios .10
308 Brendan Harris **RC** .50
309 Ramon Martinez .25
310 Terry Tiffee **RC** .40
311 Kevin Youkilis **RC** 1.00
312 Ruddy Lugo **RC** .20
313 C.J. Wilson .10
314 Mike McNutt **RC** .10
315 Jeff Clark **RC** .10
316 Mark Malaska **RC** .10
317 Doug Waechter **RC** .25
318 Derell McCall **RC** .10
319 Scott Tyler .10
320 Craig Brazell **RC** .40
321a Walter Young (Red Topps) .10
322a Marlon Byrd, Jorge Padilla (Red Topps) .10
323 Chris Snelling, Shin-Soo Choo .10
324a Hank Blalock, Mark Teixeira (Red Topps) .10
325 Josh Hamilton, Carl Crawford .20
326 Orlando Hudson, Josh Phelps .10
327 Jack Cust, Rene Reyes .10
328 Angel Berroa, Alexis Gomez .10
329 Michael Cuddyer, Michael Restovich .10
330 Juan Rivera, Marcus Thames .10
331 Brandon Puffer, Jung Bong .10
332 Mike Cameron .10
333 Shawn Green .25
334 Team Shot .10
335 Jason Giambi .25
336 Derek Lowe .10
337 Manny Ramirez, Mike Sweeney, Bernie Williams .25
338 Alfonso Soriano, Alex Rodriguez, Derek Jeter .50
339 Alex Rodriguez, Jim Thome, Rafael Palmeiro .40
340 Magglio Ordonez, Alex Rodriguez, Miguel Tejada .40
341 Pedro Martinez, Derek Lowe, Barry Zito .25
342 Pedro Martinez, Roger Clemens, Mike Mussina .25
343 Larry Walker, Vladimir Guerrero, Todd Helton .25
344 Sammy Sosa, Albert Pujols, Shawn Green .40
345 Sammy Sosa, Lance Berkman, Shawn Green .40
346 Lance Berkman, Albert Pujols, Pat Burrell .25
347 Randy Johnson, Greg Maddux, Tom Glavine .25
348 Randy Johnson, Curt Schilling, Kerry Wood .25
349 AL Divison Series .20
350 AL & NL Divison Series .20
351 AL & NL Divison Series .20
352 NL Divison Series .20
353 AL Championship Series .20
354 Postseason Highlight .20
355 NL Championship Series .10
356 Jason Giambi .25
357 Alfonso Soriano .50
358 Alex Rodriguez .75
359 Eric Chavez .10
360 Torii Hunter .10
361 Bernie Williams .20
362 Garret Anderson .10
363 Jorge Posada .20
364 Derek Lowe .10
365 Barry Zito .20
366 Manny Ramirez .25
367 Mike Scioscia .10
368a Francisco Rodriguez (Red Topps) .10
369 Andres Galarraga .10
370a Chipper Jones (Red Topps) .50
371 Chris Singleton .10
372 Cliff Floyd .10
373 Bobby Hill .10
374 Antonio Osuna .10
375 Barry Larkin .25
376 Charles Nagy .10
377 Denny Stark .10
378 Dean Palmer .10
379 Eric Owens .10
380a Randy Johnson (Red Topps) .50
381 Jeff Suppan .10
382 Eric Karros .10
383 Luis Vizcaino .10
384 Johan Santana .10
385 Javier Vazquez .10
386 John Thomson .10
387a Nick Johnson (Red Topps) .10
388 Mark Ellis .10
389 Doug Glanville .10
390a Ken Griffey Jr. (Red Topps) .75
391 Bubba Trammell .10
392 Livan Hernandez .10
393 Desi Relaford .10
394 Eli Marrero .10
395 Jared Sandberg .10
396a Barry Bonds (Red Topps) 1.50
397 Esteban Loaiza .10
398 Aaron Sele .10
399 Geoff Blum .10
400a Derek Jeter (Red Topps) 1.50
401 Eric Byrnes .10
402 Mike Timlin .10
403 Mark Kotsay .10
404 Rich Aurilia .10
405 Joel Pineiro .10
406 Chuck Finley .10
407 Bengie Molina .10
408 Steve Finley .10
409 Julio Franco .10
410 Marty Cordova .10
411 Shea Hillenbrand .10
412 Mark Bellhorn .10
413 Jon Garland .10
414 Reggie Taylor .10
415 Milton Bradley .10
416 Carlos Pena .10
417 Andy Fox .10
418 Brad Ausmus .10
419 Brent Mayne .10
420 Paul Quantrill .10
421a Carlos Delgado (Red Topps) .20
422 Kevin Mench .10
423 Joe Kennedy .10
424 Mike Crudale .10
425 Mark McLemore .10
426 Bill Mueller .10
427 Robert Mackowiak .10
428 Ricky Ledee .10
429 Ted Lilly .10
430 Sterling Hitchcock .10
431 Scott Strickland .10
432 Damion Easley .10
433a Torii Hunter (Red Topps) .25
434 Brad Radke .10
435 Geoff Jenkins .10
436 Paul Byrd .10
437 Morgan Ensberg .10
438 Mike Maroth .10
439 Mike Hampton .10
440 Adam Hyzdu .10
441 Vance Wilson .10
442 Todd Ritchie .10
443 Flash Gordon .10
444 John Burkett .10
445 Rodrigo Lopez .10
446 Tim Spooneybarger .10
447 Quinton McCracken .10
448 Tim Salmon .20
449 Jarrod Washburn .10
450a Pedro Martinez (Red Topps) .50
451 Dustan Mohr .10
452 Julio Lugo .10
453 Scott Stewart .10
454 Armando Benitez .10
455 Raul Mondesi .20
456 Robin Ventura .20
457 Bobby Abreu .20
458 Josh Fogg .20
459 Ryan Klesko .20
460 Tsuyoshi Shinjo .10
461a Jim Edmonds (Red Topps) .25
462 Cliff Politte .10
463 Chan Ho Park .10
464 John Mabry .10
465 Woody Williams .10
466 Jason Michaels .10
467 Scott Schoeneweis .10
468 Brian Anderson .10
469 Brett Tomko .10
470 Scott Erickson .10
471 Tony Clark .10
472 Danny Wright .10
473 Jason Schmidt .10
474 Scott Williamson .10
475 Einar Diaz .10
476 Jay Payton .10
477 Juan Acevedo .10
478 Ben Grieve .10
479 Raul Ibanez .10
480 Richie Sexson .25
481 Rick Reed .10
482 Pedro Astacio .10
483 Adam Piatt .10
484 Bud Smith .10
485 Tomas Perez .10
486 Adam Eaton .10
487 Rafael Palmeiro .25
488 Jason Tyner .10
489a Scott Rolen (Red Topps) .50
490 Randy Winn .10
491 Ryan Jensen .10
492 Trevor Hoffman .10
493 Craig Wilson .10
494 Jeremy Giambi .10
495 Daryle Ward .10
496 Shane Spencer .10
497 Andy Pettitte .25
498 John Franco .10
499 Masato Yoshii .10
500a Mike Piazza (Red Topps) 1.00
501 Cristian Guzman .10
502 Jose Hernandez .10
503 Octavio Dotel .10
504 Brad Penny .10
505 Jose Ortiz .10
506 Ryan Dempster .10
507 Joe Crede .10
508 Chad Hermansen .10
509 Gary Matthews Jr. .10
510 Matt Franco .10
511 Ben Weber .10
512 Dave Berg .10
513 Michael Young .10
514 Frank Catalanotto .10
515a Darin Erstad (Red Topps) .25
516 Matt Williams .10
517 B.J. Surhoff .10
518 Kerry Ligtenberg .10
519 Mike Bordick .10
520 Arthur Rhodes .10
521 Joe Girardi .10
522 D'Angelo Jimenez .10
523 Paul Konerko .10
524 Jose Macias .10
525 Joe Mays .10
526 Marquis Grissom .10
527 Neifi Perez .10
528 Preston Wilson .10
529 Jeff Weaver .10
530a Eric Chavez (Red Topps) .25
531 Placido Polanco .10
532 Ray Lankford .10
533 James Baldwin .10
534 Toby Hall .10
535 Brendan Donnelly .10
536 Benji Gil .10
537 Damian Moss .10
538 Jorge Julio .10
539 Matt Clement .10
540 Brian Moehler .10
541 Lee Stevens .10
542 Jimmy Haynes .10
543 Kevin Millar .10
544 Dave Roberts .10
545 J.C. Romero .10
546 Bartolo Colon .10
547 Roger Cedeno .10
548 Mariano Rivera .20
549 Billy Koch .10
550a Manny Ramirez (Red Topps) .50
551 Travis Lee .10
552 Oliver Perez .10
553 Tim Worrell .10
554 Rafael Soriano .10
555 Damian Miller .10
556 John Smoltz .10
557 Willis Roberts .10
558a Tim Hudson (Red Topps) .25
559 Moises Alou .20
560 Gary Glover .10
561 Corky Miller .10
562 Ben Broussard .10
563 Gabe Kapler .10
564 Chris Woodward .10
565 Paul Wilson .10
566 Todd Hollandsworth .10
567 So Taguchi .10
568 John Olerud .20
569 Reggie Sanders .10
570 Jake Peavy .10
571 Kris Benson .10
572 Todd Pratt .10
573 Ray Durham .10
574 David Wells .10
575 Chris Widger .10
576 Shawn Wooten .10
577 Tom Glavine .25
578 Antonio Alfonseca .10
579 Keith Foulke .10
580 Shawn Estes .10

581 Travis Fryman .10
582 Dmitri Young .10
583 A.J. Burnett .10
584 Richard Hidalgo .10
585a Mike Sweeney (Red Topps) .10
586 Alex Cora .10
587 Matt Stairs .10
588 Doug Mientkiewicz .10
589 Fernando Tatis .10
590 David Weathers .10
591 Cory Lidle .10
592 Dan Plesac .10
593a Jeff Bagwell (Red Topps) .50
594 Steve Sparks .10
595 Sandy Alomar Jr. .10
596 John Lackey .10
597 Rick Helling .10
598 Mark DeRosa .10
599 Carlos Lee .10
600a Garret Anderson (Red Topps) .20
601 Vinny Castilla .10
602 Ryan Drese .10
603 LaTroy Hawkins .10
604 David Bell .10
605 Freddy Garcia .10
606 Miguel Cairo .10
607 Scott Spiezio .10
608 Mike Remlinger .10
609 Tony Graffanino .10
610 Russell Branyan .10
611 Chris Magruder .10
612 Jose Contreras **RC** .75
613 Carl Pavano .10
614 Kevin Brown .10
615 Tyler Houston .10
616 A.J. Pierzynski .10
617 Tony Fiore .10
618 Peter Bergeron .10
619 Rondell White .10
620 Brett Myers .10
621 Kevin Young .10
622 Kenny Lofton .10
623 Ben Davis .10
624 J.D. Drew .10
625 Chris Gomez .10
626 Karim Garcia .10
627 Ricky Gutierrez .10
628 Mark Redman .10
629 Juan Encarnacion .10
630 Anaheim Angels .25
631 Arizona Diamondbacks .10
632 Atlanta Braves .25
633 Baltimore Orioles .10
634 Boston Red Sox .25
635 Chicago Cubs .10
636 Chicago White Sox .10
637 Cincinnati Reds .10
638 Cleveland Indians .10
639 Colorado Rockies .10
640 Detroit Tigers .10
641 Florida Marlins .10
642 Houston Astros .10
643 Kansas City Royals .10
644 Los Angeles Dodgers .10
645 Milwaukee Brewers .10
646 Minnesota Twins .10
647 Montreal Expos .10
648 New York Mets .10
649 New York Yankees .50
650 Oakland Athletics .10
651 Philadelphia Phillies .10
652 Pittsburgh Pirates .10
653 San Diego Padres .10
654 San Francisco Giants .10
655 Seattle Mariners .10
656 St. Louis Cardinals .10
657 Tampa Bay Devil Rays .10
658 Texas Rangers .10
659 Toronto Blue Jays .10
660 Bryan Bullington **RC** 1.00
661 Jeremy Guthrie .10
662 Joey Gomes .25
663 Evel Bastida-Martinez **RC** .40
664 Brian Wright **RC** .10
665 B.J. Upton .10
666 Jeff Francis .10
667 Drew Meyer .10
668 Jeremy Hermida .10
669 Khalil Greene .75
670 Darrell Rasner .10
671 Cole Hamels .50
672 James Loney .10
673 Sergio Santos .10
674 Jason Pridie .10
675 Brandon Phillips, Victor Martinez .10
676 Hee Seop Choi, Nic Jackson .10
677 Dontrelle Willis, Jason Stokes .10
678 Chad Tracy, Lyle Overbay .10
679 Joe Borchard, Corwin Malone .10
680 Joe Mauer, Justin Morneau .25
681 Drew Henson, Brandon Claussen .10
682 Chase Utley, Gavin Floyd .25
683 Taggert Bozied, Xavier Nady .25
684 Aaron Heilman, Jose Reyes .25
685 Kenny Rogers .10
686 Bengie Molina .10
687 John Olerud .10
688 Bret Boone .10
689 Eric Chavez .15
690 Alex Rodriguez .75
691 Darin Erstad .15
692 Ichiro Suzuki .50
693 Torii Hunter .15
694 Greg Maddux .50
695 Brad Ausmus .10
696 Todd Helton .20
697 Fernando Vina .10
698 Scott Rolen .25
699 Edgar Renteria .10
700 Andruw Jones .20
701 Larry Walker .10
702 Jim Edmonds .10
703 Barry Zito .10
704 Randy Johnson .40
705 Miguel Tejada .15
706 Barry Bonds .75
707 Eric Hinske .10
708 Jason Jennings .10
709 Todd Helton .20
710 Jeff Kent .10
711 Edgar Renteria .10
712 Scott Rolen .25
713 Barry Bonds .75
714 Sammy Sosa .50
715 Vladimir Guerrero .40
716 Mike Piazza .75
717 Curt Schilling .20
718 Randy Johnson .40
719 Bobby Cox .10
720 World Series Card .10
721 World Series Card .10

Black

Stars: 10-20X
Production 52 Sets

Gold

Stars: 3-6X
Production 2,003 Sets

Autographs

NM/M
Common Autograph: 8.00
HB Hank Blalock 20.00
MB Mark Buehrle 20.00
EC Eric Chavez 25.00
DE Darin Erstad 15.00
OH Orlando Hudson 10.00
AK Austin Kearns 15.00
JL Jason Lane 10.00
PL Paul LoDuca 12.00
JDM J.D. Martin 8.00
JM Joe Mauer 40.00
EM Eric Milton 10.00
NN Nick Neugebauer 10.00
MP Mark Prior 40.00
SR Scott Rolen 50.00
BS Ben Sheets 15.00
MTE Mark Teixeira 20.00
MTH Marcus Thames 8.00

Autographs Series 2

NM/M
Common Autograph: 8.00
JB Josh Beckett 30.00
LB Lance Berkman 40.00
CE Clint Everts 8.00
CF Cliff Floyd 20.00
BH Brad Hawpe 8.00
EH Eric Hinske 10.00
TH Torii Hunter 20.00
AK Austin Kearns 15.00
PK Paul Konerko 20.00
PL Paul LoDuca 15.00
MO Magglio Ordonez 20.00
JPH Josh Phelps 10.00
AP Albert Pujols 120.00
MT Miguel Tejada 30.00
BU B.J. Upton 25.00
JV Jose Vidro 10.00
DW Dontrelle Willis 25.00
BZ Barry Zito 30.00

All-Stars

NM/M
Complete Set (20): 20.00
Common Player: .50
Inserted 1:15

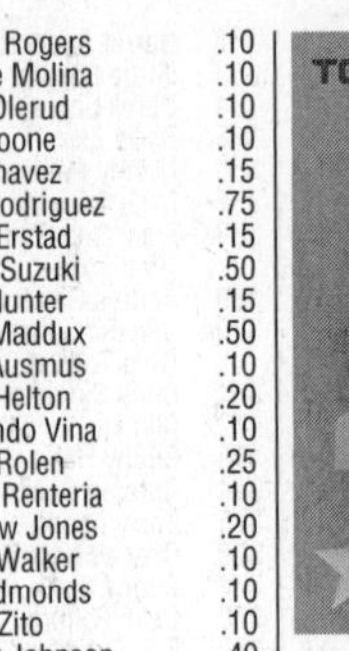

TAS1 Alfonso Soriano 1.50
TAS2 Barry Bonds 4.00
TAS3 Ichiro Suzuki 2.00
TAS4 Alex Rodriguez 3.00
TAS5 Miguel Tejada .75
TAS6 Nomar Garciaparra 2.50
TAS7 Jason Giambi 2.00
TAS8 Manny Ramirez 1.00
TAS9 Derek Jeter 4.00
TAS10 Garret Anderson .50
TAS11 Barry Zito .50
TAS12 Sammy Sosa 2.00
TAS13 Adam Dunn 1.00
TAS14 Vladimir Guerrero 1.50
TAS15 Mike Piazza 2.50
TAS16 Shawn Green .50
TAS17 Luis Gonzalez .50
TAS18 Todd Helton .75
TAS19 Torii Hunter .75
TAS20 Curt Schilling .75

Blue Backs

NM/M
Complete Set (40): 50.00
Common Player: .75
Inserted 1:12
BB1 Albert Pujols 2.00
BB2 Barry Bonds 5.00
BB3 Ichiro Suzuki 3.00
BB4 Sammy Sosa 2.50
BB5 Kazuhisa Ishii .75
BB6 Alex Rodriguez 4.00
BB7 Derek Jeter 5.00
BB8 Vladimir Guerrero 2.00
BB9 Ken Griffey Jr. 2.50
BB10 Jason Giambi 2.50
BB11 Todd Helton 1.00
BB12 Mike Piazza 3.00
BB13 Nomar Garciaparra 3.00
BB14 Chipper Jones 2.50
BB15 Ivan Rodriguez 1.00
BB16 Luis Gonzalez .75
BB17 Pat Burrell 1.00
BB18 Mark Prior 1.50
BB19 Adam Dunn 1.50
BB20 Jeff Bagwell 1.50
BB21 Austin Kearns 1.00
BB22 Alfonso Soriano 2.00
BB23 Jim Thome 1.50
BB24 Bernie Williams 1.00
BB25 Pedro J. Martinez 2.00
BB26 Lance Berkman 1.00
BB27 Randy Johnson 2.00
BB28 Rafael Palmeiro 1.00
BB29 Richie Sexson .75
BB30 Troy Glaus 1.50
BB31 Shawn Green .75
BB32 Larry Walker .75
BB33 Eric Hinske .75
BB34 Andruw Jones 1.50
BB35 Carlos Delgado 1.00
BB36 Curt Schilling 1.50
BB37 Greg Maddux 2.50
BB38 Jimmy Rollins .75
BB39 Eric Chavez 1.00
BB40 Scott Rolen 1.00

Draft Picks

NM/M
Complete Set (10): 30.00
1-5 issued in retail sets
6-10 issued in holiday sets
1 Brandon Wood 10.00
2 Ryan Wagner 5.00
3 Sean Rodriguez 3.00
4 Chris Lubanski 5.00
5 Chad Billingsley 3.00
6 Javi Herrera 3.00
7 Brian McFall 3.00
8 Nicholas Markakis 5.00
9 Adam Miller 5.00
10 Daric Barton 5.00

Flashback

NM/M
Complete Set (14): 50.00
Common Player: 2.00
HTA exclusive
GB George Brett 6.00
LD Lenny Dykstra 3.00
HK Harmon Killebrew 6.00
BM Bill Madlock 2.00
EM Eddie Mathews 4.00
DM Dale Murphy 5.00
JP Jim Palmer 3.00
MP Mike Piazza 6.00
RR Robin Roberts 3.00
AR Al Rosen 4.00
NR Nolan Ryan 10.00
TS Tom Seaver 5.00
WS Warren Spahn 4.00
CY Carl Yastrzemski 6.00

Futures Game

Flashback photos of alumni of the All-Star Futures Game are featured on this set of cards given away at the 2003 event July 13 in connection with All-Star Weekend in Chicago. The design follows the basic Topps format for 2003 and includes a special Futures Game logo.

NM/M
Complete Set (6): 5.00
Common Player: .50
1 Alfonso Soriano 2.00
2 Pat Burrell 1.00
3 Adam Dunn 1.00
4 Barry Zito .75
5 Mark Buehrle .50
6 Rafael Furcal .75

Hit Parade

NM/M
Complete Set (30): 30.00
Common Player: .50
Inserted 1:15
HP1 Barry Bonds 4.00
HP2 Sammy Sosa 2.50
HP3 Rafael Palmeiro 1.00
HP4 Fred McGriff .75
HP5 Ken Griffey Jr. 2.50
HP6 Juan Gonzalez 1.00
HP7 Andres Galarraga .50
HP8 Jeff Bagwell 1.50
HP9 Frank Thomas 1.50
HP10 Matt Williams .50
HP11 Barry Bonds 4.00
HP12 Rafael Palmeiro 1.00
HP13 Fred McGriff .75
HP14 Andres Galarraga .50
HP15 Ken Griffey Jr. 2.50
HP16 Sammy Sosa 2.50
HP17 Jeff Bagwell 1.50
HP18 Juan Gonzalez 1.00
HP19 Frank Thomas 1.50
HP20 Matt Williams .50
HP21 Rickey Henderson 1.00
HP22 Rafael Palmeiro 1.00
HP23 Roberto Alomar 1.00
HP24 Barry Bonds 4.00
HP25 Mark Grace 1.00
HP26 Fred McGriff .75
HP27 Julio Franco .50
HP28 Craig Biggio .50
HP29 Andres Galarraga .50
HP30 Barry Larkin .50

Hobby Masters

NM/M
Complete Set (20): 40.00
Common Player: 1.00
Inserted 1:18
HM1 Ichiro Suzuki 4.00
HM2 Kazuhisa Ishii 1.00
HM3 Derek Jeter 6.00
HM4 Barry Bonds 5.00
HM5 Sammy Sosa 3.00
HM6 Alex Rodriguez 5.00
HM7 Mike Piazza 4.00
HM8 Chipper Jones 3.00
HM9 Vladimir Guerrero 2.00
HM10 Nomar Garciaparra 4.00
HM11 Todd Helton 1.00
HM12 Jason Giambi 3.00
HM13 Ken Griffey Jr. 3.00
HM14 Albert Pujols 2.00
HM15 Ivan Rodriguez 1.00
HM16 Mark Prior 1.00
HM17 Adam Dunn 1.50
HM18 Randy Johnson 2.00
HM19 Pedro J. Martinez 2.00
HM20 Alfonso Soriano 3.00

Own The Game

NM/M
Complete Set (30): 30.00
Common Player: .50
Inserted 1:12
OG1 Ichiro Suzuki 3.00
OG2 Barry Bonds 4.00
OG3 Todd Helton .75
OG4 Larry Walker .75
OG5 Mike Sweeney .50
OG6 Sammy Sosa 2.50
OG7 Lance Berkman .75
OG8 Alex Rodriguez 4.00
OG9 Jim Thome 1.25
OG10 Shawn Green .75
OG11 Troy Glaus 1.00
OG12 Richie Sexson .50
OG13 Paul Konerko .50
OG14 Jason Giambi 2.50
OG15 Chipper Jones 2.50
OG16 Torii Hunter .50
OG17 Albert Pujols 1.50
OG18 Jose Vidro .50
OG19 Alfonso Soriano 2.00
OG20 Luis Castillo .50
OG21 Mike Lowell .50
OG22 Garret Anderson .50
OG23 Jimmy Rollins .50
OG24 Curt Schilling 1.00
OG25 Kazuhisa Ishii .50
OG26 Randy Johnson 1.50
OG27 Tom Glavine .75
OG28 Roger Clemens 2.50
OG29 Pedro J. Martinez 1.50
OG30 Derek Lowe .50

Prime Cuts Autograph

NM/M
Production 50 Sets
EC Eric Chavez 100.00
LB Lance Berkman 120.00
AJ Andruw Jones 100.00
CJ Chipper Jones 150.00
MO Magglio Ordonez 100.00
MT Miguel Tejada 120.00

Prime Cuts Pine Tar Series

NM/M
Pine Tar Series
Production 200 Sets
Trademark Series: 1-1.5X
Production 100 Sets
Prime Cuts Series: 1.5-2X
Production 50 Sets
RA Roberto Alomar 20.00
LB Lance Berkman 15.00
EC Eric Chavez 20.00
AD Adam Dunn 25.00
DE Darin Erstad 15.00
NG Nomar Garciaparra 40.00
JG Juan Gonzalez 15.00
TH Todd Helton 25.00
AJ Andruw Jones 20.00
CJ Chipper Jones 30.00
RP Rafael Palmeiro 20.00
MP Mike Piazza 30.00
AP Albert Pujols 40.00
AR Alex Rodriguez 25.00
IR Ivan Rodriguez 25.00
SR Scott Rolen 25.00
AS Alfonso Soriano 25.00
MT Miguel Tejada 15.00
FT Frank Thomas 30.00
MV Mo Vaughn 10.00
BW Bernie Williams 25.00

Prime Cuts Pine Tar Series 2

NM/M
Pine Tar Series:
Production 200
RA Roberto Alomar 20.00
LB Lance Berkman 15.00
HB Hank Blalock 25.00
BBO Barry Bonds 40.00
EC Eric Chavez 15.00
CD Carlos Delgado 10.00
AD Adam Dunn 25.00
NG Nomar Garciaparra 30.00
LG Luis Gonzalez 8.00
TG Tony Gwynn 20.00
RH Rickey Henderson 25.00
RJ Randy Johnson 25.00
EM Edgar Martinez 20.00
TM Tino Martinez 15.00
MO Magglio Ordonez 10.00
RP Rafael Palmeiro 15.00
JP Jorge Posada 15.00
AP Albert Pujols 40.00
MP Mark Prior 20.00
AR Alex Rodriguez 25.00
AS Alfonso Soriano 20.00
Trademark Series: 1-1.5X
Production 100
Prime Cuts: 1.5-2.5X
Production 50

2003 Topps Record Breakers

NM/M
Complete Set (50): 40.00
Common Player: .50
Inserted 1:6
JB Jeff Bagwell 1.50
LBE Lance Berkman 1.00
BB Barry Bonds 5.00
GB George Brett 2.50
LB Lou Brock .50
RCA Rod Carew .50
LC Luis Castillo .50
RC Roger Clemens 2.50
CD Carlos Delgado .50
CF Cliff Floyd .50
GF George Foster .50
AG Andres Galarraga .50
JG Jason Giambi 2.50
BG Bob Gibson 1.00
TG Troy Glaus 1.00
JGO Juan Gonzalez 1.00
LGO Luis Gonzalez .50
SG Shawn Green .75
HG Hank Greenberg .50
KG Ken Griffey Jr. 3.00
VG Vladimir Guerrero 1.50

RG	Ron Guidry	.50
TH	Todd Helton	1.00
RH	Rickey Henderson	.75
FJ	Fergie Jenkins	.50
RJ	Randy Johnson	1.50
CJ	Chipper Jones	3.00
HK	Harmon Killebrew	1.00
CK	Chuck Klein	.50
JM	Juan Marichal	.50
PM	Pedro J. Martinez	1.50
EM	Eddie Mathews	1.00
DM	Don Mattingly	4.00
FM	Fred McGriff	.50
JO	John Olerud	.50
RP	Rafael Palmeiro	1.00
MP	Mike Piazza	3.00
FR	Frank Robinson	1.00
AR	Alex Rodriguez	4.00
NR	Nolan Ryan	6.00
MSC	Mike Schmidt	3.00
CS	Curt Schilling	1.00
TS	Tom Seaver	1.00
RS	Richie Sexson	.50
GS	Gary Sheffield	.50
SS	Sammy Sosa	3.00
MS	Mike Sweeney	.50
HW	Hack Wilson	.50
PW	Preston Wilson	.50
RY	Robin Yount	1.00

Series 2

		NM/M
Complete Set (50):		40.00
Common Player:		.50
Inserted 1:6		
RA	Roberto Alomar	1.00
GA	Garret Anderson	.75
LA	Luis Aparicio	.50
JB	Jeff Bagwell	1.50
LB	Lance Berkman	1.00
CB	Craig Biggio	.75
WB	Wade Boggs	.75
BB	Barry Bonds	5.00
GB	George Brett	2.50
LBR	Lou Brock	.75
JD	Johnny Damon	.50
CD	Carlos Delgado	.50
LD	Lenny Dykstra	.50
DE	Darin Erstad	.50
BF	Bob Feller	.75
GF	George Foster	.50
NG	Nomar Garciaparra	3.00
LG	Luis Gonzalez	.50
DG	Dwight Gooden	.50
SG	Shawn Green	.75
KG	Ken Griffey Jr.	2.50
VG	Vladimir Guerrero	1.50
TG	Tony Gwynn	1.50
TH	Todd Helton	1.00
RH	Rickey Henderson	1.00
RJ	Randy Johnson	1.50
JK	Jeff Kent	.50
TK	Ted Kluszewski	.50
GM	Greg Maddux	2.50
JM	Juan Marichal	.50
EM	Edgar Martinez	.50
WM	Willie Mays	4.00
JME	Jose Mesa	.50
PM	Paul Molitor	1.00
JP	Jim Palmer	.75
TR	Tim Raines	.50
MR	Manny Ramirez	1.50
JR	Jim Rice	.50
FR	Frank Robinson	1.00
AR	Alex Rodriguez	4.00
TS	Tom Seaver	2.00
RS	Richie Sexson	.75
JS	John Smoltz	.50
SS	Sammy Sosa	2.50
WS	Willie Stargell	1.00
IS	Ichiro Suzuki	2.50
FT	Frank Thomas	1.50
JT	Jim Thome	1.50
LW	Larry Walker	.50
RY	Robin Yount	2.00

Autographs

		NM/M
Common Autograph:		
CF	Cliff Floyd	20.00
LG	Luis Gonzalez	30.00
FJ	Fergie Jenkins	25.00
CJ	Chipper Jones	75.00
HK	Harmon Killebrew	60.00
RP	Rafael Palmeiro	60.00
MS	Mike Schmidt	100.00
RS	Richie Sexson	30.00
MSW	Mike Sweeney	30.00
RY	Robin Yount	75.00

Autographs Series 2

		NM/M
Common Autograph:		25.00
Inserted 1:2,218		
LA	Luis Aparicio	40.00
LB	Lance Berkman	40.00
LBR	Lou Brock	40.00
GF	George Foster	25.00
JM	Juan Marichal	40.00
DM	Don Mattingly	125.00
WM	Willie Mays	150.00

Relics

		NM/M
Common Player:		6.00

JB	Jeff Bagwell/Jsy	8.00
LB	Lance Berkman/Bat	10.00
GB	George Brett/Bat	25.00
LC	Luis Castillo/Bat	6.00
CD	Carlos Delgado/Jsy	8.00
LGO	Luis Gonzalez/Jsy	6.00
SG	Shawn Green/Jsy	8.00
HG	Hank Greenberg/Bat	30.00
TH	Todd Helton/Jsy	10.00
RH	Rickey Henderson/Bat	15.00
CJ	Chipper Jones/Jsy	12.00
PM	Pedro Martinez/Jsy	10.00
DM	Don Mattingly/Bat	35.00
MP	Mike Piazza/Bat	15.00
FR	Frank Robinson/Bat	12.00
AR	Alex Rodriguez/Jsy	15.00
NR	Nolan Ryan/Jsy	35.00
MS	Mike Sweeney/Bat	8.00
HW	Hack Wilson/Bat	50.00
RY	Robin Yount/Jsy	15.00

Relics Series 2

		NM/M
Common Player:		5.00
WB	Wade Boggs/Bat	10.00
GB	George Brett/Bat	25.00
CD	Carlos Delgado/Jsy	6.00
DE	Darin Erstad/Jsy	8.00
LG	Luis Gonzalez/Jsy	5.00
TH	Todd Helton/Jsy	8.00
RH	Rogers Hornsby/Bat	35.00
TK	Ted Kluszewski/Bat	15.00
EM	Edgar Martinez/Bat	12.00
JR	Jim Rice/Jsy	8.00
FR	Frank Robinson/Bat	12.00
AR	Alex Rodriguez/Jsy	15.00
NRA	Nolan Ryan/Jsy	30.00
RS	Richie Sexson/Jsy	8.00
FT	Frank Thomas/Bat	10.00
RY	Robin Yount	12.00

Red Backs

		NM/M
Complete Set (40):		50.00
Common Player:		.50
Inserted 1:12		
TRB1	Nomar Garciaparra	3.00
TRB2	Ichiro Suzuki	2.50
TRB3	Alex Rodriguez	4.00
TRB4	Sammy Sosa	2.50
TRB5	Barry Bonds	5.00
TRB6	Vladimir Guerrero	1.50
TRB7	Derek Jeter	5.00
TRB8	Miguel Tejada	1.00
TRB9	Alfonso Soriano	2.00
TRB10	Manny Ramirez	1.50
TRB11	Adam Dunn	1.50
TRB12	Jason Giambi	2.50
TRB13	Mike Piazza	3.00
TRB14	Scott Rolen	1.50
TRB15	Shawn Green	.75
TRB16	Randy Johnson	1.50
TRB17	Todd Helton	1.00
TRB18	Garret Anderson	.50
TRB19	Curt Schilling	1.00
TRB20	Albert Pujols	2.00
TRB21	Chipper Jones	2.50
TRB22	Luis Gonzalez	.50
TRB23	Mark Prior	1.50
TRB24	Jim Thome	1.50
TRB25	Ivan Rodriguez	1.00
TRB26	Torii Hunter	1.00
TRB27	Lance Berkman	1.00
TRB28	Troy Glaus	1.50
TRB29	Andruw Jones	1.00
TRB30	Barry Zito	.75
TRB31	Jeff Bagwell	1.50
TRB32	Magglio Ordonez	.75
TRB33	Pat Burrell	1.50
TRB34	Mike Sweeney	.50
TRB35	Rafael Palmeiro	1.00
TRB36	Larry Walker	.50
TRB37	Carlos Delgado	.50
TRB38	Brian Giles	.50
TRB39	Pedro J. Martinez	1.50
TRB40	Greg Maddux	2.50

Nolan Ryan No-Hitters

		NM/M
Complete Set (7):		45.00
Common Ryan (1-7):		8.00
RB-NR1-7	Nolan Ryan	8.00

Nolan Ryan Record Breakers Autographs

		NM/M
Inserted 1:1,894		
HTA Exclusive		
NR	Nolan Ryan	200.00
NRA	Nolan Ryan	200.00
NRR	Nolan Ryan	200.00

Stadium Seat Relics

		NM/M
Common Player:		15.00
Inserted 1:37 Series 2 HTA		
JB	Johnny Bench	30.00
DC	Dave Concepcion	20.00
AD	Adam Dunn	20.00
KG	Ken Griffey Jr.	25.00
AK	Austin Kearns	20.00
BL	Barry Larkin	25.00
JM	Joe Morgan	15.00
PO	Paul O'Neill	15.00
TP	Tony Perez	20.00
TS	Tom Seaver	25.00

Team Topps Legends Autographs

		NM/M
Common Player:		
	Vida Blue	20.00
	Bob Feller	25.00
	Willie Mays	125.00
	Gil McDougald	12.00
	Robin Roberts	25.00
	Bobby Thomson	20.00
	Luis Tiant	8.00
	Carl Yastrzemski	50.00

Team Topps Legends Autographs Series 2

Common Player:

Turn Back The Clock Autographs

		NM/M
Common Player:		
LD	Lenny Dykstra	15.00
BM	Bill Madlock	10.00
DM	Dale Murphy	40.00
JP	Jim Palmer	20.00

2003 Topps All-Time Fan Favorites

		NM/M
Complete Set (150):		30.00
Common Player:		.25
Pack (6):		4.00
Box (24):		75.00
1	Willie Mays	3.00
2	Whitey Ford	1.00
3	Stan Musial	2.50
4	Paul Blair	.25
5	Harold Reynolds	.25
6	Bob Friend	.25
7	Rod Carew	.75
8	Kirk Gibson	.25
9	Graig Nettles	.25

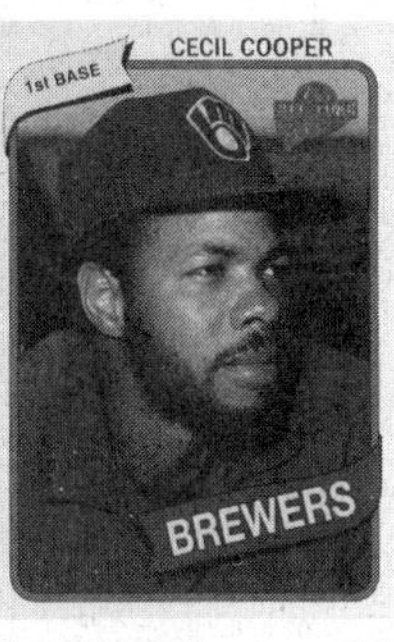

10	Ozzie Smith	1.00
11	Tony Perez	.25
12	Tim Wallach	.25
13	Bert Campaneris	.25
14	Cory Snyder	.25
15	Dave Parker	.25
16	Darrell Evans	.25
17	Joe Pepitone	.25
18	Don Sutton	.25
19	Dale Murphy	1.00
20	George Brett	2.50
21	Carlton Fisk	.50
22	Bob Watson	.25
23	Wally Joyner	.25
24	Paul Molitor	1.00
25	Keith Hernandez	.25
26	Jerry Koosman	.25
27	George Bell	.25
28	Boog Powell	.25
29	Bruce Sutter	.75
30	Ernie Banks	1.50
31	Steve Lyons	.25
32	Earl Weaver	.25
33	Dave Stieb	.25
34	Alan Trammell	.25
35	Bret Saberhagen	.25
36	J.R. Richard	.25
37	Mickey Rivers	.25
38	Juan Marichal	.75
39	Gaylord Perry	.25
40	Don Mattingly	3.00
41	Bobby Grich	.25
42	Steve Sax	.25
43	Sparky Anderson	.25
44	Luis Aparicio	.25
45	Fergie Jenkins	.50
46	Jim Palmer	.75
47	Howard Johnson	.25
48	Dwight Evans	.25
49	Bill Buckner	.25
50	Cal Ripken Jr.	4.00
51	Jose Cruz	.25
52	Tony Oliva	.25
53	Bobby Richardson	.25
54	Luis Tiant	.25
55	Warren Spahn	1.00
56	Phil Rizzuto	1.00
57	Eric Davis	.25
58	Vida Blue	.25
59	Steve Balboni	.25
60	Mike Schmidt	2.50
61	Ken Griffey Sr.	.25
62	Jim Abbott	.25
63	Whitey Herzog	.25
64	Rich "Goose" Gossage	.25
65	Tony Armas	.25
66	Bill "Moose" Skowron	.25
67	Don Newcombe	.25
68	Bill Madlock	.25
69	Lance Parrish	.25
70	Reggie Jackson	1.50
71	Willie Wilson	.25
72	Terry Pendleton	.25
73	Jimmy Piersall	.25
74	George Foster	.25
75	Bob Horner	.25
76	Chris Sabo	.25
77	Fred Lynn	.25
78	Jim Rice	.25
79	Maury Wills	.25
80	Yogi Berra	1.50
81	Johnny Sain	.25
82	Tom Lasorda	.50
83	Bill Mazeroski	.25
84	John Kruk	.25
85	Bob Feller	.75
86	Frank Robinson	.75
87	Red Schoendienst	.25
88	Gary Carter	.50
89	Andre Dawson	.50
90	Tim McCarver	.25
91	Robin Yount	1.00
92	Phil Niekro	.25
93	Joe Morgan	.25
94	Darren Daulton	.25
95	Bobby Thomson	.25
96	Alvin Davis	.25
97	Robin Roberts	.25
98	Kirby Puckett	1.50
99	Jack Clark	.25
100	Hank Aaron	3.00
101	Orlando Cepeda	.50
102	Vern Law	.25
103	Cecil Cooper	.25
104	Don Larsen	.50
105	Mario Mendoza	.25
106	Tony Gwynn	1.50
107	Ernie Harwell	.25
108a	Monte Irvin (No facsimile autograph.)	.75
108b	Monte Irvin (W/facsimile autograph.)	1.50
109	Tommy John	.25
110	Rollie Fingers	.75
111	Johnny Podres	.25
112	Jeff Reardon	.25
113	Buddy Bell	.25
114	Dwight Gooden	.50
115	Garry Templeton	.25
116	Johnny Bench	2.00
117	Joe Rudi	.25
118	Ron Guidry	.50
119	Vince Coleman	.25
120	Al Kaline	2.00
121	Carl Yastrzemski	1.50
122	Hank Bauer	.25
123	Mark Fidrych	.25
124	Paul O'Neill	.50
125	Ron Cey	.25
126	Willie McGee	.25
127	Harmon Killebrew	1.50
128	Dave Concepcion	.25
129	Harold Baines	.25
130	Lou Brock	.50
131	Lee Smith	.25
132	Willie McCovey	.75
133	Steve Garvey	.25
134	Kent Tekulve	.25
135	Tom Seaver	1.50
136	Bo Jackson	1.00
137	Walt Weiss	.25
138	Brook Jacoby	.25
139	Dennis Eckersley	.50
140	Duke Snider	1.00
141	Lenny Dykstra	.25
142	Greg Luzinski	.25
143	Jim Bunning	.25
144	Jose Canseco	.75
145	Ron Santo	.25
146	Bert Blyleven	.25
147	Wade Boggs	.75
148	Brooks Robinson	1.00
149	Ray Knight	.25
150	Nolan Ryan	4.00

Refractors

Cards (1-150):	3-6X
Production 299 Sets	

Autographs

		NM/M
Common Autograph:		8.00
SP's Production 50		
HA	Hank Aaron/SP	250.00
JA	Jim Abbott	10.00
SA	Sparky Anderson/SP	30.00
LA	Luis Aparicio	10.00
TA	Tony Armas	10.00
HBA	Harold Baines	15.00
SB	Steve Balboni	8.00
EB	Ernie Banks/SP	120.00
HB	Hank Bauer/SP	35.00
BBE	Buddy Bell	15.00
GB	George Bell	10.00
JBE	Johnny Bench/SP	100.00
YB	Yogi Berra/SP	100.00
BBI	Buddy Biancalana	8.00
PB	Paul Blair	10.00
VB	Vida Blue	15.00
BB	Bert Blyleven	15.00
WB	Wade Boggs/SP	75.00
GBR	George Brett/SP	250.00
LB	Lou Brock/SP	60.00
BBU	Bill Buckner	10.00
JB	Jim Bunning/SP	75.00
BC	Bert Campaneris	10.00
JOS	Jose Canseco/SP	60.00
RCA	Rod Carew/SP	75.00
GC	Gary Carter/SP	40.00
JCA	Joe Carter/SP	35.00
OC	Orlando Cepeda/SP	60.00
RCE	Ron Cey	10.00
JC	Jack Clark	15.00
VC	Vince Coleman	10.00
DC	Dave Concepcion/SP	35.00
CC	Cecil Cooper	10.00
JCR	Jose Cruz	10.00
RDA	Ron Darling	10.00
DD	Darren Daulton	15.00
AD	Alvin Davis	8.00
ED	Eric Davis	15.00
ADA	Andre Dawson/SP	50.00
DDE	Doug DeCinces	15.00
RD	Rob Dibble	15.00
LDU	Leon Durham	10.00
LD	Lenny Dykstra	10.00
DEC	Dennis Eckersley/SP	60.00
DE	Darrell Evans	10.00
DEV	Dwight Evans/SP	40.00
BF	Bob Feller	15.00
MF	Mark Fidrych	10.00
RF	Rollie Fingers/SP	40.00
CF	Carlton Fisk/SP	60.00
WF	Whitey Ford/SP	100.00
GF	George Foster	10.00
BFR	Bob Friend	10.00
SG	Steve Garvey	20.00
KGI	Kirk Gibson/SP	75.00
DG	Dwight Gooden/SP	30.00
RG	Rich "Goose" Gossage/SP	30.00
BGR	Bobby Grich	10.00
KG	Ken Griffey Sr./SP	30.00
RGU	Ron Guidry	15.00
TG	Tony Gwynn/SP	100.00
EH	Ernie Harwell	40.00
KH	Keith Hernandez/SP	60.00
WHE	Willie Hernandez	10.00
TH	Tom Herr	10.00
WH	Whitey Herzog	20.00
BH	Bob Horner	8.00
MI	Monte Irvin/SP	40.00
BJ	Bo Jackson/SP	100.00
RJ	Reggie Jackson/SP	100.00
BJA	Brook Jacoby	8.00
FJ	Fergie Jenkins	15.00
TJ	Tommy John	15.00
HJ	Howard Johnson	10.00
WJ	Wally Joyner	10.00
AK	Al Kaline/SP	75.00
HK	Harmon Killebrew/SP	80.00
RK	Ralph Kiner/SP	65.00
RKI	Ron Kittle	10.00
RY	Ray Knight	10.00
JK	Jerry Koosman	20.00
JKR	John Kruk/SP	60.00
CL	Carney Lansford	15.00
DL	Don Larsen	15.00
TL	Tom Lasorda/SP	40.00
VL	Vern Law	15.00
BL	Bill Lee	10.00
CLE	Chet Lemon	10.00
GL	Greg Luzinski	15.00
FL	Fred Lynn/SP	25.00
SL	Steve Lyons	15.00
BMA	Bill Madlock	10.00
JMA	Juan Marichal/SP	75.00
DON	Don Mattingly/SP	100.00
WM	Willie Mays/SP	150.00
BMZ	Bill Mazeroski/SP	50.00
TM	Tim McCarver/SP	40.00
WMC	Willie McCovey/SP	60.00
MCG	Willie McGee/SP	60.00
TMC	Tug McGraw	20.00
MM	Mario Mendoza	10.00
KM	Kevin Mitchell	10.00
PM	Paul Molitor/SP	60.00
JMO	John Montefusco	10.00
JM	Joe Morgan/SP	30.00
DM	Dale Murphy/SP	60.00
SM	Stan Musial/SP	120.00
GN	Graig Nettles	15.00
DN	Don Newcombe/SP	40.00
PN	Phil Niekro/SP	40.00
AO	Al Oliver	10.00
PO	Paul O'Neill/SP	75.00
MP	Mike Pagliarulo	10.00
JP	Jim Palmer/SP	60.00
DP	Dave Parker/SP	40.00
LP	Lance Parrish	10.00
TP	Terry Pendleton	15.00
JPE	Joe Pepitone	10.00
TPE	Tony Perez/SP	65.00
GP	Gaylord Perry	25.00
BP	Boog Powell	15.00
KP	Kirby Puckett/SP	65.00
JRE	Jeff Reardon	10.00
HR	Harold Reynolds/SP	40.00
JRI	Jim Rice/SP	45.00
JR	J.R. Richard	10.00
CR	Cal Ripken Jr./SP	225.00
MR	Mickey Rivers	10.00
PR	Phil Rizzuto/SP	75.00
RR	Robin Roberts	25.00
BRO	Brooks Robinson/SP	100.00
FR	Frank Robinson/SP	75.00
JRU	Joe Rudi	10.00
NR	Nolan Ryan/SP	200.00
BSA	Bret Saberhagen/SP	40.00
CS	Chris Sabo	8.00
RSA	Ron Santo	25.00
SS	Steve Sax	8.00

MS Mike Schmidt/SP 150.00
RS Red Schoendienst 15.00
TSE Tom Seaver/SP 100.00
KS Kevin Seitzer 10.00
BS Bill "Moose" Skowron 15.00
LS Lee Smith 10.00
OS Ozzie Smith/SP 100.00
DSN Duke Snider/SP 60.00
CN Cory Snyder 15.00
WS Warren Spahn 40.00
CSP Chris Speier 10.00
DS Dave Stieb 15.00
BSU Bruce Sutter 35.00
DSU Don Sutton/SP 40.00
KT Kent Tekulve 10.00
GT Garry Templeton 10.00
BT Bobby Thomson/SP 25.00
LT Luis Tiant/SP 40.00
AT Alan Trammell 20.00
TW Tim Wallach 10.00
BW Bob Watson 10.00
EW Earl Weaver 10.00
WW Walt Weiss 8.00
MW Maury Wills 10.00
WWI Willie Wilson/SP 25.00
CY Carl Yastrzemski/SP 150.00
SY Steve Yeager 10.00
RYO Robin Yount/SP 100.00

Best Seat Relics

BEST SEAT IN THE HOUSE

NM/M
Common Card: 20.00
BS1 Jim Palmer, Frank Robinson, Brooks Robinson 25.00
BS2 Wally Joyner, Rod Carew, Bobby Grich 20.00
BS3 Phil Garner, Willie Stargell, Dave Parker, Kent Tekulve 20.00
BS4 Rollie Fingers, Robin Yount, Paul Molitor 25.00
BS5 Phil Niekro, Dale Murphy, Bob Horner 20.00

Relics

NM/M
Common Player: 8.00
HBA Harold Baines/Bat 12.00
GBR George Brett/Jsy 25.00
JOS Jose Canseco/Bat 12.00
RCA Rod Carew/Bat 10.00
GC Gary Carter/Bat 10.00
NC Norm Cash/Jsy 25.00
VC Vince Coleman/Bat 8.00
JCR Jose Cruz/Bat 6.00
RDA Ron Darling/Jsy 8.00
ADA Andre Dawson/Bat 8.00
LD Lenny Dykstra/Bat 8.00
DEC Dennis Eckersley/Jsy 10.00
CF Curt Flood/Bat 10.00
GF George Foster/Bat 8.00
BFR Bob Friend/Jsy 6.00
SG Steve Garvey/Bat 6.00
KGI Kirk Gibson/Bat 8.00
KH Keith Hernandez/Bat 12.00
WHE Willie Hernandez/Bat 8.00
BH Bob Horner/Bat 6.00
BJ Bo Jackson/Bat 20.00
WJ Wally Joyner/Bat 8.00
GL Greg Luzinski/Bat 6.00
FL Fred Lynn/Bat 10.00
DON Don Mattingly/Bat 30.00
MCG Willie McGee/Bat 15.00
TMC Tug McGraw/Jsy 10.00
KM Kevin Mitchell/Bat 6.00
JM Joe Morgan/Bat 10.00
DM Dale Murphy/Bat 15.00
PO Paul O'Neill/Bat 8.00
DP Dave Parker/Bat 6.00
LP Lance Parrish/Bat 12.00
KP Kirby Puckett/Bat 15.00
HR Harold Reynolds/Bat 6.00
JRI Jim Rice/Bat 8.00
BR Bobby Richardson/Bat 15.00
JRU Joe Rudi/Bat 6.00
CS Chris Sabo/Bat 8.00
MS Mike Schmidt/Bat 25.00
WS Willie Stargell/Bat 12.00
AT Alan Trammell/Bat 15.00
MW Maury Wills/Bat 6.00

Team Topps Leg. Auto.

NM/M
Common Autograph: 10.00
Paul Blair 10.00
Lou Brock 30.00
Jim Bunning 15.00
Gary Carter 30.00
Rich "Goose" Gossage 15.00
Al Kaline 50.00
Willie Mays 120.00
Joe Morgan 30.00
Stan Musial 75.00
Graig Nettles 15.00
Johnny Sain 15.00
Mike Schmidt 75.00

2003 Topps Bazooka

NM/M
Complete Set (280): 40.00
Common Player: .15
Pack (8): 2.00
Box (24): 40.00
Card #7 has 31 variations.
1 Luis Castillo .15
2 Randy Winn .15
3 Orlando Hudson .15
4 Fernando Vina .15
5 Pat Burrell .25
6 Brad Wilkerson .15
7 Bazooka Joe .25
8 Javy Lopez .25
9 Juan Pierre .15
10 Hideo Nomo .40
11 Barry Larkin .25
12 Alfonso Soriano .75
13 Rodrigo Lopez .15
14 Mark Ellis .15
15 Tim Salmon .25
16 Garret Anderson .25
17 Aaron Boone .15
18 Jason Kendall .15
19 Hee Seop Choi .15
20 Jorge Posada .40
21 Sammy Sosa 1.50
22 Mark Prior .75
23 Mark Teixeira .50
24 Manny Ramirez .50
25 Jim Thome .75
26 A.J. Pierzynski .15
27 Scott Rolen .75
28 Austin Kearns .25
29 Bret Boone .15
30 Ken Griffey Jr. 1.00
31 Greg Maddux 1.00
32 Derek Lowe .15
33 David Wells .15
34 A.J. Burnett .15
35 Randall Simon .15
36 Nick Johnson .15
37 Junior Spivey .15
38 Eric Gagne .40
39 Darin Erstad .25
40 Marty Cordova .15
41 Brett Myers .15
42 Mo Vaughn .15
43 Randy Wolf .15
44 Vicente Padilla .15
45 Elmer Dessens .15
46 Jason Simontacchi .15
47 John Mabry .15
48 Torii Hunter .25
49 Lyle Overbay .15
50 Kirk Saarloos .15
51 Bernie Williams .50
52 Wade Miller .15
53 Bobby Abreu .25
54 Wilson Betemit .15
55 Edwin Almonte .15
56 Jarrod Washburn .15
57 Drew Henson .25
58 Tony Batista .15
59 Juan Rivera .15
60 Larry Walker .25
61 Brandon Phillips .15
62 Franklyn German .15
63 Victor Martinez .25
64 Moises Alou .25
65 Nomar Garciaparra 1.00
66 Willie Harris .15
67 Sean Casey .25
68 Omar Vizquel .25
69 Robert Fick .15
70 Curt Schilling .50
71 Adam Kennedy .15
72 Scott Hairston .15
73 Jimmy Journell .15
74 Rafael Furcal .25
75 Barry Zito .25
76 Ed Rogers .15
77 Cliff Floyd .15
78 Matt Clement .15
79 Mike Lowell .25
80 Randy Johnson .75
81 Craig Biggio .25
82 Carlos Beltran .50
83 Paul LoDuca .15
84 Jose Vidro .15
85 Gary Sheffield .40
86 Jacque Jones .15
87 Corey Hart .15
88 Roberto Alomar .40
89 Robin Ventura .25
90 Pedro Martinez .75
91 Scott Hatteberg .15
92 Marlon Byrd .15
93 Pokey Reese .15
94 Sean Burroughs .15
95 Magglio Ordonez .25
96 Tsuyoshi Shinjo .15
97 John Olerud .15
98 Edgar Renteria .25
99 Ben Grieve .15
100 Mariano Rivera .25
101 Ivan Rodriguez .50
102 Josh Phelps .15
103 Nobuaki Yoshida **RC** .40
104 Roy Halladay .15
105 Mark Buehrle .15
106 Chan Ho Park .15
107 Joe Kennedy .15
108 Shin-Soo Choo .15
109 Ryan Jensen .15
110 Todd Helton .50
111 Chris Duncan **RC** 1.00
112 Taggert Bozied .15
113 Sean Burnett .15
114 Mike Lieberthal .15
115 Josh Beckett .40
116 Andy Pettitte .40
117 Jose Reyes .25
118 Bartolo Colon .15
119 Justin Morneau .25
120 Lance Berkman .25
121 Mike Wodnicki **RC** .40
122 Craig Brazell **RC** .50
123 Troy Glaus .40
124 John Smoltz .25
125 Mike Sweeney .15
126 Jay Gibbons .15
127 Kerry Wood .75
128 Ellis Burks .15
129 Carlos Pena .15
130 Shawn Green .25
131 Jason Stokes .15
132 Raul Ibanez .15
133 Francisco Rodriguez .15
134 Adrian Beltre .25
135 Richie Sexson .40
136 Paul Byrd .15
137 Bobby Kielty .15
138 Dewon Brazelton .15
139 Jeremy Griffiths .15
140 Vladimir Guerrero .75
141 Jake Peavy .15
142 Bryan Bullington **RC** 1.00
143 Orlando Cabrera .15
144 Scott Erickson .15
145 Doug Mientkiewicz .15
146 Derrek Lee .25
147 Daryl Clark **RC** .40
148 Trevor Hoffman .15
149 Gabe Gross .15
150 Roger Clemens 1.50
151 Khalil Greene 1.00
152 Cory Doyne **RC** .40
153 Brandon Roberson **RC** .40
154 Josh Fogg .15
155 Eric Chavez .25
156 Kris Benson .15
157 Billy Koch .15
158 Jermaine Dye .15
159 Kip Bouknight **RC** .40
160 Brian Giles .25
161 Justin Huber .15
162 Mike Restovich .15
163 Brandon Webb **RC** .75
164 Odalis Perez .15
165 Phil Nevin .15
166 Dontrelle Willis .25
167 Aaron Heilman .15
168 Dustin Moseley **RC** .50
169 Rylan Reed **RC** .40
170 Miguel Tejada .40
171 Nic Jackson .15
172 Anthony Webster **RC** .40
173 Jorge Julio .15
174 Kevin Millwood .25
175 Brian Jordan .15
176 Terry Tiffee **RC** .40
177 Dallas McPherson .15
178 Freddy Garcia .15
179 Jamie Moyer .15
180 Rafael Palmeiro .50
181 Mike O'Keefe **RC** .40
182 Kevin Youkilis **RC** 1.00
183 Kip Wells .15
184 Joe Mauer .25
185 Edgar Martinez .25
186 Jaime Bubela **RC** .40
187 Jose Hernandez .15
188 Josh Hamilton .15
189 Matt Diaz **RC** .40
190 Chipper Jones .75
191 Kevin Mench .15
192 Joey Gomes .15
193 Shannon Stewart .15
194 Damian Miller .15
195 Mike Piazza 1.00
196 Damian Moss .15
197 Mike Fontenot .15
198 Shea Hillenbrand .15
199 Evel Bastida-Martinez **RC** .40
200 Jason Giambi .40
201 Aron Weston **RC** .40
202 Frank Thomas .50
203 Carlos Lee .15
204 C.C. Sabathia .15
205 Jim Edmonds .40
206 Jemel Spearman **RC** .40
207 Jason Jennings .15
208 Jeremy Bonderman 1.00
209 Preston Wilson .15
210 Eric Hinske .15
211 Will Smith .15
212 Matthew Hagen **RC** .40
213 Joe Randa .15
214 James Loney .15
215 Carlos Delgado .25
216 Kris Kroski **RC** .50
217 Cristian Guzman .15
218 Tomokazu Ohka .15
219 Al Leiter .15
220 Adam Dunn .50
221 Raul Mondesi .25
222 Donald Hood **RC** .40
223 Mark Mulder .25
224 Mike Williams .15
225 Ryan Klesko .25
226 Rich Aurilia .15
227 Chris Snelling .15
228 Gary Schneidmiller **RC** .40
229 Ichiro Suzuki 1.50
230 Luis Gonzalez .25
231 Rocco Baldelli .15
232 Callix Crabbe **RC** .40
233 Adrian Gonzalez .15
234 Corey Koskie .15
235 Tom Glavine .40
236 Kevin Beavers **RC** .40
237 Frank Catalanotto .15
238 Kevin Cash .15
239 Nick Trzesniak **RC** .50
240 Paul Konerko .25
241 Jose Cruz Jr. .15
242 Hank Blalock .50
243 J.D. Drew .25
244 Kazuhiro Sasaki .15
245 Jeff Bagwell .50
246 Jason Schmidt .25
247 Xavier Nady .15
248 Aramis Ramirez .40
249 Jimmy Rollins .20
250 Alex Rodriguez 1.50
251 Terrence Long .15
252 Derek Jeter 2.00
253 Edgardo Alfonzo .15
254 Toby Hall .15
255 Kazuhisa Ishii .15
256 Brad Nelson .15
257 Kevin Brown .25
258 Roy Oswalt .25
259 Mike Cameron .15
260 Juan Gonzalez .40
261 Dmitri Young .15
262 Jose Jimenez .15
263 Wily Mo Pena .25
264 Joe Borchard .15
265 Mike Mussina .50
266 Fred McGriff .25
267 Johnny Damon .25
268 Joel Pineiro .15
269 Andruw Jones .50
270 Tim Hudson .25
271 Chad Tracy .15
272 Brad Fullmer .15
273 Boof Bonser .15
274 Clint Nageotte .15
275 Jeff Kent .25
276 Tino Martinez .25
277 Matt Morris .15
278 Jonny Gomes .15
279 Benito Santiago .15
280 Albert Pujols 1.50

Mini

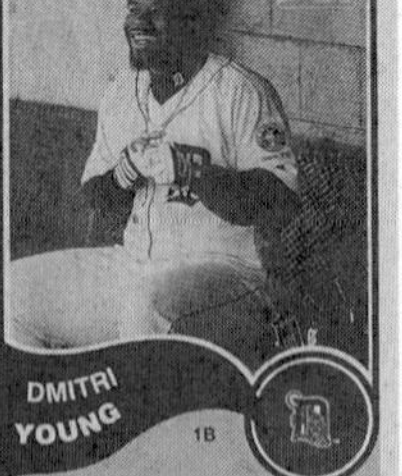

Stars: 1-30X
Inserted 1:1

Silver

Stars: 1-30X
Inserted 1:1

Blasts

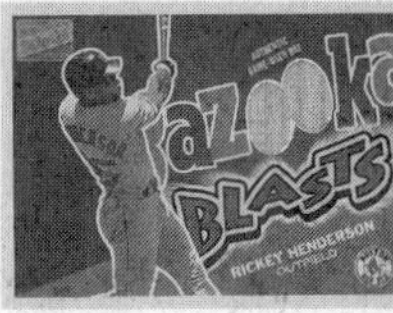

NM/M
Common Player: 4.00
Refractors: 3-4X
Production 25 Sets
RA Roberto Alomar 6.00
LB Lance Berkman 6.00
WB Wilson Betemit 4.00
JD Johnny Damon 6.00
CD Carlos Delgado 5.00
JDD J.D. Drew 8.00
DE Darin Erstad 4.00
AG Andres Galarraga 4.00
LG Luis Gonzalez 4.00
SG Shawn Green 6.00
TG Tony Gwynn 8.00
RH Rickey Henderson 10.00
DH Drew Henson 4.00
NJ Nick Johnson 4.00
CJ Chipper Jones 10.00
RK Ryan Klesko 4.00
PL Paul LoDuca 4.00
EM Edgar Martinez 8.00
TM Tino Martinez 8.00
RM Raul Mondesi 4.00
RP Rafael Palmeiro 6.00
MP Mike Piazza 12.00
JP Jorge Posada 8.00
ANR Aramis Ramirez 6.00
MR Manny Ramirez 8.00
AR Alex Rodriguez 12.00
IR Ivan Rodriguez 8.00
GS Gary Sheffield 6.00
TS Tsuyoshi Shinjo 4.00
AS Alfonso Soriano 10.00
MS Mike Sweeney 4.00
RV Robin Ventura 4.00
BW Bernie Williams 10.00

Comics

NM/M
Complete Set (12): 4.00
Common Player: .30
Inserted 1:4
Roger Clemens .40
Nomar Garciaparra .60
Jason Giambi .40
Derek Jeter .75
Randy Johnson .30
Chipper Jones .40
Mike Piazza .50
Albert Pujols .30
Alex Rodriguez .60
Alfonso Soriano .40
Sammy Sosa .40
Ichiro Suzuki .50

Piece of Americana

NM/M
Common Player: 5.00
Refractors: 3-4X
Production 25 Sets
JB Jeff Bagwell 10.00
CB Craig Biggio 5.00
BB Bret Boone 5.00
DB Dewon Brazelton 5.00
CD Carlos Delgado 5.00
AD Adam Dunn 10.00
JE Jim Edmonds 6.00
RF Rafael Furcal 5.00
NG Nomar Garciaparra 15.00
SG Shawn Green 6.00
CG Cristian Guzman 5.00
TG Tony Gwynn 10.00
THA Toby Hall 5.00
TH Todd Helton 6.00
AH Aubrey Huff 5.00
AJ Andruw Jones 5.00
CJ Chipper Jones 10.00
JK Jeff Kent 5.00
AL Al Leiter 5.00
PL Paul LoDuca 6.00
MM Mike Mussina 8.00
MO Magglio Ordonez 6.00
RP Rafael Palmeiro 6.00
MP Mike Piazza 12.00
PA Albert Pujols 10.00
IR Ivan Rodriguez 5.00
CS Curt Schilling 8.00
FT Frank Thomas 6.00
LW Larry Walker 5.00
PW Preston Wilson 5.00

Stand-Ups

NM/M
Complete Set (25): 20.00
Common Player: .40
Inserted 1:8
1 Albert Pujols 2.50
2 Alfonso Soriano 1.00
3 Ichiro Suzuki 2.00
4 Sammy Sosa 2.00
5 Randy Johnson 1.00
6 Torii Hunter .50
7 Vladimir Guerrero 1.00
8 Nomar Garciaparra 2.00
9 Alex Rodriguez 3.00
10 Troy Glaus .50
11 Greg Maddux 1.50
12 Derek Jeter 3.00
13 Lance Berkman .40
14 Larry Walker .40
15 Adam Dunn .50
16 Shawn Green .50
17 Curt Schilling .75
18 Todd Helton .75
19 Pedro Martinez 1.00
20 Pat Burrell .50
21 Miguel Tejada .50
22 Manny Ramirez 1.00
23 Mike Piazza 1.50
24 Chipper Jones 1.00
25 Jason Giambi 1.00

4-On-1 Stickers

NM/M
Complete Set (55): 10.00
Common Sticker: .20
Inserted 1:4
1 Mark Prior, Roy Oswalt, Jarrod Washburn, Barry Zito .30
2 Troy Glaus, Shea Hillenbrand, Eric Chavez, Eric Hinske .30
3 Orlando Hudson, Alfonso Soriano, Roberto Alomar, Jose Vidro .40
4 Nomar Garciaparra, Derek Jeter, Miguel Tejada, Alex Rodriguez .75
5 Jason Giambi, Jim Thome, Todd Helton, Rafael Palmeiro .40
6 Mike Williams, Trevor Hoffman, Billy Koch, John Smoltz .20

#	Players	Price
7	Jorge Posada, Mike Piazza, A.J. Pierzynski, Ivan Rodriguez	.50
8	Vladimir Guerrero, Jim Edmonds, Manny Ramirez, Brad Wilkerson	.40
9	Shawn Green, Sammy Sosa, Torii Hunter, Larry Walker	.40
10	Bernie Williams, Ken Griffey Jr., Ichiro Suzuki, Adam Dunn	.50
11	John Olerud, Mike Lieberthal, Terrence Long, Drew Henson	.20
12	Edgar Martinez, Bret Boone, Mo Vaughn, Robert Fisk	.20
13	Randy Johnson, Roger Clemens, Pedro Martinez, Greg Maddux	.40
14	Curt Schilling, Tim Hudson, Tom Glavine, Kerry Wood	.20
15	Paul Konerko, Mike Sweeney, Cristian Guzman, Scott Rolen	.20
16	Josh Phelps, Brandon Phillips, Hee Seop Choi, Hank Blalock	.20
17	Benito Santiago, Barry Larkin, Gary Sheffield, Carlos Delgado	.20
18	Juan Rivera, Jose Reyes, Sean Burroughs, Carlos Pena	.20
19	Tony Batista, Tim Salmon, Jeff Bagwell, Raul Ibanez	.25
20	Edgardo Alfonzo, Nic Jackson, Luis Castillo, Damian Miller	.20
21	David Wells, Ryan Klesko, Phil Nevin, Jeff Kent	.20
22	Derek Lowe, Vicente Padilla, Kevin Millwood, Joel Pineiro	.20
23	Fernando Vina, Darin Erstad, Jimmy Rollins, Doug Mientkiewicz	.20
24	Joe Mauer, Justin Huber, Jason Stokes, Chad Tracy	.20
25	Austin Kearns, Junior Spivey, Brett Myers, Victor Martinez	.25
26	Khalil Greene, Gabe Gross, Kevin Cash, James Loney	.20
27	Albert Pujols, Mark Buehrle, Chipper Jones, Lance Berkman	.40
28	Adam Kennedy, Craig Biggio, Johnny Damon, Randy Winn	.20
29	Brian Giles, J.D. Drew, Marlon Byrd, Joe Borchard	.20
30	Al Leiter, Mike Mussina, Bartolo Colon, Freddy Garcia	.20
31	Jason Kendall, Richie Sexson, Mike Lowell, Paul LoDuca	.20
32	Pat Burrell, Garret Anderson, Cliff Floyd, Andruw Jones	.25
33	Xavier Nady, Bobby Abreu, Taggert Bozied, Adrian Beltre	.20
34	Rocco Baldelli, Dontrelle Willis, Chris Snelling, Mark Teixeira	.20
35	Willie Harris, Nick Johnson, Jason Jennings, Kazuhisa Ishii	.20
36	Mark Mulder, Sean Burnett, Paul Byrd, Josh Beckett	.20
37	Corey Koskie, Aramis Ramirez, Tino Martinez, Moises Alou	.20
38	Jose Cruz Jr., Roy Halliday, Dewon Brazelton, Jonny Gomes	.20
39	Odalis Perez, Kevin Brown, Matt Clement, Randy Wolf	.20
40	Eric Gagne, Jose Jimenez, Franklyn German, Edwin Almonte	.20
41	Luis Gonzalez, Shannon Stewart, Brian Jordan, Juan Gonzalez	.25
42	Toby Hall, Joe Kennedy, Javier Lopez, Damian Moss	.20
43	Maggio Ordonez, Carlos Lee, Randall Simon, Dmitri Young	.20
44	Sean Casey, Aaron Boone, Jacque Jones, Michael Restovich	.20
45	Adrian Gonzalez, Corey Hart, Fred McGriff, Frank Thomas	.25
46	C.C. Sabathia, Omar Vizquel, Andy Pettitte, Robin Ventura	.20
47	Jason Schmidt, Ellis Burks, Joe Randa, Tsuyoshi Shinjo	.20
48	Mike Cameron, Pokey Reese, Jermaine Dye, Preston Wilson	.20
49	Chan Ho Park, Kazuhiro Sasaki, Tomokazu Ohka, Hideo Nomo	.20
50	Jason Simontacchi, Kip Wells, Matt Morris, Rodrigo Lopez	.20
51	Dallas McPherson, Josh Hamilton, Jeremy Bonderman, Aaron Heilman	.20
52	Nobuaki Yoshida, Chris Duncan, Craig Brazell, Bryan Bullington	.20
53	Daryl Clark, Brandon Webb, Dustin Moseley, Mike O'Keefe	.20
54	Kevin Youkilis, Jaime Bubela, Matt Diaz, Joey Gomes	.20
55	Kris Kroski, Donald Hood, Gary Schneidmiller, Callix Crabbe	.20

Chicago Cubs Reprints

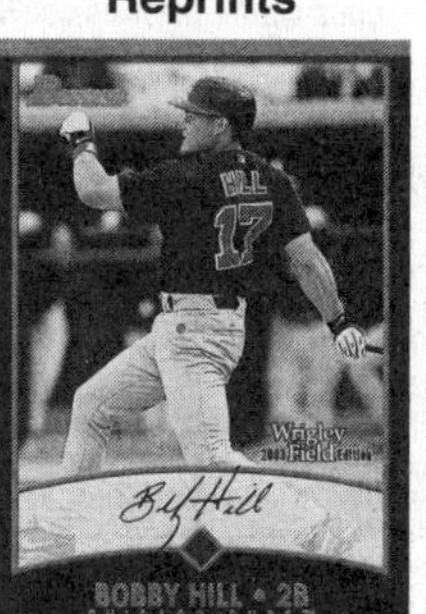

For a third year the Cubs contracted with Topps to provide a series of reprint cards for use as give-aways at special games throughout the season. Each reprint features a Wrigley Field logo on front and is sequentially numbered to 20,000 in a strip of gold foil on back. Each card was distributed in a cello wrapper with the date of the promotion and names of the sponsor(s).

		NM/M
Complete Set (6):		10.00
Common Player:		2.00
(1)	Glenn Beckert	2.00
(2)	Hee Seop Choi	2.00
(3)	Bobby Hill	2.00
(4)	Bill Madlock	2.00
(5)	Ron Santo	4.00
(6)	Steve Stone	2.00

2003 Topps Chrome

		NM/M
Complete Set (440):		160.00
Common Player:		.25
Series 1 & 2 Hobby Pack (4):		2.50
Hobby Box (24):		50.00
1	Alex Rodriguez	4.00
2	Eddie Guardado	.25
3	Curt Schilling	1.50
4	Andruw Jones	1.00
5	Magglio Ordonez	.75
6	Todd Helton	1.00
7	Odalis Perez	.25
8	Edgardo Alfonzo	.25
9	Eric Hinske	.25
10	Danny Bautista	.25
11	Sammy Sosa	2.50
12	Roberto Alomar	1.00
13	Roger Clemens	3.00
14	Austin Kearns	1.00
15	Luis Gonzalez	.50
16	Mo Vaughn	.50
17	Alfonso Soriano	1.50
18	Orlando Cabrera	.25
19	Hideo Nomo	.75
20	Omar Vizquel	.25
21	Greg Maddux	2.50
22	Fred McGriff	.50
23	Frank Thomas	1.25
24	Shawn Green	.75
25	Jacque Jones	.25
26	Bernie Williams	1.00
27	Corey Patterson	.75
28	Cesar Izturis	.25
29	Larry Walker	.75
30	Darren Dreifort	.25
31	Al Leiter	.25
32	Jason Marquis	.25
33	Sean Casey	.25
34	Craig Counsell	.25
35	Albert Pujols	3.00
36	Kyle Lohse	.25
37	Paul LoDuca	.25
38	Roy Oswalt	.50
39	Danny Graves	.25
40	Kevin Millwood	.25
41	Lance Berkman	1.00
42	Denny Hocking	.25
43	Jose Valentin	.25
44	Josh Beckett	.75
45	Nomar Garciaparra	3.00
46	Craig Biggio	.50
47	Omar Daal	.25
48	Jimmy Rollins	.50
49	Jermaine Dye	.25
50	Edgar Renteria	.50
51	Brandon Duckworth	.25
52	Luis Castillo	.25
53	Andy Ashby	.25
54	Mike Williams	.25
55	Benito Santiago	.25
56	Bret Boone	.25
57	Randy Wolf	.25
58	Ivan Rodriguez	1.50
59	Shannon Stewart	.25
60	Jose Cruz Jr.	.25
61	Billy Wagner	.25
62	Alex Gonzalez	.25
63	Ichiro Suzuki	3.00
64	Joe McEwing	.25
65	Mark Mulder	.50
66	Mike Cameron	.25
67	Corey Koskie	.25
68	Marlon Anderson	.25
69	Jason Kendall	.25
70	J.T. Snow Jr.	.25
71	Edgar Martinez	.50
72	Vernon Wells	.25
73	Vladimir Guerrero	2.00
74	Adam Dunn	1.50
75	Barry Zito	.50
76	Jeff Kent	.50
77	Russ Ortiz	.25
78	Phil Nevin	.25
79	Carlos Beltran	1.00
80	Mike Lowell	.50
81	Bob Wickman	.25
82	Junior Spivey	.25
83	Melvin Mora	.25
84	Derrek Lee	.50
85	Chuck Knoblauch	.25
86	Eric Gagne	.75
87	Orlando Hernandez	.50
88	Robert Person	.25
89	Elmer Dessens	.25
90	Wade Miller	.25
91	Adrian Beltre	.50
92	Kazuhiro Sasaki	.25
93	Timoniel Perez	.25
94	Jose Vidro	.25
95	Geronimo Gil	.25
96	Trot Nixon	.25
97	Denny Neagle	.25
98	Roberto Hernandez	.25
99	David Ortiz	1.50
100	Robb Nen	.25
101	Sidney Ponson	.25
102	Kevin Appier	.25
103	Javier Lopez	.50
104	Jeff Conine	.25
105	Mark Buehrle	.25
106	Jason Simontacchi	.25
107	Jose Jimenez	.25
108	Brian Jordan	.25
109	Brad Wilkerson	.25
110	Scott Hatteberg	.25
111	Matt Morris	.50
112	Miguel Tejada	.75
113	Rafael Furcal	.50
114	Steve Cox	.25
115	Roy Halladay	.25
116	David Eckstein	.25
117	Tomokazu Ohka	.25
118	Jack Wilson	.25
119	Randall Simon	.25
120	Jamie Moyer	.25
121	Andy Benes	.25
122	Tino Martinez	.50
123	Esteban Yan	.25
124	Jason Isringhausen	.25
125	Chris Carpenter	.25
126	Aaron Rowand	.25
127	Brandon Inge	.25
128	Jose Vizcaino	.25
129	Jose Mesa	.25
130	Troy Percival	.25
131	Jon Lieber	.25
132	Brian Giles	.50
133	Aaron Boone	.25
134	Bobby Higginson	.25
135	Luis Rivas	.25
136	Troy Glaus	1.00
137	Jim Thome	1.50
138	Ramon Martinez	.25
139	Jay Gibbons	.25
140	Mike Lieberthal	.25
141	Juan Uribe	.25
142	Gary Sheffield	.75
143	Ramon Santiago	.25
144	Ben Sheets	.50
145	Tony Armas Jr.	.25
146	Kazuhisa Ishii	.25
147	Erubiel Durazo	.25
148	Jerry Hairston Jr.	.25
149	Byung-Hyun Kim	.25
150	Marcus Giles	.25
151	Johnny Damon	.75
152	Terrence Long	.25
153	Juan Pierre	.25
154	Aramis Ramirez	.75
155	Brent Abernathy	.25
156	Ismael Valdes	.25
157	Mike Mussina	1.00
158	Ramon Hernandez	.25
159	Adam Kennedy	.25
160	Tony Womack	.25
161	Tony Batista	.25
162	Kip Wells	.25
163	Jeromy Burnitz	.25
164	Todd Hundley	.25
165	Tim Wakefield	.25
166	Derek Lowe	.25
167	Jorge Posada	.75
168	Ramon Ortiz	.25
169	Brent Butler	.25
170	Shane Halter	.25
171	Matt Lawton	.25
172	Alex Sanchez	.25
173	Eric Milton	.25
174	Vicente Padilla	.25
175	Steve Karsay	.25
176	Mark Prior	1.50
177	Kerry Wood	1.50
178	Jason LaRue	.25
179	Danys Baez	.25
180	Nick Neugebauer	.25
181	Andres Galarraga	.25
182	Jason Giambi	1.00
183	Aubrey Huff	.50
184	Juan Gonzalez	1.00
185	Ugueth Urbina	.25
186	Rickey Henderson	.75
187	Brad Fullmer	.25
188	Todd Zeile	.25
189	Jason Jennings	.25
190	Vladimir Nunez	.25
191	David Justice	.50
192	Brian Lawrence	.25
193	Pat Burrell	.50
194	Pokey Reese	.25
195	Robert Fick	.25
196	C.C. Sabathia	.25
197	Fernando Vina	.25
198	Sean Burroughs	.25
199	Ellis Burks	.25
200	Joe Randa	.25
201	Chris Duncan **RC**	8.00
202	Franklin Gutierrez **RC**	1.00
203	Adam LaRoche	.25
204	Manuel Ramirez **RC**	1.00
205	Il Kim **RC**	1.00
206	Daryl Clark **RC**	1.00
207	Sean Pierce	.25
208	Andy Marte **RC**	5.00
209	Bernie Castro **RC**	1.00
210	Jason Perry **RC**	1.00
211	Jaime Bubela **RC**	1.00
212	Alexis Rios	.25
213	Brendan Harris **RC**	2.00
214	Ramon A. Martinez **RC**	.25
215	Terry Tiffee **RC**	1.00
216	Kevin Youkilis **RC**	4.00
217	Derell McCall **RC**	1.00
218	Scott Tyler	1.00
219	Craig Brazell **RC**	2.50
220	Walter Young	1.00
221	Francisco Rodriguez	.40
222	Chipper Jones	2.00
223	Chris Singleton	.25
224	Cliff Floyd	.25
225	Bobby Hill	.25
226	Antonio Osuna	.25
227	Barry Larkin	.50
228	Dean Palmer	.25
229	Eric Owens	.25
230	Randy Johnson	1.50
231	Jeff Suppan	.25
232	Eric Karros	.25
233	Johan Santana	.25
234	Javier Vazquez	.25
235	John Thomson	.25
236	Nick Johnson	.25
237	Mark Ellis	.25
238	Doug Glanville	.25
239	Ken Griffey Jr.	2.50
240	Bubba Trammell	.25
241	Livan Hernandez	.25
242	Desi Relaford	.25
243	Eli Marrero	.25
244	Jared Sandberg	.25
245	Barry Bonds	4.00
246	Aaron Sele	.25
247	Derek Jeter	5.00
248	Eric Byrnes	.25
249	Rich Aurilia	.25
250	Joel Pineiro	.25
251	Chuck Finley	.25
252	Bengie Molina	.25
253	Steve Finley	.25
254	Marty Cordova	.25
255	Shea Hillenbrand	.25
256	Milton Bradley	.25
257	Carlos Pena	.25
258	Brad Ausmus	.25
259	Carlos Delgado	.75
260	Kevin Mench	.25
261	Joe Kennedy	.25
262	Mark McLemore	.25
263	Bill Mueller	.25
264	Ricky Ledee	.25
265	Ted Lilly	.25
266	Sterling Hitchcock	.25
267	Scott Strickland	.25
268	Damion Easley	.25
269	Torii Hunter	.50
270	Brad Radke	.25
271	Geoff Jenkins	.25
272	Paul Byrd	.25
273	Morgan Ensberg	.25
274	Mike Hampton	.25
275	Flash Gordon	.25
276	John Burkett	.25
277	Rodrigo Lopez	.25
278	Tim Spooneybarger	.25
279	Quinton McCracken	.25
280	Tim Salmon	.50
281	Jarrod Washburn	.25
282	Pedro J. Martinez	1.50
283	Julio Lugo	.25
284	Armando Benitez	.25
285	Raul Mondesi	.50
286	Robin Ventura	.25
287	Bobby Abreu	.50
288	Josh Fogg	.25
289	Ryan Klesko	.50
290	Tsuyoshi Shinjo	.25
291	Jim Edmonds	.75
292	Chan Ho Park	.25
293	John Mabry	.25
294	Woody Williams	.25
295	Scott Schoeneweis	.25
296	Brian Anderson	.25
297	Brett Tomko	.25
298	Scott Erickson	.25
299	Tony Clark	.25
300	Danny Wright	.25
301	Jason Schmidt	.75
302	Scott Williamson	.25
303	Einar Diaz	.25
304	Jay Payton	.25
305	Juan Acevedo	.25
306	Ben Grieve	.25
307	Raul Ibanez	.25
308	Richie Sexson	.75
309	Rick Reed	.25
310	Pedro Astacio	.25
311	Bud Smith	.25
312	Tomas Perez	.25
313	Adam Eaton	.25
314	Rafael Palmeiro	1.50
315	Jason Tyner	.25
316	Scott Rolen	2.00
317	Randy Winn	.25
318	Ryan Jensen	.25
319	Trevor Hoffman	.25
320	Craig Wilson	.25
321	Jeremy Giambi	.25
322	Andy Pettitte	.50
323	John Franco	.25
324	Felipe Lopez	.25
325	Mike Piazza	3.00
326	Cristian Guzman	.25
327	Jose Hernandez	.25
328	Octavio Dotel	.25
329	Brad Penny	.25
330	Charles Johnson	.25
331	Ryan Dempster	.25
332	Joe Crede	.25
333	Chad Hermansen	.25
334	Gary Matthews Jr.	.25
335	Frank Catalanotto	.25
336	Darin Erstad	.50
337	Matt Williams	.25
338	B.J. Surhoff	.25
339	Kerry Ligtenberg	.25
340	Mike Bordick	.25
341	Joe Girardi	.25
342	D'Angelo Jimenez	.25
343	Paul Konerko	.25
344	Joe Mays	.25
345	Marquis Grissom	.25
346	Neifi Perez	.25
347	Preston Wilson	.25
348	Jeff Weaver	.25
349	Eric Chavez	.50
350	Placido Polanco	.25
351	Ray Lankford	.25
352	James Baldwin	.25
353	Toby Hall	.25
354	Benji Gil	.25
355	Damian Moss	.25
356	Jorge Julio	.25
357	Matt Clement	.25
358	Lee Stevens	.25
359	Dave Roberts	.25
360	J.C. Romero	.25
361	Bartolo Colon	.25
362	Roger Cedeno	.25
363	Mariano Rivera	.50
364	Billy Koch	.25
365	Manny Ramirez	1.50
366	Travis Lee	.25
367	Oliver Perez	.25
368	Rafael Soriano	.25
369	Damian Miller	.25
370	John Smoltz	.50
371	Willis Roberts	.25
372	Tim Hudson	.50
373	Moises Alou	.50
374	Corky Miller	.25
375	Ben Broussard	.25
376	Gabe Kapler	.25
377	Chris Woodward	.25
378	Todd Hollandsworth	.25
379	So Taguchi	.25
380	John Olerud	.50
381	Reggie Sanders	.25
382	Jake Peavy	.25
383	Kris Benson	.25
384	Ray Durham	.25
385	David Wells	.25
386	Tom Glavine	.75
387	Antonio Alfonseca	.25
388	Keith Foulke	.25
389	Shawn Estes	.25
390	Mark Grace	.50
391	Dmitri Young	.25
392	A.J. Burnett	.25
393	Richard Hidalgo	.25
394	Mike Sweeney	.25
395	Doug Mientkiewicz	.25
396	Cory Lidle	.25
397	Jeff Bagwell	1.50
398	Steve Sparks	.25
399	Sandy Alomar Jr.	.25
400	John Lackey	.25
401	Rick Helling	.25
402	Carlos Lee	.25
403	Garret Anderson	.50
404	Vinny Castilla	.25
405	David Bell	.25
406	Freddy Garcia	.25
407	Scott Spiezio	.25
408	Russell Branyan	.25
409	Jose Contreras **RC**	3.00
410	Kevin Brown	.50
411	Tyler Houston	.25
412	A.J. Pierzynski	.25
413	Peter Bergeron	.25
414	Brett Myers	.25
415	Kenny Lofton	.25
416	Ben Davis	.25
417	J.D. Drew	.50
418	Ricky Gutierrez	.25
419	Mark Redman	.25
420	Juan Encarnacion	.25
421	Bryan Bullington **RC**	4.00
422	Jeremy Guthrie	.25
423	Joey Gomes	.50
424	Evel Bastida-Martinez **RC**	1.50
425	Brian Wright **RC**	1.00
426	B.J. Upton	.25
427	Jeff Francis	.25
428	Jeremy Hermida	.25
429	Khalil Greene	3.00
430	Darrell Rasner	.25
431	Brandon Phillips, Victor Martinez	.75
432	Hee Seop Choi, Nic Jackson	.75
433	Dontrelle Willis, Jason Stokes	1.00
434	Chad Tracy, Lyle Overbay	.25
435	Joe Borchard, Corwin Malone	.25
436	Joe Mauer, Justin Morneau	1.00
437	Drew Henson, Brandon Claussen	.50
438	Chase Utley, Gavin Floyd	.50
439	Taggert Bozied, Xavier Nady	.25
440	Aaron Heilman, Jose Reyes	1.50

Refractors

Stars:	1-2X
Production 699 Sets	
Gold Refractors:	1.5-3X
Production 449 Sets	

Black Refractors: 3-5X
Production 199 Sets

Uncirculated X-Fractors

Stars: 5-10X
Inserted 1:Hobby Box
Production 50 Sets

Blue Backs Relics

NM/M
Common Player: 6.00
Bat Relics Inserted 1:236
RA Roberto Alomar/Bat 10.00
JBA Jeff Bagwell/Jsy 10.00
JB Josh Beckett/Jsy 10.00
LB Lance Berkman/Bat 8.00
EC Eric Chavez/Jsy 6.00
AD Adam Dunn/Jsy 15.00
NG Nomar Garciaparra /Jsy 15.00
SG Shawn Green/Jsy 6.00
NJ Nick Johnson/Bat 8.00
PK Paul Konerko/Jsy 8.00
MO Magglio Ordonez/Jsy 8.00
MP Mike Piazza/Jsy 15.00
AP Albert Pujols/Jsy 15.00
AR Alex Rodriguez/Bat 15.00
JR Jimmy Rollins/Jsy 6.00
TS Tsuyoshi Shinjo/Bat 8.00
AS Alfonso Soriano/Bat 10.00
FT Frank Thomas/Jsy 8.00
BW Bernie Williams/Bat 10.00
KW Kerry Wood/Jsy 8.00

Record Breakers Relics Series 2

NM/M
Common Player: 5.00
JB Jeff Bagwell 8.00
BB Barry Bonds 20.00
BB2 Barry Bonds 20.00
BB3 Barry Bonds 20.00
JC Jose Canseco 10.00
RC Rod Carew 8.00
RC2 Rod Carew 8.00
DLE Dennis Eckersley 8.00
DE Darin Erstad 5.00
LG Luis Gonzalez 5.00
RH Rickey Henderson 15.00
RJ Randy Johnson 8.00
DM Don Mattingly 30.00
PM Paul Molitor 15.00
MR Manny Ramirez 15.00
HR Harold Reynolds 5.00
AR Alex Rodriguez 15.00
TS Tom Seaver 20.00
JS John Smoltz 8.00
SS Sammy Sosa 15.00
Common Player: 5.00
JB Jeff Bagwell 8.00
BB Barry Bonds 20.00
BB2 Barry Bonds 20.00
BB3 Barry Bonds 20.00
JC Jose Canseco 10.00
RC Rod Carew 8.00
RC2 Rod Carew 8.00
DLE Dennis Eckersley 8.00
DE Darin Erstad 5.00
LG Luis Gonzalez 5.00
RH Rickey Henderson 15.00
RJ Randy Johnson 8.00
DM Don Mattingly 30.00
PM Paul Molitor 15.00
MR Manny Ramirez 15.00
HR Harold Reynolds 5.00
AR Alex Rodriguez 15.00
TS Tom Seaver 20.00
JS John Smoltz 8.00
SS Sammy Sosa 15.00

Red Backs Relics

NM/M
Common Player: 5.00
Inserted 1:49
RA Roberto Alomar 8.00
GA Garret Anderson 8.00
JB Jeff Bagwell 8.00
PB Pat Burrell 5.00
AD Adam Dunn 8.00
NG Nomar Garciaparra 12.00
TH Todd Helton 8.00
TKH Torii Hunter 8.00
RJ Randy Johnson 8.00
AJ Andruw Jones 8.00
CJ Chipper Jones 10.00
PM Pedro J. Martinez 10.00
MP Mike Piazza 10.00
AP Albert Pujols 15.00
MR Manny Ramirez 8.00
AR Alex Rodriguez 10.00
SR Scott Rolen 10.00
CS Curt Schilling 8.00
AS Alfonso Soriano 10.00
MS Mike Sweeney 5.00

2003 Topps eTopps

Topps continued its on-line card program with a third annual eTopps edition in 2003. Initial Player Offerings were again made for only one week with allocations having to made for some cards in high demand. The number of each card actually sold in shown parenthetically. After the IPO, cards could be bought and sold within portfolios, or physically delivered (for a fee) for more traditional venues. The 2-1/2" x 3-1/2" cards are printed on metallic foil with vertical portrait and action photos on front. Horizontal backs have another portrait photo, a 2002 recap and 2003 "prospectus," and a few biographical bits and stats. The listings here include the initial offering price and the number of cards sold during the open ordering period. Values shown are for cards in a virtual portfolio, rather than "in hand." Taking physical possession of a card from an eTopps portfolio costs about $6 apiece.

NM/M
Complete Set (122): 275.00
Common Player: 1.50
1 Troy Glaus ($6.50 / 1,454) 1.50
2 Manny Ramirez ($6.50 / 1,970) 1.50
3 Magglio Ordonez ($6.50 / 1,007) 3.00
4 Jim Thome ($6.50 / 3,393) 1.50
5 Torii Hunter ($6.50 / 2,027) 1.50
6 Jason Giambi ($9.50 / 2,065) 1.50
7 Tim Hudson ($6.50 / 1,690) 1.50
8 Ichiro ($6.50 / 3,465) 2.50
9 Aubrey Huff ($6.50 / 3,234) 1.50
10 Alex Rodriguez ($9.50 / 2,847) 4.00
11 Francisco Rodriguez ($6.50 / 3,627) 1.50
12 Joe Borchard ($4 / 3,000) 1.50
13 Mark Teixeira ($9.50 / 5,000) 5.00
14 Marlon Byrd ($6.50 / 1,822) 1.50
15 Carlos Delgado ($6.50 / 2,500) 1.50
16 Tom Glavine ($6.50 / 2,407) 1.50
17 Curt Schilling ($6.50 / 1,333) 1.50
18 Mark Prior ($9.50 / 4,000) 1.50
19 Ken Griffey Jr. ($6.50 / 1,238) 4.00
20 Todd Helton ($6.50 / 2,315) 1.50
21 Jeff Bagwell ($6.50 / 1,678) 1.75
22 Shawn Green ($6.50 / 1,162) 1.50
23 Vladimir Guerrero ($9.50 / 2,523) 1.75
24 Roberto Alomar ($6.50 / 1,394) 1.50
25 Brian Giles ($6.50 / 1,500) 2.00
26 Barry Bonds ($9.50 / 4,000) 9.00
27 Albert Pujols ($9.50 / 3,000) 5.00
28 Nomar Garciaparra ($9.50 / 2,177) 1.50
29 Alfonso Soriano ($9.50 / 3,500) 1.50
30 Barry Zito ($6.50 / 2,500) 2.00
31 Edgar Martinez ($6.50 / 2,732) 3.00
32 Ivan Rodriguez ($6.50 / 1,436) 1.50
33 Greg Maddux ($6.50 / 2,004) 2.00
34 Sammy Sosa ($9.50 / 1,425) 2.00
35 Austin Kearns ($6.50 / 3,000) 1.50
36 Craig Biggio ($6.50 / 1,317) 1.75
37 Mike Piazza ($6.50 / 1,355) 2.25
38 Andruw Jones ($6.50 / 1,589) 2.75
39 Jeff Kent ($6.50 / 1,685) 1.50
40 Roy Oswalt ($6.50 / 2,108) 2.75
41 Miguel Tejada ($6.50 / 2,630) 1.75
42 Derek Jeter ($9.50 / 3,054) 3.75
43 Pedro Martinez ($9.50 / 1,754) 1.50
44 Jarrod Washburn ($6.50 / 1,196) 2.00
45 Randy Johnson ($9.50 / 1,117) 5.25
46 Bernie Williams ($6.50 / 1,750) 1.50
47 Chipper Jones ($6.50 / 1,443) 1.75
48 Gary Sheffield ($6.50 / 1,500) 1.75
49 Larry Walker ($6.50 / 1,001) 3.50
50 Lance Berkman ($6.50 / 1,107) 2.50
51 Garret Anderson ($6.50 / 2,647) 1.50
52 Jason Schmidt ($6.50 / 1,840) 3.25
53 Rodrigo Lopez ($4 / 1,500) 2.50
54 Oliver Perez ($4 / 1,996) 3.50
55 Derek Lowe ($6.50 / 1,434) 1.50
56 Vicente Padilla ($6.50 / 995) 3.50
57 Paul Konerko ($6.50 / 1,151) 3.00
58 Bartolo Colon ($6.50 / 2,028) 1.50
59 Omar Vizquel ($4.00 / 3,413) 2.00
60 Adam Dunn ($6.50 / 1,812) 1.50
61 Carlos Pena ($4 / 1,402) 1.50
62 Richie Sexson ($6.50 / 1,380) 2.25
63 Paul Byrd ($4 / 2,000) 1.50
64 Eric Gagne ($6.50 / 2,929) 1.50
65 Brad Radke ($4 / 827) 4.50
66 A.J. Burnett ($6.50 / 1,009) 11.50
67 Brandon Phillips ($4 / 4,000) 1.50
68 Mike Hampton ($6.50 / 763) 9.00
69 Tim Salmon ($6.50 / 1,548) 1.50
70 Roger Clemens ($9.50 / 3,000) 2.75
71 Jake Peavy ($4 / 2,500) 3.75
72 Pat Burrell ($6.50 / 1,168) 2.75
73 Ben Sheets ($4 / 1,500) 8.00
74 Fred McGriff ($6.50 / 1,323) 1.75
75 John Smoltz ($6.50 / 3,161) 5.00
76 Josh Phelps ($6.50 / 2,500) 1.50
77 John Olerud ($6.50 / 1,620) 3.00
78 Eric Chavez ($4 / 2,054) 1.50
79 Jeff Weaver ($4 / 1,877) 1.50
80 Scott Rolen ($6.50 / 2,000) 2.00
81 Carl Crawford ($6.50 / 1,518) 3.00
82 Rafael Palmeiro ($6.50 / 1,500) 1.50
83 Roy Halladay ($6.50 / 2,500) 2.50
84 Josh Beckett ($6.50 / 1,130) 4.50
85 Jorge Posada ($6.50 / 2,171) 1.50
86 Mark Mulder ($6.50 / 2,000) 1.50
87 Eric Milton ($4 / 1,758) 1.50
88 Angel Berroa ($6.50 / 1,614) 1.50
89 Jason Lane ($4 / 1,952) 1.50
90 Kerry Wood ($6.50 / 2,000) 1.50
91 Brad Wilkerson ($4 / 2,944) 1.50
92 Orlando Hudson ($4 / 2,500) 2.50
93 Mike Mussina ($6.50 / 2,000) 1.50
94 Hee Seop Choi ($6.50 / 3,000) 1.50
95 Chris Snelling ($6.50 / 2,879) 1.50
96 Tomo Ohka ($4 / 1,975) 1.50
97 Andy Pettitte ($4 / 2,367) 1.50
98 Drew Henson ($4 / 3,000) 1.50
99 Chin-Feng Chen ($4 / 2,500) 1.50
100 Jason Jennings ($6.50 / 1,761) 1.50
101 Hideki Matsui ($9 / 8,000) 2.00
102 Jose Contreras ($9.50 / 6,000) 1.50
103 Rocco Baldelli ($6.50 / 5,000) 2.25
104 Jeremy Bonderman ($6.50 / 3,000) 3.50
105 Jesse Foppert ($6.50 / 3,500) 5.00
106 Randy Wolf ($6.50 / 1,874) 1.50
107 Kevin Millwood ($6.50 / 3,000) 1.50
108 Eric Byrnes ($6.50 / 2,500) 1.50
109 Edgar Renteria ($6.50 / 2,015) 1.50
110 Jose Reyes ($6.50 / 5,000) 4.00
111 Dontrelle Willis ($6.50 / 5,000) 3.00
112 Mike Lowell ($6.50 / 2,500) 1.50
113 Jerome Williams ($6.50 / 3,000) 3.00
114 Esteban Loaiza ($6.50 / 2,364) 1.50
115 Gil Meche ($6.50 / 2,000) 1.75
116 Ty Wigginton ($4 / 2,000) 1.50
118 Brett Myers ($6.50 / 2,115) 1.50
119 Miguel Cabrera ($6.50 / 2,610) 13.50
120 Brandon Webb ($6.50 / 3,000) 1.50
121 Aaron Heilman ($6.50 / 1,229) 2.00
122 Rich Harden ($6.50 / 5,000) 2.75
123 Morgan Ensberg ($6.50 / 1,329) 2.75

All-Star Most Valuable Player

This card was offered for $5 in the weeks after the All-Star Game, with production set at 4,000.

NM/M
1 All-Star MVP (Garret Anderson) 1.50

All-Star Top Vote Getters

This card was offered for $5 in the weeks preceding the All-Star Game, with no limit set on production. The players appearing on the card were announced after the voting.

NM/M
1 Ichiro Suzuki, Albert Pujols (3,938) 4.00

Classics

Topps continued its eTopps Classics line-up in 2003 with 20 cards of former greats. Numbering and format were contiguous with the 2002 issue. Like regular eTopps cards, Classics could only be ordered during a one-week Initial Player Offering period. Cards were issued in a quantity of up to 4,000 each at $12.50. The number of cards actually sold is shown parenthetically. Fronts have a color or colorized action photo, backs have a picture of one of that player's Topps cards, along with career notes, stats, etc. Values shown are for cards in a virtual portfolio, rather than "in hand." Taking physical possession of a card from an eTopps portfolio costs about $6 apiece.

NM/M
Complete Set (20): 210.00
Common Player: 9.00
21 Gary Carter/908 9.00
22 Eddie Murray/930 12.00
23 Luis Aparicio/778 17.50
24 Lou Brock/1,135 9.00
25 George Brett/1,128 17.50
26 Bob Feller/962 10.00
27 Carlton Fisk/890 10.00
28 Willie McCovey/915 11.00
29 Willie Stargell/843 14.00
30 Roberto Clemente/ 1,664 20.00
31 Lou Gehrig/3,049 9.00
32 Johnny Bench/1,144 20.00
33 Walter Johnson/888 11.00
34 Christy Mathewson/ 868 10.00
35 Rogers Hornsby/826 12.00
36 Lefty Grove/885 9.50
37 Josh Gibson/1,133 9.00
38 Mel Ott/917 9.00
39 Nap Lajoie/886 9.00
40 Yogi Berra/1,281 9.00

Events

Highlights of the 2003 season were commemorated by Topps with the issue of special eTopps cards. Like the regular-issue eTopps, the cards were only available directly from Topps on-line. Up to 5,000 of each card were possible with an initial order price of $8 each. Only the baseball related Events cards are listed here, along with the

number of cards actually sold during the one-week ordering window. Values shown represent cards in a virtual portfolio rather than "in hand." To physically take possession of a card in a portfolio costs about $7 apiece.

NM/M
ES9 Rafael Palmeiro/1,633 (Joins 500-HR Club) 2.00
ES10 Roger Clemens/3,418 (Records 300 W's & 4000 K's) 5.00
ES11 Barry Bonds/2,649 (Establishes 500-500 Club) 6.00
ES13 Carlos Delgado/630 (Smashes 4 Home Runs) 8.00

FanFest Promos

Attendees visiting Topps' booth at the All-Star FanFest could obtain a pair of eTopps promo cards. Fronts are identical to the issued versions except for the appearance of an All-Star Game logo. Backs have an offer of $5 off an initial eTopps order.

NM/M
Luis Aparicio (Classic) 2.00
Mark Buehrle 2.00

2003 Topps Gallery

NM/M
Complete Set (200): 60.00
Common Player: .25
SP's Inserted 1:20
Pack (5): 2.50
Box (20): 45.00
1 Jason Giambi .50
1 Jason Giambi/SP/ Drk Blue Jsy 2.00
2 Miguel Tejada .50
3 Mike Lieberthal .25
4 Jason Kendall .40
5 Robb Nen .25
6 Freddy Garcia .25
7 Scott Rolen .75
8 David Wells .25
9 Rafael Palmeiro .75

10 Garret Anderson .50
11 Curt Schilling .75
12 Greg Maddux 1.00
13 Rodrigo Lopez .25
14 Nomar Garciaparra 1.50
14 N.Garciaparra/SP/ Navy Elbow Pad 4.00
15 Kerry Wood .75
16 Frank Thomas .75
17 Ken Griffey Jr. 1.00
18 Jim Thome .75
19 Todd Helton .75
20 Lance Berkman .50
21 Robert Fick .25
22 Kevin Brown .40
23 Richie Sexson .50
24 Eddie Guardado .25
25 Vladimir Guerrero 1.00
26 Mike Piazza 1.50
27 Bernie Williams .50
28 Eric Chavez .40
29 Jimmy Rollins .40
30 Ichiro Suzuki 1.50
30 Ichiro Suzuki/SP/ Black Long Shirt 3.00
31 J.D. Drew .25
32 Nick Johnson .25
33 Shannon Stewart .25
34 Tim Salmon .40
35 Andruw Jones .75
36 Jay Gibbons .25
37 Johnny Damon .50
38 Fred McGriff .40
39 Carlos Lee .25
40 Adam Dunn .75
40 Adam Dunn/SP/ Red Sleeves & Helmet 1.50
41 Jason Jennings .25
42 Mike Lowell .40
43 Mike Sweeney .25
44 Shawn Green .50
45 Doug Mientkiewicz .25
46 Bartolo Colon .40
47 Edgardo Alfonzo .25
48 Roger Clemens 2.00
49 Randy Wolf .25
50 Alex Rodriguez 2.00
50 Alex Rodriguez/SP/ Red Undershirt 4.00
51 Vernon Wells .40
52 Kenny Lofton .40
53 Mariano Rivera .40
54 Brian Jordan .25
55 Roberto Alomar .50
56 Carlos Pena .25
57 Moises Alou .40
58 John Smoltz .40
59 Adam Kennedy .25
60 Randy Johnson 1.00
61 Mark Buehrle .25
62 C.C. Sabathia .25
63 Craig Biggio .40
64 Eric Karros .25
65 Jose Vidro .25
66 Tim Hudson .40
67 Trevor Hoffman .25
68 Bret Boone .25
69 Carl Crawford .25
70 Derek Jeter 2.50
71 Troy Percival .25
72 Gary Sheffield .50
73 Rickey Henderson .50
74 Paul Konerko .25
75 Larry Walker .40
76 Pat Burrell .50
77 Brian Giles .40
78 Jeff Kent .40
79 Kazuhiro Sasaki .25
80 Chipper Jones 1.00
81 Darin Erstad .40
82 Sean Casey .40
83 Luis Gonzalez .40
84 Roy Oswalt .40
85 Dustan Mohr .25
86 Al Leiter .25
87 Mike Mussina .50
88 Vicente Padilla .25
89 Rich Aurilia .25
90 Albert Pujols 2.00
91 John Olerud .40
92 Ivan Rodriguez .75
93 Eric Hinske .25
94 Phil Nevin .25
95 Barry Zito .50
96 Armando Benitez .25
97 Torii Hunter .50
98 Paul LoDuca .25
99 Preston Wilson .40
100 Sammy Sosa 1.50
100 Sammy Sosa/SP/ No Shin Guard 4.00
101 Jarrod Washburn .25
102 Steve Finley .25
103 Cliff Floyd .25
104 Mark Prior 1.00
105 Austin Kearns .50
106 Jeff Bagwell .75
107 A.J. Pierzynski .25
108 Pedro J. Martinez 1.00
109 Orlando Cabrera .25
110 Raul Mondesi .25
111 Russ Ortiz .25
112 Ruben Sierra .25
113 Tino Martinez .25
114 Manny Ramirez .75
115 Troy Glaus .50
116 Magglio Ordonez .50
117 Omar Vizquel .40
118 Carlos Beltran .40
119 Jose Hernandez .25
120 Javier Vazquez .25
121 Jorge Posada .50
122 Aramis Ramirez .25
123 Jason Schmidt .40
124 Jamie Moyer .25
125 Jim Edmonds .50
126 Aubrey Huff .25
127 Carlos Delgado .50
128 Junior Spivey .25
129 Tom Glavine .50
130 Marty Cordova .25
131 Derek Lowe .25
132 Ellis Burks .25
133 Barry Bonds 2.50
134 Josh Beckett .25
135 Raul Ibanez .25
136 Kazuhisa Ishii .25
137 Geoff Jenkins .25
138 Eric Milton .25
139 Mo Vaughn .25
140 Mark Mulder .40
141 Bobby Abreu .40
142 Ryan Klesko .40
143 Tsuyoshi Shinjo .25
144 Jose Mesa .25
145 Shea Hillenbrand .25
146 Edgar Renteria .25
147 Juan Gonzalez .50
148 Edgar Martinez .25
149 Matt Morris .25
150 Alfonso Soriano 1.00
150 Alfonso Soriano/SP/ No Elbow Pad 2.50
151 Bryan Bullington **RC** 2.50
151 Bryan Bullington/SP/ Red Background **RC** 6.00
152 Andy Marte **RC** 3.00
152 Andy Marte/SP/ No Necklace **RC** 4.00
153 Brendan Harris **RC** 1.00
154 Juan Camacho **RC** 1.00
155 Byron Gettis 1.00
156 Daryl Clark **RC** 1.00
157 J.D. Durbin **RC** 1.50
158 Craig Brazell **RC** 1.50
158 Craig Brazell/SP/ Black Jersey **RC** 3.00
159 Jason Kubel **RC** 4.00
160 Brandon Roberson **RC** 1.00
161 Jose Contreras **RC** 2.00
162 Hanley Ramirez **RC** 5.00
163 Jaime Bubela **RC** 1.00
164 Chris Duncan **RC** 8.00
165 Tyler Johnson **RC** 1.00
166 Adam LaRoche .25
167 Walter Young .25
168 Ryan Kibler .25
169 Tommy Whiteman **RC** .25
170 Trey Hodges .25
171 Francisco Rodriguez .25
172 Jason Arnold .25
173 Brett Myers .25
174 Rocco Baldelli .50
175 Adrian Gonzalez .25
176 Dontrelle Willis 1.00
177 Kris Honel .25
178 Marlon Byrd .25
179 Aaron Heilman .25
180 Casey Kotchman .25
181 Miguel Cabrera .25
182 Hee Seop Choi .50
183 Drew Henson .25
184 Jose Reyes .50
185 Michael Cuddyer .25
186 Brandon Phillips .25
187 Victor Martinez .25
188 Joe Mauer .50
189 Hank Blalock .75
190 Mark Teixeira .25
191 Willie Mays 2.00
192 George Brett 2.00
193 Tony Gwynn 1.00
194 Carl Yastrzemski 1.00
195 Nolan Ryan 3.00
196 Reggie Jackson .75
197 Mike Schmidt 1.50
198 Cal Ripken Jr. 3.00
199 Don Mattingly 2.00
200 Tom Seaver .75

Rainbow Refractors

Stars (1-200): 2-3X
Inserted 1:1
Rookies (151-165): 1X
Inserted 1:1

Currency Collection

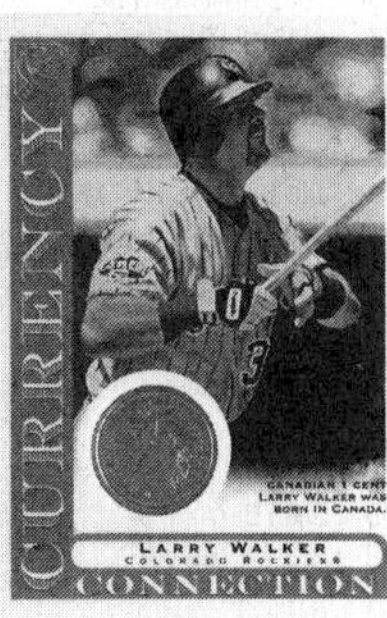

NM/M
Common Player: 4.00
Inserted 1:Box
BA Bobby Abreu 6.00
HC Hee Seop Choi 6.00
BC Bartolo Colon 4.00
LG Luis Gonzalez 4.00
VG Vladimir Guerrero 12.00
KI Kazuhisa Ishii 4.00
AJ Andruw Jones 8.00
RL Rodrigo Lopez 6.00
PM Pedro J. Martinez 10.00
RM Raul Mondesi 4.00
MO Magglio Ordonez 8.00
VP Vicente Padilla 6.00
RP Rafael Palmeiro 6.00
AP Albert Pujols 20.00
MR Manny Ramirez 8.00
ER Edgar Renteria 6.00
JR Jose Reyes 8.00
MRI Mariano Rivera 10.00
FR Francisco Rodriguez 4.00
KS Kazuhiro Sasaki 4.00
AS Alfonso Soriano 8.00
SS Sammy Sosa 15.00
IS Ichiro Suzuki 15.00
OV Omar Vizquel 10.00
LW Larry Walker 5.00

Heritage

NM/M
Complete Set (25): 75.00
Common Player: 1.50
Inserted 1:10
WB Wade Boggs 1.50
GB George Brett 8.00
JC Jose Canseco 1.50
RC Roger Clemens 6.00
AD Adam Dunn 2.00
NG Nomar Garciaparra 5.00
TG Tom Glavine 1.50
SG Shawn Green 1.50
TGW Tony Gwynn 3.00
RH Rickey Henderson 2.00
DJ Derek Jeter 8.00
RJ Randy Johnson 3.00
HK Harmon Killebrew 4.00
KR Jerry Koosman, Nolan Ryan 10.00
WM Willie Mays 8.00
HN Hideo Nomo 2.00
KP Kirby Puckett 3.00
IR Ivan Rodriguez 2.00
DS Duke Snider 2.00
AS Alfonso Soriano 3.00
IS Ichiro Suzuki 5.00
MT Miguel Tejada 1.50
JT Jim Thome 2.00
BW Bernie Williams 2.00
CY Carl Yastrzemski 3.00

Heritage Relics

NM/M
Common Player: 5.00
WB Wade Boggs 5.00
GB George Brett 20.00
JC Jose Canseco 8.00
RC Roger Clemens 15.00
SG Shawn Green 5.00
TG Tony Gwynn 10.00
RH Rickey Henderson 10.00
HK Harmon Killebrew 25.00

HN Hideo Nomo 15.00
KP Kirby Puckett 15.00

Heritage Autographed Relics

NM/M
Inserted 1:3,260
WB Wade Boggs 70.00
KP Kirby Puckett/25 80.00

Originals Relics

NM/M
Common Player: 5.00
RA Roberto Alomar 6.00
MA Moises Alou 5.00
LB Lance Berkman 5.00
BB Bret Boone 5.00
AD Adam Dunn 6.00
NG Nomar Garciaparra 12.00
LG Luis Gonzalez 5.00
SG Shawn Green 5.00
TG Tony Gwynn 8.00
TH Todd Helton 8.00
RH Rickey Henderson 8.00
DH Drew Henson 5.00
THU Torii Hunter 8.00
AJ Andruw Jones 6.00
CJ Chipper Jones 8.00
JM Joe Mauer 10.00
MO Magglio Ordonez 5.00
RP Rafael Palmeiro 8.00
MP Mike Piazza 10.00
AP Albert Pujols 15.00
MR Manny Ramirez 8.00
AR Alex Rodriguez 10.00
IR Ivan Rodriguez 8.00
GS Gary Sheffield 6.00
AS Alfonso Soriano 8.00
MT Miguel Tejada 5.00
FT Frank Thomas 8.00
JT Jim Thome 8.00
BW Bernie Williams 6.00
CY Carl Yastrzemski 20.00

HOF Edition

NM/M
Complete Set (74): 35.00
Common Player: .40
SP Variations: 2-4X
Inserted 1:1
Pack (5): 4.00
Box (20): 70.00
1 Willie Mays 2.00
2 Al Kaline 1.50
3 Hank Aaron 2.00
4 Carl Yastrzemski 1.00
5 Luis Aparicio .40
6 Sam Crawford .40
7 Tom Lasorda .40
8 John McGraw .40
9 Edd Roush .40
10 Reggie Jackson 1.00
11 Jim "Catfish" Hunter .40
12 Roberto Clemente 2.00
13 Ralph Kiner .40
14 Frankie Frisch .40
15 Nolan Ryan 4.00
16 Brooks Robinson 1.00
17 Phil Niekro .40
18 Joe Cronin .40
19 Joe Tinker .40
20 Johnny Bench 1.50
21 Harry Heilmann .40
22 Ernie Harwell .40
23 Warren Spahn 1.00
24 George Kelly .40
25 Phil Rizzuto 1.00
26 Robin Roberts .40
27 Ozzie Smith 1.00
28 Jim Palmer .40
29 Duke Snider 1.00
30 Bob Feller .40
31 Buck Leonard .40
32 Kirby Puckett 1.00
33 Monte Irvin .40
34 Chuck Klein .40
35 Willie Stargell .75
36 Juan Marichal .40
37 Lou Brock .40
38 Bucky Harris .40
39 Bobby Doerr .40
40 Lee MacPhail .40
41 Heinie Manush .40
42 George Brett 1.50
43 Harmon Killebrew 1.50
44 Whitey Ford 1.00
45 Eddie Mathews 1.50
46 Gaylord Perry .40
47 Red Schoendienst .40
48 Earl Weaver .40
49 Joe Morgan .40
50 Mike Schmidt 2.00
51 Willie McCovey .40
52 Stan Musial 2.00
53 Don Sutton .40
54 Hank Greenberg .40
55 Robin Yount 1.00
56 Tom Seaver 1.00
57 Tony Perez .40
58 George Sisler .40
59 Jim Bottomley .40
60 Yogi Berra 1.50
61 Fred Lindstrom .40
62 Napoleon Lajoie .40
63 Frank Robinson 1.00
64 Carlton Fisk .40
65 Orlando Cepeda .40
66 Fergie Jenkins .40
67 Ernie Banks 1.50
68 Bill Mazeroski .40
69 Jim Bunning .40
70 Rollie Fingers .40
71 Jimmie Foxx 1.50
72 Rod Carew .40
73 Sparky Anderson .40
74 George Kell .40

HOF Edition Refractors

Cards (1-74): 2-4X
Inserted 1:1
SP Refractors: 4-8X
Inserted 1:Box

HOF Edition Accent Mark Autograph

NM/M
Common Player:
Refractors: 1-2X
Production 25 Sets
YB Yogi Berra 65.00
BD Bobby Doerr 40.00
LM Lee MacPhail 40.00
RR Robin Roberts 40.00
RS Red Schoendienst 30.00
WS Warren Spahn 30.00

HOF Edition ARTifact Relics

NM/M
Common Player: 8.00
Refractors: 1.5-3X
Production 25 Sets
HA Hank Aaron/Bat 25.00
SA Sparky Anderson/Jsy 8.00
LA Luis Aparicio/Bat 15.00
EB Ernie Banks/Jsy 30.00
JBE Johnny Bench/Bat 12.00
JB Jim Bottomley/Bat 15.00
GB George Brett/Jsy 25.00
RCA Rod Carew/Jsy 10.00
OC Orlando Cepeda/Bat 8.00
TC Ty Cobb/Bat 80.00
EC Eddie Collins/Bat 12.00
SC Sam Crawford/Bat 20.00
BD Bobby Doerr/Jsy 15.00
CF Carlton Fisk/Bat 8.00
FF Frankie Frisch/Bat 15.00
LG Lou Gehrig/Bat 125.00
HG Hank Greenberg/Bat 25.00
BH Bucky Harris/Bat 12.00
HH Harry Heilmann/Bat 20.00
RJ Reggie Jackson/Bat 10.00
AK Al Kaline/Bat 15.00
GK George Kelly/Bat 20.00
HK Harmon Killebrew/Jsy 25.00
CK Chuck Klein/Bat 15.00
TLA Tom Lasorda/Jsy 15.00
HM Heinie Manush/Bat 15.00
EM Eddie Mathews/Jsy 30.00
WM Willie Mays/Jsy 45.00
WMC Willie McCovey/Bat 8.00
JM Joe Morgan/Bat 8.00
SM Stan Musial/Bat 20.00
PN Phil Niekro/Jsy 6.00
JP Jim Palmer/Jsy 20.00
TP Tony Perez/Bat 8.00
GP Gaylord Perry/Jsy 8.00
KP Kirby Puckett/Bat 12.00
BRO Brooks Robinson/Bat 20.00
FR Frank Robinson/Bat 10.00
JR Jackie Robinson/Bat 35.00
ER Edd Roush/Bat 20.00
BR Babe Ruth/Bat 140.00
NR Nolan Ryan/Bat 40.00
MS Mike Schmidt/Jsy 25.00
TS Tom Seaver/Bat 25.00
GS George Sisler/Bat 12.00
OS Ozzie Smith/Bat 15.00
DS Duke Snider/Bat 12.00
WS Willie Stargell/Jsy 10.00
DSU Don Sutton/Bat 8.00
JT Joe Tinker/Bat 20.00
HW Honus Wagner/Bat 140.00
PW Paul Waner/Bat 20.00
HWI Hoyt Wilhelm/Jsy 8.00
CY Carl Yastrzemski/Bat 20.00
RY Robin Yount/Bat 10.00

HOF Edition ARTifact Autograph Relics

NM/M
Common Player: 30.00
Refractors: 1-1.5X
Production 25 Sets
OC Orlando Cepeda 30.00
BD Bobby Doerr 45.00
AK Al Kaline 75.00
HK Harmon Killebrew 75.00
JM Joe Morgan 40.00
JP Jim Palmer 50.00
BRO Brooks Robinson 60.00
MS Mike Schmidt 225.00
RS Red Schoendienst 30.00
DS Duke Snider 50.00
RY Robin Yount 125.00

HOF Edition Currency Connection

NM/M
Common Player: 12.00
1:Box

EB Ernie Banks 20.00
OC Orlando Cepeda 15.00
TC Ty Cobb 40.00
BF Bob Feller 25.00
LG Lou Gehrig 35.00
HG Hank Greenberg 20.00
WM Willie Mays 20.00
WMA Willie Mays 20.00
WMC Willie McCovey 12.00
SM Stan Musial 30.00
JR Jackie Robinson 25.00
BR Babe Ruth 60.00

HOF Edition Patch Relics

NM/M
Common Player: 40.00
Production 25 Sets
GB George Brett 125.00
CH Jim "Catfish" Hunter 40.00
FJ Fergie Jenkins 40.00
HK Harmon Killebrew 80.00
TL Tom Lasorda 40.00
EM Eddie Matthews 80.00
WM Willie McCovey 40.00
JP Jim Palmer 40.00
NR Nolan Ryan 125.00
MS Mike Schmidt 125.00
OS Ozzie Smith 75.00
CY Carl Yastrzemski 80.00
RY Robin Yount 85.00

HOF Edition Team Topps Legends Autographs

NM/M
Common Player:
Vern Law 20.00
Johnny Sain 30.00

2003 Topps Heritage

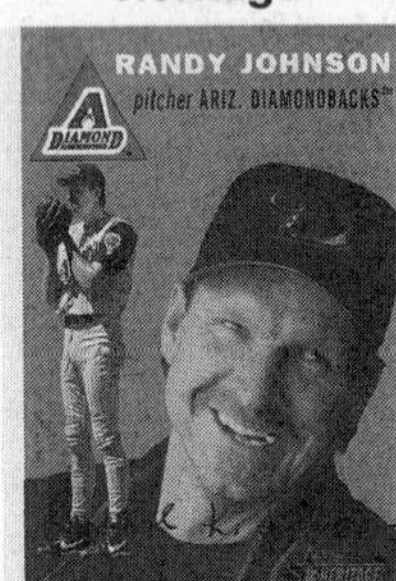

NM/M
Complete Set (430): 350.00
Common Player: .40
Common High # SP (364-430): 4.00
Pack (8): 5.00
Box (24): 100.00
1 Alex Rodriguez 3.00
1 Alex Rodriguez/ Black SP 10.00
2 Jose Cruz Jr. .40
3 Ichiro Suzuki/SP 10.00
4 Rich Aurilia .40
5 Trevor Hoffman .40
6 Brian Giles .75
6 Brian Giles/ Old Logo SP 5.00
7 Albert Pujols 2.00
7 Albert Pujols/ Black/SP 10.00
8 Vicente Padilla .40
9 Bobby Crosby .40
10 Derek Jeter 4.00
10 Derek Jeter/ Old Logo/SP 15.00
11 Pat Burrell .50
11 Pat Burrell/ Old Logo/SP 5.00
12 Armando Benitez .40
13 Javier Vazquez .40
14 Justin Morneau .75
15 Doug Mientkiewicz .40
16 Kevin Brown .40
17 Alexis Gomez .40
18 Lance Berkman .75
18 Lance Berkman/ Black/SP 5.00
19 Adrian Gonzalez .50
20 Todd Helton .75
20 Todd Helton/Black/SP 6.00
21 Carlos Pena .40
22 Matt Lawton .40
23 Elmer Dessens .40
24 Hee Seop Choi .40
25 Chris Duncan/SP **RC** 12.00
26 Ugueth Urbina .40
27 Rodrigo Lopez .40
27 Rodrigo Lopez/ Old Logo/SP 4.00
28 Damian Moss .40
29 Steve Finley .40
30 Sammy Sosa 1.50
30 Sammy Sosa/ Old Logo/SP 6.00
31 Kevin Cash .40
32 Kenny Rogers .40
33 Ben Grieve .40
34 Jason Simontacchi .40
35 Shin-Soo Choo .40
36 Freddy Garcia .40
37 Jesse Foppert .40
38 Tony LaRussa .40
39 Mark Kotsay .40
40 Barry Zito .75
41 Josh Fogg .40
42 Marlon Byrd .40
43 Marcus Thames .40
44 Al Leiter .50
45 Michael Barrett .40
46 Jake Peavy .75
47 Dustan Mohr .40
48 Alex Sanchez .40
49 Chin-Feng Chen .40
50 Kazuhisa Ishii .40
50 Kazuhisa Ishii/ Black/SP 5.00
51 Carlos Beltran .75
52 Franklin Gutierrez **RC** 1.50
53 Miguel Cabrera 1.00
54 Roger Clemens 2.50
55 Juan Cruz .40
56 Jason Young .40
57 Alex Herrera .40
58 Aaron Boone .40
59 Mark Buehrle .50
60 Larry Walker .75
61 Morgan Ensberg .40
62 Barry Larkin .75
63 Joe Borchard .40
64 Jason Dubois .40
65 Juan Acevedo .40
66 Jay Gibbons .40
67 Vinny Castilla .40
68 Jeff Mathis .40
69 Curt Schilling 1.00
70 Garret Anderson .50
71 Josh Phelps .40
72 Chan Ho Park .40
73 Edgar Renteria .50
74 Kazuhiro Sasaki .40
75 Lloyd McClendon .40
76 Jon Lieber .40
77 Rolando Viera .40
78 Jeff Conine .40
79 Kevin Millwood .40
80 Randy Johnson 1.50
80 Randy Johnson/ Black/SP 8.00
81 Troy Percival .40
82 Cliff Floyd .40
83 Tony Graffanino .40
84 Austin Kearns .50
85 Manuel Ramirez/ SP **RC** 5.00
86 Jim Tracy .40
87 Rondell White .40
88 Trot Nixon .40
89 Carlos Lee .50
90 Mike Lowell .50
91 Raul Ibanez .40
92 Ricardo Rodriguez .40
93 Ben Sheets .50
94 Jason Perry/SP **RC** 4.00
95 Mark Teixeira .75
96 Brad Fullmer .40
97 Casey Kotchman .40
98 Craig Counsell .40
99 Jason Marquis .40
100 Nomar Garciaparra 2.00
100 Nomar Garciaparra/ Old Logo/SP 5.00
101 Ed Rogers .40
102 Wilson Betemit .40
103 Wayne Lydon **RC** 1.00
104 Jack Cust .40
105 Derrek Lee .75
106 Jim Kavourias .40
107 Joe Randa .40
108 Taylor Buchholz .40
109 Gabe Kapler .40
110 Preston Wilson .40
111 Craig Biggio .50
112 Paul LoDuca .40
113 Eddie Guardado .40
114 Andres Galarraga .40
115 Edgardo Alfonzo .40
116 Robin Ventura .40
117 Jeremy Giambi .40
118 Ray Durham .40
119 Mariano Rivera .50
120 Jimmy Rollins .50
121 Dennis Tankersley .40
122 Jason Schmidt .50
123 Bret Boone .40
124 Josh Hamilton .50
125 Scott Rolen .75
126 Steve Cox .40
127 Larry Bowa .40
128 Adam LaRoche/SP 5.00
129 Ryan Klesko .40
130 Tim Hudson .50
131 Brandon Claussen .40
132 Craig Brazell/SP **RC** 4.00
133 Grady Little .40
134 Jarrod Washburn .40
135 Lyle Overbay .40
136 John Burkett .40
137 Daryl Clark **RC** .75
138 Kirk Rueter .40
139 Joe Mauer, Jake Mauer 1.00
139 Joe Mauer, Jake Mauer/Black/SP 8.00
140 Troy Glaus .75
141 Trey Hodges/SP 4.00
142 Dallas McPherson .40
143 Art Howe .40
144 Jesus Cota .40
145 J.R. House .40
146 Reggie Sanders .40
147 Clint Nageotte .40
148 Jim Edmonds .50
149 Carl Crawford .50
150 Mike Piazza 2.00
150 Mike Piazza/Black/SP 10.00
151 Seung Jun Song .40
152 Roberto Hernandez .40
153 Marquis Grissom .40
154 Billy Wagner .40
155 Josh Beckett .50
156 Randall Simon .40
156 Randall Simon/ Old Logo/SP 4.00
157 Ben Broussard .40
158 Russell Branyan .40
159 Frank Thomas 1.00
160 Alex Escobar .40
161 Mark Bellhorn .40
162 Melvin Mora .40
163 Andruw Jones .75
164 Danny Bautista .40
165 Ramon Ortiz .40
166 Wily Mo Pena .50
167 Jose Jimenez .40
168 Mark Redman .40
169 Angel Berroa .40
170 Andy Marte/SP **RC** 10.00
171 Juan Gonzalez .75
172 Fernando Vina .40
173 Joel Pineiro .40
174 Boof Bonser .40
175 Bernie Castro/SP **RC** 4.00
176 Bobby Cox .40
177 Jeff Kent .50
178 Oliver Perez .40
179 Chase Utley 1.00
180 Mark Mulder .50
181 Bobby Abreu .50
182 Ramiro Mendoza .40
183 Aaron Heilman .40
184 A.J. Pierzynski .40
185 Eric Gagne .75
186 Kirk Saarloos .40
187 Ron Gardenhire .40
188 Dmitri Young .40
189 Todd Zeile .40
190 Jim Thome 1.00
190 Jim Thome/ Old Logo/SP 8.00
191 Cliff Lee .40
192 Matt Morris .40
193 Robert Fick .40
194 C.C. Sabathia .40
195 Alexis Rios .40
196 D'Angelo Jimenez .40
197 Edgar Martinez .50
198 Robb Nen .40
199 Taggert Bozied .40
200 Vladimir Guerrero/SP 8.00
201 Walter Young/SP 4.00
202 Brendan Harris **RC** 1.00
203 Mike Hargrove .40
204 Vernon Wells .50
205 Hank Blalock .75
206 Mike Cameron .40
207 Tony Batista .40
208 Matt Williams .40
209 Tony Womack .40
210 Ramon A. Martinez **RC** .40
211 Aaron Sele .40
212 Mark Grace .75
213 Joe Crede .75
214 Ryan Dempster .40
215 Omar Vizquel .40
216 Juan Pierre .40
217 Denny Bautista .40
218 Chuck Knoblauch .40
219 Eric Karros .40
220 Victor Diaz .40
221 Jacque Jones .40
222 Jose Vidro .40
223 Joe McEwing .40
224 Nick Johnson .40
225 Eric Chavez .50
226 Jose Mesa .40
227 Aramis Ramirez .75
228 John Lackey .40
229 David Bell .40
230 John Olerud .50
231 Tino Martinez .40
232 Randy Winn .40
233 Todd Hollandsworth .40
234 Ruddy Lugo **RC** .75
235 Carlos Delgado .75
236 Chris Narveson .40
237 Tim Salmon .75
238 Orlando Palmeiro .40
239 Jeff Clark/SP **RC** 4.00
240 Byung-Hyun Kim .40
241 Mike Remlinger .40
242 Johnny Damon 1.00
243 Corey Patterson .50
244 Paul Konerko .75
245 Danny Graves .40
246 Ellis Burks .40
247 Gavin Floyd .40
248 Jaime Bubela **RC** .75
249 Sean Burroughs .40
250 Alex Rodriguez/SP 10.00
251 Gabe Gross .40
252 Rafael Palmeiro .75
253 Dewon Brazelton .40
254 Jimmy Journell .40
255 Rafael Soriano .40
256 Jerome Williams .40
257 Xavier Nady .40
258 Mike Williams .40
259 Randy Wolf .40
260 Miguel Tejada .75
260 Miguel Tejada/ Black/SP 5.00
261 Juan Rivera .40
262 Rey Ordonez .40
263 Bartolo Colon .40
264 Eric Milton .40
265 Jeffrey Hammonds .40
266 Odalis Perez .40
267 Mike Sweeney .40
268 Richard Hidalgo .40
269 Alex Gonzalez .40
270 Aaron Cook .40
271 Earl Snyder .40
272 Todd Walker .40
273 Aaron Rowand .40
274 Matt Clement .40
275 Anastacio Martinez .40
276 Mike Bordick .40
277 John Smoltz .50
278 Scott Hairston .40
279 David Eckstein .40
280 Shannon Stewart .40
281 Carl Everett .40
282 Aubrey Huff .40
283 Mike Mussina .75
284 Ruben Sierra .40
285 Russ Ortiz .40
286 Brian Lawrence .40
287 Kip Wells .40
288 Placido Polanco .40
289 Ted Lilly .40
290 Andy Pettitte .50
291 John Buck .40
292 Orlando Cabrera .40
293 Cristian Guzman .40
294 Ruben Quevedo .40
295 Cesar Izturis .40
296 Ryan Ludwick .40
297 Roy Oswalt .75
298 Jason Stokes .40
299 Mike Hampton .40
300 Pedro Martinez 1.50
301 Nic Jackson .40
302 Magglio Ordonez .50
302 Magglio Ordonez/ Old Logo/SP 5.00
303 Manny Ramirez 1.00
304 Jorge Julio .40
305 Javy Lopez .50
306 Roy Halladay .50
307 Kevin Mench .40
308 Jason Isringhausen .40
309 Carlos Guillen .40
310 Tsuyoshi Shinjo .40
311 Phil Nevin .40
312 Pokey Reese .40
313 Jorge Padilla .40
314 Jermaine Dye .40
315 David Wells .40
316 Mo Vaughn .40
317 Bernie Williams .75
318 Michael Restovich .40
319 Jose Hernandez .40
320 Richie Sexson .75
321 Daryle Ward .40
322 Luis Castillo .40
323 Rene Reyes .40
324 Victor Martinez .40
325 Adam Dunn .75
325 Adam Dunn/ Old Logo/SP 6.00
326 Corwin Malone .40
327 Kerry Wood .50
328 Rickey Henderson .75
329 Marty Cordova .40
330 Greg Maddux 2.00
331 Miguel Batista .40
332 Chris Bootcheck .40
333 Carlos Baerga .40
334 Antonio Alfonseca .40
335 Shane Halter .40
336 Juan Encarnacion .40
337 Flash Gordon .40
338 Hideo Nomo .75
339 Torii Hunter .75
340 Alfonso Soriano 1.00
340 Alfonso Soriano/ Black/SP 6.00
341 Roberto Alomar .75
342 David Justice .50
343 Mike Lieberthal .40
344 Jeff Weaver .40
345 Timoniel Perez .40
346 Travis Lee .40
347 Sean Casey .40
348 Willie Harris .40
349 Derek Lowe .40
350 Tom Glavine .75
351 Eric Hinske .40
352 Rocco Baldelli .40
353 J.D. Drew .60
354 Jamie Moyer .40
355 Todd Linden .40
356 Benito Santiago .40
357 Brad Baker .40
358 Alex Gonzalez .40
359 Brandon Duckworth .40
360 John Rheinecker .40
361 Orlando Hernandez .40
362 Pedro Astacio .40
363 Brad Wilkerson .40
364 David Ortiz 8.00
365 Geoff Jenkins 4.00
366 Brian Jordan 4.00
367 Paul Byrd 4.00
368 Jason Lane 4.00
369 Jeff Bagwell 6.00
370 Bobby Higginson 4.00
371 Juan Uribe 4.00
372 Lee Stevens 4.00
373 Jimmy Haynes 4.00
374 Jose Valentin 4.00
375 Ken Griffey Jr. 10.00
376 Shea Hillenbrand 4.00
377 Gary Matthews Jr. 4.00
378 Gary Sheffield 5.00
379 Rick Helling 4.00
380 Junior Spivey 4.00
381 Francisco Rodriguez 4.00
382 Chipper Jones 6.00
383 Orlando Hudson 4.00
384 Ivan Rodriguez 6.00
385 Chris Snelling 4.00
386 Kenny Lofton 4.00
387 Eric Cyr 4.00
388 Jason Kendall 4.00
389 Marlon Anderson 4.00
390 Billy Koch 4.00
391 Shelly Duncan 4.00
392 Jose Reyes 6.00
393 Fernando Tatis 4.00
394 Michael Cuddyer 4.00
395 Mark Prior 8.00
396 Dontrelle Willis 4.00
397 Jay Payton 4.00
398 Brandon Phillips 4.00
399 Dustin Moseley **RC** 4.00
400 Jason Giambi 5.00
401 John Mabry 4.00
402 Ron Gant 4.00
403 J.T. Snow 4.00
404 Jeff Cirillo 4.00
405 Darin Erstad 4.00
406 Luis Gonzalez 4.00
407 Marcus Giles 4.00
408 Brian Daubach 4.00
409 Moises Alou 4.00
410 Raul Mondesi 4.00
411 Adrian Beltre 4.00
412 A.J. Burnett 4.00
413 Jason Jennings 4.00
414 Edwin Almonte 4.00
415 Fred McGriff 4.00
416 Tim Raines Jr. 4.00
417 Rafael Furcal 4.00
418 Erubiel Durazo 4.00
419 Drew Henson 4.00
420 Kevin Appier 4.00
421 Chad Tracy 4.00
422 Adam Wainwright 4.00
423 Choo Freeman 4.00
424 Sandy Alomar Jr. 4.00
425 Corey Koskie 4.00
426 Jeromy Burnitz 4.00
427 Jorge Posada 6.00
428 Jason Arnold 4.00
429 Brett Myers 4.00
430 Shawn Green 5.00

Chrome

NM/M
Common Player: 1.00
Production 1,954 Sets
Refractors: 1.5-2X
Production 554 Sets
THC1 Alex Rodriguez 8.00
THC2 Ichiro Suzuki 8.00
THC3 Brian Giles 1.50
THC4 Albert Pujols 4.00
THC5 Derek Jeter 10.00
THC6 Pat Burrell 3.00
THC7 Lance Berkman 2.00
THC8 Todd Helton 2.00
THC9 Chris Duncan 20.00
THC10 Rodrigo Lopez 1.00
THC11 Sammy Sosa 5.00
THC12 Barry Zito 2.00
THC13 Marlon Byrd 1.00
THC14 Al Leiter 1.00
THC15 Kazuhisa Ishii 1.50
THC16 Franklin Gutierrez 1.00
THC17 Roger Clemens 5.00
THC18 Mark Buehrle 1.00
THC19 Larry Walker 1.50
THC20 Curt Schilling 2.50
THC21 Garret Anderson 1.50
THC22 Randy Johnson 3.00
THC23 Cliff Floyd 1.00
THC24 Austin Kearns 2.00
THC25 Manuel Ramirez 1.00
THC26 Raul Ibanez 1.00
THC27 Jason Perry 1.00
THC28 Mark Teixeira 2.00
THC29 Nomar Garciaparra 6.00
THC30 Wayne Lydon 1.00
THC31 Preston Wilson 1.00
THC32 Paul LoDuca 1.00
THC33 Edgardo Alfonzo 1.00
THC34 Jeremy Giambi 1.00
THC35 Mariano Rivera 1.50
THC36 Jimmy Rollins 2.00
THC37 Bret Boone 1.00
THC38 Scott Rolen 2.00
THC39 Adam LaRoche 1.00
THC40 Tim Hudson 1.50
THC41 Craig Brazell 1.00
THC42 Daryl Clark 1.00
THC43 Joe Mauer, Jake Mauer 3.00
THC44 Troy Glaus 2.50
THC45 Sean Pierce 1.00
THC46 Carl Crawford 1.00
THC47 Mike Piazza 6.00
THC48 Josh Beckett 1.00
THC49 Randall Simon 1.00
THC50 Frank Thomas 2.50
THC51 Andruw Jones 2.00
THC52 Andy Marte 4.00
THC53 Bernie Castro 1.00
THC54 Jim Thome 3.00
THC55 Alexis Rios 1.00
THC56 Vladimir Guerrero 4.00
THC57 Walter Young 1.00
THC58 Hank Blalock 1.50
THC59 Ramon A. Martinez 1.00
THC60 Jacque Jones 1.00
THC61 Nick Johnson 1.00
THC62 Ruddy Lugo 1.00
THC63 Carlos Delgado 1.50
THC64 Jeff Clark 1.00
THC65 Johnny Damon 1.00
THC66 Jaime Bubela 1.00
THC67 Alex Rodriguez 8.00
THC68 Rafael Palmeiro 2.00
THC69 Miguel Tejada 2.00
THC70 Bartolo Colon 1.00
THC71 Mike Sweeney 1.00
THC72 John Smoltz 1.00
THC73 Shannon Stewart 1.00
THC74 Mike Mussina 2.00
THC75 Roy Oswalt 1.50
THC76 Pedro Martinez 4.00
THC77 Magglio Ordonez 2.00
THC78 Manny Ramirez 3.00
THC79 David Wells 1.00
THC80 Richie Sexson 1.50
THC81 Adam Dunn 2.50
THC82 Greg Maddux 5.00
THC83 Alfonso Soriano 5.00
THC84 Roberto Alomar 2.00
THC85 Derek Lowe 1.00
THC86 Tom Glavine 2.00
THC87 Jeff Bagwell 2.50
THC88 Ken Griffey Jr. 6.00
THC89 Shea Hillenbrand 1.00
THC90 Gary Sheffield 1.50
THC91 Chipper Jones 5.00
THC92 Orlando Hudson 1.00
THC93 Jose Cruz Jr. 1.00
THC94 Mark Prior 2.50
THC95 Jason Giambi 5.00
THC96 Luis Gonzalez 1.50
THC97 Drew Henson 1.50
THC98 Cristian Guzman 1.00
THC99 Shawn Green 1.50
THC100 Jose Vidro 1.00

Clubhouse Collection Autographed

No Pricing
Production 25 Sets

Clubhouse Collection Relics

		NM/M
Common Player:		10.00
EB	Ernie Banks	25.00
AD	Adam Dunn	15.00
JG	Jim Gilliam	12.00
SG	Shawn Green	10.00
CJ	Chipper Jones	15.00
AK	Al Kaline	25.00
EM	Eddie Mathews	20.00
WM	Willie Mays	40.00
AP	Albert Pujols	15.00
AR	Alex Rodriguez	15.00
DS	Duke Snider	25.00
KW	Kerry Wood	10.00

Clubhouse Collection Dual Relics

		NM/M
Production 54 Sets		
SG	Duke Snider, Shawn Green	80.00
BW	Ernie Banks, Kerry Wood	80.00
MJ	Eddie Mathews, Chipper Jones	100.00

Flashbacks

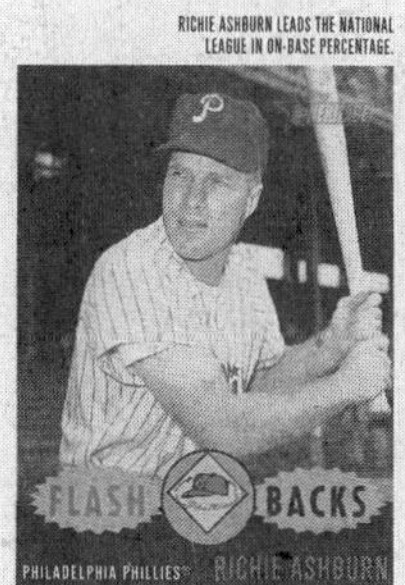

		NM/M
Complete Set (10):		12.00
Common Player:		.75
Inserted 1:12		
F1	Willie Mays	3.00
F2	Yogi Berra	2.00
F3	Ted Kluszewski	.75
F4	Stan Musial	3.00
F5	Hank Aaron	3.00
F6	Duke Snider	1.50
F7	Richie Ashburn	.75
F8	Robin Roberts	.75
F9	Mickey Vernon	.75
F10	Don Larsen	.75

Flashbacks Autographs

Production 25:

Grandstand Glory

		NM/M
Common Player:		10.00
RA	Richie Ashburn	15.00
EB	Ernie Banks	20.00
YB	Yogi Berra	20.00
DG	Dick Groat	12.00
AK	Al Kaline	15.00
TK	Ted Kluszewski	12.00
EM	Eddie Mathews	12.00
WM	Willie Mays	35.00
AP	Andy Pafko	10.00
PR	Phil Rizzuto	15.00
HS	Hank Sauer	10.00
DS	Duke Snider	15.00
WS	Warren Spahn	15.00

New Age Performers

		NM/M
Complete Set (15):		20.00
Common Player:		.75
Inserted 1:15		
NA1	Mike Piazza	3.00
NA2	Ichiro Suzuki	3.00
NA3	Derek Jeter	4.00
NA4	Alex Rodriguez	3.00
NA5	Sammy Sosa	2.00
NA6	Jason Giambi	2.00
NA7	Vladimir Guerrero	1.50
NA8	Albert Pujols	1.50
NA9	Todd Helton	.75
NA10	Nomar Garciaparra	2.50
NA11	Randy Johnson	1.50
NA12	Jim Thome	1.00
NA13	Andruw Jones	.75
NA14	Miguel Tejada	.75
NA15	Alfonso Soriano	1.50

Real One Autographs

		NM/M
Common Autograph:		15.00
Inserted 1:188		
Special Editions (Red Ink):		1.5-2X
Production 54		
HA	Hank Aaron	250.00
EB	Ernie Banks	150.00
MB	Matt Batts	25.00
HB	Hank Bauer	40.00
LB	Lance Berkman	50.00
YB	Yogi Berra	80.00
MBL	Mike Blyzka	25.00
JC	Jose Cruz Jr.	15.00
RF	Roy Face	40.00
WF	Whitey Ford	60.00
DG	Dick Groat	40.00
GH	Gene Hermanski	25.00
CH	Cal Hogue	25.00
MI	Monte Irvin	50.00
LJ	Larry Jansen	30.00
AK	Al Kaline	80.00
CK	Charlie Kress	25.00
DK	Dick Kryhoski	25.00
TL	Tom Lasorda	70.00
VL	Vern Law	30.00
DL	Don Lenhardt	25.00
DLU	Don Lund	25.00
EM	Eddie Mayo	25.00
WM	Willie Mays	200.00
MM	Mickey Micelotta	25.00
RM	Ray Murray	25.00
AP	Andy Pafko	60.00
PP	Paul Penson	30.00
JPO	Johnny Podres	40.00
JP	Joe Presko	25.00
PR	Phil Rizzuto	50.00
PRO	Preacher Roe	50.00
JR	Jimmy Rollins	25.00
BR	Bob Ross	25.00
JS	Johnny Sain	40.00
MS	Mike Sandlock	25.00
CS	Carl Scheib	25.00
BSH	Bobby Shantz	40.00
BS	Bill "Moose" Skowron	40.00
DS	Duke Snider	80.00
BT	Bob Talbot	25.00
JV	Jose Vidro	15.00
BWE	Bill Werle	25.00
LW	Leroy Wheat	25.00
JW	Jim Willis	25.00

Real One Special Edition Autographs

		NM/M
Production 54 Sets		
RO-MB	Matt Batts	50.00
RO-HB	Hank Bauer	75.00
RO-MBL	Mike Blyzka	40.00
RO-RF	Roy Face	60.00
RO-WF	Whitey Ford	120.00
RO-DG	Dick Groat	60.00
RO-MI	Monte Irvin	80.00
RO-LJ	Larry Jansen	35.00
RO-CK	Charlie Kress	60.00
RO-TL	Tom Lasorda	65.00
RO-VL	Vern Law	40.00
RO-DL	Don Lenhardt	75.00
RO-EM	Eddie Mayo	45.00
RO-MM	Mickey Micelotta	40.00
RO-RM	Ray Murray	45.00
RO-PP	Paul Penson	40.00
RO-JPO	Johnny Podres	70.00
RO-JP	Joe Presko	50.00
RO-PR	Phil Rizzuto	75.00
RO-PRO	Preacher Roe	80.00
RO-BR	Bob Ross	40.00
RO-JS	Johnny Sain	65.00
RO-MS	Mike Sandlock	50.00
RO-CS	Carl Scheib	35.00
RO-BSH	Bobby Shantz	60.00
RO-BS	Bill "Moose" Skowron	80.00
RO-BT	Bob Talbot	50.00
RO-BWE	Bill Werle	60.00
RO-LW	Leroy Wheat	50.00
RO-JW	Jim Willis	60.00

Team Legends Autographs

	NM/M
Common Autograph:	35.00
Luis Aparicio	35.00
Jim Bunning	35.00
Al Kaline	70.00
Don Larsen	40.00
Duke Snider	70.00

Then and Now

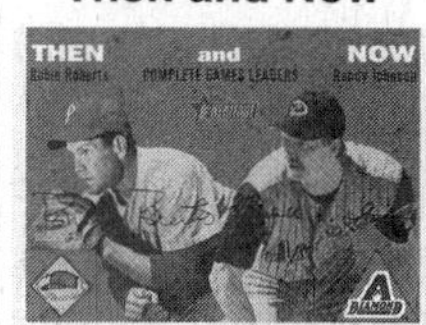

		NM/M
Complete Set (10):		12.00
Common Card:		.75
Inserted 1:15		
TN1	Ted Kluszewski, Alex Rodriguez	3.00
TN2	Ted Kluszewski, Alex Rodriguez	3.00
TN3	Robin Roberts, Randy Johnson	1.00
TN4	Don Mueller, Alfonso Soriano	1.50
TN5	Stan Musial, Garret Anderson	2.00
TN6	Minnie Minoso, Johnny Damon	.75
TN7	Robin Roberts, Randy Johnson	1.00
TN8	Duke Snider, Alex Rodriguez	3.00
TN9	Robin Roberts, Randy Johnson	1.00
TN10	Johnny Antonelli, Pedro Martinez	1.00

2003 Topps Opening Day

		NM/M
Complete Set (165):		30.00
Common Player:		.10
Pack (6):		1.00
Box (36):		30.00
1	Alex Rodriguez	1.00
2	Jarrod Washburn	.10
3	Kevin Brown	.10
4	Chipper Jones	.75
5	Ken Griffey Jr.	.75
6	Shea Hillenbrand	.10
7	Moises Alou	.20
8	Carlos Lee	.10
9	Marty Cordova	.10
10	Derek Jeter	1.50
11	Dmitri Young	.10
12	Barry Bonds	1.50
13	Jeff Bagwell	.40
14	Paul Byrd	.10
15	Carlos Delgado	.20
16	Richie Sexson	.20
17	Torii Hunter	.20
18	Bartolo Colon	.10
19	Robin Ventura	.10
20	Mike Piazza	1.00
21	Tim Hudson	.20
22	Brett Myers	.10
23	Ryan Klesko	.20
24	Tsuyoshi Shinjo	.10
25	Cliff Floyd	.10
26	Scott Rolen	.50
27	Randy Winn	.10
28	Rafael Palmeiro	.25
29	Carlos Pena	.10
30	Randy Johnson	.50
31	Jimmy Rollins	.20
32	Jermaine Dye	.10
33	Jose Vidro	.10
34	Jorge Julio	.10
35	Mark Prior	.50
36	Curt Schilling	.40
37	A.J. Pierzynski	.10
38	Andruw Jones	.25
39	Kerry Wood	.50
40	Todd Helton	.40
41	Magglio Ordonez	.20
42	Darin Erstad	.20
43	Barry Larkin	.20
44	Edgardo Alfonzo	.10
45	Jason Giambi	.25
46	Eric Chavez	.20
47	Brian Giles	.20
48	Raul Ibanez	.10
49	Edgar Renteria	.20
50	Sammy Sosa	.75
51	Bobby Hill	.10
52	A.J. Burnett	.10
53	Juan Gonzalez	.25
54	Eric Hinske	.10
55	Roberto Alomar	.25
56	Javier Lopez	.10
57	Mark Buehrle	.10
58	Garret Anderson	.20
59	Mike Hampton	.10
60	Rich Aurilia	.10
61	Brian Jordan	.10
62	Brad Wilkerson	.10
63	Geoff Jenkins	.10
64	Brad Radke	.10
65	Roger Clemens	1.00
66	Scott Hatteberg	.10
67	Mike Williams	.10
68	Steve Finley	.10
69	Benito Santiago	.10
70	John Smoltz	.20
71	Bret Boone	.10
72	Matt Morris	.10
73	Manny Ramirez	.50
74	Troy Glaus	.25
75	Austin Kearns	.25
76	Jim Thome	.50
77	Luis Gonzalez	.20
78	Freddy Garcia	.10
79	Randy Wolf	.10
80	Miguel Tejada	.25
81	Paul Konerko	.20
82	Ivan Rodriguez	.25
83	Shannon Stewart	.10
84	Rafael Furcal	.10
85	Cristian Guzman	.10
86	Mo Vaughn	.10
87	Jose Cruz Jr.	.10
88	Alfonso Soriano	.50
89	Orlando Cabrera	.10
90	Ichiro Suzuki	1.00
91	Omar Vizquel	.20
92	Hideo Nomo	.25
93	Roy Halladay	.10
94	Mike Sweeney	.10
95	Greg Maddux	.75
96	David Eckstein	.10
97	Jay Gibbons	.10
98	Andy Pettitte	.25
99	Frank Thomas	.40
100	Shawn Green	.25
101	Jacque Jones	.10
102	Pedro J. Martinez	.50
103	Mark Mulder	.20
104	Rodrigo Lopez	.10
105	Bernie Williams	.25
106	Aaron Boone	.10
107	Mike Lieberthal	.10
108	Jim Edmonds	.20
109	Tino Martinez	.20
110	Gary Sheffield	.25
111	Mike Cameron	.10
112	Jason Jennings	.10
113	Larry Walker	.20
114	Corey Koskie	.10
115	Kazuhisa Ishii	.10
116	Jose Hernandez	.10
117	Al Leiter	.10
118	David Justice	.10
119	Jason Kendall	.20
120	Edgar Martinez	.10
121	Pat Burrell	.25
122	Vladimir Guerrero	.50
123	Juan Rivera	.10
124	Byung-Hyun Kim	.10
125	Adam Dunn	.40
126	Tim Salmon	.20
127	Terrence Long	.10
128	Johnny Damon	.25
129	Aramis Ramirez	.25
130	Barry Zito	.20
131	Mike Lowell	.10
132	Adam Kennedy	.10
133	J.D. Drew	.20
134	Tony Batista	.10
135	Albert Pujols	1.50
136	Doug Mientkiewicz	.10
137	Phil Nevin	.10
138	Paul LoDuca	.10
139	Roy Oswalt	.20
140	Jeff Kent	.20
141	Robert Fick	.10
142	Aubrey Huff	.10
143	C.C. Sabathia	.10
144	Tim Wakefield	.10
145	Derek Lowe	.10
146	Kevin Millwood	.10
147	Jorge Posada	.25
148	Fernando Vina	.10
149	Junior Spivey	.10
150	Lance Berkman	.25
151	Eric Gagne	.25
152	Mariano Rivera	.20
153	Alex Sanchez	.10
154	Ellis Burks	.10
155	Josh Beckett	.10
156	Nomar Garciaparra	1.00
157	Craig Biggio	.20
158	Adrian Beltre	.25
159	Vicente Padilla	.10
160	Mike Cameron HL	.10
161	Shawn Green HL	.20
162	A's Team Shot HL	.10
163	Jason Giambi HL	.20
164	Derek Lowe HL	.10
165	Checklist	.10

Stickers

Stars: .5-1.5X
Inserted 1:1

2003 Topps Pristine

		NM/M
Complete Set (190):		
Common Player:		1.00
Common Rookie:		1.00
Common Uncommon RC:		2.50
Production 1,499		
Common Rare RC:		5.00
Production 499		
Pack (8):		30.00
Box (5):		140.00
1	Pedro J. Martinez	2.50
2	Derek Jeter	6.00
3	Alex Rodriguez	6.00
4	Miguel Tejada	1.00
5	Nomar Garciaparra	2.50
6	Austin Kearns	1.50
7	Jose Vidro	1.00
8	Bret Boone	1.00
9	Scott Rolen	2.00
10	Mike Sweeney	1.00
11	Jason Schmidt	1.00
12	Alfonso Soriano	2.50
13	Tim Hudson	1.50
14	A.J. Pierzynski	1.00
15	Lance Berkman	2.00
16	Frank Thomas	2.00
17	Gary Sheffield	1.50
18	Jarrod Washburn	1.00
19	Hideo Nomo	1.50
20	Barry Zito	1.50
21	Kevin Millwood	1.50
22	Matt Morris	1.00
23	Carl Crawford	1.00
24	Carlos Delgado	2.00
25	Mike Piazza	3.00
26	Brad Radke	1.00
27	Richie Sexson	1.50
28	Kevin Brown	1.00
29	Carlos Beltran	2.00
30	Curt Schilling	2.00
31	Chipper Jones	3.00
32	Paul Konerko	1.50
33	Larry Walker	1.50
34	Jeff Bagwell	2.00
35	Jason Giambi	1.50
36	Mark Mulder	1.50
37	Vicente Padilla	1.00
38	Kris Benson	1.00
39	Bernie Williams	1.50
40	Jim Thome	2.00
41	Roger Clemens	5.00
42	Roberto Alomar	1.50
43	Torii Hunter	1.50
44	Bobby Abreu	1.50
45	Jeff Kent	1.00
46	Roy Oswalt	1.50
47	Bartolo Colon	1.00
48	Greg Maddux	4.00
49	Tom Glavine	1.50
50	Sammy Sosa	3.00
51	Ichiro Suzuki	4.00
52	Mark Prior	1.50
53	Manny Ramirez	2.00
54	Andruw Jones	1.50
55	Randy Johnson	3.00
56	Garret Anderson	1.00
57	Roy Halladay	1.00
58	Rafael Palmeiro	2.00
59	Rocco Baldelli	1.50
60	Albert Pujols	6.00
61	Edgar Renteria	1.00
62	John Olerud	1.00
63	Rich Aurilia	1.00
64	Ryan Klesko	1.00
65	Brian Giles	1.50
66	Eric Chavez	1.50
67	Jorge Posada	1.50
68	Cliff Floyd	1.00
69	Vladimir Guerrero	2.00
70	Cristian Guzman	1.00
71	Raul Ibanez	1.00
72	Paul LoDuca	1.00
73	A.J. Burnett	1.00
74	Ken Griffey Jr.	4.00
75	Mark Buehrle	1.50
76	Moises Alou	1.50
77	Adam Dunn	2.00
78	Tony Batista	1.00
79	Troy Glaus	1.50
80	Luis Gonzalez	1.00
81	Shea Hillenbrand	1.00
82	Kerry Wood	1.00
83	Magglio Ordonez	1.00
84	Omar Vizquel	1.00
85	Bobby Higginson	1.00
86	Mike Lowell	1.00
87	Runelvys Hernandez	1.00
88	Shawn Green	1.50
89	Erubiel Durazo	1.00
90	Pat Burrell	1.50
91	Todd Helton	2.00
92	Jim Edmonds	1.50
93	Aubrey Huff	1.00
94	Eric Hinske	1.00
95	Barry Bonds	6.00
96	Willie Mays	5.00
97	Bo Jackson	2.00
98	Carl Yastrzemski	2.00
99	Don Mattingly	5.00
100	Gary Carter	1.50
101	Jose Contreras/C **RC**	2.00
102	Jose Contreras/U **RC**	4.00
103	Jose Contreras/R **RC**	8.00
104	Dan Haren/C	4.00
105	Dan Haren/U	6.00
106	Dan Haren/R	10.00
107	Michel Hernandez/C **RC**	1.00
108	Michel Hernandez/U **RC**	2.50
109	Michel Hernandez/R **RC**	5.00
110	Bobby Basham/C **RC**	1.00
111	Bobby Basham/U **RC**	2.50
112	Bobby Basham/R **RC**	5.00
113	Bryan Bullington/C **RC**	1.50
114	Bryan Bullington/U **RC**	2.50
115	Bryan Bullington/R **RC**	5.00
116	Bernie Castro/C **RC**	1.00
117	Bernie Castro/U **RC**	2.50
118	Bernie Castro/R **RC**	5.00
119	Chien-Ming Wang/C **RC**	25.00
120	Chien-Ming Wang/U **RC**	30.00
121	Chien-Ming Wang/R **RC**	40.00
122	Eric Crozier/C **RC**	1.00
123	Eric Crozier/U **RC**	2.50
124	Eric Crozier/R **RC**	5.00
125	Michael Garciaparra/C	1.00
126	Michael Garciaparra/U	2.50
127	Michael Garciaparra/R	5.00
128	Joey Gomes/C	1.00
129	Joey Gomes/U	2.50
130	Joey Gomes/R	5.00
131	Wilfredo Ledezma/C **RC**	1.00
132	Wilfredo Ledezma/U **RC**	2.50
133	Wilfredo Ledezma/R **RC**	5.00
134	Branden Florence/C **RC**	1.00
135	Branden Florence/U **RC**	2.50
136	Branden Florence/R **RC**	5.00
137	Jeremy Bonderman/C	6.00
138	Jeremy Bonderman/U	10.00
139	Jeremy Bonderman/R	15.00
140	Travis Ishikawa/C **RC**	1.00
141	Travis Ishikawa/U **RC**	2.50
142	Travis Ishikawa/R **RC**	5.00
143	Ben Francisco/C **RC**	1.00
144	Ben Francisco/U **RC**	2.50
145	Ben Francisco/R **RC**	5.00
146	Jason Kubel/C **RC**	4.00
147	Jason Kubel/U **RC**	8.00
148	Jason Kubel/R **RC**	10.00
149	Tyler Martin/C **RC**	1.00
150	Tyler Martin/U **RC**	2.50
151	Tyler Martin/R **RC**	5.00
152	Jason Perry/C	1.50
153	Jason Perry/U	3.00
154	Jason Perry/R	5.00
155	Ryan Shealy/C **RC**	4.00
156	Ryan Shealy/U **RC**	6.00
157	Ryan Shealy/R **RC**	10.00
158	Hanley Ramirez/C **RC**	12.00
159	Hanley Ramirez/U **RC**	15.00
160	Hanley Ramirez/R **RC**	25.00
161	Rajai Davis/C **RC**	1.00
162	Rajai Davis/U **RC**	2.50
163	Rajai Davis/R **RC**	5.00
164	Gary Schneidmiller/C **RC**	1.00
165	Gary Schneidmiller/U **RC**	2.50

166 Gary Schneidmiller/ R **RC** 5.00
167 Haj Turay/C **RC** 1.00
168 Haj Turay/U **RC** 2.50
169 Haj Turay/R **RC** 5.00
170 Kevin Youkilis/C **RC** 4.00
171 Kevin Youkilis/U **RC** 8.00
172 Kevin Youkilis/R **RC** 15.00
173 Shane Bazzell/C **RC** 1.00
174 Shane Bazzell/U **RC** 2.50
175 Shane Bazzell/R **RC** 5.00
176 Elizardo Ramirez/C **RC** 1.50
177 Elizardo Ramirez/U **RC** 3.00
178 Elizardo Ramirez/R **RC** 6.00
179 Robinson Cano/C **RC** 20.00
180 Robinson Cano/U **RC** 30.00
181 Robinson Cano/R **RC** 35.00
182 Nook Logan/C **RC** 1.00
183 Nook Logan/U **RC** 2.50
184 Nook Logan/R **RC** 5.00
185 Dustin McGowan/C **RC** 2.00
186 Dustin McGowan/U **RC** 5.00
187 Dustin McGowan/R **RC** 8.00
188 Ryan Howard/C 40.00
189 Ryan Howard/U 40.00
190 Ryan Howard/R 65.00

Plates

No pricing due to scarcity.
Four plates per player.

Refractors

Veterans (1-100): 4-6X
Production 99
Common RC's: .75-1.5X
Production 1,599
Uncommon RC's: 1-2X
Production 499
Rare RC's: 1.5-3X
Production 99
Veteran Gold Refrac.(1-100):4-8X
Rookie Golds (101-190): 2-4X
Production 69 Sets

Bomb Squad

NM/M
Common Player: 4.00
Refractors: No Pricing
Production 25 Sets
MO1 Moises Alou 4.00
MO2 Moises Alou 4.00
GA1 Garret Anderson 5.00
GA2 Garret Anderson 5.00
JRB Jeff Bagwell 6.00
JB Johnny Bench 10.00
LB1 Lance Berkman 5.00
LB2 Lance Berkman 5.00
HB Hank Blalock 5.00
BB Barry Bonds 15.00
GB1 George Brett 12.00
GB2 George Brett 12.00
GC Gary Carter 5.00
EC1 Eric Chavez 4.00
EC2 Eric Chavez 4.00
CC Carl Crawford 4.00
AD Adam Dunn 6.00
DE1 Darin Erstad 4.00
DE2 Darin Erstad 4.00
CF Cliff Floyd 4.00
NG1 Nomar Garciaparra 10.00
NG2 Nomar Garciaparra 10.00
JG Jason Giambi 6.00
TG1 Troy Glaus 5.00
TG2 Troy Glaus 5.00
JAG Juan Gonzalez 6.00
LG Luis Gonzalez 4.00
SG Shawn Green 5.00
VG1 Vladimir Guerrero 8.00
VG2 Vladimir Guerrero 8.00
TH Todd Helton 6.00
RH Rickey Henderson 10.00
AJ Andruw Jones 6.00
CJ Chipper Jones 8.00
JK Jeff Kent 4.00
MO Magglio Ordonez 4.00
RP Rafael Palmeiro 6.00
MP Mike Piazza 10.00
AP1 Albert Pujols 15.00
AP2 Albert Pujols 15.00
MR Manny Ramirez 6.00
AR1 Alex Rodriguez 10.00
AR2 Alex Rodriguez 10.00
TS Tim Salmon 4.00
MS1 Mike Schmidt 12.00
MS2 Mike Schmidt 12.00
GS Gary Sheffield 5.00
AS Alfonso Soriano 8.00
SS1 Sammy Sosa 10.00
SS2 Sammy Sosa 10.00
MT Miguel Tejada 4.00
FT Frank Thomas 6.00
JT Jim Thome 10.00

Borders

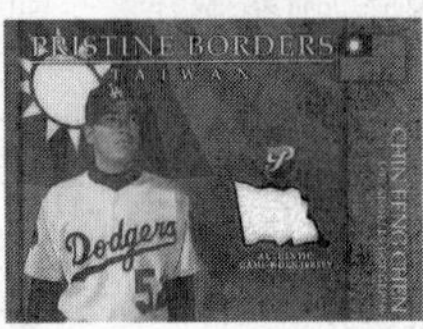

NM/M
Common Player: 4.00
Inserted 1:9
Refractors: No Pricing
Production 25 Sets
CC Chin-Feng Chen 40.00
VG Vladimir Guerrero 8.00
CG Cristian Guzman 4.00
KI Kazuhisa Ishii 4.00
AJ Andruw Jones 6.00
PM Pedro J. Martinez 8.00
MO Magglio Ordonez 4.00
AP Albert Pujols 15.00
MR Manny Ramirez 6.00
IR Ivan Rodriguez 6.00
TS Tsuyoshi Shinjo 4.00
AS Alfonso Soriano 8.00
SS Sammy Sosa 10.00
MT Miguel Tejada 4.00
BW Bernie Williams 6.00

Corners

NM/M
Common Duo: 6.00
Inserted 1:12
Refractors: No Pricing
Production 25 Sets
CD Eric Chavez, Erubiel Durazo 6.00
VG Robin Ventura, Jason Giambi 10.00
WG Matt Williams, Mark Grace 8.00
RM Scott Rolen, Tino Martinez 10.00
BM Adrian Beltre, Fred McGriff 6.00
GS Troy Glaus, Scott Spiezio 8.00
KM Corey Koskie, Doug Mientkiewicz 6.00
BT David Bell, Jim Thome 10.00
BK Sean Burroughs, Ryan Klesko 6.00
AS Edgardo Alfonzo, J.T. Snow 6.00
TP Mark Teixeira, Rafael Palmeiro 10.00

Factor

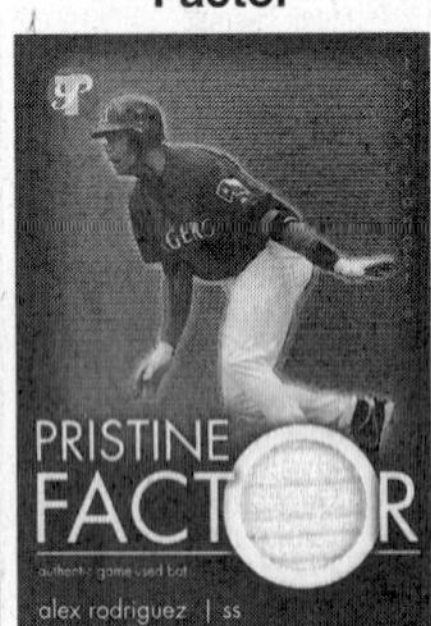

NM/M
Common Player: 4.00
Inserted 1:9
Refractors: No Pricing
Production 25 Sets
LB Lance Berkman 4.00
AD Adam Dunn 6.00
DE Darin Erstad 4.00
NG Nomar Garciaparra 10.00
JG Jason Giambi 6.00
TG Troy Glaus 5.00
VG Vladimir Guerrero 8.00
TH Todd Helton 6.00
TKH Torii Hunter 5.00
MO Magglio Ordonez 4.00
MP Mike Piazza 10.00
MR Manny Ramirez 6.00
AR Alex Rodriguez 10.00
AS Alfonso Soriano 8.00
SS Sammy Sosa 10.00

Mini

NM/M
Common Player: 1.00
RB Rocco Baldelli 1.50
BWB Bobby Basham 1.00
JB Jeremy Bonderman 4.00
BB Barry Bonds 6.00
BPB Bryan Bullington 3.00
RJC Robinson Cano 20.00
BC Bernie Castro 1.00
EC Eric Chavez 1.00
RC Roger Clemens 5.00
JC Jose Contreras 2.00
ELC Eric Crozier 1.00
RD Rajai Davis 1.00
NG Nomar Garciaparra 5.00
JG Jason Giambi 2.00
BG Brian Giles 1.50
VG Vladimir Guerrero 3.00
DH Dan Haren 4.00
MH Michel Hernandez 1.00
RH Ryan Howard 60.00
DJ Derek Jeter 6.00
AK Austin Kearns 2.00
JK Jeff Kent 1.50
JJK Jason Kubel 4.00
WL Wilfredo Ledezma 1.00
NL Nook Logan 1.00
TM Tyler Martin 1.00
DM Dustin McGowan 3.00
MO Magglio Ordonez 1.00
MJP Mike Piazza 4.00
MP Mark Prior 6.00
ER Elizardo Ramirez 1.00
AR Alex Rodriguez 6.00
RS Ryan Shealy 3.00
AS Alfonso Soriano 3.00
SS Sammy Sosa 4.00
IS Ichiro Suzuki 3.00
MT Miguel Tejada 1.50
JT Jim Thome 2.00
CW Chien-Ming Wang 40.00
KY Kevin Youkilis 6.00

Mini Autograph

NM/M
Production 100
RC Roger Clemens 125.00

Personal Endorsements

NM/M
Common Autograph: 6.00
Golds: No Pricing
Production 25 Sets
AB Andrew Brown 6.00
RYC Ryan Church 10.00
DE David Eckstein 10.00
LF Lew Ford 10.00
JG Jay Gibbons 10.00
RJH Rich Harden 25.00
KH Ken Harvey 6.00
PK Paul Konerko 20.00
ML Mike Lowell 10.00
VM Victor Martinez 20.00
BM Brett Myers 10.00
JP Josh Phelps 8.00
SR Scott Rolen 25.00
FS Felix Sanchez 6.00
KS Kelly Shoppach 15.00
MS Mike Sweeney 10.00
FV Fernando Vina 6.00

Primary Elements

NM/M
Many not priced due to scarcity.
Production 50 Sets
Refractors: No Pricing
Production 10
BRB Bret Boone 15.00
NG Nomar Garciaparra 35.00
LG Luis Gonzalez 10.00
SG Shawn Green 10.00
TH Todd Helton 20.00
TKH Torii Hunter 20.00
KI Kazuhisa Ishii 10.00
AJ Andruw Jones 15.00
CJ Chipper Jones 20.00
PM Pedro J. Martinez 20.00
MO Magglio Ordonez 10.00
RP Rafael Palmeiro 15.00
MP Mike Piazza 25.00
AR Alex Rodriguez 50.00
MT Miguel Tejada 15.00
BZ Barry Zito 15.00

Solo Bonds

NM/M
Common Bonds: 20.00
Refractors: No Pricing
Production 25
GG Barry Bonds 20.00
HR Barry Bonds 20.00
BB Barry Bonds 20.00
MVP Barry Bonds 20.00

Double Bonds

NM/M
Common Duo: 25.00
Refractors: No Pricing
Production 25
BJ Barry Bonds, Randy Johnson 50.00
BT Miguel Tejada, Barry Bonds 25.00
BM Willie Mays, Barry Bonds 75.00
BR Alex Rodriguez, Barry Bonds 35.00

2003 Topps Retired Signature Edition

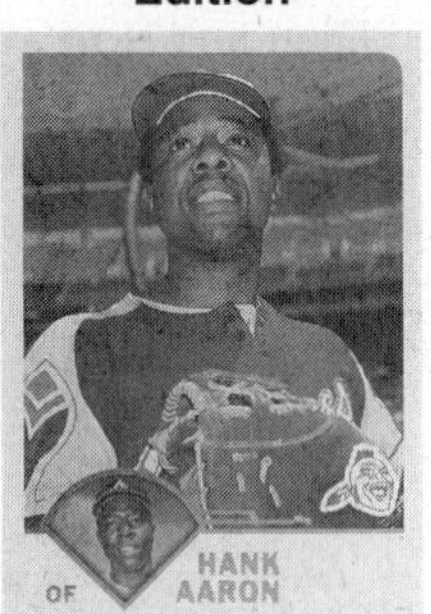

NM/M
Complete Set (110): 100.00
Common Player: .50
Pack (5): 30.00
Box (5): 120.00
1 Willie Mays 4.00
2 Tony Perez 1.00
3 Tom Seaver 2.00
4 Johnny Bench 4.00
5 Rod Carew 1.50
6 Red Schoendienst .50
7 Phil Rizzuto 1.00
8 Ozzie Smith 2.50
9 Maury Wills .50
10 Hank Aaron 4.00
11 Jim Palmer 1.00
12 Jose Cruz .50
13 Dave Parker .50
14 Don Sutton .75
15 Brooks Robinson 2.00
16 Bo Jackson 1.50
17 Andre Dawson .75
18 Fergie Jenkins .75
19 George Foster .50
20 George Brett 5.00
21 Jerry Koosman .50
22 John Kruk .50
23 Kent Tekulve .50
24 Lee Smith .50
25 Nolan Ryan 6.00
26 Paul O'Neill .50
27 Rich "Goose" Gossage .50
28 Ron Santo .50
29 Tom Lasorda .75
30 Tony Gwynn 2.00
31 Vida Blue .50
32 Whitey Herzog .50
33 Willie McGee .50
34 Bill Mazeroski .50
35 Al Kaline 3.00
36 Bobby Richardson .50
37 Carlton Fisk 1.00
38 Darrell Evans .50
39 Dave Concepcion .50
40 Cal Ripken Jr. 5.00
41 Dwight Evans .50
42 Earl Weaver .50
43 Fred Lynn .50
44 Greg Luzinski .50
45 Duke Snider 1.50
46 Hank Bauer .50
47 Jim Rice .50
48 Johnny Sain .50
49 Lenny Dykstra .50
50 Mike Schmidt 4.00
51 Orlando Cepeda 1.00
52 Ralph Kiner .75
53 Robin Roberts .50
54 Ron Guidry .50
55 Steve Garvey .50
56 Tony Oliva .50
57 Whitey Ford 1.00
58 Willie McCovey 1.00
59 Phil Niekro 1.00
60 Stan Musial 3.00
61 Rollie Fingers 1.00
62 Robin Yount 2.00
63 Alan Trammell 1.00
64 Bill Buckner .50
65 Bob Feller 1.00
66 Bruce Sutter .75
67 Dale Murphy 1.00
68 Dennis Eckersley 1.00
69 Don Newcombe .50
70 Don Mattingly 5.00
71 Dwight Gooden .75
72 Frank Robinson 1.50
73 Gary Carter .50
74 Graig Nettles .50
75 Harmon Killebrew 2.00
76 Jim Bunning .50
77 Joe Morgan 1.00
78 Joe Rudi .50
79 Jose Canseco 1.00
80 Ernie Banks 3.00
81 Luis Aparicio .50
82 Luis Tiant .50
83 Mark Fidrych .50
84 Kirk Gibson .50
85 Lou Brock 1.00
86 Juan Marichal 1.00
87 Monte Irvin 1.00
88 Paul Molitor 1.00
89 Tommy John .50
90 Warren Spahn 1.50
91 Wade Boggs 1.00
92 Reggie Jackson 2.00
93 Kirby Puckett 3.00
94 Boog Powell .50
95 Carl Yastrzemski 2.00
96 Bobby Thomson .50
97 Bill "Moose" Skowron .50
98 Bill Madlock .50
99 Sparky Anderson .50
100 Yogi Berra 2.00
101 Bobby Doerr .50
102 Gaylord Perry .50
103 George Kell .50
104 Harold Reynolds .50
105 Joe Carter .50
106 Johnny Podres .50
107 Ron Cey .50
108 Tim McCarver .50
109 Tug McGraw .50
110 Don Larsen 1.00

Black

Cards (1-110): 2-4X
Production 99 Sets

Autographs

NM/M
Common Autograph: 10.00
Inserted 1:1
Refractors: 1-2.5X
Production 25 Sets
HA Hank Aaron/30 300.00
JA Jim Abbott 20.00
SA Sparky Anderson 20.00
LA Luis Aparicio 12.00
HB Harold Baines 10.00
EB Ernie Banks/24 175.00
HBA Hank Bauer 20.00
JBE Johnny Bench 65.00
YB Yogi Berra/25 150.00
VB Vida Blue 15.00
BB Bert Blyleven 10.00
WB Wade Boggs/77 125.00
GB George Brett/25 180.00
LB Lou Brock/76 120.00
BBU Bill Buckner 10.00
JB Jim Bunning/76 100.00
JCA Jose Canseco 40.00
RCA Rod Carew 60.00
GC Gary Carter/77 100.00
JC Joe Carter 25.00
OC Orlando Cepeda/75 180.00
RCE Ron Cey 10.00
JCR Jose Cruz 10.00
AD Andre Dawson 20.00
BD Bobby Doerr 20.00
LD Lenny Dykstra 20.00
DEC Dennis Eckersley 65.00
DE Darrell Evans 10.00
DEV Dwight Evans/78 80.00
BF Bob Feller 20.00
MF Mark Fidrych 20.00
RF Rollie Fingers 25.00
CF Carlton Fisk 65.00
WF Whitey Ford 65.00
GF George Foster 10.00
SG Steve Garvey 15.00
KG Kirk Gibson 40.00
DG Dwight Gooden 30.00
RG Rich "Goose" Gossage 15.00
BGR Bobby Grich 15.00
KGR Ken Griffey Sr. 25.00
RGU Ron Guidry 35.00
TG Tony Gwynn/25 165.00
WH Whitey Herzog 15.00
BH Bob Horner 10.00
MI Monte Irvin 60.00
BJ Bo Jackson 75.00
RJ Reggie Jackson 100.00
FJ Fergie Jenkins 20.00
TJ Tommy John 25.00
AK Al Kaline 75.00
GK George Kell 30.00
HK Harmon Killebrew/76 150.00
RK Ralph Kiner 125.00
JK Jerry Koosman 25.00
JKR John Kruk 35.00
DL Don Larsen 15.00
TL Tom Lasorda/76 100.00
GL Greg Luzinski 15.00
FL Fred Lynn 20.00
BM Bill Madlock 10.00
JMA Juan Marichal 35.00
DON Don Mattingly/81 175.00
BMA Bill Mazeroski 15.00
TM Tim McCarver 25.00
WMC Willie McCovey 50.00
WMG Willie McGee 25.00
TMC Tug McGraw 50.00
PM Paul Molitor 75.00
JM Joe Morgan 35.00
DM Dale Murphy 40.00
SM Stan Musial/28 185.00
PN Phil Niekro 15.00
GN Graig Nettles 10.00
DN Don Newcombe 15.00
TO Tony Oliva 25.00
PO Paul O'Neill 50.00
JP Jim Palmer 50.00
DP Dave Parker 20.00
LP Lance Parrish 10.00
TP Terry Pendleton 10.00
TP Tony Perez 40.00
GP Gaylord Perry 10.00
JPI Jimmy Piersall 10.00
JPO Johnny Podres 10.00
BP Boog Powell 10.00
HR Harold Reynolds 20.00
JR Jim Rice 30.00
BR Bobby Richardson 15.00
CR Cal Ripken Jr./25 340.00
PR Phil Rizzuto/70 140.00
RR Robin Roberts 25.00
BRO Brooks Robinson/75 140.00
FR Frank Robinson 60.00
JRU Joe Rudi 10.00
NR Nolan Ryan/77 200.00
BSA Bret Saberhagen 25.00
RSA Ron Santo 20.00
MS Mike Schmidt/83 200.00
RS Red Schoendienst/83 100.00
TS Tom Seaver 65.00
BS Bill "Moose" Skowron 10.00
LS Lee Smith 15.00
OS Ozzie Smith 65.00
DSN Duke Snider/75 100.00
WS Warren Spahn 50.00
DS Dave Stieb 15.00
BSU Bruce Sutter 35.00
DSU Don Sutton 20.00
KT Kent Tekulve 20.00
BT Bobby Thomson 10.00
LT Luis Tiant 10.00
AT Alan Trammell 20.00
BW Bob Watson 10.00
EW Earl Weaver 12.00
MW Maury Wills 10.00
CY Carl Yastrzemski 80.00
RY Robin Yount/25 150.00

2003 Topps Total

NM/M
Complete Set (990): 125.00
Common Player: .10
Pack (10): 1.00
Box (36): 25.00
1 Brent Abernathy .10
2 Bobby Hill .10
3 Victor Martinez .10
4 Chip Ambres .10
5 Matt Anderson .10
6 Ricardo Aramboles .10
7 Carlos Pena .10
8 Aaron Guiel .10
9 Luke Allen .10
10 Francisco Rodriguez .20
11 Jason Marquis .10

12 Edwin Almonte .10
13 Grant Balfour .10
14 Adam Piatt .10
15 Andy Phillips .10
16 Adrian Beltre .10
17 Brandon Backe .10
18 Dave Berg .10
19 Brett Myers .10
20 Brian Meadows .10
21 Chin-Feng Chen .25
22 Blake Williams .10
23 Josh Bard .10
24 Josh Beckett .10
25 Kip Bouknight **RC** .20
26 Matt Childers .10
27 Adam Everett .10
28 Mike Bordick .10
29 Antonio Alfonseca .10
30 Doug Creek .10
31 J.D. Drew .20
32 Milton Bradley .10
33 David Wells .10
34 Vance Wilson .10
35 Jeff Fassero .10
36 Sandy Alomar .10
37 Ryan Vogelsong .10
38 Roger Clemens 1.25
39 Juan Gonzalez .40
40 Dustin Hermanson .10
41 Andy Ashby .10
42 Adam Hyzdu .10
43 Ben Broussard .10
44 Ryan Klesko .10
45 Chris Buglovsky .10
46 Bud Smith .10
47 Aaron Boone .10
48 Cliff Floyd .10
49 Alex Cora .10
50 Curt Schilling .40
51 Michael Cuddyer .10
52 Mike Venafro .10
53 Carlos Gullien .10
54 Angel Berroa .10
55 Eli Marrero .10
56 A.J. Burnett .10
57 Oliver Perez .10
58 Matt Morris .25
59 Valerio De Los Santos .10
60 Austin Kearns .50
61 Darren Dreifort .10
62 Jason Standridge .10
63 Carlos Silva .10
64 Moises Alou .20
65 Jason Anderson .10
66 Russell Branyan .10
67 B.J. Ryan .10
68 Cory Aldridge .10
69 Ellis Burks .10
70 Troy Glaus .50
71 Kelly Wunsch .10
72 Brad Wilkerson .10
73 Jayson Durocher .10
74 Tony Fiore .10
75 Brian Giles .25
76 Billy Wagner .10
77 Neifi Perez .10
78 Jose Valverde .10
79 Brent Butler .10
80 Mario Ramos .10
81 Kerry Robinson .10
82 Brent Mayne .10
83 Sean Casey .10
84 Danys Baez .10
85 Chase Utley .25
86 Jared Sandberg .10
87 Terrence Long .10
88 Kevin Walker .10
89 Royce Clayton .10
90 Shea Hillenbrand .10
91 Brad Lidge .10
92 Shawn Chacon .10
93 Kevin Frederick .10
94 Chris Snelling .10
95 Omar Vizquel .20
96 Joe Borchard .10
97 Matt Belisle .10
98 Steve Smyth .10
99 Raul Mondesi .20
100 Chipper Jones 1.00
101 Victor Alvarez .10
102 J.M. Gold .10
103 Willis Roberts .10
104 Eddie Guardado .10
105 Brad Voyles .10
106 Bronson Arroyo .10
107 Juan Castro .10
108 Dan Pleasac .10
109 Ramon Castro .10
110 Tim Salmon .25
111 Damion Easley .10
112 J.D. Closser .10
113 Mark Buehrle .10
114 Steve Karsay .10
115 Cristian Guerrero .10
116 Brad Ausmus .10
117 Cristian Guzman .10
118 Dan Wilson .10
119 Jake Westbrook .10
120 Manny Ramirez .50
121 Jason Giambi .75
122 Bob Wickman .10
123 Aaron Cook .10
124 Alfredo Amezaga .10
125 Corey Thurman .10
126 Brandon Puffer .10
127 Hee Seop Choi .25
128 Javier Vazquez .10
129 Carlos Valderrama .10
130 Jerome Williams .10
131 Wilson Betemit .10
132 Bruce Chen .10
133 Esteban Yan .10
134 Brandon Berger .10
135 Bill Hall .10
136 LaTroy Hawkins .10
137 Nate Cornejo .10
138 Jim Mecir .10
139 Joe Crede .10
140 Andres Galarraga .10
141 Dave Williams .10
142 Joey Eischen .10
143 Mike Timlin .10
144 Jose Cruz Jr. .10
145 Wes Helms .10
146 Brian Roberts .10
147 Bret Prinz .10
148 Brian Hunter .10
149 Chad Hermansen .10
150 Andruw Jones .40
151 Kurt Ainsworth .10
152 Clifford Bartosh .10
153 Kyle Lohse .10
154 Brian Jordan .10
155 Coco Crisp .10
156 Tomas Perez .10
157 Keith Foulke .10
158 Chris Carpenter .10
159 Mike Remlinger .10
160 Dewon Brazelton .10
161 Brook Fordyce .10
162 Rusty Greer .10
163 Scott Downs .10
164 Jason Dubois .10
165 David Coggin .10
166 Jose Hernandez .10
167 Carlos Hernandez .10
168 Matt Williams .10
169 Rheal Cormier .10
170 Duaner Sanchez .10
171 Craig Counsell .10
172 Edgar Martinez .20
173 Zack Greinke .10
174 Pedro Feliz .10
175 Randy Choate .10
176 Jon Garland .10
177 Keith Ginter .10
178 Carlos Febles .10
179 Gregor Blanco **RC** .10
180 Jack Cust .10
181 Koyie Hill .10
182 Ricky Gutierrez .10
183 Ben Grieve .10
184 Livan Hernandez .10
185 Jason Isringhausen .10
186 Gookie Dawkins .10
187 Roberto Alomar .40
188 Eric Junge .10
189 Carlos Beltran .10
190 Denny Hocking .10
191 Jason Schmidt .10
192 Cory Lidle .10
193 Robert Mackowiak .10
194 Charlton Jimerson **RC** .10
195 Darin Erstad .25
196 Jason Davis .10
197 Luis Castillo .10
198 Juan Encarnacion .10
199 Jeffrey Hammonds .10
199 .10
200 Nomar Garciaparra 1.50
201 Ryan Christianson .10
202 Willie Banks .10
203 Damian Moss .10
204 Chris Richard .10
205 Todd Hundley .10
206 Paul Bako .10
207 Adam Kennedy .10
208 Scott Hatteberg .10
209 Andy Pratt .10
210 Ken Griffey Jr. 1.00
211 Chris George .10
212 Lance Niekro .10
213 Greg Colbrunn .10
214 Herbert Perry .10
215 Cody Ransom .10
216 Craig Biggio .25
217 Miguel Batista .10
218 Alex Escobar .10
219 Willie Harris .10
220 Scott Strickland .10
221 Felix Rodriguez .10
222 Torii Hunter .25
223 Tyler Houston .10
224 Darrell May .10
225 Benito Santiago .10
226 Ryan Dempster .10
227 Andy Fox .10
228 Jung Bong .10
229 Jose Macias .10
230 Shannon Stewart .10
231 Buddy Groom .10
232 Eric Valent .10
233 Scott Schoeneweis .10
234 Corey Hart .10
235 Brett Tomko .10
236 Shane Bazzell **RC** .20
237 Tim Hummel .10
238 Al Reyes .10
239 Daryle Ward .10
240 Ismael Valdes .10
241 Brian Fuentes .10
242 Cesar Izturis .10
243 Mark Bellhorn .10
244 Geoff Jenkins .10
245 Derek Jeter 2.00
246 Anderson Machado .10
247 Dave Roberts .10
248 Jaime Cerda .10
249 Woody Williams .10
250 Vernon Wells .20
251 Jon Lieber .10
252 Franklyn German .10
253 David Segui .10
254 Freddy Garcia .10
255 James Baldwin .10
256 Tony Alvarez .10
257 Walter Young .10
258 Alex Herrera .10
259 Robert Fick .10
260 Rob Bell .10
261 Ross Gload .10
262 Dee Brown .10
263 Mike Bacsik .10
264 Corey Patterson .10
265 Marvin Bernard .10
266 Eddie Rogers .10
267 Elio Serrano .10
268 D'Angelo Jimenez .10
269 Adam Johnson .10
270 Gregg Zaun .10
271 Nick Johnson .10
272 Geoff Goetz .10
273 Ryan Drese .10
274 Eric DuBose .10
275 Barry Zito .25
276 Mike Crudale .10
277 Paul Byrd .10
278 Eric Gagne .10
279 Aramis Ramirez .10
280 Ray Durham .10
281 Tony Graffanino .10
282 Jeremy Guthrie .10
283 Erik Bedard .10
284 Vince Faison .10
285 Bobby Kielty .10
286 Francis Beltran .10
287 Alexis Gomez .10
288 Vladimir Guerrero .75
289 Kevin Appier .10
290 Gil Meche .10
291 Marquis Grissom .10
292 John Burkett .10
293 Vinny Castilla .10
294 Tyler Walker .10
295 Shane Halter .10
296 Geronimo Gil .10
297 Eric Hinske .10
298 Adam Dunn .50
299 Mike Kinkade .10
300 Mark Prior .50
301 Corey Koskie .10
302 David Dellucci .10
303 Todd Helton .40
304 Greg Miller .10
305 Delvin James .10
306 Humberto Cota .10
307 Aaron Harang .10
308 Jeremy Hill .10
309 Billy Koch .10
310 Brandon Claussen .10
311 Matt Ginter .10
312 Jason Lane .10
313 Ben Weber .10
314 Alan Benes .10
315 Oscar Herinquez .10
316 Danny Graves .10
317 Jason Johnson .10
318 Jason Grimsley .10
319 Steve Kline .10
320 Johnny Damon .10
321 Jay Gibbons .10
322 J.J. Putz .10
323 Stephen Randolph **RC** .10
324 Bobby Higginson .10
325 Kazuhisa Ishii .10
326 Carlos Lee .10
327 J.R. House .10
328 Mark Loretta .10
329 Mike Matheny .10
330 Ben Diggins .10
331 Seth Etherton .10
332 Eli Whiteside **RC** .20
333 Juan Rivera .10
334 Jeff Conine .10
335 John McDonald .10
336 Erik Hiljus .10
337 David Eckstein .10
338 Jeff Bagwell .50
339 Matt Holliday .25
340 Jeff Liefer .10
341 Greg Myers .10
342 Scott Sauerbeck .10
343 Omar Infante .10
344 Ryan Langerhans .10
345 Abraham Nunez .10
346 Mike MacDougal .10
347 Travis Phelps .10
348 Dan Reichert .10
349 Alex Rodriguez 1.50
350 Bobby Seay .10
351 Ichiro Suzuki 1.00
352 Brandon Inge .10
353 Jack Wilson .10
354 John Ennis .10
355 Jamal Strong .10
356 Jason Jennings .10
357 Jeff Kent .20
358 Scott Chiasson .10
359 Jeremy Griffiths .10
360 Paul Konerko .10
361 Jeff Austin .10
362 Todd Van Poppel .10
363 Sun-Woo Kim .10
364 Jerry Hairston .10
365 Tony Torcato .10
366 Arthur Rhodes .10
367 Jose Jimenez .10
368 Matt LeCroy .10
369 Curtis Lesanic .10
370 Ramon Vasquez .10
371 Joe Randa .10
372 John Franco .10
373 Charles Johnson .10
374 Craig Wilson .10
375 Michael Young .10
376 Mark Ellis .10
377 Joe Mauer .25
378 Checklist .10
379 Jason Kendall .10
380 Checklist .10
381 Alex Gonzalez .10
382 Flash Gordon .10
383 John Buck .10
384 Shigetoshi Hasegawa .10
385 Scott Stewart .10
386 Luke Hudson .10
387 Todd Jones .10
388 Fred McGriff .25
389 Mike Sweeney .10
390 Marlon Anderson .10
391 Terry Adams .10
392 Mark DeRosa .10
393 Doug Mientkiewicz .10
394 Miguel Cairo .10
395 Jamie Moyer .10
396 Josh Towers .10
397 Matt Clement .10
398 Bengie Molina .10
399 Marcus Thames .10
400 Nick Bierbrodt .10
401 Tim Kalita .10
402 Corwin Malone .10
403 Jesse Orosco .10
404 Brandon Phillips .10
405 Eric Cyr .10
406 Jason Michaels .10
407 Julio Lugo .10
408 Gabe Kapler .10
409 Mark Mulder .25
410 Adam Eaton .10
411 Ken Harvey .10
412 Jolbert Cabrera .10
413 Eric Milton .10
414 Josh Hall **RC** .20
415 Bob File .10
416 Brett Evert .10
417 Ron Chiavacci .10
418 Jorge De La Rosa .10
419 Quinton McCracken .10
420 Luther Hackman .10
421 Gary Knotts .10
422 Kevin Brown .20
423 Jeff Cirillo .10
424 Damaso Marte .10
425 Chan Ho Park .10
426 Nathan Haynes .10
427 Matt Lawton .10
428 Mike Stanton .10
429 Bernie Williams .40
430 Kevin Jarvis .10
431 Joe McEwing .10
432 Mark Kotsay .10
433 Juan Cruz .10
434 Russ Ortiz .10
435 Jeff Nelson .10
436 Alan Embree .10
437 Miguel Tejada .25
438 Kirk Saarloos .10
439 Cliff Lee .10
440 Ryan Ludwick .10
441 Derrek Lee .10
442 Bobby Abreu .20
443 Dustan Mohr .10
444 Nook Logan **RC** .25
445 Seth McClung .10
446 Miguel Olivo .10
447 Henry Blanco .10
448 Seung Jun Song .10
449 Kris Wilson .10
450 Xavier Nady .10
451 Corky Miller .10
452 Jim Thome .50
453 George Lombard .10
454 Rey Ordonez .10
455 Deivis Santos .10
456 Mike Myers .10
457 Edgar Renteria .10
458 Braden Looper .10
459 Guillermo Mota .10
460 Scott Rolen .50
461 Lance Berkman .10
462 Jeff Heaverlo .10
463 Ramon Hernandez .10
464 Jason Simontacchi .10
465 So Taguchi .10
466 Dave Veres .10
467 Shane Loux .10
468 Rodrigo Lopez .10
469 Bubba Trammell .10
470 Scott Sullivan .10
471 Mike Mussina .40
472 Ramon Ortiz .10
473 Lyle Overbay .10
474 Mike Lowell .10
475 Greg Vaughn .10
476 Larry Bigbie .10
477 Rey Sanchez .10
478 Magglio Ordonez .25
479 Rondell White .10
480 Jay Witasick .10
481 Jimmy Rollins .25
482 Mike Maroth .10
483 Mark Quinn .10
484 Nick Neugebauer .10
485 Victor Zambrano .10
486 Travis Lee .10
487 Bobby Bradley .10
488 Marcus Giles .10
489 Steve Trachsel .10
490 Derek Lowe .10
491 Hideo Nomo .25
492 Brad Hawpe .10
493 Jesus Medrano .10
494 Rick Ankiel .10
495 Pasqual Coco .10
496 Michael Barrett .10
497 Joe Beimel .10
498 Marty Cordova .10
499 Aaron Sele .10
500 Sammy Sosa 1.00
501 Ivan Rodriguez .40
502 Keith Osik .10
503 Hank Blalock .25
504 Craig Monroe .10
505 Junior Spivey .10
506 Edgardo Alfonzo .10
507 Alex Graman .10
508 J.J. Davis .10
509 Roger Cedeno .10
510 Joe Roa .10
511 Wily Mo Pena .10
512 Eric Munson .10
513 Arnie Munoz **RC** .10
514 Miguel Asencio .10
515 Andy Pettitte .25
516 Jim Edmonds .25
517 Jeff DaVanon .10
518 Aaron Myette .10
519 C.C. Sabathia .10
520 Gerardo Garcia .10
521 Brian Schneider .10
522 Wes Obermueller .10
523 John Mabry .10
524 Casey Fossum .10
525 Toby Hall .10
526 Denny Neagle .10
527 Willie Bloomquist .10
528 A.J. Pierzynski .10
529 Bartolo Colon .10
530 Chad Harville .10
531 Blaine Neal .10
532 Luis Terrero Jr. .10
533 Reggie Taylor .10
534 Melvin Mora .10
535 Tino Martinez .10
536 Peter Bergeron .10
537 Jorge Padilla .10
538 Oscar Villarreal **RC** .20
539 David Weathers .10
540 Mike Lamb .10
541 Greg Norton .10
542 Michael Tucker .10
543 Ben Kozlowski .10
544 Alex Sanchez .10
545 Trey Lunsford .10
546 Abraham Nunez .10
547 Mike Lincoln .10
548 Orlando Hernandez .10
549 Kevin Mench .10
550 Garret Anderson .25
551 Kyle Farnsworth .10
552 Kevin Olsen .10
553 Joel Pineiro .10
554 Jorge Julio .10
555 Jose Mesa .10
556 Jorge Posada .40
557 Jose Ortiz .10
558 Mike Tonis .10
559 Gabe White .10
560 Rafael Furcal .10
561 Matt Franco .10
562 Trey Hodges .10
563 Esteban German .10
564 Josh Fogg .10
565 Fernando Tatis .10
566 Alex Cintron .10
567 Grant Roberts .10
568 Gene Stechschulte .10
569 Rafael Palmeiro .25
570 Mike Hampton .10
571 Ben Davis .10
572 Dean Palmer .10
573 Jerrod Riggan .10
574 Nate Frese .10
575 Josh Phelps .10
576 Freddie Bynum .10
577 Morgan Ensberg .10
578 Juan Rincon .10
579 Kazuhiro Sasaki .10
580 Yorvit Torrealba .10
581 Tim Wakefield .10
582 Sterling Hitchcock .10
583 Craig Paquette .10
584 Kevin Millwood .25
585 Damian Rolls .10
586 Brad Baisley .10
587 Kyle Snyder .10
588 Paul Quantrill .10
589 Trot Nixon .10
590 J.T. Snow .10
591 Kevin Young .10
592 Tomokazu Ohka .10
593 Brian Boehringer .10
594 Danny Patterson .10
595 Jeff Tam .10
596 Anastacio Martinez .10
597 Rod Barajas .10
598 Octavio Dotel .10
599 Jason Tyner .10
600 Gary Sheffield .40
601 Ruben Quevedo .10
602 Jay Payton .10
603 Mo Vaughn .10
604 Pat Burrell .40
605 Fernando Vina .10
606 Wes Anderson .10
607 Alex Gonzalez .10
608 Ted Lilly .10
609 Nick Punto .10
610 Ryan Madson .10
611 Odalis Perez .10
612 Chris Woodward .10
613 John Olerud .25
614 Brad Cresse .10
615 Chad Zerbe .10
616 Brad Penny .10
617 Barry Larkin .40
618 Brandon Duckworth .10
619 Brad Radke .10
620 Giovanni Carrara .10
621 Juan Pierre .10
622 Rick Reed .10
623 Omar Daal .10
624 Jose Hernandez .10
625 Greg Maddux 1.00
626 Henry Mateo .10
627 Kip Wells .10
628 Kevin Cash .10
629 Mark Redman .10
630 Luis Gonzalez .25
631 Jason Conti .10
632 Ricardo Rincon .10
633 Mike Bynum .10
634 Mike Redmond .10
635 Chance Capel .10
636 Chris Widger .10
637 Michael Restovich .10
638 Mark Grudzielanek .10
639 Brandon Larson .10
640 Luis De Los Santos .10
641 Javy Lopez .20
642 Rene Reyes .10
643 Orlando Merced .10
644 Jason Phillips .10
645 Luis Ugueto .10
646 Ron Calloway .10
647 Josh Paul .10
648 Todd Greene .10
649 Joe Giradi .10
650 Todd Ritchie .10
651 Lou Merloni .10
652 Shawn Wooten .10
653 David Riske .10
654 Luis Rivas .10
655 Roy Halladay .10
656 Travis Driskill .10
657 Ricky Ledee .10
658 Tony Perez .10
659 Fernando Rodney .10
660 Trevor Hoffman .10
661 Pat Hentgen .10
662 Bret Boone .10
663 Ryan Jensen .10
664 Ricardo Rodriguez .10
665 Jeremy Lambert .10
666 Troy Percival .10
667 Jon Rauch .10
668 Mariano Rivera .25
669 Jason LaRue .10
670 J.C. Romero .10
671 Cody Ross .10
672 Eric Byrnes .10
673 Paul LoDuca .10
674 Brad Fullmer .10
675 Cliff Politte .10
676 Justin Miller .10
677 Nic Jackson .10
678 Kris Benson .10
679 Carl Sadler .10
680 Joe Nathan .10
681 Julio Santana .10
682 Wade Miller .10
683 Josh Pearce .10
684 Tony Armas .10
685 Al Leiter .10
686 Raul Ibanez .10
687 Danny Bautista .10
688 Travis Hafner .10
689 Rylan Reed **RC** .20
690 Pedro J. Martinez .75
691 Ramon Santiago .10
692 Felipe Lopez .10
693 David Ross .10
694 Chone Figgins .10
695 Antonio Osuna .10
696 Jay Powell .10
697 Roy Smith .10
698 Alexis Rios .10
699 Tanyon Sturtze .10
700 Turk Wendell .10
701 Richard Hidalgo .10
702 Joe Mays .10
703 Jorge Sosa .10
704 Eric Karros .10
705 Steve Finley .10
706 Sean Smith .10
707 Jeremy Giambi .10
708 Scott Hodges .10
709 Vicente Padilla .10
710 Bert Snow .10
711 Aaron Rowand .10
712 Dennis Tankersley .10
713 Rick Bauer .10
714 Tim Olson **RC** .25
715 Jeff Urban .10
716 Steve Sparks .10
717 Glendon Rusch .10
718 Ricky Stone .10

719 Benji Gil .10
720 Pete Walker .10
721 Tim Worrell .10
722 Michael Tejera .10
723 David Kelton .10
724 Britt Reames .10
725 John Stephens .10
726 Mark McLemore .10
727 Jeff Zimmerman .10
728 Checklist .10
729 Andres Torres .10
730 Checklist .10
731 Johan Santana .10
732 Dane Sardinha .10
733 Rodrigo Rosario .10
734 Frank Thomas .50
735 Tom Glavine .25
736 Doug Mirabelli .10
737 Juan Uribe .10
738 Ryan Anderson .10
739 Sean Burroughs .10
740 Eric Chavez .25
741 Enrique Wilson .10
742 Elmer Dessens .10
743 Marlon Byrd .10
744 Brendan Donnelly .10
745 Gary Bennett .10
746 Roy Oswalt .25
747 Andy Van Hekken .10
748 Jesus Colome .10
749 Erick Almonte .10
750 Frank Catalanotto .10
751 Matt Herges .10
752 Carlos Delgado .40
753 Ryan Franklin .10
754 Wilken Ruan .10
755 Kelvim Escobar .10
756 Tim Drew .10
757 Jarrod Washburn .10
758 Runelvys Hernandez .10
759 Cory Vance .10
760 Doug Glanville .10
761 Ryan Rupe .10
762 Jermaine Dye .10
763 Mike Cameron .10
764 Scott Erickson .10
765 Richie Sexson .25
766 Jose Vidro .10
767 Brian West .10
768 Shawn Estes .10
769 Brian Tallet .10
770 Larry Walker .25
771 Josh Hamilton .10
772 Orlando Hudson .10
773 Justin Morneau .20
774 Ryan Bukvich .10
775 Mike Gonzalez .10
776 Tsuyoshi Shinjo .10
777 Matt Mantei .10
778 Jimmy Journell .10
779 Brian Lawrence .10
780 Mike Lieberthal .10
781 Scott Mullen .10
782 Zach Day .10
783 John Thomson .10
784 Ben Sheets .10
785 Damon Minor .10
786 Jose Valentin .10
787 Armando Benitez .10
788 Jamie Walker .10
789 Preston Wilson .10
790 Josh Wilson .10
791 Phil Nevin .10
792 Roberto Hernandez .10
793 Mike Williams .10
794 Jake Peavy .10
795 Paul Shuey .10
796 Chad Bradford .10
797 Bobby Jenks .10
798 Sean Douglass .10
799 Damian Miller .10
800 Mark Wohlers .10
801 Ty Wigginton .10
802 Alfonso Soriano 1.00
803 Randy Johnson .75
804 Placido Polanco .10
805 Drew Henson .10
806 Tony Womack .10
807 Pokey Reese .10
808 Albert Pujols .75
809 Shane Reynolds .10
810 Mike Rivera .10
811 John Lackey .10
812 Brian Wright **RC** .20
813 Eric Good .10
814 Dernell Stenson .10
815 Kirk Rueter .10
816 Todd Zeile .10
817 Brad Thomas .10
818 Shawn Sedlacek .10
819 Garrett Stephenson .10
820 Mark Teixeira .25
821 Tim Hudson .25
822 Mike Koplove .10
823 Chris Reitsma .10
824 Rafael Soriano .10
825 Ugueth Urbina .10
826 Matt White .10
827 Colin Young .10
828 Pat Strange .10
829 Juan Pena .10
830 Joe Thurston .10
831 Shawn Green .25
832 Pedro Astacio .10
833 Danny Wright .10
834 Weston O'Brien **RC** .20
835 Luis Lopez .10
836 Randall Simon .10
837 Jaret Wright .10
838 Jayson Werth .10
839 Endy Chavez .10
840 Checklist .10
841 Chad Paronto .10
842 Randy Winn .10
843 Sidney Ponson .10
844 Robin Ventura .10
845 Rich Aurilia .10
846 Joaquin Benoit .10
847 Barry Bonds 2.00
848 Carl Crawford .10
849 Jeromy Burnitz .10
850 Orlando Cabrera .10
851 Luis Vizcaino .10
852 Randy Wolf .10
853 Benny Agbayani .10
854 Jeremy Affeldt .10
855 Einar Diaz .10
856 Carl Everett .10
857 Wiki Gonzalez .10
858 Steve Belcher .10
859 Travis Harper .10
860 Mike Piazza 1.25
861 Will Ohman .10
862 Eric Young .10
863 Jason Grabowski .10
864 Rett Johnson **RC** .20
865 Aubrey Huff .10
866 John Smoltz .10
867 Mickey Callaway .10
868 Joe Kennedy .10
869 Tim Redding .10
870 Colby Lewis .10
871 Salomon Torres .10
872 Marco Scutaro .10
873 Tony Batista .10
874 Dmitri Young .10
875 Scott Williamson .10
876 Scott Spezio .10
877 John Webb .10
878 Jose Acevedo .10
879 Kevin Orie .10
880 Jacque Jones .10
881 Ben Francisco **RC** .25
882 Bobby Basham **RC** .25
883 Corey Shafer **RC** .20
884 J.D. Durbin **RC** .20
885 Chien-Ming Wang **RC** 2.50
886 Adam Stern .10
887 Wayne Lydon **RC** .20
888 Derell McCall **RC** .20
889 Jon Nelson **RC** .20
890 Willie Eyre **RC** .20
891 Ramon A. Martinez **RC** .20
892 Adrian Myers **RC** .20
893 Jamie Athas **RC** .20
894 Ismael Castro **RC** .20
895 David Martinez .10
896 Terry Tiffee **RC** .20
897 Nathan Panther **RC** .25
898 Kyle Roat **RC** .20
899 Kason Gabbard **RC** .75
900 Hanley Ramirez **RC** 3.00
901 Bryan Grace **RC** .15
902 B.J. Barns **RC** .50
903 Greg Bruso **RC** .15
904 Mike Neu **RC** .15
905 Dustin Yount **RC** .50
906 Shane Victorino **RC** .20
907 Brian Burgamy **RC** .20
908 Beau Kemp **RC** .20
909 Eny Cabreja **RC** .50
910 Dexter Cooper **RC** .20
911 Chris Colton **RC** .20
912 David Cash **RC** .20
913 Bernie Castro **RC** .20
914 Luis Hodge **RC** .20
915 Jeff Clark **RC** .20
916 Jason Kubel **RC** 1.00
917 T.J. Bohn **RC** .20
918 Luke Steidlmayer **RC** .20
919 Natthew Petterson .10
920 Darrell Rasner .10
921 Scott Tyler .10
922 Gary Schneidmiller **RC** .20
923 Kerry Wood .40
924 Ryan Cameron **RC** .20
925 Wilfredo Rodriguez .10
926 Rajai Davis **RC** .20
927 Evel Bastida-Martinez **RC** .20
928 Chris Duncan **RC** 2.00
929 David Pember **RC** .20
930 Branden Florence **RC** .20
931 Eric Eckenstahler .10
932 Hong-Chih Kuo **RC** 1.00
933 Il Kim **RC** .20
934 Michael Garciaparra .50
935 Tommy Whiteman **RC** .10
936 Gary Harris **RC** .20
937 Derry Hammond .10
938 Joey Gomes .10
939 Donald Hood **RC** .20
940 Clay Hensley **RC** .50
941 David Pahucki **RC** .20
942 Wilton Reynolds **RC** .20
943 Michael Hinckley **RC** .20
944 Josh Willingham **RC** .20
945 Pete LaForest **RC** .20
946 Pete Smart .10
947 Jay Stizman .10
948 Mark Malaska **RC** .20
949 Mike Gallo **RC** .20
950 Tyler Martin **RC** .20
951 Shane Victorino .20
952 Ryan Howard 30.00
953 Daryl Clark **RC** .20
954 Dayton Buller .10
955 Carlos Zambrano .10
956 Chris Booker .10
957 Brandon Watson **RC** .20
958 Matt DeMarco **RC** .20
959 Doug Waechter **RC** .75
960 Callix Crabbe **RC** .20
961 Jairo Garcia **RC** .20
962 Jason Perry **RC** .20
963 Eric Riggs **RC** .20
964 Travis Ishikawa **RC** .40
965 Jorge Piedra **RC** .20
966 Manuel Ramirez **RC** .20
967 Tyler Johnson **RC** .20
968 Jaime Bubela **RC** .20
969 Haj Turay **RC** .20
970 Tyson Graham **RC** .20
971 David DeJesus **RC** .20
972 Franklin Gutierrez **RC** .20
973 Craig Brazell **RC** 1.00
974 Keith Stamler **RC** .20
975 Jemel Spearman **RC** .20
976 Kade Johnson **RC** .10
977 Nick Trzesniak **RC** .20
978 Bill Simon **RC** .20
979 Matthew Hagen **RC** .20
980 Kris Kroski **RC** .20
981 Prentice Redman **RC** .50
982 Kevin Randel **RC** .20
983 Thomari Stori-Harden .10
984 Brian Shackelford **RC** .20
985 Mike Adams **RC** .20
986 Brian McCann 5.00
987 Mike McNutt **RC** .20
988 Aron Weston **RC** .20
989 Dustin Moseley **RC** .20
990 Bryan Bullington **RC** 1.50

Silver

Stars (1-990): 1-2X
Inserted 1:1

Award Winners

NM/M
Complete Set (30): 20.00
Common Player: .50
Inserted 1:12
AW1 Barry Zito .75
AW2 Randy Johnson 1.50
AW3 Miguel Tejada .75
AW4 Barry Bonds 3.00
AW5 Sammy Sosa 2.00
AW6 Barry Bonds 3.00
AW7 Mike Piazza 2.50
AW8 Todd Helton .75
AW9 Jeff Kent .50
AW10 Edgar Renteria .50
AW11 Scott Rolen .75
AW12 Vladimir Guerrero 1.00
AW13 Mike Hampton .50
AW14 Jason Giambi 1.50
AW15 Alfonso Soriano 1.50
AW16 Alex Rodriguez 3.00
AW17 Eric Chavez .50
AW18 Jorge Posada .50
AW19 Bernie Williams .75
AW20 Magglio Ordonez .50
AW21 Garret Anderson .50
AW22 Manny Ramirez 1.00
AW23 Jason Jennings .50
AW24 Eric Hinske .50
AW25 Billy Koch .50
AW26 John Smoltz .50
AW27 Alex Rodriguez 3.00
AW28 Barry Bonds 3.00
AW29 Tony LaRussa .50
AW30 Mike Scioscia .50

Total Production

NM/M
Complete Set (10): 10.00
Common Player: .40
Inserted 1:18
TP1 Barry Bonds 2.50
TP2 Manny Ramirez .75
TP3 Albert Pujols 1.00
TP4 Jason Giambi 1.00
TP5 Magglio Ordonez .40
TP6 Mike Piazza 1.50
TP7 Todd Helton .75
TP8 Miguel Tejada .50
TP9 Sammy Sosa 1.50
TP10 Alex Rodriguez 2.50

Total Signatures

NM/M
Common Autograph:
Inserted 1:176
MB Marlon Byrd 10.00
EM Eli Marrero 8.00
BP Brandon Phillips 10.00
MT Marcus Thames 8.00
TT Tony Torcato 8.00

Total Topps

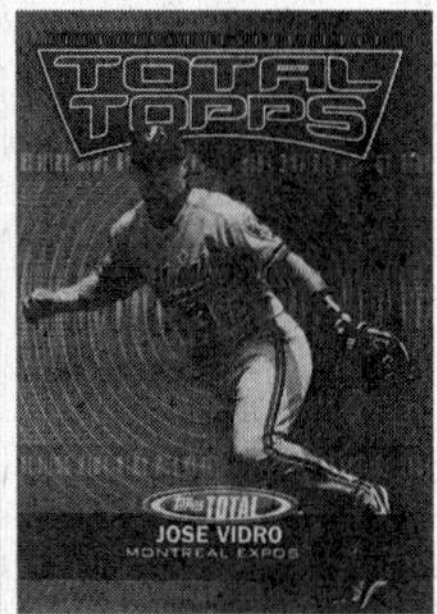

NM/M
Complete Set (50): 25.00
Common Player: .25
Inserted 1:7
TT1 Ichiro Suzuki 1.50
TT2 Alex Rodriguez 2.50
TT3 Barry Bonds 2.50
TT4 Jason Giambi 1.00
TT5 Troy Glaus .75
TT6 Greg Maddux 1.50
TT7 Albert Pujols 1.00
TT8 Randy Johnson 1.00
TT9 Chipper Jones 1.50
TT10 Magglio Ordonez .25
TT11 Jim Thome .75
TT12 Jeff Kent .40
TT13 Curt Schilling .50
TT14 Alfonso Soriano 1.00
TT15 Rafael Palmeiro .50
TT16 Carlos Delgado .50
TT17 Torii Hunter .50
TT18 Pat Burrell .50
TT19 Adam Dunn .75
TT20 Roberto Alomar .50
TT21 Eric Chavez .40
TT22 Derek Jeter 3.00
TT23 Nomar Garciaparra 2.00
TT24 Lance Berkman .40
TT25 Jim Edmonds .40
TT26 Todd Helton .75
TT27 Sammy Sosa 1.50
TT28 Phil Nevin .25
TT29 Andruw Jones .40
TT30 Barry Zito .50
TT31 Richie Sexson .40
TT32 Ken Griffey Jr. 1.50
TT33 Gary Sheffield .40
TT34 Shawn Green .40
TT35 Mike Sweeney .25
TT36 Mike Lowell .25
TT37 Larry Walker .40
TT38 Manny Ramirez .75
TT39 Miguel Tejada .40
TT40 Mike Piazza 2.00
TT41 Scott Rolen .75
TT42 Brian Giles .40
TT43 Garret Anderson .40
TT44 Vladimir Guerrero .75
TT45 Bartolo Colon .25
TT46 Jorge Posada .40
TT47 Ivan Rodriguez .50
TT48 Ryan Klesko .25
TT49 Jose Vidro .25
TT50 Pedro J. Martinez .75

2003 Topps Traded & Rookies

NM/M
Complete Set (275): 50.00
Common Player: .15
Pack (8 + 2 Chrome): 2.00
Box (24): 40.00
Chrome Cards: 2-4X
T1 Juan Pierre .15
T2 Mark Grudzielanek .15
T3 Tanyon Sturtze .15
T4 Greg Vaughn .15
T5 Greg Myers .15
T6 Randall Simon .15
T7 Todd Hundley .15
T8 Marlon Anderson .15
T9 Jeff Reboulet .15
T10 Alex Sanchez .15
T11 Mike Rivera .15
T12 Todd Walker .15
T13 Ray King .15
T14 Shawn Estes .15
T15 Gary Mathews Jr. .15
T16 Jaret Wright .15
T17 Edgardo Alfonzo .15
T18 Omar Daal .15
T19 Ryan Rupe .15
T20 Tony Clark .15
T21 Damon Minor .15
T22 Mike Stanton .15
T23 Ramon Martinez .15
T24 Armando Rios .15
T25 Johnny Estrada .15
T26 Joe Girardi .15
T27 Ivan Rodriguez .75
T28 Robert Fick .15
T29 Rick White .15
T30 Robert Person .15
T31 Alan Benes .15
T32 Chris Carpenter .40
T33 Chris Widger .15
T34 Travis Hafner .40
T35 Mike Venafro .15
T36 Jon Lieber .15
T37 Orlando Hernandez .15
T38 Aaron Myette .15
T39 Paul Bako .15
T40 Erubiel Durazo .15
T41 Mark Guthrie .15
T42 Steve Avery .15
T43 Damian Jackson .15
T44 Rey Ordonez .15
T45 John Flaherty .15
T46 Byung-Hyun Kim .15
T47 Tom Goodwin .15
T48 Elmer Dessens .15
T49 Al Martin .15
T50 Gene Kingsale .15
T51 Lenny Harris .15
T52 David Ortiz .75
T53 John Rocker .15
T54 Mike DiFelice .15
T55 Nick Bierbrodt .15
T56 Todd Zeile .15
T57 Roberto Hernandez .15
T58 Albie Lopez .15
T59 Roberto Alomar .50
T60 Russ Ortiz .15
T61 Brian Daubach .15
T62 Carl Everett .15
T63 Jeromy Burnitz .15
T64 Mark Bellhorn .15
T65 Ruben Sierra .15
T66 Mike Fetters .15
T67 Armando Benitez .15
T68 Deivi Cruz .15
T69 Jose Cruz Jr. .15
T70 Jeremy Fikac .15
T71 Jeff Kent .25
T72 Andres Galarraga .25
T73 Rickey Henderson .50
T74 Royce Clayton .15
T75 Troy O'Leary .15
T76 Ron Coomer .15
T77 Greg Colbrunn .15
T78 Wes Helms .15
T79 Kevin Millwood .25
T80 Damion Easley .15
T81 Bobby Kielty .15
T82 Keith Osik .15
T83 Ramiro Mendoza .15
T84 Shea Hillenbrand .15
T85 Shannon Stewart .15
T86 Eddie Perez .15
T87 Ugueth Urbina .15
T88 Orlando Palmeiro .15
T89 Graeme Lloyd .15
T90 John Vander Wal .15
T91 Gary Bennett .15
T92 Shane Reynolds .15
T93 Steve Parris .15
T94 Julio Lugo .15
T95 John Halama .15
T96 Carlos Baerga .15
T97 Jim Parque .15
T98 Mike Williams .15
T99 Fred McGriff .25
T100 Kenny Rogers .15
T101 Matt Herges .15
T102 Jay Bell .15
T103 Esteban Yan .15
T104 Eric Owens .15
T105 Aaron Fultz .15
T106 Rey Sanchez .15
T107 Jim Thome .75
T108 Aaron Boone .25
T109 Raul Mondesi .25
T110 Kenny Lofton .25
T111 Jose Guillen .15
T112 Aramis Ramirez .40
T113 Sidney Ponson .15
T114 Scott Williamson .15
T115 Robin Ventura .25
T116 Dusty Baker .15
T117 Felipe Alou .15
T118 Buck Showalter .15
T119 Jack McKeon .15
T120 Art Howe .15
T121 Bobby Crosby .40
T122 Adrian Gonzalez .25
T123 Kevin Cash .15
T124 Shin-Soo Choo .15
T125 Chin-Feng Chen .25
T126 Miguel Cabrera .75
T127 Jason Young .15
T128 Alex Herrera .15
T129 Jason Dubois .15
T130 Jeff Mathis .15
T131 Casey Kotchman .25
T132 Ed Rogers .15
T133 Wilson Betemit .15
T134 Jim Kavourias .15
T135 Taylor Buchholz .15
T136 Adam LaRoche .15
T137 Dallas McPherson .40
T138 Jesus Cota .15
T139 Clint Nageotte .15
T140 Boof Bonser .15
T141 Walter Young .15
T142 Joe Crede .25
T143 Denny Bautista .15
T144 Victor Diaz .15
T145 Chris Narveson .15
T146 Gabe Gross .15
T147 Jimmy Journell .15
T148 Rafael Soriano .15
T149 Jerome Williams .15
T150 Aaron Cook .15
T151 Anastacio Martinez .15
T152 Scott Hairston .15
T153 John Buck .15
T154 Ryan Ludwick .15
T155 Chris Bootcheck .15
T156 John Rheinecker .15
T157 Jason Lane .15
T158 Shelley Duncan .15
T159 Adam Wainwright .15
T160 Jason Arnold .15
T161 Jonny Gomes .15
T162 James Loney .50
T163 Mike Fontenot .15
T164 Khalil Greene 1.00
T165 Sean Burnett .15
T166 David Martinez .15
T167 Felix Pie **RC** 3.00
T168 Joe Valentine **RC** .50
T169 Brandon Webb **RC** 1.50
T170 Matt Diaz **RC** .25
T171 Lew Ford **RC** .75
T172 Jeremy Griffiths .25
T173 Matt Hensley **RC** .50
T174 Charlie Manning **RC** .25
T175 Elizardo Ramirez **RC** .75
T176 Greg Aquino **RC** .25
T177 Felix Sanchez **RC** .50
T178 Kelly Shoppach **RC** .75
T179 Bubba Nelson **RC** .50
T180 Mike O'Keefe **RC** .25
T181 Hanley Ramirez **RC** 5.00
T182 Todd Wellemeyer **RC** .50
T183 Dustin Moseley **RC** .25
T184 Eric Crozier **RC** .50
T185 Ryan Shealy **RC** 1.00
T186 Jeremy Bonderman 2.00
T187 Thomari Story-Harden **RC** .40
T188 Dusty Brown **RC** .50
T189 Rob Hammock **RC** .40
T190 Jorge Piedra **RC** .25
T191 Chris De La Cruz **RC** .25
T192 Eli Whiteside **RC** .25
T193 Jason Kubel **RC** 1.00
T194 Jon Schuerholz **RC** .25
T195 Stephen Randolph **RC** .25
T196 Andy Sisco .75
T197 Sean Smith .15
T198 Jon-Mark Sprowl **RC** .75
T199 Matt Kata **RC** .40
T200 Robinson Cano **RC** 6.00
T201 Nook Logan **RC** .25
T202 Ben Francisco **RC** .25
T203 Arnie Munoz **RC** .25
T204 Eric Chavez .15
T205 Eric Riggs **RC** .25

T206 Beau Kemp **RC** .25
T207 Travis Wong **RC** .50
T208 Dustin Yount **RC** .50
T209 Brian McCann 4.00
T210 Wilton Reynolds **RC** .25
T211 Matt Bruback **RC** .50
T212 Andrew Brown **RC** .50
T213 Edgar Gonzalez **RC** .25
T214 Eider Torres **RC** .25
T215 Aquilino Lopez **RC** .25
T216 Bobby Basham **RC** .50
T217 Tim Olson **RC** .50
T218 Nathan Panther **RC** .50
T219 Bryan Grace **RC** .25
T220 Dusty Gomon **RC** .25
T221 Wilfredo Ledezma **RC** .25
T222 Josh Willingham **RC** .75
T223 David Cash **RC** .25
T224 Oscar Villarreal **RC** .25
T225 Jeff Duncan **RC** .50
T226 Kade Johnson **RC** .25
T227 Luke Steidlmayer **RC** .25
T228 Brandon Watson **RC** .50
T229 Jose Morales .25
T230 Mike Gallo **RC** .25
T231 Tyler Adamczyk **RC** .50
T232 Adam Stern .15
T233 Brennan King **RC** .25
T234 Dan Haren 1.00
T235 Michel Hernandez **RC** .25
T236 Ben Fritz .15
T237 Clay Hensley **RC** .50
T238 Tyler Johnson **RC** .25
T239 Pete LaForest **RC** .25
T240 Tyler Martin **RC** .25
T241 J.D. Durbin **RC** .50
T242 Shane Victorino **RC** .25
T243 Rajai Davis **RC** .50
T244 Ismael Castro **RC** .25
T245 Chien-Ming Wang **RC** 4.00
T246 Travis Ishikawa **RC** .40
T247 Corey Shafer **RC** .50
T248 Gary Schneidmiller **RC** .25
T249 David Pember **RC** .25
T250 Keith Stamler **RC** .25
T251 Tyson Graham **RC** .25
T252 Ryan Cameron **RC** .25
T253 Eric Eckenstahler .25
T254 Matthew Peterson **RC** .25
T255 Dustin McGowan **RC** 1.00
T256 Prentice Redman **RC** .40
T257 Haj Turay **RC** .25
T258 Carlos Guzman **RC** .40
T259 Matt DeMarco **RC** .25
T260 Derek Michaelis **RC** .25
T261 Brian Burgamy **RC** .25
T262 Jay Sitzman **RC** .25
T263 Chris Fallon **RC** .25
T264 Mike Adams **RC** .25
T265 Clint Barmes **RC** .75
T266 Eric Reed **RC** .50
T267 Willie Eyre **RC** .25
T268 Carlos Duran **RC** .40
T269 Nick Trzesniak **RC** .25
T270 Ferdin Tejeda **RC** .50
T271 Michael Garciaparra .25
T272 Michael Hinckley **RC** .75
T273 Branden Florence **RC** .25
T274 Trent Oeltjen **RC** .40
T275 Mike Neu **RC** .25

Chrome Refractor

Stars: 4-8X
Rookies: 2-4X
Inserted 1:12

Gold

Stars: 5-10X
Rookies: 1-2.5X
Production 2003 Sets

Future Phenoms

NM/M
Common Player: 4.00
RB Rocco Baldelli 6.00
WB Wilson Betemit 4.00
HB Hank Blalock 6.00
WPB Willie Bloomquist 15.00
MB Marlon Byrd 4.00
CC Chin-Feng Chen 20.00
CDC Carl Crawford 6.00
TH Travis Hafner 6.00
TAH Trey Hodges 4.00
JM Justin Morneau 10.00
BP Brandon Phillips 4.00
MR Michael Restovich 6.00
CS Chris Snelling 4.00
MT Mark Teixeira 8.00
JT Joe Thurston 4.00

Hall of Fame

NM/M
Common Player: 8.00
GC Gary Carter 8.00
EM Eddie Murray 15.00

Hall of Fame Dual

NM/M
Complete Set (1):
CM Gary Carter, Eddie Murray 25.00

Signature Moves

NM/M
Common Player: 8.00
EA Erick Almonte 8.00
DB David Bell 10.00
JB Joe Borchard 8.00
BC Bartolo Colon 12.00
JC Jose Cruz Jr. 8.00
JJC Jack Cust 10.00
RF Robert Fick 8.00
CF Cliff Floyd 15.00
JF Jesse Foppert 10.00
JG Joey Gomes 8.00
KG Khalil Greene 25.00
JL James Loney 25.00
VM Victor Martinez 20.00
FP Felix Pie 60.00
ER Elizardo Ramirez 12.00
JR Jose Reyes 40.00
JS Jason Stokes 15.00
MT Mark Teixeira 25.00
BU B.J. Upton 25.00
WY Walter Young 10.00

Tools of the Trade

NM/M
Common Player: 4.00
EA Edgardo Alfonzo 4.00
DB David Bell 4.00
JC Jose Cruz Jr. 4.00
ED Erubiel Durazo 4.00
RD Ray Durham 4.00
RF Robert Fick 4.00
CF Cliff Floyd 4.00
AG Andres Galarraga 5.00
JG Jeremy Giambi 4.00
TG Tom Glavine 6.00
EK Eric Karros 5.00
JK Jeff Kent 5.00
KL Kenny Lofton 10.00
FL Felipe Lopez 6.00
FM Fred McGriff 6.00
KM Kevin Millar 5.00
RO Rey Ordonez 4.00
JP Juan Pierre 5.00
SH Tsuyoshi Shinjo 4.00
SS Shane Spencer 4.00
JT Jim Thome 10.00
BT Bubba Trammell 4.00
RW Rondell White 4.00
PW Preston Wilson 4.00
TZ Todd Zeile 6.00

Tools of the Trade Dual

NM/M
Common Player: 10.00
KM Kevin Millwood 10.00
IR Ivan Rodriguez 15.00
JT Jim Thome 15.00

2003 Topps Tribute

NM/M
Complete Set (110): 300.00
Common Player: 1.00
Common Auto. (101-110): 10.00
Pack (5): 35.00
Box (6): 160.00
1 Jim Thome 2.50
2 Edgardo Alfonzo 1.00
3 Edgar Martinez 1.50
4 Scott Rolen 2.50
5 Eric Hinske 1.00
6 Mark Mulder 1.50
7 Jason Giambi 2.50
8 Bernie Williams 2.00
9 Cliff Floyd 1.00
10 Ichiro Suzuki 5.00
11 Pat Burrell 1.50
12 Garret Anderson 1.50
13 Gary Sheffield 1.50
14 Johnny Damon 3.00
15 Kerry Wood 1.50
16 Bartolo Colon 1.00
17 Adam Dunn 2.00
18 Omar Vizquel 1.50
19 Todd Helton 2.00
20 Nomar Garciaparra 4.00
21 A.J. Burnett 1.00
22 Craig Biggio 1.50
23 Carlos Beltran 2.50
24 Kazuhisa Ishii 1.00
25 Vladimir Guerrero 2.50
26 Roberto Alomar 2.00
27 Roger Clemens 6.00
28 Tim Hudson 2.00
29 Brian Giles 1.50
30 Barry Bonds 8.00
31 Jim Edmonds 1.50
32 Rafael Palmeiro 2.00
33 Francisco Rodriguez 1.00
34 Andruw Jones 2.00
35 Shea Hillenbrand 1.00
36 Moises Alou 1.50
37 Luis Gonzalez 1.00
38 Darin Erstad 1.00
39 John Smoltz 1.50
40 Derek Jeter 8.00
41 Aubrey Huff 1.00
42 Eric Chavez 1.50
43 Doug Mientkiewicz 1.00
44 Lance Berkman 2.00
45 Josh Beckett 1.50
46 Austin Kearns 1.50
47 Frank Thomas 2.50
48 Pedro J. Martinez 3.00
49 Tim Salmon 1.50
50 Alex Rodriguez 8.00
51 Ryan Klesko 1.00
52 Tom Glavine 1.50
53 Shawn Green 1.50
54 Jeff Kent 1.50
55 Carlos Pena 1.00
56 Paul Konerko 1.50
57 Troy Glaus 2.00
58 Manny Ramirez 2.50
59 Jason Jennings 1.00
60 Randy Johnson 3.00
61 Ivan Rodriguez 2.00
62 Roy Oswalt 1.50
63 Kevin Brown 1.50
64 Jose Vidro 1.00
65 Jorge Posada 1.50
66 Mike Piazza 5.00
67 Bret Boone 1.50
68 Carlos Delgado 2.00
69 Jimmy Rollins 2.00
70 Alfonso Soriano 3.00
71 Greg Maddux 5.00
72 Mark Prior 2.00
73 Jeff Bagwell 2.50
74 Richie Sexson 2.00
75 Sammy Sosa 4.00
76 Curt Schilling 2.00
77 Mike Sweeney 1.00
78 Torii Hunter 1.50
79 Larry Walker 1.50
80 Miguel Tejada 1.50
81 Rich Aurilia 1.00
82 Bobby Abreu 1.50
83 Phil Nevin 1.00
84 Rodrigo Lopez 1.00
85 Chipper Jones 3.00
86 Ken Griffey Jr. 5.00
87 Mike Lowell 1.00
88 Magglio Ordonez 1.50
89 Barry Zito 1.50
90 Albert Pujols 8.00
91 Corey Shafer **RC** 2.00
92 Dan Haren 5.00
93 Jeremy Bonderman 6.00
94 Branden Florence **RC** 2.00
95 Evel Bastida-Martinez **RC** 2.00
96 Brian Wright **RC** 2.00
97 Elizardo Ramirez **RC** 2.00
98 Michael Garciaparra 2.00
99 Clay Hensley **RC** 3.00
100 Bobby Basham **RC** 2.00
101 Jose Contreras **RC** 20.00
102 Bryan Bullington **RC** 20.00
103 Joey Gomes 10.00
104 Craig Brazell **RC** 15.00
105 Andy Marte **RC** 25.00
106 Hanley Ramirez **RC** 80.00
107 Ryan Shealy **RC** 25.00
108 Daryl Clark **RC** 10.00
109 Tyler Johnson **RC** 15.00
110 Ben Francisco **RC** 10.00

Gold Proof

Cards (1-100): No Pricing
Production 25
Autos (101-110) are 1 of 1.

Red Proof

Stars (1-100): 2-4X
Production 225
Autos (101-110): 1-2.5X
Production 50

Matching Marks Dual Relics

NM/M
Common Duo: 10.00
Premiere Proofs: 1.5X
Production 50
PH Rafael Palmeiro, Rickey Henderson 15.00
GR Nomar Garciaparra, Alex Rodriguez 25.00
AP Roberto Alomar, Rafael Palmeiro 15.00
MP Fred McGriff, Rafael Palmeiro 10.00
HR Rickey Henderson, Manny Ramirez 15.00
RP Manny Ramirez, Mike Piazza 20.00
BG Jeff Bagwell, Juan Gonzalez 10.00
BP Barry Bonds, Rafael Palmeiro 35.00
SB Sammy Sosa, Jeff Bagwell 20.00
SG Alfonso Soriano, Vladimir Guerrero 15.00
PS Rafael Palmeiro, Sammy Sosa 20.00
MG Fred McGriff, Juan Gonzalez 10.00
PA Rafael Palmeiro, Roberto Alomar 15.00

Memorable Materials

NM/M
Common Player: 8.00
Premiere Proofs: 1.5X
Production 50
BB Barry Bonds 30.00
JG Jason Giambi 8.00
JG2 Jason Giambi 8.00

TG Troy Glaus 8.00
LG Luis Gonzalez 8.00
SG Shawn Green 8.00
VG Vladimir Guerrero 10.00
RH Rickey Henderson 10.00
TH Torii Hunter 8.00
AJ Andruw Jones 8.00
GM Greg Maddux 15.00
AP Albert Pujols 20.00
CR Cal Ripken Jr. 45.00
AR Alex Rodriguez 15.00
AS Alfonso Soriano 10.00
SS Sammy Sosa 15.00
SS2 Sammy Sosa 15.00
MT Miguel Tejada 8.00
KW Kerry Wood 8.00

Milestone Materials

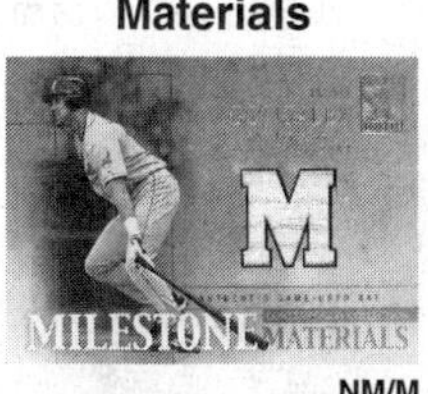

NM/M
Common Player: 8.00
Premiere Proofs: 1.5X
Production 50
RA Roberto Alomar 10.00
JB1 Jeff Bagwell 10.00
JB2 Jeff Bagwell 10.00
BB1 Barry Bonds 25.00
BB2 Barry Bonds 25.00
BB3 Barry Bonds 25.00
BB4 Barry Bonds 25.00
BB5 Barry Bonds 25.00
NG Nomar Garciaparra 20.00
JG1 Juan Gonzalez 10.00
JG2 Juan Gonzalez 10.00
VG Vladimir Guerrero 10.00
TH Todd Helton 10.00
RH1 Rickey Henderson 10.00
RH2 Rickey Henderson 10.00
RH3 Rickey Henderson 10.00
RH4 Rickey Henderson 10.00
RH5 Rickey Henderson 10.00
CJ Chipper Jones 12.00
FM1 Fred McGriff 8.00
FM2 Fred McGriff 8.00
FM3 Fred McGriff 8.00
RP1 Rafael Palmeiro 10.00
RP2 Rafael Palmeiro 10.00
RP3 Rafael Palmeiro 10.00
RP4 Rafael Palmeiro 10.00
MP1 Mike Piazza 15.00
MP2 Mike Piazza 15.00
MR1 Manny Ramirez 10.00
MR2 Manny Ramirez 10.00
AR Alex Rodriguez 15.00
SS1 Sammy Sosa 15.00
SS2 Sammy Sosa 15.00
SS3 Sammy Sosa 15.00
FT Frank Thomas 12.00

Modern Marks Autographs

NM/M
Common Autograph: 10.00
Premiere Proofs: 1.5X
Production 50
LB Lance Berkman 20.00
RC Roger Clemens 120.00
CF Cliff Floyd 10.00
EH Eric Hinske 10.00
TH Torii Hunter 15.00
PK Paul Konerko 15.00
PL Paul LoDuca 15.00
MO Magglio Ordonez 20.00

Perennial All-Stars Relics

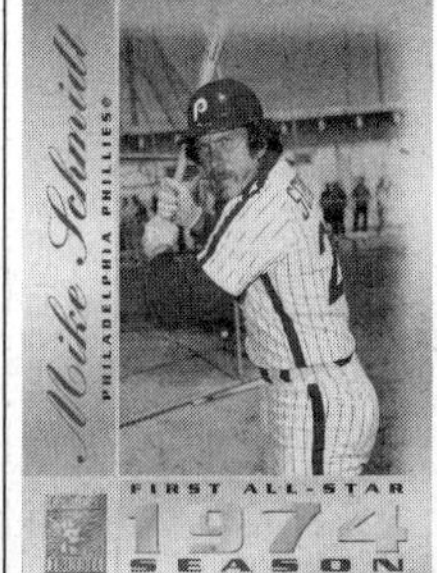

NM/M
Common Player: 8.00
Premiere Proofs: 1.5X
Production 50
RA Roberto Alomar 10.00
CB Craig Biggio 8.00
BB Barry Bonds 25.00
RC Roger Clemens 20.00
RH Rickey Henderson 15.00
CJ Chipper Jones 10.00
GM Greg Maddux 15.00
EM Edgar Martinez 15.00
EM Pedro J. Martinez 15.00
MM Mike Mussina 10.00
MP Mike Piazza 20.00
MR Manny Ramirez 10.00
AR Alex Rodriguez 15.00
IR Ivan Rodriguez 8.00
BS Benito Santiago 8.00
CS Curt Schilling 8.00
GS Gary Sheffield 8.00
JS John Smoltz 8.00
SS Sammy Sosa 20.00
FT Frank Thomas 10.00
LW Larry Walker 8.00
BW Bernie Williams 10.00

Performance Tribute Doubles

NM/M
Common Duo: 10.00
Premiere Proofs: 1.5X
Production 50
ZJ Barry Zito, Randy Johnson 15.00
SA Alfonso Soriano, Roberto Alomar 15.00
RR Cal Ripken Jr., Alex Rodriguez 60.00
RT Alex Rodriguez, Miguel Tejada 15.00
GG Luis Gonzalez, Troy Glaus 10.00
PW Albert Pujols, Kerry Wood 25.00
RG Alex Rodriguez, Nomar Garciaparra 30.00
BJ Barry Bonds, Chipper Jones 25.00
SG Sammy Sosa, Juan Gonzalez 15.00
PS Mike Piazza, Benito Santiago 15.00
PR Mike Piazza, Ivan Rodriguez 15.00
MM Pedro J. Martinez, Greg Maddux 15.00
CM Roger Clemens, Greg Maddux 35.00
JP Chipper Jones, Mike Piazza 20.00

Performance Tribute Triples

NM/M
Common Trio: 20.00
Premiere Proofs: 1.5X
Production 50
SMP Sammy Sosa, Rafael Palmeiro, Fred McGriff 25.00
CMJ Roger Clemens, Greg Maddux, Randy Johnson 30.00
RHP Manny Ramirez, Mike Piazza, Rickey Henderson 30.00
STB Sammy Sosa, Frank Thomas, Jeff Bagwell 20.00
BMP Barry Bonds, Fred McGriff, Rafael Palmeiro 30.00

Solo Bonds

NM/M
Premiere Proof: 1.5X
Production 50
SB Barry Bonds 25.00

Double Bonds

NM/M
Premiere Proof: 1.5X
Production 50
BT-DB Barry Bonds 40.00

Triple Bonds

NM/M
Premiere Proof: 1.5X
Production 50
TB Barry Bonds 60.00

Team Tribute Doubles

NM/M
Common Duo: 10.00
Premiere Proofs: 1.5X
Production 50
MS Greg Maddux, John Smoltz 35.00
IN Kazuhisa Ishii, Hideo Nomo 25.00
WH Larry Walker, Todd Helton 10.00
BB Craig Biggio, Jeff Bagwell 15.00
RP Alex Rodriguez, Rafael Palmeiro 15.00
GR Nomar Garciaparra, Manny Ramirez 20.00

Team Tribute Triples

NM/M
Common Trio: 15.00
Premiere Proofs: 1.5X
Production 50
JSJ Andruw Jones, Gary Sheffield, Chipper Jones 30.00
GRM Nomar Garciaparra, Manny Ramirez, Pedro J. Martinez 40.00
ASP Moises Alou, Sammy Sosa, Corey Patterson 30.00
TOK Frank Thomas, Magglio Ordonez, Paul Konerko 20.00
BBB Craig Biggio, Lance Berkman, Jeff Bagwell 20.00
MHM Joe Mauer, Torii Hunter, Doug Mientkiewicz 25.00
SGV Alfonso Soriano, Jason Giambi, Robin Ventura 25.00
CTM Eric Chavez, Miguel Tejada, Mark Mulder 15.00
HZM Tim Hudson, Barry Zito, Mark Mulder 25.00
TBB Jim Thome, Marlon Byrd, Pat Burrell 25.00
MOB Edgar Martinez, John Olerud, Bret Boone 20.00
PER Albert Pujols, Jim Edmonds, Scott Rolen 40.00
RGP Alex Rodriguez, Juan Gonzalez, Rafael Palmeiro 25.00
RBT Alex Rodriguez, Hank Blalock, Mark Teixeira 25.00

Tribute to the Stars

NM/M
Common Player: 10.00
Premiere Proofs: 1.5X
Production 50
RA Roberto Alomar 15.00
GA Garret Anderson 15.00
LB Lance Berkman 10.00
BB Barry Bonds 50.00
PB Pat Burrell 15.00
EC Eric Chavez 15.00
AD Adam Dunn 15.00
NG Nomar Garciaparra 40.00
TG Troy Glaus 15.00
VG Vladimir Guerrero 15.00
TH Todd Helton 15.00
RH Rickey Henderson 15.00
THU Torii Hunter 10.00
AJ Andruw Jones 10.00
CJ Chipper Jones 15.00
GM Greg Maddux 20.00
RP Rafael Palmeiro 10.00
MP Mike Piazza 20.00
AP Albert Pujols 40.00
AR Alex Rodriguez 30.00
AS Alfonso Soriano 15.00
SS Sammy Sosa 25.00
FT Frank Thomas 15.00
JT Jim Thome 15.00
LW Larry Walker 10.00

Tribute to the Stars Patchworks

NM/M
Common Player: 25.00
Production 50 Sets
JB Jeff Bagwell 35.00
BB Barry Bonds 80.00
NG Nomar Garciaparra 50.00
LG Luis Gonzalez 25.00
SG Shawn Green 25.00
TH Todd Helton 35.00
THU Torii Hunter 25.00
RJ Randy Johnson 40.00
CJ Chipper Jones 35.00
GM Greg Maddux 50.00
PM Pedro J. Martinez 40.00
RP Rafael Palmeiro 30.00
AP Albert Pujols 80.00
MR Manny Ramirez 35.00
AR Alex Rodriguez 50.00
AR2 Alex Rodriguez 50.00
CS Curt Schilling 25.00
SS Sammy Sosa 40.00
FT Frank Thomas 35.00
KW Kerry Wood 30.00

40/40 Club

NM/M
Premiere Proof: 1.5X
Production 50
CBR Jose Canseco, Barry Bonds, Alex Rodriguez 85.00

600 HR Club Relic

NM/M
Premiere Proofs: 1.5X
Production 50
Gold: No Pricing
Production One Set
HA-600 Hank Aaron 35.00
BB-600 Barry Bonds 30.00
WM-600 Willie Mays 45.00
BR-600 Babe Ruth 125.00

600 HR Club Double Relic

NM/M
Premiere Proofs: 1.5X
Production 50
BA-600 Barry Bonds, Hank Aaron 80.00
BA-600 Barry Bonds, Willie Mays 80.00
BA-600 Barry Bonds, Babe Ruth 200.00

600 HR Club Quad Relic

NM/M
Premiere Proof: 1X
Production 25
BA-600 Hank Aaron, Babe Ruth, Willie Mays, Barry Bonds 625.00

All-Star Edition

NM/M
Complete Set (50): 50.00
Common Player: 1.00
Pack (5): 40.00
Box (6): 200.00
1 Willie Mays 8.00
2 Don Mattingly 8.00
3 Hoyt Wilhelm 1.00
4 Hank Aaron 8.00
5 Hank Greenberg 1.00
6 Johnny Bench 5.00
7 Duke Snider 3.00
8 Carl Yastrzemski 3.00
9 Jim Palmer 1.00
10 Roberto Clemente 8.00
11 Mike Schmidt 8.00
12 Joe Cronin 1.00
13 Lou Brock 1.00
14 Orlando Cepeda 1.00
15 Bill Mazeroski 1.00
16 Whitey Ford 3.00
17 Rod Carew 1.00
18 Joe Morgan 1.00
19 Luis Aparicio 1.00
20 Nolan Ryan 10.00
21 Bobby Doerr 1.00
22 Dale Murphy 2.00
23 Bob Feller 1.00
24 Paul Molitor 2.00
25 Tom Seaver 3.00
26 Ozzie Smith 3.00
27 Stan Musial 6.00
28 Willie McCovey 1.00
29 Gary Carter 1.00
30 Reggie Jackson 3.00
31 Gaylord Perry 1.00
32 George Brett 8.00
33 Rocky Colavito 1.00
34 Wade Boggs 2.00
35 Cal Ripken Jr. 8.00
36 Carlton Fisk 1.00
37 Al Kaline 3.00
38 Kirby Puckett 4.00
39 Phil Rizzuto 2.00
40 Willie Stargell 1.00
41 Harmon Killebrew 3.00
42 Red Schoendienst 1.00
43 Tony Gwynn 3.00
44 Ralph Kiner 1.00
45 Yogi Berra 4.00
46 Jim "Catfish" Hunter 1.00
47 Frank Robinson 2.00
48 Ernie Banks 4.00
49 Warren Spahn 2.00
50 Brooks Robinson 3.00

All-Star Edition Premier Proof

Cards (1-50): 4-8X
Numbered to last two digits of 1st All-Star Year.

All-Star Edition All-Star Signing

NM/M
Common Autograph: 40.00
Premier Proofs: 1.5-2X
Production 25 Sets
LB Lou Brock 50.00
GC Gary Carter 40.00
OC Orlando Cepeda 40.00
AD Andre Dawson 40.00
TG Tony Gwynn 80.00
AK Al Kaline 75.00
DMA Don Mattingly 125.00
DM Dale Murphy 75.00
JP Jim Palmer 40.00
MS Mike Schmidt 100.00
DSN Duke Snider 45.00

All-Star Edition Memorable Match-up Relic

NM/M
Common Card: 50.00
Production 150 Sets
Premier Proofs: 1.5-2X
Production 25 Sets
YB Carl Yastrzemski, Johnny Bench 70.00
BS George Brett, Mike Schmidt 120.00
MJ Willie Mays, Reggie Jackson 65.00
BF Johnny Bench, Carlton Fisk 50.00
CM Gary Carter, Don Mattingly 85.00
KA Harmon Killebrew, Hank Aaron 125.00
BG Wade Boggs, Tony Gwynn 60.00
PG Kirby Puckett, Tony Gwynn 60.00
YBR Carl Yastrzemski, Lou Brock 60.00

All-Star Edition Perennial Patch Relics

NM/M
Common Player: 40.00
Production 30 Sets
WB Wade Boggs 75.00
GB George Brett 220.00
GC Gary Carter 40.00
TG Tony Gwynn 125.00
HK Harmon Killebrew 90.00
WM Willie McCovey 40.00
JM Joe Morgan 40.00
DMU Dale Murphy 120.00
CR Cal Ripken Jr. 225.00
NR Nolan Ryan/ Rangers 200.00
NRA Nolan Ryan/Astros 200.00
MS Mike Schmidt 200.00
OS Ozzie Smith 120.00
WS Willie Stargell 75.00
CY Carl Yastrzemski 190.00

All-Star Edition Tribute Relics

NM/M
Common Player: 10.00
Inserted 1:1
HA Hank Aaron 35.00
LA Luis Aparicio 10.00
EB Ernie Banks 20.00
JBE Johnny Bench 20.00
YB Yogi Berra 40.00
WB Wade Boggs 15.00
GB George Brett 20.00
LB Lou Brock/bat 30.00
LBU Lou Brock/Jersey 15.00
RCA Roy Campanella 20.00
ROD Rod Carew 15.00
GC Gary Carter 10.00
OC Orlando Cepeda 12.00
RC Roberto Clemente 60.00
TC Ty Cobb 100.00
JCR Joe Cronin 15.00
AD Andre Dawson 10.00
DD Dizzy Dean 40.00
BD Bobby Doerr 10.00
BF Bob Feller 15.00
CF Carlton Fisk 15.00
WF Whitey Ford 30.00
JF Jimmie Foxx 40.00
LG Lou Gehrig 125.00
HG Hank Greenberg 40.00
TG Tony Gwynn 20.00
RH Rogers Hornsby 40.00
CH Jim "Catfish" Hunter 20.00
RJ Reggie Jackson 15.00
AK Al Kaline 25.00
HK Harmon Killebrew 20.00
NL Napoleon Lajoie 60.00
EM Eddie Mathews 15.00
DMA Don Mattingly 30.00
WM Willie Mays 40.00
BM Bill Mazeroski 20.00
WMC Willie McCovey 18.00
JMI Johnny Mize 30.00
PM Paul Molitor 15.00
JMO Joe Morgan 10.00
TM Thurman Munson 30.00
DM Dale Murphy 50.00
SM Stan Musial 30.00
DN Don Newcombe 10.00
MO Mel Ott 30.00
JP Jim Palmer 10.00
KP Kirby Puckett 20.00
CRB Cal Ripken Jr. 40.00
PR Phil Rizzuto 15.00
BRO Brooks Robinson 15.00
FR Frank Robinson 10.00
JR Jackie Robinson 40.00
BR Babe Ruth 140.00
NR Nolan Ryan/Rangers 40.00
NRA Nolan Ryan/Astros 40.00
MS Mike Schmidt 20.00
RS Red Schoendienst 15.00
TSE Tom Seaver 25.00
OS Ozzie Smith 15.00
DSN Duke Snider 20.00
TS Tris Speaker 75.00
WST Willie Stargell 20.00
HW Honus Wagner 125.00
WHI Hoyt Wilhelm 10.00
CY Carl Yastrzemski 30.00

All-Star Edition 1st Class Cuts

NM/M
Production One Set
FC-TC Ty Cobb (3/03 Auction) 7,600
FC-JR Jackie Robinson (3/03 Auction) 3,500
FC-BR Babe Ruth (6/04 Auction) 7,300

World Series

NM/M
Complete Set (150): 150.00
Common Player: 1.00
Pack (5): 50.00
Box (6): 260.00
1 Willie Mays 8.00
2 Gary Carter 1.50
3 Yogi Berra 4.00
4 Dennis Eckersley 1.50
5 Willie McCovey 1.50
6 Willie Stargell 2.00
7 Mike Schmidt 8.00
8 Robin Yount 4.00
9 Bucky Harris 1.00
10 Carl Yastrzemski 4.00
11 Lenny Dykstra 1.00
12 Boog Powell 1.00
13 Bill Lee 1.00
14 Lou Brock 1.50
15 Bob Friend 1.00
16 Hank Greenberg 1.50
17 Maury Wills 1.00
18 Tommy Lasorda 1.00
19 Bill "Moose" Skowron 1.00
20 Frank Robinson 2.00
21 Rollie Fingers 1.00
22 Doug DeCinces 1.00
23 Eric Davis 1.00
24 Johnny Podres 1.00
25 Darrell Evans 1.00
26 Ron Cey 1.00
27 Ray Knight 1.00
28 Don Larsen 1.00
29 Harold Baines 1.00
30 Brooks Robinson 4.00
31 Wade Boggs 2.00
32 Joe Morgan 1.00
33 Kirk Gibson 1.00
34 Tommy John 1.00
35 Monte Irvin 2.00
36 Rich "Goose" Gossage 1.00
37 Tug McGraw 1.00
38 Walt Weiss 1.00
39 Bill Madlock 1.00
40 Juan Marichal 2.00
41 Willie McGee 1.00
42 Joe Cronin 1.00
43 Paul Blair 1.00
44 Norm Cash 1.00
45 Ken Griffey Sr. 1.00
46 Bret Saberhagen 1.00
47 Don Sutton 1.00
48 Kirby Puckett 4.00
49 Keith Hernandez 1.00
50 George Brett 8.00
51 Bobby Richardson 1.00
52 Jose Canseco 2.00
53 Greg Luzinski 1.00
54 Bill Mazeroski 1.00
55 Red Schoendienst 1.00
56 Graig Nettles 1.00
57 Jerry Koosman 1.00
58 Tony Perez 1.00
59 Jim Rice 1.00
60 Duke Snider 4.00
61 David Justice 1.00
62 Johnny Sain 1.00
63 Chuck Klein 1.00
64 Sparky Anderson 1.00
65 Alan Trammell 2.00
66 Willie Wilson 1.00
67 Hoyt Wilhelm 1.00
68 Joe Pepitone 1.00
69 Darren Daulton 1.00
70 Tom Seaver 4.00
71 Jim "Catfish" Hunter 1.00
72 Tim McCarver 1.00
73 Dave Parker 1.00
74 Earl Weaver 1.00
75 Ted Kluszewski 1.00
76 John Kruk 1.00
77 Dwight Evans 1.00
78 Ron Darling 1.00
79 Tony Oliva 1.00
80 Johnny Bench 5.00
81 Sam Crawford 1.00
82 Steve Yeager 1.00
83 Paul Molitor 2.00
84 Bert Campaneris 1.00
85 Mickey Rivers 1.00
86 Vince Coleman 1.00
87 Kent Tekulve 1.00
88 Dwight Gooden 1.00
89 Whitey Herzog 1.00
90 Whitey Ford 4.00
91 Warren Spahn 3.00

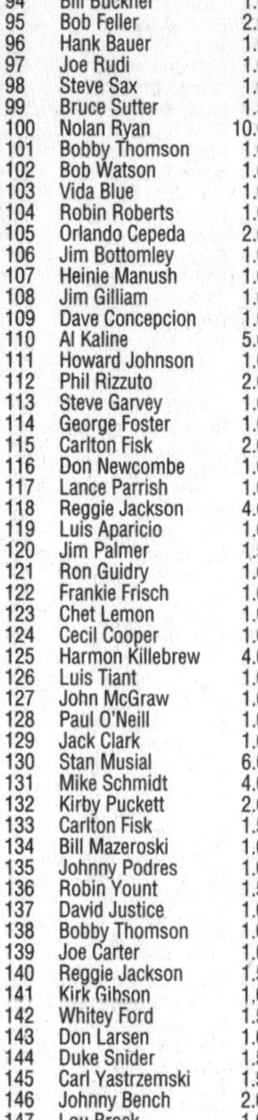

92 Fred Lynn 1.00
93 Joe Tinker 1.00
94 Bill Buckner 1.00
95 Bob Feller 2.00
96 Hank Bauer 1.00
97 Joe Rudi 1.00
98 Steve Sax 1.00
99 Bruce Sutter 1.50
100 Nolan Ryan 10.00
101 Bobby Thomson 1.00
102 Bob Watson 1.00
103 Vida Blue 1.00
104 Robin Roberts 1.00
105 Orlando Cepeda 2.00
106 Jim Bottomley 1.00
107 Heinie Manush 1.00
108 Jim Gilliam 1.00
109 Dave Concepcion 1.00
110 Al Kaline 5.00
111 Howard Johnson 1.00
112 Phil Rizzuto 2.00
113 Steve Garvey 1.00
114 George Foster 1.00
115 Carlton Fisk 2.00
116 Don Newcombe 1.00
117 Lance Parrish 1.00
118 Reggie Jackson 4.00
119 Luis Aparicio 1.00
120 Jim Palmer 1.50
121 Ron Guidry 1.00
122 Frankie Frisch 1.00
123 Chet Lemon 1.00
124 Cecil Cooper 1.00
125 Harmon Killebrew 4.00
126 Luis Tiant 1.00
127 John McGraw 1.00
128 Paul O'Neill 1.00
129 Jack Clark 1.00
130 Stan Musial 6.00
131 Mike Schmidt 4.00
132 Kirby Puckett 2.00
133 Carlton Fisk 1.50
134 Bill Mazeroski 1.00
135 Johnny Podres 1.00
136 Robin Yount 1.50
137 David Justice 1.00
138 Bobby Thomson 1.00
139 Joe Carter 1.00
140 Reggie Jackson 1.50
141 Kirk Gibson 1.00
142 Whitey Ford 1.50
143 Don Larsen 1.00
144 Duke Snider 1.50
145 Carl Yastrzemski 1.50
146 Johnny Bench 2.00
147 Lou Brock 1.00
148 Ted Kluszewski 1.00
149 Jim Palmer 1.00
150 Willie Mays 5.00

World Series Gold

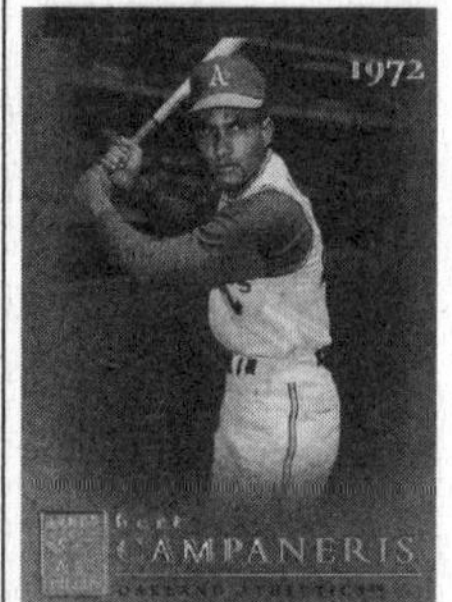

Golds (1-150): 4-8X
Production 100 Sets

World Series Relic

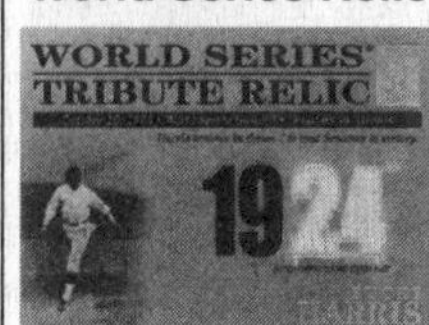

NM/M
Common Player: 10.00
Production 425 unless noted.
Golds: No Pricing
Production 25
HA Hank Aaron/50 60.00
HB Hank Bauer/50 30.00
JBE Johnny Bench 25.00
YB Yogi Berra 20.00
WB Wade Boggs 15.00
JB Jim Bottomley/50 30.00
GB George Brett 25.00
LB Lou Brock 10.00
JC Jose Canseco 15.00
NC Norm Cash/50 25.00
OC Orlando Cepeda/50 30.00
RC Roberto Clemente/ 50 120.00
TC Ty Cobb 120.00
SC Sam Crawford/50 50.00
CF Carlton Fisk 40.00

JF Jimmie Foxx/50 80.00
FF Frankie Frisch 15.00
LG Lou Gehrig/50 185.00
HG Hank Greenberg/50 60.00
TG Tony Gwynn 20.00
BH Bucky Harris 10.00
RH Rogers Hornsby 35.00
CH Jim "Catfish" Hunter 15.00
RJ Reggie Jackson 15.00
HK Harmon Killebrew 25.00
CK Chuck Klein 10.00
TK Ted Kluszewski 15.00
HM Heinie Manush/50 35.00
JM Juan Marichal 10.00
RM Roger Maris/50 75.00
BMA Billy Martin 15.00
WM Willie Mays 50.00
BM Bill Mazeroski 15.00
WMC Willie McCovey 10.00
TM Thurman Munson 30.00
SM Stan Musial 30.00
KP Kirby Puckett 20.00
CR Cal Ripken Jr. 35.00
FR Frank Robinson 15.00
JR Jackie Robinson 40.00
ER Edd Roush/50 40.00
BR Babe Ruth 140.00
MS Mike Schmidt 25.00
RS Red Schoendienst 10.00
TS Tom Seaver 15.00
OS Ozzie Smith 20.00
TSP Tris Speaker/50 90.00
WS Willie Stargell/50 30.00
BT Bobby Thomson 15.00
JT Joe Tinker 30.00
HW Honus Wagner/50 150.00
CY Carl Yastrzemski 30.00
RY Robin Yount 20.00

World Series Autographed Relic

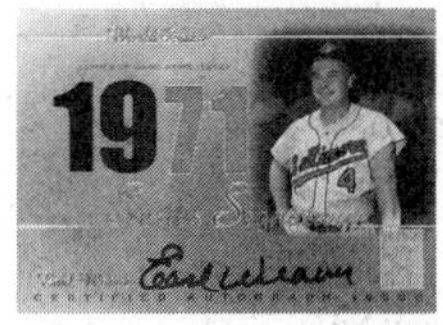

NM/M
Inserted 1:55
Golds: No Pricing
Production 25 Sets
LB Lou Brock 40.00
JC Jose Canseco 40.00
CF Carlton Fisk 120.00
HK Harmon Killebrew 75.00
WM Willie Mays 275.00
BM Bill Mazeroski 60.00
MS Mike Schmidt 100.00
BT Bobby Thomson 40.00

World Series Cut Signature Relic

No pricing due to scarcity.
Production One Set

World Series Fan Fare Relic

NM/M
Common Player: 10.00
Inserted 1:Box
HB Hank Bauer 10.00
YB Yogi Berra 20.00
WF Whitey Ford 15.00
DJ David Justice 10.00
DL Don Larsen 15.00
BM Billy Martin 15.00
DN Don Newcombe 10.00
PO Paul O'Neill 15.00
JP Johnny Podres 15.00
PR Phil Rizzuto 15.00
MS Bill "Moose" Skowron 10.00
DS Duke Snider 15.00

World Series Memorab. Match-Up Relic

NM/M
Common Player:

Varying quantities produced
GF Hank Greenberg, Frankie Frisch/34 90.00
GK Hank Greenberg, Chuck Klein/35 90.00
PR Phil Rizzuto, Willie Mays/51 150.00
FS Whitey Ford, Duke Snider/53 75.00
AS Luis Aparicio, Duke Snider/59 35.00
MF Bill Mazeroski, Whitey Ford/60 50.00
KB Al Kaline, Lou Brock/68 75.00
RS Frank Robinson, Tom Seaver/69 40.00
RBE Brooks Robinson, Johnny Bench/70 55.00
AM Sparky Anderson, Billy Martin/76 25.00
SP Willie Stargell, Jim Palmer/79 40.00
SB Mike Schmidt, George Brett/80 80.00
SY Ozzie Smith, Robin Yount/82 50.00
SRI Mike Schmidt, Cal Ripken Jr./83 120.00
TG Alan Trammell, Tony Gwynn/84 50.00
WB Mookie Wilson, Bill Buckner/86 40.00
EG Dennis Eckersley, Kirk Gibson/88 35.00

World Series Pastime Patches Relics

No pricing due to scarcity.
Production 15 Sets

World Series Series Signatures

NM/M
Common Autograph: 25.00
Golds: No Pricing
Production 25
SA Sparky Anderson 25.00
JC Joe Carter 25.00
WF Whitey Ford 60.00
SG Steve Garvey 25.00
KG Kirk Gibson 30.00
DJ David Justice 40.00
AK Al Kaline 50.00
DN Don Newcombe 40.00
JP Jim Palmer 30.00
BR Brooks Robinson 75.00
MS Bill "Moose" Skowron 25.00
AT Alan Trammell 25.00
EW Earl Weaver 25.00
MW Maury Willis 25.00
MWI Mookie Wilson 30.00

World Series Team Tribute Relic

NM/M
Common Card: 15.00
Production 275 unless noted.
YLK Carl Yastrzemski, Fred Lynn, Carlton Fisk 50.00
OSD Paul O'Neill, Chris Sabo, Eric Davis 25.00
FPG George Foster, Tony Perez, Ken Griffey Jr. 25.00
CPM Dave Concepcion, Tony Perez, Joe Morgan 50.00
KCA Al Kaline, Norm Cash 40.00
TA Alan Trammell, Sparky Anderson 15.00
GT Kirk Gibson, Alan Trammell 25.00
SB Bret Saberhagen, George Brett 40.00
CYG Ron Cey, Steve Yeager, Steve Garvey 30.00
YM Robin Yount, Paul Molitor 35.00
SRK Tom Seaver, Nolan Ryan, Jerry Koosman 50.00
HCD Keith Hernandez, Gary Carter, Lenny Dykstra 30.00
GB Lou Gehrig, Babe Ruth/25 500.00
EC Dennis Eckersley, Jose Canseco 25.00
HJ Jim "Catfish" Hunter, Reggie Jackson 30.00
SPM Willie Stargell, Dave Parker, Bill Madlock 30.00
CM Orlando Cepeda, Juan Marichal 30.00
MM Willie Mays, Willie McCovey 50.00
SMC Ozzie Smith, Willie McGee, Vince Coleman 40.00

World Series Tribute Singles

NM/M
Common Player: 8.00
Premiere Proofs: 1.5X
Production 50
TG Troy Glaus 8.00
MR Mariano Rivera 10.00

World Series Tribute Doubles

NM/M
Common Duo: 10.00
Premiere Proofs: 1.5X
Production 50
PP Jorge Posada, Andy Pettitte 15.00
WO Bernie Williams, Paul O'Neill 15.00
LP John Lackey, Troy Percival 10.00
SJ Curt Schilling, Randy Johnson 15.00
BG Barry Bonds, Troy Glaus 35.00
WG Bernie Williams, Luis Gonzalez 10.00
PC Mike Piazza, Roger Clemens 35.00

World Series Tribute Triples

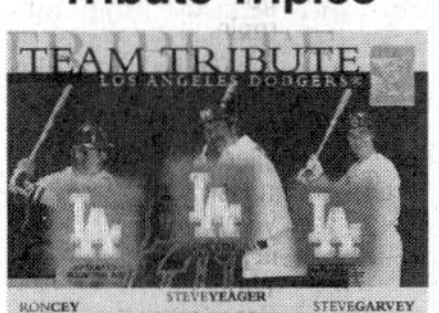

NM/M
Common Trio: 15.00
Premiere Proofs: 1.5X
Production 50
LGP John Lackey, Troy Glaus, Troy Percival 15.00
EGS Darin Erstad, Troy Glaus, Tim Salmon 15.00

2003 Topps 205

NM/M
Complete Set (335): 150.00
Common Player: .20
SP's inserted 1:5
25 variations in base set and minis
Mini-Cards(316-335): Exclusive Mini Cards
Price for minis (316-335) are Polar Bear
Series 1 or 2 Pack (8): 4.00
Series 1 or 2 Box (20): 65.00
1 Barry Bonds 2.50
1 Barry Bonds/Variation 3.00
2 Bret Boone .40
3 Albert Pujols 2.00
3 Albert Pujols/Variation 2.00
4 Carl Crawford .20
5 Bartolo Colon .20
6 Cliff Floyd .20
7 John Olerud .40
8 Jason Giambi .50
8 Jason Giambi/Variation .75
9 Edgardo Alfonzo .20
10 Ivan Rodriguez .50
11 Jim Edmonds .50
12 Mike Piazza 1.50
12 Mike Piazza/Variation 2.00
13 Greg Maddux 1.50
14 Jose Vidro .20
15 Vladimir Guerrero .75
15 Vladimir Guerrero/Variation 1.00
16 Bernie Williams .50
17 Roger Clemens 2.00
18 Miguel Tejada .50
18 Miguel Tejada/Variation .75
19 Carlos Delgado .50
20 Alfonso Soriano .75
20 Alfonso Soriano/Variation .75
21 Bobby Cox .20
22 Mike Scioscia .20
23 John Smoltz .40
24 Luis Gonzalez .40
25 Shawn Green .40
26 Raul Ibanez .20
27 Andruw Jones .50
28 Josh Beckett .40
29 Derek Lowe .20
30 Todd Helton .75
31 Barry Larkin .40
32 Jason Jennings .20
33 Darin Erstad .40
34 Magglio Ordonez .40
35 Mike Sweeney .20
36 Kazuhisa Ishii .20
37 Ron Gardenhire .20
38 Tim Hudson .40
39 Tim Salmon .20
40 Pat Burrell .40
40 Pat Burrell/Variation .50
41 Manny Ramirez .75
42 Nick Johnson .20
43 Tom Glavine .40
44 Mark Mulder .40
45 Brian Jordan .20
46 Rafael Palmeiro .50
47 Vernon Wells .40
48 Bob Brenly .20
49 C.C. Sabathia .20
50 Alex Rodriguez 2.50
50 Alex Rodriguez/Variation 2.50
51 Sammy Sosa 1.50
51 Sammy Sosa/Variation 2.00
52 Paul Konerko .20
53 Craig Biggio .40
54 Moises Alou .40
55 Johnny Damon .50
56 Torii Hunter .40
57 Omar Vizquel .40
58 Orlando Hernandez .20
59 Barry Zito .40
60 Lance Berkman .50
61 Carlos Beltran .50
62 Edgar Renteria .40
63 Ben Sheets .40
64 Doug Mientkiewicz .20
65 Troy Glaus .50
66 Preston Wilson .20
67 Kerry Wood .75
68 Frank Thomas .75
69 Jimmy Rollins .40
70 Brian Giles .40
71 Bobby Higginson .20
72 Larry Walker .40
73 Randy Johnson 1.00
74 Tony LaRussa .20
75 Derek Jeter 3.00
75 Derek Jeter/Variation 3.00
76 Bobby Abreu .40
77 Adam Dunn .75
77 Adam Dunn/Variation .75
78 Ryan Klesko .20
79 Francisco Rodriguez .20
80 Scott Rolen .75
81 Roberto Alomar .50
82 Joe Torre .50
83 Jim Thome .75
84 Kevin Millwood .20
85 J.T. Snow .20
86 Trevor Hoffman .20
87 Jay Gibbons .20
88 Mark Prior 1.00
88 Mark Prior/Variation 1.50
89 Rich Aurilia .20
90 Chipper Jones 1.00
91 Richie Sexson .50
92 Gary Sheffield .50
93 Pedro J. Martinez 1.00
94 Rodrigo Lopez .20
95 Al Leiter .20
96 Jorge Posada .50
97 Luis Castillo .20
98 Aubrey Huff .20
99 A.J. Pierzynski .20
100 Ichiro Suzuki 2.00
100 Ichiro Suzuki/Variation 2.00
101 Eric Chavez .40
102 Brett Myers .20
103 Jason Kendall .40
104 Jeff Kent .40
105 Eric Hinske .20
106 Jacque Jones .20
107 Phil Nevin .20
108 Roy Oswalt .40
109 Curt Schilling .75
110 Nomar Garciaparra 2.00
110 Nomar Garciaparra/Variation 2.00
111 Garret Anderson .40
112 Eric Gagne .40
113 Javier Vazquez .75
114 Jeff Bagwell .75
115 Mike Lowell .40
116 Carlos Pena .20
117 Ken Griffey Jr. 1.50
118 Tony Batista .20
119 Edgar Martinez .20
120 Austin Kearns .20
121 Jason Stokes .20
122 Jose Reyes .50
123 Rocco Baldelli .40
124 Joe Borchard .20
125 Joe Mauer .20
126 Gavin Floyd .20
127 Mark Teixeira .50
128 Jeremy Guthrie .20
129 B.J. Upton .40
130 Khalil Greene 2.00
131 Hanley Ramirez **RC** 3.00
132 Andy Marte **RC** 3.00
133 J.D. Durbin **RC** 1.00
134 Jason Kubel **RC** 2.00
135 Craig Brazell **RC** .75
136 Bryan Bullington **RC** 1.00
137 Jose Contreras **RC** 1.00
138 Brian Burgamy **RC** .75
139 Evel Bastida-Martinez **RC** .50
140 Joey Gomes 1.00
141 Ismael Castro **RC** .75
142 Travis Wong **RC** .75
143 Michael Garciaparra .50
144 Arnaldo Munoz **RC** .50
145 Louis Sockalexis 2.00
146 Dick Hoblitzell 1.00
147 George "Peaches" Graham .50
148 Hal Chase .50
149 John McGraw 1.00
150 Bobby Wallace .50
151 Dave Shean .20
152 Dick Hoblitzell SP 3.00
153 Hal Chase .20
154 George Wiltse .20
155 George Brett 2.00
156 Willie Mays 3.00
157 Honus Wagner SP 4.00
158 Nolan Ryan 3.00
159 Reggie Jackson 1.00
160 Mike Schmidt 1.50
161 Josh Barfield .20
162 Grady Sizemore .40
163 Justin Morneau .40
164 Laynce Nix .20
165 Zack Greinke .20
166 Victor Martinez .50
167 Jeff Mathis .20
168 Casey Kotchman .20
169 Gabe Gross .20
170 Edwin Jackson **RC** 1.50
171 Delmon Young/SP **RC** 10.00
172 Eric Duncan/SP 2.00
173 Brian Snyder/SP 1.50
174 Chris Lubanski/SP **RC** 4.00
175 Ryan Harvey/SP **RC** 5.00
176 Nicholas Markakis/SP **RC** 6.00
177 Chad Billingsley/SP **RC** 3.00
178 Elizardo Ramirez .50
179 Ben Francisco .50
180 Franklin Gutierrez/SP 4.00
181 Aaron Hill/SP 2.00
182 Kevin Correia .50
183 Kelly Shoppach **RC** .75
184 Felix Pie/SP **RC** 5.00
185 Adam Loewen/SP **RC** 5.00
186 Danny Garcia .50
187 Rickie Weeks/SP **RC** 8.00
188 Robby Hammock/SP 2.00
189 Ryan Wagner/SP **RC** 2.00
190 Matt Kata/SP 1.50
191 Bo Hart/SP **RC** 2.00
192 Brandon Webb/SP **RC** 3.00
193 Bengie Molina .20
194 Junior Spivey .20
195 Gary Sheffield .50
196 Jason Johnson .20
197 David Ortiz .75
198 Roberto Alomar .50
199 Wily Mo Pena .20
200 Sammy Sosa 2.00
201 Jay Payton .20
202 Dmitri Young .20
203 Derek Lee .40
204 Jeff Bagwell .75
204 Jeff Bagwell/Variation .75
205 Runelvys Hernandez .20
206 Kevin Brown .40
207 Wes Helms .20
208 Eddie Guardado .20
209 Orlando Cabrera .20
210 Alfonso Soriano .75
211 Ty Wigginton .20
212 Rich Harden .40
212 Rich Harden/Variation .50
213 Mike Lieberthal .20
214 Brian Giles .40
215 Jason Schmidt .40
216 Jamie Moyer .20
217 Matt Morris .20
218 Victor Zambrano .20
219 Roy Halladay .50
220 Mike Hampton .20
221 Kevin Millar .20
222 Hideo Nomo .50
223 Milton Bradley .20
224 Jose Guillen .20
225 Derek Jeter 3.00
226 Rondell White .20
227 Hank Blalock .50
227 Hank Blalock/Variation .50
228 Shigetoshi Hasegawa .20
229 Mike Mussina .50
230 Cristian Guzman .20
231 Todd Helton .75
231 Todd Helton/Variation .75
232 Kenny Lofton .40
233 Carl Everett .20
234 Shea Hillenbrand .20
235 Brad Fullmer .20
236 Bernie Williams .50
237 Vicente Padilla .20
238 Tim Worrell .20
239 Juan Gonzalez .40
240 Ichiro Suzuki 2.00
241 Aaron Boone .20
242 Shannon Stewart .20
243 Barry Zito .40
243 Barry Zito/Variation .40
244 Reggie Sanders .20
245 Scott Podsednik .40
246 Miguel Cabrera .75
247 Angel Berroa .20
248 Carlos Zambrano .40
249 Marlon Byrd .20
250 Mark Prior 1.00
251 Esteban Loaiza .20
252 David Eckstein .20
253 Alex Cintron .20
254 Melvin Mora .20
255 Russ Ortiz .20
256 Carlos Lee .20
257 Tino Martinez .20
258 Randy Wolf .20
259 Jason Phillips .20
260 Vladimir Guerrero 1.00
261 Brad Wilkerson .20
262 Ivan Rodriguez .75
263 Matt Lawton .20
264 Adam Dunn .50
265 Joe Borowski .20
266 Jody Gerut .20
267 Alex Rodriguez 2.50
268 Brendan Donnelly .20
269 Randy Johnson 1.00
269 Randy Johnson/Variation 1.00
270 Nomar Garciaparra 2.50
271 Javy Lopez .50
272 Travis Hafner .20
273 Juan Pierre .20
274 Morgan Ensberg .20
275 Albert Pujols 2.00
276 Jason LaRue .20
277 Paul LoDuca .20
278 Andy Pettitte .50
279 Mike Piazza 1.50
280 Jim Thome 1.00
280 Jim Thome/Variation 1.00
281 Marquis Grissom .20
282 Woody Williams .20
283 Curt Schilling .75
283 Curt Schilling/Variation .75
284 Chipper Jones 1.00
284 Chipper Jones/Variation 1.00
285 Deivi Cruz .20
286 Johnny Damon .50
287 Chin-Hui Tsao .20
288 Alex Gonzalez .20
289 Billy Wagner .40
290 Jason Giambi .50
291 Keith Foulke .20
292 Jerome Williams .20
293 Livan Hernandez .20
294 Aaron Guiel .20
295 Randall Simon .20
296 Byung-Hyun Kim .20
297 Jorge Julio .20
298 Miguel Batista .20
299 Rafael Furcal .40
300 Dontrelle Willis/SP 1.00
300 Dontrelle Willis/Variation 1.00
301 Alex Sanchez .20
302 Shawn Chacon .20
303 Matt Clement .20
304 Luis Matos .20
305 Steve Finley .20
306 Marcus Giles .40
307 David Wells .20
308 Jeromy Burnitz .20
309 Mike MacDougal .20
310 Mariano Rivera .40
311 Adrian Beltre .40
312 Mark Loretta .20
313 Ugueth Urbina .20
314 Bill Mueller .20
315 Johan Santana .50
316 Willie Mays 2.00
317 Delmon Young 4.00
318 Rickie Weeks 4.00
319 Ryan Wagner .50
320 Brandon Webb .50
321 Chris Lubanski 1.00
322 Ryan Harvey 3.00
323 Nicholas Markakis 1.00
324 Chad Billingsley 1.00
325 Aaron Hill .40
326 Brian Snyder .40
327 Eric Duncan .40
328 Sammy Sosa 1.50
329 Alfonso Soriano 1.00
330 Ichiro Suzuki 2.00
331 Alex Rodriguez 2.00
332 Nomar Garciaparra 2.00
333 Albert Pujols 2.00
334 Jim Thome 1.00
335 Dontrelle Willis .50

Mini Parallel

Polar Bear:	1-2X
Sovereign:	1-2X
Sovereign Green:	2-3X
American Beauty:	1-2X
Amer. Beauty Purple:	3-5X
Cycle:	1-2X
Cycle Purple:	3-5X
Drum:	2-4X
Honest:	1-2X
Honest Purple:	3-5X
Piedmont:	1-2X
Piedmont Purple:	3-5X
Sweet Caporal:	1-2X
Sweet Caporal Purple:	3-5X
Bazooka:	No Pricing
Production Five Sets	
Brooklyn:	1.5-4X
Brooklyn: Varies for common, rare & Unc.	

T-205 Autographs

		NM/M
Common Autograph:		12.00
LB	Lance Berkman	25.00
MB	Marlon Byrd	10.00
CF	Cliff Floyd	15.00
TH	Torii Hunter	15.00
PL	Paul LoDuca	15.00
MO	Magglio Ordonez	20.00
JR	Jose Reyes	30.00
SR	Scott Rolen	40.00
MS	Mike Sweeney	20.00
Series 2		
HA	Hank Aaron/50	280.00
LC	Luis Castillo	10.00
ED	Eric Duncan	20.00
RH	Rich Harden	25.00
FP	Felix Pie	40.00
RWA	Ryan Wagner	15.00
JW	Jerome Williams	20.00
DW	Dontrelle Willis	25.00

T-205 Relics

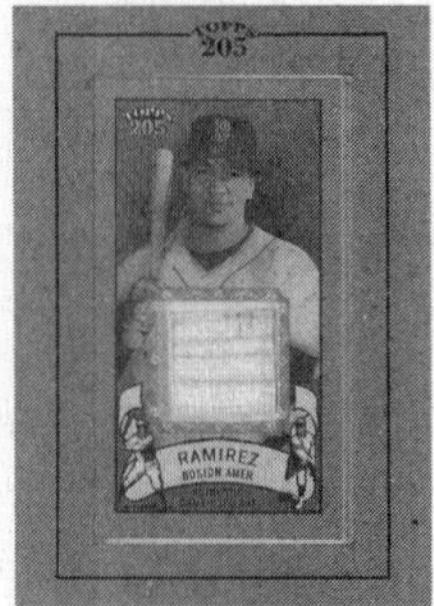

		NM/M
Common Player:		4.00
RA	Roberto Alomar/Bat	6.00
GA	Garret Anderson/Jsy	5.00
JB	Jeff Bagwell/Jsy	6.00
LB	Lance Berkman/Bat	8.00
BB	Barry Bonds	25.00
AB	A.J. Burnett/Jsy	4.00
LC	Luis Castillo/Jsy	4.00
EC	Eric Chavez/Bat	5.00
JD	Johnny Damon/Bat	6.00
AD	Adam Dunn/Bat	8.00
RF	Rafael Furcal/Bat	6.00
EG	Eric Gagne/Jsy	8.00
NG	Nomar Garciaparra/Jsy	15.00
BG	Brian Giles/Bat	5.00
LG	Luis Gonzalez/Jsy	4.00
TH	Todd Helton/Jsy	10.00
KI	Kazuhisa Ishii/Jsy	6.00
JJ	Jason Jennings/Jsy	4.00
NJ	Nick Johnson/Bat	4.00
RJ	Randy Johnson/Jsy	8.00
JK	Jeff Kent/Bat	4.00
AL	Al Leiter/Jsy	4.00
KL	Kenny Lofton/Bat	4.00
DL	Derek Lowe/Jsy	4.00
GM	Greg Maddux/Jsy	15.00
PM	Pedro Martinez/Jsy	10.00
MO	Magglio Ordonez/Jsy	4.00
RO	Roy Oswalt/Jsy	4.00
RP	Rafael Palmeiro/Jsy	6.00
TP	Troy Percival/Jsy	4.00
MP	Mike Piazza/Bat	10.00
AP	Albert Pujols/Jsy	20.00
MR	Manny Ramirez/Bat	8.00
AR	Alex Rodriguez/Jsy	10.00
SR	Scott Rolen/Bat	15.00
CS	Curt Schilling/Jsy	6.00
JS	John Smoltz/Jsy	8.00
AS	Alfonso Soriano/Jsy	10.00
MS	Mike Sweeney/Bat	4.00
JT	Jim Thome/Bat	12.00
MV	Mo Vaughn/Jsy	4.00
BW	Bernie Williams/Bat	10.00
BZ	Barry Zito/Jsy	4.00
Series 2		4.00
RA	Roberto Alomar	6.00
JB	Jeff Bagwell	8.00
RBB	Rocco Baldelli/bat	8.00
RB	Rocco Baldelli/Jsy	8.00
CB	Craig Biggio	4.00
HB	Hank Blalock	6.00
WB	Wade Boggs	15.00
BB	Bret Boone	10.00
GB	George Brett	25.00
KB	Kevin Brown	4.00
SB	Sean Burroughs	4.00
MC	Mike Cameron	4.00
JC	Jose Canseco	8.00
GC	Gary Carter	8.00
RC	Roger Clemens	15.00
CD	Carlos Delgado	6.00
BD	Brandon Duckworth	4.00
JE	Jim Edmonds	6.00
DE	Darin Erstad	4.00
RF	Rafael Furcal	4.00
NG	Nomar Garciaparra	10.00
JG	Jason Giambi	6.00
JGI	Jeremy Giambi	4.00
BG	Brian Giles	4.00
TG	Troy Glaus	6.00
JGO	Juan Gonzalez	6.00
LG	Luis Gonzalez	4.00
MG	Mark Grace	10.00
MGR	Marquis Grissom	4.00
VG	Vladimir Guerrero	8.00
CG	Cristian Guzman	4.00
RH	Rickey Henderson	8.00
RJ	Randy Johnson	8.00
AJ	Andruw Jones	6.00
CJB	Chipper Jones	8.00
KL	Kenny Lofton	4.00
GM	Greg Maddux	10.00
EM	Edgar Martinez	4.00
PM	Pedro J. Martinez	8.00
TM	Tino Martinez	6.00
FM	Fred McGriff	6.00
MM	Mark Mulder	4.00
EMU	Eddie Murray	25.00
JO	John Olerud	4.00
PO	Paul O'Neill	4.00
RP	Rafael Palmeiro	8.00
CP	Corey Patterson	10.00
BP	Brad Penny	4.00
MP	Mike Piazza	10.00
JP	Jorge Posada	15.00
APB	Albert Pujols/Bat	20.00
AP	Albert Pujols/Jsy	20.00
ARA	Aramis Ramirez	6.00
FR	Frank Robinson	15.00
AR	Alex Rodriguez	10.00
IR	Ivan Rodriguez	8.00
SR	Scott Rolen	8.00
NR	Nolan Ryan	40.00
CS	Curt Schilling	6.00
MS	Mike Schmidt	25.00
GS	Gary Sheffield	6.00
TS	Tsuyoshi Shinjo	4.00
AS	Alfonso Soriano	8.00
SS	Sammy Sosa	15.00
SST	Shannon Stewart	4.00
MT	Mark Teixeira	6.00
MTE	Miguel Tejada	6.00
FT	Frank Thomas	8.00
RV	Robin Ventura	4.00
LW	Larry Walker	4.00
VW	Vernon Wells	6.00
BW	Bernie Williams	6.00
DW	Dontrelle Willis	8.00

Team Topps Legends Autographs

	NM/M
Common Player:	
Stan Musial	65.00
Jim Palmer	20.00
Gaylord Perry	10.00
Robin Yount	75.00

Triple Folder

		NM/M
Complete Set (100):		60.00
Common Card:		.25
Inserted 1:1		
Series 1 Brooklyn Variation:		4-8X
Inserted 1:72		
Series 2 Brooklyn Variation:		2-4X
Inserted 1:29		
TF1	Barry Bonds, Jason LaRue	1.50
TF2	Alfonso Soriano, Derek Jeter	1.50
TF3	Alex Rodriguez, Miguel Tejada	1.50
TF4	Nomar Garciaparra, Derek Jeter	2.00
TF5	Omar Vizquel, Alex Rodriguez	1.50
TF6	Paul Konerko, Omar Vizquel	.25
TF7	Paul Konerko, Magglio Ordonez	.25
TF8	Doug Mientkiewicz, Darin Erstad	.25
TF9	Jason Kendall, Jimmy Rollins	.25
TF10	Shawn Green, Roberto Alomar	.25
TF11	Derek Jeter, Roberto Alomar	1.50
TF12	Bobby Abreu, Luis Castillo	.25
TF13	Randy Johnson, Curt Schilling	.75
TF14	Mike Piazza, Kerry Wood	1.00
TF15	Roger Clemens, Jorge Posada	1.00
TF16	Ichiro Suzuki, Ryan Klesko	1.00
TF17	Alfonso Soriano, Chipper Jones	1.00
TF18	Barry Bonds, Nick Johnson	1.50
TF19	Chipper Jones, Andruw Jones	.75
TF20	Bobby Abreu, Paul Konerko	.25
TF21	Rafael Palmeiro, Alex Rodriguez	1.50
TF22	Eric Hinske, Carlos Delgado	.25
TF23	Nomar Garciaparra, Jay Gibbons	1.00
TF24	Mike Piazza, Luis Gonzalez	1.00
TF25	J.T. Snow, Vladimir Guerrero	.50
TF26	Jason Giambi, Bernie Williams	.75
TF27	Miguel Tejada, Richie Sexson	.25
TF28	Doug Mientkiewicz, Jimmy Rollins	.25
TF29	Eric Chavez, Derek Jeter	2.00
TF30	Alfonso Soriano, Bret Boone	1.00
TF31	Chipper Jones, Mike Piazza	1.00
TF32	Ichiro Suzuki, Bret Boone	1.00
TF33	Bobby Abreu, Mike Piazza	1.00
TF34	Jimmy Rollins, Pat Burrell	.25
TF35	Ichiro Suzuki, Miguel Tejada	1.00
TF36	Jason LaRue, Barry Bonds	1.50
TF37	Derek Jeter, Alfonso Soriano	1.50
TF38	Miguel Tejada, Alex Rodriguez	1.50
TF39	Derek Jeter, Nomar Garciaparra	2.00
TF40	Alex Rodriguez, Omar Vizquel	1.50
TF41	Curt Schilling, Randy Johnson	.75
TF42	Jorge Posada, Roger Clemens	1.50
TF43	Ryan Klesko, Ichiro Suzuki	1.00
TF44	Nick Johnson, Barry Bonds	1.50
TF45	Alex Rodriguez, Rafael Palmeiro	1.50
TF46	Vladimir Guerrero, J.T. Snow	.50
TF47	Derek Jeter, Eric Chavez	2.00
TF48	Bret Boone, Ichiro Suzuki	1.00
TF49	Mike Piazza, Bobby Abreu	1.00
TF50	Miguel Tejada, Ichiro Suzuki	1.00
TF51	Juan Pierre, Jim Thome	.50
TF52	Kevin Millwood, Jim Thome	.50
TF53	Hank Blalock, Jorge Posada	.40
TF54	Deivi Cruz, Hank Blalock	.25
TF55	Rafael Furcal, Ty Wigginton	.25
TF56	Jim Thome, Nomar Garciaparra	1.50
TF57	Craig Biggio, Jason Giambi	.75
TF58	Aaron Boone, Jason Giambi	.75
TF59	Jason Giambi, Bernie Williams	.75
TF60	Cristian Guzman, Jody Gerut	.25
TF61	Todd Helton, Jose Reyes	.50
TF62	Derek Jeter, Hank Blalock	2.00
TF63	Mike Piazza, Jimmy Rollins	1.00
TF64	Bernie Williams, Derek Jeter	2.00
TF65	Andruw Jones, Rafael Furcal	.50
TF66	Mike Piazza, Andruw Jones	1.00
TF67	Mike Piazza, Cliff Floyd	1.00
TF68	Jason Kendall, Albert Pujols	1.50
TF69	Nomar Garciaparra, Manny Ramirez	1.50
TF70	Jorge Posada, Alex Rodriguez	1.50
TF71	Derek Jeter, Alex Rodriguez	2.00
TF72	Mike Sweeney, Alex Rodriguez	1.50
TF73	Marquis Grissom, Ivan Rodriguez	.50
TF74	Jason Phillips, Gary Sheffield	.40
TF75	Chipper Jones, Gary Sheffield	1.00
TF76	Junior Spivey, Gary Sheffield	.40
TF77	Al Leiter, Ichiro Suzuki	1.00
TF78	Jose Vidro, Jim Thome	.75
TF79	Jimmy Rollins, Paul LoDuca	.25
TF80	Alex Rodriguez, Rafael Palmeiro	1.50
TF81	Albert Pujols, Jim Edmonds	1.50
TF82	Eric Chavez, Mike Sweeney	.25
TF83	Cristian Guzman, Jimmy Rollins	.25
TF84	Alfonso Soriano, Bernie Williams	.50
TF85	Ichiro Suzuki, Derek Jeter	2.00
TF86	Jimmy Rollins, Derek Lee	.25
TF87	Shawn Green, Paul LoDuca	.25
TF88	Carlos Delgado, Jorge Posada	.50
TF89	Dmitri Young, C.C. Sabathia	.25
TF90	Dontrelle Willis, Shawn Chacon	.25
TF91	Edgar Martinez, Alex Rodriguez	1.50
TF92	Edgar Martinez, Carlos Delgado	.50
TF93	Edgar Martinez, Esteban Loaiza	.25
TF94	Roy Halladay, C.C. Sabathia	.25
TF95	Ichiro Suzuki, Albert Pujols	1.50
TF96	Ichiro Suzuki, Shigetoshi Hasegawa	1.00
TF97	Geoff Jenkins, Aaron Boone	.25
TF98	Nomar Garciaparra, Alfonso Soriano	1.50
TF99	Jorge Posada, Alfonso Soriano	.75
TF100	Vernon Wells, Garret Anderson	.25

Triple Folder Autographs

		NM/M
Inserted 1:355		
RH	Rich Harden	40.00
RW	Ryan Wagner	40.00
JW	Jerome Williams	35.00
DW	Dontrelle Willis	40.00

World Series Lineup

Inserted 1:27,440
No Pricing

2004 Topps Pre-Production

		NM/M
Complete Set (3):		4.00
Common Player:		1.00
PP1	Jason Giambi	3.00
PP2	Curt Schilling	1.50
PP3	Jimmy Rollins	1.00

2004 Topps

		NM/M
Complete Set (732):		60.00
Complete Team Factory Set (737):		75.00
Complete Factory Set (742):		75.00
Common Player:		.15
Pack (10):		2.00
Box (36):		55.00
Jumbo Box (12):		65.00
1	Jim Thome	.40
2	Aramis Ramirez	.25
3	Mark Kotsay	.15
4	Edgardo Alfonzo	.15
5	Ben Davis	.15
6	Mike Matheny	.15
8	Marlon Anderson	.15
9	Chan Ho Park	.15
10	Ichiro Suzuki	.75
11	Kevin Millwood	.25
12	Bengie Molina	.15
13	Tom Glavine	.25
14	Junior Spivey	.15
15	Marcus Giles	.15
16	David Segui	.15
17	Kevin Millar	.15
18	Corey Patterson	.15
19	Aaron Rowand	.15
20	Derek Jeter	1.00
21	Jason LaRue	.15
22	Chris Hammond	.15
23	Jay Payton	.15
24	Bobby Higginson	.15
25	Lance Berkman	.25
26	Juan Pierre	.15
27	Brent Mayne	.15
28	Fred McGriff	.25
29	Richie Sexson	.25
30	Tim Hudson	.25
31	Mike Piazza	.50
32	Brad Radke	.15
33	Jeff Weaver	.15
34	Ramon Hernandez	.15
35	David Bell	.15
36	Craig Wilson	.15
37	Jake Peavy	.15
38	Tim Worrell	.15
39	Gil Meche	.15
40	Albert Pujols	1.00
41	Michael Young	.15
42	Josh Phelps	.15
43	Brendan Donnelly	.15
44	Steve Finley	.15
45	John Smoltz	.15
46	Jay Gibbons	.15
47	Trot Nixon	.15
48	Carl Pavano	.15
49	Frank Thomas	.40
50	Mark Prior	1.00
51	Danny Graves	.15
52	Milton Bradley	.15
53	Jose Jimenez	.15
54	Shane Halter	.15
55	Mike Lowell	.15
56	Geoff Blum	.15
57	Michael Tucker	.15
58	Paul LoDuca	.15
59	Vicente Padilla	.15
60	Jacque Jones	.15
61	Fernando Tatis	.15
62	Ty Wigginton	.15
63	Pedro Astacio	.15
64	Andy Pettitte	.25
65	Terrence Long	.15
66	Cliff Floyd	.15
67	Mariano Rivera	.25
68	Mike Williams	.15
69	Marlon Byrd	.15
70	Mark Mulder	.25
71	Damian Moss	.15
72	Carlos Guillen	.15
73	Fernando Vina	.15
74	Lance Carter	.15
75	Hank Blalock	.25
76	Jimmy Rollins	.25
77	Kevin Appier	.15
78	Javy Lopez	.25
79	Jerry Hairston Jr.	.15
80	Andruw Jones	.40
81	Rodrigo Lopez	.15
82	Johnny Damon	.25
83	Hee Seop Choi	.15
84	Miguel Olivo	.15
85	Scott Sullivan	.15
86	Matt Lawton	.15
87	Juan Uribe	.15
88	Steve Sparks	.15
89	Tim Spooneybarger	.15
90	Jose Vidro	.15
91	Luis Rivas	.15
92	Hideo Nomo	.25
93	Javier Vazquez	.15
94	Al Leiter	.15
95	Darren Dreifort	.15
96	Mike DeJean	.15
97	Zach Day	.15
98	Jorge Posada	.25
99	John Halama	.15
100	Alex Rodriguez	1.00
101	Orlando Palmeiro	.15
102	Dave Berg	.15
103	Brad Fullmer	.15
104	Mike Hampton	.15
105	Willis Roberts	.15
106	Ramiro Mendoza	.15
107	Juan Cruz	.15
108	Esteban Loaiza	.15
109	Aaron Boone	.15
110	Todd Helton	.40
111	Braden Looper	.15
112	Octavio Dotel	.15
113	Mike MacDougal	.15
114	Cesar Izturis	.15
115	Johan Santana	.15
116	Jose Contreras	.25
117	Placido Polanco	.15
118	Kenny Lofton	.25
119	Adam Eaton	.15
120	Vernon Wells	.25
121	Ben Grieve	.15
122	Randy Winn	.15
123	Ismael Valdes	.15
124	Eric Owens	.15
125	Curt Schilling	.25
126	Russ Ortiz	.15
127	Mark Buehrle	.15
128	Danys Baez	.15
129	Dmitri Young	.15
130	Kazuhisa Ishii	.15
131	A.J. Pierzynski	.15
132	Michael Barrett	.15
133	Joe McEwing	.15
134	Robin Ventura	.15
135	Tom Wilson	.15
136	Carlos Zambrano	.15
137	Brett Tomko	.15
138	Jeff Nelson	.15
139	Jarrod Washburn	.15
140	Greg Maddux	.75
141	Craig Counsell	.15
142	Reggie Taylor	.15
143	Omar Vizquel	.25
144	Alex Gonzalez	.15
145	Billy Wagner	.15
146	Brian Jordan	.15
147	Wes Helms	.15
148	Kyle Lohse	.15
149	Timoniel Perez	.15
150	Jason Giambi	.50
151	Erubiel Durazo	.15
152	Mike Lieberthal	.15
153	Jason Kendall	.15
154	Xavier Nady	.15
155	Kirk Rueter	.15
156	Mike Cameron	.15
157	Miguel Cairo	.15
158	Woody Williams	.15
159	Toby Hall	.15
160	Bernie Williams	.40
161	Darin Erstad	.25
162	Matt Mantei	.15
163	Geronimo Gil	.15
164	Bill Mueller	.15
165	Damian Miller	.15
166	Tony Graffanino	.15
167	Sean Casey	.15
168	Brandon Phillips	.15

169 Mike Remlinger .15
170 Adam Dunn .25
171 Carlos Lee .15
172 Juan Encarnacion .15
173 Angel Berroa .15
174 Desi Relaford .15
175 Paul Quantrill .15
176 Ben Sheets .15
177 Eddie Guardado .15
178 Rocky Biddle .15
179 Mike Stanton .15
180 Eric Chavez .25
181 Jason Michaels .15
182 Terry Adams .15
183 Kip Wells .15
184 Brian Lawrence .15
185 Bret Boone .25
186 Tino Martinez .25
187 Aubrey Huff .15
188 Kevin Mench .15
189 Tim Salmon .25
190 Carlos Delgado .40
191 John Lackey .15
192 Oscar Villarreal .15
193 Sidney Ponson .15
194 Derek Lowe .15
195 Mark Grudzielanek .15
196 Flash Gordon .15
197 Matt Clement .15
198 Scott Williamson .15
199 Brandon Inge .15
200 Nomar Garciaparra 1.00
201 Antonio Osuna .15
202 Jose Mesa .15
203 Randall Simon .15
204 Jack Wilson .15
205 Ray Durham .15
206 Freddy Garcia .15
207 J.D. Drew .15
208 Einar Diaz .15
209 Roy Halladay .25
210 David Eckstein .15
211 Jason Marquis .15
212 Jorge Julio .15
213 Tim Wakefield .15
214 Moises Alou .25
215 Bartolo Colon .25
216 Jimmy Haynes .15
217 Preston Wilson .15
218 Luis Castillo .15
219 Richard Hidalgo .15
220 Manny Ramirez .40
221 Mike Mussina .40
222 Randy Wolf .15
223 Kris Benson .15
224 Ryan Klesko .25
225 Rich Aurilia .15
226 Kelvim Escobar .15
227 Francisco Cordero .15
228 Kazuhiro Sasaki .15
229 Danny Bautista .15
230 Rafael Furcal .15
231 Travis Driskill .15
232 Kyle Farnsworth .15
233 Jose Valentin .15
234 Felipe Lopez .15
235 C.C. Sabathia .15
236 Brad Penny .15
237 Brad Ausmus .15
238 Raul Ibanez .15
239 Adrian Beltre .15
240 Rocco Baldelli .25
241 Orlando Hudson .15
242 Dave Roberts .15
243 Doug Mientkiewicz .15
244 Brad Wilkerson .15
245 Scott Strickland .15
246 Sterling Hitchcock .15
247 Chad Bradford .15
248 Gary Bennett .15
249 Jose Cruz Jr. .15
250 Jeff Kent .25
251 Josh Beckett .25
252 Ramon Ortiz .15
253 Miguel Batista .15
254 Jung Bong .15
255 Deivi Cruz .15
256 Alex Gonzalez .15
257 Shawn Chacon .15
258 Runelvys Hernandez .15
259 Joe Mays .15
260 Eric Gagne .15
261 Dustan Mohr .15
262 Tomokazu Ohka .15
263 Eric Byrnes .15
264 Frank Catalanotto .15
265 Cristian Guzman .15
266 Orlando Cabrera .15
267 Mike Scioscia .15
268 Bob Brenly .15
269 Bobby Cox .15
270 Mike Hargrove .15
271 Grady Little .15
272 Dusty Baker .15
273 Jerry Manuel .15
274 Bob Boone .15
275 Eric Wedge .15
276 Clint Hurdle .15
277 Alan Trammell .15
278 Jack McKeon .15
279 Jimy Williams .15
280 Tony Pena .15
281 Jim Tracy .15
282 Ned Yost .15
283 Ron Gardenhire .15
284 Frank Robinson .25
285 Art Howe .15
286 Joe Torre .25

287 Ken Macha .15
288 Larry Bowa .15
289 Lloyd McClendon .15
290 Bruce Bochy .15
291 Felipe Alou .15
292 Bob Melvin .15
293 Tony LaRussa .15
294 Lou Piniella .15
295 Buck Showalter .15
296 Carlos Tosca .15
297 Anthony Acevedo **RC** .25
298 Anthony Lerew **RC** .75
299 Blake Hawksworth **RC** .50
300 Brayan Pena **RC** .50
301 Casey Myers **RC** .50
302 Craig Ansman **RC** .50
303 David Murphy .40
304 David Crouthers .15
305 Dioner Navarro **RC** .40
306 Donald Levinski .15
307 Jesse Roman **RC** .40
308 Sung Ki Jung **RC** .25
309 Jon Knott **RC** .40
310 Josh Labandeira **RC** .25
311 Kenny Perez **RC** .25
312 Khalid Ballouli **RC** .25
313 Kyle Davies **RC** .40
314 Marcus McBeth **RC** .40
315 Matt Creighton **RC** .40
316 Chris O'Riordan **RC** .50
317 Mike Gosling .15
318 Nic Ungs **RC** .40
319 Omar Falcon **RC** .40
320 Rodney Choy Foo **RC** .40
321 Tim Frend **RC** .50
322 Todd Self **RC** .50
323 Tydus Meadows **RC** .40
324 Yadier Molina **RC** .50
325 Zachary Duke **RC** 2.00
326 Zach Miner **RC** 1.00
327 Bernie Castro,
Khalil Greene .15
328 Ryan Madson,
Elizardo Ramirez .15
329 Rich Harden,
Bobby Crosby .15
330 Zack Greinke,
Jimmy Gobble .15
331 Bobby Jenks,
Casey Kotchman .15
332 Sammy Sosa .50
333 Kevin Millwood .25
334 Rafael Palmeiro .25
335 Roger Clemens .75
336 Eric Gagne .15
337 Bill Mueller,
Manny Ramirez,
Derek Jeter .50
338 Vernon Wells,
Ichiro Suzuki,
Michael Young .40
339 Alex Rodriguez,
Frank Thomas,
Carlos Delgado .50
340 Carlos Delgado,
Alex Rodriguez,
Bret Boone .50
341 Pedro Martinez,
Tim Hudson,
Esteban Loaiza .25
342 Esteban Loaiza,
Pedro Martinez,
Roy Halladay .25
343 Albert Pujols, Todd Helton,
Edgar Renteria .50
344 Albert Pujols, Todd Helton,
Juan Pierre .50
345 Jim Thome, Richie Sexson,
Javy Lopez .25
346 Preston Wilson,
Gary Sheffield,
Jim Thome .25
347 Jason Schmidt,
Kevin Brown,
Mark Prior .50
348 Kerry Wood, Mark Prior,
Javier Vazquez .50
349 AL Division Series .15
350 NL Division Series .15
351 NL Championship
Series .15
352 AL Championship
Series .25
353 AL & NL Division Series .15
354 AL Championship
Series .15
355 World Series Highlights .25
356 Carlos Delgado .25
357 Bret Boone .15
358 Alex Rodriguez .50
359 Bill Mueller .15
360 Vernon Wells .15
361 Garret Anderson .15
362 Magglio Ordonez .15
363 Jorge Posada .15
364 Roy Halladay .15
365 Andy Pettitte .15
366 Frank Thomas .25
367 Jody Gerut .15
368 Sammy Sosa .75
369 Joe Crede .15
370 Gary Sheffield .25
371 Coco Crisp .15
372 Torii Hunter .25
373 Derrek Lee .15
374 Adam Everett .15
375 Miguel Tejada .25
376 Jeremy Affeldt .15

377 Robin Ventura .15
378 Scott Podsednik .40
379 Matthew LeCroy .15
380 Vladimir Guerrero .40
381 Tony Clark .15
382 Jeff Nelson .15
383 Chris Singleton .15
384 Bobby Abreu .25
385 Josh Fogg .15
386 Trevor Hoffman .15
387 Jesse Foppert .25
388 Edgar Martinez .25
389 Edgar Renteria .25
390 Chipper Jones .50
391 Eric Munson .15
392 Dewon Brazelton .15
393 John Thomson .15
394 Chris Woodward .15
395 Aaron Sele .15
396 Elmer Dessens .15
397 Johnny Estrada .15
398 Damian Moss .15
399 Gabe Kapler .15
400 Dontrelle Willis .40
401 Troy Glaus .25
402 Raul Mondesi .20
403 Shane Reynolds .15
404 Kurt Ainsworth .15
405 Pedro J. Martinez .50
406 Eric Karros .15
407 Billy Koch .15
408 Scott Schoeneweis .15
409 Paul Wilson .15
410 Mike Sweeney .15
411 Jason Bay .15
412 Mark Redman .15
413 Jason Jennings .15
414 Rondell White .25
415 Todd Hundley .15
416 Shannon Stewart .15
417 Jae Weong Seo .15
418 Livan Hernandez .15
419 Mark Ellis .15
420 Pat Burrell .25
421 Mark Loretta .15
422 Robb Nen .15
423 Joel Pineiro .15
424 Jason Simontacchi .15
425 Sterling Hitchcock .15
426 Rey Ordonez .15
427 Greg Myers .15
428 Shane Spencer .15
429 Carlos Baerga .15
430 Garret Anderson .25
431 Horacio Ramirez .15
432 Brian Roberts .15
433 Damian Jackson .15
434 Doug Glanville .15
435 Brian Daubach .15
436 Alex Escobar .15
437 Alex Sanchez .15
438 Jeff Bagwell .40
439 Darrell May .15
440 Shawn Green .25
441 Geoff Jenkins .25
442 Endy Chavez .15
443 Nick Johnson .15
444 Jose Guillen .15
445 Tomas Perez .15
446 Phil Nevin .15
447 Jason Schmidt .25
448 Julio Mateo .15
449 So Taguchi .15
450 Randy Johnson .40
451 Paul Byrd .15
452 Chone Figgins .15
453 Larry Bigbie .15
454 Scott Williamson .15
455 Ramon Martinez .15
456 Roberto Alomar .25
457 Ryan Dempster .15
458 Ryan Ludwick .15
459 Ramon Santiago .15
460 Jeff Conine .15
461 Brad Lidge .15
462 Ken Harvey .15
463 Guillermo Mota .15
464 Rick Reed .15
465 Joey Eischen .15
466 Wade Miller .15
467 Steve Karsay .15
468 Chase Utley .25
469 Matt Stairs .15
470 Yorvit Torrealba .15
471 Joe Kennedy .15
472 Reed Johnson .15
473 Victor Zambrano .15
474 Jeff DaVanon .15
475 Luis Gonzalez .25
476 Rod Barajas .15
477 Ray King .15
478 Jack Cust .15
479 Omar Daal .15
480 Todd Walker .15
481 Shawn Estes .15
482 Chris Reitsma .15
483 Jake Westbrook .15
484 Jeremy Bonderman .15
485 A.J. Burnett .15
486 Roy Oswalt .25
487 Kevin Brown .25
488 Eric Milton .15
489 Claudio Vargas .15
490 Roger Cedeno .15
491 David Wells .15
492 Scott Hatteberg .15
493 Ricky Ledee .15
494 Eric Young .15

495 Armando Benitez .15
496 Dan Haren .15
497 Carl Crawford .15
498 Laynce Nix .15
499 Eric Hinske .15
500 Ivan Rodriguez .40
501 Scot Shields .15
502 Brandon Webb .15
503 Mark DeRosa .15
504 Jhonny Peralta .15
505 Adam Kennedy .15
506 Tony Batista .15
507 Jeff Suppan .15
508 Kenny Lofton .25
509 Scott Sullivan .15
510 Ken Griffey Jr. .60
511 Billy Traber .15
512 Larry Walker .25
513 Mike Maroth .15
514 Todd Hollandsworth .15
515 Kirk Saarloos .15
516 Carlos Beltran .25
517 Andy Ashby .15
518 Jose Macias .15
519 Karim Garcia .15
520 Jose Reyes .40
521 Brandon Duckworth .15
522 Brian Giles .25
523 J.T. Snow Jr. .15
524 Jamie Moyer .15
525 Jason Isringhausen .15
526 Julio Lugo .15
527 Mark Teixeira .25
528 Cory Lidle .15
529 Lyle Overbay .15
530 Troy Percival .15
531 Robby Hammock .15
532 Robert Fick .15
533 Jason Johnson .15
534 Brandon Lyon .15
535 Antonio Alfonseca .15
536 Tom Goodwin .15
537 Paul Konerko .15
538 D'Angelo Jimenez .15
539 Ben Broussard .15
540 Magglio Ordonez .25
541 Ellis Burks .15
542 Carlos Pena .15
543 Chad Fox .15
544 Jeriome Robertson .15
545 Travis Hafner .15
546 Joe Randa .15
547 Wil Cordero .15
548 Brady Clark .15
549 Ruben Sierra .15
550 Barry Zito .25
551 Brett Myers .15
552 Oliver Perez .15
553 Trey Hodges .15
554 Benito Santiago .15
555 David Ross .15
556 Ramon Vazquez .15
557 Joe Nathan .15
558 Dan Wilson .15
559 Garrett Stephenson .15
560 Jim Edmonds .25
561 Shawn Wooten .15
562 Matt Kata .15
563 Vinny Castilla .15
564 Marty Cordova .15
565 Aramis Ramirez .15
566 Carl Everett .15
567 Ryan Freel .15
568 Jason Davis .15
569 Mark Bellhorn .15
570 Craig Monroe .15
571 Ugueth Urbina .15
572 Tim Redding .15
573 Kevin Appier .15
574 Jeromy Burnitz .15
575 Miguel Cabrera .40
576 Orlando Hernandez .15
577 Casey Blake .15
578 Aaron Boone .15
579 Jermaine Dye .15
580 Jerome Williams .15
581 John Olerud .15
582 Scott Rolen .40
583 Bobby Kielty .15
584 Travis Lee .15
585 Jeff Cirillo .15
586 Scott Spiezio .15
587 Stephen Randolph .15
588 Melvin Mora .15
589 Mike Timlin .15
590 Kerry Wood .50
591 Tony Womack .15
592 Jody Gerut .15
593 Franklyn German .15
594 Morgan Ensberg .15
595 Odalis Perez .15
596 Michael Cuddyer .15
597 Jon Lieber .15
598 Mike Williams .15
599 Jose Hernandez .15
600 Alfonso Soriano .50
601 Marquis Grissom .15
602 Matt Morris .25
603 Damian Rolls .15
604 Juan Gonzalez .25
605 Aquilino Lopez .15
606 Jose Valverde .15
607 Scott Sauerbeck .15
608 Joe Borowski .15
609 Josh Bard .15
610 Austin Kearns .25
611 Chin-Hui Tsao .15
612 Wilfredo Ledezma .15

613 Aaron Guiel .15
614 LaTroy Hawkins .15
615 Tony Armas Jr. .15
616 Steve Trachsel .15
617 Ted Lilly .15
618 Todd Pratt .15
619 Sean Burroughs .15
620 Rafael Palmeiro .40
621 Jeremi Gonzalez .15
622 Quinton McCracken .15
623 David Ortiz .25
624 Randall Simon .15
625 Wily Mo Pena .15
626 Nate Cornejo .15
627 Brian Anderson .15
628 Corey Koskie .15
629 Keith Foulke .15
630 Rheal Cormier .15
631 Sidney Ponson .15
632 Gary Matthews Jr. .15
633 Herbert Perry .15
634 Shea Hillenbrand .15
635 Craig Biggio .25
636 Barry Larkin .25
637 Orlando Merced .15
638 Anaheim Angels .15
639 Arizona Diamondbacks .15
640 Atlanta Braves .15
641 Baltimore Orioles .15
642 Boston Red Sox .25
643 Chicago Cubs .40
644 Chicago White Sox .15
645 Cincinnati Reds .15
646 Cleveland Indians .15
647 Colorado Rockies .15
648 Detroit Tigers .15
649 Florida Marlins .15
650 Houston Astros .15
651 Kansas City Royals .15
652 Los Angeles Dodgers .15
653 Milwaukee Brewers .15
654 Minnesota Twins .15
655 Montreal Expos .15
656 New York Mets .15
657 New York Yankees .50
658 Oakland Athletics .15
659 Philadelphia Phillies .15
660 Pittsburgh Pirates .15
661 San Diego Padres .15
662 San Francisco Giants .15
663 Seattle Mariners .15
664 St. Louis Cardinals .15
665 Tampa Bay Devil Rays .15
666 Texas Rangers .15
667 Toronto Blue Jays .15
668 Kyle Sleeth .15
669 Bradley Sullivan .15
670 Carlos Quentin .50
671 Conor Jackson 1.00
672 Jeffrey Allison .15
673 Matthew Moses .25
674 Tim Stauffer .15
675 Estee Harris **RC** .25
676 David Aardsma .15
677 Omar Quintanilla .25
678 Aaron Hill .15
679 Tony Richie .15
680 Lastings Milledge 3.00
681 Brad Snyder .15
682 Jason Hirsh .50
683 Logan Kensing **RC** .40
684 Chris Lubanski .15
685 Ryan Harvey .15
686 Ryan Wagner .15
687 Rickie Weeks .50
688 Jeremy Guthrie,
Grady Sizemore .25
689 Edwin Jackson,
Greg Miller .15
690 Neal Cotts,
Jeremy Reed .15
691 Nicholas Markakis,
Adam Loewen .15
692 Delmon Young,
B.J. Upton .75
693 Nomar Garciaparra,
Alfonso Soriano .50
694 Ichiro Suzuki,
Albert Pujols .50
695 Jim Thome,
Mike Schmidt .40
696 Mike Mussina .25
697 Bengie Molina .15
698 John Olerud .15
699 Bret Boone .25
700 Eric Chavez .25
701 Alex Rodriguez .75
702 Mike Cameron .15
703 Ichiro Suzuki .75
704 Torii Hunter .25
705 Mike Hampton .15
706 Mike Matheny .15
707 Derrek Lee .15
708 Luis Castillo .15
709 Scott Rolen .40
710 Edgar Renteria .25
711 Andruw Jones .25
712 Jose Cruz Jr. .15
713 Jim Edmonds .25
714 Roy Halladay .25
715 Eric Gagne .25
716 Alex Rodriguez .75
717 Angel Berroa .15
718 Dontrelle Willis .25
719 Todd Helton .25
720 Marcus Giles .15
721 Edgar Renteria .25
722 Scott Rolen .40

723 Albert Pujols .75
724 Gary Sheffield .25
725 Javy Lopez .25
726 Eric Gagne .25
727 Randy Wolf .15
728 Bobby Cox .15
729 Scott Podsednik .40
730 World Series Game 4 .15
731 World Series Game 5 .15
732 World Series Game 6 .15
733 World Series MVP .25

Black

Black (1-733): 15-30X
Production 53 Sets

Gold

Stars (1-733): 5-10X
Production 2,004 Sets

1st Edition

NM/M
Stars: 3-5X
HTA Exclusive
1st Edition Pack (10): 3.00
1st Edition Box (20): 55.00

Team Factory Sets

NM/M
Complete Astros Set (737): 75.00
Complete Cubs Set (737): 75.00
Complete Red Sox Set
(737): 75.00
Complete Yankees Set
(737): 75.00
1 Brooks Conrad 1.00
2 Hector Giminez 1.00
3 Kevin Davidson 1.00
4 Chris Burke 3.00
5 John Buck 1.00
1 Bobby Brownlie 2.00
2 Felix Pie 3.00
3 Jon Connolly 1.00
4 David Kelton 1.00
5 Ricky Nolasco 1.00
1 David Murphy 1.00
2 Kevin Youkilis 3.00
3 Juan Cedeno 1.00
4 Matt Murton 1.00
5 Kenny Perez 1.00
1 Rudy Guillen 1.00
2 David Parrish 2.00
3 Brad Halsey 1.00
4 Hector Made 1.00
5 Robinson Cano 6.00

All-Stars

NM/M
Complete Set (20): 20.00
Common Player: .50
Inserted 1:16
TAS1 Jason Giambi 1.50
TAS2 Ichiro Suzuki 2.50
TAS3 Alex Rodriguez 3.00
TAS4 Albert Pujols 3.00
TAS5 Alfonso Soriano 1.50
TAS6 Nomar Garciaparra 2.50
TAS7 Andruw Jones 1.00
TAS8 Carlos Delgado .75
TAS9 Gary Sheffield .75
TAS10 Jorge Posada .75
TAS11 Magglio Ordonez .75
TAS12 Kerry Wood 1.50
TAS13 Garret Anderson .75
TAS14 Bret Boone .50
TAS15 Hank Blalock .75
TAS16 Mike Lowell .50
TAS17 Todd Helton 1.00
TAS18 Vernon Wells .50
TAS19 Roger Clemens 3.00
TAS20 Scott Rolen 1.50

All-Star Patch Relics

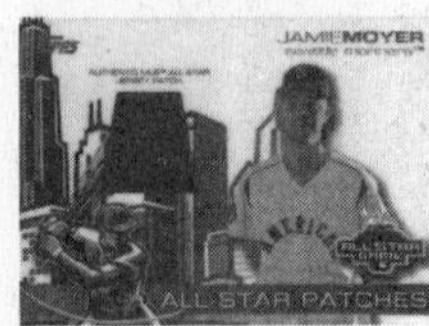

No Pricing
Inserted 1:7,698

All-Star Stitches

NM/M
Common Player: 5.00
Inserted 1:137
GA Garret Anderson 6.00
HB Hank Blalock 6.00
AB Aaron Boone 5.00
BD Brendan Donnelly 5.00
CE Carl Everett 5.00
KF Keith Foulke 5.00
RF Rafael Furcal 8.00
EGA Eric Gagne 8.00
NG Nomar Garciaparra 15.00
TG Troy Glaus 8.00
EG Eddie Guardado 5.00
SH Shigetoshi Hasegawa 5.00
TH Todd Helton 8.00
RH Ramon Hernandez 5.00
AJ Andruw Jones 8.00
EL Esteban Loàiza 5.00
PL Paul LoDuca 5.00
JL Javy Lopez 8.00
ML Mike Lowell 5.00
EM Edgar Martinez 8.00
MMO Melvin Mora 5.00
JM Jamie Moyer 5.00
MM Mark Mulder 6.00
RO Russ Ortiz 6.00
JP Jorge Posada 8.00
ER Edgar Renteria 5.00
AR Alex Rodriguez 15.00
SR Scott Rolen 10.00
JS Jason Schmidt 6.00
JV Jose Vidro 5.00
BW Billy Wagner 5.00
VW Vernon Wells 6.00
RWH Rondell White 5.00
WW Woody Williams 6.00
PW Preston Wilson 5.00
RW Randy Wolf 5.00
KW Kerry Wood 8.00

2004 Topps American Treasures Cut Signatures

No Pricing
Inserted 1:658,152

Dual

Complete Set (1):

Presidential Signatures

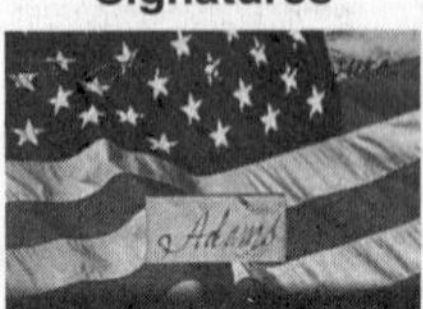

No Pricing
Production One Set

Autographs

NM/M
Common Player:
JB Josh Beckett 50.00
HB Hank Blalock 20.00
CF Cliff Floyd 8.00
JG Jay Gibbons 15.00
KG Khalil Greene 10.00
EH Eric Hinske 10.00
TH Torii Hunter 25.00
AK Austin Kearns 25.00
PK Paul Konerko 15.00
PL Paul LoDuca 10.00
ML Mike Lowell 8.00
VM Victor Martinez 20.00
MO Magglio Ordonez 15.00
JP Josh Phelps 8.00
MP Mark Prior 40.00
ER Elizardo Ramirez 8.00
BS Benito Santiago 15.00
MS Mike Sweeney 20.00
MT Mark Teixeira 25.00
BU B.J. Upton 20.00
JV Jose Vidro 8.00
Series 2
GA Garret Anderson 35.00
LB Lance Berkman 35.00
AB Aaron Boone 35.00
BB Bobby Brownlie 30.00
MC Miguel Cabrera 40.00
ZG Zack Greinke 20.00
AH Aubrey Huff 20.00
DM Dustin McGowan 15.00
SP Scott Podsednik 25.00
JP Jorge Posada 40.00
IR Ivan Rodriguez 45.00
SR Scott Rolen 30.00
DW Dontrelle Willis 30.00

Derby Digs

NM/M
Common Player: 8.00
Inserted 1:585
GA Garret Anderson 8.00
BB Bret Boone 8.00
CD Carlos Delgado 8.00
JE Jim Edmonds 8.00
JG Jason Giambi 15.00
AP Albert Pujols 25.00
RS Richie Sexson 8.00

Draft Pick Bonus

NM/M
Complete Set (15): 50.00
Complete Holiday Set (10): 30.00
Complete Retail Set (5): 20.00
1 Josh Johnson 4.00
2 Donny Lucy 4.00
3 Greg Golson 6.00
4 K.C. Herren 4.00
5 Jeff Marquez 4.00
6 Mark Rogers 8.00
7 Eric Hurley 4.00
8 Gio Gonzalez 6.00
9 Thomas Diamond 6.00
10 Matt Bush 8.00
11 Kyle Waldrop 6.00
12 Neil Walker 6.00
13 Mike Ferris 4.00
14 Ray Liotta 6.00
15 Phillip Hughes 15.00

Fall Classic Covers

NM/M
Complete Set (99): 125.00
Common Card: 2.00
Inserted 1:12
FC1903 1903 World Series 2.00
FC1905 1905 World Series 2.00
FC1906 1906 World Series 2.00
FC1907 1907 World Series 2.00
FC1908 1908 World Series 2.00
FC1909 1909 World Series 2.00
FC1910 1910 World Series 2.00
FC1911 1911 World Series 2.00
FC1912 1912 World Series 2.00
FC1913 1913 World Series 2.00
FC1914 1914 World Series 2.00
FC1915 1915 World Series 2.00
FC1916 1916 World Series 2.00
FC1917 1917 World Series 2.00
FC1918 1918 World Series 2.00
FC1919 1919 World Series 2.00
FC1920 1920 World Series 2.00
FC1921 1921 World Series 2.00
FC1922 1922 World Series 2.00
FC1923 1923 World Series 2.00
FC1924 1924 World Series 2.00
FC1925 1925 World Series 2.00
FC1926 1926 World Series 2.00
FC1927 1927 World Series 2.00
FC1928 1928 World Series 2.00
FC1929 1929 World Series 2.00
FC1930 1930 World Series 2.00
FC1931 1931 World Series 2.00
FC1932 1932 World Series 2.00
FC1933 1933 World Series 2.00
FC1934 1934 World Series 2.00
FC1935 1935 World Series 2.00
FC1936 1936 World Series 2.00
FC1937 1937 World Series 2.00
FC1938 1938 World Series 2.00
FC1939 1939 World Series 2.00
FC1940 1940 World Series 2.00
FC1941 1941 World Series 2.00
FC1942 1942 World Series 2.00
FC1943 1943 World Series 2.00
FC1944 1944 World Series 2.00
FC1945 1945 World Series 2.00
FC1946 1946 World Series 2.00
FC1947 1947 World Series 2.00
FC1948 1948 World Series 2.00
FC1949 1949 World Series 2.00
FC1950 1950 World Series 2.00
FC1951 1951 World Series 2.00
FC1952 1952 World Series 2.00
FC1953 1953 World Series 2.00
FC1954 1954 World Series 2.00
FC1955 1955 World Series 2.00
FC1956 1956 World Series 2.00
FC1957 1957 World Series 2.00
FC1958 1958 World Series 2.00
FC1959 1959 World Series 2.00
FC1960 1960 World Series 2.00
FC1961 1961 World Series 2.00
FC1962 1962 World Series 2.00
FC1963 1963 World Series 2.00
FC1964 1964 World Series 2.00
FC1965 1965 World Series 2.00
FC1966 1966 World Series 2.00
FC1967 1967 World Series 2.00
FC1968 1968 World Series 2.00
FC1969 1969 World Series 2.00
FC1970 1970 World Series 2.00
FC1971 1971 World Series 2.00
FC1972 1972 World Series 2.00
FC1973 1973 World Series 2.00
FC1974 1974 World Series 2.00
FC1975 1975 World Series 2.00
FC1976 1976 World Series 2.00
FC1977 1977 World Series 2.00
FC1978 1978 World Series 2.00
FC1979 1979 World Series 2.00
FC1980 1980 World Series 2.00
FC1981 1981 World Series 2.00
FC1982 1982 World Series 2.00
FC1983 1983 World Series 2.00
FC1984 1984 World Series 2.00
FC1985 1985 World Series 2.00
FC1986 1986 World Series 2.00
FC1987 1987 World Series 2.00
FC1988 1988 World Series 2.00
FC1989 1989 World Series 2.00
FC1990 1990 World Series 2.00
FC1991 1991 World Series 2.00
FC1992 1992 World Series 2.00
FC1993 1993 World Series 2.00
FC1995 1995 World Series 2.00
FC1996 1996 World Series 2.00
FC1997 1997 World Series 2.00
FC1998 1998 World Series 2.00
FC1999 1999 World Series 2.00
FC2000 2000 World Series 2.00
FC2001 2001 World Series 2.00
FC2002 2002 World Series 2.00
FC2003 2003 World Series 2.00

Hit Parade

NM/M
Complete Set (30): 20.00
Common Player: .50
Inserted 1:7
HP1 Sammy Sosa 3.00
HP2 Rafael Palmeiro 1.00
HP3 Fred McGriff .50
HP4 Ken Griffey Jr. 2.00
HP5 Juan Gonzalez 1.00
HP6 Frank Thomas 1.00
HP7 Andres Galarraga .50
HP8 Jim Thome 1.50
HP9 Jeff Bagwell 1.00
HP10 Mike Piazza 2.00
HP11 Rafael Palmeiro 1.00
HP12 Sammy Sosa 3.00
HP13 Fred McGriff .50
HP14 Andres Galarraga .50
HP15 Juan Gonzalez 1.00
HP16 Frank Thomas 1.00
HP17 Jeff Bagwell 1.00
HP18 Ken Griffey Jr. 2.00
HP19 Ruben Sierra .50
HP20 Ellis Burks .50
HP21 Rafael Palmeiro 1.00
HP22 Roberto Alomar .75
HP23 Julio Franco .50
HP24 Andres Galarraga .50
HP25 Fred McGriff .50
HP26 Craig Biggio .75
HP27 Barry Larkin .75
HP28 Edgar Martinez .50
HP29 Ellis Burks .50
HP30 Sammy Sosa 3.00

Hobby Masters

NM/M
Complete Set (20): 40.00
Common Player: .75
Inserted 1:12
HM1 Albert Pujols 3.00
HM2 Mark Prior 4.00
HM3 Alex Rodriguez 4.00
HM4 Nomar Garciaparra 3.00
HM5 Barry Bonds 4.00
HM6 Sammy Sosa 3.00
HM7 Alfonso Soriano 2.00
HM8 Ichiro Suzuki 2.50
HM9 Derek Jeter 4.00
HM10 Jim Thome 1.50
HM11 Jason Giambi 1.50
HM12 Mike Piazza 2.50
HM13 Barry Zito 1.00
HM14 Randy Johnson 2.00
HM15 Adam Dunn 1.00
HM16 Vladimir Guerrero 2.00
HM17 Gary Sheffield .75
HM18 Carlos Delgado 1.00
HM19 Chipper Jones 2.50
HM20 Dontrelle Willis 1.00

Own the Game

NM/M
Complete Set (30): 25.00
Common Player: .50
Inserted 1:18
OG1 Jim Thome 1.50
OG2 Albert Pujols 3.00
OG3 Alex Rodriguez 3.00
OG4 Barry Bonds 4.00
OG5 Ichiro Suzuki 2.00
OG6 Derek Jeter 3.00
OG7 Nomar Garciaparra 3.00
OG8 Alfonso Soriano 1.50
OG9 Gary Sheffield .75
OG10 Jason Giambi 1.00
OG11 Todd Helton 1.00
OG12 Garret Anderson .50
OG13 Carlos Delgado 1.00
OG14 Manny Ramirez 1.00
OG15 Richie Sexson .75
OG16 Vernon Wells .50
OG17 Preston Wilson .50
OG18 Frank Thomas 1.00
OG19 Shawn Green .75
OG20 Rafael Furcal .50
OG21 Juan Pierre .50
OG22 Javy Lopez .50
OG23 Edgar Renteria .50
OG24 Mark Prior 3.00
OG25 Pedro J. Martinez 1.50
OG26 Kerry Wood 1.00
OG27 Curt Schilling .75
OG28 Roy Halladay .50
OG29 Eric Gagne .50
OG30 Brandon Webb .50

Presidential Pastime

NM/M
Complete Set (42): 100.00
Common President: 3.00
Inserted 1:6
PP1 George Washington 8.00
PP2 John Adams 4.00
PP3 Thomas Jefferson 4.00
PP4 James Madison 4.00
PP5 James Monroe 4.00
PP6 John Quincy Adams 4.00
PP7 Andrew Jackson 3.00
PP8 Martin Van Buren 3.00
PP9 William H. Harrison 3.00
PP10 John Tyler 4.00
PP11 James K. Polk 4.00
PP12 Zachary Taylor 3.00
PP13 Millard Fillmore 3.00
PP14 Franklin Pierce 3.00
PP15 James Buchanan 3.00
PP16 Abraham Lincoln 6.00
PP17 Andrew Johnson 3.00
PP18 Ulysses S. Grant 5.00
PP19 Rutherford B. Hayes 3.00
PP20 James Garfield 3.00
PP21 Chester A. Arthur 3.00
PP22 Grover Cleveland 3.00
PP23 Benjamin Harrison 3.00
PP24 William McKinley 3.00
PP25 Theodore Roosevelt 4.00
PP26 William H. Taft 4.00
PP27 Woodrow Wilson 4.00
PP28 Warren Harding 4.00
PP29 Calvin Coolidge 4.00
PP30 Herbert Hoover 3.00
PP31 Franklin D. Roosevelt 4.00
PP32 Harry S. Truman 4.00
PP33 Dwight D. Eisenhower 4.00
PP34 John F. Kennedy 6.00
PP35 Lyndon B. Johnson 3.00
PP36 Richard Nixon 4.00
PP37 Gerald Ford 3.00
PP38 Jimmy Carter 3.00
PP39 Ronald Reagan 3.00
PP40 George H.W. Bush 3.00
PP41 Bill Clinton 4.00
PP42 George W. Bush 3.00

Presidential First Pitch Relics

NM/M
Common Player: 15.00
Inserted 1:592
GHB George H.W. Bush 25.00
GB George W. Bush 25.00
BC Bill Clinton 40.00
CC Calvin Coolidge 15.00
DE Dwight D. Eisenhower 15.00
GF Gerald Ford 30.00
WH Warren Harding 30.00
HH Herbert Hoover 30.00
LJ Lyndon B. Johnson 20.00
JK John F. Kennedy 50.00
RN Richard Nixon 30.00
RR Ronald Reagan 30.00
FR Franklin D. Roosevelt 40.00
WT William H. Taft 25.00
HT Harry S. Truman 30.00
WW Woodrow Wilson 25.00

Series Seats Relics

NM/M
Common Player: 10.00
Inserted 1:316
LA Luis Aparicio 15.00
BF Bob Feller 12.00
RJ Reggie Jackson 20.00
AK Al Kaline 20.00
HK Harmon Killebrew 25.00
WM Willie Mays 25.00
BM Bill Mazeroski 20.00
PM Paul Molitor 20.00
JP Jim Palmer 15.00
LP Lou Piniella 10.00
BP Boog Powell 10.00
BR Brooks Robinson 15.00
FR Frank Robinson 15.00
WS Warren Spahn 15.00
RY Robin Yount 20.00

Series Stitches Relics

NM/M
Common Player: 10.00
JBE Josh Beckett 10.00
JB Johnny Bench 25.00
GB George Brett 30.00
JCA Jose Canseco 15.00
GC Gary Carter 12.00
JC Joe Carter 10.00
RC Roger Clemens 20.00
LD Lenny Dykstra 15.00
SG Steve Garvey 15.00
KG Kirk Gibson 10.00
DG Dwight Gooden 15.00
RJA Reggie Jackson 20.00
RJ Randy Johnson 10.00
CJ Chipper Jones 15.00
DJ David Justice 15.00
HK Harmon Killebrew 30.00
WM Willie Mays 50.00
PO Paul O'Neill 20.00
KP Kirby Puckett 25.00
FR Frank Robinson 20.00
MS Mike Schmidt 30.00
TS Tom Seaver 25.00
AS Alfonso Soriano 15.00
RY Robin Yount 20.00

Team Topps Legends Autographs

NM/M
Inserted 1:766
SG Steve Garvey 15.00
BP Boog Powell 10.00

World Series Highlights

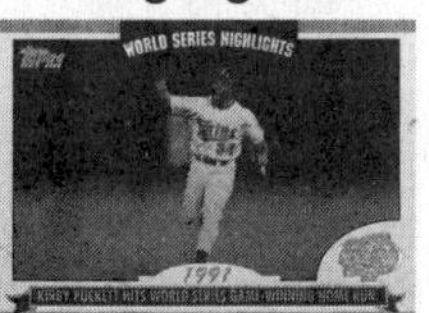

NM/M
Complete Set (30): 35.00
Common Player: 1.00
Inserted 1:18
LB Lou Brock 1.00
CF Carlton Fisk 1.50
KG Kirk Gibson 1.00
RJ Reggie Jackson 2.00
DL Don Larsen 1.00
MM Willie Mays 4.00
BM Bill Mazeroski 1.00
SM Stan Musial 3.00
JP Jim Palmer 1.00
KP Kirby Puckett 2.00
BR Brooks Robinson 2.00
MS Mike Schmidt 4.00
TS Tom Seaver 2.00
CY Carl Yastrzemski 2.00
RY Robin Yount 2.00
Series 2
DB Dusty Baker 1.00
JB Johnny Bench 2.50
JCA Jose Canseco 1.50
JC Joe Carter 1.00
WF Whitey Ford 2.00
LG Luis Gonzalez 1.00
AJ Andruw Jones 1.50
DJ David Justice 1.00
AK Al Kaline 2.00
WM Willie McCovey 1.00
JP Johnny Podres 1.00
FR Frank Robinson 1.50
OS Ozzie Smith 2.00
DS Duke Snider 1.50
BT Bobby Thomson 1.00

World Series Highlights Autographs

NM/M
Common Player:
LB Lou Brock 30.00
CF Carlton Fisk 50.00
KG Kirk Gibson 30.00
DL Don Larsen 25.00
BM Bill Mazeroski 30.00
JP Jim Palmer 25.00
BR Brooks Robinson 40.00
MS Mike Schmidt 65.00
RY Robin Yount 50.00
Series 2
DB Dusty Baker 20.00
JB Johnny Bench 50.00
WF Whitey Ford 35.00
RJ Reggie Jackson 40.00
DJ David Justice 30.00
AK Al Kaline 40.00
SM Stan Musial 75.00
JP Johnny Podres 15.00
DS Duke Snider 35.00
BT Bobby Thomson 20.00

2004 Topps All-Time Fan Favorites

NM/M
Complete Set (150): 35.00
Common Player: .25
Pack (6): 4.00
Box (24): 80.00
1 Willie Mays 2.50
2 Bob Gibson .75
3 Dave Steib .25
4 Tim McCarver .25
5 Reggie Jackson .75
6 John Candelaria .25
7 Lenny Dykstra .25

8 Tony Oliva .50
9 Frank Viola .25
10 Don Mattingly 2.50
11 Garry Maddox .25
12 Randy Jones .25
13 Joe Carter .25
14 Orlando Cepeda .50
15 Bob Sheppard .25
16 Bobby Grich .25
17 George Scott .25
18 Mickey Rivers .25
19 Ron Santo .25
20 Mike Schmidt 2.00
21 Luis Aparicio .25
22 Cesar Geronimo .25
23 Jack Morris .25
24 Jeffrey Loria .25
25 George Brett 2.00
26 Paul O'Neill .25
27 Reggie Smith .25
28 Robin Yount 1.00
29 Andre Dawson .50
30 Whitey Ford .75
31 Ralph Kiner .50
32 Will Clark .50
33 Keith Hernandez .25
34 Tony Fernandez .25
35 Willie McGee .25
36 Harmon Killebrew .75
37 Dave Kingman .25
38 Kirk Gibson .25
39 Terry Steinbach .25
40 Frank Robinson .75
41 Chet Lemon .25
42 Mike Cuellar .25
43 Darrell Evans .25
44 Don Kessinger .25
45 Dave Concepcion .25
46 Sparky Anderson .25
47 Bret Saberhagen .25
48 Brett Butler .25
49 Kent Hrbek .25
50 Hank Aaron 2.50
51 Rudolph Giuliani .25
52 Clete Boyer .25
53 Mookie Wilson .25
54 Dave Stewart .25
55 Gary Matthews .25
56 Roy Face .25
57 Vida Blue .25
58 Jimmy Key .25
59 Al Hrabosky .25
60 Al Kaline .75
61 Mike Scott .25
62 Jack McDowell .25
63 Reggie Jackson .75
64 Earl Weaver .25
65 Ernie Harwell .25
66 David Justice .25
67 Wilbur Wood .25
68 Mike Boddicker .25
69 Don Zimmer .25
70 Jim Palmer .50
71 Doug DeCinces .25
72 Ryne Sandberg 1.00
73 Don Newcombe .25
74 Denny Martinez .25
75 Carl Yastrzemski 1.50
76 Bake McBride .25
77 Andy Van Slyke .25
78 Bruce Sutter .50
79 Bobby Valentine .25
80 Johnny Bench 1.50
81 Orel Hershiser .25
82 Danny Tartabull .25
83 Lou Whitaker .25
84 Alan Trammell .50
85 Sam McDowell .25
86 Ray Knight .25
87 Fernando Valenzuela .25
88 Ben Oglivie .25
89 Billy Beane .25
90 Yogi Berra 1.00
91 Jose Canseco .50
92 Bobby Bonilla .25
93 Darren Daulton .25
94 Harold Reynolds .25
95 Lou Brock .50
96 Pete Incaviglia .25
97 Eric Gregg .25
98 Devon White .25
99 Kelly Gruber .25
100 Nolan Ryan 3.00
101 Carlton Fisk .50
102 George Foster .25
103 Dennis Eckersley .25
104 Rick Sutcliffe .25
105 Cal Ripken Jr. 3.00
106 Norm Cash .25
107 Charlie Hough .25
108 Paul Molitor .75
109 Maury Wills .25
110 Tom Seaver 1.00
111 Brooks Robinson 1.00
112 Jim Rice .25
113 Dwight Gooden .25
114 Harold Baines .25
115 Tim Raines .25
116 Roy Smalley .25
117 Richie Allen .25
118 Ron Swoboda .25
119 Ron Guidry .25
120 Duke Snider .75
121 Ferguson Jenkins .50
122 Mark Fidrych .25
123 Buddy Bell .25
124 Bo Jackson .50
125 Stan Musial 1.50
126 Jesse Barfield .25
127 Tony Gwynn 1.00
128 Phil Garner .25
129 Dale Murphy .75
130 Wade Boggs .50
131 Sid Fernandez .25
132 Monte Irvin .25
133 Peter Ueberroth .25
134 Gary Gaetti .25
135 Gorman Thomas .25
136 Davey Lopes .25
137 Sy Berger .25
138 Buck O'Neil .25
139 Herb Score .25
140 Rod Carew .75
141 Joe Buck .25
142 Willie Horton .25
143 Hal McRae .25
144 Rollie Fingers .25
145 Tom Brunansky .25
146 Fay Vincent .25
147 Gary Carter .50
148 Bobby Richardson .25
149 Steve Garvey .25
150 Don Larsen .50

Refractor

Cards (1-150): 3-6X
Production 299 Sets

Autographs

NM/M
Common Autograph: 10.00
Inserted 2:Box
SP's Noted
HA Hank Aaron/50 350.00
RA Richie Allen 15.00
SA Sparky Anderson/100 20.00
LA Luis Aparicio/100 40.00
HB Harold Baines/100 20.00
JB Jesse Barfield 10.00
BB Billy Beane/100 25.00
BBE Buddy Bell 20.00
JBE Johnny Bench/100 150.00
SB Sy Berger 50.00
YB Yogi Berra/100 90.00
VB Vida Blue 15.00
MB Mike Boddicker 15.00
WB Wade Boggs/50 100.00
BMB Bobby Bonilla 20.00
GB George Brett/50 100.00
LB Lou Brock/100 60.00
TB Tom Brunansky 25.00
JB Joe Buck/100 30.00
JCA Jose Canseco/100 65.00
RC Rod Carew/100 60.00
GC Gary Carter/50 60.00
JC Joe Carter/100 45.00
OC Orlando Cepeda/100 65.00
DC Dave Concepcion/100 40.00
DD Darren Daulton 15.00
AD Andre Dawson/100 40.00
LD Lenny Dykstra/100 20.00
DEC Dennis Eckersley/100 40.00
DE Darrell Evans 10.00
SF Sid Fernandez/100 40.00
TF Tony Fernandez 15.00
MF Mark Fidrych/100 40.00
RF Rollie Fingers/100 40.00
WF Whitey Ford/100 100.00
GF George Foster 10.00
SG Steve Garvey/100 30.00
CG Cesar Geronimo/100 65.00
BG Bob Gibson/100 90.00
DG Dwight Gooden/50 60.00
EG Eric Gregg 15.00
BGR Bobby Grich 10.00
RG Ron Guidry/100 50.00
TG Tony Gwynn/50 100.00
EH Ernie Harwell 25.00
KH Keith Hernandez/50 25.00
OH Orel Hershiser 30.00
WH Willie Horton 10.00
CH Charlie Hough 15.00
AH Al Hrabosky 15.00
PI Pete Incaviglia 20.00
MI Monte Irvin/100 25.00
BJ Bo Jackson/50 100.00
RJ2 Reggie Jackson 80.00
FJ Ferguson Jenkins 15.00
RJO Randy Jones 10.00
DJ David Justice 25.00
AK Al Kaline/50 100.00
DKE Don Kessinger 15.00
JK Jimmy Key/100 45.00
HK Harmon Killebrew/100 85.00
RK Ralph Kiner 40.00
DK Dave Kingman 40.00
RKN Ray Knight/100 40.00
DLA Don Larsen 15.00
CL Chet Lemon 15.00
DL Davey Lopes 10.00
GM Gary Mathews 10.00
DON Don Mattingly/50 125.00
WM Willie Mays/50 225.00
TM Tim McCarver 40.00
JM Jack McDowell 15.00
SM Sam McDowell/100 15.00
WMC Willie McGee/100 50.00
PM Paul Molitor/50 85.00
JMO Jack Morris 10.00
DM Dale Murphy/50 75.00
SM Stan Musial/100 100.00
BO Buck O'Neil 30.00
PO Paul O'Neill/50 60.00
BO Ben Oglivie 15.00
TO Tony Oliva 30.00
JP Jim Palmer/50 100.00
TR Tim Raines 25.00
HR Harold Reynolds/100 30.00
JR Jim Rice/100 40.00
BR Bobby Richardson 15.00
CR Cal Ripken Jr./50 200.00
MR Mickey Rivers 10.00
BRO Brooks Robinson/50 100.00
FR Frank Robinson/100 80.00
NR Nolan Ryan 175.00
BS Bret Saberhagen/100 45.00
RYN Ryne Sandberg/100 100.00
RS Ron Santo 30.00
MS Mike Schmidt/50 120.00
GS George Scott 15.00
MSC Mike Scott 10.00
TSE Tom Seaver/50 100.00
DSN Duke Snider/100 75.00
DS Dave Stewart 10.00
DST Dave Stieb 25.00
RSU Rick Sutcliffe/100 40.00
BSU Bruce Sutter 35.00
RSW Ron Swoboda 15.00
AT Alan Trammell/100 60.00
PU Peter Ueberroth/100 60.00
BV Bobby Valentine/100 50.00
AV Andy Van Slyke/100 65.00
FVI Fay Vincent/100 50.00
EW Earl Weaver 15.00
MW Maury Wills 15.00
MWI Mookie Wilson 10.00
WW Wilbur Wood 15.00
CY Carl Yastrzemski/50 100.00
RY Robin Yount/50 100.00
DZ Don Zimmer 30.00

Best Seat In The House

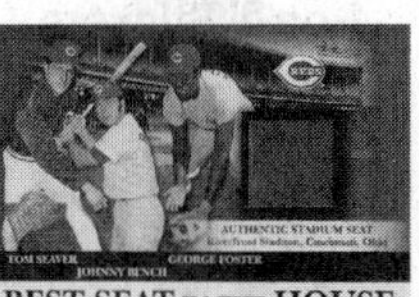

NM/M
Common Card: 15.00
BS1 Tom Seaver, Johnny Bench, George Foster 15.00
BS2 Frank Robinson, Jim Palmer, Brooks Robinson 15.00
BS3 Dave Parker, Bill Madlock, Bill Mazeroski 15.00
BS4 Kent Hrbek, Rod Carew, Harmon Killebrew 30.00

Relics

NM/M
Common Player: 5.00
WB Wade Boggs 10.00
GB George Brett 15.00
LB Lou Brock 10.00
JC Jose Canseco/Jsy 8.00
JCB Jose Canseco/Bat 8.00
GC Gary Carter 8.00
DE Dennis Eckersley 5.00
CF Carlton Fisk 10.00
GF George Foster 5.00
KG Kirk Gibson 5.00
KH Keith Hernandez 8.00
RJ Reggie Jackson 10.00
DJ David Justice 5.00
HK Harmon Killebrew 20.00
WM Willie Mays 30.00
JM Joe Morgan 5.00
GN Graig Nettles 8.00
JP Jim Palmer 8.00
DP Dave Parker 5.00
KP Kirby Puckett 10.00
HR Harold Reynolds 5.00
JR Jim Rice 5.00
BR Brooks Robinson 12.00
FRB Frank Robinson/Bat 8.00
FR Frank Robinson/Jsy 8.00
NR Nolan Ryan 25.00
BS Bret Saberhagen 5.00
MS Mike Schmidt 15.00
DS Darryl Strawberry 8.00
EW Earl Weaver 8.00
MW Maury Wills 5.00
CY Carl Yastrzemski 20.00

2004 Topps Bazooka

NM/M
Complete Set (300): 40.00
Common Player: .15
Variations (30): Same Price
Pack (8): 2.00
Box (24): 40.00
1 Bobby Abreu .25
2 Jesse Foppert .15
3 Shea Hillenbrand .15
4 Jose Lima .15
5 Manny Ramirez .50
6 Denny Neagle .15
7 Frank Thomas .50
8 A.J. Burnett .15
9 Carl Everett .15
10 Scott Podsednik .25
11 Travis Lee .15
12 Mike Mussina .40
13 Runelvys Hernandez .15
14 Shannon Stewart .15
15 Miguel Cabrera .40
16 Edgardo Alfonzo .15
17 Victor Zambrano .15
18 Rafael Furcal .25
19 Eric Hinske .15
20 Paul LoDuca .15
21 Phil Nevin .15
22 Aramis Ramirez .15
23 Jim Thome .75
24 Jeromy Burnitz .15
25 Mark Prior 1.50
26 Ramon Hernandez .15
27 Cliff Lee .15
28 Greg Myers .15
29 Robert Fick .15
30 Mike Sweeney .15
31 Carlos Zambrano .15
32 Roberto Alomar .40
33 Orlando Cabrera .25
34 Orlando Hudson .15
35 Nomar Garciaparra 1.50
36 Esteban Loaiza .15
37 Laynce Nix .15
38 Joe Randa .15
39 Juan Uribe .15
40 Pat Burrell .40
41 Steve Finley .15
42 Livan Hernandez .15
43 Al Leiter .15
44 Brett Myers .15
45 Jody Gerut .15
46 Mark Teixeira .40
47 Barry Zito .40
48 Moises Alou .25
49 Mike Cameron .15
50 Albert Pujols 1.50
51 Tim Hudson .25
52 Kenny Lofton .25
53 Trot Nixon .15
54 Tim Redding .15
55 Marlon Byrd .15
56 Javier Vazquez .25
57 Sean Burroughs .15
58 Cliff Floyd .15
59 Juan Rivera .15
60 Mike Lieberthal .15
61 Xavier Nady .15
62 Brad Radke .15
63 Miguel Tejada .40
64 Ichiro Suzuki 1.00
65 Garret Anderson .25
66 Sean Casey .15
67 Jason Giambi .75
68 Aubrey Huff .15
69 Javy Lopez .25
70 Hideo Nomo .25
71 Mark Redman .15
72 Jose Vidro .15
73 Rich Aurilia .15
74 Luis Castillo .15
75 Jay Gibbons .15
76 Torii Hunter .25
77 Derek Lowe .15
78 Wes Obermueller .15
79 Edgar Renteria .15
80 Jeff Bagwell .50
81 Fernando Vina .15
82 Frank Catalanotto .15
83 Marcus Giles .15
84 Raul Ibanez .15
85 Mike Lowell .25
86 Tomokazu Ohka .15
87 Jose Reyes .25
88 Omar Vizquel .25
89 Shawn Chacon .15
90 Rocco Baldelli .25
91 Brian Giles .25
92 Kazuhisa Ishii .15
93 Greg Maddux 1.00
94 John Olerud .25
95 Eric Chavez .25
96 Doug Waechter .15
97 Tony Batista .15
98 Jeriome Robertson .15
99 Troy Glaus .25
100 Eric Gagne .25
101 Pedro J. Martinez .75
102 Magglio Ordonez .25
103 Alex Rodriguez 2.00
104 Jason Bay .15
105 Larry Walker .25
106 Matt Clement .15
107 Tom Glavine .25
108 Geoff Jenkins .25
109 Victor Martinez .15
110 David Ortiz .15
111 Ivan Rodriguez .40
112 Jarrod Washburn .15
113 Josh Beckett .25
114 Bartolo Colon .25
115 Juan Gonzalez .40
116 Derek Jeter 2.00
117 Edgar Martinez .25
118 Ramon Ortiz .15
119 Scott Rolen .75
120 Brandon Webb .15
121 Carlos Beltran .25
122 Jose Contreras .25
123 Luis Gonzalez .25
124 Jason Johnson .15
125 Luis Matos .15
126 Russ Ortiz .15
127 Damian Rolls .15
128 David Wells .15
129 Adrian Beltre .15
130 Shawn Green .25
131 Nate Cornejo .15
132 Nick Johnson .15
133 Joe Mays .15
134 Roy Oswalt .25
135 C.C. Sabathia .15
136 Vernon Wells .25
137 Kris Benson .15
138 Carl Crawford .15
139 Ken Griffey Jr. 1.00
140 Randy Johnson .75
141 Fred McGriff .25
142 Vicente Padilla .15
143 Tim Salmon .25
144 Kip Wells .15
145 Lance Berkman .25
146 Jose Cruz Jr. .15
147 Marquis Grissom .15
148 Jacque Jones .15
149 Gil Meche .15
150 Vladimir Guerrero .75
151 Reggie Sanders .15
152 Ty Wigginton .15
153 Angel Berroa .15
154 Johnny Damon .25
155 Rafael Palmeiro .50
156 Chipper Jones .75
157 Kevin Millar .15
158 Corey Patterson .25
159 Johan Santana .15
160 Bernie Williams .40
161 Craig Biggio .25
162 Carlos Delgado .50
163 Aaron Guiel .15
164 Wade Miller .15
165 Andruw Jones .50
166 Jay Payton .15
167 Benito Santiago .15
168 Woody Williams .15
169 Casey Blake .15
170 Adam Dunn .40
171 Jose Guillen .15
172 Brian Jordan .15
173 Kevin Millwood .25
174 Carlos Pena .15
175 Curt Schilling .50
176 Jerome Williams .15
177 Hank Blalock .25
178 Erubiel Durazo .15
179 Cristian Guzman .15
180 Austin Kearns .40
181 Raul Mondesi .15
182 Andy Pettitte .25
183 Jason Schmidt .25
184 Jeremy Bonderman .15
185 Dontrelle Willis .25
186 Ray Durham .15
187 Jerry Hairston Jr. .15
188 Jason Kendall .15
189 Melvin Mora .15
190 Jeff Kent .25
191 Jae Weong Seo .15
192 Jack Wilson .15
193 Cesar Izturis .15
194 Jermaine Dye .15
195 Roy Halladay .25
196 Jason Phillips .15
197 Matt Morris .25
198 Mike Piazza 1.00
199 Richie Sexson .40
200 Alfonso Soriano .75
201 Mark Mulder .25
202 David Eckstein .15
203 Mike Hampton .15
204 Ryan Klesko .25
205 Damian Moss .15
206 Juan Pierre .15
207 Ben Sheets .25
208 Randy Winn .15
209 Bret Boone .25
210 Jim Edmonds .25
211 Rich Harden .15
212 Paul Konerko .15
213 Jamie Moyer .15
214 A.J. Pierzynski .15
215 Gary Sheffield .25
216 Randy Wolf .15
217 Kevin Brown .25
218 Morgan Ensberg .15
219 Bo Hart .15
220 Bill Mueller .15
221 Corey Koskie .15
222 Joel Pineiro .15
223 Preston Wilson .15
224 Aaron Boone .15
225 Kerry Wood .50
226 Darin Erstad .25
227 Wes Helms .15
228 Brian Lawrence .15
229 Mark Buehrle .15
230 Sammy Sosa 1.25
231 Sidney Ponson .15
232 Dmitri Young .15
233 Ellis Burks .15
234 Kelvim Escobar .15
235 Todd Helton .50
236 Matt Lawton .15
237 Eric Munson .15
238 Jorge Posada .50
239 Junior Spivey .15
240 Michael Young .15
241 Ramon Nivar .15
242 Edwin Jackson .15
243 Felix Pie .15
244 Ryan Wagner .15
245 Grady Sizemore .25
246 Bobby Jenks .15
247 Chad Billingsley .15
248 Casey Kotchman .15
249 Bobby Crosby .15
250 Khalil Greene .15
251 Danny Garcia .15
252 Nicholas Markakis .15
253 Bernie Castro .15
254 Aaron Hill .15
255 Josh Barfield .15
256 Ryan Wagner .15
257 Ryan Harvey .15
258 Jimmy Gobble .15

259 Ryan Madson .15
260 Zack Greinke .15
261 Rene Reyes .15
262 Eric Duncan .15
263 Chris Lubanski .15
264 Jeff Mathis .15
265 Rickie Weeks .25
266 Justin Morneau .25
267 Brian Snyder .15
268 Neal Cotts .15
269 Joe Borchard .15
270 Larry Bigbie .15
271 Marcus McBeth **RC** .40
272 Tydus Meadows **RC** .40
273 Zach Miner **RC** .50
274 Anthony Lerew **RC** .40
275 Yadier Molina **RC** .40
276 Jon Knott **RC** .40
277 Matthew Moses .40
278 Sung Jung **RC** .40
279 Mike Gosling .15
280 David Murphy .15
281 Tim Frend **RC** .40
282 Casey Myers **RC** .40
283 Brayan Pena **RC** .40
284 Omar Falcon **RC** .40
285 Blake Hawksworth **RC** .40
286 Jesse Roman **RC** .40
287 Kyle Davies **RC** .40
288 Matt Creighton **RC** .40
289 Rodney Choy Foo **RC** .40
290 Kyle Sleeth .15
291 Carlos Quentin .50
292 Khalid Ballouli **RC** .40
293 Tim Stauffer .15
294 Craig Ansman **RC** .40
295 Dioner Navarro **RC** .40
296 Josh Labandeira **RC** .40
297 Jeff Allison .15
298 Anthony Acevedo **RC** .40
299 Brad Sullivan .15
300 Conor Jackson .50

Red

Cards (1-300): 1-2X
Inserted 1:1

Mini

Stars (1-300): 1-2X
Inserted 1:1

Adventures

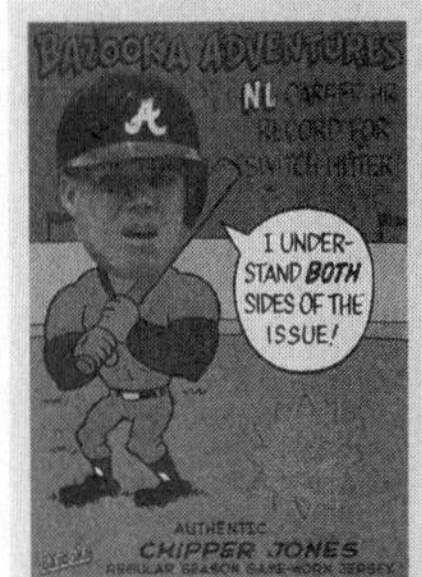

I UNDER-STAND BOTH SIDES OF THE ISSUE!

NM/M
Common Player: 4.00
EA Edgardo Alfonzo 4.00
JB Jeff Bagwell 8.00
LB Lance Berkman 6.00
CB Craig Biggio 4.00
KB Kevin Brown 4.00
PB Pat Burrell 6.00
MB Marlon Byrd 4.00
SC Sean Casey 4.00
LC Luis Castillo 4.00
EC Eric Chavez 5.00
AD1 Adam Dunn 6.00
AD2 Adam Dunn 6.00
CE Carl Everett 4.00
CF Cliff Floyd 4.00
NG Nomar Garciaparra 10.00
JG Jason Giambi 8.00
JDG Jeremy Giambi 4.00
TEG Troy Glaus 5.00
TG Tom Glavine 5.00
LG Luis Gonzalez 4.00
SG Shawn Green 5.00
BG Ben Grieve 4.00
VG Vladimir Guerrero 8.00
CG Cristian Guzman 4.00
TH Toby Hall 4.00
TAH1 Tim Hudson 4.00
TAH2 Tim Hudson 4.00
GJ Geoff Jenkins 4.00
RJ Randy Johnson 8.00
AJ Andruw Jones 6.00
CJ Chipper Jones 8.00
JK Jason Kendall 4.00
PK Paul Konerko 4.00
PL Paul LoDuca 4.00
ML Mike Lowell 4.00
GM Greg Maddux 8.00
KM Kevin Millwood 6.00
MM Mark Mulder 5.00
MCM Mike Mussina 6.00
HN Hideo Nomo 8.00
JO John Olerud 4.00
RP1 Rafael Palmeiro 6.00
RP2 Rafael Palmeiro 6.00
BP Brad Penny 4.00
MP1 Mike Piazza 10.00
MP2 Mike Piazza 10.00
AP Albert Pujols 15.00
MR Manny Ramirez 6.00
AR1 Alex Rodriguez 10.00
AR2 Alex Rodriguez 10.00
TJS Tim Salmon 5.00
CS Curt Schilling 8.00
AS Alfonso Soriano 6.00
MT Miguel Tejada 6.00
JT Jim Thome 8.00
LW Larry Walker 4.00
JW Jarrod Washburn 4.00
BW Bernie Williams 6.00
DW Dontrelle Willis 6.00
PW Preston Wilson 4.00
KW Kerry Wood 6.00
BZ Barry Zito 6.00

AUTHENTIC GAME-USED BAT
Blasts

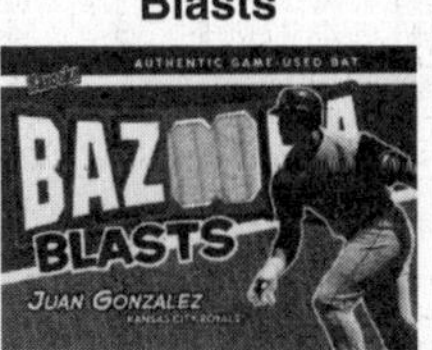

NM/M
Common Player: 4.00
RA Roberto Alomar 6.00
MA Moises Alou 4.00
RSA Rich Aurilia 4.00
JB Jeff Bagwell 8.00
RB Rocco Baldelli 8.00
TB Tony Batista 4.00
CIB Carlos Beltran 4.00
LB Lance Berkman 5.00
CB Craig Biggio 4.00
HB Hank Blalock 6.00
BB Bret Boone 5.00
JNB Jeromy Burnitz 4.00
SB Sean Burroughs 4.00
CC Carl Crawford 4.00
AD Adam Dunn 6.00
CE Carl Everett 4.00
BF Brad Fullmer 4.00
RF Rafael Furcal 5.00
AJG Andres Galarraga 4.00
NG Nomar Garciaparra 12.00
JG Jason Giambi 8.00
TG Troy Glaus 5.00
AG Adrian Gonzalez 4.00
JAG Juan Gonzalez 6.00
LG Luis Gonzalez 4.00
SG Shawn Green 6.00
MG Marquis Grissom 4.00
VG Vladimir Guerrero 8.00
CG Cristian Guzman 4.00
NH Nathan Haynes 4.00
TKH Todd Helton 6.00
AH Aubrey Huff 4.00
TH Torii Hunter 5.00
CJ Chipper Jones 8.00
PK Paul Konerko 4.00
ML Matt Lawton 4.00
CL Carlos Lee 4.00
PL Paul LoDuca 4.00
EM Edgar Martinez 4.00
TM Tino Martinez 6.00
FM Fred McGriff 5.00
DM Doug Mientkiewicz 4.00
JO John Olerud 4.00
MO Magglio Ordonez 4.00
RP Rafael Palmeiro 8.00
CP Corey Patterson 4.00
MP Mike Piazza 10.00
JP Jorge Posada 6.00
AP Albert Pujols 15.00
ANR Aramis Ramirez 4.00
MR Manny Ramirez 6.00
JR Juan Rivera 4.00
AR Alex Rodriguez 10.00
IR Ivan Rodriguez 6.00
SR Scott Rolen 8.00
TJS Tim Salmon 6.00
GS Gary Sheffield 6.00
RS Ruben Sierra 4.00
AS Alfonso Soriano 8.00
SS Shannon Stewart 4.00
ST So Taguchi 5.00
MCT Mark Teixeira 5.00
MT Miguel Tejada 5.00
FT Frank Thomas 8.00
MAT Michael Tucker 4.00
MV Mo Vaughn 4.00
OV Omar Vizquel 4.00
LW Larry Walker 5.00
VW Vernon Wells 5.00
RW Rondell White 4.00
BW Bernie Williams 6.00

Comics

ALEX RODRIGUEZ
A-ROD YOUNGEST EVER TO HIT 300 HR

NM/M
Complete Set (24): 6.00
Common Player: .25
Inserted 1:4
BC1 Garret Anderson .25
BC2 Jeff Bagwell .50
BC3 Hank Blalock .25
BC4 Roy Halladay .25
BC5 Dontrelle Willis .25
BC6 Roger Clemens .75
BC7 Carlos Delgado .40
BC8 Rafael Furcal .25
BC9 Eric Gagne .25
BC10 Nomar Garciaparra .75
BC11 Derek Jeter .75
BC12 Esteban Loaiza .25
BC13 Kevin Millwood .25
BC14 Bill Mueller .25
BC15 Rafael Palmeiro .40
BC16 Albert Pujols .75
BC17 Jose Reyes .25
BC18 Alex Rodriguez .75
BC19 Alfonso Soriano .40
BC20 Sammy Sosa .50
BC21 Ichiro Suzuki .50
BC22 Frank Thomas .40
BC23 Brad Wilkerson .25
BC24 Houston Astros .25

One-Liners

BAZOOKA ONE-LINERS
"RUN EVERYTHING OUT AND BE IN BY TWELVE."
RED SCHOENDIENST
ST. LOUIS CARDINALS

NM/M
Common Player: 5.00
DA Dick Allen 8.00
JB Johnny Bench 10.00
BB Bert Blyleven 5.00
WB1 Wade Boggs 6.00
WB2 Wade Boggs 6.00
GB George Brett 20.00
BC Bert Campaneris 5.00
RC Rod Carew 8.00
GC Gary Carter 5.00
JCA Joe Carter 5.00
OC Orlando Cepeda 5.00
RD Ron Darling 5.00
AD Andre Dawson 8.00
DE Dennis Eckersley 10.00
KG1 Kirk Gibson 5.00
KG2 Kirk Gibson 5.00
DW Dwight Gooden 5.00
KH Keith Hernandez 5.00
RJ Reggie Jackson 10.00
DJ1 David Justice 8.00
DJ2 David Justice 8.00
HK Harmon Killebrew 20.00
JK Jerry Koosman 5.00
BM Bill Madlock 5.00
WM Willie Mays 30.00
WMC Willie McGee 8.00
TM Tug McGraw 8.00
JM Joe Morgan 8.00
DM Dale Murphy 15.00
EM Eddie Murray 10.00
PN Phil Niekro 5.00
DP Dave Parker 5.00
GP Gaylord Perry 5.00
KP1 Kirby Puckett 10.00
KP2 Kirby Puckett 10.00
FR Frank Robinson 10.00
NR Nolan Ryan 15.00
BS Bret Saberhagen 5.00
RSA Ron Santo 10.00
MS Mike Schmidt 15.00
RS Red Schoendienst 5.00
TS Tom Seaver 8.00
WS Willie Stargell 8.00
CY Carl Yastrzemski 15.00
RY Robin Yount 10.00

Stand-Ups

NM/M
Complete Set (25): 20.00
Common Player: .50
Inserted 1:8
1 Jose Reyes .50
2 Jim Thome 1.00
3 Roy Halladay .50
4 Jason Giambi 1.00
5 Dontrelle Willis .50
6 Mike Piazza 1.50
7 Chipper Jones 1.00
8 Mark Prior 2.00
9 Todd Helton .75
10 Miguel Cabrera .75
11 Derek Jeter 3.00
12 Nomar Garciaparra 2.00
13 Alex Rodriguez 3.00
14 Miguel Tejada .50
15 Carlos Delgado .75
16 Pedro J. Martinez 1.00
17 Sammy Sosa 2.00
18 Ichiro Suzuki 1.50
19 Vladimir Guerrero 1.00
20 Alfonso Soriano 1.00
21 Eric Chavez .50
22 Albert Pujols 2.50
23 Ivan Rodriguez .75
24 Vernon Wells .50
25 Eric Gagne .50

Tattoos

NM/M
Complete Set (55): 8.00
Common Player: .15
Inserted 1:4
JB Jeff Bagwell .25
BAZ Bazooka Logo .15
LB Lance Berkman .15
CB Craig Biggio .15
KB Kevin Brown .15
PB Pat Burrell .15
MB Marlon Byrd .15
SC Sean Casey .15
LC Luis Castillo .15
EC Eric Chavez .15
AD Adam Dunn .15
CF Cliff Floyd .15
NG Nomar Garciaparra .75
JG Jason Giambi .40
TFG Troy Glaus .25
TG Tom Glavine .25
LG Luis Gonzalez .15
SG Shawn Green .15
VG Vladimir Guerrero .40
CG Cristian Guzman .15
TH Toby Hall .15
TAH Tim Hudson .15
GJ Geoff Jenkins .15
RJ Randy Johnson .40
AJ Andruw Jones .25
CJ Chipper Jones .40
JK Jason Kendall .15
PK Paul Konerko .15
PL Paul LoDuca .15
ML Mike Lowell .15
GM Greg Maddux .50
KM Kevin Millwood .15
MM Mark Mulder .15
MCM Mike Mussina .25
HN Hideo Nomo .15
JO John Olerud .15
RP Rafael Palmeiro .25
BP Brad Penny .15
MP Mike Piazza .50
AP Albert Pujols 1.00
MR Manny Ramirez .25
AR Alex Rodriguez 1.00
TJS Tim Salmon .25
CS Curt Schilling .25
AS Alfonso Soriano .40
MT Miguel Tejada .25
JT Jim Thome .40
TOP Topps Logo .15
LW Larry Walker .15
JW Jarrod Washburn .15
BW Bernie Williams .25
DW Dontrelle Willis .15
PW Preston Wilson .15
KW Kerry Wood .25
BZ Barry Zito .25

4-on-1 Stickers

NM/M
Complete Set (40): 8.00
Common Player: .20
Inserted 1:4
1 Rich Harden, Dontrelle Willis, Jerome Williams, Brandon Webb .20
2 Eric Duncan, Derek Jeter, Alfonso Soriano, Jason Giambi .75

3 Grady Sizemore, Rocco Baldelli, Ichiro Suzuki, Vladimir Guerrero .50
4 Roy Halladay, Pedro J. Martinez, Curt Schilling, Brett Myers .40
5 Alex Rodriguez, Angel Berroa, Jose Reyes, Khalil Greene .75
6 Kerry Wood, Adam Dunn, Jeff Kent, Scott Rolen .40
7 Miguel Cabrera, Scott Podsednik, Bo Hart, Mark Teixeira .20
8 Rickie Weeks, Josh Barfield, Albert Pujols, Vernon Wells .50
9 Torii Hunter, Garret Anderson, Bobby Abreu, Ken Griffey Jr. .40
10 Jay Gibbons, Chipper Jones, Mike Piazza, Mike Sweeney .50
11 David Ortiz, Nick Johnson, Carlos Delgado, Frank Thomas .40
12 Todd Helton, Jose Vidro, Mike Lowell, Miguel Tejada .40
13 Randy Wolf, Mark Mulder, Johan Santana, Randy Johnson .40
14 Bret Boone, Aubrey Huff, Eric Chavez, Javy Lopez .20
15 Jason Schmidt, Roy Oswalt, Joel Pineiro, Mark Prior .50
16 Kevin Millwood, Andy Pettitte, Matt Morris, Tim Hudson .20
17 Javier Vazquez, Esteban Loaiza, Orlando Cabrera, Roberto Alomar .20
18 Al Leiter, David Wells, Mike Hampton, Jarrod Washburn .20
19 Paul LoDuca, Mike Lieberthal, Brian Giles, Andruw Jones .20
20 Magglio Ordonez, Corey Patterson, Aaron Boone, Jeff Bagwell .40
21 Troy Glaus, Edgar Martinez, Manny Ramirez, Raul Ibanez .30
22 Sammy Sosa, Barry Zito, Bartolo Colon, Austin Kearns .50
23 Jim Edmonds, Gary Sheffield, Preston Wilson, Shawn Green .20
24 Bernie Williams, Juan Pierre, Josh Beckett, Mike Mussina .20
25 Ramon Hernandez, Jason Kendall, Jason Phillips, A.J. Pierzynski .20
26 Pat Burrell, Laynce Nix, Mike Cameron, Cliff Floyd .20
27 Eric Gagne, Carl Crawford, Jose Guillen, Steve Finley .20
28 Ellis Burks, Livan Hernandez, Derek Lowe, Kazuhisa Ishii .20
29 Jorge Posada, Jeff Mathis, Victor Martinez, Ivan Rodriguez .20
30 Jim Thome, Marcus Giles, Nomar Garciaparra, Hank Blalock .50
31 Edgar Renteria, Bobby Crosby, Neal Cotts, Russ Ortiz .20
32 Zack Greinke, Cristian Guzman, Cesar Izturis, Kevin Brown .20
33 Bobby Jenks, Ramon Nivar, Richie Sexson, Ryan Klesko .20
34 Omar Vizquel, Carlos Pena, Rafael Furcal, Gil Meche .20
35 Kenny Lofton, Tim Salmon, Marquis Grissom, Craig Biggio .20
36 Kyle Davies, Anthony Lerew, Brayan Pena, Sung Jung .20
37 Rodney Choy Foo, Craig Ansman, David Murphy, Matthew Moses .20
38 Carlos Quentin, Dioner Navarro, Marcus McBeth, Josh Labandeira .20
39 Kyle Sleeth, Conor Jackson, Brad Sullivan, Jeff Allison .20
40 Yadier Molina, Jon Knott, Blake Hawksworth, Tim Stauffer .20

Chicago Cubs Reprints

For a fourth year the Cubs contracted with Topps to provide a series of reprint cards for use as give-aways at special games throughout the season. Each reprint features a Wrigley Field logo on front and is sequentially numbered to 20,000 in a strip of gold foil on back. Each card was distributed in a cello wrapper with the date of the promotion and names of the sponsor(s).

NM/M
Complete Set (2): 5.00
Common Player: 2.00
(1) Shawon Dunston 2.00
(2) Mark Prior 2.00

2004 Topps Chrome

NM/M
Complete Set (466):
Common Player: .25
Common Rookie Auto. (221-246): 10.00
Inserted 1:21
Series 1 Pack (4): 3.50
Series 1 Box (20): 50.00
Series 2 Pack (4): 3.50
Series 2 Box (20): 50.00
1 Jim Thome 1.00
2 Reggie Sanders .25
3 Mark Kotsay .25
4 Edgardo Alfonzo .25
5 Tim Wakefield .25
6 Moises Alou .50
7 Jorge Julio .25
8 Bartolo Colon .50
9 Chan Ho Park .25
10 Ichiro Suzuki 3.00
11 Kevin Millwood .50
12 Preston Wilson .40
13 Tom Glavine .75
14 Junior Spivey .25
15 Marcus Giles .40
16 David Segui .25
17 Kevin Millar .25
18 Corey Patterson .40
19 Aaron Rowand .25
20 Derek Jeter 4.00
21 Luis Castillo .25
22 Manny Ramirez 1.50
23 Jay Payton .25
24 Bobby Higginson .25
25 Lance Berkman .75
26 Juan Pierre .25
27 Mike Mussina 1.00
28 Fred McGriff .50

29 Richie Sexson .75
30 Tim Hudson .50
31 Mike Piazza 2.00
32 Brad Radke .25
33 Jeff Weaver .25
34 Ramon Hernandez .25
35 David Bell .25
36 Randy Wolf .25
37 Jake Peavy .50
38 Tim Worrell .25
39 Gil Meche .25
40 Albert Pujols 4.00
41 Michael Young .25
42 Josh Phelps .25
43 Brendan Donnelly .25
44 Steve Finley .25
45 John Smoltz .50
46 Jay Gibbons .25
47 Trot Nixon .25
48 Carl Pavano .25
49 Frank Thomas 1.00
50 Mark Prior 1.00
51 Danny Graves .25
52 Milton Bradley .25
53 Kris Benson .25
54 Ryan Klesko .25
55 Mike Lowell .25
56 Geoff Blum .25
57 Michael Tucker .25
58 Paul LoDuca .25
59 Vicente Padilla .25
60 Jacque Jones .25
61 Fernando Tatis .25
62 Ty Wigginton .25
63 Rich Aurilia .25
64 Andy Pettitte .75
65 Terrence Long .25
66 Cliff Floyd .25
67 Mariano Rivera .50
68 Kelvim Escobar .25
69 Marlon Byrd .25
70 Mark Mulder .50
71 Francisco Cordero .25
72 Carlos Guillen .25
73 Fernando Vina .25
74 Lance Carter .25
75 Hank Blalock .75
76 Jimmy Rollins .50
77 Francisco Rodriguez .25
78 Javy Lopez .50
79 Jerry Hairston Jr. .25
80 Andruw Jones .75
81 Rodrigo Lopez .25
82 Johnny Damon 1.00
83 Hee Seop Choi .25
84 Kazuhiro Sasaki .25
85 Danny Bautista .25
86 Matt Lawton .25
87 Juan Uribe .25
88 Rafael Furcal .50
89 Kyle Farnsworth .25
90 Jose Vidro .25
91 Luis Rivas .25
92 Hideo Nomo .75
93 Javier Vazquez .50
94 Al Leiter .40
95 Jose Valentin .25
96 Alex Cintron .25
97 Zach Day .25
98 Jorge Posada .75
99 C.C. Sabathia .25
100 Alex Rodriguez 3.00
101 Brad Penny .25
102 Brad Ausmus .25
103 Raul Ibanez .25
104 Mike Hampton .25
105 Adrian Beltre .50
106 Ramiro Mendoza .25
107 Rocco Baldelli .75
108 Esteban Loaiza .25
109 Russell Branyan .25
110 Todd Helton 1.00
111 Braden Looper .25
112 Octavio Dotel .25
113 Mike MacDougal .25
114 Cesar Izturis .25
115 Johan Santana 1.00
116 Jose Contreras .50
117 Placido Polanco .25
118 Jason Phillips .25
119 Orlando Hudson .25
120 Vernon Wells .50
121 Ben Grieve .25
122 Dave Roberts .25
123 Ismael Valdes .25
124 Eric Owens .25
125 Curt Schilling 1.00
126 Russ Ortiz .25
127 Mark Buehrle .50
128 Doug Mientkiewicz .25
129 Dmitri Young .25
130 Kazuhisa Ishii .25
131 A.J. Pierzynski .25
132 Brad Wilkerson .25
133 Joe McEwing .25
134 Alex Cora .25
135 Jose Cruz Jr. .25
136 Carlos Zambrano .50
137 Jeff Kent .50
138 Shigetoshi Hasegawa .25
139 Jarrod Washburn .25
140 Greg Maddux 2.00
141 Josh Beckett .75
142 Miguel Batista .25
143 Omar Vizquel .40
144 Alex Gonzalez .25
145 Billy Wagner .25
146 Brian Jordan .25
147 Wes Helms .25
148 Deivi Cruz .25
149 Alex Gonzalez .25
150 Jason Giambi 1.00
151 Erubiel Durazo .25
152 Mike Lieberthal .25
153 Jason Kendall .25
154 Xavier Nady .25
155 Kirk Rueter .25
156 Mike Cameron .25
157 Miguel Cairo .25
158 Woody Williams .25
159 Toby Hall .25
160 Bernie Williams .75
161 Darin Erstad .50
162 Matt Mantei .25
163 Shawn Chacon .25
164 Bill Mueller .25
165 Damian Miller .25
166 Tony Graffanino .25
167 Sean Casey .25
168 Brandon Phillips .25
169 Runelvys Hernandez .25
170 Adam Dunn .75
171 Carlos Lee .50
172 Juan Encarnacion .25
173 Angel Berroa .25
174 Desi Relaford .25
175 Joe Mays .25
176 Ben Sheets .50
177 Eddie Guardado .25
178 Rocky Biddle .25
179 Eric Gagne .50
180 Eric Chavez .50
181 Jason Michaels .25
182 Dustan Mohr .25
183 Kip Wells .25
184 Brian Lawrence .25
185 Bret Boone .25
186 Tino Martinez .40
187 Aubrey Huff .25
188 Kevin Mench .25
189 Tim Salmon .50
190 Carlos Delgado 1.00
191 John Lackey .25
192 Eric Byrnes .25
193 Luis Matos .25
194 Derek Lowe .50
195 Mark Grudzielanek .25
196 Flash Gordon .25
197 Matt Clement .25
198 Byung-Hyun Kim .25
199 Brandon Inge .25
200 Nomar Garciaparra 1.50
201 Frank Catalanotto .25
202 Cristian Guzman .25
203 Bo Hart .25
204 Jack Wilson .25
205 Ray Durham .25
206 Freddy Garcia .25
207 J.D. Drew .50
208 Orlando Cabrera .25
209 Roy Halladay .50
210 David Eckstein .25
211 Omar Falcon **RC** 2.00
212 Todd Self **RC** 2.00
213 David Murphy 3.00
214 Dioner Navarro **RC** 4.00
215 Marcus McBeth **RC** 2.00
216 Chris O'Riordan **RC** 2.00
217 Rodney Choy Foo **RC** 2.00
218 Tim Frend **RC** 2.00
219 Yadier Molina **RC** 6.00
220 Zachary Duke **RC** 3.00
221 Anthony Lerew/ Auto. **RC** 10.00
222 Blake Hawksworth/ Auto. **RC** 15.00
223 Brayan Pena/ Auto. **RC** 10.00
224 Craig Ansman/ Auto. **RC** 10.00
225 Jon Knott/Auto. **RC** 10.00
226 Josh Labandeira/ Auto. **RC** 10.00
227 Khalid Ballouli/ Auto. **RC** 10.00
228 Kyle Davies/Auto. **RC** 15.00
229 Matt Creighton/ Auto. **RC** 15.00
230 Mike Gosling/Auto. 15.00
231 Nic Ungs/Auto. **RC** 10.00
232 Zach Miner/Auto. **RC** 10.00
233 Donald Levinski/ Auto. 10.00
234 Bradley Sullivan 15.00
235 Carlos Quentin 25.00
236 Conor Jackson 25.00
237 Estee Harris **RC** 15.00
238 Jeffrey Allison 10.00
239 Kyle Sleeth 10.00
240 Matthew Moses 15.00
241 Tim Stauffer 15.00
242 Brad Snyder 10.00
243 Jason Hirsh 15.00
244 Lastings Milledge 40.00
245 Logan Kensing **RC** 15.00
246 Kory Casto 10.00
247 David Aardsma 1.50
248 Omar Quintanilla 2.00
249 Ervin Santana **RC** 2.00
250 Merkin Valdez **RC** 2.00
251 Vito Chiaravalloti **RC** 2.00
252 Travis Blackley **RC** 2.00
253 Chris Shelton **RC** 2.00
254 Rudy Guillen **RC** 3.00
255 Bobby Brownlie **RC** 2.00
256 Paul Maholm **RC** 4.00
257 Roger Clemens 3.00
258 Laynce Nix .25
259 Eric Hinske .25
260 Ivan Rodriguez 1.00
261 Brandon Webb .50
262 Jhonny Peralta .25
263 Adam Kennedy .25
264 Tony Batista .25
265 Jeff Suppan .25
266 Kenny Lofton .50
267 Scott Sullivan .25
268 Ken Griffey Jr. 2.00
269 Billy Traber .25
270 Larry Walker .50
271 Todd Hollandsworth .25
272 Carlos Beltran 1.00
273 Carl Crawford .50
274 Karim Garcia .25
275 Jose Reyes .75
276 Brandon Duckworth .25
277 Brian Giles .50
278 J.T. Snow Jr. .25
279 Jamie Moyer .25
280 Julio Lugo .25
281 Mark Teixeira .75
282 Cory Lidle .25
283 Lyle Overbay .50
284 Troy Percival .25
285 Robby Hammock .25
286 Jason Johnson .25
287 Brandon Lyon .25
288 Antonio Alfonseca .25
289 Tom Goodwin .25
290 Paul Konerko .50
291 D'Angelo Jimenez .25
292 Ben Broussard .25
293 Magglio Ordonez .50
294 Carlos Pena .25
295 Chad Fox .25
296 Jeriome Robertson .25
297 Travis Hafner .50
298 Joe Randa .25
299 Brady Clark .25
300 Barry Zito .75
301 Ruben Sierra .25
302 Brett Myers .25
303 Oliver Perez .25
304 Benito Santiago .25
305 David Ross .25
306 Joe Nathan .25
307 Jim Edmonds .50
308 Matt Kata .25
309 Vinny Castilla .25
310 Marty Cordova .25
311 Aramis Ramirez .50
312 Carl Everett .25
313 Ryan Freel .25
314 Mark Bellhorn .25
315 Ugueth Urbina .25
316 Tim Redding .25
317 Jeromy Burnitz .25
318 Miguel Cabrera 1.00
319 Orlando Hernandez .25
320 Casey Blake .25
321 Aaron Boone .25
322 Jermaine Dye .25
323 Jerome Williams .25
324 John Olerud .50
325 Scott Rolen 1.00
326 Bobby Kielty .25
327 Travis Lee .25
328 Jeff Cirillo .25
329 Scott Spiezio .25
330 Melvin Mora .25
331 Mike Timlin .25
332 Kerry Wood .50
333 Tony Womack .25
334 Jody Gerut .25
335 Morgan Ensberg .25
336 Odalis Perez .25
337 Michael Cuddyer .25
338 Jose Hernandez .25
339 LaTroy Hawkins .25
340 Marquis Grissom .25
341 Matt Morris .50
342 Juan Gonzalez .75
343 Jose Valverde .25
344 Joe Borowski .25
345 Josh Bard .25
346 Austin Kearns .50
347 Chin-Hui Tsao .25
348 Wilfredo Ledezma .25
349 Aaron Guiel .25
350 Alfonso Soriano 1.00
351 Ted Lilly .25
352 Sean Burroughs .25
353 Rafael Palmeiro .75
354 Quinton McCracken .25
355 David Ortiz 1.00
356 Randall Simon .25
357 Wily Mo Pena .25
358 Brian Anderson .25
359 Corey Koskie .25
360 Keith Foulke .25
361 Sidney Ponson .25
362 Gary Matthews Jr. .25
363 Herbert Perry .25
364 Shea Hillenbrand .25
365 Craig Biggio .50
366 Barry Larkin .50
367 Orlando Merced .25
368 Sammy Sosa 1.50
369 Joe Crede .50
370 Gary Sheffield .75
371 Coco Crisp .25
372 Torii Hunter .50
373 Derrek Lee .75
374 Adam Everett .25
375 Miguel Tejada .75
376 Jeremy Affeldt .25
377 Robin Ventura .25
378 Scott Podsednik .75
379 Matthew LeCroy .25
380 Vladimir Guerrero 1.50
381 Steve Karsay .25
382 Jeff Nelson .25
383 Chase Utley .75
384 Bobby Abreu .50
385 Josh Fogg .25
386 Trevor Hoffman .25
387 Matt Stairs .25
388 Edgar Martinez .50
389 Edgar Renteria .50
390 Chipper Jones 1.50
391 Eric Munson .25
392 Dewon Brazelton .25
393 John Thomson .25
394 Chris Woodward .25
395 Joe Kennedy .25
396 Reed Johnson .25
397 Johnny Estrada .25
398 Damian Moss .25
399 Victor Zambrano .25
400 Dontrelle Willis .50
401 Troy Glaus .75
402 Raul Mondesi .25
403 Jeff DaVanon .25
404 Kurt Ainsworth .25
405 Pedro J. Martinez 1.50
406 Eric Karros .25
407 Billy Koch .25
408 Luis Gonzalez .50
409 Jack Cust .25
410 Mike Sweeney .25
411 Jason Bay .75
412 Mark Redman .25
413 Jason Jennings .25
414 Rondell White .50
415 Todd Hundley .25
416 Shannon Stewart .25
417 Jae Weong Seo .25
418 Livan Hernandez .25
419 Mark Ellis .25
420 Pat Burrell .50
421 Mark Loretta .25
422 Robb Nen .25
423 Joel Pineiro .25
424 Todd Walker .25
425 Jeremy Bonderman .50
426 A.J. Burnett .25
427 Greg Myers .25
428 Roy Oswalt .50
429 Carlos Baerga .25
430 Garret Anderson .50
431 Horacio Ramirez .25
432 Brian Roberts .25
433 Kevin Brown .50
434 Eric Milton .25
435 Brian Daubach .25
436 Alex Escobar .25
437 Alex Sanchez .25
438 Jeff Bagwell 1.00
439 Claudio Vargas .25
440 Shawn Green .50
441 Geoff Jenkins .25
442 David Wells .25
443 Nick Johnson .25
444 Jose Guillen .25
445 Scott Hatteberg .25
446 Phil Nevin .25
447 Jason Schmidt .50
448 Ricky Ledee .25
449 So Taguchi .25
450 Randy Johnson .75
451 Eric Young .25
452 Chone Figgins .25
453 Larry Bigbie .25
454 Scott Williamson .25
455 Ramon Martinez .25
456 Roberto Alomar .50
457 Ryan Dempster .25
458 Ryan Ludwick .25
459 Ramon Santiago .25
460 Jeff Conine .25
461 Brad Lidge .25
462 Ken Harvey .25
463 Guillermo Mota .25
464 Rick Reed .25
465 Armando Benitez .25
466 Wade Miller .25

Refractors

Cards (1-220, 247-466): 1-2X
Inserted 1:4
Rookie Auto (221-246): 1.5-2X
Production 100
Gold Refractor (1-220): 1-2X
Inserted 1:5
Rookie Gold Refractor (221-246) 2-3X
Production 50
Black Refractor (1-220): 2-4X
Inserted 1:10
Rookie Black Refractor: No Pricing
Production 25

Fashionably Great

NM/M
Common Player: 5.00
Inserted 1:Box
JB Jeff Bagwell 10.00
CB Craig Biggio 5.00
HB Hank Blalock 8.00
JBO Joe Borchard 5.00
KB Kevin Brown 5.00

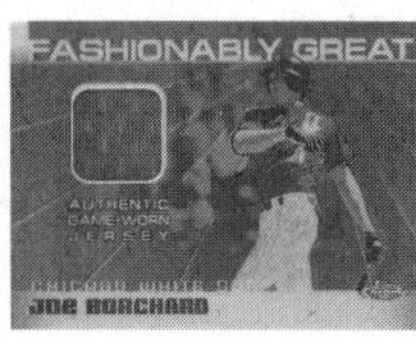

EC Eric Chavez 6.00
CD Carlos Delgado 6.00
AD Adam Dunn 6.00
FG Freddy Garcia 5.00
CF Cliff Floyd 5.00
NG Nomar Garciaparra 10.00
TH Trevor Hoffman 5.00
TH Tim Hudson 6.00
AJ Andruw Jones 6.00
CJ Chipper Jones 8.00
DL Derek Lowe 6.00
PM Pedro J. Martinez 8.00
FM Fred McGriff 8.00
MM Mark Mulder 6.00
BM Brett Myers 5.00
JO John Olerud 6.00
RP Rafael Palmeiro 8.00
WP Wily Mo Pena 5.00
MP Mike Piazza 10.00
AP Albert Pujols 15.00
MR Manny Ramirez 8.00
JR Juan Rivera 5.00
AR Alex Rodriguez 12.00
IR Ivan Rodriguez 8.00
CS Curt Schilling 6.00
JS John Smoltz 6.00
SS Sammy Sosa 12.00
MS Mike Sweeney 5.00
FT Frank Thomas 10.00
JV Jose Vidro 5.00
BW Billy Wagner 6.00
VW Vernon Wells 5.00

Handle With Care

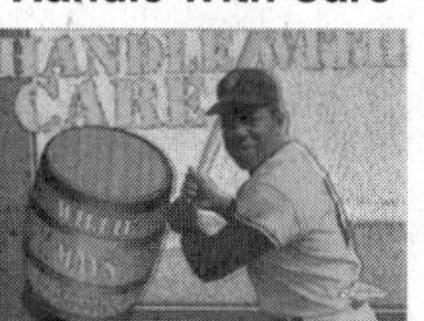

No pricing due to scarcity.
Production Five Sets

Presidential First Pitch Relics

NM/M
Common President: 10.00
Inserted 1:15
GHB George H.W. Bush 20.00
GB George W. Bush 25.00
BC Bill Clinton 20.00
CC Calvin Coolidge 20.00
DE Dwight D. Eisenhower 20.00
GF Gerald Ford 30.00
WH Warren Harding 15.00
HH Herbert Hoover 25.00
LJ Lyndon B. Johnson 30.00
RN Richard Nixon 25.00
RR Ronald Reagan 30.00
FR Franklin D. Roosevelt 20.00
WT William H. Taft 25.00
HT Harry S. Truman 25.00
WW Woodrow Wilson 10.00

Presidential Pastime Refractors

NM/M
Common President: 3.00
X-fractors: 3-5X
Inserted 1:400
PP1 George Washington 10.00
PP2 John Adams 3.00
PP3 Thomas Jefferson 6.00
PP4 James Madison 4.00
PP5 James Monroe 4.00
PP6 John Quincy Adams 4.00
PP7 Andrew Jackson 3.00
PP8 Martin Van Buren 3.00
PP9 William H. Harrison 3.00
PP10 John Tyler 3.00
PP11 James K. Polk 3.00
PP12 Zachary Taylor 3.00
PP13 Millard Fillmore 3.00
PP14 Franklin Pierce 3.00
PP15 James Buchanan 3.00
PP16 Abraham Lincoln 8.00
PP17 Andrew Johnson 3.00
PP18 Ulysses S. Grant 5.00
PP19 Rutherford B. Hayes 3.00
PP20 James Garfield 3.00
PP21 Chester A. Arthur 3.00
PP22 Grover Cleveland 3.00
PP23 Benjamin Harrison 3.00
PP24 William McKinley 3.00
PP25 Theodore Roosevelt 5.00
PP26 William H. Taft 3.00
PP27 Woodrow Wilson 3.00
PP28 Warren Harding 3.00
PP29 Calvin Coolidge 3.00
PP30 Herbert Hoover 3.00
PP31 Franklin D. Roosevelt 5.00
PP32 Harry S. Truman 3.00
PP33 Dwight D. Eisenhower 3.00
PP34 John F. Kennedy 8.00
PP35 Lyndon B. Johnson 3.00
PP36 Richard Nixon 4.00
PP37 Gerald Ford 3.00
PP38 Jimmy Carter 3.00
PP39 Ronald Reagan 3.00
PP40 George H.W. Bush 3.00
PP41 Bill Clinton 4.00
PP42 George W. Bush 3.00

Town Heroes

NM/M
Common Player: 5.00
LB Lance Berkman 5.00
EC Eric Chavez 5.00
NG Nomar Garciaparra 12.00
JG Jason Giambi 8.00
RH Rich Harden 5.00
TH Tim Hudson 5.00
CJ Chipper Jones 8.00
MM Mark Mulder 5.00
HN Hideo Nomo 8.00
RP Rafael Palmeiro 8.00
MP Mark Prior 8.00
AP Albert Pujols 15.00
MR Manny Ramirez 8.00
JR Jose Reyes 5.00
AR Alex Rodriguez 10.00
SS Sammy Sosa 15.00
SST Shannon Stewart 5.00
MT Miguel Tejada 5.00
FT Frank Thomas 8.00
KW Kerry Wood 10.00
BZ Barry Zito 6.00

2004 Topps Clubhouse Collection Relics

NM/M
Common Player: 4.00
Two Relics Per Pack
Pack (2): 18.00
Box (10): 140.00
HA Hank Aaron/113 50.00
BA Bobby Abreu 6.00
RA Roberto Alomar 6.00
EA Edgardo Alfonzo/286 4.00
TA Tony Armas Jr. 4.00
JB Jeff Bagwell 8.00
RB Rocco Baldelli 6.00
TB Tony Batista 4.00
HB Hank Bauer 10.00
JPB Josh Beckett/195 6.00
JBE Johnny Bench 10.00
AB Armando Benitez 4.00
LB Lance Berkman 6.00
YB Yogi Berra 10.00
HBL Hank Blalock 6.00
WB Wade Boggs/250 6.00
BB Bret Boone 4.00
GB George Brett 12.00
KB Kevin Brown 6.00
JBU Jeromy Burnitz 4.00
PB Pat Burrell 6.00
MB Marlon Byrd 4.00
MC Miguel Cabrera 8.00
GC Gary Carter/221 8.00
JCA Joe Carter/259 6.00
RLC Roger Cedeno 4.00
OC Orlando Cepeda 8.00
RCE Ron Cey 6.00
EC Eric Chavez 6.00
CFC Chin-Feng Chen 8.00
JC Jeff Cirillo 4.00
WC Will Clark 8.00
RC Roberto Clemente 75.00
DC Dave Concepcion 8.00
CCR Carl Crawford 4.00
CD Carlos Delgado/200 6.00
AD Adam Dunn 8.00
DE Dennis Eckersley 10.00
CE Carl Everett 4.00
SF Steve Finley 4.00
CFL Cliff Floyd 4.00
WF Whitey Ford/296 15.00
BF Brad Fullmer/200 4.00
JF Jonathan Fulton 6.00
RF Rafael Furcal 4.00
EG Eric Gagne 8.00
NG Nomar Garciaparra 12.00
JG Jason Giambi 8.00

TGL	Troy Glaus	6.00
TG	Tom Glavine	8.00
AG	Adrian Gonzalez	4.00
LG	Luis Gonzalez	4.00
JGO	Juan Gonzalez	8.00
MG	Mark Grace	8.00
SG	Shawn Green	6.00
KG	Ken Griffey Jr./200	15.00
MDG	Marquis Grissom	4.00
VG	Vladimir Guerrero	8.00
CG	Cristian Guzman	4.00
TGW	Tony Gwynn	10.00
MH	Mickey Hall	4.00
EH	Estee Harris/206	4.00
THE	Todd Helton	8.00
RHE	Rickey Henderson	10.00
RH	Ramon Hernandez	4.00
OH	Orel Hershiser	8.00
JH	James Houser/182	8.00
OHU	Orlando Hudson	4.00
TH	Tim Hudson	6.00
THU	Torii Hunter	6.00
KI	Kazuhisa Ishii	4.00
RJ	Reggie Jackson	10.00
DJ	Derek Jeter	20.00
AJ	Andruw Jones	6.00
CJ	Chipper Jones	8.00
AK	Al Kaline	15.00
JKE	Jeff Kent/200	8.00
PK	Paul Konerko	6.00
BL	Barry Larkin/200	10.00
AL	Al Leiter	4.00
SL	Steve Lerud	4.00
EL	Esteban Loaiza	4.00
PL	Paul LoDuca	4.00
JL	Javy Lopez	6.00
DL	Derek Lowe/200	4.00
CL	Chris Lubanski/209	8.00
GM	Greg Maddux	15.00
EMA	Edgar Martinez/200	6.00
PM	Pedro Martinez/200	10.00
TM	Tino Martinez	6.00
EM	Eddie Mathews/174	25.00
WM	Willie Mays	60.00
FM	Fred McGriff	6.00
KM	Kevin Millwood	4.00
MM	Mark Mulder	6.00
EMU	Eddie Murray	12.00
BM	Brett Myers	4.00
HN	Hideo Nomo/207	8.00
JO	John Olerud	6.00
MO	Magglio Ordonez	4.00
RP	Rafael Palmeiro/200	10.00
CP	Chan Ho Park	4.00
DP	Dave Parker/292	10.00
CPA	Corey Patterson/267	8.00
WP	Wily Mo Pena	8.00
TPE	Troy Percival	6.00
TP	Tony Perez	10.00
MP	Mike Piazza	10.00
JP	Jorge Posada/264	8.00
AP	Albert Pujols	15.00
ARA	Aramis Ramirez	8.00
MR	Manny Ramirez/207	8.00
JRE	Jose Reyes	6.00
CR	Cal Ripken Jr.	20.00
MRI	Mariano Rivera/239	8.00
FR	Frank Robinson	8.00
JR	Jackie Robinson/262	50.00
AR	Alex Rodriguez	15.00
IR	Ivan Rodriguez	8.00
SR	Scott Rolen	10.00
JRO	Jimmy Rollins	8.00
NR	Nolan Ryan	20.00
CS	C.C. Sabathia	4.00
TS	Tim Salmon	6.00
RSA	Ryne Sandberg	15.00
JS	Jay Sborz	6.00
CSC	Curt Schilling	8.00
MS	Mike Schmidt	15.00
RS	Richie Sexson/200	6.00
GS	Gary Sheffield	6.00
RSI	Ruben Sierra	10.00
OS	Ozzie Smith	15.00
JSM	John Smoltz	6.00
DS	Duke Snider	15.00
AS	Alfonso Soriano	6.00
SS	Sammy Sosa	12.00
WS	Willie Stargell/200	10.00
CST	Casey Stengel/217	10.00
MSW	Mike Sweeney	4.00
MTE	Miguel Tejada	6.00
MT	Mark Teixeira	6.00
FT	Frank Thomas	8.00
JT	Jim Thome	8.00
FV	Fernando Valenzuela	8.00
JVI	Jose Vidro	4.00
BWA	Billy Wagner	4.00
LW	Larry Walker	4.00
VW	Vernon Wells/200	4.00
BW	Bernie Williams	6.00
PW	Preston Wilson	4.00
JV	Javier Vazquez	6.00
CY	Carl Yastrzemski	15.00
RY	Robin Yount	12.00
BZ	Barry Zito/230	6.00

Black

Black: 2-3X
Production 25 Sets

Copper

Copper: .75-1.5X
Production 99 Sets

Red

Red: No Pricing
Production One Set

All-Star Appeal Ball

No Pricing
Production 10 Sets

All-Star Appeal Ball Auto.

NM/M

Production 30 Sets

GA	Garret Anderson	30.00
HB	Hank Blalock	35.00
JP	Jorge Posada	50.00

All-Star Appeal Base

NM/M

Common Player: 5.00
Production 65 Sets
On Deck Circle: 1X
Production 90 Sets

GA	Garret Anderson	8.00
HB	Hank Blalock	8.00
BB	Bret Boone	5.00
CD	Carlos Delgado	6.00
JE	Jim Edmonds	8.00
RF	Rafael Furcal	6.00
NG	Nomar Garciaparra	15.00
JG	Jason Giambi	8.00
TG	Troy Glaus	6.00
LG	Luis Gonzalez	6.00
TH	Todd Helton	8.00
AJ	Andruw Jones	6.00
JL	Javy Lopez	8.00
ML	Mike Lowell	6.00
EM	Edgar Martinez	8.00
MO	Magglio Ordonez	6.00
JP	Jorge Posada	8.00
AP	Albert Pujols	25.00
ER	Edgar Renteria	8.00
AR	Alex Rodriguez	15.00
SR	Scott Rolen	10.00
RS	Richie Sexson	6.00
GS	Gary Sheffield	8.00
AS	Alfonso Soriano	10.00
VW	Vernon Wells	6.00
PW	Preston Wilson	5.00

All-Star Appeal Base Auto.

NM/M

Production 50 Sets

GA	Garret Anderson	25.00
JP	Jorge Posada	35.00
GS	Gary Sheffield	25.00

All-Star Appeal On Deck Circle

NM/M

Common Player: 5.00
Production 90 Sets

GA	Garret Anderson	8.00
HB	Hank Blalock	8.00
AB	Aaron Boone	5.00
BB	Bret Boone	5.00
LC	Luis Castillo	5.00
CD	Carlos Delgado	6.00
JE	Jim Edmonds	8.00
CE	Carl Everett	5.00
RF	Rafael Furcal	6.00
NG	Nomar Garciaparra	15.00
JG	Jason Giambi	8.00
TG	Troy Glaus	6.00
LG	Luis Gonzalez	6.00
TH	Todd Helton	8.00
AJ	Andruw Jones	6.00
PL	Paul LoDuca	5.00
JL	Javy Lopez	8.00
ML	Mike Lowell	6.00
EM	Edgar Martinez	8.00
MM	Melvin Mora	5.00
MO	Magglio Ordonez	6.00
JP	Jorge Posada	8.00
AP	Albert Pujols	20.00
ER	Edgar Renteria	8.00
AR	Alex Rodriguez	15.00
SR	Scott Rolen	10.00
RS	Richie Sexson	6.00
GS	Gary Sheffield	8.00
AS	Alfonso Soriano	10.00
JV	Jose Vidro	5.00
VW	Vernon Wells	6.00
RW	Rondell White	5.00
PW	Preston Wilson	5.00

All-Star Appeal On Deck Auto

NM/M

Quantity produced listed

GA	Garret Anderson/320	15.00
HB	Hank Blalock/920	15.00
JP	Jorge Posada/420	30.00
GS	Gary Sheffield/170	25.00

Career Legends Relics

NM/M

Common Player:

BR1	Babe Ruth/60	175.00
BR2	Babe Ruth/171	150.00
BR3	Babe Ruth/45	200.00
EB1	Ernie Banks/143	15.00
EB3	Ernie Banks/47	20.00
EB6	Ernie Banks/71	15.00
LG1	Lou Gehrig/49	125.00
LG2	Lou Gehrig/184	100.00
LG3	Lou Gehrig/52	125.00
TC3	Ty Cobb/47	120.00
WM1	Willie Mays/52	70.00
WM2	Willie Mays/141	60.00

DoublePlay Relics

NM/M

Production 75 Sets

CLE	Omar Vizquel, Brandon Phillips, Travis Hafner	10.00
NYM	Ty Wigginton, Jose Reyes, Mike Piazza	25.00
NYY	Derek Jeter, Alex Rodriguez, Jason Giambi	50.00
PHI	Jimmy Rollins, David Bell, Jim Thome	20.00
SDP	Khalil Greene, Sean Burroughs, Phil Nevin	10.00

Frozen Ropes Relics

NM/M

Common Player: 5.00
Production 50 Sets

BA	Bobby Abreu	8.00
JB	Jeff Bagwell	10.00
RB	Rocco Baldelli	8.00
JBE	Johnny Bench	20.00
LB	Lance Berkman	5.00
CB	Craig Biggio	6.00
HB	Hank Blalock	10.00
WB	Wade Boggs	8.00
GC	Gary Carter	8.00
EC	Eric Chavez	8.00
ADA	Andre Dawson	8.00
AD	Adam Dunn	10.00
CE	Carl Everett	5.00
RF	Rafael Furcal	5.00
JG	Jason Giambi	8.00
LG	Luis Gonzalez	5.00
SG	Shawn Green	5.00
VG	Vladimir Guerrero	15.00
TH	Todd Helton	10.00
AH	Aubrey Huff	5.00
CJ	Chipper Jones	15.00
PK	Paul Konerko	5.00
EM	Edgar Martinez	8.00
DM	Don Mattingly	40.00
DMU	Dale Murphy	12.00
MO	Magglio Ordonez	5.00
RP	Rafael Palmeiro	10.00
MP	Mike Piazza	15.00
KP	Kirby Puckett	15.00
AP	Albert Pujols	25.00
MR	Manny Ramirez	10.00
JR	Jose Reyes	8.00
BR	Brooks Robinson	15.00
AR	Alex Rodriguez	15.00
IR	Ivan Rodriguez	10.00
RS	Ryne Sandberg	40.00
MS	Mike Schmidt	40.00
GS	Gary Sheffield	6.00
OS	Ozzie Smith	25.00
DS	Duke Snider	15.00
AS	Alfonso Soriano	10.00
SS	Sammy Sosa	15.00
MT	Miguel Tejada	8.00
JT	Jim Thome	10.00
BW	Bernie Williams	8.00
PW	Preston Wilson	5.00
CY	Carl Yastrzemski	20.00

Heart of the Line-Up Relics

NM/M

Production 100 unless noted.

ARI	Steve Finley, Richie Sexson, Luis Gonzalez	10.00
CHC	Sammy Sosa, Moises Alou, Aramis Ramirez	35.00
CHW	Magglio Ordonez, Frank Thomas, Carlos Lee/78	20.00
CIN	Ken Griffey Jr., Austin Kearns, Adam Dunn	25.00
COL	Todd Helton, Larry Walker, Preston Wilson	15.00
NYY	Alex Rodriguez, Jason Giambi, Gary Sheffield	35.00
PHI	Jim Thome, Pat Burrell, Bobby Abreu	20.00
SEA	Edgar Martinez, Bret Boone, John Olerud	10.00
STL	Albert Pujols, Jim Edmonds, Scott Rolen	40.00
TEX	Alfonso Soriano, Mark Teixeira, Hank Blalock	20.00
TOR	Vernon Wells, Carlos Delgado, Eric Hinske	10.00

Patch Place Relics

No Pricing
Production 25 or less.

Power Pieces Relics

NM/M

Quantity produced listed

CD	Carlos Delgado/25	8.00
THU	Torii Hunter/48	8.00
AJ	Andruw Jones/25	10.00
PM	Pedro Martinez/45	10.00
WM	Willie Mays/24	85.00
BM	Brett Myers/39	5.00
BP	Brad Penny/31	5.00
MP	Mike Piazza/31	40.00
NR	Nolan Ryan/34	50.00
CS	Curt Schilling/38	8.00
BZ	Barry Zito/75	6.00

2004 Topps Cracker Jack

NM/M

Complete Set with SP's (250): 160.00
Common Player: .25
Common SP: 2.00
SP's inserted 1:3
Pack (8): 3.00
Box (24): 60.00

1	Jose Reyes/SP	2.00
2	Edgar Renteria	.25
3	Albert Pujols	2.00
3	Albert Pujols/SP/Swinging	6.00
4	Garret Anderson	.50
5	Bobby Abreu	.40
6	Andruw Jones	.75
7	Jeff Kent	.40
8	Magglio Ordonez	.50
9	Kris Benson	.25
10	Luis Gonzalez	.40
11	Corey Patterson	.50
12	Connie Mack	.25
13	Vernon Wells/SP	2.00
14	Jim Edmonds	.50
15	Bret Boone	.50
16	Travis Lee	.25
17	Alex Rodriguez/SP	6.00
No #	Alex Rodriguez	2.00
18	Erubiel Durazo	.25
19	Brett Myers	.25
20	Scott Rolen/SP	3.00
21	Paul LoDuca	.25
22	Geoff Jenkins	.50
23	Charles Comiskey	.25
24	Cliff Floyd	.25
25	Jim Thome	.75
25	Jim Thome/SP/Fldg	3.00
26	Russ Ortiz	.25
27	Bill Mueller	.25
28	Kenny Lofton	.40
29	Jay Gibbons	.40
30	Ken Griffey Jr.	1.50
31	Jeff Bagwell	.75
32	Jose Lima	.25
33	Brad Radke	.25
34	Ramon Hernandez	.25
35	Brian Giles/SP	2.00
36	Jeremy Bonderman	.25
37	Jerome Williams	.25
38	Rafael Palmeiro	.50
39	Scott Podsednik	.75
40	Rafael Furcal	.40
41	Roy Oswalt	.40
42	Orlando Hudson	.25
43	Todd Helton	.75
44	Kerry Wood	1.00
45	Tom Glavine	.40
46	David Eckstein	.25
47	Trot Nixon	.25
48	Preston Wilson	.25
50	Eric Gagne/SP	3.00
51	Ichiro Suzuki/SP	5.00
52	Juan Gonzalez	.75
53	Torii Hunter	.50
54	Bartolo Colon	.40
55	Dick Hoblitzell	.25
56	Al Leiter	.25
57	Johnny Damon	.40
58	Larry Walker	.40
59	Brian Jordan	.25
60	Richie Sexson/SP	3.00
61	Orlando Cabrera	.25
62	Jason Phillips	.25
63	Phil Nevin	.25
64	John Olerud	.40
65	Miguel Tejada	.50
66	Nap Lajoie	.50
67	C.C. Sabathia	.25
68	Ty Wigginton	.25
69	Troy Glaus	.50
70	Mike Piazza	1.50
71	Craig Biggio	.40
72	Cristian Guzman	.25
73	Dmitri Young	.25
74	Roger Clemens	2.00
75	Runelvys Hernandez	.25
76	Nomar Garciaparra	2.00
77	Mark Mulder	.40
78	Derek Lowe	.40
79	Paul Konerko	.25
80	Sammy Sosa/SP	5.00
81	Vladimir Guerrero	1.00
82	Xavier Nady	.25
83	Joel Pineiro	.25
84	Chipper Jones	1.50
85	Manny Ramirez	.75
86	Burt Shotton	.25
87	Raul Ibanez/SP	2.00
88	Eric Chavez	.50
89	Frank Catalanotto	.25
90	Dontrelle Willis	.50
91	Roy Halladay	.50
92	Jermaine Dye	.25
93	Jason Kendall	.25
94	Jacque Jones	.25
95	Gary Sheffield	.50
95	Gary Sheffield/SP/Yankees	3.00
96	Mike Lieberthal	.25
97	Adam Dunn	.50
98	Carl Crawford	.25
99	Reggie Sanders	.25
100	Mark Prior/SP	6.00
101	Luis Matos	.25
102	Barry Zito	.50
103	Randy Johnson	1.00
104	Kevin Brown	.50
105	Pat Burrell	.50
106	Steve Finley	.25
107	Moises Alou	.50
108	David Ortiz/SP	3.00
109	Austin Kearns/SP	2.00
110	Carlos Beltran	.50
111	Shawn Green	.40
112	Javier Vazquez	.50
113	Hideo Nomo	.50
114	Kazuhisa Ishii	.25
115	Corey Koskie	.25
116	Kevin Millwood	.50
117	Randy Wolf	.40
118	Darin Erstad	.40
119	Fernando Vina	.25
120	Pedro J. Martinez	1.00
121	Melvin Mora	.25
122	Carl Everett	.25
123	Matt Morris	.40
124	Greg Maddux	1.50
125	Jason Schmidt	.25
126	Mark Teixeira/SP	3.00
127	Randy Winn	.25
128	Rich Aurilia	.25
129	Vicente Padilla	.25
130	Tim Hudson	.50
131	Marlon Byrd	.25
132	Jae Weong Seo	.25
133	Branch Rickey	.25
134	A.J. Pierzynski	.25
135	Ryan Klesko	.40
136	Eric Hinske	.25
137	Mike Cameron	.25
138	Roberto Alomar	.50
139	Jarrod Washburn	.25
140	Curt Schilling	.75
140	Curt Schilling/SP/Red Sox	3.00
141	Omar Vizquel	.25
142	Mike Sweeney	.25
143	Wade Miller	.25
144	Jose Vidro	.25
145	Rich Harden/SP	2.00
146	Eric Munson	.25
147	Lance Berkman	.50
148	Mark Buehrle	.25
149	Carlos Delgado	.75
150	Sean Burroughs	.25
151	Kevin Millar	.25
152	Frank Thomas	.75
153	Adrian Beltre	.25
154	Shannon Stewart	.25
155	Johan Santana	.25
156	Edgardo Alfonzo	.25
157	Jose Cruz Jr.	.25
158	Sidney Ponson	.25
159	Edgar Martinez	.50
160	Jamie Moyer	.25
161	Tony Batista	.25
162	Wes Helms	.25
163	Brandon Webb/SP	2.00
164	Gil Meche	.25
165	Marcus Giles/SP	2.00
166	Angel Berroa/SP	2.00
167	Rocco Baldelli/SP	3.00
168	Michael Young	.25
169	Esteban Loaiza	.25
170	Casey Blake	.25
171	Jody Gerut	.25
172	Bo Hart/SP	2.00
173	Kelvim Escobar	.25
174	Aaron Guiel	.25
175	Javy Lopez/SP	3.00
176	Aubrey Huff	.25
177	Hank Blalock	.50
178	Edwin Jackson	.25
178	Edwin Jackson/SP/#104	2.00
179	Delmon Young/SP	3.00
180	Bobby Jenks	.25
181	Felix Pie	.25
181	Felix Pie/SP/#80	2.00
182	Jeremy Reed/SP	2.00
183	Aaron Hill	.25
184	Casey Kotchman/SP	2.00
185	Grady Sizemore	.50
186	Joe Mauer/SP	3.00
187	Ryan Harvey	.25
188	Neal Cotts	.25
189	Victor Martinez	.25
190	Rene Reyes	.25
191	Eric Duncan	.25
192	B.J. Upton/SP	3.00
193	Khalil Greene/SP	2.00
194	Bobby Crosby	.25
195	Rickie Weeks/SP	3.00
196	Zack Greinke/SP	2.00
197	Laynce Nix	.25
198	Vito Chiaravalloti/SP **RC**	2.00
199	Estee Harris **RC**	.25
200	Jon Knott/SP **RC**	3.00
201	Dioner Navarro **RC**	.75
201	Dioner Navarro/SP/#236	2.00
202	Craig Ansman **RC**	.50
203	Travis Blackley **RC**	1.00
204	Yadier Molina **RC**	.50
205	Rodney Choy Foo **RC**	.50
206	Kyle Sleeth/SP	5.00
207	Jeff Allison	1.00
208	Josh Labandeira **RC**	.50
209	Lastings Milledge/SP	10.00
210	Rudy Guillen/SP **RC**	3.00
211	Blake Hawksworth/SP **RC**	3.00
212	David Aardsma	.50
213	Shawn Hill **RC**	.50
214	Erick Aybar/SP **RC**	3.00
215	Ervin Santana **RC**	1.00
216	Tim Stauffer/SP	3.00
217	Merkin Valdez **RC**	1.00
218	Jack McKeon	.25
219	Derrek Lee	.50
220	Josh Beckett/SP	3.00
221	Luis Castillo	.25
222	Mike Lowell	.50
223	Juan Pierre	.40
224	Ivan Rodriguez	.75
224	Ivan Rodriguez/SP/Tigers	3.00
225	A.J. Burnett	.25
226	Miguel Cabrera/SP	4.00
227	Jeffrey Loria	.25
228	Joe Torre	.50
229	Jason Giambi	.75
229	Jason Giambi/SP/Fldg	3.00
230	Aaron Boone	.25
231	Jose Contreras	.25
232	Derek Jeter/SP	6.00
233	Nick Johnson	.25
234	Mike Mussina	.75
235	Andy Pettitte	.50
236	Jorge Posada/SP	3.00
237	Alfonso Soriano	.75
238	Bernie Williams	.50

Mini

Mini: 1-2X
Mini SP: 1X
Inserted 1:Pack
Mini SPs Inserted 1:20
SP's are same as in base set.

Mini Autograph

NM/M

Common Autograph:
Inserted 1:258
95 Gary Sheffield/50 40.00
112 Javier Vazquez 15.00
163 Brandon Webb 15.00
165 Marcus Giles 12.00
221 Luis Castillo 8.00
226 Miguel Cabrera 35.00

Mini Blue

Mini Blue: 3-6X
Mini Blue SP: 1-2X
Inserted 1:10
Mini Blue SP's Inserted 1:60
SP's are same as in base set.

Mini White

No Pricing
Production One Set

Sticker

Stickers: 1X
SP Stickers: .5X
Inserted 1:Surprise Pack
SP's Inserted 1:10 Surprise Packs

Secret Surprise Signatures

NM/M

Common Autograph: 8.00
CF Cliff Floyd 15.00
BG Brian Giles 15.00
AH Aubrey Huff 15.00
ML Mike Lamb 8.00
DM Dustin McGowan 20.00
FP Felix Pie 20.00
SP Scott Podsednik 20.00
SR Scott Rolen 30.00
MV Merkin Valdez 15.00
JW Jerome Williams 20.00
DW Dontrelle Willis 30.00

Take Me Out to/Ballgame Relics

NM/M

Common Player: 5.00
BA Bobby Abreu 5.00
MA Moises Alou 6.00
GA Garret Anderson 8.00
JB Jeff Bagwell 8.00
RB Rocco Baldelli 8.00
LB Lance Berkman 5.00
AB Angel Berroa 5.00
CB Craig Biggio 5.00
HB Hank Blalock 6.00
BB1 Bret Boone/Bat 5.00
BB2 Bret Boone/Jsy 5.00
PB Pat Burrell 6.00
MC Miguel Cabrera 8.00
EC Eric Chavez 5.00
AD Adam Dunn 8.00
JE Jim Edmonds 5.00
RF Rafael Furcal 6.00
NG Nomar Garciaparra/Bat 10.00
NG Nomar Garciaparra/Jsy 10.00
JG Jason Giambi 8.00
MG Marcus Giles 5.00
TG Troy Glaus 8.00
LG Luis Gonzalez 5.00
SG Shawn Green/Bat 6.00
SG Shawn Green/Jsy 6.00
TH Todd Helton 8.00
TKH Torii Hunter 6.00
CJ Chipper Jones 8.00
PL Paul LoDuca 5.00
JL Javy Lopez/Bat 6.00
JL Javy Lopez/Jsy 6.00
MP Mike Piazza 10.00
AP Albert Pujols/Bat 15.00
AP Albert Pujols/Jsy 15.00
MR Manny Ramirez 8.00
JR Jose Reyes 6.00
AR Alex Rodriguez/Bat/Yankees 15.00
AR Alex Rodriguez/Jsy 10.00
IR Ivan Rodriguez 8.00
JRO Jimmy Rollins 5.00
AS Alfonso Soriano/Bat 8.00
AS Alfonso Soriano/Jsy 8.00
SS Sammy Sosa/Bat 10.00
SS Sammy Sosa/Jsy 10.00
MS Mike Sweeney 5.00
MT Mark Teixeira 6.00
MT Miguel Tejada 6.00
JT Jim Thome 8.00
LW Larry Walker 5.00
VW Vernon Wells 5.00
KW Kerry Wood 8.00
MY Michael Young 5.00

1,2,3 Strikes You're Out Relics

NM/M

Common Player: 4.00
JB Josh Beckett 8.00
KB Kevin Brown 6.00
EG Eric Gagne 8.00
RH Rich Harden 4.00
RJ Randy Johnson 8.00
DL Derek Lowe 6.00
PM Pedro J. Martinez 8.00
KM Kevin Millwood 6.00
MAM Mark Mulder 6.00
MM Mike Mussina 15.00
BM Brett Myers 4.00
HN Hideo Nomo 8.00
CCS C.C. Sabathia 4.00
CS Curt Schilling 15.00
JS John Smoltz 6.00
BW Billy Wagner 4.00
KW Kerry Wood 10.00
BZ Barry Zito 6.00

2004 Topps eTopps

Topps continued its on-line card program for a fourth year in 2004. Initial Player Offerings ($4.50-7.50 per card) were again made for one week, with allocations having to be made for some cards in high demand. The number of each card actually sold is shown parenthetically. After the IPO, cards could be bought and sold within portfolios, or physically delivered (for a fee) for more traditional venues. The 2-1/2" x 3-1/2" cards' fronts have an action photo at top and a strip of fading portrait photos below. Backs repeat the portrait photo, have a 2003 recap and 2004 "prospectus," and a few biographical bits and stats. New for 2004 was a subset of team cards picturing several stars. A total of 119 cards was issued, skip-numbered between 1-133. Values shown are for cards in a virtual portfolio, rather than "in hand." Taking physical possession of a card from an eTopps portfolio costs about $6 apiece.

NM/M

Complete Set (119): 175.00
Common Player: 1.50
1 Andy Pettitte/1,991 1.50
2 Jason Giambi/1,565 1.50
3 Kevin Youkilis/2,171 1.75
4 Casey Blake/1,420 1.50
5 Ryan Ludwick/1,321 1.50
6 Craig Wilson/1,544 1.50
7 Curt Schilling/2,216 1.50
8 Mark Prior/3,750 1.50
9 Casey Kotchman/2,006 1.75
10 Scott Podsednik/2,500 1.75
11 Carlos Guillen/1,541 1.50
12 Clint Nageotte/1,526 1.50
13 Melvin Mora/1,432 1.50
14 Ivan Rodriguez/2,104 1.75
15 Travis Hafner/2,500 3.00
16 Mike Piazza/2,500 1.50
17 Brian Giles/1,267 2.00
18 Derek Jeter/2,708 5.75
19 Edwin Jackson/3,655 1.50
20 Chipper Jones/2,158 1.50
21 Jody Gerut/1,436 1.50
22 Carlos Lee/1,562 2.00
23 Jason Schmidt/1,659 1.75
25 Ichiro/2,228 1.75
27 Corey Patterson/2,500 1.50
30 Kerry Wood/1,824 1.50
31 Jim Thome/1,908 1.50
32 Hideki Matsui/2,500 2.00
33 Rocco Baldelli/2,500 1.50
34 Jose Reyes/1,739) 1.50
35 Dontrelle Willis/3,750 1.50
36 Miguel Cabrera/3,750 2.00
37 Brandon Webb/2,072 1.50
38 Rich Harden/1,823 2.75
40 Vladimir Guerrero/1,913 1.50
41 Hank Blalock/3,303 1.50
42 Kazuo Matsui/5,000 1.50
43 Joe Mauer/4,888 3.00
44 Keith Foulke/1,896 1.50
45 Josh Beckett/3,178 1.50
46 Jamie Moyer/1,573 1.50
47 Victor Martinez/2,500 2.25
49 Derrek Lee/1,920 1.50
51 Roger Clemens/3,750 2.25
52 David Ortiz/1,655 2.25
53 Jason Bay/2,336 4.75
54 Erubiel Durazo/1,577 1.50
55 Gary Sheffield/1,639 1.50
56 Jeff Kent/2,036 1.50
57 Ken Harvey/1,621 1.50
58 Jason Varitek/2,698 1.50
59 Jeromy Burnitz/2,148 1.50
60 Nomar Garciaparra/2,074 1.50
61 Javy Lopez/3,204 1.50
62 Eric Gagne/2,279 1.50
63 Khalil Greene/3,456 3.00
64 Carlos Zambrano/3,492 1.50
65 Lyle Overbay/2,789 1.50
68 Laynce Nix/1,760 1.50
69 Manny Ramirez/1,909 1.75
70 Alfonso Soriano/1,820 1.50
71 Mike Lieberthal/1,479 1.50
72 Juan Pierre/2,500 1.50
73 Frank Thomas/1,835 1.50
74 Sean Casey/1,851 1.50
75 Albert Pujols/3,750 4.25
76 Bill Mueller/1,977 1.75
78 Randy Johnson/2,725 1.50
79 Carlos Beltran/2,500 1.50
80 Pedro Martinez/1,726 1.50
81 Lew Ford/1,932 1.50
82 Javier Vazquez/1,936 1.50
83 Kevin Brown/2,635 1.50
84 Johnny Estrada/1,590 1.50
85 Ken Griffey Jr./2,396 2.75
87 Jorge Posada/2,176 1.50
89 Bobby Crosby/3,498 2.50
90 Sammy Sosa/3,248 1.50
91 Shingo Takatsu/1,678 1.50
92 Akinori Otsuka/1,544 1.50
93 Michael Young/2,004 3.25
94 Aaron Miles/1,608 1.50
95 Miguel Tejada/1,548 1.50
96 Chad Tracy/2,534 2.50
99 Todd Helton/1,998 1.50
100 Alex Rodriguez/5,000 2.50
101 Bartolo Colon/1,973 1.50
102 Philadelphia Phillies/2,500 1.50
103 Seattle Mariners/2,500 1.50
104 Atlanta Braves/2,500 1.50
105 Chicago White Sox/2,458 1.50
106 Pittsburgh Pirates/2,500 1.50
107 St. Louis Cardinals/2,500 1.75
108 Houston Astros/2,500 1.50
109 Toronto Blue Jays/2,500 1.50
110 Arizona Diamondbacks/1,818 8.00
111 New York Mets/2,570 1.50
112 Minnesota Twins/2,500 1.50
113 Baltimore Orioles/2,570 1.50
114 Cleveland Indians/2,219 1.50
115 Boston Red Sox/3,750 5.25
116 Tampa Bay Devil Rays/2,191 1.50
117 Chicago Cubs/3,750 1.50
118 Texas Rangers/2,500 1.50
119 Cincinnati Reds/2,500 1.50
120 Anaheim Angels/2,500 1.50
121 Colorado Rockies/2,500 1.50
122 K.C. Royals/2,120 1.50
123 Florida Marlins/2,500 1.50
124 Oakland A's/2,375 1.50
125 L.A. Dodgers/2,155 1.50
126 Milwaukee Brewers/2,500 1.50
127 S.F. Giants/2,500 1.50
128 Montreal Expos/2,500 1.50
129 San Diego Padres/2,500 1.50
130 New York Yankees/3,750 1.50
131 Detroit Tigers/2,570 1.50
132 Matt Holliday/2,425 2.00
133 Zack Greinke/3,750 2.25

Classics

Topps continued its eTopps Classics line-up in 2004 with 20 cards of former greats. Numbering and format were contiguous with earlier issues. Like regular eTopps cards, Classics could only be ordered during a one-week Initial Player Offering period. Cards were issued in a quantity of 1,200 each at $9.50. The number of cards actually sold is shown parenthetically. Fronts have a color or colorized action photo, backs have a picture of one of that player's Topps cards, along with career notes, stats, etc. Values shown are for cards in a virtual portfolio, rather than "in hand". Taking physical possession of a card from an eTopps portfolio costs about $6 apiece.

NM/M

Complete Set (20): 175.00
Common Player: 8.00
41 Orlando Cepeda/806 10.00
42 Wade Boggs/908 10.00
43 Al Kaline/962 9.00
44 Jim Palmer/768 20.00
45 Ozzie Smith/1,161 8.00
46 Rod Carew/908 8.00
47 Paul Molitor/850 8.00
48 Hank Aaron/1,250 25.00
49 Robin Yount/1,002 8.00
50 Hank Greenberg/769 15.00
51 Robin Roberts/807 10.00
52 Casey Stengel/898 8.00
53 Cy Young/1,200 9.00
54 Thurman Munson/1,250 9.00
55 Roy Campanella/984 8.00
56 Satchel Paige/1,222 8.00
57 Tris Speaker/795 11.00
58 Jimmie Foxx/952 9.00
59 Dizzy Dean/967 9.00
60 "Cool Papa" Bell/988 8.00

Econ

A four-card set honoring local athletes was issued in conjunction with the 25th National Sports Collectors Convention and the 2nd Topps Econ in Cleveland in late July. Only one baseball player was included. Persons purchasing VIP admission packs at the show received a version of the card without the eTopps authenticity sticker on back.

NM/M

1 Bob Lemon ($5.25 / 978) 3.25
1 Bob Lemon (unstickered show version.) 2.00

Events Series

Values shown are for cards in a virtual portfolio rather than "in hand." Each card originally sold for $4.50. Quantity actually issued is shown parenthetically.

NM/M

Complete Set (12): 25.00
Common Card: 1.50
1 Alex Rodriguez, Curt Schilling/1,500 2.50
2 Albert Pujols, Carlos Beltran/1,298 2.00
3 Hideki Matsui, Mariano Rivera/1,294 1.50
4 Carlos Beltran/1,427 1.50
5 Jeff Kent, David Ortiz/1,126 1.50
6 Jim Edmonds/983 6.00
7 Derek Lowe, Johnny Damon/2,116 1.50
8 Scott Rolen, Albert Pujols/1,119 3.00
9 Mark Bellhorn, Curt Schilling/1,173 1.50
10 Pedro Martinez/1,250 1.50
11 Derek Lowe/2,565 2.00
12 Manny Ramirez/1,500 2.00

2004 Topps Heritage

NM/M

Complete Set (475): 400.00
Common Player: .40
Common SP (398-475): 4.00
Variations & SP's Inserted 1:2
Pack (8): 5.00
Box (24): 100.00
1 Jim Thome 1.50
1 Jim Thome/SP/Htg 8.00
2 Nomar Garciaparra/SP 10.00
3 Aramis Ramirez .50
4 Rafael Palmeiro/SP 6.00
5 Danny Graves .40
6 Casey Blake .40
7 Juan Uribe .40
8 Dmitri Young .40
8 Dmitri Young/SP/Old Logo 4.00
9 Billy Wagner .40
10 Jason Giambi .75
10 Jason Giambi/SP/Btg Stance 6.00
11 Carlos Beltran 1.00
12 Chad Hermansen .40
13 B.J. Upton .75
14 Dustan Mohr .40
15 Endy Chavez .40
16 Cliff Floyd .40
17 Bernie Williams .75
18 Eric Chavez .50
19 Chase Utley .75
20 Randy Johnson 1.50
21 Vernon Wells .50
22 Juan Gonzalez .75
23 Joe Kennedy .40
24 Bengie Molina .40
25 Carlos Lee .40
26 Horacio Ramirez .40
27 Anthony Acevedo **RC** 1.00
28 Sammy Sosa/SP 10.00
29 Jon Garland .40
30 Adam Dunn 1.00
30 Adam Dunn/SP/Htg 6.00
31 Aaron Rowand .40
32 Jody Gerut .40
33 Chin-Hui Tsao .40
34 Alex Sanchez .40
35 A.J. Burnett .40
36 Brad Ausmus .40
37 Blake Hawksworth **RC** 1.50
38 Francisco Rodriguez .40
39 Alex Cintron .40
40 Chipper Jones 1.50
40 Chipper Jones/SP/Fldg 6.00
41 Deivi Cruz .40
42 Bill Mueller .40
43 Joe Borowski .40
44 Jimmy Haynes .40
45 Mark Loretta .40
46 Jerome Williams .40
47 Gary Sheffield/SP 6.00
48 Richard Hidalgo .40
49 Jason Kendall .40
49 Jason Kendall/SP/Old Logo 4.00
50 Ichiro Suzuki/SP 8.00
51 Jim Edmonds .75
52 Frank Catalanotto .40
53 Jose Contreras .40
54 Mo Vaughn .40
55 Brendan Donnelly .40
56 Luis Gonzalez .50
57 Robert Fick .40
58 Laynce Nix .40
59 Johnny Damon .75
60 Magglio Ordonez .50
60 Magglio Ordonez/SP/Htg 6.00
61 Matt Clement .40
62 Ryan Ludwick .40
63 Luis Castillo .40
64 David Crouthers .40
65 Dave Berg .40
66 Kyle Davies **RC** 3.00
67 Tim Salmon .50
68 Marcus Giles .40
69 Marty Cordova .40
70 Todd Helton 1.00
70 Todd Helton/SP/Purple Jsy 6.00
71 Jeff Kent .50
72 Michael Tucker .40
73 Cesar Izturis .40
74 Paul Quantrill .40
75 Conor Jackson 3.00
76 Placido Polanco .40
77 Adam Eaton .40
78 Ramon Hernandez .40
79 Edgardo Alfonzo .40
80 Dioner Navarro **RC** 1.00
81 Woody Williams .40
82 Rey Ordonez .40
83 Randy Winn .40
84 Casey Myers **RC** 1.00
85 Rodney Choy Foo **RC** 2.00
85 Rodney Choy Foo/SP/Old Logo 6.00
86 Ray Durham .40
87 Sean Burroughs .40
88 Tim Frend **RC** 3.00
89 Shigetoshi Hasegawa .40
90 Jeff Allison .40
91 Orlando Hudson .40
92 Matt Creighton/SP **RC** 6.00
93 Tim Worrell .40
94 Kris Benson .40
95 Mike Lieberthal .40
96 David Wells .40
97 Jason Phillips .40
98 Bobby Cox .40
99 Johan Santana .75
100 Alex Rodriguez 3.00
100 Alex Rodriguez/SP/Throwing 10.00
101 John Vander Wal .40
102 Orlando Cabrera .50
103 Hideo Nomo .75
104 Todd Walker .40
105 Jason Johnson .40
106 Matt Mantei .40
107 Jarrod Washburn .40
108 Preston Wilson .40
109 Carl Pavano .40
110 Geoff Blum .40
111 Eric Gagne .50
112 Geoff Jenkins .50
113 Joe Torre .50
114 Jon Knott **RC** 1.50
115 Hank Blalock .75
116 John Olerud .50
117 Pat Burrell .75
117 Pat Burrell/Old Logo 5.00
118 Aaron Boone .40
119 Zach Day .40
120 Frank Thomas 1.00
120 Frank Thomas/Old Logo 6.00
121 Kyle Farnsworth .40
122 Derek Lowe .50
123 Zach Miner/SP **RC** 6.00
124 Matt Moses/SP 8.00
125 Jesse Roman **RC** 1.50
126 Josh Phelps .40
127 Nic Ungs **RC** 1.50
128 Dan Haren .40
129 Kirk Rueter .40
130 Jack McKeon .40
131 Keith Foulke .40

132 Garrett Stephenson .40
133 Wes Helms .40
134 Raul Ibanez .50
135 Morgan Ensberg .40
136 Jay Payton .40
137 Billy Koch .40
138 Mark Grudzielanek .40
139 Rodrigo Lopez .40
140 Corey Patterson .40
141 Troy Percival .40
142 Shea Hillenbrand .40
143 Brad Fullmer .40
144 Ricky Nolasco 1.50
145 Mark Teixeira .75
146 Tydus Meadows **RC** 1.50
147 Toby Hall .40
148 Orlando Palmeiro .40
149 Khalid Ballouli **RC** 1.50
150 Grady Little .40
151 David Eckstein .40
152 Kenny Perez **RC** 1.50
153 Ben Grieve .40
154 Ismael Valdes .40
155 Bret Boone .50
156 Jesse Foppert .40
157 Vicente Padilla .40
158 Bobby Abreu .50
159 Scott Hatteberg .40
160 Carlos Quentin 4.00
161 Anthony Lerew **RC** 1.50
162 Lance Carter .40
163 Robb Nen .40
164 Zachary Duke/SP **RC** 10.00
165 Xavier Nady .40
166 Kip Wells .40
167 Kevin Millwood .75
168 Jon Lieber .40
169 Jose Reyes .50
170 Eric Byrnes .40
171 Paul Konerko .40
172 Chris Lubanski .40
173 Jae Weong Seo .40
174 Corey Koskie .40
175 Tim Stauffer .40
176 John Lackey .40
177 Danny Bautista .40
178 Shane Reynolds .40
179 Jorge Julio .40
180 Manny Ramirez 1.00
180 Manny Ramirez/ SP/Old Logo 6.00
181 Alex Gonzalez .40
182 Moises Alou .75
182 Moises Alou/ SP/Old Logo 6.00
183 Mark Buehrle .40
184 Carlos Guillen .40
185 Nate Cornejo .40
186 Billy Traber .40
187 Jason Jennings .40
188 Eric Munson .40
189 Braden Looper .40
190 Juan Encarnacion .40
191 Dusty Baker .40
192 Travis Lee .40
193 Miguel Cairo .40
194 Rich Aurilia/SP 5.00
195 Flash Gordon .40
196 Freddy Garcia .40
197 Brian Lawrence .40
198 Jorge Posada/SP 8.00
199 Javier Vazquez .40
200 Albert Pujols 3.00
200 Albert Pujols/ SP/Old Logo 12.00
201 Victor Zambrano .40
202 Eli Marrero .40
203 Joel Pineiro .40
204 Rondell White .50
205 Craig Ansman **RC** 2.00
206 Michael Young .40
207 Carlos Baerga .40
208 Andruw Jones 1.00
209 Jerry Hairston Jr. .40
210 Shawn Green/SP 6.00
211 Ron Gardenhire .40
212 Darin Erstad .50
213 Brandon Webb .50
213 Brandon Webb/ SP/Glove In Air 6.00
214 Greg Maddux 2.00
215 Reed Johnson .40
216 John Thomson .40
217 Tino Martinez .40
218 Mike Cameron .40
219 Edgar Martinez .50
220 Eric Young .40
221 Reggie Sanders .40
222 Randy Wolf .40
223 Erubiel Durazo .40
224 Mike Mussina .75
225 Tom Glavine .75
226 Troy Glaus .75
227 Oscar Villarreal .40
228 David Segui .40
229 Jeff Suppan .40
230 Kenny Lofton .50
231 Esteban Loaiza .40
232 Felipe Lopez .40
233 Matt Lawton .40
234 Mark Bellhorn .40
235 Wilfredo Ledezma .40
236 Todd Hollandsworth .40
237 Octavio Dotel .40
238 Darren Dreifort .40
239 Paul LoDuca .40
240 Richie Sexson .75
241 Doug Mientkiewicz .40
242 Luis Rivas .40
243 Claudio Vargas .40
244 Mark Ellis .40
245 Brett Myers .40
246 Jake Peavy .40
247 Marquis Grissom .40
248 Armando Benitez .40
249 Ryan Franklin .40
250 Alfonso Soriano 1.50
250 Alfonso Soriano/ SP/Fldg 6.00
251 Tim Hudson .75
252 Shannon Stewart .40
253 A.J. Pierzynski .40
254 Runelvys Hernandez .40
255 Roy Oswalt .50
256 Shawn Chacon .40
257 Tony Graffanino .40
258 Tim Wakefield .40
259 Damian Miller .40
260 Joe Crede .40
261 Jason LaRue .40
262 Jose Jimenez .40
263 Juan Pierre .40
264 Wade Miller .40
265 Odalis Perez .40
266 Eddie Guardado .40
267 Rocky Biddle .40
268 Jeff Nelson .40
269 Terrence Long .40
270 Ramon Ortiz .40
271 Raul Mondesi .50
272 Ugueth Urbina .40
273 Jeromy Burnitz .40
274 Brad Radke .40
275 Jose Vidro .40
276 Bobby Jenks .40
277 Ty Wigginton .40
278 Jose Guillen .40
279 Delmon Young .75
280 Brian Giles .50
281 Jason Schmidt .50
282 Nicholas Markakis .40
283 Felipe Alou .40
284 Carl Crawford .40
285 Neifi Perez .40
286 Miguel Tejada .75
287 Victor Martinez .40
288 Adam Kennedy .40
289 Kerry Ligtenberg .40
290 Scott Williamson .40
291 Tony Womack .40
292 Travis Hafner .40
293 Bobby Crosby .40
294 Chad Billingsley .40
295 Russ Ortiz .40
296 John Burkett .40
297 Carlos Zambrano .40
298 Randall Simon .40
299 Juan Castro .40
300 Mike Lowell .40
301 Fred McGriff .50
302 Glendon Rusch .40
303 Sung Ki Jung **RC** .40
304 Rocco Baldelli .75
305 Fernando Vina .40
306 Gil Meche .40
307 Jose Cruz Jr. .40
308 Bernie Castro .40
309 Scott Spiezio .40
310 Paul Byrd .40
311 Jay Gibbons .50
311 Jay Gibbons/ SP/Old Logo 6.00
312 Trot Nixon .40
313 Chris O'Riordan **RC** 1.50
314 Julio Lugo .40
315 Ben Davis .40
316 Mike Williams .40
317 Trevor Hoffman .40
318 Andy Pettitte .75
319 Orlando Hernandez .40
320 Juan Rivera .40
321 Elizardo Ramirez .40
322 Junior Spivey .40
323 Tony Batista .40
324 Mike Remlinger .40
325 Alex Gonzalez .40
326 Aaron Hill .40
327 Steve Finley .40
328 Vinny Castilla .40
329 Eric Duncan .40
330 Mike Gosling .40
331 Eric Hinske .40
332 Scott Rolen 1.50
333 Benito Santiago .40
334 Jimmy Gobble .40
335 Bobby Higginson .40
336 Kelvim Escobar .40
337 Mike DeJean .40
338 Sidney Ponson .40
339 Todd Self **RC** 1.50
340 Jeff Cirillo .40
341 Jimmy Rollins .50
342 Barry Zito .75
342 Barry Zito/SP/ Green Jsy 6.00
343 Felix Pie .40
344 Matt Morris .40
345 Kazuhiro Sasaki .40
346 Jack Wilson .40
347 Nick Johnson .40
348 Wil Cordero .40
349 Ryan Madson .40
350 Torii Hunter .75
351 Andy Ashby .40
352 Aubrey Huff .40
353 Brad Lidge .40
354 Derrek Lee .40
355 Yadier Molina **RC** 2.00
356 Paul Wilson .40
357 Omar Vizquel .50
358 Rene Reyes .40
359 Marlon Anderson .40
360 Bobby Kielty .40
361 Ryan Wagner .40
361 Ryan Wagner/ SP/Old Logo 5.00
362 Justin Morneau .50
363 Shane Spencer .40
364 David Bell .40
365 Matt Stairs .40
366 Joe Borchard .40
367 Mark Redman .40
368 Dave Roberts .40
369 Desi Relaford .40
370 Rich Harden .40
371 Fernando Tatis .40
372 Eric Karros .40
373 Eric Milton .40
374 Mike Sweeney .40
375 Brian Daubach .40
376 Brian Snyder .40
377 Chris Reitsma .40
378 Kyle Lohse .40
379 Livan Hernandez .40
380 Robin Ventura .40
381 Jacque Jones .40
382 Danny Kolb .40
383 Casey Kotchman .40
384 Cristian Guzman .40
385 Josh Beckett 1.00
386 Khalil Greene .40
387 Greg Myers .40
388 Francisco Cordero .40
389 Donald Levinski .40
390 Roy Halladay .75
391 J.D. Drew .40
392 Jamie Moyer .40
393 Ken Macha .40
394 Jeff DaVanon .40
395 Matt Kata .40
396 Jack Cust .40
397 Mike Timlin .40
398 Zack Greinke 4.00
399 Byung-Hyun Kim 4.00
400 Kazuhisa Ishii 4.00
401 Brayan Pena **RC** 4.00
402 Garret Anderson 6.00
403 Kyle Sleeth 4.00
404 Javy Lopez 4.00
405 Damian Moss 4.00
406 David Ortiz 4.00
407 Pedro J. Martinez 8.00
408 Hee Seop Choi 4.00
409 Carl Everett 4.00
410 Dontrelle Willis 5.00
411 Ryan Harvey 4.00
412 Russell Branyan 4.00
413 Milton Bradley 4.00
414 Marcus McBeth **RC** 4.00
415 Carlos Pena 4.00
416 Ivan Rodriguez 6.00
417 Craig Biggio 5.00
418 Angel Berroa 4.00
419 Brian Jordan 4.00
420 Scott Podsednik 4.00
421 Omar Falcon **RC** 4.00
422 Joe Mays 4.00
423 Brad Wilkerson 4.00
424 Al Leiter 4.00
425 Derek Jeter 15.00
426 Mark Mulder 4.00
427 Marlon Byrd 4.00
428 David Murphy 4.00
429 Phil Nevin 4.00
430 J.T. Snow Jr. 4.00
431 Brad Sullivan 4.00
432 Bo Hart 4.00
433 Josh Labandeira **RC** 4.00
434 Chan Ho Park 4.00
435 Carlos Delgado 6.00
436 Curt Schilling 6.00
437 John Smoltz 5.00
438 Luis Matos 4.00
439 Mark Prior 5.00
440 Roberto Alomar 6.00
441 Coco Crisp 4.00
442 Austin Kearns 4.00
443 Larry Walker 5.00
444 Neal Cotts 4.00
445 Jeff Bagwell 6.00
446 Adrian Beltre 4.00
447 Grady Sizemore 6.00
448 Keith Ginter 4.00
449 Vladimir Guerrero 8.00
450 Lyle Overbay 4.00
451 Rafael Furcal 4.00
452 Melvin Mora 4.00
453 Kerry Wood 4.00
454 Jose Valentin 4.00
455 Ken Griffey Jr. 8.00
456 Brandon Phillips 4.00
457 Miguel Cabrera 8.00
458 Edwin Jackson 4.00
459 Eric Owens 4.00
460 Miguel Batista 4.00
461 Mike Hampton 4.00
462 Kevin Millar 4.00
463 Bartolo Colon 4.00
464 Sean Casey 4.00
465 C.C. Sabathia 5.00
466 Rickie Weeks 4.00
467 Brad Penny 4.00
468 Mike MacDougal 4.00
469 Kevin Brown 4.00
470 Lance Berkman 5.00
471 Ben Sheets 4.00
472 Mariano Rivera 5.00
473 Mike Piazza 8.00
474 Ryan Klesko 4.00
475 Edgar Renteria 4.00

Chrome

NM/M
Complete Set (110):
Common Player: 1.00
Production 1,955 Sets
Refractor: 1.5-2X
Production 555 Sets
Black Refractor: 2-4X
Production 55 Sets
THC1 Sammy Sosa 8.00
THC2 Nomar Garciaparra 8.00
THC3 Ichiro Suzuki 6.00
THC4 Rafael Palmeiro 3.00
THC5 Carlos Delgado 2.50
THC6 Troy Glaus 2.00
THC7 Jay Gibbons 1.50
THC8 Frank Thomas 3.00
THC9 Pat Burrell 2.00
THC10 Albert Pujols 8.00
THC11 Brandon Webb 1.50
THC12 Chipper Jones 4.00
THC13 Magglio Ordonez 2.00
THC14 Adam Dunn 2.00
THC15 Todd Helton 2.50
THC16 Jason Giambi 3.00
THC17 Alfonso Soriano 3.00
THC18 Barry Zito 2.00
THC19 Jim Thome 3.00
THC20 Alex Rodriguez 8.00
THC21 Hee Seop Choi 1.00
THC22 Pedro J. Martinez 3.00
THC23 Kerry Wood 3.00
THC24 Bartolo Colon 1.50
THC25 Austin Kearns 2.00
THC26 Ken Griffey Jr. 5.00
THC27 Coco Crisp 1.00
THC28 Larry Walker 1.50
THC29 Ivan Rodriguez 2.50
THC30 Dontrelle Willis 2.00
THC31 Miguel Cabrera 2.50
THC32 Jeff Bagwell 2.50
THC33 Lance Berkman 1.50
THC34 Shawn Green 1.50
THC35 Kevin Brown 1.50
THC36 Vladimir Guerrero 3.00
THC37 Mike Piazza 5.00
THC38 Derek Jeter 10.00
THC39 John Smoltz 1.50
THC40 Mark Prior 8.00
THC41 Gary Sheffield 2.00
THC42 Curt Schilling 2.00
THC43 Randy Johnson 3.00
THC44 Luis Gonzalez 1.50
THC45 Andruw Jones 2.50
THC46 Greg Maddux 5.00
THC47 Tony Batista 1.00
THC48 Esteban Loaiza 1.00
THC49 Chin-Hui Tsao 1.00
THC50 Mike Lowell 1.50
THC51 Jeff Kent 1.50
THC52 Richie Sexson 2.00
THC53 Torii Hunter 2.00
THC54 Jose Vidro 1.00
THC55 Jose Reyes 3.00
THC56 Jimmy Rollins 1.00
THC57 Bret Boone 1.50
THC58 Rocco Baldelli 2.00
THC59 Hank Blalock 2.00
THC60 Rickie Weeks 2.00
THC61 Rodney Choy Foo 1.00
THC62 Zach Miner 3.00
THC63 Brayan Pena 1.00
THC64 David Murphy 1.00
THC65 Matt Creighton 1.00
THC66 Kyle Sleeth 1.00
THC67 Matthew Moses 1.00
THC68 Josh Labandeira 1.00
THC69 Grady Sizemore 2.00
THC70 Edwin Jackson 1.00
THC71 Marcus McBeth 1.00
THC72 Bradley Sullivan 1.00
THC73 Zachary Duke 25.00
THC74 Omar Falcon 1.00
THC75 Conor Jackson 2.00
THC76 Carlos Quentin 4.00
THC77 Craig Ansman 1.00
THC78 Mike Gosling 1.00
THC79 Kyle Davies 1.00
THC80 Anthony Lerew 1.00
THC81 Sung Jung 1.00
THC82 David Crouthers 1.00
THC83 Kenny Perez 1.00
THC84 Jeffrey Allison 1.00
THC85 Nic Ungs 1.00
THC86 Donald Levinski 1.00
THC87 Anthony Acevedo 1.00
THC88 Todd Self 1.00
THC89 Tim Frend 1.00
THC90 Tydus Meadows 1.00
THC91 Khalid Ballouli 1.00
THC92 Dioner Navarro 1.00
THC93 Casey Myers 1.00
THC94 Jon Knott 1.00
THC95 Tim Stauffer 1.00
THC96 Ricky Nolasco 2.00
THC97 Blake Hawksworth 1.00
THC98 Jesse Roman 1.00
THC99 Yadier Molina 1.00
THC100 Chris O'Riordan 1.00
THC101 Cliff Floyd 1.00
THC102 Nick Johnson 1.00
THC103 Edgar Martinez 1.50
THC104 Brett Myers 1.00
THC105 Francisco Rodriguez 1.00
THC106 Scott Rolen 3.00
THC107 Mark Teixeira 2.00
THC108 Miguel Tejada 2.00
THC109 Vernon Wells 1.50
THC110 Jerome Williams 1.00

Clubhouse Collection

NM/M
Common Player: 5.00
BA Bobby Abreu 6.00
RB Rocco Baldelli 12.00
LB Lance Berkman 6.00
YB Yogi Berra 35.00
HB Hank Blalock 8.00
BB Bret Boone 6.00
KB Kevin Brown 6.00
EC Eric Chavez 5.00
RC Roger Clemens 15.00
JD Johnny Damon 10.00
AD Adam Dunn 6.00
RF Rafael Furcal 6.00
EG Eric Gagne 8.00
NG Nomar Garciaparra 15.00
JG Jason Giambi 8.00
MG Marcus Giles 8.00
TG Troy Glaus 6.00
LG Luis Gonzalez 5.00
SG Shawn Green 6.00
TH Tim Hudson 6.00
THU Torii Hunter 8.00
KI Kazuhisa Ishii 6.00
RJ Randy Johnson 10.00
AJ Andruw Jones 6.00
CJ Chipper Jones 8.00
AK Al Kaline 25.00
HK Harmon Killebrew 30.00
PL Paul LoDuca 5.00
JL Javy Lopez 6.00
GM Greg Maddux 20.00
PM Pedro J. Martinez 10.00
WM Willie Mays 100.00
FM Fred McGriff 6.00
MM Mark Mulder 5.00
SM Stan Musial 40.00
BM Brett Myers 5.00
AP Albert Pujols 15.00
MR Manny Ramirez 8.00
JRE Jose Reyes 8.00
AR Alex Rodriguez 10.00
IR Ivan Rodriguez 6.00
SRB Scott Rolen/bat 8.00
SR Scott Rolen/jsy 8.00
JR Jimmy Rollins 6.00
CS C.C. Sabathia 5.00
GS Gary Sheffield 8.00
JS John Smoltz 8.00
DS Duke Snider 30.00
AS Alfonso Soriano 10.00
SS Sammy Sosa 15.00
MS Mike Sweeney 5.00
MTE Mark Teixeira 6.00
MT Miguel Tejada/jsy 6.00
MTB Miguel Tejada/bat 8.00
JT Jim Thome 10.00
VW Vernon Wells 6.00
KW Kerry Wood 10.00
BZ Barry Zito 6.00

Clubhouse Collection Autograph

NM/M
Inserted 15,186
Production 25 Sets
WM Willie Mays 400.00

Clubhouse Collection - Dual

NM/M
Production 55 Sets
BC Yogi Berra, Roger Clemens 160.00
GS Shawn Green, Duke Snider 150.00

Doubleheader

NM/M
Complete Set (30): 50.00
Common Player: .75
Inserted 1:Box
1 Alex Rodriguez 5.00
2 Nomar Garciaparra 4.00
3 Ichiro Suzuki 4.00
4 Albert Pujols 4.00
5 Sammy Sosa 4.00
6 Derek Jeter 6.00
7 Jim Thome 2.00
8 Adam Dunn 1.00
9 Jason Giambi 2.00
10 Ivan Rodriguez 1.50
11 Todd Helton 1.50
12 Luis Gonzalez .75
13 Jeff Bagwell 1.50
14 Lance Berkman 1.00
15 Alfonso Soriano 2.00
16 Dontrelle Willis 1.00
17 Mark Prior 4.00
18 Vladimir Guerrero 2.00
19 Mike Piazza 3.00
20 Roger Clemens 4.00
21 Randy Johnson 2.00
22 Curt Schilling 1.50
23 Gary Sheffield 1.00
24 Pedro J. Martinez 2.00
25 Carlos Delgado 1.50
26 Jimmy Rollins .75
27 Andruw Jones 1.50
28 Chipper Jones 3.00
29 Rocco Baldelli 1.50
30 Hank Blalock 1.00

Flashbacks

NM/M
Complete Set (10): 8.00
Common Player: .50
Inserted 1:12
F1 Duke Snider 1.50
F2 Johnny Podres .50
F3 Don Newcombe .50
F4 Al Kaline 1.50
F5 Willie Mays 4.00
F6 Stan Musial 3.00
F7 Harmon Killebrew 2.00
F8 Herb Score .50
F9 Whitey Ford 1.00
F10 Robin Roberts .50

Flashbacks Autograph

Inserted 1:30,373

Grandstand Glory

		NM/M
Common Player:		20.00
YB	Yogi Berra	20.00
AK	Al Kaline	30.00
HK	Harmon Killebrew	30.00
SM	Stan Musial	35.00
WS	Warren Spahn	20.00

New Age Performers

		NM/M
Complete Set (15):		15.00
Common Player:		.75
Inserted 1:5		
NAP1	Jason Giambi	1.50
NAP2	Ichiro Suzuki	2.50
NAP3	Alex Rodriguez	3.00
NAP4	Alfonso Soriano	1.50
NAP5	Albert Pujols	3.00
NAP6	Nomar Garciaparra	3.00
NAP7	Mark Prior	3.00
NAP8	Derek Jeter	4.00
NAP9	Sammy Sosa	2.50
NAP10	Carlos Delgado	1.00
NAP11	Jim Thome	1.50
NAP12	Todd Helton	1.00
NAP13	Gary Sheffield	.75
NAP14	Vladimir Guerrero	1.50
NAP15	Josh Beckett	1.00

Real One Autograph

		NM/M
Common Autograph:		30.00
Inserted 1:230		
Red Autograph:		1.5-2X
Production 55		
GA	Gair Allie	50.00
EB	Ernie Banks	100.00
YB	Yogi Berra	100.00
BB	Bob Borkowski	40.00
BC	Billy Consolo	55.00
CF	Cliff Floyd	30.00
BG	Bill Glynn	45.00
JG	Johnny Gray	45.00
AH	Aubrey Huff	30.00
AK	Al Kaline	100.00
HK	Harmon Killebrew	90.00
TK	Thornton Kipper	45.00
BK	Bob Kline	45.00
SK	Steve Kraly	60.00
LL	Lou Limmer	60.00
ML	Mike Lowell	40.00
WM	Willie Mays	185.00
BM	Bob Milliken	45.00
SM	Stan Musial	140.00
DN	Don Newcombe	65.00
MO	Magglio Ordonez	35.00
JP	Jim Pearce	45.00
HP	Harry Perkowski	50.00
DP	Duane Pillette	40.00
JPO	Johnny Podres	45.00
SR	Scott Rolen	45.00
FS	Frank Smith	45.00
DS	Duke Snider	85.00
VT	"Jake" Thies	45.00
HV	Harold Valentine	45.00
DW	Dontrelle Willis	50.00
BW	Bill Wilson	40.00
TW	Tom Wright	45.00

Team Topps Legends

		NM/M
Inserted 1:505		
	Davey Johnson	12.00
	Joe Rudi	15.00

Then And Now

		NM/M
Complete Set (6):		8.00
Common Player:		1.00
Inserted 1:15		
TN1	Willie Mays, Jim Thome	4.00
TN2	Al Kaline, Albert Pujols	4.00
TN3	Duke Snider, Carlos Delgado	1.50

TN4	Robin Roberts, Roy Halladay	1.00
TN5	Don Newcombe, Johan Santana	1.00
TN6	Herb Score, Kerry Wood	1.50

National Trading Card Day

As part of its participation in NTCD on April 3, Topps issued a 12-card foil pack with four baseball player cards, two football and three each basketball and hockey, plus a header. Only the baseball players are listed here. Fronts have action photos, gold-foil highlights and a NTCD logo. Backs have recent stats, a photo portrait and biographical data.

		NM/M
Unopened Pack:		3.00
Common Player:		.25
1	Rocco Baldelli	.35
2	Mark Prior	.50
3	Dontrelle Willis	.25
4	Jason Giambi	.25

2004 Topps Opening Day

		NM/M
Complete Set (165):		25.00
Common Player:		.10
Pack (6):		1.00
Box (36):		30.00
1	Jim Thome	.50
2	Edgardo Alfonzo	.10
3	Marlon Anderson	.10
4	Ichiro Suzuki	1.00
5	Frank Thomas	.40
6	Tom Glavine	.25
7	Bo Hart	.10
8	Marcus Giles	.10
9	Kevin Millar	.10
10	Derek Jeter	1.50
11	Corey Patterson	.10
12	Jay Payton	.10
13	Lance Berkman	.20
14	Juan Pierre	.10
15	Mike Piazza	.75
16	Richie Sexson	.40
17	Tim Hudson	.25
18	Fred McGriff	.25
19	Brad Radke	.10
20	John Smoltz	.20
21	Jay Gibbons	.10
22	Michael Young	.10
23	Steve Finley	.10
24	Ramon Hernandez	.10
25	Albert Pujols	1.25
26	Trot Nixon	.10
27	Kevin Millwood	.25
28	Mark Prior	1.00
29	Mike Lowell	.20
30	Paul LoDuca	.10
31	Jacque Jones	.10
32	Ty Wigginton	.10
33	Cliff Floyd	.10
34	Marlon Byrd	.10
35	Mark Mulder	.20
36	Johnny Damon	.20
37	Jimmy Rollins	.25
38	Javy Lopez	.25
39	Andruw Jones	.40
40	Hank Blalock	.25
41	Hee Seop Choi	.10
42	Jose Vidro	.10
43	Hideo Nomo	.25
44	Javier Vazquez	.10
45	Jorge Posada	.25
46	Al Leiter	.10
47	Orlando Cabrera	.10
48	Mike Hampton	.10
49	Esteban Loaiza	.10
50	Todd Helton	.40
51	Jose Contreras	.20
52	Jason L. Phillips	.10
53	Vernon Wells	.20
54	Randy Winn	.10
55	Curt Schilling	.40
56	Mark Buehrle	.10
57	Dmitri Young	.10
58	Kazuhisa Ishii	.10
59	A.J. Pierzynski	.10
60	Greg Maddux	.75
61	Jarrod Washburn	.10
62	Omar Vizquel	.10
63	Alex Gonzalez	.10
64	Sean Casey	.10
65	Eric Chavez	.20
66	Mike Lieberthal	.10
67	Jason Kendall	.10
68	Mike Cameron	.10
69	Woody Williams	.10
70	Nomar Garciaparra	1.00
71	Bernie Williams	.25
72	Darin Erstad	.20
73	Bill Mueller	.10
74	Damian Miller	.10
75	Jason Giambi	.50
76	Adam Dunn	.25
77	Carlos Lee	.10
78	Angel Berroa	.10
79	Erubiel Durazo	.10
80	Bret Boone	.20
81	Aubrey Huff	.20
82	Carlos Delgado	.40
83	Toby Hall	.10
84	Roy Halladay	.25
85	Preston Wilson	.10
86	Bartolo Colon	.20
87	Moises Alou	.20
88	Luis Castillo	.10
89	Manny Ramirez	.40
90	Garret Anderson	.25
91	Ryan Klesko	.20
92	Rich Aurilia	.10
93	Rafael Furcal	.20
94	Rocco Baldelli	.40
95	Eric Gagne	.20
96	Jeff Kent	.20
97	Josh Beckett	.40
98	Alex Gonzalez	.10
99	Jose Cruz Jr.	.10
100	Alex Rodriguez	1.25
101	Troy Glaus	.20
102	Carlos Beltran	.20
103	Luis Gonzalez	.20
104	A.J. Burnett	.10
105	Gary Sheffield	.25
106	Benito Santiago	.10
107	Tony Batista	.10
108	David Ortiz	.20
109	Shannon Stewart	.10
110	Jim Edmonds	.25
111	Kenny Lofton	.20
112	Paul Konerko	.10
113	Rafael Palmeiro	.40
114	Pat Burrell	.25
115	Barry Zito	.25
116	Edgar Martinez	.20
117	Austin Kearns	.25
118	Geoff Jenkins	.20
119	Mike Mussina	.25
120	Alfonso Soriano	.50
121	Shea Hillenbrand	.10
122	Ivan Rodriguez	.40
123	Kerry Wood	.40
124	Scott Rolen	.50
125	Jeff Bagwell	.40
126	Roberto Alomar	.25
127	Carl Crawford	.10
128	Mike Sweeney	.10
129	Melvin Mora	.20
130	Larry Walker	.20
131	Matt Morris	.10
132	Shawn Green	.20
133	Scott Podsednik	.25
134	Phil Nevin	.10
135	Dontrelle Willis	.50
136	Torii Hunter	.25
137	Carl Everett	.10
138	Pedro J. Martinez	.50
139	Roy Oswalt	.25
140	Vladimir Guerrero	.50
141	Chipper Jones	.75
142	Jose Reyes	.25
143	Sammy Sosa	1.00
144	Nick Johnson	.10
145	Miguel Tejada	.25
146	Bobby Abreu	.20
147	Magglio Ordonez	.25
148	Sean Burroughs	.10
149	Jody Gerut	.10
150	Jermaine Dye	.10
151	Craig Biggio	.20
152	Randy Johnson	.50
153	Jeff Conine	.10
154	Edgar Renteria	.20
155	Mark Teixeira	.25
156	Eric Hinske	.10
157	Kevin Brown	.20
158	Ken Griffey Jr.	.75
159	Brandon Webb	.10
160	Brian Giles	.20
161	Jason Schmidt	.20
162	Aramis Ramirez	.10
163	Aaron Boone	.10
164	Miguel Cabrera	.40
165	Checklist	.10

Autograph

		NM/M
Common Autograph:		10.00
Inserted 1:629		
JD	Jeff Duncan	20.00
RH	Rich Harden	20.00
AT	Andres Torres	10.00
RW	Ryan Wagner	25.00
DW	Dontrelle Willis	30.00

Originals Signature Edition

		NM/M
Common Autograph:		10.00
Pack (4):		45.00
Box (6):		220.00
Second number reflects quantity produced.		
JA1	Jim Abbott 88 TR/339	20.00
SA5	Sparky Anderson 83 MG/67	15.00
SA6	Sparky Anderson 84 MG/97	15.00
SA7	Sparky Anderson 85 MG/73	15.00
LA9	Luis Aparicio 69/49	20.00
LA12	Luis Aparicio 72/15	30.00
HB2	Harold Baines 82/31	25.00
HB3	Harold Baines 83/19	30.00
HB5	Harold Baines 85/97	15.00
HB6	Harold Baines 86/93	15.00
HB7	Harold Baines 87/115	15.00
JB2	Jesse Barfield 83/45	15.00
JB4	Jesse Barfield 85/60	15.00
JB5	Jesse Barfield 86/37	15.00
JB6	Jesse Barfield 87/180	10.00
KB2	Kevin Bass 84/71	10.00
KB3	Kevin Bass 85/30	10.00
KB4	Kevin Bass 86/44	10.00
KB5	Kevin Bass 87/74	10.00
KB6	Kevin Bass 90 TR/35	10.00
BB5	Buddy Bell 79/135	15.00
BB8	Buddy Bell 82/34	15.00
BB9	Buddy Bell 83/83	10.00
BB10	Buddy Bell 84/22	15.00
BB12	Buddy Bell 86/32	15.00
GB2	George Bell 84/67	10.00
GB3	George Bell 85/32	15.00
GB4	George Bell 86/34	15.00
GB5	George Bell 87/204	10.00
JBE2	Johnny Bench 79/14	125.00
JBE5	Johnny Bench 82/16	125.00
YB10	Yogi Berra 85 MG/27	100.00
VB5	Vida Blue 79/21	20.00
VB7	Vida Blue 81/227	10.00
VB8	Vida Blue 82/53	15.00
VB9	Vida Blue 83/45	15.00
BBL4	Bert Blyleven 79/45	25.00
BBL6	Bert Blyleven 81/29	25.00
BBL8	Bert Blyleven 83/41	20.00
BBL10	Bert Blyleven 85/40	20.00
BBL11	Bert Blyleven 86/62	20.00
BBL12	Bert Blyleven 87/54	20.00
MB2	Mike Boddicker 84/56	15.00
MB3	Mike Boddicker 85/139	10.00
MB4	Mike Boddicker 86/66	10.00
MB5	Mike Boddicker 87/88	10.00
WB2	Wade Boggs 84/20	75.00
WB3	Wade Boggs 85/25	75.00
WB5	Wade Boggs 87/45	60.00
LB4	Lou Brock 70/20	50.00
LB13	Lou Brock 79/27	50.00
TB2	Tom Brunansky 83/27	15.00
TB3	Tom Brunansky 84/62	15.00
TB5	Tom Brunansky 86/28	15.00
TB6	Tom Brunansky 87/193	10.00
BU8	Bill Buckner 81/39	20.00
BU9	Bill Buckner 82/38	20.00
BU10	Bill Buckner 83/47	15.00
BU11	Bill Buckner 84/31	20.00
BU12	Bill Buckner 84 TR/24	20.00
BU13	Bill Buckner 85/80	15.00
BU14	Bill Buckner 86/63	15.00
BC5	Bert Campaneris 79/107	10.00
BC7	Bert Campaneris 84/28	15.00
JC2	John Candelaria 79/77	20.00
JC4	John Candelaria 81/19	30.00
JC5	John Candelaria 82/42	25.00
JC6	John Candelaria 83/77	20.00
JC8	John Candelaria 85/61	20.00
JC9	John Candelaria 86/36	20.00
JCA2	Jose Canseco 87/99	60.00
RC4	Rod Carew 79/29	60.00
RC6	Rod Carew 81/21	75.00
RC7	Rod Carew 82/18	75.00
GC3	Gary Carter 79/21	40.00
GC4	Gary Carter 80/24	40.00
GC5	Gary Carter 81/22	40.00
JCR2	Joe Carter 86/24	50.00
JCR3	Joe Carter 87/23	50.00
RCE3	Ron Cey 79/55	15.00
RCE6	Ron Cey 82/34	15.00
RCE7	Ron Cey 83/87	15.00
RCE8	Ron Cey 83 TR/68	15.00
RCE11	Ron Cey 86/43	15.00
VC2	Vince Coleman 87/299	15.00
VC3	Vince Coleman 88/34	20.00
VC4	Vince Coleman 91 TR/23	25.00
DC6	Dave Concepcion 80/21	40.00
DC8	Dave Concepcion 82/43	30.00
DC9	Dave Concepcion 83/34	30.00
DC10	Dave Concepcion 84/24	40.00
DC11	Dave Concepcion 85/41	30.00
DC12	Dave Concepcion 86/69	25.00
JCU8	Jose Cruz Sr. 82/28	15.00
JCU9	Jose Cruz Sr. 83/102	10.00
JCU10	Jose Cruz Sr. 84/67	10.00
JCU11	Jose Cruz Sr. 85/68	10.00
JCU12	Jose Cruz Sr. 86/31	15.00
RD3	Ron Darling 87/224	15.00
DD2	Darren Daulton 87/269	10.00
DD4	Darren Daulton 92/32	15.00
DD5	Darren Daulton 94/17	20.00
DD6	Darren Daulton 96/22	20.00
ED3	Eric Davis 87/336	15.00
AD3	Andre Dawson 80/27	25.00
AD4	Andre Dawson 81/37	25.00
AD5	Andre Dawson 82/55	20.00
AD6	Andre Dawson 83/47	20.00
AD7	Andre Dawson 84/25	25.00
AD8	Andre Dawson 85/22	25.00
AD9	Andre Dawson 86/24	25.00
DDE2	Doug DeCinces 79/38	20.00
DDE3	Doug DeCinces 80/24	20.00
DDE4	Doug DeCinces 81/24	20.00
DDE5	Doug DeCinces 82/42	20.00
DDE6	Doug DeCinces 83/75	15.00
DDE7	Doug DeCinces 84/19	20.00
DDE8	Doug DeCinces 85/54	15.00
DDE9	Doug DeCinces 86/74	15.00
BD6	Bucky Dent 82/49	20.00
BD7	Bucky Dent 83/92	15.00
BD8	Bucky Dent 84/63	15.00
RDI2	Rob Dibble 90/31	25.00
RDI3	Rob Dibble 91/62	20.00
RDI4	Rob Dibble 92/56	20.00
RDI6	Rob Dibble 93/47	15.00
RDI7	Rob Dibble 94/37	15.00
LD2	Leon Durham 82/51	10.00
LD3	Leon Durham 83/52	10.00
LD4	Leon Durham 84/151	10.00
LD7	Leon Durham 87/87	10.00
LDY2	Lenny Dykstra 87/200	15.00
LDY3	Lenny Dykstra 88/30	25.00
LDY4	Lenny Dykstra 89/17	30.00
DE3	Dennis Eckersley 79/44	40.00
DE4	Dennis Eckersley 80/40	40.00
DEV5	Darrell Evans 79/19	20.00
DEV7	Darrell Evans 81/15	20.00
DEV8	Darrell Evans 82/25	20.00
DEV9	Darrell Evans 83/63	15.00
DEV10	Darrell Evans 84/81	10.00
DEV11	Darrell Evans 85/48	15.00
DEV12	Darrell Evans 86/82	10.00
SF2	Sid Fernandez 86/18	30.00
SF3	Sid Fernandez 87/211	15.00
SF4	Sid Fernandez 93/20	25.00
TF2	Tony Fernandez 86/41	15.00
TF3	Tony Fernandez 87/228	10.00
MF3	Mark Fidrych 79/74	25.00
MF4	Mark Fidrych 80/16	40.00
CF2	Cecil Fielder 87/208	30.00
CF3	Cecil Fielder 88/26	50.00
CF4	Cecil Fielder 89/16	50.00
RF3	Rollie Fingers 79/52	20.00
RF4	Rollie Fingers 80/15	40.00
RF5	Rollie Fingers 81/18	40.00
CFI3	Carlton Fisk 79/24	60.00
CFI4	Carlton Fisk 80/32	50.00
CFI6	Carlton Fisk 82/30	50.00
GF6	George Foster 79/20	20.00
GF10	George Foster 83/39	15.00
GF11	George Foster 84/112	10.00
GF12	George Foster 85/76	10.00
GF13	George Foster 86/64	10.00
SG4	Steve Garvey 79/26	30.00
SG7	Steve Garvey 82/122	15.00
SG9	Steve Garvey 84/32	20.00
SG10	Steve Garvey 85/129	15.00
CG3	Cesar Geronimo 79/28	15.00
CG5	Cesar Geronimo 81/21	15.00
CG6	Cesar Geronimo 82/52	10.00
CG7	Cesar Geronimo 83/67	10.00
CG8	Cesar Geronimo 84/70	10.00
KGI2	Kirk Gibson 82/35	20.00
KGI3	Kirk Gibson 83/35	20.00
KGI5	Kirk Gibson 85/44	20.00
KGI6	Kirk Gibson 86/44	20.00
KGI7	Kirk Gibson 87/65	20.00
DG3	Dwight Gooden 87/52	30.00
RG7	Rich "Goose" Gossage 81/21	20.00
RG8	Rich "Goose" Gossage 82/30	20.00
RG9	Rich "Goose" Gossage 83/34	20.00
RG10	Rich "Goose" Gossage 84/90	15.00
RG12	Rich "Goose" Gossage 86/30	15.00
BG2	Bobby Grich 79/29	20.00
BG3	Bobby Grich 80/70	15.00
BG5	Bobby Grich 82/45	15.00
BG6	Bobby Grich 83/85	10.00
BG7	Bobby Grich 84/57	15.00
BG8	Bobby Grich 85/36	15.00
KG5	Ken Griffey Sr. 80/15	30.00
KG7	Ken Griffey Sr. 82/18	30.00
KG8	Ken Griffey Sr. 83/70	15.00
KG9	Ken Griffey Sr. 84/64	15.00
KG10	Ken Griffey Sr. 85/32	20.00
KG11	Ken Griffey Sr. 86 TR/32	20.00
KGU2	Kelly Gruber 88/77	10.00
KGU3	Kelly Gruber 89/44	10.00
KGU4	Kelly Gruber 90/86	10.00
KGU5	Kelly Gruber 91/52	10.00
KGU6	Kelly Gruber 92/55	10.00
KGU7	Kelly Gruber 93/26	15.00
RGU4	Ron Guidry 80/22	40.00
RGU5	Ron Guidry 81/104	20.00
RGU6	Ron Guidry 82/53	40.00
RGU7	Ron Guidry 83/46	40.00
RGU8	Ron Guidry 84/40	40.00
RGU9	Ron Guidry 85/50	40.00
TG2	Tony Gwynn 84/95	60.00

KH3 Keith Hernandez 80/38 50.00
KH4 Keith Hernandez 81/19 50.00
KH5 Keith Hernandez 82/156 20.00
KH6 Keith Hernandez 83/17 50.00
TH2 Tom Herr 81/22 15.00
TH3 Tom Herr 82/42 15.00
TH4 Tom Herr 83/80 10.00
TH5 Tom Herr 84/30 15.00
TH6 Tom Herr 85/17 15.00
TH7 Tom Herr 86/28 15.00
TH8 Tom Herr 87/134 10.00
OH2 Orel Hershiser 86/23 40.00
OH3 Orel Hershiser 87/218 20.00
WH4 Whitey Herzog 83 MG/63 10.00
WH5 Whitey Herzog 84 MG/85 10.00
WH6 Whitey Herzog 85 MG/75 10.00
WH7 Whitey Herzog 86 MG/66 10.00
WH8 Whitey Herzog 87 MG/29 15.00
WH9 Whitey Herzog 88 MG/35 15.00
BH5 Bob Horner 83/69 15.00
BH6 Bob Horner 84/63 15.00
BH8 Bob Horner 86/118 15.00
BH9 Bob Horner 87/38 15.00
CH2 Charlie Hough 83/19 20.00
CH3 Charlie Hough 84/50 10.00
CH4 Charlie Hough 85/57 10.00
CH5 Charlie Hough 86/66 10.00
CH6 Charlie Hough 87/46 10.00
CH7 Charlie Hough 88/19 20.00
CH8 Charlie Hough 91 TR/70 10.00
CH9 Charlie Hough 92/25 15.00
AH6 Al Hrabosky 78/20 20.00
AH7 Al Hrabosky 79/40 15.00
AH8 Al Hrabosky 80/61 10.00
AH9 Al Hrabosky 81/38 15.00
AH10 Al Hrabosky 82/62 10.00
AH11 Al Hrabosky 89 Sr./20 20.00
BJ2 Bo Jackson 87/100 60.00
RJ8 Reggie Jackson 82/21 75.00
RJ11 Reggie Jackson 85/17 75.00
RJ12 Reggie Jackson 86/17 75.00
BJA2 Brook Jacoby 86/133 10.00
BJA3 Brook Jacoby 87/191 10.00
FJ8 Fergie Jenkins 78/17 40.00
FJ10 Fergie Jenkins 80/37 30.00
FJ11 Fergie Jenkins 81/32 30.00
FJ12 Fergie Jenkins 82/65 20.00
FJ13 Fergie Jenkins 83/22 30.00
FJ14 Fergie Jenkins 84/42 30.00
WJ2 Wally Joyner 87/335 15.00
DJ3 David Justice 93/32 20.00
AK10 Al Kaline 67/18 120.00
AK16 Al Kaline 73/25 140.00
JK2 Jimmy Key 86/21 20.00
JK3 Jimmy Key 87/263 10.00
JK5 Jimmy Key 92/37 20.00
DK4 Dave Kingman 81/25 30.00
DK6 Dave Kingman 83/32 30.00
DK7 Dave Kingman 86/25 30.00
RK2 Ron Kittle 85/86 10.00
RK3 Ron Kittle 86/55 15.00
RK4 Ron Kittle 87/201 10.00
RKN5 Ray Knight 82/25 20.00
RKN6 Ray Knight 83/36 20.00
RKN7 Ray Knight 84/26 20.00
RKN8 Ray Knight 85/68 15.00
RKN9 Ray Knight 86/80 15.00
RKN10 Ray Knight 87 TR/90 15.00
JKR2 John Kruk 87/214 15.00
JKR3 John Kruk 92/22 35.00
CL3 Carney Lansford 81/184 10.00
CL5 Carney Lansford 83/40 15.00
CL6 Carney Lansford 85/35 15.00
CL7 Carney Lansford 86/76 10.00
CLE3 Chet Lemon 79/24 20.00
CLE6 Chet Lemon 82/23 20.00
CLE7 Chet Lemon 83/35 15.00
CLE8 Chet Lemon 84/42 15.00
CLE9 Chet Lemon 85/32 15.00
CLE10 Chet Lemon 86/136 10.00
CLE11 Chet Lemon 87/27 20.00
JL2 Jim Leyritz 91/38 10.00
JL3 Jim Leyritz 93/49 10.00
JL4 Jim Leyritz 94/16 20.00
JL6 Jim Leyritz 97/62 10.00
JL7 Jim Leyritz 98/20 20.00
JL8 Jim Leyritz 99/124 10.00
JL9 Jim Leyritz 00/40 10.00
DL4 Davey Lopes 79/71 10.00
DL5 Davey Lopes 80/19 15.00
DL7 Davey Lopes 82/17 15.00
DL8 Davey Lopes 83/65 10.00
DL10 Davey Lopes 85/24 15.00
DL11 Davey Lopes 86/40 10.00
DL12 Davey Lopes 01 MG/67 10.00
DL13 Davey Lopes 02 MG/19 15.00
GL7 Greg Luzinski 80/21 30.00
GL9 Greg Luzinski 82/34 20.00
GL10 Greg Luzinski 83/75 10.00
GL11 Greg Luzinski 84/85 10.00
GL12 Greg Luzinski 85/92 10.00
BM7 Bill Madlock 82/26 15.00
BM8 Bill Madlock 83/55 15.00
BM9 Bill Madlock 84/69 15.00
BM10 Bill Madlock 85/60 15.00
BM11 Bill Madlock 86/63 15.00
BM12 Bill Madlock 87/42 15.00
GM3 Gary Matthews Sr. 83/20 15.00
GM4 Gary Matthews Sr. 84/43 10.00
GM5 Gary Matthews Sr. 85/39 10.00
GM6 Gary Matthews Sr. 86/38 10.00
GM7 Gary Matthews Sr. 87/82 10.00
GM8 Gary Matthews Sr. 88/30 15.00
DM3 Don Mattingly 87/84 100.00
WM9 Willie Mays 72/25 300.00
TM5 Tim McCarver 79/22 20.00
JM2 Jack McDowell 89/36 20.00
JM3 Jack McDowell 90 TR/61 15.00
JM4 Jack McDowell 91/33 20.00
JM5 Jack McDowell 92/38 20.00
JM6 Jack McDowell 93/27 20.00
JM9 Jack McDowell 96/15 25.00
JM10 Jack McDowell 97/27 20.00
WMC2 Willie McGee 84/66 25.00
WMC3 Willie McGee 85/44 25.00
WMC4 Willie McGee 86/24 40.00
WMC5 Willie McGee 87/117 25.00
PM1 Paul Molitor 79/15 60.00
PM2 Paul Molitor 80/26 50.00
PM4 Paul Molitor 82/32 50.00
JMO9 Joe Morgan 81/32 30.00
JMO10 Joe Morgan 82/18 40.00
JMO11 Joe Morgan 83/49 25.00
JMO13 Joe Morgan 84/73 15.00
JMO14 Joe Morgan 85/40 25.00
DMU2 Dale Murphy 79/38 50.00
DMU6 Dale Murphy 84/29 40.00
DMU8 Dale Murphy 86/25 50.00
DMU9 Dale Murphy 87/91 20.00
SM5 Stan Musial 62/16 150.00
AO6 Al Oliver 79/42 15.00
AO8 Al Oliver 81/54 15.00
AO9 Al Oliver 82/45 15.00
AO10 Al Oliver 83/50 15.00
AO11 Al Oliver 84/51 15.00
AO12 Al Oliver 85/46 15.00
AO13 Al Oliver 86/44 15.00
PO2 Paul O'Neill 89/24 50.00
PO3 Paul O'Neill 90/18 50.00
PO4 Paul O'Neill 91/24 50.00
PO5 Paul O'Neill 97/33 40.00
JP3 Jim Palmer 80/33 30.00
JP4 Jim Palmer 81/23 30.00
JP5 Jim Palmer 82/24 30.00
DP6 Dave Parker 82/73 20.00
DP7 Dave Parker 83/30 30.00
DP9 Dave Parker 85/45 25.00
DP10 Dave Parker 86/24 30.00
BP9 Boog Powell 73/17 50.00
BP11 Boog Powell 75/19 40.00
TR2 Tim Raines 82/43 20.00
TR3 Tim Raines 83/26 25.00
TR5 Tim Raines 85/43 20.00
TR6 Tim Raines 86/21 25.00
TR7 Tim Raines 87/211 15.00
HR2 Harold Reynolds 87/255 10.00
JR7 Jim Rice 81/123 20.00
JR8 Jim Rice 82/24 35.00
JR9 Jim Rice 83/71 25.00
CR4 Cal Ripken Jr. 86/74 120.00
MR2 Mickey Rivers 79/35 15.00
MR5 Mickey Rivers 82/49 15.00
MR6 Mickey Rivers 83/79 10.00
MR7 Mickey Rivers 84/91 10.00
MR8 Mickey Rivers 85/34 15.00
BR11 Brooks Robinson 74/20 75.00
BR13 Brooks Robinson 76/17 75.00
JRU9 Joe Rudi 79/24 15.00
JRU10 Joe Rudi 80/45 15.00
JRU11 Joe Rudi 82/26 15.00
JRU12 Joe Rudi 83/75 10.00
NR5 Nolan Ryan 83/23 200.00
NR6 Nolan Ryan 84/20 200.00
NR8 Nolan Ryan 86/20 200.00
BS2 Bret Saberhagen 86/23 25.00
BS3 Bret Saberhagen 87/230 15.00
RS2 Ryne Sandberg 84/37 100.00
RS5 Ryne Sandberg 87/32 100.00
SS2 Steve Sax 83/34 15.00
SS4 Steve Sax 85/33 15.00
SS5 Steve Sax 86/45 15.00
SS6 Steve Sax 87/215 10.00
MS2 Mike Schmidt 80/100 60.00
MSC3 Mike Scott 82/32 15.00
MSC4 Mike Scott 83/55 15.00
MSC5 Mike Scott 84/28 15.00
MSC6 Mike Scott 86/73 10.00
MSC7 Mike Scott 87/36 15.00
MSC8 Mike Scott 88/21 15.00
TS2 Tom Seaver 79/44 85.00
TS4 Tom Seaver 81/16 100.00
TS5 Tom Seaver 82/25 100.00
KS2 Kevin Seitzer 88/88 10.00
KS3 Kevin Seitzer 89/39 10.00
KS4 Kevin Seitzer 90/18 15.00
KS5 Kevin Seitzer 91/39 10.00
KS6 Kevin Seitzer 92/49 10.00
KS9 Kevin Seitzer 93/38 10.00
KS10 Kevin Seitzer 94/22 15.00
KS13 Kevin Seitzer 97/24 15.00
LS5 Lee Smith 86/29 25.00
LS6 Lee Smith 87/237 15.00
LS7 Lee Smith 88/27 25.00
OS2 Ozzie Smith 81/28 60.00
OS3 Ozzie Smith 82/27 60.00
OS5 Ozzie Smith 84/19 75.00
OS6 Ozzie Smith 85/16 75.00
RM8 Reggie Smith 79/15 25.00
RM9 Reggie Smith 80/16 25.00
RM10 Reggie Smith 81/14 25.00
RM11 Reggie Smith 82/32 15.00
RM12 Reggie Smith 83/48 15.00
DS8 Duke Snider 64/18 150.00
CS2 Cory Snyder 87/291 10.00
CS3 Cory Snyder 91/39 15.00
DSW2 Dave Stewart 83/41 15.00
DSW3 Dave Stewart 84/60 15.00
DSW4 Dave Stewart 85/24 15.00
DSW5 Dave Stewart 86/53 15.00
DSW6 Dave Stewart 87/171 10.00
DSE2 Dave Stieb 81/21 35.00
DSE3 Dave Stieb 82/34 30.00
DSE4 Dave Stieb 83/70 25.00
DSE5 Dave Stieb 84/20 35.00
DSE6 Dave Stieb 85/55 25.00
DSE7 Dave Stieb 86/69 25.00
DSE8 Dave Stieb 87/75 25.00
DSR2 Darryl Strawberry 85/32 25.00
DSR3 Darryl Strawberry 86/24 25.00
DSR4 Darryl Strawberry 87/183 20.00
DSR5 Darryl Strawberry 87 AS/110 20.00
RU3 Rick Sutcliffe 82/53 20.00
RU4 Rick Sutcliffe 83/43 20.00
RU5 Rick Sutcliffe 84/33 20.00
RU6 Rick Sutcliffe 85/82 20.00
RU8 Rick Sutcliffe 87/19 25.00
BSU6 Bruce Sutter 82/111 20.00
BSU7 Bruce Sutter 83/45 25.00
BSU8 Bruce Sutter 84/24 30.00
BSU9 Bruce Sutter 85/19 35.00
BSU10 Bruce Sutter 86/78 20.00
BSU11 Bruce Sutter 87/36 25.00
KT5 Kent Tekulve 81/17 20.00
KT6 Kent Tekulve 82/36 15.00
KT7 Kent Tekulve 83/52 15.00
KT8 Kent Tekulve 84/71 15.00
KT9 Kent Tekulve 85/43 15.00
KT10 Kent Tekulve 86/57 15.00
KT11 Kent Tekulve 87/32 15.00
KT12 Kent Tekulve 88/20 20.00
LT2 Luis Tiant 68/16 40.00
LT11 Luis Tiant 79/22 30.00
LT12 Luis Tiant 80/23 30.00
LT13 Luis Tiant 81/20 30.00
LT14 Luis Tiant 82/51 15.00
LT15 Luis Tiant 83/58 15.00
AT2 Alan Trammell 80/17 30.00
AT3 Alan Trammell 81/26 30.00
AT4 Alan Trammell 82/40 30.00
AT5 Alan Trammell 83/21 30.00
AT6 Alan Trammell 84/57 30.00
AT7 Alan Trammell 85/39 30.00
AT8 Alan Trammell 86/23 30.00
AT9 Alan Trammell 87/15 30.00
AV2 Andy Van Slyke 85/35 35.00
AV3 Andy Van Slyke 86/37 35.00
AV4 Andy Van Slyke 87/178 25.00
AV5 Andy Van Slyke 87 TR/130 25.00
FV3 Frank Viola 85/25 25.00
FV4 Frank Viola 86/99 15.00
FV5 Frank Viola 87/209 15.00
TW2 Tim Wallach 83/49 15.00
TW4 Tim Wallach 85/46 15.00
TW5 Tim Wallach 86/44 15.00
TW6 Tim Wallach 87/197 10.00
BW3 Bob Watson 79/77 10.00
BW6 Bob Watson 82/23 20.00
BW7 Bob Watson 83/93 10.00
BW8 Bob Watson 84/64 10.00
BW9 Bob Watson 85/68 10.00
EW4 Earl Weaver 78 MG/52 15.00
EW5 Earl Weaver 83 MG/38 20.00
EW7 Earl Weaver 86 MG/107 15.00
EW8 Earl Weaver 87 MG/175 10.00
WW2 Walt Weiss 89/34 10.00
WW3 Walt Weiss 91/30 10.00
WW4 Walt Weiss 92/71 10.00
WW7 Walt Weiss 97/49 10.00
WW10 Walt Weiss 99/40 10.00
WW11 Walt Weiss 01/51 10.00
MW2 Mookie Wilson 82/20 20.00
MW3 Mookie Wilson 83/41 15.00
MW5 Mookie Wilson 85/51 15.00
MW6 Mookie Wilson 86/47 15.00
MW7 Mookie Wilson 87/67 15.00
CY4 Carl Yastrzemski 80/60 100.00
CY5 Carl Yastrzemski 81/35 120.00
SY5 Steve Yeager 79/23 25.00
SY9 Steve Yeager 83/80 10.00
SY12 Steve Yeager 86/47 15.00
SY13 Steve Yeager 86 TR/100 10.00
RY5 Robin Yount 80/18 100.00
RY6 Robin Yount 81/23 100.00
RY9 Robin Yount 84/15 125.00
RY11 Robin Yount 86/21 100.00

2004 Topps Pristine

NM/M
Complete Set (190):
Common Player: 1.00
Common Rookie: 1.50
Common Uncommon RC: 3.00
Production 999
Common Rare RC: 6.00
Production 499
Pack (8): 35.00
Box (5): 140.00
1 Jim Thome 2.00
2 Ryan Klesko 1.00
3 Ichiro Suzuki 4.00
4 Rocco Baldelli 1.00
5 Vernon Wells 1.00
6 Javier Vazquez 1.00
7 Billy Wagner 1.00
8 Jose Reyes 1.00
9 Lance Berkman 1.00
10 Alex Rodriguez 6.00
11 Pat Burrell 1.00
12 Mark Mulder 1.00
13 Mike Piazza 3.00
14 Miguel Cabrera 2.00
15 Larry Walker 1.00
16 Carlos Lee 1.00
17 Mark Prior 2.00
18 Pedro J. Martinez 2.00
19 Melvin Mora 1.00
20 Sammy Sosa 4.00
21 Bartolo Colon 1.00
22 Luis Gonzalez 1.00
23 Marcus Giles 1.00
24 Ken Griffey Jr. 3.00
25 Ivan Rodriguez 1.50
26 Carlos Beltran 1.50
27 Geoff Jenkins 1.00
28 Nick Johnson 1.00
29 Gary Sheffield 1.50
30 Alfonso Soriano 2.00
31 Scott Rolen 2.00
32 Garret Anderson 1.00
33 Richie Sexson 1.00
34 Curt Schilling 1.50
35 Greg Maddux 3.00
36 Adam Dunn 1.50
37 Preston Wilson 1.00
38 Josh Beckett 1.50
39 Roy Oswalt 1.00
40 Derek Jeter 6.00
41 Jason Kendall 1.00
42 Bret Boone 1.00
43 Torii Hunter 1.00
44 Roy Halladay 1.00
45 Edgar Renteria 1.00
46 Troy Glaus 1.00
47 Chipper Jones 2.00
48 Manny Ramirez 1.50
49 C.C. Sabathia 1.00
50 Albert Pujols 5.00
51 Randy Wolf 1.00
52 Eric Chavez 1.00
53 Kevin Brown 1.00
54 Cliff Floyd 1.00
55 Jeff Bagwell 1.50
56 Frank Thomas 1.50
57 David Ortiz 1.50
58 Rafael Palmeiro 1.50
59 Randy Johnson 2.00
60 Vladimir Guerrero 2.00
61 Carlos Delgado 1.00
62 Hank Blalock 1.50
63 Jim Edmonds 1.00
64 Jason Schmidt 1.00
65 Mike Lieberthal 1.00
66 Tim Hudson 1.00
67 Jorge Posada 1.00
68 Jose Vidro 1.00
69 Eric Gagne 1.00
70 Roger Clemens 5.00
71 Mike Lowell 1.00
72 Dontrelle Willis 1.00
73 Austin Kearns 1.00
74 Kerry Wood 2.00
75 Miguel Tejada 1.50
76 Bobby Abreu 1.00
77 Edgar Martinez 1.00
78 Joe Mauer 1.00
79 Mike Sweeney 1.00
80 Jason Giambi 1.00
81 Mark Teixeira 1.00
82 Aubrey Huff 1.00
83 Brian Giles 1.00
84 Barry Zito 1.00
85 Mike Mussina 1.50
86 Brandon Webb 1.00
87 Andruw Jones 1.50
88 Javy Lopez 1.00
89 Bill Mueller 1.00
90 Scott Podsednik 1.00
91 Moises Alou 1.00
92 Esteban Loaiza 1.00
93 Magglio Ordonez 1.00
94 Jeff Kent 1.00
95 Todd Helton 1.50
96 Juan Pierre 1.00
97 Jody Gerut 1.00
98 Angel Berroa 1.00
99 Shawn Green 1.00
100 Nomar Garciaparra 3.00
101 David Aardsma/C 1.50
102 David Aardsma/U 4.00
103 David Aardsma/R 8.00
104 Erick Aybar/C **RC** 5.00
105 Erick Aybar/U **RC** 10.00
106 Erick Aybar/R **RC** 15.00
107 Chad Bentz/C **RC** 1.50
108 Chad Bentz/U **RC** 3.00
109 Chad Bentz/R **RC** 6.00
110 Travis Blackley/C **RC** 1.50
111 Travis Blackley/U **RC** 3.00
112 Travis Blackley/R **RC** 6.00
113 Bobby Brownlie/C **RC** 4.00
114 Bobby Brownlie/U **RC** 6.00
115 Bobby Brownlie/R **RC** 10.00
116 Alberto Callaspo/C **RC** 1.50
117 Alberto Callaspo/U **RC** 3.00
118 Alberto Callaspo/R **RC** 6.00
119 Kazuo Matsui/C **RC** 5.00
120 Kazuo Matsui/U **RC** 8.00
121 Kazuo Matsui/R **RC** 12.00
122 Jesse Crain/C 3.00
123 Jesse Crain/U 5.00
124 Jesse Crain/R 8.00
125 Howard Kendrick/C **RC** 15.00
126 Howard Kendrick/U **RC** 20.00
127 Howard Kendrick/R **RC** 25.00
128 Blake Hawksworth/C **RC** 1.50
129 Blake Hawksworth/U **RC** 3.00
130 Blake Hawksworth/R **RC** 6.00
131 Conor Jackson/C 6.00
132 Conor Jackson/U 8.00
133 Conor Jackson/R 12.00
134 Paul Maholm/C **RC** 1.50
135 Paul Maholm/U **RC** 3.00
136 Paul Maholm/R **RC** 6.00
137 Lastings Milledge/C 8.00
138 Lastings Milledge/U 15.00
139 Lastings Milledge/R 20.00
140 Matt Moses/C 4.00
141 Matt Moses/U 6.00
142 Matt Moses/R 10.00
143 David Murphy/C 1.50
144 David Murphy/U 3.00
145 David Murphy/R 6.00
146 Dioner Navarro/C **RC** 4.00
147 Dioner Navarro/U **RC** 8.00
148 Dioner Navarro/R **RC** 10.00
149 Dustin Nippert/C **RC** 1.50
150 Dustin Nippert/U **RC** 3.00
151 Dustin Nippert/R **RC** 6.00
152 Vito Chiaravalloti/C **RC** 3.00
153 Vito Chiaravalloti/U **RC** 6.00
154 Vito Chiaravalloti/R **RC** 8.00
155 Akinori Otsuka/C **RC** 3.00
156 Akinori Otsuka/U **RC** 5.00
157 Akinori Otsuka/R **RC** 8.00
158 Casey Daigle/C **RC** 1.50
159 Casey Daigle/U **RC** 3.00
160 Casey Daigle/R **RC** 6.00
161 Carlos Quentin/C 5.00
162 Carlos Quentin/U 10.00
163 Carlos Quentin 15.00
164 Omar Quintanilla/C 4.00
165 Omar Quintanilla/U 8.00
166 Omar Quintanilla/R 12.00
167 Chris Saenz/C **RC** 1.50
168 Chris Saenz/U **RC** 3.00
169 Chris Saenz/R **RC** 6.00
170 Ervin Santana/C **RC** 1.50
171 Ervin Santana/U **RC** 3.00
172 Ervin Santana/R **RC** 6.00
173 Chris Shelton/C **RC** 4.00
174 Chris Shelton/U **RC** 8.00
175 Chris Shelton/R **RC** 10.00
176 Kyle Sleeth/C 1.50
177 Kyle Sleeth/U 3.00
178 Kyle Sleeth/R 6.00
179 Brad Snyder/C 4.00
180 Brad Snyder/U 8.00
181 Brad Snyder/R 12.00
182 Tim Stauffer/C 4.00
183 Tim Stauffer/U 8.00
184 Tim Stauffer/R 12.00
185 Shingo Takatsu/C **RC** 4.00
186 Shingo Takatsu/U **RC** 8.00
187 Shingo Takatsu/R **RC** 12.00
188 Merkin Valdez/C **RC** 1.50
189 Merkin Valdez/U **RC** 3.00
190 Merkin Valdez/R **RC** 6.00

Refractors

Veterans (1-100): 4-8X
Production 49
Common RC's: .75-1.5X
Production 999
UnCommon RC's: 1-2X
Production 399
Rare RC's: 1.5-3X
Production 49

Gold Refractors

Veterans (1-100): 4-8X
Common RC's: 4-8X
Uncommon RC's: 3-5X
Rare RC's: 1.5-3X
Production 41 Sets

Fantasy Favorite Relics

NM/M
Common Player: 4.00
Refractor: 2-4X
Production 25 Sets
MA Moises Alou 6.00
JB Jeff Bagwell 8.00
RB Rocco Baldelli 6.00
AB Angel Berroa 4.00
BB Bret Boone 4.00
JD Johnny Damon 8.00
CD Carlos Delgado 5.00
RF Rafael Furcal 4.00
RFJ Rafael Furcal 4.00
EG Eric Gagne 10.00
NG Nomar Garciaparra 10.00
SG Shawn Green 4.00
MG Mark Grudzielanek 4.00
VG Vladimir Guerrero 8.00
THE Todd Helton 8.00
TH Tim Hudson 6.00
DJ Derek Jeter 20.00
AJ Andruw Jones 6.00
CJ Chipper Jones 8.00
CK Corey Koskie 4.00
KL Kenny Lofton 4.00
PM Pedro J. Martinez 8.00
MPI Mike Piazza 10.00
MP Mark Prior 8.00

AP Albert Pujols 15.00
AR Alex Rodriguez 12.00
JR Jimmy Rollins 4.00
MT Mark Teixeira 4.00
FT Frank Thomas 8.00
JT Jim Thome 10.00
JV Jose Vidro 4.00
LW Larry Walker 4.00
BW Brandon Webb 4.00
PW Preston Wilson 4.00
KW Kerry Wood 8.00

Going, Going, Gone! Relics

NM/M
Common Player: 4.00
Refractor: 2-4X
Production 25 Sets
LB Lance Berkman 4.00
BB Bret Boone 4.00
AD Adam Dunn 8.00
JG Juan Gonzalez 6.00
LG Luis Gonzalez 4.00
VG Vladimir Guerrero 8.00
TH Todd Helton 8.00
CJ Chipper Jones 8.00
JJ Jacque Jones 4.00
JK Jeff Kent 4.00
RK Ryan Klesko 4.00
MO Magglio Ordonez 4.00
DO David Ortiz 10.00
MP Mike Piazza 10.00
AP Albert Pujols 15.00
MR Manny Ramirez 8.00
AR Alex Rodriguez 12.00
SR Scott Rolen 8.00
AS Alfonso Soriano 8.00
SS Sammy Sosa 10.00
FT Frank Thomas 8.00
JT Jim Thome 10.00
VW Vernon Wells 4.00

Key Acquisitions Relics

NM/M
Common Player: 4.00
Inserted 1:8
Refractors: 2-4X
Production 25 Sets
HC Hee Seop Choi 4.00
JG Juan Gonzalez 6.00
VG Vladimir Guerrero 8.00
JL Javy Lopez 6.00
AR Alex Rodriguez 12.00
IR Ivan Rodriguez 8.00
GS Gary Sheffield 6.00
AS Alfonso Soriano 8.00

Mini

NM/M
Common Player: 2.00
Inserted 1:5
DA David Aardsma 5.00
EA Erick Aybar 4.00
VC Vito Chiaravalloti 3.00
NG Nomar Garciaparra 4.00
JG Jason Giambi 2.00
VG Vladimir Guerrero 4.00
BH Blake Hawksworth 4.00
CJA Conor Jackson 4.00
DJ Derek Jeter 6.00
CJ Chipper Jones 3.00
HK Howard Kendrick 10.00
KM Kazuo Matsui 4.00
LM Lastings Milledge 6.00
MM Matt Moses 6.00
DM David Murphy 3.00
DN Dioner Navarro 10.00
AO Akinori Otsuka 3.00
MPI Mike Piazza 4.00
MP Mark Prior 3.00
AP Albert Pujols 6.00
AR Alex Rodriguez 6.00
KS Kyle Sleeth 4.00
SS Sammy Sosa 4.00
TS Tim Stauffer 3.00
IS Ichiro Suzuki 5.00
ST Shingo Takatsu 4.00
JT Jim Thome 3.00
MV Merkin Valdez 3.00
DW Dontrelle Willis 3.00
KW Kerry Wood 4.00

Mini Relics

NM/M
Common Player: 5.00
Inserted 1:51
JB Jeff Bagwell 20.00
EG Eric Gagne 15.00
NG Nomar Garciaparra 12.00
CJ Chipper Jones 10.00
PM Pedro J. Martinez 12.00
MPI Mike Piazza 12.00
MP Mark Prior 10.00
AP Albert Pujols 25.00
PW Preston Wilson 5.00
KW Kerry Wood 10.00

Patch Place Relics

NM/M
Common Player: 10.00
Refractor: No Pricing
Production 10 Sets
JB Jeff Bagwell 20.00
RB Rocco Baldelli 12.00
JBE Josh Beckett 15.00
BB Bret Boone 10.00
LC Luis Castillo 10.00
CC Chin-Feng Chen 40.00
CD Carlos Delgado 10.00
AD Adam Dunn 15.00
RF Rafael Furcal 10.00
EG Eric Gagne 15.00
NG Nomar Garciaparra 40.00
LG Luis Gonzalez 10.00
SG Shawn Green 10.00
THE Todd Helton 15.00
TH Tim Hudson 10.00
RJ Randy Johnson 20.00
AJ Andruw Jones 10.00
CJ Chipper Jones 15.00
AK Austin Kearns 10.00
PL Paul LoDuca 10.00
ML Mike Lowell 10.00
PM Pedro J. Martinez 20.00
MPI Mike Piazza 35.00
MP Mark Prior 15.00
AP Albert Pujols 40.00
JR Jose Reyes 15.00
JS John Smoltz 15.00
SS Sammy Sosa 20.00
FT Frank Thomas 20.00
DW Dontrelle Willis 10.00
PW Preston Wilson 10.00
KW Kerry Wood 20.00
BZ Barry Zito 15.00

Personal Endorsements

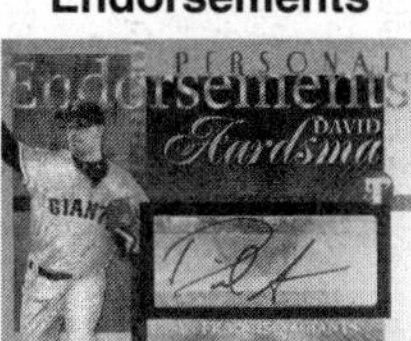

NM/M
Common Autograph: 6.00
Golds: 1.5-3X
Production 25 Sets
DA David Aardsma 15.00
GA Garret Anderson 10.00
LB Lance Berkman 20.00
HB Hank Blalock 20.00
MC Miguel Cabrera 30.00
VC Vito Chiaravalloti 10.00
BC Bobby Crosby 25.00
JF Jennie Finch 120.00
MG Marcus Giles 10.00
VG Vladimir Guerrero 50.00
EH Estee Harris 8.00
AH Aubrey Huff 8.00
CJ Conor Jackson 20.00
CL Chris Lubanski 10.00
JM Joe Mauer 35.00
WM Willie Mays 200.00
DM Dustin McGowan 6.00
BM Brett Myers 10.00
SP Scott Podsednik 10.00
JP Jorge Posada 40.00
AR Alex Rodriguez 150.00
IR Ivan Rodriguez 40.00
ES Ervin Santana 10.00
GS Gary Sheffield 40.00
GS Grady Sizemore 25.00
JV Javier Vazquez 15.00
BW Brandon Webb 6.00
DY Delmon Young 15.00

Two of a Kind Autograph

Production 13

1, 2, 3 Triple Relics

NM/M
Inserted 1:171
Refractor: 1.5-2X
Production 25 Sets
NYY Kenny Lofton, Derek Jeter, Alex Rodriguez 50.00
CHC Mark Grudzielanek, Alex Gonzalez, Sammy Sosa 40.00
BOS Johnny Damon, Bill Mueller, Nomar Garciaparra 40.00

2004 Topps Retired Signature Edition

NM/M
Complete Set (110): 125.00
Common Player: 1.00
Pack (5): 35.00
Box (5): 140.00
1 Willie Mays 6.00
2 Tony Gwynn 3.00
3 Dale Murphy 2.00
4 Lenny Dykstra 1.00
5 Johnny Bench 4.00
6 Bill Buckner 1.00
7 Ferguson Jenkins 1.50
8 George Brett 6.00
9 Ralph Kiner 2.00
10 Ernie Banks 4.00
11 Hal McRae 1.00
12 Lou Brock 2.00
13 Keith Hernandez 1.00
14 Jose Canseco 2.00
15 Whitey Ford 2.50
16 Dave Kingman 1.00
17 Tim Raines 1.00
18 Paul O'Neill 1.50
19 Lou Whitaker 1.00
20 Mike Schmidt 5.00
21 Wally Joyner 1.00
22 Kirk Gibson 1.00
23 Ryne Sandberg 5.00
24 Luis Tiant 1.00
25 Al Kaline 4.00
26 Brooks Robinson 3.00
27 Don Zimmer 1.00
28 Nolan Ryan 6.00
29 Maury Wills 1.00
30 Stan Musial 4.00
31 Garry Maddox 1.00
32 Tom Brunansky 1.00
33 Don Mattingly 5.00
34 Earl Weaver 1.00
35 Bobby Grich 1.00
36 Orlando Cepeda 1.50
37 Alan Trammell 1.50
38 Al Hrabosky 1.00
39 Davey Lopes 1.00
40 Rod Carew 2.00
41 Robin Yount 4.00
42 Dwight Gooden 1.00
43 Andre Dawson 1.50
44 Hank Aaron 6.00
45 Norm Cash 1.00
46 Reggie Jackson 2.50
47 Jim Rice 1.00
48 Carlton Fisk 2.00
49 Dave Parker 1.00
50 Cal Ripken Jr. 6.00
51 Roy Face 1.00
52 Bob Gibson 2.50
53 Jimmy Key 1.00
54 Al Oliver 1.00
55 Don Larsen 1.50
56 Tom Seaver 3.00
57 Tony Armas 1.00
58 Dave Stieb 1.00
59 Will Clark 2.00
60 Duke Snider 2.50
61 Cesar Geronimo 1.00
62 Ron Kittle 1.00
63 Ron Santo 2.00
64 Mickey Rivers 1.00
65 Jimmy Piersall 1.00
66 Ron Swoboda 1.00
67 Kent Hrbek 1.00
68 Dennis Eckersley 2.00
69 Greg Luzinski 1.00
70 Harmon Killebrew 3.00
71 Ron Guidry 1.50
72 Steve Garvey 1.00
73 Andy Van Slyke 1.00
74 Rich "Goose" Gossage 1.00
75 Ozzie Smith 3.00
76 Richie Allen 1.00
77 Vida Blue 1.00
78 Tony Oliva 1.00
79 Darryl Strawberry 1.00
80 Frank Robinson 2.00
81 Bruce Sutter 1.50
82 Dave Concepcion 1.00
83 Darrell Evans 1.00
84 Jack Morris 1.00
85 Bo Jackson 2.00
86 Orel Hershiser 1.00
87 Rob Dibble 1.00
88 Wade Boggs 2.00
89 Fernando Valenzuela 1.00
90 Jim Palmer 2.00
91 George Foster 1.00
92 Mike Scott 1.00
93 Paul Molitor 2.50
94 Gary Carter 2.00
95 Bobby Richardson 1.00
96 Rollie Fingers 1.00
97 Tim McCarver 1.00
98 John Candelaria 1.00
99 Dave Winfield 2.00
100 Yogi Berra 3.00
101 Bill Madlock 1.00
102 Jack McDowell 1.00
103 Luis Aparicio 1.00
104 Graig Nettles 1.00
105 Dave Stewart 1.00
106 Darren Daulton 1.00
107 Gary Gaetti 1.00
108 Tony Fernandez 1.00
109 Buddy Bell 1.00
110 Carl Yastrzemski 4.00

Black

Black (1-110): 4-6X
Production 99 Sets

Chrome Autographs

NM/M
Common Autograph: 10.00
Inserted 1:1
Refractor: 2-4X
SP Refractor: .75-2X
Production 25 Sets
HA Hank Aaron/SP/50 320.00
TA Tony Armas 10.00
EB Ernie Banks/SP/50 180.00
BBE Buddy Bell 12.00
JB Johnny Bench/SP/75 80.00
YB Yogi Berra/SP/75 80.00
VB Vida Blue 10.00
WB Wade Boggs 40.00
TB Tom Brunansky 10.00
BB Bill Buckner 12.00
JC John Candelaria 20.00
JCA Jose Canseco 35.00
RC Rod Carew 35.00
GC Gary Carter 20.00
OC Orlando Cepeda 15.00
DD Darren Daulton 10.00
BD Bucky Dent 10.00
RD Rob Dibble 12.00
DEC Dennis Eckersley 30.00
DE Darrell Evans 10.00
RF Roy Face 15.00
TF Tony Fernandez 10.00
WF Whitey Ford/SP/75 90.00
RF Rollie Fingers 15.00
CF Carlton Fisk 40.00
GF George Foster 12.00
CG Cesar Geronimo 25.00
BG Bob Gibson/SP/75 75.00
KG Kirk Gibson 20.00
DG Dwight Gooden/SP/75 40.00
GG Rich "Goose" Gossage 15.00
BGR Bobby Grich 10.00
TG Tony Gwynn/SP/75 75.00
OH Orel Hershiser 25.00
AH Al Hrabosky 10.00
FJ Ferguson Jenkins 15.00
WJ Wally Joyner 10.00
JK Jimmy Key 10.00
RK Ralph Kiner 50.00
RKI Ron Kittle 10.00
DL Davey Lopes 10.00
GL Greg Luzinski 15.00
BM Bill Madlock 10.00
DM Don Mattingly/SP/75 100.00
JM Jack McDowell 10.00
PM Paul Molitor 50.00
DM Dale Murphy 25.00
SM Stan Musial/SP/50 160.00
GN Graig Nettles 12.00
TO Tony Oliva 20.00
AO Al Oliver 12.00
PO Paul O'Neill 40.00
DP Dave Parker 20.00
JP Jimmy Piersall 15.00
BR Bobby Richardson 15.00
CR Cal Ripken Jr./SP/25 275.00
BRO Brooks Robinson/SP/75 90.00
FR Frank Robinson 30.00
NR Nolan Ryan/SP/25 300.00
RSA Ryne Sandberg 75.00
RS Ron Santo 20.00
MS Mike Schmidt/SP/75 150.00
TS Tom Seaver/SP/75 75.00
OS Ozzie Smith/SP/75 100.00
DSN Duke Snider/SP/50 90.00
DST Dave Stieb 12.00
DS Darryl Strawberry 30.00
BS Bruce Sutter 25.00
RS Ron Swoboda 10.00
LT Luis Tiant 10.00
AT Alan Trammell 20.00
EW Earl Weaver 10.00
MW Maury Wills 10.00
CY Carl Yastrzemski/SP/25 180.00
RY Robin Yount/SP/50 125.00
DZ Don Zimmer 20.00

Chrome Co-Signers

No Pricing
Production 25 Sets

2004 Topps Total

NM/M
Complete Set (880): 100.00
Common Player: .10
Pack (10): 1.00
Box (36): 30.00
1 Kevin Brown .25
2 Mike Mordecai .10
3 Seung Jun Song .10
4 Mike Maroth .10
5 Mike Lieberthal .10
6 Billy Koch .10
7 Mike Stanton .10
8 Brad Penny .10
9 Brooks Kieschnick .10
10 Carlos Delgado .40
11 Brady Clark .10
12 Ramon Martinez .10
13 Dan Wilson .10
14 Guillermo Mota .10
15 Trevor Hoffman .10
16 Tony Batista .10
17 Rusty Greer .10
18 David Weathers .10
19 Horacio Ramirez .10
20 Aubrey Huff .10
21 Casey Blake .10
22 Ryan Bukvich .10
23 Garrett Atkins .10
24 Jose Contreras .10
25 Chipper Jones .75
26 Neifi Perez .10
27 Scott Linebrink .10
28 Matt Kinney .10
29 Michael Restovich .10
30 Scott Rolen .75
31 John Franco .10
32 Toby Hall .10
33 Wily Mo Pena .10
34 Dennis Tankersley .10
35 Robb Nen .10
36 Jose Valverde .10
37 Chin-Feng Chen .10
38 Gary Knotts .10
39 Scott Elarton .10
40 Bret Boone .25
41 Josh Phelps .10
42 Jason Larue .10
43 Tim Redding .10
44 Greg Myers .10
45 Darin Erstad .25
46 Kip Wells .10
47 Matt Ford .10
48 Jerome Williams .10
49 Brian Meadows .10
50 Albert Pujols 1.50
51 Kirk Saarloos .10
52 Scott Eyre .10
53 John Flaherty .10
54 Rafael Soriano .10
55 Shea Hillenbrand .10
56 Kyle Farnsworth .10
57 Nate Cornejo .10
58 Kerry Robinson .10
59 Yan Vogelsong .10
60 Ryan Klesko .20
61 Luke Hudson .10
62 Justin Morneau .20
63 Frank Catalanotto .10
64 Derrick Turnbow .10
65 Marcus Giles .10
66 Mark Mulder .25
67 Matt Anderson .10
68 Mike Matheny .10
69 Brian Lawrence .10
70 Bobby Abreu .10
71 Damian Moss .10
72 Richard Hidalgo .10
73 Mark Kotsay .10
74 Mike Cameron .10
75 Troy Glaus .40
76 Matt Holliday .25
77 Byung-Hyun Kim .10
78 Aaron Sele .10
79 Danny Graves .10
80 Barry Zito .40
81 Matt LeCroy .10
82 Jason Isringhausen .10
83 Colby Lewis .10
84 Franklyn German .10
85 Luis Matos .10
86 Mike Timlin .10
87 Miguel Batista .10
88 John McDonald .10
89 Joey Eischen .10
90 Mike Mussina .50
91 Jack Wilson .20
92 Aaron Cook .10
93 John Parrish .10
94 Jose Valentin .10
95 Johnny Damon .20
96 Pat Burrell .25
97 Brendan Donnelly .10
98 Lance Carter .10
99 Omar Daal .10
100 Ichiro Suzuki 1.00
101 Robin Ventura .10
102 Brian Shouse .10
103 Kevin Jarvis .10
104 Jason Young .10
105 Moises Alou .25
106 Wes Obermueller .10
107 David Segui .10
108 Mike MacDougal .10
109 John Buck .10
110 Gary Sheffield .25
111 Yorvit Torrealba .10
112 Matt Kata .10
113 David Bell .10
114 Juan Gonzalez .40
115 Kelvim Escobar .10
116 Ruben Sierra .10
117 Todd Wellemeyer .10
118 Jamie Walker .10
119 Will Cunnane .10
120 Cliff Floyd .10
121 Aramis Ramirez .40
122 Damaso Marte .10
123 Juan Castro .10
124 Chris Woodward .10
125 Andruw Jones .50
126 Ben Weber .10
127 Dee Brown .10
128 Steve Reed .10
129 Gabe Kapler .10
130 Miguel Cabrera .75
131 Billy McMillon .10
132 Julio Mateo .10
133 Preston Wilson .10
134 Tony Clark .10
135 Carlos Lee .20
136 Carlos Baerga .10
137 Mike Crudale .10
138 David Ross .10
139 Josh Fogg .10
140 Dmitri Young .10
141 Cliff Lee .10
142 Mike Lowell .25
143 Jason Lane .10
144 Pedro Feliz .10
145 Ken Griffey Jr. 1.00
146 Dustin Hermanson .10
147 Scott Hodges .10
148 Aquilino Lopez .10
149 Wes Helms .10
150 Jason Giambi .50
151 Erasmo Ramirez .10
152 Sean Burroughs .10
153 J.T. Snow .10
154 Eddie Guardado .10
155 C.C. Sabathia .10
156 Kyle Lohse .10
157 Roberto Hernandez .10
158 Jason Simontacchi .10
159 Tim Spooneybarger .10
160 Alfonso Soriano .50
161 Mike Gonzalez .10
162 Alex Cora .10
163 Kevin Gryboski .10
164 Steve Cox .10
165 Luis Castillo .10
166 Odalis Perez .10
167 Alex Sanchez .10
168 Robert Mackowiak .10
169 Francisco Rodriguez .10
170 Roy Oswalt .25
171 Omar Infante .10
172 Ryan Jensen .10
173 Ben Broussard .10
174 Mark Hendrickson .10
175 Manny Ramirez .50
176 Rob Bell .10
177 Adam Everett .10
178 Chris George .10
179 Ricky Gutierrez .10
180 Eric Gagne .40
181 Scott Schoeneweis .10
182 Kris Benson .10
183 Amaury Telemaco .10
184 John Riedling .10
185 Juan Pierre .10
186 Ramon Ortiz .10
187 Luis Rivas .10
188 Larry Bigbie .10
189 Robby Hammock .10
190 Geoff Jenkins .20
191 Chad Cordero .10

No.	Player	Price
192	Mark Ellis	.10
193	Mark Loretta	.10
194	Ryan Drese	.10
195	Lance Berkman	.10
196	Kevin Appier	.10
197	Enrique Calero (Kiko)	.10
198	Mickey Callaway	.10
199	Chase Utley	.25
200	Nomar Garciaparra	1.00
201	Kevin Cash	.10
202	Ramiro Mendoza	.10
203	Shane Reynolds	.10
204	Chris Spurling	.10
205	Aaron Guiel	.10
206	Mark Derosa	.10
207	Adam Kennedy	.10
208	Andy Pettitte	.25
209	Rafael Palmeiro	.50
210	Luis Gonzalez	.25
211	Ryan Franklin	.10
212	Bob Wickman	.10
213	Ron Calloway	.10
214	Jae Weong Seo	.10
215	Kazuhisa Ishii	.10
216	Sterling Hitchcock	.10
217	Jimmy Gobble	.10
218	Chad Moeller	.10
219	Jake Peavy	.10
220	John Smoltz	.25
221	Erick Almonte	.10
222	David Wells	.10
223	Brad Lidge	.10
224	Carlos Zambrano	.25
225	Kerry Wood	.75
226	Alex Cintron	.10
227	Javier Lopez	.25
228	Jeremy Griffiths	.10
229	Jon Garland	.10
230	Curt Schilling	.50
231	Alex Gonzalez	.10
232	Jay Gibbons	.10
233	Damian Jackson	.10
234	Jeriome Robertson	.10
235	Johan Santana	.10
236	Jose Guillen	.10
237	Jeff Connie	.10
238	Matt Roney	.10
239	Desi Relaford	.10
240	Frank Thomas	.50
241	Danny Patterson	.10
242	Kevin Mench	.10
243	Mike Redmond	.10
244	Jeff Suppan	.10
245	Carl Everett	.10
246	Jack Cressend	.10
247	Matt Mantei	.10
248	Enrique Wilson	.10
249	Craig Counsell	.10
250	Mark Prior	1.50
251	Jared Sandberg	.10
252	Scott Strickland	.10
253	Lew Ford	.10
254	Hee Seop Choi	.10
255	Jason Phillips	.10
256	Jason Jennings	.10
257	Todd Pratt	.10
258	Matt Herges	.10
259	Kerry Ligtenberg	.10
260	Austin Kearns	.25
261	Jay Witasick	.10
262	Tony Armas Jr.	.10
263	Tom Martin	.10
264	Oliver Perez	.10
265	Jorge Posada	.40
266	Joe Beimel	.10
267	Ben Hendrickson	.10
268	Reggie Sanders	.10
269	Julio Lugo	.10
270	Josh Beckett	.40
271	Kyle Snyder	.10
272	Felipe Lopez	.10
273	Kevin Millar	.10
274	Travis Hafner	.20
275	Magglio Ordonez	.25
276	Marlon Byrd	.10
277	Scott Spiezio	.10
278	Mark Corey	.10
279	Tim Salmon	.25
280	Alex Gonzalez	.10
281	Marquis Grissom	.20
282	Miguel Olivo	.10
283	Orlando Hudson	.10
284	Rondell White	.20
285	Jermaine Dye	.10
286	Paul Shuey	.10
287	Brandon Inge	.10
288	B.J. Surhoff	.10
289	Edgar Gonzalez	.10
290	Angel Berroa	.10
291	Claudio Vargas	.10
292	Cesar Izturis	.10
293	Brandon Phillips	.10
294	Jeff Duncan	.10
295	Randy Wolf	.10
296	Barry Larkin	.25
297	Felix Rodriguez	.10
298	Robb Quinlan	.10
299	Brian Jordan	.10
300	Dontrelle Willis	.25
301	Doug Davis	.10
302	Ricky Stone	.10
303	Travis Harper	.10
304	Jaret Wright	.10
305	Edgardo Alfonzo	.10
306	Quinton McCracken	.10
307	Jason Bay	.10
308	Joe Randa	.10
309	Steve Sparks	.10
310	Roy Halladay	.25
311	Antonio Alfonseca	.10
312	Michael Cuddyer	.10
313	John Patterson	.10
314	Chris Widger	.10
315	Shigetoshi Hasegawa	.10
316	Tim Wakefield	.10
317	Scott Hatteberg	.10
318	Mike Remlinger	.10
319	Jose Vizcaino	.10
320	Rocco Baldelli	.25
321	David Riske	.10
322	Steve Karsay	.10
323	Peter Bergeron	.10
324	Jeff Weaver	.10
325	Larry Walker	.25
326	Jack Cust	.10
327	Bo Hart	.10
328	Rod Beck	.10
329	Jose Acevedo	.10
330	Hank Blalock	.40
331	Flash Gordon	.10
332	Brian Fuentes	.10
333	Tomas Perez	.10
334	Lenny Harris	.10
335	Matt Morris	.25
336	Jeremi Gonzalez	.10
337	David Eckstein	.10
338	Aaron Rowand	.10
339	Rick Bauer	.10
340	Jim Edmonds	.25
341	Joe Borowski	.10
342	Eric Dubose	.10
343	D'Angelo Jimenez	.10
344	Tomokazu Ohka	.10
345	Victor Zambrano	.10
346	Joe McEwing	.10
347	Jorge Sosa	.10
348	Keith Ginter	.10
349	A.J. Pierzynski	.10
350	Mike Sweeney	.10
351	Shawn Chacon	.10
352	Matt Clement	.25
353	Vance Wilson	.10
354	Benito Santiago	.10
355	Eric Hinske	.10
356	Vladimir Guerrero	.75
357	Kenny Rogers	.10
358	Aaron Boone	.10
359	Jay Powell	.10
360	Phil Nevin	.10
361	Willie Harris	.10
362	Ty Wigginton	.10
363	Chad Fox	.10
364	Junior Spivey	.10
365	Brandon Webb	.10
366	Brett Myers	.10
367	Alexis Gomez	.10
368	Dave Roberts	.10
369	LaTroy Hawkins	.10
370	Kevin Millwood	.25
371	Brian Schneider	.10
372	Blaine Neal	.10
373	Jeromy Burnitz	.10
374	Ted Lilly	.10
375	Shawn Green	.25
376	Carlos Pena	.10
377	Gil Meche	.10
378	Jeff Bagwell	.50
379	Alex Escobar	.10
380	Erubiel Durazo	.10
381	Cristian Guzman	.10
382	Rocky Biddle	.10
383	Craig Wilson	.25
384	Rey Sanchez	.10
385	Russ Ortiz	.10
386	Freddy Garcia	.10
387	Luis Vizcaino	.10
388	David Ortiz	.40
389	Jose Molina	.10
390	Edgar Martinez	.25
391	Nate Bump	.10
392	Brent Mayne	.10
393	Ray King	.10
394	Paul Wilson	.10
395	Melvin Mora	.10
396	Morgan Ensberg	.10
397	Ramon Hernandez	.10
398	Juan Rincon	.10
399	Ron Mahay	.10
400	Jeff Kent	.25
401	Cal Eldred	.10
402	Mike Difelice	.10
403	Valerio De Los Santos	.10
404	Steve Finley	.10
405	Trot Nixon	.25
406	Kevin Walker	.10
407	John Vander Wal	.10
408	Ray Durham	.10
409	Aaron Heilman	.10
410	Edgar Renteria	.25
411	Mike Hampton	.10
412	Kirk Rueter	.10
413	Jim Mecir	.10
414	Brian Roberts	.10
415	Paul Konerko	.10
416	Reed Johnson	.10
417	Roger Clemens	1.50
418	Coco Crisp	.10
419	Carlos Hernandez	.10
420	Scott Podsednik	.40
421	Miguel Cairo	.10
422	Abraham Nunez	.10
423	Endy Chavez	.10
424	Eric Munson	.10
425	Torii Hunter	.25
426	Ben Howard	.10
427	Chris Gomez	.10
428	Francisco Cordero	.10
429	Jeffrey Hammonds	.10
430	Shannon Stewart	.10
431	Einar Diaz	.10
432	Eric Byrnes	.10
433	Marty Cordova	.10
434	Matt Ginter	.10
435	Victor Martinez	.10
436	Geronimo Gil	.10
437	Grant Balfour	.10
438	Ramon Vazquez	.10
439	Jose Cruz	.10
440	Orlando Cabrera	.10
441	Joe Kennedy	.10
442	Scott Williamson	.10
443	Troy Percival	.10
444	Derrek Lee	.25
445	Runelvys Hernandez	.10
446	Mark Grudzielanek	.10
447	Trey Hodges	.10
448	Jimmy Haynes	.10
449	Eric Milton	.10
450	Todd Helton	.50
451	Gregg Zaun	.10
452	Woody Williams	.10
453	Todd Walker	.10
454	Gary Matthews	.10
455	Fernando Vina	.10
456	Omar Vizquel	.10
457	Roberto Alomar	.40
458	Bill Hall	.10
459	Juan Rivera	.10
460	Tom Glavine	.40
461	Ramon Castro	.10
462	Cory Vance	.10
463	Dan Miceli	.10
464	Lyle Overbay	.25
465	Craig Biggio	.25
466	Ricky Ledee	.10
467	Michael Barrett	.10
468	Jason Anderson	.10
469	Matt Stairs	.10
470	Jarrod Washburn	.10
471	Todd Hundley	.10
472	Grant Roberts	.10
473	Randy Winn	.10
474	Pat Hentgen	.10
475	Jose Vidro	.10
476	Tony Torcato	.10
477	Jeremy Affeldt	.10
478	Carlos Guillen	.10
479	Paul Quantrill	.10
480	Rafael Furcal	.10
481	Adam Melhuse	.10
482	Jerry Hairston	.10
483	Adam Bernero	.10
484	Terrence Long	.10
485	Paul Lo Duca	.10
486	Corey Koskie	.10
487	John Lackey	.10
488	Chad Zerbe	.10
489	Vinny Castilla	.10
490	Corey Patterson	.20
491	John Olerud	.20
492	Josh Bard	.10
493	Darren Dreifort	.10
494	Jason Standridge	.10
495	Ben Sheets	.25
496	Jose Castillo	.10
497	Jay Payton	.10
498	Rob Bowen	.10
499	Bobby Higginson	.10
500	Alex Rodriguez	1.50
501	Octavio Dotel	.10
502	Rheal Cormier	.10
503	Felix Heredia	.10
504	Dan Wright	.10
505	Michael Young	.10
506	Wilfredo Ledezma	.10
507	Sun-Woo Kim	.10
508	Michael Tejera	.10
509	Herbert Perry	.10
510	Esteban Loaiza	.10
511	Alan Embree	.10
512	Ben Davis	.10
513	Greg Colbrunn	.10
514	Josh Hall	.10
515	Raul Ibanez	.10
516	Jayson Werth	.10
517	Corky Miller	.10
518	Jason Marquis	.10
519	Roger Cedeno	.10
520	Adam Dunn	.50
521	Paul Byrd	.10
522	Sandy Alomar	.10
523	Salomon Torres	.10
524	John Halama	.10
525	Mike Piazza	1.00
526	Buddy Groom	.10
527	Adrian Beltre	.25
528	Chad Harville	.10
529	Javier Vazquez	.20
530	Jody Gerut	.10
531	Elmer Dessens	.10
532	B.J. Ryan	.10
533	Chad Durbin	.10
534	Doug Mirabelli	.10
535	Bernie Williams	.40
536	Jeff Davanon	.10
537	Dave Berg	.10
538	Geoff Blum	.10
539	John Thomson	.10
540	Jeremy Bonderman	.10
541	Jeff Zimmerman	.10
542	Derek Lowe	.10
543	Scot Shields	.10
544	Michael Tucker	.10
545	Tim Hudson	.40
546	Ryan Ludwick	.10
547	Rick Reed	.10
548	Placido Palanco	.10
549	Tony Graffanino	.10
550	Garret Anderson	.40
551	Timoniel Perez	.10
552	Jesus Colome	.10
553	R.A. Dickey	.10
554	Tim Worrell	.10
555	Jason Kendall	.10
556	Tom Goodwin	.10
557	Joaquin Benoit	.10
558	Stephen Randolph	.10
559	Miguel Tejada	.40
560	A.J. Burnett	.10
561	Ben Diggins	.10
562	Juan Cruz	.10
563	Zach Day	.10
564	Antonio Perez	.10
565	Jason Schmidt	.25
566	Armando Benitez	.10
567	Denny Neagle	.10
568	Eric Eckenstahler	.10
569	Chan Ho Park	.10
570	Carlos Beltran	.40
571	Brett Tomko	.10
572	Henry Mateo	.10
573	Ken Harvey	.10
574	Matt Lawton	.10
575	Mariano Rivera	.25
576	Darrell May	.10
577	Jamie Moyer	.10
578	Paul Bako	.10
579	Cory Lidle	.10
580	Jacque Jones	.10
581	Jolbert Cabrera	.10
582	Jason Grimsley	.10
583	Danny Kolb	.10
584	Billy Wagner	.10
585	Rich Aurilia	.10
586	Vicente Padilla	.10
587	Oscar Villarreal	.10
588	Rene Reyes	.10
589	Jon Lieber	.10
590	Nick Johnson	.10
591	Bobby Crosby	.10
592	Steve Trachsel	.10
593	Brian Boehringer	.10
594	Juan Uribe	.10
595	Bartolo Colon	.20
596	Bobby Hill	.10
597	Andy Van Hekken	.10
598	Carl Pavano	.10
599	Kurt Ainsworth	.10
600	Derek Jeter	2.00
601	Doug Mientkiewicz	.10
602	Orlando Pameiro	.10
603	J.C. Romero	.10
604	Scott Sullivan	.10
605	Brad Radke	.10
606	Fernando Rodney	.10
607	Jim Brower	.10
608	Josh Towers	.10
609	Brad Fullmer	.10
610	Jose Reyes	.25
611	Ryan Wagner	.10
612	Joe Mays	.10
613	Jung Bong	.10
614	Curtis Leskanic	.10
615	Al Leiter	.10
616	Wade Miller	.10
617	Keith Foulke	.10
618	Casey Fossum	.10
619	Craig Monroe	.10
620	Hideo Nomo	.25
621	Bob File	.10
622	Steve Kline	.10
623	Bobby Kielty	.10
624	Dewon Brazelton	.10
625	Eric Chavez	.25
626	Chris Carpenter	.10
627	Trever Miller	.10
628	Jason Davis	.10
629	Jose Jimenez	.10
630	Vernon Wells	.10
631	Kenny Lofton	.25
632	Chad Bradford	.10
633	Brad Wilkerson	.10
634	Pokey Reese	.10
635	Richie Sexson	.40
636	Chin-Hui Tsao	.10
637	Eli Marrero	.10
638	Chris Reitsma	.10
639	Daryle Ward	.10
640	Mark Teixeira	.25
641	Corwin Malone	.10
642	Adam Eaton	.10
643	Jimmy Rollins	.25
644	Brian Anderson	.10
645	Bill Mueller	.10
646	Jake Westbrook	.10
647	Bengie Molina	.10
648	Jorge Julio	.10
649	Billy Traber	.10
650	Randy Johnson	.75
651	Javy Lopez	.25
652	Doug Glanville	.10
653	Jeff Cirillo	.10
654	Tino Martinez	.10
655	Mark Buehrle	.10
656	Jason Michaels	.10
657	Damian Rolls	.10
658	Rosman Garcia	.10
659	Scott Hairston	.10
660	Carl Crawford	.10
661	Livan Hernandez	.10
662	Danny Bautista	.10
663	Brad Ausmus	.10
664	Juan Acevedo	.10
665	Sean Casey	.10
666	Pedro Martinez	.75
667	Milton Bradley	.10
668	Braden Looper	.10
669	Paul Abbott	.10
670	Joel Pinero	.10
671	Luis Terrero	.10
672	Rodrigo Lopez	.10
673	Joe Crede	.10
674	Mike Koplove	.10
675	Brian Giles	.25
676	Jeff Nelson	.10
677	Russell Branyan	.10
678	Mike DeJean	.10
679	Brian Daubach	.10
680	Ellis Burks	.10
681	Ryan Dempster	.10
682	Cliff Politte	.10
683	Brian Reith	.10
684	Scott Stewart	.10
685	Allan Simpson	.10
686	Shawn Estes	.10
687	Jason Johnson	.10
688	Wil Cordero	.10
689	Kelly Stinnett	.10
690	Jose Lima	.10
691	Gary Bennett	.10
692	T.J. Tucker	.10
693	Shane Spencer	.10
694	Chris Hammond	.10
695	Chris Singleton	.10
696	Xavier Nady	.10
697	Cody Ransom	.10
698	Ron Villone	.10
699	Brook Fordyce	.10
700	Sammy Sosa	1.50
701	Terry Adams	.10
702	Ricardo Rincon	.10
703	Tike Redman	.10
704	Chris Stynes	.10
705	Mark Redman	.10
706	Juan Encarnacion	.10
707	Jhonny Peralta	.10
708	Denny Hocking	.10
709	Ivan Rodriguez	.50
710	Jose Hernandez	.10
711	Brandon Duckworth	.10
712	Dave Burba	.10
713	Joe Nathan	.10
714	Dan Smith	.10
715	Karim Garcia	.10
716	Arthur Rhodes	.10
717	Shawn Wooten	.10
718	Ramon Santiago	.10
719	Luis Ugueto	.10
720	Danys Baez	.10
721	Alfredo Amezaga	.10
722	Sidney Ponson	.10
723	Joe Mauer	.50
724	Jesse Foppert	.10
725	Todd Greene	.10
726	Dan Haren	.10
727	Brandon Larson	.10
728	Bobby Jenks	.10
729	Grady Sizemore	.25
730	Ben Grieve	.10
731	Khalil Greene	.10
732	Chad Gaudin	.10
733	Johnny Estrada	.10
734	Joe Valentine	.10
735	Tim Raines	.10
736	Brandon Claussen	.10
737	Sam Marsonek	.10
738	Delmon Young	.25
739	David Dellucci	.10
740	Sergio Mitre	.10
741	Nick Neugebauer	.10
742	Laynce Nix	.10
743	Joe Thurston	.10
744	Ryan Langerhans	.10
745	Pete LaForest	.10
746	Arnie Munoz	.10
747	Rickie Weeks	.25
748	Neal Cotts	.10
749	Jonny Gomes	.10
750	Jim Thome	.75
751	Jon Rauch	.10
752	Edwin Jackson	.10
753	Ryan Madson	.10
754	Chad Tracy	.10
755	Eddie Perez	.10
756	Joe Borchard	.10
757	Jeremy Guthrie	.10
758	Jose Mesa	.10
759	Doug Waechter	.10
760	J.D. Drew	.25
761	Adam LaRoche	.10
762	Rich Harden	.10
763	Justin Speier	.10
764	Todd Zeile	.10
765	Turk Wendell	.10
766	Mark Bellhorn	.10
767	Mike Jackson	.10
768	Chone Figgins	.10
769	Mike Neu	.10
770	Greg Maddux	.10
771	Frank Brooks	.10
772	Alec Zumwalt **RC**	.25
773	Glendon Rusch	.10
774	Dustan Mohr	.10
775	Shane Halter	.10
776	Tom Wilson	.10
777	So Taguchi	.10
778	Eric Karros	.10
779	Ramon Nivar	.10
780	Marlon Anderson	.10
781	Brayan Pena **RC**	.10
782	Chris O'Riordan	.10
783	Dioner Navarro **RC**	1.50
784	Alberto Callaspo **RC**	.50
785	Hector Gimenez **RC**	.25
786	Yadier Molina **RC**	.40
787	Kevin Richardson	.25
788	Brian Pilkington	.40
789	Adam Greenberg	.50
790	Ervin Santana **RC**	1.00
791	Brent Colamarino	.75
792	Ben Himes	.10
793	Todd Self **RC**	.25
794	Brad Vericker	.25
795	Donald Kelly **RC**	.25
796	Brock Jacobsen	.25
797	Brock Peterson	.25
798	Carlos Sosa	.50
799	Chad Chop	.10
800	Matt Moses	1.00
801	Chris Aguila **RC**	.25
802	David Murphy	.50
803	Don Sutton **RC**	1.00
804	Jereme Milons	.10
805	Jon Coutlangus	.10
806	Greg Thissen	.10
807	Jose Capellan **RC**	1.00
808	Chad Santos **RC**	.10
809	Wardell Starling **RC**	.10
810	Kevin Kouzmanoff	2.00
811	Kevin Davidson	.40
812	Michael Mooney	.10
813	Rodney Choy Foo	.10
814	Reid Gorecki	.10
815	Rudy Guillen **RC**	1.00
816	Harvey Garcia	.10
817	Warner Madrigal **RC**	.50
818	Kenny Perez	.10
819	Joaquin Arias **RC**	.10
820	Benji Dequin	.40
821	Lastings Milledge	2.00
822	Blake Hawksworth **RC**	.50
823	Estee Harris **RC**	.50
824	Bobby Brownlie **RC**	.75
825	Wanell Severino **RC**	.10
826	Bobby Madritsch	.10
827	Travis Hanson	.40
828	Brandon Medders **RC**	.40
829	Kevin Howard **RC**	.50
830	Brian Steffek	.10
831	Terry Jones	.10
832	Anthony Acevedo	.40
833	Kory Casto	.10
834	Brooks Conrad	.10
835	Juan Gutierrez **RC**	.50
836	Charlie Zink **RC**	.40
837	David Aardsma	.40
838	Carl Loadenthal	.10
839	Donald Levinski	.10
840	Dustin Nippert **RC**	.75
841	Calvin Hayes	.10
842	Felix Hernandez **RC**	4.00
843	Tyler Davidson	.50
844	George Sherrill **RC**	.10
845	Craig Ansman **RC**	.10
846	Jeffrey Allison	.50
847	Tommy Murphy **RC**	.10
848	Jerome Gamble **RC**	.40
849	Jesse English **RC**	.10
850	Alex Romero **RC**	.40
851	Joel Zumaya **RC**	2.00
852	Carlos Quentin	2.00
853	Jose Valdez	.25
854	J.J. Furmaniak **RC**	.75
855	Juan Cedeno **RC**	.25
856	Kyle Sleeth	1.00
857	Joch Labandeira **RC**	.25
858	Lee Gwaltney	.10
859	Lincoln Holdzkom **RC**	.25
860	Ivan Ochoa **RC**	.10
861	Luke Anderson	.10
862	Conor Jackson	1.00
863	Matt Capps **RC**	.75
864	Merkin Valdez **RC**	.75
865	Paul Bacot	.50
866	Erick Aybar **RC**	1.00
867	Scott Proctor **RC**	1.00
868	Tim Stauffer	.50
869	Matt Creighton **RC**	.50
870	Zach Miner **RC**	1.00
871	Danny Gonzalez **RC**	.10
872	Tom Farmer	.10
873	John Santor	.10
874	Logan Kensing **RC**	.25
875	Vito Chiaravalloti **RC**	.50
876	Checklist	.10
877	Checklist	.10
878	Checklist	.10
879	Checklist	.10
880	Checklist	.10

Silver

Stars: 2-3X

Inserted 1:1

Press Plates

No Pricing

Production one for each color.

Autograph

		NM/M
Inserted 1:414		
GB	Grant Balfour	8.00
LB	Larry Bigbie	10.00
BC	Brandon Claussen	8.00

TH	Toby Hall	8.00
JJ	Jimmy Journell	8.00

Total Award Winners

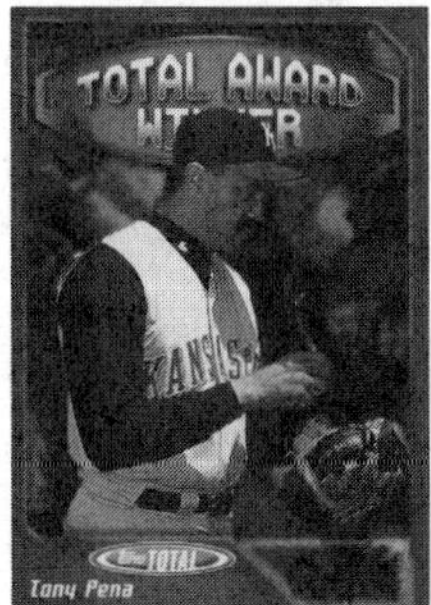

		NM/M
Complete Set (30):		20.00
Common Player:		.50
Inserted 1:12		
AW1	Roy Halladay	.50
AW2	Eric Gagne	.50
AW3	Alex Rodriguez	3.00
AW4	Albert Pujols	3.00
AW5	Alex Rodriguez	3.00
AW6	Jorge Posada	.50
AW7	Javy Lopez	.50
AW8	Carlos Delgado	.50
AW9	Todd Helton	.75
AW10	Bret Boone	.50
AW11	Jose Vidro	.50
AW12	Bill Mueller	.50
AW13	Mike Lowell	.50
AW14	Alex Rodriguez	3.00
AW15	Edgar Renteria	.50
AW16	Garret Anderson	.50
AW17	Albert Pujols	3.00
AW18	Manny Ramirez	1.00
AW19	Vernon Wells	.50
AW20	Gary Sheffield	.50
AW21	Edgar Martinez	.50
AW22	Mike Hampton	.50
AW23	Angel Berroa	.50
AW24	Dontrelle Willis	.50
AW25	Keith Foulke	.50
AW26	Eric Gagne	.50
AW27	Alex Rodriguez	3.00
AW28	Albert Pujols	3.00
AW29	Tony Pena	.50
AW30	Jack McKeon	.50

Total Production

		NM/M
Complete Set (10):		10.00
Common Player:		.50
Inserted 1:18		
TP1	Alex Rodriguez	3.00
TP2	Albert Pujols	3.00
TP3	Sammy Sosa	2.50
TP4	Carlos Delgado	.50
TP5	Gary Sheffield	.50
TP6	Manny Ramirez	1.00
TP7	Jim Thome	1.00
TP8	Todd Helton	.75
TP9	Garret Anderson	.50
TP10	Nomar Garciaparra	2.00

Total Topps

		NM/M
Complete Set (50):		25.00
Common Player:		.50
Inserted 1:7		
TT1	Derek Jeter	3.00
TT2	Jose Reyes	.50
TT3	Miguel Tejada	.50
TT4	Larry Walker	.50
TT5	Frank Thomas	.75
TT6	Carlos Delgado	.50
TT7	Vernon Wells	.50
TT8	Jeff Bagwell	.75
TT9	Jason Giambi	.75
TT10	Mike Lowell	.50
TT11	Shannon Stewart	.50
TT12	Mike Piazza	1.50
TT13	Todd Helton	.75
TT14	Austin Kearns	.50
TT15	Jim Edmonds	.50
TT16	Jose Vidro	.50
TT17	Andruw Jones	.50
TT18	Gary Sheffield	.50
TT19	Eric Chavez	.50
TT20	Magglio Ordonez	.50
TT21	Geoff Jenkins	.50
TT22	Ken Griffey Jr.	1.50
TT23	Jeff Kent	.50
TT24	Jorge Posada	.50
TT25	Albert Pujols	2.00
TT26	Javy Lopez	.50
TT27	Alfonso Soriano	1.00
TT28	Brian Giles	.50
TT29	Mike Sweeney	.50
TT30	Miguel Cabrera	1.00
TT31	Luis Gonzalez	.50
TT32	Scott Rolen	1.00
TT33	Jim Thome	1.00
TT34	Garret Anderson	.75
TT35	Vladimir Guerrero	1.00
TT36	Shawn Green	.50
TT37	Hank Blalock	.75
TT38	Marcus Giles	.50
TT39	Torii Hunter	.50
TT40	Sammy Sosa	2.00
TT41	Nomar Garciaparra	2.00
TT42	Bobby Abreu	.50
TT43	Richie Sexson	.50
TT44	Manny Ramirez	.75
TT45	Troy Glaus	.75
TT46	Preston Wilson	.50
TT47	Ivan Rodriguez	.75
TT48	Ichiro Suzuki	1.50
TT49	Chipper Jones	1.00
TT50	Alex Rodriguez	3.00

2004 Topps Traded & Rookies

		NM/M
Complete Set (220):		50.00
Common Player:		.10
Chrome cards:		2-4X
Pack (10):		4.00
Box (24):		85.00
T1	Pokey Reese	.10
T2	Tony Womack	.10
T3	Michael Barrett	.10
T4	Juan Uribe	.10
T5	J.D. Drew	.25
T6	Marlon Anderson	.10
T7	Carlos Guillen	.10
T8	Royce Clayton	.10
T9	Fernando Vina	.10
T10	Milton Bradley	.10
T11	Eddie Perez	.10
T12	Ben Grieve	.10
T13	Brian Jordan	.10
T14	Tony Graffanino	.10
T15	Billy Wagner	.10
T16	Terrence Long	.10
T17	Casey Fossum	.10
T18	Denny Hocking	.10
T19	Reggie Sanders	.10
T20	Javy Lopez	.25
T21	Jay Payton	.10
T22	Cliff Politte	.10
T23	Eddie Guardado	.10
T24	Andy Pettitte	.50
T25	Richie Sexson	.40
T26	Ronnie Belliard	.10
T27	Michael Tucker	.10
T28	Brad Fullmer	.10
T29	Orlando Palmeiro	.10
T30	Bartolo Colon	.25
T31	Larry Walker	.40
T32	Mark Kotsay	.10
T33	Jason Marquis	.10
T34	Dustan Mohr	.10
T35	Javier Vazquez	.25
T36	Nomar Garciaparra	1.50
T37	Tino Martinez	.25
T38	Hee Seop Choi	.10
T39	Damian Miller	.10
T40	Jose Lima	.10
T41	Todd Zeile	.10
T42	Raul Ibanez	.10
T43	Danys Baez	.10
T44	Tony Clark	.10
T45	Greg Maddux	1.00
T46	Craig Counsell	.10
T47	Orlando Cabrera	.25
T48	Jose Cruz Jr.	.10
T49	Kris Benson	.10
T50	Alex Rodriguez	2.00
T51	Steve Finley	.10
T52	Ramon Hernandez	.10
T53	Esteban Loaiza	.10
T54	Ugueth Urbina	.10
T55	Jeff Weaver	.10
T56	Flash Gordon	.10
T57	Jose Contreras	.10
T58	Paul LoDuca	.10
T59	Junior Spivey	.10
T60	Curt Schilling	1.00
T61	Brad Penny	.10
T62	Braden Looper	.10
T63	Miguel Cairo	.10
T64	Juan Encarnacion	.10
T65	Miguel Batista	.10
T66	Terry Francona	.10
T67	Lee Mazzilli	.10
T68	Al Pedrique	.10
T69	Ozzie Guillen	.10
T70	Phil Garner	.10
T71	Matt Bush **RC**	1.50
T72	Homer Bailey **RC**	5.00
T73	Greg Golson **RC**	2.00
T74	Kyle Waldrop **RC**	1.00
T75	Richie Robnett **RC**	1.00
T76	Jay Rainville **RC**	1.50
T77	Bill Bray **RC**	.50
T78	Phillip Hughes **RC**	10.00
T79	Scott Elbert **RC**	1.00
T80	Josh Fields **RC**	2.00
T81	Justin Orenduff **RC**	.75
T82	Dan Putnam **RC**	.75
T83	Chris Nelson **RC**	2.50
T84	Blake DeWitt **RC**	2.00
T85	J.P. Howell **RC**	1.00
T86	Huston Street **RC**	2.00
T87	Kurt Suzuki **RC**	1.50
T88	Erick San Pedro **RC**	.50
T89	Matt Tuiasosopo **RC**	1.50
T90	Matt Macri **RC**	1.00
T91	Chad Tracy	.20
T92	Scott Hairston	.20
T93	Jonny Gomes	.20
T94	Chin-Feng Chen	.20
T95	Chien-Ming Wang	.50
T96	Dustin McGowan	.20
T97	Chris Burke	.20
T98	Denny Bautista	.20
T99	Preston Larrison	.20
T100	Kevin Youkilis	.40
T101	John Maine	.20
T102	Guillermo Quiroz	.20
T103	David Krynzel	.20
T104	David Kelton	.20
T105	Edwin Encarnacion	.20
T106	Chad Gaudin	.20
T107	Sergio Mitre	.20
T108	Laynce Nix	.20
T109	David Parrish	.20
T110	Brandon Claussen	.20
T111	Frank Francisco **RC**	.25
T112	Brian Dallimore **RC**	.25
T113	Jim Crowell **RC**	.25
T114	Andres Blanco **RC**	.50
T115	Eduardo Villacis **RC**	.50
T116	Kazuhito Tadano **RC**	.50
T117	Aarom Baldiris **RC**	.25
T118	Justin Germano **RC**	.25
T119	Joey Gathright **RC**	1.00
T120	Franklyn Gracesqui **RC**	.25
T121	Chin-Lung Hu **RC**	1.00
T122	Scott Olsen **RC**	1.00
T123	Tyler Davidson	.25
T124	Fausto Carmona **RC**	.50
T125	Tim Hutting **RC**	.25
T126	Ryan Meaux **RC**	.25
T127	Jon Connolly **RC**	.75
T128	Hector Made **RC**	.75
T129	Jamie Brown **RC**	.25
T130	Paul McAnulty **RC**	.50
T131	Chris Saenz **RC**	.25
T132	Marland Williams **RC**	.25
T133	Mike Huggins **RC**	.25
T134	Jesse Crain	.50
T135	Chad Bentz **RC**	.50
T136	Kazuo Matsui **RC**	.75
T137	Paul Maholm **RC**	.75
T138	Brock Jacobsen **RC**	.25
T139	Casey Daigle **RC**	.25
T140	Nyjer Morgan **RC**	.25
T141	Tom Mastny **RC**	.50
T142	Kody Kirkland **RC**	.50
T143	Jose Capellan **RC**	.50
T144	Felix Hernandez **RC**	5.00
T145	Shawn Hill **RC**	.25
T146	Danny Gonzalez **RC**	.25
T147	Scott Dohmann **RC**	.25
T148	Tommy Murphy **RC**	.50
T149	Akinori Otsuka **RC**	.50
T150	Miguel Perez **RC**	.50
T151	Mike Rouse	.25
T152	Ramon Ramirez **RC**	.50
T153	Luke Hughes **RC**	.50
T154	Howard Kendrick **RC**	5.00
T155	Ryan Budde	.25
T156	Charlie Zink **RC**	.25
T157	Warner Madrigal **RC**	.50
T158	Jason Szuminski **RC**	.25
T159	Chad Chop **RC**	.25
T160	Shingo Takatsu **RC**	.50
T161	Matt Lemanczyk **RC**	.25
T162	Wardell Starling **RC**	.50
T163	Nick Gorneault **RC**	.25
T164	Scott Proctor **RC**	.50
T165	Brooks Conrad **RC**	.50
T166	Hector Gimenez **RC**	.50
T167	Kevin Howard **RC**	.50
T168	Vince Perkins **RC**	.50
T169	Brock Peterson **RC**	.25
T170	Chris Shelton **RC**	1.00
T171	Erick Aybar **RC**	1.00
T172	Paul Bacot **RC**	.25
T173	Matt Capps **RC**	.25
T174	Kory Casto	.25
T175	Juan Cedeno **RC**	.25
T176	Vito Chiaravalloti **RC**	.50
T177	Alec Zumwalt **RC**	.25
T178	J.J. Furmaniak **RC**	.50
T179	Lee Gwaltney **RC**	.50
T180	Donald Kelly **RC**	.25
T181	Benji DeQuin **RC**	.25
T182	Brant Colamarino **RC**	.75
T183	Juan Gutierrez **RC**	.50
T184	Carl Loadenthal **RC**	.50
T185	Ricky Nolasco	1.25
T186	Jeff Salazar **RC**	1.00
T187	Rob Tejeda **RC**	.50
T188	Alex Romero **RC**	.25
T189	Yoann Torrealba **RC**	.25
T190	Carlos Sosa **RC**	.25
T191	Tim Bittner **RC**	.50
T192	Chris Aguila **RC**	.25
T193	Jason Frasor **RC**	.25
T194	Reid Gorecki **RC**	.50
T195	Dustin Nippert **RC**	.50
T196	Javier Guzman **RC**	.25
T197	Harvey Garcia **RC**	.50
T198	Ivan Ochoa **RC**	.25
T199	Dave Wallace **RC**	.25
T200	Joel Zumaya **RC**	2.50
T201	Casey Kopitzke **RC**	.25
T202	Lincoln Holdzkom **RC**	.25
T203	Chad Santos **RC**	.25
T204	Brian Pilkington **RC**	.25
T205	Terry Jones **RC**	.25
T206	Jerome Gamble **RC**	.25
T207	Brad Eldred **RC**	.50
T208	David Pauley **RC**	1.00
T209	Kevin Davidson **RC**	.25
T210	Damaso Espino **RC**	.25
T211	Tom Farmer **RC**	.50
T212	Michael Mooney **RC**	.25
T213	James Tomlin **RC**	.25
T214	Greg Thissen **RC**	.25
T215	Calvin Hayes **RC**	.25
T216	Fernando Cortez **RC**	.25
T217	Sergio Silva **RC**	.25
T218	Jon DeVries **RC**	.25
T219	Don Sutton **RC**	1.00
T220	Leo Nunez **RC**	.25
T221	Barry Bonds HTA Redemption	5.00

Gold

Stars:	5-10X
Rookies:	2-3X
Production 2,004 Sets	

Blue Refractor

No Pricing
Production One Set

Chrome Refractor

Stars:	4-8X
Rookies:	2-4X
Inserted 1:12	

X-Fractor

No Pricing
Production 20 Sets

Printing Plates

No pricing due to scarcity.

Dual Transactions Relic

		NM/M
Common Player:		
Inserted 1:562		
RP	Rafael Palmeiro	15.00
AR	Alex Rodriguez	25.00
CS	Curt Schilling	15.00

Future Phenoms

		NM/M
Common Player:		5.00
KC	Kevin Cash	5.00
BC	Bobby Crosby	10.00
ED	Eric Duncan	5.00
AG	Adrian Gonzalez	8.00
NG	Nick Green	5.00
JH	J.J. Hardy	5.00
EJ	Edwin Jackson	5.00
MM	Mark Malaska	5.00
VM	Victor Martinez	8.00
KM	Kazuo Matsui	10.00
LM	Lastings Milledge	15.00
JM	Justin Morneau	10.00
DN	Dioner Navarro	8.00
RN	Ramon Nivar	5.00
BU	B.J. Upton	12.00
JW	Jayson Werth	10.00
DY	Delmon Young	10.00

Hall of Fame Relic

		NM/M
Common Player:		
DE	Dennis Eckersley	10.00
PM	Paul Molitor	15.00

Hall of Fame Dual Relic

		NM/M
Inserted 1:3,388		
ME	Paul Molitor, Dennis Eckersley	30.00

Signature Cuts

No Pricing
Production One Set

Signature Moves

		NM/M
Common Autograph:		10.00
MB	Milton Bradley	15.00
MK	Mark Kotsay	10.00
EM	Eli Marrero	10.00
MN	Mike Neu	10.00
AR	Alex Rodriguez	160.00
JV	Javier Vazquez	15.00
FV	Fernando Vina	10.00
AW	Adam Wainwright	35.00

Transactions Relics

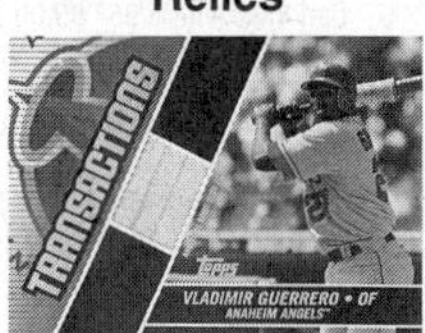

		NM/M
Common Player:		5.00
Inserted 1:106		
RA	Roberto Alomar	8.00
JB	Jeromy Burnitz	5.00
HC	Hee Seop Choi	5.00
RC	Roger Clemens	15.00
CE	Carl Everett	5.00
JG	Juan Gonzalez	8.00
VG	Vladimir Guerrero	10.00
BJ	Brian Jordan	5.00
KL	Kenny Lofton	5.00
JL	Javy Lopez	5.00
RP	Rafael Palmeiro	8.00
AP	Andy Pettitte	8.00
AR	Alex Rodriguez	25.00
IR	Ivan Rodriguez	10.00
RS	Reggie Sanders	5.00
RLS	Richie Sexson	8.00
GS	Gary Sheffield	10.00
MT	Miguel Tejada	8.00
RW	Rondell White	5.00

2004 Topps Tribute HOF

		NM/M
Complete Set (80):		120.00
Common Player:		2.00
Pack (5):		50.00
Box (6):		260.00
1	Willie Mays	8.00
2	Richie Ashburn	2.00
3	Babe Ruth	10.00
4	Lou Gehrig	8.00
5	Carl Yastrzemski	5.00
6	Fergie Jenkins	2.00
7	Cool Papa Bell	3.00
8	Johnny Bench	4.00
9	Satchel Paige	4.00
10	Ty Cobb	6.00
11	Robin Roberts	2.00
12	Eddie Mathews	3.00
13	Tom Seaver	3.00
14	Kirby Puckett	3.00
15	Stan Musial	5.00
16	Ralph Kiner	2.00
17	Reggie Jackson	3.00
18	Walter Johnson	4.00
19	Phil Niekro	2.00
20	Mike Schmidt	6.00
21	Brooks Robinson	3.00
22	Jimmie Foxx	4.00
23	Nellie Fox	2.00
24	Joe Morgan	2.00
25	Cy Young	3.00
26	Hank Greenberg	3.00
27	Josh Gibson	3.00
28	Robin Yount	5.00
29	Hoyt Wilhelm	2.00
30	Yogi Berra	3.00
31	Rollie Fingers	2.00
32	Gaylord Perry	2.00
33	Ozzie Smith	4.00
34	Jim Palmer	2.00
35	Harmon Killebrew	4.00
36	Bob Feller	2.00
37	Chuck Klein	2.00
38	Mordecai Brown	2.00
39	Napoleon Lajoie	2.00
40	Al Kaline	3.00
41	Paul Molitor	3.00
42	Jackie Robinson	5.00
43	Mel Ott	3.00
44	Hank Aaron	8.00
45	Rod Carew	2.00
46	Rogers Hornsby	3.00
47	Bob Gibson	3.00
48	Juan Marichal	2.00
49	Bill Mazeroski	2.00
50	Roberto Clemente	8.00
51	Willie McCovey	2.00
52	Red Schoendienst	2.00
53	Nolan Ryan	8.00
54	Dennis Eckersley	2.00
55	Monte Irvin	2.00
56	George Kell	2.00
57	Gary Carter	2.00
58	Tony Perez	2.00
59	Carlton Fisk	2.00
60	Duke Snider	3.00
61	Bobby Doerr	2.00
62	John McGraw	2.00
63	George Sisler	2.00
64	Orlando Cepeda	2.00
65	Earl Weaver	2.00
66	Roy Campanella	3.00
67	Tris Speaker	3.00
68	Sparky Anderson	2.00
69	Willie Stargell	2.00
70	Honus Wagner	3.00
71	Lou Brock	2.00
72	Whitey Ford	3.00
73	George Brett	8.00
74	Luis Aparicio	2.00
75	Ernie Banks	4.00
76	Jim Bunning	2.00
77	Warren Spahn	3.00
78	Jim "Catfish" Hunter	2.00
79	Pee Wee Reese	2.00
80	Frank Robinson	2.00

Gold

Gold Print Run 61-99:	2-3X
Gold p/r 36-60:	2-4X
#'d to last 2 digits of HOF induction yr	

Cooperstown Classmates Dual Cut Signature

No Pricing
Production One Set

Cooperstown Classmates Dual Relic

		NM/M
Common Duo:		20.00
Gold:		.75-1.5X
Production 25		
ME	Paul Molitor, Dennis Eckersley/75	35.00
KK	Chuck Klein, Al Kaline/75	35.00
RB	Nolan Ryan, George Brett/50	60.00
MP	Joe Morgan, Jim Palmer/75	20.00
SK	Duke Snider, Al Kaline/50	60.00
PC	Gaylord Perry, Rod Carew/50	30.00

BY	Johnny Bench, Carl Yastrzemski/75	50.00
CR	Orlando Cepeda, Nolan Ryan/75	60.00
MR	Juan Marichal, Brooks Robinson/50	35.00

Cooperstown Cut Signatures

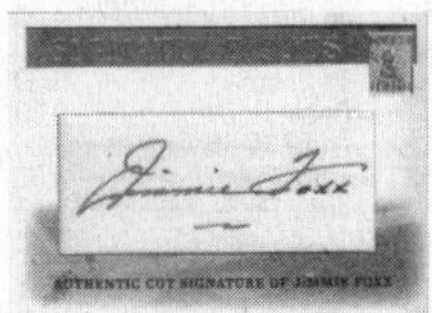

		NM/M
No Pricing		
Production One Set		
JF	Jimmie Foxx (10/05 auction)	1,940
MO	Mel Ott (8/05 auction)	2,025

Cut Signatures

No Pricing
Production One Set

Dual Cut Signatures

No Pricing
Production One Set

Hall of Fame Patches Relics

		NM/M
Common Player:		20.00
Gold:		.75-1.5X
Production 1-25		
No pricing for production 15 or less.		
GB	George Brett/50	40.00
RC	Rod Carew/100	25.00
DE	Dennis Eckersley/50	25.00
RJ	Reggie Jackson/50	25.00
FR	Frank Robinson/39	35.00
NR	Nolan Ryan/100	50.00
MS	Mike Schmidt/100	40.00
MS2	Mike Schmidt/100	40.00
RY	Robin Yount/35	40.00

Tribute Relics

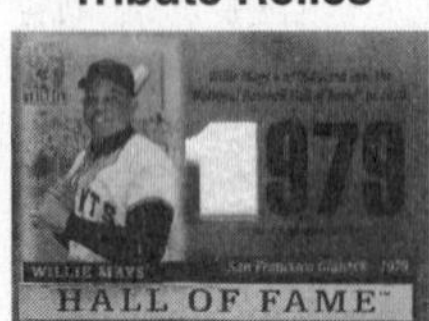

		NM/M
Common Player:		10.00
Golds:		1-30X
Production 25 Sets		
HA	Hank Aaron/Bat	30.00
JB	Johnny Bench/Jsy/250	15.00
JB2	Johnny Bench/Jsy	10.00
GB	George Brett/Jsy	15.00
GBB	George Brett/Bat	15.00
LBB	Lou Brock/Bat	10.00
GC	Gary Carter/Jsy/200	10.00
GCU	Gary Carter/Jsy	10.00
OC	Orlando Cepeda/Bat/100	20.00
RC	Roberto Clemente/Bat	50.00
TC	Ty Cobb/Jsy/20	275.00
TCB	Ty Cobb/Bat	75.00
CF	Carlton Fisk/Wall/300	20.00
WF	Whitey Ford/Jsy/50	60.00
JF	Jimmie Foxx/Bat/25	100.00
LG	Lou Gehrig/Bat/52	300.00
BG	Bob Gibson/Jsy	15.00
HG	Hank Greenberg/Bat	20.00
RH	Rogers Hornsby/Bat	40.00
RJ	Reggie Jackson/Jsy/110	15.00
RJB	Reggie Jackson/Bat/200	10.00
AK	Al Kaline/Jsy/125	20.00
AKB	Al Kaline/Bat	15.00
HK	Harmon Killebrew/Bat/135	30.00
CK	Chuck Klein/Bat/107	20.00
JMA	Juan Marichal/Jsy/125	10.00
WM1	Willie Mays/Glv/110	150.00
WM2	Willie Mays/Bat	30.00
WM3	Willie Mays/Bat	30.00
WM4	Willie Mays/Jsy	30.00
WM5	Willie Mays/Jsy	30.00
PM	Paul Molitor/Jsy	10.00
PMB	Paul Molitor/Bat	10.00
JM	Joe Morgan/Bat	10.00
SM	Stan Musial/Jsy	20.00
MO	Mel Ott/Bat/25	100.00
JP	Jim Palmer/Jsy	10.00
JP2	Jim Palmer/Jsy	10.00
KP	Kirby Puckett/Jsy/175	15.00
KPB	Kirby Puckett/Bat	10.00
BRO	Brooks Robinson/Bat	10.00
FR	Frank Robinson/Jsy	10.00
FRA	Frank Robinson/Jsy	10.00
FRB	Frank Robinson/Bat	10.00
JR	Jackie Robinson/Bat	25.00
BR	Babe Ruth/Bat/163	150.00
NR	Nolan Ryan/Jsy	25.00
NRA	Nolan Ryan/Jsy/425	25.00
NRJ	Nolan Ryan/Jsy	25.00
MS	Mike Schmidt/Jsy/50	30.00
MSB	Mike Schmidt/Bat	15.00
TS	Tom Seaver/Jsy	10.00
GS	George Sisler/Bat/455	25.00
OS	Ozzie Smith/Bat	15.00
DS	Duke Snider/Bat	10.00
TSP	Tris Speaker/Bat/85	120.00
HW	Honus Wagner/Bat/118	120.00
EW	Earl Weaver/Jsy/25	20.00
CY	Carl Yastrzemski/Wall/300	30.00
CYU	Carl Yastrzemski/Jsy	15.00
RY	Robin Yount/Jsy/50	25.00

Tribute Relic Autographs

		NM/M
Common Player:		40.00
Gold:		No Pricing
Production Five Sets		
AKB	Al Kaline/95	60.00
BRO	Brooks Robinson/95	50.00
NRJ	Nolan Ryan/95	140.00
EW	Earl Weaver/55	40.00
CYU	Carl Yastrzemski/95	85.00

World Champions Boston Red Sox

		NM/M
Complete Boxed Set (56):		25.00
Common Player:		.25
1	Bronson Arroyo	.25
2	Alan Embree	.25
3	Keith Foulke	.25
4	Curt Leskanic	.25
5	Derek Lowe	.50
6	Pedro Martinez	2.00
7	Ramiro Mendoza	.25
8	Mike Myers	.25
9	Curt Schilling	2.00
10	Mike Timlin	.25
11	Tim Wakefield	.25
12	Scott Williamson	.25
13	Doug Mirabelli	.25
14	Mark Bellhorn	.25
15	Orlando Cabrera	.50
16	Ricky Gutierrez	.25
17	Doug Mientkiewicz	.25
18	Kevin Millar	.50
19	Bill Mueller	.25
20	Pokey Reese	.25
21	Kevin Youkilis	.25
22	Johnny Damon	1.50
23	Gabe Kapler	.25
24	David McCarty	.25
25	Trot Nixon	.25
26	Manny Ramirez	2.00
27	Dave Roberts	.25
28	Ellis Burks	.25
29	David Ortiz	2.00
30	Terry Francona	.25
31	Red Sox Team Card	.50
32	Curt Schilling (Season Highlights)	1.00
33	Kevin Millar (Season Highlights)	.25
34	Manny Ramirez (Season Highlights)	1.00
35	Orlando Cabrera (Season Highlights)	.25
36	Manny Ramirez (Season Highlights)	1.00
37	Red Sox All-Stars (Season Highlights)	1.00
38	Pokey Reese (Season Highlights)	.25
39	Bill Mueller (Season Highlights)	.25
40	Curt Schilling (Postseason Highlights)	1.00
41	Pedro Martinez (Postseason Highlights)	1.00
42	David Ortiz (Postseason Highlights)	1.00
43	Kevin Millar (Postseason Highlights)	.25
44	Johnny Damon (Postseason Highlights)	1.00
45	Bill Mueller (Postseason Highlights)	.25
46	David Ortiz (Postseason Highlights)	1.00
47	Keith Foulke (Postseason Highlights)	.25
48	Curt Schilling (Postseason Highlights)	1.00
49	Game 7 Celebration	.50
50	David Ortiz (Postseason Highlights)	1.00
51	Mark Bellhorn (Postseason Highlights)	.25
52	Curt Schilling (Postseason Highlights)	1.00
53	Pedro Martinez (Postseason Highlights)	1.00
54	Red Sox Win World Series	1.00
55	Manny Ramirez (Postseason Highlights)	1.00

World Champions Boston Red Sox Team Card

		NM/M
Inserted 1:Set		
	Red Sox Team Card	1.00

Poland Spring N.Y. Yankees

This cello-wrapped stadium give-away set was sponsored by the team's bottled water concessionaire. Fronts have poses or action photos with team and sponsor logos in opposite corners. Backs have a close-up repeat of part of the front photo, along with personal data, lifetime stats and logos.

		NM/M
Complete Set (5):		10.00
Common Player:		2.00
1	Goose Gossage	2.00
2	Ron Guidry	2.00
3	Don Mattingly	6.00
4	Don Larsen	2.00
--	Sponsor's Card	.05

2005 Topps

		NM/M
Complete Set (732):		75.00
Factory Set (742):		80.00
Factory Set (737):		80.00
Common Player:		.10
Pack (10):		2.00
Box (36):		60.00
1	Alex Rodriguez	1.50
2	Placido Polanco	.10
3	Torii Hunter	.25
4	Lyle Overbay	.10
5	Johnny Damon	.40
6	Johnny Estrada	.10
8	Francisco Rodriguez	.10
9	Jason LaRue	.10
10	Sammy Sosa	1.00
11	Randy Wolf	.10
12	Jason Bay	.10
13	Tom Glavine	.25
14	Michael Tucker	.10
15	Brian Giles	.20
16	Dan Wilson	.10
17	Jim Edmonds	.40
18	Danys Baez	.10
19	Roy Halladay	.20
20	Hank Blalock	.50
21	Darin Erstad	.20
22	Robby Hammock	.10
23	Mike Hampton	.10
24	Mark Bellhorn	.10
25	Jim Thome	.50
26	Scott Schoeneweis	.10
27	Jody Gerut	.10
28	Vinny Castilla	.10
29	Luis Castillo	.10
30	Ivan Rodriguez	.50
31	Craig Biggio	.20
32	Joe Randa	.10
33	Dave Roberts	.10
34	Scott Podsednik	.10
35	Cliff Floyd	.10
36	Livan Hernandez	.10
37	Eric Byrnes	.10
38	Ricky Ledee	.10
39	Jack Wilson	.10
40	Gary Sheffield	.40
41	Chan Ho Park	.10
42	Carl Crawford	.10
43	Miguel Batista	.10
44	David Bell	.10
45	Jeff DaVanon	.10
46	Brandon Webb	.10
47	Bronson Arroyo	.10
48	Melvin Mora	.10
49	David Ortiz	.50
50	Andruw Jones	.40
51	Chone Figgins	.10
52	Danny Graves	.10
53	Preston Wilson	.10
54	Jeremy Bonderman	.10
55	Chad Fox	.10
56	Dan Miceli	.10
57	Jimmy Gobble	.10
58	Darren Dreifort	.10
59	Matt LeCroy	.10
60	Jose Vidro	.10
61	Al Leiter	.10
62	Javier Vazquez	.10
63	Erubiel Durazo	.10
64	Doug Glanville	.10
65	Scot Shields	.10
66	Edgardo Alfonzo	.10
67	Ryan Franklin	.10
68	Francisco Cordero	.10
69	Brett Myers	.10
70	Curt Schilling	.50
71	Matt Kata	.10
72	Mark DeRosa	.10
73	Rodrigo Lopez	.10
74	Tim Wakefield	.10
75	Frank Thomas	.50
76	Jimmy Rollins	.25
77	Barry Zito	.25
78	Hideo Nomo	.25
79	Brad Wilkerson	.10
80	Adam Dunn	.50
81	Billy Traber	.10
82	Fernando Vina	.10
83	Nate Robertson	.10
84	Brad Ausmus	.10
85	Mike Sweeney	.10
86	Kip Wells	.10
87	Doug Mientkiewicz	.10
88	Zach Day	.10
89	Tony Clark	.10
90	Bret Boone	.10
91	Mark Loretta	.10
92	Jerome Williams	.10
93	Randy Winn	.10
94	Marlon Anderson	.10
95	Aubrey Huff	.10
96	Kevin Mench	.10
97	Frank Catalanotto	.10
98	Flash Gordon	.10
99	Scott Hatteberg	.10
100	Albert Pujols	1.50
101	Jose Molina, Bengie Molina	.10
102	Oscar Villarreal	.10
103	Jay Gibbons	.10
104	Byung-Hyun Kim	.10
105	Joe Borowski	.10
106	Mark Grudzielanek	.10
107	Mark Buehrle	.10
108	Paul Wilson	.10
109	Ronnie Belliard	.10
110	Larry Walker	.40
111	Tim Redding	.10
112	Hee Seop Choi	.10
113	Darrell May	.10
114	Jose Hernandez	.10
115	Ben Sheets	.25
116	Johan Santana	.40
117	Billy Wagner	.20
118	Mariano Rivera	.25
119	Steve Trachsel	.10
120	Akinori Otsuka	.10
121	Bobby Kielty	.10
122	Felix Rodriguez	.10
123	Raul Ibanez	.10
124	Mike Matheny	.10
125	Vernon Wells	.10
126	Jason Isringhausen	.10
127	Jose Guillen	.10
128	Danny Bautista	.10
129	Marcus Giles	.10
130	Javy Lopez	.25
131	Kevin Millar	.10
132	Kyle Farnsworth	.10
133	Carl Pavano	.10
134	D'Angelo Jimenez	.10
135	Casey Blake	.10
136	Matt Holliday	.25
137	Bobby Higginson	.10
138	Ramon Castro	.10
139	Alex Gonzalez	.10
140	Jeff Kent	.20
141	Aaron Guiel	.10
142	Shawn Green	.25
143	Bill Hall	.10
144	Shannon Stewart	.10
145	Juan Rivera	.10
146	Ty Wigginton	.10
147	Mike Mussina	.50
148	Eric Chavez	.25
149	Randall Simon	.10
150	Vladimir Guerrero	.75
151	Alex Cintron	.10
152	Horacio Ramirez	.10
153	Sidney Ponson	.10
154	Trot Nixon	.10
155	Greg Maddux	1.00
156	Esteban Loaiza	.10
157	Ryan Freel	.10
158	Matt Lawton	.10
159	Shawn Chacon	.10
160	Josh Beckett	.25
161	Ken Harvey	.10
162	Juan Cruz	.10
163	Juan Encarnacion	.10
164	Wes Helms	.10
165	Brad Radke	.10
166	Claudio Vargas	.10
167	Mike Cameron	.10
168	Jose Contreras	.10
169	Bobby Crosby	.10
170	Mike Lieberthal	.10
171	Robert Mackowiak	.10
172	Sean Burroughs	.10
173	J.T. Snow Jr.	.10
174	Paul Konerko	.10
175	Luis Gonzalez	.10
176	John Lackey	.10
177	Antonio Alfonseca	.10
178	Brian Roberts	.10
179	Bill Mueller	.10
180	Carlos Lee	.10
181	Corey Patterson	.25
182	Sean Casey	.25
183	Cliff Lee	.10
184	Jason Jennings	.10
185	Dmitri Young	.10
186	Brad Penny	.10
187	Andy Pettitte	.25
188	Juan Gonzalez	.25
189	Paul LoDuca	.10
190	Jason Phillips	.10
191	Rocky Biddle	.10
192	Lew Ford	.10
193	Mark Mulder	.25
194	Bobby Abreu	.25
195	Jason Kendall	.10
196	Terrence Long	.10
197	A.J. Pierzynski	.10
198	Eddie Guardado	.10
199	So Taguchi	.10
200	Jason Giambi	.25
201	Tony Batista	.10
202	Kyle Lohse	.10
203	Trevor Hoffman	.10
204	Tike Redman	.10
205	Neifi Perez	.10
206	Gil Meche	.10
207	Chris Carpenter	.10
208	Josh Phelps	.10
209	Eric Young	.10
210	Doug Waechter	.10
211	Jarrod Washburn	.10
212	Chad Tracy	.10
213	John Smoltz	.25
214	Jorge Julio	.10
215	Alex Gonzalez	.10
216	Shingo Takatsu	.10
217	Jose Acevedo	.10
218	Jason Davis	.10
219	Shawn Estes	.10
220	Lance Berkman	.25
221	Carlos Guillen	.10
222	Jeremy Affeldt	.10
223	Cesar Izturis	.10
224	Scott Sullivan	.10
225	Kazuo Matsui	.25
226	Josh Fogg	.10
227	Jason Schmidt	.25
228	Jason Marquis	.10
229	Scott Spiezio	.10
230	Miguel Tejada	.40
231	Bartolo Colon	.10
232	Jose Valverde	.10
233	Derrek Lee	.25
234	Scott Williamson	.10
235	Joe Crede	.10
236	Cory Lidle	.10
237	Mike MacDougal	.10
238	Eric Gagne	.25
239	Alex Sanchez	.10
240	Miguel Cabrera	.75
241	Luis Rivas	.10
242	Adam Everett	.10
243	Jason Johnson	.10
244	Travis Hafner	.25
245	Jose Valentin	.10
246	Stephen Randolph	.10
247	Rafael Furcal	.25
248	Adam Kennedy	.10
249	Luis Matos	.10
250	Mark Prior	.75
251	Angel Berroa	.10
252	Phil Nevin	.10
253	Oliver Perez	.10
254	Orlando Hudson	.10
255	Victor Zambrano	.10
256	Khalil Greene	.25
257	Tim Worrell	.10
258	Carlos Zambrano	.25
259	Elmer Dessens	.10
260	Gerald Laird	.10
261	Jose Cruz Jr.	.10
262	Michael Barrett	.10
263	Michael Young (Uncorrected error - Photo is Rod Barajas.)	.10
264	Toby Hall	.10
265	Woody Williams	.10
266	Rich Harden	.10
267	Mike Scioscia	.10
268	Al Pedrique	.10
269	Bobby Cox	.10
270	Lee Mazzilli	.10
271	Terry Francona	.10
272	Dusty Baker	.10
273	Ozzie Guillen	.10
274	Dave Miley	.10
275	Eric Wedge	.10
276	Clint Hurdle	.10
277	Alan Trammell	.10
278	Jack McKeon	.10
279	Phil Garner	.10
280	Tony Pena	.10
281	Jim Tracy	.10
282	Ned Yost	.10
283	Ron Gardenhire	.10
284	Frank Robinson	.25
285	Art Howe	.10
286	Joe Torre	.25
287	Ken Macha	.10
288	Larry Bowa	.10
289	Lloyd McClendon	.10
290	Bruce Bochy	.10
291	Felipe Alou	.10
292	Bob Melvin	.10
293	Tony LaRussa	.10
294	Lou Piniella	.10
295	Buck Showalter	.10
296	Carlos Tosca	.10
297	Steven Doetsch **RC**	.10
298	Melky Cabrera **RC**	1.00
299	Luis Ramirez **RC**	.10
300	Chris Seddon **RC**	.10
301	Nate Schierholtz	1.00
302	Ian Kinsler **RC**	2.00
303	Brandon Moss **RC**	1.50
304	Chadd Blasko **RC**	.10
305	Jeremy West **RC**	1.00
306	Sean Marshall **RC**	.75
307	Matt DeSalvo **RC**	.50
308	Ryan Sweeney	1.50
309	Matt Lindstrom **RC**	.10
310	Ryan Goleski **RC**	.50
311	Brett Harper **RC**	.25
312	Chris Roberson **RC**	.10
313	Andre Ethier	1.50
314	Chris Denorfia **RC**	.10
315	Ian Bladergroen **RC**	.75
316	Darren Fenster **RC**	.10

317 Kevin West **RC** .10
318 Chaz Lytle **RC** .50
319 James Jurries **RC** .10
320 Matt Rogelstad **RC** .10
321 Wade Robinson **RC** .10
322 Jake Dittler .10
323 Edgar Huerta **RC** .10
324 Kole Strayhorn .10
325 Jose Vaquedano **RC** .10
326 Elvys Quezada **RC** .10
327 John Maine, Val Majewski .10
328 Rickie Weeks, J.J. Hardy .10
329 Gabe Gross, Guillermo Quiroz .10
330 David Wright, Craig Brazell 1.50
331 Dallas McPherson, Jeff Mathis .10
332 Randy Johnson .10
333 Randy Johnson .10
334 Ichiro Suzuki .10
335 Ken Griffey Jr. .10
336 Greg Maddux .10
337 Ichiro Suzuki, Melvin Mora, Vladimir Guerrero .10
338 Ichiro Suzuki, Michael Young, Vladimir Guerrero .10
339 Manny Ramirez, Paul Konerko, David Ortiz .10
340 Miguel Tejada, David Ortiz, Manny Ramirez .10
341 Johan Santana, Curt Schilling, Jake Westbrook .10
342 Johan Santana, Pedro J. Martinez, Curt Schilling .10
343 Todd Helton, Mark Loretta, Adrian Beltre .10
344 Juan Pierre, Mark Loretta, Jack Wilson .10
345 Adrian Beltre, Adam Dunn, Albert Pujols .10
346 Vinny Castilla, Scott Rolen, Albert Pujols .10
347 Jake Peavy, Randy Johnson, Ben Sheets .10
348 Randy Johnson, Ben Sheets, Jason Schmidt .10
349 Postseason Highlight .10
350 Postseason Highlight .10
351 Postseason Highlight .10
352 Postseason Highlight .10
353 Postseason Highlight .10
354 Postseason Highlight .10
355 Postseason Highlight .10
356 Paul Konerko .10
357 Alfonso Soriano .10
358 Miguel Tejada .10
359 Melvin Mora .10
360 Vladimir Guerrero .10
361 Ichiro Suzuki .10
362 Manny Ramirez .10
363 Ivan Rodriguez .10
364 Johan Santana .10
365 Paul Konerko .10
366 David Ortiz .10
367 Bobby Crosby .10
368 Sox Celebration WS4 1.50
369 Garret Anderson .25
370 Randy Johnson .75
371 Charles Thomas .10
372 Rafael Palmeiro .40
373 Kevin Youkilis .10
374 Freddy Garcia .10
375 Magglio Ordonez .10
376 Aaron Harang .10
377 Grady Sizemore .25
378 Chin-Hui Tsao .10
379 Eric Munson .10
380 Juan Pierre .10
381 Brad Lidge .10
382 Brian Anderson .10
383 Alex Cora .10
384 Brady Clark .10
385 Todd Helton .40
386 Chad Cordero .10
387 Kris Benson .10
388 Brad Halsey .10
389 Jermaine Dye .10
390 Manny Ramirez .50
391 Daryle Ward .10
392 Adam Eaton .10
393 Brett Tomko .10
394 Bucky Jacobsen .10
395 Dontrelle Willis .40
396 B.J. Upton .25
397 Rocco Baldelli .10
398 Ted Lilly .10
399 Ryan Drese .10
400 Ichiro Suzuki 1.25
401 Brendan Donnelly .10
402 Brandon Lyon .10
403 Nick Green .10
404 Jerry Hairston Jr. .10
405 Mike Lowell .10
406 Kerry Wood .50
407 Carl Everett .10
408 Hideki Matsui 1.25
409 Omar Vizquel .25
410 Joe Kennedy .10
411 Carlos Pena .10
412 Armando Benitez .10
413 Carlos Beltran .50
414 Kevin Appier .10
415 Jeff Weaver .10
416 Chad Moeller .10
417 Joe Mays .10
418 Terrmel Sledge .10
419 Richard Hidalgo .10
420 Kenny Lofton .10
421 Justin Duchscherer .10
422 Eric Milton .10
423 Jose Mesa .10
424 Ramon Hernandez .10
425 Jose Reyes .25
426 Joel Pineiro .10
427 Matt Morris .10
428 John Halama .10
429 Gary Matthews Jr. .10
430 Ryan Madson .10
431 Mark Kotsay .10
432 Carlos Delgado .10
433 Casey Kotchman .10
434 Greg Aquino .10
435 Eli Marrero .10
436 David Newhan .10
437 Mike Timlin .10
438 LaTroy Hawkins .10
439 Jose Contreras .10
440 Ken Griffey Jr. 1.00
441 C.C. Sabathia .10
442 Brandon Inge .10
443 Peter Munro .10
444 John Buck .10
445 Hee Seop Choi .10
446 Chris Capuano .10
447 Jesse Crain .10
448 Geoff Jenkins .10
449 Brian Schneider .10
450 Mike Piazza 1.00
451 Jorge Posada .40
452 Nick Swisher .10
453 Kevin Millwood .25
454 Mike Gonzalez .10
455 Jake Peavy .25
456 Dustin Hermanson .10
457 Jeremy Reed .10
458 Julian Tavarez .10
459 Geoff Blum .10
460 Alfonso Soriano .50
461 Alexis Rios .10
462 David Eckstein .10
463 Shea Hillenbrand .10
464 Russ Ortiz .10
465 Kurt Ainsworth .10
466 Orlando Cabrera .10
467 Carlos Silva .10
468 Ross Gload .10
469 Josh Phelps .10
470 Marquis Grissom .10
471 Mike Maroth .10
472 Guillermo Mota .10
473 Chris Burke .10
474 David DeJesus .10
475 Jose Lima .10
476 Cristian Guzman .10
477 Nick Johnson .10
478 Victor Zambrano .10
479 Rod Barajas .10
480 Damian Miller .10
481 Chase Utley .25
482 Todd Pratt .10
483 Sean Burnett .10
484 David Wells .10
485 Dustan Mohr .10
486 Bobby Madritsch .10
487 Ray King .10
488 Reed Johnson .10
489 R.A. Dickey .10
490 Scott Kazmir .25
491 Tony Womack .10
492 Tomas Perez .10
493 Esteban Loaiza .10
494 Tomokazu Ohka .10
495 Mike Lamb .10
496 Ramon Ortiz .10
497 Richie Sexson .40
498 J.D. Drew .25
499 David Segui .10
500 Barry Bonds 2.00
501 Aramis Ramirez .25
502 Wily Mo Pena .10
503 Jeromy Burnitz .10
504 Craig Monroe .10
505 Nomar Garciaparra 1.00
506 Brandon Backe .10
507 Marcus Thames .10
508 Derek Lowe .10
509 Doug Davis .10
510 Joe Mauer .25
511 Endy Chavez .10
512 Bernie Williams .25
513 Mark Redman .10
514 Jason Michaels .10
515 Craig Wilson .10
516 Ryan Klesko .10
517 Ray Durham .10
518 Jose Lopez .10
519 Jeff Suppan .10
520 Julio Lugo .10
521 Mike Wood .10
522 David Bush .10
523 Juan Rincon .10
524 Paul Quantrill .10
525 Marlon Byrd .10
526 Roy Oswalt .25
527 Rondell White .10
528 Troy Glaus .25
529 Scott Hairston .10
530 Chipper Jones .75
531 Daniel Cabrera .10
532 Doug Mientkiewicz .10
533 Glendon Rusch .10
534 Jon Garland .10
535 Austin Kearns .10
536 Jake Westbrook .10
537 Aaron Miles .10
538 Omar Infante .10
539 Paul LoDuca .10
540 Morgan Ensberg .10
541 Tony Graffanino .10
542 Milton Bradley .25
543 Keith Ginter .10
544 Justin Morneau .40
545 Tony Armas Jr. .10
546 Mike Stanton .10
547 Kevin Brown .10
548 Marco Scutaro .10
549 Tim Hudson .10
550 Pat Burrell .10
551 Ty Wigginton .10
552 Jeff Cirillo .10
553 Jim Brower .10
554 Jamie Moyer .10
555 Larry Walker .10
556 Dewon Brazelton .10
557 Brian Jordan .10
558 Josh Towers .10
559 Shigetoshi Hasegawa .10
560 Octavio Dotel .10
561 Travis Lee .10
562 Michael Cuddyer .10
563 Junior Spivey .10
564 Zack Greinke .10
565 Roger Clemens 1.50
566 Chris Shelton .10
567 Ugueth Urbina .10
568 Rafael Betancourt .10
569 Willie Harris .10
570 Todd Hollandsworth .10
571 Keith Foulke .10
572 Larry Bigbie .10
573 Paul Byrd .10
574 Troy Percival .10
575 Pedro Martinez .75
576 Matt Clement .10
577 Ryan Wagner .10
578 Jeff Francis .10
579 Jeff Conine .10
580 Wade Miller .10
581 Matt Stairs .10
582 Gavin Floyd .10
583 Kazuhisa Ishii .10
584 Victor Santos .10
585 Jacque Jones .10
586 Sunny Kim .10
587 Dan Kolb .10
588 Cory Lidle .10
589 Jose Castillo .10
590 Alex Gonzalez .10
591 Kirk Rueter .10
592 Jolbert Cabrera .10
593 Erik Bedard .10
594 Ben Grieve .10
595 Ricky Ledee .10
596 Mark Hendrickson .10
597 Laynce Nix .10
598 Jason Frasor .10
599 Kevin Gregg .10
600 Derek Jeter 1.50
601 Luis Terrero .10
602 Jaret Wright .10
603 Edwin Jackson .10
604 Dave Roberts .10
605 Moises Alou .25
606 Aaron Rowand .10
607 Kazuhito Tadano .10
608 Luis Gonzalez .10
609 A.J. Burnett .25
610 Jeff Bagwell .40
611 Brad Penny .10
612 Craig Counsell .10
613 Corey Koskie .10
614 Mark Ellis .10
615 Felix Rodriguez .10
616 Jay Payton .10
617 Hector Luna .10
618 Miguel Olivo .10
619 Rob Bell .10
620 Scott Rolen .50
621 Ricardo Rodriguez .10
622 Eric Hinske .10
623 Tim Salmon .10
624 Adam LaRoche .10
625 B.J. Ryan .10
626 Roberto Alomar .25
627 Steve Finley .10
628 Joe Nathan .10
629 Scott Linebrink .10
630 Vicente Padilla .10
631 Raul Mondesi .10
632 Yadier Molina .10
633 Tino Martinez .10
634 Mark Teixeira .25
635 Kelvim Escobar .10
636 Pedro Felix .10
637 Rich Aurilia .10
638 Los Angeles Angels of Anaheim .10
639 Arizona Diamondbacks .10
640 Atlanta Braves .10
641 Baltimore Orioles .10
642 Boston Red Sox .10
643 Chicago Cubs .10
644 Chicago White Sox .10
645 Cincinnati Reds .10
646 Cleveland Indians .10
647 Colorado Rockies .10
648 Detroit Tigers .10
649 Florida Marlins .10
650 Houston Astros .10
651 Kansas City Royals .10
652 Los Angeles Dodgers .10
653 Milwaukee Brewers .10
654 Minnesota Twins .10
655 Montreal Expos .10
656 New York Mets .10
657 New York Yankees .10
658 Oakland Athletics .10
659 Philadelphia Phillies .10
660 Pittsburgh Pirates .10
661 San Diego Padres .10
662 San Francisco Giants .10
663 Seattle Mariners .10
664 St. Louis Cardinals .10
665 Tampa Bay Devil Rays .10
666 Texas Rangers .10
667 Toronto Blue Jays .10
668 Billy Butler **RC** 1.50
669 Wes Swackhamer **RC** .25
670 Matt Campbell **RC** .25
671 Ryan Webb **RC** .50
672 Glen Perkins **RC** .25
673 Michael Rogers **RC** .25
674 Kevin Melillo **RC** .25
675 Erik Cordier **RC** .50
676 Landon Powell **RC** .50
677 Justin Verlander **RC** 1.00
678 Eric Nielsen **RC** .25
679 Alexander Smit **RC** .25
680 Ryan Garko **RC** .50
681 Bobby Livingston **RC** .25
682 Jeff Niemann **RC** .50
683 Wladimir Balentien **RC** .50
684 Chip Cannon **RC** .50
685 Yorman Bazardo **RC** .50
686 Michael Bourn .10
687 Andy LaRoche **RC** 2.00
688 Felix Hernandez, Justin Leone .50
689 Ryan Howard, Cole Hamels .75
690 Matt Cain, Merkin Valdez .25
691 Andy Marte, Jeff Francoeur .10
692 Chad Billingsley, Joel Guzman .10
693 Jerry Hairston Jr., Scott Hairston .10
694 Miguel Tejada, Lance Berkman .25
695 Kenny Rogers .10
696 Ivan Rodriguez .25
697 Darin Erstad .10
698 Bret Boone .10
699 Eric Chavez .10
700 Derek Jeter 1.00
701 Vernon Wells .10
702 Ichiro Suzuki .75
703 Torii Hunter .10
704 Greg Maddux .50
705 Mike Matheny .10
706 Todd Helton .25
707 Luis Castillo .10
708 Scott Rolen .40
709 Cesar Izturis .10
710 Jim Edmonds .25
711 Andruw Jones .25
712 Steve Finley .10
713 Johan Santana .40
714 Roger Clemens 1.00
715 Vladimir Guerrero .40
716 Barry Bonds 1.50
717 Bobby Crosby .10
718 Jason Bay .10
719 Albert Pujols 1.00
720 Mark Loretta .10
721 Edgar Renteria .10
722 Scott Rolen .40
723 J.D. Drew .10
724 Jim Edmonds .25
725 Johnny Estrada .10
726 Jason Schmidt .10
727 Chris Carpenter .10
728 Eric Gagne .10
729 Jason Bay .10
730 Bobby Cox .10
731 Game 1 .50
732 Game 2 .50
733 Game 3 .50
734 Game 4 .50

Black

1st Edition: 20-50X
Production 54 Sets

Gold

Stars: 5-10X
Production 2,005 Sets

1st Edition

NM/M
Stars: 3-5X
HTA Exclusive
1st Edition Pack (10): 4.00
1st Edition Box (20): 65.00

All-Stars

NM/M
Complete Set (15): 20.00
Common Player:
Inserted 1:9
TAS1 Todd Helton .75
TAS2 Albert Pujols 3.00
TAS3 Vladimir Guerrero 1.00
TAS4 Ichiro Suzuki 2.00
TAS5 Randy Johnson 1.00
TAS6 Manny Ramirez 1.00
TAS7 Sammy Sosa 2.00
TAS8 Alfonso Soriano 1.00
TAS9 Jim Thome 1.00
TAS10 Barry Bonds 3.00
TAS11 Roger Clemens 3.00
TAS12 Mike Piazza 1.50
TAS13 Derek Jeter 3.00
TAS14 Alex Rodriguez 2.50
TAS15 Carlos Beltran 1.00

All-Star Patches

No Pricing
Production 25 Sets

All-Star Stitches Relics

NM/M
Common Player: 5.00
Inserted 1:96
BA Bobby Abreu 8.00
MA Moises Alou 10.00
RB Ronnie Belliard 5.00
CB Carlos Beltran 10.00
LB Lance Berkman 10.00
HB Hank Blalock 10.00
MC Miguel Cabrera 10.00
CC Carl Crawford 5.00
JE Johnny Estrada 8.00
EG Eric Gagne 10.00
JG Jason Giambi 10.00
TG Tom Glavine 10.00
FG Flash Gordon 5.00
VG Vladimir Guerrero 10.00
KH Ken Harvey 5.00
TH Todd Helton 10.00
JK Jeff Kent 8.00
DK Danny Kolb 8.00
BL Barry Larkin 10.00
MLA Matt Lawton 5.00
TL Ted Lilly 8.00
EL Esteban Loaiza 5.00
PL Paul LoDuca 5.00
MLO Mark Loretta 8.00
ML Mike Lowell 8.00
VM Victor Martinez 10.00
MM Mark Mulder 10.00
JN Joe Nathan 8.00
DO David Ortiz 20.00
CP Carl Pavano 10.00
MP Mike Piazza 12.00
AP Albert Pujols 25.00
MR Manny Ramirez 10.00
ER Edgar Renteria 8.00
MRI Mariano Rivera 10.00
FR Francisco Rodriguez 10.00
IR Ivan Rodriguez 10.00
SR Scott Rolen 12.00
CS C.C. Sabathia 8.00
BS Ben Sheets 10.00
GS Gary Sheffield 10.00
AS Alfonso Soriano 10.00
SS Sammy Sosa 15.00
MT Miguel Tejada 10.00
JT Jim Thome 12.00
JW Jack Wilson 10.00
MY Michael Young 15.00
CZ Carlos Zambrano 10.00

Autographs

NM/M
Common Autograph:
CB Carlos Beltran 30.00
MC Miguel Cabrera 40.00
JC Jose Capellan 10.00
EC Eric Chavez 25.00
DD David DeJesus 10.00
ZG Zack Greinke 10.00
CK Casey Kotchman 10.00
JMA John Maine 30.00
DM Dallas McPherson 10.00
ARI Alexis Rios 15.00
AR Alex Rodriguez 200.00
CT Chad Tracy 10.00
VW Vernon Wells 25.00
DW David Wright 75.00
Series 2
JB Jason Bay 25.00
CB Carlos Beltran 30.00
MB Milton Bradley 25.00
BB Billy Butler 50.00
MC Matt Campbell 10.00
EC Eric Chavez 20.00
ECO Erik Cordier 10.00
CC Carl Crawford 15.00
EG Eric Gagne 30.00
FH Felix Hernandez 30.00
SK Scott Kazmir 25.00
ML Mark Loretta 15.00
GP Glen Perkins 15.00
LP Landon Powell 15.00
AR2 Alex Rodriguez/50 250.00
IR Ivan Rodriguez 50.00
MR Michael Rogers 10.00
JS Johan Santana 40.00
TS Terrmel Sledge 10.00
CW Craig Wilson 10.00

Barry Bonds Home Run Highlights

NM/M
Complete Set (330):
Common Bonds: 1.50
Inserted 1:4
BB1-BB330 Barry Bonds 1.50

Bonds MVP

NM/M
Production 25-500
BBI2 Barry Bonds/50 40.00
BBI3 Barry Bonds/100 30.00
BBI4 Barry Bonds/200 25.00
BBI5 Barry Bonds/300 20.00
BBI6 Barry Bonds/400 15.00
BBI7 Barry Bonds/500 15.00

2005 Topps Bonds MVP Autographs

No Pricing

Bonds MVP Relics

NM/M
Production 25-500
BBR3 Barry Bonds/100 50.00
BBR4 Barry Bonds/200 40.00
BBR5 Barry Bonds/300 40.00
BBR6 Barry Bonds/400 25.00
BBR7 Barry Bonds/500 25.00

Celebrity Threads Relics

NM/M
Common Player: 8.00
Inserted 1:562
CC Cesar Cedeno 8.00
CF Cecil Fielder 15.00
RF Rollie Fingers 12.00
GG Rich "Goose" Gossage 10.00
HR Harold Reynolds 8.00
MS Mike Scott 8.00
OS Ozzie Smith 25.00
DW Dave Winfield 15.00

Dem Bums

NM/M
Complete Set (13): 40.00
Common Player: 4.00
Inserted 1:12
WA Walter Alston 4.00
BB Bob Borkowski 4.00
RC Roy Campanella 6.00
RCR Roger Craig 4.00
CF Carl Furillo 4.00
JG Jim Gilliam 4.00
DH Don Hoak 4.00
JH Jim Hughes 4.00
RM Russ Meyer 4.00
JR Jackie Robinson 8.00
ER Ed Roebuck 4.00
GS George Shuba 4.00
KS Karl Spooner 4.00

Dem Bums Autographs

NM/M
Common Autograph: 30.00
CE Carl Erskine 30.00
CL Clem Labine 50.00
JP Johnny Podres 30.00
DS Duke Snider 50.00
DZ Don Zimmer 50.00

Dem Bums Cuts

No Pricing
Production One Set

Derby Digs Relics

NM/M
Common Player: 15.00

Production 100 Sets
LB Lance Berkman 15.00
HB Hank Blalock 20.00
DO David Ortiz 35.00
SS Sammy Sosa 40.00
MT Miguel Tejada 15.00
JT Jim Thome 25.00
Series 2
Production 10 Sets

Factory Set Team Bonus

NM/M
Complete Cubs Set (5): 15.00
Complete Yankees Set (5): 15.00
Complete Red Sox Set (5): 15.00
Complete Giants Set (5): 15.00
Complete Nationals Set (5): 15.00
Complete Tigers Set (5): 15.00
Issued in Team themed Factory Sets

Factory Set Draft Picks Bonus

NM/M
Complete Set (5): 20.00
One set per Factory Set
1 Beau Jones 4.00
2 Cliff Pennington 4.00
3 Chris Volstad 4.00
4 Ricky Romero 4.00
5 Jay Bruce 10.00

Factory Set First Year Draft Bonus

NM/M
Complete Set (10): 50.00
One set per Green Factory Set
1 Nick Webber 3.00
2 Aaron Thompson 4.00
3 Matt Garza 8.00
4 Tyler Greene 4.00
5 Ryan Braun 10.00
6 C.J. Henry 4.00
7 Ryan Zimmerman 20.00
8 John Mayberry Jr. 4.00
9 Cesar Carrillo 3.00
10 Mark McCormick 3.00

Factory Set First Year Player Bonus

NM/M
Complete Set (5): 15.00
Issued in Red Factory Sets
1 Bill McCarthy 4.00
2 John Hudgins 4.00
3 Kyle Nichols 4.00
4 Thomas Pauly 4.00
5 Philip Humber 4.00

Grudge Match

NM/M
Complete Set (10):
Common Duo: 1.00
Inserted 1:24
GM1 Jorge Posada, Pedro J. Martinez 2.00
GM2 Mike Piazza, Roger Clemens 3.00
GM3 Mariano Rivera, Luis Gonzalez 1.00
GM4 Carlos Zambrano, Jim Edmonds 1.00
GM5 Aaron Boone, Tim Wakefield 1.00
GM6 Manny Ramirez, Roger Clemens 3.00
GM7 Michael Tucker, Eric Gagne 1.00
GM8 Ivan Rodriguez, J.T. Snow 1.00
GM9 Alex Rodriguez, Bronson Arroyo 3.00
GM10 Corky Miller, Sammy Sosa 2.50

Hit Parade

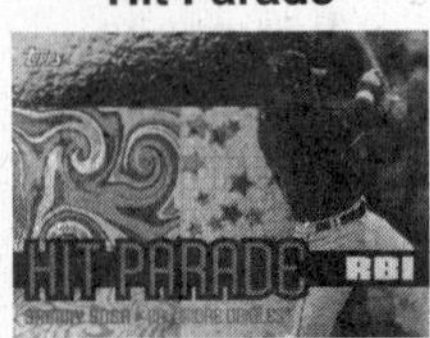

NM/M
Complete Set (30): 25.00
Common Player: .50
Inserted 1:12
HR1 Barry Bonds 4.00
HR2 Sammy Sosa 2.50
HR3 Rafael Palmeiro 1.00
HR4 Ken Griffey Jr. 2.00
HR5 Jeff Bagwell 1.00
HR6 Frank Thomas 1.00
HR7 Juan Gonzalez .75
HR8 Jim Thome 1.00
HR9 Gary Sheffield 1.00
HR10 Manny Ramirez 1.50
RBI1 Barry Bonds 4.00
RBI2 Rafael Palmeiro 1.00
RBI3 Sammy Sosa 2.50
RBI4 Jeff Bagwell 1.00
RBI5 Ken Griffey Jr. 2.00
RBI6 Frank Thomas 1.00
RBI7 Juan Gonzalez .75
RBI8 Gary Sheffield 1.00
RBI9 Ruben Sierra .50
RBI10 Manny Ramirez 1.50
HIT1 Rafael Palmeiro 1.00
HIT2 Barry Bonds 4.00
HIT3 Roberto Alomar .75
HIT4 Craig Biggio .50
HIT5 Julio Franco .50
HIT6 Steve Finley .50
HIT7 Jeff Bagwell 1.00
HIT8 B.J. Surhoff .50
HIT9 Marquis Grissom .50
HIT10 Sammy Sosa 2.50

Hobby Masters

NM/M
Complete Set (20): 25.00
Common Player: .75
Inserted 1:18
HM1 Alex Rodriguez 4.00
HM2 Sammy Sosa 2.50
HM3 Ichiro Suzuki 3.00
HM4 Albert Pujols 4.00
HM5 Derek Jeter 4.00
HM6 Jim Thome 1.50
HM7 Vladimir Guerrero 1.50
HM8 Nomar Garciaparra 2.00
HM9 Mike Piazza 2.00
HM10 Jason Giambi .75
HM11 Ivan Rodriguez 1.00
HM12 Alfonso Soriano 1.50
HM13 Dontrelle Willis .75
HM14 Chipper Jones 1.50
HM15 Mark Prior 1.50
HM16 Todd Helton 1.00
HM17 Randy Johnson 1.50
HM18 Hank Blalock 1.00
HM19 Ken Griffey Jr. 2.00
HM20 Roger Clemens 3.00

Midsummer Covers Relics

No Pricing
Production 10 Sets
Series 2
Production 10 Sets

On-Deck Relics

NM/M
Inserted 1:1,493
CB Carlos Beltran 15.00
HB Hank Blalock 12.00
TH Todd Helton 12.00
AP Albert Pujols 30.00
AR Alex Rodriguez 25.00
IR Ivan Rodriguez 15.00
SR Scott Rolen 15.00
AS Alfonso Soriano 15.00
SS Sammy Sosa 25.00
JT Jim Thome 15.00

Own The Game

NM/M
Complete Set (30): 15.00
Common Player: .50
Inserted 1:12
OG1 Ichiro Suzuki 3.00
OG2 Todd Helton 1.00
OG3 Adrian Beltre 1.00
OG4 Albert Pujols 4.00
OG5 Adam Dunn 1.00
OG6 Jim Thome 1.50
OG7 Miguel Tejada .75
OG8 David Ortiz 1.50
OG9 Manny Ramirez 1.50
OG10 Scott Rolen 1.50
OG11 Gary Sheffield .75
OG12 Vladimir Guerrero 1.50
OG13 Jim Edmonds .75
OG14 Ivan Rodriguez 1.00
OG15 Lance Berkman .50
OG16 Michael Young .50
OG17 Juan Pierre .50
OG18 Craig Biggio .50
OG19 Johnny Damon .75
OG20 Jimmy Rollins .50
OG21 Scott Podsednik .50
OG22 Bobby Abreu .50
OG23 Lyle Overbay .50
OG24 Carl Crawford .50
OG25 Mark Loretta .50
OG26 Vinny Castilla .50
OG27 Curt Schilling 1.00
OG28 Johan Santana .75
OG29 Randy Johnson 1.50
OG30 Pedro J. Martinez 1.50

Power Brokers Cut Signatures

Complete Set (51):
Common Player:

National Convention

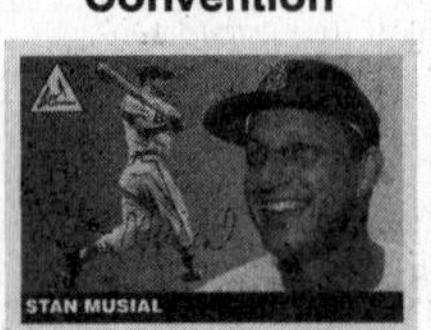

A latter-day attempt to recreate the "missing" four cards from its original high-number series, these cards were available only as a cello-wrapped set to purchasers of the VIP Attendee package at the 2005 National Sports Collectors Convention in Chicago. Cards are in the original 3-3/4" x 2-5/8" format.

NM/M
Complete Set (4): 20.00
Common Player: 3.00
175 Stan Musial 9.00
186 Whitey Ford 6.00
203 Bob Feller 5.00
209 Herb Score 3.00

Spokesman

NM/M
Complete Set (4): 10.00
Common Player: 3.00
Inserted 1:24
ARI1-4 Alex Rodriguez 3.00

Spokesman Autographs

NM/M
Production 1-200
ARA3 Alex Rodriguez/100 200.00
ARA4 Alex Rodriguez/200 180.00

Spokesman Relics

NM/M
Production 1-800
ARR2 Alex Rodriguez/50 30.00
ARR3 Alex Rodriguez/300 20.00
ARR4 Alex Rodriguez/800 20.00

Spokesman Relic

NM/M
Inserted 1:5,627
AR Alex Rodriguez 50.00

Spokesman Relic Autographs

13 Sets

Touch'em All Relics

Common Player:
Production 50 Sets
Series 2
Production 50 Sets

World Treasures

No Pricing
Production One Set

World Treasures - Dual

No Pricing
Production One Set

World Champion Red Sox Relics

NM/M
Common Player:
OC Orlando Cabrera 20.00
OC2 Orlando Cabrera 20.00
JD Johnny Damon 25.00
JD2 Johnny Damon 25.00
DL Derek Lowe 20.00
PM Pedro Martinez 20.00
DMI Doug Mientkiewicz 15.00
KM Kevin Millar 20.00
BM Bill Mueller 15.00
BM2 Bill Mueller 15.00
TN Trot Nixon 20.00
DO David Ortiz 20.00
DO2 David Ortiz 20.00
MR Manny Ramirez 25.00
MR2 Manny Ramirez 25.00
MR3 Manny Ramirez 25.00
PR Pokey Reese 15.00
DR Dave Roberts 15.00
CS Curt Schilling 25.00
KY Kevin Youkilis 15.00

1955 World Series Cut Signatures

Complete Set (21):
Common Player:

1955 World Series Dual Cut Signatures

Complete Set (3):
Common Player:
Production One Set

1955 Luis Aparicio

This original format (3-3/4" x 2-5/8") card was only available at the Chicago White Sox booth during the 2005 National Sports Collectors Convention in Chicago.

NM/M
NAT1 Luis Aparicio 7.50

2005 Topps All-Time Fan Favorites

NM/M
Complete Set (142): 40.00
Common Player: .25
Pack (6): 5.00
Box (24): 110.00
1 Andy Van Slyke .25
2 Bill Freehan .75
3 Bo Jackson .75
4 Mark Grace .50
5 Chuck Knoblauch .25
6 Candy Maldonado .25
7 David Cone .25
8 Don Mattingly 1.50
9 Darryl Strawberry .25
10 Dick Williams .25
11 Frank Robinson .75
12 Glenn Hubbard .25
13 Jim Abbott .25
14 Jeff Brantley .25
15 John Elway 2.00
16 Jim Leyland .25
17 Jesse Orosco .25
18 Joe Pepitone .25
19 J.R. Richard .25
20 Jerome Walton .25
21 Kevin Maas .25
22 Lou Brock .50
23 Lou Whitaker .25
24 Carl Erskine .25
25 John Candelaria .25
26 Mike Norris .25
27 Nolan Ryan 2.00
28 Pedro Guerrero .25
29 Roger Craig .25
30 Ron Gant .25
31 Sid Bream .25
32 Sid Fernandez .25
33 Tony LaRussa .25
34 Tom Seaver .75
35 Yogi Berra .75
36 Andre Dawson .75
37 Al Kaline .75
38 Brett Butler .25
39 Bob Gibson .75
40 Bill Mazeroski .25
41 Matty Alou .25
42 Chet Lemon .25
43 Cal Ripken Jr. 2.00
44 Dusty Baker .25
45 Dwight Gooden .25
46 Dave Winfield .50
47 Ernie Banks 1.00
48 Gary Carter .50
49 Howard Johnson .25
50 Mike Schmidt 1.50
51 Matt Williams .25
52 Ozzie Smith 1.00
53 Atlee Hammaker .25
54 Cleon Jones .25
55 Dave Johnson .25
56 Denny McLain .25
57 Don Zimmer .25
58 Gregg Jefferies .25
59 Jay Buhner .25
60 Johnny Bench .75
61 George Brett 1.50
62 Dale Murphy .50
63 Bob Welch .25
64 Paul O'Neill .25
65 Mark Lemke .25
66 Kevin McReynolds .25
67 Jesus Alou .25
68 Joe Pignatano .25
69 Jim Lonborg .25
70 Jerry Grote .25
71 Joaquin Andujar .25
72 Gary Gaetti .25
73 Edgar Martinez .25
74 Ron Darling .25
75 Duke Snider .75
76 Dave Magadan .25
77 Doug Drabek .25
78 Carl Yastrzemski 1.00
79 Mitch Williams .25
80 Marvin Miller .25
81 Michael Kay .25
82 Lonnie Smith .25
83 John Wetteland .25
84 Johnny Podres .25
85 Joe Morgan .25
86 Juan Marichal .50
87 Jeffrey Leonard .25
88 Bob Feller .50
89 Brooks Robinson .75
90 Clem Labine .25
91 Barry Lyons .25
92 Harmon Killebrew .75
93 Jim Frey .25
94 John Kruk .25
95 Ed Kranepool .25
96 Jose Oquendo .25
97 Johnny Pesky .25
98 John Tudor .25
99 Keith Hernandez .25
100 Monte Irvin .50
101 Marty Barrett .25
102 Oscar Gamble .25
103 Hank Bauer .25
104 Ron Blomberg .25
105 Rod Carew .50
106 Rick Dempsey .25
107 Walt Jocketty .25
108 Tom Kelly .25
109 Steve Carlton .50
110 Rick Monday .25
111 Rob Dibble .25
112 Shawon Dunston .25
113 Tony Gwynn .75
114 Tom Niedenfuer .25
115 Bob Dernier .25
116 Anthony Young .25
117 Reggie Jackson .75
118 Steve Garvey .25
119 Tim Raines .25
120 Whitey Ford .75
121 Rafael Santana .25
122 Scott Brosius .25
123 Stan Musial 1.50
124 Ron Santo .50
125 Wade Boggs .75
126 Jose Canseco .50
127 Brady Anderson .25
128 Vida Blue .25
129 Charlie Hough .25
130 Jim Kaat .25
131 Zane Smith .25
132 Bob Boone .25
133 Travis Fryman .25
134 Harold Baines .25
135 Orlando Cepeda .25
136 Mike Cuellar .25
137 Tito Fuentes .25
138 Daryl Boston .25
139 Jim Leyritz .25
140 Bill "Moose" Skowron .25
141 Theo Epstein .25
142 Barry Bonds 3.00

Refractor

Stars (1-142): 3-5X
Production 299 Sets

Gold Refractor

No Pricing
Production 25 Sets

Printing Plates

No Pricing
Production one set per color (4):

Autographs

NM/M
Common Autograph: 15.00
Rainbow: No Pricing
Production 10 Sets
JA Jim Abbott 30.00
JAN Joaquin Andujar 20.00
DB Dusty Baker 25.00
MB Marty Barrett 15.00
JBE Dr. Jim Beckett/SP/90 100.00
JB Johnny Bench/SP/40 125.00
YB Yogi Berra/SP/90 125.00
RB Ron Blomberg 15.00
JBR Jeff Brantley 20.00
SB Sid Bream 20.00
GB George Brett/SP/40 250.00
SBR Scott Brosius/SP/90 85.00
JBU Jay Buhner 20.00
BB Brett Butler 20.00
SC Steve Carlton/SP/90 60.00
GC Gary Carter 25.00
DC David Cone 25.00
RCR Roger Craig 25.00
RD Rick Dempsey 15.00
DD Doug Drabek 20.00
SD Shawon Dunston 20.00
JE John Elway/SP/40 250.00
BFE Bob Feller 85.00
SF Sid Fernandez 15.00
WF Whitey Ford/SP/90 150.00
BF Bill Freehan 20.00
GG Gary Gaetti 15.00
OG Oscar Gamble 15.00
RG Ron Gant/SP/90 50.00
SG Steve Garvey 50.00
BG Bob Gibson/SP/90 100.00
DG Dwight Gooden 40.00
JG Jerry Grote 30.00
TG Tony Gwynn/SP/90 125.00
AH Atlee Hammaker 15.00
GH Glenn Hubbard 20.00
MI Monte Irvin 50.00
BJ Bo Jackson 70.00
RJ Reggie Jackson/SP/40 100.00
GJ Gregg Jefferies 40.00
WJ Walt Jocketty/SP/90 60.00
DJ Dave Johnson 20.00
HJ Howard Johnson 20.00
CJ Cleon Jones 35.00
AK Al Kaline 60.00
TK Tom Kelly 25.00
HK Harmon Killebrew 85.00
CK Chuck Knoblauch 25.00
JK John Kruk 30.00
CL Clem Labine 40.00
TL Tony LaRussa 30.00
MLE Mark Lemke 15.00
CLE Chet Lemon 15.00
JLE Jim Leyland 20.00
JLO Jim Lonborg 15.00
BL Barry Lyons 15.00
KM Kevin Maas 15.00
DMA Dave Magadan 20.00
CM Candy Maldonado 15.00
JMA Juan Marichal/SP/90 140.00
EM Edgar Martinez 30.00
DM Don Mattingly 140.00
BM Bill Mazeroski 75.00
DMC Denny McLain 30.00
KMC Kevin McReynolds 15.00
MM Marvin Miller/SP/90 80.00
RM Rick Monday 30.00
DMU Dale Murphy 30.00
SM Stan Musial/SP/40 150.00
TN Tom Niedenfuer 15.00
MNO Mike Norris 15.00
PO Paul O'Neill 60.00
JO Jesse Orosco 25.00
JOQ Jose Oquendo 15.00
JPE Joe Pepitone 25.00

		NM/M
JPY	Johnny Pesky	65.00
JP	Joe Pignatano	30.00
TR	Tim Raines	25.00
JR	J.R. Richard	15.00
CR	Cal Ripken Jr./ SP/90	200.00
BR	Brooks Robinson/ SP/90	125.00
FR	Frank Robinson	100.00
NR	Nolan Ryan/SP/40	200.00
RS	Rafael Santana	20.00
RSA	Ron Santo/SP/90	75.00
MS	Mike Schmidt/ SP/40	160.00
LS	Lonnie Smith	15.00
DSN	Duke Snider/SP/40	60.00
DS	Darryl Strawberry	25.00
JT	John Tudor	35.00
AV	Andy Van Slyke	25.00
JW	Jerome Walton	15.00
BW	Bob Welch	30.00
JWE	John Wetteland	20.00
LW	Lou Whitaker/SP/90	60.00
DWI	Dick Williams/SP/90	75.00
MW	Matt Williams	25.00
MWI	Mitch Williams	25.00
DW	Dave Winfield/ SP/90	125.00
CY	Carl Yastrzemski/ SP/90	125.00
AY	Anthony Young	15.00
DZ	Don Zimmer/SP/40	50.00

Best Seat in House

NM/M

Production 125 unless noted.
Rainbow: No Pricing
Production 25 Sets

		NM/M
MFBJ	Don Mattingly, Whitey Ford, Yogi Berra, Reggie Jackson/50	50.00
RRRD	Brooks Robinson, Rick Dempsey, Frank Robinson, Cal Ripken Jr.	25.00
RR	Brooks Robinson, Cal Ripken Jr.	25.00
CR	Cal Ripken Jr., Frank Robinson	25.00
JD	Dave Johnson, Rick Dempsey	10.00
KMLW	Al Kaline, Lou Whitaker, Chet Lemon, Denny McLain	20.00

Fan Favorite Relics

NM/M

Inserted 1:Box
Rainbow: No Pricing
Production 25 Sets

		NM/M
WB	Wade Boggs/200	8.00
JCC	Jose Canseco/350	8.00
RC	Rod Carew/200	8.00
GC	Gary Carter/350	5.00
JC	Joe Carter/350	5.00
VC	Vince Coleman/200	5.00
ED	Eric Davis/200	5.00
AD	Andre Dawson/350	5.00
BD	Bucky Dent/200	5.00
LD	Lenny Dykstra/200	5.00
CF	Cecil Fielder/200	5.00
TG	Tony Gwynn/200	15.00
KH	Keith Hernandez/200	5.00
BJ	Bo Jackson/200	12.00
RJ	Reggie Jackson/350	10.00
WJ	Wally Joyner/200	5.00
WM	Willie McGee/350	5.00
DM	Dale Murphy/200	10.00
SM	Stan Musial/50	20.00
PO	Paul O'Neill/200	15.00
JR	Jim Rice/200	5.00
BR	Brooks Robinson/ 350	10.00
NR	Nolan Ryan/135	25.00
DS	Darryl Strawberry/350	5.00
BS	Bruce Sutter/350	7.50
MW	Mookie Wilson/135	5.00
CY	Carl Yastrzemski/50	25.00

League Leaders Tr-Signers

Production 50 Sets

Originals Relics

NM/M

Production 50 Sets
Actual vintage cards used.

		NM/M
WB	Wade Boggs/Bat	15.00
RC	Rod Carew/Bat	20.00
GC	Gary Carter/Bat	10.00
AD	Andre Dawson/Bat	10.00
TG	Tony Gwynn/Jsy	20.00
BJ	Bo Jackson/Jsy	25.00
RJ	Reggie Jackson/Bat	20.00
DM	Dale Murphy/Bat	15.00
JR	Jim Rice/Bat	15.00
NR	Nolan Ryan/Jsy	35.00

Rookie Dual Autograph

NM/M

Production 50 Sets

		NM/M
SC	Tom Seaver, Rod Carew	160.00

2005 Topps Bazooka

NM/M

Complete Set (220): 35.00
Common Player: .15
Common (191-220): .25
Pack (8): 2.50
Box (24): 50.00

		NM/M
1	Eric Gagne	.40
2	Aramis Ramirez	.40
3	Hank Blalock	.50
4	Jason Kendall	.15
5	Jeromy Burnitz	.15
6	Jose Guillen	.15
7	Tom Glavine	.40
8	Adrian Beltre	.25
9	Jason Bay	.25
10	Mark Teixeira	.40
11	Moises Alou	.25
12	Ronnie Belliard	.15
13	Aaron Guiel	.15
14	Vladimir Guerrero	.75
15	Scott Podsednik	.15
16	Alfonso Soriano	.75
17	Craig Wilson	.15
18	Jose Reyes	.25
19	Mark Prior	.75
20	Preston Wilson	.15
21	Shawn Green	.25
22	Troy Glaus	.25
23	Dmitri Young	.15
24	Garret Anderson	.25
25	Kazuo Matsui	.25
26	Kerry Wood	.75
27	Michael Young	.15
28	Oliver Perez	.15
29	Bartolo Colon	.15
30	Richie Sexson	.40
31	Brad Penny	.15
32	Carlos Guillen	.15
33	Carlos Zambrano	.25
34	David Wright	.50
35	Al Leiter	.25
36	Jack Wilson	.15
37	Ryan Drese	.15
38	Darin Erstad	.15
39	Derrek Lee	.25
40	Ivan Rodriguez	.50
41	Kenny Rogers	.15
42	Mike Piazza	1.00
43	Phil Nevin	.15
44	Geoff Jenkins	.15
45	Jorge Posada	.40
46	Khalil Greene	.40
47	Randy Johnson	.75
48	Rondell White	.15
49	Sammy Sosa	1.25
50	Vernon Wells	.15
51	Ben Sheets	.40
52	Brian Giles	.15
53	Carlos Delgado	.40
54	Derek Jeter	2.00
55	Jeremy Bonderman	.15
56	Magglio Ordonez	.25
57	Chad Tracy	.15
58	Kevin Brown	.15
59	Luis Castillo	.15
60	Lyle Overbay	.15
61	Mark Buehrle	.15
62	Mark Loretta	.15
63	Orlando Hudson	.15
64	Adam Dunn	.50
65	Frank Thomas	.50
66	Jake Peavy	.15
67	Jason Giambi	.40
68	Joe Mauer	.25
69	Marcus Giles	.15
70	Mike Lowell	.25
71	Roy Halladay	.15
72	Aaron Rowand	.15
73	Alex Rodriguez	1.50
74	Brian Lawrence	.15
75	Gabe Gross	.15
76	Johnny Estrada	.25
77	Justin Morneau	.40
78	Miguel Cabrera	.75
79	Alex Rios	.15
80	Gary Sheffield	.40
81	Jason Schmidt	.25
82	Juan Pierre	.15
83	Paul Konerko	.25
84	Jermaine Dye	.15
85	Rafael Furcal	.25
86	Torii Hunter	.25
87	A.J. Pierzynski	.15
88	Carl Pavano	.25
89	Carlos Lee	.25
90	J.D. Drew	.25
91	Javier Vazquez	.25
92	Lew Ford	.15
93	Ted Lilly	.15
94	Austin Kearns	.15
95	Chipper Jones	.75
96	Erubiel Durazo	.15
97	Johan Santana	.50
98	Josh Beckett	.25
99	Mariano Rivera	.25
100	Mark Mulder	.25
101	Andruw Jones	.25
102	Barry Zito	.25
103	Bret Boone	.15
104	Paul LoDuca	.15
105	Shannon Stewart	.15
106	Wily Mo Pena	.25
107	Dontrelle Willis	.25
108	Eric Chavez	.25
109	Jamie Moyer	.15
110	Joe Nathan	.15
111	Sidney Ponson	.15
112	John Smoltz	.25
113	Ichiro Suzuki	1.50
114	Javy Lopez	.25
115	Victor Martinez	.25
116	Ken Griffey Jr.	1.00
117	Lance Berkman	.25
118	Scott Hatteberg	.15
119	Jim Edmonds	.25
120	Kazuhisa Ishii	.15
121	Miguel Tejada	.40
122	Roger Clemens	2.00
123	Ryan Freel	.15
124	Albert Pujols	2.00
125	Hideo Nomo	.25
126	Mark Kotsay	.15
127	Melvin Mora	.15
128	Roy Oswalt	.25
129	Sean Casey	.25
130	Casey Blake	.15
131	Edgar Renteria	.25
132	Jeff Kent	.25
133	Rafael Palmeiro	.50
134	Tim Hudson	.25
135	Tony Batista	.15
136	Andy Pettitte	.25
137	Brian Roberts	.15
138	Jose Vidro	.15
139	Omar Vizquel	.15
140	Rich Harden	.25
141	Scott Rolen	.75
142	Carlos Beltran	.50
143	Chris Carpenter	.15
144	Manny Ramirez	.75
145	Nick Johnson	.15
146	Pat Burrell	.25
147	C.C. Sabathia	.15
148	Johnny Damon	.50
149	Juan Rivera	.15
150	Ken Harvey	.15
151	Kevin Millwood	.15
152	Larry Walker	.50
153	Aubrey Huff	.15
154	Curt Schilling	.75
155	Jake Westbrook	.15
156	Randy Wolf	.15
157	Zach Day	.15
158	Zack Greinke	.15
159	Brad Wilkerson	.15
160	Carl Crawford	.15
161	Jim Thome	.75
162	Mike Sweeney	.15
163	Pedro J. Martinez	.75
164	Travis Hafner	.15
165	Bobby Abreu	.25
166	Cliff Floyd	.15
167	David DeJesus	.15
168	David Ortiz	.75
169	Rocco Baldelli	.15
170	Todd Helton	.50
171	Dallas McPherson	.50
172	Kevin Youkilis	.15
173	Val Majewski	.15
174	Grady Sizemore	.25
175	Joey Gathright	.15
176	Rickie Weeks	.25
177	Jason Kubel	.25
178	Robinson Cano	.25
179	Nick Swisher	.25
180	Ryan Howard	.50
181	Tim Stauffer	.15
182	Merkin Valdez	.15
183	B.J. Upton	.40
184	Scott Kazmir	.40
185	Chris Burke	.25
186	Felix Hernandez	.50
187	Freddy Guzman	.15
188	Josh Labandeira	.15
189	Willy Taveras	.15
190	Casey Kotchman	.25
191	Steven Doetsch **RC**	.25
192	Melky Cabrera **RC**	.75
193	Luis Ramirez **RC**	.25
194	Chris Seddon **RC**	.40
195	Chad Orvella **RC**	.50
196	Ian Kinsler **RC**	1.50
197	Brandon Moss **RC**	1.00
198	Chadd Blasko **RC**	.50
199	Jeremy West **RC**	.75
200	Sean Marshall **RC**	.50
201	Matt DeSalvo **RC**	.50
202	Ryan Sweeney	1.50
203	Matt Lindstrom **RC**	.50
204	Ryan Goleski **RC**	.40
205	Brett Harper **RC**	.25
206	Chris Roberson **RC**	.25
207	Andre Ethier	1.00
208	Chris Denorfia **RC**	.25
209	Darren Fenster **RC**	.25
210	Elvys Quezada **RC**	.25
211	Kevin West **RC**	.50
212	Chaz Lytle **RC**	.50
213	James Jurries **RC**	.25
214	Matt Rogelstad **RC**	.25
215	Wade Robinson **RC**	.25
216	Ian Bladergroen **RC**	.75
217	Jake Dittler	.25
218	Nate McLouth **RC**	.40
219	Kole Strayhorn	.25
220	Jose Vaquedano **RC**	.25

Gold Chunks

Golds: 1-2X
Inserted 1:1

Minis

Mini: 1-2x
Inserted 1:1

Blasts

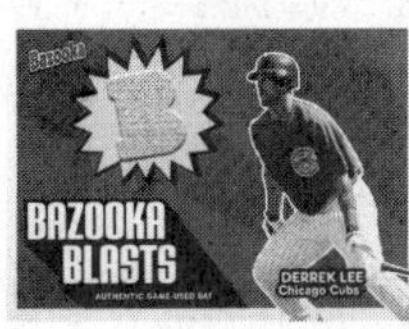

NM/M

Common Bat: 4.00

		NM/M
RA	Roberto Alomar	6.00
RB	Ron Belliard	4.00
AB	Angel Berroa	4.00
CB	Craig Biggio	8.00
HB	Hank Blalock	8.00
JB	Jeromy Burnitz	4.00
SB	Sean Burroughs	4.00
MC	Miguel Cabrera	10.00
VC	Vinny Castilla	4.00
TC	Tony Clark	4.00
JC	Jeff Conine	4.00
JCJ	Jose Cruz Jr.	4.00
AD	Adam Dunn	6.00
ME	Morgan Ensberg	4.00
DE	Darin Erstad	4.00
CE	Carl Everett	4.00
CF	Chone Figgins	4.00
JF	Julio Franco	4.00
NG	Nomar Garciaparra	8.00
AGO	Adrian Gonzalez	4.00
AG	Alex Gonzalez	4.00
LG	Luis Gonzalez	4.00
VG	Vladimir Guerrero	8.00
CGU	Carlos Guillen	4.00
CG	Cristian Guzman	4.00
TH	Todd Helton	6.00
LH	Livan Hernandez	4.00
RH	Richard Hidalgo	4.00
JK	Jeff Kent	4.00
PK	Paul Konerko	4.00
DL	Derrek Lee	4.00
ML	Mike Lowell	6.00
PM	Pedro Martinez	6.00
TM	Tino Martinez	6.00
VM	Victor Martinez	6.00
KM	Kazuo Matsui	8.00
MO	Magglio Ordonez	4.00
DO	David Ortiz	10.00
ARA	Aramis Ramirez	6.00
MR	Manny Ramirez	6.00
AR	Alex Rodriguez	20.00
CS	Curt Schilling	6.00
GS	Gary Sheffield	4.00
RS	Ruben Sierra	4.00
MT	Miguel Tejada	6.00
BU	B.J. Upton	10.00
JV	Jose Valentin	4.00
JVI	Jose Vidro	4.00
LW	Larry Walker	6.00
JW	Jayson Werth	4.00
PW	Preston Wilson	4.00
DW	David Wright	10.00
MY	Michael Young	4.00

Comics

NM/M

Complete Set (24): 8.00
Common Player: .25
Inserted 1:4

		NM/M
1	Randy Johnson	.50
2	Gary Sheffield	.25
3	Ken Griffey Jr.	.75
4	Alex Rodriguez	.75
5	Vladimir Guerrero	.50
6	David Bell	.25
7	Carlos Pena	.25
8	Eric Gagne	.25
9	Jim Thome	.50
10	Cleveland Indians	.25
11	Greg Maddux	.50
12	Miguel Tejada	.25
13	Ichiro Suzuki	.75
14	Mariano Rivera	.25
15	Juan Pierre	.25
16	Carl Crawford	.25
17	Mike Mussina	.25
18	Vladimir Guerrero	.50
19	Oliver Perez	.25
20	Ichiro Suzuki	.75
21	Johan Santana	.25
22	Kevin Brown	.25
23	Mike Piazza	.50
24	Randy Johnson	.50

Fun Facts Relics

NM/M

Common Relic: 4.00

		NM/M
HB	Harold Baines	4.00
WB	Wade Boggs	6.00
GB	George Brett	12.00
JC	Jose Canseco	8.00
RC	Rod Carew	12.00
GC	Gary Carter	4.00
DD	Darren Daulton	4.00
DE	Darrell Evans	4.00
CF	Cecil Fielder	8.00
KG	Ken Griffey Sr.	4.00
WH	Willie Horton	4.00
WJ	Wally Joyner	4.00
DJ	David Justice	4.00
DJ2	David Justice	4.00
RK	Ron Kittle	4.00
JL	Jim Leyritz	4.00
DP	Dave Parker	4.00
HR	Harold Reynolds	4.00
MR	Mickey Rivers	4.00
MS	Mike Schmidt	10.00
OS	Ozzie Smith	20.00
CS	Cory Snyder	4.00
DS	Darryl Strawberry	4.00
WW	Walt Weiss	4.00

Moments Relics

NM/M

Common Relic: 6.00

		NM/M
MB	Matt Bush	8.00
RH	Ramon Hernandez	6.00
TL	Terrence Long	6.00
MM	Mark Mulder	6.00
MP	Mike Piazza	12.00
JP	Jorge Posada	8.00
AP	Albert Pujols	25.00
AR	Alex Rodriguez	12.00
IR	Ivan Rodriguez	8.00
KR	Kenny Rogers	6.00
AS	Alfonso Soriano	6.00
MT	Mark Teixeira	6.00
FT	Frank Thomas	6.00

Tatoos

NM/M

Common Player: .25
Inserted 1:4

		NM/M
1	Alex Rodriguez	.50
2	Randy Johnson	.50
3	Jim Thome	.25
4	Pedro Martinez	.50
5	Roger Clemens	.50
6	Troy Glaus	.25
7	Todd Helton	.25
8	Albert Pujols	.50
9	Sammy Sosa	.50
10	David Wright	.50
11	Mike Piazza	.50
12	Gary Sheffield	.25
13	David Ortiz	.50
14	Hank Blalock	.25
15	Miguel Tejada	.25
16	Dontrelle Willis	.25
17	Ivan Rodriguez	.25
18	Nomar Garciaparra	.50
19	Alfonso Soriano	.25
20	Adrian Beltre	.25
21	Torii Hunter	.25
22	Brian Giles	.25
23	Chipper Jones	.50
24	Carlos Beltran	.25
25	Manny Ramirez	.50

4-on-1 Stickers

NM/M

Common Sticker: .50
Inserted 1:3 Hobby

		NM/M
1	Alex Rodriguez, Hank Blalock, Scott Rolen, Mike Lowell	1.50
2	Jorge Posada, Ivan Rodriguez, Joe Mauer, Johnny Estrada	.75
3	Ichiro Suzuki, Carlos Beltran, Jim Edmonds, Brian Giles	1.50
4	Jim Thome, Mark Teixeira, Paul Konerko, Lyle Overbay	1.00
5	Jose Reyes, Mark Loretta, Jose Vidro, Luis Castillo	.50
6	Miguel Tejada, Derek Jeter, Michael Young, Edgar Renteria	2.00
7	Roy Oswalt, Rich Harden, Johan Santana, Mark Prior	1.00
8	Mariano Rivera, Eric Gagne, Joe Nathan, John Smoltz	.50
9	Larry Walker, Carl Crawford, Preston Wilson, Garret Anderson	.50
10	Wily Mo Pena, Mark Kotsay, Alex Rios, Geoff Jenkins	.50
11	Victor Martinez, David Wright, Justin Morneau, Jason Bay	.75
12	Carlos Lee, Andruw Jones, Ronnie Belliard, Eric Chavez	.50
13	Vladimir Guerrero, Vernon Wells, Miguel Cabrera, Adrian Beltre	1.00
14	David Ortiz, Marcus Giles, Jeff Kent, Bobby Abreu	1.00
15	Juan Pierre, Torii Hunter, J.D. Drew, Austin Kearns	.50
16	Bartolo Colon, Manny Ramirez, Ken Griffey Jr., Dontrelle Willis	1.50
17	Andy Pettitte, Tim Hudson, Curt Schilling, Randy Johnson	1.00
18	Jamie Moyer, Zach Day, Al Leiter, Oliver Perez	.50
19	Kazuo Matsui, Roger Clemens, Khalil Greene, Javier Vazquez	2.00
20	Pedro Martinez, Rocco Baldelli, Mike Piazza, Melvin Mora	1.50
21	Hideo Nomo, Kazuhisa Ishii, Ken Harvey, Mike Sweeney	.50
22	Casey Blake, Ryan Freel, Bret Boone, Javy Lopez	.50
23	Craig Wilson, Shawn Green, Aramis Ramirez, Darin Erstad	.50
24	Troy Glaus, Lance Berkman, Scott Podsednik, Adam Dunn	.50
25	Albert Pujols, Gary Sheffield, Chipper Jones, Magglio Ordonez	2.00
26	Johnny Damon, Carlos Zambrano, Jason Schmidt, Ted Lilly	1.00

27 Sidney Ponson, Chris Carpenter, C.C. Sabathia, Kevin Millwood .50
28 Carl Pavano, Mark Mulder, Rafael Furcal, Jack Wilson .50
29 Jeremy Bonderman, Jake Westbrook, Zack Greinke, Tom Glavine .50
30 Omar Vizquel, Carlos Guillen, Roy Halladay, Ben Sheets .50
31 Kerry Wood, Kevin Brown, Moises Alou, Travis Hafner .75
32 Nick Johnson, Erubiel Durazo, Alfonso Soriano, Jason Giambi .75
33 Chad Tracy, Richie Sexson, Aubrey Huff, Brian Roberts .50
34 Todd Helton, Dmitri Young, Jeromy Burnitz, Jose Guillen .75
35 Juan Rivera, Shannon Stewart, Sammy Sosa, Cliff Floyd 1.00
36 Pat Burrell, Gabe Gross, Aaron Guiel, Paul LoDuca .50
37 A.J. Pierzynski, Orlando Hudson, David DeJesus, Brian Lawrence .50
38 Josh Beckett, Barry Zito, Mark Buehrle, Randy Wolf .50
39 Brad Penny, Jake Peavy, Rondell White, Brad Wilkerson .50
40 Ryan Drese, Kenny Rogers, Jermaine Dye, Lew Ford .50
41 Aaron Rowand, Jason Kendall, Tony Batista, Derrek Lee .50
42 Phil Nevin, Sean Casey, Rafael Palmeiro, Frank Thomas .75
43 Scott Hatteberg, Josh Labandeira, Jason Kubel, Nick Swisher .50
44 Freddy Guzman, Tim Stauffer, Merkin Valdez, Felix Hernandez .50
45 Willy Taveras, Grady Sizemore, Joey Gathright, Carlos Delgado .50
46 Scott Kazmir, Rickie Weeks, Dallas McPherson, Kevin Youkilis 1.00
47 Val Majewski, Casey Kotchman, Ryan Howard, Chris Burke .50
48 Robinson Cano, B.J. Upton, Jake Dittler, Ian Bladergroen 1.00
49 Brett Harper, James Jurries, Jeremy West, Matt Rogelstad 1.00
50 Darren Fenster, Nate Schierholtz, Brandon Moss, Ryan Sweeney 2.00
51 Chris Roberson, Steven Doetsch, Andre Ethier, Kevin West .50
52 Melky Cabrera, Ryan Goleski, Chris Denorfia, Chaz Lytle 1.00
53 Luis Ramirez, Matt DeSalvo, Sean Marshall, Jose Vaquedano .50
54 Chris Seddon, Chadd Blasko, Elvys Quezada, Wade Robinson .50
55 Nate McLouth, Matt Lindstrom, Kole Strayhorn, Ian Kinsler 2.50

Chicago White Sox World Series Commemorative

NM/M

Complete Boxed Set (56):
Common Card: .25
1 Mark Buehrle .50
2 A.J. Pierzynski .50
3 Juan Uribe .50
4 Tadahito Iguchi .50
5 Paul Konerko .75
6 Frank Thomas 2.50
7 Jermaine Dye .50
8 Aaron Rowand .50
9 Timo Perez .50
10 Jose Contreras .50
11 Carl Everett .50
12 Pablo Ozuna .50
13 Geoff Blum .50
14 Cliff Politte .50
15 Freddy Garcia .50
16 Bobby Jenks .50
17 Dustin Hermanson .50
18 Neal Cotts .50
19 Chris Widger .50
20 Jon Garland .50
21 Luis Vizcaino .50
22 Damaso Marte .50
23 Scott Podsednik .75
24 Willie Harris .50
25 Orlando Hernandez .50
26 Joe Crede .50
27 Ross Gload .50
28 Brian Anderson .50
29 Brandon McCarthy .50
30 Ozzie Guillen .50
31 Team Photo .50
32 Buehrle Pitches 6+ .25
33 Sox Win 99 Games .25
34 Buehrle Named Starter .25
35 Podsednik Steals 59 .25
36 Konerko Tops 40 HRs .25
37 Pierzynski Hits 2 of 5 .25
38 Chicago Socks Boston .25
39 Sox Sweep Sox .25
40 Pierzynski Safe .25
41 Paul Hits Bunyanesque Homer .25
42 It's a South Side Series .25
43 Sox Starters Win Four (Buehrle) .25
44 Sox Starters Win Four (Garland) .25
45 Sox Starters Win Four (Garcia) .25
46 Sox Starters Win Four (Contreras) .25
47 World Series Game 1 (Crede, Jenks) .25
48 World Series Game 2 (Konerko, Podsednik) .25
49 World Series Game 3 (Blum) .25
50 World Series Game 4 .25
51 World Series Game 4 (Garcia, Uribe) .25
52 Astros Get Swept .25
53 World Series Games 1, 4 (Podsednik, Dye, Iguchi) .25
54 ALCS MVP (Konerko) .25
55 World Series MVP (Dye) .25
--- Team Composite Box Topper (4-5/8" x 3-1/4") 4.00

2005 Topps Chrome

NM/M

Complete Set (472):
Common Player: .25
Common Rookie Auto. (221-252): 10.00
Inserted 1:20
Series 1 Hobby Pack (4): 3.00
Series 1 Hobby Box (20): 50.00
Series 2 Hobby Pack (4): 5.00
Series 2 Hobby Box (20): 90.00
1 Alex Rodriguez 2.50
2 Placido Polanco .25
3 Torii Hunter .50
4 Lyle Overbay .25
5 Johnny Damon .75
6 Johnny Estrada .25
7 Rich Harden .25
8 Francisco Rodriguez .25
9 Jarrod Washburn .25
10 Sammy Sosa 1.00
11 Randy Wolf .25
12 Jason Bay .50
13 Tom Glavine .50
14 Michael Tucker .25
15 Brian Giles .25
16 Chad Tracy .25
17 Jim Edmonds .50
18 John Smoltz .50
19 Roy Halladay .25
20 Hank Blalock .75
21 Darin Erstad .50
22 Todd Walker .25
23 Mike Hampton .25
24 Mark Bellhorn .25
25 Jim Thome 1.00
26 Shingo Takatsu .25
27 Jody Gerut .25
28 Vinny Castilla .25
29 Luis Castillo .25
30 Ivan Rodriguez .75
31 Craig Biggio .50
32 Joe Randa .25
33 Adrian Beltre .50
34 Scott Podsednik .25
35 Cliff Floyd .25
36 Livan Hernandez .25
37 Eric Byrnes .25
38 Jose Acevedo .25
39 Jack Wilson .25
40 Gary Sheffield .75
41 Chan Ho Park .25
42 Carl Crawford .25
43 Shawn Estes .25
44 David Bell .25
45 Jeff DaVanon .25
46 Brandon Webb .25
47 Lance Berkman .50
48 Melvin Mora .25
49 David Ortiz 1.00
50 Andruw Jones .50
51 Chone Figgins .25
52 Danny Graves .25
53 Preston Wilson .25
54 Jeremy Bonderman .25
55 Carlos Guillen .25
56 Cesar Izturis .25
57 Kazuo Matsui .25
58 Jason Schmidt .50
59 Jason Marquis .25
60 Jose Vidro .25
61 Al Leiter .40
62 Javier Vazquez .25
63 Erubiel Durazo .25
64 Scott Spiezio .25
65 Scot Shields .25
66 Edgardo Alfonzo .25
67 Miguel Tejada .50
68 Francisco Cordero .25
69 Brett Myers .25
70 Curt Schilling 1.00
71 Matt Kata .25
72 Bartolo Colon .25
73 Rodrigo Lopez .25
74 Tim Wakefield .25
75 Frank Thomas .75
76 Jimmy Rollins .50
77 Barry Zito .50
78 Hideo Nomo .50
79 Brad Wilkerson .25
80 Adam Dunn .75
81 Derrek Lee .50
82 Joe Crede .25
83 Nate Robertson .25
84 John Thomson .25
85 Mike Sweeney .25
86 Kip Wells .25
87 Eric Gagne .50
88 David Wells .25
89 Alex Sanchez .25
90 Bret Boone .25
91 Mark Loretta .25
92 Miguel Cabrera 1.00
93 Randy Winn .25
94 Adam Everett .25
95 Aubrey Huff .25
96 Kevin Mench .25
97 Frank Catalanotto .25
98 Flash Gordon .25
99 Scott Hatteberg .25
100 Albert Pujols 3.00
101 Jose Molina, Bengie Molina .25
102 Jason Johnson .25
103 Jay Gibbons .25
104 Byung-Hyun Kim .25
105 Joe Borowski .25
106 Mark Grudzielanek .25
107 Mark Buehrle .25
108 Paul Wilson .25
109 Ronnie Belliard .25
110 Reggie Sanders .25
111 Tim Redding .25
112 Brian Lawrence .25
113 Travis Hafner .40
114 Jose Hernandez .25
115 Ben Sheets .50
116 Johan Santana .75
117 Billy Wagner .40
118 Mariano Rivera .50
119 Steve Trachsel .25
120 Akinori Otsuka .25
121 Jose Valentin .25
122 Orlando Hernandez .25
123 Raul Ibanez .25
124 Mike Matheny .25
125 Vernon Wells .25
126 Jason Isringhausen .25
127 Jose Guillen .25
128 Danny Bautista .25
129 Marcus Giles .25
130 Javy Lopez .40
131 Kevin Millar .25
132 Kyle Farnsworth .25
133 Carl Pavano .25
134 Rafael Furcal .25
135 Casey Blake .25
136 Matt Holliday .50
137 Bobby Higginson .25
138 Adam Kennedy .25
139 Alex Gonzalez .25
140 Jeff Kent .40
141 Aaron Guiel .25
142 Shawn Green .40
143 Bill Hall .25
144 Shannon Stewart .25
145 Juan Rivera .25
146 Coco Crisp .25
147 Mike Mussina .50
148 Eric Chavez .50
149 Jon Lieber .25
150 Vladimir Guerrero 1.00
151 Alex Cintron .25
152 Luis Matos .25
153 Sidney Ponson .25
154 Trot Nixon .25
155 Greg Maddux 2.00
156 Edgar Renteria .50
157 Ryan Freel .25
158 Matt Lawton .25
159 Mark Prior 1.00
160 Josh Beckett .50
161 Ken Harvey .25
162 Angel Berroa .25
163 Juan Encarnacion .25
164 Wes Helms .25
165 Brad Radke .25
166 Phil Nevin .25
167 Mike Cameron .25
168 Billy Koch .25
169 Bobby Crosby .50
170 Mike Lieberthal .25
171 Robert Mackowiak .25
172 Sean Burroughs .25
173 J.T. Snow Jr. .25
174 Paul Konerko .40
175 Luis Gonzalez .25
176 John Lackey .25
177 Oliver Perez .25
178 Brian Roberts .25
179 Bill Mueller .25
180 Carlos Lee .25
181 Corey Patterson .50
182 Sean Casey .40
183 Cliff Lee .25
184 Jason Jennings .25
185 Dmitri Young .25
186 Juan Uribe .25
187 Andy Pettitte .50
188 Juan Gonzalez .50
189 Orlando Hudson .25
190 Jason Phillips .25
191 Braden Looper .25
192 Lew Ford .25
193 Mark Mulder .40
194 Bobby Abreu .40
195 Jason Kendall .25
196 Khalil Greene .50
197 A.J. Pierzynski .25
198 Tim Worrell .25
199 So Taguchi .25
200 Jason Giambi .50
201 Tony Batista .25
202 Carlos Zambrano .50
203 Trevor Hoffman .25
204 Odalis Perez .25
205 Jose Cruz Jr. .25
206 Michael Barrett .25
207 Chris Carpenter .25
208 Michael Young .25
209 Toby Hall .25
210 Woody Williams .25
211 Chris Denorfia **RC** 1.00
212 Darren Fenster **RC** 1.00
213 Elvys Quezada **RC** 2.00
214 Ian Kinsler **RC** 4.00
215 Matt Lindstrom **RC** 2.00
216 Ryan Goleski **RC** 2.00
217 Ryan Sweeney 3.00
218 Sean Marshall **RC** 1.00
219 Steven Doetsch **RC** 2.00
220 Wade Robinson **RC** 3.00
221 Andre Ethier 40.00
222 Brandon Moss **RC** 20.00
223 Chadd Blasko **RC** 10.00
224 Chris Roberson **RC** 10.00
225 Chris Seddon **RC** 10.00
226 Ian Bladergroen **RC** 15.00
227 Jake Dittler 10.00
228 Jose Vaquedano **RC** 10.00
229 Jeremy West **RC** 15.00
230 Kole Strayhorn 10.00
231 Kevin West **RC** 10.00
232 Luis Ramirez **RC** 10.00
233 Melky Cabrera **RC** 40.00
234 Nate Schierholtz 15.00
235 Billy Butler **RC** 50.00
236 Brandon Szymanski **RC** 10.00
237 Chad Orvella **RC** 10.00
238 Chip Cannon **RC** 20.00
239 Eric Nielsen **RC** 10.00
240 Erik Cordier **RC** 10.00
241 Glen Perkins **RC** 15.00
242 Justin Verlander **RC** 60.00
243 Kevin Melillo **RC** 15.00
244 Landon Powell **RC** 20.00
245 Matt Campbell **RC** 10.00
246 Michael Rogers **RC** 15.00
247 Nate McLouth **RC** 20.00
248 Scott Mathieson **RC** 10.00
249 Shane Costa 10.00
250 Tony Giarratano **RC** 10.00
251 Tyler Pelland **RC** 10.00
252 Wes Swackhamer **RC** 10.00
253 Garret Anderson .50
254 Randy Johnson 1.00
255 Charles Thomas .25
256 Rafael Palmeiro .75
257 Kevin Youkilis .25
258 Freddy Garcia .25
259 Magglio Ordonez .25
260 Aaron Harang .25
261 Grady Sizemore .50
262 Chin-Hui Tsao .25
263 Eric Munson .25
264 Juan Pierre .25
265 Brad Lidge .25
266 Brian Anderson .25
267 Todd Helton .75
268 Chad Cordero .25
269 Kris Benson .25
270 Brad Halsey .25
271 Jermaine Dye .25
272 Manny Ramirez 1.00
273 Adam Eaton .25
274 Brett Tomko .25
275 Bucky Jacobsen .25
276 Dontrelle Willis .50
277 B.J. Upton .25
278 Rocco Baldelli .25
279 Ryan Drese .25
280 Ichiro Suzuki 2.50
281 Brandon Lyon .25
282 Nick Green .25
283 Jerry Hairston .25
284 Mike Lowell .25
285 Kerry Wood 1.00
286 Omar Vizquel .25
287 Carlos Beltran .50
288 Carlos Pena .25
289 Jeff Weaver .25
290 Chad Moeller .25
291 Joe Mays .25
292 Terrmel Sledge .25
293 Richard Hidalgo .25
294 Justin Duchscherer .25
295 Eric Milton .25
296 Ramon Hernandez .25
297 Jose Reyes .50
298 Joel Pineiro .25
299 Matt Morris .25
300 John Halama .25
301 Gary Matthews .25
302 Ryan Madson .25
303 Mark Kotsay .25
304 Carlos Delgado .50
305 Casey Kotchman .25
306 Greg Aquino .25
307 LaTroy Hawkins .25
308 Jose Contreras .25
309 Ken Griffey Jr. 2.00
310 C.C. Sabathia .25
311 Brandon Inge .25
312 John Buck .25
313 Hee Seop Choi .25
314 Chris Capuano .25
315 Jesse Crain .25
316 Geoff Jenkins .25
317 Mike Piazza 2.00
318 Jorge Posada .50
319 Nick Swisher .25
320 Kevin Millwood .25
321 Mike Gonzalez .25
322 Jake Peavy .25
323 Dustin Hermanson .25
324 Jeremy Reed .25
325 Alfonso Soriano 1.00
326 Alexis Rios .25
327 David Eckstein .25
328 Shea Hillenbrand .25
329 Russ Ortiz .25
330 Kurt Ainsworth .25
331 Orlando Cabrera .25
332 Carlos Silva .25
333 Ross Gload .25
334 Josh Phelps .25
335 Mike Maroth .25
336 Guillermo Mota .25
337 Chris Burke .25
338 David DeJesus .25
339 Jose Lima .25
340 Cristian Guzman .25
341 Nick Johnson .25
342 Victor Zambrano .25
343 Rod Barajas .25
344 Damian Miller .25
345 Chase Utley .50
346 Sean Burnett .25
347 David Wells .25
348 Dustan Mohr .25
349 Bobby Madritsch .25
350 Reed Johnson .25
351 R.A. Dickey .25
352 Scott Kazmir .25
353 Tony Womack .25
354 Thomas Perez .25
355 Esteban Loaiza .25
356 Tomokazu Ohka .25
357 Ramon Ortiz .25
358 Richie Sexson .50
359 J.D. Drew .40
360 Barry Bonds 4.00
361 Aramis Ramirez .50
362 Wily Mo Pena .25
363 Jeromy Burnitz .25
364 Nomar Garciaparra 2.00
365 Brandon Backe .25
366 Derek Lowe .25
367 Doug Davis .25
368 Joe Mauer .75
369 Endy Chavez .25
370 Bernie Williams .50
371 Jason Michaels .25
372 Craig Wilson .25
373 Ryan Klesko .25
374 Ray Durham .25
375 Jose Lopez .25
376 Jeff Suppan .25
377 David Bush .25
378 Marlon Byrd .25
379 Roy Oswalt .40
380 Rondell White .25
381 Troy Glaus .50
382 Scott Hairston .25
383 Chipper Jones 1.00
384 Daniel Cabrera .25
385 Jon Garland .25
386 Austin Kearns .25
387 Jake Westbrook .25
388 Aaron Miles .25
389 Omar Infante .25
390 Paul LoDuca .25
391 Morgan Ensberg .25
392 Tony Graffanino .25
393 Milton Bradley .25
394 Keith Ginter .25
395 Justin Morneau .75
396 Tony Armas Jr. .25
397 Kevin Brown .25
398 Marco Scutaro .25
399 Tim Hudson .50
400 Pat Burrell .40
401 Jeff Cirillo .25
402 Larry Walker .50
403 Dewon Brazelton .25
404 Shigetoshi Hasegawa .25
405 Octavio Dotel .25
406 Michael Cuddyer .25
407 Junior Spivey .25
408 Zack Greinke .25
409 Roger Clemens 3.00
410 Chris Shelton .25
411 Ugueth Urbina .25
412 Rafael Betancourt .25
413 Willie Harris .25
414 Keith Foulke .25
415 Larry Bigbie .25
416 Paul Byrd .25
417 Troy Percival .25
418 Pedro J. Martinez 1.00
419 Matt Clement .25
420 Ryan Wagner .25
421 Jeff Francis .25
422 Jeff Conine .25
423 Wade Miller .25
424 Gavin Floyd .25
425 Kazuhisa Ishii .25
426 Victor Santos .25
427 Jacque Jones .25
428 Hideki Matsui 2.00
429 Cory Lidle .25
430 Jose Castillo .25
431 Alex Gonzalez .25
432 Kirk Rueter .25
433 Jolbert Cabrera .25
434 Erik Bedard .25
435 Ricky Ledee .25
436 Mark Hendrickson .25
437 Layne Nix .25
438 Jason Frasor .25
439 Kevin Gregg .25
440 Derek Jeter 3.00
441 Jaret Wright .25
442 Edwin Jackson .25
443 Moises Alou .50
444 Aaron Rowand .25
445 Kazuhito Tadano .25
446 Luis Gonzalez .40
447 A.J. Burnett .40
448 Jeff Bagwell .50
449 Brad Penny .25
450 Corey Koskie .25
451 Mark Ellis .25
452 Hector Luna .25
453 Miguel Olivo .25
454 Scott Rolen 1.00
455 Ricardo Rodriguez .25
456 Eric Hinske .25
457 Tim Salmon .25
458 Adam LaRoche .25
459 B.J. Ryan .25
460 Steve Finley .25
461 Joe Nathan .25
462 Vicente Padilla .25
463 Yadier Molina .25
464 Tino Martinez .25
465 Mark Teixeira .50
466 Kelvim Escobar .25
467 Pedro Feliz .25
468 Ryan Garko **RC** 4.00

469 Bobby Livingston **RC** 2.00
470 Yorman Bazardo **RC** 3.00
471 Michael Bourn 2.00
472 Andy LaRoche **RC** 10.00

Refractor

Refractor: 2-3X
Inserted 1:6
Rookie Auto. (221-252): 1-1.5X
Production 500

Black Refractor

Black Refractor: 3-5X
Production 225
Rookie Auto. (221-252): 1.5-3X
Production 200

Gold Refractor

No Pricing
Production One Set

X-Fractor

Cards (1-220): 5-10X
Rookie Auto. (221-234): No Pricing
Production 25 Sets

Printing Plates

No Pricing
Production one set per color.

A-Rod Throwbacks

NM/M
Common A-Rod: 3.00
ARI1-ARI4 Alex Rodriquez 3.00

Chrome The Game Relics

NM/M
Common Player: 5.00
Inserted 1:Box
JB Jeff Bagwell 8.00
WB Wade Boggs 6.00
TH Torii Hunter 5.00
MPI Mike Piazza 8.00
JP Jorge Posada 6.00
MP Mark Prior 8.00
AR Alex Rodriguez 15.00
JS John Smoltz 8.00
AS Alfonso Soriano 8.00
SS Sammy Sosa 10.00
MY Michael Young 5.00

Chrome The Game Patch Relics

NM/M
Common Player: 10.00
JB Jeff Bagwell 15.00
JBE Josh Beckett 10.00
LB Lance Berkman 10.00
BB Bret Boone 10.00
AD1 Adam Dunn 15.00
AD2 Adam Dunn 15.00
TG Troy Glaus 10.00
TH Todd Helton 15.00
KI Kazuhisa Ishii 10.00
CJ Chipper Jones 20.00
PL Paul LoDuca 10.00
ML Mike Lowell 10.00
PM Pedro Martinez 20.00
HN Hideo Nomo 20.00
MO Maggilo Ordonez 10.00
MPI Mike Piazza 20.00
AP Albert Pujols 25.00
AR Alex Rodriguez 25.00
CS C.C. Sabathia 10.00
SS Sammy Sosa 20.00
MT Mark Teixeira 15.00
FT Frank Thomas 15.00
DW Dontrelle Willis 10.00
KW Kerry Wood 20.00

Dem Bums Autographs

NM/M
Inserted 1:1,816
CE Carl Erskine 50.00
DS Duke Snider 85.00

2005 Topps Cracker Jack

NM/M
Complete Set (240):
Common Player: .25
Common SP: 3.00
Inserted 1:3
Pack (8): 4.00
Box (20): 70.00
1 David Wright/SP 8.00
2 Rafael Furcal .25
3 Alex Rodriguez 1.50
3 Alex Rodriguez/SP/Fldg 5.00
4 Victor Martinez/SP 3.00
5 Ken Griffey Jr. 1.50
6 Bobby Crosby/SP 3.00
7 Ivan Rodriguez .50
8 Darin Erstad .25
9 Javy Lopez .25
10 Brian Giles .25
11 Aaron Rowand/SP 3.00
12 Joe Torre .25
13 Zack Greinke/SP 3.00
14 Shannon Stewart .25
15 Jack Wilson .25
16 Jose Vidro .25
17 Josh Beckett .40
--- Josh Beckett (No number.) 4.00
18 Barry Zito .40
19 Bret Boone .25
20 Greg Maddux 1.00
21 Carl Crawford/SP 3.00
22 Mark Teixeira .50
23 Jason Schmidt .40
24 Kazuhisa Ishii .25
25 Mike Piazza 1.00
26 Daniel Cabrera/SP 3.00
27 Mike Lieberthal .25
28 Gil Meche .25
29 Phil Nevin .25
30 Adrian Beltre/SP 3.00
31 Chipper Jones/SP 4.00
32 Zach Day .25
33 Ben Sheets .40
34 Carlos Zambrano .40
35 Melvin Mora .25
36 Joe Mauer .75
37 Ken Harvey .25
38 Bernie Williams .40
39 Mike Maroth .25
40 Eric Chavez .40
41 Matt Lawton/SP 3.00
42 Ray Durham .25
43 Vernon Wells .25
44 Mike Lowell .25
45 Jim Thome .50
46 Joel Pineiro .25
47 Lance Berkman .40
48 Ryan Klesko .25
49 Adam Dunn .50
50 Vladimir Guerrero .75
51 Eric Gagne/SP 4.00
52 Richie Sexson .40
53 Javier Vazquez .25
54 Roy Oswalt .40
55 Carlos Delgado .50
56 John Buck/SP 3.00
57 Kenny Rogers .25
58 Sidney Ponson .25
59 Vicente Padilla .25
60 Mark Prior/SP .75
60 Mark Prior/SP/Portrait 4.00
61 A.J. Pierzynski .25
62 Aubrey Huff .25
63 Shea Hillenbrand .25
64 Carlos Guillen .25
65 Lyle Overbay .25
66 Al Leiter .25
67 Eric Hinske .25
68 Laynce Nix .25
69 Scott Hairston .25
70 Roger Clemens 2.00
71 Cesar Izturis/SP 3.00
72 Shawn Green .25
73 Marcus Giles .25
74 Rafael Palmeiro .50
75 Melky Cabrera/SP 3.00
75 Gary Sheffield/SP 4.00
76 Juan Pierre .25
77 Pat Burrell .40
78 Sean Burroughs .25
79 Frank Thomas .50
80 Andruw Jones .40
81 C.C. Sabathia .25
82 Jeff Bagwell .50
83 Tom Glavine .40
84 Craig Wilson/SP 3.00
85 Johan Santana .75
85 Johan Santana/SP/Portrait 4.00
86 Raul Ibanez .25
87 Sean Casey .25
88 Bucky Jacobsen .25
89 B.J. Upton .40
90 Bobby Abreu .40
91 Geoff Jenkins .25
92 Troy Glaus .40
93 Dontrelle Willis .40
94 Jose Lima .25
95 Rocco Baldelli .25
96 Aramis Ramirez .40
97 Paul LoDuca .25
98 Torii Hunter .40
99 Jay Payton .25
100 Carlos Beltran .50
101 Jaret Wright .25
102 Jason Bay .40
103 Cliff Floyd .25
104 Mike Sweeney .25
105 Sammy Sosa 1.50
106 Khalil Greene/SP 4.00
107 David DeJesus .25
108 Jermaine Dye .25
109 Miguel Cabrera .75
110 Miguel Tejada/SP 5.00
111 Johnny Estrada/SP 3.00
112 Ronnie Belliard/SP 3.00
113 Austin Kearns .25
114 Erubiel Durazo .25
115 Preston Wilson .25
116 Hideo Nomo .40
117 Dmitri Young .25
118 Jon Lieber .25
119 Derrek Lee .40
120 Todd Helton .50
121 Omar Vizquel .25
122 Wily Mo Pena .40
123 J.D. Drew .40
124 Matt Holliday .25
125 Ichiro Suzuki 1.50
126 Mark Buehrle/SP 3.00
127 Eric Munson .25
128 Jeff Kent .25
129 Kerry Wood .75
130 Mariano Rivera .50
131 Nick Johnson .25
132 Randy Winn .25
133 Phil Garner .25
134 Jose Reyes .50
135 Michael Young/SP 3.00
135 Ian Kinsler/SP 6.00
136 Jose Contreras .25
137 Oliver Perez .25
138 Roy Halladay .40
139 Kevin Millwood .25
140 Jorge Posada .40
141 Mike Cameron .25
142 Edgardo Alfonzo .25
143 Chris Shelton .25
144 Luis Castillo .25
145 Alfonso Soriano .75
146 Ryan Dresse/SP 3.00
147 Mark Mulder .40
148 Jason Giambi .25
149 Travis Hafner .25
150 Randy Johnson .75
151 Paul Konerko/SP 3.00
152 Mike Mussina .50
153 Brad Wilkerson .25
154 Tim Hudson .40
155 Garret Anderson .40
156 Chase Utley/SP 3.00
157 Jamie Moyer .25
158 Scott Kazmir .40
159 Brett Myers .25
160 Kazuo Matsui .25
161 Orlando Hudson .25
162 Luis Gonzalez .25
163 Kevin Youkilis .25
164 Jason Kendall/SP .25
164 Landon Powell/SP 3.00
165 Hank Blalock .50
166 Mark Loretta/SP 3.00
167 Miguel Cairo .25
168 Corey Patterson .40
169 Carlos Zambrano .25
170 Magglio Ordonez .25
171 J.T. Snow .25
172 Randy Wolf .25
173 Rich Harden .40
174 Bartolo Colon .25
175 Derek Jeter 2.00
176 Casey Kotchman/SP 3.00
177 Val Majewski .25
178 Grady Sizemore .50
179 Rickie Weeks .25
180 Robinson Cano .75
181 Nick Swisher/SP 3.00
182 Ryan Howard 1.50
183 John Van Benschoten .25
184 Delmon Young .50
185 Aaron Hill .25
186 Chris Burke/SP 3.00
187 Merkin Valdez .25
188 Jeremy Reed .25
189 Conor Jackson .25
190 Melky Cabrera .25
191 Joey Gathright/SP 3.00
192 Gavin Floyd .25
193 Joe Blanton .25
194 Jason Kubel .25
195 Jeff Francis .25
196 Angel Guzman/SP 3.00
197 Dallas McPherson .25
198 Melky Cabrera **RC** 1.50
199 Jake Dittler .25
200 Elvys Quezada **RC** .50
201 Ian Kinsler/SP **RC** 6.00
202 Nate McLouth **RC** .50
203 Chris Seddon **RC** .75
204 Chad Orvella **RC** .50
205 Ian Bladergroen **RC** 1.00
206 James Jurries/SP **RC** 4.00
207 Landon Powell **RC** .75
208 Eric Nielsen **RC** .50
209 Chris Roberson **RC** .50
210 Andre Ethier 2.00
211 Chris Denorfia/SP **RC** 4.00
212 Darren Fenster **RC** .50
213 Jeremy West **RC** 1.00
214 Sean Marshall **RC** .50
215 Ryan Sweeney 1.50
216 Steven Doetsch/SP **RC** 3.00
217 Kevin Melillo **RC** .50
218 Chip Cannon **RC** 1.00
219 Tony LaRussa .25
220 Chris Carpenter .25
221 Edgar Renteria/SP Red Sox 3.00
221 Edgar Renteria/SP Cardinals 3.00
222 Albert Pujols 2.00
223 Jim Edmonds .40
224 Jason Marquis .25
225 Scott Rolen/SP 4.00
226 Larry Walker/SP 4.00
227 Matt Morris .25
228 Mike Matheny 3.00
228 Mike Matheny/SP Cardinals 3.00
229 Jeromy Burnitz .25
230 Terry Francona .25
231 Johnny Damon/SP 4.00
232 Keith Foulke .25
233 Trot Nixon .25
234 Manny Ramirez .75
235 David Ortiz/SP 4.00
236 Pedro Martinez/SP Mets 4.00
236 Pedro J. Martinez/SP Red Sox 4.00
237 Curt Schilling .75
238 Kevin Millar .25
239 Bill Mueller .25
240 Mark Bellhorn .25
Josh Beckett/SP 3.00

Mini Blue

Stars: 8-15X
SP's: 4-6X
Production 50 Sets

Mini Grey

No Pricing
Production 25 Sets

Mini Red

Stars: 1-2X
Inserted 1:1
SP's: .75-1.5X
Inserted 1:20

Mini Stickers

Stars: 1-2X
Inserted 1:1
SP's: .75-1.5X
Inserted 1:20

Mini White

No Pricing
Production One Set

Autographs

NM/M
Production 50 Sets
Bonds Production 25
GA Garret Anderson/50 30.00
CB Carlos Beltran/50 80.00
EC Eric Chavez/50 30.00
CC Carl Crawford/50 40.00
EG Eric Gagne 40.00
AR Alex Rodriguez 250.00
CS C.C. Sabathia/50 50.00
JS Johan Santana 60.00
CW Craig Wilson/50 25.00
DW David Wright/50 150.00

Secret Surprise Autographs

NM/M
Common Auto.: 8.00
GA Garret Anderson 15.00
EC Eric Chavez 15.00
CC Carl Crawford 10.00
EG Eric Gagne 20.00
AG Angel Guzman 8.00
SK Scott Kazmir 25.00
MK Mark Kotsay/100 15.00
ML Mark Loretta/100 15.00
DM Dallas McPherson/100 15.00
KM Kevin Millar 15.00
MM Melvin Mora 15.00
CN Chris Nelson 10.00
RR Richie Robnett 10.00
AR Alex Rodriguez/100 250.00
CS C.C. Sabathia 20.00
JS Johan Santana 50.00
CT Curtis Thigpen 15.00
CW Craig Wilson 10.00
DW David Wright 50.00

Take Me Out To/Ballgame Relics

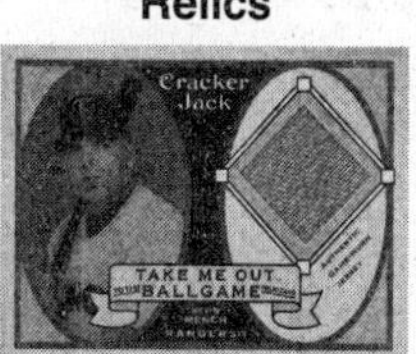

NM/M
Inserted 1:16
JB Jeff Bagwell 6.00
RB Ronnie Belliard 4.00
CB Carlos Beltran 8.00
AB Adrian Beltre 6.00
LB1 Lance Berkman 6.00
LB2 Lance Berkman 6.00
AB1 Angel Berroa 4.00
AB2 Angel Berroa 4.00
CBI Craig Biggio 6.00
HB1 Hank Blalock 8.00
HB2 Hank Blalock 8.00
HB3 Hank Blalock 8.00
SB Sean Burroughs 4.00
MC Miguel Cabrera 8.00
VC Vinny Castilla 4.00
EC1 Eric Chavez 6.00
EC2 Eric Chavez 6.00
BC Bobby Cox 6.00
CC Coco Crisp 4.00
BCR Bobby Crosby 6.00
AD Adam Dunn 8.00
JE1 Jim Edmonds 6.00
JE2 Jim Edmonds 6.00
DE Darin Erstad 4.00
JE Johnny Estrada 4.00
RF Rafael Furcal 6.00
JG Jody Gerut 4.00
JGI Jay Gibbons 4.00
MG Marcus Giles 4.00
TG Troy Glaus 6.00
LG Luis Gonzalez 4.00
NG Nick Green 4.00
SG Shawn Green 4.00
VG Vladimir Guerrero 10.00
JGU Jose Guillen 6.00
CG Cristian Guzman 4.00
TH Todd Helton 8.00
THU Torii Hunter 6.00
JJ Jacque Jones 4.00
JK Jason Kendall 4.00
BK Bobby Kielty 4.00
RK Ryan Klesko 4.00
PK Paul Konerko 4.00
MK Mark Kotsay 4.00
AL Adam LaRoche 6.00
VM Victor Martinez 6.00
KME Kevin Mench 4.00
DM Doug Mientkiewicz 4.00
KM Kevin Millar 10.00
MM Melvin Mora 6.00
PN Phil Nevin 4.00
LN Laynce Nix 4.00
MO Magglio Ordonez 4.00
DO David Ortiz 10.00
RP Rafael Palmeiro 8.00
CP Corey Patterson 6.00
MP Mike Piazza 12.00
JP1 Jorge Posada 8.00
JP2 Jorge Posada 8.00
AP Albert Pujols 20.00
MR Manny Ramirez 10.00
JR Jeremy Reed 8.00
MRE Mike Restovich 4.00
AR Alex Rodriguez 15.00
ARA Aramis Ramirez 6.00
IR1 Ivan Rodriguez 8.00
IR2 Ivan Rodriguez 8.00
RS Reggie Sanders 4.00
BS Benito Santiago 4.00
GS Gary Sheffield 8.00
AS Alfonso Soriano 8.00
MT1 Mark Teixeira 8.00
MT2 Mark Teixeira 8.00
MT3 Mark Teixeira 8.00
MTE1 Miguel Tejada 8.00
MTE2 Miguel Tejada 8.00
CT Charles Thomas 4.00
JT Jim Thome 8.00
JTO Joe Torre 10.00
OV Omar Vizquel 6.00
BW Bernie Williams 6.00
DW Dontrelle Willis 8.00
MY Michael Young 6.00

1,2,3 Strikes You're Out Relics

NM/M
Inserted 1:204
JB Josh Beckett 8.00
RD Ryan Drese 5.00
RO Russ Ortiz 5.00
BR Brad Radke 8.00
CS Curt Schilling 15.00
JW Jaret Wright 8.00

2005 Topps eTopps Alex Rodrguez Promos

NM/M
Complete Set (3): 12.00
Common Card: 4.00
1 of 100: 2X
1 of 50: 3X
AR1 Alex Rodriguez (follow-through) 4.00
AR2 Alex Rodriguez/Throwing 4.00
AR3 Alex Rodriguez/Btg 4.00

2005 Topps eTopps

Topps continued its on-line card program for a fifth year in 2005. Initial Player Offerings (about $5-7 per card) were again made for one week, with allocations having to be made for some cards in high demand. The number of each card actually sold is shown parenthetically. After the IPO, cards could be bought and sold within portfolios, or physically delivered for a fee. The 2-1/2" x 3-1/2" cards' fronts have an action photo at top and a portrait photo below. Backs repeat the portrait photo, have a 2004 recap and 2005 "prospectus," and a few biographical bits and stats. A total of 111 cards was issued, skip-numbered between 1-220. Values shown are for cards in a virtual portfolio, rather than "in hand."

NM/M
Complete Set (111): 325.00
Common Player: 1.50
1 Los Angeles Angels of Anaheim/1,018 1.50
2 Arizona Diamondbacks/1,000 1.50
3 Atlanta Braves/1,275 2.00
4 Baltimore Orioles/1,189 1.50
5 Boston Red Sox/2,538 1.50
6 Chicago Cubs/1,300 1.50
7 Chicago White Sox/1,199 2.75
8 Cincinnati Reds/770 1.50
9 Cleveland Indians/974 1.50
10 Colorado Rockies/736 1.50
11 Detroit Tigers/832 1.50
12 Florida Marlins/863 1.50
13 Houston Astros/1,227 2.00
14 Kansas City Royals/807 1.50
15 Los Angeles Dodgers/1,000 1.50
16 Milwaukee Brewers/728 1.50
17 Minnesota Twins/888 1.50
18 New York Mets/1,300 1.50
19 New York Yankees/2,600 1.75
20 Oakland Athletics/739 1.75
21 Philadelphia Phillies/090 1.50
22 Pittsburgh Pirates/776 2.00
23 San Diego Padres/818 1.50
24 San Francisco Giants/1,051 2.50
25 Seattle Mariners/800 1.50
26 St. Louis Cardinals/1,300 2.00
27 Tampa Bay Devil Rays/688 1.75
28 Texas Rangers/705 1.50
29 Toronto Blue Jays/701 1.50
30 Washington Nationals/1,300 2.00
31 Adrian Beltre/1,298 1.75
33 Albert Pujols/2,600 5.50
34 Alex Rodriguez/2,259 4.00
35 Alexis Rios/1,158 1.50
36 Alfonso Soriano/793 5.50
40 Carlos Beltran/1,630 1.75
41 Carl Crawford/820 3.00
43 Carlos Guillen/920 2.00
44 Chipper Jones/927 3.25
45 Carl Pavano/826 2.50
46 Curt Schilling/1,288 1.50
47 Derek Jeter/2,000 3.50
48 David Ortiz/981 3.50
49 David Wright/2,956 8.00
50 David Wells/851 5.00
51 Eric Gagne/688 6.00
53 Gary Sheffield/857 3.25
54 Hank Blalock/814 3.75
55 Hideki Matsui/1,200 2.00
56 Ichiro Suzuki/2,223 2.00
57 Ivan Rodriguez/773 4.00
61 Johan Santana/2,600 7.25
63 Jim Thome/750 6.50
64 Ken Griffey Jr./1,200 3.50
67 Kerry Wood/756 4.25
68 Livan Hernandez/1,200 1.50
69 Miguel Cabrera/1,200 4.00
71 Mark Prior/1,337 1.75
72 Mike Piazza/1,057 2.50
73 Manny Ramirez/1,200 2.00
74 Miguel Tejada/944 2.75
75 Mark Teixeira/1,037 4.00
77 Pedro Martinez/1,163 1.75
80 Roger Clemens/1,667 3.00
82 Randy Johnson/2,196 1.75
86 Sammy Sosa/1,200 1.50
89 Todd Helton/785 3.50
91 Vladimir Guerrero/1,036 2.50
95 Dallas McPherson/2,350 2.25
99 Andy Marte/2,000 5.25
115 Grady Sizemore/1,200 4.00
133 David DeJesus/680 9.00
142 J.J. Hardy/1,523 2.50
149 Justin Morneau/1,664 3.75
152 Chien-Ming Wang/1,200 4.00
153 Dioner Navarro/939 3.25
156 Gavin Floyd/1,485 2.00
165 David Aardsma/889 2.00
172 B.J. Upton/1,910 3.00
174 Scott Kazmir/1,760 4.25
175 Adrian Gonzalez/938 6.25
181 Brendan Harris/977 2.00
185 Tim Hudson/859 2.25
186 Mark Mulder/860 2.50
188 Jeff Bagwell/823 2.75
189 Troy Glaus/824 2.75
191 Jim Edmonds/874 4.00
193 Johnny Damon/1,415 2.00
195 Billy Wagner/939 2.25
196 Dmitri Young/778 2.75
198 David Eckstein/874 5.00
199 Tadahito Iguchi/1,200 2.50
200 Jason Bartlett/913 2.50
202 Joe Blanton/1,097 2.75
203 Huston Street/1,200 7.75
204 Clint Barmes/2,000 3.25
207 Brian Roberts/1,200 1.75
208 John Garland/1,200 2.25
209 Robinson Cano/1,200 11.00
210 Zach Duke/2,000 6.75
211a Rickie Weeks/1,675 4.50
211b Brad Eldred/849 5.00
212a Jeff Francoeur/2,000 9.50
212b Felix Hernandez/2,000 12.75
213 Jonathan Papelbon/1,500 9.00
214 Conor Jackson/1,278 3.25
215 Dan Johnson/1,000 3.25
216 Prince Fielder/2,000 15.00
217 Jeremy Hermida/1,400 4.00
219 Melky Cabrera/1,000 3.50
220 Ryan Howard/2,000 6.00

Classics

Topps continued its eTopps Classics line-up in 2005 with five cards of former greats. Numbering and format were contiguous with earlier issues. Like regular eTopps cards, Classics could only be ordered during a one-week Initial Player Offering period. Cards were issued in a quantity of up to 2,000 each at $9.50. The number of cards actually sold is shown parenthetically. Fronts have a color photo, backs have a picture of one of that player's Topps cards, along with career notes, stats, etc. Values shown are for cards in a virtual portfolio, rather than "in hand."

NM/M
Complete Set (5): 45.00
Common Player: 6.00
61 Roger Maris/2,000 9.00
62 Ryne Sandberg/1,000 9.00
63 Don Mattingly/1,000 15.00
64 Ernie Banks/1,657 6.00
65 Mark Fidrych/976 6.00

Classic Events

Great moments of late 20th Century baseball history are captured in this series. Each card has a front photo depicting the event, with a write-up on back. Cards were issued in quantities of up to nearly 1,200 each (actual number issued is shown parenthetically) at an issue price of $9.50. Values shown are for cards in "virtual portfolios" rather than "in hand."

NM/M
Complete Set (20): 145.00
Common Player: 4.00
1 Bobby Thomson/819 5.00
2 Don Larsen/713 4.50
3 Bill Mazeroski/731 7.00
4 Bucky Dent/713 5.50
5 George Brett/1,000 6.75
6 Dwight Gooden/555 11.50
7 Bob Gibson/728 7.25
8 1989 World Series/1,000 4.00
9 Kirk Gibson/714 10.00
10 Reggie Jackson/979 10.00
11 Carlton Fisk/861 5.00
12 Mookie Wilson/577 9.00
13 Yogi Berra/1,000 4.00
14 Cal Ripken Jr./1,000 16.00
15 Denny McLain/576 12.50
16 Josh Gibson/728 5.75
17 Barry Bonds/1,000 16.50
18 Joe Carter/557 7.75
19 Nolan Ryan/1,000 7.75
20 Rickey Henderson/748 8.50

Events Series

Values shown are for cards in a virtual portfolio rather than "in hand." Each card originally sold for $4.50. Quantity actually issued is shown parenthetically.

NM/M
Complete Set (21): 50.00
Common Card: 1.50
1 NL Transactions/862 1.50
2 AL Transactions/977 1.50
3 Opening Day (Hideki Matsui, Randy Johnson/1,000) 1.50
4 David Ortiz/1,000 3.00
5 Lucky #7 (David Wright/1,000) 2.50
6 Alex Rodriguez/1,000 5.50
7 Derrek Lee/1,000 1.75
8 Alex Rodriguez/1,000 6.50
9 Nationals Win 10 (Nick Johnson, Livan Hernandez/678) 3.50
10 Bob Abreu/800 2.00
11 Miguel Tejada/642 2.00
12 Rafael Palmeiro/1,000 1.50
13 Greg Maddux/1,000 6.00
14 Houston Astros (Andy Pettitte, Roger Clemens/650 2.75
15 Tony LaRussa/550 4.00
16 Jeremy Hermida/760 2.50
17 Houston Marathon (Chris Burke, Roger Clemens/1,000) 1.75
18 Complete Series (Jose Contreras, Mark Buehrle/840) 1.50
19 Houston Astros/579 3.00
20 Chicago White Sox/1,000 2.50
21 Jermaine Dye/746 2.00

2005 Topps Gallery

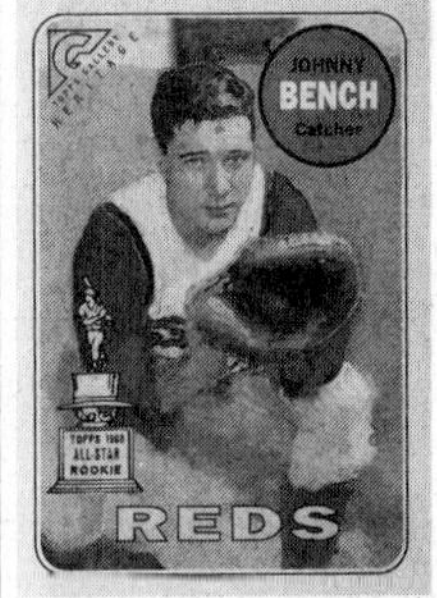

NM/M
Complete Set (195): 175.00
Common Player: .25
Common SP (151-195): 1.00
Inserted 1:1
Variations 1:40
Pack (5): 6.00
Box (20): 100.00
1 Alex Rodriguez 2.50
1 Alex Rodriguez/SP/Black Bat Glove 8.00
2 Eric Chavez .50
3 Mike Piazza 1.50
4 Bret Boone .25
5 Albert Pujols 3.00
6 Vernon Wells .25
7 Andruw Jones .50
8 Miguel Tejada .50
9 Johnny Damon .75
10 Nomar Garciaparra 2.00
11 Pat Burrell .40
12 Bartolo Colon .25
13 Johnny Estrada .25
14 Luis Gonzalez .40
15 Jay Gibbons .25
16 Curt Schilling 1.00
17 Aramis Ramirez .50
18 Frank Thomas .75
19 Adam Dunn .75
20 Sammy Sosa 2.00
21 Matt Lawton .25
22 Preston Wilson .25
23 Carlos Pena .25
24 Josh Beckett .50
25 Carlos Beltran .75
26 Juan Gonzalez .50
27 Adrian Beltre .50
28 Lyle Overbay .25
29 Justin Morneau .50
30 Derek Jeter 3.00
31 Barry Zito .50
32 Bobby Abreu .40
33 Jason Bay .25
34 Jose Reyes .50
35 Nick Johnson .25
36 Lew Ford .25
37 Scott Podsednik .25
38 Rocco Baldelli .40
39 Eric Hinske .25
40 Ichiro Suzuki 2.50
40 Ichiro Suzuki/SP/Writing On Wall 8.00
41 Larry Walker .50
42 Mark Teixeira .50
43 Khalil Greene .50
44 Edgardo Alfonzo .25
45 Javier Vazquez .25
46 Cliff Floyd .25
47 Geoff Jenkins .25
48 Ken Griffey Jr. 2.00
49 Vinny Castilla .25
50 Mark Prior 1.00
51 Jose Guillen .25
52 J.D. Drew .50
53 Rafael Palmeiro .75
54 Kevin Youkilis .25
55 Derrek Lee .50
56 Freddy Garcia .25
57 Wily Mo Pena .25
58 C.C. Sabathia .25
59 Craig Biggio .40
60 Ivan Rodriguez .75
61 Angel Berroa .25
62 Ben Sheets .50
63 Johan Santana .75
64 Al Leiter .40
65 Bernie Williams .50
66 Bobby Crosby .50
67 Jack Wilson .25
68 A.J. Pierzynski .25
69 Jimmy Rollins .50
70 Jason Giambi .50
71 Tom Glavine .50
72 Kevin Brown .25
73 B.J. Upton .50
74 Edgar Renteria .50
75 Alfonso Soriano 1.00
76 Mike Lieberthal .25
77 Kazuo Matsui .25
78 Phil Nevin .25
79 Shawn Green .40
80 Miguel Cabrera 1.00
81 Todd Helton .75
82 Magglio Ordonez .40
83 Manny Ramirez 1.00
84 Bill Mueller .25
85 Troy Glaus .50
86 Richie Sexson .50
87 Javy Lopez .40
88 David Ortiz 1.00
89 Greg Maddux 1.50
90 Vladimir Guerrero 1.00
91 Jeromy Burnitz .25
92 Jeff Kent .40
93 Travis Hafner .40
94 Mark Buehrle .25
95 Paul LoDuca .25
96 Roy Oswalt .40
97 Torii Hunter .40
98 Gary Sheffield .75
99 Erubiel Durazo .25
100 Jim Thome 1.00
100 Jim Thome/SP/Kid's Shirt Is Red 6.00
101 Ken Harvey .25
102 Shannon Stewart .25
103 Dmitri Young .25
104 Kevin Millar .50
105 Kerry Wood 1.00
106 Paul Konerko .40
107 Ronnie Belliard .25
108 Mike Lowell .40
109 Hee Seop Choi .25
110 Joe Mauer .50
111 David Wright .50
112 Jorge Posada .50
113 Tim Hudson .50
114 Brian Giles .25
115 Jason Schmidt .50
116 Aubrey Huff .25
117 Hank Blalock .75
118 Jim Edmonds .50
119 Raul Ibanez .25
120 Carlos Delgado .50
121 Craig Wilson .40
122 Ryan Klesko .25
123 Mark Mulder .50
124 Jose Vidro .25
125 Mike Sweeney .25
126 Lance Berkman .50
127 Juan Pierre .25
128 Austin Kearns .25
129 Moises Alou .50
130 Garret Anderson .50
131 Pedro J. Martinez 1.00
132 Melvin Mora .25
133 Marcus Giles .25
134 Corey Patterson .50
135 Carlos Lee .25
136 Sean Casey .40
137 Jody Gerut .25
138 Jose Valentin .25
139 Aaron Miles .25
140 Randy Johnson 1.00
141 Carlos Guillen .25
142 Dontrelle Willis .50
143 Jeff Dagwell .75
144 Jason Kendall .25
145 Mark Loretta .25
146 Scott Rolen 1.00
147 Carl Crawford .25
148 Michael Young .25
149 Jermaine Dye .25
150 Chipper Jones 1.00
151 Melky Cabrera **RC** 4.00
152 Chris Seddon **RC** 4.00
153 Nate Schierholtz 4.00
154 Ian Kinsler **RC** 8.00
154 Ian Kinsler/SP/Gold Background 20.00
155 Brandon Moss **RC** 4.00
155 Brandon Moss/SP/Red Hat 10.00
156 Chadd Blasko **RC** 2.00
157 Jeremy West **RC** 2.00
157 Jeremy West/SP/Navy Blue Jersey 6.00
158 Sean Marshall **RC** 2.00
159 Ryan Sweeney 4.00
160 Matt Lindstrom **RC** 2.00
161 Ryan Goleski **RC** 4.00
162 Brett Harper **RC** 2.00
163 Chris Roberson **RC** 3.00
164 Andre Ethier 8.00
165 Ian Bladergroen **RC** 2.00
165 Ian Bladergroen/SP/Swinging 6.00
166 James Jurries **RC** 2.00
167 Billy Butler **RC** 6.00
167 Billy Butler/SP/Black Jersey 15.00
168 Michael Rogers **RC** 3.00
168 Michael Rogers/SP/Baseball In Hand 8.00
169 Tyler Clippard **RC** 10.00
170 Luis Ramirez **RC** 3.00
171 Casey Kotchman 2.00
172 Chris Burke 2.00
173 Dallas McPherson 2.00
174 Edwin Jackson 1.00
175 Felix Hernandez 4.00
176 Gavin Floyd 1.00
177 Guillermo Quiroz 1.00
178 Jason Kubel 1.00
179 Jeff Mathis 1.00
180 Rickie Weeks 1.00
181 Ryan Howard 3.00
182 Franklin Gutierrez 1.00
183 Jeremy Reed 5.00
184 Carlos Quentin 5.00
185 Jeff Francis 5.00
186 Nolan Ryan 6.00
187 Hank Aaron 6.00
187 Hank Aaron/SP/Red 755 15.00
188 Duke Snider 4.00
189 Mike Schmidt 5.00
190 Ernie Banks 4.00
191 Frank Robinson 3.00
192 Harmon Killebrew 4.00
193 Al Kaline 3.00
194 Rod Carew 3.00
195 Johnny Bench 4.00

Artist's Proof

Stars (1-150): 2-4X
SP's (151-195): 1-2X
Inserted 1:1

Murray Olderman Sketches

No Pricing
Production One Set

Printing Plates

No Pricing
Production one for each color.

Gallo's Gallery Sketches

NM/M
Complete Set (20): 50.00
Common Player: 1.50
Inserted 1:15
HA Hank Aaron 6.00
HB Hank Blalock 1.50
NG Nomar Garciaparra 4.00
VG Vladimir Guerrero 2.00
TH Todd Helton 1.50
DJ Derek Jeter 6.00
RJ Randy Johnson 2.00
CJ Chipper Jones 2.00
MPI Mike Piazza 4.00
MP Mark Prior 2.00
AP Albert Pujols 6.00
AR Alex Rodriguez 5.00
IR Ivan Rodriguez 1.50
NR Nolan Ryan 6.00
MS Mike Schmidt 5.00
AS Alfonso Soriano 2.00
SS Sammy Sosa 4.00
IS Ichiro Suzuki 4.00
MT Miguel Tejada 1.50
JT Jim Thome 2.00

Heritage Insert

NM/M
Complete Set (25): 65.00
Common Player: 2.00
Inserted 1:15
EB Ernie Banks 4.00
CB Carlos Beltran 3.00
JB Johnny Bench 4.00
HB Hank Blalock 2.00
GB George Brett 6.00
JC Jose Canseco 2.00
BG Bob Gibson 3.00
AK Al Kaline 3.00
DM Don Mattingly 6.00
RP Rafael Palmeiro 3.00
JP Jim Palmer 2.00
AP Albert Pujols 8.00
BR Brooks Robinson 3.00
FR Frank Robinson 2.00
RR Frank Robinson, Brooks Robinson 3.00
RJ Alex Rodriguez, Derek Jeter 8.00
IR Ivan Rodriguez 3.00
NR Nolan Ryan 8.00
CS Curt Schilling 3.00
MS Mike Schmidt 5.00
TS Jim Thome, Mike Schmidt 5.00
OS Ozzie Smith 3.00
DSN Duke Snider 3.00
DS Darryl Strawberry 2.00
DW Dontrelle Willis 2.00

Heritage Relics

NM/M
Common Player: 5.00
Inserted 1:40
GB George Brett 12.00

JC Jose Canseco 8.00
DM Don Mattingly 15.00
AP Albert Pujols 15.00
AR Alex Rodriguez 15.00
IR Ivan Rodriguez 8.00
NR Nolan Ryan 20.00
OS Ozzie Smith 8.00
DS Darryl Strawberry 5.00
DW Dontrelle Willis 5.00

Heritage Relic Autographs

NM/M
Production 25 Sets
DM Don Mattingly 75.00
AR Alex Rodriguez 300.00
NR Nolan Ryan 150.00

Originals Relics

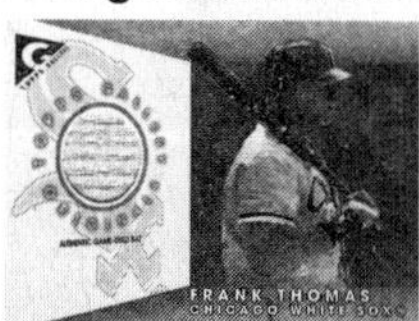

NM/M
Common Player: 4.00
Inserted 1:10
JB Jeff Bagwell 8.00
RB Rocco Baldelli 4.00
JBE Josh Beckett 4.00
LB Lance Berkman 4.00
AB Angel Berroa 4.00
HB Hank Blalock 8.00
HBB Hank Blalock 8.00
MC Miguel Cabrera 8.00
JD Johnny Damon 8.00
RD Ryan Drese 4.00
JG Jason Giambi 6.00
MG Marcus Giles 4.00
VG Vladimir Guerrero 8.00
RH Rich Harden 4.00
TH Todd Helton 8.00
CJ Chipper Jones 8.00
JL Javy Lopez 4.00
ML Mike Lowell 4.00
PM Pedro J. Martinez 8.00
KM Kazuo Matsui 6.00
LN Laynce Nix 4.00
DO David Ortiz 8.00
MP Mike Piazza 8.00
MPB Mike Piazza 8.00
MPR Mark Prior 8.00
AP Albert Pujols 15.00
MR Manny Ramirez 8.00
JR Jose Reyes 6.00
AR Alex Rodriguez 12.00
IR Ivan Rodriguez 8.00
AS Alfonso Soriano 8.00
SS Sammy Sosa 10.00
MT Mark Teixeira 4.00
MTE Miguel Tejada 6.00
FT Frank Thomas 8.00
BU B.J. Upton 4.00
BW Bernie Williams 6.00
DW Dontrelle Willis 4.00
KW Kerry Wood 8.00
MY Michael Young 4.00

Penmanship Autographs

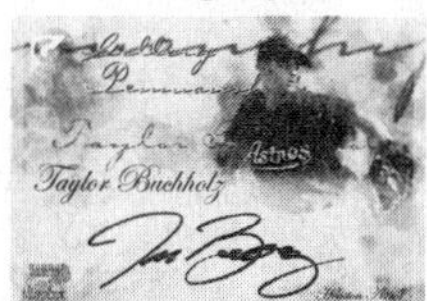

NM/M
Common Autograph: 10.00
JB Jason Bartlett 10.00
TB Taylor Buchholz 10.00
EC Eric Chavez 15.00
FH Felix Hernandez 30.00
AH Aubrey Huff 15.00
JJ Justin Jones 15.00
DM Dallas McPherson 25.00
AR Alex Rodriguez 250.00
VW Vernon Wells 10.00

2005 Topps Heritage

NM/M
Complete Set (475): 400.00
Common Player: .40
Common SP (398-475): 4.00

SP's & Variations Inserted 1:2
Pack (8): 5.00
Box (24): 100.00
1 Will Harridge .40
2 Warren Giles .40
3 Alfonso Soriano 1.00
3 Alfonso Soriano/SP/Running 5.00
4 Mark Mulder .75
5 Todd Helton/SP 5.00
6 Jason Bay .40
6 Jason Bay/SP/1956 Pirates Uniform 5.00
7 Ichiro Suzuki 2.50
7 Ichiro Suzuki/SP/Squatting On-Deck 8.00
8 Jim Tracy .40
9 Gavin Floyd .40
10 John Smoltz .75
11 Chicago Cubs .50
12 Darin Erstad .40
13 Chad Tracy .40
14 Charles Thomas .40
15 Miguel Tejada .75
16 Andre Ethier 6.00
17 Jeff Francis .40
18 Derrek Lee .75
19 Juan Uribe .40
20 Jim Edmonds/SP 5.00
21 Kenny Lofton .40
22 Brad Ausmus .40
23 Jon Garland .40
24 Edwin Jackson .40
25 Joe Mauer .75
26 Wes Helms .40
27 Brian Schneider .40
28 Kazuo Matsui .40
29 Tom Gordon .40
30 Hideo Nomo/SP 4.00
31 Albert Pujols/SP 15.00
31 Albert Pujols/SP/1956 Cards Uniform 15.00
32 Carl Crawford .40
33 Vladimir Guerrero/SP 6.00
34 Nick Green .40
35 Jay Gibbons .40
36 Kevin Youkilis .40
37 Billy Wagner .40
38 Terrence Long .40
39 Kevin Mench .40
40 Garret Anderson .50
41 Reed Johnson .40
42 Reggie Sanders .40
43 Kirk Rueter .40
44 Jay Payton .40
45 Tike Redman .40
46 Mike Lieberthal .40
47 Damian Miller .40
48 Zach Day .40
49 Juan Rincon .40
50 Jim Thome 1.00
50 Jim Thome/SP/Fldg 6.00
51 Jose Guillen .40
52 Richie Sexson .75
53 Juan Cruz .40
54 Byung-Hyun Kim .40
55 Carlos Zambrano .50
56 Carlos Lee .40
57 Adam Dunn .75
58 David Riske .40
59 Carlos Guillen .40
60 Larry Bowa .40
61 Barry Bonds 4.00
62 Chris Woodward .40
63 Matt DeSalvo **RC** 2.50
64 Brian Stavisky **RC** 1.00
65 Scot Shields .40
66 J.D. Drew .50
67 Erik Bedard .40
68 Scott Williamson .40
69 Mark Prior 1.00
69 Mark Prior/SP/1956 Cubs Uniform 6.00
69 6.00
70 Ken Griffey Jr. 2.00
71 Kazuhito Tadano .40
72 Philadelphia Phillies .40
73 Jeremy Reed .40
74 Ricardo Rodriguez .40
75 Carlos Delgado .50
76 Eric Milton .40
77 Miguel Olivo .40
78 Edgardo Alfonzo .40
78 Edgardo Alfonzo/SP/1956 Giants Uniform 4.00
79 Kazuhisa Ishii/SP 4.00
80 Jason Giambi .75
81 Cliff Floyd .40
82 Torii Hunter .50
82 Torii Hunter/SP/1956 Senators Uniform 4.00
83 Odalis Perez .40
84 Scott Podsednik .40
85 Cleveland Indians .40
86 Jeff Suppan .40
87 Ray Durham .40
88 Tyler Clippard **RC** 10.00
89 Ryan Howard 2.00
90 Cincinnati Reds .40
91 Bengie Molina .40
92 Danny Bautista .40
93 Eli Marrero .40
94 Larry Bigbie .40
95 Atlanta Braves .40
96 Merkin Valdez .40
97 Rocco Baldelli .40
98 Woody Williams .40
99 Jason Frasor .40
100 Baltimore Orioles .40
101 Ivan Rodriguez/SP 6.00
102 Joe Kennedy .40
103 Mike Lowell .50
104 Armando Benitez .40
105 Craig Biggio .50
106 David DeJesus .40
107 Adrian Beltre .75
108 Phil Nevin .40
109 Cristian Guzman .40
110 Jorge Posada/SP 6.00
111 Boston Red Sox .75
112 Jeff Mathis .40
113 Bartolo Colon .40
114 Alex Cintron .40
115 Russ Ortiz .40
116 Doug Mientkiewicz .40
117 Placido Polanco .40
118 Magglio Ordonez .40
118 Magglio Ordonez/SP/1956 White Sox Uni. 4.00
119 Chris Seddon **RC** 1.00
120 Bobby Abreu .50
121 Pittsburgh Pirates .40
122 Dallas McPherson .75
123 Rodrigo Lopez .40
124 Mark Bellhorn .40
125 Nomar Garciaparra 2.00
125 Nomar Garciaparra/SP/1956 Cubs Uniform 8.00
126 Sean Casey .40
127 Ronnie Belliard .40
128 Tom Goodwin .40
129 Preston Wilson .40
130 Andruw Jones/SP 5.00
131 Roberto Alomar .75
132 John Buck .40
133 Jason LaRue .40
134 St. Louis Cardinals .75
135 Alex Rodriguez/SP 10.00
135 Alex Rodriguez/SP/Fldg 10.00
136 Nate Robertson .40
137 Juan Pierre .40
138 Morgan Ensberg .40
139 Vinny Castilla .40
140 Jake Dittler 1.00
141 Chan Ho Park .40
142 Felix Hernandez 2.50
143 Jason Isringhausen .40
144 Dustan Mohr .40
145 Khalil Greene .75
146 Minnesota Twins .40
147 Vicente Padilla .40
148 Oliver Perez .40
149 Brian Giles .40
150 Shawn Green .40
151 Matt Lawton .40
152 Casey Blake .40
153 Frank Thomas .75
154 Orlando Hernandez .40
155 Eric Chavez .50
155 Eric Chavez/SP/1956 Kansas City Uni. 4.00
156 Chase Utley .75
157 John Olerud .40
158 Adam Eaton .40
159 Josh Fogg .40
160 Michael Tucker .40
161 Kevin Brown .40
162 Bobby Crosby .50
163 Jason Schmidt .50
164 Shannon Stewart .40
165 Tony Womack .40
166 Los Angeles Dodgers .40
167 Franklin Gutierrez .40
168 Ted Lilly .40
169 Mark Teixeira .50
170 Matt Morris .40
171 Bucky Jacobsen .40
172 Steven Doetsch **RC** 1.00
173 Jeff Weaver .40
174 Tony Graffanino .40
175 Jeff Bagwell .75
176 Carl Pavano .50
177 Junior Spivey .40
178 Carlos Silva .40
179 Tim Redding .40
180 Brett Myers .40
181 Mike Mussina .75
182 Richard Hidalgo .40
183 Nick Johnson .40
184 Lew Ford .40
185 Barry Zito .50
186 Jimmy Rollins .50
187 Jack Wilson .40
188 Chicago White Sox .40
189 Guillermo Quiroz .40
190 Mark Hendrickson .40
191 Jeremy Bonderman .40
192 Jason Jennings .40
193 Paul LoDuca .40
194 A.J. Burnett .40
195 Ken Harvey .40
196 Geoff Jenkins .40
197 Joe Mays .40
198 Jose Vidro .40
199 David Wright .75
200 Randy Johnson 1.00
201 Jeff DeVanon .40
202 Paul Byrd .40
203 David Ortiz 1.00
204 Kyle Farnsworth .40
205 Keith Foulke .40
206 Joe Crede .40
207 Austin Kearns .40
208 Jody Gerut .40
209 Shawn Chacon .40
210 Carlos Pena .40
211 Luis Castillo .40
212 Chris Denorfia **RC** 1.00
213 Detroit Tigers .40
214 Aubrey Huff .40
215 Brad Fullmer .40
216 Frank Catalanotto .40
217 Raul Ibanez .40
218 Ryan Klesko .40
219 Octavio Dotel .40
220 Robert Mackowiak .40
221 Scott Hatteberg .40
222 Pat Burrell .40
223 Bernie Williams .50
224 Kris Benson .40
225 Eric Gagne .50
226 San Francisco Giants .40
227 Roy Oswalt .40
228 Josh Beckett .50
229 Lee Mazzilli .40
230 Rickie Weeks .40
231 Troy Glaus .50
232 Chone Figgins .40
233 John Thomson .40
234 Trot Nixon .40
235 Brad Penny .40
236 Oakland Athletics .40
237 Miguel Batista .40
238 Ryan Drese .40
239 Aaron Miles .40
240 Randy Wolf .40
241 Brian Lawrence .40
242 A.J. Pierzynski .40
243 Jamie Moyer .40
244 Chris Carpenter .40
245 So Taguchi .40
246 Rob Bell .40
247 Francisco Cordero .40
248 Tom Glavine .50
249 Jermaine Dye .40
250 Cliff Lee .40
251 New York Yankees .75
252 Vernon Wells .40
253 R.A. Dickey .40
254 Larry Walker .50
255 Randy Winn .40
256 Pedro Feliz .40
257 Mark Loretta .40
258 Tim Worrell .40
259 Kip Wells .40
260 Cesar Izturis/SP 4.00
261 Carlos Beltran .75
261 Carlos Beltran/SP/Btg 6.00
262 Juan Encarnacion .40
263 Luis Gonzalez .40
264 Grady Sizemore .75
265 Paul Wilson .40
266 Mark Buehrle .40
267 Todd Hollandsworth .40
268 Orlando Cabrera .50
269 Sidney Ponson .40
270 Mike Hampton .40
271 Luis Gonzalez .50
272 Brendan Donnelly .40
273 Chipper Jones 1.00
273 Chipper Jones/SP/Blue Background 6.00
274 Brandon Webb .40
275 Marty Cordova .40
276 Greg Maddux 2.00
277 Jose Contreras .40
278 Aaron Harang .40
279 Coco Crisp .40
280 Bobby Higginson .40
281 Guillermo Mota .40
282 Andy Pettitte .50
283 Jeremy West **RC** 3.00
284 Craig Brazell .40
285 Eric Hinske .40
286 Hank Blalock .75
286 Hank Blalock/SP/Fldg 6.00
287 B.J. Upton .75
288 Jason Marquis .40
289 Matt Herges .40
290 Ramon Hernandez .40
291 Marlon Byrd .40
292 Ryan Sweeney/SP 8.00
293 Esteban Loaiza .40
294 Al Leiter .50
295 Alex Gonzalez .40
296 Johan Santana .75
296 Johan Santana/SP/1956 Senators Uniform 6.00
297 Milton Bradley .40
298 Mike Sweeney .40
299 Wade Miller .40
300 Sammy Sosa 2.00
300 Sammy Sosa/SP/Blue Jersey 8.00
301 Wily Mo Pena .40
302 Tim Wakefield .40
303 Rafael Palmeiro .75
304 Rafael Furcal .40
305 David Eckstein .40
306 David Segui .40
307 Kevin Millar .40
308 Matt Clement .40
309 Wade Robinson **RC** 1.00
310 Brad Radke .40
311 Steve Finley .40
312 Lance Berkman .50
312 Lance Berkman/SP/Fldg 5.00
313 Joe Randa .40
314 Miguel Cabrera 1.00
315 Billy Koch .40
316 Alex Sanchez .40
317 Chin-Hui Tsao .40
318 Omar Vizquel .40
319 Ryan Freel .40
320 LaTroy Hawkins .40
321 Aaron Rowand .40
322 Paul Konerko .40
323 Joe Borowski .40
324 Jarrod Washburn .40
325 Jaret Wright .40
326 Johnny Damon .75
327 Corey Patterson .50
328 Travis Hafner .40
329 Shingo Takatsu .40
330 Dmitri Young .40
331 Matt Holliday .50
332 Jeff Kent .50
333 Desi Relaford .40
334 Jose Hernandez .40
335 Lyle Overbay .40
336 Jacque Jones .40
337 Terrmel Sledge .40
338 Victor Zambrano .40
339 Gary Sheffield .75
340 Brad Wilkerson .40
341 Ian Kinsler **RC** 5.00
342 Jesse Crain .40
343 Orlando Hudson .40
344 Laynce Nix .40
345 Jose Cruz Jr. .40
346 Edgar Renteria .50
347 Eddie Guardado .40
348 Jerome Williams .40
349 Trevor Hoffman .40
350 Mike Piazza 1.50
351 Jason Kendall .40
352 Kevin Millwood .40
353 Tim Hudson .50
353 Tim Hudson/SP/1956 Braves Uniform 5.00
354 Paul Quantrill .40
355 Jon Lieber .40
356 Braden Looper .40
357 Chad Cordero .40
358 Joe Nathan .40
359 Doug Davis .40
360 Ian Bladergroen **RC** 1.00
361 Val Majewski .40
362 Francisco Rodriguez .40
363 Kelvim Escobar .40
364 Marcus Giles .40
365 Darren Fenster **RC** 1.00
366 David Bell .40
367 Shea Hillenbrand .40
368 Manny Ramirez 1.00
369 Ben Broussard .40
370 Luis Ramirez **RC** 1.00
371 Dustin Hermanson .40
372 Akinori Otsuka .40
373 Chadd Blasko **RC** 1.00
374 Delmon Young .75
375 Michael Young .40
376 Bret Boone .40
377 Jake Peavy .40
378 Matt Lindstrom **RC** 1.00
379 Sean Burroughs .40
380 Rich Harden .40
381 Chris Roberson **RC** 1.00
382 John Lackey .40
383 Johnny Estrada .40
384 Matt Rogelstad **RC** 1.00
385 Toby Hall .40
386 Adam LaRoche .40
387 Bill Hall .40
388 Tim Salmon .50
389 Curt Schilling 1.00
389 Curt Schilling/SP/Looking In 6.00
390 Michael Barrett .40
391 Jose Acevedo .40
392 Nate Schierholtz 1.00
393 J.T. Snow Jr. .40
394 Mark Redman .40
395 Ryan Madson .40
396 Kevin West **RC** 1.00
397 Ramon Ortiz .40
398 Derek Lowe 4.00
399 Kerry Wood 6.00
400 Derek Jeter 15.00
401 Livan Hernandez 4.00
402 Casey Kotchman 6.00
403 Chaz Lytle **RC** 6.00
404 Alexis Rios 5.00
405 Scott Spiezio 4.00
406 Craig Wilson 4.00
407 Felix Rodriguez 4.00
408 D'Angelo Jimenez 4.00
409 Rondell White 4.00
410 Shawn Estes 4.00
411 Troy Percival 4.00
412 Melvin Mora 4.00
413 Aramis Ramirez 6.00
414 Carl Everett 4.00
415 Elvys Quezada **RC** 6.00
416 Ben Sheets 5.00
417 Matt Stairs 4.00
418 Adam Everett 4.00
419 Jason Johnson 4.00
420 Billy Butler **RC** 15.00
421 Justin Morneau 6.00
422 Jose Reyes 6.00
423 Mariano Rivera 5.00
424 Jose Vaquedano **RC** 6.00
425 Gabe Gross 5.00
426 Scott Rolen 6.00
427 Ty Wigginton 4.00
428 James Jurries **RC** 6.00
429 Pedro J. Martinez 6.00
430 Mark Grudzielanek 4.00
431 Josh Phelps 4.00
432 Ryan Goleski **RC** 5.00
433 Mike Matheny 4.00
434 Bobby Kielty 4.00
435 Tony Batista 4.00
436 Corey Koskie 4.00
437 Brad Lidge 4.00
438 Dontrelle Willis 4.00
439 Angel Berroa 4.00
440 Jason Kubel 4.00
441 Roy Halladay 4.00
442 Brian Roberts 4.00
443 Bill Mueller 4.00
444 Adam Kennedy 4.00
445 Brandon Moss **RC** 5.00
446 Sean Burnett 4.00
447 Eric Byrnes 4.00
448 Matt Campbell **RC** 6.00
449 Ryan Webb **RC** 6.00
450 Jose Valentin 4.00
451 Jake Westbrook 4.00
452 Glen Perkins **RC** 6.00
453 Alex Gonzalez 4.00
454 Jeromy Burnitz 4.00
455 Zack Greinke 4.00
456 Sean Marshall **RC** 6.00
457 Erubiel Durazo 4.00
458 Michael Cuddyer 4.00
459 Hee Seop Choi 4.00
460 Melky Cabrera **RC** 10.00
461 Jerry Hairston Jr. 4.00
462 Moises Alou 5.00
463 Michael Rogers **RC** 6.00
464 Javy Lopez 4.00
465 Freddy Garcia 4.00
466 Brett Harper **RC** 5.00
467 Juan Gonzalez 5.00
468 Kevin Melillo **RC** 5.00
469 Todd Walker 5.00
470 C.C. Sabathia 4.00
471 Kole Strayhorn 5.00
472 Mark Kotsay 4.00
473 Javier Vazquez 4.00
474 Mike Cameron 4.00
475 Wes Swackhamer **RC** 6.00

Chrome Parallel

NM/M
Complete Set (110):
Common Player: 1.00
Production 1,956 Sets
Refractors: 1.5-2X
Production 556 Sets
Black Refractor: 3-5X
Production 56 Sets
THC1 Will Harridge 2.00
THC2 Warren Giles 2.00
THC3 Alex Rodriguez 10.00
THC4 Alfonso Soriano 5.00
THC5 Barry Bonds 12.00
THC6 Todd Helton 3.00
THC7 Kazuo Matsui 2.00
THC8 Garret Anderson 1.50
THC9 Mark Prior 5.00
THC10 Jim Thome 4.00
THC11 Jason Giambi 2.00
THC12 Ivan Rodriguez 4.00
THC13 Mike Lowell 1.00
THC14 Vladimir Guerrero 5.00
THC15 Adrian Beltre 2.00
THC16 Andruw Jones 2.00
THC17 Jose Vidro 1.00
THC18 Josh Beckett 1.50
THC19 Mike Sweeney 1.00
THC20 Sammy Sosa 6.00
THC21 Scott Rolen 5.00
THC22 Javy Lopez 1.50
THC23 Albert Pujols 12.00
THC24 Adam Dunn 3.00
THC25 Ken Griffey Jr. 6.00
THC26 Torii Hunter 1.50
THC27 Jorge Posada 2.00
THC28 Magglio Ordonez 1.00
THC29 Shawn Green 1.50
THC30 Frank Thomas 3.00
THC31 Barry Zito 1.50
THC32 David Ortiz 5.00
THC33 Pat Burrell 1.50
THC34 Luis Gonzalez 1.50
THC35 Chipper Jones 5.00
THC36 Hank Blalock 3.00
THC37 Rafael Palmeiro 3.00
THC38 Lance Berkman 2.00
THC39 Miguel Cabrera 5.00
THC40 Paul Konerko 1.00
THC41 Jeff Kent 1.50
THC42 Gary Sheffield 3.00

THC43 Mike Piazza 6.00
THC44 Bret Boone 1.00
THC45 Kerry Wood 5.00
THC46 Derek Jeter 12.00
THC47 Pedro J. Martinez 5.00
THC48 Jason Bay 2.00
THC49 Ichiro Suzuki 8.00
THC50 Miguel Tejada 3.00
THC51 Richie Sexson 2.00
THC52 Jeff Bagwell 3.00
THC53 Lew Ford 1.00
THC54 Randy Johnson 5.00
THC55 Carlos Beltran 3.00
THC56 Greg Maddux 6.00
THC57 Lyle Overbay 1.00
THC58 Michael Young 1.00
THC59 Curt Schilling 5.00
THC60 Jose Reyes 3.00
THC61 Dontrelle Willis 1.50
THC62 Nomar Garciaparra 6.00
THC63 Paul LoDuca 1.00
THC64 Larry Walker 2.00
THC65 Andre Ethier 8.00
THC66 Matt DeSalvo 5.00
THC67 Brian Stavicky 2.00
THC68 Tyler Clippard 20.00
THC69 Chris Seddon 3.00
THC70 Steven Doetsch 3.00
THC71 Chris Denorfia 2.00
THC72 Jeremy West 3.00
THC73 Ryan Sweeney 5.00
THC74 Ian Kinsler 10.00
THC75 Ian Bladergroen 4.00
THC76 Darren Fenster 4.00
THC77 Luis Ramirez 2.00
THC78 Chadd Blasko 2.00
THC79 Matt Lindstrom 2.00
THC80 Chris Roberson 3.00
THC81 Matt Rogelstad 3.00
THC82 Nate Schierholtz 4.00
THC83 Kevin West 4.00
THC84 Chaz Lytle 4.00
THC85 Elvys Quezada 4.00
THC86 Billy Butler 15.00
THC87 Jose Vaquedano 4.00
THC88 James Jurries 4.00
THC89 Ryan Goleski 4.00
THC90 Brandon Moss 4.00
THC91 Matt Campbell 4.00
THC92 Ryan Webb 5.00
THC93 Glen Perkins 5.00
THC94 Sean Marshall 4.00
THC95 Melky Cabrera 8.00
THC96 Michael Rogers 4.00
THC97 Brett Harper 4.00
THC98 Kevin Melillo 4.00
THC99 Kole Strayhorn 4.00
THC100 Wes Swackhamer 4.00
THC101 Rickie Weeks 2.00
THC102 Delmon Young 4.00
THC103 Kazuhito Tadano 1.00
THC104 Kazuhisa Ishii 1.00
THC105 David Wright 4.00
THC106 Eric Gagne 3.00
THC107 So Taguchi 1.00
THC108 B.J. Upton 4.00
THC109 Shingo Takatsu 1.00
THC110 Akinori Otsuka 1.00

Clubhouse Collection Relics

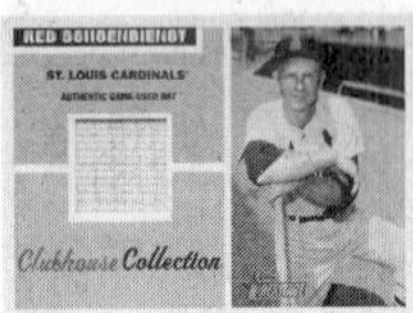

NM/M
Common Player: 5.00
LA Luis Aparicio 8.00
EB Ernie Banks 15.00
LB Lance Berkman 5.00
MC Miguel Cabrera 8.00
AK Al Kaline 15.00
HK Harmon Killebrew 15.00
AP Albert Pujols 20.00
MR Manny Ramirez 8.00
AR Alex Rodriguez 15.00
RS Red Schoendienst 8.00
GS Gary Sheffield 8.00
AS Alfonso Soriano 8.00
MT Miguel Tejada 8.00
BW Bernie Williams 5.00
DW Dontrelle Willis 5.00

Clubhouse Collection Dual Relics

NM/M
Production 56 Sets
MP Stan Musial, Albert Pujols 85.00
KR Al Kaline, Ivan Rodriguez 65.00
BG Ernie Banks, Nomar Garciaparra 85.00

Clubhouse Collection Relic Auto.

NM/M
Production 25 Sets
LA Luis Aparicio 165.00
EB Ernie Banks 200.00
AK Al Kaline 200.00
HK Harmon Killebrew 200.00
RS Red Schoendienst 165.00

Flashbacks

SEPTEMBER 30, 1956
HANK AARON WINS NL BATTING CROWN WITH .328 BATTING AVERAGE.

NM/M
Complete Set (10): 8.00
Common Player: .50
Inserted 1:12
HA Hank Aaron 4.00
LA Luis Aparicio .50
EB Ernie Banks 2.00
BF Bob Feller .50
AK Al Kaline 1.50
DL Don Larsen .50
SM Stan Musial 2.00
FR Frank Robinson 1.00
HS Herb Score .50
DS Duke Snider 1.00

Flashbacks Autographs

NM/M
Common Player:
Production 25 Sets
LA Luis Aparicio 125.00
EB Ernie Banks 200.00
BF Bob Feller 165.00
AK Al Kaline 165.00
DL Don Larsen 175.00
SM Stan Musial 200.00
FR Frank Robinson 200.00
HS Herb Score 150.00

Flashbacks Relics

SEPTEMBER 30, 1956
DUKE SNIDER'S 2 HOMERS LEAD DODGERS TO PENNANT ON LAST DAY OF SEASON.
AUTHENTIC STADIUM SEAT
EBBETS FIELD, BROOKLYN, NEW YORK

NM/M
Common Player: 8.00
Inserted 1:96
HA Hank Aaron 15.00
LA Luis Aparicio 8.00
EB Ernie Banks 15.00
BF Bob Feller 10.00
AK Al Kaline 15.00
DL Don Larsen 8.00
SM Stan Musial 15.00
FR Frank Robinson 10.00
HS Herb Score 8.00
DS Duke Snider 10.00

Flashbacks Relic Autographs

NM/M
Production 25 Sets
LA Luis Aparicio 150.00
EB Ernie Banks 200.00
BF Bob Feller 175.00

YANKEE STADIUM
BRONX, NY
AUTHENTIC STADIUM SEAT
OCTOBER 8, 1956
DON LARSEN PITCHES A PERFECT GAME IN THE WORLD SERIES

AK Al Kaline 175.00
DL Don Larsen 175.00
SM Stan Musial 200.00
FR Frank Robinson 200.00
HS Herb Score 150.00

New Age Performers

NM/M
Complete Set (15): 15.00
Common Player: 1.00
Inserted 1:15
NAP1 Alfonso Soriano 1.50
NAP2 Alex Rodriguez 3.00
NAP3 Ichiro Suzuki 3.00
NAP4 Albert Pujols 4.00
NAP5 Vladimir Guerrero 1.50
NAP6 Jim Thome 1.50
NAP7 Derek Jeter 4.00
NAP8 Sammy Sosa 2.50
NAP9 Ivan Rodriguez 1.00
NAP10 Manny Ramirez 1.50
NAP11 Todd Helton 1.50
NAP12 David Ortiz 1.50
NAP13 Gary Sheffield 1.00
NAP14 Nomar Garciaparra 2.00
NAP15 Randy Johnson 1.50

Real One Autographs

NM/M
Production 200 Sets
Red Ink: 1.5-2X
Production 56 Sets
HA Hank Aaron 250.00
JA Joe Astroth 50.00
EB Ernie Banks 125.00
YB Yogi Berra 100.00
JB Jim Brady 50.00
CD Chuck Diering 50.00
BF Bob Feller 70.00
JG Jim Greengrass 50.00
MI Monte Irvin 60.00
SJ Spook Jacobs 50.00
FM Fred Marsh 50.00
JM Jake Martin 50.00
RM Rudy Minarcin 50.00
PM Paul Minner 50.00
BN Bob Nelson 50.00
LP Laurin Pepper 40.00
LPO Leroy Powell 60.00
JSA Jose Santiago 50.00
JS Johnny Schmitz 50.00
DS Duke Snider 85.00
AS Art Swanson 50.00
BT Bill Tremel 50.00
WW Wally Westlake 50.00

Then and Now

NM/M
Complete Set (10): 8.00
Common Duo: .50
Inserted 1:15
TN1 Hank Aaron, Ichiro Suzuki 4.00
TN2 Don Newcombe, Curt Schilling 1.50
TN3 Robin Roberts, Livan Hernandez .50
TN4 Bob Friend, Livan Hernandez .50
TN5 Herb Score, Randy Johnson 1.50
TN6 Whitey Ford, Jake Peavy 1.00
TN7 Jimmy Piersall, Lyle Overbay .50
TN8 Clem Labine, Mariano Rivera .75
TN9 Bill Bruton, Carl Crawford .50
TN10 Eddie Yost, Bobby Abreu .50

2005 Topps Opening Day

NM/M
Complete Set (165): 30.00
Common Player: .15
Pack (6): 1.00
Box (36): 30.00
1 Alex Rodriguez 1.50
2 Placido Polanco .15
3 Torii Hunter .25
4 Lyle Overbay .15
5 Johnny Damon .50
6 Mike Cameron .15
7 Ichiro Suzuki 1.50
8 Francisco Rodriguez .15
9 Bobby Crosby .15
10 Sammy Sosa 1.25
11 Randy Wolf .15
12 Jason Bay .25
13 Mike Lieberthal .15
14 Paul Konerko .15
15 Brian Giles .15
16 Luis Gonzalez .25
17 Jim Edmonds .40
18 Carlos Lee .15
19 Corey Patterson .40
20 Hank Blalock .50
21 Sean Casey .25
22 Dmitri Young .25
23 Mark Mulder .25
24 Bobby Abreu .25
25 Jim Thome .50
26 Jason Kendall .15
27 Jason Giambi .25
28 Vinny Castilla .15
29 Tony Batista .15
30 Ivan Rodriguez .50
31 Craig Biggio .25
32 Chris Carpenter .15
33 Adrian Beltre .40
34 Scott Podsednik .15
35 Cliff Floyd .15
36 Chad Tracy .15
37 John Smoltz .25
38 Shingo Takatsu .15
39 Jack Wilson .15
40 Gary Sheffield .50
41 Lance Berkman .25
42 Carl Crawford .25
43 Carlos Guillen .15
44 David Bell .15
45 Kazuo Matsui .15
46 Jason Schmidt .25
47 Jason Marquis .15
48 Melvin Mora .15
49 David Ortiz .50
50 Andruw Jones .40
51 Miguel Tejada .50
52 Bartolo Colon .15
53 Derrek Lee .25
54 Eric Gagne .25
55 Miguel Cabrera .75
56 Travis Hafner .15
57 Jose Valentin .15
58 Mark Prior .75
59 Phil Nevin .15
60 Jose Vidro .15
61 Khalil Greene .25
62 Carlos Zambrano .40
63 Erubiel Durazo .15
64 Michael Young .15
65 Woody Williams .15
66 Edgardo Alfonzo .15
67 Troy Glaus .40
68 Garret Anderson .25
69 Richie Sexson .40
70 Curt Schilling .75
71 Randy Johnson .75
72 Chipper Jones .75
73 J.D. Drew .25
74 Russ Ortiz .15
75 Frank Thomas .50
76 Jimmy Rollins .25
77 Barry Zito .25
78 Rafael Palmeiro .50
79 Brad Wilkerson .15
80 Adam Dunn .50
81 Doug Mientkiewicz .15
82 Manny Ramirez .75
83 Pedro J. Martinez .75
84 Moises Alou .25
85 Mike Sweeney .15
86 Boston Red Sox WC 1.00
87 Matt Clement .15
88 Nomar Garciaparra 1.00
89 Magglio Ordonez .15
90 Bret Boone .15
91 Mark Loretta .15
92 Jose Contreras .15
93 Randy Winn .15
94 Austin Kearns .15
95 Ken Griffey Jr. 1.25
96 Jake Westbrook .15
97 Kazuhito Tadano .15
98 C.C. Sabathia .15
99 Todd Helton .50
100 Albert Pujols 2.00
101 Jose Molina .15
102 Aaron Miles .15
103 Mike Lowell .25
104 Paul LoDuca .15
105 Juan Pierre .15
106 Dontrelle Willis .40
107 Jeff Bagwell .40
108 Carlos Beltran .50
109 Ronnie Belliard .15
110 Roy Oswalt .25
111 Zack Greinke .15
112 Steve Finley .15
113 Kazuhisa Ishii .15
114 Justin Morneau .40
115 Ben Sheets .25
116 Johan Santana .50
117 Billy Wagner .15
118 Mariano Rivera .25
119 Corey Koskie .15
120 Akinori Otsuka .15
121 Joe Mauer .40
122 Jacque Jones .15
123 Joe Nathan .15
124 Nick Johnson .15
125 Vernon Wells .15
126 Mike Piazza 1.00
127 Jose Guillen .15
128 Jose Reyes .25
129 Marcus Giles .15
130 Javy Lopez .25
131 Kevin Millar .15
132 Jorge Posada .40
133 Carl Pavano .25
134 Bernie Williams .40
135 Kerry Wood .75
136 Matt Holiday .15
137 Kevin Brown .15
138 Derek Jeter 2.00
139 Barry Bonds 2.00
140 Jeff Kent .25
141 Mark Kotsay .15
142 Shawn Green .25
143 Tim Hudson .25
144 Shannon Stewart .15
145 Pat Burrell .25
146 Gavin Floyd .15
147 Mike Mussina .50
148 Eric Chavez .25
149 Jon Lieber .15
150 Vladimir Guerrero .75
151 Vicente Padilla .15
152 Ryan Klesko .15
153 Jake Peavy .25
154 Scott Rolen .75
155 Greg Maddux 1.00
156 Edgar Renteria .25
157 Larry Walker .25
158 Scott Kazmir .25
159 B.J. Upton .25
160 Mark Teixeira .50
161 Ken Harvey .15
162 Alfonso Soriano .75
163 Carlos Delgado .40
164 Alexis Rios .15
165 Checklist .15

Autographs

NM/M
Complete Set (6):
Common Player:
CC Chad Cordero 10.00
FH Felix Hernandez 25.00
AH Aaron Hill 8.00
PM Paul Maholm 8.00
OQ Omar Quintanilla 15.00
AW Anthony Whittington 8.00

MLB Game Worn Jersey Collection

NM/M
Target Retail Exclusive
37 Vladimir Guerrero 8.00
38 Albert Pujols 15.00
39 Torii Hunter 4.00
40 Alfonso Soriano 6.00
41 Bobby Abreu 6.00
42 Moises Alou 6.00
43 Sean Burroughs 4.00
44 Shannon Stewart 4.00
45 Troy Glaus 6.00
46 Fernando Vina 4.00
47 Dan Wilson 4.00
48 Paul Konerko 4.00
49 Jimmy Rollins 6.00
50 Livan Hernandez 4.00
51 Sean Casey 4.00
52 Paul LoDuca 4.00
53 Richie Sexson 6.00
54 Aubrey Huff 4.00

2005 Topps Pack Wars

NM/M
Complete Set (175): 40.00
Common Player: .25
Pack (7): 20.00

Box (7): 120.00
1 Alex Rodriguez 3.00
2 Eric Chavez .40
3 Jimmy Rollins .40
4 Jason Bay .50
5 Nomar Garciaparra 2.00
6 Melvin Mora .25
7 Bobby Abreu .50
8 Bartolo Colon .25
9 Orlando Cabrera 1.00
10 Albert Pujols 3.00
11 Barry Zito .40
12 Vernon Wells .25
13 J.D. Drew .40
14 Darin Erstad .25
15 Manny Ramirez 1.00
16 Derrek Lee .40
17 Juan Uribe .25
18 Wily Mo Pena .25
19 Jeromy Burnitz .25
20 Dontrelle Willis .25
21 Craig Biggio .40
22 Cesar Izturis .25
23 Geoff Jenkins .25
24 Joe Mauer .50
25 Derek Jeter 3.00
26 David Wright 1.00
27 Jose Vidro .25
28 Bobby Crosby .25
29 Khalil Greene .50
30 Ichiro Suzuki 2.00
31 Reggie Sanders .25
32 A.J. Pierzynski .25
33 Corey Patterson .40
34 Frank Thomas .75
35 Craig Wilson .25
36 Carl Crawford .25
37 Michael Young .25
38 Mark Kotsay .25
39 Javier Vazquez .25
40 Kazuo Matsui .25
41 Lew Ford .25
42 Corey Koskie .25
43 Larry Walker .50
44 Mike Lowell .40
45 Todd Helton .75
46 Travis Hafner .25
47 Sean Casey .25
48 Ken Griffey Jr. 1.50
49 Milton Bradley .25
50 Ivan Rodriguez .75
51 Carlos Lee .25
52 Aramis Ramirez .50
53 Curt Schilling 1.00
54 Russ Ortiz .25
55 Randy Johnson 1.00
56 Preston Wilson .25
57 Jay Gibbons .25
58 Mike Lieberthal .25
59 Johnny Damon .75
60 Mark Prior 1.00
61 Freddy Garcia .25
62 Casey Blake .25
63 Chipper Jones 1.00
64 Carlos Guillen .25
65 Juan Pierre .25
66 Tom Glavine .50
67 Alex Sanchez .25
68 Tony Batista .25
69 Paul LoDuca .25
70 Hank Blalock .75
71 Pedro Feliz .25
72 Jim Edmonds .50
73 Phil Nevin .25
74 Rocco Baldelli .25
75 Alfonso Soriano 1.00
76 David Bell .25
77 Eric Hinske .25
78 Jose Guillen .25
79 Marcus Giles .25
80 Rafael Palmeiro .75
81 Jeff Bagwell .75
82 Kerry Wood 1.00
83 Johan Santana .75
84 Troy Glaus .40
85 Andruw Jones .50
86 Barry Bonds 3.00
87 Jermaine Dye .25
88 Carlos Zambrano .50
89 Aaron Rowand .25
90 Garret Anderson .40
91 Ryan Klesko .25
92 Paul Konerko .25
93 Jeff Kent .40
94 Richie Sexson .50
95 Lyle Overbay .25
96 Torii Hunter .40
97 Mike Cameron .25

98 Eric Byrnes .25
99 Jason Kendall .25
100 Vladimir Guerrero 1.00
101 Johnny Estrada .25
102 Mark Bellhorn .25
103 Moises Alou .40
104 Ronnie Belliard .25
105 Adam Dunn .75
106 Dmitri Young .25
107 Luis Castillo .25
108 Carlos Beltran .75
109 Steve Finley .25
110 Shannon Stewart .25
111 Al Leiter .25
112 Bernie Williams .50
113 Roy Oswalt .40
114 Sean Burroughs .25
115 Randy Winn .25
116 Tony Womack .25
117 Jim Thome 1.00
118 Aubrey Huff .25
119 Bret Boone .25
120 Carlos Delgado .40
121 Jason Schmidt .50
122 Rafael Furcal .25
123 Miguel Tejada .75
124 Bill Mueller .25
125 Pedro Martinez 1.00
126 Michael Barrett .25
127 Jody Gerut .25
128 Vinny Castilla .25
129 Rondell White .25
130 Magglio Ordonez .25
131 Lance Berkman .25
132 Alex Gonzalez .25
133 Mike Sweeney .25
134 Ben Sheets .50
135 Jacque Jones .25
136 Brad Wilkerson .25
137 Cliff Floyd .25
138 Kevin Brown .25
139 Scott Hatteberg .25
140 Gary Sheffield .50
141 Justin Morneau .50
142 Scott Podsednik .25
143 Shawn Green .40
144 David Ortiz 1.00
145 Josh Beckett .50
146 Tim Hudson .50
147 Matt Lawton .25
148 Mark Buehrle .25
149 Todd Walker .25
150 Jason Giambi .50
151 Brian Giles .25
152 Erubiel Durazo .25
153 Jack Wilson .25
154 Jose Reyes .50
155 Scott Rolen 1.00
156 Raul Ibanez .25
157 Mark Teixeira .50
158 Luis Gonzalez .25
159 Javy Lopez .25
160 Greg Maddux 1.50
161 Kevin Millar .25
162 Jose Valentin .25
163 C.C. Sabathia .25
164 Carlos Pena .25
165 Miguel Cabrera 1.00
166 Adrian Beltre .50
167 Sammy Sosa 2.00
168 Nick Johnson .25
169 Jorge Posada .50
170 Mike Piazza 1.50
171 Mark Mulder .50
172 Mark Loretta .25
173 Edgardo Alfonzo .25
174 Edgar Renteria .50
175 Pat Burrell .25

Autographs

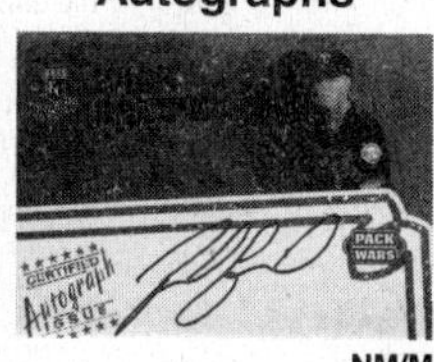

NM/M
Common Autograph: 15.00
CB Carlos Beltran 30.00
HB Hank Blalock 20.00
AB Aaron Boone 20.00
MC Miguel Cabrera 25.00
EC Eric Chavez 15.00
JE Johnny Estrada 10.00
ZG Zack Greinke 15.00
VM Victor Martinez 15.00
CS C.C. Sabathia 15.00
VW Vernon Wells 10.00
MY Michael Young 15.00

Collector Chips

NM/M
Common Player: 8.00
Inserted 1:Box
Blue: No Pricing
Production 25 Sets
Red: No Pricing
Production 10 Sets
2 Ichiro Suzuki 30.00
3 Jim Thome 20.00
4 Albert Pujols 30.00
5 Vladimir Guerrero 15.00
6 Derek Jeter 30.00
7 Sammy Sosa 20.00
9 Ivan Rodriguez 10.00
11 Nomar Garciaparra 20.00
12 Ken Griffey Jr. 20.00
13 Mark Prior 10.00
14 Todd Helton 10.00
15 Mike Piazza 20.00
16 Jorge Posada 10.00
17 Chipper Jones 10.00
18 Randy Johnson 15.00
19 Gary Sheffield 8.00
20 Mike Schmidt 25.00
21 Ernie Banks 20.00
22 Frank Robinson 20.00
23 Reggie Jackson 10.00
24 George Brett 25.00
25 Nolan Ryan 30.00

Cut Signatures

No Pricing

Relics

NM/M
Common Player: 8.00
RC Roger Clemens 12.00
NG Nomar Garciaparra 15.00
VG Vladimir Guerrero 10.00
TH Todd Helton 8.00
THB Todd Helton 8.00
CJ Chipper Jones 8.00
CJB Chipper Jones 8.00
GM Greg Maddux 10.00
PM Pedro Martinez 8.00
RP Rafael Palmeiro 8.00
MP Mike Piazza 10.00
AP Albert Pujols 15.00
MR Manny Ramirez 10.00
MRB Manny Ramirez 10.00
AR Alex Rodriguez 15.00
IR Ivan Rodriguez 8.00
SR Scott Rolen 10.00
GS Gary Sheffield 8.00
AS Alfonso Soriano 8.00
SS Sammy Sosa 10.00
FT Frank Thomas 8.00
JT Jim Thome 8.00

Relic Autographs

NM/M
Common Autograph: 15.00
Production 200 Sets
CB Carlos Beltran 40.00
HB Hank Blalock 25.00
MC Miguel Cabrera 30.00
EC Eric Chavez 20.00
JE Johnny Estrada 15.00
VM Victor Martinez 15.00
MY Michael Young 20.00

2005 Topps Pristine

NM/M
Common 1-100 .75
Common Rookie (101-130): 1.00
Common (131-180): 3.00
Production 500
Common (181-205): 10.00
Production 100
Common (206-210):
Production 49
Pack (8): 30.00
Box (5): 125.00
1 Alex Rodriguez 3.00
2 Jake Peavy .75
3 Bobby Crosby .75
4 J.D. Drew .75
5 Scott Rolen 1.50
6 Bobby Abreu .75
7 Ken Griffey Jr. 2.50
8 Jeremy Bonderman .75
9 Mike Sweeney .75
10 Mark Prior 1.50
11 Tim Hudson .75
12 Clint Barmes .75
13 Jeff Bagwell 1.00
14 Andruw Jones 1.50
15 Carlos Delgado .75
16 Rocco Baldelli .75
17 Adam Dunn 1.50
18 Greg Maddux 2.00
19 Torii Hunter .75
20 Miguel Tejada 1.50
21 Lyle Overbay .75
22 Craig Wilson .75
23 Scott Kazmir .75
24 Alex Rios .75
25 Ichiro Suzuki 3.00
26 Jorge Posada 1.00
27 Jose Reyes .75
28 Hank Blalock .75
29 Troy Glaus 1.00
30 Todd Helton 1.50
31 Javy Lopez .75
32 Barry Zito 1.00
33 Jimmy Rollins 1.00
34 Mark Loretta .75
35 Richie Sexson 1.00
36 Nick Johnson .75
37 Ivan Rodriguez 1.00
38 Jeff Kent .75
39 Jake Westbrook .75
40 Carlos Beltran 1.00
41 Rich Harden .75
42 Joe Mauer 1.00
43 Luis Gonzalez .75
44 Frank Thomas 1.00
45 Michael Young .75
46 Jason Schmidt .75
47 Eric Chavez .75
48 Vinny Castilla .75
49 John Smoltz 1.00
50 Barry Bonds 4.00
51 Jim Edmonds 1.00
52 Edgar Renteria .75
53 Jose Vidro .75
54 Chipper Jones 1.50
55 Curt Schilling 1.50
56 Victor Martinez .75
57 Josh Beckett .75
58 Derrek Lee 1.50
59 Shawn Green .75
60 Roger Clemens 4.00
61 Orlando Cabrera .75
62 Mike Piazza 2.00
63 Gary Sheffield 1.00
64 Carl Crawford .75
65 Johan Santana 1.50
66 Oliver Perez .75
67 Manny Ramirez 1.50
68 Paul Konerko 1.00
69 Preston Wilson .75
70 Sammy Sosa 2.00
71 Eric Gagne .75
72 Geoff Jenkins .75
73 Magglio Ordonez .75
74 Kerry Wood 1.00
75 Albert Pujols 4.00
76 Roy Halladay 1.00
77 Aubrey Huff .75
78 Nomar Garciaparra 1.50
79 Brian Roberts .75
80 Randy Johnson 1.50
81 Pat Burrell .75
82 Brian Giles .75
83 Mike Mussina 1.00
84 Mark Teixeira 1.00
85 Pedro Martinez 1.50
86 Jason Bay .75
87 Mark Buehrle .75
88 Rafael Furcal .75
89 Juan Pierre .75
90 Jim Thome 1.00
91 Ben Sheets 1.00
92 Alfonso Soriano 1.50
93 Adrian Beltre .75
94 Miguel Cabrera 1.50
95 Derek Jeter 4.00
96 Vernon Wells .75
97 Lance Berkman 1.00
98 Hideki Matsui 2.50
99 David Ortiz 1.50
100 Vladimir Guerrero 1.50
101 Justin Verlander **RC** 3.00
102 Billy Butler **RC** 8.00
103 Wladimir Balentien **RC** 2.00
104 Jeremy West **RC** 2.00
105 Philip Humber **RC** 3.00
106 Tyler Pelland **RC** 1.00
107 Andy LaRoche **RC** 5.00
108 Hernan Iribarren **RC** 1.00
109 Luke Scott **RC** 1.00
110 Landon Powell **RC** 1.00
111 Alexander Smit **RC** 1.00
112 Ryan Garko **RC** 1.00
113 Bear Bay **RC** 1.00
114 Ian Bladergroen **RC** 1.00
115 Manny Parra **RC** 1.00
116 Andy Sides **RC** 1.00
117 Travis Chick **RC** 1.00
118 Stefan Bailie **RC** 1.00
119 Chuck Tiffany **RC** 2.00
120 Buck Coats **RC** 1.00
121 Jeff Niemann **RC** 2.00
122 Jake Postlewait **RC** 1.00
123 Matt Campbell **RC** 1.00
124 Kevin Melillo **RC** 2.00
125 Mike Morse **RC** 3.00
126 Anthony Reyes **RC** 6.00
127 Casey McGehee **RC** 1.00
128 Cody Haerther **RC** 1.00
129 Brandon McCarthy **RC** 4.00
130 Glen Perkins **RC** 2.00
131 Moises Alou 3.00
132 Nomar Garciaparra 6.00
133 Scott Rolen 6.00
134 Miguel Tejada 4.00
135 Alex Rodriguez 10.00
136 Michael Young 3.00
137 Tim Hudson 5.00
138 Troy Glaus 3.00
139 Eric Chavez 3.00
140 David Ortiz 10.00
141 Andruw Jones 5.00
142 Richie Sexson 5.00
143 Jim Thome 5.00
144 Javy Lopez 3.00
145 Lance Berkman 3.00
146 Gary Sheffield 5.00
147 Dontrelle Willis 4.00
148 Curt Schilling 5.00
149 Jorge Posada 5.00
150 Vladimir Guerrero 8.00
151 Adam Dunn 5.00
152 Ryan Drese 3.00
153 Hank Blalock 3.00
154 Kerry Wood 4.00
155 Alfonso Soriano 5.00
156 Aramis Ramirez 4.00
157 Mark Mulder 4.00
158 Paul Konerko 4.00
159 Jim Edmonds 6.00
160 Roger Clemens 10.00
161 Mariano Rivera 6.00
162 Rafael Palmeiro 6.00
163 Mark Teixeira 6.00
164 Eric Gagne 3.00
165 Sammy Sosa 8.00
166 Brett Myers 3.00
167 Kazuhisa Ishii 3.00
168 Ken Harvey 3.00
169 Johnny Estrada 3.00
170 Todd Helton 5.00
171 Rich Harden 3.00
172 Johnny Damon 6.00
173 Manny Ramirez 6.00
174 Benito Santiago 3.00
175 Albert Pujols 15.00
176 Chipper Jones .75
177 Miguel Cabrera 8.00
178 Jeff Bagwell 5.00
179 Ivan Rodriguez 5.00
180 Mike Piazza 8.00
181 Chip Cannon **RC** 15.00
182 Erik Cordier **RC** 15.00
183 Billy Butler **RC** 40.00
184 C.J. Smith **RC** 10.00
185 Alfonso Soriano 25.00
186 Bobby Livingston **RC** 15.00
187 Wladimir B alentien **RC** 25.00
188 Mike Morse **RC** 15.00
189 Wes Swackhamer **RC** 15.00
190 Justin Verlander **RC** 50.00
191 Jake Postlewait **RC** 15.00
192 Michael Rogers **RC** 20.00
193 Matt Campbell **RC** 20.00
194 Eric Nielsen **RC** 15.00
195 Gary Sheffield 30.00
196 Glen Perkins **RC** 25.00
197 Kevin Melillo **RC** 20.00
198 Chad Orvella **RC** 10.00
199 Jeff Niemann **RC** 25.00
200 Alex Rodriguez 180.00
201 Brian Stavisky **RC** 15.00
202 Brian Miller **RC** 15.00
203 Landon Powell **RC** 20.00
204 Philip Humber **RC** 20.00
205 Mariano Rivera 100.00
206 Curt Schilling 50.00
207 Nolan Ryan 150.00

Red

Red (1-130): 2-4X
Production 66
Red (131-210): No Pricing
Production Three Sets

Uncirculated Bronze

Bronze (1-130): 1.5-3X
Production 375
Bronze (131-180): 1-1.5X
Production 100
Bronze (181-205): No Pricing
Production 18
Bronze (206-210): No Pricing
Production 10

Doubles Act Autographs

No Pricing
Production Five Sets

Fielder's Choice

No Pricing
Production Nine Sets

In The Name Patch

No Pricing
One card for each letter.

Personal Endorsements

NM/M
Common
Production 497 Sets
Uncirculated: No Pricing
Production Three Sets
MB Milton Bradley 10.00
BB Billy Butler 25.00
LC Lance Cormier 5.00
SE Scott Elbert 8.00
JF Josh Fields 5.00
LH Livan Hernandez 12.00
JPH J.P. Howell 8.00
PH Philip Humber 10.00
ZJ Zach Jackson 8.00
BJ Blake Johnson 5.00
BL Bobby Livingston 8.00
CO Chad Orvella 5.00
GP Glen Perkins 15.00
LP Landon Powell 8.00
MR Mike Rodriguez 5.00
MRO Mark Rogers 8.00
TS Terrmel Sledge 5.00
CJS C.J. Smith 5.00
JS Jeremy Sowers 10.00
JV Justin Verlander 20.00
Uncommon
Production 247 Sets
JB Jason Bay 25.00
AB Aaron Boone 10.00
MB Matt Bush 15.00
BB Billy Butler 25.00
CC Chip Cannon 8.00
CE Carl Erskine 10.00
HK Harmon Killebrew 25.00
BL Bobby Livingston 8.00
ML Mark Loretta 8.00
DO David Ortiz 40.00
CW Craig Wilson 10.00
DW David Wright 60.00
DZ Don Zimmer 15.00
Rare
Production 97 Sets
GA Garret Anderson 15.00
EB Ernie Banks 50.00
SM Stan Musial 50.00
MR Mariano Rivera 100.00
TS Tom Seaver 30.00
AS Alfonso Soriano 25.00
Scarce
Production 22 Sets

Personal Pieces

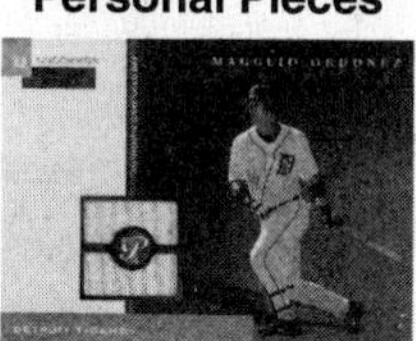

NM/M
Common
Production 425
Uncirculated: No Pricing
Production Three Sets
JB Jeff Bagwell 5.00
RB Ronnie Belliard 3.00
AB Adrian Beltre 3.00
LB Lance Berkman 5.00
HB Hank Blalock 5.00
EC Eric Chavez 3.00
RC Roger Clemens 12.00
BC Bobby Crosby 5.00
JDD J.D. Drew 3.00
AD Adam Dunn 5.00
JE Jim Edmonds 5.00
JES Johnny Estrada 3.00
JG Jason Giambi 5.00
JGI Jay Gibbons 3.00
SG Shawn Green 3.00
VG Vladimir Guerrero 8.00
CG Cristian Guzman 3.00
THA Travis Hafner 3.00
TH Todd Helton 5.00
THU Tim Hudson 5.00
AJ Andruw Jones 5.00
CJ Chipper Jones 8.00
JL Javy Lopez 3.00
ML Mark Loretta 3.00
MLO Mike Lowell 3.00
PM Pedro Martinez 8.00
VM Victor Martinez 3.00
KM Kevin Millar 3.00
MM Mark Mulder 5.00
BM Brett Myers 3.00
LN Laynce Nix 3.00
MP Mike Piazza 8.00
MPR Mark Prior 5.00
AP Albert Pujols 15.00
BR Brad Radke 3.00
MR Manny Ramirez 8.00
ER Edgar Renteria 3.00
MRI Mariano Rivera 6.00
SR Scott Rolen 5.00
CS Curt Schilling 6.00
GS Gary Sheffield 5.00
AS Alfonso Soriano 5.00
MTE Mark Teixeira 5.00
MT Miguel Tejada 5.00
FT Frank Thomas 8.00
JT Jim Thome 5.00
BJU B.J. Upton 3.00
BW Bernie Williams 5.00
KW Kerry Wood 5.00
BZ Barry Zito 3.00
Uncommon
Production 200
CB Carlos Beltran 5.00
AB Adrian Beltre 3.00
MC Miguel Cabrera 8.00
RC Roger Clemens 12.00
JE Jim Edmonds 5.00
EG Eric Gagne 3.00
TG Troy Glaus 3.00
TH Torii Hunter 3.00
AJ Andruw Jones 5.00
CJ Chipper Jones 8.00
MM Mark Mulder 5.00
MO Magglio Ordonez 3.00
DO David Ortiz 8.00
MP Mike Piazza 8.00
JP Jorge Posada 5.00
AP Albert Pujols 15.00
MR Manny Ramirez 8.00
MRI Mariano Rivera 6.00
AR Alex Rodriguez 15.00
IR Ivan Rodriguez 5.00
SR Scott Rolen 5.00
CS Curt Schilling 6.00
AS Alfonso Soriano 5.00
SS Sammy Sosa 8.00
JT Jim Thome 5.00
Rare
CB Carlos Beltran 10.00
BB Barry Bonds 40.00
RC Roger Clemens 20.00
JD Johnny Damon 12.00
EG Eric Gagne 8.00
VG Vladimir Guerrero 10.00
TH Todd Helton 10.00
PM Pedro Martinez 10.00
AP Albert Pujols 25.00
AR Alex Rodriguez 25.00
Scarce

Power Core

No Pricing
Production 3-10
Power Stick: No Pricing
Production One Set

Printing Plates

No Pricing
Production one set for each color.

Selective Swatch

No Pricing
Production One Set

Legends

NM/M
Complete Set (140):
Common Player: 1.00
Common SP (101-125): 2.00
Production 1,999
Common SP (126-135): 3.00
Production 999
Common SP (136-140): 4.00
Production 499
Pack (8): 30.00
Box (5): 120.00
1 Vida Blue 1.00
2 Bert Blyleven 1.00
3 Joe Carter 1.00
4 Bill Buckner 1.00
5 Luis Aparicio 1.00
6 Ernie Banks 2.50
7 Wade Boggs 2.00
8 George Brett 4.00
9 Lou Brock 2.00
10 Rod Carew 2.00
11 Gary Carter 1.00
12 Andre Dawson 1.00
13 Dennis Eckersley 1.00
14 Rollie Fingers 1.00
15 Steve Garvey 1.00
16 Dwight Gooden 1.00
17 Rich "Goose" Gossage 1.00
18 Ron Guidry 1.00
19 Keith Hernandez 1.00
20 Charlie Hough 1.00
21 Bo Jackson 2.50
22 Monte Irvin 2.00
23 Reggie Jackson 2.00
24 Ferguson Jenkins 1.00
25 Ralph Kiner 1.00
26 Juan Marichal 1.00
27 Stan Musial 4.00
28 Tony Oliva 1.00
29 Jim Palmer 1.50
30 Dave Parker 1.00
31 Gaylord Perry 1.00
32 Jimmy Piersall 1.00
33 Johnny Podres 1.00
34 Brooks Robinson 2.00
35 Frank Robinson 2.00
36 Nolan Ryan 5.00
37 Tom Seaver 2.00
38 Ozzie Smith 3.00
39 Duke Snider 2.00
40 Bobby Thomson 1.00
41 Carl Yastrzemski 3.00
42 Maury Wills 1.00

43 Robin Yount 3.00
44 Matt Williams 1.00
45 Orel Hershiser 1.00
46 Tim McCarver 1.00
47 Don Newcombe 1.00
48 Paul O'Neill 1.00
49 Al Kaline 2.00
50 Harmon Killebrew 2.00
51 Dave Kingman 1.00
52 Ken Griffey 1.00
53 George Foster 1.00
54 Mark Fidrych 1.00
55 Orlando Cepeda 1.00
56 Don Larsen 1.00
57 Bill Madlock 1.00
58 Dale Murphy 1.50
59 Graig Nettles 1.00
60 Phil Niekro 1.00
61 Al Oliver 1.00
62 Harold Reynolds 1.00
63 Bobby Richardson 1.00
64 Mike Scott 1.00
65 Dave Stewart 1.00
66 Rick Sutcliffe 1.00
67 Bruce Sutter 1.50
68 Luis Tiant 1.00
69 Bob Watson 1.00
70 Walt Weiss 1.00
71 Don Zimmer 1.00
72 Tommy John 1.00
73 Ray Knight 1.00
74 Jack Morris 1.00
75 Mickey Rivers 1.00
76 Lee Smith 1.00
77 Darryl Strawberry 1.00
78 David Justice 1.00
79 Wally Joyner 1.00
80 Jimmy Key 1.00
81 John Kruk 1.00
82 Greg Luzinski 1.00
83 Mookie Wilson 1.00
84 Wilbur Wood 1.00
85 Tim Raines 1.00
86 Jim Rice 1.00
87 Tony Armas 1.00
88 Harold Baines 1.00
89 Bucky Dent 1.00
90 Darrell Evans 1.00
91 Cecil Fielder 1.00
92 Jose Cruz 1.00
93 Dave Concepcion 1.00
94 Ron Cey 1.00
95 Davey Lopes 1.00
96 Boog Powell 1.00
97 Buddy Bell 1.00
98 George Bell 1.00
99 Bert Campaneris 1.00
100 Chet Lemon 1.00
101 Bo Jackson 4.00
102 Will Clark 2.00
103 Cecil Fielder 2.00
104 Ron Cey 2.00
105 Tony Gwynn 5.00
106 Orel Hershiser 2.00
107 Jimmy Key 2.00
108 Paul Molitor 3.00
109 Pete Incaviglia 2.00
110 Wally Joyner 2.00
111 Dave Kingman 2.00
112 Ron Guidry 2.00
113 Ron Darling 2.00
114 Mookie Wilson 2.00
115 Reggie Jackson 3.00
116 Walt Weiss 2.00
117 Joe Carter 2.00
118 Cory Snyder 2.00
119 Dave Winfield 3.00
120 Terry Steinbach 2.00
121 Matt Williams 2.00
122 Ozzie Smith 5.00
123 Jack McDowell 2.00
124 Bob Horner 2.00
125 Don Kessinger 2.00
126 Minnie Minoso 3.00
127 Cecil Kaiser 3.00
128 Buck O'Neil 3.00
129 Monte Irvin 4.00
130 Jim Gilliam 3.00
131 Josh Gibson 4.00
132 Ernie Banks 6.00
133 Don Newcombe 3.00
134 Red Moore 3.00
135 Willie Pope 3.00
136 Gary Carter 4.00
137 Bo Jackson 6.00
138 George Brett 8.00
139 Joe Carter 4.00
140 Nolan Ryan 8.00

Legends Refractor

Refractor (1-100): 1-1.5X
Production 549
Refractor (101-125): 1.5-2X
Production 199
Refractor (126-135): 1.5-2.5X
Production 99
Refractor (136-140): No Pricing
Production 25

Legends Refractors Gold Die-Cut

Gold (1-100): 3-4X
Gold (101-135): 1-2.5X
Gold (136-140): 1-1.5X
Production 65 Sets

Legends SuperFractor

No Pricing
Production One Set

Legends Printing Plates

No Pricing
One set produced per color.

Legends Celebrity Threads

NM/M
Inserted 1:18
Refractor: No pricing
Production 25 Sets
MM Marilyn Monroe 75.00
EP Elvis Presley 65.00

Legends Leading Indicators

NM/M
Common Player: 4.00
Refractor: No Pricing
Production one or 25.
WB Wade Boggs 10.00
RC Rod Carew 8.00
AD Andre Dawson 6.00
BF Bob Feller 10.00
CF Cecil Fielder 8.00
GF George Foster 4.00
TG Tony Gwynn 10.00
AK Al Kaline 12.00
DK Dave Kingman 6.00
RM Roger Maris 35.00
DM Don Mattingly 15.00
DBM Dale Murphy 10.00
TO Tony Oliva 6.00
PO Paul O'Neill 10.00
DP Dave Parker 4.00
GP Gaylord Perry 4.00
TR Tim Raines 4.00
TR2 Tim Raines 6.00
JR Jim Rice 4.00
NR Nolan Ryan 20.00
MS Mike Scott 4.00
TS Tom Seaver 10.00
DS Darryl Strawberry 6.00
MW Maury Wills 10.00
CY Carl Yastrzemski 15.00

Legends Personal Endorsements

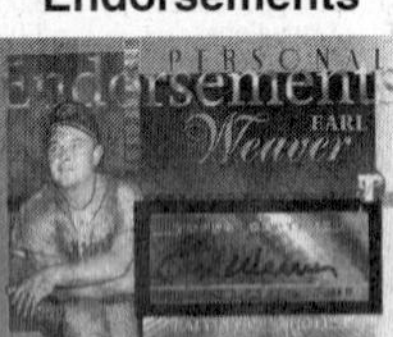

NM/M
Common Autograph: 10.00
Gold: No Pricing
Production 25 Sets
JA Jim Abbott 15.00
LA Luis Aparicio 15.00
BB Bert Blyleven 15.00
GB George Brett 50.00
GC Gary Carter 15.00
RD Ron Darling 15.00
AD Andre Dawson 15.00
DE Dennis Eckersley 15.00
DWE Darrell Evans 15.00
CF Carlton Fisk 25.00
GF George Foster 10.00
GG Rich "Goose" Gossage 10.00
BG Bobby Grich 10.00
KH Keith Hernandez 12.00
BJ Bo Jackson 60.00
RJ Reggie Jackson 50.00
AK Al Kaline 40.00
DL Don Larsen 15.00
JM Jack McDowell 10.00
SM Stan Musial 50.00
GN Graig Nettles 15.00
JO Jesse Orosco 10.00
JP Jim Palmer 15.00
JAP Jimmy Piersall 15.00
CR Cal Ripken Jr. 125.00
BR Brooks Robinson 30.00
NR Nolan Ryan 90.00
DS Duke Snider 40.00
EW Earl Weaver 15.00
CY Carl Yastrzemski 50.00
RY Robin Yount 50.00

Legends Signature Marks

NM/M
No pricing
Production One Set
RR Sugar Ray Robinson (12/05 Auction) 1,000

Legends Title Threads

NM/M
Common Player: 4.00
Refractors: No Pricing
Production 25 Sets
WB Wade Boggs 10.00
GC Gary Carter 6.00
JC Joe Carter 6.00
OC Orlando Cepeda 8.00
BD Bucky Dent 6.00
LD Lenny Dykstra 6.00
RF Rollie Fingers 8.00
GF George Foster 4.00
CS Cesar Geronimo 6.00
GG Rich "Goose" Gossage 6.00
KG Ken Griffey Sr. 6.00
OH Orel Hershiser 8.00
WH Willie Horton 10.00
MI Monte Irvin 12.00
DJ David Justice 6.00
JK Jimmy Key 6.00
EK Ed Kranepool 6.00
TM Tim McCarver 6.00
GN Graig Nettles 8.00
PO Paul O'Neill 10.00
JP Jim Palmer 8.00
DS Darryl Strawberry 6.00
MW Mookie Wilson 4.00

Legends Valuable Performances

NM/M
Common Player: 4.00
Refractor: No Pricing
Production one or 25.
YB Yogi Berra 15.00
JC Jose Canseco 10.00
AD Andre Dawson 6.00
DE Dennis Eckersley 8.00
CF Cecil Fielder 8.00
SG Steve Garvey 6.00
KH Keith Hernandez 4.00
RJ Reggie Jackson 10.00
HK Harmon Killebrew 12.00
DBM Don Mattingly 15.00
JM Joe Morgan 6.00
DM Dale Murphy 10.00
SM Stan Musial 15.00
DP Dave Parker 4.00
JR Jim Rice 8.00
CR Cal Ripken Jr. 25.00
FR Frank Robinson 8.00
MS Mike Schmidt 15.00
CY Carl Yastrzemski 15.00
RY Robin Yount 8.00

2005 Topps Retired Signature Edition

NM/M
Complete Set (110): 150.00
Common Player: 1.00
Pack (5): 30.00
Box (5): 125.00
1 Josh Gibson 1.00
2 Andre Dawson 1.00
3 Al Kaline 2.00
4 Andy Van Slyke 1.00
5 Brett Butler 1.00
6 Bob Gibson 1.50
7 Bo Jackson 2.00
8 Carlton Fisk 1.00
9 Chuck Knoblauch 1.00
10 Cal Ripken Jr. 6.00
11 Carl Yastrzemski 3.00
12 Tom Niedenfuer 1.00
13 Dennis Eckersley 1.00
14 Darryl Strawberry 1.00
15 Dwight Gooden 1.00
16 Davey Johnson 1.00
17 Don Mattingly 3.00
18 Dave Winfield 1.50
19 Don Zimmer 1.00
20 Ernie Banks 2.00
21 George Brett 3.00
22 Gary Carter 1.00
23 Gregg Jefferies 1.00
24 Harold Baines 1.00
25 Ryne Sandberg 2.00
26 Howard Johnson 1.00
27 Jim Abbott 1.00
28 Johnny Bench 2.00
29 Jay Buhner 1.00
30 Johnny Podres 1.00
31 Jose Canseco 1.50
32 Keith Hernandez 1.00
33 Lou Brock 1.00
34 Lou Whitaker 1.00
35 Mark Fidrych 1.00
36 Orlando Cepeda 1.00
37 Ozzie Smith 2.00
38 Paul O'Neill 1.00
39 Reggie Jackson 1.50
40 Sid Fernandez 1.00
41 Tony Gwynn 2.00
42 Tim Raines 1.00
43 Tom Seaver 1.50
44 Vida Blue 1.00
45 Brady Anderson 1.00
46 Bob Brenly 1.00
47 Bob Feller 1.50
48 Bill Mazeroski 1.00
49 Brooks Robinson 1.50
50 Harmon Killebrew 1.50
51 Bob Welch 1.00
52 Carl Erskine 1.00
53 Dale Murphy 1.00
54 Denny McClain 1.00
55 Dave Magadan 1.00
56 Duke Snider 1.50
57 Ed Kranepool 1.00
58 Frank Robinson 1.50
59 Jesus Alou 1.00
60 Joe Girardi 1.00
61 John Kruk 1.00
62 Jim Leyland 1.00
63 Juan Marichal 1.00
64 Johnny Pesky 1.00
65 Jesse Orosco 1.00
66 Ken Singleton 1.00
67 Matty Alou 1.00
68 Monte Irvin 1.00
69 Matt Williams 1.00
70 Pedro Guerrero 1.00
71 Ron Blomberg 1.00
72 Rod Carew 1.50
73 Rafael Santana 1.00
74 Ralph Kiner 1.00
75 Wade Boggs 1.50
76 Roger Craig 1.00
77 Robin Yount 2.00
78 Steve Carlton 1.00
79 Shawon Dunston 1.00
80 Steve Garvey 1.00
81 Stan Musial 3.00
82 Travis Fryman 1.00
83 Tito Fuentes 1.00
84 Mike Cuellar 1.00
85 Roberto Clemente 4.00
86 Whitey Ford 1.50
87 Yogi Berra 2.00
88 Atlee Hammaker 1.00
89 Bill Freehan 1.00
90 Brian Cashman 1.00
91 Bobby Richardson 1.00
92 Bob Boone 1.00
93 Charlie Hough 1.00
94 Glenn Hubbard 1.00
95 Grady Little 1.00
96 Jimmy Piersall 1.00
97 Jim Frey 1.00
98 Jerry Grote 1.00
99 Jim Leyritz 1.00
100 Nolan Ryan 5.00
101 Jim Kaat 1.00
102 Joe Pepitone 1.00
103 J.R. Richard 1.00
104 John Candelaria 1.00
105 Bill "Moose" Skowron 1.00
106 Rick Cerone 1.00
107 Ron Santo 1.00
108 Rick Dempsey 1.00
109 Roy White 1.00
110 Tippy Martinez 1.00

Black

Black (1-110): 4-6X
Production 54 Sets

Gold

Gold (1-110): 2-4X
Production 500 Sets

Holographic

No Pricing
Production One Set

Autographs

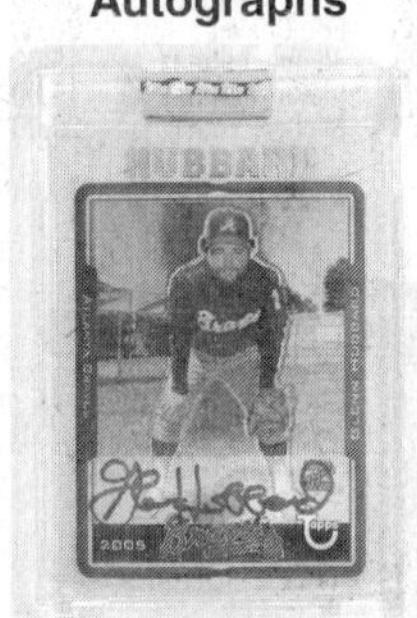

NM/M
Common Autograph: 10.00
JAA Jim Abbott 20.00
JA Jesus Alou 15.00
MA Matty Alou 15.00
BA Brady Anderson 15.00
HB Harold Baines 15.00
EB Ernie Banks 150.00
JB Johnny Bench 200.00
YB Yogi Berra 200.00
RB Ron Blomberg 15.00
VB Vida Blue 25.00
WB Wade Boggs 50.00
BRB Bob Boone 20.00
DLB Daryl Boston 10.00
BEB Bob Brenly 10.00
GB George Brett 150.00
LB Lou Brock 25.00
JCB Jay Buhner 25.00
BB Brett Butler 20.00
JRC John Candelaria 15.00
JC Jose Canseco 50.00
RCC Rod Carew 30.00
SC Steve Carlton 35.00
GC Gary Carter 20.00
BC Brian Cashman 85.00
OC Orlando Cepeda 15.00
RC Rick Cerone 15.00
RLC Roger Craig 15.00
MC Mike Cuellar 15.00
RD Ron Darling 15.00
AD Andre Dawson 25.00
RRD Rick Dempsey 15.00
BD Bob Dernier 20.00
SD Shawon Dunston 35.00
CE Carl Erskine 30.00
BF Bob Feller 30.00
SF Sid Fernandez 20.00
CF Carlton Fisk 30.00
BAF Bill Freehan 10.00
JF Jim Frey 15.00
TDF Travis Fryman 15.00
TF Tito Fuentes 15.00
REG Ron Gant 25.00
SG Steve Garvey 20.00
BG Bob Gibson 150.00
DG Dwight Gooden 20.00
JG Jerry Grote 20.00
PG Pedro Guerrero 15.00
TG Tony Gwynn 100.00
AH Atlee Hammaker 10.00
TH Toby Harrah 15.00
KH Keith Hernandez 20.00
CH Charlie Hough 10.00
GH Glenn Hubbard 10.00
MI Monte Irvin 50.00
BJ Bo Jackson 100.00
RJ Reggie Jackson 150.00
GJ Gregg Jefferies 20.00
HJ Howard Johnson 25.00
JLK Jim Kaat 15.00
AK Al Kaline 40.00
HK Harmon Killebrew 100.00
RK Ralph Kiner 35.00
EK Ed Kranepool 15.00
JK John Kruk 20.00
TL Tony LaRussa 20.00
JL Jim Leyland 15.00
JJL Jim Leyritz 15.00
GL Grady Little 15.00
JRL Jim Lonborg 15.00
DJM Dave Magadan 15.00
JM Juan Marichal 25.00
TM Tippy Martinez 10.00
DM Don Mattingly 140.00
BM Bill Mazeroski 45.00
DDM Denny McLain 20.00
DBM Dale Murphy 30.00
TN Tom Niedenfuer 15.00
PO Paul O'Neill 40.00
JO Jesse Orosco 10.00
JP Joe Pepitone 15.00
JMP Johnny Pesky 25.00
JAP Jimmy Piersall 20.00
JJP Johnny Podres 50.00
TR Tim Raines 25.00
JR J.R. Richard 20.00
BCR Bobby Richardson 20.00
CR Cal Ripken Jr. 180.00
BR Brooks Robinson 80.00
FR Frank Robinson 60.00
NR Nolan Ryan 250.00
RS Ryne Sandberg 90.00
RFS Rafael Santana 10.00
RES Ron Santo 30.00
TS Tom Seaver 100.00
MS Bill "Moose" Skowron 15.00
OS Ozzie Smith 125.00
ZS Zane Smith 10.00
DS Duke Snider 60.00
DES Darryl Strawberry 50.00
BW Bob Welch 15.00
LW Lou Whitaker 35.00
RW Roy White 15.00
MW Matt Williams 30.00
DW Dave Winfield 50.00
CY Carl Yastrzemski 120.00
AY Anthony Young 10.00
RY Robin Yount 125.00
DZ Don Zimmer 30.00

Co-Signers

NM/M
Some not priced.
BS Wade Boggs, Ryne Sandberg/49 140.00
BF Johnny Bench, Carlton Fisk/49 125.00
GF Bob Gibson, Whitey Ford/49 100.00

2005 Topps Rookie Cup

NM/M
Complete Set (160): 35.00
Common Player (1-150): .15
Common Rookie Auto. (151-160): 8.00
Inserted 1:62
Pack (7): 4.00
Box (24): 75.00
1 Pat Corrales .15
2 Ron Santo .25
3 Joe Torre .40
4 Boog Powell .15
5 Tom Tresh .15
6 Jonny Gomes .15
7 Rico Carty .15
8 Bert Campaneris .15
9 Tony Oliva .25
10 Ron Swoboda .15
11 Tony Perez .40
12 Joe Morgan .40
13 Davey Johnson .15
14 Cleon Jones .15
15 Tom Seaver .75
16 Rod Carew .50
17 Rick Monday .15
18 Johnny Bench .75
19 Bobby Cox .15
20 Jerry Koosman .15
21 Al Oliver .25
22 Lou Piniella .25
23 Larry Bowa .25
24 Chris Chambliss .15
25 Bill Buckner .15

26 Don Baylor .15
27 Buddy Bell .15
28 Carlton Fisk .50
29 Gary Mathews .15
30 Davey Lopes .15
31 Bob Boone .15
32 Bill Madlock .15
33 Claudell Washington .15
34 Jim Rice .25
35 Gary Carter .15
36 Willie Randolph .15
37 Chet Lemon .15
38 Andre Dawson .25
39 Eddie Murray .50
40 Paul Molitor .50
41 Ozzie Smith 1.00
42 Jeffrey Leonard .15
43 Lonnie Smith .15
44 Mookie Wilson .15
45 Tim Wallach .15
46 Tim Raines .25
47 Fernando Valenzuela .15
48 Cal Ripken Jr. 2.00
49 Ryne Sandberg 1.00
50 Willie McGee .15
51 Darryl Strawberry .15
52 Julio Franco .15
53 Brook Jacoby .15
54 Dwight Gooden .15
55 Roger McDowell .15
56 Ozzie Guillen .15
57 Vince Coleman .15
58 Pete Incaviglia .15
59 Wally Joyner .15
60 Jose Canseco .50
61 Cory Snyder .15
62 Devon White .15
63 Walt Weiss .15
64 Mark Grace .40
65 Ron Gant .15
66 Chris Sabo .15
67 Jay Buhner .15
68 Gary Sheffield .40
69 Gregg Jefferies .15
70 Ken Griffey Jr. 1.50
71 Tom Gordon .15
72 Jim Abbott .15
73 David Justice .25
74 Larry Walker .25
75 Sandy Alomar .15
76 Chuck Knoblauch .15
77 Jeff Bagwell .50
78 Luis Gonzalez .25
79 Ivan Rodriguez .50
80 Eric Karros .15
81 Jeff Kent .15
82 Kenny Lofton .15
83 Moises Alou .25
84 Reggie Sanders .15
85 Jeff Conine .15
86 J.T. Snow .15
87 Tim Salmon .25
88 Mike Piazza 1.00
89 Manny Ramirez .75
90 Ryan Klesko .15
91 Javy Lopez .15
92 Chipper Jones .75
93 Ray Durham .15
94 Garret Anderson .25
95 Shawn Green .15
96 Hideo Nomo .25
97 Jermaine Dye .15
98 Tony Clark .15
99 Joe Randa .15
100 Derek Jeter 2.00
101 Jason Kendall .15
102 Billy Wagner .15
103 Andruw Jones .50
104 Dmitri Young .15
105 Scott Rolen .50
106 Nomar Garciaparra .75
107 Jose Cruz Jr. .15
108 Scott Hatteberg .15
109 Mark Kotsay .15
110 Todd Helton .50
111 Miguel Cairo .15
112 Magglio Ordonez .25
113 Kerry Wood .25
114 Preston Wilson .15
115 Alex Gonzalez .15
116 Carlos Beltran .50
117 Rafael Furcal .25
118 Pat Burrell .15
119 Adam Kennedy .15
120 Terrence Long .15
121 Jay Payton .15
122 Bengie Molina .15
123 Albert Pujols 2.00
124 Craig Wilson .15
125 Alfonso Soriano .50
126 Jimmy Rollins .25
127 Adam Dunn .50
128 Ichiro Suzuki 1.50
129 Roy Oswalt .25
130 C.C. Sabathia .15
131 Brad Wilkerson .15
132 Nick Johnson .15
133 Eric Hinske .15
134 Austin Kearns .25
135 Dontrelle Willis .40
136 Mark Teixeira .50
137 Rocco Baldelli .15
138 Scott Podsednik .25
139 Brandon Webb .15
140 Jason Bay .25
141 Adam LaRoche .15
142 Khalil Greene .25
143 Joe Mauer .50
144 Matt Holliday .25
145 Chad Tracy .15
146 Garrett Atkins .15
147 Tadahito Iguchi 1.00
148 Russ Adams .15
149 Huston Street .15
150 Dan Johnson .15
151 J. Brent Cox **RC** 15.00
152 John Drennen **RC** 20.00
153 Ryan Tucker **RC** 10.00
154 Yunel Escobar **RC** 25.00
155 Jacob Marceaux **RC** 10.00
156 Mark Pawelek **RC** 25.00
157 Brandon Snyder **RC** 25.00
158 Wade Townsend **RC** 15.00
159 Troy Tulowitzki **RC** 85.00
160 Kevin Whelan **RC** 12.00

Blue

Blue (1-150): 3-6X
Blue (151-160): 1-2X
Production 50 Sets

Gold

No Pricing
Production One Set

Green

Green (1-150): 2-4X
Production 199
Green (151-160): 1-2X
Production 99

Orange

Orange (1-150): 1.5-3X
Production 399
Orange (151-160): 1X
Production 299

Red

Red (1-150): 1-2X
Production 499
Red (151-160): 1X
Production 399

Silver

No Pricing
Production One Set

Yellow

Yellow (1-150): 2-3X
Production 299
Yellow (151-160): 1X
Production 199

Printing Plates

No Pricing
Production one set per color.

Autographs

NM/M
Common Autograph:
Silver: No Pricing
Production Five Sets
Gold: No Pricing
Production One Set
JBA Jason Bay 20.00
JB Johnny Bench 65.00
AD Andre Dawson 15.00
JD Jermaine Dye 8.00
RF Rafael Furcal 12.00
MG Mark Grace 25.00
DRJ Dan Johnson 15.00
DJ Davey Johnson 8.00
AJ Andruw Jones 40.00
CJ Chipper Jones 35.00
DJ David Justice 20.00
EK Eric Karros 8.00
MK Mark Kotsay 8.00
CK Chuck Knoblauch 20.00
RM Roger McDowell 10.00
PM Paul Molitor 50.00
BP Boog Powell 15.00
MR Manny Ramirez 50.00
JR Jim Rice 30.00
RSA Ron Santo 25.00
TS Tom Seaver 50.00
GS Gary Sheffield 25.00
DS Darryl Strawberry 15.00
RS Ron Swoboda 10.00
JT Joe Torre 25.00
BW Brad Wilkerson 8.00
DW Dontrelle Willis 20.00

Dual Autographs

NM/M
Inserted 1:118
GS Mark Grace, Ron Santo 80.00
BW Jason Bay, Dontrelle Willis 50.00
WD Brad Wilkerson, Andre Dawson 50.00
CS J. Brent Cox, Tom Seaver 40.00
RTW Ryan Tucker, Dontrelle Willis 20.00
EF Yunel Escobar, Rafael Furcal 20.00
MM Jacob Marceaux, Roger McDowell 20.00
SP Brandon Snyder, Boog Powell 25.00
TS Wade Townsend, Tom Seaver 50.00
TW Troy Tulowitzki, Walt Weiss 50.00
WM Kevin Whelan, Roger McDowell 15.00

Reprints

NM/M
Complete Set (150): 60.00
Common Player: .25
Reprints: 1-2X Base Card
2 Per Hobby Pack
1 Per Retail Pack
Chrome: No Pricing
Production 25 Sets
Refractor: No Pricing
15 Sets
Chrome Gold: No Pricing
Production One Set
1 Pat Corrales/66 .25
2 Ron Santo/61 .50
3 Joe Torre/62 .75
4 Boog Powell/63 .25
5 Tom Tresh/63 .25
6 Jonny Gomes/06 .25
7 Rico Carty/65 .25
8 Bert Campaneris/65 .25
9 Tony Oliva/65 .50
10 Ron Swoboda/66 .25
11 Tony Perez/66 .75
12 Joe Morgan/66 .75
13 Davey Johnson/67 .25
14 Cleon Jones/67 .25
15 Tom Seaver/68 1.00
16 Rod Carew/68 .75
17 Rick Monday/68 .25
18 Johnny Bench/69 1.50
19 Bobby Cox/69 .25
20 Jerry Koosman/69 .25
21 Al Oliver/70 .50
22 Lou Piniella/70 .40
23 Larry Bowa/71 .40
24 Chris Chambliss/72 .25
25 Bill Buckner/72 .25
26 Don Baylor/73 .25
27 Buddy Bell/73 .25
28 Carlton Fisk/73 .75
29 Gary Mathews/74 .25
30 Davey Lopes/74 .25
31 Bob Boone/74 .25
32 Bill Madlock/75 .25
33 Claudell Washington/75 .25
34 Jim Rice/76 .40
35 Gary Carter/76 .25
36 Willie Randolph/77 .25
37 Chet Lemon/77 .25
38 Andre Dawson/78 .40
39 Eddie Murray/78 .75
40 Paul Molitor/79 .75
41 Ozzie Smith/79 1.50
42 Jeffrey Leonard/80 .25
43 Lonnie Smith/81 .25
44 Mookie Wilson/82 .25
45 Tim Wallach/82 .25
46 Tim Raines/82 .40
47 Fernando Valenzuela/82 .25
48 Cal Ripken Jr./83 3.00
49 Ryne Sandberg/84 1.50
50 Willie McGee/83 .25
51 Darryl Strawberry/84 .25
52 Julio Franco/84 .25
53 Brook Jacoby/85 .25
54 Dwight Gooden/85 .25
55 Roger McDowell/86 .25
56 Ozzie Guillen/86 .25
57 Vince Coleman/86 .25
58 Pete Incaviglia/87 .25
59 Wally Joyner/87 .25
60 Jose Canseco/87 .75
61 Cory Snyder/87 .25
62 Devon White/88 .25
63 Walt Weiss/89 .25
64 Mark Grace/89 .50
65 Ron Gant/89 .25
66 Chris Sabo/89 .25
67 Jay Buhner/89 .25
68 Gary Sheffield/90 .50
69 Gregg Jefferies/90 .25
70 Ken Griffey Jr./90 2.00
71 Tom Gordon/90 .25
72 Jim Abbott/90 .25
73 David Justice/91 .40
74 Larry Walker/91 .40
75 Sandy Alomar Jr./91 .25
76 Chuck Knoblauch/92 .25
77 Jeff Bagwell/92 .50
78 Luis Gonzalez/92 .25
79 Ivan Rodriguez/92 .50
80 Eric Karros/93 .25
81 Jeff Kent/93 .25
82 Kenny Lofton/93 .25
83 Moises Alou/93 .25
84 Reggie Sanders/93 .25
85 Jeff Conine/94 .25
86 J.T. Snow/94 .25
87 Tim Salmon/94 .25
88 Mike Piazza/94 1.50
89 Manny Ramirez/95 .75
90 Ryan Klesko/95 .25
91 Javy Lopez/95 .25
92 Chipper Jones/96 1.00
93 Ray Durham/96 .25
94 Garret Anderson/96 .25
95 Shawn Green/96 .25
96 Hideo Nomo/96 .40
97 Jermaine Dye/97 .25
98 Tony Clark/97 .25
99 Joe Randa/97 .25
100 Derek Jeter/97 3.00
101 Jason Kendall/97 .25
102 Billy Wagner/97 .25
103 Andruw Jones/98 .75
104 Dmitri Young/98 .25
105 Scott Rolen/98 .75
106 Nomar Garciaparra/98 .75
107 Jose Cruz Jr./98 .25
108 Scott Hatteberg/98 .25
109 Mark Kotsay/99 .25
110 Todd Helton/99 .50
111 Miguel Cairo/99 .25
112 Magglio Ordonez/99 .25
113 Kerry Wood/99 .40
114 Preston Wilson/00 .25
115 Alex Gonzalez/00 .25
116 Carlos Beltran/00 .50
117 Rafael Furcal/01 .25
118 Pat Burrell/01 .25
119 Adam Kennedy/01 .25
120 Terrence Long/01 .25
121 Jay Payton/01 .25
122 Bengie Molina/01 .25
123 Albert Pujols/02 3.00
124 Craig Wilson/02 .25
125 Alfonso Soriano/02 .50
126 Jimmy Rollins/02 .50
127 Adam Dunn/02 .75
128 Ichiro Suzuki/02 2.00
129 Roy Oswalt/02 .40
130 C.C. Sabathia/02 .25
131 Brad Wilkerson/03 .25
132 Nick Johnson/03 .25
133 Eric Hinske/03 .25
134 Austin Kearns/03 .25
135 Dontrelle Willis/04 .75
136 Mark Teixeira/04 .75
137 Rocco Baldelli/04 .25
138 Scott Podsednik/04 .25
139 Brandon Webb/04 .25
140 Jason Bay/05 .25
141 Adam LaRoche/05 .25
142 Khalil Greene/05 .25
143 Joe Mauer/05 .50
144 Matt Holliday/05 .25
145 Chad Tracy/05 .25
146 Garrett Atkins/06 .25
147 Tadahito Iguchi/06 1.50
148 Russ Adams/06 .25
149 Huston Street/06 .25
150 Dan Johnson/06 .25

Original Relics

No Pricing
Production 1-10

2005 Topps Total

NM/M
Complete Set (770): 120.00
Common Player: .15
Pack (10): 1.00
Box (36): 35.00
1 Rafael Furcal .15
2 Tony Clark .15
3 Hideki Matsui 1.25
4 Zach Day .15
5 Garret Anderson .40
6 B.J. Surhoff .15
7 Trevor Hoffman .15
8 Kenny Lofton .15
9 Ross Gload .15
10 Jorge Cantu .15
11 Joel Pineiro .15
12 Alex Cintron .15
13 Mike Matheny .15
14 Rod Barajas .15
15 Ray Durham .15
16 Danys Baez .15
17 Brian Schneider .15
18 Tike Redman .15
19 Ricardo Rodriguez .15
20 Mike Sweeney .15
21 Greg Myers .15
22 Chone Figgins .15
23 Brian Lawrence .15
24 Joe Nathan .15
25 Placido Polanco .15
26 Yadier Molina .15
27 Gary Bennett .15
28 Yorvit Torrealba .15
29 Javier Valentin .15
30 Jason Giambi .25
31 Brandon Claussen .15
32 Miguel Olivo .15
33 Josh Bard .15
34 Ramon Hernandez .15
35 Geoff Jenkins .15
36 Bobby Kielty .15
37 Luis A. Gonzalez .15
38 Benito Santiago .15
39 Brandon Inge .15
40 Mark Prior .50
41 Mike Lieberthal .15
42 Toby Hall .15
43 Brad Ausmus .15
44 Damian Miller .15
45 Mark Kotsay .15
46 John Buck .15
47 Oliver Perez .25
48 Matt Morris .25
49 Raul Chavez .15
50 Randy Johnson .50
51 David Bush .15
52 Jose Macias .15
53 Paul Wilson .15
54 Wilfredo Ledezma .15
55 J.D. Drew .25
56 Pedro Martinez .50
57 Josh Towers .15
58 Jamie Moyer .15
59 Scott Elarton .15
60 Ken Griffey Jr. 1.00
61 Steve Trachsel .15
62 Bubba Crosby .15
63 Michael Barrett .15
64 Odalis Perez .15
65 B.J. Upton .25
66 Eric Bruntlett .15
67 Carlos Zambrano .15
68 Brandon League .15
69 Carlos Silva .15
70 Lyle Overbay .25
71 Runelvys Hernandez .15
72 Brad Penny .15
73 Ty Wigginton .15
74 Orlando Hudson .15
75 Roy Oswalt .25
76 Jason LaRue .15
77 Ismael Valdez .15
78 Calvin Pickering .15
79 Bill Hall .15
80 Carl Crawford .15
81 Tomas Perez .15
82 Joe Kennedy .15
83 Chris Woodward .15
84 Jason Lane .15
85 Steve Finley .15
86 Jeff Francis .15
87 Felipe Lopez .15
88 Chan Ho Park .15
89 Joe Crede .15
90 Jose Vidro .15
91 Casey Kotchman .25
92 Brandon Backe .15
93 Mike Hampton .15
94 Ryan Dempster .15
95 Wily Mo Pena .25
96 Matt Holliday .25
97 A.J. Pierzynski .15
98 Jason Jennings .15
99 Eli Marrero .15
100 Carlos Beltran .40
101 Scott Kazmir .25
102 Kenny Rogers .15
103 Roy Halladay .25
104 Alex Cora .15
105 Richie Sexson .25
106 Ben Sheets .25
107 Bartolo Colon .25
108 Eddie Perez .15
109 Vicente Padilla .15
110 Sammy Sosa 1.00
111 Mark Ellis .15
112 Woody Williams .15
113 Todd Greene .15
114 Nook Logan .15
115 Francisco Rodriguez .15
116 Miguel Batista .15
117 Livan Hernandez .15
118 Chris Aguila .15
119 Coco Crisp .15
120 Jose Reyes .25
121 Ricky Ledee .15
122 Brad Radke .15
123 Carlos Guillen .15
124 Paul Bako .15
125 Tom Glavine .25
126 Chad Moeller .15
127 Mark Buehrle .25
128 Casey Blake .15
129 Juan Rivera .15
130 Preston Wilson .15
131 Nate Robertson .15
132 Julio Franco .15
133 Derek Lowe .15
134 Rob Bell .15
135 Javy Lopez .25
136 Javier Vazquez .15
137 Desi Relaford .15
138 Danny Graves .15
139 Josh Fogg .15
140 Bobby Crosby .25
141 Ramon Castro .15
142 Jerry Hairston Jr. .15
143 Morgan Ensberg .15
144 Brandon Webb .25
145 Jack Wilson .15
146 Bill Mueller .15
147 Troy Glaus .25
148 Armando Benitez .15
149 Adam LaRoche .15
150 Hank Blalock .40
151 Ryan Franklin .15
152 Kevin Millwood .15
153 Jason Marquis .15
154 Dewon Brazelton .15
155 Al Leiter .15
156 Garrett Atkins .15
157 Todd Walker .15
158 Kris Benson .15
159 Eric Milton .15
160 Bret Boone .15
161 Matthew LeCroy .15
162 Chris Widger .15
163 Ruben Gotay .15
164 Craig Monroe .15
165 Travis Hafner .15
166 Vance Wilson .15
167 Jason Grabowski .15
168 Tim Salmon .25
169 Henry Blanco .15
170 Josh Beckett .25
171 Jake Westbrook .15
172 Paul LoDuca .15
173 Julio Lugo .15
174 Juan Cruz .15
175 Mark Mulder .25
176 Juan Castro .15
177 Damion Easley .15
178 LaTroy Hawkins .15
179 Jon Lieber .25
180 Vernon Wells .25
181 Jeff DaVanon .15
182 Dustan Mohr .15
183 Ryan Freel .15
184 Doug Davis .15
185 Sean Casey .25
186 Robb Quinlan .15
187 J.D. Closser .15
188 Tim Wakefield .15
189 Brian Jordan .15
190 Adam Dunn .40
191 Antonio Perez .15
192 Brett Tomko .15
193 John Flaherty .15
194 Michael Cuddyer .15
195 Ronnie Belliard .15
196 Tony Womack .15
197 Jason Johnson .15
198 Victor Santos .15
199 Dan Haren .15
200 Derek Jeter 1.50
201 Brian Anderson .15
202 Carlos Pena .15
203 Jaret Wright .15
204 Paul Byrd .15
205 Shannon Stewart .15
206 Chris Carpenter .15
207 Matt Stairs .15
208 Brad Hawpe .15
209 Bobby Higginson .15
210 Torii Hunter .25
211 Shawn Green .25
212 Todd Hollandsworth .15
213 Scott Erickson .15
214 C.C. Sabathia .15
215 Mike Mussina .40
216 Jason Kendall .15
217 Todd Pratt .15
218 Danny Kolb .15
219 Tony Armas .15
220 Edgar Renteria .25
221 Dave Roberts .15
222 Luis Rivas .15
223 Adam Everett .15
224 Jeff Cirillo .15
225 Orlando Hernandez .15
226 Ken Harvey .15
227 Corey Patterson .25
228 Humberto Cota .15
229 A.J. Burnett .25
230 Roger Clemens 1.50
231 Joe Randa .15
232 David Dellucci .15
233 Troy Percival .15
234 Dustin Hermanson .15
235 Eric Gagne .25
236 Terry Tiffee .15
237 Tony Graffanino .15
238 Jayson Werth .15
239 Michael Sweeney .15
240 Chipper Jones .75
241 Aramis Ramirez .40
242 Frank Catalanotto .15
243 Mike Maroth .15
244 Kelvim Escobar .15
245 Bobby Abreu .25
246 Kyle Lohse .15
247 Jason Isringhausen .15
248 Jose Lima .15
249 Adrian Gonzalez .15
250 Alex Rodriguez 1.50
251 Ramon Ortiz .15
252 Frank Menechino .15
253 Keith Ginter .15
254 Kip Wells .15
255 Dmitri Young .15
256 Craig Biggio .25
257 Ramon E. Martinez .15
258 Jason Bartlett .15
259 Brad Lidge .15
260 Brian Giles .25
261 Luis Terrero .15
262 Miguel Ojeda .15
263 Rich Harden .25
264 Jacque Jones .15
265 Marcus Giles .25
266 Carlos Zambrano .25
267 Michael Tucker .15
268 Wes Obermueller .15

No.	Player	Price
269	Peter Orr	.50
270	Jim Thome	.50
271	Omar Vizquel	.25
272	Jose Valentin	.15
273	Juan Uribe	.15
274	Doug Mirabelli	.15
275	Jeff Kent	.25
276	Brad Wilkerson	.15
277	Chris Burke	.25
278	Endy Chavez	.15
279	Richard Hidalgo	.15
280	John Smoltz	.25
281	Jarrod Washburn	.15
282	Larry Bigbie	.15
283	Edgardo Alfonzo	.15
284	Cliff Lee	.15
285	Carlos Lee	.25
286	Olmedo Saenz	.15
287	Tomokazu Ohka	.15
288	Ruben Sierra	.15
289	Nick Swisher	.15
290	Frank Thomas	.40
291	Aaron Cook	.15
292	Cody McKay	.15
293	Hee Seop Choi	.15
294	Carl Pavano	.25
295	Scott Rolen	.50
296	Matt Kata	.15
297	Terrence Long	.15
298	Jimmy Gobble	.15
299	Jason Repko	.15
300	Manny Ramirez	.50
301	Dan Wilson	.15
302	Jhonny Peralta	.15
303	John Mabry	.15
304	Adam Melhuse	.15
305	Kerry Wood	.50
306	Ryan Langerhans	.15
307	Antonio Alfonseca	.15
308	Marco Scutaro	.15
309	Jamey Carroll	.15
310	Lance Berkman	.25
311	Willie Harris	.15
312	Phil Nevin	.25
313	Gregg Zaun	.15
314	Michael Ryan	.15
315	Zack Greinke	.15
316	Ted Lilly	.15
317	David Eckstein	.15
318	Tony Torcato	.15
319	Robert Mackowiak	.15
320	Mark Teixeira	.40
321	Jason Phillips	.15
322	Jeremy Reed	.15
323	Bengie Molina	.15
324	Terrmel Sledge	.15
325	Justin Morneau	.40
326	Sandy Alomar Jr.	.15
327	Jon Garland	.25
328	Jay Payton	.15
329	Tino Martinez	.25
330	Jason Bay	.25
331	Jeff Conine	.15
332	Shawn Chacon	.15
333	Angel Berroa	.15
334	Reggie Sanders	.15
335	Kevin Brown	.15
336	Brady Clark	.15
337	Casey Fossum	.15
338	Raul Ibanez	.15
339	Derrek Lee	.40
340	Victor Martinez	.25
341	Kazuhisa Ishii	.15
342	Royce Clayton	.15
343	Trot Nixon	.25
344	Eric Young	.15
345	Aubrey Huff	.15
346	Brett Myers	.25
347	Joey Gathright	.15
348	Mark Grudzielanek	.15
349	Scott Spiezio	.15
350	Eric Chavez	.25
351	Einar Diaz	.15
352	Dallas McPherson	.25
353	John Thomson	.15
354	Neifi Perez	.15
355	Larry Walker	.25
356	Billy Wagner	.25
357	Mike Cameron	.15
358	Jimmy Rollins	.25
359	Kevin Mench	.15
360	Joe Mauer	.25
361	Jose Molina	.15
362	Joe Borchard	.15
363	Kevin Cash	.15
364	Jay Gibbons	.15
365	Khalil Greene	.25
366	Justin Leone	.15
367	Eddie Guardado	.15
368	Mike Lamb	.15
369	Matt Riley	.15
370	Luis Gonzalez	.25
371	Alfredo Amezaga	.15
372	J.J. Hardy	.15
373	Hector Luna	.15
374	Greg Aquino	.15
375	Jim Edmonds	.25
376	Joe Blanton	.15
377	Russell Branyan	.15
378	J.T. Snow	.15
379	Magglio Ordonez	.25
380	Rafael Palmeiro	.40
381	Andruw Jones	.25
382	David DeJesus	.15
383	Marquis Grissom	.15
384	Bobby Hill	.15
385	Kazuo Matsui	.15
386	Mark Loretta	.15
387	Chris Shelton	.15
388	Johnny Estrada	.15
389	Adam Hyzdu	.15
390	Nomar Garciaparra	1.00
391	Mark Teahen	.15
392	Chris Capuano	.15
393	Ben Broussard	.15
394	Daniel Cabrera	.15
395	Jeremy Bonderman	.25
396	Darin Erstad	.25
397	Alex S. Gonzalez	.15
398	Kevin Millar	.15
399	Freddy Garcia	.15
400	Alfonso Soriano	.50
401	Koyie Hill	.15
402	Omar Infante	.15
403	Alex Gonzalez	.15
404	Pat Burrell	.25
405	Wes Helms	.15
406	Junior Spivey	.15
407	Joe Mays	.15
408	Jason Stanford	.15
409	Gil Meche	.15
410	Tim Hudson	.25
411	Chase Utley	.25
412	Matt Clement	.25
413	Nick Green	.15
414	Jose Vizcaino	.15
415	Ryan Klesko	.15
416	Vinny Castilla	.15
417	Brian Roberts	.40
418	Geronimo Gil	.15
419	Gary Matthews	.15
420	Jeff Weaver	.15
421	Jerome Williams	.15
422	Andy Pettitte	.40
423	Randy Wolf	.15
424	D'Angelo Jimenez	.15
425	Moises Alou	.25
426	Eric Byrnes	.15
427	Mark Redman	.15
428	Jermaine Dye	.15
429	Cory Lidle	.15
430	Jason Schmidt	.25
431	Jason W. Smith	.15
432	Jose Castillo	.15
433	Pokey Reese	.15
434	Matt Lawton	.15
435	Jose Guillen	.25
436	Craig Counsell	.15
437	Jose Hernandez	.15
438	Braden Looper	.15
439	Scott Hatteberg	.15
440	Gary Sheffield	.40
441	Gabe Gross	.15
442	Chris Gomez	.15
443	Dontrelle Willis	.40
444	Jamey Wright	.15
445	Rocco Baldelli	.15
446	Bernie Williams	.25
447	Sean Burroughs	.15
448	Willie Bloomquist	.15
449	Luis Castillo	.15
450	Mike Piazza	1.00
451	Ryan Drese	.15
452	Pedro Feliz	.15
453	Horacio Ramirez	.15
454	Luis Matos	.15
455	Craig Wilson	.15
456	Russ Ortiz	.15
457	Xavier Nady	.15
458	Hideo Nomo	.25
459	Miguel Cairo	.15
460	Mike Lowell	.25
461	Corky Miller	.15
462	Bobby Madritsch	.15
463	Jose Contreras	.15
464	Johnny Damon	.75
465	Miguel Cabrera	.50
466	Eric Hinske	.15
467	Marlon Byrd	.15
468	Aaron Miles	.15
469	Ramon Vazquez	.15
470	Michael Young	.15
471	Alex Sanchez	.15
472	Shea Hillenbrand	.15
473	Jeff Bagwell	.40
474	Erik Bedard	.15
475	Jake Peavy	.40
476	Jody Gerut	.15
477	Randy Winn	.15
478	Kevin Youkilis	.15
479	Eric Dubose	.15
480	David Wright	.75
481	Wilson Valdez	.15
482	Cliff Floyd	.15
483	Jose Mesa	.25
484	Doug Mientkiewicz	.15
485	Jorge Posada	.40
486	Sidney Ponson	.15
487	David Krynzel	.15
488	Octavio Dotel	.15
489	Matt Treanor	.15
490	Johan Santana	.40
491	John Patterson	.15
492	So Taguchi	.15
493	Carl Everett	.15
494	Jason Dubois	.15
495	Albert Pujols	1.50
496	Kirk Rueter	.15
497	Geoff Blum	.15
498	Juan Encarnacion	.15
499	Mark Hendrickson	.15
500	Barry Bonds	2.00
501	Cesar Izturis	.15
502	David Wells	.15
503	Jorge Julio	.15
504	Cristian Guzman	.15
505	Juan Pierre	.15
506	Adam Eaton	.15
507	Nick Johnson	.25
508	Mike Redmond	.15
509	Daryle Ward	.15
510	Adrian Beltre	.25
511	Laynce Nix	.15
512	Reed Johnson	.15
513	Jeremy Affeldt	.15
514	R.A. Dickey	.15
515	Alex Rios	.15
516	Orlando Palmeiro	.15
517	Mark Belhorn	.15
518	Adam Kennedy	.15
519	Curtis Granderson	.15
520	Todd Helton	.40
521	Aaron Boone	.15
522	Milton Bradley	.25
523	Timoniel Perez	.15
524	Jeff Suppan	.15
525	Austin Kearns	.15
526	Charles Thomas	.15
527	Bronson Arroyo	.15
528	Roger Cedeno	.15
529	Russ Adams	.15
530	Barry Zito	.25
531	Bob Wickman	.15
532	Deivi Cruz	.15
533	Mariano Rivera	.40
534	J.J. Davis	.15
535	Greg Maddux	1.00
536	Ryan Vogelsong	.15
537	Josh Phelps	.15
538	Scott Hairston	.15
539	Vladimir Guerrero	.75
540	Ivan Rodriguez	.50
541	David Newhan	.15
542	David Bell	.15
543	Lew Ford	.15
544	Grady Sizemore	.25
545	David Ortiz	.75
546	Jose Cruz Jr.	.15
547	Aaron Rowand	.15
548	Marcus Thames	.15
549	Scott Podsednik	.25
550	Ichiro Suzuki	1.25
551	Eduardo Perez	.15
552	Chris Snyder	.15
553	Corey Koskie	.15
554	Miguel Tejada	.50
555	Orlando Cabrera	.25
556	Rondell White	.15
557	Wade Miller	.15
558	Rodrigo Lopez	.15
559	Chad Tracy	.15
560	Paul Konerko	.25
561	Wil Cordero	.15
562	John McDonald	.15
563	Jason Ellison	.15
564	Jason Michaels	.15
565	Melvin Mora	.25
566	Ryan Church	.15
567	Ryan Ludwick	.15
568	Erubiel Durazo	.15
569	Noah Lowry	.15
570	Curt Schilling	.50
571	Esteban Loaiza	.15
572	Freddy Sanchez	.15
573	Rich Aurilia	.15
574	Travis Lee	.15
575	Dennis Tankersley, Chris George	.15
576	Jason Christiansen, Kevin Correia	.15
577	Ryan Bukvich, Randy Williams	.15
578	Terry Adams, Gavin Floyd	.15
579	Seth Etherton, Dan Meyer	.15
580	Justin Lehr, Derrick Turnbow	.15
581	Mike Gosling, Brad Halsey	.15
582	Jim Mecir, Logan Kensing	.15
583	Brad Hennessey, Jeff Fassero	.15
584	Jason Grilli, John Adkins	.15
585	Jesse Crain, Juan Rincon	.15
586	Jaime Cerda, Nate Field	.15
587	Bartolome Fortunato, Jae Weong Seo	.15
588	Frank Brooks, Yhency Brazoban	.15
589	Jamie Walker, Ugueth Urbina	.15
590	Bret Prinz, Scott Proctor	.15
591	Bob Howry, Jason Davis	.15
592	Amaury Telemaco, Tim Worrell	.15
593	Jose Acevedo, Kent Mercker	.15
594	Chris Hammond, Scott Linebrink	.15
595	Fernando Nieve, John Franco	.15
596	Mike Lincoln, Randy Flores	.15
597	Joe Borowski, Kyle Farnsworth	.15
598	Jesus Colome, Lance Carter	.15
599	Abe Alvarez, Lenny DiNardo	.15
600	Chad Bradford, Kiko Calero	.15
601	David Aardsma, Jim Brower	.15
602	Geoff Geary, Ryan Madson	.15
603	Ben Howard, Nate Bump	.15
604	Chin-Hui Tsao, Jason Young	.15
605	Aaron Harang, Ryan Wagner	.15
606	Rick Bauer, Steve Kline	.15
607	Lance Cormier, Randy Choate	.15
608	Jon Leicester, Todd Wellemeyer	.15
609	Jason Frasor, Vinnie Chulk	.15
610	Brian Fuentes, Scott Dohmann	.15
611	Matt Ginter, Tyler Yates	.15
612	Cory Stewart, Salomon Torres	.15
613	Cal Eldred, Mike Myers	.15
614	Carlos Almanzar, Doug Brocail	.15
615	George Sherrill, J.J. Putz	.15
616	Bruce Chen, Matt Riley	.15
617	Ben Weber, David Weathers	.15
618	Dennys Reyes, Rudy Seanez	.15
619	Ricardo Rincon, Tim Harikkala	.15
620	D.J. Carrasco, Shawn Camp	.15
621	Allan Simpson, Javier Lopez	.15
622	Glendon Rusch, Mike Remlinger	.15
623	Kevin Gryboski, Roman Colon	.15
624	Chris Reitsma, Tom Martin	.15
625	Chad Qualls, Dan Wheeler	.15
626	Brooks Kieschnick, Matt Wise	.15
627	Justin Speier, Kerry Ligtenberg	.15
628	Francisco Cordero, Frank Francisco	.15
629	Matt Thornton, Rafael Soriano	.15
630	Mike Stanton, Steve Karsay	.15
631	Mike MacDougal, Scott Sullivan	.15
632	Brian Bruney, Oscar Villarreal	.15
633	Jeff Bennett, Mike Adams	.15
634	Dave Borkowski, Eddy Rodriguez	.15
635	David Riske, Rafael Betancourt	.15
636	Gary Glover, Jorge De La Rosa	.15
637	Justin Wayne, Matt Perisho	.15
638	Jeff Bajenaru, Luis Vizcaino	.15
639	Erasmo Ramirez, Ron Mahay	.15
640	John Grabow, Mike Gonzalez	.15
641	J.C. Romero, Matt Guerrier	.15
642	Brandon Duckworth, Tim Redding	.15
643	Franklin Nunez, Travis Harper	.15
644	Matt Herges, Tyler Walker	.15
645	Elmer Dessens, Wilson Alvarez	.15
646	Anastacio Martinez, Mark Malaska	.15
647	Gary Knotts, Roberto Novoa	.15
648	Jairo Garcia, Justin Duchscherer	.15
649	Aaron Rakers, Todd Williams	.15
650	Paul Quantrill, Tom Gordon	.15
651	Brandon Lyon, Shawn Estes	.15
652	Gustavo Chacin, Justin Miller	.15
653	John Lackey, Scot Shields	.15
654	Bobby Seay, Jorge Sosa	.15
655	Chad Cordero, Luis Ayala	.15
656	Julio Mateo, Ron Villone	.15
657	Byung-Hyun Kim, Matt Mantei	.15
658	Cliff Politte, Damaso Marte	.15
659	Joe Valentine, Luke Hudson	.15
660	John Riedling, Todd Jones	.15
661	Aaron Heilman, Heath Bell	.15
662	Akinori Otsuka, Blaine Neal	.15
663	Joe Horgan, Joey Eischen	.15
664	Grant Balfour, J.D. Durbin	.15
665	Alan Embree, Mike Timlin	.15
666	Keith Foulke	.15
667	Aaron Fultz, Rheal Cormier	.15
668	Kevin Gregg, Scott Dunn	.15
669	Franklyn German, Steve Coyler	.15
670	Scott Eyre, Wayne Franklin	.15
671	Brian Meadows, Mike Johnston	.15
672	Guillermo Mota, Tim Spooneybarger	.15
673	B.J. Ryan, Jason Grimsley	.15
674	Neal Cotts, Shingo Takatsu	.15
675	Felix Heredia, Mike DeJean	.15
676	Brian Shackelford, Josh Hancock	.15
677	Jon Rauch, T.J. Tucker	.15
678	Brian Shouse, Nick Regilio	.15
679	Julian Tavarez, Ray King	.15
680	Mike Wuertz, Stephen Randolph	.15
681	Gabe White, Jorge Vasquez	.15
682	Jose Valverde, Mike Koplove	.15
683	Arthur Rhodes, Scott Sauerbeck	.15
684	Felix Rodriguez, Tanyon Sturtze	.15
685	Duaner Sanchez, Giovanni Carrara	.15
686	Chad Harville, Mike Gallo	.15
687	Dave Williams, Sean Burnett	.15
688	Scott Atchison, Shigetoshi Hasegawa	.15
689	Claudio Vargas, Francis Beltran	.15
690	Brendan Donnelly, Esteban Yan	.15
691	Ervin Santana, Jeff Mathis	.15
692	Bill Bray, Clint Everts	.15
693	Jason Kubel, Trevor Plouffe	.15
694	Andy Marte, Jake Stevens	.15
695	Aaron Hill, Chad Gaudin	.15
696	Carlos Quentin, Jesus Cota	.15
697	Chris Young, Thomas Diamond	.15
698	Dan Johnson, Omar Quintanilla	.15
699	John Maine, Val Majewski	.15
700	James Houser, Jonny Gomes	.15
701	David Murphy, Hanley Ramirez	.25
702	Chris Lambert, Rick Ankiel	.15
703	Angel Guzman, Felix Pie	.15
704	Merkin Valdez, Nate Schierholtz	.15
705	Arnie Munoz, Gio Gonzalez	.15
706	Felix Hernandez, Travis Blackley	.15
707	Edwin Encarnacion, Tony Blanco	.15
708	Justin Germano, Tim Stauffer	.15
709	Jeremy Guthrie, Jeremy Sowers	.15
710	Jorge Cortes, Tom Gorzelanny	.15
711	Logan Kensing, Taylor Tankersley	.15
712	Neil Walker, Paul Maholm	.15
713	Carlos Hernandez, Willy Taveras	.50
714	Greg Golson, Ryan Howard	1.00
715	Blake DeWitt, Edwin Jackson	.15
716	Dan Putnam, Huston Street	.15
717	Mark Rogers, Rickie Weeks	.25
718	Phillip Hughes, Robinson Cano	.40
719	Jay Rainville, Kyle Waldrop	.15
720	Craig Brazell, Yusmeiro Petit	.15
721	Baltazar Lopez **RC**, Matt Brown **RC**	.25
722	Brett Price **RC**, Jerry Owens **RC**	.50
723	Dan Uggla **RC**, Kyle Nichols **RC**	2.00
724	Francisco Rosario **RC**, Jayce Tingler **RC**	.25
725	Eulogio de la Cruz **RC**, Tony Giarratano **RC**	.25
726	Matt Campbell **RC**, Shane Costa **RC**	.25
727	Bill McCarthy **RC**, Martin Prado **RC**	.25
728	Edinson Volquez **RC**, Ian Kinsler **RC**	3.00
729	Lorenzo Scott **RC**, Luis Ramirez **RC**	.25
730	Chris Seddon **RC**, Elliot Johnson **RC**	.75
731	Chris Dickerson **RC**, Thomas Pauly **RC**	.15
732	Jason Motte **RC**, Stuart Pomeranz **RC**	.25
733	Jose Vaquedano **RC**, Stefan Bailie **RC**	.25
734	D.J. Houlton **RC**, Wade Robinson **RC**	.25
735	Matt DeSalvo **RC**, Melky Cabrera **RC**	1.00
736	Brian Stavisky **RC**, Landon Powell **RC**	.25
737	Scott Mathieson **RC**, Scott Mitchinson **RC**	.50
738	Bear Bay **RC**, Sean Marshall **RC**	.50
739	Brandon McCarthy **RC**, Pedro Lopez **RC**	1.50
740	Alexander Smit **RC**, Jair Jurrjens **RC**	1.00
741	Matt Rogelstad **RC**, Ryan Feierabend **RC**	.25
742	Adam Boeve **RC**, Nate McLouth **RC**	.25
743	Kevin Melillo **RC**, Michael Rogers **RC**	.25
744	Heath Totten **RC**, Matthew Kemp **RC**	2.00
745	Trevor Hutchinson **RC**, Yorman Bazardo **RC**	.15
746	Jesse Gutierrez **RC**, Tyler Pelland **RC**	.25
747	Jeremy West **RC**, Willy Mota **RC**	.25
748	Ryan Garko **RC**, Ryan Goleski **RC**	.50
749	Bryan Triplett **RC**, Jared Gothreaux **RC**	.25
750	Glen Perkins **RC**, Kevin West **RC**	.25
751	Michael Esposito **RC**, Zachary Parker **RC**	.25
752	Brian Miller **RC**, Ryan Sweeney	.25
753	Buck Coats **RC**, Casey McGehee **RC**	.25
754	Nate Cabrera **RC**, Zachary Cline **RC**	.15
755	Bobby Livingston **RC**, Mike Morse **RC**	.25
756	Brendan Ryan **RC**, Wes Swackhamer **RC**	.25
757	John Hudgins **RC**, Nick Masset **RC**	.25
758	George Kottaras **RC**, Peeter Ramos **RC**	.25
759	Elvys Quezada **RC**, T.J. Beam **RC**	.25
760	Dana Eveland **RC**, Travis Hinton **RC**	.25
761	Chris Vines **RC**, James Jurries **RC**	.25
762	Humberto Sanchez **RC**, Justin Verlander **RC**	2.00
763	Ian Bladergroen **RC**, Shawn Bowman **RC**	.50
764	J.B. Thurmond **RC**, Pat Misch **RC**	.25
765	Christian Colonel **RC**, Neil Wilson **RC**	.25
766	Checklist 1	.15
767	Checklist 2	.15
768	Checklist 3	.15
769	Checklist 4	.15
770	Checklist 5	.15

Silver

Stars: 1-30X
Inserted 1:1

Press Plates

	NM/M
Common Card Front P. Plate:	25.00
Common Card Back P. Plate:	15.00

Stars not priced.
Production one set per color (4):

Award Winners

		NM/M
Complete Set (30):		15.00
Common Player:		.25
Inserted 1:10		
AW1	Barry Bonds	2.00
AW2	Vladimir Guerrero	.75

AW3	Roger Clemens	2.00
AW4	Johan Santana	.75
AW5	Jason Bay	.25
AW6	Bobby Crosby	.25
AW7	Eric Gagne	.40
AW8	Mariano Rivera	.50
AW9	Albert Pujols	2.00
AW10	Mark Teixeira	.50
AW11	Mark Loretta	.25
AW12	Alfonso Soriano	.75
AW13	Jack Wilson	.25
AW14	Miguel Tejada	.50
AW15	Adrian Beltre	.40
AW16	Melvin Mora	.25
AW17	Barry Bonds	2.00
AW18	Jim Edmonds	.50
AW19	Bobby Abreu	.40
AW20	Manny Ramirez	.75
AW21	Gary Sheffield	.50
AW22	Vladimir Guerrero	.75
AW23	Johnny Estrada	.25
AW24	Victor Martinez	.25
AW25	Ivan Rodriguez	.50
AW26	Livan Hernandez	.25
AW27	David Ortiz	.75
AW28	Bobby Cox	.25
AW29	Buck Showalter	.25
AW30	Barry Bonds	2.00

Domination

		NM/M
Complete Set (30):		15.00
Common Player:		.25
Inserted 1:10		
40	Mark Prior	.75
50	Randy Johnson	.75
56	Pedro Martinez	.75
60	Ken Griffey Jr.	1.00
100	Carlos Beltran	.50
110	Sammy Sosa	1.50
147	Troy Glaus	.50
150	Hank Blalock	.50
180	Vernon Wells	.25
190	Adam Dunn	.50
200	Derek Jeter	2.00
230	Roger Clemens	2.00
250	Alex Rodriguez	1.50
260	Brian Giles	.25
270	Jim Thome	.75
290	Frank Thomas	.50
300	Manny Ramirez	.75
345	Aubrey Huff	.25
350	Eric Chavez	.25
400	Alfonso Soriano	.75
465	Miguel Cabrera	.75
490	Johan Santana	.50
495	Albert Pujols	2.00
500	Barry Bonds	2.00
510	Adrian Beltre	.40
520	Todd Helton	.50
575	Vladimir Guerrero	.75
540	Ivan Rodriguez	.50
545	David Ortiz	.75
554	Miguel Tejada	.50

Domination Autograph

Production 10

Production

		NM/M
Complete Set (10):		8.00
Common Player:		.40
Inserted 1:15		
AB	Adrian Beltre	.40
BB	Barry Bonds	2.00
VG	Vladimir Guerrero	.75
TH	Todd Helton	.50
AP	Albert Pujols	2.00
MR	Manny Ramirez	.75
AR	Alex Rodriguez	1.50
AS	Alfonso Soriano	.75
MT	Miguel Tejada	.50
JT	Jim Thome	.75

Signatures

		NM/M
Common Autograph:		8.00
BB	Brian Bruney	8.00
RC	Robinson Cano	35.00
JG	Joey Gathright	10.00
ZG	Zack Greinke	12.00
BM	Brett Myers	12.00
TT	Terry Tiffee	15.00
DW	David Wright	50.00

Team Checklists

		NM/M
Complete Set (30):		8.00
Common Player:		.15
3	Miguel Tejada	.50
6	Frank Thomas	.50
8	Victor Martinez	.25
9	Todd Helton	.50
10	Ivan Rodriguez	.50
11	Miguel Cabrera	.50
12	Roger Clemens	1.00
13	Zack Greinke	.15
14	Vladimir Guerrero	.50
16	Ben Sheets	.25
17	Johan Santana	.50
18	Carlos Beltran	.50
19	Alex Rodriguez	1.00
20	Eric Chavez	.25
21	Jim Thome	.50
22	Jason Bay	.25
23	Brian Giles	.25
24	Barry Bonds	1.50
25	Ichiro Suzuki	1.00
26	Albert Pujols	1.00
27	Carl Crawford	.25
28	Alfonso Soriano	.50
29	Roy Halladay	.25
30	Jose Vidro	.15
7	Adam Dunn	.50
5	Kerry Wood	.50
1	Luis Gonzalez	.25
2	John Smoltz	.25
4	David Ortiz	.50
15	Eric Gagne	.25

Total Topps

		NM/M
Complete Set (20):		12.00
Common Player:		.25
Inserted 1:15		
CB	Carlos Beltran	.50
AB	Adrian Beltre	.40
BB	Barry Bonds	2.00
EC	Eric Chavez	.25
RC	Roger Clemens	2.00
VG	Vladimir Guerrero	.75
TH	Todd Helton	.50
DJ	Derek Jeter	2.00
RJ	Randy Johnson	.75
GM	Greg Maddux	1.00
MP	Mike Piazza	1.00
AP	Albert Pujols	2.00
MR	Manny Ramirez	.75
AR	Alex Rodriguez	1.50
IR	Ivan Rodriguez	.50
JS	Johan Santana	.50
AS	Alfonso Soriano	.75
SS	Sammy Sosa	1.50
MT	Miguel Tejada	.50
JT	Jim Thome	.50

Pepcid Phillies

This special version of Topps Total cards was an August 6 stadium giveaway on Phillies Alumni Night. Except for the numbering on the backs, most cards are identical to the regular Topps Total versions. A sponsor's card was included in the cello wrapped pack.

		NM/M
Complete Set (22):		10.00
Common Player:		.50
1	Jason Michaels	.50
2	Ryan Howard, Greg Golson	1.00
3	Tim Worrell, Pedro Liriano	.50
4	Geoff Geary, Ryan Madson	.50
5	Rheal Cormier, Aaron Fultz	.50
6	Kenny Lofton	.50
7	Pat Burrell	1.00
8	Bobby Abreu	.75
9	Chase Utley	.75
10	Jim Thome	1.00
11	Jimmy Rollins	1.00
12	Tomas Perez	.50
13	David Bell	.50
14	Todd Pratt	.50
15	Mike Lieberthal	.50
16	Billy Wagner	.50
17	Cory Lidle	.50
18	Brett Myers	.50
19	Vicente Padilla	.50
20	Randy Wolf	.50
21	Jon Lieber	.50
---	Pepcid Sponsor's Card	.50

2005 Topps Turkey Red

		NM/M
Complete Set (315):		
Common Player:		.25
Common SP:		4.00
Inserted 1:4		
Pack (8):		5.00
Box (24):		100.00
1	Barry Bonds/Grey Uni/SP	15.00
1	Barry Bonds	4.00
2	Michael Young	.25
3	Jim Edmonds	.50
4	Cliff Floyd	.25
5	Roger Clemens/Blue Sky/SP	12.00
5	Roger Clemens/Yellow Sky/SP	12.00
6	Hal Chase	.25
7	Shannon Stewart	.25
8	Fred Clarke	.25
9	Travis Hafner	.50
10	Sammy Sosa/w/Name/SP	6.00
10	Sammy Sosa/w/o Name/SP	6.00
11	Jermaine Dye	.25
12	Lyle Overbay	.25
13	Oliver Perez	.25
14	Red Dooin	.25
15	Kid Elberfeld	.25
16	Mike Piazza/Blue Uni/SP	6.00
16	Mike Piazza Pinstripe	1.50
17	Bret Boone	.25
18	Hughie Jennings	.25
19	Jeff Francis	.25
20	Manny Ramirez/SP	6.00
21	Russ Ortiz	.25
22	Carlos Zambrano	.50
23	Luis Castillo	.25
24	David DeJesus	.25
25	Carlos Beltran/SP	5.00
26	Doug Davis	.25
27	Bobby Abreu	.50
28	Rich Harden/SP	4.00
29	Brian Giles	.25
30	Richie Sexson/SP	4.00
31	Nick Johnson	.25
32	Roy Halladay	.50
33	Andy Pettitte	.50
34	Miguel Cabrera	1.00
35	Jeff Kent	.25
36	Chone Figgins	.25
37	Carlos Lee	.50
38	Greg Maddux	2.00
39	Preston Wilson	.25
40	Chipper Jones	1.00
41	Coco Crisp	.25
42	Adam Dunn	.75
43	Miguel Tejada/CL	.50
44	Gary Sheffield/CL	.50
45	Javy Lopez/CL	.25
46	Scott Rolen/CL	.50
47	Todd Helton/CL	.50
48	Roger Clemens/CL	1.00
49	Jimmy Rollins/CL	.40
50	Ichiro Suzuki/CL	1.00
51	Cliff Floyd/CL	.25
52	Johan Santana/CL	.50
53	Mark Teixeira	.75
54	Chris Carpenter	.25
55	Roy Oswalt/SP	4.00
56	Casey Kotchman	.25
57	Torii Hunter	.50
58	Jose Reyes	.50
59	Wily Mo Pena/SP	4.00
60	Magglio Ordonez/SP	4.00
61	Aaron Miles	.25
62	Dallas McPherson	.25
63	Javy Lopez	.25
64	Luis Gonzalez	.25
65	David Ortiz	1.00
66	Jorge Posada	.50
67	Xavier Nady	.25
68	Larry Walker	.50
69	Mark Loretta	.25
70	Jim Thome/SP	5.00
71	Livan Hernandez	.25
72	Garrett Atkins	.25
73	Milton Bradley	.25
74	B.J. Upton	.25
75	Ichiro Suzuki/w/Name/SP	8.00
75	Ichiro Suzuki/w/o Name/SP	8.00
76	Aramis Ramirez	.25
77	Eric Milton	.25
78	Troy Glaus/SP	4.00
79	David Newhan	.25
80	Delmon Young	.50
81	Justin Morneau	.40
82	Ramon Ortiz	.25
83	Eric Chavez Blue Sky	.25
83	Eric Chavez/Purple Sky/SP	4.00
84	Sean Burroughs	.25
85	Scott Rolen/SP	6.00
86	Rocco Baldelli	.25
87	Joe Mauer/SP	5.00
88	Tony Womack	.25
89	Ken Griffey Jr.	2.00
90	Alfonso Soriano/SP	6.00
91	Paul Konerko	.25
92	Guillermo Mota	.25
93	Lance Berkman	.50
94	Mark Buehrle	.25
95	Matt Clement	.25
96	Melvin Mora	.25
97	Khalil Greene	.50
98	David Wright	1.50
99	Jack Wilson	.25
100	Alex Rodriguez/w/Bat/SP	10.00
100	Alex Rodriguez/w/Glove/SP	10.00
101	Joe Nathan	.25
102	Adrian Beltre/Grey Uni/SP	4.00
102	Adrian Beltre White Uni	.25
103	Mike Sweeney	.25
104	Brad Lidge	.25
105	Shawn Green	.25
106	Miguel Tejada/SP	5.00
107	Derrek Lee	.75
108	Eric Hinske	.25
109	Eric Byrnes	.25
110	Hideki Matsui/SP	8.00
111	Tom Glavine	.50
112	Jimmy Rollins	.40
113	Ryan Drese	.25
114	Josh Beckett	.25
115	Curt Schilling/SP	6.00
116	Jeremy Bonderman	.25
117	Hideki Matsui	.25
118	Chase Utley	.50
119	Troy Percival	.25
120	Vladimir Guerrero/w/Bat/SP	6.00
120	Vladimir Guerrero/w/Glove/SP	6.00
121	Gary Sheffield	.50
122	Jeromy Burnitz	.25
123	Javier Vazquez	.25
124	Kevin Millar	.25
125	Randy Johnson/Blue Sky	1.00
125	Randy Johnson/Purple Sky/SP	5.00
126	Pat Burrell	.25
127	Jason Schmidt	.25
128	Jose Vidro	.25
129	Kip Wells	.25
130	Ivan Rodriguez w/Cap	.75
130	Ivan Rodriguez/w/Helmet/SP	6.00
131	C.C. Sabathia	.25
132	Carlos Delgado/SP	4.00
133	Bartolo Colon	.25
134	Andruw Jones	.50
135	Kerry Wood	.50
136	Sidney Ponson	.25
137	Eric Gagne	.25
138	Rickie Weeks	.50
139	Mariano Rivera	.50
140	Bobby Crosby	.25
141	Jamie Moyer	.25
142	Corey Koskie	.25
143	John Smoltz	.50
144	Frank Thomas	.75
145	Cristian Guzman	.25
146	Paul LoDuca	.25
147	Geoff Jenkins	.25
148	Nick Swisher	.25
149	Jason Bay/SP	4.00
150	Albert Pujols/SP	10.00
151	Edwin Jackson	.25
152	Carl Crawford	.25
153	Mark Mulder	.50
154	Rafael Palmeiro	.75
155	Pedro Martinez/SP	6.00
156	Jake Westbrook	.25
157	Sean Casey	.25
158	Aaron Rowand	.25
159	J.D. Drew	.25
160	Johan Santana/Glove on Knee/SP	5.00
160	Johan Santana/Throwing/SP	5.00
161	Gavin Floyd	.25
162	Vernon Wells	.25
163	Aubrey Huff	.25
164	Jeff Bagwell	.50
165	David Wells	.25
166	Brad Penny	.25
167	Austin Kearns	.25
168	Mike Mussina	.50
169	Randy Wolf	.25
170	Tim Hudson/SP	4.00
171	Casey Blake	.25
172	Edgar Renteria	.50
173	Ben Sheets	.50
174	Kevin Brown	.25
175	Nomar Garciaparra/SP	8.00
176	Armando Benitez	.25
177	Jody Gerut	.25
178	Craig Biggio	.50
179	Omar Vizquel	.25
180	Jake Peavy	.50
181	Gustavo Chacin/SP	4.00
182	Johnny Damon	.75
183	Mike Lieberthal	.25
184	Felix Hernandez/SP	10.00
185	Zach Day/SP	4.00
186	Matt Cain	.25
187	Erubiel Durazo	.25
188	Zack Greinke	.25
189	Matt Morris	.25
190	Billy Wagner	.25
191	Al Leiter	.25
192	Miguel Olivo	.25
193	Jose Capellan/SP	4.00
194	Adam Eaton	.25
195	Steven White/SP	4.00
196	Joe Randa	.25
197	Richard Hidalgo	.25
198	Orlando Cabrera	.25
199	Joel Guzman/SP	6.00
200	Garret Anderson	.50
201	Endy Chavez	.25
202	Andy Marte	.25
203	Jose Guillen	.25
204	Victor Martinez	.25
205	Johnny Estrada	.25
206	Damian Miller	.25
207	Ken Harvey	.25
208	Ronnie Belliard	.25
209	Chan Ho Park	.25
210	Laynce Nix	.25
211	Lew Ford	.25
212	Moises Alou	.50
213	Kris Benson	.25
214	Mike Gonzalez/SP	4.00
215	Chris Burke	.25
216	Juan Pierre	.25
217	Phil Nevin	.25
218	Jerry Hairston Jr.	.25
219	Jeremy Reed	.25
220	Scott Kazmir/SP	4.00
221	Mike Maroth	.25
222	Alex Rios	.25
223	Esteban Loaiza	.25
224	Terrmel Sledge	.25
225	Mark Prior/Blue Sky/SP	5.00
225	Mark Prior/Yellow Sky/SP	5.00
226	Hank Blalock	.50
227	Craig Wilson	.25
228	Cesar Izturis	.25
229	Dmitri Young	.25
230	Derek Jeter/Blue Sky/SP	15.00
230	Derek Jeter/Purple Sky/SP	15.00
231	Mark Kotsay	.25
232	Darin Erstad	.25
233	Brandon Backe/SP	4.00
234	Mike Lowell	.25
235	Scott Podsednik	.25
236	Michael Barrett	.25
237	Chad Tracy	.25
238	David Dellucci	.25
239	Brady Clark	.25
240	Jorge Cantu	.25
241	Wilfredo Ledezma	.25
242	Morgan Ensberg	.25
243	Omar Infante	.25
244	Corey Patterson	.25
245	Matt Holliday	.50
246	Vinny Castilla	.25
247	Jason Bartlett	.25
248	Noah Lowry	.25
249	Huston Street	.25
250	Russell Branyan	.25
251	Juan Uribe	.25
252	Larry Bigbie	.25
253	Grady Sizemore	.50
254	Pedro Feliz	.25
255	Brad Wilkerson	.25
256	Brandon Inge	.25
257	Dewon Brazelton	.25
258	Rodrigo Lopez	.25
259	Jacque Jones	.25
260	Jason Giambi	.50
261	Clint Barmes	.25
262	Willy Taveras	.25
263	Marcus Giles	.25
264	Joe Blanton	.25
265	John Thomson	.25
266	Steve Finley SP	4.00
267	Kevin Millwood	.25
268	David Eckstein	.25
269	Barry Zito	.50
270	Todd Helton/Purple Sky/SP	5.00
270	Todd Helton/Yellow Sky/SP	5.00
271	Landon Powell **RC**	1.00
272	Justin Verlander **RC**	3.00
273	Wes Swackhamer **RC**	1.00
274	Wladimir Balentien **RC**	2.00
275	Philip Humber **RC**	1.00
276	Kevin Melillo **RC**	2.00
277	Billy Butler **RC**	5.00
278	Michael Rogers **RC**	1.00
279	Bobby Livingston **RC**	1.00
280	Glen Perkins **RC**	1.00
281	Michael Bourn	1.00
282	Tyler Pelland **RC**	1.00
283	Jeremy West **RC**	2.00
284	Brandon McCarthy **RC**	4.00
285	Ian Kinsler **RC**	3.00
286	Chris Roberson **RC**	1.00
287	Melky Cabrera **RC**	2.00
288	Ryan Sweeney	1.00
289	Chip Cannon **RC**	1.50
290	Andy LaRoche **RC**	5.00
291	Chuck Tiffany **RC**	1.00
292	Ian Bladergroen **RC**	1.00
293	Bear Bay **RC**	1.00
294	Hernan Iribarren **RC**	1.00
295	Stuart Pomeranz **RC**	1.00
296	Luke Scott **RC**	1.00
297	Chuck James **RC**	2.00
298	Kennard Bibbs **RC**	1.00
299	Steve Bondurant	1.50
300	Tom Oldham **RC**	1.00
301	Nolan Ryan	3.00
302	Reggie Jackson	1.00
303	Tom Seaver	1.00
304	Al Kaline	1.50
305	Cal Ripken Jr.	4.00
306	Josh Gibson	1.50
307	Frank Robinson	1.00
308	Duke Snider	1.00
309	Wade Boggs	1.50
310	Tony Gwynn	2.00
311	Carl Yastrzemski	2.00
312	Ryne Sandberg	2.00
313	Gary Carter	1.00
314	Brooks Robinson	1.50
315	Ernie Banks	1.50

Red

Stars (1-315):	1-2X
SP's:	.5-1X

White

Stars (1-315):	2-3X
SP's:	1 1.5X
Inserted 1:4	

Black

Stars (1-315):	3-5X
SP's:	1.5-2X
Inserted 1:20	

Gold

Stars (1-315):	5-10X
SP's:	3-5X
Production 50 Sets	

Suede

No Pricing
Production One Set

Autographs

		NM/M
Common Auto.:		10.00
Cards are not serial numbered		
MB	Matt Bush/17	20.00
CC	Carl Crawford/17	30.00
SE	Scott Elbert	20.00
JF	Josh Fields	15.00
EG	Eric Gagne/142	20.00
JG	Jody Gerut	10.00
JPH	J.P. Howell	15.00
ZJ	Zach Jackson	12.00
JJ	Jason Jaramillo	12.00
BJ	Blake Johnson	15.00
BM	Brett Myers/67	20.00
CN	Chris Nelson	10.00
DO	David Ortiz	50.00
ZP	Zachary Parker	12.00
DP	Dustin Pedroia	40.00
MR	Mariano Rivera/192	90.00
MRO	Mike Rodriguez	10.00
GS	Gary Sheffield	40.00
AS	Alfonso Soriano/142	40.00
JS	Jeremy Sowers	20.00

B-18 Blanket Boxloaders

		NM/M
Common Blanket		8.00
	Barry Bonds	20.00
	Roger Clemens	20.00
	Todd Helton	8.00
	Derek Jeter	20.00
	Alex Rodriguez	15.00
	Curt Schilling	12.00
	Alfonso Soriano	8.00
	Ichiro Suzuki	15.00

Cabinet Boxloaders

		NM/M
Inserted 1:Box		
BB	Barry Bonds	25.00
GB	George W. Bush	10.00
RJ	Randy Johnson	12.00
MP	Mike Piazza	12.00
AP	Albert Pujols	20.00
MR	Manny Ramirez	12.00
AR	Alex Rodriguez	20.00
SR	Scott Rolen	10.00
JS	Johan Santana	12.00
SS	Sammy Sosa	15.00
WT	William H. Taft	15.00
MT	Miguel Tejada	10.00
JT	Jim Thome	10.00
GW	George Washington	25.00

Cabinet Auto. Relics

		NM/M
Production 5-450		
MB	Matt Bush/450	25.00
CC	Carl Crawford/450	25.00
JG	Jody Gerut/450	20.00
MK	Mark Kotsay/450	30.00
BM	Brett Myers/150	40.00
DO	David Ortiz/75	100.00
MR	Mariano Rivera/25	90.00
AR	Alex Rodriguez/25	400.00
GS	Gary Sheffield/25	100.00
AS	Alfonso Soriano/75	75.00

Relics

		NM/M
Common Player:		4.00
JB	Jeff Bagwell	6.00
CB	Carlos Beltran	6.00
AB	Adrian Beltre	6.00
HB	Hank Blalock	6.00
BB	Barry Bonds	20.00
MC	Miguel Cabrera	8.00
RC	Roger Clemens	15.00
RC2	Roger Clemens	15.00
JD	Johnny Damon	10.00
JD2	Johnny Damon	10.00
VG	Vladimir Guerrero	8.00
TH	Todd Helton	6.00
CJ	Chipper Jones	8.00
ML	Mike Lowell	4.00
MM	Mark Mulder	4.00
MO	Magglio Ordonez	4.00
DO	David Ortiz	8.00
RP	Rafael Palmeiro	6.00
MP	Mike Piazza	8.00
MPR	Mark Prior	6.00
AP	Albert Pujols	15.00
MR	Manny Ramirez	8.00
AR	Alex Rodriguez	12.00
AR2	Alex Rodriguez	12.00
CS	Curt Schilling	8.00
GS	Gary Sheffield	6.00
AS	Alfonso Soriano	8.00
SS	Sammy Sosa	10.00
MTE	Mark Teixeira	6.00
MT	Miguel Tejada	8.00
JT	Jim Thome	6.00
LW	Larry Walker	4.00

2005 Topps Update

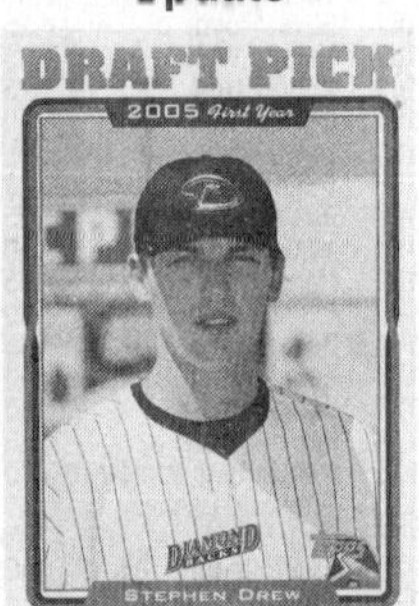

		NM/M
Complete Set (330):		35.00
Complete Factory Set (330):		40.00
Common Player:		.10
Pack (10):		2.00
Box (36):		60.00
1	Sammy Sosa	1.00
2	Jeff Francoeur	.25
3	Tony Clark	.10
4	Michael Tucker	.10
5	Mike Matheny	.10
6	Eric Young	.10
7	Jose Valentin	.10
8	Matt Lawton	.10
9	Juan Rivera	.10
10	Shawn Green	.25
11	Aaron Boone	.10
12	Woody Williams	.10
13	Brad Wilkerson	.10
14	Anthony Reyes **RC**	1.50
15	Russ Adams	.10
16	Gustavo Chacin	.10
17	Mike Restovich	.10
18	Humberto Quintero	.10
19	Matt Ginter	.10
20	Scott Podsednik	.25
21	Byung-Hyun Kim	.10
22	Orlando Hernandez	.10
23	Mark Grudzielanek	.10
24	Jody Gerut	.10
25	Adrian Beltre	.25
26	Scott Schoeneweis	.10
27	Marlon Anderson	.10
28	Jason Vargas	.10
29	Claudio Vargas	.10
30	Jason Kendall	.10
31	Aaron Small	.10
32	Juan Cruz	.10
33	Placido Polanco	.10
34	Jorge Sosa	.10
35	John Olerud	.10
36	Ryan Langerhans	.10
37	Randy Winn	.10
38	Zachary Duke	.25
39	Garrett Atkins	.10
40	Al Leiter	.10
41	Shawn Chacon	.10
42	Mark DeRosa	.10
43	Miguel Ojeda	.10
44	A.J. Pierzynski	.10
45	Carlos Lee	.10
46	LaTroy Hawkins	.10
47	Nick Green	.10
48	Shawn Estes	.10
49	Eli Marrero	.10
50	Jeff Kent	.10
51	Joe Randa	.10
52	Jose Hernandez	.10
53	Joe Blanton	.10
54	Huston Street	.10
55	Marlon Byrd	.10
56	Alex Sanchez	.10
57	Livan Hernandez	.10
58	Chris Young	.10
59	Brad Eldred	.10
60	Terrence Long	.10
61	Phil Nevin	.10
62	Kyle Farnsworth	.10
63	Jon Lieber	.10
64	Antonio Alfonseca	.10
65	Tony Graffanino	.10
66	Tadahito Iguchi **RC**	1.00
67	Brad Thompson	.10
68	Jose Vidro	.10
69	Jason Phillips	.10
70	Carl Pavano	.10
71	Pokey Reese	.10
72	Jerome Williams	.10
73	Kazuhisa Ishii	.10
74	Zach Day	.10
75	Edgar Renteria	.25
76	Mike Myers	.10
77	Jeff Cirillo	.10
78	Endy Chavez	.10
79	Jose Guillen	.10
80	Ugueth Urbina	.10
81	Vinny Castilla	.10
82	Javier Vazquez	.10
83	Willy Taveras	.10
84	Mark Mulder	.25
85	Mike Hargrove	.10
86	Buddy Bell	.10
87	Charlie Manuel	.10
88	Willie Randolph	.10
89	Bob Melvin	.10
90	Chris Lambert	.10
91	Homer Bailey	.20
92	Ervin Santana	.10
93	Bill Bray	.10
94	Thomas Diamond	.10
95	Trevor Plouffe	.10
96	James Houser	.10
97	Jake Stevens	.10
98	Anthony Whittington	.10
99	Phillip Hughes	.10
100	Greg Golson	.10
101	Paul Maholm	.10
102	Carlos Quentin	.10
103	Dan Johnson	.10
104	Mark Rogers	.10
105	Neil Walker	.10
106	Omar Quintanilla	.10
107	Blake DeWitt	.10
108	Taylor Tankersley	.10
109	David Murphy	.10
110	Felix Hernandez	.50
111	Craig Biggio	.10
112	Greg Maddux	.50
113	Bobby Abreu	.10
114	Alex Rodriguez	.75
115	Trevor Hoffman	.10
116	A.J. Pierzynski, Tadahito Iguchi	.25
117	Reggie Sanders	.10
118	Bengie Molina, Ervin Santana	.10
119	Chris Burke, Lance Berkman, Adam LaRoche	.10
120	Garret Anderson	.25
121	A.J. Pierzynski	.10
122	Paul Konerko	.25
123	Joe Crede	.10
124	Mark Buehrle, Jon Garland	.10
125	Freddy Garcia, Jose Contreras	.10
126	Reggie Sanders	.10
127	Roy Oswalt	.10
128	Roger Clemens	.75
129	Albert Pujols	.75
130	Roy Oswalt	.25
131	Joe Crede, Bobby Jenks	.10
132	Paul Konerko, Scott Podsednik	.25
133	Geoff Blum	.10
134	White Sox Sweep	.10
135	Alex Rodriguez, David Ortiz, Manny Ramirez	.50
136	Michael Young, Alex Rodriguez, Vladimir Guerrero	.50
137	David Ortiz, Mark Teixeira, Manny Ramirez	.25
138	Bartolo Colon, Jon Garland, Cliff Lee	.10
139	Kevin Millwood, Johan Santana, Mark Buehrle	.10
140	Johan Santana, Randy Johnson, John Lackey	.25
141	Andruw Jones, Derrek Lee, Albert Pujols	.50
142	Derek Lee, Albert Pujols, Miguel Cabrera	.50
143	Andruw Jones, Albert Pujols, Pat Burrell	.50
144	Dontrelle Willis, Chris Carpenter, Roy Oswalt	.25
145	Roger Clemens, Andy Pettitte, Dontrelle Willis	.50
146	Jake Peavy, Chris Carpenter, Pedro Martinez	.25
147	Mark Teixeira	.25
148	Brian Roberts	.10
149	Michael Young	.10
150	Alex Rodriguez	1.00
151	Johnny Damon	.25
152	Vladimir Guerrero	.25
153	Manny Ramirez	.25
154	David Ortiz	.25
155	Mariano Rivera	.25
156	Joe Nathan	.10
157	Albert Pujols	1.00
158	Jeff Kent	.10
159	Felipe Lopez	.10
160	Morgan Ensberg	.10
161	Miguel Cabrera	.25
162	Ken Griffey Jr.	.50
163	Andruw Jones	.25
164	Paul LoDuca	.10
165	Chad Cordero	.10
166	Ken Griffey Jr.	.50
167	Jason Giambi	.10
168	Willy Taveras	.10
169	Huston Street	.10
170	Chris Carpenter	.10
171	Bartolo Colon	.10
172	Bobby Cox	.10
173	Ozzie Guillen	.10
174	Andruw Jones	.25
175	Johnny Damon	.25
176	Alex Rodriguez	1.00
177	David Ortiz	.25
178	Manny Ramirez	.25
179	Miguel Tejada	.25
180	Vladimir Guerrero	.25
181	Mark Teixeira	.25
182	Ivan Rodriguez	.25
183	Brian Roberts	.10
184	Mark Buehrle	.10
185	Bobby Abreu	.25
186	Carlos Beltran	.25
187	Albert Pujols	1.00
188	Derrek Lee	.25
189	Jim Edmonds	.25
190	Aramis Ramirez	.10
191	Mike Piazza	.50
192	Jeff Kent	.10
193	David Eckstein	.10
194	Chris Carpenter	.10
195	Bobby Abreu	.10
196	Ivan Rodriguez	.25
197	Carlos Lee	.10
198	David Ortiz	.25
199	Hee Seop Choi	.10
200	Andruw Jones	.25
201	Mark Teixeira	.25
202	Jason Bay	.10
203	Hanley Ramirez	.50
204	Shin-Soo Choo	.10
205	Justin Huber	.10
206	Nelson Cruz **RC**	.50
207	Edwin Encarnacion	.10
208	Miguel Montero **RC**	.50
209	William Bergolla	.10
210	Luis Montanez	.10
211	Francisco Liriano	.50
212	Kevin Thompson	.10
213	B.J. Upton	.10
214	Conor Jackson	.10
215	Delmon Young	.25
216	Andy LaRoche	.50
217	Ryan Garko	.10
218	Josh Barfield	.10
219	Chris Young	.10
220	Justin Verlander	.25
221	Drew Anderson **RC**	.25
222	Luis Hernandez **RC**	.25
223	Jim Burt **RC**	.25
224	Mike Morse **RC**	.25
225	Elliot Johnson **RC**	.50
226	C.J. Smith **RC**	.25
227	Casey McGehee **RC**	.25
228	Brian Miller **RC**	.15
229	Chris Vines **RC**	.40
230	D.J. Houlton **RC**	.25
231	Chuck Tiffany **RC**	.40
232	Humberto Sanchez **RC**	.75
233	Baltazar Lopez **RC**	.25
234	Russell Martin **RC**	1.00
235	Dana Eveland **RC**	.25
236	Johan Silva **RC**	.25
237	Adam Harben **RC**	1.00
238	Brian Bannister **RC**	.25
239	Adam Boeve **RC**	.25
240	Tom Oldham **RC**	.25
241	Cody Haerther **RC**	.25
242	Dan Santin **RC**	.25
243	Daniel Haigwood **RC**	.25
244	Craig Tatum **RC**	.25
245	Martin Prado **RC**	.40
246	Errol Simonitsch **RC**	.40
247	Lorenzo Scott **RC**	.25
248	Hayden Penn **RC**	.40
249	Heath Totten **RC**	.25
250	Nick Masset **RC**	.25
251	Pedro Lopez **RC**	.25
252	Benjamin Harrison	.15
253	Michael Spidale **RC**	.25
254	Jeremy Harts **RC**	.25
255	Danny Zell **RC**	.40
256	Kevin Collins **RC**	.15
257	Tony Arnerich **RC**	.15
258	Matt Albers **RC**	.50
259	Ricky Barrett **RC**	.25
260	Hernan Iribarren **RC**	.40
261	Sean Tracey **RC**	.25
262	Jerry Owens **RC**	.40
263	Steve Nelson **RC**	.25
264	Brandon McCarthy **RC**	1.00
265	David Shepard **RC**	.25
266	Steve Bondurant **RC**	.25
267	Billy Sadler	.15
268	Ryan Feierabend **RC**	.25
269	Stuart Pomeranz **RC**	.40
270	Shaun Marcum	.25
271	Erik Schindewolf **RC**	.25
272	Stefan Bailie **RC**	.15
273	Mike Esposito **RC**	.25
274	Buck Coats **RC**	.40
275	Andy Sides **RC**	.25
276	Micah Schnurstein **RC**	.40
277	Jesse Gutierrez **RC**	.25
278	Jake Postlewait **RC**	.25
279	Willy Mota **RC**	.50
280	Ryan Speier **RC**	.25
281	Frank Mata **RC**	.25
282	Jair Jurrjens **RC**	1.00
283	Nick Touchstone **RC**	.25
284	Matthew Kemp **RC**	1.50
285	Vinny Rottino **RC**	.40
286	J.B. Thurmond **RC**	.40
287	Kelvin Pichardo **RC**	.25
288	Scott Mitchinson **RC**	.25
289	Darwinson Salazar **RC**	.25
290	George Kottaras **RC**	.50
291	Ken Durost **RC**	.40
292	Jonathan Sanchez **RC**	.50
293	Brandon Moorhead **RC**	.25
294	Kennard Bibbs **RC**	.25
295	David Gassner **RC**	.40
296	Micah Furtado **RC**	.25
297	Ismael Ramirez **RC**	.25
298	Carlos Gonzalez **RC**	1.50
299	Brandon Sing **RC**	.50
300	Jason Motte **RC**	.25
301	Chuck James **RC**	1.00
302	Andy Santana **RC**	.25
303	Manny Parra **RC**	.40
304	Chris Young **RC**	1.00
305	Juan Senreiso **RC**	.25
306	Franklin Morales **RC**	1.00
307	Jared Gothreaux **RC**	.15
308	Jayce Tingler **RC**	.25
309	Matt Brown **RC**	.25
310	Frank Diaz **RC**	.40
311	Stephen Drew **RC**	2.00
312	Jered Weaver **RC**	4.00
313	Ryan Braun **RC**	4.00
314	John Mayberry Jr. **RC**	.75
315	Aaron Thompson **RC**	1.00
316	Cesar Carrillo **RC**	.50
317	Jacoby Ellsbury **RC**	6.00
318	Matt Garza **RC**	5.00
319	Cliff Pennington **RC**	.75
320	Colby Rasmus **RC**	2.00
321	Chris Volstad **RC**	1.00
322	Ricky Romero **RC**	.50
323	Ryan Zimmerman **RC**	3.00
324	C.J. Henry **RC**	.75
325	Jay Bruce **RC**	3.00
326	Beau Jones **RC**	.50
327	Mark McCormick **RC**	.50
328	Eli Iorg **RC**	.50
329	Andrew McCutchen **RC**	1.00
330	Mike Costanzo **RC**	.50

Blue

No Pricing
Production One Set

Gold

Gold Rookies:	2-4X
Gold Stars:	4-8X
Production 2,005 Sets	

All-Star Patches

		NM/M
Common Player:		15.00
BA	Bobby Abreu/65	15.00
MA	Moises Alou/65	20.00
JB	Jason Bay/50	20.00
CB	Carlos Beltran/60	25.00
MB	Mark Buehrle/60	20.00
MC	Miguel Cabrera/70	30.00
CC	Chris Carpenter/70	20.00
MCL	Matt Clement/70	15.00
BC	Bartolo Colon/60	15.00
CCO	Chad Cordero/65	15.00
JD	Johnny Damon/60	25.00
DE	David Eckstein/65	20.00
JE	Jim Edmonds/50	20.00
ME	Morgan Ensberg/60	15.00
JG	Jon Garland/70	20.00
LG	Luis Gonzalez/70	15.00
LH	Livan Hernandez/50	15.00
JI	Jason Isringhausen/65	15.00
AJ	Andruw Jones/70	25.00
JK	Jeff Kent/65	20.00
PK	Paul Konerko/70	20.00
CL	Carlos Lee/65	20.00
DL	Derrek Lee/65	20.00
BL	Brad Lidge/65	15.00
FL	Felipe Lopez/35	20.00
MM	Melvin Mora/30	20.00
JN	Joe Nathan/65	15.00
DO	David Ortiz/70	25.00
RO	Roy Oswalt/60	20.00
JP	Jake Peavy/60	20.00
MP	Mike Piazza/50	30.00
SP	Scott Podsednik/65	20.00
AP	Albert Pujols/35	50.00
ARA	Aramis Ramirez/60	20.00
MR	Manny Ramirez/65	25.00
MRI	Mariano Rivera/65	30.00
AR	Alex Rodriguez/50	30.00
KR	Kenny Rogers/50	15.00
JS	Johan Santana/60	30.00
GS	Gary Sheffield/50	20.00
JSM	John Smoltz/65	30.00
IS	Ichiro Suzuki/50	40.00
MTE	Mark Teixeira/60	20.00
MT	Miguel Tejada/60	20.00
BW	Billy Wagner/50	15.00
DW	Dontrelle Willis/60	20.00
MY	Michael Young/50	20.00

All-Star Stitches

		NM/M
Common Player:		4.00
BA	Bobby Abreu/B	4.00
MA	Moises Alou/C	6.00
JB	Jason Bay/C	4.00
CB	Carlos Beltran/D	6.00
MB	Mark Buehrle/B	4.00
MC	Miguel Cabrera/E	8.00
CC	Chris Carpenter/E	4.00
LC	Luis Castillo/B	4.00
MCL	Matt Clement/B	4.00
BC	Bartolo Colon/D	4.00
CCO	Chad Cordero/D	4.00
JD	Johnny Damon/B	8.00
DE	David Eckstein/B	4.00
JE	Jim Edmonds/A	6.00
ME	Morgan Ensberg/B	4.00
JG	Jon Garland/E	4.00
LG	Luis Gonzalez/C	4.00
LH	Livan Hernandez	4.00
JI	Jason Isringhausen/E	4.00
AJ	Andruw Jones/C	6.00
JK	Jeff Kent/C	4.00
PK	Paul Konerko/A	4.00
CL	Carlos Lee/E	4.00
DL	Derrek Lee/F	6.00
BL	Brad Lidge/D	4.00
FL	Felipe Lopez/B	4.00
MM	Melvin Mora/B	4.00
JN	Joe Nathan/C	4.00
DO	David Ortiz/E	8.00
RO	Roy Oswalt/A	4.00
JP	Jake Peavy/D	4.00
MP	Mike Piazza/E	8.00
SP	Scott Podsednik/A	4.00
AP	Albert Pujols/E	20.00
ARA	Aramis Ramirez/E	4.00
MR	Manny Ramirez/E	8.00
MRI	Mariano Rivera	6.00
BR	Brian Roberts/C	4.00
AR	Alex Rodriguez/D	15.00
IR	Ivan Rodriguez/A	6.00
KR	Kenny Rogers/A	4.00
JS	Johan Santana/C	6.00
GS	Gary Sheffield/D	6.00
JSM	John Smoltz/D	6.00
IS	Ichiro Suzuki/A	20.00
MTE	Mark Teixeira/C	6.00
MT	Miguel Tejada/B	6.00
BW	Billy Wagner/C	4.00
DW	Dontrelle Willis/F	6.00
MY	Michael Young/A	4.00

Derby Digs Jersey

		NM/M
Production 100 Sets		
BA	Bobby Abreu	25.00
JB	Jason Bay	15.00
AJ	Andruw Jones	25.00
CL	Carlos Lee	10.00
DO	David Ortiz	25.00
IR	Ivan Rodriguez	25.00
MT	Mark Teixeira	25.00

Hall of Fame Bat

		NM/M
Complete Set (2):		
WB	Wade Boggs/A	10.00
RS	Ryne Sandberg/B	15.00

Hall of Fame Dual Bat

		NM/M
Production 200 Sets		
BS	Wade Boggs, Ryne Sandberg	25.00

Legendary Sacks

		NM/M
Production 300 Sets		
JA	Jim Abbott	6.00
AD	Andre Dawson	6.00
MF	Mark Fidrych	4.00
RF	Rollie Fingers	4.00
BJ	Bo Jackson	8.00
HR	Harold Reynolds	4.00
OS	Ozzie Smith	8.00

LW Lou Whitaker 4.00
DW Dave Winfield 8.00

Midsummer Covers

NM/M
Production 150 Sets
CB Carlos Beltran 15.00
RC Roger Clemens 25.00
VG Vladimir Guerrero 25.00
DL Derrek Lee 15.00
AP Albert Pujols 40.00
BR Brian Roberts 10.00
AR Alex Rodriguez 30.00
IS Ichiro Suzuki 50.00
MT Miguel Tejada 15.00
DW Dontrelle Willis 10.00

Printing Plates

No Pricing
Production one set per color.

Signature Moves

NM/M
Production 15-475 Sets
Red Foil: No Pricing
Production 25 Sets
MA Matt Albers/475 15.00
TC Travis Chick/475 8.00
TG Troy Glaus/275 20.00
TH Tim Hudson/275 25.00
KI Kazuhisa Ishii/275 15.00
GK George Kottaras/475 15.00
BL Bobby Livingston/475 10.00
MM Mark Mulder/275 25.00
GP Glen Perkins/275 15.00
JP Jake Postlewait/275 10.00
HS Humberto Sanchez 30.00
BS Benito Santiago 20.00
RS Richie Sexson/275 25.00
CJS C.J. Smith/475 10.00
JV Justin Verlander/275 35.00
TW Tony Womack 15.00

Touch Em All Base

NM/M
Production 1,000 Sets
VG Vladimir Guerrero 10.00
DL Derrek Lee 8.00
DO David Ortiz 10.00
AP Albert Pujols 20.00
MR Manny Ramirez 10.00
AR Alex Rodriguez 15.00
IR Ivan Rodriguez 8.00
GS Gary Sheffield 6.00
IS Ichiro Suzuki 20.00
MT Miguel Tejada 10.00

Washington Nationals Inaugural Lineup

NM/M
Inserted 1:10
Ball Relics: No Pricing
Production Five Sets
VC Vinny Castilla .50
JG Jose Guillen 1.00
CG Cristian Guzman .50
LH Livan Hernandez .50
NJ Nick Johnson .50
BS Brian Schneider .50
TS Terrmel Sledge .50
JV Jose Vidro .50
BW Brad Wilkerson .50
TEAM Team Photo 1.00

2005 Topps Chrome Update

NM/M
Complete Set (237):
Common Player: .25
Common Rookie (106-215): .50
Common Rk Auto. (221-237): 10.00
Pack (4): 4.00
Box (20): 70.00
UH1 Sammy Sosa 1.00
UH2 Jeff Francoeur .50
UH3 Tony Clark .25
UH4 Michael Tucker .25
UH5 Mike Matheny .25
UH6 Eric Young .25
UH7 Jose Valentin .25
UH8 Matt Lawton .25
UH9 Juan Rivera .25
UH10 Shawn Green .50
UH11 Aaron Boone .25
UH12 Woody Williams .25
UH13 Brad Wilkerson .25
UH14 Anthony Reyes **RC** 3.00
UH15 Gustavo Chacin .25
UH16 Mike Restovich .25
UH17 Humberto Quintero .25
UH18 Matt Ginter .25
UH19 Scott Podsednik .25
UH20 Byung-Hyun Kim .25
UH21 Orlando Hernandez .25
UH22 Mark Grudzielanek .25
UH23 Jody Gerut .25
UH24 Adrian Beltre .50
UH25 Scott Schoeneweis .25
UH26 Marlon Anderson .25
UH27 Jason Vargas .25
UH28 Claudio Vargas .25
UH29 Jason Kendall .25
UH30 Aaron Small .25
UH31 Juan Cruz .25
UH32 Placido Polanco .25
UH33 Jorge Sosa .25
UH34 John Olerud .25
UH35 Ryan Langerhans .25
UH36 Randy Winn .25
UH37 Zachary Duke .50
UH38 Garrett Atkins .25
UH39 Al Leiter .25
UH40 Shawn Chacon .25
UH41 Mark DeRosa .25
UH42 Miguel Ojeda .25
UH43 A.J. Pierzynski .25
UH44 Carlos Lee .25
UH45 LaTroy Hawkins .25
UH46 Nick Green .25
UH47 Shawn Estes .25
UH48 Eli Marrero .25
UH49 Jeff Kent .25
UH50 Joe Randa .25
UH51 Jose Hernandez .25
UH52 Joe Blanton .25
UH53 Huston Street .25
UH54 Marlon Byrd .25
UH55 Alex Sanchez .25
UH56 Livan Hernandez .25
UH57 Chris Young .25
UH58 Brad Eldred .25
UH59 Terrence Long .25
UH60 Phil Nevin .25
UH61 Kyle Farnsworth .25
UH62 Jon Lieber .25
UH63 Antonio Alfonseca .25
UH64 Tony Graffanino .25
UH65 Tadahito Iguchi 1.00
UH66 Brad Thompson .25
UH67 Jose Vidro .25
UH68 Jason Phillips .25
UH69 Carl Pavano .25
UH70 Pokey Reese .25
UH71 Jerome Williams .25
UH72 Kazuhisa Ishii .25
UH73 Felix Hernandez .50
UH74 Edgar Renteria .25
UH75 Mike Myers .25
UH76 Jeff Cirillo .25
UH77 Endy Chavez .25
UH78 Jose Guillen .25
UH79 Ugueth Urbina .25
UH80 Zach Day .25
UH81 Javier Vazquez .25
UH82 Willy Taveras .25
UH83 Mark Mulder .50
UH84 Vinny Castilla .25
UH85 Russ Adams .25
UH86 Homer Bailey .25
UH87 Ervin Santana .25
UH88 Bill Bray .25
UH89 Thomas Diamond .25
UH90 Trevor Plouffe .25
UH91 James Houser .25
UH92 Jake Stevens .25
UH93 Anthony Whittington .25
UH94 Phillip Hughes .25
UH95 Greg Golson .25
UH96 Paul Maholm .25
UH97 Carlos Quentin .25
UH98 Dan Johnson .25
UH99 Mark Rogers .25
UH100 Neil Walker .25
UH101 Omar Quintanilla .25
UH102 Blake DeWitt .25
UH103 Taylor Tankersley .25
UH104 David Murphy .25
UH105 Chris Lambert .25
UH106 Drew Anderson **RC** .50
UH107 Luis Hernandez **RC** .50
UH108 Jim Burt **RC** .50
UH109 Mike Morse **RC** .50
UH110 Elliot Johnson **RC** 2.00
UH111 C.J. Smith **RC** .50
UH112 Casey McGehee **RC** .50
UH113 Brian Miller **RC** .50
UH114 Chris Vines **RC** .50
UH115 D.J. Houlton **RC** .50
UH116 Chuck Tiffany **RC** 2.00
UH117 Humberto Sanchez **RC** 3.00
UH118 Baltazar Lopez **RC** .50
UH119 Russell Martin **RC** 4.00
UH120 Dana Eveland **RC** 1.00
UH121 Johan Silva **RC** .50
UH122 Adam Harben **RC** 1.00
UH123 Brian Bannister **RC** 1.50
UH124 Adam Boeve **RC** .75
UH125 Tom Oldham **RC** .75
UH126 Cody Haerther **RC** 1.50
UH127 Dan Santin **RC** .75
UH128 Daniel Haigwood **RC** 1.00
UH129 Craig Tatum **RC** .50
UH130 Martin Prado **RC** .75
UH131 Errol Simonitsch **RC** .50
UH132 Lorenzo Scott **RC** .75
UH133 Hayden Penn **RC** 1.00
UH134 Heath Totten **RC** .50
UH135 Nick Masset **RC** .50
UH136 Pedro Lopez **RC** .75
UH137 Benjamin Harrison **RC** .50
UH138 Michael Spidale **RC** .50
UH139 Jeremy Harts **RC** .50
UH140 Danny Zell **RC** .50
UH141 Kevin Collins **RC** .50
UH142 Tony Arnerich **RC** .50
UH143 Matt Albers **RC** 2.50
UH144 Ricky Barrett **RC** .50
UH145 Hernan Iribarren **RC** .75
UH146 Sean Tracey **RC** .50
UH147 Jerry Owens **RC** 1.00
UH148 Steve Nelson **RC** .50
UH149 Brandon McCarthy **RC** 2.00
UH150 David Shepard **RC** .75
UH151 Steve Bondurant **RC** .75
UH152 Billy Sadler .75
UH153 Ryan Feierabend **RC** .75
UH154 Stuart Pomeranz **RC** .75
UH155 Shawn Marcum **RC** 1.00
UH156 Erik Schindewolf **RC** .50
UH157 Stefan Bailie **RC** .50
UH158 Mike Esposito **RC** .50
UH159 Buck Coats **RC** .75
UH160 Andy Sides **RC** .50
UH161 Micah Schnurstein **RC** .75
UH162 Jesse Gutierrez **RC** .50
UH163 Jake Postlewait **RC** .50
UH164 Willy Mota **RC** .50
UH165 Ryan Speier **RC** .50
UH166 Frank Mata **RC** .50
UH167 Jair Jurrjens **RC** 3.00
UH168 Nick Touchstone **RC** .50
UH169 Matthew Kemp **RC** 6.00
UH170 Vinny Rottino **RC** .50
UH171 J.B. Thurmond **RC** .50
UH172 Kelvin Pichardo **RC** .50
UH173 Scott Mitchinson **RC** .50
UH174 Darwinson Salazar **RC** .50
UH175 George Kottaras **RC** 1.50
UH176 Ken Durost **RC** .75
UH177 Jonathan Sanchez **RC** 2.00
UH178 Brandon Moorhead **RC** .75
UH179 Kennard Bibbs **RC** .75
UH180 David Gassner **RC** .50
UH181 Micah Furtado **RC** .50
UH182 Ismael Ramirez **RC** .50
UH183 Carlos Gonzalez **RC** 5.00
UH184 Brandon Sing **RC** .75
UH185 Jason Motte **RC** .50
UH186 Chuck James **RC** 3.00
UH187 Andy Santana **RC** .50
UH188 Manny Parra **RC** 1.00
UH189 Chris Young **RC** 5.00
UH190 Juan Senreiso **RC** .50
UH191 Franklin Morales **RC** 3.00
UH192 Jared Gothreaux **RC** .50
UH193 Jayce Tingler **RC** .50
UH194 Matt Brown **RC** .50
UH195 Frank Diaz **RC** 1.50
UH196 Stephen Drew **RC** 8.00
UH197 Jered Weaver **RC** 10.00
UH198 Ryan Braun **RC** 25.00
UH199 John Mayberry Jr. **RC** 2.50
UH200 Aaron Thompson **RC** 2.00
UH201 Ben Copeland **RC** 4.00
UH202 Jacoby Ellsbury **RC** 25.00
UH203 Garrett Olson **RC** 1.50
UH204 Cliff Pennington **RC** 2.00
UH205 Colby Rasmus **RC** 10.00
UH206 Chris Volstad **RC** 3.00
UH207 Ricky Romero **RC** 2.00
UH208 Ryan Zimmerman **RC** 10.00
UH209 C.J. Henry **RC** 2.00
UH210 Nelson Cruz **RC** 1.00
UH211 Josh Wall **RC** 1.50
UH212 Nick Webber **RC** .50
UH213 Paul Kelly **RC** 1.00
UH214 Kyle Winters **RC** 1.50
UH215 Mitch Boggs **RC** .75
UH216 Craig Biggio .50
UH217 Greg Maddux 1.00
UH218 Bobby Abreu .25
UH219 Alex Rodriguez 2.00
UH220 Trevor Hoffman .25
UH221 Trevor Bell **RC** 20.00
UH222 Jay Bruce **RC** 120.00
UH223 Travis Buck **RC** 20.00
UH224 Cesar Carrillo **RC** 15.00
UH225 Mike Costanzo **RC** 25.00
UH226 Brent Cox **RC** 10.00
UH227 Matt Garza **RC** 30.00
UH228 Josh Geer **RC** 10.00
UH229 Tyler Greene **RC** 10.00
UH230 Eli Iorg **RC** 10.00
UH231 Craig Italiano **RC** 15.00
UH232 Beau Jones **RC** 15.00
UH233 Mark McCormick **RC** 10.00
UH234 Andrew McCutchen **RC** 40.00
UH235 Micah Owings **RC** 25.00
UH236 Cesar Ramos **RC** 10.00
UH237 Chaz Roe **RC** 10.00

Refractor

Stars (1-105): 2-3X
Rookies (106-215): 1-2X
Inserted 1:5
Refractor Auto (221-237): 1-1.5X
Production 500

Black Refractor

Black (1-105): 2-4X
Black (106-215): 2-3X
Production 250
Black Auto (221-237): 1-2.5X
Production 200

Gold SuperFractor

No Pricing
Production One Set

Red X-Fractor

Red (1-105): 4-8X
Red (106-215): 6-12X
Production 65
Red Auto (221-237): No Pricing
Production 25

Barry Bonds Home Run History

NM/M
Complete Set (15): 40.00
Common Bonds: 3.00
Inserted 1:12
Refractor: 1-2X
Inserted 1:71
Black Refractor: 2-3X
Production 200 Sets
Red X-Fractor: 4-6X
Production 25 Sets
Gold Super: No Pricing
Production One Set
BB1 Barry Bonds 3.00
BB25 Barry Bonds 3.00
BB50 Barry Bonds 3.00
BB75 Barry Bonds 3.00
BB100 Barry Bonds 3.00
BB125 Barry Bonds 3.00
BB150 Barry Bonds 3.00
BB175 Barry Bonds 3.00
BB200 Barry Bonds 3.00
BB225 Barry Bonds 3.00
BB250 Barry Bonds 3.00
BB275 Barry Bonds 3.00
BB300 Barry Bonds 3.00
BB325 Barry Bonds 3.00
BB350 Barry Bonds 3.00

Printing Plates

No Pricing
Production one set per color.

Washington Nationals Commemorative Set

NM/M
Complete Boxed Set (55): 20.00
Common Player: .50
1 Nationals Logo .50
2 Jose Vidro .75
3 Joe Horgan .50
4 Danny Rueckel .50
5 Wil Cordero .50
6 Cristian Guzman .75
7 Alex Escobar .50
8 Tony Armas Jr. .50
9 Zach Day .50
10 Jamey Carroll .50
11 Nick Johnson .75
12 John Patterson .50
13 Josh Karp .50
14 Brendan Harris .50
15 Gary Bennett .50
16 Terrmel Sledge .50
17 Tomo Ohka .50
18 Chad Cordero .50
19 Luis Ayala .50
20 Tony Blanco .50
21 Endy Chavez .75
22 George Arias .50
23 Chad Durbin .50
24 Phil Hiatt .50
25 Henry Mateo .50
26 Livan Hernandez .50
27 Larry Broadway .60
28 T.J. Tucker .50
29 J.J. Davis .50
30 Brian Schneider .50
31 Vinny Castilla .50
32 Michael Hinckley .50
33 Brandon Watson .50
34 Claudio Vargas .50
35 Ryan Church .50
36 Jose Guillen .65
37 Gary Majewski .50
38 Jon Rauch .50
39 Brad Wilkerson .50
40 Francis Beltran .50
41 Esteban Loaiza .50
42 Carlos Baerga .50
43 Sunny Kim .50
44 Ian Desmond .50
45 Jeffrey Hammonds .50
46 Hector Carrasco .50
47 Drew McMillan .50
48 Jared Sandberg .50
49 Frank Robinson 1.00
50 RFK Stadium .50
51 Senators Become Twins in 1961 .50
52 Senators Move to Texas in 1972 .50
53 Nationals Top Orioles .50
54 First Moves (Vinny Castilla, Jose Guillen) .50
55 First Moves (Cristian Guzman, Esteban Loaiza) .50

Emerald Nuts S.F. Giants

The first 20,000 fans at the August 28 game at SBC Park received this foil-wrapped team set. High-gloss fronts are bordered in black with gold-foil highlights. Backs have a portrait photo, stats and career highlights. Cards are numbered with GTS prefix.

NM/M
Complete Set (31): 7.50
Common Player: .25
1 Barry Bonds 3.00
2 Armando Benitez .25
3 Edgardo Alfonzo .25
4 Kirk Rueter .25
5 Ray Durham .25
6 Michael Tucker .25
7 Noah Lowry .25
8 Jason Christiansen .25
9 J.T. Snow .35
10 Jason Schmidt .35
11 Pedro Feliz .25
12 Brett Tomko .25
13 Jeff Fassero .25
14 Mike Matheny .25
15 Omar Vizquel .25
16 Lance Niekro .25
17 Scott Eyre .25
18 Jesse Foppert .25
19 Deivi Cruz .25
20 Moises Alou .35
21 Scott Munter .25
22 Todd Linden .25
23 Marquis Grissom .25
24 Jason Ellison .25
25 Tyler Walker .25
26 LaTroy Hawkins .25
27 Yorvit Torrealba .25
28 Felipe Alou .35
29 Coaches (Joe Lefebvre, Luis Pujols, Gene Glynn) .25
30 Coaches (Dave Righetti, Ron Wotus, Mark Gardner) .25
--- Checklist .25

Poland Spring Yankees Legends

Stadium giveaway July 30.

NM/M
Complete Set (5): 6.00
Common Player: 2.00
1 Paul O'Neill 2.00
2 Hank Bauer 2.00
3 Bill "Moose" Skowron 2.00
4 Graig Nettles 2.00
-- Sponsor's Card .10

2006 Topps

NM/M
Complete Set (659): 60.00
Complete Hobby Set (664): 75.00
Complete Holiday Set (659): 75.00
Complete Cardinals Set (664): 75.00
Complete Cubs Set (664): 75.00
Complete Pirates Set (664): 75.00
Complete Red Sox Set (664): 75.00
Complete Yankees Set (664): 75.00
Common Player: .10
Pack (10): 2.00
Box (36): 60.00
Jumbo Pack (35): 6.00
Jumbo Box (12): 60.00
1 Alex Rodriguez 1.50
2 Jose Valentin .10
3 Garrett Atkins .10
4 Scott Hatteberg .10
5 Carl Crawford .25
6 Armando Benitez .10
7 Mickey Mantle 5.00
8 Mike Morse .10
9 Damian Miller .10
10 Clint Barmes .10
11 Michael Barrett .10
12 Coco Crisp .10
13 Tadahito Iguchi .25
14 Chris Snyder .10
15 Brian Roberts .10
16 David Wright 1.00
17 Victor Santos .10
18 Trevor Hoffman .10
19 Jeremy Reed .10
20 Bobby Abreu .25
21 Lance Berkman .25
22 Zach Day .10
23 Jonny Gomes .10
24 Jason Marquis .10
25 Chipper Jones .50
26 Scott Hairston .10
27 Ryan Dempster .10
28 Brandon Inge .10
29 Aaron Harang .10
30 Jon Garland .10
31 Pokey Reese .10
32 Mike MacDougal .10
33 Mike Lieberthal .10
34 Cesar Izturis .10
35 Brad Wilkerson .10
36 Jeff Suppan .10
37 Adam Everett .10
38 Bengie Molina .10
39 Rickie Weeks .25
40 Jorge Posada .25
41 Rheal Cormier .10
42 Reed Johnson .10
43 Laynce Nix .10
44 Carl Everett .10
45 Greg Maddux 1.00
46 Jeff Francis .10
47 Felipe Lopez .10
48 Dan Johnson .10
49 Humberto Cota .10
50 Manny Ramirez .50
51 Juan Uribe .10
52 Jaret Wright .10
53 Tomokazu Ohka .10
54 Mike Matheny .10
55 Joe Mauer .25
56 Jarrod Washburn .10
57 Randy Winn .10
58 Pedro Feliz .10
59 Kenny Rogers .10
60 Rocco Baldelli .10
61 Eric Hinske .10
62 Damaso Marte .10
63 Desi Relaford .10
64 Juan Encarnacion .10
65 Nomar Garciaparra .50
66 Shawn Estes .10
67 Brian Jordan .10
68 Steve Kline .10
69 Braden Looper .10
70 Carlos Lee .10
71 Tom Glavine .25
72 Craig Biggio .25
73 Steve Finley .10
74 David Newhan .10
75 Eric Gagne .20
76 Tony Graffanino .10
77 Dallas McPherson .10
78 Nick Punto .10
79 Mark Kotsay .10
80 Kerry Wood .25
81 Kyle Farnsworth .10
82 Huston Street .20
83 Endy Chavez .10
84 So Taguchi .10
85 Hank Blalock .25

86 Brad Radke .10
87 Chien-Ming Wang .50
88 B.J. Surhoff .10
89 Glendon Rusch .10
90 Mark Buehrle .25
91 Rafael Betancourt .10
92 Lance Cormier .10
93 Alex Gonzalez .10
94 Matt Stairs .10
95 Andy Pettitte .25
96 Jesse Crain .10
97 Kenny Lofton .10
98 Geoff Blum .10
99 Mark Redman .10
100 Barry Bonds 1.50
101 Chad Orvella .10
102 Xavier Nady .10
103 Junior Spivey .10
104 Bernie Williams .25
105 Victor Martinez .25
106 Nook Logan .10
107 Mark Teahen .10
108 Mike Lamb .10
109 Jayson Werth .10
110 Mariano Rivera .25
111 Erubiel Durazo .10
112 Ryan Vogelsong .10
113 Bobby Madritsch .10
114 Travis Lee .10
115 Adam Dunn .40
116 David Riske .10
117 Troy Percival .10
118 Chad Tracy .20
119 Andy Marte .20
120 Edgar Renteria .20
121 Jason Giambi .25
122 Justin Morneau .40
123 J.T. Snow .10
124 Danys Baez .10
125 Carlos Delgado .25
126 John Buck .10
127 Shannon Stewart .10
128 Mike Cameron .10
129 Joe McEwing .10
130 Richie Sexson .25
131 Rod Barajas .10
132 Russ Adams .10
133 J.D. Closser .10
134 Ramon Ortiz .10
135 Josh Beckett .25
136 Ryan Freel .10
137 Victor Zambrano .10
138 Ronnie Belliard .10
139 Jason Michaels .10
140 Brian Giles .20
141 Randy Wolf .10
142 Robinson Cano .40
143 Joe Blanton .10
144 Esteban Loaiza .10
145 Troy Glaus .25
146 Matt Clement .10
147 Geoff Jenkins .10
148 John Thomson .10
149 A.J. Pierzynski .10
150 Pedro Martinez .50
151 Roger Clemens 1.50
152 Jack Wilson .10
153 Ray King .10
154 Ryan Church .10
155 Paul LoDuca .10
156 Dan Wheeler .10
157 Carlos Zambrano .25
158 Mike Timlin .10
159 Brandon Claussen .10
160 Travis Hafner .25
161 Chris Shelton .10
162 Rafael Furcal .26
163 Flash Gordon .10
164 Noah Lowry .10
165 Larry Walker .25
166 Dave Roberts .10
167 Scott Schoeneweis .10
168 Julian Tavarez .10
169 Jhonny Peralta .25
170 Vernon Wells .25
171 Jorge Cantu .20
172 Todd Greene .10
173 Willy Taveras .10
174 Corey Patterson .10
175 Ivan Rodriguez .40
176 Bobby Kielty .10
177 Jose Reyes .25
178 Barry Zito .25
179 Deivi Cruz .10
180 Mark Teixeira .50
181 Chone Figgins .10
182 Aaron Rowand .10
183 Tim Wakefield .10
184 Mike Maroth .10
185 Johnny Damon .50
186 Vicente Padilla .10
187 Ryan Klesko .10
188 Gary Matthews .10
189 Jose Mesa .10
190 Nick Johnson .10
191 Freddy Garcia .10
192 Larry Bigbie .10
193 Chris Ray .10
194 Torii Hunter .25
195 Mike Sweeney .10
196 Brad Penny .10
197 Jason Frasor .10
198 Kevin Mench .10
199 Adam Kennedy .10
200 Albert Pujols 1.50
201 Jody Gerut .10
202 Luis Gonzalez .10
203 Zack Greinke .10
204 Miguel Cairo .10
205 Jimmy Rollins .25
206 Edgardo Alfonzo .10
207 Billy Wagner .10
208 B.J. Ryan .10
209 Orlando Hudson .10
210 Preston Wilson .10
211 Melvin Mora .10
212 Bill Mueller .10
213 Javy Lopez .10
214 Wilson Betemit .10
215 Garret Anderson .10
216 Russell Branyan .10
217 Jeff Weaver .10
218 Doug Mientkiewicz .10
219 Mark Ellis .10
220 Jason Bay .25
221 Adam LaRoche .10
222 C.C. Sabathia .10
223 Humberto Quintero .10
224 Bartolo Colon .20
225 Ichiro Suzuki 1.00
226 Brett Tomko .10
227 Corey Koskie .10
228 David Eckstein .10
229 Cristian Guzman .10
230 Jeff Kent .25
231 Chris Capuano .10
232 Rodrigo Lopez .10
233 Jason Phillips .10
234 Luis Rivas .10
235 Cliff Floyd .10
236 Gil Meche .10
237 Adam Eaton .10
238 Matt Morris .25
239 Kyle Davies .10
240 David Wells .10
241 John Smoltz .25
242 Felix Hernandez .50
243 Kenny Rogers .10
244 Mark Teixeira .25
245 Orlando Hudson .10
246 Derek Jeter 1.00
247 Eric Chavez .20
248 Torii Hunter .10
249 Vernon Wells .10
250 Ichiro Suzuki .50
251 Greg Maddux .50
252 Mike Matheny .10
253 Derrek Lee .25
254 Luis Castillo .10
255 Omar Vizquel .10
256 Mike Lowell .10
257 Andruw Jones .25
258 Jim Edmonds .20
259 Bobby Abreu .20
260 Bartolo Colon .10
261 Chris Carpenter .10
262 Alex Rodriguez 1.00
263 Albert Pujols 1.00
264 Huston Street .10
265 Ryan Howard .50
266 Bob Melvin .10
267 Bobby Cox .10
268 Baltimore Orioles .10
269 Boston Red Sox .25
270 Chicago White Sox .25
271 Dusty Baker .10
272 Jerry Narron .10
273 Cleveland Indians .10
274 Clint Hurdle .10
275 Detroit Tigers .10
276 Jack McKeon .10
277 Phil Garner .10
278 Kansas City Royals .10
279 Jim Tracy .10
280 Angels .10
281 Milwaukee Brewers .10
282 Minnesota Twins .10
283 Willie Randolph .10
284 New York Yankees .50
285 Oakland Athletics .10
286 Charlie Manuel .10
287 Pete Mackanin .10
288 Bruce Bochy .10
289 Felipe Alou .10
290 Seattle Mariners .10
291 Tony LaRussa .10
292 Tampa Bay Devil Rays .10
293 Texas Rangers .10
294 Toronto Blue Jays .10
295 Frank Robinson .25
296 Anderson Hernandez **(RC)** .10
297b Alex Gordon (Cut-out card.) 80.00
298 Jason Botts **(RC)** .10
299 Jeff Mathis **(RC)** .10
300 Ryan Garko **(RC)** .10
301 Charlton Jimerson **(RC)** .10
302 Chris Denorfia **(RC)** .10
303 Anthony Reyes **(RC)** .10
304 Bryan Bullington **(RC)** .10
305 Chuck James **(RC)** .10
306 Danny Sandoval **RC** .25
307 Walter Young **(RC)** .10
308 Fausto Carmona **(RC)** .10
309 Francisco Liriano **(RC)** 1.00
310 Hong-Chih Kuo **(RC)** .10
311 Joe Saunders **(RC)** .10
312 John Koronka **(RC)** .10
313 Robert Andino **RC** .25
314 Shaun Marcum **(RC)** .10
315 Tom Gorzelanny **(RC)** .10
316 Craig Breslow **RC** .25
317 Chris Demaria **RC** .50
318 Brayan Pena **(RC)** .10
319 Rich Hill **(RC)** .25
320 Rick Short **RC** .25
321 C.J. Wilson **(RC)** .10
322 Marshall McDougall **(RC)** .10
323 Darrell Rasner **(RC)** .10
324 Brandon Watson **(RC)** .10
325 Paul McAnulty **(RC)** .10
326 Derek Jeter, Alex Rodriguez .50
327 Miguel Tejada, Melvin Mora .25
328 Marcus Giles, Chipper Jones .25
329 Manny Ramirez, David Ortiz .25
330 Michael Barrett, Greg Maddux .25
331 Matt Holliday .25
332 Orlando Cabrera .10
333 Ryan Langerhans .10
334 Lew Ford .10
335 Mark Prior .40
336 Ted Lilly .10
337 Michael Young .10
338 Livan Hernandez .10
339 Yadier Molina .10
340 Eric Chavez .25
341 Miguel Batista .10
342 Bruce Chen .10
343 Sean Casey .10
344 Doug Davis .10
345 Andruw Jones .40
346 Hideki Matsui 1.00
347 Joe Randa .10
348 Reggie Sanders .10
349 Jason Jennings .10
350 Joe Nathan .10
351 Jose Lopez .10
352 John Lackey .10
353 Claudio Vargas .10
354 Grady Sizemore .25
355 Jonathan Papelbon **(RC)** 3.00
356 Luis Matos .10
357 Orlando Hernandez .10
358 Jamie Moyer .10
359 Chase Utley .25
360 Moises Alou .25
361 Chad Cordero .10
362 Brian McCann .10
363 Jermaine Dye .10
364 Ryan Madson .10
365 Aramis Ramirez .25
366 Matt Treanor .10
367 Ray Durham .10
368 Khalil Greene .10
369 Mike Hampton .10
370 Mike Mussina .25
371 Brad Hawpe .10
372 Marlon Byrd .10
373 Woody Williams .10
374 Victor Diaz .10
375 Brady Clark .10
376 Luis Gonzalez .10
377 Raul Ibanez .10
378 Tony Clark .10
379 Shawn Chacon .10
380 Marcus Giles .10
381 Odalis Perez .10
382 Steve Trachsel .10
383 Russ Ortiz .10
384 Toby Hall .10
385 Bill Hall .10
386 Luke Hudson .10
387 Ken Griffey Jr. 1.00
388 Tim Hudson .25
389 Brian Moehler .10
390 Jake Peavy .25
391 Casey Blake .10
392 Sidney Ponson .10
393 Brian Schneider .10
394 J.J. Hardy .10
395 Austin Kearns .25
396 Pat Burrell .25
397 Jason Vargas .10
398 Ryan Howard .75
399 Joe Crede .10
400 Vladimir Guerrero .50
401 Roy Halladay .25
402 David Dellucci .10
403 Brandon Webb .10
404 Marlon Anderson .10
405 Miguel Tejada .25
406 Ryan Doumit .10
407 Kevin Youkilis .10
408 Jon Lieber .10
409 Edwin Encarnacion .10
410 Miguel Cabrera .50
411 A.J. Burnett .10
412 David Bell .10
413 Gregg Zaun .10
414 Lance Niekro .10
415 Shawn Green .10
416 Roberto Hernandez .10
417 Jay Gibbons .10
418 Johnny Estrada .10
419 Omar Vizquel .10
420 Gary Sheffield .25
421 Brad Halsey .10
422 Aaron Cook .10
423 David Ortiz .50
424 Tony Womack .10
425 Joe Kennedy .10
426 Dustin McGowan .10
427 Carl Pavano .10
428 Nick Green .10
429 Francisco Cordero .10
430 Octavio Dotel .10
431 Julio Franco .10
432 Brett Myers .10
433 Casey Kotchman .10
434 Frank Catalanotto .10
435 Paul Konerko .25
436 Keith Foulke .10
437 Juan Rivera .10
438 Todd Pratt .10
439 Ben Broussard .10
440 Scott Kazmir .25
441 Rich Aurilia .10
442 Craig Monroe .10
443 Danny Kolb .10
444 Curtis Granderson .20
445 Jeff Francoeur .20
446 Dustin Hermanson .10
447 Jacque Jones .10
448 Bobby Crosby .10
449 Jason LaRue .10
450 Derrek Lee .40
451 Curt Schilling .50
452 Jake Westbrook .10
453 Daniel Cabrera .10
454 Bobby Jenks .10
455 Dontrelle Willis .25
456 Brad Lidge .10
457 Shea Hillenbrand .10
458 Luis Castillo .10
459 Mark Hendrickson .10
460 Randy Johnson .50
461 Placido Polanco .10
462 Aaron Boone .10
463 Todd Walker .10
464 Nick Swisher .10
465 Joel Pineiro .10
466 Jay Payton .10
467 Cliff Lee .10
468 Johan Santana .50
469 Josh Willingham **(RC)** .10
470 Jeremy Bonderman .10
471 Runelvys Hernandez .10
472 Duaner Sanchez .10
473 Jason Lane .10
474 Trot Nixon .10
475 Ramon Hernandez .10
476 Mike Lowell .10
477 Chan Ho Park .10
478 Doug Waechter .10
479 Carlos Silva .10
480 Jose Contreras .10
481 Vinny Castilla .10
482 Chris Reitsma .10
483 Jose Guillen .10
484 Aaron Hill .10
485 Kevin Millwood .10
486 Wily Mo Pena .10
487 Rich Harden .10
488 Chris Carpenter .25
489 Jason Bartlett .10
490 Magglio Ordonez .20
491 John Rodriguez .10
492 Bob Wickman .10
493 Eddie Guardado .10
494 Kip Wells .10
495 Adrian Beltre .20
496 Jose Capellan **(RC)** .10
497 Scott Podsednik .20
498 Brad Thompson .10
499 Aaron Heilman .10
500 Derek Jeter 1.50
501 Emil Brown .10
502 Morgan Ensberg .20
503 Nate Bump .10
504 Phil Nevin .10
505 Jason Schmidt .20
506 Michael Cuddyer .10
507 John Patterson .10
508 Danny Haren .10
509 Freddy Sanchez .10
510 J.D. Drew .25
511 Dmitri Young .10
512 Eric Milton .10
513 Ervin Santana .10
514 Mark Loretta .10
515 Mark Grudzielanek .10
516 Derrick Turnbow .10
517 Danny Bautista .10
518 Lyle Overbay .10
519 Julio Lugo .10
520 Carlos Beltran .40
521 Jose Cruz Jr. .10
522 Jason Isringhausen .10
523 Bronson Arroyo .10
524 Ben Sheets .20
525 Zachary Duke .10
526 Ryan Wagner .10
527 Jose Vidro .10
528 Doug Mirabelli .10
529 Kris Benson .10
530 Carlos Guillen .10
531 Juan Pierre .10
532 Scot Shields .10
533 Scott Hatteberg .10
534 Tim Stauffer .10
535 Jim Edmonds .25
536 Scott Eyre .10
537 Ben Johnson **(RC)** .10
538 Mark Mulder .25
539 Juan Rincon .10
540 Gustavo Chacin .10
541 Oliver Perez .10
542 Chris Young .10
543 Edinson Volquez .10
544 Mark Bellhorn .10
545 Kelvim Escobar .10
546 Andrew Sisco .10
547 Derek Lowe .10
548 Sean Burroughs .10
549 Erik Bedard .10
550 Alfonso Soriano .40
551 Matt Murton .10
552 Eric Byrnes .10
553 Chris Duffy .10
554 Kazuo Matsui .10
555 Scott Rolen .40
556 Robert Mackowiak .10
557 Chris Burke .10
558 Jeromy Burnitz .10
559 Jerry Hairston Jr. .10
560 Jim Thome .40
561 Miguel Olivo .10
562 Jose Castillo .10
563 Brad Ausmus .10
564 Yorvit Torrealba .10
565 David DeJesus .10
566 Paul Byrd .10
567 Brandon Backe .10
568 Aubrey Huff .10
569 Mike Jacobs **(RC)** .10
570 Todd Helton .40
571 Angel Berroa .10
572 Todd Jones .10
573 Jeff Bagwell .25
574 Darin Erstad .10
575 Roy Oswalt .25
576 Rondell White .10
577 Alex Rios .10
578 Wes Helms .10
579 Javier Vazquez .10
580 Frank Thomas .40
581 Brian Fuentes .10
582 Francisco Rodriguez .10
583 Craig Counsell .10
584 Jorge Sosa .10
585 Mike Piazza .50
586 Mike Scioscia .10
587 Joe Torre .25
588 Ken Macha .10
589 John Gibbons .10
590 Joe Maddon .10
591 Eric Wedge .10
592 Mike Hargrove .10
593 Sam Perlozzo .10
594 Buck Showalter .10
595 Terry Francona .10
596 Buddy Bell .10
597 Jim Leyland .10
598 Ron Gardenhire .10
599 Ozzie Guillen .10
600 Ned Yost .10
601 Atlanta Braves .10
602 Philadelphia Phillies .10
603 New York Mets .10
604 Washington Nationals .10
605 Florida Marlins .10
606 Houston Astros .10
607 Chicago Cubs .25
608 St. Louis Cardinals .25
609 Pittsburgh Pirates .10
610 Cincinnati Reds .10
611 Colorado Rockies .10
612 Los Angeles Dodgers .25
613 San Francisco Giants .10
614 San Diego Padres .10
615 Arizona Diamondbacks .10
616 Kenji Johjima **RC** 2.00
617 Ryan Zimmerman **(RC)** 2.00
618 Craig Hansen **RC** 1.50
619 Joey Devine **RC** .25
620 Hanley Ramirez **(RC)** .50
621 Scott Olsen **(RC)** .25
622 Jason Bergmann **RC** .25
623 Geovany Soto **(RC)** .10
624 J.J. Furmaniak **(RC)** .10
625 Jeremy Accardo **RC** .25
626 Mark Woodyard **(RC)** .10
627 Matt Capps **(RC)** .10
628 Tim Corcoran **RC** .25
629 Ryan Jorgensen **RC** .25
630 Ronny Paulino **(RC)** .10
631 Dan Uggla **(RC)** .50
632 Ian Kinsler **(RC)** .25
633 Josh Barfield **(RC)** .25
634 Reggie Abercrombie **(RC)** .25
635 Joel Zumaya **(RC)** 1.00
636 Matt Cain **(RC)** .25
637 Conor Jackson **(RC)** .10
638 Bryan Anderson **(RC)** .10
639 Prince Fielder **(RC)** 1.00
640 Jeremy Hermida **(RC)** .25
641 Justin Verlander **(RC)** 1.00
642 Brian Bannister **(RC)** .10
643 Willie Eyre **(RC)** .10
644 Ricky Nolasco **(RC)** .10
645 Paul Maholm **(RC)** .10
646 Johnny Damon, Jason Giambi .25
647 Rondell White, Lew Ford .10
648 Orlando Hernandez, Orlando Hudson .10
649 Adam Dunn, Ken Griffey Jr. .25
650 Pat Burrell, Mike Lieberthal .10
651 Jose Reyes, Kazuo Matsui .10
652 Hank Blalock, Michael Young .10
653 Prince Fielder, Rickie Weeks .50
654 Travis Lee, Rocco Baldelli .10
655 Derrick Lee, Aramis Ramirez .25
656 Grady Sizemore, Aaron Boone .25
657 Luis Gonzalez, Shawn Green, Koyie Hill .10
658 Ivan Rodriguez, Carlos Guillen .10
659 Alex Rodriguez, Gary Sheffield .25
660 Ervin Santana, Francisco Rodriguez .10

Black

Stars: 15-25X
Production 55 Sets
HTA Exclusive

eTopps Classics

Topps continued its eTopps Classics line-up in 2006 with cards of former greats. The format was the same as earlier issues. Like regular eTopps cards, Classics could only be ordered during a one-week Initial Player Offering period. Cards were issued in a quantity of up to 3,000 each at $9.50-12.50. The number of cards actually sold is shown parenthetically. Fronts have a color or colorized action photo, backs have a picture of one of that player's Topps cards, along with career notes, stats, etc. Values shown are for cards in a virtual portfolio, rather than "in hand." Taking physical possession of a card from an eTopps portfolio costs about $6 apiece.

Complete Set (xx):
Common Player:

Gold

Stars: 5-10X
Production 2,006 Sets

Platinum

No Pricing
Production One Set

Factory Set Rookie Bonus

NM/M

1-5 issued in retail factory sets
6-10 issued in hobby factory sets
11-20 issued in holiday factory sets

1 Nicholas Markakis 5.00
2 Kelly Shoppach 3.00
3 Jordan Tata 3.00
4 Ruddy Lugo 3.00
5 Josh Wilson 3.00
6 Fernando Nieve 3.00
7 Sendy Rleal 3.00
8 Jason Kubel 3.00
9 James Loney 5.00
10 Fabio Castro 3.00
11 Jonathan Broxton 3.00
12 Eliezer Alfonzo 3.00
13 Jason Hirsh 3.00
14 Rajai Davis 3.00
15 Henry Owens 5.00
16 Kevin Frandsen 3.00
17 Matt Garza 5.00
18 Chris Duncan 3.00
19 Chris Coste 3.00
20 Jeff Karstens 5.00

Factory Set Team Bonus

NM/M

Issued in specified factory team sets.

BRS1 Jonathan Papelbon 10.00
BRS2 Manny Ramirez 5.00
BRS3 David Ortiz 5.00
BRS4 Josh Beckett 3.00
BRS5 Curt Schilling 4.00

CC1 Sean Marshall 3.00
CC2 Freddie Bynum 3.00
CC3 Derrek Lee 4.00
CC4 Juan Pierre 3.00
CC5 Carlos Zambrano 3.00
NYY1 Wilbert Nieves 3.00
NYY2 Alex Rodriguez 6.00
NYY3 Derek Jeter 8.00
NYY4 Mariano Rivera 5.00
NYY5 Randy Johnson 5.00
PP1 Matt Capps 3.00
PP2 Paul Maholm 3.00
PP3 Nate McLouth 3.00
PP4 John Van Benschoten 3.00
PP5 Jason Bay 3.00
SLC1 Adam Wainwright 4.00
SLC2 Skip Schumaker 3.00
SLC3 Albert Pujols 10.00
SLC4 Jim Edmonds 3.00
SLC5 Scott Rolen 5.00

Autographs

NM/M

Common Player:
WB Wade Boggs/250 50.00
JB Jason Botts 10.00
MB Milton Bradley 20.00
CB Craig Breslow 10.00
FC Fausto Carmona 15.00
BC Brian Cashman/100 175.00
EC Eric Chavez/200 60.00
LC Lance Cormier 15.00
NC Nelson Cruz 8.00
DD Doug DeVore 8.00
TE Theo Epstein/100 120.00
RG Ryan Garko 20.00
AG Alex Gordon 100.00
CG Carlos Guillen 20.00
LH Livan Hernandez 10.00
RH Rich Hill 30.00
CJ Chuck James 25.00
JJ Josh Johnson 15.00
AL Anthony Lerew 10.00
FL Francisco Liriano 30.00
JM Jeff Mathis 15.00
GN Graig Nettles 25.00
SO Scott Olsen 15.00
TO Tim Olson 8.00
DO David Ortiz/100 100.00
HR Horacio Ramirez 10.00
DR Darrell Rasner 10.00
ARE Anthony Reyes 25.00
CR Cal Ripken Jr./100 200.00
AR Alex Rodriguez/100 450.00
RS Ryne Sandberg/100 140.00
GS Gary Sheffield/200 60.00
TS Terrmel Sledge 15.00
BW Brad Wilkerson 15.00
DW Dave Winfield/100 150.00
MY Michael Young 25.00

Series 2

GA Garrett Atkins 20.00
CB Clint Barmes 15.00
JB Jose Bautista 15.00
BB Barry Bonds/120 400.00
RC Robinson Cano 50.00
GC Gary Carter/250 40.00
BC Brandon Claussen 10.00
DD Doug Drabek/250 20.00
JF Jeff Francis 20.00
DJ Dan Johnson 15.00
AJ Andruw Jones/50 50.00
SK Scott Kazmir 25.00
DL Derrek Lee/250 50.00
BM Brandon McCarthy 15.00
CO Chad Orvella 10.00
JP Jonathan Papelbon 60.00
WP Wily Mo Pena/250 30.00
BR Brian Roberts/250 40.00
DSN Duke Snider/250 60.00
DS Darryl Strawberry/250 25.00
CV Claudio Vargas 15.00
RZ Ryan Zimmerman 50.00

Hit Parade

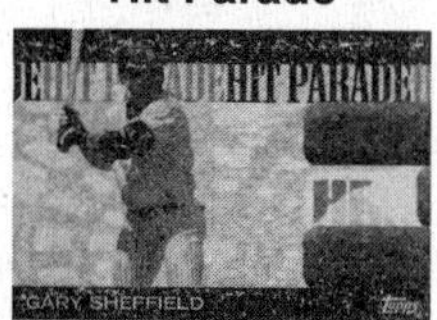

NM/M

Common Player: .50
RB11 Barry Bonds 3.00
RB12 Ken Griffey Jr. 2.00
RB13 Jeff Bagwell .75
RB14 Gary Sheffield .75
RB15 Frank Thomas .75
RB16 Manny Ramirez 1.00
RB17 Ruben Sierra .50
RB18 Jeff Kent .50
RB19 Luis Gonzalez .50
RBI10 Alex Rodriguez 3.00
HR1 Barry Bonds 3.00
HR2 Ken Griffey Jr. 2.00
HR3 Jeff Bagwell .75
HR4 Gary Sheffield .75
HR5 Frank Thomas .75
HR6 Manny Ramirez 1.00
HR7 Jim Thome 1.00
HR8 Alex Rodriguez 3.00
HR9 Mike Piazza 1.00
HR10 Carlos Delgado .75
HT1 Craig Biggio .50
HT2 Barry Bonds 3.00
HT3 Julio Franco .50
HT4 Steve Finley .50
HT5 Gary Sheffield .75
HT6 Jeff Bagwell .75
HT7 Ken Griffey Jr. 2.00
HT8 Omar Vizquel .50
HT9 Marquis Grissom .50
HT10 Bernie Williams .50

Hobby Masters

NM/M

Complete Set (20): 20.00
Common Player: .75
Inserted 1:18
HM1 Derrek Lee 1.00
HM2 Albert Pujols 4.00
HM3 Nomar Garciaparra 1.00
HM4 Alfonso Soriano .75
HM5 Derek Jeter 4.00
HM6 Miguel Tejada 1.00
HM7 Alex Rodriguez 4.00
HM8 Jim Edmonds .75
HM9 Mark Prior 1.00
HM10 Roger Clemens 4.00
HM11 Randy Johnson 1.50
HM12 Manny Ramirez 1.50
HM13 Curt Schilling 1.50
HM14 Vladimir Guerrero 1.50
HM15 Barry Bonds 4.00
HM16 Ichiro Suzuki 2.50
HM17 Pedro Martinez 1.50
HM18 Carlos Beltran 1.00
HM19 David Ortiz 1.50
HM20 Andruw Jones 1.00

King of England Cut Sig

Production One

Mantle Homerun History

NM/M

Inserted 1:4
MHR1 Mickey Mantle 2.00
Common Mantle: 2.00
MHR2-MHR101 Mickey Mantle 2.00

Mantle Homerun History Relic

Inserted 1:4,540
Series 2
Production Seven Sets

Mantle Homerun History Cut Signature

Production One

Opening Day

NM/M

Common Team: .50
WI Chicago White Sox 2.00
MN New York Mets 2.00
RR Texas Rangers 1.00
BP Milwaukee Brewers .50
RC Cincinnati Reds 1.00
PC Philadelphia Phillies 1.00
OD Baltimore Orioles 1.00
RD Colorado Rockies .50
DB Los Angeles Dodgers 2.00
RT Kansas City Royals .50
MA Seattle Mariners 1.00
AM Houston Astros 1.00
PG San Diego Padres 1.00
AY Oakland Athletics 2.00
JT Toronto Blue Jays 1.00

Own the Game

NM/M

Complete Set (30): 20.00
Common Player: .50
Inserted 1:12
OG1 Derrek Lee 1.00
OG2 Michael Young .75
OG3 Albert Pujols 3.00
OG4 Roger Clemens 3.00
OG5 Andy Pettitte .75
OG6 Dontrelle Willis .75
OG7 Michael Young .75
OG8 Ichiro Suzuki 2.00
OG9 Derek Jeter 3.00
OG10 Andruw Jones .75
OG11 Alex Rodriguez 3.00
OG12 David Ortiz 1.00
OG13 David Ortiz 1.00
OG14 Manny Ramirez 1.00
OG15 Mark Teixeira 1.00
OG16 Albert Pujols 3.00
OG17 Alex Rodriguez 3.00
OG18 Derek Jeter 3.00
OG19 Chad Cordero .50
OG20 Francisco Rodriguez .50
OG21 Mariano Rivera .75
OG22 Chone Figgins .50
OG23 Jose Reyes .75
OG24 Scott Podsednik .50
OG25 Jake Peavy .75
OG26 Johan Santana 1.00
OG27 Pedro Martinez 1.00
OG28 Dontrelle Willis .75
OG29 Chris Carpenter .50
OG30 Bartolo Colon .50

Signers of the Declaration of Independence

NM/M

Complete Set (56): 80.00
Common Signer: 1.50
Inserted 1:4
JA John Adams 3.00
SA Samuel Adams 3.00
JB Josiah Bartlett 1.50
CB Carter Braxton 1.50
CC Charles Carroll 1.50
SC Samuel Chase 1.50
AC Abraham Clark 1.50
GC George Clymer 1.50
WE William Ellery 1.50
WF William Floyd 1.50
BF Benjamin Franklin 4.00
EG Elbridge Gerry 1.50
BG Button Gwinnett 1.50
LH Lyman Hall 1.50
JH John Hancock 3.00
BH Benjamin Harrison 1.50
JHA John Hart 1.50
JHE Joseph Hewes 1.50
TH Thomas Heyward Jr. 1.50
WH William Hooper 1.50
SH Stephen Hopkins 1.50
FH Francis Hopkinson 1.50
SHU Samuel Huntington 1.50
TJ Thomas Jefferson 4.00
FLL Francis Lightfoot Lee 1.50
RHL Richard Henry Lee 1.50
FL Francis Lewis 1.50
PL Philip Livingston 1.50
TL Thomas Lynch Jr. 1.50
TM Thomas McKean 1.50
AM Arthur Middleton 1.50
LM Lewis Morris 1.50
RM Robert Morris 1.50
JM John Morton 1.50
TN Thomas Nelson Jr. 1.50
WP William Paca 1.50
RTP Robert Treat Paine 1.50
JP John Penn 1.50
GRE George Read 1.50
CR Caesar Rodney 1.50
GR George Ross 1.50
BR Benjamin Rush 1.50
ER Edward Rutledge 1.50
RS Roger Sherman 1.50
JS James Smith 1.50
RST Richard Stockton 1.50
TS Thomas Stone 1.50
GT George Taylor 1.50
MT Matthew Thornton 1.50
GW George Walton 1.50
WW William Whipple 1.50
WWI William Williams 1.50
JW James Wilson 1.50
JWI John Witherspoon 1.50
OW Oliver Wolcott 1.50
GWY George Wythe 1.50

Declaration of Independence Cuts

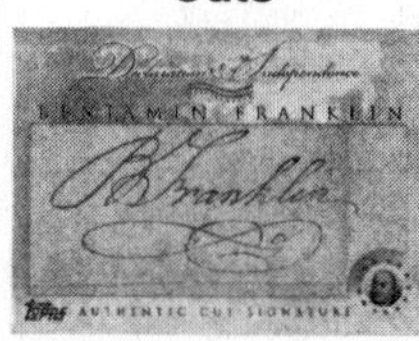

No Pricing
Production One Set

Signers of the Constitution

NM/M

Common Signer: 1.50
Inserted 1:8
AB Abraham Baldwin 1.50
RB Richard Bassett 1.50
GB Gunning Bedford Jr. 1.50
JB John Blair 1.50
WB William Blount 1.50
DB David Brearly 1.50
JBR Jacob Broom 1.50
PB Pierce Butler 1.50
DC Daniel Carroll 1.50
GC George Clymer 1.50
JD Jonathan Dayton 1.50
JDI John Dickinson 1.50
WF William Few 1.50
TF Thomas Fitzsimons 1.50
BF Benjamin Franklin 4.00
NG Nicholas Gilman 1.50
NGO Nathaniel Gorham 1.50
AH Alexander Hamilton 3.00
JI Jared Ingersoll 1.50
DJ Daniel of St. Thomas Jenifer 1.50
WJ William Samuel Johnson 1.50
RK Rufus King 1.50
JL John Langdon 1.50
WL William Livingston 1.50
JM James Madison 2.00
JMC James McHenry 1.50
TM Thomas Mifflin 1.50
GM Gouverneur Morris 1.50
RM Robert Morris 1.50
WP William Paterson 1.50
CCP Charles Cotesworth Pinckney 1.50
CP Charles Pinckney 1.50
GR George Read 1.50
JR John Rutledge 1.50
RS Roger Sherman 1.50
RDS Richard Dobbs Spaight 1.50
GW George Washington 4.00
HW Hugh Williamson 1.50
JW James Wilson 1.50

Signers of the Constitution Cut Signatures

(No Pricing)

Stars

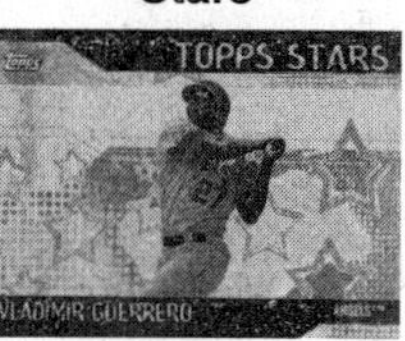

NM/M

Common Player: .75
BB Barry Bonds 3.00
MC Miguel Cabrera 1.00
RC Roger Clemens 3.00
VG Vladimir Guerrero 1.00
TH Todd Helton .75
DJ Derek Jeter 3.00
PM Pedro Martinez 1.00
HM Hideki Matsui 2.00
DO David Ortiz 1.00
AP Albert Pujols 3.00
MR Manny Ramirez 1.00
AR Alex Rodriguez 3.00
AS Alfonso Soriano .75
IS Ichiro Suzuki 2.00
MT Miguel Tejada .75

2006 Topps Trading Places

NM/M

Common Player: .50
MB Milton Bradley .50
CC Coco Crisp .50
JD Johnny Damon 1.00
CD Carlos Delgado .75
JDN Juan Encarnacion .50
RF Rafael Furcal .50
NG Nomar Garciaparra 1.00
TG Troy Glaus .50
RH Ramon Hernandez .50
KL Kenny Lofton .50
BM Bill Mueller .50
CP Corey Patterson .50
MJP Mike Piazza 1.00
JP Juan Pierre .50
ER Edgar Renteria .50
AS Alfonso Soriano .75
FT Frank Thomas .75
JT Jim Thome 1.00
BW Brad Wilkerson .50
PW Preston Wilson .50

Autographs

NM/M

Autographed Relics: No Pricing
Production 25 Sets
JE Johnny Estrada 10.00
KJ Kenji Johjima 140.00
PL Paul LoDuca 20.00
ML Mike Lowell 25.00
BR B.J. Ryan 30.00
TS Terrmel Sledge 10.00
BW Billy Wagner 30.00

Autographed Relics

No Pricing
Production 25 Sets

Relics

NM/M

Common Player: 4.00
MB Milton Bradley 4.00
CC Coco Crisp 6.00
JD Johnny Damon 15.00
JE Johnny Estrada 6.00
NG Nomar Garciaparra 15.00
RH Ramon Hernandez 4.00
KJ Kenji Johjima 15.00
PL Paul LoDuca 6.00
KL Kenny Lofton 6.00
ML Mike Lowell 10.00
BM Bill Mueller 4.00
CP Corey Patterson 8.00
JP Juan Pierre 6.00
ER Edgar Renteria 6.00
BR B.J. Ryan 4.00
TS Terrmel Sledge 4.00
AS Alfonso Soriano 8.00
FT Frank Thomas 8.00
JT Jim Thome 10.00
BW Billy Wagner 6.00
BW Brad Wilkerson 4.00
PW Preston Wilson 4.00

2006 Topps The Mantle Collection

NM/M

Complete Set (10): 65.00
Common Mantle: 8.00
Inserted 1:36
Black: No Pricing
Production Seven Sets
MM2005 Mickey Mantle 8.00
MM2004 Mickey Mantle 8.00
MM2003 Mickey Mantle 8.00
MM2002 Mickey Mantle 8.00
MM2001 Mickey Mantle 8.00
MM2000 Mickey Mantle 8.00
MM1999 Mickey Mantle 8.00
MM1998 Mickey Mantle 8.00
MM1997 Mickey Mantle 8.00
MM1996 Mickey Mantle 8.00

Gold

NM/M

Varying quantities produced
MM2005 Mickey Mantle/977 30.00
MM2004 Mickey Mantle/877 30.00
MM2003 Mickey Mantle/777 40.00
MM2002 Mickey Mantle/677 40.00
MM2001 Mickey Mantle/577 50.00
MM2000 Mickey Mantle/477 50.00
MM1999 Mickey Mantle/377 50.00
MM1998 Mickey Mantle/277 60.00
MM1997 Mickey Mantle/177 100.00
MM1996 Mickey Mantle/77 150.00

Relics

NM/M

Production 77-167
Gold:
Black: No Pricing
Production Seven Sets
MM2005 Mickey Mantle/167 160.00
MM2004 Mickey Mantle/157 160.00
MM2003 Mickey Mantle/147 160.00
MM2002 Mickey Mantle/137 160.00
MM2001 Mickey Mantle/127 200.00
MM2000 Mickey Mantle/117 200.00
MM1999 Mickey Mantle/107 200.00
MM1998 Mickey Mantle/97 200.00
MM1997 Mickey Mantle/87 200.00
MM1996 Mickey Mantle/77 200.00

Rookie of the Week

NM/M

Issued one per week via HTA shops
1 Mickey Mantle 10.00
2 Barry Bonds 3.00
3 Roger Clemens 3.00
4 Ernie Banks 2.00
5 Nolan Ryan 5.00
6 Albert Pujols 4.00
7 Roberto Clemente 5.00
8 Frank Robinson 1.50
9 Brooks Robinson 1.50
10 Harmon Killebrew 1.50
11 Reggie Jackson 1.50
12 George Brett 3.00
13 Ichiro Suzuki 3.00
14 Cal Ripken Jr. 6.00
15 Tom Seaver 1.50
16 Johnny Bench 1.50
17 Mike Schmidt 2.00
18 Derek Jeter 5.00
19 Bob Gibson 1.50
20 Ozzie Smith 2.00
21 Rickey Henderson 1.50
22 Tony Gwynn 1.50
23 Wade Boggs 1.50
24 Ryne Sandberg 3.00
25 Mickey Mantle 10.00

Walmart Cards

NM/M

Complete Set (18): 25.00
Common Player: .50
WM1 Stan Musial 2.00
WM2 Ted Williams 3.00
WM3 Yogi Berra 2.00
WM5 Mickey Mantle 10.00
WM6 Mickey Mantle 10.00
WM7 Alex Rodriguez 3.00
WM9 Gary Carter .50
WM10 Roy Oswalt .50
WM13 Carlos Lee .50
WM14 Johan Santana 1.00
WM15 Roberto Clemente 3.00
WM16 Carl Yastrzemski 1.50
WM21 Chipper Jones 1.00
WM22 Ichiro Suzuki 2.00
WM23 Bobby Abreu .50
WM24 Tom Seaver 1.00
WM25 Alfonso Soriano .75
WM26 Andruw Jones 1.00
WM28 Adam Dunn .75
WM30 Mark Teixeira 1.00
WM31 Albert Pujols 3.00
WM32 Cal Ripken Jr. 4.00
WM33 Ryne Sandberg 2.00
WM34 Don Mattingly 2.00
WM35 Roger Clemens 3.00
WM36 Jose Reyes .50
WM38 Derrek Lee 1.00
WM39 Miguel Cabrera 1.00
WM41 Barry Bonds 3.00
WM42 Barry Bonds 3.00
WM44 Livan Hernandez .50
WM45 Derek Jeter 3.00
WM46 David Ortiz 1.00
WM48 Ivan Rodriguez .75
WM52 Alex Rodriguez 3.00
WM53 Vladimir Guerrero 1.00

World Series Relics

NM/M

Common Player:
MB Mark Buehrle/Glv/100 200.00
JC Joe Crede 35.00
JD Jermaine Dye 20.00
CEB Carl Everett 15.00
CEU Carl Everett/Uni./100 90.00
JG Jon Garland 20.00
WH Willie Harris 10.00
TI Tadahito Iguchi 25.00
BJ Bobby Jenks/Glv/100 275.00
PKB Paul Konerko 15.00
PKU Paul Konerko 15.00
TP Timoniel Perez 15.00
AP A.J. Pierzynski 20.00
SP Scott Podsednik 25.00
AR Aaron Rowand 25.00
FT Frank Thomas 20.00
JU Juan Uribe 20.00

2K6 Promo Cards

NM/M
Complete Set (11): 10.00
Common Player: .75
Inserted 1:18
1 Derek Jeter 3.00
2 Andruw Jones 1.00
3 Miguel Cabrera 1.00
4 Derrek Lee 1.00
5 Mariano Rivera .75
6 Ivan Rodriguez .75
7 Vladimir Guerrero 1.00
8 Albert Pujols 3.00
9 Alex Rodriguez 3.00
10 Alfonso Soriano .75
11 Dontrelle Willis .75

Bonds Home Run History

NM/M
Complete Set (48): 35.00
Common Bonds: 1.00
Inserted 1:4
BB661-BB708 Barry Bonds 1.00

AFLAC

NM/M
Common Player: 15.00
BB Blake Beavan 50.00
BK Brett Krill 40.00
CC Christian Colon 40.00
CR Cameron Rupp 25.00
DB Drake Britton 15.00
DD Derek Dietrich 25.00
DM D.J. LeMahieu 25.00
DR Danny Rams 25.00
ED Evan Danieli 30.00
EG Erik Goeddel 30.00
FF Freddie Freeman 25.00
GP Greg Peavey 30.00
HM Hunter Morris 40.00
JG Jon Gilmore 25.00
JH Jason Heyward 65.00
JL Joe Leftridge 20.00
JS Josh Smoker 40.00
JT John Tolisano 25.00
JV Josh Vitters 125.00
KB Kyle Blair 15.00
KK Kevin Keyes 15.00
MB Madison Bumgarner 75.00
MH Matt Harvey 60.00
MM Michael Main 40.00
NN Nick Noonan 15.00
NR Neil Ramirez 25.00
PD Paul Demny 15.00
RP Rick Porcello 75.00
RS Robert Stock 50.00
SB Steven Brooks 25.00
SS Sequoyah Stonecipher 75.00
TA Tim Alderson 25.00
YG Yasmani Grandal 25.00

2006 Topps Allen & Ginter

NM/M
Complete Set (350):
Common Player: .25
Common SP: .50
SP's Inserted 1:2
Pack (7): 9.00
Box (24): 180.00
1 Albert Pujols 3.00
2 Aubrey Huff .25
3 Mark Teixeira .75
4 Vernon Wells .50
5 Ken Griffey Jr./SP 4.00
6 Nick Swisher .25
7 Jose Reyes .50
8 David Wright 2.00
9 Vladimir Guerrero 1.00
10 Andruw Jones .75
11 Ramon Hernandez .25
12 Miguel Tejada .75
13 Juan Pierre .25
14 Jim Thome .75
15 Austin Kearns/SP .50
16 Jhonny Peralta .25
17 Clint Barmes .25
18 Angel Berroa .25
19 Nomar Garciaparra 1.00
20 Joe Nathan .25
21 Brandon Webb .25
22 Chad Tracy .25
23 Derek Jeter 3.00
24 Conor Jackson **(RC)** .50
25 Jason Giambi/SP 1.00
26 Johnny Estrada .25
27 Luis Gonzalez .40
28 Javier Vazquez .25
29 Orlando Hudson .25
30 Shawn Green .40
31 Mark Buehrle .40
32 Wily Mo Pena .25
33 C.C. Sabathia .25
34 Ronnie Belliard .25
35 Travis Hafner/SP 1.00
36 Mike Jacobs **(RC)** .50
37 Roy Oswalt .50
38 Zack Greinke .25
39 J.D. Drew .40
40 Jeff Kent .40
41 Ben Sheets .40
42 Luis Castillo .25
43 Carlos Delgado .75
44 Cliff Floyd .25
45 Danny Haren/SP .50
46 Bobby Abreu .50
47 Jeromy Burnitz .25
48 Khalil Greene .25
49 Moises Alou .25
50 Alex Rodriguez/SP 5.00
51 Ervin Santana/SP .50
52 Bartolo Colon/SP .50
53 John Smoltz/SP 1.00
54 David Ortiz/SP 2.00
55 Hideki Matsui/SP 3.00
56 Jermaine Dye/SP .50
57 Victor Martinez/SP .50
58 Willy Taveras/SP .50
59 Brady Clark/SP .50
60 Justin Morneau .50
61 Xavier Nady .25
62 Rich Harden .25
63 Jack Wilson .25
64 Brian Giles .25
65 Jon Lieber/SP .50
66 Dan Johnson .25
67 Billy Wagner .25
68 Rickie Weeks .40
69 Chris Ray **(RC)** .50
70 Chris Shelton .25
71 Dmitri Young .25
72 Ivan Rodriguez .75
73 Jeremy Bonderman .50
74 Justin Verlander **(RC)** 1.00
75 Randy Johnson 1.00
76 Magglio Ordonez .25
77 Brandon Inge .25
78 Placido Polanco .25
79 Ryan Howard 1.00
80 Jason Bay .50
81 Sean Casey .25
82 Jeremy Hermida **(RC)** .50
83 Mike Cameron .25
84 Trevor Hoffman .25
85 Mike Matheny/SP .50
86 Steve Finley .25
87 Adam Everett .25
88 Jason Isringhausen .25
89 Jonny Gomes .25
90 Barry Zito .50
91 Bobby Crosby .25
92 Eric Chavez .25
93 Frank Thomas .75
94 Huston Street .25
95 Jorge Posada .50
96 Casey Kotchman .25
97 Darin Erstad .25
98 Chipper Jones 1.00
99 Jeff Francoeur .40
100 Barry Bonds 3.00
101 Alfonso Soriano 1.00
102 Brandon Claussen .25
103 Aaron Boone .25
104 Roger Clemens 3.00
105 Andy Pettitte/SP .75
106 Nick Johnson .25
107 Tom Gordon .25
108 Orlando Hernandez .25
109 Francisco Rodriguez .25
110 Orlando Cabrera .25
111 Edgar Renteria .40
112 Tim Hudson .50
113 Coco Crisp .25
114 Matt Clement .25
115 Greg Maddux/SP 3.00
116 Paul Konerko .50
117 Felipe Lopez .25
118 Garrett Atkins .25
119 Akinori Otsuka .25
120 Craig Biggio .50
121 Danys Baez .25
122 Brad Penny .25
123 Eric Gagne .25
124 Lew Ford .25
125 Mariano Rivera/SP 1.00
126 Carlos Beltran .75
127 Pedro Martinez 1.00
128 Todd Helton .75
129 Aaron Rowand .25
130 Mike Lieberthal .25
131 Oliver Perez .25
132 Ryan Klesko .25
133 Randy Winn .25
134 Yuniesky Betancourt .25
135 David Eckstein/SP .50
136 Chad Orvella .25
137 Toby Hall .25
138 Hank Blalock .50
139 B.J. Ryan .25
140 Roy Halladay .50
141 Livan Hernandez .25
142 John Patterson .25
143 Bengie Molina .25
144 Brad Wilkerson .25
145 Jorge Cantu/SP .50
146 Mark Mulder .50
147 Felix Hernandez .50
148 Paul LoDuca .25
149 Prince Fielder **(RC)** 4.00
150 Johnny Damon/SP 2.00
151 Ryan Langerhans/SP .50
152 Kris Benson/SP .50
153 Curt Schilling/SP 2.00
154 Manny Ramirez/SP 2.00
155 Robinson Cano/SP 1.50
156 Derrek Lee/SP 1.50
157 A.J. Pierzynski/SP .50
158 Adam Dunn/SP 1.00
159 Cliff Lee/SP .50
160 Grady Sizemore .50
161 Jeff Francis .25
162 Dontrelle Willis .50
163 Brad Ausmus .25
164 Preston Wilson .25
165 Derek Lowe/SP .50
166 Chris Capuano .25
167 Joe Mauer .50
168 Torii Hunter .40
169 Chase Utley .75
170 Zachary Duke .25
171 Jason Schmidt .40
172 Adrian Beltre .25
173 Eddie Guardado .25
174 Richie Sexson .50
175 Miguel Cabrera/SP 2.00
176 Julio Lugo .25
177 Francisco Cordero .25
178 Kevin Millwood .25
179 A.J. Burnett .25
180 Jose Guillen .25
181 Larry Bigbie .25
182 Raul Ibanez .25
183 Jake Peavy .50
184 Pat Burrell .50
185 Tom Glavine/SP .75
186 J.J. Hardy .25
187 Emil Brown .25
188 Lance Berkman .50
189 Marcus Giles .25
190 Scott Podsednik .25
191 Chone Figgins .25
192 Melvin Mora .25
193 Mark Loretta .25
194 Carlos Zambrano .40
195 Chien-Ming Wang .75
196 Mark Prior .50
197 Bobby Jenks .50
198 Brian Fuentes .25
199 Garret Anderson .25
200 Ichiro Suzuki 2.00
201 Brian Roberts .25
202 Jason Kendall .25
203 Milton Bradley .25
204 Jimmy Rollins .50
205 Brett Myers/SP .50
206 Joe Randa .25
207 Mike Piazza 1.00
208 Matt Morris .25
209 Omar Vizquel .25
210 Jeremy Reed .25
211 Chris Carpenter .50
212 Jim Edmonds .50
213 Scott Kazmir .50
214 Travis Lee .25
215 Michael Young/SP .75
216 Rod Barajas .25
217 Gustavo Chacin .25
218 Lyle Overbay .25
219 Troy Glaus .50
220 Chad Cordero .25
221 Jose Vidro .25
222 Scott Rolen .75
223 Carl Crawford .25
224 Rocco Baldelli .25
225 Mike Mussina .50
226 Kelvim Escobar .25
227 Corey Patterson .25
228 Javy Lopez .25
229 Jonathan Papelbon/SP **(RC)** 5.00
230 Aramis Ramirez .50
231 Tadahito Iguchi .50
232 Morgan Ensberg .50
233 Mark Grudzielanek .25
234 Mike Sweeney .25
235 Shawn Chacon/SP .50
236 Nick Punto .25
237 Geoff Jenkins .25
238 Carlos Lee .50
239 David DeJesus .25
240 Brad Lidge .25
241 Bob Wickman .25
242 Jon Garland .25
243 Kerry Wood .25
244 Bronson Arroyo .25
245 Matt Holliday/SP .50
246 Josh Beckett .50
247 Johan Santana .75
248 Rafael Furcal .25
249 Shannon Stewart .25
250 Gary Sheffield .50
251 Josh Barfield **(RC)** .50
252 Kenji Johjima **RC** 2.00
253 Ian Kinsler **(RC)** .50
254 Brian Anderson **(RC)** .50
255 Matt Cain **(RC)** 1.00
256 Josh Willingham/SP **(RC)** .50
257 John Koronka **(RC)** .50
258 Chris Duffy **(RC)** .50
259 Brian McCann **(RC)** .50
260 Hanley Ramirez **(RC)** 1.00
261 Hong-Chih Kuo **(RC)** .50
262 Francisco Liriano **(RC)** 5.00
263 Anderson Hernandez **(RC)** .50
264 Ryan Zimmerman **(RC)** 4.00
265 Brian Bannister/SP **(RC)** .50
266 Nolan Ryan 2.00
267 Frank Robinson 1.00
268 Roberto Clemente 3.00
269 Hank Greenberg .50
270 Napoleon Lajoie .50
271 Lloyd Waner .25
272 Paul Waner .25
273 Frankie Frisch .25
274 Bill "Moose" Skowron .25
275 Mickey Mantle 6.00
276 Brooks Robinson 1.00
277 Carl Yastrzemski 1.00
278 Johnny Pesky .25
279 Stan Musial 1.50
280 Bill Mazeroski .50
281 Harmon Killebrew .75
282 Monte Irvin .50
283 Bob Gibson 1.00
284 Ted Williams 2.00
285 Yogi Berra/SP 2.00
286 Ernie Banks 1.00
287 Bobby Doerr .25
288 Josh Gibson .50
289 Bob Feller .25
290 Cal Ripken Jr. 3.00
291 Bobby Cox .25
292 Terry Francona .25
293 Dusty Baker .25
294 Ozzie Guillen .25
295 Jim Leyland .50
296 Willie Randolph .25
297 Joe Torre .50
298 Felipe Alou .25
299 Tony LaRussa .25
300 Frank Robinson .50
301 Mike Tyson 2.00
302 Duke Paoa Kahanamoku .25
303 Jennie Finch 2.00
304 Brandi Chastain .25
305 Danica Patrick/SP 10.00
306 Wendy Guey .25
307 Hulk Hogan .25
308 Carl Lewis .25
309 John Wooden .25
310 Randy Couture .25
311 Andy Irons .25
312 Takeru Kobayashi .25
313 Leon Spinks .25
314 Jim Thorpe 1.00
315 Jerry Bailey/SP .50
316 Adrian C. Anson .25
317 John M. Ward .25
318 Mike Kelly .25
319 Cpt. Jack Glasscock .25
320 Aaron Hill .25
321 Derrick Turnbow .25
322 Nicholas Markakis .25
323 Brad Hawpe .25
324 Kevin Mench .25
325 John Lackey/SP .50
326 Chester A. Arthur .25
327 Ulysses S. Grant .50
328 Abraham Lincoln 1.00
329 Grover Cleveland .25
330 Benjamin Harrison .25
331 Theodore Roosevelt .50
332 Rutherford B. Hayes .25
333 Chancellor Otto Von Bismarck .25
334 Kaiser Wilhelm II .25
335 Queen Victoria/SP .50
336 Pope Leo XIII .50
337 Thomas Edison .50
338 Orville Wright .50
339 Wilbur Wright .50
340 Nathaniel Hawthorne .25
341 Herman Melville .25
342 Stonewall Jackson .50
343 Robert E. Lee .50
344 Andrew Carnegie .25
345 John Rockefeller/SP .50
346 Bob Fitzsimmons .25
347 Billy the Kid .25
348 Buffalo Bill .25
349 Jesse James .25
350 Statue of Liberty .25

Mini

Mini: 2-4X
SP's: 1-2X
Mini SP's Inserted 1:13
Mini (351-375): No Pricing
#'s 351-375 Inserted In Rip Cards
Allen & Ginter Back: 3-6X
Inserted 1:5
A & G Back SP's: 2-3X
Inserted 1:65
Bazooka Mini: No Pricing
Production 25 Sets
Black Mini: 5-10X
Inserted 1:10
Black SP: 3-5X
Inserted 1:130
Wood: No Pricing
Production One Set

Printing Plates

No Pricing
Production one set per color.

Relics

NM/M
Common Player: 4.00
CBA Clint Barmes 4.00
CB Carlos Beltran 10.00
BB Barry Bonds 20.00
MB Mark Buehrle 8.00
GWB George W. Bush 300.00
MC Miguel Cabrera 10.00
RC Robinson Cano 20.00
JC Jorge Cantu 6.00
EC Eric Chavez 6.00
BC Bobby Crosby 4.00
JD Johnny Damon 12.00
CD Carlos Delgado 8.00
ZD Zachary Duke 8.00
JDY Jermaine Dye 8.00
JF Jeff Francoeur 15.00
JG Jonny Gomes 6.00
VG Vladimir Guerrero 10.00
TH Travis Hafner 10.00
FH Felix Hernandez 8.00
MH Matt Holliday 8.00
RH Ryan Howard 30.00
JFK John F. Kennedy 375.00
PK Paul Konerko 10.00
HCK Hong-Chih Kuo 20.00
RL Ryan Langerhans 8.00
MM Mickey Mantle 125.00
PM Pedro Martinez 10.00
VM Victor Martinez 8.00
HM Hideki Matsui 15.00
BM Brandon McCarthy 4.00
DO David Ortiz 15.00
Ro Roy Oswalt 6.00
JP Jake Peavy 6.00
APE Andy Pettitte 6.00
MPZ Mike Piazza 10.00
MP Mark Prior 8.00
AP Albert Pujols 20.00
MR Manny Ramirez 10.00
AR Alex Rodriguez 20.00
JS Johan Santana 10.00
CS Curt Schilling 10.00
GS Gary Sheffield 8.00
HS Huston Street 6.00
NS Nick Swisher 8.00
WT Willy Taveras 6.00
MT Miguel Tejada 10.00
FT Frank Thomas 8.00
JT Jim Thome 10.00
CU Chase Utley 15.00
CMW Chien-Ming Wang 50.00
DWI Dontrelle Willis 8.00
DW David Wright 15.00

Autographs

NM/M
Cards are not serial numbered.
JB Jerry Bailey/200 80.00
JBA Josh Barfield 20.00
CB Clint Barmes 15.00
BB Barry Bonds/25 500.00
MC Miguel Cabrera/100 150.00
RC Robinson Cano 60.00
BC Brandi Chastain/200 75.00
EC Eric Chavez 15.00
RA Randy Couture 80.00
BF Bob Feller 75.00
PF Prince Fielder 100.00
JF Jennie Finch/200 140.00
LF Lew Ford 10.00
JG Jonny Gomes 15.00
VG Vladimir Guerrero/50 200.00
WG Wendy Guey 30.00
TG Tony Gwynn/50 250.00
TH Travis Hafner 30.00
HH Hulk Hogan/200 200.00
RH Ryan Howard 150.00
AI Andy Irons/200 40.00
KJ Kenji Johjima/50 275.00
SK Scott Kazmir 30.00
TK Takeru Kobayashi/200 125.00
DL Derrek Lee 50.00
CL Carl Lewis/200 120.00
FL Francisco Liriano 50.00
VM Victor Martinez 25.00
SM Stan Musial/50 375.00
DP Danica Patrick/100 500.00
WMP Wily Mo Pena 20.00
CR Cal Ripken Jr./50 300.00
AR Alex Rodriguez/50 400.00
BJR B.J. Ryan 15.00
NR Nolan Ryan/50 350.00
ES Ervin Santana 15.00
JS Johan Santana/100 125.00
GS Gary Sheffield/50 140.00
OS Ozzie Smith/75 200.00
LS Leon Spinks/200 75.00
HS Huston Street 40.00
MT Mike Tyson/200 275.00
CU Chase Utley 75.00
BW Billy Wagner 25.00
CMW Chien-Ming Wang/100 400.00
DWI Dontrelle Willis/100 40.00
JW John Wooden/200 200.00
DW David Wright 140.00
CY Carl Yastrzemski/50 320.00
MY Michael Young 35.00
RZ Ryan Zimmerman 60.00

Dick Perez Sketches

NM/M
Common Player .25
Inserted 1:1
Originals: No Pricing
Production One Set
ARI Shawn Green .25
ATL Andruw Jones .50
BAL Miguel Tejada .50
BOS David Ortiz 1.00
CHC Derrek Lee .50
CHW Paul Konerko .50
CIN Ken Griffey Jr. 1.00
CLE Travis Hafner .50
COL Todd Helton .50
DET Ivan Rodriguez .50
FLA Miguel Cabrera .75
HOU Lance Berkman .25
KC Mike Sweeney .25
LAA Vladimir Guerrero .75
LAD Rafael Furcal .25
MIL Carlos Lee .25
MIN Johan Santana .50
NYM David Wright 1.00
NYY Alex Rodriguez 2.00
OAK Huston Street .25
PHI Bobby Abreu .50
PIT Jason Bay .50
SDP Jake Peavy .50

SEA Ichiro Suzuki 1.50
SFG Barry Bonds 2.00
STL Albert Pujols 2.00
TAM Aubrey Huff .25
TEX Mark Teixeira .50
TOR Vernon Wells .25
WAS Alfonso Soriano .75

Postcards

NM/M

Inserted 1:2 Hobby Boxes
BB Barry Bonds 4.00
JG Josh Gibson 2.00
KG Ken Griffey Jr. 3.00
VG Vladimir Guerrero 2.00
DJ Derek Jeter 4.00
MM Mickey Mantle 10.00
DO David Ortiz 2.00
AP Albert Pujols 4.00
MR Manny Ramirez 2.00
CR Cal Ripken Jr. 6.00
AR Alex Rodriguez 4.00
I Ichiro Suzuki 3.00
MT Miguel Tejada 1.50
TW Ted Williams 4.00
DW David Wright 3.00

Personalized Postcards

One Set Produced

Allen & Ginter N43

NM/M

Inserted 1:2 Hobby Boxes
1 Alex Rodriguez 4.00
2 Barry Bonds 4.00
3 Albert Pujols 4.00
4 Josh Gibson 2.00
5 Nolan Ryan 4.00
6 Ichiro Suzuki 3.00
7 Mickey Mantle 10.00
8 Ted Williams 4.00
9 David Wright 3.00
10 Ken Griffey Jr. 3.00
11 Mark Teixeira 1.50
12 Adrian C. Anson 2.00
13 Mike Tyson 3.00
14 Kenji Johjima 2.00
15 Ryan Zimmerman 2.00

Allen & Ginter N43 Autos

Production 10 Sets

Allen & Ginter N43 Relics

NM/M

Production 50 Sets
AP Albert Pujols 100.00
JG Josh Gibson 250.00

Rip Card

NM/M

All prices for unripped cards.
1-4: Production 10 Sets
5-9: Production 15 Sets
10-19: Production 25 Sets
20-50: Production 99 Sets
RIP20 Kenji Johjima 100.00
RIP21 Cap Anson 100.00
RIP22 Ryan Zimmerman 100.00
RIP23 Andruw Jones 100.00
RIP24 Barry Bonds 150.00
RIP25 Cal Ripken Jr. 150.00
RIP26 David Ortiz 100.00
RIP27 Hideki Matsui 150.00
RIP28 Ken Griffey Jr. 100.00
RIP29 Manny Ramirez 100.00
RIP30 Mickey Mantle 200.00
RIP31 Alex Rodriguez 150.00
RIP32 Miguel Cabrera 100.00
RIP33 Miguel Tejada 100.00
RIP34 Pedro Martinez 100.00
RIP35 Albert Pujols 150.00
RIP36 Alex Rodriguez 150.00
RIP37 Alex Rodriguez, Derek Jeter 150.00
RIP38 Barry Bonds 150.00
RIP39 Derek Jeter 180.00
RIP40 Ichiro Suzuki 150.00
RIP41 Ichiro Suzuki, Hideki Matsui 150.00
RIP42 Josh Gibson 150.00
RIP43 Mickey Mantle 200.00
RIP44 Jonathan Papelbon 100.00
RIP45 Mickey Mantle, Ted Williams 200.00
RIP46 Albert Pujols 150.00
RIP47 Roberto Clemente 150.00
RIP48 Roger Clemens 150.00
RIP49 Ted Williams 150.00
RIP50 Vladimir Guerrero 100.00

2006 Topps Bazooka

NM/M

Complete Set (220): 30.00
Common Player: .10
Pack (8): 2.50
Box (24): 50.00
1 Josh Gibson .50
2 Scott Podsednik .10
3 Sammy Sosa .75
4 Ivan Rodriguez .40
5 Derek Jeter 1.50
6 Manny Ramirez .50
7 Nook Logan .10
8 Adam Dunn .40
9 Travis Hafner .25
10 Felix Hernandez .40
11 Larry Bigbie .10
12 Magglio Ordonez .10
13 Josh Beckett .25
14 Mike Sweeney .10
15 Mickey Mantle 2.00
16 Grady Sizemore .25
17 Brian Fuentes .10
18 Wily Mo Pena .10
19 Morgan Ensberg .10
20 Tim Hudson .25
21 Justin Verlander **(RC)** .25
22 Jermaine Dye .10
23 Miguel Cabrera .50
24 Greg Maddux 1.00
25 Jason Giambi .25
26 Ben Sheets .25
27 Brad Radke .10
28 Torii Hunter .25
29 Mike Piazza .75
30 Jason Kendall .10
31 Pat Burrell .25
32 Khalil Greene .10
33 Brian Roberts .25
34 C.C. Sabathia .10
35 Mike Mussina .40
36 Bob Wickman .10
37 Dmitri Young .10
38 Dontrelle Willis .25
39 David DeJesus .10
40 J.D. Drew .25
41 Chad Tracy .10
42 Joe Mauer .25
43 Melvin Mora .10
44 Carlos Zambrano .25
45 Mariano Rivera .25
46 Coco Crisp .10
47 Derrek Lee .50
48 Cliff Floyd .10
49 Willy Taveras .10
50 Albert Pujols 1.50
51 Aaron Boone .10
52 Mark Mulder .25
53 Brad Wilkerson .10
54 Hank Blalock .25
55 Hideki Matsui 1.00
56 Victor Martinez .10
57 Jeremy Bonderman .10
58 Felipe Lopez .10
59 Paul LoDuca .10
60 Derek Lowe .10
61 Luis Gonzalez .10
62 Paul Konerko .25
63 Miguel Tejada .40
64 Jeromy Burnitz .10
65 Orlando Hernandez .10
66 Curt Schilling .50
67 Joe Nathan .10
68 Jose Reyes .25
69 David Wright .75
70 Eric Chavez .25
71 Rich Harden .25
72 A.J. Pierzynski .10
73 Trevor Hoffman .10
74 Adrian Beltre .25
75 Alex Rodriguez 1.50
76 Larry Walker .25
77 Jorge Cantu .10
78 Mark Teixeira .40
79 Jeff Bagwell .40
80 Jeff Francoeur .50
81 Ichiro Suzuki 1.00
82 Jhonny Peralta .10
83 Todd Helton .40
84 Brad Penny .10
85 Shawn Chacon .10
86 Billy Wagner .10
87 Jason Schmidt .25
88 Austin Kearns .10
89 Chris Carpenter .10
90 Chipper Jones .50
91 Shawn Green .25
92 A.J. Burnett .10
93 Joe Crede .10
94 Mark Prior .40
95 Andy Pettitte .25
96 Edgar Renteria .10
97 Roy Halladay .25
98 Eric Milton .10
99 Craig Biggio .25
100 Barry Bonds 1.50
101 Troy Glaus .10
102 Aaron Rowand .10
103 Aramis Ramirez .25
104 Nomar Garciaparra .50
105 Randy Johnson .50
106 David Ortiz .50
107 Vinny Castilla .10
108 Carl Crawford .25
109 Zachary Duke .10
110 Barry Zito .25
111 Darin Erstad .10
112 Chris Capuano .10
113 Javy Lopez .10
114 Lew Ford .10
115 Robinson Cano .25
116 Ronnie Belliard .10
117 Placido Polanco .10
118 Rickie Weeks .25
119 Brad Lidge .10
120 Andruw Jones .40
121 Nick Swisher .10
122 Bartolo Colon .10
123 Juan Pierre .10
124 Johan Santana .50
125 Jorge Posada .25
126 Jeff Francis .10
127 Matt Holliday .25
128 Carlos Delgado .25
129 Zack Greinke .10
130 Lyle Overbay .10
131 Conor Jackson **(RC)** .10
132 Mark Buehrle .25
133 Chone Figgins .10
134 Pedro Martinez .50
135 Roger Clemens 1.50
136 Raul Ibanez .10
137 Jim Edmonds .25
138 Michael Young .10
139 Preston Wilson .10
140 Rafael Furcal .10
141 Bobby Abreu .25
142 Tadahito Iguchi .25
143 B.J. Ryan .10
144 Francisco Rodriguez .10
145 J.T. Snow .10
146 Aubrey Huff .10
147 Mike Morse .10
148 Jason Bay .25
149 Roy Oswalt .25
150 Carlos Beltran .40
151 Carlos Lee .25
152 Emil Brown .10
153 Craig Monroe .10
154 Kris Benson .10
155 Gary Sheffield .40
156 Jake Peavy .25
157 David Eckstein .10
158 Tom Glavine .25
159 Jeff Kent .25
160 Livan Hernandez .10
161 Orlando Hudson .10
162 Randy Winn .10
163 Jimmy Rollins .20
164 Luis Castillo .10
165 Nick Johnson .10
166 Johnny Damon .50
167 Eric Gagne .25
168 Geoff Jenkins .10
169 Mike Cameron .10
170 Marcus Giles .10
171 Huston Street .25
172 Moises Alou .25
173 Scott Rolen .50
174 Jose Vidro .10
175 Alfonso Soriano .40
176 Toby Hall .10
177 Orlando Cabrera .10
178 Brian Giles .10
179 Erubiel Durazo .10
180 Matt Morris .10
181 Jack Wilson .10
182 Brady Clark .10
183 Shannon Stewart .10
184 Kerry Wood .25
185 Carl Pavano .10
186 Chase Utley .25
187 Omar Vizquel .10
188 Vladimir Guerrero .50
189 Richie Sexson .25
190 John Smoltz .25
191 Garret Anderson .10
192 Jon Garland .10
193 Julio Lugo .10
194 Rocco Baldelli .10
195 Jaret Wright .10
196 Matt Clement .10
197 Vernon Wells .10
198 Sean Casey .10
199 Lance Berkman .25
200 Justin Morneau .20
201 Shaun Marcum **(RC)** .20
202 Chuck James **(RC)** .20
203 Hong-Chih Kuo **(RC)** .20
204 Darrell Rasner **(RC)** .20
205 Anthony Reyes **(RC)** .25
206 Francisco Liriano **(RC)** .50
207 Joe Saunders **(RC)** .20
208 Fausto Carmona **(RC)** .20
209 Charlton Jimerson **(RC)** .20
210 Bryan Bullington **(RC)** .20
211 Tom Gorzelanny **(RC)** .20
212 Anderson Hernandez **(RC)** .20
213 Ryan Garko **(RC)** .20
214 John Koronka **(RC)** .20
215 Chris Denorfia **(RC)** .20
216 Jeff Mathis **(RC)** .20
217 Jose Bautista **(RC)** .20
218 Danny Sandoval **RC** .20
219 Robert Andino **RC** .20
220 Justin Huber **(RC)** .20

Gold

Stars: 1-2X
Inserted 1:1

Autographs

NM/M

BM Brandon McCarthy 12.00
KM Kevin Millar 20.00
MM Mike Morse 15.00
VZ Victor Zambrano 15.00

Bazooka Basics

NM/M

BA Bobby Abreu 4.00
LB Lance Berkman 6.00
CB Craig Biggio 4.00
HB Hank Blalock 4.00
SB Sean Burroughs 4.00
MC Miguel Cabrera 8.00
JD Johnny Damon 8.00
CD Carlos Delgado 4.00
EG Eric Gagne 6.00
MG Marcus Giles 4.00
MH Matt Holliday 4.00
TH Tim Hudson 6.00
AJ Andruw Jones 6.00
CJ Chipper Jones 8.00
ML Mike Lowell 4.00
PM Pedro Martinez 10.00
MM Mark Mulder 4.00
MMU Mike Mussina 6.00
AP Albert Pujols 15.00
MR Manny Ramirez 4.00
JR Jose Reyes 4.00
BR Brian Roberts 4.00
CS Curt Schilling 8.00
MT Mark Teixeira 6.00
BW Bernie Williams 6.00
DW Dontrelle Willis 6.00

Bazooka Blasts

NM/M

BA Bobby Abreu 4.00
MA Moises Alou 4.00
JB Jason Bay 8.00
CB Carlos Beltran 6.00
HB Hank Blalock 4.00
BB Barry Bonds 20.00
CC Coco Crisp 4.00
JD Johnny Damon 8.00
JD J.D. Drew 4.00
AD Adam Dunn 6.00
CF Cliff Floyd 4.00
TG Troy Glaus 4.00
VG Vladimir Guerrero 6.00
GJ Geoff Jenkins 4.00
AJ Andruw Jones 6.00
CJ Chipper Jones 8.00
PK Paul Konerko 6.00
DL Derrek Lee 6.00
PL Paul LoDuca 4.00
ML Mark Loretta 4.00
MM Mickey Mantle/100 175.00
VM Victor Martinez 4.00
TN Trot Nixon 4.00
DO David Ortiz 8.00
CP Corey Patterson 4.00
MP Mike Piazza 8.00
AR Aramis Ramirez 6.00
AR Alex Rodriguez 15.00
GS Gary Sheffield 6.00
SS Sammy Sosa 8.00
MT Miguel Tejada 8.00
JT Jim Thome 6.00
PW Preston Wilson 4.00
DW David Wright 10.00

Bazooka Rewind

NM/M

CB Clint Barmes 4.00
WB William Bergolla 4.00
LB Lance Berkman 4.00

CBI Craig Biggio 6.00
JB Jason Botts 4.00
PB Pat Burrell 4.00
RC Robinson Cano 15.00
SC Shin-Soo Choo 4.00
CC Carl Crawford 6.00
NC Nelson Cruz 6.00
JDA Johnny Damon 8.00
JD Jermaine Dye 4.00
CE Carl Everett 4.00
RG Ryan Garko 4.00
JG Jon Garland 4.00
MG Mark Grudzielanek 4.00
JG Jose Guillen 4.00
CG Cristian Guzman 4.00
JH Justin Huber 4.00
MJ Mike Jacobs 8.00
NJ Nick Johnson 4.00
AJ Andruw Jones 6.00
AK Adam Kennedy 4.00
PK Paul Konerko 6.00
AML Adam LaRoche 4.00
CL Carlos Lee 4.00
FL Francisco Liriano 8.00
LM Luis Montanez 4.00
MM Miguel Montero 4.00
AP A.J. Pierzynski 6.00
SP Scott Podsednik 6.00
HR Hanley Ramirez 4.00
MR Manny Ramirez 8.00
ER Edgar Renteria 4.00
BR Brian Roberts 4.00
AR Alex Rodriguez 15.00
JR Jimmy Rollins 4.00
AR Aaron Rowand 4.00
TS Terrmel Sledge 4.00
WT Willy Taveras 4.00
FT Frank Thomas 6.00
KT Kevin Thompson 4.00
CU Chase Utley 8.00
JV Justin Verlander 6.00
RW Rickie Weeks 6.00
DW Dontrelle Willis 6.00
CY Chris Young 4.00

Comics

NM/M

Complete Set (24): 10.00
Common Player: .25
Inserted 1:4
1 Greg Maddux 1.00
2 Alex Rodriguez 1.00
3 Trevor Hoffman .25
4 Rafael Palmeiro .50
5 Roy Oswalt .25
6 Bobby Abreu .25
7 Miguel Tejada .50
8 Vladimir Guerrero .50
9 Mark Teixeira .25
10 Zachary Duke .25
11 Xavier Nady .25
12 Alex Rodriguez 1.00
13 Jeremy Hermida .25
14 Craig Biggio .25
15 Manny Ramirez .50
16 Texas Rangers .25
17 Oakland A's .25
18 Alex Rodriguez 1.00
19 Jason Giambi .50
20 Aaron Small .25
21 Jimmy Rollins .25
22 Roger Clemens 1.00
23 White Sox/Mariners .50
24 Andruw Jones .50

Fortune

Stars: 1-2X
Inserted 1:1

Mickey Mantle Oversized Reprint

NM/M

1952 Mickey Mantle 40.00
1953 Mickey Mantle 30.00
1956 Mickey Mantle 25.00
1957 Mickey Mantle 25.00
1958 Mickey Mantle 25.00
1959 Mickey Mantle 25.00
1960 Mickey Mantle 25.00
1961 Mickey Mantle 25.00
1962 Mickey Mantle 25.00
1963 Mickey Mantle 20.00
1964 Mickey Mantle 25.00
1965 Mickey Mantle 25.00
1966 Mickey Mantle 25.00
1967 Mickey Mantle 25.00
1968 Mickey Mantle 25.00
1969 Mickey Mantle 25.00

Stamps

NM/M

Complete Set (30): 15.00
Common Player: .50
Inserted 1:3 Hobby
1 Bobby Abreu .50
2 Lance Berkman .50
3 Hank Blalock .50
4 Barry Bonds 2.00
5 Mark Buehrle .50
6 Miguel Cabrera 1.00
7 Jim Edmonds .50
8 Morgan Ensberg .50
9 Jeff Francoeur .50
10 Roy Halladay .50
11 Tim Hudson .50
12 Derek Jeter 2.00
13 Andruw Jones .75
14 Chipper Jones 1.00
15 Derrek Lee .75
16 Mickey Mantle 3.00
17 Victor Martinez .50
18 Justin Morneau .50
19 Manny Ramirez 1.00
20 Brian Roberts .50
21 Alex Rodriguez 2.00
22 Ivan Rodriguez .50
23 Johan Santana .50
24 Alfonso Soriano .50
25 Huston Street .50
26 Ichiro Suzuki 1.00
27 Mark Teixeira .50
28 Miguel Tejada .50
29 Rickie Weeks .50
30 Dontrelle Willis .50

4-on-1 Stickers

NM/M

1 Josh Gibson, Mickey Mantle, Alex Rodriguez, Barry Bonds 2.00
2 Jason Giambi, David Ortiz, Carlos Delgado, Jeff Bagwell .75
3 Vernon Wells, Shannon Stewart, Carl Crawford, Torii Hunter .50
4 Jason Kendall, Javy Lopez, Joe Mauer, Jorge Posada .50
5 Roger Clemens, Andy Pettitte, Mike Mussina, Orlando Hernandez 1.00
6 Ivan Rodriguez, Rafael Palmeiro, Alfonso Soriano, Hank Blalock .50
7 Pedro Martinez, Curt Schilling, Matt Clement, Derek Lowe .75
8 J.D. Drew, Andruw Jones, Gary Sheffield, Vladimir Guerrero .50
9 Tim Hudson, Greg Maddux, Tom Glavine, John Smoltz .75
10 Justin Morneau, Albert Pujols, Mark Teixeira, Derrek Lee 1.00
11 B.J. Ryan, Bob Wickman, Mariano Rivera, Trevor Hoffman .50
12 Mike Morse, Mike Cameron, Mike Piazza, Mike Sweeney .75

13 Michael Young, Jimmy Rollins, David Eckstein, Orlando Cabrera .50
14 A.J. Burnett, A.J. Pierzynski, C.C. Sabathia, J.T. Snow .50
15 Hideki Matsui, Ichiro Suzuki, Tadahito Iguchi, Chase Utley 1.00
16 Barry Zito, Zachary Duke, Zack Greinke, Jeff Francis .50
17 Mark Buehrle, Mark Mulder, Mark Prior, Marcus Giles .75
18 Sammy Sosa, Manny Ramirez, Bobby Abreu, Wily Mo Pena .75
19 Scott Podsednik, Preston Wilson, Juan Pierre, Carlos Beltran .50
20 Francisco Rodriguez, Billy Wagner, Huston Street, Joe Nathan .50
21 Melvin Mora, Morgan Ensberg, Scott Rolen, Eric Chavez .50
22 Garret Anderson, Jim Edmonds, Johnny Damon, Moises Alou .50
23 Derek Jeter, Edgar Renteria, Miguel Tejada, Julio Lugo 1.00
24 Felix Hernandez, Dontrelle Willis, Rich Harden, Brian Fuentes .50
25 Bartolo Colon, Jason Schmidt, Jeremy Bonderman, Carlos Zambrano .50
26 Randy Johnson, Johan Santana, Roy Halladay, Chris Carpenter .75
27 Roy Oswalt, Shawn Chacon, Kris Benson, Josh Beckett .50
28 Jose Reyes, Felipe Lopez, Rafael Furcal, Jhonny Peralta .50
29 Justin Verlander, Kerry Wood, Livan Hernandez, Matt Morris .50
30 Khalil Greene, Nomar Garciaparra, Omar Vizquel, Jack Wilson .50
31 Pat Burrell, Rocco Baldelli, Shawn Green, Jason Bay .50
32 Brad Lidge, Brad Penny, Brad Radke, Brian Roberts .50
33 Jeff Francoeur, Willy Taveras, Rickie Weeks, Robinson Cano .50
34 Geoff Jenkins, Lance Berkman, Larry Bigbie, Matt Holliday .50
35 Paul LoDuca, Toby Hall, Victor Martinez, Carlos Lee .50
36 Aramis Ramirez, Chipper Jones, David Wright, Troy Glaus .75
37 Randy Winn, Brad Wilkerson, Craig Monroe, Aaron Rowand .50
38 Aaron Boone, Adrian Beltre, Vinny Castilla, Chone Figgins .50
39 Larry Walker, Cliff Floyd, Luis Gonzalez, Adam Dunn .50
40 Ronnie Belliard, Jeff Kent, Jorge Cantu, Placido Polanco .50
41 Craig Biggio, Jose Vidro, Luis Castillo, Orlando Hudson .50
42 Grady Sizemore, Lew Ford, Nick Swisher, Brian Giles .50
43 David DeJesus, Emil Brown, Coco Crisp, Jeromy Burnitz .50
44 Eric Gagne, Eric Milton, Jake Peavy, Jaret Wright .50
45 Aubrey Huff, Austin Kearns, Brady Clark, Nook Logan .50
46 Ben Sheets, Carl Pavano, Chris Capuano, Jon Garland .50
47 Darin Erstad, Dmitri Young, Erubiel Durazo, Travis Hafner .50
48 Magglio Ordonez, Miguel Cabrera, Jermaine Dye, Conor Jackson .50
49 Richie Sexson, Sean Casey, Chad Tracy, Lyle Overbay .50
50 Nick Johnson, Paul Konerko, Raul Ibanez, Todd Helton .50
51 Shaun Marcum, Chuck James, Hong-Chih Kuo, Darrell Rasner .50
52 Anthony Reyes, Francisco Liriano, Joe Saunders, Fausto Carmona .50
53 Charlton Jimerson, Bryan Bullington, Tom Gorzelanny, Anderson Hernandez .50
54 Ryan Garko, John Koronka, Chris Denorfia, Jeff Mathis .50
55 Jose Bautista, Danny Sandoval, Robert Andino, Alex Gordon .50

2006 Topps Chrome

NM/M

Complete Set (354):
Common Player: .25
Common Auto. (331-354): 10.00
Pack (4): 3.50
Box (24): 70.00
1 Alex Rodriguez 3.00
2 Garrett Atkins .25
3 Carl Crawford .50
4 Clint Barmes .25
5 Tadahito Iguchi .50
6 Brian Roberts .40
7 Mickey Mantle 8.00
8 David Wright 2.00
9 Jeremy Reed .25
10 Bobby Abreu .50
11 Lance Berkman .50
12 Jonny Gomes .50
13 Jason Marquis .25
14 Chipper Jones 1.00
15 Jon Garland .25
16 Brad Wilkerson .25
17 Rickie Weeks .25
18 Jorge Posada .50
19 Greg Maddux 2.00
20 Jeff Francis .25
21 Felipe Lopez .25
22 Dan Johnson .25
23 Manny Ramirez 1.00
24 Joe Mauer .75
25 Randy Winn .25
26 Pedro Feliz .25
27 Kenny Rogers .25
28 Rocco Baldelli .25
29 Nomar Garciaparra 1.00
30 Carlos Lee .50
31 Tom Glavine .50
32 Craig Biggio .40
33 Steve Finley .25
34 Eric Gagne .40
35 Dallas McPherson .25
36 Mark Kotsay .25
37 Kerry Wood .25
38 Huston Street .25
39 Hank Blalock .50
40 Brad Radke .25
41 Chien-Ming Wang .75
42 Mark Buehrle .40
43 Andy Pettitte .50
44 Bernie Williams .50
45 Victor Martinez .50
46 Darin Erstad .40
47 Gustavo Chacin .25
48 Carlos Guillen .25
49 Lyle Overbay .25
50 Barry Bonds 3.00
51 Nook Logan .25
52 Mark Teahen .25
53 Mike Lamb .25
54 Jayson Werth .25
55 Mariano Rivera .50
56 Julio Lugo .25
57 Adam Dunn .75
58 Troy Percival .25
59 Chad Tracy .25
60 Edgar Renteria .50
61 Jason Giambi .75
62 Justin Morneau .50
63 Carlos Delgado .75
64 John Buck .25
65 Shannon Stewart .25
66 Mike Cameron .25
67 Richie Sexson .50
68 Russ Adams .25
69 Josh Beckett .25
70 Ryan Freel .25
71 Victor Zambrano .25
72 Ronnie Belliard .25
73 Brian Giles .40
74 Randy Wolf .25
75 Robinson Cano .75
76 Joe Blanton .25
77 Esteban Loaiza .25
78 Troy Glaus .50
79 Matt Clement .25
80 Geoff Jenkins .25
81 Roy Oswalt .50
82 A.J. Pierzynski .25
83 Pedro Martinez 1.00
84 Roger Clemens 3.00
85 Jack Wilson .25
86 Mike Piazza 1.00
87 Paul LoDuca .25
88 Jeff Bagwell .50
89 Carlos Zambrano .50
90 Brandon Claussen .25
91 Travis Hafner .50
92 Chris Shelton .25
93 Rafael Furcal .40
94 Frank Thomas .75
95 Noah Lowry .25
96 Jhonny Peralta .25
97 Vernon Wells .50
98 Jorge Cantu .25
99 Willy Taveras .25
100 Ivan Rodriguez .75
101 Jose Reyes .75
102 Barry Zito .50
103 Mark Teixeira .75
104 Chone Figgins .25
105 Todd Helton .75
106 Tim Wakefield .25
107 Mike Maroth .25
108 Johnny Damon 1.00
109 David DeJesus .25
110 Ryan Klesko .25
111 Nick Johnson .25
112 Freddy Garcia .25
113 Torii Hunter .50
114 Mike Sweeney .25
115 Scott Rolen 1.00
116 Jim Thome .75
117 Adam Kennedy .25
118 Albert Pujols 3.00
119 Kazuo Matsui .25
120 Zack Greinke .25
121 Jimmy Rollins .50
122 Edgar Alfonzo .25
123 Billy Wagner .25
124 B.J. Ryan .25
125 Orlando Hudson .25
126 Preston Wilson .25
127 Melvin Mora .25
128 Alfonso Soriano .75
129 Javy Lopez .25
130 Wilson Betemit .25
131 Garret Anderson .25
132 Jason Bay .50
133 Adam LaRoche .25
134 C.C. Sabathia .25
135 Bartolo Colon .25
136 Ichiro Suzuki 2.00
137 Jim Edmonds .50
138 David Eckstein .25
139 Cristian Guzman .25
140 Jeff Kent .40
141 Chris Capuano .25
142 Cliff Floyd .25
143 Zachary Duke .25
144 Matt Morris .25
145 Jose Vidro .25
146 David Wells .25
147 John Smoltz .50
148 Felix Hernandez .50
149 Orlando Cabrera .25
150 Mark Prior .50
151 Ted Lilly .25
152 Michael Young .25
153 Livan Hernandez .25
154 Yadier Molina .25
155 Eric Chavez .25
156 Miguel Batista .25
157 Ben Sheets .40
158 Oliver Perez .25
159 Doug Davis .25
160 Andruw Jones .75
161 Hideki Matsui 1.50
162 Reggie Sanders .25
163 Joe Nathan .25
164 John Lackey .25
165 Matt Murton .25
166 Grady Sizemore .75
167 Brad Thompson .25
168 Kevin Millwood .25
169 Orlando Hernandez .25
170 Mark Mulder .25
171 Chase Utley .75
172 Moises Alou .50
173 Wily Mo Pena .25
174 Brian McCann .25
175 Jermaine Dye .25
176 Ryan Madson .25
177 Aramis Ramirez .50
178 Khalil Greene .25
179 Mike Hampton .25
180 Mike Mussina .50
181 Rich Harden .25
182 Woody Williams .25
183 Chris Carpenter .50
184 Brady Clark .25
185 Luis Gonzalez .25
186 Raul Ibanez .25
187 Magglio Ordonez .25
188 Adrian Beltre .25
189 Marcus Giles .25
190 Odalis Perez .25
191 Derek Jeter 3.00
192 Jason Schmidt .50
193 Toby Hall .25
194 Danny Haren .25
195 Tim Hudson .50
196 Jake Peavy .50
197 Casey Blake .25
198 J.D. Drew .25
199 Ervin Santana .25
200 J.J. Hardy .25
201 Austin Kearns .25
202 Pat Burrell .25
203 Jason Vargas .25
204 Ryan Howard 1.50
205 Joe Crede .25
206 Vladimir Guerrero 1.00
207 Roy Halladay .50
208 David Dellucci .25
209 Brandon Webb .25
210 Ryan Church .25
211 Miguel Tejada .75
212 Mark Loretta .25
213 Kevin Youkilis .50
214 Jon Lieber .25
215 Miguel Cabrera 1.00
216 A.J. Burnett .25
217 David Bell .25
218 Eric Byrnes .25
219 Lance Niekro .25
220 Shawn Green .25
221 Ken Griffey Jr. 2.00
222 Johnny Estrada .25
223 Omar Vizquel .25
224 Gary Sheffield .50
225 Brad Halsey .25
226 Aaron Cook .25
227 David Ortiz 1.00
228 Scott Kazmir .50
229 Dustin McGowan .25
230 Gregg Zaun .25
231 Carlos Beltran .75
232 Bob Wickman .25
233 Brett Myers .25
234 Casey Kotchman .25
235 Jeff Francoeur .25
236 Paul Konerko .50
237 Juan Rivera .25
238 Bobby Crosby .25
239 Derrek Lee .75
240 Curt Schilling 1.00
241 Jake Westbrook .25
242 Dontrelle Willis .25
243 Brad Lidge .25
244 Randy Johnson 1.00
245 Nick Swisher .50
246 Johan Santana .75
247 Jeremy Bonderman .50
248 Ramon Hernandez .25
249 Mike Lowell .25
250 Javier Vazquez .25
251 Jose Contreras .25
252 Aubrey Huff .25
253 Kenny Rogers .25
254 Mark Teixeira .50
255 Orlando Hudson .25
256 Derek Jeter 2.00
257 Eric Chavez .25
258 Torii Hunter .25
259 Vernon Wells .25
260 Ichiro Suzuki 1.00
261 Greg Maddux 1.00
262 Mike Matheny .25
263 Derrek Lee .50
264 Luis Castillo .25
265 Omar Vizquel .25
266 Mike Lowell .25
267 Andruw Jones .50
268 Jim Edmonds .25
269 Bobby Abreu .25
270 Bartolo Colon .25
271 Chris Carpenter .25
272 Alex Rodriguez 2.00
273 Albert Pujols 2.00
274 Huston Street .25
275 Ryan Howard .75
276 Chris Denorfia **(RC)** .50
277 John Van Benschoten **(RC)** .50
278 Russell Martin **(RC)** .50
279 Fausto Carmona **(RC)** .50
280 Freddie Bynum **(RC)** .50
281 Kelly Shoppach **(RC)** .50
282 Chris Demaria **RC** .50
283 Jordan Tata **RC** .50
284 Ryan Zimmerman **(RC)** 6.00
285 Kenji Johjima **RC** 5.00
285 Kenji Johjima/ Auto. **RC** 75.00
286 Ruddy Lugo **(RC)** .50
287 Tommy Murphy **(RC)** .50
288 Bobby Livingston **RC** .50
289 Anderson Hernandez **RC** .50
290 Brian Slocum **(RC)** .50
291 Sendy Rleal **RC** .50
292 Ryan Spilborghs **(RC)** .50
293 Brandon Fahey **RC** 1.00
294 Jason Kubel **(RC)** .50
295 James Loney **(RC)** .50
296 Jeremy Accardo **RC** .50
297 Fabio Castro **RC** .50
298 Matt Capps **(RC)** .75
299 Casey Janssen **RC** 1.00
300 Martin Prado **(RC)** 1.00
301 Ronny Paulino **(RC)** 1.00
302 Josh Barfield **(RC)** .50
303 Joel Zumaya **(RC)** 2.00
304 Matt Cain **(RC)** 1.00
305 Conor Jackson **(RC)** .50
306 Brian Anderson **(RC)** .50
307 Prince Fielder **(RC)** 4.00
308 Jeremy Hermida **(RC)** .75
309 Justin Verlander **(RC)** 4.00
310 Brian Bannister **(RC)** .50
311 Josh Willingham **(RC)** .50
312 John Rheinecker **(RC)** .50
313 Nicholas Markakis **(RC)** .75
314 Jonathan Papelbon **(RC)** 8.00
315 Mike Jacobs **(RC)** .50
316 Jose Capellan **(RC)** .50
317 Michael Napoli **RC** 4.00
318 Ricky Nolasco **(RC)** .50
319 Ben Johnson **(RC)** .50
320 Paul Maholm **(RC)** .50
321 Drew Meyer **(RC)** .50
322 Jeff Mathis **(RC)** .50
323 Fernando Nieve **(RC)** .50
324 John Koronka **(RC)** .50
325 Wilbert Nieves **(RC)** .50
326 Nate McLouth **(RC)** 1.00
327 Howard Kendrick **(RC)** 4.00
328 Sean Marshall **(RC)** 1.50
329 Brandon Watson **(RC)** .50
330 Skip Schumaker **(RC)** .50
331 Ryan Garko **(RC)** 15.00
332 Jason Bergmann **RC** 15.00
333 Chuck James **(RC)** 15.00
334 Adam Wainwright **(RC)** 20.00
335 Daniel Ortmeier **(RC)** 10.00
336 Francisco Liriano **(RC)** 30.00
337 Craig Breslow **RC** 10.00
338 Darrell Rasner **(RC)** 15.00
339 Jason Botts **(RC)** 10.00
340 Ian Kinsler **(RC)** 30.00
341 Joey Devine **RC** 10.00
342 Miguel Perez **(RC)** 10.00
343 Scott Olsen **(RC)** 15.00
344 Tyler Johnson **(RC)** 10.00
345 Anthony Lerew **(RC)** 10.00
346 Nelson Cruz **(RC)** 15.00
347 Willie Eyre **(RC)** 10.00
348 Josh Johnson **(RC)** 15.00
349 Shawn Marcum **(RC)** 15.00
350 Dustin Nippert **(RC)** 15.00
351 Josh Wilson **(RC)** 10.00
352 Hanley Ramirez **(RC)** 25.00
353 Reggie Abercrombie **(RC)** 15.00
354 Dan Uggla **(RC)** 30.00

Refractors

Cards (1-330): 2-3X
Inserted 1:4
Rookie Auto. (331-354): 1-1.5X
Production 500

Black Refractors

Cards (1-330): 3-5X
Production 549
Rookie Auto. (331-354): 1.5-2X
Production 200

Blue Refractors

Cards (1-330): 2-4X
Inserted 1:8

Gold Super-Fractor

No Pricing
Production One Set

Red Refractors

Cards (1-330): 4-8X
Production 90
Rookie Auto. (331-354): No Pricing
Production 25

X-Fractor

Cards (1-330): 2-4X
Inserted 1:6 Retail

Printing Plates

No Pricing
Production one set per color.

Bonds Home Run History

NM/M

Common Bonds: 2.00
Inserted 1:6
Refractors: 2-4X
Production 500 Sets
Black Refractor: 3-5X
Production 200 Sets
Red Refractor: 10-20X
Production 25 Sets
BBC375 Barry Bonds 2.00
BBC400 Barry Bonds 2.00
BBC425 Barry Bonds 2.00
BBC450 Barry Bonds 2.00
BBC475 Barry Bonds 2.00
BBC500 Barry Bonds 2.00
BBC525 Barry Bonds 2.00
BBC550 Barry Bonds 2.00
BBC575 Barry Bonds 2.00
BBC600 Barry Bonds 2.00
BBC625 Barry Bonds 2.00
BBC650 Barry Bonds 2.00
BBC675 Barry Bonds 2.00
BBC700 Barry Bonds 2.00

Mantle Home Run History

NM/M

Common Mantle: 3.00
Inserted 1:6
Refractor: 2-4X
Production 500 Sets
Black Refractor: 3-5X
Production 200 Sets
Red Refractor: 15-20X
Production 25 Sets
MHRC1 Mickey Mantle 3.00
MHRC7 Mickey Mantle 3.00
MHRC10 Mickey Mantle 3.00
MHRC20 Mickey Mantle 3.00
MHRC30 Mickey Mantle 3.00
MHRC40 Mickey Mantle 3.00
MHRC40 Mickey Mantle 3.00
MHRC50 Mickey Mantle 3.00
MHRC60 Mickey Mantle 3.00
MHRC70 Mickey Mantle 3.00
MHRC80 Mickey Mantle 3.00
MHRC90 Mickey Mantle 3.00
MHRC100 Mickey Mantle 3.00
MHRC110 Mickey Mantle 3.00

Signers of the Constitution

NM/M

Common Signer: 1.50
Inserted 1:7
Refractors: 1-2X
Inserted 1:11
AB Abraham Baldwin 1.50
RB Richard Bassett 1.50
GB Gunning Bedford Jr. 1.50
JB John Blair 1.50
WB William Blount 1.50
DB David Brearly 1.50
JBR Jacob Broom 1.50
PB Pierce Butler 1.50
DC Daniel Carroll 1.50
GC George Clymer 1.50
JD Jonathan Dayton 1.50
JDI John Dickinson 1.50
WF William Few 1.50
TF Thomas Fitzsimons 1.50
BF Benjamin Franklin 4.00
NG Nicholas Gilman 1.50
NGO Nathaniel Gorham 1.50
AH Alexander Hamilton 3.00
JI Jared Ingersoll 1.50
DJ Daniel of St. Thomas Jenifer 1.50
WJ William Samuel Johnson 1.50
RK Rufus King 1.50
JL John Langdon 1.50
WL William Livingston 1.50
JM James Madison 2.00
JMC James McHenry 1.50
TM Thomas Mifflin 1.50
GM Gouverneur Morris 1.50
RM Robert Morris 1.50
WP William Paterson 1.50
CCP Charles Cotesworth Pinckney 1.50
CP Charles Pinckney 1.50

GR George Read 1.50
JR John Rutledge 1.50
RS Roger Sherman 1.50
RDS Richard Dobbs Spaight 1.50
GW George Washington 4.00
HW Hugh Williamson 1.50
JW James Wilson 1.50

Signers of Declaration/ Independence

NM/M
Common Signer: 1.50
Inserted 1:5
Refractors: 1-2X
Inserted 1:9
JA John Adams 2.00
SA Samuel Adams 1.50
JB Josiah Bartlett 1.50
CB Carter Braxton 1.50
CC Charles Carroll 1.50
SC Samuel Chase 1.50
AC Abraham Clark 1.50
GC George Clymer 1.50
WE William Ellery 1.50
WF William Floyd 1.50
BF Benjamin Franklin 4.00
EG Elbridge Gerry 1.50
BG Button Gwinnett 1.50
LH Lyman Hall 1.50
JH John Hancock 3.00
BH Benjamin Harrison 1.50
JHA John Hart 1.50
JHE Joseph Hewes 1.50
TH Thomas Heyward Jr. 1.50
WH William Hooper 1.50
SH Stephen Hopkins 1.50
FH Francis Hopkinson 1.50
SHU Samuel Huntington 1.50
TJ Thomas Jefferson 4.00
FL Francis Lewis 1.50
FLL Francis Lightfoot Lee 1.50
RHL Richard Henry Lee 1.50
PL Philip Livingston 1.50
TL Thomas Lynch Jr. 1.50
TM Thomas McKean 1.50
AM Arthur Middleton 1.50
LM Lewis Morris 1.50
RM Robert Morris 1.50
JM John Morton 1.50
TN Thomas Nelson Jr. 1.50
WP William Paca 1.50
RTP Robert Treat Paine 1.50
JP John Penn 1.50
GRE George Read 1.50
CR Caesar Rodney 1.50
GR George Ross 1.50
BR Benjamin Rush 1.50
ER Edward Rutledge 1.50
RS Roger Sherman 1.50
JS James Smith 1.50
RST Richard Stockton 1.50
TS Thomas Stone 1.50
GT George Taylor 1.50
MT Matthew Thornton 1.50
GW George Walton 1.50
WW William Whipple 1.50
WWI William Williams 1.50
JW James Wilson 1.50
JWI John Witherspoon 1.50
OW Oliver Wolcott 1.50
GWY George Wythe 1.50

2006 Topps Co-Signers

NM/M
Complete Set (120):
Common Player (1-100): .25
Common Auto. (101-120): 10.00
Pack (6): 12.00
Box (12): 130.00
Note: Each parallel has three versions.
1 Albert Pujols 3.00
2 Roger Clemens 3.00
3 Paul Konerko .50
4 Jeff Francoeur .25
5 Miguel Tejada .75
6 Curt Schilling 1.00
7 Mickey Mantle 4.00
8 Miguel Cabrera 1.00
9 Derrek Lee 1.00
10 Jeff Kent .50
11 Gary Sheffield .50
12 Rich Harden .25
13 Scott Rolen .75
14 David Wright 1.50
15 Troy Glaus .25
16 Torii Hunter .25
17 Nolan Ryan 2.00
18 Alfonso Soriano .75
19 Hank Blalock .50
20 Chase Utley .50
21 Ryan Howard .75
22 Robinson Cano 1.00
23 Derek Jeter 3.00
24 Huston Street .25
25 Jason Giambi .50
26 Rafael Furcal .25
27 Rickie Weeks .25
28 Ivan Rodriguez .50
29 Travis Hafner .50
30 Greg Maddux 2.00
31 Andruw Jones .75
32 Andy Pettitte .50
33 Scott Podsednik .25
34 Francisco Rodriguez .25
35 Josh Beckett .25
36 Lance Berkman .50
37 Roy Oswalt .50
38 Pedro Martinez 1.00
39 Jimmy Rollins .50
40 Johan Santana .75
41 Randy Johnson 1.00
42 Mariano Rivera .50
43 Nick Johnson .25
44 Josh Gibson .50
45 Shawn Green .25
46 Adrian Beltre .25
47 Johnny Damon 1.00
48 Joe Mauer .50
49 Todd Helton .50
50 Alex Rodriguez 2.50
51 Jake Peavy .50
52 David Ortiz 1.00
53 Mark Buehrle .50
54 Eric Gagne .25
55 Hideki Matsui 1.50
56 Bobby Abreu .50
57 Victor Martinez .50
58 Brian Roberts .25
59 Chipper Jones 1.00
60 Carlos Beltran .75
61 Tim Hudson .50
62 Carlos Lee .50
63 Barry Zito .50
64 Moises Alou .50
65 Mark Teixeira .75
66 Lyle Overbay .25
67 Kerry Wood .50
68 B.J. Ryan .25
69 Jim Edmonds .50
70 Carlos Delgado .50
71 Magglio Ordonez .25
72 Juan Pierre .25
73 Manny Ramirez 1.00
74 Dontrelle Willis .50
75 Ichiro Suzuki 2.00
76 Nomar Garciaparra 1.00
77 Zachary Duke .25
78 Chris Carpenter .50
79 A.J. Burnett .25
80 Scott Kazmir .25
81 Carl Crawford .25
82 Mark Prior .50
83 Adam Dunn .75
84 Justin Morneau .50
85 Morgan Ensberg .25
86 Pat Burrell .25
87 Paul LoDuca .25
88 Jason Bay .50
89 Aubrey Huff .25
90 Kevin Millwood .25
91 Vernon Wells .25
92 Javy Lopez .25
93 Michael Young .25
94 Felix Hernandez .50
95 Ken Griffey Jr. 2.00
96 Bartolo Colon .25
97 Billy Wagner .25
98 Vladimir Guerrero 1.00
99 Jose Reyes .75
100 Barry Bonds 3.00
101 Anthony LeRew **(RC)** 10.00
102 Ryan Zimmerman/ 440 **(RC)** 40.00
103 Craig Hansen/ 250 **RC** 25.00
104 Francisco Liriano **(RC)** 30.00
105 Jason Botts **(RC)** 10.00
106 Josh Johnson **(RC)** 15.00
107 Hanley Ramirez **(RC)** 30.00
108 Adam Wainwright **(RC)** 20.00
109 Kenji Johjima/ 200 **RC** 100.00
110 Daniel Ortmeier **(RC)** 10.00
111 Darrell Rasner **(RC)** 15.00
112 Chuck James **(RC)** 15.00
113 Nelson Cruz **(RC)** 15.00
114 Hong-Chih Kuo **(RC)** 25.00
115 Ryan Garko **(RC)** 15.00
116 R. Abercrombie **(RC)** 15.00
117 Ian Kinsler **(RC)** 25.00
118 Joel Zumaya **(RC)** 25.00
119 Willie Eyre **(RC)** 15.00
120 Dan Uggla **(RC)** 20.00

Bronze

Bronze (1-100): 2-3X
Production 150 Sets

Blue

Blue (1-100): 2-3X
Production 125 Sets

Gold

Gold (1-100): 2-3X
Production 115 Sets

Hyper Silver - Bronze

Hyper Silver/Bronze (1-100): 2-3X
Production 75 Sets

Hyper Silver - Blue

Hyper Silver/Blue: No Pricing
Production 10 Sets

Hyper Silver - Gold

Hyper Silver/Gold: No Pricing
Production Five Sets

Hyper Silver - Red

Hyper Silver/Red: No Pricing
Production 25 Sets

Silver - Bronze

Silver/Bronze (1-100): 2-3X
Production 125 Sets

Silver - Blue

Silver/Blue (1-100): 2-3X
Production 75 Sets

Silver - Gold

Silver/Gold (1-100): 3-4X
Production 50 Sets

Silver - Red

Silver/Red (1-100): 2-3X
Production 100 Sets

Dual Autographs

NM/M
Cards are not serial #'d.
CS2 David Wright, Alex Rodriguez/25 275.00
CS3 Victor Martinez, Kenji Johjima/25 75.00
CS4 Kenji Johjima, Felix Hernandez/18 200.00
CS5 David Ortiz, Manny Ramirez/25 150.00
CS6 Nolan Ryan, Roger Clemens/25 350.00
CS7 David Ortiz, Albert Pujols/25 350.00
CS8 Chipper Jones, Dale Murphy/25 100.00
CS11 Stan Musial, Albert Pujols/20 500.00
CS15 Prince Fielder, Ryan Zimmerman 100.00
CS16 Cal Ripken Jr., Ozzie Smith/25 275.00
CS18 Don Larsen, Yogi Berra/25 200.00
CS19 Mike Schmidt, Brooks Robinson/25 125.00
CS20 Ryan Zimmerman, Wade Boggs/25 75.00
CS22 Ryan Howard, Derrek Lee/75 80.00
CS23 Jeff Mathis, Chris Snyder 15.00
CS25 Ray Knight, Keith Hernandez/100 25.00
CS26 Mike Schmidt, Chase Utley/25 100.00
CS27 Billy Wagner, Paul LoDuca/50 70.00
CS28 Tony Gwynn, Wade Boggs/25 140.00
CS30 Dwight Gooden, Darryl Strawberry/50 40.00
CS31 Ryan Howard, Huston Street 60.00
CS32 Mariano Rivera, Huston Street/25 140.00
CS33 Prince Fielder, Ryan Howard/50 80.00
CS34 Robinson Cano, Chase Utley/75 60.00
CS36 David Justice, Chipper Jones/25 80.00
CS37 Jose Reyes, David Wright/50 200.00
CS38 Jeff Mathis, Ryan Garko 15.00
CS39 Brandon McCarthy, Pedro Lopez 15.00
CS40 David Justice, Dale Murphy/100 50.00
CS42 Joe Mauer, Francisco Liriano 75.00
CS44 Ryan Zimmerman, David Wright/100 125.00
CS45 Rick Rhoden, Dave Parker/100 40.00
CS46 Jonathan Papelbon, Craig Breslow 50.00
CS48 Dan Johnson, Prince Fielder/100 40.00
CS49 Victor Martinez, Ryan Garko 20.00
CS50 Ben Hendrickson, Anthony Reyes 15.00
CS51 Nelson Cruz, Prince Fielder/100 40.00
CS52 Jonathan Papelbon, Anthony Reyes 50.00
CS53 Ben Hendrickson, Rich Hill 20.00
CS54 Shin-Soo Choo, Kenji Johjima/25 85.00
CS55 Francisco Liriano, Johan Santana/100 100.00
CS56 Brandon McCarthy, Zachary Duke 15.00
CS57 Josh Johnson, Scott Olsen 15.00
CS58 Tommy John, Bob Welch 15.00
CS59 Roy White, Joe Pepitone 25.00
CS60 Cecil Fielder, Prince Fielder 70.00
CS62 Conor Jackson, Ryan Howard 60.00
CS63 Dontrelle Willis, Zachary Duke/50 30.00
CS64 Mariano Rivera, Billy Wagner/25 150.00
CS65 Hong-Chih Kuo, Shin-Soo Choo 30.00
CS66 Jim Leyritz, Cecil Fielder 50.00
CS67 Scott Kazmir, Francisco Liriano 50.00
CS68 Scott Kazmir, Roy Oswalt/50 50.00
CS69 Chuck James, Anthony LeRew 15.00
CS70 Cecil Fielder, Ryan Howard 60.00
CS71 Chien-Ming Wang, Hong-Chih Kuo/25 200.00
CS72 Shin-Soo Choo, Chien-Ming Wang/50 160.00
CS73 Nelson Cruz, Jason Botts 15.00
CS74 Francisco Liriano, Ervin Santana 30.00
CS75 Adam Wainwright, Anthony Reyes 30.00
CS76 Ervin Santana, Scott Kazmir 30.00
CS77 Robinson Cano, Gary Sheffield 60.00
CS78 David Wright, Miguel Cabrera/50 120.00
CS79 Dan Johnson, Conor Jackson 15.00
CS80 Frank Tanana, Mickey Tettleton 15.00
CS81 Andruw Jones, Chipper Jones 75.00
CS82 Morgan Ensberg, Roy Oswalt 25.00
CS83 Michael Young, Ozzie Smith 50.00
CS84 Grady Sizemore, Nick Swisher 40.00
CS85 Garrett Atkins, Clint Barmes 20.00

Dual Cut Signatures

No Pricing

Solo Sigs

NM/M
Cards are not serial #'d.
CB Clint Barmes 10.00
CBR Craig Breslow 10.00
RC Robinson Cano 50.00
GC Gustavo Chacin 10.00
SSC Shin-Soo Choo 15.00
JC Jack Clark 10.00
AD Andre Dawson 10.00
ZD Zachary Duke 15.00
CF Cecil Fielder 20.00
PF Prince Fielder/250 50.00
RHI Rich Hill 30.00
RH Ryan Howard/100 75.00
DJ Dan Johnson/250 10.00
CJ Chipper Jones/25 80.00
AK Al Kaline/100 50.00
SK Scott Kazmir 20.00
DL Don Larsen 20.00
DLE Derrek Lee/50 40.00
VM Victor Martinez/50 25.00
JM Jeff Mathis 10.00
DM Don Mattingly/50 120.00
JMA Joe Mauer/75 40.00
CM Craig Monroe 10.00
SO Scott Olsen 15.00
DO David Ortiz/25 60.00
JP Jonathan Papelbon 60.00
ARE Anthony Reyes 15.00
RR Rick Rhoden 10.00
CR Cal Ripken Jr./20 200.00
AR Alex Rodriguez/20 200.00
NR Nolan Ryan/20 125.00
ES Ervin Santana/250 10.00
JS Johan Santana/50 40.00
CS Chris Snyder 8.00
DS Darryl Strawberry 15.00
HS Huston Street/250 20.00
DWI Dontrelle Willis 20.00
DW David Wright/75 80.00

2006 Topps Heritage

NM/M
Complete Set (485):
Common Player: .40
Common SP: 4.00
Pack (8): 5.00
Box (24): 100.00
1 David Ortiz/SP 8.00
2 Mike Piazza/SP 8.00
3 Daryle Ward .40
4 Rafael Furcal .40
5 Derrek Lowe .40
6 Eric Chavez .75
7 Juan Uribe .40
8 C.C. Sabathia .40
9 Sean Casey .40
10 Barry Bonds/SP 15.00
11 Gary Sheffield .40
12 Ted Lilly .40
13 Lew Ford .40
14 Tom Gordon .40
15 Curt Schilling .40
16 Jason Kendall .40
17 Frank Catalanotto .40
18 Pedro Martinez/SP 8.00
19 David Dellucci .40
20 Andruw Jones 1.00
20 Andruw Jones w/Seats/SP 6.00
21 Brad Halsey .40
22 Vernon Wells .40
23 Derek Jeter 4.00
23 Derek Jeter/ Blue Letter/SP 15.00
24 Todd Helton 1.00
25 Randy Johnson/SP 8.00
26 Jay Gibbons .40
27 Joe Mays .40
28 Paul Konerko .75
29 Lyle Overbay .40
30 Jorge Posada .75
31 Brandon Webb .40
32 Marcus Giles .40
33 J.T. Snow .40
34 Todd Walker .40
35 Wily Mo Pena/SP 5.00
36 Carlos Delgado .75
37 David Wright 2.00
38 Shea Hillenbrand .40
39 Daniel Cabrera .40
40 Trevor Hoffman .40
41 Matt Morris .40
42 Mariano Rivera .75
43 Jeff Bagwell 1.00
44 J.D. Drew .40
45 Carl Pavano .40
46 Placido Polanco .40
47 Adrian Beltre .75
48 J.D. Closser .40
49 Paul LoDuca .40
50 Scott Rolen 1.00
51 Bernie Williams .75
52 Jose Guillen .40
53 Aubrey Huff .40
54 Greg Maddux 2.50
55 Derrek Lee/SP 8.00
56 Hideki Matsui 2.50
57 Jose Bautista .40
58 Kyle Farnsworth .40
59 Nate Robertson .40
60 Sammy Sosa 1.50
61 Javier Vazquez .40
62 Jeff Mathis **(RC)** .40
63 Mark Buehrle .75
64 Orlando Hernandez .40
65 Brandon Claussen .40
66 Miguel Batista .40
67 Eddie Guardado .40
68 Alex Gonzalez .40
69 Kris Benson .40
70 Bobby Abreu/SP 6.00
71 Vinny Castilla .40
72 Ben Broussard .40
73 Travis Hafner 1.00
74 Dmitri Young .40
75 Alex S. Gonzalez .40
76 Jason Bay/SP 6.00
77 Charlton Jimerson .40
78 Ryan Garko **(RC)** .50
79 Lance Berkman .75
80 Tim Hudson .75
80 Tim Hudson/ Blue Letter/SP 5.00
81 Guillermo Mota .40
82 Chris Young .40
83 Brad Lidge .40
84 A.J. Pierzynski .40
85 Maicer Izturis .40
86 Vladimir Guerrero 1.50
87 J.J. Hardy .40
88 Cesar Izturis .40
89 Mark Ellis .40
90 Chipper Jones 1.50
91 Chris Snelling/SP 4.00
92 Jose Reyes .75
93 Mike Lieberthal .40
94 Octavio Dotel .40
95 Alex Rodriguez/ Fldg/SP 10.00
95 Alex Rodriguez with bat/SP 10.00
96 Brett Myers .40
97 New York Yankees 1.00
98 Ryan Klesko .40
99 Brian Jordan/SP 4.00
100 William Harridge, Warren Giles .40
101 Adam Eaton .40
102 Aaron Boone .40
103 Alex Rios .40
104 Andy Pettitte .75
105 Barry Zito .75
106 Bengie Molina/SP 4.00
107 Austin Kearns .50
108 Adam Everett .40
109 A.J. Burnett .40
110 Mark Prior 1.00
111 Russ Ortiz .40
112 Adam Dunn 1.00
113 Byung-Hyun Kim .40
114 Atlanta Braves .50
115 Carlos Silva .40
116 Chad Cordero .40
117 Chone Figgins .40
118 Chris Reitsma .40
119 Coco Crisp .40
120 David DeJesus .40
121 Chris Snyder .40
122 Brad Eldred .40
123 Humberto Cota/SP 5.00
124 Erubiel Durazo .40
125 Josh Beckett .75
126 Kenny Lofton .40
127 Joe Nathan/SP 5.00
128 Bryan Bullington .40
129 Jim Thome 1.00
130 Shawn Green .75
131 LaTroy Hawkins .40
132 Mark Kotsay .40
133 Matt Lawton .40
134 Luis Castillo .40
135 Michael Barrett .40
136 Preston Wilson .40
137 Orlando Cabrera .40
138 Chuck James **(RC)** .40
139 Raul Ibanez .40
140 Frank Thomas 1.00
141 Orlando Hudson .40
142 Scott Kazmir .40
143 Steve Finley .40
144 Danny Sandoval **RC** 1.00
145 Javy Lopez .40
146 Tony Giarratano .40
147 Terrence Long .40
148 Victor Martinez .40
149 Toby Hall .40
150 Fausto Carmona **(RC)** .40
151 Tim Wakefield .40
152 Troy Percival .40
153 Chris Denorfia **(RC)** .40
154 Junior Spivey .40
155 Desi Relaford .40
156 Francisco Liriano **(RC)** .75
157 Corey Koskie .40
158 Chris Carpenter .40
159 Robert Andino **RC** 1.00
160 Cliff Floyd .40
161 Pittsburgh Pirates .40
162 Anderson Hernandez **(RC)** .40
163 Mike Maroth .40
164 Aaron Rowand .40
165 Albert Pujols 4.00
165 Albert Pujols/ Red Shirt/SP 15.00
166 David Bell .40
167 Angel Berroa .40
168 B.J. Ryan .40
169 Bartolo Colon .40
170 Hong-Chih Kuo .40
171 Cincinnati Reds .40
172 Bill Mueller .40
173 John Koronka **(RC)** .40
174 Billy Wagner .40
175 Zack Greinke .40
176 Rick Short **RC** 1.00
177 Yadier Molina .40
178 Willy Taveras .40
179 Wes Helms .40
180 Wade Miller .40
181 Luis Gonzalez .40

No.	Player	Price
182	Carlos Zambrano	.40
183	Chicago Cubs	.50
184	Victor Santos	.40
185	Tyler Walker	.40
186	Bobby Crosby	.40
187	Trot Nixon	.40
188	Nick Johnson	.40
189	Nick Swisher	.40
190	Brian Roberts	.40
191	Nomar Garciaparra	1.50
192	Oliver Perez	.40
193	Ramon Hernandez	.40
194	Randy Winn	.40
195	Ryan Church	.40
196	Ryan Wagner	.40
197	Todd Hollandsworth	.40
198	Detroit Tigers	.40
199	Tino Martinez	.40
200	Roger Clemens	4.00
200	Roger Clemens/ Red Shirt/SP	12.00
201	Shawn Estes	.40
202	Justin Morneau	.75
203	Jeff Francis	.40
204	Oakland Athletics	.40
205	Jeff Francoeur	.75
206	C.J. Wilson	.40
207	Francisco Rodriguez	.40
208	Edgardo Alfonzo	.40
209	David Eckstein	.40
210	Cory Lidle	.40
211	Chase Utley	.75
212	Rocco Baldelli	.40
212	Rocco Baldelli/ Blue Letter/SP	5.00
213	So Taguchi	.40
214	Philadelphia Phillies	.40
215	Brad Hawpe	.40
216	Walter Young	.40
217	Tom Gorzelanny **(RC)**	.40
218	Shaun Marcum **(RC)**	.40
219	Ryan Howard	2.00
220	Damian Jackson	.40
221	Craig Counsell	.40
222	Damian Miller	.40
223	Derrick Turnbow	.40
224	Hank Blalock	.75
225	Brayan Pena	.40
226	Grady Sizemore	1.00
227	Ivan Rodriguez	1.00
228	Jason Isringhausen	.40
229	Brian Fuentes	.40
230	Jason Phillips	.40
231	Jason Schmidt	.75
232	Javier Valentin	.40
233	Jeff Kent	.75
234	John Buck	.40
235	Mike Matheny	.40
236	Jorge Cantu	.40
237	Jose Castillo	.40
238	Kenny Rogers	.40
239	Kerry Wood	.75
240	Kevin Mench	.40
241	Tim Stauffer	.40
242	Eric Milton	.40
243	St. Louis Cardinals	.75
244	Shawn Chacon	.40
245	Mike Jacobs **(RC)**	.40
246	Ryan Dempster	.40
247	Todd Jones	.40
248	Tom Glavine	.75
249	Tony Graffanino	.40
250	Ichiro Suzuki	2.50
251	Baltimore Orioles	.50
252	Brad Radke	.40
253	Brad Wilkerson	.40
254	Carlos Lee	.40
255	Alex Gordon/ Cut-Out	125.00
256	Gustavo Chacin	.40
257	Jermaine Dye	.40
258	Jose Mesa	.40
259	Julio Lugo	.40
260	Mark Redman	.40
261	Brandon Watson **(RC)**	.40
262	Pedro Feliz	.40
263	Esteban Loaiza	.40
264	Anthony Reyes	.40
265	Jose Contreras/SP	6.00
266	Tadahito Iguchi/SP	8.00
267	Mark Loretta/SP	6.00
268	Ray Durham/SP	4.00
269	Neifi Perez/SP	4.00
270	Washington Nationals	.40
271	Troy Glaus/SP	6.00
272	Matt Holliday/SP	6.00
273	Kevin Millwood/SP	5.00
274	Jon Lieber/SP	4.00
275	Cleveland Indians	.40
276	Jeremy Reed/SP	4.00
277	Garrett Atkins/SP	4.00
278	Geoff Jenkins/SP	4.00
279	Joey Gathright/SP	4.00
280	Ben Sheets/SP	6.00
281	Melvin Mora/SP	4.00
282	Jonathan Papelbon/ SP **(RC)**	10.00
283	John Smoltz/SP	5.00
284	Jake Peavy/SP	5.00
285	Felix Hernandez/SP	6.00
286	Alfonso Soriano/SP	6.00
287	Bronson Arroyo/SP	4.00
288	Adam LaRoche/SP	5.00
289	Aramis Ramirez/SP	5.00
290	Brad Hennessey/SP	4.00
291	Conor Jackson/ SP **(RC)**	4.00
292	Rod Barajas/SP	4.00
293	Chris Young/SP	4.00
294	Jeremy Bonderman/ SP	4.00
295	Jack Wilso/ SP	4.00
296	Jay Payton/SP	4.00
297	Danys Baez/SP	4.00
298	Jose Lima/SP	4.00
299	Luis A. Gonzalez/SP	4.00
300	Mike Sweeney/SP	4.00
301	Nelson Cruz/SP **(RC)**	6.00
302	Eric Gagne/SP	5.00
303	Juan Castro/SP	4.00
304	Joe Mauer/SP	6.00
305	Richie Sexson/SP	5.00
306	Roy Oswalt/SP	5.00
307	Rickie Weeks/SP	5.00
308	Pat Borders/SP	4.00
309	Mike Morse/SP	4.00
310	Matt Stairs/SP	4.00
311	Chad Tracy/SP	4.00
312	Matt Cain/SP **(RC)**	6.00
313	Mark Mulder/SP	5.00
314	Mark Grudzielanek/SP	4.00
315	Johnny Damon/SP	8.00
316	Casey Kotchman/SP	4.00
317	San Francisco Giants	.40
318	Chris Burke/SP	4.00
319	Carl Crawford/SP	4.00
320	Edgar Renteria/SP	5.00
321	Chan Ho Park/SP	4.00
322	Boston Red Sox	6.00
323	Robinson Cano/SP	8.00
324	Los Angeles Dodgers	.40
325	Miguel Tejada/ w/bat/SP	6.00
325	Miguel Tejada/ Hand Up/SP	6.00
326	Jimmy Rollins/SP	5.00
327	Juan Pierre/SP	4.00
328	Dan Johnson/SP	4.00
329	Chicago White Sox	.40
330	Pat Burrell/SP	5.00
331	Ramon Ortiz/SP	4.00
332	Rondell White/SP	4.00
333	David Wells/SP	4.00
334	Michael Young/SP	6.00
335	Mike Mussina/SP	6.00
336	Moises Alou/SP	5.00
337	Scott Podsednik/SP	5.00
338	Rich Harden/SP	6.00
339	Mark Teahen/SP	4.00
340	Jacque Jones/SP	4.00
341	Jason Giambi/SP	6.00
342	Bill Hall/SP	4.00
343	Jon Garland/SP	6.00
344	Dontrelle Willis/SP	6.00
345	Danny Haren/SP	4.00
346	Brian Giles/SP	4.00
347	Brad Penny/SP	4.00
348	Brandon McCarthy/SP	6.00
349	Chien-Ming Wang/SP	7.00
350	Torii Hunter/ Blue Letter/SP	5.00
350	Torii Hunter/ Red/Blue Letter/SP	5.00
351	Yhency Brazoban/SP	4.00
352	Rodrigo Lopez/SP	4.00
353	Paul McAnulty	.40
354	Francisco Cordero	.40
355	Brandon Inge	.40
356	Jason Lane	.40
357	Brian Schneider	.40
358	Dustin Hermanson	.40
359	Eric Hinske	.40
360	Jarrod Washburn	.40
361	Jayson Werth	.40
362	Craig Breslow **RC**	1.00
363	Jeff Weaver	.40
364	Jeromy Burnitz	.40
365	Jhonny Peralta	.75
366	Joe Crede	.40
367	Johan Santana	1.50
368	Jose Valentin	.40
369	Keith Foulke	.40
370	Larry Bigbie	.40
371	Manny Ramirez	1.50
372	Jim Edmonds	.75
373	Horacio Ramirez	.40
374	Garret Anderson	.75
375	Felipe Lopez	.75
376	Eric Byrnes	.40
377	Darin Erstad	.75
378	Carlos Zambrano	.75
379	Craig Biggio	.75
380	Darrell Rasner **(RC)**	.40
381	Dave Roberts	.40
382	Hanley Ramirez **(RC)**	.75
383	Geoff Blum	.40
384	Joel Pineiro	.40
385	Kip Wells	.40
386	Kelvim Escobar	.40
387	John Patterson	.40
388	Jody Gerut	.40
389	Marshall McDougall	.40
390	Mike MacDougal	.40
391	Orlando Palmeiro	.40
392	Rich Aurilia	.40
393	Ronnie Belliard	.40
394	Rich Hill	.50
395	Scott Hatteberg	.40
396	Ryan Langerhans	.40
397	Richard Hidalgo	.40
398	Omar Vizquel	.40
399	Mike Lowell	.40
400	Astros' Aces/SP	8.00
401	Mike Cameron	.40
402	Matt Clement	.40
403	Miguel Cabrera	1.50
404	Milton Bradley	.40
405	Laynce Nix	.40
406	Robert Mackowiak	.40
407	White Sox Power Hitters/SP	10.00
408	Mark Teixeira	1.00
409	Brady Clark	.40
410	Johnny Estrada	.40
411	Juan Encarnacion	.40
412	Morgan Ensberg	.40
413	Nook Logan	.40
414	Phil Nevin	.40
415	Reggie Sanders	.40
416	Roy Halladay	.75
417	Livan Hernandez	.40
418	Jose Vidro	.40
419	Shannon Stewart	.40
420	Brian Bruney	.40
421	Royce Clayton	.40
422	Chris Demaria **RC**	1.50
423	Eduardo Perez	.40
424	Jeff Suppan	.40
425	Jaret Wright	.40
426	Joe Randa	.40
427	Bobby Kielty	.40
428	Jason Ellison	.40
429	Gregg Zaun	.40
430	Runelvys Hernandez	.40
431	Joe McEwing	.40
432	Jason LaRue	.40
433	Aaron Miles	.40
434	Adam Kennedy	.40
435	Ambiorix Burgos	.40
436	Armando Benitez	.40
437	Brad Ausmus	.40
438	Brandon Backe	.40
439	Brian Anderson **(RC)**	.40
440	Bruce Chen	.40
441	Carlos Guillen	.40
442	Casey Blake	.40
443	Chris Capuano	.40
444	Chris Duffy	.40
445	Chris Ray	.40
446	Clint Barmes	.40
447	Andrew Sisco	.40
448	Dallas McPherson	.40
449	Tanyon Sturtze	.40
450	Carlos Beltran	1.50
451	Jason Vargas	.40
452	Ervin Santana	.40
453	Jason Marquis	.40
454	Juan Rivera	.40
455	Jake Westbrook	.40
456	Jason Johnson	.40
457	Joe Blanton	.40
458	Kevin Millar	.40
459	John Thomson	.40
460	J.P. Howell	.40
461	Justin Verlander **(RC)**	.40
462	Kelly Johnson	.40
463	Kyle Davies	.40
464	Lance Niekro	.40
465	Magglio Ordonez	.40
466	Melky Cabrera	.40
467	Nick Punto	.40
468	Paul Byrd	.40
469	Randy Wolf	.40
470	Ruben Gotay	.40
471	Ryan Madson	.40
472	Victor Diaz	.40
473	Xavier Nady	.40
474	Zachary Duke	.40
475	Huston Street	.75
475	Huston Street/ Blue Letter/SP	6.00
476	Brad Thompson	.40
477	Jonny Gomes	.40
478	B.J. Upton	.40
479	Jamey Carroll	.40
480	Mike Hampton	.40
481	Tony Clark	.40
482	Antonio Alfonseca	.40
483	Justin Duchscherer	.40
484	Mike Timlin	.40
485	Joe Saunders	.40

Chrome

		NM/M
Common Player:		2.00
Production 1,957 Sets		
Refractor:		1.5-2X
Production 557 Sets		
Black Refractor:		3-6X
Production 57 Sets		
1	Rafael Furcal	2.00
2	C.C. Sabathia	2.00
3	Sean Casey	2.00
4	Gary Sheffield	3.00
5	William Harridge, Warren Giles	2.00
6	Curt Schilling	3.00
7	Jay Gibbons	2.00
8	Paul Konerko	3.00
9	Lyle Overbay	2.00
10	Jorge Posada	3.00
11	Todd Walker	2.00
12	Carlos Delgado	3.00
13	David Wright	6.00
14	Matt Morris	2.00
15	Mariano Rivera	3.00
16	Jeff Bagwell	3.00
17	Carl Pavano	2.00
18	Adrian Beltre	3.00
19	Scott Rolen	4.00
20	Aubrey Huff	2.00
21	Hideki Matsui	6.00
22	Andruw Jones	3.00
23	Sammy Sosa	4.00
24	Mark Buehrle	3.00
25	Orlando Hernandez	2.00
26	Travis Hafner	3.00
27	Vladimir Guerrero	4.00
28	Chipper Jones	4.00
29	Jose Reyes	3.00
30	Roger Clemens	8.00
31	Aaron Boone	2.00
32	Andy Pettitte	3.00
33	David DeJesus	2.00
34	Shawn Green	2.00
35	Luis Castillo	2.00
36	Frank Thomas	3.00
37	Javy Lopez	2.00
38	Victor Martinez	2.00
39	Tim Wakefield	2.00
40	Cliff Floyd	2.00
41	Bartolo Colon	2.00
42	Billy Wagner	2.00
43	Dmitri Young	2.00
44	Mark Prior	3.00
45	Nick Johnson	2.00
46	Brian Roberts	2.00
47	Nomar Garciaparra	4.00
48	Jorge Cantu	2.00
49	Jeff Francoeur	3.00
50	Barry Bonds	10.00
51	Francisco Rodriguez	2.00
52	Rocco Baldelli	2.00
53	Ryan Howard	5.00
54	Hank Blalock	2.00
55	Ivan Rodriguez	3.00
56	Jason Schmidt	2.00
57	Jeff Kent	2.00
58	Jose Castillo	2.00
59	Kerry Wood	3.00
60	Chase Utley	2.00
61	Shawn Chacon	2.00
62	Tom Glavine	2.00
63	Ichiro Suzuki	6.00
64	Carlos Lee	2.00
65	Jeff Weaver	2.00
66	Jeromy Burnitz	2.00
67	Jhonny Peralta	2.00
68	Johan Santana	3.00
69	Keith Foulke	2.00
70	Manny Ramirez	4.00
71	Jim Edmonds	3.00
72	Garret Anderson	2.00
73	Felipe Lopez	2.00
74	Craig Biggio	2.00
75	Ryan Langerhans	2.00
76	Mike Cameron	2.00
77	Matt Clement	2.00
78	Miguel Cabrera	3.00
79	Mark Teixeira	3.00
80	Johnny Estrada	2.00
81	Nook Logan	2.00
82	Livan Hernandez	2.00
83	Roy Halladay	3.00
84	Jose Vidro	2.00
85	Shannon Stewart	2.00
86	Brian Bruney	2.00
87	Jaret Wright	2.00
88	Gregg Zaun	2.00
89	Jason LaRue	2.00
90	Adam Kennedy	2.00
91	Armando Benitez	2.00
92	Chris Ray	2.00
93	Clint Barmes	2.00
94	Ervin Santana	2.00
95	Justin Verlander	2.00
96	Magglio Ordonez	2.00
97	Todd Helton	3.00
98	Zachary Duke	2.00
99	Huston Street	2.00
100	Alex Rodriguez	8.00
101	Mike Hampton	2.00
102	Tony Clark	2.00
104	Barry Zito	2.00
105	Anderson Hernandez	2.00
106	B.J. Upton	2.00
107	Albert Pujols	10.00
108	Tim Hudson	3.00
109	Derek Jeter	10.00
110	Greg Maddux	6.00

Clubhouse Collection Relics

		NM/M
Common Player:		4.00
CB	Clint Barmes	6.00
BB	Barry Bonds	25.00
MC	Miguel Cabrera	8.00
RC	Robinson Cano	15.00
EC	Eric Chavez	4.00
SC	Shin-Soo Choo	4.00
CC	Carl Crawford	4.00
JD	Johnny Damon	6.00
JD2	Johnny Damon	6.00
AD	Adam Dunn	6.00
JE	Jim Edmonds	6.00
ME	Morgan Ensberg	4.00
JF	Jeff Francis	4.00
EG	Eric Gagne	4.00
KG	Khalil Greene	4.00
VG	Vladimir Guerrero	8.00
MH	Matt Holliday	8.00
TI	Tadahito Iguchi	10.00
CJ	Conor Jackson	4.00
AJ	Andruw Jones	6.00
AK	Al Kaline	20.00
DL	Derrek Lee	8.00
MM	Mickey Mantle	200.00
PM	Pedro Martinez	8.00
BM	Bill Mazeroski	30.00
MMU	Mark Mulder	4.00
SM	Stan Musial	35.00
DO	David Ortiz	10.00
JP	Jake Peavy	4.00
MP	Mike Piazza	8.00
AP	Albert Pujols	20.00
MR	Manny Ramirez	8.00
MR2	Manny Ramirez	8.00
BR	Brian Roberts	4.00
BR2	Brian Roberts	4.00
BRO	Brooks Robinson	30.00
FR	Frank Robinson	20.00
AR	Alex Rodriguez	20.00
AR2	Alex Rodriguez	20.00
JS	Johan Santana	6.00
CS	Curt Schilling	8.00
GS	Gary Sheffield	6.00
AS	Alfonso Soriano	6.00
MTE	Mark Teixeira	6.00
MT	Miguel Tejada	6.00
RW	Rickie Weeks	6.00
DWI	Dontrelle Willis	6.00
DW	David Wright	10.00

Clubhouse Collection Relic Auto.

		NM/M
Production 25 Sets		
CCA-3	Brooks Robinson	125.00
CCA-4	Al Kaline	200.00
CCA-5	Stan Musial	250.00

Clubhouse Collection Dual Relics

		NM/M
Production 57 Sets		
BR	Brooks Robinson, Brian Roberts	75.00
MR	Mickey Mantle, Alex Rodriguez	250.00
MP	Stan Musial, Albert Pujols	150.00

Clubhouse Collection Cut Sig. Relic

Production One Set

Flashbacks

		NM/M
Complete Set (10):		10.00
Common Player:		.50
Inserted 1:12		
EB	Ernie Banks	1.50
YB	Yogi Berra	1.50
WF	Whitey Ford	1.00
AK	Al Kaline	1.50
MM	Mickey Mantle	5.00
BM	Bill Mazeroski	.50
SM	Stan Musial	1.50
BRI	Bobby Richardson	.50
BR	Brooks Robinson	1.00
FR	Frank Robinson	1.00

Flashbacks Autographs

No Pricing
Production 25 Sets

Flashbacks Relics

		NM/M
EB	Ernie Banks	15.00
YB	Yogi Berra	20.00
WF	Whitey Ford	20.00
AK	Al Kaline	15.00
MM	Mickey Mantle	40.00
BM	Bill Mazeroski	10.00
SM	Stan Musial	50.00
BRI	Bobby Richardson	15.00
BR	Brooks Robinson	10.00
FR	Frank Robinson	10.00

Flashbacks Relic Autographs

No Pricing
Production 25 Sets

New Age Performers

		NM/M
Complete Set (15):		20.00
Common Player:		1.00
Inserted 1:15		
BB	Barry Bonds	4.00
MC	Miguel Cabrera	1.50
RC	Roger Clemens	4.00
VG	Vladimir Guerrero	1.50
CL	Carlos Lee	1.00
DL	Derrek Lee	1.50
PM	Pedro Martinez	1.50
DO	David Ortiz	1.50
GM	Mark Prior	1.00
AP	Albert Pujols	4.00
MR	Manny Ramirez	1.50
AR	Alex Rodriguez	4.00
GS	Gary Sheffield	1.00
I	Ichiro Suzuki	2.50
MT	Mark Teixeira	1.50

Real One Autographs

		NM/M
Production 200 Sets		
Red Ink:		1.5-2X
Production 57 Sets		
EB	Ernie Banks	120.00
YB	Yogi Berra	120.00
TB	Tommy Byrne	60.00
BC	Bob Chakales	50.00
JAC	Jack Collum	40.00
JCR	Jack Crimian	50.00
JD	Jack Dittmer	60.00
WF	Whitey Ford	100.00
DK	Don Kaiser	40.00
NK	Nellie King	50.00
LK	Lou Kretlow	50.00
PL	Paul LaPalme	50.00
JM	Joe Margoneri	60.00
WM	Windy McCall	40.00
JRM	John (Red) Murff	50.00
SM	Stan Musial	150.00
RN	Ron Negray	40.00
EOB	Eddie O'Brien	50.00
KO	Karl Olson	50.00
EO	Ernie Oravetz	50.00
MP	Mel Parnell	60.00
JP	Jim Pyburn	50.00
DR	Dusty Rhodes	50.00
FR	Frank Robinson	100.00
JSM	Jim Small	50.00
DS	Duke Snider	140.00
JSN	Jerry Snyder	60.00
CT	Charles Thompson	50.00
BW	Bob Wiesler	60.00

Real One Cut Signatures

Production One Set

Then and Now

		NM/M
Complete Set (10):		20.00
Common Duo:		1.00
Inserted 1:15		
TN1	Mickey Mantle, Alex Rodriguez	6.00
TN2	Ted Williams, Michael Young	3.00
TN3	Mickey Mantle, Jason Giambi	6.00
TN4	Luis Aparicio, Chone Figgins	1.00
TN5	Ted Williams, Alex Rodriguez	4.00
TN6	Stan Musial, Derrek Lee	2.00
TN7	Stan Musial, Derrek Lee	2.00
TN8	Red Schoendienst, Derrek Lee	1.50
TN9	Johnny Podres, Roger Clemens	4.00
TN10	Clem Labine, Chad Cordero	1.00

2006 Topps Opening Day

NM/M
Complete Set (165): 25.00
Common Player: .10
Pack (6): 1.00
Box (36): 30.00
1 Alex Rodriguez 1.50
2 Jhonny Peralta .20
3 Garrett Atkins .10
4 Vernon Wells .25
5 Carl Crawford .25
6 Josh Beckett .25
7 Mickey Mantle 3.00
8 Willy Taveras .10
9 Ivan Rodriguez .40
10 Clint Barmes .10
11 Jose Reyes .25
12 Travis Hafner .40
13 Tadahito Iguchi .25
14 Barry Zito .25
15 Brian Roberts .25
16 David Wright 1.00
17 Mark Teixeira .50
18 Roy Halladay .25
19 Scott Rolen .40
20 Bobby Abreu .25
21 Lance Berkman .25
22 Moises Alou .20
23 Chone Figgins .10
24 Aaron Rowand .10
25 Chipper Jones .50
26 Johnny Damon .50
27 Matt Clement .10
28 Nick Johnson .10
29 Freddy Garcia .10
30 Jon Garland .10
31 Torii Hunter .20
32 Mike Sweeney .10
33 Mike Lieberthal .10
34 Rafael Furcal .20
35 Brad Wilkerson .10
36 Brad Penny .10
37 Jorge Cantu .10
38 Paul Konerko .25
39 Rickie Weeks .25
40 Jorge Posada .25
41 Albert Pujols 1.50
42 Zack Greinke .10
43 Jimmy Rollins .25
44 Mark Prior .40
45 Greg Maddux 1.00
46 Jeff Francis .10
47 Felipe Lopez .10
48 Dan Johnson .10
49 B.J. Ryan .10
50 Manny Ramirez .50
51 Melvin Mora .20
52 Javy Lopez .10
53 Garret Anderson .20
54 Jason Bay .25
55 Joe Mauer .20
56 C.C. Sabathia .10
57 Bartolo Colon .20
58 Ichiro Suzuki 1.00
59 Andruw Jones .50
60 Rocco Baldelli .10
61 Jeff Kent .20
62 Cliff Floyd .10
63 John Smoltz .25
64 Shawn Green .20
65 Nomar Garciaparra .50
66 Miguel Cabrera .50
67 Vladimir Guerrero .50
68 Gary Sheffield .25
69 Jake Peavy .25
70 Carlos Lee .20
71 Tom Glavine .25
72 Craig Biggio .25
73 Steve Finley .10
74 Adrian Beltre .10
75 Eric Gagne .10
76 Aubrey Huff .10
77 Livan Hernandez .10
78 Scott Podsednik .10
79 Todd Helton .40
80 Kerry Wood .25
81 Randy Johnson .50
82 Huston Street .20
83 Pedro Martinez .50
84 Roger Clemens 1.50
85 Hank Blalock .20
86 Carlos Beltran .40
87 Chien-Ming Wang .25
88 Rich Harden .25
89 Mike Mussina .25
90 Mark Buehrle .25
91 Michael Young .20
92 Mark Mulder .20
93 Khalil Greene .10
94 Johan Santana .50
95 Andy Pettitte .25
96 Derek Jeter 1.50
97 Jack Wilson .10
98 Ben Sheets .25
99 Miguel Tejada .40
100 Barry Bonds 1.50
101 Dontrelle Willis .20
102 Curt Schilling .50
103 Jose Contreras .10
104 Jeremy Bonderman .10
105 David Ortiz .50
106 Lyle Overbay .10
107 Robinson Cano .25
108 Tim Hudson .25
109 Paul LoDuca .10
110 Mariano Rivera .25
111 Derrek Lee .50
112 Morgan Ensberg .20
113 Wily Mo Pena .10
114 Roy Oswalt .20
115 Adam Dunn .40
116 Hideki Matsui 1.00
117 Pat Burrell .25
118 Jason Schmidt .20
119 Alfonso Soriano .40
120 Aramis Ramirez .25
121 Jason Giambi .25
122 Orlando Hernandez .10
123 Magglio Ordonez .10
124 Troy Glaus .20
125 Carlos Delgado .25
126 Kevin Millwood .20
127 Shannon Stewart .10
128 Luis Castillo .10
129 Jim Edmonds .25
130 Richie Sexson .25
131 Dmitri Young .10
132 Russ Adams .10
133 Nick Swisher .10
134 Jermaine Dye .10
135 Anderson Hernandez **(RC)** .10
136 Justin Huber **(RC)** .10
137 Jason Botts **(RC)** .10
138 Jeff Mathis **(RC)** .10
139 Ryan Garko **(RC)** .10
140 Charlton Jimerson **(RC)** .10
141 Chris Denorfia **(RC)** .10
142 Anthony Reyes **(RC)** .10
143 Bryan Bullington **(RC)** .10
144 Chuck James **(RC)** .10
145 Danny Sandoval **RC** .25
146 Walter Young **(RC)** .10
147 Fausto Carmona **(RC)** .10
148 Francisco Liriano **(RC)** .25
149 Hong-Chih Kuo **(RC)** .10
150 Joe Saunders **(RC)** .10
151 John Koronka **(RC)** .10
152 Robert Andino **RC** .25
153 Shaun Marcum **(RC)** .10
154 Tom Gorzelanny **(RC)** .10
155 Craig Breslow **RC** .25
156 Chris Demaria **RC** .50
157 Brayan Pena **(RC)** .10
158 Rich Hill **(RC)** .25
159 Rick Short **RC** .25
160 Darrell Rasner **(RC)** .10
161 C.J. Wilson **(RC)** .10
162 Brandon Watson **(RC)** .10
163 Paul McAnulty **(RC)** .10
164 Marshall McDougall **(RC)** .10
165 Checklist .10

Red Foil

Red: 2-3X
Production 2,006 Sets

Printing Plates

No Pricing
Production one set per color.

Autographs

NM/M
BE Brad Eldred 15.00
JE Johnny Estrada 20.00
TH Toby Hall 10.00
MK Mark Kotsay 10.00
EM Eli Marrero 10.00
VZ Victor Zambrano 10.00

Relics

NM/M
Common Team: 25.00
WI Chicago White Sox 40.00
MN New York Mets 40.00
RR Texas Rangers 30.00
BP Milwaukee Brewers 25.00
RC Cincinnati Reds 30.00
PC Philadelphia Phillies 40.00
OD Baltimore Orioles 25.00
RD Colorado Rockies 25.00
DB Los Angeles Dodgers 40.00
RT Kansas City Royals 25.00
MA Seattle Mariners 30.00
AM Houston Astros 30.00
PG San Diego Padres 40.00
AY Oakland Athletics 40.00
JT Toronto Blue Jays 30.00

SI For Kids

NM/M
1 Vladimir Guerrero .50
2 Marcus Giles .15
3 Michael Young .15
4 Derek Jeter 1.50
5 Barry Bonds 1.50
6 Ivan Rodriguez .40
7 Miguel Cabrera .50
8 Jim Edmonds .25
9 Jack Wilson .15
10 Khalil Greene .15
11 Miguel Tejada .40
12 Eric Chavez .25
13 Shannon Stewart .15
14 Julio Lugo .15
15 Andruw Jones .50
16 Nick Johnson, Randy Johnson .50
17 Tadahito Iguchi, Ivan Rodriguez .25
18 Roy Oswalt, Jose Reyes .25
19 Manny Ramirez, Ronnie Belliard .50
20 Todd Helton, Khalil Greene .25
21 David Ortiz, Dontrelle Willis .50
22 Ichiro Suzuki, Johnny Damon .75
23 Craig Biggio, Jack Wilson .15
24 Brian Roberts, Richie Sexson .25
25 Chipper Jones, Marcus Giles .50

2006 Topps Sterling

NM/M
Common Player: 10.00
Production 250 Sets
Box (Five Cards): 300.00
1-19 Barry Bonds 10.00
20-39 Mickey Mantle 25.00
40-43 Josh Gibson 30.00
44-53 Rickey Henderson 10.00
54-62 Ted Williams 15.00
63-67 Roberto Clemente 25.00
68-77 Nolan Ryan 20.00
78-96 Cal Ripken Jr. 20.00
97-101 Stan Musial 15.00
102-106 Reggie Jackson 15.00
107-111 Johnny Bench 15.00
112-121 George Brett 15.00
122-131 Don Mattingly 15.00
132-136 Roger Maris 20.00
137-146 Rod Carew 10.00
147-151 Yogi Berra 15.00
152-156 Mike Schmidt 15.00
157-175 Carl Yastrzemski 15.00
176-185 Tony Gwynn 15.00
186-190 Ryne Sandberg 15.00
191-200 Ozzie Smith 15.00

Framed Burgundy

Burgundy (1-200): 3-5X
Production 10 Sets

Framed Silver

No Pricing
Production One Set

Framed White

White (1-200): 1-1.5X
Production 50 Sets

Baseball Cut Signatures

NM/M
SA Sparky Anderson 40.00
LA Luis Aparicio 40.00
LB Lou Brock 50.00
RC Rod Carew 50.00
SC Steve Carlton 50.00
GC Gary Carter 50.00
OC Orlando Cepeda 35.00
DE Dennis Eckersley 40.00
BF Bob Feller 40.00
RF Rollie Fingers 40.00
CF Carlton Fisk 60.00
BG Bob Gibson 50.00
MI Monte Irvin 40.00
AK Al Kaline 60.00
GK George Kell 40.00
HK Harmon Killebrew 70.00
RK Ralph Kiner 50.00
JM Juan Marichal 40.00
JMO Joe Morgan 50.00
PN Phil Niekro 40.00
JP Jim Palmer 40.00
TP Tony Perez 40.00
GP Gaylord Perry 40.00
RR Robin Roberts 40.00
BR Brooks Robinson 60.00
FR Frank Robinson 60.00
RS Ryne Sandberg 80.00
MS Mike Schmidt 75.00
RSH Red Schoendienst 60.00
DS Duke Snider 75.00
EW Earl Weaver 30.00
RY Robin Yount 70.00

Career Stats Relics

No Pricing
Production 10 Sets
Prime: No Pricing
Production One Set
Sterling Silver: No Pricing
Production One Set

Career Stats Relics Autographs

Production 10 Sets
Prime: No Pricing
Production One Set
Sterling Silver: No Pricing
Production One Set

Cut from the Same Cloth Signatures

Production 1-5

Cut Signatures

NM/M
46 Elmer Valo 80.00
53 Carl Furillo 100.00
61 Hal Newhouser 60.00
64 Dick Sisler 65.00
65 Frank Shea 75.00
66 Monty Stratton 80.00
67 Lloyd Waner 150.00
68 Sal Maglie 70.00
69 Waite Hoyt 80.00
70 Warren Spahn 100.00
72 A.B. Chandler 60.00
73 Al Barlick 75.00
74 Bill Dickey 100.00
75 Bill Terry 80.00
76 Billy Herman 75.00
77 Bob Lemon 60.00
78 Buck Leonard 80.00
79 Charles Gehringer 100.00
81 Earl Averill 60.00
82 Hoyt Wilhelm 80.00
83 Jim "Catfish" Hunter 100.00
84 Joe Sewell 80.00
85 Judy Johnson 80.00
86 Carl Hubbell 85.00
87 Lou Boudreau 65.00
88 Luke Appling 80.00
89 Ray Dandridge 75.00
90 Rick Ferrell 60.00
91 Stan Coveleski 75.00
92 Willie Stargell 120.00

Five Relics

Production 10 Sets
Prime: No Pricing
Production 10 Sets
Sterling Silver: No Pricing
Production One Set

Five Relics Autographs

Production 10 Sets
Prime: No Pricing
Production 10 Sets
Sterling Silver: No Pricing
Production One Set

Josh Gibson Bat Barrel

Production One

Jumbo Jersey

Production 10 Sets
Prime: No Pricing
Production One Set
Patch: No Pricing
Production 10 Sets
Sterling Silver: No Pricing
Production One Set

Moments Relics

NM/M
Production 10 Sets
Prime: No Pricing
Production One Set
BB Barry Bonds HR 1 75.00
BB Barry Bonds HR 2 75.00
BB Barry Bonds HR 3 75.00
BB Barry Bonds HR 4 75.00
BB Barry Bonds HR 5 75.00
BB Barry Bonds HR 6 75.00
BB Barry Bonds HR 7 75.00
BB Barry Bonds HR 8 75.00
BB Barry Bonds HR 9 75.00
BB Barry Bonds HR 1 75.00
BB Barry Bonds HR 2 75.00
BB Barry Bonds HR 3 75.00
BB Barry Bonds HR 4 75.00
BB Barry Bonds HR 5 75.00
BB Barry Bonds HR 6 75.00
BB Barry Bonds HR 7 75.00
BB Barry Bonds HR 8 75.00
BB Barry Bonds HR 1 75.00
BB Barry Bonds HR 2 75.00
BB Barry Bonds HR 3 75.00
BB Barry Bonds HR 4 75.00
BB Barry Bonds HR 5 75.00
BB Barry Bonds HR 6 75.00
BB Barry Bonds HR 7 75.00
BB Barry Bonds HR 8 75.00
BB Barry Bonds 75.00
BB Barry Bonds/1993 75.00
BB Barry Bonds/1994 75.00
BB Barry Bonds/1995 75.00
BB Barry Bonds/1996 75.00
BB Barry Bonds/1997 75.00
BB Barry Bonds/1998 75.00
BB Barry Bonds/1999 75.00
BB Barry Bonds/1993 75.00
BB Barry Bonds/2001 75.00
BB Barry Bonds/2002 75.00
BB Barry Bonds/2003 75.00
BB Barry Bonds/2004 75.00
BB Barry Bonds/1993 75.00
BB Barry Bonds/1994 75.00
BB Barry Bonds/1995 75.00
BB Barry Bonds/1996 75.00
BB Barry Bonds/1997 75.00
BB Barry Bonds/1998 75.00
BB Barry Bonds/2000 75.00
BB Barry Bonds/2001 75.00
BB Barry Bonds/2002 75.00
BB Barry Bonds/2003 75.00
BB Barry Bonds/2004 75.00
BB Barry Bonds/2002 75.00
BB Barry Bonds/2004 75.00
BB Barry Bonds/1993 75.00
BB Barry Bonds/1994 75.00
BB Barry Bonds/1996 75.00
BB Barry Bonds/1997 75.00
BB Barry Bonds/2000 75.00
BB Barry Bonds/2001 75.00
BB Barry Bonds/2002 75.00
BB Barry Bonds/2003 75.00
BB Barry Bonds/2004 75.00
BB Barry Bonds/1993 75.00
BB Barry Bonds/2001 75.00
BB Barry Bonds/2002 75.00
BB Barry Bonds/2003 75.00
BB Barry Bonds/2004 75.00
MM Mickey Mantle WS HR 1 350.00
MM Mickey Mantle WS HR 2 350.00
MM Mickey Mantle WS HR 3 350.00
MM Mickey Mantle WS HR 4 350.00
MM Mickey Mantle WS HR 5 350.00
MM Mickey Mantle WS HR 6 350.00
MM Mickey Mantle WS HR 7 350.00
MM Mickey Mantle WS HR 8 350.00
MM Mickey Mantle WS HR 9 350.00
MM Mickey Mantle WS HR 10 350.00
MM Mickey Mantle WS HR 11 350.00
MM Mickey Mantle WS HR 12 350.00
MM Mickey Mantle WS HR 13 350.00
MM Mickey Mantle WS HR 14 350.00
MM Mickey Mantle WS HR 15 350.00
MM Mickey Mantle WS HR 16 350.00
MM Mickey Mantle WS HR 17 350.00
MM Mickey Mantle WS HR 18 350.00
MM Mickey Mantle/1952 350.00
MM Mickey Mantle/1956 350.00
MM Mickey Mantle/1957 350.00
MM Mickey Mantle/1962 350.00
MM Mickey Mantle/1953 350.00
MM Mickey Mantle/1954 350.00
MM Mickey Mantle/1955 350.00
MM Mickey Mantle/1958 350.00
MM Mickey Mantle/1959 350.00
MM Mickey Mantle/1960 350.00
MM Mickey Mantle/1961 350.00
MM Mickey Mantle/1963 350.00
MM Mickey Mantle/1964 350.00
MM Mickey Mantle/1965 350.00
MM Mickey Mantle/1967 350.00
MM Mickey Mantle/1968 350.00
MM Mickey Mantle HR 1 350.00
MM Mickey Mantle HR 7 350.00
MM Mickey Mantle HR 10 350.00
MM Mickey Mantle HR 2 350.00
MM Mickey Mantle HR 3 350.00
MM Mickey Mantle HR 4 350.00
MM Mickey Mantle HR 5 350.00
MM Mickey Mantle HR 6 350.00
MM Mickey Mantle HR 8 350.00
MM Mickey Mantle HR 9 350.00
MM Mickey Mantle HR 11 350.00
MM Mickey Mantle HR 12 350.00
MM Mickey Mantle HR 13 350.00
MM Mickey Mantle HR 14 350.00
MM Mickey Mantle HR 15 350.00
MM Mickey Mantle HR 16 350.00
MM Mickey Mantle HR 17 350.00
MM Mickey Mantle HR 18 350.00
MM Mickey Mantle HR 19 350.00
MM Mickey Mantle HR 20 350.00
MM Mickey Mantle HR 25 350.00
MM Mickey Mantle HR 21 350.00
MM Mickey Mantle HR 22 350.00
MM Mickey Mantle HR 23 350.00
MM Mickey Mantle HR 24 350.00
MM Mickey Mantle HR 26 350.00
MM Mickey Mantle HR 27 350.00
MM Mickey Mantle HR 28 350.00
MM Mickey Mantle HR 29 350.00
MM Mickey Mantle HR 30 350.00
MM Mickey Mantle HR 31 350.00
MM Mickey Mantle HR 32 350.00
MM Mickey Mantle HR 33 350.00
MM Mickey Mantle HR 34 350.00
MM Mickey Mantle HR 35 350.00
MM Mickey Mantle HR 36 350.00
MM Mickey Mantle HR 37 350.00
MM Mickey Mantle HR 38 350.00
MM Mickey Mantle HR 39 350.00
MM Mickey Mantle HR 40 350.00
MM Mickey Mantle HR 50 350.00
MM Mickey Mantle HR 60 350.00
MM Mickey Mantle HR 41 350.00
MM Mickey Mantle HR 42 350.00
MM Mickey Mantle HR 43 350.00
MM Mickey Mantle HR 44 350.00
MM Mickey Mantle HR 45 350.00
MM Mickey Mantle HR 46 350.00
MM Mickey Mantle HR 47 350.00
MM Mickey Mantle HR 48 350.00
MM Mickey Mantle HR 49 350.00
MM Mickey Mantle HR 51 350.00
MM Mickey Mantle HR 52 350.00
MM Mickey Mantle HR 53 350.00
MM Mickey Mantle HR 54 350.00
MM Mickey Mantle HR 55 350.00
MM Mickey Mantle HR 56 350.00
MM Mickey Mantle HR 57 350.00
MM Mickey Mantle HR 58 350.00
MM Mickey Mantle HR 59 350.00
MM Mickey Mantle HR 75 350.00
MM Mickey Mantle HR 61 350.00
MM Mickey Mantle HR 62 350.00
MM Mickey Mantle HR 63 350.00
MM Mickey Mantle HR 64 350.00
MM Mickey Mantle HR 65 350.00
MM Mickey Mantle HR 66 350.00

MM Mickey Mantle HR 67 350.00
MM Mickey Mantle HR 68 350.00
MM Mickey Mantle HR 69 350.00
MM Mickey Mantle HR 70 350.00
MM Mickey Mantle HR 71 350.00
MM Mickey Mantle HR 72 350.00
MM Mickey Mantle HR 73 350.00
MM Mickey Mantle HR 74 350.00
MM Mickey Mantle HR 76 350.00
MM Mickey Mantle HR 77 350.00
MM Mickey Mantle HR 78 350.00
MM Mickey Mantle HR 79 350.00
MM Mickey Mantle HR 80 350.00
MM Mickey Mantle HR 90 350.00
MM Mickey Mantle HR 81 350.00
MM Mickey Mantle HR 82 350.00
MM Mickey Mantle HR 83 350.00
MM Mickey Mantle HR 84 350.00
MM Mickey Mantle HR 85 350.00
MM Mickey Mantle HR 86 350.00
MM Mickey Mantle HR 87 350.00
MM Mickey Mantle HR 88 350.00
MM Mickey Mantle HR 89 350.00
MM Mickey Mantle HR 91 350.00
MM Mickey Mantle HR 92 350.00
MM Mickey Mantle HR 93 350.00
MM Mickey Mantle HR 94 350.00
MM Mickey Mantle HR 95 350.00
MM Mickey Mantle HR 96 350.00
MM Mickey Mantle HR 97 350.00
MM Mickey Mantle HR 98 350.00
MM Mickey Mantle HR 99 350.00
MM Mickey Mantle HR 100 350.00
JG Josh Gibson 500.00
JG Josh Gibson 500.00
JG Josh Gibson 500.00
JG Josh Gibson 500.00
JG Josh Gibson 500.00
JG Josh Gibson 500.00
JG Josh Gibson 500.00
JG Josh Gibson 500.00
RH Rickey Henderson/1980 60.00
RH Rickey Henderson/1981 60.00
RH Rickey Henderson/1982 60.00
RH Rickey Henderson/1983 60.00
RH Rickey Henderson/1984 60.00
RH Rickey Henderson/1990 60.00
RH Rickey Henderson/1998 60.00
RH Rickey Henderson/1989 60.00
RH Rickey Henderson/1991 60.00
RH Rickey Henderson/1985 60.00
RH Rickey Henderson/1986 60.00
RH Rickey Henderson/1987 60.00
RH Rickey Henderson/1980 60.00
RH Rickey Henderson/1983 60.00
RH Rickey Henderson/1990 60.00
RH Rickey Henderson/1982 60.00
RH Rickey Henderson/1984 60.00
RH Rickey Henderson/1991 60.00
RH Rickey Henderson/1985 60.00
RH Rickey Henderson/1987 60.00
RH Rickey Henderson/1986 60.00
RH Rickey Henderson/1988 60.00
RH Rickey Henderson/1981 60.00
RH Rickey Henderson/1990 60.00
RH Rickey Henderson/1989 60.00
RH Rickey Henderson/1986 60.00
RH Rickey Henderson/1985 60.00
RH Rickey Henderson/1983 60.00
RH Rickey Henderson/1998 60.00
RH Rickey Henderson/1982 60.00
RH Rickey Henderson/1989 60.00
RH Rickey Henderson/1990 60.00
RH Rickey Henderson/1981 60.00
RH Rickey Henderson/1985 60.00
TW Ted Williams 0.406 150.00
TW Ted Williams 0.5 150.00
TW Ted Williams 0.308 150.00
TW Ted Williams 0.341 150.00
TW Ted Williams 0.421 150.00
TW Ted Williams 0.436 150.00
TW Ted Williams 0.42 150.00
TW Ted Williams 0.405 150.00
TW Ted Williams 0.397 150.00
TW Ted Williams 0.4 150.00
TW Ted Williams 0.414 150.00
TW Ted Williams 0.409 150.00
TW Ted Williams 0.411 150.00
TW Ted Williams 0.399 150.00
TW Ted Williams 0.404 150.00
TW Ted Williams HR 1 150.00
TW Ted Williams HR 10 150.00
TW Ted Williams HR 20 150.00
TW Ted Williams HR 30 150.00
TW Ted Williams HR 36 150.00
TW Ted Williams HR 1 150.00
TW Ted Williams HR 10 150.00
TW Ted Williams HR 20 150.00
TW Ted Williams HR 30 150.00
TW Ted Williams HR 32 150.00
RC Roberto Clemente HIT 1 200.00
RC Roberto Clemente HIT 2 200.00
RC Roberto Clemente HIT 3 200.00
RC Roberto Clemente HIT 4 200.00
RC Roberto Clemente HIT 5 200.00
RC Roberto Clemente HIT 6 200.00
RC Roberto Clemente HIT 7 200.00
RC Roberto Clemente HIT 8 200.00
RC Roberto Clemente HIT 9 200.00
RC Roberto Clemente HIT 10 200.00
RC Roberto Clemente HIT 11 200.00
RC Roberto Clemente HIT 12 200.00
RC Roberto Clemente HIT 21 200.00
RC Roberto Clemente HIT 13 200.00
RC Roberto Clemente HIT 14 200.00
RC Roberto Clemente HIT 15 200.00
RC Roberto Clemente HIT 16 200.00
RC Roberto Clemente HIT 17 200.00
RC Roberto Clemente HIT 18 200.00
RC Roberto Clemente HIT 19 200.00
RC Roberto Clemente HIT 20 200.00
RC Roberto Clemente/1966 200.00
RC Roberto Clemente/1971 200.00
RC Roberto Clemente/1972 200.00
RC Roberto Clemente/1961 200.00
RC Roberto Clemente/1962 200.00
RC Roberto Clemente/1963 200.00
RC Roberto Clemente/1964 200.00
RC Roberto Clemente/1965 200.00
RC Roberto Clemente/1967 200.00
RC Roberto Clemente/1968 200.00
RC Roberto Clemente/1969 200.00
RC Roberto Clemente/1970 200.00
NR Nolan Ryan SO 1 100.00
NR Nolan Ryan SO 50 100.00
NR Nolan Ryan SO 100 100.00
NR Nolan Ryan SO 200 100.00
NR Nolan Ryan SO 10 100.00
NR Nolan Ryan SO 20 100.00
NR Nolan Ryan SO 30 100.00
NR Nolan Ryan SO 40 100.00
NR Nolan Ryan SO 60 100.00
NR Nolan Ryan SO 70 100.00
NR Nolan Ryan SO 80 100.00
NR Nolan Ryan SO 90 100.00
NR Nolan Ryan SO 125 100.00
NR Nolan Ryan SO 150 100.00
NR Nolan Ryan SO 175 100.00
NR Nolan Ryan SO 225 100.00
NR Nolan Ryan SO 300 100.00
NR Nolan Ryan SO 350 100.00
NR Nolan Ryan SO 380 100.00
NR Nolan Ryan SO 382 100.00
NR Nolan Ryan SO 383 100.00
NR Nolan Ryan SO 250 100.00
NR Nolan Ryan SO 275 100.00
NR Nolan Ryan SO 310 100.00
NR Nolan Ryan SO 320 100.00
NR Nolan Ryan SO 330 100.00
NR Nolan Ryan SO 340 100.00
NR Nolan Ryan SO 360 100.00
NR Nolan Ryan SO 370 100.00
NR Nolan Ryan SO 375 100.00
NR Nolan Ryan NO HIT 1 100.00
NR Nolan Ryan NO HIT 2 100.00
NR Nolan Ryan NO HIT 3 100.00
NR Nolan Ryan NO HIT 4 100.00
NR Nolan Ryan NO HIT 5 100.00
NR Nolan Ryan NO HIT 6 100.00
NR Nolan Ryan NO HIT 7 100.00
CR Cal Ripken Jr./1983 100.00
CR Cal Ripken Jr./1985 100.00
CR Cal Ripken Jr./1987 100.00
CR Cal Ripken Jr./1989 100.00
CR Cal Ripken Jr./1991 100.00
CR Cal Ripken Jr./1993 100.00
CR Cal Ripken Jr./1995 100.00
CR Cal Ripken Jr./1997 100.00
CR Cal Ripken Jr./1999 100.00
CR Cal Ripken Jr./2001 100.00
CR Cal Ripken Jr./1984 100.00
CR Cal Ripken Jr./1986 100.00
CR Cal Ripken Jr./1988 100.00
CR Cal Ripken Jr./1990 100.00
CR Cal Ripken Jr./1992 100.00
CR Cal Ripken Jr./1994 100.00
CR Cal Ripken Jr./1996 100.00
CR Cal Ripken Jr./1998 100.00
CR Cal Ripken Jr./2000 100.00
CR Cal Ripken Jr./1984 100.00
CR Cal Ripken Jr./1986 100.00
CR Cal Ripken Jr./1991 100.00
CR Cal Ripken Jr./1994 100.00
CR Cal Ripken Jr./1983 100.00
CR Cal Ripken Jr./1985 100.00
CR Cal Ripken Jr./1989 100.00
CR Cal Ripken Jr./1993 100.00
CR Cal Ripken Jr. HIT 1 100.00
CR Cal Ripken Jr. 1,000 100.00
CR Cal Ripken Jr. 1,500 100.00
CR Cal Ripken Jr. 2,000 100.00
CR Cal Ripken Jr. 2,500 100.00
CR Cal Ripken Jr. 2,900 100.00
CR Cal Ripken Jr. 3,000 100.00
CR Cal Ripken Jr. 3,184 100.00
CR Cal Ripken Jr. 100 100.00
CR Cal Ripken Jr. 200 100.00
CR Cal Ripken Jr. 300 100.00
CR Cal Ripken Jr. 400 100.00
CR Cal Ripken Jr. 500 100.00
CR Cal Ripken Jr. 2,100 100.00
CR Cal Ripken Jr. 2,200 100.00
CR Cal Ripken Jr. 2,300 100.00
CR Cal Ripken Jr. 2,400 100.00
CR Cal Ripken Jr. 2,600 100.00
CR Cal Ripken Jr. 2,700 100.00
CR Cal Ripken Jr. 2,800 100.00
CR Cal Ripken Jr. HR 1 100.00
CR Cal Ripken Jr. HR 100 100.00
CR Cal Ripken Jr. HR 200 100.00
CR Cal Ripken Jr. HR 300 100.00
CR Cal Ripken Jr. HR 400 100.00
CR Cal Ripken Jr. HR 431 100.00
CR Cal Ripken Jr. HR 10 100.00
CR Cal Ripken Jr. HR 25 100.00
CR Cal Ripken Jr. HR 50 100.00
CR Cal Ripken Jr. HR 75 100.00
CR Cal Ripken Jr. HR 125 100.00
CR Cal Ripken Jr. HR 150 100.00
CR Cal Ripken Jr. HR 175 100.00
CR Cal Ripken Jr. HR 225 100.00
CR Cal Ripken Jr. HR 250 100.00
CR Cal Ripken Jr. HR 275 100.00
CR Cal Ripken Jr. HR 325 100.00
CR Cal Ripken Jr. HR 350 100.00
CR Cal Ripken Jr. HR 375 100.00
CR Cal Ripken Jr. HR 425 100.00
CR Cal Ripken Jr. GM 1 100.00
CR Cal Ripken Jr. 500 100.00
CR Cal Ripken Jr. 1,000 100.00
CR Cal Ripken Jr. 2,000 100.00
CR Cal Ripken Jr. 2,130 100.00
CR Cal Ripken Jr. 2,131 100.00
CR Cal Ripken Jr. 2,632 100.00
CR Cal Ripken Jr. 100 100.00
CR Cal Ripken Jr. 200 100.00
CR Cal Ripken Jr. 300 100.00
CR Cal Ripken Jr. 400 100.00
CR Cal Ripken Jr. 600 100.00
CR Cal Ripken Jr. 700 100.00
CR Cal Ripken Jr. 800 100.00
CR Cal Ripken Jr. 900 100.00
CR Cal Ripken Jr. 1,250 100.00
CR Cal Ripken Jr. 1,500 100.00
CR Cal Ripken Jr. 1,750 100.00
CR Cal Ripken Jr. 2,500 100.00
CR Cal Ripken Jr. 2,600 100.00
SM Stan Musial/1943 75.00
SM Stan Musial/1946 75.00
SM Stan Musial/1948 75.00
SM Stan Musial/1950 75.00
SM Stan Musial/1952 75.00
SM Stan Musial/1942 75.00
SM Stan Musial/1944 75.00
SM Stan Musial/1947 75.00
SM Stan Musial/1949 75.00
SM Stan Musial/1951 75.00
SM Stan Musial/1954 75.00
SM Stan Musial/1956 75.00
SM Stan Musial/1958 75.00
SM Stan Musial/1960 75.00
SM Stan Musial/1962 75.00
SM Stan Musial/1953 75.00
SM Stan Musial/1955 75.00
SM Stan Musial/1957 75.00
SM Stan Musial 1959 75.00
SM Stan Musial/1961 75.00
RJ Reggie Jackson HR 1 60.00
RJ Reggie Jackson HR 100 60.00
RJ Reggie Jackson HR 200 60.00
RJ Reggie Jackson HR 250 60.00
RJ Reggie Jackson HR 300 60.00
RJ Reggie Jackson HR 350 60.00
RJ Reggie Jackson HR 400 60.00
RJ Reggie Jackson HR 450 60.00
RJ Reggie Jackson HR 550 60.00
RJ Reggie Jackson HR 25 60.00
RJ Reggie Jackson HR 50 60.00
RJ Reggie Jackson HR 75 60.00
RJ Reggie Jackson HR 150 60.00
JB Johnny Bench/1968 65.00
JB Johnny Bench/1969 65.00
JB Johnny Bench/1971 65.00
JB Johnny Bench/1973 65.00
JB Johnny Bench/1975 65.00
JB Johnny Bench/1976 65.00
GB George Brett HIT 1 60.00
GB George Brett HIT 3 60.00
GB George Brett HIT 5 60.00
GB George Brett HIT 7 60.00
GB George Brett HIT 10 60.00
GB George Brett HIT 12 60.00
GB George Brett HIT 15 60.00
GB George Brett HIT 16 60.00
GB George Brett HIT 17 60.00
GB George Brett HIT 18 60.00
GB George Brett HIT 2 60.00
GB George Brett HIT 4 60.00
GB George Brett HIT 6 60.00
GB George Brett HIT 8 60.00
GB George Brett HIT 9 60.00
GB George Brett HIT 11 60.00
GB George Brett HIT 13 60.00
GB George Brett HIT 14 60.00
GB George Brett/1976 60.00
GB George Brett/1980 60.00
GB George Brett/1990 60.00
GB George Brett/1976 60.00
GB George Brett/1977 60.00
GB George Brett/1979 60.00
GB George Brett/1981 60.00
GB George Brett/1983 60.00
GB George Brett/1985 60.00
GB George Brett/1988 60.00
GB George Brett/1978 60.00
GB George Brett/1980 60.00
GB George Brett/1982 60.00
GB George Brett/1984 60.00
GB George Brett/1986 60.00
GB George Brett/1980 60.00
GB George Brett/1985 60.00
GB George Brett/1988 60.00
RM Roger Maris HR 1 125.00
RM Roger Maris HR 2 125.00
RM Roger Maris HR 5 125.00
RM Roger Maris HR 9 125.00
RM Roger Maris HR 10 125.00
RM Roger Maris HR 15 125.00
RM Roger Maris HR 3 125.00
RM Roger Maris HR 4 125.00
RM Roger Maris HR 6 125.00
RM Roger Maris HR 7 125.00
RM Roger Maris HR 8 125.00
RM Roger Maris HR 11 125.00
RM Roger Maris HR 12 125.00
RM Roger Maris HR 13 125.00
RM Roger Maris HR 14 125.00
RM Roger Maris HR 20 125.00
RM Roger Maris HR 25 125.00
RM Roger Maris HR 30 125.00
RM Roger Maris HR 16 125.00
RM Roger Maris HR 17 125.00
RM Roger Maris HR 18 125.00
RM Roger Maris HR 19 125.00
RM Roger Maris HR 21 125.00
RM Roger Maris HR 22 125.00
RM Roger Maris HR 23 125.00
RM Roger Maris HR 24 125.00
RM Roger Maris HR 26 125.00
RM Roger Maris HR 27 125.00
RM Roger Maris HR 28 125.00
RM Roger Maris HR 29 125.00
YB Yogi Berra 1951 75.00
YB Yogi Berra 1951 75.00
YB Yogi Berra 1954 75.00
YB Yogi Berra 1955 75.00
MS Mike Schmidt HR 1 50.00
MS Mike Schmidt HR 2 50.00
MS Mike Schmidt HR 3 50.00
MS Mike Schmidt HR 4 50.00
CY Carl Yastrzemski HR 1 60.00
CY Carl Yastrzemski HR 5 60.00
CY Carl Yastrzemski HR 10 60.00
CY Carl Yastrzemski HR 15 60.00
CY Carl Yastrzemski HR 2 60.00
CY Carl Yastrzemski HR 3 60.00
CY Carl Yastrzemski HR 4 60.00
CY Carl Yastrzemski HR 6 60.00
CY Carl Yastrzemski HR 7 60.00
CY Carl Yastrzemski HR 8 60.00
CY Carl Yastrzemski HR 9 60.00
CY Carl Yastrzemski HR 11 60.00
CY Carl Yastrzemski HR 12 60.00
CY Carl Yastrzemski HR 13 60.00
CY Carl Yastrzemski HR 14 60.00
CY Carl Yastrzemski HR 20 60.00
CY Carl Yastrzemski HR 25 60.00
CY Carl Yastrzemski HR 30 60.00
CY Carl Yastrzemski HR 16 60.00
CY Carl Yastrzemski HR 17 60.00
CY Carl Yastrzemski HR 18 60.00
CY Carl Yastrzemski HR 19 60.00
CY Carl Yastrzemski HR 21 60.00
CY Carl Yastrzemski HR 22 60.00
CY Carl Yastrzemski HR 23 60.00
CY Carl Yastrzemski HR 24 60.00
CY Carl Yastrzemski HR 26 60.00
CY Carl Yastrzemski HR 27 60.00
CY Carl Yastrzemski HR 28 60.00
CY Carl Yastrzemski HR 29 60.00
CY Carl Yastrzemski HR 35 60.00
CY Carl Yastrzemski HR 40 60.00
CY Carl Yastrzemski HR 44 60.00
CY Carl Yastrzemski HR 31 60.00
CY Carl Yastrzemski HR 32 60.00
CY Carl Yastrzemski HR 33 60.00
CY Carl Yastrzemski HR 34 60.00
CY Carl Yastrzemski HR 36 60.00
CY Carl Yastrzemski HR 37 60.00
CY Carl Yastrzemski HR 38 60.00
CY Carl Yastrzemski HR 39 60.00
CY Carl Yastrzemski HR 41 60.00
CY Carl Yastrzemski HR 42 60.00
CY Carl Yastrzemski HR 43 60.00
CY Carl Yastrzemski/1961 60.00
CY Carl Yastrzemski/1964 60.00
CY Carl Yastrzemski/1966 60.00
CY Carl Yastrzemski/1967 60.00
CY Carl Yastrzemski/1970 60.00
CY Carl Yastrzemski/1972 60.00
CY Carl Yastrzemski/1962 60.00
CY Carl Yastrzemski/1963 60.00
CY Carl Yastrzemski/1965 60.00
CY Carl Yastrzemski/1968 60.00
CY Carl Yastrzemski/1969 60.00
CY Carl Yastrzemski/1971 60.00
CY Carl Yastrzemski/1973 60.00
CY Carl Yastrzemski/1975 60.00
CY Carl Yastrzemski/1977 60.00
CY Carl Yastrzemski/1980 60.00
CY Carl Yastrzemski/1983 60.00
CY Carl Yastrzemski/1974 60.00
CY Carl Yastrzemski/1976 60.00
CY Carl Yastrzemski/1978 60.00
CY Carl Yastrzemski/1979 60.00
CY Carl Yastrzemski/1981 60.00
CY Carl Yastrzemski/1982 60.00
CY Carl Yastrzemski/1963 60.00
CY Carl Yastrzemski/1965 60.00
CY Carl Yastrzemski/1966 60.00
CY Carl Yastrzemski/1967 60.00
CY Carl Yastrzemski/1968 60.00
CY Carl Yastrzemski/1969 60.00
CY Carl Yastrzemski/1970 60.00
CY Carl Yastrzemski/1971 60.00
CY Carl Yastrzemski/1972 60.00
CY Carl Yastrzemski/1973 60.00
CY Carl Yastrzemski/1974 60.00
CY Carl Yastrzemski/1975 60.00
CY Carl Yastrzemski/1976 60.00
CY Carl Yastrzemski/1977 60.00
CY Carl Yastrzemski/1978 60.00
CY Carl Yastrzemski/1979 60.00
CY Carl Yastrzemski/1982 60.00
CY Carl Yastrzemski/1983 60.00
TG Tony Gwynn/1984 60.00
TG Tony Gwynn/1987 60.00
TG Tony Gwynn/1988 60.00
TG Tony Gwynn/1989 60.00
TG Tony Gwynn/1994 60.00
TG Tony Gwynn/1995 60.00
TG Tony Gwynn/1996 60.00
TG Tony Gwynn/1997 60.00
RS Ryne Sandberg/1984 70.00
RS Ryne Sandberg/1988 70.00
RS Ryne Sandberg/1990 70.00
RS Ryne Sandberg/1992 70.00
RS Ryne Sandberg/1983 70.00
RS Ryne Sandberg/1985 70.00
RS Ryne Sandberg/1987 70.00
RS Ryne Sandberg/1989 70.00

Moments Relics Autographs

NM/M

Production 10 Sets
Prime: No Pricing
Production One Set
RH Rickey Henderson/1980 125.00
RH Rickey Henderson/1981 125.00

RH	Rickey Henderson/1982	125.00
RH	Rickey Henderson/1983	125.00
RH	Rickey Henderson/1984	125.00
RH	Rickey Henderson/1990	125.00
RH	Rickey Henderson/1998	125.00
RH	Rickey Henderson/1985	125.00
RH	Rickey Henderson/1986	125.00
RH	Rickey Henderson/1987	125.00
RH	Rickey Henderson/1980	125.00
RH	Rickey Henderson/1983	125.00
RH	Rickey Henderson/1990	125.00
RH	Rickey Henderson/1985	125.00
RH	Rickey Henderson/1987	125.00
RH	Rickey Henderson/1981	125.00
RH	Rickey Henderson/1990	125.00
RH	Rickey Henderson/1986	125.00
RH	Rickey Henderson/1983	125.00
RH	Rickey Henderson/1998	125.00
RH	Rickey Henderson/1990	125.00
NR	Nolan Ryan SO 1	300.00
NR	Nolan Ryan SO 50	300.00
NR	Nolan Ryan SO 100	300.00
NR	Nolan Ryan SO 200	300.00
NR	Nolan Ryan SO 300	300.00
NR	Nolan Ryan SO 350	300.00
NR	Nolan Ryan SO 380	300.00
NR	Nolan Ryan SO 382	300.00
NR	Nolan Ryan SO 383	300.00
NR	Nolan Ryan NO HIT 1	300.00
NR	Nolan Ryan NO HIT 2	300.00
NR	Nolan Ryan NO HIT 3	300.00
NR	Nolan Ryan NO HIT 4	300.00
NR	Nolan Ryan NO HIT 5	300.00
NR	Nolan Ryan NO HIT 6	300.00
NR	Nolan Ryan NO HIT 7	300.00
CR	Cal Ripken Jr./1983	300.00
CR	Cal Ripken Jr./1985	300.00
CR	Cal Ripken Jr./1987	300.00
CR	Cal Ripken Jr./1989	300.00
CR	Cal Ripken Jr./1991	300.00
CR	Cal Ripken Jr./1993	300.00
CR	Cal Ripken Jr./1995	300.00
CR	Cal Ripken Jr./1997	300.00
CR	Cal Ripken Jr./1999	300.00
CR	Cal Ripken Jr./2001	300.00
CR	Cal Ripken Jr./1984	300.00
CR	Cal Ripken Jr./1986	300.00
CR	Cal Ripken Jr./1991	300.00
CR	Cal Ripken Jr./1994	300.00
CR	Cal Ripken Jr. HIT 1	300.00
CR	Cal Ripken Jr./1,000	300.00
CR	Cal Ripken Jr./1,500	300.00
CR	Cal Ripken Jr./1,500	300.00
CR	Cal Ripken Jr./2,000	300.00
CR	Cal Ripken Jr./2,500	300.00
CR	Cal Ripken Jr./2,900	300.00
CR	Cal Ripken Jr./3,000	300.00
CR	Cal Ripken Jr./3,184	300.00
CR	Cal Ripken Jr. HR 1	300.00
CR	Cal Ripken Jr. HR 100	300.00
CR	Cal Ripken Jr. HR 200	300.00
CR	Cal Ripken Jr. HR 300	300.00
CR	Cal Ripken Jr. HR 400	300.00
CR	Cal Ripken Jr. HR 431	300.00
CR	Cal Ripken Jr. GM 1	300.00
CR	Cal Ripken Jr./500	300.00
CR	Cal Ripken Jr./1,000	300.00
CR	Cal Ripken Jr./2,000	300.00
CR	Cal Ripken Jr./2,130	300.00
CR	Cal Ripken Jr./2,131	300.00
CR	Cal Ripken Jr./2,632	300.00
SM	Stan Musial/1941	150.00
SM	Stan Musial/1943	150.00
SM	Stan Musial/1946	150.00
SM	Stan Musial/1948	150.00
SM	Stan Musial/1950	150.00
SM	Stan Musial/1952	150.00
SM	Stan Musial/1954	150.00
SM	Stan Musial/1956	150.00
SM	Stan Musial/1958	150.00
SM	Stan Musial/1960	150.00
SM	Stan Musial/1962	150.00
SM	Stan Musial/1963	150.00
RJ	Reggie Jackson HR 1	150.00
RJ	Reggie Jackson HR 100	150.00
RJ	Reggie Jackson HR 200	150.00
RJ	Reggie Jackson HR 250	150.00
RJ	Reggie Jackson HR 300	150.00
RJ	Reggie Jackson HR 350	150.00
RJ	Reggie Jackson HR 400	150.00
RJ	Reggie Jackson HR 450	150.00
RJ	Reggie Jackson HR 500	150.00
RJ	Reggie Jackson HR 550	150.00
RJ	Reggie Jackson HR 563	150.00
RJ	Reggie Jackson WS HR 1	150.00
RJ	Reggie Jackson WS HR 2	150.00
RJ	Reggie Jackson WS HR 3	150.00
RJ	Reggie Jackson 500 HR	150.00
JB	Johnny Bench/1968	150.00
JB	Johnny Bench/1969	150.00
JB	Johnny Bench/1970	150.00
JB	Johnny Bench/1971	150.00
JB	Johnny Bench/1972	150.00
JB	Johnny Bench/1973	150.00
JB	Johnny Bench/1974	150.00
JB	Johnny Bench/1975	150.00
JB	Johnny Bench/1976	150.00
JB	Johnny Bench/1977	150.00
JB	Johnny Bench/1975	150.00
JB	Johnny Bench/1976	150.00
GB	George Brett HIT 1	150.00
GB	George Brett HIT 3	150.00
GB	George Brett HIT 5	150.00
GB	George Brett HIT 7	150.00
GB	George Brett HIT 10	150.00
GB	George Brett HIT 12	150.00
GB	George Brett HIT 15	150.00
GB	George Brett HIT 16	150.00
GB	George Brett HIT 17	150.00
GB	George Brett HIT 18	150.00
GB	George Brett/1976	150.00
GB	George Brett/1980	150.00
GB	George Brett/1990	150.00
GB	George Brett/1976	150.00
GB	George Brett/1977	150.00
GB	George Brett/1979	150.00
GB	George Brett/1981	150.00
GB	George Brett/1983	150.00
GB	George Brett/1985	150.00
GB	George Brett/1988	150.00
DM	Don Mattingly GS 1	140.00
DM	Don Mattingly GS 2	140.00
DM	Don Mattingly GS 3	140.00
DM	Don Mattingly GS 4	140.00
DM	Don Mattingly GS 5	140.00
DM	Don Mattingly GS 6	140.00
DM	Don Mattingly HR 1	140.00
DM	Don Mattingly HR 2	140.00
DM	Don Mattingly HR 3	140.00
DM	Don Mattingly HR 4	140.00
DM	Don Mattingly HR 5	140.00
DM	Don Mattingly HR 6	140.00
DM	Don Mattingly HR 7	140.00
DM	Don Mattingly HR 8	140.00
DM	Don Mattingly HR 9	140.00
DM	Don Mattingly/1985	140.00
DM	Don Mattingly/1986	140.00
DM	Don Mattingly/1987	140.00
DM	Don Mattingly/1988	140.00
DM	Don Mattingly/1989	140.00
DM	Don Mattingly/1991	140.00
DM	Don Mattingly/1992	140.00
DM	Don Mattingly/1993	140.00
DM	Don Mattingly/1994	140.00
DM	Don Mattingly/1984	140.00
DM	Don Mattingly/1985	140.00
DM	Don Mattingly/1986	140.00
DM	Don Mattingly/1987	140.00
DM	Don Mattingly/1988	140.00
DM	Don Mattingly/1989	140.00
DM	Don Mattingly HR 1	140.00
DM	Don Mattingly HR 2	140.00
DM	Don Mattingly HR 3	140.00
DM	Don Mattingly HR 4	140.00
DM	Don Mattingly HR 5	140.00
DM	Don Mattingly HR 6	140.00
DM	Don Mattingly HR 7	140.00
DM	Don Mattingly HR 8	140.00
DM	Don Mattingly HR 9	140.00
RC	Rod Carew/1967	80.00
RC	Rod Carew/1968	80.00
RC	Rod Carew/1969	80.00
RC	Rod Carew/1970	80.00
RC	Rod Carew/1971	80.00
RC	Rod Carew/1972	80.00
RC	Rod Carew/1973	80.00
RC	Rod Carew/1974	80.00
RC	Rod Carew/1975	80.00
RC	Rod Carew/1976	80.00
RC	Rod Carew/1977	80.00
RC	Rod Carew/1978	80.00
RC	Rod Carew/1979	80.00
RC	Rod Carew/1980	80.00
RC	Rod Carew/1981	80.00
RC	Rod Carew/1982	80.00
RC	Rod Carew/1983	80.00
RC	Rod Carew/1984	80.00
RC	Rod Carew SH 1	80.00
RC	Rod Carew SH 2	80.00
RC	Rod Carew SH 3	80.00
RC	Rod Carew SH 4	80.00
RC	Rod Carew SH 5	80.00
RC	Rod Carew SH 6	80.00
RC	Rod Carew SH 7	80.00
RC	Rod Carew 100	80.00
RC	Rod Carew 200	80.00
RC	Rod Carew 300	80.00
RC	Rod Carew 400	80.00
RC	Rod Carew 500	80.00
RC	Rod Carew 600	80.00
RC	Rod Carew 700	80.00
RC	Rod Carew 800	80.00
RC	Rod Carew 900	80.00
RC	Rod Carew 1969	80.00
RC	Rod Carew 1972	80.00
RC	Rod Carew 1973	80.00
RC	Rod Carew 1974	80.00
RC	Rod Carew 1975	80.00
RC	Rod Carew 1977	80.00
RC	Rod Carew 1978	80.00
YB	Yogi Berra 1947	160.00
YB	Yogi Berra 1949	160.00
YB	Yogi Berra 1950	160.00
YB	Yogi Berra 1951	160.00
YB	Yogi Berra 1952	160.00
YB	Yogi Berra 1953	160.00
YB	Yogi Berra 1956	160.00
YB	Yogi Berra 1958	160.00
YB	Yogi Berra 1961	160.00
YB	Yogi Berra 1962	160.00
YB	Yogi Berra 1948	160.00
YB	Yogi Berra 1949	160.00
YB	Yogi Berra 1950	160.00
YB	Yogi Berra 1951	160.00
YB	Yogi Berra 1952	160.00
YB	Yogi Berra 1953	160.00
YB	Yogi Berra 1954	160.00
YB	Yogi Berra 1955	160.00
YB	Yogi Berra 1956	160.00
YB	Yogi Berra 1957	160.00
YB	Yogi Berra 1958	160.00
YB	Yogi Berra 1959	160.00
YB	Yogi Berra 1960	160.00
YB	Yogi Berra 1961	160.00
YB	Yogi Berra 1962	160.00
MS	Mike Schmidt HR 1	140.00
MS	Mike Schmidt HR 2	140.00
MS	Mike Schmidt HR 3	140.00
MS	Mike Schmidt HR 4	140.00
MS	Mike Schmidt HIT 1	140.00
MS	Mike Schmidt HIT 2	140.00
MS	Mike Schmidt HIT 3	140.00
MS	Mike Schmidt HIT 4	140.00
MS	Mike Schmidt HIT 5	140.00
MS	Mike Schmidt HIT 6	140.00
MS	Mike Schmidt HIT 7	140.00
MS	Mike Schmidt HIT 8	140.00
MS	Mike Schmidt RUN 1	140.00
MS	Mike Schmidt RUN 2	140.00
MS	Mike Schmidt RUN 3	140.00
MS	Mike Schmidt RUN 4	140.00
MS	Mike Schmidt RUN 5	140.00
MS	Mike Schmidt RUN 6	140.00
CY	Carl Yastrzemski HR 1	125.00
CY	Carl Yastrzemski HR 5	125.00
CY	Carl Yastrzemski HR 10	125.00
CY	Carl Yastrzemski HR 15	125.00
CY	Carl Yastrzemski HR 20	125.00
CY	Carl Yastrzemski HR 25	125.00
CY	Carl Yastrzemski HR 30	125.00
CY	Carl Yastrzemski HR 35	125.00
CY	Carl Yastrzemski HR 40	125.00
CY	Carl Yastrzemski HR 44	125.00
CY	Carl Yastrzemski 1961	125.00
CY	Carl Yastrzemski 1964	125.00
CY	Carl Yastrzemski 1966	125.00
CY	Carl Yastrzemski 1967	125.00
CY	Carl Yastrzemski 1970	125.00
CY	Carl Yastrzemski 1972	125.00
CY	Carl Yastrzemski 1973	125.00
CY	Carl Yastrzemski 1975	125.00
CY	Carl Yastrzemski 1977	125.00
CY	Carl Yastrzemski 1980	125.00
CY	Carl Yastrzemski 1983	125.00
CY	Carl Yastrzemski 1963	125.00
CY	Carl Yastrzemski 1965	125.00
CY	Carl Yastrzemski 1966	125.00
CY	Carl Yastrzemski/1967	125.00
CY	Carl Yastrzemski/1968	125.00
CY	Carl Yastrzemski/1969	125.00
CY	Carl Yastrzemski/1970	125.00
CY	Carl Yastrzemski/1971	125.00
CY	Carl Yastrzemski/1972	125.00
CY	Carl Yastrzemski/1973	125.00
CY	Carl Yastrzemski/1974	125.00
CY	Carl Yastrzemski/1975	125.00
CY	Carl Yastrzemski/1976	125.00
CY	Carl Yastrzemski/1977	125.00
CY	Carl Yastrzemski/1978	125.00
CY	Carl Yastrzemski/1979	125.00
CY	Carl Yastrzemski/1982	125.00
CY	Carl Yastrzemski/1983	125.00
TG	Tony Gwynn/1983	120.00
TG	Tony Gwynn/1984	120.00
TG	Tony Gwynn/1985	120.00
TG	Tony Gwynn/1986	120.00
TG	Tony Gwynn/1987	120.00
TG	Tony Gwynn/1988	120.00
TG	Tony Gwynn/1989	120.00
TG	Tony Gwynn/1990	120.00
TG	Tony Gwynn/1991	120.00
TG	Tony Gwynn/1992	120.00
TG	Tony Gwynn/1993	120.00
TG	Tony Gwynn/1994	120.00
TG	Tony Gwynn/1994	120.00
TG	Tony Gwynn/1995	120.00
TG	Tony Gwynn/1996	120.00
TG	Tony Gwynn/1997	120.00
TG	Tony Gwynn/1998	120.00
TG	Tony Gwynn/1999	120.00
TG	Tony Gwynn/2000	120.00
TG	Tony Gwynn/2001	120.00
TG	Tony Gwynn/1984	120.00
TG	Tony Gwynn/1987	120.00
TG	Tony Gwynn/1988	120.00
\G	Tony Gwynn/1989	120.00
TG	Tony Gwynn/1994	120.00
TG	Tony Gwynn/1995	120.00
TG	Tony Gwynn/1996	120.00
TG	Tony Gwynn/1997	120.00
TG	Tony Gwynn/1984	120.00
TG	Tony Gwynn/1985	120.00
TG	Tony Gwynn/1986	120.00
TG	Tony Gwynn/1987	120.00
TG	Tony Gwynn/1989	120.00
TG	Tony Gwynn/1990	120.00
TG	Tony Gwynn/1991	120.00
TG	Tony Gwynn/1992	120.00
TG	Tony Gwynn/1993	120.00
TG	Tony Gwynn/1994	120.00
TG	Tony Gwynn/1995	120.00
TG	Tony Gwynn/1996	120.00
TG	Tony Gwynn/1997	120.00
TG	Tony Gwynn/1998	120.00
TG	Tony Gwynn/1999	120.00
TG	Tony Gwynn/1984	120.00
TG	Tony Gwynn/1986	120.00
TG	Tony Gwynn/1987	120.00
TG	Tony Gwynn/1989	120.00
TG	Tony Gwynn/1994	120.00
TG	Tony Gwynn/1995	120.00
TG	Tony Gwynn/1997	120.00
RS	Ryne Sandberg/1984	150.00
RS	Ryne Sandberg/1985	150.00
RS	Ryne Sandberg/1988	150.00
RS	Ryne Sandberg/1989	150.00
RS	Ryne Sandberg/1990	150.00
RS	Ryne Sandberg/1991	150.00
RS	Ryne Sandberg/1992	150.00
RS	Ryne Sandberg/1983	150.00
RS	Ryne Sandberg/1984	150.00
RS	Ryne Sandberg/1985	150.00
RS	Ryne Sandberg/1986	150.00
RS	Ryne Sandberg/1987	150.00
RS	Ryne Sandberg/1988	150.00
RS	Ryne Sandberg/1989	150.00
RS	Ryne Sandberg/1990	150.00
RS	Ryne Sandberg/1991	150.00
OS	Ozzie Smith/1980	100.00
OS	Ozzie Smith/1981	100.00
OS	Ozzie Smith/1982	100.00
OS	Ozzie Smith/1983	100.00
OS	Ozzie Smith/1984	100.00
OS	Ozzie Smith/1985	100.00
OS	Ozzie Smith/1986	100.00
OS	Ozzie Smith/1987	100.00
OS	Ozzie Smith/1988	100.00
OS	Ozzie Smith/1989	100.00
OS	Ozzie Smith/1990	100.00
OS	Ozzie Smith/1991	100.00
OS	Ozzie Smith/1992	100.00
OS	Ozzie Smith 2B 1	100.00
OS	Ozzie Smith 2B 2	100.00
OS	Ozzie Smith 2B 3	100.00
OS	Ozzie Smith 2B 4	100.00
OS	Ozzie Smith 2B 5	100.00
OS	Ozzie Smith 2B 6	100.00
OS	Ozzie Smith 2B 7	100.00
OS	Ozzie Smith 2B 8	100.00
OS	Ozzie Smith 2B 9	100.00
OS	Ozzie Smith 2B 10	100.00
OS	Ozzie Smith 2B 11	100.00
OS	Ozzie Smith 2B 12	100.00
OS	Ozzie Smith 2B 13	100.00
OS	Ozzie Smith 2B 14	100.00
OS	Ozzie Smith 2B 15	100.00
OS	Ozzie Smith 2B 16	100.00
OS	Ozzie Smith 2B 17	100.00
OS	Ozzie Smith 2B 18	100.00
OS	Ozzie Smith 2B 19	100.00
OS	Ozzie Smith 2B 20	100.00
OS	Ozzie Smith 2B 21	100.00
OS	Ozzie Smith 2B 22	100.00
OS	Ozzie Smith 2B 23	100.00
OS	Ozzie Smith 2B 24	100.00
OS	Ozzie Smith 2B 25	100.00
OS	Ozzie Smith 2B 26	100.00
OS	Ozzie Smith 2B 27	100.00
OS	Ozzie Smith 2B 28	100.00
OS	Ozzie Smith 2B 29	100.00
OS	Ozzie Smith 2B 30	100.00
OS	Ozzie Smith 2B 31	100.00
OS	Ozzie Smith 2B 32	100.00
OS	Ozzie Smith 2B 33	100.00
OS	Ozzie Smith 2B 34	100.00
OS	Ozzie Smith 2B 35	100.00
OS	Ozzie Smith 2B 36	100.00
OS	Ozzie Smith 2B 37	100.00
OS	Ozzie Smith 2B 38	100.00
OS	Ozzie Smith 2B 39	100.00
OS	Ozzie Smith 2B 40	100.00

Moments Relics Cut Signatures

Production 10 Sets
Prime: No Pricing
Production One Set

Quad Relics

Production 10 Sets
Prime: No Pricing
Production 10 Sets
Sterling Silver: No Pricing
Production One Set

Quad Relics Autographs

Production 10 Sets
Prime: No Pricing
Production 10 Sets
Sterling Silver: No Pricing
Production One Set

Season Stats Relics

Production 10 Sets
Prime: No Pricing
Production One Set
Sterling Silver: No Pricing
Production One Set

Season Stats Relics Autographs

Production 10 Sets
Prime: No Pricing
Production One Set
Sterling Silver: No Pricing
Production One Set

Six Relics

Production 10 Sets
Prime: No Pricing
Production 10 Sets
Sterling Silver: No Pricing
Production One Set

Six Relics Autographs

Production 10 Sets
Prime: No Pricing
Production 10 Sets
Sterling Silver: No Pricing
Production One Set

Triple Relics Autographs

Production 10 Sets
Prime: No Pricing
Production 10 Sets
Sterling Silver: No Pricing
Production One Set

2006 Topps Triple Threads

		NM/M
	Complete Set (120):	
	Common (1-100):	.50
	Common (101-120):	
	Production 225	
	Pack (6):	140.00
	Box (2):	270.00
1	Hideki Matsui	3.00
2	Josh Gibson	2.00
3	Roger Clemens	4.00
4	Paul Konerko	1.00
5	Brooks Robinson	1.00
6	Stan Musial	2.00
7	Dontrelle Willis	.75
8	Yogi Berra	1.50
9	John Smoltz	.75
10	Brian Roberts	.75
11	Gary Sheffield	.75
12	Wade Boggs	1.00
13	Alex Rodriguez	4.00
14	Ernie Banks	2.00
15	Ichiro Suzuki	3.00
16	Whitey Ford	1.00
17	Vladimir Guerrero	1.50
18	Tadahito Iguchi	.50
19	Robin Yount	1.50
20	Jason Schmidt	.50
21	Roberto Clemente	3.00
22	Andruw Jones	1.00
23	Don Mattingly	2.00
24	Joe Mauer	.50
25	Barry Bonds	4.00
26	Johnny Damon	1.50
27	Chris Carpenter	.75
28	Garret Anderson	.50
29	Scott Rolen	1.50
30	Tim Hudson	.75
31	Dave Winfield	.75
32	Steve Carlton	.75
33	Miguel Tejada	1.00
34	Nolan Ryan	3.00
35	Mark Buehrle	.75
36	Travis Hafner	1.00
37	Rickie Weeks	.75
38	Sammy Sosa	1.50
39	Carlos Beltran	1.00
40	Todd Helton	1.00
41	Tom Seaver	1.00
42	Ted Williams	3.00
43	Alfonso Soriano	1.00
44	Reggie Jackson	1.00
45	Pedro Martinez	1.50
46	Randy Johnson	1.50
47	Ted Williams	3.00
48	Torii Hunter	.50
49	Manny Ramirez	1.50
50	George Brett	3.00
51	Chipper Jones	1.50
52	Nomar Garciaparra	1.50
53	Richie Sexson	.75
54	David Ortiz	1.50
55	Derek Jeter	4.00
56	Mickey Mantle	8.00
57	Michael Young	.75
58	Aramis Ramirez	.75
59	Bartolo Colon	.50
60	Troy Glaus	.75
61	Carlos Delgado	.75
62	Mike Sweeney	.50
63	Jorge Cantu	.50
64	Mike Mussina	.75
65	Hank Blalock	.75
66	Frank Robinson	1.50
67	Carl Yastrzemski	2.00
68	Adam Dunn	1.00
69	Eric Chavez	.75
70	Curt Schilling	1.50
71	Jeff Francoeur	.50
72	C.C. Sabathia	.50
73	Roy Oswalt	.75
74	Carlos Lee	.50
75	Barry Zito	.75
76	Derrek Lee	1.00
77	Greg Maddux	3.00
78	Ivan Rodriguez	.75
79	Jeff Kent	.75
80	Gary Carter	.75
81	Jose Reyes	.75
82	Johan Santana	1.50
83	Magglio Ordonez	.50
84	Mark Prior	1.00
85	Johnny Bench	2.00
86	Vernon Wells	.75
87	Mark Mulder	.75
88	Cal Ripken Jr.	6.00
89	Mark Teixeira	1.00
90	Miguel Cabrera	1.50
91	Duke Snider	1.00
92	Jason Giambi	1.00
93	Albert Pujols	4.00
94	Carl Crawford	.75
95	Jim Edmonds	.75
96	Jose Contreras	.50
97	Victor Martinez	.75
98	Jeremy Bonderman	.50
99	Lance Berkman	.75
100	Rocco Baldelli	.50
101	Zachary Duke	20.00
102	Felix Hernandez	40.00
103	Dan Johnson	15.00
104	Brandon McCarthy	20.00
105	Huston Street	25.00
106	Robinson Cano	50.00
107	Jason Bay	25.00
108	Ryan Howard	100.00
109	Ervin Santana	15.00
110	Rich Harden	15.00
111	Aaron Hill	15.00
112	David Wright	75.00
113	Rich Hill **(RC)**	40.00

114 Nelson Cruz **(RC)** 20.00
115 Francisco Liriano **(RC)** 50.00
116 Hong-Chih Kuo **(RC)** 75.00
117 Ryan Garko **(RC)** 25.00
118 Craig Hansen **RC** 30.00
119 Shin-Soo Choo **(RC)** 20.00
120 Darrell Rasner **(RC)** 20.00

Sepia Tone

Sepia (1-100): 3-4X
Production 150
Sepia (101-120): 1X
Production 125

Emerald

Emerald (1-100): 4-6X
Production 99
Emerald (101-120): 1X
Production 75

Gold

Gold (1-100): 5-10X
Gold (101-120): 1-1.5X
Production 50 Sets

Sapphire

Sapphire (1-100): 8-15X
Sapphire (101-120): 1-2X
Production 25 Sets

Platinum

Platinum: No Pricing
Production One Set

Printing Plates

No Pricing
Production one set per color.

Heroes

NM/M

Inserted 1:Pack
Die-cut: 2-3X
Production 50 Sets
Autograph: No Pricing
Production Three Sets
MM1 Mickey Mantle 8.00
MM2 Mickey Mantle 8.00
MM3 Mickey Mantle 8.00
MM4 Mickey Mantle 8.00
MM5 Mickey Mantle 8.00
MM6 Mickey Mantle 8.00
MM7 Mickey Mantle 8.00
MM8 Mickey Mantle 8.00
MM9 Mickey Mantle 8.00
MM10 Mickey Mantle 8.00
TW1 Ted Williams 5.00
TW2 Ted Williams 5.00
TW3 Ted Williams 5.00
TW4 Ted Williams 5.00
TW5 Ted Williams 5.00
TW1 Ted Williams 5.00
TW2 Ted Williams 5.00
TW3 Ted Williams 5.00
TW4 Ted Williams 5.00
TW5 Ted Williams 5.00
FR1 Frank Robinson 4.00
FR2 Frank Robinson 4.00
FR3 Frank Robinson 4.00
FR4 Frank Robinson 4.00
FR5 Frank Robinson 4.00
FR6 Frank Robinson 4.00
FR7 Frank Robinson 4.00
FR8 Frank Robinson 4.00
FR9 Frank Robinson 4.00
FR10 Frank Robinson 4.00
CY1 Carl Yastrzemski 4.00
CY2 Carl Yastrzemski 4.00
CY3 Carl Yastrzemski 4.00
CY4 Carl Yastrzemski 4.00
CY5 Carl Yastrzemski 4.00
CY6 Carl Yastrzemski 4.00
CY7 Carl Yastrzemski 4.00
CY8 Carl Yastrzemski 4.00
CY9 Carl Yastrzemski 4.00
CY10 Carl Yastrzemski 4.00

Heroes Co-Signer Autographs

No Pricing
Production Three Sets

Heroes Quad Signers

Production One Card

Heroes Cut Signatures

Production One Set

Triple Signed Hides

Production One Set

Triple Relic

NM/M

Production 18 Sets
Gold: No Pricing
Production Nine Sets
Platinum: No Pricing
Production Three Sets
1 Adam Dunn 30.00
2 Adam Dunn 30.00
3 Adrian Beltre 20.00
4 Adrian Beltre 20.00
5 Al Kaline 35.00
6 Al Kaline 35.00
7 Al Kaline 35.00
8 Joe Torre 25.00
9 Albert Pujols 90.00
10 Alex Rodriguez 100.00
11 Ichiro Suzuki 125.00
12 Alex Rodriguez 100.00
13 Alex Rodriguez 100.00
14 Alex Rodriguez 100.00
15 Alex Rodriguez 100.00
16 Alex Rodriguez 100.00
17 Alex Rodriguez 100.00
18 Alfonso Soriano 25.00
19 Dwight Gooden 25.00
20 Barry Bonds 100.00
21 Alfonso Soriano 25.00
22 Ozzie Smith 50.00
23 Andruw Jones 50.00
24 Andruw Jones 50.00
25 Andy Pettitte 30.00
26 Andy Pettitte 30.00
27 Aramis Ramirez 25.00
28 B.J. Upton 25.00
29 Barry Bonds 100.00
30 Vladimir Guerrero 35.00
31 Barry Bonds 100.00
32 Barry Bonds 100.00
33 Barry Bonds 100.00
34 Barry Bonds 100.00
35 Barry Bonds 100.00
36 Barry Bonds 100.00
37 Eric Chavez 25.00
38 Barry Zito 25.00
39 Ben Sheets 25.00
40 Bill Mazeroski 40.00
41 Bob Feller 30.00
42 Bobby Abreu 25.00
43 Bobby Cox 25.00
44 Bobby Doerr 20.00
45 Brad Lidge 20.00
46 Brian Giles 20.00
47 Brian Roberts 25.00
48 Michael Young 20.00
49 Cal Ripken Jr. 100.00
50 Cal Ripken Jr. 100.00
51 Carl Yastrzemski 50.00
52 Carl Yastrzemski 50.00
53 Carl Yastrzemski 50.00
54 Carlos Beltran 30.00
55 Carlos Beltran 30.00
56 Carlos Delgado 30.00
57 Carlton Fisk 40.00
58 Carlton Fisk 40.00
59 Carlton Fisk 40.00
60 Chipper Jones 50.00
61 Chipper Jones 50.00
62 Chipper Jones 50.00
63 Chris Carpenter 25.00
64 Craig Biggio 30.00
65 Craig Biggio 30.00
66 Curt Schilling 35.00
67 Curt Schilling 35.00
68 Curt Schilling 35.00
69 Curt Schilling 35.00
70 Sammy Sosa 50.00
71 Darryl Strawberry 25.00
72 Darryl Strawberry 25.00
73 Alex Rodriguez 100.00
74 Dave Winfield 30.00
75 Dave Winfield 30.00
76 Jorge Posada 30.00
77 David Ortiz 35.00
78 David Ortiz 35.00
79 Derrek Lee 35.00
80 Don Mattingly 40.00
81 Don Mattingly 40.00
82 Don Mattingly 40.00
83 Dontrelle Willis 25.00
84 Dontrelle Willis 25.00
85 Duke Snider 35.00
86 Dwight Gooden 25.00
87 Cal Ripken Jr. 100.00
88 David Ortiz 35.00
89 Ernie Banks 40.00
90 Ernie Banks 40.00
91 Ernie Banks 40.00
92 Frank Robinson 35.00
93 Frank Robinson 35.00
94 Frankie Frisch 30.00
95 Gary Carter 25.00
96 Mickey Mantle 200.00
97 Gary Sheffield 35.00
98 George Brett 50.00
99 George Brett 50.00
100 Greg Maddux 50.00
101 Hank Blalock 25.00
102 Hank Greenberg 65.00
103 Hank Greenberg 65.00
104 Hideki Matsui 80.00
105 Hideki Matsui 80.00
106 Hideki Matsui 80.00
107 Ichiro Suzuki 125.00
108 Johnny Bench 40.00
109 Ichiro Suzuki 125.00
110 Ivan Rodriguez 30.00
111 Ivan Rodriguez 30.00
112 Ivan Rodriguez 30.00
113 Ivan Rodriguez 30.00
114 Jake Peavy 20.00
115 Javy Lopez 20.00
116 Jeff Bagwell 35.00
117 Jim Edmonds 25.00
118 Jim Thome 30.00
119 Joe Mauer 20.00
120 Alex Rodriguez 100.00
121 Johan Santana 30.00
122 Johan Santana 30.00
123 Sean Burroughs 15.00
124 Johnny Bench 40.00
125 Johnny Damon 30.00
126 Jon Garland 20.00
127 Jon Garland 20.00
128 Jorge Posada 30.00
129 Manny Ramirez 30.00
130 Jose Canseco 25.00
131 Jose Reyes 25.00
132 Juan Marichal 25.00
133 Kerry Wood 25.00
134 Kerry Wood 25.00
135 Albert Pujols 90.00
136 Lance Berkman 30.00
137 Lloyd Waner 75.00
138 Lloyd Waner 75.00
139 Lou Brock 25.00
140 Miguel Tejada 25.00
141 Manny Ramirez 30.00
142 Mariano Rivera 35.00
143 Mariano Rivera 35.00
144 Mark Buehrle 30.00
145 Mark Mulder 25.00
146 Mark Mulder 25.00
147 Mark Prior 30.00
148 Mark Teixeira 30.00
149 Michael Young 20.00
150 Dale Murphy 35.00
151 Barry Zito 25.00
152 Mickey Mantle 200.00
153 Mickey Mantle 200.00
154 Mickey Mantle 200.00
155 Mickey Mantle 200.00
156 Miguel Cabrera 30.00
157 Miguel Tejada 25.00
158 Vladimir Guerrero 35.00
159 Miguel Tejada 25.00
160 Miguel Tejada 25.00
161 Mike Mussina 25.00
162 Mike Mussina 25.00
163 Mike Piazza 60.00
164 Gary Sheffield 35.00
165 Mike Piazza 60.00
166 Mike Schmidt 40.00
167 Mike Schmidt 40.00
168 Mike Schmidt 40.00
169 Monte Irvin 30.00
170 Morgan Ensberg 25.00
171 Lance Berkman 30.00
172 Nolan Ryan 65.00
173 Nolan Ryan 65.00
174 Nolan Ryan 65.00
175 Albert Pujols 90.00
176 Dave Winfield 30.00
177 Ozzie Smith 40.00
178 Pat Burrell 30.00
179 Paul Konerko 20.00
180 Paul Konerko 20.00
181 Paul Konerko 20.00
182 Paul Molitor 30.00
183 Pedro Martinez 35.00
184 Pedro Martinez 35.00
185 Pedro Martinez 35.00
186 Randy Johnson 35.00
187 Randy Johnson 35.00
188 Reggie Jackson 40.00
189 Reggie Jackson 40.00
190 Rickey Henderson 40.00
191 Rickey Henderson 40.00
192 Rickey Henderson 40.00
193 Rickey Henderson 40.00
194 Rickie Weeks 25.00
195 Rickie Weeks 25.00
196 Roberto Clemente 125.00
197 Roberto Clemente 125.00
198 Robin Yount 40.00
199 Rod Carew 30.00
200 Roger Clemens 60.00
201 Roger Clemens 60.00
202 Roger Clemens 60.00
203 Roger Clemens 60.00
204 Roger Clemens 60.00
205 Roger Clemens 60.00
206 Roy Halladay 25.00
207 Roy Oswalt 25.00
208 Roy Oswalt 25.00
209 Ryne Sandberg 60.00
210 Ryne Sandberg 60.00
211 Nolan Ryan 65.00
212 Sammy Sosa 60.00
213 Sammy Sosa 60.00
214 Sammy Sosa 60.00
215 Sammy Sosa 60.00
216 Scott Rolen 40.00
217 Scott Rolen 40.00
218 Orlando Cepeda 25.00
219 Stan Musial 50.00
220 Steve Carlton 25.00
221 Steve Carlton 25.00
222 Steve Carlton 25.00
223 Steve Garvey 20.00
224 Tadahito Iguchi 30.00
225 Ted Williams 80.00
226 Ted Williams 80.00
227 Tim Hudson 20.00
228 Tim Hudson 20.00
229 Todd Helton 25.00
230 Todd Helton 25.00
231 Todd Helton 25.00
232 Tom Seaver 40.00
233 Tony Gwynn 40.00
234 Tony Gwynn 40.00
235 Tony Gwynn 40.00
236 Torii Hunter 20.00
237 Torii Hunter 20.00
238 Travis Hafner 35.00
239 Mike Piazza 60.00
240 Albert Pujols 90.00
241 Wade Boggs 30.00
242 Willie Stargell 40.00
243 Willie Stargell 40.00
244 Willie Stargell 40.00
245 Willy Taveras 25.00

Triple Relic Combo

NM/M

Production 18 Sets
Gold: No Pricing
Production Nine Sets
Platinum: No Pricing
Production Three Sets
1 Albert Pujols, Alex Rodriguez, Barry Bonds 100.00
2 Alex Rodriguez, Barry Bonds, Albert Pujols 100.00
3 Albert Pujols, Alex Rodriguez, Manny Ramirez 100.00
4 Albert Pujols, Barry Bonds, Ted Williams 125.00
5 Alex Rodriguez, Barry Bonds, Chipper Jones 75.00
6 Alex Rodriguez, Roberto Clemente, Barry Bonds 125.00
7 Alex Rodriguez, Vladimir Guerrero, Ichiro Suzuki 80.00
8 Alex Rodriguez, Stan Musial, Ted Williams 120.00
9 Andruw Jones, Alfonso Soriano, Vladimir Guerrero 40.00
10 Barry Bonds, Ichiro Suzuki, Roberto Clemente 150.00
11 Barry Bonds, Lloyd Waner, Roberto Clemente 160.00
12 Barry Bonds, Manny Ramirez, Andruw Jones 60.00
13 Barry Bonds, Manny Ramirez, Ted Williams 100.00
14 Barry Bonds, Roberto Clemente, Willie Stargell 125.00
15 Carl Yastrzemski, Paul Molitor, Manny Ramirez 40.00
16 Don Mattingly, Paul Molitor, Manny Ramirez 40.00
17 Don Mattingly, Rod Carew, Tony Gwynn 70.00
18 Gary Sheffield, Vladimir Guerrero, Ivan Rodriguez 30.00
19 Hank Greenberg, Stan Musial, Ted Williams 125.00
20 Ichiro Suzuki, Chipper Jones, Barry Bonds 80.00
21 Ichiro Suzuki, Ted Williams, Roberto Clemente 150.00
22 Joe Morgan, Paul Molitor, Gary Carter 35.00
23 Manny Ramirez, Vladimir Guerrero, Roberto Clemente 90.00
24 Mike Piazza, Paul Molitor, Rickey Henderson 40.00
26 Paul Molitor, Andruw Jones, Robin Yount 40.00
27 Paul Molitor, Andruw Jones, Alfonso Soriano 35.00
28 Reggie Jackson, Vladimir Guerrero, Andruw Jones 35.00
29 Rickey Henderson, Wade Boggs, Tony Gwynn 60.00
31 Stan Musial, Ted Williams, Tony Gwynn 70.00
32 Ted Williams, Ichiro Suzuki, Wade Boggs 140.00
33 Albert Pujols, Ted Williams, Mickey Mantle 250.00
34 Andruw Jones, George Brett, Chipper Jones 60.00
35 Greg Maddux, Nolan Ryan, Steve Carlton 60.00
36 Greg Maddux, Steve Carlton, Tom Seaver 50.00
37 Nolan Ryan, Steve Carlton, Tom Seaver 50.00
38 Nolan Ryan, Tom Seaver, Roger Clemens 60.00
39 Roger Clemens, Nolan Ryan, Tom Seaver 60.00
40 Barry Bonds, Rickey Henderson, Tony Gwynn 60.00
41 Cal Ripken Jr., Carl Yastrzemski, Paul Molitor 60.00
42 Cal Ripken Jr., George Brett, Roberto Clemente 100.00
43 Cal Ripken Jr., George Brett, Tony Gwynn 85.00
44 Cal Ripken Jr., Paul Molitor, Rickey Henderson 85.00
45 Cal Ripken Jr., Paul Molitor, Tony Gwynn 80.00
46 George Brett, Cal Ripken Jr., Rod Carew 80.00
47 George Brett, Cal Ripken Jr., Rod Carew 80.00
48 George Brett, Robin Yount, Rod Carew 50.00
49 George Brett, Tony Gwynn, Wade Boggs 60.00
50 George Brett, Tony Gwynn, Wade Boggs 60.00
51 Paul Molitor, Robin Yount, Wade Boggs 40.00
52 Paul Waner, Rickey Henderson, Stan Musial 60.00
53 Paul Waner, Rickey Henderson, Wade Boggs 50.00
54 Paul Waner, Rod Carew, Wade Boggs 50.00
55 Rickey Henderson, Stan Musial, Wade Boggs 50.00
56 Roberto Clemente, Robin Yount, Rod Carew 80.00
57 Roberto Clemente, Robin Yount, Rod Carew 90.00
58 Roberto Clemente, Robin Yount, Tony Gwynn 90.00
59 Rod Carew, Stan Musial, Tony Gwynn 50.00
60 Stan Musial, Tony Gwynn, Wade Boggs 50.00
61 Wade Boggs 30.00
62 Barry Bonds, Mickey Mantle, Frank Robinson 140.00
63 Barry Bonds, Ted Williams, Mickey Mantle 160.00
64 Barry Bonds, Frank Robinson, Reggie Jackson 70.00
65 Barry Bonds, Frank Robinson, Harmon Killebrew 60.00
66 Frank Robinson, Barry Bonds, Mike Schmidt 60.00
67 Frank Robinson, Harmon Killebrew, Mickey Mantle 150.00
68 Josh Gibson, Barry Bonds, Mickey Mantle 200.00
69 Josh Gibson, Barry Bonds, Ted Williams 150.00
70 Mike Schmidt, Harmon Killebrew, Reggie Jackson 75.00
71 Dave Winfield, Vladimir Guerrero, Reggie Jackson 50.00
72 Rod Carew, Reggie Jackson, Vladimir Guerrero 30.00
73 Andruw Jones, Chipper Jones, Jeff Francoeur 30.00
74 Bobby Cox, Andruw Jones, Chipper Jones 50.00
75 Chipper Jones, Greg Maddux, Andruw Jones 50.00
76 Brian Roberts, Sammy Sosa, Miguel Tejada 40.00
77 Brooks Robinson, Cal Ripken Jr., Jim Palmer 65.00
78 Brooks Robinson, Jim Palmer, Frank Robinson 40.00
79 Cal Ripken Jr., Brooks Robinson, Miguel Tejada 50.00
80 Cal Ripken Jr., Frank Robinson, Sammy Sosa 80.00
81 Frank Robinson, Reggie Jackson, Brooks Robinson 75.00
82 Jim Palmer, Frank Robinson, Reggie Jackson 60.00
83 Jim Palmer, Reggie Jackson, Sammy Sosa 50.00
84 Jim Palmer, Sammy Sosa, Miguel Tejada 40.00
85 Miguel Tejada, Brian Roberts, Cal Ripken Jr. 80.00
86 Reggie Jackson, Frank Robinson, Sammy Sosa 50.00
87 Bobby Doerr, Carl Yastrzemski, Ted Williams 80.00
88 Carl Yastrzemski, David Ortiz, Manny Ramirez 60.00
89 Carl Yastrzemski, Ted Williams, David Ortiz 80.00
90 Carl Yastrzemski, Ted Williams, Manny Ramirez 80.00
91 Curt Schilling, David Ortiz, Johnny Damon 40.00
92 Curt Schilling, David Ortiz, Manny Ramirez 40.00
93 Curt Schilling, Manny Ramirez, Johnny Damon 40.00
94 David Ortiz, Johnny Damon, Manny Ramirez 50.00
95 Johnny Damon, Manny Ramirez, Ted Williams 60.00
96 Manny Ramirez, David Ortiz, Pedro Martinez 40.00
97 Manny Ramirez, Ted Williams, David Ortiz 60.00
98 Pedro Martinez, Roger Clemens, Manny Ramirez 50.00
99 Greg Maddux, Randy Johnson, Roger Clemens 50.00
100 Johan Santana, Pedro Martinez, Roger Clemens 60.00
101 Roger Clemens 50.00
102 Roger Clemens 50.00
103 Randy Johnson, Curt Schilling, Roger Clemens 75.00
104 Derrek Lee, Aramis Ramirez, Mark Prior 35.00
105 Derrek Lee, Ryne Sandberg, Sammy Sosa 65.00
106 Ernie Banks, Ryne Sandberg, Derrek Lee 60.00
107 Ernie Banks, Ryne Sandberg, Sammy Sosa 60.00
108 Greg Maddux, Ryne Sandberg, Ernie Banks 75.00
109 Mark Prior, Kerry Wood, Greg Maddux 60.00
110 Sammy Sosa, Ernie Banks, Derrek Lee 60.00
111 Frank Robinson, Joe Morgan, Johnny Bench 40.00
112 Johnny Bench, Frank Robinson, Tom Seaver 50.00
113 Johnny Bench, Tom Seaver, Joe Morgan 50.00
114 Jermaine Dye, Scott Podsednik, Tadahito Iguchi 40.00
115 Jim Thome, Paul Konerko, Tadahito Iguchi 60.00
116 Jon Garland, Scott Podsednik, Mark Buehrle 25.00
117 Jon Garland, Tadahito Iguchi, Mark Buehrle 30.00
118 Paul Konerko, Sammy Sosa, Carlton Fisk 40.00
119 Paul Konerko, Tadahito Iguchi, Jermaine Dye 40.00
120 Al Kaline, Ivan Rodriguez, Hank Greenberg 60.00
121 Greg Maddux, Johan Santana, Roger Clemens 60.00
122 Juan Marichal, Nolan Ryan, Roger Clemens 80.00
123 Nolan Ryan, Randy Johnson, Whitey Ford 60.00
124 Cal Ripken Jr., Ozzie Smith, Mike Schmidt 60.00
125 Mike Schmidt, Cal Ripken Jr., Ozzie Smith 60.00
126 Al Kaline, Frank Robinson, Paul Waner 50.00

127 Al Kaline, Harmon Killebrew, Frank Robinson 75.00
128 Al Kaline, Mickey Mantle, Reggie Jackson 125.00
129 Al Kaline, Reggie Jackson, Stan Musial 60.00
130 Al Kaline, Robin Yount, Paul Waner 40.00
131 Barry Bonds, Chipper Jones, Manny Ramirez 65.00
132 Bob Feller, Juan Marichal, Nolan Ryan 60.00
133 Bob Feller, Whitey Ford, Steve Carlton 40.00
134 Bobby Doerr, Ted Williams, Wade Boggs 80.00
135 Brooks Robinson, Ozzie Smith, Ryne Sandberg 50.00
136 Carl Yastrzemski, George Brett, Paul Molitor 50.00
137 Carlton Fisk, Carl Yastrzemski, Wade Boggs 75.00
138 Joe Morgan, George Brett, Mike Schmidt 50.00
139 Yogi Berra, Carlton Fisk, Gary Carter 50.00
140 Andy Pettitte, Nolan Ryan, Brad Lidge 50.00
141 Andy Pettitte, Nolan Ryan, Randy Johnson 50.00
142 Andy Pettitte, Nolan Ryan, Roger Clemens 60.00
143 Andy Pettitte, Randy Johnson, Brad Lidge 30.00
144 Andy Pettitte, Roy Oswalt, Roger Clemens 50.00
145 Brad Lidge, Roy Oswalt, Andy Pettitte 35.00
146 Craig Biggio, Jeff Bagwell, Lance Berkman 40.00
147 Nolan Ryan, Roger Clemens, Randy Johnson 80.00
148 Roger Clemens, Brad Lidge, Andy Pettitte 50.00
149 Roger Clemens, Randy Johnson, Andy Pettitte 50.00
150 Ichiro Suzuki, Hideki Matsui 160.00
151 Ichiro Suzuki, Hideki Matsui, Kazuo Matsui 140.00
152 Ichiro Suzuki, Tadahito Iguchi, Hideki Matsui 150.00
153 Eric Gagne, Mike Piazza, Duke Snider 100.00
154 Gary Sheffield, Rickie Weeks, Paul Molitor 40.00
155 Paul Molitor, Gary Sheffield, Robin Yount 35.00
156 Robin Yount, Paul Molitor, Rickie Weeks 40.00
157 Harmon Killebrew, Rod Carew, Johan Santana 40.00
158 Harmon Killebrew, Torii Hunter, Rod Carew 40.00
159 Johan Santana, Joe Mauer, Torii Hunter 35.00
160 Paul Molitor, Rod Carew, Harmon Killebrew 40.00
161 Albert Pujols, Ichiro Suzuki, Barry Bonds 180.00
162 Alex Rodriguez, Barry Bonds, George Brett 60.00
163 Alex Rodriguez, Barry Bonds, Mickey Mantle 150.00
164 Alex Rodriguez, Ichiro Suzuki, Mickey Mantle 180.00
165 Alex Rodriguez, Reggie Jackson, Yogi Berra 50.00
166 Alex Rodriguez, Ted Williams, Mickey Mantle 200.00
167 Alex Rodriguez, Yogi Berra, Don Mattingly 60.00
168 Alex Rodriguez, Barry Bonds, Don Mattingly 70.00
169 Alex Rodriguez, Cal Ripken Jr., Miguel Tejada 60.00
170 Barry Bonds, Harmon Killebrew, Reggie Jackson 70.00
171 Barry Bonds, Roberto Clemente, Willie Stargell 120.00
172 Barry Bonds, Alex Rodriguez, Albert Pujols 100.00
173 Barry Bonds, Cal Ripken Jr., Mickey Mantle 200.00
174 Barry Bonds, Josh Gibson, Albert Pujols 120.00
175 Barry Bonds, Vladimir Guerrero, Ichiro Suzuki 75.00
176 Brooks Robinson, George Brett, Mike Schmidt 60.00
177 Cal Ripken Jr., Barry Bonds, Ichiro Suzuki 120.00
178 Cal Ripken Jr., Don Mattingly, George Brett 90.00
179 Cal Ripken Jr., George Brett, Don Mattingly 90.00
180 Cal Ripken Jr., Mike Schmidt, Don Mattingly 100.00
181 Cal Ripken Jr., Roger Clemens, Don Mattingly 125.00
182 Chipper Jones, Dale Murphy, Don Mattingly 75.00
183 Don Mattingly, Mickey Mantle, Reggie Jackson 150.00
184 George Brett, Johnny Bench, Mike Schmidt 60.00
185 George Brett, Johnny Bench, Mike Schmidt 60.00
186 Ichiro Suzuki, Barry Bonds, Mickey Mantle 180.00
187 Ivan Rodriguez, Vladimir Guerrero, Miguel Tejada 35.00
188 Ivan Rodriguez, Yogi Berra, Johnny Bench 50.00
189 Ivan Rodriguez, Yogi Berra, Johnny Bench 50.00
190 Johnny Bench, Mike Piazza, Yogi Berra 50.00
191 Mickey Mantle, Barry Bonds, Ted Williams 200.00
192 Mickey Mantle, Ichiro Suzuki, Roberto Clemente 200.00
193 Mickey Mantle, Roberto Clemente, Stan Musial 200.00
194 Mickey Mantle, Ted Williams, Roberto Clemente 220.00
195 Mickey Mantle, Vladimir Guerrero, Roberto Clemente 200.00
196 Miguel Tejada, Reggie Jackson, Rickey Henderson 40.00
197 Reggie Jackson, Alex Rodriguez, Yogi Berra 50.00
198 Roberto Clemente, Mickey Mantle, Barry Bonds 180.00
199 Buck O'Neil, Josh Gibson, Monte Irvin 100.00
200 Carlos Beltran, Carlos Delgado, David Wright 60.00
201 Carlos Beltran, Carlos Delgado, Jose Reyes 50.00
202 Carlos Beltran, David Wright, Pedro Martinez 60.00
203 Darryl Strawberry, Dwight Gooden, Gary Carter 30.00
204 David Wright, Carlos Beltran, Mike Piazza 60.00
205 David Wright, Mike Piazza, Jose Reyes 75.00
206 Jose Reyes, Kazuo Matsui, David Wright 40.00
207 Alex Rodriguez, Don Mattingly, Mickey Mantle 180.00
208 Alex Rodriguez, Hideki Matsui, Joe Torre 80.00
209 Alex Rodriguez, Hideki Matsui, Mickey Mantle 200.00
210 Don Mattingly, Mickey Mantle, Roger Clemens 200.00
211 Hideki Matsui, Gary Sheffield, Alex Rodriguez 50.00
212 Hideki Matsui, Gary Sheffield, Jorge Posada 50.00
213 Jorge Posada, Roger Clemens, Mike Mussina 75.00
214 Mickey Mantle, Whitey Ford, Yogi Berra 200.00
215 Mike Mussina, Whitey Ford, Roger Clemens 65.00
216 Roger Clemens, Mickey Mantle, Alex Rodriguez 200.00
217 Wade Boggs, Joe Torre, Alfonso Soriano 30.00
218 Barry Zito, Mark Mulder, Tim Hudson 25.00
219 Jose Canseco, Reggie Jackson, Rickey Henderson 40.00
220 Mark Mulder, Miguel Tejada, Tim Hudson 40.00
221 Bobby Abreu, Pat Burrell, Jim Thome 40.00
222 Curt Schilling, Mike Schmidt, Steve Carlton 50.00
223 Mike Schmidt, Pat Burrell, Scott Rolen 50.00
224 Barry Bonds, Roberto Clemente, Josh Gibson 150.00
225 Paul Waner, Roberto Clemente, Lloyd Waner 150.00
226 Willie Stargell, Bill Mazeroski, Roberto Clemente 140.00
227 Albert Pujols, Carlos Beltran, Dontrelle Willis 60.00
228 Albert Pujols, Dontrelle Willis, Ichiro Suzuki 90.00
229 Cal Ripken Jr., Albert Pujols, Orlando Cepeda 90.00
230 Cal Ripken Jr., Carlton Fisk, Tom Seaver 80.00
231 Cal Ripken Jr., Rod Carew, Carlton Fisk 75.00
232 Cal Ripken Jr., Rod Carew, Carlton Fisk 75.00
233 Jeff Bagwell, Albert Pujols, Mike Piazza 100.00
234 Mike Piazza, Jeff Bagwell, Scott Rolen 80.00
235 Rickey Henderson, Steve Garvey, Tony Gwynn 50.00
236 Adrian Beltre, Ichiro Suzuki, Alex Rodriguez 80.00
237 Ichiro Suzuki, Alex Rodriguez, Randy Johnson 100.00
238 Barry Bonds, Juan Marichal, Orlando Cepeda 75.00
239 Juan Marichal, Monte Irvin, Orlando Cepeda 40.00
240 Orlando Cepeda, Monte Irvin, Barry Bonds 60.00
241 Albert Pujols, Frankie Frisch, Stan Musial 120.00
242 Albert Pujols, Mark Mulder, Scott Rolen 65.00
243 Scott Rolen, Jim Edmonds, Albert Pujols 75.00
244 Stan Musial, Ozzie Smith, Albert Pujols 120.00
245 Alex Rodriguez, Ivan Rodriguez, Alfonso Soriano 50.00
246 Alex Rodriguez, Mark Teixeira, Alfonso Soriano 50.00
247 Alex Rodriguez, Nolan Ryan, Alfonso Soriano 60.00
248 Alfonso Soriano, Hank Blalock, Mark Teixeira 30.00
249 Alfonso Soriano, Hank Blalock, Michael Young 25.00
250 Mark Teixeira, Alfonso Soriano, Michael Young 30.00

Triple Relic Autograph

NM/M

Production 18 Sets
Gold: No Pricing
Production Nine Sets
Platinum: No Pricing
Production Three Sets

1 Albert Pujols 475.00
2 Albert Pujols 475.00
3 Albert Pujols 475.00
4 Alex Rodriguez 275.00
5 Alex Rodriguez 275.00
6 Alex Rodriguez 275.00
7 Derrek Lee 60.00
8 Barry Bonds 400.00
9 Ben Sheets 400.00
10 Ben Sheets 400.00
11 Brad Lidge 35.00
12 Brad Lidge 35.00
13 Cal Ripken Jr. 220.00
14 Cal Ripken Jr. 220.00
15 Cal Ripken Jr. 220.00
16 Carl Yastrzemski 100.00
17 Carl Yastrzemski 100.00
18 Carl Yastrzemski 100.00
19 Chase Utley 65.00
20 Chase Utley 65.00
21 Chien-Ming Wang 750.00
22 Chien-Ming Wang 400.00
23 Chien-Ming Wang 400.00
24 Chien-Ming Wang 400.00
25 Chris Carpenter 100.00
26 Chris Carpenter 100.00
27 Clint Barmes 25.00
28 Clint Barmes 25.00
29 Conor Jackson 30.00
30 Conor Jackson 30.00
31 David Ortiz 125.00
32 Don Mattingly 140.00
33 Don Mattingly 140.00
34 Don Mattingly 140.00
35 Duke Snider 75.00
36 Duke Snider 75.00
37 Ernie Banks 120.00
38 Frank Robinson 65.00
39 Frank Robinson 65.00
40 Frank Robinson 65.00
41 Garrett Atkins 35.00
42 Garrett Atkins 35.00
43 Derrek Lee 60.00
44 Derrek Lee 60.00
45 Derrek Lee 60.00
46 J.J. Hardy 40.00
47 J.J. Hardy 40.00
48 Jake Peavy 40.00
49 Jake Peavy 40.00
50 Jeff Francis 30.00
51 Jeff Francis 30.00
52 Joe Mauer 50.00
53 Joe Mauer 50.00
54 Joey Devine 25.00
55 Joey Devine 25.00
56 Johan Santana 60.00
57 Johan Santana 60.00
58 Johan Santana 60.00
59 Johan Santana 60.00
60 Johnny Bench 80.00
61 Johnny Bench 80.00
62 Johnny Bench 80.00
63 Johnny Damon 80.00
64 Jonny Gomes 40.00
65 Jonny Gomes 40.00
66 Jose Reyes 50.00
67 Jose Reyes 50.00
68 Justin Morneau 40.00
69 Justin Morneau 40.00
70 Lou Brock 60.00
71 Lou Brock 60.00
72 Lou Brock 60.00
73 Lou Brock 60.00
74 Manny Ramirez 100.00
75 Mariano Rivera 150.00
76 Mark Prior 50.00
77 Miguel Cabrera 70.00
78 Miguel Cabrera 70.00
79 Miguel Cabrera 70.00
80 Miguel Cabrera 70.00
81 Mike Schmidt 100.00
82 Mike Schmidt 100.00
83 Mike Schmidt 100.00
84 Morgan Ensberg 35.00
85 Morgan Ensberg 35.00
86 Nick Swisher 60.00
87 Nick Swisher 60.00
88 Nolan Ryan 150.00
89 Nolan Ryan 150.00
90 Nolan Ryan 150.00
91 Zachary Duke 30.00
92 Zachary Duke 30.00
93 Ozzie Smith 80.00
94 Ozzie Smith 80.00
95 Ozzie Smith 80.00
96 Pedro Martinez 125.00
97 Robin Yount 75.00
98 Robin Yount 75.00
99 Robin Yount 75.00
100 Rod Carew 50.00
101 Rod Carew 50.00
102 Rod Carew 50.00
103 Rod Carew 50.00
104 Roger Clemens 180.00
105 Roger Clemens 180.00
106 Ryan Langerhans 40.00
107 Ryan Langerhans 40.00
108 Ryne Sandberg 100.00
109 Ryne Sandberg 100.00
110 Ryne Sandberg 100.00
111 Scott Kazmir 50.00
112 Scott Kazmir 50.00
113 Stan Musial 100.00
114 Stan Musial 100.00
115 Stan Musial 100.00
116 Steve Carlton 50.00
117 Steve Carlton 50.00
118 Steve Carlton 50.00
119 Steve Garvey 50.00
120 Steve Garvey 50.00
121 Tony Gwynn 100.00
122 Tony Gwynn 100.00
123 Tony Gwynn 100.00
124 Travis Hafner 50.00
125 Travis Hafner 50.00
126 Victor Martinez 50.00
127 Victor Martinez 50.00
128 Wade Boggs 60.00
129 Wade Boggs 60.00
130 Wade Boggs 60.00

Triple Relic Combos Autograph

NM/M

Production 18 Sets
Gold: No Pricing
Production Nine Sets
Platinum: No Pricing
Production Three Sets

1 Albert Pujols, Barry Bonds, Alex Rodriguez 1,000
2 Felix Hernandez, Alex Rodriguez, Shin-Soo Choo 150.00
3 Nolan Ryan, Roger Clemens, Felix Hernandez 300.00
4 Johnny Damon, Alex Rodriguez, Robinson Cano 300.00
5 Manny Ramirez, Carl Yastrzemski, David Ortiz 250.00
6 Michael Young, Cal Ripken Jr., Ozzie Smith 300.00
7 Brian Roberts, Cal Ripken Jr., Frank Robinson 250.00
8 Stan Musial, Ozzie Smith, Lou Brock 180.00
9 Ozzie Smith, Stan Musial, Lou Brock 180.00
10 Tony Gwynn, Stan Musial, Rod Carew 180.00
11 Brooks Robinson, Cal Ripken Jr., Brian Roberts 200.00
12 Rod Carew, Robin Yount, Paul Molitor 120.00
13 Derrek Lee, Ryne Sandberg, Mark Prior 180.00
14 Chien-Ming Wang, Steve Carlton, Dontrelle Willis 275.00
15 Brad Lidge, Mariano Rivera, Huston Street 180.00
16 Morgan Ensberg, Wade Boggs, David Wright 120.00
17 Ben Sheets, Steve Carlton, Felix Hernandez 80.00
18 Victor Martinez, Johnny Bench, Joe Mauer 125.00
19 David Wright, Mike Schmidt, Aaron Hill 160.00
20 Chase Utley, Mike Schmidt, Ryan Howard 200.00
21 Felix Hernandez, Steve Carlton, Brandon McCarthy 75.00
22 David Wright, Miguel Cabrera, Jason Bay 140.00
23 Robinson Cano, Don Mattingly, Chien-Ming Wang 350.00
24 Justin Morneau, Don Mattingly, Travis Hafner 100.00
25 Steve Garvey, Don Mattingly, Dan Johnson 100.00
26 Travis Hafner, Miguel Cabrera, Jason Bay 100.00
27 Ben Sheets, Johan Santana, Jake Peavy 75.00
28 Ervin Santana, Johan Santana, Ben Sheets 70.00
29 Chris Carpenter, Johan Santana, Rich Harden 120.00
30 Zachary Duke, Johan Santana, Brandon McCarthy 75.00

2006 Topps Turkey Red

NM/M

Complete Set (316-630):
Common Player: .25
Common SP: 4.00
Inserted 1:4
Pack (8): 4.50
Box (24): 90.00

316 Alex Rodriguez 3.00
316 Alex Rodriguez/Rangers/SP 8.00
316 Alex Rodriguez/M's/SP 8.00
317 Jeff Francoeur/SP 4.00
318 Shawn Green .25
319 Daniel Cabrera .25
320 Craig Biggio .50
321 Jeremy Bonderman .40
322 Mark Kotsay .25
323 Cliff Floyd .25
324 Jimmy Rollins .40
325 Magglio Ordonez .25
325 Magglio Ordonez/W. Sox/SP 4.00
326 C.C. Sabathia .25
327 Oliver Perez .25
328 Orlando Hudson .25
329 Chris Ray .25
330 Manny Ramirez 1.00
331 Paul Konerko .50
332 Joe Mauer/SP 5.00
333 Jorge Posada .50
334 Mark Ellis .25
335 A.J. Burnett .25
336 Mike Sweeney .25
337 Shannon Stewart .25
338 Jake Peavy/SP 4.00
339 Carlos Delgado/Mets/SP 5.00
339 Carlos Delgado/B. Jays/SP 5.00
340 Brian Roberts .25
341 Dontrelle Willis .50
342 Aaron Rowand .25
343 Richie Sexson .50
343 Richie Sexson/Brewers/SP 4.00
344 Chris Carpenter .75
345 Carlos Zambrano .40
346 Nomar Garciaparra 1.00
347 Carlos Lee .40
348 Preston Wilson .25
348 Preston Wilson/Marlins/SP 4.00
349 Mariano Rivera .50
350 Ichiro Suzuki/SP 8.00
351 Mike Piazza 1.00
351 Mike Piazza/Mets/SP 4.00
352 Jason Schmidt .25
353 Jeff Weaver .25
354 Rocco Baldelli .25
355 Adam Dunn .75
356 Jeromy Burnitz .25
357 Chris Shelton/SP 4.00
358 Chone Figgins/SP 4.00
359 Javier Vazquez .25
360 Chipper Jones 1.00
361 Frank Thomas 1.00
362 Mark Loretta .25
363 Hideki Matsui 2.00
364 J.J. Hardy/SP 4.00
365 Todd Helton .75
366 Reggie Sanders .25
367 Jay Gibbons .25
368 Johnny Estrada .25
369 Grady Sizemore .75
370 Jim Thome 1.00
371 Ivan Rodriguez .75
372 Jason Bay .75
373 Carl Crawford .50
374 Adrian Beltre .25
375 Derrek Lee/SP 6.00
376 Miguel Olivo .25
377 Roy Oswalt .50
378 Coco Crisp .25
379 Moises Alou .40
380 Kevin Millwood .25
381 Mark Grudzielanek .25
382 Justin Morneau .75
383 Austin Kearns .40
384 Brad Penny .25
385 Troy Glaus .50
386 Cliff Lee .25
387 Armando Benitez .25
388 Clint Barmes .25
389 Orlando Cabrera .25
390 Jim Edmonds/SP 4.00
391 Jermaine Dye .25
392 Morgan Ensberg/SP 4.00
393 Paul LoDuca .25
394 Eric Chavez .25
395 Greg Maddux/SP 8.00
396 Jack Wilson .25
397 Omar Vizquel .25
398 Joe Nathan .25
399 Bobby Abreu .50
400 Barry Bonds/SP 8.00
401 Gary Sheffield .50
402 John Patterson .25
403 J.D. Drew .25
404 Bruce Chen .25
405 Johnny Damon 1.00
406 Aubrey Huff .25
407 Mark Mulder .40
408 Jamie Moyer .25
409 Carlos Guillen .25
410 Andruw Jones/SP 5.00
411 Jhonny Peralta/SP 4.00

412 Doug Davis .25
413 Aaron Miles .25
414 Jon Lieber .25
415 Aaron Hill .25
416 Josh Beckett/SP 4.00
417 Bobby Crosby .25
418 Noah Lowry/SP 4.00
419 Sidney Ponson .25
420 Luis Castillo .25
421 Brad Wilkerson .25
422 Felix Hernandez/SP 4.00
423 Vinny Castilla .25
424 Tom Glavine .50
425 Vladimir Guerrero 1.00
426 Javy Lopez .25
427 Ronnie Belliard .25
428 Dmitri Young .25
429 Johan Santana 1.00
430 David Ortiz/Red Sox/SP 5.00
430 David Ortiz/Twins/SP 5.00
431 Ben Sheets .50
432 Matt Holliday .50
433 Brian McCann .50
434 Joe Blanton .25
435 Sean Casey .25
436 Brad Lidge .25
437 Chad Tracy .25
438 Brett Myers .25
439 Matt Morris .25
440 Brian Giles .25
441 Zachary Duke .25
442 Jose Lopez .25
443 Kris Benson .25
444 Jose Reyes/SP 5.00
445 Travis Hafner .75
446 Orlando Hernandez .25
447 Edgar Renteria .40
448 Scott Podsednik .25
449 Nick Swisher/SP 4.00
450 Derek Jeter 8.00
451 Scott Kazmir 4.00
452 Hank Blalock .50
453 Jake Westbrook .25
454 Miguel Cabrera 1.00
455 Ken Griffey Jr. 2.00
455 Ken Griffey Jr./M's/SP 8.00
456 Rafael Furcal .50
457 Lance Berkman .50
458 Aramis Ramirez .50
459 Xavier Nady .25
459 Xavier Nady/Padres/SP 4.00
460 Randy Johnson 1.00
460 Randy Johnson/Astros/SP 6.00
461 Khalil Greene .25
462 Bartolo Colon .25
463 Mike Lowell .25
464 David DeJesus .25
465 Ryan Howard/SP 8.00
466 Tim Salmon/SP 4.00
467 Mark Buehrle/SP 4.00
468 Curtis Granderson .25
469 Kerry Wood .50
470 Miguel Tejada .75
471 Geoff Jenkins .25
472 Jeremy Reed .25
473 David Eckstein .25
474 Lyle Overbay .25
475 Michael Young .25
476 Nick Johnson/Nats/SP 4.00
476 Nick Johnson/Yanks/SP 4.00
477 Carlos Beltran 1.00
478 Huston Street .25
479 Brandon Webb .25
480 Phil Nevin .25
481 Ryan Madson/SP 4.00
482 Jason Giambi 1.00
483 Angel Berroa .25
484 Casey Blake .25
485 Pat Burrell .50
486 B.J. Ryan .25
487 Torii Hunter .25
488 Garret Anderson .25
489 Chase Utley/SP 6.00
490 Matt Murton .25
491 Rich Harden .25
492 Garrett Atkins .25
493 Tadahito Iguchi/SP 5.00
494 Jarrod Washburn .25
495 Carl Everett .25
496 Kameron Loe .25
497 Jorge Cantu/SP 4.00
498 Chris Young .25
499 Marcus Giles .25
500 Albert Pujols 3.00
501 Alfonso Soriano/Nats/SP 5.00
501 Alfonso Soriano/Yanks/SP 5.00
502 Randy Winn .25
503 Roy Halladay .50
504 Victor Martinez .25
505 Pedro Martinez 1.00
506 Rickie Weeks .40
507 Dan Johnson .25
508 Tim Hudson .50
508 Tim Hudson/A's/SP 4.00
509 Mark Prior .75
510 Melvin Mora .25
511 Matt Clement .25
512 Brandon Inge .25
513 Mike Mussina .75
514 Mike Cameron .25
515 Barry Zito .50
516 Luis Gonzalez .25
517 Jose Castillo .25
518 Andy Pettitte .50
519 Wily Mo Pena .25
520 Billy Wagner .25
521 Ervin Santana/SP 4.00
522 Juan Pierre .25
523 Danny Haren .25
524 Adrian Gonzalez/SP 4.00
525 Robinson Cano .75
526 Jeff Kent .40
527 Cory Sullivan .25
528 Joe Crede/SP 4.00
529 John Smoltz .50
530 David Wright 2.00
531 Chad Cordero .25
532 Scott Rolen/SP 5.00
533 Edwin Jackson .25
534 Doug Mientkiewicz .25
535 Mark Teixeira/SP 5.00
536 Kelvim Escobar .25
537 Alex Rios .25
538 Jose Vidro .25
539 Alex Gonzalez .25
540 Yadier Molina .25
541 Ronny Cedeno/SP 4.00
542 Mark Hendrickson .25
543 Russ Adams .25
544 Chris Capuano .25
545 Raul Ibanez .25
546 Vicente Padilla .25
547 Chris Duffy .25
548 Bengie Molina .25
549 Chien-Ming Wang .75
550 Curt Schilling .25
551 Craig Wilson .25
552 Mike Lieberthal .25
553 Kazuo Matsui .25
554 Jeff Francis .25
555 Brady Clark .25
556 Willy Taveras .25
557 Mike Maroth .25
558 Bernie Williams .50
559 Edwin Encarnacion .25
560 Vernon Wells .25
561 Livan Hernandez/Nats .25
561 Livan Hernandez/Giants/SP 4.00
562 Kenny Rogers .25
563 Steve Finley .25
564 Trot Nixon .25
565 Jonny Gomes/SP 4.00
566 Brandon Phillips .25
567 Shawn Chacon .25
568 David Bush .25
569 Jose Guillen .25
570 Gustavo Chacin .25
571 A. Rod Safe at the Plate/CL 1.00
572 Pujols At Bat/CL 1.00
573 Bonds On Deck/CL 1.00
574 Breaking Up Two/CL .25
575 Conference On The Mound/CL .25
576 Touch Em All/CL .50
577 Avoiding The Runner/CL .25
578 Bunting The Runner Over/CL .25
579 In The Hole/CL .25
580 Jeter Steals Third/CL 1.00
581 Nolan Ryan 2.00
582 Cal Ripken Jr. 3.00
583 Carl Yastrzemski 1.00
584 Duke Snider 1.00
585 Tom Seaver 1.00
586 Mickey Mantle 5.00
587 Jim Palmer .50
588 Gary Carter .25
589 Stan Musial 1.50
590 Luis Aparicio .25
591 Prince Fielder **(RC)** 4.00
592 Conor Jackson **(RC)** .50
593 Jeremy Hermida **(RC)** 1.00
594 Jeff Mathis **(RC)** .50
595 Alay Soler **RC** 1.00
596 Ryan Spilborghs **(RC)** .50
597 Chuck James **(RC)** 1.00
598 Josh Barfield **(RC)** 1.00
599 Ian Kinsler **(RC)** .50
600 Val Majewski **(RC)** .50
601 Brian Slocum **(RC)** .50
602 Matthew Kemp **(RC)** 2.00
603 Nate McLouth **(RC)** .50
604 Sean Marshall **(RC)** .50
605 Brian Bannister **(RC)** .50
606 Ryan Zimmerman **(RC)** 4.00
607 Kendry Morales **(RC)** 1.00
608 Jonathan Papelbon **(RC)** 4.00
609 Matt Cain **(RC)** 1.00
610 Anderson Hernandez **(RC)** .50
611 Jose Capellan **(RC)** .50
612 Lastings Milledge **(RC)** 2.00
613 Francisco Liriano **(RC)** 4.00
614 Hanley Ramirez **(RC)** 2.00
615 Bryan Anderson **(RC)** .50
616 Reggie Abercrombie **(RC)** .50
617 Erick Aybar **(RC)** .50
618 James Loney **(RC)** 1.00
619 Joel Zumaya **(RC)** .50
620 Travis Ishikawa **(RC)** .50
621 Jason Kubel **(RC)** .50
622 Drew Meyer **(RC)** .50
623 Kenji Johjima **RC** 4.00
624 Fausto Carmona **(RC)** .50
625 Nicholas Markakis **(RC)** .50
626 John Rheinecker **(RC)** .50
627 Melky Cabrera **(RC)** .50
628 Mike Pelfrey **RC** 5.00
629 Dan Uggla **(RC)** 1.00
630 Justin Verlander **(RC)** 4.00

Black

Stars (316-630): 3-5X
SP's: 1.5-2X
Inserted 1:20

Gold

Stars (316-630): 5-10X
SP's: 3-5X
Inserted 1:60

Red

Stars (316-630): 1-2X
SP's: .5-1X

Suede

No Pricing
Production One Set

White

Stars (316-630): 2-3X
SP's: 1X
Inserted 1:4

Autographs

NM/M
Common Auto.: 8.00
Suede: No Pricing
Production One Set
GA Garrett Atkins 15.00
JB Josh Barfield 15.00
CB Clint Barmes 10.00
MC Miguel Cabrera 50.00
RC Robinson Cano 60.00
JG Jonny Gomes 25.00
RH Ryan Howard 100.00
CJA Conor Jackson 15.00
KJ Kenji Johjima 90.00
DJ Dan Johnson 15.00
CJ Chipper Jones 60.00
DL Derrek Lee 40.00
PL Paul LoDuca 25.00
BM Brian McCann 30.00
BMC Brandon McCarthy Exch 15.00
MM Mike Morse 10.00
RO Roy Oswalt 25.00
AR Alex Rodriguez 250.00
JS Johan Santana Exch 65.00
HS Huston Street Exch 25.00
NS Nick Swisher Exch 20.00
CV Claudio Vargas Exch 8.00
DW David Wright 85.00

Autographs Black

NM/M
Production 15 or 99
GA Garrett Atkins/99 15.00
JB Josh Barfield/99 20.00
CB Clint Barmes/99 15.00
CJA Conor Jackson/99 20.00
DJ Dan Johnson/99 15.00
BM Brian McCann/99 40.00
BMC Brandon McCarthy/99 Exch 15.00
MM Mike Morse/99 30.00
NS Nick Swisher/99 Exch 20.00
CV Claudio Vargas/99 Exch 15.00

Autographs Gold

NM/M
Production 5 or 25
JB Josh Barfield/25 40.00
BM Brian McCann/25 75.00
MM Mike Morse/25 30.00
NS Nick Swisher/25 Exch 30.00

Autographs Red

NM/M
Production 50 or 475
GA Garrett Atkins/475 15.00
JB Josh Barfield/475 15.00
CB Clint Barmes/475 15.00
MC Miguel Cabrera/50 60.00
RC Robinson Cano/50 100.00
JG Jonny Gomes/50 30.00
RH Ryan Howard/50 125.00
CJA Conor Jackson/475 15.00
KJ Kenji Johjima/50 100.00
DJ Dan Johnson/475 15.00
CJ Chipper Jones/50 100.00
DL Derrek Lee/50 40.00
PL Paul LoDuca/50 30.00
BM Brian McCann/475 30.00
BMC Brandon McCarthy/475 Exch 15.00
MM Mike Morse/475 10.00
RO Roy Oswalt/50 30.00
AR Alex Rodriguez/50 250.00
JS Johan Santana/50 Exch 75.00
HS Huston Street/50 Exch 30.00
NS Nick Swisher/475 Exch 20.00
CV Claudio Vargas/475 Exch 8.00
DW David Wright/50 100.00

Autographs White

NM/M
Production 25 or 100
GA Garrett Atkins/200 15.00
JB Josh Barfield/200 20.00
CB Clint Barmes/200 15.00
CJA Conor Jackson/200 15.00
DJ Dan Johnson/200 15.00
BM Brandon McCarthy/200 Exch 15.00
BMC Brandon McCarthy/200 Exch 15.00
MM Mike Morse/200 10.00
NS Nick Swisher/200 Exch 20.00
CV Claudio Vargas/200 Exch 10.00

B-18 Blankets

NM/M
Inserted 1:2 Boxes
Original B-18 Blanket: No Pricing
Inserted 1:159 Boxes
BB1 Barry Bonds/White 15.00
BB2 Barry Bonds/Red 15.00
VG1 Vladimir Guerrero/White 10.00
VG2 Vladimir Guerrero/Green 10.00
KJ1 Kenji Johjima/White 10.00
KJ2 Kenji Johjima/Green 10.00
DL1 Derrek Lee/White 10.00
DL2 Derrek Lee/Red 10.00
MM1 Mickey Mantle/White 25.00
MM2 Mickey Mantle/Blue 25.00
HM1 Hideki Matsui/White 10.00
HM2 Hideki Matsui/Blue 10.00
DO1 David Ortiz/White 10.00
DO2 David Ortiz/Orange 10.00
MR1 Manny Ramirez/White 10.00
MR2 Manny Ramirez/Orange 10.00
AR1 Alex Rodriguez/White 15.00
AR2 Alex Rodriguez/Blue 15.00
IS1 Ichiro Suzuki/White 10.00
IS2 Ichiro Suzuki/Green 10.00

Cabinet

NM/M
Common Player:
Inserted 1:2 Boxes
Cabinet Original: No Pricing
Inserted 1:4,340 Boxes
Suede: No Pricing
Inserted 1:634 Boxes
JB Josh Barfield 10.00
JBE Josh Beckett 10.00
BB Barry Bonds 25.00
JC Jorge Cantu 10.00
CCA Chris Carpenter 10.00
GC Gary Carter 10.00
CC Carl Crawford 10.00
JD Johnny Damon 20.00
CD Carlos Delgado 10.00
PF Prince Fielder 20.00
JF Jeff Francoeur 15.00
NG Nomar Garciaparra 15.00
TG Troy Glaus 10.00
JG Jonny Gomes 10.00
KG Ken Griffey Jr. 20.00
RH Ryan Howard 20.00
DJ Derek Jeter 30.00
NJ Nick Johnson 10.00
RJ Randy Johnson 20.00
AJ Andruw Jones 15.00
DL Derrek Lee 10.00
FL Francisco Liriano 10.00
MM Mickey Mantle 50.00
NM Nicholas Markakis 10.00
PM Pedro Martinez 15.00
HM Hideki Matsui 15.00
DO David Ortiz 20.00
JPA Jonathan Papelbon 25.00
JP Jake Peavy 10.00
MP Mike Piazza 15.00
AP Albert Pujols 30.00
AR Alex Rodriguez 25.00
IR Ivan Rodriguez 10.00
JR Jimmy Rollins 15.00
NR Nolan Ryan 25.00
JS Johan Santana 15.00
DS Duke Snider 20.00
AS Alfonso Soriano 20.00
IS Ichiro Suzuki 20.00
JT Jim Thome 15.00
DW David Wright 15.00
CY Carl Yastrzemski 25.00

Cabinet Auto Relics

No Pricing
Inserted 1:86 Boxes
Suede: No Pricing
Production One Set

Cabinet Auto Relics Dual

No Pricing
Inserted 1:1,368 Boxes
Suede: No Pricing
Production One Set

Relics

NM/M
Common Player: 4.00
Red: 1-1.5X
Production 150 Sets
White: 1.5-2X
Production 99 Sets
Black: 2-3X
Production 50 Sets
Gold: 2-4X
Production 25 Sets
Suede: No Pricing
Production One Set
CBA Clint Barmes 6.00
CB Carlos Beltran 8.00
LB Lance Berkman 6.00
HB Hank Blalock 4.00
MC Miguel Cabrera 8.00
RC Robinson Cano 15.00
CC Chris Carpenter 8.00
EC Eric Chavez 6.00
JC Jose Contreras 6.00
JD Johnny Damon 15.00
CD Carlos Delgado 6.00
JE Jim Edmonds 6.00
ME Morgan Ensberg 4.00
JF Jeff Francoeur 8.00
JG Jon Garland 4.00
VG Vladimir Guerrero 8.00
RHA Roy Halladay 6.00
RIH Rich Harden 8.00
JH Jeremy Hermida 6.00
RH Ryan Howard 25.00
TH Torii Hunter 6.00
CJ Andruw Jones 6.00
CJ Chipper Jones 10.00
PK Paul Konerko 8.00
DL Derrek Lee 8.00
BL Brad Lidge 6.00
PL Paul LoDuca 4.00
PM Pedro Martinez 10.00
HM Hideki Matsui 15.00
JM Joe Mauer 10.00
MM Mike Mussina 10.00
DO David Ortiz 15.00
RO Roy Oswalt 6.00
APE Andy Pettitte 6.00
MP Mike Piazza 10.00
AP Albert Pujols 20.00
MR Manny Ramirez 10.00
JR Jose Reyes 8.00
MRI Mariano Rivera 15.00
BR Brian Roberts 6.00
AR Alex Rodriguez 15.00
JS Johan Santana 10.00
IS Ichiro Suzuki 25.00
MT Mark Teixeira 8.00
BW Bernie Williams 8.00
DWI Dontrelle Willis 6.00
DW David Wright 15.00

2006 Topps Updates & Highlights

NM/M
Complete Factory Set (333): 40.00
Complete Set (330): 30.00
Common Player: .10
UH1 Austin Kearns .20
UH2 Adam Eaton .10
UH3 Juan Encarnacion .10
UH4 Jarrod Washburn .10
UH5 Alex Gonzalez .10
UH6 Toby Hall .10
UH7 Preston Wilson .10
UH8 Ramon Ortiz .10
UH9 Jason Michaels .10
UH10 Jeff Weaver .10
UH11 Russell Branyan .10
UH12 Brett Tomko .10
UH13 Doug Mientkiewicz .10
UH14 David Wells .10
UH15 Corey Koskie .10
UH16 Russ Ortiz .10
UH17 Carlos Pena .10
UH18 Mark Hendrickson .10
UH19 Julian Tavarez .10
UH20 Jeff Conine .10
UH21 Dioner Navarro .10
UH22 Bob Wickman .10
UH23 Felipe Lopez .10
UH24 Eddie Guardado .10
UH25 David Dellucci .10
UH26 Ryan Wagner .10
UH27 Nick Green .10
UH28 Gary Majewski .10
UH29 Shea Hillenbrand .10
UH30 Jae Weong Seo .10
UH31 Royce Clayton .10
UH32 David Riske .10
UH33 Joey Gathright .10
UH34 Robinson Tejeda .10
UH35 Edwin Jackson .10
UH36 Aubrey Huff .10
UH37 Akinori Otsuka .10
UH38 Juan Castro .10
UH39 Zach Day .10
UH40 Jeremy Accardo .10
UH41 Shawn Green .10
UH42 Kazuo Matsui .10
UH43 J.J. Putz .10
UH44 David Ross .10
UH45 Scott Williamson .10
UH46 Joe Borchard .10
UH47 Elmer Dessens .10
UH48 Odalis Perez .10
UH49 Kelly Shoppach .10
UH50 Brandon Phillips .10
UH51 Guillermo Mota .10
UH52 Alex Cintron .10
UH53 Denny Bautista .10
UH54 Josh Bard .10
UH55 Julio Lugo .10
UH56 Doug Mirabelli .10
UH57 Kip Wells .10
UH58 Adrian Gonzalez .10
UH59 Shawn Chacon .10
UH60 Marcus Thames .10
UH61 Craig Wilson .10
UH62 Cory Sullivan .10
UH63 Ben Broussard .10
UH64 Todd Walker .10
UH65 Greg Maddux 1.00
UH66 Xavier Nady .10
UH67 Oliver Perez .10
UH68 Sean Casey .10
UH69 Kyle Lohse .10
UH70 Carlos Lee .20
UH71 Rheal Cormier .10
UH72 Ronnie Belliard .10
UH73 Cory Lidle .10
UH74 David Bell .10
UH75 Wilson Betemit .10
UH76 Danys Baez .10
UH77 Mike Stanton .10
UH78 Kevin Mench .10
UH79 Sandy Alomar .10
UH80 Cesar Izturis .10
UH81 Jeremy Affeldt .10
UH82 Matt Stairs .10
UH83 Hector Luna .10
UH84 Tony Graffanino .10
UH85 J.P. Howell .10
UH86 Bengie Molina .10
UH87 Maicer Izturis .10
UH88 Marco Scutaro .10
UH89 Daryle Ward .10
UH90 Sal Fasano .10
UH91 Oscar Villarreal .10
UH92 Gabe Gross .10
UH93 Phil Nevin .10
UH94 Damon Hollins .10
UH95 Juan Cruz .10
UH96 Marlon Anderson .10
UH97 Jason Davis .10
UH98 Ryan Shealy .10
UH99 Francisco Cordero .10
UH100 Bobby Abreu .25
UH101 Roberto Hernandez .10
UH102 Gary Bennett .10
UH103 Aaron Sele .10
UH104 Nook Logan .10
UH105 Alfredo Amezaga .10
UH106 Chris Woodward .10
UH107 Kevin Jarvis .10
UH108 B.J. Upton .10
UH109 Alan Embree .10
UH110 Milton Bradley .10
UH111 Peter Orr .10
UH112 Jeff Cirillo .10
UH113 Corey Patterson .10
UH114 Josh Paul .10
UH115 Fernando Rodney .10
UH116 Jerry Hairston .10
UH117 Scott Proctor .10
UH118 Ambiorix Burgos .10
UH119 Jose Bautista .10
UH120 Livan Hernandez .10
UH121 John McDonald .10
UH122 Ronny Cedeno .10

UH123 Nate Robertson .10
UH124 Jamey Carroll .10
UH125 Alex Escobar .10
UH126 Endy Chavez .10
UH127 Jorge Julio .10
UH128 Kenny Lofton .10
UH129 Matt Diaz .10
UH130 David Bush .10
UH131 Jose Molina .10
UH132 Mike MacDougal .10
UH133 Benjamin Zobrist **(RC)** .50
UH134 Shane Komine **RC** .25
UH135 Casey Janssen **RC** .50
UH136 Kevin Frandsen **(RC)** .25
UH137 John Rheinecker **(RC)** .25
UH138 Matthew Kemp **(RC)** .75
UH139 Scott Mathieson **(RC)** .25
UH140 Jered Weaver **(RC)** .75
UH141 Joel Guzman **(RC)** .25
UH142 Anibal Sanchez **(RC)** .50
UH143 Melky Cabrera **(RC)** .50
UH144 Howie Kendrick **(RC)** .50
UH145 Cole Hamels **(RC)** 1.00
UH146 Willy Aybar **(RC)** .25
UH147 James Shields **RC** .50
UH148 Kevin Thompson **(RC)** .25
UH149 Jon Lester **(RC)** 1.00
UH150 Stephen Drew **(RC)** .75
UH151 Andre Ethier **(RC)** .50
UH152 Jordan Tata **RC** .50
UH153 Michael Napoli **RC** .50
UH154 Kason Gabbard **(RC)** .25
UH155 Lastings Milledge **(RC)** .50
UH156 Erick Aybar **(RC)** .25
UH157 Fausto Carmona **(RC)** .25
UH158 Russell Martin **(RC)** .50
UH159 David Pauley **(RC)** .25
UH160 Andy Marte **(RC)** .25
UH161 Carlos Quentin **(RC)** .25
UH162 Franklin Gutierrez **(RC)** .25
UH163 Taylor Buchholz **(RC)** .25
UH164 Josh Johnson **(RC)** .25
UH165 Chad Billingsley **(RC)** .50
UH166 Kendry Morales **(RC)** .25
UH167 Adam Loewen **(RC)** .25
UH168 Yusmeiro Petit **(RC)** .25
UH169 Matt Albers **(RC)** .25
UH170 John Maine **(RC)** .25
UH171 Alex Rodriguez .75
UH172 Mike Piazza .40
UH173 Cory Sullivan .10
UH174 Anibal Sanchez .10
UH175 Trevor Hoffman .10
UH176 Barry Bonds .75
UH177 Derek Jeter .75
UH178 Jose Reyes .25
UH179 Manny Ramirez .25
UH180 Vladimir Guerrero .25
UH181 Mariano Rivera .25
UH182 Postseason Highlights .25
UH183 Postseason Highlights .25
UH184 Postseason Highlights .25
UH185 Postseason Highlights .25
UH186 Postseason Highlights .25
UH187 Postseason Highlights .25
UH188 Postseason Highlights .25
UH189 Postseason Highlights .25
UH190 Postseason Highlights .25
UH191 Postseason Highlights .25
UH192 Postseason Highlights .25
UH193 Postseason Highlights .25
UH194 Postseason Highlights .25
UH195 Postseason Highlights .25
UH196 Postseason Highlights .25
UH197 Postseason Highlights .25
UH198 Postseason Highlights .25
UH199 Postseason Highlights .25
UH200 Postseason Highlights .25
UH201 Postseason Highlights .25
UH202 David Ortiz, Jermaine Dye, Travis Hafner .25
UH203 Joe Mauer, Derek Jeter, Robinson Cano .50
UH204 David Ortiz, Justin Morneau, Raul Ibanez .25
UH205 Carl Crawford, Chone Figgins, Ichiro Suzuki .50
UH206 Johan Santana, Chien-Ming Wang, Jon Garland .50
UH207 Johan Santana, Roy Halladay, C.C. Sabathia .25
UH208 Johan Santana, Jeremy Bonderman, John Lackey .25
UH209 Francisco Rodriguez, Bobby Jenks, B.J. Ryan .10
UH210 Ryan Howard, Albert Pujols, Alfonso Soriano 1.00
UH211 Freddy Sanchez, Miguel Cabrera, Albert Pujols .50
UH212 Ryan Howard, Albert Pujols, Lance Berkman 1.00
UH213 Jose Reyes, Juan Pierre, Hanley Ramirez .40
UH214 Derek Lowe, Brandon Webb, Carlos Zambrano .10
UH215 Roy Oswalt, Chris Carpenter, Brandon Webb .10
UH216 Aaron Harang, Jake Peavy, John Smoltz .10
UH217 Trevor Hoffman, Billy Wagner, Joe Borowski .10
UH218 Ichiro Suzuki .50
UH219 Derek Jeter .75
UH220 Alex Rodriguez .75
UH221 David Ortiz .25
UH222 Vladimir Guerrero .25
UH223 Ivan Rodriguez .25
UH224 Vernon Wells .10
UH225 Mark Loretta .10
UH226 Kenny Rogers .10
UH227 Alfonso Soriano .25
UH228 Carlos Beltran .25
UH229 Albert Pujols .75
UH230 Jason Bay .25
UH231 Edgar Renteria .10
UH232 David Wright .50
UH233 Chase Utley .25
UH234 Paul LoDuca .10
UH235 Brad Penny .10
UH236 Derrick Turnbow .10
UH237 Mark Redman .10
UH238 Francisco Liriano .25
UH239 A.J. Pierzynski .10
UH240 Grady Sizemore .25
UH241 Jose Contreras .10
UH242 Jermaine Dye .10
UH243 Jason Schmidt .10
UH244 Nomar Garciaparra .25
UH245 Scott Kazmir .10
UH246 Johan Santana .25
UH247 Chris Capuano .10
UH248 Magglio Ordonez .10
UH249 Gary Matthews .10
UH250 Carlos Lee .10
UH251 David Eckstein .10
UH252 Michael Young .10
UH253 Matt Holliday .25
UH254 Lance Berkman .25
UH255 Scott Rolen .25
UH256 Bronson Arroyo .10
UH257 Barry Zito .10
UH258 Brian McCann .10
UH259 Jose Lopez .10
UH260 Chris Carpenter .25
UH261 Roy Halladay .10
UH262 Jim Thome .25
UH263 Dan Uggla .10
UH264 Mariano Rivera .25
UH265 Roy Oswalt .20
UH266 Tom Gordon .10
UH267 Troy Glaus .10
UH268 Bobby Jenks .10
UH269 Freddy Sanchez .10
UH270 Paul Konerko .25
UH271 Joe Mauer .25
UH272 B.J. Ryan .10
UH273 Ryan Howard .75
UH274 Brian Fuentes .10
UH275 Miguel Cabrera .25
UH276 Brandon Webb .10
UH277 Mark Buehrle .10
UH278 Trevor Hoffman .10
UH279 Jonathan Papelbon .25
UH280 Andruw Jones .25
UH281 Miguel Tejada .20
UH282 Carlos Zambrano .20
UH283 Ryan Howard .75
UH284 David Wright .50
UH285 Miguel Cabrera .25
UH286 David Ortiz .25
UH287 Jermaine Dye .10
UH288 Miguel Tejada .25
UH289 Lance Berkman .25
UH290 Troy Glaus .10
UH291 David Wright, Tom Glavine .25
UH292 Ryan Howard, Tom Gordon .50
UH293 Miguel Cabrera, Dontrelle Willis .25
UH294 Andruw Jones, John Smoltz .25
UH295 Alfonso Soriano .25
UH296 Albert Pujols, Chris Carpenter .50
UH297 Adam Dunn, Bronson Arroyo .10
UH298 Lance Berkman, Roy Oswalt .25
UH299 Chris Capuano, Prince Fielder .50
UH300 Freddy Sanchez, Jason Bay .10
UH301 Carlos Zambrano, Juan Pierre .10
UH302 Adrian Gonzalez, Trevor Hoffman .10
UH303 Derek Lowe, Rafael Furcal .10
UH304 Omar Vizquel, Jason Schmidt .10
UH305 Brandon Webb, Chad Tracy .10
UH306 Matt Holliday, Garrett Atkins .25
UH307 Alex Rodriguez, Chien-Ming Wang .50
UH308 Curt Schilling, David Ortiz .25
UH309 Roy Halladay, Vernon Wells .10
UH310 Miguel Tejada, Erik Bedard .10
UH311 Carl Crawford, Scott Kazmir .10
UH312 Jeremy Bonderman, Magglio Ordonez .10
UH313 Justin Morneau, Johan Santana .25
UH314 Jon Garland, Jermaine Dye .10
UH315 Travis Hafner, C.C. Sabathia .10
UH316 Emil Brown, Mark Grudzielanek .10
UH317 Frank Thomas, Barry Zito .25
UH318 Jered Weaver, Vladimir Guerrero .25
UH319 Michael Young, Gary Matthews .10
UH320 Ichiro Suzuki, J.J. Putz .50
UH321 Derek Jeter, Robinson Cano .50
UH232 Mark Mulder, Chris Carpenter .25
UH323 Trevpr Schmidt, Jason Schmidt .10
UH324 David Wright, Paul LoDuca .25
UH325 Lance Berkman, Roy Oswalt .25
UH326 Derek Jeter, Jose Reyes .50
UH327 David Wright, Cliff Floyd .25
UH328 Johan Santana, Francisco Liriano .25
UH329 Stephen Drew, J.D. Drew .25
UH330 Jeff Weaver .25

Black

Black: 15-25X
Production 55 Sets

Gold

Gold: 5-10X
Production 2,006 Sets

First Edition

1st Edition: 4-6X
Inserted 1:Hobby Box

Platinum

Production One Set

All-Star Autographs

No Pricing
Production 25 Sets

All-Star Stitches

NM/M
Common Player: 4.00
Inserted 1:43
Patch: No Pricing
Production 10 Sets
BA Bronson Arroyo 8.00
JB Jason Bay 15.00
CB Carlos Beltran 10.00
LB Lance Berkman 10.00
MB Mark Buehrle 8.00
MC Miguel Cabrera 10.00
RC Robinson Cano 10.00
CFC Chris Capuano 4.00
CC Chris Carpenter 10.00
JC Jose Contreras 8.00
JD Jermaine Dye 6.00
DE David Eckstein 20.00
BF Brian Fuentes 4.00
TEG Troy Glaus 6.00
TMG Tom Glavine 8.00
TG Tom Gordon 4.00
VG Vladimir Guerrero 8.00
RH Roy Halladay 6.00
TH Trevor Hoffman 6.00
MH Matt Holliday 6.00
RJH Ryan Howard 25.00
BJ Bobby Jenks 4.00
AJ Andruw Jones 10.00
SK Scott Kazmir 6.00
PK Paul Konerko 6.00
CL Carlos Lee 8.00
PL Paul LoDuca 6.00
JL Jose Lopez 6.00
ML Mark Loretta 6.00
GM Gary Matthews 6.00
JM Joe Mauer 10.00
BM Brian McCann 15.00
MO Magglio Ordonez 8.00
DO David Ortiz 15.00
RO Roy Oswalt 6.00
JP Jonathan Papelbon 20.00
BP Brad Penny 4.00
AJP A.J. Pierzynski 4.00
AP Albert Pujols 25.00
MAR Mark Redman 4.00
ER Edgar Renteria 6.00
JR Jose Reyes 15.00
MR Mariano Rivera 10.00
AR Alex Rodriguez 15.00
IR Ivan Rodriguez 8.00
KR Kenny Rogers 8.00
SR Scott Rolen 8.00
BR B.J. Ryan 4.00
FS Freddy Sanchez 8.00
JS Johan Santana 10.00
JDS Jason Schmidt 8.00
GS Grady Sizemore 10.00
AS Alfonso Soriano 8.00
MT Miguel Tejada 8.00
JT Jim Thome 10.00
DT Derrick Turnbow 6.00
DU Dan Uggla 10.00
CU Chase Utley 10.00
BW Brandon Webb 10.00
VW Vernon Wells 8.00
DW David Wright 20.00
MY Michael Young 6.00
CZ Carlos Zambrano 8.00

All-Star Patches

No Pricing
Production 10 Sets

Barry Bonds HR History

NM/M
Common Bonds HR History: 1.00
Inserted 1:6
Autographs: No Pricing
Production Five Sets
BB709-BB734 Barry Bonds 1.00

Barry Bonds 715

NM/M
Inserted 1:36
715-BBBarry Bonds 3.00

Barry Bonds 715 Relic

NM/M
Production 715
Barry Bonds 35.00

Chrome RC Box Topper

NM/M
Production 599
Inserted one per box.
Refractors: 2-4X
Production 25 Sets
1 Aaron Zobrist 3.00
2 Shane Komine 3.00
3 Casey Janssen 3.00
4 Kevin Frandsen 5.00
5 John Rheinecker 3.00
6 Matthew Kemp 8.00
7 Scott Mathieson 5.00
8 Jered Weaver 8.00
9 Joel Guzman 5.00
10 Anibal Sanchez 5.00
11 Melky Cabrera 6.00
12 Howie Kendrick 6.00
13 Cole Hamels 8.00
14 Willy Aybar 3.00
15 James Shields 3.00
16 Kevin Thompson 5.00
17 Jon Lester 15.00
18 Stephen Drew 6.00
19 Andre Ethier 8.00
20 Jordan Tata 3.00
21 Michael Napoli 6.00
22 Kason Gabbard 5.00
23 Lastings Milledge 5.00
24 Erick Aybar 3.00
25 Fausto Carmona 3.00
26 Russell Martin 5.00
27 David Pauley 3.00
28 Andy Marte 5.00
29 Carlos Quentin 5.00
30 Franklin Gutierrez 5.00
31 Taylor Buchholz 5.00
32 Josh Johnson 5.00
33 Chad Billingsley 6.00
34 Kendry Morales 3.00
35 Adam Loewen 5.00
36 Yusmeiro Petit 5.00
37 Matt Albers 3.00
38 John Maine 5.00
39 Josh Willingham 5.00
40 Taylor Tankersley 5.00
41 Pat Neshek 30.00
42 Francisco Rosario 3.00
43 Matt Smith 5.00
44 Jonathan Sanchez 5.00
45 Chris Demaria 3.00
46 Manuel Corpas 5.00
47 Kevin Reese 3.00
48 Brent Clevlen 3.00
49 Anderson Hernandez 3.00
50 Chris Roberson 5.00

Derby Digs Relics

NM/M
Inserted 1:4,200
JD Jermaine Dye 25.00
TG Troy Glaus 25.00

Mickey Mantle HR History

NM/M
Common Mantle (102-201): 2.00
Inserted 1:4

Mickey Mantle HR History Relics

NM/M
Common Mantle: 140.00
Production Seven Sets

Midsummer Covers

No Pricing
Production 10 Sets

Rookie Debut

NM/M
Common Player: 1.00
Inserted 1:4
RD1 Joel Zumaya 2.00
RD2 Ian Kinsler 2.00
RD3 Kenji Johjima 3.00
RD4 Josh Barfield 1.00
RD5 Nicholas Markakis 2.00
RD6 Dan Uggla 2.00
RD7 Eric Reed 1.00
RD8 Carlos Martinez 1.00
RD9 Angel Pagan 1.50
RD10 Jason Childers 1.00
RD11 Ruddy Lugo 1.00
RD12 James Loney 2.50
RD13 Fernando Nieve 1.00
RD14 Reggie Abercrombie 1.00
RD15 Boone Logan 1.00
RD16 Brian Bannister 1.00
RD17 Ricky Nolasco 1.50
RD18 Willie Eyre 1.00
RD19 Fabio Castro 1.00
RD20 Jordan Tata 1.00
RD21 Taylor Buchholz 1.50
RD22 Sean Marshall 1.00
RD23 John Rheinecker 1.00
RD24 Casey Janssen 1.00
RD25 Russell Martin 1.50
RD26 Yusmeiro Petit 1.50
RD27 Kendry Morales 1.50
RD28 Alay Soler 1.00
RD29 Jered Weaver 3.00
RD30 Matthew Kemp 2.00
RD31 Enrique Gonzalez 1.00
RD32 Lastings Milledge 2.00
RD33 James Shields 1.00
RD34 David Pauley 1.00
RD35 Zach Jackson 1.00
RD36 Zach Miner 1.00
RD37 Jon Lester 3.00
RD38 Chad Billingsley 2.00
RD39 Scott Thorman 1.00
RD40 Anibal Sanchez 2.00
RD41 Mike Thompson 1.00
RD42 T.J. Beam 1.00
RD43 Stephen Drew 3.00
RD44 Joe Saunders 1.00
RD45 Carlos Quentin 1.50

Rookie Debut Autographs

NM/M
Common Autograph: 15.00
RA Reggie Abercrombie 15.00
MA Matt Albers 20.00
FC Fausto Carmona 15.00
FF Emiliano Fruto 15.00
IK Ian Kinsler 20.00
JL Jon Lester 35.00
BL Bobby Livingston 15.00
AL Adam Loewen 40.00
MN Michael Napoli 30.00
RN Ricky Nolasco 15.00
YP Yusmeiro Petit 15.00
MP Martin Prado 20.00
JS Jeremy Sowers 15.00
ST Scott Thorman 20.00

Signature Moves

NM/M
Common Autograph:
AH Aubrey Huff 20.00
JL Julio Lugo 20.00
BP Brandon Phillips 20.00
BW Brad Wilkerson 10.00
CW Craig Wilson 10.00

Touch 'Em All Relics

NM/M
Inserted 1:610
CB Carlos Beltran 20.00
RH Ryan Howard 30.00
JM Joe Mauer 20.00
DO David Ortiz 20.00
AP Albert Pujols 30.00
AR Alex Rodriguez 25.00
IS Ichiro Suzuki 25.00
MT Miguel Tejada 10.00
DW David Wright 25.00
MY Michael Young 8.00

2006 Topps 1952 Edition

NM/M
Complete Set (312):
Common Player: .25
Common SP (276-312): 5.00
Common 52 Logo Variation: 4.00
Inserted 1:5
Pack (8): 4.50
Box (20): 80.00
1 Howie Kendrick **(RC)** 1.50
2 Enrique Gonzalez **(RC)** .25
3 Chuck James **(RC)** .75
4 Chris Britton **RC** .50
5 David Pauley **(RC)** .50
6 Angel Pagan **(RC)** .25
7 Pat Neshek **RC** 6.00
8 Walter Young **(RC)** .25

#	Player	NM/M
9	Chris Denorfia **(RC)**	.25
10	Rafael Perez **RC**	.50
11	Ryan Spilborghs **(RC)**	.25
12	Jon Huber **RC**	.50
13	Jordan Tata **RC**	.50
14	Eric Reed **(RC)**	.25
15	Norris Hopper **RC**	.75
16	Scott Olsen **(RC)**	.25
17	Fernando Nieve **(RC)**	.25
18	Chris Booker **(RC)**	.25
19	Chad Billingsley **(RC)**	.75
20	Carlos Villanueva **RC**	.75
21	Craig Hansen **RC**	1.50
22	David Gassner **(RC)**	.25
23	Mike Pelfrey **RC**	4.00
24	Matt Smith **(RC)**	1.00
25	Chris Roberson **(RC)**	.50
26	John Van Benschoten **(RC)**	.25
27	Kevin Frandsen **(RC)**	.25
28	Les Walrond **(RC)**	.50
29	James Shields **RC**	.50
30	Russell Martin **(RC)**	.50
31	Benjamin Zobrist **(RC)**	.25
32	John Rheinecker **(RC)**	.25
33	Francisco Rosario **(RC)**	.25
34	Santiago Ramirez **(RC)**	.25
35	Michael Napoli **RC**	1.50
36	Tony Pena **(RC)**	.25
37	Jeff Karstens **RC**	1.00
37	Jeff Karstens 52 logo/SP **RC**	5.00
38	Phil Stockman **(RC)**	.25
39	Kurt Birkins **RC**	1.00
40	Dustin Pedroia **(RC)**	.50
41	Buck Coats **(RC)**	.25
42	Jim Johnson **RC**	1.00
43	Angel Guzman **(RC)**	.25
44	Kelly Shoppach **(RC)**	.25
45	Josh Wilson **(RC)**	.25
46	Jack Hannahan **RC**	.75
47	Ricky Nolasco **(RC)**	.25
48	T.J. Bohn **(RC)**	.25
49	Joel Zumaya **(RC)**	1.00
50	Philip Barzilla **RC**	.75
51	Justin Huber **(RC)**	.25
52	Willy Aybar **(RC)**	.25
52	Willy Aybar 52 logo/SP **(RC)**	4.00
53	Tony Gwynn Jr. **(RC)**	.50
54	Chris Barnwell **RC**	.50
55	Henry Owens **RC**	.75
56	Jeff Bajenaru **(RC)**	.25
57	Jonah Bayliss **RC**	.50
58	Joshua Sharpless **RC**	.50
59	Eliezer Alfonzo **RC**	.50
60	Bobby Livingston **(RC)**	.25
61	John Gall **(RC)**	.25
62	Ruddy Lugo **(RC)**	.25
63	Fabio Castro **RC**	.50
64	Casey Janssen **RC**	.75
65	Mike O'Connor **RC**	.50
66	Kendry Morales **(RC)**	.50
67	James Hoey **RC**	.75
68	Dustin Moseley **(RC)**	.25
69	Peter Moylan **RC**	1.00
70	Manny Delcarmen **(RC)**	.50
71	Rich Hill **(RC)**	.40
72	Boone Logan **RC**	.50
73	Cody Ross **(RC)**	.25
74	Fausto Carmona **(RC)**	.25
75	Ramon Ramirez **(RC)**	.25
76	Zach Miner **(RC)**	.25
77	Hanley Ramirez **(RC)**	.50
78	Josh Johnson **(RC)**	.25
79	Taylor Buchholz **(RC)**	.25
80	Joe Nelson **(RC)**	.25
81	Hong-Chih Kuo **(RC)**	.50
82	Chris Mabeus **(RC)**	.25
83	Willie Eyre **(RC)**	.25
84	John Maine **(RC)**	.25
85	Yurendell DeCaster **(RC)**	.25
86	Mike Thompson **RC**	.50
87	Brian Wilson **RC**	.50
88	Matt Cain **(RC)**	.50
88	Matt Cain 52 logo/SP **(RC)**	8.00
89	Josh Rupe **RC**	.25
90	Tyler Johnson **(RC)**	.25
91	Jason Childers **RC**	.50
92	Wes Littleton **(RC)**	.25
93	Ty Taubenheim **RC**	.50
94	Saul Rivera **(RC)**	.25
95	Reggie Willits **(RC)**	1.50
96	Carlos Quentin **(RC)**	.50
97	Macay McBride **(RC)**	.25
98	Brandon Fahey **RC**	.50
99	Sean Marshall **(RC)**	.25
100	Sean Tracey **(RC)**	.25
101	Brian Slocum **(RC)**	.25
102	Choo Freeman **(RC)**	.25
103	Brent Clevlen **(RC)**	.25
104	Josh Willingham **(RC)**	.25
105	Chris Resop **(RC)**	.25
106	Chris Sampson **RC**	1.50
107	James Loney **(RC)**	.50
107	James Loney 52 logo/SP **(RC)**	8.00
108	Matthew Kemp **(RC)**	.50
109	Jason Kubel **(RC)**	.25
110	Brian Bannister **(RC)**	4.00
111	Kevin Thompson **(RC)**	.25
112	Jeremy Brown **(RC)**	.25
113	Brian Sanches **(RC)**	.25
114	Nate McLouth **(RC)**	.25
115	Ben Johnson **(RC)**	.25
116	Jonathan Sanchez **(RC)**	.25
117	Mark Lowe **(RC)**	.25
118	Skip Schumaker **(RC)**	.25
119	Jason Hammel **(RC)**	.25
120	Drew Meyer **(RC)**	.25
121	Melvin Dorta **RC**	.50
122	Jeff Mathis **(RC)**	.25
123	Davis Romero **(RC)**	.25
124	Joey Devine **RC**	.50
125	Sendy Rleal **RC**	.50
126	Freddie Bynum **(RC)**	.25
127	Bryan Anderson **(RC)**	.25
128	Jeremy Sowers **(RC)**	.25
129	Ryan Shealy **(RC)**	.25
130	Reggie Abercrombie **(RC)**	.25
131	Matt Albers **(RC)**	.25
132	Lastings Milledge **(RC)**	.50
133	Robert Andino **RC**	.50
134	Chris Demaria **RC**	.50
135	Boof Bonser **(RC)**	.25
136	Alay Soler **RC**	.50
137	Wilbert Nieves **(RC)**	.25
138	Mike Rouse **(RC)**	.25
139	Carlos Ruiz **(RC)**	.25
140	Matt Capps **(RC)**	.25
141	Travis Ishikawa **(RC)**	.25
142	Josh Kinney **RC**	1.50
143	Josh Rupe **(RC)**	.25
144	Shaun Marcum **(RC)**	.25
145	Jason Bergmann **(RC)**	.25
146	Tommy Murphy **(RC)**	.25
147	Martin Prado **(RC)**	.25
148	Val Majewski **(RC)**	.25
149	Ian Kinsler **(RC)**	.25
150	Joe Winkelsas **(RC)**	.25
151	Agustin Montero **(RC)**	.25
152	Joe Inglett **RC**	1.00
153	Manuel Corpas **RC**	.50
154	Yusmeiro Petit **(RC)**	.25
155	Mark Woodyard **(RC)**	.25
156	Jeff Fulchino **RC**	.50
157	Stephen Andrade **(RC)**	.25
158	Tim Hamulack **(RC)**	.25
159	Colter Bean **(RC)**	.25
160	Anderson Hernandez **(RC)**	.25
161	Kevin Reese **(RC)**	.25
162	Jason Windsor **(RC)**	.25
163	Paul Maholm **(RC)**	.25
163	Paul Maholm 52 logo/SP **(RC)**	4.00
164	Jeremy Accardo **RC**	.50
165	Joel Guzman **(RC)**	.25
166	Erick Aybar **(RC)**	.25
167	Scott Thorman **(RC)**	.25
168	Adam Loewen **(RC)**	.25
169	Carlos Marmol **RC**	.50
170	Bill Bray **(RC)**	.25
171	Edward Mujica **RC**	.50
172	Jeremy Hermida **(RC)**	.50
173	Taylor Tankersley **(RC)**	.25
174	Bobby Keppel **(RC)**	.25
175	Chris Young **(RC)**	.50
176	Josh Rabe **RC**	1.50
177	T.J. Beam **(RC)**	.25
178	Shane Komine **RC**	1.00
178	Shane Komine 52 logo/SP	6.00
179	Scott Mathieson **(RC)**	.25
180	Josh Barfield **(RC)**	.25
181	Justin Knoedler **(RC)**	.25
182	Emiliano Fruto **RC**	.50
183	Adam Wainwright **(RC)**	.25
184	Nick Masset **(RC)**	.25
185	Ryan Roberts **RC**	.50
186	Brandon Watson **(RC)**	.25
187	Chris Bootcheck **(RC)**	.25
188	Daniel Ortmeier **(RC)**	.25
189	Kevin Barry **(RC)**	.25
190	Cory Morris **RC**	.50
191	Kason Gabbard **(RC)**	.25
192	Tom Mastny **(RC)**	.25
193	David Aardsma **(RC)**	.25
194	Anthony Reyes **(RC)**	.25
195	Mike Jacobs **(RC)**	.25
196	Conor Jackson **(RC)**	.25
197	Kenji Johjima **RC**	3.00
198	Jack Taschner **(RC)**	.25
199	Renyel Pinto **(RC)**	.25
200	Chad Santos **(RC)**	.25
201	Aaron Rakers **(RC)**	.25
202	Franklin Gutierrez **(RC)**	.25
203	Chris Coste **RC**	1.50
204	Chris Iannetta **RC**	.50
205	Michael Vento **(RC)**	.25
206	Ryan O'Malley **RC**	1.00
207	Jason Botts **(RC)**	.25
208	John Hattig Jr. **(RC)**	.25
209	Brandon Harper **RC**	.50
210	Ryan Theriot **(RC)**	1.00
211	Travis Hughes **(RC)**	.25
212	Paul Hoover **(RC)**	.25
213	Bryan Pena **(RC)**	.25
214	Craig Breslow **RC**	.75
215	Eude Brito **(RC)**	.25
216	Melky Cabrera **(RC)**	.50
216	Melky Cabrera 52 logo/SP **(RC)**	8.00
217	Jonathan Broxton **(RC)**	5.00
217	Jonathan Broxton 52 logo/SP **(RC)**	8.00
218	Bryan Corey **(RC)**	.25
219	Ron Flores **RC**	.50
220	Andrew Brown **(RC)**	.25
221	Jaime Bubela **(RC)**	.25
222	Jason Bulger **(RC)**	.25
223	Alberto Callaspo **(RC)**	.25
224	Jose Capellan **(RC)**	.25
225	Cole Hamels **(RC)**	.50
225	Cole Hamels 52 logo/SP **(RC)**	6.00
226	Bernie Castro **(RC)**	.25
227	Shin-Soo Choo **(RC)**	.25
228	Doug Clark **(RC)**	.25
229	Roy Corcoran **RC**	.50
230	Tim Corcoran **RC**	.75
231	Nelson Cruz **(RC)**	.25
232	Rajai Davis **(RC)**	.25
233	Chris Duncan **(RC)**	.25
233	Chris Duncan 52 logo/SP **(RC)**	5.00
234	Scott Dunn **(RC)**	.25
235	Mike Esposito **(RC)**	.25
236	Scott Feldman **RC**	.50
237	Luis Figueroa **RC**	.50
238	Bartolome Fortunato **(RC)**	.25
239	Alejandro Freire **RC**	.50
240	J.J. Furmaniak **(RC)**	.25
241	Nicholas Markakis **(RC)**	.50
242	Matt Garza **(RC)**	1.00
243	Justin Germano **(RC)**	.25
244	Alexis Gomez **(RC)**	.25
245	Tom Gorzelanny **(RC)**	.25
246	Dan Uggla **(RC)**	.25
247	Jeremy Guthrie **(RC)**	.25
248	Stephen Drew **(RC)**	1.00
249	Brendan Harris **(RC)**	.25
250	Jeff Harris **RC**	.50
251	Corey Hart **(RC)**	.25
252	Chris Heintz **(RC)**	.25
253	Prince Fielder **(RC)**	1.00
254	Francisco Liriano **(RC)**	.50
255	Jason Hirsh **(RC)**	.25
256	J.R. House **(RC)**	.25
257	Zach Jackson **(RC)**	.25
258	Charlton Jimerson **(RC)**	.25
259	Greg Jones **(RC)**	.25
260	Mitch Jones **(RC)**	.25
261	Ryan Jorgensen **RC**	.50
262	Logan Kensing **(RC)**	.25
263	John Koronka **(RC)**	.25
264	Anthony Lerew **(RC)**	.25
265	Anibal Sanchez **(RC)**	.25
266	Juan Mateo **RC**	.50
267	Paul McAnulty **(RC)**	.25
268	Dustin McGowan **(RC)**	.25
269	Marty McLeary **(RC)**	.25
270	Ryan Zimmerman **(RC)**	2.00
271	Dustin Nippert **(RC)**	.25
272	Eric O'Flaherty **RC**	.50
273	Ronny Paulino **(RC)**	.25
274	Tony Pena **(RC)**	.25
275	Hayden Penn **(RC)**	.25
276	Miguel Perez **(RC)**	5.00
277	Paul Phillips **(RC)**	5.00
278	Omar Quintanilla **(RC)**	5.00
279	Guillermo Quiroz **(RC)**	5.00
280	Darrell Rasner **(RC)**	5.00
281	Kenny Ray **(RC)**	5.00
282	Royce Ring **(RC)**	5.00
283	Brian Rogers **(RC)**	5.00
284	Ed Rogers **(RC)**	5.00
285	Danny Sandoval **RC**	6.00
286	Joe Saunders **(RC)**	5.00
287	Chris Schroder **RC**	5.00
288	Mike Smith **(RC)**	5.00
289	Travis Smith **(RC)**	5.00
290	Geovany Soto **(RC)**	5.00
291	Brian Sweeney **(RC)**	5.00
292	Jon Switzer **(RC)**	5.00
293	Joe Thurston **(RC)**	5.00
294	Jermaine Van Buren **(RC)**	5.00
295	Ryan Garko **(RC)**	5.00
296	Cla Meredith **(RC)**	5.00
297	Luke Scott **(RC)**	5.00
298	Andy Marte **(RC)**	5.00
299	Jered Weaver **(RC)**	10.00
300	Freddy Guzman **(RC)**	5.00
301	Jonathan Papelbon **(RC)**	10.00
302	John-Ford Griffin **(RC)**	5.00
303	Jon Lester **RC**	8.00
304	Shawn Hill **(RC)**	5.00
305	Brian Myrow **RC**	6.00
306	Anderson Garcia **RC**	6.00
307	Andre Ethier **(RC)**	6.00
308	Ben Hendrickson **(RC)**	5.00
309	Alejandro Machado **(RC)**	6.00
310	Justin Verlander **(RC)**	8.00
311	Mickey Mantle/Blue	40.00
311	Mickey Mantle/Black	20.00
311	Mickey Mantle/Green	20.00
311	Mickey Mantle/ Orange	20.00
311	Mickey Mantle/Red	20.00
311	Mickey Mantle/ Yellow	20.00
312	Steve Stemle **RC**	5.00

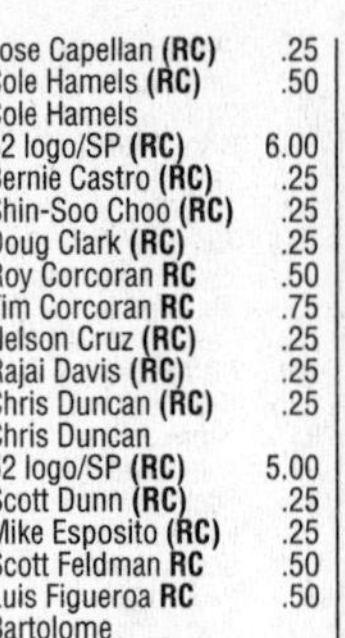

Chrome

		NM/M
Common Player:		1.50
Production 1,952 Sets		
Refractor:		2-3X
Production 552 Sets		
Gold Refractor:		4-6X
Production 52 Sets		
1	Howie Kendrick	2.00
2	David Pauley	1.50
3	Chris Denorfia	1.50
4	Jordan Tata	2.00
5	Fernando Nieve	1.50
6	Craig Hansen	2.00
7	Mickey Mantle	25.00
8	James Shields	2.00
9	Francisco Rosario	1.50
10	Jeff Karstens	1.50
11	Buck Coats	2.00
12	Josh Wilson	1.50
13	Joel Zumaya	2.00
14	Tony Gwynn Jr.	2.00
15	Jonah Bayliss	1.50
16	John Gall	1.50
17	Mike O'Connor	1.50
18	Peter Moylan	1.50
19	Cody Ross	1.50
20	Hanley Ramirez	3.00
21	Hong-Chih Kuo	3.00
22	Yurendell DeCaster	1.50
23	Sean Green	1.50
24	Ty Taubenheim	1.50
25	Macay McBride	1.50
26	Brian Slocum	1.50
27	Chris Resop	1.50
28	Jason Kubel	1.50
29	Brian Sanches	1.50
30	Mark Lowe	1.50
31	Melvin Dorta	1.50
32	Sendy Rleal	1.50
33	Ryan Shealy	1.50
34	Robert Andino	1.50
35	Wilbert Nieves	1.50
36	Travis Ishikawa	1.50
37	Jason Bergmann	1.50
38	Ian Kinsler	2.00
39	Manuel Corpas	1.50
40	Stephen Andrade	1.50
41	Kevin Reese	1.50
42	Joel Guzman	1.50
43	Carlos Marmol	2.00
44	Taylor Tankersley	1.50
45	T.J. Beam	1.50
46	Justin Knoedler	1.50
47	Ryan Roberts	1.50
48	Kevin Barry	1.50
49	David Aardsma	1.50
50	Kenji Johjima	3.00
51	Aaron Rakers	1.50
52	Michael Vento	1.50
53	Brandon Harper	1.50
54	Brayan Pena	1.50
55	Jonathan Broxton	2.00
56	Jaime Bubela	1.50
57	Cole Hamels	5.00
58	Roy Corcoran	1.50
59	Chris Duncan	4.00
60	Luis Figueroa	1.50
61	Kendry Morales	1.50
62	Tom Gorzelanny	1.50
63	Brendan Harris	1.50
64	Anibal Sanchez	1.50
65	Zach Jackson	1.50
66	Ryan Jorgensen	1.50
67	Josh Johnson	2.00
68	Marty McLeary	1.50
69	Ronny Paulino	1.50
70	Tyler Johnson	1.50
2	Reggie Abercrombie	1.50
72	Nicholas Markakis	5.00
73	J.J. Furmaniak	2.00
74	Prince Fielder	5.00
75	Enrique Gonzalez	1.50
76	Angel Pagan	1.50
77	Rafael Perez	2.00
78	Eric Reed	1.50
79	Chris Booker	1.50
80	David Gassner	1.50
81	John Van Benschoten	1.50
82	Russell Martin	2.00
83	Santiago Ramirez	1.50
84	Phil Stockman	1.50
85	Jim Johnson	1.50
86	Jack Hannahan	1.50
87	Philip Barzilla	1.50
88	Chris Barnwell	1.50
89	Joshua Sharpless	1.50
90	Chris Roberson	2.00

Debut Flashbacks

		NM/M
Common Player:		2.00
Chrome:		1.5-2X
Production 1,952 Sets		
Refractor:		2-3X
Production 552 Sets		
Gold Refractor:		4-6X
Production 52 Sets		
1	Dontrelle Willis	2.00
2	Carlos Beltran	3.00
3	Albert Pujols	8.00
4	Ichiro Suzuki	5.00
5	Mike Piazza	4.00
6	Nomar Garciaparra	3.00
7	Scott Rolen	3.00
8	Mariano Rivera	3.00
9	David Ortiz	4.00
10	Johnny Damon	4.00
11	Tom Glavine	3.00
12	David Wright	5.00
13	Greg Maddux	5.00
14	Manny Ramirez	4.00
15	Alex Rodriguez	6.00
16	Roger Clemens	6.00
17	Alfonso Soriano	3.00
18	Frank Thomas	3.00
19	Chipper Jones	4.00
20	Ivan Rodriguez	3.00

Dynamic Duos

		NM/M
Common Duo:		1.00
Inserted 1:4		
1	Stephen Drew, Carlos Quentin	2.00
2	Jonathan Papelbon, Jon Lester	3.00
3	Joel Zumaya, Justin Verlander	4.00
4	Dan Uggla, Hanley Ramirez	1.50
5	Jonathan Broxton, Chad Billingsley	1.00
6	Francisco Liriano, Matt Garza	1.50
7	Lastings Milledge, John Maine	1.50
8	Chris Coste, Cole Hamels	2.00
9	Michael Napoli, Howie Kendrick	1.50
10	Joe Inglett, Andy Marte	1.00
11	Jeremy Hermida, Josh Willingham	1.00
12	Matthew Kemp, James Loney	1.50
13	Andre Ethier, Russell Martin	1.50
14	Melky Cabrera, Jeff Karstens	1.50
15	Ricky Nolasco, Scott Olsen, Josh Johnson, Anibal Sanchez	1.50

Autograph

		NM/M
Common Auto.:		10.00
Red Ink:		2-3X
Production 52 Sets		
RA	Reggie Abercrombie	10.00
MA	Matt Albers	10.00
BA	Brian Anderson	10.00
EA	Erick Aybar	10.00
BPB	Brian Bannister	10.00
TJB	T.J. Bohn	10.00
BB	Boof Bonser	25.00
WB	Bill Bray	15.00
MC	Melky Cabrera	30.00
MTC	Matt Cain	35.00
FC	Fabio Castro	10.00
BC	Buck Coats	10.00
YD	Yurendell DeCaster	10.00
SD	Stephen Drew	35.00
KF	Kevin Frandsen	10.00
EF	Emiliano Fruto	10.00
MG	Matt Garza	25.00
EG	Enrique Gonzalez	10.00
FG	Franklin Gutierrez	10.00
AG	Angel Guzman	10.00
JG	Joel Guzman	10.00
CI	Chris Iannetta	15.00
CHJ	Chuck James	15.00
JWK	Jeff Karstens	25.00
MK	Matthew Kemp	20.00
HK	Howie Kendrick	30.00
JK	Josh Kinney	10.00
HCK	Hong-Chih Kuo	40.00
AL	Anthony Lerew	10.00
CM	Chris Mabeus	10.00
TM	Tom Mastny	15.00
SM	Scott Mathieson	10.00
JM	Jeff Mathis	10.00
KM	Kendry Morales	15.00
EM	Edward Mujica	10.00
MN	Michael Napoli	15.00
RO	Ryan O'Malley	15.00
AP	Angel Pagan	10.00
JP	Jonathan Papelbon	40.00
YP	Yusmeiro Petit	15.00
AS	Anibal Sanchez	15.00
JFS	Joe Saunders	15.00
JS	Joshua Sharpless	15.00
BS	Brian Slocum	15.00
DU	Dan Uggla	25.00
JVB	John Van Benschoten	10.00
JV	Justin Verlander	50.00
JW	Jered Weaver	40.00
RZ	Ryan Zimmerman	60.00
BZ	Benjamin Zobrist	10.00
JZ	Joel Zumaya	50.00

Ticket to Stardom Relics

No Pricing
Production 10 Sets

2007 Topps

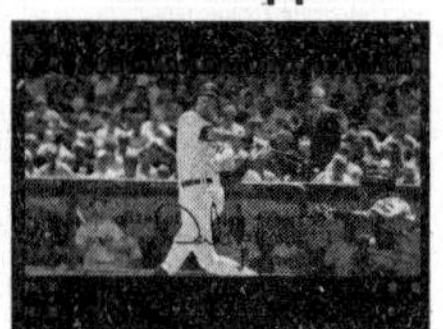

		NM/M
Complete Set (661):		75.00
Common Player:		.10
Series 1 Hobby Pack (10):		3.00
Series 1 Hobby Box (36):		100.00
Series 1 Jumbo Pack (50):		15.00
Series 1 Jumbo Box (10):		140.00
Series 1 Rack Pack (22):		5.00
Series 1 Rack Box (24):		100.00
Series 2 Hobby Pack (10):		2.00
Series 2 Hobby Box (36):		60.00
Series 2 Jumbo Pack (50):		10.00
Series 2 Jumbo Box (10):		90.00
Series 2 Rack Pack (22):		4.00
Series 2 Rack Box (24):		85.00
Series 1 Variations:		No Pricing
Inserted 1:3700 Wal-Mart		
1	John Lackey	.10
2	Nick Swisher	.25
3	Brad Lidge	.10
4	Bengie Molina	.10
5	Bobby Abreu	.25
6	Edgar Renteria	.25
7	Mickey Mantle	5.00
8	Preston Wilson	.10
9	Ryan Dempster	.10
10	C.C. Sabathia	.10
11	Julio Lugo	.10
12	J.D. Drew	.25
13	Miguel Batista	.10
14	Eliezer Alfonzo	.10
15	Andrew Miller **RC**	3.00
15	Andrew Miller Posed **RC**	.10
16	Yuniesky Betancourt	.10
17	Saul Rivera	.10
18	Orlando Hernandez	.10
19	Alfredo Amezaga	.10
20	Delmon Young Face Right **(RC)**	.50
20	Delmon Young Face Left **(RC)**	.10
21	Javy Lopez	.10
22	Corey Patterson	.10
23	Josh Bard	.10
24	Tom Gordon	.10
25	Gary Matthews	.10
26	Jason Jennings	.10
27	Joey Gathright	.10
28	Brandon Inge	.10
29	Pat Neshek	.10
30	Bronson Arroyo	.10

31 Jay Payton .10
32 Andy Pettitte .25
33 Ervin Santana .25
34 Paul Konerko .25
35 Joel Zumaya .25
36 Gregg Zaun .10
37 Tony Gwynn .50
38 Adam LaRoche .10
39 Jim Edmonds .25
40 Derek Jeter 15.00
41 Rich Hill .25
42 Livan Hernandez .10
43 Aubrey Huff .10
44 Todd Greene .10
45 Andre Ethier .25
46 Jeremy Sowers .10
47 Ben Broussard .10
48 Darren Oliver .10
49 Nook Logan .10
50 Miguel Cabrera .50
51 Carlos Lee .25
52 José Castillo .10
53 Mike Piazza .75
54 Daniel Cabrera .10
55 Cole Hamels .40
56 Mark Loretta .10
57 Brian Fuentes .10
58 Todd Coffey .10
59 Brent Clevlen .10
60 John Smoltz .25
61 Ross Gload .10
62 Dan Wheeler .10
63 Scott Proctor .10
64 Bobby Kielty .10
65 Dan Uggla .25
66 Lyle Overbay .10
67 Geoff Jenkins .10
68 Michael Barrett .10
69 Casey Fossum .10
70 Ivan Rodriguez .40
71 Jose Lopez .10
72 Jake Westbrook .10
73 Moises Alou .25
74 Jose Valverde .10
75 Jered Weaver .25
76 Lastings Milledge .25
77 Austin Kearns .10
78 Adam Loewen .10
79 Josh Barfield .10
80 Johan Santana .40
81 Ian Kinsler .10
82 Ian Snell .10
83 Mike Lowell .10
84 Elizardo Ramirez .10
85 Scott Rolen .40
86 Shannon Stewart .10
87 Alexis Gomez .10
88 Jimmy Gobble .10
89 Jamey Carroll .10
90 Chipper Jones .50
91 Carlos Silva .10
92 Joe Crede .25
93 Michael Napoli .10
94 Willy Travis .10
95 Rafael Furcal .25
96 Phil Nevin .10
97 David Bush .10
98 Marcus Giles .10
99 Joe Blanton .10
100 Dontrelle Willis .25
101 Scott Kazmir .25
102 Jeff Kent .25
103 Pedro Feliz .10
104 Johnny Estrada .10
105 Travis Hafner .25
106 Ryan Garko .10
107 Rafael Soriano .10
108 Wes Helms .10
109 Billy Wagner .10
110 Aaron Rowand .10
111 Felipe Lopez .10
112 Jeff Conine .10
113 Nicholas Markakis .25
114 John Koronka .10
115 B.J. Ryan .10
116 Tim Wakefield .10
117 David Ross .10
118 Emil Brown .10
119 Michael Cuddyer .10
120 Jason Giambi .40
121 Alex Cintron .10
122 Luke Scott .10
123 Chone Figgins .10
124 Huston Street .10
125 Carlos Delgado .40
126 Daryle Ward .10
127 Chris Duncan .10
128 Damian Miller .10
129 Aramis Ramirez .25
130 Albert Pujols 1.50
131 Chris Snyder .10
132 Ray Durham .10
133 Franklin Gutierrez .10
134 Mike Jacobs .10
135 Troy Tulowitzki **(RC)** .50
135 Troy Tulowitzki Throw **(RC)** .10
136 Jon Rauch .10
137 Jay Gibbons .10
138 Adrian Gonzalez .10
139 Randy Wolf .10
140 Freddy Sanchez .10
141 Rich Aurilia .10
142 Trot Nixon .10
143 Vicente Padilla .10
144 Jack Wilson .10
145 Jake Peavy .25
146 Luke Hudson .10
147 Javier Vazquez .10
148 Scott Podsednik .10
149 Ivan Rodriguez, Magglio Ordonez .25
150 Todd Helton .40
151 Kendry Morales .10
152 Adam Everett .10
153 Bob Wickman .10
154 Bill Hall .25
155 Jeremy Bonderman .25
156 Ryan Theriot .10
157 Rocco Baldelli .25
158 Noah Lowry .10
159 Jason Michaels .10
160 Justin Verlander .50
161 Eduardo Perez .10
162 Chris Ray .10
163 Dave Roberts .10
164 Zachary Duke .10
165 Mark Buehrle .10
166 Hank Blalock .25
167 Royce Clayton .10
168 Mark Teahen .10
169 Todd Jones .10
170 Chien-Ming Wang .50
171 Nick Punto .10
172 Morgan Ensberg .10
173 Robert Mackowiak .10
174 Frank Catalanotto .10
175 Matt Murton .10
176 Alfonso Soriano, Carlos Beltran .40
177 Francisco Cordero .10
178 Jason Marquis .10
179 Joe Nathan .10
180 Roy Halladay .25
181 Melvin Mora .10
182 Ramon Ortiz .10
183 Jose Valentin .10
184 Gil Meche .10
185 B.J. Upton .25
186 Grady Sizemore .40
187 Matt Cain .25
188 Eric Byrnes .10
189 Carl Crawford .25
190 J.J. Putz .10
191 Cla Meredith .10
192 Matt Capps .10
193 Rod Barajas .10
194 Edwin Encarnacion .10
195 James Loney .10
196 Johnny Damon .50
197 Freddy Garcia .10
198 Mike Redmond .10
199 Ryan Shealy .10
200 Carlos Beltran .40
201 Chuck James .10
202 Mark Ellis .10
203 Brad Ausmus .10
204 Juan Rivera .10
205 Cory Sullivan .10
206 Ben Sheets .25
207 Mark Mulder .10
208 Carlos Quentin .10
209 Jonathan Broxton .10
210 Kazuo Matsui .10
211 Armando Benitez .10
212 Richie Sexson .40
213 Josh Johnson .10
214 Brian Schneider .10
215 Craig Monroe .10
216 Chris Duffy .10
217 Chris Coste .10
218 Clay Hensley .10
219 Chris Gomez .10
220 Hideki Matsui .75
221 Robinson Tejeda .10
222 Scott Hatteberg .10
223 Jeff Francis .10
224 Matt Thornton .10
225 Robinson Cano .40
226 New York Yankees 1.00
227 Oakland A's .25
228 St. Louis Cardinals .50
229 Minnesota Twins .25
230 Barry Zito .25
231 Baltimore Orioles .25
232 Seattle Mariners .25
233 Houston Astros .25
234 Florida Marlins .25
235 Reed Johnson .10
236 Toronto Blue Jays .25
237 Cincinnati Reds .25
238 Philadelphia Phillies .25
239 Anaheim Angels .25
240 Chris Carpenter .25
241 Atlanta Braves .25
242 Washington Nationals .25
243 Joe Torre .50
244 Tampa Bay Devil Rays .25
245 Chad Tracey .10
246 Mike Hargrove .10
247 Mike Scioscia .10
248 Ron Gardenhire .10
249 Tony LaRussa .10
250 Anibal Sanchez .10
251 Charlie Manuel .10
252 John Gibbons .10
253 Ken Macha .10
254 Jerry Narron .10
255 Brad Penny .10
256 Bobby Cox .10
257 Bob Melvin .10
258 Mike Hargrove .10
259 Phil Garner .10
260 David Wright 1.00
261 Vinny Rottino **(RC)** .25
262 Ryan Braun **(RC)** 2.00
263 Kevin Kouzmanoff **(RC)** .50
264 David Murphy **(RC)** .25
265 Jimmy Rollins .25
266 Joe Maddon .10
267 Grady Little .10
268 Ryan Sweeney **(RC)** .25
269 Fred Lewis **(RC)** .25
270 Alfonso Soriano .50
271 Delwyn Young **(RC)** .25
271 Delwyn Young Swing **(RC)** .10
272 Jeff Salazar **(RC)** .25
273 Miguel Montero **(RC)** .25
274 Shawn Riggans **(RC)** .25
275 Greg Maddux 1.00
276 Brian Stokes **(RC)** .25
277 Philip Humber **(RC)** .25
278 Scott Moore **(RC)** .25
279 Adam Lind **(RC)** .25
280 Curt Schilling .50
281 Chris Narveson **(RC)** .25
282 Oswaldo Navarro **RC** .50
283 Drew Anderson **(RC)** .25
284 Jerry Owens **(RC)** .25
285 Randy Johnson .50
286 Joaquin Arias **(RC)** .25
287 Jose Garcia **(RC)** .25
288 Shane Youman **RC** .50
289 Brian Burres **(RC)** .25
290 Matt Holliday .25
291 Ryan Feierabend **(RC)** .25
292 Josh Fields **(RC)** .25
292 Josh Fields Running **(RC)** .10
293 Glen Perkins **(RC)** .25
294 Mike Rabelo **RC** .50
295 Jorge Posada .25
296 Ubaldo Jimenez **(RC)** .25
297 Brad Ausmus .10
298 Eric Chavez .25
299 Orlando Hudson .10
300 Vladimir Guerrero .50
301 Derek Jeter 1.00
302 Scott Rolen .25
303 Mark Grudzielanek .10
304 Kenny Rogers .10
305 Frank Thomas .25
306 Mike Cameron .10
307 Torii Hunter .10
308 Albert Pujols 1.00
309 Mark Teixeira .25
310 Jonathan Papelbon .50
311 Greg Maddux .50
312 Carlos Beltran .25
313 Ichiro Suzuki .75
314 Andruw Jones .25
315 Manny Ramirez .50
316 Vernon Wells .25
317 Omar Vizquel .10
318 Ivan Rodriguez .25
319 Brandon Webb .25
320 Magglio Ordonez .25
321 Johan Santana .25
322 Ryan Howard 1.00
323 Justin Morneau .25
324 Hanley Ramirez .40
325 Joe Mauer .25
326 Justin Verlander .25
327 Derek Jeter, Bobby Abreu .50
328 Carlos Delgado, David Wright .50
329 Yadier Molina, Albert Pujols .50
330 Ryan Howard .50
331 Kelly Johnson .10
332 Chris Young .10
333 Mark Kotsay .10
334 A.J. Burnett .10
335 Brian McCann .10
336 Woody Williams .10
337 Jason Isringhausen .10
338 Juan Pierre .10
339 Jonny Gomes .10
340 Roger Clemens 1.50
341 Akinori Iwamura **RC** 1.50
342 Bengie Molina .10
343 Shin-Soo Choo .10
344 Kenji Johjima .25
345 Joe Borowski .10
346 Shawn Green .25
347 Chicago Cubs .10
348 Rodrigo Lopez .10
349 Brian Giles .25
350 Chase Utley .50
351 Mark DeRosa .25
352 Carl Pavano .10
353 Kyle Lohse .10
354 Chris Iannetta .10
355 Oliver Perez .10
356 Curtis Granderson .10
357 Sean Casey .10
358 Jason Tyner .10
359 Jon Garland .10
360 David Ortiz .75
361 Adam Kennedy .10
362 Chris Burke .10
363 Bobby Crosby .10
364 Conor Jackson .10
365 Tim Hudson .25
366 Rickie Weeks .25
367 Cristian Guzman .10
368 Mark Prior .25
369 Benjamin Zobrist .10
370 Troy Glaus .25
371 Kenny Lofton .25
372 Shane Victorino .25
373 Cliff Lee .10
374 Adrian Beltre .25
375 Miguel Olivo .10
376 Endy Chavez .10
377 Zack Segovia **(RC)** .25
378 Ramon Hernandez .10
379 Chris Young .25
380 Jason Schmidt .25
381 Ronny Paulino .10
382 Kevin Millwood .10
383 Jon Lester .25
384 Alex Gonzalez .10
385 Brad Hawpe .10
386 Placido Polanco .10
387 Nate Robertson .10
388 Torii Hunter .25
389 Gavin Floyd .10
390 Roy Oswalt .40
391 Kelvim Escobar .10
392 Craig Wilson .10
393 Milton Bradley .10
394 Aaron Hill .10
395 Matt Diaz .10
396 Chris Capuano .10
397 Juan Encarnacion .10
398 Jacque Jones .10
399 James Shields .10
400 Ichiro Suzuki .75
401 Matthew Kemp .10
402 Matt Morris .10
403 Casey Blake .10
404 Corey Hart .10
405 Josh Willingham .10
406 Ryan Madson .10
407 Nick Johnson .10
408 Kevin Millar .10
409 Khalil Greene .10
410 Tom Glavine .25
411 Jason Bay .25
412 Gerald Laird .10
413 Coco Crisp .10
414 Brandon Phillips .10
415 Aaron Cook .10
416 Mark Redman .10
417 Mike Maroth .10
418 Boof Bonser .10
419 Jorge Cantu .10
420 Jeff Weaver .10
421 Melky Cabrera .25
422 Francisco Rodriguez .10
423 Mike Lamb .10
424 Danny Haren .25
425 Tomokazu Ohka .10
426 Jeff Francoeur .25
427 Randy Wolf .10
428 So Taguchi .10
429 Carlos Zambrano .25
430 Justin Morneau .50
431 Luis Gonzalez .25
432 Takashi Saito .25
433 Brandon Morrow **RC** .75
434 Victor Martinez .25
435 Felix Hernandez .25
436 Ricky Nolasco .10
437 Paul LoDuca .10
438 Chad Cordero .10
439 Miguel Tejada .40
440 Mark Teixeira .40
441 Pat Burrell .25
442 Paul Maholm .10
443 Mike Cameron .25
444 Josh Beckett .25
445 Pablo Ozuna .10
446 Jaret Wright .10
447 Angel Berroa .10
448 Fernando Rodney .10
449 Francisco Liriano .25
450 Ken Griffey Jr. 1.00
451 Bobby Jenks .10
452 Mike Mussina .40
453 Howie Kendrick .25
454 Milwaukee Brewers .10
455 Dan Johnson .10
456 Ted Lilly .10
457 Mike Hampton .10
458 J.J. Hardy .25
459 Jeff Suppan .10
460 Jose Reyes 1.00
461 Jae Weong Seo .10
462 Edgar Gonzalez .10
463 Russell Martin .25
464 Omar Vizquel .10
465 Jhonny Peralta .25
466 Raul Ibanez .10
467 Hanley Ramirez .50
468 Kerry Wood .25
469 Ryan Church .10
470 Gary Sheffield .40
471 David Wells .10
472 David Dellucci .10
473 Xavier Nady .10
474 Michael Young .25
475 Kevin Youkilis .40
476 Aaron Harang .10
477 Brian Lawrence .10
478 Octavio Dotel .10
479 Chris Shelton .10
480 Matt Garza .25
481 Jim Thome .40
482 Jose Contreras .10
483 Kris Benson .10
484 John Maine .10
485 Tadahito Iguchi .10
486 Wandy Rodriguez .10
487 Eric Chavez .25
488 Vernon Wells .25
489 Doug Davis .10
490 Andruw Jones .40
491 David Eckstein .10
492 Michael Barrett .10
493 Greg Norton .10
494 Orlando Hudson .10
495 Wilson Betemit .10
496 Ryan Klesko .10
497 Fausto Carmona .10
498 Jarrod Washburn .10
499 Aaron Boone .10
500 Pedro Martinez .50
501 Mike O'Connor .10
502 Brian Roberts .25
503 Jeff Cirillo .10
504 Brett Myers .25
505 Jose Bautista .10
506 Akinori Otsuka .10
507 Shea Hillenbrand .10
508 Ryan Langerhans .10
509 Josh Fogg .10
510 Alex Rodriguez 1.50
511 Kenny Rogers .10
512 Jason Kubel .10
513 Jermaine Dye .25
514 Mark Grudzielanek .10
515 Josh Phelps .10
516 Bartolo Colon .25
517 Craig Biggio .25
518 Esteban Loaiza .10
519 Alex Rios .25
520 Adam Dunn .40
521 Derrick Turnbow .10
522 Anthony Reyes .10
523 Derrek Lee .40
524 Ty Wigginton .10
525 Jeremy Hermida .10
526 Derek Lowe .25
527 Randy Winn .10
528 Paul Byrd .10
529 Chris Snelling .10
530 Brandon Webb .25
531 Julio Franco .10
532 Jose Vidro .10
533 Erik Bedard .25
534 Terrmel Sledge .10
535 Jon Lieber .10
536 Tom Gorzelanny .10
537 Kip Wells .10
538 Wily Mo Pena .10
539 Eric Milton .10
540 Chad Billingsley .10
541 David DeJesus .10
542 Omar Infante .10
543 Rondell White .10
544 Juan Uribe .10
545 Miguel Cairo .10
546 Orlando Cabrera .25
547 Byung-Hyun Kim .10
548 Jason Kendall .10
549 Horacio Ramirez .10
550 Trevor Hoffman .25
551 Ronnie Belliard .10
552 Chris Woodward .10
553 Ramon Martinez .10
554 Elizardo Ramirez .10
555 Andy Marte .10
556 John Patterson .10
557 Scott Olsen .10
558 Steve Trachsel .10
559 Doug Mientkiewicz .10
560 Randy Johnson .50
561 Chan Ho Park .10
562 Jamie Moyer .10
563 Mike Gonzalez .10
564 Nelson Cruz .10
565 Alex Cora .10
566 Ryan Freel .10
567 Chris Stewart **RC** .50
568 Carlos Guillen .10
569 Jason Bartlett .10
570 Mariano Rivera .40
571 Norris Hopper .10
572 Alex Escobar .10
573 Gustavo Chacin .10
574 Brandon McCarthy .10
575 Seth McClung .10
576 Yuniesky Betancourt .10
577 Jason LaRue .10
578 Dustin Pedroia .25
579 Taylor Tankersley .10
580 Garret Anderson .10
581 Mike Sweeney .10
582 Scott Thorman .10
583 Joe Inglett .10
584 Clint Barmes .10
585 Willie Bloomquist .10
586 Willy Aybar .10
587 Brian Bannister .10
588 Jose Guillen .10
589 Brad Wilkerson .10
590 Lance Berkman .25
591 Toronto Blue Jays .10
592 Florida Marlins .10
593 Washington Nationals .10
594 Los Angeles Angels .10
595 Cleveland Indians .10
596 Texas Rangers .10
597 Detroit Tigers .10
598 Arizona Diamondbacks .10
599 Kansas City Royals .10
600 Ryan Zimmerman .40
601 Colorado Rockies .10
602 Minnesota Twins .10
603 Los Angeles Dodgers .10
604 San Diego Padres .10
605 Bruce Bochy .10
606 Ron Washington .10
607 Manny Acta .10
608 Sam Perlozzo .10
609 Terry Francona .10
610 Jim Leyland .10
611 Eric Wedge .10
612 Ozzie Guillen .10
613 Buddy Bell .10
614 Bob Geren .10
615 Lou Piniella .10
616 Fredi Gonzalez .10
617 Ned Yost .10
618 Willie Randolph .10
619 Bud Black .10
620 Garrett Atkins .10
621 Alexi Casilla **RC** .25
622 Matt Chico **(RC)** .25
623 Alejandro De Aza **RC** .75
624 Jeremy Brown .10
625 Josh Hamilton **(RC)** .50
626 Doug Slaten **RC** .50
627 Andy Cannizaro **RC** .50
628 Juan Salas **(RC)** .25
629 Levale Speigner **RC** .50
630 Daisuke Matsuzaka **RC** 6.00
631 Elijah Dukes **RC** 1.00
632 Kevin Cameron **RC** .50
633 Juan Perez **RC** .50
634 Alex Gordon **RC** 4.00
635 Juan Lara **RC** .50
636 Mike Rabelo **RC** .50
637 Justin Hampson **(RC)** .25
638 Cesar Jimenez **RC** .50
639 Joe Smith **RC** .50
640 Kei Igawa **RC** 1.00
641 Hideki Okajima **RC** 2.00
642 Sean Henn **(RC)** .25
643 Jay Marshall **RC** .50
644 Jared Burton **RC** .50
645 Angel Sanchez **RC** .50
646 Devern Hansack **RC** 1.00
647 Juan Morillo **(RC)** .25
648 Hector Gimenez **(RC)** .25
649 Brian Barden **RC** .50
650 Alex Rodriguez, Jason Giambi 1.00
651 Jason Michaels, Travis Hafner .25
652 J. Johnson, Miguel Olivo .10
653 Sean Casey, Placido Polanco .10
654 Ivan Rodriguez, Fernando Rodney .25
655 Dan Uggla, H. Ramirez .25
656 Carlos Beltran, Jose Reyes .50
657 Alex Rodriguez, Derek Jeter 1.00
658 Aaron Rowand, Jimmy Rollins .25
659 Angel Berroa, Andres Blanco .10
660 Yadier Molina .10
661 Barry Bonds 2.00

Copper

Copper: 25-50X
Production 56 Sets

Gold

Gold: 8-15X
Production 2,007 Sets

Platinum

No Pricing
Production One Set

1st Edition

1st Edition: 5-10X
Hobby Exclusive 1:36

Red Back

Red Back (1-330): 1-2.5X
Inserted 2:Hobby, 10:HTA

Printing Plates

Production one set per color

All-Stars

NM/M
Complete Set (12): 15.00
Common Player: 1.00
Inserted 1:Rack Pack
1 Alfonso Soriano 2.00
2 Paul Konerko 1.50
3 Carlos Beltran 2.00
4 Troy Glaus 1.00
5 Jason Bay 1.50
6 Vladimir Guerrero 2.50
7 Chase Utley 3.00
8 Michael Young 1.00
9 David Wright 3.00
10 Gary Matthews 1.00
11 Brad Penny 1.00
12 Roy Halladay 1.00

All-Star Rookies

NM/M
Complete Set (10): 12.00
Common Player: 1.50
Inserted 1:Rack Pack
1 Prince Fielder 2.00
2 Dan Uggla 1.50
3 Ryan Zimmerman 2.00
4 Hanley Ramirez 2.00
5 Melky Cabrera 1.50
6 Andre Ethier 1.50
7 Nicholas Markakis 1.50

8 Justin Verlander 2.00
9 Francisco Liriano 2.00
10 Russell Martin 1.50

A-Rod Road to 500

NM/M
Series 1 A-Rod (1-25): 3.00
Series 2 A-Rod (201-225): 3.00

A-Rod Road to 500 Autographs

Production One Set

Distinguished Service

NM/M
Complete Set (20): 25.00
Common Player: 2.00
Inserted 1:12 Hobby, 1:12 HTA
1 Duke Snider 3.00
2 Yogi Berra 3.00
3 Bob Feller 2.00
4 Bobby Doerr 2.00
5 Monte Irvin 2.00
6 Dwight D. Eisenhower 2.00
7 George Marshall 2.00
8 Franklin D. Roosevelt 2.00
9 Harry S. Truman 2.00
10 Douglas MacArthur 2.00
11 Ralph Kiner 2.00
12 Hank Sauer 2.00
13 Elmer Valo 2.00
14 Bob Lemon 2.00
15 Hoyt Wilhelm 2.00
16 James Doolittle 2.00
17 Curtis Lemay 2.00
18 Omar Bradley 2.00
19 Chester Nimitz 2.00
20 Mark Clark 2.00
21 Joe DiMaggio 4.00
22 Warren Spahn 3.00
23 Stan Musial 3.00
24 Red Schoendienst 2.00
25 Ted Williams 4.00
26 Winston Churchill 3.00
27 Charles de Gaulle 2.00
28 George Bush 2.00
29 John F. Kennedy 3.00
30 Richard Bong 2.00

Distinguished Service Autograph

NM/M
Inserted 1:20,000 Hobby
BD Bobby Doerr 50.00
BF Bob Feller 60.00
DS Duke Snider 75.00
MI Monte Irvin 50.00
RK Ralph Kiner 75.00

Distinguished Service Cut Signatures

Production One Set

Generation Now

NM/M
All Ryan Howard's: 2.00
All Chase Utley's: 1.00
All C. Ming Wang's: 3.00
All Mike Napoli's: .50
All Justin Morneau's: 1.00
All David Wright's: 2.00
All Jered Weaver's: 1.00
All Andre Ethier's: 1.00
All Ryan Zimmerman's: 1.00
All Delmon Young's: 1.00
All Russell Martin's: .75
All Justin Verlander's: 1.00
All Hanley Ramirez's: 1.00
All Nick Markakis's: 1.00
All Nick Swisher's: .75

Generation Now Autographs

Production One Set

Highlights Autographs

NM/M
Short prints are not serial #'d.
JH John Hattig Jr. 8.00
AM Andrew Miller 50.00
AS Anibal Sanchez 10.00
MN Michael Napoli 10.00
JL James Loney 20.00
MH Matt Holliday 25.00
TT Troy Tulowitzki 30.00
HR Hanley Ramirez 20.00
JF Josh Fields 15.00
CQ Carlos Quentin 15.00
MG Matt Garza 15.00
JM John Maine 35.00
MP Mike Piazza/50 120.00
TH Travis Hafner 25.00
KM Kevin Mench 10.00
CU Chase Utley 50.00
DW David Wright 75.00
JM Justin Morneau 25.00
JS Johan Santana/250 60.00
MC Miguel Cabrera/250 35.00
DY Delmon Young 30.00
DWW Dontrelle Willis 20.00
CW Chien-Ming Wang/100 250.00
JS John Smoltz/250 50.00
AS Alfonso Soriano/100 100.00
DO David Ortiz/100 80.00
RH Ryan Howard/100 100.00
AR Alex Rodriguez/25 250.00
EF Emiliano Fruto 10.00
RZ Ryan Zimmerman 30.00
Series 2
AB Aaron Boone 10.00
AJ Andruw Jones 35.00
AP Albert Pujols 250.00
AR Anthony Reyes 15.00
CG Curtis Granderson 30.00
CW Craig Wilson 15.00
DO David Ortiz 80.00
DT Derrick Turnbow 15.00
DU Dan Uggla 20.00
DW David Wright 50.00
DWW Dontrelle Willis 20.00
EC Endy Chavez 40.00
ES Ervin Santana 15.00
JT Jim Thome 40.00
JD Johnny Damon 100.00
JG Jon Garland 15.00
JV Justin Verlander 50.00
JZ Joel Zumaya 20.00
KE Kelvim Escobar 20.00
KM Kendry Morales 10.00
LM Lastings Milledge 20.00
MC Melky Cabrera 25.00
MTC Matt Cain 20.00
PL Paul LoDuca 40.00
RC Robinson Cano 30.00
RH Ryan Howard 100.00
RM Russell Martin 20.00
RZ Ryan Zimmerman 30.00
SC Shawn Chacon 10.00
SP Scott Podsednik 15.00
SR Shawn Riggans 10.00
SSC Shin-Soo Choo 20.00
ST Steve Trachsel 25.00
TG Tom Glavine 75.00
VG Vladimir Guerrero 150.00

Highlights Relics

NM/M
Common Player: 5.00
AP Albert Pujols 25.00
AR Alex Rodriguez 20.00
AS Alfonso Soriano 15.00
BM Brian McCann 15.00
CB Carlos Beltran 10.00
CD Carlos Delgado 8.00
CQ Carlos Quentin 10.00
CB Craig Biggio 10.00
CS Curt Schilling 10.00
DO David Ortiz 10.00
DW Dontrelle Willis 8.00
ER Edgar Renteria 5.00
FT Frank Thomas 10.00
GS Gary Sheffield 8.00
IS Ichiro Suzuki 25.00
IR Ivan Rodriguez 10.00
JB Jason Bay 10.00
JPM Joe Mauer 15.00
JAS Johan Santana 20.00
JS John Smoltz 10.00
JR Jose Reyes 15.00
JM Justin Morneau 15.00
MO Magglio Ordonez 5.00
MAR Manny Ramirez 10.00
MR Mariano Rivera 15.00
MT Miguel Tejada 8.00
PK Paul Konerko 10.00
RC Robinson Cano 15.00
RO Roy Oswalt 8.00
RH Ryan Howard 20.00
SK Scott Kazmir 8.00
SR Scott Rolen 10.00
TG Tom Glavine 8.00
TG Troy Glaus 5.00
VW Vernon Wells 8.00
Series 2
AB Adrian Beltre 5.00
AER Alex Rodriguez 20.00
AJ Andruw Jones 8.00
ALR Anthony Reyes 5.00
AP Albert Pujols 25.00
AR Aramis Ramirez 8.00
AS Alfonso Soriano 10.00
CJ Chipper Jones 10.00
DE David Eckstein 20.00
DO David Ortiz 15.00
DW David Wright 15.00
DWW Dontrelle Willis 8.00
GA Garrett Atkins 5.00
GS Grady Sizemore 10.00
JD Jermaine Dye 5.00
JDD Johnny Damon 15.00
JT Jim Thome 10.00
JV Justin Verlander 20.00
LB Lance Berkman 8.00
MC Matt Cain 8.00
MCT Mark Teixeira 8.00
MEC Melky Cabrera 10.00
MR Manny Ramirez 10.00
MT Miguel Tejada 8.00
NS Nick Swisher 8.00
PK Paul Konerko 8.00
PM Pedro Martinez 8.00
RC Robinson Cano 15.00
RH Roy Halladay 10.00
RJH Ryan Howard 20.00
SK Scott Kazmir 8.00
TG Tom Glavine 10.00
VG Vladimir Guerrero 8.00
VW Vernon Wells 8.00

Hit Parade

NM/M
Inserted 1:9
1 Barry Bonds 2.00
2 Ken Griffey Jr. 1.50
3 Frank Thomas 1.00
4 Jim Thome .75
5 Manny Ramirez 1.00
6 Alex Rodriguez 2.00
7 Gary Sheffield .75
8 Mike Piazza 1.00
9 Carlos Delgado .75
10 Chipper Jones 1.00
11 Barry Bonds 2.00
12 Ken Griffey Jr. 1.50
13 Frank Thomas 1.00
14 Manny Ramirez 1.00
15 Gary Sheffield .75
16 Jeff Kent .50
17 Alex Rodriguez 2.00
18 Luis Gonzalez .50
19 Jim Thome .75
20 Mike Piazza 1.00
21 Craig Biggio .50
22 Barry Bonds 2.00
23 Julio Franco .50
24 Steve Finley .50
25 Omar Vizquel .50
26 Ken Griffey Jr. 1.50
27 Gary Sheffield .75
28 Luis Gonzalez .50
29 Ivan Rodriguez .75
30 Bernie Williams .50

Hobby Masters

NM/M
Common Player: .50
Inserted 1:6
1 David Wright 3.00
2 Albert Pujols 4.00
3 David Ortiz 1.50
4 Ryan Howard 3.00
5 Alfonso Soriano 1.50
6 Delmon Young 1.50
7 Jered Weaver 1.50
8 Derek Jeter 4.00
9 Freddy Sanchez .50
10 Alex Rodriguez 3.00
11 Johan Santana 1.50
12 Ichiro Suzuki 2.50
13 Andruw Jones 1.50
14 Vladimir Guerrero 1.50
15 Miguel Cabrera 1.50
16 Todd Helton 1.00
17 Manny Ramirez 1.50
18 Carlos Beltran 1.50
19 Justin Morneau 1.00
20 Francisco Liriano 1.00

Home Run Derby

NM/M
Production 999 Sets
DO David Ortiz 4.00
RH Ryan Howard 8.00
JD Jermaine Dye 2.00
AP Albert Pujols 10.00
TH Travis Hafner 2.00
AS Alfonso Soriano 4.00
JT Jim Thome 3.00
LB Lance Berkman 2.00
FT Frank Thomas 4.00
CB Carlos Beltran 4.00
TG Troy Glaus 2.00
AJ Andruw Jones 4.00
JG Jason Giambi 3.00
AD Adam Dunn 3.00
PK Paul Konerko 2.00
CD Carlos Delgado 3.00
MR Manny Ramirez 4.00
AR Aramis Ramirez 3.00
AER Alex Rodriguez 10.00
JB Jason Bay 2.00
NS Nick Swisher 2.00
BH Bill Hall 2.00
JM Justin Morneau 4.00
MH Matt Holliday 2.00
RS Richie Sexson 2.00
AL Adam LaRoche 2.00
VG Vladimir Guerrero 4.00
CU Chase Utley 4.00
RI Raul Ibanez 2.00
GA Garrett Atkins 2.00
MT Mark Teixeira 4.00
PB Pat Burrell 2.00
VW Vernon Wells 2.00
PF Prince Fielder 10.00
TKH Torii Hunter 3.00
CL Carlos Lee 2.00
CM Craig Monroe 2.00
KG Ken Griffey Jr. 10.00
JC Joe Crede 2.00
DU Dan Uggla 2.00
GS Grady Sizemore 4.00
MC Miguel Cabrera 4.00
MOT Miguel Tejada 3.00
DW David Wright 8.00
DY Delmon Young 4.00
MMT Marcus Thames 2.00
JDD Johnny Damon 4.00
JF Jeff Francoeur 3.00
AB Adrian Beltre 2.00
MP Mike Piazza 4.00

In The Name

Production One Set

Josh Gibson HR History

NM/M
Common Gibson: 1.00
Inserted 1:9

Mickey Mantle Home Run History

NM/M
Common Mantle HR History: 2.00
Inserted 1:9 Hobby

Mickey Mantle Home Run History Relics

NM/M
Common Mantle: 150.00
Production Seven Sets

Opening Day

NM/M
Inserted 1:12
1 New York Mets, St. Louis Cardinals 2.00
2 Atlanta Braves, Philadelphia Phillies 1.00
3 Florida Marlins, Washington Nationals 1.00
4 Tampa Bay Devil Rays, New York Yankees 2.00
5 Toronto Blue Jays, Detroit Tigers 1.00
6 Cleveland Indians, Chicago White Sox 1.00
7 Los Angeles Dodgers, Milwaukee Brewers 1.00
8 Chicago Cubs, Cincinnati Reds 1.00
9 Arizona Diamondbacks, Colorado Rockies 1.00
10 Boston Red Sox, Kansas City Royals 2.00
11 Oakland Athletics, Seattle Mariners 1.00
12 Baltimore Orioles, Minnesota Twins 1.00
13 Pittsburgh Pirates, Houston Astros 1.00
14 Texas Rangers, Anaheim Angels 1.00
15 San Diego Padres, San Francisco Giants 1.00

Own The Game

NM/M
Common Player: .50
Inserted 1:6
1 Ryan Howard 2.50
2 David Ortiz 1.00
3 Alfonso Soriano 1.00
4 Albert Pujols 3.00
5 Lance Berkman .75
6 Jermaine Dye .50
7 Travis Hafner .75
8 Jim Thome 1.00
9 Carlos Beltran 1.00
10 Adam Dunn .75
11 Ryan Howard 2.50
12 David Ortiz 1.00
13 Albert Pujols 3.00
14 Lance Berkman .75
15 Justin Morneau .75
16 Andruw Jones 1.00
17 Jermaine Dye .50
18 Travis Hafner .75
19 Alex Rodriguez 3.00
20 David Wright 2.00
21 Johan Santana 1.00
22 Chris Carpenter .75
23 Brandon Webb .50
24 Roy Oswalt .75
25 Josh Johnson .50

Ted Williams 406

NM/M
Complete Set (18): 30.00
Common Williams: 2.50
Inserted 1:4 Target

The Mickey Mantle Story

NM/M
Complete Set (30): 40.00
Common Mantle: 3.00

The Streak

NM/M
Common Joe DiMaggio (1-56): 1.50
Inserted 1:9

The Streak Before The Streak

NM/M
Common Joe DiMaggio (1-61): 1.50
Inserted 1:9

Topps Stars

NM/M
Inserted 1:9
1 Ryan Howard 1.50
2 Alfonso Soriano 1.00
3 Todd Helton .75
4 Johan Santana .75
5 David Wright 1.50
6 Albert Pujols 2.00
7 Daisuke Matsuzaka 3.00
8 Miguel Cabrera 1.00
9 David Ortiz 1.00
10 Alex Rodriguez 2.00
11 Vladimir Guerrero 1.00
12 Ichiro Suzuki 1.50
13 Derek Jeter 2.00
14 Lance Berkman .50
15 Ryan Zimmerman .50

Trading Places

NM/M
Inserted 1:9
1 Jeff Weaver .50
2 Frank Thomas 1.00
3 Mike Piazza 1.00
4 Alfonso Soriano 1.00
5 Freddy Garcia .50
6 Jason Marquis .50
7 Ted Lilly .50
8 Mark Loretta .50
9 Marcus Giles .50
10 Barry Zito .50
11 Andy Pettitte .75
12 J.D. Drew .50
13 Gary Matthews .50
14 Jay Payton .50
15 Aubrey Huff .50
16 Brian Bannister .50
17 Jeff Conine .50
18 Gary Sheffield .75
19 Shea Hillenbrand .50
20 Wes Helms .50
21 Frank Catalanotto .50
22 Adam LaRoche .50
23 Mike Gonzalez .50
24 Greg Maddux 1.50
25 Jason Schmidt .50

Trading Places Autographs

NM/M
AL Adam LaRoche 15.00
BB Brian Bannister 20.00
FC Frank Catalanotto 15.00
FG Freddy Garcia 20.00
GS Gary Sheffield 40.00
JS Jason Schmidt 20.00
MG Mike Gonzalez 10.00
SH Shea Hillenbrand 15.00
WH Wes Helms 15.00

Trading Places Relics

NM/M
AP Andy Pettitte 10.00
AS Alfonso Soriano 10.00
BZ Barry Zito 8.00
FT Frank Thomas 10.00
GM Greg Maddux 20.00
GS Gary Sheffield 15.00
JW Jeff Weaver 8.00
MG Marcus Giles 5.00
ML Mark Loretta 8.00
MP Mike Piazza 20.00

Unlock the Mick

NM/M
Complete Set (5):
Common Mantle: 2.00
Inserted 1:18
1-5 Mickey Mantle 2.00

Wal-Mart

NM/M
Complete Set (18): 40.00
Common Player: 1.50
Three per $9.99 Wal-Mart box.
1 Frank Thomas 3.00
2 Mike Piazza 3.00
3 Ivan Rodriguez 2.00
4 David Ortiz 3.00
5 David Wright 4.00
6 Greg Maddux 4.00
7 Mickey Mantle 8.00
8 Jose Reyes 4.00
9 John Smoltz 1.50
10 Jim Edmonds 1.50
11 Ryan Howard 4.00
12 Miguel Cabrera 3.00
13 Carlos Delgado 2.00
14 Miguel Tejada 2.00
15 Ichiro Suzuki 4.00
16 Albert Pujols 5.00
17 Derek Jeter 5.00
18 Vladimir Guerrero 3.00

World Champion Relics

NM/M
Production 100 Sets
Cards are not serial #'d
1 Jeff Weaver 60.00
2 Chris Duncan 60.00
3 Chris Carpenter 75.00
4 Yadier Molina 40.00
5 Albert Pujols 160.00
6 Jim Edmonds 65.00
7 Ronnie Belliard 50.00
8 So Taguchi 80.00
9 Juan Encarnacion 50.00
10 Scott Rolen 75.00
11 Anthony Reyes 60.00
12 Preston Wilson 50.00
13 Jeff Suppan 60.00
14 Adam Wainwright 120.00
15 David Eckstein 100.00

1952 Mickey Mantle Reprint Relic

Production 52

1953 Mickey Mantle Reprint Relic

Production 53

2007 Topps Allen & Ginter

NM/M
Complete Set (390):
Common player: .25
Mini Exclusives (351-390): No pricing
Inserted in Rip Cards
Common SP: 2.00
Inserted 1:2
Pack (8): 5.00
Box (24): 110.00
1 Ryan Howard 3.00
2 Mike Gonzalez .25
3 Austin Kearns .25
4 Josh Hamilton **(RC)** .50
5 Stephen Drew/SP 2.00
6 Matt Murton .25
7 Mickey Mantle 5.00
8 Howie Kendrick .25
9 Alexander Graham Bell .25
10 Jason Bay .50
11 Hank Blalock .50
12 Johan Santana .75
13 Eleanor Roosevelt .25
14 Kei Igawa **RC** 1.00
15 Jeff Francoeur .50
16 Carl Crawford .50
17 Jhonny Peralta .25
18 Mariano Rivera .50
19 Mario Andretti .25
20 Vladimir Guerrero .75
21 Adam Wainwright .50
22 Huston Street .25
23 Cael Sanderson .25
24 Susan B. Anthony .25
25 Jay Payton .25
26 P.T. Barnum .25
27 Scott Podsednik .25
28 Willie Randolph .25
29 Sean Casey .25
30 Eiffel Tower .25
31 Kenji Johjima .25
32 Felix Hernandez .50
33 Elijah Dukes **RC** 1.00
34 Mark Grudzielanek .25
35 J.D. Drew .25
36 Kevin Kouzmanoff **(RC)** .50
37 Jonathan Papelbon .50
38 Bobby Crosby .25
39 Brooklyn Bridge .25
40 Adam Dunn .50
41 Lyle Overbay .25
42 Brian Fuentes .25
43 Scott Rolen/SP 3.00
44 Matt Lindstrom **(RC)** .50
45 Carlos Zambrano .50
46 Cole Hamels .50
47 Matthew Kemp .25
48 Gary Matthews/SP 2.00
49 J.J. Putz .25
50 Albert Pujols 2.00
51 Danny Haren .25
52 Aaron Harang .25
53 Ferris Wheel .25
54 Juan Rivera .25
55 Ken Griffey Jr. 1.50
56 Chien-Ming Wang 1.00
57 Sean Henn **(RC)** .50
58 Mike Mussina/SP 3.00

59 Ian Snell .25
60 Josh Barfield .25
61 Justin Morneau .75
62 Dwight D. Eisenhower .25
63 Bengie Molina/SP 2.00
64 Brett Myers .25
65 Andy Marte .25
66 Bill Hall .25
67 Ryan Shealy .25
68 Joe Scott .25
69 Mike Rabelo **RC** .50
70 Jermaine Dye .50
71 Andre Ethier .25
72 Bruce Lee 1.00
73 Nick Punto .25
74 Ervin Santana .25
75 Troy Tulowitzki **(RC)** 1.00
76 Garret Anderson .25
77 Ryan Freel .25
78 Carlos Guillen .50
79 John Smoltz .50
80 Chase Utley .75
81 Mike Sweeney .25
82 Joe Frazier 1.00
83 Brad Lidge .25
84 Casey Blake .25
85 Ivan Rodriguez .50
86 Roy Oswalt .50
87 Akinori Iwamura **RC** 2.00
88 Francisco Rodriguez .25
89 John Lackey .25
90 Miguel Cabrera .75
91 Kevin Mench .25
92 Victor Martinez .50
93 Chad Tracy .25
94 Charlie Manuel .25
95 Hanley Ramirez .75
96 Dontrelle Willis .50
97 Doug Slaten **RC** .50
98 Noah Lowry .25
99 Shawn Green .25
100 David Ortiz 1.00
101 Mark Reynolds **RC** 2.00
102 Preston Wilson .25
103 Mohandas Gandhi .25
104 Jeff Kent .50
105 Lance Berkman .50
106 C.C. Sabathia .50
107 Jason Varitek/SP 3.00
108 Mark Twain .25
109 Melvin Mora .25
110 Michael Young/SP 2.00
111 Scott Hatteberg .25
112 Erik Bedard .50
113 Sitting Bull .25
114 Homer Bailey **(RC)** 1.00
115 Mark Teahen .25
116 Ryan Braun **(RC)** 3.00
117 John Miles .25
118 Coco Crisp .25
119 Hunter Pence/SP **(RC)** 6.00
120 Delmon Young **(RC)** 1.00
121 Aramis Ramirez .50
122 Magglio Ordonez .50
123 Tadahito Iguchi .25
124 Mark Selby .25
125 Gil Meche .25
126 Curt Schilling .75
127 Brandon Phillips .25
128 Milton Bradley .25
129 Craig Monroe .25
130 Jason Schmidt/SP 2.00
131 Nick Markakis .50
132 Paul Konerko .50
133 Carlos Gomez **RC** 1.50
134 Garrett Atkins .25
135 Jered Weaver .50
136 Edgar Renteria .50
137 Jason Isringhausen/SP 2.00
138 Ray Durham .25
139 Bob Baffert .25
140 Nick Swisher .25
141 Brian McCann .50
142 Orlando Hudson .25
143 Brian Bannister .25
144 Manny Acta .25
145 Jose Vidro .25
146 Carlos Quentin .25
147 Billy Butler **(RC)** 1.00
148 Kenny Rogers .25
149 Tom Gordon .25
150 Derek Jeter 2.00
151 Bob Wickman .25
152 Carlos Lee SP 2.00
153 Willy Taveras .25
154 Paul LoDuca .25
155 Ben Sheets .50
156 Brian Roberts .50
157 Freddy Adu .25
158 Jason Kendall .25
159 Michael Barrett/SP 2.00
160 Frank Thomas .75
161 Manny Ramirez .75
162 Stanley Glenn .25
163 Robinson Cano .50
164 Phil Hughes **(RC)** 2.00
165 Joe Mauer .50
166 Derrek Lee .75
167 Jeff Weaver .25
168 Joe Smith **RC** .50
169 Louis Pasteur .25
170 Gary Sheffield .50
171 Luis Castillo .25
172 Joe Torre .50
173 Andy LaRoche **(RC)** .50
174 Jamie Fischer .25
175 Carlos Beltran .50
176 Bronson Arroyo .25
177 Rafael Furcal .50
178 Juan Pierre/SP 2.00
179 Matt Cain .50
180 Alfonso Soriano .75
181 Joe Borowski .25
182 Conor Jackson .25
183 Groundhog Day .25
184 Pat Burrell .25
185 Troy Glaus .50
186 Joel Zumaya .25
187 Russell Martin .50
188 Josh Willingham .25
189 Jarrod Saltalamacchia **(RC)** .50
190 Scott Kazmir .50
191 Jeremy Hermida .25
192 Tower Bridge .25
193 Rich Hill SP 2.00
194 Francisco Cordero/SP 2.00
195 Mike Piazza 1.00
196 Brad Ausmus .25
197 Greg Louganis .25
198 Frank Catalanotto .25
199 Alejandro De Aza **RC** 1.00
200 David Wright 1.00
201 Freddy Sanchez .25
202 Shea Hillenbrand .25
203 Justin Verlander/SP 3.00
204 Alex Gordon **RC** 5.00
205 Jimmy Rollins .50
206 Mike Napoli .25
207 Chris Burke .25
208 Chipper Jones .75
209 Randy Johnson .75
210 Daisuke Matsuzaka **RC** 5.00
211 Orlando Cabrera .25
212 B.J. Upton .50
213 Lou Piniella .25
214 Mike Cameron .25
215 Luis Gonzalez .25
216 Rickie Weeks .25
217 Hideki Okajima **RC** 2.00
218 Johnny Estrada .25
219 Dan Uggla/SP 2.00
220 Ryan Zimmerman .50
221 Tony Gwynn Jr. .25
222 Rocco Baldelli/SP 2.00
223 Xavier Nady .25
224 Josh Bard/SP 2.00
225 Raul Ibanez .25
226 Chris Carpenter .50
227 Matt DeSalvo **(RC)** .50
228 Jack the Ripper .25
229 Eric Chavez .25
230 Jose Reyes 1.00
231 Glen Perkins **(RC)** .50
232 Gregg Zaun .25
233 Jim Thome .75
234 Joe Crede .25
235 Barry Zito .50
236 Yoel Hernandez **RC** 1.00
237 Kelly Johnson .25
238 Chris Young .50
239 Fyodor Dostoevsky .25
240 Miguel Tejada .50
241 Doug Mientkiewicz .25
242 Bobby Jenks .25
243 Brad Hawpe/SP 2.00
244 Jay Marshall **RC** .50
245 Brad Penny .25
246 Johnny Damon .75
247 Dave Roberts .25
248 Ron Washington .25
249 Mike Aponte .25
250 Brandon Webb .50
251 Andy Pettitte .50
252 Bud Black .25
253 Mike Cuddyer .25
254 Chris Stewart **RC** .50
255 Mark Teixeira .75
256 Hideki Matsui 1.50
257 Curtis Granderson .50
258 A.J. Pierzynski .25
259 Tony LaRussa .25
260 Andruw Jones .75
261 Torii Hunter .50
262 Mark Loretta .25
263 Jim Edmonds/SP 2.00
264 Aaron Rowand .25
265 Roy Halladay .50
266 Freddy Garcia .25
267 Reggie Sanders .25
268 Washington Monument .25
269 Franklin D. Roosevelt .25
270 Alex Rodriguez 2.00
271 Wes Helms .25
272 Mia Hamm .50
273 Jorge Posada .50
274 Tim Lincecum **RC** 5.00
275 Bobby Abreu .50
276 Zachary Duke .25
277 Carlos Delgado .50
278 Julio Juarez .25
279 Brandon Inge .25
280 Todd Helton .50
281 Marcus Giles .25
282 Josh Johnson .25
283 Chris Capuano .25
284 B.J. Ryan .25
285 Nick Johnson .25
286 Khalil Greene .25
287 Travis Hafner .50
288 Ted Lilly .25
289 Jim Leyland .25
290 Prince Fielder 1.00
291 Trevor Hoffman .25
292 Brian Giles .25
293 Omar Vizquel .25
294 Julio Lugo .25
295 Jake Peavy .50
296 Adrian Beltre .25
297 Josh Beckett .50
298 Harry S. Truman .25
299 Mark Buehrle .25
300 Ichiro Suzuki 1.50
301 Chris Duncan/SP 2.00
302 Augie Garrido/SP 2.00
303 Tyler Clippard/SP **(RC)** 2.00
304 Ramon Hernandez .25
305 Jeremy Bonderman .50
306 Morgan Ensberg/SP 2.00
307 J.J. Hardy/SP 2.00
308 Mark Zupan/SP 2.00
309 Laila Ali/SP 4.00
310 Greg Maddux/SP 4.00
311 David Ross .25
312 Chris Duffy .25
313 Moises Alou .50
314 Yadier Molina .25
315 Corey Patterson .25
316 Dan O'Brien/SP 2.00
317 Michael Bourn/SP **(RC)** 2.00
318 Jonny Gomes/SP 2.00
319 Ken Jennings/SP 2.00
320 Barry Bonds/SP 5.00
321 Gary Hall Jr./SP 2.00
322 Kerri Walsh/SP 2.00
323 Craig Biggio .50
324 Ian Kinsler .25
325 Grady Sizemore/SP 3.00
326 Alex Rios/SP 3.00
327 Ted Toles/SP 2.00
328 Jason Jennings .25
329 Vernon Wells .50
330 Bob Geren/SP 2.00
331 Dennis Rodman/SP 2.00
332 Tom Glavine .50
333 Pedro Martinez .75
334 Gustavo Molina/SP **RC** 3.00
335 Bartolo Colon/SP 2.00
336 Misty May-Treanor/SP 2.00
337 Randy Winn .25
338 Eric Byrnes .50
339 Jason McElwain/SP 2.00
340 Placido Polanco/SP 2.00
341 Adrian Gonzalez .50
342 Chad Coredo .25
343 Jeff Francis .25
344 Lastings Milledge .25
345 Sammy Sosa/SP 3.00
346 Jacque Jones .25
347 Anibal Sanchez .25
348 Roger Clemens/SP 4.00
349 Jesse Litsch/SP **RC** 2.00
350 Adam LaRoche/SP 2.00

Mini

Mini: 2-3X
Mini (351-390): No Pricing
#'s 351-390 Inserted in Rip Cards
Allen & Ginter Back: 3-4X
Inserted 1:5
Black Border: 4-6X
Inserted 1:10
No Number: 10-20X
Production 50 Sets
Bazooka Mini: No Pricing
Production 25 Sets
Wood: No Pricing
Production One Set

Printing Plates

Production one set per color.

Autographs

NM/M
Short-prints are noted.
Red Ink: No Pricing
Production 10 Sets
CS Cael Sanderson/200 120.00
MS Mark Selby/200 75.00
SJF Joe Frazier/120 350.00
DR Dennis Rodman/200 160.00
MZ Mark Zupan/200 85.00
FA Freddy Adu/200 125.00
BB Bob Baffert/200 120.00
TT Ted Toles/200 100.00
KJ Ken Jennings/200 120.00
GH Gary Hall Jr./200 80.00
DO Dan O'Brien/200 75.00
JF Jamie Fischer/200 80.00
GL Greg Louganis/200 100.00
MA Mike Aponte/200 60.00
JJ Julio Juarez/200 60.00
KW Kerri Walsh/200 100.00
LA Laila Ali/200 200.00
TS Tommie Smith/200 120.00
MGA Mario Andretti/200 180.00
AG Augie Garrido/200 100.00
JMC Jason McElwain/200 100.00
SG Stanley Glenn/200 125.00
JMM John Miles/200 125.00
JBS Joe Scott/200 120.00
MH Mia Hamm/200 220.00
MMT Misty May-Treanor/200 100.00
BC Brian Cashman/100 250.00
CMW Chien-Ming Wang/200 375.00
AI Akinori Iwamura 50.00
RH Ryan Howard/100 125.00
HR Hanley Ramirez 50.00
HK Howie Kendrick 25.00
AR Alex Rodriguez/225 300.00
DW David Wright/200 150.00
RM Russell Martin 40.00
AE Andre Ethier 40.00
JT Jim Thome/100 80.00
JM Justin Morneau 40.00
ES Ervin Santana 20.00
BH Bill Hall 30.00
CH Cole Hamels 75.00
MEI Maicer Izturis 20.00
CG Curtis Granderson 50.00
AG2 Adrian Gonzalez 25.00
TT Troy Tulowitzki 50.00
VW Vernon Wells 30.00
JS Johan Santana/100 150.00
JP Jonathan Papelbon 50.00
MC Miguel Cabrera 100 60.00
BPB Brian Bannister 25.00
TH Torii Hunter 30.00
RZ Ryan Zimmerman 65.00
NM Nicholas Markakis 50.00
JH Jeremy Hermida 25.00
MN Mike Napoli 25.00
NL Nook Logan 20.00

Cut Signatures

Production One Set

Dick Perez Sketch Cards

NM/M
Complete Set (30): 15.00
Common Player: .50
Inserted 1:1
Dick Perez Originals: No Pricing
Production One Set
1 Brandon Webb .50
2 Chipper Jones 1.00
3 Nick Markakis .50
4 Daisuke Matsuzaka 2.00
5 Alfonso Soriano 1.00
6 Jermaine Dye .50
7 Adam Dunn .50
8 Grady Sizemore 1.00
9 Troy Tulowitzki .50
10 Gary Sheffield .75
11 Hanley Ramirez .75
12 Carlos Lee .50
13 Mark Teahen .50
14 Gary Matthews .50
15 Andre Ethier .50
16 Prince Fielder 1.50
17 Joe Mauer .75
18 Jose Reyes 1.00
19 Derek Jeter 2.00
20 Nick Swisher .50
21 Ryan Howard 1.50
22 Freddy Sanchez .50
23 Greg Maddux 1.50
24 Raul Ibanez .50
25 Barry Zito .50
26 Jim Edmonds .50
27 Delmon Young .50
28 Michael Young .50
29 Roy Halladay .50
30 Ryan Zimmerman .75

Mini Flags

NM/M
Common Card: 2.00
1 Angola 2.00
2 Argentina 2.00
3 Australia 2.00
4 Austria 2.00
5 Belgium 2.00
6 Brazil 2.00
7 Bulgaria 2.00
8 Canada 2.00
9 Chile 2.00
10 China 2.00
11 Colombia 2.00
12 Costa Rica 2.00
13 Denmark 2.00
14 Dominican Republic 2.00
15 Ecuador 2.00
16 Egypt 2.00
17 France 2.00
18 Germany 2.00
19 Greece 2.00
20 Greenland 2.00
21 Honduras 2.00
22 Iceland 2.00
23 India 2.00
24 Indonesia 2.00
25 Ireland 2.00
26 Israel 2.00
27 Italy 2.00
28 Ivory Coast 2.00
29 Jamaica 2.00
30 Japan 2.00
31 Kenya 2.00
32 Mexico 2.00
33 Morocco 2.00
34 Netherlands 2.00
35 Nigeria 2.00
36 Norway 2.00
37 Panama 2.00
38 Peru 2.00
39 Phillipines 2.00
40 Portugal 2.00
41 Puerto Rico 2.00
42 Russian Federation 2.00
43 Spain 2.00
44 Switzerland 2.00
45 Taiwan 2.00
46 Thailand 2.00
47 Turkey 2.00
48 United Arab Emirates 2.00
49 United Kingdom 2.00
50 United States 2.00

Mini Snakes

NM/M
Common Mini Snake: 25.00
1 Arizona Coral Snake 25.00
2 Copperhead 25.00
3 Black Mamba 25.00
4 King Cobra 25.00
5 Cottonmouth 25.00

Mini Emperors

NM/M
Common Emperor: 5.00
1 Julius Caesar 5.00
2 Caesar Augustus 5.00
3 Tiberius 5.00
4 Caligula 5.00
5 Claudius 5.00
6 Nero 5.00
7 Titus 5.00
8 Hadrian 5.00
9 Marcus Aurelius 5.00
10 Septimus Severus 5.00

National Pride Box Loaders

NM/M
Common Card: 5.00
Inserted 1:Box
1 Kei Igawa, Daisuke Matsuzaka, Hideki Matsui, Ichiro Suzuki 8.00
2 Hideki Okajima, Akinori Iwamura, Kenji Johjima, Tadahito Iguchi 6.00
3 Bobby Abreu, Miguel Cabrera, Felix Hernandez, Johan Santana 5.00
4 Shin-Soo Choo, Chan Ho Park, Byung-Hyun Kim, Jae-Kuk Ryu 5.00
5 Jason Bay, Russell Martin, Justin Morneau, Rich Harden 6.00
6 Hanley Ramirez, Manny Ramirez, Aramis Ramirez, Vladimir Guerrero 8.00
7 Jose Reyes, Pedro Martinez, David Ortiz, Albert Pujols 8.00
8 Carlos Beltran, Carlos Delgado, Ivan Rodriguez, Jorge Posada 6.00
9 Prince Fielder, Alex Rodriguez, Ryan Howard, David Wright 8.00
10 Brandon Webb, Justin Verlander, Greg Maddux, John Smoltz 5.00

N43 Box Loader

NM/M
Common Player: 4.00
Inserted 1:Box
AR Alex Rodriguez 8.00
RH Ryan Howard 6.00
DW David Wright 6.00
IS Ichiro Suzuki 6.00
AP Albert Pujols 8.00
DM Daisuke Matsuzaka 10.00
VG Vladimir Guerrero 4.00
BB Barry Bonds 8.00
PF Prince Fielder 6.00
RZ Ryan Zimmerman 4.00
DJ Ch Felicity's Diamond Jim 15.00
BL Bruce Lee 10.00
MA Mario Andretti 4.00
GL Greg Louganis 4.00
JF Joe Frazier 6.00

N43 Box Loader Autographs

Production 10 Sets

N43 Box Loader Relics

Production 25 Sets

Relics

NM/M
Common Relic: 5.00
KJ Ken Jennings/250 40.00
JF Jamie Fischer/250 30.00
TS Tommie Smith/250 50.00
KW Kerri Walsh/250 60.00
LA Laila Ali/250 50.00
JJ Julio Juarez/250 25.00
MH Mia Hamm/250 70.00
BL Bruce Lee/250 300.00
DO Dan O'Brien/250 20.00
SJF Joe Frazier/250 80.00
GH Gary Hall Jr./250 50.00
AL Adam LaRoche 8.00
AP Albert Pujols 30.00
AR Aramis Ramirez 8.00
CB Carlos Beltran 8.00
CC Carl Crawford 8.00
CK Casey Kotchman 5.00
EC Eric Chavez 5.00
EG Eric Gagne 8.00
HB Hank Blalock 5.00
HR Hanley Ramirez 8.00
JB Jason Bay 5.00
JG Jason Giambi 8.00
MC1 Miguel Cabrera 10.00
MC2 Miguel Cabrera 10.00
MG Marcus Giles 5.00
MMU Mark Mulder 5.00
MCM Mike Mussina 8.00
MP Mike Piazza 15.00
MR Manny Ramirez 10.00
MT Miguel Tejada 8.00
NS Nick Swisher 5.00
PF Prince Fielder 20.00
PK Paul Konerko 8.00
RC Robinson Cano 20.00
RH Rich Harden 8.00
RW Randy Winn 5.00
SD Stephen Drew 8.00
SP Scott Podsednik 8.00
SR1 Scott Rolen 8.00
SR2 Scott Rolen 8.00
TG Troy Glaus 5.00
VG Vladimir Guerrero 10.00
DAO David Ortiz/250 20.00
AER Alex Rodriguez/250 30.00
BB Barry Bonds/250 35.00
MM Mickey Mantle/250 150.00
BR Brian Roberts 8.00
BZ Barry Zito 5.00
CMS Curt Schilling 10.00
DW Dontrelle Willis 5.00
IR Ivan Rodriguez 8.00
PL Paul LoDuca 5.00
CLC Coco Crisp 8.00
CP Corey Patterson 5.00
CT Chad Tracy 5.00
DL Derrek Lee 8.00
RA Rich Aurilia 5.00
SS Sammy Sosa 10.00
TN Trot Nixon 5.00
BC Brian Cashman/250 35.00
AS Arthur Shorin/50 150.00
KO Keith Olbermann/100 150.00

Rip Cards

NM/M
Production 10-99 75.00
1 Grady Sizemore/90 125.00
2 Miguel Cabrera/75 125.00
3 Adam Dunn/95 100.00
4 Jose Reyes/99 150.00
5 Alfonso Soriano/90 125.00
6 Chase Utley/99 125.00
7 Frank Thomas/95 150.00
8 Andruw Jones/95 125.00
9 Nick Markakis/75 100.00
10 Felix Hernandez/99 125.00
11 Jered Weaver/99 125.00
12 Ivan Rodriguez/99 125.00
13 Joe Mauer/99 100.00
14 Derek Jeter/99 180.00
17 Miguel Tejada/95 100.00
18 Vladimir Guerrero/75 125.00
19 Greg Maddux/99 150.00
20 Michael Young/99 100.00
21 Barry Zito/99 100.00
22 Russell Martin/95 150.00
23 Daisuke Matsuzaka/99 180.00
24 Stephen Drew/95 100.00
25 Alex Rodriguez/99 150.00
26 J.D. Drew/99 100.00
27 Paul Konerko/99 100.00
28 Josh Hamilton/90 100.00
29 Mike Piazza/99 125.00
31 Carl Crawford/99 100.00
32 Adam LaRoche/99 100.00
33 Bill Hall/95 100.00
34 Scott Kazmir/95 100.00
35 Gary Matthews/99 100.00
36 Gary Sheffield/99 125.00
37 Francisco Rodriguez/95 100.00
38 Todd Helton/99 100.00
40 David Wright/99 150.00
42 Barry Bonds/99 180.00
43 Johan Santana/75 125.00
44 Albert Pujols/90 200.00
45 Carlos Lee/99 75.00
46 Cole Hamels/95 125.00
47 Prince Fielder/99 125.00
48 Hanley Ramirez/99 125.00
49 Ryan Zimmerman/90 125.00
50 Kei Igawa/75 100.00

2007 Topps Chrome

NM/M
Complete Set (363):
Common Player: .25

Common RC Auto.
(331-363): 10.00
Pack (4): 3.00
Box (24): 60.00
1 Nick Swisher .50
2 Bobby Abreu .50
3 Edgar Renteria .50
4 Mickey Mantle 5.00
5 Preston Wilson .25
6 C.C. Sabathia .50
7 Julio Lugo .25
8 J.D. Drew .50
9 Jason Varitek .50
10 Orlando Hernandez .25
11 Corey Patterson .25
12 Josh Bard .25
13 Gary Matthews .25
14 Jason Jennings .25
15 Bronson Arroyo .25
16 Andy Pettitte .50
17 Ervin Santana .25
18 Paul Konerko .50
19 Adam LaRoche .25
20 Jim Edmonds .50
21 Derek Jeter 3.00
22 Aubrey Huff .25
23 Andre Ethier .25
24 Jeremy Sowers .25
25 Miguel Cabrera 1.00
26 Carlos Lee .50
27 Mike Piazza 1.00
28 Cole Hamels .75
29 Mark Loretta .25
30 John Smoltz .50
31 Dan Uggla .25
32 Lyle Overbay .25
33 Michael Barrett .25
34 Ivan Rodriguez .75
35 Jake Westbrook .25
36 Moises Alou .50
37 Jered Weaver .50
38 Lastings Milledge .50
39 Austin Kearns .25
40 Adam Loewen .25
41 Josh Barfield .25
42 Johan Santana 1.00
43 Ian Kinsler .25
44 Mike Lowell .50
45 Scott Rolen .75
46 Chipper Jones 1.00
47 Joe Crede .25
48 Rafael Furcal .25
49 David Bush .25
50 Marcus Giles .25
51 Joe Blanton .25
52 Dontrelle Willis .25
53 Scott Kazmir .50
54 Jeff Kent .50
55 Travis Hafner .50
56 Ryan Garko .25
57 Nicholas Markakis .50
58 Michael Cuddyer .25
59 Jason Giambi .75
60 Chone Figgins .25
61 Carlos Delgado .75
62 Aramis Ramirez .50
63 Albert Pujols 3.00
64 Gary Sheffield .75
65 Adrian Gonzalez .50
66 Prince Fielder 1.50
67 Freddy Sanchez .25
68 Jack Wilson .25
69 Jake Peavy .50
70 Javier Vazquez .25
71 Todd Helton .75
72 Bill Hall .25
73 Jeremy Bonderman .50
74 Rocco Baldelli .25
75 Noah Lowry .25
76 Justin Verlander .75
77 Mark Buehrle .50
78 Hank Blalock .25
79 Mark Teahen .25
80 Chien-Ming Wang 1.00
81 Roy Halladay .50
82 Melvin Mora .25
83 Grady Sizemore .75
84 Matt Cain .50
85 Carl Crawford .50
86 Johnny Damon .75
87 Freddy Garcia .25
88 Ryan Shealy .25
89 Carlos Beltran .75
90 Chuck James .25
91 Ben Sheets .50
92 Mark Mulder .25
93 Carlos Quentin .25
94 Richie Sexson .50
95 Brian Schneider .25
96 Hideki Matsui 2.00
97 Robinson Tejeda .25
98 Scott Hatteberg .25
99 Jeff Francis .25
100 Robinson Cano .50
101 Barry Zito .50
102 Reed Johnson .25
103 Chris Carpenter .50
104 Chad Tracy .25
105 Anibal Sanchez .25
106 Brad Penny .25
107 David Wright 2.00
108 Jimmy Rollins .75
109 Alfonso Soriano 1.00
110 Greg Maddux 2.00
111 Curt Schilling .75
112 Stephen Drew .25
113 Matt Holliday .50
114 Jorge Posada .50
115 Vladimir Guerrero 1.00
116 Frank Thomas .75
117 Jonathan Papelbon .50
118 Manny Ramirez 1.00
119 Magglio Ordonez .50
120 Joe Mauer .50
121 Ryan Howard 2.00
122 Chris Young .50
123 A.J. Burnett .25
124 Brian McCann .50
125 Juan Pierre .25
126 Jonny Gomes .25
127 Roger Clemens 2.50
128 Chad Billingsley .25
129 Kenji Johjima .25
130 Brian Giles .25
131 Chase Utley 1.00
132 Carl Pavano .25
133 Curtis Granderson .50
134 Sean Casey .25
135 Jon Garland .25
136 David Ortiz 1.00
137 Bobby Crosby .25
138 Conor Jackson .25
139 Tim Hudson .50
140 Rickie Weeks .25
141 Mark Prior .25
142 Benjamin Zobrist .25
143 Troy Glaus .50
144 Cliff Lee .25
145 Adrian Beltre .50
146 Endy Chavez .25
147 Ramon Hernandez .25
148 Chris Young .50
149 Jason Schmidt .25
150 Kevin Millwood .25
151 Placido Polanco .25
152 Torii Hunter .50
153 Roy Oswalt .50
154 Kelvim Escobar .25
155 Milton Bradley .25
156 Chris Capuano .25
157 Juan Encarnacion .25
158 Ichiro Suzuki 2.00
159 Matthew Kemp .50
160 Matt Morris .25
161 Casey Blake .25
162 Josh Willingham .25
163 Nick Johnson .25
164 Khalil Greene .25
165 Tom Glavine .75
166 Jason Bay .50
167 Brandon Phillips .25
168 Jorge Cantu .25
169 Jeff Weaver .25
170 Melky Cabrera .25
171 Danny Haren .25
172 Jeff Francoeur .50
173 Randy Wolf .25
174 Carlos Zambrano .50
175 Justin Morneau .75
176 Takashi Saito .25
177 Victor Martinez .50
178 Felix Hernandez .50
179 Paul LoDuca .25
180 Miguel Tejada .75
181 Mark Teixeira .75
182 Pat Burrell .25
183 Mike Cameron .25
184 Josh Beckett .50
185 Francisco Liriano .50
186 Ken Griffey Jr. 2.00
187 Mike Mussina .50
188 Howie Kendrick .25
189 Ted Lilly .25
190 Mike Hampton .25
191 Jeff Suppan .25
192 Jose Reyes 2.00
193 Russell Martin .50
194 Jhonny Peralta .50
195 Raul Ibanez .25
196 Hanley Ramirez 1.00
197 Kerry Wood .25
198 Gary Sheffield .50
199 David Dellucci .25
200 Xavier Nady .25
201 Michael Young .50
202 Kevin Youkilis .50
203 Aaron Harang .25
204 Mario Garza .50
205 Jim Thome .50
206 Jose Contreras .25
207 Tadahito Iguchi .25
208 Eric Chavez .25
209 Vernon Wells .50
210 Doug Davis .25
211 Andruw Jones .75
212 David Eckstein .25
213 J.J. Hardy .25
214 Orlando Hudson .25
215 Pedro Martinez 1.00
216 Brian Roberts .50
217 Brett Myers .25
218 Alex Rodriguez 3.00
219 Kenny Rogers .25
220 Jason Kubel .25
221 Jermaine Dye .25
222 Bartolo Colon .25
223 Craig Biggio .50
224 Alex Rios .25
225 Adam Dunn .75
226 Anthony Reyes .25
227 Derrek Lee .50
228 Jeremy Hermida .25
229 Derek Lowe .25
230 Randy Winn .25
231 Brandon Webb .25
232 Jose Vidro .25
233 Erik Bedard .50
234 Jon Lieber .25
235 Wily Mo Pena .25
236 Kelly Johnson .25
237 David DeJesus .25
238 Andy Marte .25
239 Scott Olsen .25
240 Randy Johnson 1.00
241 Nelson Cruz .25
242 Carlos Guillen .25
243 Brandon McCarthy .25
244 Garret Anderson .25
245 Mike Sweeney .25
246 Brian Bannister .25
247 Jose Guillen .25
248 Brad Wilkerson .25
249 Lance Berkman .50
250 Ryan Zimmerman .50
251 Garrett Atkins .50
252 Johan Santana 1.00
253 Brandon Webb .50
254 Justin Verlander .75
255 Hanley Ramirez 1.00
256 Justin Morneau .75
257 Ryan Howard 2.00
258 Eric Chavez .25
259 Scott Rolen .75
260 Derek Jeter 3.00
261 Omar Vizquel .25
262 Mark Grudzielanek .25
263 Orlando Hudson .25
264 Mark Teixeira .50
265 Albert Pujols 3.00
266 Ivan Rodriguez .75
267 Brad Ausmus .25
268 Torii Hunter .50
269 Mike Cameron .25
270 Ichiro Suzuki 2.00
271 Carlos Beltran .75
272 Vernon Wells .50
273 Andruw Jones .50
274 Kenny Rogers .25
275 Greg Maddux 2.00
276 Danny Putnam **(RC)** 1.00
277 Chase Wright **RC** 2.00
278 Zach McClellan **RC** 1.00
279 Jamie Vermilyea **RC** 1.00
280 Felix Pie **(RC)** 2.00
281 Phil Hughes **(RC)** 5.00
282 Jon Knott **(RC)** 1.00
283 Micah Owings **(RC)** 1.00
284 Devern Hansack **RC** 2.00
285 Andy Cannizaro **RC** 1.00
286 Lee Gardner **(RC)** 1.00
287 Josh Hamilton **(RC)** 2.00
288 Angel Sanchez/
Auto. **RC** 10.00
289 J.D. Durbin **(RC)** 1.00
290 Jamie Burke **(RC)** 1.00
291 Joseph Bisenius **RC** 1.00
292 Rick Vanden Hurk **RC** 2.00
293 Brian Barden **RC** 1.00
294 Levale Speigner **RC** 1.00
295 Kevin Cameron **RC** 1.00
296 Donald Kelly **(RC)** 1.00
297 Hideki Okajima **RC** 3.00
298 Andrew Miller **RC** 5.00
299 Delmon Young **(RC)** 1.00
300 Vinny Rottino **(RC)** 1.00
301 Philip Humber **(RC)** 1.00
302 Drew Anderson **(RC)** 1.00
303 Jerry Owens **(RC)** 1.00
304 Jose Garcia **RC** 1.00
305 Shane Youman **RC** 1.00
306 Ryan Feierabend **(RC)** 1.00
307 Mike Rabelo **RC** 1.00
308 Josh Fields **(RC)** 1.00
309 Jon Coutlangus **(RC)** 1.00
310 Travis Buck **(RC)** 1.00
311 Doug Slaten **RC** 1.00
312 Ryan Braun **RC** 1.00
313 Juan Salas **(RC)** 1.00
314 Matt Lindstrom **(RC)** 1.00
315 Cesar Jimenez **RC** 1.00
316 Jay Marshall **RC** 1.00
317 Jared Burton **RC** 1.00
318 Juan Perez **RC** 1.00
319 Elijah Dukes **RC** 2.00
320 Juan Lara **RC** 1.00
321 Justin Hampson **(RC)** 1.00
322 Kei Igawa **RC** 2.00
323 Zack Segovia **(RC)** 1.00
324 Alejandro De Aza **RC** 1.00
325 Brandon Morrow **RC** 2.00
326 Gustavo Molina **RC** 1.00
327 Joe Smith **RC** 1.00
328 Jesus Flores **RC** 2.00
329 Jeff Baker **(RC)** 1.00
330 Daisuke Matsuzaka
RC 10.00
331 Troy Tulowitzki/
Auto. **(RC)** 25.00
332 John Danks/
Auto. **RC** 20.00
333 Kevin Kouzmanoff/
Auto. **(RC)** 15.00
334 David Murphy/
Auto. **(RC)** 15.00
335 Ryan Sweeney/
Auto. **(RC)** 15.00
336 Fred Lewis/
Auto. **(RC)** 15.00
337 Delwyn Young/
Auto. **(RC)** 15.00
338 Matt Chico/
Auto. **(RC)** 10.00
339 Miguel Montero/
Auto. **(RC)** 10.00
340 Shawn Riggans/
Auto. **(RC)** 10.00
341 Brian Stokes/
Auto. **(RC)** 10.00
342 Scott Moore/
Auto. **(RC)** 10.00
343 Adam Lind/Auto.**(RC)** 15.00
344 Chris Narveson/
Auto. **(RC)** 10.00
345 Alex Gordon/
Auto. **RC** 50.00
346 Joaquin Arias/
Auto. **(RC)** 10.00
347 Brian Burres/
Auto. **(RC)** 10.00
348 Glen Perkins/
Auto. **(RC)** 10.00
349 Ubaldo Jimenez/
Auto. **(RC)** 15.00
350 Chris Stewart/
Auto. **RC** 10.00
351 Beltran Perez/
Auto. **(RC)** 10.00
352 Dennis Sarfate/
Auto. **(RC)** 10.00
353 Carlos Maldonado/
Auto. **(RC)** 10.00
354 Mitch Maier/Auto. **RC** 10.00
355 Kory Casto/
Auto. **(RC)** 10.00
356 Juan Morillo/
Auto. **(RC)** 10.00
357 Hector Gimenez/
Auto. **(RC)** 10.00
358 Alexi Casilla/Auto. **RC** 15.00
359 Michael Bourn/
Auto. **(RC)** 15.00
360 Sean Henn/
Auto. **(RC)** 10.00
361 Tim Gradoville/
Auto. **RC** 10.00
362 Akinori Iwamura/
Auto. **RC** 30.00
363 Oswaldo Navarro/
Auto. **RC** 10.00

Refractor

Refractor (1-330): 2-3X
Ref. RC Auto.
(288, 331-363): 1-1.5X
Auto. Production 500

Red Refractor

Red Ref. (1-330): 4-8X
Production 99
Red Auto. (288, 331-363): 3-4X
Auto. Production 25

White Refractor

White Ref. (1-330): 3-4X
Production 660
White Auto.
(288, 331-363): 1-1.5X
Auto production 200

Printing Plates

Production one set per color.

A-Rod Road to 500

NM/M
Complete Set (226-250): 40.00
Common A-Rod: 2.00

A-Rod Road to 500 Autographs

NM/M
Production One Set 40.00

Generation Now

NM/M
Common Player: .50
Refractor: 2-3X
Production 500 Sets
White Refractor: 3-4X
Production 200 Sets
Red Refractor: 3-5X
Production 99 Sets
GN201 Ryan Howard 2.00
GN203 Ryan Howard 2.00
GN204 Ryan Howard 2.00
GN205 Ryan Howard 2.00
GN208 Ryan Howard 2.00
GN209 Chase Utley 2.00
GN210 Chien-Ming Wang 3.00
GN211 Mike Napoli .50
GN213 Justin Morneau 2.00
GN214 Justin Morneau 2.00
GN215 Justin Morneau 2.00
GN216 Justin Morneau 2.00
GN217 Jered Weaver 1.00
GN218 Andre Ethier 1.00
GN219 Ryan Zimmerman 1.00
GN238 Ryan Zimmerman 1.00
GN264 Ryan Zimmerman 1.00
GN265 Delmon Young 1.00
GN269 Delmon Young 1.00
GN274 Delmon Young 1.00
GN278 Delmon Young 1.00
GN279 Russell Martin 1.00
GN280 Russell Martin 1.00
GN281 Russell Martin 1.00
GN282 Russell Martin 1.00
GN283 Justin Verlander 1.50
GN292 Justin Verlander 1.50
GN297 Justin Verlander 1.50
GN298 Justin Verlander 1.50
GN299 Hanley Ramirez 1.50
GN308 Hanley Ramirez 1.50
GN318 Hanley Ramirez 1.50
GN328 Hanley Ramirez 1.50
GN338 Hanley Ramirez 1.50
GN349 Hanley Ramirez 1.50
GN350 Nicholas Markakis 1.00
GN359 Nicholas Markakis 1.00
GN360 Nick Swisher .50
GN364 Nick Swisher .50
GN379 Nick Swisher .50
GN394 Nick Swisher .50

Mickey Mantle Home Run History

NM/M
Common Mantle: 2.00
Refractor: 2-3X
Production 500 Sets
White Refractor: 3-5X
Production 200 Sets
Red Refractor: 4-8X
Production 99 Sets

The Mickey Mantle Story

NM/M
Complete Set (30): 50.00
Common Mantle: 2.00
Refractor: 2-3X
Production 500 Sets
White Refractor: 3-4X
Production 200 Sets
Red Refractor: 3-6X
Production 99 Sets
1-30 Mickey Mantle 2.00

2007 Topps Co-Signers

NM/M
Complete Set (122):
Common Player: .25
Common RC Auto.: 10.00
Pack (6): 10.00
Box (12): 100.00
1 Ryan Howard 2.00
2 Jered Weaver .50
3 Brian McCann .25
4 Garrett Atkins .25
5 Travis Hafner .50
6 Jason Schmidt .50
7 Curtis Granderson .25
8 Ben Sheets .50
9 Chien-Ming Wang 1.50
10 Francisco Liriano .50
11 Freddy Sanchez .25
12 Roy Oswalt .75
13 Jim Edmonds .50
14 Matt Cain .50
15 Jake Peavy .75
16 Ryan Zimmerman .75
17 Troy Glaus .50
18 Kenji Johjima .50
19 Curt Schilling 1.00
20 Alfonso Soriano 1.00
21 Adam Dunn .75
22 Hanley Ramirez .75
23 Mark Teahen .25
24 Todd Helton .75
25 Alex Rodriguez 3.00
26 Mike Mussina .75
27 Jason Bay .50
28 Carl Crawford .50
29 Vernon Wells .50
30 Rich Harden .25
31 Justin Morneau 1.00
32 Andre Ethier .25
33 Ramon Hernandez .25
34 Erik Bedard .50
35 Vladimir Guerrero 1.00
36 Stephen Drew .50
37 Felix Hernandez .50
38 C.C. Sabathia .50
39 Adrian Gonzalez .50
40 Prince Fielder 1.00
41 Carlos Delgado .75
42 Jimmy Rollins .75
43 Raul Ibanez .25
44 Jorge Cantu .25
45 Michael Young .50
46 Austin Kearns .25
47 Ivan Rodriguez .75
48 Chad Billingsley .25
49 David Ortiz 1.00
50 David Wright 1.50
51 Justin Verlander .75
52 Nicholas Markakis .50
53 Miguel Cabrera 1.00
54 Lance Berkman .50
55 Robinson Cano .75
56 Jon Lieber .25
57 Andruw Jones .75
58 Danny Haren .50
59 Grady Sizemore .75
60 Gary Sheffield .75
61 Paul LoDuca .25
62 Cole Hamels 1.00
63 Richie Sexson .50
64 David Eckstein .25
65 Carlos Zambrano .50
66 Scott Kazmir .25
67 Anthony Reyes .25
68 Mark Kotsay .25
69 Miguel Tejada .75
70 Pedro Martinez 1.00
71 Jack Wilson .25
72 Joe Mauer .75
73 Brian Giles .25
74 Jonathan Papelbon 1.00
75 Albert Pujols 3.00
76 Nick Swisher .25
77 Bill Hall .50
78 Jose Contreras .25
79 David DeJesus .25
80 Bobby Abreu .50
81 John Smoltz .50
82 Chipper Jones 1.00
83 Mark Buehrle .25
84 Josh Barfield .25
85 Derrek Lee .75
86 Jim Thome .75
87 Kenny Rogers .25
88 Jeremy Sowers .25
89 Brandon Webb .50
90 Roy Halladay .50
91 Tadahito Iguchi .25
92 Jeff Kent .50
93 Johnny Damon 1.00
94 Daisuke Matsuzaka **RC** 5.00
95 Mark Teixeira .75
96a Delmon Young **RC** 2.00
96b Delmon Young/Auto. 25.00
97a Jeff Baker **RC** 1.00
97b Jeff Baker/Auto. 10.00
98a Michael Bourn **(RC)** 1.00
98b Michael Bourn/Auto. 10.00
99a Ubaldo Jimenez **RC** 1.00
99b Ubaldo Jimenez/
Auto. 10.00
100a Andrew Miller **(RC)** 5.00
100b Andrew Miller/Auto. 35.00
101 Angel Sanchez/
Auto. **(RC)** 10.00
102 Troy Tulowitzki/
Auto. **(RC)** 25.00
103 Joaquin Arias/
Auto. **RC** 10.00
104 Beltran Perez/
Auto. **RC** 10.00
105 Josh Fields/Auto. **RC** 10.00
106 Hector Gimenez/
Auto. **RC** 10.00
107 Kevin Kouzmanoff/
Auto. **RC** 15.00
108 Miguel Montero/
Auto. **RC** 10.00
109 Philip Humber/
Auto. **RC** 15.00
110 Jerry Owens/
Auto. **RC** 15.00
111 Shawn Riggans/
Auto. **RC** 10.00
112 Brian Stokes/
Auto. **RC** 10.00
113 Scott Moore/
Auto. **RC** 10.00
114 David Murphy/
Auto. **(RC)** 10.00
115 Mitch Maier/Auto. **RC** 10.00
116 Adam Lind/Auto. **RC** 15.00
117 Adam Lind/Auto. **RC** 10.00
118 Dennis Sarfate/
Auto. **RC** 10.00
119 Elijah Dukes/
Auto. **(RC)** 15.00
120 Josh Hamilton/
Auto. **RC** 20.00
121 Alex Gordon/
Auto. **RC** 60.00
122 Barry Bonds 3.00

Bronze

Bronze Non-Auto.: 2-3X
Bronze RC Auto.: 1X
Production 250 Sets

Blue

Blue Non-Auto.: 2-3X
Blue RC Auto.: 1X
Production 225 Sets

Gold

Gold Non-Auto.: 2-3X
Gold RC Auto.: 1X
Production 200 Sets

Red

Red Non-Auto.: 2-3X
Production 299 Sets
Red RC Auto.: 1X
Production 275 Sets

Silver-Red

Silver Red Non-Auto.: 2-3X
Silver Red RC Auto.: 1X
Production 175 Sets

Silver-Bronze

Silver Bronze Non-Auto.: 2-4X
Silver Bronze RC Auto.: 1-1.5X
Production 150 Sets

Silver-Blue

Silver Blue Non-Auto.: 2-4X
Silver Blue RC Auto.: 1-1.5X
Production 125 Sets

Silver-Gold

Silver Gold Non-Auto.: 2-4X
Silver Gold RC Auto.: 1-1.5X
Production 100 Sets

Hyper Silver-Red

Hyper Silver Red Non-Auto.: 2-4X
Hyper Silver Red RC Auto.: 1-1.5X
Production 75 Sets

Hyper Silver-Bronze

Hyper Silver Bronze Non-Auto.: 3-4X
Hyper Silver Bronze Auto.: 1-2X
Production 50 Sets

Hyper Silver Blue

No Pricing
Production 25 Sets

Hyper Silver Gold

No Pricing
Production Five Sets

Hyper Plaid Silver

No Pricing
Production One Set

Printing Plates

No Pricing
Production one set per color.

A-Rod Road to 500

NM/M
Common A-Rod: 3.00
2:Box
Autograph: No Pricing
Production One Set

Cut Signatures Dual

Production One Set

Dual Autograph

NM/M
Common Dual Auto.: 10.00
AH Garrett Atkins, Matt Holliday 30.00
AI Matt Albers, Chris Iannetta 10.00
AS Matt Albers, Brian Slocum 10.00
BB Brian Bannister, Floyd Bannister 20.00
BDE Erik Bedard, Zachary Duke 20.00
BG Jeremy Bonderman, Curtis Granderson 30.00
BS Jeff Baker, Jeff Salazar 10.00
BV Jeremy Bonderman, Justin Verlander 50.00
CC Melky Cabrera, Robinson Cano 60.00
CJ Chris Carpenter, Tyler Johnson 40.00
CK Robinson Cano, Chuck Knoblauch 40.00
CM Fabio Castro, Scott Mathieson 15.00
CW Miguel Cabrera, Dontrelle Willis 30.00
CY Alberto Callaspo, Chris Young 20.00
CZ Alberto Callaspo, Benjamin Zobrist 15.00
GB Garrett Atkins, Clint Barmes 15.00
GC Curtis Granderson, Melky Cabrera 25.00
GM Hector Gimenez, Miguel Montero 15.00
GS Dwight Gooden, Darryl Strawberry 40.00
HH Bill Hall, J.J. Hardy 30.00
HO Ryan Howard, David Ortiz 100.00
IK Chris Iannetta, Matthew Kemp 15.00
IM Chris Iannetta, Miguel Montero 15.00
JJ Andruw Jones, David Justice 50.00
JS Ubaldo Jimenez, Dennis Sarfate 10.00
JY Conor Jackson, Chris Young 25.00
KA Howie Kendrick, Erick Aybar 25.00
KF Kevin Kouzmanoff, Josh Fields 20.00
KG Matthew Kemp, Franklin Gutierrez 15.00
KM Josh Kinney, Tom Mastny 15.00
KMA Jeff Karstens, Scott Mathieson 15.00
KZ Austin Kearns, Ryan Zimmerman 25.00
LG Adam LaRoche, Tom Gorzelanny 20.00
LK Francisco Liriano, Jim Kaat 20.00
LL Tony Larussa, Jim Leyland 50.00
LP Francisco Liriano, Jonathan Papelbon 35.00
LV Francisco Liriano, Justin Verlander 40.00
LY Adam Lind, Delmon Young 20.00
MB Nicholas Markakis, Brian Roberts 30.00
MC Omar Minaya, Brian Cashman 60.00
MCA Nicholas Markakis, Melky Cabrera 30.00
MG Craig Monroe, Curtis Granderson 30.00
MH John Maine, Philip Humber 30.00
MM Lastings Milledge, John Maine 25.00
MMA David Murphy, Mitch Maier 15.00
MP Andrew Miller, Glen Perkins 30.00
MQ Nicholas Markakis, Carlos Quentin 20.00
MS Justin Morneau, Nick Swisher 30.00
MSL Tom Mastny, Brian Slocum 10.00
MW Lastings Milledge, David Wright 50.00
OB Jerry Owens, Michael Bourn 15.00
PC Angel Pagan, Buck Coats 15.00
PS Yusmeiro Petit, Anibal Sanchez 15.00
PV Jonathan Papelbon, Justin Verlander 50.00
SH Jonathan Sanchez, Brad Hennessey 15.00
SM Freddy Sanchez, Joe Mauer 30.00
SMA Chris Stewart, Carlos Maldonado 15.00
SR Brian Stokes, Shawn Riggans 15.00
VF Justin Verlander, Mark Fidrych 50.00
VM John Van Benschoten, Scott Mathieson 15.00
VP Jason Varitek, Jorge Posada 80.00
WC David Wright, Robinson Cano 80.00
WS Dontrelle Willis, Anibal Sanchez 20.00
YL Chris Young, Nook Logan 15.00
YU Delmon Young, B.J. Upton 35.00
ZG Benjamin Zobrist, Joel Guzman 15.00

Moon Shots Autographs

NM/M
Common Auto.: 80.00
BA Buzz Aldrin 200.00
WC Walt Cunningham 80.00
WS Wally Schirra 180.00
RC Robert Crippen 80.00
CD Charles Duke 80.00
AW Alfred Worden 90.00
EM Edgar Mitchell 80.00
FH Fred Haise 100.00
RG Richard Gordon 100.00
SC Scott Carpenter 100.00

Moon Shots Autographs Dual

NM/M
Common Dual Auto.: 100.00
AC Garrett Atkins, Scott Carpenter 100.00
AD Andre Dawson, Alfred Worden 140.00
DG Jermaine Dye, Richard Gordon 100.00
HC Ryan Howard, W. Cunningham 140.00
OS David Ortiz, Wally Schirra 150.00
RA Alex Rodriguez, Buzz Aldrin 375.00
SC Alfonso Soriano, Robert Crippen 150.00
SH Duke Snider, Fred Haise 160.00
WD David Wright, Charles Duke 180.00
WM Dave Winfield, Edgar Mitchell 125.00

Solo Sigs

NM/M
Common Autograph: 10.00
AH Aaron Hill 10.00
AL Anthony Lerew 10.00
AS Anibal Sanchez 10.00
BB Boof Bonser 10.00
CB Clint Barmes 10.00
CH Cole Hamels 35.00
CJ Chuck James 10.00
CQ Carlos Quentin 15.00
DH Dave Henderson 10.00
DU Dan Uggla 15.00
ES Ervin Santana 15.00
FL Francisco Liriano 20.00
FS Freddy Sanchez 15.00
GA Garrett Atkins 10.00
HK Howie Kendrick 20.00
HM Hideki Matsui 250.00
HR Hanley Ramirez 20.00
JM Justin Morneau 30.00
JS Jeremy Sowers 10.00
MC Matt Cain 20.00
MH Matt Holliday 35.00
NM Nicholas Markakis 25.00
RC Robinson Cano 30.00
RCE Ronny Cedeno 10.00
RG Ryan Garko 10.00
RH Ryan Howard 60.00
RR Rick Rhoden 10.00
VG Vladimir Guerrero 50.00

Tri-Signers

NM/M
Inserted 1:288
ANS Joaquin Arias, Oswaldo Navarro, Angel Sanchez 20.00
CPC Melky Cabrera, Wily Mo Pena, Miguel Cabrera 40.00
HLC Brad Hennessey, J. Sanchez, Matt Cain 40.00
JGK Conor Jackson, Ryan Garko, Howie Kendrick 40.00
JHS Chuck James, Cole Hamels, Jeremy Sowers 50.00
LNB Francisco Liriano, Joe Nathan, Boof Bonser 50.00
MAR Justin Morneau, Garrett Atkins, Brian Roberts 40.00
MLM Justin Morneau, Francisco Liriano, Matt Garza 60.00
MLP Justin Morneau, Francisco Liriano, Glen Perkins 50.00
MSG Justin Morneau, Nick Swisher, Adrian Gonzalez 50.00
MYT Andrew Miller, Delmon Young, Troy Tulowitzki 60.00
OPV David Ortiz, Jonathan Papelbon, Jason Varitek 150.00
OWH David Ortiz, David Wright, Ryan Howard 150.00
QJY Carlos Quentin, Conor Jackson, Chris Young 40.00
RCC Alex Rodriguez, Melky Cabrera, Robinson Cano 250.00
RWH Alex Rodriguez, David Wright, Ryan Howard 250.00
SHH Huston Street, Rich Harden, Danny Haren 50.00
TPW Taylor Tankersley, Yusmeiro Petit, Dontrelle Willis 35.00
URW Dan Uggla, Hanley Ramirez, Dontrelle Willis 50.00

Yankees Cut Signatures

Production One Set

2007 Topps Heritage

NM/M
Complete Set (495): 325.00
Common Player: .40
Common SP: 5.00
Inserted 1:2
Common Variation: 5.00
Inserted 1:6
Pack (8): 3.00
Box (24): 65.00
1 David Ortiz 1.50
2 Roger Clemens 3.00
2 Roger Clemens/Yellow Team Name/SP 15.00
3 David Wells .40
4 Ronny Paulino/SP 5.00
5 Derek Jeter/SP 15.00
6 Felix Hernandez 2.00
7 Todd Helton 1.00
8 David Eckstein .40
8 David Eckstein/Yellow Name/SP 5.00
9 Craig Wilson .40
10 John Smoltz .75
11 Robert Mackowiak .40
11 Robert Mackowiak/Yellow Team Name/SP 5.00
12 Scott Hatteberg .40
13 Wilfredo Ledezma/SP 5.00
13 Wilfredo Ledezma/Yellow Team Name/SP 5.00
14 Bobby Abreu/SP 8.00
15 Austin Kearns .40
16 Wilson Betemit .40
17 Darren Oliver .40
18 Josh Beckett .40
19 San Francisco Giants .40
20 Robinson Cano 1.00
20 Robinson Cano/Yellow Team Name/SP 8.00
21 Matt Cain 1.00
22 Jason Kendall/SP 5.00
23 Mark Kotsay/SP 5.00
23 Mark Kotsay/Yellow Name/SP 5.00
24 Yadier Molina .40
24 Yadier Molina/Yellow Name/SP 5.00
25 Brad Penny .40
26 Adrian Gonzalez .50
27 Danny Haren .40
28 Brian Giles .50
29 Jose Lopez .40
30 Ichiro Suzuki 2.50
30 Ichiro Suzuki/Yellow Name/SP 10.00
31 Beltran Perez/SP **(RC)** 5.00
32 Brad Hawpe/SP 5.00
33 Jim Thome 1.50
33 Jim Thome/Yellow Team Name/SP 8.00
34 Mark DeRosa .40
35 Woody Williams .40
35 Woody Williams/Yellow Team Name/SP 5.00
36 Luis Gonzalez .40
37 Billy Sadler **(RC)** 1.00
38 Dave Roberts .40
39 Mitch Maier **(RC)** 1.00
40 Francisco Cordero/SP 5.00
41 Anthony Reyes/SP 8.00
42 Russell Martin .40
43 Scott Proctor .40
44 Washington Nationals .40
45 Shane Victorino .40
46 Joel Zumaya 1.00
46 Joel Zumaya/Yellow Name/SP 5.00
47 Delmon Young **(RC)** 1.00
48 Alex Rios .40
49 Willy Taveras/SP 5.00
50 Mark Buehrle/SP 5.00
50 Mark Buehrle/Yellow Team Name/SP 5.00
51 Livan Hernandez .40
52 Jason Bay 1.00
52 Jason Bay/Yellow Team Name/SP 5.00
53 Jose Valentin .40
53 Jose Valentin/Yellow Name/SP 5.00
54 Kevin Reese .40
55 Felipe Lopez .40
56 Ryan Sweeney **(RC)** 1.00
57 Kelvim Escobar .40
57 Kelvim Escobar/Yellow Name/SP 5.00
58 Nick Swisher/SP 5.00
58 Nick Swisher/Yellow Team Name/SP 8.00
59 Kevin Millwood/SP 5.00
60 Preston Wilson .40
60 Preston Wilson/Yellow Name/SP 5.00
61 Mariano Rivera .75
61 Mariano Rivera/Yellow Name/SP 8.00
62 Josh Barfield .40
63 Ryan Freel .40
64 Tim Hudson .75
65 Chris Narveson **(RC)** 1.00
65 Chris Narveson/Yellow Name/SP 5.00
66 Matt Murton .40
67 Melvin Mora/SP 5.00
68 Jason Jennings/SP 5.00
69 Emil Brown .40
70 Magglio Ordonez .40
70 Magglio Ordonez/Yellow Name/SP 5.00
71 Los Angeles Dodgers .40
72 Huston Street .40
73 David Ross .40
74 Juan Uribe .40
75 Scott Podsednik .40
76 Cole Hamels/SP 8.00
76 Cole Hamels/Yellow Team Name/SP 8.00
77 Rafael Furcal/SP 5.00
77 Rafael Furcal/Yellow Team Name/SP 5.00
78 Ryan Theriot .40
78 Ryan Theriot/Yellow Name/SP 5.00
79 Corey Patterson .40
79 Corey Patterson/Yellow Team Name/SP 5.00
80 Jered Weaver .40
81 Stephen Drew .75
81 Stephen Drew/Yellow Team Name/SP 8.00
82 Adam Kennedy .40
83 Tony Gwynn Jr. .40
84 Erik Bedard .40
85 Omar Vizquel/SP 5.00
85 Omar Vizquel/Yellow Team Name/SP 5.00
86 Fred Lewis/SP **(RC)** 5.00
87 Brad Radke .40
87 Shawn Chacon/Yellow Name/SP 5.00
88 Frank Catalanotto .40
89 Orlando Hudson .40
90 Pat Burrell .40
91 David DeJesus .40
92 David Wright 2.50
92 David Wright/Yellow Name/SP 10.00
93 Conor Jackson .40
94 Xavier Nady/SP 5.00
95 Bill Hall/SP 8.00
96 Andre Ethier .75
97 Jeff Suppan .40
97 Jeff Suppan/Yellow Name/SP 5.00
98 Ryan Zimmerman .75
98 Ryan Zimmerman/Yellow Name/SP 8.00
99 Yuniesky Betancourt .40
100 Jose Contreras .40
100 Jose Contreras/Yellow Team Name/SP 5.00
101 Miguel Cairo .40
101 Miguel Cairo/Yellow Name/SP 5.00
102 Brian Roberts .40
103 Carl Crawford/SP 8.00
104 Mike Lamb/SP 5.00
105 Mark Ellis .40
106 Scott Rolen 1.50
107 Garrett Atkins .40
108 Hanley Ramirez .75
108 Hanley Ramirez/Yellow Team Name/SP 8.00
109 Trot Nixon .40
110 Edgar Renteria .40
111 Jeff Francis .40
112 Marcus Thames/SP 5.00
113 Brian Burres/SP **(RC)** 5.00
114 Brian Schneider .40
115 Jeremy Bonderman .75
116 Ryan Madson .40
117 Gerald Laird .40
118 Roy Halladay .75
119 Victor Martinez .40
120 Greg Maddux 2.50
121 Jay Payton/SP 5.00
122 Jacque Jones/SP 5.00
123 Juan Lara **RC** 1.00
124 Derrick Turnbow .40
125 Adam Everett .40
126 Michael Cuddyer .40
127 Gil Meche .40
128 Willy Aybar .40
129 Jerry Owens **RC** 1.00
130 Manny Ramirez/SP 10.00
131 Howie Kendrick/SP 8.00
132 Byung-Hyun Kim .40
133 Kevin Kouzmanoff **(RC)** 1.00
134 Philadelphia Phillies .40
135 Joe Blanton .40
136 Ray Durham .40
137 Luke Hudson .40
138 Eric Byrnes .40
139 Ryan Braun SP **(RC)** 8.00
140 Johnny Damon/SP 10.00
141 Ambiorix Burgos .40
142 Hideki Matsui .40
143 Josh Johnson .40
144 Miguel Cabrera .40
146 Delwyn Young **(RC)** 1.00
147 Chuck James .40
148 Morgan Ensberg .40
149 Jose Vidro/SP 5.00
150 Alex Rodriguez/SP 15.00
151 Carlos Maldonado **(RC)** 1.00
152 Jason Schmidt .40
153 Alex Escobar .40
154 Chris Gomez .40
155 Endy Chavez .40
156 Kris Benson .40
157 Bronson Arroyo .40
158 Cleveland Indians/SP 8.00
159 Chris Ray/SP 5.00
160 Richie Sexson .40
161 Huston Street .40
162 Kevin Youkilis .40
163 Armando Benitez .40
164 Vinny Rottino **(RC)** 1.00
165 Garret Anderson .40
166 Todd Greene .40
167 Brian Stokes/SP **(RC)** 5.00
168 Albert Pujols/SP 15.00
169 Todd Coffey .40
170 Jason Michaels .40
171 David Dellucci .40
172 Eric Milton .40
173 Austin Kearns .40
174 Kansas City Royals .40
175 Andy Cannizaro **RC** 2.00
176 David Weathers/SP 5.00
177 Jermaine Dye/SP 5.00
178 Wily Mo Pena .40
179 Chris Burke .40
180 Jeff Weaver .40
181 Juan Encarnacion .40
182 Jeremy Hermida .40
183 Tim Wakefield .40
184 Rich Hill .50
185 Aaron Hill SP 5.00
186 Scot Shields/SP 5.00
187 Randy Johnson .40
188 Dan Johnson .40
189 Sean Marshall .40
190 Marcus Giles .40
191 Jonathan Broxton .40
192 Mike Piazza .40
193 Carlos Quentin .40
194 Derek Lowe/SP 5.00
195 Russell Branyan/SP 5.00
196 Jason Marquis .40
197 Khalil Greene .40
198 Ryan Dempster .40
199 Ronnie Belliard .40
200 Josh Fogg .40
201 Carlos Lee .40
202 Chris Denorfia .40
203 Kendry Morales/SP 5.00
204 Rafael Soriano/SP 5.00
205 Brandon Phillips .40
206 Andrew Miller **RC** 5.00
207 John Koronka .40
208 Luis Castillo .40
209 Angel Guzman .40
210 Jim Edmonds .40
211 Patrick Misch **(RC)** 1.00
212 Ty Wigginton/SP 5.00
213 Brandon Inge/SP 5.00
214 Royce Clayton .40
215 Ben Broussard .40
216 St. Louis Cardinals .40
217 Mark Mulder .40
218 Kenji Johjima .40
219 Joe Crede .40
220 Danny Haren .40
221 Josh Fields/SP **(RC)** 8.00
222 Pat Neshek/SP 10.00
223 Reed Johnson .40
224 Mike Mussina .40
225 Randy Winn .40
226 Brian Rogers **(RC)** .40
227 Juan Rivera .40
228 Shawn Green .40
229 Mike Napoli .40
230 Chase Utley/SP 10.00
231 John Nelson/SP **(RC)** 10.00
232 Casey Blake .40
233 Lyle Overbay .40
234 Adam LaRoche .40
235 Jeff Weaver .40
236 Johnny Estrada .40
237 James Shields .40
238 Jose Castillo .40
239 Doug Davis/SP 5.00
240 Jason Giambi/SP 8.00
241 Mike Gonzalez .40
242 Scott Downs .40
243 Joe Inglett .40
244 Matthew Kemp .40
245 Ted Lilly .40
246 New York Yankees .40
247 Jamey Carroll .40
248 Adam Wainwright/SP 8.00
249 Matt Thornton/SP 5.00
250 Alfonso Soriano .40
251 Tom Gordon .40
252 Dennis Sarfate **(RC)** .40
253 Zachary Duke .40
254 Hank Blalock .40
255 Johan Santana .40
256 Chicago White Sox .40
257 Aaron Cook/SP 5.00
258 Cliff Lee/SP 5.00
259 Miguel Tejada .40
260 Mike Lowell .40
261 Ian Snell .40
262 Jason Tyner .40
263 Troy Tulowitzki **(RC)** .75
264 Ervin Santana .40
265 Jon Lester .40
266 Andy Pettitte/SP 8.00
267 A.J. Pierzynski/SP 5.00
268 Rich Aurilia .40
269 Phil Nevin .40
270 Tom Glavine .40
271 Chris Coste .40
272 Moises Alou .40
273 J.D. Drew .40
274 Abraham Nunez .40
275 Jorge Posada/SP 8.00
276 Jeff Conine/SP 5.00
277 Chad Cordero .40
278 Nick Johnson .40
279 Kevin Millar .40
280 Mark Grudzielanek .40
281 Chris Stewart **RC** 1.00
282 Nate Robertson .40
283 Drew Anderson **(RC)** 1.00
284 Doug Mientkiewicz/SP 5.00
285 Ken Griffey Jr./SP 10.00
286 Cory Sullivan .40
287 Chris Carpenter .40
288 Gary Matthews .40
289 Justin Verlander, Jeff Weaver .40
290 Vicente Padilla .40
291 Chris Roberson .40
292 Chris Young .40
293 Ryan Garko/SP 5.00
294 Miguel Batista/SP 5.00
295 B.J. Upton .40
296 Justin Verlander .40
297 Benjamin Zobrist .40
298 Ben Sheets .40
299 Eric Chavez .40
300 William Harridge, Warren Giles .40

301 Placido Polanco .40
302 Angel Sanchez/SP **RC** 5.00
303 Freddy Sanchez/SP 5.00
304 Magglio Ordonez, Carlos Guillen .40
305 A.J. Burnett .40
306 Juan Perez **RC** 1.00
307 Chris Britton .40
308 Jon Garland .40
309 Pedro Feliz .40
310 Ryan Howard .40
311 Aaron Harang/SP 5.00
312 Boston Red Sox/SP 8.00
313 Chad Billingsley .40
314 Bobby Cox, Chipper Jones .40
315 Johan Santana .40
316 Juan Pierre .40
317 Luke Scott .40
318 Javier Valentin .40
319 Mark Loretta .40
320 Kenny Lofton/SP 5.00
321 Vladimir Guerrero/SP, Ivan Rodriguez/SP 8.00
322 Josh Willingham .40
323 Lance Berkman .40
324 Anibal Sanchez .40
325 Maicer Izturis .40
326 Brett Myers .40
327 Chicago Cubs .40
328 Francisco Liriano .40
329 Craig Monroe/SP 5.00
330 Paul LoDuca/SP 5.00
331 Steve Trachsel .40
332 Bernie Williams .40
333 Carlos Guillen .40
334 Johan Santana, Francisco Liriano .40
335 David Bush .40
336 Carlos Beltran .40
337 Jason Isringhausen .40
338 Todd Walker/SP 5.00
339 Jarrod Washburn/SP 5.00
340 Brandon Webb .40
341 Pittsburgh Pirates .40
342 Derrick Turnbow .40
343 Chad Santos .40
344 Brad Lidge .40
345 Brad Ausmus .40
346 Carlos Delgado .40
347 Boone Logan/SP 5.00
348 Jimmy Rollins/SP 8.00
349 Orlando Hernandez .40
350 Gary Sheffield .40
351 Albert Pujols, Yadier Molina, Jim Edmonds, Chris Duncan .40
352 Jake Peavy .40
353 Jason Varitek .40
354 Freddy Garcia .40
355 Matt Diaz .40
356 Bernie Castro/SP 5.00
357 Eric Stults/SP **RC** 5.00
358 John Lackey .40
359 Bobby Jenks .40
360 Mark Teixeira .40
361 Jonathan Papelbon .40
362 Paul Konerko .40
363 Erik Bedard .40
364 Eliezer Alfonzo .40
365 Fernando Rodney/SP 5.00
366 Chris Duncan/SP 8.00
367 Jose Diaz **RC** 1.00
368 Travis Hafner .40
369 Matt Capps .40
370 Ivan Rodriguez .40
371 David Murphy **(RC)** 1.00
372 Carlos Zambrano .40
373 Chris Iannetta .40
374 Jose Mesa/SP 5.00
375 Michael Young/SP 8.00
376 Bill Bray .40
377 Milwaukee Brewers .40
378 Robert Mackowiak .40
379 Barry Zito .40
380 Clay Hensley .40
381 J.J. Putz .40
382 C.C. Sabathia .40
383 Eduardo Perez/SP 5.00
384 Scott Moore/SP **(RC)** 8.00
385 Scott Olsen .40
386 Ryan Howard, Chase Utley .40
387 Aaron Rowand .40
388 Mike Rouse .40
389 Alexis Gomez .40
390 Brian McCann .40
391 Ryan Shealy .40
392 Shane Youman/SP **RC** 8.00
393 Melky Cabrera/SP 8.00
394 Jeremy Sowers .40
395 Casey Janssen .40
396 Miguel Perez .40
397 Detroit Tigers .40
398 Reggie Abercrombie .40
399 Ricky Nolasco .40
400 Tadahito Iguchi .40
401 Jose Reyes/SP 10.00
402 Juan Encarnacion/SP 5.00
403 Brandon Harper .40
404 Torii Hunter .40
405 Dan Uggla .40
406 Orlando Cabrera .40
407 Jose Capellan .40
408 Baltimore Orioles .40
409 Frank Thomas .40
410 Francisco Rodriguez/SP 5.00
411 Ian Kinsler/SP 5.00
412 Billy Wagner .40
413 Andy Marte .40
414 Mike Jacobs .40
415 Raul Ibanez .40
416 Jhonny Peralta .40
417 Chris Young .40
418 Albert Pujols, Craig Monroe .40
419 Scott Kazmir/SP 5.00
420 Norris Hopper/SP 8.00
421 Chris Capuano .40
422 Troy Glaus .40
423 Roy Oswalt .40
424 Grady Sizemore .40
425 Chone Figgins .40
426 Chad Tracy .40
427 Brian Fuentes .40
428 Cincinnati Reds/SP 8.00
429 Ramon Hernandez/SP 5.00
430 Mike Cameron .40
431 Dontrelle Willis .40
432 Joshua Sharpless .40
433 Adrian Beltre .40
434 Curtis Granderson .40
435 B.J. Ryan .40
436 Ryan Howard, David Wright .40
437 Vernon Wells/SP 8.00
438 Vladimir Guerrero/SP 8.00
439 Jake Westbrook .40
440 Chipper Jones .40
441 James Loney .40
442 St. Louis Cardinals .40
443 Oswaldo Navarro .40
444 Joe Mauer .40
445 Miguel Montero .40
446 Franklin Gutierrez/SP 5.00
447 Mark Redman/SP 5.00
448 Mike Rabelo **RC** 1.00
449 Philip Humber .40
450 Justin Morneau .40
451 Hector Gimenez .40
452 Matt Holliday .50
453 Akinori Otsuka .40
454 Prince Fielder .50
455 Chien-Ming Wang/SP 10.00
456 Shawn Riggans/SP 8.00
457 John Maine .40
458 Adam Lind **(RC)** 1.00
459 Ubaldo Jimenez .40
460 Drew Anderson .40
461 Cla Meredith .40
462 Joaquin Arias .40
463 Kenny Rogers .40
464 Jose Garcia/SP 5.00
465 Pedro Martinez/SP 8.00
466 Jeff Salazar .40
467 Glen Perkins **(RC)** .40
468 Travis Ishikawa .40
469 Joe Borowski .40
470 Jeremy Brown .40
471 Andre Ethier .40
472 Taylor Tankersley .40
473 Lastings Milledge/SP 8.00
474 Brian Sanchez/SP 8.00
475 Ozzie Guillen, Phil Garner .40
476 Albert Pujols .40
477 David Ortiz .40
478 Chase Utley .40
479 Mark Loretta .40
480 David Wright .40
481 Alex Rodriguez .40
482 Edgar Rontoria/SP 5.00
483 Derek Jeter/SP 15.00
484 Alfonso Soriano .40
485 Vladimir Guerrero .40
486 Carlos Beltran .40
487 Vernon Wells .40
488 Jason Bay .40
489 Ichiro Suzuki .40
490 Paul LoDuca .40
491 Ivan Rodriguez/SP 8.00
492 Brad Penny/SP 5.00
493 Roy Halladay .40
494 Brian Fuentes .40
495 Kenny Rogers .40

Chrome

NM/M

Common Player: 2.00
Production 1,958 Sets
Refractors: 1.5-2X
Production 558 Sets
Black Refractors: 3-6X
Production 58 Sets
1 David Ortiz 6.00
2 John Smoltz 3.00
4 Brian Giles 2.00
5 Billy Sadler 4.00
6 Joel Zumaya 4.00
7 Felipe Lopez 3.00
8 Tim Hudson 3.00
9 David Ross 2.00
10 Adam Kennedy 2.00
11 David DeJesus 2.00
12 Jose Contreras 2.00
13 Trot Nixon 2.00
14 Roy Halladay 2.00
15 Gil Meche 2.00
16 Ray Durham 2.00
17 Delwyn Young 2.00
18 Endy Chavez 2.00
19 Vinny Rottino 3.00
20 Austin Kearns 3.00
21 Jeremy Hermida 3.00
22 Jonathan Broxton 4.00
23 Josh Fogg 2.00
24 Angel Guzman 4.00
25 Kenji Johjima 4.00
26 Juan Rivera 2.00
27 Johnny Estrada 2.00
28 Ted Lilly 2.00
29 Hank Blalock 3.00
30 Troy Tulowitzki 5.00
31 Moises Alou 3.00
32 Chris Stewart 2.00
33 Vicente Padilla 2.00
34 Eric Chavez 3.00
35 Jon Garland 2.00
36 Luke Scott 3.00
37 Brett Myers 5.00
38 David Bush 2.00
39 Brad Lidge 2.00
40 Jason Varitek 5.00
41 Paul Konerko 4.00
42 David Murphy 2.00
43 Clay Hensley 2.00
44 Alexis Gomez 2.00
45 Reggie Abercrombie 2.00
46 Jose Capellan 2.00
47 Jhonny Peralta 3.00
48 Chone Figgins 3.00
49 Curtis Granderson 4.00
50 Oswaldo Navarro 3.00
51 Matt Holliday 4.00
52 Cla Meredith 2.00
53 Jeremy Brown 3.00
54 Mark Loretta 2.00
55 Jason Bay 4.00
56 Roger Clemens 8.00
57 Robert Mackowiak 2.00
58 Robinson Cano 6.00
59 Jose Lopez 3.00
60 Dave Roberts 2.00
61 Delmon Young 6.00
62 Ryan Sweeney 2.00
63 Chris Narveson 3.00
64 Juan Uribe 2.00
65 Tony Gwynn Jr. 2.00
66 David Wright 8.00
67 Miguel Cairo 2.00
68 Edgar Renteria 2.00
69 Victor Martinez 3.00
70 Willy Aybar 2.00
71 Luke Hudson 2.00
72 Chuck James 3.00
73 Kris Benson 2.00
74 Garret Anderson 2.00
76 Tim Wakefield 2.00
77 Mike Piazza 6.00
78 Carlos Lee 4.00
79 Jim Edmonds 4.00
80 Joe Crede 4.00
81 Shawn Green 3.00
82 James Shields 2.00
84 Johan Santana 8.00
85 Ervin Santana 3.00
86 J.D. Drew 4.00
87 Nate Robertson 3.00
88 Chris Roberson 3.00
90 Pedro Feliz 2.00
91 Javier Valentin 2.00
93 Carlos Beltran 5.00
94 Brad Ausmus 2.00
95 Freddy Garcia 2.00
96 Erik Bedard 4.00
97 Carlos Zambrano 4.00
98 J.J. Putz 2.00
99 Brian McCann 4.00
100 Ricky Nolasco 2.00
102 Chris Young 4.00
103 Chad Tracy 2.00
104 B.J. Ryan 2.00
105 Joe Mauer 5.00
106 Akinori Otsuka 2.00
107 Joaquin Arias 2.00
108 Andre Ethier 4.00
109 David Wright 10.00
110 Ichiro Suzuki 8.00

A-Rod Road to 500

NM/M

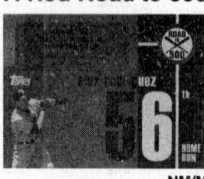

Common A-Rod: 3.00
Inserted 1:24
Autograph: No Pricing
Production 1 Set
51-75 Alex Rodriguez 3.00

Clubhouse Collection

NM/M

Common Player: 8.00
SM Stan Musial 30.00
DS Duke Snider 20.00
FR Frank Robinson 20.00
BR Brooks Robinson 15.00
YB Yogi Berra 25.00
AK Al Kaline 20.00
AW Adam Wainwright 15.00
AJP Albert Pujols 20.00
AR Alex Rodriguez 20.00
ALR Anthony Reyes 10.00
BU B.J. Upton 8.00
BZ Barry Zito 8.00
BS Ben Sheets 10.00
BW Billy Wagner 8.00
BR Brian Roberts 10.00
CU Chase Utley 15.00
CJ Chipper Jones 15.00
CC Chris Carpenter 15.00
CD Chris Duncan 10.00
CJ Conor Jackson 10.00
DE David Eckstein 20.00
DO David Ortiz 15.00
DW David Wright 30.00
DY Delmon Young 10.00
DWW Dontrelle Willis 8.00
DM Doug Mientkiewicz 8.00
ER Edgar Renteria 8.00
EC Eric Chavez 8.00
ES Ervin Santana 8.00
FL Francisco Liriano 10.00
GS Gary Sheffield 10.00
HB Hank Blalock 8.00
IR Ivan Rodriguez 10.00
JS Jeff Suppan 10.00
JW Jeff Weaver 8.00
JR Jimmy Rollins 10.00
JD Johnny Damon 15.00
JRP Jorge Posada 10.00
JBR Jose Reyes 20.00
JV Jose Vidro 8.00
JP Juan Pierre 8.00
JM Justin Morneau 15.00
LB Lance Berkman 10.00
LG Luis Gonzalez 8.00
MO Magglio Ordonez 8.00
MR Manny Ramirez 10.00
MK Mark Kotsay 8.00
MT Mark Teixeira 10.00
MM Melvin Mora 8.00
MC Miguel Cabrera 10.00
MOT Miguel Tejada 8.00
MP Mike Piazza 15.00
MA Moises Alou 8.00
NS Nick Swisher 10.00
OV Omar Vizquel 8.00
PB Pat Burrell 10.00
PP Placido Polanco 8.00
RF Rafael Furcal 8.00
RS Richie Sexson 10.00
RB Ronnie Belliard 8.00
RH Ryan Howard 30.00
TH Todd Helton 10.00
TKH Torii Hunter 10.00
VM Victor Martinez 8.00
YM Yadier Molina 15.00

Clubhouse Collection Dual Relic

NM/M

Production 58 Sets
MP Stan Musial, Albert Pujols 180.00
KR Al Kaline, Ivan Rodriguez 80.00

Clubhouse Coll. Relic Autograph

Production 25 Sets

Felt Team Emblem

NM/M

Inserted 1:Box
Los Angeles Dodgers 3.00
Washington Senators 3.00
San Francisco Giants 3.00
Boston Red Sox 5.00
Cincinnati Redlegs 3.00
Pittsburgh Pirates 3.00
Milwaukee Braves 3.00
Chicago Cubs 5.00
Baltimore Orioles 3.00
New York Yankees 5.00
Cleveland Indians 3.00
St. Louis Cardinals 5.00
Kansas City Athletics 3.00
Detroit Tigers 3.00
Chicago White Sox 3.00
Philadelphia Phillies 3.00

Flashbacks

NM/M

Common Player: 1.00
Inserted 1:12
SM Stan Musial 2.00
AK Al Kaline 2.00
BR Brooks Robinson 2.00
RS Red Schoendienst 1.00
LA Luis Aparicio 1.00
WS Warren Spahn 2.00
HS Hank Sauer 1.00
LB Lew Burdette 1.00
EY Eddie Yost 1.00
JB Jim Bunning 1.00

Flashback Autograph

No Pricing
Production 25 Sets

Flashbacks Relics

NM/M

Common Player: 20.00
SM Stan Musial 30.00
AK Al Kaline 25.00
BR Brooks Robinson 25.00
RS Red Schoendienst 20.00
WS Warren Spahn 25.00
LB Lew Burdette 25.00
EY Eddie Yost 20.00
JB Jim Bunning 20.00

Flashbacks Relic Autograph

Production 25 Sets

2007 Topps Heritage Dual Flashbacks

Production 10 Sets

New Age Performers

NM/M

Common Player: 1.00
Inserted 1:15
RH Ryan Howard 3.00
AR Alex Rodriguez 3.00
AS Alfonso Soriano 2.00
DO David Ortiz 2.00
TH Trevor Hoffman 1.00
DJ Derek Jeter 4.00
AAS Anibal Sanchez 1.00
RC Roger Clemens 3.00
JS Johan Santana 2.00
AP Albert Pujols 4.00
CJ Chipper Jones 2.00
FT Frank Thomas 2.00
IR Ivan Rodriguez 1.50
IS Ichiro Suzuki 3.00
CB Craig Biggio 1.00

Real One Autographs

NM/M

Common Autograph:
Red Ink: 1.5-2X
Production 58 Sets
AK Al Kaline 150.00
BH Bob Henrich 60.00
BM Bobby Morgan 70.00
BP Buddy Pritchard 65.00
BR Brooks Robinson 100.00
BT Bill Taylor 50.00
BW Bill Wight 50.00
CH Chuck Harmon 60.00
CJD Jim Derrington 65.00
CR Charley Rabe 60.00
DM Dave Melton 60.00
DS Duke Snider 100.00
DW David Wright 140.00
DWW Dontrelle Willis 50.00
DY Delmon Young 60.00
DZ Don Zimmer 50.00
EM Ed Mayer 60.00
GK George Kell 75.00
HP Harding Peterson 60.00
JC Joe Caffie 60.00
JD Joe Durham 70.00
JL Joe Lonnett 50.00
JM Justin Morneau 00.00
JP Johnny Podres 60.00
LA Luis Aparicio 80.00
LM Lloyd Merritt 60.00
LS Lou Sleater 60.00
MB Milt Bolling 60.00
MEB Mack Burk 60.00
OH Orlando Hudson 40.00
PS Paul Smith 60.00
RC Ray Crone 60.00
RH Ryan Howard 250.00
RS Red Schoendienst 85.00
SP Stan Palys 60.00
TT Tim Thompson 50.00

Then and Now

NM/M

Common Player: 1.00
Inserted 1:15
RH Ryan Howard 3.00
DO David Ortiz 2.00
JM Joe Mauer 1.50
JR Jose Reyes 2.00
JS Johan Santana 2.00
AH Aaron Harang 1.00
IS Ichiro Suzuki 3.00
TH Travis Hafner 1.50
FR Francisco Rodriguez 1.00
CW Chien-Ming Wang 2.00

1958 A.L. Home Run Champion

NM/M

Common Mantle: 3.00
Inserted 1:6
1-42 Mickey Mantle 3.00

1958 Cut Signatures

Production One Set

2007 Topps Moments & Milestones

NM/M

Complete Set (193):
Common Player: .50
Production 150 Sets
Pack (6): 9.00
Box (18): 140.00
1 Albert Pujols (37/5550) 4.00
2 Albert Pujols (130/19500) 4.00
3 Albert Pujols (194/29100) 4.00
4 Albert Pujols (112/16800) 4.00
5 Albert Pujols (47/7050) 4.00
6 Ichiro Suzuki (242/36300) 2.50
7 Ichiro Suzuki (34/5100) 2.50
8 Ichiro Suzuki (8/1200) 2.50
9 Ichiro Suzuki (56/8400) 2.50
10 Ichiro Suzuki (69/10350) 2.50
11 Ichiro Suzuki (8/1200) 2.50
12 Greg Maddux (20/3000) 3.00
13 Greg Maddux (199/29850) 3.00
14 Greg Maddux (20/3000) 3.00
15 Greg Maddux (197/29550) 3.00
16 Roger Clemens (24/3600) 3.00
17 Roger Clemens (10/1500) 3.00
18 Roger Clemens (238/35700) 3.00
19 Roger Clemens (20/3000) 3.00
20 Roger Clemens (256/38400) 3.00
21 Chipper Jones (45/6750) 1.50
22 Chipper Jones (110/16500) 1.50
23 Chipper Jones (181/27150) 1.50
24 Chipper Jones (116/17400) 1.50
25 Chipper Jones (41/6150) 1.50
26 Chipper Jones (25/3750) 1.50
27 Alex Rodriguez (47/7050) 4.00
28 Alex Rodriguez (118/17700) 4.00
29 Alex Rodriguez (181/27150) 4.00
30 Alex Rodriguez (124/18600) 4.00
31 Alex Rodriguez (30/4500) 4.00
32 Alex Rodriguez (17/2550) 4.00
33 Alex Rodriguez (48/7200) 4.00
34 Alex Rodriguez (130/19500) 4.00
35 Alex Rodriguez (194/29100) 4.00
36 Alex Rodriguez (124/18600) 4.00
37 Alex Rodriguez (29/4350) 4.00
38 Alex Rodriguez (21/3150) 4.00
39 Vladimir Guerrero (39/5850) 1.50
40 Vladimir Guerrero (126/18900) 1.50
41 Vladimir Guerrero (206/30900) 1.50
42 Vladimir Guerrero (124/18600) 1.50
43 Vladimir Guerrero (39/5850) 1.50
44 Vladimir Guerrero (13/1950) 1.50
45 Ken Griffey Jr. (56/8400) 3.00
46 Ken Griffey Jr. (147/22050) 3.00
47 Ken Griffey Jr. (185/27750) 3.00
48 Barry Zito (23/3450) .75
49 Barry Zito (182/27300) .75
50 Randy Johnson (18/2700) 1.50
51 Randy Johnson (294/44100) 1.50
52 Randy Johnson (6/900) 1.50
53 Randy Johnson (3/450) 1.50
54 Randy Johnson (17/2550) 1.50
55 Randy Johnson (364/54600) 1.50

56 Randy Johnson (12/1800) 1.50
57 Randy Johnson (2/300) 1.50
58 Prince Fielder (35/5250) 2.00
59 Prince Fielder (81/12150) 2.00
60 Dan Uggla (26/3900) .50
61 Dan Uggla (27/4050) .50
62 Dan Uggla (172/25800) .50
63 Justin Verlander (17/2550) 1.50
64 Justin Verlander (124/18600) 1.50
65 Francisco Liriano (12/1800) 1.50
66 Francisco Liriano (144/21600) 1.50
67 Ryan Zimmerman (176/26400) 1.00
68 Ryan Zimmerman (110/16500) 1.00
69 Ryan Zimmerman (84/12600) 1.00
70 Hanley Ramirez (51/7650) 1.50
71 Hanley Ramirez (119/17850) 1.50
72 Hanley Ramirez (185/27750) 1.50
73 Russ Martin (65/9750) 1.00
74 Russ Martin (26/3900) 1.00
75 Mickey Mantle (173/25950) 5.00
76 Mickey Mantle (121/18150) 5.00
77 Mickey Mantle (146/21900) 5.00
78 Mickey Mantle (94/14100) 5.00
79 Mike Piazza (35/5250) 1.50
80 Mike Piazza (112/16800) 1.50
81 Derek Jeter (10/1500) 4.00
82 Derek Jeter (78/1700) 4.00
83 Derek Jeter (183/27450) 4.00
84 Dontrelle Willis (14/2100) .75
85 Dontrelle Willis (142/21300) .75
86 Dontrelle Willis (2/300) .75
87 Bobby Crosby (22/3300) .50
88 Bobby Crosby (64/9600) .50
89 Ryan Howard (22/3300) 3.00
90 Ryan Howard (63/9450) 3.00
91 Curt Schilling (21/3150) 1.50
92 Curt Schilling (203/30450) 1.50
93 Andruw Jones (52/7800) 1.50
94 Andruw Jones (128/19200) 1.50
95 Andruw Jones (11/1650) 1.50
96 Hideki Matsui (23/3450) 2.50
97 Hideki Matsui (116/17400) 2.50
98 Hideki Matsui (192/28800) 2.50
99 David Wright (27/4050) 2.50
100 David Wright (102/15300) 2.50
101 David Wright (42/6300) 2.50
102 David Wright (17/2550) 2.50
103 David Ortiz (75/11250) 2.00
104 David Wright (47/7050) 2.00
105 David Ortiz (11/1650) 2.00
106 Frank Thomas (38/5700) 1.50
107 Frank Thomas (101/15150) 1.50
108 Craig Biggio (40/6000) 1.00
109 Miguel Cabrera (33/4950) 2.00
110 Miguel Cabrera (116/17400) 2.00
111 Vernon Wells (12/1800) 1.00
112 Michael Young (24/3600) 1.00
113 Michael Young (40/6000) 1.00
114 Joe Mauer (144/21600) 1.50
115 Gary Sheffield (34/5100) 1.00
116 Jim Edmonds (42/6300) 1.00
117 Jorge Posada (19/2850) 1.00
118 Jorge Posada (23/3450) 1.00
119 Pat Burrell (32/4800) .75
120 Adam Dunn (40/6000) 1.00
121 Johnny Damon (35/5250) 2.00
122 Scott Rolen (34/5100) 1.50
123 Paul Konerko (6/900) 1.00
124 Roy Halladay (22/3300) 1.00
125 Grady Sizemore (22/3300) 1.50
126 Grady Sizemore (37/5550) 1.50
127 John Smoltz (24/3600) 1.00
128 Jeff Kent (29/4350) .75
129 Billy Wagner (38/5700) .50
130 Mark Prior (18/2700) .75
131 Eric Chavez (32/4800) .75
132 Jimmy Rollins (41/6150) 1.50
133 Manny Ramirez (7/1050) 1.50
134 Manny Ramirez (45/6750) 1.50
135 Manny Ramirez (144/21600) 1.50
136 Derrek Lee (46/6900) 1.50
137 Derrek Lee (107/16050) 1.50
138 Tom Glavine (14/2100) 1.00
139 Tom Glavine (20/3000) 1.00
140 Jose Reyes (17/2550) 2.00
141 Pedro Martinez (15/2250) 1.50
142 Pedro Martinez (208/31200) 1.50
143 Mark Teixeira (43/6450) 1.00
144 Jake Peavy (13/1950) 1.00
145 Carlos Lee (32/4800) .75
146 Josh Beckett (16/2400) .75
147 Johan Santana (20/3000) 2.00
148 Todd Helton (33/4950) 1.50
149 Mariano Rivera (43/6450) 1.50
150 Travis Hafner (33/4950) 1.50
151 Jason Bay (24/3600) 1.00
152 Bobby Abreu (30/4500) 1.00
153 Mike Mussina (13/1950) 1.00
154 Miguel Tejada (34/5100) 1.00
155 Miguel Tejada (150/22500) 1.00
156 Robinson Cano (14/2100) 1.50
157 Robinson Cano (34/5100) 1.50
158 Ryan Zimmerman (23/3450) 1.00
159 Carlos Beltran (16/2400) 1.50
160 Carlos Beltran (17/2550) 1.50
161 Roger Clemens (18/2700) 3.00
162 Roger Clemens (218/32700) 3.00
163 Mickey Mantle (52/7800) 5.00
164 Mickey Mantle (130/19500) 5.00
165 Mickey Mantle (188/28200) 5.00
166 Mickey Mantle (132/19800) 5.00
167 Mickey Mantle (42/6300) 5.00
168 Mickey Mantle (97/14550) 5.00
169 Mickey Mantle (127/19050) 5.00
170 Daisuke Matsuzaka **RC** 150.00
171 Daisuke Matsuzaka **RC** 150.00
172 Daisuke Matsuzaka **RC** 150.00
173 Delmon Young **(RC)** 5.00
174 Delmon Young **(RC)** 5.00
175 Delmon Young **(RC)** 5.00
176 Andrew Miller **RC** 30.00
177 Andrew Miller **RC** 30.00
178 Andrew Miller **RC** 25.00
179 Troy Tulowitzki **(RC)** 5.00
180 Troy Tulowitzki **(RC)** 5.00
181 Troy Tulowitzki **(RC)** 5.00
182 Josh Fields **(RC)** 5.00
183 Josh Fields **(RC)** 5.00
184 Josh Fields **(RC)** 5.00
185 Jeff Baker **(RC)** 5.00
186 Jeff Baker **(RC)** 5.00
187 Jeff Baker **(RC)** 5.00
188 Philip Humber **(RC)** 5.00
189 Philip Humber **(RC)** 5.00
190 Philip Humber **(RC)** 5.00
191 Kevin Kouzmanoff **(RC)** 5.00
192 Kevin Kouzmanoff **(RC)** 5.00
193 Kevin Kouzmanoff **(RC)** 5.00

Black

Stars: 2-3X
Production 29 Sets

Red

No Pricing
Production One Set

Printing Plates

No Pricing
Production one set per color.

A-Rod Road to 500

NM/M
Common A-Rod (101-125): 3.00
Inserted 2:Box

A-Rod Road to 500 Auto.

NM/M
Production One Set 3.00

Milestone Autographs

NM/M
Common Auto.: 15.00
Black: 1-1.5X
Production 40 Sets
Red: No Pricing
Production One Set
AJ Andruw Jones/100 50.00
AR Alex Rodriguez/100 180.00
BP Brandon Phillips 15.00
BR Brian Roberts 15.00
CJ Conor Jackson 15.00
DO David Ortiz 60.00
DW David Wright 60.00
GA Garrett Atkins 15.00
GS Gary Sheffield/100 35.00
HS Huston Street/200 20.00
JF Jeff Francoeur 50.00
JG Jason Giambi/100 50.00
JJG Jonny Gomes 15.00
JL Julio Lugo 15.00
JP Jonathan Papelbon 40.00
JR Jose Reyes/200 70.00
JS Jeremy Sowers 15.00
KJ Kenji Johjima 35.00
KM Kendry Morales 15.00
LM Lastings Milledge 20.00
MK Matthew Kemp 15.00
MN Mike Napoli 15.00
MP Martin Prado 15.00
NS Nick Swisher 15.00
RH Ryan Howard/200 75.00
RP Ronny Paulino 15.00
TH Travis Hafner 20.00
VG Vladimir Guerrero/100 50.00
WP Wily Mo Pena/100 20.00

Rookie Autographs

NM/M
Common Auto.: 10.00
Black: 2-3X
Production 40 Sets
Red: No Pricing
Production One Set
AL Adam Lind 15.00
AM Andrew Miller 40.00
DM David Murphy 10.00
HG Hector Gimenez 10.00
JA Joaquin Arias 10.00
KK Kevin Kouzmanoff 15.00
MB Michael Bourn 10.00
MM Miguel Montero 10.00
SR Shawn Riggans 10.00
TT Troy Tulowitzki 30.00

2007 Topps Opening Day

NM/M
Complete Set (220): 35.00
Common Player: .15
Pack (6): 1.25
Box (36): 40.00
1 Bobby Abreu .25
2 Mike Piazza .75
3 Jake Westbrook .15
4 Zachary Duke .15
5 David Wright 1.00
6 Adrian Gonzalez .25
7 Mickey Mantle 3.00
8 Bill Hall .25
9 Robinson Cano .25
10 Dontrelle Willis .25
11 J.D. Drew .25
12 Paul Konerko .25
13 Austin Kearns .15
14 Mike Lowell .15
15 Magglio Ordonez .15
16 Rafael Furcal .25
17 Matt Cain .25
18 Craig Monroe .15
19 Matt Holliday .25
20 Edgar Renteria .25
21 Mark Buehrle .15
22 Carlos Quentin .15
23 C.C. Sabathia .25
24 Nicholas Markakis .25
25 Chipper Jones .50
26 Jason Giambi .40
27 Barry Zito .25
28 Jake Peavy .25
29 Hank Blalock .25
30 Johnny Damon .50
31 Chad Tracy .15
32 Nick Swisher .25
33 Willy Taveras .15
34 Chuck James .25
35 Carlos Delgado .40
36 Livan Hernandez .15
37 Freddy Garcia .15
38 Bronson Arroyo .15
39 Jack Wilson .15
40 Dan Uggla .15
41 Chris Carpenter .50
42 Jorge Posada .25
43 Joe Mauer .40
44 Corey Patterson .15
45 Chien-Ming Wang .50
46 Derek Jeter 1.50
47 Carlos Beltran .50
48 Jim Edmonds .25
49 Jeremy Sowers .15
50 Randy Johnson .50
51 Jered Weaver .25
52 Josh Barfield .15
53 Scott Rolen .40
54 Ryan Shealy .15
55 Freddy Sanchez .15
56 Javier Vazquez .15
57 Jeremy Bonderman .25
58 Miguel Cabrera .50
59 Kazuo Matsui .15
60 Curt Schilling .50
61 Alfonso Soriano .50
62 Orlando Hernandez .15
63 Joe Blanton .15
64 Aramis Ramirez .25
65 Ben Sheets .25
66 Jimmy Rollins .25
67 Mark Loretta .15
68 Cole Hamels .25
69 Albert Pujols 1.50
70 Moises Alou .25
71 Mark Teahen .15
72 Roy Halladay .25
73 Cory Sullivan .15
74 Frank Thomas .50
75 Ryan Howard 1.50
76 Rocco Baldelli .25
77 Manny Ramirez .50
78 Ray Durham .15
79 Gary Sheffield .40
80 Jay Gibbons .15
81 Todd Helton .40
82 Gary Matthews .15
83 Brandon Inge .15
84 Jonathan Papelbon .40
85 John Smoltz .25
86 Chone Figgins .15
87 Hideki Matsui .75
88 Carlos Lee .25
89 Jose Reyes .75
90 Lyle Overbay .25
91 Johan Santana .50
92 Ian Kinsler .15
93 Scott Kazmir .25
94 Hanley Ramirez .40
95 Greg Maddux 1.00
96 Johnny Estrada .15
97 B.J. Upton .25
98 Francisco Liriano .25
99 Chase Utley .50
100 Preston Wilson .15
101 Marcus Giles .15
102 Jeff Kent .25
103 Grady Sizemore .50
104 Ken Griffey Jr. 1.00
105 Garret Anderson .15
106 Brian McCann .25
107 Jon Garland .15
108 Troy Glaus .25
109 Brandon Webb .25
110 Jason Schmidt .25
111 Ramon Hernandez .15
112 Justin Morneau .50
113 Mike Cameron .15
114 Andruw Jones .40
115 Russell Martin .15
116 Vernon Wells .15
117 Orlando Hudson .15
118 Derek Lowe .15
119 Alex Rodriguez 1.50
120 Chad Billingsley .15
121 Kenji Johjima .15
122 Nick Johnson .15
123 Danny Haren .25
124 Mark Teixeira .40
125 Jeff Francoeur .25
126 Ted Lilly .15
127 Jhonny Peralta .15
128 Aaron Harang .15
129 Ryan Zimmerman .25
130 Jermaine Dye .15
131 Orlando Cabrera .25
132 Juan Pierre .15
133 Brian Giles .25
134 Jason Bay .25
135 David Ortiz .50
136 Chris Capuano .15
137 Carlos Zambrano .25
138 Luis Gonzalez .15
139 Jeff Weaver .15
140 Lance Berkman .25
141 Raul Ibanez .15
142 Jim Thome .40
143 Jose Contreras .15
144 David Eckstein .15
145 Adam Dunn .40
146 Alex Rios .15
147 Garrett Atkins .25
148 A.J. Burnett .15
149 Jeremy Hermida .15
150 Conor Jackson .15
151 Adrian Beltre .25
152 Torii Hunter .25
153 Andrew Miller **RC** 2.00
154 Ichiro Suzuki 1.00
155 Mark Redman .15
156 Paul LoDuca .15
157 Xavier Nady .15
158 Stephen Drew .25
159 Eric Chavez .25
160 Pedro Martinez .50
161 Derrek Lee .40
162 David DeJesus .15
163 Troy Tulowitzki **(RC)** .50
164 Vinny Rottino **(RC)** .25
165 Philip Humber **(RC)** .25
166 Jerry Owens **(RC)** .25
167 Ubaldo Jimenez **(RC)** .25
168 Michael Young .25
169 Ryan Braun **(RC)** .25
170 Kevin Kouzmanoff **(RC)** .25
171 Oswaldo Navarro **RC** .25
172 Miguel Montero **(RC)** .25
173 Roy Oswalt .25
174 Shane Youman **RC** .25
175 Josh Fields **(RC)** .25
176 Adam Lind **(RC)** .25
177 Miguel Tejada .40
178 Delwyn Young **(RC)** .25
179 Scott Moore **(RC)** .25
180 Fred Lewis **(RC)** .25
181 Glen Perkins **(RC)** .25
182 Vladimir Guerrero .50
183 Drew Anderson **(RC)** .25
184 Jeff Salazar **(RC)** .25
185 Tom Gordon .15
186 The Bird .15
187 Justin Verlander .40
188 Delmon Young **(RC)** .50
189 Homer .15
190 Wally the Green Monster .15
191 Southpaw .15
192 Dinger .15
193 Carl Crawford .15
194 Slider .15
195 Gapper .15
196 Paws .15
197 Billy the Marlin .15
198 Ivan Rodriguez .15
199 Slugger .15
200 Junction Jack .15
201 Bernie the Brewer .15
202 Travis Hafner .40
203 Stomper .15
204 Mr. Met .15
205 The Moose .15
206 Phillie Phanatic .15
207 Prince Fielder .50
208 Julio Lugo .15
209 Pirate Parrot .15
210 Joel Zumaya .25
211 Swinging Friar .15
212 Jay Payton .15
213 Lou Seal .15
214 Fredbird .15
215 Screech .15
216 TC Bear .15
217 Andre Ethier .15
218 Ervin Santana .15
219 Melvin Mora .15
220 Checklist .15

Autographs

NM/M
Common Auto.: 15.00
EF Emiliano Fruto 20.00
HK Howie Kendrick 40.00
JT Jordan Tata 25.00
JM Juan Morillo 15.00
MC Matt Cain 20.00
MK Matthew Kemp 25.00
MN Mike Napoli 20.00
OH Orlando Hudson 20.00
RM Robert Mackowiak 15.00
SS Shannon Stewart 15.00

A-Rod Road to 500

NM/M
Common A-Rod (76-100): 3.00

A-Rod Road to 500 Autograph

Production One Set

Diamond Stars

NM/M
Common Player: .25
1 Ryan Howard 1.50
2 Alfonso Soriano .75
3 Alex Rodriguez 1.50
4 David Ortiz .75
5 Raul Ibanez .25
6 Matt Holliday .50
7 Delmon Young .50
8 Derrick Turnbow .25
9 Freddy Sanchez .50
10 Troy Glaus .50
11 A.J. Pierzynski .25
12 Dontrelle Willis .50
13 Justin Morneau .75
14 Jose Reyes 1.00
15 Derek Jeter 1.50
16 Ivan Rodriguez .50
17 Jay Payton .25
18 Adrian Gonzalez .25
19 David Eckstein .25
20 Chipper Jones .75
21 Aramis Ramirez .50
22 David Wright 1.00
23 Mark Teixeira .50
24 Stephen Drew .50
25 Ichiro Suzuki 1.00

Movie Gallery

NM/M
Alex Rodriguez 1.00

Puzzle

NM/M
Complete Puzzle: 10.00
Common Player: .25
1 Adam Dunn .25
2 Adam Dunn .25
3 Miguel Tejada .25
4 Miguel Tejada .25
5 Hanley Ramirez .25
6 Hanley Ramirez .25
7 Johan Santana .50
8 Johan Santana .50
9 Brandon Webb .25
10 Brandon Webb .25
11 David Wright .75
12 David Wright .75
13 Alex Rodriguez .75
14 Alex Rodriguez .75
15 Ryan Howard .75
16 Ryan Howard .75
17 Albert Pujols 1.00
18 Albert Pujols 1.00
19 Andruw Jones .50
20 Andruw Jones .50
21 Alfonso Soriano .50
22 Alfonso Soriano .50
23 Vladimir Guerrero .50
24 Vladimir Guerrero .50
25 David Ortiz .50
26 David Ortiz .50
27 Ichiro Suzuki .75
28 Ichiro Suzuki .75

2007 Topps Sterling

NM/M
Common Mantle (1-24): 12.00
Common Bonds (25-48): 10.00
Common Ichiro (49-56): 8.00
Common Yastrzemski (57-64): 8.00
Common David Wright (65-76): 8.00
Common Clemente (77-81): 15.00
Common Johan Santana (82-89): 8.00
Common Morneau (90-101): 6.00
Common R. Jackson (102-109): 6.00
Common Clemens (110-117): 8.00
Common T. Williams (118-122): 10.00
Common Berra (123-130): 8.00
Common Matsui (131-135): 8.00
Common R. Howard (136-143): 8.00
Common Gwynn (144-151): 8.00
Common Ortiz (152-159): 8.00
Common Seaver (160-167): 6.00
Common Pujols (168-175): 10.00
Common Musial (176-183): 8.00
Common Wang (184-191): 10.00
Common Sandberg (192-199): 8.00
Common Ryan (200-207): 15.00
Common Gibson (208-215): 6.00
Common Maris (216-220): 8.00
Common Ramirez (221-228): 8.00
Common Schmidt (229-236): 8.00
Common A-Rod (237-244): 10.00
Common Matsuzaka (245-249): 15.00
Common DiMaggio (250-254): 10.00
Production 250 Sets
1-24 Mickey Mantle 12.00
25-48 Barry Bonds 10.00
49-56 Ichiro Suzuki 8.00

57-64 Carl Yastrzemski 8.00
65-76 David Wright 8.00
77-81 Roberto Clemente 15.00
82-89 Johan Santana 8.00
90-101 Justin Morneau 6.00
102-109 Reggie Jackson 6.00
110-117 Roger Clemens 8.00
118-122 Ted Williams 10.00
123-130 Yogi Berra 8.00
131-135 Hideki Matsui 8.00
136-143 Ryan Howard 8.00
144-151 Tony Gwynn 8.00
152-159 David Ortiz 8.00
160-167 Tom Seaver 6.00
168-175 Albert Pujols 10.00
176-183 Stan Musial 8.00
184-191 Chien-Ming Wang 10.00
192-199 Ryne Sandberg 8.00
200-207 Nolan Ryan 15.00
208-215 Bob Gibson 6.00
216-220 Roger Maris 8.00
221-228 Manny Ramirez 8.00
229-236 Mike Schmidt 8.00
237-244 Alex Rodriguez 10.00
245-249 Daisuke Matsuzaka RC 15.00
250-254 Joe DiMaggio 10.00

Framed Burgundy

Burgundy: 3-4X
Production 14 Sets

Cherry Wood

Production One Set

Framed Gold

Gold: 4-5X
Production Nine Sets

Sterling Silver

Production One Set

White Suede

White Suede: 1-2X
Production 50 Sets

Bat Barrels

No Pricing
Production One Set

Career Stats Relics Autographs Quad

NM/M
Production 10 Sets
1-5 Carl Yastrzemski 75.00
6-16 David Wright 120.00
17-22 Johan Santana 100.00
23-33 Justin Morneau 50.00
34-39 Reggie Jackson 60.00
40 Roger Clemens 100.00
41-48 Yogi Berra 120.00
50-56 Ryan Howard 100.00
57-62 Tony Gwynn 100.00
63-66 David Ortiz 100.00
67-73 Tom Seaver 80.00
74 Albert Pujols 300.00
75-80 Stan Musial 120.00
81-86 Chien-Ming Wang 200.00
87-92 Ryne Sandberg 120.00
93-98 Nolan Ryan 150.00
99-104 Bob Gibson 60.00
105-108 Manny Ramirez 75.00
109-113 Mike Schmidt 80.00
114-120 Alex Rodriguez 250.00

Career Stats Relics Auto. Triples

NM/M
Production 10 Sets
1 Barry Bonds 250.00
2-7 Carl Yastrzemski 75.00
8-17 David Wright 100.00
18-24 Johan Santana 75.00
25-34 Justin Morneau 50.00
35-40 Reggie Jackson 60.00
41 Roger Clemens 100.00
42-48 Yogi Berra 100.00
49-54 Ryan Howard 100.00
55-61 Tony Gwynn 100.00
62-64 David Ortiz 80.00
65-70 Tom Seaver 80.00
71 Albert Pujols 250.00
72-77 Stan Musial 100.00
78-83 Chien-Ming Wang 200.00
84-89 Ryne Sandberg 100.00
90-95 Nolan Ryan 120.00
96-102 Bob Gibson 60.00
103-108 Manny Ramirez 60.00
109-113 Mike Schmidt 80.00
114-120 Alex Rodriguez 250.00

Career Stats Relics Five

NM/M
Production 10 Sets
1-10 Mickey Mantle 180.00
11-21 Barry Bonds 50.00
22-25 Ichiro Suzuki 100.00
26 Carl Yastrzemski 50.00
27 David Wright 75.00
28-30 Roberto Clemente 140.00
31 Justin Morneau 25.00
32-34 Roger Clemens 40.00
35-37 Ted Williams 100.00
38 Yogi Berra 50.00
39-40 Hideki Matsui 75.00
41 Ryan Howard 50.00
42 Tony Gwynn 40.00
43 David Ortiz 50.00
44 Tom Seaver 40.00
45-48 Albert Pujols 60.00
49 Chien-Ming Wang 75.00
50 Ryne Sandberg 40.00
51 Nolan Ryan 80.00
52 Bob Gibson 40.00
53 Roger Maris 80.00
54 Roger Maris 80.00
55-56 Manny Ramirez 40.00
57 Mike Schmidt 60.00
58 Alex Rodriguez 100.00
59 Daisuke Matsuzaka 80.00
60 Joe DiMaggio 125.00

Career Stats Relics Quad

NM/M
Production 10 Sets
1-10 Mickey Mantle 180.00
11 Mickey Mantle 50.00
12-21 Barry Bonds 50.00
22 Barry Bonds 100.00
23-25 Ichiro Suzuki 100.00
26 Ichiro Suzuki 50.00
27 Ichiro Suzuki 75.00
28 Carl Yastrzemski 140.00
29 David Wright 140.00
30 Roberto Clemente 140.00
31 Roberto Clemente 25.00
32 Johan Santana 40.00
33 Justin Morneau 40.00
34 Reggie Jackson 40.00
35-36 Roger Clemens 100.00
37 Ted Williams 100.00
38 Ted Williams 50.00
39-40 Hideki Matsui 75.00
41 Ryan Howard 50.00
42 David Ortiz 40.00
43 David Ortiz 50.00
44 Tom Seaver 40.00
45-48 Albert Pujols 60.00
49 Stan Musial 50.00
50 Ryne Sandberg 75.00
51 Nolan Ryan 40.00
52 Bob Gibson 40.00
53-54 Roger Maris 80.00
55-56 Manny Ramirez 75.00
57 Mike Schmidt 80.00
58 Alex Rodriguez 100.00
59 Daisuke Matsuzaka 100.00
60 Joe DiMaggio 100.00

Career Stats Relics Six

NM/M
Production 10 Sets
1-10 Mickey Mantle 180.00
11-20 Barry Bonds 50.00
21-24 Ichiro Suzuki 120.00
25 Carl Yastrzemski 60.00
26 David Wright 80.00
27-28 Roberto Clemente 160.00
29 Roberto Clemente 160.00
30 Johan Santana 30.00
31 Justin Morneau 30.00
32-35 Reggie Jackson 50.00
36-38 Ted Williams 125.00
39 Yogi Berra 60.00
40 Hideki Matsui 80.00
41 Tony Gwynn 50.00
42 David Ortiz 60.00
43-45 Albert Pujols 60.00
46 Stan Musial 60.00
47 Chien-Ming Wang 80.00
48 Ryne Sandberg 50.00
49 Nolan Ryan 80.00
50 Bob Gibson 50.00
51-53 Roger Maris 80.00
54-56 Manny Ramirez 50.00
57 Mike Schmidt 75.00
58 Alex Rodriguez 100.00
59 Daisuke Matsuzaka 120.00
60 Joe DiMaggio 125.00

Career Stats Relics Triple

NM/M
Production 10 Sets
1-11 Mickey Mantle 125.00
12-22 Barry Bonds 40.00
23-27 Ichiro Suzuki 100.00
28 Carl Yastrzemski 40.00
29 David Wright 50.00
30-31 Roberto Clemente 100.00
32 Justin Morneau 25.00
33 Reggie Jackson 30.00
34-36 Roger Clemens 40.00
37-38 Ted Williams 80.00
39 Yogi Berra 50.00
40-41 Hideki Matsui 60.00
42 Tony Gwynn 40.00
43-45 David Ortiz 50.00
46 Tom Seaver 40.00
47-49 Albert Pujols 50.00
50 Stan Musial 50.00
51 Ryne Sandberg 40.00
52 Nolan Ryan 60.00
53 Bob Gibson 30.00
54-56 Roger Maris 75.00
57-58 Mike Schmidt 65.00
59 Daisuke Matsuzaka 80.00
60-64 Joe DiMaggio 100.00

Cut Signatures

No Pricing
Production One Set

Jumbo Swatch

No Pricing
Production 10 Sets
Autographs: No Pricing
Production 10 Sets

Letter Patch

Production one per letter.
Total print run listed

Moments Relics Autographs Eight

No Pricing
Production 10 Sets

Moments Relics Autographs Quad

NM/M
Production 10 Sets
1 Barry Bonds 250.00
2-9 Carl Yastrzemski 75.00
10-20 David Wright 120.00
21 Johan Santana 100.00
22 Johan Santana 28.00
23-27 Johan Santana 100.00
28-38 Justin Morneau 50.00
39-46 Reggie Jackson 60.00
47-48 Roger Clemens 100.00
49-55 Yogi Berra 120.00
56-63 Ryan Howard 100.00
64-70 Tony Gwynn 100.00
71-74 David Ortiz 100.00
75-81 Tom Seaver 80.00
82 Albert Pujols 300.00
83-89 Stan Musial 120.00
90-97 Chien-Ming Wang 200.00
98-104 Ryne Sandberg 120.00
105-112 Nolan Ryan 150.00
113-120 Bob Gibson 60.00
121-128 Manny Ramirez 75.00
129-133 Mike Schmidt 80.00
134-140 Alex Rodriguez 250.00

Moments Relics Autographs Triple

NM/M
1 Barry Bonds 250.00
2-9 Carl Yastrzemski 75.00
10-20 David Wright 100.00
21-27 Johan Santana 75.00
28-38 Justin Morneau 50.00
39-45 Reggie Jackson 60.00
46-47 Roger Clemens 100.00
48-55 Yogi Berra 100.00
56-62 Ryan Howard 100.00
63-70 Tony Gwynn 100.00
71-72 David Ortiz 80.00
73-80 Tom Seaver 80.00
81 Albert Pujols 80.00
82-89 Stan Musial 100.00
90-96 Chien-Ming Wang 200.00
97-104Ryno Sandberg 100.00
105-111Nolan Ryan 120.00
112-119Bob Gibson 60.00
120-126Manny Ramirez 60.00
127-133Mike Schmidt 80.00
134-140Alex Rodriguez 250.00

Moments Relics Eight

NM/M
Production 10 Sets
1-2 Mickey Mantle 300.00
3-4 Barry Bonds 200.00
11-12 Hideki Matsui 150.00

Moments Relics Five

NM/M
Production 10 Sets
1-15 Mickey Mantle 180.00
16-30 Barry Bonds 50.00
31-34 Ichiro Suzuki 100.00
35 Carl Yastrzemski 50.00
36 David Wright 75.00
37-39 Roberto Clemente 140.00
40 Johan Santana 30.00
41 Justin Morneau 25.00
42-44 Roger Clemens 40.00
45-49 Ted Williams 100.00
50 Ryan Howard 50.00
51 David Ortiz 50.00
52 Tom Seaver 40.00
53-56 Albert Pujols 60.00
57 Stan Musial 60.00
58 Chien-Ming Wang 75.00
59 Nolan Ryan 80.00
60 Bob Gibson 50.00
61-63 Roger Maris 80.00
64-65 Manny Ramirez 40.00
66 Mike Schmidt 60.00
67 Alex Rodriguez 100.00
68-70 Daisuke Matsuzaka 80.00
71 Joe DiMaggio 125.00

Moments Relics Quad

NM/M
Production 10 Sets
1-15 Mickey Mantle 180.00
16-17 Mickey Mantle 50.00
18-30 Barry Bonds 50.00
31-32 Barry Bonds 100.00
33-34 Ichiro Suzuki 100.000
35 Ichiro Suzuki 50.00
36 Ichiro Suzuki 75.00
37 Ichiro Suzuki 140.00
38 Carl Yastrzemski 50.00
39 David Wright 60.00
40-41 Roberto Clemente 125.00
42 Johan Santana 30.00
43 Justin Morneau 25.00
44-46 Roger Clemens 40.00
47-48 Ted Williams 100.00
50-51 Hideki Matsui 75.00
53-54 David Ortiz 50.00
55 Tom Seaver 40.00
56-58 Albert Pujols 50.00
59 Stan Musial 50.00
60 Bob Gibson 40.00
61-62 Roger Maris 80.00
63-64 Mike Schmidt 75.00
65-68 Daisuke Matsuzaka 80.00
69-71 Joe DiMaggio 100.00

Moments Relics Six

NM/M
Production 10 Sets
1-15 Mickey Mantle 180.00
16-29 Barry Bonds 50.00
30-33 Ichiro Suzuki 100.00
34 David Wright 80.00
35-37 Roberto Clemente 160.00
38 Johan Santana 30.00
39 Justin Morneau 30.00
40 Reggie Jackson 50.00
41-45 Roger Clemens 50.00
46-48 Ted Williams 125.00
49-50 Hideki Matsui 80.00
51 Ron Howard 50.00
52-55 David Ortiz 60.00
56-60 Albert Pujols 60.00
61 Chien-Ming Wang 80.00
62 Ryne Sanberg 50.00
63 Nolan Ryan 80.00
64-66 Roger Maris 80.00
67 Mike Schmidt 75.00
68 Alex Rodriguez 100.00
69-70 Daisuke Matsuzaka 120.00
71 Joe DiMaggio 125.00

Moments Relics Triple

NM/M
Production 10 Sets
1-17 Mickey Mantle 125.00
18-32 Barry Bonds 40.00
33-36 Ichiro Suzuki 100.00
37 David Wright 50.00
38-39 Roberto Clemente 100.00
40 Justin Morneau 25.00
41 Reggie Jackson 30.00
42-44 Roger Clemens 40.00
45-46 Ted Williams 80.000
47 Yogi Berra 50.00
48-49 Hideki Matsui 60.00
50 Tony Gwynn 40.00
51-54 David Ortiz 50.00
55 Tom Seaver 40.00
56-58 Albert Pujols 50.00
59 Stan Musial 50.00
60 Bob Gibson 30.00
61-62 Roger Maris 75.00
63 Mike Schmidt 65.00
64-67 Daisuke Matsuzaka 80.00
68-72 Joe DiMaggio 100.00

Stardom Relics Autographs Eight

No Pricing
Production 10 Sets

Stardom Relics Autograhs Quad

NM/M
Production 10 Sets
1 Barry Bonds 250.00
2-8 Carl Yastrzemski 75.00
9-19 David Wright 120.00
20-27 Johan Santana 100.00
28-38 Justin Morneau 50.00
39-45 Reggie Jackson 60.00
46-47 Roger Clemens 100.00
48-54 Yogi Berra 120.00
56-63 Ryan Howard 100.00
64-70 Tony Gwynn 100.00
71-74 David Ortiz 100.00
75-81 Tom Seaver 80.00
82 Albert Pujols 300.00
83-89 Stan Musial 120.00
90-97 Chien-Ming Wang 200.00
98-104 Ryne Sandberg 120.00
105-111 Nolan Ryan 150.00
112-118 Bob Gibson 60.00
119-125 Manny Ramirez 75.00
126-132 Mike Schmidt 80.00
133-140 Alex Rodriguez 250.00

Stardom Relics Autographs Triple

NM/M
1 Barry Bonds 250.00
2-9 Carl Yastrzemski 75.00
10-20 David Wright 100.00
21-27 Johan Santana 75.00
28-38 Justin Morneau 50.00
39-46 Reggie Jackson 60.00
47-48 Roger Clemens 100.00
49-55 Yogi Berra 100.00
56-62 Ryan Howard 100.00
63-69 Tony Gwynn 100.00
70-72 David Ortiz 80.00
73 Tom Seaver 80.00
74 David Ortiz 80.00
75-79 Tom Seaver 80.00
80 Albert Pujols 250.00
81-88 Stan Musial 100.00
89-95 Chien-Ming Wang 200.00
96-103 Ryne Sandberg 100.00
104-111 Nolan Ryan 120.00
112-119 Bob Gibson 60.00
120-126 Manny Ramirez 60.00
127-133 Mike Schmidt 80.00
134-140 Alex Rodriguez 250.00

Stardom Relics Eight

NM/M
Production 10 Sets
1-2 Mickey Mantle 350.00
3-4 Barry Bonds 200.00
10-11 Hideki Matsui 125.00
14-15 David Ortiz 75.00

Stardom Relics Five

NM/M
Production 10 Sets
1-14 Mickey Mantle 180.00
15-29 Barry Bonds 50.00
30-33 Ichiro Suzuki 100.00
34 Carl Yastrzemski 50.00
35 David Wright 75.00
36-38 Roberto Clemente 140.00
39 Johan Santana 30.00
40 Justin Morneau 25.00
41 Reggie Jackson 40.00
42-44 Roger Clemens 40.00
45-47 Ted Williams 100.00
48 Yogi Berra 50.00
49-50 Hideki Matsui 75.00
51 Ryan Howard 50.00
52 Tony Gwynn 40.00
53 David Ortiz 50.00
54-57 Albert Pujols 60.00
58 Chien-Ming Wang 75.00
59 Nolan Ryan 80.00
60 Bob Gibson 40.00
61-63 Roger Maris 80.00
64-65 Manny Ramirez 40.00
66 Mike Schmidt 60.00
67 Alex Rodriguez 100.00
68-70 Daisuke Matsuzaka 80.00
71 Joe DiMaggio 125.00

Stardom Relics Quad

NM/M
Production 10 Sets
1-17 Mickey Mantle 180.00
18-32 Barry Bonds 50.00
33-37 Ichiro Suzuki 100.00
38 Carl Yastrzemski 50.00
39-40 Roberto Clemente 125.00
41 Johan Santana 30.00
42-44 Roger Clemens 40.00
45-46 Ted Williams 100.00
47 Yogi Berra 50.00
48-49 Hideki Matsui 75.00
50 Ryan Howard 50.00
51 Tony Gwynn 40.00
52-54 David Ortiz 50.00
55 Tom Seaver 40.00
56-58 Albert Pujols 50.00
59 Chien-Ming Wang 75.00
60 Ryne Sandberg 40.00
61 Bob Gibson 40.00
62-63 Roger Maris 80.00
64 Alex Rodriguez 60.00
65-68 Daisuke Matsuzaka 80.00
69-71 Joe DiMaggio 100.00

Stardom Relics Six

NM/M
Production 10 Sets
1-14 Mickey Mantle 180.00
15-28 Barry Bonds 50.00
29-32 Ichiro Suzuki 120.00
33 David Wright 80.00
34-36 Roberto Clemente 160.00
37 Johan Santana 30.00
38 Justin Morneau 30.00
39 Reggie Jackson 50.00
40-44 Roger Clemens 50.00
45-47 Ted Williams 125.00
48-49 Hideki Matsui 80.00
50 Ryan Howard 60.00
51-54 David Ortiz 60.00
55-59 Albert Pujols 60.00
60 Chien-Ming Wang 80.00
61 Ryne Sandberg 50.00
62 Nolan Ryan 80.00
63-65 Roger Maris 80.00
66 Mike Schmidt 75.00
67 Alex Rodriguez 100.00
68-69 Daisuke Matsuzaka 120.00
70 Joe DiMaggio 125.00

Stardom Relics Triple

NM/M
Production 10 Sets
1-17 Mickey Mantle 125.00
18-32 Barry Bonds 40.00
33-37 Ichiro Suzuki 100.00
38 Carl Yastrzemski 40.00
39 David Wright 50.00
40-41 Roberto Clemente 100.00
42 Justin Morneau 25.00
43-45 Roger Clemens 40.00
46-47 Ted Williams 80.00
48 Yogi Berra 50.00
49-51 Hideki Matsui 60.00
51-54 David Ortiz 50.00
55 Tom Seaver 40.00
56-58 Albert Pujols 50.00
59 Stan Musial 50.00
60 Nolan Ryan 60.00
61 Bob Gibson 30.00
62-63 Roger Maris 75.00
64-67 Daisuke Matsuzaka 80.00
68 Joe DiMaggio 100.00
69 Joe DiMaggio 100.00
70 Joe DiMaggio 100.00
71 Joe DiMaggio 100.00
72 Joe DiMaggio 100.00

2007 Topps Triple Threads

NM/M
Complete Set (189):
Common Player (1-125): 1.00
Production 1,350
Common Auto. (126-189): 10.00
Production 99
Pack (6): 100.00
Box (2): 200.00
1 Alex Rodriguez 6.00
2 Barry Zito 1.50
3 Corey Patterson 1.00
4 Roberto Clemente 5.00
5 David Wright 3.00
6 Dontrelle Willis 1.50
7 Mickey Mantle 8.00
8 Adam Dunn 2.00
9 Richie Ashburn 2.00
10 Ryan Howard 5.00
11 Miguel Tejada 2.00
12 Ernie Banks 4.00
13 Ken Griffey Jr. 5.00
14 Johnny Bench 3.00
15 Ichiro Suzuki 4.00
16 Gil Meche 1.00
17 Kazuo Matsui 1.00
18 Matt Holliday 1.50
19 Juan Pierre 1.00
20 Yogi Berra 3.00
21 Bill Hall 1.00
22 Wade Boggs 2.00
23 Jason Bay 1.50
24 Troy Glaus 1.50
25 Paul Konerko 1.50
26 Rod Carew 2.00
27 Jay Gibbons 1.00
28 Frank Thomas 3.00
29 Joe Mauer 2.00
30 Carlos Beltran 2.00
31 Frank Robinson 3.00
32 Bobby Abreu 1.50
33 Roy Oswalt 1.50
34 Edgar Renteria 1.50
35 Magglio Ordonez 1.50
36 Mike Piazza 4.00
37 Trevor Hoffman 1.50
38 Eddie Mathews 3.00
39 Albert Pujols 6.00
40 Dennis Eckersley 1.50
41 Andruw Jones 2.00
42 Alfonso Soriano 2.00
43 Bob Feller 2.00
44 J.D. Drew 1.50
45 Jason Schmidt 1.00
46 Vladimir Guerrero 3.00
47 Reggie Jackson 3.00
48 Lance Berkman 1.50
49 Michael Young 1.50
50 Carlton Fisk 2.00
51 Brandon Webb 1.00
52 Adrian Beltre 1.00
53 Hideki Matsui 4.00
54 Bronson Arroyo 1.00
55 Tony Gwynn 3.00
56 Ray Durham 1.00
57 Garrett Atkins 1.50
58 Nolan Ryan 4.00
59 Daisuke Matsuzaka RC 25.00
60 Todd Helton 2.00
61 Carl Crawford 1.50
62 Jake Peavy 2.00
63 Rafael Furcal 1.50

64 Joe Morgan 2.00
65 Greg Maddux 4.00
66 Luis Aparicio 1.50
67 Derrek Lee 2.00
68 Johnny Damon 2.00
69 Mike Lowell 1.00
70 Roger Maris 4.00
71 Vernon Wells 1.50
72 Monte Irvin 2.00
73 Jermaine Dye 1.50
74 Miguel Cabrera 3.00
75 Barry Bonds 6.00
76 Stan Musial 3.00
77 Derek Lowe 1.00
78 Don Mattingly 5.00
79 Lyle Overbay 1.00
80 Chien-Ming Wang 5.00
81 Carlos Zambrano 1.50
82 Kei Igawa **RC** 5.00
83 Cole Hamels 2.00
84 Gary Sheffield 2.00
85 Nick Johnson 1.00
86 Brooks Robinson 3.00
87 Curt Schilling 3.00
88 Ryne Sandberg 3.00
89 Mike Cameron 1.00
90 Mike Schmidt 3.00
91 Chris Carpenter 2.00
92 Scott Rolen 2.00
93 Rocco Baldelli 1.50
94 C.C. Sabathia 1.50
95 Jeff Francis 1.00
96 Ozzie Smith 3.00
97 Aramis Ramirez 1.50
98 Aaron Harang 1.00
99 Duke Snider 3.00
100 David Ortiz 3.00
101 Raul Ibanez 1.00
102 Bruce Sutter 1.00
103 Gary Matthews 1.00
104 Chipper Jones 3.00
105 Craig Biggio 1.50
106 Roy Halladay 1.50
107 Hoyt Wilhelm 1.00
108 Manny Ramirez 3.00
109 Randy Johnson 3.00
110 Carl Yastrzemski 3.00
111 Mark Teixeira 2.00
112 Derek Jeter 6.00
113 Stephen Drew 1.50
114 Darryl Strawberry 1.50
115 Travis Hafner 1.50
116 Torii Hunter 1.50
117 Jim Edmonds 1.50
118 John Smoltz 1.50
119 Bo Jackson 3.00
120 Roger Clemens 5.00
121 Pedro Martinez 3.00
122 Rickey Henderson 2.00
123 Ivan Rodriguez 2.00
124 Robin Yount 3.00
125 Johan Santana 2.00
126a Robinson Cano 40.00
126b Robinson Cano 40.00
127a Jose Reyes 75.00
127b Jose Reyes 75.00
128a Justin Morneau 35.00
128b Justin Morneau 35.00
129a Curtis Granderson 30.00
129b Curtis Granderson 30.00
130a Justin Verlander 50.00
130b Justin Verlander 50.00
131 Prince Fielder 65.00
132a Ryan Zimmerman 40.00
132b Ryan Zimmerman 40.00
133 Mike Napoli 20.00
134 Melky Cabrera 30.00
135 Jonathan Papelbon 40.00
136a Nicholas Markakis 30.00
136b Nicholas Markakis 30.00
137 B.J. Upton 25.00
138a Joel Zumaya 30.00
138b Joel Zumaya 30.00
140 Nick Swisher 25.00
141 Andre Ethier 25.00
142a Jered Weaver 30.00
142b Jered Weaver 30.00
143 Matt Cain 25.00
144 Lastings Milledge 25.00
145 Brian McCann 35.00
146 Shin-Soo Choo 20.00
147a Dan Uggla 25.00
147b Dan Uggla 25.00
148 Hanley Ramirez 30.00
149 Russell Martin 40.00
150 Francisco Liriano 30.00
151 Anthony Reyes 10.00
152 Josh Barfield 20.00
153 Anibal Sanchez 20.00
154 Jeremy Hermida 15.00
155 Kendry Morales 15.00
156 Matthew Kemp 30.00
157 Freddy Sanchez 20.00
158 Howie Kendrick 25.00
159 Scott Thorman 20.00
160 Franklin Gutierrez 20.00
161 Jason Bartlett 15.00
162 Chris Duncan 50.00
163 Maicer Izturis 20.00
164 Jason Botts 20.00
165 Tony Gwynn Jr. 30.00
166 Jorge Cantu 10.00
167 Adam Jones 30.00
168 Edinson Volquez 15.00
169 Joey Gathright 20.00
170 Carlos Marmol 30.00
171 Benjamin Zobrist 15.00
172 Josh Willingham 20.00
173 Brad Thompson 20.00
174a Chris Ray 20.00
174b Ervin Santana 20.00
175 Ronny Paulino 15.00
176 Tyler Johnson 20.00
177 J.J. Hardy 40.00
178 Adrian Gonzalez 25.00
179 Scott Kazmir 30.00
180 Juan Morillo **(RC)** 10.00
181a Shawn Riggans **(RC)** 15.00
181b Shawn Riggans **(RC)** 15.00
182 Brian Stokes **(RC)** 20.00
183 Delmon Young **(RC)** 35.00
184a Troy Tulowitzki **(RC)** 60.00
184b Troy Tulowitzki **(RC)** 60.00
185 Adam Lind **(RC)** 20.00
186 David Murphy **(RC)** 20.00
187a Philip Humber **(RC)** 25.00
187b Philip Humber **(RC)** 25.00
188a Andrew Miller **RC** 60.00
188b Andrew Miller **RC** 60.00
189a Glen Perkins **(RC)** 20.00
189b Glen Perkins **(RC)** 20.00

Sepia

Sepia (1-125): 1-2X
Production 559 Sets
Autos. (126-189): 1X
Production 75 Sets

Emerald

Emerald (1-125): 2-3X
Production 239 Sets
Autos. (126-189): 1-1.5X
Production 50 Sets

Gold

Gold (1-125): 3-4X
Production 99 Sets
Autos. (126-189): 1-2X
Production 25 Sets

Sapphire

Sapphire (1-125): 4-8X
Production 25 Sets
Autos. (126-189): No Pricing
Production 10 Sets

Platinum

Production One Set

Printing Plates

Production one set per color.

All-Star Triple Patches

No Pricing
Production Nine Sets
Platinum: No Pricing
Production One Set

Bat-Barrels

No Pricing

Logo Man

No Pricing
Production One Set

Relics

NM/M
Common Player: 20.00
Production 36 Sets
Sepia: 1X
Production 27 Sets
Emerald: 1-1.5X
Production 18 Sets
Gold: No Pricing
Production Nine Sets
Sapphire: No Pricing
Production Three Sets
Platinum: No Pricing
Production One Set
1-3 Carl Yastrzemski 30.00
4-9 Roberto Clemente 100.00
10-15 Alex Rodriguez 50.00
16-21 Ryan Howard 40.00
22-24 Chien-Ming Wang 100.00
25-27 Ichiro Suzuki 80.00
28-30 Hideki Matsui 60.00
31-33 Luis Aparicio 20.00
34-36 Joe DiMaggio 100.00
37-39 Ted Williams 100.00
40-48 Mickey Mantle 150.00
49-51 David Ortiz 30.00
52-54 Albert Pujols 50.00
55-57 Justin Morneau 25.000
58-63 Nolan Ryan 50.00
64-66 Manny Ramirez 20.00
67-69 Roger Maris 80.00
70-72 Daisuke Matsuzaka 100.00
73-75 Brian Cashman 25.00
76-78 Ernie Banks 40.00
79-81 Stan Musial 50.00
82-84 Duke Snider 30.00
85-87 Yogi Berra 50.00
88-90 Harmon Killebrew 40.00
91-93 Joe Mauer 25.00
94-96 Alfonso Soriano 25.00
97-102 Reggie Jackson 35.00
103-105 Vladimir Guerrero 20.00
106-108 Pedro Martinez 30.00
109-111 Roger Clemens 40.00
112-114 Randy Johnson 25.00
115-117 Don Mattingly 50.00
121a Barry Bonds 100.00
121b Bruce Sutter 20.00
122a Barry Bonds 100.00
122b Bruce Sutter 20.00
123a Barry Bonds 100.00
123b Bruce Sutter 20.00
124-126 John F. Kennedy 200.00
127-129 Johnny Bench 35.00
130-132 Mark Teixeira 20.00
133-135 Johan Santana 30.00
136-138 Alex Rodriguez 50.00
139-141 Brooks Robinson 30.00
142-144 Rickey Henderson 30.00
145-147 Ozzie Smith 50.00
148-150 Chipper Jones 30.00

Relics Autographs

NM/M
Production 18 Sets
Gold: No Pricing
Production Nine Sets
Sapphire: No Pricing
Production Three Sets
Platinum: No Pricing
Production One Set
1-3 Alex Rodriguez 275.00
4-6 Chien-Ming Wang 450.00
7-9 David Ortiz 100.00
10-12 Manny Ramirez 75.00
13-15 Johnny Damon 75.00
16-18 Miguel Tejada 50.00
19-21 Carl Crawford 40.00
22-24 Johan Santana 60.00
25-27 Francisco Liriano 30.00
28-30 Bob Feller 60.00
31-33 Vladimir Guerrero 75.00
34-36 Ernie Banks 150.00
37-39 Yogi Berra 100.00
40-42 Nolan Ryan 150.00
43-45 Ozzie Smith 100.00
46-48 David Wright 100.00
49-51 Albert Pujols 350.00
52-54 Ryan Howard 120.00
55 Don Mattingly 100.00
56 Don Mattingly 100.00
57 Don Mattingly 100.00
58-60 Brooks Robinson 60.00
61-63 Robin Yount 75.00
64-66 Mike Schmidt 100.00
67-69 Carl Yastrzemski 100.00
70-72 Wade Boggs 65.00
73-75 Andre Dawson 50.00
76-78 Reggie Jackson 75.00
79-81 Miguel Cabrera 60.00
82-84 Tom Seaver 75.00
85-87 Ralph Kiner 65.00
88-90 Chipper Jones 100.00
91-93 Andruw Jones 60.00
94-96 Dontrelle Willis 40.00
97-99 Bob Gibson 80.00
100-102 Johnny Bench 85.00
103-105 Joe Morgan 50.00
106-108 Ryne Sandberg 120.00
109-111 Dwight Gooden 40.00
112-114 Johnny Podres 60.00
115-117 Monte Irvin 50.00
118-120 Orlando Cepeda 50.00
121-123 Bo Jackson 140.00
124-126 Gary Sheffield 60.00
127-129 Tom Glavine 100.00
130-132 Tony LaRussa 40.00
133-135 Jim Leyland 50.00
136-138 Joe Torre 60.00
139-141 Gary Carter 75.00
142-144 Roy Oswalt 50.00
145-147 Carlos Delgado 50.00
148-150 Jason Varitek 75.00
151-153 Bobby Abreu 50.00
154-156 Juan Marichal 60.00
157-159 Frank Robinson 65.00
160-162 Jorge Posada 80.00
163-165 Luis Aparicio 50.00
166-168 Carlton Fisk 50.00
169-171 Dale Murphy 80.00
172-174 Mark Teixeira 60.00
175-177 Darryl Strawberry 50.00
178-180 Justin Morneau 50.00

Relics Combos Autographs

NM/M
Production 36 Sets
Sepia: 1X
Production 27 Sets
Emerald: 1-1.5X
Production 18 Sets
Gold: No Pricing
Production Nine Sets
Sapphire: No Pricing
Production Three Sets
Platinum: No Pricing
Production One Set
1 Brooks Robinson, Robin Yount, Johnny Bench 125.00
2 Reggie Jackson, Joe Morgan, Ryne Sandberg 125.00
3 Tom Seaver, Bob Gibson, Nolan Ryan 180.00
4 Albert Pujols, Alex Rodriguez, Vladimir Guerrero 375.00
5 Tom Seaver, Roger Clemens, Dwight Gooden 160.00
6 Johan Santana, Tom Glavine, Roger Clemens 200.00
7 Alex Rodriguez, Chien-Ming Wang, Don Mattingly 300.00
8 Ryan Howard, Mike Schmidt, Bobby Abreu 150.00
9 Ryan Howard, David Ortiz, Albert Pujols 350.00
10 Alex Rodriguez, David Wright, Jose Reyes 300.00
11 Miguel Cabrera, Manny Ramirez, David Ortiz 125.00
12 Justin Verlander, Jered Weaver, Chien-Ming Wang 250.00
13 Ralph Kiner, Duke Snider, Yogi Berra 125.00
14 Ryan Howard, Alex Rodriguez, Andruw Jones 260.00
15 Adam Lind, Brian Stokes, David Murphy 30.00
16 Andrew Miller, Brian Stokes, Glen Perkins 50.00
17 Shawn Riggans, Troy Tulowitzki, Andrew Miller 80.00
18 Glen Perkins, Lastings Milledge, Troy Tulowitzki 50.00

Relics Combos

NM/M
Production 36 Sets
Sepia: 1X
Production 27 Sets
Emerald: 1-1.5X
Production 18 Sets
Gold: No Pricing
Production Nine Sets
Sapphire: No Pricing
Production Three Sets
Platinum: No Pricing
Production One Set
1 Albert Pujols, Manny Ramirez, David Ortiz 40.00
2 Albert Pujols, Pedro Martinez, Vladimir Guerrero 40.00
3 Ivan Rodriguez, Carlos Delgado, Roberto Clemente 60.00
4 Roberto Clemente, Bernie Williams, Carlos Beltran 65.00
5 Jose Reyes, Alfonso Soriano, Miguel Tejada 30.00
6 Carl Crawford, Jose Reyes, Juan Pierre 25.00
7 Hideki Matsui, Ichiro Suzuki, So Taguchi 60.00
8 Miguel Cabrera, Johan Santana, Bobby Abreu 25.00
9 Alex Rodriguez, Mariano Rivera, Hideki Matsui 60.00
10 Reggie Jackson, Alex Rodriguez, Don Mattingly 50.00
11 Yogi Berra, Don Mattingly, Reggie Jackson 75.00
12 David Ortiz, Wade Boggs, Manny Ramirez 25.00
13 David Ortiz, Manny Ramirez, Pedro Martinez 30.00
14 Miguel Tejada, Eddie Murray, Brooks Robinson 30.00
15 Joe Mauer, Justin Morneau, Johan Santana 30.00
16 Harmon Killebrew, Joe Mauer, Justin Morneau 40.00
17 Justin Verlander, Ivan Rodriguez, Joel Zumaya 25.00
18 Barry Zito, Dennis Eckersley, Huston Street 20.00
19 Reggie Jackson, Rod Carew, Vladimir Guerrero 30.00
20 Vladimir Guerrero, Pedro Martinez, Moises Alou 30.00
21 Michael Young, Mark Teixeira, Alex Rodriguez 40.00
22 Edgar Martinez, Ichiro Suzuki, Alex Rodriguez 70.00
23 David Wright, Carlos Delgado, Jose Reyes 40.00
24 Jose Reyes, Pedro Martinez, David Wright 50.00
25 Jose Reyes, Carlos Beltran, David Wright 40.00
26 Ryan Howard, Chase Utley, Jimmy Rollins 50.00
27 Jeff Francoeur, Chipper Jones, Brian McCann 30.00
28 John Smoltz, Tom Glavine, Greg Maddux 40.00
29 Chipper Jones, Jeff Francoeur, Andruw Jones 40.00
30 Nolan Ryan, Pedro Martinez, Tom Seaver 50.00
31 Mike Schmidt, Jim Thome, Ryan Howard 40.00
32 Stan Musial, Albert Pujols, Ozzie Smith 60.00
33 Albert Pujols, David Eckstein, Jim Edmonds 50.00
34 Lance Berkman, Roy Oswalt, Craig Biggio 25.00
35 Roger Clemens, Roy Oswalt, Nolan Ryan 40.00
36 Frank Robinson, Joe Morgan, Johnny Bench 30.00
37 Paul Molitor, Prince Fielder, Robin Yount 40.00
38 Ernie Banks, Alfonso Soriano, Ryne Sandberg 50.00
39 Andre Ethier, Matthew Kemp, Jered Weaver 25.00
40 Chien-Ming Wang, Alex Rodriguez, Mariano Rivera 100.00
41 Albert Pujols, Ichiro Suzuki, Vladimir Guerrero 50.00
42 Albert Pujols, Alex Rodriguez, Ichiro Suzuki 75.00
43 Ryan Howard, Justin Morneau, Albert Pujols 50.00
44 Albert Pujols, Roberto Clemente, Ichiro Suzuki 100.00
45 Albert Pujols, Roberto Clemente, Mickey Mantle 150.00
46 Joe DiMaggio, Mickey Mantle, Alex Rodriguez 150.00
47 Ted Williams, Joe DiMaggio, Mickey Mantle 200.00
48 Roberto Clemente, Mickey Mantle, Reggie Jackson 125.00
49 Stan Musial, Roberto Clemente, Frank Robinson 100.00
50 Albert Pujols, Johnny Bench, Mickey Mantle 100.00
51 Carl Yastrzemski, Ted Williams, Mickey Mantle 140.00
52 Brandon Webb, Tom Seaver, Johan Santana 30.00
53 Roger Clemens, Dwight Gooden, Pedro Martinez 40.00
54 Johan Santana, Greg Maddux, Roger Clemens 35.00
55 Johan Santana, Pedro Martinez, Roger Clemens 30.00
56 Randy Johnson, Roger Clemens, Tom Glavine 30.00
57 Justin Verlander, Ryan Howard, Ichiro Suzuki 50.00
58 Dontrelle Willis, Carlos Beltran, Jason Bay 20.00
59 Albert Pujols, Scott Rolen, Ryan Howard 40.00
60 Roberto Clemente, Joe DiMaggio, Mickey Mantle 200.00
61 Stan Musial, Ernie Banks, Mickey Mantle 140.00
62 Mike Schmidt, Joe Morgan, Johnny Bench 35.00
63 George Brett, Robin Yount, Ozzie Smith 60.00
64 Albert Pujols, Ichiro Suzuki, Rod Carew 50.00
65 Alfonso Soriano, Mickey Mantle, Alex Rodriguez 100.00
66 Don Mattingly, Wade Boggs, Tony Gwynn 50.00
67 Rod Carew, Vladimir Guerrero, Garret Anderson 25.00
68 Tony Gwynn, Wade Boggs, George Brett 50.00
69 Vladimir Guerrero, Alfonso Soriano, Bobby Abreu 30.00
70 Darryl Strawberry, Carlos Beltran, Howard Johnson 30.00
71 Jim Thome, Manny Ramirez, Frank Thomas 30.00
72 Mickey Mantle, Mike Piazza, Mike Schmidt 120.00
73 Carl Yastrzemski, Alex Rodriguez, Dave Winfield 50.00
74 Johan Santana, Pedro Martinez, Roger Clemens 30.00
75 Greg Maddux, Nolan Ryan, Tom Seaver 60.00
76 Bob Gibson, Dwight Gooden, Greg Maddux 50.00
77 Roberto Clemente, Reggie Jackson, Manny Ramirez 75.00
78 Johnny Podres, Don Larsen, Lew Burdette 30.00
79 Ichiro Suzuki, Kenji Johjima, Tadahito Iguchi 70.00
80 Paul Molitor, Jimmy Rollins, Chase Utley 35.00
81 Gary Carter, Paul LoDuca, Mike Piazza 60.00
82 George Brett, Alex Rodriguez, David Wright 50.00
83 Hoyt Wilhelm, Phil Niekro, Tim Wakefield 35.00
84 Franklin D. Roosevelt, Harry S. Truman, Dwight D. Eisenhower 80.00
85 Ichiro Suzuki, Eric Chavez, Torii Hunter 50.00
86 Richard Nixon, Ronald Reagan, George W. Bush 100.00
87 John Smoltz, Carlos Delgado, Edgar Martinez 30.00
88 Manny Ramirez, Vladimir Guerrero, David Ortiz 30.00
89 Livan Hernandez, Orel Hershiser, Willie Stargell 20.00
90 David Ortiz, Ryan Howard, Albert Pujols 50.00
91 Chien-Ming Wang, Johan Santana, Jon Garland 80.00
92 Deion Sanders, Bo Jackson, Brian Jordan 60.00
93 Franklin D. Roosevelt, John F. Kennedy, Bill Clinton 125.00
94 Vladimir Guerrero, Ichiro Suzuki, Vernon Wells 50.00
95 Jim Thome, Jermaine Dye, Paul Konerko 25.00
96 A.J. Pierzynski, Kelvim Escobar, Josh Paul 20.00
97 Joe Carter, Rickey Henderson, Paul Molitor 50.00
98 Kirk Gibson, Dennis Eckersley 25.00
99 Luis Castillo, Moises Alou, Mark Prior 20.00
100 Mookie Wilson, Ray Knight, Bill Buckner 50.00

Relics Combos Double

NM/M
Production 36 Sets
Sepia: No Pricing
Production 27 Sets
Emerald: 1-1.5X
Production 18 Sets
Gold: No Pricing
Production Nine Sets
Sapphire: No Pricing
Production Three Sets
Platinum: No Pricing

Production One Set
1 Mickey Mantle, Joe DiMaggio 250.00
2 Alex Rodriguez, Chien-Ming Wang, Johnny Damon, Manny Ramirez, David Ortiz, Jason Varitek 100.00
3 David Wright, Carlos Beltran, Tom Glavine, Chipper Jones, Andruw Jones, John Smoltz 50.00
4 David Wright 50.00
5 Albert Pujols 70.00
6 Chien-Ming Wang 100.00
7 David Wright, Ryan Howard 60.00
8 Alex Rodriguez 70.00
9 Ryan Howard 60.00
10 Ichiro Suzuki 100.00
11 Albert Pujols, Pedro Martinez, David Ortiz, Vladimir Guerrero, Manny Ramirez, Alfonso Soriano 70.00
12 Ichiro Suzuki, So Taguchi, Hideki Matsui, Kazuo Matsui, Tadahito Iguchi, Kenji Johjima 140.00
13 Roberto Clemente, Ivan Rodriguez, Carlos Beltran, Bernie Williams, Carlos Delgado, Javy Lopez 125.00
14 Johan Santana, Miguel Cabrera, Bobby Abreu, Omar Vizquel, Ozzie Guillen, Luis Aparicio 50.00
15 Mickey Mantle, Joe DiMaggio, Ted Williams, Ernie Banks, Yogi Berra, Stan Musial 200.00
16 Mickey Mantle, Albert Pujols, Vladimir Guerrero, Ted Williams, Roberto Clemente, Joe DiMaggio 200.00
17 Mickey Mantle, Alex Rodriguez, Don Mattingly, Yogi Berra, Chien-Ming Wang, Reggie Jackson 200.00
18 Carl Yastrzemski, Manny Ramirez, David Ortiz, Pedro Martinez, Johnny Damon, Carlton Fisk 60.00
19 Justin Morneau, Torii Hunter, Joe Mauer, Johan Santana, Francisco Liriano, Harmon Killebrew 60.00
20 Justin Verlander, Joel Zumaya, Curtis Granderson, Magglio Ordonez, Ivan Rodriguez, Kenny Rogers 50.00
21 Nick Swisher, Huston Street, Reggie Jackson, Barry Zito, Jose Canseco, Dennis Eckersley 40.00
22 Vladimir Guerrero, Rod Carew, Jered Weaver, Reggie Jackson, Garret Anderson, Francisco Rodriguez 50.00
23 Vladimir Guerrero, Pedro Martinez, Moises Alou, Gary Carter, Andre Dawson, Randy Johnson 50.00
24 Nolan Ryan, Mark Teixeira, Michael Young, Alex Rodriguez, Ivan Rodriguez, Hank Blalock 65.00
25 Kenji Johjima, Ichiro Suzuki, Alex Rodriguez, Randy Johnson, Edgar Martinez, Richie Sexson 90.00
26 David Wright, Jose Reyes, Carlos Beltran, Pedro Martinez, Tom Glavine, Carlos Delgado 75.00
27 David Eckstein, Albert Pujols, Chris Carpenter, Stan Musial, Ozzie Smith, Jim Edmonds 75.00
28 Nolan Ryan, Andy Pettitte, Roger Clemens, Roy Oswalt, Lance Berkman, Craig Biggio 75.00
29 Ryan Howard, Chase Utley, Mike Schmidt, Jimmy Rollins, Richie Ashburn, Steve Carlton 100.00
30 Jeff Francoeur, Brian McCann, Chipper Jones, Andruw Jones, John Smoltz, Tim Hudson 70.00
31 Alfonso Soriano, Ernie Banks, Ryne Sandberg, Kerry Wood, Mark Prior, Andre Dawson 60.00
32 David Wright, Justin Morneau, Ryan Howard, Chien-Ming Wang, Chase Utley, Jose Reyes 75.00
33 David Ortiz 35.00
34 Roger Maris, Stan Musial, Roberto Clemente, Ernie Banks, Johnny Bench, Carl Yastrzemski 150.00
35 Albert Pujols, Jim Edmonds, Scott Rolen, Ivan Rodriguez, Kenny Rogers, Magglio Ordonez 50.00
36 Derrek Lee, Juan Pierre, Greg Maddux, Paul Konerko, Jermaine Dye, Jim Thome 60.00
37 David Wright, Paul LoDuca, Jose Reyes, Alex Rodriguez, Jason Giambi, Johnny Damon 75.00
38 Joe Mauer, Freddy Sanchez, Robinson Cano, Miguel Cabrera, Albert Pujols, Miguel Cabrera 75.00
39 Ryan Howard, David Ortiz, Albert Pujols, Alfonso Soriano, Lance Berkman, Jermaine Dye 75.00
40 Ryan Howard, Albert Pujols, David Ortiz, Lance Berkman, Justin Morneau, Andruw Jones 75.00
41 Johan Santana, Roy Oswalt, Chris Carpenter, Brandon Webb, Roy Halladay, C.C. Sabathia 50.00
42 Chien-Ming Wang, Johan Santana, Jon Garland, Randy Johnson, Kenny Rogers, Freddy Garcia 85.00
43 Johan Santana, Aaron Harang, Jake Peavy, John Smoltz, Carlos Zambrano, Jeremy Bonderman 50.00
44 Jeff Suppan, Roy Oswalt, Albert Pujols, Placido Polanco, Paul Konerko, David Ortiz 50.00
45 Orlando Cepeda, Monte Irvin, Bobby Thomson, Duke Snider, Johnny Podres, Don Zimmerman 75.00
46 Ryne Sandberg, Wade Boggs, Dennis Eckersley, Paul Molitor, Gary Carter, Eddie Murray 70.00
47 Jermaine Dye, Paul Konerko, A.J. Pierzynski, Craig Biggio, Lance Berkman, Morgan Ensberg 50.00
48 Roger Clemens, Randy Johnson, Greg Maddux, Curt Schilling, Pedro Martinez, John Smoltz 85.00
49 David Wright, Brooks Robinson, George Brett, Mike Schmidt, Alex Rodriguez, Eddie Murray 80.00
50 Alfonso Soriano, Bobby Abreu, Carlos Beltran, Vladimir Guerrero, Alex Rodriguez, Preston Wilson 70.00

Triple Signed Hide

Production One Set

2007 Topps Turkey Red

NM/M
Complete Set (186):
Common Player: .25
Common SP: 4.00
Inserted 1:4
Pack (8): 4.00
Box (24): 85.00
1 Ryan Howard 2.00
1 Ryan Howard/SP Ad Back 8.00
2 Dontrelle Willis .25
3 Matt Cain .50
4 John Maine .50
5 Cole Hamels .75
6 Corey Patterson .25
7 Mickey Mantle/SP 25.00
8 Johan Santana/CL .75
9 Josh Beckett .75
10 Jimmy Rollins 1.00
11 Kenji Johjima .50
12 Orlando Hernandez .25
13 Jorge Posada/CL .50
14 Ivan Rodriguez .75
15 Ichiro Suzuki 2.00
15 Ichiro Suzuki/SP Ad Back 6.00
16 Ken Griffey Jr./CL 1.00
17 Stephen Drew .25
18 B.J. Upton .50
19 Mickey Mantle 3.00
20 Alex Rodriguez 3.00
20 Alex Rodriguez/SP Ad Back 8.00
21 Adam Dunn .75
22 Adam Lind SP **(RC)** 6.00
23 Adrian Gonzalez .50
24 Akinori Iwamura **RC** 2.00
25 Albert Pujols 3.00
25 Albert Pujols/SP Ad Back 8.00
26 Frank Thomas 1.00
27 Roy Halladay .50
28 Alejandro De Aza **RC** .50
29 Alex Gordon **RC** 4.00
30 Barry Bonds 3.00
31 Andrew Miller **RC** 4.00
32 Andruw Jones .75
33 Kurt Suzuki/SP **(RC)** 5.00
34 Mickey Mantle 3.00
35 Andy Pettitte .50
36 Tadahito Iguchi .50
37 Edgar Renteria .50
38 Tim Hudson .50
39 Micah Owings **(RC)** .50
40 Chipper Jones 1.00
40 Chipper Jones/SP Ad Back 6.00
41 Barry Zito .50
42 Daisuke Matsuzaka CL 2.00
43 Jarrod Saltalamacchia/SP **(RC)** 6.00
44 Bill Hall .25
45 Billy Butler **(RC)** 1.00
46 Billy Wagner .25
47 Rich Harden SP 4.00
48 Albert Pujols/CL 1.00
49 Brandon Inge .25
50 Jason Giambi .50
51 Brandon Webb .75
52 Brandon Wood **(RC)** 1.00
53 Carl Crawford/CL .50
54 Brian Giles .25
55 Josh Hamilton **(RC)** 1.00
56 Chase Utley 1.50
56 Chase Utley/SP Ad Back 6.00
57 Miguel Montero **(RC)** .50
58 Carl Crawford .50
59 Carlos Beltran 1.00
60 Mariano Rivera .50
61 Carlos Delgado .75
62 Carlos Lee SP 5.00
63 Carlos Zambrano/SP 5.00
64 Miguel Tejada .50
65 Mike Cameron .25
66 Chase Utley/SP 8.00
67 Chase Wright **RC** 1.00
68 Chien-Ming Wang 1.00
69 Nick Swisher .50
70 David Wright 1.50
71 Mike Piazza/SP 5.00
72 Chris Carpenter 1.00
73 Mark Buehrle/SP 4.00
74 Torii Hunter/SP 5.00
75 Tyler Clippard **(RC)** .50
76 Nicholas Markakis .50
77 Mickey Mantle 3.00
78 Curt Schilling 1.00
79 Curtis Granderson .75
80 Craig Biggio .50
81 Juan Pierre .50
82 Dallas Braden/SP **RC** 4.00
83 Dan Haren/SP 6.00
84 Dan Uggla .50
85 Danny Putnam **(RC)** .50
86 David DeJesus .25
87 David Eckstein .25
88 Tim Lincecum **RC** 6.00
89 Johnny Damon/SP 6.00
90 Justin Morneau 1.00
91 Delmon Young **(RC)** 1.00
92 Homer Bailey **(RC)** 1.00
93 Carlos Gomez **RC** 1.00
94 Josh Fields SP **(RC)** 4.00
95 Derek Jeter 3.00
95 Derek Jeter/SP Ad Back 8.00
96 Derrek Lee .75
97 Donald Kelly **(RC)** .50
98 Doug Slaten **RC** .50
99 Dustin Moseley .25
100 Gary Sheffield .75
101 Orlando Hudson/SP 4.00
102 Elijah Dukes **RC** 1.00
103 Eric Byrnes/SP 4.00
104 Eric Chavez .50
105 Phil Hughes **(RC)** 1.00
105 Phil Hughes/SP Ad Back 6.00
106 Felix Hernandez/SP 4.00
106 Felix Hernandez/SP Ad Back 6.00
107 Mickey Mantle 3.00
108 Felix Pie **(RC)** 1.00
109 Derek Jeter CL 1.00
110 Daisuke Matsuzaka **RC** 5.00
110 Daisuke Matsuzaka/SP Ad Back **RC** 10.00
111 Francisco Rodriguez .50
112 Ramon Hernandez .25
113 Randy Johnson 1.00
114 Gary Matthews .25
115 Prince Fielder 1.00
116 Vladimir Guerrero/CL .50
117 Mickey Mantle 3.00
118 Hideki Matsui 2.00
119 Hideki Okajima **RC** 1.00
120 Manny Ramirez 1.00
121 Hunter Pence/SP **(RC)** 10.00
122 Roy Oswalt .50
123 Josh Willingham/SP 4.00
124 Tom Gordon/SP 4.00
125 Michael Young .50
126 J.D. Drew .25
127 Ryan Zimmerman .50
128 James Shields/SP 4.00
129 Jack Wilson .25
130 David Ortiz 1.00
130 David Ortiz/SP Ad Back 6.00
131 Jose Reyes/CL .50
132 Jamie Vermilyea **RC** .50
133 Jason Bay .50
134 Scott Kazmir/SP 4.00
135 Jason Isringhausen/SP 4.00
136 Jason Marquis/SP 4.00
137 Jason Schmidt .50
138 Shawn Green .25
139 Jeff Francoeur/SP 5.00
140 Alfonso Soriano 1.00
141 Kevin Kouzmanoff **(RC)** .50
142 Jered Weaver .50
143 Todd Helton/SP 5.00
144 Jermaine Dye .50
145 Jim Thome .75
146 Tom Glavine/SP 5.00
147 Joe Mauer .75
148 Joe Nathan .50
149 Joe Smith **RC** .50
150 Ken Griffey Jr. 2.00
150 Ken Griffey Jr./SP Ad Back 6.00
151 Grady Sizemore 1.00
152 Sammy Sosa SP 5.00
153 Andy LaRoche **(RC)** 1.00
154 Travis Buck **(RC)** .50
155 Alex Rios .50
156 Travis Hafner .50
157 Jake Peavy .50
158 Jeff Kent .50
159 Johan Santana 1.00
159 Johan Santana/SP Ad Back 5.00
160 Ivan Rodriguez .75
161 Trevor Hoffman .50
162 Troy Glaus .50
163 Troy Tulowitzki **(RC)** 1.00
164 Jorge Posada .50
165 Kei Igawa/SP **RC** 5.00
166 Jose Reyes 1.00
167 Mickey Mantle 3.00
168 Chase Utley/CL .50
169 Justin Verlander .50
170 Hanley Ramirez 1.00
171 Kelly Johnson/SP 4.00
172 Kelvin Jimenez **RC** .50
173 Roger Clemens 2.00
174 Khalil Greene/SP 5.00
175 Lance Berkman .50
176 Hanley Ramirez/CL .50
177 Kyle Kendrick **RC** 2.00
178 Magglio Ordonez .50
179 Marcus Giles/SP 4.00
180 Miguel Cabrera 1.00
180 Miguel Cabrera/SP Ad Back 5.00
181 Mark Teahen .25
182 Mark Teixeira/SP 5.00
183 Matt Chico SP **(RC)** 4.00
184 Matt Holliday .75
185 Vladimir Guerrero 1.00
185 Vladimir Guerrero/SP Ad Back 5.00
186 Yovani Gallardo **(RC)** 1.00

Chrome

Chrome: 2-3X
Chrome SP's: 1X
Production 1,999 Sets

Chrome Refractors

Refractors: 3-4X
Refractor SP's: 1-2X
Production 999 Sets

Chrome Black Refractors

Refractors: 5-10X
Refractor SP's: 2-4X
Production 99 Sets

A-Rod Road to 500

Common A-Rod (301-325):
Inserted 2:Box

A-Rod Road to 500 Autographs

Production One Set

Cabinet

NM/M
Common Player: 3.00
Inserted 1:Box
JB Jason Bay 5.00
LB Lance Berkman 6.00
MC Miguel Cabrera 6.00
CC Chris Carpenter 8.00
SD Stephen Drew 4.00
ED Elijah Dukes 4.00
JD Jermaine Dye 4.00
AD Adam Dunn 4.00
PF Prince Fielder 15.00
JF Jeff Francoeur 10.00
AG Alex Gordon 10.00
KG Ken Griffey Jr. 15.00
VG Vladimir Guerrero 8.00
FH Felix Hernandez 5.00
RH Ryan Howard 15.00
KI Kei Igawa 4.00
AI Akinori Iwamura 3.00
DJ Derek Jeter 20.00
AJ Andruw Jones 5.00
CL Carlos Lee 4.00
MM Mickey Mantle 25.00
NM Nicholas Markakis 8.00
DM Daisuke Matsuzaka 15.00
JM Joe Mauer 5.00
JEM Justin Morneau 5.00
HO Hideki Okajima 8.00
DO David Ortiz 15.00
MP Mike Piazza 10.00
AP Albert Pujols 20.00
HR Hanley Ramirez 10.00
MR Manny Ramirez 10.00
JR Jose Reyes 15.00
AR Alex Rodriguez 20.00
FR Francisco Rodriguez 4.00
IR Ivan Rodriguez 5.00
JS Johan Santana 8.00
JDS Jason Schmidt 3.00
GS Grady Sizemore 10.00
AS Alfonso Soriano 8.00
IS Ichiro Suzuki 15.00
MT Miguel Tejada 5.00
TT Troy Tulowitzki 8.00
CU Chase Utley 10.00
JV Justin Verlander 5.00
CW Chien-Ming Wang 8.00
BW Brandon Webb 4.00
DW David Wright 15.00
DY Delmon Young 5.00
MY Michael Young 5.00
RZ Ryan Zimmerman 10.00
BZ Barry Zito 3.00

Cabinet Dick Perez Autographs

NM/M
Production 25 Sets
JB Jason Bay 30.00
LB Lance Berkman 30.00
MC Miguel Cabrera 30.00
CC Chris Carpenter 30.00
SD Stephen Drew 25.00
ED Elijah Dukes 20.00
AD Adam Dunn 25.00
JD Jermaine Dye 30.00
PF Prince Fielder 40.00
JF Jeff Francoeur 30.00
AG Alex Gordon 35.00
KG Ken Griffey Jr. 50.00
VG Vladimir Guerrero 30.00
FH Felix Hernandez 30.00
RH Ryan Howard 40.00
KI Kei Igawa 25.00
AI Akinori Iwamura 30.00
AJ Andruw Jones 30.00
CL Carlos Lee 30.00
MM Mickey Mantle 100.00
NM Nicholas Markakis 30.00
JM Joe Mauer 30.00
JEM Justin Morneau 30.00
HO Hideki Okajima 30.00
DO David Ortiz 50.00
MP Mike Piazza 40.00
AP Albert Pujols 80.00
HR Hanley Ramirez 40.00
MR Manny Ramirez 30.00
JR Jose Reyes 40.00
AR Alex Rodriguez 80.00
FR Francisco Rodriguez 25.00
IR Ivan Rodriguez 30.00
JS Johan Santana 30.00
JDS Jason Schmidt 25.00
GS Grady Sizemore 40.00
AS Alfonso Soriano 50.00
IS Ichiro Suzuki 80.00
MT Miguel Tejada 30.00
TT Troy Tulowitzki 30.00
CU Chase Utley 50.00
JV Justin Verlander 30.00
CW Chien-Ming Wang 50.00
BW Brandon Webb 30.00
DW David Wright 50.00
DY Delmon Young 30.00
MY Michael Young 30.00
RZ Ryan Zimmerman 30.00
BZ Barry Zito 30.00

Chromographs

NM/M
Common Autograph: 10.00
AG Alex Gordon 50.00
AK Austin Kearns 15.00
AR Alex Rodriguez 250.00
BJ Bobby Jenks 25.00
BW Brad Wilkerson 10.00
CAH Clay Hensley 10.00
CG Curtis Granderson 75.00
CH Cole Hamels 40.00
CJ Chuck James 15.00
DE Darin Erstad 15.00
DU Dan Uggla 20.00
EC Eric Chavez 20.00
FP Felix Pie 20.00
GS Gary Sheffield 40.00
HCK Hong-Chih Kuo 25.00
HR Hanley Ramirez 30.00
JB Jason Bay 40.00
JD Johnny Damon 40.00
JM John Maine 25.00
JZ Joel Zumaya 20.00
KE Kelvim Escobar 15.00
LM Lastings Milledge 20.00
MC Melky Cabrera 30.00
MG Mike Gonzalez 10.00
NM Nicholas Markakis 25.00
NR Nate Robertson 20.00
PL Paul LoDuca 15.00
RC Robinson Cano 40.00
RH Ryan Howard 80.00
RJH Rich Hill 20.00
RM Robert Mackowiak 15.00
RNM Russell Martin 25.00
SC Sean Casey 25.00
SP Scott Podsednik 15.00
SV Shane Victorino 25.00
TG Tony Gwynn Jr. 20.00
WN Wilbert Nieves 10.00

Presidents

NM/M
Common President: 1.00
Inserted 1:12
1 George Washington 4.00
2 John Adams 2.00
3 Thomas Jefferson 3.00
4 James Madison 2.00
5 James Monroe 2.00
6 John Quincy Adams 2.00
7 Andrew Jackson 2.00
8 Martin Van Buren 1.00
9 William H. Harrison 1.00
10 John Tyler 1.00
11 James K. Polk 1.00
12 Zachary Taylor 1.00
13 Millard Fillmore 1.00
14 Franklin Pierce 1.00
15 James Buchanan 1.00
16 Abraham Lincoln 4.00
17 Andrew Johnson 1.00
18 Ulysses S. Grant 2.00
19 Rutherford B. Hayes 1.00
20 James Garfield 1.00
21 Chester A. Arthur 1.00
22 Grover Cleveland 1.00
23 Benjamin Harrison 1.00
24 Grover Cleveland 1.00
25 William McKinley 1.00
26 Theodore Roosevelt 3.00
27 William H. Taft 1.00
28 Woodrow Wilson 1.00
29 Warren G. Harding 1.00
30 Calvin Coolidge 1.00
31 Herbert Hoover 1.00
32 Franklin D. Roosevelt 3.00
33 Harry S. Truman 2.00
34 Dwight D. Eisenhower 3.00
35 John F. Kennedy 4.00
36 Lyndon B. Johnson 1.00
37 Richard Nixon 2.00
38 Gerald Ford 1.00
39 Jimmy Carter 2.00
40 Ronald Reagan 2.00
41 George H.W. Bush 2.00
42 Bill Clinton 2.00
43 George W. Bush 2.00

Relics

NM/M
Common Relic: 4.00
AB Adrian Beltre 4.00
AD Adam Dunn 6.00
AH Aaron Harang 4.00

AJ1	Andruw Jones	6.00
AJ2	Andruw Jones	6.00
AM	Andrew Miller	8.00
ANB	Angel Berroa	4.00
AS	Alfonso Soriano	10.00
BB	Barry Bonds	30.00
BC	Bobby Crosby	4.00
BJR	B.J. Ryan	4.00
BR	Brian Roberts	6.00
BS	Brian Stokes	4.00
BT	Brad Thompson	4.00
BW	Brandon Webb	6.00
BZ	Benjamin Zobrist	6.00
CB1	Carlos Beltran	8.00
CB2	Carlos Beltran	8.00
CC	Coco Crisp	6.00
CD	Carlos Delgado	8.00
CH	Cole Hamels	10.00
CJ	Chipper Jones	10.00
CJC	Chris Carpenter	8.00
CL	Carlos Lee	6.00
CR	Chris Ray	4.00
CS	C.C. Sabathia	6.00
DN	Dioner Navarro	4.00
DO	David Ortiz	10.00
DR	Darrell Rasner	4.00
DU	Dan Uggla	6.00
DW	David Wright	15.00
DWA	Daryle Ward	4.00
DWW	Dontrelle Willis	6.00
DY	Delmon Young	6.00
ES	Ervin Santana	4.00
GP	Glen Perkins	4.00
HB	Hank Blalock	8.00
HR	Hanley Ramirez	10.00
IR	Ivan Rodriguez	8.00
IS	Ichiro Suzuki	20.00
JB	Josh Beckett	6.00
JC	Jorge Cantu	4.00
JD	Jermaine Dye	6.00
JE	Jim Edmonds	6.00
JF	Jeff Francoeur	15.00
JG	Jon Garland	4.00
JH	Josh Hamilton	8.00
JK	Jeff Kent	4.00
JM	Justin Morneau	8.00
JP	Josh Paul	4.00
JPM	Joe Mauer	6.00
JR	Jose Reyes	10.00
JRB	Jason Bay	6.00
JS	John Smoltz	8.00
JV2	Jason Varitek	10.00
JW	Jered Weaver	8.00
JZ	Joel Zumaya	8.00
KM	Kazuo Matsui	6.00
LB	Lance Berkman	6.00
LC	Luis Castillo	4.00
MC	Melky Cabrera	8.00
ME	Morgan Ensberg	4.00
MG	Marcus Giles	4.00
MJC	Miguel Cairo	4.00
MM	Mickey Mantle	125.00
MP	Mike Piazza	10.00
MR	Manny Ramirez	8.00
MT	Miguel Tejada	6.00
MY	Michael Young	6.00
NM	Nicholas Markakis	20.00
NP	Neifi Perez	4.00
NS	Nick Swisher	6.00
PM	Pedro Martinez	8.00
PP	Placido Polanco	6.00
RB1	Rocco Baldelli	4.00
RB2	Rocco Baldelli	4.00
RH	Ryan Howard	15.00
RJH	Rich Hill	6.00
RK	Ryan Klesko	4.00
RS	Reggie Sanders	4.00
RZ	Ryan Zimmerman	10.00
SR	Scott Rolen	8.00
SS	Sammy Sosa	8.00
ST	So Taguchi	4.00
TB	Travis Buck	4.00
TH	Travis Hafner	8.00
TI	Tadahito Iguchi	6.00
TJ	Tyler Johnson	8.00
VG	Vladimir Guerrero	8.00
VW	Vernon Wells	6.00

Silks

		NM/M
Common Player:		15.00
Production 99 Sets		
AD	Adam Dunn	15.00
AI	Akinori Iwamura	15.00
AIR	Alex Rios	15.00
AP	Albert Pujols	50.00
AR	Alex Rodriguez	50.00
AS	Alfonso Soriano	20.00
BB	Billy Butler	20.00
BLB	Barry Bonds	40.00
CH	Cole Hamels	25.00
CJ	Chipper Jones	25.00
CS	C.C. Sabathia	15.00
CY	Adrian Gonzalez	15.00
DH	Danny Haren	15.00
DJ	Derek Jeter	50.00
DM	Daisuke Matsuzaka	80.00
DO	David Ortiz	30.00
DU	Dan Uggla	15.00
DW	David Wright	30.00
DWW	Dontrelle Willis	20.00
EB	Erik Bedard	20.00
GS	Grady Sizemore	25.00
HP	Hunter Pence	30.00
HR	Hanley Ramirez	20.00
IS	Ichiro Suzuki	50.00
JAS	John Smoltz	20.00
JB	Josh Beckett	20.00
JBR	Jose Reyes	25.00
JD	Jermaine Dye	15.00
JH	J.J. Hardy	15.00
JL	John Lackey	15.00
JM	Justin Morneau	20.00
JP	Jake Peavy	20.00
JR	Jimmy Rollins	25.00
JRB	Jason Bay	15.00
JS	Johan Santana	25.00
JV	Justin Verlander	25.00
KG	Ken Griffey Jr.	40.00
MAR	Manny Ramirez	25.00
MH	Matt Holliday	25.00
MM	Mickey Mantle	80.00
MO	Magglio Ordonez	25.00
MR	Mark Reynolds	15.00
MT	Mark Teixeira	20.00
NS	Nick Swisher	20.00
PF	Prince Fielder	30.00
RH	Ryan Howard	40.00
RM	Russell Martin	20.00
RZ	Ryan Zimmerman	25.00
TH	Torii Hunter	15.00
VG	Vladimir Guerrero	15.00

2007 Topps Update

		NM/M
Complete Set (330):		40.00
Common player:		.10
Pack (10):		2.00
Box (36):		65.00
1	Tony Armas Jr.	.10
2	Shannon Stewart	.10
3	Jason Marquis	.10
4	Josh Wilson	.10
5	Steve Trachsel	.10
6	J.D. Drew	.25
7	Ronnie Belliard	.10
8	Trot Nixon	.10
9	Adam LaRoche	.25
10	Mark Loretta	.10
11	Matt Morris	.10
12	Marlon Anderson	.10
13	Jorge Julio	.10
14	Brady Clark	.10
15	David Wells	.10
16	Francisco Rosario	.10
17	Jason Ellison	.10
18	Adam Jones	.10
19	Russell Branyan	.10
20	Rob Bowen	.10
21	J.D. Durbin	.10
22	Jeff Salazar	.10
23	Tadahito Iguchi	.10
24	Brad Hennessey	.10
25	Mark Hendrickson	.10
26	Kameron Loe	.10
27	Yusmeiro Petit	.10
28	Olmedo Saenz	.10
29	Carlos Silva	.10
30	Kevin Frandsen	.10
31	Tony Pena	.10
32	Russ Ortiz	.10
33	Hong-Chih Kuo	.10
34	Paul McAnulty	.10
35	Hiram Bocachica	.10
36	Justin Germano	.10
37	Jason Simontacchi	.10
38	Jose Cruz	.10
39	Wilfredo Ledezma	.10
40	Chris Denorfia	.10
41	Ryan Langerhans	.10
42	Chris Snelling	.10
43	Ubaldo Jimenez	.10
44	Scott Spiezio	.10
45	Byung-Hyun Kim	.10
46	Brandon Lyon	.10
47	Scott Hairston	.10
48	Chad Durbin	.10
49	Sammy Sosa	.50
50	Jason Smith	.10
51	Zack Greinke	.10
52	Armando Benitez	.10
53	Randy Messenger	.10
54	Mark Teixeira	.50
55	Mike Maroth	.10
56	Jamie Burke	.10
57	Carlos Marmol	.10
58	David Weathers	.10
59	Ryan Doumit	.10
60	Michael Barrett	.10
61	Shawn Chacon	.10
62	Mike Fontenot	.10
63	Cesar Izturis	.10
64	Cliff Floyd	.10
65	Angel Pagan	.10
66	Aaron Miles	.10
67	Tony Graffanino	.10
68	Kevin Mench	.10
69	Claudio Vargas	.10
70	Jose Capellan	.10
71	A.J. Pierzynski	.10
72	Darin Erstad	.10
73	Boone Logan	.10
74	Luis Castillo	.10
75	Marcus Thames	.10
76	Neifi Perez	.10
77	Esteban German	.10
78	Tony Pena	.10
79	Adam Wainwright	.25
80	Reggie Sanders	.10
81	Kelly Shoppach	.10
82	Rafael Betancourt	.10
83	Tom Mastny	.10
84	Kyle Farnsworth	.10
85	Rick Ankiel	.25
86	Kevin Thompson	.10
87	Jeff Karstens	.10
88	Eric Hinske	.10
89	Doug Mirabelli	.10
90	Julian Tavarez	.10
91	Carlos Pena	.25
92	Brendan Harris	.10
93	Chris Sampson	.10
94	Al Reyes	.10
95	Dmitri Young	.10
96	Jason Bergmann	.10
97	Shawn Hill	.10
98	Greg Dobbs	.10
99	Carlos Ruiz	.10
100	Abraham Nunez	.10
100b	Jacoby Ellsbury **(RC)**	150.00
101	Jayson Werth	.10
102	Adam Eaton	.10
103	Antonio Alfonseca	.10
104	Jorge Sosa	.10
105	Ramon Castro	.10
106	Ruben Gotay	.10
107	Damion Easley	.10
108	David Newhan	.10
109	Jason Wood	.10
110	Reggie Abercrombie	.10
111	Kevin Gregg	.10
112	Henry Owens	.10
113	Willie Harris	.10
114	Peter Orr	.10
115	Casey Janssen	.10
116	Jason Frasor	.10
117	Jeremy Accardo	.10
118	John McDonald	.10
119	Matt Stairs	.10
120	Jason Phillips	.10
121	Justin Duchscherer	.10
122	Rich Harden	.10
123	Jack Cust	.10
124	Lenny DiNardo	.10
125	Joe Kennedy	.10
126	Chad Gaudin	.10
127	Marco Scutaro	.10
128	Brad Thompson	.10
129	Dustin Moseley	.10
130	Eric Gagne	.10
131	Marlon Byrd	.10
132	Scot Shields	.10
133	Victor Diaz	.10
134	Reggie Willits	.25
135	Jose Molina	.10
136	Ramon Vazquez	.10
137	Erick Aybar	.10
138	Sean Marshall	.25
139	Casey Kotchman	.25
140	Ryan Spilborghs	.10
141	Cameron Maybin **RC**	2.50
142	Jeremy Guthrie	.10
143	Jeff Baker	.10
144	Edwin Jackson	.10
145	Macay McBride	.10
146	Freddie Bynum	.10
147	Eric Patterson	.10
148	Dustin McGowan	.10
149	Homer Bailey **(RC)**	1.00
150	Ryan Braun **(RC)**	2.50
151	Tony Abreu **RC**	.50
152	Tyler Clippard **(RC)**	.50
153	Mark Reynolds **RC**	1.00
154	Jesse Litsch **RC**	.50
155	Carlos Gomez **RC**	2.00
156	Matt DeSalvo **(RC)**	.50
157	Andy LaRoche **(RC)**	1.00
158	Tim Lincecum **RC**	5.00
159	Jarrod Saltalamacchia **(RC)**	.50
160	Hunter Pence **(RC)**	2.00
161	Brandon Wood **(RC)**	.50
162	Phil Hughes **(RC)**	2.00
163	Rocky Cherry **RC**	.50
164	Chase Wright **RC**	.50
165	Dallas Braden **RC**	.50
166	Felix Pie **(RC)**	.50
167	Zach McClellan **RC**	.50
168	Rick Vanden Hurk **RC**	.50
169	Micah Owings **(RC)**	.50
170	Jon Coutlangus **(RC)**	.25
171	Andrew Sonnanstine **RC**	.50
172	Yunel Escobar **(RC)**	.25
173	Kevin Slowey **(RC)**	.50
174	Curtis Thigpen **(RC)**	.25
175	Masumi Kuwata **RC**	2.00
176	Kurt Suzuki **(RC)**	.50
177	Travis Buck **(RC)**	.25
178	Matt Lindstrom **(RC)**	.25
179	Jesus Flores **RC**	.50
180	Joakim Soria **RC**	.50
181	Nathan Haynes **RC**	.25
182	Matthew Brown **RC**	.50
183	Travis Metcalf **RC**	.50
184	Yovani Gallardo **(RC)**	1.00
185	Nate Schierholtz **(RC)**	.25
186	Kyle Kendrick **RC**	1.00
187	Kevin Melillo **(RC)**	.25
188	Ryan Rowland-Smith	.25
189	Lee Gronkiewicz **RC**	.50
190	Eulogio De La Cruz **(RC)**	.25
191	Brett Carroll **RC**	.50
192	Terry Evans **RC**	.50
193	Chase Headley **(RC)**	.25
194	Guillermo Rodriguez **RC**	.50
195	Marcus McBeth **(RC)**	.25
196	Brian Wolfe **(RC)**	.25
197	Troy Cate **RC**	.50
198	Mike Zagurski **RC**	.50
199	Yoel Hernandez	.25
200	Brad Salmon **RC**	.50
201	Alberto Arias **RC**	.50
202	Danny Putnam **(RC)**	.25
203	Jamie Vermilyea **RC**	.50
204	Kyle Lohse	.10
205	Sammy Sosa	.25
206	Tom Glavine	.25
207	Prince Fielder	.50
208	Mark Buehrle	.10
209	Troy Tulowitzki	1.00
210	Daisuke Matsuzaka **RC**	5.00
211	Randy Johnson	.50
212	Justin Verlander	.50
213	Trevor Hoffman	.10
214	Alex Rodriguez	1.00
215	Ivan Rodriguez	.25
216	David Ortiz	.50
217	Placido Polanco	.10
218	Derek Jeter	1.00
219	Alex Rodriguez	1.00
220	Vladimir Guerrero	.50
221	Magglio Ordonez	.25
222	Ichiro Suzuki	.75
223	Russell Martin	.25
224	Prince Fielder	.50
225	Chase Utley	.50
226	Jose Reyes	.50
227	David Wright	.50
228	Carlos Beltran	.25
229	Barry Bonds	1.00
230	Ken Griffey Jr.	.75
231	Torii Hunter	.25
232	Jonathan Papelbon	.25
233	J.J. Putz	.10
234	Francisco Rodriguez	.10
235	C.C. Sabathia	.25
236	Johan Santana	.50
237	Justin Verlander	.25
238	Francisco Cordero	.10
239	Mike Lowell	.25
240	Cole Hamels	.25
241	Trevor Hoffman	.10
242	Manny Ramirez	.50
243	Jake Peavy	.25
244	Brad Penny	.10
245	Takashi Saito	.10
246	Ben Sheets	.25
247	Hideki Okajima	.25
248	Roy Oswalt	.25
249	Billy Wagner	.10
250	Carl Crawford	.25
251	Chris Young	.10
252	Brian McCann	.10
253	Derrek Lee	.25
254	Albert Pujols	1.00
255	Dmitri Young	.10
256	Orlando Hudson	.10
257	J.J. Hardy	.25
258	Miguel Cabrera	.50
259	Freddy Sanchez	.10
260	Matt Holliday	.25
261	Carlos Lee	.25
262	Aaron Rowand	.10
263	Alfonso Soriano	.50
264	Victor Martinez	.25
265	Jorge Posada	.25
266	Justin Morneau	.25
267	Brian Roberts	.25
268	Carlos Guillen	.10
269	Grady Sizemore	.50
270	Josh Beckett	.25
271	Danny Haren	.10
272	Bobby Jenks	.10
273	John Lackey	.10
274	Gil Meche	.10
275	Mike Fontenot, Khalil Greene	.10
276	Alex Rodriguez, Russell Martin	.50
277	Troy Tulowitzki, Jose Reyes	.50
278	Jorge Posada, Derek Jeter, Alex Rodriguez	1.00
279	Chase Utley, Ichiro Suzuki	.50
280	Carl Crawford, Carlos Guillen	.10
281	Cole Hamels, Russell Martin	.25
282	Jonathan Papelbon, Jorge Posada	.25
283	Carl Crawford, Victor Martinez	.25
284	Alfonso Soriano, J.J. Hardy	.25
285	Justin Morneau	.25
286	Prince Fielder	.50
287	Alex Rios	.25
288	Vladimir Guerrero	.50
289	Albert Pujols	1.00
290	Ryan Howard	.75
291	Magglio Ordonez	.25
292	Matt Holliday	.25
293	Wilson Betemit	.10
294	Todd Wellemeyer	.10
295	Scott Baker	.10
296	Edgar Gonzalez	.10
297	J.P. Howell	.10
298	Shaun Marcum	.10
299	Edinson Volquez	.10
300	Kason Gabbard	.10
301	Bob Howry	.10
302	J.A. Happ	.10
303	Scott Feldman	.10
304	D'Angelo Jimenez	.10
305	Orlando Palmeiro	.10
306	Paul Bako	.10
307	Kyle Davies	.10
308	Gabe Gross	.10
309	John Wasdin	.10
310	Jon Knott	.10
311	Josh Phelps	.10
312	Joba Chamberlain **RC**	8.00
312	Joba Chamberlain Reverse Negative	150.00
313	Octavio Dotel	.10
314	Craig Monroe	.10
315	Edward Mujica	.10
316	Brandon Watson	.10
317	Chris Schroder	.10
318	Scott Proctor	.10
319	Ty Wigginton	.10
320	Troy Percival	.10
321	Scott Linebrink	.10
322	David Murphy	.10
323	Jorge Cantu	.10
324	Dan Wheeler	.10
325	Jason Kendall	.10
326	Milton Bradley	.10
327	Justin Upton **RC**	3.00
328	Kenny Lofton	.10
329	Roger Clemens	1.00
330	Brian Burres	.10
SQ1	Poley Walnuts	40.00

1st Edition

1st Edition: 5-10X
Hobby Exclusive 1:36

Copper

Copper: 25-50X
Production 56 Sets

Gold

Gold: 8-15X
Production 2,007 Sets

Platinum

No Pricing
Production One Set

Red Back

Red Back (1-330): 1-2.5X
Inserted 2:Hobby, 10:HTA

Printing Plates

Production one set per color.

Barry Bonds Home Run King Relic Auto

Production 20

A-Rod Road to 500

	NM/M
A-Rod (376-400):	3.00

A-Rod Road to 500 Autographs

Production One Set

Generation Now

	NM/M
All Ryan Zimmerman's:	1.00
All Justin Verlander's:	1.00
All Prince Fielder's:	2.00
All Ian Kinsler's:	1.00
All Kenji Johjima's:	1.00
All Jonathan Papelbon's:	1.00
All Jose Reyes':	2.00
All Curtis Granderson's:	1.00
All Josh Barfield's:	.50

Barry Bonds Home Run King Relic

		NM/M
Production 756		
HRK	Barry Bonds	50.00

Mickey Mantle Home Run History Relics

	NM/M
Common Mantle:	125.00
Production Seven Sets	

1954 Mickey Mantle Reprint Relic

Production 54

Generation Now Autographs

Production One Set

Mickey Mantle Home Run History

	NM/M
Common Mantle HR History:	2.00
Inserted 1:9 Hobby	

Barry Bonds Home Run History

	NM/M
Common Bonds (735-756):	3.00
Inserted 1:12	

Barry Bonds Home Run King

		NM/M
Inserted 1:36		
HRK	Barry Bonds	5.00

Mickey Mantle Story

	NM/M
Complete Set (15):	30.00
Common Mantle:	3.00
Inserted 1:18	

Chrome

		NM/M
Common player:		5.00
Production 415 sets		
1	Homer Bailey	10.00
2	Ryan Braun	25.00
3	Tony Abreu	5.00
4	Tyler Clippard	8.00
5	Mark Reynolds	10.00
6	Jesse Litsch	5.00
7	Carlos Gomez	15.00
8	Matt DeSalvo	5.00
9	Andy LaRoche	10.00
10	Tim Lincecum	20.00
11	Jarrod Saltalamacchia	15.00
12	Hunter Pence	20.00
13	Brandon Wood	8.00
14	Phil Hughes	15.00
15	Rocky Cherry	5.00
16	Chase Wright	5.00
17	Dallas Braden	5.00
18	Felix Pie	5.00
19	Zach McClellan	5.00
20	Rick Vanden Hurk	5.00
21	Micah Owings	8.00
22	Jon Coutlangus	5.00
23	Andrew Sonnanstine	5.00
24	Yunel Escobar	5.00
25	Kevin Slowey	10.00
26	Curtis Thigpen	5.00
27	Masumi Kuwata	15.00
28	Kurt Suzuki	5.00
29	Travis Buck	5.00
30	Matt Lindstrom	5.00
31	Jesus Flores	5.00
32	Joakim Soria	5.00
33	Nathan Haynes	5.00
34	Matthew Brown	5.00
35	Travis Metcalf	5.00
36	Yovani Gallardo	8.00
37	Nate Schierholtz	5.00
38	Kyle Kendrick	10.00
39	Kevin Melillo	5.00
40	Cameron Maybin	25.00
41	Lee Gronkiewicz	5.00
42	Eulogio De La Cruz	5.00
43	Brett Carroll	5.00
44	Terry Evans	5.00
45	Chase Headley	5.00
46	Guillermo Rodriguez	5.00
47	Marcus McBeth	5.00
48	Brian Wolfe	5.00
49	Troy Cate	5.00
50	Justin Upton	30.00
51	Joba Chamberlain	60.00
52	Brad Salmon	5.00
53	Alberto Arias	5.00
54	Danny Putnam	5.00
55	Jamie Vermilyea	5.00

Target

Common Mantle:
Target Exclusive

World Series Watch

NM/M

Inserted 1:36
1 New York Mets 1.00
2 Detroit Tigers 1.00
3 Boston Red Sox 5.00
4 Milwaukee Brewers 1.00
5 Cleveland Indians 1.00
6 Angels 1.00
7 San Diego Padres 1.00
8 Los Angeles Dodgers 1.00
9 Philadelphia Phillies 1.00
10 Chicago Cubs 1.00
11 St. Louis Cardinals 1.00
12 Arizona Diamondbacks 1.00
13 New York Yankees 1.00
14 Seattle Mariners 1.00
15 Atlanta Braves 1.00

Highlights Autographs

NM/M

Some not priced due to scarcity
DW David Wright 75.00
RH Ryan Howard 60.00
AR Alex Rodriguez 200.00
JT Jim Thome 60.00
AP Albert Pujols 200.00
AJ Andruw Jones 30.00
AG Alex Gordon 35.00
GS Gary Sheffield 30.00
JS Jarrod Saltalamacchia 20.00
CJ Conor Jackson 15.00
RC Robinson Cano 30.00
PF Prince Fielder 40.00
AE Andre Ethier 15.00
JR Jimmy Rollins 40.00
AL Anthony Lerew 10.00
FC Francisco Cordero 15.00
BB Brian Bruney 20.00
AH Aaron Heilman 15.00
CS C.C. Sabathia 20.00
TT Troy Tulowitzki 25.00
RB Rod Barajas 10.00
RW Ron Washington 10.00
AC Asdrubal Cabrera 20.00
DE Damion Easley 15.00
MC Miguel Cairo 10.00

All-Star Stitches

NM/M

Common Player: 8.00
Inserted 1:45
Patch: No Pricing
Production 10 Sets
AIR Alex Rios 10.00
AP Albert Pujols 25.00
AR Alex Rodriguez 25.00
ARR Aaron Rowand 10.00
BF Brian Fuentes 8.00
BJ Bobby Jenks 10.00
BM Brian McCann 15.00
BR Brian Roberts 8.00
BS Ben Sheets 10.00
BW Brandon Webb 10.00
CB Carlos Beltran 10.00
CC Carl Crawford 10.00
CH Cole Hamels 15.00
CL Carlos Lee 10.00
CS C.C. Sabathia 15.00
CU Chase Utley 15.00
CY Chris Young 8.00
DO David Ortiz 15.00
DW David Wright 15.00
DY Dmitri Young 8.00
FR Francisco Rodriguez 8.00
FC Francisco Cordero 8.00
FS Freddy Sanchez 10.00
GM Gil Meche 8.00
GS Grady Sizemore 15.00
HO Hideki Okajima 20.00
IR Ivan Rodriguez 10.00
IS Ichiro Suzuki 30.00
JB Josh Beckett 20.00
JEP Jake Peavy 10.00
JH J.J. Hardy 10.00
JL John Lackey 10.00
JM Justin Morneau 10.00
JP J.J. Putz 8.00
JR Jose Reyes 20.00
JRP Jorge Posada 10.00
JRV Jose Valverde 8.00
JS Johan Santana 10.00
JV Justin Verlander 10.00
MH Matt Holliday 10.00
ML Mike Lowell 10.00
MR Manny Ramirez 15.00
OH Orlando Hudson 8.00
PF Prince Fielder 15.00
RH Ryan Howard 20.00
RM Russell Martin 15.00
RO Roy Oswalt 10.00
TH Torii Hunter 10.00
TS Takashi Saito 15.00
TWH Trevor Hoffman 8.00
VM Victor Martinez 10.00

All-Star Dual Stitches

Production 25 Sets

All-Star Triple Stitches

Production 25 Sets

2007 Topps 1952 Edition

NM/M

Complete set (221):
Common RC: .25
Common Action Variation:
Inserted 1:6 Hobby
Common SP (208-221): 4.00
Inserted 1:6 Hobby
Hobby Pack (8): 5.00
Hobby Box (20): 90.00
1 Akinori Iwamura **RC** 1.00
2 Angel Sanchez **RC** .50
3 Luis Hernandez **(RC)** .25
4 Joaquin Arias **(RC)** .25
5 Troy Tulowitzki **(RC)** 2.00
5 Troy Tulowitzki/ Action SP 5.00
6 Jesus Flores **RC** .50
7 Mickey Mantle 3.00
8 Kory Casto **(RC)** .25
9 Tony Abreu **RC** .50
10 Kevin Kouzmanoff **(RC)** .50
11 Travis Buck **(RC)** .25
12 Kurt Suzuki **(RC)** .25
13 Matt DeSalvo **(RC)** .25
14 Jerry Owens **(RC)** .25
15 Alex Gordon **RC** 3.00
16 Jeff Baker **(RC)** .25
17 Ben Francisco **(RC)** .25
18 Nate Schierholtz **(RC)** .25
19 Nathan Haynes **(RC)** .25
20 Ryan Braun **RC** 3.00
20 Ryan Braun Action SP 8.00
21 Brian Barden **RC** .50
22 Sean Barker **RC** .50
23 Alejandro De Aza **RC** .50
24 Jamie Burke **(RC)** .25
25 Michael Bourn **(RC)** .25
26 Jeff Salazar **(RC)** .25
27 Chase Headley **(RC)** .25
28 Chris Basak **RC** .50
29 Mike Fontenot **(RC)** .25
30 Hunter Pence **(RC)** 3.00
30 Hunter Pence/ Action SP 8.00
31 Masumi Kuwata **RC** 1.00
32 Ryan Rowland-Smith **RC** .50
33 Tyler Clippard **(RC)** .25
34 Matt Lindstrom **(RC)** .25
35 Fred Lewis **(RC)** .25
36 Brett Carroll **RC** .50
37 Alexi Casilla **RC** .50
38 Nick Gorneault **(RC)** .25
39 Dennis Sarfate **(RC)** .25
40 Felix Pie **(RC)** .25
41 Miguel Montero **(RC)** .25
42 Danny Putnam **(RC)** .25
43 Shane Youman **(RC)** .25
44 Andy LaRoche **(RC)** 1.00
45 Jarrod Saltalamacchia **(RC)** .50
46 Kei Igawa **RC** 1.00
47 Don Kelly **(RC)** .25
48 Fernando Cortez **(RC)** .25
49 Travis Metcalf **RC** .50
50 Daisuke Matsuzaka **RC** 4.00
50 Daisuke Matsuzaka/ Action/SP 8.00
51 Edwar Ramirez **RC** .50
52 Ryan Sweeney **(RC)** .25
53 Shawn Riggans **(RC)** .25
54 Billy Sadler **(RC)** .25
55 Billy Butler **(RC)** .50
56 Andy Cavazos **RC** .50
57 Sean Henn **(RC)** .25
58 Brian Esposito **(RC)** .25
59 Brandon Morrow **RC** .50
60 Adam Lind **(RC)** .25
61 Joe Smith **RC** .50
62 Chris Stewart **RC** .50
63 Eulogio De La Cruz **(RC)** .25
64 Sean Gallagher **(RC)** .25
65 Carlos Gomez **RC** 1.00
66 Jailen Peguero **RC** .50
67 Juan Perez **RC** .50
68 Levale Speigner **RC** .50
69 Jamie Vermilyea **RC** .50
70 Delmon Young **(RC)** .50
70 Delmon Young/ Action/SP 3.00
71 Jo Jo Reyes **(RC)** .25
72 Zack Segovia **(RC)** .25
73 Andrew Sonnanstine **RC** .50
74 Chase Wright **RC** 1.00
75 Josh Fields **(RC)** .25
76 Jon Knott **(RC)** .25
77 Guillermo Rodriguez **RC** .50
78 Jon Coutlangus **(RC)** .25
79 Kevin Cameron **RC** .50
80 Mark Reynolds **RC** .50
81 Brian Stokes **(RC)** .25
82 Alberto Arias **RC** .50
83 Yoel Hernandez **RC** .50
84 David Murphy **(RC)** .25
85 Josh Hamilton **(RC)** .50
86 Justin Hampson **(RC)** .25
87 Doug Slaten **RC** .50
88 Joseph Bisenius **RC** .50
89 Troy Cate **RC** .50
90 Homer Bailey **(RC)** 1.00
91 Jacoby Ellsbury **(RC)** 5.00
92 Devern Hansack **RC** .50
93 Zach McClellan **RC** .50
94 Vinny Rottino **(RC)** .25
95 Elijah Dukes **RC** .50
96 Ryan Braun **RC** .50
97 Lee Gardner **(RC)** .25
98 Joakim Soria **RC** .50
99 Jason Miller **(RC)** .25
100 Hideki Okajima **RC** 1.00
100 Hideki Okajima/ Action/SP 4.00
101 John Danks **RC** .50
102 Garrett Jones **(RC)** .25
103 Jensen Lewis **RC** .50
104 Clay Rapada **RC** .50
105 Kyle Kendrick **RC** .50
106 Eric Stults **RC** .50
107 Jared Burton **RC** .50
108 Julio DePaula **RC** .50
109 Jesse Litsch **RC** .50
110 Micah Owings **(RC)** .25
111 Cory Doyne **(RC)** .25
112 Jay Marshall **RC** .50
113 Mike Schultz **RC** .50
114 Juan Salas **(RC)** .25
115 Matt Chico **(RC)** .25
116 Brad Salmon **RC** .50
117 Jeff Bailey **(RC)** .25
118 Gustavo Molina **RC** .50
119 Billy Burres **(RC)** .25
120 Yovani Gallardo **(RC)** 2.00
121 Hector Gimenez **(RC)** .25
122 Kelvin Jimenez **RC** .50
123 Rick Vanden Hurk **RC** .50
124 Billy Petrick **(RC)** .25
125 Andrew Miller **RC** 3.00
126 Rocky Cherry **RC** .50
127 Jordan DeJong **RC** .50
128 Eric Hull **RC** .50
129 Kevin Mahar **RC** .50
130 Tim Lincecum **RC** 3.00
130 Tim Lincecum/ Action/SP 8.00
131 Garrett Olson **(RC)** .25
132 Neal Musser **RC** .50
133 Mike Rabelo **RC** .50
134 Dennis Dove **(RC)** .25
135 J.D. Durbin **(RC)** .25
136 Jose Garcia **RC** .50
137 Marcus McBeth **(RC)** .25
138 Curtis Thigpen **(RC)** .25
139 Mike Zagurski **RC** .50
140 Kevin Slowey **(RC)** .25
141 Dewon Day **RC** .50
142 Glen Perkins **(RC)** .25
143 Brian Wolfe **(RC)** .25
144 Dallas Braden **RC** .50
145 J.A. Happ **(RC)** .25
146 Lee Gronkiewicz **RC** .50
147 Cesar Jimenez **RC** .50
148 Mark McLemore **(RC)** .25
149 Connor Robertson **RC** .50
150 Phil Hughes **(RC)** 3.00
150 Phil Hughes/Action/SP 6.00
151 Matthew Brown **RC** .50
152 Ryan Feierabend **(RC)** .25
153 Brendan Ryan **(RC)** .25
154 Terry Evans **RC** .50
155 Eric Patterson **(RC)** .25
156 Patrick Misch **(RC)** .25
157 Darren Clarke **RC** .50
158 Kevin Melillo **(RC)** .25
159 Edwin Bellorin **RC** .50
160 Ubaldo Jimenez **(RC)** .25
161 Ryan Budde **(RC)** .25
162 Brian Buscher **RC** .50
163 Juan Gutierrez **RC** .50
164 Franklin Morales **(RC)** .25
165 Carmen Pignatiello **(RC)** .25
166 Jair Jurrjens **(RC)** .25
167 Manny Acosta **(RC)** .25
168 Ian Stewart **(RC)** .25
169 Daniel Barone **(RC)** .25
170 Justin Upton **RC** 3.00
170 Justin Upton/ Action/SP 8.00
171 Tommy Watkins **RC** .50
172 Ross Wolf **RC** .50
173 Jack Cassel **RC** .50
174 Asdrubal Cabrera **RC** 1.00
175 Mauro Zarate **RC** .50
176 Aaron Laffey **RC** .50
177 Marcus Gwyn **RC** .50
178 Danny Richar **RC** .50
179 Joel Hanrahan **(RC)** .25
180 Cameron Maybin **RC** 2.00
181 John Lannan **RC** .50
182 Shelley Duncan **(RC)** .25
183 Brandon Wood **(RC)** .50
184 Delwyn Young **(RC)** .25
185 Manny Parra **(RC)** .25
186 Ehren Wassermann **RC** .50
187 Jose Reyes **RC** .50
188 Jose Ascanio **RC** .50
190 Alvin Colina **RC** .50
190 Joba Chamberlain/ Action/SP 20.00
191 Yunel Escobar **(RC)** .25
192 Carlos Maldonado **(RC)** .25
193 Dan Meyer **(RC)** .25
194 Scott Moore **(RC)** .25
195 Romulo Sanchez **RC** .50
196 Tom Shearn **(RC)** .25
197 Craig Stansberry **(RC)** .25
201 Joba Chamberlain **RC** 6.00
202 John Nelson/SP **(RC)** 5.00
203 Phil Dumatrait **(RC)** .25
204 Brandon Moss **(RC)** .25
205 Beltran Perez **(RC)** .25
206 Drew Anderson **RC** .50
207 Brett Campbell **RC** .50
208 Andy Cannizaro/SP **RC** 8.00
209 Travis Chick/SP **(RC)** 5.00
210 Francisco Cruceta/ SP **(RC)** 4.00
211 Jose Diaz/SP **(RC)** 4.00
212 Jeff Fiorentino/ SP **(RC)** 5.00
213 Tim Gradoville/SP **RC** 4.00
214 Kevin Hooper/SP **(RC)** 4.00
215 Philip Humber/ SP **(RC)** 5.00
216 Juan Lara/SP **RC** 5.00
217 Mitch Maier/SP **RC** 4.00
218 Juan Morillo/SP **(RC)** 4.00
219 A.J. Murray/SP **RC** 5.00
220 Chris Narveson/ SP **(RC)** 5.00
221 Oswaldo Navarro/ SP **RC** 6.00

Black Back

Black Backs: 2-4X
Inserted 1:6 Hobby

A-Rod Road to 500

NM/M

A-Rod (476-500): 3.00

A-Rod Road to 500 Autograph

NM/M

Production One Set 3.00

Chrome

NM/M

Common player: 1.50
Production 1,952 Sets
Refractor: 2-3X
Production 552 Sets
Gold Refractor: 4-6X
Production 52 Sets
1 Akinori Iwamura 2.00
2 Angel Sanchez 1.50
3 Luis Hernandez 1.50
4 Troy Tulowitzki 5.00
5 Joaquin Arias 1.50
6 Jesus Flores 1.50
7 Brandon Wood 2.00
8 Kory Casto 1.50
9 Kevin Kouzmanoff 2.00
10 Tony Abreu 1.50
11 Travis Buck 1.50
12 Kurt Suzuki 1.50
13 Alejandro De Aza 1.50
14 Alex Gordon 6.00
15 Jerry Owens 1.50
16 Ryan Braun 8.00
17 Michael Bourn 1.50
18 Hunter Pence 6.00
19 Jeff Baker 1.50
20 Ben Francisco 1.50
21 Nate Schierholtz 1.50
22 Nathan Haynes 1.50
23 Andrew Miller 4.00
24 Sean Barker 1.50
25 Matt DeSalvo 1.50
26 Fred Lewis 1.50
27 Jamie Burke 1.50
28 Jeff Salazar 1.50
29 Chase Headley 1.50
30 Chris Basak 1.50
31 Mike Fontenot 1.50
32 Felix Pie 2.00
33 Masumi Kuwata 1.50
34 Daisuke Matsuzaka 8.00
35 Tim Lincecum 6.00
36 Jarrod Saltalamacchia 3.00
37 Tyler Clippard 2.00
38 Billy Butler 4.00
39 Matt Lindstrom 1.50
40 Brett Carroll 1.50
41 Alexi Casilla 1.50
42 Nick Gorneault 1.50
43 Matt Chico 1.50
44 Adam Lind 1.50
45 Miguel Montero 1.50
46 Danny Putnam 1.50
47 Delmon Young 2.00
48 Josh Fields 1.50
49 Carlos Gomez 3.00
50 Mark Reynolds 3.00
51 Shane Youman 2.00
52 Andy LaRoche 3.00
53 Kei Igawa 1.50
54 Don Kelly 1.50
55 Cameron Maybin 5.00
56 Travis Metcalf 1.50
57 Ubaldo Jimenez 1.50
58 Ryan Sweeney 1.50
59 Shawn Riggans 1.50
60 Jacoby Ellsbury 15.00
61 Andy Cavazos 1.50
62 Justin Hamilton 3.00
63 Homer Bailey 3.00
64 Sean Henn 1.50
65 Elijah Dukes 1.50
66 Brian Esposito 1.50
67 Brandon Morrow 1.50
68 Joe Smith 1.50
69 Chris Stewart 1.50
70 Eulogio De La Cruz 1.50
71 Sean Gallagher 1.50
72 Jailen Peguero 1.50
73 Juan Perez 1.50
74 Levale Speigner 1.50
75 Jamie Vermilyea 1.50
76 Hideki Okajima 2.00
77 Eric Patterson 1.50
78 Zack Segovia 1.50
79 Kyle Kendrick 1.50
80 Andrew Sonnanstine 1.50
81 Chase Wright 1.50
82 Jon Knott 1.50
83 Guillermo Rodriguez 1.50
84 Jon Coutlangus 1.50
85 Kevin Cameron 1.50
86 Brian Stokes 1.50
87 Alberto Arias 1.50
88 Delwyn Young 1.50
89 David Murphy 1.50
90 Micah Owings 1.50
91 Yovani Gallardo 4.00
92 Justin Hampson 1.50
93 Doug Slaten 1.50
94 Justin Upton 5.00
95 Joba Chamberlain 20.00

Dynamic Duos

NM/M

Common Duo: 1.00
Inserted 1:4
1 Tim Lincecum, Nate Schierholtz 2.00
2 Joba Chamberlain, Phil Hughes 8.00
3 Ryan Braun, Yovani Gallardo 3.00
4 Kyle Kendrick, Michael Bourn 1.00
5 Delmon Young, Elijah Dukes 1.00
6 Hideki Okajima, Daisuke Matsuzaka 5.00
7 Justin Upton, Mark Reynolds 2.00
8 Eric Patterson, Felix Pie 1.00
9 Josh Hamilton, Homer Bailey 1.50
10 Ubaldo Jimenez, Troy Tulowitzki 2.00
11 Alex Gordon, Billy Butler 3.00
12 Delwyn Young, Andy LaRoche 2.00
13 Andrew Miller, Cameron Maybin 2.00
14 Joe Smith, Carlos Gomez 1.00
15 David Murphy, Jarrod Saltalamacchia 1.00

Debut Flashbacks

NM/M

Complete Set (15): 10.00
Common player: .50
Inserted 1:6
Chrome: 2X
Production 1,952 Sets
Refractor: 3-4X
Production 552 Sets
Gold Refractor: 4-8X
Production 52 Sets
1 Vladimir Guerrero 1.50
2 Ken Griffey Jr. 3.00
3 Pedro Martinez 1.50
4 Carlos Delgado .75
5 Gary Sheffield 1.00
6 Curt Schilling 1.00
7 Jorge Posada .75
8 Miguel Tejada .75
9 Trevor Hoffman .50
10 Francisco Cordero .50
11 Travis Hafner .75
12 Paul LoDuca .50
13 Jimmy Rollins 1.50
14 Magglio Ordonez .75
15 Jim Edmonds .50

Signatures

NM/M

Common Auto.: 5.00
Red Ink: 1.5-2X
Production 52 sets
AA Alberto Arias 5.00
AC Alexi Casilla 8.00
AG Alex Gordon 50.00
AI Akinori Iwamura 25.00
AL Andy LaRoche 25.00
AM Andrew Miller 30.00
AS Angel Sanchez 5.00
ASL Aaron Laffey 15.00
BB Brian Barden 8.00
BC Brett Carroll 8.00
BE Brian Esposito 8.00
BF Ben Francisco 8.00
BP Ben Petrick 10.00
BPB Brian Buscher 10.00
BS Brian Stokes 8.00
BW Brian Wolfe 8.00
CD Cory Doyne 8.00
CM Cameron Maybin 50.00
CS Chris Stewart 15.00
CW Chase Wright 20.00
DC Darren Clarke 8.00
ER Edwar Ramirez 15.00
FL Fred Lewis 20.00
FP Felix Pie 25.00
GS Gary Sheffield/SP 60.00
HO Hideki Okajima 60.00
HP Hunter Pence 50.00
JA Joaquin Arias 15.00
JB Jared Burton 20.00
JC Jon Coutlangus 15.00
JCH Joba Chamberlain 200.00
JH Joel Hanrahan 20.00
JJR Jo Jo Reyes 20.00
JL Jensen Lewis 10.00
JM Jason Miller 10.00
JRB Joseph Bisenius 8.00
JSS Jarrod Saltalamacchia 25.00
JU Justin Upton 60.00
KK Kevin Kouzmanoff 20.00
KS Kurt Suzuki 15.00
LS Levale Speigner 8.00
MB Michael Bourn 15.00
MBB Matthew Brown 8.00
ML Matt Lindstrom 10.00
MM Mark McLemore 8.00
NG Nick Gorneault 25.00
NH Nathan Haynes 8.00
PD Phil Dumatrait 10.00
PH Phil Hughes 80.00
RB Ryan Braun 60.00
RC Rocky Cherry 20.00
RDB Ryan Budde 10.00
RZB Ryan Braun 10.00
TB Travis Buck 15.00
TC Tyler Clippard 25.00
TL Tim Lincecum 75.00
TM Travis Metcalf 30.00
TPC Troy Cate 8.00
YG Yovani Gallardo 30.00
ZS Zack Segovia 10.00

Signatures Combos

NM/M

Production 25 sets
LO Tim Lincecum, Hideki Okajima 125.00
ML Andrew Miller, Matt Lindstrom 60.00
OI Hideki Okajima, Akinori Iwamura 125.00
LB Matt Lindstrom, Michael Bourn 40.00

Diamond Debut Tix Relics

Production 20 Sets

Highlights Autographs

NM/M

Short prints are not serial #'d.
JH John Hattig Jr. 8.00
AM Andrew Miller 50.00
AS Anibal Sanchez 10.00
MN Michael Napoli 10.00
JL James Loney 20.00
MH Matt Holliday 25.00
TT Troy Tulowitzki 30.00
HR Hanley Ramirez 20.00
JF Josh Fields 15.00
CQ Carlos Quentin 15.00
MG Matt Garza 15.00
JM John Maine 35.00
MP Mike Piazza/50 120.00
TH Travis Hafner 25.00
KM Kevin Mench 10.00
CU Chase Utley 50.00
DW David Wright 75.00
JM Justin Morneau 25.00
JS Johan Santana/250 60.00
MC Miguel Cabrera/250 35.00
DY Delmon Young 30.00
DWW Dontrelle Willis 20.00
CW Chien-Ming Wang/100 250.00
JS John Smoltz/250 50.00
AS Alfonso Soriano/100 100.00
DO David Ortiz/100 80.00
RH Ryan Howard/100 100.00
AR Alex Rodriguez/25 250.00
EF Emiliano Fruto 10.00
RZ Ryan Zimmerman 30.00
Series 2
AB Aaron Boone 10.00
AJ Andruw Jones 35.00
AP Albert Pujols 250.00
AR Anthony Reyes 15.00
CG Curtis Granderson 30.00
CW Craig Wilson 15.00
DO David Ortiz 80.00
DT Derrick Turnbow 15.00
DU Dan Uggla 20.00
DW David Wright 50.00
DWW Dontrelle Willis 20.00
EC Endy Chavez 40.00
ES Ervin Santana 15.00
JT Jim Thome 40.00
JD Johnny Damon 100.00
JG Jon Garland 15.00
JV Justin Verlander 50.00
JZ Joel Zumaya 20.00
KE Kelvim Escobar 20.00
KM Kendry Morales 10.00
LM Lastings Milledge 20.00
MC Melky Cabrera 25.00

MTC Matt Cain 20.00
PL Paul LoDuca 40.00
RC Robinson Cano 30.00
RH Ryan Howard 100.00
RM Russell Martin 20.00
RZ Ryan Zimmerman 30.00
SC Shawn Chacon 10.00
SP Scott Podsednik 15.00
SR Shawn Riggans 10.00
SSC Shin-Soo Choo 20.00
ST Steve Trachsel 25.00
TG Tom Glavine 75.00
VG Vladimir Guerrero 150.00

Highlights Relics

NM/M
Common Player: 5.00
AP Albert Pujols 25.00
AR Alex Rodriguez 20.00
AS Alfonso Soriano 15.00
BM Brian McCann 15.00
CB Carlos Beltran 10.00
CD Carlos Delgado 8.00
CQ Carlos Quentin 10.00
CB Craig Biggio 10.00
CS Curt Schilling 10.00
DO David Ortiz 10.00
DW Dontrelle Willis 8.00
ER Edgar Renteria 5.00
FT Frank Thomas 10.00
GS Gary Sheffield 8.00
IS Ichiro Suzuki 25.00
IR Ivan Rodriguez 10.00
JB Jason Bay 10.00
JPM Joe Mauer 15.00
JAS Johan Santana 20.00
JS John Smoltz 10.00
JR Jose Reyes 15.00
JM Justin Morneau 15.00
MO Magglio Ordonez 5.00
MAR Manny Ramirez 10.00
MR Mariano Rivera 15.00
MT Miguel Tejada 8.00
PK Paul Konerko 10.00
RC Robinson Cano 15.00
RO Roy Oswalt 8.00
RH Ryan Howard 20.00
SK Scott Kazmir 8.00
SR Scott Rolen 10.00
TG Tom Glavine 8.00
TG Troy Glaus 5.00
VW Vernon Wells 8.00

Series 2
AB Adrian Beltre 5.00
AER Alex Rodriguez 20.00
AJ Andruw Jones 8.00
ALR Anthony Reyes 5.00
AP Albert Pujols 25.00
AR Aramis Ramirez 8.00
AS Alfonso Soriano 10.00
CJ Chipper Jones 10.00
DE David Eckstein 20.00
DO David Ortiz 15.00
DW David Wright 15.00
DWW Dontrelle Willis 8.00
GA Garrett Atkins 5.00
GS Grady Sizemore 10.00
JD Jermaine Dye 5.00
JDD Johnny Damon 15.00
JT Jim Thome 10.00
JV Justin Verlander 20.00
LB Lance Berkman 8.00
MC Matt Cain 8.00
MCT Mark Teixeira 8.00
MEC Melky Cabrera 10.00
MR Manny Ramirez 10.00
MT Miguel Tejada 8.00
NS Nick Swisher 8.00
PK Paul Konerko 8.00
PM Pedro Martinez 8.00
RC Robinson Cano 15.00
RH Roy Halladay 10.00
RJH Ryan Howard 20.00
SK Scott Kazmir 8.00
TG Tom Glavine 10.00
VG Vladimir Guerrero 8.00
VW Vernon Wells 8.00

2008 Topps

NM/M
Complete Set (330): 30.00
Common Player: .10
Hobby Pack (10): 2.00
Hobby Box (36): 60.00
1 Alex Rodriguez 1.50
2 Barry Zito .10
3 Jeff Suppan .10
4 Rick Ankiel .25
5 Scott Kazmir .25
6 Felix Pie .10
7 Mickey Mantle 4.00
8 Stephen Drew .25
9 Randy Wolf .10
10 Miguel Cabrera .50
11 Yorvit Torrealba .10
12 Jason Bartlett .10
13 Kendry Morales .10
14 Lenny DiNardo .10
15 Magglio Ordonez, Ichiro Suzuki, Placido Polanco .50
16 Kevin Gregg .10
17 Cristian Guzman .10
18 J.D. Durbin .10
19 Robinson Tejeda .10
20 Daisuke Matsuzaka 1.00
21 Edwin Encarnacion .10
22 Ron Washington .10
23 Chin-Lung Hu **RC** .25
24 Alex Rodriguez, Magglio Ordonez, Vladimir Guerrero .50
25 Kazuo Matsui .10
26 Manny Ramirez .50
27 Bob Melvin .10
28 Kyle Kendrick .10
29 Anibal Sanchez .10
30 Jimmy Rollins .50
31 Ronny Paulino .10
32 Howie Kendrick .10
33 Joe Mauer .25
34 Aaron Cook .10
35 Cole Hamels .25
36 Brendan Harris .10
37 Jason Marquis .10
38 Preston Wilson .10
39 Yovani Gallardo .25
40 Miguel Tejada .25
41 Rich Aurilia .10
42 Corey Hart .25
43 Ryan Dempster .10
44 Jonathan Broxton .10
45 Dontrelle Willis .10
46 Zack Greinke .10
47 Orlando Cabrera .25
48 Zachary Duke .10
49 Orlando Hernandez .10
50 Jake Peavy .25
51 Erik Bedard .25
52 Trevor Hoffman .10
53 Hank Blalock .10
54 Victor Martinez .25
55 Chris Young .10
56 Seth Smith **RC** .25
57 Wladimir Balentien **RC** .25
58 Matt Holliday, Ryan Howard, Miguel Cabrera .50
59 Grady Sizemore .50
60 Jose Reyes .50
61 Alex Rodriguez, Carlos Pena, David Ortiz .50
62 Rich Thompson **RC** .25
63 Jason Michaels .10
64 Mike Lowell .10
65 Billy Wagner .10
66 Brad Wilkerson .10
67 Wes Helms .10
68 Kevin Millar .10
69 Bobby Cox .10
70 Dan Uggla .10
71 Jarrod Washburn .10
72 Mike Piazza .40
73 Mike Napoli .10
74 Garrett Atkins .25
75 Felix Hernandez .25
76 Ivan Rodriguez .25
77 Angel Guzman .10
78 Radhames Liz **RC** .50
79 Omar Vizquel .10
80 Alex Rios .25
81 Ray Durham .10
82 So Taguchi .10
83 Mark Reynolds .10
84 Brian Fuentes .10
85 Jason Bay .25
86 Scott Podsednik .10
87 Maicer Izturis .10
88 Jack Cust .10
89 Josh Willingham .10
90 Vladimir Guerrero .50
91 Marcus Giles .10
92 Ross Detwiler **RC** 1.00
93 Kenny Lofton .10
94 Bud Black .10
95 John Lackey .10
96 Sam Fuld **RC** .50
97 Clint Sammons **RC** .25
98 Ryan Howard, Chase Utley .50
99 David Ortiz, Manny Ramirez .25
100 Ryan Howard .75
101 Ryan Braun .50
102 Ross Ohlendorf **RC** .50
103 Jonathan Albaladejo **RC** 1.00
104 Kevin Youkilis .25
105 Roger Clemens 1.00
106 Josh Bard .10
107 Shawn Green .10
108 B.J. Ryan .10
109 Joe Nathan .10
110 Justin Morneau .40
111 Ubaldo Jimenez .10
112 Jacque Jones .10
113 Kevin Frandsen .10
114 Mike Fontenot .10
115 Johan Santana .50
116 Chuck James .10
117 Boof Bonser .10
118 Marco Scutaro .10
119 Jeremy Hermida .10
120 Andruw Jones .25
121 Mike Cameron .10
122 Jason Varitek .25
123 Terry Francona .10
124 Bob Geren .10
125 Tim Hudson .25
126 Brandon Jones **RC** .50
127 Steve Pearce **RC** 1.00
128 Kenny Lofton .10
129 Kevin Hart **RC** .25
130 Justin Upton .50
131 Norris Hopper .10
132 Ramon Vazquez .10
133 Mike Bacsik .10
134 Matt Stairs .10
135 Brad Penny .10
136 Robinson Cano .40
137 Jamey Carroll .10
138 Dan Wheeler .10
139 Johnny Estrada .10
140 Brandon Webb .25
141 Ryan Klesko .10
142 Chris Duncan .10
143 Willie Harris .10
144 Jerry Owens .10
145 Magglio Ordonez .25
146 Aaron Hill .10
147 Marlon Anderson .10
148 Gerald Laird .10
149 Luke Hochevar **RC** 1.00
150 Alfonso Soriano .40
151 Adam Loewen .10
152 Bronson Arroyo .10
153 Luis Mendoza **RC** .50
154 David Ross .10
155 Carlos Zambrano .25
156 Brandon McCarthy .10
157 Tim Redding .10
158 Jose Bautista .10
159 Luke Scott .10
160 Ben Sheets .25
161 Matt Garza .10
162 Andy LaRoche .25
163 Doug Davis .10
164 Nate Schierholtz .10
165 Tim Lincecum .25
166 Andrew Sonnanstine .10
167 Jason Hirsh .10
168 Phil Hughes .25
169 Adam Lind .10
170 Scott Rolen .25
171 John Maine .10
172 Chris Ray .10
173 Jamie Moyer .10
174 Julian Tavarez .10
175 Delmon Young .25
176 Troy Patton **RC** .25
177 Josh Anderson **RC** .50
178 Dustin Pedroia .25
179 Chris Young .25
180 Jose Valverde .10
181 Joe Borowski, Bobby Jenks, J.J. Putz .10
182 Billy Buckner **RC** .25
183 Paul Byrd .10
184 Tadahito Iguchi .10
185 Yunel Escobar .10
186 Lastings Milledge .10
187 Dustin McGowan .10
188 Kei Igawa .10
189 Esteban German .10
190 Russell Martin .25
191 Orlando Hudson .10
192 Jim Edmonds .10
193 J.J. Hardy .10
194 Chad Billingsley .10
195 Todd Helton .25
196 Ross Gload .10
197 Melky Cabrera .25
198 Shannon Stewart .10
199 Adrian Beltre .25
200 Manny Ramirez .40
201 Matt Capps .10
202 Mike Lamb .10
203 Jason Tyner .10
204 Rafael Furcal .10
205 Gil Meche .10
206 Geoff Jenkins .10
207 Jeff Kent .10
208 David DeJesus .10
209 Andy Phillips .10
210 Mark Teahen .10
211 Lyle Overbay .10
212 Moises Alou .10
213 Michael Barrett .10
214 C.J. Wilson .10
215 Bobby Jenks .10
216 Ryan Garko .10
217 Josh Beckett .40
218 Clint Hurdle .10
219 Kevin Kouzmanoff .25
220 Roy Oswalt .25
221 Ian Snell .10
222 Mark Grudzielanek .10
223 Odalis Perez .10
224 Mark Buehrle .10
225 Hunter Pence .25
226 Kurt Suzuki .10
227 Alfredo Amezaga .10
228 Geoff Blum .10
229 Dustin Pedroia .25
230 Roy Halladay .25
231 Casey Blake .10
232 Clay Buchholz **RC** .50
233 Jimmy Rollins .50
234 Boston Red Sox .25
234 Boston Red Sox with Giuliani 15.00
235 Rich Harden .10
236 Joe Koshansky **RC** .25
237 Eric Wedge .10
238 Shane Victorino .10
239 Richie Sexson .25
240 Jim Thome .25
241 Ervin Santana .10
242 Manny Acta .10
243 Akinori Iwamura .10
244 Adam Wainwright .10
245 Danny Haren .10
246 Jason Isringhausen .10
247 Edgar Gonzalez .10
248 Jose Contreras .10
249 Chris Sampson .10
250 Jonathan Papelbon .25
251 Dan Johnson .10
252 Dmitri Young .10
253 Bronson Sardinha **RC** .25
254 David Murphy .10
255 Brandon Phillips .10
256 Alex Rodriguez 1.00
257 Austin Kearns, Dmitri Young .10
258 Manny Ramirez, Kevin Youkilis .25
259 Emilio Bonifacio **RC** .50
260 Chad Cordero .10
261 Josh Barfield .10
262 Brett Myers .10
263 Nook Logan .10
264 Byung-Hyun Kim .10
265 Fredi Gonzalez .10
266 Ryan Doumit .10
267 Chris Burke .10
268 Daric Barton **RC** .25
269 James Loney .25
270 C.C. Sabathia .25
271 Chad Tracy .10
272 Anthony Reyes .10
273 Rafael Soriano .10
274 Jermaine Dye .10
275 C.C. Sabathia .25
276 Brad Ausmus .10
277 Aubrey Huff .10
278 Xavier Nady .10
279 Damion Easley .10
280 Willie Randolph .10
281 Carlos Ruiz .10
282 Jon Lester .10
283 Jorge Sosa .10
284 Lance Broadway **RC** .25
285 Tony LaRussa .10
286 Jeff Clement **RC** .25
287 Justin Morneau, Johan Santana, Joe Mauer .25
288 Ivan Rodriguez, Justin Verlander .25
289 Justin Ruggiano **RC** .50
290 Edgar Renteria .10
291 Eugenio Velez **RC** .50
292 Mark Loretta .10
293 Gavin Floyd .10
294 Brian McCann .25
295 Tim Wakefield .10
296 Paul Konerko .25
297 Jorge Posada .25
298 Prince Fielder, Ryan Howard, Adam Dunn .50
299 Cesar Izturis .10
300 Chien-Ming Wang .50
301 Chris Duffy .10
302 Horacio Ramirez .10
303 Jose Lopez .10
304 Jose Vidro .10
305 Carlos Delgado .25
306 Scott Olsen .10
307 Shawn Hill .10
308 Felipe Lopez .10
309 Ryan Church .10
310 Kelvim Escobar .10
311 Jeremy Guthrie .10
312 Ramon Hernandez .10
313 Kameron Loe .10
314 Ian Kinsler .10
315 David Weathers .10
316 Scott Hatteberg .10
317 Cliff Lee .10
318 Ned Yost .10
319 Joey Votto **RC** .50
320 Ichiro Suzuki 1.00
321 J.R. Towles **RC** 1.00
322 Scott Kazmir, Johan Santana, Erik Bedard .25
323 Jose Valverde, Francisco Cordero, Trevor Hoffman .10
324 Jake Peavy .25
325 Jim Leyland .10
326 Matt Holliday, Chipper Jones, Hanley Ramirez .25
327 Jake Peavy, Aaron Harang, John Smoltz .25
328 Nyjer Morgan **RC** .50
329 Lou Piniella .10
330 Curtis Granderson .25

Gold

Gold: 8-15X
Production 2,007 Sets

Black

Black: 25-50X
Production 57 Sets

Platinum

No Pricing
Production One Set

Printing Plates

No Pricing
Production one set per color.

Mickey Mantle Home Run History

NM/M
Common Mantle (502-536): 2.00
Inserted 1:9

The Mickey Mantle Story

NM/M
Complete Set (10): 20.00
Common Mantle: 3.00
Inserted 1:18

Own the Game

NM/M
Complete Set (25): 10.00
Common Player: .50
Inserted 1:6
1 Alex Rodriguez 2.00
2 Prince Fielder 1.00
3 Ryan Howard 1.00
4 Carlos Pena .50
5 Adam Dunn .50
6 Matt Holliday .75
7 David Ortiz 1.00
8 Jim Thome .50
9 Lance Berkman .50
10 Miguel Cabrera .75
11 Alex Rodriguez 2.00
12 Magglio Ordonez .50
13 Matt Holliday .75
14 Ryan Howard 1.00
15 Vladimir Guerrero .75
16 Carlos Pena .50
17 Mike Lowell .50
18 Miguel Cabrera .75
19 Prince Fielder 1.00
20 Carlos Lee .50
21 Jake Peavy .50
22 John Lackey .50
23 Brandon Webb .50
24 Brad Penny .50
25 Fausto Carmona .50

Year In Review

NM/M
Complete Set (60): 30.00
Common Player: .25
Inserted 1:6
1 Paul LoDuca .25
2 Felix Hernandez .50
3 Ian Snell .25
4 Carlos Beltran .50
5 Daisuke Matsuzaka 1.00
6 Jose Reyes 1.00
7 Alex Rodriguez 2.00
8 Scott Kazmir .50
9 Adam Everett .25
10 Josh Beckett, Josh Hamilton .50
11 Craig Monroe .25
12 Justin Morneau .50
13 Roy Halladay .50
14 Jeff Suppan .25
15 Marco Scutaro .25
16 Ivan Rodriguez .50
17 Dmitri Young .25
18 Mark Buehrle .25
19 Alex Rodriguez 2.00
20 Joe Saunders .25
21 Russell Martin .50
22 Manny Ramirez .50
23 Chase Utley .75
24 Travis Hafner .50
25 Jake Peavy .50
26 Shawn Hill .25
27 Daisuke Matsuzaka 1.00
28 Matt Belisle .25
29 Troy Tulowitzki .50
30 Andruw Jones .50
31 Phil Hughes .50
32 Derrek Lee .50
33 Ichiro Suzuki 1.50
34 Julio Franco .25
35 Chien-Ming Wang .75
36 Hideki Matsui 1.00
37 Brad Penny .25
38 Jack Wilson .25
39 Francisco Cordero .25
40 Omar Vizquel .25
41 Tim Lincecum .50
42 Bartolo Colon .25
43 Fred Lewis .25
44 Jeff Kent .25
45 Randy Johnson .75
46 Rafael Furcal .25
47 Delmon Young .50
48 Andrew Miller .50
49 David Ortiz, Mike Lowell 1.00
50 Justin Verlander .50
51 C.C. Sabathia .50
52 Felipe Lopez .25
53 Oliver Perez .25
54 John Smoltz .50
55 Mark Reynolds .25
56 Jeremy Accardo .25
57 Todd Helton .50
58 Adrian Beltre .25
59 Carlos Delgado .50
60 Chris Young .50

Topps 50th Anniversary All-Rookie Team

NM/M
Complete Set (55): 50.00
Common Player: .50
Inserted 1:5
1 Darryl Strawberry .50
2 Gary Sheffield .75
3 Dwight Gooden .50
4 Melky Cabrera .75
5 Gary Carter .50
6 Lou Piniella .50
7 David Justice .50
8 Andre Dawson .75
9 Mark Ellis .50
10 Dave Johnson .50
11 Jermaine Dye .50
12 Dan Johnson .50
13 Alfonso Soriano .75
14 Prince Fielder 1.50
15 Hanley Ramirez 1.00
16 Matt Holliday .75
17 Justin Verlander 1.00
18 Mark Teixeira .75
19 Julio Franco .50
20 Ivan Rodriguez .75
21 Jason Bay .75
22 Brandon Webb .75
23 Dontrelle Willis .50
24 Brad Wilkerson .50
25 Dan Uggla .50
26 Ozzie Smith 1.00
27 Andruw Jones .75
28 Garret Anderson .50
29 Jimmy Rollins 1.00
30 Brian McCann .50
31 Scott Podsednik .50
32 Garrett Atkins .50
33 Billy Wagner .50
34 Chipper Jones 1.00
35 Roger McDowell .50
36 Austin Kearns .50
37 Boog Powell .50
38 Ron Swoboda .50
39 Roy Oswalt .75
40 Mike Piazza 1.00
41 Albert Pujols 3.00
42 Ichiro Suzuki 2.00
43 C.C. Sabathia .75
44 Todd Helton .75
45 Scott Rolen .75
46 Derek Jeter 3.00
47 Shawn Green .50
48 Manny Ramirez 1.00
49 Tom Seaver 1.00
50 Kenny Lofton .50
51 Francisco Liriano .75
52 Ryan Zimmerman .75
53 Jeff Francoeur .75
54 Joe Mauer .75
55 Magglio Ordonez .75

Trading Card History

NM/M
Common player: .50
Inserted 1:12
1 Jacoby Ellsbury 1.00
2 Joba Chamberlain 1.00
3 Daisuke Matsuzaka 1.00
4 Prince Fielder 1.00
5 Clay Buchholz 1.00
6 Alex Rodriguez 2.00
7 Mickey Mantle 2.00
8 Ryan Braun 1.00
9 Albert Pujols 2.00
10 Joe Mauer .50
11 Jose Reyes 1.00
12 Joey Votto .25
13 Johan Santana .75
14 Hunter Pence .50
15 Hideki Okajima .50
16 Cameron Maybin .50
17 Roger Clemens 1.50
18 Tim Lincecum .50
19 Mark Teixeira, Jeff Francoeur .50
20 Justin Upton .50
21 Alfonso Soriano .75
22 Pedro Martinez .75
23 Chien-Ming Wang .75
24 Ichiro Suzuki 1.50
25 Grady Sizemore .75

Campaign 2008

NM/M
Common Candidate: 1.00
Inserted 1:9
JB Joseph Biden 1.00
HC Hillary Clinton 3.00
JE John Edwards 2.00
RG Rudy Giuliani 2.00
MH Mike Huckabee 1.00
DK Dennis Kucininch 1.00
JM John McCain 3.00
BO Barack Obama 6.00
RP Ron Paul 1.00
BR Bill Richardson 1.00
MR Mitt Romney 1.00
FT Fred Thompson 2.00

World Champion Autograph Relics

		NM/M
Production 50 Sets		
2	Hideki Okajima	150.00
3	Curt Schilling	150.00
4	Jason Varitek	150.00
5	Mike Lowell	150.00
6	Jacoby Ellsbury	300.00
7	Dustin Pedroia	200.00
9	Julio Lugo	100.00
10	Manny Ramirez	225.00

2007 Highlight Autographs

		NM/M
Common Auto:		10.00
AS	Alfonso Soriano	50.00
CMW	Chien-Ming Wang	125.00
GS	Gary Sheffield	40.00
JD	Johnny Damon	50.00
JP	Jake Peavy	30.00
JV	Jason Varitek	50.00
MR	Manny Ramirez	80.00
RJC	Robinson Cano	40.00
VG	Vladimir Guerrero	50.00
BP	Brad Penny	25.00
DH	Danny Haren	25.00
DW	David Wright	60.00
HR	Hanley Ramirez	40.00
JBR	Jose Reyes	60.00
JR	Jimmy Rollins	50.00
JTD	Jermaine Dye	20.00
MY	Michael Young	20.00
PF	Prince Fielder	65.00
CB	Clay Buchholz	80.00
CP	Carlos Pena	20.00
ED	Eulogio de la Cruz	15.00
ES	Ervin Santana	10.00
FC	Fausto Carmona	20.00
FS	Freddy Sanchez	15.00
JF	Josh Fields	15.00
JL	John Lackey	15.00
LC	Luis Castillo	15.00
MG	Matt Garza	15.00
NM	Nicholas Markakis	20.00
RM	Russell Martin	20.00
WN	Wilbert Nieves	15.00
YG	Yovani Gallardo	20.00
HK	Howie Kendrick	15.00
JB	John Buck	10.00
JM	Jose Molina	10.00
RC	Ramon Castro	10.00
RH	Rich Hill	20.00
CV	Carlos Villanueva	10.00
DM	Dustin Moseley	10.00
MB	Mike Bacsik	10.00
ME	Mark Ellis	10.00
RJM	Randy Messenger	10.00
SM	Scott Moore	10.00
TG	Tom Gorzelanny	15.00
UJ	Ubaldo Jimenez	10.00
AL	Adam Lind	10.00
JA	Josh Anderson	15.00
DB	Daric Barton	15.00
LB	Lance Broadway	10.00
SF	Sam Fuld	20.00
NJM	Nyjer Morgan	20.00
SS	Seth Smith	15.00

Topps 50th Anniversary All-Rookie Team Autos

25 Sets

World Champion Relics

		NM/M
Production 100 Sets		
1	Josh Beckett	60.00
2	Hideki Okajima	50.00
3	Curt Schilling	60.00
4	Jason Varitek	60.00
5	Mike Lowell	60.00
6	Jacoby Ellsbury	80.00
7	Dustin Pedroia	70.00
8	Jonathan Papelbon	60.00
9	Julio Lugo	30.00
10	Manny Ramirez	50.00
11	David Ortiz	60.00
12	Eric Gagne	40.00
13	Jon Lester	50.00
14	J.D. Drew	50.00
15	Kevin Youkilis	50.00

2007 Highlight Relics

		NM/M
Common Relic:		5.00
CB	Carlos Beltran	10.00
DO	David Ortiz	15.00
DW	David Wright	10.00
IR	Ivan Rodriguez	8.00
LB	Lance Berkman	8.00
MT	Miguel Tejada	5.00
TH	Todd Helton	8.00
JV	Justin Verlander	15.00
MH	Matt Holliday	8.00
AP	Albert Pujols	20.00
VG	Vladimir Guerrero	8.00
JR	Jose Reyes	10.00
PF	Prince Fielder	15.00
CC	Carl Crawford	5.00
MR	Manny Ramirez	8.00
IS	Ichiro Suzuki	20.00
EC	Eric Chavez	5.00
CM	Cameron Maybin	10.00
CS	Curt Schilling	8.00
DWW	Dontrelle Willis	5.00

In The Name Relics

No Pricing

Topps 50th Anniversary All-Rookie Team Relics

		NM/M
Production 50 sets		
DS	Darryl Strawberry	20.00
AD	Andre Dawson	40.00
DW	Dontrelle Willis	10.00
MP	Mike Piazza	40.00
TS	Tom Seaver	40.00
OS	Ozzie Smith	40.00
IR	Ivan Rodriguez	25.00
DG	Dwight Gooden	15.00
GC	Gary Carter	20.00
AS	Alfonso Soriano	30.00
IS	Ichiro Suzuki	40.00
MH	Matt Holliday	25.00
JR	Jimmy Rollins	30.00
PF	Prince Fielder	40.00
DJ	David Justice	20.00
JV	Justin Verlander	40.00
AJ	Andruw Jones	20.00
CJ	Chipper Jones	30.00
RO	Roy Oswalt	20.00
BW	Brandon Webb	25.00

Commemorative Patch Relics

		NM/M
Production 499-539		
AIR	Alex Rios	15.00
AP	Albert Pujols	20.00
AR	Alex Rodriguez	25.00
BW	Brandon Webb	10.00
CC	Carl Crawford	8.00
CH	Cole Hamels	20.00
CMS	Curt Schilling	15.00
CS	C.C. Sabathia	15.00
CU	Chase Utley	20.00
DAO	David Ortiz	30.00
DO	David Ortiz	15.00
DP	Dustin Pedroia	25.00
DW	David Wright	20.00
GS	Grady Sizemore	15.00
HO	Hideki Okajima	20.00
IS	Ichiro Suzuki	30.00
JAV	Jason Varitek	20.00
JB	Josh Beckett	25.00
JCL	Julio Lugo	15.00
JDD	J.D. Drew	20.00
JE	Jacoby Ellsbury	40.00
JL	Jon Lester	25.00
JM	Justin Morneau	20.00
JP	Jake Peavy	15.00
JR	Jose Reyes	15.00
JRP	Jonathan Papelbon	25.00
JV	Justin Verlander	15.00
KY	Kevin Youkilis	20.00
MH	Matt Holliday	15.00
ML	Mike Lowell	25.00
MR	Manny Ramirez	20.00
MT	Mike Timlin	15.00
PF	Prince Fielder	20.00
RH	Ryan Howard	25.00
RM	Russell Martin	15.00

The Presidential Stamp Collection

		NM/M
Production 90 Sets		
GW1	George Washington	50.00
GW2	George Washington	50.00
GW3	George Washington	50.00
GW4	George Washington	50.00
GW5	George Washington	50.00
GW6	George Washington	50.00
TJ1	Thomas Jefferson	60.00
TJ2	Thomas Jefferson	60.00
TJ3	Thomas Jefferson	60.00
TJ4	Thomas Jefferson	60.00
JM1	James Monroe	60.00
JQA1	John Quincy Adams	60.00
AJ1	Andrew Jackson	60.00
WHH1	William Henry Harrison	40.00
JT1	John Tyler	60.00
ZT1	Zachary Taylor	50.00
JB1	James Buchanan	50.00
AL1	Abraham Lincoln	60.00
AL2	Abraham Lincoln	60.00
AL3	Abraham Lincoln	60.00
JG1	James Garfield	50.00
BH1	Benjamin Harrison	50.00
TR1	Teddy Roosevelt	60.00
WW1	Woodrow Wilson	60.00
WGH1	Warren G. Harding	50.00
HH1	Herbert Hoover	40.00
FDR1	Franklin Delano Roosevelt	50.00
DDE1	Dwight D. Eisenhower	60.00
JFK1	John F. Kennedy	100.00
JFK2	John F. Kennedy	100.00

2008 Topps Heritage

		NM/M
Complete Set (500):		275.00
Common Player:		.40
Common SP:		5.00
Inserted 1:3		
Common Black Back:		3.00
Pack (8):		3.50
Box (24):		75.00
1	Vladimir Guerrero	1.00
2	Placido Polanco	.40
2	Placido Polanco/ Black Back	3.00
3	Eric Byrnes	.50
3	Eric Byrnes/ Black back	4.00
4	Mark Teixeira	.75
5	Javier Vazquez	.40
5	Javier Vazquez/ Black back	3.00
6	Jacoby Ellsbury	2.00
7	Joey Gathright	.40
7	Joey Gathright/ Black back	3.00
8	Philadelphia Phillies	.75
8	Philadelphia Phillies/ Black back	4.00
9	Andre Ethier	.40
9	Andre Ethier/ Black back	3.00
10	Alex Rodriguez	3.00
11	Luke Scott/SP	5.00
12	Curt Schilling	1.00
12	Curt Schilling/ Black back	4.00
13	Billy Wagner	.40
13	Billy Wagner/ Black back	3.00
14	Gary Matthews Jr.	.40
14	Gary Matthews Jr./ Black back	3.00
15	Sean Marshall	.50
16	Ichiro Suzuki	2.00
16	Ichiro Suzuki/ Black back	5.00
17	Jason Bay, Freddy Sanchez, Jack Wilson	.40
18	Dontrelle Willis	.40
18	Dontrelle Willis/ Black back	3.00
19	Josh Willingham	.40
20	Jeff Kent	.50
21	Troy Tulowitzki	.75
21	Troy Tulowitzki/ Black back	4.00
22	Brian Fuentes	.40
22	Brian Fuentes/ Black back	3.00
23	Robinson Cano	.75
23	Robinson Cano/ Black back	4.00
24	Felix Hernandez	.75
24	Felix Hernandez/ Black back	4.00
25	Edwin Encarnacion	.40
26	Fausto Carmona	.40
27	Greg Maddux	1.50
28	Ivan Rodriguez	.75
28	Ivan Rodriguez/ Black back	4.00
29	Joe Nathan	.40
30	Paul Konerko	.75
31	Nook Logan	.40
32	Derek Lowe	.40
33	Jose Lopez	.40
34	Magglio Ordonez, Curtis Granderson	.50
34	Ordonez, Granderson/ Black back	3.00
35	Adam LaRoche	.40
35	Adam LaRoche/ Black back	3.00
36	Kenny Lofton	.40
37	Matt Capps	.40
38	Mark Reynolds	.40
39	Joe Mauer	.50
40	Tim Hudson	.50
40	Tim Hudson/ Black back	3.00
41	Kelvim Escobar	.40
41	Kelvim Escobar/ Black back	3.00
42	Jason Jennings	.40
42	Jason Jennings/ Black back	3.00
43	Victor Martinez	.75
44	Jason Kendall	.40
45	Chris Ray	.40
45	Chris Ray/Black back	3.00
46	Jason Bergmann	.40
47	Jason Marquis	.40
48	Baltimore Orioles	.50
49	Bill Hall	.40
49	Bill Hall/Black back	3.00
50	Ken Griffey Jr.	2.00
51	Chad Cordero	.40
52	Omar Vizquel	.40
52	Omar Vizquel/ Black back	3.00
53	Jim Edmonds	.50
54	Justin Upton	1.00
54	Justin Upton/ Black back	4.00
55	Josh Beckett	1.00
56	Jeff Francis	.40
57	Brad Lidge	.40
57	Brad Lidge/Black back	3.00
58	Paul LoDuca	.40
58	Paul LoDuca/ Black back	3.00
59	John Patterson	.40
60	Andy Pettitte	.75
60	Andy Pettitte/ Black back	3.00
61	Brendan Harris	.40
61	Brendan Harris/ Black back	3.00
62	Chris Young	.50
62	Chris Young/ Black back	3.00
63	Eric Chavez	.40
64	Francisco Rodriguez	.50
65	Jason Giambi	.75
65	Jason Giambi/ Black back	3.00
66	B.J. Ryan	.40
67	Rich Hill	.50
67	Rich Hill/Black back	3.00
68	Derek Jeter	3.00
69	San Francisco Giants	.50
69	San Francisco Giants/ Black back	3.00
70	Carlos Guillen	.50
71	Trevor Hoffman	.40
71	Trevor Hoffman/ Black back	.40
72	Zachary Duke	.40
73	Dustin Pedroia	.50
74	Ryan Zimmerman, Dmitri Young	.50
75	Cole Hamels	.75
76	Carlos Delgado	.50
77	Jonathan Broxton	.40
78	Josh Hamilton	.50
78	Josh Hamilton/ Black back	4.00
79	Mark Loretta	.40
79	Mark Loretta/ Black back	3.00
80	Grady Sizemore	1.00
81	Torii Hunter	.75
81	Torii Hunter/ Black back	3.00
82	Carlos Beltran	1.00
82	Carlos Beltran/ Black back	4.00
83	Jason Isringhausen	.40
83	Jason Isringhausen/ Black back	3.00
84	Brad Penny	.40
84	Brad Penny/ Black back	3.00
85	Jayson Werth	.40
86	Alex Gordon	.75
87	David DeJesus	.40
88	Clay Buchholz	.75
89	Conor Jackson	.40
90	Hideki Matsui	1.50
90	Hideki Matsui/ Black back	5.00
91	Matt Garza	.40
91	Matt Garza/Black back	3.00
92	Phil Hughes	1.00
92	Phil Hughes/ Black back	5.00
93	Mike Piazza	.75
94	Chicago White Sox	.40
94	Chicago White Sox/ Black back	3.00
95	Buddy Carlyle	.40
96	Mark DeRosa	.40
97	Brandon Webb	.75
98	Jon Garland	.40
98	Jon Garland/ Black back	3.00
99	Mariano Rivera	.75
100	Jack Cust	.40
101	Carlos Ruiz	.40
102	Moises Alou	.50
102	Moises Alou/ Black back	3.00
103	Bengie Molina	.40
104	Adam Jones	.40
105	Alfonso Soriano	1.00
106	Troy Glaus	.75
107	John Maine	.50
108	Pat Burrell	.50
109	David Eckstein	.40
110	Homer Bailey	.50
111	Cincinnati Reds	.50
112	Corey Hart	.50
113	Orlando Hernandez	.50
114	Orlando Cabrera	.50
115	Ryan Garko	.40
116	Wladimir Balentien	.40
116	Wladimir Balentien/ Black back	3.00
117	Daric Barton	.40
117	Daric Barton/ Black back	3.00
118	Emilio Bonifacio **RC**	.75
119	Lance Broadway **RC**	.75
120	Jeff Clement	.40
121	David Davidson **RC**	.40
122	Ross Detwiler **RC**	1.00
122	Ross Detwiler/ Black back	3.00
123	Sam Fuld **RC**	1.00
124	Armando Galarraga	.40
125	Harvey Garcia	.40
126	Daniel Giese	.40
126	Daniel Giese/ Black back	3.00
127	Alberto Gonzalez **RC**	.50
127	Alberto Gonzalez/ Black back	3.00
128	Kevin Hart	.40
129	Luke Hochevar **RC**	.75
129	Luke Hochevar/ Black back	4.00
130	Chin-Lung Hu	.40
130	Chin-Lung Hu/ Black back	3.00
131	Brandon Jones **RC**	.75
132	Joe Koshansky	.40
133	Radhames Liz **RC**	.50
134	Donny Lucy	.40
135	Mitch Stetter **RC**	.50
135	Mitch Stetter/ Black back	3.00
136	Nyjer Morgan	.40
137	Ross Ohlendorf **RC**	.40
138	Steve Pearce **RC**	1.00
139	Jeff Ridgway	.40
140	Bronson Sardinha	.40
141	Seth Smith	.40
142	Rich Thompson	.40
143	Erick Threets	.40
144	J.R. Towles **RC**	1.00
145	Eugenio Velez **RC**	.50
146	Joey Votto	.40
147	Alfonso Soriano, Aramis Ramirez, Derrek Lee	.50
148	Hunter Pence	.75
149	Barry Zito	.40
150	Albert Pujols	3.00
150	Albert Pujols/ Black back	6.00
151	Sammy Sosa	.40
152	Brian Bannister	.40
153	Reggie Willits	.40
154	Bobby Abreu	.75
155	Johnny Damon	.75
155	Johnny Damon/ Black back	4.00
156	Brandon Webb, Jake Peavy	.50
157	Aramis Ramirez	.75
158	Mark Buehrle	.40
159	David Weathers	.40
160	Jack Wilson	.40
161	Josh Fogg	.40
162	Garrett Atkins	.40
163	Brad Ausmus	.40
164	Gil Meche	.40
165	Jeff Francoeur	.50
166	Grady Sizemore, Travis Hafner, Victor Martinez	.50
167	Juan Pierre	.40
168	Rafael Furcal	.40
169	J.J. Hardy	.40
170	Nicholas Markakis	.50
171	Delmon Young	.50
172	Oakland A's	.40
173	Ronny Paulino	.40
173	Ronny Paulino/ Black back	3.00
174	Mike Cameron	.40
174	Mike Cameron/ Black back	3.00
175	Jeff Weaver	.40
175	Jeff Weaver/ Black back	3.00
176	Preston Wilson	.40
176	Preston Wilson/ Black back	3.00
177	Robinson Tejeda	.40
177	Robinson Tejeda/ Black back	3.00
178	Adam Lind	.40
178	Adam Lind/Black back	3.00
179	Austin Kearns	.40
179	Austin Kearns/ Black back	3.00
180	Jorge Posada	.75
180	Jorge Posada/ Black back	4.00
181	Tadahito Iguchi	.40
182	Matt Cain	.50
183	Yuniesky Betancourt	.40
184	Bronson Arroyo	.40
185	Brad Hawpe	.40
185	Brad Hawpe/ Black back	3.00
186	Rickie Weeks	.50
186	Rickie Weeks/ Black back	3.00
187	Carlos Silva	.40
187	Carlos Silva/ Black back	3.00
188	Adrian Gonzalez	.50
189	Kenji Johjima	.50
190	Chris Duncan	.40
191	James Shields	.50
192	Akinori Iwamura	.50
193	David Murphy	.40
194	Alex Rios	.75
195	Carlos Quentin	.40
195	Carlos Quentin/ Black back	3.00
196	Jose Valverde	.40
196	Jose Valverde/ Black back	3.00
197	Derrek Lee	.75
197	Derrek Lee/Black back	4.00
198	Jerry Owens	.40
198	Jerry Owens/ Black back	3.00
199	Russell Martin	.75
200	Yovani Gallardo	.75
201	Johan Santana	1.00
202	Nick Swisher	.50
203	So Taguchi	.40
204	Justin Morneau	.75
205	Milton Bradley	.40
206	Jake Westbrook	.40
207	Dave Roberts	.40
208	Billy Butler	.40
209	Lance Berkman	.75
210	J.J. Putz	.40
210	J.J. Putz/Black back	3.00
211	Mike Sweeney	.40
211	Mike Sweeney/ Black back	3.00
212	Andruw Jones, Chipper Jones	.50
213	Ricky Nolasco	.40
214	Andy LaRoche	.50
215	Ray Durham	.40
216	Francisco Cordero	.40
217	Jered Weaver	.50
218	Rafael Soriano	.40
219	Orlando Hudson	.40
220	Mike Lowell	.50
221	Chris Snyder	.40
222	Cesar Izturis	.40
223	St. Louis Cardinals	.50
224	David Wright	1.50
224	David Wright/ Black back	5.00
225	Pedro Martinez	1.00
225	Pedro Martinez/ Black back	4.00
226	Rich Harden	.40
226	Rich Harden/ Black back	3.00
227	Shane Victorino	.50
227	Shane Victorino/ Black back	3.00
228	Andrew Miller	.50
228	Andrew Miller/ Black back	3.00
229	Chris Young	.50
230	Andruw Jones	.50
231	Kevin Gregg/SP	5.00
232	C.C. Sabathia	.75
233	Hanley Ramirez	1.00
234	Wandy Rodriguez	.40
235	Roy Oswalt	.75
236	Mark Grudzielanek	.40
237	Derek Jeter, Chien-Ming Wang, Robinson Cano	1.00
238	Todd Helton	.75
239	Zack Greinke	.40
240	Carlos Gomez	.40
241	Lastings Milledge	.40
242	Huston Street	.40
243	Danny Haren	.40
244	Carlos Pena	.75
245	Brad Wilkerson	.40
246	Roy Halladay	.40
247	Dmitri Young	.40
248	Boston Red Sox	1.00
249	Jonathan Papelbon	.75
250	Felix Pie	.40
251	Alex Gonzalez	.40
252	Bobby Crosby	.40
253	Justin Ruggiano **RC**	.75
254	Freddy Garcia	.40
255	Khalil Greene	.50
256	Rich Aurilia	.40
257	Jarrod Washburn	.40
258	B.J. Upton	.50
259	Michael Young	.40
260	Carlos Zambrano	.75
261	Livan Hernandez	.40
262	Derek Lowe, Brad Penny, Chad Billingsley	.40
262	Lowe, Penny, Billingsley/ Black back	3.00
263	Melky Cabrera	.50
263	Melky Cabrera/ Black back	3.00
264	Shannon Stewart	.40
264	Shannon Stewart/ Black back	3.00
265	Aaron Rowand	.50
265	Aaron Rowand/ Black back	3.00
266	Matt Morris	.40
266	Matt Morris/ Black back	3.00
267	Xavier Nady	.50
267	Xavier Nady/ Black back	3.00
268	Jim Thome	.75
269	Horacio Ramirez	.40
270	Prince Fielder	1.00
271	Andy Phillips	.40
272	Aaron Harang	.40
273	Josh Barfield	.40
274	Ubaldo Jimenez	.40
275	Anibal Sanchez	.40
276	Carlos Lee	.50
277	Mark Teahen	.40
278	Delwyn Young	.40
279	Kurt Suzuki	.40
280	Nate Schierholtz	.40
281	Raul Ibanez	.40
282	Jose Vidro	.40
283	Miguel Cabrera	1.00

283	Miguel Cabrera/Black back	4.00
284	Luis Gonzalez	.40
284	Luis Gonzalez/Black back	3.00
285	Chad Billingsley	.40
285	Chad Billingsley/Black back	3.00
286	Tony Gwynn Jr.	.40
286	Tony Gwynn Jr./Black back	3.00
287	Matthew Kemp	.75
288	James Loney	.50
289	Brett Myers	.40
290	Nate McLouth	.40
291	Matt Chico, Jason Bergmann	.40
291	Matt Chico, Jason Bergmann/Black back	3.00
292	Chad Tracy	.40
293	Edgar Renteria	.40
294	Jay Payton	.40
295	Josh Johnson	.40
296	Josh Banks	.40
297	Bill Murphy	.40
298	Ben Sheets	.50
299	Jose Reyes	1.00
300	Chase Utley	1.00
301	Ronnie Belliard	.40
301	Ronnie Belliard/Black back	3.00
302	Wily Mo Pena	.40
303	Tim Lincecum	.75
304	Chicago Cubs	.75
305	John Lackey	.40
306	Stephen Drew	.75
307	Kelly Johnson	.40
308	Daisuke Matsuzaka	2.00
309	Craig Monroe	.40
310	Jerry Owens	.40
311	Jeff Suppan	.40
312	Tom Glavine	.75
313	Kei Igawa	.40
314	Mark Kotsay	.40
315	Jacque Jones/SP	5.00
316	Melvin Mora	.40
317	Matt Holliday, Hanley Ramirez	.75
318	Jarrod Saltalamacchia	.50
319	A.J. Burnett	.40
320	Casey Kotchman	.40
321	Randy Winn	.40
321	Randy Winn/Black back	3.00
322	Richie Sexson	.50
322	Richie Sexson/Black back	3.00
323	Juan Encarnacion	.40
323	Juan Encarnacion/Black back	3.00
324	Rick Ankiel	.50
324	Rick Ankiel/Black back	3.00
325	Dan Wheeler	.40
325	Dan Wheeler/Black back	3.00
326	Brian Roberts	.50
327	David Ortiz	1.00
328	Garret Anderson	.40
329	Detroit Tigers	.50
330	Ty Wigginton	.40
330	Ty Wigginton/Black back	3.00
331	Travis Hafner	.50
332	Howie Kendrick	.50
332	Howie Kendrick/Black back	3.00
333	Kevin Kouzmanoff	.50
333	Kevin Kouzmanoff/Black back	3.00
334	Matt Holliday	.75
334	Matt Holliday/Black back	4.00
335	Brandon Phillips	.50
335	Brandon Phillips/Black back	3.00
336	Ian Kinsler	.50
336	Ian Kinsler/Black back	3.00
337	Lyle Overbay	.50
337	Lyle Overbay/Black back	3.00
338	Justin Verlander	.75
338	Justin Verlander/Black back	4.00
339	Ian Snell	.50
340	Hank Blalock	.50
341	Vernon Wells	.50
342	Matt Chico	.40
343	Tim Wakefield	.40
344	Michael Bourn	.40
345	Chris Carpenter	.50
346	Josh Beckett, Daisuke Matsuzaka	1.00
347	Chuck James	.40
347	Chuck James/Black back	3.00
348	Joba Chamberlain	3.00
349	Erik Bedard	.75
350	Jimmy Rollins	.75
350	Jimmy Rollins/Black back	4.00
351	Anthony Reyes	.40
352	Carl Crawford	.50
353	Jeremy Hermida	.40
354	Ervin Santana	.40
355	Edgar Gonzalez	.40
356	Yunel Escobar	.40
357	Yorvit Torrealba	.40
358	Hideki Okajima	.50
359	Paul Byrd	.40
360	Magglio Ordonez	.50
360	Magglio Ordonez/Black back	3.00
361	Joe Borowski	.40
362	Clint Sammons	.40
363	Chris Duffy	.40
364	Fred Lewis	.40
365	Adrian Beltre	.50
366	Alex Rodriguez	3.00
367	Troy Tulowitzki	.75
368	Prince Fielder	1.00
369	Clay Buchholz	.75
370	Justin Verlander	.75
370	Justin Verlander/Black back	4.00
371	Pedro Martinez	1.00
371	Pedro Martinez/Black back	4.00
372	Ryan Howard	1.00
372	Ryan Howard/Black back	5.00
373	Ichiro Suzuki	2.00
374	Kenny Lofton	.40
375	Manny Ramirez	.75
376	Randy Johnson	1.00
377	Chris Capuano	.40
378	Johnny Estrada	.40
379	Franklin Morales	.40
380	Ryan Howard	1.00
381	Casey Blake/SP	5.00
382	Coco Crisp	.40
383	John Maine, Willie Randolph	.40
384	Jeremy Guthrie	.40
385	Geoff Jenkins	.40
386	Marlon Byrd	.40
387	Jeremy Bonderman	.50
388	Ryan Howard	1.00
389	Joe Girardi	.40
390	Ryan Braun	1.00
391	Ryan Zimmerman	.75
392	Dustin Pedroia, Kevin Youkilis, Mike Lowell	.50
393	Pittsburgh Pirates	.40
394	Ryan Spilborghs	.40
395	Eric Gagne	.40
396	Joe Blanton	.40
397	Washington Nationals	.40
398	Ryan Church	.40
399	Ted Lilly	.40
400	Manny Ramirez	.75
401	Chad Gaudin	.40
402	Dustin McGowan	.40
403	Scott Baker	.40
404	Franklin Gutierrez	.40
405	David Bush	.40
406	Aubrey Huff	.40
407	Jermaine Dye	.40
408	Chase Utley, Jimmy Rollins	.75
409	Jon Lester/SP	5.00
410	Aaron Cook	.40
411	Sergio Mitre	.40
412	Jason Bartlett	.40
413	Edwin Jackson	.40
414	J.D. Drew	.40
415	Freddy Sanchez	.40
415	Freddy Sanchez/Black back	3.00
416	Asdrubal Cabrera	.40
417	Nate Robertson	.40
418	Shaun Marcum	.40
419	Noah Lowry	.40
420	Atlanta Braves	.50
421	Jamie Moyer	.40
422	Michael Cuddyer	.40
423	Randy Wolf	.40
424	Juan Uribe	.40
425	Brian McCann	.50
426	Kyle Lohse/SP	5.00
427	Doug Davis/SP	5.00
428	Ian Snell, Tom Gorzelanny, Matt Capps/SP	5.00
429	Miguel Batista/SP	5.00
430	Chien-Ming Wang/SP	10.00
431	Jeff Salazar/SP	5.00
432	Yadier Molina/SP	5.00
433	Adam Wainwright/SP	5.00
434	Scott Kazmir/SP	5.00
435	Adam Dunn/SP	6.00
436	Ryan Freel/SP	5.00
437	Jhonny Peralta/SP	5.00
438	Kazuo Matsui/SP	5.00
439	Daniel Cabrera	.40
440	John Smoltz	.75
441	Emil Brown/SP	5.00
442	Gary Sheffield/SP	5.00
443	Jake Peavy/SP	8.00
444	Scott Rolen/SP	5.00
445	Kason Gabbard/SP	5.00
446	Aaron Hill/SP	5.00
447	Felipe Lopez/SP	5.00
448	Dan Uggla/SP	5.00
449	Willy Taveras/SP	5.00
450	Chipper Jones/SP	6.00
451	Josh Anderson/SP	5.00
452	Eric Byrnes, Chris Young, Justin Upton/SP	5.00
453	Braden Looper/SP	5.00
454	Brandon Inge/SP	5.00
455	Brian Giles/SP	5.00
456	Corey Patterson/SP	5.00
457	Los Angeles Dodgers/SP	5.00
458	Sean Casey/SP	5.00
459	Pedro Feliz/SP	5.00
460	Tom Gorzelanny	.40
461	Chone Figgins/SP	5.00
462	Kyle Kendrick/SP	5.00
463	Tony Pena/SP	5.00
464	Marcus Giles/SP	5.00
465	Augie Ojeda/SP	5.00
466	Micah Owings/SP	5.00
467	Ryan Theriot/SP	5.00
468	Shawn Green/SP	5.00
469	Frank Thomas/SP	6.00
470	Lenny DiNardo/SP	5.00
471	Jose Bautista/SP	5.00
472	Manny Corpas/SP	5.00
473	Kevin Millwood/SP	5.00
474	Kevin Youkilis/SP	5.00
475	Jose Contreras/SP	5.00
476	Cleveland Indians	.50
477	Julio Lugo/SP	5.00
478	Jason Bay	.75
479	Tony LaRussa/SP	5.00
480	Jim Leyland/SP	5.00
481	Derrek Lee/SP	6.00
482	Justin Morneau/SP	6.00
483	Orlando Hudson/SP	5.00
484	Brian Roberts/SP	5.00
485	Miguel Cabrera/SP	6.00
486	Mike Lowell/SP	5.00
487	J.J. Hardy/SP	5.00
488	Carlos Guillen/SP	5.00
489	Ken Griffey Jr./SP	8.00
490	Vladimir Guerrero/SP	6.00
491	Alfonso Soriano/SP	6.00
492	Ichiro Suzuki/SP	8.00
493	Matt Holliday/SP	6.00
494	Magglio Ordonez/SP	5.00
495	Brian McCann/SP	5.00
496	Victor Martinez/SP	5.00
497	Brad Penny/SP	5.00
498	Josh Beckett/SP	6.00
499	Cole Hamels/SP	6.00
500	Justin Verlander/SP	6.00

New Age Performers

NM/M

Complete Set (15): 12.00
Common Player: .50
Inserted 1:15

1	Magglio Ordonez	1.00
2	Ichiro Suzuki	2.00
3	Matt Holliday	1.00
4	Prince Fielder	1.00
5	David Wright	2.00
6	Jake Peavy	.75
7	Alex Rodriguez	3.00
8	John Lackey	.50
9	Vladimir Guerrero	1.00
10	Ryan Howard	1.00
11	Brandon Webb	.50
12	Manny Ramirez	1.00
13	Josh Beckett	1.00
14	Jimmy Rollins	1.00
15	David Ortiz	1.00

Then & Now

NM/M

Complete Set (10): 12.00
Common Duo: 1.00
Inserted 1:15

1	Alex Rodriguez, Eddie Mathews	3.00
2	Alex Rodriguez, Ernie Banks	3.00
3	Magglio Ordonez, Orlando Cepeda	1.00
4	Jose Reyes, Luis Aparicio	1.50
5	David Ortiz, Mickey Mantle	3.00
6	Erik Bedard, Johnny Podres	1.00
7	Josh Beckett, Early Wynn	1.00
8	Ichiro Suzuki, Minnie Minoso	2.00
9	David Ortiz, Frank Robinson	1.50
10	Jake Peavy, Don Drysdale	1.00

Flashbacks

NM/M

Complete Set (10): 10.00
Common Player: .50
Inserted 1:12

1	Minnie Minoso	.50
2	Luis Aparicio	.50
3	Ernie Banks	1.50
4	Bill Mazeroski	.50
5	Bob Gibson	1.50
6	Frank Robinson	1.50
7	Brooks Robinson	1.50
8	Mickey Mantle	3.00
9	Orlando Cepeda	.50
10	Eddie Mathews	1.50

News Flashbacks

NM/M

Complete Set (10): 10.00
Common Card: 1.00
Inserted 1:12

1	Alaska becomes 49th State	1.00
2	The Day the Music Died	1.00
3	Castro becomes Prime Minister of Cuba	1.00
4	Dalai Lama flees to India	1.00
5	NASA 1st 7 Astronauts	1.00
6	Nixon and Khrushchev	1.00
7	Hawaii becomes 50th State	1.00
8	USSR's Luna 2	1.00
9	In Cold Blood murders committed	1.00
10	Antarctic Treaty	1.00

Autographs

NM/M

Inserted 1:247
Red Ink: 1.5X
Production 59 Sets

MB	Mike Baxes	50.00
BB	Bob Blaylock	60.00
JB	Jim Bolger	60.00
TC	Tom Carroll	50.00
PC	Phil Clark	50.00
CE	Carl Erskine	60.00
RH	Russ Heman	50.00
RJ	Randy Jackson	60.00
TK	Ted Kazanski	50.00
CK	Chick King	50.00
KL	Ken Lehman	50.00
MM	Morrie Martin	60.00
BM	Bob Martyn	50.00
LM	Les Moss	60.00
JO	Johnny O'Brien	50.00
HP	Herb Plews	50.00
JP	J.W. Porter	60.00
TQ	Tom Qualters	50.00
BR	Bill Renna	50.00
BS	Bob Smith	50.00
BSP	Bob Speake	60.00
LT	Lee Tate	50.00
VV	Vito Valentinetti	40.00
GEZ	Gus Zernial	60.00
GZ	George Zuverink	60.00
MIM	Minnie Minoso	65.00
YB	Yogi Berra	120.00
LA	Luis Aparicio	80.00
WM	Bill Mazeroski	85.00
JC	Joba Chamberlain	150.00
FS	Freddy Sanchez	40.00
AR	Aramis Ramirez	40.00
SP	Scott Podsednik	40.00

Dual Autographs

Production 25 Sets

Flashbacks Autographs

NM/M

Production 25 Sets 10.00

1959 Cut Signatures

Production One Set

Clubhouse Collection

NM/M

Common Player: 5.00

MIM	Minnie Minoso	25.00
YB	Yogi Berra	25.00
LA	Luis Aparicio	15.00
BG	Bob Gibson	20.00
WM	Bill Mazeroski	20.00
AD	Adam Dunn	8.00
AJ	Andruw Jones	8.00
AR	Aramis Ramirez	10.00
BA	Bobby Abreu	8.00
CC	Carl Crawford	8.00
CB	Carlos Beltran	8.00
CD	Carlos Delgado	8.00
CL	Carlos Lee	5.00
CAB	Craig Biggio	8.00
DL	Derrek Lee	8.00
DO	David Ortiz	15.00
DY	Dmitri Young	5.00
EC	Eric Chavez	5.00
FT	Frank Thomas	10.00
GA	Garret Anderson	5.00
HB	Hank Blalock	5.00
IR	Ivan Rodriguez	8.00
JE	Jim Edmonds	5.00
JS	John Smoltz	8.00
JD	Johnny Damon	10.00
JP	Jorge Posada	5.00
JV	Justin Verlander	10.00
LB	Lance Berkman	8.00
MC	Miguel Cabrera	10.00
MT	Miguel Tejada	5.00
MM	Mike Mussina	8.00
PM	Pedro Martinez	8.00
RS	Richie Sexson	5.00
RO	Roy Oswalt	8.00
RH	Ryan Howard	15.00
RZ	Ryan Zimmerman	8.00
SG	Shawn Green	5.00
TH	Todd Helton	8.00
TKH	Torii Hunter	8.00
TLH	Travis Hafner	8.00

Clubhouse Collection Dual Relics

NM/M

Production 59 Sets

MB	Bill Mazeroski, Jason Bay	125.00
BL	Ernie Banks, Derrek Lee	150.00
GE	Bob Gibson, Jim Edmonds	125.00
MH	Minnie Minoso, Travis Hafner	125.00
AK	Luis Aparicio, Paul Konerko	80.00

Flashbacks Relics

NM/M

Common Player:

MIM	Minnie Minoso	20.00
LA	Luis Aparicio	15.00
EB	Ernie Banks	25.00
WM	Bill Mazeroski	20.00
BG	Bob Gibson	20.00
FR	Frank Robinson	20.00
BR	Brooks Robinson	20.00
MM	Mickey Mantle	50.00
OC	Orlando Cepeda	20.00
EM	Eddie Mathews	20.00

Flashbacks Dual Relics

No Pricing
Production 10 Sets

Clubhouse Collection Relic Auto.

NM/M

Production 25 Sets

BG	Bob Gibson	250.00
JC	Joba Chamberlain	280.00

Flashbacks Stadium Relics

NM/M

Common player:

MM	Minnie Minoso	20.00
LA	Luis Aparicio	15.00
EB	Ernie Banks	25.00
WM	Bill Mazeroski	20.00
BG	Bob Gibson	20.00

Advertising Panels

NM/M

Common Panel: 3.00

1959 Topps Originals

See 1959 Topps pricing.

1984 Toronto Blue Jays Fire Safety

This 35-card set was issued in conjuction with the Toronto Sun newspaper and various Ontario area fire departments. The cards feature full-color action photos on the fronts, along with the player name, number and position. Rather than the customary wide white border on front, the Blue Jays fire safety set features bright blue borders. The card backs include brief player biographies and a fire safety tip. The 2-1/2" x 3-1/2" cards were distributed five at a time at two-week intervals during the summer of 1984.

NM/M

Complete Set (35): 6.00
Common Player: .25

1	Tony Fernandez	.30
3	Jimy Williams	.25
4	Alfredo Griffin	.25
5	Rance Mulliniks	.25
6	Bobby Cox	.50
7	Damaso Garcia	.25
8	John Sullivan	.25
9	Rick Leach	.25
10	Dave Collins	.25
11	George Bell	.40
12	Ernie Whitt	.25
13	Buck Martinez	.25
15	Lloyd Moseby	.25
16	Garth Iorg	.25
17	Kelly Gruber	.25
18	Jim Clancy	.25
23	Mitch Webster	.25
24	Willie Aikens	.25
25	Roy Lee Jackson	.25
26	Willie Upshaw	.25
27	Jimmy Key	.50
29	Jesse Barfield	.25
31	Jim Acker	.25
33	Doyle Alexander	.25
34	Stan Clarke	.25
35	Bryan Clark	.25
37	Dave Stieb	.40
38	Jim Gott	.25
41	Al Widmar	.25
42	Billy Smith	.25
43	Cito Gaston	.25
44	Cliff Johnson	.25
48	Luis Leal	.25
53	Dennis Lamp	.25
---	Team Logo/Checklist	.25

1985 Toronto Blue Jays Fire Safety

The Toronto Blue Jays issued a 35-card fire safety set for the second year in a row in 1985. Cards feature players, coaches, manager, checklist and team picture. The full-color photos are on the card fronts with a blue border. The backs feature player stats and a safety tip. The cards measure 2-1/2" x 3-1/2" and were distributed throughout the Province of Ontario, Canada.

NM/M

Complete Set (36): 5.00
Common Player: .25

1	Tony Fernandez	.30
3	Jimy Williams	.25
4	Manny Lee	.25
5	Rance Mulliniks	.25
6	Bobby Cox	.40
7	Damaso Garcia	.25
8	John Sullivan	.25
11	George Bell	.30
12	Ernie Whitt	.25
13	Buck Martinez	.25
15	Lloyd Moseby	.25
16	Garth Iorg	.25
17	Kelly Gruber	.25
18	Jim Clancy	.25
22	Jimmy Key	.35
23	Mitch Webster	.25
24	Willie Aikens	.25
25	Len Matuszek	.25
26	Willie Upshaw	.25
28	Lou Thornton	.25
29	Jesse Barfield	.25
30	Ron Musselman	.25
31	Jim Acker	.25
33	Doyle Alexander	.25
36	Bill Caudill	.25
37	Dave Stieb	.30
41	Al Widmar	.25
42	Billy Smith	.25
43	Cito Gaston	.25
44	Jeff Burroughs	.25
46	Gary Lavelle	.25
48	Luis Leal	.25
50	Tom Henke	.30
53	Dennis Lamp	.25
---	Team Logo/Checklist	.25
---	Team Photo/Schedule	.25

1986 Toronto Blue Jays Fire Safety

This was the third consecutive year the Toronto Blue Jays issued a fire safety set of

36 baseball cards. The cards were given out at many fire stations in Ontario, Canada. The cards are printed in full color and include players and other personnel. The set was co-sponsored by the local fire departments, Bubble Yum and the Toronto Star. The cards measure 2-1/2" x 3-1/2".

		NM/M
Complete Set (36):		6.00
Common Player:		.25
1	Tony Fernandez	.30
3	Jimy Williams	.25
5	Rance Mulliniks	.25
7	Damaso Garcia	.25
8	John Sullivan	.25
9	Rick Leach	.25
11	George Bell	.30
12	Ernie Whitt	.25
13	Buck Martinez	.25
15	Lloyd Moseby	.25
16	Garth Iorg	.25
17	Kelly Gruber	.25
18	Jim Clancy	.25
22	Jimmy Key	.30
23	Cecil Fielder	2.00
24	John McLaren	.25
25	Steve Davis	.25
26	Willie Upshaw	.25
29	Jesse Barfield	.25
31	Jim Acker	.25
33	Doyle Alexander	.25
36	Bill Caudill	.25
37	Dave Stieb	.30
38	Mark Eichhorn	.25
39	Don Gordon	.25
41	Al Widmar	.25
42	Billy Smith	.25
43	Cito Gaston	.25
44	Cliff Johnson	.25
46	Gary Lavelle	.25
49	Tom Filer	.25
50	Tom Henke	.25
53	Dennis Lamp	.25
54	Jeff Hearron	.25
---	Team Photo	.25
---	10th Anniversary Logo Card	.25

1987 Toronto Blue Jays Fire Safety

For the fourth consecutive year, the Toronto Blue Jays issued a fire safety set of 36 cards. As in 1986, the set was sponsored by the local fire departments and governing agencies, Bubble Yum and the Toronto Star. The card fronts feature a full-color photo surrounded by a white border. The backs carry a fire safety tip and logos of all sponsors, plus player personal data and statistics. Produced on thin stock, cards in the set are the standard 2-1/2" x 3-1/2" size.

		NM/M
Complete Set (36):		6.00
Common Player:		.25
1	Tony Fernandez	.30
3	Jimy Williams	.25
5	Rance Mulliniks	.25
8	John Sullivan	.25
9	Rick Leach	.25
10	Mike Sharperson	.25
11	George Bell	.30
12	Ernie Whitt	.25
15	Lloyd Moseby	.25
16	Garth Iorg	.25
17	Kelly Gruber	.25
18	Jim Clancy	.25
19	Fred McGriff	2.00
22	Jimmy Key	.30
23	Cecil Fielder	.50
24	John McLaren	.25
26	Willie Upshaw	.25
29	Jesse Barfield	.25
31	Duane Ward	.25
33	Joe Johnson	.25
35	Jeff Musselman	.25
37	Dave Stieb	.30
38	Mark Eichhorn	.25
40	Rob Ducey	.25
41	Al Widmar	.25
42	Billy Smith	.25
43	Cito Gaston	.25
45	Jose Nunez	.25
46	Gary Lavelle	.25
47	Matt Stark	.25
48	Craig McMurtry	.25
50	Tom Henke	.25
54	Jeff Hearron	.25
55	John Cerutti	.25
---	Logo/Won-Loss Record	.25
---	Team Photo/Checklist	.25

1988 Toronto Blue Jays Fire Safety

This 36-card set features action photos on 3-1/2" x 5" cards with white borders. Card numbers (player's uniform #) appear lower-left; team logo lower-right; player's name and position are printed bottom center. Card backs are blue on white and include personal and career info, 1987 and career stats, sponsor logos and a fire safety tip. The set includes 34 player cards, a team photo checklist card and a team logo card with a year-by-year won/loss record. The set was sponsored by the Ontario Fire Chief Association, Ontario's Solicitor General, The Toronto Star and Bubble Yum and was distributed free as part of a community service project. At least some of the cards have been seen in a blank-back version, apparently used to answer fans autograph requests.

		NM/M
Complete Set (36):		5.00
Common Player:		.25
1	Tony Fernandez	.30
2	Nelson Liriano	.25
3	Jimy Williams	.25
4	Manny Lee	.25
5	Rance Mulliniks	.25
6	Silvestre Campusano	.25
7	John McLaren	.25
8	John Sullivan	.25
9	Rick Leach	.25
10	Pat Borders	.30
11	George Bell	.30
12	Ernie Whitt	.25
13	Jeff Musselman	.25
15	Lloyd Moseby	.25
16	Todd Stottlemyre	.75
17	Kelly Gruber	.25
18	Jim Clancy	.25
19	Fred McGriff	.75
21	Juan Beniquez	.25
22	Jimmy Key	.30
23	Cecil Fielder	.30
29	Jesse Barfield	.25
31	Duane Ward	.25
36	David Wells	1.00
37	Dave Stieb	.30
38	Mark Eichhorn	.25
40	Rob Ducey	.25
41	Al Widmar	.25
42	Billy Smith	.25
43	Cito Gaston	.25
46	Mike Flanagan	.25
50	Tom Henke	.25
55	John Cerutti	.25
57	Winston Llenas	.25
---	Team Photo	.25
---	Team Logo	.25

1989 Toronto Blue Jays Fire Safety

The 1989 Blue Jays safety set consists of 36 standard-size cards co-sponsored by the Ontario Association of Fire Chiefs, Oh Henry! candy bars and A&P supermarkets. Card fronts feature color photos with the player's uniform number in large type in the upper left corner. His name and position are to the right above the photo. The Blue Jays "On the Move" logo is centered at the bottom. The backs of the cards include fire safety messages.

		NM/M
Complete Set (36):		6.00
Common Player:		.25
1	Tony Fernandez	.30
2	Nelson Liriano	.25
3	Jimy Williams	.25
4	Manny Lee	.25
5	Rance Mulliniks	.25
6	Silvestre Campusano	.25
7	John McLaren	.25
8	John Sullivan	.25
9	Bob Brenly	.25
10	Pat Borders	.25
11	George Bell	.30
12	Ernie Whitt	.25
13	Jeff Musselman	.25
15	Lloyd Moseby	.25
16	Greg Myers	.25
17	Kelly Gruber	.25
18	Tom Lawless	.25
19	Fred McGriff	.50
22	Jimmy Key	.30
25	Mike Squires	.25
26	Sal Butera	.25
29	Jesse Barfield	.25
30	Todd Stottlemyre	.35
31	Duane Ward	.25
36	David Wells	.50
37	Dave Steib	.30
40	Rob Ducey	.25
41	Al Widman	.25
43	Cito Gaston	.25
44	Frank Wills	.25
45	Jose Nunez	.25
46	Mike Flanagan	.25
50	Tom Henke	.25
55	John Cerutti	.25
---	Team Photo	.25
---	Team Logo	.25

1990 Toronto Blue Jays Fire Safety

This 35-card set was co-sponsored by the Ontario Association of Fire Chiefs, The Ministry of the Solicitor General, A & P/Dominion, Oh Henry, and the Toronto Blue Jays. The card fronts feature full-color photos on white stock and display a special Blue Jays fan club logo in the upper left corner. The flip sides feature biographical information, statistics, and a fire fact. The cards are checklisted here by uniform number.

		NM/M
Complete Set (35):		6.00
Common Player:		.25
1	Tony Fernandez	.30
2	Nelson Liriano	.25
3	Mookie Wilson	.25
4	Manny Lee	.25
5	Rance Mulliniks	.25
7	John McLaren	.25
8	John Sullivan	.25
9	John Olerud	2.00
10	Pat Borders	.25
11	George Bell	.30
15	Gene Tenace	.25
18	Tom Lawless	.25
19	Fred McGriff	.50
21	Greg Myers	.25
22	Jimmy Key	.30
23	Alex Sanchez	.25
24	Glenallen Hill	.25
25	Mike Squires	.25
26	Ozzie Virgil	.25
27	Willie Blair	.25
28	Al Leiter	.30
30	Todd Stottlemyre	.30
31	Duane Ward	.25
34	Jim Acker	.25
36	David Wells	.50
37	Dave Steib	.30
39	Paul Kilgus	.25
42	Galen Cisco	.25
43	Cito Gaston	.25
44	Frank Wills	.25
47	Junior Felix	.25
50	Tom Henke	.25
55	John Cerutti	.25
---	Skydome/Checklist	.25
---	Logo/Schedule	.25

1991 Toronto Blue Jays Fire Safety

The Blue Jays played host to the 1991 All-Star Game and the team's annual fire safety set prominently featured that honor. A headercard with the Jays All-Star logo was included in the set and each card carried the logo in full color on the front. The 2-1/2" x 3-1/2" cards have a color action photo at top which bleeds off the top and sides. Beneath the photo is a white border with the player's name, position and uniform number. Backs are printed in black-and-white and have a few biographical notes, 1990 and career stats, a Fire Fact safety message and logos of the cards' sponsors.

		NM/M
Complete Set (36):		6.00
Common Player:		.25
3	Mookie Wilson	.25
4	Manuel Lee	.25
5	Rance Mulliniks	.25
6	Mike Squires	.25
7	Rich Hacker	.25
8	John Sullivan	.25
9	John Olerud	.50
10	Pat Borders	.25
12	Roberto Alomar	3.00
13	Kenny Williams	.25
15	Pat Tabler	.25
17	Kelly Gruber	.25
18	Gene Tenace	.25
20	Rob Ducey	.25
21	Greg Myers	.25
22	Jimmy Key	.30
23	Mark Whiten	.25
24	Glenallen Hill	.25
25	Devon White	.35
28	Al Leiter	.30
29	Joe Carter	.50
30	Todd Stottlemyre	.30
31	Duane Ward	.25
34	Jim Acker	.25
35	Denis Boucher	.25
36	David Wells	.45
37	Dave Steib	.30
42	Galen Cisco	.25
43	Cito Gaston	.25
44	Frank Wills	.25
46	Ken Dayley	.25
50	Tom Henke	.25
56	Hector Torres	.25
88	Rene Gonzales	.25
---	BJ Birdy (Mascot)	.25
---	All-Star Season Header/Checklist Card	.25

1992 Toronto Blue Jays Fire Safety

Hidden amid the myriad sponsors' logos on the backs of these cards is a fire safety message. The 2-1/2" x 3-1/2" cards are printed on thin cardboard and feature color player photos on front, along with a red, white and blue "Toronto Blue Jays Fanatic" logo. Fronts also carry uniform numbers, by which the set is checklisted here. Backs are printed in black-and-white with a few biographical details, 1991 and career stats.

		NM/M
Complete Set (36):		8.00
Common Player:		.25
1	Eddie Zosky	.25
2	Manuel Lee	.25
3	Bob Bailor	.25
4	Alfredo Griffin	.25
5	Rance Mulliniks	.25
7	Rich Hacker	.25
8	John Sullivan	.25
9	John Olerud	.50
10	Pat Borders	.25
12	Roberto Alomar	1.00
14	Derek Bell	.25
15	Pat Tabler	.25
17	Kelly Gruber	.25
18	Gene Tenace	.25
20	Rob Ducey	.25
21	Greg Myers	.25
22	Jimmy Key	.35
23	Candy Maldonado	.25
24	Turner Ward	.25
25	Devon White	.30
29	Joe Carter	.35
30	Todd Stottlemyre	.30
31	Duane Ward	.25
32	Dave Winfield	1.50
36	David Wells	.45
37	Dave Steib	.30
39	Larry Hisle	.25
40	Mike Timlin	.25
42	Galen Cisco	.25
43	Cito Gaston	.25
45	Bob MacDonald	.25
46	Ken Dayley	.25
47	Jack Morris	.25
50	Tom Henke	.25
66	Juan Guzman	.25
---	Checklist	.25

1993 Toronto Blue Jays Fire Safety

The Blue Jays produced a fire safety set for the 10th year in a row in 1993. In the first year of offering the item as a boxed set, the cards feature a full-bleed color photo on the

front, with the player's name printed in white over a blue stripe across the top of the card. The Blue Jay's 1992 World Champions logo appears in the upper left corner. Cards are checklisted here by uniform number.

		NM/M
Complete Set (36):		6.00
Common Player:		.25
1	Eddie Zosky	.25
2	Luis Sojo	.25
3	Bob Bailor	.25
4	Alfredo Griffin	.25
5	Domingo Martinez	.25
7	Rich Hacker	.25
8	John Sullivan	.25
9	John Olerud	.40
10	Pat Borders	.25
11	Darnell Coles	.25
12	Roberto Alomar	.75
14	Darrin Jackson	.25
16	Tom Quinlin	.25
18	Gene Tenace	.25
19	Paul Molitor	1.50
22	Dick Schofield	.25
24	Turner Ward	.25
25	Devon White	.30
27	Randy Knorr	.25
28	Al Leiter	.30
29	Joe Carter	.30
30	Todd Stottlemyre	.30
31	Duane Ward	.25
33	Ed Sprague	.25
34	Dave Stewart	.25
39	Larry Hisle	.25
40	Mike Timlin	.25
41	Pat Hentgen	.25
42	Galen Cisco	.25
43	Cito Gaston	.25
46	Ken Davley	.25
47	Jack Morris	.25
48	Mark Eichhorn	.25
50	Danny Cox	.25
66	Juan Guzman	.25
---	World's Champion Trophy/Checklist	.25

2002 Toronto Blue Jays Team Issue

This boxed set was a stadium giveaway. It features current players, coaches and a handful of "alumni." Backs have Major League stats, biographical data and either 2001 highlights or a short biography.

		NM/M
Complete Set (34):		10.00
Common Player:		.35
2	Dave Berg	.35
5	Chris Woodward	.35
6	Joe Lawrence	.35
7	Felipe Lopez	.35
9	Darrin Fletcher	.35
10	Vernon Wells	.50
11	Eric Hinske	.50
14	Carlos Tosca	.35
15	Tom Wilson	.35
19	Cliff Politte	.35
20	Ken Huckaby	.35
21	Esteban Loaiza	.35

23	Jose Cruz Jr.	.35
24	Shannon Stewart	.45
25a	Carlos Delgado	.50
25b	Devon White	.35
26	Cris Carpenter	.35
29	Scott Eyre	.35
32	Roy Halladay	.45
35	Corey Thurman	.35
39	Steve Parris	.35
40	Scott Cassidy	.35
41	Pete Walker	.35
43	Cito Gaston	.35
44	Luke Prokopec	.35
45	Kelvim Escobar	.35
47a	Jack Morris	.35
47b	Gil Patterson	.35
49	Felix Heredia	.35
50	Tom Henke	.35
52	Bruce Walton	.35
53	John Gibbons	.35
55	Brian Butterfield	.35
56	Mike Barnett	.35

1987 Toys "R" Us

Marked as a collectors' edition set and titled "Baseball Rookies," the 1987 Toys "R" Us issue was produced by Topps for the toy store chain. The set is comprised of 33 glossy-coated cards, each measuring 2-1/2" x 3-1/2". The card fronts are very colorful, employing nine different colors including deep black borders. The backs, printed in blue and orange, contain career highlights and composite minor and major league statistics. The set was distributed in a specially designed box and sold for $1.99 in retail outlets.

		NM/M
Complete Set (33):		15.00
Common Player:		.10
1	Andy Allanson	.10
2	Paul Assenmacher	.10
3	Scott Bailes	.10
4	Barry Bonds	12.50
5	Jose Canseco	.50
6	John Cerutti	.10
7	Will Clark	.10
8	Kal Daniels	.10
9	Jim Deshaies	.10
10	Mark Eichhorn	.10
11	Ed Hearn	.10
12	Pete Incaviglia	.10
13	Bo Jackson	.50
14	Wally Joyner	.10
15	Charlie Kerfeld	.10
16	Eric King	.10
17	John Kruk	.10
18	Barry Larkin	.10
19	Mike LaValliere	.10
20	Greg Mathews	.10
21	Kevin Mitchell	.10
22	Dan Plesac	.10
23	Bruce Ruffin	.10
24	Ruben Sierra	.10
25	Cory Snyder	.10
26	Kurt Stillwell	.10
27	Dale Sveum	.10
28	Danny Tartabull	.10
29	Andres Thomas	.10
30	Robby Thompson	.10
31	Jim Traber	.10
32	Mitch Williams	.10
33	Todd Worrell	.10

1988 Toys "R" Us Rookies

This 33-card boxed edition was produced by Topps for exclusive distribution at Toys "R" Us stores. The glossy standard-size cards spotlight rookies in both close-ups and action photos on a bright blue background inlaid with yellow. The Toys "R" Us logo frames the top left corner, above a

curving white banner that reads "Topps 1988 Collectors' Edition Rookies." A black Topps logo hugs the upper right-hand edge of the photo. The player name, red-lettered on a tube of yellow, frames the bottom. Card backs are horizontal, blue and pink on a bright pink background and include the player name, personal information and career highlights and stats.

		NM/M
Complete Set (33):		3.00
Common Player:		.10
1	Todd Benzinger	.10
2	Bob Brower	.10
3	Jerry Browne	.10
4	DeWayne Buice	.10
5	Ellis Burks	.10
6	Ken Caminiti	.10
7	Casey Candaele	.10
8	Dave Cone	.10
9	Kelly Downs	.10
10	Mike Dunne	.10
11	Ken Gerhart	.10
12	Mike Greenwell	.10
13	Mike Henneman	.10
14	Sam Horn	.10
15	Joe Magrane	.10
16	Fred Manrique	.10
17	John Marzano	.10
18	Fred McGriff	.10
19	Mark McGwire	2.50
20	Jeff Musselman	.10
21	Randy Myers	.10
22	Matt Nokes	.10
23	Al Pedrique	.10
24	Luis Polonia	.10
25	Billy Ripken	.10
26	Benny Santiago	.10
27	Kevin Seitzer	.10
28	John Smiley	.10
29	Mike Stanley	.10
30	Terry Steinbach	.10
31	B.J. Surhoff	.10
32	Bobby Thigpen	.10
33	Devon White	.10

1989 Toys "R" Us Rookies

This glossy set of 33 top rookies was produced by Topps for the Toys "R" Us chain and was sold in a special box. Each player's name and position appear below the full-color photo, while the Toys "R" Us logo and "Topps 1989 Collector's Edition" appear along the top. Major and minor league stats are on the back. The set is numbered alphabetically.

		NM/M
Complete Set (33):		3.00
Common Player:		.10
1	Roberto Alomar	.50
2	Brady Anderson	.10
3	Tim Belcher	.10
4	Damon Berryhill	.10
5	Jay Buhner	.10
6	Sherman Corbett	.10
7	Kevin Elster	.10
8	Cecil Espy	.10
9	Dave Gallagher	.10
10	Ron Gant	.10
11	Paul Gibson	.10
12	Mark Grace	.50
13	Bryan Harvey	.10
14	Darrin Jackson	.10
15	Gregg Jefferies	.10
16	Ron Jones	.10
17	Ricky Jordan	.10
18	Roberto Kelly	.10
19	Al Leiter	.10
20	Jack McDowell	.10
21	Melido Perez	.10
22	Jeff Pico	.10
23	Jody Reed	.10
24	Chris Sabo	.10
25	Nelson Santovenia	.10
26	Mackey Sasser	.10
27	Mike Schooler	.10
28	Gary Sheffield	1.50
29	Pete Smith	.10
30	Pete Stanicek	.10
31	Jeff Treadway	.10
32	Walt Weiss	.10
33	Dave West	.10

1990 Toys "R" Us Rookies

This 33-card set marks the fourth straight year that Topps has produced a set to be sold exclusively at Toys "R" Us stores. The card fronts contain full-color photos of 1989 rookies. The flip sides are horizontal and provide both minor and major league totals. The complete set is packaged in a special box which features a checklist on the back.

		NM/M
Complete Set (33):		3.00
Common Player:		.10
1	Jim Abbott	.10
2	Eric Anthony	.10
3	Joey Belle	.50
4	Andy Benes	.10
5	Greg Briley	.10
6	Kevin Brown	.10
7	Mark Carreon	.10
8	Mike Devereaux	.10
9	Junior Felix	.10
10	Mark Gardner	.10
11	Bob Geren	.10
12	Tom Gordon	.10
13	Ken Griffey Jr.	2.50
14	Pete Harnisch	.10
15	Ken Hill	.10
16	Gregg Jefferies	.10
17	Derek Lilliquist	.10
18	Carlos Martinez	.10
19	Ramon Martinez	.10
20	Bob Milacki	.10
21	Gregg Olson	.10
22	Kenny Rogers	.10
23	Alex Sanchez	.10
24	Gary Sheffield	.10
25	Dwight Smith	.10
26	Billy Spiers	.10
27	Greg Vaughn	.10
28	Robin Ventura	.10
29	Jerome Walton	.10
30	Dave West	.10
31	John Wetteland	.10
32	Craig Worthington	.10
33	Todd Zeile	.10

1991 Toys "R" Us Rookies

Produced by Topps, this 33-card set features baseball's top young players. The cards are styled much like past Toys "R" Us issues featuring glossy photos. The backs are printed horizontally and include player information and

statistics. This set is the fifth of its kind produced by Topps for Toys "R" Us.

		NM/M
Complete Set (33):		3.00
Common Player:		.10
1	Sandy Alomar, Jr.	.10
2	Kevin Appier	.10
3	Steve Avery	.10
4	Carlos Baerga	.10
5	Alex Cole	.10
6	Pat Combs	.10
7	Delino DeShields	.10
8	Travis Fryman	.10
9	Marquis Grissom	.10
10	Mike Harkey	.10
11	Glenallen Hill	.10
12	Jeff Huson	.10
13	Felix Jose	.10
14	Dave Justice	.50
15	Dana Kiecker	.10
16	Kevin Maas	.10
17	Ben McDonald	.10
18	Brian McRae	.10
19	Kent Mercker	.10
20	Hal Morris	.10
21	Chris Nabholz	.10
22	Tim Naehring	.10
23	Jose Offerman	.10
24	John Olerud	.25
25	Scott Radinsky	.10
26	Bill Sampen	.10
27	Frank Thomas	1.50
28	Randy Tomlin	.10
29	Greg Vaughn	.10
30	Robin Ventura	.10
31	Larry Walker	.50
32	Wally Whitehurst	.10
33	Todd Zeile	.10

1993 Toys "R" Us Topps Stadium Club

Featuring subsets labeled "Young Stars," "Future Stars" and "Rookie Stars," this 100-card set was sold in a plastic replica of a Toys "R" Us store, packaged with a dozen "Master Photos." Similar to regular 1993 Topps Stadium Club cards, the Toys "R" Us version features full-bleed photos on front, highlighed with goil-foil and a color Toys "R" Us logo in one of the upper corners. Backs have a background of a cloud-filled blue sky and green grass. A small player photo is at upper-right. Back information offers a few personal details, 1992 and career stats and a few career highlights. At bottom are the logos of all involved parties. The cards are UV-coated front and back. Each card is designated on the front as "Rookie Star," "Young Star" or "Future Star" in gold foil.

		NM/M
Unopened Set (100+12):		10.00
Complete Set (100):		6.00
Common Player:		.05
1	Ken Griffey Jr.	1.50
2	Chad Curtis	.05
3	Mike Bordick	.05
4	Ryan Klesko	.05
5	Pat Listach	.05
6	Jim Bullinger	.05
7	Tim Laker	.05
8	Mike Devereaux	.05
9	Kevin Young	.05
10	John Valentin	.05
11	Pat Mahomes	.05
12	Todd Hundley	.05
13	Roberto Alomar	.25
14	David Justice	.05
15	Mike Perez	.05
16	Royce Clayton	.05
17	Ryan Thompson	.05
18	Dave Hollins	.05
19	Brien Taylor	.05
20	Melvin Nieves	.05
21	Rheal Cormier	.05
22	Mike Piazza	1.50
23	Larry Walker	.05
24	Tim Wakefield	.05
25	Tim Costo	.05
26	Pedro Munoz	.05
27	Reggie Sanders	.05
28	Arthur Rhodes	.05
29	Scott Cooper	.05
30	Marquis Grissom	.05
31	Dave Nilsson	.05
32	John Patterson	.05
33	Ivan Rodriguez	.50
34	Andy Stankiewicz	.05
35	Bret Boone	.05
36	Gerald Williams	.05
37	Mike Mussina	.45
38	Henry Rodriguez	.05
39	Chuck Knoblauch	.05
40	Bob Wickman	.05
41	Donovan Osborne	.05
42	Mike Timlin	.05
43	Damion Easley	.05
44	Pedro Astacio	.05
45	David Segui	.05
46	Willie Greene	.05
47	Mike Trombley	.05
48	Bernie Williams	.05
49	Eric Anthony	.05
50	Tim Naehring	.05
51	Carlos Baerga	.05
52	Brady Anderson	.05
53	Mo Vaughn	.05
54	Willie Banks	.05
55	Mark Wohlers	.05
56	Jeff Bagwell	.75
57	Frank Seminara	.05
58	Robin Ventura	.05
59	Alan Embree	.05
60	Rey Sanchez	.05
61	Delino DeShields	.05
62	Todd Van Poppel	.05
63	Eric Karros	.05
64	Gary Sheffield	.35
65	Dan Wilson	.05
66	Frank Thomas	.75
67	Tim Salmon	.05
68	Dan Smith	.05
69	Kenny Lofton	.05
70	Carlos Garcia	.05
71	Scott Livingstone	.05
72	Sam Militello	.05
73	Juan Guzman	.05
74	Greg Colbrunn	.05
75	David Hulse	.05
76	Rusty Meacham	.05
77	Dave Fleming	.05
78	Rene Arocha	.05
79	Derrick May	.05
80	Cal Eldred	.05
81	Bernard Gilkey	.05
82	Deion Sanders	.05
83	Reggie Jefferson	.05
84	Jeff Kent	.05
85	Juan Gonzalez	.35
86	Bill Ashley	.05
87	Travis Fryman	.05
88	Roberto Hernandez	.05
89	Hipolito Pichardo	.05
90	Wil Cordero	.05
91	John Jaha	.05
92	Javy Lopez	.05
93	Derek Bell	.05
94	Jeff Juden	.05
95	Steve Avery	.05
96	Moises Alou	.05
97	Brian Jordan	.05
98	Brian Williams	.05
99	Bob Zupcic	.05
100	Ray Lankford	.05

Master Photos

Each boxed set of Toys "R" Us Stadium Club cards comes with a set of 12 Master Photos. Similar to the regular 1993 S.C. Master Photos, they feature at center a larger 2-3/4" x 3-3/4"), uncropped version of the photo used on the Toys "R" Us card. A gold holographic box on the photo delineates the dimensions of the

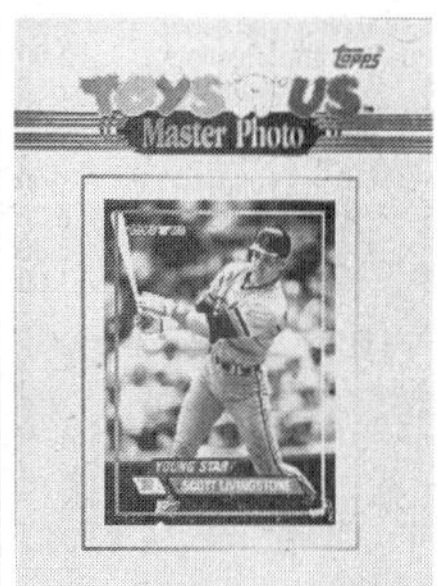

regular card, while another separates the photo from the 5" by 7" white background. Topps, Toys "R" Us, and Master Photo logos appear at the top of the card. Blank white backs have a few logos and copyrights printed in black.

		NM/M
Complete Set (12):		4.00
Common Player:		.25
(1)	Willie Greene	.25
(2)	Frank Thomas	1.00
(3)	Chuck Knoblauch	.25
(4)	Marquis Grissom	.25
(5)	Scott Livingstone	.25
(6)	Ken Griffey Jr.	2.00
(7)	Carlos Baerga	.25
(8)	Ivan Rodriguez	.75
(9)	Moises Alou	.25
(10)	Sam Militello	.25
(11)	Eric Anthony	.25
(12)	Gary Sheffield	.50

Ty Cobb

This special gold-foil bordered card was available exclusively at TRU stores as part of a package of 65 plastic sheets sold by Megacards. The card is in the design of the contemporary Conlon Collection issue from Megacards and features on its front the classic photo of Cobb sliding into base. On the back, Conlon describes how he came to take the photo.

	NM/M
Ty Cobb	4.00

1992 Triple Play Previews

To introduce its base-brand Triple Play set in 1992, Donruss issued these preview cards. The format and photos on the previews are exactly like the issued versions; backs, however, differ in the numbering "X of 8" and the appearance of the word "PREVIEW" between the MLBPA and MLB logos at bottom.

		NM/M
Complete Set (8):		25.00
Common Player:		1.00
1	Ken Griffey Jr.	9.00
2	Darryl Strawberry	1.00

3 Andy Van Slyke (Little Hotshots) 1.00
4 Don Mattingly 7.50
5 Awesome Action (Gary Carter, Steve Finley) 1.00
6 Frank Thomas 5.00
7 Kirby Puckett 6.00
8 Fun at the Ballpark 1.00

1992 Triple Play

This set was released only in wax pack form. Cards feature red borders. Boyhood photos, mascots and ballparks are among the featured cards. This set was designed to give collectors an alternative product to the high-end card sets. The cards are standard size.

NM/M
Complete Set (264): 6.00
Common Player: .05
Wax Pack (12): .40
Wax Box (36): 7.50
1 SkyDome .05
2 Tom Foley .05
3 Scott Erickson .05
4 Matt Williams .05
5 Dave Valle .05
6 Andy Van Slyke (Little Hotshot) .05
7 Tom Glavine .25
8 Kevin Appier .05
9 Pedro Guerrero .05
10 Terry Steinbach .05
11 Terry Mulholland .05
12 Mike Boddicker .05
13 Gregg Olson .05
14 Tim Burke .05
15 Candy Maldonado .05
16 Orlando Merced .05
17 Robin Ventura .05
18 Eric Anthony .05
19 Greg Maddux .60
20 Erik Hanson .05
21 Bob Ojeda .05
22 Nolan Ryan 1.00
23 Dave Righetti .05
24 Reggie Jefferson .05
25 Jody Reed .05
26 Awesome Action (Steve Finley, Gary Carter) .10
27 Chili Davis .05
28 Hector Villanueva .05
29 Cecil Fielder .05
30 Hal Morris .05
31 Barry Larkin .05
32 Bobby Thigpen .05
33 Andy Benes .05
34 Harold Baines .05
35 David Cone .05
36 Mark Langston .05
37 Bryan Harvey .05
38 John Kruk .05
39 Scott Sanderson .05
40 Lonnie Smith .05
41 Awesome Action (Rex Hudler) .05
42 George Bell .05
43 Steve Finley .05
44 Mickey Tettleton .05
45 Robby Thompson .05
46 Pat Kelly .05
47 Marquis Grissom .05
48 Tony Pena .05
49 Alex Cole .05
50 Steve Buechele .05
51 Ivan Rodriguez .45
52 John Smiley .05
53 Gary Sheffield .25
54 Greg Olson .05
55 Ramon Martinez .05
56 B.J. Surhoff .05
57 Bruce Hurst .05
58 Todd Stottlemyre .05
59 Brett Butler .05
60 Glenn Davis .05
61 Awesome Action (Glenn Braggs, Kirt Manwaring) .05
62 Lee Smith .05
63 Rickey Henderson .45
64 Fun at the Ballpark (David Cone, Jeff Innis, John Franco) .05
65 Rick Aguilera .05
66 Kevin Elster .05
67 Dwight Evans .05
68 Andujar Cedeno .05
69 Brian McRae .05
70 Benito Santiago .05
71 Randy Johnson .45
72 Roberto Kelly .05
73 Awesome Action (Juan Samuel) .05
74 Alex Fernandez .05
75 Felix Jose .05
76 Brian Harper .05
77 Scott Sanderson (Little Hotshot) .05
78 Ken Caminiti .05
79 Mo Vaughn .05
80 Roger McDowell .05
81 Robin Yount .45
82 Dave Magadan .05
83 Julio Franco .05
84 Roberto Alomar .25
85 Steve Avery .05
86 Travis Fryman .05
87 Fred McGriff .05
88 Dave Stewart .05
89 Larry Walker .05
90 Chris Sabo .05
91 Chuck Finley .05
92 Dennis Martinez .05
93 Jeff Johnson .05
94 Len Dykstra .05
95 Mark Whiten .05
96 Wade Taylor .05
97 Lance Dickson .05
98 Kevin Tapani .05
99 Awesome Action (Luis Polonia, Tony Phillips) .05
100 Milt Cuyler .05
101 Willie McGee .05
102 Awesome Action (Tony Fernandez, Ryne Sandberg) .15
103 Albert Belle .05
104 Todd Hundley .05
105 Ben McDonald .05
106 Doug Drabek .05
107 Tim Raines .05
108 Joe Carter .05
109 Reggie Sanders .05
110 John Olerud .05
111 Darren Lewis .05
112 Juan Gonzalez .25
113 Awesome Action (Andre Dawson) .05
114 Mark Grace .05
115 George Brett .65
116 Barry Bonds 1.00
117 Lou Whitaker .05
118 Jose Oquendo .05
119 Lee Stevens .05
120 Phil Plantier .05
121 Awesome Action (Devon White, Matt Merullo) .05
122 Greg Vaughn .05
123 Royce Clayton .05
124 Bob Welch .05
125 Juan Samuel .05
126 Ron Gant .05
127 Edgar Martinez .05
128 Andy Ashby .05
129 Jack McDowell .05
130 Awesome Action (Dave Henderson, Jerry Browne) .05
131 Leo Gomez .05
132 Checklist 1-88 .05
133 Phillie Phanatic .05
134 Bret Barbarie .05
135 Kent Hrbek .05
136 Hall of Fame .05
137 Omar Vizquel .05
138 The Famous Chicken .05
139 Terry Pendleton .05
140 Jim Eisenreich .05
141 Todd Zeile .05
142 Todd Van Poppel .05
143 Darren Daulton .05
144 Mike Macfarlane .05
145 Luis Mercedes .05
146 Trevor Wilson .05
147 Dave Steib .05
148 Andy Van Slyke .05
149 Carlton Fisk .45
150 Craig Biggio .05
151 Joe Girardi .05
152 Ken Griffey Jr. .65
153 Jose Offerman .05
154 Bobby Witt .05
155 Will Clark .05
156 Steve Olin .05
157 Greg Harris .05
158 Dale Murphy (Little Hotshot) .05
159 Don Mattingly .65
160 Shawon Dunston .05
161 Bill Gullickson .05
162 Paul O'Neill .05
163 Norm Charlton .05
164 Bo Jackson .10
165 Tony Fernandez .05
166 Dave Henderson .05
167 Dwight Gooden .05
168 Junior Felix .05
169 Lance Parrish .05
170 Pat Combs .05
171 Chuck Knoblauch .05
172 John Smoltz .05
173 Wrigley Field .05
174 Andre Dawson .25
175 Pete Harnisch .05
176 Alan Trammell .05
177 Kirk Dressendorfer .05
178 Matt Nokes .05
179 Wil Cordero .05
180 Scott Cooper .05
181 Glenallen Hill .05
182 John Franco .05
183 Rafael Palmeiro .40
184 Jay Bell .05
185 Bill Wegman .05
186 Deion Sanders .05
187 Darryl Strawberry .05
188 Jaime Navarro .05
189 Darren Jackson .05
190 Eddie Zosky .05
191 Mike Scioscia .05
192 Chito Martinez .05
193 Awesome Action (Pat Kelly, Ron Tingley) .05
194 Ray Lankford .05
195 Dennis Eckersley .35
196 Awesome Action (Ivan Calderon, Mike Maddux) .05
197 Shane Mack .05
198 Checklist 89-176 .05
199 Cal Ripken, Jr. 1.00
200 Jeff Bagwell .45
201 David Howard .05
202 Kirby Puckett .60
203 Harold Reynolds .05
204 Jim Abbott .05
205 Mark Lewis .05
206 Frank Thomas .45
207 Rex Hudler .05
208 Vince Coleman .05
209 Delino DeShields .05
210 Luis Gonzalez .05
211 Wade Boggs .60
212 Orel Hershiser .05
213 Cal Eldred .05
214 Jose Canseco .25
215 Jose Guzman .05
216 Roger Clemens .65
217 Dave Justice .05
218 Tony Phillips .05
219 Tony Gwynn .60
220 Mitch Williams .05
221 Bill Sampen .05
222 Billy Hatcher .05
223 Gary Gaetti .05
224 Tim Wallach .05
225 Kevin Maas .05
226 Kevin Brown .05
227 Sandy Alomar .05
228 John Habyan .05
229 Ryne Sandberg .60
230 Greg Gagne .05
231 Autographs (Mark McGwire) .40
232 Mike LaValliere .05
233 Mark Gubicza .05
234 Lance Parrish (Little Hotshot) .05
235 Carlos Baerga .05
236 Howard Johnson .05
237 Mike Mussina .25
238 Ruben Sierra .05
239 Lance Johnson .05
240 Devon White .05
241 Dan Wilson .05
242 Kelly Gruber .05
243 Brett Butler (Little Hotshot) .05
244 Ozzie Smith .60
245 Chuck McElroy .05
246 Shawn Boskie .05
247 Mark Davis .05
248 Bill Landrum .05
249 Frank Tanana .05
250 Darryl Hamilton .05
251 Gary DiSarcina .05
252 Mike Greenwell .05
253 Cal Ripken, Jr. (Little Hotshot) .35
254 Paul Molitor .45
255 Tim Teufel .05
256 Chris Hoiles .05
257 Rob Dibble .05
258 Sid Bream .05
259 Chito Martinez .05
260 Dale Murphy .15
261 Greg Hibbard .05
262 Mark McGwire .75
263 Oriole Park .05
264 Checklist 177-264 .05

Gallery of Stars

Two levels of scarcity are represented in this insert issue. Cards #1-6 (all cards have a GS prefix to the card number) feature in their new uniforms players who changed teams for 1993. Those inserts were found in the standard Triple Play foil packs and are somewhat more common than cards #7-12, which were found only in jumbo packs and which feature a better selection of established stars and rookies. All of the inserts feature the artwork of Dick Perez, with player portraits set against a colorful background. Silver-foil accents highlight the front design. Backs are red with a white "tombstone" containing a career summary.

NM/M
Complete Set (12): 4.00
Common Player: .15
1 Bobby Bonilla .15
2 Wally Joyner .15
3 Jack Morris .15
4 Steve Sax .15
5 Danny Tartabull .15
6 Frank Viola .15
7 Jeff Bagwell .60
8 Ken Griffey Jr. 1.00
9 David Justice .15
10 Ryan Klesko .15
11 Cal Ripken, Jr. 1.50
12 Frank Thomas .75

1993 Triple Play Promos

This set was given to dealers to preview the 1993 Donruss Triple Play issue. Cards are virtually identical to the regular-issue cards except for a large promotional sample notation printed on back.

NM/M
Complete Set (12): 100.00
Common Player: 5.00
1 Ken Griffey Jr. 25.00
2 Roberto Alomar 6.00
3 Cal Ripken, Jr. 40.00
4 Eric Karros 5.00
5 Cecil Fielder 5.00
6 Gary Sheffield 7.50
7 Darren Daulton 5.00
8 Andy Van Slyke 5.00
9 Dennis Eckersley 10.00
10 Ryne Sandberg 25.00
11 Mark Grace (Little Hotshots) 5.00
12 Awesome Action #1 (Luis Polonia, David Segui) 5.00

1993 Triple Play

For the second year, Leaf-Donruss used the "Triple Play" brand name for its base-level card set aimed at the younger collector. The 264-card set was available in several types of retail packaging and included a number of special subsets, such as childhood photos (labeled LH - Little Hotshots - in the checklist) and insert sets. Checklist card #264 incorrectly shows card #129, Joe Robbie Stadium, as #259. There is a second card, "Equipment," which also bears #129. An "Action Baseball" scratch-off game card was included in each foil pack.

NM/M
Complete Set (264): 10.00
Common Player: .05
Wax Pack (12): .60
Wax Box (36): 15.00
1 Ken Griffey Jr. .50
2 Roberto Alomar .10
3 Cal Ripken, Jr. .75
4 Eric Karros .05
5 Cecil Fielder .05
6 Gary Sheffield .15
7 Darren Daulton .05
8 Andy Van Slyke .05
9 Dennis Eckersley .20
10 Ryne Sandberg .35
11 Mark Grace (Little Hotshots) .05
12 Awesome Action #1 (Luis Polonia, David Segui) .05
13 Mike Mussina .15
14 Vince Coleman .05
15 Rafael Belliard .05
16 Ivan Rodriguez .20
17 Eddie Taubensee .05
18 Cal Eldred .05
19 Rick Wilkins .05
20 Edgar Martinez .05
21 Brian McRae .05
22 Darren Holmes .05
23 Mark Whiten .05
24 Todd Zeile .05
25 Scott Cooper .05
26 Frank Thomas .25
27 Wil Cordero .05
28 Juan Guzman .05
29 Pedro Astacio .05
30 Steve Avery .05
31 Barry Larkin .05
32 President Clinton 2.00
33 Scott Erickson .05
34 Mike Devereaux .05
35 Tino Martinez .05
36 Brent Mayne .05
37 Tim Salmon .05
38 Dave Hollins .05
39 Royce Clayton .05
40 Shawon Dunston .05
41 Eddie Murray .25
42 Larry Walker .05
43 Jeff Bagwell .25
44 Milt Cuyler .05
45 Mike Bordick .05
46 Mike Greenwell .05
47 Steve Sax .05
48 Chuck Knoblauch .05
49 Charles Nagy .05
50 Tim Wakefield .05
51 Tony Gwynn .35
52 Rob Dibble .05
53 Mickey Morandini .05
54 Steve Hosey .05
55 Mike Piazza .50
56 Bill Wegman .05
57 Kevin Maas .05
58 Gary DiSarcina .05
59 Travis Fryman .05
60 Ruben Sierra .05
61 Awesome Action #2 (Ken Caminiti) .05
62 Brian Jordan .05
63 Scott Chiamparino .05
64 Awesome Action #3 (Mike Bordick, George Brett) .05
65 Carlos Garcia .05
66 Checklist 1-66 .05
67 John Smoltz .05
68 Awesome Action #4 (Mark McGwire, Brian Harper) .20
69 Kurt Stillwell .05
70 Chad Curtis .05
71 Rafael Palmeiro .20
72 Kevin Young .05
73 Glenn Davis .05
74 Dennis Martinez .05
75 Sam Militello .05
76 Mike Morgan .05
77 Frank Thomas (Little Hotshots) .20
78 Staying Fit (Bip Roberts, Mike Devereaux) .05
79 Steve Buechele .05
80 Carlos Baerga .05
81 Robby Thompson .05
82 Kirk McCaskill .05
83 Lee Smith .05
84 Gary Scott .05
85 Tony Pena .05
86 Howard Johnson .05
87 Mark McGwire .60
88 Bip Roberts .05
89 Devon White .05
90 John Franco .05
91 Tom Browning .05
92 Mickey Tettleton .05
93 Jeff Conine .05
94 Albert Belle .05
95 Fred McGriff .05
96 Nolan Ryan .75
97 Paul Molitor (Little Hotshots) .10
98 Juan Bell .05
99 Dave Fleming .05
100 Craig Biggio .05
101a Andy Stankiewicz (White name on front.) .05
101b Andy Stankiewicz (Red name on front.) .25
102 Delino DeShields .05
103 Damion Easley .05
104 Kevin McReynolds .05
105 David Nied .05
106 Rick Sutcliffe .05
107 Will Clark .05
108 Tim Raines .05
109 Eric Anthony .05
110 Mike LaValliere .05
111 Dean Palmer .05
112 Eric Davis .05
113 Damon Berryhill .05
114 Felix Jose .05
115 Ozzie Guillen .05
116 Pat Listach .05
117 Tom Glavine .15
118 Roger Clemens .40
119 Dave Henderson .05
120 Don Mattingly .40
121 Orel Hershiser .05
122 Ozzie Smith .35
123 Joe Carter .05
124 Bret Saberhagen .05
125 Mitch Williams .05
126 Jerald Clark .05
127 Mile High Stadium .05
128 Kent Hrbek .05
129a Equipment (Curt Schilling, Mark Whiten) .05
129b Joe Robbie Stadium .05
130 Gregg Jefferies .05
131 John Orton .05
132 Checklist 67-132 .05
133 Bret Boone .05
134 Pat Borders .05
135 Gregg Olson .05
136 Brett Butler .05
137 Rob Deer .05
138 Darrin Jackson .05
139 John Kruk .05
140 Jay Bell .05
141 Bobby Witt .05
142 New Cubs (Dan Plesac, Randy Myers, Jose Guzman) .05
143 Wade Boggs (Little Hotshots) .15
144 Awesome Action #5 (Kenny Lofton) .05
145 Ben McDonald .05
146 Dwight Gooden .05
147 Terry Pendleton .05
148 Julio Franco .05
149 Ken Caminiti .05
150 Greg Vaughn .05
151 Sammy Sosa .35
152 David Valle .05
153 Wally Joyner .05
154 Dante Bichette .05
155 Mark Lewis .05
156 Bob Tewksbury .05
157 Billy Hatcher .05
158 Jack McDowell .05
159 Marquis Grissom .05
160 Jack Morris .05
161 Ramon Martinez .05
162 Deion Sanders .05
163 Tim Belcher .05
164 Mascots .05
165 Scott Leius .05
166 Brady Anderson .05
167 Randy Johnson .25
168 Mark Gubicza .05
169 Chuck Finley .05
170 Terry Mulholland .05
171 Matt Williams .05
172 Dwight Smith .05
173 Bobby Bonilla .05
174 Ken Hill .05
175 Doug Jones .05
176 Tony Phillips .05
177 Terry Steinbach .05
178 Frank Viola .05
179 Robin Ventura .05
180 Shane Mack .05
181 Kenny Lofton .05
182 Jeff King .05
183 Tim Teufel .05
184 Chris Sabo .05
185 Lenny Dykstra .05
186 Trevor Wilson .05
187 Darryl Strawberry .05
188 Robin Yount .25
189 Bob Wickman .05
190 Luis Polonia .05
191 Alan Trammell .05
192 Bob Welch .05
193 Awesome Action #6 .05
194 Tom Pagnozzi .05
195 Bret Barberie .05
196 Awesome Action #7 (Mike Scioscia) .05
197 Randy Tomlin .05
198 Checklist 133-198 .05
199 Ron Gant .05
200 Awesome Action #8 (Roberto Alomar) .05

#	Player	NM/M
201	Andy Benes	.05
202	Pepper	.05
203	Steve Finley	.05
204	Steve Olin	.05
205	Chris Hoiles	.05
206	John Wetteland	.05
207	Danny Tartabull	.05
208	Bernard Gilkey	.05
209	Tom Glavine (Little Hotshots)	.05
210	Benito Santiago	.05
211	Mark Grace	.05
212	Glenallen Hill	.05
213	Jeff Brantley	.05
214	George Brett	.40
215	Mark Lemke	.05
216	Ron Karkovice	.05
217	Tom Brunansky	.05
218	Todd Hundley	.05
219	Rickey Henderson	.25
220	Joe Oliver	.05
221	Juan Gonzalez	.15
222	John Olerud	.05
223	Hal Morris	.05
224	Lou Whitaker	.05
225	Bryan Harvey	.05
226	Mike Gallego	.05
227	Willie McGee	.05
228	Jose Oquendo	.05
229	Darren Daulton (Little Hotshots)	.05
230	Curt Schilling	.10
231	Jay Buhner	.05
232	New Astros (Doug Drabek, Greg Swindell)	.05
233	Jaime Navarro	.05
234	Kevin Appier	.05
235	Mark Langston	.05
236	Jeff Montgomery	.05
237	Joe Girardi	.05
238	Ed Sprague	.05
239	Dan Walters	.05
240	Kevin Tapani	.05
241	Pete Harnisch	.05
242	Al Martin	.05
243	Jose Canseco	.15
244	Moises Alou	.05
245	Mark McGwire (Little Hotshots)	.25
246	Luis Rivera	.05
247	George Bell	.05
248	B.J. Surhoff	.05
249	Dave Justice	.05
250	Brian Harper	.05
251	Sandy Alomar, Jr.	.05
252	Kevin Brown	.05
253	New Dodgers (Tim Wallach, Jody Reed, Todd Worrell)	.05
254	Ray Lankford	.05
255	Derek Bell	.05
256	Joe Grahe	.05
257	Charlie Hayes	.05
258	New Yankees (Wade Boggs, Jim Abbott)	.25
259	Joe Robbie Stadium	.05
260	Kirby Puckett	.35
261	Fun at the Ballpark (Jay Bell, Vince Coleman)	.05
262	Bill Swift	.05
263	Fun at the Ballpark (Roger McDowell)	.05
264	Checklist 199-264	.05

Action Baseball

These game folders were inserted in each 1993 Triple Play foil pack. Because collation of the folders was very bad, few collectors bothered to save them. Measuring 2-1/2" x 5", fronts have an action photo of an unnamed player. Printed over the bottom of the photo are two full-color team logos, with a white "Versus" between. Inside the folder is a baseball diamond diagram, a three-inning scoreboard, rules for playing the game and 32 scratch-off squares for playing. Backs have a number designating the folder as "of 30."

#	Player	NM/M
	Complete Set (30):	3.00
	Common Player:	.10
1	Andy Van Slyke	.10
2	Bobby Bonilla	.10
3	Ozzie Smith	.30
4	Ryne Sandberg	.30
5	Darren Daulton	.10
6	Larry Walker	.10
7	Eric Karros	.10
8	Barry Larkin	.10
9	Deion Sanders	.10
10	Gary Sheffield	.20
11	Will Clark	.10
12	Jeff Bagwell	.25
13	Roberto Alomar	.15
14	Roger Clemens	.35
15	Cecil Fielder	.10
16	Robin Yount	.25
17	Cal Ripken, Jr.	.50
18	Carlos Baerga	.10
19	Don Mattingly	.35
20	Kirby Puckett	.30
21	Frank Thomas	.25
22	Juan Gonzalez	.15
23	Mark McGwire	.45
24	Ken Griffey Jr.	.40
25	Wally Joyner	.10
26	Chad Curtis	.10
27	Batting glove	.10
28	Juan Guzman	.10
29	Dave Justice	.10
30	Joe Carter	.10

Gallery

The Gallery of Stars cards were found as random inserts in Triple Play jumbo packs. The cards feature Dick Perez painted representations of the players.

#	Player	NM/M
	Complete Set (10):	7.00
	Common Player:	.50
1	Barry Bonds	3.00
2	Andre Dawson	.65
3	Wade Boggs	1.50
4	Greg Maddux	1.50
5	Dave Winfield	1.00
6	Paul Molitor	1.00
7	Jim Abbott	.50
8	J.T. Snow	.50
9	Benito Santiago	.50
10	David Nied	.50

League Leaders

These "double-headed" cards feature one player on each side. The six cards were random inserts in Triple Play retail packs.

#	Player	NM/M
	Complete Set (6):	7.00
	Common Player:	.50
1	Barry Bonds, Dennis Eckersley	3.50
2	Greg Maddux, Dennis Eckersley	2.00
3	Eric Karros, Pat Listach	.50
4	Fred McGriff, Juan Gonzalez	.75
5	Darren Daulton, Cecil Fielder	.50
6	Gary Sheffield, Edgar Martinez	.65

Nicknames

Popular nicknames of 10 of the game's top stars are featured in silver foil on this insert set found in Triple Play foil packs.

#	Player	NM/M
	Complete Set (10):	10.00
	Common Player:	.75
1	Frank Thomas (Big Hurt)	1.25
2	Roger Clemens (Rocket)	2.00
3	Ryne Sandberg (Ryno)	1.50
4	Will Clark (Thrill)	.75
5	Ken Griffey Jr. (Junior)	3.00
6	Dwight Gooden (Doc)	.75
7	Nolan Ryan (Express)	4.00
8	Deion Sanders (Prime Time)	.75
9	Ozzie Smith (Wizard)	1.50
10	Fred McGriff (Crime Dog)	.75

1994 Triple Play Promos

This set was given to dealers to preview the 1994 Donruss Triple Play issue. Cards are virtually identical to the regular-issue cards except for a large black "Promotional Sample" printed diagonally in black on both front and back. Cards are numbered as "X of 10" on the promos.

#	Player	NM/M
	Complete Set (10):	9.00
	Common Player:	.50
1	Juan Gonzalez	.60
2	Frank Thomas	.85
3	Barry Bonds	3.00
4	Ken Griffey Jr.	1.50
5	Paul Molitor	.75
6	Mike Piazza	1.50
7	Tim Salmon	.50
8	Lenny Dykstra	.50
9	Don Mattingly	1.25
10	Greg Maddux	1.00

1994 Triple Play

Triple Play cards returned for a third year in 1994, this time with a borderless design. According to company officials, production was less than 1994 Donruss Series I baseball, which was roughly 17,500 20-box cases. In the regular-issue 300-card set, 10 players from each team were featured, along with a 17-card Rookie Review subset and several insert sets.

#	Player	NM/M
	Complete Set (300):	7.50
	Common Player:	.05
	Wax Pack (12):	.50
	Wax Box (36):	12.00
1	Mike Bordick	.05
2	Dennis Eckersley	.35
3	Brent Gates	.05
4	Rickey Henderson	.40
5	Mark McGwire	.65
6	Troy Neel	.05
7	Craig Paquette	.05
8	Ruben Sierra	.05
9	Terry Steinbach	.05
10	Bobby Witt	.05
11	Chad Curtis	.05
12	Chili Davis	.05
13	Gary DiSarcina	.05
14	Damion Easley	.05
15	Chuck Finley	.05
16	Joe Grahe	.05
17	Mark Langston	.05
18	Eduardo Perez	.05
19	Tim Salmon	.05
20	J.T. Snow	.05
21	Jeff Bagwell	.40
22	Craig Biggio	.05
23	Ken Caminiti	.05
24	Andujar Cedeno	.05
25	Doug Drabek	.05
26	Steve Finley	.05
27	Luis Gonzalez	.05
28	Pete Harnisch	.05
29	Darryl Kile	.05
30	Mitch Williams	.05
31	Roberto Alomar	.20
32	Joe Carter	.05
33	Juan Guzman	.05
34	Pat Hentgen	.05
35	Paul Molitor	.40
36	John Olerud	.05
37	Ed Sprague	.05
38	Dave Stewart	.05
39	Duane Ward	.05
40	Devon White	.05
41	Steve Avery	.05
42	Jeff Blauser	.05
43	Ron Gant	.05
44	Tom Glavine	.20
45	Dave Justice	.05
46	Greg Maddux	.45
47	Fred McGriff	.05
48	Terry Pendleton	.05
49	Deion Sanders	.05
50	John Smoltz	.05
51	Ricky Bones	.05
52	Cal Eldred	.05
53	Darryl Hamilton	.05
54	John Jaha	.05
55	Pat Listach	.05
56	Jaime Navarro	.05
57	Dave Nilsson	.05
58	B.J. Surhoff	.05
59	Greg Vaughn	.05
60	Robin Yount	.40
61	Bernard Gilkey	.05
62	Gregg Jefferies	.05
63	Brian Jordan	.05
64	Ray Lankford	.05
65	Tom Pagnozzi	.05
66	Ozzie Smith	.45
67	Bob Tewksbury	.05
68	Allen Watson	.05
69	Mark Whiten	.05
70	Todd Zeile	.05
71	Steve Buechele	.05
72	Mark Grace	.05
73	Jose Guzman	.05
74	Derrick May	.05
75	Mike Morgan	.05
76	Randy Myers	.05
77	Ryne Sandberg	.45
78	Sammy Sosa	.50
79	Jose Vizcaino	.05
80	Rick Wilkins	.05
81	Pedro Astacio	.05
82	Brett Butler	.05
83	Delino DeShields	.05
84	Orel Hershiser	.05
85	Eric Karros	.05
86	Ramon Martinez	.05
87	Jose Offerman	.05
88	Mike Piazza	.50
89	Darryl Strawberry	.05
90	Tim Wallach	.05
91	Moises Alou	.05
92	Wil Cordero	.05
93	Jeff Fassero	.05
94	Darrin Fletcher	.05
95	Marquis Grissom	.05
96	Ken Hill	.05
97	Mike Lansing	.05
98	Kirk Rueter	.05
99	Larry Walker	.05
100	John Wetteland	.05
101	Rod Beck	.05
102	Barry Bonds	.75
103	John Burkett	.05
104	Royce Clayton	.05
105	Darren Lewis	.05
106	Kirt Manwaring	.05
107	Willie McGee	.05
108	Bill Swift	.05
109	Robby Thompson	.05
110	Matt Williams	.05
111	Sandy Alomar Jr.	.05
112	Carlos Baerga	.05
113	Albert Belle	.05
114	Wayne Kirby	.05
115	Kenny Lofton	.05
116	Jose Mesa	.05
117	Eddie Murray	.40
118	Charles Nagy	.05
119	Paul Sorrento	.05
120	Jim Thome	.35
121	Rich Amaral	.05
122	Eric Anthony	.05
123	Mike Blowers	.05
124	Chris Bosio	.05
125	Jay Buhner	.05
126	Dave Fleming	.05
127	Ken Griffey Jr.	.50
128	Randy Johnson	.40
129	Edgar Martinez	.05
130	Tino Martinez	.05
131	Bret Barberie	.05
132	Ryan Bowen	.05
133	Chuck Carr	.05
134	Jeff Conine	.05
135	Orestes Destrade	.05
136	Chris Hammond	.05
137	Bryan Harvey	.05
138	Dave Magadan	.05
139	Benito Santiago	.05
140	Gary Sheffield	.30
141	Bobby Bonilla	.05
142	Jeromy Burnitz	.05
143	Dwight Gooden	.05
144	Todd Hundley	.05
145	Bobby Jones	.05
146	Jeff Kent	.05
147	Joe Orsulak	.05
148	Bret Saberhagen	.05
149	Pete Schourek	.05
150	Ryan Thompson	.05
151	Brady Anderson	.05
152	Harold Baines	.05
153	Mike Devereaux	.05
154	Chris Hoiles	.05
155	Ben McDonald	.05
156	Mark McLemore	.05
157	Mike Mussina	.25
158	Rafael Palmeiro	.40
159	Cal Ripken, Jr.	.75
160	Chris Sabo	.05
161	Brad Ausmus	.05
162	Derek Bell	.05
163	Andy Benes	.05
164	Doug Brocail	.05
165	Archi Cianfrocco	.05
166	Ricky Gutierrez	.05
167	Tony Gwynn	.45
168	Gene Harris	.05
169	Pedro Martinez	.40
170	Phil Plantier	.05
171	Darren Daulton	.05
172	Mariano Duncan	.05
173	Len Dykstra	.05
174	Tommy Greene	.05
175	Dave Hollins	.05
176	Danny Jackson	.05
177	John Kruk	.05
178	Terry Mulholland	.05
179	Curt Schilling	.20
180	Kevin Stocker	.05
181	Jay Bell	.05
182	Steve Cooke	.05
183	Carlos Garcia	.05
184	Joel Johnston	.05
185	Jeff King	.05
186	Al Martin	.05
187	Orlando Merced	.05
188	Don Slaught	.05
189	Andy Van Slyke	.05
190	Kevin Young	.05
191	Kevin Brown	.05
192	Jose Canseco	.25
193	Will Clark	.05
194	Juan Gonzalez	.20
195	Tom Henke	.05
196	David Hulse	.05
197	Dean Palmer	.05
198	Roger Pavlik	.05
199	Ivan Rodriguez	.35
200	Kenny Rogers	.05
201	Roger Clemens	.45
202	Scott Cooper	.05
203	Andre Dawson	.20
204	Mike Greenwell	.05
205	Billy Hatcher	.05
206	Jeff Russell	.05
207	Aaron Sele	.05
208	John Valentin	.05
209	Mo Vaughn	.05
210	Frank Viola	.05
211	Rob Dibble	.05
212	Willie Greene	.05
213	Roberto Kelly	.05
214	Barry Larkin	.05
215	Kevin Mitchell	.05
216	Hal Morris	.05
217	Joe Oliver	.05
218	Jose Rijo	.05
219	Reggie Sanders	.05
220	John Smiley	.05
221	Dante Bichette	.05
222	Ellis Burks	.05
223	Andres Galarraga	.05
224	Joe Girardi	.05
225	Charlie Hayes	.05
226	Darren Holmes	.05
227	Howard Johnson	.05
228	Roberto Mejia	.05
229	David Nied	.05
230	Armando Reynoso	.05
231	Kevin Appier	.05
232	David Cone	.05
233	Greg Gagne	.05
234	Tom Gordon	.05
235	Felix Jose	.05
236	Wally Joyner	.05
237	Jose Lind	.05
238	Brian McRae	.05
239	Mike MacFarlane	.05
240	Jeff Montgomery	.05
241	Eric Davis	.05
242	John Doherty	.05
243	Cecil Fielder	.05
244	Travis Fryman	.05
245	Bill Gullickson	.05
246	Mike Henneman	.05
247	Tony Phillips	.05
248	Mickey Tettleton	.05
249	Alan Trammell	.05
250	Lou Whitaker	.05
251	Rick Aguilera	.05
252	Scott Erickson	.05
253	Kent Hrbek	.05
254	Chuck Knoblauch	.05
255	Shane Mack	.05
256	Dave McCarty	.05
257	Pat Meares	.05
258	Kirby Puckett	.45
259	Kevin Tapani	.05
260	Dave Winfield	.40
261	Wilson Alvarez	.05
262	Jason Bere	.05
263	Alex Fernandez	.05
264	Ozzie Guillen	.05
265	Roberto Hernandez	.05
266	Lance Johnson	.05
267	Jack McDowell	.05
268	Tim Raines	.05
269	Frank Thomas	.40
270	Robin Ventura	.05
271	Jim Abbott	.05
272	Wade Boggs	.45
273	Mike Gallego	.05
274	Pat Kelly	.05
275	Jimmy Key	.05
276	Don Mattingly	.50
277	Paul O'Neill	.05
278	Mike Stanley	.05
279	Danny Tartabull	.05
280	Bernie Williams	.05
281	Chipper Jones	.45
282	Ryan Klesko	.05
283	Javier Lopez	.05
284	Jeffrey Hammonds	.05
285	Jeff McNeely	.05
286	Manny Ramirez	.40
287	Billy Ashley	.05
288	Raul Mondesi	.05
289	Cliff Floyd	.05
290	Rondell White	.05
291	Steve Karsay	.05
292	Midre Cummings	.05
293	Salomon Torres	.05
294	J.R. Phillips	.05
295	Marc Newfield	.05
296	Carlos Delgado	.30
297	Butch Huskey	.05
298	Checklist (Frank Thomas)	.05
299	Checklist (Barry Bonds)	.05
300	Checklist (Juan Gonzalez)	.05

Bomb Squad

Ten of the top major league home run hitters are included in this insert set. Fronts feature sepia-toned player photos within a wide brown frame. Gold foil enhances the typography. Backs have a white background with representations of vintage airplanes. A bar chart at left gives the player's home run totals by year. A small color portrait photo is at upper-right. Below are a few words about his homer history.

		NM/M
Complete Set (10):		5.00
Common Player:		.25
1	Frank Thomas	1.00
2	Cecil Fielder	.25
3	Juan Gonzalez	.45
4	Barry Bonds	2.50
5	Dave Justice	.25
6	Fred McGriff	.25
7	Ron Gant	.25
8	Ken Griffey Jr.	1.50
9	Albert Belle	.25
10	Matt Williams	.25

Medalists

Statistical performance over the 1992-93 seasons was used to rank the players appearing in the Medalists insert set. Horizontal format cards have photos of the first, second and third place winners in appropriate boxes of gold, silver and bronze foil. "Medalists," the "medals" and "Triple Play 94" are embossed on the front. Backs have color action photos of each player along with team logos and a few stats.

		NM/M
Complete Set (15):		10.00
Common Player:		.50
1	A.L. Catchers (Chris Hoiles, Mickey Tettleton, Brian Harper)	.50
2	N.L. Catchers (Darren Daulton, Rick Wilkins, Kirt Manwaring)	.50
3	A.L. First Basemen (Frank Thomas, Rafael Palmeiro, John Olerud)	1.00
4	N.L. First Basemen (Mark Grace, Fred McGriff, Jeff Bagwell)	1.00
5	A.L. Second Basemen (Roberto Alomar, Carlos Baerga, Lou Whitaker)	.50
6	N.L. Second Basemen (Ryne Sandberg, Craig Biggio, Robby Thompson)	1.25
7	A.L. Shortstops (Tony Fernandez, Cal Ripken, Jr., Alan Trammell)	2.00
8	N.L. Shortstops (Barry Larkin, Jay Bell, Jeff Blauser)	.50
9	A.L. Third Basemen (Robin Ventura, Travis Fryman, Wade Boggs)	1.25
10	N.L. Third Basemen (Terry Pendleton, Dave Hollins, Gary Sheffield)	.50
11	A.L. Outfielders (Ken Griffey Jr., Kirby Puckett, Albert Belle)	1.50
12	N.L. Outfielders (Barry Bonds, Andy Van Slyke, Len Dykstra)	2.00
13	A.L. Starters (Jack McDowell, Kevin Brown, Randy Johnson)	.60
14	N.L. Starters (Greg Maddux, Jose Rijo, Billy Swift)	1.25
15	Designated Hitters (Paul Molitor, Dave Winfield, Harold Baines)	.60

Nicknames

Eight of baseball's most colorful team nicknames are featured in this insert set.

Fronts feature a background photo representative of the nickname, with a player photo is superimposed over that. Backs have another player photo and a history of the team's nickname.

		NM/M
Complete Set (8):		10.00
Common Player:		.75
1	Cecil Fielder	.75
2	Ryne Sandberg	1.50
3	Gary Sheffield	.90
4	Joe Carter	.75
5	John Olerud	.75
6	Cal Ripken, Jr.	3.00
7	Mark McGwire	2.50
8	Gregg Jefferies	.75

1990 Tropicana Team Mets

In 1990, Tropicana orange juice took over as sponsor of the junior Mets fan club. One of the membership perks was a nine-card sheet. Action photos were surrounded by team-color stripes of blue and orange and a white outer border. Backs have Team Mets and Tropicana logos, 1989 highlights and stats, career numbers and personal data. Individual cards measure 2-1/2" x 3-1/2", though they are not often sold other than as an original 7-1/2" x 10-1/2" sheet. Cards are checklisted here on the basis of uniform numbers found on the cards' fronts.

		NM/M
Complete Set (9):		4.00
Common Player:		.50
9	Gregg Jefferies	.50
16	Dwight Gooden	.50
18	Darryl Strawberry	.50
20	Howard Johnson	.50
21	Kevin Elster	.50
25	Keith Miller	.50
29	Frank Viola	.50
44	David Cone	.50
50	Sid Fernandez	.50

1991 Tropicana Team Mets

This nine-card sheet was a perk for members of the junior Mets fan club - Team Mets. Sponsored by Tropicana fruit juices for the second straight year, the 2-1/2" x 3-1/2" individual cards on the 7-1/2" x 10-1/2" sheet feature color action photos of the players, surrounded by team-color blue and orange stripes and an outer white border. Backs have 1990 highlights and

stats, career stats and biographical details, along with the Team Mets and Tropicana logos. Cards are checklisted here according to the uniform numbers found on the front.

		NM/M
Complete Set (9):		4.00
Common Player:		.50
2	Mackey Sasser	.50
9	Gregg Jefferies	.50
10	Dave Magadan	.50
16	Dwight Gooden	.50
20	Howard Johnson	.50
22	Kevin McReynolds	.50
29	Frank Viola	.50
31	John Franco	.50
44	David Cone	.50

1983 True Value White Sox

Issued by the White Sox and True Value hardware stores, these 2-5/8" x 4-1/8" cards are among the scarcer early 1980s regional sets. The issue was originally scheduled as part of a promotion in which cards were given out at special Tuesday night games. The idea was sound, but rainouts forced the cancellation of some games so those scheduled cards were never given out. They were, however, smuggled out to hobby channels making it possible, although not easy, to assemble complete sets. The cards feature a large color photo with a wide white border. A team logo is at lower-left while the player's name, position and uniform number are in the lower-right. Backs feature a True Value ad along with statistics. The three cards which were never given out through the normal channels are considered scarcer than the others. They are Marc Hill, Harold Baines and Salome Barojas.

		NM/M
Complete Set (23):		12.00
Common Player:		.25
1	Scott Fletcher	.25
2	Harold Baines	3.50
5	Vance Law	.25
7	Marc Hill	2.00
10	Tony LaRussa	.40
11	Rudy Law	.25
14	Tony Bernazard	.25
17	Jerry Hairston Sr.	.25
19	Greg Luzinski	.25
24	Floyd Bannister	.25
25	Mike Squires	.25
30	Salome Barojas	2.00
31	LaMarr Hoyt	.25
34	Richard Dotson	.25
36	Jerry Koosman	.25
40	Britt Burns	.25
41	Dick Tidrow	.25
42	Ron Kittle	.25
44	Tom Paciorek	.25
45	Kevin Hickey	.25
53	Dennis Lamp	.25
67	Jim Kern	.25
72	Carlton Fisk	1.50

1984 True Value White Sox

True Value hardware stores and the White Sox gave the Tuesday night baseball card promotion at Comiskey Park another try in 1984. The cards measure 2-5/8" x 4-1/8". In addition to the players, there are cards for manager Tony LaRussa, the coaching staff, and former Sox greats Luis Aparicio and Minnie Minoso. Card design is very similar to the 1983 cards. As the cards were given out two at a time, it was very difficult to acquire a complete set. Additionally, as numbers available vary because of attendance, some cards are scarcer than others.

		NM/M
Complete Set (30):		25.00
Common Player:		.50
1	Scott Fletcher	.50
3	Harold Baines	1.00
5	Vance Law	.50
7	Marc Hill	.50
8	Dave Stegman	.50
10	Tony LaRussa	1.00
11	Rudy Law	.50
16	Julio Cruz	.50
17	Jerry Hairston Sr.	.50
19	Greg Luzinski	.50
20	Jerry Dybzinski	.50
24	Floyd Bannister	.50
25	Mike Squires	.50
27	Ron Reed	.50
29	Greg Walker	.50
30	Salome Barojas	.50
31	LaMarr Hoyt	.50
32	Tim Hulett	.50
34	Richard Dotson	.50
40	Britt Burns	.50
41	Tom Seaver	5.00
42	Ron Kittle	.50
44	Tom Paciorek	.50
50	Juan Agosto	.50
59	Tom Brennan	.50
72	Carlton Fisk	3.00
---	Minnie Minoso	3.00
---	Luis Aparicio	3.00
---	Nancy Faust (organist)	1.00
---	The Coaching Staff (Ed Brinkman, Dave Duncan, Art Kusnyer, Tony LaRussa, Jim Leyland, Dave Nelson, Joe Nossek)	.50

1986 True Value

A 30-card set of 2-1/2" x 3-1/2" cards was available in three-card folders at True Value hardware stores with a purchase of $5 or more. Fronts feature a portrait flanked by stars with balls and bats at the bottom. The player's ID and a Major League Players Association logo are at bottom. Team insignia have been removed from the uniforms. Backs feature some personal information and brief 1985 statistics. Along with the player cards, the folders contained a sweepstakes card offering trips to post-season games and other prizes.

		NM/M
Complete Panel Set (10):		6.00
Complete Singles Set (30):		5.00
Common Player:		.05
	Panel (1)	.50
1	Pedro Guerrero	.05
2	Steve Garvey	.10
3	Eddie Murray	.25
	Panel (2)	1.25
4	Pete Rose	.60
5	Don Mattingly	.50
6	Fernando Valenzuela	.05
	Panel (3)	.50
7	Jim Rice	.15
8	Kirk Gibson	.05
9	Ozzie Smith	.35
	Panel (4)	.75
10	Dale Murphy	.15
11	Robin Yount	.25
12	Tom Seaver	.25
	Panel (5)	.75
13	Reggie Jackson	.35
14	Ryne Sandberg	.35
15	Bruce Sutter	.25
	Panel (6)	.75
16	Gary Carter	.25
17	George Brett	.50
18	Rick Sutcliffe	.05
	Panel (7)	.25
19	Dave Steib	.05
20	Buddy Bell	.05
21	Alvin Davis	.05
	Panel (8)	1.00
22	Cal Ripken Jr.	.75
23	Bill Madlock	.05
24	Kent Hrbek	.05
	Panel (9)	1.00
25	Lou Whitaker	.05
26	Nolan Ryan	.75
27	Dwayne Murphy	.05
	Panel (10)	1.00
28	Mike Schmidt	.50
29	Andre Dawson	.15
30	Wade Boggs	.35

U

1991 Ultra

This 400-card set was originally going to be called the Elite set, but Fleer chose to use the Ultra label. The card fronts feature gray borders surrounding full-color action photos. The backs feature three player photos and statistics. Hot Prospects and Great Performers are among the special cards featured within the set.

		NM/M
Complete Set (400):		12.00
Common Player:		.05
Wax Pack (14):		.50
Wax Box (36):		9.00
1	Steve Avery	.05
2	Jeff Blauser	.05
3	Francisco Cabrera	.05
4	Ron Gant	.05
5	Tom Glavine	.25
6	Tommy Gregg	.05
7	Dave Justice	.05
8	Oddibe McDowell	.05
9	Greg Olson	.05
10	Terry Pendleton	.05
11	Lonnie Smith	.05
12	John Smoltz	.05
13	Jeff Treadway	.05
14	Glenn Davis	.05
15	Mike Devereaux	.05
16	Leo Gomez	.05
17	Chris Hoiles	.05
18	Dave Johnson	.05
19	Ben McDonald	.05
20	Randy Milligan	.05
21	Gregg Olson	.05
22	Joe Orsulak	.05
23	Bill Ripken	.05
24	Cal Ripken, Jr.	1.50
25	David Segui	.05
26	Craig Worthington	.05
27	Wade Boggs	.60
28	Tom Bolton	.05
29	Tom Brunansky	.05
30	Ellis Burks	.05
31	Roger Clemens	.65
32	Mike Greenwell	.05
33	Greg Harris	.05
34	Daryl Irvine	.05
35	Mike Marshall	.05
36	Tim Naehring	.05
37	Tony Pena	.05
38	Phil Plantier **RC**	.05
39	Carlos Quintana	.05
40	Jeff Reardon	.05
41	Jody Reed	.05
42	Luis Rivera	.05
43	Jim Abbott	.05
44	Chuck Finley	.05
45	Bryan Harvey	.05
46	Donnie Hill	.05
47	Jack Howell	.05
48	Wally Joyner	.05
49	Mark Langston	.05
50	Kirk McCaskill	.05
51	Lance Parrish	.05
52	Dick Schofield	.05
53	Lee Stevens	.05
54	Dave Winfield	.50
55	George Bell	.05
56	Damon Berryhill	.05
57	Mike Bielecki	.05
58	Andre Dawson	.25
59	Shawon Dunston	.05
60	Joe Girardi	.05
61	Mark Grace	.05
62	Mike Harkey	.05
63	Les Lancaster	.05
64	Greg Maddux	.60
65	Derrick May	.05
66	Ryne Sandberg	.60
67	Luis Salazar	.05
68	Dwight Smith	.05
69	Hector Villanueva	.05
70	Jerome Walton	.05
71	Mitch Williams	.05
72	Carlton Fisk	.50
73	Scott Fletcher	.05
74	Ozzie Guillen	.05
75	Greg Hibbard	.05
76	Lance Johnson	.05
77	Steve Lyons	.05
78	Jack McDowell	.05
79	Dan Pasqua	.05
80	Melido Perez	.05
81	Tim Raines	.05
82	Sammy Sosa	.60
83	Cory Snyder	.05
84	Bobby Thigpen	.05
85	Frank Thomas	.50
86	Robin Ventura	.05
87	Todd Benzinger	.05
88	Glenn Braggs	.05
89	Tom Browning	.05
90	Norm Charlton	.05
91	Eric Davis	.05
92	Rob Dibble	.05
93	Bill Doran	.05
94	Mariano Duncan	.05
95	Billy Hatcher	.05
96	Barry Larkin	.05
97	Randy Myers	.05
98	Hal Morris	.05
99	Joe Oliver	.05
100	Paul O'Neill	.05
101a	Jeff Reed	.05
101b	Beau Allred (Should be #104.)	.05
102	Jose Rijo	.05
103a	Chris Sabo	.05
103b	Carlos Baerga (Should be #106.)	.05
105	Sandy Alomar,Jr.	.05
107	Albert Belle	.05
108	Jerry Browne	.05
109	Tom Candiotti	.05
110	Alex Cole	.05
111a	John Farrell	.05
111b	Chris James (Should be #114.)	.05
112	Felix Fermin	.05
113	Brook Jacoby	.05
115	Doug Jones	.05
116a	Steve Olin	.05
116b	Mitch Webster (Should be #119.)	.05
117	Greg Swindell	.05
118	Turner Ward	.05
120	Dave Bergman	.05
121	Cecil Fielder	.05
122	Travis Fryman	.05
123	Mike Henneman	.05
124	Lloyd Moseby	.05

125	Dan Petry	.05
126	Tony Phillips	.05
127	Mark Salas	.05
128	Frank Tanana	.05
129	Alan Trammell	.05
130	Lou Whitaker	.05
131	Eric Anthony	.05
132	Craig Biggio	.05
133	Ken Caminiti	.05
134	Casey Candaele	.05
135	Andujar Cedeno	.05
136	Mark Davidson	.05
137	Jim Deshaies	.05
138	Mark Portugal	.05
139	Rafael Ramirez	.05
140	Mike Scott	.05
141	Eric Yelding	.05
142	Gerald Young	.05
143	Kevin Appier	.05
144	George Brett	.65
145	Jeff Conine **RC**	.40
146	Jim Eisenreich	.05
147	Tom Gordon	.05
148	Mark Gubicza	.05
149	Bo Jackson	.10
150	Brent Mayne	.05
151	Mike Macfarlane	.05
152	Brian McRae **RC**	.10
153	Jeff Montgomery	.05
154	Bret Saberhagen	.05
155	Kevin Seitzer	.05
156	Terry Shumpert	.05
157	Kurt Stillwell	.05
158	Danny Tartabull	.05
159	Tim Belcher	.05
160	Kal Daniels	.05
161	Alfredo Griffin	.05
162	Lenny Harris	.05
163	Jay Howell	.05
164	Ramon Martinez	.05
165	Mike Morgan	.05
166	Eddie Murray	.50
167	Jose Offerman	.05
168	Juan Samuel	.05
169	Mike Scioscia	.05
170	Mike Sharperson	.05
171	Darryl Strawberry	.05
172	Greg Brock	.05
173	Chuck Crim	.05
174	Jim Gantner	.05
175	Ted Higuera	.05
176	Mark Knudson	.05
177	Tim McIntosh	.05
178	Paul Molitor	.50
179	Dan Plesac	.05
180	Gary Sheffield	.35
181	Bill Spiers	.05
182	B.J. Surhoff	.05
183	Greg Vaughn	.05
184	Robin Yount	.50
185	Rick Aguilera	.05
186	Greg Gagne	.05
187	Dan Gladden	.05
188	Brian Harper	.05
189	Kent Hrbek	.05
190	Gene Larkin	.05
191	Shane Mack	.05
192	Pedro Munoz	.05
193	Al Newman	.05
194	Junior Ortiz	.05
195	Kirby Puckett	.60
196	Kevin Tapani	.05
197	Dennis Boyd	.05
198	Tim Burke	.05
199	Ivan Calderon	.05
200	Delino DeShields	.05
201	Mike Fitzgerald	.05
202	Steve Frey	.05
203	Andres Galarraga	.05
204	Marquis Grissom	.05
205	Dave Martinez	.05
206	Dennis Martinez	.05
207	Junior Noboa	.05
208	Spike Owen	.05
209	Scott Ruskin	.05
210	Tim Wallach	.05
211	Daryl Boston	.05
212	Vince Coleman	.05
213	David Cone	.05
214	Ron Darling	.05
215	Kevin Elster	.05
216	Sid Fernandez	.05
217	John Franco	.05
218	Dwight Gooden	.05
219	Tom Herr	.05
220	Todd Hundley	.05
221	Gregg Jefferies	.05
222	Howard Johnson	.05
223	Dave Magadan	.05
224	Kevin McReynolds	.05
225	Keith Miller	.05
226	Mackey Sasser	.05
227	Frank Viola	.05
228	Jesse Barfield	.05
229	Greg Cadaret	.05
230	Alvaro Espinoza	.05
231	Bob Geren	.05
232	Lee Guetterman	.05
233	Mel Hall	.05
234	Andy Hawkins	.05
235	Roberto Kelly	.05
236	Tim Leary	.05
237	Jim Leyritz	.05
238	Kevin Maas	.05
239	Don Mattingly	.65
240	Hensley Meulens	.05
241	Eric Plunk	.05
242	Steve Sax	.05
243	Todd Burns	.05
244	Jose Canseco	.35
245	Dennis Eckersley	.40
246	Mike Gallego	.05
247	Dave Henderson	.05
248	Rickey Henderson	.50
249	Rick Honeycutt	.05
250	Carney Lansford	.05
251	Mark McGwire	1.00
252	Mike Moore	.05
253	Terry Steinbach	.05
254	Dave Stewart	.05
255	Walt Weiss	.05
256	Bob Welch	.05
257	Curt Young	.05
258	Wes Chamberlain	.05
259	Pat Combs	.05
260	Darren Daulton	.05
261	Jose DeJesus	.05
262	Len Dykstra	.05
263	Charlie Hayes	.05
264	Von Hayes	.05
265	Ken Howell	.05
266	John Kruk	.05
267	Roger McDowell	.05
268	Mickey Morandini	.05
269	Terry Mulholland	.05
270	Dale Murphy	.15
271	Randy Ready	.05
272	Dickie Thon	.05
273	Stan Belinda	.05
274	Jay Bell	.05
275	Barry Bonds	1.50
276	Bobby Bonilla	.05
277	Doug Drabek	.05
278	Carlos Garcia **RC**	.05
279	Neal Heaton	.05
280	Jeff King	.05
281	Bill Landrum	.05
282	Mike LaValliere	.05
283	Jose Lind	.05
284	Orlando Merced **RC**	.10
285	Gary Redus	.05
286	Don Slaught	.05
287	Andy Van Slyke	.05
288	Jose DeLeon	.05
289	Pedro Guerrero	.05
290	Ray Lankford	.05
291	Joe Magrane	.05
292	Jose Oquendo	.05
293	Tom Pagnozzi	.05
294	Bryn Smith	.05
295	Lee Smith	.05
296	Ozzie Smith	.60
297	Milt Thompson	.05
298	Craig Wilson **RC**	.05
299	Todd Zeile	.05
300	Shawn Abner	.05
301	Andy Benes	.05
302	Paul Faries	.05
303	Tony Gwynn	.60
304	Greg Harris	.05
305	Thomas Howard	.05
306	Bruce Hurst	.05
307	Craig Lefferts	.05
308	Fred McGriff	.05
309	Dennis Rasmussen	.05
310	Bip Roberts	.05
311	Benito Santiago	.05
312	Garry Templeton	.05
313	Ed Whitson	.05
314	Dave Anderson	.05
315	Kevin Bass	.05
316	Jeff Brantley	.05
317	John Burkett	.05
318	Will Clark	.05
319	Steve Decker	.05
320	Scott Garrelts	.05
321	Terry Kennedy	.05
322	Mark Leonard	.05
323	Darren Lewis	.05
324	Greg Litton	.05
325	Willie McGee	.05
326	Kevin Mitchell	.05
327	Don Robinson	.05
328	Andres Santana	.05
329	Robby Thompson	.05
330	Jose Uribe	.05
331	Matt Williams	.05
332	Scott Bradley	.05
333	Henry Cotto	.05
334	Alvin Davis	.05
335	Ken Griffey Sr.	.05
336	Ken Griffey Jr.	.75
337	Erik Hanson	.05
338	Brian Holman	.05
339	Randy Johnson	.50
340	Edgar Martinez	.05
341	Tino Martinez	.05
342	Pete O'Brien	.05
343	Harold Reynolds	.05
344	David Valle	.05
345	Omar Vizquel	.05
346	Brad Arnsberg	.05
347	Kevin Brown	.05
348	Julio Franco	.05
349	Jeff Huson	.05
350	Rafael Palmeiro	.40
351	Geno Petralli	.05
352	Gary Pettis	.05
353	Kenny Rogers	.05
354	Jeff Russell	.05
355	Nolan Ryan	1.50
356	Ruben Sierra	.05
357	Bobby Witt	.05
358	Roberto Alomar	.15
359	Pat Borders	.05
360	Joe Carter	.05
361	Kelly Gruber	.05
362	Tom Henke	.05
363	Glenallen Hill	.05
364	Jimmy Key	.05
365	Manny Lee	.05
366	Rance Mulliniks	.05
367	John Olerud	.05
368	Dave Stieb	.05
369	Duane Ward	.05
370	David Wells	.05
371	Mark Whiten	.05
372	Mookie Wilson	.05
373	Willie Banks	.05
374	Steve Carter	.05
375	Scott Chiamparino	.05
376	Steve Chitren	.05
377	Darrin Fletcher	.05
378	Rich Garces	.05
379	Reggie Jefferson	.05
380	Eric Karros **RC**	.50
381	Pat Kelly	.05
382	Chuck Knoblauch	.05
383	Denny Neagle	.05
384	Dan Opperman	.05
385	John Ramos	.05
386	Henry Rodriguez **RC**	.05
387	Mo Vaughn	.05
388	Gerald Williams	.05
389	Mike York	.05
390	Eddie Zosky	.05
391	Barry Bonds (Great Performer)	.75
392	Cecil Fielder (Great Performer)	.05
393	Rickey Henderson (Great Performer)	.25
394	Dave Justice (Great Performer)	.05
395	Nolan Ryan (Great Performer)	.75
396	Bobby Thigpen (Great Performer)	.05
397	Checklist	.05
398	Checklist	.05
399	Checklist	.05
400	Checklist	.05

Gold

A pair of action photos flanking and below a portrait in a home plate frame at top-center are featured on these cards. Background is a graduated gold coloring. The Fleer Ultra Team logo is in the upper-left corner. Backs have narrative career information. The Puckett and Sandberg cards feature incorrect historical information on the backs.

		NM/M
Complete Set (10):		5.00
Common Player:		.15
1	Barry Bonds	2.50
2	Will Clark	.15
3	Doug Drabek	.15
4	Ken Griffey Jr.	1.50
5	Rickey Henderson	.75
6	Bo Jackson	.25
7	Ramon Martinez	.15
8	Kirby Puckett	1.00
9	Chris Sabo	.15
10	Ryne Sandberg	1.00

Update

This 120-card set was produced as a supplement to the premier Fleer Ultra set. Cards feature the same style as the regular Fleer Ultra cards. The cards were sold only as complete sets in full color, shrinkwrapped boxes.

		NM/M
Complete Set (120):		15.00
Common Player:		.05
1	Dwight Evans	.05
2	Chito Martinez	.05
3	Bob Melvin	.05
4	Mike Mussina **RC**	3.00
5	Jack Clark	.05
6	Dana Kiecker	.05
7	Steve Lyons	.05
8	Gary Gaetti	.05
9	Dave Gallagher	.05
10	Dave Parker	.05
11	Luis Polonia	.05
12	Luis Sojo	.05
13	Wilson Alvarez	.05
14	Alex Fernandez	.05
15	Craig Grebeck	.05
16	Ron Karkovice	.05
17	Warren Newson	.05
18	Scott Radinsky	.05
19	Glenallen Hill	.05
20	Charles Nagy	.05
21	Mark Whiten	.05
22	Milt Cuyler	.05
23	Paul Gibson	.05
24	Mickey Tettleton	.05
25	Todd Benzinger	.05
26	Storm Davis	.05
27	Kirk Gibson	.05
28	Bill Pecota	.05
29	Gary Thurman	.05
30	Darryl Hamilton	.05
31	Jaime Navarro	.05
32	Willie Randolph	.05
33	Bill Wegman	.05
34	Randy Bush	.05
35	Chili Davis	.05
36	Scott Erickson	.05
37	Chuck Knoblauch	.05
38	Scott Leius	.05
39	Jack Morris	.05
40	John Habyan	.05
41	Pat Kelly	.05
42	Matt Nokes	.05
43	Scott Sanderson	.05
44	Bernie Williams	.05
45	Harold Baines	.05
46	Brook Jacoby	.05
47	Ernest Riles	.05
48	Willie Wilson	.05
49	Jay Buhner	.05
50	Rich DeLucia	.05
51	Mike Jackson	.05
52	Bill Krueger	.05
53	Bill Swift	.05
54	Brian Downing	.05
55	Juan Gonzalez	.75
56	Dean Palmer	.05
57	Kevin Reimer	.05
58	Ivan Rodriguez **RC**	6.00
59	Tom Candiotti	.05
60	Juan Guzman	.05
61	Bob MacDonald	.05
62	Greg Myers	.05
63	Ed Sprague	.05
64	Devon White	.05
65	Rafael Belliard	.05
66	Juan Berenguer	.05
67	Brian Hunter	.05
68	Kent Mercker	.05
69	Otis Nixon	.05
70	Danny Jackson	.05
71	Chuck McElroy	.05
72	Gary Scott	.05
73	Heathcliff Slocumb	.05
74	Chico Walker	.05
75	Rick Wilkins	.05
76	Chris Hammond	.05
77	Luis Quinones	.05
78	Herm Winningham	.05
79	Jeff Bagwell **RC**	6.00
80	Jim Corsi	.05
81	Steve Finley	.05
82	Luis Gonzalez **RC**	1.00
83	Pete Harnisch	.05
84	Darryl Kile	.05
85	Brett Butler	.05
86	Gary Carter	1.00
87	Tim Crews	.05
88	Orel Hershiser	.05
89	Bob Ojeda	.05
90	Bret Barberie	.05
91	Barry Jones	.05
92	Gilberto Reyes	.05
93	Larry Walker	.05
94	Hubie Brooks	.05
95	Tim Burke	.05
96	Rick Cerone	.05
97	Jeff Innis	.05
98	Wally Backman	.05
99	Tommy Greene	.05
100	Ricky Jordan	.05
101	Mitch Williams	.05
102	John Smiley	.05
103	Randy Tomlin	.05
104	Gary Varsho	.05
105	Cris Carpenter	.05
106	Ken Hill	.05
107	Felix Jose	.05
108	Omar Oliveras **RC**	.05
109	Gerald Perry	.05
110	Jerald Clark	.05
111	Tony Fernandez	.05
112	Darrin Jackson	.05
113	Mike Maddux	.05
114	Tim Teufel	.05
115	Bud Black	.05
116	Kelly Downs	.05
117	Mike Felder	.05
118	Willie McGee	.05
119	Trevor Wilson	.05
120	Checklist	.05

1992 Ultra Pre-Production Samples

These cards were produced and distributed to hobby dealers to give them a preview of Ultra's second-year offering. Cards are virtually identical to the issued versions except for a white oval on back which has a "1992 / PRE-PRODUCTION / SAMPLE" notice printed in black. Each card (except the Gwynn) can also be found in a version with no card number on back; they are worth a small premium over the numbered promos. Two strips were issued, each with a different Gwynn card.

		NM/M
Uncut Strip:		25.00
Complete Set (6):		25.00
Common Player:		1.00
118	Todd Van Poppel	1.00
180	Rey Sanchez	1.00
271	Ozzie Smith	7.50
288	Royce Clayton	1.00
6/25	Roger Clemens (Award Winners)	10.00
2/10	Tony Gwynn (Commermorative Series)	7.50
7/10	Tony Gwynn (Commemorative Series)	7.50

1992 Ultra

Fleer released its second annual Ultra set in 1992. Card fronts feature full-color action photos with a marble accent at the card bottom. The flip sides are horizontal with two additional player photos. Many insert sets were randomly included in foil packs as premiums. These included rookie, All-Star and award winners, among others. A two-card Tony Gwynn send-away set was also available through an offer from Fleer. For $1 and 10 Ultra wrappers, collectors could receive the Gwynn cards. The set is numbered by team; cards #1-300 comprise Series I, cards #301-600 are Series II.

		NM/M
Complete Set (600):		12.00
Common Player:		.05
Ser. 1 or 2 Pack (14):		.60
Ser. 1 or 2 Box (36):		12.50
Tony Gwynn Auto.		60.00
1	Glenn Davis	.05
2	Mike Devereaux	.05
3	Dwight Evans	.05
4	Leo Gomez	.05
5	Chris Hoiles	.05
6	Sam Horn	.05
7	Chito Martinez	.05
8	Randy Milligan	.05
9	Mike Mussina	.30
10	Billy Ripken	.05
11	Cal Ripken, Jr.	1.00
12	Tom Brunansky	.05
13	Ellis Burks	.05
14	Jack Clark	.05
15	Roger Clemens	.60
16	Mike Greenwell	.05
17	Joe Hesketh	.05
18	Tony Pena	.05
19	Carlos Quintana	.05
20	Jeff Reardon	.05
21	Jody Reed	.05
22	Luis Rivera	.05
23	Mo Vaughn	.05
24	Gary DiSarcina	.05
25	Chuck Finley	.05
26	Gary Gaetti	.05
27	Bryan Harvey	.05
28	Lance Parrish	.05
29	Luis Polonia	.05
30	Dick Schofield	.05
31	Luis Sojo	.05
32	Wilson Alvarez	.05
33	Carlton Fisk	.40
34	Craig Grebeck	.05
35	Ozzie Guillen	.05
36	Greg Hibbard	.05
37	Charlie Hough	.05
38	Lance Johnson	.05
39	Ron Karkovice	.05
40	Jack McDowell	.05
41	Donn Pall	.05
42	Melido Perez	.05
43	Tim Raines	.05
44	Frank Thomas	.40
45	Sandy Alomar, Jr.	.05
46	Carlos Baerga	.05
47	Albert Belle	.05
48	Jerry Browne	.05
49	Felix Fermin	.05
50	Reggie Jefferson	.05
51	Mark Lewis	.05
52	Carlos Martinez	.05
53	Steve Olin	.05
54	Jim Thome	.35
55	Mark Whiten	.05
56	Dave Bergman	.05
57	Milt Cuyler	.05
58	Rob Deer	.05
59	Cecil Fielder	.05
60	Travis Fryman	.05
61	Scott Livingstone	.05
62	Tony Phillips	.05
63	Mickey Tettleton	.05
64	Alan Trammell	.05
65	Lou Whitaker	.05
66	Kevin Appier	.05
67	Mike Boddicker	.05
68	George Brett	.60
69	Jim Eisenreich	.05
70	Mark Gubicza	.05
71	David Howard	.05
72	Joel Johnston	.05
73	Mike Macfarlane	.05
74	Brent Mayne	.05
75	Brian McRae	.05
76	Jeff Montgomery	.05
77	Terry Shumpert	.05
78	Don August	.05
79	Dante Bichette	.05
80	Ted Higuera	.05
81	Paul Molitor	.40
82	Jamie Navarro	.05
83	Gary Sheffield	.30
84	Bill Spiers	.05
85	B.J. Surhoff	.05
86	Greg Vaughn	.05
87	Robin Yount	.40
88	Rick Aguilera	.05
89	Chili Davis	.05
90	Scott Erickson	.05
91	Brian Harper	.05
92	Kent Hrbek	.05
93	Chuck Knoblauch	.05
94	Scott Leius	.05
95	Shane Mack	.05
96	Mike Pagliarulo	.05
97	Kirby Puckett	.50
98	Kevin Tapani	.05
99	Jesse Barfield	.05
100	Alvaro Espinoza	.05
101	Mel Hall	.05
102	Pat Kelly	.05
103	Roberto Kelly	.05
104	Kevin Maas	.05
105	Don Mattingly	.60
106	Hensley Meulens	.05

No.	Player	Price
107	Matt Nokes	.05
108	Steve Sax	.05
109	Harold Baines	.05
110	Jose Canseco	.30
111	Ron Darling	.05
112	Mike Gallego	.05
113	Dave Henderson	.05
114	Rickey Henderson	.40
115	Mark McGwire	.75
116	Terry Steinbach	.05
117	Dave Stewart	.05
118	Todd Van Poppel	.05
119	Bob Welch	.05
120	Greg Briley	.05
121	Jay Buhner	.05
122	Rich DeLucia	.05
123	Ken Griffey Jr.	.65
124	Erik Hanson	.05
125	Randy Johnson	.40
126	Edgar Martinez	.05
127	Tino Martinez	.05
128	Pete O'Brien	.05
129	Harold Reynolds	.05
130	Dave Valle	.05
131	Julio Franco	.05
132	Juan Gonzalez	.20
133	Jeff Huson	.05
134	Mike Jeffcoat	.05
135	Terry Mathews	.05
136	Rafael Palmeiro	.35
137	Dean Palmer	.05
138	Geno Petralli	.05
139	Ivan Rodriguez	.35
140	Jeff Russell	.05
141	Nolan Ryan	1.00
142	Ruben Sierra	.05
143	Roberto Alomar	.15
144	Pat Borders	.05
145	Joe Carter	.05
146	Kelly Gruber	.05
147	Jimmy Key	.05
148	Manny Lee	.05
149	Rance Mulliniks	.05
150	Greg Myers	.05
151	John Olerud	.05
152	Dave Stieb	.05
153	Todd Stottlemyre	.05
154	Duane Ward	.05
155	Devon White	.05
156	Eddie Zosky	.05
157	Steve Avery	.05
158	Rafael Belliard	.05
159	Jeff Blauser	.05
160	Sid Bream	.05
161	Ron Gant	.05
162	Tom Glavine	.25
163	Brian Hunter	.05
164	Dave Justice	.05
165	Mark Lemke	.05
166	Greg Olson	.05
167	Terry Pendleton	.05
168	Lonnie Smith	.05
169	John Smoltz	.05
170	Mike Stanton	.05
171	Jeff Treadway	.05
172	Paul Assenmacher	.05
173	George Bell	.05
174	Shawon Dunston	.05
175	Mark Grace	.05
176	Danny Jackson	.05
177	Les Lancaster	.05
178	Greg Maddux	.50
179	Luis Salazar	.05
180	Rey Sanchez	.05
181	Ryne Sandberg	.50
182	Jose Vizcaino	.05
183	Chico Walker	.05
184	Jerome Walton	.05
185	Glenn Braggs	.05
186	Tom Browning	.05
187	Rob Dibble	.05
188	Bill Doran	.05
189	Chris Hammond	.05
190	Billy Hatcher	.05
191	Barry Larkin	.05
192	Hal Morris	.05
193	Joe Oliver	.05
194	Paul O'Neill	.05
195	Jeff Reed	.05
196	Jose Rijo	.05
197	Chris Sabo	.05
198	Jeff Bagwell	.40
199	Craig Biggio	.05
200	Ken Caminiti	.05
201	Andujar Cedeno	.05
202	Steve Finley	.05
203	Luis Gonzalez	.05
204	Pete Harnisch	.05
205	Xavier Hernandez	.05
206	Darryl Kile	.05
207	Al Osuna	.05
208	Curt Schilling	.25
209	Brett Butler	.05
210	Kal Daniels	.05
211	Lenny Harris	.05
212	Stan Javier	.05
213	Ramon Martinez	.05
214	Roger McDowell	.05
215	Jose Offerman	.05
216	Juan Samuel	.05
217	Mike Scioscia	.05
218	Mike Sharperson	.05
219	Darryl Strawberry	.05
220	Delino DeShields	.05
221	Tom Foley	.05
222	Steve Frey	.05
223	Dennis Martinez	.05
224	Spike Owen	.05
225	Gilberto Reyes	.05
226	Tim Wallach	.05
227	Daryl Boston	.05
228	Tim Burke	.05
229	Vince Coleman	.05
230	David Cone	.05
231	Kevin Elster	.05
232	Dwight Gooden	.05
233	Todd Hundley	.05
234	Jeff Innis	.05
235	Howard Johnson	.05
236	Dave Magadan	.05
237	Mackey Sasser	.05
238	Anthony Young	.05
239	Wes Chamberlain	.05
240	Darren Daulton	.05
241	Len Dykstra	.05
242	Tommy Greene	.05
243	Charlie Hayes	.05
244	Dave Hollins	.05
245	Ricky Jordan	.05
246	John Kruk	.05
247	Mickey Morandini	.05
248	Terry Mulholland	.05
249	Dale Murphy	.25
250	Jay Bell	.05
251	Barry Bonds	1.00
252	Steve Buechele	.05
253	Doug Drabek	.05
254	Mike LaValliere	.05
255	Jose Lind	.05
256	Lloyd McClendon	.05
257	Orlando Merced	.05
258	Don Slaught	.05
259	John Smiley	.05
260	Zane Smith	.05
261	Randy Tomlin	.05
262	Andy Van Slyke	.05
263	Pedro Guerrero	.05
264	Felix Jose	.05
265	Ray Lankford	.05
266	Omar Olivares	.05
267	Jose Oquendo	.05
268	Tom Pagnozzi	.05
269	Bryn Smith	.05
270	Lee Smith	.05
271	Ozzie Smith	.50
272	Milt Thompson	.05
273	Todd Zeile	.05
274	Andy Benes	.05
275	Jerald Clark	.05
276	Tony Fernandez	.05
277	Tony Gwynn	.50
278	Greg Harris	.05
279	Thomas Howard	.05
280	Bruce Hurst	.05
281	Mike Maddux	.05
282	Fred McGriff	.05
283	Benito Santiago	.05
284	Kevin Bass	.05
285	Jeff Brantley	.05
286	John Burkett	.05
287	Will Clark	.05
288	Royce Clayton	.05
289	Steve Decker	.05
290	Kelly Downs	.05
291	Mike Felder	.05
292	Darren Lewis	.05
293	Kirt Manwaring	.05
294	Willie McGee	.05
295	Robby Thompson	.05
296	Matt Williams	.05
297	Trevor Wilson	.05
298	Checklist 1-108 (Sandy Alomar, Jr.)	.05
299	Checklist 109-208 (Rey Sanchez)	.05
300	Checklist 209-300 (Nolan Ryan)	.25
301	Brady Anderson	.05
302	Todd Frohwirth	.05
303	Ben McDonald	.05
304	Mark McLemore	.05
305	Jose Mesa	.05
306	Bob Milacki	.05
307	Gregg Olson	.05
308	David Segui	.05
309	Rick Sutcliffe	.05
310	Jeff Tackett	.05
311	Wade Boggs	.50
312	Scott Cooper	.05
313	John Flaherty	.05
314	Wayne Housie	.05
315	Peter Hoy	.05
316	John Marzano	.05
317	Tim Naehring	.05
318	Phil Plantier	.05
319	Frank Viola	.05
320	Matt Young	.05
321	Jim Abbott	.05
322	Hubie Brooks	.05
323	Chad Curtis **RC**	.25
324	Alvin Davis	.05
325	Junior Felix	.05
326	Von Hayes	.05
327	Mark Langston	.05
328	Scott Lewis	.05
329	Don Robinson	.05
330	Bobby Rose	.05
331	Lee Stevens	.05
332	George Bell	.05
333	Esteban Beltre	.05
334	Joey Cora	.05
335	Alex Fernandez	.05
336	Roberto Hernandez	.05
337	Mike Huff	.05
338	Kirk McCaskill	.05
339	Dan Pasqua	.05
340	Scott Radinsky	.05
341	Steve Sax	.05
342	Bobby Thigpen	.05
343	Robin Ventura	.05
344	Jack Armstrong	.05
345	Alex Cole	.05
346	Dennis Cook	.05
347	Glenallen Hill	.05
348	Thomas Howard	.05
349	Brook Jacoby	.05
350	Kenny Lofton	.05
351	Charles Nagy	.05
352	Rod Nichols	.05
353	Junior Ortiz	.05
354	Dave Otto	.05
355	Tony Perezchica	.05
356	Scott Scudder	.05
357	Paul Sorrento	.05
358	Skeeter Barnes	.05
359	Mark Carreon	.05
360	John Doherty	.05
361	Dan Gladden	.05
362	Bill Gullickson	.05
363	Shawn Hare	.05
364	Mike Henneman	.05
365	Chad Kreuter	.05
366	Mark Leiter	.05
367	Mike Munoz	.05
368	Kevin Ritz	.05
369	Mark Davis	.05
370	Tom Gordon	.05
371	Chris Gwynn	.05
372	Gregg Jefferies	.05
373	Wally Joyner	.05
374	Kevin McReynolds	.05
375	Keith Miller	.05
376	Rico Rossy	.05
377	Curtis Wilkerson	.05
378	Ricky Bones	.05
379	Chris Bosio	.05
380	Cal Eldred	.05
381	Scott Fletcher	.05
382	Jim Gantner	.05
383	Darryl Hamilton	.05
384	Doug Henry	.05
385	Pat Listach **RC**	.05
386	Tim McIntosh	.05
387	Edwin Nunez	.05
388	Dan Plesac	.05
389	Kevin Seitzer	.05
390	Franklin Stubbs	.05
391	William Suero	.05
392	Bill Wegman	.05
393	Willie Banks	.05
394	Jarvis Brown	.05
395	Greg Gagne	.05
396	Mark Guthrie	.05
397	Bill Krueger	.05
398	Pat Mahomes **RC**	.05
399	Pedro Munoz	.05
400	John Smiley	.05
401	Gary Wayne	.05
402	Lenny Webster	.05
403	Carl Willis	.05
404	Greg Cadaret	.05
405	Steve Farr	.05
406	Mike Gallego	.05
407	Charlie Hayes	.05
408	Steve Howe	.05
409	Dion James	.05
410	Jeff Johnson	.05
411	Tim Leary	.05
412	Jim Leyritz	.05
413	Melido Perez	.05
414	Scott Sanderson	.05
415	Andy Stankiewicz	.05
416	Mike Stanley	.05
417	Danny Tartabull	.05
418	Lance Blankenship	.05
419	Mike Bordick	.05
420	Scott Brosius **RC**	.05
421	Dennis Eckersley	.35
422	Scott Hemond	.05
423	Carney Lansford	.05
424	Henry Mercedes	.05
425	Mike Moore	.05
426	Gene Nelson	.05
427	Randy Ready	.05
428	Bruce Walton	.05
429	Willie Wilson	.05
430	Rich Amaral	.05
431	Dave Cochrane	.05
432	Henry Cotto	.05
433	Calvin Jones	.05
434	Kevin Mitchell	.05
435	Clay Parker	.05
436	Omar Vizquel	.05
437	Floyd Bannister	.05
438	Kevin Brown	.05
439	John Cangelosi	.05
440	Brian Downing	.05
441	Monty Fariss	.05
442	Jose Guzman	.05
443	Donald Harris	.05
444	Kevin Reimer	.05
445	Kenny Rogers	.05
446	Wayne Rosenthal	.05
447	Dickie Thon	.05
448	Derek Bell	.05
449	Juan Guzman	.05
450	Tom Henke	.05
451	Candy Maldonado	.05
452	Jack Morris	.05
453	David Wells	.05
454	Dave Winfield	.40
455	Juan Berenguer	.05
456	Damon Berryhill	.05
457	Mike Bielecki	.05
458	Marvin Freeman	.05
459	Charlie Leibrandt	.05
460	Kent Mercker	.05
461	Otis Nixon	.05
462	Alejandro Pena	.05
463	Ben Rivera	.05
464	Deion Sanders	.10
465	Mark Wohlers	.05
466	Shawn Boskie	.05
467	Frank Castillo	.05
468	Andre Dawson	.25
469	Joe Girardi	.05
470	Chuck McElroy	.05
471	Mike Morgan	.05
472	Ken Patterson	.05
473	Bob Scanlan	.05
474	Gary Scott	.05
475	Dave Smith	.05
476	Sammy Sosa	.50
477	Hector Villanueva	.05
478	Scott Bankhead	.05
479	Tim Belcher	.05
480	Freddie Benavides	.05
481	Jacob Brumfield	.05
482	Norm Charlton	.05
483	Dwayne Henry	.05
484	Dave Martinez	.05
485	Bip Roberts	.05
486	Reggie Sanders	.05
487	Greg Swindell	.05
488	Ryan Bowen	.05
489	Casey Candaele	.05
490	Juan Guerrero	.05
491	Pete Incaviglia	.05
492	Jeff Juden	.05
493	Rob Murphy	.05
494	Mark Portugal	.05
495	Rafael Ramirez	.05
496	Scott Servais	.05
497	Ed Taubensee	.05
498	Brian Williams	.05
499	Todd Benzinger	.05
500	John Candelaria	.05
501	Tom Candiotti	.05
502	Tim Crews	.05
503	Eric Davis	.05
504	Jim Gott	.05
505	Dave Hansen	.05
506	Carlos Hernandez	.05
507	Orel Hershiser	.05
508	Eric Karros	.05
509	Bob Ojeda	.05
510	Steve Wilson	.05
511	Moises Alou	.05
512	Bret Barberie	.05
513	Ivan Calderon	.05
514	Gary Carter	.40
515	Archi Cianfrocco	.05
516	Jeff Fassero	.05
517	Darrin Fletcher	.05
518	Marquis Grissom	.05
519	Chris Haney	.05
520	Ken Hill	.05
521	Chris Nabholz	.05
522	Bill Sampen	.05
523	John VanderWal	.05
524	David Wainhouse	.05
525	Larry Walker	.05
526	John Wetteland	.05
527	Bobby Bonilla	.05
528	Sid Fernandez	.05
529	John Franco	.05
530	Dave Gallagher	.05
531	Paul Gibson	.05
532	Eddie Murray	.40
533	Junior Noboa	.05
534	Charlie O'Brien	.05
535	Bill Pecota	.05
536	Willie Randolph	.05
537	Bret Saberhagen	.05
538	Dick Schofield	.05
539	Pete Schourek	.05
540	Ruben Amaro	.05
541	Andy Ashby	.05
542	Kim Batiste	.05
543	Cliff Brantley	.05
544	Mariano Duncan	.05
545	Jeff Grotewold	.05
546	Barry Jones	.05
547	Julio Peguero	.05
548	Curt Schilling	.25
549	Mitch Williams	.05
550	Stan Belinda	.05
551	Scott Bullett	.05
552	Cecil Espy	.05
553	Jeff King	.05
554	Roger Mason	.05
555	Paul Miller	.05
556	Denny Neagle	.05
557	Vocente Palacios	.05
558	Bob Patterson	.05
559	Tom Prince	.05
560	Gary Redus	.05
561	Gary Varsho	.05
562	Juan Agosto	.05
563	Cris Carpenter	.05
564	Mark Clark **RC**	.05
565	Jose DeLeon	.05
566	Rich Gedman	.05
567	Bernard Gilkey	.05
568	Rex Hudler	.05
569	Tim Jones	.05
570	Donovan Osborne	.05
571	Mike Perez	.05
572	Gerald Perry	.05
573	Bob Tewksbury	.05
574	Todd Worrell	.05
575	Dave Eiland	.05
576	Jeremy Hernandez	.05
577	Craig Lefferts	.05
578	Jose Melendez	.05
579	Randy Myers	.05
580	Gary Pettis	.05
581	Rich Rodriguez	.05
582	Gary Sheffield	.30
583	Craig Shipley	.05
584	Kurt Stillwell	.05
585	Tim Teufel	.05
586	Rod Beck **RC**	.05
587	Dave Burba	.05
588	Craig Colbert	.05
589	Bryan Hickerson	.05
590	Mike Jackson	.05
591	Mark Leonard	.05
592	Jim McNamara	.05
593	John Patterson	.05
594	Dave Righetti	.05
595	Cory Snyder	.05
596	Bill Swift	.05
597	Ted Wood	.05
598	Checklist 301-403 (Scott Sanderson)	.05
599	Checklist 404-498 (Junior Ortiz)	.05
600	Checklist 499-600 (Mike Morgan)	.05

All-Rookies

The 10 promising rookies in this set could be found on special cards inserted in Ultra Series 2 foil packs.

		NM/M
Complete Set (10):		2.00
Common Player:		.25
1	Eric Karros	.35
2	Andy Stankiewicz	.25
3	Gary DiSarcina	.25
4	Archi Cianfrocco	.25
5	Jim McNamara	.25
6	Chad Curtis	.25
7	Kenny Lofton	.35
8	Reggie Sanders	.25
9	Pat Mahomes	.25
10	Donovan Osborne	.25

All-Stars

An All-Star team from each league, with two pitchers, could be assembled by collecting these inserts from Ultra Series 2 foil packs.

		NM/M
Complete Set (20):		7.50
Common Player:		.15
1	Mark McGwire	1.25
2	Roberto Alomar	.30
3	Cal Ripken, Jr.	1.50
4	Wade Boggs	.75
5	Mickey Tettleton	.15
6	Ken Griffey Jr.	1.00
7	Roberto Kelly	.15
8	Kirby Puckett	.75
9	Frank Thomas	.65
10	Jack McDowell	.15
11	Will Clark	.15
12	Ryne Sandberg	.75
13	Barry Larkin	.15
14	Gary Sheffield	.35
15	Tom Pagnozzi	.15
16	Barry Bonds	1.50
17	Deion Sanders	.15
18	Darryl Strawberry	.15
19	David Cone	.15
20	Tom Glavine	.30

Winners

The 25 cards in this insert issue were randomly packaged with Series 1 Ultra. One of the Cal Ripken cards (#21) can be found with a photo made from a reversed negative, as well as with the proper orientation. Neither version carries a premium.

		NM/M
Complete Set (26):		10.00
Common Player:		.20
1	Jack Morris	.20
2	Chuck Knoblauch	.20
3	Jeff Bagwell	.75
4	Terry Pendleton	.20
5	Cal Ripken, Jr.	2.00
6	Roger Clemens	1.25
7	Tom Glavine	.35
8	Tom Pagnozzi	.20
9	Ozzie Smith	1.00
10	Andy Van Slyke	.20
11	Barry Bonds	2.00
12	Tony Gwynn	1.00
13	Matt Williams	.20
14	Will Clark	.20
15	Robin Ventura	.20
16	Mark Langston	.20
18	Devon White	.20
19	Don Mattingly	1.25
20	Roberto Alomar	.40
21a	Cal Ripken, Jr. (Reversed negative.)	2.00
21b	Cal Ripken, Jr. (Correct)	2.00
22	Ken Griffey Jr.	1.50
23	Kirby Puckett	1.00
24	Greg Maddux	1.00
25	Ryne Sandberg	1.00

Tony Gwynn

This 12-card subset of Ultra's spokesman features 10 cards which were available as inserts in Series I foil packs, plus two cards labeled "Special No. 1" and "Special No. 2" which could only be obtained in a send-away offer. Some 2,000 of these cards carry a "certified" Gwynn autograph. Not part of the issue, but similar in format were a pair of extra Tony Gwynn cards. One pictures him with Fleer CEO Paul Mullan, the other shows him with the poster child for Casa de Amparo, a children's shelter in San Diego County.

		NM/M
Complete Set (12):		9.00
Common Card:		.75
Certified Autograph Card:		60.00
1	Tony Gwynn/Fldg	.75
2	Tony Gwynn/Btg	.75
3	Tony Gwynn/Fldg	.75
4	Tony Gwynn/Btg	.75

5 Tony Gwynn (Base-running.) .75
6 Tony Gwynn (Awards) .75
7 Tony Gwynn/Bunting .75
8 Tony Gwynn/Btg .75
9 Tony Gwynn/Running .75
10 Tony Gwynn/Btg .75
1 Tony Gwynn/Btg 2.00
2 Tony Gwynn/Fldg 2.00
--- Tony Gwynn, Paul Mullan 3.00
--- Tony Gwynn (Casa de Amparo) 7.50

1993 Ultra

The first series of 300 cards retains Fleer's successful features from 1992, including additional gold foil stamping, UV coating, and team color-coded marbled bars on the fronts. The backs feature a stylized ballpark background, which creates a 3-D effect, stats and portrait and an action photo. Dennis Eckersley is featured in a limited-edition "Career Highlights" set and personally autographed more than 2,000 of his cards, to be randomly inserted into both series' packs. A 10-card Home Run Kings subset and 25-card Ultra Awards Winners subset were also randomly inserted in packs. Ultra Rookies cards are included in both series. Ultra's second series has three limited-edition subsets: Ultra All-Stars, Ultra All-Rookie Team, and Strikeout Kings, plus cards featuring Colorado Rockies and Florida Marlins players.

	NM/M
Complete Set (650):	15.00
Common Player:	.05
Series 1 or 2 Pack (14):	.75
Series 1 or 2 Wax Box (36):	15.00

1 Steve Avery .05
2 Rafael Belliard .05
3 Damon Berryhill .05
4 Sid Bream .05
5 Ron Gant .05
6 Tom Glavine .20
7 Ryan Klesko .05
8 Mark Lemke .05
9 Javier Lopez .05
10 Greg Olson .05
11 Terry Pendleton .05
12 Deion Sanders .05
13 Mike Stanton .05
14 Paul Assenmacher .05
15 Steve Buechele .05
16 Frank Castillo .05
17 Shawon Dunston .05
18 Mark Grace .05
19 Derrick May .05
20 Chuck McElroy .05
21 Mike Morgan .05
22 Bob Scanlan .05
23 Dwight Smith .05
24 Sammy Sosa .60
25 Rick Wilkins .05
26 Tim Belcher .05
27 Jeff Branson .05
28 Bill Doran .05
29 Chris Hammond .05
30 Barry Larkin .05
31 Hal Morris .05
32 Joe Oliver .05
33 Jose Rijo .05
34 Bip Roberts .05
35 Chris Sabo .05
36 Reggie Sanders .05
37 Craig Biggio .05
38 Ken Caminiti .05
39 Steve Finley .05
40 Luis Gonzalez .05
41 Juan Guerrero .05
42 Pete Harnisch .05
43 Xavier Hernandez .05
44 Doug Jones .05
45 Al Osuna .05
46 Eddie Taubensee .05
47 Scooter Tucker .05
48 Brian Williams .05
49 Pedro Astacio .05
50 Rafael Bournigal .05
51 Brett Butler .05
52 Tom Candiotti .05
53 Eric Davis .05
54 Lenny Harris .05
55 Orel Hershiser .05
56 Eric Karros .05
57 Pedro Martinez .50
58 Roger McDowell .05
59 Jose Offerman .05
60 Mike Piazza .75
61 Moises Alou .05
62 Kent Bottenfield .05
63 Archi Cianfrocco .05
64 Greg Colbrunn .05
65 Wil Cordero .05
66 Delino DeShields .05
67 Darrin Fletcher .05
68 Ken Hill .05
69 Chris Nabholz .05
70 Mel Rojas .05
71 Larry Walker .05
72 Sid Fernandez .05
73 John Franco .05
74 Dave Gallagher .05
75 Todd Hundley .05
76 Howard Johnson .05
77 Jeff Kent .05
78 Eddie Murray .50
79 Bret Saberhagen .05
80 Chico Walker .05
81 Anthony Young .05
82 Kyle Abbott .05
83 Ruben Amaro Jr. .05
84 Juan Bell .05
85 Wes Chamberlain .05
86 Darren Daulton .05
87 Mariano Duncan .05
88 Dave Hollins .05
89 Ricky Jordan .05
90 John Kruk .05
91 Mickey Morandini .05
92 Terry Mulholland .05
93 Ben Rivera .05
94 Mike Williams .05
95 Stan Belinda .05
96 Jay Bell .05
97 Jeff King .05
98 Mike LaValliere .05
99 Lloyd McClendon .05
100 Orlando Merced .05
101 Zane Smith .05
102 Randy Tomlin .05
103 Andy Van Slyke .05
104 Tim Wakefield .05
105 John Wehner .05
106 Bernard Gilkey .05
107 Brian Jordan .05
108 Ray Lankford .05
109 Donovan Osborne .05
110 Tom Pagnozzi .05
111 Mike Perez .05
112 Lee Smith .05
113 Ozzie Smith .60
114 Bob Tewksbury .05
115 Todd Zeile .05
116 Andy Benes .05
117 Greg Harris .05
118 Darrin Jackson .05
119 Fred McGriff .05
120 Rich Rodriguez .05
121 Frank Seminara .05
122 Gary Sheffield .35
123 Craig Shipley .05
124 Kurt Stillwell .05
125 Dan Walters .05
126 Rod Beck .05
127 Mike Benjamin .05
128 Jeff Brantley .05
129 John Burkett .05
130 Will Clark .05
131 Royce Clayton .05
132 Steve Hosey .05
133 Mike Jackson .05
134 Darren Lewis .05
135 Kirt Manwaring .05
136 Bill Swift .05
137 Robby Thompson .05
138 Brady Anderson .05
139 Glenn Davis .05
140 Leo Gomez .05
141 Chito Martinez .05
142 Ben McDonald .05
143 Alan Mills .05
144 Mike Mussina .30
145 Gregg Olson .05
146 David Segui .05
147 Jeff Tackett .05
148 Jack Clark .05
149 Scott Cooper .05
150 Danny Darwin .05
151 John Dopson .05
152 Mike Greenwell .05
153 Tim Naehring .05
154 Tony Pena .05
155 Paul Quantrill .05
156 Mo Vaughn .05
157 Frank Viola .05
158 Bob Zupcic .05
159 Chad Curtis .05
160 Gary DiScarcina .05
161 Damion Easley .05
162 Chuck Finley .05
163 Tim Fortugno .05
164 Rene Gonzales .05
165 Joe Grahe .05
166 Mark Langston .05
167 John Orton .05
168 Luis Polonia .05
169 Julio Valera .05
170 Wilson Alvarez .05
171 George Bell .05
172 Joey Cora .05
173 Alex Fernandez .05
174 Lance Johnson .05
175 Ron Karkovice .05
176 Jack McDowell .05
177 Scott Radinsky .05
178 Tim Raines .05
179 Steve Sax .05
180 Bobby Thigpen .05
181 Frank Thomas .50
182 Sandy Alomar Jr. .05
183 Carlos Baerga .05
184 Felix Fermin .05
185 Thomas Howard .05
186 Mark Lewis .05
187 Derek Lilliquist .05
188 Carlos Martinez .05
189 Charles Nagy .05
190 Scott Scudder .05
191 Paul Sorrento .05
192 Jim Thome .40
193 Mark Whiten .05
194 Milt Cuyler .05
195 Rob Deer .05
196 John Doherty .05
197 Travis Fryman .05
198 Dan Gladden .05
199 Mike Henneman .05
200 John Kiely .05
201 Chad Kreuter .05
202 Scott Livingstone .05
203 Tony Phillips .05
204 Alan Trammell .05
205 Mike Boddicker .05
206 George Brett .65
207 Tom Gordon .05
208 Mark Gubicza .05
209 Gregg Jefferies .05
210 Wally Joyner .05
211 Kevin Koslofski .05
212 Brent Mayne .05
213 Brian McRae .05
214 Kevin McReynolds .05
215 Rusty Meacham .05
216 Steve Shifflett .05
217 James Austin .05
218 Cal Eldred .05
219 Darryl Hamilton .05
220 Doug Henry .05
221 John Jaha .05
222 Dave Nilsson .05
223 Jesse Orosco .05
224 B.J. Surhoff .05
225 Greg Vaughn .05
226 Bill Wegman .05
227 Robin Yount .50
228 Rick Aguilera .05
229 J.T. Bruett .05
230 Scott Erickson .05
231 Kent Hrbek .05
232 Terry Jorgensen .05
233 Scott Leius .05
234 Pat Mahomes .05
235 Pedro Munoz .05
236 Kirby Puckett .60
237 Kevin Tapani .05
238 Lenny Webster .05
239 Carl Willis .05
240 Mike Gallego .05
241 John Habyan .05
242 Pat Kelly .05
243 Kevin Maas .05
244 Don Mattingly .65
245 Hensley Meulens .05
246 Sam Militello .05
247 Matt Nokes .05
248 Melido Perez .05
249 Andy Stankiewicz .05
250 Randy Velarde .05
251 Bob Wickman .05
252 Bernie Williams .05
253 Lance Blankenship .05
254 Mike Bordick .05
255 Jerry Browne .05
256 Ron Darling .05
257a Dennis Eckersley .40
257b Dennis Eckersley (Wt. 195; no "MLBPA" on back - unmarked sample card.) 1.50
257c Dennis Eckersley (Wt. 195; no "Printed in USA" on back - unmarked sample card.) 1.50
258 Rickey Henderson .50
259 Vince Horsman .05
260 Troy Neel .05
261 Jeff Parrett .05
262 Terry Steinbach .05
263 Bob Welch .05
264 Bobby Witt .05
265 Rich Amaral .05
266 Bret Boone .05
267 Jay Buhner .05
268 Dave Fleming .05
269 Randy Johnson .50
270 Edgar Martinez .05
271 Mike Schooler .05
272 Russ Swan .05
273 Dave Valle .05
274 Omar Vizquel .05
275 Kerry Woodson .05
276 Kevin Brown .05
277 Julio Franco .05
278 Jeff Frye .05
279 Juan Gonzalez .25
280 Jeff Huson .05
281 Rafael Palmeiro .40
282 Dean Palmer .05
283 Roger Pavlik .05
284 Ivan Rodriguez .40
285 Kenny Rogers .05
286 Derek Bell .05
287 Pat Borders .05
288 Joe Carter .05
289 Bob MacDonald .05
290 Jack Morris .05
291 John Olerud .05
292 Ed Sprague .05
293 Todd Stottlemyre .05
294 Mike Timlin .05
295 Duane Ward .05
296 David Wells .05
297 Devon White .05
298 Checklist (Ray Lankford) .05
299 Checklist (Bobby Witt) .05
300 Checklist (Mike Piazza) .40
301 Steve Bedrosian .05
302 Jeff Blauser .05
303 Francisco Cabrera .05
304 Marvin Freeman .05
305 Brian Hunter .05
306 Dave Justice .05
307 Greg Maddux .60
308 Greg McMichael **RC** .05
309 Kent Mercker .05
310 Otis Nixon .05
311 Pete Smith .05
312 John Smoltz .05
313 Jose Guzman .05
314 Mike Harkey .05
315 Greg Hibbard .05
316 Candy Maldonado .05
317 Randy Myers .05
318 Dan Plesac .05
319 Rey Sanchez .05
320 Ryne Sandberg .60
321 Tommy Shields **RC** .05
322 Jose Vizcaino .05
323 Matt Walbeck **RC** .05
324 Willie Wilson .05
325 Tom Browning .05
326 Tim Costo .05
327 Rob Dibble .05
328 Steve Foster .05
329 Roberto Kelly .05
330 Randy Milligan .05
331 Kevin Mitchell .05
332 Tim Pugh **RC** .05
333 Jeff Reardon .05
334 John Roper **RC** .05
335 Juan Samuel .05
336 John Smiley .05
337 San Wilson .05
338 Scott Aldred .05
339 Andy Ashby .05
340 Freddie Benavides .05
341 Dante Bichette .05
342 Willie Blair .05
343 Daryl Boston .05
344 Vinny Castilla .05
345 Jerald Clark .05
346 Alex Cole .05
347 Andres Galarraga .05
348 Joe Girardi .05
349 Ryan Hawblitzel **RC** .05
350 Charlie Hayes .05
351 Butch Henry .05
352 Darren Holmes .05
353 Dale Murphy .20
354 David Nied .05
355 Jeff Parrett .05
356 Steve Reed **RC** .05
357 Bruce Ruffin .05
358 Danny Sheaffer **RC** .05
359 Bryn Smith .05
360 Jim Tatum **RC** .05
361 Eric Young .05
362 Gerald Young .05
363 Luis Aquino .05
364 Alex Arias **RC** .05
365 Jack Armstrong .05
366 Bret Barberie .05
367 Ryan Bowen .05
368 Greg Briley .05
369 Cris Carpenter .05
370 Chuck Carr .05
371 Jeff Conine **RC** .25
372 Steve Decker .05
373 Orestes Destrade .05
374 Monty Fariss .05
375 Junior Felix .05
376 Chris Hammond .05
377 Bryan Harvey .05
378 Trevor Hoffman **RC** .25
379 Charlie Hough .05
380 Joe Klink .05
381 Richie Lewis **RC** .05
382 Dave Magadan .05
383 Bob McClure .05
384 Scott Pose **RC** .05
385 Rich Renteria **RC** .05
386 Benito Santiago .05
387 Walt Weiss .05
388 Nigel Wilson .05
389 Eric Anthony .05
390 Jeff Bagwell .50
391 Andujar Cedeno .05
392 Doug Drabek .05
393 Darryl Kile .05
394 Mark Portugal .05
395 Karl Rhodes .05
396 Scott Servais .05
397 Greg Swindell .05
398 Tom Goodwin .05
399 Kevin Gross .05
400 Carlos Hernandez .05
401 Ramon Martinez .05
402 Raul Mondesi .05
403 Jody Reed .05
404 Mike Sharperson .05
405 Cory Snyder .05
406 Darryl Strawberry .05
407 Rick Trlicek **RC** .05
408 Tim Wallach .05
409 Todd Worrell .05
410 Tavo Alvarez .05
411 Sean Berry **RC** .05
412 Frank Bolick **RC** .05
413 Cliff Floyd .05
414 Mike Gardiner .05
415 Marquis Grissom .05
416 Tim Laker **RC** .05
417 Mike Lansing **RC** .10
418 Dennis Martinez .05
419 John Vander Wal .05
420 John Wetteland .05
421 Rondell White .05
422 Bobby Bonilla .05
423 Jeromy Burnitz .05
424 Vince Burnitz **RC** .05
425 Mike Draper **RC** .05
426 Tony Fernandez .05
427 Dwight Gooden .05
428 Jeff Innis .05
429 Bobby Jones .05
430 Mike Maddux .05
431 Charlie O'Brien .05
432 Joe Orsulak .05
433 Pete Schourek .05
434 Frank Tanana .05
435 Ryan Thompson **RC** .05
436 Kim Batiste .05
437 Mark Davis .05
438 Jose DeLeon .05
439 Len Dykstra .05
440 Jim Eisenreich .05
441 Tommy Greene .05
442 Pete Incaviglia .05
443 Danny Jackson .05
444 Todd Pratt **RC** .05
445 Curt Schilling .20
446 Milt Thompson .05
447 David West .05
448 Mitch Williams .05
449 Steve Cooke .05
450 Carlos Garcia .05
451 Al Martin .05
452 Blas Minor **RC** .05
453 Dennis Moeller .05
454 Denny Neagle .05
455 Don Slaught .05
456 Lonnie Smith .05
457 Paul Wagner .05
458 Bob Walk .05
459 Kevin Young .05
460 Rene Arocha **RC** .05
461 Brian Barber .05
462 Rheal Cormier .05
463 Gregg Jefferies .05
464 Joe Magrane .05
465 Omar Olivares .05
466 Geronimo Pena .05
467 Allen Watson .05
468 Mark Whiten .05
469 Derek Bell .05
470 Phil Clark .05
471 Pat Gomez **RC** .05
472 Tony Gwynn .60
473 Jeremy Hernandez .05
474 Bruce Hurst .05
475 Phil Plantier .05
476 Scott Sanders **RC** .05
477 Tim Scott **RC** .05
478 Darrell Sherman **RC** .05
479 Guillermo Velasquez .05
480 Tim Worrell **RC** .05
481 Todd Benzinger .05
482 Bud Black .05
483 Barry Bonds 1.50
484 Dave Burba .05
485 Bryan Hickerson .05
486 Dave Martinez .05
487 Willie McGee .05
488 Jeff Reed .05
489 Kevin Rogers .05
490 Matt Williams .05
491 Trevor Wilson .05
492 Harold Baines .05
493 Mike Devereaux .05
494 Todd Frohwirth .05
495 Chris Hoiles .05
496 Luis Mercedes .05
497 Sherman Obando **RC** .05
498 Brad Pennington **RC** .05
499 Harold Reynolds .05
500 Arthur Rhodes .05
501 Cal Ripken, Jr. 1.50
502 Rick Sutcliffe .05
503 Fernando Valenzuela .05
504 Mark Williamson .05
505 Scott Bankhead .05
506 Greg Blosser .05
507 Ivan Calderon .05
508 Roger Clemens .65
509 Andre Clemens .05
510 Scott Fletcher .05
511 Greg Harris .05
512 Billy Hatcher .05
513 Bob Melvin .05
514 Carlos Quintana .05
515 Luis Rivera .05
516 Jeff Russell .05
517 Ken Ryan **RC** .05
518 Chili Davis .05
519 Jim Edmonds **RC** 1.50
520 Gary Gaetti .05
521 Torey Lovullo .05
522 Tony Percival **RC** .05
523 Tim Salmon .05
524 Scott Sanderson .05
525 J.T. Snow **RC** .75
526 Jerome Walton .05
527 Jason Bere .05
528 Rod Bolton **RC** .05
529 Ellis Burks .05
530 Carlton Fisk .50
531 Craig Grebeck .05
532 Ozzie Guillen .05
533 Roberto Hernandez .05
534 Bo Jackson .10
535 Kirk McCaskill .05
536 Dave Stieb .05
537 Robin Ventura .05
538 Albert Belle .05
539 Mike Bielecki .05
540 Glenallen Hill .05
541 Reggie Jefferson .05
542 Kenny Lofton .05
543 Jeff Mutis **RC** .05
544 Junior Ortiz .05
545 Manny Ramirez .50
546 Jeff Treadway .05
547 Kevin Wickander .05
548 Cecil Fielder .05
549 Kirk Gibson .05
550 Greg Gohr **RC** .05
551 David Haas .05
552 Bill Krueger .05
553 Mike Moore .05
554 Mickey Tettleton .05
555 Lou Whitaker .05
556 Kevin Appier .05
557 Billy Brewer **RC** .05
558 David Cone .05
559 Greg Gagne .05
560 Mark Gardner .05
561 Phil Hiatt .05
562 Felix Jose .05
563 Jose Lind .05
564 Mike Macfarlane .05
565 Keith Miller .05
566 Jeff Montgomery .05
567 Hipolito Pechardo .05
568 Ricky Bones .05
569 Tom Brunansky .05
570 Joe Kmak **RC** .05
571 Pat Listach .05
572 Graeme Lloyd **RC** .05
573 Carlos Maldonado **RC** .05
574 Josias Manzanillo .05
575 Matt Mieske .05
576 Kevin Reimer .05
577 Bill Spiers .05
578 Dickie Thon .05
579 Willie Banks .05
580 Jim Deshaies .05
581 Mark Guthrie .05
582 Brian Harper .05
583 Chuck Knoblauch .05
584 Gene Larkin .05
585 Shane Mack .05
586 David McCarty .05
587 Mike Pagliarulo .05
588 Mike Trombley .05
589 Dave Winfield .50
590 Jim Abbott .05
591 Wade Boggs .60
592 Russ Davis **RC** .05
593 Steve Farr .05
594 Steve Howe .05
595 Mike Humphreys **RC** .05
596 Jimmy Key .05
597 Jim Leyritz .05
598 Bobby Munoz **RC** .05
599 Paul O'Neill .05
600 Spike Owen .05
601 Mike Stanley .05
602 Danny Tartabull .05
603 Scott Brosius .05
604 Storm Davis .05
605 Eric Fox .05
606 Goose Gossage .05
607 Scott Hammond .05
608 Dave Henderson .05
609 Mark McGwire 1.00
610 Mike Mohler **RC** .05
611 Edwin Nunez .05
612 Kevin Seitzer .05
613 Ruben Sierra .05
614 Chris Bosio .05
615 Norm Charlton .05
616 Jim Converse **RC** .05
617 John Cummings **RC** .05
618 Mike Felder .05
619 Ken Griffey Jr. .75
620 Mike Hampton .05
621 Erik Hanson .05
622 Bill Haselman .05
623 Tino Martinez .05
624 Lee Tinsley .05
625 Fernando Vina **RC** .05
626 David Wainhouse **RC** .05

627	Jose Canseco	.30
628	Benji Gil	.05
629	Tom Henke	.05
630	David Hulse **RC**	.05
631	Manuel Lee	.05
632	Craig Lefferts	.05
633	Robb Nen **RC**	.05
634	Gary Redus	.05
635	Bill Ripken	.05
636	Nolan Ryan	1.50
637	Dan Smith	.05
638	Matt Whiteside **RC**	.05
639	Roberto Alomar	.25
640	Juan Guzman	.05
641	Pat Hentgen	.05
642	Darrin Jackson	.05
643	Randy Knorr	.05
644	Domingo Martinez **RC**	.05
645	Paul Molitor	.50
646	Dick Schofield	.05
647	Dave Stewart	.05
648	Checklist (Rey Sanchez)	.05
649	Checklist (Jeremy Hernandez)	.05
650	Checklist (Junior Ortiz)	.05

All-Rookies

These insert cards are foil stamped on both sides and were randomly inserted into Series 2 packs. The cards have black fronts, with six different colors of type. The player's uniform number and position are located in the upper-right corner. The player's name and Ultra logo are gold-foil stamped. Backs have a black background with a player photo and career summary.

		NM/M
Complete Set (10):		4.00
Common Player:		.25
1	Rene Arocha	.25
2	Jeff Conine	.25
3	Phil Hiatt	.25
4	Mike Lansing	.25
5	Al Martin	.25
6	David Nied	.25
7	Mike Piazza	3.00
8	Tim Salmon	.50
9	J.T. Snow	.45
10	Kevin Young	.25

All-Stars

This 20-card set features 10 of the top players from each league. Cards were randomly inserted into Series II packs and are foil stamped on both sides.

		NM/M
Complete Set (20):		17.50
Common Player:		.25
1	Darren Daulton	.25
2	Will Clark	.35
3	Ryne Sandberg	1.50
4	Barry Larkin	.25
5	Gary Sheffield	.40
6	Barry Bonds	3.00
7	Ray Lankford	.25
8	Larry Walker	.25
9	Greg Maddux	1.50
10	Lee Smith	.25
11	Ivan Rodriguez	.75
12	Mark McGwire	2.50
13	Carlos Baerga	.25
14	Cal Ripken, Jr.	3.00
15	Edgar Martinez	.25
16	Juan Gonzalez	1.00
17	Ken Griffey Jr.	2.00
18	Kirby Puckett	1.50
19	Frank Thomas	1.25
20	Mike Mussina	.65

Award Winners

This insert set features 18 Top Glove players (nine from each league), two rookies of the year, three MVPs (both leagues and World Series), both Cy Young Award winners and one Player of the Year. All cards are UV coated and foil stamped on both sides and were found in Series I packs. Two formats are seen. Cards #1-18 are horizontal with player portrait and action photos on a marbled black background. Gold-foil graphics identify the player. Cards #19-25 are verticial with a black background that has "Fleer Ultra Award Winners" splashed around in trendy colors. The Ultra logo, player's name and his award are spelled out in gold foil. Horizontally arranged backs share many of their respective front elements, and have a summary of the season's performance which led to the award. There is a close-up player photo, as well.

		NM/M
Complete Set (25):		12.00
Common Player:		.25
1	Greg Maddux	.75
2	Tom Pagnozzi	.25
3	Mark Grace	.25
4	Jose Lind	.25
5	Terry Pendleton	.25
6	Ozzie Smith	.75
7	Barry Bonds	2.00
8	Andy Van Slyke	.25
9	Larry Walker	.25
10	Mark Langston	.25
11	Ivan Rodriguez	.60
12	Don Mattingly	.75
13	Roberto Alomar	.35
14	Robin Ventura	.25
15	Cal Ripken, Jr.	2.00
16	Ken Griffey Jr.	1.00
17	Kirby Puckett	.75
18	Devon White	.25
19	Pat Listach	.25
20	Eric Karros	.25
21	Pat Borders	.25
22	Greg Maddux	.75
23	Dennis Eckersley	.60
24	Barry Bonds	2.00
25	Gary Sheffield	.45

Career Highlights Promo Sheet

To introduce its "Career Highlights" insert cards in Fleer and Fleer Ultra, the company distributed this promo sheet picturing one card each from the Tom Glavine and Dennis Eckersley sets, overprinted with a gray "PROMOTIONAL SAMPLE" across front and back. A third panel on the sheet provides details of the mail-in offer through which additional cards from the sets could be ordered. The sheet measures 7-1/2"x3-1/2".

	NM/M
Three-Panel Strip:	2.50

Dennis Eckersley Career Highlights

This limited-edition subset chronicles Dennis Eckersley's illustrious career. Cards, which are UV coated and silver foil-stamped on both sides, were randomly inserted into both series' packs. Eckersley autographed more than 2,000 of the cards, which were also randomly inserted into packs. By sending in 10 Fleer Ultra wrappers plus $1, collectors could receive two additional Eckersley cards which were not available in regular packs. Card fronts have a color action photo, the background of which has been colorized into shades of purple. A black marble strip at bottom has the city name and years he was with the team in silver foil. A large black marble box in one corner has the "Dennis Eckersley Career High lights" logo in silver foil. On back, a purple box is dropped out of a color photo, and silver-foil typography describes some phrase of Eck's career.

		NM/M
Complete Set (12):		6.00
Common Card:		.50
Autographed Card:		35.00
1	"Perfection" (A's 1987-92)	.50
2	"The Kid" (Indians 1975-77)	.50
3	"The Warrior" (Indians 1975-77)	.50
4	"Beantown Blazer" (Red Sox 1978-84)	.50
5	"Eckspeak" (Red Sox 1978-84)	.50
6	"Down to Earth" (Red Sox 1978-84)	.50
7	"Wrigley Bound" (Cubs 1984-86)	.50
8	"No Relief" (A's 1987-92)	.50
9	"In Control" (A's 1987-92)	.50
10	"Simply the Best" (A's 1987-92)	.50
11	"Reign of Perfection" (A's 1987-92)	.50
12	"Leaving His Mark" (A's 1987-92)	.50

Commemorative

Photos of Fleer's CEO and the company's spokesman, 1992 Cy Young/MVP winner Dennis Eckersley are superimposed on a background of Oakland-Alameda Country Stadium on this promo card. The back gives details of the forthcoming 1993 Fleer Ultra issue.

	NM/M
Dennis Eckersley, Paul Mullan	5.00

Home Run Kings

This insert set features top home run kings. Cards, which are UV coated and have gold foil stamping on both sides, were inserts in Series I packs.

		NM/M
Complete Set (10):		8.00
Common Player:		.50
1	Juan Gonzalez	.65
2	Mark McGwire	2.50
3	Cecil Fielder	.50
4	Fred McGriff	.50
5	Albert Belle	.50
6	Barry Bonds	2.50
7	Joe Carter	.50
8	Gary Sheffield	.65
9	Darren Daulton	.50
10	Dave Hollins	.50

Performers

An Ultra Performers set of Fleer Ultra baseball cards was offered directly to collectors in 1993. The set, available only by mail, was limited to 150,000 sets. The cards featured gold-foil stamping and UV coating on each side and a six-photo design, including five on the front of the card. Each card was identified on the back by set serial number jet-printed in black in a strip at bottom.

		NM/M
Complete Set (10):		5.00
Common Player:		.25
1	Barry Bonds	2.50
2	Juan Gonzalez	.30
3	Ken Griffey Jr.	1.00
4	Eric Karros	.25
5	Pat Listach	.25
6	Greg Maddux	.75
7	David Nied	.25
8	Gary Sheffield	.40
9	J.T. Snow	.25
10	Frank Thomas	.65

Strikeout Kings

Five of baseball's top strikeout pitchers are featured in this second-series Ultra insert set. Cards are UV coated and foil stamped on both sides. Each card front has a picture of a pitcher winding up to throw. A baseball is in the background, with the pitcher in the forefront.

		NM/M
Complete Set (5):		7.50
Common Player:		.25
1	Roger Clemens	2.50
2	Juan Guzman	.25
3	Randy Johnson	1.25
4	Nolan Ryan	5.00
5	John Smoltz	.50

1994 Ultra

Issued in two series of 300 cards each, Ultra for 1994 represented a new highwater mark in production values for a mid-priced brand. Each side of the basic cards is UV coated and gold-foil embossed. Fronts feature full-bleed action photos. At bottom the player name, team, position and Fleer Ultra logo appear in gold foil above a gold-foil strip. Some rookie cards are specially designated with a large gold "ROOKIE" above the Ultra logo. Backs feature a basic background that is team color coordinated. Three more player action photos are featured on the back, along with a team logo and a modicum of stats and personal data. There is a gold stripe along the left edge and the player's name and card number appear in gold in the lower-left corner. The set features seven types of insert cards, packaged one per pack.

		NM/M
Complete Set (600):		15.00
Common Player:		.05
Series 1 or 2 Pack (14):		.50
Series 1 or 2 Wax Box (36):		15.00
1	Jeffrey Hammonds	.05
2	Chris Hoiles	.05
3	Ben McDonald	.05
4	Mark McLemore	.05
5	Alan Mills	.05
6	Jamie Moyer	.05
7	Brad Pennington	.05
8	Jim Poole	.05
9	Cal Ripken, Jr.	1.50
10	Jack Voigt	.05
11	Roger Clemens	.65
12	Danny Darwin	.05
13	Andre Dawson	.25
14	Scott Fletcher	.05
15	Greg Harris	.05
16	Billy Hatcher	.05
17	Jeff Russell	.05
18	Aaron Sele	.05
19	Mo Vaughn	.05
20	Mike Butcher	.05
21	Rod Correia	.05
22	Steve Frey	.05
23	Phil Leftwich **RC**	.05
24	Torey Lovullo	.05
25	Ken Patterson	.05
26	Eduardo Perez	.05
27	Tim Salmon	.05
28	J.T. Snow	.05
29	Chris Turner	.05
30	Wilson Alvarez	.05
31	Jason Bere	.05
32	Joey Cora	.05
33	Alex Fernandez	.05
34	Roberto Hernandez	.05
35	Lance Johnson	.05
36	Ron Karkovice	.05
37	Kirk McCaskill	.05
38	Jeff Schwarz	.05
39	Frank Thomas	.50
40	Sandy Alomar Jr.	.05
41	Albert Belle	.05
42	Felix Fermin	.05
43	Wayne Kirby	.05
44	Tom Kramer	.05
45	Kenny Lofton	.05
46	Jose Mesa	.05
47	Eric Plunk	.05
48	Paul Sorrento	.05
49	Jim Thome	.35
50	Bill Wertz	.05
51	John Doherty	.05
52	Cecil Fielder	.05
53	Travis Fryman	.05
54	Chris Gomez	.05
55	Mike Henneman	.05
56	Chad Kreuter	.05
57	Bob MacDonald	.05
58	Mike Moore	.05
59	Tony Phillips	.05
60	Lou Whitaker	.05
61	Kevin Appier	.05
62	Greg Gagne	.05
63	Chris Gwynn	.05
64	Bob Hamelin	.05
65	Chris Haney	.05
66	Phil Hiatt	.05
67	Felix Jose	.05
68	Jose Lind	.05
69	Mike Macfarlane	.05
70	Jeff Montgomery	.05
71	Hipolito Pichardo	.05
72	Juan Bell	.05
73	Cal Eldred	.05
74	Darryl Hamilton	.05
75	Doug Henry	.05
76	Mike Ignasiak	.05
77	John Jaha	.05
78	Graeme Lloyd	.05
79	Angel Miranda	.05
80	Dave Nilsson	.05
81	Troy O'Leary	.05
82	Kevin Reimer	.05
83	Willie Banks	.05
84	Larry Casian	.05
85	Scott Erickson	.05
86	Eddie Guardado	.05
87	Kent Hrbek	.05
88	Terry Jorgensen	.05
89	Chuck Knoblauch	.05
90	Pat Meares	.05
91	Mike Trombley	.05
92	Dave Winfield	.50
93	Wade Boggs	.60
94	Scott Kamieniecki	.05
95	Pat Kelly	.05
96	Jimmy Key	.05
97	Jim Leyritz	.05
98	Bobby Munoz	.05
99	Paul O'Neill	.05
100	Melido Perez	.05
101	Mike Stanley	.05
102	Danny Tartabull	.05
103	Bernie Williams	.05
104	Kurt Abbott **RC**	.05
105	Mike Bordick	.05
106	Ron Darling	.05
107	Brent Gates	.05
108	Miguel Jimenez	.05
109	Steve Karsay	.05
110	Scott Lydy	.05
111	Mark McGwire	1.00
112	Troy Neel	.05
113	Craig Paquette	.05
114	Bob Welch	.05
115	Bobby Witt	.05
116	Rich Amaral	.05
117	Mike Blowers	.05
118	Jay Buhner	.05
119	Dave Fleming	.05
120	Ken Griffey Jr.	.75
121	Tino Martinez	.05
122	Marc Newfield	.05
123	Ted Power	.05
124	Mackey Sasser	.05
125	Omar Vizquel	.05
126	Kevin Brown	.05
127	Juan Gonzalez	.25
128	Tom Henke	.05
129	David Hulse	.05
130	Dean Palmer	.05
131	Roger Pavlik	.05
132	Ivan Rodriguez	.40
133	Kenny Rogers	.05
134	Doug Strange	.05
135	Pat Borders	.05
136	Joe Carter	.05
137	Darnell Coles	.05
138	Pat Hentgen	.05
139	Al Leiter	.05
140	Paul Molitor	.50
141	John Olerud	.05
142	Ed Sprague	.05
143	Dave Stewart	.05
144	Mike Timlin	.05
145	Duane Ward	.05
146	Devon White	.05
147	Steve Avery	.05
148	Steve Bedrosian	.05
149	Damon Berryhill	.05
150	Jeff Blauser	.05
151	Tom Glavine	.20
152	Chipper Jones	.60
153	Mark Lemke	.05
154	Fred McGriff	.05

155 Greg McMichael .05
156 Deion Sanders .05
157 John Smoltz .05
158 Mark Wohlers .05
159 Jose Bautista .05
160 Steve Buechele .05
161 Mike Harkey .05
162 Greg Hibbard .05
163 Chuck McElroy .05
164 Mike Morgan .05
165 Kevin Roberson .05
166 Ryne Sandberg .60
167 Jose Vizcaino .05
168 Rick Wilkins .05
169 Willie Wilson .05
170 Willie Greene .05
171 Roberto Kelly .05
172 Larry Luebbers .05
173 Kevin Mitchell .05
174 Joe Oliver .05
175 John Roper .05
176 Johnny Ruffin .05
177 Reggie Sanders .05
178 John Smiley .05
179 Jerry Spradlin .05
180 Freddie Benavides .05
181 Dante Bichette .05
182 Willie Blair .05
183 Kent Bottenfield .05
184 Jerald Clark .05
185 Joe Girardi .05
186 Roberto Mejia .05
187 Steve Reed .05
188 Armando Reynoso .05
189 Bruce Ruffin .05
190 Eric Young .05
191 Luis Aquino .05
192 Bret Barberie .05
193 Ryan Bowen .05
194 Chuck Carr .05
195 Orestes Destrade .05
196 Richie Lewis .05
197 Dave Magadan .05
198 Bob Natal .05
199 Gary Sheffield .30
200 Matt Turner .05
201 Darrell Whitmore .05
202 Eric Anthony .05
203 Jeff Bagwell .50
204 Andujar Cedeno .05
205 Luis Gonzalez .05
206 Xavier Hernandez .05
207 Doug Jones .05
208 Darryl Kile .05
209 Scott Servais .05
210 Greg Swindell .05
211 Brian Williams .05
212 Pedro Astacio .05
213 Brett Butler .05
214 Omar Daal .05
215 Jim Gott .05
216 Raul Mondesi .05
217 Jose Offerman .05
218 Mike Piazza .75
219 Cory Snyder .05
220 Tim Wallach .05
221 Todd Worrell .05
222 Moises Alou .05
223 Sean Berry .05
224 Wil Cordero .05
225 Jeff Fassero .05
226 Darrin Fletcher .05
227 Cliff Floyd .05
228 Marquis Grissom .05
229 Ken Hill .05
230 Mike Lansing .05
231 Kirk Rueter .05
232 John Wetteland .05
233 Rondell White .05
234 Tim Bogar .05
235 Jeromy Burnitz .05
236 Dwight Gooden .05
237 Todd Hundley .05
238 Jeff Kent .05
239 Josias Manzanillo .05
240 Joe Orsulak .05
241 Ryan Thompson .05
242 Kim Batiste .05
243 Darren Daulton .05
243a Darren Daulton (Promotional Sample) 1.00
244 Tommy Greene .05
245 Dave Hollins .05
246 Pete Incaviglia .05
247 Danny Jackson .05
248 Ricky Jordan .05
249 John Kruk .05
249a John Kruk (Promotional Sample) 1.00
250 Mickey Morandini .05
251 Terry Mulholland .05
252 Ben Rivera .05
253 Kevin Stocker .05
254 Jay Bell .05
255 Steve Cooke .05
256 Jeff King .05
257 Al Martin .05
258 Danny Miceli .05
259 Blas Minor .05
260 Don Slaught .05
261 Paul Wagner .05
262 Tim Wakefield .05
263 Kevin Young .05
264 Rene Arocha .05
265 Richard Batchelor **RC** .05
266 Gregg Jefferies .05
267 Brian Jordan .05
268 Jose Oquendo .05
269 Donovan Osborne .05
270 Erik Pappas .05
271 Mike Perez .05
272 Bob Tewksbury .05
273 Mark Whiten .05
274 Todd Zeile .05
275 Andy Ashby .05
276 Brad Ausmus .05
277 Phil Clark .05
278 Jeff Gardner .05
279 Ricky Gutierrez .05
280 Tony Gwynn .60
281 Tim Mauser .05
282 Scott Sanders .05
283 Frank Seminara .05
284 Wally Whitehurst .05
285 Rod Beck .05
286 Barry Bonds 1.50
287 Dave Burba .05
288 Mark Carreon .05
289 Royce Clayton .05
290 Mike Jackson .05
291 Darren Lewis .05
292 Kirt Manwaring .05
293 Dave Martinez .05
294 Billy Swift .05
295 Salomon Torres .05
296 Matt Williams .05
297 Checklist 1-103 (Joe Orsulak) .05
298 Checklist 104-201 (Pete Incaviglia) .05
299 Checklist 202-300 (Todd Hundley) .05
300 Checklist - Inserts (John Doherty) .05
301 Brady Anderson .05
302 Harold Baines .05
303 Damon Buford .05
304 Mike Devereaux .05
305 Sid Fernandez .05
306 Rick Krivda .05
307 Mike Mussina .30
308 Rafael Palmeiro .40
309 Arthur Rhodes .05
310 Chris Sabo .05
311 Lee Smith .05
312 Gregg Zaun **RC** .05
313 Scott Cooper .05
314 Mike Greenwell .05
315 Tim Naehring .05
316 Otis Nixon .05
317 Paul Quantrill .05
318 John Valentin .05
319 Dave Valle .05
320 Frank Viola .05
321 Brian Anderson **RC** .10
322 Garret Anderson .05
323 Chad Curtis .05
324 Chili Davis .05
325 Gary DiSarcina .05
326 Damion Easley .05
327 Jim Edmonds .05
328 Chuck Finley .05
329 Joe Grahe .05
330 Bo Jackson .10
331 Mark Langston .05
332 Harold Reynolds .05
333 James Baldwin .05
334 Ray Durham **RC** .50
335 Julio Franco .05
336 Craig Grebeck .05
337 Ozzie Guillen .05
338 Joe Hall .05
339 Darrin Jackson .05
340 Jack McDowell .05
341 Tim Raines .05
342 Robin Ventura .05
343 Carlos Baerga .05
344 Derek Lilliquist .05
345 Dennis Martinez .05
346 Jack Morris .05
347 Eddie Murray .50
348 Chris Nabholz .05
349 Charles Nagy .05
350 Chad Ogea .05
351 Manny Ramirez .50
352 Omar Vizquel .05
353 Tim Belcher .05
354 Eric Davis .05
355 Kirk Gibson .05
356 Rick Greene .05
357 Mickey Tettleton .05
358 Alan Trammell .05
359 David Wells .05
360 Stan Belinda .05
361 Vince Coleman .05
362 David Cone .05
363 Gary Gaetti .05
364 Tom Gordon .05
365 Dave Henderson .05
366 Wally Joyner .05
367 Brent Mayne .05
368 Brian McRae .05
369 Michael Tucker .05
370 Ricky Bones .05
371 Brian Harper .05
372 Tyrone Hill .05
373 Mark Kiefer .05
374 Pat Listach .05
375 Mike Matheny **RC** .10
376 Jose Mercedes **RC** .05
377 Jody Reed .05
378 Kevin Seitzer .05
379 B.J. Surhoff .05
380 Greg Vaughn .05
381 Turner Ward .05
382 Wes Weger **RC** .05
383 Bill Wegman .05
384 Rick Aguilera .05
385 Rich Becker .05
386 Alex Cole .05
387 Steve Dunn .05
388 Keith Garagozzo **RC** .05
389 LaTroy Hawkins **RC** .05
390 Shane Mack .05
391 David McCarty .05
392 Pedro Munoz .05
393 Derek Parks **RC** .05
394 Kirby Puckett .60
395 Kevin Tapani .05
396 Matt Walbeck .05
397 Jim Abbott .05
398 Mike Gallego .05
399 Xavier Hernandez .05
400 Don Mattingly .65
401 Terry Mulholland .05
402 Matt Nokes .05
403 Luis Polonia .05
404 Bob Wickman .05
405 Mark Acre .05
406 Fausto Cruz **RC** .05
407 Dennis Eckersley .45
408 Rickey Henderson .50
409 Stan Javier .05
410 Carlos Reyes **RC** .05
411 Ruben Sierra .05
412 Terry Steinbach .05
413 Bill Taylor .05
414 Todd Van Poppel .05
415 Eric Anthony .05
416 Bobby Ayala .05
417 Chris Bosio .05
418 Tim Davis .05
419 Randy Johnson .50
420 Kevin King .05
421 Anthony Manahan **RC** .05
422 Edgar Martinez .05
423 Keith Mitchell .05
424 Roger Salkeld .05
425 Mac Suzuki **RC** .05
426 Dan Wilson .05
427 Duff Brumley **RC** .05
428 Jose Canseco .30
429 Will Clark .05
430 Steve Dreyer .05
431 Rick Helling .05
432 Chris James .05
433 Matt Whiteside .05
434 Roberto Alomar .20
435 Scott Brow .05
436 Domingo Cedeno **RC** .05
437 Carlos Delgado .35
438 Juan Guzman .05
439 Paul Spoljaric .05
440 Todd Stottlemyre .05
441 Woody Williams .05
442 Dave Justice .05
443 Mike Kelly .05
444 Ryan Klesko .05
445 Javier Lopez .05
446 Greg Maddux .60
447 Kent Mercker .05
448 Charlie O'Brien .05
449 Terry Pendleton .05
450 Mike Stanton .05
451 Tony Tarasco .05
452 Terrell Wade **RC** .05
453 Willie Banks .05
454 Shawon Dunston .05
455 Mark Grace .05
456 Jose Guzman .05
457 Jose Hernandez .05
458 Glenallen Hill .05
459 Blaise Ilsley .05
460 Brooks Kieschnick **RC** .05
461 Derrick May .05
462 Randy Myers .05
463 Karl Rhodes .05
464 Sammy Sosa .60
465 Steve Trachsel **RC** .10
466 Anthony Young .05
467 Eddie Zambrano **RC** .05
468 Bret Boone .05
469 Tom Browning .05
470 Hector Carrasco **RC** .05
471 Rob Dibble .05
472 Erik Hanson .05
473 Thomas Howard .05
474 Barry Larkin .05
475 Hal Morris .05
476 Jose Rijo .05
477 John Burke .05
478 Ellis Burks .05
479 Marvin Freeman .05
480 Andres Galarraga .05
481 Greg Harris .05
482 Charlie Hayes .05
483 Darren Holmes .05
484 Howard Johnson .05
485 Marcus Moore **RC** .05
486 David Nied .05
487 Mark Thompson .05
488 Walt Weiss .05
489 Kurt Abbott .05
490 Matias Carrillo .05
491 Jeff Conine .05
492 Chris Hammond .05
493 Bryan Harvey .05
494 Charlie Hough .05
495 Yorkis Perez **RC** .05
496 Pat Rapp .05
497 Benito Santiago .05
498 David Weathers .05
499 Craig Biggio .05
500 Ken Caminiti .05
501 Doug Drabek .05
502 Tony Eusebio **RC** .10
503 Steve Finley .05
504 Pete Harnisch .05
505 Brian Hunter .05
506 Domingo Jean .05
507 Todd Jones .05
508 Orlando Miller .05
509 James Mouton .05
510 Roberto Petagine .05
511 Shane Reynolds .05
512 Mitch Williams .05
513 Billy Ashley .05
514 Tom Candiotti .05
515 Delino DeShields .05
516 Kevin Gross .05
517 Orel Hershiser .05
518 Eric Karros .05
519 Ramon Martinez .05
520 Chan Ho Park **RC** .75
521 Henry Rodriguez .05
522 Joey Eischen .05
523 Rod Henderson .05
524 Pedro Martinez .50
525 Mel Rojas .05
526 Larry Walker .05
527 Gabe White **RC** .10
528 Bobby Bonilla .05
529 Jonathan Hurst .05
530 Bobby Jones .05
531 Kevin McReynolds .05
532 Bill Pulsipher .05
533 Bret Saberhagen .05
534 David Segui .05
535 Pete Smith .05
536 Kelly Stinnett **RC** .05
537 Dave Telgheder .05
538 Quilvio Veras **RC** .05
539 Jose Vizcaino .05
540 Pete Walker .05
541 Ricky Bottalico .05
542 Wes Chamberlain .05
543 Mariano Duncan .05
544 Len Dykstra .05
545 Jim Eisenreich .05
546 Phil Geisler **RC** .05
547 Wayne Gomes **RC** .10
548 Doug Jones .05
549 Jeff Juden .05
550 Mike Lieberthal .05
551 Tony Longmire **RC** .05
552 Tom Marsh .05
553 Bobby Munoz .05
554 Curt Schilling .15
555 Carlos Garcia .05
556 Ravelo Manzanillo **RC** .05
557 Orlando Merced .05
558 Will Pennyfeather **RC** .05
559 Zane Smith .05
560 Andy Van Slyke .05
561 Rick White .05
562 Luis Alicea .05
563 Brian Barber **RC** .05
564 Clint Davis **RC** .05
565 Bernard Gilkey .05
566 Ray Lankford .05
567 Tom Pagnozzi .05
568 Ozzie Smith .60
569 Rick Sutcliffe .05
570 Allen Watson .05
571 Dmitri Young .05
572 Derek Bell .05
573 Andy Benes .05
574 Archi Cianfrocco .05
575 Joey Hamilton .05
576 Gene Harris .05
577 Trevor Hoffman .05
578 Tim Hyers **RC** .05
579 Brian Johnson **RC** .05
580 Keith Lockhart **RC** .05
581 Pedro Martinez .05
582 Ray McDavid .05
583 Phil Plantier .05
584 Bip Roberts .05
585 Dave Staton .05
586 Todd Benzinger .05
587 John Burkett .05
588 Bryan Hickerson .05
589 Willie McGee .05
590 John Patterson .05
591 Mark Portugal .05
592 Kevin Rogers .05
593 Joe Rosselli **RC** .05
594 Steve Soderstrom **RC** .05
595 Robby Thompson .05
596 125th Anniversary card .05
597 Checklist .05
598 Checklist .05
599 Checklist .05
600 Checklist .05

All-Rookie Team

A stylized sunrise landscape is the background for this insert set featuring top rookies and inserted into Ultra Series II packs at the rate of about one per 10. Backs repeat the motif with an action photo. Both sides are gold-foil enhanced and UV-coated.

NM/M

Complete Set (10): 4.00
Common Player: .35
1 Kurt Abbott .35

2 Carlos Delgado 3.00
3 Cliff Floyd .35
4 Jeffrey Hammonds .35
5 Ryan Klesko .35
6 Javier Lopez .35
7 Raul Mondesi .35
8 James Mouton .35
9 Chan Ho Park .50
10 Dave Staton .35

All-Rookie Team Supers

This super-size (3-1/2" x 5-1/2") version of the Fleer Ultra II insert set featuring top rookies was included one per case of hobby packaging. Cards are identical to the smaller version. Both sides are gold-foil enhanced and UV-coated.

NM/M

Complete Set (10): 5.00
Common Player: .50
1 Kurt Abbott .50
2 Carlos Delgado 3.00
3 Cliff Floyd .50
4 Jeffrey Hammonds .50
5 Ryan Klesko .50
6 Javier Lopez .50
7 Raul Mondesi .50
8 James Mouton .50
9 Chan Ho Park .75
10 Dave Staton .50

All-Stars

Fleer's opinion of the top 20 players in 1994 are featured in this most common of the Series II Ultra insert sets. Silver-foil highlights enhance the chase cards, found, according to stated odds, once per three packs, on average. National Leaguers have purple backgrounds front and back, American Leaguers have red.

NM/M

Complete Set (20): 5.00
Common Player: .15
1 Chris Hoiles .15
2 Frank Thomas .35
3 Roberto Alomar .20
4 Cal Ripken, Jr. 1.00
5 Robin Ventura .15
6 Albert Belle .15
7 Juan Gonzalez .20
8 Ken Griffey Jr. .50
9 John Olerud .15
10 Jack McDowell .15
11 Mike Piazza .50
12 Fred McGriff .15
13 Ryne Sandberg .40
14 Jay Bell .15
15 Matt Williams .15
16 Barry Bonds 1.00
17 Len Dykstra .15
18 Dave Justice .15
19 Tom Glavine .20
20 Greg Maddux .40

Award Winners

The most common of the Fleer Ultra insert sets for 1994 is the 25-card "Award Winners." Horizontal format cards feature front and back background with a gold-embossed look. A player action photo appears on the front. A gold-foil seal on the front has a symbolic player representation flanked by the pictured player's name and award. A gold Fleer Ultra logo is at top. Backs have a player portrait photo and a write-up about the award. The name of the award and the player's name appear in gold foil at the top. Stated odds of finding an Award Winners card were one in three packs.

NM/M

Complete Set (25): 5.00
Common Player: .10
1 Ivan Rodriguez .25
2 Don Mattingly .45
3 Roberto Alomar .20
4 Robin Ventura .10
5 Omar Vizquel .10
6 Ken Griffey Jr. .50
7 Kenny Lofton .10
8 Devon White .10
9 Mark Langston .10
10 Kirt Manwaring .10
11 Mark Grace .10
12 Robby Thompson .10
13 Matt Williams .10
14 Jay Bell .10
15 Barry Bonds .60
16 Marquis Grissom .10
17 Larry Walker .10
18 Greg Maddux .40
19 Frank Thomas .35
20 Barry Bonds .60
21 Paul Molitor .35
22 Jack McDowell .10
23 Greg Maddux .40
24 Tim Salmon .10
25 Mike Piazza .50

Career Achievement Awards

The outstanding careers of five of baseball's top veteran stars are recognized in this chase set, inserted on average once every 21 packs of Ultra Series II. The gold-highlighted horizontal fronts combine a current color photo with a background single-tint photo from the player's earlier days. Backs flip-flop the photo use, with the current photo in the background and the earlier photo in full color in the foreground. The gold Ultra Career Achievement Award seal is repeated on back, as well.

NM/M

Complete Set (5): 4.00

Common Player:		.50
1	Joe Carter	.50
2	Paul Molitor	.75
3	Cal Ripken, Jr.	2.00
4	Ryne Sandberg	1.00
5	Dave Winfield	.75

Firemen

Ten of the major leagues' leading relief pitchers are featured in this Ultra insert set. Cards have an action photo of the player superimposed over a background photo of a fire truck. A shield at top, in gold foil, has a smoke-eater's helmet, stylized flames and proclaims the player an "Ultra Fireman." Backs are horizontal in format and feature the pumper's control panel in the background photo. A color player portrait photo appears on one side, with a description of his relief role and successes in a whitened box. Fireman cards are found, on average, once per 11 packs, according to stated odds.

		NM/M
Complete Set (10):		2.00
Common Player:		.25
1	Jeff Montgomery	.25
2	Duane Ward	.25
3	Tom Henke	.25
4	Roberto Hernandez	.25
5	Dennis Eckersley	1.25
6	Randy Myers	.25
7	Rod Beck	.25
8	Bryan Harvey	.25
9	John Wetteland	.25
10	Mitch Williams	.25

Hitting Machines

A heavy metal background of gears and iron-letter logo is featured in this insert set honoring the game's top hitters. The cards turn up about once in every five packs of Ultra Series II. Both front and back are highlighted in silver foil.

		NM/M
Complete Set (10):		4.00
Common Player:		.15
1	Roberto Alomar	.25
2	Carlos Baerga	.15
3	Barry Bonds	2.00
4	Andres Galarraga	.15
5	Juan Gonzalez	.25
6	Tony Gwynn	.50
7	Paul Molitor	.40
8	John Olerud	.15
9	Mike Piazza	.75
10	Frank Thomas	.40

Home Run Kings

One of two high-end insert sets in '94 Ultra is the 12-card "Home Run Kings" found exclusively in 14-card foil packs, on an average of once per 36-pack box. Featuring the technology Fleer calls "etched metallization," the cards have a black background with a red and blue foil representation of

a batter. An action photo of a player taking a mighty cut or starting his home-run trot is featured. A large gold-foil "Home Run King" crown-and-shield device are in an upper corner, while the Ultra logo and player name are in gold foil at bottom. Backs have a white background with the red and blue batter symbol. The player's name appears in gold foil at the top, along with a portrait photo and a summary of his home run prowess.

		NM/M
Complete Set (12):		15.00
Common Player:		.75
1	Juan Gonzalez	1.00
2	Ken Griffey Jr.	2.50
3	Frank Thomas	2.00
4	Albert Belle	.75
5	Rafael Palmeiro	1.50
6	Joe Carter	.75
7	Barry Bonds	4.00
8	Dave Justice	.75
9	Matt Williams	.75
10	Fred McGriff	.75
11	Ron Gant	.75
12	Mike Piazza	2.50

League Leaders

Arguably the least attractive of the '94 Ultra inserts are the "League Leaders." Fronts feature a full-bleed action photo on which the bottom has been re-colored to a team hue giving the effect of teal, purple and magenta miasmas rising from the turf. An Ultra logo appears in gold foil in an upper corner, with the player's name in gold foil at about the dividing line between the natural color and colorized portions of the photo. A large "League Leader" appears in the bottom half of the photo, with the category led printed in the lower-left. Backs repeat the team color at top, fading to white at the bottom. In gold foil are "League Leader" and the category. A portrait photo appears at bottom. Several paragraphs detail the league leading performance of the previous season.

		NM/M
Complete Set (10):		3.00
Common Player:		.25
1	John Olerud	.25
2	Rafael Palmeiro	1.00
3	Kenny Lofton	.25
4	Jack McDowell	.25
5	Randy Johnson	1.50
6	Andres Galarraga	.25
7	Len Dykstra	.25
8	Chuck Carr	.25
9	Tom Glavine	.35
10	Jose Rijo	.25

On-Base Leaders

One of the lesser-known, but most valuable, stats - on-base percentage - is featured in this subset found exclusively in 17-card packs, at the rate of about one per 37 packs. The fronts feature color photos against a stat-filled printed-foil background.

		NM/M
Complete Set (12):		25.00
Common Player:		1.50
1	Roberto Alomar	2.00
2	Barry Bonds	6.50
3	Len Dykstra	1.50
4	Andres Galarraga	1.50
5	Mark Grace	1.50
6	Ken Griffey Jr.	5.00
7	Gregg Jefferies	1.50
8	Orlando Merced	1.50
9	Paul Molitor	3.50
10	John Olerud	1.50
11	Tony Phillips	1.50
12	Frank Thomas	3.50

Phillies Finest

As a tribute to two of Fleer's home-team heroes, the Philadelphia-based card company created an Ultra insert set featuring 12 cards each of "Phillies Finest," John Kruk and Darren Daulton. Twenty of the cards were issued as Series 1 and 2 inserts, about one in every eight packs, while four were available only by a mail-in offer. Fronts feature action photos with large block letters popping out of the background. The Ultra logo and player name appear in gold foil. Backs have portrait photos and career summaries, with the player's name and card number in gold foil. Daulton and Kruk each autographed 1,000 of the inserts. Stated odds of finding the autographed cards were one in 11,000 packs. Values listed are per card.

		NM/M
Complete Set (24):		4.00
Common Player:		.25
Autographed Daulton:		45.00
Autographed Kruk:		30.00
1-5	Darren Daulton	.25
6-10	John Kruk	.25
11-15	Darren Daulton	.25
16-20	John Kruk	.25
9a	John Kruk (PROMOTIONAL SAMPLE)	1.50
1M, 3M	Darren Daulton	.75
2M, 4M	John Kruk	.75

RBI Kings

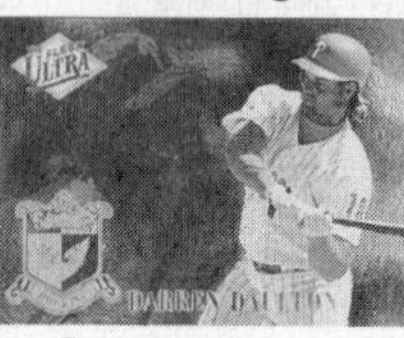

Exclusive to the 19-card jumbo packs of Fleer Ultra are a series of 12 "RBI Kings" insert cards, found, according to stated odds, one per 36 packs. The horizontal-format card front uses Fleer's "etched metallized" technology to produce a sepia-toned background action photo, in front of which is a color player photo. An Ultra logo appears in gold foil in an upper corner while a fancy shield-and-scroll "RBI King" logo and the player's name are in gold at the bottom. Backs repeat the basic front motif and include a color player portrait photo, his name in gold foil and a paragraph justifying his selection as an RBI King.

		NM/M
Complete Set (12):		16.00
Common Player:		1.00
1	Albert Belle	1.00
2	Frank Thomas	2.50
3	Joe Carter	1.00
4	Juan Gonzalez	1.25
5	Cecil Fielder	1.00
6	Carlos Baerga	1.00
7	Barry Bonds	5.00
8	David Justice	1.00
9	Ron Gant	1.00
10	Mike Piazza	3.50
11	Matt Williams	1.00
12	Darren Daulton	1.00

Rising Stars

An outer space background printed on metallic foil sets this chase set apart from most of the rest of the Ultra Series II inserts. The silver-foil enhanced cards of projected superstars of tomorrow are found on average once every 37 packs.

		NM/M
Complete Set (12):		15.00
Common Player:		1.00
1	Carlos Baerga	1.00
2	Jeff Bagwell	5.00
3	Albert Belle	1.00
4	Cliff Floyd	1.00
5	Travis Fryman	1.00
6	Marquis Grissom	1.00
7	Kenny Lofton	1.00
8	John Olerud	1.00
9	Mike Piazza	7.50
10	Kirk Rueter	1.00
11	Tim Salmon	1.00
12	Aaron Sele	1.00

Second Year Standouts

Approximately once every 11 packs, the Ultra insert find is a "Second Year Standout" card. Ten of the game's sophomore stars are featured. Fronts feature a pair of action photos against a team-color background. Gold-foil highlights are the Ultra logo, the player's name

and a "Second Year Standout" shield. The shield and player name are repeated in gold foil on the back, as is the team color background. There is a player portrait photo at bottom and a summary of the player's 1993 season.

		NM/M
Complete Set (10):		5.00
Common Player:		.25
1	Jason Bere	.25
2	Brent Gates	.25
3	Jeffrey Hammonds	.25
4	Tim Salmon	.50
5	Aaron Sele	.25
6	Chuck Carr	.25
7	Jeff Conine	.25
8	Greg McMichael	.25
9	Mike Piazza	4.00
10	Kevin Stocker	.25

Strikeout Kings

A gold-foil "Strikeout Kings" crown-and-shield logo is featured on the front of this chase set. Cards are found on average once per seven packs. Each of the cards features the K-king in sequential action photos. Backs have a larger action photo with a large version of the Strikeout King shield in the background.

		NM/M
Complete Set (5):		2.00
Common Player:		.25
1	Randy Johnson	.75
2	Mark Langston	.25
3	Greg Maddux	1.00
4	Jose Rijo	.25
5	John Smoltz	.25

1995 Ultra

A clean design enhanced with three different colors of metallic foil graphics is featured on the basic cards of 1995 Fleer Ultra. Two series of 250 cards each were issued with cards arranged alphabetically within team, also sequenced alphabetically. Fronts have a gold-foil Ultra logo in an upper corner, with the player's name and team logo in a team-color coded foil at bottom. There are no other graphic elements on the borderless photos. Backs have a large photo rendered in a single color, again team-coded. A postage-stamp sized color photo in one corner is flanked by a few vital stats in silver foil. Career and '94 stats are printed at bottom, enhanced by the foil color from the front. Cards were issued in 12-card retail and hobby packs at $1.99 and jumbo pre-priced ($2.69) magazine packs. Each pack contains one of the several insert series from the appropriate series.

		NM/M
Complete Set (450):		10.00
Common Player:		.05
Gold Medallion:		2X
Series 1 or 2 Pack (12):		.50
Series 1 or 2 Wax Box (36):		12.50
1	Brady Anderson	.05
2	Sid Fernandez	.05
3	Jeffrey Hammonds	.05
4	Chris Hoiles	.05
5	Ben McDonald	.05
6	Mike Mussina	.35
7	Rafael Palmeiro	.65
8	Jack Voigt	.05
9	Wes Chamberlain	.05
10	Roger Clemens	1.00
11	Chris Howard	.05
12	Tim Naehring	.05
13	Otis Nixon	.05
14	Rich Rowland	.05
15	Ken Ryan	.05
16	John Valentin	.05
17	Mo Vaughn	.05
18	Brian Anderson	.05
19	Chili Davis	.05
20	Damion Easley	.05
21	Jim Edmonds	.05
22	Mark Langston	.05
23	Tim Salmon	.05
24	J.T. Snow	.05
25	Chris Turner	.05
26	Wilson Alvarez	.05
27	Joey Cora	.05
28	Alex Fernandez	.05
29	Roberto Hernandez	.05
30	Lance Johnson	.05
31	Ron Karkovice	.05
32	Kirk McCaskill	.05
33	Tim Raines	.05
34	Frank Thomas	.75
35	Sandy Alomar	.05
36	Albert Belle	.05
37	Mark Clark	.05
38	Kenny Lofton	.05
39	Eddie Murray	.75
40	Eric Plunk	.05
41	Manny Ramirez	.75
42	Jim Thome	.60
43	Omar Vizquel	.05
44	Danny Bautista	.05
45	Junior Felix	.05
46	Cecil Fielder	.05
47	Chris Gomez	.05
48	Chad Kreuter	.05
49	Mike Moore	.05
50	Tony Phillips	.05
51	Alan Trammell	.05
52	David Wells	.05
53	Kevin Appier	.05
54	Billy Brewer	.05
55	David Cone	.05
56	Greg Gagne	.05
57	Bob Hamelin	.05
58	Jose Lind	.05
59	Brent Mayne	.05
60	Brian McRae	.05
61	Terry Shumpert	.05
62	Ricky Bones	.05
63	Mike Fetters	.05
64	Darryl Hamilton	.05
65	John Jaha	.05
66	Graeme Lloyd	.05
67	Matt Mieske	.05
68	Kevin Seitzer	.05
69	Jose Valentin	.05
70	Turner Ward	.05
71	Rick Aguilera	.05
72	Rich Becker	.05
73	Alex Cole	.05
74	Scott Leius	.05
75	Pat Meares	.05
76	Kirby Puckett	1.00
77	Dave Stevens	.05
78	Kevin Tapani	.05
79	Matt Walbeck	.05
80	Wade Boggs	1.00
81	Scott Kamieniecki	.05
82	Pat Kelly	.05
83	Jimmy Key	.05
84	Paul O'Neill	.05
85	Luis Polonia	.05
86	Mike Stanley	.05

No.	Player	Value
87	Danny Tartabull	.05
88	Bob Wickman	.05
89	Mark Acre	.05
90	Geronimo Berroa	.05
91	Mike Bordick	.05
92	Ron Darling	.05
93	Stan Javier	.05
94	Mark McGwire	1.50
95	Troy Neel	.05
96	Ruben Sierra	.05
97	Terry Steinbach	.05
98	Eric Anthony	.05
99	Chris Bosio	.05
100	Dave Fleming	.05
101	Ken Griffey Jr.	1.25
102	Reggie Jefferson	.05
103	Randy Johnson	.75
104	Edgar Martinez	.05
105	Bill Risley	.05
106	Dan Wilson	.05
107	Cris Carpenter	.05
108	Will Clark	.05
109	Juan Gonzalez	.40
110	Rusty Greer	.05
111	David Hulse	.05
112	Roger Pavlik	.05
113	Ivan Rodriguez	.75
114	Doug Strange	.05
115	Matt Whiteside	.05
116	Roberto Alomar	.20
117	Brad Cornett	.05
118	Carlos Delgado	.45
119	Alex Gonzalez	.05
120	Darren Hall	.05
121	Pat Hentgen	.05
122	Paul Molitor	.75
123	Ed Sprague	.05
124	Devon White	.05
125	Tom Glavine	.25
126	Dave Justice	.05
127	Roberto Kelly	.05
128	Mark Lemke	.05
129	Greg Maddux	1.00
130	Charles Johnson	.05
131	Kent Mercker	.05
132	Charlie O'Brien	.05
133	John Smoltz	.05
134	Willie Banks	.05
135	Steve Buechele	.05
136	Kevin Foster	.05
137	Glenallen Hill	.05
138	Ray Sanchez	.05
139	Sammy Sosa	1.00
140	Steve Trachsel	.05
141	Rick Wilkins	.05
142	Jeff Brantley	.05
143	Hector Carrasco	.05
144	Kevin Jarvis	.05
145	Barry Larkin	.05
146	Chuck McElroy	.05
147	Jose Rijo	.05
148	Johnny Ruffin	.05
149	Deion Sanders	.05
150	Eddie Taubensee	.05
151	Dante Bichette	.05
152	Ellis Burks	.05
153	Joe Girardi	.05
154	Charlie Hayes	.05
155	Mike Kingery	.05
156	Steve Reed	.05
157	Kevin Ritz	.05
158	Bruce Ruffin	.05
159	Eric Young	.05
160	Kurt Abbott	.05
161	Chuck Carr	.05
162	Chris Hammond	.05
163	Bryan Harvey	.05
164	Terry Mathews	.05
165	Yorkis Perez	.05
166	Pat Rapp	.05
167	Gary Sheffield	.40
168	Dave Weathers	.05
169	Jeff Bagwell	.75
170	Ken Caminiti	.05
171	Doug Drabek	.05
172	Steve Finley	.05
173	John Hudek	.05
174	Todd Jones	.05
175	James Mouton	.05
176	Shane Reynolds	.05
177	Scott Servais	.05
178	Tom Candiotti	.05
179	Omar Daal	.05
180	Darren Dreifort	.05
181	Eric Karros	.05
182	Ramon Martinez	.05
183	Raul Mondesi	.05
184	Henry Rodriguez	.05
185	Todd Worrell	.05
186	Moises Alou	.05
187	Sean Berry	.05
188	Wil Cordero	.05
189	Jeff Fassero	.05
190	Darrin Fletcher	.05
191	Butch Henry	.05
192	Ken Hill	.05
193	Mel Rojas	.05
194	John Wetteland	.05
195	Bobby Bonilla	.05
196	Rico Brogna	.05
197	Bobby Jones	.05
198	Jeff Kent	.05
199	Josias Manzanillo	.05
200	Kelly Stinnett	.05
201	Ryan Thompson	.05
202	Jose Vizcaino	.05
203	Lenny Dykstra	.05
204	Jim Eisenreich	.05
205	Dave Hollins	.05
206	Mike Lieberthal	.05
207	Mickey Morandini	.05
208	Bobby Munoz	.05
209	Curt Schilling	.20
210	Heathcliff Slocumb	.05
211	David West	.05
212	Dave Clark	.05
213	Steve Cooke	.05
214	Midre Cummings	.05
215	Carlos Garcia	.05
216	Jeff King	.05
217	Jon Lieber	.05
218	Orlando Merced	.05
219	Don Slaught	.05
220	Rick White	.05
221	Rene Arocha	.05
222	Bernard Gilkey	.05
223	Brian Jordan	.05
224	Tom Pagnozzi	.05
225	Vicente Palacios	.05
226	Geronimo Pena	.05
227	Ozzie Smith	1.00
228	Allen Watson	.05
229	Mark Whiten	.05
230	Brad Ausmus	.05
231	Derek Bell	.05
232	Andy Benes	.05
233	Tony Gwynn	1.00
234	Joey Hamilton	.05
235	Luis Lopez	.05
236	Pedro A. Martinez	.05
237	Scott Sanders	.05
238	Eddie Williams	.05
239	Rod Beck	.05
240	Dave Burba	.05
241	Darren Lewis	.05
242	Kirt Manwaring	.05
243	Mark Portugal	.05
244	Darryl Strawberry	.05
245	Robby Thompson	.05
246	William Van Landingham	.05
247	Matt Williams	.05
248	Checklist	.05
249	Checklist	.05
250	Checklist	.05
251	Harold Baines	.05
252	Bret Barberie	.05
253	Armando Benitez	.05
254	Mike Devereaux	.05
255	Leo Gomez	.05
256	Jamie Moyer	.05
257	Arthur Rhodes	.05
258	Cal Ripken Jr.	2.00
259	Luis Alicea	.05
260	Jose Canseco	.45
261	Scott Cooper	.05
262	Andre Dawson	.25
263	Mike Greenwell	.05
264	Aaron Sele	.05
265	Garret Anderson	.05
266	Chad Curtis	.05
267	Gary DiSarcina	.05
268	Chuck Finley	.05
269	Rex Hudler	.05
270	Andrew Lorraine	.05
271	Spike Owen	.05
272	Lee Smith	.05
273	Jason Bere	.05
274	Ozzie Guillen	.05
275	Norberto Martin	.05
276	Scott Ruffcorn	.05
277	Robin Ventura	.05
278	Carlos Baerga	.05
279	Jason Grimsley	.05
280	Dennis Martinez	.05
281	Charles Nagy	.05
282	Paul Sorrento	.05
283	Dave Winfield	.75
284	John Doherty	.05
285	Travis Fryman	.05
286	Kirk Gibson	.05
287	Lou Whitaker	.05
288	Gary Gaetti	.05
289	Tom Gordon	.05
290	Mark Gubicza	.05
291	Wally Joyner	.05
292	Mike Macfarlane	.05
293	Jeff Montgomery	.05
294	Jeff Cirillo	.05
295	Cal Eldred	.05
296	Pat Listach	.05
297	Jose Mercedes	.05
298	Dave Nilsson	.05
299	Duane Singleton	.05
300	Greg Vaughn	.05
301	Scott Erickson	.05
302	Denny Hocking	.05
303	Chuck Knoblauch	.05
304	Pat Mahomes	.05
305	Pedro Munoz	.05
306	Erik Schullstrom	.05
307	Jim Abbott	.05
308	Tony Fernandez	.05
309	Sterling Hitchcock	.05
310	Jim Leyritz	.05
311	Don Mattingly	1.00
312	Jack McDowell	.05
313	Melido Perez	.05
314	Bernie Williams	.05
315	Scott Brosius	.05
316	Dennis Eckersley	.65
317	Brent Gates	.05
318	Rickey Henderson	.75
319	Steve Karsay	.05
320	Steve Ontiveros	.05
321	Bill Taylor	.05
322	Todd Van Poppel	.05
323	Bob Welch	.05
324	Bobby Ayala	.05
325	Mike Blowers	.05
326	Jay Buhner	.05
327	Felix Fermin	.05
328	Tino Martinez	.05
329	Marc Newfield	.05
330	Greg Pirkl	.05
331	Alex Rodriguez	1.50
332	Kevin Brown	.05
333	John Burkett	.05
334	Jeff Frye	.05
335	Kevin Gross	.05
336	Dean Palmer	.05
337	Joe Carter	.05
338	Shawn Green	.35
339	Juan Guzman	.05
340	Mike Huff	.05
341	Al Leiter	.05
342	John Olerud	.05
343	Dave Stewart	.05
344	Todd Stottlemyre	.05
345	Steve Avery	.05
346	Jeff Blauser	.05
347	Chipper Jones	1.00
348	Mike Kelly	.05
349	Ryan Klesko	.05
350	Javier Lopez	.05
351	Fred McGriff	.05
352	Jose Oliva	.05
353	Terry Pendleton	.05
354	Mike Stanton	.05
355	Tony Tarasco	.05
356	Mark Wohlers	.05
357	Jim Bullinger	.05
358	Shawon Dunston	.05
359	Mark Grace	.05
360	Derrick May	.05
361	Randy Myers	.05
362	Karl Rhodes	.05
363	Bret Boone	.05
364	Brian Dorsett	.05
365	Ron Gant	.05
366	Brian R. Hunter	.05
367	Hal Morris	.05
368	Jack Morris	.05
369	John Roper	.05
370	Reggie Sanders	.05
371	Pete Schourek	.05
372	John Smiley	.05
373	Marvin Freeman	.05
374	Andres Galarraga	.05
375	Mike Munoz	.05
376	David Nied	.05
377	Walt Weiss	.05
378	Greg Colbrunn	.05
379	Jeff Conine	.05
380	Charles Johnson	.05
381	Kurt Miller	.05
382	Robb Nen	.05
383	Benito Santiago	.05
384	Craig Biggio	.05
385	Tony Eusebio	.05
386	Luis Gonzalez	.05
387	Brian L. Hunter	.05
388	Darryl Kile	.05
389	Orlando Miller	.05
390	Phil Plantier	.05
391	Greg Swindell	.05
392	Billy Ashley	.05
393	Pedro Astacio	.05
394	Brett Butler	.05
395	Delino DeShields	.05
396	Orel Hershiser	.05
397	Garey Ingram	.05
398	Chan Ho Park	.05
399	Mike Piazza	1.25
400	Ismael Valdes	.05
401	Tim Wallach	.05
402	Cliff Floyd	.05
403	Marquis Grissom	.05
404	Mike Lansing	.05
405	Pedro Martinez	.75
406	Kirk Rueter	.05
407	Tim Scott	.05
408	Jeff Shaw	.05
409	Larry Walker	.05
410	Rondell White	.05
411	John Franco	.05
412	Todd Hundley	.05
413	Jason Jacome	.05
414	Joe Orsulak	.05
415	Bret Saberhagen	.05
416	David Segui	.05
417	Darren Daulton	.05
418	Mariano Duncan	.05
419	Tommy Greene	.05
420	Gregg Jefferies	.05
421	John Kruk	.05
422	Kevin Stocker	.05
423	Jay Bell	.05
424	Al Martin	.05
425	Denny Neagle	.05
426	Zane Smith	.05
427	Andy Van Slyke	.05
428	Paul Wagner	.05
429	Tom Henke	.05
430	Danny Jackson	.05
431	Ray Lankford	.05
432	John Mabry	.05
433	Bob Tewksbury	.05
434	Todd Zeile	.05
435	Andy Ashby	.05
436	Andujar Cedeno	.05
437	Donnie Elliott	.05
438	Bryce Florie	.05
439	Trevor Hoffman	.05
440	Melvin Nieves	.05
441	Bip Roberts	.05
442	Barry Bonds	2.00
443	Royce Clayton	.05
444	Mike Jackson	.05
445	John Patterson	.05
446	J.R. Phillips	.05
447	Bill Swift	.05
448	Checklist	.05
449	Checklist	.05
450	Checklist	.05

Gold Medallion

Less than 10 percent of the production run of Fleer Ultra (regular and insert sets) was produced in a special parallel Gold Medallion edition. On these special cards an embossed round gold seal replaces the Fleer Ultra logo in the upper corner. One Gold Medallion card was inserted into each Ultra foil pack.

	NM/M
Complete Set (450):	60.00
Common Player:	.25
Stars/Rookies:	2X

All-Rookies

Enlarged pieces of the central color action photo, set on a white background, make up the front design on these inserts. The player's name, card title and Ultra logo are printed in silver foil. Horizontal backs have another color photo, which is also repeated in single-color fashion. A career summary is printed over the larger photo. The All-Rookie inserts are found only in 12-card packs, at the rate of about one per four packs.

		NM/M
Complete Set (10):		2.25
Common Player:		.15
Gold Medallion:		2X
1	Cliff Floyd	.15
2	Chris Gomez	.15
3	Rusty Greer	.15
4	Bob Hamelin	.15
5	Joey Hamilton	.15
6	John Hudek	.15
7	Ryan Klesko	.15
8	Raul Mondesi	.15
9	Manny Ramirez	2.00
10	Steve Trachsel	.15

All-Stars

Twenty of the top players in the majors were chosen as Ultra All-Stars in this Series II chase set. Fronts have a color player photo at left. At right is a second photo, printed in only one color. A large "ALL-STAR" is at bottom, with the player's name above and team

below in silver foil. An Ultra logo is at left. Backs have another color photo, with a '94 season summary printed in a black panel at right. These cards were found one per five packs, on average.

		NM/M
Complete Set (20):		7.50
Common Player:		.15
Gold Medallion:		2X
1	Moises Alou	.15
2	Albert Belle	.15
3	Craig Biggio	.15
4	Wade Boggs	.60
5	Barry Bonds	1.50
6	David Cone	.15
7	Ken Griffey Jr.	.75
8	Tony Gwynn	.60
9	Chuck Knoblauch	.15
10	Barry Larkin	.15
11	Kenny Lofton	.15
12	Greg Maddux	.60
13	Fred McGriff	.15
14	Paul O'Neill	.15
15	Mike Piazza	.75
16	Kirby Puckett	.60
17	Cal Ripken Jr.	1.50
18	Ivan Rodriguez	.45
19	Frank Thomas	.50
20	Matt Williams	.15

Award Winners

Various official and unofficial award winners from the 1994 season are featured in this Series I insert set. Horizontal cards have a color player photo on the right side, with a single-color, vertically compressed action photo at left. The player's award is printed in a white strip at top, while his name and team logo, along with the Ultra logo, are at bottom. All front typography is in gold foil. Backs repeat the compressed photo at left, combined with another color photo at right. A season summary is printed over the photo at left. The Award Winners inserts were common to all types of packaging, found at the rate of about one per four packs.

		NM/M
Complete Set (25):		6.00
Common Player:		.10
Gold Medallion:		2X
1	Ivan Rodriguez	.30
2	Don Mattingly	.65
3	Roberto Alomar	.20
4	Wade Boggs	.60
5	Omar Vizquel	.10
6	Ken Griffey Jr.	.75
7	Kenny Lofton	.10
8	Devon White	.10
9	Mark Langston	.10
10	Tom Pagnozzi	.10
11	Jeff Bagwell	.45
12	Craig Biggio	.10
13	Matt Williams	.10
14	Barry Larkin	.10
15	Barry Bonds	1.00
16	Marquis Grissom	.10
17	Darren Lewis	.10
18	Greg Maddux	.60
19	Frank Thomas	.45
20	Jeff Bagwell	.45
21	David Cone	.10
22	Greg Maddux	.60
23	Bob Hamelin	.10
24	Raul Mondesi	.10
25	Moises Alou	.10

Golden Prospects

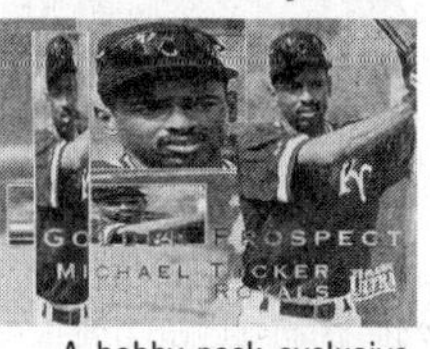

A hobby-pack exclusive, found at the rate of one per eight packs on average in Series I. Fronts feature a player photo at right, with three horizontally and vertically compressed versions of the same photo at right. The photo's background has been rendered in a single color. All typography - Ultra logo, card title, name and team - is in gold foil. Backs are also horizontal and have a color player photo and career summary.

		NM/M
Complete Set (10):		5.00
Common Player:		.10
Gold Medallion:		2X
1	James Baldwin	.10
2	Alan Benes	.10
3	Armando Benitez	.10
4	Ray Durham	.10
5	LaTroy Hawkins	.10
6	Brian Hunter	.10
7	Derek Jeter	3.00
8	Charles Johnson	.10
9	Alex Rodriguez	2.00
10	Michael Tucker	.10

Gold Medallion Rookies Mail-in

This set of 20 was available only by mailing in 10 Fleer Ultra wrappers plus $5.95. A reported 100,000 sets were produced. The cards are in the same format as the regular-issue Fleer Ultra. Each card has a team logo, player name and "ROOKIE" notation in gold foil at bottom, and the round Gold Medallion seal in an upper-corner of the borderless game-action photo front. Backs have two more action photos, a large one in one-color and a small one in full-color. Much of the typography on back is rendered in gold foil. Card numbers have an M prefix.

		NM/M
Complete Set (20):		3.00
Common Player:		.10
M-1	Manny Alexander	.10
M-2	Edgardo Alfonzo	.10
M-3	Jason Bates	.10
M-4	Andres Berumen	.10
M-5	Darren Bragg	.10
M-6	Jamie Brewington	.10
M-7	Jason Christiansen	.10
M-8	Brad Clontz	.10
M-9	Marty Cordova	.10
M-10	Johnny Damon	1.50
M-11	Vaughn Eshelman	.10
M-12	Chad Fonville	.10
M-13	Curtis Goodwin	.10
M-14	Tyler Green	.10
M-15	Bob Higginson	.10
M-16	Jason Isringhausen	.10
M-17	Hideo Nomo	1.50
M-18	Jon Nunnally	.10
M-19	Carlos Perez	.10
M-20	Julian Tavarez	.10

Hitting Machines

Various mechanical devices and dynamics make up the letters of "HITTING MACHINE" behind the color player action photo in this insert set. Both of those elements, along with the gold-foil player name, team and Ultra logo are in UV-coated contrast to the matte-finish gray background. Backs are also horizontal in format and feature a portrait photo at right, against a gray-streaked background. A career summary is printed at right. The Hitting Machines series is found only in Series II Ultra retail packs, at the rate of one card per eight packs, on average.

		NM/M
Complete Set (10):		6.00
Common Player:		.40
Gold Medallion:		2X
1	Jeff Bagwell	.65
2	Albert Belle	.25
3	Dante Bichette	.25
4	Barry Bonds	2.50
5	Jose Canseco	.50
6	Ken Griffey Jr.	1.00
7	Tony Gwynn	.75
8	Fred McGriff	.25
9	Mike Piazza	1.00
10	Frank Thomas	.65

Home Run Kings

Retail packaging of Fleer Ultra Series I was the hiding place for this sluggers' chase set. An average of one out of eight packs yielded a Home Run King insert. Fronts have a photo of the player's home run cut, while large letters "H," "R" and "K" are stacked vertically down one side. All front typography is in gold foil. Backs have another batting photo and a couple of sentences of recent career slugging prowess.

		NM/M
Complete Set (10):		7.50
Common Player:		.25
Gold Medallion:		2X
1	Ken Griffey Jr.	2.00
2	Frank Thomas	.75
3	Albert Belle	.25
4	Jose Canseco	.50
5	Cecil Fielder	.25
6	Matt Williams	.25
7	Jeff Bagwell	.75
8	Barry Bonds	3.00
9	Fred McGriff	.25
10	Andres Galarraga	.25

League Leaders

Top performers in major statistical categories are featured in this Series I insert. Cards were seeded in all types of Ultra packaging at the rate of about one card per three packs. Cards have a horizontal orientation with a color player action photo printed over a black logo of the appropriate league. American Leaguers' cards have a light brown overall background color, National Leaguers have dark green. The player's name, team and Ultra logos, and box with his league-leading category are printed in silver foil. The background from the front is carried over to the back, where a color portrait photo is at left, and a '94 season summary printed at right.

		NM/M
Complete Set (10):		2.50
Common Player:		.15
Gold Medallion:		2X
1	Paul O'Neill	.15
2	Kenny Lofton	.15
3	Jimmy Key	.15
4	Randy Johnson	.50
5	Lee Smith	.15
6	Tony Gwynn	.75
7	Craig Biggio	.15
8	Greg Maddux	.75
9	Andy Benes	.15
10	John Franco	.15

On-Base Leaders

Numerous smaller versions in several sizes of the central action photo against a graduated color background from the front design of this Series II insert set. The player name, card title and Ultra logo are printed in gold foil down one side. Backs have a horizontal player photo with a large team logo at top, a smaller version at bottom and a 1994 season summary. One out of eight (on average) prepriced packs yielded an On-Base Leaders insert.

		NM/M
Complete Set (10):		15.00
Common Player:		1.00
Gold Medallion:		2X
1	Jeff Bagwell	2.00
2	Albert Belle	1.00
3	Craig Biggio	1.00
4	Wade Boggs	2.50
5	Barry Bonds	6.00
6	Will Clark	1.00
7	Tony Gwynn	2.50
8	Dave Justice	1.00
9	Paul O'Neill	1.00
10	Frank Thomas	2.00

Power Plus

The scarcest of the Series I Ultra inserts are the Power Plus cards, printed on 100% etched foil and inserted at the rate of less than one per box. Fronts have a player action photo overprinted on a background of "POWER PLUS" logos in various metallic colors. A team logo and player name are at bottom in gold foil, as is the Ultra logo at top. Backs are conventionally

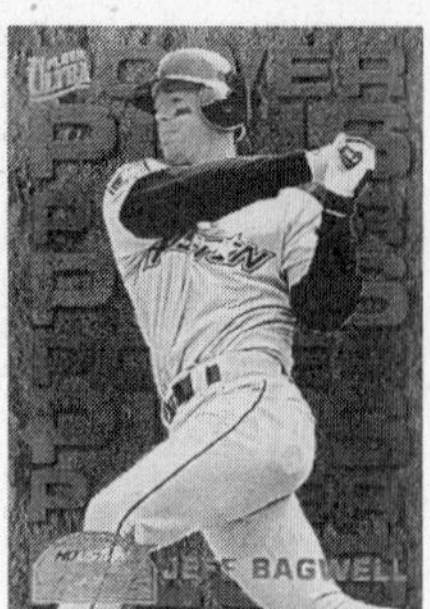

printed and have a player photo on one side and season summary on the other.

		NM/M
Complete Set (6):		7.50
Common Player:		.50
Gold Medallion:		2X
1	Albert Belle	.50
2	Ken Griffey Jr.	2.00
3	Frank Thomas	1.00
4	Jeff Bagwell	1.00
5	Barry Bonds	4.00
6	Matt Williams	.50

RBI Kings

A bright aura surrounds the central player action photo on these cards, separating the player image from an indistinct colored background. At center is a large gold-foil "RBI KING" with the player's name above and team below. Backs have a similar design with a white box at bottom covering the player's RBI abilities. This set is found only in Series I jumbo packs, at an average rate of one per eight packs.

		NM/M
Complete Set (10):		12.00
Common Player:		.50
Gold Medallion:		2X
1	Kirby Puckett	3.00
2	Joe Carter	.50
3	Albert Belle	.50
4	Frank Thomas	2.00
5	Julio Franco	.50
6	Jeff Bagwell	2.00
7	Matt Williams	.50
8	Dante Bichette	.50
9	Fred McGriff	.50
10	Mike Piazza	4.00

Rising Stars

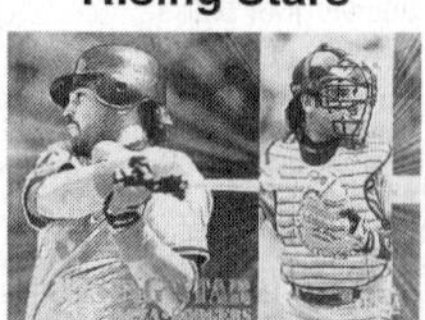

The top of the line among Series II chase cards is this set printed on 100% etched foil and seeded at the rate of less than one per box, on average. Horizontal-format cards have two player photos on a background of multi-colored rays. The Ultra logo, card title, player name and team are printed in gold foil. Backs repeat the colored rays, have another player photo and a career summary.

		NM/M
Complete Set (9):		7.00
Common Player:		.50
Gold Medallion:		2X
1	Moises Alou	.50
2	Jeff Bagwell	1.50
3	Albert Belle	.65
4	Juan Gonzalez	1.50
5	Chuck Knoblauch	.50
6	Kenny Lofton	.50
7	Raul Mondesi	.50
8	Mike Piazza	2.50
9	Frank Thomas	1.50

1995 Ultra Second Year Standouts

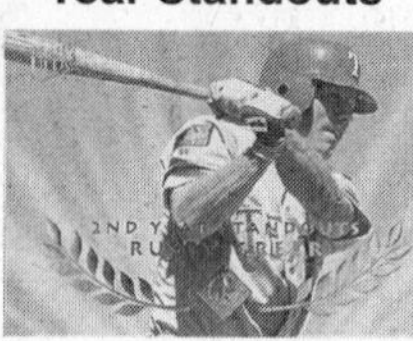

Fifteen of the game's sophomore stars are featured in this Series I insert set. Horizontal-format cards have player action photos front and back set against a background of orange and yellow rays. Besides the player name, card title and Ultra logo in gold-foil, the front features a pair of leafed branches flanking a team logo, all in embossed gold-foil. Backs have a career summary. The series was seeded at the average rate of one per six packs.

		NM/M
Complete Set (15):		3.50
Common Player:		.15
Gold Medallion:		2X
1	Cliff Floyd	.15
2	Chris Gomez	.15
3	Rusty Greer	.15
4	Darren Hall	.15
5	Bob Hamelin	.15
6	Joey Hamilton	.15
7	Jeffrey Hammonds	.15
8	John Hudek	.15
9	Ryan Klesko	.15
10	Raul Mondesi	.15
11	Manny Ramirez	3.00
12	Bill Risley	.15
13	Steve Trachsel	.15
14	William Van Landingham	.15
15	Rondell White	.15

Strikeout Kings

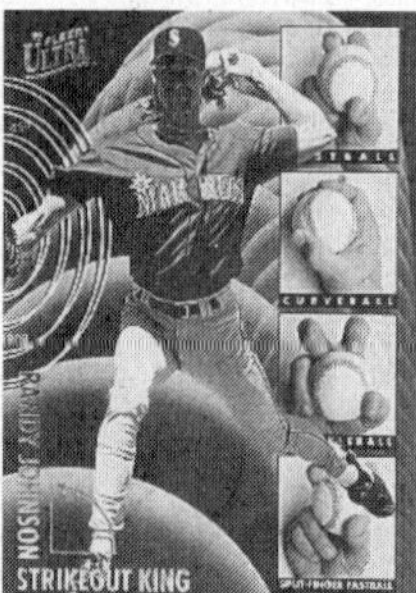

A purple background with several types of concentric and overlapping circular designs in white are the background of this Series II chase set. An action color photo of the K-King is at center, while down one side are stacked photos of the grips used for various pitches. The player name, card title and Ultra logo are in silver foil. Backs have a portrait photo and career summary with purple circles behind and a black background. Stated odds of finding a Strikeout King card are one in five packs, on average.

		NM/M
Complete Set (6):		3.00
Common Player:		.10
Gold Medallion:		2X
1	Andy Benes	.10
2	Roger Clemens	1.50
3	Randy Johnson	.75
4	Greg Maddux	1.00
5	Pedro Martinez	.75
6	Jose Rijo	.10

1996 Ultra Promotional Samples

A six-page glossy folder which was die-cut to hold three sample cards introduced Fleer's Ultra line for 1996. The fronts of all three cards are similar in format to the issued versions, but only the back of the basic-card sample replicates the issued version. Backs of the chase card samples contained product information.

		NM/M
Complete Set (8):		7.50
Common Player:		1.00
(1)	Ken Griffey Jr. (basic card)	1.50
(2)	Matt Williams (basic card)	1.00
(3)	Barry Bonds (HR King)	2.50
(4)	Frank Thomas (HR King)	1.25
(5)	Roberto Alomar (Prime Leather)	1.00
(6)	Cal Ripken Jr. (Prime Leather)	2.50
2	Tony Gwynn (Season Crown)	1.50
4	Kenny Lofton (Season Crown)	1.00

1996 Ultra

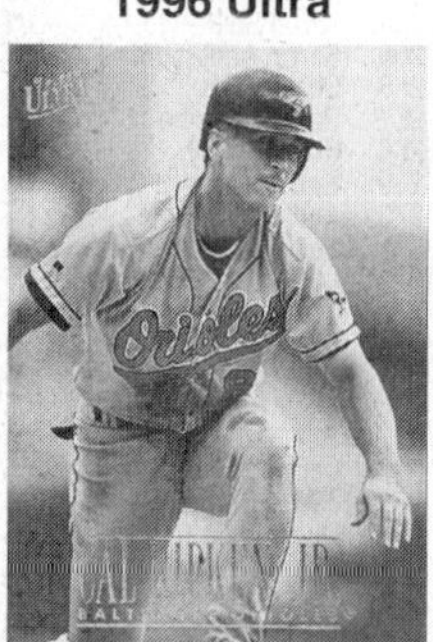

A 40% thicker cardboard stock and silver-foil highlights are featured in this year's edition. Fronts are very basic with a borderless action photo and silver-foil graphics. Backs feature a three-photo montage along with 1995 and career stats. The set was released in two 300-card series; each card is also reprinted as part of a limited-edition Gold Medallion parallel set. One Gold Medallion card is found in every pack. Each series has eight insert sets. Series 1 inserts are RBI Kings, Home Run Kings, Fresh Foundations, Diamond Producers, Power Plus, Season Crowns, Golden Prospects and Prime Leather. Series 2 inserts are Call to the Hall, Golden Prospects, Hitting Machines, On-Base Leaders, RESPECT, Rawhide, Rising Stars and Thunderclap. Checklist cards were also randomly inserted into packs from both series.

		NM/M
Complete Set (600):		22.50
Common Player:		.05
Gold Medallions:		2X
Series 1 or 2 Pack (12):		1.25
Series 1 or 2 Wax Box (24):		20.00
1	Manny Alexander	.05
2	Brady Anderson	.05
3	Bobby Bonilla	.05
4	Scott Erickson	.05
5	Curtis Goodwin	.05
6	Chris Hoiles	.05
7	Doug Jones	.05
8	Jeff Manto	.05
9	Mike Mussina	.35
10	Rafael Palmeiro	.50
11	Cal Ripken Jr.	1.50
12	Rick Aguilera	.05
13	Luis Alicea	.05
14	Stan Belinda	.05
15	Jose Canseco	.40
16	Roger Clemens	.85
17	Mike Greenwell	.05
18	Mike Macfarlane	.05
19	Tim Naehring	.05
20	Troy O'Leary	.05
21	John Valentin	.05
22	Mo Vaughn	.05
23	Tim Wakefield	.05
24	Brian Anderson	.05
25	Garret Anderson	.05
26	Chili Davis	.05
27	Gary DiSarcina	.05
28	Jim Edmonds	.05
29	Jorge Fabregas	.05
30	Chuck Finley	.05
31	Mark Langston	.05
32	Troy Percival	.05
33	Tim Salmon	.05
34	Lee Smith	.05
35	Wilson Alvarez	.05
36	Ray Durham	.05
37	Alex Fernandez	.05
38	Ozzie Guillen	.05
39	Roberto Hernandez	.05
40	Lance Johnson	.05
41	Ron Karkovice	.05
42	Lyle Mouton	.05
43	Tim Raines	.05
44	Frank Thomas	.60
45	Carlos Baerga	.05
46	Albert Belle	.05
47	Orel Hershiser	.05
48	Kenny Lofton	.05
49	Dennis Martinez	.05
50	Jose Mesa	.05
51	Eddie Murray	.60
52	Chad Ogea	.05
53	Manny Ramirez	.60
54	Jim Thome	.50
55	Omar Vizquel	.05
56	Dave Winfield	.60
57	Chad Curtis	.05
58	Cecil Fielder	.05
59	John Flaherty	.05
60	Travis Fryman	.05
61	Chris Gomez	.05
62	Bob Higginson	.05
63	Felipe Lira	.05
64	Brian Maxcy	.05
65	Alan Trammell	.05
66	Lou Whitaker	.05
67	Kevin Appier	.05
68	Gary Gaetti	.05
69	Tom Goodwin	.05
70	Tom Gordon	.05
71	Jason Jacome	.05
72	Wally Joyner	.05
73	Brent Mayne	.05
74	Jeff Montgomery	.05
75	Jon Nunnally	.05
76	Joe Vitiello	.05
77	Ricky Bones	.05
78	Jeff Cirillo	.05
79	Mike Fetters	.05
80	Darryl Hamilton	.05
81	David Hulse	.05
82	Dave Nilsson	.05
83	Kevin Seitzer	.05
84	Steve Sparks	.05
85	B.J. Surhoff	.05
86	Jose Valentin	.05
87	Greg Vaughn	.05
88	Marty Cordova	.05
89	Chuck Knoblauch	.05
90	Pat Meares	.05
91	Pedro Munoz	.05
92	Kirby Puckett	.75
93	Brad Radke	.05
94	Scott Stahoviak	.05
95	Dave Stevens	.05
96	Mike Trombley	.05
97	Matt Walbeck	.05
98	Wade Boggs	.75
99	Russ Davis	.05
100	Jim Leyritz	.05
101	Don Mattingly	.85
102	Jack McDowell	.05
103	Paul O'Neill	.05
104	Andy Pettitte	.30
105	Mariano Rivera	.15
106	Ruben Sierra	.05
107	Darryl Strawberry	.05
108	John Wetteland	.05
109	Bernie Williams	.05
110	Geronimo Berroa	.05
111	Scott Brosius	.05
112	Dennis Eckersley	.50
113	Brent Gates	.05
114	Rickey Henderson	.60
115	Mark McGwire	1.25

116 Ariel Prieto .05
117 Terry Steinbach .05
118 Todd Stottlemyre .05
119 Todd Van Poppel .05
120 Steve Wojciechowski .05
121 Rich Amaral .05
122 Bobby Ayala .05
123 Mike Blowers .05
124 Chris Bosio .05
125 Joey Cora .05
126 Ken Griffey Jr. 1.00
127 Randy Johnson .60
128 Edgar Martinez .05
129 Tino Martinez .05
130 Alex Rodriguez 1.25
131 Dan Wilson .05
132 Will Clark .05
133 Jeff Frye .05
134 Benji Gil .05
135 Juan Gonzalez .30
136 Rusty Greer .05
137 Mark McLemore .05
138 Roger Pavlik .05
139 Ivan Rodriguez .50
140 Kenny Rogers .05
141 Mickey Tettleton .05
142 Roberto Alomar .20
143 Joe Carter .05
144 Tony Castillo .05
145 Alex Gonzalez .05
146 Shawn Green .35
147 Pat Hentgen .05
148 Sandy Martinez **RC** .05
149 Paul Molitor .60
150 John Olerud .05
151 Ed Sprague .05
152 Jeff Blauser .05
153 Brad Clontz .05
154 Tom Glavine .30
155 Marquis Grissom .05
156 Chipper Jones .75
157 David Justice .05
158 Ryan Klesko .05
159 Javier Lopez .05
160 Greg Maddux .75
161 John Smoltz .05
162 Mark Wohlers .05
163 Jim Bullinger .05
164 Frank Castillo .05
165 Shawon Dunston .05
166 Kevin Foster .05
167 Luis Gonzalez .05
168 Mark Grace .05
169 Rey Sanchez .05
170 Scott Servais .05
171 Sammy Sosa .75
172 Ozzie Timmons .05
173 Steve Trachsel .05
174 Bret Boone .05
175 Jeff Branson .05
176 Jeff Brantley .05
177 Dave Burba .05
178 Ron Gant .05
179 Barry Larkin .05
180 Darren Lewis .05
181 Mark Portugal .05
182 Reggie Sanders .05
183 Pete Schourek .05
184 John Smiley .05
185 Jason Bates .05
186 Dante Bichette .05
187 Ellis Burks .05
188 Vinny Castilla .05
189 Andres Galarraga .05
190 Darren Holmes .05
191 Armando Reynoso .05
192 Kevin Ritz .05
193 Bill Swift .05
194 Larry Walker .05
195 Kurt Abbott .05
196 John Burkett .05
197 Greg Colbrunn .05
198 Jeff Conine .05
199 Andre Dawson .25
200 Chris Hammond .05
201 Charles Johnson .05
202 Robb Nen .05
203 Terry Pendleton .05
204 Quilvio Veras .05
205 Jeff Bagwell .60
206 Derek Bell .05
207 Doug Drabek .05
208 Tony Eusebio .05
209 Mike Hampton .05
210 Brian Hunter .05
211 Todd Jones .05
212 Orlando Miller .05
213 James Mouton .05
214 Shane Reynolds .05
215 Dave Veres .05
216 Billy Ashley .05
217 Brett Butler .05
218 Chad Fonville .05
219 Todd Hollandsworth .05
220 Eric Karros .05
221 Ramon Martinez .05
222 Raul Mondesi .05
223 Hideo Nomo .30
224 Mike Piazza 1.00
225 Kevin Tapani .05
226 Ismael Valdes .05
227 Todd Worrell .05
228 Moises Alou .05
229 Wil Cordero .05
230 Jeff Fassero .05
231 Darrin Fletcher .05
232 Mike Lansing .05
233 Pedro Martinez .60
234 Carlos Perez .05
235 Mel Rojas .05
236 David Segui .05
237 Tony Tarasco .05
238 Rondell White .05
239 Edgardo Alfonzo .05
240 Rico Brogna .05
241 Carl Everett .05
242 Todd Hundley .05
243 Butch Huskey .05
244 Jason Isringhausen .05
245 Bobby Jones .05
246 Jeff Kent .05
247 Bill Pulsipher .05
248 Jose Vizcaino .05
249 Ricky Bottalico .05
250 Darren Daulton .05
251 Jim Eisenreich .05
252 Tyler Green .05
253 Charlie Hayes .05
254 Gregg Jefferies .05
255 Tony Longmire .05
256 Michael Mimbs .05
257 Mickey Morandini .05
258 Paul Quantrill .05
259 Heathcliff Slocumb .05
260 Jay Bell .05
261 Jacob Brumfield .05
262 Angelo Encarnacion **RC** .05
263 John Ericks .05
264 Mark Johnson .05
265 Esteban Loaiza .05
266 Al Martin .05
267 Orlando Merced .05
268 Dan Miceli .05
269 Denny Neagle .05
270 Brian Barber .05
271 Scott Cooper .05
272 Tripp Cromer .05
273 Bernard Gilkey .05
274 Tom Henke .05
275 Brian Jordan .05
276 John Mabry .05
277 Tom Pagnozzi .05
278 Mark Petkovsek **RC** .05
279 Ozzie Smith .75
280 Andy Ashby .05
281 Brad Ausmus .05
282 Ken Caminiti .05
283 Glenn Dishman .05
284 Tony Gwynn .75
285 Joey Hamilton .05
286 Trevor Hoffman .05
287 Phil Plantier .05
288 Jody Reed .05
289 Eddie Williams .05
290 Barry Bonds 1.50
291 Jamie Brewington .05
292 Mark Carreon .05
293 Royce Clayton .05
294 Glenallen Hill .05
295 Mark Leiter .05
296 Kirt Manwaring .05
297 J.R. Phillips .05
298 Deion Sanders .05
299 William Van Landingham .05
300 Matt Williams .05
301 Roberto Alomar .20
302 Armando Benitez .05
303 Mike Devereaux .05
304 Jeffrey Hammonds .05
305 Jimmy Haynes .05
306 Scott McClain **RC** .05
307 Kent Mercker .05
308 Randy Myers .05
309 B.J. Surhoff .05
310 Tony Tarasco .05
311 David Wells .05
312 Wil Cordero .05
313 Alex Delgado .05
314 Tom Gordon .05
315 Dwayne Hosey .05
316 Jose Malave .05
317 Kevin Mitchell .05
318 Jamie Moyer .05
319 Aaron Sele .05
320 Heathcliff Slocumb .05
321 Mike Stanley .05
322 Jeff Suppan .05
323 Jim Abbott .05
324 George Arias .05
325 Todd Greene .05
326 Bryan Harvey .05
327 J.T. Snow .05
328 Randy Velarde .05
329 Tim Wallach .05
330 Harold Baines .05
331 Jason Bere .05
332 Darren Lewis .05
333 Norberto Martin .05
334 Tony Phillips .05
335 Bill Simas .05
336 Chris Snopek .05
337 Kevin Tapani .05
338 Danny Tartabull .05
339 Robin Ventura .05
340 Sandy Alomar .05
341 Julio Franco .05
342 Jack McDowell .05
343 Charles Nagy .05
344 Julian Tavarez .05
345 Kimera Bartee .05
346 Greg Keagle .05
347 Mark Lewis .05
348 Jose Lima .05
349 Melvin Nieves .05
350 Mark Parent .05
351 Eddie Williams .05
352 Johnny Damon .30
353 Sal Fasano .05
354 Mark Gubicza .05
355 Bob Hamelin .05
356 Chris Haney .05
357 Keith Lockhart .05
358 Mike Macfarlane .05
359 Jose Offerman .05
360 Bip Roberts .05
361 Michael Tucker .05
362 Chuck Carr .05
363 Bobby Hughes .05
364 John Jaha .05
365 Mark Loretta .05
366 Mike Matheny .05
367 Ben McDonald .05
368 Matt Mieske .05
369 Angel Miranda .05
370 Fernando Vina .05
371 Rick Aguilera .05
372 Rich Becker .05
373 LaTroy Hawkins .05
374 Dave Hollins .05
375 Roberto Kelly .05
376 Matt Lawton **RC** .25
377 Paul Molitor .60
378 Dan Naulty **RC** .05
379 Rich Robertson .05
380 Frank Rodriguez .05
381 David Cone .05
382 Mariano Duncan .05
383 Andy Fox **RC** .05
384 Joe Girardi .05
385 Dwight Gooden .05
386 Derek Jeter 1.50
387 Pat Kelly .05
388 Jimmy Key .05
389 Matt Luke **RC** .05
390 Tino Martinez .05
391 Jeff Nelson .05
392 Melido Perez .05
393 Tim Raines .05
394 Ruben Rivera .05
395 Kenny Rogers .05
396 Tony Batista **RC** .25
397 Allen Battle .05
398 Mike Bordick .05
399 Steve Cox .05
400 Jason Giambi .40
401 Doug Johns .05
402 Pedro Munoz .05
403 Phil Plantier .05
404 Scott Spiezio .05
405 George Williams .05
406 Ernie Young .05
407 Darren Bragg .05
408 Jay Buhner .05
409 Norm Charlton .05
410 Russ Davis .05
411 Sterling Hitchcock .05
412 Edwin Hurtado .05
413 Raul Ibanez **RC** .05
414 Mike Jackson .05
415 Luis Sojo .05
416 Paul Sorrento .05
417 Bob Wolcott .05
418 Damon Buford .05
419 Kevin Gross .05
420 Darryl Hamilton .05
421 Mike Henneman .05
422 Ken Hill .05
423 Dean Palmer .05
424 Bobby Witt .05
425 Tilson Brito .05
426 Giovanni Carrara .05
427 Domingo Cedeno .05
428 Felipe Crespo .05
429 Carlos Delgado .40
430 Juan Guzman .05
431 Erik Hanson .05
432 Marty Janzen **RC** .05
433 Otis Nixon .05
434 Robert Perez .05
435 Paul Quantrill .05
436 Bill Risley .05
437 Steve Avery .05
438 Jermaine Dye .05
439 Mark Lemke .05
440 Marty Malloy **RC** .05
441 Fred McGriff .05
442 Greg McMichael .05
443 Wonderful Monds .05
444 Eddie Perez .05
445 Jason Schmidt .05
446 Terrell Wade .05
447 Terry Adams .05
448 Scott Bullett .05
449 Robin Jennings **RC** .05
450 Doug Jones .05
451 Brooks Kieschnick .05
452 Dave Magadan .05
453 Jason Maxwell **RC** .05
454 Brian McRae .05
455 Rodney Myers .05
456 Jaime Navarro .05
457 Ryne Sandberg .75
458 Vince Coleman .05
459 Eric Davis .05
460 Steve Gibralter .05
461 Thomas Howard .05
462 Mike Kelly .05
463 Hal Morris .05
464 Eric Owens .05
465 Jose Rijo .05
466 Chris Sabo .05
467 Eddie Taubensee .05
468 Trenidad Hubbard .05
469 Curt Leskanic .05
470 Quinton McCracken .05
471 Jayhawk Owens .05
472 Steve Reed .05
473 Bryan Rekar .05
474 Bruce Ruffin .05
475 Bret Saberhagen .05
476 Walt Weiss .05
477 Eric Young .05
478 Kevin Brown .05
479 Al Leiter .05
480 Pat Rapp .05
481 Gary Sheffield .35
482 Devon White .05
483 Bob Abreu .05
484 Sean Berry .05
485 Craig Biggio .05
486 Jim Dougherty .05
487 Richard Hidalgo .05
488 Darryl Kile .05
489 Derrick May .05
490 Greg Swindell .05
491 Rick Wilkins .05
492 Mike Blowers .05
493 Tom Candiotti .05
494 Roger Cedeno .05
495 Delino DeShields .05
496 Greg Gagne .05
497 Karim Garcia .10
498 Wilton Guerrero **RC** .05
499 Chan Ho Park .05
500 Israel Alcantara .05
501 Shane Andrews .05
502 Yamil Benitez .05
503 Cliff Floyd .05
504 Mark Grudzielanek .05
505 Ryan McGuire .05
506 Sherman Obando .05
507 Jose Paniagua .05
508 Henry Rodriguez .05
509 Kirk Rueter .05
510 Juan Acevedo .05
511 John Franco .05
512 Bernard Gilkey .05
513 Lance Johnson .05
514 Rey Ordonez .05
515 Robert Person .05
516 Paul Wilson .05
517 Toby Borland .05
518 David Doster **RC** .05
519 Lenny Dykstra .05
520 Sid Fernandez .05
521 Mike Grace **RC** .05
522 Rich Hunter **RC** .05
523 Benito Santiago .05
524 Gene Schall .05
525 Curt Schilling .15
526 Kevin Sefcik **RC** .05
527 Lee Tinsley .05
528 David West .05
529 Mark Whiten .05
530 Todd Zeile .05
531 Carlos Garcia .05
532 Charlie Hayes .05
533 Jason Kendall .05
534 Jeff King .05
535 Mike Kingery .05
536 Nelson Liriano .05
537 Dan Plesac .05
538 Paul Wagner .05
539 Luis Alicea .05
540 David Bell .05
541 Alan Benes .05
542 Andy Benes .05
543 Mike Busby **RC** .05
544 Royce Clayton .05
545 Dennis Eckersley .50
546 Gary Gaetti .05
547 Ron Gant .05
548 Aaron Holbert .05
549 Ray Lankford .05
550 T.J. Mathews .05
551 Willie McGee .05
552 Miguel Mejia **RC** .05
553 Todd Stottlemyre .05
554 Sean Bergman .05
555 Willie Blair .05
556 Andujar Cedeno .05
557 Steve Finley .05
558 Rickey Henderson .60
559 Wally Joyner .05
560 Scott Livingstone .05
561 Marc Newfield .05
562 Bob Tewksbury .05
563 Fernando Valenzuela .05
564 Rod Beck .05
565 Doug Creek .05
566 Shawon Dunston .05
567 Osvaldo Fernandez **RC** .20
568 Stan Javier .05
569 Marcus Jensen .05
570 Steve Scarsone .05
571 Robby Thompson .05
572 Allen Watson .05
573 Roberto Alomar (Ultra Stars) .10
574 Jeff Bagwell (Ultra Stars) .30
575 Albert Belle (Ultra Stars) .05
576 Wade Boggs (Ultra Stars) .40
577 Barry Bonds (Ultra Stars) .75
578 Juan Gonzalez (Ultra Stars) .15
579 Ken Griffey Jr. (Ultra Stars) .50
580 Tony Gwynn (Ultra Stars) .40
581 Randy Johnson (Ultra Stars) .30
582 Chipper Jones (Ultra Stars) .40
583 Barry Larkin (Ultra Stars) .05
584 Kenny Lofton (Ultra Stars) .05
585 Greg Maddux (Ultra Stars) .40
586 Raul Mondesi (Ultra Stars) .05
587 Mike Piazza (Ultra Stars) .50
588 Cal Ripken Jr. (Ultra Stars) .75
589 Tim Salmon (Ultra Stars) .05
590 Frank Thomas (Ultra Stars) .35
591 Mo Vaughn (Ultra Stars) .05
592 Matt Williams (Ultra Stars) .05
593 Marty Cordova (Raw Power) .05
594 Jim Edmonds (Raw Power) .05
595 Cliff Floyd (Raw Power) .05
596 Chipper Jones (Raw Power) .40
597 Ryan Klesko (Raw Power) .05
598 Raul Mondesi (Raw Power) .05
599 Manny Ramirez (Raw Power) .30
600 Ruben Rivera (Raw Power) .05

Gold Medallion

Limited to less than 10 percent of the regular edition's production, the Gold Medallion parallel set replaces the front photo's background with gold foil featuring a large embossed Fleer Ultra Gold Medallion seal at center. One Gold Medallion card is found in each foil pack.

NM/M
Complete Set (600): 75.00
Common Player: .25

Call to the Hall

Ten probable future Hall of Famers are featured on these cards, which use classic style original illustrations of the players. The cards were seeded one per every 24 Series 2 packs.

NM/M
Complete Set (10): 10.00
Common Player: 1.00
Gold Medallion Edition: 2X
1 Barry Bonds 3.00
2 Ken Griffey Jr. 2.00
3 Tony Gwynn 1.25
4 Rickey Henderson 1.00
5 Greg Maddux 1.25
6 Eddie Murray 1.00
7 Cal Ripken Jr. 3.00
8 Ryne Sandberg 1.25
9 Ozzie Smith 1.25
10 Frank Thomas 1.00

Checklists

Fleer Ultra featured 10 checklist cards that were inserted every four packs. These cards featured a superstar player on the front and, throughout the set, a full checklist of all cards in the 1996 Ultra set on the back.

NM/M
Complete Set (20): 9.00
Common Player: .15
1 Jeff Bagwell .50
2 Barry Bonds 1.00
3 Juan Gonzalez .25
4 Ken Griffey Jr. .65
5 Chipper Jones .60
6 Mike Piazza .65
7 Manny Ramirez .50
8 Cal Ripken Jr. 1.00
9 Frank Thomas .50
10 Matt Williams .15
1 Albert Belle .15
2 Cecil Fielder .15
3 Ken Griffey Jr. .65
4 Tony Gwynn .60
5 Derek Jeter 1.00
6 Jason Kendall .15
7 Ryan Klesko .15
8 Greg Maddux .60
9 Cal Ripken Jr. 1.00
10 Frank Thomas .50

Diamond Dust

This card commemorates Cal Ripken's history-making 1995 record of playing in 2,131 consecutive regular-season games. Horizontal in format, the front has a color action photo of Ripken on a simulated leather background. Back has a photo of Ripken on the night he set the new record. Sandwiched between front and back is a dime-sized plastic capsule of dirt certified, according to the facsimile autograph of the team's head groundskeeper, to have been used on the infield at Oriole Park in Camden Yards during the 1995 season. Two versions of the card were made. A hand-numbered version limited to 2,131 was offered direct to dealers for $39.99. An unnumbered version was available to collectors as a wrapper redemption for $24.99.

NM/M
Cal Ripken Jr. (Numbered) 40.00
Cal Ripken Jr. (Unnumbered) 20.00

Diamond Producers

A horizontal layout and two versions of the same photo printed on holographic foil are

featured in this insert set. Stated odds of finding a Diamond Producers card are one per every 20 Series I packs.

		NM/M
Complete Set (12):		15.00
Common Player:		.50
Gold Medallions:		2X
1	Albert Belle	.50
2	Barry Bonds	3.00
3	Ken Griffey Jr.	2.00
4	Tony Gwynn	1.50
5	Greg Maddux	1.50
6	Hideo Nomo	.75
7	Mike Piazza	2.00
8	Kirby Puckett	1.50
9	Cal Ripken Jr.	3.00
10	Frank Thomas	1.25
11	Mo Vaughn	.50
12	Matt Williams	.50

Fresh Foundations

Rising stars who can carry their teams' fortunes into the next century are featured in this foil-printed insert set, found on average of one card per every three Series I foil packs.

		NM/M
Complete Set (10):		2.00
Common Player:		.15
Gold Medallions:		2X
1	Garret Anderson	.15
2	Marty Cordova	.15
3	Jim Edmonds	.15
4	Brian Hunter	.15
5	Chipper Jones	.50
6	Ryan Klesko	.15
7	Raul Mondesi	.15
8	Hideo Nomo	.25
9	Manny Ramirez	.40
10	Rondell White	.15

Golden Prospects, Series 1

A hobby-pack-only insert, these horizontal format cards have rainbow foil ballpark backgrounds and feature 1996's rookie crop. They are found on average of one per every five Series I packs.

		NM/M
Complete Set (10):		7.00
Common Player:		.25
Gold Medallions:		2X
1	Yamil Benitez	.25
2	Alberto Castillo	.25
3	Roger Cedeno	.25
4	Johnny Damon	1.00
5	Micah Franklin	.25
6	Jason Giambi	1.00
7	Jose Herrera	.25
8	Derek Jeter	5.00
9	Kevin Jordan	.25
10	Ruben Rivera	.25

Golden Prospects, Series 2

The Golden Prospects insert series continued with 15 more young stars found exclusively in Series 2 hobby packs, though in much lower numbers than the Series 1 inserts.

		NM/M
Complete Set (15):		10.00
Common Player:		1.00
Gold Medallions:		2X
1	Bob Abreu	1.50
2	Israel Alcantara	1.00
3	Tony Batista	1.00
4	Mike Cameron	1.00
5	Steve Cox	1.00
6	Jermaine Dye	1.00
7	Wilton Guerrero	1.00
8	Richard Hidalgo	1.00
9	Raul Ibanez	1.00
10	Marty Janzen	1.00
11	Robin Jennings	1.00
12	Jason Maxwell	1.00
13	Scott McClain	1.00
14	Wonderful Monds	1.00
15	Chris Singleton	1.00

Hitting Machines

These die-cut 1996 Fleer Ultra Series II insert cards showcase the heaviest hitters on cards featuring a machine-gear design. The cards were seeded one per every 288 Series II packs.

		NM/M
Complete Set (10):		35.00
Common Player:		2.00
Gold Medallion:		2X
1	Albert Belle	2.00
2	Barry Bonds	12.00
3	Juan Gonzalez	2.50
4	Ken Griffey Jr.	6.00
5	Edgar Martinez	2.00
6	Rafael Palmeiro	3.00
7	Mike Piazza	6.00
8	Tim Salmon	2.00
9	Frank Thomas	4.00
10	Matt Williams	2.00

Home Run Kings Exchange Cards

Printed on cardboard, these super-scarce inserts are found at the rate of only one per 75 packs. Because of quality control problems, the cards were initially released as exchange cards, with instructions on back for a mail-in redemption offer for the actual wooden card. The redemption period expired Dec. 1, 1996.

		NM/M
Complete Set (12):		20.00
Common Player:		.75
1	Albert Belle	.75
2	Dante Bichette	.75
3	Barry Bonds	5.00
4	Jose Canseco	1.50
5	Juan Gonzalez	1.25
6	Ken Griffey Jr.	3.00
7	Mark McGwire	4.00
8	Manny Ramirez	2.50
9	Tim Salmon	.75
10	Frank Thomas	2.50
11	Mo Vaughn	.75
12	Matt Williams	.75

Home Run Kings

Printed on a thin wood veneer, these super-scarce inserts are seeded one per every 75 Series 1 packs. Because of quality control problems, the cards were initially released as exchange cards, with instructions on back for a mail-in redemption offer for the actual wooden card.

		NM/M
Complete Set (12):		50.00
Common Player:		2.50
Gold Medallions:		2X
1	Albert Belle	2.50
2	Dante Bichette	2.50
3	Barry Bonds	12.50
4	Jose Canseco	5.00
5	Juan Gonzalez	3.00
6	Ken Griffey Jr.	9.00
7	Mark McGwire	10.00
8	Manny Ramirez	6.50
9	Tim Salmon	2.50
10	Frank Thomas	6.50
11	Mo Vaughn	2.50
12	Matt Williams	2.50

On-Base Leaders

These 1996 Fleer Ultra Series II inserts feature 10 of the game's top on-base leaders. The cards were seeded one per every four packs.

		NM/M
Complete Set (10):		4.50
Common Player:		.25
Gold Medallion:		2X
1	Wade Boggs	.75
2	Barry Bonds	2.00
3	Tony Gwynn	.75
4	Rickey Henderson	.60
5	Chuck Knoblauch	.25
6	Edgar Martinez	.25
7	Mike Piazza	1.00
8	Tim Salmon	.25
9	Frank Thomas	.60
10	Jim Thome	.50

Power Plus

Etched-foil backgrounds, multiple player photos and a horizontal format are featured in this chase set. Stated odds of finding one of the dozen Power Plus cards are one per every 10 Series I packs.

		NM/M
Complete Set (12):		10.00
Common Player:		.40
Gold Medallions:		2X
1	Jeff Bagwell	1.25
2	Barry Bonds	3.00
3	Ken Griffey Jr.	2.00
4	Raul Mondesi	.40
5	Rafael Palmeiro	1.00
6	Mike Piazza	2.00
7	Manny Ramirez	1.25
8	Tim Salmon	.40
9	Reggie Sanders	.40
10	Frank Thomas	1.25
11	Larry Walker	.40
12	Matt Williams	.40

Prime Leather

An embossed leather-feel background is featured on these cards of top fielders, seeded one per every eight Series I packs, on average.

		NM/M
Complete Set (18):		17.50
Common Player:		.50
Gold Medallions:		2X
1	Ivan Rodriguez	1.50
2	Will Clark	.50
3	Roberto Alomar	.65
4	Cal Ripken Jr.	4.00
5	Wade Boggs	2.00
6	Ken Griffey Jr.	2.50
7	Kenny Lofton	.50
8	Kirby Puckett	2.00
9	Tim Salmon	.65
10	Mike Piazza	2.50
11	Mark Grace	.50
12	Craig Biggio	.50
13	Barry Larkin	.50
14	Matt Williams	.50
15	Barry Bonds	4.00
16	Tony Gwynn	2.00
17	Brian McRae	.50
18	Raul Mondesi	.50

Rawhide

Ten top fielders are featured on these 1996 Fleer Ultra Series II inserts. The cards were seeded one per every eight packs.

		NM/M
Complete Set (10):		10.00
Common Player:		.45
Gold Medallion:		2X
1	Roberto Alomar	.65
2	Barry Bonds	3.00
3	Mark Grace	.45
4	Ken Griffey Jr.	1.50
5	Kenny Lofton	.45
6	Greg Maddux	1.00
7	Raul Mondesi	.45
8	Mike Piazza	1.50
9	Cal Ripken Jr.	3.00
10	Matt Williams	.45

RBI Kings

Retail packs are the exclusive provenance of this 10-card set of top RBI men. Stated odds of finding an RBI King card are one per every five Series I packs.

		NM/M
Complete Set (10):		4.00
Common Player:		.10
Gold Medallions:		2X
1	Derek Bell	.10
2	Albert Belle	.10
3	Dante Bichette	.10
4	Barry Bonds	2.00
5	Jim Edmonds	.15
6	Manny Ramirez	1.00
7	Reggie Sanders	.10
8	Sammy Sosa	1.50
9	Frank Thomas	1.00
10	Mo Vaughn	.10

R-E-S-P-E-C-T

These cards feature 10 players held in high esteem by their major league peers. The cards were seeded one per every 18 1996 Ultra Series II packs.

		NM/M
Complete Set (10):		20.00
Common Player:		.50
Gold Medallion:		2X
1	Joe Carter	.50
2	Ken Griffey Jr.	3.00
3	Tony Gwynn	2.50
4	Greg Maddux	2.50
5	Eddie Murray	2.00
6	Kirby Puckett	2.50
7	Cal Ripken Jr.	5.00
8	Ryne Sandberg	2.50
9	Frank Thomas	2.00
10	Mo Vaughn	.50

Rising Stars

Ten of baseball's best young players are spotlighted on these 1996 Fleer Ultra Series II inserts. Cards were seeded one per every four packs.

		NM/M
Complete Set (10):		4.00
Common Player:		.20
Gold Medallion:		2X
1	Garret Anderson	.20
2	Marty Cordova	.20
3	Jim Edmonds	.35
4	Cliff Floyd	.20
5	Brian Hunter	.20
6	Chipper Jones	2.00
7	Ryan Klesko	.20
8	Hideo Nomo	.65
9	Manny Ramirez	1.25
10	Rondell White	.20

Season Crowns

Large coats-of-arms printed on "Ultra Crystal" clear plastic are the background for player action photos in this insert set. Odds of one per every 10 Series II packs were stated.

		NM/M
Complete Set (10):		12.50
Common Player:		.75
Gold Medallions:		2X
1	Barry Bonds	4.00
2	Tony Gwynn	2.00
3	Randy Johnson	1.25
4	Kenny Lofton	.75
5	Greg Maddux	2.00
6	Edgar Martinez	.75
7	Hideo Nomo	1.00
8	Cal Ripken Jr.	4.00
9	Frank Thomas	1.25
10	Tim Wakefield	.75

Thunderclap

The active career home run leaders are featured in this retail-exclusive Ultra insert set. Seeded only one per 72 packs, the Thunderclap cards have action photos on front with simulated lightning in the background and other graphic highlights rendered in holographic foil. Backs have a large portrait photo and career summary. Each of these scarce retail inserts can also be found in an even more elusive Gold Medallion version.

		NM/M
Complete Set (20):		45.00
Common Player:		1.00
Gold Medallion:		2X
1	Albert Belle	1.00
2	Barry Bonds	7.50
3	Bobby Bonilla	1.00
4	Jose Canseco	1.50
5	Joe Carter	1.00
6	Will Clark	1.00
7	Andre Dawson	1.50
8	Cecil Fielder	1.00
9	Andres Galarraga	1.00
10	Juan Gonzalez	1.50
11	Ken Griffey Jr.	5.00
12	Fred McGriff	1.00
13	Mark McGwire	6.00
14	Eddie Murray	2.50
15	Rafael Palmeiro	2.00
16	Kirby Puckett	4.00
17	Cal Ripken Jr.	7.50
18	Ryne Sandberg	4.00
19	Frank Thomas	2.50
20	Matt Williams	1.00

1997 Ultra Promo Strip

To introduce the concept of its new non-parallel parallel set, Fleer issued this three-card promo strip picturing regular (left), Gold Medallion (center) and Platinum Medallion (right) Cal Ripken, Jr., cards. Fronts have a "PROMOTIONAL SAMPLE," overprint in foil to match the cards' graphic highlights (silver, gold and prismatic). Backs, which have stats only through the 1995 season, have the same overprint in red.

NM/M
Three-Card Strip: 10.00

1997 Ultra

Ultra was issued in a 300-card Series 1 and 252-card Series 2, each with two parallel editions, Gold and Platinum, which feature "G" and "P" prefixes on the card number, respectively. Cards were issued in 10-card packs. Player names and the Ultra logo are in silver holographic foil. Backs contains complete year-by-year statistics, plus two photos of the player. This also marked the first time that the Gold and Platinum parallel sets displayed a different photo than the base cards. Inserts in Ultra included: Rookie Reflections, Double Trouble, Checklists, Season Crowns, RBI Kings, Power Plus, Fielder's Choice, Diamond Producers, HR Kings, and Baseball Rules.

NM/M
Complete Set (553): 80.00
Common Player: .05
Gold Medallion: 3X
Platinum Medallion: 25X
Series 1 Wax Pack (10): 1.25
Series 1 Wax Box (24): 20.00
Series 2 Wax Pack (10): 5.00
Series 2 Wax Box (24): 90.00

1 Roberto Alomar .25
2 Brady Anderson .05
3 Rocky Coppinger .05
4 Jeffrey Hammonds .05
5 Chris Hoiles .05
6 Eddie Murray .75
7 Mike Mussina .45
8 Jimmy Myers .05
9 Randy Myers .05
10 Arthur Rhodes .05
11 Cal Ripken Jr. 2.50
12 Jose Canseco .50
13 Roger Clemens 1.25
14 Tom Gordon .05
15 Jose Malave .05
16 Tim Naehring .05
17 Troy O'Leary .05
18 Bill Selby .05
19 Heathcliff Slocumb .05
20 Mike Stanley .05
21 Mo Vaughn .05
22 Garret Anderson .05
23 George Arias .05
24 Chili Davis .05
25 Jim Edmonds .05
26 Darin Erstad .25
27 Chuck Finley .05
28 Todd Greene .05
29 Troy Percival .05
30 Tim Salmon .05
31 Jeff Schmidt .05
32 Randy Velarde .05
33 Shad Williams .05
34 Wilson Alvarez .05
35 Harold Baines .05
36 James Baldwin .05
37 Mike Cameron .05
38 Ray Durham .05
39 Ozzie Guillen .05
40 Roberto Hernandez .05
41 Darren Lewis .05
42 Jose Munoz .05
43 Tony Phillips .05
44 Frank Thomas .75
45 Sandy Alomar Jr. .05
46 Albert Belle .05
47 Mark Carreon .05
48 Julio Franco .05
49 Orel Hershiser .05
50 Kenny Lofton .05
51 Jack McDowell .05
52 Jose Mesa .05
53 Charles Nagy .05
54 Manny Ramirez .75
55 Julian Tavarez .05
56 Omar Vizquel .05
57 Raul Casanova .05
58 Tony Clark .05
59 Travis Fryman .05
60 Bob Higginson .05
61 Melvin Nieves .05
62 Curtis Pride .05
63 Justin Thompson .05
64 Alan Trammell .05
65 Kevin Appier .05
66 Johnny Damon .35
67 Keith Lockhart .05
68 Jeff Montgomery .05
69 Jose Offerman .05
70 Bip Roberts .05
71 Jose Rosado .05
72 Chris Stynes .05
73 Mike Sweeney .05
74 Jeff Cirillo .05
75 Jeff D'Amico .05
76 John Jaha .05
77 Scott Karl .05
78 Mike Matheny .05
79 Ben McDonald .05
80 Matt Mieske .05
81 Marc Newfield .05
82 Dave Nilsson .05
83 Jose Valentin .05
84 Fernando Vina .05
85 Rick Aguilera .05
86 Marty Cordova .05
87 Chuck Knoblauch .05
88 Matt Lawton .05
89 Pat Meares .05
90 Paul Molitor .75
91 Greg Myers .05
92 Dan Naulty .05
93 Kirby Puckett 1.00
94 Frank Rodriguez .05
95 Wade Boggs 1.00
96 Cecil Fielder .05
97 Joe Girardi .05
98 Dwight Gooden .05
99 Derek Jeter 2.50
100 Tino Martinez .05
101 Ramiro Mendoza **RC** .05
102 Andy Pettitte .20
103 Mariano Rivera .15
104 Ruben Rivera .05
105 Kenny Rogers .05
106 Darryl Strawberry .05
107 Bernie Williams .05
108 Tony Batista .05
109 Geronimo Berroa .05
110 Bobby Chouinard .05
111 Brent Gates .05
112 Jason Giambi .60
113 Damon Mashore **RC** .05
114 Mark McGwire 2.00
115 Scott Spiezio .05
116 John Wasdin .05
117 Steve Wojciechowski .05
118 Ernie Young .05
119 Norm Charlton .05
120 Joey Cora .05
121 Ken Griffey Jr. 1.50
122 Sterling Hitchcock .05
123 Raul Ibanez .05
124 Randy Johnson .75
125 Edgar Martinez .05
126 Alex Rodriguez 2.00
127 Matt Wagner .05
128 Bob Wells .05
129 Dan Wilson .05
130 Will Clark .05
131 Kevin Elster .05
132 Juan Gonzalez .40
133 Rusty Greer .05
134 Darryl Hamilton .05
135 Mike Henneman .05
136 Ken Hill .05
137 Mark McLemore .05
138 Dean Palmer .05
139 Roger Pavlik .05
140 Ivan Rodriguez .65
141 Joe Carter .05
142 Carlos Delgado .50
143 Alex Gonzalez .05
144 Juan Guzman .05
145 Pat Hentgen .05
146 Marty Janzen .05
147 Otis Nixon .05
148 Charlie O'Brien .05
149 John Olerud .05
150 Robert Perez .05
151 Jermaine Dye .05
152 Tom Glavine .30
153 Andruw Jones .75
154 Chipper Jones 1.00
155 Ryan Klesko .05
156 Javier Lopez .05
157 Greg Maddux 1.00
158 Fred McGriff .05
159 Wonderful Monds .05
160 John Smoltz .05
161 Terrell Wade .05
162 Mark Wohlers .05
163 Brant Brown .05
164 Mark Grace .05
165 Tyler Houston .05
166 Robin Jennings .05
167 Jason Maxwell .05
168 Ryne Sandberg 1.00
169 Sammy Sosa 1.00
170 Amaury Telemaco .05
171 Steve Trachsel .05
172 Pedro Valdes **RC** .05
173 Tim Belk .05
174 Bret Boone .05
175 Jeff Brantley .05
176 Eric Davis .05
177 Barry Larkin .05
178 Chad Mottola .05
179 Mark Portugal .05
180 Reggie Sanders .05
181 John Smiley .05
182 Eddie Taubensee .05
183 Dante Bichette .05
184 Ellis Burks .05
185 Andres Galarraga .05
186 Curt Leskanic .05
187 Quinton McCracken .05
188 Jeff Reed .05
189 Kevin Ritz .05
190 Walt Weiss .05
191 Jamey Wright .05
192 Eric Young .05
193 Kevin Brown .05
194 Luis Castillo .05
195 Jeff Conine .05
196 Andre Dawson .25
197 Charles Johnson .05
198 Al Leiter .05
199 Ralph Milliard .05
200 Robb Nen .05
201 Edgar Renteria .05
202 Gary Sheffield .40
203 Bob Abreu .10
204 Jeff Bagwell .75
205 Derek Bell .05
206 Sean Berry .05
207 Richard Hidalgo .05
208 Todd Jones .05
209 Darryl Kile .05
210 Orlando Miller .05
211 Shane Reynolds .05
212 Billy Wagner .05
213 Donne Wall .05
214 Roger Cedeno .05
215 Greg Gagne .05
216 Karim Garcia .10
217 Wilton Guerrero .05
218 Todd Hollandsworth .05
219 Ramon Martinez .05
220 Raul Mondesi .05
221 Hideo Nomo .40
222 Chan Ho Park .05
223 Mike Piazza 1.50
224 Ismael Valdes .05
225 Moises Alou .05
226 Derek Aucoin .05
227 Yamil Benitez .05
228 Jeff Fassero .05
229 Darrin Fletcher .05
230 Mark Grudzielanek .05
231 Barry Manuel .05
232 Pedro Martinez .75
233 Henry Rodriguez .05
234 Ugueth Urbina .05
235 Rondell White .05
236 Carlos Baerga .05
237 John Franco .05
238 Bernard Gilkey .05
239 Todd Hundley .05
240 Butch Huskey .05
241 Jason Isringhausen .05
242 Lance Johnson .05
243 Bobby Jones .05
244 Alex Ochoa .05
245 Rey Ordonez .05
246 Paul Wilson .05
247 Ron Blazier .05
248 David Doster .05
249 Jim Eisenreich .05
250 Mike Grace .05
251 Mike Lieberthal .05
252 Wendell Magee .05
253 Mickey Morandini .05
254 Ricky Otero .05
255 Scott Rolen .60
256 Curt Schilling .20
257 Todd Zeile .05
258 Jermaine Allensworth .05
259 Trey Beamon .05
260 Carlos Garcia .05
261 Mark Johnson .05
262 Jason Kendall .05
263 Jeff King .05
264 Al Martin .05
265 Denny Neagle .05
266 Matt Ruebel .05
267 Marc Wilkins **RC** .05
268 Alan Benes .05
269 Dennis Eckersley .65
270 Ron Gant .05
271 Aaron Holbert .05
272 Brian Jordan .05
273 Ray Lankford .05
274 John Mabry .05
275 T.J. Mathews .05
276 Ozzie Smith 1.00
277 Todd Stottlemyre .05
278 Mark Sweeney .05
279 Andy Ashby .05
280 Steve Finley .05
281 John Flaherty .05
282 Chris Gomez .05
283 Tony Gwynn 1.00
284 Joey Hamilton .05
285 Rickey Henderson .75
286 Trevor Hoffman .05
287 Jason Thompson .05
288 Fernando Valenzuela .05
289 Greg Vaughn .05
290 Barry Bonds 2.50
291 Jay Canizaro .05
292 Jacob Cruz .05
293 Shawon Dunston .05
294 Shawn Estes .05
295 Mark Gardner .05
296 Marcus Jensen .05
297 Bill Mueller **RC** .35
298 Chris Singleton .05
299 Allen Watson .05
300 Matt Williams .05
301 Rod Beck .05
302 Jay Bell .05
303 Shawon Dunston .05
304 Reggie Jefferson .05
305 Darren Oliver .05
306 Benito Santiago .05
307 Gerald Williams .05
308 Damon Buford .05
309 Jeromy Burnitz .05
310 Sterling Hitchcock .05
311 Dave Hollins .05
312 Mel Rojas .05
313 Robin Ventura .05
314 David Wells .05
315 Cal Eldred .05
316 Gary Gaetti .05
317 John Hudek .05
318 Brian Johnson .05
319 Denny Neagle .05
320 Larry Walker .05
321 Russ Davis .05
322 Delino DeShields .05
323 Charlie Hayes .05
324 Jermaine Dye .05
325 John Ericks .05
326 Jeff Fassero .05
327 Nomar Garciaparra 1.00
328 Willie Greene .05
329 Greg McMichael .05
330 Damion Easley .05
331 Ricky Bones .05
332 John Burkett .05
333 Royce Clayton .05
334 Greg Colbrunn .05
335 Tony Eusebio .05
336 Gregg Jefferies .05
337 Wally Joyner .05
338 Jim Leyritz .05
339 Paul O'Neill .05
340 Bruce Ruffin .05
341 Michael Tucker .05
342 Andy Benes .05
343 Craig Biggio .05
344 Rex Hudler .05
345 Brad Radke .05
346 Deion Sanders .05
347 Moises Alou .05
348 Brad Ausmus .05
349 Armando Benitez .05
350 Mark Gubicza .05
351 Terry Steinbach .05
352 Mark Whiten .05
353 Ricky Bottalico .05
354 Brian Giles **RC** .75
355 Eric Karros .05
356 Jimmy Key .05
357 Carlos Perez .05
358 Alex Fernandez .05
359 J.T. Snow .05
360 Bobby Bonilla .05
361 Scott Brosius .05
362 Greg Swindell .05
363 Jose Vizcaino .05
364 Matt Williams .05
365 Darren Daulton .05
366 Shane Andrews .05
367 Jim Eisenreich .05
368 Ariel Prieto .05
369 Bob Tewksbury .05
370 Mike Bordick .05
371 Rheal Cormier .05
372 Cliff Floyd .05
373 David Justice .05
374 John Wetteland .05
375 Mike Blowers .05
376 Jose Canseco .50
377 Roger Clemens 1.25
378 Kevin Mitchell .05
379 Todd Zeile .05
380 Jim Thome .60
381 Turk Wendell .05
382 Rico Brogna .05
383 Eric Davis .05
384 Mike Lansing .05
385 Devon White .05
386 Marquis Grissom .05
387 Todd Worrell .05
388 Jeff Kent .05
389 Mickey Tettleton .05
390 Steve Avery .05
391 David Cone .05
392 Scott Cooper .05
393 Lee Stevens .05
394 Kevin Elster .05
395 Tom Goodwin .05
396 Shawn Green .25
397 Pete Harnisch .05
398 Eddie Murray .75
399 Joe Randa .05
400 Scott Sanders .05
401 John Valentin .05
402 Todd Jones .05
403 Terry Adams .05
404 Brian Hunter .05
405 Pat Listach .05
406 Kenny Lofton .05
407 Hal Morris .05
408 Ed Sprague .05
409 Rich Becker .05
410 Edgardo Alfonzo .05
411 Albert Belle .05
412 Jeff King .05
413 Kirt Manwaring .05
414 Jason Schmidt .05
415 Allen Watson .05
416 Lee Tinsley .05
417 Brett Butler .05
418 Carlos Garcia .05
419 Mark Lemke .05
420 Jaime Navarro .05
421 David Segui .05
422 Ruben Sierra .05
423 B.J. Surhoff .05
424 Julian Tavarez .05
425 Billy Taylor .05
426 Ken Caminiti .05
427 Chuck Carr .05
428 Benji Gil .05
429 Terry Mulholland .05
430 Mike Stanton .05
431 Wil Cordero .05
432 Chili Davis .05
433 Mariano Duncan .05
434 Orlando Merced .05
435 Kent Mercker .05
436 John Olerud .05
437 Quilvio Veras .05
438 Mike Fetters .05
439 Glenallen Hill .05
440 Dill Swift .05
441 Tim Wakefield .05
442 Pedro Astacio .05
443 Vinny Castilla .05
444 Doug Drabek .05
445 Alan Embree .05
446 Lee Smith .05
447 Darryl Hamilton .05
448 Brian McRae .05
449 Mike Timlin .05
450 Bob Wickman .05
451 Jason Dickson .05
452 Chad Curtis .05
453 Mark Leiter .05
454 Damon Berryhill .05
455 Kevin Orie .05
456 Dave Burba .05
457 Chris Holt .05
458 Ricky Ledee **RC** .10
459 Mike Devereaux .05
460 Pokey Reese .05
461 Tim Raines .05
462 Ryan Jones .05
463 Shane Mack .05
464 Darren Dreifort .05
465 Mark Parent .05
466 Mark Portugal .05
467 Dante Powell .05
468 Craig Grebeck .05
469 Ron Villone .05
470 Dmitri Young .05
471 Shannon Stewart .05
472 Rick Helling .05
473 Bill Haselman .05
474 Albie Lopez .05
475 Glendon Rusch .05
476 Derrick May .05
477 Chad Ogea .05
478 Kirk Reuter .05
479 Chris Hammond .05
480 Russ Johnson .05
481 James Mouton .05
482 Mike Macfarlane .05
483 Scott Ruffcorn .05
484 Jeff Frye .05
485 Richie Sexson .05
486 Emil Brown **RC** .05
487 Desi Wilson .05
488 Brent Gates .05
489 Tony Graffanino .05
490 Dan Miceli .05
491 Orlando Cabrera **RC** .65
492 Tony Womack **RC** .20
493 Jerome Walton .05
494 Mark Thompson .05
495 Jose Guillen .05
496 Willie Blair .05
497 T.J. Staton **RC** .05
498 Scott Kamieniecki .05
499 Vince Coleman .05
500 Jeff Abbott .05
501 Chris Widger .05
502 Kevin Tapani .05
503 Carlos Castillo **RC** .05
504 Luis Gonzalez .05
505 Tim Belcher .05
506 Armando Reynoso .05
507 Jamie Moyer .05
508 Randall Simon **RC** .05
509 Vladimir Guerrero .75
510 Wady Almonte **RC** .05
511 Dustin Hermanson .05
512 Deivi Cruz **RC** .25
513 Luis Alicea .05
514 Felix Heredia **RC** .15
515 Don Slaught .05
516 Shigetosi Hasegawa .05
517 Matt Walbeck .05
518 David Arias **RC** (Last name actually Ortiz.) 40.00
519 Brady Raggio **RC** .05
520 Rudy Pemberton .05
521 Wayne Kirby .05
522 Calvin Maduro .05
523 Mark Lewis .05
524 Mike Jackson .05
525 Sid Fernandez .05
526 Mike Bielecki .05
527 Bubba Trammell **RC** .05
528 Brent Brede **RC** .05
529 Matt Morris .05
530 Joe Borowski .05
531 Orlando Miller .05
532 Jim Bullinger .05
533 Robert Person .05
534 Doug Glanville .05
535 Terry Pendleton .05
536 Jorge Posada .05
537 Marc Sagmoen **RC** .05
538 Fernando Tatis **RC** .20
539 Aaron Sele .05
540 Brian Banks .05
541 Derrek Lee .50
542 John Wasdin .05
543 Justin Towle **RC** .05
544 Pat Cline .05
545 Dave Magadan .05
546 Jeff Blauser .05
547 Phil Nevin .05
548 Todd Walker .05
549 Elieser Marrero .05
550 Bartolo Colon .05
551 Jose Cruz Jr. **RC** .50
552 Todd Dunwoody .05
553 Hideki Irabu **RC** .25

Gold Medallion Edition

A new concept in parallel editions was debuted by Ultra in Series I. While sharing the card numbers with regular-issue Ultra cards, the Gold Medallion Edition features a "G" prefix to the card number and gold-foil highlights on front. Unlike past parallels, however, the '97 Ultra Gold Medallion and Platinum Medallion inserts share a photograph which is entirely different from the regular Ultra base cards. Gold Medallion Edition cards are identified as such in the lower-right corner and were inserted at a rate of one per pack.

NM/M
Complete Set (553): 100.00
Common Player: .25
Stars/Rookies: 3X

Platinum Medallion Edition

A new concept in parallel editions was debuted by Ultra in Series I. While sharing the card numbers with regular-issue Ultra cards, the Platinum Medallion Edition features a "P" prefix to the card number and holographic-foil highlights on front. Unlike past parallels, however, the '97 Ultra Gold Medallion and Platinum Medallion inserts share

a photograph which is entirely different from the regular Ultra base cards are identified as such in the lower-right corner and were inserted at a rate of one per 100 packs.

	NM/M
Common Player:	2.00
Stars/Rookies:	25X

Baseball Rules!

Baseball Rules was a 10-card insert that was found only in retail packs at a rate of one per 36 packs. The cards are die-cut with a player in front of a mound of baseballs with embossed seams on the front, while each card back explains a baseball term or rule.

		NM/M
Complete Set (10):		45.00
Common Player:		.50
1	Barry Bonds	10.00
2	Ken Griffey Jr.	6.00
3	Derek Jeter	10.00
4	Chipper Jones	5.00
5	Greg Maddux	5.00
6	Mark McGwire	7.50
7	Troy Percival	.50
8	Mike Piazza	6.00
9	Cal Ripken Jr.	10.00
10	Frank Thomas	4.00

Checklists

There are 10 Checklist cards in each series of Ultra baseball covering all regular-issue cards and inserts. The front of the card features a superstar, while the back contains a portion of the set checklist. The cards have the player's name and "CHECKLIST" in bold, all caps across the bottom in silver foil.

		NM/M
Complete Set (20):		5.00
Common Player:		.05
1	Dante Bichette	.05
2	Barry Bonds	.75
3	Ken Griffey Jr.	.35
4	Greg Maddux	.25
5	Mark McGwire	.50
6	Mike Piazza	.35
7	Cal Ripken Jr.	.75
8	John Smoltz	.05
9	Sammy Sosa	.25
10	Frank Thomas	.20
1	Andruw Jones	.20
2	Ken Griffey Jr.	.35
3	Frank Thomas	.20
4	Alex Rodriguez	.60
5	Cal Ripken Jr.	.75
6	Mike Piazza	.35
7	Greg Maddux	.25
8	Chipper Jones	.25
9	Derek Jeter	.75
10	Juan Gonzalez	.10

Diamond Producers

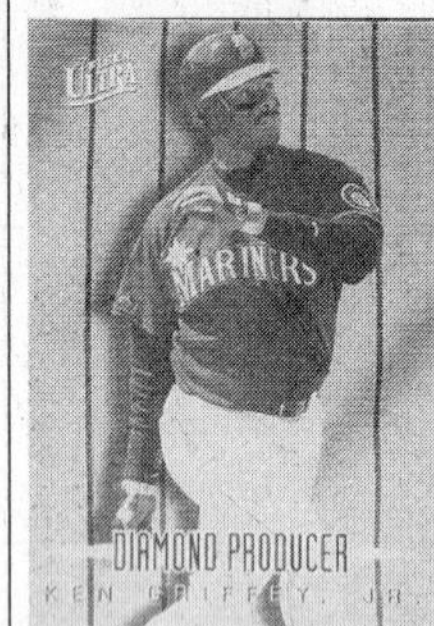

Printed on textured, uniform-like matterial, this 12-card insert contains some of the most consistent producers in baseball. Horizontal backs are conventionally printed with another color player photo on a pin-striped background and a few words about him. This was the most difficult insert Ultra foil-pack insert, with a ratio of one per 288.

		NM/M
Complete Set (12):		110.00
Common Player:		2.50
1	Jeff Bagwell	7.00
2	Barry Bonds	20.00
3	Ken Griffey Jr.	12.50
4	Chipper Jones	10.00
5	Kenny Lofton	2.50
6	Greg Maddux	10.00
7	Mark McGwire	15.00
8	Mike Piazza	12.50
9	Cal Ripken Jr.	20.00
10	Alex Rodriguez	15.00
11	Frank Thomas	7.50
12	Matt Williams	2.50

Double Trouble

Double Trouble is a 20-card, team color coded set pairing two stars from the same team on a horizontal front. These inserts were found every four packs.

		NM/M
Complete Set (20):		10.00
Common Player:		.15
1	Roberto Alomar, Cal Ripken Jr.	1.50
2	Mo Vaughn, Jose Canseco	.40
3	Jim Edmonds, Tim Salmon	.15
4	Harold Baines, Frank Thomas	.50
5	Albert Belle, Kenny Lofton	.15
6	Chuck Knoblauch, Marty Cordova	.15
7	Andy Pettitte, Derek Jeter	1.50
8	Jason Giambi, Mark McGwire	1.00
9	Ken Griffey Jr., Alex Rodriguez	1.00
10	Juan Gonzalez, Will Clark	.30
11	Greg Maddux, Chipper Jones	.60
12	Mark Grace, Sammy Sosa	.60
13	Dante Bichette, Andres Galarraga	.15
14	Jeff Bagwell, Derek Bell	.50
15	Hideo Nomo, Mike Piazza	.75
16	Henry Rodriguez, Moises Alou	.15
17	Rey Ordonez, Alex Ochoa	.15
18	Ray Lankford, Ron Gant	.15
19	Tony Gwynn, Rickey Henderson	.60
20	Barry Bonds, Matt Williams	1.50

Fame Game

This eight-card hobby-exclusive insert showcases players who have displayed Hall of Fame potential. The player photo on front and Fame Game logo are embossed and highlighted in gold and silver foil. Backs have a color portrait photo and a few words about the player. Cards were inserted 1:8 packs.

		NM/M
Complete Set (18):		20.00
Common Player:		.35
1	Ken Griffey Jr.	1.75
2	Frank Thomas	1.00
3	Alex Rodriguez	2.00
4	Cal Ripken Jr.	3.00
5	Mike Piazza	1.75
6	Greg Maddux	1.25
7	Derek Jeter	3.00
8	Jeff Bagwell	1.00
9	Juan Gonzalez	.50
10	Albert Belle	.35
11	Tony Gwynn	1.25
12	Mark McGwire	2.00
13	Andy Pettitte	.45
14	Kenny Lofton	.35
15	Roberto Alomar	.40
16	Ryne Sandberg	1.25
17	Barry Bonds	3.00
18	Eddie Murray	1.00

Fielder's Choice

Fielder's Choice highlights 18 of the top defensive players in baseball. Fronts of the horizontal cards have a leather look and feel and are highlighted in gold foil. Backs are conventionally printed with another player photo and some words about his fielding ability. Fielder's Choice inserts were found every 144 packs.

		NM/M
Complete Set (18):		80.00
Common Player:		1.00
1	Roberto Alomar	1.50
2	Jeff Bagwell	6.00
3	Wade Boggs	7.50
4	Barry Bonds	15.00
5	Mark Grace	1.00
6	Ken Griffey Jr.	10.00
7	Marquis Grissom	1.00
8	Charles Johnson	1.00
9	Chuck Knoblauch	1.00
10	Barry Larkin	1.00
11	Kenny Lofton	1.00
12	Greg Maddux	7.50
13	Raul Mondesi	1.00
14	Rey Ordonez	1.00
15	Cal Ripken Jr.	15.00
16	Alex Rodriguez	12.50
17	Ivan Rodriguez	5.00
18	Matt Williams	1.00

Golden Prospects

This 10-card set was exclusive to hobby shop packs and highlighted the top young players in baseball. Action photos on front and portraits on back are set on a sepia background. Cards were inserted 1:4 packs.

		NM/M
Complete Set (10):		3.00
Common Player:		.25
1	Andruw Jones	1.50
2	Vladimir Guerrero	1.50
3	Todd Walker	.25
4	Karim Garcia	.25
5	Kevin Orie	.25
6	Brian Giles	.25
7	Jason Dickson	.25
8	Jose Guillen	.25
9	Ruben Rivera	.25
10	Derrek Lee	1.00

Hitting Machines

This 36-card insert was only found in hobby packs and showcases the game's top hitters. Cards were inserted at a ratio of 1:36 packs.

		NM/M
Complete Set (18):		60.00
Common Player:		1.00
1	Andruw Jones	3.00
2	Ken Griffey Jr.	5.00
3	Frank Thomas	3.00
4	Alex Rodriguez	6.50
5	Cal Ripken Jr.	9.00
6	Mike Piazza	5.00
7	Derek Jeter	9.00
8	Albert Belle	1.00
9	Tony Gwynn	4.00
10	Jeff Bagwell	3.00
11	Mark McGwire	6.50
12	Kenny Lofton	1.00
13	Manny Ramirez	3.00
14	Roberto Alomar	1.25
15	Ryne Sandberg	4.00
16	Eddie Murray	3.00
17	Sammy Sosa	4.00
18	Ken Caminiti	1.00

HR Kings

HR Kings are printed on clear plastic with transparent refractive holofoil crowns and other objects in the plastic. Backs contain a white silhouette of the player with career summary and logos within the figure. Stated odds of finding an HR King card were one per 36 packs.

		NM/M
Complete Set (12):		30.00
Common Player:		1.00
1	Albert Belle	1.00
2	Barry Bonds	7.50
3	Juan Gonzalez	1.50
4	Ken Griffey Jr.	4.50
5	Todd Hundley	1.00
6	Ryan Klesko	1.00
7	Mark McGwire	6.00
8	Mike Piazza	4.50
9	Sammy Sosa	3.50
10	Frank Thomas	2.50
11	Mo Vaughn	1.00
12	Matt Williams	1.00

Leather Shop

Baseball's best fielders are honored in this 12-card hobby-exclusive insert. Cards were inserted at a ratio of 1:6 packs and feature an embossed grain-like finish on the fronts.

		NM/M
Complete Set (12):		9.00
Common Player:		.25
1	Ken Griffey Jr.	1.25
2	Alex Rodriguez	1.50
3	Cal Ripken Jr.	2.00
4	Derek Jeter	2.00
5	Juan Gonzalez	.45
6	Tony Gwynn	1.00
7	Jeff Bagwell	.75
8	Roberto Alomar	.40
9	Ryne Sandberg	1.00
10	Ken Caminiti	.25
11	Kenny Lofton	.25
12	John Smoltz	.25

Power Plus Series 1

Series 1 Power Plus is a 12-card insert utilizing silver rainbow holofoil in the background, with the featured player in the foreground. Backs have another action photo and the player's credentials. The insert captures power hitters that also excel in other areas of the game. Power Plus inserts can be found every 24 packs.

		NM/M
Complete Set (12):		15.00
Common Player:		.50
1	Jeff Bagwell	.75
2	Barry Bonds	3.00
3	Juan Gonzalez	.60
4	Ken Griffey Jr.	1.50
5	Chipper Jones	1.00
6	Mark McGwire	2.00
7	Mike Piazza	1.50
8	Cal Ripken Jr.	3.00
9	Alex Rodriguez	2.00
10	Sammy Sosa	1.00
11	Frank Thomas	.75
12	Matt Williams	.50

Power Plus Series 2

Similar in design to the Power Plus insert in Series I, this 12-card insert salutes the game's top sluggers and was found only in hobby packs. Cards were inserted at a ratio of 1:8 packs. Front design features gold holographic foil graphics. Backs have another photo and a description of the player's skills.

		NM/M
Complete Set (12):		6.50
Common Player:		.25
1	Ken Griffey Jr.	.75
2	Frank Thomas	.50
3	Alex Rodriguez	1.00
4	Cal Ripken Jr.	1.50
5	Mike Piazza	.75
6	Chipper Jones	.65
7	Albert Belle	.25
8	Juan Gonzalez	.35
9	Jeff Bagwell	.50
10	Mark McGwire	1.00
11	Mo Vaughn	.25
12	Barry Bonds	1.50

RBI Kings

Ten different players are featured in RBI Kings, which contain a metallic paisley background, with an English shield of armor and latin words in the background. RBI Kings were inserted every 18 packs of Series I.

		NM/M
Complete Set (10):		12.50
Common Player:		.75
1	Jeff Bagwell	1.50
2	Albert Belle	.75
3	Dante Bichette	.75
4	Barry Bonds	4.00
5	Jay Buhner	.75
6	Juan Gonzalez	1.00
7	Ken Griffey Jr.	2.50
8	Sammy Sosa	2.00
9	Frank Thomas	1.50
10	Mo Vaughn	.75

Rookie Reflections

Rookie Reflections features 10 of the 1996 season's top first-year stars. Cards are inserted every four packs. Front features an action photo on a black-and-silver starburst pattern. Horizontal backs have another photo and a career summary of the prospect.

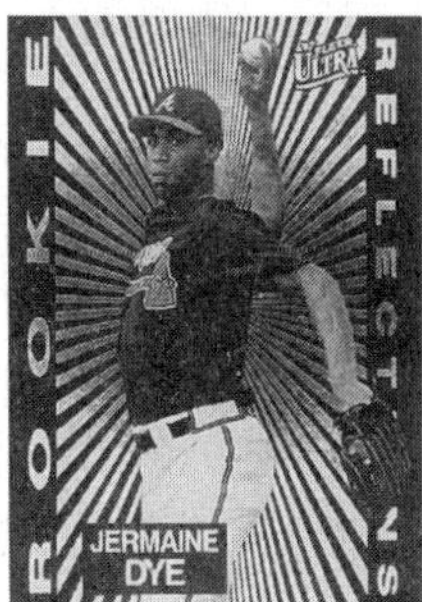

		NM/M
Complete Set (10):		3.50
Common Player:		.25
1	James Baldwin	.25
2	Jermaine Dye	.25
3	Darin Erstad	.40
4	Todd Hollandsworth	.25
5	Derek Jeter	3.00
6	Jason Kendall	.25
7	Alex Ochoa	.25
8	Rey Ordonez	.25
9	Edgar Renteria	.25
10	Scott Rolen	.50

Season Crowns

Season Crowns were found at a rate of one per eight packs of Ultra I Baseball. This etched, silver-foil insert contained 12 statistical leaders and award winners from the 1996 season.

		NM/M
Complete Set (12):		10.00
Common Player:		.50
1	Albert Belle	.50
2	Dante Bichette	.50
3	Barry Bonds	3.00
4	Kenny Lofton	.50
5	Edgar Martinez	.50
6	Mark McGwire	2.00
7	Andy Pettitte	.50
8	Mike Piazza	1.50
9	Alex Rodriguez	2.00
10	John Smoltz	.50
11	Sammy Sosa	1.25
12	Frank Thomas	1.00

Starring Role

Another hobby-exclusive insert, these 12 cards salute baseball's clutch performers and were found 1:288 packs.

		NM/M
Complete Set (12):		175.00
Common Player:		7.50
1	Andruw Jones	12.00
2	Ken Griffey Jr.	20.00
3	Frank Thomas	12.00
4	Alex Rodriguez	25.00
5	Cal Ripken Jr.	30.00
6	Mike Piazza	20.00
7	Greg Maddux	15.00
8	Chipper Jones	15.00
9	Derek Jeter	30.00
10	Juan Gonzalez	9.00
11	Albert Belle	7.50
12	Tony Gwynn	15.00

Thunderclap

This 10-card hobby-exclusive insert showcases hitters who strike fear in opposing pitchers. Cards were inserted 1:18 packs. Fronts are highlighted by streaks of gold prismatic foil lightning in a stormy sky. Backs have another player photo and a few words about him.

		NM/M
Complete Set (10):		20.00
Common Player:		.75
1	Barry Bonds	5.00
2	Mo Vaughn	.75
3	Mark McGwire	4.00
4	Jeff Bagwell	1.50
5	Juan Gonzalez	1.00
6	Alex Rodriguez	4.00
7	Chipper Jones	2.50
8	Ken Griffey Jr.	3.00
9	Mike Piazza	3.00
10	Frank Thomas	2.00

Top 30

This 30-card insert was found only in retail store packs and salutes the 30 most collectible players in the game. Cards were inserted one per pack. A Top 30 Gold Medallion parallel set, die-cut around the top, was also produced and inserted 1:18 packs.

		NM/M
Complete Set (30):		12.00
Common Player:		.20
Gold Medallions:		6X
1	Andruw Jones	.75
2	Ken Griffey Jr.	1.25
3	Frank Thomas	.75
4	Alex Rodriguez	1.50
5	Cal Ripken Jr.	2.00
6	Mike Piazza	1.25
7	Greg Maddux	1.00
8	Chipper Jones	1.00
9	Derek Jeter	2.00
10	Juan Gonzalez	.40
11	Albert Belle	.20
12	Tony Gwynn	1.00
13	Jeff Bagwell	.75
14	Mark McGwire	1.50
15	Andy Pettitte	.30
16	Mo Vaughn	.20
17	Kenny Lofton	.20
18	Manny Ramirez	.75
19	Roberto Alomar	.40
20	Ryne Sandberg	1.00
21	Hideo Nomo	.40
22	Barry Bonds	2.00
23	Eddie Murray	.75
24	Ken Caminiti	.20
25	John Smoltz	.20
26	Pat Hentgen	.20
27	Todd Hollandsworth	.20
28	Matt Williams	.20
29	Bernie Williams	.20
30	Brady Anderson	.20

FanFest Larry Doby

In the same basic style as its regular-issue Ultra baseball series of 1997, Fleer issued a special Larry Doby card in conjunction with the All-Star FanFest in Cleveland, recognizing Doby's 50th anniversary of breaking the American League color barrier. The card has a black-and-white batting pose of Doby on front with his name, team and Fleer Ultra logo in red-shaded silver holographic foil. A color All-Star Game logo also appears on front. Backs have a red duotone photo of Doby fielding, his career stats and a few words about his career.

	NM/M
Larry Doby	4.00

1998 Ultra

Ultra was released in two series with a total of 501 cards; 250 in Series 1 and 251 in Series 2. Ten-card packs carried an SRP of $2.59. There were three parallel sets: Gold Medallion, Platinum Medallion and Masterpieces. Series 1 has 210 regular cards, 25 Prospects (seeded 1:4 packs), 10 Season's Crowns (1:12) and five Checklists (1:8). Series 2 has 202 regular cards, 25 Pizzazz (1:4), 20 New Horizons and three checklists. Series 2 also added a Mike Piazza N.Y. Mets card as #501, inserted every 20 packs. Inserts in Series 1 include: Big Shots, Double Trouble, Kid Gloves, Back to the Future, Artistic Talents, Fall Classics, Power Plus, Prime Leather, Diamond Producers, Diamond Ink and Million Dollar Moments. Series 2 included: Notables, Rocket to Stardom, Millennium Men, Win Now, Ticket Studs, Diamond Immortals, Diamond Ink, Top 30 and 750 sequentially numbered Alex Rodriguez autographed promo cards.

		NM/M
Complete Set (501):		75.00
Common Player:		.05
Alex Rodriguez Autograph (750):		50.00
Pack (10):		1.25
Wax Box (24):		20.00
1	Ken Griffey Jr.	1.25
2	Matt Morris	.05
3	Roger Clemens	1.00
4	Matt Williams	.05
5	Roberto Hernandez	.05
6	Rondell White	.05
7	Tim Salmon	.05
8	Brad Radke	.05
9	Brett Butler	.05
10	Carl Everett	.05
11	Chili Davis	.05
12	Chuck Finley	.05
13	Darryl Kile	.05
14	Deivi Cruz	.05
15	Gary Gaetti	.05
16	Matt Stairs	.05
17	Pat Meares	.05
18	Will Cunnane	.05
19	Steve Woodard **RC**	.15
20	Andy Ashby	.05
21	Bobby Higginson	.05
22	Brian Jordan	.05
23	Craig Biggio	.05
24	Jim Edmonds	.05
25	Ryan McGuire	.05
26	Scott Hatteberg	.05
27	Willie Greene	.05
28	Albert Belle	.05
29	Ellis Burks	.05
30	Hideo Nomo	.40
31	Jeff Bagwell	.75
32	Kevin Brown	.05
33	Nomar Garciaparra	1.00
34	Pedro Martinez	.75
35	Raul Mondesi	.05
36	Ricky Bottalico	.05
37	Shawn Estes	.05
38	Shawon Dunston	.05
39	Terry Steinbach	.05
40	Tom Glavine	.25
41	Todd Dunwoody	.05
42	Deion Sanders	.05
43	Gary Sheffield	.45
44	Mike Lansing	.05
45	Mike Lieberthal	.05
46	Paul Sorrento	.05
47	Paul O'Neill	.05
48	Tom Goodwin	.05
49	Andruw Jones	.75
50	Barry Bonds	2.00
51	Bernie Williams	.05
52	Jeremi Gonzalez	.05
53	Mike Piazza	1.25
54	Russ Davis	.05
55	Vinny Castilla	.05
56	Rod Beck	.05
57	Andres Galarraga	.05
58	Ben McDonald	.05
59	Billy Wagner	.05
60	Charles Johnson	.05
61	Fred McGriff	.05
62	Dean Palmer	.05
63	Frank Thomas	.75
64	Ismael Valdes	.05
65	Mark Bellhorn	.05
66	Jeff King	.05
67	John Wetteland	.05
68	Mark Grace	.05
69	Mark Kotsay	.05
70	Scott Rolen	.60
71	Todd Hundley	.05
72	Todd Worrell	.05
73	Wilson Alvarez	.05
74	Bobby Jones	.05
75	Jose Canseco	.50
76	Kevin Appier	.05
77	Neifi Perez	.05
78	Paul Molitor	.75
79	Quilvio Veras	.05
80	Randy Johnson	.75
81	Glendon Rusch	.05
82	Curt Schilling	.15
83	Alex Rodriguez	1.50
84	Rey Ordonez	.05
85	Jeff Juden	.05
86	Mike Cameron	.05
87	Ryan Klesko	.05
88	Trevor Hoffman	.05
89	Chuck Knoblauch	.05
90	Larry Walker	.05
91	Mark McLemore	.05
92	B.J. Surhoff	.05
93	Darren Daulton	.05
94	Ray Durham	.05
95	Sammy Sosa	1.00
96	Eric Young	.05
97	Gerald Williams	.05
98	Javy Lopez	.05
99	John Smiley	.05
100	Juan Gonzalez	.40
101	Shawn Green	.30
102	Charles Nagy	.05
103	David Justice	.05
104	Joey Hamilton	.05
105	Pat Hentgen	.05
106	Raul Casanova	.05
107	Tony Phillips	.05
108	Tony Gwynn	1.00
109	Will Clark	.05
110	Jason Giambi	.50
111	Jay Bell	.05
112	Johnny Damon	.30
113	Alan Benes	.05
114	Jeff Suppan	.05
115	Kevin Polcovich **RC**	.05
116	Shigetosi Hasegawa	.05
117	Steve Finley	.05
118	Tony Clark	.05
119	David Cone	.05
120	Jose Guillen	.05
121	Kevin Millwood **RC**	1.00
122	Greg Maddux	1.00
123	Dave Nilsson	.05
124	Hideki Irabu	.05
125	Jason Kendall	.05
126	Jim Thome	.60
127	Delino DeShields	.05
128	Edgar Renteria	.05
129	Edgardo Alfonzo	.05
130	J.T. Snow	.05
131	Jeff Abbott	.05
132	Jeffrey Hammonds	.05
133	Rich Loiselle	.05
134	Vladimir Guerrero	.75
135	Jay Buhner	.05
136	Jeff Cirillo	.05
137	Jeromy Burnitz	.05
138	Mickey Morandini	.05
139	Tino Martinez	.05
140	Jeff Shaw	.05
141	Rafael Palmeiro	.65
142	Bobby Bonilla	.05
143	Cal Ripken Jr.	2.00
144	Chad Fox **RC**	.05
145	Dante Bichette	.05
146	Dennis Eckersley	.65
147	Mariano Rivera	.15
148	Mo Vaughn	.05
149	Reggie Sanders	.05
150	Derek Jeter	2.00
151	Rusty Greer	.05
152	Brady Anderson	.05
153	Brett Tomko	.05
154	Jaime Navarro	.05
155	Kevin Orie	.05
156	Roberto Alomar	.20
157	Edgar Martinez	.05
158	John Olerud	.05
159	John Smoltz	.05
160	Ryne Sandberg	1.00
161	Billy Taylor	.05
162	Chris Holt	.05
163	Damion Easley	.05
164	Darin Erstad	.25
165	Joe Carter	.05
166	Kelvim Escobar	.05
167	Ken Caminiti	.05
168	Pokey Reese	.05
169	Ray Lankford	.05
170	Livan Hernandez	.05
171	Steve Kline	.05
172	Tom Gordon	.05
173	Travis Fryman	.05
174	Al Martin	.05
175	Andy Pettitte	.25
176	Jeff Kent	.05
177	Jimmy Key	.05
178	Mark Grudzielanek	.05
179	Tony Saunders	.05
180	Barry Larkin	.05
181	Bubba Trammell	.05
182	Carlos Delgado	.50
183	Carlos Baerga	.05
184	Derek Bell	.05
185	Henry Rodriguez	.05
186	Jason Dickson	.05
187	Ron Gant	.05
188	Tony Womack	.05
189	Justin Thompson	.05
190	Fernando Tatis	.05
191	Mark Wohlers	.05
192	Takashi Kashiwada	.05
193	Garret Anderson	.05
194	Jose Cruz, Jr.	.05
195	Ricardo Rincon	.05
196	Tim Naehring	.05
197	Moises Alou	.05
198	Eric Karros	.05
199	John Jaha	.05
200	Marty Cordova	.05
201	Travis Lee	.10
202	Mark Davis	.05
203	Vladimir Nunez	.05
204	Stanton Cameron	.05
205	Mike Stoner **RC**	.05
206	Rolando Arrojo **RC**	.40
207	Rick White	.05
208	Luis Polonia	.05
209	Greg Blosser	.05
210	Cesar Devarez	.05
211	Jeff Bagwell (Season Crown)	1.00
212	Barry Bonds (Season Crown)	3.00
213	Roger Clemens (Season Crown)	1.75
214	Nomar Garciaparra (Season Crown)	1.50
215	Ken Griffey Jr. (Season Crown)	2.00
216	Tony Gwynn (Season Crown)	1.50
217	Randy Johnson (Season Crown)	1.00
218	Mark McGwire (Season Crown)	3.00
219	Scott Rolen (Season Crown)	.75
220	Frank Thomas (Season Crown)	1.25
221	Matt Perisho (Prospect)	.25
222	Wes Helms (Prospect)	.25
223	David Dellucci **RC** (Prospect)	.25
224	Todd Helton (Prospect)	1.00
225	Brian Rose (Prospect)	.25
226	Aaron Boone (Prospect)	.25
227	Keith Foulke (Prospect)	.25
228	Homer Bush (Prospect)	.25
229	Shannon Stewart (Prospect)	.25
230	Richard Hidalgo (Prospect)	.25
231	Russ Johnson (Prospect)	.25
232	Henry Blanco **RC** (Prospect)	.25
233	Paul Konerko (Prospect)	.35
234	Antone Williamson (Prospect)	.25
235	Shane Bowers **RC** (Prospect)	.25
236	Jose Vidro (Prospect)	.25
237	Derek Wallace (Prospect)	.25
238	Ricky Ledee (Prospect)	.25
239	Ben Grieve (Prospect)	.25
240	Lou Collier (Prospect)	.25
241	Derrek Lee (Prospect)	.65
242	Ruben Rivera (Prospect)	.25
243	Jorge Velandia (Prospect)	.25
244	Andrew Vessel (Prospect)	.25
245	Chris Carpenter (Prospect)	.25
246	Checklist (Ken Griffey Jr.)	.65
247	Checklist (Andruw Jones)	.50
248	Checklist (Alex Rodriguez)	.75
249	Checklist (Frank Thomas)	.60
250	Checklist (Cal Ripken Jr.)	1.00
251	Carlos Perez	.05
252	Larry Sutton	.05
253	Brad Rigby	.05
254	Wally Joyner	.05
255	Todd Stottlemyre	.05
256	Nerio Rodriguez	.05
257	Jeff Frye	.05
258	Pedro Astacio	.05
259	Cal Eldred	.05
260	Chili Davis	.05
261	Freddy Garcia	.05
262	Bobby Witt	.05
263	Michael Coleman	.05
264	Mike Caruso	.05
265	Mike Lansing	.05
266	Dennis Reyes	.05
267	F.P. Santangelo	.05
268	Darryl Hamilton	.05
269	Mike Fetters	.05
270	Charlie Hayes	.05
271	Royce Clayton	.05
272	Doug Drabek	.05
273	James Baldwin	.05
274	Brian Hunter	.05
275	Chan Ho Park	.05
276	John Franco	.05
277	David Wells	.05
278	Eli Marrero	.05
279	Kerry Wood	.40
280	Donnie Sadler	.05
281	Scott Winchester **RC**	.05
282	Hal Morris	.05
283	Brad Fullmer	.05
284	Bernard Gilkey	.05
285	Ramiro Mendoza	.05
286	Kevin Brown	.05
287	David Segui	.05
288	Willie McGee	.05
289	Darren Oliver	.05
290	Antonio Alfonseca	.05
291	Eric Davis	.05
292	Mickey Morandini	.05
293	Frank Catalanotto **RC**	.20
294	Derrek Lee	.50
295	Todd Zeile	.05
296	Chuck Knoblauch	.05
297	Wilson Delgado	.05
298	Raul Ibanez	.05
299	Orel Hershiser	.05
300	Ozzie Guillen	.05
301	Aaron Sele	.05
302	Joe Carter	.05
303	Darryl Kile	.05
304	Shane Reynolds	.05
305	Todd Dunn	.05
306	Bob Abreu	.10
307	Doug Strange	.05
308	Jose Canseco	.50
309	Lance Johnson	.05
310	Harold Baines	.05
311	Todd Pratt	.05
312	Greg Colbrunn	.05
313	Masato Yoshii **RC**	.25
314	Felix Heredia	.05
315	Dennis Martinez	.05
316	Geronimo Berroa	.05
317	Darren Lewis	.05
318	Billy Ripken	.05
319	Enrique Wilson	.05
320	Alex Ochoa	.05
321	Doug Glanville	.05
322	Mike Stanley	.05
323	Gerald Williams	.05
324	Pedro Martinez	.75
325	Jaret Wright	.05
326	Terry Pendleton	.05
327	LaTroy Hawkins	.05

328	Emil Brown	.05
329	Walt Weiss	.05
330	Omar Vizquel	.05
331	Carl Everett	.05
332	Fernando Vina	.05
333	Mike Blowers	.05
334	Dwight Gooden	.05
335	Mark Lewis	.05
336	Jim Leyritz	.05
337	Kenny Lofton	.05
338	John Halama **RC**	.05
339	Jose Valentin	.05
340	Desi Relaford	.05
341	Dante Powell	.05
342	Ed Sprague	.05
343	Reggie Jefferson	.05
344	Mike Hampton	.05
345	Marquis Grissom	.05
346	Heathcliff Slocumb	.05
347	Francisco Cordova	.05
348	Ken Cloude	.05
349	Benito Santiago	.05
350	Denny Neagle	.05
351	Sean Casey	.15
352	Robb Nen	.05
353	Orlando Merced	.05
354	Adrian Brown	.05
355	Gregg Jefferies	.05
356	Otis Nixon	.05
357	Michael Tucker	.05
358	Eric Milton	.05
359	Travis Fryman	.05
360	Gary DiSarcina	.05
361	Mario Valdez	.05
362	Craig Counsell	.05
363	Jose Offerman	.05
364	Tony Fernandez	.05
365	Jason McDonald	.05
366	Sterling Hitchcock	.05
367	Donovan Osborne	.05
368	Troy Percival	.05
369	Henry Rodriguez	.05
370	Dmitri Young	.05
371	Jay Powell	.05
372	Jeff Conine	.05
373	Orlando Cabrera	.10
374	Butch Huskey	.05
375	Mike Lowell **RC**	.50
376	Kevin Young	.05
377	Jamie Moyer	.05
378	Jeff D'Amico	.05
379	Scott Erickson	.05
380	Magglio Ordonez **RC**	2.50
381	Melvin Nieves	.05
382	Ramon Martinez	.05
383	A.J. Hinch	.05
384	Jeff Brantley	.05
385	Kevin Elster	.05
386	Allen Watson	.05
387	Moises Alou	.05
388	Jeff Blauser	.05
389	Pete Harnisch	.05
390	Shane Andrews	.05
391	Rico Brogna	.05
392	Stan Javier	.05
393	David Howard	.05
394	Darryl Strawberry	.05
395	Kent Mercker	.05
396	Juan Encarnacion	.05
397	Sandy Alomar	.05
398	Al Leiter	.05
399	Tony Graffanino	.05
400	Terry Adams	.05
401	Bruce Aven	.05
402	Derrick Gibson	.05
403	Jose Cabrera	.05
404	Rich Becker	.05
405	David Ortiz	.50
406	Brian McRae	.05
407	Bobby Estalella	.05
408	Bill Mueller	.05
409	Dennis Eckersley	.65
410	Sandy Martinez	.05
411	Jose Vizcaino	.05
412	Jermaine Allensworth	.05
413	Miguel Tejada	.20
414	Turner Ward	.05
415	Glenallen Hill	.05
416	Lee Stevens	.05
417	Cecil Fielder	.05
418	Ruben Sierra	.05
419	Jon Nunnally	.05
420	Rod Myers	.05
421	Dustin Hermanson	.05
422	James Mouton	.05
423	Dan Wilson	.05
424	Roberto Kelly	.05
425	Antonio Osuna	.05
426	Jacob Cruz	.05
427	Brent Mayne	.05
428	Matt Karchner	.05
429	Damian Jackson	.05
430	Roger Cedeno	.05
431	Rickey Henderson	.75
432	Joe Randa	.05
433	Greg Vaughn	.05
434	Andres Galarraga	.05
435	Rod Beck	.05
436	Curtis Goodwin	.05
437	Brad Ausmus	.05
438	Bob Hamelin	.05
439	Todd Walker	.05
440	Scott Brosius	.05
441	Lenny Dykstra	.05
442	Abraham Nunez	.05
443	Brian Johnson	.05
444	Randy Myers	.05
445	Bret Boone	.15
446	Oscar Henriquez	.05
447	Mike Sweeney	.05
448	Kenny Rogers	.05
449	Mark Langston	.05
450	Luis Gonzalez	.05
451	John Burkett	.05
452	Bip Roberts	.05
453	Travis Lee (New Horizons)	.15
454	Felix Rodriguez (New Horizons)	.05
455	Andy Benes (New Horizons)	.05
456	Willie Blair (New Horizons)	.05
457	Brian Anderson (New Horizons)	.05
458	Jay Bell (New Horizons)	.05
459	Matt Williams (New Horizons)	.05
460	Devon White (New Horizons)	.05
461	Karim Garcia (New Horizons)	.10
462	Jorge Fabregas (New Horizons)	.05
463	Wilson Alvarez (New Horizons)	.05
464	Roberto Hernandez (New Horizons)	.05
465	Tony Saunders (New Horizons)	.05
466	Rolando Arrojo **RC** (New Horizons)	.35
467	Wade Boggs (New Horizons)	1.00
468	Fred McGriff (New Horizons)	.05
469	Paul Sorrento (New Horizons)	.05
470	Kevin Stocker (New Horizons)	.05
471	Bubba Trammell (New Horizons)	.05
472	Quinton McCracken (New Horizons)	.05
473	Checklist (Ken Griffey Jr.)	.65
474	Checklist (Cal Ripken Jr.)	1.00
475	Checklist (Frank Thomas)	.60
476	Ken Griffey Jr. (Pizzazz)	1.75
477	Cal Ripken Jr. (Pizzazz)	3.00
478	Frank Thomas (Pizzazz)	1.25
479	Alex Rodriguez (Pizzazz)	2.00
480	Nomar Garciaparra (Pizzazz)	1.50
481	Derek Jeter (Pizzazz)	3.00
482	Andruw Jones (Pizzazz)	1.00
483	Chipper Jones (Pizzazz)	1.50
484	Greg Maddux (Pizzazz)	1.50
485	Mike Piazza (Pizzazz)	1.75
486	Juan Gonzalez (Pizzazz)	.60
487	Jose Cruz (Pizzazz)	.50
488	Jaret Wright (Pizzazz)	.50
489	Hideo Nomo (Pizzazz)	.60
490	Scott Rolen (Pizzazz)	.65
491	Tony Gwynn (Pizzazz)	1.50
492	Roger Clemens (Pizzazz)	1.60
493	Darin Erstad (Pizzazz)	.50
494	Mark McGwire (Pizzazz)	2.00
495	Jeff Bagwell (Pizzazz)	1.00
496	Mo Vaughn (Pizzazz)	.50
497	Albert Belle (Pizzazz)	.50
498	Kenny Lofton (Pizzazz)	.50
499	Ben Grieve (Pizzazz)	.50
500	Barry Bonds (Pizzazz)	2.50
501	Mike Piazza (Mets)	1.50

Gold Medallion

This parallel to the Ultra set is found seeded on a one per pack ratio. Cards are similar to the regular-issue Ultra except for a gold presentation of the embossed player name on front and a shower of gold specks in the photo background. Backs have a "G" suffix to the card number and a "GOLD MEDALLION EDITION" notation at bottom. The short-printed subset cards from the regular Ultra edition are not short-printed in Gold Medallion.

	NM/M
Common Player:	.25
Stars/RC's:	2X
Checklists:	2X
Season Crowns:	1X
Prospects:	1X
Pizzazz:	1X

Platinum Medallion

Insertion odds on this super-scarce insert set are not given but each card is produced and serially numbered in an edition of only 100 (Series 1) or 98 (Series 2). Fronts are similar to regular Ultra cards except the photo is black-and-white and the name is rendered in silver prismatic foil. Backs are in color with the serial number printed in silver foil at bottom. Series 2 checklist cards #473-475 were not printed in Platinum, and the short-prints from the regular issue are not short-printed in this parallel edition.

	NM/M
Common Player:	5.00
Stars/RC's:	25X
Checklists:	25X
Season Crowns:	8X
Prospects:	8X
Pizzazz:	8X

Masterpiece

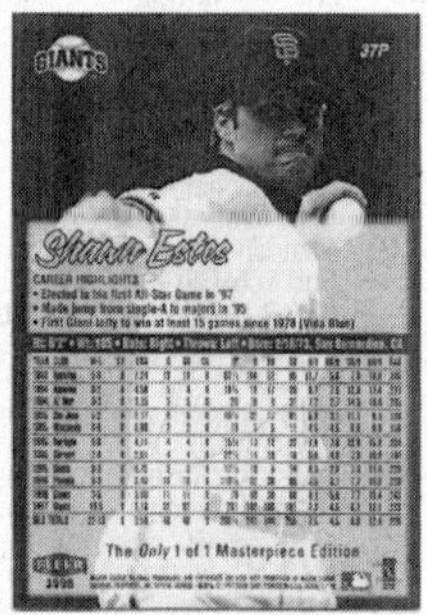

This top of the line parallel to '98 Ultra consists of a 1 of 1 version of each regular card.

	NM/M
Common Player:	50.00

Artistic Talents

This 18-card insert featured top players in the game on a canvas-like surface with the insert name in silver holographic letters across the top. The backs are done in black and white and numbered with an "AT" suffix.

		NM/M
Complete Set (18):		12.00
Common Player:		.40
Inserted 1:8		
1	Ken Griffey Jr.	1.00
2	Andruw Jones	.60
3	Alex Rodriguez	1.25
4	Frank Thomas	.60
5	Cal Ripken Jr.	1.50
6	Derek Jeter	1.50
7	Chipper Jones	.75
8	Greg Maddux	.75
9	Mike Piazza	1.00
10	Albert Belle	.40
11	Darin Erstad	.50
12	Juan Gonzalez	.50
13	Jeff Bagwell	.60
14	Tony Gwynn	.75
15	Mark McGwire	1.25
16	Scott Rolen	.50
17	Barry Bonds	1.50
18	Kenny Lofton	.40

Back to the Future

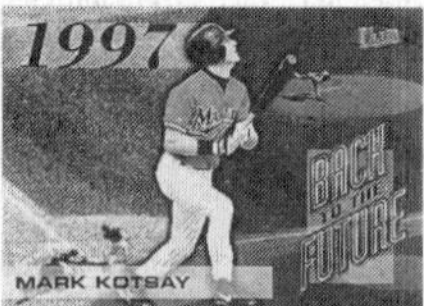

This 15-card insert was printed in a horizontal format with a baseball field background. Cards were numbered with a "BF" suffix.

		NM/M
Complete Set (15):		4.00
Common Player:		.10
Inserted 1:6		
1	Andruw Jones	.50
2	Alex Rodriguez	1.00
3	Derek Jeter	1.60
4	Darin Erstad	.25
5	Mike Cameron	.10
6	Scott Rolen	.35
7	Nomar Garciaparra	.75
8	Hideki Irabu	.10
9	Jose Cruz, Jr.	.10
10	Vladimir Guerrero	.50
11	Mark Kotsay	.10
12	Tony Womack	.10
13	Jason Dickson	.10
14	Jose Guillen	.10
15	Tony Clark	.10

Big Shots

Big Shots is a 15-card insert displaying some of the top home run hitters in baseball. A generic stadium is pictured across the bottom with the insert name running up the left side. Cards are numbered with a "BS" suffix and inserted one per four Series 1 packs.

		NM/M
Complete Set (15):		4.00
Common Player:		.10
Inserted 1:4		
1	Ken Griffey Jr.	.75
2	Frank Thomas	.35
3	Chipper Jones	.50
4	Albert Belle	.10
5	Juan Gonzalez	.25
6	Jeff Bagwell	.35
7	Mark McGwire	1.00
8	Barry Bonds	1.50
9	Manny Ramirez	.35
10	Mo Vaughn	.10
11	Matt Williams	.10
12	Jim Thome	.30
13	Tino Martinez	.10
14	Mike Piazza	.75
15	Tony Clark	.10

Diamond Immortals

This Series 2 insert showcases 15 top players on an intricate silver holographic foil design. Cards are numbered with a "DI" suffix.

		NM/M
Complete Set (15):		330.00
Common Player:		7.50
Inserted 1:288		
1	Ken Griffey Jr.	30.00
2	Frank Thomas	12.50
3	Alex Rodriguez	40.00
4	Cal Ripken Jr.	50.00
5	Mike Piazza	30.00
6	Mark McGwire	40.00
7	Greg Maddux	20.00
8	Andruw Jones	12.50
9	Chipper Jones	20.00
10	Derek Jeter	50.00
11	Tony Gwynn	20.00
12	Juan Gonzalez	9.00
13	Jose Cruz	7.50
14	Roger Clemens	25.00
15	Barry Bonds	50.00

Diamond Producers

This 15-card insert captures players on a prismatic silver design, with a wood backdrop and a black felt frame around the border. Cards were seeded one per 288 Series 1 packs and numbered with a "DP" suffix.

		NM/M
Complete Set (15):		180.00
Common Player:		7.50
Inserted 1:288		
1	Ken Griffey Jr.	30.00
2	Andruw Jones	12.50
3	Alex Rodriguez	40.00
4	Frank Thomas	12.50
5	Cal Ripken Jr.	50.00
6	Derek Jeter	50.00
7	Chipper Jones	20.00
8	Greg Maddux	20.00
9	Mike Piazza	30.00
10	Juan Gonzalez	9.00
11	Jeff Bagwell	12.50
12	Tony Gwynn	20.00
13	Mark McGwire	40.00
14	Barry Bonds	50.00
15	Jose Cruz, Jr.	7.50

Double Trouble

Double Trouble includes 20 cards and pairs teammates on a horizontal format with the team's logo and the insert name featured in a silver holographic circle in the middle.

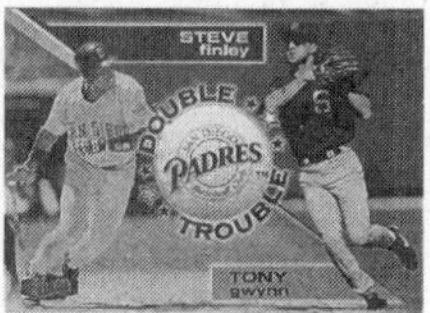

These are numbered with a "DT" suffix and exclusive to Series 1 packs.

		NM/M
Complete Set (20):		12.00
Common Player:		.15
Inserted 1:4		
1	Ken Griffey Jr., Alex Rodriguez	1.25
2	Vladimir Guerrero, Pedro Martinez	.60
3	Andruw Jones, Kenny Lofton	.60
4	Chipper Jones, Greg Maddux	.65
5	Derek Jeter, Tino Martinez	1.50
6	Frank Thomas, Albert Belle	.60
7	Cal Ripken Jr., Roberto Alomar	1.50
8	Mike Piazza, Hideo Nomo	1.00
9	Darin Erstad, Jason Dickson	.15
10	Juan Gonzalez, Ivan Rodriguez	.25
11	Jeff Bagwell, Darryl Kile	.60
12	Tony Gwynn, Steve Finley	.65
13	Mark McGwire, Ray Lankford	1.00
14	Barry Bonds, Jeff Kent	1.50
15	Andy Pettitte, Bernie Williams	.25
16	Mo Vaughn, Nomar Garciaparra	.65
17	Matt Williams, Jim Thome	.15
18	Hideki Irabu, Mariano Rivera	.25
19	Roger Clemens, Jose Cruz, Jr.	.75
20	Manny Ramirez, David Justice	.60

Fall Classics

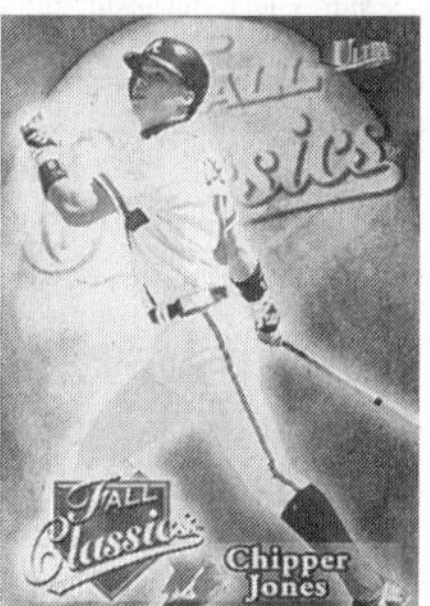

This Series 1 insert pictures 15 stars on a green holographic background. They are numbered with a "FC" suffix.

		NM/M
Complete Set (15):		35.00
Common Player:		1.00
Inserted 1:18		
1	Ken Griffey Jr.	3.00
2	Andruw Jones	1.50
3	Alex Rodriguez	4.00
4	Frank Thomas	1.50
5	Cal Ripken Jr.	5.00
6	Derek Jeter	5.00
7	Chipper Jones	2.00
8	Greg Maddux	2.00
9	Mike Piazza	4.00
10	Albert Belle	1.00
11	Juan Gonzalez	1.00
12	Jeff Bagwell	1.50
13	Tony Gwynn	2.00
14	Mark McGwire	3.00
15	Barry Bonds	5.00

Kid Gloves

Kid Gloves features top fielders on an embossed glove background. Exclusive to Series 1 packs, they are numbered with a "KG" suffix.

		NM/M
Complete Set (12):		9.00
Common Player:		.25
Inserted 1:8		
1	Andruw Jones	.75
2	Alex Rodriguez	2.00

3	Derek Jeter	3.00
4	Chipper Jones	1.00
5	Darin Erstad	.35
6	Todd Walker	.25
7	Scott Rolen	.65
8	Nomar Garciaparra	1.00
9	Jose Cruz, Jr.	.25
10	Charles Johnson	.25
11	Rey Ordonez	.25
12	Vladimir Guerrero	.75

Millennium Men

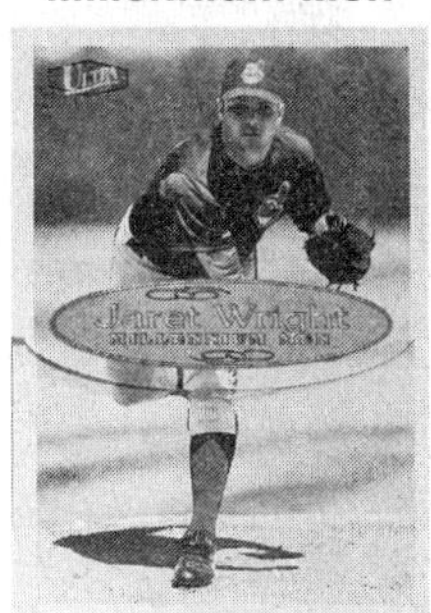

Millenium Men is a hobby-only insert exclusive to Series 2 packs. The tri-fold cards feature an embossed wax seal design and can be unfolded to reveal another shot of the player, team logo and statistics. They are numbered with a "MM" suffix.

		NM/M
Complete Set (15):		30.00
Common Player:		.75
Inserted 1:35		
1	Jose Cruz	.75
2	Ken Griffey Jr.	3.50
3	Cal Ripken Jr.	6.00
4	Derek Jeter	6.00
5	Andruw Jones	2.00
6	Alex Rodriguez	4.50
7	Chipper Jones	2.50
8	Scott Rolen	1.00
9	Nomar Garciaparra	2.50
10	Frank Thomas	2.00
11	Mike Piazza	3.50
12	Greg Maddux	2.50
13	Juan Gonzalez	1.00
14	Ben Grieve	.75
15	Jaret Wright	.75

Notables

This insert pictures a player on a holographic background with either an American League or National League logo in the background. Notables were seeded in Series 2 packs and numbered with a "N" suffix.

		NM/M
Complete Set (20):		13.50
Common Player:		.20
Inserted 1:4		
1	Frank Thomas	.50
2	Ken Griffey Jr.	1.25
3	Edgar Renteria	.20
4	Albert Belle	.20
5	Juan Gonzalez	.30
6	Jeff Bagwell	.50
7	Mark McGwire	1.50
8	Barry Bonds	2.25
9	Scott Rolen	.40
10	Mo Vaughn	.20
11	Andruw Jones	.50
12	Chipper Jones	.75
13	Tino Martinez	.20
14	Mike Piazza	1.25
15	Tony Clark	.20
16	Jose Cruz	.20
17	Nomar Garciaparra	.75
18	Cal Ripken Jr.	2.25
19	Alex Rodriguez	1.50
20	Derek Jeter	2.25

Power Plus

This insert is exclusive to Series 1 packs. Cards picture the player on an embossed blue background featuring plus signs. These are numbered with a "PP" suffix.

		NM/M
Complete Set (10):		16.00
Common Player:		1.00
Inserted 1:36		
1	Ken Griffey Jr.	4.00
2	Andruw Jones	2.00
3	Alex Rodriguez	3.00
4	Frank Thomas	2.00
5	Mike Piazza	3.00
6	Albert Belle	1.00
7	Juan Gonzalez	1.25
8	Jeff Bagwell	2.00
9	Barry Bonds	5.00
10	Jose Cruz, Jr.	1.00

Prime Leather

This insert features top fielders on a leather-like card stock, with a large baseball in the background. Cards are seeded in Series 1 packs and numbered with a "PL" suffix.

		NM/M
Complete Set (18):		135.00
Common Player:		2.00
Inserted 1:144		
1	Ken Griffey Jr.	12.50
2	Andruw Jones	7.50
3	Alex Rodriguez	15.00
4	Frank Thomas	7.50
5	Cal Ripken Jr.	20.00
6	Derek Jeter	20.00
7	Chipper Jones	10.00
8	Greg Maddux	10.00
9	Mike Piazza	12.50
10	Albert Belle	2.00
11	Darin Erstad	3.00
12	Juan Gonzalez	3.00
13	Jeff Bagwell	7.50
14	Tony Gwynn	10.00
15	Roberto Alomar	2.50
16	Barry Bonds	20.00
17	Kenny Lofton	2.00
18	Jose Cruz, Jr.	2.00

Rocket to Stardom

This insert set is exclusive to Series 2 packs. Cards are in black-and- white and are die-cut, embossed and numbered with an "RS" suffix.

		NM/M
Complete Set (15):		15.00
Common Player:		.75
Inserted 1:20		
1	Ben Grieve	.75
2	Magglio Ordonez	4.00
3	Travis Lee	1.00
4	Carl Pavano	.75
5	Brian Rose	.75
6	Brad Fullmer	.75
7	Michael Coleman	.75
8	Juan Encarnacion	.75
9	Karim Garcia	1.00
10	Todd Helton	7.50
11	Richard Hildalgo	.75
12	Paul Konerko	1.50
13	Rod Myers	.75
14	Jaret Wright	.75
15	Miguel Tejada	1.50

Ticket Studs

Fifteen players are featured on fold-out ticket-like cards in Ticket Studs. The cards arrive folded across the middle and open to reveal a full-length shot of the player with prismatic team color stripes over a white background that has section, seat and row numbers. Cards were inserted in Series 2 packs and are numbered with a "TS" suffix.

		NM/M
Complete Set (15):		150.00
Common Player:		2.50
Inserted 1:144		
1	Travis Lee	3.00
2	Tony Gwynn	12.00
3	Scott Rolen	6.00
4	Nomar Garciaparra	12.00
5	Mike Piazza	15.00
6	Mark McGwire	17.50
7	Ken Griffey Jr.	15.00
8	Juan Gonzalez	5.00
9	Jose Cruz	2.50
10	Frank Thomas	9.00
11	Derek Jeter	20.00
12	Chipper Jones	12.00
13	Cal Ripken Jr.	20.00
14	Andruw Jones	9.00
15	Alex Rodriguez	17.50

Top 30

Top 30 is a retail-only insert found only in Series 2.

		NM/M
Complete Set (30):		20.00
Common Player:		.15
Inserted 1:1 R		
1	Barry Bonds	2.00
2	Ivan Rodriguez	.65
3	Kenny Lofton	.15
4	Albert Belle	.15
5	Mo Vaughn	.15
6	Jeff Bagwell	.75
7	Mark McGwire	1.50
8	Darin Erstad	.35
9	Roger Clemens	1.00
10	Tony Gwynn	1.00
11	Scott Rolen	.45
12	Hideo Nomo	.35
13	Juan Gonzalez	.35
14	Mike Piazza	1.25
15	Greg Maddux	1.00
16	Chipper Jones	1.00
17	Andruw Jones	.75
18	Derek Jeter	2.00
19	Nomar Garciaparra	1.00
20	Alex Rodriguez	1.50
21	Frank Thomas	.75
22	Cal Ripken Jr	2.00
23	Ken Griffey Jr.	1.25
24	Jose Cruz Jr.	.15
25	Jaret Wright	.15
26	Travis Lee	.30
27	Wade Boggs	1.00
28	Chuck Knoblauch	.15
29	Joe Carter	.15
30	Ben Grieve	.15

Win Now

This Series 2 insert has top players printed on plastic card stock, with a color shot of the player on the left side and a close-up shot on the right with black lines through it. Cards are numbered with a "WN" suffix.

		NM/M
Complete Set (20):		100.00
Common Player:		2.50
Inserted 1:72		
1	Alex Rodriguez	10.00
2	Andruw Jones	4.00
3	Cal Ripken Jr.	12.50
4	Chipper Jones	5.00
5	Darin Erstad	3.00
6	Derek Jeter	12.50
7	Frank Thomas	4.00
8	Greg Maddux	5.00
9	Hideo Nomo	3.00
10	Jeff Bagwell	4.00
11	Jose Cruz	2.50
12	Juan Gonzalez	3.00
13	Ken Griffey Jr.	7.50
14	Mark McGwire	10.00
15	Mike Piazza	7.50
16	Mo Vaughn	2.50
17	Nomar Garciaparra	5.00
18	Roger Clemens	6.00
19	Scott Rolen	3.00
20	Tony Gwynn	5.00

1999 Ultra Sample Sheet

This six-card sheet was issued to introduce potential customers to '99 Ultra's base cards. The sheet measures 7-1/2" x 7". Cards are virtually identical to the issued version, except for the diagonal black-and-white "PROMOTIONAL SAMPLE" overprint on front and back.

	NM/M
Complete Sheet:	5.00

1999 Ultra

Base cards feature the full career stats by year in 15 categories and career highlights. There are short-printed subsets including Season Crowns (216-225) found 1:8 packs and Prospects (226-250) found 1:4 packs. Card fronts feature full bleed photography, and metallic foil stamping. There are three parallel versions Gold Medallion seeded 1 per pack with Prospects 1:40 and Season Crowns 1:80. Platinum Medallions are numbered to 99 with Prospects numbered to 65 and Season Crowns numbered to 50 sets. One of One Masterpiece parallels also exist. Packs consist of 10 cards with a S.R.P. of $2.69.

		NM/M
Complete Set (250):		35.00
Common Player:		.05
Common Season Crown:		.25
Inserted 1:8		
Common Prospect:		.25
Inserted 1:4		
Gold Medallion (1-215):		2X
Inserted 1:1		
Gold Medall. Prospect:		4X
Inserted 1:40		
Gold Medall. Season Crown:		3X
Inserted 1:80		
Platinums (1-215):		25X
Production 99 Sets		
Platinum Prospects:		6X
Production 65 Sets		
Platinum Season Crowns:		20X
Production 50 Sets		
Pack (10):		1.50
Wax Box (24):		25.00
1	Greg Maddux	1.00
2	Greg Vaughn	.05
3	John Wetteland	.05
4	Tino Martinez	.05
5	Todd Walker	.05
6	Troy O'Leary	.05
7	Barry Larkin	.05
8	Mike Lansing	.05
9	Delino DeShields	.05
10	Brett Tomko	.05
11	Carlos Perez	.05
12	Mark Langston	.05
13	Jamie Moyer	.05
14	Jose Guillen	.05
15	Bartolo Colon	.05
16	Brady Anderson	.05
17	Walt Weiss	.05
18	Shane Reynolds	.05
19	David Segui	.05
20	Vladimir Guerrero	.75
21	Freddy Garcia	.05
22	Carl Everett	.05
23	Jose Cruz Jr.	.05
24	David Ortiz	.40
25	Andruw Jones	.75
26	Darren Lewis	.05
27	Ray Lankford	.05
28	Wally Joyner	.05
29	Charles Johnson	.05
30	Derek Jeter	2.00
31	Sean Casey	.10
32	Bobby Bonilla	.05
33	Todd Zeile	.05
34	Todd Helton	.65
35	David Wells	.05
36	Darin Erstad	.30
37	Ivan Rodriguez	.65
38	Antonio Osuna	.05
39	Mickey Morandini	.05
40	Rusty Greer	.05
41	Rod Beck	.05
42	Larry Sutton	.05
43	Edgar Renteria	.05
44	Otis Nixon	.05
45	Eli Marrero	.05
46	Reggie Jefferson	.05
47	Trevor Hoffman	.05
48	Andres Galarraga	.05
49	Scott Brosius	.05
50	Vinny Castilla	.05
51	Bret Boone	.05
52	Masato Yoshii	.05
53	Matt Williams	.05
54	Robin Ventura	.05
55	Jay Powell	.05
56	Dean Palmer	.05
57	Eric Milton	.05
58	Willie McGee	.05
59	Tony Gwynn	1.00
60	Tom Gordon	.05
61	Dante Bichette	.05
62	Jaret Wright	.05
63	Devon White	.05
64	Frank Thomas	.75
65	Mike Piazza	1.25
66	Jose Offerman	.05
67	Pat Meares	.05
68	Brian Meadows	.05
69	Nomar Garciaparra	1.00
70	Mark McGwire	1.50
71	Tony Graffanino	.05
72	Ken Griffey Jr.	1.25
73	Ken Caminiti	.05
74	Todd Jones	.05
75	A.J. Hinch	.05
76	Marquis Grissom	.05
77	Jay Buhner	.05
78	Albert Belle	.05
79	Brian Anderson	.05
80	Quinton McCracken	.05
81	Omar Vizquel	.05
82	Todd Stottlemyre	.05
83	Cal Ripken Jr.	2.00
84	Maggio Ordonez	.30
85	John Olerud	.05
86	Hal Morris	.05
87	Derrek Lee	.40
88	Doug Glanville	.05
89	Marty Cordova	.05
90	Kevin Brown	.05
91	Kevin Young	.05
92	Rico Brogna	.05
93	Wilson Alvarez	.05
94	Bob Wickman	.05
95	Jim Thome	.50
96	Mike Mussina	.35
97	Al Leiter	.05
98	Travis Lee	.10
99	Jeff King	.05
100	Kerry Wood	.40
101	Cliff Floyd	.05
102	Jose Valentin	.05
103	Manny Ramirez	.75
104	Butch Huskey	.05
105	Scott Erickson	.05
106	Ray Durham	.05
107	Johnny Damon	.30
108	Craig Counsell	.05
109	Rolando Arrojo	.05
110	Bob Abreu	.05
111	Tony Womack	.05
112	Mike Stanley	.05
113	Kenny Lofton	.05
114	Eric Davis	.05
115	Jeff Conine	.05
116	Carlos Baerga	.05
117	Rondell White	.05
118	Billy Wagner	.05
119	Ed Sprague	.05
120	Jason Schmidt	.05
121	Edgar Martinez	.05
122	Travis Fryman	.05
123	Armando Benitez	.05
124	Matt Stairs	.05
125	Roberto Hernandez	.05
126	Jay Bell	.05
127	Justin Thompson	.05
128	John Jaha	.05
129	Mike Caruso	.05
130	Miguel Tejada	.20
131	Geoff Jenkins	.05
132	Wade Boggs	1.00
133	Andy Benes	.05
134	Aaron Sele	.05
135	Bret Saberhagen	.05
136	Mariano Rivera	.15
137	Neifi Perez	.05
138	Paul Konerko	.15

139	Barry Bonds	2.00
140	Garret Anderson	.05
141	Bernie Williams	.05
142	Gary Sheffield	.40
143	Rafael Palmeiro	.65
144	Orel Hershiser	.05
145	Craig Biggio	.05
146	Dmitri Young	.05
147	Damion Easley	.05
148	Henry Rodriguez	.05
149	Brad Radke	.05
150	Pedro Martinez	.75
151	Mike Lieberthal	.05
152	Jim Leyritz	.05
153	Chuck Knoblauch	.05
154	Darryl Kile	.05
155	Brian Jordan	.05
156	Chipper Jones	1.00
157	Pete Harnisch	.05
158	Moises Alou	.05
159	Ismael Valdes	.05
160	Stan Javier	.05
161	Mark Grace	.05
162	Jason Giambi	.40
163	Chuck Finley	.05
164	Juan Encarnacion	.05
165	Chan Ho Park	.05
166	Randy Johnson	.75
167	J.T. Snow	.05
168	Tim Salmon	.05
169	Brian Hunter	.05
170	Rickey Henderson	.75
171	Cal Eldred	.05
172	Curt Schilling	.25
173	Alex Rodriguez	1.50
174	Dustin Hermanson	.05
175	Mike Hampton	.05
176	Shawn Green	.30
177	Roberto Alomar	.20
178	Sandy Alomar Jr.	.05
179	Larry Walker	.05
180	Mo Vaughn	.05
181	Raul Mondesi	.05
182	Hideki Irabu	.05
183	Jim Edmonds	.05
184	Shawn Estes	.05
185	Tony Clark	.05
186	Dan Wilson	.05
187	Michael Tucker	.05
188	Jeff Shaw	.05
189	Mark Grudzielanek	.05
190	Roger Clemens	1.00
191	Juan Gonzalez	.40
192	Sammy Sosa	1.00
193	Troy Percival	.05
194	Robb Nen	.05
195	Dill Mueller	.05
196	Ben Grieve	.05
197	Luis Gonzalez	.05
198	Will Clark	.05
199	Jeff Cirillo	.05
200	Scott Rolen	.50
201	Reggie Sanders	.05
202	Fred McGriff	.05
203	Denny Neagle	.05
204	Brad Fullmer	.05
205	Royce Clayton	.05
206	Jose Canseco	.50
207	Jeff Bagwell	.75
208	Hideo Nomo	.40
209	Karim Garcia	.15
210	Kenny Rogers	.05
211	Checklist (Kerry Wood)	.25
212	Checklist (Alex Rodriguez)	.75
213	Checklist (Cal Ripken Jr.)	1.00
214	Checklist (Frank Thomas)	.50
215	Checklist (Ken Griffey Jr.)	.65
216	Alex Rodriguez (Season Crowns)	1.00
217	Greg Maddux (Season Crowns)	.50
218	Juan Gonzalez (Season Crowns)	.20
219	Ken Griffey Jr. (Season Crowns)	.75
220	Kerry Wood (Season Crowns)	.25
221	Mark McGwire (Season Crowns)	1.00
222	Mike Piazza (Season Crowns)	.75
223	Rickey Henderson (Season Crowns)	.40
224	Sammy Sosa (Season Crowns)	.50
225	Travis Lee (Season Crowns)	.25
226	Gabe Alvarez (Prospects)	.25
227	Matt Anderson (Prospects)	.25
228	Adrian Beltre (Prospects)	.35
229	Orlando Cabrera (Prospects)	.35
230	Orlando Hernandez (Prospects)	.25
231	Aramis Ramirez (Prospects)	.25
232	Troy Glaus (Prospects)	1.00
233	Gabe Kapler (Prospects)	.25
234	Jeremy Giambi (Prospects)	.25
235	Derrick Gibson (Prospects)	.25
236	Carlton Loewer (Prospects)	.25
237	Mike Frank (Prospects)	.25
238	Carlos Guillen (Prospects)	.25
239	Alex Gonzalez (Prospects)	.25
240	Enrique Wilson (Prospects)	.25
241	J.D. Drew (Prospects)	.75
242	Bruce Chen (Prospects)	.25
243	Ryan Minor (Prospects)	.25
244	Preston Wilson (Prospects)	.35
245	Josh Booty (Prospects)	.25
246	Luis Ordaz (Prospects)	.25
247	George Lombard (Prospects)	.25
248	Matt Clement (Prospects)	.25
249	Eric Chavez (Prospects)	.35
250	Corey Koskie (Prospects)	.30

Gold Medallion

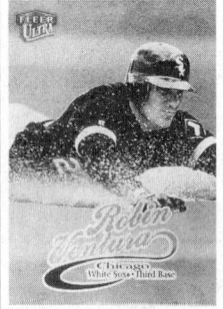

The basic cards (#1-215) in this parallel set are found one per pack, while the short-printed versions are seen one per 40 packs (Prospects) or one per 80 packs (Season Crowns). Sharing the photos and format of the regular-issue cards, these inserts have a gold-foil background on front. On back, "GOLD MEDALLION EDITION" is printed in gold foil.

	NM/M
Common Player (1-215):	.25
Stars/RC's:	2X
Season Crowns (216-225):	4X
Prospects (226-250):	3X

Platinum Medallion

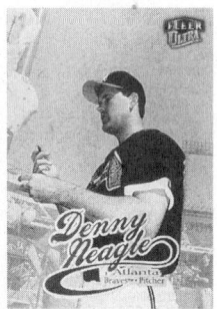

The basic cards (#1-215) in this parallel set are found in an individually serial numbered edition of 99. The short-printed cards were released in editions of 65 (Prospects) and 50 (Season Crowns). Sharing the photos and format of the regular-issue cards, these inserts have a silver-foil background on front. On back, "PLATINUM MEDALLION" is printed in silver foil along with the serial number.

	NM/M
Common Player (1-215):	5.00
Stars/RC's:	25X
Season Crowns (216-225):	20X
Prospects (226-250):	6X

Masterpiece

This top of the line parallel to '99 Ultra consists of a 1 of 1 version of each regular card.

	NM/M
Common Player:	50.00

Book On

This set features insider scouting reports on the game's best players, utilizing embossing and gold foil stamping.

		NM/M
Complete Set (20):		13.50
Common Player:		.25
Inserted 1:6		
1	Kerry Wood	.35
2	Ken Griffey Jr.	1.00
3	Frank Thomas	.65
4	Albert Belle	.25
5	Juan Gonzalez	.35
6	Jeff Bagwell	.65
7	Mark McGwire	1.25
8	Barry Bonds	1.50
9	Andruw Jones	.65
10	Mo Vaughn	.25
11	Scott Rolen	.40
12	Travis Lee	.25
13	Tony Gwynn	.75
14	Greg Maddux	.75
15	Mike Piazza	1.00
16	Chipper Jones	.75
17	Nomar Garciaparra	.75
18	Cal Ripken Jr.	1.50
19	Derek Jeter	1.50
20	Alex Rodriguez	1.25

Damage Inc.

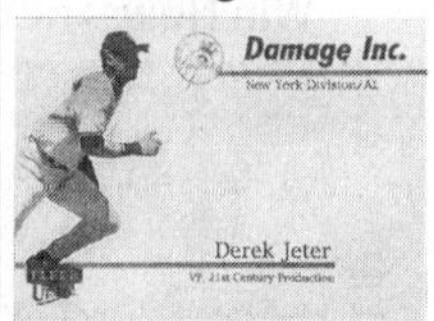

This insert set has a business card design, for players who mean business.

		NM/M
Complete Set (15):		50.00
Common Player:		1.00
Inserted 1:72		
1	Alex Rodriguez	5.00
2	Greg Maddux	3.50
3	Cal Ripken Jr.	7.50
4	Chipper Jones	3.50
5	Derek Jeter	7.50
6	Frank Thomas	2.50
7	Juan Gonzalez	1.50
8	Ken Griffey Jr.	4.00
9	Kerry Wood	1.25
10	Mark McGwire	5.00
11	Mike Piazza	4.00
12	Nomar Garciaparra	3.50
13	Scott Rolen	1.50
14	Tony Gwynn	3.50
15	Travis Lee	1.00

Diamond Producers

This die-cut set uses full-foil plastic with custom embossing.

		NM/M
Complete Set (10):		140.00
Common Player:		6.00
Inserted 1:288		
1	Ken Griffey Jr.	17.50
2	Frank Thomas	12.00
3	Alex Rodriguez	20.00
4	Cal Ripken Jr.	25.00
5	Mike Piazza	17.50
6	Mark McGwire	20.00
7	Greg Maddux	15.00
8	Kerry Wood	6.00
9	Chipper Jones	15.00
10	Derek Jeter	25.00

RBI Kings

Found exclusively in retail packs, this set showcases baseball's top run producers.

		NM/M
Complete Set (30):		12.00
Common Player:		.15
Inserted 1:1 R		
1	Rafael Palmeiro	.40
2	Mo Vaughn	.15
3	Ivan Rodriguez	.40
4	Barry Bonds	1.25
5	Albert Belle	.15
6	Jeff Bagwell	.45
7	Mark McGwire	1.00
8	Darin Erstad	.25
9	Manny Ramirez	.45
10	Chipper Jones	.60
11	Jim Thome	.40
12	Scott Rolen	.35
13	Tony Gwynn	.60
14	Juan Gonzalez	.25
15	Mike Piazza	.75
16	Sammy Sosa	.60
17	Andruw Jones	.45
18	Derek Jeter	1.25
19	Nomar Garciaparra	.60
20	Alex Rodriguez	1.00
21	Frank Thomas	.45
22	Cal Ripken Jr.	1.25
23	Ken Griffey Jr.	.75
24	Travis Lee	.25
25	Paul O'Neill	.15
26	Greg Vaughn	.15
27	Andres Galarraga	.15
28	Tino Martinez	.15
29	Jose Canseco	.30
30	Ben Grieve	.15

Thunderclap

This set highlights the top hitters in the game. Card fronts feature a lightning bolt in the background.

		NM/M
Complete Set (15):		35.00
Common Player:		.75
Inserted 1:36		
1	Alex Rodriguez	4.00
2	Andruw Jones	1.50
3	Cal Ripken Jr.	6.00
4	Chipper Jones	2.50
5	Darin Erstad	.75
6	Derek Jeter	6.00
7	Frank Thomas	1.50
8	Jeff Bagwell	1.50
9	Juan Gonzalez	.75
10	Ken Griffey Jr.	3.00
11	Mark McGwire	4.00
12	Mike Piazza	3.00
13	Travis Lee	.75
14	Nomar Garciaparra	2.50
15	Scott Rolen	1.00

World Premiere

This set highlights rookies who made debuts in 1998.

		NM/M
Complete Set (15):		8.00
Common Player:		.50
Inserted 1:18		
1	Gabe Alvarez	.50
2	Kerry Wood	1.50
3	Orlando Hernandez	.60
4	Mike Caruso	.50
5	Matt Anderson	.50
6	Randall Simon	.50
7	Adrian Beltre	.65
8	Scott Elarton	.50
9	Karim Garcia	.60
10	Mike Frank	.50
11	Richard Hidalgo	.50
12	Paul Konerko	.60
13	Travis Lee	.65
14	J.D. Drew	1.50
15	Miguel Tejada	.75

2000 Ultra Sample

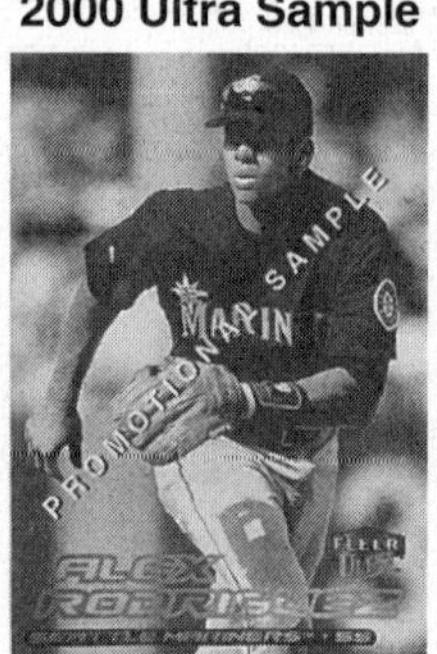

Product spokesman Alex Rodriguez is featured on the promo card for 2000 Ultra. Virtually identical in format to the issued version, the card has a "PROMOTIONAL SAMPLE" overprint diagonally on front and back.

		NM/M
1	Alex Rodriguez	2.00

2000 Ultra

The 300-card base set features a borderless design with silver holographic foil stamping on the card front. Card backs have an action image along with complete year-by-year statistics. The base set includes a 50-card short-printed Prospects (1:4) subset. A Masterpiece one-of-one parallel was produced.

		NM/M
Complete Set (300):		35.00
Common Player:		.10
Common Player (251-300):		.50
Inserted 1:4		
Pack (10):		2.00
Wax Box (24):		35.00
1	Alex Rodriguez	1.50
2	Shawn Green	.25
3	Magglio Ordonez	.25
4	Tony Gwynn	.75
5	Joe McEwing	.10
6	Jose Rosado	.10
7	Sammy Sosa	1.00
8	Gary Sheffield	.25
9	Mickey Morandini	.10
10	Mo Vaughn	.15
11	Todd Hollandsworth	.10
12	Tom Gordon	.10
13	Charles Johnson	.10
14	Derek Bell	.10
15	Kevin Young	.10
16	Jay Buhner	.15
17	J.T. Snow	.10
18	Jay Bell	.10
19	John Rocker	.10
20	Ivan Rodriguez	.40
21	Pokey Reese	.10
22	Paul O'Neill	.20
23	Ronnie Belliard	.10
24	Ryan Rupe	.10
25	Travis Fryman	.20
26	Trot Nixon	.10
27	Wally Joyner	.10
28	Andy Pettitte	.25
29	Dan Wilson	.10
30	Orlando Hernandez	.20
31	Dmitri Young	.10
32	Edgar Renteria	.10
33	Eric Karros	.20
34	Fernando Seguignol	.10
35	Jason Kendall	.20
36	Jeff Shaw	.10
37	Matt Lawton	.10
38	Robin Ventura	.20
39	Scott Williamson	.10
40	Ben Grieve	.10
41	Billy Wagner	.10
42	Javy Lopez	.20
43	Joe Randa	.10
44	Neifi Perez	.10
45	David Justice	.20
46	Ray Durham	.10
47	Dustin Hermanson	.10
48	Andres Galarraga	.20
49	Brad Fullmer	.10
50	Nomar Garciaparra	1.50
51	David Cone	.15
52	David Nilsson	.10
53	David Wells	.10
54	Miguel Tejada	.25
55	Ismael Valdes	.10
56	Jose Lima	.10
57	Juan Encarnacion	.10
58	Fred McGriff	.20
59	Kenny Rogers	.10
60	Vladimir Guerrero	.75
61	Benito Santiago	.10
62	Chris Singleton	.10
63	Carlos Lee	.10
64	Sean Casey	.20
65	Tom Goodwin	.10
66	Todd Hundley	.10
67	Ellis Burks	.10
68	Tim Hudson	.25
69	Matt Stairs	.10
70	Chipper Jones	1.00
71	Craig Biggio	.20
72	Brian Rose	.10
73	Carlos Delgado	.40
74	Eddie Taubensee	.10
75	John Smoltz	.20
76	Ken Caminiti	.15
77	Rafael Palmeiro	.40
78	Sidney Ponson	.10
79	Todd Helton	.50
80	Juan Gonzalez	.50
81	Bruce Aven	.10
82	Desi Relaford	.10
83	Johnny Damon	.20
84	Albert Belle	.15
85	Mark McGwire	1.50
86	Rico Brogna	.10
87	Tom Glavine	.25
88	Harold Baines	.10
89	Chad Allen	.10
90	Barry Bonds	2.00
91	Mark Grace	.25
92	Paul Byrd	.10
93	Roberto Alomar	.40
94	Roberto Hernandez	.10
95	Steve Finley	.10
96	Bret Boone	.20
97	Charles Nagy	.10
98	Eric Chavez	.20
99	Jamie Moyer	.10
100	Ken Griffey Jr.	1.00
101	J.D. Drew	.20
102	Todd Stottlemyre	.10
103	Tony Fernandez	.10
104	Jeromy Burnitz	.10
105	Jeremy Giambi	.10
106	Livan Hernandez	.10

107 Marlon Anderson .10
108 Troy Glaus .50
109 Troy O'Leary .10
110 Scott Rolen .50
111 Bernard Gilkey .10
112 Brady Anderson .15
113 Chuck Knoblauch .10
114 Jeff Weaver .10
115 B.J. Surhoff .10
116 Alex Gonzalez .10
117 Vinny Castilla .10
118 Tim Salmon .20
119 Brian Jordan .10
120 Corey Koskie .10
121 Dean Palmer .10
122 Gabe Kapler .15
123 Jim Edmonds .25
124 John Jaha .10
125 Mark Grudzielanek .10
126 Mike Bordick .10
127 Mike Lieberthal .10
128 Pete Harnisch .10
129 Russ Ortiz .10
130 Kevin Brown .20
131 Troy Percival .10
132 Alex Gonzalez .10
133 Bartolo Colon .10
134 John Valentin .10
135 Jose Hernandez .10
136 Marquis Grissom .10
137 Wade Boggs .25
138 Dante Bichette .10
139 Bobby Higginson .10
140 Frank Thomas .50
141 Geoff Jenkins .20
142 Jason Giambi .50
143 Jeff Cirillo .10
144 Sandy Alomar Jr. .10
145 Luis Gonzalez .20
146 Preston Wilson .20
147 Carlos Beltran .10
148 Greg Vaughn .10
149 Carlos Febles .10
150 Jose Canseco .40
151 Kris Benson .10
152 Chuck Finley .10
153 Michael Barrett .10
154 Rey Ordonez .10
155 Adrian Beltre .20
156 Andruw Jones .50
157 Barry Larkin .20
158 Brian Giles .20
159 Carl Everett .10
160 Manny Ramirez .50
161 Darryl Kile .10
162 Edgar Martinez .15
163 Jeff Kent .20
164 Matt Williams .20
165 Mike Piazza 1.00
166 Pedro J. Martinez .75
167 Ray Lankford .10
168 Roger Cedeno .10
169 Ron Coomer .10
170 Cal Ripken Jr. 2.00
171 Jose Offerman .10
172 Kenny Lofton .20
173 Kent Bottenfield .10
174 Kevin Millwood .20
175 Omar Daal .10
176 Orlando Cabrera .20
177 Pat Hentgen .10
178 Tino Martinez .20
179 Tony Clark .10
180 Roger Clemens 1.25
181 Brad Radke .10
182 Darin Erstad .20
183 Jose Jimenez .10
184 Jim Thome .50
185 John Wetteland .10
186 Justin Thompson .10
187 John Hamala .10
188 Lee Stevens .10
189 Miguel Cairo .10
190 Mike Mussina .40
191 Raul Mondesi .15
192 Armando Rios .10
193 Trevor Hoffman .10
194 Tony Batista .10
195 Will Clark .40
196 Brad Ausmus .10
197 Chili Davis .10
198 Cliff Floyd .10
199 Curt Schilling .25
200 Derek Jeter 2.00
201 Henry Rodriguez .10
202 Jose Cruz Jr. .10
203 Omar Vizquel .20
204 Randy Johnson .75
205 Reggie Sanders .10
206 Al Leiter .10
207 Damion Easley .10
208 David Bell .10
209 Fernando Tatis .10
210 Kerry Wood .25
211 Kevin Appier .10
212 Mariano Rivera .20
213 Mike Caruso .10
214 Moises Alou .20
215 Randy Winn .10
216 Roy Halladay .20
217 Shannon Stewart .10
218 Todd Walker .10
219 Jim Parque .10
220 Travis Lee .10
221 Andy Ashby .10
222 Ed Sprague .10
223 Larry Walker .20
224 Rick Helling .10
225 Rusty Greer .10
226 Todd Zeile .10
227 Freddy Garcia .15
228 Hideo Nomo .40
229 Marty Cordova .10
230 Greg Maddux 1.00
231 Rondell White .20
232 Paul Konerko .15
233 Warren Morris .10
234 Bernie Williams .40
235 Bobby Abreu .20
236 John Olerud .25
237 Doug Glanville .10
238 Eric Young .10
239 Robb Nen .10
240 Jeff Bagwell .50
241 Sterling Hitchcock .10
242 Todd Greene .10
243 Bill Mueller .10
244 Rickey Henderson .25
245 Chan Ho Park .10
246 Jason Schmidt .10
247 Jeff Zimmerman .10
248 Jermaine Dye .10
249 Randall Simon .10
250 Richie Sexson .40
251 Micah Bowie .50
252 Joe Nathan .50
253 Chris Woodward .50
254 Lance Berkman .75
255 Ruben Mateo .50
256 Russell Branyan .50
257 Randy Wolf .75
258 A.J. Burnett .75
259 Mark Quinn .50
260 Buddy Carlyle .50
261 Ben Davis .50
262 Yamid Haad .50
263 Mike Colangelo .50
264 Rick Ankiel .75
265 Jacque Jones .75
266 Kelly Dransfeldt .50
267 Matt Riley .50
268 Adam Kennedy .50
269 Octavio Dotel .50
270 Francisco Cordero .50
271 Wilton Veras .50
272 Calvin Pickering .50
273 Alex Sanchez .50
274 Tony Armas Jr. .50
275 Pat Burrell 1.00
276 Chad Meyers .50
277 Ben Petrick .50
278 Ramon Hernandez .50
279 Ed Yarnall .50
280 Erubiel Durazo .50
281 Vernon Wells 1.00
282 Gary Matthews .50
283 Kip Wells .50
284 Peter Bergeron .50
285 Travis Dawkins .50
286 Jorge Toca .50
287 Cole Liniak .50
288 Chad Hermansen .50
289 Eric Gagne .50
290 Chad Hutchinson .50
291 Eric Munson .50
292 Wiki Gonzalez .50
293 Alfonso Soriano 1.50
294 Trent Durrington .50
295 Ben Molina .50
296 Aaron Myette .50
297 Willi Mo Pena .75
298 Kevin Barker .50
299 Geoff Blum .50
300 Josh Beckett .75

Gold Medallion

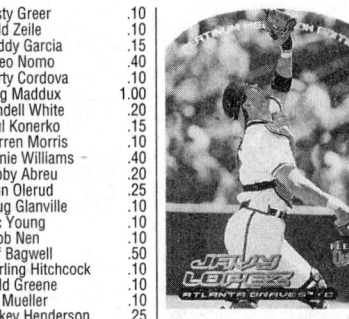

A parallel to the 300-card base set these have gold foil stamping over a metallic gold background. Cards 1-250 are seeded one per pack, Prospects 251-300 are seeded 1:24 packs. Card backs are numbered with a "G" suffix.

Stars: 2X
Inserted 1:1
Prospects (251-300): 2-4X
Inserted 1:24

Platinum Medallion

Platinum Medallion are a parallel to the 300-card base set and are die-cut like the Gold Medallion parallel inserts. Card fronts are stamped with silver foil over a metallic silver background. Card backs are serially numbered with cards 1-250 limited to 50 sets and Prospects limited to 25 numbered sets. Card backs are numbered with a "P" suffix.

Stars: 15-30X
Production 50 Sets
Prospects (251-300): 4-8X
Production 25 Sets

Masterpiece Edition

Masterpiece Edition is a 1 of 1 parallel to the 300-card base set and are "tombstone" die-cut like the Gold and Platinum Medallion inserts. Card fronts are stamped with purple foil over a metallic purple background. Card backs are overprinted with "The only 1 of 1 Masterpiece."

Club 3000

This three-card set is die-cut around the number 3,000 and commemorates 3,000 hit club members Wade Boggs, Tony Gwynn and Carl Yastrzemski. These were seeded 1:24 packs.

	NM/M
Common Player:	3.00
Inserted 1:24	
Wade Boggs	2.00
Tony Gwynn	3.00
Carl Yastrzemski	3.00

Club 3000 Memorabilia

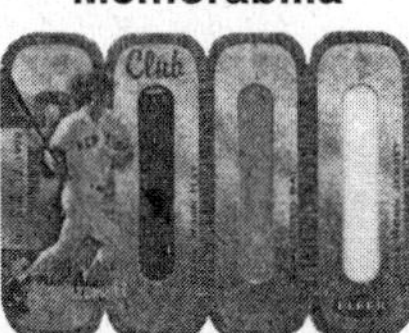

Each featured player has a total of four different memorabilia based inserts: hat, jersey, bat/jersey and bat/hat/jersey.

	NM/M
Wade Boggs/Bat/250	20.00
Wade Boggs/Hat/100	40.00
Wade Boggs/Jsy/440	20.00
Wade Boggs/ Bat/Jsy/100	40.00
Wade Boggs/ Bat/Hat/Jsy/25	150.00
Tony Gwynn/Bat/260	40.00
Tony Gwynn/Hat/115	60.00
Tony Gwynn/Jsy/450	25.00
Tony Gwynn/ Bat/Jsy/100	65.00
Tony Gwynn/ Bat/Hat/Jsy/25	375.00
Carl Yastrzemski/ Bat/250	40.00
Carl Yastrzemski/ Hat/100	60.00
Carl Yastrzemski/ Jsy/440	25.00
Carl Yastrzemski/ Bat/Jsy/100	75.00
Carl Yastrzemski/ Bat/Hat/Jsy/25	300.00

Crunch Time

This 15-card insert set is printed on suede stock with gold foil stamping. These were seeded 1:72 packs and numbered with a "CT" suffix on the card back.

		NM/M
Complete Set (15):		50.00
Common Player:		2.00
Inserted 1:72		
1	Nomar Garciaparra	8.00
2	Ken Griffey Jr.	5.00
3	Mark McGwire	8.00
4	Alex Rodriguez	8.00
5	Derek Jeter	8.00
6	Sammy Sosa	6.00
7	Mike Piazza	5.00
8	Cal Ripken Jr.	10.00
9	Frank Thomas	3.00
10	Juan Gonzalez	3.00
11	J.D. Drew	2.00
12	Greg Maddux	5.00
13	Tony Gwynn	3.00
14	Vladimir Guerrero	3.00
15	Ben Grieve	2.00

Diamond Mine

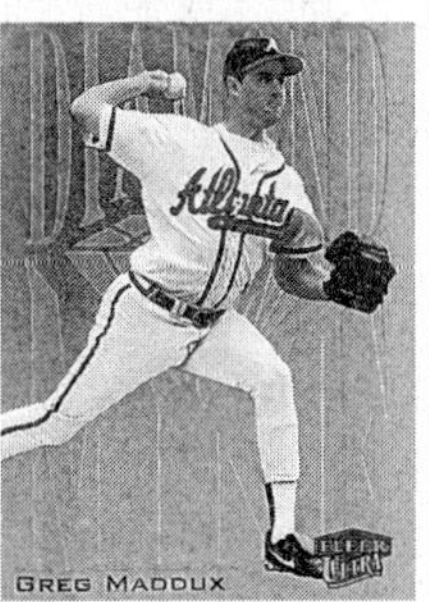

These were printed on a silver foil card front with Diamond Mine stamped in the background of the player image. These were inserted 1:6 packs and numbered with a "DM" suffix on the card back.

		NM/M
Complete Set (15):		20.00
Common Player:		1.00
Inserted 1:6		
1	Greg Maddux	1.50
2	Mark McGwire	2.00
3	Ken Griffey Jr.	1.50
4	Cal Ripken Jr.	3.00
5	Nomar Garciaparra	2.50
6	Mike Piazza	2.00
7	Alex Rodriguez	2.50
8	Frank Thomas	1.00
9	Juan Gonzalez	1.00
10	Derek Jeter	2.50
11	Tony Gwynn	1.00
12	Chipper Jones	1.50
13	Sammy Sosa	2.00
14	Roger Clemens	1.50
15	Vladimir Guerrero	1.00

Feel the Game

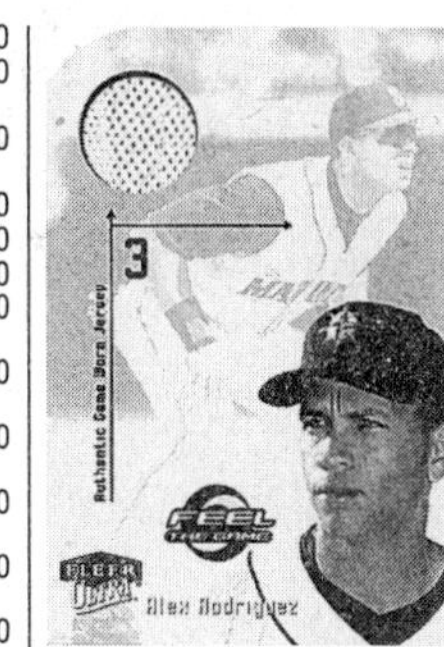

These memorabilia based inserts have a piece of game worn jersey or batting glove embedded into the card front.

	NM/M
Common Player:	5.00
Roberto Alomar	10.00
J.D. Drew	5.00
Tony Gwynn/SP	40.00
Randy Johnson	20.00
Greg Maddux	20.00
Edgar Martinez	10.00
Pedro Martinez	20.00
Kevin Millwood	10.00
Cal Ripken Jr.	40.00
Alex Rodriguez	25.00
Scott Rolen	10.00
Curt Schilling	10.00
Chipper Jones	20.00
Frank Thomas/SP	40.00
Robin Ventura	5.00

Fresh Ink

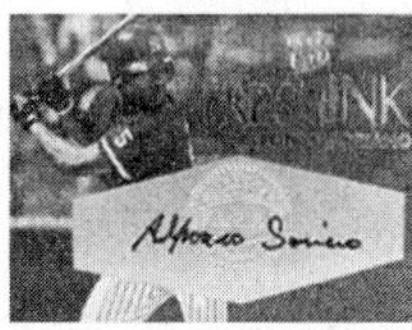

These autographed cards have the words "Fresh Ink" printed continually in the background image of the player. The signature is in a designated blank box intended for the autograph. Production numbers vary from player to player and are listed in parentheses after the player name.

		NM/M
Common Player:		5.00
1	Bobby Abreu/400	10.00
2	Chad Allen/1,000	5.00
3	Marlon Anderson/ 1,000	5.00
4	Glen Barker/1,000	5.00
5	Michael Barrett/1,000	5.00
6	Carlos Beltran/1,000	15.00
7	Adrian Beltre/1,000	8.00
8	Wade Boggs/250	40.00
9	Barry Bonds/250	150.00
10	Peter Bergeron/1,000	5.00
11	Pat Burrell/500	20.00
12	Roger Cedeno/500	5.00
13	Eric Chavez/750	10.00
14	Bruce Chen/600	5.00
15	Johnny Damon/750	8.00
16	Ben Davis/1,000	5.00
17	Carlos Delgado/300	10.00
18	Einar Diaz/1,000	5.00
19	Octavio Dotel/1,000	6.00
20	J.D. Drew/600	8.00
21	Scott Elarton/1,000	5.00
22	Freddy Garcia/500	8.00
23	Jeremy Giambi/1,000	5.00
24	Troy Glaus/500	20.00
25	Shawn Green/350	30.00
26	Tony Gwynn/250	50.00
27	Richard Hidalgo/500	8.00
28	Bobby Higginson/ 1,000	6.00
29	Tim Hudson/1,000	10.00
30	Norm Hutchins/1,000	5.00
31	Derek Jeter/95	200.00
32	Randy Johnson/150	50.00
33	Gabe Kapler/750	8.00
34	Jason Kendall/400	8.00
35	Paul Konerko/500	8.00
36	Matt Lawton/1,000	6.00
37	Carlos Lee/1,000	8.00
38	Jose Macias/1,000	5.00
39	Greg Maddux/250	65.00
40	Ruben Mateo/250	8.00
41	Kevin Millwood/500	10.00
42	Warren Morris/1,000	5.00
43	Eric Munson/1,000	6.00
44	Heath Murray/1,000	5.00
45	Joe Nathan/1,000	5.00
46	Magglio Ordonez/350	10.00
47	Angel Pena/1,000	5.00
48	Cal Ripken Jr./350	125.00
49	Alex Rodriguez/350	80.00
50	Scott Rolen/250	35.00
51	Ryan Rupe/1,000	5.00
52	Curt Schilling/375	25.00
53	Randall Simon/1,000	5.00
54	Alfonso Soriano/ 1,000	60.00
55	Shannon Stewart/300	5.00
56	Miguel Tejada/1,000	25.00
57	Frank Thomas/150	60.00
58	Jeff Weaver/1,000	6.00
59	Randy Wolf/1,000	8.00
60	Ed Yarnall/1,000	5.00
61	Kevin Young/1,000	5.00
62	Tony Gwynn, Wade Boggs, Nolan Ryan/100	450.00
63	Rick Ankiel/500	5.00

Swing King

Printed on a clear, plastic stock this 10-card set features the top hitters in the game. Card fronts also utilize silver foil stamping. These were seeded 1:24 packs and are numbered on the card back with a "SK" suffix.

		NM/M
Complete Set (10):		20.00
Common Player:		1.00
Inserted 1:24		
1	Cal Ripken Jr.	4.00
2	Nomar Garciaparra	3.00
3	Frank Thomas	1.00
4	Tony Gwynn	1.50
5	Ken Griffey Jr.	2.00
6	Chipper Jones	2.00
7	Mark McGwire	3.00
8	Sammy Sosa	2.50
9	Derek Jeter	3.00
10	Alex Rodriguez	3.00

Ultra Talented

Available exclusively in hobby packs these were printed on a holofoil background with gold foil stamping. Each card is serially numbered to 100 and are numbered on the card back with a "UT" suffix.

		NM/M
Common Player:		5.00
Production 100 Sets		
1	Sammy Sosa	15.00
2	Derek Jeter	20.00
3	Alex Rodriguez	20.00
4	Mike Piazza	15.00
5	Ken Griffey Jr.	15.00
6	Nomar Garciaparra	20.00
7	Mark McGwire	20.00
8	Cal Ripken Jr.	25.00
9	Frank Thomas	8.00
10	J.D. Drew	5.00

World Premiere

This insert set highlights ten young potential stars on a die-cut, silver foil etched design. These were inserted 1:12 packs and are numbered with a "WP" suffix on the card back.

	NM/M
Complete Set (10):	5.00

Common Player: .50
Inserted 1:12
1 Ruben Mateo .50
2 Lance Berkman 1.00
3 Octavio Dotel .50
4 Ben Davis .50
5 Warren Morris .50
6 Carlos Beltran .75
7 Rick Ankiel .50
8 Adam Kennedy .50
9 Tim Hudson 1.00
10 Jorge Toca .50

2001 Ultra

NM/M
Complete Set (275): 65.00
Common Player: .15
Common Prospect (251-275): 1.00
Inserted 1:4
Pack (10): 3.00
Box (24): 55.00
1 Pedro Martinez .75
2 Derek Jeter 2.00
3 Cal Ripken Jr. 2.00
4 Alex Rodriguez 1.50
5 Vladimir Guerrero .75
6 Troy Glaus .40
7 Sammy Sosa 1.25
8 Mike Piazza 1.00
9 Tony Gwynn .75
10 Tim Hudson .25
11 John Flaherty .15
12 Jeff Cirillo .15
13 Ellis Burks .15
14 Carlos Lee .15
15 Carlos Beltran .25
16 Ruben Rivera .15
17 Richard Hidalgo .15
18 Omar Vizquel .25
19 Michael Barrett .15
20 Jose Canseco .40
21 Jason Giambi .50
22 Greg Maddux 1.00
23 Charles Johnson .15
24 Sandy Alomar .15
25 Rick Ankiel .15
26 Richie Sexson .40
27 Matt Williams .25
28 Joe Girardi .15
29 Jason Kendall .25
30 Brad Fullmer .15
31 Alex Gonzalez .15
32 Rick Helling .15
33 Mike Mussina .50
34 Joe Randa .15
35 J.T. Snow .15
36 Edgardo Alfonzo .15
37 Dante Bichette .15
38 Brad Ausmus .15
39 Bobby Abreu .25
40 Warren Morris .15
41 Tony Womack .15
42 Russell Branyan .15
43 Mike Lowell .15
44 Mark Grace .40
45 Jeromy Burnitz .15
46 J.D. Drew .25
47 David Justice .25
48 Alex Gonzalez .15
49 Tino Martinez .25
50 Raul Mondesi .25
51 Rafael Furcal .25
52 Marquis Grissom .15
53 Kevin Young .15
54 Jon Lieber .15
55 Henry Rodriguez .15
56 Dave Burba .15
57 Shannon Stewart .15
58 Preston Wilson .15
59 Paul O'Neill .25
60 Jimmy Haynes .15
61 Darryl Kile .15
62 Bret Boone .25
63 Bartolo Colon .25
64 Andres Galarraga .25
65 Trot Nixon .15
66 Steve Finley .15
67 Shawn Green .30
68 Robert Person .15
69 Kenny Rogers .15
70 Bobby Higginson .15
71 Barry Larkin .30
72 Al Martin .15
73 Tom Glavine .40
74 Rondell White .15
75 Ray Lankford .15
76 Moises Alou .25
77 Matt Clement .15
78 Geoff Jenkins .25
79 David Wells .15
80 Chuck Finley .15
81 Andy Pettitte .25
82 Travis Fryman .25
83 Ron Coomer .15
84 Mark McGwire 1.50
85 Kerry Wood .50
86 Jorge Posada .40
87 Jeff Bagwell .50
88 Andruw Jones .50
89 Ryan Klesko .25
90 Mariano Rivera .25
91 Lance Berkman .25
92 Kenny Lofton .25
93 Jacque Jones .15
94 Eric Young .15
95 Edgar Renteria .15
96 Chipper Jones 1.00
97 Todd Helton .50
98 Shawn Estes .15
99 Mark Mulder .25
100 Lee Stevens .15
101 Jermaine Dye .15
102 Greg Vaughn .15
103 Chris Singleton .15
104 Brady Anderson .15
105 Terrence Long .15
106 Quilvio Veras .15
107 Magglio Ordonez .40
108 Johnny Damon .25
109 Jeffrey Hammonds .15
110 Fred McGriff .25
111 Carl Pavano .15
112 Bobby Estalella .15
113 Todd Hundley .15
114 Scott Rolen .75
115 Robin Ventura .25
116 Pokey Reese .15
117 Luis Gonzalez .25
118 Jose Offerman .15
119 Edgar Martinez .25
120 Dean Palmer .15
121 David Segui .15
122 Troy O'Leary .15
123 Tony Batista .15
124 Todd Zeile .15
125 Randy Johnson .75
126 Luis Castillo .15
127 Kris Benson .15
128 John Olerud .25
129 Eric Karros .25
130 Eddie Taubensee .15
131 Neifi Perez .15
132 Matt Stairs .15
133 Luis Alicea .15
134 Jeff Kent .25
135 Javier Vazquez .15
136 Garret Anderson .25
137 Frank Thomas .50
138 Carlos Febles .15
139 Albert Belle .15
140 Tony Clark .15
141 Pat Burrell .50
142 Mike Sweeney .15
143 Jay Buhner .15
144 Gabe Kapler .15
145 Derek Bell .15
146 B.J. Surhoff .15
147 Adam Kennedy .15
148 Aaron Boone .15
149 Todd Stottlemyre .15
150 Roberto Alomar .40
151 Orlando Hernandez .25
152 Jason Varitek .15
153 Gary Sheffield .40
154 Cliff Floyd .15
155 Chad Hermansen .15
156 Carlos Delgado .50
157 Aaron Sele .15
158 Sean Casey .15
159 Ruben Mateo .15
160 Mike Bordick .15
161 Mike Cameron .15
162 Doug Glanville .15
163 Damion Easley .15
164 Carl Everett .25
165 Bengie Molina .15
166 Adrian Beltre .25
167 Tom Goodwin .15
168 Rickey Henderson .40
169 Mo Vaughn .25
170 Mike Lieberthal .15
171 Ken Griffey Jr. 1.00
172 Juan Gonzalez .50
173 Ivan Rodriguez .50
174 Al Leiter .25
175 Vinny Castilla .15
176 Peter Bergeron .15
177 Pedro Astacio .15
178 Paul Konerko .15
179 Mitch Meluskey .15
180 Kevin Millwood .25
181 Ben Grieve .15
182 Barry Bonds 2.00
183 Rusty Greer .15
184 Miguel Tejada .40
185 Mark Quinn .15
186 Larry Walker .25
187 Jose Valentin .15
188 Jose Vidro .15
189 Delino DeShields .15
190 Darin Erstad .25
191 Bill Mueller .15
192 Ray Durham .15
193 Ken Caminiti .15
194 Jim Thome .75
195 Javy Lopez .25
196 Fernando Vina .15
197 Eric Chavez .25
198 Eric Owens .15
199 Brad Radke .15
200 Travis Lee .15
201 Tim Salmon .25
202 Rafael Palmeiro .50
203 Nomar Garciaparra 1.50
204 Mike Hampton .15
205 Kevin Brown .25
206 Juan Encarnacion .15
207 Danny Graves .15
208 Carlos Guillen .15
209 Phil Nevin .15
210 Matt Lawton .15
211 Manny Ramirez .50
212 James Baldwin .15
213 Fernando Tatis .15
214 Craig Biggio .25
215 Brian Jordan .15
216 Bernie Williams .40
217 Ryan Dempster .15
218 Roger Clemens 1.50
219 Jose Cruz Jr. .15
220 John Valentin .15
221 Dmitri Young .15
222 Curt Schilling .40
223 Jim Edmonds .30
224 Chan Ho Park .15
225 Brian Giles .25
226 Jimmy Anderson .15
227 Adam Piatt .15
228 Kenny Kelly .15
229 Randy Choate .15
230 Eric Cammack .15
231 Yovanny Lara .15
232 Wayne Franklin .15
233 Cameron Cairncross .15
234 J.C. Romero .15
235 Geraldo Guzman .15
236 Morgan Burkhart .15
237 Pascual Coco .15
238 John Parrish .15
239 Keith McDonald .15
240 Carlos Casimiro .15
241 Daniel Garibay .15
242 Sang-Hoon Lee .15
243 Hector Ortiz .15
244 Jeff Sparks .15
245 Jason Boyd .15
246 Mark Buehrle .15
247 Adam Melhuse .15
248 Kane Davis .15
249 Mike Darr .15
250 Vicente Padilla .15
251 Barry Zito (Prospects) 4.00
252 Tim Drew (Prospects) 1.00
253 Luis Matos (Prospects) 2.00
254 Alex Cabrera (Prospects) 1.00
255 Jon Garland (Prospects) 1.00
256 Milton Bradley (Prospects) 1.50
257 Juan Pierre (Prospects) 2.00
258 Ismael Villegas (Prospects) 1.00
259 Eric Munson (Prospects) 1.00
260 Tomas De La Rosa (Prospects) 1.00
261 Chris Richard (Prospects) 1.00
262 Jason Tyner (Prospects) 1.00
263 B.J. Waszgis (Prospects) 1.00
264 Jason Marquis (Prospects) 1.00
265 Dusty Allen (Prospects) 1.00
266 Corey Patterson (Prospects) 2.00
267 Eric Byrnes (Prospects) 2.00
268 Xavier Nady (Prospects) 2.00
269 George Lombard (Prospects) 1.00
270 Timoniel Perez (Prospects) 1.00
271 Gary Matthews Jr. (Prospects) 1.00
272 Chad Durbin (Prospects) 1.00
273 Tony Armas Jr. (Prospects) 2.00
274 Francisco Cordero (Prospects) 1.00
275 Alfonso Soriano (Prospects) 5.00

Gold Medallion

Stars (1-250): 1-2X
Inserted 1:1
Prospects (251-275): 1-2X
Inserted 1:24

Platinum Medallion

Stars (1-250): 15-25X
Production 50 Sets
Prospects (251-275): 5-10X
Production 25 Sets

Autographics

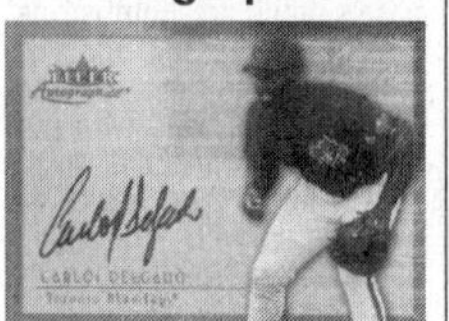

NM/M
Common Player: 5.00
Inserted 1:48
Silvers: 1-1.5X
Production 250 Sets
1 Roberto Alomar 25.00
2 Jimmy Anderson 5.00
3 Lance Berkman 15.00
4 Barry Bonds 150.00
5 Roosevelt Brown 5.00
6 Jeromy Burnitz 5.00
7 Pat Burrell 10.00
8 Alex Cabrera 5.00
9 Eric Chavez 10.00
10 Joe Crede 5.00
11 Johnny Damon 30.00
12 Carlos Delgado 10.00
13 Adam Dunn 20.00
14 Jim Edmonds 15.00
15 Chad Green 5.00
16 Dustin Hermanson 5.00
17 Randy Johnson 50.00
18 Corey Lee 5.00
19 Derrek Lee 25.00
20 Terrence Long 5.00
21 Julio Lugo 5.00
22 Edgar Martinez 20.00
23 Justin Miller 5.00
24 Russ Ortiz 5.00
25 Pablo Ozuna 5.00
26 Adam Piatt 5.00
27 Mark Redman 5.00
28 Richie Sexson 15.00
29 Gary Sheffield 15.00
30 Alfonso Soriano 25.00
31 Jose Vidro 8.00
32 Vernon Wells 10.00
33 Preston Wilson 10.00
34 Jamey Wright 5.00
35 Julio Zuleta 5.00

Decade of Dominance

NM/M
Complete Set (15): 15.00
Common Player: .50

Inserted 1:8
1 Barry Bonds 3.00
2 Mark McGwire 2.00
3 Sammy Sosa 2.00
4 Ken Griffey Jr. 1.50
5 Cal Ripken Jr. 3.00
6 Tony Gwynn 1.00
7 Albert Belle .50
8 Frank Thomas 1.00
9 Randy Johnson 1.00
10 Juan Gonzalez .75
11 Greg Maddux 1.50
12 Craig Biggio .50
13 Edgar Martinez .50
14 Roger Clemens 2.00
15 Andres Galarraga .50

Fall Classics

NM/M
Complete Set (37): 150.00
Common Player: 2.00
Inserted 1:20
1 Jackie Robinson 8.00
2 Enos Slaughter 2.00
3 Mariano Rivera 2.00
4 Hank Bauer 2.00
5 Cal Ripken Jr. 12.00
6 Babe Ruth 15.00
7 Thurman Munson 5.00
8 Tom Glavine 3.00
9 Fred Lynn 2.00
10 Johnny Bench 6.00
11 Tony Lazzeri 2.00
12 Al Kaline 5.00
13 Reggie Jackson 5.00
14 Derek Jeter 10.00
15 Willie Stargell 3.00
16 Roy Campanella 4.00
17 Phil Rizzuto 4.00
18 Roberto Clemente 12.00
19 Carlton Fisk 4.00
20 Duke Snider 4.00
21 Ted Williams 12.00
22 Bill Skowron 2.00
23 Bucky Dent 2.00
24 Mike Schmidt 8.00
25 Lou Brock 3.00
26 Whitey Ford 5.00
27 Brooks Robinson 4.00
28 Roberto Alomar 4.00
29 Yogi Berra 5.00
30 Joe Carter 2.00
31 Bill Mazeroski 2.00
32 Bob Gibson 3.00
33 Hank Greenberg 4.00
34 Andruw Jones 4.00
35 Bernie Williams 3.00
36 Don Larsen 3.00
37 Billy Martin 3.00

Fall Classics Memorabilia

NM/M
Common Player: 10.00
Inserted 1:288
1 Jackie Robinson/Pants 80.00
2 Enos Slaughter/Bat 15.00
3 Mariano Rivera/Jsy 15.00
4 Hank Bauer/Bat 10.00
5 Cal Ripken Jr./Jsy 40.00
6 Thurman Munson/Bat 25.00
7 Tom Glavine/Jsy 15.00
8 Fred Lynn/Bat 10.00
9 Babe Ruth/Bat 200.00
10 Tony Lazzeri/Bat 10.00
11 Al Kaline/Jsy 20.00
12 Reggie Jackson/Jsy 20.00
13 Derek Jeter/Jsy 40.00
14 Willie Stargell/Bat 15.00
15 Roy Campanella/Bat 50.00
16 Phil Rizzuto/Bat 20.00
17 Roberto Clemente/Bat 120.00
18 Carlton Fisk/Jsy 20.00
19 Duke Snider/Bat 25.00
20 Ted Williams/Bat 120.00
21 Bill Skowron/Bat 10.00
22 Bucky Dent/Bat 10.00
23 Mike Schmidt/Jsy 40.00
24 Lou Brock/Jersey 15.00
25 Brooks Robinson/Bat 20.00
26 Johnny Bench/Jsy 25.00

Fall Classics Memorabilia Autographs

No pricing due to scarcity.

Feel the Game

NM/M
Common Player: 5.00
Inserted 1:48
Golds: 2X
Production 50 Sets
1 Moises Alou 5.00
2 Brady Anderson 5.00
3 Adrian Beltre 5.00
4 Carlos Delgado 8.00
5 J.D. Drew 5.00
6 Jermaine Dye 5.00
7 Jason Giambi 8.00
8 Richard Hidalgo 5.00
9 Chipper Jones 10.00
10 Eric Karros 5.00
11 Raul Mondesi 5.00
12 Chan Ho Park 5.00
13 Ivan Rodriguez 8.00
14 Matt Stairs 5.00
15 Frank Thomas 8.00
16 Jose Vidro 5.00
17 Matt Williams 5.00
18 Preston Wilson 5.00

Power Plus

NM/M
Complete Set (10): 15.00
Common Player: 1.00
Inserted 1:24
1 Vladimir Guerrero 1.50
2 Mark McGwire 3.00
3 Mike Piazza 2.00
4 Derek Jeter 4.00
5 Chipper Jones 2.00
6 Carlos Delgado 1.00
7 Sammy Sosa 2.00
8 Ken Griffey Jr. 2.00
9 Nomar Garciaparra 2.50
10 Alex Rodriguez 3.00

Season Pass

Complete Set (6):
Common Player:

The Greatest Hits of ...

NM/M
Complete Set (10): 10.00

Common Player:		.50
Inserted 1:12		
1	Mark McGwire	2.00
2	Alex Rodriguez	2.00
3	Ken Griffey Jr.	1.50
4	Ivan Rodriguez	.75
5	Cal Ripken Jr.	3.00
6	Todd Helton	.75
7	Derek Jeter	3.00
8	Pedro Martinez	1.00
9	Tony Gwynn	1.00
10	Jim Edmonds	.50

Tomorrow's Legends

		NM/M
Complete Set (15):		10.00
Common Player:		.25
Inserted 1:4		
1	Rick Ankiel	.25
2	J.D. Drew	.40
3	Carlos Delgado	.75
4	Todd Helton	.75
5	Andruw Jones	.75
6	Troy Glaus	.75
7	Jermaine Dye	.25
8	Vladimir Guerrero	1.00
9	Brian Giles	.25
10	Scott Rolen	.75
11	Darin Erstad	.40
12	Derek Jeter	3.00
13	Alex Rodriguez	3.00
14	Pat Burrell	.50
15	Nomar Garciaparra	2.00

2002 Ultra

		NM/M
Complete Set (285):		100.00
Common Player:		.15
Common SP (201-285):		.50
Inserted 1:4		
Pack (10):		2.00
Box (24):		40.00
1	Jeff Bagwell	.50
2	Derek Jeter	2.00
3	Alex Rodriguez	1.50
4	Eric Chavez	.40
5	Tsuyoshi Shinjo	.15
6	Chris Stynes	.15
7	Ivan Rodriguez	.50
8	Cal Ripken Jr.	2.00
9	Freddy Garcia	.15
10	Chipper Jones	.75
11	Hideo Nomo	.40
12	Rafael Furcal	.25
13	Preston Wilson	.15
14	Jimmy Rollins	.25
15	Cristian Guzman	.15
16	Garret Anderson	.40
17	Todd Helton	.50
18	Moises Alou	.25
19	Tony Gwynn	.75
20	Jorge Posada	.40
21	Sean Casey	.25
22	Kazuhiro Sasaki	.15
23	Ray Lankford	.15
24	Manny Ramirez	.50
25	Barry Bonds	2.00
26	Fred McGriff	.25
27	Vladimir Guerrero	.75
28	Jermaine Dye	.15
29	Adrian Beltre	.25
30	Ken Griffey Jr.	1.00
31	Ramon Hernandez	.15
32	Kerry Wood	.75
33	Greg Maddux	1.00
34	Rondell White	.15
35	Mike Mussina	.50
36	Jim Edmonds	.40
37	Scott Rolen	.75
38	Mike Lowell	.25
39	Al Leiter	.25
40	Tony Clark	.15
41	Joe Mays	.15
42	Mo Vaughn	.25
43	Geoff Jenkins	.25
44	Curt Schilling	.50
45	Pedro Martinez	.75
46	Andy Pettitte	.40
47	Tim Salmon	.25
48	Carl Everett	.15
49	Lance Berkman	.25
50	Troy Glaus	.40
51	Ichiro Suzuki	1.00
52	Alfonso Soriano	.75
53	Tomo Ohka	.15
54	Dean Palmer	.15
55	Kevin Brown	.25
56	Albert Pujols	1.50
57	Homer Bush	.15
58	Tim Hudson	.40
59	Frank Thomas	.50
60	Joe Randa	.15
61	Chan Ho Park	.15
62	Bobby Higginson	.15
63	Bartolo Colon	.15
64	Aramis Ramirez	.40
65	Jeff Cirillo	.15
66	Roberto Alomar	.50
67	Mark Kotsay	.15
68	Mike Cameron	.15
69	Mike Hampton	.15
70	Trot Nixon	.15
71	Juan Gonzalez	.50
72	Damian Rolls	.15
73	Brad Fullmer	.15
74	David Ortiz	.25
75	Brandon Inge	.15
76	Orlando Hernandez	.15
77	Matt Stairs	.15
78	Jay Gibbons	.15
79	Greg Vaughn	.15
80	Brady Anderson	.15
81	Jim Thome	.75
82	Ben Sheets	.40
83	Rafael Palmeiro	.50
84	Edgar Renteria	.25
85	Doug Mientkiewicz	.15
86	Raul Mondesi	.15
87	Shane Reynolds	.15
88	Steve Finley	.15
89	Jose Cruz Jr.	.15
90	Edgardo Alfonzo	.15
91	Jose Valentin	.15
92	Mark McGwire	2.00
93	Mark Grace	.40
94	Mike Lieberthal	.15
95	Barry Larkin	.25
96	Chuck Knoblauch	.15
97	Deivi Cruz	.15
98	Jeromy Burnitz	.15
99	Shannon Stewart	.15
100	David Wells	.15
101	Brook Fordyce	.15
102	Rusty Greer	.15
103	Andruw Jones	.50
104	Jason Kendall	.15
105	Nomar Garciaparra	1.25
106	Shawn Green	.25
107	Craig Biggio	.25
108	Masato Yoshii	.15
109	Ben Petrick	.15
110	Gary Sheffield	.40
111	Travis Lee	.15
112	Matt Williams	.25
113	Billy Wagner	.15
114	Robin Ventura	.15
115	Jerry Hairston Jr.	.15
116	Paul LoDuca	.15
117	Darin Erstad	.25
118	Ruben Sierra	.15
119	Ricky Gutierrez	.15
120	Bret Boone	.25
121	John Rocker	.15
122	Roger Clemens	1.50
123	Eric Karros	.15
124	J.D. Drew	.25
125	Carlos Delgado	.40
126	Jeffrey Hammonds	.15
127	Jeff Kent	.25
128	David Justice	.25
129	Cliff Floyd	.15
130	Omar Vizquel	.25
131	Matt Morris	.25
132	Rich Aurilia	.15
133	Larry Walker	.25
134	Miguel Tejada	.25
135	Eric Young	.15
136	Aaron Sele	.15
137	Eric Milton	.15
138	Travis Fryman	.15
139	Magglio Ordonez	.25
140	Sammy Sosa	1.50
141	Pokey Reese	.15
142	Adam Eaton	.15
143	Adam Kennedy	.15
144	Mike Piazza	1.00
145	Larry Barnes	.15
146	Darryl Kile	.15
147	Tom Glavine	.25
148	Ryan Klesko	.15
149	Jose Vidro	.15
150	Joe Kennedy	.15
151	Bernie Williams	.40
152	C.C. Sabathia	.15
153	Alex Ochoa	.15
154	A.J. Pierzynski	.15
155	Johnny Damon	.25
156	Omar Daal	.15
157	A.J. Burnett	.15
158	Eric Munson	.15
159	Fernando Vina	.15
160	Chris Singleton	.15
161	Juan Pierre	.15
162	John Olerud	.25
163	Randy Johnson	.75
164	Paul Konerko	.25
165	Tino Martinez	.25
166	Richard Hidalgo	.15
167	Luis Gonzalez	.25
168	Ben Grieve	.15
169	Matt Lawton	.15
170	Gabe Kapler	.25
171	Mariano Rivera	.25
172	Kenny Lofton	.25
173	Brian Jordan	.15
174	Brian Giles	.25
175	Mark Quinn	.15
176	Neifi Perez	.15
177	Ellis Burks	.15
178	Bobby Abreu	.40
179	Jeff Weaver	.15
180	Andres Galarraga	.25
181	Javy Lopez	.25
182	Todd Walker	.15
183	Fernando Tatis	.15
184	Charles Johnson	.15
185	Pat Burrell	.40
186	Jay Bell	.15
187	Aaron Boone	.15
188	Jason Giambi	.50
189	Jay Payton	.15
190	Carlos Lee	.15
191	Phil Nevin	.15
192	Mike Sweeney	.15
193	J.T. Snow	.15
194	Dmitri Young	.15
195	Richie Sexson	.40
196	Derrek Lee	.25
197	Corey Koskie	.15
198	Edgar Martinez	.25
199	Wade Miller	.15
200	Tony Batista	.15
201	John Olerud	.50
202	Bret Boone	.50
203	Cal Ripken Jr.	3.00
204	Alex Rodriguez	2.50
205	Ichiro Suzuki	2.00
206	Manny Ramirez	.75
207	Juan Gonzalez	.75
208	Ivan Rodriguez	.75
209	Roger Clemens	2.00
210	Edgar Martinez	.50
211	Todd Helton	.75
212	Jeff Kent	.50
213	Chipper Jones	1.00
214	Rich Aurilia	.50
215	Barry Bonds	3.00
216	Sammy Sosa	2.00
217	Luis Gonzalez	.50
218	Mike Piazza	2.00
219	Randy Johnson	1.00
220	Larry Walker	.50
221	Todd Helton, Juan Uribe	.50
222	Pat Burrell, Eric Valent	.50
223	Edgar Martinez, Ichiro Suzuki	2.00
224	Ben Grieve, Jason Tyner	.50
225	Mark Quinn, Dee Brown	.50
226	Cal Ripken Jr., Brian Roberts	3.00
227	Cliff Floyd, Abraham Nunez	.50
228	Jeff Bagwell, Adam Everett	.75
229	Mark McGwire, Albert Pujols	3.00
230	Doug Mientkiewicz, Luis Rivas	.50
231	Juan Gonzalez, Danny Peoples	.75
232	Kevin Brown, Luke Prokopec	.50
233	Richie Sexson, Ben Sheets	.50
234	Jason Giambi, Jason Hart	.75
235	Barry Bonds, Carlos Valderrama	3.00
236	Tony Gwynn, Cesar Crespo	1.00
237	Ken Griffey Jr., Adam Dunn	1.50
238	Frank Thomas, Joe Crede	.75
239	Derek Jeter, Drew Henson	3.00
240	Chipper Jones, Wilson Betemit	1.00
241	Luis Gonzalez, Junior Spivey	.50
242	Bobby Higginson, Andres Torres	.50
243	Carlos Delgado, Vernon Wells	.50
244	Sammy Sosa, Corey Patterson	2.00
245	Nomar Garciaparra, Shea Hillenbrand	2.00
246	Alex Rodriguez, Jason Romano	2.50
247	Troy Glaus, David Eckstein	.75
248	Mike Piazza, Alex Escobar	2.00
249	Brian Giles, Jack Wilson	.50
250	Vladimir Guerrero, Scott Hodges	1.00
251	Bud Smith	1.00
252	Juan Diaz	1.00
253	Wilkin Ruan	1.00
254	Chris Spurling **RC**	1.00
255	Toby Hall	1.00
256	Jason Jennings	1.00
257	George Perez	1.00
258	D'Angelo Jimenez	1.00
259	Jose Acevedo	1.00
260	Josue Perez	1.00
261	Brian Rogers	1.00
262	Carlos Maldonado	1.00
263	Travis Phelps	1.00
264	Rob Mackowiak	1.50
265	Ryan Drese	1.00
266	Carlos Garcia	1.00
267	Alexis Gomez	1.00
268	Jeremy Affeldt	1.00
269	Scott Podsednik	3.00
270	Adam Johnson	1.00
271	Pedro Santana	1.00
272	Les Walrond	1.00
273	Jackson Melian	1.00
274	Carlos Hernandez	1.00
275	Mark Nussbeck **RC**	1.00
276	Cory Aldridge	1.00
277	Troy Mattes	1.00
278	Brent Abernathy	1.00
279	J.J. Davis	1.00
280	Brandon Duckworth	1.00
281	Kyle Lohse	1.00
282	Justin Kaye	1.00
283	Cody Ransom	1.00
284	Dave Williams	1.00
285	Luis Lopez	1.00

Gold Medallion

Stars (1-200):	2-3X
Inserted 1:1	
Stars (201-250):	2-4X
Inserted 1:24	
Prospects (251-285):	4-8X
Production 100	

Fall Classic

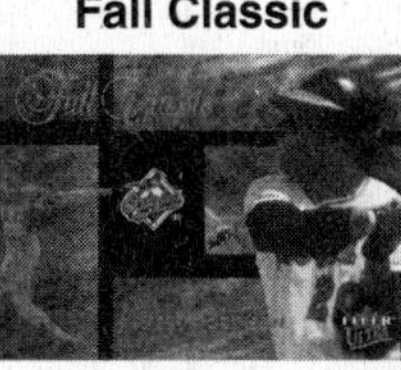

		NM/M
Complete Set (39):		180.00
Common Player:		2.50
Inserted 1:20		
1FC	Ty Cobb	10.00
2FC	Lou Gehrig	10.00
3FC	Babe Ruth	15.00
4FC	Stan Musial	8.00
5FC	Ted Williams	12.00
6FC	Dizzy Dean	6.00
7FC	Mickey Cochrane	2.50
8FC	Jimmie Foxx	8.00
9FC	Mel Ott	5.00
10FC	Rogers Hornsby	6.00
11FC	Hank Aaron	10.00
12FC	Clete Boyer	2.50
13FC	George Brett	10.00
14FC	Bob Gibson	5.00
15FC	Carlton Fisk	4.00
16FC	Johnny Bench	8.00
17FC	Rusty Staub	2.50
18FC	Willie McCovey	2.50
19FC	Paul Molitor	5.00
20FC	Jim Palmer	4.00
21FC	Frank Robinson	5.00
22FC	Derek Jeter	10.00
23FC	Earl Weaver	2.50
24FC	Lefty Grove	2.50
25FC	Tony Perez	2.50
26FC	Reggie Jackson	5.00
27FC	Sparky Anderson	2.50
28FC	Casey Stengel	2.50
29FC	Roy Campanella	6.00
30FC	Roberto Clemente	10.00
31FC	Don Drysdale	6.00
32FC	Joe Morgan	4.00
33FC	Eddie Murray	5.00
34FC	Nolan Ryan	15.00
35FC	Tom Seaver	8.00
36FC	Bill Mazeroski	2.50
37FC	Jackie Robinson	8.00
38FC	Kirk Gibson	2.50
39FC	Robin Yount	8.00

Fall Classic Autographs

		NM/M
Common Autograph:		10.00
Inserted 1:240		
1	Sparky Anderson	15.00
2	Johnny Bench/SP	40.00
3	George Brett/SP	80.00
4	Carlton Fisk	25.00
5	Bob Gibson	25.00
6	Kirk Gibson	15.00
7	Reggie Jackson/SP	40.00
9	Bill Mazeroski	20.00
10	Willie McCovey/SP	30.00
11	Joe Morgan	15.00
12	Eddie Murray/SP	40.00
14	Jim Palmer	15.00
15	Tony Perez	15.00
16	Frank Robinson	20.00
17	Nolan Ryan/SP	175.00
18	Tom Seaver/SP	30.00
19	Earl Weaver	10.00
20	Robin Yount/SP	50.00

Fall Classic Game-Used

Twenty-six players or managers who have had a role in World Series history are included in this insert series found at the announced rate of about one per 113 packs. Some players' cards can be found with more than one type of game-used memorabilia and in varying rates of production (some with as few as 21 pieces reported by the manufacturerand shown here). Players are checklisted alphabetically.

	NM/M
Inserted 1:113	
Sparky Anderson/Pants	5.00
Johnny Bench/Jsy	15.00
Johnny Bench/Pants	10.00
George Brett/Bat	15.00
George Brett/Blue Jesy/65	45.00
George Brett/White Jsy	15.00
Roy Campanella/Bat/21	225.00
Carlton Fisk/Bat/42	35.00
Carlton Fisk/Jersey	8.00
Jimmie Foxx/Bat	35.00
Bob Gibson/Jsy	10.00
Kirk Gibson/Bat	5.00
Reggie Jackson/Bat	10.00
Reggie Jackson/Jsy/73	20.00
Derek Jeter/Pants	30.00
Willie McCovey/Jsy	5.00
Paul Molitor/Bat	10.00
Paul Molitor/Jsy	10.00
Joe Morgan/Bat	8.00
Joe Morgan/Jsy	8.00
Eddie Murray/Bat	10.00
Eddie Murray/Jsy/91	35.00
Jim Palmer/Gray Jsy/85	20.00
Jim Palmer/White Jsy	5.00
Tony Perez/Bat	8.00
Frank Robinson/Bat/40	25.00
Jackie Robinson/Jsy	50.00
Babe Ruth/Bat/44	200.00
Nolan Ryan/Pants	30.00
Tom Seaver/Jsy	10.00
Earl Weaver/Jsy	5.00
Ted Williams/Bat/30	200.00
Ted Williams/Jsy	75.00
Robin Yount/Bat	10.00
Robin Yount/Gray Jsy	10.00
Robin Yount/White Jsy/30	30.00

Glove Works

		NM/M
Complete Set (15):		25.00
Common Player:		1.00
Inserted 1:20		
1GW	Andruw Jones	1.50
2GW	Derek Jeter	6.00
3GW	Cal Ripken Jr.	8.00
4GW	Larry Walker	1.00
5GW	Chipper Jones	2.00
6GW	Barry Bonds	6.00
7GW	Scott Rolen	2.00
8GW	Jim Edmonds	1.00
9GW	Robin Ventura	1.00
10GW	Darin Erstad	1.00
11GW	Barry Larkin	1.00
12GW	Raul Mondesi	1.00
13GW	Mark Grace	1.50
14GW	Bernie Williams	1.00
15GW	Ivan Rodriguez	1.50

Glove Works Game Worn

	NM/M
Common Player:	10.00
Production 450 Sets	
Platinum (25 Sets) randomly inserted.	
Derek Jeter	35.00
Cal Ripken Jr.	50.00
Barry Bonds	40.00
Robin Ventura	10.00
Barry Larkin/SP	15.00
Raul Mondesi	10.00
Ivan Rodriguez	15.00

Hitting Machine

		NM/M
Complete Set (25):		60.00
Common Player:		1.00
Inserted 1:20		
1HM	Frank Thomas	2.00
2HM	Derek Jeter	8.00
3HM	Vladimir Guerrero	3.00
4HM	Jim Edmonds	1.50
5HM	Mike Piazza	5.00
6HM	Ivan Rodriguez	2.00
7HM	Chipper Jones	3.00
8HM	Tony Gwynn	3.00
9HM	Manny Ramirez	2.00
10HM	Andruw Jones	2.00
11HM	Carlos Delgado	1.50
12HM	Bernie Williams	1.50
13HM	Larry Walker	1.00
14HM	Juan Gonzalez	2.00
15HM	Ichiro Suzuki	5.00
16HM	Albert Pujols	6.00
17HM	Barry Bonds	8.00
18HM	Cal Ripken Jr.	8.00
19HM	Edgar Martinez	1.50
20HM	Luis Gonzalez	1.00
21HM	Moises Alou	1.50
22HM	Roberto Alomar	2.00
23HM	Todd Helton	2.00
24HM	Rafael Palmeiro	2.00
25HM	Bobby Abreu	1.50

Hitting Machine Game Worn

	NM/M
Common Player:	8.00
Inserted 1:81	
Platinum (25 Sets) randomly inserted.	
Frank Thomas	15.00
Derek Jeter	25.00

Jim Edmonds 10.00
Mike Piazza 15.00
Ivan Rodriguez 15.00
Chipper Jones 15.00
Tony Gwynn 15.00
Manny Ramirez 10.00
Andruw Jones 10.00
Carlos Delgado 10.00
Bernie Williams 10.00
Larry Walker 8.00
Juan Gonzalez 10.00
Albert Pujols 30.00
Barry Bonds 25.00
Cal Ripken Jr. 40.00
Edgar Martinez 10.00
Luis Gonzalez 8.00
Moises Alou 10.00
Roberto Alomar 15.00
Todd Helton 15.00
Rafael Palmeiro 10.00
Bobby Abreu 10.00

On the Road Game-Used

NM/M
Common Player: 10.00
Inserted 1:93
Platinum (25 Sets) randomly inserted.
Derek Jeter 30.00
Ivan Rodriguez 10.00
Carlos Delgado 8.00
Larry Walker 8.00
Roberto Alomar 15.00
Tony Gwynn 15.00
Greg Maddux 20.00
Barry Bonds 30.00
Todd Helton 15.00
Kazuhiro Sasaki 10.00
Jeff Bagwell 15.00
Omar Vizquel 8.00
Chan Ho Park 10.00
Tom Glavine 10.00

Rising Stars

NM/M
Complete Set (15): 15.00
Common Player: .50
Inserted 1:12
1RS Ichiro Suzuki 2.50
2RS Derek Jeter 4.00
3RS Albert Pujols 3.00
4RS Jimmy Rollins 1.00
5RS Adam Dunn 1.00
6RS Sean Casey 1.00
7RS Kerry Wood 2.00
8RS Tsuyoshi Shinjo .50
9RS Shea Hillenbrand .50
10RS Pat Burrell 1.00
11RS Ben Sheets 1.00
12RS Alfonso Soriano 1.50
13RS J.D. Drew 1.00
14RS Kazuhiro Sasaki .50
15RS Corey Patterson .75

Rising Stars Game Worn

NM/M
Common Player: 20.00
Production 100 Sets
Platinum (25 Sets) randomly seeded.
Derek Jeter 75.00
Albert Pujols 50.00
Tsuyoshi Shinjo 25.00
Alfonso Soriano 25.00
J.D. Drew 25.00
Kazuhiro Sasaki 20.00

2003 Ultra

NM/M
Complete Set (250): 75.00
Common Player: .15
Common SP (201-250): .50
Inserted 1:4
Hobby Pack (10): 2.00
Hobby Box (24): 35.00
1 Barry Bonds 2.00
2 Derek Jeter 2.50
3 Ichiro Suzuki 1.50
4 Mike Lowell .15
5 Hideo Nomo .50
6 Javier Vazquez .15
7 Jeremy Giambi .15
8 Jamie Moyer .15
9 Rafael Palmeiro .40
10 Magglio Ordonez .25
11 Trot Nixon .15
12 Luis Castillo .15
13 Paul Byrd .15
14 Adam Kennedy .15
15 Trevor Hoffman .15
16 Matt Morris .15
17 Nomar Garciaparra 1.50
18 Matt Lawton .15
19 Carlos Beltran .15
20 Jason Giambi 1.25
21 Brian Giles .25
22 Jim Edmonds .25
23 Garret Anderson .25
24 Tony Batista .15
25 Aaron Boone .15
26 Mike Hampton .15
27 Billy Wagner .15
28 Kazuhisa Ishii .15
29 Al Leiter .25
30 Pat Burrell .40
31 Jeff Kent .25
32 Randy Johnson .75
33 Ray Durham .15
34 Josh Beckett .15
35 Cristian Guzman .15
36 Roger Clemens 1.25
37 Freddy Garcia .15
38 Roy Halladay .15
39 David Eckstein .15
40 Jerry Hairston Jr. .15
41 Barry Larkin .25
42 Larry Walker .25
43 Craig Biggio .25
44 Edgardo Alfonzo .15
45 Marlon Byrd .15
46 J.T. Snow .15
47 Juan Gonzalez .50
48 Ramon Ortiz .15
49 Jay Gibbons .15
50 Adam Dunn .60
51 Juan Pierre .15
52 Jeff Bagwell .60
53 Kevin Brown .15
54 Pedro Astacio .15
55 Mike Lieberthal .15
56 Johnny Damon .15
57 Tim Salmon .25
58 Mike Bordick .15
59 Ken Griffey Jr. 1.50
60 Jason Jennings .15
61 Lance Berkman .50
62 Jeromy Burnitz .15
63 Jimmy Rollins .25
64 Tsuyoshi Shinjo .15
65 Alex Rodriguez 2.00
66 Greg Maddux 1.25
67 Mark Prior .40
68 Mike Maroth .15
69 Geoff Jenkins .15
70 Tony Armas Jr. .15
71 Jermaine Dye .15
72 Albert Pujols .75
73 Shannon Stewart .15
74 Troy Glaus .60
75 Brook Fordyce .15
76 Juan Encarnacion .15
77 Todd Hollandsworth .15
78 Roy Oswalt .25
79 Paul LoDuca .15
80 Mike Piazza 1.50
81 Bobby Abreu .15
82 Sean Burroughs .15
83 Randy Winn .15
84 Curt Schilling .50
85 Chris Singleton .15
86 Sean Casey .25
87 Todd Zeile .15
88 Richard Hidalgo .15
89 Roberto Alomar .50
90 Tim Hudson .25
91 Ryan Klesko .15
92 Greg Vaughn .15
93 Tony Womack .15
94 Fred McGriff .25
95 Tom Glavine .40
96 Todd Walker .15
97 Travis Fryman .15
98 Shane Reynolds .15
99 Shawn Green .25
100 Mo Vaughn .25
101 Adam Piatt .15
102 Deivi Cruz .15
103 Steve Cox .15
104 Luis Gonzalez .25
105 Russell Branyan .15
106 Daryle Ward .15
107 Mariano Rivera .25
108 Phil Nevin .15
109 Ben Grieve .15
110 Moises Alou .15
111 Omar Vizquel .25
112 Joe Randa .15
113 Jorge Posada .40
114 Mark Kotsay .15
115 Ryan Rupe .15
116 Javy Lopez .15
117 Corey Patterson .15
118 Bobby Higginson .15
119 Jose Vidro .15
120 Barry Zito .25
121 Matt Morris .15
122 Gary Sheffield .25
123 Kerry Wood .15
124 Brandon Inge .15
125 Jose Hernandez .15
126 Michael Barrett .15
127 Miguel Tejada .40
128 Edgar Renteria .15
129 Junior Spivey .15
130 Jose Valentin .15
131 Derrek Lee .15
132 A.J. Pierzynski .15
133 Mike Mussina .50
134 Bret Boone .15
135 Chan Ho Park .15
136 Steve Finley .15
137 Mark Buehrle .15
138 A.J. Burnett .15
139 Ben Sheets .15
140 David Ortiz .15
141 Nick Johnson .15
142 Randall Simon .15
143 Carlos Delgado .40
144 Darin Erstad .25
145 Shea Hillenbrand .15
146 Todd Helton .40
147 Preston Wilson .15
148 Eric Gagne .15
149 Vladimir Guerrero .75
150 Brandon Duckworth .15
151 Rich Aurilia .15
152 Ivan Rodriguez .50
153 Andruw Jones .50
154 Carlos Lee .15
155 Robert Fick .15
156 Jacque Jones .15
157 Bernie Williams .50
158 John Olerud .25
159 Eric Hinske .15
160 Matt Clement .15
161 Dmitri Young .15
162 Torii Hunter .15
163 Carlos Pena .15
164 Mike Cameron .15
165 Raul Mondesi .15
166 Pedro J. Martinez .75
167 Bob Wickman .15
168 Mike Sweeney .15
169 David Wells .15
170 Jason Kendall .15
171 Tino Martinez .15
172 Matt Williams .15
173 Frank Thomas .60
174 Cliff Floyd .15
175 Corey Koskie .15
176 Orlando Hernandez .15
177 Edgar Martinez .15
178 Richie Sexson .25
179 Manny Ramirez .60
180 Jim Thome .50
181 Andy Pettitte .40
182 Aramis Ramirez .15
183 J.D. Drew .25
184 Brian Jordan .15
185 Sammy Sosa 1.25
186 Jeff Weaver .15
187 Jeffrey Hammonds .15
188 Eric Milton .15
189 Eric Chavez .25
190 Kazuhiro Sasaki .15
191 Jose Cruz Jr. .15
192 Derek Lowe .15
193 C.C. Sabathia .15
194 Adrian Beltre .15
195 Alfonso Soriano 1.00
196 Jack Wilson .15
197 Fernando Vina .15
198 Chipper Jones 1.25
199 Paul Konerko .15
200 Rusty Greer .15
201 Jason Giambi 2.00
202 Alfonso Soriano 2.00
203 Shea Hillenbrand .50
204 Alex Rodriguez 3.00
205 Jorge Posada .60
206 Ichiro Suzuki 3.00
207 Manny Ramirez 1.00
208 Torii Hunter .50
209 Todd Helton .75
210 Roberto Alomar .75
211 Scott Rolen .75
212 Jimmy Rollins .50
213 Mike Piazza 3.00
214 Barry Bonds 3.00
215 Sammy Sosa 2.00
216 Vladimir Guerrero 1.50
217 Lance Berkman .75
218 Derek Jeter 4.00
219 Nomar Garciaparra 3.00
220 Luis Gonzalez .75
221 Kazuhisa Ishii 1.00
222 Satoru Komiyama .50
223 So Taguchi .50
224 Jorge Padilla .50
225 Ben Howard .50
226 Jason Simontacchi .50
227 Barry Wesson .50
228 Howie Clark .50
229 Aaron Guiel .50
230 Oliver Perez .75
231 David Ross .50
232 Julius Matos .50
233 Chris Snelling .50
234 Rodrigo Lopez .50
235 Wilbert Nieves .50
236 Brendan Donnelly .50
237 Aaron Cook .50
238 Anderson Machado .50
239 Corey Thurman .50
240 Tyler Yates .50
241 Coco Crisp 4.00
242 Andy Van Hekken 1.50
243 Jim Rushford 2.00
244 Jeriome Robertson 1.00
245 Shane Nance 1.00
246 Kevin Cash .50
247 Kirk Saarloos 1.50
248 Josh Bard 2.00
249 David Pember **RC** 1.00
250 Freddy Sanchez 1.50

Gold Medallion

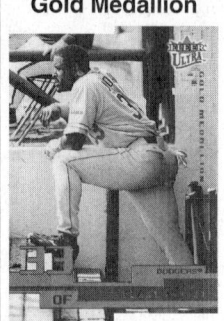

Stars (1-200): 2-3X
Inserted 1:1
Stars (201-220): 3-4X
Inserted 1:24
Rookies (221-250): 1-30X
Inserted 1:24

Back 2 Back

NM/M
Complete Set (17): 60.00
Common Player: 2.00
Production 1,000 Sets
1B2B Derek Jeter 10.00
2B2B Barry Bonds 8.00
3B2B Mike Piazza 6.00
4B2B Alex Rodriguez 8.00
5B2B Todd Helton 2.00
6B2B Edgar Martinez 2.00
7B2B Chipper Jones 5.00
8B2B Shawn Green 2.00
9B2B Chan Ho Park 2.00
10B2B Preston Wilson 2.00
11B2B Manny Ramirez 3.00
12B2B Aramis Ramirez 2.00
13B2B Pedro J. Martinez 4.00
14B2B Ivan Rodriguez 2.00
15B2B Ichiro Suzuki 6.00
16B2B Sammy Sosa 5.00
17B2B Jason Giambi 5.00

Back 2 Back Memorabilia

NM/M
Common Player: 5.00
Production 500 Sets
Golds: 1.5-3X
Production 50 Sets
Derek Jeter 25.00
Barry Bonds/Bat 20.00
Mike Piazza/Jsy 12.00
Alex Rodriguez/Jsy 12.00
Todd Helton/Jsy 8.00
Edgar Martinez/Jsy 6.00
Chipper Jones/Jsy 15.00
Shawn Green/Jsy 6.00
Chan Ho Park/Bat 6.00
Preston Wilson/Jsy 5.00
Manny Ramirez/Jsy 8.00
Aramis Ramirez/Jsy 5.00
Pedro Martinez/Jsy 10.00
Ivan Rodriguez/Jsy 8.00
Ichiro Suzuki/Base 15.00
Sammy Sosa/Base 10.00
Jason Giambi/Base 8.00

Double Up

NM/M
Complete Set (16): 30.00
Common Card: 1.00
Inserted 1:8
1DU Derek Jeter, Mike Piazza 4.00
2DU Alex Rodriguez, Rafael Palmeiro 3.00
3DU Chipper Jones, Andruw Jones 2.00
4DU Derek Jeter, Alex Rodriguez 4.00

5DU Nomar Garciaparra, Derek Jeter 4.00
6DU Barry Bonds, Jason Giambi 3.00
7DU Ichiro Suzuki, Hideo Nomo 3.00
8DU Randy Johnson, Curt Schilling 1.00
9DU Pedro J. Martinez, Nomar Garciaparra 2.50
10DU Roger Clemens, Kevin Brown 2.00
11DU Nomar Garciaparra, Manny Ramirez 2.50
12DU Kazuhiro Sasaki, Hideo Nomo 1.00
13DU Mike Piazza, Ivan Rodriguez 3.00
14DU Ichiro Suzuki, Ken Griffey Jr. 3.00
15DU Barry Bonds, Sammy Sosa 3.00
16DU Alfonso Soriano, Roberto Alomar 2.00

Double Up Memorabilia

NM/M
Common Card: 15.00
Production 100 Sets
Derek Jeter, Mike Piazza 50.00
Alex Rodriguez, Rafael Palmeiro 25.00
Chipper Jones, Andruw Jones 15.00
Derek Jeter, Alex Rodriguez 50.00
Nomar Garciaparra, Derek Jeter 50.00
Barry Bonds, Jason Giambi 30.00
Ichiro Suzuki, Hideo Nomo 80.00
Randy Johnson, Curt Schilling 20.00
Pedro J. Martinez, Nomar Garciaparra 30.00
Roger Clemens, Kevin Brown 25.00
Nomar Garciaparra, Manny Ramirez 25.00
Kazuhiro Sasaki, Hideo Nomo 50.00
Mike Piazza, Ivan Rodriguez 25.00
Ichiro Suzuki, Ken Griffey Jr. 50.00
Barry Bonds, Sammy Sosa 40.00
Alfonso Soriano, Roberto Alomar 25.00

Moonshots

NM/M
Complete Set (20): 30.00
Common Player: .75
Inserted 1:12
1M Mike Piazza 4.00
2M Alex Rodriguez 4.00
3M Manny Ramirez 1.50
4M Ivan Rodriguez 1.00
5M Luis Gonzalez .75
6M Shawn Green .75
7M Barry Bonds 5.00
8M Jason Giambi 3.00
9M Nomar Garciaparra 4.00
10M Edgar Martinez .75
11M Mo Vaughn .75
12M Chipper Jones 3.00
13M Todd Helton 1.00
14M Raul Mondesi .75
15M Preston Wilson .75
16M Rafael Palmeiro 1.00
17M Jim Edmonds .75
18M Bernie Williams 1.00
19M Vladimir Guerrero 2.00
20M Alfonso Soriano 2.00

Moonshots Memorabilia

NM/M
Common Player: 4.00
Inserted 1:20
Mike Piazza/Jsy 12.00
Alex Rodriguez/Jsy 12.00
Manny Ramirez/Jsy 5.00
Ivan Rodriguez/Jsy 5.00
Luis Gonzalez/Jsy 4.00
Shawn Green/Jsy 4.00
Barry Bonds/Jsy 12.00
Jason Giambi/Base 8.00
Nomar Garciaparra/Jsy 12.00
Edgar Martinez/Jsy 5.00
Mo Vaughn/Jsy 4.00
Chipper Jones/Jsy 8.00
Todd Helton/Jsy 6.00
Raul Mondesi/Jsy 5.00
Preston Wilson/Jsy 4.00
Rafael Palmeiro/Jsy 5.00
Jim Edmonds/Jsy 5.00
Bernie Williams/Jsy 6.00
Vladimir Guerrero/Base 5.00
Alfonso Soriano/Jsy 8.00

Photo Effex

NM/M
Complete Set (20): 45.00
Common Player: 1.00
Inserted 1:12
Golds: 6-12X
Production 25 Sets
1PE Derek Jeter 6.00
2PE Barry Bonds 5.00
3PE Sammy Sosa 3.00
4PE Troy Glaus 1.50
5PE Albert Pujols 2.00
6PE Alex Rodriguez 5.00
7PE Ichiro Suzuki 4.00
8PE Greg Maddux 3.00
9PE Nomar Garciaparra 4.00
10PE Jeff Bagwell 1.50
11PE Chipper Jones 3.00
12PE Mike Piazza 4.00
13PE Randy Johnson 2.00
14PE Vladimir Guerrero 2.00
15PE Alfonso Soriano 3.00
16PE Lance Berkman 1.00
17PE Todd Helton 1.00
18PE Mike Lowell 1.00
19PE Carlos Delgado 1.00
20PE Jason Giambi 3.00

When it was a Game

NM/M
Complete Set (40): 125.00
Common Player: 2.00
Inserted 1:20
1WG Derek Jeter 10.00

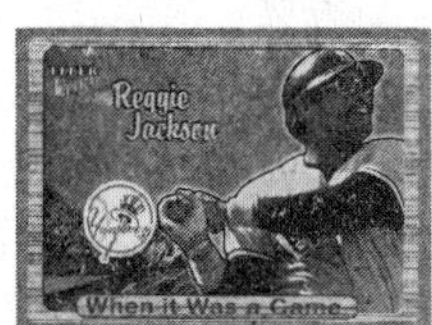

2WG Barry Bonds 8.00
3WG Luis Aparicio 2.00
4WG Richie Ashburn 2.00
5WG Ernie Banks 5.00
6WG Enos Slaughter 3.00
7WG Yogi Berra 5.00
8WG Lou Boudreau 2.00
9WG Lou Brock 4.00
10WG Jim Bunning 2.00
11WG Rod Carew 4.00
12WG Orlando Cepeda 2.00
13WG Larry Doby 4.00
14WG Bobby Doerr 2.00
15WG Bob Feller 3.00
16WG Brooks Robinson 5.00
17WG Rollie Fingers 2.00
18WG Whitey Ford 3.00
19WG Bob Gibson 4.00
20WG Jim "Catfish" Hunter 3.00
21WG Nolan Ryan 15.00
22WG Reggie Jackson 5.00
23WG Fergie Jenkins 3.00
24WG Al Kaline 6.00
25WG Mike Schmidt 8.00
26WG Harmon Killebrew 8.00
27WG Ralph Kiner 4.00
28WG Willie Stargell 4.00
29WG Billy Williams 2.00
30WG Tom Seaver 5.00
31WG Juan Marichal 3.00
32WG Eddie Mathews 6.00
33WG Willie McCovey 4.00
34WG Joe Morgan 4.00
35WG Stan Musial 8.00
36WG Robin Roberts 4.00
37WG Robin Yount 8.00
38WG Jim Palmer 3.00
39WG Phil Rizzuto 4.00
40WG Pee Wee Reese 4.00

When it was a Game Autograph

No Pricing

When it was a Game Memorabilia

NM/M

Common Player:
Varying quantities produced
Derek Jeter/Jsy/200 35.00
Barry Bonds/Bat/200 25.00
Yogi Berra/100 35.00
Larry Doby/Bat/150 20.00
Catfish Hunter/Jsy 8.00
Reggie Jackson/Bat 12.00
Tom Seaver/Jsy 15.00
Juan Marichal/Jsy 8.00
Eddie Mathews/Bat 25.00
Willie McCovey/Jsy/150 15.00
Joe Morgan/Jsy/200 10.00
Jim Palmer/Jsy/300 10.00

All-Vet Phillies Team

At the Phillies Sept. 28 final game at Veterans Stadium, this cello-wrapped set of the greatest players to appear for the home team in that era was issued as a stadium give away. Fronts have gold-foil highlights on borderless game-action photos. Backs have personal data, full or partial major league stats and an assortment of licensor and sponsor logos.

NM/M

Complete Set (13): 6.00
Common Player: .50
1 Steve Carlton 1.00
2 Darren Daulton .50
3 John Kruk .50
4 Juan Samuel .50
5 Mike Schmidt 3.00
6 Larry Bowa .50
7 Greg Luzinski .50
8 Garry Maddox .50
9 Bobby Abreu .50
10 Tug McGraw .50
11 Curt Schilling .75
12 Dallas Green .50
--- Header Card .05

2004 Ultra

NM/M

Complete Set (220): 45.00
Common Player: .15
Common All-Rookie (201-220): .50
Common Player (221-295): .25
Minor Stars (221-295): .40
Unlisted Stars (221-295): .60
Common Player (296-382): 2.00
Inserted 2:1
Common Player (383-395): 15.00
Production 500 Sets
Pack (8): 3.00
Box (24): 60.00
1 Magglio Ordonez .40
2 Bobby Abreu .25
3 Eric Munson .15
4 Eric Byrnes .15
5 Bartolo Colon .25
6 Juan Encarnacion .15
7 Jody Gerut .15
8 Eddie Guardado .15
9 Shea Hillenbrand .15
10 Andruw Jones .50
11 Carlos Lee .15
12 Pedro J. Martinez .75
13 Barry Larkin .25
14 Angel Berroa .15
15 Edgar Martinez .25
16 Sidney Ponson .15
17 Mariano Rivera .25
18 Richie Sexson .40
19 Frank Thomas .50
20 Jerome Williams .15
21 Barry Zito .40
22 Roberto Alomar .50
23 Rocky Biddle .15
24 Orlando Cabrera .25
25 Placido Polanco .15
26 Morgan Ensberg .15
27 Jason Giambi .75
28 Jim Thome .75
29 Vladimir Guerrero .75
30 Tim Hudson .40
31 Jacque Jones .15
32 Derrek Lee .25
33 Rafael Palmeiro .40
34 Mike Mussina .40
35 Corey Patterson .15
36 Mike Cameron .15
37 Ivan Rodriguez .50
38 Ben Sheets .15
39 Woody Williams .15
40 Ichiro Suzuki 1.00
41 Moises Alou .25
42 Craig Biggio .25
43 Jorge Posada .40
44 Craig Monroe .15
45 Darin Erstad .25
46 Jay Gibbons .25
47 Aaron Guiel .15
48 Travis Lee .15
49 Jorge Julio .15
50 Torii Hunter .25
51 Luis Matos .15
52 Brett Myers .15
53 Sean Casey .25
54 Mark Prior 1.50
55 Alex Rodriguez 1.50
56 Gary Sheffield .40
57 Jason Varitek .15
58 Dontrelle Willis .40
59 Garret Anderson .25
60 Casey Blake .15
61 Jay Payton .15
62 Carl Crawford .15
63 Carl Everett .15
64 Marcus Giles .15
65 Jose Guillen .15
66 Eric Karros .15
67 Mike Lieberthal .15
68 Hideki Matsui 3.00
69 Xavier Nady .15
70 Hank Blalock .40
71 Albert Pujols 1.50
72 Jose Cruz Jr. .15
73 Randall Simon .15
74 Javier Vazquez .15
75 Preston Wilson .15
76 Danys Baez .15
77 Alex Cintron .15
78 Jake Peavy .15
79 Scott Rolen .50
80 Robert Fick .15
81 Brian Giles .25
82 Roy Halladay .25
83 Kazuhisa Ishii .15
84 Austin Kearns .40
85 Paul LoDuca .15
86 Darrell May .15
87 Phil Nevin .15
88 Carlos Pena .15
89 Manny Ramirez .50
90 C.C. Sabathia .15
91 John Smoltz .25
92 Jose Vidro .15
93 Randy Wolf .15
94 Jeff Bagwell .50
95 Barry Bonds 2.00
96 Frank Catalanotto .15
97 Zach Day .15
98 David Ortiz .15
99 Troy Glaus .40
100 Bo Hart .15
101 Geoff Jenkins .25
102 Jason Kendall .15
103 Esteban Loiaza .15
104 Doug Mientkiewicz .15
105 Trot Nixon .15
106 Troy Percival .15
107 Aramis Ramirez .15
108 Alex Sanchez .15
109 Alfonso Soriano .75
110 Omar Vizquel .25
111 Kerry Wood .50
112 Rocco Baldelli .15
113 Bret Boone .25
114 Shawn Chacon .15
115 Carlos Delgado .50
116 Shawn Green .40
117 Tim Worrell .15
118 Tom Glavine .25
119 Shigetoshi Hasegawa .15
120 Derek Jeter 2.00
121 Jeff Kent .25
122 Braden Looper .15
123 Kevin Millwood .25
124 Hideo Nomo .40
125 Jason Phillips .15
126 Tim Redding .15
127 Reggie Sanders .15
128 Sammy Sosa 1.25
129 Billy Wagner .25
130 Miguel Batista .15
131 Milton Bradley .15
132 Eric Chavez .25
133 J.D. Drew .15
134 Keith Foulke .15
135 Luis Gonzalez .25
136 LaTroy Hawkins .15
137 Randy Johnson .75
138 Byung-Hyun Kim .15
139 Javy Lopez .25
140 Melvin Mora .15
141 Aubrey Huff .15
142 Mike Piazza 1.00
143 Mark Redman .15
144 Kazuhiro Sasaki .15
145 Shannon Stewart .15
146 Larry Walker .25
147 Dmitri Young .15
148 Josh Beckett .50
149 Jae Weong Seo .15
150 Hee Seop Choi .15
151 Adam Dunn .40
152 Rafael Furcal .25
153 Juan Gonzalez .50
154 Todd Helton .50
155 Carlos Zambrano .15
156 Ryan Klesko .25
157 Mike Lowell .25
158 Jamie Moyer .15
159 Russ Ortiz .15
160 Juan Pierre .15
161 Edgar Renteria .25
162 Curt Schilling .40
163 Mike Sweeney .15
164 Brandon Webb .15
165 Michael Young .15
166 Carlos Beltran .25
167 Sean Burroughs .15
168 Luis Castillo .15
169 David Eckstein .15
170 Eric Gagne .25
171 Chipper Jones 1.00
172 Livan Hernandez .15
173 Nick Johnson .15
174 Corey Koskie .15
175 Jason Schmidt .15
176 Bill Mueller .15
177 Steve Finley .15
178 A.J. Pierzynski .15
179 Rene Reyes .15
180 Jason Johnson .15
181 Mark Teixeira .15
182 Kip Wells .15
183 Mike MacDougal .15
184 Lance Berkman .25
185 Victor Zambrano .15
186 Roger Clemens 1.50
187 Jim Edmonds .25
188 Nomar Garciaparra 1.50
189 Ken Griffey Jr. 1.00
190 Richard Hidalgo .15
191 Cliff Floyd .15
192 Greg Maddux 1.00
193 Mark Mulder .25
194 Roy Oswalt .25
195 Marlon Byrd .15
196 Jose Reyes .25
197 Kevin Brown .25
198 Miguel Tejada .25
199 Vernon Wells .25
200 Joel Pineiro .15
201 Rickie Weeks 5.00
202 Chad Gaudin 1.50
203 Ryan Wagner 1.50
204 Chris Bootcheck .50
205 Koyie Hill .50
206 Jeff Duncan 1.00
207 Rich Harden 1.00
208 Edwin Jackson .50
209 Robby Hammock .50
210 Khalil Greene .50
211 Chien-Ming Wang .50
212 Prentice Redman .50
213 Todd Wellemeyer .50
214 Clint Barmes 1.00
215 Matt Kata .50
216 Jon Leicester .50
217 Jeremy Guthrie .50
218 Chin-Hui Tsao 1.50
219 Dan Haren 1.00
220 Delmon Young 5.00
221 Vladimir Guerrero 1.00
222 Andy Pettitte .60
223 Gary Sheffield .60
224 Javier Vazquez .25
225 Alex Rodriguez 2.50
226 Billy Wagner .25
227 Miguel Tejada .60
228 Greg Maddux 1.50
229 Ivan Rodriguez .60
230 Roger Clemens 2.50
231 Alfonso Soriano 1.00
232 Miguel Cabrera .75
233 Javy Lopez .40
234 David Wells .25
235 Eric Milton .25
236 Armando Benitez .25
237 Mike Cameron .25
238 J.D. Drew .40
239 Carlos Beltran .60
240 Bartolo Colon .40
241 Jose Guillen .25
242 Kevin Brown .40
243 Carlos Guillen .25
244 Kenny Lofton .25
245 Pokey Reese .25
246 Rafael Palmeiro .75
247 Nomar Garciaparra 2.50
248 Hee Seop Choi .25
249 Juan Uribe .25
250 Nick Johnson .25
251 Scott Podsednik .25
252 Richie Sexson .60
253 Keith Foulke .25
254 Jaret Wright .25
255 Johnny Estrada .25
256 Michael Barrett .25
257 Bernie Williams .60
258 Octavio Dotel .25
259 Jeromy Burnitz .25
260 Kevin Youkilis .25
261 Derrek Lee .40
262 Jack Wilson .25
263 Craig Wilson .25
264 Richard Hidalgo .25
265 Royce Clayton .25
266 Curt Schilling .60
267 Joe Mauer .75
268 Bobby Crosby .25
269 Zack Greinke .25
270 Victor Martinez .25
271 Pedro Feliz .25
272 Tony Batista .25
273 Casey Kotchman .25
274 Freddy Garcia .25
275 Adam Everett .25
276 Alexis Rios .25
277 Lew Ford .25
278 Adam LaRoche .25
279 Lyle Overbay .25
280 Juan Gonzalez .40
281 A.J. Pierzynski .25
282 Scott Hairston .25
283 Danny Bautista .25
284 Brad Penny .25
285 Paul Konerko .25
286 Matt Lawton .25
287 Carl Pavano .25
288 Pat Burrell .40
289 Kenny Rogers .25
290 Laynce Nix .25
291 Johnny Damon .40
292 Paul Wilson .25
293 Vinny Castilla .25
294 Aaron Miles .25
295 Ken Harvey .25
296 Onil Joseph **RC** 2.00
297 Kazuhito Tadano **RC** 3.00
298 Jeff Bennett **RC** 2.00
299 Chad Bentz **RC** 3.00
300 Akinori Otsuka **RC** 2.00
301 Jon Knott **RC** 3.00
302 Ian Snell **RC** 3.00
303 Fernando Nieve **RC** 2.00
304 Mike Rouse 2.00
305 Dennis Sarfate **RC** 2.00
306 Josh Labandeira **RC** 3.00
307 Chris Oxspring **RC** 2.00
308 Alfredo Simon **RC** 2.00
309 Rusty Tucker **RC** 2.00
310 Lincoln Holdzkom **RC** 2.00
311 Justin Leone **RC** 2.00
312 Jorge Sequea **RC** 2.00
313 Brian Dallimore **RC** 2.00
314 Tim Bittner **RC** 2.00
315 Ronny Cedeno **RC** 2.00
316 Justin Hampson **RC** 2.00
317 Ryan Wing 2.00
318 Mariano Gomez **RC** 2.00
319 Carlos Vasquez **RC** 2.00
320 Casey Daigle **RC** 2.00
321 Renyel Pinto **RC** 2.00
322 Chris Shelton **RC** 4.00
323 Mike Gosling 2.00
324 Aarom Baldiris **RC** 2.00
325 Ramon Ramirez **RC** 2.00
326 Roberto Novoa **RC** 2.00
327 Sean Henn 2.00
328 Nick Regilio **RC** 2.00
329 David Crouthers 2.00
330 Greg Dobbs **RC** 2.00
331 Angel Chavez **RC** 2.00
332 Luis A. Gonzalez **RC** 2.00
333 Justin Knoedler **RC** 2.00
334 Jason Frasor **RC** 2.00
335 Jerry Gil **RC** 2.00
336 Carlos Hines **RC** 2.00
337 Ivan Ochoa **RC** 3.00
338 Jose Capellan **RC** 3.00
339 Hector Gimenez **RC** 2.00
340 Shawn Hill **RC** 3.00
341 Freddy Guzman **RC** 2.00
342 Scott Proctor **RC** 2.00
343 Frank Francisco **RC** 2.00
344 Brandon Medders **RC** 2.00
345 Andy Green **RC** 2.00
346 Eddy Rodriguez **RC** 2.00
347 Tim Hamulack **RC** 2.00
348 Mike Wuertz **RC** 2.00
349 Arnie Munoz 2.00
350 Enemencio Pacheco **RC** 2.00
351 Dusty Bergman **RC** 2.00
352 Charles Thomas **RC** 5.00
353 William Bergolla **RC** 2.00
354 Ramon Castro **RC** 2.00
355 Justin Lehr **RC** 2.00
356 Lino Urdaneta **RC** 2.00
357 Donnie Kelly **RC** 2.00
358 Kevin Cave **RC** 2.00
359 Franklyn Gracesqui **RC** 2.00
360 Chris Aguila **RC** 2.00
361 Jorge Vasquez **RC** 2.00
362 Andres Blanco **RC** 2.00
363 Orlando Rodriguez **RC** 2.00
364 Colby Miller **RC** 2.00
365 Shawn Camp **RC** 2.00
366 Jake Woods 2.00
367 George Sherrill **RC** 2.00
368 Justin Huisman **RC** 2.00
369 Jimmy Serrano **RC** 3.00
370 Mike Johnston **RC** 3.00
371 Ryan Meaux **RC** 2.00
372 Scott Dohmann **RC** 2.00
373 Brad Halsey **RC** 5.00
374 Joey Gathright **RC** 3.00
375 Yadier Molina **RC** 3.00
376 Travis Blackley **RC** 2.00
377 Steve Andrade **RC** 2.00
378 Phil Stockman **RC** 2.00
379 Roman Colon **RC** 2.00
380 Jesse Crain 2.00
381 Edwardo Sierra **RC** 2.00
382 Justin Germano **RC** 2.00
383 Kazuo Matsui **RC** 30.00
384 Shingo Takatsu **RC** 20.00
385 John Gall **RC** 15.00
386 Chris Saenz **RC** 15.00
387 Merkin Valdez **RC** 20.00
388 Jamie Brown **RC** 15.00
389 Jason Bartlett **RC** 20.00
390 David Aardsma **RC** 20.00
391 Scott Kazmir 30.00
392 David Wright 40.00
393 Dioner Navarro **RC** 30.00
394 B.J. Upton 25.00
395 Gavin Floyd 30.00

Gold Medallion

Cards (1-200): 2-3X
Inserted 1:1
All-Rookies (201-220): 3-4X
Inserted 1:8
Cards (221-295): .75-1.5X
Inserted 1:1
Cards (296-382): .75-1.25X
Cards (383-395): .25-.75X
Inserted 1:4

Platinum Medallion

Cards (1-200): 8-15X
All-Rookies (201-220): 5-10X
Production 66 Sets
Cards (221-295): 4-8X
Cards (296-382): 2-4X
Production 100 Sets
Cards (383-395): No Pricing
Production 13 Sets

Diamond Producers

NM/M

Complete Set (10): 60.00
Common Player: 4.00
Inserted 1:144
1DP Greg Maddux 8.00
2DP Dontrelle Willis 4.00
3DP Jim Thome 5.00
4DP Alfonso Soriano 6.00
5DP Alex Rodriguez 10.00
6DP Sammy Sosa 10.00
7DP Nomar Garciaparra 10.00
8DP Derek Jeter 15.00
9DP Adam Dunn 4.00
10DP Mark Prior 8.00

Diamond Producers Memorabilia

NM/M

Production 1,000 Sets
Dontrelle Willis 15.00
Alfonso Soriano 10.00
Alex Rodriguez 10.00
Sammy Sosa 10.00
Nomar Garciaparra 10.00
Derek Jeter 15.00
Mark Prior 10.00

Diamond Producers UltraSwatch

NM/M

Numbered to Jersey #.
Dontrelle Willis/35 25.00

Hitting Machines

NM/M

Common Player: 3.00
Inserted 1:12
Die-Cut: 1-2X
1HM Albert Pujols 6.00
2HM Ken Griffey Jr. 4.00
3HM Vladimir Guerrero 3.50
4HM Mike Piazza 4.00
5HM Ichiro Suzuki 5.00
6HM Miguel Cabrera 3.00
7HM Hideki Matsui 6.00
8HM Nomar Garciaparra 6.00
9HM Derek Jeter 8.00
10HM Chipper Jones 4.00

Hitting Machines Game-Used Silver

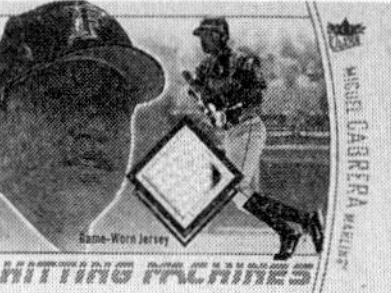

NM/M

Common Player: 8.00
Inserted 1:74
Gold: 1-30X
Production 50 Sets
Platinum: No Pricing
Production 10 Sets
JB Jeff Bagwell 10.00

MC Miguel Cabrera 10.00
AD Adam Dunn 8.00
VG Vladimir Guerrero 10.00
TH Todd Helton 10.00
CJ Chipper Jones 12.00
HM Hideki Matsui 20.00
MP Mike Piazza 12.00
AP Albert Pujols 12.00
FT Frank Thomas 10.00

HR Kings

NM/M
Complete Set (10): 35.00
Inserted 1:96
Golds: 2-3X
Production 50 Sets
1HK Barry Bonds 8.00
2HK Albert Pujols 6.00
3HK Jason Giambi 3.00
4HK Jeff Bagwell 2.00
5HK Ken Griffey Jr. 4.00
6HK Alex Rodriguez 6.00
7HK Sammy Sosa 5.00
8HK Alfonso Soriano 3.00
9HK Chipper Jones 4.00
10HK Mike Piazza 4.00

Legendary 13 Memorabilia

Numbered to 13 each.
Each player's jersey swatch on each card
Masterpiece 1/1 auto. by named player.
Inserted 1:192 Series 2 Hobby

Legendary 13 Memorabilia Autographs

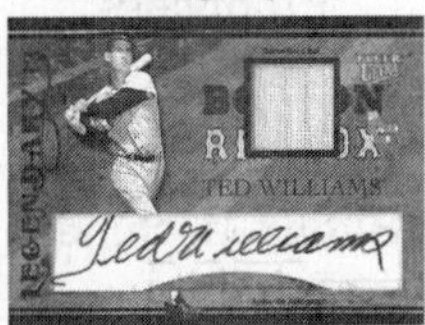

NM/M
Numbered to five each.
Masterpiece: 1/1
Numbered with "L13A-" prefix
Limited pricing due to scarcity.
TW Ted Williams 900.00

Legendary 13 Memorabilia Gold

Numbered to uniform #.
Jersey, patch or bat swatch on each.
Masterpiece: 1/1
No pricing due to scarcity.

Legendary 13 Dual Memorabilia Autographs

Numbered to three each.
Masterpiece 1/1
No pricing due to scarcity.

Legendary 13 Dual Memorabilia Gold

Numbered to 22 each.
Jersey, patch or bat swatches on each.
Platinum numbered to 10 each.
Masterpiece 1/1
Numbered with "L13D-" prefix.
No pricing due to scarcity.

Performers

NM/M
Complete Set (15): 12.00
Common Player: .50
Inserted 1:6
1UP Ichiro Suzuki 1.50
2UP Albert Pujols 2.00
3UP Barry Bonds 3.00
4UP Hideki Matsui 2.00
5UP Randy Johnson 1.00

6UP Jason Giambi 1.00
7UP Pedro J. Martinez 1.00
8UP Hank Blalock .50
9UP Chipper Jones 1.50
10UP Mike Piazza 1.50
11UP Derek Jeter 3.00
12UP Vladimir Guerrero 1.00
13UP Barry Zito .75
14UP Rocco Baldelli .50
15UP Hideo Nomo .75

Performers Memorabilia

NM/M
Common Player: 6.00
Production 500 Sets
Albert Pujols 15.00
Barry Bonds/base 15.00
Randy Johnson 8.00
Jason Giambi 8.00
Pedro J. Martinez 10.00
Hank Blalock 6.00
Chipper Jones 10.00
Mike Piazza 10.00
Derek Jeter 15.00
Vladimir Guerrero 8.00
Rocco Baldelli 10.00
Hideo Nomo 15.00

Performers UltraSwatch

NM/M
Numbered to Jersey #.
Randy Johnson/51 15.00
Pedro Martinez/45 20.00
Mike Piazza/31 25.00
Vladimir Guerrero/27 20.00

RBI Kings

NM/M
Complete Set (10): 15.00
Inserted 1:32
Golds: 3-4X
Production 50 Sets
1RK Hideki Matsui 4.00
2RK Albert Pujols 4.00
3RK Todd Helton 1.50
4RK Jim Thome 1.50
5RK Carlos Delgado 1.50
6RK Alex Rodriguez 4.00
7RK Barry Bonds 5.00
8RK Manny Ramirez 1.50
9RK Vladimir Guerrero 1.50
10RK Nomar Garciaparra 4.00

Season Crowns Autograph

NM/M
Common Player: 15.00
Production 150 Sets
Golds: No Pricing
Production 25 Sets
Rocco Baldelli 35.00
Hank Blalock 15.00
Bo Hart 30.00
Aubrey Huff 15.00
Chipper Jones 60.00
Austin Kearns 15.00
Mike Lowell 15.00
Corey Patterson 20.00
Carlos Pena 15.00
Jose Reyes 30.00
Scott Rolen 20.00
Miguel Tejada 25.00
Brandon Webb 15.00
Rickie Weeks 50.00
Dontrelle Willis 35.00

Season Crowns Memorabilia

NM/M
Common Player: 4.00
Production 399 Sets

Golds: 1-2X
Production 99 Sets
Platinums: No Pricing
Production 25 Sets
Adam Dunn 6.00
Carlos Pena 4.00
Torii Hunter 8.00
Gary Sheffield 8.00
Sean Casey 4.00
Lance Berkman 4.00
Tom Glavine 6.00
Sean Burroughs 4.00
Shawn Green 6.00
Jason Kendall 4.00
Vladimir Guerrero 10.00
Todd Helton 8.00
Tim Hudson 8.00
Troy Glaus 6.00
Larry Walker 4.00
Carlos Beltran 6.00
Hideo Nomo 10.00
Kazuhiro Sasaki 4.00
Mike Piazza 10.00
Scott Rolen 8.00
Carlos Delgado 6.00
Andruw Jones 8.00
Alfonso Soriano 10.00
Angel Berroa 4.00
Brandon Webb 6.00
Jason Giambi 8.00
Pedro J. Martinez 10.00
Manny Ramirez 8.00
Alex Rodriguez 10.00
Derek Jeter 15.00
Mark Mulder 6.00
Greg Maddux 10.00
Sammy Sosa 15.00
Jim Thome 10.00
Hank Blalock 6.00
Roberto Alomar 8.00
Omar Vizquel 5.00
Austin Kearns 8.00
Jeff Bagwell 8.00
Frank Thomas 8.00
Randy Johnson 8.00
Rocco Baldelli 12.00
Albert Pujols 15.00
Jose Reyes 8.00
Dontrelle Willis 12.00
Hideki Matsui/Base 20.00
Barry Bonds/Base 15.00
Ichiro Suzuki/Base 15.00
Chipper Jones 10.00
Roger Clemens 15.00

Strikeout Kings

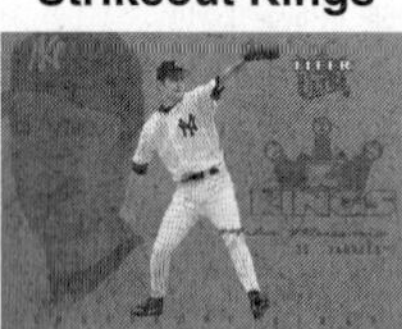

NM/M
Complete Set (10): 10.00
Common Player: .75
Inserted 1:24
Golds: 3-5X
Production 50 Sets
1KK Randy Johnson 1.50
2KK Pedro J. Martinez 1.50
3KK Curt Schilling 1.00
4KK Roger Clemens 3.00
5KK Mike Mussina 1.00
6KK Roy Halladay .75
7KK Kerry Wood 1.00
8KK Dontrelle Willis 1.00
9KK Greg Maddux 2.00
10KK Mark Prior 2.00

Turn Back the Clock

NM/M
Common Player: 1.50
Inserted 1:6
1 Roger Clemens 5.00
2 Alex Rodriguez 5.00
3 Randy Johnson 2.00
4 Pedro Martinez 2.00
5 Alfonso Soriano 2.00
6 Curt Schilling 1.50
7 Miguel Tejada 1.50
8 Scott Rolen 2.00

9 Jim Thome 2.00
10 Manny Ramirez 1.50
11 Vladimir Guerrero 2.00
12 Tom Glavine 1.50
13 Andy Pettitte 1.50
14 Ivan Rodriguez 1.50
15 Jason Giambi 2.00
16 Rafael Palmeiro 2.00
17 Greg Maddux 3.00
18 Hideo Nomo 1.50
19 Mike Mussina 1.50
20 Sammy Sosa 4.00

Turn Back the Clock Game-Used Copper

NM/M
Common Player: 8.00
Production 399 Sets
Silver: .75-1.5X
Production 199 Sets
Gold: 1-2X
Production 99 Sets
Platinum Patch: 2-5X
Production 29 Sets
RC Roger Clemens 12.00
JG Jason Giambi 10.00
TG Tom Glavine 8.00
VG Vladimir Guerrero 10.00
RJ Randy Johnson 10.00
GM Greg Maddux 12.00
PR Pedro Martinez 10.00
MM Mike Mussina 8.00
HM Hideo Nomo 8.00
RP Rafael Palmeiro 10.00
AP Andy Pettitte 8.00
MR Manny Ramirez 10.00
IR Ivan Rodriguez 8.00
SR Scott Rolen 10.00
CS Curt Schilling 8.00
AS Alfonso Soriano 10.00
SS Sammy Sosa 12.00
MT Miguel Tejada 8.00
JT Jim Thome 10.00

3 Kings

NM/M
Production 33 Sets
Mike Piazza, Roger Clemens, Alex Rodriguez 70.00
Albert Pujols, Mark Prior, Todd Helton 50.00
Alfonso Soriano, Dontrelle Willis, Albert Pujols 60.00
P. Martinez, Sammy Sosa, Albert Pujols 70.00
Randy Johnson, Albert Pujols, Todd Helton 50.00
Dontrelle Willis, Chipper Jones, Albert Pujols 60.00
Dontrelle Willis, Jeff Bagwell, Jim Thome 40.00
Greg Maddux, Jason Giambi, Manny Ramirez 50.00

2005 Ultra

NM/M
Common Player (1-200): .15
Minor Stars (1-200): .25
Unlisted Stars (1-200): .50
Common Player (201-220): 2.00
Minor Stars (201-220): 3.00
Inserted 1:4
Pack (8): 3.50
Box (24): 75.00
1 Andy Pettitte .40
2 Jose Cruz .15
3 Cliff Floyd .25
4 Paul Konerko .15
5 Joe Mauer .75
6 Scott Spiezio .15
7 Ben Sheets .25
8 Kerry Wood .50
9 Carl Pavano .15
10 Matt Morris .15
11 Kazuo Matsui .75
12 Ivan Rodriguez .40
13 Victor Martinez .15
14 Justin Morneau .25
15 Adam Everett .15
16 Carl Crawford .15
17 David Ortiz .25
18 Jason Giambi .75
19 Derrek Lee .25
20 Magglio Ordonez .25
21 Bobby Abreu .25
22 Milton Bradley .15
23 Jeff Bagwell .50
24 Jim Edmonds .25
25 Garret Anderson .25
26 Jacque Jones .15
27 Ted Lilly .15
28 Greg Maddux 1.00
29 Jermaine Dye .15
30 Bill Mueller .15
31 Roy Oswalt .25
32 Tony Womack .15
33 Andruw Jones .50
34 Tom Glavine .25
35 Mariano Rivera .25
36 Sean Casey .15
37 Edgardo Alfonzo .15
38 Brad Penny .15
39 Johan Santana .15
40 Mark Teixeira .25
41 Manny Ramirez .50
42 Gary Sheffield .40
43 Matt Lawton .15
44 Troy Percival .15
45 Rocco Baldelli .40
46 Doug Mientkiewicz .15
47 Corey Patterson .15
48 Austin Kearns .15
49 Edgar Martinez .25
50 Brad Radke .15
51 Barry Larkin .25
52 Chone Figgins .15
53 Alexis Rios .15
54 Alex Rodriguez 1.50
55 Vinny Castilla .15
56 Javier Vazquez .15
57 Javy Lopez .25
58 Mike Cameron .15
59 Brian Giles .25
60 Dontrelle Willis .25
61 Rafael Furcal .15
62 Trot Nixon .15
63 Mark Mulder .25
64 Josh Beckett .50
65 J.D. Drew .25
66 Brandon Webb .15
67 Wade Miller .15
68 Lyle Overbay .15
69 Pedro J. Martinez .75
70 Rich Harden .15
71 Al Leiter .15
72 Adam Eaton .15
73 Mike Sweeney .15
74 Steve Finley .15
75 Kris Benson .15
76 Jim Thome .75
77 Juan Pierre .15
78 Bartolo Colon .25
79 Carlos Delgado .50
80 Jack Wilson .15
81 Ken Harvey .15
82 Nomar Garciaparra 1.50
83 Paul LoDuca .15
84 Cesar Izturis .15
85 Adrian Beltre .25
86 Brian Roberts .15
87 David Eckstein .15
88 Jimmy Rollins .25
89 Roger Clemens 1.00
90 Randy Johnson .75
91 Orlando Hudson .15
92 Tim Hudson .25
93 Dmitri Young .15
94 Chipper Jones 1.00
95 John Smoltz .25
96 Billy Wagner .15
97 Hideo Nomo .25
98 Sammy Sosa 1.25
99 Darin Erstad .25
100 Todd Helton .50
101 Aubrey Huff .15
102 Alfonso Soriano .75
103 Jose Vidro .15
104 Carlos Lee .15
105 Corey Koskie .15
106 Bret Boone .25
107 Torii Hunter .40
108 Aramis Ramirez .15
109 Chase Utley .15
110 Reggie Sanders .15
111 Livan Hernandez .15
112 Jeromy Burnitz .15
113 Carlos Zambrano .15
114 Hank Blalock .40
115 Sidney Ponson .15
116 Zack Greinke .15
117 Trevor Hoffman .15
118 Jeff Kent .25
119 Richie Sexson .40
120 Melvin Mora .15
121 Eric Chavez .25
122 Miguel Cabrera .50
123 Ryan Freel .15
124 Russ Ortiz .15
125 Craig Wilson .15
126 Craig Biggio .25
127 Curt Schilling .40
128 Kazuhisa Ishii .15
129 Marquis Grissom .15
130 Bernie Williams .40
131 Travis Hafner .15
132 Hee Seop Choi .15
133 Scott Rolen .15
134 Tony Batista .75
135 Frank Thomas .15
136 Jason Varitek .50
137 Ichiro Suzuki 1.25
138 Junior Spivey .15
139 Adam Dunn .40
140 Jorge Posada .40
141 Edgar Renteria .15
142 Hideki Matsui 1.50
143 Carlos Guillen .15
144 Jody Gerut .15
145 Wily Mo Pena .15
146 Derek Jeter 2.00
147 C.C. Sabathia .15
148 Geoff Jenkins .25
149 Albert Pujols 1.50
150 Eric Munson .15
151 Moises Alou .25
152 Jerry Hairston .15
153 Ray Durham .15
154 Mike Piazza 1.00
155 Omar Vizquel .25
156 A.J. Pierzynski .15
157 Michael Young .15
158 Jason Bay .15
159 Mark Loretta .15
160 Shawn Green .25
161 Luis Gonzalez .25
162 Johnny Damon .25
163 Eric Milton .15
164 Mike Lowell .15
165 Jose Guillen .15
166 Eric Hinske .15
167 Jason Kendall .25
168 Carlos Beltran .40
169 Johnny Estrada .15
170 Scott Hatteberg .15
171 Laynce Nix .15
172 Eric Gagne .25
173 Richard Hidalgo .15
174 Bobby Crosby .15
175 Woody Williams .15
176 Justin Leone .15
177 Orlando Cabrera .15
178 Mark Prior 1.50
179 Jorge Julio .15
180 Jamie Moyer .15
181 Jose Reyes .40
182 Ken Griffey Jr. 1.00
183 Mike Lieberthal .15
184 Kenny Rogers .15
185 Mike Mussina .40
186 Preston Wilson .15
187 Khalil Greene .50
188 Angel Berroa .15
189 Miguel Tejada .40
190 Freddy Garcia .15
191 Pat Burrell .25
192 Luis Castillo .15
193 Vladimir Guerrero .75
194 Roy Halladay .25
195 Barry Zito .40
196 Lance Berkman .25
197 Rafael Palmeiro .50
198 Nate Robertson .15
199 Jason Schmidt .25
200 Scott Podsednik .15
201 Casey Kotchman 3.00
202 Scott Kazmir 4.00
203 Bucky Jacobsen 4.00
204 Jeff Keppinger 3.00
205 David Bush 2.00
206 Gavin Floyd 5.00
207 David Wright 8.00
208 B.J. Upton 3.00
209 David Aardsma 2.00
210 Jason Bartlett 3.00
211 Dioner Navarro 3.00
212 Jason Kubel 3.00
213 Ryan Howard 3.00
214 Charles Thomas **RC** 2.00
215 Freddy Guzman 2.00
216 Brad Halsey 3.00
217 Joey Gathright 2.00
218 Jeff Francis 2.00
219 Terry Tiffee 2.00
220 Nick Swisher 5.00

Gold

Cards 1-200: 1-30X
Inserted 1:1
Cards 201-220: .5-1X
Inserted 1:8

Platinum

Cards 1-200: 5-8X
Cards 201-220: 3-5X
Production 50 Sets

Follow the Leader

NM/M
Common Player: 1.50
Inserted 1:6
Copper Game-Used: 3-5X
Inserted 1:72 (Hobby Only)
Red Game-Used: 2-4X
Inserted 1:48 (Retail Only)
Gold Game-Used: 4-6X
Production 250 Sets
Platinum Game-Used: 5-8X
Production 99 Sets
Ultra Game-Used:
Numbered 26-51: 5-10X
Numbered 25 or less: No Pricing
Production to player's jersey number.
1 Roger Clemens 3.00
2 Albert Pujols 3.00
3 Sammy Sosa 2.50
4 Manny Ramirez 1.50
5 Vladimir Guerrero 2.00
6 Ivan Rodriguez 1.50
7 Mike Piazza 2.00
8 Scott Rolen 2.00
9 Ichiro Suzuki 2.50
10 Randy Johnson 2.00
11 Mark Prior 2.00
12 Jim Thome 2.00
13 Greg Maddux 2.00
14 Pedro J. Martinez 2.00
15 Miguel Cabrera 1.50

HR Kings

NM/M
Common Player: 2.50
Inserted 1:96
Ultra Kings Gold: 1-30X
Production 50 Sets
1 Jim Thome 4.00
2 David Ortiz 3.00
3 Adam Dunn 3.00
4 Albert Pujols 8.00
5 Manny Ramirez 3.50
6 Vladimir Guerrero 4.00
7 Miguel Tejada 3.00
8 Rafael Palmeiro 3.50
9 Mark Teixeira 2.50
10 Sammy Sosa 6.00
11 Frank Thomas 3.50
12 Pat Burrell 2.50
13 Adrian Beltre 2.50
14 Miguel Cabrera 3.50
15 Gary Sheffield 3.00

RBI Kings

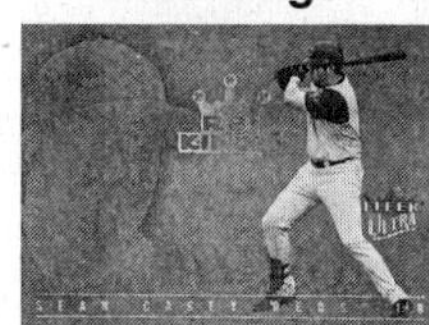

NM/M
Common Player: 2.50
Inserted 1:32
Ultra Kings Gold: 2-4X
Production 50 Sets
1 Sean Casey 2.50
2 Ivan Rodriguez 2.50
3 Mike Piazza 4.00
4 Todd Helton 3.00
5 Scott Rolen 3.50
6 Hideki Matsui 6.00
7 Gary Sheffield 2.50
8 Alfonso Soriano 3.50
9 Bobby Abreu 2.50
10 Lance Berkman 2.50
11 Miguel Tejada 2.50
12 Travis Hafner 2.50
13 Hank Blalock 2.50
14 Jeff Bagwell 3.00
15 Chipper Jones 4.00

Season Crown Autographs Copper

NM/M
Common Player: 20.00
Stated Production 199 Sets
All 199 cards not released for some players.
31 Roy Oswalt/50 25.00
80 Jack Wilson/199 20.00
125 Craig Wilson/130 20.00
157 Michael Young/150 20.00

Season Crown Autographs Gold

NM/M
Common Player: 20.00
Stated Production 99 Sets
All 99 cards not released for some players.
21 Roy Oswalt/99 20.00
50 Brad Radke/89 20.00
51 Barry Larkin/99 25.00
62 Trot Nixon/37 25.00
70 Rich Harden/41 20.00
80 Jack Wilson/99 20.00
88 Jimmy Rollins/45 25.00
121 Eric Chavez/69 20.00
125 Craig Wilson/99 20.00
157 Michael Young/99 20.00
200 Scott Podsednik/99 20.00

Season Crown Autographs Platinum

NM/M
Common Player: 25.00
Stated Production 50 Sets
All 50 cards not released for some players.
Masterpiece: No Pricing
Production One Set
20 Magglio Ordonez/50 25.00
25 Garret Anderson/50 25.00
31 Roy Oswalt/50 25.00
40 Mark Teixeira/50 30.00
50 Brad Radke/50 25.00
51 Barry Larkin/50 30.00
62 Trot Nixon/50 25.00
70 Rich Harden/50 25.00
80 Jack Wilson/50 25.00
87 David Eckstein/45 25.00
88 Jimmy Rollins/50 25.00
96 Billy Wagner/50 30.00
116 Zack Greinke/49 25.00
121 Eric Chavez/50 25.00
125 Craig Wilson/50 25.00
157 Michael Young/50 25.00
161 Luis Gonzalez/50 25.00
185 Mike Mussina/50 30.00
195 Barry Zito/50 25.00
199 Jason Schmidt/50 25.00
200 Scott Podsednik/50 25.00
201 Casey Kotchman/50 25.00

Season Crowns Copper Game-Used

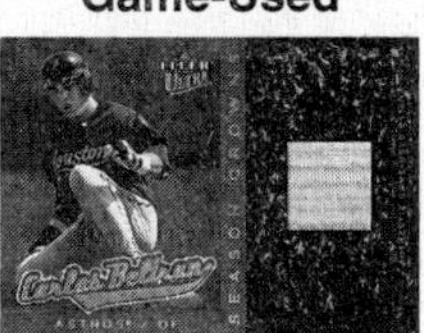

NM/M
Common Player: 5.00
Production 399 Sets
Gold: .75-1.5X
Production 99 Sets
Platinum: No Pricing
Production 25 Sets
1 Andy Pettitte/Jsy 8.00
3 Cliff Floyd/Jsy 5.00
7 Ben Sheets/Jsy 5.00
8 Kerry Wood/Jsy 8.00
11 Kazuo Matsui/Bat 15.00
13 Victor Martinez/Jsy 5.00
17 David Carr/Jsy 8.00
20 Magglio Ordonez/Bat 5.00
21 Bobby Abreu/Bat 5.00
24 Jim Edmonds/Jsy 5.00
31 Roy Oswalt/Jsy 5.00
33 Andruw Jones/Jsy 8.00
34 Tom Glavine/Bat 5.00
36 Sean Casey/Jsy 5.00
37 Edgardo Alfonzo/Bat 5.00
41 Manny Ramirez/Bat 8.00
42 Gary Sheffield/Bat 8.00
45 Rocco Baldelli/Jsy 8.00
48 Austin Kearns/Jsy 5.00
49 Edgar Martinez/Jsy 5.00
60 Dontrelle Willis/Jsy 5.00
65 J.D. Drew/Jsy 5.00
70 Rich Harden/Jsy 5.00
71 Al Leiter/Jsy 5.00
80 Jack Wilson/Bat 5.00
93 Dmitri Young/Bat 5.00
94 Chipper Jones/Bat 10.00
97 Hideo Nomo/Jsy 8.00
98 Sammy Sosa/Bat 12.00
100 Todd Helton/Bat 8.00
102 Alfonso Soriano/Bat 8.00
107 Torii Hunter/Jsy 8.00
114 Hank Blalock/Bat 8.00
119 Richie Sexson/Jsy 8.00
121 Eric Chavez/Jsy 5.00
130 Bernie Williams/Bat 8.00
135 Frank Thomas/Bat 8.00
139 Adam Dunn/Bat 8.00
142 Hideki Matsui/Bat 15.00
144 Jody Gerut/Bat 8.00
154 Mike Piazza/Bat 10.00
158 Jason Bay/Bat 8.00
162 Johnny Damon/Jsy 10.00
168 Carlos Beltran/Bat 8.00
173 Richard Hidalgo/Jsy 5.00
181 Jose Reyes/Bat 6.00
187 Khalil Greene/Jsy 15.00
191 Pat Burrell/Bat 8.00
193 Vladimir Guerrero/Bat 8.00
197 Rafael Palmeiro/Jsy 8.00

Strikeout Kings

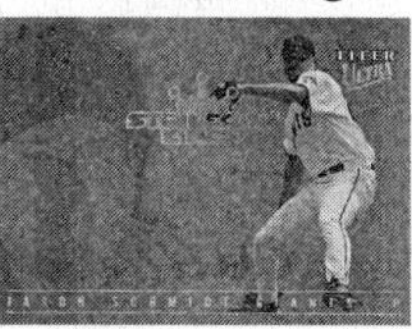

NM/M
Common Player: 2.50
Inserted 1:24
Ultra Kings Gold: 2-4X
Production 50 Sets
1 Pedro J. Martinez 3.50
2 Randy Johnson 3.50
3 Mark Mulder 2.50
4 Barry Zito 2.50
5 Roger Clemens 6.00
6 Mark Prior 5.00
7 Ben Sheets 2.50
8 Curt Schilling 2.50
9 Billy Wagner 2.50
10 Eric Gagne 2.50
11 Josh Beckett 3.00
12 Kerry Wood 3.00
13 Jason Schmidt 2.50
14 Roy Halladay 2.50
15 Greg Maddux 4.00

Ultra Kings Game-Used Gold

NM/M
Common Player: 8.00
Production 150 Sets
Ultra Swatch
Numbered 51-75: .75-1.5X
Numbered 26-50: 1-2X
Numbered 25 or less: No Pricing
Production to player's jersey number.
Platinum: No Pricing
Production 25 Sets
1 Pedro J. Martinez 12.00
2 Randy Johnson 12.00
3 Mark Mulder 8.00
4 Barry Zito 8.00
5 Roger Clemens 25.00
6 Mark Prior 20.00
7 Ben Sheets 8.00
8 Curt Schilling 8.00
9 Billy Wagner 8.00
10 Eric Gagne 8.00
11 Josh Beckett 10.00
12 Kerry Wood 10.00
13 Jason Schmidt 8.00
14 Roy Halladay 8.00
15 Greg Maddux 15.00
16 Sean Casey 8.00
17 Ivan Rodriguez 8.00
18 Mike Piazza 15.00
19 Todd Helton 10.00
20 Scott Rolen 12.00
21 Hideki Matsui 30.00
22 Gary Sheffield 8.00
23 Alfonso Soriano 12.00
24 Bobby Abreu 8.00
25 Lance Berkman 8.00
26 Miguel Tejada 8.00
27 Travis Hafner 8.00
28 Hank Blalock 8.00
29 Jeff Bagwell 10.00
30 Chipper Jones 15.00
31 Jim Thome 12.00
32 David Ortiz 8.00
33 Adam Dunn 8.00
34 Albert Pujols 25.00
35 Manny Ramirez 10.00
36 Vladimir Guerrero 12.00
37 Miguel Tejada 8.00
38 Rafael Palmeiro 10.00
39 Mark Teixeira 8.00
40 Sammy Sosa 20.00
41 Frank Thomas 10.00
42 Pat Burrell 8.00
43 Adrian Beltre 8.00
44 Miguel Cabrera 10.00
45 Gary Sheffield 8.00

Ultra 3 Kings Triple Swatch

NM/M
Common Card: 40.00
Production 33 Sets
1 Greg Maddux, Mark Prior, Kerry Wood 75.00
2 Mark Teixeira, Hank Blalock, Alfonso Soriano 40.00
3 Jeff Bagwell, Roger Clemens, Lance Berkman 60.00
4 Jim Thome, Pat Burrell, Billy Wagner 40.00
5 Gary Sheffield, Hideki Matsui, Mike Piazza 75.00
6 Scott Rolen, Chipper Jones, Adrian Beltre 40.00
7 Albert Pujols, Adam Dunn, Miguel Cabrera 50.00
8 Curt Schilling, Pedro J. Martinez, Manny Ramirez 60.00
9 Randy Johnson, Greg Maddux, Pedro J. Martinez 50.00
10 Josh Beckett, Miguel Cabrera, Ivan Rodriguez 40.00

2006 Ultra

NM/M
Complete Set (251): 60.00
Common Player: .15
Common SP (201-250): .50
Inserted 1:4
Pack (8): 3.00
Box (24): 65.00
1 Vladimir Guerrero .75
2 Bartolo Colon .15
3 Francisco Rodriguez .15
4 Darin Erstad .15
5 Chone Figgins .15
6 Bengie Molina .15
7 Roger Clemens 2.00
8 Lance Berkman .25
9 Morgan Ensberg .15
10 Roy Oswalt .25
11 Andy Pettitte .25
12 Craig Biggio .25
13 Eric Chavez .25
14 Barry Zito .25
15 Huston Street .15
16 Bobby Crosby .15
17 Nick Swisher .25
18 Rich Harden .15
19 Vernon Wells .25
20 Roy Halladay .25
21 Alex Rios .15
22 Orlando Hudson .15
23 Shea Hillenbrand .15
24 Gustavo Chacin .15
25 Chipper Jones .75
26 Andruw Jones .50
27 Jeff Francoeur .15
28 John Smoltz .25
29 Tim Hudson .25
30 Marcus Giles .15
31 Carlos Lee .25
32 Ben Sheets .25
33 Rickie Weeks .25
34 Chris Capuano .15
35 Geoff Jenkins .15
36 Brady Clark .15
37 Albert Pujols 2.00
38 Jim Edmonds .25
39 Chris Carpenter .25
40 Mark Mulder .25
41 Yadier Molina .15
42 Scott Rolen .75
43 Derrek Lee .50
44 Mark Prior .50
45 Aramis Ramirez .25
46 Carlos Zambrano .25
47 Greg Maddux 1.50
48 Nomar Garciaparra .75
49 Jonny Gomes .25
50 Carl Crawford .25
51 Scott Kazmir .25
52 Jorge Cantu .15
53 Julio Lugo .15
54 Aubrey Huff .15
55 Luis Gonzalez .15
56 Brandon Webb .25
57 Troy Glaus .25
58 Shawn Green .15
59 Craig Counsell .15
60 Conor Jackson **(RC)** .15
61 Jeff Kent .25
62 Eric Gagne .15
63 J.D. Drew .25
64 Milton Bradley .15
65 Jeff Weaver .15
66 Cesar Izturis .15
67 Jason Schmidt .15
68 Moises Alou .25
69 Pedro Feliz .15
70 Randy Winn .15
71 Omar Vizquel .15
72 Noah Lowry .15
73 Travis Hafner .40
74 Victor Martinez .25
75 C.C. Sabathia .15
76 Grady Sizemore .40
77 Coco Crisp .15
78 Cliff Lee .15
79 Raul Ibanez .15
80 Ichiro Suzuki 1.00
81 Richie Sexson .25
82 Felix Hernandez .25
83 Adrian Beltre .15
84 Jamie Moyer .15
85 Miguel Cabrera .75
86 A.J. Burnett .15
87 Juan Pierre .15
88 Carlos Delgado .50
89 Dontrelle Willis .25
90 Juan Encarnacion .15
91 Carlos Beltran .50
92 Jose Reyes .50
93 David Wright .75
94 Tom Glavine .25
95 Mike Piazza .75
96 Pedro Martinez .75
97 Ryan Zimmerman **(RC)** .15
98 Nick Johnson .15
99 Jose Vidro .15
100 Jose Guillen .15
101 Livan Hernandez .15
102 John Patterson .15
103 Miguel Tejada .25
104 Melvin Mora .15
105 Brian Roberts .15
106 Erik Bedard .15
107 Javy Lopez .15
108 Rodrigo Lopez .15
109 Jake Peavy .25
110 Mike Cameron .15
111 Mark Loretta .15
112 Brian Giles .25
113 Trevor Hoffman .15
114 Ramon Hernandez .15
115 Bobby Abreu .25
116 Chase Utley .40
117 Pat Burrell .25
118 Jimmy Rollins .40
119 Ryan Howard .75
120 Billy Wagner .15
121 Jason Bay .40
122 Oliver Perez .15
123 Jack Wilson .15
124 Zachary Duke .15
125 Robert Mackowiak .15
126 Freddy Sanchez .15
127 Mark Teixeira .50
128 Michael Young .25
129 Alfonso Soriano .50
130 Hank Blalock .25
131 Kenny Rogers .15
132 Kevin Mench .15
133 Manny Ramirez .75
134 Josh Beckett .25
135 David Ortiz .75
136 Johnny Damon .75
137 Edgar Renteria .25
138 Curt Schilling .75
139 Ken Griffey Jr. 1.50
140 Adam Dunn .50
141 Felipe Lopez .15
142 Wily Mo Pena .15
143 Aaron Harang .15
144 Sean Casey .15
145 Todd Helton .50
146 Garrett Atkins .15
147 Matt Holliday .25
148 Jeff Francis .15
149 Clint Barmes .15
150 Luis Gonzalez .15
151 Mike Sweeney .15
152 Zack Greinke .15
153 Angel Berroa .15
154 Emil Brown .15
155 David DeJesus .15
156 Ivan Rodriguez .50
157 Jeremy Bonderman .15
158 Brandon Inge .15
159 Craig Monroe .15
160 Chris Shelton .15
161 Dmitri Young .15
162 Johan Santana .50
163 Joe Mauer .50
164 Torii Hunter .25
165 Shannon Stewart .15
166 Scott Baker .15
167 Brad Radke .15
168 Jon Garland .15
169 Tadahito Iguchi .15
170 Paul Konerko .25
171 Scott Podsednik .15
172 Mark Buehrle .25
173 Joe Crede .15
174 Derek Jeter 2.00
175 Alex Rodriguez 1.50
176 Hideki Matsui 1.00
177 Randy Johnson .75
178 Gary Sheffield .40
179 Mariano Rivera .40
180 Jason Giambi .40
181 Joey Devine **RC** .50
182 Alejandro Freire **RC** .75
183 Craig Hansen **RC** 2.00
184 Robert Andino **RC** .50
185 Ryan Jorgensen **RC** .50
186 Chris Demaria **RC** .50
187 Jonah Bayliss **RC** .50
188 Ryan Theriot **(RC)** .25
189 Steve Stemle **RC** .50
190 Brian Myrow **RC** .50
191 Chris Heintz **RC** .50
192 Ron Flores **RC** .50
193 Danny Sandoval **RC** .50
194 Craig Breslow **RC** 1.00
195 Jeremy Accardo **RC** .50
196 Jeff Harris **RC** .50
197 Tim Corcoran **RC** .50
198 Scott Feldman **RC** 1.00
199 Robinson Cano .50
200 Jason Bergmann **RC** 3.00
201 Ken Griffey Jr. 4.00
202 Frank Thomas 1.00
203 Chipper Jones 2.00
204 Tony Clark .50
205 Mike Lieberthal .50
206 Manny Ramirez 2.00
207 Phil Nevin .50
208 Derek Jeter 6.00
209 Preston Wilson .50
210 Billy Wagner .50
211 Alex Rodriguez 6.00
212 Trot Nixon 1.00
213 Jaret Wright .50
214 Nomar Garciaparra 2.00
215 Paul Konerko 1.00
216 Paul Wilson .50
217 Dustin Hermanson .50
218 Todd Walker .50
219 Matt Morris .50
220 Darin Erstad .50
221 Todd Helton 1.50
222 Geoff Jenkins .50
223 Eric Chavez 1.00
224 Kris Benson .50
225 Jon Garland .50
226 Troy Glaus 1.00
227 Vernon Wells 1.00
228 Michael Cuddyer .50
229 Justin Verlander **(RC)** 2.00
230 Pat Burrell 2.00
231 Mark Mulder 1.00
232 Corey Patterson 1.00
233 J.D. Drew 1.00
234 Austin Kearns 1.00
235 Felipe Lopez .50
236 Sean Burroughs .50
237 Ben Sheets 1.00
238 Brett Myers .50
239 Josh Beckett 1.00
240 Barry Zito 1.00
241 Adrian Gonzalez .50
242 Rocco Baldelli .50
243 Chris Burke .50
244 Joe Mauer 2.00
245 Mark Prior 1.00
246 Mark Teixeira 2.00
247 Khalil Greene .50
248 Zack Greinke .50
249 Prince Fielder **(RC)** 6.00
250 Rickie Weeks 1.00
251 Kenji Johjima **RC** 20.00

Gold

Gold (1-200): 2-3X
Inserted 1:1
Gold (201-251): 2-3X
Inserted 1:13

AUTOGRAPHics

No Pricing

Diamond Producers

NM/M
Complete Set (25): 15.00
Common Player: .50

DP1 Derek Jeter 3.00
DP2 Chipper Jones 1.00
DP3 Jim Edmonds .75
DP4 Ken Griffey Jr. 2.00
DP5 David Ortiz 1.00
DP6 Manny Ramirez 1.00
DP7 Mark Teixeira .75
DP8 Alex Rodriguez 3.00
DP9 Jeff Kent .50
DP10 Albert Pujols 3.00
DP11 Todd Helton .75
DP12 Miguel Cabrera 1.00
DP13 Hideki Matsui 2.00
DP14 Derek Lee .75
DP15 Vladimir Guerrero 1.00
DP16 Miguel Tejada .75
DP17 Jorge Cantu .50
DP18 Travis Hafner .75
DP19 Pat Burrell .50
DP20 Bobby Abreu .50
DP21 David Wright 2.00
DP22 Jason Bay .75
DP23 Adam Dunn .75
DP24 Eric Chavez .50
DP25 Paul Konerko .50

Feel the Game

NM/M
Common Player: 4.00
BA Bobby Abreu 6.00
JB Josh Beckett 6.00
CB Carlos Beltran 8.00
AB Adrian Beltre 6.00
EC Eric Chavez 4.00
MC Matt Clement/SP 8.00
CD Carlos Delgado 6.00
BG Brian Giles 4.00
TG Troy Glaus 6.00
SG Shawn Green 4.00
KG Ken Griffey Jr. 20.00
VG Vladimir Guerrero 8.00
FH Felix Hernandez 8.00
DJ Derek Jeter 20.00
RJ Randy Johnson/SP 10.00
AJ Andruw Jones 8.00
CJ Chipper Jones 8.00
GM Greg Maddux 10.00
MO Magglio Ordonez 4.00
MP Mike Piazza 10.00
AP Albert Pujols 20.00
MR Manny Ramirez 10.00
JR Jose Reyes/SP 8.00
IR Ivan Rodriguez 6.00
RS Richie Sexson 6.00
AS Alfonso Soriano 8.00
MT Miguel Tejada 8.00
FT Frank Thomas/SP 8.00
PW Preston Wilson 4.00
DW David Wright 15.00

Home Run Kings

NM/M
Complete Set (15): 10.00
Common Player: .50
HRK1 Albert Pujols 3.00
HRK2 Ken Griffey Jr. 2.00
HRK3 Andruw Jones 1.00
HRK4 Alex Rodriguez 3.00
HRK5 David Ortiz 1.00
HRK6 Manny Ramirez 1.00
HRK7 Derrek Lee .75
HRK8 Mark Teixeira .75
HRK9 Adam Dunn .75
HRK10 Paul Konerko .50
HRK11 Richie Sexson .50
HRK12 Alfonso Soriano .75
HRK13 Vladimir Guerrero 1.00
HRK14 Gary Sheffield .75
HRK15 Mike Piazza 1.00

Midsummer Classic Kings

NM/M
Complete Set (10): 10.00
Common Player: .50
MCK1 Ken Griffey Jr. 2.00
MCK2 Mike Piazza 1.00
MCK3 Derek Jeter 3.00
MCK4 Roger Clemens 3.00
MCK5 Randy Johnson 1.00
MCK6 Miguel Tejada .75
MCK7 Alfonso Soriano .75
MCK8 Garret Anderson .50
MCK9 Pedro Martinez 1.00
MCK10 Ivan Rodriguez .75

RBI Kings

NM/M
Complete Set (20): 15.00
Common Player: .50
RBI1 Ken Griffey Jr. 2.00
RBI2 David Ortiz 1.00
RBI3 Manny Ramirez 1.00
RBI4 Mark Teixeira .75
RBI5 Alex Rodriguez 3.00
RBI6 Andruw Jones 1.00
RBI7 Jeff Bagwell .75
RBI8 Gary Sheffield .75
RBI9 Richie Sexson .50
RBI10 Jeff Kent .50
RBI11 Albert Pujols 3.00
RBI12 Todd Helton .75
RBI13 Miguel Cabrera 1.00
RBI14 Hideki Matsui 2.00
RBI15 Carlos Delgado .75
RBI16 Carlos Lee .50
RBI17 Derrek Lee .75
RBI18 Vladimir Guerrero 1.00
RBI19 Luis Gonzalez .50
RBI20 Mike Piazza 1.00

Strikeout Kings

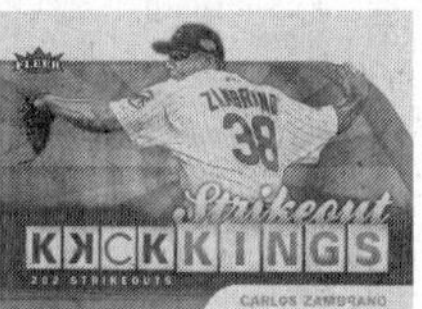

NM/M
Complete Set (10): 8.00
Common Player: .50
SOK1 Roger Clemens 3.00
SOK2 Johan Santana 1.00
SOK3 Jake Peavy .50
SOK4 Randy Johnson 1.00
SOK5 Curt Schilling 1.00
SOK6 Chris Carpenter .75
SOK7 Pedro Martinez 1.00
SOK8 Mark Prior .75
SOK9 Carlos Zambrano .50
SOK10 John Smoltz .50

Fine Fabrics

NM/M
BA Bobby Abreu 6.00
JB Josh Beckett 6.00
CB Carlos Beltran 8.00
AB Adrian Beltre 6.00
HB Hank Blalock 6.00
SB Sean Burroughs 4.00
EC Eric Chavez 4.00
RC Roger Clemens/SP 15.00
MC Matt Clement 4.00
BC Bobby Crosby 4.00
CD Carlos Delgado 6.00
JD J.D. Drew 4.00
AD Adam Dunn 8.00
SF Steve Finley 4.00
JG Jason Giambi 10.00
BG Brian Giles 4.00
TG Troy Glaus 6.00
SG Shawn Green 4.00
KH Khalil Greene/SP 8.00
KG Ken Griffey Jr. 20.00
VG Vladimir Guerrero 8.00
TH Travis Hafner 8.00
FH Felix Hernandez 8.00
RH Ramon Hernandez 4.00
RY Ryan Howard 15.00
DJ Derek Jeter 20.00
RJ Randy Johnson/SP 10.00
AJ Andruw Jones 8.00
CJ Chipper Jones 8.00
JK Jeff Kent 4.00
RK Ryan Klesko 4.00
DL Derrek Lee 8.00
GM Greg Maddux 10.00
MO Magglio Ordonez 4.00
DO David Ortiz 8.00
CP Corey Patterson 6.00
MP Mike Piazza 10.00
JP Jorge Posada 8.00
AP Albert Pujols 20.00
MR Manny Ramirez 10.00
JR Jose Reyes 8.00
BR Brian Roberts 6.00
IR Ivan Rodriguez 6.00
SR Scott Rolen 10.00
RS Richie Sexson 6.00
JS John Smoltz 8.00
AS Alfonso Soriano 8.00
SS Sammy Sosa 10.00
HS Huston Street 4.00
TX Mark Teixeira 8.00
MT Miguel Tejada 8.00
FT Frank Thomas 8.00
CU Chase Utley 15.00
VW Vernon Wells 6.00
BW Bernie Williams 6.00
WI Dontrelle Willis 6.00
PW Preston Wilson 4.00
KW Kerry Wood 6.00
DW David Wright 15.00
BZ Barry Zito 6.00

Rising Stars

NM/M
Complete Set (10): 10.00
Common Player: .50
URS1 Ryan Howard 3.00
URS2 Huston Street .50
URS3 Jeff Francoeur .75
URS4 Felix Hernandez 1.50
URS5 Chase Utley 2.00
URS6 Robinson Cano 1.00
URS7 Zachary Duke .50
URS8 Scott Kazmir 1.00
URS9 Willy Taveras .50
URS10 Tadahito Iguchi 1.00

2007 Ultra

NM/M
Complete Set (250):
Common player (1-200): .15
Common RC (201-250): 1.00
Hobby SE Pack (15): 12.00
Hobby SE Box (5): 55.00
1 Brandon Webb .25
2 Randy Johnson .75
3 Conor Jackson .15
4 Stephen Drew .25
5 Eric Byrnes .25
6 Carlos Quentin .25
7 Andruw Jones .50
8 Chipper Jones .75
9 Jeff Francoeur .50
10 Tim Hudson .25
11 John Smoltz .50
12 Ed Renteria .25
13 Erik Bedard .25
14 Kris Benson .15
15 Miguel Tejada .50
16 Nicholas Markakis .25
17 Brian Roberts .25
18 Melvin Mora .15
19 Aubrey Huff .15
20 Curt Schilling .75
21 Jonathan Papelbon 1.00
22 Josh Beckett .50
23 Jason Varitek .25
24 David Ortiz 1.00
25 Manny Ramirez .75
26 J.D. Drew .15
27 Carlos Zambrano .25
28 Derrek Lee .50
29 Aramis Ramirez .50
30 Alfonso Soriano .75
31 Rich Hill .15
32 Jacque Jones .15
33 A.J. Pierzynski .15
34 Jermaine Dye .25
35 Paul Konerko .25
36 Bobby Jenks .15
37 Jon Garland .15
38 Mark Buehrle .25
39 Tadahito Iguchi .15
40 Adam Dunn .50
41 Ken Griffey Jr. 1.50
42 Aaron Harang .15
43 Bronson Arroyo .15
44 Ryan Freel .15
45 Brandon Phillips .25
46 Grady Sizemore 1.00
47 Travis Hafner .25
48 Victor Martinez .25
49 Jhonny Peralta .25
50 C.C. Sabathia .25
51 Jeremy Sowers .15
52 Ryan Garko .15
53 Garrett Atkins .25
54 Willy Taveras .15
55 Todd Helton .50
56 Jeff Francis .15
57 Brad Hawpe .15
58 Matt Holliday .50
59 Justin Verlander .75
60 Jeremy Bonderman .50
61 Magglio Ordonez .50
62 Ivan Rodriguez .50
63 Gary Sheffield .50
64 Kenny Rogers .15
65 Brandon Inge .15
66 Anibal Sanchez .15
67 Scott Olsen .15
68 Dontrelle Willis .25
69 Dan Uggla .15
70 Hanley Ramirez 1.00
71 Miguel Cabrera 1.00
72 Jeremy Hermida .15
73 Roy Oswalt .50
74 Brad Lidge .15
75 Lance Berkman .50
76 Carlos Lee .50
77 Morgan Ensberg .15
78 Craig Biggio .50
79 Reggie Sanders .15
80 Mike Sweeney .15
81 Mark Teahen .15
82 John Buck .15
83 Mark Grudzielanek .15
84 Gary Matthews .25
85 Vladimir Guerrero 1.00
86 Garret Anderson .25
87 Howie Kendrick .25
88 Jered Weaver .50
89 Chone Figgins .25
90 Bartolo Colon .15
91 Francisco Rodriguez .25
92 Nomar Garciaparra .75
93 Andre Ethier .15
94 Rafael Furcal .25
95 Jeff Kent .50
96 Derek Lowe .25
97 Jason Schmidt .25
98 Takashi Saito .15
99 Ben Sheets .25
100 Prince Fielder 1.00
101 Bill Hall .25
102 Rickie Weeks .25
103 Francisco Cordero .15
104 J.J. Hardy .25
105 Johan Santana .75
106 Justin Morneau .50
107 Joe Mauer .25
108 Joe Nathan .15
109 Torii Hunter .25
110 Michael Cuddyer .15
111 Boof Bonser .15
112 Tom Glavine .50
113 Pedro Martinez .75
114 Billy Wagner .15
115 Jose Reyes 1.00
116 David Wright 1.00
117 Carlos Delgado .50
118 Carlos Beltran .50
119 Alex Rodriguez 2.00
120 Chien-Ming Wang 1.00
121 Mariano Rivera .50
122 Bobby Abreu .50
123 Hideki Matsui 1.50
124 Johnny Damon .75
125 Robinson Cano .75
126 Derek Jeter 2.00
127 Nick Swisher .25
128 Eric Chavez .15
129 Jason Kendall .15
130 Bobby Crosby .15
131 Huston Street .15
132 Danny Haren .15
133 Rich Harden .15
134 Mike Piazza .75
135 Chase Utley 1.00
136 Jimmy Rollins .75
137 Aaron Rowand .25
138 Jamie Moyer .15
139 Cole Hamels .50
140 Pat Burrell .25
141 Ryan Howard 1.50
142 Freddy Sanchez .15
143 Zachary Duke .15
144 Ian Snell .15
145 Jack Wilson .15
146 Jason Bay .25
147 Albert Pujols 2.00
148 Scott Rolen .50
149 Jim Edmonds .25
150 Chris Carpenter .50
151 Yadier Molina .15
152 Adam Wainwright .25
153 David Eckstein .15
154 Trevor Hoffman .15
155 Brian Giles .15
156 Adrian Gonzalez .25
157 Jake Peavy .50
158 Khalil Greene .25
159 Chris Young .25
160 Greg Maddux 1.00
161 Mike Cameron .15
162 Matt Cain .15
163 Matt Morris .15
164 Pedro Feliz .15
165 Omar Vizquel .15
166 Randy Winn .15
167 Barry Zito .25
168 Adrian Beltre .15
169 Yuniesky Betancourt .15
170 Richie Sexson .25
171 Raul Ibanez .15
172 Kenji Johjima .25
173 Ichiro Suzuki 1.50
174 Felix Hernandez .50
175 Scott Kazmir .25
176 Carl Crawford .25
177 B.J. Upton .25
178 James Shields .15
179 Rocco Baldelli .15
180 Jorge Cantu .15
181 Ty Wigginton .15
182 Mark Teixeira .50
183 Hank Blalock .25
184 Ian Kinsler .25
185 Michael Young .25
186 Vicente Padilla .15
187 Akinori Otsuka .15
188 Kenny Lofton .15
189 A.J. Burnett .15
190 Roy Halladay .25
191 B.J. Ryan .15
192 Vernon Wells .25
193 Alex Rios .50
194 Troy Glaus .25
195 Frank Thomas .75
196 Ryan Zimmerman .50
197 Michael O'Connor .15
198 Chad Cordero .15
199 Nick Johnson .15
200 Felipe Lopez .15
201 Miguel Montero 1.00
202 Doug Slaten **RC** 1.00
203 Joseph Bisenius **RC** 1.00
204 Jared Burton **RC** 1.00
205 Kevin Cameron **RC** 1.00
206 Matt Chico **(RC)** 1.00
207 Chris Stewart **RC** 1.00
208 Joe Smith **RC** 2.00
209 Zack Segovia **(RC)** 1.00
210 John Danks **RC** 2.00
211 Lee Gardner **(RC)** 1.00
212 Jeff Baker **(RC)** 2.00
213 Jamie Burke **(RC)** 1.00
214 Phil Hughes **(RC)** 4.00
215 Mike Rabelo **RC** 1.00
216 Jose Garcia **RC** 1.00
217 Hector Gimenez **(RC)** 1.00
218 Jesus Flores **RC** 1.00
219 Brandon Morrow **RC** 3.00
220 Hideki Okajima **RC** 3.00
221 Jay Marshall **RC** 1.00
222 Matt Lindstrom **(RC)** 1.00
223 Juan Salas **(RC)** 1.00
224 Juan Perez **RC** 1.00
225 Sean Henn **(RC)** 1.00
226 Travis Buck **(RC)** 1.00
227 Gustavo Molina **RC** 1.00
228 Hunter Pence **(RC)** 6.00
229 Michael Bourn **(RC)** 1.00
230 Brian Barden **RC** 1.00
231 Donald Kelly **(RC)** 1.00
232 Joakim Soria **RC** 3.00
233 Cesar Jimenez **RC** 1.00
234 Levale Speigner **RC** 2.00
235 Micah Owings **(RC)** 1.00
236 Brian Stokes **(RC)** 1.00
237 Joaquin Arias **(RC)** 1.00
238 Josh Hamilton **(RC)** 2.00
239 Daisuke Matsuzaka **RC** 5.00
240 Alejandro De Aza **RC** 1.00
241 Kory Casto **(RC)** 1.00
242 Troy Tulowitzki **(RC)** 4.00
243 Akinori Iwamura **RC** 2.00
244 Angel Sanchez **RC** 1.00
245 Ryan Braun **(RC)** 8.00
246 Alex Gordon **RC** 5.00
247 Elijah Dukes **RC** 1.00
248 Kei Igawa **RC** 1.00
249 Kevin Kouzmanoff **(RC)** 1.00
250 Delmon Young **(RC)** 1.00

Printing Plates

Production one set per color.

Gold

Gold (1-200): 2-3X
Gold RC (201-250): 1X
Inserted 1:10 Hobby

Retail

Retail (1-200): .5X
Retail RC (201-250): .5X

Iron Man

NM/M
Common Ripken (1-50): 3.00
Autograph: No Pricing
Production 10 Sets

Autographics

NM/M
Common Auto:
AG Alex Gordon/499 40.00
AH Aaron Harang/499 15.00
CH Clay Hensley/499 10.00
JA Jason Bay/499 15.00
JB Joe Blanton/499 10.00
JE Johnny Estrada/132 10.00
JS Johan Santana/173 30.00
KG Khalil Greene/499 15.00
KI Kei Igawa/199 25.00

Dual Materials

NM/M
Common Player: 5.00
Production 160 unless noted.
Gold: 1-1.5x
Production 20-75
Patch: No Pricing
Production 25 Sets
AB A.J. Burnett 5.00
AE Andre Ethier 5.00
AJ Andruw Jones 8.00
AK Austin Kearns 5.00
AL Adam LaRoche 5.00
AN Garret Anderson 5.00
AP Albert Pujols 20.00
AS Anibal Sanchez 5.00
BA Bobby Abreu 5.00
BC Bobby Crosby 5.00
BE Adrian Beltre 5.00
BG Brian Giles 5.00
BI Craig Biggio 8.00
BJ Bobby Jenks 5.00
BL Brad Lidge 5.00
BM Brandon McCarthy 5.00
BR Brian Roberts 8.00
BS Ben Sheets 5.00
DW Drandon Wobb 5.00
CA Carlos Beltran 10.00
CB Chris Burke 5.00
CC Carl Crawford 5.00
CF Chone Figgins 5.00
CH Chris Carpenter 8.00
CJ Conor Jackson 5.00
CK Casey Kotchman 5.00
CL Carlos Lee 8.00
CP Corey Patterson 5.00
CR Coco Crisp 5.00
CS C.C. Sabathia 8.00
CU Curt Schilling 10.00
DJ Derek Jeter 20.00
DL Derek Lowe 8.00
DO David Ortiz 10.00
DR J.D. Drew 5.00
DU Dan Uggla 5.00
DW David Wells 5.00
ED Jim Edmonds 5.00
ES Ervin Santana 5.00
FG Freddy Garcia 5.00
FH Felix Hernandez 10.00
GA Garrett Atkins 5.00
GJ Geoff Jenkins 5.00
GM Greg Maddux 15.00
GS Gary Sheffield 10.00
HE Todd Helton 10.00
HO Trevor Hoffman 8.00
HR Hanley Ramirez 10.00
HU Torii Hunter 8.00
IS Ian Snell 5.00
JB Jeremy Bonderman 8.00
JC Chipper Jones 10.00
JD Jermaine Dye 8.00
JG Jonny Gomes 5.00
JH J.J. Hardy 8.00
JJ Josh Johnson 5.00
JK Jeff Kent 8.00
JM Justin Morneau 10.00
JN Joe Nathan 5.00
JO Josh Beckett 15.00
JP Jorge Posada 10.00
JS James Shields 8.00
JV Jason Varitek 10.00
JW Josh Willingham 5.00
KG Khalil Greene 8.00
KW Kerry Wood 5.00
LB Lance Berkman 8.00
LE Derrek Lee 10.00
LG Luis Gonzalez 5.00
LM Lastings Milledge 8.00
LS Luke Scott 5.00
MC Matt Cain 8.00
ME Melky Cabrera 10.00
MH Matt Holliday 8.00
MI Mike Mussina 10.00
MM Melvin Mora 5.00
MO Magglio Ordonez 8.00
MR Manny Ramirez 10.00
MS Mike Sweeney 5.00
MT Miguel Tejada 8.00
MU Mark Mulder 5.00
PE Andy Pettitte 8.00
PF Prince Fielder 15.00
PJ Jhonny Peralta 5.00
RH Rich Harden 5.00

SC	Jason Schmidt	5.00
SI	Grady Sizemore	20.00
SO	Scott Olsen	5.00
TE	Mark Teixeira	10.00
TH	Travis Hafner	8.00
TW	Tim Wakefield	5.00
VG	Vladimir Guerrero	10.00
VM	Victor Martinez	8.00
VW	Vernon Wells	5.00
WI	Dontrelle Willis	5.00
ZD	Zachary Duke	5.00

Faces of the Game Materials

		NM/M
Common Jersey:		5.00
AB	Adrian Beltre	5.00
AJ	Andruw Jones	8.00
BS	Ben Sheets	8.00
CJ	Chipper Jones	8.00
CS	C.C. Sabathia	5.00
CU	Chase Utley	10.00
DJ	Derek Jeter	20.00
FR	Francisco Rodriguez	5.00
GM	Greg Maddux	10.00
HU	Torii Hunter	5.00
JB	Jason Bay	5.00
JG	Jason Giambi	8.00
KG	Ken Griffey Jr.	15.00
LG	Luis Gonzalez	5.00
MC	Miguel Cabrera	8.00
MP	Mike Piazza	8.00
MR	Mariano Rivera	8.00
OV	Omar Vizquel	5.00
TG	Tom Glavine	8.00
TH	Trevor Hoffman	5.00

Feel the Game Materials

		NM/M
Common Jersey:		5.00
AP	Albert Pujols	20.00
BA	Bobby Abreu	5.00
BR	Brian Roberts	5.00
BW	Brandon Webb	5.00
CC	Chris Carpenter	8.00
CJ	Chipper Jones	8.00
CR	Carl Crawford	5.00
CS	Curt Schilling	8.00
CU	Chase Utley	10.00
CZ	Carlos Zambrano	8.00
DJ	Derek Jeter	20.00
DW	Dontrelle Willis	5.00
EC	Eric Chavez	5.00
GS	Grady Sizemore	10.00
HR	Hanley Ramirez	8.00
IR	Ivan Rodriguez	8.00
JM	Justin Morneau	8.00
JP	Jonathan Papelbon	10.00
JR	Jose Reyes	10.00
JS	John Smoltz	8.00
KJ	Ken Griffey Jr.	15.00
KJ	Kenji Johjima	8.00
LB	Lance Berkman	5.00
LG	Luis Gonzalez	5.00
MC	Miguel Cabrera	8.00
RC	Robinson Cano	10.00
RJ	Randy Johnson	8.00
SA	Johan Santana	8.00
SC	Jason Schmidt	5.00
VG	Vladimir Guerrero	8.00

Hitting Machines Materials

		NM/M
Common Jersey:		5.00
AR	Aramis Ramirez	8.00
AS	Alfonso Soriano	8.00
BI	Craig Biggio	8.00
CB	Carlos Beltran	8.00
DO	David Ortiz	8.00
FS	Freddy Sanchez	5.00
FT	Frank Thomas	10.00
JK	Jeff Kent	5.00
JM	Joe Mauer	8.00
JT	Jim Thome	8.00
MT	Mark Teixeira	8.00
NS	Nick Swisher	5.00
TE	Miguel Tejada	5.00
TG	Troy Glaus	5.00
TH	Todd Helton	8.00

Strike Zone Materials

		NM/M
Common Player:		5.00
BZ	Barry Zito	5.00
CC	C.C. Sabathia	5.00
CZ	Carlos Zambrano	8.00
DW	Dontrelle Willis	5.00
JS	Johan Santana	8.00
JV	Justin Verlander	8.00
MM	Mike Mussina	8.00
PM	Pedro Martinez	8.00
RH	Roy Halladay	8.00
RO	Roy Oswalt	8.00

Swing Kings Materials

		NM/M
Common Player:		5.00
AD	Adam Dunn	8.00
AJ	Andruw Jones	8.00
AP	Albert Pujols	20.00
AR	Aramis Ramirez	8.00
AS	Alfonso Soriano	8.00
CB	Carlos Beltran	8.00
CL	Carlos Lee	5.00
DJ	Derek Jeter	20.00
DO	David Ortiz	8.00
FT	Frank Thomas	10.00
GS	Gary Sheffield	8.00
HE	Todd Helton	8.00
JM	Joe Mauer	8.00
JR	Jose Reyes	10.00
JT	Jim Thome	8.00
KG	Ken Griffey Jr.	15.00
MC	Miguel Cabrera	8.00
MR	Manny Ramirez	8.00
MT	Miguel Tejada	5.00
NG	Nomar Garciaparra	8.00
PB	Pat Burrell	5.00
TE	Mark Teixeira	8.00
TH	Travis Hafner	5.00
VG	Vladimir Guerrero	8.00
VW	Vernon Wells	5.00

Ultragraphs

		NM/M
Common Auto:		8.00
AK	Austin Kearns/499	10.00
AL	Adam LaRoche/499	8.00
AN	Garret Anderson/499	10.00
BB	Boof Bonser/499	10.00
GA	Garrett Atkins/499	10.00
JJ	Jorge Julio/499	8.00
JN	Joe Nathan/299	10.00
JW	Jered Weaver/499	10.00
MM	Mark Mulder/319	8.00
RW	Rickie Weeks/499	10.00
TH	Travis Hafner/499	10.00
ZG	Zack Greinke/199	8.00

Faces of the Game

		NM/M
Common Player:		.50
AB	Adrian Beltre	.50
AJ	Andruw Jones	.75
BS	Ben Sheets	.50
CJ	Chipper Jones	1.00
CS	C.C. Sabathia	.75
CU	Chase Utley	1.00
DJ	Derek Jeter	3.00
FR	Francisco Rodriguez	.50
GM	Greg Maddux	2.00
HO	Trevor Hoffman	.50
JB	Jason Bay	.75
JG	Jason Giambi	.75
KG	Ken Griffey Jr.	2.00
LG	Luis Gonzalez	.50
MC	Miguel Cabrera	1.00
MP	Mike Piazza	1.00
MR	Mariano Rivera	.75
OV	Omar Vizquel	.50
TG	Tom Glavine	.75
TH	Torii Hunter	.50

Feel the Game

		NM/M
Common Player:		.50
AP	Albert Pujols	3.00
BA	Bobby Abreu	.50
BR	Brian Roberts	.50
BW	Brandon Webb	.50
CC	Chris Carpenter	.75
CJ	Chipper Jones	1.00
CR	Carl Crawford	.50
CS	Curt Schilling	1.00
CZ	Carlos Zambrano	.50
DJ	Derek Jeter	3.00
DW	Dontrelle Willis	.50
EC	Eric Chavez	.50
GS	Grady Sizemore	1.00
HR	Hanley Ramirez	1.00
IR	Ivan Rodriguez	.75
JM	Justin Morneau	.75
JP	Jonathan Papelbon	.75
JR	Jose Reyes	2.00
JS	John Smoltz	.75
KG	Ken Griffey Jr.	2.00
KJ	Kenji Johjima	.50
LB	Lance Berkman	.50
LG	Luis Gonzalez	.50
MC	Miguel Cabrera	1.00
RC	Robinson Cano	1.00
RJ	Randy Johnson	1.00
SA	Johan Santana	1.00
SC	Jason Schmidt	.50
VG	Vladimir Guerrero	1.00

Hitting Machines

		NM/M
Common Player:		.50
AR	Aramis Ramirez	.75
AS	Alfonso Soriano	1.00
BI	Craig Biggio	.50
CB	Carlos Beltran	1.00
DO	David Ortiz	1.00
FS	Freddy Sanchez	.50
FT	Frank Thomas	1.00
JK	Jeff Kent	.75
JM	Joe Mauer	.75
JT	Jim Thome	.75
MT	Mark Teixeira	1.00
NS	Nick Swisher	.50
TE	Miguel Tejada	.75
TG	Troy Glaus	.75
TH	Todd Helton	.75

Lucky 13 Rookies Autographs

		NM/M
Quantity produced listed		10.00
Parallel:		1-1.5x
Production 99 or 199		
238	Josh Hamilton/499	30.00
241	Kory Casto/499	10.00
242	Troy Tulowitzki/499	40.00
245	Ryan Braun/499	100.00
246	Alex Gordon/499	40.00
248	Kei Igawa/299	40.00
249	Kevin Kouzmanoff/499	15.00

Lucky 13 Rookies Auto.-Retail

		NM/M
Common Autograph:		10.00
238	Josh Hamilton	30.00
241	Kory Casto	10.00
242	Troy Tulowitzki	40.00
246	Alex Gordon/SP	30.00
248	Kei Igawa/SP	40.00
249	Kevin Kouzmanoff	15.00

Stike Zone

		NM/M
Common Player:		.50
BZ	Barry Zito	.50
CC	C.C. Sabathia	.75
CZ	Carlos Zambrano	.75
DW	Dontrelle Willis	.50
JS	Johan Santana	1.00
JV	Justin Verlander	1.00
MM	Mike Mussina	.75
PM	Pedro Martinez	1.00
RH	Roy Halladay	.75
RO	Roy Oswalt	.75

Swing Kings

		NM/M
Common Player:		.50
AD	Adam Dunn	.75
AJ	Andruw Jones	1.00
AP	Albert Pujols	3.00
AR	Aramis Ramirez	.75
AS	Alfonso Soriano	1.00
CB	Carlos Beltran	.75
CL	Carlos Lee	.75
DJ	Derek Jeter	3.00
DO	David Ortiz	1.00
FT	Frank Thomas	1.00
GS	Gary Sheffield	.75
HE	Todd Helton	.75
JM	Joe Mauer	.75
JR	Jose Reyes	2.00
JT	Jim Thome	.75
KG	Ken Griffey Jr.	2.00
MC	Miguel Cabrera	1.00
MR	Manny Ramirez	1.00
MT	Miguel Tejada	.75
NG	Nomar Garciaparra	1.00
PB	Pat Burrell	.75
TE	Mark Teixeira	.75
TH	Travis Hafner	.75
VG	Vladimir Guerrero	1.00
VW	Vernon Wells	.50

Rookies Auto.

		NM/M
Production 299 Unless Noted		
Parallel:		1x
Production 99-349		
201	Miguel Montero	10.00
202	Doug Slaten	10.00
203	Joseph Bisenius	10.00
204	Jared Burton	10.00
205	Kevin Cameron	10.00
206	Matt Chico	10.00
207	Chris Stewart	10.00
209	Zack Segovia	15.00
210	John Danks	15.00
213	Jamie Burke	15.00
215	Mike Rabelo	15.00
217	Hector Gimenez	10.00
219	Brandon Morrow	25.00
221	Jay Marshall	10.00
225	Sean Henn	10.00
226	Travis Buck	10.00
227	Gustavo Molina	10.00
229	Michael Bourn	15.00
232	Joakim Soria	25.00
234	Levale Speigner	10.00
236	Brian Stokes	10.00
237	Joaquin Arias	10.00

Rookies Auto.-Retail

		NM/M
Common Autograph:		10.00
201	Miguel Montero	10.00
202	Doug Slaten	10.00
204	Jared Burton/SP	10.00
205	Kevin Cameron/SP	10.00
206	Matt Chico	10.00
207	Chris Stewart	10.00
209	Zack Segovia	10.00
215	Mike Rabelo	15.00
217	Hector Gimenez	10.00
225	Sean Henn	10.00
229	Michael Bourn/SP	15.00
234	Levale Speigner	10.00
236	Brian Stokes	10.00
237	Joaquin Arias	10.00

1989 Upper Deck Promos

In 1988 Upper Deck produced a two-card test set to be distributed as samples for the 1989 set; 18,000 of each card were produced. The cards were distributed to dealers at the 1988 National Sports Collectors Convention. Two other variations of the promo cards exist. Both variations involve differences in where the hologram was placed. Fewer than 5,000 of one of the hologram variations exist, while less than 1,000 of the third variation exist. Joyner and Buice were selected for the promo cards because of a reported investment interest in Upper Deck; they were later required to sell their interest in the card company due to their active-player status.

		NM/M
Complete Set A (2):		5.00
Complete Set B (2):		9.00
Complete Set C (2):		15.00
1a	DeWayne Buice (1/2" x 3/16" hologram at bottom)	2.00
1b	DeWayne Buice (Hologram extends to bottom edge.)	3.00
1c	DeWayne Buice (Hologram at top.)	5.00
700a	Wally Joyner (1/2" x 3/16" hologram at bottom)	2.50
700b	Wally Joyner (Hologram extends to bottom edge.)	6.00
700c	Wally Joyner (Hologram at top.)	10.00

1989 Upper Deck Show Samples

At the Nov. 26-27, 1988 Anaheim card show, Upper Deck distributed samples of its forthcoming premiere set. While card fronts are nearly identical to the same players' issued versions (except they lack the position indicator at top-right), the bbacks are blank, also lacking the hologram. All cards in this sample distribution are from the range of card numbers between 206-250, in five contiguous groups of five, with gaps of five between them. The samples are listed here in alphabetical order. Uncut sheets of the samples were reported to be widely available at the show.

	NM/M
Complete Set (25):	90.00
Common Player:	3.00
Uncut Sheet (25):	100.00
Mike Aldrete	3.00
Andy Allanson	3.00
Scott Bailes	3.00
Phil Bradley	3.00
Scott Bradley	3.00
Jay Buhner	3.00
Brett Butler	3.00
John Candelaria	3.00
Bruce Fields	3.00
Von Hayes	3.00
Rickey Henderson	15.00
Steve Jeltz	3.00
Tommy John	4.50
Ron Kittle	3.00
Bob Melvin	3.00
Lance Parrish	3.00
Willie Randolph	4.50
Harold Reynolds	3.00
Rafael Santana	3.00
Rod Scurry	3.00
Chris Speier	3.00
Greg Swindell	3.00
Kent Tekulve	3.00
Matt Williams	3.00
Paul Zuvella	3.00

1989 Upper Deck

This premiere "Collector's Choice" issue from Upper Deck contains 700 cards (2-1/2" x 3-1/2") with full-color photos on both sides. The first 26 cards feature Star Rookies. The set also includes 26 special portrait cards with team checklist backs and seven numberical checklist cards. Major 1988 award winners (Cy Young, Rookie of Year, MVP) are honored on 10 cards in the set, in addition to their individual player cards. There are also special cards for the Most Valuable Players in both League Championship series and the World Series. The card fronts feature player photos framed by a white border. A vertical brown and green artist's rendition of the runner's lane that leads from home plate to first base is found along the right margin. Backs carry full-color action poses that fill the card back, except for a compact (yet complete) stats chart. A high-number series, cards 701-800, featuring rookies and traded players, was released in mid-season in foil packs mixed within the complete set, in boxed complete sets and in high number set boxes.

		NM/M
Unopened Fact. Set (800):		80.00
Complete Set (800):		45.00
Complete Low Set (700):		40.00
Complete High Set (100):		5.00
Common Player:		.05
Low Foil Pack (15):		4.00
Low Foil Box (36):		100.00
High Foil Pack (15):		2.00
High Foil Box (36):		60.00
1	Ken Griffey Jr. **RC**	40.00
2	Luis Medina **RC**	.05
3	Tony Chance **RC**	.05
4	Dave Otto **RC**	.05
5	Sandy Alomar, Jr. **RC**	1.00
6	Rolando Roomes **RC**	.05
7	David West **RC**	.05
8	Cris Carpenter **RC**	.05
9	Gregg Jefferies	.25
10	Doug Dascenzo **RC**	.05
11	Ron Jones **RC**	.05
12	Luis de los Santos **RC**	.05
13a	Gary Sheffield **RC** ("SS" upside-down)	8.00
13b	Gary Sheffield **RC** ("SS" correct)	8.00
14	Mike Harkey **RC**	.05
15	Lance Blankenship **RC**	.05
16	William Brennan **RC**	.05
17	John Smoltz	.05
18	Ramon Martinez **RC**	.25
19	Mark Lemke **RC**	.05
20	Juan Bell **RC**	.05
21	Rey Palacios **RC**	.05
22	Felix Jose **RC**	.05
23	Van Snider **RC**	.05
24	Dante Bichette **RC**	.75
25	Randy Johnson **RC**	10.00
26	Carlos Quintana **RC**	.05
27	Star Rookie Checklist 1-26	.05
28	Mike Schooler **RC**	.05
29	Randy St. Claire	.05
30	Jerald Clark **RC**	.05
31	Kevin Gross	.05
32	Dan Firova **RC**	.05
33	Jeff Calhoun	.05
34	Tommy Hinzo	.05
35	Ricky Jordan **RC**	.05
36	Larry Parrish	.05
37	Bret Saberhagen	.05
38	Mike Smithson	.05
39	Dave Dravecky	.05
40	Ed Romero	.05
41	Jeff Musselman	.05
42	Ed Hearn	.05
43	Rance Mulliniks	.05
44	Jim Eisenreich	.05
45	Sil Campusano **RC**	.05
46	Mike Krukow	.05
47	Paul Gibson **RC**	.05
48	Mike LaCoss	.05
49	Larry Herndon	.05
50	Scott Garrelts	.05
51	Dwayne Henry	.05
52	Jim Acker	.05
53	Steve Sax	.05
54	Pete O'Brien	.05
55	Paul Runge	.05
56	Rick Rhoden	.05
57	John Dopson **RC**	.05
58	Casey Candaele	.05
59	Dave Righetti	.05
60	Joe Hesketh	.05
61	Frank DiPino	.05
62	Tim Laudner	.05
63	Jamie Moyer	.05
64	Fred Toliver	.05
65	Mitch Webster	.05
66	John Tudor	.05
67	John Cangelosi	.05
68	Mike Devereaux	.05
69	Brian Fisher	.05
70	Mike Marshall	.05
71	Zane Smith	.05
72a	Brian Holton (Ball not visible on card front, photo a ctually Shawn Hillegas.)	.75
72b	Brian Holton (Ball visible, correct photo.)	.05
73	Jose Guzman	.05
74	Rick Mahler	.05
75	John Shelby	.05
76	Jim Deshaies	.05
77	Bobby Meacham	.05
78	Bryn Smith	.05
79	Joaquin Andujar	.05
80	Richard Dotson	.05
81	Charlie Lea	.05
82	Calvin Schiraldi	.05
83	Les Straker	.05
84	Les Lancaster	.05
85	Allan Anderson	.05
86	Junior Ortiz	.05
87	Jesse Orosco	.05
88	Felix Fermin	.05
89	Dave Anderson	.05
90	Rafael Belliard	.05
91	Franklin Stubbs	.05
92	Cecil Espy	.05
93	Albert Hall	.05
94	Tim Leary	.05
95	Mitch Williams	.05
96	Tracy Jones	.05
97	Danny Darwin	.05
98	Gary Ward	.05
99	Neal Heaton	.05
100	Jim Pankovits	.05
101	Bill Doran	.05
102	Tim Wallach	.05
103	Joe Magrane	.05
104	Ozzie Virgil	.05
105	Alvin Davis	.05
106	Tom Brookens	.05
107	Shawon Dunston	.05
108	Tracy Woodson	.05
109	Nelson Liriano	.05
110	Devon White	.05
111	Steve Balboni	.05
112	Buddy Bell	.05
113	German Jimenez **RC**	.05
114	Ken Dayley	.05
115	Andres Galarraga	.05
116	Mike Scioscia	.05

No.	Player	Value
117	Gary Pettis	.05
118	Ernie Whitt	.05
119	Bob Boone	.05
120	Ryne Sandberg	1.50
121	Bruce Benedict	.05
122	Hubie Brooks	.05
123	Mike Moore	.05
124	Wallace Johnson	.05
125	Bob Horner	.05
126	Chili Davis	.05
127	Manny Trillo	.05
128	Chet Lemon	.05
129	John Cerutti	.05
130	Orel Hershiser	.05
131	Terry Pendleton	.05
132	Jeff Blauser	.05
133	Mike Fitzgerald	.05
134	Henry Cotto	.05
135	Gerald Young	.05
136	Luis Salazar	.05
137	Alejandro Pena	.05
138	Jack Howell	.05
139	Tony Fernandez	.05
140	Mark Grace	.05
141	Ken Caminiti	.05
142	Mike Jackson	.05
143	Larry McWilliams	.05
144	Andres Thomas	.05
145	Nolan Ryan	2.00
146	Mike Davis	.05
147	DeWayne Buice	.05
148	Jody Davis	.05
149	Jesse Barfield	.05
150	Matt Nokes	.05
151	Jerry Reuss	.05
152	Rick Cerone	.05
153	Storm Davis	.05
154	Marvell Wynne	.05
155	Will Clark	.05
156	Luis Aguayo	.05
157	Willie Upshaw	.05
158	Randy Bush	.05
159	Ron Darling	.05
160	Kal Daniels	.05
161	Spike Owen	.05
162	Luis Polonia	.05
163	Kevin Mitchell	.05
164	Dave Gallagher **RC**	.05
165	Benito Santiago	.05
166	Greg Gagne	.05
167	Ken Phelps	.05
168	Sid Fernandez	.05
169	Bo Diaz	.05
170	Cory Snyder	.05
171	Eric Show	.05
172	Robby Thompson	.05
173	Marty Barrett	.05
174	Dave Henderson	.05
175	Ozzie Guillen	.05
176	Barry Lyons	.05
177	Kelvin Torve **RC**	.05
178	Don Slaught	.05
179	Steve Lombardozzi	.05
180	Chris Sabo **RC**	.05
181	Jose Uribe	.05
182	Shane Mack	.05
183	Ron Karkovice	.05
184	Todd Benzinger	.05
185	Dave Stewart	.05
186	Julio Franco	.05
187	Ron Robinson	.05
188	Wally Backman	.05
189	Randy Velarde	.05
190	Joe Carter	.05
191	Bob Welch	.05
192	Kelly Paris	.05
193	Chris Brown	.05
194	Rick Reuschel	.05
195	Roger Clemens	1.60
196	Dave Concepcion	.05
197	Al Newman	.05
198	Brook Jacoby	.05
199	Mookie Wilson	.05
200	Don Mattingly	1.60
201	Dick Schofield	.05
202	Mark Gubicza	.05
203	Gary Gaetti	.05
204	Dan Pasqua	.05
205	Andre Dawson	.35
206	Chris Speier	.05
207	Kent Tekulve	.05
208	Rod Scurry	.05
209	Scott Bailes	.05
210	Rickey Henderson	1.00
211	Harold Baines	.05
212	Tony Armas	.05
213	Kent Hrbek	.05
214	Darrin Jackson	.05
215	George Brett	1.60
216	Rafael Santana	.05
217	Andy Allanson	.05
218	Brett Butler	.05
219	Steve Jeltz	.05
220	Jay Buhner	.05
221	Bo Jackson	.15
222	Angel Salazar	.05
223	Kirk McCaskill	.05
224	Steve Lyons	.05
225	Bert Blyleven	.05
226	Scott Bradley	.05
227	Bob Melvin	.05
228	Ron Kittle	.05
229	Phil Bradley	.05
230	Tommy John	.05
231	Greg Walker	.05
232	Juan Berenguer	.05
233	Pat Tabler	.05
234	Terry Clark **RC**	.05
235	Rafael Palmeiro	.75
236	Paul Zuvella	.05
237	Willie Randolph	.05
238	Bruce Fields	.05
239	Mike Aldrete	.05
240	Lance Parrish	.05
241	Greg Maddux	1.50
242	John Moses	.05
243	Melido Perez	.05
244	Willie Wilson	.05
245	Mark McLemore	.05
246	Von Hayes	.05
247	Matt Williams	.05
248	John Candelaria	.05
249	Harold Reynolds	.05
250	Greg Swindell	.05
251	Juan Agosto	.05
252	Mike Felder	.05
253	Vince Coleman	.05
254	Larry Sheets	.05
255	George Bell	.05
256	Terry Steinbach	.05
257	Jack Armstrong **RC**	.05
258	Dickie Thon	.05
259	Ray Knight	.05
260	Darryl Strawberry	.05
261	Doug Sisk	.05
262	Alex Trevino	.05
263	Jeff Leonard	.05
264	Tom Henke	.05
265	Ozzie Smith	1.50
266	Dave Bergman	.05
267	Tony Phillips	.05
268	Mark Davis	.05
269	Kevin Elster	.05
270	Barry Larkin	.05
271	Manny Lee	.05
272	Tom Brunansky	.05
273	Craig Biggio	.05
274	Jim Gantner	.05
275	Eddie Murray	1.00
276	Jeff Reed	.05
277	Tim Teufel	.05
278	Rick Honeycutt	.05
279	Guillermo Hernandez	.05
280	John Kruk	.05
281	Luis Alicea **RC**	.15
282	Jim Clancy	.05
283	Billy Ripken	.05
284	Craig Reynolds	.05
285	Robin Yount	1.00
286	Jimmy Jones	.05
287	Ron Oester	.05
288	Terry Leach	.05
289	Dennis Eckersley	.75
290	Alan Trammell	.05
291	Jimmy Key	.05
292	Chris Bosio	.05
293	Jose DeLeon	.05
294	Jim Traber	.05
295	Mike Scott	.05
296	Roger McDowell	.05
297	Garry Templeton	.05
298	Doyle Alexander	.05
299	Nick Esasky	.05
300	Mark McGwire	1.75
301	Darryl Hamilton **RC**	.05
302	Dave Smith	.05
303	Rick Sutcliffe	.05
304	Dave Stapleton	.05
305	Alan Ashby	.05
306	Pedro Guerrero	.05
307	Ron Guidry	.05
308	Steve Farr	.05
309	Curt Ford	.05
310	Claudell Washington	.05
311	Tom Prince	.05
312	Chad Kreuter **RC**	.15
313	Ken Oberkfell	.05
314	Jerry Browne	.05
315	R.J. Reynolds	.05
316	Scott Bankhead	.05
317	Milt Thompson	.05
318	Mario Diaz	.05
319	Bruce Ruffin	.05
320	Dave Valle	.05
321a	Gary Varsho **RC** (Batting righty on card back, photo actually Mike Bielecki.)	1.00
321b	Gary Varsho **RC** (Batting lefty on card back, correct photo.)	.05
322	Paul Mirabella	.05
323	Chuck Jackson	.05
324	Drew Hall	.05
325	Don August	.05
326	Israel Sanchez **RC**	.05
327	Denny Walling	.05
328	Joel Skinner	.05
329	Danny Tartabull	.05
330	Tony Pena	.05
331	Jim Sundberg	.05
332	Jeff Robinson	.05
333	Odibbe McDowell	.05
334	Jose Lind	.05
335	Paul Kilgus	.05
336	Juan Samuel	.05
337	Mike Campbell	.05
338	Mike Maddux	.05
339	Darnell Coles	.05
340	Bob Dernier	.05
341	Rafael Ramirez	.05
342	Scott Sanderson	.05
343	B.J. Surhoff	.05
344	Billy Hatcher	.05
345	Pat Perry	.05
346	Jack Clark	.05
347	Gary Thurman	.05
348	Timmy Jones **RC**	.05
349	Dave Winfield	1.00
350	Frank White	.05
351	Dave Collins	.05
352	Jack Morris	.05
353	Eric Plunk	.05
354	Leon Durham	.05
355	Ivan DeJesus	.05
356	Brian Holman **RC**	.05
357a	Dale Murphy (Reversed negative.)	20.00
357b	Dale Murphy (Corrected)	.25
358	Mark Portugal	.05
359	Andy McGaffigan	.05
360	Tom Glavine	.25
361	Keith Moreland	.05
362	Todd Stottlemyre	.05
363	Dave Leiper	.05
364	Cecil Fielder	.05
365	Carmelo Martinez	.05
366	Dwight Evans	.05
367	Kevin McReynolds	.05
368	Rich Gedman	.05
369	Len Dykstra	.05
370	Jody Reed	.05
371	Jose Canseco	.60
372	Rob Murphy	.05
373	Mike Henneman	.05
374	Walt Weiss	.05
375	Rob Dibble **RC**	.05
376	Kirby Puckett	1.50
377	Denny Martinez	.05
378	Ron Gant	.05
379	Brian Harper	.05
380	Nelson Santovenia **RC**	.05
381	Lloyd Moseby	.05
382	Lance McCullers	.05
383	Dave Stieb	.05
384	Tony Gwynn	1.50
385	Mike Flanagan	.05
386	Bob Ojeda	.05
387	Bruce Hurst	.05
388	Dave Magadan	.05
389	Wade Boggs	1.50
390	Gary Carter	1.00
391	Frank Tanana	.05
392	Curt Young	.05
393	Jeff Treadway	.05
394	Darrell Evans	.05
395	Glenn Hubbard	.05
396	Chuck Cary	.05
397	Frank Viola	.05
398	Jeff Parrett	.05
399	Terry Blocker **RC**	.05
400	Dan Gladden	.05
401	Louie Meadows **RC**	.05
402	Tim Raines	.05
403	Joey Meyer	.05
404	Larry Andersen	.05
405	Rex Hudler	.05
406	Mike Schmidt	1.60
407	John Franco	.05
408	Brady Anderson	.05
409	Don Carman	.05
410	Eric Davis	.05
411	Bob Stanley	.05
412	Pete Smith	.05
413	Jim Rice	.25
414	Bruce Sutter	.75
415	Oil Can Boyd	.05
416	Ruben Sierra	.05
417	Mike LaValliere	.05
418	Steve Buechele	.05
419	Gary Redus	.05
420	Scott Fletcher	.05
421	Dale Sveum	.05
422	Bob Knepper	.05
423	Luis Rivera	.05
424	Ted Higuera	.05
425	Kevin Bass	.05
426	Ken Gerhart	.05
427	Shane Rawley	.05
428	Paul O'Neill	.05
429	Joe Orsulak	.05
430	Jackie Gutierrez	.05
431	Gerald Perry	.05
432	Mike Greenwell	.05
433	Jerry Royster	.05
434	Ellis Burks	.05
435	Ed Olwine	.05
436	Dave Rucker	.05
437	Charlie Hough	.05
438	Bob Walk	.05
439	Bob Brower	.05
440	Barry Bonds	2.00
441	Tom Foley	.05
442	Rob Deer	.05
443	Glenn Davis	.05
444	Dave Martinez	.05
445	Bill Wegman	.05
446	Lloyd McClendon	.05
447	Dave Schmidt	.05
448	Darren Daulton	.05
449	Frank Williams	.05
450	Don Aase	.05
451	Lou Whitaker	.05
452	Goose Gossage	.05
453	Ed Whitson	.05
454	Jim Walewander	.05
455	Damon Berryhill	.05
456	Tim Burke	.05
457	Barry Jones	.05
458	Joel Youngblood	.05
459	Floyd Youmans	.05
460	Mark Salas	.05
461	Jeff Russell	.05
462	Darrell Miller	.05
463	Jeff Kunkel	.05
464	Sherman Corbett **RC**	.05
465	Curtis Wilkerson	.05
466	Bud Black	.05
467	Cal Ripken, Jr.	2.00
468	John Farrell	.05
469	Terry Kennedy	.05
470	Tom Candiotti	.05
471	Roberto Alomar	.20
472	Jeff Robinson	.05
473	Vance Law	.05
474	Randy Ready	.05
475	Walt Terrell	.05
476	Kelly Downs	.05
477	Johnny Paredes **RC**	.05
478	Shawn Hillegas	.05
479	Bob Brenly	.05
480	Otis Nixon	.05
481	Johnny Ray	.05
482	Geno Petralli	.05
483	Stu Cliburn	.05
484	Pete Incaviglia	.05
485	Brian Downing	.05
486	Jeff Stone	.05
487	Carmen Castillo	.05
488	Tom Niedenfuer	.05
489	Jay Bell	.05
490	Rick Schu	.05
491	Jeff Pico **RC**	.05
492	Mark Parent **RC**	.05
493	Eric King	.05
494	Al Nipper	.05
495	Andy Hawkins	.05
496	Daryl Boston	.05
497	Ernie Riles	.05
498	Pascual Perez	.05
499	Bill Long	.05
500	Kirt Manwaring	.05
501	Chuck Crim	.05
502	Candy Maldonado	.05
503	Dennis Lamp	.05
504	Glenn Braggs	.05
505	Joe Price	.05
506	Ken Williams	.05
507	Bill Pecota	.05
508	Rey Quinones	.05
509	Jeff Bittiger **RC**	.05
510	Kevin Seitzer	.05
511	Steve Bedrosian	.05
512	Todd Worrell	.05
513	Chris James	.05
514	Jose Oquendo	.05
515	David Palmer	.05
516	John Smiley	.05
517	Dave Clark	.05
518	Mike Dunne	.05
519	Ron Washington	.05
520	Bob Kipper	.05
521	Lee Smith	.05
522	Juan Castillo	.05
523	Don Robinson	.05
524	Kevin Romine	.05
525	Paul Molitor	1.00
526	Mark Langston	.05
527	Donnie Hill	.05
528	Larry Owen	.05
529	Jerry Reed	.05
530	Jack McDowell	.05
531	Greg Mathews	.05
532	John Russell	.05
533	Dan Quisenberry	.05
534	Greg Gross	.05
535	Danny Cox	.05
536	Terry Francona	.05
537	Andy Van Slyke	.05
538	Mel Hall	.05
539	Jim Gott	.05
540	Doug Jones	.05
541	Criag Lefferts	.05
542	Mike Boddicker	.05
543	Greg Brock	.05
544	Atlee Hammaker	.05
545	Tom Bolton	.05
546	Mike Macfarlane **RC**	.25
547	Rich Renteria **RC**	.05
548	John Davis	.05
549	Floyd Bannister	.05
550	Mickey Brantley	.05
551	Duane Ward	.05
552	Dan Petry	.05
553	Mickey Tettleton	.05
554	Rick Leach	.05
555	Mike Witt	.05
556	Sid Bream	.05
557	Bobby Witt	.05
558	Tommy Herr	.05
559	Randy Milligan	.05
560	Jose Cecena **RC**	.05
561	Mackey Sasser	.05
562	Carney Lansford	.05
563	Rick Aguilera	.05
564	Ron Hassey	.05
565	Dwight Gooden	.05
566	Paul Assenmacher	.05
567	Neil Allen	.05
568	Jim Morrison	.05
569	Mike Pagliarulo	.05
570	Ted Simmons	.05
571	Mark Thurmond	.05
572	Fred McGriff	.05
573	Wally Joyner	.05
574	Jose Bautista **RC**	.05
575	Kelly Gruber	.05
576	Cecilio Guante	.05
577	Mark Davidson	.05
578	Bobby Bonilla	.05
579	Mike Stanley	.05
580	Gene Larkin	.05
581	Stan Javier	.05
582	Howard Johnson	.05
583a	Mike Gallego (Photo on card back reversed.)	.75
583b	Mike Gallego (Correct photo.)	.05
584	David Cone	.05
585	Doug Jennings **RC**	.05
586	Charlie Hudson	.05
587	Dion James	.05
588	Al Leiter	.05
589	Charlie Puleo	.05
590	Roberto Kelly	.05
591	Thad Bosley	.05
592	Pete Stanicek	.05
593	Pat Borders **RC**	.25
594	Bryan Harvey **RC**	.05
595	Jeff Ballard	.05
596	Jeff Reardon	.05
597	Doug Drabek	.05
598	Edwin Correa	.05
599	Keith Atherton	.05
600	Dave LaPoint	.05
601	Don Baylor	.05
602	Tom Pagnozzi	.05
603	Tim Flannery	.05
604	Gene Walter	.05
605	Dave Parker	.05
606	Mike Diaz	.05
607	Chris Gwynn	.05
608	Odell Jones	.05
609	Carlton Fisk	1.00
610	Jay Howell	.05
611	Tim Crews	.05
612	Keith Hernandez	.05
613	Willie Fraser	.05
614	Jim Eppard	.05
615	Jeff Hamilton	.05
616	Kurt Stillwell	.05
617	Tom Browning	.05
618	Jeff Montgomery	.05
619	Jose Rijo	.05
620	Jamie Quirk	.05
621	Willie McGee	.05
622	Mark Grant	.05
623	Bill Swift	.05
624	Orlando Mercado	.05
625	John Costello **RC**	.05
626	Jose Gonzalez	.05
627a	Bill Schroeder (Putting on shin guards on card back, photo actually Ronn Reynolds.)	.75
627b	Bill Schroeder (Arms crossed on card back, correct photo.)	.05
628a	Fred Manrique (Throwing on card back, photo actually Ozzie Guillen.)	.75
628b	Fred Manrique (Batting on card back, correct photo.)	.05
629	Ricky Horton	.05
630	Dan Plesac	.05
631	Alfredo Griffin	.05
632	Chuck Finley	.05
633	Kirk Gibson	.05
634	Randy Myers	.05
635	Greg Minton	.05
636	Herm Winningham	.05
637	Charlie Leibrandt	.05
638	Tim Birtsas	.05
639	Bill Buckner	.05
640	Danny Jackson	.05
641	Greg Booker	.05
642	Jim Presley	.05
643	Gene Nelson	.05
644	Rod Booker	.05
645	Dennis Rasmussen	.05
646	Juan Nieves	.05
647	Bobby Thigpen	.05
648	Tim Belcher	.05
649	Mike Young	.05
650	Ivan Calderon	.05
651	Oswaldo Peraza **RC**	.05
652a	Pat Sheridan (No position on front.)	8.00
652b	Pat Sheridan (Position on front.)	.05
653	Mike Morgan	.05
654	Mike Heath	.05
655	Jay Tibbs	.05
656	Fernando Valenzuela	.05
657	Lee Mazzilli	.05
658	Frank Viola	.05
659	Jose Canseco	.60
660	Walt Weiss	.05
661	Orel Hershiser	.05
662	Kirk Gibson	.05
663	Chris Sabo	.05
664	Dennis Eckersley	.75
665	Orel Hershiser	.05
666	Kirk Gibson	.05
667	Orel Hershiser	.05
668	Wally Joyner (TC)	.05
669	Nolan Ryan (TC)	1.00
670	Jose Canseco (TC)	.30
671	Fred McGriff (TC)	.05
672	Dale Murphy (TC)	.20
673	Paul Molitor (TC)	.50
674	Ozzie Smith (TC)	.75
675	Ryne Sandberg (TC)	.40
676	Kirk Gibson (TC)	.05
677	Andres Galarraga (TC)	.05
678	Will Clark (TC)	.05
679	Cory Snyder (TC)	.05
680	Alvin Davis (TC)	.05
681	Darryl Strawberry (TC)	.05
682	Cal Ripken, Jr. (TC)	1.00
683	Tony Gwynn (TC)	.40
684	Mike Schmidt (TC)	.85
685	Andy Van Slyke (TC)	.05
686	Ruben Sierra (TC)	.05
687	Wade Boggs (TC)	.40
688	Eric Davis (TC)	.05
689	George Brett (TC)	.85
690	Alan Trammell (TC)	.05
691	Frank Viola (TC)	.05
692	Harold Baines (TC)	.05
693	Don Mattingly (TC)	.85
694	Checklist 1-100	.05
695	Checklist 101-200	.05
696	Checklist 201-300	.05
697	Checklist 301-400	.05
698	Checklist 401-500	.05
699	Checklist 501-600	.05
700	Checklist 601-700	.05
701	Checklist 701-800	.05
702	Jessie Barfield	.05
703	Walt Terrell	.05
704	Dickie Thon	.05
705	Al Leiter	.05
706	Dave LaPoint	.05
707	Charlie Hayes **RC**	.05
708	Andy Hawkins	.05
709	Mickey Hatcher	.05
710	Lance McCullers	.05
711	Ron Kittle	.05
712	Bert Blyleven	.05
713	Rick Dempsey	.05
714	Ken Williams	.05
715	Steve Rosenberg **RC**	.05
716	Joe Skalski **RC**	.05
717	Spike Owen	.05
718	Todd Burns	.05
719	Kevin Gross	.05
720	Tommy Herr	.05
721	Rob Ducey	.05
722	Gary Green **RC**	.05
723	Gregg Olson **RC**	.10
724	Greg Harris **RC**	.05
725	Craig Worthington **RC**	.05
726	Tom Howard **RC**	.05
727	Dale Mohorcic	.05
728	Rich Yett	.05
729	Mel Hall	.05
730	Floyd Youmans	.05
731	Lonnie Smith	.05
732	Wally Backman	.05
733	Trevor Wilson	.05
734	Jose Alvarez	.05
735	Bob Milacki **RC**	.05
736	Tom Gordon **RC**	.50
737	Wally Whitehurst **RC**	.05
738	Mike Aldrete	.05
739	Keith Miller	.05
740	Randy Milligan	.05
741	Jeff Parrett	.05
742	Steve Finley **RC**	.75
743	Junior Felix **RC**	.05
744	Pete Harnisch **RC**	.25
745	Bill Spiers **RC**	.05
746	Hensley Meulens **RC**	.05
747	Juan Bell	.05
748	Steve Sax	.05
749	Phil Bradley	.05
750	Rey Quinones	.05
751	Tommy Gregg **RC**	.05
752	Kevin Brown **RC**	.25
753	Derek Lilliquist **RC**	.05
754	Todd Zeile **RC**	.75
755	Jim Abbott	.05
756	Ozzie Canseco **RC**	.05
757	Nick Esasky	.05
758	Mike Moore	.05
759	Rob Murphy	.05
760	Rick Mahler	.05
761	Fred Lynn	.05
762	Kevin Blankenship **RC**	.05
763	Eddie Murray	1.00
764	Steve Searcy **RC**	.05
765	Jerome Walton **RC**	.05
766	Erik Hanson **RC**	.05
767	Bob Boone	.05
768	Edgar Martinez **RC**	.05
769	Jose DeJesus **RC**	.05
770	Greg Briley **RC**	.05
771	Steve Peters **RC**	.05
772	Rafael Palmeiro	.75
773	Jack Clark	.05
774	Nolan Ryan	2.00
775	Lance Parrish	.05
776	Joe Girardi **RC**	.30
777	Willie Randolph	.05
778	Mitch Williams	.05
779	Dennis Cook **RC**	.05
780	Dwight Smith **RC**	.05
781	Lenny Harris **RC**	.10
782	Torey Lovullo **RC**	.05
783	Norm Charlton **RC**	.15
784	Chris Brown	.05
785	Todd Benzinger	.05
786	Shane Rawley	.05
787	Omar Vizquel **RC**	2.00
788	LaVel Freeman **RC**	.05
789	Jeffrey Leonard	.05
790	Eddie Williams **RC**	.05
791	Jamie Moyer	.05
792	Bruce Hurst	.05
793	Julio Franco	.05
794	Claudell Washington	.05
795	Jody Davis	.05
796	Oddibe McDowell	.05
797	Paul Kilgus	.05
798	Tracy Jones	.05
799	Steve Wilson **RC**	.05
800	Pete O'Brien	.05

1990 Upper Deck

Tom Gordon

Following the success of its first issue, Upper Deck released another 800-card set in 1990. The cards feature full-color photos on both sides in the standard 2-1/2" x 3-1/2" format. The artwork of Vernon Wells Sr. is featured on the front of all team checklist cards. The 1990 set also introduces two new Wells illustrations - a tribute to Mike Schmidt upon his retirement and one commemorating Nolan Ryan's 5,000 career strikeouts. The cards are similar in design to the 1989 issue. The high-number series (701-800) was released as a boxed set, in factory sets and in foil packs at mid-season. Cards #101-199 can be found either with or without the copyright line on back; no premium attaches to either.

		NM/M
	Unopened Factory Set (800):	20.00
	Complete Set (800):	15.00
	Complete Low Set (700):	12.00
	Complete High Set (100):	5.00
	Common Player:	.05
	Low or High Foil Pack (15):	.50
	Low or High Foil Box (36):	12.00
1	Star Rookie Checklist	.05
2	Randy Nosek **RC**	.05
3	Tom Drees **RC**	.05
4	Curt Young	.05
5	Angels checklist (Devon White)	.05
6	Luis Salazar	.05
7	Phillies checklist (Von Hayes)	.05
8	Jose Bautista	.05
9	Marquis Grissom **RC**	.50
10	Dodgers checklist (Orel Hershiser)	.05
11	Rick Aguilera	.05
12	Padres checklist (Benito Santiago)	.05
13	Deion Sanders	.10
14	Marvell Wynne	.05
15	David West	.05
16	Pirates checklist (Bobby Bonilla)	.05
17	Sammy Sosa **RC**	5.00
18	Yankees checklist (Steve Sax)	.05
19	Jack Howell	.05
20	Mike Schmidt Retires (Mike Schmidt)	.75
21	Robin Ventura	.05
22	Brian Meyer **RC**	.05
23	Blaine Beatty **RC**	.05
24	Mariners checklist (Ken Griffey Jr.)	.50
25	Greg Vaughn	.05
26	Xavier Hernandez **RC**	.05
27	Jason Grimsley **RC**	.05
28	Eric Anthony **RC**	.05
29	Expos checklist (Tim Raines)	.05
30	David Wells	.05
31	Hal Morris **RC**	.05
32	Royals checklist (Bo Jackson)	.10
33	Kelly Mann **RC**	.05
34	Nolan Ryan 5000 Strikeouts (Nolan Ryan)	1.00
35	Scott Service **RC**	.05
36	Athletics checklist (Mark McGwire)	.50
37	Tino Martinez	.05
38	Chili Davis	.05
39	Scott Sanderson	.05
40	Giants checklist (Kevin Mitchell)	.05
41	Tigers checklist (Lou Whitaker)	.05
42	Scott Coolbaugh **RC**	.05
43	Jose Cano **RC**	.05
44	Jose Vizcaino **RC**	.10
45	Bob Hamelin **RC**	.05
46	Jose Offerman **RC**	.15
47	Kevin Blankenship	.05
48	Twins checklist (Kirby Puckett)	.40
49	Tommy Greene **RC**	.05
50	N.L. Top Vote Getter (Will Clark)	.05
51	Rob Nelson **RC**	.05
52	Chris Hammond **RC**	.15
53	Indians checklist (Joe Carter)	.05
54a	Ben McDonald **RC** (Orioles Logo)	1.00
54b	Ben McDonald **RC** (Star Rookie logo)	.25
55	Andy Benes	.05
56	John Olerud **RC**	1.00
57	Red Sox checklist (Roger Clemens)	.45
58	Tony Armas	.05
59	George Canale **RC**	.05
60a	Orioles checklist (Mickey Tettleton (#683 Jamie Weston))	1.00
60b	Orioles checklist (Mickey Tettleton (#683 Mickey Weston))	.05
61	Mike Stanton **RC**	.05
62	Mets checklist (Dwight Gooden)	.05
63	Kent Mercker **RC**	.10
64	Francisco Cabrera **RC**	.05
65	Steve Avery	.05
66	Jose Canseco	.35
67	Matt Merullo **RC**	.05
68	Cardinals checklist (Vince Coleman)	.05
69	Ron Karkovice	.05
70	Kevin Maas **RC**	.05
71	Dennis Cook	.05
72	Juan Gonzalez **RC**	2.00
73	Cubs checklist (Andre Dawson)	.10
74	Dean Palmer **RC**	.25
75	A.L. Top Vote Getter (Bo Jackson)	.10
76	Rob Richie **RC**	.05
77	Bobby Rose **RC**	.05
78	Brian DuBois **RC**	.05
79	White Sox checklist (Ozzie Guillen)	.05
80	Gene Nelson	.05
81	Bob McClure	.05
82	Rangers checklist (Julio Franco)	.05
83	Greg Minton	.05
84	Braves checklist (John Smoltz)	.05
85	Willie Fraser	.05
86	Neal Heaton	.05
87	Kevin Tapani **RC**	.05
88	Astros checklist (Mike Scott)	.05
89a	Jim Gott (Incorrect photo.)	1.00
89b	Jim Gott (Correct photo.)	.05
90	Lance Johnson	.05
91	Brewers checklist (Robin Yount)	.35
92	Jeff Parrett	.05
93	Julio Machado **RC**	.05
94	Ron Jones	.05
95	Blue Jays checklist (George Bell)	.05
96	Jerry Reuss	.05
97	Brian Fisher	.05
98	Kevin Ritz **RC**	.05
99	Reds checklist (Barry Larkin)	.05
100	Checklist 1-100	.05
101	Gerald Perry	.05
102	Kevin Appier	.05
103	Julio Franco	.05
104	Craig Biggio	.05
105	Bo Jackson	.10
106	Junior Felix **RC**	.05
107	Mike Harkey **RC**	.05
108	Fred McGriff	.05
109	Rick Sutcliffe	.05
110	Pete O'Brien	.05
111	Kelly Gruber	.05
112	Pat Borders	.05
113	Dwight Evans	.05
114	Dwight Gooden	.05
115	Kevin Batiste **RC**	.05
116	Eric Davis	.05
117	Kevin Mitchell	.05
118	Ron Oester	.05
119	Brett Butler	.05
120	Danny Jackson	.05
121	Tommy Gregg	.05
122	Ken Caminiti	.05
123	Kevin Brown	.05
124	George Brett	.85
125	Mike Scott	.05
126	Cory Snyder	.05
127	George Bell	.05
128	Mark Grace	.05
129	Devon White	.05
130	Tony Fernandez	.05
131	Don Aase	.05
132	Rance Mulliniks	.05
133	Marty Barrett	.05
134	Nelson Liriano	.05
135	Mark Carreon **RC**	.05
136	Candy Maldonado	.05
137	Tim Birtsas	.05
138	Tom Brookens	.05
139	John Franco	.05
140	Mike LaCoss	.05
141	Jeff Treadway	.05
142	Pat Tabler	.05
143	Darrell Evans	.05
144	Rafael Ramirez	.05
145	Oddibe McDowell	.05
146	Brian Downing	.05
147	Curtis Wilkerson	.05
148	Ernie Whitt	.05
149	Bill Schroeder	.05
150	Domingo Ramos	.05
151	Rick Honeycutt	.05
152	Don Slaught	.05
153	Mitch Webster	.05
154	Tony Phillips	.05
155	Paul Kilgus	.05
156	Ken Griffey Jr.	1.50
157	Gary Sheffield	.35
158	Wally Backman	.05
159	B.J. Surhoff	.05
160	Louie Meadows	.05
161	Paul O'Neill	.05
162	Jeff McKnight **RC**	.05
163	Alvaro Espinoza **RC**	.05
164	Scott Scudder **RC**	.05
165	Jeff Reed	.05
166	Gregg Jefferies	.05
167	Barry Larkin	.05
168	Gary Carter	.60
169	Robby Thompson	.05
170	Rolando Roomes	.05
171	Mark McGwire	1.50
172	Steve Sax	.05
173	Mark Williamson	.05
174	Mitch Williams	.05
175	Brian Holton	.05
176	Rob Deer	.05
177	Tim Raines	.05
178	Mike Felder	.05
179	Harold Reynolds	.05
180	Terry Francona	.05
181	Chris Sabo	.05
182	Darryl Strawberry	.05
183	Willie Randolph	.05
184	Billy Ripken	.05
185	Mackey Sasser	.05
186	Todd Benzinger	.05
187	Kevin Elster	.05
188	Jose Uribe	.05
189	Tom Browning	.05
190	Keith Miller	.05
191	Don Mattingly	.85
192	Dave Parker	.05
193	Roberto Kelly	.05
194	Phil Bradley	.05
195	Ron Hassey	.05
196	Gerald Young	.05
197	Hubie Brooks	.05
198	Bill Doran	.05
199	Al Newman	.05
200	Checklist 101-200	.05
201	Terry Puhl	.05
202	Frank DiPino	.05
203	Jim Clancy	.05
204	Bob Ojeda	.05
205	Alex Trevino	.05
206	Dave Henderson	.05
207	Henry Cotto	.05
208	Rafael Belliard	.05
209	Stan Javier	.05
210	Jerry Reed	.05
211	Doug Dascenzo	.05
212	Andres Thomas	.05
213	Greg Maddux	.75
214	Mike Schooler	.05
215	Lonnie Smith	.05
216	Jose Rijo	.05
217	Greg Gagne	.05
218	Jim Gantner	.05
219	Allan Anderson	.05
220	Rick Mahler	.05
221	Jim Deshaies	.05
222	Keith Hernandez	.05
223	Vince Coleman	.05
224	David Cone	.05
225	Ozzie Smith	.75
226	Matt Nokes	.05
227	Barry Bonds	2.00
228	Felix Jose	.05
229	Dennis Powell	.05
230	Mike Gallego	.05
231	Shawon Dunston	.05
232	Ron Gant	.05
233	Omar Vizquel	.05
234	Derek Lilliquist	.05
235	Erik Hanson	.05
236	Kirby Puckett	.75
237	Bill Spiers	.05
238	Dan Gladden	.05
239	Bryan Clutterbuck **RC**	.05
240	John Moses	.05
241	Ron Darling	.05
242	Joe Magrane	.05
243	Dave Magadan	.05
244	Pedro Guerrero	.05
245	Glenn Davis	.05
246	Terry Steinbach	.05
247	Fred Lynn	.05
248	Gary Redus	.05
249	Kenny Williams	.05
250	Sid Bream	.05
251	Bob Welch	.05
252	Bill Buckner	.05
253	Carney Lansford	.05
254	Paul Molitor	.60
255	Jose DeJesus	.05
256	Orel Hershiser	.05
257	Tom Brunansky	.05
258	Mike Davis	.05
259	Jeff Ballard	.05
260	Scott Terry	.05
261	Sid Fernandez	.05
262	Mike Marshall	.05
263	Howard Johnson	.05
264	Kirk Gibson	.05
265	Kevin McReynolds	.05
266	Cal Ripken, Jr.	2.00
267	Ozzie Guillen	.05
268	Jim Traber	.05
269	Bobby Thigpen	.05
270	Joe Orsulak	.05
271	Bob Boone	.05
272	Dave Stewart	.05
273	Tim Wallach	.05
274	Luis Aquino	.05
275	Mike Moore	.05
276	Tony Pena	.05
277	Eddie Murray	.60
278	Milt Thompson	.05
279	Alejandro Pena	.05
280	Ken Dayley	.05
281	Carmen Castillo	.05
282	Tom Henke	.05
283	Mickey Hatcher	.05
284	Roy Smith **RC**	.05
285	Manny Lee	.05
286	Dan Pasqua	.05
287	Larry Sheets	.05
288	Garry Templeton	.05
289	Eddie Williams	.05
290	Brady Anderson	.05
291	Spike Owen	.05
292	Storm Davis	.05
293	Chris Bosio	.05
294	Jim Eisenreich	.05
295	Don August	.05
296	Jeff Hamilton	.05
297	Mickey Tettleton	.05
298	Mike Scioscia	.05
299	Kevin Hickey **RC**	.05
300	Checklist 201-300	.05
301	Shawn Abner	.05
302	Kevin Bass	.05
303	Bip Roberts **RC**	.05
304	Joe Girardi	.05
305	Danny Darwin	.05
306	Mike Heath	.05
307	Mike Macfarlane	.05
308	Ed Whitson	.05
309	Tracy Jones	.05
310	Scott Fletcher	.05
311	Darnell Coles	.05
312	Mike Brumley	.05
313	Bill Swift	.05
314	Charlie Hough	.05
315	Jim Presley	.05
316	Luis Polonia	.05
317	Mike Morgan	.05
318	Lee Guetterman	.05
319	Jose Oquendo	.05
320	Wayne Tollenson	.05
321	Jody Reed	.05
322	Damon Berryhill	.05
323	Roger Clemens	.85
324	Ryne Sandberg	.75
325	Benito Santiago	.05
326	Bret Saberhagen	.05
327	Lou Whitaker	.05
328	Dave Gallagher	.05
329	Mike Pagliarulo	.05
330	Doyle Alexander	.05
331	Jeffrey Leonard	.05
332	Torey Lovullo	.05
333	Pete Incaviglia	.05
334	Rickey Henderson	.60
335	Rafael Palmeiro	.50
336	Ken Hill **RC**	.05
337	Dave Winfield	.60
338	Alfredo Griffin	.05
339	Andy Hawkins	.05
340	Ted Power	.05
341	Steve Wilson	.05
342	Jack Clark	.05
343	Ellis Burks	.05
344	Tony Gwynn	.75
345	Jerome Walton	.05
346	Roberto Alomar	.20
347	Carlos Martinez **RC**	.05
348	Chet Lemon	.05
349	Willie Wilson	.05
350	Greg Walker	.05
351	Tom Bolton	.05
352	German Gonzalez **RC**	.05
353	Harold Baines	.05
354	Mike Greenwell	.05
355	Ruben Sierra	.05
356	Andres Galarraga	.05
357	Andre Dawson	.25
358	Jeff Brantley **RC**	.05
359	Mike Bielecki	.05
360	Ken Oberkfell	.05
361	Kurt Stillwell	.05
362	Brian Holman	.05
363	Kevin Seitzer	.05
364	Alvin Davis	.05
365	Tom Gordon	.05
366	Bobby Bonilla	.05
367	Carlton Fisk	.60
368	Steve Carter **RC**	.05
369	Joel Skinner	.05
370	John Cangelosi	.05
371	Cecil Espy	.05
372	Gary Wayne **RC**	.05
373	Jim Rice	.20
374	Mike Dyer **RC**	.05
375	Joe Carter	.05
376	Dwight Smith	.05
377	John Wetteland **RC**	.15
378	Ernie Riles	.05
379	Otis Nixon	.05
380	Vance Law	.05
381	Dave Bergman	.05
382	Frank White	.05
383	Scott Bradley	.05
384	Israel Sanchez	.05
385	Gary Pettis	.05
386	Donn Pall **RC**	.05
387	John Smiley	.05
388	Tom Candiotti	.05
389	Junior Ortiz	.05
390	Steve Lyons	.05
391	Brian Harper	.05
392	Fred Manrique	.05
393	Lee Smith	.05
394	Jeff Kunkel	.05
395	Claudell Washington	.05
396	John Tudor	.05
397	Terry Kennedy	.05
398	Lloyd McClendon	.05
399	Craig Lefferts	.05
400	Checklist 301-400	.05
401	Keith Moreland	.05
402	Rich Gedman	.05
403	Jeff Robinson	.05
404	Randy Ready	.05
405	Rick Cerone	.05
406	Jeff Blauser	.05
407	Larry Andersen	.05
408	Joe Boever	.05
409	Felix Fermin	.05
410	Glenn Wilson	.05
411	Rex Hudler	.05
412	Mark Grant	.05
413	Dennis Martinez	.05
414	Darrin Jackson	.05
415	Mike Aldrete	.05
416	Roger McDowell	.05
417	Jeff Reardon	.05
418	Darren Daulton	.05
419	Tim Laudner	.05
420	Don Carman	.05
421	Lloyd Moseby	.05
422	Doug Drabek	.05
423	Lenny Harris	.05
424	Jose Lind	.05
425	Dave Johnson **RC**	.05
426	Jerry Browne	.05
427	Eric Yelding **RC**	.05
428	Brad Komminsk **RC**	.05
429	Jody Davis	.05
430	Mariano Duncan **RC**	.05
431	Mark Davis	.05
432	Nelson Santovenia	.05
433	Bruce Hurst	.05
434	Jeff Huson **RC**	.05
435	Chris James	.05
436	Mark Guthrie **RC**	.05
437	Charlie Hayes **RC**	.05
438	Shane Rawley	.05
439	Dickie Thon	.05
440	Juan Berenguer	.05
441	Kevin Romine	.05
442	Bill Landrum	.05
443	Todd Frohwirth	.05
444	Craig Worthington	.05
445	Fernando Valenzuela	.05
446	Albert Belle	.05
447	Ed Whited **RC**	.05
448	Dave Smith	.05
449	Dave Clark	.05
450	Juan Agosto	.05
451	Dave Valle	.05
452	Kent Hrbek	.05
453	Von Hayes	.05
454	Gary Gaetti	.05
455	Greg Briley	.05
456	Glenn Braggs	.05
457	Kirt Manwaring	.05
458	Mel Hall	.05
459	Brook Jacoby	.05
460	Pat Sheridan	.05
461	Rob Murphy	.05
462	Jimmy Key	.05
463	Nick Esasky	.05
464	Rob Ducey	.05
465	Carlos Quintana	.05
466	Larry Walker **RC**	1.00
467	Todd Worrell	.05
468	Kevin Gross	.05
469	Terry Pendleton	.05
470	Dave Martinez	.05
471	Gene Larkin	.05
472	Len Dykstra	.05
473	Barry Lyons	.05
474	Terry Mulholland **RC**	.05
475	Chip Hale **RC**	.05
476	Jesse Barfield	.05
477	Dan Plesac	.05
478a	Scott Garrelts (Photo actually Bill Bathe.)	1.00
478b	Scott Garrelts (Correct photo.)	.05
479	Dave Righetti	.05
480	Gus Polidor **RC**	.05
481	Mookie Wilson	.05
482	Luis Rivera	.05
483	Mike Flanagan	.05
484	Dennis "Oil Can" Boyd	.05
485	John Cerutti	.05
486	John Costello	.05
487	Pascual Perez	.05
488	Tommy Herr	.05
489	Tom Foley	.05
490	Curt Ford	.05
491	Steve Lake	.05
492	Tim Teufel	.05
493	Randy Bush	.05
494	Mike Jackson	.05
495	Steve Jeltz	.05
496	Paul Gibson	.05
497	Steve Balboni	.05
498	Bud Black	.05
499	Dale Sveum	.05
500	Checklist 401-500	.05
501	Timmy Jones	.05
502	Mark Portugal	.05
503	Ivan Calderon	.05
504	Rick Rhoden	.05
505	Willie McGee	.05
506	Kirk McCaskill	.05
507	Dave LaPoint	.05
508	Jay Howell	.05
509	Johnny Ray	.05
510	Dave Anderson	.05
511	Chuck Crim	.05
512	Joe Hesketh	.05
513	Dennis Eckersley	.40
514	Greg Brock	.05
515	Tim Burke **RC**	.05
516	Frank Tanana	.05
517	Jay Bell	.05
518	Guillermo Hernandez	.05
519	Randy Kramer **RC**	.05
520	Charles Hudson	.05
521	Jim Corsi **RC**	.05
522	Steve Rosenberg	.05
523	Cris Carpenter	.05
524	Matt Winters **RC**	.05
525	Melido Perez	.05
526	Chris Gwynn **RC**	.05
527	Bert Blyleven	.05
528	Chuck Cary **RC**	.05
529	Daryl Boston	.05
530	Dale Mohorcic	.05
531	Geronimo Berroa **RC**	.05
532	Edgar Martinez	.05
533	Dale Murphy	.20
534	Jay Buhner	.05
535	John Smoltz	.05
536	Andy Van Slyke	.05
537	Mike Henneman **RC**	.05
538	Miguel Garcia **RC**	.05
539	Frank Williams **RC**	.05
540	R.J. Reynolds	.05
541	Shawn Hillegas **RC**	.05
542	Walt Weiss	.05
543	Greg Hibbard **RC**	.05
544	Nolan Ryan	2.00
545	Todd Zeile	.05
546	Hensley Meulens	.05
547	Tim Belcher **RC**	.05
548	Mike Witt	.05
549	Greg Cadaret **RC**	.05
550	Franklin Stubbs	.05
551	Tony Castillo **RC**	.05
552	Jeff Robinson	.05
553	Steve Olin **RC**	.05
554	Alan Trammell	.05
555	Wade Boggs	.75
556	Will Clark	.05
557	Jeff King	.05
558	Mike Fitzgerald	.05
559	Ken Howell **RC**	.05
560	Bob Kipper	.05
561	Scott Bankhead **RC**	.05
562a	Jeff Innis **RC** (Photo actually David West.)	1.00
562b	Jeff Innis **RC** (Correct photo.)	.05
563	Randy Johnson	.60
564	Wally Whithurst **RC**	.05
565	Gene Harris **RC**	.05
566	Norm Charlton **RC**	.05
567	Robin Yount	.60
568	Joe Oliver **RC**	.05
569	Mark Parent	.05
570	John Farrell **RC**	.05
571	Tom Glavine	.20
572	Rod Nichols **RC**	.05
573	Jack Morris	.05
574	Greg Swindell **RC**	.05
575	Steve Searcy **RC**	.05
576	Ricky Jordan **RC**	.05
577	Matt Williams	.05
578	Mike LaValliere **RC**	.05
579	Bryn Smith	.05
580	Bruce Ruffin **RC**	.05
581	Randy Myers	.05
582	Rick Wrona **RC**	.05
583	Juan Samuel	.05
584	Les Lancaster **RC**	.05
585	Jeff Musselman	.05
586	Rob Dibble **RC**	.05
587	Eric Show	.05
588	Jesse Orosco	.05
589	Herm Winningham	.05
590	Andy Allanson	.05
591	Dion James	.05
592	Carmelo Martinez **RC**	.05
593	Luis Quinones **RC**	.05
594	Dennis Rasmussen **RC**	.05
595	Rich Yett	.05
596	Bob Walk **RC**	.05
597a	Andy McGaffigan (Player #48, photo actually Rich Thompson.)	.75

597b	Andy McGaffigan (Player #27, correct photo.)	.05
598	Billy Hatcher **RC**	.05
599	Bob Knepper	.05
600	Checklist 501-600	.05
601	Joey Cora **RC**	.05
602	Steve Finley **RC**	.20
603	Kal Daniels	.05
604	Gregg Olson	.05
605	Dave Steib	.05
606	Kenny Rogers **RC**	.05
607	Zane Smith	.05
608	Bob Geren **RC**	.05
609	Chad Kreuter	.05
610	Mike Smithson **RC**	.05
611	Jeff Wetherby **RC**	.05
612	Gary Mielke **RC**	.05
613	Pete Smith	.05
614	Jack Daugherty **RC**	.05
615	Lance McCullers	.05
616	Don Robinson **RC**	.05
617	Jose Guzman	.05
618	Steve Bedrosian **RC**	.05
619	Jamie Moyer	.05
620	Atlee Hammaker **RC**	.05
621	Rick Luecken **RC**	.05
622	Greg W. Harris **RC**	.05
623	Pete Harnisch	.05
624	Jerald Clark **RC**	.05
625	Jack McDowell	.05
626	Frank Viola	.05
627	Ted Higuera	.05
628	Marty Pevey **RC**	.05
629	Bill Wegman	.05
630	Eric Plunk **RC**	.05
631	Drew Hall	.05
632	Doug Jones **RC**	.05
633	Geno Petralli	.05
634	Jose Alvarez **RC**	.05
635	Bob Milacki	.05
636	Bobby Witt **RC**	.05
637	Trevor Wilson	.05
638	Jeff Russell **RC**	.05
639	Mike Krukow	.05
640	Rick Leach **RC**	.05
641	Dave Schmidt	.05
642	Terry Leach **RC**	.05
643	Calvin Schiraldi	.05
644	Bob Melvin **RC**	.05
645	Jim Abbott	.05
646	Jaime Navarro **RC**	.05
647	Mark Langston	.05
648	Juan Nieves **RC**	.05
649	Damaso Garcia	.05
650	Charlie O'Brien **RC**	.05
651	Eric King	.05
652	Mike Boddicker	.05
653	Duane Ward	.05
654	Bob Stanley	.05
655	Sandy Alomar, Jr.	.05
656	Danny Tartabull	.05
657	Randy McCament	.05
658	Charlie Leibrandt	.05
659	Dan Quisenberry	.05
660	Paul Assenmacher **RC**	.05
661	Walt Terrell	.05
662	Tim Leary	.05
663	Randy Milligan	.05
664	Bo Diaz **RC**	.05
665	Mark Lemke	.05
666	Jose Gonzalez **RC**	.05
667	Chuck Finley	.05
668	John Kruk	.05
669	Dick Schofield	.05
670	Tim Crews	.05
671	John Dopson	.05
672	John Orton **RC**	.05
673	Eric Hetzel **RC**	.05
674	Lance Parrish	.05
675	Ramon Martinez	.05
676	Mark Gubicza	.05
677	Greg Litton	.05
678	Greg Mathews	.05
679	Dave Dravecky	.05
680	Steve Farr **RC**	.05
681	Mike Devereaux	.05
682	Ken Griffey Sr.	.05
683a	Jamie Weston **RC** (First name incorrect.)	1.00
683b	Mickey Weston **RC** (Corrected)	.05
684	Jack Armstrong	.05
685	Steve Buechele	.05
686	Bryan Harvey	.05
687	Lance Blankenship	.05
688	Dante Bichette	.05
689	Todd Burns **RC**	.05
690	Dan Petry	.05
691	Kent Anderson **RC**	.05
692	Todd Stottlemyre	.05
693	Wally Joyner	.05
694	Mike Rochford **RC**	.05
695	Floyd Bannister	.05
696	Rick Reuschel	.05
697	Jose DeLeon **RC**	.05
698	Jeff Montgomery	.05
699	Kelly Downs	.05
700a	Checklist 601-700 (#683 Jamie Weston)	.05
700b	Checklist 601-700 (# 683 Mickey Weston)	.05
701	Jim Gott	.05
702	"Rookie Threats" (Delino DeShields, Larry Walker, Marquis Grissom)	.25
703	Alejandro Pena	.05
704	Willie Randolph	.05
705	Tim Leary	.05
706	Chuck McElroy **RC**	.05
707	Gerald Perry **RC**	.05
708	Tom Brunansky	.05
709	John Franco	.05
710	Mark Davis	.05
711	Dave Justice **RC**	1.50
712	Storm Davis	.05
713	Scott Ruskin **RC**	.05
714	Glenn Braggs	.05
715	Kevin Bearse **RC**	.05
716	Jose Nunez **RC**	.05
717	Tim Layana **RC**	.05
718	Greg Myers **RC**	.05
719	Pete O'Brien	.05
720	John Candelaria	.05
721	Craig Grebeck	.05
722	Shawn Boskie **RC**	.05
723	Jim Leyritz **RC**	.10
724	Bill Sampen **RC**	.05
725	Scott Radinsky **RC**	.05
726	Todd Hundley **RC**	.25
727	Scott Hemond **RC**	.05
728	Lenny Webster **RC**	.05
729	Jeff Reardon	.05
730	Mitch Webster	.05
731	Brian Bohanon **RC**	.05
732	Rick Parker **RC**	.05
733	Terry Shumpert **RC**	.05
734a	Nolan Ryan (300-win stripe on front)	1.50
734b	Nolan Ryan (No stripe.)	4.00
735	John Burkett	.05
736	Derrick May **RC**	.05
737	Carlos Baerga **RC**	.05
738	Greg Smith **RC**	.05
739	Joe Kraemer **RC**	.05
740	Scott Sanderson **RC**	.05
741	Hector Villanueva **RC**	.05
742	Mike Fetters **RC**	.05
743	Mark Gardner **RC**	.05
744	Matt Nokes **RC**	.05
745	Dave Winfield	.60
746	Delino DeShields **RC**	.15
747	Dann Howitt **RC**	.05
748	Tony Pena	.05
749	Oil Can Boyd	.05
750	Mike Benjamin **RC**	.05
751	Alex Cole **RC**	.05
752	Eric Gunderson **RC**	.05
753	Howard Farmer **RC**	.05
754	Joe Carter	.05
755	Ray Lankford **RC**	.25
756	Sandy Alomar,Jr.	.05
757	Alex Sanchez **RC**	.05
758	Nick Esasky	.05
759	Stan Belinda **RC**	.05
760	Jim Presley **RC**	.05
761	Gary DiSarcina **RC**	.05
762	Wayne Edwards **RC**	.05
763	Pat Combs **RC**	.05
764	Mickey Pina **RC**	.05
765	Wilson Alvarez **RC**	.25
766	Dave Parker	.05
767	Mike Blowers **RC**	.05
768	Tony Phillips	.05
769	Pascual Perez	.05
770	Gary Pettis	.05
771	Fred Lynn	.05
772	Mel Rojas **RC**	.10
773	David Segui **RC**	.25
774	Gary Carter	.60
775	Rafael Valdez **RC**	.05
776	Glenallen Hill **RC**	.05
777	Keith Hernandez	.05
778	Billy Hatcher	.05
779	Marty Clary **RC**	.05
780	Candy Maldonado **RC**	.05
781	Mike Marshall	.05
782	Billy Jo Robidoux **RC**	.05
783	Mark Langston	.05
784	Paul Sorrento **RC**	.05
785	Dave Hollins **RC**	.05
786	Cecil Fielder	.05
787	Matt Young	.05
788	Jeff Huson	.05
789	Lloyd Moseby	.05
790	Ron Kittle	.05
791	Hubie Brooks	.05
792	Craig Lefferts	.05
793	Kevin Bass	.05
794	Bryn Smith **RC**	.05
795	Juan Samuel	.05
796	Sam Horn	.05
797	Randy Myers	.05
798	Chris James **RC**	.05
799	Bill Gullickson	.05
800	Checklist 701-800	.05

Baseball Heroes Reggie Jackson

This Baseball Heroes set is devoted to Reggie Jackson. The cards, numbered 1-9, are the first in a continuing series of cards issued in subsequent years. An unnumbered cover card that says "Baseball Heroes" was also issued. The Jackson cards were randomly inserted in high number foil packs only. Jackson also autographed 2,500 numbered cards, which were randomly included in high number packs.

		NM/M
	Complete Set (10):	5.00
	Common Player:	.50
	Autographed Card:	100.00
1	1969 Emerging Superstar (Reggie Jackson)	.50
2	1973 An MVP Year (Reggie Jackson)	.50
3	1977 "Mr. October" (Reggie Jackson)	.50
4	1978 Jackson vs. Welch (Reggie Jackson)	.50
5	1982 Under the Halo (Reggie Jackson)	.50
6	1984 500! (Reggie Jackson)	.50
7	1986 Moving Up the List (Reggie Jackson)	.50
8	1987 A Great Career Ends (Reggie Jackson)	.50
9	Heroes Checklist 1-9 (Reggie Jackson)	.50
----	Header Card	.50

Black-Box Variations

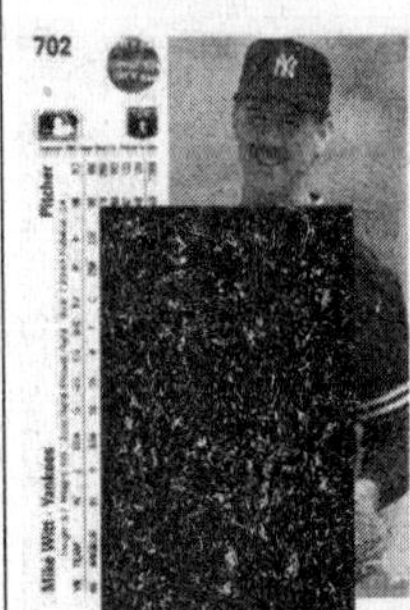

It appears that card #702 in 1990 UD was originally intended to be Mike Witt, but that it was replaced by a "Rookie Threats" card picturing three Expos. At least a few examples of the Witt card, factory cancelled with a large black ink box on back, have made their way into the market, along with a #800 checklist card naming Witt as #702.

		NM/M
702	Mike Witt	450.00
800	Checklist 701-800	250.00

1991 Upper Deck

More than 110 rookies are included among the first 700 cards in the 1991 Upper Deck set. A 100-card high-number series was released in late summer. Cards feature top quality white stock and color photos on front and back. A nine-card "Baseball Heroes" bonus set honoring Nolan Ryan, is among the many insert specials in the '91 UD set. Others include a card of Chicago Bulls superstar Michael Jordan. Along with the Ryan bonus cards, 2,500 cards personally autographed and numbered by Ryan were randomly inserted. Upper Deck cards are packaged in tamper-proof foil packs. Each pack contains 15 cards and a 3-1/2" x 2-1/2" 3-D team logo hologram sticker.

		NM/M
	Unopened Factory Set (800):	15.00
	Complete Set (800):	10.00
	Complete Low Series (700):	9.00
	Complete High Series (100):	1.00
	Common Player:	.05
	Low or High Wax Pack (15):	.60
	Low or High Wax Box (36):	13.50
1	Star Rookie Checklist	.05
2	Phil Plantier **RC**	.05
3	D.J. Dozier **RC**	.05
4	Dave Hansen **RC**	.05
5	Mo Vaughn **RC**	.10
6	Leo Gomez **RC**	.05
7	Scott Aldred **RC**	.05
8	Scott Chiamparino **RC**	.05
9	Lance Dickson **RC**	.05
10	Sean Berry **RC**	.05
11	Bernie Williams **RC**	.25
12	Brian Barnes **RC**	.05
13	Narciso Elvira **RC**	.05
14	Mike Gardiner **RC**	.05
15	Greg Colbrunn **RC**	.05
16	Bernard Gilkey **RC**	.05
17	Mark Lewis **RC**	.05
18	Mickey Morandini **RC**	.05
19	Charles Nagy **RC**	.05
20	Geronimo Pena **RC**	.05
21	Henry Rodriguez **RC**	.05
22	Scott Cooper **RC**	.05
23	Andujar Cedeno **RC**	.05
24	Eric Karros **RC**	.25
25	Steve Decker **RC**	.05
26	Kevin Belcher **RC**	.05
27	Jeff Conine **RC**	.25
28	Oakland Athletics checklist (Dave Stewart)	.05
29	Chicago White Sox checklist (Carlton Fisk)	.20
30	Texas Rangers checklist (Rafael Palmeiro)	.20
31	California Angels checklist (Chuck Finley)	.05
32	Seattle Mariners checklist (Harold Reynolds)	.05
33	Kansas City Royals checklist (Bret Saberhagen)	.05
34	Minnesota Twins checklist (Gary Gaetti)	.05
35	Scott Leius	.05
36	Neal Heaton	.05
37	Terry Lee **RC**	.05
38	Gary Redus	.05
39	Barry Jones	.05
40	Chuck Knoblauch	.05
41	Larry Andersen	.05
42	Darryl Hamilton	.05
43	Boston Red Sox checklist (Mike Greenwell)	.05
44	Toronto Blue Jays checklist (Kelly Gruber)	.05
45	Detroit Tigers checklist (Jack Morris)	.05
46	Cleveland Indians checklist (Sandy Alomar Jr.)	.05
47	Baltimore Orioles checklist (Gregg Olson)	.05
48	Milwaukee Brewers checklist (Dave Parker)	.05
49	New York Yankees checklist (Roberto Kelly)	.05
50	Top Prospect '91 checklist	.05
51	Kyle Abbott **RC** (Top Prospect)	.10
52	Jeff Juden **RC** (Top Prospect)	.05
53	Todd Van Poppel **RC** (Top Prospect)	.10
54	Steve Karsay **RC** (Top Prospect)	.10
55	Chipper Jones **RC** (Top Prospect)	3.00
56	Chris Johnson **RC** (Top Prospect)	.05
57	John Ericks **RC** (Top Prospect)	.05
58	Gary Scott **RC** (Top Prospect)	.05
59	Kiki Jones **RC** (Top Prospect)	.05
60	Wil Cordero **RC** (Top Prospect)	.05
61	Royce Clayton **RC** (Top Prospect)	.05
62	Tim Costo **RC** (Top Prospect)	.05
63	Roger Salkeld **RC** (Top Prospect)	.05
64	Brook Fordyce **RC** (Top Prospect)	.05
65	Mike Mussina **RC** (Top Prospect)	1.00
66	Dave Staton **RC** (Top Prospect)	.05
67	Mike Lieberthal **RC** (Top Prospect)	.50
68	Kurt Miller **RC** (Top Prospect)	.05
69	Dan Peltier **RC** (Top Prospect)	.05
70	Greg Blosser **RC** (Top Prospect)	.05
71	Reggie Sanders **RC** (Top Prospect)	.25
72	Brent Mayne **RC** (Top Prospect)	.05
73	Rico Brogna **RC** (Top Prospect)	.05
74	Willie Banks **RC** (Top Prospect)	.05
75	Len Brutcher **RC** (Top Prospect)	.05
76	Pat Kelly **RC** (Top Prospect)	.05
77	Cincinnati Reds checklist (Chris Sabo)	.05
78	Los Angeles Dodgers checklist (Ramon Martinez)	.05
79	San Francisco Giants checklist (Matt Williams)	.05
80	San Diego Padres checklist (Roberto Alomar)	.05
81	Houston Astros checklist (Glenn Davis)	.05
82	Atlanta Braves checklist (Ron Gant)	.05
83	"Fielder's Feat" (Cecil Fielder)	.05
84	Orlando Merced **RC**	.10
85	Domingo Ramos	.05
86	Tom Bolton	.05
87	Andres Santana **RC**	.05
88	John Dopson **RC**	.05
89	Kenny Williams	.05
90	Marty Barrett	.05
91	Tom Pagnozzi	.05
92	Carmelo Martinez	.05
93	"Save Master" (Bobby Thigpen)	.05
94	Pittsburgh Pirates checklist (Barry Bonds)	.50
95	New York Mets checklist (Gregg Jefferies)	.05
96	Montreal Expos checklist (Tim Wallach)	.05
97	Philadelphia Phillies checklist (Lenny Dykstra)	.05
98	St. Louis Cardinals checklist (Pedro Guerrero)	.05
99	Chicago Cubs checklist (Mark Grace)	.05
100	Checklist 1-100	.05
101	Kevin Elster	.05
102	Tom Brookens	.05
103	Mackey Sasser	.05
104	Felix Fermin **RC**	.05
105	Kevin McReynolds	.05
106	Dave Steib	.05
107	Jeffrey Leonard	.05
108	Dave Henderson	.05
109	Sid Bream	.05
110	Henry Cotto	.05
111	Shawon Dunston	.05
112	Mariano Duncan **RC**	.05
113	Joe Girardi	.05
114	Billy Hatcher	.05
115	Greg Maddux	.50
116	Jerry Browne **RC**	.05
117	Juan Samuel	.05
118	Steve Olin	.05
119	Alfredo Griffin	.05
120	Mitch Webster **RC**	.05
121	Joel Skinner	.05
122	Frank Viola	.05
123	Cory Snyder	.05
124	Howard Johnson	.05
125	Carlos Baerga	.05
126	Tony Fernandez	.05
127	Dave Stewart	.05
128	Jay Buhner	.05
129	Mike LaValliere	.05
130	Scott Bradley	.05
131	Tony Phillips	.05
132	Ryne Sandberg	.50
133	Paul O'Neill	.05
134	Mark Grace	.05
135	Chris Sabo	.05
136	Ramon Martinez	.05
137	Brook Jacoby	.05
138	Candy Maldonado	.05
139	Mike Scioscia	.05
140	Chris James **RC**	.05
141	Craig Worthington	.05
142	Manny Lee	.05
143	Tim Raines	.05
144	Sandy Alomar, Jr.	.05
145	John Olerud	.05
146	Ozzie Canseco **RC**	.05
147	Pat Borders	.05
148	Harold Reynolds	.05
149	Tom Henke	.05
150	R.J. Reynolds	.05
151	Mike Gallego	.05
152	Bobby Bonilla	.05
153	Terry Steinbach	.05
154	Barry Bonds	1.00
155	Jose Canseco	.30
156	Gregg Jefferies	.05
157	Matt Williams	.05
158	Craig Biggio	.05
159	Daryl Boston	.05
160	Ricky Jordan	.05
161	Stan Belinda	.05
162	Ozzie Smith	.50
163	Tom Brunansky	.05
164	Todd Zeile	.05
165	Mike Greenwell	.05
166	Kal Daniels	.05
167	Kent Hrbek	.05
168	Franklin Stubbs	.05
169	Dick Schofield	.05
170	Junior Ortiz	.05
171	Hector Villanueva **RC**	.05
172	Dennis Eckersley	.35
173	Mitch Williams	.05
174	Mark McGwire	.75
175	Fernando Valenzuela	.05
176	Gary Carter	.40
177	Dave Magadan	.05
178	Robby Thompson	.05
179	Bob Ojeda	.05
180	Ken Caminiti	.05
181	Don Slaught	.05
182	Luis Rivera	.05
183	Jay Bell	.05
184	Jody Reed	.05
185	Wally Backman	.05
186	Dave Martinez	.05
187	Luis Polonia	.05
188	Shane Mack	.05
189	Spike Owen	.05
190	Scott Bailes	.05
191	John Russell	.05
192	Walt Weiss	.05
193	Jose Oquendo	.05
194	Carney Lansford	.05
195	Jeff Huson	.05
196	Keith Miller	.05
197	Eric Yelding	.05
198	Ron Darling	.05
199	John Kruk	.05
200	Checklist 101-200	.05
201	John Shelby	.05
202	Bob Geren	.05
203	Lance McCullers	.05
204	Alvaro Espinoza	.05
205	Mark Salas	.05
206	Mike Pagliarulo	.05
207	Jose Uribe	.05
208	Jim Deshaies **RC**	.05
209	Ron Karkovice	.05
210	Rafael Ramirez	.05
211	Donnie Hill	.05
212	Brian Harper **RC**	.05
213	Jack Howell	.05
214	Wes Gardner	.05
215	Tim Burke	.05
216	Doug Jones **RC**	.05
217	Hubie Brooks	.05
218	Tom Candiotti	.05
219	Gerald Perry	.05
220	Jose DeLeon **RC**	.05
221	Wally Whitehurst	.05
222	Alan Mills **RC**	.05
223	Alan Trammell	.05
224	Dwight Gooden	.05
225	Travis Fryman	.05
226	Joe Carter	.05
227	Julio Franco	.05
228	Craig Lefferts	.05
229	Gary Pettis	.05
230	Dennis Rasmussen	.05
231a	Brian Downing (No position on front.)	2.00
231b	Brian Downing (DH on front)	.05
232	Carlos Quintana **RC**	.05
233	Gary Gaetti	.05
234	Mark Langston	.05
235	Tim Wallach	.05
236	Greg Swindell	.05
237	Eddie Murray	.40
238	Jeff Manto **RC**	.05
239	Lenny Harris	.05
240	Jesse Orosco	.05
241	Scott Lusader	.05
242	Sid Fernandez	.05
243	Jim Leyritz	.05
244	Cecil Fielder	.05
245	Darryl Strawberry	.05
246	Frank Thomas **RC**	.50
247	Kevin Mitchell	.05
248	Lance Johnson **RC**	.05
249	Rick Rueschel	.05
250	Mark Portugal	.05
251	Derek Lilliquist	.05
252	Brian Holman **RC**	.05
253	Rafael Valdez	.05
254	R.J. Surhoff	.05
255	Tony Gwynn	.50
256	Andy Van Slyke	.05
257	Todd Stottlemyre	.05
258	Jose Lind	.05
259	Greg Myers	.05
260	Jeff Ballard **RC**	.05
261	Bobby Thigpen	.05
262	Jimmy Kremers **RC**	.05
263	Robin Ventura	.05
264	John Smoltz	.05
265	Sammy Sosa	.50

#	Player	NM/M
266	Gary Sheffield	.30
267	Len Dykstra	.05
268	Bill Spiers	.05
269	Charlie Hayes	.05
270	Brett Butler	.05
271	Bip Roberts	.05
272	Rob Deer	.05
273	Fred Lynn	.05
274	Dave Parker	.05
275	Andy Benes	.05
276	Glenallen Hill **RC**	.05
277	Steve Howard **RC**	.05
278	Doug Drabek	.05
279	Joe Oliver	.05
280	Todd Benzinger	.05
281	Eric King	.05
282	Jim Presley	.05
283	Ken Patterson **RC**	.05
284	Jack Daugherty **RC**	.05
285	Ivan Calderon	.05
286	Edgar Diaz **RC**	.05
287	Kevin Bass	.05
288	Don Carman **RC**	.05
289	Greg Brock	.05
290	John Franco	.05
291	Joey Cora	.05
292	Bill Wegman	.05
293	Eric Show	.05
294	Scott Bankhead	.05
295	Garry Templeton	.05
296	Mickey Tettleton	.05
297	Luis Sojo	.05
298	Jose Rijo	.05
299	Dave Johnson	.05
300	Checklist 201-300	.05
301	Mark Grant	.05
302	Pete Harnisch	.05
303	Greg Olson	.05
304	Anthony Telford **RC**	.05
305	Lonnie Smith	.05
306	Chris Hoiles	.05
307	Bryn Smith	.05
308	Mike Devereaux	.05
309a	Milt Thompson ("86" in stats obscured by "bull's eye")	.50
309b	Milt Thompson ("86" visible)	.05
310	Bob Melvin	.05
311a	Luis Salazar (Circled dot over "i" in Luis on back.)	2.00
311b	Luis Salazar (Corrected)	.05
312	Ed Whitson **RC**	.05
313	Charlie Hough	.05
314	Dave Clark	.05
315	Eric Gunderson **RC**	.05
316	Dan Petry	.05
317	Dante Bichette	.05
318	Mike Heath	.05
319	Damon Berryhill	.05
320	Walt Terrell	.05
321	Scott Fletcher	.05
322	Dan Plesac	.05
323	Jack McDowell	.05
324	Paul Molitor	.40
325	Ozzie Guillen	.05
326	Gregg Olson	.05
327	Pedro Guerrero	.05
328	Bob Milacki **RC**	.05
329	John Tudor	.05
330	Steve Finley	.05
331	Jack Clark	.05
332	Jerome Walton	.05
333	Andy Hawkins	.05
334	Derrick May	.05
335	Roberto Alomar	.20
336	Jack Morris	.05
337	Dave Winfield	.40
338	Steve Searcy	.05
339	Chili Davis	.05
340	Larry Sheets	.05
341	Ted Higuera	.05
342	David Segui **RC**	.10
343	Greg Cadaret	.05
344	Robin Yount	.40
345	Nolan Ryan	1.00
346	Ray Lankford	.05
347	Cal Ripken, Jr.	1.00
348	Lee Smith	.05
349	Brady Anderson	.05
350	Frank DiPino	.05
351	Hal Morris	.05
352	Deion Sanders	.10
353	Barry Larkin	.05
354	Don Mattingly	.60
355	Eric Davis	.05
356	Jose Offerman	.05
357	Mel Rojas	.05
358	Rudy Seanez **RC**	.05
359	Oil Can Boyd	.05
360	Nelson Liriano	.05
361	Ron Gant	.05
362	Howard Farmer **RC**	.05
363	Dave Justice	.05
364	Delino DeShields	.05
365	Steve Avery	.05
366	David Cone	.05
367	Lou Whitaker	.05
368	Von Hayes	.05
369	Frank Tanana	.05
370	Tim Teufel	.05
371	Randy Myers	.05
372	Roberto Kelly	.05
373	Jack Armstrong	.05
374	Kelly Gruber	.05
375	Kevin Maas	.05
376	Randy Johnson	.40
377	David West	.05
378	Brent Knackert **RC**	.05
379	Rick Honeycutt	.05
380	Kevin Gross	.05
381	Tom Foley	.05
382	Jeff Blauser	.05
383	Scott Ruskin **RC**	.05
384	Andres Thomas **RC**	.05
385	Dennis Martinez	.05
386	Mike Henneman	.05
387	Felix Jose	.05
388	Alejandro Pena	.05
389	Chet Lemon	.05
390	Craig Wilson **RC**	.05
391	Chuck Crim	.05
392	Mel Hall	.05
393	Mark Knudson	.05
394	Norm Charlton	.05
395	Mike Felder	.05
396	Tim Layana **RC**	.05
397	Steve Frey **RC**	.05
398	Bill Doran	.05
399	Dion James	.05
400	Checklist 301-400	.05
401	Ron Hassey	.05
402	Don Robinson	.05
403	Gene Nelson	.05
404	Terry Kennedy	.05
405	Todd Burns	.05
406	Roger McDowell	.05
407	Bob Kipper	.05
408	Darren Daulton	.05
409	Chuck Cary	.05
410	Bruce Ruffin	.05
411	Juan Berenguer	.05
412	Gary Ward	.05
413	Al Newman	.05
414	Danny Jackson	.05
415	Greg Gagne	.05
416	Tom Herr	.05
417	Jeff Parrett	.05
418	Jeff Reardon	.05
419	Mark Lemke	.05
420	Charlie O'Brien **RC**	.05
421	Willie Randolph	.05
422	Steve Bedrosian	.05
423	Mike Moore	.05
424	Jeff Brantley **RC**	.05
425	Bob Welch	.05
426	Terry Mulholland	.05
427	Willie Blair **RC**	.05
428	Darrin Fletcher **RC**	.05
429	Mike Witt	.05
430	Joe Boever	.05
431	Tom Gordon	.05
432	Pedro Munoz **RC**	.05
433	Kevin Seitzer	.05
434	Kevin Tapani	.05
435	Bret Saberhagen	.05
436	Ellis Burks	.05
437	Chuck Finley	.05
438	Mike Boddicker	.05
439	Francisco Cabrera	.05
440	Todd Hundley	.05
441	Kelly Downs	.05
442	Dann Howitt **RC**	.05
443	Scott Garrelts	.05
444	Rickey Henderson	.40
445	Will Clark	.05
446	Ben McDonald	.05
447	Dale Murphy	.20
448	Dave Righetti	.05
449	Dickie Thon	.05
450	Ted Power	.05
451	Scott Coolbaugh	.05
452	Dwight Smith	.05
453	Pete Incaviglia	.05
454	Andre Dawson	.25
455	Ruben Sierra	.05
456	Andres Galarraga	.05
457	Alvin Davis	.05
458	Tony Castillo	.05
459	Pete O'Brien	.05
460	Charlie Leibrandt	.05
461	Vince Coleman	.05
462	Steve Sax	.05
463	Omar Oliveras **RC**	.05
464	Oscar Azocar **RC**	.05
465	Joe Magrane **RC**	.05
466	Karl Rhodes **RC**	.05
467	Benito Santiago	.05
468	Joe Klink **RC**	.05
469	Sil Campusano **RC**	.05
470	Mark Parent	.05
471	Shawn Boskie **RC**	.05
472	Kevin Brown	.05
473	Rick Sutcliffe	.05
474	Rafael Palmeiro	.35
475	Mike Harkey	.05
476	Jaime Navarro	.05
477	Marquis Grissom	.05
478	Marty Clary	.05
479	Greg Briley **RC**	.05
480	Tom Glavine	.25
481	Lee Guetterman	.05
482	Rex Hudler	.05
483	Dave LaPoint **RC**	.05
484	Terry Pendleton	.05
485	Jesse Barfield	.05
486	Jose DeJesus	.05
487	Paul Abbott **RC**	.05
488	Ken Howell	.05
489	Greg W. Harris	.05
490	Roy Smith	.05
491	Paul Assenmacher	.05
492	Geno Petralli	.05
493	Steve Wilson	.05
494	Kevin Reimer **RC**	.05
495	Bill Long	.05
496	Mike Jackson **RC**	.05
497	Oddibe McDowell	.05
498	Bill Swift	.05
499	Jeff Treadway	.05
500	Checklist 401-500	.05
501	Gene Larkin	.05
502	Bob Boone	.05
503	Allan Anderson	.05
504	Luis Aquino **RC**	.05
505	Mark Guthrie	.05
506	Joe Orsulak	.05
507	Dana Kiecker **RC**	.05
508	Dave Gallagher **RC**	.05
509	Greg A. Harris	.05
510	Mark Williamson	.05
511	Casey Candaele	.05
512	Mookie Wilson	.05
513	Dave Smith	.05
514	Chuck Carr **RC**	.05
515	Glenn Wilson	.05
516	Mike Fitzgerald **RC**	.05
517	Devon White	.05
518	Dave Hollins	.05
519	Mark Eichhorn	.05
520	Otis Nixon	.05
521	Terry Shumpert **RC**	.05
522	Scott Erickson **RC**	.15
523	Danny Tartabull	.05
524	Orel Hershiser	.05
525	George Brett	.60
526	Greg Vaughn	.05
527	Tim Naehring **RC**	.05
528	Curt Schilling **RC**	.25
529	Chris Bosio	.05
530	Sam Horn	.05
531	Mike Scott	.05
532	George Bell	.05
533	Eric Anthony	.05
534	Julio Valera **RC**	.05
535	Glenn Davis	.05
536	Larry Walker	.05
537	Pat Combs	.05
538	Chris Nabholz **RC**	.05
539	Kirk McCaskill	.05
540	Randy Ready	.05
541	Mark Gubicza	.05
542	Rick Aguilera	.05
543	Brian McRae **RC**	.05
544	Kirby Puckett	.50
545	Bo Jackson	.10
546	Wade Boggs	.50
547	Tim McIntosh **RC**	.05
548	Randy Milligan **RC**	.05
549	Dwight Evans	.05
550	Billy Ripken	.05
551	Erik Hanson	.05
552	Lance Parrish	.05
553	Tino Martinez	.05
554	Jim Abbott	.05
555	Ken Griffey Jr.	.65
556	Milt Cuyler **RC**	.05
557	Mark Leonard **RC**	.05
558	Jay Howell	.05
559	Lloyd Moseby	.05
560	Chris Gwynn	.05
561	Mark Whiten **RC**	.05
562	Harold Baines	.05
563	Junior Felix	.05
564	Darren Lewis	.05
565	Fred McGriff	.05
566	Kevin Appier	.05
567	Luis Gonzalez **RC**	1.00
568	Frank White	.05
569	Juan Agosto	.05
570	Mike Macfarlane	.05
571	Bert Blyleven	.05
572	Ken Griffey Sr.	.05
573	Lee Stevens **RC**	.05
574	Edgar Martinez	.05
575	Wally Joyner	.05
576	Tim Belcher	.05
577	John Burkett	.05
578	Mike Morgan	.05
579	Paul Gibson	.05
580	Jose Vizcaino **RC**	.05
581	Duane Ward	.05
582	Scott Sanderson	.05
583	David Wells	.05
584	Willie McGee	.05
585	John Cerutti	.05
586	Danny Darwin	.05
587	Kurt Stillwell	.05
588	Rich Gedman	.05
589	Mark Davis	.05
590	Bill Gullickson	.05
591	Matt Young	.05
592	Bryan Harvey **RC**	.05
593	Omar Vizquel	.05
594	Scott Lewis **RC**	.05
595	Dave Valle	.05
596	Tim Crews **RC**	.05
597	Mike Bielecki	.05
598	Mike Sharperson	.05
599	Dave Bergman	.05
600	Checklist 501-600	.05
601	Steve Lyons	.05
602	Bruce Hurst	.05
603	Donn Pall	.05
604	Jim Vatcher **RC**	.05
605	Dan Pasqua	.05
606	Kenny Rogers	.05
607	Jeff Schulz **RC**	.05
608	Brad Arnsberg **RC**	.05
609	Willie Wilson	.05
610	Jamie Moyer	.05
611	Ron Oester	.05
612	Dennis Cook **RC**	.05
613	Rick Mahler	.05
614	Bill Landrum	.05
615	Scott Scudder	.05
616	Tom Edens **RC**	.05
617	"1917 Revisited" (Chicago White Sox team photo.)	.05
618	Jim Gantner	.05
619	Darrel Akerfelds **RC**	.05
620	Ron Robinson	.05
621	Scott Radinsky	.05
622	Pete Smith	.05
623	Melido Perez	.05
624	Jerald Clark **RC**	.05
625	Carlos Martinez	.05
626	Wes Chamberlain **RC**	.05
627	Bobby Witt	.05
628	Ken Dayley **RC**	.05
629	John Barfield **RC**	.05
630	Bob Tewksbury	.05
631	Glenn Braggs	.05
632	Jim Neidlinger **RC**	.05
633	Tom Browning	.05
634	Kirk Gibson	.05
635	Rob Dibble	.05
636	"Stolen Base Leaders" (Lou Brock, Rickey Henderson)	.15
637	Jeff Montgomery	.05
638	Mike Schooler	.05
639	Storm Davis	.05
640	Rich Rodriguez **RC**	.05
641	Phil Bradley	.05
642	Kent Mercker	.05
643	Carlton Fisk	.40
644	Mike Bell	.05
645	Alex Fernandez **RC**	.05
646	Juan Gonzalez	.30
647	Ken Hill	.05
648	Jeff Russell	.05
649	Chuck Malone **RC**	.05
650	Steve Buechele	.05
651	Mike Benjamin	.05
652	Tony Pena	.05
653	Trevor Wilson	.05
654	Alex Cole	.05
655	Roger Clemens	.60
656	"The Bashing Years" (Mark McGwire)	.50
657	Joe Grahe **RC**	.05
658	Jim Eisenreich	.05
659	Dan Gladden	.05
660	Steve Farr **RC**	.05
661	Bill Sampen **RC**	.05
662	Dave Rohde **RC**	.05
663	Mark Gardner	.05
664	Mike Simms **RC**	.05
665	Moises Alou	.05
666	Mickey Hatcher	.05
667	Jimmy Key	.05
668	John Wetteland	.05
669	John Smiley	.05
670	Jim Acker	.05
671	Pascual Perez	.05
672	Reggie Harris **RC**	.05
673	Matt Nokes	.05
674	Rafael Novoa **RC**	.05
675	Hensley Meulens	.05
676	Jeff M. Robinson **RC**	.05
677	"Ground Breaking" (New Comiskey Park)	.15
678	Johnny Ray	.05
679	Greg Hibbard	.05
680	Paul Sorrento	.05
681	Mike Marshall	.05
682	Jim Clancy	.05
683	Rob Murphy	.05
684	Dave Schmidt **RC**	.05
685	Jeff Gray **RC**	.05
686	Mike Hartley **RC**	.05
687	Jeff King	.05
688	Stan Javier **RC**	.05
689	Bob Walk	.05
690	Jim Gott	.05
691	Mike LaCoss	.05
692	John Farrell	.05
693	Tim Leary	.05
694	Mike Walker **RC**	.05
695	Eric Plunk	.05
696	Mike Fetters	.05
697	Wayne Edwards	.05
698	Tim Drummond **RC**	.05
699	Willie Fraser	.05
700	Checklist 601-700	.05
701	Mike Heath	.05
702	"Rookie Threats" (Luis Gonzalez, Karl Rhodes, Jeff Bagwell)	.45
703	Jose Mesa	.05
704	Dave Smith **RC**	.05
705	Danny Darwin	.05
706	Rafael Belliard	.05
707	Rob Murphy	.05
708	Terry Pendleton	.05
709	Mike Pagliarulo	.05
710	Sid Bream	.05
711	Junior Felix	.05
712	Dante Bichette	.05
713	Kevin Gross	.05
714	Luis Sojo	.05
715	Bob Ojeda	.05
716	Julio Machado **RC**	.05
717	Steve Farr	.05
718	Franklin Stubbs	.05
719	Mike Boddicker	.05
720	Willie Randolph	.05
721	Willie McGee	.05
722	Chili Davis	.05
723	Danny Jackson	.05
724	Cory Snyder	.05
725	"MVP Lineup" (Andre Dawson, George Bell, Ryne Sandberg)	.20
726	Rob Deer	.05
727	Rich DeLucia **RC**	.05
728	Mike Perez **RC**	.05
729	Mickey Tettleton	.05
730	Mike Blowers	.05
731	Gary Gaetti	.05
732	Brett Butler	.05
733	Dave Parker	.05
734	Eddie Zosky **RC**	.05
735	Jack Clark	.05
736	Jack Morris	.05
737	Kirk Gibson	.05
738	Steve Bedrosian	.05
739	Candy Maldonado	.05
740	Matt Young	.05
741	Rich Garces **RC**	.05
742	George Bell	.05
743	Deion Sanders	.10
744	Bo Jackson	.10
745	Luis Mercedes **RC**	.05
746	Reggie Jefferson **RC**	.05
747	Pete Incaviglia	.05
748	Chris Hammond	.05
749	Mike Stanton	.05
750	Scott Sanderson	.05
751	Paul Faries **RC**	.05
752	Al Osuna **RC**	.05
753	Steve Chitren **RC**	.05
754	Tony Fernandez	.05
755	Jeff Bagwell **RC**	1.50
756	Kirk Dressendorfer **RC**	.05
757	Glenn Davis	.05
758	Gary Carter	.40
759	Zane Smith	.05
760	Vance Law	.05
761	Denis Boucher **RC**	.05
762	Turner Ward **RC**	.05
763	Roberto Alomar	.20
764	Albert Belle	.05
765	Joe Carter	.05
766	Pete Schourek **RC**	.05
767	Heathcliff Slocumb **RC**	.05
768	Vince Coleman	.05
769	Mitch Williams	.05
770	Brian Downing	.05
771	Dana Allison **RC**	.05
772	Pete Harnisch	.05
773	Tim Raines	.05
774	Darryl Kile **RC**	.05
775	Fred McGriff	.05
776	Dwight Evans	.05
777	Joe Slusarski	.05
778	Dave Righetti	.05
779	Jeff Hamilton	.05
780	Ernest Riles	.05
781	Ken Dayley	.05
782	Eric King	.05
783	Devon White	.05
784	Beau Allred **RC**	.05
785	Mike Timlin **RC**	.05
786	Ivan Calderon	.05
787	Hubie Brooks	.05
788	Juan Agosto **RC**	.05
789	Barry Jones	.05
790	Wally Backman	.05
791	Jim Presley	.05
792	Charlie Hough	.05
793	Larry Andersen	.05
794	Steve Finley	.05
795	Shawn Abner	.05
796	Jeff M. Robinson	.05
797	Joe Bitker **RC**	.05
798	Eric Show	.05
799	Bud Black	.05
800	Checklist 701-800	.05
SP1	Michael Jordan	3.00
SP2	"A Day to Remember" (Rickey Henderson, Nolan Ryan)	1.00
HH1	Hank Aaron (Hologram)	1.00

Baseball Heroes Hank Aaron

This set devoted to Hank Aaron is numbered 19-27 and includes an unnumbered "Baseball Heroes" cover card. The cards are found in foil and jumbo packs of Upper Deck high-number cards.

		NM/M
Complete Set (10):		4.00
Common Aaron:		.50
Autographed Card:		180.00
Aaron Header:		1.00
19	1954 Rookie Year	.50
20	1957 MVP	.50
21	1966 Move to Atlanta	.50
22	1970 3,000	.50
23	1974 715	.50
24	1975 Return to Milwaukee	.50
25	1976 755	.50
26	1982 Hall of Fame	.50
27	Checklist - Heroes 19-27	.50

Baseball Heroes Nolan Ryan

This set devoted to Nolan Ryan is numbered 10-18 and includes an unnumbered "Baseball Heroes" cover card. The cards are found in low-number foil and jumbo boxes. One out of every hundred of the autographed cards was specially inscribed "Strike Out King."

		NM/M
Complete Set (10):		3.00
Common Player:		.50
Ryan Header Card:		1.00
Autographed Card:		200.00
"Strike Out King" Auto.:		575.00
10	1968 Victory #1	.50
11	1973 A Career Year	.50
12	1975 Double Milestone	.50
13	1979 Back Home	.50
14	1981 All-Time Leader	.50
15	1989 5,000	.50
16	1990 The Sixth	.50
17	1990 ... and Still Counting	.50
18	Checklist - Heroes 10-18	.50

Heroes of Baseball

This four-card set features three members of Baseball's Hall of Fame: Harmon Killebrew, Gaylord Perry and Ferguson Jenkins. Each has a card for himself, plus there's a card which features all three players. The cards were found in specially-marked low number foil packs. The cards are numbered H1-H4. Upper Deck also produced 3,000 autographed and numbered cards for each player.

		NM/M
Complete Set (4):		7.00
Common Card:		2.00
1	Harmon Killebrew	2.00
1a	Harmon Killebrew/ Auto.	10.00
2	Gaylord Perry	2.00
2a	Gaylord Perry/Auto.	10.00
3	Ferguson Jenkins	2.00
3a	Ferguson Jenkins/ Auto.	10.00
4	Gaylord Perry, Ferguson Jenkins, Harmon Killebrew	2.00

Silver Sluggers

Each year the "Silver Slugger" award is presented to the player at each position with the highest batting average in each league. Upper Deck produced special cards in honor of the 1990 season award winners. The cards were randomly inserted in jumbo packs of Upper Deck cards. The cards feature a "SS" designation along with the card number. The cards are designed like the regular issue Upper Deck cards from 1991, but feature a Silver Slugger bat along the left border of the card.

		NM/M
Complete Set (18):		5.00
Common Player:		.15
1	Julio Franco	.15
2	Alan Trammell	.15
3	Rickey Henderson	.75
4	Jose Canseco	.50
5	Barry Bonds	2.00
6	Eddie Murray	.75
7	Kelly Gruber	.15
8	Ryne Sandberg	1.00
9	Darryl Strawberry	.15
10	Ellis Burks	.15
11	Lance Parrish	.15
12	Cecil Fielder	.15
13	Matt Williams	.15
14	Dave Parker	.15
15	Bobby Bonilla	.15
16	Don Robinson	.15
17	Benito Santiago	.15
18	Barry Larkin	.15

Final Edition

Upper Deck surprised the hobby with the late-season release of this 100-card boxed set. The cards are numbered with an "F" designation. A special "Minor League Diamond Skills" subset (cards #1-21) features several top prospects. An All-Star subset (cards #79-99) is also included in this set. The cards are styled like the regular 1991 Upper Deck issue. Special team hologram cards are included with the set.

		NM/M
Complete Set (100):		9.00
Common Player:		.05
1	Ryan Klesko, Reggie Sanders (Minor League Diamond Skills Checklist)	.10
2	Pedro Martinez **RC**	5.00
3	Lance Dickson **RC**	.05
4	Royce Clayton	.05
5	Scott Bryant **RC**	.05
6	Dan Wilson **RC**	.05
7	Dmitri Young **RC**	.50
8	Ryan Klesko **RC**	.50
9	Tom Goodwin **RC**	.05
10	Rondell White **RC**	.25
11	Reggie Sanders	.05
12	Todd Van Poppel	.05
13	Arthur Rhodes **RC**	.05
14	Eddie Zosky	.05
15	Gerald Williams **RC**	.05
16	Robert Eenhoorn **RC**	.05
17	Jim Thome **RC**	3.00
18	Marc Newfield **RC**	.05
19	Kerwin Moore **RC**	.05
20	Jeff McNeely **RC**	.05
21	Frankie Rodriguez	.05
22	Andy Mota **RC**	.05
23	Chris Haney **RC**	.05
24	Kenny Lofton **RC**	.25
25	Dave Nilsson **RC**	.05
26	Derek Bell	.05
27	Frank Castillo **RC**	.05
28	Candy Maldonado	.05
29	Chuck McElroy	.05
30	Chito Martinez **RC**	.05
31	Steve Howe **RC**	.05
32	Freddie Benavides **RC**	.05
33	Scott Kamieniecki	.05
34	Denny Neagle **RC**	.05
35	Mike Humphreys **RC**	.05
36	Mike Remlinger **RC**	.05
37	Scott Coolbaugh	.05
38	Darren Lewis	.05
39	Thomas Howard **RC**	.05
40	John Candelaria	.05
41	Todd Benzinger	.05
42	Wilson Alvarez	.05
43	Patrick Lennon **RC**	.05
44	Rusty Meacham **RC**	.05
45	Ryan Bowen **RC**	.05
46	Rick Wilkins **RC**	.10
47	Ed Sprague **RC**	.05
48	Bob Scanlan **RC**	.05
49	Tom Candiotti	.05
50	Dennis Martinez (Perfecto)	.05
51	Oil Can Boyd	.05
52	Glenallen Hill	.05
53	Scott Livingstone **RC**	.05
54	Brian Hunter **RC**	.05
55	Ivan Rodriguez **RC**	1.50
56	Keith Mitchell **RC**	.05
57	Roger McDowell	.05
58	Otis Nixon	.05
59	Juan Bell **RC**	.05
60	Bill Krueger	.05
61	Chris Donnels **RC**	.05
62	Tommy Greene	.05
63	Doug Simons **RC**	.05
64	Andy Ashby **RC**	.15
65	Anthony Young **RC**	.05
66	Kevin Morton **RC**	.05
67	Bret Barberie **RC**	.05
68	Scott Servais **RC**	.05
69	Ron Darling	.05
70	Vicente Palacios	.05
71	Tim Burke **RC**	.05
72	Gerald Alexander **RC**	.05
73	Reggie Jefferson	.05
74	Dean Palmer	.05
75	Mark Whiten	.05
76	Randy Tomlin **RC**	.05
77	Mark Wohlers **RC**	.05
78	Brook Jacoby	.05
79	Ken Griffey Jr., Ryne Sandberg (All-Star Checklist)	.25
80	Jack Morris/AS	.05
81	Sandy Alomar, Jr./AS	.05
82	Cecil Fielder/AS	.05
83	Roberto Alomar/AS	.10
84	Wade Boggs/AS	.25
85	Cal Ripken, Jr./AS	.60
86	Rickey Henderson/AS	.15
87	Ken Griffey Jr./AS	.60
88	Dave Henderson/AS	.05
89	Danny Tartabull/AS	.05
90	Tom Glavine/AS	.10
91	Benito Santiago/AS	.05
92	Will Clark/AS	.05
93	Ryne Sandberg/AS	.50
94	Chris Sabo/AS	.05
95	Ozzie Smith/AS	.50
96	Ivan Calderon/AS	.05
97	Tony Gwynn/AS	.25
98	Andre Dawson/AS	.05
99	Bobby Bonilla/AS	.05
100	Checklist	.05

Comic Ball 2 Promos

Among the most sought-after promo cards in the promo-card mania that marked the 1991 National Sports Collectors Convention in Anaheim, Calif., was this set of Upper Deck preview cards for its Comic Ball 2 set. One card was given out each day of the National, from July 4-7, with the giveaway date noted in a banner at top. Fronts picture Reggie Jackson and Nolan Ryan with various Looney Tunes cartoon characters. Backs have information on the upcoming Comic Ball 2 issue against a cartoon puzzle background.

	NM/M
Complete Set (4):	6.00
Common Player:	1.00
7/4/91 Nolan Ryan (w/ Bugs Bunny, Daffy Duck)	2.50
7/5/91 Reggie Jackson (w/ Taz)	1.00
7/6/91 Nolan Ryan (w/ Speedy Gonzalez)	2.50
7/7/91 Reggie Jackson (w/ Sylvester, Elmer Fudd)	1.00

Comic Ball 2

Despite featuring two popular superstars on dozens of the cards, this 198-piece issue has found little favor with collectors. Most cards are arranged in 18-card sequences which tell a baseball-related cartoon tale starring Bugs Bunny, Daffy Duck, Wile E. Coyote and the rest of the Looney Tune characters. Actual-photo "guest appearances" by Nolan Ryan and Reggie Jackson highlight these presentations. There are also "Seventh Inning Stretch" cards featuring the ballplayers in scenes with the cartoon figures. When arranged in nine-pocket plastic sheets, card backs form a cartoon picture puzzle. Cards are typical Upper Deck quality with semi-gloss front and back surfaces and a circular hologram on the backs in the standard 2-1/2" x 3-1/2" format. Nine hologram stickers featuring Ryan and Jackson along with the cartoon characters were produced as random pack inserts. Because the cards are licensed by Major League Baseball, the players and cartoon critters are depicted in Major League uniforms.

	NM/M
Complete Set (198):	5.00
Common Card, Cartoon:	.05
Common Card, Ryan/Jackson:	.10
Hologram Sticker:	2.00
Wax Pack:	.50
Wax Box (36):	7.50

Comic Ball 2 Holograms

Nine silver-foil hologram stickers combine photos of Reggie Jackson and/or Nolan Ryan with various Warner Brothers cartoon stars and were issued as random pack inserts in Comic Ball 2. The 2-1/2" x 3-1/2" round-cornered stickers are blank-backed and unnumbered.

		NM/M
Complete Set (9):		17.50
Common Player:		3.00
(1)	Reggie Jackson (w/Daffy)	3.00
(2)	Reggie Jackson (w/Speedy)	3.00
(3)	Reggie Jackson (w/Sylvester)	3.00
(4)	Reggie Jackson (w/Taz)	3.00
(5)	Reggie Jackson, Nolan Ryan (w/Roadrunner & Wile)	3.00
(6)	Nolan Ryan (w/Bugs)	3.00
(7)	Nolan Ryan (w/Sylvester)	3.00
(8)	Nolan Ryan (w/?)	3.00
(9)	Nolan Ryan (w/?)	3.00

1992 Upper Deck

Upper Deck introduced a new look in 1992. The baseline style was no longer used. The cards feature full-color action photos on white stock, with the player's name and the Upper Deck logo along the top border. The team name is in the photo's bottom-right corner. Once again a 100-card high number series was released in late summer. Ted Williams autographed 2,500 Baseball Heroes cards which were randomly inserted into packs. Subsets featured in the 1992 issue include Star Rookies and Top Prospects. Cards originating from factory sets have gold-foil holograms on back, rather than silver.

		NM/M
Unopened Fact. Set (800):		20.00
Complete Set (800):		15.00
Common Player:		.05
Low or High Pack (15):		.50
Low or High Box (36):		12.50
Jumbo Pack (27):		1.00
Jumbo Box (20):		16.00
Bench/Morgan Auto.		75.00
Ted Williams Auto.		425.00
1	Star Rookie Checklist (Ryan Klesko, Jim Thome)	.25
2	Royce Clayton/SR	.05
3	Brian Jordan/SR **RC**	.30
4	Dave Fleming/SR **RC**	.05
5	Jim Thome/SR	.40
6	Jeff Juden/SR	.05
7	Roberto Hernandez/SR **RC**	.15
8	Kyle Abbott/SR **RC**	.05
9	Chris George/SR **RC**	.05
10	Rob Maurer/SR **RC**	.05
11	Donald Harris/SR **RC**	.05
12	Ted Wood/SR **RC**	.05
13	Patrick Lennon/SR **RC**	.05
14	Willie Banks/SR	.05
15	Roger Salkeld/SR **RC**	.05
16	Wil Cordero/SR	.05
17	Arthur Rhodes/SR **RC**	.05
18	Pedro Martinez/SR	.40
19	Andy Ashby/SR **RC**	.10
20	Tom Goodwin	.05
21	Braulio Castillo/SR **RC**	.05
22	Todd Van Poppel/SR	.05
23	Brian Williams/SR **RC**	.05
24	Ryan Klesko/SR	.05
25	Kenny Lofton/SR	.05
26	Derek Bell/SR	.05
27	Reggie Sanders/SR	.05
28	Dave Winfield (Winfield's 400th)	.25
29	Atlanta Braves Checklist (Dave Justice)	.05
30	Cincinnati Reds Checklist (Rob Dibble)	.05
31	Houston Astros Checklist (Craig Biggio **RC**)	.05
32	Los Angeles Dodgers Checklist (Eddie Murray)	.20
33	San Diego Padres Checklist (Fred McGriff)	.05
34	San Francisco Giants Checklist (Willie McGee)	.05
35	Chicago Cubs Checklist (Shawon Dunston)	.05
36	Montreal Expos Checklist (Delino DeShields)	.05
37	New York Mets Checklist (Howard Johnson)	.05
38	Philadelphia Phillies Checklist (John Kruk)	.05
39	Pittsburgh Pirates Checklist (Doug Drabek)	.05
40	St. Louis Cardinals Checklist (Todd Zeile)	.05
41	Steve Avery (Playoff Perfection)	.05
42	Jeremy Hernandez **RC**	.05
43	Doug Henry **RC**	.05
44	Chris Donnels **RC**	.05
45	Mo Sanford **RC**	.05
46	Scott Kamieniecki **RC**	.10
47	Mark Lemke	.05
48	Steve Farr	.05
49	Francisco Oliveras	.05
50	Ced Landrum **RC**	.05
51	Top Prospect Checklist (Rondell White, Marc Newfield)	.05
52	Eduardo Perez **RC** (Top Prospect)	.10
53	Tom Nevers **RC** (Top Prospect)	.05
54	David Zancanaro **RC** (Top Prospect)	.05
55	Shawn Green **RC** (Top Prospect)	1.50
56	Mark Wohlers **RC** (Top Prospect)	.05
57	Dave Nilsson (Top Prospect)	.05
58	Dmitri Young (Top Prospect)	.05
59	Ryan Hawblitzel **RC** (Top Prospect)	.05
60	Raul Mondesi (Top Prospect)	.05
61	Rondell White (Top Prospect)	.05
62	Steve Hosey (Top Prospect)	.05
63	Manny Ramirez **RC** (Top Prospect)	2.00
64	Marc Newfield (Top Prospect)	.05
65	Jeromy Burnitz (Top Prospect)	.05
66	Mark Smith **RC** (Top Prospect)	.05
67	Joey Hamilton **RC** (Top Prospect)	.10
68	Tyler Green **RC** (Top Prospect)	.05
69	John Farrell **RC** (Top Prospect)	.05
70	Kurt Miller **RC** (Top Prospect)	.05
71	Jeff Plympton **RC** (Top Prospect)	.05
72	Dan Wilson (Top Prospect)	.05
73	Joe Vitiello **RC** (Top Prospect)	.05
74	Rico Brogna (Top Prospect)	.05
75	David McCarty **RC** (Top Prospect)	.05
76	Bob Wickman **RC** (Top Prospect)	.05
77	Carlos Rodriguez **RC** (Top Prospect)	.05
78	Jim Abbott (Stay in School)	.05
79	Bloodlines (Pedro Martinez, Ramon Martinez)	.25
80	Bloodlines (Kevin Mitchell, Keith Mitchell)	.05
81	Bloodlines (Sandy Jr. & Roberto Alomar, Sandy Jr. & Roberto Alomar)	.10
82	Bloodlines (Cal Jr. & Billy Ripken, Cal Jr. & Billy Ripken)	.40
83	Bloodlines (Tony & Chris Gwynn, Tony & Chris Gwynn)	.20
84	Bloodlines (Dwight Gooden, Gary Sheffield)	.15
85	Bloodlines (Ken, Sr.; Ken, Jr.; & Craig Griffey, Ken, Sr.; Ken, Jr.; & Craig Griffey, Ken, Sr.; Ken, Jr.; & Craig Griffey)	.30
86	California Angels Checklist (Jim Abbott)	.05
87	Chicago White Sox Checklist (Frank Thomas)	.25
88	Kansas City Royals Checklist (Danny Tartabull)	.05
89	Minnesota Twins Checklist (Scott Erickson)	.05
90	Oakland Athletics Checklist (Rickey Henderson)	.25
91	Seattle Mariners Checklist (Edgar Martinez)	.05
92	Texas Rangers Checklist (Nolan Ryan)	.50
93	Baltimore Orioles Checklist (Ben McDonald)	.05
94	Boston Red Sox Checklist (Ellis Burks)	.05
95	Cleveland Indians Checklist (Greg Swindell)	.05
96	Detroit Tigers Checklist (Cecil Fielder)	.05
97	Milwaukee Brewers Checklist (Greg Vaughn)	.05
98	New York Yankees Checklist (Kevin Maas)	.05
99	Toronto Blue Jays Checklist (Dave Steib)	.05
100	Checklist 1-100	.05
101	Joe Oliver	.05
102	Hector Villanueva	.05
103	Ed Whitson	.05
104	Danny Jackson	.05
105	Chris Hammond	.05
106	Ricky Jordan	.05
107	Kevin Bass	.05
108	Darrin Fletcher	.05
109	Junior Ortiz	.05
110	Tom Bolton	.05
111	Jeff King	.05
112	Dave Magadan	.05
113	Mike LaValliere	.05
114	Hubie Brooks	.05
115	Jay Bell	.05
116	David Wells	.05
117	Jim Leyritz	.05
118	Manuel Lee	.05
119	Alvaro Espinoza	.05
120	B.J. Surhoff	.05
121	Hal Morris	.05
122	Shawon Dunston	.05
123	Chris Sabo	.05
124	Andre Dawson	.25
125	Eric Davis	.05
126	Chili Davis	.05
127	Dale Murphy	.15
128	Kirk McCaskill	.05
129	Terry Mulholland	.05
130	Rick Aguilera	.05
131	Vince Coleman	.05
132	Andy Van Slyke	.05
133	Gregg Jefferies	.05
134	Barry Bonds	1.00
135	Dwight Gooden	.05
136	Dave Stieb	.05
137	Albert Belle	.05
138	Teddy Higuera	.05
139	Jesse Barfield	.05
140	Pat Borders	.05
141	Bip Roberts	.05
142	Rob Dibble	.05
143	Mark Grace	.05
144	Barry Larkin	.05
145	Ryne Sandberg	.50
146	Scott Erickson	.05
147	Luis Polonia	.05
148	John Burkett	.05
149	Luis Sojo	.05
150	Dickie Thon	.05
151	Walt Weiss	.05
152	Mike Scioscia	.05
153	Mark McGwire	.75
154	Matt Williams	.05
155	Rickey Henderson	.40
156	Sandy Alomar, Jr.	.05
157	Brian McRae	.05
158	Harold Baines	.05
159	Kevin Appier	.05
160	Felix Fermin	.05
161	Leo Gomez	.05
162	Craig Biggio	.05
163	Ben McDonald	.05
164	Randy Johnson	.40
165	Cal Ripken, Jr.	1.00
166	Frank Thomas	.40
167	Delino DeShields	.05
168	Greg Gagne	.05
169	Ron Karkovice	.05
170	Charlie Leibrandt	.05
171	Dave Righetti	.05
172	Dave Henderson	.05
173	Steve Decker	.05
174	Darryl Strawberry	.05
175	Will Clark	.05
176	Ruben Sierra	.05
177	Ozzie Smith	.50
178	Charles Nagy	.05
179	Gary Pettis	.05
180	Kirk Gibson	.05
181	Randy Milligan	.05
182	Dave Valle	.05

183 Chris Hoiles .05
184 Tony Phillips .05
185 Brady Anderson .05
186 Scott Fletcher .05
187 Gene Larkin .05
188 Lance Johnson .05
189 Greg Olson .05
190 Melido Perez .05
191 Lenny Harris .05
192 Terry Kennedy .05
193 Mike Gallego .05
194 Willie McGee .05
195 Juan Samuel .05
196 Jeff Huson .05
197 Alex Cole .05
198 Ron Robinson .05
199 Joel Skinner .05
200 Checklist 101-200 .05
201 Kevin Reimer .05
202 Stan Belinda .05
203 Pat Tabler .05
204 Jose Guzman .05
205 Jose Lind .05
206 Spike Owen .05
207 Joe Orsulak .05
208 Charlie Hayes .05
209 Mike Devereaux .05
210 Mike Fitzgerald .05
211 Willie Randolph .05
212 Rod Nichols .05
213 Mike Boddicker .05
214 Bill Spiers .05
215 Steve Olin .05
216 David Howard **RC** .05
217 Gary Varsho .05
218 Mike Harkey .05
219 Luis Aquino .05
220 Chuck McElroy **RC** .05
221 Doug Drabek .05
222 Dave Winfield .40
223 Rafael Palmeiro .35
224 Joe Carter .05
225 Bobby Bonilla .05
226 Ivan Calderon .05
227 Gregg Olson .05
228 Tim Wallach .05
229 Terry Pendleton .05
230 Gilberto Reyes **RC** .05
231 Carlos Baerga .05
232 Greg Vaughn .05
233 Bret Saberhagen .05
234 Gary Sheffield .30
235 Mark Lewis .05
236 George Bell .05
237 Danny Tartabull .05
238 Willie Wilson .05
239 Doug Dascenzo .05
240 Bill Pecota .05
241 Julio Franco .05
242 Ed Sprague .05
243 Juan Gonzalez .20
244 Chuck Finley .05
245 Ivan Rodriguez .35
246 Len Dykstra .05
247 Deion Sanders .10
248 Dwight Evans .05
249 Larry Walker .05
250 Billy Ripken .05
251 Mickey Tettleton .05
252 Tony Pena .05
253 Benito Santiago .05
254 Kirby Puckett .50
255 Cecil Fielder .05
256 Howard Johnson .05
257 Andujar Cedeno .05
258 Jose Rijo .05
259 Al Osuna .05
260 Todd Hundley .05
261 Orel Hershiser .05
262 Ray Lankford .05
263 Robin Ventura .05
264 Felix Jose .05
265 Eddie Murray .40
266 Kevin Mitchell .05
267 Gary Carter .40
268 Mike Benjamin .05
269 Dick Schofield .05
270 Jose Uribe .05
271 Pete Incaviglia .05
272 Tony Fernandez .05
273 Alan Trammell .05
274 Tony Gwynn .50
275 Mike Greenwell .05
276 Jeff Bagwell .40
277 Frank Viola .05
278 Randy Myers .05
279 Ken Caminiti .05
280 Bill Doran .05
281 Dan Pasqua .05
282 Alfredo Griffin .05
283 Jose Oquendo .05
284 Kal Daniels .05
285 Bobby Thigpen .05
286 Robby Thompson .05
287 Mark Eichhorn .05
288 Mike Felder .05
289 Dave Gallagher .05
290 Dave Anderson .05
291 Mel Hall .05
292 Jerald Clark .05
293 Al Newman .05
294 Rob Deer .05
295 Matt Nokes .05
296 Jack Armstrong .05
297 Jim Deshaies .05
298 Jeff Innis .05
299 Jeff Reed .05
300 Checklist 201-300 .05
301 Lonnie Smith .05
302 Jimmy Key .05
303 Junior Felix .05
304 Mike Heath .05
305 Mark Langston .05
306 Greg W. Harris .05
307 Brett Butler .05
308 Luis Rivera **RC** .05
309 Bruce Ruffin .05
310 Paul Faries .05
311 Terry Leach .05
312 Scott Brosius **RC** .10
313 Scott Leius .05
314 Harold Reynolds .05
315 Jack Morris .05
316 David Segui .05
317 Bill Gullickson .05
318 Todd Frohwirth .05
319 Mark Leiter **RC** .05
320 Jeff M. Robinson .05
321 Gary Gaetti .05
322 John Smoltz .05
323 Andy Benes .05
324 Kelly Gruber .05
325 Jim Abbott .05
326 John Kruk .05
327 Kevin Seitzer .05
328 Darrin Jackson .05
329 Kurt Stillwell **RC** .05
330 Mike Maddux .05
331 Dennis Eckersley .35
332 Dan Gladden .05
333 Jose Canseco .30
334 Kent Hrbek .05
335 Ken Griffey Sr. .05
336 Greg Swindell .05
337 Trevor Wilson **RC** .05
338 Sam Horn .05
339 Mike Henneman .05
340 Jerry Browne .05
341 Glenn Braggs .05
342 Tom Glavine .20
343 Wally Joyner .05
344 Fred McGriff .05
345 Ron Gant .05
346 Ramon Martinez .05
347 Wes Chamberlain .05
348 Terry Shumpert .05
349 Tim Teufel .05
350 Wally Backman .05
351 Joe Girardi .05
352 Devon White .05
353 Greg Maddux .50
354 Ryan Bowen **RC** .05
355 Roberto Alomar .20
356 Don Mattingly .60
357 Pedro Guerrero .05
358 Steve Sax .05
359 Joey Cora .05
360 Jim Gantner .05
361 Brian Barnes **RC** .05
362 Kevin McReynolds .05
363 Bret Barberie **RC** .05
364 David Cone .05
365 Dennis Martinez .05
366 Brian Hunter **RC** .05
367 Edgar Martinez .05
368 Steve Finley .05
369 Greg Briley .05
370 Jeff Blauser .05
371 Todd Stottlemyre .05
372 Luis Gonzalez .05
373 Rick Wilkins .05
374 Darryl Kile **RC** .05
375 John Olerud .05
376 Lee Smith .05
377 Kevin Maas .05
378 Dante Bichette .05
379 Tom Pagnozzi .05
380 Mike Flanagan .05
381 Charlie O'Brien .05
382 Dave Martinez .05
383 Keith Miller .05
384 Scott Ruskin .05
385 Kevin Elster .05
386 Alvin Davis .05
387 Casey Candaele .05
388 Pete O'Brien .05
389 Jeff Treadway **RC** .05
390 Scott Bradley .05
391 Mookie Wilson .05
392 Jimmy Jones .05
393 Candy Maldonado .05
394 Eric Yelding .05
395 Tom Henke .05
396 Franklin Stubbs .05
397 Milt Thompson .05
398 Mark Carreon .05
399 Randy Velarde .05
400 Checklist 301-400 .05
401 Omar Vizquel .05
402 Joe Boever .05
403 Bill Krueger .05
404 Jody Reed .05
405 Mike Schooler **RC** .05
406 Jason Grimsley .05
407 Greg Myers .05
408 Randy Ready .05
409 Mike Timlin **RC** .15
410 Mitch Williams .05
411 Garry Templeton .05
412 Greg Cadaret .05
413 Donnie Hill .05
414 Wally Whitehurst .05
415 Scott Sanderson .05
416 Thomas Howard .05
417 Neal Heaton .05
418 Charlie Hough .05
419 Jack Howell .05
420 Greg Hibbard .05
421 Carlos Quintana .05
422 Kim Batiste **RC** .05
423 Paul Molitor .40
424 Ken Griffey Jr. .65
425 Phil Plantier .05
426 Denny Neagle .05
427 Von Hayes .05
428 Shane Mack .05
429 Darren Daulton .05
430 Dwayne Henry .05
431 Lance Parrish .05
432 Mike Humphreys **RC** .05
433 Tim Burke .05
434 Bryan Harvey .05
435 Pat Kelly .05
436 Ozzie Guillen .05
437 Bruce Hurst .05
438 Sammy Sosa .50
439 Dennis Rasmussen .05
440 Ken Patterson .05
441 Jay Buhner .05
442 Pat Combs .05
443 Wade Boggs .50
444 George Brett .60
445 Mo Vaughn .05
446 Chuck Knoblauch .05
447 Tom Candiotti .05
448 Mark Portugal .05
449 Mickey Morandini .05
450 Duane Ward .05
451 Otis Nixon .05
452 Bob Welch .05
453 Rusty Meacham .05
454 Keith Mitchell .05
455 Marquis Grissom .05
456 Robin Yount .40
457 Harvey Pulliam **RC** .05
458 Jose DeLeon **RC** .05
459 Mark Gubicza .05
460 Darryl Hamilton .05
461 Tom Browning .05
462 Monty Fariss .05
463 Jerome Walton .05
464 Paul O'Neill .05
465 Dean Palmer .05
466 Travis Fryman .05
467 John Smiley .05
468 Lloyd Moseby .05
469 John Wehner **RC** .05
470 Skeeter Barnes **RC** .05
471 Steve Chitren .05
472 Kent Mercker .05
473 Terry Steinbach .05
474 Andres Galarraga .05
475 Steve Avery .05
476 Tom Gordon .05
477 Cal Eldred .05
478 Omar Olivares **RC** .05
479 Julio Machado .05
480 Bob Milacki .05
481 Les Lancaster .05
482 John Candelaria .05
483 Brian Downing .05
484 Roger McDowell .05
485 Scott Scudder .05
486 Zane Smith .05
487 John Cerutti .05
488 Steve Buechele .05
489 Paul Gibson .05
490 Curtis Wilkerson .05
491 Marvin Freeman .05
492 Tom Foley .05
493 Juan Berenguer .05
494 Ernest Riles .05
495 Sid Bream .05
496 Chuck Crim .05
497 Mike Macfarlane .05
498 Dale Sveum .05
499 Storm Davis .05
500 Checklist 401-500 .05
501 Jeff Reardon .05
502 Shawn Abner .05
503 Tony Fossas .05
504 Cory Snyder .05
505 Matt Young .05
506 Allan Anderson **RC** .05
507 Mark Lee .05
508 Gene Nelson .05
509 Mike Pagliarulo .05
510 Rafael Belliard .05
511 Jay Howell .05
512 Bob Tewksbury .05
513 Mike Morgan .05
514 John Franco .05
515 Kevin Gross .05
516 Lou Whitaker .05
517 Orlando Merced .05
518 Todd Benzinger .05
519 Gary Redus .05
520 Walt Terrell .05
521 Jack Clark .05
522 Dave Parker .05
523 Tim Naehring .05
524 Mark Whiten .05
525 Ellis Burks .05
526 Frank Castillo **RC** .05
527 Brian Harper .05
528 Brook Jacoby .05
529 Rick Sutcliffe .05
530 Joe Klink .05
531 Terry Bross .05
532 Jose Offerman .05
533 Todd Zeile .05
534 Eric Karros .05
535 Anthony Young **RC** .05
536 Milt Cuyler .05
537 Randy Tomlin .05
538 Scott Livingstone **RC** .05
539 Jim Eisenreich .05
540 Don Slaught .05
541 Scott Cooper .05
542 Joe Grahe **RC** .05
543 Tom Brunansky .05
544 Eddie Zosky .05
545 Roger Clemens .60
546 Dave Justice .05
547 Dave Stewart .05
548 David West .05
549 Dave Smith .05
550 Dan Plesac .05
551 Alex Fernandez .05
552 Bernard Gilkey .05
553 Jack McDowell .05
554 Tino Martinez .05
555 Bo Jackson .10
556 Bernie Williams .05
557 Mark Gardner .05
558 Glenallen Hill .05
559 Oil Can Boyd .05
560 Chris James .05
561 Scott Servais **RC** .05
562 Rey Sanchez **RC** .05
563 Paul McClellan **RC** .05
564 Andy Mota **RC** .05
565 Darren Lewis .05
566 Jose Melendez **RC** .05
567 Tommy Greene .05
568 Rich Rodriguez .05
569 Heathcliff Slocumb **RC** .05
570 Joe Hesketh **RC** .05
571 Carlton Fisk .40
572 Erik Hanson .05
573 Wilson Alvarez .05
574 Rheal Cormier **RC** .05
575 Tim Raines .05
576 Bobby Witt .05
577 Roberto Kelly .05
578 Kevin Brown .05
579 Chris Nabholz .05
580 Jesse Orosco .05
581 Jeff Brantley .05
582 Rafael Ramirez .05
583 Kelly Downs .05
584 Mike Simms .05
585 Mike Remlinger **RC** .05
586 Dave Hollins .05
587 Larry Andersen .05
588 Mike Gardiner .05
589 Craig Lefferts .05
590 Paul Assenmacher **RC** .05
591 Bryn Smith .05
592 Donn Pall .05
593 Mike Jackson .05
594 Scott Radinsky .05
595 Brian Holman .05
596 Geronimo Pena .05
597 Mike Jeffcoat .05
598 Carlos Martinez **RC** .05
599 Geno Petralli .05
600 Checklist 501-600 .05
601 Jerry Don Gleaton .05
602 Adam Peterson **RC** .05
603 Craig Grebeck .05
604 Mark Guthrie .05
605 Frank Tanana .05
606 Hensley Meulens **RC** .05
607 Mark Davis .05
608 Eric Plunk .05
609 Mark Williamson .05
610 Lee Guetterman **RC** .05
611 Bobby Rose .05
612 Bill Wegman .05
613 Mike Hartley .05
614 Chris Beasley **RC** .05
615 Chris Bosio .05
616 Henry Cotto .05
617 Chico Walker **RC** .05
618 Russ Swan **RC** .05
619 Bob Walk .05
620 Billy Swift .05
621 Warren Newson **RC** .05
622 Steve Bedrosian **RC** .05
623 Ricky Bones **RC** .05
624 Kevin Tapani .05
625 Juan Guzman **RC** .05
626 Jeff Johnson **RC** .05
627 Jeff Montgomery .05
628 Ken Hill .05
629 Gary Thurman .05
630 Steve Howe **RC** .05
631 Jose DeJesus .05
632 Bert Blyleven .05
633 Jaime Navarro .05
634 Lee Stevens **RC** .05
635 Pete Harnisch .05
636 Bill Landrum .05
637 Rich DeLucia .05
638 Luis Salazar **RC** .05
639 Rob Murphy .05
640 A.L. Diamond Skills Checklist (Rickey Henderson, Jose Canseco) .05
641 Roger Clemens (Diamond Skills) .40
642 Jim Abbott (Diamond Skills) .05
643 Travis Fryman (Diamond Skills) .05
644 Jesse Barfield (Diamond Skills) .05
645 Cal Ripken, Jr. (Diamond Skills) .50
646 Wade Boggs (Diamond Skills) .35
647 Cecil Fielder (Diamond Skills) .05
648 Rickey Henderson (Diamond Skills) .20
649 Jose Canseco (Diamond Skills) .15
650 Ken Griffey Jr. (Diamond Skills) .45
651 Kenny Rogers .05
652 Luis Mercedes **RC** .05
653 Mike Stanton .05
654 Glenn Davis .05
655 Nolan Ryan 1.00
656 Reggie Jefferson .05
657 Javier Ortiz **RC** .05
658 Greg A. Harris .05
659 Mariano Duncan .05
660 Jeff Shaw .05
661 Mike Moore .05
662 Chris Haney **RC** .05
663 Joe Slusarski **RC** .05
664 Wayne Housie **RC** .05
665 Carlos Garcia .05
666 Bob Ojeda .05
667 Bryan Hickerson **RC** .05
668 Tim Belcher .05
669 Ron Darling .05
670 Rex Hudler **RC** .05
671 Sid Fernandez .05
672 Chito Martinez **RC** .05
673 Pete Schourek **RC** .05
674 Armando Reynoso **RC** .05
675 Mike Mussina .30
676 Kevin Morton **RC** .05
677 Norm Charlton .05
678 Danny Darwin .05
679 Eric King .05
680 Ted Power .05
681 Barry Jones .05
682 Carney Lansford .05
683 Mel Rojas .05
684 Rick Honeycutt .05
685 Jeff Fassero **RC** .05
686 Cris Carpenter **RC** .05
687 Tim Crews .05
688 Scott Terry .05
689 Chris Gwynn .05
690 Gerald Perry .05
691 John Barfield .05
692 Bob Melvin .05
693 Juan Agosto .05
694 Alejandro Pena **RC** .05
695 Jeff Russell .05
696 Carmelo Martinez .05
697 Bud Black .05
698 Dave Otto **RC** .05
699 Billy Hatcher .05
700 Checklist 601-700 .05
701 Clemente Nunez **RC** .05
702 "Rookie Threats" (Donovan Osborne, Brian Jordan, Mark Clark) .05
703 Mike Morgan .05
704 Keith Miller .05
705 Kurt Stillwell .05
706 Damon Berryhill .05
707 Von Hayes .05
708 Rick Sutcliffe .05
709 Hubie Brooks .05
710 Ryan Turner **RC** .05
711 N.L. Diamond Skills Checklist (Barry Bonds, Andy Van Slyke) .30
712 Jose Rijo (Diamond Skills) .05
713 Tom Glavine (Diamond Skills) .05
714 Shawon Dunston (Diamond Skills) .05
715 Andy Van Slyke (Diamond Skills) .05
716 Ozzie Smith (Diamond Skills) .35
717 Tony Gwynn (Diamond Skills) .35
718 Will Clark (Diamond Skills) .05
719 Marquis Grissom (Diamond Skills) .05
720 Howard Johnson (Diamond Skills) .05
721 Barry Bonds (Diamond Skills) .50
722 Kirk McCaskill .05
723 Sammy Sosa .50
724 George Bell .05
725 Gregg Jefferies .05
726 Gary DiSarcina **RC** .05
727 Mike Bordick .05
728 Eddie Murray (400 Home Run Club) .20
729 Rene Gonzales .05
730 Mike Bielecki .05
731 Calvin Jones **RC** .05
732 Jack Morris .05
733 Frank Viola .05
734 Dave Winfield .40
735 Kevin Mitchell .05
736 Billy Swift .05
737 Dan Gladden .05
738 Mike Jackson .05
739 Mark Carreon .05
740 Kirt Manwaring .05
741 Randy Myers .05
742 Kevin McReynolds .05
743 Steve Sax .05
744 Wally Joyner .05
745 Gary Sheffield .25
746 Danny Tartabull .05
747 Julio Valera .05
748 Denny Neagle .05
749 Lance Blankenship .05
750 Mike Gallego .05
751 Bret Saberhagen .05
752 Ruben Amaro **RC** .05
753 Eddie Murray .40
754 Kyle Abbott **RC** .05
755 Bobby Bonilla .05
756 Eric Davis .05
757 Eddie Taubensee **RC** .05
758 Andres Galarraga .05
759 Pete Incaviglia .05
760 Tom Candiotti .05
761 Tim Belcher .05
762 Ricky Bones .05
763 Bip Roberts .05
764 Pedro Munoz .05
765 Greg Swindell .05
766 Kenny Lofton .05
767 Gary Carter .40
768 Charlie Hayes .05
769 Dickie Thon .05
770 Diamond Debuts Checklist (Donovan Osborne) .05
771 Bret Boone (Diamond Debuts) .10
772 Archi Cianfrocco **RC** (Diamond Debuts) .05
773 Mark Clark **RC** (Diamond Debuts) .05
774 Chad Curtis **RC** (Diamond Debuts) .20
775 Pat Listach **RC** (Diamond Debuts) .05
776 Pat Mahomes **RC** (Diamond Debuts) .05
777 Donovan Osborne **RC** (Diamond Debuts) .05
778 John Patterson **RC** (Diamond Debuts) .05
779 Andy Stankiewicz **RC** (Diamond Debuts) .05
780 Turk Wendell **RC** (Diamond Debuts) .10
781 Bill Krueger .05
782 Rickey Henderson (Grand Theft) .20
783 Kevin Seitzer .05
784 Dave Martinez .05
785 John Smiley .05
786 Matt Stairs .05
787 Scott Scudder .05
788 John Wetteland .05
789 Jack Armstrong .05
790 Ken Hill .05
791 Dick Schofield .05
792 Mariano Duncan .05
793 Bill Pecota .05
794 Mike Kelly **RC** .05
795 Willie Randolph .05
796 Butch Henry **RC** .05
797 Carlos Hernandez **RC** .05
798 Doug Jones .05
799 Melido Perez .05
800 Checklist .05
SP3 "Prime Time's Two" (Deion Sanders) .25
SP4 "Mr. Baseball" (Tom Selleck, Frank Thomas) 2.00
HH2 Ted Williams (Hologram) 2.00

Baseball Heroes Bench/Morgan

This set is devoted to two of the vital cogs in Cincinnati's Big Red Machine: Hall of Famers Johnny Bench and Joe Morgan. Cards, numbered 37-45, were included in high number packs. An unnumbered cover card was also produced. Both players autographed 2,500 of card #45, the painting of the Reds duo by sports artist Vernon Wells.

		NM/M
Complete Set (10):		4.00
Common Card:		.50
Autographed Card:		65.00
---	Header Card	.75
37	1968 Rookie of the Year (Johnny Bench)	.75
38	1968-77 Ten Straight Gold Gloves (Johnny Bench)	.75
39	1970 & 1972 MVP (Johnny Bench)	.75

40	1965 Rookie Year (Joe Morgan)	.50
41	1975-76 Back-to-Back MVP (Joe Morgan)	.50
42	1980-83 The Golden Years (Joe Morgan)	.50
43	1972-79 Big Red Machine (Johnny Bench, Joe Morgan)	.60
44	1989 & 1990 Hall of Fame (Johnny Bench, Joe Morgan)	.60
45	Checklist - Heroes 37-45 (Johnny Bench, Joe Morgan)	.60

Bench-Morgan Box Bottoms

The eight Heroes of Baseball high-number cards featuring Johnny Bench and/or Joe Morgan were also issued in a box-bottom version measuring about 5" x 7". The blank-back box bottoms are listed here according to the corresponding number of the regular-size cards.

		NM/M
Complete Set (8):		7.00
Common Card:		1.00
(37)	1968 Rookie of the Year (Johnny Bench)	1.00
(38)	1968-77 Ten Straight Gold Gloves (Johnny Bench)	1.00
(39)	1970 & 1972 MVP (Johnny Bench)	1.00
(40)	1965 Rookie Year (Joe Morgan)	1.00
(41)	1975-76 Back-to-Back MVP (Joe Morgan)	1.00
(42)	1980-83 The Golden Years (Joe Morgan)	1.00
(43)	1972-79 Big Red Machine (Johnny Bench, Joe Morgan)	1.00
(44)	1989 & 1990 Hall of Fame (Johnny Bench, Joe Morgan)	1.00

Baseball Heroes Ted Williams

This Baseball Heroes set devoted to Ted Williams continues where previous efforts left off by numbering it from 28-36. An unnumbered "Baseball Heroes" cover card is also included. Cards were found in low-number foil and jumbo packs. Williams also autographed 2,500 cards, which were numbered and randomly inserted in low-number packs.

		NM/M
Complete Set (10):		3.00
Common Player:		.50
Autographed Card:		425.00
---	Header Card	.75
28	1939 Rookie Year (Ted Williams)	.50
29	1941 .406! (Ted Williams)	.50
30	1942 Triple Crown Year (Ted Williams)	.50
31	1946 & 1949 MVP (Ted Williams)	.50
32	1947 Second Triple Crown (Ted Williams)	.50
33	1950s Player of the Decade (Ted Williams)	.50
34	1960 500 Home Run Club (Ted Williams)	.50
35	1966 Hall of Fame (Ted Williams)	.50
36	Checklist - Heroes 28-36 (Ted Williams)	.50

Ted Williams Box Bottoms

Foil-pack boxes of low-number 1992 Upper Deck baseball featured on their bottom an oversize reproduction of the front of one of the Ted Williams "Baseball Heroes" insert cards. Eight different box-bottom cards were produced, measuring 5" x 7" and printed on a mottled orange background. The box-bottom cards are blank-backed and unnumbered. They are checklisted here according to the card numbers of the regular-size version.

		NM/M
Complete Set (8):		6.00
Common Player:		1.00
(28)	1939 - Rookie Year (Ted Williams)	1.00
(29)	1941 - .406 (Ted Williams)	1.00
(30)	1942 - Triple Crown Year (Ted Williams)	1.00
(31)	1946, 1949 - MVP (Ted Williams)	1.00
(32)	1947 - Second Triple Crown (Ted Williams)	1.00
(33)	1950s - Player of the Decade (Ted Williams)	1.00
(34)	1960 - 500 Hokme Run Club (Ted Williams)	1.00
(35)	1966 - Hall of Fame (Ted Williams)	1.00

College POY Holograms

This three-card hologram set features the College Player of the Year winners from 1989-91. Cards were randomly inserted in high number foil packs and have a CP prefix for numbering.

		NM/M
Complete Set (3):		.75
Common Player:		.25
1	David McCarty	.25
2	Mike Kelly	.25
3	Ben McDonald	.25

Hall of Fame Heroes

This set features three top players from the 1970s: Vida Blue, Lou Brock and Rollie Fingers. The cards continue from last year's set by using numbers H5-H8. The three players are each on one card; the fourth card features all three. They were found in low-number foil packs and specially-marked jumbo packs. Both

types of packs could also contain autographed cards; each player signed 3,000 cards.

		NM/M
Complete Set (4):		2.50
Common Player:		.50
5	Vida Blue	.50
5a	Vida Blue/Auto.	20.00
6	Lou Brock	1.00
6a	Lou Brock/Auto.	35.00
7	Rollie Fingers	.50
7a	Rollie Fingers/Auto.	30.00
8	Vida Blue, Lou Brock, Rollie Fingers	1.00

Heroes Highlights

Special packaging of 1992 Upper Deck high numbers produced for sales to dealers at its Heroes of Baseball show series included these cards of former players as inserts. Cards have a Heroes Highlights banner including the player's name and the date of his career highlight beneath the photo. In a tombstone frame on back, the highlight is chronicled. Cards are numbered alphabetically by player name, with the card number carrying an HI prefix.

		NM/M
Complete Set (10):		4.00
Common Player:		.45
1	Bobby Bonds	.45
2	Lou Brock	.45
3	Rollie Fingers	.45
4	Bob Gibson	.45
5	Reggie Jackson	.75
6	Gaylord Perry	.45
7	Robin Roberts	.45
8	Brooks Robinson	.45
9	Billy Williams	.45
10	Ted Williams	2.00

Home Run Heroes

This 26-card set features a top home run hitter from each major league team. The cards, numbered HR1-HR26, were found in low-number jumbo packs, one per pack.

		NM/M
Complete Set (26):		5.00
Common Player:		.15
1	Jose Canseco	.45
2	Cecil Fielder	.15
3	Howard Johnson	.15
4	Cal Ripken, Jr.	1.50
5	Matt Williams	.15
6	Joe Carter	.15
7	Ron Gant	.15
8	Frank Thomas	.75
9	Andre Dawson	.40
10	Fred McGriff	.15
11	Danny Tartabull	.15
12	Chili Davis	.15
13	Albert Belle	.15
14	Jack Clark	.15
15	Paul O'Neill	.15
16	Darryl Strawberry	.15
17	Dave Winfield	.75
18	Jay Buhner	.15
19	Juan Gonzalez	.25
20	Greg Vaughn	.15
21	Barry Bonds	1.50
22	Matt Nokes	.15
23	John Kruk	.15
24	Ivan Calderon	.15
25	Jeff Bagwell	.75
26	Todd Zeile	.15

Scouting Report

These cards were randomly inserted in Upper Deck high-number jumbo packs. The set is numbered SR1-SR25 and features 25 top prospects, including 1992 Rookies of the Year Pat Listach and Eric Karros. "Scouting Report" is written down the side on the front in silver lettering. The back features a clipboard which shows a photo, a player profile and a major league scouting report.

		NM/M
Complete Set (25):		2.00
Common Player:		.25
1	Andy Ashby	.25
2	Willie Banks	.25
3	Kim Batiste	.25
4	Derek Bell	.25
5	Archi Cianfrocco	.25
6	Royce Clayton	.25
7	Gary DiSarcina	.25
8	Dave Fleming	.25
9	Butch Henry	.25
10	Todd Hundley	.25
11	Brian Jordan	.25
12	Eric Karros	.25
13	Pat Listach	.25
14	Scott Livingstone	.25
15	Kenny Lofton	.25
16	Pat Mahomes	.25
17	Denny Neagle	.25
18	Dave Nilsson	.25
19	Donovan Osborne	.25
20	Reggie Sanders	.25
21	Andy Stankiewicz	.25
22	Jim Thome	1.50
23	Julio Valera	.25
24	Mark Wohlers	.25
25	Anthony Young	.25

Ted Williams' Best Hitters/Future

Twenty of the best hitters in baseball according to legend Ted Williams are featured in this special insert set from Upper Deck. The cards are styled much like the 1992 FanFest cards and showcase each chosen player. Each card is numbered with a "T" designation.

		NM/M
Complete Set (20):		3.00
Common Player:		.12
1	Wade Boggs	.50
2	Barry Bonds	1.00
3	Jose Canseco	.25
4	Will Clark	.10
5	Cecil Fielder	.10
6	Tony Gwynn	.50
7	Rickey Henderson	.40
8	Fred McGriff	.10
9	Kirby Puckett	.50
10	Ruben Sierra	.10
11	Roberto Alomar	.20
12	Jeff Bagwell	.40
13	Albert Belle	.10
14	Juan Gonzalez	.20
15	Ken Griffey Jr.	.75
16	Chris Hoiles	.10
17	Dave Justice	.10
18	Phil Plantier	.10
19	Frank Thomas	.40
20	Robin Ventura	.10

FanFest

This 54-card boxed set was made available through special offers at the 1992 National Sports Collectors Convention and at the 1992 All-Star FanFest in San Diego. Card fronts feature a glossy UV finish, silver-foil stamping and the All-Star FanFest logo. The card backs include a player profile. Both "Future Heroes" and past and present "All-Star Heroes" are featured. The complete set was packaged in an attractive blue box with white pinstripes.

		NM/M
Complete Set (54):		6.00
Common Player:		.10
1	Steve Avery	.10
2	Ivan Rodriguez	.60
3	Jeff Bagwell	.75
4	Delino DeShields	.10
5	Royce Clayton	.10
6	Robin Ventura	.10
7	Phil Plantier	.10
8	Ray Lankford	.10
9	Juan Gonzalez	.40
10	Frank Thomas	.75
11	Roberto Alomar	.30
12	Sandy Alomar, Jr.	.10
13	Wade Boggs	1.25
14	Barry Bonds	2.50
15	Bobby Bonilla	.10
16	George Brett	1.50
17	Jose Canseco	.60
18	Will Clark	.10
19	Roger Clemens	1.50
20	Eric Davis	.10
21	Rob Dibble	.10
22	Cecil Fielder	.10
23	Dwight Gooden	.10
24	Ken Griffey Jr.	2.00
25	Tony Gwynn	1.25
26	Bryan Harvey	.10
27	Rickey Henderson	.75
28	Howard Johnson	.10
29	Wally Joyner	.10
30	Barry Larkin	.10
31	Don Mattingly	1.50
32	Mark McGwire	2.25
33	Dale Murphy	.30
34	Rafael Palmeiro	.60
35	Kirby Puckett	1.25
36	Cal Ripken, Jr.	2.50
37	Nolan Ryan	2.50
38	Chris Sabo	.10
39	Ryne Sandberg	1.25
40	Benito Santiago	.10
41	Ruben Sierra	.10
42	Ozzie Smith	1.25
43	Darryl Strawberry	.10
44	Robin Yount	.75
45	Rollie Fingers	.20
46	Reggie Jackson	1.25
47	Billy Williams	.20
48	Lou Brock	.20
49	Gaylord Perry	.20
50	Ted Williams	2.00
51	Brooks Robinson	.50
52	Bob Gibson	.20
53	Bobby Bonds	.10
54	Robin Roberts	.20

FanFest Gold

One out of every 60 sets of Upper Deck FanFest All-Stars was produced with gold-foil printing highlights rather than silver. The sets were randomly inserted into cases.

	NM/M
Complete Set (54):	30.00
Common Player:	.25

FanFest Ted Williams Super

This large-format (8-1/2" x 11") card is essentially an enlargement of Ted Williams' card issued with the FanFest All-Star Heroes boxed set by UD. The Williams super cards were distributed at the FanFest event and are serially numbered on back within an edition of 2,500.

	NM/M
Ted Williams	25.00

MVP Holograms

State of the art holography is presented in this 54-card plastic-cased set featuring a top pitcher and a top position player from each major league team, plus 1991 MVPs Terry Pendleton and Cal Ripken, Jr. The hologram on the front of each card feature a closeup and a field-action photo of the player; his name and position are in a strip at bottom. Full-color backs have a player photo on the right and career summary on the left. A custom album for the set was available via a mail offer for $10. Each set includes a numbered certificate of authenticity, verifying its position within a total issue of 216,000 sets.

		NM/M
Complete Set (54):		6.00
Common Player:		.10
1	A.L. Checklist (Cal Ripken, Jr.)	.40
2	N.L. Checkklist (Terry Pendleton)	.10

3 Jim Abbott .10
4 Roberto Alomar .25
5 Kevin Appier .10
6 Steve Avery .10
7 Jeff Bagwell .40
8 Albert Belle .10
9 Andy Benes .10
10 Wade Boggs .50
11 Barry Bonds 1.00
12 George Brett .60
13 Ivan Calderon .10
14 Jose Canseco .30
15 Will Clark .10
16 Roger Clemens .60
17 David Cone .10
18 Doug Drabek .10
19 Dennis Eckersley .35
20 Scott Erickson .10
21 Cecil Fielder .10
22 Ken Griffey Jr. .75
23 Bill Gullickson .10
24 Juan Guzman .10
25 Pete Harnisch .10
26 Howard Johnson .10
27 Randy Johnson .40
28 John Kruk .10
29 Barry Larkin .10
30 Greg Maddux .50
31 Dennis Martinez .10
32 Ramon Martinez .10
33 Don Mattingly .60
34 Jack McDowell .10
35 Fred McGriff .10
36 Paul Molitor .40
37 Charles Nagy .10
38 Gregg Olson .10
39 Terry Pendleton .10
40 Luis Polonia .10
41 Kirby Puckett .50
42 Dave Righetti .10
43 Jose Rijo .10
44 Cal Ripken, Jr. 1.00
45 Nolan Ryan 1.00
46 Ryne Sandberg .50
47 Scott Sanderson .10
48 Ruben Sierra .10
49 Lee Smith .10
50 Ozzie Smith .50
51 Darryl Strawberry .10
52 Frank Thomas .40
53 Bill Wegman .10
54 Mitch Williams .10

Comic Ball 3

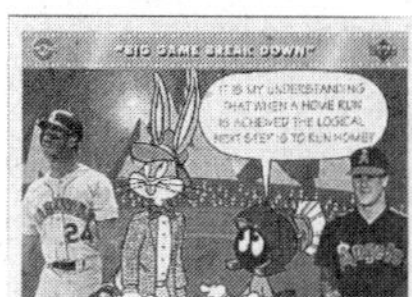

The third series of Comic Ball cards was issued in 1992 and was the second to combine photos of real ballplayers with Looney Tune cartoon characters in several cartoon strip-style series. Players featured in the set with Bugs, Taz and the gang were Jim Abbott and the Ken Griffeys, Sr. and Jr. Each of the 198 regular cards features a puzzle-piece back. A special album to house the set was sold separately. A series of holograms which also combined the players and cartoon figures was issued as pack inserts.

	NM/M
Complete Set (198):	6.00
Common Card:	.05
Hologram:	1.00

Comic Ball 3 Holograms

These blank-back holograms which combine player pictures with those of cartoon characters were issued as inserts in Comic Ball 3 foil packs.

	NM/M
Common Hologram:	.50
(1) Jim Abbott (w/Tweety)	1.00
(2) Jim Abbott (w/Taz)	1.00
(3) Ken Griffey Jr. (w/Bugs)	2.00
(4) Ken Griffey Jr. (w/Wile E. Coyote)	2.00
(5) Chuck Jones (Artist) (w/Bugs)	.50

1993 Upper Deck

Upper Deck introduced its 1993 set in a two-series format to adjust to expansion. Cards 1-420 make up the first series.

Special subsets in Series 1 include rookies, teammates and community heroes. Fronts feature color player photos surrounded by a white border. Backs feature vertical photos, a change from the past, and more complete statistics than Upper Deck had in the past. The hologram appears in the lower-left corner on the card back. One out of 20 factory sets featured cards with gold, rather than silver, holograms.

	NM/M
Unopened Fact. Set (840):	30.00
Complete Set (840):	25.00
Common Player:	.05
Gold Hologram:	4X
Series 1 or 2 Pack (15):	.75
Series 1 or 2 Wax Box (36):	17.50
Jumbo Pack, USA (27):	1.50
Jumbo Box, USA (20):	17.50
Jumbo Pack, Canada (23):	2.00
Jumbo Box, Canada (20):	20.00

1 Tim Salmon (Checklist) .05
2 Mike Piazza/SR 1.25
3 Rene Arocha/SR **RC** .05
4 Willie Greene/SR **RC** .05
5 Manny Alexander/SR **RC** .05
6 Dan Wilson/SR .05
7 Dan Smith/SR **RC** .05
8 Kevin Rogers/SR **RC** .05
9 Nigel Wilson/SR **RC** .05
10 Joe Vitko/SR **RC** .05
11 Tim Costo/SR **RC** .05
12 Alan Embree/SR .05
13 Jim Tatum/SR **RC** .05
14 Cris Colon/SR **RC** .05
15 Steve Hosey/SR **RC** .05
16 Sterling Hitchcock/SR **RC** .15
17 Dave Mlicki/SR **RC** .05
18 Jessie Hollins/SR **RC** .05
19 Bobby J. Jones/SR **RC** .05
20 Kurt Miller/SR **RC** .05
21 Melvin Nieves/SR **RC** .05
22 Billy Ashley/SR **RC** .05
23 J.T. Snow/SR **RC** .50
24 Chipper Jones/SR .85
25 Tim Salmon/SR .25
26 Tim Pugh/SR **RC** .05
27 David Nied/SR .05
28 Mike Trombley/SR **RC** .05
29 Javier Lopez/SR .05
30 Community Heroes Checklist (Jim Abbott) .05
31 Jim Abbott (Community Heroes) .05
32 Dale Murphy (Community Heroes) .10
33 Tony Pena (Community Heroes) .05
34 Kirby Puckett (Community Heroes) .40
35 Harold Reynolds (Community Heroes) .05
36 Cal Ripken, Jr. (Community Heroes) .65
37 Nolan Ryan (Community Heroes) .65
38 Ryne Sandberg (Community Heroes) .35
39 Dave Stewart (Community Heroes) .05
40 Dave Winfield (Community Heroes) .25
41 Teammates Checklist (Joe Carter, Mark McGwire) .50
42 Blockbuster Trade (Joe Carter, Roberto Alomar) .05
43 Brew Crew (Pat Listach, Robin Yount, Paul Molitor) .15
44 Iron and Steal (Brady Anderson, Cal Ripken, Jr.) .45
45 Youthful Tribe (Albert Belle, Sandy Alomar Jr., Jim Thome, Carlos Baerga, Kenny Lofton) .25
46 Motown Mashers (Cecil Fielder, Mickey Tettleton) .05
47 Yankee Pride (Roberto Kelly, Don Mattingly) .45
48 Boston Cy Sox (Frank Viola, Roger Clemens) .30
49 Bash Brothers (Ruben Sierra, Mark McGwire) .50
50 Twin Titles (Kent Hrbek, Kirby Puckett) .35
51 Southside Sluggers (Robin Ventura, Frank Thomas) .35
52 Latin Stars (Jose Canseco, Ivan Rodriguez, Rafael Palmeiro, Juan Gonzalez) .35
53 Lethal Lefties (Mark Langston, Jim Abbott, Chuck Finley) .05
54 Royal Family (Gregg Jefferies, George Brett, Wally Joyner) .35
55 Pacific Sox Exchange (Kevin Mitchell, Jay Buhner, Ken Griffey Jr.) .40
56 George Brett .85
57 Scott Cooper .05
58 Mike Maddux .05
59 Rusty Meacham **RC** .05
60 Wil Cordero .05
61 Tim Teufel .05
62 Jeff Montgomery .05
63 Scott Livingstone **RC** .05
64 Doug Dascenzo .05
65 Bret Boone .05
66 Tim Wakefield **RC** .10
67 Curt Schilling .20
68 Frank Tanana .05
69 Len Dykstra .05
70 Derek Lilliquist .05
71 Anthony Young **RC** .05
72 Hipolito Pichardo **RC** .05
73 Rod Beck **RC** .05
74 Kent Hrbek .05
75 Tom Glavine .20
76 Kevin Brown .05
77 Chuck Finley .05
78 Bob Walk .05
79 Rheal Cormier .05
80 Rick Sutcliffe .05
81 Harold Baines .05
82 Lee Smith .05
83 Geno Petralli .05
84 Jose Oquendo .05
85 Mark Gubicza .05
86 Mickey Tettleton .05
87 Bobby Witt .05
88 Mark Lewis .05
89 Kevin Appier .05
90 Mike Stanton .05
91 Rafael Belliard .05
92 Kenny Rogers .05
93 Randy Velarde .05
94 Luis Sojo .05
95 Mark Leiter .05
96 Jody Reed .05
97 Pete Harnisch .05
98 Tom Candiotti .05
99 Mark Portugal .05
100 Dave Valle .05
101 Shawon Dunston .05
102 B.J. Surhoff .05
103 Jay Bell .05
104 Sid Bream .05
105 Checklist 1-105 (Frank Thomas) .35
106 Mike Morgan .05
107 Bill Doran .05
108 Lance Blankenship .05
109 Mark Lemke .05
110 Brian Harper .05
111 Brady Anderson .05
112 Bip Roberts .05
113 Mitch Williams .05
114 Craig Biggio .05
115 Eddie Murray .65
116 Matt Nokes .05
117 Lance Parrish .05
118 Bill Swift .05
119 Jeff Innis .05
120 Mike LaValliere .05
121 Hal Morris .05
122 Walt Weiss .05
123 Ivan Rodriguez .60
124 Andy Van Slyke .05
125 Roberto Alomar .20
126 Robby Thompson .05
127 Sammy Sosa .75
128 Mark Langston .05
129 Jerry Browne .05
130 Chuck McElroy .05
131 Frank Viola .05
132 Leo Gomez .05
133 Ramon Martinez .05
134 Don Mattingly .85
135 Roger Clemens .85
136 Rickey Henderson .65
137 Darren Daulton .05
138 Ken Hill .05
139 Ozzie Guillen .05
140 Jerald Clark .05
141 Dave Fleming .05
142 Delino DeShields .05
143 Matt Williams .05
144 Larry Walker .05
145 Ruben Sierra .05
146 Ozzie Smith .75
147 Chris Sabo .05
148 Carlos Hernandez **RC** .05
149 Pat Borders .05
150 Orlando Merced .05
151 Royce Clayton .05
152 Kurt Stillwell .05
153 Dave Hollins .05
154 Mike Greenwell .05
155 Nolan Ryan 1.50
156 Felix Jose .05
157 Junior Felix .05
158 Derek Bell .05
159 Steve Buechele .05
160 John Burkett .05
161 Pat Howell **RC** .05
162 Milt Cuyler .05
163 Terry Pendleton .05
164 Jack Morris .05
165 Tony Gwynn .75
166 Deion Sanders .10
167 Mike Devereaux .05
168 Ron Darling .05
169 Orel Hershiser .05
170 Mike Jackson .05
171 Doug Jones .05
172 Dan Walters **RC** .05
173 Darren Lewis .05
174 Carlos Baerga .05
175 Ryne Sandberg .75
176 Gregg Jefferies .05
177 John Jaha .05
178 Luis Polonia .05
179 Kirt Manwaring .05
180 Mike Magnante .05
181 Billy Ripken .05
182 Mike Moore .05
183 Eric Anthony .05
184 Lenny Harris .05
185 Tony Pena .05
186 Mike Felder .05
187 Greg Olson .05
188 Rene Gonzales .05
189 Mike Bordick .05
190 Mel Rojas .05
191 Todd Frohwirth .05
192 Darryl Hamilton .05
193 Mike Fetters .05
194 Omar Olivares **RC** .05
195 Tony Phillips .05
196 Paul Sorrento .05
197 Trevor Wilson .05
198 Kevin Gross .05
199 Ron Karkovice .05
200 Brook Jacoby .05
201 Mariano Duncan .05
202 Dennis Cook .05
203 Daryl Boston .05
204 Mike Perez .05
205 Manuel Lee .05
206 Steve Olin .05
207 Charlie Hough .05
208 Scott Scudder .05
209 Charlie O'Brien .05
210 Checklist 106-210 (Barry Bonds) .60
211 Jose Vizcaino .05
212 Scott Leius .05
213 Kevin Mitchell .05
214 Brian Barnes .05
215 Pat Kelly .05
216 Chris Hammond .05
217 Rob Deer .05
218 Cory Snyder .05
219 Gary Carter .65
220 Danny Darwin .05
221 Tom Gordon .05
222 Gary Sheffield .40
223 Joe Carter .05
224 Jay Buhner .05
225 Jose Offerman .05
226 Jose Rijo .05
227 Mark Whiten .05
228 Randy Milligan .05
229 Bud Black .05
230 Gary DiSarcina .05
231 Steve Finley .05
232 Dennis Martinez .05
233 Mike Mussina .30
234 Joe Oliver .05
235 Chad Curtis .05
236 Shane Mack .05
237 Jaime Navarro .05
238 Brian McRae .05
239 Chili Davis .05
240 Jeff King .05
241 Dean Palmer .05
242 Danny Tartabull .05
243 Charles Nagy .05
244 Ray Lankford .05
245 Barry Larkin .05
246 Steve Avery .05
247 John Kruk .05
248 Derrick May .05
249 Stan Javier .05
250 Roger McDowell .05
251 Dan Gladden .05
252 Wally Joyner .05
253 Pat Listach .05
254 Chuck Knoblauch .05
255 Sandy Alomar Jr. .05
256 Jeff Bagwell .65
257 Andy Stankiewicz .05
258 Darrin Jackson .05
259 Brett Butler .05
260 Joe Orsulak .05
261 Andy Benes .05
262 Kenny Lofton .05
263 Robin Ventura .05
264 Ron Gant .05
265 Ellis Burks .05
266 Juan Guzman .05
267 Wes Chamberlain .05
268 John Smiley .05
269 Franklin Stubbs .05
270 Tom Browning .05
271 Dennis Eckersley .60
272 Carlton Fisk .65
273 Lou Whitaker .05
274 Phil Plantier .05
275 Bobby Bonilla .05
276 Ben McDonald .05
277 Bob Zupcic .05
278 Terry Steinbach .05
279 Terry Mulholland .05
280 Lance Johnson .05
281 Willie McGee .05
282 Bret Saberhagen .05
283 Randy Myers .05
284 Randy Tomlin .05
285 Mickey Morandini .05
286 Brian Williams .05
287 Tino Martinez .05
288 Jose Melendez .05
289 Jeff Huson .05
290 Joe Grahe .05
291 Mel Hall .05
292 Otis Nixon .05
293 Todd Hundley .05
294 Casey Candaele .05
295 Kevin Seitzer .05
296 Eddie Taubensee .05
297 Moises Alou .05
298 Scott Radinsky .05
299 Thomas Howard .05
300 Kyle Abbott .05
301 Omar Vizquel .05
302 Keith Miller .05
303 Rick Aguilera .05
304 Bruce Hurst .05
305 Ken Caminiti .05
306 Mike Pagiarulo .05
307 Frank Seminara .05
308 Andre Dawson .30
309 Jose Lind .05
310 Joe Boever .05
311 Jeff Parrett **RC** .05
312 Alan Mills .05
313 Kevin Tapani .05
314 Darryl Kile .05
315 Checklist 211-315 (Will Clark) .05
316 Mike Sharperson .05
317 John Orton .05
318 Bob Tewksbury .05
319 Xavier Hernandez .05
320 Paul Assenmacher .05
321 John Franco .05
322 Mike Timlin .05
323 Jose Guzman .05
324 Pedro Martinez .65
325 Bill Spiers .05
326 Melido Perez .05
327 Mike Macfarlane .05
328 Ricky Bones .05
329 Scott Bankhead .05
330 Rich Rodriguez .05
331 Geronimo Pena .05
332 Bernie Williams .05
333 Paul Molitor .65
334 Roger Mason .05
335 David Cone .05
336 Randy Johnson .65
337 Pat Mahomes .05
338 Erik Hanson .05
339 Duane Ward .05
340 Al Martin .05
341 Pedro Munoz .05
342 Greg Colbrunn .05
343 Julio Valera .05
344 John Olerud .05
345 George Bell .05
346 Devon White .05
347 Donovan Osborne .05
348 Mark Gardner .05
349 Zane Smith .05
350 Wilson Alvarez .05
351 Kevin Koslofski **RC** .05
352 Roberto Hernandez .05
353 Glenn Davis .05
354 Reggie Sanders .05
355 Ken Griffey Jr. 1.00
355a Ken Griffey Jr. (Promo, 1992-dated hologram on back.) 3.00
355b Ken Griffey Jr. (8-1/2" x 11" limited edition of 1,000) 15.00
356 Marquis Grissom .05
357 Jack McDowell .05
358 Jimmy Key .05
359 Stan Belinda .05
360 Gerald Williams .05
361 Sid Fernandez .05
362 Alex Fernandez .05
363 John Smoltz .05
364 Travis Fryman .05
365 Jose Canseco .50
366 Dave Justice .05
367 Pedro Astacio **RC** .10
368 Tim Belcher .05
369 Steve Sax .05
370 Gary Gaetti .05
371 Jeff Frye .05
372 Bob Wickman .05
373 Ryan Thompson **RC** .05
374 David Hulse **RC** .05
375 Cal Eldred .05
376 Ryan Klesko .05
377 Damion Easley **RC** .10
378 John Kiely **RC** .05
379 Jim Bullinger **RC** .05
380 Brian Bohanon .05
381 Rod Brewer .05
382 Fernando Ramsey **RC** .05
383 Sam Militello .05
384 Arthur Rhodes .05
385 Eric Karros .05
386 Rico Brogna .05
387 John Valentin **RC** .10
388 Kerry Woodson **RC** .05
389 Ben Rivera **RC** .05
390 Matt Whiteside **RC** .05
391 Henry Rodriguez .05
392 John Wetteland .05
393 Kent Mercker .05
394 Bernard Gilkey .05
395 Doug Henry .05
396 Mo Vaughn .05
397 Scott Erickson .05
398 Bill Gullickson .05
399 Mark Guthrie .05
400 Dave Martinez .05
401 Jeff Kent **RC** .50
402 Chris Hoiles .05
403 Mike Henneman .05
404 Chris Nabholz .05
405 Tom Pagnozzi .05
406 Kelly Gruber .05
407 Bob Welch .05
408 Frank Castillo .05
409 John Dopson .05
410 Steve Farr .05
411 Henry Cotto .05
412 Bob Patterson .05
413 Todd Stottlemyre .05
414 Greg A. Harris .05
415 Denny Neagle .05
416 Bill Wegman .05
417 Willie Wilson .05
418 Terry Leach .05
419 Willie Randolph .05
420 Checklist 316-420 (Mark McGwire) .65
421 Calvin Murray (Top Prospects Checklist) .05
422 Pete Janicki **RC** (Top Prospect) .05
423 Todd Jones **RC** (Top Prospect) .05
424 Mike Neill (Top Prospect) .05
425 Carlos Delgado (Top Prospect) .40
426 Jose Oliva (Top Prospect) .05
427 Tyrone Hill (Top Prospect) .05
428 Dmitri Young (Top Prospect) .05
429 Derek Wallace **RC** (Top Prospect) .05
430 Michael Moore **RC** (Top Prospect) .05
431 Cliff Floyd (Top Prospect) .05
432 Calvin Murray (Top Prospect) .05
433 Manny Ramirez (Top Prospect) .75
434 Marc Newfield (Top Prospect) .05
435 Charles Johnson (Top Prospect) .05
436 Butch Huskey (Top Prospect) .05
437 Brad Pennington (Top Prospect) .05
438 Ray McDavid **RC** (Top Prospect) .05
439 Chad McConnell (Top Prospect) .05
440 Midre Cummings **RC** (Top Prospect) .05
441 Benji Gil (Top Prospect) .05
442 Frank Rodriguez (Top Prospect) .05
443 Chad Mottola **RC** (Top Prospect) .05
444 John Burke **RC** (Top Prospect) .05
445 Michael Tucker (Top Prospect) .05
446 Rick Greene (Top Prospect) .05
447 Rich Becker (Top Prospect) .05
448 Mike Robertson (Top Prospect) .05
449 Derek Jeter **RC** (Top Prospect) 10.00
450 Checklist 451-470 Inside the Numbers (David McCarty, Ivan Rodriguez) .05
451 Jim Abbott (Inside the Numbers) .05
452 Jeff Bagwell (Inside the Numbers) .40

453 Jason Bere (Inside the Numbers) .05
454 Delino DeShields (Inside the Numbers) .05
455 Travis Fryman (Inside the Numbers) .05
456 Alex Gonzalez (Inside the Numbers) .05
457 Phil Hiatt (Inside the Numbers) .05
458 Dave Hollins (Inside the Numbers) .05
459 Chipper Jones (Inside the Numbers) .65
460 Dave Justice (Inside the Numbers) .05
461 Ray Lankford (Inside the Numbers) .05
462 David McCarty (Inside the Numbers) .05
463 Mike Mussina (Inside the Numbers) .15
464 Jose Offerman (Inside the Numbers) .05
465 Dean Palmer (Inside the Numbers) .05
466 Geronimo Pena (Inside the Numbers) .05
467 Eduardo Perez (Inside the Numbers) .05
468 Ivan Rodriguez (Inside the Numbers) .25
469 Reggie Sanders (Inside the Numbers) .05
470 Bernie Williams (Inside the Numbers) .05
471 Checklist 472-485 Team Stars (Barry Bonds, Matt Williams, Will Clark) .45
472 Strike Force (John Smoltz, Steve Avery, Greg Maddux, Tom Glavine) .10
473 Red October (Jose Rijo, Rob Dibble, Roberto Kelly, Reggie Sanders, Barry Larkin) .10
474 Four Corners (Gary Sheffield, Phil Plantier, Tony Gwynn, Fred McGriff) .20
475 Shooting Stars (Doug Drabek, Craig Biggio, Jeff Bagwell) .15
476 Giant Sticks (Will Clark, Barry Bonds, Matt Williams) .40
477 Boyhood Friends (Darryl Strawberry, Eric Davis) .05
478 Rock Solid (Dante Bichette, David Nied, Andres Galarraga) .05
479 Inaugural Catch (Dave Magadan, Orestes Destrade, Bret Barbarie, Jeff Conine) .05
480 Steel City Champions (Tim Wakefield, Andy Van Slyke, Jay Bell) .05
481 "Les Grandes Etoiles" (Marquis Grissom, Delino DeShields, Dennis Martinez, Larry Walker) .05
482 Runnin' Redbirds (Geronimo Pena, Ray Lankford, Ozzie Smith, Bernard Gilkey) .10
483 Ivy Leaguers (Ryne Sandberg, Mark Grace, Randy Myers) .15
484 Big Apple Power Switch (Eddie Murray, Bobby Bonilla, Howard Johnson) .10
485 Hammers & Nails (John Kruk, Dave Hollins, Darren Daulton, Len Dykstra) .05
486 Barry Bonds (Award Winners) .60
487 Dennis Eckersley (Award Winners) .30
488 Greg Maddux (Award Winners) .40
489 Dennis Eckersley (Award Winners) .30
490 Eric Karros (Award Winners) .05
491 Pat Listach (Award Winners) .05
492 Gary Sheffield (Award Winners) .10
493 Mark McGwire (Award Winners) .75
494 Gary Sheffield (Award Winners) .10
495 Edgar Martinez (Award Winners) .05
496 Fred McGriff (Award Winners) .05
497 Juan Gonzalez (Award Winners) .20
498 Darren Daulton (Award Winners) .05
499 Cecil Fielder (Award Winners) .05
500 Checklist 501-510 Diamond Debuts (Brent Gates) .05
501 Tavo Alvarez (Diamond Debuts) .05
502 Rod Bolton (Diamond Debuts) .05
503 John Cummings **RC** (Diamond Debuts) .05
504 Brent Gates (Diamond Debuts) .05
505 Tyler Green (Diamond Debuts) .05
506 Jose Martinez **RC** (Diamond Debuts) .05
507 Troy Percival (Diamond Debuts) .05
508 Kevin Stocker (Diamond Debuts) .05
509 Matt Walbeck **RC** (Diamond Debuts) .10
510 Rondell White (Diamond Debuts) .05
511 Billy Ripken .05
512 Mike Moore .05
513 Jose Lind .05
514 Chito Martinez .05
515 Jose Guzman .05
516 Kim Batiste .05
517 Jeff Tackett .05
518 Charlie Hough .05
519 Marvin Freeman .05
520 Carlos Martinez .05
521 Eric Young .05
522 Pete Incaviglia .05
523 Scott Fletcher .05
524 Orestes Destrade .05
525 Checklist 421-525 (Ken Griffey Jr.) .40
526 Ellis Burks .05
527 Juan Samuel .05
528 Dave Magadan .05
529 Jeff Parrett .05
530 Bill Krueger .05
531 Frank Bolick .05
532 Alan Trammell .05
533 Walt Weiss .05
534 David Cone .05
535 Greg Maddux .75
536 Kevin Young .05
537 Dave Hansen .05
538 Alex Cole .05
539 Greg Hibbard .05
540 Gene Larkin .05
541 Jeff Reardon .05
542 Felix Jose .05
543 Jimmy Key .05
544 Reggie Jefferson .05
545 Gregg Jefferies .05
546 Dave Stewart .05
547 Tim Wallach .05
548 Spike Owen .05
549 Tommy Greene .05
550 Fernando Valenzuela .05
551 Rich Amaral .05
552 Bret Barberie .05
553 Edgar Martinez .05
554 Jim Abbott .05
555 Frank Thomas .65
556 Wade Boggs .75
557 Tom Henke .05
558 Milt Thompson .05
559 Lloyd McClendon .05
560 Vinny Castilla .05
561 Ricky Jordan .05
562 Andujar Cedeno .05
563 Greg Vaughn .05
564 Cecil Fielder .05
565 Kirby Puckett .75
566 Mark McGwire 1.25
567 Barry Bonds 1.50
568 Jody Reed .05
569 Todd Zeile .05
570 Mark Carreon .05
571 Joe Girardi .05
572 Luis Gonzalez .05
573 Mark Grace .05
574 Rafael Palmeiro .60
575 Darryl Strawberry .05
576 Will Clark .05
577 Fred McGriff .05
578 Kevin Reimer .05
579 Dave Righetti .05
580 Juan Bell .05
581 Jeff Brantley .05
582 Brian Hunter .05
583 Tim Naehring .05
584 Glenallen Hill .05
585 Cal Ripken, Jr. 1.50
586 Albert Belle .05
587 Robin Yount .65
588 Chris Bosio .05
589 Pete Smith .05
590 Chuck Carr .05
591 Jeff Blauser .05
592 Kevin McReynolds .05
593 Andres Galarraga .05
594 Kevin Maas .05
595 Eric Davis .05
596 Brian Jordan .05
597 Tim Raines .05
598 Rick Wilkins .05
599 Steve Cooke .05
600 Mike Gallego .05
601 Mike Munoz .05
602 Luis Rivera .05
603 Junior Ortiz .05
604 Brent Mayne .05
605 Luis Alicea .05
606 Damon Berryhill .05
607 Dave Henderson .05
608 Kirk McCaskill .05
609 Jeff Fassero .05
610 Mike Harkey .05
611 Francisco Cabrera .05
612 Rey Sanchez .05
613 Scott Servais .05
614 Darrin Fletcher .05
615 Felix Fermin .05
616 Kevin Seitzer .05
617 Bob Scanlan .05
618 Billy Hatcher .05
619 John Vander Wal .05
620 Joe Hesketh .05
621 Hector Villanueva .05
622 Randy Milligan .05
623 Tony Tarasco **RC** .05
624 Russ Swan .05
625 Willie Wilson .05
626 Frank Tanana .05
627 Pete O'Brien .05
628 Lenny Webster .05
629 Mark Clark .05
630 Checklist 526-630 (Roger Clemens) .40
631 Alex Arias .05
632 Chris Gwynn .05
633 Tom Bolton .05
634 Greg Briley .05
635 Kent Bottenfield .05
636 Kelly Downs .05
637 Manuel Lee .05
638 Al Leiter .05
639 Jeff Gardner .05
640 Mike Gardiner .05
641 Mark Gardner .05
642 Jeff Branson .05
643 Paul Wagner .05
644 Sean Berry .05
645 Phil Hiatt .05
646 Kevin Mitchell .05
647 Charlie Hayes .05
648 Jim Deshaies .05
649 Dan Pasqua .05
650 Mike Maddux .05
651 Domingo Martinez **RC** .05
652 Greg McMichael **RC** .05
653 Eric Wedge **RC** .05
654 Mark Whiten .05
655 Bobby Kelly .05
656 Julio Franco .05
657 Gene Harris .05
658 Pete Schourek .05
659 Mike Bielecki .05
660 Ricky Gutierrez .05
661 Chris Hammond .05
662 Tim Scott .05
663 Norm Charlton .05
664 Doug Drabek .05
665 Dwight Gooden .05
666 Jim Gott .05
667 Randy Myers .05
668 Darren Holmes .05
669 Tim Spehr .05
670 Bruce Ruffin .05
671 Bobby Thigpen .05
672 Tony Fernandez .05
673 Darrin Jackson .05
674 Gregg Olson .05
675 Rob Dibble .05
676 Howard Johnson .05
677 Mike Lansing **RC** .15
678 Charlie Leibrandt .05
679 Kevin Bass .05
680 Hubie Brooks .05
681 Scott Brosius .05
682 Randy Knorr .05
683 Dante Bichette .05
684 Bryan Harvey .05
685 Greg Gohr .05
686 Willie Banks .05
687 Robb Nen .05
688 Mike Scioscia .05
689 John Farrell .05
690 John Candelaria .05
691 Damon Buford .05
692 Todd Worrell .05
693 Pat Hentgen .05
694 John Smiley .05
695 Greg Swindell .05
696 Derek Bell .05
697 Terry Jorgensen .05
698 Jimmy Jones .05
699 David Wells .05
700 Dave Martinez .05
701 Steve Bedrosian .05
702 Jeff Russell .05
703 Joe Magrane .05
704 Matt Mieske .05
705 Paul Molitor .65
706 Dale Murphy .15
707 Steve Howe .05
708 Greg Gagne .05
709 Dave Eiland .05
710 David West .05
711 Luis Aquino .05
712 Joe Orsulak .05
713 Eric Plunk .05
714 Mike Felder .05
715 Joe Klink .05
716 Lonnie Smith .05
717 Monty Fariss .05
718 Craig Lefferts .05
719 John Habyan .05
720 Willie Blair .05
721 Darnell Coles .05
722 Mark Williamson .05
723 Bryn Smith .05
724 Greg W. Harris .05
725 Graeme Lloyd **RC** .05
726 Cris Carpenter .05
727 Chico Walker .05
728 Tracy Woodson .05
729 Jose Uribe .05
730 Stan Javier .05
731 Jay Howell .05
732 Freddie Benavides .05
733 Jeff Reboulet .05
734 Scott Sanderson .05
735 Checklist 631-735 (Ryne Sandberg) .20
736 Archi Cianfrocco .05
737 Daryl Boston .05
738 Craig Grebeck .05
739 Doug Dascenzo .05
740 Gerald Young .05
741 Candy Maldonado .05
742 Joey Cora .05
743 Don Slaught .05
744 Steve Decker .05
745 Blas Minor .05
746 Storm Davis .05
747 Carlos Quintana .05
748 Vince Coleman .05
749 Todd Burns .05
750 Steve Frey .05
751 Ivan Calderon .05
752 Steve Reed **RC** .05
753 Danny Jackson .05
754 Jeff Conine .05
755 Juan Gonzalez .35
756 Mike Kelly .05
757 John Doherty .05
758 Jack Armstrong .05
759 John Wehner .05
760 Scott Bankhead .05
761 Jim Tatum .05
762 Scott Pose **RC** .05
763 Andy Ashby .05
764 Ed Sprague .05
765 Harold Baines .05
766 Kirk Gibson .05
767 Troy Neel .05
768 Dick Schofield .05
769 Dickie Thon .05
770 Butch Henry .05
771 Junior Felix .05
772 Ken Ryan **RC** .05
773 Trevor Hoffman .05
774 Phil Plantier .05
775 Bo Jackson .10
776 Benito Santiago .05
777 Andre Dawson .25
778 Bryan Hickerson .05
779 Dennis Moeller .05
780 Ryan Bowen .05
781 Eric Fox .05
782 Joe Kmak .05
783 Mike Hampton .05
784 Darrell Sherman **RC** .05
785 J.T. Snow .05
786 Dave Winfield .65
787 Jim Austin .05
788 Craig Shipley .05
789 Greg Myers .05
790 Todd Benzinger .05
791 Cory Snyder .05
792 David Segui .05
793 Armando Reynoso .05
794 Chili Davis .05
795 Dave Nilsson .05
796 Paul O'Neill .05
797 Jerald Clark .05
798 Jose Mesa .05
799 Brian Holman .05
800 Jim Eisenreich .05
801 Mark McLemore .05
802 Luis Sojo .05
803 Harold Reynolds .05
804 Dan Plesac .05
805 Dave Stieb .05
806 Tom Brunansky .05
807 Kelly Gruber .05
808 Bob Ojeda .05
809 Dave Burba .05
810 Joe Boever .05
811 Jeremy Hernandez .05
812 Angels Checklist (Tim Salmon) .05
813 Astros Checklist (Jeff Bagwell) .35
814 Athletics Checklist (Mark McGwire) .75
815 Blue Jays Checklist (Roberto Alomar) .10
816 Braves Checklist (Steve Avery) .05
817 Brewers Checklist (Pat Listach) .05
818 Cardinals Checklist (Gregg Jefferies) .05
819 Cubs Checklist (Sammy Sosa) .40
820 Dodgers Checklist (Darryl Strawberry) .05
821 Expos Checklist (Dennis Martinez) .05
822 Giants Checklist (Robby Thompson) .05
823 Indians Checklist (Albert Belle) .05
824 Mariners Checklist (Randy Johnson) .30
825 Marlins Checklist (Nigel Wilson) .05
826 Mets Checklist (Bobby Bonilla) .05
827 Orioles Checklist (Glenn Davis) .05
828 Padres Checklist (Gary Sheffield) .10
829 Phillies Checklist (Darren Daulton) .05
830 Pirates Checklist (Jay Bell) .05
831 Rangers Checklist (Juan Gonzalez) .20
832 Red Sox Checklist (Andre Dawson) .10
833 Reds Checklist (Hal Morris) .05
834 Rockies Checklist (David Nied) .05
835 Royals Checklist (Felix Jose) .05
836 Tigers Checklist (Travis Fryman) .05
837 Twins Checklist (Shane Mack) .05
838 White Sox Checklist (Robin Ventura) .05
839 Yankees Checklist (Danny Tartabull) .05
840 Checklist 736-840 (Roberto Alomar) .10
SP5 3,000 Hits (Robin Yount, George Brett) .50
SP6 Nolan Ryan 1.50

Gold Holograms

Unlike 1992, when gold holograms were found on the back of every card originating in a factory set, in 1993 the use of gold holograms was limited to just one factory set per 20-set case, creating a scarce parallel version.

NM/M

Complete Fact. Set (840): 200.00
Common Player: .50

Baseball Heroes Reggie Jackson Supers

Upper Deck issued a large version of its 1990 Heroes Reggie Jackson cards that was available in retail outlets. Just as in the case of the regular issue Jackson insert cards, there are 10 cards (nine numbered and one unnumbered header card). The cards are 3-1/2" x 5" and identical to the smaller Heroes cards in every other respect. Each of the individual cards carries a sequential number out of a limit of 10,000. The cards were sold one to a package that also included two packs of 1993 Upper Deck cards for about $5.

NM/M

Complete Set (10): 25.00
Common Card: 3.00
1 1969 Emerging Superstar (Reggie Jackson) 3.00
2 1973 An MVP Year (Reggie Jackson) 3.00
3 1977 "Mr. October" (Reggie Jackson) 3.00
4 1978 Jackson vs. Welch (Reggie Jackson) 3.00
5 1982 Under the Halo (Reggie Jackson) 3.00
6 1984 500! (Reggie Jackson) 3.00
7 1986 Moving Up the List (Reggie Jackson) 3.00
8 1987 A Great Career Ends (Reggie Jackson) 3.00
9 Heroes Checklist (Reggie Jackson) 3.00
--- Header Card 3.00

Baseball Heroes Willie Mays

This 10-card insert set includes eight individually-titled cards, an illustrated checklist and one header card. The set is a continuation of Upper Deck's previous Heroes efforts, honoring greats such as Hank Aaron, Nolan Ryan and Reggie Jackson, and is numbered 46-54. Cards were randomly inserted into Series 1 foil packs.

NM/M

Complete Set (10): 4.00
Common Card: .50
Header Card: 1.00
46 1951 Rookie-of-the-Year .50
47 1954 The Catch .50
48 1956-57 30-30 Club .50
49 1961 Four-Homer Game .50
50 1965 Most Valuable Player .50
51 1969 600-Home Run Club .50
52 1972 New York Homecoming .50
53 1979 Hall of Fame .50
54 Checklist - Heroes 46-54 .50

Clutch Performers

Reggie Jackson has selected the players who perform the best under pressure for this 20-card insert set. Cards were available only in Series II retail packs and use the prefix "R" for numbering. Fronts have a black bottom panel with "Clutch Performers" printed in dark gray. Jackson's facsimile autograph is overprinted in gold foil. On back, under a second player photo, is Jackson's picture and his assessment of the player. There are a few lines of stats to support the player's selection to this exclusive company.

NM/M

Complete Set (20): 8.00

Common Player:		.25
1	Roberto Alomar	.30
2	Wade Boggs	1.00
3	Barry Bonds	2.50
4	Jose Canseco	.40
5	Joe Carter	.25
6	Will Clark	.25
7	Roger Clemens	1.25
8	Dennis Eckersley	.60
9	Cecil Fielder	.25
10	Juan Gonzalez	.60
11	Ken Griffey Jr.	2.00
12	Rickey Henderson	.75
13	Barry Larkin	.25
14	Don Mattingly	1.25
15	Fred McGriff	.25
16	Terry Pendleton	.25
17	Kirby Puckett	1.00
18	Ryne Sandberg	1.00
19	John Smoltz	.25
20	Frank Thomas	.75

Future Heroes

This insert set includes eight player cards, a checklist and an unnumbered header card. The cards are numbered 55-63 as a continuation of previous Heroes sets, but this one features more than one player; previous sets featured only one player. Card fronts have a Future Heroes logo and a facsimile autograph. The player's name is revealed using a peeled-back paper effect. Cards were randomly inserted in Series II foil packs.

		NM/M
Complete Set (10):		5.00
Common Player:		.50
Header Card:		.25
55	Roberto Alomar	.50
56	Barry Bonds	2.50
57	Roger Clemens	1.00
58	Juan Gonzalez	.50
59	Ken Griffey Jr.	1.50
60	Mark McGwire	2.00
61	Kirby Puckett	.85
62	Frank Thomas	.75
63	Checklist	.05

Highlights

These 20 insert cards commemorate highlights from the 1992 season. Cards, which were randomly inserted in Series II packs, have a '92 Season Highlights logo on the bottom, with the player's name inside a banner trailing from the logo. The date of the significant event is under the player's name. Card backs have the logo at the top and are numbered with an "HI" prefix. A headline describes what highlight occurred, while the text describes the event.

		NM/M
Complete Set (20):		20.00
Common Player:		.25
1	Roberto Alomar	.50
2	Steve Avery	.25
3	Harold Baines	.25
4	Damon Berryhill	.25
5	Barry Bonds	7.50
6	Bret Boone	.25
7	George Brett	4.00
8	Francisco Cabrera	.25
9	Ken Griffey Jr.	5.00
10	Rickey Henderson	2.00
11	Kenny Lofton	.25
12	Mickey Morandini	.25
13	Eddie Murray	2.00
14	David Nied	.25
15	Jeff Reardon	.25
16	Bip Roberts	.25
17	Nolan Ryan	7.50
18	Ed Sprague	.25
19	Dave Winfield	2.00
20	Robin Yount	2.00

Home Run Heroes

This 28-card insert set features the top home run hitters from each team for 1992. Cards, inserted in Series I jumbo packs, are numbered with an "HR" prefix. The card fronts have "Home Run Heroes" printed vertically at the left edge and an embossed bat with the player's name and Upper Deck trademark at bottom. Backs have a purple or pink posterized photo and a few words about the player.

		NM/M
Complete Set (28):		7.50
Common Player:		.15
1	Juan Gonzalez	.50
2	Mark McGwire	2.25
3	Cecil Fielder	.15
4	Fred McGriff	.15
5	Albert Belle	.15
6	Barry Bonds	2.50
7	Joe Carter	.15
8	Darren Daulton	.15
9	Ken Griffey Jr.	2.00
10	Dave Hollins	.15
11	Ryne Sandberg	1.00
12	George Bell	.15
13	Danny Tartabull	.15
14	Mike Devereaux	.15
15	Greg Vaughn	.15
16	Larry Walker	.15
17	Dave Justice	.15
18	Terry Pendleton	.15
19	Eric Karros	.15
20	Ray Lankford	.15
21	Matt Williams	.15
22	Eric Anthony	.15
23	Bobby Bonilla	.15
24	Kirby Puckett	1.00
25	Mike Macfarlane	.15
26	Tom Brunansky	.15
27	Paul O'Neill	.15
28	Gary Gaetti	.15

Iooss Collection

Sports photographer Walter Iooss Jr. has captured 26 current players in this insert set featuring their candid portraits. Cards have full-bleed photos and gold foil stamping. Backs have biographical sketches and are numbered using a WI prefix. They are available in Series I retail packs.

		NM/M
Complete Set (27):		10.00
Common Player:		.25
Header Card:		.25
1	Tim Salmon	.25
2	Jeff Bagwell	.75
3	Mark McGwire	1.50
4	Roberto Alomar	.35
5	Steve Avery	.25
6	Paul Molitor	.75
7	Ozzie Smith	1.00
8	Mark Grace	.25
9	Eric Karros	.25
10	Delino DeShields	.25
11	Will Clark	.25
12	Albert Belle	.35
13	Ken Griffey Jr.	1.50
14	Howard Johnson	.25
15	Cal Ripken, Jr.	2.00
16	Fred McGriff	.25
17	Darren Daulton	.25
18	Andy Van Slyke	.25
19	Nolan Ryan	2.00
20	Wade Boggs	1.00
21	Barry Larkin	.25
22	George Brett	1.25
23	Cecil Fielder	.25
24	Kirby Puckett	1.00
25	Frank Thomas	.75
26	Don Mattingly	1.25

Iooss Collection Supers

Upper Deck issued a series of 27 individually numbered oversized cards identical to the Iooss Collection inserts from the regular 1993 Upper Deck set. The cards are 3-1/2" x 5" and each is numbered on back to a limit of 10,000. The cards were available in retail outlets such as WalMart, packaged in blister packs with two foil packs of 1993 Upper Deck cards for around $5. Authetically autographed and numbered (on card fronts) of some players' cards were sold by Upper Deck Authenticated.

		NM/M
Complete Set (27):		20.00
Common Player:		.50
Header Card:		.50
1	Tim Salmon	.50
2	Jeff Bagwell	1.00
3	Mark McGwire	2.00
4	Roberto Alomar	.75
5	Steve Avery	.50
6	Paul Molitor	1.00
7	Ozzie Smith	1.25
8	Mark Grace	.50
9	Eric Karros	.50
10	Delino DeShields	.50
11	Will Clark	.50
12	Albert Belle	.50
13	Ken Griffey Jr.	2.00
14	Howard Johnson	.50
15	Cal Ripken, Jr.	2.50
16	Fred McGriff	.50
17	Darren Daulton	.50
18	Andy Van Slyke	.50
19	Nolan Ryan	2.50
20	Wade Boggs	1.25
21	Barry Larkin	.50
22	George Brett	1.50
23	Cecil Fielder	.50
24	Kirby Puckett	1.25
25	Frank Thomas	1.00
26	Don Mattingly	1.50

On Deck

These UV-coated cards feature 25 of the game's top players. Each card has a full-bleed photo on the front and questions and answers on the back. Available only in Series II jumbo packs, the cards have a D prefix for numbering.

		NM/M
Complete Set (25):		10.00
Common Player:		.15
1	Jim Abbott	.15
2	Roberto Alomar	.25
3	Carlos Baerga	.15
4	Albert Belle	.15
5	Wade Boggs	1.00
6	George Brett	1.25
7	Jose Canseco	.45
8	Will Clark	.15
9	Roger Clemens	1.25
10	Dennis Eckersley	.65
11	Cecil Fielder	.15
12	Juan Gonzalez	.40
13	Ken Griffey Jr.	1.50
14	Tony Gwynn	1.00
15	Bo Jackson	.20
16	Chipper Jones	1.00
17	Eric Karros	.15
18	Mark McGwire	2.00
19	Kirby Puckett	1.00
20	Nolan Ryan	2.50
21	Tim Salmon	.15
22	Ryne Sandberg	1.00
23	Darryl Strawberry	.15
24	Frank Thomas	.75
25	Andy Van Slyke	.15

Supers

A series of six 1993 Upper Deck cards and one from 1991 was re-issued in an 8-1/2" x 11" format, though the manner of distribution is unclear. The cards are virtually identical in design to the regularly issued versions, except for the size, the lack of a hologram on back, and a 1993 dated seal with an individual serial number. The Ryan card was issued in an edition of 5,000, the Karros and Finley cards were issued in an edition of 2,500; the others were limited to 1,000 each.

		NM/M
Complete Set (7):		24.00
Common Card:		3.00
6	Kirby Puckett (Triple Crown Contender)	4.50
10	Barry Bonds/SP	7.50
24	Eric Karros/1991	3.00
75	Tom Glavine/1993	3.00
77	Chuck Finley	3.00
155	Nolan Ryan	7.50
199	Roger Clemens/SP	5.00

Then And Now

This 18-card lithogram set features both Hall of Famers and current players. The cards feature a combination of four-color player photos and a holographic background. They were random inserts in both Series I and Series II packs. Numbering includes the prefix TN. A limited edition of 2,500 supersize 5" by 7" Mickey Mantle Then And Now cards was created for sale through Upper Deck Authenticated.

		NM/M
Complete Set (18):		30.00
Common Player:		.75
1	Wade Boggs	2.00
2	George Brett	2.50
3	Rickey Henderson	1.25
4	Cal Ripken, Jr.	4.00
5	Nolan Ryan	4.00
6	Ryne Sandberg	2.00
7	Ozzie Smith	2.00
8	Darryl Strawberry	.75
9	Dave Winfield	1.25
10	Dennis Eckersley	1.00
11	Tony Gwynn	2.00
12	Howard Johnson	.75
13	Don Mattingly	2.50
14	Eddie Murray	1.25
15	Robin Yount	1.25
16	Reggie Jackson	2.00
17	Mickey Mantle	6.00
17a	Mickey Mantle (5" x 7")	13.50
18	Willie Mays	3.00

Triple Crown Contenders

These insert cards were available in 1993 Upper Deck Series I foil packs sold by hobby dealers. The set features 10 players who are candidates to win baseball's Triple Crown. Card fronts have a crown and the player's name at the bottom. Backs put that material at the top and explain why the player might lead the league in home runs, batting average and runs batted in.

		NM/M
Complete Set (10):		6.00
Common Player:		.25
1	Barry Bonds	1.50
2	Jose Canseco	.45
3	Will Clark	.25
4	Ken Griffey Jr.	1.25
5	Fred McGriff	.25
6	Kirby Puckett	.75
7	Cal Ripken, Jr.	1.50
8	Gary Sheffield	.35
9	Frank Thomas	.60
10	Larry Walker	.25

5th Anniversary

This 15-card insert set replicates 15 of Upper Deck's most popular cards from its first five years. Foil stamping and a fifth-anniversary logo appear on the cards, which are otherwise reproductions of the originals. The prefix A appears before each card number. The cards were available in Series II hobby packs only.

		NM/M
Complete Set (15):		7.00
Common Player:		.25
1	Ken Griffey Jr.	1.50
2	Gary Sheffield	.35
3	Roberto Alomar	.35
4	Jim Abbott	.25
5	Nolan Ryan	2.00
6	Juan Gonzalez	.35
7	Dave Justice	.25
8	Carlos Baerga	.25
9	Reggie Jackson	1.00
10	Eric Karros	.25
11	Chipper Jones	1.00
12	Ivan Rodriguez	.50
13	Pat Listach	.25
14	Frank Thomas	.90
15	Tim Salmon	.25

5th Anniversary Supers

This set of oversized (3-1/2" x 5") cards is simply an enlarged version of the Upper Deck 5th Anniversary subset that was inserted with the company's 1993 cards. There are 15 cards in the set, which are reprinted versions of some of the most popular cards in the last five years from Upper Deck. Each of the cards carries a number on the back out of an edition of 10,000. The cards were sold individually in blister packs at retail outlets along with two packs of 1993 Upper Deck.

		NM/M
Complete Set (15):		17.50
Common Player:		1.00
1	Ken Griffey Jr.	2.50
2	Gary Sheffield	1.25
3	Roberto Alomar	1.25
4	Jim Abbott	1.00
5	Nolan Ryan	3.00
6	Juan Gonzalez	1.25
7	David Justice	1.00
8	Carlos Baerga	1.00
9	Reggie Jackson	2.00
10	Eric Karros	1.00
11	Chipper Jones	2.00
12	Ivan Rodriguez	1.50
13	Pat Listach	1.00
14	Frank Thomas	1.75
15	Tim Salmon	1.00

Heroes of Baseball Previews

This four-card preview set was produced in conjunction with the All-Star FanFest in Baltimore to re-introduce the concept of T202-style "triplefolder" baseball cards. The preview set came in a specially decorated box. The 5-1/4" x 2-1/4" cards feature Ted Williams, Mickey Mantle and Reggie Jackson in various combinations of photos and artwork on each card. Backs are printed in red and gold and include an in-field-shaped hologram. Written summaries of the players and their careers are featured. Cards have an "HOB" prefix to their number. A special offering of uncut 27" x 20" sheets containing eight complete sets of the preview cards was sold by UD Authenticated in a numbered edition of 2,000.

		NM/M
Complete Set (4):		5.00
Common Card:		1.00
Uncut UDA Sheet:		20.00

1 Triple Threat (Mickey Mantle, Ted Williams) 2.00
2 Changing of the Guard (Mickey Mantle, Reggie Jackson) 1.50
3 Night and Day (Reggie Jackson, Ted Williams) 1.00
4 Hall-of-Fame Trio (Reggie Jackson, Mickey Mantle, Ted Williams) 1.50

All-Time Heroes

This 1993 set pays homage to one of the classiest, turn-of-the-century card sets, the T202 Hassan Triple Folders. The All-Time Heroes cards are 2-1/4" x 5-1/4" and feature two side panels and a larger middle panel, which features an action shot of the player. A portrait of the player and the Baseball Assistance Team (BAT) logo flank the action photo. Card backs have a biography and career summary. A Classic Combinations subset of 35 cards features artwork or photographs of two or more great players together, plus individual photos on the side panels. Production was limited to 5,140 numbered cases of 12-card foil packs. Ten T202 reprints were also produced and were randomly inserted in the foil packs.

NM/M
Complete Set (165): 35.00
Common Player: .10
Wax Pack (12): 2.00
Wax Box (24): 30.00
1 Hank Aaron 2.00
2 Tommie Agee .10
3 Bob Allison .10
4 Matty Alou .10
5 Sal Bando .10
6 Hank Bauer .15
7 Don Baylor .10
8 Glenn Beckert .10
9 Yogi Berra .50
10 Buddy Biancalana .10
11 Jack Billingham .10
12 Joe Black .10
13 Paul Blair .10
14 Steve Blass .10
15 Ray Boone .10
16 Lou Boudreau .10
17 Ken Brett .10
18 Nellie Briles .10
19 Bobby Brown .10
20 Bill Buckner .10
21 Don Buford .10
22 Al Bumbry .10
23 Lew Burdette .10
24 Jeff Burroughs .10
25 Johnny Callison .10
26 Bert Campaneris .10
27 Rico Carty .10
28 Dave Cash .10
29 Cesar Cedeno .10
30 Frank Chance .25
31 Joe Charboneau .15
32 Ty Cobb 2.00
33 Jerry Coleman .10
34 Cecil Cooper .10
35 Frankie Crossetti .10
36 Alvin Dark .10
37 Tommy Davis .10
38 Dizzy Dean .25
39 Doug DeCinces .10
40 Bucky Dent .10
41 Larry Dierker .10
42 Larry Doby .20
43 Moe Drabowsky .10
44 Dave Dravecky .10
45 Del Ennis .10
46 Carl Erskine .10
47 Johnny Evers .25
48 Elroy Face .10
49 Rick Ferrell .10
50 Mark Fidrych .15
51 Curt Flood .10
52 Whitey Ford .50
53 George Foster .10
54 Jimmie Foxx .25
55 Jim Fregosi .10
56 Phil Garner .10
57 Ralph Garr .10
58 Lou Gehrig 2.00
59 Bobby Grich .10
60 Jerry Grote .10
61 Harvey Haddix .10
62 Toby Harrah .10
63 Bud Harrelson .10
64 Jim Hegan .10
65 Gil Hodges .25
66 Ken Holtzman .10
67 Bob Horner .10
68 Rogers Hornsby .25
69 Carl Hubbell .25
70 Ron Hunt .10
71 Monte Irvin .10
72a Reggie Jackson (Regular issue, black printing on back.) .50
72b Reggie Jackson (Dealer promo, red printing on back.) 6.00
73 Larry Jansen .10
74 Ferguson Jenkins .10
75 Tommy John .10
76 Cliff Johnson .10
77 Davey Johnson .10
78 Walter Johnson .45
79 George Kell .10
80 Don Kessinger .10
81 Vern Law .10
82 Dennis Leonard .10
83 Johnny Logan .10
84 Mickey Lolich .10
85 Jim Lonborg .10
86 Bill Madlock .10
87 Mickey Mantle 4.00
88 Billy Martin .25
89 Christy Mathewson .45
90 Lee May .10
91 Willie Mays 2.00
92 Bill Mazeroski .25
93 Gil McDougald .15
94 Sam McDowell .10
95 Minnie Minoso .15
96 Johnny Mize .25
97 Rick Monday .10
98 Wally Moon .10
99 Manny Mota .10
100 Bobby Murcer .10
101 Ron Necciai .10
102 Al Oliver .10
103 Mel Ott .15
104 Mel Parnell .10
105 Jimmy Piersall .10
106 Johnny Podres .15
107 Bobby Richardson .15
108 Robin Roberts .15
109 Al Rosen .10
110 Babe Ruth 3.00
111 Joe Sambito .10
112 Manny Sanguillen .10
113 Ron Santo .10
114 Bill Skowron .15
115 Enos Slaughter .15
116 Warren Spahn .20
117 Tris Speaker .20
118 Frank Thomas .15
119 Bobby Thomson .10
120 Andre Thornton .10
121 Marv Throneberry .10
122 Luis Tiant .10
123 Joe Tinker .25
124 Honus Wagner .50
125 Bill White .10
126 Ted Williams 1.00
127 Earl Wilson .10
128 Joe Wood .10
129 Cy Young .40
130 Richie Zisk .10
131 Babe Ruth, Lou Gehrig 2.00
132 Ted Williams, Rogers Hornsby 1.00
133 Lou Gehrig, Babe Ruth 2.00
134 Babe Ruth, Mickey Mantle 3.00
135 Mickey Mantle, Reggie Jackson 1.00
136 Mel Ott, Carl Hubbell .15
137 Mickey Mantle, Willie Mays 2.00
138 Cy Young, Walter Johnson .25
139 Honus Wagner, Rogers Hornsby .25
140 Mickey Mantle, Whitey Ford 2.00
141 Mickey Mantle, Billy Martin 2.00
142 Cy Young, Walter Johnson .25
143 Christy Mathewson, Walter Johnson .25
144 Warren Spahn, Christy Mathewson .15
145 Honus Wagner, Ty Cobb .50
146 Babe Ruth, Ty Cobb 1.00
147 Joe Tinker, Johnny Evers .15
148 Johnny Evers, Frank Chance .15
149 Hank Aaron, Babe Ruth 1.00
150 Willie Mays, Hank Aaron 1.00
151 Babe Ruth, Willie Mays 1.00
152 Babe Ruth, Whitey Ford 1.00
153 Larry Doby, Minnie Minoso .25
154 Joe Black, Monte Irvin .10
155 Joe Wood, Christy Mathewson .15
156 Christy Mathewson, Cy Young .25
157 Cy Young, Joe Wood .15
158 Cy Young, Whitey Ford .20
159 Cy Young, Ferguson Jenkins .15
160 Ty Cobb, Rogers Hornsby .45
161 Tris Speaker, Ted Williams 1.00
162 Rogers Hornsby, Ted Williams 1.00
163 Willie Mays, Monte Irvin .50
164 Willie Mays, Bobby Thomson .50
165 Reggie Jackson, Mickey Mantle 2.00

All-Time Heroes T202 Reprints

A series of 10 reprints of the classic 1912 Hassan "Triplefolders" baseball cards on which the All-Time Heroes set was patterned was included as random inserts in the Upper Deck Old-Timers set. The reprints measure 5-1/4" x 2-1/4" (same as the originals). The Hassan cigarette ads on the backs of the originals have been replaced on the reprints by an Upper Deck hologram and the logos of the card company, B.A.T., Major League Baseball and the Cooperstown Collection. The Hassan cards are known as T202, their designation in the "American Card Catalog." The reprints are unnumbered and are checklisted here alphabetically in order of the player appearing on the left end of each card.

NM/M
Complete Set (10): 10.00
Common Player: .50
(1) Art Devlin, Christy Mathewson 1.00
(2) Hugh Jennings, Ty Cobb 2.00
(3) John Kling, Cy Young 1.00
(4) Jack Knight, Walter Johnson .75
(5) John McGraw, Hugh Jennings .50
(6) George Moriarty, Ty Cobb 2.00
(7) Charley O'Leary, Ty Cobb 2.00
(8) Charley O'Leary, Ty Cobb 2.00
(9) Joe Tinker, Frank Chance 1.00
(10) Joe Wood, Tris Speaker .50

Diamond Gallery

Utilizing something the company calls lithogram technology, Upper Deck produced a 36-card set that combines four-color photography and a holographic image. The set features one star from each of the 28 teams, along with a subset spotlighting top rookies from 1993 and cards saluting Nolan Ryan, Rickey Henderson and Ozzie Smith. The set comes in a specially designed box, with a numbered checklist card. The set was limited to a total of 123,600.

NM/M
Complete Set (36): 6.00
Common Player: .10
1 Tim Salmon .10
2 Jeff Bagwell .30
3 Mark McGwire .75
4 Roberto Alomar .25
5 Terry Pendleton .10
6 Robin Yount .30
7 Ray Lankford .10
8 Ryne Sandberg .40
9 Darryl Strawberry .10
10 Marquis Grissom .10
11 Barry Bonds 1.00
12 Carlos Baerga .10
13 Ken Griffey Jr. .65
14 Benito Santiago .10
15 Dwight Gooden .10
16 Cal Ripken, Jr. 1.00
17 Tony Gwynn .40
18 Dave Hollins .10
19 Andy Van Slyke .10
20 Juan Gonzalez .25
21 Roger Clemens .50
22 Barry Larkin .10
23 Dave Nied .10
24 George Brett .50
25 Travis Fryman .10
26 Kirby Puckett .40
27 Frank Thomas .30
28 Don Mattingly .50
29 Rickey Henderson .30
30 Nolan Ryan 1.00
31 Ozzie Smith .40
32 Wil Cordero .10
33 Phil Hiatt .10
34 Mike Piazza .65
35 J.T. Snow .10
36 Kevin Young .10

Fun Packs

Aimed at the younger audience, this product features 150 "regular" player cards and 75 specialty cards in a variety of subsets, plus two different types of insert cards. Basic player cards feature a photo (generally in action) on a background of purple, green and red, highlighted by yellow and orange stripes. On back is a white panel on red, yellow and orange blended stripes. In the panel are a cartoon, a trivia question and answer, brief biographical details, stats, and career summary. The basic player cards are arranged within the set alphabetically by team. The teams are also arranged alphabetically by nickname. Leading off each team's roster is a "Glow Stars" sticker, featuring a player photo against a particolored background. The area around the photo is die-cut to allow the picture to be separated from the background and stuck to a wall, where the white and green outlines glow in the dark. Cards #1-9 and designated "Stars of Tomorrow." Both front and back have a background of a star-studded purple sky. Cards #10-21 are "Hot Shots" - heat-sensitive cards. When touched the black textured ink surrounding the player photo turns clear, revealing a colored pattern beneath. The Hot Shot cards were available only via mail-in redemption. Cards #22-27 are "Kid Stars" and feature a childhood photo. Cards #28-37 are checklisted as "Upper Deck Heroes," though that designation does not appear on the cards. The subset is done in comic-book art style. Cards #216-220 are double-size (2-1/2"x7") "Fold-outs." The five checklist cards which conclude the set have player photos on front.

NM/M
Complete Set (225): 15.00
Common Player: .05
Wax Pack (6): .50
Wax Box (36): 15.00
1 Wil Cordero (Stars of Tomorrow) .05
2 Brent Gates (Stars of Tomorrow) .05
3 Benji Gil (Stars of Tomorrow) .05
4 Phil Hiatt (Stars of Tomorrow) .05
5 David McCarty (Stars of Tomorrow) .05
6 Mike Piazza (Stars of Tomorrow) 1.50
7 Tim Salmon (Stars of Tomorrow) .05
8 J.T. Snow **RC** (Stars of Tomorrow) .50
9 Kevin Young (Stars of Tomorrow) .05
10 Roberto Alomar (Hot Shots) .25
11 Barry Bonds (Hot Shots) 1.50
12 Jose Canseco (Hot Shots) .35
13 Will Clark (Hot Shots) .10
14 Roger Clemens (Hot Shots) .75
15 Juan Gonzalez (Hot Shots) .25
16 Ken Griffey Jr. (Hot Shots) 1.00
17 Mark McGwire (Hot Shots) 1.25
18 Nolan Ryan (Hot Shots) 1.50
19 Ryne Sandberg (Hot Shots) .65
20 Gary Sheffield (Hot Shots) .30
21 Frank Thomas (Hot Shots) .60
22 Roberto Alomar (Kid Stars) .10
23 Roger Clemens (Kid Stars) .45
24 Ken Griffey Jr. (Kid Stars) .50
25 Gary Sheffield (Kid Stars) .15
26 Nolan Ryan (Kid Stars) .75
27 Frank Thomas (Kid Stars) .40
28 Reggie Jackson (Heroes) .45
29 Roger Clemens (Heroes) .45
30 Ken Griffey Jr. (Heroes) .50
31 Bo Jackson (Heroes) .10
32 Cal Ripken, Jr. (Heroes) .75
33 Nolan Ryan (Heroes) .75
34 Deion Sanders (Heroes) .10
35 Ozzie Smith (Heroes) .40
36 Frank Thomas (Heroes) .35
37 Tim Salmon (Glow Stars) .05
38 Chili Davis .05
39 Chuck Finley .05
40 Mark Langston .05
41 Luis Polonia .05
42 Jeff Bagwell (Glow Stars) .30
43 Jeff Bagwell .50
44 Craig Biggio .05
45 Ken Caminiti .05
46 Doug Drabek .05
47 Steve Finley .05
48 Mark McGwire (Glow Stars) .65
49 Dennis Eckersley .45
50 Rickey Henderson .50
51 Mark McGwire 1.25
52 Ruben Sierra .05
53 Terry Steinbach .05
54 Roberto Alomar (Glow Stars) .10
55 Roberto Alomar .20
56 Joe Carter .05
57 Juan Guzman .05
58 Paul Molitor .50
59 Jack Morris .05
60 John Olerud .05
61 Tom Glavine (Glow Stars) .10
62 Steve Avery .05
63 Tom Glavine .20
64 Dave Justice .05
65 Greg Maddux .65
66 Terry Pendleton .05
67 Deion Sanders .10
68 John Smoltz .05
69 Robin Yount (Glow Stars) .30
70 Cal Eldred .05
71 Pat Listach .05
72 Greg Vaughn .05
73 Robin Yount .50
74 Ozzie Smith (Glow Stars) .45
75 Gregg Jefferies .05
76 Ray Lankford .05
77 Lee Smith .05
78 Ozzie Smith .65
79 Bob Tewksbury .05
80 Ryne Sandberg (Glow Stars) .35
81 Mark Grace .05
82 Mike Morgan .05
83 Randy Myers .05
84 Ryne Sandberg .65
85 Sammy Sosa .65
86 Eric Karros (Glow Stars) .05
87 Brett Butler .05
88 Orel Hershiser .05
89 Eric Karros .05
90 Ramon Martinez .05
91 Jose Offerman .05
92 Darryl Strawberry .05
93 Marquis Grissom (Glow Stars) .05
94 Delino DeShields .05
95 Marquis Grissom .05
96 Ken Hill .05
97 Dennis Martinez .05
98 Larry Walker .05
99 Barry Bonds (Glow Stars) .65
100 Barry Bonds 1.50
101 Will Clark .05
102 Bill Swift .05
103 Robby Thompson .05
104 Matt Williams .05
105 Carlos Baerga (Glow Stars) .05
106 Sandy Alomar, Jr. .05
107 Carlos Baerga .05
108 Albert Belle .05
109 Kenny Lofton .05
110 Charles Nagy .05
111 Ken Griffey Jr. (Glow Stars) .50
112 Jay Buhner .05
113 Dave Fleming .05
114 Ken Griffey Jr. 1.00
115 Randy Johnson .50
116 Edgar Martinez .05
117 Benito Santiago (Glow Stars) .05
118 Bret Barberie .05
119 Jeff Conine .05
120 Brian Harvey .05
121 Benito Santiago .05
122 Walt Weiss .05
123 Dwight Gooden (Glow Stars) .05
124 Bobby Bonilla .05
125 Tony Fernandez .05
126 Dwight Gooden .05
127 Howard Johnson .05
128 Eddie Murray .50
129 Bret Saberhagen .05
130 Cal Ripken, Jr. (Glow Stars) .75
131 Brady Anderson .05
132 Mike Devereaux .05
133 Ben McDonald .05
134 Mike Mussina .30
135 Cal Ripken, Jr. 1.50
136 Fred McGriff (Glow Stars) .05
137 Andy Benes .05
138 Tony Gwynn .65
139 Fred McGriff .05
140 Phil Plantier .05
141 Gary Sheffield .25
142 Darren Daulton (Glow Stars) .05
143 Darren Daulton .05
144 Len Dykstra .05
145 Dave Hollins .05
146 John Kruk .05
147 Mitch Williams .05
148 Andy Van Slyke (Glow Stars) .05
149 Jay Bell .05
150 Zane Smith .05
151 Andy Van Slyke .05
152 Tim Wakefield .05
153 Juan Gonzalez (Glow Stars) .15
154 Kevin Brown .05
155 Jose Canseco .35
156 Juan Gonzalez .25
157 Rafael Palmeiro .40
158 Dean Palmer .05
159 Ivan Rodriguez .45
160 Nolan Ryan 1.50
161 Roger Clemens (Glow Stars) .50
162 Roger Clemens .75
163 Andre Dawson .25
164 Mike Greenwell .05
165 Tony Pena .05
166 Frank Viola .05
167 Barry Larkin (Glow Stars) .05
168 Rob Dibble .05
169 Roberto Kelly .05
170 Barry Larkin .05
171 Kevin Mitchell .05
172 Bip Roberts .05
173 Andres Galarraga (Glow Stars) .05
174 Dante Bichette .05

175 Jerald Clark .05
176 Andres Galarraga .05
177 Charlie Hayes .05
178 David Nied .05
179 David Cone (Glow Stars) .05
180 Kevin Appler .05
181 George Brett .75
182 David Cone .05
183 Felix Jose .05
184 Wally Joyner .05
185 Cecil Fielder (Glow Stars) .05
186 Cecil Fielder .05
187 Travis Fryman .05
188 Tony Phillips .05
189 Mickey Tettleton .05
190 Lou Whitaker .05
191 Kirby Puckett (Glow Stars) .35
192 Scott Erickson .05
193 Chuck Knoblauch .05
194 Shane Mack .05
195 Kirby Puckett .65
196 Dave Winfield .50
197 Frank Thomas (Glow Stars) .40
198 George Bell .05
199 Bo Jackson .10
200 Jack McDowell .05
201 Tim Raines .05
202 Frank Thomas .50
203 Robin Ventura .05
204 Jim Abbott (Glow Stars) .05
205 Jim Abbott .05
206 Wade Boggs .65
207 Jimmy Key .05
208 Don Mattingly .75
209 Danny Tartabull .05
210 Brett Butler (All-Star Advice) .05
211 Tony Gwynn (All-Star Advice) .35
212 Rickey Henderson (All-Star Advice) .25
213 Ramon Martinez (All-Star Advice) .05
214 Nolan Ryan (All-Star Advice) .75
215 Ozzie Smith (All-Star Advice) .35
216 Marquis Grissom (Fold-Out) .05
217 Dean Palmer (Fold-Out) .05
218 Cal Ripken, Jr. (Fold-Out) .75
219 Deion Sanders (Fold-Out) .05
220 Darryl Strawberry (Fold-Out) .05
221 David McCarty (Checklist) .05
222 Barry Bonds (Checklist) .65
223 Juan Gonzalez (Checklist) .15
224 Ken Griffey Jr. (Checklist) .50
225 Frank Thomas (Checklist) .25
Trade Upper Deck ("Hot Shots" redemption card) .05

Fun Packs Mascot Madness

Upper Deck's high-tech lithogram process of combining color photos and holograms was used to create the five-card "Mascot Madness" inserts which were randomly found in Fun Packs. Backs have a description of the mascot and explain his role with the team.

		NM/M
Complete Set (5):		2.50
Common Card:		.50
1	Phillie Phanatic	.50
2	Pirate Parrot	.50
3	Fredbird	.50
4	BJ Birdy	.50
5	Youppi (Mascot)	.50

Fun Packs All-Star Scratch-Off

Randomly inserted into Fun Packs was a series of nine "All-Star Scratch-Off" game cards. Fronts and backs have a star-studded blue background. Inside the folded, double-size (2-1/2" x 7") cards

are American and National League line-ups which can be used to play a baseball game, the rules of which are explained on the card backs. On front are photos of two of the players in the line-up, matched by position from each league. The inserts are numbered with an "AS" prefix.

		NM/M
Complete Set (9):		5.00
Common Player:		.25
1	Fred McGriff, Frank Thomas	.45
2	Darren Daulton, Ivan Rodriguez	.35
3	Mark McGwire, Will Clark	1.25
4	Ryne Sandberg, Roberto Alomar	.50
5	Robin Ventura, Terry Pendleton	.25
6	Cal Ripken Jr., Ozzie Smith	1.50
7	Barry Bonds, Juan Gonzalez	1.50
8	Marquis Grissom, Ken Griffey Jr.	1.00
9	Tony Gwynn, Kirby Puckett	.50

1994 Upper Deck

Upper Deck's 1994 offering was a typical presentation, combining high-quality regular-issue cards with innovative subsets and high-tech chase cards. Series 1, besides the standard player cards, features subsets including Star Rookies with metallic borders, "Fantasy Team" stars, Home Field Advantage cards showcasing National League stadiums, and, stars under the age of 25 in a subset titled, "The Future is Now." Regular-issue cards feature a color photo on front and a second, black-and-white version of the same photo at left in a vertically stretched format. The player's name, team and Upper Deck logo appear on front in copper foil. Backs have a color photo, stats and an infield-shaped hologram. Series 2 offered in addition to regular cards, subsets of American League Home Field Advantage cards, a group of "Classic Alumni" minor league players, a selection of "Diamond Debuts" cards and a group of "Top Prospects." Series 1 retail packaging contained a special Mickey Mantle/Ken Griffey, Jr. card that could be found bearing either one or both of the players' autographs in an edition of 1,000 each. Series 2 retail packs offered a chance to find an autographed version of Alex Rodriguez' Classic Alumni card.

	NM/M
Complete Set (550):	30.00
Complete Series 1 (280):	25.00
Complete Series 2 (270):	5.00
Common Player:	.05
Series 1 Hobby Pack (12):	2.50
Series 1 Hobby Box (36):	65.00
Series 1 Retail Pack (12):	2.00
Series 1 Retail Box (36):	40.00
Series 2 Hobby Pack (12):	.75
Series 2 Hobby Box (36):	20.00
Series 2 Retail Pack (12):	1.25
Series 2 Retail Box (36):	25.00

1 Brian Anderson/SR **RC** .15
2 Shane Andrews/SR .05
3 James Baldwin/SR .05
4 Rich Becker/SR .05
5 Greg Blosser/SR .05
6 Ricky Bottalico/SR **RC** .05
7 Midre Cummings/SR .05
8 Carlos Delgado/SR .50
9 Steve Dreyer/SR **RC** .05
10 Joey Eischen/SR **RC** .05
11 Carl Everett/SR .05
12 Cliff Floyd/SR .05
13 Alex Gonzalez/SR .05
14 Jeff Granger/SR .05
15 Shawn Green/SR .35
16 Brian Hunter/SR .05
17 Butch Huskey/SR .05
18 Mark Hutton/SR .05
19 Michael Jordan/SR **RC** 5.00
20 Steve Karsay/SR .05
21 Jeff McNeely/SR .05
22 Marc Newfield/SR .05
23 Manny Ramirez/SR .60
24 Alex Rodriguez/SR **RC** 20.00
25 Scott Ruffcorn/SR .05
26 Paul Spoljaric/SR .05
27 Salomon Torres/SR **RC** .05
28 Steve Trachsel/SR .05
29 Chris Turner/SR **RC** .05
30 Gabe White/SR .05
31 Randy Johnson (Fantasy Team) .40
32 John Wetteland (Fantasy Team) .05
33 Mike Piazza (Fantasy Team) .65
34 Rafael Palmeiro (Fantasy Team) .35
35 Roberto Alomar (Fantasy Team) .10
36 Matt Williams (Fantasy Team) .05
37 Travis Fryman (Fantasy Team) .05
38 Barry Bonds (Fantasy Team) 1.00
39 Marquis Grissom (Fantasy Team) .05
40 Albert Belle (Fantasy Team) .05
41 Steve Avery (Future/Now) .05
42 Jason Bere (Future/Now) .05
43 Alex Fernandez (Future/Now) .05
44 Mike Mussina (Future/Now) .15
45 Aaron Sele (Future/Now) .05
46 Rod Beck (Future/Now) .05
47 Mike Piazza (Future/Now) .65
48 John Olerud (Future/Now) .05
49 Carlos Baerga (Future/Now) .05
50 Gary Sheffield (Future/Now) .20
51 Travis Fryman (Future/Now) .05
52 Juan Gonzalez (Future/Now) .20
53 Ken Griffey Jr. (Future/Now) .65
54 Tim Salmon (Future/Now) .05
55 Frank Thomas (Future/Now) .45
56 Tony Phillips .05
57 Julio Franco .05
58 Kevin Mitchell .05
59 Raul Mondesi .05
60 Rickey Henderson .75
61 Jay Buhner .05
62 Bill Swift .05
63 Brady Anderson .05
64 Ryan Klesko .05
65 Darren Daulton .05
66 Damion Easley .05
67 Mark McGwire 1.50
68 John Roper .05
69 Dave Telgheder .05
70 Dave Nied .05
71 Mo Vaughn .05
72 Tyler Green .05
73 Dave Magadan .05
74 Chili Davis .05
75 Archi Cianfrocco .05
76 Joe Girardi .05
77 Chris Hoiles .05
78 Ryan Bowen .05
79 Greg Gagne .05
80 Aaron Sele .05
81 Dave Winfield .75
82 Chad Curtis .05
83 Andy Van Slyke .05
84 Kevin Stocker .05
85 Deion Sanders .05
86 Bernie Williams .05
87 John Smoltz .05
88 Ruben Santana **RC** .05
89 Dave Stewart .05
90 Don Mattingly 1.00
91 Joe Carter .05
92 Ryne Sandberg .90
93 Chris Gomez .05
94 Tino Martinez .05
95 Terry Pendleton .05
96 Andre Dawson .25
97 Wil Cordero .05
98 Kent Hrbek .05
99 John Olerud .05
100 Kirt Manwaring .05
101 Tim Bogar .05
102 Mike Mussina .30
103 Nigel Wilson .05
104 Ricky Gutierrez .05
105 Roberto Mejia .05
106 Tom Pagnozzi .05
107 Mike Macfarlane .05
108 Jose Bautista .05
109 Luis Ortiz .05
110 Brent Gates .05
111 Tim Salmon .05
112 Wade Boggs .90
113 Tripp Cromer **RC** .05
114 Denny Hocking .05
115 Carlos Baerga .05
116 J.R. Phillips **RC** .05
117 Bo Jackson .10
118 Lance Johnson .05
119 Bobby Jones .05
120 Bobby Witt .05
121 Ron Karkovice .05
122 Jose Vizcaino .05
123 Danny Darwin .05
124 Eduardo Perez .05
125 Brian Looney .05
126 Pat Hentgen .05
127 Frank Viola .05
128 Darren Holmes .05
129 Wally Whitehurst .05
130 Matt Walbeck .05
131 Albert Belle .05
132 Steve Cooke .05
133 Kevin Appier .05
134 Joe Oliver .05
135 Benji Gil .05
136 Steve Buechele .05
137 Devon White .05
138 Sterling Hitchcock .05
139 Phil Leftwich **RC** .05
140 Jose Canseco .45
141 Rick Aguilera .05
142 Rod Beck .05
143 Jose Rijo .05
144 Tom Glavine .25
145 Phil Plantier .05
146 Jason Bere .05
147 Jamie Moyer .05
148 Wes Chamberlain .05
149 Glenallen Hill .05
150 Mark Whiten .05
151 Bret Barberie .05
152 Chuck Knoblauch .05
153 Trevor Hoffman .05
154 Rick Wilkins .05
155 Juan Gonzalez .40
156 Ozzie Guillen .05
157 Jim Eisenreich .05
158 Pedro Astacio .05
159 Joe Magrane .05
160 Ryan Thompson .05
161 Jose Lind .05
162 Jeff Conine .05
163 Todd Benzinger .05
164 Roger Salkeld .05
165 Gary DiSarcina .05
166 Kevin Gross .05
167 Charlie Hayes .05
168 Tim Costo .05
169 Wally Joyner .05
170 Johnny Ruffin .05
171 Kirk Rueter **RC** .10
172 Len Dykstra .05
173 Ken Hill .05
174 Mike Bordick .05
175 Billy Hall .05
176 Rob Butler .05
177 Jay Bell .05
178 Jeff Kent .05
179 David Wells .05
180 Dean Palmer .05
181 Mariano Duncan .05
182 Orlando Merced .05
183 Brett Butler .05
184 Milt Thompson .05
185 Chipper Jones .90
186 Paul O'Neill .05
187 Mike Greenwell .05
188 Harold Baines .05
189 Todd Stottlemyre .05
190 Jeromy Burnitz .05
191 Rene Arocha .05
192 Jeff Fassero .05
193 Robby Thompson .05
194 Greg W. Harris .05
195 Todd Van Poppel .05
196 Jose Guzman .05
197 Shane Mack .05
198 Carlos Garcia .05
199 Kevin Roberson .05
200 David McCarty .05
201 Alan Trammell .05
202 Chuck Carr .05
203 Tommy Greene .05
204 Wilson Alvarez .05
205 Dwight Gooden .05
206 Tony Tarasco .05
207 Darren Lewis .05
208 Eric Karros .05
209 Chris Hammond .05
210 Jeffrey Hammonds .05
211 Rich Amaral .05
212 Danny Tartabull .05
213 Jeff Russell .05
214 Dave Staton .05
215 Kenny Lofton .05
216 Manuel Lee .05
217 Brian Koelling .05
218 Scott Lydy .05
219 Tony Gwynn .90
220 Cecil Fielder .05
221 Royce Clayton .05
222 Reggie Sanders .05
223 Brian Jordan .05
224 Ken Griffey Jr. 1.25
224a Ken Griffey Jr. (Promo Card) 3.00
225 Fred McGriff .05
226 Felix Jose .05
227 Brad Pennington .05
228 Chris Bosio .05
229 Mike Stanley .05
230 Willie Greene .05
231 Alex Fernandez .05
232 Brad Ausmus .05
233 Darrell Whitmore .05
234 Marcus Moore .05
235 Allen Watson .05
236 Jose Offerman .05
237 Rondell White .05
238 Jeff King .05
239 Luis Alicea .05
240 Dan Wilson .05
241 Ed Sprague .05
242 Todd Hundley .05
243 Al Martin .05
244 Mike Lansing .05
245 Ivan Rodriguez .65
246 Dave Fleming .05
247 John Doherty .05
248 Mark McLemore .05
249 Bob Hamelin .05
250 Curtis Pride **RC** .05
251 Zane Smith .05
252 Eric Young .05
253 Brian McRae .05
254 Tim Raines .05
255 Javier Lopez .05
256 Melvin Nieves .05
257 Randy Myers .05
258 Willie McGee .05
259 Jimmy Key .05
260 Tom Candiotti .05
261 Eric Davis .05
262 Craig Paquette .05
263 Robin Ventura .05
264 Pat Kelly .05
265 Gregg Jefferies .05
266 Cory Snyder .05
267 Dave Justice (Home Field Advantage) .05
268 Sammy Sosa (Home Field Advantage) .45
269 Barry Larkin (Home Field Advantage) .05
270 Andres Galarraga (Home Field Advantage) .05
271 Gary Sheffield (Home Field Advantage) .20
272 Jeff Bagwell (Home Field Advantage) .40
273 Mike Piazza (Home Field Advantage) .65
274 Larry Walker (Home Field Advantage) .05
275 Bobby Bonilla (Home Field Advantage) .05
276 John Kruk (Home Field Advantage) .05
277 Jay Bell (Home Field Advantage) .05
278 Ozzie Smith (Home Field Advantage) .45
279 Tony Gwynn (Home Field Advantage) .45
280 Barry Bonds (Home Field Advantage) 1.00
281 Cal Ripken, Jr. (Home Field Advantage) 1.00
282 Mo Vaughn (Home Field Advantage) .05
283 Tim Salmon (Home Field Advantage) .05
284 Frank Thomas (Home Field Advantage) .40
285 Albert Belle (Home Field Advantage) .05
286 Cecil Fielder (Home Field Advantage) .05
287 Wally Joyner (Home Field Advantage) .05
288 Greg Vaughn (Home Field Advantage) .05
289 Kirby Puckett (Home Field Advantage) .45
290 Don Mattingly (Home Field Advantage) .50
291 Terry Steinbach (Home Field Advantage) .05
292 Ken Griffey Jr. (Home Field Advantage) .90
293 Juan Gonzalez (Home Field Advantage) .20
294 Paul Molitor (Home Field Advantage) .40
295 Tavo Alvarez (Classic Alumni) .05
296 Matt Brunson (Classic Alumni) .05
297 Shawn Green (Classic Alumni) .20
298 Alex Rodriguez (Classic Alumni) 2.00
299 Shannon Stewart (Classic Alumni) .05
300 Frank Thomas .75
301 Mickey Tettleton .05
302 Pedro Munoz .05
303 Jose Valentin .05
304 Orestes Destrade .05
305 Pat Listach .05
306 Scott Brosius .05
307 Kurt Miller **RC** .05
308 Rob Dibble .05
309 Mike Blowers .05
310 Jim Abbott .05
311 Mike Jackson .05
312 Craig Biggio .05
313 Kurt Abbott **RC** .05
314 Chuck Finley .05
315 Andres Galarraga .05
316 Mike Moore .05
317 Doug Strange .05
318 Pedro J. Martinez .75
319 Kevin McReynolds .05
320 Greg Maddux .90
321 Mike Henneman .05
322 Scott Leius .05
323 John Franco .05
324 Jeff Blauser .05
325 Kirby Puckett .90
326 Darryl Hamilton .05
327 John Smiley .05
328 Derrick May .05
329 Jose Vizcaino .05
330 Randy Johnson .75
331 Jack Morris .05
332 Graeme Lloyd .05
333 Dave Valle .05
334 Greg Myers .05
335 John Wetteland .05
336 Jim Gott .05
337 Tim Naehring .05
338 Mike Kelly .05
339 Jeff Montgomery .05
340 Rafael Palmeiro .65
341 Eddie Murray .75
342 Xavier Hernandez .05
343 Bobby Munoz .05
344 Bobby Bonilla .05
345 Travis Fryman .05
346 Steve Finley .05
347 Chris Sabo .05
348 Armando Reynoso .05
349 Ramon Martinez .05
350 Will Clark .05
351 Moises Alou .05
352 Jim Thome .50
353 Bob Tewksbury .05
354 Andujar Cedeno .05
355 Orel Hershiser .05
356 Mike Devereaux .05
357 Mike Perez .05
358 Dennis Martinez .05
359 Dave Nilsson .05
360 Ozzie Smith .90
361 Eric Anthony .05
362 Scott Sanders .05
363 Paul Sorrento .05
364 Tim Belcher .05
365 Dennis Eckersley .60
366 Mel Rojas .05
367 Tom Henke .05
368 Randy Tomlin .05
369 B.J. Surhoff .05
370 Larry Walker .05
371 Joey Cora .05
372 Mike Harkey .05
373 John Valentin .05
374 Doug Jones .05
375 Dave Justice .05
376 Vince Coleman .05
377 David Hulse .05
378 Kevin Seitzer .05
379 Pete Harnisch .05
380 Ruben Sierra .05
381 Mark Lewis .05
382 Bip Roberts .05
383 Paul Wagner .05
384 Stan Javier .05
385 Barry Larkin .05
386 Mark Portugal .05
387 Roberto Kelly .05
388 Andy Benes .05
389 Felix Fermin .05
390 Marquis Grissom .05
391 Troy Neel .05

392 Chad Kreuter .05
393 Gregg Olson .05
394 Charles Nagy .05
395 Jack McDowell .05
396 Luis Gonzalez .05
397 Benito Santiago .05
398 Chris James .05
399 Terry Mulholland .05
400 Barry Bonds 2.00
401 Joe Grahe .05
402 Duane Ward .05
403 John Burkett .05
404 Scott Servais .05
405 Bryan Harvey .05
406 Bernard Gilkey .05
407 Greg McMichael .05
408 Tim Wallach .05
409 Ken Caminiti .05
410 John Kruk .05
411 Darrin Jackson .05
412 Mike Gallego .05
413 David Cone .05
414 Lou Whitaker .05
415 Sandy Alomar Jr. .05
416 Bill Wegman .05
417 Pat Borders .05
418 Roger Pavlik .05
419 Pete Smith .05
420 Steve Avery .05
421 David Segui .05
422 Rheal Cormier .05
423 Harold Reynolds .05
424 Edgar Martinez .05
425 Cal Ripken, Jr. 2.00
426 Jaime Navarro .05
427 Sean Berry .05
428 Bret Saberhagen .05
429 Bob Welch .05
430 Juan Guzman .05
431 Cal Eldred .05
432 Dave Hollins .05
433 Sid Fernandez .05
434 Willie Banks .05
435 Darryl Kile .05
436 Henry Rodriguez .05
437 Tony Fernandez .05
438 Walt Weiss .05
439 Kevin Tapani .05
440 Mark Grace .05
441 Brian Harper .05
442 Kent Mercker .05
443 Anthony Young .05
444 Todd Zeile .05
445 Greg Vaughn .05
446 Ray Lankford .05
447 David Weathers .05
448 Bret Boone .05
449 Charlie Hough .05
450 Roger Clemens 1.00
451 Mike Morgan .05
452 Doug Drabek .05
453 Danny Jackson .05
454 Dante Bichette .05
455 Roberto Alomar .20
456 Ben McDonald .05
457 Kenny Rogers .05
458 Bill Gullickson .05
459 Darrin Fletcher .05
460 Curt Schilling .20
461 Billy Hatcher .05
462 Howard Johnson .05
463 Mickey Morandini .05
464 Frank Castillo .05
465 Delino DeShields .05
466 Gary Gaetti .05
467 Steve Farr .05
468 Roberto Hernandez .05
469 Jack Armstrong .05
470 Paul Molitor .75
471 Melido Perez .05
472 Greg Hibbard .05
473 Jody Reed .05
474 Tom Gordon .05
475 Gary Sheffield .35
476 John Jaha .05
477 Shawon Dunston .05
478 Reggie Jefferson .05
479 Don Slaught .05
480 Jeff Bagwell .75
481 Tim Pugh .05
482 Kevin Young .05
483 Ellis Burks .05
484 Greg Swindell .05
485 Mark Langston .05
486 Omar Vizquel .05
487 Kevin Brown .05
488 Terry Steinbach .05
489 Mark Lemke .05
490 Matt Williams .05
491 Pete Incaviglia .05
492 Karl Rhodes .05
493 Shawn Green .30
494 Hal Morris .05
495 Derek Bell .05
496 Luis Polonia .05
497 Otis Nixon .05
498 Ron Darling .05
499 Mitch Williams .05
500 Mike Piazza 1.25
501 Pat Meares .05
502 Scott Cooper .05
503 Scott Erickson .05
504 Jeff Juden .05
505 Lee Smith .05
506 Bobby Ayala .05
507 Dave Henderson .05
508 Erik Hanson .05
509 Bob Wickman .05
510 Sammy Sosa .90
511 Hector Carrasco (Diamond Debuts) .05
512 Tim Davis (Diamond Debuts) .05
513 Joey Hamilton (Diamond Debuts) .05
514 Robert Eenhoorn (Diamond Debuts) .05
515 Jorge Fabregas (Diamond Debuts) .05
516 Tim Hyers (Diamond Debuts) .05
517 John Hudek (Diamond Debuts) .05
518 James Mouton **RC** (Diamond Debuts) .05
519 Herbert Perry (Diamond Debuts) .05
520 Chan Ho Park **RC** (Diamond Debuts) .75
521 Bill VanLandingham (Diamond Debuts) .05
522 Paul Shuey (Diamond Debuts) .05
523 Ryan Hancock **RC** (Top Prospects) .05
524 Billy Wagner **RC** (Top Prospects) .25
525 Jason Giambi (Top Prospects) .50
526 Jose Silva **RC** (Top Prospects) .05
527 Terrell Wade **RC** (Top Prospects) .05
528 Todd Dunn (Top Prospects) .05
529 Alan Benes **RC** (Top Prospects) .05
530 Brooks Kieschnick **RC** (Top Prospects) .05
531 Todd Hollandsworth (Top Prospects) .05
532 Brad Fullmer **RC** (Top Prospects) .15
533 Steve Soderstrom **RC** (Top Prospects) .05
534 Daron Kirkreit (Top Prospects) .05
535 Arquimedez Pozo **RC** (Top Prospects) .05
536 Charles Johnson (Top Prospects) .05
537 Preston Wilson (Top Prospects) .10
538 Alex Ochoa (Top Prospects) .05
539 Derrek Lee **RC** (Top Prospects) 3.00
540 Wayne Gomes **RC** (Top Prospects) .05
541 Jermaine Allensworth **RC** (Top Prospects) .05
542 Mike Bell **RC** (Top Prospects) .05
543 Trot Nixon **RC** (Top Prospects) 1.25
544 Pokey Reese (Top Prospects) .05
545 Neifi Perez **RC** (Top Prospects) .05
546 Johnny Damon (Top Prospects) .30
547 Matt Brunson (Top Prospects) .05
548 LaTroy Hawkins **RC** (Top Prospects) .05
549 Eddie Pearson **RC** (Top Prosepcts) .05
550 Derek Jeter (Top Prospects) 2.00

Electric Diamond

Each of the regular-issue and subset cards from 1994 Upper Deck was also produced in a limited edition premium insert "Electric Diamond" version. Where the regular cards have the Upper Deck logo, player and team name in copper foil, the Electric Diamond version has those elements in a silver prismatic foil, along with an "Electric Diamond" identification line next to the UD logo. Backs are identical to the regular cards. (Forty-five of the first series cards can be found with player names on back in either silver or copper.) Electric Diamond cards are found, on average, about every other pack.

	NM/M
Complete Set (550):	75.00
Common Player:	.25
Stars:	1.5X

Baseball Heroes Mickey Mantle

Mickey Mantle Baseball Hero is a 10-card set that chronicles his career. The cards, which include an unnumbered header card, were randomly inserted into both hobby and retail packs of Series II Upper Deck Baseball. This set starts with his rookie season in 1951 and concludes with his induction into The Hall of Fame. It is numbered 64-72 and was the eighth in the continuing "Baseball Heroes" series, which began in 1990.

		NM/M
Complete Set (10):		25.00
Common Card:		3.00
64	1951 - The Early Years (Mickey Mantle)	3.00
65	1953 - Tape Measure Home Runs (Mickey Mantle)	3.00
66	1956 - Triple Crown Season (Mickey Mantle)	3.00
67	1957 - 2nd Consecutive MVP (Mickey Mantle)	3.00
68	1961 - Chases The Babe (Mickey Mantle)	3.00
69	1964 - Series Home Run Record (Mickey Mantle)	3.00
70	1967 - 500th Home Run (Mickey Mantle)	3.00
71	1974: Hall of Fame (Mickey Mantle)	3.00
72	Mickey Mantle/Portrait	3.00
----	Header Card (Mickey Mantle)	5.00

Diamond Collection

The premium chase cards in 1994 Upper Deck are a series of Diamond Collection cards issued in regional subsets. Ten cards are found unique to each of three geographic areas of distribution. Western region cards carry a "W" prefix to the card number, Central cards have a "C" prefix and Eastern cards have an "E" prefix. The region is also indicated in silver-foil printing on the front of the card, with a large "W," "C" or "E" in a compass design. The player's name and team are presented in a foil strip at bottom. A "Diamond Collection" logo is shown in embossed-look typography in the background. Diamond Collection cards are inserted only in hobby packs.

		NM/M
Complete Set (30):		40.00
Common Player:		.50
Complete Central (10):		20.00
1	Michael Jordan	10.00
2	Jeff Bagwell	2.00
3	Barry Larkin	1.00
4	Kirby Puckett	4.00
5	Manny Ramirez	3.00
6	Ryne Sandberg	3.00
7	Ozzie Smith	3.00
8	Frank Thomas	3.00
9	Andy Van Slyke	.50
10	Robin Yount	3.00
Complete East (10):		12.00
1	Roberto Alomar	1.00
2	Roger Clemens	4.00
3	Len Dykstra	.50
4	Cecil Fielder	.50
5	Cliff Floyd	.50
6	Dwight Gooden	.50
7	Dave Justice	.50
8	Don Mattingly	3.00
9	Cal Ripken, Jr.	6.00
10	Gary Sheffield	1.00
Complete West (10):		15.00
1	Barry Bonds	5.00
2	Andres Galarraga	.50
3	Juan Gonzalez	1.00
4	Ken Griffey Jr.	4.00
5	Tony Gwynn	2.50
6	Rickey Henderson	1.50
7	Bo Jackson	1.00
8	Mark McGwire	3.00
9	Mike Piazza	3.00
10	Tim Salmon	.50

Jumbo Checklists

Each hobby foil box of 1994 Upper Deck cards contains one jumbo checklist card. Each of the 5" x 7" cards features Ken Griffey, Jr. There is a large color action photo along with a hologram of the player on front, highlighted by copper-foil printing. Backs have one of four checklists and are numbered with a "CL" prefix.

		NM/M
Complete Set (4):		4.00
Common Card:		1.00
1	Numerical Checklist (Ken Griffey Jr.)	1.00
2	Alphabetical Checklist (Ken Griffey Jr.)	1.00
3	Team Checklist (Ken Griffey Jr.)	1.00
4	Insert Checklist (Ken Griffey Jr.)	1.00

Mickey Mantle's Long Shots

Retail packaging was the exclusive venue for this insert set of contemporary long-ball sluggers. Horizontal fronts feature game-action photos with holographic foil rendering of the background. In one of the lower corners appears the logo "1994 Mickey Mantle's Long Shots." Backs have a color player photo at top, with a photo of Mantle beneath and a statement by him about the featured player. Previous season and career stats are included. Cards are numbered with an "MM" prefix. Besides the 20 current player cards there is a Mickey Mantle card and two trade cards which could be redeemed for complete insert card sets.

		NM/M
Complete Set (21):		20.00
Common Player:		.50
Electric Diamonds:		1X
(1)	Mickey Mantle Trade Card (Silver): (Redeemable for 21-card Mantle Long Shots set.)	4.00
(2)	Mickey Mantle Trade Card (Blue): (Redeemable for Electric Diamond version Mantle Long Shots set.)	4.00
1	Jeff Bagwell	1.50
2	Albert Belle	.50
3	Barry Bonds	4.00
4	Jose Canseco	.75
5	Joe Carter	.50
6	Carlos Delgado	.75
7	Cecil Fielder	.50
8	Cliff Floyd	.50
9	Juan Gonzalez	.75
10	Ken Griffey Jr.	2.50
11	David Justice	.50
12	Fred McGriff	.50
13	Mark McGwire	3.00
14	Dean Palmer	.50
15	Mike Piazza	2.50
16	Manny Ramirez	1.50
17	Tim Salmon	.50
18	Frank Thomas	1.50
19	Mo Vaughn	.50
20	Matt Williams	.50
21	Header (Mickey Mantle)	4.00

Mantle-Griffey Autographed Inserts

First series retail packs of '94 UD were the exclusive venue for a special card featuring spokesmen Ken Griffey Jr. and Mickey Mantle. The front has a painting of the two stars. On back are career highlights and a comparison of the players' first five seasons. A large numbered elliptical hologram on back authenticates the autographs. One thousand cards were issued with either or both signatures.

		NM/M
KG1	Ken Griffey Jr., Mickey Mantle (Griffey Autograph)	250.00
MM1	Ken Griffey Jr., Mickey Mantle (Mantle Autograph)	650.00
GM1	Ken Griffey Jr., Mickey Mantle (Both Autographs)	1,150

Next Generation

Next Generation linked 18 top stars with all-time greats, using the HoloView printing technology. Next Generation Electric Diamond Trade Cards could be redeemed for a complete set of Electic Diamond versions of the Next Generation set. The insert cards were a retail-only find at a rate of one per 20 packs, while the Electric Diamond Trade card was inserted one per case.

		NM/M
Complete Set (18):		100.00
Common Player:		1.50
1	Roberto Alomar	2.50
2	Carlos Delgado	4.00
3	Cliff Floyd	1.50
4	Alex Gonzalez	1.50
5	Juan Gonzalez	3.00
6	Ken Griffey Jr.	10.00
7	Jeffrey Hammonds	1.50
8	Michael Jordan	30.00
9	Dave Justice	1.50
10	Ryan Klesko	1.50
11	Javier Lopez	1.50
12	Raul Mondesi	1.50
13	Mike Piazza	10.00
14	Kirby Puckett	7.50
15	Manny Ramirez	6.50
16	Alex Rodriguez	30.00
17	Tim Salmon	1.50
18	Gary Sheffield	4.00
	ED Trade Card (Ken Griffey Jr.)	30.00

Alex Rodriguez Autograph

Available exclusively in Series 2 retail packaging was this special version of A-Rod's Classic Alumni card. The card is authentically signed in blue Sharpie and carries on its back an authentication hologram.

		NM/M
A298	Alex Rodriguez/Auto. (Classic Alumni)	500.00

SP Insert

Fifteen SP Preview cards were inserted into Series II packs of Upper Deck baseball. The cards were inserted with regional distribution and gave collectors a chance to see what the SP super-premium cards would look like. There were five cards available in the East, Central and West and were inserted at a rate of about one per 36 packs. Most of the preview inserts have different front and back photos than the regularly issued SPs, along with other differences in typography and graphics elements.

		NM/M
Complete Set (15):		60.00
Common Player:		.50
EASTERN REGION		
1	Roberto Alomar	1.00
2	Cliff Floyd	.50
3	Javier Lopez	.50
4	Don Mattingly	6.00
5	Cal Ripken, Jr.	10.00
CENTRAL REGION		
1	Jeff Bagwell	3.00
2	Michael Jordan	10.00
3	Kirby Puckett	6.00
4	Manny Ramirez	3.00
5	Frank Thomas	4.00
WESTERN REGION		
1	Barry Bonds	10.00
2	Juan Gonzalez	1.50
3	Ken Griffey Jr.	5.00
4	Mike Piazza	5.00
5	Tim Salmon	.50

Ken Griffey Jr. 5th Anniversary Jumbo

The origins of this card are unknown. Besides producing 15-card sets of top players in a black-bordered 5th Anniversary insert set in regular and 3-1/2" x 5-1/2" formats, UD issued an 8-1/2" x 11" 5th Anniversary card of Griffey. In virtually all respects except size, the jumbo card is identical to the others. It is, however, numbered on back from within an edition of 5,000.

NM/M
Ken Griffey Jr. 20.00

All-Stars

Produced in commemoration of the 1994 All-Star Game, this boxed set features photography by Walter Iooss, Jr. on most cards, shown to its best advantage on a large 3-1/2" x 5" format. The front of each card has a foil seal of the Pittsburgh All-Star Game logo. On most sets, the seal is in green foil; every 40th set has the seals in gold. The left side of the card backs features a smaller version of the front photo and a few sentences about the player. Some cards feature a second, larger photo of the player on back, but most have a photo and write-up of a teammate. The last six cards in the set honor the 125th anniversary of professional baseball. An album to house the set was made available for $10 via a mail-in offer card in the set.

NM/M
Complete Set (48): 9.00
Common Player: .15
Gold: 4X
1 Ken Griffey Jr. 1.00
2 Ruben Sierra, Todd Van Poppel .15
3 Bryan Harvey, Gary Sheffield .35
4 Gregg Jefferies, Brian Jordan .15
5 Ryne Sandberg .75
6 Matt Williams, John Burkett .15
7 Darren Daulton, John Kruk .15
8 Don Mattingly, Wade Boggs .75
9 Pat Listach, Greg Vaughn .15
10 Tim Salmon, Eduardo Perez .25
11 Fred McGriff, Tom Glavine .25
12 Mo Vaughn, Andre Dawson .35
13 Brian McRae, Kevin Appier .15
14 Kirby Puckett, Kent Hrbek .75
15 Cal Ripken, Jr. 2.00
16 Roberto Alomar, Paul Molitor .65
17 Tony Gwynn, Phil Plantier .75
18 Greg Maddux, Steve Avery .75
19 Mike Mussina, Chris Hoiles .50
20 Randy Johnson .65
21 Roger Clemens, Aaron Sele .75
22 Will Clark, Dean Palmer .25
23 Cecil Fielder, Travis Fryman .15
24 John Olerud, Joe Carter .15
25 Juan Gonzalez .65
26 Jose Rijo, Barry Larkin .15
27 Andy Van Slyke, Jeff King .15
28 Larry Walker, Marquis Grissom .15
29 Kenny Lofton, Albert Belle .25
30 Mark Grace, Sammy Sosa 1.00
31 Mike Piazza 1.00
32 Ramon Martinez, Orel Hershiser .15
33 Dave Justice, Terry Pendleton .15
34 Ivan Rodriguez, Jose Canseco .50
35 Barry Bonds 2.00
36 Jeff Bagwell, Craig Biggio .65
37 Jay Bell, Orlando Merced .15
38 Jeff Kent, Dwight Gooden .15
39 Andres Galarraga, Charlie Hayes .15
40 Frank Thomas .70
41 Bobby Bonilla .15
42 Jack McDowell, Tim Raines .15
43 1869 Red Stockings .15
44 Ty Cobb .50
45 Babe Ruth 1.50
46 Mickey Mantle 2.50
47 Reggie Jackson .50
48 Ken Griffey Jr. 1.00
48a Ken Griffey Jr. (Promo Card) 1.00

All-Time Heroes

The All-Time Heroes set provided collectors with both Ted Williams cards from Topps 1954 reprint set, from which they were absent due to a contractual obligation between Ted Williams and the Upper Deck Co. An agreement between Topps and Upper Deck allowed both Williams' cards to be offered in the All-Time Heroes set. There is also a 1954 Mickey Mantle inserted that has no number, but bears the same design as original 1954 Topps cards. The basic All-Time Heroes of Baseball set contains 225 cards. The cards were patterned after cards from the early 60's, with black borders across the top and bottom. Black-and-white photographs give the 2-1/2" x 3-1/2" cards a nostalgic appearance. All-Time Heroes also has autographed cards of Mantle, Brett, Jackson and Seaver, along with a Next in Line insert set and a parallel, bronze-foil 125th anniversary set. Cards #1-18 comprise an Off the Wire subset. Cards #101-125 are a Major League 125th Anniversary subset. Cards #151-177 are a Diamond Legends subset. Cards #208-224 are a subset titled Heroes of Baseball.

NM/M
Complete Set (225): 20.00
Common Player: .10
Wax Box: 65.00
1 Ted Williams (OTW) .75
2 Johnny Vander Meer (OTW) .10
3 Lou Brock (OTW) .10
4 Lou Gehrig (OTW) .75
5 Hank Aaron (OTW) .50
6 Tommie Agee (OTW) .10
7 Mickey Mantle (OTW) 1.50
8 Bill Mazeroski (OTW) .30
9 Reggie Jackson, Bud Harrelson (OTW) .20
10 Willie Mays, Mickey Mantle (OTW) 1.25
11 Roy Campanella (OTW) .20
12 Harvey Haddix (OTW) .10
13 Jimmy Piersall (OTW) .10
14 Enos Slaughter (OTW) .10
15 Nolan Ryan (OTW) .75
16 Bobby Thomson (OTW) .10
17 Willie Mays (OTW) .50
18 Bucky Dent (OTW) .10
19 Joe Garagiola .20
20 George Brett .75
21 Cecil Cooper .10
22 Ray Boone .10
23 King Kelly .10
24 Willie Mays 1.00
25 Napoleon Lajoie .10
26 Gil McDougald .10
27 Nelson Briles .10
28 Bucky Dent .10
29 Manny Sanguillen .10
30 Ty Cobb 1.00
31 Jim Grant .10
32 Del Ennis .10
33 Ron Hunt .10
34 Nolan Ryan 1.50
35 Christy Mathewson .75
36 Robin Roberts .10
37 Frank Crosetti .10
38 Johnny Vander Meer .10
39 Virgil Trucks .10
40 Lou Gehrig 1.50
41 Luke Appling .10
42 Rico Petrocelli .10
43 Harry Walker .10
44 Reggie Jackson .65
44a Reggie Jackson (Promo card.) 4.00
45 Mel Ott .10
46 Phil Cavaretta .10
47 Larry Doby .10
48 Johnny Mize .10
49 Ralph Kiner .10
50 Ted Williams 1.50
51 Bobby Thomson .10
52 Joe Black .10
53 Monte Irvin .10
54 Bill Virdon .10
55 Honus Wagner 1.00
56 Herb Score .10
57 Jerry Coleman .10
58 Jimmie Foxx .30
59 Elroy Face .10
60 Babe Ruth 2.00
61 Jimmy Piersall .10
62 Ed Charles .10
63 Johnny Podres .10
64 Charlie Neal .10
65 Bill White .10
66 Bill Skowron .10
67 Al Rosen .10
68 Eddie Lopat .10
69 Bud Harrelson .10
70 Steve Carlton .10
71 Vida Blue .10
72 Don Newcombe .10
73 Al Bumbry .10
74 Bill Madlock .10
(75) Checklist 1-75 (Hank Aaron) .50
76 Bill Mazeroski .50
77 Ron Cey .10
78 Tommy John .10
79 Lou Brock .10
80 Walter Johnson .75
81 Harvey Haddix .10
82 Al Oliver .10
83 Johnny Logan .10
84 Dave Dravecky .10
85 Tony Oliva .10
86 Dave Kingman .10
87 Luis Tiant .10
88 Sal Bando .10
89 Cesar Cedeno .10
90 Warren Spahn .10
91 Mickey Lolich .10
92 Lew Burdette .10
93 Hank Bauer .10
94 Marv Throneberry .10
95 Willie Stargell .10
96 George Kell .10
97 Fergie Jenkins .10
98 Al Kaline .10
99 Billy Martin .10
100 Mickey Mantle 3.00
101 1869 - Red Stockings (125th) .20
102 1892 (King Kelly (125th)) .10
103 1901 (Nap Lajoie (125th)) .10
104 1905 (Christy Mathewson (125th)) .40
105 1910 (Cy Young (125th)) .40
106 1915 (Ty Cobb (125th)) .75
(107) Checklist 136-180 (Reggie Jackson) .40
108 1924 (Rogers Hornsby (125th)) .10
109 1926 (Walter Johnson (125th)) .40
110 1927 (Babe Ruth (125th)) 1.00
111 1930 (Hack Wilson (125th)) .10
112 1939 (Lou Gehrig (125th)) .75
113 1941 (Ted Williams (125th)) .75
113a 1941 (Ted Williams (125th)(Autographed edition of 2,500.) 250.00
114 1949 (Yogi Berra (125th)) .30
115 1951 (Bobby Thomson (125th)) .10
116 1953 (Mickey Mantle (125th)) 1.50
117 1954 (Willie Mays (125th)) .50
118 1960 (Bill Mazeroski (125th)) .30
119 1967 (Bob Gibson (125th)) .10
120 1969 Miracle Mets (125th) .50
121 1974 (Hank Aaron (125th)) .50
122 1977 (Reggie Jackson (125th)) .40
123 1980 (George Brett (125th)) .20
124 1982 (Steve Carlton (125th)) .10
125 1991 (Nolan Ryan (125th)) .75
126 Frank Thomas .10
127 Sam McDowell .10
128 Jim Lonberg .10
129 Bert Campaneris .10
130 Bob Gibson .10
131 Bobby Richardson .10
132 Bobby Grich .10
133 Billy Pierce .10
134 Enos Slaughter .10
(135) Checklist 181-225 (Honus Wagner) .50
136 Orlando Cepeda .10
137 Rennie Stennett .10
138 Gene Alley .10
139 Manny Mota .10
140 Rogers Hornsby .10
141 Joe Charboneau .20
142 Rick Farrell .10
143 Toby Harrah .10
144 Hank Aaron 1.00
145 Yogi Berra .50
146 Whitey Ford .50
147 Roy Campanella .50
148 Graig Nettles .10
149 Bobby Brown .10
150 Checklist 76-150 (Willie Mays) .50
151 Cy Young/DL .40
152 Walter Johnson/DL .40
153 Christy Mathewson/DL .40
154 Warren Spahn/DL .10
155 Steve Carlton/DL .10
156 Bob Gibson/DL .10
157 Whitey Ford/DL .30
158 Yogi Berra/DL .30
159 Roy Campanella/DL .30
160 Lou Gehrig/DL .75
161 Johnny Mize/DL .10
162 Rogers Hornsby/DL .10
163 Honus Wagner/DL .50
164 Hank Aaron/DL .50
165 Babe Ruth/DL 1.00
166 Willie Mays/DL .50
167 Reggie Jackson/DL .40
168 Mickey Mantle/DL 1.50
169 Jimmie Foxx/DL .10
170 Ted Williams/DL .75
171 Mel Ott/DL .10
172 Willie Stargell/DL .10
173 Al Kaline/DL .10
174 Ty Cobb/DL .75
175 Napoleon Lajoie/DL .10
176 Lou Brock/DL .10
177 Tom Seaver/DL .10
178 Mark Fidrych .20
179 Don Baylor .10
180 Tom Seaver .10
181 Jerry Grote .10
182 George Foster .10
183 Buddy Bell .10
184 Ralph Garr .10
185 Steve Garvey .10
186 Joe Torre .10
187 Carl Erskine .10
188 Tommy Davis .10
189 Bill Buckner .10
190 Hack Wilson .10
191 Steve Bass .10
192 Ken Brett .10
193 Lee May .10
194 Bob Horner .10
195 Boog Powell .10
196 Darrell Evans .10
197 Paul Blair .10
198 Johnny Callison .10
199 Jimmie Reese .10
200 Cy Young .75
201 Ron Santo .10
202 Rico Carty .10
203 Ron Necciai .10
204 Lou Boudreau .10
205 Minnie Minoso .10
206 Eddie Yost .10
207 Tommie Agee .10
208 Dave Kingman (Heroes) .10
209 Tony Oliva (Heroes) .10
210 Reggie Jackson (Heroes) .40
211 Paul Blair (Heroes) .10
212 Fergie Jenkins (Heroes) .10
213 Steve Garvey (Heroes) .10
214 Bert Campaneris (Heroes) .10
215 Orlando Cepeda (Heroes) .10
216 Bill Madlock (Heroes) .10
217 Rennie Stennett (Heroes) .10
218 Frank Thomas (Heroes) .10
219 Bob Gibson (Heroes) .10
220 Lou Brock (Heroes) .10
221 Rico Carty (Heroes) .10
222 Mickey Mantle (Heroes) 1.50
223 Robin Roberts (Heroes) .10
224 Manny Sanguillen (Heroes) .10
225 Checklist 151-225 (Mickey Mantle) 1.50

All-Time Heroes 125th Anniversary

This parallel set was issued at the rate of one card per pack of Upper Deck All-Time Heroes cards. They are identical to the regular-issue version except for the presence on front of bronze-foil stamping which reads, "Major League Baseball / 125th Anniversary."

NM/M
Complete Set (225): 40.00
Common Player: .25
Stars: 2X
15 Nolan Ryan/OTW (Overprint at left.) 1.00
15 Nolan Ryan/OTW (Overprint at right.) 1.00

All-Time Heroes Autographs

Four players' autographed cards were randomly inserted into packs of All-Time Heroes at a reported rate of about 1:385. Seaver, Jackson and Mantle signed 1,000 each, Brett signed 2,000.

NM/M
Complete Set (4): 650.00
Common Player: 45.00
(1) Mickey Mantle 550.00
(2) Reggie Jackson 40.00
(3) George Brett 60.00
(4) Tom Seaver 25.00

All-Time Heroes Next In Line

The Next in Line insert set includes 20 top minor leaguers. These cards were randomly inserted into every 39 packs with only 2,500 of each card produced.

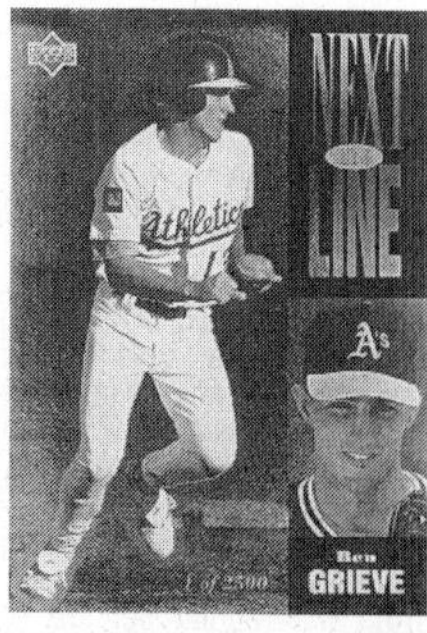

NM/M
Complete Set (20): 40.00
Common Player: 1.00
1 Mike Bell 1.00
2 Alan Benes 1.00
3 D.J. Boston 1.00
4 Johnny Damon 5.00
5 Brad Fullmer 1.00
6 LaTroy Hawkins 1.00
7 Derek Jeter 25.00
8 Daron Kirkreit 1.00
9 Trot Nixon 3.00
10 Alex Ochoa 1.00
11 Kirk Presley 1.00
12 Jose Silva 1.00
13 Terrell Wade 1.00
14 Billy Wagner 1.50
15 Glenn Williams 1.00
16 Preston Wilson 1.50
17 Wayne Gomes 1.00
18 Ben Grieve 1.00
19 Dustin Hermanson 1.00
20 Paul Wilson 1.00

All-Time Heroes 1954 Topps Archives

Two cards that were not included in the Topps 1954 Archives Set and one that wasn't even in the original 1954 set were randomly inserted into All-Time Heroes foil packs. Both Ted Williams cards, numbers 1 and 250, were left out of the Archives set because of contractual obligations of Williams with Upper Deck. In addition, a Mickey Mantle card with the original 1954 design was randomly inserted. Mantle was signed exclusively with Bowman in 1954 and 1955, and therefore, was not in either Topps set.

NM/M
Complete Set (3): 150.00
1 Ted Williams 50.00
250 Ted Williams 50.00
259 Mickey Mantle 75.00

American Epic

Baseball, The American Epic traces the history of the game, highlighting players, personalities, events and stadiums that have contributed to the national pastime. The set was patterned after a 1994 18-hour TV documentary. This boxed set contains 80 cards. It explains the roots of the game and showcases some of baseball's great players and events. Each set contains a randomly inserted card of either Michael Jordan, Babe Ruth or Mickey Mantle. Cards from the regular set are in black-and-white, with the player name and the featured year running down the left side in white print. Card backs contain half color, depending on what "inning" the card is from, and half white. The color side tells a story, the white side gives statistics and highlights.

NM/M
Complete Set (81): 12.50
Common Player: .15
1 1880s - Our Game .15
2 1845 - Alexander Cartwright .15
3 1857 - Henry Chadwick .15
4 1866 - The Fair Sex .15
5 1869 - Harry Wright .15
6 1876 - Albert Goodwill Spalding .15
7 1883 - Cap Anson .15
8 1884 - Moses Fleetwood Walker .25
9 1886 - King Kelly .15
10 1890 - John Montgomery Ward .15
11 1909 - Ty Cobb .75
12 1904 - John McGraw .15
13 1904 - Rube Waddell .15
14 1905 - Christy Mathewson .25
15 1907 - Walter Johnson .25
16 1908 - Alta Weiss .15
17 1908 - Fred Merkle .15
18 1908 - Take Me Out To The Ball Game .15
19 1909 - John Henry Lloyd .15
20 1909 - Honus Wagner .40
21 1915 - Woodrow Wilson .15
22 1910 - Napoleon Lajoie .15
23 1911 - Addie Joss .15
24 1912 - Joe Wood .15
25 1912 - Royal Rooters .15
26 1913 - Ebbets Field .15
27 1914 - Johnny Evers .15
28 1918 - World War II .15
29 1919 - Joe Jackson .75
30 1927 - Babe Ruth 1.50
31 1920 - Rube Foster .15
32 1920 - Ray Chapman .15
33 1921 - Kenesaw M. Landis .15
34 1923 - Yankee Stadium .15
35 1924 - Rogers Hornsby .15
36 1923 - Warren G. Harding .15
37 1925 - Lou Gehrig .75
38 1926 - Grover C. Alexander .15
39 1929 - House of David .15
40 1933 - Satchel Paige .40
41 1931 - Lefty Grove .15
42 1932 - Jimmie Foxx .15
43 1932 - Connie Mack .15
44 1937 - Josh Gibson .15
45 1934 - Dizzy Dean .15
46 1934 - Carl Hubbell .15
47 1937 - Franklin D. Roosevelt .15
48 1938 - Bob Feller .15
49 1939 - Cool Papa Bell .15
50 1947 - Jackie Robinson .75
51 1941 - Ted Williams .75
52 1941 - Sym-Phony Band .15
53 1944 - Annabel Lee .15
54 1945 - Hank Greenberg .15
55 1947 - Branch Rickey .15
56 1948 - Harry S. Truman .15
57 1953 - Casey Stengel .15
58 1951 - Bobby Thomson .15
59 1952 - Dwight D. Eisenhower .15
60 1952 - Mario Cuomo .15
61 1952 - Buck O'Neil .15
62 1955 - Yogi Berra .25
63 1956 - Mickey Mantle 2.00
64 1956 - Don Larsen .15
65 1961 - John F. Kennedy .15
66 1960 - Bill Mazeroski .15
67 1961 - Roger Maris .25
68 1966 - Frank Robinson .15
69 1969 - Bob Gibson .15
70 1970 - Tom Seaver .15
71 1969 - Curt Flood .15
72 1972 - Roberto Clemente .75
73 1975 - Luis Tiant .15
74 1975 - Marvin Miller .15
75 1977 - Reggie Jackson .25
76 1979 - Willie Stargell .15
77 1985 - Pete Rose .75
78 1994 - Bill Clinton .15
79 1991 - Nolan Ryan .75
80 1993 - George Brett .25
--- Checklist .08

American Epic Inserts

In addition to the regular 80-card set, each boxed set contains one special insert card, depending on where it was purchased. At retail locations, an additional Babe Ruth card was included. Michael Jordan was included in sets purchased through direct mail outlets. Mickey Mantle was featured in sets purchased from QVC (sets purchased from Upper Deck Authenticated included an autographed card of Mantle). The inserts are numbered BC1- BC3.

NM/M
Complete Set (3): 6.00
Common Player: 2.00
1 Mickey Mantle 2.00
2 Michael Jordan 2.00
3 Babe Ruth 2.00

American Epic Little Debbie Mail-in

Fifteen of the cards from Upper Deck's "An American Epic" card set were chosen for use in a mail-in promotion with Little Debbie snack cakes. These cards are identical to the Epic versions except for the card numbers, which include an "LD" prefix. The back of card LD1 is a checklist for the set and includes a Little Debbie logo. Sets sold for about $4, with proofs of purchase.

NM/M
Complete Set (15): 4.50
Common Player: .25
1 Our Game/Checklist .05
2 Alexander Cartwright .25
3 King Kelly .25
4 John McGraw .25
5 Christy Mathewson .40
6 Walter Johnson .40
7 Ted Williams .75
8 Annabel Lee .25
9 Jackie Robinson .50
10 Bobby Thomson .25
11 Buck O'Neil .25
12 Mickey Mantle 1.50
13 Bob Gibson .25
14 Curt Flood .25
15 Reggie Jackson .40

Fun Packs

In its second year this product aimed at the young collector again offered a basic set of some 160 players, sur-

rounded by several special subsets. The first nine cards feature Stars of Tomorrow. There is a group of 18 Stand Out cards on which the background can be folded to create a player figure. Profiles cards feature playing tips from six young stars. A group of nine Headline Stars cards features two players on each which fold back to reveal a holographic photo. What's the Call cards offer game problems and cartoon caricatures of nine players. There are nine Fold Outs cards which open to reveal action photos. The subsets concluded with seven heat-activated Fun Cards on which the background temporarily appears when body heat is applied. Each five-card foil pack also includes a scratch-off game card; one for each major league team and one All-Star team for each league.

NM/M
Complete Set (240): 35.00
Common Player: .05
Wax Box: 15.00
1 Manny Ramirez (Stars of Tomorrow) .75
2 Cliff Floyd (Stars of Tomorrow) .05
3 Rondell White (Stars of Tomorrow) .05
4 Carlos Delgado (Stars of Tomorrow) .50
5 Chipper Jones (Stars of Tomorrow) 1.25
6 Javier Lopez (Stars of Tomorrow) .05
7 Ryan Klesko (Stars of Tomorrow) .05
8 Steve Karsay (Stars of Tomorrow) .05
9 Rich Becker (Stars of Tomorrow) .05
10 Gary Sheffield .35
11 Jeffrey Hammonds .05
12 Roberto Alomar .20
13 Brent Gates .05
14 Andres Galarraga .05
15 Tim Salmon .05
16 Dwight Gooden .05
17 Mark Grace .05
18 Andy Van Slyke .05
19 Juan Gonzalez .40
20 Mickey Tettleton .05
21 Roger Clemens 1.25
22 Will Clark .05
23 Dave Justice .05
24 Ken Griffey Jr. 1.50
24a Ken Griffey Jr. (Promo Card) 1.50
25 Barry Bonds 2.50
26 Bill Swift .05
27 Fred McGriff .05
28 Randy Myers .05
29 Joe Carter .05
30 Nigel Wilson .05
31 Mike Piazza 1.50
32 Dave Winfield .75
33 Steve Avery .05
34 Kirby Puckett .90
35 Frank Thomas .75
36 Aaron Sele .05
37 Ricky Gutierrez .05
38 Curt Schilling .25
39 Mike Greenwell .05
40 Andy Benes .05
41 Kevin Brown .05
42 Mo Vaughn .05
43 Dennis Eckersley .60
44 Ken Hill .05
45 Cecil Fielder .05
46 Bobby Jones .05
47 Tom Glavine .25
48 Wally Joyner .05
49 Ellis Burks .05
50 Jason Bere .05
51 Randy Johnson .75
52 Darryl Kile .05
53 Jeff Montgomery .05
54 Alex Fernandez .05
55 Kevin Appier .05
56 Brian McRae .05
57 John Wetteland .05
58 Bob Tewksbury .05
59 Todd Van Poppel .05
60 Ryne Sandberg .90
61 Bret Barberie .05
62 Phil Plantier .05
63 Chris Hoiles .05
64 Tony Phillips .05
65 Salomon Torres .05
66 Juan Guzman .05
67 Paul O'Neill .05
68 Dante Bichette .05
69 Len Dykstra .05
70 Ivan Rodriguez .65
71 Dean Palmer .05
72a Brett Butler .05
72b Phil Hiatt (Checklisted as #172.) .05
73 Rick Aguilera .05
74 Robby Thompson .05
75 Jim Abbott .05
76 Al Martin .05
77 Roberto Hernandez .05
78 Jay Buhner .05
79 Devon White .05
80 Travis Fryman .05
81 Jeromy Burnitz .05
82 John Burkett .05
83 Orlando Merced .05
84 Jose Rijo .05
85 Eddie Murray .75
86 Howard Johnson .05
87 Chuck Carr .05
88 Pedro J. Martinez .75
89 Charlie Hayes .05
90 Matt Williams .05
91 Steve Finley .05
92 Pat Listach .05
93 Sandy Alomar, Jr. .05
94 Delino DeShields .05
95 Rod Beck .05
97 Todd Zeile (Checklisted as #96.) .05
98a Darryl Hamilton .05
98b Duane Ward (Checklisted as #97.) .05
99 John Olerud .05
100 Andre Dawson .25
101 Ozzie Smith .90
102 Rick Wilkins .05
103 Alan Trammell .05
104 Jeff Blauser .05
105 Bret Boone .05
106 J.T. Snow .05
107 Kenny Lofton .05
108 Cal Ripken, Jr. 2.50
109 Carlos Baerga .05
110 Bip Roberts .05
111 Barry Larkin .05
112 Mark Langston .05
113 Ozzie Guillen .05
114 Chad Curtis .05
115 Dave Hollins .05
116 Reggie Sanders .05
117 Jeff Conine .05
118 Mark Whiten .05
119 Tony Gwynn .90
120 John Kruk .05
121 Eduardo Perez .05
122 Walt Weiss .05
123 Don Mattingly 1.00
124 Rickey Henderson .75
125 Mark McGwire 2.00
126 Wade Boggs .90
127 Bobby Bonilla .05
128 Jeff King .05
129 Jack McDowell .05
130 Albert Belle .05
131 Greg Maddux .90
132 Dennis Martinez .05
133 Jose Canseco .40
134 Bryan Harvey .05
135 Dave Fleming .05
136 Larry Walker .05
137 Ken Caminiti .05
138 Doug Drabek .05
139 Ron Gant .05
140 Darren Daulton .05
141 Ruben Sierra .05
142 Kirk Rueter .05
143 Raul Mondesi .05
144 Greg Vaughn .05
145 Danny Tartabull .05
146 Eric Karros .05
147 Chuck Knoblauch .05
148 Mike Mussina .30
149 Brady Anderson .05
150 Paul Molitor .75
151 Bo Jackson .10
152 Jeff Bagwell .75
153 Gregg Jefferies .05
154 Rafael Palmeiro .65
155 Orel Hershiser .05
156 Derek Bell .05
157 Jeff Kent .05
158 Craig Biggio .05
159 Marquis Grissom .05
160 Matt Mieske .05
161 Jay Bell .05
162 Sammy Sosa .90
163 Robin Ventura .05
164 Deion Sanders .05
165 Jimmy Key .05
166 Cal Eldred .05
167 David McCarty .05
168 Carlos Garcia .05
169 Willie Greene .05
170 Michael Jordan **RC** 2.50
171 Roberto Mejia .05
173 Marc Newfield .05
174 Kevin Stocker .05
175 Randy Johnson (Standouts) .40
176 Ivan Rodriguez (Standouts) .30
177 Frank Thomas (Standouts) .45
178 Roberto Alomar (Standouts) .10
179 Travis Fryman (Standouts) .05
180 Cal Ripken, Jr. (Standouts) 1.25
181 Juan Gonzalez (Standouts) .30
182 Ken Griffey Jr. (Standouts) .75
183 Albert Belle (Standouts) .05
184 Greg Maddux (Standouts) .50
185 Mike Piazza (Standouts) .75
186 Fred McGriff (Standouts) .05
187 Robby Thompson (Standouts) .05
188 Matt Williams (Standouts) .05
189 Jeff Blauser (Standouts) .05
190 Barry Bonds (Standouts) 1.25
191 Len Dykstra (Standouts) .05
192 Dave Justice (Standouts) .05
193 Ken Griffey Jr. (Profiles) .75
194 Barry Bonds (Profiles) 1.25
195 Frank Thomas (Profiles) .45
196 Juan Gonzalez (Profiles) .30
197 Randy Johnson (Profiles) .40
198 Chuck Carr (Profiles) .05
199 Barry Bonds, Juan Gonzalez (Headline Stars) 1.00
200 Ken Griffey Jr., Don Mattingly (Headline Stars) .75
201 Roberto Alomar, Carlos Baerga (Headline Stars) .10
202 Dave Winfield, Robin Yount (Headline Stars) .40
203 Mike Piazza, Tim Salmon (Headline Stars) .75
204 Albert Belle, Frank Thomas (Headline Stars) .45
205 Cliff Floyd, Rondell White (Headline Stars) .05
206 Kirby Puckett, Tony Gwynn (Headline Stars) .50
207 Roger Clemens, Greg Maddux (Headline Stars) .50
208 Mike Piazza (What's The Call) .75
209 Jose Canseco (What's The Call) .20
210 Frank Thomas (What's The Call) .45
211 Roberto Alomar (What's The Call) .10
212 Barry Bonds (What's The Call) 1.25
213 Rickey Henderson (What's The Call) .40
214 John Kruk (What's The Call) .05
215 Juan Gonzalez (What's The Call) .40
216 Ken Griffey Jr. (What's The Call) .75
217 Roberto Alomar (Foldouts) .10
218 Craig Biggio (Foldouts) .05
219 Cal Ripken, Jr. (Foldouts) 1.25
220 Mike Piazza (Foldouts) .75
221 Brent Gates (Foldouts) .05
222 Walt Weiss (Foldouts) .05
223 Bobby Bonilla (Foldouts) .05
224 Ken Griffey Jr. (Foldouts) .75
225 Barry Bonds (Foldouts) 1.25
226 Barry Bonds (Fun Cards) 1.25
227 Joe Carter (Fun Cards) .05
228 Mike Greenwell (Fun Cards) .05
229 Ken Griffey Jr. (Fun Cards) .75
230 John Kruk (Fun Cards) .05
231 Mike Piazza (Fun Cards) .75
232 Kirby Puckett (Fun Cards) .50
233 John Smoltz (Fun Cards) .05
234 Rick Wilkins (Fun Cards) .05
235 Checklist 1-40 (Ken Griffey Jr.) .65
236 Checklist 41-80 (Frank Thomas) .45
237 Checklist 81-120 (Barry Bonds) 1.00
238 Checklist 121-160 (Mike Piazza) .65
239 Checklist 161-200 (Tim Salmon) .05
240 Checklist 201-240 (Juan Gonzalez) .35

Scratch-off Game Cards:
(1) National League .05
(2) Atlanta Braves .05
(3) Chicago Cubs .05
(4) Cincinnati Reds .05
(5) Colorado Rockies .05
(6) Florida Marlins .05
(7) Houston Astros .05
(8) Los Angeles Dodgers .05
(9) Montreal Expos .05
(10) New York Mets .05
(11) Philadelphia Phillies .05
(12) Pittsburgh Pirates .05
(13) St. Louis Cardinals .05
(14) San Diego Padres .05
(15) San Francisco Giants .05

GM "Baseball" Previews

This nine-card set is closely related to the 80-card issue subsequently released in conjunction with the public television series "Baseball" by Ken Burns. This preview issue, carrying the logo of General Motors (principal sponsor of the TV series), was issued in cello and foil packs and was available, generally with a test drive, at GM automobile dealerships. Card backs have some biographical and statistical highlights and a career summary.

NM/M
Complete Set (9): 6.00
Common Player: .50
1 Hank Aaron 1.25
2 Roberto Clemente 1.50
3 Ty Cobb .50
4 Hank Greenberg .50
5 Mickey Mantle 3.00
6 Satchel Paige .50
7 Jackie Robinson .75
8 Babe Ruth 2.00
9 Ted Williams 1.00

GTS Mickey Mantle Phone Cards

Upper Deck and Global Telecommunication Solutions combined to produce this set of phone cards paralleling the Mantle Heroes insert cards found in the regular UD issue. The phone cards were sold in two series of five cards each for $59.95 per series. Fronts of the 2-1/8" x 3-3/8" plastic cards feature black-and-white or color photos of Mantle, along with mention of a career highlight. Backs are printed in black and have instructions for use of the card. A card picturing the 1869 Cincinnati Red Stockings was included as a random insert in the first series of Mantle phone card sets.

NM/M

Complete Set (10): 20.00
Common Card: 3.00
(1) Mickey Mantle/Portrait 3.00
(2) Mickey Mantle (1951: The Early Years) 3.00
(3) Mickey Mantle (1953: Tape Measure Home Runs) 3.00
(4) Mickey Mantle (1956: Triple Crown Season) 3.00
(5) Mickey Mantle (1957: Second Consecutive MVP) 3.00
(6) Mickey Mantle (1961: Chasing the Babe) 3.00
(7) Mickey Mantle (1964: Series Home Run Record) 3.00
(8) Mickey Mantle (1967: 500th Home Run) 3.00
(9) Mickey Mantle (1974: Hall of Fame) 3.00
(10) Mickey Mantle/Portrait 3.00
(11) 1869 Cincinnati Red Stockings 10.00

1995 Upper Deck

Issued in two series of 225 base cards each, with loads of subsets and inserts, the 1995 Upper Deck set was a strong collector favorite from the outset. Basic cards feature a borderless front photo with the player's name and UD logo in bronze foil. Backs have another large color photo, recent stats and career totals and appropriate logos, along with the infield-shaped hologram. Subsets in each series include Star Rookies and Top Prospects, each with special designs highlighting the game's young stars. Series I has a "'90s Midpoint Analysis" subset studying the decade's superstars, and Series II has another hot rookies' subset, Diamond Debuts. The set closes with a five-card "Final Tribute" subset summarizing the careers of five recently retired superstars. Retail and hobby versions were sold with each featuring some unique insert cards. Basic packaging of each type was the 12-card foil pack at $1.99, though several other configurations were also released.

NM/M

Complete Set (450): 20.00
Common Player: .05
Electric Diamond: 2X
Electric Diamond Golds: 8X
Series 1 or 2 Pack (12): .85
Series 1 or 2 Wax Box (36): 20.00
1 Ruben Rivera (Top Prospect) .05
2 Bill Pulsipher (Top Prospect) .05
3 Ben Grieve (Top Prospect) .05
4 Curtis Goodwin (Top Prospect) .05
5 Damon Hollins (Top Prospect) .05
6 Todd Greene (Top Prospect) .05
7 Glenn Williams (Top Prospect) .05
8 Bret Wagner (Top Prospect) .05
9 Karim Garcia **RC** (Top Prospect) .50
10 Nomar Garciaparra (Top Prospect) 1.00
11 Raul Casanova **RC** (Top Prospect) .10
12 Matt Smith (Top Prospect) .05
13 Paul Wilson (Top Prospect) .05
14 Jason Isringhausen (Top Prospect) .05
15 Reid Ryan (Top Prospect) .05
16 Lee Smith .05
17 Chili Davis .05
18 Brian Anderson .05
19 Gary DiSarcina .05
20 Bo Jackson .10
21 Chuck Finley .05
22 Darryl Kile .05
23 Shane Reynolds .05
24 Tony Eusebio .05
25 Craig Biggio .05
26 Doug Drabek .05
27 Brian L. Hunter .05
28 James Mouton .05
29 Geronimo Berroa .05
30 Rickey Henderson .75
31 Steve Karsay .05
32 Steve Ontiveros .05
33 Ernie Young .05
34 Dennis Eckersley .65
35 Mark McGwire 1.50
36 Dave Stewart .05
37 Pat Hentgen .05
38 Carlos Delgado .45
39 Joe Carter .05
40 Roberto Alomar .20
41 John Olerud .05
42 Devon White .05
43 Roberto Kelly .05
44 Jeff Blauser .05
45 Fred McGriff .05
46 Tom Glavine .25
47 Mike Kelly .05
48 Javy Lopez .05
49 Greg Maddux 1.00
50 Matt Mieske .05
51 Troy O'Leary .05
52 Jeff Cirillo .05
53 Cal Eldred .05
54 Pat Listach .05
55 Jose Valentin .05
56 John Mabry .05
57 Bob Tewksbury .05
58 Brian Jordan .05
59 Gregg Jefferies .05
60 Ozzie Smith 1.00
61 Geronimo Pena .05
62 Mark Whiten .05
63 Rey Sanchez .05
64 Willie Banks .05
65 Mark Grace .05
66 Randy Myers .05
67 Steve Trachsel .05
68 Derrick May .05
69 Brett Butler .05
70 Eric Karros .05
71 Tim Wallach .05
72 Delino DeShields .05
73 Darren Dreifort .05
74 Orel Hershiser .05
75 Billy Ashley .05
76 Sean Berry .05
77 Ken Hill .05
78 John Wetteland .05
79 Moises Alou .05
80 Cliff Floyd .05
81 Marquis Grissom .05
82 Larry Walker .05
83 Rondell White .05
84 William Van Landingham .05
85 Matt Williams .05
86 Rod Beck .05
87 Darren Lewis .05
88 Robby Thompson .05
89 Darryl Strawberry .05
90 Kenny Lofton .05
91 Charles Nagy .05
92 Sandy Alomar Jr. .05
93 Mark Clark .05
94 Dennis Martinez .05
95 Dave Winfield .75
96 Jim Thome .60
97 Manny Ramirez .75
98 Goose Gossage .05
99 Tino Martinez .05
100 Ken Griffey Jr. 1.25
100a Ken Griffey Jr./OPS 2.00
101 Greg Maddux (Analysis: '90s Midpoint) .50
102 Randy Johnson (Analysis: '90s Midpoint) .40
103 Barry Bonds (Analysis: '90s Midpoint) 1.00
104 Juan Gonzalez (Analysis: '90s Midpoint) .20
105 Frank Thomas (Analysis: '90s Midpoint) .40
106 Matt Williams (Analysis: '90s Midpoint) .05
107 Paul Molitor (Analysis: '90s Midpoint) .40
108 Fred McGriff (Analysis: '90s Midpoint) .05
109 Carlos Baerga (Analysis: '90s Midpoint) .05
110 Ken Griffey Jr. (Analysis: '90s Midpoint) .65
111 Reggie Jefferson .05
112 Randy Johnson .75
113 Marc Newfield .05
114 Robb Nen .05
115 Jeff Conine .05
116 Kurt Abbott .05
117 Charlie Hough .05
118 Dave Weathers .05
119 Juan Castillo .05
120 Bret Saberhagen .05
121 Rico Brogna .05
122 John Franco .05
123 Todd Hundley .05
124 Jason Jacome .05
125 Bobby Jones .05
126 Bret Barberie .05
127 Ben McDonald .05
128 Harold Baines .05
129 Jeffrey Hammonds .05
130 Mike Mussina .30
131 Chris Hoiles .05
132 Brady Anderson .05
133 Eddie Williams .05
134 Andy Benes .05
135 Tony Gwynn 1.00
136 Bip Roberts .05
137 Joey Hamilton .05
138 Luis Lopez .05
139 Ray McDavid .05
140 Lenny Dykstra .05
141 Mariano Duncan .05
142 Fernando Valenzuela .05
143 Bobby Munoz .05
144 Kevin Stocker .05
145 John Kruk .05
146 Jon Lieber .05
147 Zane Smith .05
148 Steve Cooke .05
149 Andy Van Slyke .05
150 Jay Bell .05
151 Carlos Garcia .05
152 John Dettmer .05
153 Darren Oliver .05
154 Dean Palmer .05
155 Otis Nixon .05
156 Rusty Greer .05
157 Rick Helling .05
158 Jose Canseco .40
159 Roger Clemens 1.00
160 Andre Dawson .25
161 Mo Vaughn .05
162 Aaron Sele .05
163 John Valentin .05
164 Brian Hunter .05
165 Bret Boone .05
166 Hector Carrasco .05
167 Pete Schourek .05
168 Willie Greene .05
169 Kevin Mitchell .05
170 Deion Sanders .05
171 John Roper .05
172 Charlie Hayes .05
173 David Nied .05
174 Ellis Burks .05
175 Dante Bichette .05
176 Marvin Freeman .05
177 Eric Young .05
178 David Cone .05
179 Greg Gagne .05
180 Bob Hamelin .05
181 Wally Joyner .05
182 Jeff Montgomery .05
183 Jose Lind .05
184 Chris Gomez .05
185 Travis Fryman .05
186 Kirk Gibson .05
187 Mike Moore .05
188 Lou Whitaker .05
189 Sean Bergman .05
190 Shane Mack .05
191 Rick Aguilera .05
192 Denny Hocking .05
193 Chuck Knoblauch .05
194 Kevin Tapani .05
195 Kent Hrbek .05
196 Ozzie Guillen .05
197 Wilson Alvarez .05
198 Tim Raines .05
199 Scott Ruffcorn .05
200 Michael Jordan 2.00
201 Robin Ventura .05
202 Jason Bere .05
203 Darrin Jackson .05
204 Russ Davis .05
205 Jimmy Key .05
206 Jack McDowell .05
207 Jim Abbott .05
208 Paul O'Neill .05
209 Bernie Williams .05
210 Don Mattingly 1.00
211 Orlando Miller/SR .05
212 Alex Gonzalez/SR .05
213 Terrell Wade/SR .05
214 Jose Oliva/SR .05
215 Alex Rodriguez/SR 1.50
216 Garret Anderson/SR .05
217 Alan Benes/SR .05
218 Armando Benitez/SR .05
219 Dustin Hermanson/SR .05
220 Charles Johnson/SR .05
221 Julian Tavarez/SR .05
222 Jason Giambi/SR .50
223 LaTroy Hawkins/SR .05
224 Todd Hollandsworth/SR .05
225 Derek Jeter/SR 2.00
226 Hideo Nomo/SR **RC** 2.00
227 Tony Clark/SR .05
228 Roger Cedeno/SR .05
229 Scott Stahoviak/SR .05
230 Michael Tucker/SR .05
231 Joe Rosselli/SR .05
232 Antonio Osuna/SR .05
233 Bobby Higginson/SR **RC** .25
234 Mark Grudzielanek/SR **RC** .25
235 Ray Durham/SR .05
236 Frank Rodriguez/SR .05
237 Quilvio Veras/SR .05
238 Darren Bragg/SR .05
239 Ugueth Urbina/SR .05
240 Jason Bates/SR .05
241 David Bell (Diamond Debuts) .05
242 Ron Villone (Diamond Debuts) .05
243 Joe Randa (Diamond Debuts) .05
244 Carlos Perez **RC** (Diamond Debuts) .05
245 Brad Clontz (Diamond Debuts) .05
246 Steve Rodriguez (Diamond Debuts) .05
247 Joe Vitiello (Diamond Debuts) .05
248 Ozzie Timmons (Diamond Debuts) .05
249 Rudy Pemberton (Diamond Debuts) .05
250 Marty Cordova (Diamond Debuts) .05
251 Tony Graffanino (Top Prospect) .05
252 Mark Johnson **RC** (Top Prospect) .05
253 Tomas Perez **RC** (Top Prospect) .05
254 Jimmy Hurst (Top Prospect) .05
255 Edgardo Alfonzo (Top Prospect) .05
256 Jose Malav e (Top Prospect) .05
257 Brad Radke **RC** (Top Prospect) .30
258 Jon Nunnally (Top Prospect) .05
259 Dilson Torres (Top Prospect) .05
260 Esteban Loaiza (Top Prospect) .05
261 Freddy Garcia **RC** (Top Prospect) .05
262 Don Wengert (Top Prospect) .05
263 Robert Person **RC** (Top Prospect) .05
264 Tim Unroe **RC** (Top Prospect) .05
265 Juan Acevedo (Top Prospect) .05
266 Eduardo Perez .05
267 Tony Phillips .05
268 Jim Edmonds .05
269 Jorge Fabregas .05
270 Tim Salmon .05
271 Mark Langston .05
272 J.T. Snow .05
273 Phil Plantier .05
274 Derek Bell .05
275 Jeff Bagwell .75
276 Luis Gonzalez .05
277 John Hudek .05
278 Todd Stottlemyre .05
279 Mark Acre .05
280 Ruben Sierra .05
281 Mike Bordick .05
282 Ron Darling .05
283 Brent Gates .05
284 Todd Van Poppel .05
285 Paul Molitor .75
286 Ed Sprague .05
287 Juan Guzman .05
288 David Cone .05
289 Shawn Green .30
290 Marquis Grissom .05
291 Kent Mercker .05
292 Steve Avery .05
293 Chipper Jones 1.00
294 John Smoltz .05
295 Dave Justice .05
296 Ryan Klesko .05
297 Joe Oliver .05
298 Ricky Bones .05
299 John Jaha .05
300 Greg Vaughn .05
301 Dave Nilsson .05
302 Kevin Seitzer .05
303 Bernard Gilkey .05
304 Allen Battle .05
305 Ray Lankford .05
306 Tom Pagnozzi .05
307 Allen Watson .05
308 Danny Jackson .05
309 Ken Hill .05
310 Todd Zeile .05
311 Kevin Roberson .05
312 Steve Buechele .05
313 Rick Wilkins .05
314 Kevin Foster .05
315 Sammy Sosa 1.00
316 Howard Johnson .05
317 Greg Hansell .05
318 Pedro Astacio .05
319 Rafael Bournigal .05
320 Mike Piazza 1.25
321 Ramon Martinez .05
322 Raul Mondesi .05
323 Ismael Valdes .05
324 Wil Cordero .05
325 Tony Tarasco .05
326 Roberto Kelly .05
327 Jeff Fassero .05
328 Mike Lansing .05
329 Pedro J. Martinez .75
330 Kirk Rueter .05
331 Glenallen Hill .05
332 Kirt Manwaring .05
333 Royce Clayton .05
334 J.R. Phillips .05
335 Barry Bonds 2.00
336 Mark Portugal .05
337 Terry Mulholland .05
338 Omar Vizquel .05
339 Carlos Baerga .05
340 Albert Belle .05
341 Eddie Murray .75
342 Wayne Kirby .05
343 Chad Ogea .05
344 Tim Davis .05
345 Jay Buhner .05
346 Bobby Ayala .05
347 Mike Blowers .05
348 Dave Fleming .05
349 Edgar Martinez .05
350 Andre Dawson .30
351 Darrell Whitmore .05
352 Chuck Carr .05
353 John Burkett .05
354 Chris Hammond .05
355 Gary Sheffield .40
356 Pat Rapp .05
357 Greg Colbrunn .05
358 David Segui .05
359 Jeff Kent .05
360 Bobby Bonilla .05
361 Pete Harnisch .05
362 Ryan Thompson .05
363 Jose Vizcaino .05
364 Brett Butler .05
365 Cal Ripken Jr. 2.00
366 Rafael Palmeiro .65
367 Leo Gomez .05
368 Andy Van Slyke .05
369 Arthur Rhodes .05
370 Ken Caminiti .05
371 Steve Finley .05
372 Melvin Nieves .05
373 Andujar Cedeno .05
374 Trevor Hoffman .05
375 Fernando Valenzuela .05
376 Ricky Bottalico .05
377 Dave Hollins .05
378 Charlie Hayes .05
379 Tommy Greene .05
380 Darren Daulton .05
381 Curt Schilling .25
382 Midre Cummings .05
383 Al Martin .05
384 Jeff King .05
385 Orlando Merced .05
386 Denny Neagle .05
387 Don Slaught .05
388 Dave Clark .05
389 Kevin Gross .05
390 Will Clark .05
391 Ivan Rodriguez .65
392 Benji Gil .05
393 Jeff Frye .05
394 Kenny Rogers .05
395 Juan Gonzalez .40
396 Mike Macfarlane .05
397 Lee Tinsley .05
398 Tim Naehring .05
399 Tim Vanegmond .05
400 Mike Greenwell .05
401 Ken Ryan .05
402 John Smiley .05
403 Tim Pugh .05
404 Reggie Sanders .05
405 Barry Larkin .05
406 Hal Morris .05
407 Jose Rijo .05
408 Lance Painter .05
409 Joe Girardi .05
410 Andres Galarraga .05
411 Mike Kingery .05
412 Roberto Mejia .05
413 Walt Weiss .05
414 Bill Swift .05
415 Larry Walker .05
416 Billy Brewer .05
417 Pat Borders .05
418 Tom Gordon .05
419 Kevin Appier .05
420 Gary Gaetti .05
421 Greg Gohr .05
422 Felipe Lira .05
423 John Doherty .05
424 Chad Curtis .05
425 Cecil Fielder .05
426 Alan Trammell .05
427 David McCarty .05
428 Scott Erickson .05
429 Pat Mahomes .05
430 Kirby Puckett 1.00
431 Dave Stevens .05
432 Pedro Munoz .05
433 Chris Sabo .05
434 Alex Fernandez .05
435 Frank Thomas .75
436 Roberto Hernandez .05
437 Lance Johnson .05
438 Jim Abbott .05
439 John Wetteland .05
440 Melido Perez .05
441 Tony Fernandez .05
442 Pat Kelly .05
443 Mike Stanley .05
444 Danny Tartabull .05
445 Wade Boggs 1.00
446 Robin Yount (Final Tribute) .75
447 Ryne Sandberg (Final Tribute) 1.00
448 Nolan Ryan (Final Tribute) 2.00
449 George Brett (Final Tribute) 1.00
450 Mike Schmidt (Final Tribute) 1.00

Electric Diamond

Included as an insert at the rate of one per retail foil pack and two per jumbo pack, this set parallels the regular issue. The only differences are that the Electric Diamond cards utilize silver-foil highlights on front, compared to the copper foil on the regular cards. The Electric Diamond cards also include a home-plate shaped logo printed in silver foil in one of the upper corners.

NM/M

Complete Set (1-450): 60.00
Common Player: .25
Stars/Rookies: 2X

Electric Diamond Gold

A parallel set of a parallel set, the Electric Diamond Gold cards were found at an average rate of one per 36 retail packs. They differ from the standard ED inserts in that the home plate-shaped Electric Diamond logo in the upper corner and the player's name at bottom are printed in gold foil, rather than the silver of the ED cards or the copper of the regular-issue UD cards.

NM/M

Complete Set (450): 650.00
Common Player: 2.00
Stars/Rookies: 8X

Update Trade Cards

Inserted into Series 2 at the rate of about one per 11 packs was this five-card series of trade cards. Each card could be mailed in with $2 to receive nine cards from a special UD Update set picturing traded or free agent players in the uniforms of their new teams. The front of each trade card pictures one of the traded players in his old uniform against a red and blue background. Backs have instructions for redeeming the trade cards. The mail-in offer expired Feb. 1, 1996. Cards are numbered with a "TC" prefix.

		NM/M
Complete Set (5):		6.00
Common Player:		1.00
1	Orel Hershiser	1.00
2	Terry Pendleton	1.00
3	Benito Santiago	1.00
4	Kevin Brown	1.00
5	Gregg Jefferies	1.00

Update

These cards depicting traded and free agent players in the uniforms of their new 1995 teams were available only by redeeming trade cards found in Series 2 packs. Each trade-in card was good for one nine-card segment of the Update series when sent with $2 prior to the Feb. 1, 1996 deadline. Update cards share the same format as the regular 1995 Upper Deck set.

		NM/M
Complete Set (45):		7.50
Common Player:		.25
451	Jim Abbott	.25
452	Danny Tartabull	.25
453	Ariel Prieto	.25
454	Scott Cooper	.25
455	Tom Henke	.25
456	Todd Zeile	.25
457	Brian McRae	.25
458	Luis Gonzalez	.25
459	Jaime Navarro	.25
460	Todd Worrell	.25
461	Roberto Kelly	.25
462	Chad Fonville	.25
463	Shane Andrews	.25
464	David Segui	.25
465	Deion Sanders	.50
466	Orel Hershiser	.25
467	Ken Hill	.25
468	Andy Benes	.25
469	Terry Pendleton	.25
470	Bobby Bonilla	.25
471	Scott Erickson	.25
472	Kevin Brown	.25
473	Glenn Dishman	.25
474	Phil Plantier	.25
475	Gregg Jefferies	.25
476	Tyler Green	.25
477	Heathcliff Slocumb	.25
478	Mark Whiten	.25
479	Mickey Tettleton	.25
480	Tim Wakefield	.25
481	Vaughn Eshelman	.25
482	Rick Aguilera	.25
483	Erik Hanson	.25
484	Willie McGee	.25
485	Troy O'Leary	.25
486	Benito Santiago	.25
487	Darren Lewis	.25
488	Dave Burba	.25
489	Ron Gant	.25
490	Bret Saberhagen	.25
491	Vinny Castilla	.25
492	Frank Rodriguez	.25
493	Andy Pettitte	5.00
494	Ruben Sierra	.25
495	David Cone	.25

Autograph Trade Cards

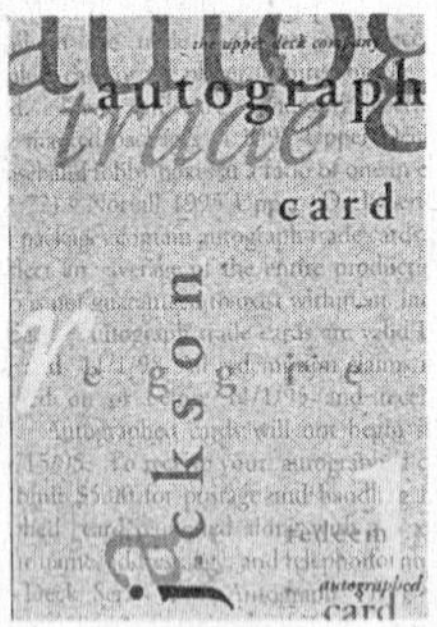

On the average of once every 72 packs (two boxes) of Series II hobby, a trade card good for an autographed player card could be found as an insert. The cards feature the player name, but no picture, on front, while the reverse has instructions for redeeming the card for a $5 fee. The autograph trade cards expired on Nov. 1, 1995.

		NM/M
Complete Set (5):		15.00
Common Player:		2.00
(1)	Roger Clemens	4.00
(2)	Reggie Jackson	3.00
(3)	Willie Mays	6.00
(4)	Raul Mondesi	2.00
(5)	Frank Robinson	3.00

Autograph Redemption Cards

These cards were sent to collectors who redeemed Autograph Trade cards found in Series II Upper Deck baseball. A certificate of authenticity with a holographic serial number matching that on the card back was issued with each card.

		NM/M
Complete Set (5):		220.00
Common Player:		15.00
AC1	Reggie Jackson	20.00
AC2	Willie Mays	100.00
AC3	Frank Robinson	30.00
AC4	Roger Clemens	125.00
AC5	Raul Mondesi	10.00

Autographed Jumbos

By sending in quantities of foil wrappers from Upper Deck baseball cards, collectors could receive a jumbo 5" x 7" blow-up of a player's card. The offer was limited to 8,000 Roger Clemens cards (Series I) and 6,000 Alex Rodriguez cards (Series II). Each card bears a serial number hologram on back and comes with a matching Upper Deck Authenticated auhtenticity guarantee card.

		NM/M
Complete Set (2):		100.00
(1)	Roger Clemens	50.00
(2)	Alex Rodriguez	75.00

Award Winners Predictors (Hobby)

Candidates for 1995 MVP and Rookie of the Year in each league are featured in the interactive insert series called Predictors. Twenty potential award winners were released in each of Series 1 and 2 at the rate of one per 30 packs on average. Cards feature on front a player photo inside a diamond cutout on a rich looking black and marbled background. In gold foil are his name and team at top, and "PREDICTOR" and the category at bottom. Backs feature game rules and details for redeeming the card if the pictured player wins the specified award. Winners could trade in the card for a foil-enhanced set of Predictor cards. The trade-in offer expired at the end of 1995. Cards are numbered with a "H" prefix.

		NM/M
Complete Set (40):		50.00
Common Player:		.50
Winner Exchange Cards:		2X
1	Albert Belle	.50
2	Juan Gonzalez	1.50
3	Ken Griffey Jr.	3.00
4	Kirby Puckett	2.50
5	Frank Thomas	2.00
6	Jeff Bagwell	2.00
7	Barry Bonds	5.00
8	Mike Piazza	3.00
9	Matt Williams	.50
10	1995 MVP Long Shot (Winner)	.50
11	Armando Benitez	.50
12	Alex Gonzalez	.50
13	Shawn Green	1.50
14	Derek Jeter	5.00
15	Alex Rodriguez	4.00
16	Alan Benes	.50
17	Brian L. Hunter	.50
18	Charles Johnson	.50
19	Jose Oliva	.50
20	1995 ROY Long Shot	.50
21	Cal Ripken Jr.	5.00
22	Don Mattingly	2.75
23	Roberto Alomar	.75
24	Kenny Lofton	.50
25	Will Clark	.50
26	Mark McGwire	4.00
27	Greg Maddux	2.50
28	Fred McGriff	.50
29	Andres Galarraga	.50
30	Jose Canseco	1.50
31	Ray Durham	.50
32	Mark Grudzielanek	.50
33	Scott Ruffcorn	.50
34	Michael Tucker	.50
35	Garret Anderson	.50
36	Darren Bragg	.50
37	Quilvio Veras	.50
38	Hideo Nomo (Winner)	4.00
39	Chipper Jones	2.50
40	Marty Cordova (Winner)	1.50

Baseball Heroes Babe Ruth

In the 100th anniversary year of his birth, Babe Ruth was the featured star in Upper Deck continuing "Heroes" insert set. Ten cards, including an unnumbered header, were issued in Series 2 packs. The cards featured colorized photos printed on metallic foil on the front. Backs have stats and/or biographical data. On average, one Babe Ruth Heroes card is found per 34 packs.

		NM/M
Complete Set (10):		45.00
Common Card:		6.00
73	1914-18 Pitching Career (Babe Ruth)	6.00
74	1919 - Move to Outfield (Babe Ruth)	6.00
75	1920 - Renaissance Man (Babe Ruth)	6.00
76	1923 - House That Ruth Built (Babe Ruth)	6.00
77	1927 - 60-Homer Season (Babe Ruth)	6.00
78	1928 - Three-Homer Game (Babe Ruth)	6.00
79	1932 - The Called Shot (Babe Ruth)	6.00
80	1930-35 - Milestones (Babe Ruth)	6.00
81	1935 - The Last Hurrah (Babe Ruth)	6.00
---	Header Card	7.50

Checklists

Upscale checklists for the 1995 UD set were part of the insert card program, seeded about one per 17 packs, on average. Horizontally formatted fronts are printed on metallic foil and include a career highlight of the pictured player. Backs have the checklist data. Five checklists were issued in each of Series I and Series II.

		NM/M
Complete Set (10):		3.00
Common Player:		.25
1	Checklist 1-75 (Montreal Expos)	.25
2	Checklist 76-150 (Fred McGriff)	.25
3	Checklist 151-225 (John Valentin (unassisted triple play))	.25
4	Special Edition Checklist (Greg Maddux)	.75
5	Special Edition Checklist 69-135 (Kenny Rogers (perfect game))	.25
1	Checklist 226-300 (Cecil Fielder)	.25
2	Checklist 301-375 (Tony Gwynn)	.75
3	Checklist 376-450 (Greg Maddux)	.75
4	Special Edition Checklist 136-203 (Randy Johnson)	.50
5	Special Edition Checklist 204-270 (Mike Schmidt)	.75

League Leaders Predictors (Retail)

Candidates for the Triple Crown categories of league leaders in hits, home runs and RBIs are featured in this retail-only insert set, found at the average rate of one per 30 packs in both Series 1 and 2. If the player pictured on the card front won the category specified on his card, it could be redeemed for a special foil-enhanced version of the subset prior to the Dec. 31, 1995 deadline. Cards are numbered with a "R" prefix.

		NM/M
Complete Set (60):		65.00
Common Player:		.50
Winner Exchange Cards:		2X
1	Albert Belle (Winner)	1.50
2	Jose Canseco	1.50
3	Juan Gonzalez	1.00
4	Ken Griffey Jr.	3.00
5	Frank Thomas	2.00
6	Jeff Bagwell	2.00
7	Barry Bonds	5.00
8	Fred McGriff	.50
9	Matt Williams	.50
10	1995 Home Run Long Shot (Winner)	.50
11	Albert Belle (Winner)	1.50
12	Joe Carter	.50
13	Cecil Fielder	.50
14	Kirby Puckett	2.50
15	Frank Thomas	2.00
16	Jeff Bagwell	2.00
17	Barry Bonds	5.00
18	Mike Piazza	3.00
19	Matt Williams	.50
20	1995 RBI Long Shot (Winner)	.50
21	Wade Boggs	2.50
22	Kenny Lofton	.50
23	Paul Molitor	2.00
24	Paul O'Neill	.50
25	Frank Thomas	2.00
26	Jeff Bagwell	2.00
27	Tony Gwynn (Winner)	5.00
28	Gregg Jefferies	.50
29	Hal Morris	.50
30	1995 Batting Long Shot (Winner)	.50
31	Joe Carter	.50
32	Cecil Fielder	.50
33	Rafael Palmeiro	1.50
34	Larry Walker	.50
35	Manny Ramirez	2.00
36	Tim Salmon	.50
37	Mike Piazza	3.00
38	Andres Galarraga	.50
39	Dave Justice	.50
40	Gary Sheffield	1.50
41	Juan Gonzalez	1.00
42	Jose Canseco	1.50
43	Will Clark	.50
44	Rafael Palmeiro	1.50
45	Ken Griffey Jr.	3.00
46	Ruben Sierra	.50
47	Larry Walker	.50
48	Fred McGriff	.50
49	Dante Bichette (Winner)	.50
50	Darren Daulton	.50
51	Will Clark	.50
52	Ken Griffey Jr.	3.00
53	Don Mattingly	2.75
54	John Olerud	.50
55	Kirby Puckett	2.50
56	Raul Mondesi	.50
57	Moises Alou	.50
58	Bret Boone	.50
59	Albert Belle	.50
60	Mike Piazza	3.00

Steal of a Deal

A horizontal format with an action photo printed over a green foil background and a large bronze seal indicating how the player was acquired are featured in this 15-card insert set. The front has a terra-cotta border, which is carried over to the back. A large green box on back details the transaction and describes why it can be categorized as a "steal" for the player's new team. These top-of-the-line chase cards were seeded in both hobby and retail packs of Series I at the average rate of one per 34 packs. Cards are numbered with a "SD" prefix.

		NM/M
Complete Set (15):		25.00
Common Player:		1.00
1	Mike Piazza	6.00
2	Fred McGriff	1.00
3	Kenny Lofton	1.00
4	Jose Oliva	1.00
5	Jeff Bagwell	3.00
6	Roberto Alomar, Joe Carter	1.00
7	Steve Karsay	1.00
8	Ozzie Smith	4.00
9	Dennis Eckersley	2.00
10	Jose Canseco	1.50
11	Carlos Baerga	1.00
12	Cecil Fielder	1.00
13	Don Mattingly	5.00
14	Bret Boone	1.00
15	Michael Jordan	10.00

Special Edition

Printed on metallic foil on front, and inserted into hobby packs only at the rate of one per pack, this insert set is found in both Series 1 (#1-135) and Series 2 (#136-270). A silver stripe at top has the name of the issue and the issuer, while stacked black and silver bars at bottom have the player name, team and position. Backs are conventionally printed and have another color photo, career data and 1994 and lifetime stats.

		NM/M
Complete Set (270):		60.00
Common Player:		.10
Gold:		3X
1	Cliff Floyd	.10
2	Wil Cordero	.10
3	Pedro Martinez	1.50
4	Larry Walker	.10
5	Derek Jeter	4.00
6	Mike Stanley	.10
7	Melido Perez	.10
8	Jim Leyritz	.10
9	Danny Tartabull	.10
10	Wade Boggs	2.00
11	Ryan Klesko	.10
12	Steve Avery	.10
13	Damon Hollins	.10
14	Chipper Jones	2.00
15	Dave Justice	.10
16	Glenn Williams	.10
17	Jose Oliva	.10
18	Terrell Wade	.10
19	Alex Fernandez	.10
20	Frank Thomas	1.50
21	Ozzie Guillen	.10
22	Roberto Hernandez	.10
23	Albie Lopez	.10
24	Eddie Murray	1.50
25	Albert Belle	.10

26 Omar Vizquel .10
27 Carlos Baerga .10
28 Jose Rijo .10
29 Hal Morris .10
30 Reggie Sanders .10
31 Jack Morris .10
32 Raul Mondesi .10
33 Karim Garcia .15
34 Todd Hollandsworth .10
35 Mike Piazza 2.50
36 Chan Ho Park .10
37 Ramon Martinez .10
38 Kenny Rogers .10
39 Will Clark .10
40 Juan Gonzalez .75
41 Ivan Rodriguez 1.25
42 Orlando Miller .10
43 John Hudek .10
44 Luis Gonzalez .10
45 Jeff Bagwell 1.50
46 Cal Ripken Jr. 4.00
47 Mike Oquist .10
48 Armando Benitez .10
49 Ben McDonald .10
50 Rafael Palmeiro 1.25
51 Curtis Goodwin .10
52 Vince Coleman .10
53 Tom Gordon .10
54 Mike Macfarlane .10
55 Brian McRae .10
56 Matt Smith .10
57 David Segui .10
58 Paul Wilson .10
59 Bill Pulsipher .10
60 Bobby Bonilla .10
61 Jeff Kent .10
62 Ryan Thompson .10
63 Jason Isringhausen .10
64 Ed Sprague .10
65 Paul Molitor 1.50
66 Juan Guzman .10
67 Alex Gonzalez .10
68 Shawn Green .50
69 Mark Portugal .10
70 Barry Bonds 4.00
71 Robby Thompson .10
72 Royce Clayton .10
73 Ricky Bottalico .10
74 Doug Jones .10
75 Darren Daulton .10
76 Gregg Jefferies .10
77 Scott Cooper .10
78 Nomar Garciaparra 2.00
79 Ken Ryan .10
80 Mike Greenwell .10
81 LaTroy Hawkins .10
82 Rich Becker .10
83 Scott Erickson .10
84 Pedro Munoz .10
85 Kirby Puckett 2.00
86 Orlando Merced .10
87 Jeff King .10
88 Midre Cummings .10
89 Bernard Gilkey .10
90 Ray Lankford .10
91 Todd Zeile .10
92 Alan Benes .10
93 Bret Wagner .10
94 Rene Arocha .10
95 Cecil Fielder .10
96 Alan Trammell .10
97 Tony Phillips .10
98 Junior Felix .10
99 Brian Harper .10
100 Greg Vaughn .10
101 Ricky Bones .10
102 Walt Weiss .10
103 Lance Painter .10
104 Roberto Mejia .10
105 Andres Galarraga .10
106 Todd Van Poppel .10
107 Ben Grieve .10
108 Brent Gates .10
109 Jason Giambi 1.00
110 Ruben Sierra .10
111 Terry Steinbach .10
112 Chris Hammond .10
113 Charles Johnson .10
114 Jesus Tavarez .10
115 Gary Sheffield .40
116 Chuck Carr .10
117 Bobby Ayala .10
118 Randy Johnson 1.50
119 Edgar Martinez .10
120 Alex Rodriguez 3.00
121 Kevin Foster .10
122 Kevin Roberson .10
123 Sammy Sosa 2.00
124 Steve Trachsel .10
125 Eduardo Perez .10
126 Tim Salmon .10
127 Todd Greene .10
128 Jorge Fabregas .10
129 Mark Langston .10
130 Mitch Williams .10
131 Raul Casanova .10
132 Mel Nieves .10
133 Andy Benes .10
134 Dustin Hermanson .10
135 Trevor Hoffman .10
136 Mark Grudzielanek .10
137 Ugueth Urbina .10
138 Moises Alou .10
139 Roberto Kelly .10
140 Rondell White .10
141 Paul O'Neill .10
142 Jimmy Key .10
143 Jack McDowell .10
144 Ruben Rivera .10
145 Don Mattingly 2.25
146 John Wetteland .10
147 Tom Glavine .25
148 Marquis Grissom .10
149 Javy Lopez .10
150 Fred McGriff .10
151 Greg Maddux 2.00
152 Chris Sabo .10
153 Ray Durham .10
154 Robin Ventura .10
155 Jim Abbott .10
156 Jimmy Hurst .10
157 Tim Raines .10
158 Dennis Martinez .10
159 Kenny Lofton .10
160 Dave Winfield 1.50
161 Manny Ramirez 1.50
162 Jim Thome 1.00
163 Barry Larkin .10
164 Bret Boone .10
165 Deion Sanders .10
166 Ron Gant .10
167 Benito Santiago .10
168 Hideo Nomo .75
169 Billy Ashley .10
170 Roger Cedeno .10
171 Ismael Valdes .10
172 Eric Karros .10
173 Rusty Greer .10
174 Rick Helling .10
175 Nolan Ryan 4.00
176 Dean Palmer .10
177 Phil Plantier .10
178 Darryl Kile .10
179 Derek Bell .10
180 Doug Drabek .10
181 Craig Biggio .10
182 Kevin Brown .10
183 Harold Baines .10
184 Jeffrey Hammonds .10
185 Chris Hoiles .10
186 Mike Mussina .50
187 Bob Hamelin .10
188 Jeff Montgomery .10
189 Michael Tucker .10
190 George Brett 2.25
191 Edgardo Alfonzo .10
192 Brett Butler .10
193 Bobby Jones .10
194 Todd Hundley .10
195 Bret Saberhagen .10
196 Pat Hentgen .10
197 Roberto Alomar .30
198 David Cone .10
199 Carlos Delgado 1.00
200 Joe Carter .10
201 William Van Landingham .10
202 Rod Beck .10
203 J.R. Phillips .10
204 Darren Lewis .10
205 Matt Williams .10
206 Lenny Dykstra .10
207 Dave Hollins .10
208 Mike Schmidt 2.25
209 Charlie Hayes .10
210 Mo Vaughn .10
211 Jose Malave .10
212 Roger Clemens 2.25
213 Jose Canseco .75
214 Mark Whiten .10
215 Marty Cordova .10
216 Rick Aguilera .10
217 Kevin Tapani .10
218 Chuck Knoblauch .10
219 Al Martin .10
220 Jay Bell .10
221 Carlos Garcia .10
222 Freddy Garcia .10
223 Jon Lieber .10
224 Danny Jackson .10
225 Ozzie Smith 2.00
226 Brian Jordan .10
227 Ken Hill .10
228 Scott Cooper .10
229 Chad Curtis .10
230 Lou Whitaker .10
231 Kirk Gibson .10
232 Travis Fryman .10
233 Jose Valentin .10
234 Dave Nilsson .10
235 Cal Eldred .10
236 Matt Mieske .10
237 Bill Swift .10
238 Marvin Freeman .10
239 Jason Bates .10
240 Larry Walker .10
241 David Nied .10
242 Dante Bichette .10
243 Dennis Eckersley 1.25
244 Todd Stottlemyre .10
245 Rickey Henderson 1.50
246 Geronimo Berroa .10
247 Mark McGwire 3.00
248 Quilvio Veras .10
249 Terry Pendleton .10
250 Andre Dawson .30
251 Jeff Conine .10
252 Kurt Abbott .10
253 Jay Buhner .10
254 Darren Bragg .10
255 Ken Griffey Jr. 2.50
256 Tino Martinez .10
257 Mark Grace .10
258 Ryne Sandberg 2.00
259 Randy Myers .10
260 Howard Johnson .10
261 Lee Smith .10
262 J.T. Snow .10
263 Chili Davis .10
264 Chuck Finley .10
265 Eddie Williams .10
266 Joey Hamilton .10
267 Ken Caminiti .10
268 Andujar Cedeno .10
269 Steve Finley .10
270 Tony Gwynn 2.00

Special Edition Gold

An insert set within an insert set, gold-foil enhanced versions of the Special Edition cards were seeded into hobby packs at the rate of about one per box. The substitution of gold ink for silver is also carried over onto the background of the card back.

	NM/M
Complete Set (270):	350.00
Common Player:	1.50
Stars/Rookies:	3X

Cal Ripken Commemorative Jumbo

To commemorate Cal Ripken's 2,131st consecutive game, UD issued this 5" x 3" die-cut card. Five thousand of the cards were issued with silver foil highlights; 2,131 with gold trim. Each card is serially numbered in the lower-right corner on back.

	NM/M
Cal Ripken Jr. (Silver edition of 5,000.)	10.00
Cal Ripken Jr. (Gold edition of 2,131.)	13.50

Sports Drink Reggie Jackson

UD partnered with Energy Foods to produce "Upper Deck Authentic Sports Drink." Each $2.99 six pack contained a cello-wrapped Reggie Jackson card. The cards are 2-1/2" x 3-1/2" and have a color photo on front on which the team logos have been removed. Backs has a subdued photo of a player swinging a bat with a stadium scene in the background. A few career highlights are presented along with the sports drink logo and UD hologram. Each card could also be found in a version with a gold-foil facsimile autograph on front.

		NM/M
Complete Set (3):		5.00
Common Card:		2.00
Gold:		1-1.5X
1/3	Reggie Jackson (Swinging bat.)	2.00
2/3	Reggie Jackson/ Portrait	2.00
3/3	Reggie Jackson (Batting follow-thru.)	2.00

Eagle Snacks Ballpark Legends

Nine Hall of Famers comprise this set which was produced by UD for the Eagle snack food company. Sets were available via mail-in redemption for proofs of purchase and $1. Fronts have sepia photos on which uniform logos have been removed. The Eagle Ballpark Legends is at upper-left, the UD logo is at lower-left, followed by the player name. Backs of the 2-1/2" x 3-1/2" cards have career summary and personal data. Autographed cards of Harmon Killebrew were random inserts.

		NM/M
Complete Set (9):		3.00
Common Player:		.25
1	Nolan Ryan	1.00
2	Reggie Jackson	.50
3	Tom Seaver	.50
4	Harmon Killebrew	.25
4a	Harmon Killebrew (autographed)	20.00
5	Ted Williams	.75
6	Whitey Ford	.50
7	Al Kaline	.50
8	Willie Stargell	.25
9	Bob Gibson	.25

GTS Phone Cards

In conjunction with Global Telecommunications Service, Upper Deck issued a series of 15 phone cards described as being the first licensed by Major League Baseball and the Player's Association. Measuring about 2-1/8" x 3-3/8" with round corners, the cards were printed on heavy plastic and utilized the basic format and photos from the players' 1994 Upper Deck baseball cards. Issue price, with phone time, was $12 each. Cards are numbered with a "MLB" prefix.

		NM/M
Complete Set (15):		21.00
Common Player:		1.00
01	Tony Gwynn	2.00
02	Fred McGriff	1.00
03	Frank Thomas	1.50
04	Ken Griffey Jr.	2.50
05	Cecil Fielder	1.00
06	Barry Bonds	3.00
07	Don Mattingly	2.25
08	Dave Justice	1.00
09	Roger Clemens	2.25
10	Cal Ripken Jr.	3.00
11	Roberto Alomar	1.25
12	Gary Sheffield	1.25
13	Jeff Bagwell	1.50
14	Kirby Puckett	2.00
15	Ozzie Smith	2.00

Metallic Impressions Michael Jordan

Michael Jordan's brief, highly publicized baseball career is chronicled in this metallic card set produced for UD by Metallic Impressions and sold in a special lithographed tin box. Each of the 2-5/8" x 3-9/16" cards has a gold-tone rolled edge. Fronts feature photos of Jordan in action. Backs have another photo and a career summary in a horizontal format. Cards are numbered with a "JT" prefix.

		NM/M
Complete Boxed Set (5):		7.50
Common Card:		1.50
1	Starting Out (Michael Jordan)	1.50
2	West to Arizona (Michael Jordan)	1.50
3	Hitting (Michael Jordan)	1.50
4	Baserunning (Michael Jordan)	1.50
5	Fielding (Michael Jordan)	1.50

Metallic Impressions Mickey Mantle

Sharing the card-front images with the UD phone cards of 1994, these metal cards trace the career of Mickey Mantle. Sold in an embossed metal box, the cards measure 2-5/8" x 3-9/16" and have rolled gold-tone metal borders. Fronts have black-and-white or color photos of Mantle. Backs have a career summary in a red box against a background of pin-striped flannel, along with a small color photo of Mantle. The issue was reportedly limited to 19,950 sets.

		NM/M
Complete Boxed Set (10):		17.50
Common Player:		3.00
1	The Commerce Comet (Mickey Mantle)	3.00
2	1951 - The Early Years (Mickey Mantle)	3.00
3	1953 - Tape-Measure Home Runs (Mickey Mantle)	3.00
4	1956 - Triple Crown Season (Mickey Mantle)	3.00
5	1957 - Second Consecutive MVP (Mickey Mantle)	3.00
6	1961 - Chasing the Babe (Mickey Mantle)	3.00
7	1964 - Series Home Run Record (Mickey Mantle)	3.00
8	1967 - 500th Home Run (Mickey Mantle)	3.00
9	1974 - Hall of Famer (Mickey Mantle)	3.00
10	Checklist (Mickey Mantle)	3.00

1996 Upper Deck Promo

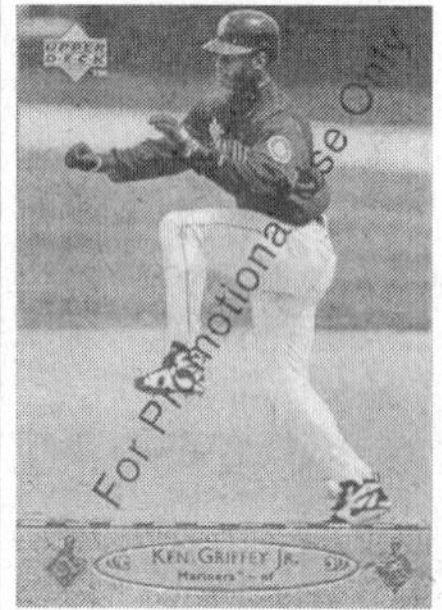

To debut its 1996 issue, Upper Deck issued this sample card. It is identical in format to the regular-issue card, except that it is numbered 100 and overprinted diagonally on each side, "For Promotional Use Only."

		NM/M
100	Ken Griffey Jr.	2.00

1996 Upper Deck

Upper Deck Series 1 consists of 240 base cards. There are 187 regular player cards plus subsets of Star Rookies, Young at Heart, Beat the Odds, Milestones, Post-season, checklists, and expansion logos. The issue was marketed in 10-card foil packs in hobby and retail versions Series 1 insert sets are Blue Chip Prospects, Future Shock and Power Driven. Cal Ripken Jr. Collection cards are inserted in both series, as are Retail Predictor (home runs, batting average and RBIs) and Hobby Predictor (Player of the Month, Pitcher of the Month and rookie hits leaders) cards. Series 2 has 240 cards, including subsets for Star Rookies, Diamond Debuts, Strange But True, Managerial Salutes and Best of a Generation. Insert sets include Hot Commodities, Hideo Nomo Highlights, Run Producers and the Lovero Collection. Factory sets comprising both regular series and the Update series were issued in two serially numbered versions, a regular boxed set in an edition of 15,000 and a wooden boxed set numbered to 500.

NM/M
Unopened Wood Box Set (510): 40.00
Unopened Fact. Set (510): 35.00
Complete Set (480): 20.00
Common Player: .05
Wax Pack (10): .75
Wax Box (32): 17.50
1 Cal Ripken Jr. (Milestones) 1.00
2 Eddie Murray (Milestones) .40
3 Mark Wohlers .05
4 Dave Justice .05
5 Chipper Jones 1.00
6 Javier Lopez .05
7 Mark Lemke .05
8 Marquis Grissom .05
9 Tom Glavine .25
10 Greg Maddux 1.00
11 Manny Alexander .05
12 Curtis Goodwin .05
13 Scott Erickson .05
14 Chris Hoiles .05
15 Rafael Palmeiro .65
16 Rick Krivda .05
17 Jeff Manto .05
18 Mo Vaughn .05
19 Tim Wakefield .05
20 Roger Clemens 1.00
21 Tim Naehring .05
22 Troy O'Leary .05
23 Mike Greenwell .05
24 Stan Belinda .05
25 John Valentin .05
26 J.T. Snow .05
27 Gary DiSarcina .05
28 Mark Langston .05
29 Brian Anderson .05
30 Jim Edmonds .05
31 Garret Anderson .05
32 Orlando Palmeiro .05
33 Brian McRae .05
34 Kevin Foster .05
35 Sammy Sosa 1.00
36 Todd Zeile .05
37 Jim Bullinger .05
38 Luis Gonzalez .05
39 Lyle Mouton .05
40 Ray Durham .05
41 Ozzie Guillen .05
42 Alex Fernandez .05
43 Brian Keyser .05
44 Robin Ventura .05
45 Reggie Sanders .05
46 Pete Schourek .05
47 John Smiley .05
48 Jeff Brantley .05
49 Thomas Howard .05
50 Bret Boone .05
51 Kevin Jarvis .05
52 Jeff Branson .05
53 Carlos Baerga .05
54 Jim Thome .50
55 Manny Ramirez .75
56 Omar Vizquel .05
57 Jose Mesa .05
58 Julian Tavarez .05
59 Orel Hershiser .05
60 Larry Walker .05
61 Bret Saberhagen .05
62 Vinny Castilla .05
63 Eric Young .05
64 Bryan Rekar .05
65 Andres Galarraga .05
66 Steve Reed .05
67 Chad Curtis .05
68 Bobby Higginson .05
69 Phil Nevin .05
70 Cecil Fielder .05
71 Felipe Lira .05
72 Chris Gomez .05
73 Charles Johnson .05
74 Quilvio Veras .05
75 Jeff Conine .05
76 John Burkett .05
77 Greg Colbrunn .05
78 Terry Pendleton .05
79 Shane Reynolds .05
80 Jeff Bagwell .75
81 Orlando Miller .05
82 Mike Hampton .05
83 James Mouton .05
84 Brian L. Hunter .05
85 Derek Bell .05
86 Kevin Appier .05
87 Joe Vitiello .05
88 Wally Joyner .05
89 Michael Tucker .05
90 Johnny Damon .20
91 Jon Nunnally .05
92 Jason Jacome .05
93 Chad Fonville .05
94 Chan Ho Park .05
95 Hideo Nomo .40
96 Ismael Valdes .05
97 Greg Gagne .05
98 Diamondbacks-Devil Rays (Expansion Card) .10
99 Raul Mondesi .05
100 Dave Winfield (Young at Heart) .75
101 Dennis Eckersley (Young at Heart) .35
102 Andre Dawson (Young at Heart) .15
103 Dennis Martinez (Young at Heart) .05
104 Lance Parrish (Young at Heart) .05
105 Eddie Murray (Young at Heart) .40
106 Alan Trammell (Young at Heart) .05
107 Lou Whitaker (Young at Heart) .05
108 Ozzie Smith (Young at Heart) .50
109 Paul Molitor (Young at Heart) .40
110 Rickey Henderson (Young at Heart) .40
111 Tim Raines (Young at Heart) .05
112 Harold Baines (Young at Heart) .05
113 Lee Smith (Young at Heart) .05
114 Fernando Valenzuela (Young at Heart) .05
115 Cal Ripken Jr. (Young at Heart) 1.00
116 Tony Gwynn (Young at Heart) .50
117 Wade Boggs (Young at Heart) .50
118 Todd Hollandsworth .05
119 Dave Nilsson .05
120 Jose Valentin **RC** .05
121 Steve Sparks .05
122 Chuck Carr .05
123 John Jaha .05
124 Scott Karl .05
125 Chuck Knoblauch .05
126 Brad Radke .05
127 Pat Meares .05
128 Ron Coomer .05
129 Pedro Munoz .05
130 Kirby Puckett 1.00
131 David Segui .05
132 Mark Grudzielanek .05
133 Mike Lansing .05
134 Sean Berry .05
135 Rondell White .05
136 Pedro Martinez .75
137 Carl Everett .05
138 Dave Mlicki .05
139 Bill Pulsipher .05
140 Jason Isringhausen .05
141 Rico Brogna .05
142 Edgardo Alfonzo .05
143 Jeff Kent .05
144 Andy Pettitte .25
145 Mike Piazza (Beat the Odds) .65
146 Cliff Floyd (Beat the Odds) .05
147 Jason Isringhausen (Beat the Odds) .05
148 Tim Wakefield (Beat the Odds) .05
149 Chipper Jones (Beat the Odds) .50
150 Hideo Nomo (Beat the Odds) .20
151 Mark McGwire (Beat the Odds) .75
152 Ron Gant (Beat the Odds) .05
153 Gary Gaetti (Beat the Odds) .05
154 Don Mattingly 1.00
155 Paul O'Neill .05
156 Derek Jeter 2.00
157 Joe Girardi .05
158 Ruben Sierra .05
159 Jorge Posada .05
160 Geronimo Berroa .05
161 Steve Ontiveros .05
162 George Williams .05
163 Doug Johns .05
164 Ariel Prieto .05
165 Scott Brosius .05
166 Mike Bordick .05
167 Tyler Green .05
168 Mickey Morandini .05
169 Darren Daulton .05
170 Gregg Jefferies .05
171 Jim Eisenreich .05
172 Heathcliff Slocumb .05
173 Kevin Stocker .05
174 Esteban Loaiza .05
175 Jeff King .05
176 Mark Johnson .05
177 Denny Neagle .05
178 Orlando Merced .05
179 Carlos Garcia .05
180 Brian Jordan .05
181 Mike Morgan .05
182 Mark Petkovsek .05
183 Bernard Gilkey .05
184 John Mabry .05
185 Tom Henke .05
186 Glenn Dishman .05
187 Andy Ashby .05
188 Bip Roberts .05
189 Melvin Nieves .05
190 Ken Caminiti .05
191 Brad Ausmus .05
192 Deion Sanders .05
193 Jamie Brewington .05
194 Glenallen Hill .05
195 Barry Bonds 2.00
196 William Van Landingham .05
197 Mark Carreon .05
198 Royce Clayton .05
199 Joey Cora .05
200 Ken Griffey Jr. 1.25
201 Jay Buhner .05
202 Alex Rodriguez 1.50
203 Norm Charlton .05
204 Andy Benes .05
205 Edgar Martinez .05
206 Juan Gonzalez .40
207 Will Clark .05
208 Kevin Gross .05
209 Roger Pavlik .05
210 Ivan Rodriguez .65
211 Rusty Greer .05
212 Angel Martinez .05
213 Tomas Perez .05
214 Alex Gonzalez .05
215 Joe Carter .05
216 Shawn Green .30
217 Edwin Hurtado .05
218 Edgar Martinez, Tony Pena (Post Season Checklist) .05
219 Chipper Jones, Barry Larkin (Post Season Checklist) .05
220 Orel Hershiser (Post Season Checklist) .05
221 Mike Devereaux (Post Season Checklist) .05
222 Tom Glavine (Post Season Checklist) .05
223 Karim Garcia/SR .10
224 Arquimedez Pozo/SR .05
225 Billy Wagner/SR .05
226 John Wasdin/SR .05
227 Jeff Suppan/SR .05
228 Steve Gibralter/SR .05
229 Jimmy Haynes/SR .05
230 Ruben Rivera/SR .05
231 Chris Snopek/SR .05
232 Alex Ochoa/SR .05
233 Shannon Stewart/SR .05
234 Quinton McCracken/SR .05
235 Trey Beamon/SR .05
236 Billy McMillon/SR .05
237 Steve Cox/SR .05
238 George Arias/SR .05
239 Yamil Benitez/SR .05
240 Todd Greene/SR .05
241 Jason Kendall/SR .05
242 Brooks Kieschnick/SR .05
243 Osvaldo Fernandez/SR **RC** .15
244 Livan Hernandez/SR **RC** .35
245 Rey Ordonez/SR .05
246 Mike Grace/SR **RC** .05
247 Jay Canizaro/SR .05
248 Bob Wolcott/SR .05
249 Jermaine Dye/SR .05
250 Jason Schmidt/SR .05
251 Mike Sweeney/SR **RC** 1.00
252 Marcus Jensen/SR .05
253 Mendy Lopez/SR .05
254 Wilton Guerrero/SR **RC** .10
255 Paul Wilson/SR .05
256 Edgar Renteria/SR .05
257 Richard Hidalgo/SR .05
258 Bob Abreu/SR .10
259 Robert Smith **RC** (Diamond Debuts) .05
260 Sal Fasano (Diamond Debuts) .05
261 Enrique Wilson (Diamond Debuts) .05
262 Rich Hunter **RC** (Diamond Debuts) .05
263 Sergio Nunez (Diamond Debuts) .05
264 Dan Serafini (Diamond Debuts) .05
265 David Doster **RC** (Diamond Debuts) .05
266 Ryan McGuire (Diamond Debuts) .05
267 Scott Spiezio (Diamond Debuts) .05
268 Rafael Orellano (Diamond Debuts) .05
269 Steve Avery .05
270 Fred McGriff .05
271 John Smoltz .05
272 Ryan Klesko .05
273 Jeff Blauser .05
274 Brad Clontz .05
275 Roberto Alomar .20
276 B.J. Surhoff .05
277 Jeffrey Hammonds .05
278 Brady Anderson .05
279 Bobby Bonilla .05
280 Cal Ripken Jr. 2.00
281 Mike Mussina .30
282 Wil Cordero .05
283 Mike Stanley .05
284 Aaron Sele .05
285 Jose Canseco .40
286 Tom Gordon .05
287 Heathcliff Slocumb .05
288 Lee Smith .05
289 Troy Percival .05
290 Tim Salmon .05
291 Chuck Finley .05
292 Jim Abbott .05
293 Chili Davis .05
294 Steve Trachsel .05
295 Mark Grace .05
296 Rey Sanchez .05
297 Scott Servais .05
298 Jaime Navarro .05
299 Frank Castillo .05
300 Frank Thomas .75
301 Jason Bere .05
302 Danny Tartabull .05
303 Darren Lewis .05
304 Roberto Hernandez .05
305 Tony Phillips .05
306 Wilson Alvarez .05
307 Jose Rijo .05
308 Hal Morris .05
309 Mark Portugal .05
310 Barry Larkin .05
311 Dave Burba .05
312 Eddie Taubensee .05
313 Sandy Alomar Jr. .05
314 Dennis Martinez .05
315 Albert Belle .15
316 Eddie Murray .75
317 Charles Nagy .05
318 Chad Ogea .05
319 Kenny Lofton .05
320 Dante Bichette .05
321 Armando Reynoso .05
322 Walt Weiss .05
323 Ellis Burks .05
324 Kevin Ritz .05
325 Bill Swift .05
326 Jason Bates .05
327 Tony Clark .05
328 Travis Fryman .05
329 Mark Parent .05
330 Alan Trammell .05
331 C.J. Nitkowski .05
332 Jose Lima .05
333 Phil Plantier .05
334 Kurt Abbott .05
335 Andre Dawson .25
336 Chris Hammond .05
337 Robb Nen .05
338 Pat Rapp .05
339 Al Leiter .05
340 Gary Sheffield .35
341 Todd Jones .05
342 Doug Drabek .05
343 Greg Swindell .05
344 Tony Eusebio .05
345 Craig Biggio .05
346 Darryl Kile .05
347 Mike Macfarlane .05
348 Jeff Montgomery .05
349 Chris Haney .05
350 Bip Roberts .05
351 Tom Goodwin .05
352 Mark Gubicza .05
353 Joe Randa .05
354 Ramon Martinez .05
355 Eric Karros .05
356 Delino DeShields .05
357 Brett Butler .05
358 Todd Worrell .05
359 Mike Blowers .05
360 Mike Piazza 1.25
361 Ben McDonald .05
362 Ricky Bones .05
363 Greg Vaughn .05
364 Matt Mieske .05
365 Kevin Seitzer .05
366 Jeff Cirillo .05
367 LaTroy Hawkins .05
368 Frank Rodriguez .05
369 Rick Aguilera .05
370 Roberto Alomar (Best of a Generation) .15
371 Albert Belle (Best of a Generation) .05
372 Wade Boggs (Best of a Generation) .50
373 Barry Bonds (Best of a Generation) 1.00
374 Roger Clemens (Best of a Generation) .65
375 Dennis Eckersley (Best of a Generation) .35
376 Ken Griffey Jr. (Best of a Generation) .65
377 Tony Gwynn (Best of a Generation) .50
378 Rickey Henderson (Best of a Generation) .40
379 Greg Maddux (Best of a Generation) .50
380 Fred McGriff (Best of a Generation) .05
381 Paul Molitor (Best of a Generation) .40
382 Eddie Murray (Best of a Generation) .40
383 Mike Piazza (Best of a Generation) .65
384 Kirby Puckett (Best of a Generation) .50
385 Cal Ripken Jr. (Best of a Generation) 1.00
386 Ozzie Smith (Best of a Generation) .50
387 Frank Thomas (Best of a Generation) .45
388 Matt Walbeck .05
389 Dave Stevens .05
390 Marty Cordova .05
391 Darrin Fletcher .05
392 Cliff Floyd .05
393 Mel Rojas .05
394 Shane Andrews .05
395 Moises Alou .05
396 Carlos Perez .05
397 Jeff Fassero .05
398 Bobby Jones .05
399 Todd Hundley .05
400 John Franco .05
401 Jose Vizcaino .05
402 Bernard Gilkey .05
403 Pete Harnisch .05
404 Pat Kelly .05
405 David Cone .05
406 Bernie Williams .05
407 John Wetteland .05
408 Scott Kamieniecki .05
409 Tim Raines .05
410 Wade Boggs 1.00
411 Terry Steinbach .05
412 Jason Giambi .40
413 Todd Van Poppel .05
414 Pedro Munoz .05
415 Eddie Murray-1990 (Strange But True) .40
416 Dennis Eckersley-1990 (Strange But True) .35
417 Bip Roberts-1992 (Strange But True) .05
418 Glenallen Hill-1992 (Strange But True) .05
419 John Hudek-1994 (Strange But True) .05
420 Derek Bell-1995 (Strange But True) .05
421 Larry Walker-1995 (Strange But True) .05
422 Greg Maddux-1995 (Strange But True) .50
423 Ken Caminiti-1995 (Strange But True) .05
424 Brent Gates .05
425 Mark McGwire 1.50
426 Mark Whiten .05
427 Sid Fernandez .05
428 Ricky Bottalico .05
429 Mike Mimbs .05
430 Lenny Dykstra .05
431 Todd Zeile .05
432 Benito Santiago .05
433 Danny Miceli .05
434 Al Martin .05
435 Jay Bell .05
436 Charlie Hayes .05
437 Mike Kingery .05
438 Paul Wagner .05
439 Tom Pagnozzi .05
440 Ozzie Smith 1.00
441 Ray Lankford .05
442 Dennis Eckersley .65
443 Ron Gant .05
444 Alan Benes .05
445 Rickey Henderson .75
446 Jody Reed .05
447 Trevor Hoffman .05
448 Andujar Cedeno .05
449 Steve Finley .05
450 Tony Gwynn 1.00
451 Joey Hamilton .05
452 Mark Leiter .05
453 Rod Beck .05
454 Kirt Manwaring .05
455 Matt Williams .05
456 Robby Thompson .05
457 Shawon Dunston .05
458 Russ Davis .05
459 Paul Sorrento .05
460 Randy Johnson .75
461 Chris Bosio .05
462 Luis Sojo .05
463 Sterling Hitchcock .05
464 Benji Gil .05
465 Mickey Tettleton .05
466 Mark McLemore .05
467 Darryl Hamilton .05
468 Ken Hill .05
469 Dean Palmer .05
470 Carlos Delgado .40
471 Ed Sprague .05
472 Otis Nixon .05
473 Pat Hentgen .05
474 Juan Guzman .05
475 John Olerud .05
476 Checklist (Buck Showalter) .05
477 Checklist (Bobby Cox) .05
478 Checklist (Tommy Lasorda) .05
479 Checklist (Jim Leyland) .05
480 Checklist (Sparky Anderson) .05

Update

Available only via a mail-in wrapper redemption or in factory sets, this update set offers cards of players who changed teams after the base card set was issued, as well as a few rookies and others. Cards share the earlier issue's format and are numbered with a "U" suffix.

NM/M
Complete Set (30): 8.00
Common Player: .25
481 Randy Myers .25
482 Kent Mercker .25
483 David Wells .35
484 Kevin Mitchell .25
485 Randy Velarde .25
486 Ryne Sandberg 4.00
487 Doug Jones .25
488 Terry Adams .25
489 Kevin Tapani .25
490 Harold Baines .25
491 Eric Davis .25
492 Julio Franco .25
493 Jack McDowell .25
494 Devon White .25
495 Kevin Brown .35
496 Rick Wilkins .25
497 Sean Berry .25
498 Keith Lockhart .25
499 Mark Loretta .25
500 Paul Molitor 2.50
501 Roberto Kelly .25
502 Lance Johnson .25
503 Tino Martinez .25
504 Kenny Rogers .25
505 Todd Stottlemyre .25
506 Gary Gaetti .25
507 Royce Clayton .25
508 Andy Benes .25
509 Wally Joyner .25
510 Erik Hanson .25

A Cut Above

Blue Chip Prospects

Twenty top young stars who could make a major impact in the major leagues in upcoming seasons are featured in this insert set. Each card is highlighted with blue-foil printing and double die-cut technology, which includes a zig-zag pattern around the top and a die-cut around both bottom corners. The cards are found one per 20 packs in Series 1 foil packs. Cards are numbered with a "BC" prefix.

NM/M
Complete Set (20): 50.00
Common Player: 1.00
1 Hideo Nomo 4.00
2 Johnny Damon 3.50
3 Jason Isringhausen 1.00
4 Bill Pulsipher 1.00
5 Marty Cordova 1.00
6 Michael Tucker 1.00
7 John Wasdin 1.00
8 Karim Garcia 1.50
9 Ruben Rivera 1.00
10 Chipper Jones 10.00
11 Billy Wagner 1.00
12 Brooks Kieschnick 1.00

13	Alex Ochoa	1.00
14	Roger Cedeno	1.00
15	Alex Rodriguez	15.00
16	Jason Schmidt	1.00
17	Derek Jeter	20.00
18	Brian L. Hunter	1.00
19	Garret Anderson	1.00
20	Manny Ramirez	7.50

Diamond Destiny

This late-season release is found exclusively in retail foil packs labeled "Upper Deck Tech." They are inserted at a rate of one per pack, sold with eight regular 1996 Upper Deck cards at a suggested retail of around $3. The cards have three versions of the same action photo; in color and black-and-white on front, and in black-and-white on back. A large team logo also appears on front and back. In the upper half of the card is a 1-3/16" diameter round color transparency portrait of the player. The basic version of this chase set had bronze foil highlights. Parallel silver and gold versions are found on average of one per 35 and one per 143 packs, respectively. Cards are numbered with a "DD" prefix.

		NM/M
Complete Set (Bronze):		35.00
Common Player (Bronze):		.30
Silver:		6X
Gold:		12X
1	Chipper Jones	1.50
2	Fred McGriff	.30
3	Ryan Klesko	.30
4	John Smoltz	.30
5	Greg Maddux	1.50
6	Cal Ripken Jr.	3.00
7	Roberto Alomar	.45
8	Eddie Murray	1.25
9	Brady Anderson	.30
10	Mo Vaughn	.30
11	Roger Clemens	1.75
12	Darin Erstad	.60
13	Sammy Sosa	1.50
14	Frank Thomas	1.25
15	Barry Larkin	.30
16	Albert Belle	.30
17	Manny Ramirez	1.25
18	Kenny Lofton	.30
19	Dante Bichette	.30
20	Gary Sheffield	.75
21	Jeff Bagwell	1.25
22	Hideo Nomo	.65
23	Mike Piazza	2.00
24	Kirby Puckett	1.50
25	Paul Molitor	1.25
26	Chuck Knoblauch	.30
27	Wade Boggs	1.50
28	Derek Jeter	3.00
29	Rey Ordonez	.30
30	Mark McGwire	2.50
31	Ozzie Smith	1.50
32	Tony Gwynn	1.50
33	Barry Bonds	3.00
34	Matt Williams	.30
35	Ken Griffey Jr.	2.00
36	Jay Buhner	.30
37	Randy Johnson	1.25
38	Alex Rodriguez	2.00
39	Juan Gonzalez	.65
40	Joe Carter	.30

Future Stock

Future Stock inserts are found on average of one per six packs of Series 1, highlighting 20 top young stars on a die-cut design. Each card has a blue border, vertical photo and silver-foil stamping on the front. Cards are numbered with a "FS" prefix.

		NM/M
Complete Set (20):		4.00
Common Player:		.25
1	George Arias	.25
2	Brian Barnes	.25
3	Trey Beamon	.25
4	Yamil Benitez	.25
5	Jamie Brewington	.25
6	Tony Clark	.25
7	Steve Cox	.25
8	Carlos Delgado	.75
9	Chad Fonville	.25
10	Steve Gibralter	.25
11	Curtis Goodwin	.25
12	Todd Greene	.25
13	Jimmy Haynes	.25
14	Quinton McCracken	.25
15	Billy McMillon	.25
16	Chan Ho Park	.25
17	Arquimedez Pozo	.25
18	Chris Snopek	.25
19	Shannon Stewart	.25
20	Jeff Suppan	.25

Gameface

This insert was exclusive to $1.50 Wal-Mart retail packs. Fronts have an action photo vignetted in white with a gold-foil Gameface logo. Backs have another photo and a few sentences about the player. One Gameface card was found in each pack.

		NM/M
Complete Set (10):		6.00
Common Player:		.15
1	Ken Griffey Jr.	1.00
2	Frank Thomas	.65
3	Barry Bonds	1.50
4	Albert Belle	.15
5	Cal Ripken Jr.	1.50
6	Mike Piazza	1.00
7	Chipper Jones	.75
8	Matt Williams	.15
9	Hideo Nomo	.40
10	Greg Maddux	.75

Hobby Predictor

These inserts depict 60 top players as possible winners in the categories of Player of the Month, Pitcher of the Month and Rookie Hits Leader. If the pictured player won that category any month of the season the card was redeemable for a 10-card set with a different look, action photos and printed on silver-foil stock. Hobby Predictor inserts are found on average once per dozen packs in both series. Winning cards are indicated by (W).

		NM/M
Complete Set (60):		35.00
Common Player:		.40
H1	Albert Belle	.40
H2	Kenny Lofton	.40
H3	Rafael Palmeiro	.65
H4	Ken Griffey Jr.	2.00
H5	Tim Salmon	.40
H6	Cal Ripken Jr.	3.00
H7	Mark McGwire/W	4.50
H8	Frank Thomas/W	1.25
H9	Mo Vaughn/W	.60
H10	Player of the Month Long Shot/W	.40
H11	Roger Clemens	1.75
H12	David Cone	.40
H13	Jose Mesa	.40
H14	Randy Johnson	.75
H15	Steve Finley	.40
H16	Mike Mussina	.50
H17	Kevin Appier	.40
H18	Kenny Rogers	.40
H19	Lee Smith	.40
H20	Pitcher of the Month Long Shot/W	.40
H21	George Arias	.40
H22	Jose Herrera	.40
H23	Tony Clark	.40
H24	Todd Greene	.40
H25	Derek Jeter/W	6.00
H26	Arquimedez Pozo	.40
H27	Matt Lawton	.40
H28	Shannon Stewart	.40
H29	Chris Snopek	.40
H30	Rookie Hits Long Shot	.40
H31	Jeff Bagwell/W	1.25
H32	Dante Bichette	.40
H33	Barry Bonds/W	6.00
H34	Tony Gwynn	1.50
H35	Chipper Jones	1.50
H36	Eric Karros	.40
H37	Barry Larkin	.40
H38	Mike Piazza	2.00
H39	Matt Williams	.40
H40	Player of the Month Long Shot/W	.40
H41	Osvaldo Fernandez	.40
H42	Tom Glavine	.60
H43	Jason Isringhausen	.40
H44	Greg Maddux	1.50
H45	Pedro Martinez	.75
H46	Hideo Nomo	.60
H47	Pete Schourek	.40
H48	Paul Wilson	.40
H49	Mark Wohlers	.40
H50	Pitcher of the Month Long Shot	.40
H51	Bob Abreu	.40
H52	Trey Beamon	.40
H53	Yamil Benitez	.40
H54	Roger Cedeno/W	.60
H55	Todd Hollandsworth	.40
H56	Marvin Benard	.40
H57	Jason Kendall	.40
H58	Brooks Kieschnick	.40
H59	Rey Ordonez/W	.60
H60	Rookie Hits Long Shot/W	.40

Hobby Predictor Redemption

Persons who redeemed winning cards from UD's interactive Predictor insert series received a 10-card set of the top players in various statistical categories. The redemption cards are similar in format to the Predictor cards, but have fronts printed on silver-foil. In place of the contest rules found on the backs of Predictor cards, the redemption cards have a career summary.

		NM/M
Complete Set (60):		45.00
Common Player:		.50
H1	Albert Belle	.50
H2	Kenny Lofton	.50
H3	Rafael Palmeiro	.75
H4	Ken Griffey Jr.	2.50
H5	Tim Salmon	.50
H6	Cal Ripken Jr.	4.00
H7	Mark McGwire	3.00
H8	Frank Thomas	1.00
H9	Mo Vaughn	.50
H10	Player of the Month Long Shot	.50
H11	Roger Clemens	2.25
H12	David Cone	.50
H13	Jose Mesa	.50
H14	Randy Johnson	1.00
H15	Steve Finley	.50
H16	Mike Mussina	.65
H17	Kevin Appier	.50
H18	Kenny Rogers	.50
H19	Lee Smith	.50
H20	Pitcher of the Month Long Shot	.50
H21	George Arias	.50
H22	Jose Herrera	.50
H23	Tony Clark	.50
H24	Todd Greene	.50
H25	Derek Jeter	4.00
H26	Arquimedez Pozo	.50
H27	Matt Lawton	.50
H28	Shannon Stewart	.50
H29	Chris Snopek	.50
H30	Rookie Hits Long Shot	.50
H31	Jeff Bagwell	1.00
H32	Dante Bichette	.50
H33	Barry Bonds	4.00
H34	Tony Gwynn	2.00
H35	Chipper Jones	2.00
H36	Eric Karros	.50
H37	Barry Larkin	.50
H38	Mike Piazza	2.50
H39	Matt Williams	.50
H40	Player of the Month Long Shot	.50
H41	Osvaldo Fernandez	.50
H42	Tom Glavine	.65
H43	Jason Isringhausen	.50
H44	Greg Maddux	2.00
H45	Pedro Martinez	1.00
H46	Hideo Nomo	.65
H47	Pete Schourek	.50
H48	Paul Wilson	.50
H49	Mark Wohlers	.50
H50	Pitcher of the Month Long Shot	.50
H51	Bob Abreu	.50
H52	Trey Beamon	.50
H53	Yamil Benitez	.50
H54	Roger Cedeno	.50
H55	Todd Hollandsworth	.50
H56	Marvin Benard	.50
H57	Jason Kendall	.50
H58	Brooks Kieschnick	.50
H59	Rey Ordonez	.50
H60	Rookie Hits Long Shot	.50

Hot Commodities

These 20 die-cut cards were seeded one per every 37 1996 Upper Deck Series 2 packs. Cards are numbered with a "HC" prefix.

		NM/M
Complete Set (20):		30.00
Common Player:		.75
1	Ken Griffey Jr.	3.00
2	Hideo Nomo	1.50
3	Roberto Alomar	1.50
4	Paul Wilson	.75
5	Albert Belle	.75
6	Manny Ramirez	2.25
7	Kirby Puckett	2.50
8	Johnny Damon	2.00
9	Randy Johnson	2.25
10	Greg Maddux	2.50
11	Chipper Jones	2.50
12	Barry Bonds	5.00
13	Mo Vaughn	.75
14	Mike Piazza	3.00
15	Cal Ripken Jr.	5.00
16	Tim Salmon	.75
17	Sammy Sosa	2.50
18	Kenny Lofton	.75
19	Tony Gwynn	2.50
20	Frank Thomas	2.25

Lovero Collection

Every sixth pack of 1996 Upper Deck Series II has a V.J. Lovero insert card. This 20-card set features unique shots from Lovero, one of the most well-known photographers in the country. Some of the cards feature Randy Johnson wearing a conehead, Frank Thomas blowing a bubble while throwing the ball, and Jay Buhner and his child both chewing on a bat. Cards are numbered with a "VJ" prefix.

		NM/M
Complete Set (20):		17.50
Common Player:		.25
1	Rod Carew	1.00
2	Hideo Nomo	.50
3	Derek Jeter	3.00
4	Barry Bonds	3.00
5	Greg Maddux	1.50
6	Mark McGwire (W/Will Clark.)	2.50
7	Jose Canseco	.50
8	Ken Caminiti	.25
9	Raul Mondesi	.25
10	Ken Griffey Jr.	2.50
11	Jay Buhner	.25
12	Randy Johnson	1.00
13	Roger Clemens	2.00
14	Brady Anderson	.25
15	Frank Thomas	1.00
16	Angels Outfielders	.25
17	Mike Piazza	2.50
18	Dante Bichette	.25
19	Tony Gwynn	1.50
20	Jim Abbott	.25

Nomo Highlights

The 1995 rookie season of Los Angeles Dodgers' pitcher Hideo Nomo is recapped in this five-card 1996 Upper Deck insert set. The cards were seeded one per every 23 Series 2 packs. A 5" x 7" version of each card was also issued as a retail box insert. Values are the same as for small cards.

		NM/M
Complete Set (5):		3.00
Common Card:		.75
1-5	Hideo Nomo	.75

Power Driven

Twenty of the game's top power hitters are analyzed in depth by baseball writer Peter Gammons on these Series 1 insert cards. Found once per 36 packs, on average, the cards are printed on an embossed light F/X design. Cards are numbered with a "PD" prefix.

		NM/M
Complete Set (20):		24.00
Common Player:		.30
1	Albert Belle	.30
2	Barry Bonds	5.00
3	Jay Buhner	.30
4	Jose Canseco	.75
5	Cecil Fielder	.30
6	Juan Gonzalez	.75
7	Ken Griffey Jr.	3.00
8	Eric Karros	.30
9	Fred McGriff	.30
10	Mark McGwire	4.00
11	Rafael Palmeiro	1.25
12	Mike Piazza	3.00
13	Manny Ramirez	1.50
14	Tim Salmon	.30
15	Reggie Sanders	.30
16	Sammy Sosa	2.50
17	Frank Thomas	1.50
18	Mo Vaughn	.30
19	Larry Walker	.30
20	Matt Williams	.30

Retail Predictor

Retail Predictor inserts feature 60 possible winners in the categories of monthly leader in home runs, batting average and RBIs. If the pictured player led a category in any month, his card was redeemable for a 10-card set featuring action photos on silver foil. Retail Predictors are found on average once per 12 packs in each series. Winning cards are indicated by (W).

		NM/M
Complete Set (60):		40.00
Common Player:		.40
R1	Albert Belle/W	.60
R2	Jay Buhner/W	.60
R3	Juan Gonzalez	.50
R4	Ken Griffey Jr.	2.00
R5	Mark McGwire/W	4.00
R6	Rafael Palmeiro	.65
R7	Tim Salmon	.40
R8	Frank Thomas	1.00
R9	Mo Vaughn/W	.60
R10	Home Run Long Shot/W	.40
R11	Albert Belle/W	.60
R12	Jay Buhner	.40
R13	Jim Edmonds	.40
R14	Cecil Fielder	.40
R15	Ken Griffey Jr.	2.00
R16	Edgar Martinez	.40
R17	Manny Ramirez	.75
R18	Frank Thomas	1.00
R19	Mo Vaughn/W	.60
R20	RBI Long Shot/W	.40
R21	Roberto Alomar/W	1.00
R22	Carlos Baerga	.40
R23	Wade Boggs	1.50
R24	Ken Griffey Jr.	2.00
R25	Chuck Knoblauch	.40
R26	Kenny Lofton	.40
R27	Edgar Martinez	.40
R28	Tim Salmon	.40
R29	Frank Thomas	1.00
R30	Batting Average Long Shot/W	.40
R31	Dante Bichette	.40
R32	Barry Bonds/W	4.50
R33	Ron Gant	.40
R34	Chipper Jones	1.50
R35	Fred McGriff	.40
R36	Mike Piazza	2.00
R37	Sammy Sosa	1.50
R38	Larry Walker	.40
R39	Matt Williams	.40
R40	Home Run Long Shot	.40
R41	Jeff Bagwell/W	1.25

R42 Dante Bichette .40
R43 Barry Bonds/W 4.50
R44 Jeff Conine .40
R45 Andres Galarraga .40
R46 Mike Piazza 2.00
R47 Reggie Sanders .40
R48 Sammy Sosa 1.50
R49 Matt Williams .40
R50 RBI Long Shot .40
R51 Jeff Bagwell .75
R52 Derek Bell .40
R53 Dante Bichette .40
R54 Craig Biggio .40
R55 Barry Bonds 2.50
R56 Bret Boone .40
R57 Tony Gwynn 1.50
R58 Barry Larkin .40
R59 Mike Piazza/W 3.50
R60 AVG Long Shot .40

Retail Predictor Redemption

Persons who redeemed winning cards from UD's interactive Predictor insert series received a 10-card set of the top players in various statistical categories. The redemption cards are similar in format to the Predictor cards, but have fronts printed on silver-foil. In place of the contest rules found on the backs of Predictor cards, the redemption cards have a career summary.

NM/M

Complete Set (60): 25.00
Common Player: .25
R1 Albert Belle .25
R2 Jay Buhner .25
R3 Juan Gonzalez .35
R4 Ken Griffey Jr. 1.00
R5 Mark McGwire 1.50
R6 Rafael Palmeiro .50
R7 Tim Salmon .25
R8 Frank Thomas .60
R9 Mo Vaughn .25
R10 Home Run Long Shot .25
R11 Albert Belle .25
R12 Jay Buhner .25
R13 Jim Edmonds .25
R14 Cecil Fielder .25
R15 Ken Griffey Jr. 1.00
R16 Edgar Martinez .25
R17 Manny Ramirez .60
R18 Frank Thomas .60
R19 Mo Vaughn .25
R20 RBI Long Shot .25
R21 Roberto Alomar .35
R22 Carlos Baerga .25
R23 Wade Boggs .75
R24 Ken Griffey Jr. 1.00
R25 Chuck Knoblauch .25
R26 Kenny Lofton .25
R27 Edgar Martinez .25
R28 Tim Salmon .25
R29 Frank Thomas .60
R30 Batting Average Long Shot .25
R31 Dante Bichette .25
R32 Barry Bonds 2.00
R33 Ron Gant .25
R34 Chipper Jones .75
R35 Fred McGriff .25
R36 Mike Piazza 1.00
R37 Sammy Sosa .75
R38 Larry Walker .25
R39 Matt Williams .25
R40 Home Run Long Shot .25
R41 Jeff Bagwell .60
R42 Dante Bichette .25
R43 Barry Bonds 2.00
R44 Jeff Conine .25
R45 Andres Galarraga .25
R46 Mike Piazza 1.00
R47 Reggie Sanders .25
R48 Sammy Sosa .75
R49 Matt Williams .25
R50 RBI Long Shot .25
R51 Jeff Bagwell .60
R52 Derek Bell .25
R53 Dante Bichette .25
R54 Craig Biggio .25
R55 Barry Bonds 2.00
R56 Bret Boone .25
R57 Tony Gwynn .75
R58 Barry Larkin .25
R59 Mike Piazza 1.00
R60 AVG Long Shot .25

Cal Ripken Collection

Part of a cross-brand insert set, four cards are included as Series I inserts at the rate of one per 24 packs. Five cards are also included in Series II, one per every 23 packs. They chronicle Cal Ripken's career and highlights.

NM/M

Complete Set (8): 12.50
Common Card: 2.00

Header: 2.00
5-8 Cal Ripken Jr. 2.00
13-17 Cal Ripken Jr. 2.00

Cal Ripken Collection Supers

The career of Cal Ripken Jr. to the point of his 2,131st consecutive major league game is chronicled in this boxed set of 3-1/2" x 5" cards. The tale is told in reverse order, with card #1 marking the record and #22 detailing Ripken's first major league experience. Fronts have photos of Ripken in various stages of his career and feature a gold-foil facsimile autograph. Backs have a green and black background with a portrait of Ripken at top. At center are a few sentences about his career and a season's stats.

NM/M

Complete Set (22): 10.00
Common Card: .75
1 Cal Ripken Jr. .75
2 Cal Ripken Jr. (w/Barry Bonds) 1.00
3-21 Cal Ripken Jr. .75
22 Cal Ripken Jr. (w/Eddie Murray) .75

Run Producers

These double die-cut, embossed and color foil-stamped cards feature 20 of the game's top RBI men. The cards were seeded one per every 71 packs of 1996 Upper Deck Series II. Cards are numbered with a "RP" prefix.

NM/M

Complete Set (20): 50.00
Common Player: 1.00
1 Albert Belle 1.00
2 Dante Bichette 1.00
3 Barry Bonds 10.00
4 Jay Buhner 1.00
5 Jose Canseco 2.00
6 Juan Gonzalez 1.50
7 Ken Griffey Jr. 6.00
8 Tony Gwynn 5.00
9 Kenny Lofton 1.00
10 Edgar Martinez 1.00
11 Fred McGriff 1.00
12 Mark McGwire 7.50
13 Rafael Palmeiro 2.50
14 Mike Piazza 6.00
15 Manny Ramirez 3.00
16 Tim Salmon 1.00
17 Sammy Sosa 5.00
18 Frank Thomas 3.00
19 Mo Vaughn 1.00
20 Matt Williams 1.00

All-Star Supers

The starting line-ups of the 1996 All-Star Game are featured in super-size (3-1/2" x 5") versions of their 1996 Upper Deck cards in this special boxed set sold at Wal-Mart late in the year for around $18. Other than a large silver-foil All-Star Game logo in the lower-left corner of each photo, these cards are identical to the regular-issue versions, right down to the silver- and bronze-foil highlights on front and the card numbers on back.

NM/M

Complete Set (18): 7.50
Common Player: .25
80 Jeff Bagwell .75
195 Barry Bonds 2.00
200 Ken Griffey Jr. 1.25
271 John Smoltz .25
275 Roberto Alomar .45
280 Cal Ripken Jr. 2.00
300 Frank Thomas .75
310 Barry Larkin .25
313 Sandy Alomar Jr. .25
315 Albert Belle .25
317 Charles Nagy .25
319 Kenny Lofton .25
320 Dante Bichette .25
345 Craig Biggio .25
360 Mike Piazza 1.25
410 Wade Boggs 1.00
450 Tony Gwynn 1.00
466 Matt Williams .25

Ken Griffey Jr. All-Star

Junior's seventh All-Star team selection was marked with the issue of this special jumbo (3-1/2" x 5") card. The front has an action photo with the 1996 All-Star Game logo and is highlighted in silver foil, including a reproduction of his autograph. The top is die-cut. On back is a portrait photo with Griffey's All-Star history overprinted, and a serial number from within an edition of 2,500. The card was an exclusive to a TV shopping network.

NM/M

Ken Griffey Jr. 12.00

Ken Griffey Jr. 22kt Gold

This standard-size card has a gold-foil facsimile autograph on front and is serially numbered on back from within an edition of 5,000. A certificate of authenticity accompanied the card when sold new.

NM/M

Ken Griffey Jr. 7.50

National Heroes

Two baseball stars are included in this series of collector issues believed to have been a TV shop-at-home exclusive. Measuring 3-1/2" x 5", the cards are die-cut into a torn ticket shape. Fronts have color action photos on a gold-foil background. Two versions of each card were issued, an edition of 5,000 unsigned cards and an autographed edition serially numbered on front to a limit of 250.

NM/M

Complete Set (2): 20.00
Complete Set, Autographed (2): 190.00
(1) Ken Griffey Jr. 7.50
(1a) Ken Griffey Jr./Auto. 90.00
(2) Cal Ripken Jr. 10.00
(2a) Cal Ripken Jr./Auto. 100.00

Hideo Nomo R.O.Y.

The Japanese pitcher's 1995 Rookie of the Year season was commemorated with this large-format (3-1/2" x 5"), die-cut card sold only via TV shopping programs. The card has an action photo of Nomo on front and is highlighted in gold foil, including a replica of his autograph. On back is an action photo, major league career summary and stats and a serial number from within an edition of 5,000 pieces.

NM/M

Hideo Nomo 15.00

Meet the Stars

These 7" x 5" cards were issued in conjunction with UD's "Meet the Stars" promotion.

NM/M

Complete Set (2): 12.00
(1) Dynamic Debut - 1989 (Ken Griffey Jr.) 5.00
(2) Magic Memories - 1995 (Ken Griffey Jr.) 5.00

Statistics Leaders Supers

National League and American League winners of important statistical categories, along with major award winners for the 1996 season are featured in this boxed set of large-format (3-1/2" x 5") cards. Besides the size, these cards differ from the regular-issue 1996 UD cards of the same players only in the addition of a silver-foil award shield on front and the card number on back. Players with multiple awards have identical cards. The set was sold only at retail outlets with a suggested price of about $20.

NM/M

Complete Set (23): 4.00
Common Player: .15
1 Alex Rodriguez (AL Batting) 1.50
2 Tony Gwynn (NL Batting) .60
3 Mark McGwire (AL HR) 1.50
4 Andres Galarraga (NL HR) .15
5 Albert Belle (AL RBI) .15
6 Andres Galarraga (NL RBI) .15
7 Kenny Lofton (AL Steals) .15
8 Eric Young (NL Steals) .15
9 Andy Pettitte (AL Wns) .25
10 John Smoltz (NL Wins) .15
11 Roger Clemens (AL Ks) .75
12 John Smoltz (NL Ks) .15
13 Juan Guzman (AL ERA) .15
14 Kevin Brown (NL ERA) .15
15 John Wetteland (AL Saves) .15
16 Jeff Brantley (NL Saves) .15
17 Todd Worrell (NL Saves) .15
18 Derek Jeter (AL ROY) 2.00
19 Todd Hollandsworth (NL ROY) .15
20 Juan Gonzalez (AL MVP) .30
21 Ken Caminiti (NL MVP) .15
22 Pat Hentgen (AL CY) .15
23 John Smoltz (NL CY) .15

1997 Upper Deck

The 520-card set was issued in two series in 12-card packs. Base card fronts fea-

ture a game-action shot with the player's name near the bottom edge above a bronze-foil, wood-grain stripe. A team logo is in the lower-left corner in silver foil. Each card front has the date of the game pictured with a brief description. Backs contain more detailed game highlight descriptions and statistics, along with a small action shot in the upper-left quadrant. Series 1 subsets are: Jackie Robinson Tribute (1-9), Strike Force (65-72), Defensive Gems (136-153), Global Impact (181-207), Season Highlights Checklist (214-222) and Star Rookies (223-240). A 30-card update to Series 1 was released early in the season featuring 1996 post-season highlights and star rookies. Those card faces have red or purple borders and are numbered 241 to 270. Second series subsets include Star Rookie (271-288), Season Highlights (316-324), Capture the Flag (370-387), the short-printed (about one per seven packs) Griffey Hot List (415-424), and Diamond Debuts (469-483). A second update set of 30 was released near the end of the 1997 season, numbered 521-550 and featuring traded players and rookies. Both of the update sets were available only via a mail-in redemption offer.

NM/M

Complete Set (550): 75.00
Complete Series 1 Set (240): 35.00
Complete Update Set (241-270): 5.00
Complete Series 2 Set (271-520): 35.00
Complete Update Set (521-550): 7.50
Common Player: .05
Series 1 or 2 Pack (12): 1.50
Series 1 or 2 Wax Box (28): 25.00
1-9 Jackie Robinson .50
10 Chipper Jones 1.00
11 Marquis Grissom .05
12 Jermaine Dye .05
13 Mark Lemke .05
14 Terrell Wade .05
15 Fred McGriff .05
16 Tom Glavine .20
17 Mark Wohlers .05
18 Randy Myers .05
19 Roberto Alomar .25
20 Cal Ripken Jr. 2.00
21 Rafael Palmeiro .65
22 Mike Mussina .30
23 Brady Anderson .05
24 Jose Canseco .50
25 Mo Vaughn .05
26 Roger Clemens 1.00
27 Tim Naehring .05
28 Jeff Suppan .05
29 Troy Percival .05
30 Sammy Sosa 1.00
31 Amaury Telemaco .05
32 Rey Sanchez .05
33 Scott Servais .05
34 Steve Trachsel .05
35 Mark Grace .05
36 Wilson Alvarez .05
37 Harold Baines .05
38 Tony Phillips .05
39 James Baldwin .05
40 Frank Thomas (Wrong (Ken Griffey Jr.'s) vital data.) .85
41 Lyle Mouton .05
42 Chris Snopek .05
43 Hal Morris .05

44 Eric Davis .05
45 Barry Larkin .05
46 Reggie Sanders .05
47 Pete Schourek .05
48 Lee Smith .05
49 Charles Nagy .05
50 Albert Belle .05
51 Julio Franco .05
52 Kenny Lofton .05
53 Orel Hershiser .05
54 Omar Vizquel .05
55 Eric Young .05
56 Curtis Leskanic .05
57 Quinton McCracken .05
58 Kevin Ritz .05
59 Walt Weiss .05
60 Dante Bichette .05
61 Marc Lewis .05
62 Tony Clark .05
63 Travis Fryman .05
64 John Smoltz (Strike Force) .05
65 Greg Maddux (Strike Force) .50
66 Tom Glavine (Strike Force) .10
67 Mike Mussina (Strike Force) .15
68 Andy Pettitte (Strike Force) .15
69 Mariano Rivera (Strike Force) .10
70 Hideo Nomo (Strike Force) .20
71 Kevin Brown (Strike Force) .05
72 Randy Johnson (Strike Force) .40
73 Felipe Lira .05
74 Kimera Bartee .05
75 Alan Trammell .05
76 Kevin Brown .05
77 Edgar Renteria .05
78 Al Leiter .05
79 Charles Johnson .05
80 Andre Dawson .25
81 Billy Wagner .05
82 Donne Wall .05
83 Jeff Bagwell .75
84 Keith Lockhart .05
85 Jeff Montgomery .05
86 Tom Goodwin .05
87 Tim Belcher .05
88 Mike Macfarlane .05
89 Joe Randa .05
90 Brett Butler .05
91 Todd Worrell .05
92 Todd Hollandsworth .05
93 Ismael Valdes .05
94 Hideo Nomo .40
95 Mike Piazza 1.25
96 Jeff Cirillo .05
97 Ricky Bones .05
98 Fernando Vina .05
99 Ben McDonald .05
100 John Jaha .05
101 Mark Loretta .05
102 Paul Molitor .75
103 Rick Aguilera .05
104 Marty Cordova .05
105 Kirby Puckett 1.00
106 Dan Naulty .05
107 Frank Rodriguez .05
108 Shane Andrews .05
109 Henry Rodriguez .05
110 Mark Grudzielanek .05
111 Pedro Martinez .75
112 Ugueth Urbina .05
113 David Segui .05
114 Rey Ordonez .05
115 Bernard Gilkey .05
116 Butch Huskey .05
117 Paul Wilson .05
118 Alex Ochoa .05
119 John Franco .05
120 Dwight Gooden .05
121 Ruben Rivera .05
122 Andy Pettitte .20
123 Tino Martinez .05
124 Bernie Williams .05
125 Wade Boggs 1.00
126 Paul O'Neill .05
127 Scott Brosius .05
128 Ernie Young .05
129 Doug Johns .05
130 Geronimo Berroa .05
131 Jason Giambi .50
132 John Wasdin .05
133 Jim Eisenreich .05
134 Ricky Otero .05
135 Ricky Bottalico .05
136 Mark Langston (Defensive Gems) .05
137 Greg Maddux (Defensive Gems) .50
138 Ivan Rodriguez (Defensive Gems) .35
139 Charles Johnson (Defensive Gems) .05
140 J.T. Snow (Defensive Gems) .05
141 Mark Grace (Defensive Gems) .05
142 Roberto Alomar (Defensive Gems) .15
143 Craig Biggio (Defensive Gems) .05
144 Ken Caminiti (Defensive Gems) .05
145 Matt Williams (Defensive Gems) .05
146 Omar Vizquel (Defensive Gems) .05
147 Cal Ripken Jr. (Defensive Gems) 1.00
148 Ozzie Smith (Defensive Gems) .40
149 Rey Ordonez (Defensive Gems) .05
150 Ken Griffey Jr. (Defensive Gems) .65
151 Devon White (Defensive Gems) .05
152 Barry Bonds (Defensive Gems) 1.00
153 Kenny Lofton (Defensive Gems) .05
154 Mickey Morandini .05
155 Gregg Jefferies .05
156 Curt Schilling .20
157 Jason Kendall .05
158 Francisco Cordova .05
159 Dennis Eckersley .65
160 Ron Gant .05
161 Ozzie Smith 1.00
162 Brian Jordan .05
163 John Mabry .05
164 Andy Ashby .05
165 Steve Finley .05
166 Fernando Valenzuela .05
167 Archi Cianfrocco .05
168 Wally Joyner .05
169 Greg Vaughn .05
170 Barry Bonds 2.00
171 William Van Landingham .05
172 Marvin Benard .05
173 Rich Aurilia .05
174 Jay Canizaro .05
175 Ken Griffey Jr. 1.25
176 Bob Wells .05
177 Jay Buhner .05
178 Sterling Hitchcock .05
179 Edgar Martinez .05
180 Rusty Greer .05
181 Dave Nilsson (Global Impact) .05
182 Larry Walker (Global Impact) .05
183 Edgar Renteria (Global Impact) .05
184 Rey Ordonez (Global Impact) .05
185 Rafael Palmeiro (Global Impact) .35
186 Osvaldo Fernandez (Global Impact) .05
187 Raul Mondesi (Global Impact) .05
188 Manny Ramirez (Global Impact) .40
189 Sammy Sosa (Global Impact) .50
190 Robert Eenhoorn (Global Impact) .05
191 Devon White (Global Impact) .05
192 Hideo Nomo (Global Impact) .20
193 Mac Suzuki (Global Impact) .05
194 Chan Ho Park (Global Impact) .05
195 Fernando Valenzuela (Global Impact) .05
196 Andruw Jones (Global Impact) .40
197 Vinny Castilla (Global Impact) .05
198 Dennis Martinez (Global Impact) .05
199 Ruben Rivera (Global Impact) .05
200 Juan Gonzalez (Global Impact) .20
201 Roberto Alomar (Global Impact) .30
202 Edgar Martinez (Global Impact) .05
203 Ivan Rodriguez (Global Impact) .35
204 Carlos Delgado (Global Impact) .20
205 Andres Galarraga (Global Impact) .05
206 Ozzie Guillen (Global Impact) .05
207 Midre Cummings (Global Impact) .05
208 Roger Pavlik .05
209 Darren Oliver .05
210 Dean Palmer .05
211 Ivan Rodriguez .65
212 Otis Nixon .05
213 Pat Hentgen .05
214 Ozzie Smith, Andre Dawson, Kirby Puckett CL (Season Highlights) .10
215 Barry Bonds, Gary Sheffield, Brady Anderson (Checklist/Season Highlights) .25
216 Ken Caminiti (Checklist/Season Highlights) .05
217 John Smoltz (Checklist/Season Highlights) .05
218 Eric Young (Checklist/Season Highlights) .05
219 Juan Gonzalez (Checklist/Season Highlights) .10
220 Eddie Murray (Checklist/Season Highlights) .15
221 Tommy Lasorda (Checklist/Season Highlights) .05
222 Paul Molitor (Checklist/Season Highlights) .15
223 Luis Castillo .05
224 Justin Thompson .05
225 Rocky Coppinger .05
226 Jermaine Allensworth .05
227 Jeff D'Amico .05
228 Jamey Wright .05
229 Scott Rolen .60
230 Darin Erstad .25
231 Marty Janzen .05
232 Jacob Cruz .05
233 Raul Ibanez .05
234 Nomar Garciaparra 1.00
235 Todd Walker .05
236 Brian Giles **RC** .75
237 Matt Beech .05
238 Mike Cameron .05
239 Jose Paniagua .05
240 Andruw Jones .75
241 Brant Brown/SR .25
242 Robin Jennings/SR .25
243 Willie Adams/SR .25
244 Ken Caminiti (Division Series) .25
245 Brian Jordan (Division Series) .25
246 Chipper Jones (Division Series) 2.50
247 Juan Gonzalez (Division Series) 1.00
248 Bernie Williams (Division Series) .25
249 Roberto Alomar (Division Series) .30
250 Bernie Williams (Post-Season) .25
251 David Wells (Post-Season) .25
252 Cecil Fielder (Post-Season) .25
253 Darryl Strawberry (Post-Season) .25
254 Andy Pettitte (Post-Season) .40
255 Javier Lopez (Post-Season) .25
256 Gary Gaetti (Post-Season) .25
257 Ron Gant (Post-Season) .25
258 Brian Jordan (Post-Season) .25
259 John Smoltz (Post-Season) .25
260 Greg Maddux (Post-Season) 2.50
261 Tom Glavine (Post-Season) .45
262 Chipper Jones (World Series) 2.50
263 Greg Maddux (World Series) 2.50
264 David Cone (World Series) .25
265 Jim Leyritz (World Series) .25
266 Andy Pettitte (World Series) .40
267 John Wetteland (World Series) .25
268 Dario Veras/SR **RC** .25
269 Neifi Perez/SR .25
270 Bill Mueller/SR .25
271 Vladimir Guerrero/SR .75
272 Dmitri Young/SR .05
273 Nerio Rodriguez/SR **RC** .05
274 Kevin Orie/SR .05
275 Felipe Crespo/SR .05
276 Danny Graves/SR .05
277 Roderick Myers/SR .05
278 Felix Heredia/SR **RC** .25
279 Ralph Milliard/SR .05
280 Greg Norton/SR .05
281 Derek Wallace/SR .05
282 Trot Nixon/SR .10
283 Bobby Chouinard/SR .05
284 Jay Witasick/SR .05
285 Travis Miller/SR .05
286 Brian Bevil/SR .05
287 Bobby Estalella/SR .05
288 Steve Soderstrom/SR .05
289 Mark Langston .05
290 Tim Salmon .05
291 Jim Edmonds .05
292 Garret Anderson .05
293 George Arias .05
294 Gary DiSarcina .05
295 Chuck Finley .05
296 Todd Greene .05
297 Randy Velarde .05
298 David Justice .05
299 Ryan Klesko .05
300 John Smoltz .05
301 Javier Lopez .05
302 Greg Maddux 1.00
303 Denny Neagle .05
304 B.J. Surhoff .05
305 Chris Hoiles .05
306 Eric Davis .05
307 Scott Erickson .05
308 Mike Bordick .05
309 John Valentin .05
310 Heathcliff Slocumb .05
311 Tom Gordon .05
312 Mike Stanley .05
313 Reggie Jefferson .05
314 Darren Bragg .05
315 Troy O'Leary .05
316 John Mabry (Season Highlight) .05
317 Mark Whiten (Season Highlight) .05
318 Edgar Martinez (Season Highlight) .05
319 Alex Rodriguez (Season Highlight) .75
320 Mark McGwire (Season Highlight) .75
321 Hideo Nomo (Season Highlight) .20
322 Todd Hundley (Season Highlight) .05
323 Barry Bonds (Season Highlight) 1.00
324 Andruw Jones (Season Highlight) .40
325 Ryne Sandberg 1.00
326 Brian McRae .05
327 Frank Castillo .05
328 Shawon Dunston .05
329 Ray Durham .05
330 Robin Ventura .05
331 Ozzie Guillen .05
332 Roberto Hernandez .05
333 Albert Belle .25
334 Dave Martinez .05
335 Willie Greene .05
336 Jeff Brantley .05
337 Kevin Jarvis .05
338 John Smiley .05
339 Eddie Taubensee .05
340 Bret Boone .05
341 Kevin Seitzer .05
342 Jack McDowell .05
343 Sandy Alomar Jr. .05
344 Chad Curtis .05
345 Manny Ramirez .75
346 Chad Ogea .05
347 Jim Thome .05
348 Mark Thompson .05
349 Ellis Burks .05
350 Andres Galarraga .05
351 Vinny Castilla .05
352 Kirt Manwaring .05
353 Larry Walker .05
354 Omar Olivares .05
355 Bobby Higginson .05
356 Melvin Nieves .05
357 Brian Johnson .05
358 Devon White .05
359 Jeff Conine .05
360 Gary Sheffield .35
361 Robb Nen .05
362 Mike Hampton .05
363 Bob Abreu .10
364 Luis Gonzalez .05
365 Derek Bell .05
366 Sean Berry .05
367 Craig Biggio .05
368 Darryl Kile .05
369 Shane Reynolds .05
370 Jeff Bagwell (Capture the Flag) .40
371 Ron Gant (Capture the Flag) .05
372 Andy Benes (Capture the Flag) .05
373 Gary Gaetti (Capture the Flag) .05
374a Ramon Martinez (Capture the Flag)(Gold back.)) .05
374b Ramon Martinez (Capture the Flag)(White back.)) .05
375 Raul Mondesi (Capture the Flag) .05
376a Steve Finley (Capture the Flag)(Gold back.)) .05
376b Steve Finley (Capture the Flag)(White back.)) .05
377 Ken Caminiti (Capture the Flag) .05
378 Tony Gwynn (Capture the Flag) .40
379 Dario Veras (Capture the Flag) .05
380 Andy Pettitte (Capture the Flag) .10
381 Ruben Rivera (Capture the Flag) .05
382 David Cone (Capture the Flag) .05
383 Roberto Alomar (Capture the Flag) .20
384 Edgar Martinez (Capture the Flag) .05
385 Ken Griffey Jr. (Capture the Flag) .65
386 Mark McGwire (Capture the Flag) .75
387 Rusty Greer (Capture the Flag) .05
388 Jose Rosado .05
389 Kevin Appier .05
390 Johnny Damon .25
391 Jose Offerman .05
392 Michael Tucker .05
393 Craig Paquette .05
394 Bip Roberts .05
395 Ramon Martinez .05
396 Greg Gagne .05
397 Chan Ho Park .05
398 Karim Garcia .10
399 Wilton Guerrero .05
400 Eric Karros .05
401 Raul Mondesi .05
402 Matt Mieske .05
403 Mike Fetters .05
404 Dave Nilsson .05
405 Jose Valentin .05
406 Scott Karl .05
407 Marc Newfield .05
408 Cal Eldred .05
409 Rich Becker .05
410 Terry Steinbach .05
411 Chuck Knoblauch .05
412 Pat Meares .05
413 Brad Radke .05
415a Kirby Puckett (Should be #414.) 1.00
415b Andruw Jones (Griffey Hot List) 1.50
416 Chipper Jones (Griffey Hot List) 2.00
417 Mo Vaughn (Griffey Hot List) .50
418 Frank Thomas (Griffey Hot List) 1.50
419 Albert Belle (Griffey Hot List) .50
420 Mark McGwire (Griffey Hot List) 3.00
421 Derek Jeter (Griffey Hot List) 4.50
422 Alex Rodriguez (Griffey Hot List) 3.00
423 Juan Gonzalez (Griffey Hot List) .75
424 Ken Griffey Jr. (Griffey Hot List) 2.50
425 Rondell White .05
426 Darrin Fletcher .05
427 Cliff Floyd .05
428 Mike Lansing .05
429 F.P. Santangelo .05
430 Todd Hundley .05
431 Mark Clark .05
432 Pete Harnisch .05
433 Jason Isringhausen .05
434 Bobby Jones .05
435 Lance Johnson .05
436 Carlos Baerga .05
437 Mariano Duncan .05
438 David Cone .05
439 Mariano Rivera .15
440 Derek Jeter 2.00
441 Joe Girardi .05
442 Charlie Hayes .05
443 Tim Raines .05
444 Darryl Strawberry .05
445 Cecil Fielder .05
446 Ariel Prieto .05
447 Tony Batista .05
448 Brent Gates .05
449 Scott Spiezio .05
450 Mark McGwire 1.50
451 Don Wengert .05
452 Mike Lieberthal .05
453 Lenny Dykstra .05
454 Rex Hudler .05
455 Darren Daulton .05
456 Kevin Stocker .05
457 Trey Beamon .05
458 Midre Cummings .05
459 Mark Johnson .05
460 Al Martin .05
461 Kevin Elster .05
462 Jon Lieber .05
463 Jason Schmidt .05
464 Paul Wagner .05
465 Andy Benes .05
466 Alan Benes .05
467 Royce Clayton .05
468 Gary Gaetti .05
469 Curt Lyons (Diamond Debuts) .05
470 Eugene Kingsale (Diamond Debuts) .05
471 Damian Jackson (Diamond Debuts) .05
472 Wendell Magee (Diamond Dubuts) .05
473 Kevin L. Brown (Diamond Debuts) .05
474 Raul Casanova (Diamond Debuts) .05
475 Ramiro Mendoza **RC** (Diamond Debuts) .25
476 Todd Dunn (Diamond Debuts) .05
477 Chad Mottola (Diamond Debuts) .05
478 Andy Larkin (Diamond Debuts) .05
479 Jaime Bluma (Diamond Debuts) .05
480 Mac Suzuki (Diamond Debuts) .05
481 Brian Banks (Diamond Debuts) .05
482 Desi Wilson (Diamond Debuts) .05
483 Einar Diaz (Diamond Debuts) .05
484 Tom Pagnozzi .05
485 Ray Lankford .05
486 Todd Stottlemyre .05
487 Donovan Osborne .05
488 Trevor Hoffman .05
489 Chris Gomez .05
490 Ken Caminiti .05
491 John Flaherty .05
492 Tony Gwynn 1.00
493 Joey Hamilton .05
494 Rickey Henderson .75
495 Glenallen Hill .05
496 Rod Beck .05
497 Osvaldo Fernandez .05
498 Rick Wilkins .05
499 Joey Cora .05
500 Alex Rodriguez 1.50
501 Randy Johnson .75
502 Paul Sorrento .05
503 Dan Wilson .05
504 Jamie Moyer .05
505 Will Clark .05
506 Mickey Tettleton .05
507 John Burkett .05
508 Ken Hill .05
509 Mark McLemore .05
510 Juan Gonzalez .40
511 Bobby Witt .05
512 Carlos Delgado .40
513 Alex Gonzalez .05
514 Shawn Green .25
515 Joe Carter .05
516 Juan Guzman .05
517 Charlie O'Brien .05
518 Ed Sprague .05
519 Mike Timlin .05
520 Roger Clemens 1.00
521 Eddie Murray 2.00
522 Jason Dickson .25
523 Jim Leyritz .25
524 Michael Tucker .25
525 Kenny Lofton .25
526 Jimmy Key .25
527 Mel Rojas .25
528 Deion Sanders .25
529 Bartolo Colon .25
530 Matt Williams .25
531 Marquis Grissom .25
532 David Justice .25
533 Bubba Trammell **RC** .35
534 Moises Alou .25
535 Bobby Bonilla .25
536 Alex Fernandez .25
537 Jay Bell .25
538 Chili Davis .25
539 Jeff King .25
540 Todd Zeile .25
541 John Olerud .25
542 Jose Guillen .25
543 Derrek Lee 1.00
544 Dante Powell .25
545 J.T. Snow .25
546 Jeff Kent .25
547 Jose Cruz Jr. **RC** .75
548 John Wetteland .25
549 Orlando Merced .25
550 Hideki Irabu **RC** .50

Amazing Greats

The 20-card, regular-sized insert set was included every 138 packs of 1997 Upper Deck baseball. The cards include real wood with two player shots imaged on the card front. The team logo appears in the upper right corner of the horizontal card. The cards are numbered with the "AG" prefix.

		NM/M
Complete Set (20):		140.00
Common Player:		2.50
1	Ken Griffey Jr.	12.50
2	Roberto Alomar	3.00
3	Alex Rodriguez	15.00
4	Paul Molitor	7.50
5	Chipper Jones	10.00
6	Tony Gwynn	10.00
7	Kenny Lofton	2.50
8	Albert Belle	2.50
9	Matt Williams	2.50
10	Frank Thomas	7.50
11	Greg Maddux	10.00
12	Sammy Sosa	10.00

13	Kirby Puckett	10.00
14	Jeff Bagwell	7.50
15	Cal Ripken Jr.	20.00
16	Manny Ramirez	7.50
17	Barry Bonds	20.00
18	Mo Vaughn	2.50
19	Eddie Murray	7.50
20	Mike Piazza	12.50

Blue Chip Prospects

This 20-card insert was found in packs of Series II and features a die-cut design. Cards appear to have a photo slide attached to them featuring a portrait shot of the promising youngster depicted on the card. A total of 500 of each card were produced. Cards are numbered with a "BC" prefix.

		NM/M
Common Player:		6.00
Production 500 Sets		
1	Andruw Jones	25.00
2	Derek Jeter	60.00
3	Scott Rolen	15.00
4	Manny Ramirez	25.00
5	Todd Walker	6.00
6	Rocky Coppinger	6.00
7	Nomar Garciaparra	30.00
8	Darin Erstad	7.50
9	Jermaine Dye	6.00
10	Vladimir Guerrero	25.00
11	Edgar Renteria	6.00
12	Bob Abreu	7.50
13	Karim Garcia	6.00
14	Jeff D'Amico	6.00
15	Chipper Jones	30.00
16	Todd Hollandsworth	6.00
17	Andy Pettitte	9.00
18	Ruben Rivera	6.00
19	Jason Kendall	6.00
20	Alex Rodriguez	40.00

Game Jersey

The three-card, regular-sized set was inserted every 800 packs of Upper Deck Series I. The cards contained a square of the player's game-used jersey, and carried a "GJ" card number prefix.

		NM/M
Complete Set (3):		160.00
Common Player:		15.00
GJ1	Ken Griffey Jr.	135.00
GJ2	Tony Gwynn	25.00
GJ3	Rey Ordonez	15.00

Hot Commodities

This 20-card insert from Series II features a flame pattern behind the image of the player depicted on the front of the card. Odds of finding a card were 1:13 packs. Cards are numbered with a "HC" prefix.

		NM/M
Complete Set (20):		20.00
Common Player:		.30
1	Alex Rodriguez	2.00
2	Andruw Jones	1.00
3	Derek Jeter	2.50
4	Frank Thomas	1.00
5	Ken Griffey Jr.	1.50
6	Chipper Jones	1.25
7	Juan Gonzalez	.50
8	Cal Ripken Jr.	2.50
9	John Smoltz	.30
10	Mark McGwire	2.00
11	Barry Bonds	2.50
12	Albert Belle	.30
13	Mike Piazza	1.50
14	Manny Ramirez	1.00
15	Mo Vaughn	.30
16	Tony Gwynn	1.25
17	Vladimir Guerrero	1.00
18	Hideo Nomo	.50
19	Greg Maddux	1.25
20	Kirby Puckett	1.25

Long Distance Connection

This 20-card insert from Series II features the top home run hitters in the game. Odds of finding a card were 1:35 packs. Cards are numbered with a "LD" prefix.

		NM/M
Complete Set (20):		32.50
Common Player:		.60
1	Mark McGwire	4.00
2	Brady Anderson	.60
3	Ken Griffey Jr.	3.00
4	Albert Belle	.60
5	Juan Gonzalez	1.25
6	Andres Galarraga	.60
7	Jay Buhner	.60
8	Mo Vaughn	.60
9	Barry Bonds	5.00
10	Gary Sheffield	1.25
11	Todd Hundley	.60
12	Frank Thomas	2.00
13	Sammy Sosa	2.50
14	Rafael Palmeiro	1.75
15	Alex Rodriguez	4.00
16	Mike Piazza	3.00
17	Ken Caminiti	.60
18	Chipper Jones	2.50
19	Manny Ramirez	2.00
20	Andruw Jones	2.00

Memorable Moments

This issue was a one per pack insert in special Series 1 and 2 Collector's Choice six-card retail packs. In standard 2-1/2" x 3-1/2", the cards are die-cut at top and bottom in a wave pattern. Fronts, highlighted in matte bronze foil, have action photos and a career highlight. Backs have another photo and a more complete explanation of the Memorable Moment.

		NM/M
Complete Set (20):		20.00
Common Player:		.50
1	Andruw Jones	.75
2	Chipper Jones	1.00
3	Cal Ripken Jr.	2.50
4	Frank Thomas	.75
5	Manny Ramirez	.75
6	Mike Piazza	1.50
7	Mark McGwire	2.00
8	Barry Bonds	2.50
9	Ken Griffey Jr.	1.50
10	Alex Rodriguez	2.00
1	Ken Griffey Jr.	1.50
2	Albert Belle	.50
3	Derek Jeter	2.50
4	Greg Maddux	1.00
5	Tony Gwynn	1.00
6	Ryne Sandberg	1.00
7	Juan Gonzalez	.60
8	Roger Clemens	1.25
9	Jose Cruz Jr.	.50
10	Mo Vaughn	.50

Power Package

The 20-card, regular-sized, die-cut set was inserted every 23 packs of 1997 Upper Deck baseball. The player's name is printed in gold foil along the top border of the card face, which also features Light F/X. The die-cut cards have a silver-foil border and team-color frame with a "Power Package" logo in gold foil centered on the bottom border. The card backs have a short highlight in a brown box bordered by team colors and are numbered with the "PP" prefix.

		NM/M
Complete Set (20):		30.00
Common Player:		1.00
1	Ken Griffey Jr.	3.50
2	Joe Carter	1.00
3	Rafael Palmeiro	1.75
4	Jay Buhner	1.00
5	Sammy Sosa	3.00
6	Fred McGriff	1.00
7	Jeff Bagwell	2.00
8	Albert Belle	1.00
9	Matt Williams	1.00
10	Mark McGwire	4.00
11	Gary Sheffield	1.25
12	Tim Salmon	1.00
13	Ryan Klesko	1.00
14	Manny Ramirez	2.00
15	Mike Piazza	3.50
16	Barry Bonds	5.00
17	Mo Vaughn	1.00
18	Jose Canseco	1.25
19	Juan Gonzalez	1.25
20	Frank Thomas	2.00

Power Package Jumbos

Unlike the regular Power Package inserts found in Series 1 packs, these jumbo versions are not die-cut. The 5" x 7" jumbos are found one per retail foil box of Series 1. Cards are numbered with a "PP" prefix.

		NM/M
Complete Set (20):		30.00
Common Player:		1.00
1	Ken Griffey Jr.	3.50
2	Joe Carter	1.00
3	Rafael Palmeiro	1.75
4	Jay Buhner	1.00
5	Sammy Sosa	3.00
6	Fred McGriff	1.00
7	Jeff Bagwell	2.00
8	Albert Belle	1.00
9	Matt Williams	1.00
10	Mark McGwire	4.00
11	Gary Sheffield	1.25
12	Tim Salmon	1.00
13	Ryan Klesko	1.00
14	Manny Ramirez	2.00
15	Mike Piazza	3.50
16	Barry Bonds	5.00
17	Mo Vaughn	1.00
18	Jose Canseco	1.25
19	Juan Gonzalez	1.25
20	Frank Thomas	2.00

Predictor

A new concept in interactive cards was UD's Series II Predictor inserts. Each player's card has four scratch-off baseball bats at the top-right. Under each bat is printed a specific accomplishment - hit for cycle, CG shutout, etc. - If the player attained that goal during the '97 season, and if the collector had scratched off the correct bat among the four, the Predictor card could be redeemed (with $2) for a premium TV cel card of the player. Thus if the player made one of his goals, the collector had a 25 percent chance of choosing the right bat. Two goals gave a 50 percent chance, etc. The Predictor cards have color action photos of the players at the left end of the horizontal format. The background at left and bottom is a red scorecard motif. Behind the bats is a black-and-white stadium scene. Backs repeat the red scorecard design with contest rules printed in white. A (W) in the checklist here indicates the player won one or more of his goals making his cards eligible for redemption. The redemption period ended Nov. 22, 1997. Values shown are for unscratched cards.

		NM/M
Complete Set (30):		15.00
Common Player:		.10
Values for unscratched cards.		
1	Andruw Jones	.40
2	Chipper Jones	.50
3	Greg Maddux/W	1.00
4	Fred McGriff/W	.25
5	John Smoltz/W	.25
6	Brady Anderson/W	.25
7	Cal Ripken Jr./W	2.00
8	Mo Vaughn/W	.25
9	Sammy Sosa	.50
10	Albert Belle/W	.25
11	Frank Thomas	.40
12	Kenny Lofton/W	.25
13	Jim Thome	.30
14	Dante Bichette/W	.25
15	Andres Galarraga	.10
16	Gary Sheffield	.25
17	Hideo Nomo/W	.40
18	Mike Piazza/W	1.25
19	Derek Jeter/W	2.00
20	Bernie Williams	.10
21	Mark McGwire/W	1.50
22	Ken Caminiti/W	.25
23	Tony Gwynn/W	1.00
24	Barry Bonds/W	2.00
25	Jay Buhner/W	.25
26	Ken Griffey Jr./W	1.25
27	Alex Rodriguez/W	1.50
28	Juan Gonzalez/W	.40
29	Dean Palmer/W	.25
30	Roger Clemens/W	1.00

Predictor Prize Cards

Persons who redeemed winning Predictor scratch-off cards prior to the Nov. 22, 1997 deadline received a premium version of that player's card. A $2 per card handling fee was charged. The Predictor prize cards are in a format similar to the scratch-off cards, with a red background on front and back depicting the motif of a baseball score card. The prize cards are printed on plastic in 3-1/2" x 2-1/2" format. Fronts have a player portrait photo at left. At right is a large semi-circular mirrored window with an action photo visible when held to the light. Backs have a few stats, copyright data, logos, etc., with a reverse image in the window. Card fronts were covered with a sheet of peel-off protection plastic. The prize cards are numbered on back with a "P" prefix.

		NM/M
Complete Set (22):		35.00
Common Player:		.60
3	Greg Maddux	2.50
4	Fred McGriff	.60
5	John Smoltz	.60
6	Brady Anderson	.60
7	Cal Ripken Jr.	5.00
8	Mo Vaughn	.60
11	Frank Thomas	1.75
12	Kenny Lofton	.60
14	Dante Bichette	.60
17	Hideo Nomo	1.00
18	Mike Piazza	3.00
19	Derek Jeter	5.00
21	Mark McGwire	4.00
22	Ken Caminiti	.60
23	Tony Gwynn	2.50
24	Barry Bonds	5.00
25	Jay Buhner	.60
26	Ken Griffey Jr.	3.00
27	Alex Rodriguez	4.00
28	Juan Gonzalez	1.00
29	Dean Palmer	.60
30	Roger Clemens	2.75

Rock Solid Foundation

The 20-card, regular-sized set was inserted every seven packs of 1997 Upper Deck baseball. The card fronts feature rainbow foil with the player's name in silver foil along the top border. The team logo appears in gold foil in the lower right corner with "Rock Solid Foundation" also printed in gold foil over a marbled background. The card backs have the same marbled background with a close-up shot on the

upper half. A short text is also included and the cards are numbered with the "RS" prefix.

		NM/M
Complete Set (20):		7.50
Common Player:		.15
1	Alex Rodriguez	1.50
2	Rey Ordonez	.15
3	Derek Jeter	2.00
4	Darin Erstad	.35
5	Chipper Jones	1.25
6	Johnny Damon	.35
7	Ryan Klesko	.15
8	Charles Johnson	.15
9	Andy Pettitte	.30
10	Manny Ramirez	.75
11	Ivan Rodriguez	.65
12	Jason Kendall	.15
13	Rondell White	.15
14	Alex Ochoa	.15
15	Javy Lopez	.15
16	Pedro Martinez	.75
17	Carlos Delgado	.50
18	Paul Wilson	.15
19	Alan Benes	.15
20	Raul Mondesi	.15

Run Producers

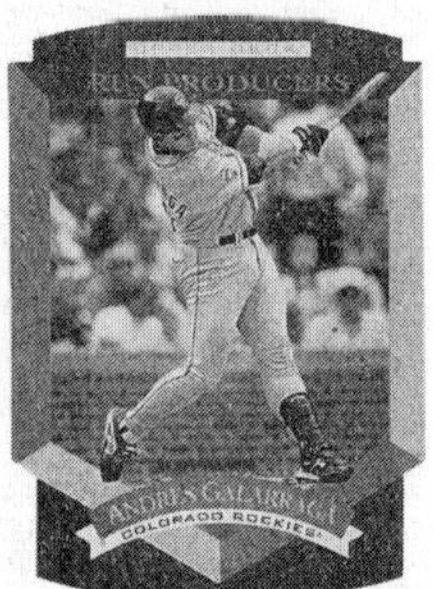

A 24-card insert found in Series II, Run Producers salutes the top offensive players in the game. Cards were inserted 1:69 packs. Die-cut into a shield shape, the cards have an action photo in a home-plate shaped center section and several colors of foil highlights. Backs have recent stats and career highlights. Cards are numbered with a "RP" prefix.

		NM/M
Complete Set (24):		45.00
Common Player:		.50
1	Ken Griffey Jr.	5.00
2	Barry Bonds	7.50
3	Albert Belle	.50
4	Mark McGwire	6.00
5	Frank Thomas	3.00
6	Juan Gonzalez	1.50
7	Brady Anderson	.50
8	Andres Galarraga	.50
9	Rafael Palmeiro	2.50
10	Alex Rodriguez	6.00
11	Jay Buhner	.50
12	Gary Sheffield	1.50
13	Sammy Sosa	4.00
14	Dante Bichette	.50
15	Mike Piazza	5.00
16	Manny Ramirez	3.00
17	Kenny Lofton	.50
18	Mo Vaughn	.50
19	Tim Salmon	.50
20	Chipper Jones	4.00
21	Jim Thome	2.00
22	Ken Caminiti	.50
23	Jeff Bagwell	3.00
24	Paul Molitor	3.00

Star Attractions

These die-cut cards were inserted one per pack of retail "Memorabila Madness" Collector's Choice (#11-20) and

Upper Deck (#1-10) cards. Fronts have action photos, backs have portrait photos. A gold version of the inserts was exclusive to retail packaging.

		NM/M
Complete Set (20):		30.00
Common Player:		.30
Gold:		1.5X
1	Ken Griffey Jr.	3.00
2	Barry Bonds	5.00
3	Jeff Bagwell	2.00
4	Nomar Garciaparra	2.50
5	Tony Gwynn	2.50
6	Roger Clemens	2.75
7	Chipper Jones	2.50
8	Tino Martinez	.30
9	Albert Belle	.30
10	Kenny Lofton	.30
11	Alex Rodriguez	4.00
12	Mark McGwire	4.00
13	Cal Ripken Jr.	5.00
14	Larry Walker	.30
15	Mike Piazza	3.00
16	Frank Thomas	2.00
17	Juan Gonzalez	.65
18	Greg Maddux	2.50
19	Jose Cruz Jr.	.30
20	Mo Vaughn	.30

Ticket to Stardom

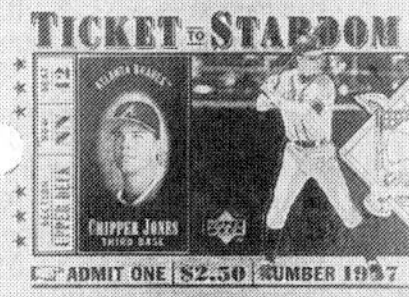

The 20-card, regular-sized, die-cut set was inserted every 34 packs of 1997 Upper Deck baseball. Card fronts have a gold-foil border on three sides with a portrait and action photo. Half of the player's league emblem appears on either the left or right border of the horizontal cards, as two cards can be placed together to form a "ticket." The card backs feature an in-depth text with the same headshot as the card front and are numbered with the "TS" prefix.

		NM/M
Complete Set (20):		35.00
Common Player:		.75
1	Chipper Jones	5.00
2	Jermaine Dye	.75
3	Rey Ordonez	.75
4	Alex Ochoa	.75
5	Derek Jeter	7.50
6	Ruben Rivera	.75
7	Billy Wagner	.75
8	Jason Kendall	.75
9	Darin Erstad	1.00
10	Alex Rodriguez	6.00
11	Bob Abreu	.75
12	Richard Hidalgo	.75
13	Karim Garcia	1.00
14	Andruw Jones	4.00
15	Carlos Delgado	1.50
16	Rocky Coppinger	.75
17	Jeff D'Amico	.75
18	Johnny Damon	2.00
19	John Wasdin	.75
20	Manny Ramirez	4.00

Ticket to Stardom Retail

Double-size "full ticket" versions of Upper Deck's Series 1 Ticket to Stardom inserts were produced as an incentive for collectors to buy a boxed three-pack of Collector's Choice cards in a special retail-only packaging. Unlike the insert Ticket cards which feature only one player and measure 3-1/2" x 2-1/2", the retail version measures 5" x 2-1/2" and features two players. The basic format of the retail cards follows the inserts, with gold-foil background, a vignetted player portrait at one end with an action photo toward center and a league logo at center. Arrangement of graphics on the retail ticket prevent unscrupulous persons from cutting them in half and passing them off as the more valuable insert cards. Backs repeat the player portrait photo and present a career summary. Cards are numbered in the upper-left corner. Seven players were dropped from the original Ticket checklist and replaced in the retail issue with new faces. Cards are numbered with a "TS" prefix.

		NM/M
Complete Set (10):		24.00
Common Player:		1.50
1	Chipper Jones, Andruw Jones	4.00
2	Rey Ordonez, Kevin Orie	1.50
3	Derek Jeter, Nomar Garciaparra	6.00
4	Billy Wagner, Jason Kendall	1.50
5	Darin Erstad, Alex Rodriguez	5.00
6	Bob Abreu, Jose Guillen	1.50
7	Wilton Guerrero, Vladimir Guerrero	3.00
8	Carlos Delgado, Rocky Coppinger	2.00
9	Jason Dickson, Johnny Damon	2.00
10	Bartolo Colon, Manny Ramirez	3.00

Ken Griffey Jr. Highlight Reel

Using its trademarked Diamond Vision technology to provide action scenes on these 5" x 3-1/2" plastic cards. Each card has two scenes which go into action as the angle of vision is changed. Cards were sold in retail outlets in plastic blister packs at a suggested $9.99 price.

		NM/M
Complete Set (5):		12.50
Common Card:		3.00
1	Record Setter (Ken Griffey Jr.)	3.00
2	Long Distance Connection (Ken Griffey Jr.)	3.00
3	Home Run Derby (Ken Griffey Jr.)	3.00
4	Swing for the Ages (Ken Griffey Jr.)	3.00
5	Postseason Power (Ken Griffey Jr.)	3.00

Tony Gwynn Commemorative

Tony Gwynn's record-tying eighth batting title in 1997 is commemorated on this 3-1/2" x 4-7/8" card marketed by UD Authenticated. The card has a batting pose on front with a die-cut background of bats citing the year and average of each of his batting titles. The back has three color photos and is numbered within an edition of 2,500.

	NM/M
Tony Gwynn	7.50

Home Team Heroes

These large-format cards were issued both as a 12-card boxed set (original price about $20) and as a blister-pack insert to enhance the sales of special Collector's Choice team sets at Wal-Mart. Each $4.99 pack contains a 14-card team set and a Home Team Heroes card of one of 12 teams, plus a random assortment of Collector's Choice cards. The Heroes cards are 5" x 3-1/2" with a die-cut pattern at top. Fronts are rendered in team colors with two player action photos superimposed on a background of the players' home ballpark. The ballpark scene is executed in etched silver foil and there are silver-foil graphics around the card front. Backs are conventionally printed with small photos and a few sentences about each player.

		NM/M
Complete Set (12):		10.00
Common Player:		.50
1	Alex Rodriguez, Ken Griffey Jr.	2.00
2	Bernie Williams, Derek Jeter	2.50
3	Bernard Gilkey, Randy Hundley	.50
4	Hideo Nomo, Mike Piazza	1.50
5	Andruw Jones, Chipper Jones	1.00
6	John Smoltz, Greg Maddux	1.00
7	Mike Mussina, Cal Ripken Jr.	2.50
8	Andres Galarraga, Dante Bichette	.50
9	Juan Gonzalez, Ivan Rodriguez	.65
10	Albert Belle, Frank Thomas	.75
11	Jim Thome, Manny Ramirez	.75
12	Ken Caminiti, Tony Gwynn	1.00

Jackie Robinson Jumbos

The nine Jackie Robinson commemorative cards which lead off the '97 Upper Deck set were also issued in a large-format (3-1/2" x 5") version as a complete boxed set. The jumbos are printed in sepia tones on gold-foil backgrounds and, like the standard-size cards, are highlighted with silver-foil graphics on front. Backs are also identical to the regular cards. Complete sets only were sold in a gold-foil stamped box with the 50th anniversary logo.

		NM/M
Complete Set (10):		13.50
Common Player:		2.00
1	The Beginnings (Jackie Robinson)	2.00
2	Breaking the Barrier (Jackie Robinson)	2.00
3	The MVP Season (Jackie Robinson)	2.00
4	The '51 Season (Jackie Robinson)	2.00
5	The '52 and '53 Seasons (Jackie Robinson)	2.00
6	The '54 Season (Jackie Robinson)	2.00
7	The '55 Season (Jackie Robinson)	2.00
8	The '56 Season (Jackie Robinson)	2.00
9	The Hall of Fame (Jackie Robinson)	2.00
--	Checklist	.10

Jackie Robinson Tribute

This retail exclusive card commemorates the 50th anniversary of Robinson's major league debut. The 5" x 3-1/2" card has a tombstone contour top edge and a sepia photo on front of Robinson at bat. Also on front are 50th anniversary and UD logos and a large gold-foil facsimile autograph. Back has a photo of Robinson sliding into home plate, his career stats and a serial number from within an edition of 5,000.

	NM/M
Jackie Robinson	3.50

1997 Upper Deck UD3

Released in April, this 60-card set is broken down into three different 20-card subsets, each utilizing a different print technology. There are 20 PROmotion cards (Light F/X cards featuring a special foil stock), 20 Future Impact cards (Cel-Chrome cards that feature a 3-D image on transparent chromium), and 20 Homerun Heroes (Electric Wood cards printed on an embossed wood/paper stock). Cards were sold in three-card packs (with one subset card per pack) for $3.99 each. Inserts include Superb Signatures, Generation Next and Marquee Attraction.

		NM/M
Complete Set (60):		30.00
Common Player:		.15
Pack (3):		1.50
Wax Box (24):		30.00
1	Mark McGwire	2.50
2	Brady Anderson	.15
3	Ken Griffey Jr.	2.00
4	Albert Belle	.15
5	Andres Galarraga	.15
6	Juan Gonzalez	.40
7	Jay Buhner	.15
8	Mo Vaughn	.15
9	Barry Bonds	3.00
10	Gary Sheffield	.40
11	Todd Hundley	.15
12	Ellis Burks	.15
13	Ken Caminiti	.15
14	Vinny Castilla	.15
15	Sammy Sosa	1.50
16	Frank Thomas	.75
17	Rafael Palmeiro	.65
18	Mike Piazza	2.00
19	Matt Williams	.15
20	Eddie Murray	.75
21	Roger Clemens	1.75
22	Tim Salmon	.15
23	Robin Ventura	.15
24	Ron Gant	.15
25	Cal Ripken Jr.	3.00
26	Bernie Williams	.15
27	Hideo Nomo	.40
28	Ivan Rodriguez	.65
29	John Smoltz	.15
30	Paul Molitor	.75
31	Greg Maddux	1.50
32	Raul Mondesi	.15
33	Roberto Alomar	.25
34	Barry Larkin	.15
35	Tony Gwynn	1.50
36	Jim Thome	.60
37	Kenny Lofton	.15
38	Jeff Bagwell	.75
39	Ozzie Smith	1.50
40	Kirby Puckett	1.50
41	Andruw Jones	.75
42	Vladimir Guerrero	.75
43	Edgar Renteria	.15
44	Luis Castillo	.15
45	Darin Erstad	.30
46	Nomar Garciaparra	1.50
47	Todd Greene	.15
48	Jason Kendall	.15
49	Rey Ordonez	.15
50	Alex Rodriguez	2.50
51	Manny Ramirez	.75
52	Todd Walker	.15
53	Ruben Rivera	.15
54	Andy Pettitte	.30
55	Derek Jeter	3.00
56	Todd Hollandsworth	.15
57	Rocky Coppinger	.15
58	Scott Rolen	.60
59	Jermaine Dye	.15
60	Chipper Jones	1.50

Generation Next

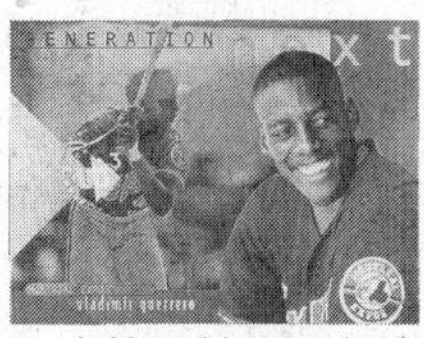

A 20-card insert saluting the game's up-and-coming stars with two different photos of the player on each card front. Odds of finding these cards were 1:11 packs. Cards are numbered with a "GN" prefix.

		NM/M
Complete Set (20):		35.00
Common Player:		1.00
1	Alex Rodriguez	5.00
2	Vladimir Guerrero	2.50
3	Luis Castillo	1.00
4	Rey Ordonez	1.00
5	Andruw Jones	2.50
6	Darin Erstad	1.25
7	Edgar Renteria	1.00
8	Jason Kendall	1.00
9	Jermaine Dye	1.00
10	Chipper Jones	3.00
11	Rocky Coppinger	1.00
12	Andy Pettitte	1.25
13	Todd Greene	1.00
14	Todd Hollandsworth	1.00
15	Derek Jeter	6.00
16	Ruben Rivera	1.00
17	Todd Walker	1.00
18	Nomar Garciaparra	3.00
19	Scott Rolen	2.00
20	Manny Ramirez	2.50

Marquee Attraction

The game's top names are featured in this insert set, inserted 1:144 packs. Cards featured a peel-off protector that would expose a holographic image on the card fronts. Cards are numbered with a "MA" prefix.

		NM/M
Complete Set (10):		40.00
Common Player:		1.25
1	Ken Griffey Jr.	6.00
2	Mark McGwire	7.50
3	Juan Gonzalez	1.75
4	Barry Bonds	9.00
5	Frank Thomas	2.50
6	Albert Belle	1.25
7	Mike Piazza	6.00
8	Cal Ripken Jr.	9.00
9	Mo Vaughn	1.25
10	Alex Rodriguez	7.50

Superb Signatures

Autographed cards of Ken Griffey Jr., Ken Caminiti, Vladimir Guerrero, and Derek Jeter were inserted 1:1,500 packs.

		NM/M
Complete Set (4):		450.00
Common Autograph:		15.00
1	Ken Caminiti	45.00
2	Ken Griffey Jr.	150.00
3	Vladimir Guerrero	50.00
4	Derek Jeter	225.00

Pepsi Mariners Insert

Though unmarked as such, this set was sponsored by Pepsi with single cards inserted into 12-packs of soda in the Northwest. Format of the cards is similar to UD's regular 1996 issue, with borderless color photos on front and back. At bottom-front is a Mariners-blue foil area with the player identification. Backs differ from the regular '96 UD cards in the use of a "M" prefix to the card number.

		NM/M
Complete Set (19):		12.00
Common Player:		.25
1	Joey Cora	.25
2	Ken Griffey Jr.	5.00
3	Jay Buhner	.50
4	Alex Rodriguez	6.00
5	Norm Charlton	.25
6	Edgar Martinez	.50
7	Paul Sorrento	.25
8	Randy Johnson	2.00
9	Rich Amaral	.25
10	Russ Davis	.25
11	Bob Wolcott	.25
12	Jamie Moyer	.25
13	Bob Wells	.25
14	Makoto Suzuki	.25
15	Dan Wilson	.25
16	Tim Davis	.25
17	Bobby Ayala	.25
18	Salomon Torres	.25
19	Raul Ibanez	.25

Pepsi Mariners SGA

This team set, sponsored by Pepsi, was a stadium give-away to the first 20,000 fans

attending the July 12 game at the Kingdome. Format of the cards is similar to UD's regular 1996 issue, with borderless color photos on front and back. At bottom-front is a Mariners-blue foil area with the player identification. Backs differ from the regular '96 UD cards in the use of a "P" prefix to the card number and the inclusion of a Pepsi logo at lower-left.

		NM/M
Complete Set (21):		12.00
Common Player:		.25
1	Joey Cora	.25
2	Ken Griffey Jr.	5.00
3	Jay Buhner	.50
4	Alex Rodriguez	6.00
5	Norm Charlton	.25
6	Edgar Martinez	.50
7	Paul Sorrento	.25
8	Randy Johnson	2.00
9	Rich Amaral	.25
10	Russ Davis	.25
11	Greg McCarthy	.25
12	Jamie Moyer	.25
13	Jeff Fassero	.25
14	Scott Sanders	.25
15	Dan Wilson	.25
16	Mike Blowers	.25
17	Bobby Ayala	.25
18	Brent Gates	.25
19	John Marzano	.25
20	Lou Piniella	.25
---	Pepsi header card/ coupon	.05

Shimano

Tony Gwynn

Two ballplayers are included with four professional fishermen in this set produced by Upper Deck as a premium with the purchase of Shimano fishing reels. Fronts have pictures of the fishermen displaying their trophy. Backs have a portrait photo, baseball and fishing stats and data.

		NM/M
5	Jay Buhner	3.00
6	Tony Gwynn	30.00

1998 Upper Deck

Upper Deck Baseball was released in three series. Series 1 consists of 270 base cards, with five subsets. Inserts included A Piece of the Action, Amazing Greats, National Pride, Ken Griffey Jr.'s Home Run Chronicles and 10th Anniversary Preview. The 270-card Series 2 also has five subsets. Inserts include Prime Nine, Ken Griffey Jr.'s Home Run Chronicles, Tape Measure Titans, Blue Chip Prospects,

Clearly Dominant and A Piece of the Action. The third series, Upper Deck Rookie Edition, has a 210-card base set. Cards #601-630, the Eminent Prestige subset, are short-printed, about one per four packs. Mike Piazza's card in Series 3 can be found depicting him either as a Marlin or a Met. Insert sets were Ken Griffey Jr. Game Jersey, Game Jersey Rookie Cards, Unparalleled, Destination Stardom, All-Star Credentials and Retrospectives.

	NM/M
Complete Set (750):	100.00
Complete Series 1 Set (270):	25.00
Complete Series 2 Set (270):	25.00
Complete Series 3 Set (210):	75.00
Common Emminent Prestige (601-630):	.25
Common Player:	.05
Series 1 or 2 Pack (12):	1.50
Series 3 Pack (10):	1.50
Series 1 or 2 Wax Box (24):	35.00
Series 3 Wax Box (24):	35.00

1 Tino Martinez (History in the Making) .05
2 Jimmy Key (History in the Making) .05
3 Jay Buhner (History in the Making) .05
4 Mark Gardner (History in the Making) .05
5 Greg Maddux (History in the Making) .25
6 Pedro Martinez (History in the Making) .20
7 Hideo Nomo, Shigetosi Hasegawa (History in the Making) .25
8 Sammy Sosa (History in the Making) .35
9 Mark McGwire (Griffey Hot List) .50
10 Ken Griffey Jr. (Griffey Hot List) .45
11 Larry Walker (Griffey Hot List) .05
12 Tino Martinez (Griffey Hot List) .05
13 Mike Piazza (Griffey Hot List) .40
14 Jose Cruz, Jr. (Griffey Hot List) .05
15 Tony Gwynn (Griffey Hot List) .25
16 Greg Maddux (Griffey Hot List) .25
17 Roger Clemens (Griffey Hot List) .35
18 Alex Rodriguez (Griffey Hot List) .50
19 Shigetosi Hasegawa .05
20 Eddie Murray .50
21 Jason Dickson .05
22 Darin Erstad .25
23 Chuck Finley .05
24 Dave Hollins .05
25 Garret Anderson .05
26 Michael Tucker .05
27 Kenny Lofton .05
28 Javier Lopez .05
29 Fred McGriff .05
30 Greg Maddux .65
31 Jeff Blauser .05
32 John Smoltz .05
33 Mark Wohlers .05
34 Scott Erickson .05
35 Jimmy Key .05
36 Harold Baines .05
37 Randy Myers .05
38 B.J. Surhoff .05
39 Eric Davis .05
40 Rafael Palmeiro .35
41 Jeffrey Hammonds .05
42 Mo Vaughn .05
43 Tom Gordon .05
44 Tim Naehring .05
45 Darren Bragg .05
46 Aaron Sele .05
47 Troy O'Leary .05
48 John Valentin .05
49 Doug Glanville .05
50 Ryne Sandberg .65
51 Steve Trachsel .05
52 Mark Grace .05
53 Kevin Foster .05
54 Kevin Tapani .05
55 Kevin Orie .05
56 Lyle Mouton .05
57 Ray Durham .05
58 Jaime Navarro .05
59 Mike Cameron .05
60 Albert Belle .05
61 Doug Drabek .05
62 Chris Snopek .05
63 Eddie Taubensee .05
64 Terry Pendleton .05
65 Barry Larkin .05
66 Willie Greene .05
67 Deion Sanders .05
68 Pokey Reese .05
69 Jeff Shaw .05
70 Jim Thome .35
71 Orel Hershiser .05
72 Omar Vizquel .05
73 Brian Giles .05
74 David Justice .05
75 Bartolo Colon .05
76 Sandy Alomar Jr. .05
77 Neifi Perez .05
78 Eric Young .05
79 Vinny Castilla .05
80 Dante Bichette .05
81 Quinton McCracken .05
82 Jamey Wright .05
83 John Thomson .05
84 Damion Easley .05
85 Justin Thompson .05
86 Willie Blair .05
87 Raul Casanova .05
88 Bobby Higginson .05
89 Bubba Trammell .05
90 Tony Clark .05
91 Livan Hernandez .05
92 Charles Johnson .05
93 Edgar Renteria .05
94 Alex Fernandez .05
95 Gary Sheffield .30
96 Moises Alou .05
97 Tony Saunders .05
98 Robb Nen .05
99 Darryl Kile .05
100 Craig Biggio .05
101 Chris Holt .05
102 Bob Abreu .10
103 Luis Gonzalez .05
104 Billy Wagner .05
105 Brad Ausmus .05
106 Chili Davis .05
107 Tim Belcher .05
108 Dean Palmer .05
109 Jeff King .05
110 Jose Rosado .05
111 Mike Macfarlane .05
112 Jay Bell .05
113 Todd Worrell .05
114 Chan Ho Park .05
115 Raul Mondesi .05
116 Brett Butler .05
117 Greg Gagne .05
118 Hideo Nomo .25
119 Todd Zeile .05
120 Eric Karros .05
121 Cal Eldred .05
122 Jeff D'Amico .05
123 Antone Williamson .05
124 Doug Jones .05
125 Dave Nilsson .05
126 Gerald Williams .05
127 Fernando Vina .05
128 Ron Coomer .05
129 Matt Lawton .05
130 Paul Molitor .50
131 Todd Walker .05
132 Rick Aguilera .05
133 Brad Radke .05
134 Bob Tewksbury .05
135 Vladimir Guerrero .50
136 Tony Gwynn (Define The Game) .25
137 Roger Clemens (Define The Game) .35
138 Dennis Eckersley (Define The Game) .15
139 Brady Anderson (Define The Game) .05
140 Ken Griffey Jr. (Define The Game) .40
141 Derek Jeter (Define The Game) .75
142 Ken Caminiti (Define The Game) .05
143 Frank Thomas (Define The Game) .20
144 Barry Bonds (Define The Game) .75
145 Cal Ripken Jr. (Define The Game) .75
146 Alex Rodriguez (Define The Game) .50
147 Greg Maddux (Define The Game) .25
148 Kenny Lofton (Define The Game) .05
149 Mike Piazza (Define The Game) .40
150 Mark McGwire (Define The Game) .50
151 Andruw Jones (Define The Game) .20
152 Rusty Greer (Define The Game) .05
153 F.P. Santangelo (Define The Game) .05
154 Mike Lansing .05
155 Lee Smith .05
156 Carlos Perez .05
157 Pedro Martinez .50
158 Ryan McGuire .05
159 F.P. Santangelo .05
160 Rondell White .05
161 Takashi Kashiwada **RC** .05
162 Butch Huskey .05
163 Edgardo Alfonzo .05
164 John Franco .05
165 Todd Hundley .05
166 Rey Ordonez .05
167 Armando Reynoso .05
168 John Olerud .05
169 Bernie Williams .05
170 Andy Pettitte .15
171 Wade Boggs .65
172 Paul O'Neill .05
173 Cecil Fielder .05
174 Charlie Hayes .05
175 David Cone .05
176 Hideki Irabu .05
177 Mark Bellhorn .05
178 Steve Karsay .05
179 Damon Mashore .05
180 Jason McDonald .05
181 Scott Spiezio .05
182 Ariel Prieto .05
183 Jason Giambi .30
184 Wendell Magee .05
185 Rico Brogna .05
186 Garrett Stephenson .05
187 Wayne Gomes .05
188 Ricky Bottalico .05
189 Mickey Morandini .05
190 Mike Lieberthal .05
191 Kevin Polcovich **RC** .05
192 Francisco Cordova .05
193 Kevin Young .05
194 Jon Lieber .05
195 Kevin Elster .05
196 Tony Womack .05
197 Lou Collier .05
198 Mike Defelice **RC** .05
199 Gary Gaetti .05
200 Dennis Eckersley .40
201 Alan Benes .05
202 Willie McGee .05
203 Ron Gant .05
204 Fernando Valenzuela .05
205 Mark McGwire 1.00
206 Archi Cianfrocco .05
207 Andy Ashby .05
208 Steve Finley .05
209 Quilvio Veras .05
210 Ken Caminiti .05
211 Rickey Henderson .50
212 Joey Hamilton .05
213 Derrek Lee .30
214 Bill Mueller .05
215 Shawn Estes .05
216 J.T. Snow .05
217 Mark Gardner .05
218 Terry Mulholland .05
219 Dante Powell .05
220 Jeff Kent .05
221 Jamie Moyer .05
222 Joey Cora .05
223 Jeff Fassero .05
224 Dennis Martinez .05
225 Ken Griffey Jr. .75
226 Edgar Martinez .05
227 Russ Davis .05
228 Dan Wilson .05
229 Will Clark .05
230 Ivan Rodriguez .40
231 Benji Gil .05
232 Lee Stevens .05
233 Mickey Tettleton .05
234 Julio Santana .05
235 Rusty Greer .05
236 Bobby Witt .05
237 Ed Sprague .05
238 Pat Hentgen .05
239 Kevin Escobar .05
240 Joe Carter .05
241 Carlos Delgado .25
242 Shannon Stewart .05
243 Benito Santiago .05
244 Tino Martinez (Season Highlights) .05
245 Ken Griffey Jr. (Season Highlights) .40
246 Kevin Brown (Season Highlights) .05
247 Ryne Sandberg (Season Highlights) .35
248 Mo Vaughn (Season Highlights) .05
249 Darryl Hamilton (Season Highlights) .05
250 Randy Johnson (Season Highlights) .20
251 Steve Finley (Season Highlights) .05
252 Bobby Higginson (Season Highlights) .05
253 Brett Tomko/SR .05
254 Mark Kotsay/SR .05
255 Jose Guillen/SR .05
256 Elieser Marrero/SR .05
257 Dennis Reyes/SR .05
258 Richie Sexson/SR .05
259 Pat Cline/SR .05
260 Todd Helton/SR .50
261 Juan Melo/SR .05
262 Matt Morris/SR .05
263 Jeremi Gonzalez/SR .05
264 Jeff Abbott/SR .05
265 Aaron Boone/SR .05
266 Todd Dunwoody/SR .05
267 Jaret Wright/SR .05
268 Derrick Gibson/SR .05
269 Mario Valdez/SR .05
270 Fernando Tatis/SR .05
271 Craig Counsell/SR .05
272 Brad Rigby/SR .05
273 Danny Clyburn/SR .05
274 Brian Rose/SR .05
275 Miguel Tejada/SR .15
276 Jason Varitek/SR .05
277 David Dellucci/SR **RC** .15
278 Michael Coleman/SR .05
279 Adam Riggs/SR .05
280 Ben Grieve/SR .05
281 Brad Fullmer/SR .05
282 Ken Cloude/SR .05
283 Tom Evans/SR .05
284 Kevin Millwood/SR **RC** .75
285 Paul Konerko/SR .15
286 Juan Encarnacion/SR .05
287 Chris Carpenter/SR .05
288 Tom Fordham/SR .05
289 Gary DiSarcina .05
290 Tim Salmon .05
291 Troy Percival .05
292 Todd Greene .05
293 Ken Hill .05
294 Dennis Springer .05
295 Jim Edmonds .05
296 Allen Watson .05
297 Brian Anderson .05
298 Keith Lockhart .05
299 Tom Glavine .20
300 Chipper Jones .65
301 Randall Simon .05
302 Mark Lemke .05
303 Ryan Klesko .05
304 Denny Neagle .05
305 Andruw Jones .50
306 Mike Mussina .30
307 Brady Anderson .05
308 Chris Hoiles .05
309 Mike Bordick .05
310 Cal Ripken Jr. 1.50
311 Geronimo Berroa .05
312 Armando Benitez .05
313 Roberto Alomar .25
314 Tim Wakefield .05
315 Reggie Jefferson .05
316 Jeff Frye .05
317 Scott Hatteberg .05
318 Steve Avery .05
319 Robinson Checo .05
320 Nomar Garciaparra .65
321 Lance Johnson .05
322 Tyler Houston .05
323 Mark Clark .05
324 Terry Adams .05
325 Sammy Sosa .65
326 Scott Servais .05
327 Manny Alexander .05
328 Norberto Martin .05
329 Scott Eyre **RC** .05
330 Frank Thomas .50
331 Robin Ventura .05
332 Matt Karchner .05
333 Keith Foulke .05
334 James Baldwin .05
335 Chris Stynes .05
336 Bret Boone .05
337 Jon Nunnally .05
338 Dave Burba .05
339 Eduardo Perez .05
340 Reggie Sanders .05
341 Mike Remlinger .05
342 Pat Watkins .05
343 Chad Ogea .05
344 John Smiley .05
345 Kenny Lofton .05
346 Jose Mesa .05
347 Charles Nagy .05
348 Bruce Aven .05
349 Enrique Wilson .05
350 Manny Ramirez .50
351 Jerry DiPoto .05
352 Ellis Burks .05
353 Kirt Manwaring .05
354 Vinny Castilla .05
355 Larry Walker .05
356 Kevin Ritz .05
357 Pedro Astacio .05
358 Scott Sanders .05
359 Deivi Cruz .05
360 Brian L. Hunter .05
361 Pedro Martinez (History in the Making) .20
362 Tom Glavine (History in the Making) .05
363 Willie McGee (History in the Making) .05
364 J.T. Snow (History in the Making) .05
365 Rusty Greer (History in the Making) .05
366 Mike Grace (History in the Making) .05
367 Tony Clark (History in the Making) .05
368 Ben Grieve (History in the Making) .05
369 Gary Sheffield (History in the Making) .10
370 Joe Oliver .05
371 Todd Jones .05
372 Frank Catalanotto **RC** .10
373 Brian Moehler .05
374 Cliff Floyd .05
375 Bobby Bonilla .05
376 Al Leiter .05
377 Josh Booty .05
378 Darren Daulton .05
379 Jay Powell .05
380 Felix Heredia .05
381 Jim Eisenreich .05
382 Richard Hidalgo .05
383 Mike Hampton .05
384 Shane Reynolds .05
385 Jeff Bagwell .50
386 Derek Bell .05
387 Ricky Gutierrez .05
388 Bill Spiers .05
389 Jose Offerman .05
390 Johnny Damon .25
391 Jermaine Dye .05
392 Jeff Montgomery .05
393 Glendon Rusch .05
394 Mike Sweeney .05
395 Kevin Appier .05
396 Joe Vitiello .05
397 Ramon Martinez .05
398 Darren Dreifort .05
399 Wilton Guerrero .05
400 Mike Piazza .75
401 Eddie Murray .50
402 Ismael Valdes .05
403 Todd Hollandsworth .05
404 Mark Loretta .05
405 Jeromy Burnitz .05
406 Jeff Cirillo .05
407 Scott Karl .05
408 Mike Matheny .05
409 Jose Valentin .05
410 John Jaha .05
411 Terry Steinbach .05
412 Torii Hunter .05
413 Pat Meares .05
414 Marty Cordova .05
415 Jaret Wright (Postseason Headliners) .05
416 Mike Mussina (Postseason Headliners) .10
417 John Smoltz (Postseason Headliners) .05
418 Devon White (Postseason Headliners) .05
419 Denny Neagle (Postseason Headliners) .05
420 Livan Hernandez (Postseason Headliners) .05
421 Kevin Brown (Postseason Headliners) .05
422 Marquis Grissom (Postseason Headliners) .05
423 Mike Mussina (Postseason Headliners) .10
424 Eric Davis (Postseason Headliners) .05
425 Tony Fernandez (Postseason Headliners) .05
426 Moises Alou (Postseason Headliners) .05
427 Sandy Alomar Jr. (Postseason Headliners) .05
428 Gary Sheffield (Postseason Headliners) .10
429 Jaret Wright (Postseason Headliners) .05
430 Livan Hernandez (Postseason Headliners) .05
431 Chad Ogea (Postseason Headliners) .05
432 Edgar Renteria (Postseason Headliners) .05
433 LaTroy Hawkins .05
434 Rich Robertson .05
435 Chuck Knoblauch .05
436 Jose Vidro .05
437 Dustin Hermanson .05
438 Jim Bullinger .05
439 Orlando Cabrera/SR .10
440 Vladimir Guerrero .50
441 Ugueth Urbina .05
442 Brian McRae .05
443 Matt Franco .05
444 Bobby Jones .05
445 Bernard Gilkey .05
446 Dave Mlicki .05
447 Brian Bohanon .05
448 Mel Rojas .05
449 Tim Raines .05
450 Derek Jeter 1.50
451 Roger Clemens (Upper Echelon) .35
452 Nomar Garciaparra (Upper Echelon) .35
453 Mike Piazza (Upper Echelon) .40

No.	Player	Price
454	Mark McGwire (Upper Echelon)	.50
455	Ken Griffey Jr. (Upper Echelon)	.40
456	Larry Walker (Upper Echelon)	.05
457	Alex Rodriguez (Upper Echelon)	.50
458	Tony Gwynn (Upper Echelon)	.25
459	Frank Thomas (Upper Echelon)	.20
460	Tino Martinez	.05
461	Chad Curtis	.05
462	Ramiro Mendoza	.05
463	Joe Girardi	.05
464	David Wells	.05
465	Mariano Rivera	.15
466	Willie Adams	.05
467	George Williams	.05
468	Dave Telgheder	.05
469	Dave Magadan	.05
470	Matt Stairs	.05
471	Billy Taylor	.05
472	Jimmy Haynes	.05
473	Gregg Jefferies	.05
474	Midre Cummings	.05
475	Curt Schilling	.15
476	Mike Grace	.05
477	Mark Leiter	.05
478	Matt Beech	.05
479	Scott Rolen	.35
480	Jason Kendall	.05
481	Esteban Loaiza	.05
482	Jermaine Allensworth	.05
483	Mark Smith	.05
484	Jason Schmidt	.05
485	Jose Guillen	.05
486	Al Martin	.05
487	Delino DeShields	.05
488	Todd Stottlemyre	.05
489	Brian Jordan	.05
490	Ray Lankford	.05
491	Matt Morris	.05
492	Royce Clayton	.05
493	John Mabry	.05
494	Wally Joyner	.05
495	Trevor Hoffman	.05
496	Chris Gomez	.05
497	Sterling Hitchcock	.05
498	Pete Smith	.05
499	Greg Vaughn	.05
500	Tony Gwynn	.65
501	Will Cunnane	.05
502	Darryl Hamilton	.05
503	Brian Johnson	.05
504	Kirk Rueter	.05
505	Barry Bonds	1.50
506	Osvaldo Fernandez	.05
507	Stan Javier	.05
508	Julian Tavarez	.05
509	Rich Aurilia	.05
510	Alex Rodriguez	1.00
511	David Segui	.05
512	Rich Amaral	.05
513	Raul Ibanez	.05
514	Jay Buhner	.05
515	Randy Johnson	.50
516	Heathcliff Slocumb	.05
517	Tony Saunders	.05
518	Kevin Elster	.05
519	John Burkett	.05
520	Juan Gonzalez	.25
521	John Wetteland	.05
522	Domingo Cedeno	.05
523	Darren Oliver	.05
524	Roger Pavlik	.05
525	Jose Cruz Jr.	.05
526	Woody Williams	.05
527	Alex Gonzalez	.05
528	Robert Person	.05
529	Juan Guzman	.05
530	Roger Clemens	.70
531	Shawn Green	.20
532	Cordova, Ricon, Smith (Season Highlights)	.05
533	Nomar Garciaparra (Season Highlights)	.35
534	Roger Clemens (Season Highlights)	.35
535	Mark McGwire (Season Highlights)	.50
536	Larry Walker (Season Highlights)	.05
537	Mike Piazza (Season Highlights)	.40
538	Curt Schilling (Season Highlights)	.05
539	Tony Gwynn (Season Highlights)	.25
540	Ken Griffey Jr. (Season Highlights)	.40
541	Carl Pavano/SR	.05
542	Shane Monahan/SR	.05
543	Gabe Kapler/SR **RC**	.25
544	Eric Milton/SR	.05
545	Gary Matthews Jr/ SR **RC**	.05
546	Mike Kinkade/SR **RC**	.25
547	Ryan Christenson/ SR **RC**	.10
548	Corey Koskie/SR **RC**	.25
549	Norm Hutchins/SR	.05
550	Russell Branyan/SR	.05
551	Masato Yoshii/SR **RC**	.25
552	Jesus Sanchez/SR **RC**	.05
553	Anthony Sanders/SR	.05
554	Edwin Diaz/SR	.05
555	Gabe Alvarez/SR	.05
556	Carlos Lee/SR **RC**	.25
557	Mike Darr/SR	.05
558	Kerry Wood/SR	.20
559	Carlos Guillen/SR	.05
560	Sean Casey/SR	.15
561	Manny Aybar/SR **RC**	.05
562	Octavio Dotel/SR	.05
563	Jarrod Washburn/SR	.05
564	Mark L. Johnson/SR	.05
565	Ramon Hernandez/SR	.05
566	Rich Butler/SR **RC**	.05
567	Mike Caruso/SR	.05
568	Cliff Politte/SR	.05
569	Scott Elarton/SR	.05
570	Magglio Ordonez/ SR **RC**	1.50
571	Adam Butler/SR **RC**	.05
572	Marlon Anderson/SR	.05
573	Julio Ramirez/SR **RC**	.05
574	Darron Ingram/SR **RC**	.05
575	Bruce Chen/SR	.05
576	Steve Woodard/SR **RC**	.05
577	Hiram Bocachica/SR	.05
578	Kevin Witt/SR	.05
579	Javier Vazquez/SR	.10
580	Alex Gonzalez/SR	.05
581	Brian Powell/SR	.05
582	Wes Helms/SR	.05
583	Ron Wright/SR	.05
584	Rafael Medina/SR	.05
585	Daryle Ward/SR	.05
586	Geoff Jenkins/SR	.05
587	Preston Wilson/SR	.10
588	Jim Chamblee/SR **RC**	.05
589	Mike Lowell/SR **RC**\	.75
590	A.J. Hinch/SR	.05
591	Francisco Cordero/ SR **RC**	.10
592	Rolando Arrojo/SR **RC**	.25
593	Braden Looper/SR	.05
594	Sidney Ponson/SR	.05
595	Matt Clement/SR	.05
596	Carlton Loewer/SR	.05
597	Brian Meadows/SR	.05
598	Danny Klassen/SR	.05
599	Larry Sutton/SR	.05
600	Travis Lee/SR	.15
601	Randy Johnson (Eminent Prestige)	1.50
602	Greg Maddux (Eminent Prestige)	2.00
603	Roger Clemens (Eminent Prestige)	2.25
604	Jaret Wright (Eminent Prestige)	.25
605	Mike Piazza (Eminent Prestige)	2.50
606	Tino Martinez (Eminent Prestige)	.25
607	Frank Thomas (Eminent Prestige)	1.50
608	Mo Vaughn (Eminent Prestige)	.25
609	Todd Helton (Eminent Prestige)	1.00
610	Mark McGwire (Eminent Prestige)	3.00
611	Jeff Bagwell (Eminent Prestige)	1.50
612	Travis Lee (Eminent Prestige)	.40
613	Scott Rolen (Eminent Prestige)	1.00
614	Cal Ripken Jr. (Eminent Prestige)	4.00
615	Chipper Jones (Eminent Prestige)	2.00
616	Nomar Garciaparra (Eminent Prestige)	2.00
617	Alex Rodriguez (Eminent Prestige)	3.00
618	Derek Jeter (Eminent Prestige)	4.00
619	Tony Gwynn (Eminent Prestige)	2.00
620	Ken Griffey Jr. (Eminent Prestige)	2.50
621	Kenny Lofton (Eminent Prestige)	.25
622	Juan Gonzalez (Eminent Prestige)	.75
623	Jose Cruz Jr. (Eminent Prestige)	.25
624	Larry Walker (Eminent Prestige)	.25
625	Barry Bonds (Eminent Prestige)	4.00
626	Ben Grieve (Eminent Prestige)	.25
627	Andruw Jones (Eminent Prestige)	1.50
628	Vladimir Guerrero (Eminent Prestige)	1.50
629	Paul Konerko (Eminent Prestige)	.50
630	Paul Molitor (Eminent Prestige)	1.50
631	Cecil Fielder	.05
632	Jack McDowell	.05
633	Mike James	.05
634	Brian Anderson	.05
635	Jay Bell	.05
636	Devon White	.05
637	Andy Stankiewicz	.05
638	Tony Batista	.05
639	Omar Daal	.05
640	Matt Williams	.05
641	Brent Brede	.05
642	Jorge Fabregas	.05
643	Karim Garcia	.10
644	Felix Rodriguez	.05
645	Andy Benes	.05
646	Willie Blair	.05
647	Jeff Suppan	.05
648	Yamil Benitez	.05
649	Walt Weiss	.05
650	Andres Galarraga	.05
651	Doug Drabek	.05
652	Ozzie Guillen	.05
653	Joe Carter	.05
654	Dennis Eckersley	.40
655	Pedro Martinez	.50
656	Jim Leyritz	.05
657	Henry Rodriguez	.05
658	Rod Beck	.05
659	Mickey Morandini	.05
660	Jeff Blauser	.05
661	Ruben Sierra	.05
662	Mike Sirotka	.05
663	Pete Harnisch	.05
664	Damian Jackson	.05
665	Dmitri Young	.05
666	Steve Cooke	.05
667	Geronimo Berroa	.05
668	Shawon Dunston	.05
669	Mike Jackson	.05
670	Travis Fryman	.05
671	Dwight Gooden	.05
672	Paul Assenmacher	.05
673	Eric Plunk	.05
674	Mike Lansing	.05
675	Darryl Kile	.05
676	Luis Gonzalez	.05
677	Frank Castillo	.05
678	Joe Randa	.05
679	Bip Roberts	.05
680	Derrek Lee	.30
681a	Mike Piazza (Marlins)	2.00
681b	Mike Piazza (Mets)	1.00
682	Sean Berry	.05
683	Ramon Garcia	.05
684	Carl Everett	.05
685	Moises Alou	.05
686	Hal Morris	.05
687	Jeff Conine	.05
688	Gary Sheffield	.25
689	Jose Vizcaino	.05
690	Charles Johnson	.05
691	Bobby Bonilla	.05
692	Marquis Grissom	.05
693	Alex Ochoa	.05
694	Mike Morgan	.05
695	Orlando Merced	.05
696	David Ortiz	.30
697	Brent Gates	.05
698	Otis Nixon	.05
699	Trey Moore	.05
700	Derrick May	.05
701	Rich Becker	.05
702	Al Leiter	.05
703	Chili Davis	.05
704	Scott Brosius	.05
705	Chuck Knoblauch	.05
706	Kenny Rogers	.05
707	Mike Blowers	.05
708	Mike Fetters	.05
709	Tom Candiotti	.05
710	Rickey Henderson	.50
711	Bob Abreu	.05
712	Mark Lewis	.05
713	Doug Glanville	.05
714	Desi Relaford	.05
715	Kent Mercker	.05
716	J. Kevin Brown	.05
717	James Mouton	.05
718	Mark Langston	.05
719	Greg Myers	.05
720	Orel Hershiser	.05
721	Charlie Hayes	.05
722	Robb Nen	.05
723	Glenallen Hill	.05
724	Tony Saunders	.05
725	Wade Boggs	.65
726	Kevin Stocker	.05
727	Wilson Alvarez	.05
728	Albie Lopez	.05
729	Dave Martinez	.05
730	Fred McGriff	.05
731	Quinton McCracken	.05
732	Bryan Rekar	.05
733	Paul Sorrento	.05
734	Roberto Hernandez	.05
735	Bubba Trammell	.05
736	Miguel Cairo	.05
737	John Flaherty	.05
738	Terrell Wade	.05
739	Roberto Kelly	.05
740	Mark Mclemore (McLemore)	.05
741	Danny Patterson	.05
742	Aaron Sele	.05
743	Tony Fernandez	.05
744	Randy Myers	.05
745	Jose Canseco	.30
746	Darrin Fletcher	.05
747	Mike Stanley	.05
748	Marquis Grissom (Season Highlights)	.05
749	Fred McGriff (Season Highlights)	.05
750	Travis Lee (Season Highlights)	.05

Amazing Greats

The 30-card Amazing Greats insert is printed on acetate. The cards are labeled "One of 2,000." A die-cut parallel was sequentially numbered to 250. Amazing Greats was an insert in Upper Deck Series One packs. Cards carry an "AG" prefix.

		NM/M
Complete Set (30):		75.00
Common Player:		.60
Die-Cuts (250):		8X
1	Ken Griffey Jr.	5.00
2	Derek Jeter	7.50
3	Alex Rodriguez	6.00
4	Paul Molitor	3.00
5	Jeff Bagwell	3.00
6	Larry Walker	.60
7	Kenny Lofton	.60
8	Cal Ripken Jr.	7.50
9	Juan Gonzalez	1.50
10	Chipper Jones	4.00
11	Greg Maddux	4.00
12	Roberto Alomar	1.25
13	Mike Piazza	5.00
14	Andres Galarraga	.60
15	Barry Bonds	7.50
16	Andy Pettitte	1.25
17	Nomar Garciaparra	4.00
18	Hideki Irabu	.60
19	Tony Gwynn	4.00
20	Frank Thomas	3.00
21	Roger Clemens	4.50
22	Sammy Sosa	5.00
23	Jose Cruz, Jr.	.60
24	Manny Ramirez	3.00
25	Mark McGwire	6.00
26	Randy Johnson	3.00
27	Mo Vaughn	.60
28	Gary Sheffield	1.50
29	Andruw Jones	3.00
30	Albert Belle	.60

A Piece of the Action

A Piece of the Action was inserted in Series 1, 2 and 3 packs. Series 1 featured 10 cards: five with a piece of game-used jersey and five with a piece of game-used bat. Series 2 offered a piece of game-used bat and jersey on four cards. Series 3 inserts featured a piece of jersey only. The cards were inserted one per 2,500 packs in Series 1 and 2; the insertion rate in Series 3 was not revealed.

		NM/M
Complete Set (14):		250.00
Common Player:		5.00
Inserted 1:2,500		
(1)	Jay Buhner/Bat	25.00
(2)	Tony Gwynn/Bat	25.00
(3)	Tony Gwynn/Jsy	25.00
(4)	Todd Hollandsworth/ Bat	5.00
(5)	Todd Hollandsworth/ Jsy	5.00
(6)	Greg Maddux/Jsy	40.00
(7)	Alex Rodriguez/Bat	40.00
(8)	Alex Rodriguez/Jsy	40.00
(9)	Gary Sheffield/Bat	15.00
(10)	Gary Sheffield/Jsy	15.00
RA	Roberto Alomar	35.00
JB	Jay Buhner	10.00
AJ	Andruw Jones	40.00
GS	Gary Sheffield	15.00

Blue Chip Prospects

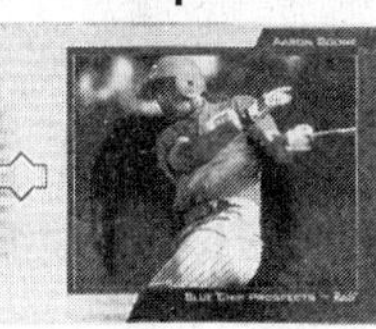

Inserted in Series 2 packs, these inserts are printed on die-cut acetate. The cards are sequentially numbered to 2,000. They carry a "BC" prefix.

		NM/M
Complete Set (30):		75.00
Common Player:		2.00
1	Nomar Garciaparra	8.00
2	Scott Rolen	5.00
3	Jason Dickson	2.00
4	Darin Erstad	3.00
5	Brad Fullmer	2.00
6	Jaret Wright	2.00
7	Justin Thompson	2.00
8	Matt Morris	2.00
9	Fernando Tatis	2.00
10	Alex Rodriguez	12.00
11	Todd Helton	6.50
12	Andy Pettitte	2.50
13	Jose Cruz Jr.	2.00
14	Mark Kotsay	2.00
15	Derek Jeter	15.00
16	Paul Konerko	3.00
17	Todd Dunwoody	2.00
18	Vladimir Guerrero	6.00
19	Miguel Tejada	5.00
20	Chipper Jones	8.00
21	Kevin Orie	2.00
22	Juan Encarnacion	2.00
23	Brian Rose	2.00
24	Andruw Jones	6.00
25	Livan Hernandez	2.00
26	Brian Giles	2.00
27	Brett Tomko	2.00
28	Jose Guillen	2.00
29	Aaron Boone	2.00
30	Ben Grieve	2.00

Clearly Dominant

Clearly Dominant was an insert in Series 2. Printed on Light F/X plastic stock, the 30-card set is sequentially numbered to 250. They carry a "CD" prefix.

		NM/M
Complete Set (30):		300.00
Common Player:		3.00
Production 250 Sets		
1	Mark McGwire	25.00
2	Derek Jeter	30.00
3	Alex Rodriguez	25.00
4	Paul Molitor	12.00
5	Jeff Bagwell	12.00
6	Ivan Rodriguez	10.00
7	Kenny Lofton	3.00
8	Cal Ripken Jr.	30.00
9	Albert Belle	3.00
10	Chipper Jones	15.00
11	Gary Sheffield	5.00
12	Roberto Alomar	4.00
13	Mo Vaughn	3.00
14	Andres Galarraga	3.00
15	Nomar Garciaparra	15.00
16	Randy Johnson	12.00
17	Mike Mussina	6.00
18	Greg Maddux	15.00
19	Tony Gwynn	15.00
20	Frank Thomas	12.00
21	Roger Clemens	17.50
22	Dennis Eckersley	10.00
23	Juan Gonzalez	6.00
24	Tino Martinez	3.00
25	Andruw Jones	12.00
26	Larry Walker	3.00
27	Ken Caminiti	3.00
28	Mike Piazza	20.00
29	Barry Bonds	30.00
30	Ken Griffey Jr.	20.00

Ken Griffey Jr.'s HR Chronicles

Griffey's Home Run Chronicles was inserted in both Series 1 and 2 packs. Series 1 had cards spotlighting one of Junior's first 30 home runs of the 1997 season. Series 2 had 26 cards highlighting the rest of his 1997 home run output. In both series, the cards were inserted one per nine packs. Cards are numbered "XX of 56" and printed on silver-metallic foil on front.

	NM/M
Complete Set (56):	45.00
Common Card:	1.00
Inserted 1:9	

National Pride

National Pride is a 42-card insert printed on die-cut rainbow foil. The set honors the nationality of the player with their country's flag in the background. The cards were inserted one per 24 packs. Cards are numbered with a "NP" prefix.

		NM/M
Complete Set (42):		65.00
Common Player:		.75
1	Dave Nilsson	.75
2	Larry Walker	.75
3	Edgar Renteria	.75
4	Jose Canseco	1.25
5	Rey Ordonez	.75
6	Rafael Palmeiro	2.50
7	Livan Hernandez	.75
8	Andruw Jones	3.00
9	Manny Ramirez	3.00
10	Sammy Sosa	4.00
11	Raul Mondesi	.75
12	Moises Alou	.75
13	Pedro Martinez	3.00
14	Vladimir Guerrero	3.00
15	Chili Davis	.75
16	Hideo Nomo	1.50
17	Hideki Irabu	.75
18	Shigetosi Hasegawa	.75
19	Takashi Kashiwada	.75
20	Chan Ho Park	.75
21	Fernando Valenzuela	.75
22	Vinny Castilla	.75
23	Armando Reynoso	.75
24	Karim Garcia	1.00
25	Marvin Benard	.75
26	Mariano Rivera	1.00
27	Juan Gonzalez	1.50
28	Roberto Alomar	1.00
29	Ivan Rodriguez	2.50
30	Carlos Delgado	1.00
31	Bernie Williams	.75
32	Edgar Martinez	.75
33	Frank Thomas	3.00
34	Barry Bonds	7.50
35	Mike Piazza	5.00
36	Chipper Jones	4.00
37	Cal Ripken Jr.	7.50
38	Alex Rodriguez	6.00
39	Ken Griffey Jr.	5.00
40	Andres Galarraga	.75
41	Omar Vizquel	.75
42	Ozzie Guillen	.75

Prime Nine

Nine of the most popular players are featured in this insert set. The cards are printed on silver-foil stock and inserted 1:5 in Series 2 packs.

		NM/M
Complete Set (60):		50.00
Common Griffey:		1.00
Common Piazza:		1.25
Common Thomas:		.60
Common McGwire:		1.25
Common Ripken:		1.75
Common Gonzalez:		.50
Common Gwynn:		.70
Common Bonds:		1.75
Common Maddux:		.70
Inserted 1:5		
PN1	Ken Griffey Jr./ 1989-1992	1.00
PN2	Ken Griffey Jr./1993	1.00
PN3	Ken Griffey Jr./1994	1.00
PN4	Ken Griffey Jr./1995	1.00
PN5	Ken Griffey Jr./1996	1.00
PN6	Ken Griffey Jr./1997	1.00
PN7	Ken Griffey Jr./1997	1.00
PN8	Mike Piazza/1991	1.00
PN9	Mike Piazza/1992	1.00
PN10	Mike Piazza/1993	1.00
PN11	Mike Piazza/1994	1.00
PN12	Mike Piazza/1995	1.00
PN13	Mike Piazza/1996	1.00
PN14	Mike Piazza/1997)	1.00
PN15	Frank Thomas/1991	.60
PN16	Frank Thomas/1992	.60
PN17	Frank Thomas/1993	.60
PN18	Frank Thomas/1994	.60
PN19	Frank Thomas/1995	.60
PN20	Frank Thomas/1996	.60
PN21	Frank Thomas/1997	.60
PN22	Mark McGwire/1987	1.25
PN23	Mark McGwire/ 1988-1990	1.25
PN24	Mark McGwire/1992	1.25
PN25	Mark McGwire/ 1995-1996	1.25
PN26	Mark McGwire/1997	1.25
PN27	Mark McGwire/1997	1.25
PN28	Mark McGwire/1997	1.25
PN29	Cal Ripken Jr./1982	1.75
PN30	Cal Ripken Jr./1983	1.75
PN31	Cal Ripken Jr./1989	1.75
PN32	Cal Ripken Jr./1991	1.75
PN33	Cal Ripken Jr./1995	1.75
PN34	Cal Ripken Jr./1996	1.75
PN35	Cal Ripken Jr./1997	1.75
PN36	Juan Gonzalez/1992	.50
PN37	Juan Gonzalez/1993	.50
PN38	Juan Gonzalez/1994	.50
PN39	Juan Gonzalez/1995	.50
PN40	Juan Gonzalez/1996	.50
PN41	Juan Gonzalez/1996	.50
PN42	Juan Gonzalez/1997	.50
PN43	Tony Gwynn/1984	.75
PN44	Tony Gwynn/ 1987-1989	.75
PN45	Tony Gwynn/ 1990-1993	.75
PN46	Tony Gwynn/1994	.75
PN47	Tony Gwynn/1996	.75
PN48	Tony Gwynn/1997	.75
PN49	Tony Gwynn/1997	.75
PN50	Barry Bonds/ 1986-1992	1.75
PN51	Barry Bonds/ 1990-1993	1.75
PN52	Barry Bonds/1993	1.75
PN53	Barry Bonds/1994	1.75
PN54	Barry Bonds/1996	1.75
PN55	Barry Bonds/1997	1.75
PN56	Greg Maddux/1992	.75
PN57	Greg Maddux/ 1993-1994	.75
PN58	Greg Maddux/1995	.75
PN59	Greg Maddux/1996	.75
PN60	Greg Maddux/1997	.75

Tape Measure Titans

Tape Measure Titans is a 30-card insert seeded 1:23 in Series 2. The set honors the game's top home run hitters. A

parallel gold version was also created with each card serially numbered to 2,667 on front.

		NM/M
Complete Set (30):		45.00
Common Player:		.40
Inserted 1:23		
Gold:		1.5X
1	Mark McGwire	5.00
2	Andres Galarraga	.40
3	Jeff Bagwell	2.00
4	Larry Walker	.40
5	Frank Thomas	2.50
6	Rafael Palmeiro	1.50
7	Nomar Garciaparra	4.00
8	Mo Vaughn	.40
9	Albert Belle	.60
10	Ken Griffey Jr.	4.00
11	Manny Ramirez	2.00
12	Jim Thome	.40
13	Tony Clark	.40
14	Juan Gonzalez	2.00
15	Mike Piazza	4.00
16	Jose Canseco	1.00
17	Jay Buhner	.40
18	Alex Rodriguez	5.00
19	Jose Cruz Jr.	.40
20	Tino Martinez	.40
21	Carlos Delgado	.75
22	Andruw Jones	2.00
23	Chipper Jones	3.00
24	Fred McGriff	.40
25	Matt Williams	.40
26	Sammy Sosa	4.00
27	Vinny Castilla	.40
28	Tim Salmon	.60
29	Ken Caminiti	.40
30	Barry Bonds	6.00

10th Anniversary Preview

10th Anniversary Preview is a 60-card set. The foil cards have the same design as the 1989 Upper Deck base cards. The set was inserted one per five packs. Retail versions have the words "PREVIEW EDITION" stamped vertically in gold foil at left. While scarcer than the hobby version, they do not command a premium.

		NM/M
Complete Set (60):		45.00
Common Player:		.30
1	Greg Maddux	2.00
2	Mike Mussina	.50
3	Roger Clemens	2.25
4	Hideo Nomo	.75
4	David Cone	.30
6	Tom Glavine	.45
7	Andy Pettitte	.60
8	Jimmy Key	.30
9	Randy Johnson	1.50
10	Dennis Eckersley	1.00
11	Lee Smith	.30
12	John Franco	.30
13	Randy Myers	.30
14	Mike Piazza	2.50
15	Ivan Rodriguez	1.25
16	Todd Hundley	.30
17	Sandy Alomar Jr.	.30
18	Frank Thomas	1.50
19	Rafael Palmeiro	1.25
20	Mark McGwire	3.00
21	Mo Vaughn	.30
22	Fred McGriff	.30
23	Andres Galarraga	.30
24	Mark Grace	.30
25	Jeff Bagwell	1.50
26	Roberto Alomar	.45
27	Chuck Knoblauch	.30
28	Ryne Sandberg	2.00
29	Eric Young	.30
30	Craig Biggio	.30
31	Carlos Baerga	.30
32	Robin Ventura	.30
33	Matt Williams	.30
34	Wade Boggs	2.00
35	Dean Palmer	.30
36	Chipper Jones	2.00
37	Vinny Castilla	.30
38	Ken Caminiti	.30
39	Omar Vizquel	.30
40	Cal Ripken Jr.	3.50
41	Derek Jeter	3.50
42	Alex Rodriguez	3.00
43	Barry Larkin	.30
44	Mark Grudzielanek	.30
45	Albert Belle	.30
46	Manny Ramirez	1.50
47	Jose Canseco	.75
48	Ken Griffey Jr.	2.50
49	Juan Gonzalez	.75
50	Kenny Lofton	.30
51	Sammy Sosa	2.00
52	Larry Walker	.30
53	Gary Sheffield	.60
54	Rickey Henderson	1.50
55	Tony Gwynn	2.00
56	Barry Bonds	3.50
57	Paul Molitor	1.50
58	Edgar Martinez	.30
59	Chili Davis	.30
60	Eddie Murray	1.50

Jumbos

For $3 and 10 foil-pack wrappers, collectors could receive this set of large-format (3-1/2" x 5") cards in a mail-in redemption. The cards are identical to the standard-size versions.

		NM/M
Complete Set (15):		6.00
Common Player:		.25
27	Kenny Lofton	.25
30	Greg Maddux	.75
40	Rafael Palmeiro	.50
50	Ryne Sandberg	.75
60	Albert Belle	.25
65	Barry Larkin	.25
67	Deion Sanders	.25
95	Gary Sheffield	.40
130	Paul Molitor	.60
135	Vladimir Guerrero	.60
176	Hideki Irabu	.25
205	Mark McGwire	2.00
211	Rickey Henderson	.60
225	Ken Griffey Jr.	1.50
230	Ivan Rodriguez	.50

5x7 Inserts

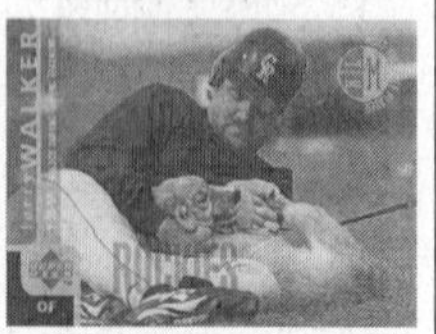

Each box of specially marked Series 2 retail packs contains one of these oversize (5" x 7") versions of UD cards. Besides being four times the size of the regular cards, the jumbo versions do not have the metallic-foil highlights on front nor the hologram on back.

		NM/M
Complete Set (10):		30.00
Common Player:		1.00
310	Cal Ripken Jr.	6.00
320	Nomar Garciaparra	3.00
330	Frank Thomas	2.50
355	Larry Walker	1.00
385	Jeff Bagwell	2.50
400	Mike Piazza	4.00
450	Derek Jeter	6.00
500	Tony Gwynn	3.00
510	Alex Rodriguez	5.00
530	Roger Clemens	3.50

Richie Ashburn Tribute

As part of the company's participation at SportsFest in May 1998, the company issued a tribute card for Phillies Hall of Famer and broadcasting great Richie Ashburn. The card front features a color action photo, part of which is repeated on the back along with Ashburn's career stats and highlights.

		NM/M
1	Richie Ashburn	4.00

Ken Griffey Most Memorable Home Runs

This retail-exclusive boxed set features 11 large-format (3-1/2" x 5") cards depicting Junior's key home runs. The cards have brushed gold-foil graphic highlights on front and a large photo with details of the memorable home run on back. Each card in the set also exists in an autographed and numbered edition of 10 which were randomly inserted. The set was originally sold with a 4" x 6" lucite card holder for about $12.

		NM/M
Complete Set (11):		7.50
Common Card:		1.00
Autographed Card:		225.00
1	Ken Griffey Jr. (First ML HR)	1.00
2	Ken Griffey Jr. (Father-son HRs)	1.00
3	Ken Griffey Jr. (1992 All-Star HR)	1.00
4	Ken Griffey Jr. (HR in eight straight)	1.00
5	Ken Griffey Jr. (32 HR in June 1994)	1.00
6	Ken Griffey Jr. (Game-winning HR)	1.00
7	Ken Griffey Jr. (5th Divison Series HR)	1.00
8	Ken Griffey Jr. (April record)	1.00
9	Ken Griffey Jr. (50th HR in 1997)	1.00
10	Ken Griffey Jr. (56th in 1997)	1.00
11	Ken Griffey Jr. (300th)	1.00

Mark McGwire's Chase for 62

This boxed set chronicles the Cardinal slugger's quest for the single-season home run record. Sold only as a boxed set of 30 cards in standard 2-1/2" x 3-1/2" format, plus a 3-1/2" x 5" card picturing home runs No. 61 and 62, these sets were offered only on a television home shopping show (individually serial numbered red box) and in selected retail stores (unnumbered yellow box). The cards in each version are identical. Issue price was about $20. Card fronts have color poses or action photos at right; at left is a monochrome portrait photo in red. Backs repeat the large front photo, also in red monochrome, and have a few words about a McGwire homer or other highlight. Each card has a silver-foil UD logo on front and a diamond-shaped hologram on back.

		NM/M
Complete Boxed Set:		7.50
Common Card:		.50
1-30	Mark McGwire	.50
---	Mark McGwire (3-1/2" x 5" HR #61/62)	3.00

Mark McGwire - Sept. 8, 1998

This is one of many special issues from Upper Deck commemorating McGwire's record-breaking 1998 season. Most such cards were produced for retail-only sales, or for home shopping television shows. This blank-back, round-cornered card is 5" x 3" and has flicker-action scenes of Big Mac's home run swing and his salute to the crowd following his historic blast.

	NM/M
Mark McGwire	6.00

Mark McGwire 70/62 Home Runs

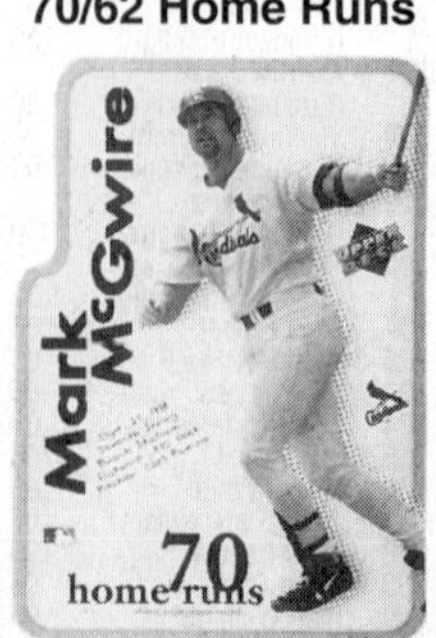

This 3-1/2" x 5" die-cut card was one of many special issues from UD commemorating McGwire's record-breaking season in 1998. This card is highlighted on front with red foil and has a photo of the player with details of his 70th HR. On back in similar format is another photo and details of his 62nd home run, along with a serial number from wihtin the edition of 17,000.

	NM/M
Mark McGwire	4.00

PowerDeck Audio Card

A late-1990s reinvention of the "talking" baseball card, this was the first application of UD's "PowerDeck" technology to the trading card field. Specially marked hobby boxes of '98 UD baseball could contain one of three Ken Griffey, Jr., audio cards. The cards are standard 2-1/2" x 3-1/2" and were made to be inserted into a "dummy" plastic disc which could then be played in any audio CD, offering comments from Griffey, trivia, and career highlights. Insertion rate of each of the Griffey cards varies and is detailed in the listings.

		NM/M
Complete Set (3):		45.00
Common Card:		2.00
(1)	Ken Griffey Jr. (Gray jersey, 1:46 packs.)	3.00
(2)	Ken Griffey Jr. (Blue jersey, 1:500 packs.)	12.00
(3)	Ken Griffey Jr. (White jersey, 1:2,400 packs.)	35.00

Rookie Edition Preview

		NM/M
Complete Set (10):		5.00
Common Player:		.50
1	Nomar Garciaparra	2.00
2	Scott Rolen	1.00
3	Mark Kotsay	.50
4	Todd Helton	1.50
5	Paul Konerko	.60
6	Juan Encarnacion	.50
7	Brad Fullmer	.50
8	Miguel Tejada	.65
9	Richard Hidalgo	.50
10	Ben Grieve	.50

Rookie Edition A Piece of the Action

A Piece of the Action consists of five Game Jersey cards. Three rookie Game Jersey cards were sequentially numbered to 200, while a Ken Griffey Jr. Game Jersey card was numbered to 300. Griffey also signed and hand-numbered 24 Game Jersey cards.

		NM/M
Common Card:		15.00
KG	Ken Griffey Jr./300	100.00
KGS	Ken Griffey Jr./ Auto./24	300.00
BG	Ben Grieve/200	15.00
JC	Jose Cruz Jr./200	15.00
TL	Travis Lee/200	15.00

Rookie Edition All-Star Credentials

All-Star Credentials is a 30-card insert seeded 1:9. It features the game's top players.

		NM/M
Complete Set (30):		25.00
Common Player:		.25
Inserted 1:9		
AS1	Ken Griffey Jr.	1.50
AS2	Travis Lee	.40
AS3	Ben Grieve	.25
AS4	Jose Cruz Jr.	.25
AS5	Andruw Jones	.75
AS6	Craig Biggio	.25
AS7	Hideo Nomo	.40
AS8	Cal Ripken Jr.	2.50
AS9	Jaret Wright	.25
AS10	Mark McGwire	2.00
AS11	Derek Jeter	2.50
AS12	Scott Rolen	.60
AS13	Jeff Bagwell	.75
AS14	Manny Ramirez	.75
AS15	Alex Rodriguez	2.00
AS16	Chipper Jones	1.00
AS17	Larry Walker	.25
AS18	Barry Bonds	2.50
AS19	Tony Gwynn	1.00
AS20	Mike Piazza	1.50
AS21	Roger Clemens	1.25
AS22	Greg Maddux	1.00
AS23	Jim Thome	.60
AS24	Tino Martinez	.25
AS25	Nomar Garciaparra	1.00
AS26	Juan Gonzalez	.40
AS27	Kenny Lofton	.25
AS28	Randy Johnson	.75
AS29	Todd Helton	.65
AS30	Frank Thomas	.75

Rookie Edition Destination Stardom

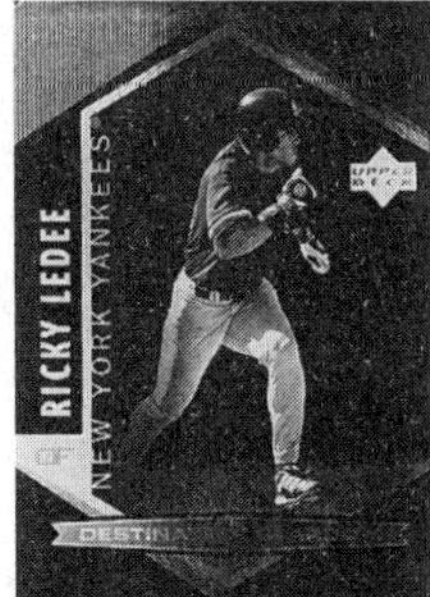

This 60-card insert features top young players. Fronts are printed on a foil background. The insertion rate was one card per five packs. Cards have a "DS" prefix to the card number.

		NM/M
Complete Set (60):		40.00
Common Player:		.50
Inserted 1:5		
1	Travis Lee	.75
2	Nomar Garciaparra	3.50
3	Alex Gonzalez	.50
4	Richard Hidalgo	.50
5	Jaret Wright	.50
6	Mike Kinkade	.50
7	Matt Morris	.50
8	Gary Mathews Jr.	.50
9	Brett Tomko	.50
10	Todd Helton	2.00
11	Scott Elarton	.50
12	Scott Rolen	1.50
13	Jose Cruz Jr.	.50
14	Jarrod Washburn	.50
15	Sean Casey	.50
16	Magglio Ordonez	2.00
17	Gabe Alvarez	.50
18	Todd Dunwoody	.50
19	Kevin Witt	.50
20	Ben Grieve	.50
21	Daryle Ward	.50
22	Matt Clement	.50
23	Carlton Loewer	.50
24	Javier Vazquez	.50
25	Paul Konerko	.75
26	Preston Wilson	.60
27	Wes Helms	.50
28	Derek Jeter	5.00
29	Corey Koskie	.50
30	Russell Branyan	.50
31	Vladimir Guerrero	2.50
32	Ryan Christenson	.50
33	Carlos Lee	.60
34	David Dellucci	.50
35	Bruce Chen	.50
36	Ricky Ledee	.50
37	Ron Wright	.50
38	Derrek Lee	1.50
39	Miguel Tejada	.75
40	Brad Fullmer	.50
41	Rich Butler	.50
42	Chris Carpenter	.50
43	Alex Rodriguez	4.00
44	Darron Ingram	.50
45	Kerry Wood	1.50
46	Jason Varitek	.50
47	Ramon Hernandez	.50
48	Aaron Boone	.50
49	Juan Encarnacion	.50
50	A.J. Hinch	.50
51	Mike Lowell	.60
52	Fernando Tatis	.50
53	Jose Guillen	.50
54	Mike Caruso	.50
55	Carl Pavano	.50
56	Chris Clemons	.50
57	Mark L. Johnson	.50
58	Ken Cloude	.50
59	Rolando Arrojo	.50
60	Mark Kotsay	.50

Rookie Edition Eminent Prestige 5x7

This 4X super-size (5" x 7") version is a partial parallel of the Rookie Edition Eminent Prestige subset. It was available only in specially marked retail packaging.

		NM/M
Complete Set (10):		25.00
Common Player:		2.00
605	Mike Piazza	3.50
607	Frank Thomas	2.50
610	Mark McGwire	4.00
611	Jeff Bagwell	2.50
612	Travis Lee	2.00
614	Cal Ripken Jr.	5.00
616	Nomar Garciaparra	3.00
617	Alex Rodriguez	4.00
619	Tony Gwynn	3.00
620	Ken Griffey Jr.	3.50

Rookie Edition Retrospectives

Retrospectives is a 30-card insert seeded 1:24. The cards offer a look back at the careers of baseball's top stars.

		NM/M
Complete Set (30):		55.00
Common Player:		.50
Inserted 1:24		
1	Dennis Eckersley	2.50
2	Rickey Henderson	3.00
3	Harold Baines	.50
4	Cal Ripken Jr.	7.50
5	Tony Gwynn	4.00
6	Wade Boggs	4.00
7	Orel Hershiser	.50
8	Joe Carter	.50
9	Roger Clemens	4.50
10	Barry Bonds	7.50
11	Mark McGwire	6.00
12	Greg Maddux	4.00
13	Fred McGriff	.50
14	Rafael Palmeiro	3.00
15	Craig Biggio	.50
16	Brady Anderson	.50
17	Randy Johnson	3.00
18	Gary Sheffield	1.00
19	Albert Belle	.50
20	Ken Griffey Jr.	5.00
21	Juan Gonzalez	1.50
22	Larry Walker	.50
23	Tino Martinez	.50
24	Frank Thomas	3.00
25	Jeff Bagwell	3.00
26	Kenny Lofton	.50
27	Mo Vaughn	.50
28	Mike Piazza	5.00
29	Alex Rodriguez	6.00
30	Chipper Jones	4.00

Rookie Edition Unparalleled

Unparalleled is a 20-card, hobby-only insert. The set consists of holo-pattern foil-stamped cards. They were inserted one per 72 packs.

		NM/M
Complete Set (20):		75.00
Common Player:		1.00
Inserted 1:72		
1	Ken Griffey Jr.	6.00
2	Travis Lee	1.50
3	Ben Grieve	1.00
4	Jose Cruz Jr.	1.00
5	Nomar Garciaparra	5.00
6	Hideo Nomo	1.75
7	Kenny Lofton	1.00
8	Cal Ripken Jr.	10.00
9	Roger Clemens	5.50
10	Mike Piazza	6.00
11	Jeff Bagwell	3.50
12	Chipper Jones	5.00
13	Greg Maddux	5.00
14	Randy Johnson	3.50
15	Alex Rodriguez	7.50
16	Barry Bonds	10.00
17	Frank Thomas	3.50
18	Juan Gonzalez	1.75
19	Tony Gwynn	5.00
20	Mark McGwire	7.50

1998 Upper Deck Special F/X

Special F/X is a retail-only product. The 150-card set consists of 125 regular cards, the 15-card Star Rookies subset and a 10-card subset called Ken Griffey Jr.'s Hot List. The base cards are printed on 20-point stock. The only insert is Power Zone which has four levels: Level One, Level Two - October-best, Level Three - Power Driven and Level Four - Superstar Xcitement.

		NM/M
Complete Set (150):		30.00
Common Player:		.05
1	Ken Griffey Jr. (Griffey Hot List)	1.00
2	Mark McGwire (Griffey Hot List)	1.25
3	Alex Rodriguez (Griffey Hot List)	2.50
4	Larry Walker (Griffey Hot List)	.05
5	Tino Martinez (Griffey Hot List)	.05
6	Mike Piazza (Griffey Hot List)	2.50
7	Jose Cruz Jr. (Griffey Hot List)	.05
8	Greg Maddux (Griffey Hot List)	.75
9	Tony Gwynn (Griffey Hot List)	.75
10	Roger Clemens (Griffey Hot List)	1.75
11	Jason Dickson	.05
12	Darin Erstad	.25
13	Chuck Finley	.05
14	Dave Hollins	.05
15	Garret Anderson	.05
16	Michael Tucker	.05
17	Javier Lopez	.05
18	John Smoltz	.05
19	Mark Wohlers	.05
20	Greg Maddux	1.50
21	Scott Erickson	.05
22	Jimmy Key	.05
23	B.J. Surhoff	.05
24	Eric Davis	.05
25	Rafael Palmeiro	.75
26	Tim Naehring	.05
27	Darren Bragg	.05
28	Troy O'Leary	.05
29	John Valentin	.05
30	Mo Vaughn	.05
31	Mark Grace	.05
32	Kevin Foster	.05
33	Kevin Tapani	.05
34	Kevin Orie	.05
35	Albert Belle	.05
36	Ray Durham	.05
37	Jaime Navarro	.05
38	Mike Cameron	.05
39	Eddie Taubensee	.05
40	Barry Larkin	.05
41	Willie Greene	.05
42	Jeff Shaw	.05
43	Omar Vizquel	.05
44	Brian Giles	.05
45	Jim Thome	.60
46	David Justice	.05
47	Sandy Alomar Jr.	.05
48	Neifi Perez	.05
49	Dante Bichette	.05
50	Vinny Castilla	.05
51	John Thomson	.05
52	Damion Easley	.05
53	Justin Thompson	.05
54	Bobby Higginson	.05
55	Tony Clark	.05
56	Charles Johnson	.05
57	Edgar Renteria	.05
58	Alex Fernandez	.05
59	Gary Sheffield	.50
60	Livan Hernandez	.05
61	Craig Biggio	.05
62	Chris Holt	.05
63	Billy Wagner	.05
64	Brad Ausmus	.05
65	Dean Palmer	.05
66	Tim Belcher	.05
67	Jeff King	.05
68	Jose Rosado	.05
69	Chan Ho Park	.05
70	Raul Mondesi	.05
71	Hideo Nomo	.50
72	Todd Zeile	.05
73	Eric Karros	.05
74	Cal Eldred	.05
75	Jeff D'Amico	.05
76	Doug Jones	.05
77	Dave Nilsson	.05
78	Todd Walker	.05
79	Rick Aguilera	.05
80	Paul Molitor	1.00
81	Brad Radke	.05
82	Vladimir Guerrero	1.00
83	Carlos Perez	.05
84	F.P. Santangelo	.05
85	Rondell White	.05
86	Butch Huskey	.05
87	Edgardo Alfonzo	.05
88	John Franco	.05
89	John Olerud	.05
90	Todd Hundley	.05
91	Bernie Williams	.05
92	Andy Pettitte	.30
93	Paul O'Neill	.05
94	David Cone	.05
95	Jason Giambi	.50
96	Damon Mashore	.05
97	Scott Spiezio	.05
98	Ariel Prieto	.05
99	Rico Brogna	.05
100	Mike Lieberthal	.05
101	Garrett Stephenson	.05
102	Ricky Bottalico	.05
103	Kevin Polcovich	.05
104	Jon Lieber	.05
105	Kevin Young	.05
106	Tony Womack	.05
107	Gary Gaetti	.05
108	Alan Benes	.05
109	Willie McGee	.05
110	Mark McGwire	2.50
111	Ron Gant	.05
112	Andy Ashby	.05
113	Steve Finley	.05
114	Quilvio Veras	.05
115	Ken Caminiti	.05
116	Joey Hamilton	.05
117	Bill Mueller	.05
118	Mark Gardner	.05
119	Shawn Estes	.05
120	J.T. Snow	.05
121	Dante Powell	.05
122	Jeff Kent	.05
123	Jamie Moyer	.05
124	Joey Cora	.05
125	Ken Griffey Jr.	2.00
126	Jeff Fassero	.05
127	Edgar Martinez	.05
128	Will Clark	.05
129	Lee Stevens	.05
130	Ivan Rodriguez	.75
131	Rusty Greer	.05
132	Ed Sprague	.05
133	Pat Hentgen	.05
134	Shannon Stewart	.05
135	Carlos Delgado	.40
136	Brett Tomko/SR	.05
137	Jose Guillen/SR	.05
138	Elieser Marrero/SR	.05
139	Dennis Reyes/SR	.05
140	Mark Kotsay/SR	.05
141	Richie Sexson/SR	.05
142	Todd Helton/SR	.75
143	Jeremi Gonzalez/SR	.05
144	Jeff Abbott/SR	.05
145	Matt Morris/SR	.05
146	Aaron Boone/SR	.05
147	Todd Dunwoody/SR	.05
148	Mario Valdez/SR	.05
149	Fernando Tatis/SR	.05
150	Jaret Wright/SR	.05

OctoberBest

OctoberBest is Level Two of the Power Zone insert. This 20-card insert is die-cut and printed on silver foil. Inserted one per 34 packs, the set features the postseason exploits of 20 players from Power Zone Level One.

		NM/M
Complete Set (15):		40.00
Common Player:		1.00
Inserted 1:34		
PZ1	Frank Thomas	3.00
PZ2	Juan Gonzalez	1.50
PZ3	Mike Piazza	5.00
PZ4	Mark McGwire	6.00
PZ5	Jeff Bagwell	3.00
PZ6	Barry Bonds	7.50
PZ7	Ken Griffey Jr.	5.00
PZ8	John Smoltz	1.00
PZ9	Andruw Jones	3.00
PZ10	Greg Maddux	4.00
PZ11	Sandy Alomar Jr.	1.00
PZ12	Roberto Alomar	1.25
PZ13	Chipper Jones	4.00
PZ14	Kenny Lofton	1.00
PZ15	Tom Glavine	1.25

Power Driven

Power Driven is Level Three of the Power Zone insert. Inserted 1:69, the set features the top 10 power hitters from Power Zone Level Two. The cards feature gold Light F/X technology.

		NM/M
Complete Set (10):		40.00
Common Player:		1.50
Inserted 1:69		
PZ1	Frank Thomas	4.50
PZ2	Juan Gonzalez	2.50
PZ3	Mike Piazza	6.00
PZ4	Larry Walker	1.50
PZ5	Mark McGwire	7.50
PZ6	Jeff Bagwell	4.50
PZ7	Mo Vaughn	1.50
PZ8	Barry Bonds	10.00
PZ9	Tino Martinez	1.50
PZ10	Ken Griffey Jr.	6.00

Power Zone

Power Zone Level One is seeded one per seven packs. The cards are printed using silver Light F/X technology.

		NM/M
Complete Set (20):		40.00
Common Player:		.50
Inserted 1:7		
PZ1	Jose Cruz Jr.	.50
PZ2	Frank Thomas	2.50
PZ3	Juan Gonzalez	1.25
PZ4	Mike Piazza	4.50
PZ5	Mark McGwire	4.50
PZ6	Barry Bonds	6.00
PZ7	Greg Maddux	3.00
PZ8	Alex Rodriguez	4.50
PZ9	Nomar Garciaparra	3.00
PZ10	Ken Griffey Jr.	3.50
PZ11	John Smoltz	.50
PZ12	Andruw Jones	2.50
PZ13	Sandy Alomar Jr.	.50
PZ14	Roberto Alomar	1.00
PZ15	Chipper Jones	3.00
PZ16	Kenny Lofton	.50
PZ17	Larry Walker	.50
PZ18	Jeff Bagwell	2.50
PZ19	Mo Vaughn	.50
PZ20	Tom Glavine	1.00

Superstar Xcitement

Printed on Light F/X gold foil, this 10-card set features the same players as the Power Driven insert. This set is Power Zone Level Four and is sequentially numbered to 250.

		NM/M
Complete Set (10):		275.00
Common Player:		10.00
Production 250 Sets		
PZ1	Jose Cruz Jr.	10.00
PZ2	Frank Thomas	25.00
PZ3	Juan Gonzalez	10.00
PZ4	Mike Piazza	40.00
PZ5	Mark McGwire	45.00
PZ6	Barry Bonds	50.00
PZ7	Greg Maddux	35.00
PZ8	Alex Rodriguez	45.00

PZ9 Nomar Garciaparra 35.00
PZ10 Ken Griffey Jr. 40.00

1998 Upper Deck UD 3

The 270-card base set of UD 3 is actually three levels of the same 90 players. Light FX cards comprise #1-90. The first 30 cards are Future Impact players. Cards #31-60 are Power Corps and cards #61-90 are The Establishment. Cards #91-180 repeat the three subsets in Embossed technology while the final 90 cards repeat the basic sequence in Rainbow technology. Because each subset at each level is seeded at a different rate, few collectors bother to try to understand the relative scarcities and the issue is largely ignored. The insertion ratio for each tier is shown in the checklist. UD 3 was offered in three-card packs at an SRP of $3.99.

NM/M

Complete Set (270): 200.00
Common Future Impact (1-30): .50
Inserted 1:12
Die-Cuts (2,000 Sets): 1X
Common Power Corps (31-60): .25
Inserted 1:1
Die-Cuts (2,000 Sets): 3X
Common Establishment (61-90): .25
Inserted 1:6
Die-Cuts (2,000 Sets): 2X
Common Future Impact Embossed (91-120): .25
Inserted 1:6
Die-Cuts (1,000 Sets): 3X
Common Power Corps Embossed (121-150): .25
Inserted 1:4
Die-Cuts (1,000 Sets): 6X
Common Establishment Embossed (151-180): .25
Inserted 1:1
Die-Cuts (1,000 Sets): 12X
Common Future Impact Rainbow (181-210): .25
Inserted 1:1
Die-Cuts (100 Sets): 15X
Common Power Corps Rainbow (211-240): .50
Inserted 1:12
Die-Cuts (100 Sets): 8X
Common Establishment Rainbow (241-270): .75
Inserted 1:24
Die-Cuts (100 Sets): 5X
Pack (3): 1.00
Wax Box (24): 20.00
1 Travis Lee .50
2 A.J. Hinch .50
3 Mike Caruso .50
4 Miguel Tejada .75
5 Brad Fullmer .50
6 Eric Milton .50
7 Mark Kotsay .50
8 Darin Erstad .75
9 Magglio Ordonez 1.00
10 Ben Grieve .50
11 Brett Tomko .50
12 Mike Kinkade **RC** .75
13 Rolando Arrojo .50
14 Todd Helton 1.00
15 Scott Rolen 1.00
16 Bruce Chen .50
17 Daryle Ward .50
18 Jaret Wright .50
19 Sean Casey .65
20 Paul Konerko .65
21 Kerry Wood 1.00
22 Russell Branyan .50
23 Gabe Alvarez .50
24 Juan Encarnacion .50
25 Andruw Jones 1.50
26 Vladimir Guerrero 1.50
27 Eli Marrero .50
28 Matt Clement .50
29 Gary Matthews Jr. .50
30 Derrek Lee 1.50
31 Ken Caminiti .25
32 Gary Sheffield .25
33 Jay Buhner .25
34 Ryan Klesko .25
35 Nomar Garciaparra .75
36 Vinny Castilla .25
37 Tony Clark .25
38 Sammy Sosa .75
39 Tino Martinez .25
40 Mike Piazza 1.00
41 Manny Ramirez .65
42 Larry Walker .25
43 Jose Cruz Jr. .25
44 Matt Williams .25
45 Frank Thomas .65
46 Jim Edmonds .25
47 Raul Mondesi .25
48 Alex Rodriguez 1.50
49 Albert Belle .25
50 Mark McGwire 1.50
51 Tim Salmon .25
52 Andres Galarraga .25
53 Jeff Bagwell .65
54 Jim Thome .50
55 Barry Bonds 2.50
56 Carlos Delgado .40
57 Mo Vaughn .25
58 Chipper Jones .75
59 Juan Gonzalez .40
60 Ken Griffey Jr. 1.00
61 David Cone .25
62 Hideo Nomo .75
63 Edgar Martinez .25
64 Fred McGriff .25
65 Cal Ripken Jr. 4.00
66 Todd Hundley .25
67 Barry Larkin .25
68 Dennis Eckersley 1.00
69 Randy Johnson 1.50
70 Paul Molitor 1.50
71 Eric Karros .25
72 Rafael Palmeiro 1.00
73 Chuck Knoblauch .25
74 Ivan Rodriguez 1.25
75 Greg Maddux 2.00
76 Dante Bichette .25
77 Brady Anderson .25
78 Craig Biggio .25
79 Derek Jeter 4.00
80 Roger Clemens 2.25
81 Roberto Alomar .40
82 Wade Boggs 2.00
83 Charles Johnson .25
84 Mark Grace .25
85 Kenny Lofton .25
86 Mike Mussina 1.00
87 Pedro Martinez 1.50
88 Curt Schilling .50
89 Bernie Williams .25
90 Tony Gwynn 2.00
91 Travis Lee .40
92 A.J. Hinch .25
93 Mike Caruso .25
94 Miguel Tejada .40
95 Brad Fullmer .25
96 Eric Milton .25
97 Mark Kotsay .25
98 Darin Erstad 1.00
99 Magglio Ordonez 1.00
100 Ben Grieve .25
101 Brett Tomko .25
102 Mike Kinkade **RC** .40
103 Rolando Arrojo .25
104 Todd Helton 1.00
105 Scott Rolen 1.00
106 Bruce Chen .25
107 Daryle Ward .25
108 Jaret Wright .25
109 Sean Casey .25
110 Paul Konerko .40
111 Kerry Wood 1.00
112 Russell Branyan .25
113 Gabe Alvarez .25
114 Juan Encarnacion .25
115 Andruw Jones 1.50
116 Vladimir Guerrero 1.50
117 Eli Marrero .25
118 Matt Clement .25
119 Gary Matthews Jr. .25
120 Derrek Lee 1.00
121 Ken Caminiti .25
122 Gary Sheffield .50
123 Jay Buhner .25
124 Ryan Klesko .25
125 Nomar Garciaparra 1.50
126 Vinny Castilla .25
127 Tony Clark .25
128 Sammy Sosa 1.50
129 Tino Martinez .25
130 Mike Piazza 2.00
131 Manny Ramirez 1.00
132 Larry Walker .25
133 Jose Cruz Jr. .25
134 Matt Williams .25
135 Frank Thomas 1.00
136 Jim Edmonds .25
137 Raul Mondesi .25
138 Alex Rodriguez 3.00
139 Albert Belle .25
140 Mark McGwire 3.00
141 Tim Salmon .25
142 Andres Galarraga .25
143 Jeff Bagwell 1.00
144 Jim Thome .75
145 Barry Bonds 5.00
146 Carlos Delgado .50
147 Mo Vaughn .25
148 Chipper Jones 1.50
149 Juan Gonzalez .50
150 Ken Griffey Jr. 2.00
151 David Cone .25
152 Hideo Nomo .40
153 Edgar Martinez .25
154 Fred McGriff .25
155 Cal Ripken Jr. 2.00
156 Todd Hundley .25
157 Barry Larkin .25
158 Dennis Eckersley .65
159 Randy Johnson .75
160 Paul Molitor .75
161 Eric Karros .25
162 Rafael Palmeiro .65
163 Chuck Knoblauch .25
164 Ivan Rodriguez .65
165 Greg Maddux 1.00
166 Dante Bichette .25
167 Brady Anderson .25
168 Craig Biggio .25
169 Derek Jeter 2.00
170 Roger Clemens 1.25
171 Roberto Alomar .30
172 Wade Boggs 1.00
173 Charles Johnson .25
174 Mark Grace .25
175 Kenny Lofton .25
176 Mike Mussina .40
177 Pedro Martinez .75
178 Curt Schilling .40
179 Bernie Williams .25
180 Tony Gwynn 1.00
181 Travis Lee .40
182 A.J. Hinch .25
183 Mike Caruso .25
184 Miguel Tejada .40
185 Brad Fullmer .25
186 Eric Milton .25
187 Mark Kotsay .25
188 Darin Erstad .50
189 Magglio Ordonez 1.25
190 Ben Grieve .25
191 Brett Tomko .25
192 Mike Kinkade **RC** .40
193 Rolando Arrojo .25
194 Todd Helton .65
195 Scott Rolen .60
196 Bruce Chen .25
197 Daryle Ward .25
198 Jaret Wright .25
199 Sean Casey .40
200 Paul Konerko .40
201 Kerry Wood .60
202 Russell Branyan .25
203 Gabe Alvarez .25
204 Juan Encarnacion .25
205 Andruw Jones 1.50
206 Vladimir Guerrero 1.50
207 Eli Marrero .25
208 Matt Clement .25
209 Gary Matthews Jr. .25
210 Derrek Lee 1.00
211 Ken Caminiti .50
212 Gary Sheffield 1.00
213 Jay Buhner .50
214 Ryan Klesko .50
215 Nomar Garciaparra 3.00
216 Vinny Castilla .50
217 Tony Clark .50
218 Sammy Sosa 3.00
219 Tino Martinez .50
220 Mike Piazza 4.00
221 Manny Ramirez 2.00
222 Larry Walker .50
223 Jose Cruz Jr. .50
224 Matt Williams .50
225 Frank Thomas 2.00
226 Jim Edmonds .50
227 Raul Mondesi .50
228 Alex Rodriguez 6.00
229 Albert Belle .50
230 Mark McGwire 6.00
231 Tim Salmon .50
232 Andres Galarraga .50
233 Jeff Bagwell 2.00
234 Jim Thome 1.50
235 Barry Bonds 9.00
236 Carlos Delgado .75
267 Mo Vaughn .50
238 Chipper Jones 3.00
239 Juan Gonzalez 1.00
240 Ken Griffey Jr. 4.00
241 David Cone .75
242 Hideo Nomo 1.50
243 Edgar Martinez .75
244 Fred McGriff .75
245 Cal Ripken Jr. 12.00
246 Todd Hundley .75
247 Barry Larkin .75
248 Dennis Eckersley 3.00
249 Randy Johnson 4.50
250 Paul Molitor 4.50
251 Eric Karros .75
252 Rafael Palmeiro 3.50
253 Chuck Knoblauch .75
254 Ivan Rodriguez 4.00
255 Greg Maddux 6.00
256 Dante Bichette .75
257 Brady Anderson .75
258 Craig Biggio .75
259 Derek Jeter 12.00
260 Roger Clemens 6.50
261 Roberto Alomar 1.25
262 Wade Boggs 6.00
263 Charles Johnson .75
264 Mark Grace .75
265 Kenny Lofton .75
266 Mike Mussina 1.25
267 Pedro Martinez 4.50
268 Curt Schilling 1.50
269 Bernie Williams .75
270 Tony Gwynn 6.00

Die-Cut

Die-cut versions of all 270 cards in UD 3 were available in three sequentially numbered tiers. Light FX were numbered to 2,000 sets; Embossed cards were numbered to 1,000 and Rainbow cards were numbered to 100.

Light FX Die-Cuts (2,000 Each)
Future Impact (1-30): .75X
Power Corps (31-60): 3X
Establishment (61-90): 2X
Embossed Die-Cuts (1,000 Each)
Future Impact (91-120): 1X
Power Corps (121-150): 3X
Establishment (151-180): 6X
Rainbow Die-Cuts (100 Each)
Future Impact (181-210): 20X
Power Corps (211-240): 4X
Establishment (241-270): 12X

Power Corps Jumbos

Ten of the Power Corps cards from UD 3 were selected to be reproduced in jumbo 4X (5" x 7") format as box-toppers for special retail packaging of UD 3.

NM/M

Complete Set (10): 60.00
Common Player: 2.50
35 Ken Griffey Jr. 7.50
38 Sammy Sosa 6.00
40 Mike Piazza 7.50
45 Frank Thomas 5.00
48 Alex Rodriguez 10.00
50 Mark McGwire 10.00
55 Barry Bonds 12.50
58 Chipper Jones 6.00
59 Juan Gonzalez 2.50
60 Ken Griffey Jr. 7.50

1998 UD Retro

The 129-card set is comprised of 99 regular player cards and 30 Futurama subset cards. Card fronts have a white border encasing the player photo. Retro is packaged in a lunchbox featuring one of six players. Each lunchbox contains 24 six-card packs.

NM/M

Complete Set (129): 15.00
Common Player: .05
Pack (6): 2.25
Lunchbox (24): 40.00
1 Jim Edmonds .05
2 Darin Erstad .25
3 Tim Salmon .05
4 Jay Bell .05
5 Matt Williams .05
6 Andres Galarraga .05
7 Andruw Jones .60
8 Chipper Jones .75
9 Greg Maddux .75
10 Rafael Palmeiro .50
11 Cal Ripken Jr. 2.00
12 Brooks Robinson .15
13 Nomar Garciaparra .75
14 Pedro Martinez .60
15 Mo Vaughn .05
16 Ernie Banks .50
17 Mark Grace .05
18 Gary Matthews .05
19 Sammy Sosa .75
20 Albert Belle .05
21 Carlton Fisk .15
22 Frank Thomas .60
23 Ken Griffey Sr. .05
24 Paul Konerko .15
25 Barry Larkin .05
26 Sean Casey .10
27 Tony Perez .05
28 Bob Feller .15
29 Kenny Lofton .05
30 Manny Ramirez .60
31 Jim Thome .45
32 Omar Vizquel .05
33 Dante Bichette .05
34 Larry Walker .05
35 Tony Clark .05
36 Damion Easley .05
37 Cliff Floyd .05
38 Livan Hernandez .05
39 Jeff Bagwell .60
40 Craig Biggio .05
41 Al Kaline .15
42 Johnny Damon .20
43 Dean Palmer .05
44 Charles Johnson .05
45 Eric Karros .05
46 Gaylord Perry .05
47 Raul Mondesi .05
48 Gary Sheffield .30
49 Eddie Mathews .15
50 Warren Spahn .15
51 Jeromy Burnitz .05
52 Jeff Cirillo .05
53 Marquis Grissom .05
54 Paul Molitor .60
55 Kirby Puckett .75
56 Brad Radke .05
57 Todd Walker .05
58 Vladimir Guerrero .60
59 Brad Fullmer .05
60 Rondell White .05
61 Bobby Jones .05
62 Hideo Nomo .30
63 Mike Piazza 1.00
64 Tom Seaver .15
65 Frank J. Thomas .05
66 Yogi Berra .50
67 Derek Jeter 2.00
68 Tino Martinez .05
69 Paul O'Neill .05
70 Andy Pettitte .20
71 Rollie Fingers .05
72 Rickey Henderson .60
73 Matt Stairs .05
74 Scott Rolen .50
75 Curt Schilling .25
76 Jose Guillen .05
77 Jason Kendall .05
78 Lou Brock .10
79 Bob Gibson .10
80 Ray Lankford .05
81 Mark McGwire 1.50
83 Kevin Brown .05
84 Ken Caminiti .05
85 Tony Gwynn .75
86 Greg Vaughn .05
87 Barry Bonds 2.00
88 Willie Stargell .10
89 Willie McCovey .10
90 Ken Griffey Jr. 1.00
91 Randy Johnson .60
92 Alex Rodriguez 1.50
93 Quinton McCracken .05
94 Fred McGriff .05
95 Juan Gonzalez .30
96 Ivan Rodriguez .50
97 Nolan Ryan 1.50
98 Jose Canseco .45
99 Roger Clemens .90
100 Jose Cruz Jr. .05
101 Justin Baughman **RC** .05
102 David Dellucci **RC** (Futurama) .15
103 Travis Lee (Futurama) .15
104 Troy Glaus **RC** (Futurama) 1.00
105 Kerry Wood (Futurama) .40
106 Mike Caruso (Futurama) .05
107 Jim Parque **RC** (Futurama) .10
108 Brett Tomko (Futurama) .05
109 Russell Branyan (Futurama) .05
110 Jaret Wright (Futurama) .05
111 Todd Helton (Futurama) .60
112 Gabe Alvarez (Futurama) .05
113 Matt Anderson **RC** (Futurama) .10
114 Alex Gonzalez (Futurama) .05
115 Mark Kotsay (Futurama) .10
116 Derrek Lee (Futurama) .50
117 Richard Hidalgo (Futurama) .05
118 Adrian Beltre (Futurama) .10
119 Geoff Jenkins (Futurama) .05
120 Eric Milton (Futurama) .05
121 Brad Fullmer (Futurama) .05
122 Vladimir Guerrero (Futurama) .60
123 Carl Pavano (Futurama) .05
124 Orlando Hernandez **RC** (Futurama) .25
125 Ben Grieve (Futurama) .05
126 A.J. Hinch (Futurama) .05
127 Matt Clement (Futurama) .05
128 Gary Matthews Jr. **RC** (Futurama) .05
129 Aramis Ramirez (Futurama) .05
130 Rolando Arrojo (Futurama) .05

Big Boppers

The game's heavy hitters are the focus of this insert set. Cards have a color action photo on a sepia background. Each card is individually serial numbered in red foil in the upper-right, within an edition of 500. Backs repeat part of the front photo, in sepia only, and have recent stats and hitting highlights. Cards are numbered with a "B" prefix.

NM/M

Complete Set (30): 80.00
Common Player: 1.00
Production 500 Sets
B1 Darin Erstad 1.50
B2 Rafael Palmeiro 3.00
B3 Cal Ripken Jr. 10.00
B4 Nomar Garciaparra 5.00
B5 Mo Vaughn 1.00
B6 Frank Thomas 4.00
B7 Albert Belle 1.00
B8 Jim Thome 2.50
B9 Manny Ramirez 4.00
B10 Tony Clark 1.00
B11 Tino Martinez 1.00
B12 Ben Grieve 1.00
B13 Ken Griffey Jr. 6.00
B14 Alex Rodriguez 7.50
B15 Jay Buhner 1.00
B16 Juan Gonzalez 2.00
B17 Jose Cruz Jr. 1.00
B18 Jose Canseco 2.50
B19 Travis Lee 1.50
B20 Chipper Jones 5.00
B21 Andres Galarraga 1.00
B22 Andruw Jones 4.00
B23 Sammy Sosa 5.00
B24 Vinny Castilla 1.00
B25 Larry Walker 1.00
B26 Jeff Bagwell 4.00
B27 Gary Sheffield 2.00
B28 Mike Piazza 6.00
B29 Mark McGwire 7.50
B30 Barry Bonds 10.00

Groovy Kind of Glove

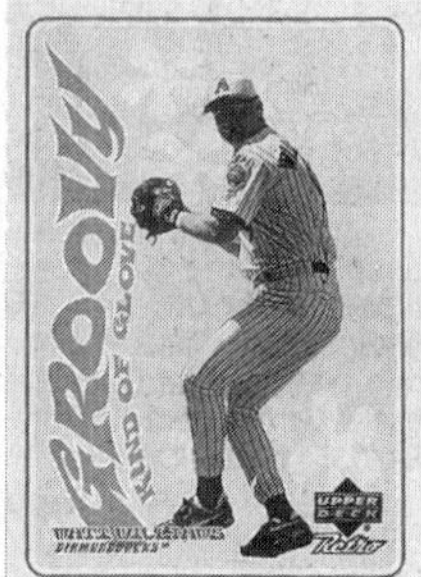

This 30-card set showcases baseball's top defensive players on a psychadelic, wavy and colorful background. They were inserted 1:7 packs.

NM/M

Complete Set (30): 50.00

Common Player: .60
Inserted 1:7

G1	Roberto Alomar	1.00
G2	Cal Ripken Jr.	7.50
G3	Nomar Garciaparra	3.50
G4	Frank Thomas	2.25
G5	Robin Ventura	.60
G6	Omar Vizquel	.60
G7	Kenny Lofton	.60
G8	Ben Grieve	.60
G9	Alex Rodriguez	6.00
G10	Ken Griffey Jr.	5.00
G11	Ivan Rodriguez	1.50
G12	Travis Lee	.75
G13	Matt Williams	.60
G14	Greg Maddux	3.50
G15	Andres Galarraga	.60
G16	Andruw Jones	2.25
G17	Kerry Wood	1.25
G18	Mark Grace	.60
G19	Craig Biggio	.60
G20	Charles Johnson	.60
G21	Raul Mondesi	.60
G22	Mike Piazza	5.00
G23	Rey Ordonez	.60
G24	Derek Jeter	7.50
G25	Scott Rolen	1.25
G26	Mark McGwire	6.00
G27	Ken Caminiti	.60
G28	Tony Gwynn	3.50
G29	J.T. Snow	.60
G30	Barry Bonds	7.50

Legendary Cut

This insert features an actual Babe Ruth cut signature and is limited to a total of three cards.

NM/M

LC Babe Ruth (Three issued; 1/04 Auction.) 9,500

New Frontier

This set spotlights 30 of baseball's top young prospects and is limited to 1,000 sequentially numbered sets.

NM/M

Complete Set (30): 45.00
Common Player: 1.00
Production 1,000 Sets

NF1	Justin Baughman	1.00
NF2	David Dellucci	1.00
NF3	Travis Lee	1.50
NF4	Troy Glaus	6.00
NF5	Mike Caruso	1.00
NF6	Jim Parque	1.00
NF7	Kerry Wood	2.00
NF8	Brett Tomko	1.00
NF9	Russell Branyan	1.00
NF10	Jaret Wright	1.00
NF11	Todd Helton	5.00
NF12	Gabe Alvarez	1.00
NF13	Matt Anderson	1.00
NF14	Alex Gonzalez	1.00
NF15	Mark Kotsay	1.00
NF16	Derrek Lee	3.00
NF17	Richard Hidalgo	1.00
NF18	Adrian Beltre	2.00
NF19	Geoff Jenkins	1.00
NF20	Eric Milton	1.00
NF21	Brad Fullmer	1.00
NF22	Vladimir Guerrero	6.00
NF23	Carl Pavano	1.00
NF24	Orlando Hernandez	1.25
NF25	Ben Grieve	1.00
NF26	A.J. Hinch	1.00
NF27	Matt Clement	1.00
NF28	Gary Matthews	1.00
NF29	Aramis Ramirez	1.00
NF30	Rolando Arrojo	1.00

1998 UD Retro Quantum Leap

This 30-card insert set highlights the technilogical advancements of Upper Deck products on a horizontal format. A total of 50 serially numbered sets were produced.

NM/M

Common Player: 15.00
Production 50 Sets

Q1	Darin Erstad	20.00
Q2	Cal Ripken Jr.	100.00
Q3	Nomar Garciaparra	50.00
Q4	Frank Thomas	40.00
Q5	Kenny Lofton	15.00
Q6	Ben Grieve	15.00
Q7	Ken Griffey Jr.	60.00
Q8	Alex Rodriguez	75.00
Q9	Juan Gonzalez	20.00
Q10	Jose Cruz Jr.	15.00
Q11	Roger Clemens	55.00
Q12	Travis Lee	15.00
Q13	Chipper Jones	50.00
Q14	Greg Maddux	50.00
Q15	Kerry Wood	20.00
Q16	Jeff Bagwell	40.00
Q17	Mike Piazza	60.00
Q18	Scott Rolen	30.00
Q19	Mark McGwire	75.00
Q20	Tony Gwynn	50.00
Q21	Larry Walker	15.00
Q22	Derek Jeter	100.00
Q23	Sammy Sosa	50.00
Q24	Barry Bonds	100.00
Q25	Mo Vaughn	15.00
Q26	Roberto Alomar	20.00
Q27	Todd Helton	30.00
Q28	Ivan Rodriguez	30.00
Q29	Vladimir Guerrero	40.00
Q30	Albert Belle	15.00

Sign of the Times

This retro-style autographed 31-card set features both retired legends and current players. They were inserted 1:36 packs.

NM/M

Common Autograph: 7.50
Inserted 1:36

EB	Ernie Banks/300	40.00
YB	Yogi Berra/150	60.00
RB	Russell Branyan/750	8.00
LB	Lou Brock/300	25.00
JC	Jose Cruz Jr./300	8.00
RF	Rollie Fingers/600	10.00
BF	Bob Feller/600	20.00
CF	Carlton Fisk/600	30.00
BGi	Bob Gibson/300	30.00
BGr	Ben Grieve/300	5.00
KGj	Ken Griffey Jr./100	185.00
KGs	Ken Griffey Sr./600	10.00
TG	Tony Gwynn/200	35.00
AK	Al Kaline/600	30.00
PK	Paul Konerko/750	15.00
TLe	Travis Lee/300	8.00
EM	Eddie Mathews/600	60.00
GMj	Gary Matthews Jr./750	8.00
GMs	Gary Matthews/600	8.00
WM	Willie McCovey/600	30.00
TP	Tony Perez/600	20.00
GP	Gaylord Perry/1,000	10.00
KP	Kirby Puckett/450	80.00
BR	Brooks Robinson/300	30.00
SR	Scott Rolen/300	20.00
NR	Nolan Ryan/500	100.00
TS	Tom Seaver/300	30.00
WS	Warren Spahn/600	40.00
WiS	Willie Stargell/600	50.00
FT	Frank Thomas/600	15.00
KW	Kerry Wood/200	25.00

Time Capsule

Another retro-styled card that featured current stars who were destined to earn a place in baseball history. They were inserted 1:2 packs.

NM/M

Complete Set (50): 35.00
Common Player: .25
Inserted 1:2

TC1	Mike Mussina	.50
TC2	Rafael Palmeiro	.65
TC3	Cal Ripken Jr.	3.00
TC4	Nomar Garciaparra	1.50
TC5	Pedro Martinez	1.00
TC6	Mo Vaughn	.25
TC7	Albert Belle	.25
TC8	Frank Thomas	1.00
TC9	David Justice	.25
TC10	Kenny Lofton	.25
TC11	Manny Ramirez	1.00
TC12	Jim Thome	.60
TC13	Derek Jeter	3.00
TC14	Tino Martinez	.25
TC15	Ben Grieve	.25
TC16	Rickey Henderson	1.00
TC17	Ken Griffey Jr.	2.00
TC18	Randy Johnson	1.00
TC19	Alex Rodriguez	2.50
TC20	Wade Boggs	1.50
TC21	Fred McGriff	.25
TC22	Juan Gonzalez	.50
TC23	Ivan Rodriguez	.75
TC24	Nolan Ryan	2.50
TC25	Jose Canseco	.50
TC26	Roger Clemens	1.75
TC27	Jose Cruz Jr.	.25
TC28	Travis Lee	.40
TC29	Matt Williams	.25
TC30	Andres Galarraga	.25
TC31	Andruw Jones	1.00
TC32	Chipper Jones	1.50
TC33	Greg Maddux	1.50
TC34	Kerry Wood	.50
TC35	Barry Larkin	.25
TC36	Dante Bichette	.25
TC37	Larry Walker	.25
TC38	Livan Hernandez	.25
TC39	Jeff Bagwell	1.00
TC40	Craig Biggio	.25
TC41	Charles Johnson	.25
TC42	Gary Sheffield	.50
TC43	Marquis Grissom	.25
TC44	Mike Piazza	2.00
TC45	Scott Rolen	.65
TC46	Curt Schilling	.40
TC47	Mark McGwire	2.50
TC48	Ken Caminiti	.25
TC49	Tony Gwynn	1.50
TC50	Barry Bonds	3.00

Lunchbox

Lunchboxes were the form of packaging for UD Retro. Six different players are featured with each lunchbox containing 24 six-card packs, with a SRP of $4.99.

NM/M

Complete Set (6): 40.00
Common Lunchbox: 4.00

Nomar Garciaparra	6.00
Ken Griffey Jr.	7.50
Chipper Jones	6.00
Travis Lee	4.00
Mark McGwire	10.00
Cal Ripken Jr.	12.00

1999 Upper Deck

Released in two series, base card fronts feature a textured silver border along the left and right sides. The player name and Upper Deck logo also are stamped in silver foil. Backs have a small photo, with stats and career highlights. Randomly seeded in packs are 100 Ken Griffey Jr. rookie cards that were bought back by Upper Deck from the hobby and autographed. Upper Deck also re-inserted one pack of '89 Upper Deck inside every hobby box. Ten-card hobby packs carry a S.R.P. of $2.99. Cards #256-265 were never produced.

NM/M

Complete Set (525): 45.00
Complete Series 1 (255): 25.00
Complete Series 2 (270): 20.00
Common Player: .05
Exclusive Stars/RC's: 15X
Production 100 each
Pack (10): 1.50
Wax Box (24): 35.00

1	Troy Glaus/SR	.60
2	Adrian Beltre/SR	.25
3	Matt Anderson/SR	.05
4	Eric Chavez/SR	.15
5	Jin Cho/SR	.05
6	Robert Smith/SR **RC**	.05
7	George Lombard/SR	.05
8	Mike Kinkade/SR	.05
9	Seth Greisinger/SR	.05
10	J.D. Drew/SR	.50
11	Aramis Ramirez/SR	.05
12	Carlos Guillen/SR	.05
13	Justin Baughman/SR	.05
14	Jim Parque/SR	.05
15	Ryan Jackson/SR	.05
16	Ramon Martinez/SR	.05
17	Orlando Hernandez/SR	.05
18	Jeremy Giambi/SR	.05
19	Gary DiSarcina	.05
20	Darin Erstad	.25
21	Troy Glaus	.50
22	Chuck Finley	.05
23	Dave Hollins	.05
24	Troy Percival	.05
25	Tim Salmon	.05
26	Brian Anderson	.05
27	Jay Bell	.05
28	Andy Benes	.05
29	Brent Brede	.05
30	David Dellucci	.05
31	Karim Garcia	.10
32	Travis Lee	.20
33	Andres Galarraga	.05
34	Ryan Klesko	.05
35	Keith Lockhart	.05
36	Kevin Millwood	.05
37	Denny Neagle	.05
38	John Smoltz	.05
39	Michael Tucker	.05
40	Walt Weiss	.05
41	Dennis Martinez	.05
42	Javy Lopez	.05
43	Brady Anderson	.05
44	Harold Baines	.05
45	Mike Bordick	.05
46	Roberto Alomar	.20
47	Scott Erickson	.05
48	Mike Mussina	.30
49	Cal Ripken Jr.	2.00
50	Darren Bragg	.05
51	Dennis Eckersley	.50
52	Nomar Garciaparra	.75
53	Scott Hatteberg	.05
54	Troy O'Leary	.05
55	Bret Saberhagen	.05
56	John Valentin	.05
57	Rod Beck	.05
58	Jeff Blauser	.05
59	Brant Brown	.05
60	Mark Clark	.05
61	Mark Grace	.05
62	Kevin Tapani	.05
63	Henry Rodriguez	.05
64	Mike Cameron	.05
65	Mike Caruso	.05
66	Ray Durham	.05
67	Jaime Navarro	.05
68	Magglio Ordonez	.30
69	Mike Sirotka	.05
70	Sean Casey	.15
71	Barry Larkin	.05
72	Jon Nunnally	.05
73	Paul Konerko	.15
74	Chris Stynes	.05
75	Brett Tomko	.05
76	Dmitri Young	.05
77	Sandy Alomar	.05
78	Bartolo Colon	.05
79	Travis Fryman	.05
80	Brian Giles	.05
81	David Justice	.05
82	Omar Vizquel	.05
83	Jaret Wright	.05
84	Jim Thome	.40
85	Charles Nagy	.05
86	Pedro Astacio	.05
87	Todd Helton	.50
88	Darryl Kile	.05
89	Mike Lansing	.05
90	Neifi Perez	.05
91	John Thomson	.05
92	Larry Walker	.05
93	Tony Clark	.05
94	Deivi Cruz	.05
95	Damion Easley	.05
96	Brian L. Hunter	.05
97	Todd Jones	.05
98	Brian Moehler	.05
99	Gabe Alvarez	.05
100	Craig Counsell	.05
101	Cliff Floyd	.05
102	Livan Hernandez	.05
103	Andy Larkin	.05
104	Derrek Lee	.35
105	Brian Meadows	.05
106	Moises Alou	.05
107	Sean Berry	.05
108	Craig Biggio	.05
109	Ricky Gutierrez	.05
110	Mike Hampton	.05
111	Jose Lima	.05
112	Billy Wagner	.05
113	Hal Morris	.05
114	Johnny Damon	.30
115	Jeff King	.05
116	Jeff Montgomery	.05
117	Glendon Rusch	.05
118	Larry Sutton	.05
119	Bobby Bonilla	.05
120	Jim Eisenreich	.05
121	Eric Karros	.05
122	Matt Luke	.05
123	Ramon Martinez	.05
124	Gary Sheffield	.40
125	Eric Young	.05
126	Charles Johnson	.05
127	Jeff Cirillo	.05
128	Marquis Grissom	.05
129	Jeromy Burnitz	.05
130	Bob Wickman	.05
131	Scott Karl	.05
132	Mark Loretta	.05
133	Fernando Vina	.05
134	Matt Lawton	.05
135	Pat Meares	.05
136	Eric Milton	.05
137	Paul Molitor	.60
138	David Ortiz	.35
139	Todd Walker	.05
140	Shane Andrews	.05
141	Brad Fullmer	.05
142	Vladimir Guerrero	.60
143	Dustin Hermanson	.05
144	Ryan McGuire	.05
145	Ugueth Urbina	.05
146	John Franco	.05
147	Butch Huskey	.05
148	Bobby Jones	.05
149	John Olerud	.05
150	Rey Ordonez	.05
151	Mike Piazza	1.25
152	Hideo Nomo	.30
153	Masato Yoshii	.05
154	Derek Jeter	2.00
155	Chuck Knoblauch	.05
156	Paul O'Neill	.05
157	Andy Pettitte	.20
158	Mariano Rivera	.15
159	Darryl Strawberry	.05
160	David Wells	.05
161	Jorge Posada	.05
162	Ramiro Mendoza	.05
163	Miguel Tejada	.15
164	Ryan Christenson	.05
165	Rickey Henderson	.60
166	A.J. Hinch	.05
167	Ben Grieve	.05
168	Kenny Rogers	.05
169	Matt Stairs	.05
170	Bob Abreu	.05
171	Rico Brogna	.05
172	Doug Glanville	.05
173	Mike Grace	.05
174	Desi Relaford	.05
175	Scott Rolen	.40
176	Jose Guillen	.05
177	Francisco Cordova	.05
178	Al Martin	.05
179	Jason Schmidt	.05
180	Turner Ward	.05
181	Kevin Young	.05
182	Mark McGwire	1.50
183	Delino DeShields	.05
184	Eli Marrero	.05
185	Tom Lampkin	.05
186	Ray Lankford	.05
187	Willie McGee	.05
188	Matt Morris	.05
189	Andy Ashby	.05
190	Kevin Brown	.05
191	Ken Caminiti	.05
192	Trevor Hoffman	.05
193	Wally Joyner	.05
194	Greg Vaughn	.05
195	Danny Darwin	.05
196	Shawn Estes	.05
197	Orel Hershiser	.05
198	Jeff Kent	.05
199	Bill Mueller	.05
200	Robb Nen	.05
201	J.T. Snow	.05
202	Ken Cloude	.05
203	Russ Davis	.05
204	Jeff Fassero	.05
205	Ken Griffey Jr.	1.00
206	Shane Monahan	.05
207	David Segui	.05
208	Dan Wilson	.05
209	Wilson Alvarez	.05
210	Wade Boggs	.75
211	Miguel Cairo	.05
212	Bubba Trammell	.05
213	Quinton McCracken	.05
214	Paul Sorrento	.05
215	Kevin Stocker	.05
216	Will Clark	.05
217	Rusty Greer	.05
218	Rick Helling	.05
219	Mike McLemore	.05
220	Ivan Rodriguez	.50
221	John Wetteland	.05
222	Jose Canseco	.40
223	Roger Clemens	.85
224	Carlos Delgado	.25
225	Darrin Fletcher	.05
226	Alex Gonzalez	.05
227	Jose Cruz Jr.	.05
228	Shannon Stewart	.05
229	Rolando Arrojo (Foreign Focus)	.05
230	Livan Hernandez (Foreign Focus)	.05
231	Orlando Hernandez (Foreign Focus)	.05
232	Raul Mondesi (Foreign Focus)	.05
233	Moises Alou (Foreign Focus)	.05
234	Pedro Martinez (Foreign Focus)	.30
235	Sammy Sosa (Foreign Focus)	.50
236	Vladimir Guerrero (Foreign Focus)	.40
237	Bartolo Colon (Foreign Focus)	.05
238	Miguel Tejada (Foreign Focus)	.05
239	Ismael Valdes (Foreign Focus)	.05
240	Mariano Rivera (Foreign Focus)	.05
241	Jose Cruz Jr. (Foreign Focus)	.05
242	Juan Gonzalez (Foreign Focus)	.20
243	Ivan Rodriguez (Foreign Focus)	.15
244	Sandy Alomar (Foreign Focus)	.05
245	Roberto Alomar (Foreign Focus)	.10
246	Magglio Ordonez (Foreign Focus)	.05
247	Kerry Wood (Highlights Checklist)	.10
248	Mark McGwire (Highlights Checklist)	.75
249	David Wells (Highlights Checklist)	.05
250	Rolando Arrojo (Highlights Checklist)	.05
251	Ken Griffey Jr. (Highlights Checklist)	.65
252	Trevor Hoffman (Highlights Checklist)	.05
253	Travis Lee (Highlights Checklist)	.05
254	Roberto Alomar (Highlights Checklist)	.10
255	Sammy Sosa (Highlights Checklist)	.50
266	Pat Burrell/SR **RC**	2.00
267	Shea Hillenbrand/SR **RC**	.65
268	Robert Fick/SR	.05
269	Roy Halladay/SR	.05
270	Ruben Mateo/SR	.05
271	Bruce Chen/SR	.05
272	Angel Pena/SR	.05
273	Michael Barrett/SR	.05
274	Kevin Witt/SR	.05
275	Damon Minor/SR	.05
276	Ryan Minor/SR	.05
277	A.J. Pierzynski/SR	.05
278	A.J. Burnett/SR **RC**	.50
279	Dermal Brown/SR	.05
280	Joe Lawrence/SR	.05
281	Derrick Gibson/SR	.05
282	Carlos Febles/SR	.05
283	Chris Haas/SR	.05
284	Cesar King/SR	.05
285	Calvin Pickering/SR	.05
286	Mitch Meluskey/SR	.05
287	Carlos Beltran/SR	.50
288	Ron Belliard/SR	.05
289	Jerry Hairston Jr./SR	.05
290	Fernando Seguignol/SR	.05
291	Kris Benson/SR	.05
292	Chad Hutchinson/SR **RC**	.05
293	Jarrod Washburn	.05
294	Jason Dickson	.05
295	Mo Vaughn	.05
296	Garrett Anderson	.05
297	Jim Edmonds	.05
298	Ken Hill	.05
299	Shigetosi Hasegawa	.05
300	Todd Stottlemyre	.05
301	Randy Johnson	.60
302	Omar Daal	.05
303	Steve Finley	.05
304	Matt Williams	.05
305	Danny Klassen	.05
306	Tony Batista	.05
307	Brian Jordan	.05
308	Greg Maddux	.75
309	Chipper Jones	.75
310	Bret Boone	.05
311	Ozzie Guillen	.05
312	John Rocker	.05
313	Tom Glavine	.25
314	Andruw Jones	.60
315	Albert Belle	.05
316	Charles Johnson	.05

317	Will Clark	.05
318	B.J. Surhoff	.05
319	Delino DeShields	.05
320	Heathcliff Slocumb	.05
321	Sidney Ponson	.05
322	Juan Guzman	.05
323	Reggie Jefferson	.05
324	Mark Portugal	.05
325	Tim Wakefield	.05
326	Jason Varitek	.05
327	Jose Offerman	.05
328	Pedro Martinez	.60
329	Trot Nixon	.05
330	Kerry Wood	.30
331	Sammy Sosa	.75
332	Glenallen Hill	.05
333	Gary Gaetti	.05
334	Mickey Morandini	.05
335	Benito Santiago	.05
336	Jeff Blauser	.05
337	Frank Thomas	.65
338	Paul Konerko	.15
339	Jaime Navarro	.05
340	Carlos Lee	.05
341	Brian Simmons	.05
342	Mark Johnson	.05
343	Jeff Abbot	.05
344	Steve Avery	.05
345	Mike Cameron	.05
346	Michael Tucker	.05
347	Greg Vaughn	.05
348	Hal Morris	.05
349	Pete Harnisch	.05
350	Denny Neagle	.05
351	Manny Ramirez	.60
352	Roberto Alomar	.20
353	Dwight Gooden	.05
354	Kenny Lofton	.05
355	Mike Jackson	.05
356	Charles Nagy	.05
357	Enrique Wilson	.05
358	Russ Branyan	.05
359	Richie Sexson	.05
360	Vinny Castilla	.05
361	Dante Bichette	.05
362	Kirt Manwaring	.05
363	Darryl Hamilton	.05
364	Jamey Wright	.05
365	Curt Leskanic	.05
366	Jeff Reed	.05
367	Bobby Higginson	.05
368	Justin Thompson	.05
369	Brad Ausmus	.05
370	Dean Palmer	.05
371	Gabe Kapler	.05
372	Juan Encarnacion	.05
373	Karim Garcia	.10
374	Alex Gonzalez	.05
375	Braden Looper	.05
376	Preston Wilson	.05
377	Todd Dunwoody	.05
378	Alex Fernandez	.05
379	Mark Kotsay	.05
380	Mark Mantei	.05
381	Ken Caminiti	.05
382	Scott Elarton	.05
383	Jeff Bagwell	.60
384	Derek Bell	.05
385	Ricky Gutierrez	.05
386	Richard Hildalgo	.05
387	Shane Reynolds	.05
388	Carl Everett	.05
389	Scott Service	.05
390	Jeff Suppan	.05
391	Joe Randa	.05
392	Kevin Appier	.05
393	Shane Halter	.05
394	Chad Kreuter	.05
395	Mike Sweeney	.05
396	Kevin Brown	.05
397	Devon White	.05
398	Todd Hollandsworth	.05
399	Todd Hundley	.05
400	Chan Ho Park	.05
401	Mark Grudzielanek	.05
402	Raul Mondesi	.05
403	Ismael Valdes	.05
404	Rafael Roque	.05
405	Sean Berry	.05
406	Kevin Barker	.05
407	Dave Nilsson	.05
408	Geoff Jenkins	.05
409	Jim Abbott	.05
410	Bobby Hughes	.05
411	Corey Koskie	.05
412	Rick Aguilera	.05
413	LaTroy Hawkins	.05
414	Ron Coomer	.05
415	Denny Hocking	.05
416	Marty Cordova	.05
417	Terry Steinbach	.05
418	Rondell White	.05
419	Wilton Guerrero	.05
420	Shane Andrews	.05
421	Orlando Cabrera	.05
422	Carl Pavano	.05
423	Jeff Vasquez	.05
424	Chris Widger	.05
425	Robin Ventura	.05
426	Rickey Henderson	.60
427	Al Leiter	.05
428	Bobby Jones	.05
429	Brian McRae	.05
430	Roger Cedeno	.05
431	Bobby Bonilla	.05
432	Edgardo Alfonzo	.05
433	Bernie Williams	.05
434	Ricky Ledee	.05
435	Chili Davis	.05
436	Tino Martinez	.05
437	Scott Brosius	.05
438	David Cone	.05
439	Joe Girardi	.05
440	Roger Clemens	.85
441	Chad Curtis	.05
442	Hideki Irabu	.05
443	Jason Giambi	.40
444	Scott Spezio	.05
445	Tony Phillips	.05
446	Ramon Hernandez	.05
447	Mike Macfarlane	.05
448	Tom Candiotti	.05
449	Billy Taylor	.05
450	Bobby Estella	.05
451	Curt Schilling	.25
452	Carlton Loewer	.05
453	Marlon Anderson	.05
454	Kevin Jordan	.05
455	Ron Gant	.05
456	Chad Ogea	.05
457	Abraham Nunez	.05
458	Jason Kendall	.05
459	Pat Meares	.05
460	Brant Brown	.05
461	Brian Giles	.05
462	Chad Hermansen	.05
463	Freddy Garcia	.05
464	Edgar Renteria	.05
465	Fernando Tatis	.05
466	Eric Davis	.05
467	Darren Bragg	.05
468	Donovan Osborne	.05
469	Manny Aybar	.05
470	Jose Jimenez	.05
471	Kent Mercker	.05
472	Reggie Sanders	.05
473	Ruben Rivera	.05
474	Tony Gwynn	.75
475	Jim Leyritz	.05
476	Chris Gomez	.05
477	Matt Clement	.05
478	Carlos Hernandez	.05
479	Sterling Hitchcock	.05
480	Ellis Burks	.05
481	Barry Bonds	2.00
482	Marvin Bernard	.05
483	Kirk Rueter	.05
484	F.P. Santangelo	.05
485	Stan Javier	.05
486	Jeff Kent	.05
487	Alex Rodriguez	1.50
488	Tom Lampkin	.05
489	Jose Mesa	.05
490	Jay Buhner	.05
491	Edgar Martinez	.05
492	Butch Huskey	.05
493	John Mabry	.05
494	Jamie Moyer	.05
495	Roberto Hernandez	.05
496	Tony Saunders	.05
497	Fred McGriff	.05
498	Dave Martinez	.05
499	Jose Canseco	.40
500	Rolando Arrojo	.05
501	Esteban Yan	.05
502	Juan Gonzalez	.30
503	Rafael Palmeiro	.50
504	Aaron Sele	.05
505	Royce Clayton	.05
506	Todd Zeile	.05
507	Tom Goodwin	.05
508	Lee Stevens	.05
509	Esteban Loaiza	.05
510	Joey Hamilton	.05
511	Homer Bush	.05
512	Willie Greene	.05
513	Shawn Green	.25
514	David Wells	.05
515	Kelvim Escobar	.05
516	Tony Fernandez	.05
517	Pat Hentgen	.05
518	Mark McGwire (Arms Race)	.75
519	Ken Griffey Jr. (Arms Race)	.65
520	Sammy Sosa (Arms Race)	.50
521	Juan Gonzalez (Arms Race)	.20
522	J.D. Drew (Arms Race)	.10
523	Chipper Jones (Arms Race)	.40
524	Alex Rodriguez (Arms Race)	.75
525	Mike Piazza (Arms Race)	.65
526	Nomar Garciaparra (Arms Race)	.50
527	Season Highlights Checklist (Mark McGwire)	.75
528	Season Highlights Checklist (Sammy Sosa)	.50
529	Season Highlights Checklist (Scott Brosius)	.05
530	Season Highlights Checklist (Cal Ripken Jr.)	1.00
531	Season Highlights Checklist (Barry Bonds)	1.00
532	Season Highlights Checklist (Roger Clemens)	.40
533	Season Highlights Checklist (Ken Griffey Jr.)	.65
534	Season Highlights Checklist (Alex Rodriguez)	.75
535	Season Highlights Checklist (Curt Schilling)	.05

Exclusives

Randomly inserted into hobby packs, this parallel issue is individually serial numbered on back from within an edition of 100 of each card. Besides the serial number, the inserts are readily apparent by the use of copper metallic foil graphic highlights on front. Series 1 Exclusive cards have the serial number on back in gold foil; Series 2 Exclusives have the number ink-jetted in black. A green-foil parallel of the parallel was issued in quantities of just one card each for Series 1, and 10 cards each for Series 2.

	NM/M
Common Player:	3.00
Stars/Rookies:	15X
Greens (1-255):	Values Undetermined
Greens (266-535):	100X

Crowning Glory

These double-sided cards feature players who reached milestones during the '98 season. There are three cards in the set, with four different versions of each card. The regular version is seeded 1:23 packs. Doubles are numbered to 1,000, Triples numbered to 25 and Home Runs are limited to one each.

		NM/M
Complete Set (3):		22.50
Common Player:		6.00
Inserted 1:23		
Doubles (1,000 Sets):		2X
Triples (25 Sets):		8X
Home Runs (1 Set):	Values Undetermined	
CG1	Roger Clemens, Kerry Wood	6.00
CG2	Mark McGwire, Barry Bonds	12.00
CG3	Ken Griffey Jr., Mark McGwire	7.50

Forte

This 30-card set features the top players in the game, highlighted by blue holofoil treatment. Numbers on card backs have an "F" prefix and are seeded 1:23 packs. There are also die-cut parallels to Forte: Double, Triple and Home Run. Doubles are sequentially numbered to 2,000 sets, Triples are limited to 100 numbered sets and Home Runs are limited to 10 numbered sets.

		NM/M
Complete Set (30):		50.00
Common Player:		.50
Inserted 1:23		
Doubles (2,000 Sets):		3X
Triples (100):		15X
Quadruples (10):		40X
1	Darin Erstad	1.50
2	Troy Glaus	1.50
3	Mo Vaughn	.50
4	Greg Maddux	2.50
5	Andres Galarraga	.50
6	Chipper Jones	2.50
7	Cal Ripken Jr.	5.00
8	Albert Belle	.50
9	Nomar Garciaparra	2.50
10	Sammy Sosa	2.50
11	Kerry Wood	1.00
12	Frank Thomas	2.00
13	Jim Thome	1.50
14	Jeff Bagwell	2.00
15	Vladimir Guerrero	2.00
16	Mike Piazza	3.00
17	Derek Jeter	5.00
18	Ben Grieve	.50
19	Eric Chavez	.50
20	Scott Rolen	1.50
21	Mark McGwire	4.00
22	J.D. Drew	1.00
23	Tony Gwynn	2.50
24	Barry Bonds	5.00
25	Alex Rodriguez	4.00
26	Ken Griffey Jr.	3.00
27	Ivan Rodriguez	1.50
28	Juan Gonzalez	1.00
29	Roger Clemens	2.75
30	Andruw Jones	2.00

Game Jersey

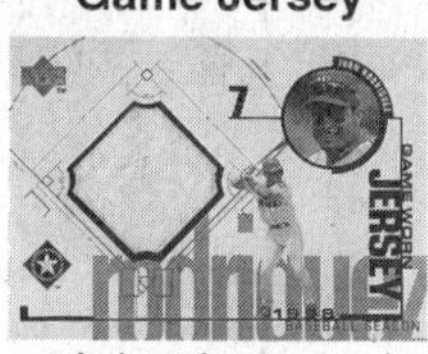

A piece of game-worn jersey is framed by a baseball diamond schematic. A round portrait photo appears at top-right, along with the player's uniform number. A small action photo is at bottom center. Backs have another round portrait photo and a statement of authenticity. Game Jersey cards bearing an H1 or H2 designation were hobby-only inserts at a rate of one per 288 packs in the appropriate series. Cards with an HR1 or HR2 notation were found in both hobby and retail packs at a rate of 1:2,500. Autographed versions of some cards were produced, with the edition number noted.

		NM/M
Common Player:		4.50
AB	Adrian Beltre H1	10.00
EC	Eric Chavez H2	6.00
JD	J.D. Drew H2	10.00
JDs	J.D. Drew/ Auto./8 H2	150.00
DE	Darin Erstad H1	10.00
BF	Brad Fullmer H2	4.50
JG	Juan Gonzalez HR1	15.00
BG	Ben Grieve H1	6.00
KG	Ken Griffey Jr. H1	20.00
KGs	Ken Griffey Jr./ Auto./24 H1	150.00
JR	Ken Griffey Jr. HR2	20.00
JRs	Ken Griffey Jr./ Auto./24 HR2	150.00
TGw	Tony Gwynn H2	15.00
TH	Todd Helton H2	15.00
CJ	Charles Johnson HR1	6.00
CJ	Chipper Jones H2	15.00
TL	Travis Lee H1	6.00
GM	Greg Maddux HR2	15.00
MP	Mike Piazza HR1	20.00
MR	Manny Ramirez H2	10.00
AR	Alex Rodriguez HR1	25.00
IR	Ivan Rodriguez H1	7.50
NRa	Nolan Ryan/ Astros H2	25.00
NRas	Nolan Ryan H2/ Auto./34	450.00
NRb	Nolan Ryan/ Rangers HR2	25.00
SS	Sammy Sosa H2	20.00
BT	Bubba Trammell H2	6.00
FT	Frank Thomas HR2	15.00
KW	Kerry Wood HR1	15.00
KWs	Kerry Wood/ Auto./34 HR1	150.00

Grand Slam Record Breakers

These gold-foil accented cards were inserts in a limited distribution retail packaging.

		NM/M
Complete Set (10):		7.50
Common Player:		.50
G1	Mark McGwire	1.50
G2	Sammy Sosa	1.50
G3	Ken Griffey Jr.	1.50
G4	Roger Clemens	1.00
G5	Kerry Wood	.75
G6	Cal Ripken Jr.	2.00
G7	Barry Bonds	2.00
G8	David Wells	.50
G9	Sammy Sosa	1.50
G10	Mark McGwire	1.50

Homerun Heroes

These gold-foil enhanced cards were inserted one per specially marked five-card foil pack, plus one as a topper in each tin can of this retail exclusive product. The first six players on the checklist were featured on the cans in which the cards were sold.

		NM/M
Complete Set (10):		10.00
Common Player:		.50
Complete Set Cans (6):		10.00
Common Player Can:		2.00
H1	Ken Griffey Jr.	1.25
H2	Mark McGwire	2.00
H3	Sammy Sosa	1.00
H4	Troy Glaus	.75
H5	Mike Piazza	2.00
H6	Chipper Jones	1.00
H7	Vladimir Guerrero	.75
H8	Frank Thomas	.75
H9	Juan Gonzalez	.50
H10	Alex Rodriguez	2.00
1	Ken Griffey Jr.	2.50
2	Mark McGwire	2.50
3	Sammy Sosa	2.00
4	Troy Glaus	1.50
5	Mike Piazza	2.50
6	Chipper Jones	2.00

Home Run Heroes

These cards were part of an unannounced multi-manufacturer (Fleer, Upper Deck, Topps, Pacific) insert program which was exclusive to Wal-Mart. Each company produced cards of Mark McGwire and Sammy Sosa, along with two other premier sluggers. Each company's cards share a "Power Elite" logo at top and "Home Run Heroes" logo vertically at right.

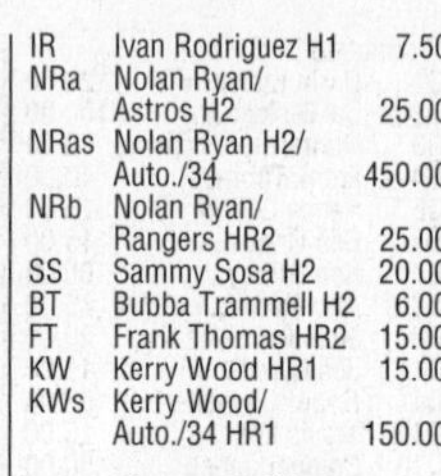

		NM/M
Complete Set (4):		5.00
Common Player:		1.00
5	Mark McGwire	2.00
6	Sammy Sosa	1.25
7	Ken Griffey Jr.	1.50
8	Frank Thomas	1.00

Immaculate Perception

Done in a horizontal format, this 27-card set features baseball's most celebrated players. Card fronts are enhanced with copper and silver foil stamping, encasing the player's image. The cards are numbered with an I prefix and are seeded 1:23 packs. There are also three parallel versions: Doubles numbered to 1,000, Triples numbered to 25 and Home Runs which are limited to one.

		NM/M
Complete Set (27):		45.00
Common Player:		.25
Inserted 1:23		
Doubles (1,000 Sets):		1.5X
Triples (25):		8X
Home Runs (1):	Values Undetermined	
I1	Jeff Bagwell	2.00
I2	Craig Biggio	.25
I3	Barry Bonds	5.00
I4	Roger Clemens	2.75
I5	Jose Cruz Jr.	.25
I6	Nomar Garciaparra	2.50
I7	Tony Clark	.25
I8	Ben Grieve	.25
I9	Ken Griffey Jr.	3.00
I10	Tony Gwynn	2.50
I11	Randy Johnson	2.00
I12	Chipper Jones	2.50
I13	Travis Lee	.40
I14	Kenny Lofton	.25
I15	Greg Maddux	2.50
I16	Mark McGwire	4.00
I17	Hideo Nomo	1.00
I18	Mike Piazza	3.00
I19	Manny Ramirez	2.00
I20	Cal Ripken Jr.	5.00
I21	Alex Rodriguez	4.00
I22	Scott Rolen	1.50
I23	Frank Thomas	2.00
I24	Kerry Wood	1.00
I25	Larry Walker	.25
I26	Vinny Castilla	.25
I27	Derek Jeter	5.00

Opening Season Superstars

These gold-foil enhanced cards were inserted one per specially marked five-card foil pack, in limited retail-exclusive distribution.

		NM/M
Complete Set (10):		10.00
Common Player:		.50
S1	Ken Griffey Jr.	1.50
S2	Mark McGwire	1.50
S3	Sammy Sosa	1.00

S4 Cal Ripken Jr. 2.00
S5 Nomar Garciaparra 1.00
S6 Alex Rodriguez 1.50
S7 Kerry Wood .50
S8 Juan Gonzalez .50
S9 Derek Jeter 2.00
S10 Greg Maddux 1.00

Piece of History 500 Club Babe Ruth

Limited to a reported 50 pieces and inserted into Series 2 Upper Deck packs, this card differs from the Piece of History Ruth bat cards on the photos used and the 500 Club notation.

NM/M
BR Babe Ruth/50 4,000

Babe Ruth Piece of History Bat

Limited to approximately 400, this card has an imbedded chip of a bat from an actual game-used Louisville Slugger swung by the Bambino himself. A "signed" version of this card also exists, which incorporates a cut signature of Ruth along with a piece of his game-used bat; only three exist.

NM/M
PH Babe Ruth/Bat 900.00
PHLC Babe Ruth Legendary Cut Auto. 25,000

Textbook Excellence

This 30-card set features the game's most fundamentally sound performers. Card fronts have a photo of the featured player on a silver-foil stamped grid background. Vertically at left is player identification on a brown background. These are seeded 1:23 packs. Three hobby-only parallels were also issued: Double, Triple and Home Run. Doubles are numbered to 2,000 sets, Triples are limited to 100 numbered sets and Home Runs are limited to 10 numbered sets. Cards are numbered with a "T" prefix.

NM/M
Complete Set (30): 12.50
Common Player: .25
Inserted 1:4
Doubles (2,000 Sets): 1.5X
Triples (100): 5X
Quadruples (10): 40X
T1 Mo Vaughn .25
T2 Greg Maddux .75
T3 Chipper Jones .75
T4 Andruw Jones .60
T5 Cal Ripken Jr. 2.00
T6 Albert Belle .25
T7 Roberto Alomar .30
T8 Nomar Garciaparra .75
T9 Kerry Wood .30
T10 Sammy Sosa .75
T11 Greg Vaughn .25
T12 Jeff Bagwell .60
T13 Kevin Brown .25
T14 Vladimir Guerrero .60
T15 Mike Piazza 1.00
T16 Bernie Williams .25
T17 Derek Jeter 2.00
T18 Ben Grieve .25
T19 Eric Chavez .25
T29 Scott Rolen .50
T21 Mark McGwire 1.50
T22 David Wells .25
T23 J.D. Drew .50
T24 Tony Gwynn .75
T25 Barry Bonds 2.00
T26 Alex Rodriguez 1.50
T27 Ken Griffey Jr. 1.00
T28 Juan Gonzalez .30
T29 Ivan Rodriguez .50
T30 Roger Clemens .85

View to a Thrill

This 30-card set focuses on baseball's best overall athletes. There are two photos of the featured player on the card front, highlighted by silver foil and some embossing. These are inserted 1:7 packs. Numbered parallel sets were produced of: Doubles (2,000), Triples (100) and Quadruples (10).

NM/M
Complete Set (30): 25.00
Common Player: .35
Inserted 1:7
Doubles (2,000 Sets): 1.5X
Triples (100): 4X
Quadruples (10): 30X
V1 Mo Vaughn .35
V2 Darin Erstad .40
V3 Travis Lee .40
V4 Chipper Jones 1.50
V5 Greg Maddux 1.50
V6 Gabe Kapler .35
V7 Cal Ripken Jr. 3.00
V8 Nomar Garciaparra 1.50
V9 Kerry Wood .40
V10 Frank Thomas 1.00
V11 Manny Ramirez 1.00
V12 Larry Walker .35
V13 Tony Clark .35
V14 Jeff Bagwell 1.00
V15 Craig Biggio .35
V16 Vladimir Guerrero 1.00
V17 Mike Piazza 2.00
V18 Bernie Williams .35
V19 Derek Jeter 3.00
V20 Ben Grieve .35
V21 Eric Chavez .35
V22 Scott Rolen .65
V23 Mark McGwire 2.50
V24 Tony Gwynn 1.50
V25 Barry Bonds 3.00
V26 Ken Griffey Jr. 2.00
V27 Alex Rodriguez 2.50
V28 J.D. Drew .65
V29 Juan Gonzalez .50
V30 Roger Clemens 1.75

Wonder Years

These inserts look like a throwback to the groovin' '70s, with brightly striped green and pink borders. "Wonder Years" is across the top of the front in yellow.

Backs have the player's three best seasons' stats along with a mention of a milestone. The cards are numbered with a WY prefix and are seeded 1:7 packs. There are three parallel versions: Doubles numbered to 1,000, Triples numbered to 25 and Home Runs that are limited to one.

NM/M
Complete Set (30): 30.00
Common Player: .50
Inserted 1:7
Doubles (2,000): 2.5X
Triples (50): 10X
Home Runs (1): Values Undetermined
WY1 Kerry Wood .75
WY2 Travis Lee .65
WY3 Jeff Bagwell 1.50
WY4 Barry Bonds 4.00
WY5 Roger Clemens 2.25
WY6 Jose Cruz Jr. .50
WY7 Andres Galarraga .50
WY8 Nomar Garciaparra 2.00
WY9 Juan Gonzalez .75
WY10 Ken Griffey Jr. 2.50
WY11 Tony Gwynn 2.00
WY12 Derek Jeter 4.00
WY13 Randy Johnson 1.50
WY14 Andruw Jones 1.50
WY15 Chipper Jones 2.00
WY16 Kenny Lofton .50
WY17 Greg Maddux 2.00
WY18 Tino Martinez .50
WY19 Mark McGwire 3.00
WY20 Paul Molitor 1.50
WY21 Mike Piazza 2.50
WY22 Manny Ramirez 1.50
WY23 Cal Ripken Jr. 4.00
WY24 Alex Rodriguez 3.00
WY25 Sammy Sosa 2.00
WY26 Frank Thomas 1.50
WY27 Mo Vaughn .50
WY28 Larry Walker .50
WY29 Scott Rolen 1.00
WY30 Ben Grieve .50

10th Anniversary Team

This 30-card set commemorates Upper Deck's 10th Anniversary, as collectors selected their favorite players for this set. Regular versions are seeded 1:4 packs, Doubles numbered to 4,000, Triples numbered to 100 and Home Runs which are limited to one set.

NM/M
Complete Set (30): 20.00
Common Player: .15
Inserted 1:4
Doubles (4,000 Sets): 2X
Triples (100): 6X
Home Runs (1): Values Undetermined
X1 Mike Piazza 1.50
X2 Mark McGwire 2.00
X3 Roberto Alomar .30
X4 Chipper Jones 1.00
X5 Cal Ripken Jr. 3.00
X6 Ken Griffey Jr. 1.50
X7 Barry Bonds 3.00
X8 Tony Gwynn 1.00
X9 Nolan Ryan 3.00
X10 Randy Johnson .75
X11 Dennis Eckersley .65
X12 Ivan Rodriguez .65
X13 Frank Thomas .75
X14 Craig Biggio .15
X15 Wade Boggs 1.00
X16 Alex Rodriguez 2.00
X17 Albert Belle .15
X18 Juan Gonzalez .40
X19 Rickey Henderson .75
X20 Greg Maddux 1.00
X21 Tom Glavine .35
X22 Randy Myers .15
X23 Sandy Alomar .15
X24 Jeff Bagwell .75
X25 Derek Jeter 3.00
X26 Matt Williams .15
X27 Kenny Lofton .15
X28 Sammy Sosa 1.00
X29 Larry Walker .15
X30 Roger Clemens 1.25

Ken Griffey Jr. Supers

These large-format (5"x 7") reproductions of each of Junior's regular-issue UD cards from 1989-98 were issued as a Wal-Mart exclusive in Series 1 UD baseball. Autographed versions of the super-sized Griffey cards were also found in the boxes. The supers were also distributed at the July 1999 National Sports Collectors Convention as a wrapper-redemption premium at the card company's booth. Other than the lack of a hologram on back, the cards are identical 4X blowups of the issued cards.

NM/M
Complete Set (10): 15.00
Common Card: 2.00
Autographed Card: 75.00
1 Ken Griffey Jr./1989 5.00
156 Ken Griffey Jr./1990 2.00
555 Ken Griffey Jr./1991 2.00
424 Ken Griffey Jr/1992 2.00
355 Ken Griffey Jr./1993 2.00
224 Ken Griffey Jr./1994 2.00
100 Ken Griffey Jr./1995 2.00
200 Ken Griffey Jr./1996 2.00
175 Ken Griffey Jr./1997 2.00
225 Ken Griffey Jr./1998 2.00

Ken Griffey Jr. 1989 Buyback Autograph

One hundred authentically autographed 1989 Ken Griffey Jr. Upper Deck rookie cards were seeded into Series 1 packs. UD bought the cards on the open market, had them autographed by Griffey and added a diamond-shaped authentication hologram on back

NM/M
Ken Griffey Jr./100 1,250

1999 Upper Deck Black Diamond

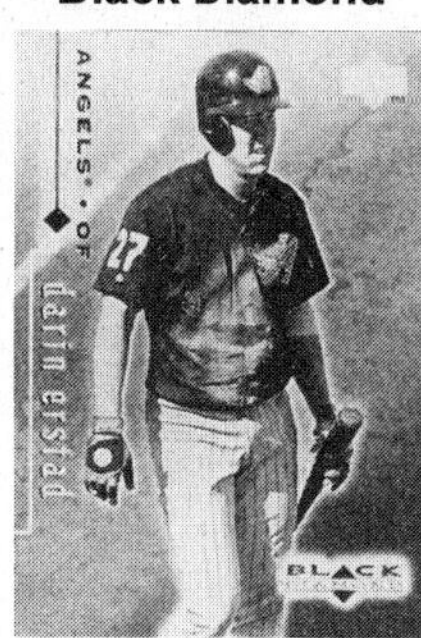

This 120-card base set features metallic foil fronts, while card backs have the featured player's vital information along with a close-up photo. The Diamond Debut subset (91-120) are short-printed and seeded 1:4 packs.

NM/M
Complete Set (120): 30.00
Common Player: .10
Common Diamond Debut (91-120): .25
Inserted 1:4
Double Diamonds (3,000 Each): 3X
Double Diamond Debuts (2,500): 2X
Triple Diamonds (1,500): 6X
Triple Diamond Debuts (1,000): 3X
Pack (6): 2.00
Wax Box (30): 40.00
1 Darin Erstad .25
2 Tim Salmon .10
3 Jim Edmonds .10
4 Matt Williams .10
5 David Dellucci .10
6 Jay Bell .10
7 Andres Galarraga .10
8 Chipper Jones 1.00
9 Greg Maddux 1.00
10 Andruw Jones .75
11 Cal Ripken Jr. 2.50
12 Rafael Palmeiro .65
13 Brady Anderson .10
14 Mike Mussina .40
15 Nomar Garciaparra 1.00
16 Mo Vaughn .10
17 Pedro Martinez .75
18 Sammy Sosa 1.00
19 Henry Rodriguez .10
20 Frank Thomas .75
21 Magglio Ordonez .40
22 Albert Belle .10
23 Paul Konerko .20
24 Sean Casey .10
25 Jim Thome .60
26 Kenny Lofton .10
27 Sandy Alomar Jr. .10
28 Jaret Wright .10
29 Larry Walker .10
30 Todd Helton .65
31 Vinny Castilla .10
32 Tony Clark .10
33 Damion Easley .10
34 Mark Kotsay .10
35 Derrek Lee .50
36 Moises Alou .10
37 Jeff Bagwell .75
38 Craig Biggio .10
39 Randy Johnson .75
40 Dean Palmer .10
41 Johnny Damon .35
42 Chan Ho Park .10
43 Raul Mondesi .10
44 Gary Sheffield .40
45 Jeromy Burnitz .10
46 Marquis Grissom .10
47 Jeff Cirillo .10
48 Paul Molitor .75
49 Todd Walker .10
50 Vladimir Guerrero .75
51 Brad Fullmer .10
52 Mike Piazza 1.50
53 Hideo Nomo .40
54 Carlos Baerga .10
55 John Olerud .10
56 Derek Jeter 2.50
57 Hideki Irabu .10
58 Tino Martinez .10
59 Bernie Williams .10
60 Miguel Tejada .25
61 Ben Grieve .10
62 Jason Giambi .55
63 Scott Rolen .60
64 Doug Glanville .10
65 Desi Relaford .10
66 Tony Womack .10
67 Jason Kendall .10
68 Jose Guillen .10
69 Tony Gwynn 1.00
70 Ken Caminiti .10
71 Greg Vaughn .10
72 Kevin Brown .10
73 Barry Bonds 2.50
74 J.T. Snow .10
75 Jeff Kent .10
76 Ken Griffey Jr. 1.50
77 Alex Rodriguez 2.00
78 Edgar Martinez .10
79 Jay Buhner .10
80 Mark McGwire 2.00
81 Delino DeShields .10
82 Brian Jordan .10
83 Quinton McCracken .10
84 Fred McGriff .10
85 Juan Gonzalez .40
86 Ivan Rodriguez .65
87 Will Clark .10
88 Roger Clemens 1.25
89 Jose Cruz Jr. .10
90 Babe Ruth 2.00
91 Troy Glaus (Diamond Debut) 1.00
92 Jarrod Washburn (Diamond Debut) .25
93 Travis Lee (Diamond Debut) .75
94 Bruce Chen (Diamond Debut) .25
95 Mike Caruso (Diamond Debut) .25
96 Jim Parque (Diamond Debut) .25
97 Kerry Wood (Diamond Debut) .50
98 Jeremy Giambi (Diamond Debut) .25
99 Matt Anderson (Diamond Debut) .25
100 Seth Greisinger (Diamond Debut) .25
101 Gabe Alvarez (Diamond Debut) .25
102 Rafael Medina (Diamond Debut) .25
103 Daryle Ward (Diamond Debut) .25
104 Alex Cora (Diamond Debut) .25
105 Adrian Beltre (Diamond Debut) .50
106 Geoff Jenkins (Diamond Debut) .25
107 Eric Milton (Diamond Debut) .25
108 Carl Pavano (Diamond Debut) .25
109 Eric Chavez (Diamond Debut) .50
110 Orlando Hernandez (Diamond Debut) .25
111 A.J. Hinch (Diamond Debut) .25
112 Carlton Loewer (Diamond Debut) .25
113 Aramis Ramirez (Diamond Debut) .25
114 Cliff Politte (Diamond Debut) .25
115 Matt Clement (Diamond Debut) .25
116 Alex Gonzalez (Diamond Debut) .25
117 J.D. Drew (Diamond Debut) .75
118 Shane Monahan (Diamond Debut) .25
119 Rolando Arrojo (Diamond Debut) .25
120 George Lombard (Diamond Debut) .25

Double Diamond

Double Diamonds are the most common parallels to the Black Diamond base set. Cards feature a red metallic-foil background or highlights. Regular-player cards (#1-90) are serially numbered on back from within

an edition of 3,000 each. Diamond Debut cards (#91-120) are individually numbered within an edition of 2,500 each.

	NM/M
Complete Set (120):	200.00
Common Player (1-90):	.25
Common Diamond Debut (91-120):	1.00
Stars (1-90):	3X
Diamond Debuts (91-120):	2X

Triple Diamond

Triple Diamonds are the mid-level of scarcity among the parallel inserts to the Black Diamond base cards. They feature yellow metallic-foil backgrounds (1-90) and highlights (91-120). Regular-player cards are serially numbered on back from within an edition of 1,500 each. Diamond Debut cards are individually numbered within an edition of 1,000 each.

	NM/M
Common Player (1-90):	1.00
Common Diamond Debut (91-120):	1.50
Stars (1-90):	6X
Diamond Debuts (91-120):	3X

Quadruple Diamond

Quadruple Diamonds are the scarcest of the parallel inserts to the Black Diamond base cards. The regular player cards (#1-90) feature a green metallic-foil background and are serially numbered on back from within an edition of 150 each. Diamond Debut cards (#91-120) also feature green foil highlights on front and are individually numbered within an edition of 100 each. Quad Diamond cards of Sosa, Griffey and McGwire were limited to the number of home runs each hit the previous season.

		NM/M
Common Player (1-90):		4.00
Production 150 each.		
Common Diamond Debut (91-120):		6.00
Production 100 each.		
Stars (1-90):		25X
Diamond Debuts (91-120):		8X
18	Sammy Sosa/66	50.00
76	Ken Griffey Jr. /56	60.00
80	Mark McGwire/70	75.00

A Piece of History

This six-card set features green metallic foil fronts with a diamond-shaped piece of game-used bat from the featured player embedded on the card front. No insertion ratio was released.

		NM/M
Common Player:		5.00
JG	Juan Gonzalez	7.50
TG	Tony Gwynn	10.00
BW	Bernie Williams	5.00
MM	Mark McGwire	200.00
MV	Mo Vaughn	5.00
SS	Sammy Sosa	25.00

Diamond Dominance

This 30-card set features full-bleed metallic foil fronts and includes the top stars of the game along with Babe Ruth. Each card is numbered with a "D" prefix and is limited to 1,500 sequentially numbered sets.

		NM/M
Complete Set (30):		65.00
Common Player:		.50
Production 1,500 Sets		
D01	Kerry Wood	1.00
D02	Derek Jeter	6.00
D03	Alex Rodriguez	5.00
D04	Frank Thomas	2.00
D05	Jeff Bagwell	2.00
D06	Mo Vaughn	.50
D07	Ivan Rodriguez	1.50
D08	Cal Ripken Jr.	6.00
D09	Rolando Arrojo	.50
D10	Chipper Jones	3.00
D11	Kenny Lofton	.50
D12	Paul Konerko	.75
D13	Mike Piazza	4.00
D14	Ben Grieve	.50
D15	Nomar Garciaparra	3.00
D16	Travis Lee	.65
D17	Scott Rolen	1.00
D18	Juan Gonzalez	1.00
D19	Tony Gwynn	3.00
D20	Tony Clark	.50
D21	Roger Clemens	3.50
D22	Sammy Sosa	3.00
D23	Larry Walker	.50
D24	Ken Griffey Jr.	4.00
D25	Mark McGwire	5.00
D26	Barry Bonds	6.00
D27	Vladimir Guerrero	2.00
D28	Tino Martinez	.50
D29	Greg Maddux	3.00
D30	Babe Ruth	5.00

Mystery Numbers

The player's card number determines scarcity in this hobby-only insert set. The basic set has an action photo set against a silver-foil background of repated numerals. Backs have a portrait photo and significant stat numbers from the 1998 season. Each

base Mystery Numbers card is individually numbered within an edition of 100 cards times the card number within the 30-card set (i.e., card #24 has an edition of 2,400) for a total of 46,500 cards. An emerald version of the Mystery Numbers cards has a total issue of 465 cards, with cards issued to a limit of the player's card number multiplied by 1.

		NM/M
Complete Set (30):		100.00
Common Player:		.75
M1	Babe Ruth/100	25.00
M2	Ken Griffey Jr./200	12.50
M3	Kerry Wood/300	4.00
M4	Mark McGwire/400	12.50
M5	Alex Rodriguez/500	12.50
M6	Chipper Jones/600	6.00
M7	Nomar Garciaparra/700	6.00
M8	Derek Jeter/800	10.00
M9	Mike Piazza/900	6.00
M10	Roger Clemens/1,000	4.50
M11	Greg Maddux/1,100	4.00
M12	Scott Rolen/1,200	1.25
M13	Cal Ripken Jr./1,300	7.50
M14	Ben Grieve/1,400	.75
M15	Troy Glaus/1,500	3.00
M16	Sammy Sosa/1,600	4.50
M17	Darin Erstad/1,700	1.25
M18	Juan Gonzalez/1,800	1.25
M19	Pedro Martinez/1,900	1.50
M20	Larry Walker/2,000	.75
M21	Vladimir Guerrero/2,100	1.50
M22	Jeff Bagwell/2,200	1.50
M23	Jaret Wright/2,300	.75
M24	Travis Lee/2,400	.75
M25	Barry Bonds/2,500	6.00
M26	Orlando Hernandez/2,600	.75
M27	Frank Thomas/2,700	1.50
M28	Tony Gwynn/2,800	2.00
M29	Andres Galarraga/2,900	.75
M30	Craig Biggio/3,000	.75

Piece of History 500 Club

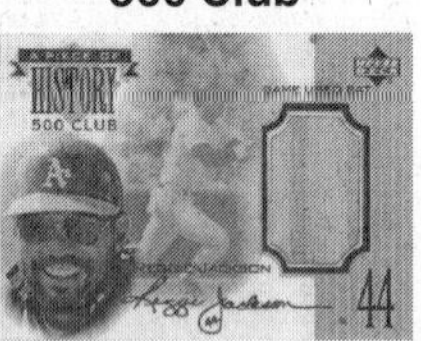

A veneer of lumber from one of Mr. October's war clubs is included in this special insert card. A facsimile autograph is also featured on front. A premium version with an authentic autograph serially numbered from within an edition of 44 (his uniform number) was also issued. Backs have a congratulatory authentication message from Upper Deck CEO Richard McWilliam.

	NM/M
Reggie Jackson	165.00
Reggie Jackson/ Auto.	500.00

1999 Upper Deck Century Legends

The first 47 cards in the 131-card set are taken from The Sporting News' list of Baseball's 100 Greatest Players. Each card bears a Sporting News photo of the featured player and his ranking in silver and copper foil. The next 50

cards tout Upper Deck's rankings of the Top 50 contemporary players. Rounding out the base set are two subsets: 21st Century Phenoms and Century Memories. Because of contractual problems, cards #11, 25, 26 and 126 were never issued. A die-cut parallel version of each card, serially numbered to 100 each, was produced as the "Century Collection."

		NM/M
Complete Set (131):		20.00
Common Player:		.10
Century Collection:		20X
Production 100 Sets		
Pack (5):		3.00
Wax Box (24):		60.00
1	Babe Ruth (Top 50)	2.00
1	Babe Ruth (SAMPLE overprint on back.)	2.00
2	Willie Mays (Top 50)	1.00
3	Ty Cobb (Top 50)	1.00
4	Walter Johnson (Top 50)	.40
5	Hank Aaron (Top 50)	1.00
6	Lou Gehrig (Top 50)	1.50
7	Christy Mathewson (Top 50)	.40
8	Ted Williams (Top 50)	1.25
9	Rogers Hornsby (Top 50)	.25
10	Stan Musial (Top 50)	.65
12	Grover Alexander (Top 50)	.25
13	Honus Wagner (Top 50)	.40
14	Cy Young (Top 50)	.40
15	Jimmie Foxx (Top 50)	.25
16	Johnny Bench (Top 50)	.50
17	Mickey Mantle (Top 50)	2.00
18	Josh Gibson (Top 50)	.25
19	Satchel Paige (Top 50)	.50
20	Roberto Clemente (Top 50)	1.50
21	Warren Spahn (Top 50)	.20
22	Frank Robinson (Top 50)	.20
23	Lefty Grove (Top 50)	.20
24	Eddie Collins (Top 50)	.10
27	Tris Speaker (Top 50)	.25
28	Mike Schmidt (Top 50)	.50
29	Napoleon LaJoie (Top 50)	.20
30	Steve Carlton (Top 50)	.25
31	Bob Gibson (Top 50)	.25
32	Tom Seaver (Top 50)	.25
33	George Sisler (Top 50)	.10
34	Barry Bonds (Top 50)	1.50
35	Joe Jackson (Top 50)	1.25
36	Bob Feller (Top 50)	.25
37	Hank Greenberg (Top 50)	.25
38	Ernie Banks (Top 50)	.40
39	Greg Maddux (Top 50)	.75
40	Yogi Berra (Top 50)	.40
41	Nolan Ryan (Top 50)	2.00
42	Mel Ott (Top 50)	.25
43	Al Simmons (Top 50)	.10
44	Jackie Robinson (Top 50)	1.25
45	Carl Hubbell (Top 50)	.25
46	Charley Gehringer (Top 50)	.10
47	Buck Leonard (Top 50)	.10
48	Reggie Jackson (Top 50)	.40
49	Tony Gwynn (Top 50)	.75
50	Roy Campanella (Top 50)	.40
51	Ken Griffey Jr. (Contemporaries)	1.00
52	Barry Bonds (Contemporaries)	1.50
53	Roger Clemens (Contemporaries)	.85
54	Tony Gwynn (Contemporaries)	.75
55	Cal Ripken Jr. (Contemporaries)	1.50
56	Greg Maddux (Contemporaries)	.75
57	Frank Thomas (Contemporaries)	.65
58	Mark McGwire (Contemporaries)	1.25
59	Mike Piazza (Contemporaries)	1.00
60	Wade Boggs (Contemporaries)	.75
61	Alex Rodriguez (Contemporaries)	1.25
62	Juan Gonzalez (Contemporaries)	.30
63	Mo Vaughn (Contemporaries)	.10
64	Albert Belle (Contemporaries)	.10
65	Sammy Sosa (Contemporaries)	.75
66	Nomar Garciaparra (Contemporaries)	.75
67	Derek Jeter (Contemporaries)	1.50
68	Kevin Brown (Contemporaries)	.10
69	Jose Canseco (Contemporaries)	.35
70	Randy Johnson (Contemporaries)	.60
71	Tom Glavine (Contemporaries)	.25
72	Barry Larkin (Contemporaries)	.10
73	Curt Schilling (Contemporaries)	.25
74	Moises Alou (Contemporaries)	.10
75	Fred McGriff (Contemporaries)	.10
76	Pedro Martinez (Contemporaries)	.65
77	Andres Galarraga (Contemporaries)	.10
78	Will Clark (Contemporaries)	.10
79	Larry Walker (Contemporaries)	.10
80	Ivan Rodriguez (Contemporaries)	.50
81	Chipper Jones (Contemporaries)	.75
82	Jeff Bagwell (Contemporaries)	.60
83	Craig Biggio (Contemporaries)	.10
84	Kerry Wood (Contemporaries)	.35
85	Roberto Alomar (Contemporaries)	.20
86	Vinny Castilla (Contemporaries)	.10
87	Kenny Lofton (Contemporaries)	.10
88	Rafael Palmeiro (Contemporaries)	.50
89	Manny Ramirez (Contemporaries)	.60
90	David Wells (Contemporaries)	.10
91	Mark Grace (Contemporaries)	.10
92	Bernie Williams (Contemporaries)	.10
93	David Cone (Contemporaries)	.10
94	John Olerud (Contemporaries)	.10
95	John Smoltz (Contemporaries)	.10
96	Tino Martinez (Contemporaries)	.10
97	Raul Mondesi (Contemporaries)	.10
98	Gary Sheffield (Contemporaries)	.35
99	Orel Hershiser (Contemporaries)	.10
100	Rickey Henderson (Contemporaries)	.65
101	J.D. Drew (21st Century Phenoms)	.50
102	Troy Glaus (21st Century Phenoms)	.50
103	Nomar Garciaparra (21st Century Phenoms)	.75
104	Scott Rolen (21st Century Phenoms)	.45
105	Ryan Minor (21st Century Phenoms)	.10
106	Travis Lee (21st Century Phenoms)	.20
107	Roy Halladay (21st Century Phenoms)	.10
108	Carlos Beltran (21st Century Phenoms)	.50
109	Alex Rodriguez (21st Century Phenoms)	1.25
110	Eric Chavez (21st Century Phenoms)	.20
111	Vladimir Guerrero (21st Century Phenoms)	.60
112	Ben Grieve (21st Century Phenoms)	.15
113	Kerry Wood (21st Century Phenoms)	.30
114	Alex Gonzalez (21st Century Phenoms)	.10
115	Darin Erstad (21st Century Phenoms)	.30
116	Derek Jeter (21st Century Phenoms)	1.50
117	Jaret Wright (21st Century Phenoms)	.10
118	Jose Cruz Jr. (21st Century Phenoms)	.10
119	Chipper Jones (21st Century Phenoms)	.75
120	Gabe Kapler (21st Century Phenoms)	.10
121	Satchel Paige (Century Memories)	.50
122	Willie Mays (Century Memories)	1.00
123	Roberto Clemente (Century Memories)	1.50
124	Lou Gehrig (Century Memories)	1.50
125	Mark McGwire (Century Memories)	1.25
127	Bob Gibson (Century Memories)	.25
128	Johnny Vander Meer (Century Memories)	.10
129	Walter Johnson (Century Memories)	.25
130	Ty Cobb (Century Memories)	.75
131	Don Larsen (Century Memories)	.20
132	Jackie Robinson (Century Memories)	1.00
133	Tom Seaver (Century Memories)	.25
134	Johnny Bench (Century Memories)	.35
135	Frank Robinson (Century Memories)	.25

All-Century Team

This 10-card set highlights Upper Deck's all-time all-star team. These were seeded 1:23 packs.

		NM/M
Complete Set (10):		30.00
Common Player:		2.50
Inserted 1:23		
1	Babe Ruth	7.50
2	Ty Cobb	3.50
3	Willie Mays	3.50
4	Lou Gehrig	6.00
5	Jackie Robinson	5.00
6	Mike Schmidt	2.50
7	Ernie Banks	2.50
8	Johnny Bench	2.50
9	Cy Young	2.50
10	Lineup Sheet	.25

Century Artifacts

A total of nine cards were inserted, redeemable for memorabilia from some of the top players of the century. Due to the limited nature of these one-of-one inserts and the fact that most or all were redeemed, no pricing is assigned. Each cut signature was framed with the player's Century Legends card.

Century MVPs

This collection selects 100 cards from Upper Deck's '99 MVP brand and adds a rainbow-foil shift to each card. These are limited to only one numbered set.

One Set Produced
Values Undetermined

Epic Milestones

This nine-card set showcases nine of the most impressive milestones established in major league history. Each card is numbered with an "EM" prefix and are seeded

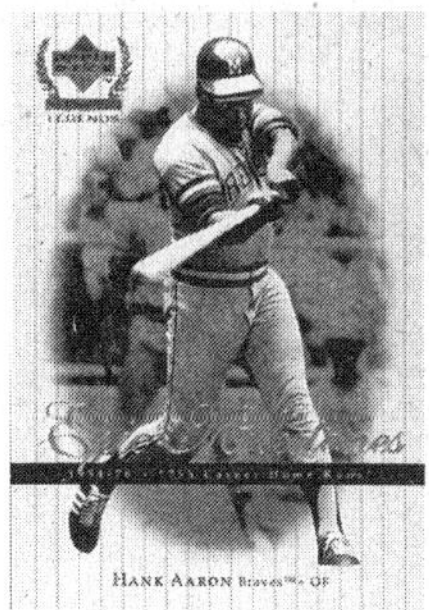

1:12 packs. Because of a contractual dispute, card #1 was never issued.

		NM/M
Complete Set (9):		5.00
Common Player:		.25
Inserted 1:12		
2	Jackie Robinson	.75
3	Nolan Ryan	1.00
4	Mark McGwire	.75
5	Roger Clemens	.60
6	Sammy Sosa	.50
7	Cal Ripken Jr.	1.00
8	Rickey Henderson	.25
9	Hank Aaron	.75
10	Barry Bonds	1.00

Epic Signatures

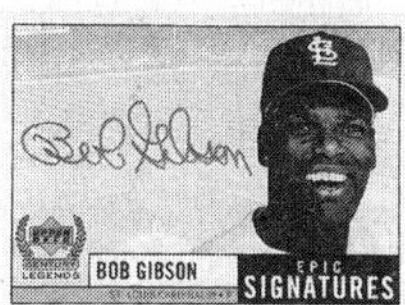

This 30-card set features autographs from retired and current stars on a horizonal format. A player portrait appears over a ballpark background on front. The portrait is repeated on back with a statement of authenticity. Cards are numbered with player initials. These autographed cards are seeded 1:24 packs. Exchange cards of Fisk, Bench, Berra and McCovey were originally inserted into packs and had to be mailed in for the autographed card. They are valued about 10 percent of the corresponding signed card.

		NM/M
Common Player:		10.00
Inserted 1:24		
EB	Ernie Banks	65.00
JB	Johnny Bench	40.00
YB	Yogi Berra	50.00
BB	Barry Bonds	180.00
SC	Steve Carlton	20.00
BD	Bucky Dent	10.00
BF	Bob Feller	15.00
CF	Carlton Fisk	25.00
BG	Bob Gibson	25.00
JG	Juan Gonzalez	20.00
Jr.	Ken Griffey Jr.	100.00
Sr.	Ken Griffey Sr.	10.00
VG	Vladimir Guerrero	30.00
TG	Tony Gwynn	40.00
RJ	Reggie Jackson	40.00
HK	Harmon Killebrew	30.00
DL	Don Larsen	15.00
GM	Greg Maddux	100.00
EMa	Eddie Mathews	80.00
BM	Bill Mazeroski	30.00
WMc	Willie McCovey	20.00
SM	Stan Musial	80.00
FR	Frank Robinson	30.00
AR	Alex Rodriguez	150.00
NR	Nolan Ryan	150.00
MS	Mike Schmidt	50.00
TS	Tom Seaver	40.00
WS	Warren Spahn	60.00
FT	Frank Thomas	50.00
BT	Bobby Thomson	10.00

Century Epic Signatures

This 32-card autographed set features signatures from retired and current stars. The cards have a horizontal format and have gold foil stamping. Each card is hand numbered to 100.

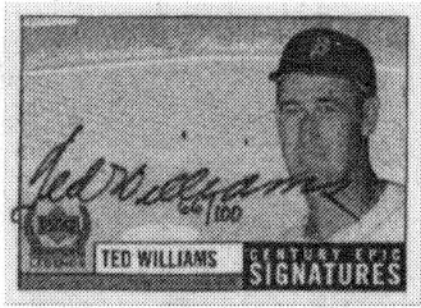

		NM/M
Common Player:		20.00
Production 100 Sets		
EB	Ernie Banks	85.00
JB	Johnny Bench	90.00
YB	Yogi Berra	75.00
BB	Barry Bonds	240.00
SC	Steve Carlton	50.00
BD	Bucky Dent	20.00
BF	Bob Feller	50.00
CF	Carlton Fisk	40.00
BG	Bob Gibson	60.00
JG	Juan Gonzalez	60.00
Jr.	Ken Griffey Jr.	165.00
Sr.	Ken Griffey Sr.	20.00
VG	Vladimir Guerrero	70.00
TG	Tony Gwynn	90.00
RJ	Reggie Jackson	60.00
HK	Harmon Killebrew	75.00
DL	Don Larsen	30.00
GM	Greg Maddux	150.00
EMa	Eddie Mathews	90.00
WM	Willie Mays	300.00
BM	Bill Mazeroski	25.00
WMc	Willie McCovey	50.00
SM	Stan Musial	100.00
FR	Frank Robinson	50.00
AR	Alex Rodriguez	200.00
NR	Nolan Ryan	200.00
MS	Mike Schmidt	125.00
TS	Tom Seaver	75.00
WS	Warren Spahn	80.00
FT	Frank Thomas	80.00
BT	Bobby Thomson	20.00
TW	Ted Williams	750.00

Jerseys of the Century

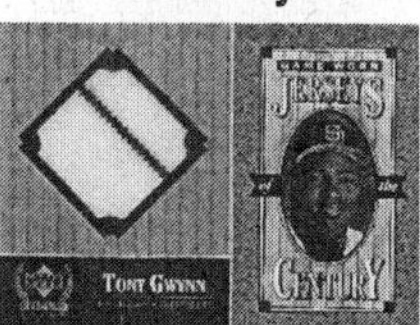

This nine-card set features a swatch of game-worn jersey from the featured current and retired player.

		NM/M
Common Player:		12.50
Inserted 1:418		
GB	George Brett	25.00
RC	Roger Clemens	25.00
TG	Tony Gwynn	20.00
GM	Greg Maddux	20.00
EM	Eddie Murray	15.00
NR	Nolan Ryan	90.00
MS	Mike Schmidt	25.00
OZ	Ozzie Smith	20.00
DW	Dave Winfield	15.00

Legendary Cuts

A total of nine of these one-fo-one inserts exist. These are actual "cut" signatures from some of baseball's all-time greats.

		NM/M
Values Undetermined		
CY	Cy Young (11/00 Auction)	1,850

Memorable Shots

This 10-card insert set focuses on the most memorable home runs launched during this century. The player's image is framed in an embossed foil, frame-like design. These are seeded 1:12 packs, each card back is numbered with an "HR" prefix.

		NM/M
Complete Set (10):		15.00
Common Player:		.50
Inserted 1:12		
1	Babe Ruth	5.00
2	Bobby Thomson	1.00
3	Kirk Gibson	.50
4	Carlton Fisk	.50
5	Bill Mazeroski	1.00
6	Bucky Dent	.50
7	Mark McGwire	2.00
8	Mickey Mantle	5.00
9	Joe Carter	.50
10	Mark McGwire	2.00

500 Club Piece History

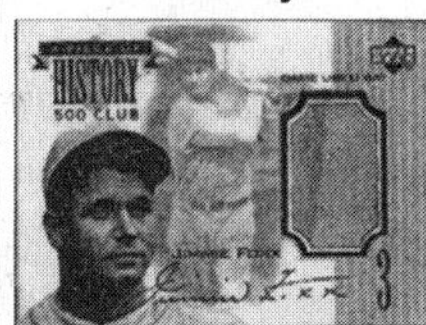

This Jimmie Foxx insert has a piece of of a game-used Louisville Slugger once swung by Foxx, embedded into the card front. An estimated 350 cards of this one exist.

		NM/M
JF	Jimmie Foxx	125.00

1999 Upper Deck Challengers for 70

Celebrating Mark McGwire's record-setting season of 1998, and featuring those who would chase his single-season home run crown in 1999, Upper Deck issued this specialty product. The base set of 90 cards is fractured into subsets of Power Elite (#1-10), Power Corps (#11-40), Rookie Power (#41-45), and Home Run Highlights (#46-90). Several styles of inserts and numbered parallels were included in the 5-card foil packs. A parallel set with each card serially numbered to 600 was also issued, titled "Challengers Edition".

		NM/M
Complete Set (90):		15.00
Common Player:		.05
Challenger's Edition (600 Sets):		5X
Pack (5):		2.00
Wax Box (20):		25.00
1	Mark McGwire (Power Elite)	1.50
2	Sammy Sosa (Power Elite)	1.00
3	Ken Griffey Jr. (Power Elite)	1.25
4	Alex Rodriguez (Power Elite)	1.50
5	Albert Belle (Power Elite)	.05
6	Mo Vaughn (Power Elite)	.05
7	Mike Piazza (Power Elite)	1.25
8	Frank Thomas (Power Elite)	.75
9	Juan Gonzalez (Power Elite)	.35
10	Barry Bonds (Power Elite)	2.00
11	Rafael Palmeiro (Power Corps)	.60
12	Jose Canseco (Power Corps)	.50
13	Nomar Garciaparra (Power Corps)	1.00
14	Carlos Delgado (Power Corps)	.20
15	Brian Jordan (Power Corps)	.05
16	Vladimir Guerrero (Power Corps)	.65
17	Vinny Castilla (Power Corps)	.05
18	Chipper Jones (Power Corps)	1.00
19	Jeff Bagwell (Power Corps)	.65
20	Moises Alou (Power Corps)	.05
21	Tony Clark (Power Corps)	.05
22	Jim Thome (Power Corps)	.50
23	Tino Martinez (Power Corps)	.05
24	Greg Vaughn (Power Corps)	.05
25	Javy Lopez (Power Corps)	.05
26	Jeromy Burnitz (Power Corps)	.05
27	Cal Ripken Jr. (Power Corps)	2.00
28	Manny Ramirez (Power Corps)	.65
29	Darin Erstad (Power Corps)	.25
30	Ken Caminiti (Power Corps)	.05
31	Edgar Martinez (Power Corps)	.05
32	Ivan Rodriguez (Power Corps)	.60
33	Larry Walker (Power Corps)	.05
34	Todd Helton (Power Corps)	.60
35	Andruw Jones (Power Corps)	.65
36	Ray Lankford (Power Corps)	.05
37	Travis Lee (Power Corps)	.10
38	Raul Mondesi (Power Corps)	.05
39	Scott Rolen (Power Corps)	.50
40	Ben Grieve (Power Corps)	.05
41	J.D. Drew (Rookie Power)	.50
42	Troy Glaus (Rookie Power)	.60
43	Eric Chavez (Rookie Power)	.10
44	Gabe Kapler (Rookie Power)	.05
45	Michael Barrett (Rookie Power)	.05
46	Mark McGwire (HR Highlights)	.75
47	Jose Canseco (HR Highlights)	.25
48	Greg Vaughn (HR Highlights)	.05
49	Albert Belle (HR Highlights)	.05
50	Mark McGwire (HR Highlights)	.75
51	Vinny Castilla (HR Highlights)	.05
52	Vladimir Guerrero (HR Highlights)	.35
53	Andres Galarraga (HR Highlights)	.05
54	Rafael Palmeiro (HR Highlights)	.30
55	Juan Gonzalez (HR Highlights)	.20
56	Ken Griffey Jr. (HR Highlights)	.60
57	Barry Bonds (HR Highlights)	1.00
58	Mo Vaughn (HR Highlights)	.05
59	Nomar Garciaparra (HR Highlights)	.50
60	Tino Martinez (HR Highlights)	.05
61	Mark McGwire (HR Highlights)	.75
62	Mark McGwire (HR Highlights)	.75
63	Mark McGwire (HR Highlights)	.75
64	Mark McGwire (HR Highlights)	.75
65	Mark McGwire (HR Highlights)	.75
66	Sammy Sosa (HR Highlights)	.50
67	Mark McGwire (HR Highlights)	.75
68	Mark McGwire (HR Highlights)	.75
69	Mark McGwire (HR Highlights)	.75
70	Mark McGwire (HR Highlights)	.75
71	Mark McGwire (HR Highlights)	.75
72	Scott Brosius (HR Highlights)	.05
73	Tony Gwynn (HR Highlights)	.40
74	Chipper Jones (HR Highlights)	.50
75	Jeff Bagwell (HR Highlights)	.35
76	Moises Alou (HR Highlights)	.05
77	Manny Ramirez (HR Highlights)	.35
78	Carlos Delgado (HR Highlights)	.05
79	Kerry Wood (HR Highlights)	.20
80	Ken Griffey Jr. (HR Highlights)	.60
81	Cal Ripken Jr. (HR Highlights)	1.00
82	Alex Rodriguez (HR Highlights)	.75
83	Barry Bonds (HR Highlights)	1.00
84	Ken Griffey Jr. (HR Highlights)	.60
85	Travis Lee (HR Highlights)	.15
86	George Lombard (HR Highlights)	.05
87	Michael Barrett (HR Highlights)	.05
88	Jeremy Giambi (HR Highlights)	.05
89	Troy Glaus (HR Highlights)	.30
90	J.D. Drew (HR Highlights)	.25

Challengers Insert

Found one per pack, this insert series identifies 30 top contenders for the 1999 home run crown. Action photos on front are highlighted by red graphics and silver-foil. Backs repeat a detail of the front photo and present a capsule of the player's 1998 season. Cards have a "C" prefix to the number. A parallel edition, utilizing refractive foil details on front, is serially numbered within an edition of 70 each.

		NM/M
Complete Set (30):		9.00
Common Player:		.15
Parallel Edition (70 Sets):		15X
1	Mark McGwire	1.00
2	Sammy Sosa	.65
3	Ken Griffey Jr.	.75
4	Alex Rodriguez	1.00
5	Albert Belle	.15
6	Mo Vaughn	.15
7	Mike Piazza	.75
8	Frank Thomas	.50
9	Juan Gonzalez	.25
10	Barry Bonds	1.50
11	Rafael Palmeiro	.35
12	Nomar Garciaparra	.65
13	Vladimir Guerrero	.45
14	Vinny Castilla	.15
15	Chipper Jones	.60
16	Jeff Bagwell	.45
17	Moises Alou	.15
18	Tony Clark	.15
19	Jim Thome	.35
20	Tino Martinez	.15
21	Greg Vaughn	.15
22	Manny Ramirez	.45
23	Darin Erstad	.25
24	Ken Caminiti	.15
25	Ivan Rodriguez	.35
26	Andruw Jones	.45
27	Travis Lee	.25
28	Scott Rolen	.35
29	Ben Grieve	.15
30	J.D. Drew	.35

Longball Legends

Top home-run threats are featured in this insert series. The action photos on front are

repeated in a diffused version on back, where they are joined by a second photo and a bargraph of the player's home run production in recent seasons. Cards have an "L" prefix to the number. Stated odds of picking a Longball Legends card are one per 39 packs.

		NM/M
Complete Set (30):		20.00
Common Player:		.50
1	Ken Griffey Jr.	1.50
2	Mark McGwire	2.00
3	Sammy Sosa	1.00
4	Cal Ripken Jr.	2.50
5	Barry Bonds	2.50
6	Larry Walker	.50
7	Fred McGriff	.50
8	Alex Rodriguez	2.00
9	Frank Thomas	.75
10	Juan Gonzalez	.60
11	Jeff Bagwell	.75
12	Mo Vaughn	.50
13	Albert Belle	.50
14	Mike Piazza	1.50
15	Vladimir Guerrero	.75
16	Chipper Jones	1.00
17	Ken Caminiti	.50
18	Rafael Palmeiro	.65
19	Nomar Garciaparra	1.00
20	Jim Thome	.60
21	Edgar Martinez	.50
22	Ivan Rodriguez	.65
23	Andres Galarraga	.50
24	Scott Rolen	.60
25	Darin Erstad	.65
26	Moises Alou	.50
27	J.D. Drew	.65
28	Andruw Jones	.75
29	Manny Ramirez	.75
30	Tino Martinez	.50

Mark on History

The details of Mark McGwire's successful assault on the single-season home run record are captured in this 25-card insert set, found on average of one per five packs. Cards have action photos set against a split red-and-black background and are highlighted in red metallic foil. Backs have details of the home run featured on front, a quote from McGwire and another photo. Cards have an "M" prefix to the number. A parallel edition number to 70 was also issued.

	NM/M
Complete Set (25):	25.00
Common McGwire:	1.50
Parallel:	8X
01-25 Mark McGwire	1.50

Piece of History 500

A piece of game-used bat from 500-HR club member Harmon Killebrew is featured

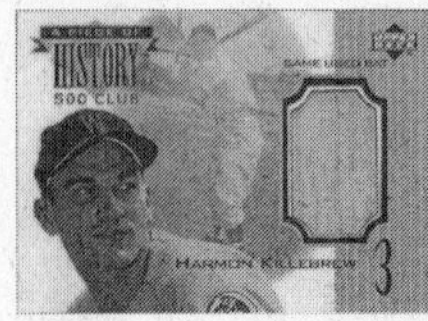

on these inserts. Only 350 cards were issued, along with three (his uniform number) authentically autographed versions. Backs have an action photo and a congratulatory authentication message from UD CEO Richard McWilliam.

	NM/M
Harmon Killebrew	120.00
Harmon Killebrew/Auto.	450.00

Swinging/Fences

Fifteen top sluggers are included in this insert set. The players' power swing is captured on a muted textured-look background. Back has a color portrait photo and an "S" prefix to the card number. Stated insertion rate is one per 19 packs.

		NM/M
Complete Set (15):		15.00
Common Player:		.50
1	Ken Griffey Jr.	1.50
2	Mark McGwire	2.00
3	Sammy Sosa	1.25
4	Alex Rodriguez	2.00
5	Nomar Garciaparra	1.25
6	J.D. Drew	.75
7	Vladimir Guerrero	1.00
8	Ben Grieve	.50
9	Chipper Jones	1.25
10	Gabe Kapler	.50
11	Travis Lee	.60
12	Todd Helton	.75
13	Juan Gonzalez	.60
14	Mike Piazza	1.50
15	Mo Vaughn	.50

Autographed Swinging

A total of 2,700 autographed versions of Swinging for the Fences inserts were featured in the Challengers for 70 issue. Only six of the 15 players' cards were included in this premium version.

		NM/M
Complete Set (6):		200.00
Common Player:		5.00
JR	Ken Griffey Jr.	95.00
VG	Vladimir Guerrero	25.00
TH	Todd Helton	15.00
GK	Gabe Kapler	5.00
TL	Travis Lee	7.50
AR	Alex Rodriguez	90.00

1999 Upper Deck UD Choice Previews

A month prior to the release of its new UD Choice brand baseball series, Upper Deck issued this 55-card Preview version. Sold in five-card cello packs for about 75 cents only at retail outlets, the cards are identical to the issued versions of the same players except for the appearance at top front of a gold foil-stamped "PREVIEW."

		NM/M
Complete Set (55):		16.00
Common Player:		.10
46	Tim Salmon	.10
48	Chuck Finley	.10
50	Matt Williams	.10
52	Travis Lee	.20
54	Andres Galarraga	.10
56	Greg Maddux	.75
58	Cal Ripken Jr.	1.50
60	Rafael Palmeiro	.50
62	Nomar Garciaparra	.75
64	Pedro Martinez	.60
66	Kerry Wood	.35
67	Sammy Sosa	.75
70	Albert Belle	.10
72	Frank Thomas	.60
74	Pete Harnisch	.10
76	Manny Ramirez	.60
78	Travis Fryman	.10
80	Kenny Lofton	.10
82	Larry Walker	.10
84	Gabe Alvarez	.10
86	Damion Easley	.10
88	Mark Kotsay	.10
90	Jeff Bagwell	.60
93	Craig Biggio	.10
94	Larry Sutton	.10
96	Johnny Damon	.30
98	Gary Sheffield	.35
100	Mark Grudzielanek	.10
102	Jeff Cirillo	.10
104	Mark Loretta	.10
106	David Ortiz	.40
108	Brad Fullmer	.10
110	Vladimir Guerrero	.60
112	Brian McRae	.10
114	Rey Ordonez	.10
115	Derek Jeter	1.50
118	Paul O'Neill	.10
120	A.J. Hinch	.10
122	Miguel Tejada	.15
124	Scott Rolen	.45
126	Bobby Abreu	.10
128	Jason Kendall	.10
130	Mark McGwire	1.25
132	Eli Marrero	.10
136	Kevin Brown	.10
137	Tony Gwynn	.75
138	Bill Mueller	.10
140	Barry Bonds	1.50
142	Ken Griffey Jr.	1.00
143	Alex Rodriguez	1.25
146	Rolando Arrojo	.10
148	Quinton McCracken	.10
150	Will Clark	.10
152	Juan Gonzalez	.30
154	Carlos Delgado	.25

1999 Upper Deck UD Choice

The 155-card base set consists of 110 regular player cards and two subsets, 27 Star Rookies and 18 Cover Glory subset cards. Card fronts have a white border, with the Upper Deck UD Choice logo on the bottom right of the front. Card backs have complete year-by-year stats along with some vital information. Each pack contains 12 cards. A parallel version also exists, called Prime Choice Reserve and are numbered to 100.

		NM/M
Complete Set (155):		7.50
Common Player:		.03
Prime Choice Reserve Stars:		10X
Production 100 Sets		
Pack (12):		.50
Wax Box (36):		10.00
1	Gabe Kapler (Rookie Class)	.05
2	Jin Ho Cho (Rookie Class)	.05
3	Matt Anderson (Rookie Class)	.05
4	Ricky Ledee (Rookie Class)	.05
5	Bruce Chen (Rookie Class)	.05
6	Alex Gonzalez (Rookie Class)	.05
7	Ryan Minor (Rookie Class)	.05
8	Michael Barrett (Rookie Class)	.05
9	Carlos Beltran (Rookie Class)	.50
10	Ramon Martinez (Rookie Class)	.05
11	Dermal Brown (Rookie Class)	.05
12	Robert Fick (Rookie Class)	.05
13	Preston Wilson (Rookie Class)	.05
14	Orlando Hernandez (Rookie Class)	.05
15	Troy Glaus (Rookie Class)	.65
16	Calvin Pickering (Rookie Class)	.05
17	Corey Koskie (Rookie Class)	.05
18	Fernando Seguignol (Rookie Class)	.05
19	Carlos Guillen (Rookie Class)	.05
20	Kevin Witt (Rookie Class)	.05
21	Mike Kinkade (Rookie Class)	.05
22	Eric Chavez (Rookie Class)	.15
23	Mike Lowell (Rookie Class)	.10
24	Adrian Beltre (Rookie Class)	.10
25	George Lombard (Rookie Class)	.05
26	Jeremy Giambi (Rookie Class)	.06
27	J.D. Drew (Rookie Class)	.40
28	Mark McGwire (Cover Glory)	.60
29	Kerry Wood (Cover Glory)	.15
30	David Wells (Cover Glory)	.05
31	Juan Gonzalez (Cover Glory)	.15
32	Randy Johnson (Cover Glory)	.35
33	Derek Jeter (Cover Glory)	.75
34	Tony Gwynn (Cover Glory)	.45
35	Greg Maddux (Cover Glory)	.45
36	Cal Ripken Jr. (Cover Glory)	.75
37	Ken Griffey Jr. (Cover Glory)	.50
38	Bartolo Colon (Cover Glory)	.05
39	Troy Glaus (Cover Glory)	.30
40	Ben Grieve (Cover Glory)	.05
41	Roger Clemens (Cover Glory)	.50
42	Chipper Jones (Cover Glory)	.45
43	Scott Rolen (Cover Glory)	.25
44	Nomar Garciaparra (Cover Glory)	.45
45	Sammy Sosa (Cover Glory)	.45
46	Tim Salmon	.05
47	Darin Erstad	.25
48	Chuck Finley	.05
49	Garrett Anderson	.05
50	Matt Williams	.05
51	Jay Bell	.05
52	Travis Lee	.10
53	Andruw Jones	.65
54	Andres Galarraga	.05
55	Chipper Jones	.75
56	Greg Maddux	.75
57	Javy Lopez	.05
58	Cal Ripken Jr.	1.50
59	Brady Anderson	.05
60	Rafael Palmeiro	.50
61	B.J. Surhoff	.05
62	Nomar Garciaparra	.75
63	Troy O'Leary	.05
64	Pedro Martinez	.65
65	Jason Varitek	.05
66	Kerry Wood	.35
67	Sammy Sosa	.75
68	Mark Grace	.05
69	Mickey Morandini	.05
70	Albert Belle	.05
71	Mike Caruso	.05
72	Frank Thomas	.65
73	Sean Casey	.10
74	Pete Harnisch	.05
75	Dmitri Young	.05
76	Manny Ramirez	.65
77	Omar Vizquel	.05
78	Travis Fryman	.05
79	Jim Thome	.40
80	Kenny Lofton	.05
81	Todd Helton	.50
82	Larry Walker	.05
83	Vinny Castilla	.05
84	Gabe Alvarez	.05
85	Tony Clark	.05
86	Damion Easley	.05
87	Livan Hernandez	.05
88	Mark Kotsay	.05
89	Cliff Floyd	.05
90	Jeff Bagwell	.65
91	Moises Alou	.05
92	Randy Johnson	.65
93	Craig Biggio	.05
94	Larry Sutton	.05
95	Dean Palmer	.05
96	Johnny Damon	.20
97	Charles Johnson	.05
98	Gary Sheffield	.25
99	Raul Mondesi	.05
100	Mark Grudzielanek	.05
101	Jeromy Burnitz	.05
102	Jeff Cirillo	.05
103	Jose Valentin	.05
104	Mark Loretta	.05
105	Todd Walker	.05
106	David Ortiz	.35
107	Brad Radke	.05
108	Brad Fullmer	.05
109	Rondell White	.05
110	Vladimir Guerrero	.65
111	Mike Piazza	1.00
112	Brian McRae	.05
113	John Olerud	.05
114	Rey Ordonez	.05
115	Derek Jeter	1.50
116	Bernie Williams	.05
117	David Wells	.05
118	Paul O'Neill	.05
119	Tino Martinez	.05
120	A.J. Hinch	.05
121	Jason Giambi	.30
122	Miguel Tejada	.10
123	Ben Grieve	.05
124	Scott Rolen	.50
125	Desi Relaford	.05
126	Bobby Abreu	.10
127	Jose Guillen	.05
128	Jason Kendall	.05
129	Aramis Ramirez	.05
130	Mark McGwire	1.25
131	Ray Lankford	.05
132	Eli Marrero	.05
133	Wally Joyner	.05
134	Greg Vaughn	.05
135	Trevor Hoffman	.05
136	Kevin Brown	.05
137	Tony Gwynn	.75
138	Bill Mueller	.05
139	Ellis Burks	.05
140	Barry Bonds	1.50
141	Robb Nen	.05
142	Ken Griffey Jr.	1.00
143	Alex Rodriguez	1.25
144	Jay Buhner	.05
145	Edgar Martinez	.05
146	Rolando Arrojo	.05
147	Robert Smith	.05
148	Quinton McCracken	.05
149	Ivan Rodriguez	.50
150	Will Clark	.05
151	Mark McLemore	.05
152	Juan Gonzalez	.35
153	Jose Cruz Jr.	.05
154	Carlos Delgado	.25
155	Roger Clemens	.85

Prime Choice Reserve

Each card in the UD Choice set is also found in a parallel version with the words "Prime Choice Reserve" repeated in the background of

the photo in refractive foil. On back, the parallels are individually serial numbered within an edition of 100 each.

	NM/M
Common Player:	2.50
Stars:	10X

All-Star Game '99

These super-size (3-1/2" x 5") versions of 1999 UD Choice cards were issued as a boxed set exclusively for retail outlet sales. The cards are in a format identical to the regular-issue UD Choice except for a large All-Star Game logo in one of the upper corners. Fronts have game-action photos; backs have a small portrait, major league stats and career highlights. The set was sold in a green-foil enhanced box with a special card commemorating the 1999 game July 13 in Boston.

		NM/M
Complete Set (21):		12.50
Common Player:		.35
1	Kenny Lofton	.35
2	Pedro Martinez	.75
3	Nomar Garciaparra	1.00
4	Ken Griffey Jr.	1.25
5	Derek Jeter	2.00
6	Manny Ramirez	.75
7	Ivan Rodriguez	.65
8	Bernie Williams	.35
9	Cal Ripken Jr.	2.00
10	Jim Thome	.60
11	Mike Piazza	1.25
12	Jeff Bagwell	.75
13	Craig Biggio	.35
14	Mark McGwire	1.50
15	Matt Williams	.35
16	Chipper Jones	1.00
17	Tony Gwynn	1.00
18	Sammy Sosa	1.00
19	Raul Mondesi	.35
20	Larry Walker	.35
---	Header Card	.05

Mini Bobbing Head

Inserted 1:5 packs, some of the game's best players can be assembled into a miniature bobbing head figure by following the instructions on the card backs.

	NM/M
Complete Set (30):	15.00
Common Player:	.25

Inserted 1:5		
B1	Randy Johnson	.50
B2	Troy Glaus	.50
B3	Chipper Jones	.65
B4	Cal Ripken Jr.	1.50
B5	Nomar Garciaparra	.65
B6	Pedro Martinez	.50
B7	Kerry Wood	.35
B8	Sammy Sosa	.65
B9	Frank Thomas	.50
B10	Paul Konerko	.35
B11	Omar Vizquel	.25
B12	Kenny Lofton	.25
B13	Gabe Kapler	.25
B14	Adrian Beltre	.35
B15	Orlando Hernandez	.25
B16	Derek Jeter	1.50
B17	Mike Piazza	.75
B18	Tino Martinez	.25
B19	Ben Grieve	.25
B20	Rickey Henderson	.50
B21	Scott Rolen	.40
B22	Aramis Ramirez	.25
B23	Greg Vaughn	.25
B24	Tony Gwynn	.65
B25	Barry Bonds	1.50
B26	Alex Rodriguez	1.00
B27	Ken Griffey Jr.	.75
B28	Mark McGwire	1.00
B29	J.D. Drew	.45
B30	Juan Gonzalez	.30

Piece of History 500 Club

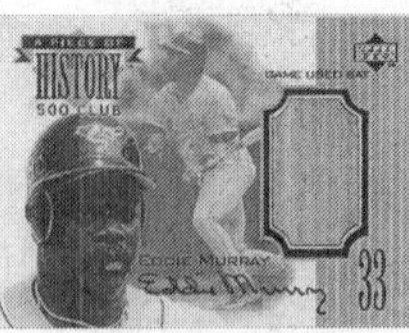

A piece from an Eddie Murray game-used bat was incorporated into each of these cards, which are limited to 350.

		NM/M
EM	Eddie Murray/350	150.00

StarQuest

This four-tiered 30-card set features four different colors for each of the levels. Singles are seeded one per pack and have blue foil etching, Doubles (1:8) have green foil etching, Triples (1:23) have red foil etching and Home Runs are limited to 100 numbered sets with gold foil etching.

		NM/M
Complete Set (30):		7.50
Common Player:		.10
Inserted 1:1		
Green (1:8):		1.5X
Red (1:23):		3X
Gold (100 Sets):		50X
SQ1	Ken Griffey Jr.	.60
SQ2	Sammy Sosa	.50
SQ3	Alex Rodriguez	.75
SQ4	Derek Jeter	1.00
SQ5	Troy Glaus	.35
SQ6	Mike Piazza	.60
SQ7	Barry Bonds	1.00
SQ8	Tony Gwynn	.50
SQ9	Juan Gonzalez	.20
SQ10	Chipper Jones	.50
SQ11	Greg Maddux	.50
SQ12	Randy Johnson	.40
SQ13	Roger Clemens	.55
SQ14	Ben Grieve	.10
SQ15	Nomar Garciaparra	.50
SQ16	Travis Lee	.15
SQ17	Frank Thomas	.40
SQ18	Vladimir Guerrero	.40
SQ19	Scott Rolen	.30
SQ20	Ivan Rodriguez	.35
SQ21	Cal Ripken Jr.	1.00
SQ22	Mark McGwire	.75
SQ23	Jeff Bagwell	.40

SQ24	Tony Clark	.10
SQ25	Kerry Wood	.25
SQ26	Kenny Lofton	.10
SQ27	Adrian Beltre	.15
SQ28	Larry Walker	.10
SQ29	Curt Schilling	.25
SQ30	Jim Thome	.40

Yard Work

This 30-card set showcases the top power hitters in the game. The right side of the card is covered in bronze foil and stamped with Yard Work. They are numbered with a Y-prefix and seeded 1:13 packs.

		NM/M
Complete Set (30):		20.00
Common Player:		.35
Inserted 1:13		
Y1	Andres Galarraga	.35
Y2	Chipper Jones	1.50
Y3	Rafael Palmeiro	.75
Y4	Nomar Garciaparra	1.50
Y5	Sammy Sosa	1.50
Y6	Frank Thomas	1.00
Y7	J.D. Drew	.75
Y8	Albert Belle	.35
Y9	Jim Thome	.60
Y10	Manny Ramirez	1.00
Y11	Larry Walker	.35
Y12	Vinny Castilla	.35
Y13	Tony Clark	.35
Y14	Jeff Bagwell	1.00
Y15	Moises Alou	.35
Y16	Dean Palmer	.35
Y17	Gary Sheffield	.50
Y18	Vladimir Guerrero	1.00
Y19	Mike Piazza	1.75
Y20	Tino Martinez	.35
Y21	Ben Grieve	.35
Y22	Greg Vaughn	.35
Y23	Ken Caminiti	.35
Y24	Barry Bonds	3.00
Y25	Ken Griffey Jr.	1.75
Y26	Alex Rodriguez	2.25
Y27	Mark McGwire	2.25
Y28	Juan Gonzalez	.50
Y29	Jose Canseco	.50
Y30	Jose Cruz Jr.	.35

1999 Upper Deck Encore

Encore is a 180-card partial parallel of Upper Deck Series 1, utilizing a special holo-foil treatment on each card. The Encore set consists of 90 base cards and three short-printed subsets: 45 Star Rookies (1:4), 30 Homer Odyssey (1:6) and 15 Stroke of Genius (1:8).

		NM/M
Complete Set (180):		75.00
Common Player (1-90):		.05
Common Player (91-135):		.25
Inserted 1:4		
Common Player (136-165):		.35
Inserted 1:6		
Common Player (166-180):		.50
Inserted 1:8		
Gold (1-90):		10X
Gold (91-135):		1.5X
Gold (136-165):		3X
Gold (166-180):		4X
Production 125 Sets		
Pack (6):		1.50
Wax Box (24):		25.00
1	Darin Erstad	.25
2	Mo Vaughn	.05
3	Travis Lee	.15
4	Randy Johnson	.60
5	Matt Williams	.05
6	John Smoltz	.05
7	Greg Maddux	.75
8	Chipper Jones	.75
9	Tom Glavine	.25
10	Andruw Jones	.60
11	Cal Ripken Jr.	1.50
12	Mike Mussina	.30
13	Albert Belle	.05
14	Nomar Garciaparra	.75
15	Jose Offerman	.05
16	Pedro Martinez	.60
17	Trot Nixon	.10
18	Kerry Wood	.40
19	Sammy Sosa	.75
20	Frank Thomas	.60
21	Paul Konerko	.15
22	Sean Casey	.15
23	Barry Larkin	.05
24	Greg Vaughn	.05
25	Travis Fryman	.05
26	Jaret Wright	.05
27	Jim Thome	.45
28	Manny Ramirez	.60
29	Roberto Alomar	.20
30	Kenny Lofton	.05
31	Todd Helton	.60
32	Larry Walker	.05
33	Vinny Castilla	.05
34	Dante Bichette	.05
35	Tony Clark	.05
36	Dean Palmer	.05
37	Gabe Kapler	.05
38	Juan Encarnacion	.05
39	Alex Gonzalez	.05
40	Preston Wilson	.05
41	Mark Kotsay	.05
42	Moises Alou	.05
43	Craig Biggio	.05
44	Ken Caminiti	.05
45	Jeff Bagwell	.60
46	Johnny Damon	.30
47	Gary Sheffield	.25
48	Kevin Brown	.05
49	Raul Mondesi	.05
50	Jeff Cirillo	.05
51	Jeromy Burnitz	.05
52	Todd Walker	.05
53	Corey Koskie	.05
54	Brad Fullmer	.05
55	Vladimir Guerrero	.60
56	Mike Piazza	1.25
57	Robin Ventura	.05
58	Rickey Henderson	.60
59	Derek Jeter	1.50
60	Paul O'Neill	.05
61	Bernie Williams	.05
62	Tino Martinez	.05
63	Roger Clemens	.85
64	Ben Grieve	.05
65	Jason Giambi	.35
66	Bob Abreu	.10
67	Scott Rolen	.40
68	Curt Schilling	.25
69	Marlon Anderson	.05
70	Kevin Young	.05
71	Jason Kendall	.05
72	Brian Giles	.05
73	Mark McGwire	1.25
74	Fernando Tatis	.05
75	Eric Davis	.05
76	Trevor Hoffman	.05
77	Tony Gwynn	.75
78	Matt Clement	.05
79	Robb Nen	.05
80	Barry Bonds	1.50
81	Ken Griffey Jr.	1.00
82	Alex Rodriguez	1.25
83	Wade Boggs	.75
84	Fred McGriff	.05
85	Jose Canseco	.30
86	Ivan Rodriguez	.50
87	Juan Gonzalez	.30
88	Rafael Palmeiro	.50
89	Carlos Delgado	.25
90	David Wells	.05
91	Troy Glaus/SR	1.00
92	Adrian Beltre/SR	.50
93	Matt Anderson/SR	.25
94	Eric Chavez/SR	.40
95	Jeff Weaver/SR **RC**	.50
96	Warren Morris/SR	.25
97	George Lombard/SR	.25
98	Mike Kinkade/SR	.25
99	Kyle Farnsworth/SR **RC**	.25
100	J.D. Drew/SR	.50
101	Joe McEwing/SR **RC**	.50
102	Carlos Guillen/SR	.25
103	Kelly Dransfeldt/SR **RC**	.25
104	Eric Munson/SR **RC**	.50
105	Armando Rios/SR	.25
106	Ramon Martinez/SR	.25
107	Orlando Hernandez/SR	.45
108	Jeremy Giambi/SR	.25
109	Pat Burrell/SR **RC**	2.50
110	Shea Hillenbrand/ SR **RC**	1.00
111	Billy Koch/SR	.25
112	Roy Halladay/SR	.35
113	Ruben Mateo/SR	.25
114	Bruce Chen/SR	.25
115	Angel Pena/SR	.25
116	Michael Barrett/SR	.25
117	Kevin Witt/SR	.25
118	Damon Minor/SR	.25
119	Ryan Minor/SR	.25
120	A.J. Pierzynski/SR	.25
121	A.J. Burnett/SR **RC**	.50
122	Christian Guzman/SR	.25
123	Joe Lawrence/SR	.25
124	Derrick Gibson/SR	.25
125	Carlos Febles/SR	.25
126	Chris Haas/SR	.25
127	Cesar King/SR	.25
128	Calvin Pickering/SR	.25
129	Mitch Meluskey/SR	.25
130	Carlos Beltran/SR	1.00
131	Ron Belliard/SR	.25
132	Jerry Hairston Jr./SR	.25
133	Fernando Seguignol/SR	.25
134	Kris Benson/SR	.25
135	Chad Hutchinson/ SR **RC**	.25
136	Ken Griffey Jr. (Homer Odyssey)	1.50
137	Mark McGwire (Homer Odyssey)	2.00
138	Sammy Sosa (Homer Odyssey)	1.25
139	Albert Belle (Homer Odyssey)	.35
140	Mo Vaughn (Homer Odyssey)	.35
141	Alex Rodriguez (Homer Odyssey)	2.00
142	Manny Ramirez (Homer Odyssey)	.75
143	J.D. Drew (Homer Odyssey)	.50
144	Juan Gonzalez (Homer Odyssey)	.45
145	Vladimir Guerrero (Homer Odyssey)	.75
146	Fernando Tatis (Homer Odyssey)	.35
147	Mike Piazza (Homer Odyssey)	2.00
148	Barry Bonds (Homer Odyssey)	2.50
149	Ivan Rodriguez (Homer Odyssey)	.60
150	Jeff Bagwell (Homer Odyssey)	.75
151	Raul Mondesi (Homer Odyssey)	.35
152	Nomar Garciaparra (Homer Odyssey)	1.25
153	Jose Canseco (Homer Odyssey)	.50
154	Greg Vaughn (Homer Odyssey)	.35
155	Scott Rolen (Homer Odyssey)	.50
156	Vinny Castilla (Homer Odyssey)	.35
157	Troy Glaus (Homer Odyssey)	.65
158	Craig Biggio (Homer Odyssey)	.35
159	Tino Martinez (Homer Odyssey)	.35
160	Jim Thome (Homer Odyssey)	.60
161	Frank Thomas (Homer Odyssey)	1.00
162	Tony Clark (Homer Odyssey)	.35
163	Ben Grieve (Homer Odyssey)	.35
164	Matt Williams (Homer Odyssey)	.35
165	Derek Jeter (Homer Odyssey)	2.50
166	Ken Griffey Jr. (Strokes of Genius)	2.00
167	Tony Gwynn (Strokes of Genius)	1.50
168	Mike Piazza (Strokes of Genius)	2.00
169	Mark McGwire (Strokes of Genius)	2.50
170	Sammy Sosa (Strokes of Genius)	1.50
171	Juan Gonzalez (Strokes of Genius)	.60
172	Mo Vaughn (Strokes of Genius)	.50
173	Derek Jeter (Strokes of Genius)	3.00
174	Bernie Williams (Strokes of Genius)	.50
175	Ivan Rodriguez (Strokes of Genius)	.75
176	Barry Bonds (Strokes of Genius)	3.00
177	Scott Rolen (Strokes of Genius)	.75
178	Larry Walker (Strokes of Genius)	.50
179	Chipper Jones (Strokes of Genius)	1.50
180	Alex Rodriguez (Strokes of Genius)	2.50

FX Gold

This is a 180-card parallel to the base set featuring gold holo-foil treatment and limited to 125 sequentially numbered sets.

	NM/M
Common Player:	1.00
Gold (1-90):	10X
Gold (91-135):	1.5X
Gold (136-165):	3X
Gold (166-180):	4X

Batting Practice Caps

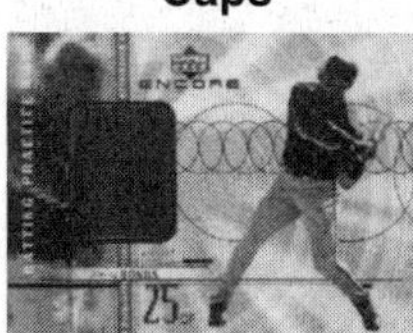

This 15-card set features actual swatch pieces of the highlighted players' batting practice cap embedded into each card. These are seeded 1:750 packs.

		NM/M
Complete Set (15):		85.00
Common Player:		4.00
Inserted 1:750		
CB	Carlos Beltran	8.00
BB	Barry Bonds	30.00
VC	Vinny Castilla	4.00
EC	Eric Chavez	6.00
TC	Tony Clark	4.00
JD	J.D. Drew	6.00
VG	Vladimir Guerrero	8.00
TG	Tony Gwynn	15.00
TH	Todd Helton	8.00
GK	Gabe Kapler	4.00
JK	Jason Kendall	4.00
DP	Dean Palmer	4.00
BH	Frank Thomas	8.00
GV	Greg Vaughn	4.00
TW	Todd Walker	4.00

Driving Forces

This 15-card set is highlighted by holo-foil treatment on the card fronts on a thick card stock. Baseball's top performers are featured in this set and are seeded 1:23 packs. A Gold parallel exists and is limited to 10 sets.

		NM/M
Complete Set (15):		30.00
Common Player:		1.00
Inserted 1:23		
Gold (10 Sets):		30X
D1	Ken Griffey Jr.	3.00
D2	Mark McGwire	4.00
D3	Sammy Sosa	2.50
D4	Albert Belle	1.00
D5	Alex Rodriguez	4.00
D6	Mo Vaughn	1.00
D7	Juan Gonzalez	1.00
D8	Jeff Bagwell	2.00
D9	Mike Piazza	3.00
D10	Frank Thomas	2.00
D11	Barry Bonds	5.00
D12	Vladimir Guerrero	2.00
D13	Chipper Jones	2.50
D14	Tony Gwynn	2.50
D15	J.D. Drew	1.50

McGwired!

This 10-card set salutes baseball's reigning single season home run king. These are seeded 1:23 packs. A gold parallel also is randomly seeded and is limited to 500 sequentially numbered sets. A small photo of the pitcher McGwire hit the historic home run off of is pictured as well.

		NM/M
Complete Set (10):		12.50
Common Card:		1.50
Inserted 1:23		
Parallel:		2X
Production 500 Sets		
1	Mark McGwire, Carl Pavano	1.50
2	Mark McGwire, Michael Morgan	1.50
3	Mark McGwire, Steve Trachsel	1.50
4	Mark McGwire	2.50
5	Mark McGwire	2.50
6	Mark McGwire, Scott Elarton	1.50
7	Mark McGwire, Jim Parque	1.50
8	Mark McGwire	2.50
9	Mark McGwire, Rafael Roque	1.50
10	Mark McGwire, Jaret Wright	1.50

Pure Excitement

This 30-card set features Light F/X technology and includes the top players in baseball. These are seeded 1:7 packs.

		NM/M
Complete Set (30):		35.00
Common Player:		.50
Inserted 1:7		
1	Mo Vaughn	.50
2	Darin Erstad	.75
3	Travis Lee	.65
4	Chipper Jones	1.50
5	Greg Maddux	1.50
6	Gabe Kapler	.50
7	Cal Ripken Jr.	4.00
8	Nomar Garciaparra	1.50
9	Kerry Wood	.75
10	Frank Thomas	1.00
11	Manny Ramirez	1.00
12	Larry Walker	.50
13	Tony Clark	.50
14	Jeff Bagwell	1.00
15	Craig Biggio	.50
16	Vladimir Guerrero	1.00
17	Mike Piazza	2.00
18	Bernie Williams	.60
19	Derek Jeter	4.00
20	Ben Grieve	.60
21	Eric Chavez	.60
22	Scott Rolen	.75
23	Mark McGwire	3.00
24	Tony Gwynn	1.50
25	Barry Bonds	4.00
26	Ken Griffey Jr.	2.00
27	Alex Rodriguez	3.00
28	J.D. Drew	.75
29	Juan Gonzalez	.60
30	Roger Clemens	1.75

Rookie Encore

This 10-card set highlights the top rookie prospects in 1999, including J.D. Drew and Gabe Kapler. These are seeded 1:23 packs. A parallel version is also randomly seeded and limited to 500 sequentially numbered sets.

		NM/M
Complete Set (10):		17.50
Common Player:		1.00
Inserted 1:23		
FX Gold:		2X
Production 500 Sets		
1	J.D. Drew	2.00
2	Eric Chavez	1.00
3	Gabe Kapler	1.00
4	Bruce Chen	1.00
5	Carlos Beltran	3.00
6	Troy Glaus	5.00
7	Roy Halladay	1.00
8	Adrian Beltre	2.00
9	Michael Barrett	1.00
10	Pat Burrell	5.00

UD Authentics

This six-card autographed set features signatures of Griffey Jr. and Nomar Garciaparra. These are seeded 1:288 packs.

		NM/M
Complete Set (6):		130.00
Common Player:		5.00
Inserted 1:288		
MB	Michael Barrett	4.00
PB	Pat Burrell	10.00
JD	J.D. Drew	12.00
NG	Nomar Garciaparra	70.00
TG	Troy Glaus	12.00
JR	Ken Griffey Jr.	90.00

Upper Realm

This 15-card set focuses on the top stars of the game. Card fronts utilize holo-foil treatment, with the initials UR lightly foiled. Card backs are numbered with a "U" prefix and are seeded 1:11 packs.

		NM/M
Complete Set (15):		13.00
Common Player:		.30
Inserted 1:11		
1	Ken Griffey Jr.	1.25
2	Mark McGwire	1.50
3	Sammy Sosa	.75
4	Tony Gwynn	.75

5	Alex Rodriguez	1.50
6	Juan Gonzalez	.40
7	J.D. Drew	.50
8	Roger Clemens	.85
9	Greg Maddux	.75
10	Randy Johnson	.60
11	Mo Vaughn	.30
12	Derek Jeter	2.00
13	Vladimir Guerrero	.60
14	Cal Ripken Jr.	2.00
15	Nomar Garciaparra	.75

2K Countdown

This set recognizes the countdown to the next century with a salute to baseball's next century of superstars including Derek Jeter and Alex Rodriguez. These are done on a horizontal format and inserted 1:11 packs.

		NM/M
Complete Set (10):		16.00
Common Player:		.75
Inserted 1:11		
1	Ken Griffey Jr.	2.00
2	Derek Jeter	3.00
3	Mike Piazza	2.00
4	J.D. Drew	.75
5	Vladimir Guerrero	1.00
6	Chipper Jones	1.50
7	Alex Rodriguez	2.50
8	Nomar Garciaparra	1.50
9	Mark McGwire	2.50
10	Sammy Sosa	1.50

Ken Griffey Jr. Santa Hat Card

A swatch of red velvet, ostensibly from "a special holiday-worn Santa hat," is featured on this card given to customers and associates of UD. The standard-size card is highlighted in gold-foil front and back and features pictures of the spokesman in a Santa hat on each side, as well.

		NM/M
HH-1	Ken Griffey Jr.	40.00

1999 Upper Deck HoloGrFX Sample

Numbered 60, rather than 56 as in the regular-issue version, this card, which also bears a white "SAMPLE" notation on back, was issued to preview the new UD brand.

		NM/M
60	Ken Griffey Jr.	2.50

1999 Upper Deck HoloGrFX

HoloGrFX was distributed exclusively to retail and the base set is comprised of 60 base cards, each utilizing holographic technology. A parallel gold-enhanced AUsome version is found about once every eight packs.

		NM/M
Complete Set (60):		12.00
Common Player:		.10
AUsome:		1.5X
Inserted 1:8		
Pack (3):		1.00
Wax Box (36):		20.00
1	Mo Vaughn	.10
2	Troy Glaus	.60
3	Tim Salmon	.10
4	Randy Johnson	.65
5	Travis Lee	.25
6	Chipper Jones	.75
7	Greg Maddux	.75
8	Andruw Jones	.65
9	Tom Glavine	.25
10	Cal Ripken Jr.	1.50
11	Albert Belle	.10
12	Nomar Garciaparra	.75
13	Pedro J. Martinez	.65
14	Sammy Sosa	.75
15	Frank Thomas	.65
16	Greg Vaughn	.10
17	Kenny Lofton	.10
18	Jim Thome	.50
19	Manny Ramirez	.65
20	Todd Helton	.60
21	Larry Walker	.10
22	Tony Clark	.10
23	Juan Encarnacion	.10
24	Mark Kotsay	.10
25	Jeff Bagwell	.65
26	Craig Biggio	.10
27	Ken Caminiti	.10
28	Carlos Beltran	.50
29	Jeremy Giambi	.10
30	Raul Mondesi	.10
31	Kevin Brown	.10
32	Jeromy Burnitz	.10
33	Corey Koskie	.10
34	Todd Walker	.10
35	Vladimir Guerrero	.65
36	Mike Piazza	1.00
37	Robin Ventura	.10
38	Derek Jeter	1.50
39	Roger Clemens	.85
40	Bernie Williams	.10
41	Orlando Hernandez	.10
42	Ben Grieve	.10
43	Eric Chavez	.15
44	Scott Rolen	.45
45	Pat Burrell **RC**	1.50
46	Warren Morris	.10
47	Jason Kendall	.10
48	Mark McGwire	1.25
49	J.D. Drew	.50
50	Tony Gwynn	.75
51	Trevor Hoffman	.10
52	Barry Bonds	1.50
53	Ken Griffey Jr.	1.00
54	Alex Rodriguez	1.25
55	Jose Canseco	.35
56	Juan Gonzalez	.30
57	Ivan Rodriguez	.60
58	Rafael Palmeiro	.60
59	David Wells	.10
60	Carlos Delgado	.25

Future Fame

This six-card set focuses on players who are destined for Hall of Fame greatness. Card fronts feature a horizontal format on a die-cut design. These are seeded 1:34 packs. A parallel Gold (AU) version is also randomly seeded in every 1:432 packs.

		NM/M
Complete Set (6):		15.00
Common Player:		2.50
Inserted 1:34		
Gold:		2X
Inserted 1:210		
1	Tony Gwynn	2.50
2	Cal Ripken Jr.	5.00
3	Mark McGwire	4.00
4	Ken Griffey Jr.	3.50
5	Greg Maddux	2.50
6	Roger Clemens	3.00

Launchers

This 15-card set highlights the top home run hitters on holographic patterned foil fronts, including McGwire and Sosa. These are seeded 1:3 packs. A Gold (AU) parallel version is also seeded 1:105 packs.

		NM/M
Complete Set (15):		20.00
Common Player:		.50
Inserted 1:3		
Gold:		2X
Inserted 1:105		
1	Mark McGwire	3.00
2	Ken Griffey Jr.	2.50
3	Sammy Sosa	2.00
4	J.D. Drew	.75
5	Mo Vaughn	.50
6	Juan Gonzalez	.50
7	Mike Piazza	2.50
8	Alex Rodriguez	3.00
9	Chipper Jones	2.00
10	Nomar Garciaparra	2.00
11	Vladimir Guerrero	1.00
12	Albert Belle	.50
13	Barry Bonds	4.00
14	Frank Thomas	1.00
15	Jeff Bagwell	1.00

StarView

This nine-card set highlights the top players in the game on a rainbow foil, full bleed design. These are seeded 1:17 packs. A Gold parallel version is also randomly seeded 1:210 packs.

		NM/M
Complete Set (9):		25.00
Common Player:		2.50
Inserted 1:17		
Gold:		2X
Inserted 1:210		
1	Mark McGwire	5.00
2	Ken Griffey Jr.	4.00
3	Sammy Sosa	2.50
4	Nomar Garciaparra	2.50
5	Roger Clemens	3.00
6	Greg Maddux	2.50
7	Mike Piazza	4.00
8	Alex Rodriguez	5.00
9	Chipper Jones	2.50

UD Authentics

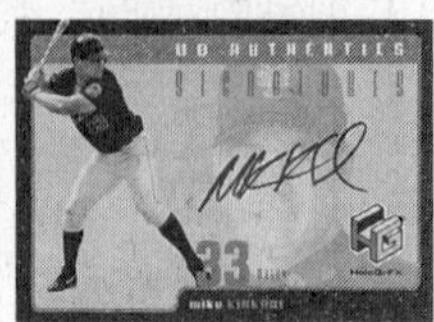

This autographed set is done on a horizontal format, with the player signature across the front of a shadow image of the featured player in the background.

		NM/M
Common Player:		4.00
Inserted 1:431		
CB	Carlos Beltran	25.00
BC	Bruce Chen	4.00
JD	J.D. Drew	12.00
AG	Alex Gonzalez	4.00
JR	Ken Griffey Jr.	80.00
CJ	Chipper Jones	50.00
GK	Gabe Kapler	6.00
MK	Mike Kinkade	4.00
CK	Corey Koskie	7.50
GL	George Lombard	4.00
RM	Ryan Minor	4.00
SM	Shane Monahan	4.00

500 Club Piece of History

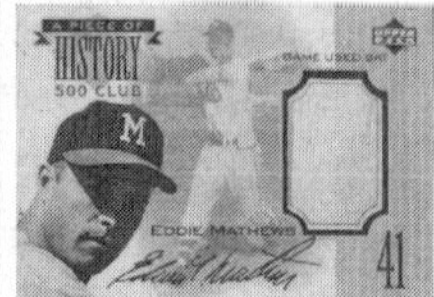

This two card collection features game-used bat chips from bats swung by Willie McCovey and Eddie Mathews embedded into each card. 350 cards of each player exist. Each player also autographed these inserts to their respective jersey numbers: McCovey (44) and Mathews (41).

	NM/M
Eddie Mathews/350	150.00
Eddie Mathews/ Auto./41	550.00
Willie McCovey/350	120.00
Willie McCovey/ Auto./44	650.00

Hitter.Net Ted Williams

To promote Ted Williams; web site, UD issued this card to persons attending the 1999 All-Star Game July 13 at Fenway Park in Boston. Enclosed in a cellophane wrapper, the 2-1/2" x 3-1/2" card has a sepia photo of a young Williams superimposed on an aerial view of the ballpark. There is a facsimile autograph on front as well as the hitter.net logo. On back are various advertisements for the service, along with a photo of an autographed baseball.

		NM/M
9	Ted Williams	7.50

1999 UD Ionix

Ionix is a 90-card set that includes a 30-card "Techno" short-printed subset (1:4 packs). Four-card packs sold for $4.99. The first 60 cards of the set are included in a parallel set in which the photo from the back of the regular card was put on the front of a rainbow-foil Reciprocal card. These cards are sequentially numbered to 750. The Techno subset cards were also paralleled on a Reciprocal version sequentially numbered to 100. Due to an error, all Techno card numbers bear the "R" prefix intended for the Reciprocals; actual Reciprocal cards also bear a dot-matrix serial number on front.

		NM/M
Complete Set (90):		45.00
Common Player (1-60):		.25
Common Techno (61-90):		.50
Inserted 1:4		
Reciprocals (1-60):		3X
Production 750 Sets		
Techno Reciprocals (61-90):		1.5X
Production 100 Sets		
Pack (4):		2.00
Wax Box (20):		25.00
1	Troy Glaus	.60
2	Darin Erstad	.50
3	Travis Lee	.35
4	Matt Williams	.25
5	Chipper Jones	.75
6	Greg Maddux	.75
7	Andruw Jones	.65
8	Andres Galarraga	.25
9	Tom Glavine	.35
10	Cal Ripken Jr.	2.00
11	Ryan Minor	.25
12	Nomar Garciaparra	1.00
13	Mo Vaughn	.25
14	Pedro Martinez	.65
15	Sammy Sosa	.75
16	Kerry Wood	.50
17	Albert Belle	.25
18	Frank Thomas	.65
19	Sean Casey	.25
20	Kenny Lofton	.25
21	Manny Ramirez	.65
22	Jim Thome	.60
23	Bartolo Colon	.25
24	Jaret Wright	.25
25	Larry Walker	.25
26	Tony Clark	.25
27	Gabe Kapler	.25
28	Edgar Renteria	.25
29	Randy Johnson	.65
30	Craig Biggio	.25
31	Jeff Bagwell	.65
32	Moises Alou	.25
33	Johnny Damon	.50
34	Adrian Beltre	.35
35	Jeromy Burnitz	.25
36	Todd Walker	.25
37	Corey Koskie	.25
38	Vladimir Guerrero	.65
39	Mike Piazza	1.00
40	Hideo Nomo	.35
41	Derek Jeter	2.00
42	Tino Martinez	.25
43	Orlando Hernandez	.25
44	Ben Grieve	.25
45	Rickey Henderson	.65
46	Scott Rolen	.60
47	Curt Schilling	.35
48	Aramis Ramirez	.25
49	Tony Gwynn	.75
50	Kevin Brown	.25
51	Barry Bonds	2.00
52	Ken Griffey Jr.	1.00
53	Alex Rodriguez	1.50
54	Mark McGwire	1.50
55	J.D. Drew	.60
56	Rolando Arrojo	.25
57	Ivan Rodriguez	.60
58	Juan Gonzalez	.35
59	Roger Clemens	.85
60	Jose Cruz Jr.	.25
61	Travis Lee (Techno)	.65
62	Andres Galarraga (Techno)	.50
63	Andruw Jones (Techno)	1.50
64	Chipper Jones (Techno)	2.00
65	Greg Maddux (Techno)	2.00
66	Cal Ripken Jr. (Techno)	4.00
67	Nomar Garciaparra (Techno)	2.00
68	Mo Vaughn (Techno)	.50
69	Sammy Sosa (Techno)	2.00
70	Frank Thomas (Techno)	1.50
71	Kerry Wood (Techno)	.75
72	Kenny Lofton (Techno)	.50
73	Manny Ramirez (Techno)	1.50
74	Larry Walker (Techno)	.50
75	Jeff Bagwell (Techno)	1.50
76	Randy Johnson (Techno)	1.50
77	Paul Molitor (Techno)	1.50
78	Derek Jeter (Techno)	4.00
79	Tino Martinez (Techno)	.50
80	Mike Piazza (Techno)	2.50
81	Ben Grieve (Techno)	.50
82	Scott Rolen (Techno)	.75
83	Mark McGwire (Techno)	3.00
84	Tony Gwynn (Techno)	2.00
85	Barry Bonds (Techno)	4.00
86	Ken Griffey Jr. (Techno)	2.50
87	Alex Rodriguez (Techno)	3.00
88	Juan Gonzalez (Techno)	.75
89	Roger Clemens (Techno)	2.25
90	J.D. Drew (Techno)	1.00
100	Ken Griffey Jr. (SAMPLE)	2.50

Reciprocal

Reciprocal is a parallel of the Ionix base set in which the front and back photos have been switched. Card numbers carry an "R" prefix. The first 60 Reciprocal parallels were produced in an edition of 750 each; the Techno subset Reciprocals (#61-90) are an edition of just 100 each.

Stars (1-60):	3X
Stars (61-90):	1.5X

Cyber

This insert set consisted of 25-cards of baseball's superstars and red-hot rookies. One card was inserted every 53 packs.

		NM/M
Complete Set (25):		125.00
Common Player:		2.00
C01	Ken Griffey Jr.	8.00
C02	Cal Ripken Jr.	12.50
C03	Frank Thomas	5.00
C04	Greg Maddux	6.50
C05	Mike Piazza	8.00
C06	Alex Rodriguez	10.00
C07	Chipper Jones	6.50
C08	Derek Jeter	12.50
C09	Mark McGwire	10.00
C10	Juan Gonzalez	2.50
C11	Kerry Wood	2.50
C12	Tony Gwynn	6.50
C13	Scott Rolen	4.00
C14	Nomar Garciaparra	6.50
C15	Roger Clemens	7.00
C16	Sammy Sosa	6.50
C17	Travis Lee	2.00
C18	Ben Grieve	2.00
C19	Jeff Bagwell	5.00
C20	Ivan Rodriguez	4.00
C21	Barry Bonds	12.50
C22	J.D. Drew	4.00
C23	Kenny Lofton	2.00
C24	Andruw Jones	5.00
C25	Vladimir Guerrero	5.00

HoloGrFX

This insert set consisted of 10-cards, and featured only the best players in the game. The cards in this set were holographically enhanced. These cards were rare with one card inserted every 1,500 packs.

		NM/M
Complete Set (10):		800.00
Common Player:		50.00
Inserted 1:1,500		
HG01	Ken Griffey Jr.	100.00
HG02	Cal Ripken Jr.	150.00
HG03	Frank Thomas	75.00
HG04	Greg Maddux	90.00
HG05	Mike Piazza	100.00
HG06	Alex Rodriguez	125.00
HG07	Chipper Jones	90.00
HG08	Derek Jeter	150.00
HG09	Mark McGwire	125.00
HG10	Juan Gonzalez	50.00

Hyper

This insert set featured the top players in baseball, and consisted of 20-cards. Hyper cards were inserted one per nine packs.

		NM/M
Complete Set (20):		37.00
Common Player:		.75
Inserted 1:9		
H01	Ken Griffey Jr.	3.00
H02	Cal Ripken Jr.	4.50
H03	Frank Thomas	1.50
H04	Greg Maddux	2.25
H05	Mike Piazza	3.00
H06	Alex Rodriguez	3.75
H07	Chipper Jones	2.25
H08	Derek Jeter	4.50
H09	Mark McGwire	3.75
H10	Juan Gonzalez	.75
H11	Kerry Wood	1.00
H12	Tony Gwynn	2.25
H13	Scott Rolen	1.00
H14	Nomar Garciaparra	2.25
H15	Roger Clemens	2.75
H16	Sammy Sosa	2.25
H17	Travis Lee	1.00
H18	Ben Grieve	.75
H19	Jeff Bagwell	1.50
H20	J.D. Drew	1.00

Nitro

Baseball's ten most collectible players are featured in this 10-card insert set. Each card features Ionix technology with rainbow foil and a unique color pattern. Nitro cards were inserted one per 18 packs.

		NM/M
Complete Set (10):		18.00
Common Player:		1.00
Inserted 1:18		
N01	Ken Griffey Jr.	2.50
N02	Cal Ripken Jr.	4.00
N03	Frank Thomas	1.50
N04	Greg Maddux	2.00
N05	Mike Piazza	2.50
N06	Alex Rodriguez	3.00
N07	Chipper Jones	2.00
N08	Derek Jeter	4.00
N09	Mark McGwire	3.00
N10	J.D. Drew	1.00

Warp Zone

This 15-card insert set contained a special holographic foil enhancement. Warp Zone cards were inserted one per 216 packs.

		NM/M
Complete Set (15):		195.00
Common Player:		6.00
Inserted 1:216		
WZ1	Ken Griffey Jr.	20.00
WZ2	Cal Ripken Jr.	30.00
WZ3	Frank Thomas	10.00
WZ4	Greg Maddux	15.00
WZ5	Mike Piazza	20.00
WZ6	Alex Rodriguez	25.00
WZ7	Chipper Jones	15.00
WZ8	Derek Jeter	30.00
WZ9	Mark McGwire	25.00
WZ10	Juan Gonzalez	6.00
WZ11	Kerry Wood	6.00
WZ12	Tony Gwynn	15.00
WZ13	Scott Rolen	6.00
WZ14	Nomar Garciaparra	15.00
WZ15	J.D. Drew	6.00

500 Club Piece of History

These cards feature an actual piece of game-used bat from one of Hall-of-Famer Frank Robinson's Louisville Sluggers. Approximately 350 were made. Robinson also autographed 20 of his Piece of History inserts.

		NM/M
FR	Frank Robinson/350	165.00
FRA	Frank Robinson/ Auto. 20	650.00

Mark McGwire Tribute Lunchbox

One of many special issues produced by Upper Deck in celebration of McGwire's short-lived season home run record, this 30-card set was sold in a metal lunchbox. Each 2-1/2" x 3-1/2" card has a large action photo on front and a small round portrait, along with the card title. The back has the same photos, with the large photo in a ghosted image as a background for the desciption of the highight presented on the card.

		NM/M
Complete Boxed Set (30):		10.00
Common Card:		.50
1-30	Mark McGwire	.50

Mark McGwire 70 HR - A New Record

This is one of many special issues from Upper Deck commemorating McGwire's record-breaking 1998 season. Most such cards were produced for retail-only sales, or for home shopping television shows. This blank-back, round-cornered card is 3-1/2" x 2-1/2" and has a flicker-action scene of Big Mac's home run swing.

	NM/M
Mark McGwire	4.00

Mark McGwire 500 Home Run Card Set

This TV-exclusive product depicts milestone home runs leading up to Big Mac's 500th career clout on Aug. 5, 1999. Sold in a shrink-wrapped decorative box, the basic design of the 2-1/2" x 3-1/2" cards has a central photo, usually an action shot, with a black pinstriped border at left and a red striped border at right. The word "MILESTONES" appears at the top of the picture. In a gray tab at left is a date or year, while his name is in a matching black tab at right. A silver-foil UD logo is at bottom. Backs have a grainy red monochromatic background photo on which are overprinted the details of the pictured blast, along with appropriate logos. Some cards have a silver-foil home run number printed on front. A special card pictures his 1st and 500th career homers. Issue price was about $30.

		NM/M
Complete Boxed Set (30):		7.00
Common Card:		.35
1-30	Mark McGwire	.35

1999 Upper Deck MVP Samples

		NM/M
S3	Ken Griffey Jr.	2.00
S3	Ken Griffey Jr. (Silver signature.)	2.00

1999 Upper Deck MVP

Card fronts of the 220-card set feature silver foil stamping and a white border. Backs feature year-by-year statistics, a small photo of the featured player and a brief career note. MVP was distributed in 36-pack boxes, with a SRP of $1.59 for 10-card packs.

		NM/M
Complete Set (220):		10.00
Common Player:		.05
Silver Script:		1X
Inserted 1:2		
Gold Script:		10X
Production 100 Sets		
Super Script:		30X
Production 25 Sets		
Pack (10):		1.00
Wax Box (36):		20.00
1	Mo Vaughn	.05
2	Tim Belcher	.05
3	Jack McDowell	.05
4	Troy Glaus	.60
5	Darin Erstad	.40
6	Tim Salmon	.15
7	Jim Edmonds	.05
8	Randy Johnson	.60
9	Steve Finley	.05
10	Travis Lee	.15
11	Matt Williams	.05
12	Todd Stottlemyre	.05
13	Jay Bell	.05
14	David Dellucci	.05
15	Chipper Jones	.75
16	Andruw Jones	.60
17	Greg Maddux	.75
18	Tom Glavine	.25
19	Javy Lopez	.05
20	Brian Jordan	.05
21	George Lombard	.05
22	John Smoltz	.05
23	Cal Ripken Jr.	1.50
24	Charles Johnson	.05
25	Albert Belle	.15
26	Brady Anderson	.05
27	Mike Mussina	.35
28	Calvin Pickering	.05
29	Ryan Minor	.05
30	Jerry Hairston Jr.	.05
31	Nomar Garciaparra	1.00
32	Pedro Martinez	.60
33	Jason Varitek	.05
34	Troy O'Leary	.05
35	Donnie Sadler	.05
36	Mark Portugal	.05
37	John Valentin	.05
38	Kerry Wood	.35
39	Sammy Sosa	1.00
40	Mark Grace	.10
41	Henry Rodriguez	.05
42	Rod Beck	.05
43	Benito Santiago	.05
44	Kevin Tapani	.05
45	Frank Thomas	.60
46	Mike Caruso	.05
47	Magglio Ordonez	.40
48	Paul Konerko	.05
49	Ray Durham	.05
50	Jim Parque	.05
51	Carlos Lee	.05
52	Denny Neagle	.05
53	Pete Harnisch	.05
54	Michael Tucker	.05
55	Sean Casey	.15
56	Eddie Taubensee	.05
57	Barry Larkin	.05
58	Pokey Reese	.05
59	Sandy Alomar	.05
60	Roberto Alomar	.25
61	Bartolo Colon	.05
62	Kenny Lofton	.05
63	Omar Vizquel	.05
64	Travis Fryman	.05
65	Jim Thome	.05
66	Manny Ramirez	.60
67	Jaret Wright	.05
68	Darryl Kile	.05
69	Kirt Manwaring	.05
70	Vinny Castilla	.05
71	Todd Helton	.60
72	Dante Bichette	.05
73	Larry Walker	.05
74	Derrick Gibson	.05
75	Gabe Kapler	.05
76	Dean Palmer	.05
77	Matt Anderson	.05
78	Bobby Higginson	.05
79	Damion Easley	.05
80	Tony Clark	.05
81	Juan Encarnacion	.05
82	Livan Hernandez	.05
83	Alex Gonzalez	.05
84	Preston Wilson	.05
85	Derrek Lee	.05
86	Mark Kotsay	.05
87	Todd Dunwoody	.05
88	Cliff Floyd	.05
89	Ken Caminiti	.05
90	Jeff Bagwell	.60
91	Moises Alou	.05
92	Craig Biggio	.05
93	Billy Wagner	.05
94	Richard Hidalgo	.05
95	Derek Bell	.05
96	Hipolito Pichardo	.05
97	Jeff King	.05
98	Carlos Beltran	.40
99	Jeremy Giambi	.05
100	Larry Sutton	.05
101	Johnny Damon	.20
102	Dee Brown	.05
103	Kevin Brown	.10
104	Chan Ho Park	.05
105	Raul Mondesi	.05
106	Eric Karros	.05
107	Adrian Beltre	.15
108	Devon White	.05
109	Gary Sheffield	.35
110	Sean Berry	.05
111	Alex Ochoa	.05
112	Marquis Grissom	.05
113	Fernando Vina	.05
114	Jeff Cirillo	.05
115	Geoff Jenkins	.05
116	Jeromy Burnitz	.05
117	Brad Radke	.05
118	Eric Milton	.05
119	A.J. Pierzynski	.05
120	Todd Walker	.05
121	David Ortiz	.05
122	Corey Koskie	.05
123	Vladimir Guerrero	.60
124	Rondell White	.05
125	Brad Fullmer	.05
126	Ugueth Urbina	.05
127	Dustin Hermanson	.05
128	Michael Barrett	.05
129	Fernando Seguignol	.05
130	Mike Piazza	1.00
131	Rickey Henderson	.60
132	Rey Ordonez	.05
133	John Olerud	.05
134	Robin Ventura	.05
135	Hideo Nomo	.60
136	Mike Kinkade	.05
137	Al Leiter	.05
138	Brian McRae	.05
139	Derek Jeter	1.50
140	Bernie Williams	.15
141	Paul O'Neill	.05
142	Scott Brosius	.05
143	Tino Martinez	.05
144	Roger Clemens	.85
145	Orlando Hernandez	.10
146	Mariano Rivera	.10
147	Ricky Ledee	.05
148	A.J. Hinch	.05
149	Ben Grieve	.10
150	Eric Chavez	.15
151	Miguel Tejada	.15
152	Matt Stairs	.05
153	Ryan Christenson	.05
154	Jason Giambi	.35
155	Curt Schilling	.25
156	Scott Rolen	.45
157	Pat Burrell **RC**	1.50
158	Doug Glanville	.05
159	Bobby Abreu	.05
160	Rico Brogna	.05
161	Ron Gant	.05
162	Jason Kendall	.05
163	Aramis Ramirez	.05
164	Jose Guillen	.05
165	Emil Brown	.05
166	Pat Meares	.05
167	Kevin Young	.05
168	Brian Giles	.05
169	Mark McGwire	1.25
170	J.D. Drew	.40
171	Edgar Renteria	.05
172	Fernando Tatis	.05
173	Matt Morris	.05
174	Eli Marrero	.05
175	Ray Lankford	.05
176	Tony Gwynn	.75
177	Sterling Hitchcock	.05
178	Ruben Rivera	.05
179	Wally Joyner	.05
180	Trevor Hoffman	.05
181	Jim Leyritz	.05
182	Carlos Hernandez	.05
183	Barry Bonds	1.50
184	Ellis Burks	.05
185	F.P. Santangelo	.05
186	J.T. Snow	.05
187	Ramon Martinez	.05
188	Jeff Kent	.05
189	Robb Nen	.05
190	Ken Griffey Jr.	1.00
191	Alex Rodriguez	1.25
192	Shane Monahan	.05
193	Carlos Guillen	.05
194	Edgar Martinez	.05
195	David Segui	.05
196	Jose Mesa	.05
197	Jose Canseco	.35
198	Rolando Arrojo	.05
199	Wade Boggs	.75
200	Fred McGriff	.05
201	Quinton McCracken	.05
202	Bobby Smith	.05
203	Bubba Trammell	.05
204	Juan Gonzalez	.60
205	Ivan Rodriguez	.45
206	Rafael Palmeiro	.45
207	Royce Clayton	.05
208	Rick Helling	.05
209	Todd Zeile	.05
210	Rusty Greer	.05
211	David Wells	.05
212	Roy Halladay	.05
213	Carlos Delgado	.25
214	Darrin Fletcher	.05
215	Shawn Green	.15
216	Kevin Witt	.05
217	Jose Cruz Jr.	.05
218	Checklist (Ken Griffey Jr.)	.45
219	Checklist (Sammy Sosa)	.45
220	Checklist (Mark McGwire)	.50

Scripts/Super Scripts

Three different parallels of the 220 base cards in MVP are inserted bearing a metallic-foil facsimile autograph on front. Silver Script cards are found about every other pack. Gold Script cards are hobby-only and serially numbered to 100 apiece. Also hobby-only are

Super Script versions on which the autograph is in holographic foil and the cards are numbered on the back to 25 apiece.

Silver Script:	1X
Gold Script:	10X
Super Script:	30X

All-Star Game

In conjunction with FanFest held in Boston prior to the All-Star Game, UD issued a set of specially marked versions of its MVP issue. It was reported that 15,000 three-card packs were distributed at the show, with some cards reportedly short-printed. The cards have a format virtually identical to the regular-issue MVP cards, except for the presence on front of a bright silver-foil All-Star logo and an AS prefix to the card number on back.

		NM/M
Complete Set (30):		12.50
Common Player:		.25
1	Mo Vaughn	.25
2	Randy Johnson	.60
3	Chipper Jones	.75
4	Greg Maddux	.75
5	Cal Ripken Jr.	2.00
6	Albert Belle	.35
7	Nomar Garciaparra	1.00
8	Pedro Martinez	.60
9	Sammy Sosa	1.00
10	Frank Thomas	.60
11	Sean Casey	.35
12	Roberto Alomar	.30
13	Manny Ramirez	.60
14	Larry Walker	.25
15	Jeff Bagwell	.60
16	Craig Biggio	.25
17	Raul Mondesi	.25
18	Vladimir Guerrero	.60
19	Mike Piazza	1.00
20	Derek Jeter	2.00
21	Roger Clemens	.85
22	Scott Rolen	.40
23	Mark McGwire	1.50
24	Tony Gwynn	.75
25	Barry Bonds	2.00
26	Ken Griffey Jr.	1.00
27	Alex Rodriguez	1.50
28	Jose Canseco	.40
29	Juan Gonzalez	.60
30	Ivan Rodriguez	.50

Dynamics

This 15-card set features holofoil treatment on the card fronts with silver foil stamping. Card backs are numbered with a "D" prefix and are inserted 1:28 packs.

		NM/M
Complete Set (15):		17.50
Common Player:		.60
Inserted 1:28		
1	Ken Griffey Jr.	2.00
2	Alex Rodriguez	2.50
3	Nomar Garciaparra	2.00
4	Mike Piazza	2.00
5	Mark McGwire	2.25
6	Sammy Sosa	2.00
7	Chipper Jones	1.50
8	Mo Vaughn	.60
9	Tony Gwynn	1.50
10	Vladimir Guerrero	1.25
11	Derek Jeter	3.00
12	Jeff Bagwell	1.25
13	Cal Ripken Jr.	3.00
14	Juan Gonzalez	1.25
15	J.D. Drew	.90

Game Used Souvenirs

This set has a piece of game-used bat from the featured player embedded into each card. These are found exclusively in hobby packs at a rate of 1:144 packs.

		NM/M
Complete Set (9):		75.00
Common Player:		5.00
Inserted 1:144		
JB	Jeff Bagwell	8.00
BB	Barry Bonds	20.00
JD	J.D. Drew	8.00
KGj	Ken Griffey Jr.	15.00
CJ	Chipper Jones	10.00
MP	Mike Piazza	15.00
CR	Cal Ripken Jr.	20.00
SR	Scott Rolen	8.00
MV	Mo Vaughn	5.00

Signed Game Used Souvenirs

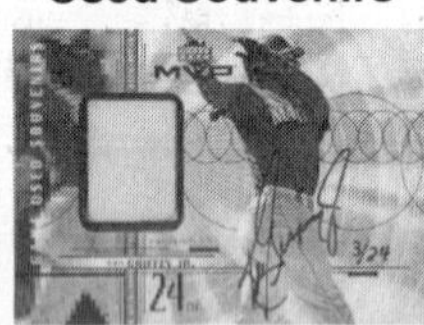

Ken Griffey Jr. and Chipper Jones both signed their Game Used Souvenir inserts to their jersey number, Griffey (24) and Jones (10). These were seeded exclusively in hobby packs.

		NM/M
KGj	Ken Griffey Jr.	300.00
CJ	Chipper Jones	200.00

Power Surge

This 15-card set features baseball's top home run hitters, utilizing rainbow-foil technology. Card backs are numbered with a "P" prefix and are seeded 1:9 packs.

		NM/M
Complete Set (15):		12.50
Common Player:		.50
Inserted 1:9		
1	Mark McGwire	1.50
2	Sammy Sosa	1.25
3	Ken Griffey Jr.	1.25
4	Alex Rodriguez	1.50
5	Juan Gonzalez	.75
6	Nomar Garciaparra	1.25
7	Vladimir Guerrero	.75
8	Chipper Jones	1.00
9	Albert Belle	.50
10	Frank Thomas	.75
11	Mike Piazza	1.25
12	Jeff Bagwell	.75
13	Manny Ramirez	.75
14	Mo Vaughn	.50
15	Barry Bonds	2.00

ProSign

This 30-card autographed set is randomly seeded exclusively in retail packs

at a rate of 1:216 packs. Card backs are numbered with the featured player's initials.

		NM/M
Common Autograph:		5.00
Inserted 1:216 R		
MA	Matt Anderson	5.00
CB	Carlos Beltran	15.00
RB	Russ Branyan	5.00
EC	Eric Chavez	10.00
BC	Bruce Chen	5.00
BF	Brad Fuller	5.00
NG	Nomar Garciaparra	80.00
JG	Jeremy Giambi	5.00
DG	Derrick Gibson	5.00
CG	Chris Gomez	5.00
AG	Alex Gonzalez	5.00
BG	Ben Grieve	5.00
JR.	Ken Griffey Jr.	80.00
RH	Richard Hidalgo	5.00
SH	Shea Hillenbrand	10.00
CJ	Chipper Jones/SP	50.00
GK	Gabe Kapler	6.00
SK	Scott Karl	5.00
CK	Corey Koskie	7.50
RL	Ricky Ledee	5.00
ML	Mike Lincoln	5.00
GL	George Lombard	5.00
MLo	Mike Lowell	7.50
RM	Ryan Minor	5.00
SM	Shane Monahan	5.00
AN	Abraham Nunez	5.00
JP	Jim Parque	5.00
CP	Calvin Pickering	5.00
JRa	Jason Rakers	5.00
RR	Ruben Rivera	5.00
IR	Ivan Rodriguez/SP	50.00
KW	Kevin Witt	5.00

Scout's Choice

Utilizing Light F/X technology, this 15-card set highlights the top young prospects in the game. Card backs are numbered with an "SC" prefix and are seeded 1:9 packs.

		NM/M
Complete Set (15):		5.00
Common Player:		.25
Inserted 1:9		
1	J.D. Drew	.65
2	Ben Grieve	.35
3	Troy Glaus	1.50
4	Gabe Kapler	.25
5	Carlos Beltran	.45
6	Aramis Ramirez	.25
7	Pat Burrell	1.00
8	Kerry Wood	.65
9	Ryan Minor	.25
10	Todd Helton	1.00
11	Eric Chavez	.35
12	Russ Branyon	.25
13	Travis Lee	.35
14	Ruben Mateo	.25
15	Roy Halladay	.35

Super Tools

This 15-card insert set focuses on baseball's top stars and utilizes holo foil technology on the card fronts. Card backs are numbered with a "T" prefix and are seeded 1:14 packs.

		NM/M
Complete Set (15):		25.00
Common Player:		.50
Inserted 1:14		
1	Ken Griffey Jr.	2.50
2	Alex Rodriguez	3.00
3	Sammy Sosa	2.00
4	Derek Jeter	4.00
5	Vladimir Guerrero	1.50
6	Ben Grieve	.50
7	Mike Piazza	2.50
8	Kenny Lofton	.50
9	Barry Bonds	4.00
10	Darin Erstad	1.00
11	Nomar Garciaparra	2.00
12	Cal Ripken Jr.	4.00
13	J.D. Drew	1.00
14	Larry Walker	.50
15	Chipper Jones	2.00

Swing Time

This 12-card set focuses on top hitters in the game and points out three aspects why the featured player is such a successful hitter. Printed on a full foiled front these are seeded 1:6 packs. Cards are numbered with an "S" prefix.

		NM/M
Complete Set (12):		5.00
Common Player:		.35
Inserted 1:6		
1	Ken Griffey Jr.	.75
2	Mark McGwire	1.00
3	Sammy Sosa	.60
4	Tony Gwynn	.60
5	Alex Rodriguez	1.00
6	Nomar Garciaparra	.60
7	Barry Bonds	1.50
8	Frank Thomas	.50
9	Chipper Jones	.60
10	Ivan Rodriguez	.35
11	Mike Piazza	.75
12	Derek Jeter	1.50

500 Club Piece of History

This insert has a piece of game-used bat once swung by Mike Schmidt embedded into each card. A total of 350 of this insert was produced. Schmidt also signed 20 of the inserts.

	NM/M
Mike Schmidt/350	160.00
Mike Schmidt/ Auto./20	1,250

1999 Upper Deck Ovation

Cards 1-60 in the base set have the look and feel of an actual baseball. A player photo is in the foreground with a partial image of a baseball in the background on the card front. Cards 61-90 make up two subsets: World Premiere (61-80) is a 20-card collection consisting of 20 rookie prospects and Superstar Spotlight (81-90) is a

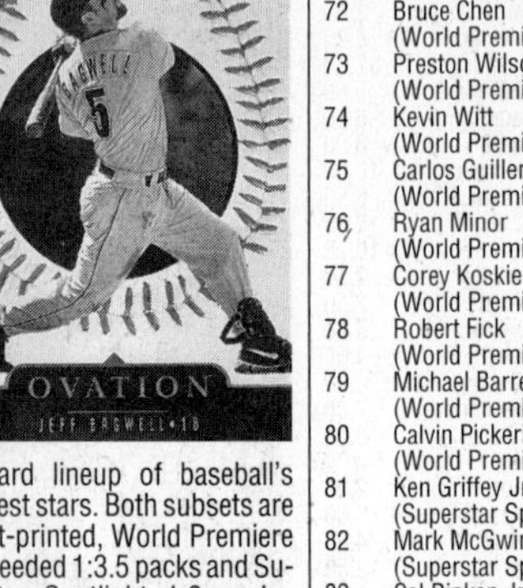

10-card lineup of baseball's biggest stars. Both subsets are short-printed, World Premiere are seeded 1:3.5 packs and Superstar Spotlight 1:6 packs. Five-card packs carry a S.R.P. of $3.99 per pack.

		NM/M
Complete Set (90):		20.00
Common Player:		.05
Common World Premiere:		.15
Inserted 1:3.5		
Common Superstar Spotlight:		.60
Inserted 1:6		
Pack (5):		2.00
Box (20):		30.00
1	Ken Griffey Jr.	1.50
2	Rondell White	.05
3	Tony Clark	.05
4	Barry Bonds	2.50
5	Larry Walker	.05
6	Greg Vaughn	.05
7	Mark Grace	.05
8	John Olerud	.05
9	Matt Williams	.05
10	Craig Biggio	.05
11	Quinton McCracken	.05
12	Kerry Wood	.35
13	Derek Jeter	2.50
14	Frank Thomas	.75
15	Tino Martinez	.05
16	Albert Belle	.05
17	Ben Grieve	.05
18	Cal Ripken Jr.	2.50
19	Johnny Damon	.30
20	Jose Cruz Jr.	.05
21	Barry Larkin	.05
22	Jason Giambi	.45
23	Sean Casey	.10
24	Scott Rolen	.60
25	Jim Thome	.45
26	Curt Schilling	.25
27	Moises Alou	.05
28	Alex Rodriguez	2.00
29	Mark Kotsay	.05
30	Darin Erstad	.25
31	Mike Mussina	.30
32	Todd Walker	.05
33	Nomar Garciaparra	1.00
34	Vladimir Guerrero	.75
35	Jeff Bagwell	.75
36	Mark McGwire	2.00
37	Travis Lee	.15
38	Dean Palmer	.05
39	Fred McGriff	.05
40	Sammy Sosa	1.00
41	Mike Piazza	1.50
42	Andres Galarraga	.05
43	Pedro Martinez	.75
44	Juan Gonzalez	.40
45	Greg Maddux	1.00
46	Jeromy Burnitz	.05
47	Roger Clemens	1.25
48	Vinny Castilla	.05
49	Kevin Brown	.05
50	Mo Vaughn	.05
51	Raul Mondesi	.05
52	Randy Johnson	.75
53	Ray Lankford	.05
54	Jaret Wright	.05
55	Tony Gwynn	1.00
56	Chipper Jones	1.00
57	Gary Sheffield	.40
58	Ivan Rodriguez	.65
59	Kenny Lofton	.05
60	Jason Kendall	.05
61	J.D. Drew (World Premiere)	.75
62	Gabe Kapler (World Premiere)	.15
63	Adrian Beltre (World Premiere)	.40
64	Carlos Beltran (World Premiere)	.50
65	Eric Chavez (World Premiere)	.35
66	Mike Lowell (World Premiere)	.25
67	Troy Glaus (World Premiere)	1.00
68	George Lombard (World Premiere)	.15
69	Alex Gonzalez (World Premiere)	.15
70	Mike Kinkade (World Premiere)	.15
71	Jeremy Giambi (World Premiere)	.15
72	Bruce Chen (World Premiere)	.15
73	Preston Wilson (World Premiere)	.25
74	Kevin Witt (World Premiere)	.15
75	Carlos Guillen (World Premiere)	.15
76	Ryan Minor (World Premiere)	.15
77	Corey Koskie (World Premiere)	.15
78	Robert Fick (World Premiere)	.15
79	Michael Barrett (World Premiere)	.15
80	Calvin Pickering (World Premiere)	.15
81	Ken Griffey Jr. (Superstar Spotlight)	1.00
82	Mark McGwire (Superstar Spotlight)	1.50
83	Cal Ripken Jr. (Superstar Spotlight)	2.00
84	Derek Jeter (Superstar Spotlight)	2.00
85	Chipper Jones (Superstar Spotlight)	.75
86	Nomar Garciapparra (Garciaparra) (Superstar Spotlight)	.75
87	Sammy Sosa (Superstar Spotlight)	.75
88	Juan Gonzalez (Superstar Spotlight)	.30
89	Mike Piazza (Superstar Spotlight)	1.00
90	Alex Rodriguez (Superstar Spotlight)	1.50

Standing Ovation

Stars (1-60):	3X
World Premiere (61-80):	1.5X
Superstar Spotlight (81-90):	2X
Production 500 Sets	

Curtain Calls

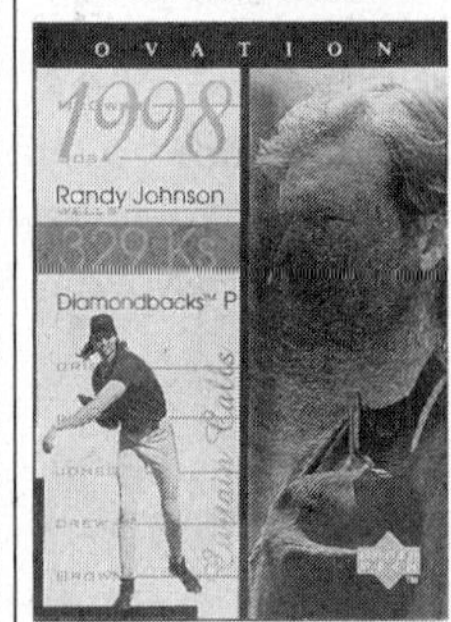

This 20-card set focuses on the most memorable accomplishments posted during the '98 season. Card fronts have two images of the player, one on the right half and a smaller image on the bottom left. Copper foil stamping is used to enhance the card front. These are numbered with a "R" prefix and are seeded 1:8 packs.

		NM/M
Complete Set (20):		20.00
Common Player:		.25
Inserted 1:8		
R1	Mark McGwire	2.00
R2	Sammy Sosa	1.00
R3	Ken Griffey Jr.	1.50
R4	Alex Rodriguez	2.00
R5	Roger Clemens	1.25
R6	Cal Ripken Jr.	2.50
R7	Barry Bonds	2.50
R8	Kerry Wood	.40
R9	Nomar Garciaparra	1.00
R10	Derek Jeter	2.50
R11	Juan Gonzalez	.50

R12 Greg Maddux 1.00
R13 Pedro Martinez 1.00
R14 David Wells .25
R15 Moises Alou .25
R16 Tony Gwynn 1.00
R17 Albert Belle .25
R18 Mike Piazza 1.50
R19 Ivan Rodriguez .65
R20 Randy Johnson .75

Major Production

This 20-card set utilizes thermography technology to simulate the look and feel of home plate and highlights some of the game's most productive players. These are inserted 1:45 packs and are numbered with an "S" prefix.

NM/M
Complete Set (20): 45.00
Common Player: .75
Inserted 1:45
S1 Mike Piazza 4.00
S2 Mark McGwire 5.00
S3 Chipper Jones 3.00
S4 Cal Ripken Jr. 6.00
S5 Ken Griffey Jr. 4.00
S6 Barry Bonds 6.00
S7 Tony Gwynn 3.00
S8 Randy Johnson 2.50
S9 Ivan Rodriguez 2.00
S10 Frank Thomas 2.50
S11 Alex Rodriguez 5.00
S12 Albert Belle .75
S13 Juan Gonzalez 1.25
S14 Greg Maddux 3.00
S15 Jeff Bagwell 2.50
S16 Derek Jeter 6.00
S17 Matt Williams .75
S18 Kenny Lofton .75
S19 Sammy Sosa 3.00
S20 Roger Clemens 3.50

Piece of History

This 16-card set has actual pieces of game-used bat, from the featured player, imbedded into the card. These are inserted 1:247 packs. Ben Grieve autographed 25 versions of his Piece of History insert cards. Although there is no regular Piece of History Kerry Wood card, Upper Deck inserted 25 autographed Piece of History game-used baseball cards. These have a piece of one of Wood's game-hurled baseballs from the 1998 season.

NM/M
Common Player: 5.00
Inserted 1:247
BB Barry Bonds 25.00
CJ Chipper Jones 15.00
BW Bernie Williams 5.00
KGj Ken Griffey Jr. 20.00
NG Nomar Garciaparra 15.00
JG Juan Gonzalez 5.00
DJ Derek Jeter 25.00
SS Sammy Sosa 15.00
TG Tony Gwynn 15.00
AR Alex Rodriguez 20.00
CR Cal Ripken Jr. 25.00
BG Ben Grieve 5.00
VG Vladimir Guerrero 10.00
MP Mike Piazza 20.00
BGAU Ben Grieve/Auto./25 30.00
KWAU Kerry Wood/Auto./25 50.00

ReMarkable

This three-tiered 15-card insert showcases Mark McGwire's historic '98 season. Cards #1-5 are Bronze and inserted 1:9 packs; cards #6-10 are Silver and inserted 1:25 packs; and cards #11-15 are Gold and inserted 1:99 packs.

NM/M
Complete Set (15): 20.00
Common #1-5: 1.50
Inserted 1:9
Common #6-10: 2.25
Inserted 1:25
Common # 11-15 3.00
Inserted 1:99
MM1-5 Mark McGwire 1.50
MM6-9 Mark McGwire 3.00
MM10-15 Mark McGwire 3.00

500 Club Piece of History

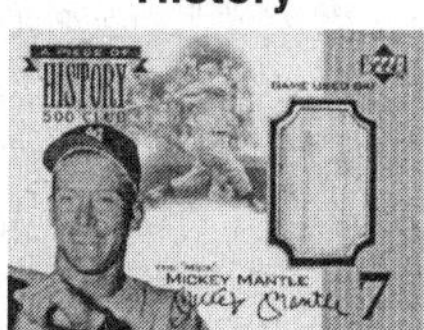

Each of these cards actually has a piece of game-used Louisville Slugger, once swung by Mickey Mantle, embedded. Approximately 350 cards exist. There is also one card with a cut signature of Mantle and a piece of his game-used bat on it.

NM/M
MIC-P Mickey Mantle/350 600.00
Mickey Mantle/ Bat/Auto. 8,000

1999 Upper Deck PowerDeck

This 25-card set is comprised of 25 digital PowerDeck interactive trading cards, complete with video and audio content. There is also a parallel "paper" version of the base set called Auxiliary Power. Each digital card includes 32 megabytes of information and is compatible with almost any internet ready computer. One PowerDeck digital card comes in every three-card pack.

NM/M
Complete Set (25): 20.00
Common Player: .50
Pack (3): 1.50
Wax Box (24): 20.00
1 Ken Griffey Jr. 2.00
2 Mark McGwire 2.50
3 Cal Ripken Jr. 3.00
4 Sammy Sosa 1.50
5 Derek Jeter 3.00
6 Mike Piazza 2.00
7 Nomar Garciaparra 1.50
8 Greg Maddux 1.50
9 Tony Gwynn 1.50
10 Roger Clemens 1.75
11 Scott Rolen 1.00
12 Alex Rodriguez 2.50
13 Manny Ramirez 1.25
14 Chipper Jones 1.50
15 Juan Gonzalez .65
16 Ivan Rodriguez 1.00
17 Frank Thomas 1.25
18 Mo Vaughn .50
19 Barry Bonds 3.00
20 Vladimir Guerrero 1.25
21 Jose Canseco .65
22 Jeff Bagwell 1.25
23 Pedro Martinez 1.25
24 Gabe Kapler .50
25 J.D. Drew .75
--- Checklist .10

Auxiliary Power

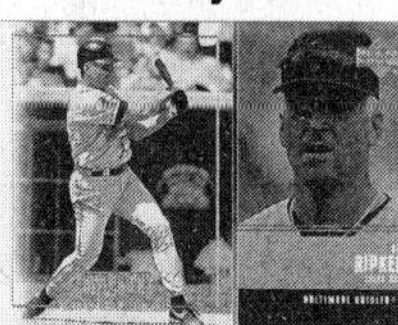

A "paper" parallel version of the 25-card digital set. These have a horizontal format with silver-foil graphics. Backs repeat the front portrait photo along with the player's past five years of statistics and a brief career highlight. Card numbers are prefixed with "AUX-."

NM/M
Complete Set (25): 6.00
Common Player: .10
1 Ken Griffey Jr. .50
2 Mark McGwire .60
3 Cal Ripken Jr. .75
4 Sammy Sosa .40
5 Derek Jeter .75
6 Mike Piazza .50
7 Nomar Garciaparra .40
8 Greg Maddux .40
9 Tony Gwynn .40
10 Roger Clemens .45
11 Scott Rolen .25
12 Alex Rodriguez .60
13 Manny Ramirez .30
14 Chipper Jones .40
15 Juan Gonzalez .15
16 Ivan Rodriguez .25
17 Frank Thomas .30
18 Mo Vaughn .10
19 Barry Bonds .75
20 Vladimir Guerrero .30
21 Jose Canseco .20
22 Jeff Bagwell .30
23 Pedro Martinez .30
24 Gabe Kapler .10
25 J.D. Drew .25

Most Valuable Performances

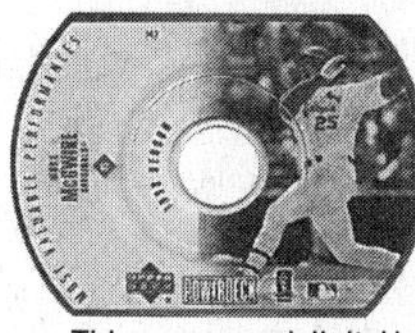

This seven-card digital insert set consists of capturing true MVP performances from some of baseball's greatest players. These were seeded 1:287 packs.

NM/M
Complete Set (7): 75.00
Common Player: 6.00
Inserted 1:287
1 Sammy Sosa 10.00
2 Barry Bonds 20.00
3 Cal Ripken Jr. 20.00
4 Juan Gonzalez 6.00
5 Ken Griffey Jr. 12.50
6 Roger Clemens 10.00
7 Mark McGwire, Sammy Sosa 12.50

MVP Auxiliary

A "paper" parallel version of the digital set, these also were inserted 1:287 packs. They have a horizontal format using silver holofoil and also have different photos from the digital version.

NM/M
Complete Set (7): 60.00
Common Player: 4.00
Inserted 1:287
1 Sammy Sosa 7.50
2 Barry Bonds 15.00
3 Cal Ripken Jr. 15.00
4 Juan Gonzalez 4.00
5 Ken Griffey Jr. 10.00
6 Roger Clemens 7.50
7 Mark McGwire, Sammy Sosa 12.50

Powerful Moments

This six-card digital interactive set has game-action footage pinpointing specific milestones in each of the featured players' careers. These were inserted 1:7 packs.

NM/M
Complete Set (6): 10.00
Common Player: 1.00
Inserted 1:7
1 Mark McGwire 2.00
2 Sammy Sosa 1.00
3 Cal Ripken Jr. 3.00
4 Ken Griffey Jr. 1.50
5 Derek Jeter 3.00
6 Alex Rodriguez 2.00

Powerful Moments Auxiliary

This "paper" parallel version of the digital set is also inserted 1:7 packs on a horizontal format. Different photos were used from the digital set.

NM/M
Complete Set (6): 10.00
Common Player: 1.00
Inserted 1:7
Gold (one each):VALUE UNDETERMINED
1 Mark McGwire 2.00
2 Sammy Sosa 1.00
3 Cal Ripken Jr. 3.00
4 Ken Griffey Jr. 1.50
5 Derek Jeter 3.00
6 Alex Rodriguez 2.00

Time Capsule

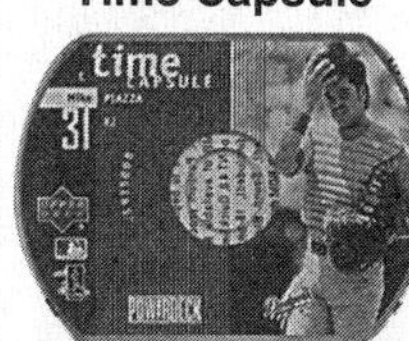

Six MLB Rookies of the Year are honored in this digital set with the digital content going back to the rookie seasons of the featured players. These were seeded 1:23 packs.

NM/M
Complete Set (6): 12.50
Common Player: 1.00
Inserted 1:23
1 Ken Griffey Jr. 2.50
2 Mike Piazza 2.50
3 Mark McGwire 3.00
4 Derek Jeter 4.00
5 Jose Canseco 1.00
6 Nomar Garciaparra 2.00

Time Capsule-Auxiliary Power

This "paper' parallel set of the digital version utilizes a similar design as the digital insert and uses different photos as well. Horizontal fronts have a thin vertical monochromatic portrait at left. At right is an action photos set on a metallized background. Backs repeat the front portrait and have a screen simulation along with stats and data. These were inserted 1:23 packs.

NM/M
Complete Set (6): 15.00
Common Player: 1.00
Inserted 1:23
Gold (One of each.): Values Undetermined
1 Ken Griffey Jr. 2.50
2 Mike Piazza 2.50
3 Mark McGwire 3.00
4 Derek Jeter 4.00
5 Jose Canseco 1.00
6 Nomar Garciaparra 2.00

A Season to Remember

This special box-topper CD insert presents audio-visual highlights of the 1999 season, featuring players like David Cone, Ken Griffey, Jr., Mark McGwire, Tony Gwynn, Wade Boggs, Sammy Sosa and Cal Ripken, Jr. McGwire is pictured on this CD hitting his 500th home run.

NM/M
Mark McGwire 3.00

Athletes of the Century

Babe Ruth was baseball's representative in a four-sport set of CD "cards" produced by Upper Deck.

NM/M
Babe Ruth 1.00

World Series Power Deck

This CD-ROM card titled "Season to Remember" was distributed at Yankee Stadium during Game 4 of the 1999 World Series and features highlights of the Yankees championship season.

NM/M
Season to Remember (1999 Yankees) 12.00

1999 UD Retro

The 110-card base set is comprised of 88 current stars and 22 retired greats. Card fronts have a tan, speckled border while card backs have a year-by-year compilation of the player's stats along with a career note. Retro is packaged in lunchboxes, 24 packs to a box with an S.R.P. of $4.99 per six-card pack.

NM/M
Complete Set (110): 15.00
Common Player: .05
Gold: 12X
Production 250 Sets
Platinum 1/1: Values Undetermined
Wax Pack (6): 2.50
Lunchbox (24): 45.00
1 Mo Vaughn .05
2 Troy Glaus .65
3 Tim Salmon .05
4 Randy Johnson .75
5 Travis Lee .15
6 Matt Williams .05
7 Greg Maddux .85
8 Chipper Jones .85
9 Andruw Jones .75
10 Tom Glavine .25
11 Javy Lopez .05
12 Albert Belle .05
13 Cal Ripken Jr. 2.00
14 Brady Anderson .05
15 Nomar Garciaparra .85
16 Pedro J. Martinez .75
17 Sammy Sosa .85
18 Mark Grace .05
19 Frank Thomas .75
20 Ray Durham .05
21 Sean Casey .10
22 Greg Vaughn .05
23 Barry Larkin .05
24 Manny Ramirez .75
25 Jim Thome .50
26 Jaret Wright .05
27 Kenny Lofton .05
28 Larry Walker .05
29 Todd Helton .65
30 Vinny Castilla .05
31 Tony Clark .05
32 Juan Encarnacion .05
33 Dean Palmer .05
34 Mark Kotsay .05
35 Alex Gonzalez .05
36 Shane Reynolds .05
37 Ken Caminiti .05
38 Jeff Bagwell .75
39 Craig Biggio .05
40 Carlos Febles .05
41 Carlos Beltran .35
42 Jeremy Giambi .05
43 Raul Mondesi .05
44 Adrian Beltre .10
45 Kevin Brown .05
46 Jeromy Burnitz .05
47 Jeff Cirillo .05
48 Corey Koskie .05
49 Todd Walker .05
50 Vladimir Guerrero .75
51 Michael Barrett .05
52 Mike Piazza 1.00
53 Robin Ventura .05
54 Edgardo Alfonzo .05
55 Derek Jeter 2.00
56 Roger Clemens .90
57 Tino Martinez .05
58 Orlando Hernandez .05
59 Chuck Knoblauch .05
60 Bernie Williams .05
61 Eric Chavez .10
62 Ben Grieve .05
63 Jason Giambi .40
64 Scott Rolen .60
65 Curt Schilling .25
66 Bobby Abreu .10
67 Jason Kendall .05
68 Kevin Young .05
69 Mark McGwire 1.50
70 J.D. Drew .60
71 Eric Davis .05
72 Tony Gwynn .85
73 Trevor Hoffman .05
74 Barry Bonds 2.00
75 Robb Nen .05
76 Ken Griffey Jr. 1.00
77 Alex Rodriguez 1.50
78 Jay Buhner .05
79 Carlos Guillen .05
80 Jose Canseco .40
81 Bobby Smith .05
82 Juan Gonzalez .40
83 Ivan Rodriguez .65
84 Rafael Palmeiro .65
85 Rick Helling .05
86 Jose Cruz Jr. .05
87 David Wells .05
88 Carlos Delgado .20
89 Nolan Ryan 1.50
90 George Brett .90
91 Robin Yount .50
92 Paul Molitor .50
93 Dave Winfield .50
94 Steve Garvey .25
95 Ozzie Smith .85
96 Ted Williams 1.50
97 Don Mattingly .90
98 Mickey Mantle 2.50
99 Harmon Killebrew .25
100 Rollie Fingers .10
101 Kirk Gibson .05
102 Bucky Dent .05
103 Willie Mays 1.00
104 Babe Ruth 1.50
105 Gary Carter .50
106 Reggie Jackson .85
107 Frank Robinson .25
108 Ernie Banks .50
109 Eddie Murray .50
110 Mike Schmidt .90

Gold/Platinum

This is a 110-card parallel to the base set. Cards have a gold-tone front and are sequentially numbered to 250 sets. A one-of-one Platinum parallel to the base set also is randomly seeded.

	NM/M
Common Gold:	1.00
Gold Stars:	15X
Platinum 1/1: Values Undetemined	

Distant Replay

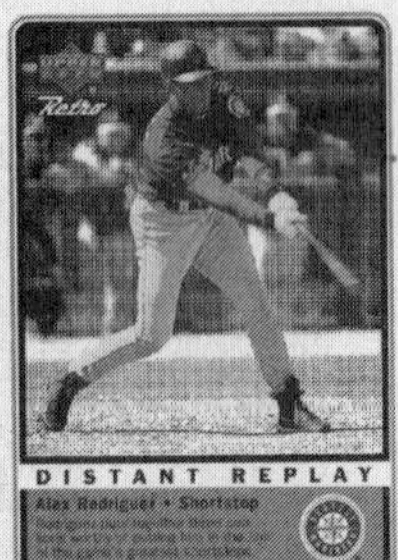

This 15-card set recounts the most memorable plays from the 1998 season. Card fronts have a black-and-white photo of the player and along the bottom of the photo a date of the memorable play and brief description are given. These are seeded 1:8 packs. A parallel version, Level 2, is also randomly seeded, limited to 100 sequentially numbered sets.

		NM/M
Complete Set (15):		30.00
Common Player:		1.00
Inserted 1:8		
Level 2:		6X
Production 100 Sets		
1	Ken Griffey Jr.	2.50
2	Mark McGwire	3.00
3	Cal Ripken Jr.	4.00
4	Greg Maddux	2.00
5	Nomar Garciaparra	2.00
6	Roger Clemens	2.25
7	Alex Rodriguez	3.00
8	Frank Thomas	1.50
9	Mike Piazza	2.50
10	Chipper Jones	2.00
11	Juan Gonzalez	1.00
12	Tony Gwynn	2.00
13	Barry Bonds	4.00
14	Ivan Rodriguez	1.00
15	Derek Jeter	4.00

INKredible

INKredible is an autographed insert set that consists of both current players and retired stars. Card fronts have a small photo in the upper left portion of the featured player and a large signing area. These are seeded 1:23 packs.

		NM/M
Common Player:		4.00
Inserted 1:23		
CBe	Carlos Beltran	30.00
GB	George Brett/SP	80.00
PB	Pat Burrell	10.00
SC	Sean Casey	10.00
TC	Tony Clark	4.00
BD	Bucky Dent	8.00
DE	Darin Erstad	15.00
RF	Rollie Fingers	8.00
SG	Steve Garvey	10.00
KG	Kirk Gibson	10.00
RG	Rusty Greer	4.00
JR	Ken Griffey Jr.	80.00
TG	Tony Gwynn	30.00
CJ	Chipper Jones	30.00
GK	Gabe Kapler	5.00
HK	Harmon Killebrew	30.00
FL	Fred Lynn	10.00
DM	Don Mattingly	50.00
PM	Paul Molitor	20.00
EM	Eddie Murray/SP	50.00
PO	Paul O'Neill	15.00
AP	Angel Pena	4.00
MR	Manny Ramirez	30.00
IR	Ivan Rodriguez	25.00
NR	Nolan Ryan	150.00
OZ	Ozzie Smith	30.00
DWe	David Wells	15.00
BW	Bernie Williams	40.00
DW	Dave Winfield	20.00
RY	Robin Yount	35.00

INKredible Level 2

A parallel to INKredible autographed inserts, these are hand-numbered to the featured player's jersey number.

		NM/M
Common Player:		10.00
Limited to player's jersey #.		
CBe	Carlos Beltran/36	60.00
PB	Pat Burrell/76	50.00
SC	Sean Casey/21	40.00
TC	Tony Clark/17	20.00
BD	Bucky Dent/20	25.00
DE	Darin Erstad/17	50.00
RF	Rollie Fingers/34	25.00
KG	Kirk Gibson/23	30.00
RG	Rusty Greer/29	20.00
JR	Ken Griffey Jr./24	200.00
TG	Tony Gwynn/19	150.00
GK	Gabe Kapler/23	40.00
FL	Fred Lynn/19	30.00
DM	Don Mattingly/23	200.00
EM	Eddie Murray/33	80.00
PO	Paul O'Neill/21	50.00
AP	Angel Pena/36	10.00
MR	Manny Ramirez/24	80.00
NR	Nolan Ryan/34	400.00
DWe	David Wells/33	25.00
BW	Bernie Williams/51	60.00
DW	Dave Winfield/31	60.00
RY	Robin Yount/19	90.00

Old/New School

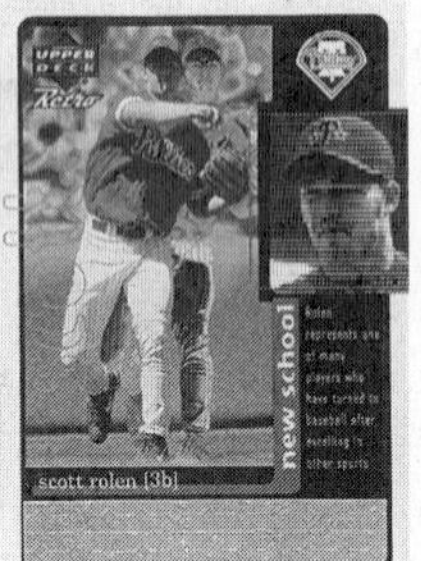

This 30-card insert set captures 15 Old School players and 15 New School players. Each card is sequentially numbered to 1,000. A parallel version is also randomly seeded and is limited to 50 sequentially numbered sets. Old School cards are basically black-and-white with color graphic highlights on front and back. New School cards have multiple computer-enhanced color photos and silver-foil highlights.

		NM/M
Complete Set (30):		35.00
Common Player:		.40
Production 1,000 Sets		
Level 2:		5X
Production 50 Sets		
1	Ken Griffey Jr.	2.50
2	Alex Rodriguez	3.00
3	Frank Thomas	1.50
4	Cal Ripken Jr.	4.00
5	Chipper Jones	2.00
6	Craig Biggio	.40
7	Greg Maddux	2.00
8	Jeff Bagwell	1.50
9	Juan Gonzalez	.75
10	Mark McGwire	3.00
11	Mike Piazza	2.50
12	Mo Vaughn	.40
13	Roger Clemens	2.25
14	Sammy Sosa	2.00
15	Tony Gwynn	2.00
16	Gabe Kapler	.40
17	J.D. Drew	1.00
18	Pat Burrell	1.00
19	Roy Halladay	.40
20	Jeff Weaver	.40
21	Troy Glaus	1.00
22	Vladimir Guerrero	1.50
23	Michael Barrett	.40
24	Carlos Beltran	.40
25	Scott Rolen	1.00
26	Nomar Garciaparra	2.00
27	Warren Morris	.40
28	Alex Gonzalez	.40
29	Kyle Farnsworth	.40
30	Derek Jeter	4.00

Piece of History 500 Club

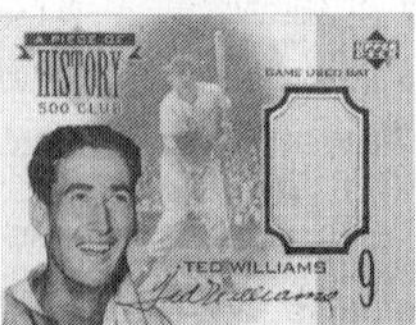

Each one of these inserts features a piece of game-used bat swung by Ted Williams embedded into each card. A total of 350 of these were issued. Williams also autographed nine of the 500 Club Piece of History cards.

		NM/M
TW	Ted Williams/350	250.00

Throwback Attack

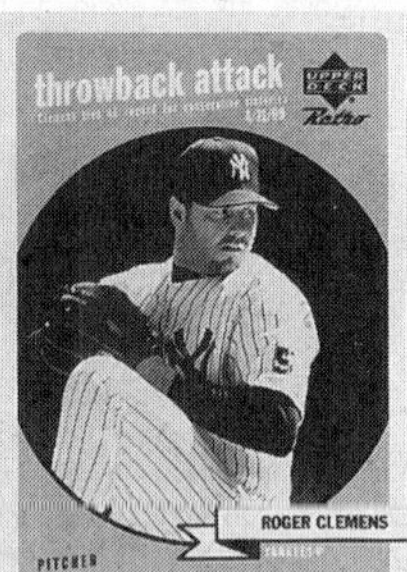

These inserts have a "Retro" look, borrowing heavily from 1959 Topps. Highlighting top players, the set features card fronts with a circular player photo on a bright orange background. At top in white is, "throwback attack." There is a white border. Backs have a ghosted image of the front photo and career highlights. Cards are numbered with a "T" prefix and are seeded 1:5 packs. A parallel version is also randomly seeded and limited to 500 numbered sets.

		NM/M
Complete Set (15):		20.00
Common Player:		.50
Inserted 1:5		
Level 2:		3X
Production 500 Sets		
1	Ken Griffey Jr.	2.00
2	Mark McGwire	2.50
3	Sammy Sosa	1.25
4	Roger Clemens	1.50
5	J.D. Drew	.75
6	Alex Rodriguez	2.50
7	Greg Maddux	1.25
8	Mike Piazza	2.00
9	Juan Gonzalez	.50
10	Mo Vaughn	.50
11	Cal Ripken Jr.	3.00
12	Frank Thomas	1.00
13	Nomar Garciaparra	1.25
14	Vladimir Guerrero	1.00
15	Tony Gwynn	1.25

Lunchbox

Lunchboxes were the packaging for UD Retro. Each lunchbox contains 24 six-card packs and features 16 different current or retired baseball legends including Babe Ruth.

	NM/M
Complete Set (17):	140.00
Common Lunchbox:	7.50
One dual-player per case.	
Roger Clemens	7.50
Ken Griffey Jr.	7.50
Mickey Mantle	10.00
Mark McGwire	10.00
Mike Piazza	7.50
Alex Rodriguez	7.50
Babe Ruth	10.00
Sammy Sosa	7.50
Ted Williams	10.00
Ken Griffey Jr., Mark McGwire	12.50
Ken Griffey Jr., Babe Ruth	12.50
Ken Griffey Jr., Ted Williams	12.50
Mickey Mantle, Babe Ruth	15.00
Mark McGwire, Mickey Mantle	15.00
Mark McGwire, Babe Ruth	15.00
Mark McGwire, Ted Williams	15.00

1999 Upper Deck Ultimate Victory

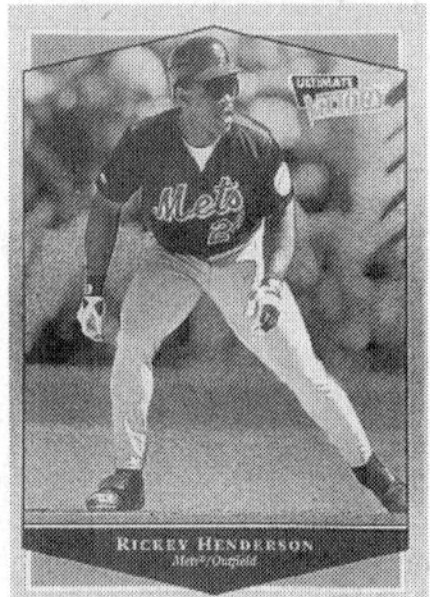

The 180-card base set includes two 30-card short-printed (1:4) subsets: McGwire Magic (151-180) and 1999 Rookie (121-150). The base cards have a silver foil border with the featured players' last five seasons of statistics along with a brief career highlight. There are two parallels randomly inserted: Victory Collection and Ultimate Collection. Victory Collection is seeded 1:12 packs with a holographic, prismatic look. Ultimate Collection has a gold holographic, prismatic look and are serially numbered "xxx/100" on the card front.

		NM/M
Complete Set (180):		125.00
Common Player:		.10
Common 99 Rookie (121-150):		.50
Common McGwire Magic (151-180):		1.00
Victory (1-120):		3.5X
Victory SP (121-180):		2X
Inserted 1:12		
Ultimate (1-120):		12X
Ultimate SP (121-180):		5X
Production 100 Sets		
Pack (5):		4.50
Wax Box (24):		75.00
1	Troy Glaus	.65
2	Tim Salmon	.10
3	Mo Vaughn	.10
4	Garret Anderson	.10
5	Darin Erstad	.30
6	Randy Johnson	.75
7	Matt Williams	.10
8	Travis Lee	.25
9	Jay Bell	.10
10	Steve Finley	.10
11	Luis Gonzalez	.10
12	Greg Maddux	1.00
13	Chipper Jones	1.00
14	Javy Lopez	.10
15	Tom Glavine	.35
16	John Smoltz	.10
17	Cal Ripken Jr.	3.00
18	Charles Johnson	.10
19	Albert Belle	.10
20	Mike Mussina	.40
21	Pedro Martinez	.75
22	Nomar Garciaparra	1.00
23	Jose Offerman	.10
24	Sammy Sosa	1.00
25	Mark Grace	.10
26	Kerry Wood	.35
27	Frank Thomas	.75
28	Ray Durham	.10
29	Paul Konerko	.20
30	Pete Harnisch	.10
31	Greg Vaughn	.10
32	Sean Casey	.20
33	Manny Ramirez	.75
34	Jim Thome	.65
35	Sandy Alomar	.10
36	Roberto Alomar	.30
37	Travis Fryman	.10
38	Kenny Lofton	.10
39	Omar Vizquel	.10
40	Larry Walker	.10
41	Todd Helton	.65
42	Vinny Castilla	.10
43	Tony Clark	.10
44	Juan Encarnacion	.10
45	Dean Palmer	.10
46	Damion Easley	.10
47	Mark Kotsay	.10
48	Cliff Floyd	.10
49	Jeff Bagwell	.75
50	Ken Caminiti	.10
51	Craig Biggio	.10
52	Moises Alou	.10
53	Johnny Damon	.35
54	Larry Sutton	.10
55	Kevin Brown	.10
56	Adrian Beltre	.25
57	Raul Mondesi	.10
58	Gary Sheffield	.50
59	Jeromy Burnitz	.10
60	Sean Berry	.10
61	Jeff Cirillo	.10
62	Brad Radke	.10
63	Todd Walker	.10
64	Matt Lawton	.10
65	Vladimir Guerrero	.75
66	Rondell White	.10
67	Dustin Hermanson	.10
68	Mike Piazza	2.00
69	Rickey Henderson	.75
70	Robin Ventura	.10
71	John Olerud	.10
72	Derek Jeter	3.00
73	Roger Clemens	1.25
74	Orlando Hernandez	.10
75	Paul O'Neill	.10
76	Bernie Williams	.10
77	Chuck Knoblauch	.10
78	Tino Martinez	.10
79	Jason Giambi	.50
80	Ben Grieve	.10
81	Matt Stairs	.10
82	Scott Rolen	.60
83	Ron Gant	.10
84	Bobby Abreu	.10
85	Curt Schilling	.35
86	Brian Giles	.10
87	Jason Kendall	.10
88	Kevin Young	.10
89	Mark McGwire	2.00
90	Fernando Tatis	.10
91	Ray Lankford	.10
92	Eric Davis	.10
93	Tony Gwynn	1.00
94	Reggie Sanders	.10
95	Wally Joyner	.10
96	Trevor Hoffman	.10
97	Robb Nen	.10
98	Barry Bonds	3.00
99	Jeff Kent	.10
100	J.T. Snow	.10
101	Ellis Burks	.10
102	Ken Griffey Jr.	1.50
103	Alex Rodriguez	2.00
104	Jay Buhner	.10
105	Edgar Martinez	.10
106	David Bell	.10
107	Bobby Smith	.10
108	Wade Boggs	1.00
109	Fred McGriff	.10
110	Rolando Arrojo	.10
111	Jose Canseco	.50
112	Ivan Rodriguez	.65
113	Juan Gonzalez	.40
114	Rafael Palmeiro	.65
115	Rusty Greer	.10
116	Todd Zeile	.10
117	Jose Cruz Jr.	.10
118	Carlos Delgado	.35
119	Shawn Green	.30
120	David Wells	.10
121	Eric Munson **RC** (99 Rookie)	2.50
122	Lance Berkman (99 Rookie)	2.00
123	Ed Yarnall (99 Rookie)	.50
124	Jacque Jones (99 Rookie)	1.00
125	Kyle Farnsworth (99 Rookie)	1.00
126	Ryan Rupe (99 Rookie)	1.00
127	Jeff Weaver **RC** (99 Rookie)	2.00
128	Gabe Kapler (99 Rookie)	.50
129	Alex Gonzalez (99 Rookie)	.50
130	Randy Wolf (99 Rookie)	1.00
131	Ben Davis (99 Rookie)	.50
132	Carlos Beltran (99 Rookie)	2.00
133	Jim Morris (99 Rookie)	2.00
134	Jeff Zimmerman (99 Rookie)	2.00
135	Bruce Aven (99 Rookie)	.50
136	Alfonso Soriano **RC** (99 Rookie)	50.00
137	Tim Hudson **RC** (99 Rookie)	15.00
138	Josh Beckett **RC** (99 Rookie)	50.00
139	Michael Barrett (99 Rookie)	.50
140	Eric Chavez (99 Rookie)	1.00
141	Pat Burrell **RC** (99 Rookie)	10.00
142	Kris Benson (99 Rookie)	1.00
143	J.D. Drew (99 Rookie)	2.00
144	Matt Clement (99 Rookie)	1.00
145	Rick Ankiel **RC** (99 Rookie)	15.00
146	Vernon Wells (99 Rookie)	1.00
147	Ruben Mateo (99 Rookie)	.50
148	Roy Halladay (99 Rookie)	1.00
149	Joe McEwing (99 Rookie)	.50
150	Freddy Garcia **RC** (99 Rookie)	8.00
151	Mark McGwire (McGwire Magic)	1.00
152	Mark McGwire (McGwire Magic)	1.00
153	Mark McGwire (McGwire Magic)	1.00
154	Mark McGwire (McGwire Magic)	1.00
155	Mark McGwire (McGwire Magic)	1.00
156	Mark McGwire (McGwire Magic)	1.00
157	Mark McGwire (McGwire Magic)	1.00
158	Mark McGwire (McGwire Magic)	1.00
159	Mark McGwire (McGwire Magic)	1.00
160	Mark McGwire (McGwire Magic)	1.00
161	Mark McGwire (McGwire Magic)	1.00
162	Mark McGwire (McGwire Magic)	1.00
163	Mark McGwire (McGwire Magic)	1.00
164	Mark McGwire (McGwire Magic)	1.00
165	Mark McGwire (McGwire Magic)	1.00
166	Mark McGwire (McGwire Magic)	1.00
167	Mark McGwire (McGwire Magic)	1.00
168	Mark McGwire (McGwire Magic)	1.00
169	Mark McGwire (McGwire Magic)	1.00
170	Mark McGwire (McGwire Magic)	1.00
171	Mark McGwire (McGwire Magic)	1.00
172	Mark McGwire (McGwire Magic)	1.00
173	Mark McGwire (McGwire Magic)	1.00
174	Mark McGwire (McGwire Magic)	1.00
175	Mark McGwire (McGwire Magic)	1.00
176	Mark McGwire (McGwire Magic)	1.00
177	Mark McGwire (McGwire Magic)	1.00
178	Mark McGwire (McGwire Magic)	1.00
179	Mark McGwire (McGwire Magic)	1.00
180	Mark McGwire (McGwire Magic)	1.00

Victory Collection

This parallel of the base set features a prismatic foil design on front. The cards are found on average of one per 12 packs. A 1-of-1 edition also exists, but is not priced here due to rarity and demand variability.

	NM/M
Common Player (1-120, 151-180):	1.00
Common Player (121-150):	5.00
Stars (1-120):	3.5X
Stars (121-150):	2X

Ultimate Collection

This parallel insert set is individually serial numbered on front from within an edition of 100 cards each. Card fronts have silver holographic prismatic foil background and a silver-foil serial number. Backs are identical to the regular-issue cards.

	NM/M
Common Player (1-120, 151-180):	2.00
Common Player (121-150):	12.00
Stars (1-120):	12X
Stars (121-150):	5X

Bleacher Reachers

This 11-card set focuses on the hitters who were vying for the 1999 home run title. They have a horizontal format with a holographic foil card front. Card backs have a small photo along with three-year statistical totals. They are numbered with a "BR" prefix and were inserted 1:23 packs.

		NM/M
Complete Set (11):		20.00
Common Player:		.75
Inserted 1:23		
1	Ken Griffey Jr.	2.50
2	Mark McGwire	3.00
3	Sammy Sosa	2.00
4	Barry Bonds	4.00
5	Nomar Garciaparra	2.00
6	Juan Gonzalez	.75
7	Jose Canseco	.75
8	Manny Ramirez	1.50
9	Mike Piazza	2.50
10	Jeff Bagwell	1.50
11	Alex Rodriguez	3.00

Fame-Used Memorabilia

This four-card set has a piece of game-used bat embedded into each card, from either George Brett, Robin Yount, Nolan Ryan or Orlando Cepeda. Approximately 350 bat cards of each player were produced.

		NM/M
Complete Set (4):		50.00
Common Player:		7.50
Production 350 Cards		
GB	George Brett	20.00
OC	Orlando Cepeda	7.50
NR	Nolan Ryan	25.00
RY	Robin Yount	10.00

Fame-Used Combo

This insert has a piece of game-used bat from each of the 1999 Hall of Fame inductees and is limited to 99 sequentially numbered singles.

		NM/M
Edition of 99:		
HOF	Nolan Ryan, George Brett, Robin Yount, Orlando Cepeda	250.00

Frozen Ropes

This 10-card set spotlights baseball's top hitters and are seeded 1:23 packs.

		NM/M
Complete Set (10):		15.00
Common Player:		.50
Inserted 1:23		
1	Ken Griffey Jr.	2.00
2	Mark McGwire	2.50
3	Sammy Sosa	1.50
4	Derek Jeter	3.00
5	Tony Gwynn	1.50
6	Nomar Garciaparra	1.50
7	Alex Rodriguez	2.50
8	Mike Piazza	2.00
9	Mo Vaughn	.50
10	Craig Biggio	.50

STATure

This 15-card set highlights players with outstanding statistical achievements. The featured stat for the player runs down the right side of the card. Fronts are printed on metallic foil with a textured pattern behind the player photo. Conventionally printed backs repeat the front design numbered with an "S" prefix. These were seeded 1:6 packs.

		NM/M
Complete Set (15):		9.00
Common Player:		.30
Inserted 1:6		
1	Ken Griffey Jr.	.75
2	Mark McGwire	1.00
3	Sammy Sosa	.65
4	Nomar Garciaparra	.65
5	Roger Clemens	.65
6	Greg Maddux	.65
7	Alex Rodriguez	1.00
8	Derek Jeter	1.50
9	Juan Gonzalez	.30
10	Manny Ramirez	.50
11	Mike Piazza	.75
12	Tony Gwynn	.65
13	Chipper Jones	.65
14	Pedro Martinez	.50
15	Frank Thomas	.50

Tribute 1999

This four-card set is devoted to 1999's Hall of Fame inductees. Card fronts have a horizontal format over a holographic foil design. Card backs have the featured players' year-by-year statistics and are numbered with a "T" prefix.

		NM/M
Complete Set (4):		5.00
Common Player:		1.00
Inserted 1:11		
1	Nolan Ryan	2.00
2	Robin Yount	1.50
3	George Brett	1.50
4	Orlando Cepeda	1.00

Ultimate Competitors

This 12-card set has a close-up photo, along with two miniature action photos in the foreground, all printed on silver foil. Backs repeat the front photos and have a few words about the player's competitive desire. These were seeded 1:23 packs and are numbered with a "U" prefix on the card back.

		NM/M
Complete Set (12):		20.00
Common Player:		.60
Inserted 1:23		
1	Ken Griffey Jr.	3.00
2	Roger Clemens	2.50
3	Scott Rolen	1.00
4	Greg Maddux	2.00
5	Mark McGwire	4.00
6	Derek Jeter	5.00
7	Randy Johnson	1.50
8	Cal Ripken Jr.	5.00
9	Craig Biggio	.50
10	Kevin Brown	.50
11	Chipper Jones	2.00
12	Vladimir Guerrero	1.50

Ultimate Hit Men

This insert set spotlights the eight candidates who competed for the 1999 batting titles. Inserted on the average of 1:23 packs they were numbered with an "H" prefix on the card back.

		NM/M
Complete Set (8):		15.00
Common Player:		1.00
Inserted 1:23		
1	Tony Gwynn	2.00
2	Cal Ripken Jr.	4.00
3	Wade Boggs	2.00
4	Larry Walker	1.00
5	Alex Rodriguez	3.00
6	Derek Jeter	4.00
7	Ivan Rodriguez	1.25
8	Ken Griffey Jr.	2.50

Victory

This 470-card base set is printed on 20-point stock and has a white border with UV coating. The set consists of a number of subsets including, 30-card Mark McGwire Magic, 30 team checklist cards, 50 '99 rookies, 15 Power Trip, 20 Rookie Flashback, 15 Big Play Makers and 10 History in the Making. Twelve-card packs had an SRP of $.99.

		NM/M
Complete Set (470):		30.00
Common Player:		.05
Pack (12):		.75
Wax Box (36):		20.00
1	Anaheim Angels (Team Checklist)	.05
2	Mark Harriger **RC** (99 Rookie)	.10
3	Mo Vaughn (Power Trip)	.05
4	Darin Erstad (Big Play Makers)	.10
5	Troy Glaus	.45
6	Tim Salmon	.05
7	Mo Vaughn	.05
8	Darin Erstad	.25
9	Garret Anderson	.05
10	Todd Greene	.05
11	Troy Percival	.05
12	Chuck Finley	.05
13	Jason Dickson	.05
14	Jim Edmonds	.05
15	Arizona Diamondbacks (Team Checklist)	.05
16	Randy Johnson	.50
17	Matt Williams	.05
18	Travis Lee	.15
19	Jay Bell	.05
20	Tony Womack	.05
21	Steve Finley	.05
22	Bernard Gilkey	.05
23	Tony Batista	.05
24	Todd Stottlemyre	.05
25	Omar Daal	.05
26	Atlanta Braves (Team Checklist)	.05
27	Bruce Chen (99 Rookie)	.05
28	George Lombard (99 Rookie)	.05
29	Chipper Jones (Power Trip)	.35
30	Chipper Jones (Big Play Makers)	.35
31	Greg Maddux	.65
32	Chipper Jones	.65
33	Javy Lopez	.05
34	Tom Glavine	.25
35	John Smoltz	.05
36	Andruw Jones	.50
37	Brian Jordan	.05
38	Walt Weiss	.05
39	Bret Boone	.05
40	Andres Galarraga	.05
41	Baltimore Orioles (Team Checklist)	.05
42	Ryan Minor (99 Rookie)	.05
43	Jerry Hairston Jr. (99 Rookie)	.05
44	Calvin Pickering (99 Rookie)	.05
45	Cal Ripken Jr. (History in the Making)	.75
46	Cal Ripken Jr.	1.50
47	Charles Johnson	.05
48	Albert Belle	.05
49	Delino DeShields	.05
50	Mike Mussina	.30
51	Scott Erickson	.05
52	Brady Anderson	.05
53	B.J. Surhoff	.05
54	Harold Baines	.05
55	Will Clark	.05
56	Boston Red Sox (Team Checklist)	.05
57	Shea Hillenbrand **RC** (99 Rookie)	.50
58	Trot Nixon (99 Rookie)	.10
59	Jin Ho Cho (99 Rookie)	.05
60	Nomar Garciaparra (Power Trip)	.35
61	Nomar Garciaparra (Big Play Makers)	.35
62	Pedro Martinez	.50
63	Nomar Garciaparra	.65
64	Jose Offerman	.05
65	Jason Varitek	.05
66	Darren Lewis	.05
67	Troy O'Leary	.05
68	Donnie Sadler	.05
69	John Valentin	.05
70	Tim Wakefield	.05
71	Bret Saberhagen	.05
72	Chicago Cubs (Team Checklist)	.05
73	Kyle Farnsworth **RC** (99 Rookie)	.10
74	Sammy Sosa (Power Trip)	.35
75	Sammy Sosa (Big Play Makers)	.35
76	Sammy Sosa (History in the Making)	.35
77	Kerry Wood (History in the Making)	.10
78	Sammy Sosa	.65
79	Mark Grace	.05
80	Kerry Wood	.25
81	Kevin Tapani	.05
82	Benito Santiago	.05
83	Gary Gaetti	.05
84	Mickey Morandini	.05
85	Glenallen Hill	.05
86	Henry Rodriguez	.05
87	Rod Beck	.05
88	Chicago White Sox (Team Checklist)	.05
89	Carlos Lee (99 Rookie)	.10
90	Mark Johnson (99 Rookie)	.05
91	Frank Thomas (Power Trip)	.30
92	Frank Thomas	.50
93	Jim Parque	.05
94	Mike Sirotka	.05
95	Mike Caruso	.05
96	Ray Durham	.05
97	Magglio Ordonez	.25
98	Paul Konerko	.15
99	Bob Howry	.05
100	Brian Simmons	.05
101	Jaime Navarro	.05
102	Cincinnati Reds (Team Checklist)	.05
103	Denny Neagle	.05
104	Pete Harnisch	.05
105	Greg Vaughn	.05
106	Brett Tomko	.05
107	Mike Cameron	.05
108	Sean Casey	.10
109	Aaron Boone	.05
110	Michael Tucker	.05
111	Dmitri Young	.05
112	Barry Larkin	.05
113	Cleveland Indians (Team Checklist)	.05
114	Russ Branyan (99 Rookie)	.05
115	Jim Thome (Power Trip)	.20
116	Manny Ramirez (Power Trip)	.25
117	Manny Ramirez	.50
118	Jim Thome	.40
119	David Justice	.05
120	Sandy Alomar	.05
121	Roberto Alomar	.20
122	Jaret Wright	.05
123	Bartolo Colon	.05
124	Travis Fryman	.05
125	Kenny Lofton	.05
126	Omar Vizquel	.05
127	Colorado Rockies (Team Checklist)	.05
128	Derrick Gibson (99 Rookie)	.05
129	Larry Walker (Big Play Makers)	.05
130	Larry Walker	.05
131	Dante Bichette	.05
132	Todd Helton	.45
133	Neifi Perez	.05
134	Vinny Castilla	.05
135	Darryl Kile	.05
136	Pedro Astacio	.05
137	Darryl Hamilton	.05
138	Mike Lansing	.05
139	Kirt Manwaring	.05
140	Detroit Tigers (Team Checklist)	.05
141	Jeff Weaver **RC** (99 Rookie)	.50
142	Gabe Kapler (99 Rookie)	.05
143	Tony Clark (Power Trip)	.05
144	Tony Clark	.05
145	Juan Encarnacion	.05
146	Dean Palmer	.05
147	Damion Easley	.05
148	Bobby Higginson	.05
149	Karim Garcia	.05
150	Justin Thompson	.05
151	Matt Anderson	.05
152	Willie Blair	.05
153	Brian Hunter	.05
154	Florida Marlins (Team Checklist)	.05
155	Alex Gonzalez (99 Rookie)	.05
156	Mark Kotsay	.05
157	Livan Hernandez	.05
158	Cliff Floyd	.05
159	Todd Dunwoody	.05
160	Alex Fernandez	.05
161	Mark Mantei	.05
162	Derrek Lee	.40
163	Kevin Orie	.05
164	Craig Counsell	.05
165	Rafael Medina	.05
166	Houston Astros (Team Checklist)	.05
167	Daryle Ward (99 Rookie)	.05
168	Mitch Meluskey (99 Rookie)	.05
169	Jeff Bagwell (Power Trip)	.25
170	Jeff Bagwell	.50
171	Ken Caminiti	.05
172	Craig Biggio	.05
173	Derek Bell	.05
174	Moises Alou	.05
175	Billy Wagner	.05
176	Shane Reynolds	.05
177	Carl Everett	.05
178	Scott Elarton	.05
179	Richard Hidalgo	.05
180	Kansas City Royals (Team Checklist)	.05
181	Carlos Beltran (99 Rookie)	.60
182	Carlos Febles (99 Rookie)	.05
183	Jeremy Giambi (99 Rookie)	.05
184	Johnny Damon	.30
185	Joe Randa	.05
186	Jeff King	.05
187	Hipolito Pichardo	.05
188	Kevin Appier	.05
189	Chad Kreuter	.05
190	Rey Sanchez	.05
191	Larry Sutton	.05
192	Jeff Montgomery	.05
193	Jermaine Dye	.05
194	Los Angeles Dodgers (Team Checklist)	.05
195	Adam Riggs (99 Rookie)	.05
196	Angel Pena (99 Rookie)	.05
197	Todd Hundley	.05
198	Kevin Brown	.05
199	Ismael Valdes	.05
200	Chan Ho Park	.05
201	Adrian Beltre	.15
202	Mark Grudzielanek	.05
203	Raul Mondesi	.05
204	Gary Sheffield	.35
205	Eric Karros	.05
206	Devon White	.05
207	Milwaukee Brewers (Team Checklist)	.05
208	Ron Belliard (99 Rookie)	.05
209	Rafael Roque (99 Rookie)	.05
210	Jeromy Burnitz	.05
211	Fernando Vina	.05
212	Scott Karl	.05
213	Jim Abbott	.05
214	Sean Berry	.05
215	Marquis Grissom	.05
216	Geoff Jenkins	.05
217	Jeff Cirillo	.05
218	Dave Nilsson	.05
219	Jose Valentin	.05
220	Minnesota Twins (Team Checklist)	.05
221	Corey Koskie (99 Rookie)	.05
222	Christian Guzman (99 Rookie)	.05
223	A.J. Pierzynski (99 Rookie)	.05
224	David Ortiz	.05
225	Brad Radke	.05
226	Todd Walker	.05
227	Matt Lawton	.05
228	Rick Aguilera	.05
229	Eric Milton	.05

230 Marty Cordova .05
231 Torii Hunter .05
232 Ron Coomer .05
233 LaTroy Hawkins .05
234 Montreal Expos (Team Checklist) .05
235 Fernando Seguignol (99 Rookie) .05
236 Michael Barrett (99 Rookie) .05
237 Vladimir Guerrero (Big Play Makers) .25
238 Vladimir Guerrero .50
239 Brad Fullmer .05
240 Rondell White .05
241 Ugueth Urbina .05
242 Dustin Hermanson .05
243 Orlando Cabrera .05
244 Wilton Guerrero .05
245 Carl Pavano .05
246 Javier Vasquez .05
247 Chris Widger .05
248 New York Mets (Team Checklist) .05
249 Mike Kinkade (99 Rookie) .05
250 Octavio Dotel (99 Rookie) .05
251 Mike Piazza (Power Trip) .40
252 Mike Piazza .75
253 Rickey Henderson .50
254 Edgardo Alfonzo .05
255 Robin Ventura .05
256 Al Leiter .05
257 Brian McRae .05
258 Rey Ordonez .05
259 Bobby Bonilla .05
260 Orel Hershiser .05
261 John Olerud .05
262 New York Yankees (Team Checklist) .05
263 Ricky Ledee (99 Rookie) .05
264 Bernie Williams (Big Play Makers) .05
265 Derek Jeter (Big Play Makers) .75
266 Scott Brosius (History in the Making) .05
267 Derek Jeter 1.50
268 Roger Clemens .65
269 Orlando Hernandez .05
270 Scott Brosius .05
271 Paul O'Neill .05
272 Bernie Williams .05
273 Chuck Knoblauch .05
274 Tino Martinez .05
275 Mariano Rivera .10
276 Jorge Posada .05
277 Oakland Athletics (Team Checklist) .05
278 Eric Chavez (99 Rookie) .15
279 Ben Grieve (History in the Making) .05
280 Jason Giambi .30
281 John Jaha .05
282 Miguel Tejada .15
283 Ben Grieve .05
284 Matt Stairs .05
285 Ryan Christenson .05
286 A.J. Hinch .05
287 Kenny Rogers .05
288 Tom Candiotti .05
289 Scott Spezio .05
290 Philadelphia Phillies (Team Checklist) .05
291 Pat Burrell **RC** (99 Rookie) 1.50
292 Marlon Anderson (99 Rookie) .05
293 Scott Rolen (Big Play Makers) .20
294 Scott Rolen .40
295 Doug Glanville .05
296 Rico Brogna .05
297 Ron Gant .05
298 Bobby Abreu .05
299 Desi Relaford .05
300 Curt Schilling .25
301 Chad Ogea .05
302 Kevin Jordan .05
303 Carlton Loewer .05
304 Pittsburgh Pirates (Team Checklist) .05
305 Kris Benson (99 Rookie) .05
306 Brian Giles .05
307 Jason Kendall .05
308 Jose Guillen .05
309 Pat Meares .05
310 Brant Brown .05
311 Kevin Young .05
312 Ed Sprague .05
313 Francisco Cordova .05
314 Aramis Ramirez .05
315 Freddy Garcia .05
316 Saint Louis Cardinals (Team Checklist) .05
317 J.D. Drew (99 Rookie) .40
318 Chad Hutchinson **RC** (99 Rookie) .05
319 Mark McGwire (Power Trip) .50
320 J.D. Drew (Power Trip) .20
321 Mark McGwire (Big Play Makers) .50
322 Mark McGwire (History in the Making) .50
323 Mark McGwire 1.00
324 Fernando Tatis .05
325 Edgar Renteria .05
326 Ray Lankford .05
327 Willie McGee .05
328 Ricky Bottalico .05
329 Eli Marrero .05
330 Matt Morris .05
331 Eric Davis .05
332 Darren Bragg .05
333 Padres (Team Checklist) .05
334 Matt Clement (99 Rookie) .05
335 Ben Davis (99 Rookie) .05
336 Gary Matthews Jr. (99 Rookie) .05
337 Tony Gwynn (Big Play Makers) .35
338 Tony Gwynn (History in the Making) .35
339 Tony Gwynn .65
340 Reggie Sanders .05
341 Ruben Rivera .05
342 Wally Joyner .05
343 Sterling Hitchcock .05
344 Carlos Hernandez .05
345 Andy Ashby .05
346 Trevor Hoffman .05
347 Chris Gomez .05
348 Jim Leyritz .05
349 San Francisco Giants (Team Checklist) .05
350 Armando Rios (99 Rookie) .05
351 Barry Bonds (Power Trip) .75
352 Barry Bonds (Big Play Makers) .75
353 Barry Bonds (History in the Making) .75
354 Robb Nen .05
355 Bill Mueller .05
356 Barry Bonds 1.50
357 Jeff Kent .05
358 J.T. Snow .05
359 Ellis Burks .05
360 F.P. Santangelo .05
361 Marvin Benard .05
362 Stan Javier .05
363 Shawn Estes .05
364 Seattle Mariners (Team Checklist) .05
365 Carlos Guillen (99 Rookie) .05
366 Ken Griffey Jr. (Power Trip) .40
367 Alex Rodriguez (Power Trip) .50
368 Ken Griffey Jr. (Big Play Makers) .40
369 Alex Rodriguez (Big Play Makers) .50
370 Ken Griffey Jr. (History in the Making) .40
371 Alex Rodriguez (History in the Making) .50
372 Ken Griffey Jr. .75
373 Alex Rodriguez 1.00
374 Jay Buhner .05
375 Edgar Martinez .05
376 Jeff Fassero .05
377 David Bell .05
378 David Segui .05
379 Russ Davis .05
380 Dan Wilson .05
381 Jamie Moyer .05
382 Tampa Bay Devil Rays (Team Checklist) .05
383 Roberto Hernandez .05
384 Bobby Smith .05
385 Wade Boggs .65
386 Fred McGriff .05
387 Rolando Arrojo .05
388 Jose Canseco .35
389 Wilson Alvarez .05
390 Kevin Stocker .05
391 Miguel Cairo .05
392 Quinton McCracken .05
393 Texas Rangers (Team Checklist) .05
394 Ruben Mateo (99 Rookie) .05
395 Cesar King (99 Rookie) .05
396 Juan Gonzalez (Power Trip) .15
397 Juan Gonzalez (Big Play Makers) .15
398 Ivan Rodriguez .40
399 Juan Gonzalez .25
400 Rafael Palmeiro .40
401 Rick Helling .05
402 Aaron Sele .05
403 John Wetteland .05
404 Rusty Greer .05
405 Todd Zeile .05
406 Royce Clayton .05
407 Tom Goodwin .05
408 Toronto Blue Jays (Team Checklist) .05
409 Kevin Witt (99 Rookie) .05
410 Roy Halladay (99 Rookie) .05
411 Jose Cruz Jr. .05
412 Carlos Delgado .30
413 Willie Greene .05
414 Shawn Green .25
415 Homer Bush .05
416 Shannon Stewart .05
417 David Wells .05
418 Kelvim Escobar .05
419 Joey Hamilton .05
420 Alex Gonzalez .05
421 Mark McGwire (McGwire Magic) .20
422 Mark McGwire (McGwire Magic) .20
423 Mark McGwire (McGwire Magic) .20
424 Mark McGwire (McGwire Magic) .20
425 Mark McGwire (McGwire Magic) .20
426 Mark McGwire (McGwire Magic) .20
427 Mark McGwire (McGwire Magic) .20
428 Mark McGwire (McGwire Magic) .20
429 Mark McGwire (McGwire Magic) .20
430 Mark McGwire (McGwire Magic) .20
431 Mark McGwire (McGwire Magic) .20
432 Mark McGwire (McGwire Magic) .20
433 Mark McGwire (McGwire Magic) .20
434 Mark McGwire (McGwire Magic) .20
435 Mark McGwire (McGwire Magic) .20
436 Mark McGwire (McGwire Magic) .20
437 Mark McGwire (McGwire Magic) .20
438 Mark McGwire (McGwire Magic) .20
439 Mark McGwire (McGwire Magic) .20
440 Mark McGwire (McGwire Magic) .20
441 Mark McGwire (McGwire Magic) .20
442 Mark McGwire (McGwire Magic) .20
443 Mark McGwire (McGwire Magic) .20
444 Mark McGwire (McGwire Magic) .20
445 Mark McGwire (McGwire Magic) .20
446 Mark McGwire (McGwire Magic) .20
447 Mark McGwire (McGwire Magic) .20
448 Mark McGwire (McGwire Magic) .20
449 Mark McGwire (McGwire Magic) .20
450 Mark McGwire (McGwire Magic) .20
451 Chipper Jones '93 (Rookie Flashback) .35
452 Cal Ripken Jr. '81 (Rookie Flashback) .75
453 Roger Clemens '84 (Rookie Flashback) .40
454 Wade Boggs '82 (Rookie Flashback) .35
455 Greg Maddux '86 (Rookie Flashback) .35
456 Frank Thomas '90 (Rookie Flashback) .30
457 Jeff Bagwell '91 (Rookie Flashback) .25
458 Mike Piazza '92 (Rookie Flashback) .45
459 Randy Johnson '88 (Rookie Flashback) .25
460 Mo Vaughn '91 (Rookie Flashback) .05
461 Mark McGwire '86 (Rookie Flashback) .50
462 Rickey Henderson '79 (Rookie Flashback) .25
463 Barry Bonds '86 (Rookie Flashback) .75
464 Tony Gwynn '82 (Rookie Flashback) .35
465 Ken Griffey Jr. '89 (Rookie Flashback) .45
466 Alex Rodriguez '94 (Rookie Flashback) .50
467 Sammy Sosa '89 (Rookie Flashback) .35
468 Juan Gonzalez '89 (Rookie Flashback) .15
469 Kevin Brown '86 (Rookie Flashback) .05
470 Fred McGriff '86 .05

2000 Upper Deck

Released in two 270-card series the base cards feature full- bleed fronts with gold foil etching and stamping. Card backs have complete year-by-year statistics.

NM/M

Complete Set (540): 40.00

Complete Series I (270): 20.00
Complete Series II (270): 20.00
Common Player: .15
Silver Stars: 5-10X
Rookies: 2-4X
Hobby Pack (10): 3.00
Hobby Box (24): 55.00

1 Rick Ankiel/SR .20
2 Vernon Wells/SR .50
3 Ryan Andersonv .15
4 Ed Yarnall/SR .15
5 Brian McNichol/SR .15
6 Ben Petrick/SR .15
7 Kip Wells/SR .15
8 Eric Munson/SR .20
9 Matt Riley/SR .15
10 Peter Bergeron/SR .15
11 Eric Gagne/SR .25
12 Ramon Ortiz/SR .25
13 Josh Beckett/SR .50
14 Alfonso Soriano/SR 1.50
15 Jorge Toca/SR .15
16 Buddy Carlyle/SR .15
17 Chad Hermansen/SR .15
18 Matt Perisho/SR .15
19 Tomokazu Ohka/SR **RC** .75
20 Jacque Jones/SR .15
21 Josh Paul/SR .15
22 Dermal Brown/SR .15
23 Adam Kennedy/SR .15
24 Chad Harville/SR .15
25 Calvin Murray/SR .15
26 Chad Meyers/SR .15
27 Brian Cooper/SR .15
28 Troy Glaus .50
29 Ben Molina .15
30 Troy Percival .15
31 Ken Hill .15
32 Chuck Finley .15
33 Todd Greene .15
34 Tim Salmon .25
35 Gary DiSarcina .15
36 Luis Gonzalez .25
37 Tony Womack .15
38 Omar Daal .15
39 Randy Johnson .50
40 Erubiel Durazo .20
41 Jay Bell .15
42 Steve Finley .15
43 Travis Lee .15
44 Greg Maddux 1.00
45 Bret Boone .25
46 Brian Jordan .15
47 Kevin Millwood .25
48 Odalis Perez .25
49 Javy Lopez .25
50 John Smoltz .25
51 Bruce Chen .15
52 Albert Belle .15
53 Jerry Hairston Jr. .15
54 Will Clark .40
55 Sidney Ponson .15
56 Charles Johnson .15
57 Cal Ripken Jr. 2.00
58 Ryan Minor .15
59 Mike Mussina .40
60 Tom Gordon .15
61 Jose Offerman .15
62 Trot Nixon .15
63 Pedro Martinez .75
64 John Valentin .15
65 Jason Varitek .15
66 Juan Pena .15
67 Troy O'Leary .15
68 Sammy Sosa 1.25
69 Henry Rodriguez .15
70 Kyle Farnsworth .15
71 Glenallen Hill .15
72 Lance Johnson .15
73 Mickey Morandini .15
74 Jon Lieber .15
75 Kevin Tapani .15
76 Carlos Lee .15
77 Ray Durham .15
78 Jim Parque .15
79 Bob Howry .15
80 Magglio Ordonez .25
81 Paul Konerko .20
82 Mike Caruso .15
83 Chris Singleton .15
84 Sean Casey .20
85 Barry Larkin .25
86 Pokey Reese .15
87 Eddie Taubensee .15
88 Scott Williamson .15
89 Jason LaRue .15
90 Aaron Boone .20
91 Jeffrey Hammonds .15
92 Omar Vizquel .20
93 Manny Ramirez .50
94 Kenny Lofton .20
95 Jaret Wright .15
96 Einar Diaz .15
97 Charles Nagy .15
98 David Justice .25
99 Richie Sexson .25
100 Steve Karsay .15
101 Todd Helton .50
102 Dante Bichette .15
103 Larry Walker .25
104 Pedro Astacio .15
105 Neifi Perez .15
106 Brian Bohanon .15
107 Edgard Clemente .15
108 Dave Veres .15
109 Gabe Kapler .15
110 Juan Encarnacion .15
111 Jeff Weaver .15
112 Damion Easley .15
113 Justin Thompson .15
114 Brad Ausmus .15
115 Frank Catalanotto .15
116 Todd Jones .15
117 Preston Wilson .25
118 Cliff Floyd .15
119 Mike Lowell .15
120 Jorge Fabregas .15
121 Alex Gonzalez .15
122 Braden Looper .15
123 Bruce Aven .15
124 Richard Hidalgo .15
125 Mitch Meluskey .15
126 Jeff Bagwell .50
127 Jose Lima .15
128 Derek Bell .15
129 Billy Wagner .15
130 Shane Reynolds .15
131 Moises Alou .25
132 Carlos Beltran .25
133 Carlos Febles .15
134 Jermaine Dye .15
135 Jeremy Giambi .15
136 Joe Randa .15
137 Jose Rosado .15
138 Chad Kreuter .15
139 Jose Vizcaino .15
140 Adrian Beltre .25
141 Kevin Brown .25
142 Ismael Valdes .15
143 Angel Pena .15
144 Chan Ho Park .15
145 Mark Grudzielanek .15
146 Jeff Shaw .15
147 Geoff Jenkins .20
148 Jeromy Burnitz .15
149 Hideo Nomo .25
150 Ron Belliard .15
151 Sean Berry .15
152 Mark Loretta .15
153 Steve Woodard .15
154 Joe Mays .15
155 Eric Milton .15
156 Corey Koskie .15
157 Ron Coomer .15
158 Brad Radke .15
159 Terry Steinbach .15
160 Christian Guzman .15
161 Vladimir Guerrero .50
162 Wilton Guerrero .15
163 Michael Barrett .15
164 Chris Widger .15
165 Fernando Seguignol .15
166 Ugueth Urbina .15
167 Dustin Hermanson .15
168 Kenny Rogers .15
169 Edgardo Alfonzo .15
170 Orel Hershiser .15
171 Robin Ventura .20
172 Octavio Dotel .15
173 Rickey Henderson .25
174 Roger Cedeno .15
175 John Olerud .25
176 Derek Jeter 2.00
177 Tino Martinez .25
178 Orlando Hernandez .20
179 Chuck Knoblauch .15
180 Bernie Williams .40
181 Chili Davis .15
182 David Cone .20
183 Ricky Ledee .15
184 Paul O'Neill .25
185 Jason Giambi .50
186 Eric Chavez .25
187 Matt Stairs .15
188 Miguel Tejada .25
189 Olmedo Saenz .15
190 Tim Hudson .40
191 John Jaha .15
192 Randy Velarde .15
193 Rico Brogna .15
194 Mike Lieberthal .20
195 Marlon Anderson .15
196 Bobby Abreu .25
197 Ron Gant .15
198 Randy Wolf .15
199 Desi Relaford .15
200 Doug Glanville .15
201 Warren Morris .15
202 Kris Benson .15
203 Kevin Young .15
204 Brian Giles .25
205 Jason Schmidt .15
206 Ed Sprague .15
207 Francisco Cordova .15
208 Mark McGwire 2.00
209 Jose Jimenez .15
210 Fernando Tatis .15
211 Kent Bottenfield .15
212 Eli Marrero .15
213 Edgar Renteria .15
214 Joe McEwing .15
215 J.D. Drew .20
216 Tony Gwynn .75
217 Gary Matthews Jr. .15
218 Eric Owens .15
219 Damian Jackson .15
220 Reggie Sanders .15
221 Trevor Hoffman .15
222 Ben Davis .15
223 Shawn Estes .15
224 F.P. Santangelo .15
225 Livan Hernandez .15
226 Ellis Burks .15
227 J.T. Snow .15
228 Jeff Kent .25
229 Robb Nen .15
230 Marvin Benard .15
231 Ken Griffey Jr. 1.00
232 John Halama .15
233 Gil Meche .15
234 David Bell .15
235 Brian L. Hunter .15
236 Jay Buhner .25
237 Edgar Martinez .25
238 Jose Mesa .15
239 Wilson Alvarez .15
240 Wade Boggs .40
241 Fred McGriff .25
242 Jose Canseco .40
243 Kevin Stocker .15
244 Roberto Hernandez .15
245 Bubba Trammell .15
246 John Flaherty .15
247 Ivan Rodriguez .40
248 Rusty Greer .15
249 Rafael Palmeiro .40
250 Jeff Zimmerman .15
251 Royce Clayton .15
252 Todd Zeile .15
253 John Wetteland .15
254 Ruben Mateo .15
255 Kelvim Escobar .15
256 David Wells .15
257 Shawn Green .40
258 Homer Bush .15
259 Shannon Stewart .15
260 Carlos Delgado .50
261 Roy Halladay .25
262 Fernando Tatis CL .15
263 Jose Jimenez CL .15
264 Tony Gwynn CL .40
265 Wade Boggs CL .25
266 Cal Ripken Jr. CL 1.00
267 David Cone CL .15
268 Mark McGwire CL .75
269 Pedro Martinez CL .40
270 Nomar Garciaparra CL .75
271 Nick Johnson/SR .40
272 Mark Quinn/SR .15
273 Roosevelt Brown/SR .15
274 Adam Everett/SR .15
275 Jason Marquis/SR .15
276 Kazuhiro Sasaki/SR **RC** 1.50
277 Aaron Myette/SR .15
278 Danys Baez/SR **RC** .50
279 Travis Dawkins/SR .15
280 Mark Mulder/SR .25
281 Chris Haas/SR .15
282 Milton Bradley/SR .15
283 Brad Penny/SR .15
284 Rafael Furcal/SR .25
285 Luis Matos/SR **RC** 1.00
286 Victor Santos/SR .15
287 Rico Washington/SR **RC** .15
288 Rob Bell/SR .15
289 Joe Crede/SR .15
290 Pablo Ozuna/SR .15
291 Wascar Serrano/SR **RC** .15
292 Sang-Hoon Lee/SR **RC** .25
293 Chris Wakeland/SR .15
294 Luis Rivera/SR .15
295 Mike Lamb/SR **RC** .20
296 Wily Pena/SR .20
297 Mike Meyers/SR **RC** .15
298 Mo Vaughn .20
299 Darin Erstad .25
300 Garret Anderson .25
301 Tim Belcher .15
302 Scott Spiezio .15
303 Kent Bottenfield .15
304 Orlando Palmeiro .15
305 Jason Dickson .15
306 Matt Williams .20
307 Brian Anderson .15
308 Hanley Frias .15
309 Todd Stottlemyre .15
310 Matt Mantei .15
311 David Dellucci .15
312 Armando Reynoso .15
313 Bernard Gilkey .15
314 Chipper Jones 1.00
315 Tom Glavine .25
316 Quilvio Veras .15
317 Andruw Jones .50
318 Bobby Bonilla .15
319 Reggie Sanders .15
320 Andres Galarraga .20
321 George Lombard .15
322 John Rocker .15
322 Wally Joyner .15
324 B.J. Surhoff .15
325 Scott Erickson .15

No.	Player	Price
326	Delino DeShields	.15
327	Jeff Conine	.15
328	Mike Timlin	.15
329	Brady Anderson	.15
330	Mike Bordick	.15
331	Harold Baines	.15
332	Nomar Garciaparra	1.50
333	Bret Saberhagen	.15
334	Ramon Martinez	.15
335	Donnie Sadler	.15
336	Wilton Veras	.15
337	Mike Stanley	.15
338	Brian Rose	.15
339	Carl Everett	.15
340	Tim Wakefield	.15
341	Mark Grace	.25
342	Kerry Wood	.30
343	Eric Young	.15
344	Jose Nieves	.15
345	Ismael Valdes	.15
346	Joe Girardi	.15
347	Damon Buford	.15
348	Ricky Gutierrez	.15
349	Frank Thomas	.50
350	Brian Simmons	.15
351	James Baldwin	.15
352	Brook Fordyce	.15
353	Jose Valentin	.15
354	Mike Sirotka	.15
355	Greg Norton	.15
356	Dante Bichette	.15
357	Deion Sanders	.25
358	Ken Griffey Jr.	1.00
359	Denny Neagle	.15
360	Dmitri Young	.15
361	Pete Harnisch	.15
362	Michael Tucker	.15
363	Roberto Alomar	.40
364	Dave Roberts	.15
365	Jim Thome	.50
366	Bartolo Colon	.15
367	Travis Fryman	.20
368	Chuck Finley	.15
369	Russell Branyan	.15
370	Alex Ramirez	.15
371	Jeff Cirillo	.15
372	Jeffrey Hammonds	.15
373	Scott Karl	.15
374	Brent Mayne	.15
375	Tom Goodwin	.15
376	Jose Jimenez	.15
377	Rolando Arrojo	.15
378	Terry Shumpert	.15
379	Juan Gonzalez	.50
380	Bobby Higginson	.15
381	Tony Clark	.15
382	Dave Mlicki	.15
383	Deivi Cruz	.15
384	Brian Moehler	.15
385	Dean Palmer	.15
386	Luis Castillo	.15
387	Mike Redmond	.15
388	Alex Fernandez	.15
389	Brant Brown	.15
390	Dave Berg	.15
391	A.J. Burnett	.15
392	Mark Kotsay	.15
393	Craig Biggio	.20
394	Daryle Ward	.15
395	Lance Berkman	.25
396	Roger Cedeno	.15
397	Scott Elarton	.15
398	Octavio Dotel	.15
399	Ken Caminiti	.15
400	Johnny Damon	.25
401	Mike Sweeney	.15
402	Jeff Suppan	.15
403	Rey Sanchez	.15
404	Blake Stein	.15
405	Ricky Bottalico	.15
406	Jay Witasick	.15
407	Shawn Green	.40
408	Orel Hershiser	.15
409	Gary Sheffield	.40
410	Todd Hollandsworth	.15
411	Terry Adams	.15
412	Todd Hundley	.15
413	Eric Karros	.15
414	F.P. Santangelo	.15
415	Alex Cora	.15
416	Marquis Grissom	.15
417	Henry Blanco	.15
418	Jose Hernandez	.15
419	Kyle Peterson	.15
420	John Snyder **RC**	.15
421	Bob Wickman	.15
422	Jamey Wright	.15
423	Chad Allen	.15
424	Todd Walker	.15
425	J.C. Romero **RC**	.15
426	Butch Huskey	.15
427	Jacque Jones	.15
428	Matt Lawton	.15
429	Rondell White	.25
430	Jose Vidro	.15
431	Hideki Irabu	.15
432	Javier Vazquez	.15
433	Lee Stevens	.15
434	Mike Thurman	.15
435	Geoff Blum	.15
436	Mike Hampton	.15
437	Mike Piazza	1.00
438	Al Leiter	.15
439	Derek Bell	.15
440	Armando Benitez	.15
441	Rey Ordonez	.15
442	Todd Zeile	.15
443	Roger Clemens	1.25
444	Ramiro Mendoza	.15
445	Andy Pettitte	.25
446	Scott Brosius	.15
447	Mariano Rivera	.25
448	Jim Leyritz	.15
449	Jorge Posada	.25
450	Omar Olivares	.15
451	Ben Grieve	.15
452	A.J. Hinch	.15
453	Gil Heredia	.15
454	Kevin Appier	.15
455	Ryan Christenson	.15
456	Ramon Hernandez	.15
457	Scott Rolen	.50
458	Alex Arias	.15
459	Andy Ashby	.15
460		.15
461	Robert Person	.15
462	Paul Byrd	.15
463	Curt Schilling	.25
464	Mike Jackson	.15
465	Jason Kendall	.25
466	Pat Meares	.15
467	Bruce Aven	.15
468	Todd Ritchie	.15
469	Wil Cordero	.15
470	Aramis Ramirez	.15
471	Andy Benes	.15
472	Ray Lankford	.15
473	Fernando Vina	.15
474a	Jim Edmonds	.25
474b	Kevin Jordan (Should be #460.)	.15
475	Craig Paquette	.15
476	Pat Hentgen	.15
477	Darryl Kile	.15
478	Sterling Hitchcock	.15
479	Ruben Rivera	.15
480	Ryan Klesko	.15
481	Phil Nevin	.15
482	Woody Williams	.15
483	Carlos Hernandez	.15
484	Brian Meadows	.15
485	Bret Boone	.25
486	Barry Bonds	1.50
487	Russ Ortiz	.15
488	Bobby Estalella	.15
489	Rich Aurilia	.15
490	Bill Mueller	.15
491	Joe Nathan	.15
492	Russ Davis	.15
493	John Olerud	.25
494	Alex Rodriguez	1.50
495	Fred Garcia	.15
496	Carlos Guillen	.15
497	Aaron Sele	.15
498	Brett Tomko	.15
499	Jamie Moyer	.15
500	Mike Cameron	.15
501	Vinny Castilla	.15
502	Gerald Williams	.15
503	Mike DiFelice	.15
504	Ryan Rupe	.15
505	Greg Vaughn	.15
506	Miguel Cairo	.15
507	Juan Guzman **RC**	.15
508	Jose Guillen	.15
509	Gabe Kapler	.15
510	Rick Helling	.15
511	David Segui	.15
512	Doug Davis	.15
513	Justin Thompson	.15
514	Chad Curtis	.15
515	Tony Batista	.15
516	Billy Koch	.15
517	Raul Mondesi	.20
518	Joey Hamilton	.15
519	Darrin Fletcher	.15
520	Brad Fullmer	.15
521	Jose Cruz Jr.	.15
522	Kevin Witt	.15
523	Mark McGwire (All-UD Team)	1.00
524	Roberto Alomar (All-UD Team)	.25
525	Chipper Jones (All-UD Team)	.50
526	Derek Jeter (All-UD Team)	1.00
527	Ken Griffey Jr. (All-UD Team)	.50
528	Sammy Sosa (All-UD Team)	.75
529	Manny Ramirez (All-UD Team)	.40
530	Ivan Rodriguez (All-UD Team)	.25
531	Pedro J. Martinez (All-UD Team)	.40
532	Mariano Rivera (Season Highlights Checklist)	.15
533	Sammy Sosa (Season Highlights Checklist)	.75
534	Cal Ripken Jr. (Season Highlights Checklist)	1.00
535	Vladimir Guerrero (Season Highlights Checklist)	.40
536	Tony Gwynn (Season Highlights Checklist)	.25
537	Mark McGwire (Season Highlights Checklist)	1.00
538	Bernie Williams (Season Highlights Checklist)	.25
539	Pedro J. Martinez (Season Highlights Checklist)	.40
540	Ken Griffey Jr. (Season Highlights Checklist)	.50

Exclusives

Labeled "UD Exclusives," these parallel sets were issued in two versions, silvers numbered to 100 each, and golds which were 1-of-1. Except for the appropriately colored foil highlights on front and dot-matrix serial number, the Exclusives are identical to the regular-issue cards. They were inserted exclusively into hobby packs. Because of their rarity and variable demand, the unique gold cards are not priced.

	NM/M
Common Silver Exclusive:	1.00
Silver Stars/Rookies:	8X

Cooperstown Calling

This insert set features players deemed by Upper Deck as future Hall of Famers. Card fronts feature silver holo-foil with gold foil stamping. Card backs are numbered with a "CC" prefix and are seeded 1:23 packs.

		NM/M
Complete Set (15):		25.00
Common Player:		.75
Inserted 1:23		
1	Roger Clemens	3.00
2	Cal Ripken Jr.	5.00
3	Ken Griffey Jr.	3.00
4	Mike Piazza	3.00
5	Tony Gwynn	2.00
6	Sammy Sosa	2.50
7	Jose Canseco	1.00
8	Larry Walker	.75
9	Barry Bonds	4.00
10	Greg Maddux	2.50
11	Derek Jeter	5.00
12	Mark McGwire	4.00
13	Randy Johnson	2.00
14	Frank Thomas	1.50
15	Jeff Bagwell	1.50

e-Card

Randomly inserted in series 2 packs, each e-card has an ID number stamped on the card front that can be entered on Upper Deck's website. Collectors then find out if that card "evolves" into a signature card, jersey card or a signed jersey card. They are seeded 1:9 packs and are numbered with an "E" prefix on the card back.

		NM/M
Complete Set (6):		10.00
Common Player:		1.00
Inserted 1:12		
1	Ken Griffey Jr.	2.00
2	Alex Rodriguez	3.00
3	Cal Ripken Jr.	3.00
4	Jeff Bagwell	1.00
5	Barry Bonds	3.00
6	Manny Ramirez	1.00

eVolve Jersey

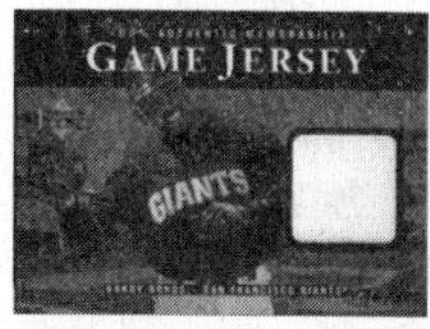

		NM/M
Common Player:		15.00
Production 300 Sets		
1	Ken Griffey Jr.	30.00
2	Alex Rodriguez	40.00
3	Cal Ripken Jr.	50.00
4	Jeff Bagwell	15.00
5	Barry Bonds	40.00
6	Manny Ramirez	20.00

eVolve Signed Jersey

		NM/M
Common Player:		80.00
Production 50 Sets		
1	Ken Griffey Jr.	150.00
2	Alex Rodriguez	150.00
3	Cal Ripken Jr.	200.00
4	Jeff Bagwell	60.00
5	Barry Bonds	150.00
6	Manny Ramirez	60.00

eVolve Signature

		NM/M
Common Player:		40.00
Production 200 Sets		
1	Ken Griffey Jr.	85.00
2	Alex Rodriguez	85.00
3	Cal Ripken Jr.	150.00
4	Jeff Bagwell	40.00
5	Barry Bonds	120.00
6	Manny Ramirez	40.00

Faces of the Game

Randomly inserted in Series 1 at a rate of 1:11 packs, card fronts feature a close-up photo of the featured player with bronze foil etching and stamping. Backs are numbered with an "F" prefix. Two parallel versions are available, Silvers are serially numbered to 100 and golds limited to one set.

		NM/M
Complete Set (20):		30.00
Common Player:		.75
Inserted 1:11		
Silver:		4-8X
Production 100 Sets		
1	Ken Griffey Jr.	2.50
2	Mark McGwire	3.00
3	Sammy Sosa	2.00
4	Alex Rodriguez	3.00
5	Manny Ramirez	1.00
6	Derek Jeter	4.00
7	Jeff Bagwell	1.00
8	Roger Clemens	2.00
9	Scott Rolen	.75
10	Tony Gwynn	1.50
11	Nomar Garciaparra	2.50
12	Randy Johnson	1.50
13	Greg Maddux	2.00
14	Mike Piazza	2.50
15	Frank Thomas	1.00
16	Cal Ripken Jr.	4.00
17	Ivan Rodriguez	.75
18	Mo Vaughn	.75
19	Chipper Jones	2.00
20	Sean Casey	.75

Five-Tool Talents

Randomly inserted in series 2 at a rate of 1:11 packs, this 15-card set spotlights players who have "five tools." Card fronts have silver holo-foil throughout with silver foil stamping. Card backs are numbered with an "FT" prefix.

		NM/M
Complete Set (15):		15.00
Common Player:		.50
Inserted 1:11		
1	Vladimir Guerrero	1.50
2	Barry Bonds	3.00
3	Jason Kendall	.50
4	Derek Jeter	4.00
5	Ken Griffey Jr.	2.50
6	Andruw Jones	.75
7	Bernie Williams	.75
8	Jose Canseco	.75
9	Scott Rolen	.75
10	Shawn Green	.50
11	Nomar Garciaparra	2.50
12	Jeff Bagwell	1.00
13	Larry Walker	.75
14	Chipper Jones	2.00
15	Alex Rodriguez	3.00

Game Balls

These inserts feature a piece of game-used baseball embedded into the card from the featured player. Card backs are numbered with the featured player's initials and are found on the average of 1:287 series 2 packs.

		NM/M
Common Player:		10.00
JB	Jeff Bagwell	10.00
RC	Roger Clemens	30.00
KG	Ken Griffey Jr.	25.00
VG	Vladimir Guerrero	15.00
TG	Tony Gwynn	25.00
DJ	Derek Jeter	40.00
CJ	Chipper Jones	20.00
GM	Greg Maddux	20.00
MM	Mark McGwire	50.00
AR	Alex Rodriguez	30.00
BW	Bernie Williams	10.00

Game Jersey

These have a piece of game-used jersey from the featured player embedded into the card. This regular version is found both in hobby and retail packs at a rate of 1:2,500 packs.

		NM/M
Common Player:		10.00
Inserted 1:2,500		
JC	Jose Canseco	15.00
JG	Juan Gonzalez	15.00
VG	Vladimir Guerrero	20.00
TH	Todd Helton	15.00
CJ	Chipper Jones	25.00
GK	Gabe Kapler	10.00
GM	Greg Maddux	35.00
MR	Manny Ramirez	20.00
CR	Cal Ripken Jr.	60.00
GV	Greg Vaughn	10.00

Game Jersey Series 2

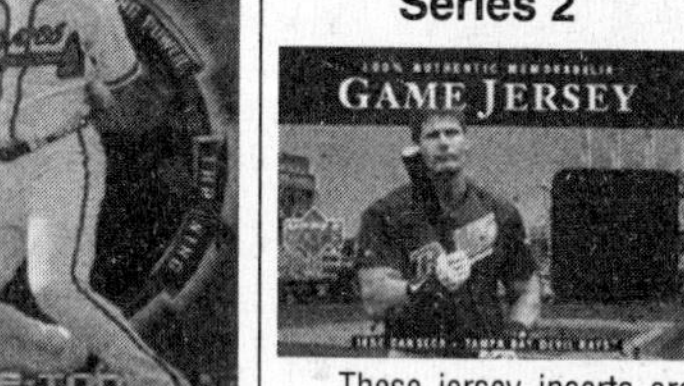

These jersey inserts are found in both hobby and retail packs and are seeded 1:287 packs.

		NM/M
Common Player:		10.00
AR	Alex Rodriguez	30.00
TG	Tony Gwynn	20.00
FT	Frank Thomas	15.00
MW	Matt Williams	10.00
JT	Jim Thome	15.00
MV	Mo Vaughn	10.00
TGl	Tom Glavine	15.00
BG	Ben Grieve	10.00
TrG	Troy Glaus	15.00
RJ	Randy Johnson	20.00
KM	Kevin Millwood	10.00
KG	Ken Griffey Jr.	25.00
AB	Albert Belle	10.00
DC	David Cone	10.00
MH	Mike Hampton	10.00
EC	Eric Chavez	10.00
EM	Edgar Martinez	15.00
PW	Preston Wilson	10.00
RV	Robin Ventura	10.00

Game Jersey Hobby

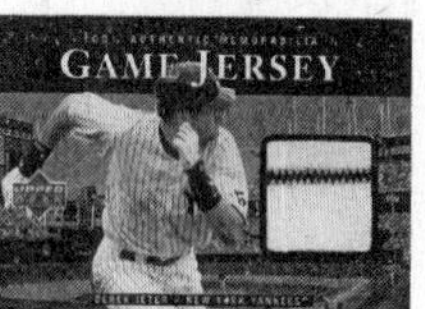

These game-used memorabilia inserts were found exclusively in series 1 packs at a rate of 1:288.

		NM/M
Common Player:		10.00
Inserted 1:288		
JB	Jeff Bagwell	15.00
TG	Troy Glaus	15.00
CY	Tom Glavine	10.00
Jr.	Ken Griffey Jr.	25.00
DJ	Derek Jeter	40.00
PM	Pedro J. Martinez	20.00
MP	Mike Piazza	30.00
AR	Alex Rodriguez	30.00
FT	Frank Thomas	15.00
LW	Larry Walker	10.00

Game Jersey Auto. Hobby Series 2

Found exclusively in series 2 packs these autographed game- used memorabilia inserts are found only in hobby packs at a rate of 1:287.

		NM/M
Common Player:		30.00
H-KG	Ken Griffey Jr.	100.00
H-CR	Cal Ripken Jr.	150.00
H-DJ	Derek Jeter	150.00
H-IR	Ivan Rodriguez	40.00
H-AR	Alex Rodriguez	100.00
H-MR	Manny Ramirez	50.00
H-JC	Jose Canseco	30.00
H-BB	Barry Bonds	180.00
H-SR	Scott Rolen	40.00
H-PO	Paul O'Neill	40.00
H-JK	Jason Kendall	30.00
H-VG	Vladimir Guerrero	50.00
H-JB	Jeff Bagwell	40.00

Game Jersey Patch

Inserted in Series 1 packs at a rate of 1:10,000, these memorabilia inserts have a piece of game-used uniform patch embedded. A 1-of-1 patch of each player was also issued, but cannot be priced due to rarity.

		NM/M
Common Player:		40.00
Inserted 1:10,000		
JB	Jeff Bagwell	60.00
JC	Jose Canseco	60.00
TG	Troy Glaus	50.00
CY	Tom Glavine	60.00
Jr.	Ken Griffey Jr.	100.00
VG	Vladimir Guerrero	100.00
TH	Todd Helton	60.00
DJ	Derek Jeter	150.00
CJ	Chipper Jones	75.00
GK	Gabe Kapler	40.00
GM	Greg Maddux	100.00
PM	Pedro J. Martinez	100.00
MP	Mike Piazza	100.00
MR	Manny Ramirez	80.00
CR	Cal Ripken Jr.	200.00
AR	Alex Rodriguez	125.00
FT	Frank Thomas	80.00
GV	Greg Vaughn	40.00
LW	Larry Walker	50.00

Game Jersey Patch Series 2

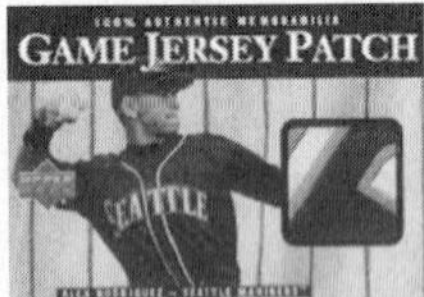

Inserted in Series 2 packs, these memorabilia inserts have a game-used uniform patch embedded and are seeded 1:7,500 packs. A limited one-of-one patch insert for each player is also randomly seeded and are not priced due to their limited nature.

		NM/M
Common Player:		50.00
JB	Jeff Bagwell	75.00
BB	Barry Bonds	200.00
JC	Jose Canseco	75.00
TGl	Troy Glaus	75.00
KG	Ken Griffey Jr.	125.00
VG	Vladimir Guerrero	100.00
TG	Tony Gwynn	100.00
DJ	Derek Jeter	150.00
RJ	Randy Johnson	100.00
AJ	Andruw Jones	80.00
CJ	Chipper Jones	100.00
GM	Greg Maddux	100.00
PM	Pedro Martinez	100.00
MR	Manny Ramirez	100.00
CR	Cal Ripken Jr.	200.00
SR	Scott Rolen	75.00
AR	Alex Rodriguez	150.00
IR	Ivan Rodriguez	90.00
FT	Frank Thomas	100.00
MV	Mo Vaughn	50.00
MW	Matt Williams	50.00

Hit Brigade

Fifteen of the game's top hitters are featured on a full foiled front with bronze foil stamping. Card backs are numbered with an "H" prefix and are found in series 1 packs at a rate of 1:8. Two parallels are randomly inserted: Silvers are serial numbered to 100 and Golds are limited to one set.

		NM/M
Complete Set (15):		15.00
Common Player:		.50
Inserted 1:8		
Silver:		5-10X
Production 100 Sets		
1	Ken Griffey Jr.	2.00
2	Tony Gwynn	1.00
3	Alex Rodriguez	2.50
4	Derek Jeter	3.00
5	Mike Piazza	2.00
6	Sammy Sosa	1.50
7	Juan Gonzalez	.75
8	Scott Rolen	.50
9	Nomar Garciaparra	2.00
10	Barry Bonds	2.50
11	Craig Biggio	.50
12	Chipper Jones	1.50
13	Frank Thomas	.75
14	Larry Walker	.50
15	Mark McGwire	2.50

Hot Properties

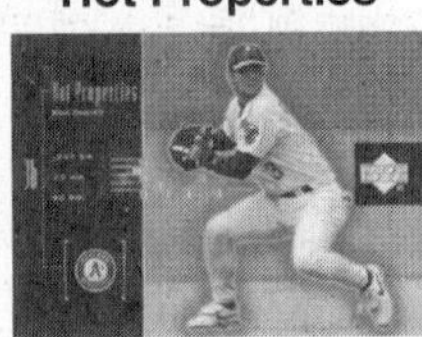

This set spotlights rookies and prospects who have a bright future. Card fronts have a horizontal format on a holo-foiled stock with silver foil stamping. Card backs are numbered with an "HP" prefix and are found in series 2 packs at a rate of 1:11.

		NM/M
Complete Set (15):		10.00
Common Player:		.50
Inserted 1:11		
1	Carlos Beltran	1.00
2	Rick Ankiel	.50
3	Sean Casey	1.00
4	Preston Wilson	1.00
5	Vernon Wells	1.00
6	Pat Burrell	1.50
7	Eric Chavez	1.00
8	J.D. Drew	1.00
9	Alfonso Soriano	2.00
10	Gabe Kapler	.50
11	Rafael Furcal	1.00
12	Ruben Mateo	.50
13	Corey Koskie	.75
14	Kip Wells	.50
15	Ramon Ortiz	.75

The People's Choice

This 15-card set is printed on a full holo-foiled front with gold foil stamping. Card backs are numbered with a "PC" prefix and are seeded 1:23 packs.

		NM/M
Complete Set (15):		20.00
Common Player:		.75
Inserted 1:23		
1	Mark McGwire	3.00
2	Nomar Garciaparra	3.00
3	Derek Jeter	3.00
4	Shawn Green	.75
5	Manny Ramirez	1.00
6	Pedro Martinez	1.50
7	Ivan Rodriguez	.75
8	Alex Rodriguez	3.00
9	Juan Gonzalez	1.00
10	Ken Griffey Jr.	2.00
11	Sammy Sosa	2.50
12	Jeff Bagwell	1.00
13	Chipper Jones	2.00
14	Cal Ripken Jr.	4.00
15	Mike Piazza	2.00

Pennant Driven

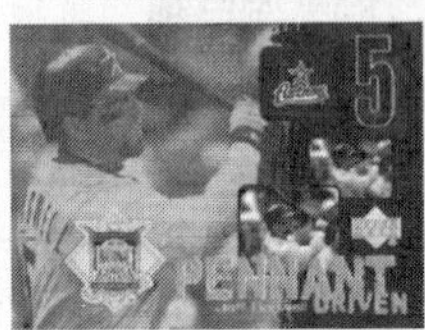

This 10-card horizontal set has a holo-foiled card front with silver foil stamping. Card backs are numbered with a "PD" prefix and are seeded 1:4 packs.

		NM/M
Complete Set (10):		8.00
Common Player:		.50
Inserted 1:4		
1	Derek Jeter	2.00
2	Roberto Alomar	.50
3	Chipper Jones	1.50
4	Jeff Bagwell	.75
5	Roger Clemens	1.00
6	Nomar Garciaparra	1.50
7	Manny Ramirez	.75
8	Mike Piazza	1.50
9	Ivan Rodriguez	.75
10	Randy Johnson	.75

Piece of History-500 Club

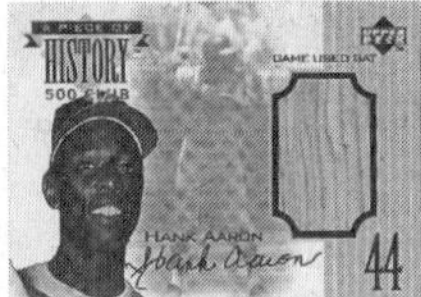

This card features a piece of a game-used Louisville Slugger once swung by Aaron. Approximately 350 cards were produced. Also randomly inserted are 44 autographed versions.

		NM/M
755HR	Hank Aaron	275.00
HAAU	Hank Aaron/ Auto./44	900.00

Power Deck

Collectors need access to a CD-ROM in order to enjoy these interactive cards. Found exclusively in hobby packs cards 1-8 are seeded 1:23 packs and cards 9-11 are found 1:287 packs.

		NM/M
Complete Set (11):		60.00
Common Player:		2.50
Inserted 1:23		
1	Ken Griffey Jr.	5.00
2	Cal Ripken Jr.	7.50
3	Mark McGwire	6.00
4	Tony Gwynn	3.50
5	Roger Clemens	3.50
6	Alex Rodriguez	6.00
7	Sammy Sosa	3.50
8	Derek Jeter	7.50
9	Ken Griffey Jr.	25.00
10	Mark McGwire	30.00
11	Reggie Jackson	15.00

Power MARK

		NM/M
Complete Set (10):		25.00
Common McGwire:		3.00
Inserted 1:23		
Silver:		5-10X
Production 100 Sets		
1-10	Mark McGwire	3.00

Power Rally

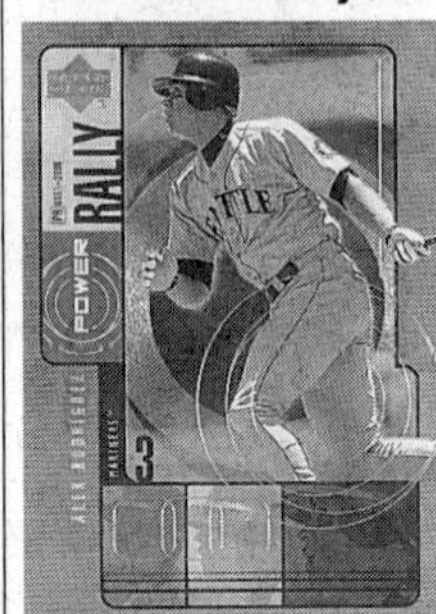

This 15-card set highlights the top hitters and are numbered with an "P" prefix on the card back. They are found 1:11 packs. Two parallel version are also seeded: Coppers are limited to 100 serial numbered sets and Golds are limited to one set.

		NM/M
Complete Set (15):		20.00
Common Player:		.75
Inserted 1:11		
Silver:		4-8X
Production 100 Sets		
1	Ken Griffey Jr.	2.50
2	Mark McGwire	3.00
3	Sammy Sosa	2.00
4	Jose Canseco	.75
5	Juan Gonzalez	1.00
6	Bernie Williams	.75
7	Jeff Bagwell	1.00
8	Chipper Jones	2.00
9	Vladimir Guerrero	1.50
10	Mo Vaughn	.75
11	Derek Jeter	4.00
12	Mike Piazza	2.50
13	Barry Bonds	3.00
14	Alex Rodriguez	3.00
15	Nomar Garciaparra	2.50

Prime Performers

This 10-card set has a horizontal format on a full holo foiled front, with silver foil etching and stamping. Card backs are numbered with a "PP" prefix and found 1:8 packs.

		NM/M
Complete Set (10):		10.00
Common Player:		.50
Inserted 1:8		
1	Manny Ramirez	.75
2	Pedro Martinez	1.00
3	Carlos Delgado	.50
4	Ken Griffey Jr.	2.00
5	Derek Jeter	3.00
6	Chipper Jones	1.50
7	Sean Casey	.50
8	Shawn Green	.50
9	Sammy Sosa	1.50
10	Alex Rodriguez	2.50

STATitude

This 30-card set spotlights the most statistically dominant players on a horizontal format with silver foil stamping. Card backs are numbered with an "S" prefix and are inserted 1:4. Two parallel versions are randomly inserted: Coppers are limited to 100 serial numbered sets and Golds are limited to one set.

		NM/M
Complete Set (30):		25.00
Common Player:		.40
Inserted 1:4		
Silver:		5-10X
Production 100 Sets		
1	Mo Vaughn	.40
2	Matt Williams	.40
3	Travis Lee	.40
4	Chipper Jones	1.50
5	Greg Maddux	1.50
6	Gabe Kapler	.40
7	Cal Ripken Jr.	3.00
8	Nomar Garciaparra	2.00
9	Sammy Sosa	1.50
10	Frank Thomas	.75
11	Manny Ramirez	.75
12	Larry Walker	.50
13	Ivan Rodriguez	.50
14	Jeff Bagwell	.75
15	Craig Biggio	.50
16	Vladimir Guerrero	1.00
17	Mike Piazza	2.00
18	Bernie Williams	.50
19	Derek Jeter	3.00
20	Jose Canseco	.50
21	Eric Chavez	.50
22	Scott Rolen	.50
23	Mark McGwire	2.50
24	Tony Gwynn	1.00
25	Barry Bonds	2.50
26	Ken Griffey Jr.	2.00
27	Alex Rodriguez	2.50
28	J.D. Drew	.50
29	Juan Gonzalez	.50
30	Roger Clemens	1.50

2K Plus

This 12-card set showcases the talents of baseball's next millennium. They are numbered with an "2K" prefix on the card back and are seeded 1:23 packs. Two parallel versions are also randomly inserted: Coppers are limited to 100 serial numbered sets and Golds are limited on one set produced.

		NM/M
Complete Set (12):		15.00
Common Player:		.50
Inserted 1:23		
Silver:		5-10X
Production 100 Sets		
1	Ken Griffey Jr.	2.00
2	J.D. Drew	.50
3	Derek Jeter	3.00
4	Nomar Garciaparra	3.00
5	Pat Burrell	.75
6	Ruben Mateo	.50
7	Carlos Beltran	.50
8	Vladimir Guerrero	1.00
9	Scott Rolen	1.00
10	Chipper Jones	2.00
11	Alex Rodriguez	3.00
12	Magglio Ordonez	.75

3,000 Hit Club Series 1

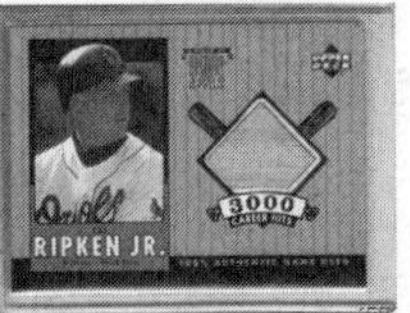

Game-used memorabilia from Orioles teammates Ripken and Murray were inserted in the cross-brand 3,000 Hit Club inserts in Series 1 UD.

		NM/M
CR-B	Cal Ripken Jr./ Bat/350	25.00
CR-J	Cal Ripken Jr./ Jsy/350	25.00
CR-JB	Cal Ripken Jr./ Jsy/Bat/100	150.00
EM-B	Eddie Murray/ Bat/350	10.00
EM-J	Eddie Murray/Jsy/350	8.00
EM-JB	Eddie Murray/ J/y/Bat/100	60.00

3,000 Hit Club Series 2

This cross-brand series spotlights Hank Aaron. The series includes a Jersey card (350 produced), Bat card (350 produced), Jersey/Bat combo (100 produced) and Autographed Jersey/Bat combo (44 produced).

		NM/M
HA-B	Hank Aaron/ Bat/350	50.00
HA-JB	Hank Aaron/ Bat/Jsy/100	100.00
HA-J	Hank Aaron/ Jsy/350	50.00
HA-JBS	Hank Aaron/ Auto. Bat/Jsy/44	700.00

2000 Upper Deck Black Diamond

The base set consists of 120-cards, including a 30 card Diamond Debut (91-120) subset that are seeded 1:4 packs. Card fronts are full foiled with silver etching. Card backs have the player's past five years of statistics, a brief career note and small photo.

		NM/M
Complete Set (120):		25.00
Common Player:		.15
Common Diamond Debut:		.50
Pack (6):		1.50
Wax Box (24):		30.00
1	Darin Erstad	.25
2	Tim Salmon	.20
3	Mo Vaughn	.20
4	Matt Williams	.25
5	Travis Lee	.15

6 Randy Johnson .75
7 Tom Glavine .40
8 Chipper Jones 1.50
9 Greg Maddux 1.50
10 Andruw Jones .50
11 Brian Jordan .15
12 Cal Ripken Jr. 2.50
13 Albert Belle .20
14 Mike Mussina .50
15 Nomar Garciaparra 2.00
16 Troy O'Leary .15
17 Pedro J. Martinez 1.00
18 Sammy Sosa 1.50
19 Henry Rodriguez .15
20 Frank Thomas .75
21 Magglio Ordonez .40
22 Greg Vaughn .15
23 Barry Larkin .25
24 Sean Casey .25
25 Jim Thome .75
26 Kenny Lofton .25
27 Roberto Alomar .50
28 Manny Ramirez .75
29 Larry Walker .25
30 Todd Helton .75
31 Gabe Kapler .15
32 Tony Clark .15
33 Dean Palmer .15
34 Cliff Floyd .15
35 Alex Gonzalez .15
36 Moises Alou .25
37 Jeff Bagwell .75
38 Craig Biggio .25
39 Richard Hidalgo .15
40 Carlos Beltran .25
41 Johnny Damon .25
42 Adrian Beltre .25
43 Gary Sheffield .40
44 Kevin Brown .25
45 Jeromy Burnitz .15
46 Jeff Cirillo .15
47 Joe Mays .15
48 Todd Walker .15
49 Vladimir Guerrero .75
50 Michael Barrett .15
51 Rickey Henderson .40
52 Mike Piazza 1.50
53 Robin Ventura .25
54 John Olerud .25
55 Edgardo Alfonzo .15
56 Derek Jeter 2.00
57 Orlando Hernandez .15
58 Tino Martinez .25
59 Bernie Williams .50
60 Roger Clemens 1.50
61 Eric Chavez .25
62 Ben Grieve .15
63 Jason Giambi 1.00
64 Scott Rolen .50
65 Bobby Abreu .25
66 Curt Schilling .40
67 Mike Lieberthal .15
68 Warren Morris .15
69 Brian Giles .25
70 Eric Owens .15
71 Tony Gwynn 1.00
72 Reggie Sanders .15
73 Barry Bonds 2.00
74 J.T. Snow .15
75 Jeff Kent .25
76 Ken Griffey Jr. 1.50
77 Alex Rodriguez 2.00
78 Edgar Martinez .15
79 Jay Buhner .15
80 Mark McGwire 2.00
81 J.D. Drew .25
82 Eric Davis .15
83 Fernando Tatis .15
84 Wade Boggs .50
85 Fred McGriff .25
86 Juan Gonzalez .75
87 Ivan Rodriguez .50
88 Rafael Palmeiro .50
89 Shawn Green .40
90 Carlos Delgado .60
91 Pat Burrell (Diamond Debut) 1.00
92 Eric Munson (Diamond Debut) .50
93 Jorge Toca (Diamond Debut) .50
94 Rick Ankiel (Diamond Debut) .50
95 Tony Armas Jr. (Diamond Debut) .75
96 Byung-Hyun Kim (Diamond Debut) .75
97 Alfonso Soriano (Diamond Debut) 3.00
98 Mark Quinn (Diamond Debut) .50
99 Ryan Rupe (Diamond Debut) .50
100 Adam Kennedy (Diamond Debut) .50
101 Jeff Weaver (Diamond Debut) .75
102 Ramon Ortiz (Diamond Debut) .75
103 Eugene Kingsale (Diamond Debut) .50
104 Josh Beckett (Diamond Debut) 1.00
105 Eric Gagne (Diamond Debut) 1.00
106 Peter Bergeron (Diamond Debut) .50
107 Erubiel Durazo (Diamond Debut) .75
108 Chad Meyers (Diamond Debut) .50
109 Kip Wells (Diamond Debut) .50
110 Chad Harville (Diamond Debut) .50
111 Matt Riley (Diamond Debut) .50
112 Ben Petrick (Diamond Debut) .50
113 Ed Yarnall (Diamond Debut) .50
114 Calvin Murray (Diamond Debut) .50
115 Vernon Wells (Diamond Debut) 1.00
116 A.J. Burnett (Diamond Debut) .75
117 Jacque Jones (Diamond Debut) .75
118 Francisco Cordero (Diamond Debut) .50
119 Tomokazu Ohka **RC** (Diamond Debut) 1.50
120 Julio Ramirez (Diamond Debut) .50

Reciprocal Cut

A parallel to the 120-card base set, the die-cut design can be used to differentiate them from base cards. Card backs are also numbered with an "R" prefix. Cards 1-90 are found 1:7 packs and Diamond Debuts (91-120) are seeded 1:12 packs.

Stars (1-90): 2-5X
Diamond Debuts 1-1.5X
1-90 inserted 1:7
Diamond Debuts Inserted 1:12

Final Cut

A parallel to the 120-card base set the die-cut design can be used to distinguish them from base cards, the card backs are also numbered with an "F" prefix. Each card is serial numbered within an edition of 100 sets.

Stars (1-90): 5-10X
Diamond Debuts: 2-4X
Production 100 Sets

A Piece of History Single

These memorabilia inserts have a piece of game-used bat embedded into the card front and are seeded 1:179 packs.

NM/M
Common Player: 8.00
Inserted 1:179
AB Albert Belle 8.00
BB Barry Bonds 40.00
JC Jose Canseco 10.00
DE Darin Erstad 8.00
JR Ken Griffey Jr. 25.00
VG Vladimir Guerrero 15.00
TG Tony Gwynn 20.00
TH Todd Helton 10.00
DJ Derek Jeter 40.00
AJ Andruw Jones 10.00
CJ Chipper Jones 20.00
TL Travis Lee 8.00
RM Raul Mondesi 8.00
MP Mike Piazza 25.00
CAL Cal Ripken Jr. 50.00
AR Alex Rodriguez 25.00
IR Ivan Rodriguez 10.00
SR Scott Rolen 10.00
MV Mo Vaughn 8.00

A Piece of History Double

These memorabilia inserts have two pieces of game-used bat embedded into the card front and are a parallel to the single set. They are inserted 1:1,079 packs.

NM/M
Common Player: 10.00
Inserted 1:1079
AB Albert Belle 10.00
BB Barry Bonds 75.00
JC Jose Canseco 20.00
DE Darin Erstad 15.00
JR Ken Griffey Jr. 50.00
VG Vladimir Guerrero 30.00
TG Tony Gwynn 40.00
TH Todd Helton 15.00
DJ Derek Jeter 75.00
AJ Andruw Jones 15.00
CJ Chipper Jones 40.00
TL Travis Lee 10.00
RM Raul Mondesi 10.00
MP Mike Piazza 50.00
CAL Cal Ripken Jr. 80.00
AR Alex Rodriguez 50.00
IR Ivan Rodriguez 15.00
SR Scott Rolen 15.00
MV Mo Vaughn 10.00

Barrage

This 10-card set features a prismatic background with silver foil stamping. Card backs are numbered with a "B" prefix and are seeded 1:29 packs.

NM/M
Complete Set (10): 15.00
Common Player: 1.00
Inserted 1:29
1 Mark McGwire 3.00
2 Ken Griffey Jr. 2.00
3 Sammy Sosa 2.50
4 Jeff Bagwell 1.00
5 Juan Gonzalez 1.00
6 Alex Rodriguez 3.00
7 Manny Ramirez 1.00
8 Ivan Rodriguez 1.00
9 Chipper Jones 2.00
10 Mike Piazza 2.00

Constant Threat

A 10-card set spotlighting the top hitters in the game. Card backs are numbered with a "T" prefix and are seeded 1:29 packs.

NM/M
Complete Set (10): 20.00
Common Player: 1.00
Inserted 1:29
1 Ken Griffey Jr. 2.00
2 Vladimir Guerrero 1.00
3 Alex Rodriguez 3.00
4 Sammy Sosa 2.50
5 Juan Gonzalez 1.00
6 Derek Jeter 3.00
7 Nomar Garciaparra 3.00
8 Barry Bonds 4.00
9 Chipper Jones 2.00
10 Mike Piazza 2.00

Diamonation

This 10-card set has a holo-foil background with gold foil etching and stamping. Card backs are numbered with a "D" prefix and have an insertion ratio of 1:4 packs.

NM/M
Complete Set (10): 6.00
Common Player: .50
Inserted 1:4
1 Ken Griffey Jr. 1.00
2 Randy Johnson 1.00
3 Mark McGwire 1.50
4 Manny Ramirez .75
5 Scott Rolen .75
6 Bernie Williams .75
7 Roger Clemens 1.50
8 Mo Vaughn .50
9 Frank Thomas .75
10 Sean Casey .50

Diamond Gallery

This 10-card set spotlights the featured player in a baseball diamond frame with a prismatic background. Gold foil etching and stamping is also used throughout. Card backs are numbered with a "G" prefix and are seeded 1:14 packs.

NM/M
Complete Set (10): 20.00
Common Player: 1.50
Inserted 1:14
1 Derek Jeter 3.00
2 Alex Rodriguez 3.00
3 Nomar Garciaparra 3.00
4 Cal Ripken Jr. 4.00
5 Sammy Sosa 2.50
6 Tony Gwynn 1.50
7 Mark McGwire 3.00
8 Roger Clemens 2.50
9 Greg Maddux 2.00
10 Pedro Martinez 1.50

DiamondMight

DiamondMight's have a horizontal format, utilizing holo-foil and gold foil stamp-

ing. Card backs are numbered with an "M" prefix and are seeded 1:14 packs.

NM/M
Complete Set (10): 15.00
Common Player: 1.00
Inserted 1:14
1 Ken Griffey Jr. 2.00
2 Mark McGwire 3.00
3 Sammy Sosa 2.50
4 Manny Ramirez 1.00
5 Jeff Bagwell 1.00
6 Frank Thomas 1.00
7 Mike Piazza 2.00
8 Juan Gonzalez 1.00
9 Barry Bonds 4.00
10 Alex Rodriguez 3.00

Diamonds in the Rough

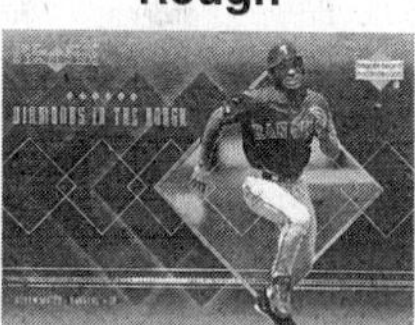

This 10-card set has a horizontal format utilizing holo-foil and gold foil stamping. Card backs are numbered with an "R" prefix and seeded 1:9 packs.

NM/M
Complete Set (10): 8.00
Common Player: .75
Inserted 1:9
1 Pat Burrell 2.00
2 Eric Munson .75
3 Alfonso Soriano 3.00
4 Ruben Mateo .75
5 A.J. Burnett 1.00
6 Ben Davis .75
7 Lance Berkman 1.50
8 Ed Yarnall .75
9 Rick Ankiel .75
10 Ryan Bradley .75

500 Club Piece of History

These Reggie Jackson inserts are part of a cross brand insert series paying tribute to baseball's 500 home run club members. These have a piece of Jackson's game-used bat embedded. An autographed version signed to his jersey number (44) are also randomly inserted.

NM/M
Reggie Jackson 165.00
Reggie Jackson/Auto./44 500.00

Rookie Edition

NM/M
Complete Set (154): 200.00
Common Player: .15
Common Rookie Gem (91-120): 4.00
Production 1,000
Rookie Jersey Gems (121-136):
Inserted 1:24
USA Authentics (137-154):
Inserted 1:96
Golds (1-90): 2-4X
Gold Gems (91-120): 1X
Gold Jerseys (121-136): 1-2X
Pack (6): 2.00
Box (24): 40.00
1 Troy Glaus .75
2 Mo Vaughn .40
3 Darin Erstad .40
4 Jason Giambi .40
5 Tim Hudson .25
6 Ben Grieve .25
7 Eric Chavez .25
8 Tony Batista .15
9 Carlos Delgado .60
10 David Wells .15
11 Greg Vaughn .15
12 Fred McGriff .25
13 Manny Ramirez .75
14 Roberto Alomar .60
15 Jim Thome .40
16 Alex Rodriguez 2.50
17 Edgar Martinez .15
18 John Olerud .20
19 Albert Belle .40
20 Mike Mussina .40
21 Cal Ripken Jr. 2.50
22 Ivan Rodriguez .75
23 Rafael Palmeiro .40
24 Pedro J. Martinez .75
25 Nomar Garciaparra 2.00
26 Carl Everett .15
27 Jermaine Dye .15
28 Mike Sweeney .15
29 Juan Gonzalez .75
30 Bobby Higginson .15
31 Dean Palmer .15
32 Jacque Jones .15
33 Eric Milton .15
34 Matt Lawton .15
35 Magglio Ordonez .25
36 Paul Konerko .15
37 Frank Thomas 1.00
38 Ray Durham .15
39 Roger Clemens 1.00
40 Derek Jeter 2.50
41 Bernie Williams .50
42 Jose Canseco .40
43 Craig Biggio .25
44 Richard Hidalgo .15
45 Jeff Bagwell .75
46 Greg Maddux 1.50
47 Chipper Jones 1.50
48 Rafael Furcal .25
49 Andruw Jones .50
50 Geoff Jenkins .25
51 Jeromy Burnitz .15
52 Mark McGwire 3.00
53 Rick Ankiel .50
54 Jim Edmonds .25
55 Kerry Wood .25
56 Sammy Sosa 2.00
57 Matt Williams .25
58 Randy Johnson .75
59 Steve Finley .15
60 Curt Schilling .15
61 Kevin Brown .15
62 Gary Sheffield .30
63 Shawn Green .30
64 Jose Vidro .15
65 Vladimir Guerrero 1.00
66 Jeff Kent .15
67 Barry Bonds 1.00
68 Ryan Dempster .15
69 Cliff Floyd .15
70 Preston Wilson .15
71 Mike Piazza 2.00
72 Al Leiter .15
73 Edgardo Alfonzo .25
74 Derek Bell .15
75 Ryan Klesko .15
76 Tony Gwynn 1.00
77 Bobby Abreu .15
78 Pat Burrell .50
79 Scott Rolen .50
80 Mike Lieberthal .15
81 Jason Kendall .15
82 Brian Giles .25
83 Ken Griffey Jr. 2.00
84 Pokey Reese .15
85 Dmitri Young .15
86 Sean Casey .15
87 Jeff Cirillo .15
88 Todd Helton .75
89 Jeffrey Hammonds .15
90 Larry Walker .30
91 Barry Zito **RC** 15.00
92 Keith Ginter **RC** 6.00
93 Dane Sardinha **RC** 4.00
94 Kenny Kelly **RC** 4.00
95 Ryan Kohlmeier **RC** 4.00
96 Leo Estrella **RC** 4.00
97 Danys Baez **RC** 4.00
98 Paul Rigdon **RC** 4.00
99 Mike Lamb **RC** 4.00
100 Aaron McNeal **RC** 4.00
101 Juan Pierre **RC** 6.00
102 Rico Washington **RC** 4.00
103 Luis Matos **RC** 8.00
104 Adam Bernero **RC** 4.00
105 Wascar Serrano **RC** 4.00

106 Chris Richard **RC** 4.00
107 Justin Miller **RC** 4.00
108 Julio Zuleta **RC** 4.00
109 Alex Cabrera **RC** 4.00
110 Gene Stechschulte **RC** 4.00
111 Tony Mota **RC** 4.00
112 Tomokazu Ohka **RC** 4.00
113 Geraldo Guzman **RC** 4.00
114 Scott Downs **RC** 4.00
115 Timoniel Perez **RC** 4.00
116 Chad Durbin **RC** 4.00
117 Sun-Woo Kim **RC** 4.00
118 Tomas de la Rosa **RC** 4.00
119 Javier Cardona **RC** 4.00
120 Kazuhiro Sasaki **RC** 6.00
121 Brad Cresse **RC** (Rookie Jersey Gems) 5.00
122 Matt Wheatland **RC** (Rookie Jersey Gems) 5.00
123 Joe Torres **RC** (Rookie Jersey Gems) 5.00
124 Dave Krynzel **RC** (Rookie Jersey Gems) 5.00
125 Ben Diggins **RC** (Rookie Jersey Gems) 5.00
126 Sean Burnett **RC** (Rookie Jersey Gems) 8.00
127 David Espinosa **RC** (Rookie Jersey Gems) 5.00
128 Scott Heard **RC** (Rookie Jersey Gems) 5.00
129 Daylan Holt **RC** (Rookie Jersey Gems) 5.00
130 Koyie Hill **RC** (Rookie Jersey Gems) 5.00
131 Mark Buehrle **RC** (Rookie Jersey Gems) 15.00
132 Xavier Nady **RC** (Rookie Jersey Gems) 8.00
133 Mike Tonis **RC** (Rookie Jersey Gems) 5.00
134 Matt Ginter **RC** (Rookie Jersey Gems) 5.00
135 Lorenzo Barcelo **RC** (Rookie Jersey Gems) 5.00
136 Cory Vance **RC** (Rookie Jersey Gems) 5.00
137 Sean Burroughs (USA Authentics) 8.00
138 Todd Williams (USA Authentics) 5.00
139 Brad Wilkerson **RC** (USA Authentics) 5.00
140 Ben Sheets **RC** (USA Authentics) 20.00
141 Kurt Ainsworth **RC** (USA Authentics) 8.00
142 Anthony Sanders (USA Authentics) 5.00
143 Ryan Franklin (USA Authentics) 5.00
144 Shane Hearns **RC** (USA Authentics) 5.00
145 Roy Oswalt **RC** (USA Authentics) 20.00
146 Jon Rauch **RC** (USA Authentics) 5.00
147 Brent Abernathy **RC** (USA Authentics) 5.00
148 Ernie Young (USA Authentics) 5.00
149 Chris George (USA Authentics) 5.00
150 Gookie Dawkins (USA Authentics) 5.00
151 Adam Everett (USA Authentics) 5.00
152 John Cotton **RC** (USA Authentics) 5.00
153 Pat Borders (USA Authentics) 5.00
154 Doug Mientkiewicz (USA Authentics) 5.00

Rookie Edition Authentics

NM/M

Jeter Authentic Pinstripes
APJ Derek Jeter/Jsy/1,000 35.00
APB Derek Jeter/Bat/1,000 35.00
APC Derek Jeter/Cap/200 70.00
APG Derek Jeter/Glv/200 80.00

Rookie Edition Combos

NM/M

Random game-used inserts.
25 produced of each combo bat
100 produced of combo jersey
JDM Derek Jeter, Joe DiMaggio, Mickey Mantle/Bat 925.00
JWO Derek Jeter, Bernie Williams, Paul O'Neill/Jsy 150.00

Rookie Edition Diamonation

NM/M

Complete Set (9): 10.00
Common Player: .50
Inserted 1:12
1 Pedro J. Martinez 1.00
2 Derek Jeter 2.50
3 Jason Giambi 1.00
4 Todd Helton .75
5 Nomar Garciaparra 2.50
6 Randy Johnson 1.00
7 Jeff Bagwell .75
8 Cal Ripken Jr. 3.00
9 Ivan Rodriguez .50

Rookie Edition Diamond Gallery

NM/M

Complete Set (6): 10.00
Common Player: 1.00
Inserted 1:20
1 Sammy Sosa 2.00
2 Barry Bonds 3.00
3 Vladimir Guerrero 1.00
4 Cal Ripken Jr. 3.00
5 Mike Piazza 1.50
6 Mark McGwire 2.00

2000 UD Black Diamond Rookie Edition Diamond Might

NM/M

Complete Set (9): 10.00
Common Player: .50
Inserted 1:12
1 Mark McGwire 2.50
2 Mike Piazza 1.50
3 Frank Thomas .75
4 Ken Griffey Jr. 1.50
5 Sammy Sosa 2.00
6 Alex Rodriguez 2.50
7 Carlos Delgado .50
8 Vladimir Guerrero 1.00
9 Barry Bonds 3.00

Rookie Edition Diamond Skills

NM/M

Complete Set (6): 8.00
Common Player: .75
Inserted 1:20
1 Alex Rodriguez 2.50
2 Chipper Jones 1.50
3 Ken Griffey Jr. 1.50
4 Pedro J. Martinez 1.00

5 Ivan Rodriguez .75
6 Derek Jeter 2.50

Brooklyn Dodgers Master Collection

Following on the success of its Yankees Master Collection, UD produced a more limited edition set featuring the Brooklyn Dodgers. Only 250 numbered boxed sets were produced. Each set includes 15 base cards, 11 Legends of Flatbush memorabilia/autograph cards and a mystery pack containing a premium memorabilia/autograph card. The set concentrates on Dodgers of the 1950s, along with Zach Wheat. The set was issued in a laser-engraved wooden box.

NM/M

Complete Unopened Set: 1,250
Complete Opened Set: 800.00

Brooklyn Dodgers Master Collection Base Set

Portrait and action photos are combined on a horizontal format for the base cards in the Dodgers Masters Collection. Cards are numbered on back with a "BD" prefix.

NM/M

Complete Set (15): 230.00
Common Player: 10.00
1 Jackie Robinson 50.00
2 Duke Snider 25.00
3 Pee Wee Reese 25.00
4 Gil Hodges 25.00
5 Carl Furillo 15.00
6 Don Newcombe 10.00
7 Sandy Koufax 50.00
8 Roy Campanella 25.00
9 Jim Gilliam 10.00
10 Don Drysdale 20.00
11 Sandy Amoros 10.00
12 Joe Black 10.00
13 Carl Erskine 10.00
14 Johnny Podres 10.00
15 Zack Wheat 10.00

Brooklyn Dodgers Master Collection Legends

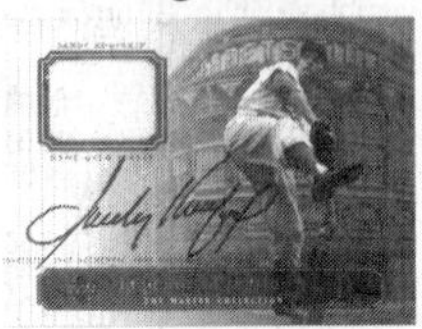

The "Legends of Flatbush" are remembered in this series of memorabilia cards inserted into each Dodgers Master Collection. Each card's number has a "LOF" prefix.

NM/M

Complete Set (11): 800.00
Common Player: 20.00
1 Gil Hodges/Bat 35.00
2 Jackie Robinson/Bat 100.00
3 Pee Wee Reese/Bat 30.00
4 Jim Gilliam/Bat 20.00
5 Roy Campanella/Bat 50.00
6 Zack Wheat/Bat 20.00
7 Carl Furillo/Bat 40.00
8 Don Newcombe (Bat/Autograph) 45.00
9 Duke Snider/Bat/Auto. 80.00
10 Don Drysdale/Jsy 40.00
11 Sandy Koufax/Jsy/Auto. 650.00

Brooklyn Dodgers Master Collection Mystery Pack

Each of the Master Collection sets included a sealed mystery pack containing a premium autograph/memorabilia card. Numbers produced are indicated where known.

NM/M

VALUES UNDETERMINED
JR-BC Jackie Robinson/Bat/5 (Cut sig.) 3,500
PW-BC Pee Wee Reese/Bat/8 (Cut sig.) 325.00

2000 Upper Deck Gold Reserve

Gold Reserve is primarily a retail product that has virtually the same design as regular 2000 Upper Deck base cards. The set consists of 300-cards each with the Upper Deck logo and the featured player's last name stamped in gold foil. Above the player name "Gold Reserve" is stamped in gold foil. The Fantastic Finds subset (268-297) are serial stamped within an edition of 2,500 for each of the subset cards.

NM/M

Complete Set (300): 75.00
Common Player: .15
Common 268-297: 3.00
Production 2,500 Sets
Pack (10): 2.00
Box (24): 40.00
1 Mo Vaughn .20
2 Darin Erstad .25
3 Garret Anderson .25
4 Troy Glaus .50
5 Troy Percival .15
6 Kent Bottenfield .15
7 Orlando Palmeiro .15
8 Tim Salmon .25
9 Jason Giambi .75
10 Eric Chavez .25
11 Matt Stairs .15
12 Miguel Tejada .40
13 Tim Hudson .25
14 John Jaha .15
15 Ben Grieve .15
16 Kevin Appier .15
17 David Wells .15
18 Jose Cruz Jr. .15
19 Homer Bush .15
20 Shannon Stewart .15
21 Carlos Delgado .50
22 Roy Halladay .25
23 Tony Batista .15
24 Raul Mondesi .25
25 Fred McGriff .25
26 Jose Canseco .40
27 Roberto Hernandez .15
28 Vinny Castilla .15
29 Gerald Williams .15
30 Ryan Rupe .15
31 Greg Vaughn .15
32 Miguel Cairo .15
33 Roberto Alomar .40
34 Jim Thome .50
35 Bartolo Colon .15
36 Omar Vizquel .25
37 Manny Ramirez .50
38 Chuck Finley .15
39 Travis Fryman .25
40 Kenny Lofton .25
41 Richie Sexson .40
42 Charles Nagy .15
43 John Halama .15
44 David Bell .15
45 Jay Buhner .15
46 Edgar Martinez .15
47 Alex Rodriguez 1.50
48 Fred Garcia .15
49 Aaron Sele .15
50 Jamie Moyer .15
51 Mike Cameron .15
52 Albert Belle .20
53 Jerry Hairston Jr. .15
54 Sidney Ponson .15
55 Cal Ripken Jr. 2.00
56 Mike Mussina .40
57 B.J. Surhoff .15
58 Brady Anderson .15
59 Mike Bordick .15
60 Ivan Rodriguez .40
61 Rusty Greer .15
62 Rafael Palmeiro .40
63 John Wetteland .15
64 Ruben Mateo .15
65 Gabe Kapler .15
66 David Segui .15
67 Justin Thompson .15
68 Rick Helling .15
69 Jose Offerman .15
70 Trot Nixon .15
71 Pedro Martinez .75
72 Jason Varitek .15
73 Troy O'Leary .15
74 Nomar Garciaparra 1.50
75 Carl Everett .15
76 Wilton Veras .15
77 Tim Wakefield .15
78 Ramon Martinez .15
79 Johnny Damon .25
80 Mike Sweeney .15
81 Rey Sanchez .15
82 Carlos Beltran .25
83 Carlos Febles .15
84 Jermaine Dye .15
85 Joe Randa .15
86 Jose Rosado .15
87 Jeff Suppan .15
88 Juan Encarnacion .15
89 Damion Easley .15
90 Brad Ausmus .15
91 Todd Jones .15
92 Juan Gonzalez .50
93 Bobby Higginson .15
94 Tony Clark .15
95 Brian Moehler .15
96 Dean Palmer .15
97 Joe Mays .15
98 Eric Milton .15
99 Corey Koskie .15
100 Ron Coomer .15
101 Brad Radke .15
102 Todd Walker .15
103 Butch Huskey .15
104 Jacque Jones .15
105 Frank Thomas .50
106 Mike Sirotka .15
107 Carlos Lee .15
108 Ray Durham .15
109 Bob Howry .15
110 Maggio Ordonez .25
111 Paul Konerko .15
112 Chris Singleton .15
113 James Baldwin .15
114 Derek Jeter 2.00
115 Tino Martinez .25
116 Orlando Hernandez .25
117 Chuck Knoblauch .15
118 Bernie Williams .50
119 David Cone .25
120 Paul O'Neill .25
121 Roger Clemens 1.25
122 Mariano Rivera .25
123 Ricky Ledee .15
124 Richard Hidalgo .25
125 Jeff Bagwell .50
126 Jose Lima .15
127 Billy Wagner .15
128 Shane Reynolds .15
129 Moises Alou .25
130 Craig Biggio .25
131 Roger Cedeno .15
132 Octavio Dotel .15
133 Greg Maddux 1.00
134 Brian Jordan .15
135 Kevin Millwood .25
136 Javy Lopez .25
137 Bruce Chen .15
138 Chipper Jones 1.00
139 Tom Glavine .40
140 Andruw Jones .40
141 Andres Galarraga .25
142 Reggie Sanders .15
143 Geoff Jenkins .25
144 Jeromy Burnitz .15
145 Ron Belliard .15
146 Mike Loretta .15
147 Steve Woodard .15
148 Marquis Grissom .15
149 Bob Wickman .15
150 Mark McGwire 1.50
151 Fernando Tatis .15
152 Edgar Renteria .15
153 J.D. Drew .20
154 Ray Lankford .15
155 Fernando Vina .15
156 Pat Hentgen .15
157 Jim Edmonds .25
158 Mark Grace .25
159 Kerry Wood .40
160 Eric Young .15
161 Ismael Valdes .15
162 Sammy Sosa 1.25
163 Henry Rodriguez .15
164 Kyle Farnsworth .15
165 Glenallen Hill .15
166 Jon Lieber .15
167 Luis Gonzalez .25
168 Tony Womack .15
169 Omar Daal .15
170 Randy Johnson .75
171 Erubiel Durazo .15
172 Jay Bell .15
173 Steve Finley .15
174 Travis Lee .15
175 Matt Williams .25
176 Matt Mantei .15
177 Adrian Beltre .25
178 Kevin Brown .25
179 Chan Ho Park .15
180 Mark Grudzielanek .15
181 Jeff Shaw .15
182 Shawn Green .25
183 Gary Sheffield .40
184 Todd Hundley .15
185 Eric Karros .25
186 Kevin Elster .15
187 Vladimir Guerrero .75
188 Michael Barrett .15
189 Chris Widger .15
190 Ugueth Urbina .15
191 Dustin Hermanson .15
192 Rondell White .15
193 Jose Vidro .15
194 Hideki Irabu .15
195 Lee Stevens .15
196 Livan Hernandez .15
197 Ellis Burks .15
198 J.T. Snow .15
199 Jeff Kent .25
200 Robb Nen .15
201 Marvin Benard .15
202 Barry Bonds 1.50
203 Russ Ortiz .15
204 Rich Aurilia .15
205 Joe Nathan .15
206 Preston Wilson .25
207 Cliff Floyd .15
208 Mike Lowell .15
209 Ryan Dempster .15
210 Luis Castillo .15
211 Alex Fernandez .15
212 Mark Kotsay .15
213 Brant Brown .15
214 Edgardo Alfonzo .15
215 Robin Ventura .25
216 Rickey Henderson .25
217 Mike Hampton .15
218 Mike Piazza 1.00
219 Al Leiter .15
220 Derek Bell .15
221 Armando Benitez .15
222 Rey Ordonez .15
223 Todd Zeile .15
224 Tony Gwynn .75
225 Eric Owens .15
226 Damian Jackson .15
227 Trevor Hoffman .15
228 Ben Davis .15
229 Sterling Hitchcock .15
230 Ruben Rivera .15
231 Ryan Klesko .15
232 Phil Nevin .15
233 Mike Lieberthal .15
234 Bobby Abreu .25
235 Doug Glanville .15
236 Rico Brogna .15
237 Scott Rolen .50
238 Andy Ashby .15
239 Robert Person .15
240 Curt Schilling .25
241 Mike Jackson .15
242 Warren Morris .15
243 Kris Benson .15
244 Kevin Young .15
245 Brian Giles .25
246 Jason Schmidt .15
247 Jason Kendall .25
248 Todd Ritchie .15
249 Wil Cordero .15
250 Aramis Ramirez .15
251 Sean Casey .25
252 Barry Larkin .25
253 Pokey Reese .15
254 Scott Williamson .15
255 Aaron Boone .25
256 Dante Bichette .15
257 Ken Griffey Jr. 1.00
258 Denny Neagle .15
259 Dmitri Young .15
260 Todd Helton .50
261 Larry Walker .25
262 Pedro Astacio .15
263 Neifi Perez .15
264 Jeff Cirillo .15

265 Jeffrey Hammonds .15
266 Tom Goodwin .15
267 Rolando Arrojo .15
268 Rick Ankiel (Fantastic Finds) 3.00
269 Pat Burrell (Fantastic Finds) 4.00
270 Eric Munson (Fantastic Finds) 3.00
271 Rafael Furcal (Fantastic Finds) 3.00
272 Brad Penny (Fantastic Finds) 3.00
273 Adam Kennedy (Fantastic Finds) 3.00
274 Mike Lamb **RC** (Fantastic Finds) 3.00
275 Matt Riley (Fantastic Finds) 3.00
276 Eric Gagne (Fantastic Finds) 5.00
277 Kazuhiro Sasaki **RC** (Fantastic Finds) 3.00
278 Julio Lugo (Fantastic Finds) 3.00
279 Kip Wells (Fantastic Finds) 3.00
280 Danys Baez **RC** (Fantastic Finds) 3.00
281 Josh Beckett (Fantastic Finds) 4.00
282 Alfonso Soriano (Fantastic Finds) 4.00
283 Vernon Wells (Fantastic Finds) 4.00
284 Nick Johnson (Fantastic Finds) 3.00
285 Ramon Ortiz (Fantastic Finds) 3.00
286 Peter Bergeron (Fantastic Finds) 3.00
287 Wascar Serrano **RC** (Fantastic Finds) 3.00
288 Josh Paul (Fantastic Finds) 3.00
289 Mark Quinn (Fantastic Finds) 3.00
290 Jason Marquis (Fantastic Finds) 3.00
291 Rob Bell (Fantastic Finds) 3.00
292 Pablo Ozuna (Fantastic Finds) 3.00
293 Milton Bradley (Fantastic Finds) 3.00
294 Roosevelt Brown (Fantastic Finds) 3.00
295 Terrence Long (Fantastic Finds) 3.00
296 Chad Durbin **RC** (Fantastic Finds) 3.00
297 Matt LeCroy (Fantastic Finds) 3.00
298 Ken Griffey Jr. (Checklist) .50
299 Mark McGwire (Checklist) .75
300 Derek Jeter (Checklist) 1.00

Game-Used Ball

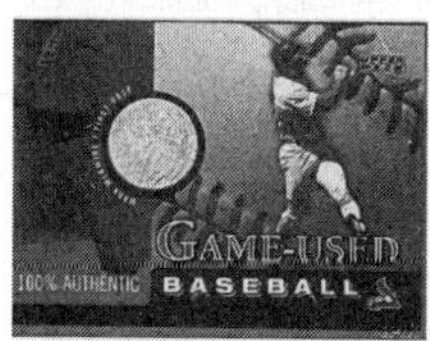

NM/M
Common Player: 10.00
Inserted 1:480
JB Jeff Bagwell 25.00
BB Barry Bonds 70.00
SC Sean Casey 10.00
RC Roger Clemens 35.00
NG Nomar Garciaparra 40.00
SG Shawn Green 10.00
KG Ken Griffey Jr. 30.00
TG Tony Gwynn 25.00
DJ Derek Jeter 60.00
AJ Andruw Jones 15.00
CJ Chipper Jones 30.00
GM Greg Maddux 30.00
MM Mark McGwire 60.00
MP Mike Piazza 30.00
MR Manny Ramirez 15.00
IR Ivan Rodriguez 15.00
SR Scott Rolen 10.00
GS Gary Sheffield 10.00
SS Sammy Sosa 30.00
BW Bernie Williams 10.00

Setting the Standard

This 15-card set spotlights the top hitters and are inserted 1:11 packs. Card fronts feature gold foil stamping and card backs are numbered with an "S" prefix.

NM/M
Complete Set (15): 25.00

Common Player: .50
Inserted 1:11
1 Tony Gwynn 1.50
2 Manny Ramirez 1.00
3 Derek Jeter 3.00
4 Cal Ripken Jr. 4.00
5 Mo Vaughn .50
6 Jose Canseco .75
7 Barry Bonds 4.00
8 Nomar Garciaparra 3.00
9 Juan Gonzalez 1.00
10 Mark McGwire 3.00
11 Alex Rodriguez 3.00
12 Jeff Bagwell 1.00
13 Ken Griffey Jr. 2.00
14 Frank Thomas 1.00
15 Sammy Sosa 2.50

Solid Gold Gallery

This 12-card set features close-up shots of the featured player accentuated by gold foil stamping. Card backs are numbered with a "G" prefix, these were seeded 1:13 packs.

NM/M
Complete Set (12): 20.00
Common Player: 1.00
Inserted 1:13
1 Ken Griffey Jr. 2.00
2 Alex Rodriguez 3.00
3 Mike Piazza 2.00
4 Sammy Sosa 2.50
5 Derek Jeter 3.00
6 Jeff Bagwell 1.00
7 Mark McGwire 3.00
8 Cal Ripken Jr. 4.00
9 Pedro Martinez 1.50
10 Chipper Jones 2.00
11 Ivan Rodriguez 1.00
12 Vladimir Guerrero 1.00

UD Authentics

NM/M
Inserted 1:480
CB Carlos Beltran 40.00
JC Jose Canseco 35.00
SG Shawn Green 20.00
TG Tony Gwynn 30.00
CJ Chipper Jones 60.00
MR Manny Ramirez 25.00
CR Cal Ripken Jr. 100.00
AR Alex Rodriguez 80.00
IR Ivan Rodriguez 20.00

UD Authentics Gold

Values Undetermined

24-Karat Gems

This 15-card set features gold foil stamping on the front and are numbered on the back with a "K" prefix. They are found on the average of 1:7 packs.

NM/M
Complete Set (15): 12.00
Common Player: .50
Inserted 1:7
1 Pedro Martinez 1.50
2 Scott Rolen 1.00
3 Jason Giambi 1.50
4 Jeromy Burnitz .50
5 Rafael Palmeiro 1.00
6 Rick Ankiel .50
7 Carlos Beltran .75
8 Derek Jeter 3.00
9 Jason Kendall .50
10 Chipper Jones 2.00
11 Carlos Delgado 1.00
12 Alex Rodriguez 3.00
13 Randy Johnson 1.50
14 Tony Gwynn 1.50
15 Shawn Green .75

3,000 Hit Club

This on-going cross brand insert series features Al Kaline. Each card features a piece of Kaline's game-used bat, he also signed six cards.

NM/M
AK-B Al Kaline Bat/400 20.00

2000 Upper Deck Hitter's Club

The 90-card base set includes only hitters and features past and current stars. The base set consists of 50 regular cards, 25 Why 3K?, and 15 Hitting the Show subset cards. Card backs of the 50 regular cards have complete year-by- year statistics.

NM/M
Complete Set (90): 20.00
Common Player: .15
Pack (5): 1.50
Wax Box (24): 25.00
1 Mo Vaughn .20
2 Troy Glaus .40
3 Jeff Bagwell .50
4 Craig Biggio .25
5 Jason Giambi .75
6 Eric Chavez .25
7 Carlos Delgado .50
8 Chipper Jones 1.00
9 Andruw Jones .50
10 Andres Galarraga .20
11 Jeromy Burnitz .15
12 Mark McGwire 1.50
13 Mark Grace .25
14 Sammy Sosa 1.25
15 Jose Canseco .40
16 Vinny Castilla .15
17 Matt Williams .25
18 Gary Sheffield .25
19 Shawn Green .25
20 Vladimir Guerrero .50
21 Barry Bonds 1.50
22 Manny Ramirez .50
23 Roberto Alomar .40
24 Jim Thome .50
25 Ken Griffey Jr. 1.00
26 Alex Rodriguez 1.50
27 Edgar Martinez .15
28 Preston Wilson .25
29 Mike Piazza 1.00
30 Robin Ventura .25
31 Albert Belle .20
32 Cal Ripken Jr. 2.00
33 Tony Gwynn .75
34 Scott Rolen .50
35 Bob Abreu .25
36 Brian Giles .25
37 Ivan Rodriguez .40
38 Rafael Palmeiro .40
39 Nomar Garciaparra 1.50
40 Sean Casey .20
41 Larry Walker .25
42 Todd Helton .50
43 Carlos Beltran .25
44 Dean Palmer .15
45 Juan Gonzalez .50
46 Corey Koskie .15
47 Frank Thomas .50
48 Magglio Ordonez .25
49 Derek Jeter 2.00
50 Bernie Williams .40
51 Paul Waner (Why 3k?) .25
52 Honus Wagner (Why 3k?) .50
53 Tris Speaker (Why 3k?) .25
54 Nap Lajoie (Why 3k?) .25
55 Eddie Collins (Why 3k?) .25
56 Roberto Clemente (Why 3k?) 1.00
57 Ty Cobb (Why 3k?) 1.50
58 Cap Anson (Why 3k?) .50
59 Robin Yount (Why 3k?) .50
60 Carl Yastrzemski (Why 3k?) .50
61 Dave Winfield (Why 3k?) .25
62 Stan Musial (Why 3k?) 1.00
63 Eddie Murray (Why 3k?) .40
64 Paul Molitor (Why 3k?) .50
65 Willie Mays (Why 3k?) 1.50
66 Al Kaline (Why 3k?) .50
67 Tony Gwynn (Why 3k?) .75
68 Rod Carew (Why 3k?) .40
69 Lou Brock (Why 3k?) .25
70 George Brett (Why 3k?) 1.00
71 Wade Boggs (Why 3k?) .25
72 Hank Aaron (Why 3k?) 1.50
73 Jorge Luis Toca (Hitting the Show) .15
74 J.D. Drew (Hitting the Show) .15
75 Pat Burrell (Hitting the Show) .25
76 Vernon Wells (Hitting the Show) .25
77 Julio Ramirez (Hitting the Show) .15
78 Gabe Kapler (Hitting the Show) .15
79 Erubiel Durazo (Hitting the Show) .15
80 Lance Berkman (Hitting the Show) .25
81 Peter Bergeron (Hitting the Show) .15
82 Alfonso Soriano (Hitting the Show) .75
83 Jacque Jones (Hitting the Show) .15
84 Ben Petrick (Hitting the Show) .15
85 Jerry Hairston Jr. (Hitting the Show) .15
86 Kevin Witt (Hitting the Show) .15
87 Dermal Brown (Hitting the Show) .15
88 Chad Hermansen (Hitting the Show) .15
89 Ruben Mateo (Hitting the Show) .15
90 Checklist (Ken Griffey Jr.) .50

Accolades

These inserts have a full foiled front with gold foil stamping. Card backs are numbered with an "A" prefix and are seeded 1:11 packs.

NM/M
Complete Set (10): 12.00
Common Player: .75
Inserted 1:11
1 Robin Yount 1.00
2 Tony Gwynn 1.00
3 Sammy Sosa 2.00
4 Mike Piazza 1.50
5 Cal Ripken Jr. 3.00

6 Mark McGwire 2.50
7 Barry Bonds 2.50
8 Wade Boggs .75
9 Ken Griffey Jr. 1.50
10 Willie Mays 2.00

Autographs

Former and current players are featured in this signature set, which are seeded 1:215 packs. Card backs are numbered with the featured player's initials.

NM/M
Common Player: 15.00
Inserted 1:215
HA Hank Aaron #44 240.00
WB Wade Boggs #12 30.00
GB George Brett #5 80.00
Lou Lou Brock #20 15.00
Rod Rod Carew #29 15.00
TG Tony Gwynn #19 40.00
Al Al Kaline #6 30.00
WM Willie Mays #24 150.00
PM Paul Molitor #4 30.00
EM Eddie Murray #33 30.00
Man Stan Musial #6 75.00
Cal Cal Ripken Jr. #8 150.00
DW Dave Winfield #31 20.00
Yaz Carl Yastrzemski #7 60.00
RY Robin Yount #19 40.00

Epic Performances

This 10-card set (#EP2 was not issued) showcases some of baseball's top performances on a fully foiled card front with gold-foil stamping. Card backs are numbered with an "EP" prefix.

NM/M
Complete Set (10): 12.00
Common Player: 1.00
Inserted 1:3
1 Mark McGwire 2.50
3 Sammy Sosa 2.00
4 Ken Griffey Jr. 1.50
5 Carl Yastrzemski 1.00
6 Tony Gwynn 1.00
7 Nomar Garciaparra 2.50
8 Cal Ripken Jr. 3.00
9 George Brett 1.50
10 Hank Aaron 2.00
11 Wade Boggs 1.00

Eternals

These inserts were printed on a fully foiled front with "Eternals" printed a number of times in the background. The player name and Upper Deck logo are stamped in gold foil at bottom. Card backs are numbered with an "E" prefix.

NM/M
Complete Set (10): 20.00
Common Player: 1.00
Inserted 1:23
1 Cal Ripken Jr. 4.00
2 Mark McGwire 3.00
3 Ken Griffey Jr. 2.00
4 Nomar Garciaparra 3.00
5 Tony Gwynn 1.50
6 Derek Jeter 3.00
7 Jose Canseco 1.00
8 Mike Piazza 2.00
9 Alex Rodriguez 3.00
10 Barry Bonds 4.00

Generations of Excellence

This 10-card insert set features two players who are linked either by team or position. Gold-foil stamping is used throughout. Card backs are numbered with a "GE" prefix.

NM/M
Complete Set (10): 15.00
Common Card: 1.00
Inserted 1:6
1 Cal Ripken Jr., Eddie Murray 3.00
2 Vladimir Guerrero, Roberto Clemente 2.00
3 George Brett, Robin Yount 2.00
4 Barry Bonds, Willie Mays 3.00
5 Chipper Jones, Hank Aaron 2.00
6 Mark McGwire, Sammy Sosa 2.00
7 Tony Gwynn, Wade Boggs 1.00
8 Rickey Henderson, Lou Brock 1.00
9 Derek Jeter, Nomar Garciaparra 3.00
10 Alex Rodriguez, Ken Griffey Jr. 2.50

On Target

This 10-card set is printed on a full foiled front with silver foil stamping. Card backs are numbered with an "OT" prefix and are seeded 1:23 packs.

NM/M
Complete Set (10): 12.00
Common Player: .50
Inserted 1:23
1 Nomar Garciaparra 3.00
2 Sean Casey .50
3 Alex Rodriguez 3.00
4 Troy Glaus 1.00

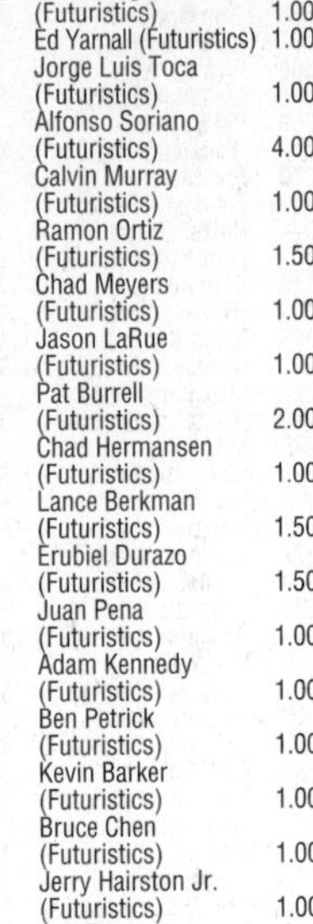

5 Ivan Rodriguez 1.00
6 Chipper Jones 2.00
7 Manny Ramirez 1.00
8 Derek Jeter 3.00
9 Vladimir Guerrero 1.00
10 Scott Rolen 1.00

The Hitters' Club

These inserts are seeded 1:95 packs and are numbered on the back with an "HC" prefix.

NM/M
Complete Set (10): 60.00
Common Player: 3.00
1 Rod Carew 5.00
2 Alex Rodriguez 15.00
3 Willie Mays 10.00
4 George Brett 10.00
5 Tony Gwynn 8.00
6 Stan Musial 8.00
7 Frank Thomas 5.00
8 Wade Boggs 3.00
9 Larry Walker 3.00
10 Nomar Garciaparra 15.00

3,000 Hit Club

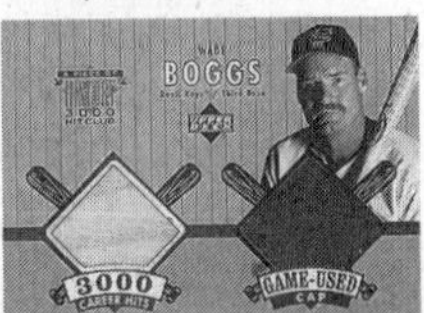

Upper Deck's cross brand series pays tribute to players who have reached 3,000 hits. Hitter's Club features Wade Boggs and Tony Gwynn inserts with Bat, Bat and Cap and Autographed versions randomly inserted.

NM/M
Common Player: 25.00
WB Wade Boggs/Bat/350 25.00
WB Wade Boggs/ Bat & Cap/50 65.00
TG Tony Gwynn/Bat/350 25.00
TG Tony Gwynn/ Bat & Cap/50 100.00
TG Tony Gwynn/AU/19 550.00
GB Tony Gwynn, Wade Boggs/Bat/99 85.00

2000 Upper Deck HoloGrFX

The base set consists of 90-cards on a horizontal format. The cards have a holo-foil front utilizing HoloGrFX technology.

NM/M
Complete Set (90): 20.00
Common Player: .15
Pack (4): 1.50
Wax Box (32): 25.00
1 Mo Vaughn .20
2 Troy Glaus .50
3 Daryle Ward .15
4 Jeff Bagwell .50
5 Craig Biggio .25
6 Jose Lima .15
7 Jason Giambi .75
8 Eric Chavez .25
9 Tim Hudson .25
10 Raul Mondesi .25
11 Carlos Delgado .50
12 David Wells .15
13 Chipper Jones 1.00
14 Greg Maddux 1.00
15 Andruw Jones .50
16 Brian Jordan .15
17 Jeromy Burnitz .15
18 Ron Belliard .15
19 Mark McGwire 1.50
20 Fernando Tatis .15
21 J.D. Drew .25
22 Sammy Sosa 1.00
23 Mark Grace .40
24 Greg Vaughn .15
25 Jose Canseco .40
26 Vinny Castilla .15
27 Fred McGriff .25
28 Matt Williams .25
29 Randy Johnson .75
30 Erubiel Durazo .15
31 Shawn Green .25
32 Gary Sheffield .40
33 Kevin Brown .25
34 Vladimir Guerrero .50
35 Michael Barrett .15
36 Russ Ortiz .15
37 Barry Bonds 1.50
38 Jeff Kent .25
39 Kenny Lofton .25
40 Manny Ramirez .50
41 Roberto Alomar .40
42 Richie Sexson .25
43 Edgar Martinez .25
44 Alex Rodriguez 1.50
45 Fred Garcia .15
46 Preston Wilson .15
47 Alex Gonzalez .15
48 Mike Hampton .15
49 Mike Piazza 1.00
50 Robin Ventura .25
51 Edgardo Alfonzo .15
52 Albert Belle .15
53 Cal Ripken Jr. 2.00
54 B.J. Surhoff .15
55 Tony Gwynn .75
56 Trevor Hoffman .15
57 Mike Lieberthal .15
58 Scott Rolen .50
59 Bob Abreu .25
60 Curt Schilling .40
61 Jason Kendall .25
62 Brian Giles .25
63 Kris Benson .15
64 Rafael Palmeiro .40
65 Ivan Rodriguez .50
66 Gabe Kapler .40
67 Nomar Garciaparra 1.50
68 Pedro Martinez .75
69 Troy O'Leary .15
70 Barry Larkin .25
71 Dante Bichette .15
72 Sean Casey .20
73 Ken Griffey Jr. 1.00
74 Jeff Cirillo .15
75 Todd Helton .50
76 Larry Walker .25
77 Carlos Beltran .25
78 Jermaine Dye .15
79 Juan Gonzalez .50
80 Juan Encarnacion .15
81 Dean Palmer .15
82 Corey Koskie .15
83 Eric Milton .15
84 Frank Thomas .50
85 Magglio Ordonez .25
86 Carlos Lee .15
87 Derek Jeter 2.00
88 Tino Martinez .25
89 Bernie Williams .50
90 Roger Clemens 1.50

A Piece of the Series

This inserts have a piece of game-used base from a 1999 World Series game embedded. These were inserted at a rate of 1:215 packs.

NM/M
Common Player: 5.00
Inserted 1:215
1 Derek Jeter 40.00
2 Chipper Jones 20.00
3 Roger Clemens 30.00
4 Greg Maddux 30.00
5 Bernie Williams 10.00
6 Andruw Jones 10.00
7 Tino Martinez 8.00
8 Brian Jordan 5.00
9 Mariano Rivera 8.00
11 Paul O'Neill 8.00
12 Tom Glavine 10.00

A Piece of Series Autograph

This is an autographed parallel of the Piece of Series insert set that is limited to 25 sets.

NM/M
Common Player: 40.00
Production 25 Sets

PSA1 Derek Jeter 300.00
PSA2 Chipper Jones 125.00
PSA3 Roger Clemens 220.00
PSA4 Greg Maddux 220.00
PSA6 Andruw Jones 85.00
PSA7 Tino Martinez 65.00
PSA8 Brian Jordan 40.00
PSA11 Paul O'Neill 75.00
PSA12 Tom Glavine 100.00

Bomb Squad

This set highlights top home run hitters in a horizontal format with complete holo-foiled fronts. Card backs are numbered with a "BS" prefix.

NM/M
Complete Set (6): 15.00
Common Player: 2.00
Inserted 1:34
1 Ken Griffey Jr. 2.00
2 Mark McGwire 3.00
3 Chipper Jones 2.00
4 Alex Rodriguez 3.00
5 Sammy Sosa 2.50
6 Barry Bonds 4.00

Future Fame

This six-card set has a horizontal format that is completely holo-foiled with silver foil stamping. Card backs are numbered with an "FF" prefix and seeded 1:34 packs.

NM/M
Complete Set (6): 10.00
Common Player: 2.00
Inserted 1:34
1 Cal Ripken Jr. 4.00
2 Mark McGwire 3.00
3 Greg Maddux 2.00
4 Tony Gwynn 1.50
5 Ken Griffey Jr. 2.00
6 Roger Clemens 2.50

Longball Legacy

This 15-card set spotlights the top home run hitters on a horizontal format and completely holo-foiled. Card backs are numbered with an "LL" prefix and seeded 1:6 packs.

NM/M
Complete Set (15): 15.00
Common Player: .50
Inserted 1:6
1 Mike Piazza 2.00
2 Ivan Rodriguez .75
3 Jeff Bagwell 1.00
4 Alex Rodriguez 3.00
5 Jose Canseco .75
6 Mark McGwire 3.00
7 Scott Rolen .75
8 Carlos Delgado .75
9 Mo Vaughn .50
10 Manny Ramirez 1.00
11 Matt Williams .50
12 Sammy Sosa 2.50
13 Ken Griffey Jr. 2.00
14 Nomar Garciaparra 3.00
15 Larry Walker .50

Stars of the System

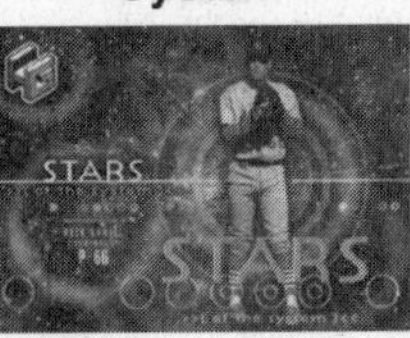

This 10-card set features some of baseball's top prospects on a horizontal format. The fronts are completely holo-foiled with silver foil stamping. Card backs are numbered with an "SS" prefix and seeded 1:8 packs.

NM/M
Complete Set (10): 8.00
Common Player: .75
Inserted 1:8
1 Rick Ankiel .75
2 Alfonso Soriano 2.00
3 Vernon Wells 1.00
4 Ben Petrick .75
5 Francisco Cordero .75
6 Matt Riley .75
7 A.J. Burnett 1.00
8 Pat Burrell 1.50
9 Ed Yarnall .75
10 Dermal Brown .75

StarView

This eight-card set features top stars on a horizontal format. Card backs are numbered with an "SV" prefix and inserted 1:11 packs.

NM/M
Complete Set (8): 15.00
Common Player: 2.00
Inserted 1:11
1 Ken Griffey Jr. 2.00
2 Nomar Garciaparra 3.00
3 Chipper Jones 2.00
4 Mark McGwire 3.00
5 Sammy Sosa 2.50
6 Derek Jeter 4.00
7 Mike Piazza 2.00
8 Alex Rodriguez 3.00

3,000 Hit Club

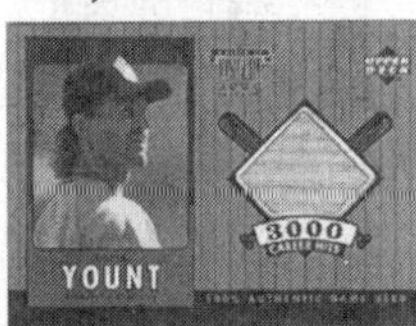

Upper Deck pays tribute to members of the 3,000 Hit Club with this cross-brand insert series. Robin Yount and George Brett are featured on a game-used bat card (350 produced), game-used jersey card (350 produced), a bat combo of both players (99 produced) and an autographed combo (10 produced).

NM/M
Common Card: 20.00
RY Robin Yount/Bat/350 20.00
RYJ Robin Yount/ Jsy/350 20.00
GB George Brett/Bat/350 35.00
GBJ George Brett/ Jsy/350 35.00
BY George Brett, Robin Yount/Bat/99 120.00
BYJ George Brett, Robin Yount/Jsy/99 120.00

2000 UD Ionix

The base set consists of 90 cards, including a 30-card Futuristics subset that were seeded 1:4 packs. A Reciprocal parallel to the base set are also randomly inserted. The cards can distinguished by a

holo-foiled front and the number on the back has an "R" prefix. Reciprocals 1-60 are found 1:4 packs, while Futuristics Reciprocals are found on the average of 1:11 packs.

NM/M
Complete Set (90): 50.00
Common Player: .15
Common Futuristic: 1.00
Inserted 1:4
Reciprocal (1-60): 1.5-2X
Reciprocal (61-90): 1-1.5X
Inserted 1:4
Future Recip. 1:11
Pack (4): 2.00
Wax Box (24): 35.00
1 Mo Vaughn .20
2 Troy Glaus .75
3 Jeff Bagwell .75
4 Craig Biggio .40
5 Jose Lima .15
6 Jason Giambi 1.00
7 Tim Hudson .40
8 Shawn Green .50
9 Carlos Delgado .75
10 Chipper Jones 1.50
11 Andruw Jones .75
12 Greg Maddux 1.50
13 Jeromy Burnitz .15
14 Mark McGwire 2.00
15 J.D. Drew .25
16 Sammy Sosa 2.00
17 Jose Canseco .50
18 Fred McGriff .40
19 Randy Johnson .75
20 Matt Williams .25
21 Kevin Brown .40
22 Gary Sheffield .40
23 Vladimir Guerrero .75
24 Barry Bonds 2.50
25 Jim Thome .75
26 Manny Ramirez .75
27 Roberto Alomar .50
28 Kenny Lofton .25
29 Ken Griffey Jr. 1.50
30 Alex Rodriguez 2.50
31 Alex Gonzalez .15
32 Preston Wilson .15
33 Mike Piazza 1.50
34 Robin Ventura .25
35 Cal Ripken Jr. 2.50
36 Albert Belle .20
37 Tony Gwynn 1.00
38 Scott Rolen .75
39 Curt Schilling .50
40 Brian Giles .25
41 Juan Gonzalez .75
42 Ivan Rodriguez .75
43 Rafael Palmeiro .60
44 Pedro J. Martinez 1.00
45 Nomar Garciaparra 2.00
46 Sean Casey .25
47 Aaron Boone .25
48 Barry Larkin .40
49 Larry Walker .25
50 Vinny Castilla .20
51 Carlos Beltran .25
52 Gabe Kapler .15
53 Dean Palmer .15
54 Eric Milton .15
55 Corey Koskie .15
56 Frank Thomas .75
57 Magglio Ordonez .40
58 Roger Clemens 2.00
59 Bernie Williams .75
60 Derek Jeter 2.50
61 Josh Beckett (Futuristics) 1.50
62 Eric Munson (Futuristics) 1.00
63 Rick Ankiel (Futuristics) 1.00
64 Matt Riley (Futuristics) 1.00
65 Robert Ramsay (Futuristics) 1.00
66 Vernon Wells (Futuristics) 2.00
67 Eric Gagne (Futuristics) 1.50
68 Robert Fick (Futuristics) 1.50
69 Mark Quinn (Futuristics) 1.00
70 Kip Wells (Futuristics) 1.00
71 Peter Bergeron (Futuristics) 1.00
72 Ed Yarnall (Futuristics) 1.00
73 Jorge Luis Toca (Futuristics) 1.00
74 Alfonso Soriano (Futuristics) 4.00
75 Calvin Murray (Futuristics) 1.00
76 Ramon Ortiz (Futuristics) 1.50
77 Chad Meyers (Futuristics) 1.00
78 Jason LaRue (Futuristics) 1.00
79 Pat Burrell (Futuristics) 2.00
80 Chad Hermansen (Futuristics) 1.00
81 Lance Berkman (Futuristics) 1.50
82 Erubiel Durazo (Futuristics) 1.50
83 Juan Pena (Futuristics) 1.00
84 Adam Kennedy (Futuristics) 1.00
85 Ben Petrick (Futuristics) 1.00
86 Kevin Barker (Futuristics) 1.00
87 Bruce Chen (Futuristics) 1.00
88 Jerry Hairston Jr. (Futuristics) 1.00
89 A.J. Burnett (Futuristics) 1.00
90 Gary Matthews Jr. (Futuristics) 1.00

Atomic

This 15-card insert set has a horizontal format on a holo-foil front. Card backs are numbered with an "A" prefix and are found 1:8 packs.

NM/M
Complete Set (15): 25.00
Common Player: 1.00
Inserted 1:8
1 Pedro J. Martinez 1.50
2 Mark McGwire 3.00
3 Ken Griffey Jr. 2.00
4 Jeff Bagwell 1.00
5 Greg Maddux 2.00
6 Derek Jeter 3.00
7 Cal Ripken Jr. 4.00
8 Manny Ramirez 1.00
9 Randy Johnson 1.50
10 Nomar Garciaparra 3.00
11 Tony Gwynn 1.50
12 Bernie Williams 1.00
13 Mike Piazza 2.00
14 Roger Clemens 3.00
15 Alex Rodriguez 3.00

Awesome Powers

The title of this insert set is a takeoff from the Austin Powers movie that was popular at the time of this release. The cards have a holo-foil front with a "groovin" '70s backdrop. Card backs are numbered with an "AP" prefix.

NM/M
Complete Set (15): 50.00
Common Player: 1.00
Inserted 1:23
1 Ken Griffey Jr. 4.00
2 Mike Piazza 4.00
3 Carlos Delgado 2.00
4 Mark McGwire 6.00

5	Chipper Jones	4.00
6	Scott Rolen	2.00
7	Cal Ripken Jr.	8.00
8	Alex Rodriguez	6.00
9	Larry Walker	1.00
10	Sammy Sosa	5.00
11	Barry Bonds	6.00
12	Nomar Garciaparra	6.00
13	Jose Canseco	1.50
14	Manny Ramirez	2.00
15	Jeff Bagwell	2.00

BIOrhythm

This 15-card set has a holo-foil front and are seeded 1:11 packs. Card backs have a brief career note and are numbered with a "B" prefix.

		NM/M
Complete Set (15):		25.00
Common Player:		.50
Inserted 1:11		
1	Randy Johnson	1.50
2	Derek Jeter	3.00
3	Sammy Sosa	2.50
4	Jose Lima	.50
5	Chipper Jones	2.00
6	Barry Bonds	4.00
7	Ken Griffey Jr.	2.00
8	Nomar Garciaparra	3.00
9	Frank Thomas	1.00
10	Pedro Martinez	1.50
11	Larry Walker	.50
12	Greg Maddux	2.00
13	Alex Rodriguez	3.00
14	Mark McGwire	3.00
15	Cal Ripken Jr.	4.00

Pyrotechnics

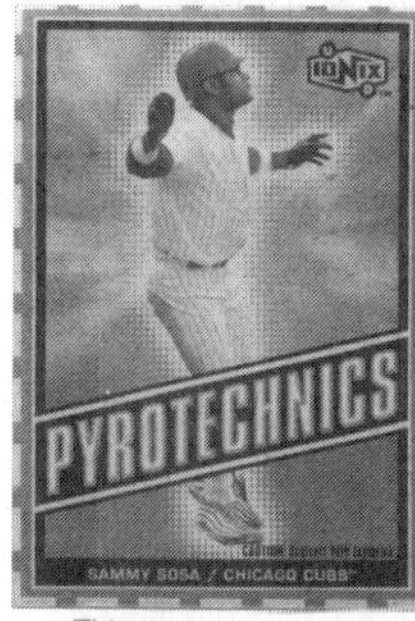

This 15-card set has a holo-foiled front with an insertion ratio of 1:72 packs. Card backs are numbered with a "P" prefix.

		NM/M
Complete Set (15):		125.00
Common Player:		5.00
Inserted 1:72		
1	Roger Clemens	12.00
2	Chipper Jones	10.00
3	Alex Rodriguez	15.00
4	Jeff Bagwell	5.00
5	Mark McGwire	15.00
6	Pedro Martinez	6.00
7	Manny Ramirez	5.00
8	Cal Ripken Jr.	20.00
9	Mike Piazza	10.00
10	Derek Jeter	15.00
11	Ken Griffey Jr.	10.00
12	Frank Thomas	5.00
13	Sammy Sosa	12.00
14	Nomar Garciaparra	15.00
15	Greg Maddux	10.00

Shockwave

Baseball's top hitters are spotlighted on a holo-foil front. They are found on the average of 1:4 packs and are numbered on the card back with an "S" prefix.

		NM/M
Complete Set (15):		15.00
Common Player:		.50
Inserted 1:4		
1	Mark McGwire	2.00
2	Sammy Sosa	2.00
3	Manny Ramirez	1.00
4	Ken Griffey Jr.	1.50
5	Vladimir Guerrero	1.00
6	Barry Bonds	2.50
7	Albert Belle	.50
8	Ivan Rodriguez	1.00
9	Chipper Jones	1.50
10	Mo Vaughn	.50
11	Jose Canseco	.75
12	Jeff Bagwell	1.00
13	Matt Williams	.50
14	Alex Rodriguez	2.50
15	Carlos Delgado	.75

UD Authentics

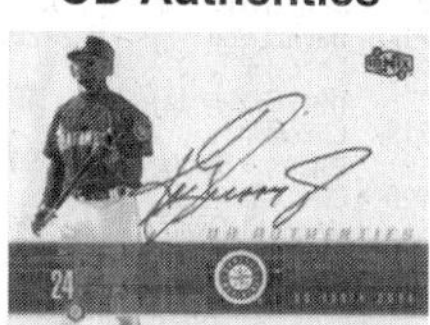

These autographed inserts have a horizontal format and are found on the average of 1:144 packs.

		NM/M
Common Player:		10.00
Inserted 1:144		
CBE	Carlos Beltran	30.00
AB	Adrian Beltre	15.00
PB	Pat Burrell	15.00
JC	Jose Canseco	25.00
SC	Sean Casey	15.00
BD	Ben Davis	10.00
SG	Shawn Green	20.00
JR	Ken Griffey Jr.	100.00
VG	Vladimir Guerrero	30.00
DJ	Derek Jeter	100.00
GK	Gabe Kapler	10.00
RM	Ruben Mateo	10.00
RB	Joe McEwing	10.00
MR	Manny Ramirez	35.00
SR	Scott Rolen	30.00
MW	Matt Williams	15.00

Warp Zone

This 15-card set has a holo-foiled front with an insertion ratio of 1:288 packs. Card backs are numbered with a "WZ" prefix.

		NM/M
Complete Set (15):		250.00
Common Player:		8.00
Inserted 1:288		
1	Cal Ripken Jr.	30.00
2	Barry Bonds	30.00
3	Ken Griffey Jr.	20.00
4	Nomar Garciaparra	25.00
5	Chipper Jones	20.00
6	Ivan Rodriguez	8.00
7	Greg Maddux	20.00
8	Derek Jeter	25.00
9	Mike Piazza	20.00
10	Sammy Sosa	20.00
11	Roger Clemens	20.00
12	Alex Rodriguez	25.00
13	Vladimir Guerrero	10.00
14	Pedro Martinez	10.00
15	Mark McGwire	25.00

3,000 Hit Club

Upper Deck's cross-brand insert series paying tribute to baseball's 3,000 Hit Club members spotlights Roberto Clemente in UD Ionix. Three versions were randomly inserted: A game-used bat card, bat/cut signature card and a cut signature card.

		NM/M
RC1	Roberto Clemente/ Bat/350	125.00

2000 Upper Deck Legends

The 135-card base set consists of 90 regular player cards, 30 20th Century Legends (1:5) and 15 Generation Y2K (1:9). The base cards have a full foiled front with silver foil stamping. Card backs have complete year-by-year statistics.

		NM/M
Complete Set (135):		80.00
Common Player:		.15
Common Y2K:		.75
Inserted 1:9		
Common 20th Century Legend		1.00
Inserted 1:5		
Pack (7):		5.00
Box (24):		90.00
1	Darin Erstad	.25
2	Troy Glaus	.75
3	Mo Vaughn	.20
4	Craig Biggio	.25
5	Jeff Bagwell	.75
6	Reggie Jackson	1.00
7	Tim Hudson	.25
8	Jason Giambi	1.00
9	Hank Aaron	2.00
10	Greg Maddux	1.50
11	Chipper Jones	1.50
12	Andres Galarraga	.25
13	Robin Yount	.50
14	Jeromy Burnitz	.15
15	Paul Molitor	.50
16	David Wells	.15
17	Carlos Delgado	.75
18	Ernie Banks	.75
19	Sammy Sosa	2.00
20	Kerry Wood	.40
21	Stan Musial	.75
22	Bob Gibson	.50
23	Mark McGwire	2.00
24	Fernando Tatis	.15
25	Randy Johnson	1.00
26	Matt Williams	.40
27	Jackie Robinson	2.00
28	Sandy Koufax	1.50
29	Shawn Green	.40
30	Kevin Brown	.25
31	Gary Sheffield	.40
32	Greg Vaughn	.15
33	Jose Canseco	.50
34	Gary Carter	.15
35	Vladimir Guerrero	.75
36	Willie Mays	2.00
37	Barry Bonds	2.00
38	Jeff Kent	.25
39	Bob Feller	.40
40	Roberto Alomar	.50
41	Jim Thome	.75
42	Manny Ramirez	.75
43	Alex Rodriguez	2.00
44	Preston Wilson	.15
45	Tom Seaver	.75
46	Robin Ventura	.15
47	Mike Piazza	1.50
48	Mike Hampton	.15
49	Brooks Robinson	.75
50	Frank Robinson	.75
51	Cal Ripken Jr.	2.50
52	Albert Belle	.20
53	Eddie Murray	.40
54	Tony Gwynn	1.00
55	Roberto Clemente	1.50
56	Willie Stargell	.25
57	Brian Giles	.25
58	Jason Kendall	.25
59	Mike Schmidt	1.00
60	Bob Abreu	.25
61	Scott Rolen	.50
62	Curt Schilling	.40
63	Johnny Bench	1.00
64	Sean Casey	.15
65	Barry Larkin	.25
66	Ken Griffey Jr.	1.50
67	George Brett	1.50
68	Carlos Beltran	.15
69	Nolan Ryan	3.00
70	Ivan Rodriguez	.75
71	Rafael Palmeiro	.40
72	Larry Walker	.25
73	Todd Helton	.75
74	Jeff Cirillo	.15
75	Carl Everett	.15
76	Nomar Garciaparra	2.00
77	Pedro Martinez	1.00
78	Harmon Killebrew	.50
79	Corey Koskie	.15
80	Ty Cobb	2.00
81	Dean Palmer	.15
82	Juan Gonzalez	.75
83	Carlton Fisk	.15
84	Frank Thomas	.75
85	Magglio Ordonez	.25
86	Lou Gehrig	2.00
87	Babe Ruth	3.00
88	Derek Jeter	2.50
89	Roger Clemens	1.50
90	Bernie Williams	.50
91	Rick Ankiel (Generation Y2K)	.75
92	Kip Wells (Generation Y2K)	.75
93	Pat Burrell (Generation Y2K)	1.50
94	Mark Quinn (Generation Y2K)	.75
95	Ruben Mateo (Generation Y2K)	.75
96	Adam Kennedy (Generation Y2K)	.75
97	Brad Penny (Generation Y2K)	.75
98	Kazuhiro Sasaki **RC** (Generation Y2K)	2.00
99	Peter Bergeron (Generation Y2K)	.75
100	Rafael Furcal (Generation Y2K)	1.00
101	Eric Munson (Generation Y2K)	.75
102	Nick Johnson (Generation Y2K)	1.00
103	Rob Bell (Generation Y2K)	.75
104	Vernon Wells (Generation Y2K)	1.00
105	Ben Petrick (Generation Y2K)	.75
106	Babe Ruth (20th Century Legends)	8.00
107	Mark McGwire (20th Century Legends)	6.00
108	Nolan Ryan (20th Century Legends)	8.00
109	Hank Aaron (20th Century Legends)	5.00
110	Barry Bonds (20th Century Legends)	6.00
111	Nomar Garciaparra (20th Century Legends)	5.00
112	Roger Clemens (20th Century Legends)	5.00
113	Johnny Bench (20th Century Legends)	2.50
114	Alex Rodriguez (20th Century Legends)	6.00
115	Cal Ripken Jr. (20th Century Legends)	8.00
116	Willie Mays (20th Century Legends)	6.00
117	Mike Piazza (20th Century Legends)	4.00
118	Reggie Jackson (20th Century Legends)	2.00
119	Tony Gwynn (20th Century Legends)	3.00
120	Cy Young (20th Century Legends)	2.00
121	George Brett (20th Century Legends)	4.00
122	Greg Maddux (20th Century Legends)	4.00
123	Yogi Berra (20th Century Legends)	2.00
124	Sammy Sosa (20th Century Legends)	5.00
125	Randy Johnson (20th Century Legends)	2.50
126	Bob Gibson (20th Century Legends)	2.00
127	Lou Gehrig (20th Century Legends)	6.00
128	Ken Griffey Jr. (20th Century Legends)	4.00
129	Derek Jeter (20th Century Legends)	6.00
130	Mike Schmidt (20th Century Legends)	3.00
131	Pedro Martinez (20th Century Legends)	2.50
132	Jackie Robinson (20th Century Legends)	5.00
133	Jose Canseco (20th Century Legends)	1.00
134	Ty Cobb (20th Century Legends)	5.00
135	Stan Musial (20th Century Legends)	3.00

Gold

Gold graphic enhancements are featured on this parallel edition. On back, a dot-matrix printed "1/1" attests to the status of these cards as unique specimens. Because only one of each card was produced, attaching values can be problematic. Values shown here represent specimens offered at auction shortly after the cards were issued.

		NM/M
Common Player:		75.00
10	Greg Maddux	340.00
13	Robin Yount	450.00
15	Paul Molitor	450.00
31	Gary Sheffield	175.00
36	Willie Mays	1,175
53	Eddie Murray	1,000
82	Juan Gonzalez	230.00
87	Babe Ruth	2,025
89	Roger Clemens	250.00
107	Mark McGwire (20th Century Legends)	1,580
119	Tony Gwynn (20th Century Legends)	190.00
126	Bob Gibson (20th Century Legends)	275.00
130	Mike Schmidt (20th Century Legends)	900.00

Commemorative Collection

A metallized photo background on front distinguishes these 1-of-100 inserts from their base-card parallels. Backs have an ink-jetted serial number from within each card's edition of 100.

Stars (1-90):	4-8X
Y2K:	1-2X
20th Century Legends:	2-3X
Production 100 Sets	

Defining Moments

This 10-card set highlights the featured player's greatest baseball moment with a date stamped in gold foil on the front and a description of the moment on the back. Card backs are numbered with a "DM" prefix and seeded 1:12 packs.

		NM/M
Complete Set (10):		20.00
Common Player:		1.00
Inserted 1:12		
1	Reggie Jackson	1.50
2	Hank Aaron	3.00
3	Babe Ruth	4.00
4	Cal Ripken Jr.	4.00
5	Carlton Fisk	1.00
6	Ken Griffey Jr.	2.00
7	Nolan Ryan	4.00
8	Roger Clemens	2.50
9	Willie Mays	3.00
10	Mark McGwire	3.00

Eternal Glory

This six-card set has a full holo-foiled front with gold foil stamping. Card backs are numbered with an "EG" prefix and are inserted 1:24 packs.

		NM/M
Complete Set (7):		15.00
Common Player:		2.00
Inserted 1:24		
1	Nolan Ryan	4.00
2	Ken Griffey Jr.	2.00
4	Sammy Sosa	2.50
5	Derek Jeter	4.00
6	Willie Mays	3.00
7	Roger Clemens	3.00

Legendary Jerseys

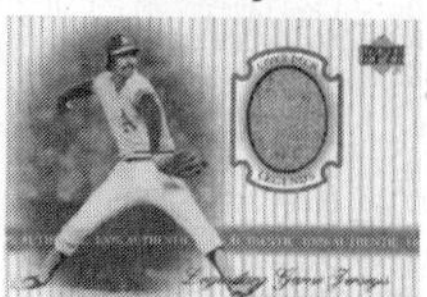

This game-used memorabilia insert set has a swatch of game- used jersey embedded and were inserted 1:48 packs.

		NM/M
Common Player:		8.00
Inserted 1:48		
HA	Hank Aaron	40.00
JB	Jeff Bagwell	10.00
JB	Johnny Bench	20.00
WB	Wade Boggs	10.00
BaB	Barry Bonds	40.00
BoB	Bobby Bonds	8.00
GB	George Brett	30.00
LB	Lou Brock	8.00
JC	Jose Canseco	10.00
RC	Roger Clemens	30.00
DC	Dave Concepcion	8.00
DD	Don Drysdale	25.00
RF	Rollie Fingers	8.00
LG	Lou Gehrig/Pants	250.00
BG	Bob Gibson/Pants	20.00
KG	Ken Griffey Jr.	35.00
TG	Tony Gwynn	20.00
RJ	Reggie Jackson	10.00
DJ	Derek Jeter	40.00
RaJ	Randy Johnson	20.00
CJ	Chipper Jones	20.00
SK	Sandy Koufax	250.00
SK	Sandy Koufax/ Auto./32	1,200
GM	Greg Maddux	30.00
MM	Mickey Mantle	150.00
RM	Roger Maris/Pants	60.00
EM	Eddie Mathews	20.00
WM	Willie Mays/SP/29	675.00
BM	Bill Mazeroski	8.00
WMc	Willie McCovey	10.00
TM	Thurman Munson	30.00
DM	Dale Murphy	10.00
SM	Stan Musial/SP/28	650.00
JP	Jim Palmer	8.00
GP	Gaylord Perry	8.00
MR	Manny Ramirez	10.00

CR Cal Ripken Jr. 40.00
BR Brooks Robinson 20.00
FR Frank Robinson 10.00
AR Alex Rodriguez 35.00
NR Nolan Ryan 40.00
MS Mike Schmidt 25.00
TS Tom Seaver 20.00
OS Ozzie Smith 20.00
WS Willie Stargell 8.00
FT Frank Thomas 10.00
JT Joe Torre 8.00
EW Earl Weaver 8.00
MW Matt Williams 8.00
MW Maury Wills 8.00
DW Dave Winfield 10.00

Legendary Signatures

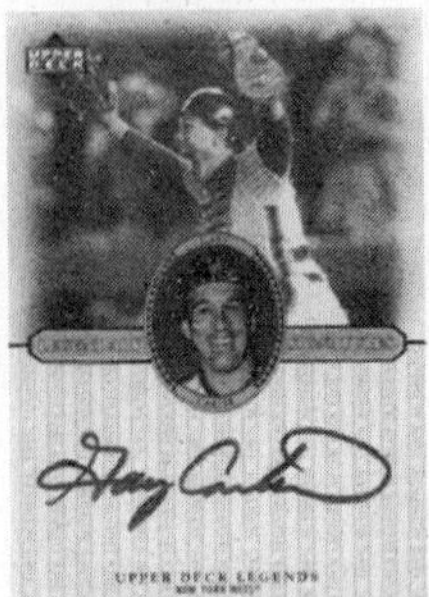

These autographed inserts are signed in blue Sharpie on the bottom panel. A Gold parallel version is also randomly seeded which has gold-foil stamping and is individually numbered to 50.

NM/M
Common Player: 8.00
Inserted 1:23
Golds: 1-2X
Production 50 Sets
HA Hank Aaron/SP/94 275.00
JB Johnny Bench 30.00
BB Bobby Bonds 8.00
LB Lou Brock 8.00
GB George Brett 60.00
JC Jose Canseco 20.00
GC Gary Carter 10.00
SC Sean Casey 8.00
RC Roger Clemens 80.00
DC Dave Concepcion 8.00
AD Andre Dawson 10.00
KG Ken Griffey Jr. 85.00
VG Vladimir Guerrero 30.00
TG Tony Gwynn 40.00
RJ Reggie Jackson 20.00
DJ Derek Jeter/SP/61 400.00
RaJ Randy Johnson 50.00
CJ Chipper Jones 35.00
HK Harmon Killebrew 25.00
FL Fred Lynn 8.00
DM Dale Murphy 15.00
SM Stan Musial 50.00
PN Phil Niekro 8.00
JP Jim Palmer 10.00
MP Mike Piazza 120.00
MR Manny Ramirez/SP/141 60.00
CR Cal Ripken Jr. 120.00
AR Alex Rodriguez 85.00
IR Ivan Rodriguez 25.00
NR Nolan Ryan 85.00
MS Mike Schmidt 50.00
TS Tom Seaver 30.00
OS Ozzie Smith 40.00
WS Willie Stargell 60.00
FT Frank Thomas 30.00
AT Alan Trammell 10.00
BW Matt Williams 8.00

Ones for the Ages

This seven-card set has a holo-foiled front with gold foil etching and stamping. The player image is in a classic picture framed design. Card backs are numbered with an "O" prefix and seeded 1:24 packs.

NM/M
Complete Set (7): 15.00
Inserted 1:24
01 Ty Cobb 2.50
02 Cal Ripken Jr. 4.00
03 Babe Ruth 4.00
04 Jackie Robinson 2.50
05 Mark McGwire 3.00
06 Alex Rodriguez 3.00
07 Mike Piazza 4.00

Reflections in Time

This 10-card horizontal insert set features two players, past and present, linked by significant events or statistics. Card fronts are completely holo-foiled with gold foil stamping. Card backs are numbered with an "R" prefix and inserted 1:12 packs.

NM/M
Complete Set (10): 25.00
Common Player: 2.00
Inserted 1:12
1 Ken Griffey Jr., Hank Aaron 3.00
2 Sammy Sosa, Roberto Clemente 3.00
3 Roger Clemens, Nolan Ryan 4.00
4 Ivan Rodriguez, Johnny Bench 2.00
5 Alex Rodriguez, Ernie Banks 3.00
6 Tony Gwynn, Stan Musial 2.00
7 Barry Bonds, Willie Mays 4.00
8 Cal Ripken Jr., Lou Gehrig 4.00
9 Chipper Jones, Mike Schmidt 2.50
10 Mark McGwire, Babe Ruth 4.00

UD Millennium Team

This nine-card set has a complete holo-foiled front with silver foil stamping. The set is Upper Deck's selections for the all-time 20th century team and are inserted 1:4 packs. Card backs are numbered with an "UD" prefix.

NM/M
Complete Set (10): 15.00
Common Player: 1.50
Inserted 1:4
1 Mark McGwire 2.00
2 Jackie Robinson 2.00
3 Mike Schmidt 1.50
4 Cal Ripken Jr. 3.00
5 Babe Ruth 3.00
7 Willie Mays 2.00
8 Johnny Bench 1.50
9 Nolan Ryan 3.00
10 Ken Griffey Jr. 1.50

3,000 Hit Club

Upper Deck's continuing series pays tribute to Carl Yastrzemski and Paul Molitor. The series includes 350 Bat cards, 350 Jersey cards, 100 Bat/Jersey combo cards and eight au-

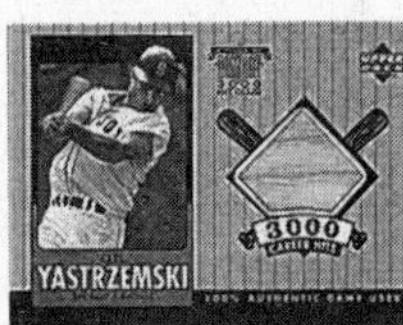

tographed Bat/Jersey combo cards from Yastrzemski and 350 Bat cards from Molitor.

NM/M
CY Carl Yastrzemski/Bat/350 30.00
CY Carl Yastrzemski/Jsy/350 30.00
CY Carl Yastrzemski/Bat/Jsy/100 80.00

2000 Upper Deck MVP

The base set consists of 220-cards with a white bordered design and bronze foil stamping. Card backs have a maximum of 10 year-by-year statistics.

NM/M
Complete Set (220): 20.00
Common Player: .10
Pack (10): 1.25
Wax Box (28): 25.00
1 Garret Anderson .25
2 Mo Vaughn .15
3 Tim Salmon .20
4 Ramon Ortiz .10
5 Darin Erstad .25
6 Troy Glaus .50
7 Troy Percival .10
8 Jeff Bagwell .50
9 Ken Caminiti .10
10 Daryle Ward .10
11 Craig Biggio .25
12 Jose Lima .10
13 Moises Alou .20
14 Octavio Dotel .10
15 Ben Grieve .10
16 Jason Giambi .50
17 Tim Hudson .20
18 Eric Chavez .20
19 Matt Stairs .10
20 Miguel Tejada .25
21 John Jaha .10
22 Chipper Jones 1.00
23 Kevin Millwood .20
24 Brian Jordan .10
25 Andruw Jones .25
26 Andres Galarraga .20
27 Greg Maddux 1.00
28 Reggie Sanders .10
29 Javy Lopez .20
30 Jeromy Burnitz .10
31 Kevin Barker .10
32 Jose Hernandez .10
33 Ron Belliard .10
34 Henry Blanco .10
35 Marquis Grissom .10
36 Geoff Jenkins .20
37 Carlos Delgado .50
38 Raul Mondesi .20
39 Roy Halladay .20
40 Tony Batista .10
41 David Wells .10
42 Shannon Stewart .10
43 Vernon Wells .20
44 Sammy Sosa 1.00
45 Ismael Valdes .10
46 Joe Girardi .10
47 Mark Grace .20
48 Henry Rodriguez .10
49 Kerry Wood .25
50 Eric Young .10
51 Mark McGwire 2.00
52 Daryle Kile .10
53 Fernando Vina .10
54 Ray Lankford .10
55 J.D. Drew .20
56 Fernando Tatis .10
57 Rick Ankiel .10
58 Matt Williams .20
59 Erubiel Durazo .15
60 Tony Womack .10
61 Jay Bell .10
62 Randy Johnson .75
63 Steve Finley .10
64 Matt Mantei .10
65 Luis Gonzalez .20
66 Gary Sheffield .25
67 Eric Gagne .10
68 Adrian Beltre .20
69 Mark Grudzielanek .10
70 Kevin Brown .20
71 Chan Ho Park .10
72 Shawn Green .40
73 Vinny Castilla .15
74 Fred McGriff .25
75 Wilson Alvarez .10
76 Greg Vaughn .10
77 Gerald Williams .10
78 Ryan Rupe .10
79 Jose Canseco .25
80 Vladimir Guerrero .50
81 Dustin Hermanson .10
82 Michael Barrett .10
83 Rondell White .20
84 Tony Armas Jr. .10
85 Wilton Guerrero .10
86 Jose Vidro .10
87 Barry Bonds 1.50
88 Russ Ortiz .10
89 Ellis Burks .10
90 Jeff Kent .20
91 Russ Davis .10
92 J.T. Snow .10
93 Roberto Alomar .40
94 Manny Ramirez .50
95 Chuck Finley .10
96 Kenny Lofton .20
97 Jim Thome .50
98 Bartolo Colon .20
99 Omar Vizquel .20
100 Richie Sexson .25
101 Mike Cameron .10
102 Brett Tomko .10
103 Edgar Martinez .20
104 Alex Rodriguez 1.50
105 John Olerud .20
106 Fred Garcia .10
107 Kazuhiro Sasaki **RC** 1.00
108 Preston Wilson .20
109 Luis Castillo .10
110 A.J. Burnett .10
111 Mike Lowell .10
112 Cliff Floyd .10
113 Brad Penny .10
114 Alex Gonzalez .10
115 Mike Piazza 1.00
116 Derek Bell .10
117 Edgardo Alfonzo .10
118 Rickey Henderson .20
119 Todd Zeile .10
120 Mike Hampton .10
121 Al Leiter .20
122 Robin Ventura .20
123 Cal Ripken Jr. 1.50
124 Mike Mussina .40
125 B.J. Surhoff .10
126 Jerry Hairston Jr. .10
127 Brady Anderson .10
128 Albert Belle .10
129 Sidney Ponson .10
130 Tony Gwynn .75
131 Ryan Klesko .10
132 Sterling Hitchcock .10
133 Eric Owens .10
134 Trevor Hoffman .10
135 Al Martin .10
136 Bret Boone .25
137 Brian Giles .25
138 Chad Hermansen .10
139 Kevin Young .10
140 Kris Benson .10
141 Warren Morris .10
142 Jason Kendall .20
143 Wil Cordero .10
144 Scott Rolen .50
145 Curt Schilling .40
146 Doug Glanville .10
147 Mike Lieberthal .10
148 Mike Jackson .10
149 Rico Brogna .10
150 Andy Ashby .10
151 Bob Abreu .20
152 Sean Casey .20
153 Pete Harnisch .10
154 Dante Bichette .10
155 Pokey Reese .10
156 Aaron Boone .20
157 Ken Griffey Jr. 1.00
158 Barry Larkin .25
159 Scott Williamson .10
160 Carlos Beltran .20
161 Jermaine Dye .10
162 Jose Rosado .10
163 Joe Randa .10
164 Johnny Damon .20
165 Mike Sweeney .10
166 Mark Quinn .10
167 Ivan Rodriguez .40
168 Rusty Greer .10
169 Ruben Mateo .10
170 Doug Davis .10
171 Gabe Kapler .10
172 Justin Thompson .10
173 Rafael Palmeiro .40
174 Larry Walker .20
175 Neifi Perez .10
176 Rolando Arrojo .10
177 Jeffrey Hammonds .10
178 Todd Helton .50
179 Pedro Astacio .10
180 Jeff Cirillo .10
181 Pedro Martinez .75
182 Carl Everett .10
183 Troy O'Leary .10
184 Nomar Garciaparra 1.25
185 Jose Offerman .10
186 Bret Saberhagen .10
187 Trot Nixon .10
188 Jason Varitek .10
189 Todd Walker .10
190 Eric Milton .10
191 Chad Allen .10
192 Jacque Jones .10
193 Brad Radke .10
194 Corey Koskie .10
195 Joe Mays .10
196 Juan Gonzalez .50
197 Jeff Weaver .10
198 Juan Encarnacion .10
199 Deivi Cruz .10
200 Damion Easley .10
201 Tony Clark .10
202 Dean Palmer .10
203 Frank Thomas .50
204 Carlos Lee .10
205 Mike Sirotka .10
206 Kip Wells .10
207 Magglio Ordonez .20
208 Paul Konerko .20
209 Chris Singleton .10
210 Derek Jeter 1.50
211 Tino Martinez .25
212 Mariano Rivera .20
213 Roger Clemens .75
214 Nick Johnson .25
215 Paul O'Neill .20
216 Bernie Williams .40
217 David Cone .20
218 Checklist (Ken Griffey Jr.) .50
219 Checklist (Sammy Sosa) .50
220 Checklist (Mark McGwire) .75

Silver

A parallel to the 220-card base set. These 1:2 pack inserts can be distinguished from the base cards by the silver foil stamping and a silver foiled facsimile signature of the featured player on the card bottom.

Stars: 1-2X
Inserted 1:2

Gold

A parallel to the base set, these can be distinguished from base cards with gold script stamping. Each card is also serial numbered on the card front within an edition of 50 sets.

Stars: 10-20X
Production 50 Sets

Super

A parallel to the 220-card base set, these inserts can be distinguished from the base cards by the holo-foil stamping used on the Upper Deck logo and the featured player's

facsimile signature on the card bottom. The card fronts are also serial numbered within an edition of 25 sets.

Stars: 15-30X
Production 25 Sets

All-Star Game

NM/M
Complete Set (30): 25.00
Common Player: .25
AS1 Mo Vaughn .25
AS2 Jeff Bagwell .75
AS3 Jason Giambi .75
AS4 Chipper Jones 1.50
AS5 Greg Maddux 1.00
AS6 Tony Batista .25
AS7 Sammy Sosa 2.00
AS8 Mark McGwire 2.50
AS9 Randy Johnson .75
AS10 Shawn Green .50
AS11 Greg Vaughn .25
AS12 Vladimir Guerrero .75
AS13 Barry Bonds 2.50
AS14 Manny Ramirez .75
AS15 Alex Rodriguez 2.50
AS16 Preston Wilson .25
AS17 Mike Piazza 1.50
AS18 Cal Ripken Jr. 3.00
AS19 Tony Gwynn 1.00
AS20 Scott Rolen .75
AS21 Ken Griffey Jr. 1.50
AS22 Carlos Beltran .25
AS23 Ivan Rodriguez .60
AS24 Larry Walker .25
AS25 Nomar Garciaparra 2.00
AS26 Pedro Martinez .75
AS27 Juan Gonzalez .75
AS28 Frank Thomas .75
AS29 Derek Jeter 2.50
AS30 Bernie Williams .50

Drawing Power

This seven-card set has a holo-foil front with silver foil stamping. Card backs are numbered with a "DP" prefix.

NM/M
Complete Set (7): 12.00
Common Player: 1.00
Inserted 1:28
1 Mark McGwire 3.00
2 Ken Griffey Jr. 2.00
3 Mike Piazza 2.00
4 Chipper Jones 2.00
5 Nomar Garciaparra 3.00
6 Sammy Sosa 2.50
7 Jose Canseco 1.00

Game Used Souvenirs

These memorabilia inserts feature a game-used piece of glove embedded and are found exclusively in hobby packs at a rate of 1:130 packs.

NM/M
Common Glove: 8.00
Inserted 1:130
RA Roberto Alomar 15.00
JB Jeff Bagwell 20.00

AB	Albert Belle	8.00
BB	Barry Bonds	65.00
JC	Jose Canseco	15.00
WC	Will Clark	20.00
AF	Alex Fernandez	8.00
JG	Jason Giambi	15.00
TGl	Troy Glaus	15.00
AG	Alex Gonzalez	8.00
BG	Ben Grieve	8.00
KG	Ken Griffey Jr.	40.00
VG	Vladimir Guerrero	15.00
TG	Tony Gwynn	30.00
AJ	Andruw Jones	15.00
CJ	Chipper Jones	30.00
KL	Kenny Lofton	8.00
RM	Raul Mondesi	8.00
PO	Paul O'Neill	10.00
RP	Rafael Palmeiro	15.00
MR	Manny Ramirez	15.00
CR	Cal Ripken Jr.	65.00
AR	Alex Rodriguez	40.00
IR	Ivan Rodriguez	15.00
NR	Nolan Ryan	65.00
TS	Tim Salmon	8.00
LW	Larry Walker	8.00
BW	Bernie Williams	15.00
MW	Matt Williams	8.00

Game Used Souvenirs - Bats

These memorabilia inserts have a piece of game-used bat embedded and are seeded exclusively in hobby packs at a rate of 1:130 packs.

		NM/M
Common Bat:		8.00
Inserted 1:130		
BB	Barry Bonds	40.00
JC	Jose Canseco	8.00
KG	Ken Griffey Jr.	20.00
VG	Vladimir Guerrero	10.00
TG	Tony Gwynn	15.00
CJ	Chipper Jones	15.00
MR	Manny Ramirez	10.00
AR	Alex Rodriguez	20.00
IR	Ivan Rodriguez	8.00
BW	Bernie Williams	10.00

Game Used Souvenirs - Bats Auto.

Production 25 Sets
Values Undetermined

Prolifics

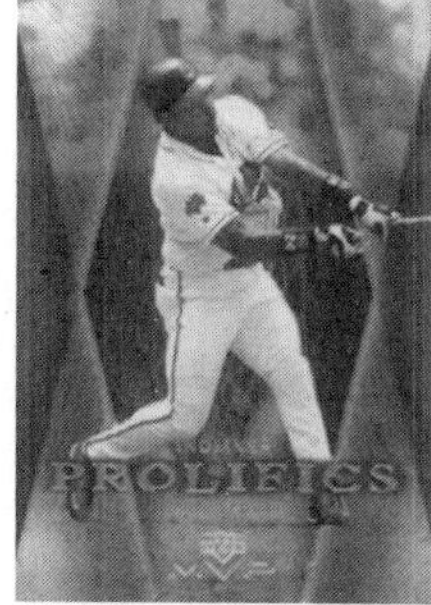

This seven-card set features a full holo-foiled front with silver foil stamping and are seeded 1:28 packs. Card backs are numbered with a "P" prefix.

		NM/M
Complete Set (7):		10.00
Common Player:		.50
Inserted 1:28		
1	Manny Ramirez	1.00
2	Vladimir Guerrero	1.00
3	Derek Jeter	3.00
4	Pedro Martinez	1.50
5	Shawn Green	.50
6	Alex Rodriguez	3.00
7	Cal Ripken Jr.	4.00

ProSign

These autographed inserts are found exclusively in retail packs at a rate of 1:216.

		NM/M
Common Player:		5.00
Inserted 1:216 R		

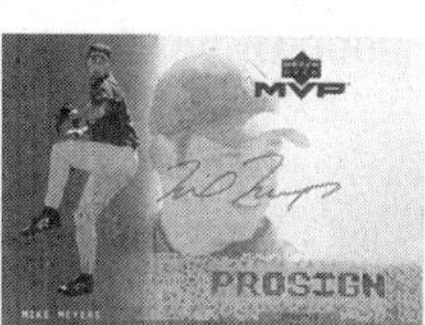

RA	Rick Ankiel	5.00
MB	Michael Barrett	5.00
RB	Rob Bell	5.00
CB	Carlos Beltran	20.00
LB	Lance Berkman	15.00
RB	Rico Brogna	5.00
SC	Sean Casey	8.00
DD	Doug Davis	5.00
ED	Erubiel Durazo	8.00
RF	Robert Fick	8.00
NG	Nomar Garciaparra	65.00
AG	Alex Gonzalez	8.00
KG	Ken Griffey Jr.	60.00
TG	Tony Gwynn	40.00
TH	Tim Hudson	15.00
DJ	Derek Jeter	80.00
CJ	Chipper Jones	50.00
MM	Mike Meyers	5.00
EM	Eric Milton	8.00
JM	Jim Morris	5.00
WM	Warren Morris	5.00
TN	Trot Nixon	8.00
BP	Ben Petrick	5.00
AP	Adam Piatt	5.00
MP	Mike Piazza	60.00
MQ	Mark Quinn	5.00
MR	Manny Ramirez	25.00
RR	Rob Ramsay	5.00
MRe	Mike Redmond	5.00
MRi	Mariano Rivera	15.00
AR	Alex Rodriguez	65.00
MS	Mike Sweeney	8.00
BT	Bubba Trammell	5.00
JV	Jose Vidro	8.00
DW	Daryle Ward	5.00
KW	Kip Wells	8.00
SW	Scott Williamson	5.00
PW	Preston Wilson	8.00
KW	Kevin Witt	5.00
TW	Tony Womack	8.00
EY	Ed Yarnall	5.00
JZ	Jeff Zimmerman	5.00

Pure Grit

These 1:6 pack inserts have a full holo-foiled front with silver foil stamping. Card backs are numbered with a "G" prefix.

		NM/M
Complete Set (10):		10.00
Common Player:		.50
Inserted 1:6		
1	Derek Jeter	2.00
2	Kevin Brown	.50
3	Craig Biggio	.50
4	Ivan Rodriguez	.75
5	Scott Rolen	.75
6	Carlos Beltran	.50
7	Ken Griffey Jr.	1.50
8	Cal Ripken Jr.	2.50
9	Nomar Garciaparra	2.00
10	Randy Johnson	1.00

Scout's Choice

This ten-card set spotlights some of the best prospects in 2000. The inserts have a full holo-foiled front with silver foil stamping. Card backs are numbered with an "SC" prefix and are seeded 1:14 packs.

		NM/M
Complete Set (10):		8.00
Common Player:		.50
Inserted 1:14		
1	Rick Ankiel	.50
2	Vernon Wells	1.00
3	Pat Burrell	1.50
4	Travis Dawkins	.50
5	Eric Munson	.50
6	Nick Johnson	1.00
7	Dermal Brown	.50
8	Alfonso Soriano	2.00
9	Ben Petrick	.50
10	Adam Everett	.50

Second Season Standouts

This 10-card set has a full holo-foiled card front with silver foil stamping. Card backs are numbered with an "SS" prefix and inserted 1:6 packs.

		NM/M
Complete Set (10):		6.00
Common Player:		.25
Inserted 1:6		
1	Pedro Martinez	1.00
2	Mariano Rivera	.40
3	Orlando Hernandez	.25
4	Ken Caminiti	.25
5	Bernie Williams	.50
6	Jim Thome	.75
7	Nomar Garciaparra	2.00
8	Edgardo Alfonzo	.25
9	Derek Jeter	2.50
10	Kevin Millwood	.40

3,000 Hit Club

Upper Deck used this cross-brand insert series to salute the players who accomplished 3,000 hits in their career. Stan Musial is featured and offers a game-used memorabilia bat, jersey, jersey/bat combo and combo autograph versions.

		NM/M
Common Player:		
SM	Stan Musial/Jsy-350	30.00
SM	Stan Musial/Bat-350	30.00
SM	Stan Musial/ Jsy/Bat-100	80.00

2000 UD N.Y. Yankees Master Collection

The most popular franchise in sports history was the subject of this Master Collection limited to 500 numbered sets. Issued in a serially-numbered mahogany box with pewter team-logo inlay, each set includes 25 cards honoring the Yankees' World Championships between 1923-1999. There is also a "Team of the Century" card set with 10 game-used bat cards and a special Gehrig commemorative. Each set also includes a Mystery Pack containing one of 14 autographed memorabilia cards. Retail price at time of issue was around $6,000. Because unopened sets may contain one of the better "Mystery Pack" cards, they maintain a significant premium.

	NM/M
Complete Boxed Set, Unopened:	3,250
Complete Boxed Set, Opened:	1,650
N.Y. Yankees Master Collection Wood Box	100.00

Mystery Cards

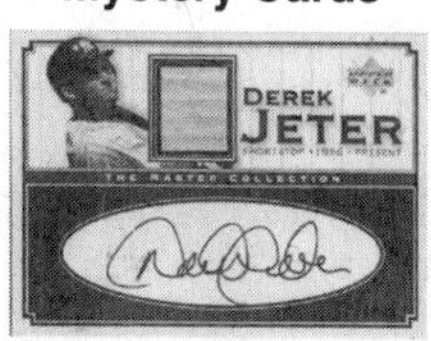

Each Master Collection set contains one foil-pack Mystery Card ranging from autographed player memorabilia-cards to cut signatures. The Gehrig, Mantle, Martin, Munson and Ruth cards are each uniquely numbered on back with the player's initials or initials plus "C" (for cut signature) as a prefix. The Berra, Ford, Jackson and Jeter cards are not "numbered," but are identified by player initials and type of memorabilia. The number issued of each card is shown in parentheses. Some cards remain unpriced due to rarity.

		NM/M
Unopened Mystery Pack:		600.00
BM	Billy Martin/2/Bat/Cut (8/05 Auction)	615.00
BR	Babe Ruth/3/Bat/Cut	9,500
BR-C	Babe Ruth/3/Cut	7,500
DJ-B	Derek Jeter/ 100/Bat/Auto.	450.00
DJ-J	Derek Jeter/ 100/Jsy/Auto.	500.00
LG-C	Lou Gehrig/2/Cut	3,000
MM	Mickey Mantle/7/ Bat/Cut	4,000
RJ-B	Reggie Jackson/ 100/Bat/Auo.	400.00
WF-J	Whitey Ford/ 100/Jsy/Auto.	450.00
YB-B	Yogi Berra/80/ Bat/Auto.	450.00

Team of the Century

An 11-player "Team of the Century" card set within the Yankees Master Collection features game-used bat cards from 10 of the players and a special Lou Gehrig commemorative card (Upper Deck could not get a Gehrig gamer to cut up for the cards). Each card carries an individual serial number from an edition of 500 each.

		NM/M
Complete Set (11):		1,575
Common Player:		35.00
ATY1	Babe Ruth	400.00
ATY2	Mickey Mantle	550.00
ATY3	Reggie Jackson	135.00
ATY4	Don Mattingly	135.00
ATY5	Billy Martin	90.00
ATY6	Graig Nettles	55.00
ATY7	Derek Jeter	110.00
ATY8	Yogi Berra	135.00
ATY9	Thurman Munson	145.00
ATY10	Whitey Ford	110.00
ATY11	Lou Gehrig	35.00

World Series Champions

Each of the Yankees' 25 World Series Championships between 1923-1999 is marked with one of these "base" cards in the Master Collection. Fronts of the 2-1/2" x 3-1/2" cards have black-and-white or color poses or action photos highlighted with holographic foil. Backs have a portrait photo, a World Series summary and the player's career and Series stats. Each card is serially numbered within an edition of 500.

		NM/M
Complete Set (25):		480.00
Common Player:		12.50
NYY1	Babe Ruth/1923	50.00
NYY2	Lou Gehrig/1927	35.00
NYY3	Tony Lazzeri/1928	12.50
NYY4	Babe Ruth/1932	50.00
NYY5	Lou Gehrig/1936	35.00
NYY6	Lefty Gomez/1937	25.00
NYY7	Bill Dickey/1938	25.00
NYY8	Bill Dickey/1939	25.00
NYY9	Tommy Henrich/ 1941	17.50
NYY10	Spud Chandler/ 1943	12.50
NYY11	Tommy Henrich/ 1947	17.50
NYY12	Phil Rizzuto/1949	25.00
NYY13	Whitey Ford/1950	25.00
NYY14	Yogi Berra/1951	30.00
NYY15	Casey Stengel/1952	17.50
NYY16	Billy Martin/1953	17.50
NYY17	Don Larsen/1956	22.00
NYY18	Elston Howard/1958	12.50
NYY19	Roger Maris/1961	30.00
NYY20	Mickey Mantle/1962	50.00
NYY21	Reggie Jackson/1977	30.00
NYY22	Bucky Dent/1978	15.00
NYY23	Derek Jeter/1996	25.00
NYY24	Derek Jeter/1998	25.00
NYY25	Derek Jeter/1999	25.00

Opening Day 2K

As part of a multi-manufacturer promotion, UD issued eight cards of an "Opening Day 2K" set. Packages containing some of the 32 cards in the issue were distributed by MLB teams early in the season. The cards were also available exclusively as inserts in Upper Deck Victory and Hitters Club packs sold at K-Mart stores early in the season. The Upper Deck OD2K cards have gold-foil graphic highlights on front. Backs have a monochromatic version of the front photo and are numbered with an "OD" prefix.

		NM/M
Complete Set (8):		6.00
Common Player:		.50
17	Ken Griffey Jr.	1.50
18	Sammy Sosa	1.00
19	Pedro Martinez	.75
20	Manny Ramirez	.65
21	Shawn Green	.65
22	Carlos Beltran	.40
23	Juan Gonzalez	.50
24	Jeromy Burnitz	.50

2000 Upper Deck Ovation

The base set consists of 90-cards, including a 20-card World Premiere subset and 10-card Superstar Spotlight subset. World Premiere's are found 1:3 packs and Superstar Spotlight's 1:6 packs. Card fronts are embossed, intended to resemble the feel of a baseball and also has silver foil stamping.

		NM/M
Complete Set (90):		65.00
Common Player:		.25
Common World Prem. (61-80):		1.00
Inserted 1:3		
Common Super. Spot (81-90):		1.50
Inserted 1:6		
Pack (5):		2.00
Wax Box (20):		30.00
1	Mo Vaughn	.25
2	Troy Glaus	.75
3	Jeff Bagwell	.75
4	Craig Biggio	.40
5	Mike Hampton	.25
6	Jason Giambi	.75
7	Tim Hudson	.40
8	Chipper Jones	1.50
9	Greg Maddux	1.50
10	Kevin Millwood	.40
11	Brian Jordan	.25
12	Jeromy Burnitz	.25
13	David Wells	.25
14	Carlos Delgado	.75
15	Sammy Sosa	2.50
16	Mark McGwire	3.00
17	Matt Williams	.25
18	Randy Johnson	.75
19	Erubiel Durazo	.40
20	Kevin Brown	.40
21	Shawn Green	.75
22	Gary Sheffield	.50
23	Jose Canseco	.50
24	Vladimir Guerrero	1.00
25	Barry Bonds	3.00
26	Manny Ramirez	.75
27	Roberto Alomar	.75
28	Richie Sexson	.40
29	Jim Thome	.75
30	Alex Rodriguez	2.50
31	Ken Griffey Jr.	1.50
32	Preston Wilson	.25

33	Mike Piazza	1.50
34	Al Leiter	.25
35	Robin Ventura	.25
36	Cal Ripken Jr.	3.00
37	Albert Belle	.25
38	Tony Gwynn	1.00
39	Brian Giles	.40
40	Jason Kendall	.40
41	Scott Rolen	.75
42	Bob Abreu	.40
43	Ken Griffey Jr.	1.50
44	Sean Casey	.25
45	Carlos Beltran	.40
46	Gabe Kapler	.25
47	Ivan Rodriguez	.75
48	Rafael Palmeiro	.50
49	Larry Walker	.40
50	Nomar Garciaparra	2.00
51	Pedro J. Martinez	1.00
52	Eric Milton	.25
53	Juan Gonzalez	.75
54	Tony Clark	.25
55	Frank Thomas	.75
56	Magglio Ordonez	.40
57	Roger Clemens	1.50
58	Derek Jeter	2.50
59	Bernie Williams	.50
60	Orlando Hernandez	.40
61	Rick Ankiel (World Premiere)	1.00
62	Josh Beckett (World Premiere)	1.50
63	Vernon Wells (World Premiere)	1.50
64	Alfonso Soriano (World Premiere)	3.00
65	Pat Burrell (World Premiere)	2.00
66	Eric Munson (World Premiere)	1.00
67	Chad Hutchinson (World Premiere)	1.00
68	Eric Gagne (World Premiere)	1.00
69	Peter Bergeron (World Premiere)	1.00
70	Ryan Anderson (Supposed to have been withdrawn, all known cards have embossed UD racing mark.)	300.00
71	A.J. Burnett (World Premiere)	1.00
72	Jorge Luis Toca (World Premiere)	1.00
73	Matt Riley (World Premiere)	1.00
74	Chad Hermansen (World Premiere)	1.00
75	Doug Davis (World Premiere)	1.00
76	Jim Morris (World Premiere)	1.00
77	Ben Petrick (World Premiere)	1.00
78	Mark Quinn (World Premiere)	1.00
79	Ed Yarnall (World Premiere)	1.00
80	Ramon Ortiz (World Premiere)	1.00
81	Ken Griffey Jr. (Superstar Spotlight)	3.00
82	Mark McGwire (Superstar Spotlight)	5.00
83	Derek Jeter (Superstar Spotlight)	5.00
84	Jeff Bagwell (Superstar Spotlight)	1.50
85	Nomar Garciaparra (Superstar Spotlight)	5.00
86	Sammy Sosa (Superstar Spotlight)	4.00
87	Mike Piazza (Superstar Spotlight)	3.00
88	Alex Rodriguez (Superstar Spotlight)	5.00
89	Cal Ripken Jr. (Superstar Spotlight)	6.00
90	Pedro Martinez (Superstar Spotlight)	2.00

Standing Ovation

A parallel to the 120-card base set, these are identical to the base cards besides the holographic silver stamping on the card front and the backs serially numbered to 50.

Stars (1-60):	8-15X
World Prem. (61-80):	2-3X
Super. Spot. (81-90):	3-5X
Production 50 Sets	

A Piece of History

These memorabilia inserts feature a piece of game-used bat embedded and are limited to 400 sets produced.

		NM/M
Common Player:		5.00
Production 400 Sets		
JB	Jeff Bagwell	10.00
CB	Carlos Beltran	10.00
SC	Sean Casey	5.00
KG	Ken Griffey Jr.	25.00
DJ	Derek Jeter	35.00
TG	Tony Gwynn	15.00
AJ	Andruw Jones	10.00
CJ	Chipper Jones	20.00
RP	Rafael Palmeiro	10.00
MP	Mike Piazza	20.00
MR	Manny Ramirez	10.00
CR	Cal Ripken Jr.	35.00
AR	Alex Rodriguez	25.00
SR	Scott Rolen	15.00
SS	Sammy Sosa	25.00
FT	Frank Thomas	10.00

A Piece of History - Signed

Values Undetermined

Center Stage

Ten of baseball's top performers are highlighted on a card that features gold foil stamping and etching. Card backs are numbered with an "CS" prefix and are seeded 1:9 packs. Two parallels to this insert set are randomly inserted: Golds are found 1:39 packs and Rainbows are seeded 1:99 packs.

		NM/M
Complete Set (10):		20.00
Common Player:		1.00
Inserted 1:9		
Gold:		2X
Inserted 1:39		
Rainbow:		3-4X
Inserted 1:99		
1	Jeff Bagwell	1.00
2	Ken Griffey Jr.	2.00
3	Nomar Garciaparra	3.00
4	Mike Piazza	2.00
5	Mark McGwire	3.00
6	Alex Rodriguez	3.00
7	Cal Ripken Jr.	4.00
8	Derek Jeter	3.00
9	Chipper Jones	2.00
10	Sammy Sosa	2.50

Curtain Calls

This 20-card set features gold foil stamping and highlights some memorable playoff moments. Card backs are numbered with a "CC" prefix.

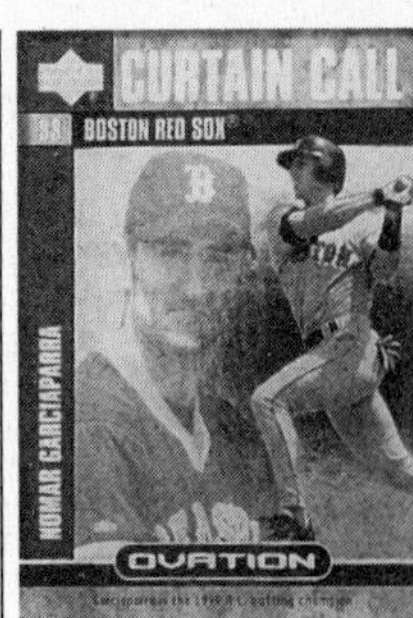

		NM/M
Complete Set (20):		15.00
Common Player:		.50
Inserted 1:3		
1	David Cone	.50
2	Mark McGwire	2.00
3	Sammy Sosa	2.00
4	Eric Milton	.50
5	Bernie Williams	.75
6	Tony Gwynn	1.00
7	Nomar Garciaparra	2.00
8	Manny Ramirez	1.00
9	Wade Boggs	.50
10	Randy Johnson	1.00
11	Cal Ripken Jr.	3.00
12	Pedro J. Martinez	1.00
13	Alex Rodriguez	2.00
14	Fernando Tatis	.50
15	Vladimir Guerrero	1.00
16	Robin Ventura	.50
17	Larry Walker	.50
18	Carlos Beltran	.50
19	Jose Canseco	.75
20	Ken Griffey Jr.	1.50

Diamond Futures

This 10-card set highlights some of baseball's top prospects on a full foiled front with silver foil stamping. Card backs are numbered with a "DM" prefix.

		NM/M
Complete Set (10):		8.00
Common Player:		.50
Inserted 1:6		
1	J.D. Drew	.75
2	Alfonso Soriano	2.50
3	Preston Wilson	1.00
4	Erubiel Durazo	.75
5	Rick Ankiel	.50
6	Octavio Dotel	.50
7	A.J. Burnett	.50
8	Carlos Beltran	.75
9	Vernon Wells	1.00
10	Troy Glaus	2.00

Lead Performers

Upper Deck chose 10 players for this set who are thought of as leaders on and off the field. Card fronts have silver foil stamping and card backs are numbered with an "LP" prefix.

		NM/M
Complete Set (10):		20.00
Common Player:		1.00
Inserted 1:19		
1	Mark McGwire	3.00
2	Derek Jeter	3.00
3	Vladimir Guerrero	1.00
4	Mike Piazza	2.00
5	Cal Ripken Jr.	4.00
6	Sammy Sosa	2.50
7	Jeff Bagwell	1.00
8	Nomar Garciaparra	3.00
9	Chipper Jones	2.00
10	Ken Griffey Jr.	2.00

Super Signatures

This two-card insert set features Ken Griffey Jr. and Mike Piazza. Spotlighting the autographs of Griffey and Piazza, Super Signatures is issued in three versions: Silver, numbered to 100; Gold, numbered to 50; and Rainbow, numbered to 10.

		NM/M
Common Card:		
KG	Ken Griffey/Gold/50	180.00
KG	Ken Griffey/ Silver/100	100.00
MP	Mike Piazza/Gold/50	180.00
MP	Mike Piazza/ Silver/100	150.00

Superstar Theatre

This 20-card set is printed on a full foiled card front enhanced by silver foil stamping and etching. Card backs are numbered with an "ST" prefix.

		NM/M
Complete Set (20):		20.00
Common Player:		.50
Inserted 1:19		
1	Ivan Rodriguez	1.00
2	Brian Giles	.50
3	Bernie Williams	1.00
4	Greg Maddux	2.00
5	Frank Thomas	1.00
6	Sean Casey	.50
7	Mo Vaughn	.50
8	Carlos Delgado	1.00
9	Tony Gwynn	1.50
10	Pedro Martinez	1.50
11	Scott Rolen	1.00
12	Mark McGwire	3.00
13	Manny Ramirez	1.00
14	Rafael Palmeiro	.75
15	Jose Canseco	.75
16	Randy Johnson	1.50
17	Gary Sheffield	.75
18	Larry Walker	.50
19	Barry Bonds	4.00
20	Roger Clemens	3.00

3,000 Hit Club

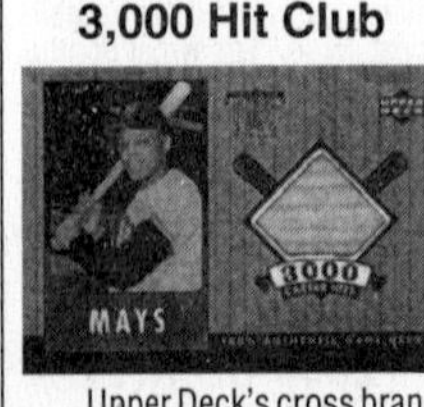

Upper Deck's cross brand insert series pays tribute to members of the elite 3,000 Hit Club. Ovation features Willie Mays in the series, which has four versions: Bat card, 300 produced; Jersey card, 350 produced; Bat/Jersey combo, 50 produced; and Bat/Jersey autograph, 24 produced.

		NM/M
1	Willie Mays/Jsy/350	40.00
2	Willie Mays/Bat/300	40.00
3	Willie Mays/ Jsy/Bat/50	180.00
4	Willie Mays/ Jersey/Bat/Auto./24	675.00

2000 Upper Deck PowerDeck

		NM/M
Complete Set (12):		50.00
Common Card:		3.00
Pack (1):		4.00
Box:		40.00
1	Sammy Sosa	6.00
2	Ken Griffey Jr.	6.00
3	Mark McGwire	8.00
4	Derek Jeter	6.00
5	Alex Rodriguez	8.00
6	Nomar Garciaparra	6.00
7	Mike Piazza	5.00
8	Cal Ripken Jr.	8.00
9	Ivan Rodriguez	3.00
10	Chipper Jones	5.00
11	Pedro Martinez	3.00
12	Manny Ramirez	3.00

Magical Moments

		NM/M
Inserted 1:10 H		
KG	Ken Griffey Jr.	6.00
CR	Cal Ripken Jr.	10.00

Magical Moments Autograph

		NM/M
Each signed 50 cards.		
KG	Ken Griffey Jr.	180.00
CR	Cal Ripken Jr.	275.00

Power Trio

		NM/M
Complete Set (3):		15.00
Common Player:		5.00
Inserted 1:7		
PT1	Derek Jeter	6.00
PT2	Ken Griffey Jr.	5.00
PT3	Mark McGwire	6.00

2000 Upper Deck Pros and Prospects

The 132-card base set consists of 90 regular player cards, a 30-card Prospective Superstars subset and a 12-card Pro- Fame subset. Prospective Superstars are serially numbered to 1,350 and Pro-Fame are serially numbered to 1,000. Card fronts have a white-bordered design with silver foil stamping. Both subsets are serially numbered on the card front.

		NM/M
Complete Set (132):		300.00
Common Player (1-90):		.15
Common (91-120):		5.00
Production 1,350 Sets		
Common (121-132):		4.00
Production 1,000 Sets		
Pack (5):		2.50
Box (24):		40.00
1	Darin Erstad	.40
2	Troy Glaus	.75
3	Mo Vaughn	.20
4	Jason Giambi	.75
5	Tim Hudson	.25
6	Ben Grieve	.15
7	Eric Chavez	.25
8	Shannon Stewart	.15
9	Raul Mondesi	.25
10	Carlos Delgado	.75
11	Jose Canseco	.40
12	Fred McGriff	.25
13	Greg Vaughn	.15
14	Manny Ramirez	.75
15	Roberto Alomar	.50
16	Jim Thome	.75
17	Alex Rodriguez	2.50
18	Fred Garcia	.15
19	John Olerud	.25
20	Cal Ripken Jr.	2.50
21	Albert Belle	.20
22	Mike Mussina	.40
23	Ivan Rodriguez	.50
24	Rafael Palmeiro	.50
25	Ruben Mateo	.15
26	Gabe Kapler	.15
27	Pedro Martinez	1.00
28	Nomar Garciaparra	2.00
29	Carl Everett	.15
30	Carlos Beltran	.25
31	Jermaine Dye	.15
32	Johnny Damon	.25
33	Juan Gonzalez	.75
34	Juan Encarnacion	.15
35	Dean Palmer	.15
36	Jacque Jones	.15
37	Matt Lawton	.15
38	Frank Thomas	.75
39	Paul Konerko	.15
40	Maggio Ordonez	.25
41	Derek Jeter	2.00
42	Bernie Williams	.50
43	Mariano Rivera	.25
44	Roger Clemens	1.50
45	Jeff Bagwell	.75
46	Craig Biggio	.25
47	Richard Hidalgo	.25
48	Chipper Jones	1.50
49	Andres Galarraga	.25
50	Andruw Jones	.50
51	Greg Maddux	1.50
52	Jeromy Burnitz	.15
53	Geoff Jenkins	.25
54	Mark McGwire	2.00
55	Jim Edmonds	.25
56	Fernando Tatis	.15
57	J.D. Drew	.15
58	Sammy Sosa	2.00
59	Kerry Wood	.50
60	Randy Johnson	.75
61	Matt Williams	.25
62	Erubiel Durazo	.15
63	Shawn Green	.25
64	Kevin Brown	.25
65	Gary Sheffield	.25
66	Adrian Beltre	.25
67	Vladimir Guerrero	.75
68	Jose Vidro	.15
69	Barry Bonds	2.00
70	Jeff Kent	.25
71	Preston Wilson	.15
72	Ryan Dempster	.15
73	Mike Lowell	.15
74	Mike Piazza	1.50
75	Robin Ventura	.25
76	Edgardo Alfonzo	.15
77	Derek Bell	.15
78	Tony Gwynn	1.00
79	Matt Clement	.15
80	Scott Rolen	.75
81	Bobby Abreu	.25
82	Curt Schilling	.40
83	Brian Giles	.25
84	Jason Kendall	.25
85	Kris Benson	.15
86	Ken Griffey Jr.	1.50
87	Sean Casey	.25
88	Pokey Reese	.15
89	Larry Walker	.25
90	Todd Helton	.75
91	Rick Ankiel (Prospective Superstars)	5.00
92	Milton Bradley (Prospective Superstars)	5.00
93	Vernon Wells (Prospective Superstars)	6.00
94	Rafael Furcal (Prospective Superstars)	6.00
95	Kazuhiro Sasaki **RC** (Prospective Superstars)	8.00
96	Joe Torres **RC** (Prospective Superstars)	5.00
97	Adam Kennedy (Prospective Superstars)	5.00
98	Adam Piatt (Prospective Superstars)	5.00
99	Matt Wheatland **RC** (Prospective Superstars)	5.00
100	Alex Cabrera **RC** (Prospective Superstars)	5.00
101	Barry Zito **RC** (Prospective Superstars)	25.00
102	Mike Lamb **RC** (Prospective Superstars)	5.00
103	Scott Heard **RC** (Prospective Superstars)	5.00
104	Danys Baez **RC** (Prospective Superstars)	8.00
105	Matt Riley (Prospective Superstars)	5.00
106	Mark Mulder (Prospective Superstars)	6.00

107 Wilfredo Rodriguez **RC** (Prospective Superstars) 5.00
108 Luis Matos **RC** (Prospective Superstars) 10.00
109 Alfonso Soriano (Prospective Superstars) 8.00
110 Pat Burrell (Prospective Superstars) 6.00
111 Mike Tonis **RC** (Prospective Superstars) 5.00
112 Aaron McNeal **RC** (Prospective Superstars) 5.00
113 Dave Krynzel **RC** (Prospective Superstars) 8.00
114 Josh Beckett (Prospective Superstars) 5.00
115 Sean Burnett **RC** (Prospective Superstars) 8.00
116 Eric Munson (Prospective Superstars) 5.00
117 Scott Downs **RC** (Prospective Superstars) 5.00
118 Brian Tollberg **RC** (Prospective Superstars) 5.00
119 Nick Johnson (Prospective Superstars) 5.00
120 Leo Estrella **RC** (Prospective Superstars) 5.00
121 Ken Griffey Jr. (Pro Fame) 8.00
122 Frank Thomas (Pro Fame) 4.00
123 Cal Ripken Jr. (Pro Fame) 15.00
124 Ivan Rodriguez (Pro Fame) 4.00
125 Derek Jeter (Pro Fame) 12.00
126 Mark McGwire (Pro Fame) 12.00
127 Pedro Martinez (Pro Fame) 5.00
128 Chipper Jones (Pro Fame) 8.00
129 Sammy Sosa (Pro Fame) 10.00
130 Alex Rodriguez (Pro Fame) 10.00
131 Vladimir Guerrero (Pro Fame) 4.00
132 Jeff Bagwell (Pro Fame) 4.00

Future Forces

This 10-card set highlights top prospects on a card front featuring gold foil stamping and etching. Card backs are numbered with an "F" prefix.

		NM/M
Complete Set (10):		5.00
Common Player:		.50
Inserted 1:6		
1	Pat Burrell	2.00
2	Brad Penny	.50
3	Rick Ankiel	.50
4	Adam Kennedy	.50
5	Eric Munson	.50
6	Rafael Furcal	.75
7	Mark Mulder	.75
8	Vernon Wells	.75
9	Matt Riley	.50
10	Nick Johnson	.75

ProMotion

This 10-card set spotlights some of baseball's best all- around talents using gold foil stamping. Card backs are numbered with a "P" prefix and are seeded 1:6 packs.

		NM/M
Complete Set (10):		15.00
Common Player:		.75

Inserted 1:6		
1	Derek Jeter	3.00
2	Mike Piazza	1.50
3	Mark McGwire	2.50
4	Ivan Rodriguez	.75
5	Kerry Wood	.75
6	Nomar Garciaparra	2.00
7	Sammy Sosa	2.00
8	Alex Rodriguez	2.50
9	Ken Griffey Jr.	1.50
10	Vladimir Guerrero	1.00

Rare Breed

Baseball's top performers are spotlighted in this 12-card set on a full foiled silver front with gold foil stamping. Card backs are numbered with an "R" prefix and are inserted 1:12 packs.

		NM/M
Complete Set (12):		15.00
Common Player:		.50
Inserted 1:12		
1	Mark McGwire	3.00
2	Frank Thomas	1.00
3	Mike Piazza	2.00
4	Barry Bonds	4.00
5	Manny Ramirez	1.00
6	Ken Griffey Jr.	2.00
7	Nomar Garciaparra	3.00
8	Randy Johnson	1.50
9	Vladimir Guerrero	1.00
10	Jeff Bagwell	1.00
11	Rick Ankiel	.50
12	Alex Rodriguez	3.00

Signed Game-Worn Jerseys

Each of these Game Jersey cards has a piece of jersey swatch and autograph from the featured player. A Level 2 "Gold" version is limited to the player's corresponding uniform number.

		NM/M
Common Player:		25.00
Inserted 1:96		
BB	Barry Bonds	200.00
JC	Jose Canseco	40.00
JD	J.D. Drew	25.00
TG	Tom Glavine	40.00
LG	Luis Gonzalez	25.00
KG	Ken Griffey Jr.	100.00
TG	Tony Gwynn	50.00
DJ	Derek Jeter/SP	350.00
RJ	Randy Johnson	80.00
CJ	Chipper Jones	50.00
KL	Kenny Lofton	25.00
CR	Cal Ripken Jr.	140.00
AR	Alex Rodriguez	120.00
IR	Ivan Rodriguez	40.00
SR	Scott Rolen	50.00
GS	Gary Sheffield	40.00
FT	Frank Thomas	40.00
MV	Mo Vaughn	25.00
RV	Robin Ventura	25.00
MW	Matt Williams	25.00
PW	Preston Wilson	25.00

The Best in the Bigs

This 10-card set spotlights baseball's best performers on a white bordered design with gold foil stamping. Card backs are numbered with a "B" prefix.

		NM/M
Complete Set (10):		15.00
Common Player:		1.00
Inserted 1:12		
1	Sammy Sosa	2.50
2	Tony Gwynn	1.50
3	Pedro Martinez	1.50
4	Mark McGwire	3.00
5	Chipper Jones	2.00
6	Derek Jeter	3.00
7	Ken Griffey Jr.	2.00
8	Cal Ripken Jr.	4.00
9	Greg Maddux	2.00
10	Ivan Rodriguez	1.00

3,000 Hit Club

Upper Deck's continuing series features Lou Brock and Rod Carew. The series features 350 numbered bat cards, 350 numbered jersey cards and 100 numbered bat/jersey combos. Each player also signed the bat/jersey combos to their jersey number, as Brock signed 20 and Carew 29.

	NM/M
Lou Brock/Bat/350	20.00
Lou Brock/Jsy/350	20.00
Lou Brock/ Bat/Jsy/100	40.00
Rod Carew/Bat/350	20.00
Rod Carew/Jsy/350	20.00
Rod Carew/ Bat/Jsy/100	40.00

2000 Upper Deck Rookie Update

		NM/M
Common Player:		.25
Common Rookie:		5.00
Pack (4):		4.50
Box (15):		50.00

SP Authentic Update
(136-164) Production 1,700

136 Barry Zito **RC** (Future Watch) 25.00
137 Aaron McNeal **RC** (Future Watch) 5.00
138 Teofilo Perez (Future Watch) 5.00
139 Sun-Woo Kim **RC** (Future Watch) 5.00
140 Xavier Nady **RC** (Future Watch) 15.00
141 Matt Wheatland **RC** (Future Watch) 5.00
142 Brent Abernathy **RC** (Future Watch) 5.00
143 Cory Vance **RC** (Future Watch) 5.00
144 Scott Heard **RC** (Future Watch) 5.00
145 Mike Meyers **RC** (Future Watch) 5.00
146 Ben Diggins **RC** (Future Watch) 5.00
147 Luis Matos **RC** (Future Watch) 5.00
148 Ben Sheets **RC** (Future Watch) 15.00
149 Kurt Ainsworth **RC** (Future Watch) 5.00
150 Dave Krynzel **RC** (Future Watch) 5.00
151 Alex Cabrera **RC** (Future Watch) 5.00
152 Mike Tonis **RC** (Future Watch) 5.00
153 Dane Sardinha **RC** (Future Watch) 5.00
154 Keith Ginter **RC** (Future Watch) 5.00
155 David Espinosa **RC** (Future Watch) 5.00
156 Joe Torres **RC** (Future Watch) 5.00
157 Daylan Holt **RC** (Future Watch) 5.00
158 Koyie Hill **RC** (Future Watch) 5.00
159 Brad Wilkerson **RC** (Future Watch) 8.00
160 Juan Pierre **RC** (Future Watch) 10.00
161 Matt Ginter **RC** (Future Watch) 5.00
162 Dane Artman **RC** (Future Watch) 5.00
163 Jon Rauch **RC** (Future Watch) 5.00
164 Sean Burnett **RC** (Future Watch) 5.00

166	Darin Erstad	.50
167	Ben Grieve	.25
168	David Wells	.25
169	Fred McGriff	.40
170	Bob Wickman	.25
171	Al Martin	.25
172	Melvin Mora	.25
173	Ricky Ledee	.25
174	Dante Bichette	.25
175	Mike Sweeney	.25
176	Bobby Higginson	.25
177	Matt Lawton	.25
178	Charles Johnson	.25
179	David Justice	.50
180	Richard Hidalgo	.40
181	B.J. Surhoff	.25
182	Richie Sexson	.50
183	Jim Edmonds	.50
184	Rondell White	.25
185	Curt Schilling	.50
186	Tom Goodwin	.25
187	Jose Vidro	.25
188	Ellis Burks	.25
189	Henry Rodriguez	.25
190	Mike Bordick	.25
191	Eric Owens	.25
192	Travis Lee	.25
193	Kevin Young	.25
194	Aaron Boone	.40
195	Todd Hollandsworth	.25

SPx Update
(121-135, 182-196) 1,600
(136-151) Production 1,500

Common Autograph		10.00
121	Brad Wilkerson **RC**	15.00
122	Roy Oswalt **RC**	125.00
123	Wascar Serrano **RC**	5.00
124	Sean Burnett **RC**	10.00
125	Alex Cabrera **RC**	5.00
126	Timoniel Perez **RC**	5.00
127	Juan Pierre **RC**	10.00
128	Daylan Holt **RC**	5.00
129	Tomokazu Ohka **RC**	5.00
130	Kazuhiro Sasaki **RC**	10.00
131	Kurt Ainsworth **RC**	10.00
132	Brent Abernathy **RC**	5.00
133	Danys Baez **RC**	5.00
134	Brad Cresse **RC**	5.00
135	Ryan Franklin	5.00
136	Mike Lamb **RC**	10.00
137	David Espinosa **RC**	5.00
138	Matt Wheatland **RC**	5.00
139	Xavier Nady **RC**	30.00
140	Scott Heard **RC**	5.00
141	Pascual Coco **RC**	5.00
142	Justin Miller **RC**	5.00
143	Dave Krynzel **RC**	10.00
144	Dane Sardinha **RC**	5.00
145	Ben Sheets **RC**	40.00
146	Leo Estrella **RC**	10.00
147	Ben Diggins **RC**	10.00
148	Barry Zito **RC**	40.00
149	Joe Torres **RC**	10.00
150	Mike Meyers **RC**	10.00
151	Kris Wilson **RC**	10.00
152	Darin Erstad	.50
153	Richard Hidalgo	.40
154	Eric Chavez	.50
155	B.J. Surhoff	.25
156	Richie Sexson	.75
157	Raul Mondesi	.50
158	Rondell White	.50
159	Jim Edmonds	.75
160	Curt Schilling	.75
161	Tom Goodwin	.25
162	Fred McGriff	.50
163	Jose Vidro	.25
164	Ellis Burks	.25
165	David Segui	.25
166	Aaron Sele	.25
167	Henry Rodriguez	.25
168	Mike Bordick	.25
169	Mike Mussina	1.00
170	Ryan Klesko	.25
171	Kevin Young	.25
172	Travis Lee	.25
173	Aaron Boone	.50
174	Jermaine Dye	.25
175	Ricky Ledee	.25
176	Jeffrey Hammonds	.25
177	Carl Everett	.25
178	Matt Lawton	.25
179	Bobby Higginson	.25
180	Charles Johnson	.25
181	David Justice	.75
182	Joey Nation **RC**	4.00
183	Rico Washington **RC**	4.00
184	Luis Matos **RC**	10.00
185	Chris Wakeland	4.00
186	Sun-Woo Kim **RC**	4.00
187	Keith Ginter **RC**	5.00
188	Geraldo Guzman **RC**	4.00
189	Jay Spurgeon **RC**	4.00
190	Jace Brewer **RC**	4.00
191	Juan Guzman **RC**	4.00
192	Ross Gload **RC**	4.00
193	Paxton Crawford **RC**	4.00
194	Ryan Kohlmeier **RC**	4.00
195	Julio Zuleta **RC**	4.00
196	Matt Ginter **RC**	4.00

UD Pros & Prospects Update
(133-162) Production 1,600

133	Dane Artman **RC**	5.00
134	Juan Pierre **RC**	8.00
135	Jace Brewer **RC**	5.00
136	Sun-Woo Kim **RC**	6.00
137	Jon Rauch **RC**	6.00
138	Juan Guzman **RC**	5.00
139	Daylan Holt **RC**	5.00
140	Rico Washington **RC**	5.00
141	Ben Diggins **RC**	8.00
142	Mike Meyers **RC**	5.00
143	Chris Wakeland	5.00
144	Cory Vance **RC**	5.00
145	Keith Ginter **RC**	8.00
146	Koyie Hill **RC**	8.00
147	Julio Zuleta **RC**	5.00
148	Geraldo Guzman **RC**	5.00
149	Jay Spurgeon **RC**	5.00
150	Ross Gload **RC**	5.00
151	Ben Sheets **RC**	15.00
152	Josh Kalinowski **RC**	6.00
153	Kurt Ainsworth **RC**	5.00
154	Paxton Crawford **RC**	5.00
155	Xavier Nady **RC**	8.00
156	Brad Wilkerson **RC**	10.00
157	Kris Wilson **RC**	5.00
158	Paul Rigdon **RC**	5.00
159	Ryan Kohlmeier **RC**	5.00
160	Dane Sardinha **RC**	5.00
161	Javier Cardona **RC**	5.00
162	Brad Cresse **RC**	5.00
163	Ron Gant	.25
164	Mark Mulder	.50
165	David Wells	.25
166	Jason Tyner	.25
167	David Segui	.25
168	Al Martin	.25
169	Melvin Mora	.25
170	Ricky Ledee	.25
171	Rolando Arrojo	.25
172	Mike Sweeney	.25
173	Bobby Higginson	.25
174	Eric Milton	.25
175	Charles Johnson	.25
176	David Justice	.50
177	Moises Alou	.50
178	Andy Ashby	.25
179	Richie Sexson	.75
180	Will Clark	.75
181	Rondell White	.40
182	Curt Schilling	.75
183	Tom Goodwin	.25
184	Lee Stevens	.25
185	Ellis Burks	.25
186	Henry Rodriguez	.25
187	Mike Bordick	.25
188	Ryan Klesko	.50
189	Travis Lee	.25
190	Kevin Young	.25
191	Barry Larkin	.75
192	Jeff Cirillo	.25

Winning Materials

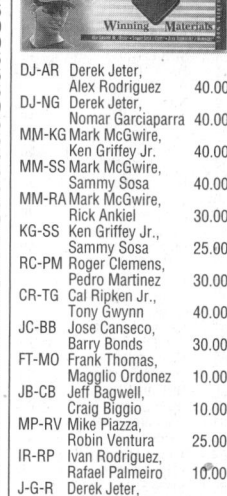

		NM/M
Common Card:		10.00
Inserted 1:15		
NG-PM	Nomar Garciaparra, Pedro Martinez	40.00
DJ-AR	Derek Jeter, Alex Rodriguez	40.00
DJ-NG	Derek Jeter, Nomar Garciaparra	40.00
MM-KG	Mark McGwire, Ken Griffey Jr.	40.00
MM-SS	Mark McGwire, Sammy Sosa	40.00
MM-RA	Mark McGwire, Rick Ankiel	30.00
KG-SS	Ken Griffey Jr., Sammy Sosa	25.00
RC-PM	Roger Clemens, Pedro Martinez	30.00
CR-TG	Cal Ripken Jr., Tony Gwynn	40.00
JC-BB	Jose Canseco, Barry Bonds	30.00
FT-MO	Frank Thomas, Magglio Ordonez	10.00
JB-CB	Jeff Bagwell, Craig Biggio	10.00
MP-RV	Mike Piazza, Robin Ventura	25.00
IR-RP	Ivan Rodriguez, Rafael Palmeiro	10.00
J-G-R	Derek Jeter, Nomar Garciaparra, Alex Rodriguez	75.00
G-S-R	Ken Griffey Jr., Sammy Sosa, Alex Rodriguez	40.00

Winning Materials Gold

		NM/M
Common Player:		5.00
JC	John Cotton	5.00
BS	Ben Sheets	15.00
SB	Sean Burroughs	8.00
MN	Mike Neill	5.00
DM	Doug Mientkiewicz	8.00
EY	Ernie Young	5.00
GD	Travis Dawkins, Mike Kinkade	5.00
BS	Sean Burroughs, Ben Sheets	15.00
AE	Brent Abernathy, Adam Everett	5.00
EY	Brad Wilkerson, Ernie Young	8.00

2000 Upper Deck Ultimate Victory

		NM/M
Complete Set (120):		200.00
Common Player:		.15
Common Ultimate Rookie (91-120):		4.00
Varying Production Levels		
Pack (5):		1.50
Box (24):		25.00
1	Mo Vaughn	.20
2	Darin Erstad	.40
3	Troy Glaus	.75
4	Adam Kennedy	.15
5	Jason Giambi	.75
6	Ben Grieve	.15
7	Terrence Long	.15
8	Tim Hudson	.25
9	David Wells	.15
10	Carlos Delgado	.75
11	Shannon Stewart	.15
12	Greg Vaughn	.15
13	Gerald Williams	.15
14	Manny Ramirez	.75
15	Roberto Alomar	.60
16	Jim Thome	.75
17	Edgar Martinez	.25
18	Alex Rodriguez	2.50
19	Matt Riley	.15
20	Cal Ripken Jr.	2.50
21	Mike Mussina	.50
22	Albert Belle	.20
23	Ivan Rodriguez	.75

24 Rafael Palmeiro .50
25 Nomar Garciaparra 2.00
26 Pedro Martinez 1.00
27 Carl Everett .15
28 Tomokazu Ohka **RC** .40
29 Jermaine Dye .15
30 Johnny Damon .25
31 Dean Palmer .15
32 Juan Gonzalez .75
33 Eric Milton .15
34 Matt Lawton .15
35 Frank Thomas .75
36 Paul Konerko .15
37 Magglio Ordonez .25
38 Jon Garland .15
39 Derek Jeter 2.50
40 Roger Clemens 1.50
41 Bernie Williams .50
42 Nick Johnson .15
43 Julio Lugo .15
44 Jeff Bagwell .75
45 Richard Hidalgo .15
46 Chipper Jones 1.50
47 Greg Maddux 1.50
48 Andruw Jones .50
49 Andres Galarraga .25
50 Rafael Furcal .50
51 Jeromy Burnitz .15
52 Geoff Jenkins .25
53 Mark McGwire 2.00
54 Jim Edmonds .25
55 Rick Ankiel .15
56 Sammy Sosa 2.00
57 Julio Zuleta **RC** .25
58 Kerry Wood .40
59 Randy Johnson .75
60 Matt Williams .25
61 Steve Finley .15
62 Gary Sheffield .40
63 Kevin Brown .25
64 Shawn Green .25
65 Milton Bradley .15
66 Vladimir Guerrero .75
67 Jose Vidro .15
68 Barry Bonds 2.00
69 Jeff Kent .25
70 Preston Wilson .15
71 Mike Lowell .15
72 Mike Piazza 2.00
73 Robin Ventura .25
74 Edgardo Alfonzo .15
75 Jay Payton .15
76 Tony Gwynn 1.00
77 Adam Eaton .15
78 Phil Nevin .15
79 Scott Rolen .75
80 Bob Abreu .25
81 Pat Burrell .50
82 Brian Giles .25
83 Jason Kendall .25
84 Kris Benson .15
85 Gookie Dawkins .15
86 Ken Griffey Jr. 1.50
87 Barry Larkin .40
88 Larry Walker .25
89 Todd Helton .75
90 Ben Petrick .15
91 Alex Cabrera 3,500 **RC** (Ultimate Rookie 2000) 4.00
92 Matt Wheatland 1,000 **RC** (Ultimate Rookie 2000) 4.00
93 Joe Torres 1,000 **RC** (Ultimate Rookie 2000) 4.00
94 Xavier Nady 1,000 **RC** (Ultimate Rookie 2000) 12.00
95 Kenny Kelly 3,500 **RC** (Ultimate Rookie 2000) 4.00
96 Matt Ginter 3,500 **RC** (Ultimate Rookie 2000) 4.00
97 Ben Diggins 1,000 **RC** (Ultimate Rookie 2000) 8.00
98 Danys Baez 3,500 **RC** (Ultimate Rookie 2000) 6.00
99 Daylan Holt 2,500 **RC** (Ultimate Rookie 2000) 4.00
100 Kazuhiro Sasaki 3,500 **RC** (Ultimate Rookie 2000) 5.00
101 Dane Artman 2,500 **RC** (Ultimate Rookie 2000) 4.00
102 Mike Tonis 1,000 **RC** (Ultimate Rookie 2000) 4.00
103 Timoniel Perez 2,500 **RC** (Ultimate Rookie 2000) 4.00
104 Barry Zito 2,500 **RC** (Ultimate Rookie 2000) 20.00
105 Koyie Hill 2,500 **RC** (Ultimate Rookie 2000) 4.00
106 Brad Wilkerson 2,500 **RC** (Ultimate Rookie 2000) 8.00
107 Juan Pierre 3,500 **RC** (Ultimate Rookie 2000) 8.00
108 Aaron McNeal 3,500 **RC** (Ultimate Rookie 2000) 4.00
109 Jay Spurgeon 3,500 **RC** (Ultimate Rookie 2000) 4.00
110 Sean Burnett 1,000 **RC** (Ultimate Rookie 2000) 8.00
111 Luis Matos 3,500 **RC** (Ultimate Rookie 2000) 8.00
112 Dave Krynzel 1,000 **RC** (Ultimate Rookie 2000) 6.00
113 Scott Heard 1,000 **RC** (Ultimate Rookie 2000) 4.00
114 Ben Sheets 2,500 **RC** (Ultimate Rookie 2000) 15.00
115 Dane Sardinha 1,000 **RC** (Ultimate Rookie 2000) 4.00
116 David Espinosa 1,000 **RC** (Ultimate Rookie 2000) 4.00
117 Leo Estrella 3,500 **RC** (Ultimate Rookie 2000) 4.00
118 Kurt Ainsworth 2,500 **RC** (Ultimate Rookie 2000) 4.00
119 Jon Rauch 2,500 **RC** (Ultimate Rookie 2000) 4.00
120 Ryan Franklin 2,500 (Ultimate Rookie 2000) 4.00

Collection

Parallel 25 Stars: 20-40X
Rookies (91-120): 2-4X
Production 25 Sets
Parallel 100 Stars: 4-8X
Rookies (91-120): 1-2X
Production 100 Sets
Parallel 250 Stars: 2-4X
Rookies (91-120): 1-2X
Production 250 Sets

Diamond Dignitaries

NM/M
Complete Set (10): 20.00
Common Player: 1.00
Inserted 1:23
1 Ken Griffey Jr. 2.00
2 Nomar Garciaparra 3.00
3 Chipper Jones 2.00
4 Ivan Rodriguez 1.00
5 Mark McGwire 3.00
6 Cal Ripken Jr. 4.00
7 Vladimir Guerrero 1.00
8 Alex Rodriguez 3.00
9 Sammy Sosa 2.50
10 Derek Jeter 3.00

HOF Game Jersey

NM/M
Common Card: 8.00
SA Sparky Anderson 8.00
CF Carlton Fisk 10.00
TP Tony Perez 8.00

HOF Game Jersey Combo

NM/M
UV-C Sparky Anderson, Carlton Fisk, Tony Perez 40.00

Lasting Impressions

NM/M
Complete Set (10): 15.00
Common Player: 1.00
Inserted 1:11
1 Barry Bonds 3.00
2 Mike Piazza 2.00
3 Manny Ramirez 1.00
4 Pedro J. Martinez 1.50
5 Mark McGwire 2.00

6 Ken Griffey Jr. 2.00
7 Ivan Rodriguez 1.00
8 Jeff Bagwell 1.00
9 Randy Johnson 1.50
10 Alex Rodriguez 3.00

Starstruck

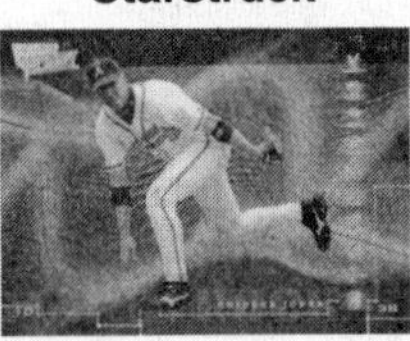

NM/M
Complete Set (10): 20.00
Common Player: 1.00
Inserted 1:11
1 Alex Rodriguez 3.00
2 Frank Thomas 1.00
3 Derek Jeter 3.00
4 Mark McGwire 3.00
5 Nomar Garciaparra 3.00
6 Chipper Jones 2.00
7 Cal Ripken Jr. 4.00
8 Sammy Sosa 2.00
9 Vladimir Guerrero 1.00
10 Ken Griffey Jr. 2.00

Victory

Victory offers no inserts just your standard 440-card base set that features a white bordered design, with two player images on the card front. The base set includes three subsets: Rookie 2000 (331-370); Big Play Makers (371-390) and JUNIOR Circuit (391-440).

NM/M
Complete Set (440): 20.00
Complete Factory Set (466): 25.00
Common Player: .10
Common Griffey (391-440): .50
Common USA (441-466): .40
Pack (12): 1.00
Wax Box (36): 25.00
1 Mo Vaughn .15
2 Garret Anderson .20
3 Tim Salmon .20
4 Troy Percival .10
5 Orlando Palmeiro .10
6 Darin Erstad .20
7 Ramon Ortiz .10
8 Ben Molina .10
9 Troy Glaus .40
10 Jim Edmonds .20
11 Mo Vaughn, Troy Percival .15
12 Craig Biggio .25
13 Roger Cedeno .10
14 Shane Reynolds .10
15 Jeff Bagwell .50
16 Octavio Dotel .10
17 Moises Alou .20
18 Jose Lima .10
19 Ken Caminiti .15
20 Richard Hidalgo .10
21 Billy Wagner .10
22 Lance Berkman .20
23 Jeff Bagwell, Jose Lima .25
24 Jason Giambi .50
25 Randy Velarde .10
26 Miguel Tejada .25
27 Matt Stairs .10
28 A.J. Hinch .10
29 Olmedo Saenz .10
30 Ben Grieve .10
31 Ryan Christenson .10
32 Eric Chavez .20
33 Tim Hudson .20
34 John Jaha .10
35 Jason Giambi, Matt Stairs .25
36 Raul Mondesi .20
37 Tony Batista .10
38 David Wells .10
39 Homer Bush .10
40 Carlos Delgado .40
41 Billy Koch .10
42 Darrin Fletcher .10
43 Tony Fernandez .10
44 Shannon Stewart .10
45 Roy Halladay .20
46 Chris Carpenter .10
47 Carlos Delgado, David Wells .20
48 Chipper Jones 1.00
49 Greg Maddux 1.00
50 Andruw Jones .40
51 Andres Galarraga .20
52 Tom Glavine .20
53 Brian Jordan .10
54 John Smoltz .15
55 John Rocker .10
56 Javy Lopez .15
57 Eddie Perez .10
58 Kevin Millwood .20
59 Chipper Jones, Greg Maddux .50
60 Jeromy Burnitz .10
61 Steve Woodard .10
62 Ron Belliard .10
63 Geoff Jenkins .20
64 Bob Wickman .10
65 Marquis Grissom .10
66 Henry Blanco .10
67 Mark Loretta .10
68 Alex Ochoa .10
69 Marquis Grissom, Jeromy Burnitz .10
70 Mark McGwire 1.50
71 Edgar Renteria .10
72 Dave Veres .10
73 Eli Marrero .10
74 Fernando Tatis .10
75 J.D. Drew .20
76 Ray Lankford .10
77 Daryle Kile .10
78 Kent Bottenfield .10
79 Joe McEwing .10
80 Mark McGwire, Ray Lankford .75
81 Sammy Sosa 1.25
82 Jose Nieves .10
83 Jon Lieber .10
84 Henry Rodriguez .10
85 Mark Grace .20
86 Eric Young .10
87 Kerry Wood .25
88 Ismael Valdes .10
89 Glenallen Hill .10
90 Sammy Sosa, Mark Grace .60
91 Greg Vaughn .10
92 Fred McGriff .20
93 Ryan Rupe .10
94 Bubba Trammell .10
95 Miguel Cairo .10
96 Roberto Hernandez .10
97 Jose Canseco .40
98 Wilson Alvarez .10
99 John Flaherty .10
100 Vinny Castilla .15
101 Jose Canseco, Roberto Hernandez .25
102 Randy Johnson .50
103 Matt Williams .15
104 Matt Mantei .10
105 Steve Finley .10
106 Luis Gonzalez .20
107 Travis Lee .10
108 Omar Daal .10
109 Jay Bell .10
110 Erubiel Durazo .10
111 Tony Womack .10
112 Todd Stottlemyre .10
113 Randy Johnson, Matt Williams .25
114 Gary Sheffield .25
115 Adrian Beltre .10
116 Kevin Brown .20
117 Todd Hundley .10
118 Eric Karros .20
119 Shawn Green .40
120 Chan Ho Park .10
121 Mark Grudzielanek .10
122 Todd Hollandsworth .10
123 Jeff Shaw .10
124 Darren Dreifort .10
125 Gary Sheffield, Kevin Brown .15
126 Vladimir Guerrero .50
127 Michael Barrett .10
128 Dustin Hermanson .10
129 Jose Vidro .10
130 Chris Widger .10
131 Mike Thurman .10
132 Wilton Guerrero .10
133 Brad Fullmer .10
134 Rondell White .20
135 Ugueth Urbina .10
136 Vladimir Guerrero, Rondell White .40
137 Barry Bonds 1.50
138 Russ Ortiz .10
139 J.T. Snow .10
140 Joe Nathan .10
141 Rich Aurilia .10
142 Jeff Kent .20
143 Armando Rios .10
144 Ellis Burks .10
145 Robb Nen .10
146 Marvin Benard .10
147 Barry Bonds, Russ Ortiz .75
148 Manny Ramirez .50
149 Bartolo Colon .10
150 Kenny Lofton .20
151 Sandy Alomar Jr. .10
152 Travis Fryman .15
153 Omar Vizquel .15
154 Roberto Alomar .40
155 Richie Sexson .25
156 David Justice .20
157 Jim Thome .50
158 Manny Ramirez, Roberto Alomar .25
159 Ken Griffey Jr. 1.00
160 Edgar Martinez .15
161 Fred Garcia .10
162 Alex Rodriguez 1.50
163 John Halama .10
164 Russ Davis .10
165 David Bell .10
166 Gil Meche .10
167 Jamie Moyer .10
168 John Olerud .20
169 Ken Griffey Jr., Fred Garcia .50
170 Preston Wilson .20
171 Antonio Alfonseca .10
172 A.J. Burnett .10
173 Luis Castillo .10
174 Mike Lowell .10
175 Alex Fernandez .10
176 Mike Redmond .10
177 Alex Gonzalez .10
178 Vladimir Nunez .10
179 Mark Kotsay .10
180 Preston Wilson, Luis Castillo .10
181 Mike Piazza 1.00
182 Darryl Hamilton .10
183 Al Leiter .20
184 Robin Ventura .20
185 Rickey Henderson .20
186 Rey Ordonez .10
187 Edgardo Alfonzo .10
188 Derek Bell .10
189 Mike Hampton .10
190 Armando Benitez .10
191 Mike Piazza, Rickey Henderson .50
192 Cal Ripken Jr. 1.50
193 B.J. Surhoff .10
194 Mike Mussina .40
195 Albert Belle .15
196 Jerry Hairston Jr. .10
197 Will Clark .20
198 Sidney Ponson .10
199 Brady Anderson .10
200 Scott Erickson .10
201 Ryan Minor .10
202 Cal Ripken Jr., Albert Belle .75
203 Tony Gwynn .75
204 Bret Boone .20
205 Ryan Klesko .10
206 Ben Davis .10
207 Matt Clement .10
208 Eric Owens .10
209 Trevor Hoffman .10
210 Sterling Hitchcock .10
211 Phil Nevin .10
212 Tony Gwynn, Trevor Hoffman .40
213 Scott Rolen .50
214 Bob Abreu .20
215 Curt Schilling .25
216 Rico Brogna .10
217 Robert Person .10
218 Doug Glanville .10
219 Mike Lieberthal .10
220 Andy Ashby .10
221 Randy Wolf .10
222 Bob Abreu, Curt Schilling .20
223 Brian Giles .20
224 Jason Kendall .20
225 Kris Benson .10
226 Warren Morris .10
227 Kevin Young .10
228 Al Martin .10
229 Wil Cordero .10
230 Bruce Aven .10
231 Todd Ritchie .10
232 Jason Kendall, Brian Giles .10
233 Ivan Rodriguez .50
234 Rusty Greer .10
235 Ruben Mateo .10
236 Justin Thompson .10
237 Rafael Palmeiro .25
238 Chad Curtis .10
239 Royce Clayton .10
240 Gabe Kapler .10
241 Jeff Zimmerman .10
242 John Wetteland .10
243 Ivan Rodriguez, Rafael Palmeiro .25
244 Nomar Garciaparra 1.25
245 Pedro Martinez .75
246 Jose Offerman .10
247 Jason Varitek .10
248 Troy O'Leary .10
249 John Valentin .10
250 Trot Nixon .10
251 Carl Everett .10
252 Wilton Veras .10
253 Bret Saberhagen .10
254 Nomar Garciaparra, Pedro J. Martinez .60
255 Sean Casey .10
256 Barry Larkin .25
257 Pokey Reese .10
258 Pete Harnisch .10
259 Aaron Boone .20
260 Dante Bichette .10
261 Scott Williamson .10
262 Steve Parris .10
263 Dmitri Young .10
264 Mike Cameron .10
265 Sean Casey, Scott Williamson .10
266 Larry Walker .25
267 Rolando Arrojo .10
268 Pedro Astacio .10
269 Todd Helton .50
270 Jeff Cirillo .10
271 Neifi Perez .10
272 Brian Bohanon .10
273 Jeffrey Hammonds .10
274 Tom Goodwin .10
275 Larry Walker, Todd Helton .25
276 Carlos Beltran .15
277 Jermaine Dye .10
278 Mike Sweeney .10
279 Joe Randa .10
280 Jose Rosado .10
281 Carlos Febles .10
282 Jeff Suppan .10
283 Johnny Damon .20
284 Jeremy Giambi .10
285 Mike Sweeney, Carlos Beltran .10
286 Tony Clark .10
287 Damion Easley .10
288 Jeff Weaver .10
289 Dean Palmer .10
290 Juan Gonzalez .50
291 Juan Encarnacion .10
292 Todd Jones .10
293 Karim Garcia .10
294 Deivi Cruz .10
295 Dean Palmer, Juan Encarnacion .10
296 Corey Koskie .10
297 Brad Radke .10
298 Doug Mientkiewicz .10
299 Ron Coomer .10
300 Joe Mays .10
301 Eric Milton .10
302 Jacque Jones .10
303 Chad Allen .10
304 Cristian Guzman .10
305 Jason Ryan .10
306 Todd Walker .10
307 Corey Koskie, Eric Milton .10
308 Frank Thomas .50
309 Paul Konerko .10
310 Mike Sirotka .10
311 Jim Parque .10
312 Magglio Ordonez .25
313 Bob Howry .10
314 Carlos Lee .10
315 Ray Durham .10
316 Chris Singleton .10
317 Brook Fordyce .10
318 Frank Thomas, Magglio Ordonez .25
319 Derek Jeter 1.50
320 Roger Clemens 1.00
321 Paul O'Neill .20
322 Bernie Williams .40
323 Mariano Rivera .20
324 Tino Martinez .20
325 David Cone .20
326 Chuck Knoblauch .10
327 Darryl Strawberry .20
328 Orlando Hernandez .10
329 Ricky Ledee .10
330 Derek Jeter, Bernie Williams .75
331 Pat Burrell (Rookie 2000) .50
332 Alfonso Soriano (Rookie 2000) .75
333 Josh Beckett (Rookie 2000) .25
334 Matt Riley (Rookie 2000) .15
335 Brian Cooper (Rookie 2000) .10
336 Eric Munson (Rookie 2000) .20
337 Vernon Wells (Rookie 2000) .25
338 Juan Pena (Rookie 2000) .10
339 Mark DeRosa (Rookie 2000) .10

340 Kip Wells (Rookie 2000) .10
341 Roosevelt Brown (Rookie 2000) .10
342 Jason LaRue (Rookie 2000) .10
343 Ben Petrick (Rookie 2000) .10
344 Mark Quinn (Rookie 2000) .10
345 Julio Ramirez (Rookie 2000) .10
346 Rod Barajas (Rookie 2000) .10
347 Robert Fick (Rookie 2000) .10
348 David Newhan (Rookie 2000) .10
349 Eric Gagne (Rookie 2000) .15
350 Jorge Toca (Rookie 2000) .10
351 Mitch Meluskey (Rookie 2000) .10
352 Ed Yarnall (Rookie 2000) .10
353 Chad Hermansen (Rookie 2000) .10
354 Peter Bergeron (Rookie 2000) .10
355 Dermal Brown (Rookie 2000) .10
356 Adam Kennedy (Rookie 2000) .10
357 Kevin Barker (Rookie 2000) .10
358 Francisco Cordero (Rookie 2000) .10
359 Travis Dawkins (Rookie 2000) .10
360 Jeff Williams (Rookie 2000) .10
361 Chad Hutchinson (Rookie 2000) .10
362 D'Angelo Jimenez (Rookie 2000) .10
363 Derrick Gibson (Rookie 2000) .10
364 Calvin Murray (Rookie 2000) .10
365 Doug Davis (Rookie 2000) .10
366 Rob Ramsay **RC** (Rookie 2000) .20
367 Mark Redman (Rookie 2000) .10
368 Rick Ankiel (Rookie 2000) .10
369 Domingo Guzman (Rookie 2000) .10
370 Eugene Kingsale (Rookie 2000) .10
371 Nomar Garciaparra (Big Play Makers) .75
372 Ken Griffey Jr. (Big Play Makers) .50
373 Randy Johnson (Big Play Makers) .25
374 Jeff Bagwell (Big Play Makers) .25
375 Ivan Rodriguez (Big Play Makers) .25
376 Derek Jeter (Big Play Makers) .75
377 Carlos Beltran (Big Play Makers) .10
378 Vladimir Guerrero (Big Play Makers) .40
379 Sammy Sosa (Big Play Makers) .60
380 Barry Bonds (Big Play Makers) .75
381 Pedro Martinez (Big Play Makers) .40
382 Chipper Jones (Big Play Makers) .50
383 Mo Vaughn (Big Play Makers) .10
384 Mike Piazza (Big Play Makers) .50
385 Alex Rodriguez (Big Play Makers) .75
386 Manny Ramirez (Big Play Makers) .25
387 Mark McGwire (Big Play Makers) .75
388 Tony Gwynn (Big Play Makers) .40
389 Sean Casey (Big Play Makers) .10
390 Cal Ripken Jr. (Big Play Makers) .75
391-440 Ken Griffey Jr. .40
441 Tommy Lasorda .50
442 Sean Burroughs .75
443 Rick Krivda .40
444 Ben Sheets **RC** 1.50
445 Pat Borders .40
446 Brent Abernathy **RC** .75
447 Tim Young .40
448 Adam Everett .50
449 Anthony Sanders .40
450 Ernie Young .40
451 Brad Wilkerson **RC** 1.50
452 Kurt Ainsworth 1.00
453 Ryan Franklin .40
454 Todd Williams .40
455 Jon Rauch **RC** .50
456 Roy Oswalt **RC** 5.00
457 Shane Heams .50
458 Chris George .50
459 Bobby Seay .40
460 Mike Kinkade .40
461 Marcus Jensen .40
462 Travis Dawkins .50
463 Doug Mientkiewicz .40
464 John Cotton .40
465 Mike Neill .40
466 Team Photo USA 2.50

2000 Upper Deck Yankees Legends Sample

This promo card was issued to preview the Yankees Legends set. With silver-foil graphics on front, it is identical in design to the base cards in the regularly issued version. Back has a "SAMPLE" overprint across the stats.

		NM/M
NY7	Mickey Mantle	5.00

2000 Upper Deck Yankees Legends

		NM/M
Complete Set (90):		20.00
Common Player:		.15
Pack (5):		6.00
Box (24):		100.00
1	Babe Ruth	2.00
2	Mickey Mantle	2.00
3	Lou Gehrig	2.00
4	Joe DiMaggio	2.00
5	Yogi Berra	.75
6	Don Mattingly	1.00
7	Reggie Jackson	.75
8	Dave Winfield	.40
9	Bill Skowron	.15
10	Willie Randolph	.15
11	Phil Rizzuto	.50
12	Tony Kubek	.15
13	Thurman Munson	1.00
14	Roger Maris	1.00
15	Billy Martin	.40
16	Elston Howard	.15
17	Graig Nettles	.15
18	Whitey Ford	.50
19	Earl Combes	.15
20	Tony Lazzeri	.15
21	Bob Meusel	.15
22	Joe Gordon	.15
23	Jerry Coleman	.15
24	Joe Torre	.50
25	Bucky Dent	.15
26	Don Larsen	.40
27	Bobby Richardson	.15
28	Ron Guidry	.15
29	Bobby Murcer	.15
30	Tommy Henrich	.15
31	Hank Bauer	.15
32	Joe Pepitone	.15
33	Clete Boyer	.15
34	Chris Chambliss	.15
35	Tommy John	.15
36	Goose Gossage	.15
37	Red Ruffing	.15
38	Charlie Keller	.15
39	Billy Gardner	.15
40	Hector Lopez	.15
41	Cliff Johnson	.15
42	Oscar Gamble	.15
43	Allie Reynolds	.15
44	Mickey Rivers	.15
45	Bill Dickey	.40
46	Dave Righetti	.15
47	Mel Stottlemyre	.15
48	Waite Hoyt	.15
49	Lefty Gomez	.15
50	Wade Boggs	.50
51	Billy Martin (Magic Numbers)	.25
52	Babe Ruth (Magic Numbers)	1.00
53	Lou Gehrig (Magic Numbers)	1.00
54	Joe DiMaggio (Magic Numbers)	1.00
55	Mickey Mantle (Magic Numbers)	1.00
56	Yogi Berra (Magic Numbers)	.40
57	Bill Dickey (Magic Numbers)	.25
58	Roger Maris (Magic Numbers)	.50
59	Phil Rizzuto (Magic Numbers)	.25
60	Thurman Munson (Magic Numbers)	.50
61	Whitey Ford (Magic Numbers)	.25
62	Don Mattingly (Magic Numbers)	.50
63	Elston Howard (Magic Numbers)	.15
64	Casey Stengel (Magic Numbers)	.15
65	Reggie Jackson (Magic Numbers)	.50
66	Babe Ruth/1923 (The Championship Years)	1.00
67	Lou Gehrig/1927 (The Championship Years)	1.00
68	Tony Lazzeri/1928 (The Championship Years)	.15
69	Babe Ruth/1932 (The Championship Years)	1.00
70	Lou Gehrig/1936 (The Championship Years)	1.00
71	Lefty Gomez/1937 (The Championship Years)	.15
72	Bill Dickey/1938(The Championship Years)	.25
73	Tommy Henrich/1939 (The Championship Years)	.15
74	Joe DiMaggio/1941 (The Championship Years)	1.00
75	Spud Chandler/1943 (The Championship Years)	.15
76	Tommy Henrich/1947 (The Championship Years)	.15
77	Phil Rizzuto/1949 (The Championship Years)	.25
78	Whitey Ford/1950 (The Championship Years)	.25
79	Yogi Berra/1951 (The Championship Years)	.40
80	Casey Stengel/1952 (The Championship Years)	.15
81	Billy Martin/1953 (The Championship Years)	.25
82	Don Larsen/1956 (The Championship Years)	.25
83	Elston Howard/1958 (The Championship Years)	.15
84	Roger Maris/1961 (The Championship Years)	.50
85	Mickey Mantle/1962 (The Championship Years)	1.00
86	Reggie Jackson/1977 (The Championship Years)	.50
87	Bucky Dent/1978 (The Championship Years)	.15
88	Wade Boggs/1996 (The Championship Years)	.25
89	Joe Torre/1998 (The Championship Years)	.25
90	Joe Torre/1999 (The Championship Years)	.25

DiMaggio Memorabilia

		NM/M
YLB-JD	Joe DiMaggio/Bat	125.00
YLG-JD	Joe DiMaggio/56 (Gold Bat)	200.00
YLC-JD	Joe DiMaggio/Bat/5 (Cut Sig.)	650.00

Legendary Lumber

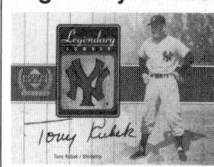

		NM/M
Common Player:		5.00
Inserted 1:23		
HB	Hank Bauer	8.00
YB	Yogi Berra	20.00
PB	Paul Blair	5.00
CB	Clete Boyer	5.00
CC	Chris Chambliss	8.00
JC	Joe Collins	5.00
BD	Bucky Dent	8.00
JD	Joe DiMaggio	140.00
OG	Oscar Gamble	5.00
BG	Billy Gardner	5.00
TH	Tommy Henrich	5.00
RH	Ralph Houk	8.00
EH	Elston Howard	8.00
RJ	Reggie Jackson	20.00
TJ	Tommy John	8.00
CJ	Cliff Johnson	5.00
CK	Charlie Keller	5.00
TK	Tony Kubek	8.00
HL	Hector Lopez	5.00
MM	Mickey Mantle	165.00
RM	Roger Maris	70.00
DM	Don Mattingly	45.00
TM	Thurman Munson	35.00
BM	Bobby Murcer	8.00
GN	Graig Nettles	10.00
JP	Joe Pepitone	6.00
WR	Willie Randolph	6.00
MR	Mickey Rivers	5.00
BR	Babe Ruth	185.00
MS	Moose Skowron	6.00
DW	Dave Winfield	15.00

Leg. Lumber/ Sign. Cut

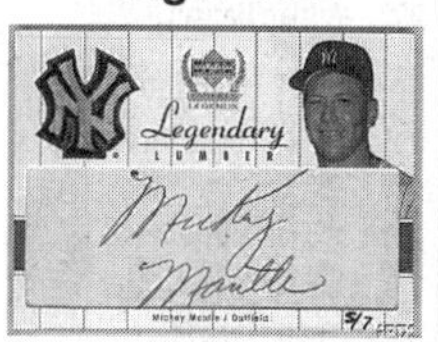

		NM/M
MM-LC	Mickey Mantle/7	4,000

Legendary Pinstripes

		NM/M
Common Player:		20.00
Inserted 1:144		
BD	Bucky Dent	20.00
WF	Whitey Ford	50.00
LG	Lou Gehrig	300.00
GG	Goose Gossage	20.00
RG	Ron Guidry	20.00
TH	Tommy Henrich	20.00
EH	Elston Howard	20.00
RJ	Reggie Jackson	40.00
HL	Hector Lopez	20.00
MM	Mickey Mantle	250.00
RM	Roger Maris	75.00
BM	Billy Martin	40.00
DM	Don Mattingly	60.00
TM	Thurman Munson	75.00
JP	Joe Pepitone	20.00
AR	Allie Reynolds	20.00
BR	Bobby Richardson	20.00
PR	Phil Rizzuto	40.00
DW	Dave Winfield	40.00

Auto. Legend. Pinstripe

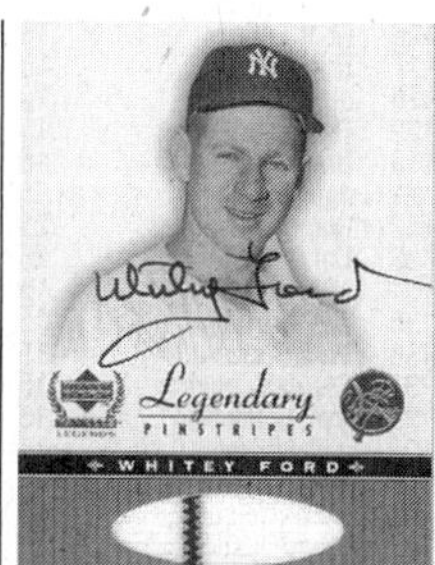

		NM/M
Common Player:		30.00
BD	Bucky Dent	30.00
WF	Whitey Ford	60.00
GG	Goose Gossage	30.00
RG	Ron Guidry	35.00
TH	Tommy Henrich	30.00
GM	Gil MacDougald	30.00
DM	Don Mattingly	150.00
JP	Joe Pepitone	30.00
PR	Phil Rizzuto	60.00
DW	Dave Winfield	35.00

Monument Park

		NM/M
Complete Set (6):		20.00
Common Player:		1.50
Inserted 1:23		3.00
1	Lou Gehrig	6.00
2	Babe Ruth	6.00
3	Mickey Mantle	6.00
4	Joe DiMaggio	6.00
5	Thurman Munson	3.00
6	Elston Howard	1.50

Murderer's Row

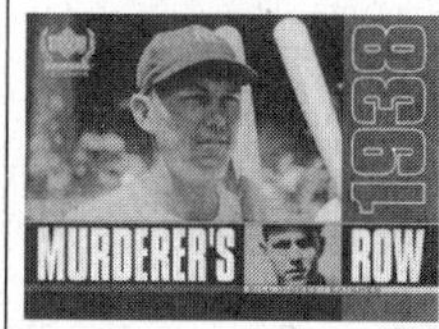

		NM/M
Complete Set (10):		17.50
Common Player:		1.50
Inserted 1:11		
1	Tony Lazzeri	1.50
2	Babe Ruth	6.00
3	Bob Meusel	1.50
4	Lou Gehrig	6.00
5	Joe Dugan	1.50
6	Bill Dickey	1.50
7	Waite Hoyt	1.50
8	Red Ruffing	1.50
9	Earl Combes	1.50
10	Lefty Gomez	1.50

Pride of the Pinstripes

		NM/M
Complete Set (6):		17.50
Common Player:		2.50
Inserted 1:23		
1	Babe Ruth	6.00
2	Mickey Mantle	6.00
3	Joe DiMaggio	5.00
4	Lou Gehrig	5.00
5	Reggie Jackson	2.50
6	Yogi Berra	2.50

The Golden Years

		NM/M
Complete Set (10):		20.00
Common Player:		1.50
Inserted 1:11		
1	Joe DiMaggio	6.00

2	Phil Rizzuto	2.50
3	Yogi Berra	3.00
4	Billy Martin	2.50
5	Whitey Ford	2.50
6	Roger Maris	5.00
7	Mickey Mantle	7.50
8	Elston Howard	1.50
9	Tommy Henrich	1.50
10	Joe Gordon	1.50

The New Dynasty

		NM/M
Complete Set (10):		15.00
Common Player:		1.50
Inserted 1:11		
1	Reggie Jackson	3.50
2	Graig Nettles	1.50
3	Don Mattingly	6.50
4	Goose Gossage	1.50
5	Dave Winfield	3.00
6	Chris Chambliss	1.50
7	Thurman Munson	4.00
8	Willie Randolph	1.50
9	Ron Guidry	2.50
10	Bucky Dent	2.50

22kt Gold Ken Griffey Jr. Rookie Card

A 22-karat gold embossed card replicating in all important details the 1989 Upper Deck Ken Griffey Jr. rookie card was issued by UD. The card was accompanied by a commemorative collectors' sheet describing the original rookie card and the gold version. The gold card was offered to members of UD's Collectors Club for $24.

		NM/M
1	Ken Griffey Jr.	24.00

2001 Upper Deck

		NM/M
Complete Set (450):		125.00
Complete Series 1 (270):		25.00
Complete Series 2 (180):		100.00
Common Player:		.15
Series 1 Pack (10):		2.00
Series 1 Box (24):		35.00
Series 2 Pack (10):		6.00
Series 2 Box (24):		120.00
1	Jeff DaVanon/SR	.25
2	Aubrey Huff/SR	.25
3	Pascual Coco/SR	.25
4	Barry Zito/SR	.75
5	Augie Ojeda/SR	.25
6	Chris Richard/SR	.25
7	Josh Phelps/SR	.25
8	Kevin Nicholson/SR	.25

9 Juan Guzman/SR .25
10 Brandon Kolb/SR .25
11 Johan Santana/SR 4.00
12 Josh Kalinowski/SR .25
13 Tike Redman/SR .25
14 Ivanon Coffie/SR .25
15 Chad Durbin/SR .25
16 Derrick Turnbow/SR .25
17 Scott Downs/SR .25
18 Jason Grilli/SR .25
19 Mark Buehrle/SR .25
20 Paxton Crawford/SR .25
21 Bronson Arroyo/SR .25
22 Tomas de la Rosa/SR .25
23 Paul Rigdon/SR .25
24 Rob Ramsay/SR .25
25 Damian Rolls/SR .25
26 Jason Conti/SR .25
27 John Parrish/SR .25
28 Geraldo Guzman/SR .25
29 Tony Mota/SR .25
30 Luis Rivas/SR .25
31 Brian Tollberg/SR .25
32 Adam Bernero/SR .25
33 Michael Cuddyer/SR .25
34 Josue Espada/SR .25
35 Joe Lawrence/SR .25
36 Chad Moeller/SR .25
37 Nick Bierbrodt/SR .25
38 Dewayne Wise/SR .25
39 Javier Cardona/SR .25
40 Hiram Bocachica/SR .25
41 Giuseppe Chiaramonte/SR .25
42 Alex Cabrera/SR .25
43 Jimmy Rollins/SR .40
44 Pat Flury/SR **RC** .25
45 Leo Estrella/SR .25
46 Darin Erstad .40
47 Seth Etherton .15
48 Troy Glaus .40
49 Brian Cooper .15
50 Tim Salmon .25
51 Adam Kennedy .15
52 Bengie Molina .15
53 Jason Giambi .50
54 Miguel Tejada .40
55 Tim Hudson .25
56 Eric Chavez .25
57 Terrence Long .15
58 Jason Isringhausen .15
59 Ramon Hernandez .15
60 Raul Mondesi .25
61 David Wells .15
62 Shannon Stewart .15
63 Tony Batista .15
64 Brad Fullmer .15
65 Chris Carpenter .15
66 Homer Bush .15
67 Gerald Williams .15
68 Miguel Cairo .15
69 Ryan Rupe .15
70 Greg Vaughn .15
71 John Flaherty .15
72 Dan Wheeler .15
73 Fred McGriff .25
74 Roberto Alomar .40
75 Bartolo Colon .25
76 Kenny Lofton .25
77 David Segui .15
78 Omar Vizquel .25
79 Russ Branyan .15
80 Chuck Finley .15
81 Manny Ramirez .50
82 Alex Rodriguez 1.50
83 John Halama .15
84 Mike Cameron .15
85 David Bell .15
86 Jay Buhner .15
87 Aaron Sele .15
88 Rickey Henderson .40
89 Brook Fordyce .15
90 Cal Ripken Jr. 2.00
91 Mike Mussina .40
92 Delino DeShields .15
93 Melvin Mora .15
94 Sidney Ponson .15
95 Brady Anderson .15
96 Ivan Rodriguez .50
97 Ricky Ledee .15
98 Rick Helling .15
99 Ruben Mateo .15
100 Luis Alicea .15
101 John Wetteland .15
102 Mike Lamb .15
103 Carl Everett .15
104 Troy O'Leary .15
105 Wilton Veras .15
106 Pedro Martinez .75
107 Rolando Arrojo .15
108 Scott Hatteberg .15
109 Jason Varitek .15
110 Jose Offerman .15
111 Carlos Beltran .25
112 Johnny Damon .25
113 Mark Quinn .15
114 Rey Sanchez .15
115 Mac Suzuki .15
116 Jermaine Dye .15
117 Chris Fussell .15
118 Jeff Weaver .15
119 Dean Palmer .15
120 Robert Fick .15
121 Brian Moehler .15
122 Damion Easley .15
123 Juan Encarnacion .15
124 Tony Clark .15
125 Cristian Guzman .15
126 Matt LeCroy .15
127 Eric Milton .15
128 Jay Canizaro .15
129 David Ortiz .15
130 Brad Radke .15
131 Jacque Jones .15
132 Magglio Ordonez .25
133 Carlos Lee .15
134 Mike Sirotka .15
135 Ray Durham .15
136 Paul Konerko .15
137 Charles Johnson .15
138 James Baldwin .15
139 Jeff Abbott .15
140 Roger Clemens 1.50
141 Derek Jeter 2.00
142 David Justice .25
143 Ramiro Mendoza .15
144 Chuck Knoblauch .15
145 Orlando Hernandez .25
146 Alfonso Soriano .75
147 Jeff Bagwell .50
148 Julio Lugo .15
149 Mitch Meluskey .15
150 Jose Lima .15
151 Richard Hidalgo .15
152 Moises Alou .25
153 Scott Elarton .15
154 Andruw Jones .50
155 Quilvio Veras .15
156 Greg Maddux 1.00
157 Brian Jordan .15
158 Andres Galarraga .20
159 Kevin Millwood .25
160 Rafael Furcal .25
161 Jeromy Burnitz .15
162 Jimmy Haynes .15
163 Mark Loretta .15
164 Ron Belliard .15
165 Richie Sexson .40
166 Kevin Barker .15
167 Jeff D'Amico .15
168 Rick Ankiel .15
169 Mark McGwire 1.50
170 J.D. Drew .25
171 Eli Marrero .15
172 Darryl Kile .15
173 Edgar Renteria .15
174 Will Clark .40
175 Eric Young .15
176 Mark Grace .40
177 Jon Lieber .15
178 Damon Buford .15
179 Kerry Wood .50
180 Rondell White .15
181 Joe Girardi .15
182 Curt Schilling .40
183 Randy Johnson .75
184 Steve Finley .15
185 Kelly Stinnett .15
186 Jay Bell .15
187 Matt Mantei .15
188 Luis Gonzalez .25
189 Shawn Green .25
190 Todd Hundley .15
191 Chan Ho Park .25
192 Adrian Beltre .25
193 Mark Grudzielanek .15
194 Gary Sheffield .40
195 Tom Goodwin .15
196 Lee Stevens .15
197 Javier Vazquez .15
198 Milton Bradley .15
199 Vladimir Guerrero .75
200 Carl Pavano .15
201 Orlando Cabrera .15
202 Tony Armas Jr. .15
203 Jeff Kent .25
204 Calvin Murray .15
205 Ellis Burks .15
206 Barry Bonds 2.00
207 Russ Ortiz .15
208 Marvin Benard .15
209 Joe Nathan .15
210 Preston Wilson .15
211 Cliff Floyd .15
212 Mike Lowell .15
213 Ryan Dempster .15
214 Brad Penny .15
215 Mike Redmond .15
216 Luis Castillo .15
217 Derek Bell .15
218 Mike Hampton .25
219 Todd Zeile .15
220 Robin Ventura .25
221 Mike Piazza 1.00
222 Al Leiter .25
223 Edgardo Alfonzo .15
224 Mike Bordick .15
225 Phil Nevin .15
226 Ryan Klesko .25
227 Adam Eaton .15
228 Eric Owens .15
229 Tony Gwynn .75
230 Matt Clement .15
231 Wiki Gonzalez .15
232 Robert Person .15
233 Doug Glanville .15
234 Scott Rolen .50
235 Mike Lieberthal .15
236 Randy Wolf .15
237 Bobby Abreu .25
238 Pat Burrell .40
239 Bruce Chen .15
240 Kevin Young .15
241 Todd Ritchie .15
242 Adrian Brown .15
243 Chad Hermansen .15
244 Warren Morris .15
245 Kris Benson .15
246 Jason Kendall .25
247 Pokey Reese .15
248 Rob Bell .15
249 Ken Griffey Jr. 1.00
250 Sean Casey .15
251 Aaron Boone .15
252 Pete Harnisch .15
253 Barry Larkin .40
254 Dmitri Young .15
255 Todd Hollandsworth .15
256 Pedro Astacio .15
257 Todd Helton .50
258 Terry Shumpert .15
259 Neifi Perez .15
260 Jeffrey Hammonds .15
261 Ben Petrick .15
262 Mark McGwire .75
263 Derek Jeter 1.00
264 Sammy Sosa .75
265 Cal Ripken Jr. 1.00
266 Pedro J. Martinez .40
267 Barry Bonds 1.00
268 Fred McGriff .20
269 Randy Johnson .40
270 Darin Erstad .25
271 Ichiro Suzuki/SR **RC** 15.00
272 Wilson Betemit/SR **RC** .50
273 Corey Patterson/SR .25
274 Sean Douglass/SR **RC** .25
275 Mike Penney/SR **RC** .25
276 Nate Teut/SR **RC** .25
277 Ricardo Rodriguez/SR **RC** .25
278 Brandon Duckworth/SR **RC** .50
279 Rafael Soriano/SR **RC** .75
280 Juan Diaz/SR **RC** .25
281 Horacio Ramirez/SR **RC** .75
282 Tsuyoshi Shinjo/SR **RC** .50
283 Keith Ginter/SR .25
284 Esix Snead/SR **RC** .25
285 Erick Almonte/SR **RC** .25
286 Travis Hafner/SR **RC** 3.00
287 Jason Smith/SR **RC** .25
288 Jackson Melian/SR **RC** .25
289 Tyler Walker/SR **RC** .25
290 Jason Standridge/SR .25
291 Juan Uribe/SR **RC** .50
292 Adrian Hernandez/SR **RC** .25
293 Jason Michaels/SR **RC** .25
294 Jason Hart/SR .15
295 Albert Pujols/SR **RC** 80.00
296 Morgan Ensberg/SR **RC** 2.00
297 Brandon Inge/SR .25
298 Jesus Colome/SR .25
299 Kyle Kessel/SR **RC** .25
300 Timo Perez/SR .25
301 Mo Vaughn .20
302 Ismael Valdes .25
303 Glenallen Hill .15
304 Garret Anderson .40
305 Johnny Damon .25
306 Jose Ortiz .15
307 Mark Mulder .25
308 Adam Piatt .15
309 Gil Heredia .15
310 Mike Sirotka .15
311 Carlos Delgado .50
312 Alex Gonzalez .15
313 Jose Cruz Jr. .15
314 Darrin Fletcher .15
315 Ben Grieve .15
316 Vinny Castilla .15
317 Wilson Alvarez .15
318 Brent Abernathy .15
319 Ellis Burks .15
320 Jim Thome .75
321 Juan Gonzalez .50
322 Ed Taubensee .15
323 Travis Fryman .25
324 John Olerud .25
325 Edgar Martinez .25
326 Fred Garcia .15
327 Bret Boone .25
328 Kazuhiro Sasaki .15
329 Albert Belle .15
330 Mike Bordick .15
331 David Segui .15
332 Pat Hentgen .15
333 Alex Rodriguez 1.50
334 Andres Galarraga .25
335 Gabe Kapler .15
336 Ken Caminiti .15
337 Rafael Palmeiro .50
338 Manny Ramirez .50
339 David Cone .15
340 Nomar Garciaparra 1.50
341 Trot Nixon .15
342 Derek Lowe .15
343 Roberto Hernandez .15
344 Mike Sweeney .15
345 Carlos Febles .15
346 Jeff Suppan .15
347 Roger Cedeno .15
348 Bobby Higginson .15
349 Deivi Cruz .15
350 Mitch Meluskey .15
351 Matt Lawton .15
352 Mark Redman .15
353 Jay Canizaro .15
354 Corey Koskie .15
355 Matt Kinney .15
356 Frank Thomas .50
357 Sandy Alomar Jr. .15
358 David Wells .15
359 Jim Parque .15
360 Chris Singleton .15
361 Tino Martinez .15
362 Paul O'Neill .25
363 Mike Mussina .40
364 Bernie Williams .50
365 Andy Pettitte .40
366 Mariano Rivera .25
367 Brad Ausmus .15
368 Craig Biggio .25
369 Lance Berkman .25
370 Shane Reynolds .15
371 Chipper Jones 1.00
372 Tom Glavine .40
373 B.J. Surhoff .15
374 John Smoltz .25
375 Rico Brogna .15
376 Geoff Jenkins .25
377 Jose Hernandez .15
378 Tyler Houston .15
379 Henry Blanco .15
380 Jeffrey Hammonds .15
381 Jim Edmonds .25
382 Fernando Vina .15
383 Andy Benes .15
384 Ray Lankford .15
385 Dustin Hermanson .15
386 Todd Hundley .15
387 Sammy Sosa 1.50
388 Tom Gordon .15
389 Bill Mueller .15
390 Ron Coomer .15
391 Matt Stairs .15
392 Mark Grace .40
393 Matt Williams .25
394 Todd Stottlemyre .15
395 Tony Womack .15
396 Erubiel Durazo .15
397 Reggie Sanders .15
398 Andy Ashby .15
399 Eric Karros .15
400 Kevin Brown .25
401 Darren Dreifort .15
402 Fernando Tatis .15
403 Jose Vidro .15
404 Peter Bergeron .15
405 Geoff Blum .15
406 J.T. Snow .15
407 Livan Hernandez .15
408 Robb Nen .15
409 Bobby Estalella .15
410 Rich Aurilia .15
411 Eric Davis .15
412 Charles Johnson .15
413 Alex Gonzalez .15
414 A.J. Burnett .15
415 Antonio Alfonseca .15
416 Derek Lee .15
417 Jay Payton .15
418 Kevin Appier .15
419 Steve Trachsel .15
420 Rey Ordonez .15
421 Darryl Hamilton .15
422 Ben Davis .15
423 Damian Jackson .15
424 Mark Kotsay .15
425 Trevor Hoffman .15
426 Travis Lee .15
427 Omar Daal .15
428 Paul Byrd .15
429 Reggie Taylor .15
430 Brian Giles .25
431 Derek Bell .15
432 Francisco Cordova .15
433 Pat Meares .15
434 Scott Williamson .15
435 Jason LaRue .15
436 Michael Tucker .15
437 Wilton Guerrero .15
438 Mike Hampton .15
439 Ron Gant .15
440 Jeff Cirillo .15
441 Denny Neagle .15
442 Larry Walker .40
443 Juan Pierre .15
444 Todd Walker .15
445 Jason Giambi .40
446 Jeff Kent .15
447 Mariano Rivera .15
448 Edgar Martinez .15
449 Troy Glaus .25
450 Alex Rodriguez .75

Exclusives

Silver Stars: 8-15X
Production 100 Sets
Gold Stars: 15-30X
Production 25 Sets

All-Star Heroes Base Cards

NM/M

Quantity produced listed
DJ Derek Jeter/2000 20.00
MP Mike Piazza/1996 10.00

All-Star Heroes Bat Cards

NM/M

Common Player: 10.00
RoC Roberto Clemente/1961 75.00
KG Ken Griffey Jr./1992 20.00
TP Tony Perez/1967 10.00
CR Cal Ripken Jr/1991 40.00
AR Alex Rodriguez/1998 20.00
BR Babe Ruth/1933 175.00

All-Star Heroes Jersey Cards

NM/M

Common Player: 10.00
RC Roger Clemens/1986 20.00
JD Joe DiMaggio/36 300.00
TG Tony Gwynn/1994 10.00
RJ Randy Johnson/1993 10.00
ASH-MM Mickey Mantle/54 400.00
ASH-SS Sammy Sosa/2000 20.00

All-Star Salute

NM/M

Common Player: 10.00
Inserted 1:288
HA Hank Aaron/Bat 35.00
HA Hank Aaron/Jsy 35.00
LA Luis Aparicio/Jsy 10.00
JB Johnny Bench/Bat 20.00
JB Johnny Bench/Jsy 20.00
LB Lou Brock/Bat 15.00
RC Roberto Clemente/Jsy 125.00
RJ Reggie Jackson/Jsy 20.00
TM Thurman Munson/Jsy 35.00
BR Brooks Robinson/Bat 20.00
FR Frank Robinson/Jsy 15.00
TS Tom Seaver/Jsy 20.00

Big League Beat

NM/M

Complete Set (20): 15.00
Common Player: .50
Inserted 1:3
1 Barry Bonds 2.00
2 Nomar Garciaparra 1.50
3 Mark McGwire 1.50
4 Roger Clemens 1.25
5 Chipper Jones 1.00
6 Jeff Bagwell .50
7 Sammy Sosa 1.50
8 Cal Ripken Jr. 2.00
9 Randy Johnson .75
10 Carlos Delgado .50
11 Manny Ramirez .50
12 Derek Jeter 2.00
13 Tony Gwynn .75
14 Pedro J. Martinez .75
15 Jose Canseco .50
16 Frank Thomas .75
17 Alex Rodriguez 1.50
18 Bernie Williams .50
19 Greg Maddux 1.00
20 Rafael Palmeiro .50

Big League Challenge Jerseys

NM/M

Common Player: 5.00
Inserted 1:288
BB Barry Bonds 40.00
JC Jose Canseco 8.00
JE Jim Edmonds 8.00
TF Steve Finley 5.00
TG Troy Glaus 8.00
TH Todd Helton 10.00
RH Richard Hidalgo 5.00
RP Rafael Palmeiro 10.00
MP Mike Piazza 20.00
GS Gary Sheffield 8.00
FT Frank Thomas 10.00

Classic Midsummer Moments

NM/M

Complete Set (20): 25.00
Common Player: .50
Inserted 1:12
CM1 Joe DiMaggio/1936 3.00
CM2 Joe DiMaggio/1951 3.00
CM3 Mickey Mantle/1952 4.00
CM4 Mickey Mantle/1968 4.00
CM5 Roger Clemens/1986 2.50
CM6 Mark McGwire/1987 2.50
CM7 Cal Ripken Jr./1991 3.00
CM8 Ken Griffey Jr./1992 1.50
CM9 Randy Johnson/1993 1.00
CM10 Tony Gwynn/1994 1.00
CM11 Fred McGriff/1994 .50
CM12 Hideo Nomo/1995 .75
CM13 Jeff Conine/1995 .50
CM14 Mike Piazza/1996 1.50
CM15 Sandy Alomar Jr./1997 .50
CM16 Alex Rodriguez/1998 2.50
CM17 Roberto Alomar/1998 .75
CM18 Pedro Martinez/1999 1.00
CM19 Andres Galarraga/2000 .50
CM20 Derek Jeter/2000 2.50

Joe DiMaggio Bat Cards - Hawaii

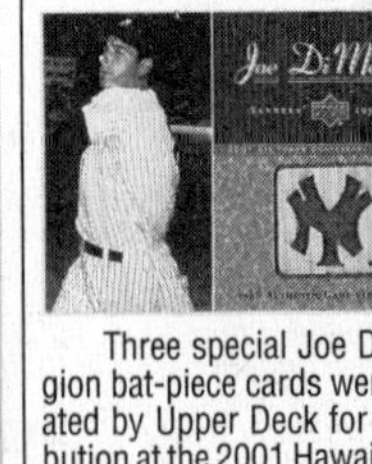

Three special Joe DiMaggio bat-piece cards were created by Upper Deck for distribution at the 2001 Hawaii trade show. Most cards have a photo of the player on left-front with a small piece of game-used bat, either the "NY" logo or the surrounding area. These cards are numbered on back within an edition of 450 pieces. An even more limited card has both a bat piece and a cut-signature autograph on front, along with a small photo portrait. On back, these cards are numbered within an edition of just five.

NM/M

KY-JD1 Joe DiMaggio/Auto. (Bat piece.) 2,250
KY-JD2 Joe DiMaggio (Bat piece.) 125.00

e-Card

NM/M

Complete Set (6): 10.00
Common Player: 1.00
Inserted 1:12
1 Andruw Jones 1.00
2 Alex Rodriguez 3.00
3 Frank Thomas 1.50

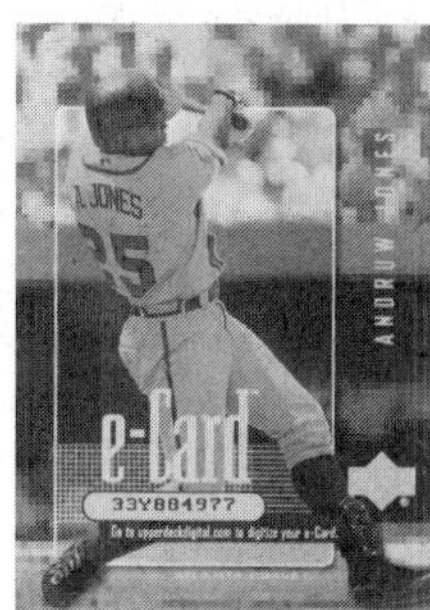

4 Todd Helton 1.50
5 Troy Glaus 1.00
6 Barry Bonds 4.00

eVolve Jersey

Because of the addition of Suzuki and Sosa cards after the initial checklist was promulgated by Upper Deck, and the possibility that cards on the initial list may have been deleted, the accuracy of this list cannot be verified. Card numbers have an "EJ-" prefix. Production was reported as 300 of each card.

		NM/M
Common Player:		10.00
BB	Barry Bonds	30.00
TG	Troy Glaus	8.00
TH	Todd Helton	10.00
AJ	Andruw Jones	10.00
AR	Alex Rodriguez	25.00
SS	Sammy Sosa	15.00
IS	Ichiro Suzuki	50.00
FT	Frank Thomas	15.00

eVolve Jersey Autograph

Because of the addition of Suzuki and Sosa cards after the initial checklist was promulgated by Upper Deck, and the possibility that cards on the initial list may have been deleted, the accuracy of this list cannot be verified. Cards have an "ESJ-" prefix. The edition is limited to 50 numbered cards each.

		NM/M
Common Player:		50.00
BB	Barry Bonds	180.00
TG	Troy Glaus	50.00
TH	Todd Helton	50.00
AJ	Andruw Jones	50.00
AR	Alex Rodriguez	120.00
SS	Sammy Sosa	180.00
IS	Ichiro Suzuki	300.00
FT	Frank Thomas	75.00

eVolve Signature

Because of the addition of Suzuki and Sosa cards after the initial checklist was promulgated by Upper Deck, and the possibility that cards on the initial list may have been deleted, the accuracy of this list cannot be verified. Cards have an "ES-" prefix to their number. Production was reported as 200 of each card.

		NM/M
Common Player:		35.00
BB	Barry Bonds	200.00
TG	Troy Glaus	35.00
TH	Todd Helton	35.00
AJ	Andruw Jones	35.00
AR	Alex Rodriguez	75.00
SS	Sammy Sosa	150.00
IS	Ichiro Suzuki	250.00
FT	Frank Thomas	40.00

2001 Upper Deck Game Jersey

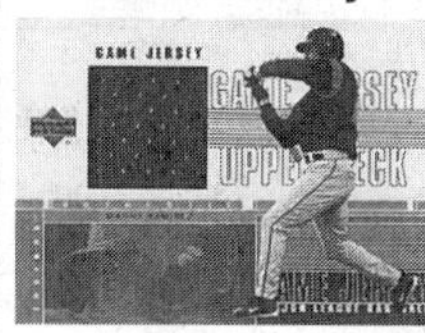

		NM/M
Common Player:		8.00
Inserted 1:288		
KG	Ken Griffey Jr.	30.00
TG	Tony Gwynn	20.00
TH	Todd Helton	12.00
TiH	Tim Hudson	10.00
DJ	Derek Jeter	50.00
AJ	Andruw Jones	10.00
SK	Sandy Koufax	100.00
PO	Paul O'Neill	10.00
MR	Manny Ramirez	10.00
CR	Cal Ripken Jr.	60.00
AR	Alex Rodriguez	40.00
IR	Ivan Rodriguez	10.00
NRa	Nolan Ryan	65.00
NRr	Nolan Ryan	65.00
FT	Fernando Tatis	8.00
RV	Robin Ventura	8.00
BW	Bernie Williams	10.00
MW	Matt Williams	8.00

Autograph

		NM/M
Print Runs Listed		
KG	Ken Griffey/30	250.00
RA	Rick Ankiel/66	25.00
SK	Sandy Koufax/32	900.00
JP	Javy Lopez/8	110.00
NRa	Nolan Ryan/ Mets/30	350.00
NRr	Nolan Ryan/ Angels/30	350.00
RV	Robin Ventura/4	50.00
MW	Matt Williams/9	200.00

Auto. Series 2

		NM/M
Common Player:		30.00
Inserted 1:288 H		
JB	Johnny Bench	50.00
BB	Barry Bonds	200.00
JC	Jose Canseco	40.00
RC	Roger Clemens	125.00
TG	Troy Glaus	30.00
KG	Ken Griffey Jr.	100.00
AJ	Andruw Jones	40.00
CJ	Chipper Jones	50.00
CR	Cal Ripken Jr./SP	200.00
AR	Alex Rodriguez	100.00
IR	Ivan Rodriguez/SP	75.00
NR	Nolan Ryan	150.00
GS	Gary Sheffield	30.00
SS	Sammy Sosa/SP	150.00

Hobby Autograph

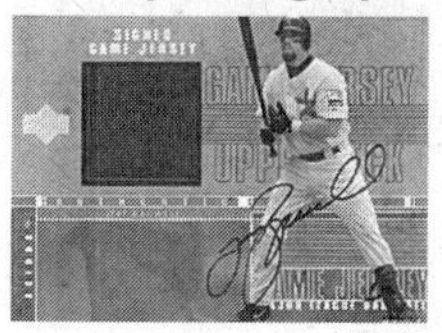

		NM/M
Common Player:		15.00
Inserted 1:288		
RA	Rick Ankiel	15.00
JB	Jeff Bagwell	40.00
BB	Barry Bonds	180.00
JC	Jose Canseco	50.00
SC	Sean Casey	25.00
JD	J.D. Drew	30.00
JG	Jason Giambi	30.00
SG	Shawn Green	30.00
KG	Ken Griffey Jr.	100.00
MH	Mike Hampton	20.00
RJ	Randy Johnson	75.00
JL	Javy Lopez	20.00
GM	Greg Maddux	125.00
RP	Rafael Palmeiro	40.00
AR	Alex Rodriguez	125.00
NRm	Nolan Ryan	125.00
NRa	Nolan Ryan	125.00
FT	Frank Thomas	50.00

Combo

		NM/M
Production 50 Sets		
BB-KG	Barry Bonds, Ken Griffey Jr.	100.00
IR-RP	Ivan Rodriguez, Rafael Palmeiro	25.00
DJ-AR	Derek Jeter, Alex Rodriguez	100.00
MM-KG	Mickey Mantle, Ken Griffey Jr.	250.00
TG-CR	Tony Gwynn, Cal Ripken Jr.	100.00
NR-AR	Nolan Ryan/ Astros/Rangers	100.00
NR-MA	Nolan Ryan/ Mets/Astros	100.00
RJ-GM	Randy Johnson, Greg Maddux	50.00
VG-MR	Vladimir Guerrero, Manny Ramirez	40.00
BB-JC	Barry Bonds, Jose Canseco	80.00
FT-JB	Frank Thomas, Jeff Bagwell	40.00
AJ-KG	Andruw Jones, Ken Griffey Jr.	60.00

Combo Autograph

Production 10 Sets
Values Undetermined

Patch

		NM/M
Common Player:		40.00
Production 25 Sets		
RA	Rick Ankiel	40.00
JB	Jeff Bagwell	60.00
BB	Barry Bonds	150.00
JC	Jose Canseco	50.00
JG	Jason Giambi	50.00
KG	Ken Griffey Jr.	75.00
TG	Tony Gwynn	75.00
DJ	Derek Jeter	125.00
RP	Rafael Palmeiro	60.00
CR	Cal Ripken Jr.	150.00
AR	Alex Rodriguez	100.00
IR	Ivan Rodriguez	60.00
NRa	Nolan Ryan	150.00
NRr	Nolan Ryan	150.00
FT	Frank Thomas	60.00

Patch Gold

		NM/M
Production 25 Sets		
BB	Barry Bonds	200.00
JC	Jose Canseco	100.00
JG	Jason Giambi	100.00
KG	Ken Griffey Jr.	150.00
TG	Tony Gwynn	100.00
DJ	Derek Jeter	200.00
CR	Cal Ripken Jr.	200.00
NRa	Nolan Ryan	200.00
NRr	Nolan Ryan	200.00
FT	Frank Thomas	90.00

Patch Autograph

		NM/M
Print Runs Listed		
RA	Rick Ankiel /66	65.00
KG	Ken Griffey Jr /30	600.00

2001 Upper Deck Game-Used Ball

		NM/M
Common Player:		10.00
Production 100 Sets		
RA	Rick Ankiel	10.00
JB	Jeff Bagwell	15.00
BB	Barry Bonds	50.00
JG	Jason Giambi	15.00
SG	Shawn Green	10.00
KG	Ken Griffey Jr.	35.00
ToG	Tony Gwynn	25.00
DJ	Derek Jeter	60.00
RJ	Randy Johnson	25.00
AJ	Andruw Jones	15.00
MM	Mark McGwire	75.00
AR	Alex Rodriguez	40.00
IR	Ivan Rodriguez	15.00
SS	Sammy Sosa	40.00

Series 2

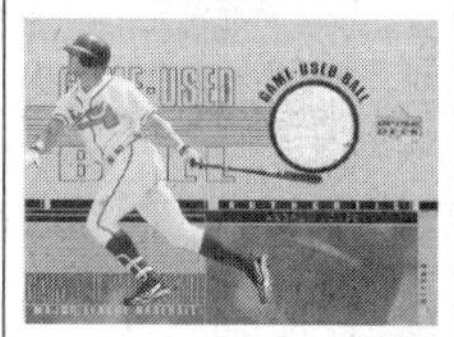

		NM/M
Common Player:		5.00
Inserted 1:288		
JB	Jeff Bagwell	10.00
BB	Barry Bonds	30.00
RC	Roger Clemens	20.00
NG	Nomar Garciaparra	30.00
KG	Ken Griffey Jr.	20.00
VG	Vladimir Guerrero	10.00
DJ	Derek Jeter	30.00
AJ	Andruw Jones	8.00
CJ	Chipper Jones	10.00
JK	Jeff Kent	5.00
MM	Mark McGwire	40.00
MP	Mike Piazza	20.00
CR	Cal Ripken Jr.	25.00
MR	Mariano Rivera	8.00
AR	Alex Rodriguez	20.00
GS	Gary Sheffield	8.00
SS	Sammy Sosa	20.00
BW	Bernie Williams	10.00

Autographs

		NM/M
Production 25 Sets		
RA	Rick Ankiel	40.00
JB	Jeff Bagwell	60.00
BB	Barry Bonds	150.00
JG	Jason Giambi	75.00
KG	Ken Griffey Jr.	90.00
SG	Shawn Green	60.00
TH	Todd Helton	60.00
RJ	Randy Johnson	90.00
AR	Alex Rodriguez	80.00

Home Run Explosion

		NM/M
Complete Set (15):		20.00
Common Player:		.50
Inserted 1:12		
1	Mark McGwire	3.00
2	Chipper Jones	2.00
3	Jeff Bagwell	1.00
4	Carlos Delgado	1.00
5	Barry Bonds	4.00
6	Troy Glaus	1.00
7	Sammy Sosa	2.50
8	Alex Rodriguez	3.00
9	Mike Piazza	2.00
10	Vladimir Guerrero	1.50
11	Ken Griffey Jr.	2.00
12	Frank Thomas	1.00
13	Ivan Rodriguez	1.00
14	Jason Giambi	1.00
15	Carl Everett	.50

Home Run Derby Heroes

		NM/M
Complete Set (10):		25.00
Common Player:		1.00
Inserted 1:36		
HD1	Mark McGwire/1999	5.00
HD2	Sammy Sosa/2000	3.00
HD3	Frank Thomas/1996	2.00
HD4	Cal Ripken Jr./1991	5.00
HD5	Tino Martinez/1997	1.00
HD6	Ken Griffey Jr./1999	3.00
HD7	Barry Bonds/1996	5.00
HD8	Albert Belle/1995	1.00
HD9	Mark McGwire/1992	5.00
HD10	Juan Gonzalez/1993	2.00

Midseason Superstar Summit

		NM/M
Complete Set (15):		25.00
Common Player:		.75
Inserted 1:24		
MS1	Derek Jeter	5.00
MS2	Sammy Sosa	3.00
MS3	Jeff Bagwell	1.50
MS4	Tony Gwynn	1.50
MS5	Alex Rodriguez	4.00
MS6	Greg Maddux	2.50
MS7	Jason Giambi	1.50
MS8	Mark McGwire	4.00
MS9	Barry Bonds	5.00
MS10	Ken Griffey Jr.	3.00
MS11	Carlos Delgado	1.50
MS12	Troy Glaus	1.00
MS13	Todd Helton	1.50
MS14	Manny Ramirez	1.50
MS15	Jeff Kent	.75

Most Wanted

		NM/M
Complete Set (15):		20.00
Common Player:		.75
Inserted 1:14 Series 1		
MW1	Mark McGwire	2.50
MW2	Cal Ripken Jr.	3.00
MW3	Ivan Rodriguez	.75
MW4	Pedro Martinez	1.00
MW5	Sammy Sosa	2.00
MW6	Tony Gwynn	1.00
MW7	Vladimir Guerrero	1.00
MW8	Derek Jeter	3.00
MW9	Mike Piazza	1.50
MW10	Chipper Jones	1.50
MW11	Alex Rodriguez	2.50
MW12	Barry Bonds	3.00
MW13	Jeff Bagwell	.75
MW14	Frank Thomas	.75
MW15	Nomar Garciaparra	2.00

Rookie Roundup

		NM/M
Complete Set (10):		5.00
Common Player:		.50
Inserted 1:6		
1	Rick Ankiel	.50
2	Adam Kennedy	.50
3	Mike Lamb	.50
4	Adam Eaton	.50
5	Rafael Furcal	.75
6	Pat Burrell	1.50
7	Adam Piatt	.50
8	Eric Munson	.50
9	Brad Penny	.50
10	Mark Mulder	.75

Subway Series Heroes - Hawaii

These cards were created for the Kit Young Hawaii trade show and were distributed on a one-per-day basis and as a complete set in a special engraved plexiglass frame measuring 8-1/2" x 6-7/8". Cards have black-and-white portrait or action photos. On a photo of a 1956 World Series scoreboard is a genuine autograph. Backs have career highlights, an authentication message, logos and are numbered from within an edition of 450 of each card.

		NM/M
Complete Set in Frame:		110.00
Complete Card Set (4):		75.00
Common Player:		20.00
KY-SS1	Don Larsen	20.00
KY-SS2	Whitey Ford	35.00
KY-SS3	Johnny Podres	20.00
KY-SS4	Duke Snider	35.00

Subway Series Jersey Cards

		NM/M
Common Player:		5.00
Inserted 1:144		
SS-EA	Edgardo Alfonzo	5.00
SS-RC	Roger Clemens	40.00
SS-JF	John Franco	5.00
SS-OH	Orlando Hernandez	8.00
SS-AL	Al Leiter	5.00
SS-PO	Paul O'Neill	10.00
SS-JP	Jay Payton	5.00
SS-TP	Timo Perez	5.00
SS-AP	Andy Pettitte	15.00
SS-BW	Bernie Williams	15.00

Superstar Summit

		NM/M
Complete Set (15):		25.00
Common Player:		1.00
Inserted 1:12		
1	Derek Jeter	4.00
2	Randy Johnson	1.50
3	Barry Bonds	4.00
4	Frank Thomas	1.00

5 Cal Ripken Jr. 4.00
6 Pedro J. Martinez 1.50
7 Ivan Rodriguez 1.00
8 Mike Piazza 2.00
9 Mark McGwire 3.00
10 Manny Ramirez 1.00
11 Ken Griffey Jr. 2.00
12 Sammy Sosa 2.50
13 Alex Rodriguez 3.00
14 Chipper Jones 2.00
15 Nomar Garciaparra 2.50

The Franchise

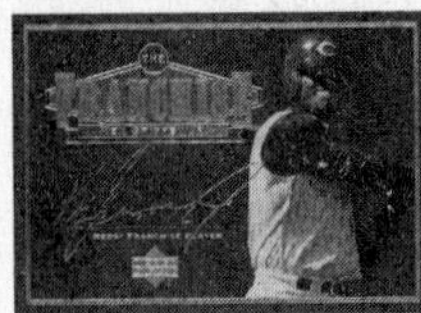

NM/M
Complete Set (10): 25.00
Common Player: 1.50
Inserted 1:36
F1 Frank Thomas 1.50
F2 Mark McGwire 5.00
F3 Ken Griffey Jr. 3.00
F4 Manny Ramirez 1.50
F5 Alex Rodriguez 5.00
F6 Greg Maddux 3.00
F7 Sammy Sosa 4.00
F8 Derek Jeter 6.00
F9 Mike Piazza 3.00
F10 Vladimir Guerrero 2.00

The People's Choice

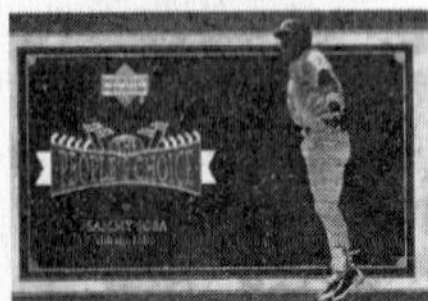

NM/M
Complete Set (15): 35.00
Common Player: 1.50
Inserted 1:24
PC1 Alex Rodriguez 5.00
PC2 Ken Griffey Jr. 3.00
PC3 Mark McGwire 5.00
PC4 Todd Helton 1.50
PC5 Manny Ramirez 1.50
PC6 Mike Piazza 3.00
PC7 Vladimir Guerrero 2.00
PC8 Randy Johnson 2.00
PC9 Cal Ripken Jr. 6.00
PC10 Andruw Jones 1.50
PC11 Sammy Sosa 4.00
PC12 Derek Jeter 6.00
PC13 Pedro Martinez 2.00
PC14 Frank Thomas 1.50
PC15 Nomar Garciaparra 4.00

UD Game-Worn Patch

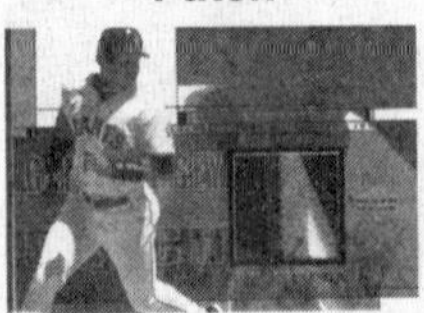

NM/M
Common Player: 60.00
P-JB Johnny Bench 120.00
P-BB Barry Bonds 150.00
P-KG Ken Griffey Jr. 100.00
P-CJ Chipper Jones 60.00
P-CR Cal Ripken Jr. 150.00
P-AR Alex Rodriguez 125.00
P-IR Ivan Rodriguez 60.00
P-NR Nolan Ryan 150.00
P-SS Sammy Sosa 100.00

Cincinnati Reds Team Set

This boxed set has 20 player cards in standard 2-1/2" x 3-1/2" format and a 3-1/2" x 5" checklist/team history card. Cards have borderless action photos on front with an Upper Deck Collectibles logo at top-left. At bottom are the team and player name, position and uniform number. Backs have a smaller version of the front photo, some biographical and career notes and 1999-2000 stats. Cards are numbered with a "CR" prefix.

NM/M
Complete Set (21): 7.50
Common Player: .50
1 Ken Griffey Jr. 3.00
2 Dmitri Young .50
3 Michael Tucker .50
4 Aaron Boone .75
5 Barry Larkin 1.00
6 Pokey Reese .50
7 Sean Casey 1.00
8 Jason LaRue .50
9 Scott Williamson .50
10 Pete Harnisch .50
11 Danny Graves .50
12 Rob Bell .50
13 Gookie Dawkins .50
14 Kelly Stinnett .50
15 Leo Estrella .50
16 Wilton Guerrero .50
17 Elmer Dessens .65
18 Seth Etherton .65
19 Donnie Sadler .50
20 Scott Sullivan .50
21 Checklist .50

2001 Upper Deck Decade

NM/M
Complete Set (180): 25.00
Common Player: .15
Pack (5): 1.50
Box (24): 30.00
1 Nolan Ryan 3.00
2 Don Baylor .15
3 Bobby Grich .15
4 Reggie Jackson .50
5 Jim "Catfish" Hunter .25
6 Gene Tenace .15
7 Rollie Fingers .25
8 Sal Bando .15
9 Bert Campaneris .15
10 John Mayberry .15
11 Rico Carty .15
12 Gaylord Perry .25
13 Andre Thornton .15
14 Buddy Bell .15
15 Dennis Eckersley .25
16 Ruppert Jones .15
17 Brooks Robinson .75
18 Tommy Davis .15
19 Eddie Murray .25
20 Boog Powell .15
21 Al Oliver .15
22 Jeff Burroughs .15
23 Mike Hargrove .15
24 Dwight Evans .15
25 Fred Lynn .15
26 Rico Petrocelli .15
27 Carlton Fisk .50
28 Luis Aparicio .15
29 Amos Otis .15
30 Hal McRae .15
31 Jason Thompson .15
32 Al Kaline .75
33 Jim Perry .15
34 Bert Blyleven .15
35 Harmon Killebrew 1.00
36 Wilbur Wood .15
37 Jim Kaat .15
38 Ron Guidry .15
39 Thurman Munson 1.00
40 Graig Nettles .15
41 Bobby Murcer .15
42 Chris Chambliss .15
43 Roy White .15
44 J.R. Richard .15
45 Jose Cruz .15
46 Hank Aaron 2.00
47 Phil Niekro .15
48 Bob Horner .15
49 Darryl Evans .15
50 Gorman Thomas .15
51 Don Money .15
52 Robin Yount .75
53 Joe Torre .25
54 Tim McCarver .15
55 Lou Brock .40
56 Keith Hernandez .15
57 Bill Madlock .15
58 Ron Santo .15
59 Billy Williams .15
60 Ferguson Jenkins .25
61 Steve Garvey .15
62 Bill Russell .15
63 Maury Wills .25
64 Ron Cey .15
65 Manny Mota .15
66 Ron Fairly .15
67 Steve Rogers .15
68 Gary Carter .15
69 Andre Dawson .25
70 Bobby Bonds .25
71 Jack Clark .15
72 Willie McCovey .15
73 Tom Seaver 1.00
74 Bud Harrelson .15
75 Dave Kingman .15
76 Jerry Koosman .15
77 Jon Matlack .15
78 Randy Jones .15
79 Ozzie Smith 1.00
80 Garry Maddox .15
81 Mike Schmidt 1.00
82 Greg Luzinski .15
83 Tug McGraw .15
84 Willie Stargell .75
85 Dave Parker .15
86 Roberto Clemente 2.00
87 Johnny Bench 1.50
88 Joe Morgan .40
89 George Foster .15
90 Ken Griffey Sr. .15
91 Carlton Fisk/1972 (1970s Rookie Flashbacks) .50
92 Andre Dawson/1977 (1970s Rookie Flashbacks) .25
93 Fred Lynn/1975 (1970s Rookie Flashbacks) .15
94 Eddie Murray/1977 (1970s Rookie Flashbacks) .25
95 Bob Horner/1978 (1970s Rookie Flashbacks) .15
96 Jon Matlack/1972 (1970s Rookie Flashbacks) .15
97 Mike Hargrove/1974 (1970s Rookie Flashbacks) .15
98 Robin Yount/1974 (1970s Rookie Flashbacks) .50
99 Mike Schmidt/1972 (1970s Rookie Flashbacks) .50
100 Gary Carter/1974 (1970s Rookie Flashbacks) .15
101 Ozzie Smith/1978 (1970s Rookie Flashbacks) .50
102 Paul Molitor/1978 (1970s Rookie Flashbacks) .50
103 Dennis Eckersley 1975 (1970s Rookie Flashbacks) .25
104 Dale Murphy/1976 (1970s Rookie Flashbacks) .15
105 Bert Blyleven/1970 (1970s Rookie Flashbacks) .15
106 Thurman Munson/1970 (1970s Rookie Flashbacks) .75
107 Dave Parker/1973 (1970s Rookie Flashbacks) .15
108 Jack Clark/1975 (1970s Rookie Flashbacks) .15
109 Keith Hernandez/1974 (1970s Rookie Flashbacks) .15
110 Ron Cey/1971 (1970s Rookie Flashbacks) .15
111 Billy Williams/1970 (Decade Dateline) .15
112 Tom Seaver/1970 (Decade Dateline) .75
113 Reggie Jackson/1971 (Decade Dateline) .75
114 Barry Bonds/1971 (Decade Dateline) .15
115 Willie Stargell/1971 (Decade Dateline) .40
116 Harmon Killebrew/1971 (Decade Dateline) .50
117 Roberto Clemente/1972 (Decade Dateline) 1.00
118 Wilbur Wood/1972 (Decade Dateline) .15
119 Billy Williams/1972 (Decade Dateline) .15
120 Nolan Ryan/1973 (Decade Dateline) 1.50
121 Ron Blomberg/1973 (Decade Dateline) .15
122 Hank Aaron/1974 (Decade Dateline) 1.00
123 Lou Brock/1974 (Decade Dateline) .25
124 Al Kaline/1974 (Decade Dateline) .40
125 Brooks Robinson/1975 (Decade Dateline) .40
126 Bill Madlock/1975 (Decade Dateline) .15
127 Rennie Stennett/1975 (Decade Dateline) .15
128 Carlton Fisk/1975 (Decade Dateline) .40
129 Chris Chambliss/1976 (Decade Dateline) .15
130 Ruppert Jones/1977 (Decade Dateline) .15
131 Ron Fairly/1977 (Decade Dateline) .15
132 George Foster/1977 (Decade Dateline) .15
133 Reggie Jackson/1977 (Decade Dateline) .75
134 Ron Guidry/1978 (Decade Dateline) .15
135 Gaylord Perry/1978 (Decade Dateline) .15
136 Bucky Dent/1978 (Decade Dateline) .15
137 Dave Kingman/1979 (Decade Dateline) .15
138 Lou Brock/1979 (Decade Dateline) .15
139 Thurman Munson/1979 (Decade Dateline) .75
140 Willie Stargell/1979 (Decade Dateline) .40
141 Johnny Bench/1970 NL MVP (1970s Award Winners) .75
142 Boog Powell/1970 AL MVP (1970s Award Winners) .15
143 Jim Perry/1970 AL CY (1970s Award Winners) .15
144 Joe Torre/1971 NL MVP (1970s Award Winners) .15
145 Chris Chambliss/1971 AL ROY (1970s Award Winners) .15
146 Ferguson Jenkins/1971 NL CY (1970s Award Winners) .15
147 Carlton Fisk/1972 AL ROY (1970s Award Winners) .40
148 Gaylord Perry/1972 AL CY (1970s Award Winners) .15
149 Johnny Bench/1972 NL MVP (1970s Award Winners) .75
150 Reggie Jackson/1973 AL MVP (1970s Award Winners) .75
151 Tom Seaver/1973 NL CY (1970s Award Winners) .75
152 Thurman Munson/1973 AL GG (1970s Award Winners) .75
153 Steve Garvey/1974 NL MVP (1970s Award Winners) .15
154 Jim "Catfish" Hunter/1974 AL CY (1970s Award Winners) .15
155 Mike Hargrove/1974 AL ROY (1970s Award Winners) .15
156 Joe Morgan/1975 NL MVP (1970s Award Winners) .15
157 Fred Lynn/1975 AL MVP & ROY (1970s Award Winners) .15
158 Tom Seaver/1975 NL CY (1970s Award Winners) .75
159 Thurman Munson/1976 AL MVP (1970s Award Winners) .75
160 Randy Jones/1976 NL CY (1970s Award Winners) .15
161 Joe Morgan/1976 NL ROY (1970s Award Winners) .15
162 George Foster/1977 NL MVP (1970s Award Winners) .15
163 Eddie Murray/1977 AL ROY (1970s Award Winners) .25
164 Andre Dawson/1977 NL ROY (1970s Award Winners) .25
165 Gaylord Perry/1978 NL CY (1970s Award Winners) .15
166 Ron Guidry/1978 AL CY (1970s Award Winners) .15
167 Dave Parker/1978 NL MVP (1970s Award Winners) .15
168 Don Baylor/1979 AL MVP (1970s Award Winners) .15
169 Bruce Sutter/1979 NL CY (1970s Award Winners) .30
170 Willie Stargell/1979 NL co-MVP (1970s Award Winners) .40
171 Brooks Robinson/1970 (1970s World Series Highlights) .50
172 Roberto Clemente/1971 (1970s World Series Highlights) 1.00
173 Gene Tenace/1972 (1970s World Series Highlights) .15
174 Reggie Jackson/1973 (1970s World Series Highlights) .75
175 Rollie Fingers/1974 (1970s World Series Highlights) .15
176 Carlton Fisk/1975 (1970s World Series Highlights) .40
177 Johnny Bench/1976 (1970s World Series Highlights) .75
178 Reggie Jackson/1977 (1970s World Series Highlights) .75
179 Bucky Dent/1978 (1970s World Series Highlights) .15
180 Willie Stargell/1979 (1970s World Series Highlights) .40

Bellbottomed Bashers

NM/M
Complete Set (10): 12.00
Common Player: 1.00
Inserted 1:14
BB1 Reggie Jackson 2.00
BB2 Gorman Thomas 1.00
BB3 Willie McCovey 1.50
BB4 Willie Stargell 1.50
BB5 Mike Schmidt 3.00
BB6 George Foster 1.00
BB7 Johnny Bench 2.50
BB8 Dave Kingman 1.00
BB9 Graig Nettles 1.00
BB10 Steve Garvey 1.00

Decade Dynasties

NM/M
Complete Set (10): 15.00
Common Player: 1.00
Inserted 1:14
D1 Boog Powell 1.00
D2 Johnny Bench 3.00
D3 Willie Stargell 1.50
D4 Jim "Catfish" Hunter 1.00
D5 Steve Garvey 1.00
D6 Carlton Fisk 2.00
D7 Mike Schmidt 4.00
D8 Hal McRae 1.00
D9 Tom Seaver 3.00
D10 Reggie Jackson 2.50

Game-Used Bat

NM/M
Common Player: 5.00
Inserted 1:24 H
HA Hank Aaron 40.00
DB Don Baylor 5.00
BB Bobby Bonds 5.00
GC Gary Carter 0.00
JaC Jack Clark 5.00
RC Roberto Clemente/243 100.00
DC Dave Concepcion 5.00
JoC Jose Cruz 5.00
TD Tommy Davis 5.00
AD Andre Dawson 8.00
DaE Darryl Evans 5.00
DwE Dwight Evans 5.00
CF Carlton Fisk 10.00
GF George Foster 5.00
SG Steve Garvey 5.00
BG Bobby Grich 5.00
KG Ken Griffey Sr. 5.00
BH Bud Harrelson/290 5.00
KH Keith Hernandez/243 20.00
RH Ron Hunt 5.00
ReJ Reggie Jackson 15.00
RaJ Randy Jones 5.00
GL Greg Luzinski 5.00
FL Fred Lynn 5.00
GM Garry Maddox 5.00
BiM Bill Madlock 5.00
TiM Tim McCarver 5.00
TuM Tug McGraw/97 25.00
HM Hal McRae 5.00
RM Rick Monday 5.00
WM Willie Montanez 5.00
JM Joe Morgan 5.00
BoM Bobby Murcer 20.00
EM Eddie Murray 10.00
GN Graig Nettles/219 15.00
AO Al Oliver 5.00
DP Dave Parker 5.00
BP Boog Powell 5.00
WR Willie Randolph 5.00
BR Bill Russell 5.00
NR Nolan Ryan 50.00
RS Ron Santo 5.00
ToS Tom Seaver/121 20.00
OS Ozzie Smith 15.00
RW Roy White 5.00
MW Maury Wills 5.00
DW Dave Winfield 8.00

Game-Used Bat Combo

NM/M
Common Card: 20.00
Inserted 1:336
NYY Reggie Jackson, Graig Nettles, Chris Chambliss, Roy White 40.00
LA Steve Garvey, Ron Cey, Bill Russell, Rick Monday 25.00
NYM Tom Seaver, Bud Harrelson, Ron Hunt, Tug McGraw 50.00
CIN Johnny Bench, George Foster, Ken Griffey Sr., Joe Morgan 50.00
ROY Andre Dawson, Fred Lynn, Carlton Fisk, Eddie Murray 40.00
MVPN Johnny Bench, Steve Garvey, Willie Stargell, George Foster 50.00
BAT Keith Hernandez, Bill Madlock, Fred Lynn, Dave Parker 20.00
GGA Carlton Fisk, Graig Nettles, Bobby Grich, Fred Lynn 25.00
GGN Johnny Bench, Roberto Clemente, Dave Concepcion, Garry Maddox 100.00
WS72 Reggie Jackson, Bert Campaneris, Dave Concepcion, Johnny Bench/97 80.00
WS73 Reggie Jackson, Bert Campaneris, Tom Seaver, Bud Harrelson 40.00
WS74 Reggie Jackson, Bert Campaneris, Steve Garvey, Ron Cey 40.00
WS75 Carlton Fisk, Fred Lynn, George Foster, Joe Morgan 40.00
WS76 Chris Chambliss, Graig Nettles, Johnny Bench, Ken Griffey Sr./97 80.00
WS77 Reggie Jackson, Graig Nettles, Steve Garvey, Ron Cey 40.00
WS78 Graig Nettles, Chris Chambliss, Bill Russell, Ron Cey/238 50.00
ASMV Bill Madlock, Joe Morgan, Steve Garvey, Dave Parker 40.00
RY Chris Chambliss, Reggie Jackson, Roy White, Hal McRae/238 40.00
RD George Foster, Joe Morgan, Ron Cey, Bill Russell 25.00

Game-Used Jersey

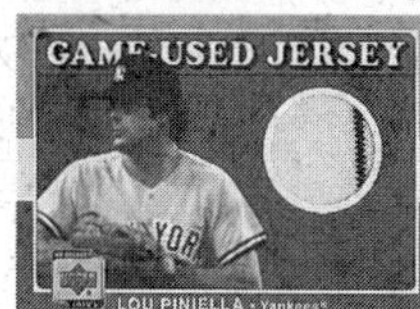

		NM/M
Common Player:		8.00
Inserted 1:168		
HA	Hank Aaron	40.00
LA	Luis Aparicio	8.00
JB	Johnny Bench	15.00
RC	Roberto Clemente	100.00
WD	Willie Davis	8.00
RF	Rollie Fingers	8.00
CF	Carlton Fisk	10.00
RG	Ron Guidry	8.00
BH	Burt Hooton	8.00
CH	Jim "Catfish" Hunter	10.00
RJ	Reggie Jackson	15.00
JKa	Jim Kaat	8.00
JKo	Jerry Koosman	8.00
BM	Bill Madlock	8.00
JM	Jon Matlack	8.00
TM	Tug McGraw	8.00
BM	Bobby Murcer	15.00
JP	Jim Perry	8.00
LP	Lou Piniella	10.00
WR	Willie Randolph	8.00
NR	Nolan Ryan/50	75.00
TS	Tom Seaver	20.00
WS	Willie Stargell	10.00
MW	Maury Wills	8.00

Game-Used Jersey Autograph

		NM/M
Common Autograph:		20.00
Inserted 1:168 H		
HA	Hank Aaron/97	200.00
LA	Luis Aparicio	30.00
SB	Sal Bando	20.00
JB	Johnny Bench	70.00
RF	Rollie Fingers	25.00
CF	Carlton Fisk/243	40.00
KG	Ken Griffey Sr.	20.00
RG	Ron Guidry	30.00
BH	Burt Hooton	20.00
RJ	Reggie Jackson/291	65.00
JKa	Jim Kaat	25.00
JKo	Jerry Koosman	20.00
BM	Bill Madlock	20.00
TM	Tug McGraw	20.00
BM	Bobby Murcer	50.00
RP	Rico Petrocelli	25.00
NR	Nolan Ryan/291	125.00
MW	Maury Wills	20.00

Game-Used Patch

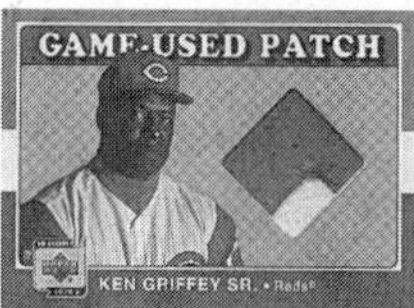

Inserted 1:7,500
No pricing due to scarcity.

The Arms Race

		NM/M
Complete Set (10):		10.00
Common Player:		.50
Inserted 1:14		
AR1	Nolan Ryan	4.00
AR2	Ferguson Jenkins	1.00
AR3	Jim "Catfish" Hunter	1.00
AR4	Tom Seaver	2.00
AR5	Randy Jones	.50
AR6	J.R. Richard	.50
AR7	Rollie Fingers	1.00
AR8	Gaylord Perry	.75
AR9	Ron Guidry	.75
AR10	Phil Niekro	.75

'70s Disco Era Dandies

		NM/M
Complete Set (6):		5.00
Common Player:		.50
Inserted 1:23		
DE1	Mike Schmidt	2.00
DE2	Johnny Bench	1.00
DE3	Lou Brock	.50
DE4	Reggie Jackson	2.00
DE5	Willie Stargell	.50
DE6	Tom Seaver	1.00

'70s Super Powers

		NM/M
Complete Set (6):		12.00
Common Player:		1.50
Inserted 1:24		
SP1	Reggie Jackson	3.00
SP2	Joe Morgan	1.50
SP3	Willie Stargell	2.00
SP4	Willie McCovey	1.50
SP5	Mike Schmidt	4.00
SP6	Nolan Ryan	5.00

2001 Upper Deck Evolution

		NM/M
Complete Set (120):		125.00
Common Player:		.15
Common SP (91-120):		3.00
Production 2,250		
Pack (5):		2.00
Box (24):		40.00
1	Darin Erstad	.25
2	Troy Glaus	.50
3	Jason Giambi	.50
4	Tim Hudson	.40
5	Jermaine Dye	.15
6	Barry Zito	.40
7	Carlos Delgado	.50
8	Shannon Stewart	.15
9	Jose Cruz Jr.	.15
10	Greg Vaughn	.15
11	Juan Gonzalez	.50
12	Roberto Alomar	.50
13	Omar Vizquel	.25
14	Jim Thome	.50
15	Edgar Martinez	.25
16	John Olerud	.25
17	Kazuhiro Sasaki	.15
18	Cal Ripken Jr.	2.00
19	Alex Rodriguez	1.50
20	Ivan Rodriguez	.50
21	Rafael Palmeiro	.50
22	Pedro Martinez	.75
23	Nomar Garciaparra	1.50
24	Manny Ramirez	.50
25	Carl Everett	.15
26	Mark Quinn	.15
27	Mike Sweeney	.15
28	Neifi Perez	.15
29	Tony Clark	.15
30	Eric Milton	.15
31	Doug Mientkiewicz	.15
32	Corey Koskie	.15
33	Frank Thomas	.50
34	David Wells	.15
35	Magglio Ordonez	.40
36	Derek Jeter	2.00
37	Mike Mussina	.40
38	Bernie Williams	.50
39	Roger Clemens	1.50
40	David Justice	.25
41	Jeff Bagwell	.50
42	Richard Hidalgo	.25
43	Wade Miller	.15
44	Chipper Jones	1.00
45	Greg Maddux	1.00
46	Andruw Jones	.50
47	Rafael Furcal	.25
48	Geoff Jenkins	.25
49	Jeromy Burnitz	.15
50	Ben Sheets	.25
51	Richie Sexson	.40
52	Mark McGwire	1.50
53	Jim Edmonds	.40
54	Darryl Kile	.15
55	J.D. Drew	.25
56	Sammy Sosa	1.50
57	Kerry Wood	.50
58	Randy Johnson	.75
59	Luis Gonzalez	.25
60	Matt Williams	.25
61	Kevin Brown	.25
62	Gary Sheffield	.40
63	Shawn Green	.40
64	Chan Ho Park	.15
65	Vladimir Guerrero	.75
66	Jose Vidro	.15
67	Fernando Tatis	.15
68	Barry Bonds	2.00
69	Jeff Kent	.25
70	Russ Ortiz	.15
71	Preston Wilson	.15
72	Ryan Dempster	.15
73	Charles Johnson	.15
74	Mike Piazza	1.00
75	Edgardo Alfonzo	.15
76	Robin Ventura	.25
77	Jay Payton	.15
78	Tony Gwynn	.75
79	Phil Nevin	.15
80	Pat Burrell	.40
81	Scott Rolen	.50
82	Bob Abreu	.25
83	Brian Giles	.25
84	Jason Kendall	.25
85	Ken Griffey Jr.	1.00
86	Barry Larkin	.40
87	Sean Casey	.25
88	Todd Helton	.50
89	Larry Walker	.25
90	Mike Hampton	.15
91	Ichiro Suzuki **RC**	20.00
92	Albert Pujols **RC**	40.00
93	Wilson Betemit **RC**	3.00
94	Jay Gibbons **RC**	8.00
95	Juan Uribe **RC**	5.00
96	Morgan Ensberg **RC**	8.00
97	Christian Parker **RC**	3.00
98	Tsuyoshi Shinjo **RC**	4.00
99	Jack Wilson **RC**	8.00
100	Donaldo Mendez **RC**	3.00
101	Ryan Freel **RC**	4.00
102	Juan Diaz **RC**	3.00
103	Horacio Ramirez **RC**	8.00
104	Ricardo Rodriguez **RC**	3.00
105	Erick Almonte **RC**	3.00
106	Josh Towers **RC**	3.00
107	Adrian Hernandez **RC**	3.00
108	Brandon Duckworth **RC**	4.00
109	Travis Hafner **RC**	10.00
110	Martin Vargas **RC**	3.00
111	Kris Keller **RC**	3.00
112	Brian Lawrence **RC**	3.00
113	Esix Snead **RC**	3.00
114	Wilken Ruan **RC**	3.00
115	Jose Mieses **RC**	3.00
116	Johnny Estrada **RC**	8.00
117	Elpidio Guzman **RC**	3.00
118	Sean Douglass **RC**	3.00
119	Billy Sylvester **RC**	3.00
120	Bret Prinz **RC**	3.00

Autographed Bat/Jersey

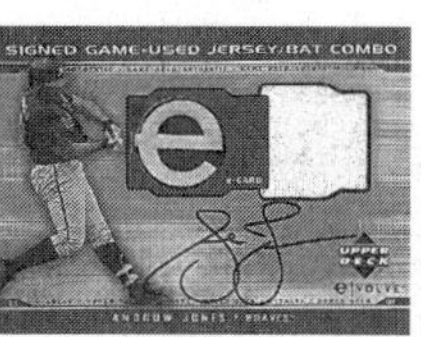

		NM/M
Common Player:		25.00
RB	Russell Branyan	25.00
PB	Pat Burrell	40.00
CD	Carlos Delgado	40.00
JD	J.D. Drew	25.00
JaG	Jason Giambi	65.00
SG	Shawn Green	40.00
KG	Ken Griffey Jr.	100.00
AJ	Andruw Jones	50.00
CJ	Chipper Jones	60.00
JK	Jason Kendall	30.00
CR	Cal Ripken Jr.	150.00
AR	Alex Rodriguez	150.00
GS	Gary Sheffield	50.00
SS	Sammy Sosa	200.00
IS	Ichiro Suzuki	300.00

Game-Used Bat Cards

		NM/M
Common Player:		5.00
Winners Evolve Into Bat/Jsy Auto.		
Inserted 1:120		
RB	Russell Branyan	5.00
PB	Pat Burrell	8.00
CD	Carlos Delgado	8.00
JD	J.D. Drew	5.00
JaG	Jason Giambi	8.00
KG	Ken Griffey Jr.	20.00
AJ	Andruw Jones	8.00
JK	Jason Kendall	5.00
AR	Alex Rodriguez	15.00
GS	Gary Sheffield	6.00

Game-Used Jersey Cards

		NM/M
Common Player:		5.00
Inserted 1:120		
RB	Russell Branyan	5.00
PB	Pat Burrell	8.00
JD	J.D. Drew	5.00
JaG	Jason Giambi	10.00
BG	Brian Giles	6.00
TG	Troy Glaus	8.00
SG	Shawn Green	6.00
KG	Ken Griffey Jr.	20.00
AJ	Andruw Jones	8.00
CJ	Chipper Jones	10.00
JK	Jason Kendall	5.00
CR	Cal Ripken Jr.	30.00
AR	Alex Rodriguez	15.00
GS	Gary Sheffield	8.00
SS	Sammy Sosa	15.00

Ichiro Suzuki All-Star Game

		NM/M
Random inserts		
51B	Ichiro Suzuki/Bronze	8.00
51S	Ichiro Suzuki/Silver/2001	20.00
51G	Ichiro Suzuki/Gold/51	120.00

UD Classics

		NM/M
Complete Set (15):		15.00
Common Player:		.50
Prices for unscratched cards.		
Winners Evolve Into Game Jersey.		
Inserted 1:4		
EC1	Ken Griffey Jr.	3.00
EC2	Gary Sheffield	.75
EC3	Randy Johnson	1.50
EC4	Sammy Sosa	3.00
EC5	Carlos Delgado	1.00
EC6	Ichiro Suzuki	3.00
EC7	Andruw Jones	1.00
EC8	Chipper Jones	2.00
EC9	Kazuhiro Sasaki	.50
EC10	Shawn Green	.75
EC11	Alex Rodriguez	3.00
EC12	Brian Giles	.75
EC13	J.D. Drew	.50
EC14	Pat Burrell	1.00
EC15	Ivan Rodriguez	1.00

UD Classics Jersey

	NM/M
Common Player:	1.00

Prices for unscratched cards.
Winners evolve into Game Jersey.

2001 Upper Deck Gold Glove

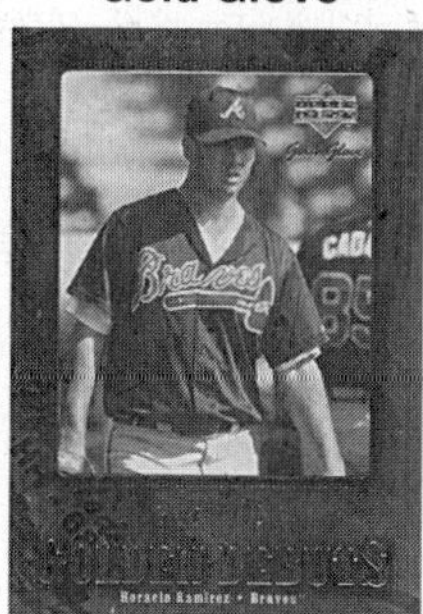

		NM/M
Common Player:		.25
Common SP (91-129):		4.00
Production 1,000		
Common SP (130-135):		8.00
Production 500		
Pack (4):		8.00
Box (20):		140.00
1	Troy Glaus	1.00
2	Darin Erstad	.50
3	Jason Giambi	1.00
4	Tim Hudson	.50
5	Jermaine Dye	.25
6	Raul Mondesi	.25
7	Carlos Delgado	1.00
8	Shannon Stewart	.25
9	Greg Vaughn	.25
10	Aubrey Huff	.25
11	Juan Gonzalez	1.00
12	Roberto Alomar	1.00
13	Omar Vizquel	.25
14	Jim Thome	1.00
15	John Olerud	.50
16	Edgar Martinez	.50
17	Kazuhiro Sasaki	.25
18	Aaron Sele	.25
19	Cal Ripken Jr.	4.00
20	Chris Richard	.25
21	Ivan Rodriguez	1.00
22	Rafael Palmeiro	.75
23	Alex Rodriguez	3.00
24	Pedro Martinez	1.50
25	Nomar Garciaparra	3.00
26	Manny Ramirez	1.00
27	Neifi Perez	.25
28	Mike Sweeney	.25
29	Bobby Higginson	.25
30	Dean Palmer	.25
31	Tony Clark	.25
32	Doug Mientkiewicz	.25
33	Brad Radke	.25
34	Joe Mays	.25
35	Frank Thomas	1.00
36	Magglio Ordonez	.50
37	Carlos Lee	.25
38	Bernie Williams	1.00
39	Mike Mussina	1.00
40	Derek Jeter	4.00
41	Roger Clemens	2.50
42	Craig Biggio	.40
43	Jeff Bagwell	1.00
44	Lance Berkman	.50
45	Andruw Jones	1.00
46	Greg Maddux	2.00
47	Chipper Jones	2.00
48	Geoff Jenkins	.40
49	Ben Sheets	.25
50	Jeromy Burnitz	.25
51	Jim Edmonds	.50
52	Mark McGwire	3.00
53	Mike Matheny	.25
54	J.D. Drew	.50
55	Sammy Sosa	2.50
56	Kerry Wood	.75
57	Fred McGriff	.40
58	Randy Johnson	1.50
59	Steve Finley	.25
60	Mark Grace	.75
61	Matt Williams	.40
62	Luis Gonzalez	.40
63	Shawn Green	.40
64	Kevin Brown	.40
65	Gary Sheffield	.50
66	Vladimir Guerrero	1.25
67	Tony Armas Jr.	.25
68	Barry Bonds	4.00
69	J.T. Snow	.25
70	Jeff Kent	.25
71	Charles Johnson	.25
72	Preston Wilson	.25
73	Cliff Floyd	.25
74	Robin Ventura	.25
75	Mike Piazza	2.00
76	Edgardo Alfonzo	.25
77	Tony Gwynn	1.50
78	Ryan Klesko	.50
79	Scott Rolen	1.00
80	Mike Lieberthal	.25
81	Pat Burrell	.75
82	Jason Kendall	.25
83	Brian Giles	.50
84	Ken Griffey Jr.	2.50
85	Barry Larkin	.50
86	Pokey Reese	.25
87	Larry Walker	.40
88	Mike Hampton	.25
89	Juan Pierre	.25
90	Todd Helton	1.00
91	Mike Penney **RC**	4.00
92	Wilkin Ruan **RC**	4.00
93	Greg Miller **RC**	4.00
94	Johnny Estrada **RC**	8.00
95	Tsuyoshi Shinjo **RC**	4.00
96	Josh Towers **RC**	4.00
97	Horacio Ramirez **RC**	6.00
98	Ryan Freel **RC**	4.00
99	Morgan Ensberg **RC**	8.00
100	Adrian Hernandez **RC**	8.00
101	Juan Uribe **RC**	6.00
102	Jose Mieses **RC**	4.00
103	Jack Wilson **RC**	8.00
104	Cesar Crespo **RC**	4.00
105	Bud Smith **RC**	4.00
106	Erick Almonte **RC**	4.00
107	Elpidio Guzman **RC**	4.00
108	Brandon Duckworth **RC**	4.00
109	Juan Diaz **RC**	4.00
110	Kris Keller **RC**	4.00
111	Jason Michaels **RC**	4.00
112	Bret Prinz **RC**	4.00
113	Henry Mateo **RC**	4.00
114	Ricardo Rodriguez **RC**	4.00
115	Travis Hafner **RC**	20.00
116	Nate Teut **RC**	4.00
117	Alexis Gomez **RC**	4.00
118	Billy Sylvester **RC**	4.00
119	Adam Pettyjohn **RC**	4.00
120	Josh Fogg **RC**	4.00
121	Juan Cruz **RC**	4.00
122	Carlos Valderrama **RC**	4.00
123	Jay Gibbons **RC**	8.00
124	Donaldo Mendez **RC**	4.00
125	William Ortega **RC**	4.00
126	Sean Douglass **RC**	4.00
127	Christian Parker **RC**	4.00
128	Grant Balfour **RC**	4.00
129	Joe Kennedy **RC**	4.00
130	Albert Pujols **RC**	140.00
131	Wilson Betemit **RC**	10.00
132	Mark Teixeira **RC**	50.00
133	Mark Prior **RC**	20.00
134	Dewon Brazelton **RC**	10.00
135	Ichiro Suzuki **RC**	60.00

Limited

Stars (1-90):	4-8X
Rookies (91-135):	.75-1.5X
Production 100 Sets	

Finite

Stars (1-90): 15-25X
Rookies (91-135): 3-5X
Production 25 Sets

Batting Gloves

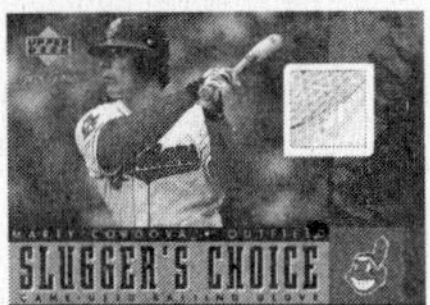

NM/M
Common Player: 5.00
Inserted 1:20
BA Bobby Abreu 8.00
BA Brady Anderson 5.00
TB Tony Batista 5.00
BB Barry Bonds 30.00
MC Marty Cordova 5.00
JC Jose Cruz 5.00
RF Rafael Furcal 8.00
AG Andres Galarraga 5.00
JG Juan Gonzalez 8.00
KGR Ken Griffey Jr./Reds 20.00
KGM Ken Griffey Jr. 20.00
CJ Chipper Jones 10.00
EM Edgar Martinez 8.00
PO Paul O'Neill 8.00
RP Rafael Palmeiro 10.00
NP Neifi Perez 5.00
MR Manny Ramirez 8.00
ARR Alex Rodriguez/Rangers 20.00
ARM Alex Rodriguez/M's 20.00
HR Henry Rodriguez 5.00
IR Ivan Rodriguez 8.00
GS Gary Sheffield 8.00
SS Sammy Sosa 15.00
FT Fernando Tatis 5.00
MT Miguel Tejada 8.00

Fielder's Gloves

NM/M
Common Player: 6.00
Inserted 1:60
GA Garret Anderson/100 15.00
CB Craig Biggio 15.00
JBi Johnny Blanchard 10.00
BB Barry Bonds 50.00
KC Ken Caminiti 10.00
RCa Roy Campanella 60.00
GC Gary Carter 10.00
RCe Roger Cedeno 10.00
JD Johnny Damon 15.00
LD Leon Day/100 60.00
OD Octavio Dotel 6.00
JE Jim Edmonds 15.00
DE Dock Ellis 10.00
AF Alex Fernandez 6.00
CF Cliff Floyd 10.00
NF Nellie Fox 25.00
RF Rafael Furcal 10.00
AG Alex Gonzalez 6.00
BG Ben Grieve 8.00
KG Ken Griffey Jr. 30.00
MG Marquis Grissom 8.00
LG Lefty Grove 100.00
THe Todd Helton 20.00
OH Orlando Hernandez 8.00
THo Todd Hollandsworth 8.00
HI Hideki Irabu 8.00
JI Jason Isringhausen 10.00
RJ Reggie Jackson 20.00
CJ Chipper Jones 25.00
JKa Jim Kaat 10.00
JKe Jason Kendall 10.00
RK Ryan Klesko 8.00
HK Harvey Kuenn 15.00
CL Carlos Lee 8.00
KL Kenny Lofton 10.00
JL Javy Lopez 10.00
GL Greg Luzinski 10.00
EM Edgar Martinez 15.00
PM Pedro Martinez 25.00
JO John Olerud 10.00
PO Paul O'Neill 15.00
RP Rafael Palmeiro 15.00
CP Chan Ho Park 10.00
MP Mike Piazza 30.00
MR Manny Ramirez 25.00
FR Frank Robinson 15.00
AR Alex Rodriguez 30.00
IR Ivan Rodriguez 15.00
TS Tim Salmon 8.00
AS Aaron Sele 6.00
GS Gary Sheffield 10.00
OS Ozzie Smith 40.00
SS Sammy Sosa 30.00
I Ichiro Suzuki 250.00
FT Frank Thomas 20.00
OV Omar Vizquel 15.00
DW Dave Winfield 20.00
MY Masato Yoshii 10.00

Fielder's Gloves Autograph

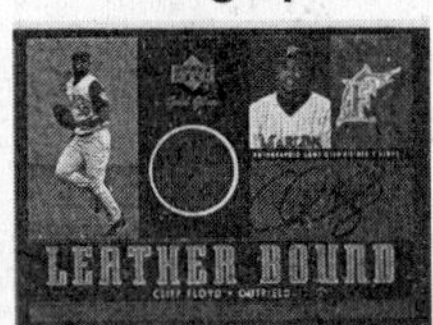

NM/M
Inserted 1:240
JD Johnny Damon 50.00
CF Cliff Floyd 20.00
RF Rafael Furcal 25.00
RP Ken Griffey Jr./49 150.00
RJ Reggie Jackson/68 60.00
JK Jim Kaat 25.00
JK Jason Kendall 20.00
RK Ryan Klesko 20.00
KL Kenny Lofton 20.00
JL Javy Lopez 20.00
GL Greg Luzinski 20.00
EM Edgar Martinez 50.00
JO John Olerud 25.00
PO Paul O'Neill 50.00
FR Frank Robinson 50.00
IR Ivan Rodriguez 60.00
OS Ozzie Smith 85.00
FT Frank Thomas 60.00
DW Dave Winfield 50.00

Game-Used Ball

NM/M
Common Player: 5.00
Inserted 1:20
GC Ken Griffey Jr., Sean Casey 20.00
RR Alex Rodriguez, Ivan Rodriguez 20.00
SW Sammy Sosa, Rondell White 15.00
MP Mark McGwire, Albert Pujols 75.00
RE Manny Ramirez, Carl Everett 15.00
GE Troy Glaus, Darin Erstad 8.00
GT Jason Giambi, Miguel Tejada 10.00
IO Ichiro Suzuki, John Olerud 40.00
RP Ivan Rodriguez, Rafael Palmeiro 10.00
GV Vladimir Guerrero, Jose Vidro 10.00
PS Mike Piazza, Tsuyoshi Shinjo 20.00
JJ Chipper Jones, Andruw Jones 15.00
RB Scott Rolen, Pat Burrell 10.00
WF Preston Wilson, Cliff Floyd 5.00
JF Andruw Jones, Rafael Furcal 10.00
BB Jeff Bagwell, Lance Berkman 15.00
PE Albert Pujols, Jim Edmonds 35.00
JB Geoff Jenkins, Jeromy Burnitz 5.00
KG Jason Kendall, Brian Giles 5.00
BK Barry Bonds, Jeff Kent 25.00
NK Phil Nevin, Ryan Klesko 5.00
SG Gary Sheffield, Shawn Green 8.00
GG Luis Gonzalez, Mark Grace 10.00
HW Todd Helton, Larry Walker 10.00
WP Larry Walker, Juan Pierre 5.00
AG Roberto Alomar, Juan Gonzalez 10.00
VM Greg Vaughn, Fred McGriff 5.00
RB Cal Ripken Jr., Tony Batista 30.00
DM Carlos Delgado, Raul Mondesi 8.00
MG Doug Mientkiewicz, Cristian Guzman 5.00
TO Frank Thomas, Magglio Ordonez 10.00
HC Bobby Higginson, Tony Clark 5.00
SB Mike Sweeney, Carlos Beltran 5.00
MO Edgar Martinez, John Olerud 8.00
EA Darin Erstad, Garret Anderson 8.00
TC Miguel Tejada, Eric Chavez 8.00
PR Rafael Palmeiro, Alex Rodriguez 20.00
BA Pat Burrell, Bobby Abreu 8.00
FJ Cliff Floyd, Charles Johnson 5.00
VP Robin Ventura, Mike Piazza 15.00
WS Kerry Wood, Sammy Sosa 20.00
DP J.D. Drew, Albert Pujols 40.00
BH Lance Berkman, Richard Hidalgo 8.00
BS Jeromy Burnitz, Richie Sexson 5.00
LG Barry Larkin, Ken Griffey Jr. 20.00
GR Brian Giles, Aramis Ramirez 5.00
JG Randy Johnson, Luis Gonzalez 15.00
GB Shawn Green, Adrian Beltre 8.00
KA Jeff Kent, Rich Aurilia 5.00
GK Tony Gwynn, Ryan Klesko 15.00
MJ Greg Maddux, Chipper Jones 20.00
HH Mike Hampton, Todd Helton 10.00
SV Tsuyoshi Shinjo, Robin Ventura 5.00
GJ Cristian Guzman, Jacque Jones 5.00
CJ Roger Clemens, Derek Jeter 125.00

Jerseys

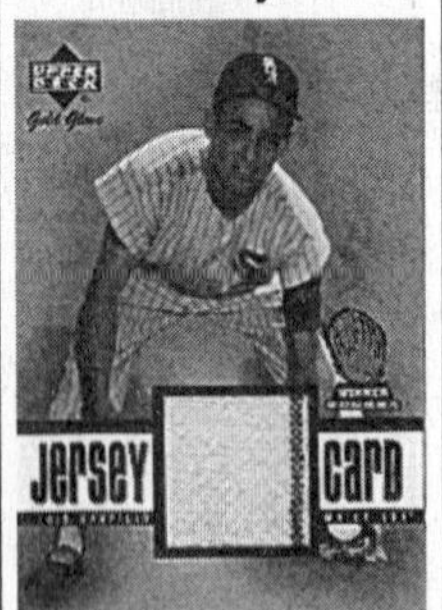

NM/M
Common Player: 5.00
Inserted 1:20
LA Luis Aparicio 5.00
JB Jeff Bagwell 8.00
BB Barry Bonds 25.00
GC Gary Carter 5.00
CC Cesar Cedeno 5.00
DE Darin Erstad 6.00
CF Carlton Fisk 8.00
MG Mark Grace 8.00
SG Shawn Green 5.00
KG Ken Griffey Jr. 20.00
RG Ron Guidry 5.00
AJ Andruw Jones 8.00
JK Jim Kaat 5.00
GM Greg Maddux 15.00
MM Mickey Mantle 175.00
RM Roger Maris 75.00
DM Don Mattingly 30.00
TM Thurman Munson 60.00
MM Mike Mussina 10.00
RP Rafael Palmeiro 10.00
BR Bobby Richardson 8.00
CR Cal Ripken Jr. 35.00
IR Ivan Rodriguez 10.00
OS Ozzie Smith 15.00
IS Ichiro Suzuki 65.00
OV Omar Vizquel 8.00
BW Bernie Williams 8.00

2001 Upper Deck Hall of Famers

NM/M
Complete Set (90): 25.00
Common Player: .15
Hobby Pack (5): 4.00
Box (24): 80.00
1 Reggie Jackson .75
2 Hank Aaron 1.50
3 Eddie Mathews .75
4 Warren Spahn .40
5 Robin Yount .40
6 Lou Brock .25
7 Dizzy Dean .15
8 Bob Gibson .40
9 Stan Musial .75
10 Enos Slaughter .15
11 Rogers Hornsby .40
12 Ernie Banks .50
13 Ferguson Jenkins .15
14 Roy Campanella .75
15 Pee Wee Reese .15
16 Jackie Robinson 1.50
17 Juan Marichal .15
18 Christy Mathewson .15
19 Willie Mays 1.50
20 Hoyt Wilhelm .15
21 Buck Leonard .15
22 Bob Feller .40
23 Cy Young .40
24 Satchel Paige .40
25 Tom Seaver .50
26 Brooks Robinson .40
27 Mike Schmidt .75
28 Roberto Clemente 1.50
29 Ralph Kiner .15
30 Willie Stargell .50
31 Honus Wagner .75
32 Josh Gibson .40
33 Nolan Ryan 1.50
34 Carlton Fisk .15
35 Jimmie Foxx .75
36 Johnny Bench .75
37 Joe Morgan .40
38 George Brett .75
39 Walter Johnson .40
40 Cool Papa Bell .15
41 Ty Cobb 1.00
42 Al Kaline .15
43 Harmon Killebrew .15
44 Luis Aparicio .15
45 Yogi Berra .75
46 Joe DiMaggio 1.50
47 Whitey Ford .25
48 Lou Gehrig 2.00
49 Mickey Mantle 2.00
50 Babe Ruth 2.00
51 Josh Gibson (Origins of the Game) .15
52 Honus Wagner (Origins of the Game) .20
53 Hoyt Wilhelm (Origins of the Game) .15
54 Cy Young (Origins of the Game) .20
55 Walter Johnson (Origins of the Game) .20
56 Satchel Paige (Origins of the Game) .25
57 Rogers Hornsby (Origins of the Game) .20
58 Christy Mathewson (Origins of the Game) .15
59 Tris Speaker (Origins of the Game) .20
60 Nap Lajoie (Origins of the Game) .15
61 Mickey Mantle (The National Pastime) 1.00
62 Jackie Robinson (The National Pastime) .75
63 Nolan Ryan (The National Pastime) .75
64 Josh Gibson (The National Pastime) .20
65 Yogi Berra (The National Pastime) .40
66 Brooks Robinson (The National Pastime) .20
67 Stan Musial (The National Pastime) .40
68 Mike Schmidt (The National Pastime) .40
69 Joe DiMaggio (The National Pastime) 1.00
70 Ernie Banks (The National Pastime) .25
71 Willie Stargell (The National Pastime) .25
72 Johnny Bench (The National Pastime) .40
73 Willie Mays (The National Pastime) .75
74 Satchel Paige (The National Pastime) .25
75 Bob Gibson (The National Pastime) .20
76 Harmon Killebrew (The National Pastime) .15
77 Al Kaline (The National Pastime) .15
78 Carlton Fisk (The National Pastime) .15
79 Tom Seaver (The National Pastime) .25
80 Reggie Jackson (The National Pastime) .40
81 Bob Gibson (The Hall of Records) .20
82 Nolan Ryan (The Hall of Records) .75
83 Walter Johnson (The Hall of Records) .20
84 Stan Musial (The Hall of Records) .40
85 Josh Gibson (The Hall of Records) .20
86 Cy Young (The Hall of Records) .20
87 Joe DiMaggio (The Hall of Records) 1.00
88 Hoyt Wilhelm (The Hall of Records) .15
89 Lou Brock (The Hall of Records) .15
90 Mickey Mantle (The Hall of Records) 1.00

Coop. Coll. Game Bat

NM/M
Common Player: 5.00
Inserted 1:24
HA Hank Aaron 30.00
LA Luis Aparicio 5.00
EB Ernie Banks 15.00
JB Johnny Bench 15.00
YB Yogi Berra 10.00
JBo Jim Bottomley 5.00
GB George Brett 20.00
RC Roy Campanella 30.00
OC Orlando Cepeda 5.00
RC Roberto Clemente/SP/409 120.00
JD Joe DiMaggio 100.00
CF Carlton Fisk 10.00
RF Rollie Fingers 5.00
JF Jimmie Foxx 50.00
HG Hank Greenberg 40.00
RH Rogers Hornsby 100.00
RJ Reggie Jackson 15.00
GK George Kell 5.00
RK Ralph Kiner 10.00
MM Mickey Mantle 125.00
WM Willie Mays 30.00
JM Johnny Mize 10.00
JMo Joe Morgan 5.00
MO Mel Ott 50.00
JP Jim Palmer/SP/372 50.00
TP Tony Perez 5.00
BR Brooks Robinson 10.00
FR Frank Robinson 10.00
JR Jackie Robinson/SP/371 175.00
BR Babe Ruth 200.00
NR Nolan Ryan 50.00
RS Red Schoendienst 5.00
ES Enos Slaughter 5.00
DS Duke Snider 10.00
WS Willie Stargell 5.00
BW Billy Williams 5.00
EW Early Wynn 5.00
RY Robin Yount 15.00

Coop. Coll. Game Jersey

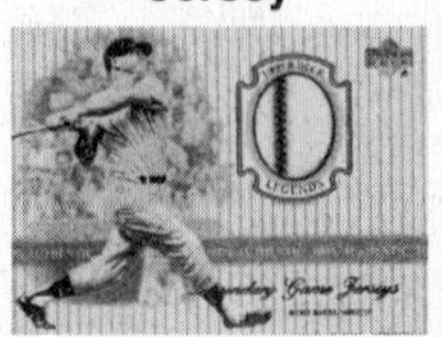

NM/M
Common Player: 10.00
Inserted 1:168
LA Luis Aparicio 10.00
OC Orlando Cepeda 10.00
RC Roberto Clemente 100.00
JD Joe DiMaggio 100.00
DD Don Drysdale/SP/49 200.00
LG Lou Gehrig/SP/194 250.00
MM Mickey Mantle/SP/216 250.00
WM Willie Mays 80.00
JM Joe Morgan 10.00
TP Tony Perez 10.00
PW Pee Wee Reese 15.00
BR Brooks Robinson 20.00
FR Frank Robinson 10.00
NR Nolan Ryan 30.00
TS Tom Seaver 15.00
DS Duke Snider/SP/267 50.00
WS Willie Stargell 15.00
DSu Don Sutton 10.00

Coop. Coll. Jersey Auto.

NM/M
Common Autograph: 40.00
Inserted 1:504
LA Luis Aparicio 40.00
OC Orlando Cepeda 40.00
RJ Reggie Jackson 75.00
EB Ernie Banks 90.00
JM Joe Morgan 40.00
TP Tony Perez 40.00
GB George Brett 125.00
BR Brooks Robinson 80.00
FR Frank Robinson 60.00
NR Nolan Ryan 175.00
TS Tom Seaver 75.00
DS Duke Snider 65.00
WS Willie Stargell 75.00
DSu Don Sutton 40.00

Hall of Fame Gallery

NM/M
Complete Set (15): 25.00
Common Player: 1.00
Inserted 1:6
1 Reggie Jackson 1.50
2 Tom Seaver 1.50
3 Bob Gibson 1.50
4 Jackie Robinson 3.00
5 Joe DiMaggio 3.00
6 Ernie Banks 1.50
7 Mickey Mantle 4.00
8 Willie Mays 3.00
9 Cy Young 1.50
10 Nolan Ryan 4.00
11 Johnny Bench 1.50
12 Yogi Berra 1.50
13 Satchel Paige 1.00
14 George Brett 2.00
15 Stan Musial 2.00

Mantle Pinstripes Excl.

NM/M
Complete Set (56): 75.00
Common Mantle: 2.00
One Pack/Box

Mantle Pinstripe Memor.

NM/M
Print Runs Listed
MMB Mickey Mantle/Bat/100 100.00
MMCJ Mickey Mantle, Joe DiMaggio/Jsy/50 300.00
MMJ Mickey Mantle/Jsy/100 125.00

The Class of '36

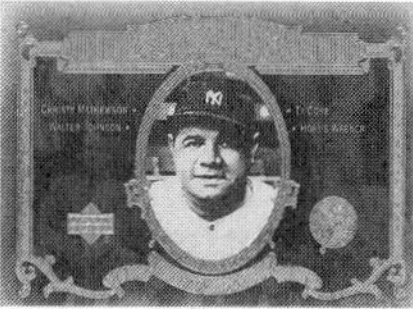

NM/M
Complete Set (5): 8.00
Common Player: 1.50
Inserted 1:17
1 Ty Cobb 2.00
2 Babe Ruth 5.00
3 Christy Mathewson 1.50
4 Walter Johnson 1.50
5 Honus Wagner 1.50

The Endless Summer

NM/M
Complete Set (11): 15.00
Common Player: 1.00
Inserted 1:8
1 Mickey Mantle 4.00
2 Yogi Berra 1.00
3 Mike Schmidt 2.50
4 Jackie Robinson 2.50
5 Johnny Bench 1.50
6 Tom Seaver 1.50
7 Ernie Banks 1.50
8 Harmon Killebrew 1.00
9 Joe DiMaggio 3.00
10 Willie Mays 3.00
11 Brooks Robinson 1.00

20th Century Showcase

NM/M
Complete Set (11): 15.00
Common Player: 1.00
Inserted 1:8
1 Cy Young 1.00
2 Joe DiMaggio 3.00
3 Harmon Killebrew 1.00
4 Stan Musial 2.00
5 Mickey Mantle 4.00
6 Satchel Paige 1.00
7 Nolan Ryan 4.00
8 Bob Gibson 1.00
9 Ernie Banks 1.50
10 Mike Schmidt 2.00
11 Willie Mays 3.00

2001 Upper Deck Legends

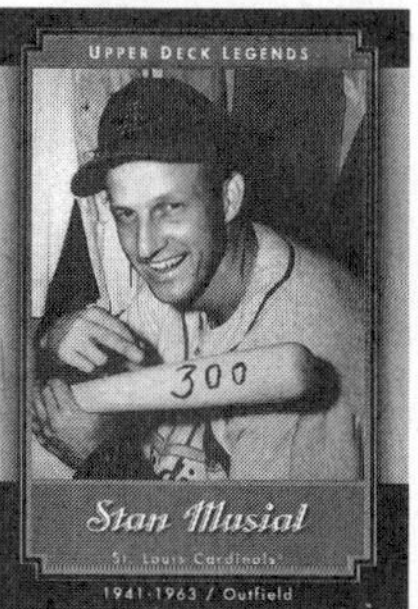

NM/M
Complete Set (90): 20.00
Common Player: .20
Pack (5): 4.00
Box (24): 80.00
1 Darin Erstad .40
2 Troy Glaus .75
3 Nolan Ryan 3.00
4 Reggie Jackson .50
5 Jim "Catfish" Hunter .20
6 Jason Giambi .50
7 Tim Hudson .30
8 Miguel Tejada .30
9 Carlos Delgado .30
10 Shannon Stewart .20
11 Greg Vaughn .20
12 Larry Doby .20
13 Jim Thome .40
14 Juan Gonzalez .75
15 Roberto Alomar .50
16 Edgar Martinez .20
17 John Olerud .40
18 Eddie Murray .40
19 Cal Ripken Jr. 2.50
20 Alex Rodriguez 2.00
21 Ivan Rodriguez .75
22 Rafael Palmeiro .40
23 Jimmie Foxx .50
24 Cy Young .50
25 Manny Ramirez .75
26 Pedro Martinez 1.00
27 Nomar Garciaparra 2.00
28 George Brett 1.00
29 Mike Sweeney .20
30 Jermaine Dye .20
31 Ty Cobb 1.50
32 Dean Palmer .20
33 Harmon Killebrew .50
34 Matt Lawton .20
35 Luis Aparicio .20
36 Frank Thomas .75
37 Magglio Ordonez .20
38 David Wells .20
39 Mickey Mantle 3.00
40 Joe DiMaggio 3.00
41 Roger Maris .75
42 Babe Ruth 3.00
43 Derek Jeter 2.50
44 Roger Clemens 1.00
45 Bernie Williams .50
46 Jeff Bagwell .75
47 Richard Hidalgo .40
48 Warren Spahn .40
49 Greg Maddux 1.50
50 Chipper Jones 1.50
51 Andruw Jones .50
52 Robin Yount .50
53 Jeromy Burnitz .20
54 Jeffrey Hammonds .20
55 Ozzie Smith .50
56 Stan Musial 1.00
57 Mark McGwire 2.50
58 Jim Edmonds .30
59 Sammy Sosa 1.50
60 Ernie Banks .50
61 Kerry Wood .50
62 Randy Johnson .75
63 Luis Gonzalez .40
64 Don Drysdale .50
65 Jackie Robinson 2.00
66 Gary Sheffield .20
67 Kevin Brown .20
68 Vladimir Guerrero 1.00
69 Willie Mays 1.50
70 Mel Ott .20
71 Jeff Kent .20
72 Barry Bonds 1.00
73 Preston Wilson .20
74 Ryan Dempster .40
75 Tom Seaver .40
76 Mike Piazza 2.00
77 Robin Ventura .20
78 Dave Winfield .40
79 Tony Gwynn 1.00
80 Bob Abreu .20
81 Scott Rolen .40
82 Mike Schmidt .75
83 Roberto Clemente 1.50
84 Brian Giles .20
85 Ken Griffey Jr. 2.00
86 Frank Robinson .40
87 Johnny Bench .75
88 Todd Helton .75
89 Larry Walker .40
90 Mike Hampton .20

Fiorentino Collection

NM/M
Complete Set (14): 40.00
Common Player: 1.50
Inserted 1:12
F1 Babe Ruth 6.00
F2 Satchel Paige 1.50
F3 Joe DiMaggio 5.00
F4 Willie Mays 4.00
F5 Ty Cobb 3.00
F6 Nolan Ryan 5.00
F7 Lou Gehrig 5.00
F8 Jackie Robinson 4.00
F9 Hank Aaron 4.00
F10 Roberto Clemente 4.00
F11 Stan Musial 3.00
F12 Johnny Bench 2.00
F13 Honus Wagner 1.50
F14 Reggie Jackson 1.50

Legendary Cuts

NM/M
Most not priced due to scarcity.
C-TC Ty Cobb/3 3,150
C-BRu Babe Ruth/7 6,000

Legendary Game Jerseys

NM/M
Common Player: 5.00
Inserted 1:24
HA Hank Aaron 40.00
JB Jeff Bagwell 8.00
EB Ernie Banks 15.00
YB Yogi Berra 10.00
BB Barry Bonds 25.00
JC Jose Canseco 10.00
RCl Roger Clemens 20.00
RoC Roberto Clemente/195 170.00
JD Joe DiMaggio/245 175.00
KG Ken Griffey Jr. 15.00
TG Tony Gwynn 10.00
RJa Reggie Jackson 10.00
RJo Randy Johnson 10.00
CJ Chipper Jones 10.00
GM Greg Maddux 15.00
MM Mickey Mantle/245 200.00
RM Roger Maris/343 65.00
PM Pedro Martinez 10.00
WM Willie Mays 30.00
SM Stan Musial/490 30.00
MP Mike Piazza 20.00
MR Manny Ramirez 8.00
CR Cal Ripken Jr. 30.00
AR Alex Rodriguez 20.00
IR Ivan Rodriguez 8.00
NR Nolan Ryan 50.00
KS Kazuhiro Sasaki 5.00
TS Tom Seaver 15.00
GS Gary Sheffield 5.00
OS Ozzie Smith 15.00
SS Sammy Sosa 15.00
DW Dave Winfield 5.00
RY Robin Yount 12.00

Legendary Jerseys Auto.

NM/M
Inserted 1:288
EB Ernie Banks 75.00
RC Roger Clemens/211 100.00
KG Ken Griffey Jr. 80.00
RJ Reggie Jackson/224 60.00
SM Stan Musial/266 100.00
AR Alex Rodriguez 85.00
NR Nolan Ryan 125.00
TS Tom Seaver 60.00
OS Ozzie Smith 60.00
SS Sammy Sosa/91 175.00

Legendary Jerseys Gold

NM/M
Common Player: 30.00
Production 25 Sets
RCl Roger Clemens 75.00
RoC Roberto Clemente 180.00
KG Ken Griffey Jr. 75.00
RJ Reggie Jackson 40.00
WM Willie Mays 120.00
AR Alex Rodriguez 75.00
NR Nolan Ryan 100.00
SS Sammy Sosa 75.00
DW Dave Winfield 30.00

Legendary Jerseys Gold Auto.

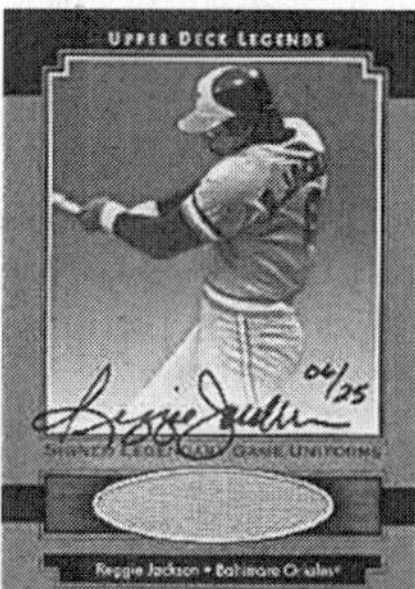

No pricing due to scarcity.
Production 25 Sets

Legendary Lumber

NM/M
Common Player: 5.00
Inserted 1:24
HA Hank Aaron 30.00
LA Luis Aparicio 5.00
EB Ernie Banks/80 50.00
JB Johnny Bench 15.00
BB Barry Bonds 25.00
RCa Roy Campanella/335 40.00
JC Jose Canseco 8.00
RCl Roger Clemens 20.00
RoC Roberto Clemente/170 120.00
JD Joe DiMaggio 85.00
JF Jimmie Foxx/351 50.00
KG Ken Griffey Jr. 15.00
TG Tony Gwynn 10.00
RJ Reggie Jackson 10.00
RJ Randy Johnson 10.00
AJ Andruw Jones 8.00
CJ Chipper Jones 10.00
MM Mickey Mantle 150.00
RM Roger Maris 40.00
WM Willie Mays 30.00
EM Eddie Murray 8.00
MO Mel Ott/355 40.00
MP Mike Piazza 15.00
AP Albert Pujols 45.00
MR Manny Ramirez 8.00
FR Frank Robinson 8.00
CR Cal Ripken Jr. 40.00
AR Alex Rodriguez 15.00
IR Ivan Rodriguez 8.00
GS Gary Sheffield 5.00
OS Ozzie Smith 10.00
SS Sammy Sosa 15.00

Legendary Lumber Auto.

NM/M
Common Player: 25.00
Inserted 1:288
LA Luis Aparicio 25.00
EB Ernie Banks 65.00
RC Roger Clemens/227 100.00
KG Ken Griffey Jr. 80.00
TG Tony Gwynn 60.00
RJ Reggie Jackson/211 65.00
EM Eddie Murray 40.00
AR Alex Rodriguez 100.00
SS Sammy Sosa/66 240.00

Legendary Lumber Gold

NM/M
Common Player: 25.00
Production 25 Sets
RC Roger Clemens 75.00
RC Roberto Clemente 180.00
KG Ken Griffey Jr. 75.00
RJ Reggie Jackson 40.00
WM Willie Mays 120.00
AR Alex Rodriguez 75.00
GS Gary Sheffield 25.00
SS Sammy Sosa 75.00

Legendary Lumber Gold Auto.

No pricing due to scarcity.
Production 25 Sets

Reflections

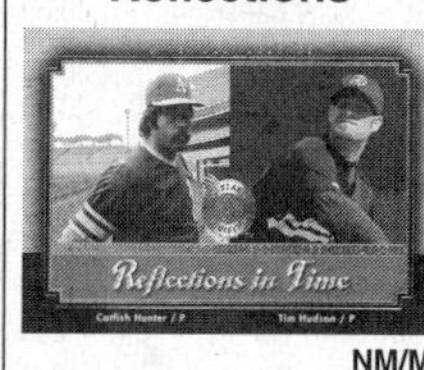

NM/M
Complete Set (10): 25.00
Common Card: 1.00
Inserted 1:18
R1 Bernie Williams, Mickey Mantle 6.00
R2 Pedro Martinez, Cy Young 2.00
R3 Barry Bonds, Willie Mays 5.00
R4 Scott Rolen, Mike Schmidt 3.00
R5 Mark McGwire, Stan Musial 4.00
R6 Ken Griffey Jr., Frank Robinson 3.00
R7 Sammy Sosa, Andre Dawson 3.00
R8 Kevin Brown, Don Drysdale 1.50
R9 Jason Giambi, Reggie Jackson 1.50
R10 Tim Hudson, Jim "Catfish" Hunter 1.00

2001 Upper Deck Legends of New York

The greatest players, teams and events of 20th Century Major League baseball in New York City are featured in this specialty set. The 200-card base set is comprised of a number of different subsets. The front of each card in the base set has an area of flocking in team colors.

NM/M
Complete Set (200): 40.00
Common Player: .20
Pack (5): 2.50
Box (24): 50.00
1 Billy Herman .20
2 Carl Erskine .20
3 Burleigh Grimes .20
4 Don Newcombe .20
5 Gil Hodges .75
6 Pee Wee Reese .75
7 Jackie Robinson 2.00
8 Duke Snider 1.00
9 Jim Gilliam .20
10 Roy Campanella 1.50
11 Carl Furillo .20
12 Casey Stengel .75
13 Casey Stengel .40
14 Billy Herman .20
15 Jackie Robinson 1.00
16 Jackie Robinson 1.00
17 Gil Hodges .40
18 Carl Furillo .20
19 Roy Campanella .50
20 Don Newcombe .40
21 Duke Snider .75
22 Casey Stengel .40
23 Burleigh Grimes .20
24 Pee Wee Reese .50
25 Jackie Robinson 1.00
26 Jackie Robinson 1.00
27 Carl Erskine .20
28 Roy Campanella .75
29 Duke Snider .75
30 Rube Marquard .20
31 Ross Youngs .20
32 Bobby Thomson .20
33 Christy Mathewson 1.00
34 Carl Hubbell .20
35 Hoyt Wilhelm .20
36 Johnny Mize .40
37 John McGraw .20
38 Monte Irvin .50
39 Travis Jackson .20
40 Mel Ott 1.00
41 Dusty Rhodes .20
42 Leo Durocher .50
43 John McGraw .20
44 Christy Mathewson .50
45 The Polo Grounds .20
46 Travis Jackson .20
47 Mel Ott .50
48 Johnny Mize .20
49 Leo Durocher .30
50 Bobby Thomson .20
51 Monte Irvin .30
52 Bobby Thomson .20
53 Christy Mathewson .50
54 Christy Mathewson .50
55 Christy Mathewson .50
56 John McGraw .20
57 John McGraw .20
58 John McGraw .20
59 Travis Jackson .20
60 Mel Ott .50
61 Mel Ott .50
62 Carl Hubbell .20
63 Bobby Thomson .20
64 Monte Irvin .20
65 Al Weis .20
66 Donn Clendenon .20
67 Ed Kranepool .20
68 Gary Carter .20
69 Tommie Agee .20
70 Jon Matlack .20
71 Ken Boswell .20
72 Len Dykstra .20
73 Nolan Ryan 3.00

74 Ray Sadecki .20
75 Ron Darling .20
76 Ron Swoboda .20
77 Dwight Gooden .20
78 Tom Seaver 1.00
79 Wayne Garrett .20
80 Casey Stengel .50
81 Tom Seaver .50
82 Tommie Agee .20
83 Tom Seaver .50
84 Yogi Berra .50
85 Yogi Berra .50
86 Tom Seaver .50
87 Dwight Gooden .20
88 Gary Carter .20
89 Ron Darling .20
90 Tommie Agee .20
91 Tom Seaver .50
92 Gary Carter .20
93 Len Dykstra .20
94 Babe Ruth 3.00
95 Bill Dickey .50
96 Rich "Goose" Gossage .20
97 Casey Stengel .50
98 Jim "Catfish" Hunter .75
99 Charlie Keller .20
100 Chris Chambliss .20
101 Don Larsen .40
102 Dave Winfield .75
103 Don Mattingly 2.00
104 Elston Howard .20
105 Frankie Crosetti .20
106 Hank Bauer .20
107 Joe DiMaggio 3.00
108 Graig Nettles .20
109 Lefty Gomez .20
110 Phil Rizzuto 1.00
111 Lou Gehrig 2.00
112 Lou Piniella .20
113 Mickey Mantle 3.00
114 Red Rolfe .20
115 Reggie Jackson 1.00
116 Roger Maris 1.50
117 Ray White .20
118 Thurman Munson 1.50
119 Tom Tresh .20
120 Tommy Henrich .20
121 Waite Hoyt .20
122 Willie Randolph .20
123 Whitey Ford .75
124 Yogi Berra 1.00
125 Babe Ruth 1.50
126 Babe Ruth 1.50
127 Lou Gehrig 1.25
128 Babe Ruth 1.50
129 Joe DiMaggio 1.50
130 Joe DiMaggio 1.50
131 Mickey Mantle 1.50
132 Roger Marris .75
133 Mickey Mantle 1.50
134 Reggie Jackson .75
135 Babe Ruth 1.50
136 Babe Ruth 1.50
137 Babe Ruth 1.50
138 Lefty Gomez .20
139 Lou Gehrig 1.25
140 Lou Gehrig 1.25
141 Joe DiMaggio 1.50
142 Joe DiMaggio 1.50
143 Casey Stengel .40
144 Mickey Mantle 1.50
145 Yogi Berra .50
146 Mickey Mantle 1.50
147 Elston Howard .40
148 Whitey Ford .50
149 Reggie Jackson .50
150 Reggie Jackson .50
151 John McGraw, Babe Ruth 1.00
152 Babe Ruth, John McGraw 1.00
153 Lou Gehrig, Mel Ott .75
154 Joe DiMaggio, Mel Ott 1.00
155 Joe DiMaggio, Billy Herman 1.00
156 Joe DiMaggio, Jackie Robinson 1.50
157 Mickey Mantle, Bobby Thomson 1.00
158 Yogi Berra, Pee Wee Reese .75
159 Roy Campanella, Mickey Mantle 1.00
160 Don Larsen, Duke Snider .50
161 Christy Mathewson .75
162 Christy Mathewson .50
163 Rube Marquard .20
164 Christy Mathewson .50
165 John McGraw .20
166 Burleigh Grimes .20
167 Babe Ruth 1.50
168 Burleigh Grimes .20
169 Babe Ruth 1.50
170 John McGraw .40
171 Lou Gehrig 1.25
172 Babe Ruth 1.50
173 Babe Ruth 1.50
174 Carl Hubbell .20
175 Joe DiMaggio 1.50
176 Lou Gehrig 1.25
177 Leo Durocher .40
178 Mel Ott .50
179 Joe DiMaggio 1.50
180 Jackie Robinson 1.00
181 Babe Ruth 1.50
182 Bobby Thomson .20
183 Joe DiMaggio 1.50
184 Mickey Mantle 1.50
185 Monte Irvin .20
186 Roy Campanella .50
187 Duke Snider .50
188 Dusty Rhodes .20
189 Yogi Berra .50
190 Mickey Mantle 1.50
191 Mickey Mantle 1.50
192 Casey Stengel .40
193 Tom Seaver .50
194 Mickey Mantle 1.50
195 Tommie Agee .20
196 Tom Seaver .50
197 Chris Chambliss .20
198 Reggie Jackson .50
199 Reggie Jackson .50
200 Gary Carter .20

Bat Cards

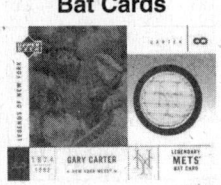

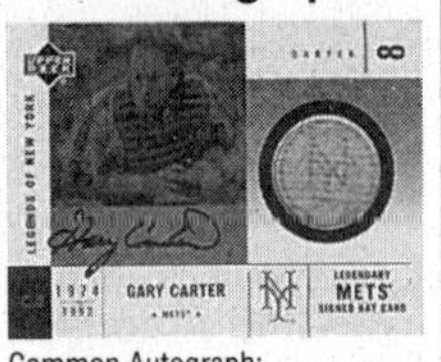

NM/M
Common Player: 5.00
Inserted 1:24
DODGERS
JG Jim Gilliam 10.00
BH Billy Herman 8.00
DN Don Newcombe/67 40.00
GIANTS
BTh Bobby Thomson 25.00
METS
KB Ken Boswell 5.00
GC Gary Carter 15.00
LD Len Dykstra 5.00
WG Wayne Garrett 8.00
EK Ed Kranepool 10.00
JM J.C. Martin 8.00
NR Nolan Ryan 40.00
TS Tom Seaver 20.00
RSw Ron Swoboda 8.00
AW Al Weis 5.00
YANKEES
HB Hank Bauer 10.00
YB Yogi Berra 15.00
CC Chris Chambliss/130 15.00
BD Bill Dickey 15.00
TH Tommy Henrich 8.00
EH Elston Howard 10.00
RJ Reggie Jackson 15.00
CK Charlie Keller 8.00
MM Mickey Mantle/134 200.00
RM Roger Maris/60 85.00
DM Don Mattingly 30.00
TM Thurman Munson 20.00
LP Lou Piniella 8.00
MR Mickey Rivers 5.00
BR Babe Ruth/107 250.00
TT Tom Tresh 10.00
DW Dave Winfield 10.00

Bat Autographs

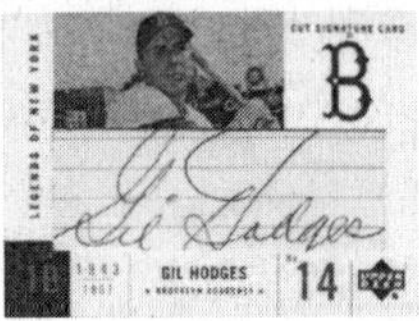

NM/M
Common Autograph:
DODGERS
DN Don Newcombe 30.00
METS
GC Gary Carter 40.00
DC Donn Clendenon 30.00
NR Nolan Ryan/129 200.00
TS Tom Seaver/89 100.00
YANKEES
YB Yogi Berra 75.00
CC Chris Chambliss 30.00
RJ Reggie Jackson/123 75.00
DM Don Mattingly 100.00
MR Mickey Rivers 25.00
RW Roy White 25.00

Cut Signatures

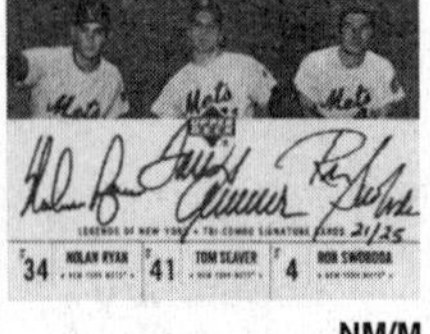

NM/M
Most not priced due to scarcity.
LC-JD Joe DiMaggio (38 Issued) 1,000

Combination Signatures

NM/M
Common Card: 75.00

NP Don Newcombe, Johnny Podres 85.00
WM Dave Winfield, Don Mattingly 200.00
RS Nolan Ryan, Tom Seaver 400.00
LB Don Larsen, Yogi Berra 150.00
GJ Ron Guidry, Tommy John 60.00
CN Chris Chambliss, Graig Nettles 60.00
RD Willie Randolph, Bucky Dent 60.00
RW Mickey Rivers, Roy White 60.00
WJ Dave Winfield, Reggie Jackson 150.00

Triple-Combination Signatures

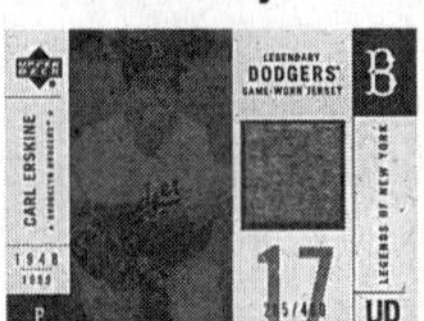

NM/M
Production 25 Sets
S-NPE Don Newcombe, Johnny Podres, Carl Erskine 175.00
S-WMN Dave Winfield, Don Mattingly, Graig Nettles 175.00
S-RSS Nolan Ryan, Tom Seaver, Ron Swoboda 450.00
S-LBP Don Larsen, Yogi Berra, Joe Pepitone 125.00
S-GJG Ron Guidry, Tommy John, Rich "Goose" Gossage 100.00
S-CND Chris Chambliss, Graig Nettles, Bucky Dent 100.00
S-LRG Sparky Lyle, Dave Righetti, Rich "Goose" Gossage 100.00

Dodgers Game Jersey

NM/M
Common Player: 5.00
Gold Edition of 400: 1.25X
HB Hank Behrman 5.00
CD Chuck Dressen 5.00
CE Carl Erskine 10.00
SJ Spider Jurgenson 5.00
JR Jackie Robinson/126 120.00

Giants Game Jersey

NM/M
Complete Set (1):
CM Christy Mathewson/63 350.00

Mets Game Jersey

NM/M
Common Player: 5.00
Gold Edition of 400: 1.25X
RD Ron Darling 5.00
JM Jon Matlack 5.00
RS Ray Sadecki 5.00
TS Tom Seaver 15.00
CS Casey Stengel 8.00
JT Joe Torre 5.00

Yankees Game Jersey

NM/M
Common Player: 5.00
Gold Edition of 400: 1.25X
HB Hank Bauer 8.00
FC Frank Crosetti 10.00
TH Tommy Henrich 10.00
EH Elston Howard 10.00
CH Jim "Catfish" Hunter 10.00
DM Duke Maas 5.00
MM Mickey Mantle/63 250.00
LM Lindy McDaniel 5.00
TM Thurman Munson 30.00
GN Graig Nettles 10.00
PN Phil Niekro 10.00
JP Joe Pepitone 5.00
WR Willie Randolph 8.00
RR Red Rolfe 5.00
BT Bob Turley 8.00
DW Dave Winfield 15.00

Signed Game Jersey

NM/M
Common Autograph: 15.00
DODGERS
CE Carl Erskine 50.00
JP Johnny Podres/193 50.00
METS
GF George Foster/196 30.00
NR Nolan Ryan/47 200.00
CS Craig Swan 30.00
YANKEES
YG Yogi Berra/73 125.00
BD Bucky Dent 30.00
RG Rich Gossage/145 40.00
RG Ron Guidry 50.00
TJ Tommy John 30.00
DL Don Larsen 60.00
HL Hector Lopez/195 15.00
SL Sparky Lyle 30.00
DM Don Mattingly/72 125.00
PN Phil Niekro/195 40.00
GN Graig Nettles 30.00
JP Joe Pepitone 30.00
WR Willie Randolph 30.00

Ebbets Field G-U Base

NM/M
Complete Set (1):
JR Jackie Robinson/100 50.00
JR Jackie Robinson/Silver/50 60.00
JR Jackie Robinson/Gold/25 75.00

Ebbets Field Seat

NM/M
Complete Set (1):
JR Jackie Robinson 50.00

Shea Stadium G-U Base

NM/M
Quantity produced listed
TS Tom Seaver/100 25.00
TS Tom Seaver/Silver/50 40.00
TS Tom Seaver/Gold/25 50.00

United We Stand

Images from the aftermath of the 9/11/01 terrorist attack on New York's World Trade Center are featured in this insert series found in the UD Legends of New York issue. Red, white and blue stars and stripes are the background on card backs for a message from Upper Deck concerning relief efforts.

NM/M
Complete Set (15): 10.00
Common Card: 1.00
Inserted 1:12
USA1-USA15 United We Stand 1.00

Yankee Stadium Seat

Complete Set (1):

Los Angeles Dodgers Team Set

This boxed set has 20 player cards in standard 2-1/2" x 3-1/2" format and a 3-1/2" x 5" checklist. Cards have borderless action photos on front with an Upper Deck Collectibles logo at top-left. At bottom are the team and player name, position and uniform number. Backs have a smaller version of the front photo, some biographical and career notes and 1999-2000 stats. Cards are numbered with an "LA" prefix.

NM/M
Complete Set (21): 10.00
Common Player: .50
1 Gary Sheffield 1.00
2 Shawn Green 1.00
3 Kevin Brown .50
4 Adrian Beltre .75
5 Eric Karros .50
6 Darren Dreifort .50
7 Chan Ho Park .50
8 Alex Cora .50
9 Mark Grudzielanek .50
10 Paul LoDuca .75
11 Dave Hansen .50
12 Tom Goodwin .50
13 Ramon Martinez .50
14 Luke Prokopec .50
15 Chad Kreuter .50
16 Jeff Shaw .50
17 Eric Gagne .75
18 Andy Ashby .50
19 F.P. Santangelo .50
20 Mike Fetters .50
21 Checklist .50

2001 Upper Deck MVP

NM/M
Complete Set (330): 35.00
Common Player: .10
Pack (8): 1.50
Box (24): 30.00
1 Mo Vaughn .10
2 Troy Percival .10
3 Adam Kennedy .10
4 Darin Erstad .25
5 Tim Salmon .10
6 Bengie Molina .10
7 Troy Glaus .40
8 Garret Anderson .25
9 Ismael Valdes .10
10 Glenallen Hill .10
11 Tim Hudson .25
12 Eric Chavez .20
13 Johnny Damon .20
14 Barry Zito .40
15 Jason Giambi .40
16 Terrence Long .10
17 Jason Hart .10
18 Jose Ortiz .10
19 Miguel Tejada .25
20 Jason Isringhausen .10
21 Adam Piatt .10
22 Jeremy Giambi .10
23 Tony Batista .10
24 Darrin Fletcher .10
25 Mike Sirotka .10
26 Carlos Delgado .40
27 Billy Koch .10
28 Shannon Stewart .10
29 Raul Mondesi .15
30 Brad Fullmer .10
31 Jose Cruz Jr. .10
32 Kelvim Escobar .10
33 Greg Vaughn .10
34 Aubrey Huff .10
35 Albie Lopez .10
36 Gerald Williams .10
37 Ben Grieve .10
38 John Flaherty .10
39 Fred McGriff .15
40 Ryan Rupe .10
41 Travis Harper .10
42 Steve Cox .10
43 Roberto Alomar .40
44 Jim Thome .50
45 Russell Branyan .10
46 Bartolo Colon .20
47 Omar Vizquel .15
48 Travis Fryman .15
49 Kenny Lofton .15
50 Chuck Finley .10
51 Ellis Burks .10
52 Eddie Taubensee .10
53 Juan Gonzalez .40
54 Edgar Martinez .20
55 Aaron Sele .10
56 John Olerud .20
57 Jay Buhner .10
58 Mike Cameron .10
59 John Halama .10
60 Ichiro Suzuki **RC** 8.00
61 David Bell .10

62 Freddy Garcia .10
63 Carlos Guillen .10
64 Bret Boone .20
65 Al Martin .10
66 Cal Ripken Jr. 1.50
67 Delino DeShields .10
68 Chris Richard .10
69 Sean Douglass **RC** .25
70 Melvin Mora .10
71 Luis Matos .10
72 Sidney Ponson .10
73 Mike Bordick .10
74 Brady Anderson .10
75 David Segui .10
76 Jeff Conine .10
77 Alex Rodriguez 1.25
78 Gabe Kapler .10
79 Ivan Rodriguez .40
80 Rick Helling .10
81 Kenny Rogers .10
82 Andres Galarraga .15
83 Rusty Greer .10
84 Justin Thompson .10
85 Ken Caminiti .10
86 Rafael Palmeiro .40
87 Ruben Mateo .10
88 Travis Hafner **RC** 1.00
89 Manny Ramirez .40
90 Pedro Martinez .50
91 Carl Everett .10
92 Dante Bichette .10
93 Derek Lowe .10
94 Jason Varitek .10
95 Nomar Garciaparra 1.25
96 David Cone .10
97 Tomokazu Ohka .10
98 Troy O'Leary .10
99 Trot Nixon .10
100 Jermaine Dye .10
101 Joe Randa .10
102 Jeff Suppan .10
103 Roberto Hernandez .10
104 Mike Sweeney .10
105 Mac Suzuki .10
106 Carlos Febles .10
107 Jose Rosado .10
108 Mark Quinn .10
109 Carlos Beltran .20
110 Dean Palmer .10
111 Mitch Meluskey .10
112 Bobby Higginson .10
113 Brandon Inge .10
114 Tony Clark .10
115 Brian Moehler .10
116 Juan Encarnacion .10
117 Damion Easley .10
118 Roger Cedeno .10
119 Jeff Weaver .10
120 Matt Lawton .10
121 Jay Canizaro .10
122 Eric Milton .10
123 Corey Koskie .10
124 Mark Redman .10
125 Jacque Jones .10
126 Brad Radke .10
127 Cristian Guzman .10
128 Joe Mays .10
129 Denny Hocking .10
130 Frank Thomas .40
131 David Wells .10
132 Ray Durham .10
133 Paul Konerko .10
134 Joe Crede .10
135 Jim Parque .10
136 Carlos Lee .10
137 Magglio Ordonez .25
138 Sandy Alomar Jr. .10
139 Chris Singleton .10
140 Jose Valentin .10
141 Roger Clemens 1.00
142 Derek Jeter 1.50
143 Orlando Hernandez .15
144 Tino Martinez .10
145 Bernie Williams .40
146 Jorge Posada .25
147 Mariano Rivera .20
148 David Justice .20
149 Paul O'Neill .15
150 Mike Mussina .25
151 Christian Parker **RC** .10
152 Andy Pettitte .25
153 Alfonso Soriano .50
154 Jeff Bagwell .40
155 Morgan Ensberg **RC** .50
156 Daryle Ward .15
157 Craig Biggio .20
158 Richard Hidalgo .10
159 Shane Reynolds .10
160 Scott Elarton .10
161 Julio Lugo .10
162 Moises Alou .20
163 Lance Berkman .10
164 Chipper Jones .75
165 Greg Maddux 1.00
166 Javy Lopez .15
167 Andruw Jones .40
168 Rafael Furcal .25
169 Brian Jordan .10
170 Wes Helms .10
171 Tom Glavine .25
172 B.J. Surhoff .10
173 John Smoltz .10
174 Quilvio Veras .10
175 Rico Brogna .10
176 Jeromy Burnitz .10
177 Jeff D'Amico .10
178 Geoff Jenkins .20
179 Henry Blanco .10
180 Mark Loretta .10
181 Richie Sexson .25
182 Jimmy Haynes .10
183 Jeffrey Hammonds .10
184 Ron Belliard .10
185 Tyler Houston .10
186 Mark McGwire 1.00
187 Rick Ankiel .10
188 Darryl Kile .10
189 Jim Edmonds .25
190 Mike Matheny .10
191 Edgar Renteria .10
192 Ray Lankford .10
193 Garrett Stephenson .10
194 J.D. Drew .20
195 Fernando Vina .10
196 Dustin Hermanson .10
197 Sammy Sosa 1.00
198 Corey Patterson .25
199 Jon Lieber .10
200 Kerry Wood .40
201 Todd Hundley .10
202 Kevin Tapani .10
203 Rondell White .10
204 Eric Young .10
205 Matt Stairs .10
206 Bill Mueller .10
207 Randy Johnson .50
208 Mark Grace .25
209 Jay Bell .10
210 Curt Schilling .25
211 Erubiel Durazo .10
212 Luis Gonzalez .20
213 Steve Finley .10
214 Matt Williams .20
215 Reggie Sanders .10
216 Tony Womack .10
217 Gary Sheffield .25
218 Kevin Brown .15
219 Adrian Beltre .20
220 Shawn Green .20
221 Darren Dreifort .10
222 Chan Ho Park .10
223 Eric Karros .15
224 Alex Cora .10
225 Mark Grudzielanek .10
226 Andy Ashby .10
227 Vladimir Guerrero .75
228 Tony Armas Jr. .10
229 Fernando Tatis .10
230 Jose Vidro .10
231 Javier Vazquez .10
232 Lee Stevens .10
233 Milton Bradley .10
234 Carl Pavano .10
235 Peter Bergeron .10
236 Wilton Guerrero .10
237 Ugueth Urbina .10
238 Barry Bonds 1.50
239 Livan Hernandez .10
240 Jeff Kent .15
241 Pedro Feliz .10
242 Bobby Estalella .10
243 J.T. Snow .10
244 Shawn Estes .10
245 Robb Nen .10
246 Rich Aurilia .10
247 Russ Ortiz .10
248 Preston Wilson .10
249 Brad Penny .10
250 Cliff Floyd .10
251 A.J. Burnett .10
252 Mike Lowell .10
253 Luis Castillo .10
254 Ryan Dempster .10
255 Derrek Lee .10
256 Charles Johnson .10
257 Pablo Ozuna .10
258 Antonio Alfonseca .10
259 Mike Piazza 1.00
260 Robin Ventura .10
261 Al Leiter .15
262 Timoniel Perez .10
263 Edgardo Alfonzo .10
264 Jay Payton .10
265 Tsuyoshi Shinjo **RC** .75
266 Todd Zeile .10
267 Armando Benitez .10
268 Glendon Rusch .10
269 Rey Ordonez .10
270 Kevin Appier .10
271 Tony Gwynn .50
272 Phil Nevin .10
273 Mark Kotsay .10
274 Ryan Klesko .20
275 Adam Eaton .10
276 Mike Darr .10
277 Damian Jackson .10
278 Woody Williams .10
279 Chris Gomez .10
280 Trevor Hoffman .10
281 Xavier Nady .15
282 Scott Rolen .40
283 Bruce Chen .10
284 Pat Burrell .30
285 Mike Lieberthal .10
286 Brandon Duckworth **RC** .40
287 Travis Lee .10
288 Bobby Abreu .10
289 Jimmy Rollins .25
290 Robert Person .10
291 Randy Wolf .10
292 Jason Kendall .10
293 Derek Bell .10
294 Brian Giles .25
295 Kris Benson .10
296 John Vander Wal .10
297 Todd Ritchie .10
298 Warren Morris .10
299 Kevin Young .10
300 Francisco Cordova .10
301 Aramis Ramirez .10
302 Ken Griffey Jr. 1.00
303 Pete Harnisch .10
304 Aaron Boone .10
305 Sean Casey .20
306 Jackson Melian **RC** .40
307 Rob Bell .10
308 Barry Larkin .25
309 Dmitri Young .10
310 Danny Graves .10
311 Pokey Reese .10
312 Leo Estrella .10
313 Todd Helton .40
314 Mike Hampton .15
315 Juan Pierre .10
316 Brent Mayne .10
317 Larry Walker .25
318 Denny Neagle .10
319 Jeff Cirillo .10
320 Pedro Astacio .10
321 Todd Hollandsworth .10
322 Neifi Perez .10
323 Ron Gant .10
324 Todd Walker .10
325 Alex Rodriguez/CL .50
326 Ken Griffey Jr./CL .50
327 Mark McGwire/CL .50
328 Pedro Martinez/CL .30
329 Derek Jeter/CL .75
330 Mike Piazza/CL .40

Authentic Griffey

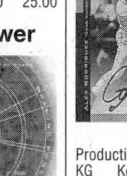

NM/M
Inserted 1:288
AGS Ken Griffey Jr./Auto. 125.00
AGJ Ken Griffey Jr./Jsy 15.00
AGC Ken Griffey Jr./Cap 40.00
AGB Ken Griffey Jr./Bat 15.00
AGU Ken Griffey Jr./Unif. 15.00
AGGS Ken Griffey/ Gold/Auto./30 250.00
AGGJ Ken Griffey Jr./ Gold Jsy/30 75.00
AGGC Ken Griffey/ Gold Cap/30 75.00
AGGB Ken Griffey/ Gold Bat/30 75.00
CGR Ken Griffey Jr., Alex Rodriguez/100 35.00
CGS Ken Griffey Jr., Sammy Sosa/100 35.00
CGT Ken Griffey Jr., Frank Thomas/100 25.00

Drawing Power

NM/M
Complete Set (10): 10.00
Common Player: .75
Inserted 1:12
DP1 Mark McGwire 2.00
DP2 Vladimir Guerrero 1.00
DP3 Manny Ramirez .75
DP4 Frank Thomas .75
DP5 Ken Griffey Jr. 1.50
DP6 Alex Rodriguez 2.50
DP7 Mike Piazza 1.50
DP8 Derek Jeter 3.00
DP9 Sammy Sosa 2.00
DP10 Todd Helton .75

Mantle Pinstripes Exclusive

NM/M
Complete Set (56): 75.00
Common Mantle: 2.00
One Pack/Box

Mantle Pinstripes Excl. Memorabilia

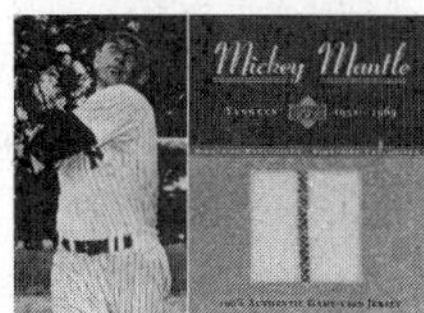

NM/M
Print Runs Listed
MMCJ3Mickey Mantle, Ken Griffey Jr./50 200.00
MMJ3 Mickey Mantle/Jsy/100 125.00

Souvenirs Batting Gloves

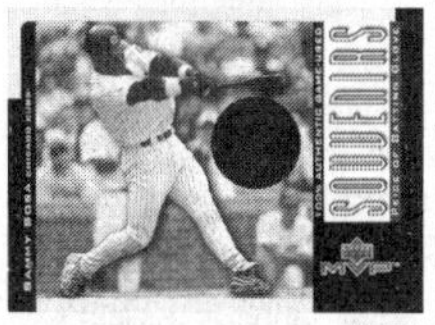

NM/M
Common Player: 8.00
Inserted 1:96 H 20.00
BB Barry Bonds 40.00
TrG Troy Glaus 10.00
JG Juan Gonzalez 10.00
KG Ken Griffey Jr. 20.00
ToG Tony Gwynn/200 30.00
CJ Chipper Jones 15.00
JL Javy Lopez 8.00
GM Greg Maddux/95 60.00
EM Edgar Martinez 8.00
FM Fred McGriff 8.00
RP Rafael Palmeiro 15.00
CR Cal Ripken Jr. 50.00
AR Alex Rodriguez 20.00
IR Ivan Rodriguez 10.00
SS Sammy Sosa 20.00
MT Miguel Tejada 8.00
FT Frank Thomas 10.00
MV Mo Vaughn 8.00

Souvenirs Batting Gloves Autographs

NM/M
Production 25 Sets
KG Ken Griffey Jr. 150.00
ToG Tony Gwynn 80.00
CR Cal Ripken Jr. 250.00
AR Alex Rodriguez 150.00
IR Ivan Rodriguez 80.00
SS Sammy Sosa 250.00
FT Frank Thomas 80.00

Souvenirs Two-Player Bat Combo

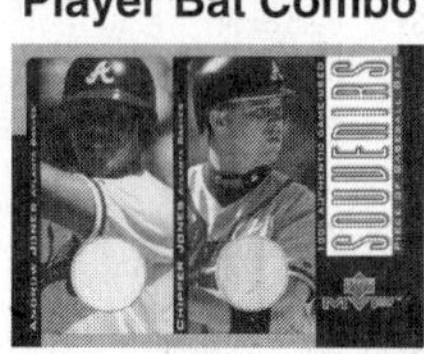

NM/M
Common Combo: 10.00
Inserted 1:144
TS Frank Thomas, Sammy Sosa 25.00
RR Alex Rodriguez, Ivan Rodriguez 25.00
TG Jim Thome, Ken Griffey Jr. 25.00
GS Ken Griffey Jr., Sammy Sosa 30.00
WA Kerry Wood, Rick Ankiel 10.00
3K Tony Gwynn, Cal Ripken Jr. 40.00
DV Carlos Delgado, Jose Vidro 10.00
JJ Andruw Jones, Chipper Jones 20.00
HR Jose Canseco, Ken Griffey Jr. 20.00
JF Chipper Jones, Rafael Furcal 15.00
OW Paul O'Neill, Bernie Williams 10.00
TO Frank Thomas, Magglio Ordonez 15.00
RM Alex Rodriguez, Edgar Martinez 20.00
RP Ivan Rodriguez, Rafael Palmeiro 15.00

Souvenirs Two-Player Bat Autograph

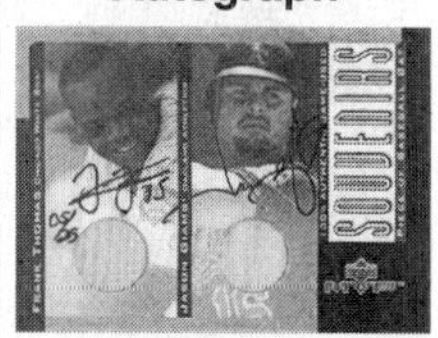

NM/M
Production 25 Sets
RG Alex Rodriguez, Ken Griffey Jr. 250.00
SG Sammy Sosa, Ken Griffey Jr. 300.00
RR Alex Rodriguez, Ivan Rodriguez 200.00
JG Chipper Jones, Troy Glaus 125.00
TS Frank Thomas, Sammy Sosa 275.00
GD Jason Giambi, Carlos Delgado 75.00
3K Cal Ripken Jr., Tony Gwynn 300.00
TG Frank Thomas, Jason Giambi 85.00
HH Todd Helton, Mike Hampton 60.00

Souvenirs Three Player Bat Combo

No pricing due to scarcity.
Production 25 Sets

Super Tools

NM/M
Complete Set (20): 20.00
Common Player: .50
Inserted 1:6
ST1 Ken Griffey Jr. 1.50
ST2 Carlos Delgado .75
ST3 Alex Rodriguez 2.50
ST4 Troy Glaus .75
ST5 Jeff Bagwell .75
ST6 Ichiro Suzuki 3.00
ST7 Derek Jeter 3.00
ST8 Jim Edmonds .50
ST9 Vladimir Guerrero 1.00
ST10 Jason Giambi .75
ST11 Todd Helton .75
ST12 Cal Ripken Jr. 3.00
ST13 Barry Bonds 3.00
ST14 Nomar Garciaparra 2.00
ST15 Randy Johnson 1.00
ST16 Jermaine Dye .50
ST17 Andruw Jones .75
ST18 Ivan Rodriguez .75
ST19 Sammy Sosa 2.00
ST20 Pedro Martinez 1.00

2001 Upper Deck Ovation

NM/M
Complete Set (90): 100.00
Common Player: .20
Common WP (61-90): 3.00
WP Production 2,000
Pack (5): 5.00
Box (20): 80.00
1 Troy Glaus .50
2 Darin Erstad .40
3 Jason Giambi .50
4 Tim Hudson .40
5 Eric Chavez .30
6 Carlos Delgado .50

7 David Wells .20
8 Greg Vaughn .20
9 Omar Vizquel .20
10 Jim Thome .50
11 Roberto Alomar .40
12 John Olerud .30
13 Edgar Martinez .20
14 Cal Ripken Jr. 2.00
15 Alex Rodriguez 1.50
16 Ivan Rodriguez .50
17 Manny Ramirez .50
18 Nomar Garciaparra 1.50
19 Pedro Martinez .75
20 Jermaine Dye .20
21 Juan Gonzalez .50
22 Matt Lawton .20
23 Frank Thomas .50
24 Magglio Ordonez .40
25 Bernie Williams .40
26 Derek Jeter 2.00
27 Roger Clemens 1.50
28 Jeff Bagwell .50
29 Richard Hidalgo .20
30 Chipper Jones 1.00
31 Greg Maddux 1.00
32 Andruw Jones .50
33 Jeromy Burnitz .20
34 Mark McGwire 1.50
35 Jim Edmonds .40
36 Sammy Sosa 1.50
37 Kerry Wood .50
38 Randy Johnson .75
39 Steve Finley .20
40 Gary Sheffield .40
41 Kevin Brown .40
42 Shawn Green .40
43 Vladimir Guerrero .75
44 Jose Vidro .20
45 Barry Bonds 2.00
46 Jeff Kent .30
47 Preston Wilson .20
48 Luis Castillo .20
49 Mike Piazza 1.00
50 Edgardo Alfonzo .20
51 Tony Gwynn .75
52 Ryan Klesko .30
53 Scott Rolen .50
54 Bob Abreu .30
55 Jason Kendall .20
56 Brian Giles .30
57 Ken Griffey Jr. 1.00
58 Barry Larkin .40
59 Todd Helton .50
60 Mike Hampton .20
61 Corey Patterson (World Premiere) 3.00
62 Timoniel Perez (World Premiere) 3.00
63 Toby Hall (World Premiere) 3.00
64 Brandon Inge (World Premiere) 3.00
65 Joe Crede (World Premiere) 3.00
66 Xavier Nady (World Premiere) 3.00
67 Adam Pettyjohn **RC** (World Premiere) 3.00
68 Keith Ginter (World Premiere) 3.00
69 Brian Cole (World Premiere) 3.00
70 Tyler Walker **RC** (World Premiere) 3.00
71 Juan Uribe **RC** (World Premiere) 5.00
72 Alex Hernandez (World Premiere) 3.00
73 Leo Estrella (World Premiere) 3.00
74 Joey Nation (World Premiere) 3.00
75 Aubrey Huff (World Premiere) 3.00
76 Ichiro Suzuki **RC** (World Premiere) 75.00
77 Jay Spurgeon (World Premiere) 3.00
78 Sun-Woo Kim (World Premiere) 3.00
79 Pedro Feliz (World Premiere) 3.00
80 Pablo Ozuna (World Premiere) 3.00
81 Hiram Bocachica (World Premiere) 3.00
82 Brad Wilkerson (World Premiere) 3.00

83 Rocky Biddle (World Premiere) 3.00
84 Aaron McNeal (World Premiere) 3.00
85 Adam Bernero (World Premiere) 3.00
86 Danys Baez (World Premiere) 3.00
87 Dee Brown (World Premiere) 3.00
88 Jimmy Rollins (World Premiere) 4.00
89 Jason Hart (World Premiere) 3.00
90 Ross Gload (World Premiere) 3.00

A Piece of History

NM/M
Common Player: 5.00
Inserted 1:40
RA Rick Ankiel 5.00
JB Johnny Bench 15.00
BB Barry Bonds 30.00
KB Kevin Brown 5.00
JC Jose Canseco 8.00
RC Roger Clemens 15.00
DC David Cone 5.00
CD Carlos Delgado 8.00
JD Joe DiMaggio 100.00
DD Don Drysdale/SP 25.00
DE Darin Erstad 5.00
RF Rollie Fingers/SP 8.00
CF Carlton Fisk 10.00
RF Rafael Furcal 5.00
TrG Troy Glaus 8.00
TG Tom Glavine 8.00
SG Shawn Green 5.00
KG Ken Griffey Jr. 15.00
KGs Ken Griffey Sr. 5.00
MH Mike Hampton 5.00
RJ Randy Johnson 10.00
AJ Andruw Jones 8.00
CJ Chipper Jones 10.00
GM Greg Maddux 15.00
MM Mickey Mantle 125.00
JP Jim Palmer 10.00
CR Cal Ripken Jr. 30.00
BR Brooks Robinson 15.00
AR Alex Rodriguez 15.00
IR Ivan Rodriguez 8.00
NR Nolan Ryan/SP 120.00
TS Tom Seaver 10.00
GS Gary Sheffield 5.00
OS Ozzie Smith/SP 20.00
SS Sammy Sosa 15.00
FT Frank Thomas 8.00
BW Bernie Williams 8.00
MW Matt Williams 5.00
EW Early Wynn 5.00

A Piece of History Autograph

Common Player:
Values Undetermined

POH Combo Cards

Production 25 Sets
Values Undetermined

Curtain Calls

NM/M
Complete Set (10): 10.00
Common Player: .50
Inserted 1:7
1 Sammy Sosa 2.00
2 Darin Erstad .50
3 Barry Bonds 2.50
4 Todd Helton .75
5 Mike Piazza 1.50
6 Ken Griffey Jr. 1.50
7 Nomar Garciaparra 2.00
8 Carlos Delgado .75
9 Jason Giambi .75
10 Alex Rodriguez 2.00

DiMaggio Pinstripes Exclusive

NM/M
Complete Set (56): 60.00
Common DiMaggio: 1.50
One Pack/Box

DiMaggio Pinstripes Memorabilia

NM/M
Print runs listed: 150.00
JDB Joe DiMaggio/Bat/100 75.00
JDCJ Joe DiMaggio, Mickey Mantle/Jsy/50 300.00
JDJ Joe DiMaggio/Jsy/100 100.00

Lead Performers

NM/M
Complete Set (11): 15.00
Common Player: 1.00
Inserted 1:12
1 Mark McGwire 3.00
2 Derek Jeter 4.00
3 Alex Rodriguez 3.00
4 Frank Thomas 1.00
5 Sammy Sosa 2.50
6 Mike Piazza 2.00
7 Vladimir Guerrero 1.50
8 Pedro Martinez 1.50
9 Carlos Delgado 1.00
10 Ken Griffey Jr. 2.00
11 Jeff Bagwell 1.00

Superstar Theatre

NM/M
Complete Set (11): 20.00
Common Player: 1.00
Inserted 1:12
1 Nomar Garciaparra 2.50
2 Ken Griffey Jr. 2.00
3 Frank Thomas 1.00
4 Derek Jeter 4.00
5 Mike Piazza 2.00
6 Sammy Sosa 2.00
7 Barry Bonds 4.00
8 Alex Rodriguez 3.00
9 Todd Helton 1.00

10 Mark McGwire 3.00
11 Jason Giambi 1.00

2001 Upper Deck Pros & Prospects

NM/M
Complete Set (141):
Common Player: .15
Common (91-135): 4.00
Production 1,250
Common (136-141): 8.00
Production 500
Pack (5): 6.00
Box (24): 120.00
1 Troy Glaus .50
2 Darin Erstad .25
3 Tim Hudson .40
4 Jason Giambi .50
5 Jermaine Dye .15
6 Barry Zito .40
7 Carlos Delgado .50
8 Shannon Stewart .15
9 Raul Mondesi .15
10 Greg Vaughn .15
11 Ben Grieve .15
12 Roberto Alomar .40
13 Juan Gonzalez .50
14 Jim Thome .50
15 C.C. Sabathia .15
16 Edgar Martinez .25
17 Kazuhiro Sasaki .15
18 Aaron Sele .15
19 John Olerud .25
20 Cal Ripken Jr. 2.00
21 Rafael Palmeiro .50
22 Ivan Rodriguez .50
23 Alex Rodriguez 1.50
24 Manny Ramirez .50
25 Pedro Martinez .75
26 Carl Everett .15
27 Nomar Garciaparra 1.50
28 Neifi Perez .15
29 Mike Sweeney .15
30 Bobby Higginson .15
31 Tony Clark .15
32 Doug Mientkiewicz .15
33 Cristian Guzman .15
34 Brad Radke .15
35 Magglio Ordonez .40
36 Carlos Lee .15
37 Frank Thomas .50
38 Roger Clemens 1.50
39 Bernie Williams .50
40 Derek Jeter 2.00
41 Tino Martinez .25
42 Wade Miller .15
43 Jeff Bagwell .50
44 Lance Berkman .25
45 Richard Hidalgo .15
46 Greg Maddux 1.00
47 Andruw Jones .50
48 Chipper Jones 1.00
49 Rafael Furcal .25
50 Jeromy Burnitz .15
51 Geoff Jenkins .25
52 Ben Sheets .25
53 Mark McGwire 1.50
54 Jim Edmonds .40
55 J.D. Drew .25
56 Fred McGriff .25
57 Sammy Sosa 1.50
58 Kerry Wood .50
59 Randy Johnson .75
60 Luis Gonzalez .25
61 Curt Schilling .25
62 Kevin Brown .25
63 Shawn Green .25
64 Gary Sheffield .40
65 Vladimir Guerrero .75
66 Jose Vidro .15
67 Barry Bonds 2.00
68 Jeff Kent .25
69 Rich Aurilia .15
70 Preston Wilson .15
71 Charles Johnson .15
72 Cliff Floyd .15
73 Mike Piazza 1.00
74 Al Leiter .25
75 Matt Lawton .15
76 Tony Gwynn .75
77 Ryan Klesko .25
78 Phil Nevin .15
79 Scott Rolen .50
80 Pat Burrell .40
81 Jimmy Rollins .25
82 Jason Kendall .25
83 Brian Giles .25
84 Aramis Ramirez .15
85 Ken Griffey Jr. 1.00
86 Barry Larkin .40
87 Sean Casey .25
88 Larry Walker .25
89 Todd Helton .50
90 Mike Hampton .15
91 Juan Cruz **RC** 4.00
92 Brian Lawrence **RC** 4.00
93 Brandon Lyon **RC** 4.00
94 Adrian Hernandez **RC** 4.00
95 Jose Mieses **RC** 4.00
96 Juan Uribe 4.00
97 Morgan Ensberg **RC** 8.00
98 Wilson Betemit **RC** 8.00
99 Ryan Freel **RC** 4.00
100 Jack Wilson **RC** 8.00
101 Cesar Crespo **RC** 4.00
102 Bret Prinz **RC** 4.00
103 Horacio Ramirez **RC** 8.00
104 Elpidio Guzman **RC** 4.00
105 Josh Towers **RC** 4.00
106 Brandon Duckworth **RC** 4.00
107 Esix Snead **RC** 4.00
108 Billy Sylvester **RC** 4.00
109 Alexis Gomez **RC** 4.00
110 Johnny Estrada **RC** 8.00
111 Joe Kennedy **RC** 4.00
112 Travis Hafner **RC** 25.00
113 Martin Vargas **RC** 4.00
114 Jay Gibbons **RC** 8.00
115 Andres Torres **RC** 4.00
116 Sean Douglass **RC** 4.00
117 Juan Diaz **RC** 4.00
118 Greg Miller **RC** 4.00
119 Carlos Valderrama **RC** 4.00
120 William Ortega **RC** 4.00
121 Josh Fogg **RC** 4.00
122 Wilken Ruan **RC** 4.00
123 Kris Keller **RC** 4.00
124 Erick Almonte **RC** 4.00
125 Ricardo Rodriguez **RC** 4.00
126 Grant Balfour **RC** 4.00
127 Nick Maness **RC** 4.00
128 Jeremy Owens **RC** 4.00
129 Doug Nickle **RC** 4.00
130 Bert Snow **RC** 4.00
131 Jason Smith **RC** 4.00
132 Henry Mateo **RC** 4.00
133 Mike Penney **RC** 4.00
134 Bud Smith **RC** 4.00
135 Junior Spivey **RC** 6.00
136 Ichiro Suzuki **RC** 90.00
137 Albert Pujols **RC** 180.00
138 Mark Teixeira **RC** 100.00
139 Dewon Brazelton **RC** 8.00
140 Mark Prior **RC** 25.00
141 Tsuyoshi Shinjo **RC** 8.00

Bats

NM/M
Common Card: 4.00
Inserted 1:24
Golds: 3-5X
Production 25 Sets
WI Bernie Williams, Ichiro Suzuki 35.00
RG Manny Ramirez, Juan Gonzalez 8.00
RP Ivan Rodriguez, Mike Piazza 15.00
BT Jeff Bagwell, Frank Thomas 8.00
GBo Ken Griffey Jr., Barry Bonds 35.00
SG Sammy Sosa, Luis Gonzalez 15.00
KA Jeff Kent, Roberto Alomar 4.00
RF Alex Rodriguez, Rafael Furcal 15.00
PT Rafael Palmeiro, Jim Thome 10.00
JP Chipper Jones, Albert Pujols 40.00
GBu Shawn Green, Jeromy Burnitz 4.00
JL Andruw Jones, Kenny Lofton 6.00
MJ Greg Maddux, Randy Johnson 15.00

Legends Bats

NM/M
Common Card: 15.00
Inserted 1:216
Gold: 3-5X
Production 25 Sets
RF Manny Ramirez, Carlton Fisk 15.00
BY Jeromy Burnitz, Robin Yount 15.00
WJ Bernie Williams, Reggie Jackson 15.00
RG Cal Ripken Jr., Tony Gwynn 50.00

Franchise Building Blocks

NM/M
Complete Set (30): 25.00
Common Player: .50
Inserted 1:6
F1 Darin Erstad, Elpidio Guzman .50
F2 Jason Giambi, Jason Hart 1.00
F3 Carlos Delgado, Vernon Wells .75
F4 Greg Vaughn, Aubrey Huff .50
F5 Jim Thome, C.C. Sabathia 1.00
F6 Edgar Martinez, Ichiro Suzuki 3.00
F7 Cal Ripken Jr., Josh Towers 3.00
F8 Ivan Rodriguez, Carlos Pena 1.00
F9 Nomar Garciaparra, Dernell Stenson 2.00
F10 Mike Sweeney, Dee Brown .50
F11 Bobby Higginson, Brandon Inge .50
F12 Brad Radke, Adam Johnson .50
F13 Frank Thomas, Joe Crede 1.00
F14 Derek Jeter, Nick Johnson 3.00
F15 Jeff Bagwell, Morgan Ensberg 1.00
F16 Chipper Jones, Wilson Betemit 1.50
F17 Jeromy Burnitz, Ben Sheets .50
F18 Mark McGwire, Albert Pujols 3.00
F19 Sammy Sosa, Corey Patterson 2.00
F20 Luis Gonzalez, Jack Cust .50
F21 Kevin Brown, Luke Prokopec .50
F22 Vladimir Guerrero, Wilken Ruan 1.00
F23 Barry Bonds, Carlos Valderrama 3.00
F24 Preston Wilson, Abraham Nunez .50
F25 Mike Piazza, Alex Escobar 1.50
F26 Tony Gwynn, Xavier Nady 1.00
F27 Scott Rolen, Jimmy Rollins 1.00
F28 Jason Kendall, Jack Wilson .50
F29 Ken Griffey Jr., Adam Dunn 1.50
F30 Todd Helton, Juan Uribe 1.00

Ichiro World Tour

NM/M
Complete Set (15): 25.00
Common Ichiro: 2.00
Inserted 1:12
WT1-WT15 Ichiro Suzuki 2.00

Specialty Jersey

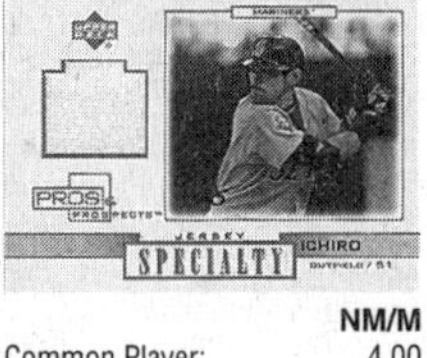

NM/M
Common Player: 4.00
Inserted 1:24
Golds: 3-5X
Production 25 Sets
RA Roberto Alomar 6.00
BB Barry Bonds 25.00
JE Jim Edmonds 4.00
JG Juan Gonzalez 6.00
SG Shawn Green 4.00
TG Tony Gwynn 10.00
RJ Randy Johnson 10.00
CR Cal Ripken Jr. 30.00
AR Alex Rodriguez 15.00
SR Scott Rolen 8.00
SS Sammy Sosa 15.00
I Ichiro 60.00
JT Jim Thome 8.00
LW Larry Walker 4.00

Then & Now Jersey

NM/M
Common Player: 4.00
Inserted 1:24
Golds: 3-5X
Production 25 Sets
RA Rick Ankiel 4.00
BB Barry Bonds 30.00
KB Kevin Brown 6.00
RC Roger Clemens 20.00
JE Jim Edmonds 6.00
FG Freddy Garcia 4.00
JGi Jason Giambi 8.00
JGo Juan Gonzalez 8.00
KG Ken Griffey Jr. 20.00
RJ Randy Johnson 10.00
GM Greg Maddux 20.00
PM Pedro Martinez 10.00
XN Xavier Nady 4.00
PN Phil Nevin 4.00
MP Mike Piazza 15.00
MR Manny Ramirez 8.00
AR Alex Rodriguez 15.00
CS Curt Schilling 6.00
GS Gary Sheffield 6.00
RV Robin Ventura 4.00

Then & Now Combo Jersey

NM/M
Complete Set (1):
NR Nolan Ryan 100.00

2001 Upper Deck Prospect Premieres

NM/M
Complete Set (90): 100.00
Common Player: .25
Common Auto. SP (91-102): 10.00
Auto. Production 1,000
Pack (4): 8.00
Box (18): 125.00
1 Jeff Mathis **RC** 1.00
2 Jake Woods **RC** .25
3 Dallas McPherson **RC** 1.00
4 Steven Shell **RC** .25
5 Ryan Budde **RC** .25

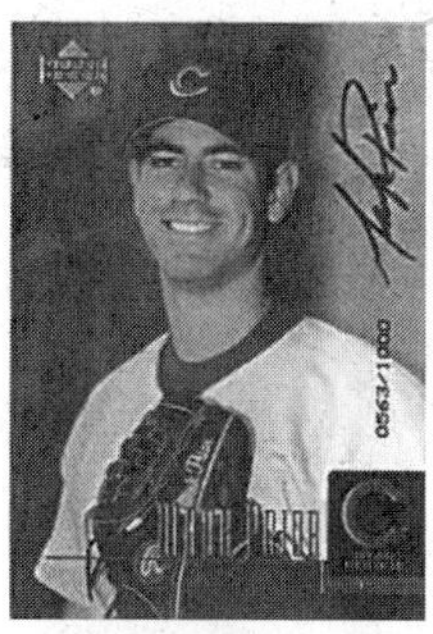

6 Kirk Saarloos RC .40
7 Ryan Stegall RC .25
8 Bobby Crosby RC 2.00
9 J.T. Stotts RC .25
10 Neal Cotts RC .75
11 Jeremy Bonderman RC 3.00
12 Brandon League RC .40
13 Tyrell Godwin RC .25
14 Gabe Gross RC 1.00
15 Chris Neylan RC .25
16 Michael Rouse RC .25
17 Macay McBride RC .25
18 Josh Burrus RC .25
19 Adam Stern RC .25
20 Richard Lewis RC .40
21 Cole Barthel RC .50
22 Mike Jones RC .25
23 J.J. Hardy RC 3.00
24 Brad Nelson RC 1.00
25 Justin Pope RC .25
26 Dan Haren RC 2.00
27 Andy Sisco RC .50
28 Ryan Theriot RC 2.50
29 Ricky Nolasco RC 1.00
30 Jon Switzer RC .25
31 Justin Wechsler RC .25
32 Mike Gosling RC .25
33 Scott Hairston RC 1.00
34 Brian Pilkington RC .25
35 Kole Strayhorn RC .25
36 David Taylor RC .25
37 Donald Levinski RC .25
38 Mike Hinckley RC .50
39 Nick Long RC .25
40 Brad Hennessey RC .25
41 Noah Lowry RC 2.00
42 Josh Cram RC .25
43 Jesse Foppert RC .50
44 Julian Benavidez RC .25
45 Daniel Denham RC .25
46 Travis Foley RC .40
47 Mike Conroy RC .25
48 Jake Dittler RC .25
49 Rene Rivera RC .25
50 John Cole RC .25
51 Lazaro Abreu RC .25
52 David Wright RC 30.00
53 Aaron Heilman RC .40
54 Lenny DiNardo RC .25
55 Alhaji Turay RC .40
56 Chris Smith RC .25
57 Rommie Lewis RC .25
58 Bryan Bass RC .25
59 David Crouthers RC .25
60 Josh Barfield RC 2.00
61 Jake Peavy RC 4.00
62 Ryan Howard RC 50.00
63 Gavin Floyd RC 1.50
64 Mike Floyd RC .25
65 Stefan Bailie RC .25
66 Jon DeVries RC .25
67 Steve Kelly RC .25
68 Alan Moye RC .25
69 Justin Gillman RC .25
70 Jayson Nix RC 1.00
71 John Draper RC .25
72 Kenny Baugh RC .25
73 Michael Woods RC .25
74 Preston Larrison RC .25
75 Matt Coenen RC .25
76 Scott Tyler RC .50
77 Jose Morales RC .25
78 Corwin Malone RC .50
79 Dennis Ulacia RC .40
80 Andy Gonzalez RC .25
81 Kris Honel RC 1.00
82 Wyatt Allen RC .25
83 Ryan Wing RC .25
84 Sean Henn RC .40
85 John-Ford Griffin RC .50
86 Bronson Sardinha RC .50
87 Jon Skaggs RC .25
88 Shelley Duncan RC .25
89 Jason Arnold RC .75
90 Aaron Rifkin RC .50
91 Colt Griffin RC 10.00
92 J.D. Martin RC 10.00
93 Justin Wayne RC 10.00
94 John VanBenschotten RC 15.00
95 Chris Burke RC 25.00
96 Casey Kotchman RC 40.00
97 Michael Garciaparra RC 10.00
98 Jake Gautreau RC 10.00
99 Jerome Williams RC 10.00
100 Greg Nash RC 10.00
101 Joe Borchard RC 15.00
102 Mark Prior RC 80.00

Heroes of Baseball Bat

NM/M
Common Player: 4.00
Inserted 1:18
DB Don Baylor 4.00
WB Wade Boggs 8.00
BB Bill Buckner 4.00
GC Gary Carter 8.00
DE Dwight Evans 4.00
SG Steve Garvey 4.00
KiG Kirk Gibson 4.00
KeG Ken Griffey Sr. 4.00
RJ Reggie Jackson 10.00
DL Davey Lopes 4.00
FL Fred Lynn 4.00
BM Bill Madlock 4.00
TM Tim McCarver 4.00
JM Joe Morgan 4.00
MM Manny Mota 4.00
EM Eddie Murray 8.00
AO Al Oliver 4.00
DP Dave Parker 4.00
TP Tony Perez 4.00
KP Kirby Puckett 15.00
OS Ozzie Smith 10.00
DW Dave Winfield 8.00

HOB Bat Autograph

Production 25 Sets
Values Undetermined

HOB Dual Combo Jersey

NM/M
Common Duo: 8.00
Inserted 1:144
BH Bryan Bass, J.J. Hardy 10.00
DG Shelley Duncan, Tyrell Godwin 8.00
GS Steve Garvey, Reggie Smith 10.00
HB Aaron Heilman, Jeremy Bonderman 10.00
JJ Michael Jordan, Michael Jordan 100.00
SG Jon Switzer, Mike Gosling 8.00
WP Dave Winfield, Kirby Puckett 20.00

HOB Dual Combo Jersey Auto

Values Undetermined

HOB Triple Combo Jersey

NM/M
Common Card:
Inserted 1:144
BKH Bobby Crosby, Michael Garciaparra, Bronson Sardinha 15.00
BBC Chris Burke, Bryan Bass, Bubba Crosby 10.00
GGH Jake Gautreau, Tyrell Godwin, Aaron Heilman 8.00
GMS Colt Griffin, J.D. Martin, Jon Switzer 8.00
GKB Gabe Gross, Casey Kotchman, Kenny Baugh 10.00
JMD Michael Jordan, Mickey Mantle, Joe DiMaggio 350.00
JPW Michael Jordan, Kirby Puckett, Dave Winfield 40.00
MMD Roger Maris, Mickey Mantle, Joe DiMaggio 700.00
VPJ John VanBenschotten, Mark Prior, Mike Jones 25.00

HOB Triple Combo Jersey Auto

Values Undetermined

MJ Grandslam Bat

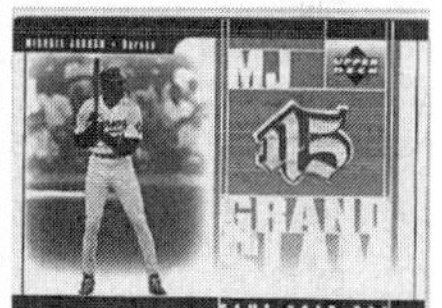

NM/M
Common MJ: 25.00
MJ1-4 Michael Jordan 25.00
MJ5 Michael Jordan (White Sox) 40.00

Tribute to 42

NM/M
Inserted 1:750
42-B Jackie Robinson/Bat 40.00
42-J Jackie Robinson/Jsy 60.00
42-C Jackie Robinson/Cut 500.00
42-B Jackie Robinson/Bat/42 100.00
42-J Jackie Robinson/Jsy/42 100.00

2001 UD Reserve

NM/M
Complete Set (210):
Common Player: .15
Common SP (181-210): 3.00
Production 2,500
Pack (5): 3.00
Box (24): 60.00
1 Darin Erstad .25
2 Tim Salmon .25
3 Bengie Molina .15
4 Troy Glaus .50
5 Glenallen Hill .15
6 Garret Anderson .25
7 Jason Giambi .50
8 Johnny Damon .25
9 Eric Chavez .25
10 Tim Hudson .25
11 Miguel Tejada .25
12 Barry Zito .25
13 Jose Ortiz .15
14 Tony Batista .15
15 Carlos Delgado .50
16 Shannon Stewart .15
17 Raul Mondesi .15
18 Ben Grieve .15
19 Aubrey Huff .15
20 Greg Vaughn .15
21 Fred McGriff .25
22 Gerald Williams .15
23 Bartolo Colon .25
24 Roberto Alomar .40
25 Jim Thome .50
26 Omar Vizquel .25
27 Juan Gonzalez .50
28 Ellis Burks .15
29 Edgar Martinez .25
30 Aaron Sele .15
31 Jay Buhner .15
32 Mike Cameron .15
33 Kazuhiro Sasaki .15
34 John Olerud .25
35 Cal Ripken Jr. 2.00
36 Brady Anderson .15
37 Pat Hentgen .15
38 Chris Richard .15
39 Jerry Hairston Jr. .15
40 Mike Bordick .15
41 Ivan Rodriguez .50
42 Rick Helling .15
43 Rafael Palmeiro .50
44 Alex Rodriguez 1.50
45 Andres Galarraga .25
46 Rusty Greer .15
47 Ruben Mateo .15
48 Ken Caminiti .15
49 Nomar Garciaparra 1.50
50 Pedro Martinez .75
51 Manny Ramirez .50
52 Carl Everett .15
53 Dante Bichette .15
54 Hideo Nomo .40
55 Mike Sweeney .15
56 Carlos Beltran .25
57 Jeff Suppan .15
58 Jermaine Dye .15
59 Mark Quinn .15
60 Joe Randa .15
61 Bobby Higginson .15
62 Tony Clark .15
63 Brian Moehler .15
64 Dean Palmer .15
65 Brandon Inge .15
66 Damion Easley .15
67 Brad Radke .15
68 Corey Koskie .15
69 Cristian Guzman .15
70 Eric Milton .15
71 Jacque Jones .15
72 Matt Lawton .15
73 Frank Thomas .50
74 David Wells .15
75 Magglio Ordonez .25
76 Paul Konerko .15
77 Sandy Alomar Jr. .15
78 Ray Durham .15
79 Roger Clemens 1.50
80 Bernie Williams .50
81 Derek Jeter 2.00
82 David Justice .25
83 Paul O'Neill .25
84 Mike Mussina .40
85 Jorge Posada .40
86 Jeff Bagwell .50
87 Richard Hidalgo .15
88 Craig Biggio .25
89 Scott Elarton .15
90 Moises Alou .25
91 Greg Maddux 1.00
92 Rafael Furcal .25
93 Andruw Jones .50
94 Tom Glavine .25
95 Chipper Jones 1.00
96 Javy Lopez .25
97 Richie Sexson .40
98 Jeromy Burnitz .15
99 Jeff D'Amico .15
100 Jeffrey Hammonds .15
101 Geoff Jenkins .25
102 Ben Sheets .25
103 Mark McGwire 1.50
104 Rick Ankiel .15
105 Darryl Kile .15
106 Edgar Renteria .15
107 Jim Edmonds .25
108 J.D. Drew .25
109 Sammy Sosa 1.50
110 Corey Patterson .25
111 Kerry Wood .50
112 Todd Hundley .15
113 Rondell White .15
114 Matt Stairs .15
115 Randy Johnson .75
116 Mark Grace .40
117 Steve Finley .15
118 Luis Gonzalez .25
119 Matt Williams .25
120 Curt Schilling .40
121 Gary Sheffield .40
122 Kevin Brown .25
123 Shawn Green .25
124 Eric Karros .15
125 Chan Ho Park .15
126 Adrian Beltre .25
127 Vladimir Guerrero .75
128 Fernando Tatis .15
129 Lee Stevens .15
130 Jose Vidro .15
131 Peter Bergeron .15
132 Michael Barrett .15
133 Jeff Kent .25
134 Russ Ortiz .15
135 Barry Bonds 2.00
136 J.T. Snow .15
137 Livan Hernandez .15
138 Rich Aurilia .15
139 Preston Wilson .15
140 Mike Lowell .15
141 Ryan Dempster .15
142 Charles Johnson .15
143 Matt Clement .15
144 Luis Castillo .15
145 Mike Piazza 1.00
146 Al Leiter .15
147 Robin Ventura .25
148 Jay Payton .15
149 Todd Zeile .15
150 Edgardo Alfonzo .15
151 Tony Gwynn .75
152 Ryan Klesko .25
153 Phil Nevin .15
154 Mark Kotsay .15
155 Trevor Hoffman .15
156 Damian Jackson .15
157 Scott Rolen .50
158 Mike Lieberthal .15
159 Bruce Chen .15
160 Bobby Abreu .25
161 Pat Burrell .40
162 Travis Lee .15
163 Jason Kendall .15
164 Derek Bell .15
165 Kris Benson .15
166 Kevin Young .15
167 Brian Giles .25
168 Pat Meares .15
169 Sean Casey .25
170 Pokey Reese .15
171 Pete Harnisch .15
172 Barry Larkin .25
173 Ken Griffey Jr. 1.00
174 Dmitri Young .15
175 Mike Hampton .15
176 Todd Helton .50
177 Jeff Cirillo .15
178 Denny Neagle .15
179 Larry Walker .25
180 Todd Hollandsworth .15
181 Ichiro Suzuki RC (Rookie Reserve) 35.00
182 Wilson Betemit RC (Rookie Reserve) 6.00
183 Adrian Hernandez RC (Rookie Reserve) 3.00
184 Travis Hafner RC (Rookie Reserve) 15.00
185 Sean Douglass RC (Rookie Reserve) 3.00
186 Juan Diaz RC (Rookie Reserve) 3.00
187 Horacio Ramirez RC (Rookie Reserve) 5.00
188 Morgan Ensberg RC (Rookie Reserve) 10.00
189 Brandon Duckworth RC (Rookie Reserve) 3.00
190 Jack Wilson RC (Rookie Reserve) 8.00
191 Erick Almonte RC (Rookie Reserve) 3.00
192 Ricardo Rodriguez RC (Rookie Reserve) 3.00
193 Elpidio Guzman RC (Rookie Reserve) 3.00
194 Juan Uribe RC (Rookie Reserve) 5.00
195 Ryan Freel RC (Rookie Reserve) 4.00
196 Christian Parker RC (Rookie Reserve) 3.00
197 Jackson Melian RC (Rookie Reserve) 3.00
198 Jose Mieses RC (Rookie Reserve) 3.00
199 Andres Torres RC (Rookie Reserve) 3.00
200 Jason Smith RC (Rookie Reserve) 3.00
201 Johnny Estrada RC (Rookie Reserve) 6.00
202 Cesar Crespo RC (Rookie Reserve) 3.00
203 Carlos Valderrama RC (Rookie Reserve) 3.00
204 Albert Pujols RC (Rookie Reserve) 100.00
205 Wilken Ruan RC (Rookie Reserve) 3.00
206 Josh Fogg RC (Rookie Reserve) 4.00
207 Bert Snow RC (Rookie Reserve) 3.00
208 Brian Lawrence RC (Rookie Reserve) 5.00
209 Esix Snead RC (Rookie Reserve) 3.00
210 Tsuyoshi Shinjo RC (Rookie Reserve) 4.00

Big Game Reserve

NM/M
Complete Set (10): 15.00
Common Player: 1.00
Inserted 1:24
BG1 Alex Rodriguez 3.00
BG2 Ken Griffey Jr. 2.00
BG3 Mark McGwire 3.00
BG4 Derek Jeter 4.00
BG5 Sammy Sosa 2.50
BG6 Pedro Martinez 1.50
BG7 Jason Giambi 1.00
BG8 Todd Helton 1.00
BG9 Carlos Delgado 1.00
BG10 Mike Piazza 2.00

G-U Reserve Base/Ball Duo

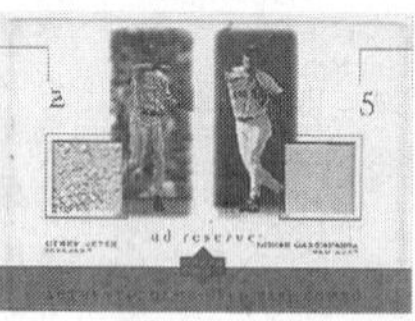

NM/M
Inserted 1:240
JR Derek Jeter, Alex Rodriguez 50.00
JP Derek Jeter, Mike Piazza 60.00
MP Mark McGwire, Mike Piazza 100.00
MJ Mark McGwire, Derek Jeter 100.00
RM Alex Rodriguez, Mark McGwire 100.00
CR Roger Clemens, Alex Rodriguez 40.00
ST Sammy Sosa, Frank Thomas 40.00
GD Vladimir Guerrero, Carlos Delgado 20.00
BH Barry Bonds, Todd Helton 35.00
MG Mark McGwire, Ken Griffey Jr. 40.00
GS Ken Griffey Jr., Sammy Sosa 20.00
GJ Ken Griffey Jr., Derek Jeter 35.00
JN Chipper Jones, Nomar Garciaparra 20.00
NJ Nomar Garciaparra, Derek Jeter 35.00
GR Nomar Garciaparra, Alex Rodriguez 30.00

G-U Reserve Base/Ball trio

NM/M
Inserted 1:480
JRG Derek Jeter, Alex Rodriguez, Nomar Garciaparra 50.00
SGM Sammy Sosa, Ken Griffey Jr., Mark McGwire 65.00
PRS Mike Piazza, Alex Rodriguez, Sammy Sosa 40.00
GSG Ken Griffey Jr., Sammy Sosa, Vladimir Guerrero 30.00
THM Frank Thomas, Todd Helton, Mark McGwire 65.00
CMJ Roger Clemens, Pedro Martinez, Derek Jeter 45.00
BSH Barry Bonds, Gary Sheffield, Todd Helton 40.00

GPJ Vladimir Guerrero, Mike Piazza, Chipper Jones 30.00
MJR Mark McGwire, Derek Jeter, Alex Rodriguez 75.00
JGS Derek Jeter, Ken Griffey Jr., Sammy Sosa 45.00

G-U Reserve Base/Ball Quad

NM/M
Production 50 Sets
SGRM Sammy Sosa, Ken Griffey Jr., Alex Rodriguez, Mark McGwire 175.00
GPJG Vladimir Guerrero, Mike Piazza, Chipper Jones, Nomar Garciaparra 65.00
THMJ Frank Thomas, Todd Helton, Mark McGwire, Derek Jeter 90.00
GBJE Ken Griffey Jr., Barry Bonds, Andruw Jones, Jim Edmonds 75.00
PMJR Mike Piazza, Mark McGwire, Derek Jeter, Alex Rodriguez 150.00

Jerseys Duo

NM/M
Common Duo: 15.00
Inserted 1:240
HG Tim Hudson, Jason Giambi 25.00
BK Barry Bonds, Jeff Kent 40.00
JJ Andruw Jones, Chipper Jones 25.00
GE Troy Glaus, Darin Erstad 15.00
WO David Wells, Magglio Ordonez 15.00
WE Bernie Williams, Jim Edmonds 15.00
DG Carlos Delgado, Jason Giambi 20.00
GK Jason Giambi, Jeff Kent 20.00
JW Randy Johnson, David Wells 25.00
JG Chipper Jones, Troy Glaus 25.00
SB Gary Sheffield, Barry Bonds 40.00
HE Todd Helton, Darin Erstad 20.00
RB Alex Rodriguez, Tony Batista 25.00
GW Brian Giles, Bernie Williams 15.00
SG Sammy Sosa, Troy Glaus 30.00

Jerseys Trio

NM/M
Common Trio: 25.00
Inserted 1:480
GHD Jason Giambi, Todd Helton, Carlos Delgado 30.00
RSS Alex Rodriguez, Sammy Sosa, Gary Sheffield 50.00
WEJ Bernie Williams, Jim Edmonds, Andruw Jones 25.00
HJW Tim Hudson, Randy Johnson, David Wells 30.00
SOD Sammy Sosa, Magglio Ordonez, Carlos Delgado 40.00
GGR Jason Giambi, Troy Glaus, Alex Rodriguez 40.00
BWD Tony Batista, Bernie Williams, Carlos Delgado 25.00
BSH Barry Bonds, Gary Sheffield, Todd Helton 50.00
WSH David Wells, Sammy Sosa, Todd Helton 40.00
EKE Darin Erstad, Jeff Kent, Jim Edmonds 25.00

Jerseys Quad

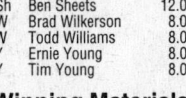

NM/M
Common Quad: 25.00
Production 50 Sets
DRGS Carlos Delgado, Alex Rodriguez, Troy Glaus, Sammy Sosa 40.00
GWBG Jason Giambi, Bernie Williams, Barry Bonds, Brian Giles 75.00
HKEJ Todd Helton, Jeff Kent, Jim Edmonds, Chipper Jones 40.00
HKEJ Gary Sheffield, Magglio Ordonez, Darin Erstad, Tony Batista 25.00
JRSB Andruw Jones, Alex Rodriguez, Sammy Sosa, Barry Bonds 100.00

The New Order

NM/M
Complete Set (10): 15.00
Common Player: .75
Inserted 1:24
NO1 Vladimir Guerrero 1.50
NO2 Andruw Jones 1.00
NO3 Corey Patterson .75
NO4 Derek Jeter 4.00
NO5 Alex Rodriguez 3.00
NO6 Pat Burrell .75
NO7 Ichiro Suzuki 5.00
NO8 Barry Zito .75
NO9 Rafael Furcal .75
NO10 Troy Glaus 1.00

UD Royalty

NM/M
Complete Set (10): 15.00
Common Player: 1.00
Inserted 1:24
R1 Ken Griffey Jr. 2.00
R2 Derek Jeter 4.00
R3 Alex Rodriguez 3.00
R4 Sammy Sosa 2.50
R5 Mark McGwire 3.00
R6 Mike Piazza 2.00
R7 Vladimir Guerrero 1.50
R8 Chipper Jones 2.00
R9 Frank Thomas 1.00
R10 Nomar Garciaparra 3.00

2001 Upper Deck Rookie Update

NM/M
Common Player: .25
Common Rookie:
Pack (4): 17.00
Box (18): 260.00
Sweet Spot
Common SP (121-150): 3.00
Production 1,500
91 Garret Anderson .50
92 Jermaine Dye .25
93 Shannon Stewart .25
94 Ben Grieve .25
95 Juan Gonzalez .75
96 Bret Boone .50
97 Tony Batista .25
98 Rafael Palmeiro 1.00
99 Carl Everett .25
100 Mike Sweeney .25
101 Tony Clark .25
102 Doug Mientkiewicz .25
103 Jose Canseco .50
104 Mike Mussina .75
105 Lance Berkman .50
106 Andruw Jones .75
107 Geoff Jenkins .40
108 Matt Morris .25
109 Fred McGriff .40
110 Luis Gonzalez .50
111 Kevin Brown .25
112 Tony Armas Jr. .25
113 John Vander Wal .25
114 Cliff Floyd .25
115 Matt Lawton .25
116 Phil Nevin .25
117 Pat Burrell .50
118 Aramis Ramirez .25
119 Sean Casey .40
120 Larry Walker .40
121 Albert Pujols **RC** 200.00
122 Johnny Estrada **RC** 8.00
123 Wilson Betemit **RC** 3.00
124 Adrian Hernandez **RC** 3.00
125 Morgan Ensberg **RC** 15.00
126 Horacio Ramirez **RC** 6.00
127 Josh Towers **RC** 6.00
128 Juan Uribe **RC** 5.00
129 Wilken Ruan **RC** 3.00
130 Andres Torres **RC** 3.00
131 Brian Lawrence **RC** 4.00
132 Ryan Freel **RC** 4.00
133 Brandon Duckworth **RC** 4.00
134 Juan Diaz **RC** 3.00
135 Rafael Soriano **RC** 6.00
136 Ricardo Rodriguez **RC** 3.00
137 Bud Smith **RC** 3.00
138 Mark Teixeira **RC** 70.00
139 Mark Prior **RC** 25.00
140 Jackson Melian **RC** 3.00
141 Dewon Brazelton **RC** 3.00
142 Greg Miller **RC** 3.00
143 Billy Sylvester **RC** 3.00
144 Elpidio Guzman **RC** 3.00
145 Jack Wilson **RC** 8.00
146 Jose Mieses **RC** 3.00
147 Brandon Lyon **RC** 3.00
148 Tsuyoshi Shinjo **RC** 4.00
149 Juan Cruz **RC** 3.00
150 Jay Gibbons **RC** 8.00
SPx
Common (181-205) 3.00
Production 1,500
Cards (206-210) Autographed
151 Garret Anderson .50
152 Jermaine Dye .25
153 Shannon Stewart .25
154 Toby Hall .25
155 C.C. Sabathia .25
156 Bret Boone .50
157 Tony Batista .25
158 Gabe Kapler .25
159 Carl Everett .25
160 Mike Sweeney .25
161 Dean Palmer .25
162 Doug Mientkiewicz .25
163 Carlos Lee .25
164 Mike Mussina .75
165 Lance Berkman .50
166 Ken Caminiti .25
167 Ben Sheets .40
168 Matt Morris .25
169 Fred McGriff .40
170 Curt Schilling .50
171 Paul LoDuca .25
172 Javier Vazquez .25
173 Rich Aurilia .25
174 A.J. Burnett .25
175 Al Leiter .40
176 Mark Kotsay .25
177 Jimmy Rollins .40
178 Aramis Ramirez .25
179 Aaron Boone .25
180 Jeff Cirillo .25
181 Johnny Estrada **RC** 10.00
182 Dave Williams **RC** 3.00
183 Donaldo Mendez **RC** 3.00
184 Junior Spivey **RC** 8.00
185 Jay Gibbons **RC** 10.00
186 Kyle Lohse **RC** 8.00
187 Willie Harris **RC** 3.00
188 Juan Cruz **RC** 5.00
189 Joe Kennedy **RC** 3.00
190 Duaner Sanchez **RC** 3.00
191 Jorge Julio **RC** 5.00
192 Cesar Crespo **RC** 3.00
193 Casey Fossum **RC** 5.00
194 Brian Roberts **RC** 15.00
195 Troy Mattes **RC** 3.00
196 Rob Mackowiak **RC** 3.00
197 Tsuyoshi Shinjo **RC** 8.00
198 Nick Punto **RC** 3.00
199 Wilmy Caceres **RC** 3.00
200 Jeremy Affeldt **RC** 3.00
201 Bret Prinz **RC** 3.00
202 Delvin James **RC** 3.00
203 Luis Pineda **RC** 3.00
204 Matt White **RC** 3.00
205 Brandon Knight **RC** 3.00
206 Albert Pujols **RC** 600.00
207 Mark Teixeira **RC** 150.00
208 Mark Prior **RC** 60.00
209 Dewon Brazelton **RC** 10.00
210 Bud Smith **RC** 8.00
SP Authentic
Common (211-240): 4.00
Production 1,500
181 Garrett Anderson .50
182 Jermaine Dye .25
183 Shannon Stewart .25
184 Ben Grieve .25
185 Ellis Burks .25
186 John Olerud .50
187 Tony Batista .25
188 Ruben Sierra .25
189 Carl Everett .25
190 Neifi Perez .25
191 Tony Clark .25
192 Doug Mientkiewicz .25
193 Carlos Lee .25
194 Jorge Posada .50
195 Lance Berkman .50
196 Ken Caminiti .25
197 Ben Sheets .50
198 Matt Morris .25
199 Fred McGriff .40
200 Mark Grace .50
201 Paul LoDuca .25
202 Tony Armas, Jr. .25
203 Andres Galarraga .40
204 Cliff Floyd .25
205 Matt Lawton .25
206 Ryan Klesko .40
207 Jimmy Rollins .25
208 Aramis Ramirez .25
209 Aaron Boone .25
210 Jose Ortiz .25
211 Mark Prior **RC** 60.00
212 Mark Teixeira **RC** 125.00
213 Bud Smith **RC** 4.00
214 Wilmy Caceres **RC** 4.00
215 Dave Williams **RC** 4.00
216 Delvin James **RC** 4.00
217 Endy Chavez **RC** 4.00
218 Doug Nickle **RC** 4.00
219 Bret Prinz **RC** 4.00
220 Troy Mattes **RC** 4.00
221 Duaner Sanchez **RC** 4.00
222 Dewon Brazelton **RC** 4.00
223 Brian Bowles **RC** 4.00
224 Donaldo Mendez **RC** 4.00
225 Jorge Julio **RC** 6.00
226 Matt White **RC** 4.00
227 Casey Fossum **RC** 6.00
228 Mike Rivera **RC** 4.00
229 Joe Kennedy **RC** 4.00
230 Kyle Lohse **RC** 6.00
231 Juan Cruz **RC** 4.00
232 Jeremy Affeldt **RC** 4.00
233 Brandon Lyon **RC** 4.00
234 Brian Roberts **RC** 15.00
235 Willie Harris **RC** 4.00
236 Pedro Santana **RC** 4.00
237 Rafael Soriano **RC** 6.00
238 Steve Green **RC** 4.00
239 Junior Spivey **RC** 6.00
240 Rob Mackowiak **RC** 4.00

Ichiro ROY

NM/M
Complete Set (51): 35.00
Common Ichiro: 1.00
1-51 Ichiro Suzuki 1.00

Ichiro ROY Game Jersey

NM/M
Numbers 1-12 Production 100 50.00
Numbers 13-17 Production 50 75.00
Numbers 18-19 Production 25 150.00
J-I1-12 Ichiro Suzuki 50.00
J-I13-17 Ichiro Suzuki 75.00
J-I18-19 Ichiro Suzuki 150.00

Ichiro ROY Game-Used Bat

NM/M
Numbers 1-12 Production 100 50.00
Numbers 13-17 Production 50 75.00
Numbers 18-19 Production 25 150.00
B-I1-12 Ichiro Suzuki 50.00
B-I13-17 Ichiro Suzuki 75.00
B-I18-19 Ichiro Suzuki 150.00

SP Chirography

NM/M
Common Autograph: 15.00
Production 250
Silver: .75-1.5X
Production 100
Gold: No Pricing
Production 25 Sets
LB Lance Berkman/100 10.00
KG Ken Griffey Jr./250 90.00
TG Tony Gwynn/250 30.00
TG Tony Gwynn/100 40.00
MS Doug Mientkiewicz/100 15.00
JP Jorge Posada/250 25.00
JP Jorge Posada/10 30.00
CR Cal Ripken Jr. 100.00
MS Mike Sweeney/100 15.00

SP Chirography - Ichiro

Available only as a redemption in UD Rookie Update. Three versions were produced, an unnumbered autographed card, a Silver parallel autograph numbered to 100 and a Gold autograph parallel numbered to 25.

NM/M
Ichiro (Unnumbered) 300.00
Ichiro/Silver/100 500.00

USA Touch of Gold

NM/M
Common Autograph: 8.00
Production 500 Sets
BA Brent Abernathy 8.00
KU Kurt Ainsworth 10.00
PB Pat Borders 8.00
SB Sean Burroughs 12.00
JC John Cotton 8.00
TD Gookie Dawkins 8.00
AE Adam Everett 8.00
RF Ryan Franklin 8.00
CG Chris George 8.00
SH Shane Heams 8.00
MJ Marcus Jensen 8.00
MK Mike Kinkade 8.00
RK Rick Krivda 8.00
DM Doug Mientkiewicz 12.00
MN Mike Neill 8.00
RO Roy Oswalt 20.00
JR Jon Rauch 8.00
AS Anthony Sanders 8.00
BSe Bobby Seay 8.00
BSh Ben Sheets 12.00
BW Brad Wilkerson 8.00
TW Todd Williams 8.00
EY Ernie Young 8.00
TY Tim Young 8.00

Winning Materials 2-Player

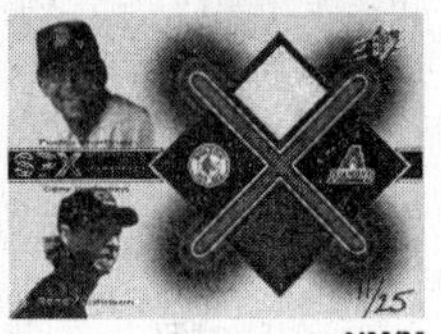

NM/M
Common Card: 10.00
Inserted 1:15
BB-LG Barry Bonds, Luis Gonzalez 25.00
JG-BB Jason Giambi, Barry Bonds 25.00
IR-AR Ivan Rodriguez, Alex Rodriguez 25.00
AP-JE Albert Pujols, Jim Edmonds 35.00
GS-SG Gary Sheffield, Shawn Green 15.00
MP-EA Mike Piazza, Edgardo Alfonzo 20.00
LW-TH Larry Walker, Todd Helton 15.00
MR-JG Manny Ramirez, Juan Gonzalez 15.00
TG-CR Tony Gwynn, Cal Ripken Jr. 40.00
SR-BA Scott Rolen, Bobby Abreu 15.00
JB-CB Jeff Bagwell, Craig Biggio 20.00
KG-SC Ken Griffey Jr., Sean Casey 25.00
EM-JM Eric Milton, Joe Mays 10.00
HN-MY Hideo Nomo, Masato Yoshii 20.00
TS-HN Tsuyoshi Shinjo, Hideo Nomo 15.00
CS-RJ Curt Schilling, Randy Johnson 20.00
AS-KS Aaron Sele, Kazuhiro Sasaki 10.00
PM-RJ Pedro Martinez, Randy Johnson 15.00
BW-MR Bernie Williams, Mariano Rivera 15.00
TG-X2 Tony Gwynn 15.00
CR-X2 Cal Ripken Jr. 40.00
JB-RY Jeromy Burnitz, Robin Yount 15.00
CR-EM Cal Ripken Jr., Eddie Murray 30.00
TG-DW Tony Gwynn, Dave Winfield 15.00
FT-MO Frank Thomas, Magglio Ordonez 15.00
PM-GM Pedro Martinez, Greg Maddux 20.00
BW-RJ Bernie Williams, Reggie Jackson 20.00
SS-EB Sammy Sosa, Ernie Banks 30.00
CP-FV Chan Ho Park, Fernando Valenzuela 10.00

Winning Materials 3-Player Jersey

NM/M
Common Card: 10.00
Inserted 1:15
KBA Jeff Kent, Barry Bonds, Rich Aurilia 25.00
JAF Chipper Jones, Andruw Jones, Rafael Furcal 15.00
GZH Jason Giambi, Barry Zito, Tim Hudson 15.00
SKB Gary Sheffield, Eric Karros, Kevin Brown 10.00
SSM Aaron Sele, Ichiro Suzuki, Edgar Martinez 40.00
HDG Todd Helton, Carlos Delgado, Jason Giambi 15.00
VRF Omar Vizquel, Alex Rodriguez, Rafael Furcal 25.00
SYN Kazuhiro Sasaki, Masato Yoshii, Hideo Nomo 20.00

BTD Jeff Bagwell, Frank Thomas, Carlos Delgado 15.00
BGG Barry Bonds, Luis Gonzalez, Ken Griffey Jr. 30.00
RPK Ivan Rodriguez, Mike Piazza, Jason Kendall 20.00
PPV Jay Payton, Mike Piazza, Robin Ventura 15.00
CHN Roger Clemens, Tim Hudson, Hideo Nomo 20.00
PWO Andy Pettitte, Bernie Williams, Paul O'Neill 20.00
TDK Frank Thomas, Ray Durham, Paul Konerko 15.00
SJC Curt Schilling, Randy Johnson, Roger Clemens 20.00
DEA J.D. Drew, Jim Edmonds, Bobby Abreu 15.00
DOP Carlos Delgado, Magglio Ordonez, Albert Pujols 35.00
TGA Jim Thome, Juan Gonzalez, Roberto Alomar 15.00
GWS Luis Gonzalez, Matt Williams, Curt Schilling 20.00
MGJ Greg Maddux, Tom Glavine, Andruw Jones 20.00

2001 Upper Deck Sweet Spot

NM/M
Complete Set (90): 200.00
Common Player: .25
Common Sweet Beginnings: 5.00
(61-90) Production 1,000
Pack (4): 15.00
Box (18): 250.00
1 Troy Glaus .75
2 Darin Erstad .50
3 Jason Giambi .75
4 Tim Hudson .50
5 Ben Grieve .25
6 Carlos Delgado .75
7 David Wells .25
8 Greg Vaughn .25
9 Roberto Alomar .75
10 Jim Thome .75
11 John Olerud .50
12 Edgar Martinez .40
13 Cal Ripken Jr. 3.00
14 Albert Belle .25
15 Ivan Rodriguez .75
16 Alex Rodriguez 2.50
17 Pedro Martinez 1.00
18 Nomar Garciaparra 2.00
19 Manny Ramirez .75
20 Jermaine Dye .25
21 Juan Gonzalez .75
22 Dean Palmer .25
23 Matt Lawton .25
24 Eric Milton .25
25 Frank Thomas .75
26 Magglio Ordonez .50
27 Derek Jeter 3.00
28 Bernie Williams .75
29 Roger Clemens 2.00
30 Jeff Bagwell .75
31 Richard Hidalgo .25
32 Chipper Jones 1.50
33 Greg Maddux 1.50
34 Richie Sexson .50
35 Jeromy Burnitz .25
36 Mark McGwire 2.50
37 Jim Edmonds .50
38 Sammy Sosa 2.00
39 Randy Johnson 1.00
40 Steve Finley .25
41 Gary Sheffield .50
42 Shawn Green .50
43 Vladimir Guerrero 1.00
44 Jose Vidro .25
45 Barry Bonds 3.00
46 Jeff Kent .40
47 Preston Wilson .25
48 Luis Castillo .25
49 Mike Piazza 1.50
50 Edgardo Alfonzo .25
51 Tony Gwynn 1.00
52 Ryan Klesko .40
53 Scott Rolen .75
54 Bob Abreu .40
55 Jason Kendall .40
56 Brian Giles .40
57 Ken Griffey Jr. 1.50
58 Barry Larkin .50
59 Todd Helton .75
60 Mike Hampton .25
61 Corey Patterson (Sweet Beginnings) 5.00
62 Ichiro Suzuki **RC** (Sweet Beginnings) 160.00
63 Jason Grilli (Sweet Beginnings) 5.00
64 Brian Cole (Sweet Beginnings) 5.00
65 Juan Pierre (Sweet Beginnings) 5.00
66 Matt Ginter (Sweet Beginnings) 5.00
67 Jimmy Rollins (Sweet Beginnings) 8.00
68 Jason Smith **RC** (Sweet Beginnings) 5.00
69 Israel Alcantara (Sweet Beginnings) 5.00
70 Adam Pettyjohn **RC** (Sweet Beginnings) 5.00
71 Luke Prokopec (Sweet Beginnings) 5.00
72 Barry Zito (Sweet Beginnings) 5.00
73 Keith Ginter (Sweet Beginnings) 5.00
74 Sun-Woo Kim (Sweet Beginnings) 5.00
75 Ross Gload (Sweet Beginnings) 5.00
76 Matt Wise (Sweet Beginnings) 5.00
77 Aubrey Huff (Sweet Beginnings) 5.00
78 Ryan Franklin (Sweet Beginnings) 5.00
79 Brandon Inge (Sweet Beginnings) 5.00
80 Wes Helms (Sweet Beginnings) 5.00
81 Junior Spivey **RC** (Sweet Beginnings) 8.00
82 Ryan Vogelsong (Sweet Beginnings) 5.00
83 John Parrish (Sweet Beginnings) 5.00
84 Joe Crede (Sweet Beginnings) 5.00
85 Damian Rolls (Sweet Beginnings) 5.00
86 Esix Snead **RC** (Sweet Beginnings) 5.00
87 Rocky Biddle (Sweet Beginnings) 5.00
88 Brady Clark (Sweet Beginnings) 5.00
89 Timoniel Perez (Sweet Beginnings) 5.00
90 Jay Spurgeon (Sweet Beginnings) 5.00

Big League Challenge

NM/M
Complete Set (20): 20.00
Common Player: .50
Inserted 1:6
1 Mark McGwire 2.50
2 Richard Hidalgo .50
3 Alex Rodriguez 2.50
4 Shawn Green .75
5 Frank Thomas 1.00
6 Chipper Jones 1.50
7 Rafael Palmeiro 1.00
8 Troy Glaus 1.00
9 Mike Piazza 1.50
10 Andruw Jones 1.00
11 Todd Helton 1.00
12 Jason Giambi 1.00
13 Sammy Sosa 2.00
14 Carlos Delgado 1.00
15 Barry Bonds 3.00
16 Jose Canseco .75
17 Jim Edmonds .75
18 Manny Ramirez 1.00
19 Gary Sheffield .75
20 Nomar Garciaparra 2.00

DiMaggio Pinstripes Excl.

NM/M
Complete Set (56): 60.00
Common DiMaggio: 1.50
One Pack/Box

DiMaggio Pinstripes Memor.

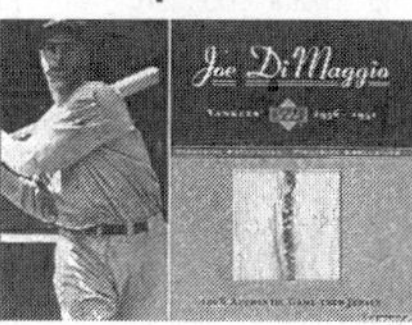

NM/M
Print Runs Listed: 150.00
JDB Joe DiMaggio/Bat/100 80.00
JDCJ Joe DiMaggio, Lou Gehrig/Jsy/50 600.00
JDJ Joe DiMaggio/Jsy/100 100.00

Game Jerseys

NM/M
Common Player: 8.00
Inserted 1:18
BB Barry Bonds 25.00
JC Jose Canseco 8.00
RC Roger Clemens 20.00
RC Roberto Clemente 125.00
JD Joe DiMaggio 80.00
KG Ken Griffey Jr. 20.00
RJ Randy Johnson 10.00
AJ Andruw Jones 8.00
CJ Chipper Jones 10.00
MM Mickey Mantle 150.00
WM Willie Mays 100.00
SM Stan Musial 65.00
CR Cal Ripken Jr. 40.00
AR Alex Rodriguez 20.00
IR Ivan Rodriguez 8.00
NR Nolan Ryan 65.00
DS Duke Snider 10.00
SS Sammy Sosa 20.00
IS Ichiro Suzuki 100.00
FT Frank Thomas 10.00

S.S. Game-Used Bases Tier 1

NM/M
Common Card: 5.00
BH Barry Bonds, Todd Helton 25.00
MG Mark McGwire, Ken Griffey Jr. 60.00
JG Chipper Jones, Nomar Garciaparra 20.00
GD Vladimir Guerrero, Carlos Delgado 8.00
ST Sammy Sosa, Frank Thomas 20.00
SR Gary Sheffield, Alex Rodriguez 15.00
GR Tony Gwynn, Ivan Rodriguez 10.00
PJ Mike Piazza, Derek Jeter 30.00
HG Jeffrey Hammonds, Troy Glaus 5.00
JGi Randy Johnson, Jason Giambi 8.00
BD Jeff Bagwell, Jermaine Dye 8.00
RR Scott Rolen, Cal Ripken Jr. 25.00
GR Ken Griffey Jr., Manny Ramirez 15.00
RJ Alex Rodriguez, Derek Jeter 40.00
MP Mark McGwire, Timoniel Perez 35.00
CP Roger Clemens, Mike Piazza 20.00

S.S. Game-Used Bases Tier 2

NM/M
Common Card: 20.00
Production 50 Sets
BHK Barry Bonds, Todd Helton, Jeff Kent 75.00
MGE Mark McGwire, Ken Griffey Jr., Bobby Edmonds 120.00
JGJ Chipper Jones, Nomar Garciaparra, Andruw Jones 60.00
GDM Vladimir Guerrero, Carlos Delgado, Raul Mondesi 20.00
STO Sammy Sosa, Frank Thomas, Magglio Ordonez 50.00
SRM Gary Sheffield, Alex Rodriguez, Edgar Martinez 50.00
GRP Tony Gwynn, Ivan Rodriguez, Rafael Palmeiro 40.00
PJW Mike Piazza, Derek Jeter, Bernie Williams 75.00
HGH Jeffrey Hammonds, Troy Glaus, Todd Helton 20.00
JGC Randy Johnson, Jason Giambi, Eric Chavez 25.00
BDH Jeff Bagwell, Jermaine Dye, Richard Hidalgo 20.00
RRB Scott Rolen, Cal Ripken Jr., Albert Belle 75.00
GRT Ken Griffey Jr., Manny Ramirez, Jim Thome 50.00

Game-Used Bat

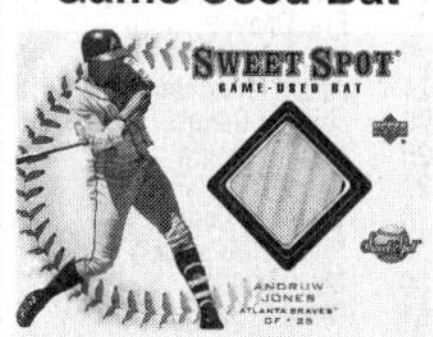

NM/M
Common Player: 5.00
Inserted 1:18
HA Hank Aaron 60.00
RA Rick Ankiel 5.00
BB Barry Bonds 25.00
JC Jose Canseco 8.00
TC Ty Cobb 175.00
JD Joe DiMaggio 80.00
KG Ken Griffey Jr. 15.00
RJ Reggie Jackson 10.00
AJ Andruw Jones 10.00
MM Mickey Mantle 140.00
WM Willie Mays 75.00
SM Stan Musial 50.00
CR Cal Ripken Jr. 40.00
AR Alex Rodriguez 20.00
IR Ivan Rodriguez 8.00
NR Nolan Ryan 65.00
GS Gary Sheffield 8.00
SS Sammy Sosa 20.00
FT Frank Thomas 10.00

Players Party

NM/M
Complete Set (10): 10.00
Common Player: .75
Inserted 1:12
1 Derek Jeter 3.00
2 Randy Johnson 1.00
3 Frank Thomas 1.00
4 Nomar Garciaparra 2.00
5 Ken Griffey Jr. 1.50
6 Carlos Delgado .75
7 Mike Piazza 1.50
8 Barry Bonds 3.00
9 Sammy Sosa 2.00
10 Pedro Martinez 1.00

Signatures

NM/M
Common Player: 20.00
RAl Roberto Alomar 40.00
RAn Rick Ankiel 20.00
JB Jeff Bagwell/SP/214 120.00
DB Dusty Baker 20.00
DB Don Baylor 20.00
BB Buddy Bell 20.00
AB Albert Belle 25.00
MB Milton Bradley 20.00
PB Pat Burrell 30.00
JC Jose Canseco 60.00
CB Chris Chambliss 20.00
RC Roger Clemens 140.00
CD Carlos Delgado 30.00
JD Joe DiMaggio/SP/150 600.00
DE Darin Erstad 25.00
RF Rafael Furcal 25.00
JG Joe Garagiola 50.00
JG Jason Giambi 50.00
TGl Troy Glaus 40.00
SG Shawn Green 30.00
KG Ken Griffey/SP/100 350.00
TGw Tony Gwynn 110.00
AH Art Howe 20.00
TH Tim Hudson 30.00
DJ Davey Johnson 20.00
RJ Randy Johnson 85.00
AJ Andruw Jones 50.00
CJ Chipper Jones 80.00
ML Mike Lamb 20.00
TL Tony LaRussa 20.00
DL Davey Lopes 20.00
BM Bill Madlock 20.00
MM Mickey Mantle/SP/10 3,500
WM Willie Mays 200.00
HM Hal McRae 20.00
SM Stan Musial 120.00
PO Paul O'Neill 50.00
LP Lou Piniella 25.00
JR Jim Rice 25.00
AR Alex Rodriguez/SP/154 200.00
IR Ivan Rodriguez/SP/150 100.00
BR Babe Ruth/SP/1 (8/03 Auction) 12,000
NR Nolan Ryan 200.00
GS Gary Sheffield 30.00
SS Sammy Sosa/SP/148 250.00
FT Frank Thomas 60.00
AT Alan Trammell 25.00
BV Bobby Valentine 20.00
RV Robin Ventura 20.00
MW Matt Williams 25.00

Texas Rangers Team Set

This set was produced for sale by the team, retailing for about $15 at souvenir outlets. Standard-size cards have game-action photos on front. Backs repeat part of the photo and have personal data, stats and logos. Card numbers carry a "TR" prefix.

NM/M
Complete Set (20): 15.00
Common Player: .50
1 Alex Rodriguez 3.00
2 Rafael Palmeiro 1.50
3 Ivan Rodriguez 1.50
4 Andres Galarraga .50
5 Ken Caminiti .50
6 Ruben Mateo .50
7 Rusty Greer .50
8 Rick Helling .50
9 Gabe Kapler .50
10 Kenny Rogers .50
11 Randy Velarde .50
12 Doug Davis .50
13 Bill Haselman .50
14 Tim Crabtree .50
15 Darren Oliver .50
16 Jeff Zimmerman .50
17 Ricky Ledee .50
18 Mark Petkovsek .50
19 Frank Catalanotto .50
20 Nolan Ryan 5.00

2001 Upper Deck Ultimate Collection

NM/M
Common Player: 1.00
Common SP (91-100): 5.00
Production 1,000
Common SP (101-110): 5.00
Production 750
Common (111-120): 20.00
Production 250
Pack (4): 160.00
Box (4): 575.00
1 Troy Glaus 2.50
2 Darin Erstad 1.50
3 Jason Giambi 3.00
4 Barry Zito 2.00
5 Tim Hudson 2.00
6 Miguel Tejada 1.50
7 Carlos Delgado 2.50
8 Shannon Stewart 1.00
9 Greg Vaughn 1.00
10 Toby Hall 1.00
11 Roberto Alomar 2.00
12 Juan Gonzalez 2.50
13 Jim Thome 3.00
14 Edgar Martinez 1.50
15 Freddy Garcia 1.00
16 Bret Boone 1.50
17 Kazuhiro Sasaki 1.00
18 Cal Ripken Jr. 10.00
19 Tim Raines Jr. 1.00
20 Alex Rodriguez 8.00
21 Ivan Rodriguez 2.50
22 Rafael Palmeiro 2.50
23 Pedro Martinez 3.00
24 Nomar Garciaparra 6.00
25 Manny Ramirez 2.50
26 Hideo Nomo 2.00
27 Mike Sweeney 1.00
28 Carlos Beltran 1.50
29 Tony Clark 1.00
30 Dean Palmer 1.00
31 Doug Mientkiewicz 1.00
32 Cristian Guzman 1.00
33 Corey Koskie 1.00
34 Frank Thomas 3.00
35 Magglio Ordonez 1.50
36 Jose Canseco 2.00
37 Roger Clemens 6.00
38 Derek Jeter 10.00
39 Bernie Williams 2.00
40 Mike Mussina 2.00
41 Tino Martinez 1.00
42 Jeff Bagwell 2.50
43 Lance Berkman 2.00
44 Roy Oswalt 1.50
45 Chipper Jones 5.00
46 Greg Maddux 5.00
47 Andruw Jones 2.50
48 Tom Glavine 2.00
49 Richie Sexson 2.00
50 Jeromy Burnitz 1.00
51 Ben Sheets 1.00
52 Mark McGwire 8.00
53 Matt Morris 1.00
54 Jim Edmonds 2.00
55 J.D. Drew 1.50
56 Sammy Sosa 6.00
57 Fred McGriff 1.00
58 Kerry Wood 2.50
59 Randy Johnson 3.00
60 Luis Gonzalez 2.00
61 Curt Schilling 2.00

62 Shawn Green 1.50
63 Kevin Brown 1.50
64 Gary Sheffield 2.00
65 Vladimir Guerrero 3.00
66 Barry Bonds 10.00
67 Jeff Kent 1.50
68 Rich Aurilia 1.00
69 Cliff Floyd 1.00
70 Charles Johnson 1.00
71 Josh Beckett 2.00
72 Mike Piazza 5.00
73 Edgardo Alfonzo 1.00
74 Robin Ventura 1.00
75 Tony Gwynn 2.50
76 Ryan Klesko 1.50
77 Phil Nevin 1.00
78 Scott Rolen 2.50
79 Bobby Abreu 1.00
80 Jimmy Rollins 1.50
81 Brian Giles 1.50
82 Jason Kendall 1.00
83 Aramis Ramirez 1.00
84 Ken Griffey Jr. 6.00
85 Adam Dunn 2.00
86 Sean Casey 1.50
87 Barry Larkin 2.00
88 Larry Walker 1.50
89 Mike Hampton 1.00
90 Todd Helton 2.50
91 Ken Harvey 5.00
92 William Ortega **RC** 5.00
93 Juan Diaz **RC** 5.00
94 Greg Miller **RC** 5.00
95 Brandon Berger **RC** 5.00
96 Brandon Lyon **RC** 5.00
97 Jay Gibbons **RC** 20.00
98 Rob Mackowiak **RC** 5.00
99 Erick Almonte **RC** 5.00
100 Jason Middlebrook **RC** 5.00
101 Johnny Estrada **RC** 10.00
102 Juan Uribe **RC** 10.00
103 Travis Hafner **RC** 30.00
104 Morgan Ensberg **RC** 20.00
105 Mike Rivera **RC** 5.00
106 Josh Towers **RC** 5.00
107 Adrian Hernandez **RC** 5.00
108 Rafael Soriano **RC** 10.00
109 Jackson Melian **RC** 5.00
110 Wilken Ruan **RC** 5.00
111 Albert Pujols **RC** 600.00
112 Tsuyoshi Shinjo **RC** 15.00
113 Brandon Duckworth **RC** 20.00
114 Juan Cruz **RC** 20.00
115 Dewon Brazelton **RC** 20.00
116 Mark Prior/Auto. **RC** 200.00
117 Mark Teixeira/Auto. **RC** 300.00
118 Wilson Betemit/Auto. **RC** 25.00
119 Bud Smith/Auto. **RC** 20.00
120 Ichiro Suzuki/Auto. **RC** 1,500

Ichiro

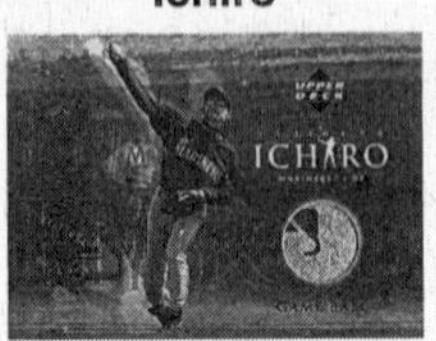

NM/M
Pricing not available for all Ichiro's.
B-IA Ichiro Suzuki/Bat Away 65.00
B-IH Ichiro Suzuki/Bat Home 65.00
B-IS Ichiro Suzuki/Bat/250 80.00
B-IG Ichiro Suzuki/Bat/200 90.00
SB-I Ichiro Suzuki/Bat/Auto./50 675.00
J-IA Ichiro Suzuki/Jsy/Away 50.00
J-IH Ichiro Suzuki/Jsy/Home 50.00
J-IS Ichiro Suzuki/Jsy/250 75.00
J-IG Ichiro Suzuki/Jsy/200 85.00
SJ-I Ichiro Suzuki/Jsy/Auto./50 675.00
UB-I Ichiro Suzuki/Base 25.00
UB-IC Ichiro Suzuki/Base/150 80.00
UB-IS Ichiro Suzuki/Base/50 100.00
BB-I Ichiro Suzuki/Ball 60.00
BB-IC Ichiro Suzuki/Ball/150 85.00
BB-IS Ichiro Suzuki/Ball/50 100.00
SBB-I Ichiro Suzuki/Ball/Auto./25 675.00
C-I Ichiro Suzuki/Glv/75 180.00
BG-I Ichiro Suzuki/Bat/Glv/75 180.00

Game Jersey

NM/M
Common Player: 10.00
Inserted 1:2
RA Roberto Alomar 20.00
JB Jeff Bagwell 20.00
BB Barry Bonds 50.00

JC Jose Canseco 10.00
RC Roger Clemens 40.00
CD Carlos Delgado 10.00
DE Darin Erstad 10.00
JaG Jason Giambi 20.00
JG Juan Gonzalez 20.00
LG Luis Gonzalez 10.00
SG Shawn Green 10.00
KG Ken Griffey Jr. 40.00
TG Tony Gwynn 20.00
TH Todd Helton 15.00
RJ Randy Johnson 15.00
AJ Andruw Jones 10.00
CJ Chipper Jones 15.00
GM Greg Maddux 40.00
MO Magglio Ordonez 10.00
MP Mike Piazza 30.00
AP Albert Pujols 75.00
CR Cal Ripken Jr. 75.00
AR Alex Rodriguez 40.00
IR Ivan Rodriguez 15.00
SR Scott Rolen 15.00
GS Gary Sheffield 10.00
SS Sammy Sosa 40.00
FT Frank Thomas 15.00
LW Larry Walker 10.00
BW Bernie Williams 10.00

Magic Numbers

NM/M
Common Player: 10.00
Production 150
Coppers #'d to 24 not priced.
Silvers #'d to 20 not priced.
Golds #'d to 15 not priced.
RA Roberto Alomar 20.00
JB Jeff Bagwell 20.00
BB Barry Bonds 50.00
JC Jose Canseco 15.00
RC Roger Clemens 50.00
CD Carlos Delgado 15.00
DE Darin Erstad 10.00
JaG Jason Giambi 20.00
JG Juan Gonzalez 15.00
LG Luis Gonzalez 10.00
SG Shawn Green 10.00
KG Ken Griffey Jr. 40.00
TG Tony Gwynn 20.00
TH Todd Helton 15.00
RJ Randy Johnson 15.00
AJ Andruw Jones 10.00
CJ Chipper Jones 15.00
GM Greg Maddux 40.00
MO Magglio Ordonez 10.00
MP Mike Piazza 30.00
AP Albert Pujols 75.00
CR Cal Ripken Jr. 90.00
AR Alex Rodriguez 40.00
IR Ivan Rodriguez 15.00
SR Scott Rolen 15.00
GS Gary Sheffield 10.00
SS Sammy Sosa 40.00
FT Frank Thomas 15.00
LW Larry Walker 10.00
BW Bernie Williams 10.00

Ultimate Signatures

NM/M
Common Autograph: 20.00
Inserted 1:4
Silvers #'d to 24 not priced.
Golds #'d to 15 not priced.
RA Roberto Alomar 40.00
EB Ernie Banks 30.00
BaB Barry Bonds 200.00
RC Roger Clemens 100.00
CD Carlos Delgado 15.00
CF Carlton Fisk 40.00
JaG Jason Giambi 25.00
TGl Tom Glavine 40.00
LG Luis Gonzalez 25.00
KG Ken Griffey Jr. 100.00
TG Tony Gwynn 60.00
RK Ryan Klesko 20.00
SK Sandy Koufax 275.00
EM Edgar Martinez 30.00
TP Tony Perez 20.00
KP Kirby Puckett 50.00
CR Cal Ripken Jr. 125.00
AR Alex Rodriguez 80.00
IR Ivan Rodriguez 50.00
TS Tom Seaver 40.00
GS Gary Sheffield 30.00
DS Duke Snider 35.00
SS Sammy Sosa 120.00
FT Frank Thomas 40.00
JT Jim Thome 50.00
RY Robin Yount 60.00

Victory

NM/M
Complete Set (660): 50.00
Common Player: .15
1 Troy Glaus .50
2 Scott Spiezio .15
3 Gary DiSarcina .15
4 Darin Erstad .20
5 Tim Salmon .20
6 Troy Percival .15
7 Ramon Ortiz .15
8 Orlando Palmeiro .15
9 Tim Belcher .15
10 Mo Vaughn .15
11 Bengie Molina .15
12 Benji Gil .15
13 Scott Schoeneweis .15
14 Garret Anderson .15
15 Matt Wise .15
16 Adam Kennedy .15
17 Jarrod Washburn .15
18 Darin Erstad, Troy Percival .15
19 Jason Giambi .20
20 Tim Hudson .20
21 Ramon Hernandez .15
22 Eric Chavez .15
23 Gil Heredia .15
24 Jason Isringhausen .15
25 Jeremy Giambi .15
26 Miguel Tejada .15
27 Barry Zito .50
28 Terrence Long .15
29 Ryan Christenson .15
30 Mark Mulder .15
31 Olmedo Saenz .15
32 Adam Piatt .15
33 Ben Grieve .20
34 Omar Olivares .15
35 John Jaha .15
36 Jason Giambi, Tim Hudson .15
37 Carlos Delgado .40
38 Esteban Loaiza .15
39 Brad Fullmer .15
40 David Wells .15
41 Chris Woodward .15
42 Billy Koch .15
43 Shannon Stewart .15
44 Chris Carpenter .15
45 Steve Parris .15
46 Darrin Fletcher .15
47 Joey Hamilton .15
48 Jose Cruz Jr. .15
49 Vernon Wells .15
50 Raul Mondesi .15
51 Kelvim Escobar .15
52 Tony Batista .15
53 Alex Gonzalez .15
54 Carlos Delgado, David Wells .20
55 Greg Vaughn .15
56 Albie Lopez .15
57 Randy Winn .15
58 Ryan Rupe .15
59 Steve Cox .15
60 Vinny Castilla .15
61 Jose Guillen .15
62 Wilson Alvarez .15
63 Bryan Rekar .15
64 Gerald Williams .15
65 Esteban Yan .15
66 Felix Martinez .15
67 Fred McGriff .20
68 John Flaherty .15
69 Jason Tyner .15
70 Russ Johnson .15
71 Roberto Hernandez .15
72 Greg Vaughn, Albie Lopez .15
73 Eddie Taubensee .15
74 Bob Wickman .15
75 Ellis Burks .15
76 Kenny Lofton .20
77 Einar Diaz .15
78 Travis Fryman .15
79 Omar Vizquel .15
80 Jason Bere .15
81 Bartolo Colon .15
82 Jim Thome .20
83 Roberto Alomar .40
84 Chuck Finley .15
85 Steve Woodard .15
86 Russ Branyan .15
87 Dave Burba .15
88 Jaret Wright .15
89 Jacob Cruz .15
90 Steve Karsay .15
91 Manny Ramirez, Bartolo Colon .20
92 Raul Ibanez .15
93 Freddy Garcia .15
94 Edgar Martinez .15
95 Jay Buhner .15
96 Jamie Moyer .15
97 John Olerud .20
98 Aaron Sele .15
99 Kazuhiro Sasaki .20
100 Mike Cameron .15
101 John Halama .15
102 David Bell .15
103 Gil Meche .15
104 Carlos Guillen .15
105 Mark McLemore .15
106 Stan Javier .15
107 Al Martin .15
108 Dan Wilson .15
109 Alex Rodriguez, Kazuhiro Sasaki .50
110 Cal Ripken Jr. 1.50
111 Delino DeShields .15
112 Sidney Ponson .15
113 Albert Belle .15
114 Jose Mercedes .15
115 Scott Erickson .15
116 Jerry Hairston Jr. .15
117 Brook Fordyce .15
118 Luis Matos .15
119 Eugene Kingsale .15
120 Jeff Conine .15
121 Chris Richard .15
122 Fernando Lunar .15
123 John Parrish .15
124 Brady Anderson .15
125 Ryan Kohlmeier .15
126 Melvin Mora .15
127 Albert Belle, Jose Mercedes .15
128 Ivan Rodriguez .50
129 Justin Thompson .15
130 Kenny Rogers .15
131 Rafael Palmeiro .30
132 Rusty Greer .15
133 Gabe Kapler .15
134 John Wetteland .15
135 Mike Lamb .15
136 Doug Davis .15
137 Ruben Mateo .15
138 Alex Rodriguez 1.25
139 Chad Curtis .15
140 Rick Helling .15
141 Ryan Glynn .15
142 Andres Galarraga .25
143 Ricky Ledee .15
144 Frank Catalanotto .15
145 Rafael Palmeiro, Rick Helling .20
146 Pedro Martinez .60
147 Wilton Veras .15
148 Manny Ramirez .50
149 Rolando Arrojo .15
150 Nomar Garciaparra 1.00
151 Darren Lewis .15
152 Troy O'Leary .15
153 Tomokazu Ohka .15
154 Carl Everett .15
155 Jason Varitek .15
156 Frank Castillo .15
157 Pete Schourek .15
158 Jose Offerman .15
159 Derek Lowe .15
160 John Valentin .15
161 Dante Bichette .15
162 Trot Nixon .15
163 Nomar Garciaparra, Pedro Martinez .25
164 Jermaine Dye .15
165 Dave McCarty .15
166 Jose Rosado .15
167 Mike Sweeney .15
168 Rey Sanchez .15
169 Jeff Suppan .15
170 Chad Durbin .15
171 Carlos Beltran .15
172 Brian Meadows .15
173 Todd Dunwoody .15
174 Johnny Damon .15
175 Blake Stein .15
176 Carlos Febles .15
177 Joe Randa .15
178 Makoto Suzuki .15
179 Mark Quinn .15
180 Gregg Zaun .15
181 Mike Sweeney, Jeff Suppan .15
182 Juan Gonzalez .50
183 Dean Palmer .15
184 Wendell Magee .15
185 Todd Jones .15
186 Bobby Higginson .15
187 Brian Moehler .15
188 Juan Encarnacion .15
189 Tony Clark .15
190 Rich Becker .15
191 Roger Cedeno .15
192 Mitch Meluskey .15
193 Shane Halter .15
194 Jeff Weaver .15
195 Deivi Cruz .15
196 Damion Easley .15
197 Robert Fick .15
198 Matt Anderson .15
199 Bobby Higginson, Brian Moehler .15
200 Brad Radke .15
201 Mark Redman .15
202 Corey Koskie .15
203 Matt Lawton .15
204 Eric Milton .15
205 Chad Moeller .15
206 Jacque Jones .15
207 Matt Kinney .15
208 Jay Canizaro .15
209 Torii Hunter .15
210 Ron Coomer .15
211 Chad Allen .15
212 Denny Hocking .15
213 Cristian Guzman .15
214 LaTroy Hawkins .15
215 Joe Mays .15
216 David Ortiz .15
217 Matt Lawton, Eric Milton .15
218 Frank Thomas .60
219 Jose Valentin .15
220 Mike Sirotka .15
221 Kip Wells .15
222 Magglio Ordonez .25
223 Herbert Perry .15
224 James Baldwin .15
225 Jon Garland .15
226 Sandy Alomar .15
227 Chris Singleton .15
228 Keith Foulke .15
229 Paul Konerko .15
230 Jim Parque .15
231 Greg Norton .15
232 Carlos Lee .15
233 Cal Eldred .15
234 Ray Durham .15
235 Jeff Abbott .15
236 Frank Thomas, Mike Sirotka .20
237 Derek Jeter 1.50
238 Glenallen Hill .15
239 Roger Clemens 1.00
240 Bernie Williams .40
241 David Justice .25
242 Luis Sojo .15
243 Orlando Hernandez .20
244 Mike Mussina .25
245 Jorge Posada .20
246 Andy Pettitte .20
247 Paul O'Neill .20
248 Scott Brosius .15
249 Alfonso Soriano .50
250 Mariano Rivera .20
251 Chuck Knoblauch .20
252 Ramiro Mendoza .15
253 Tino Martinez .15
254 David Cone .15
255 Derek Jeter, Andy Pettitte .40
256 Jeff Bagwell .50
257 Lance Berkman .50
258 Craig Biggio .20
259 Scott Elarton .15
260 Bill Spiers .15
261 Moises Alou .15
262 Billy Wagner .15
263 Shane Reynolds .15
264 Tony Eusebio .15
265 Julio Lugo .15
266 Jose Lima .15
267 Octavio Dotel .15
268 Brad Ausmus .15
269 Daryle Ward .15
270 Glen Barker .15
271 Wade Miller .15
272 Richard Hidalgo .25
273 Chris Truby .15
274 Jeff Bagwell, Scott Elarton .25
275 Greg Maddux .75
276 Chipper Jones .75
277 Tom Glavine .25
278 Brian Jordan .15
279 Andruw Jones .40
280 Kevin Millwood .15
281 Rico Brogna .15
282 George Lombard .15
283 Reggie Sanders .15
284 John Rocker .15
285 Rafael Furcal .25
286 John Smoltz .15
287 Javy Lopez .15
288 Walt Weiss .15
289 Quilvio Veras .15
290 Eddie Perez .15
291 B.J. Surhoff .15
292 Chipper Jones, Tom Glavine .25
293 Jeromy Burnitz .15
294 Charlie Hayes .15
295 Jeff D'Amico .15
296 Jose Hernandez .15
297 Richie Sexson .15
298 Tyler Houston .15
299 Paul Rigdon .15
300 Jamey Wright .15
301 Mark Loretta .15
302 Geoff Jenkins .20
303 Luis Lopez .15
304 John Snyder .15
305 Henry Blanco .15
306 Curtis Leskanic .15
307 Ron Belliard .15
308 Jimmy Haynes .15
309 Marquis Grissom .15
310 Geoff Jenkins, Jeff D'Amico .15
311 Mark McGwire 1.00
312 Rick Ankiel .20
313 Dave Veres .15
314 Carlos Hernandez .15
315 Jim Edmonds .20
316 Andy Benes .15
317 Garrett Stephenson .15
318 Ray Lankford .15
319 Dustin Hermanson .15
320 Steve Kline .15
321 Mike Matheny .15
322 Edgar Renteria .15
323 J.D. Drew .15
324 Craig Paquette .15
325 Darryl Kile .15
326 Fernando Vina .15
327 Eric Davis .15
328 Placido Polanco .15
329 Jim Edmonds, Darryl Kile .15
330 Sammy Sosa 1.00
331 Rick Aguilera .15
332 Willie Greene .15
333 Kerry Wood .20
334 Todd Hundley .15
335 Rondell White .20
336 Julio Zuleta .15
337 Jon Lieber .15
338 Joe Girardi .15
339 Damon Buford .15
340 Kevin Tapani .15
341 Ricky Gutierrez .15
342 Bill Mueller .15
343 Ruben Quevedo .15
344 Eric Young .15
345 Gary Matthews Jr. .15
346 Daniel Garibay .15
347 Sammy Sosa, Jon Lieber .30
348 Randy Johnson .50
349 Matt Williams .20
350 Kelly Stinnett .15
351 Brian Anderson .15
352 Steve Finley .15
353 Curt Schilling .20
354 Erubiel Durazo .15
355 Todd Stottlemyre .15
356 Mark Grace .20
357 Luis Gonzalez .20
358 Danny Bautista .15
359 Matt Mantei .15
360 Tony Womack .15
361 Armando Reynoso .15
362 Greg Colbrunn .15
363 Jay Bell .15
364 Byung-Hyun Kim .15
365 Luis Gonzalez, Randy Johnson .20
366 Gary Sheffield .20
367 Eric Karros .15
368 Jeff Shaw .15
369 Jim Leyritz .15
370 Kevin Brown .20
371 Alex Cora .15
372 Andy Ashby .15
373 Eric Gagne .15
374 Chan Ho Park .15
375 Shawn Green .20
376 Kevin Elster .15
377 Mark Grudzielanek .15
378 Darren Dreifort .15
379 Dave Hansen .15
380 Bruce Aven .15
381 Adrian Beltre .20
382 Tom Goodwin .15
383 Gary Sheffield, Chan Ho Park .15
384 Vladimir Guerrero .60
385 Ugueth Urbina .15
386 Michael Barrett .15
387 Geoff Blum .15
388 Fernando Tatis .15
389 Carl Pavano .15
390 Jose Vidro .15
391 Orlando Cabrera .15
392 Terry Jones .15
393 Mike Thurman .15
394 Lee Stevens .15
395 Tony Armas Jr. .15
396 Wilton Guerrero .15
397 Peter Bergeron .15
398 Milton Bradley .15
399 Javier Vazquez .15
400 Fernando Seguignol .15
401 Vladimir Guerrero, Dustin Hermanson .25
402 Barry Bonds .60
403 Russ Ortiz .15
404 Calvin Murray .15
405 Armando Rios .15
406 Livan Hernandez .15
407 Jeff Kent .20
408 Bobby Estalella .15
409 Felipe Crespo .15
410 Shawn Estes .15
411 J.T. Snow .15

#	Player	Price
412	Marvin Benard	.15
413	Joe Nathan	.15
414	Robb Nen	.15
415	Shawon Dunston	.15
416	Mark Gardner	.15
417	Kirk Rueter	.15
418	Rich Aurilia	.15
419	Doug Mirabelli	.15
420	Russ Davis	.15
421	Barry Bonds, Livan Hernandez	.30
422	Cliff Floyd	.15
423	Luis Castillo	.15
424	Antonio Alfonseca	.15
425	Preston Wilson	.15
426	Ryan Dempster	.15
427	Jesus Sanchez	.15
428	Derrek Lee	.15
429	Brad Penny	.15
430	Mark Kotsay	.15
431	Alex Fernandez	.15
432	Mike Lowell	.15
433	Chuck Smith	.15
434	Alex Gonzalez	.15
435	Dave Berg	.15
436	A.J. Burnett	.15
437	Charles Johnson	.15
438	Reid Cornelius	.15
439	Mike Redmond	.15
440	Preston Wilson, Ryan Dempster	.15
441	Mike Piazza	.75
442	Kevin Appier	.15
443	Jay Payton	.15
444	Steve Trachsel	.15
445	Al Leiter	.20
446	Joe McEwing	.15
447	Armando Benitez	.15
448	Edgardo Alfonzo	.15
449	Glendon Rusch	.15
450	Mike Bordick	.15
451	Lenny Harris	.15
452	Matt Franco	.15
453	Darryl Hamilton	.15
454	Bobby J. Jones	.15
455	Robin Ventura	.15
456	Todd Zeile	.15
457	John Franco	.15
458	Mike Piazza, Al Leiter	.40
459	Tony Gwynn	.75
460	John Mabry	.15
461	Trevor Hoffman	.15
462	Phil Nevin	.15
463	Ryan Klesko	.15
464	Wiki Gonzalez	.15
465	Matt Clement	.15
466	Alex Arias	.15
467	Woody Williams	.15
468	Ruben Rivera	.15
469	Sterling Hitchcock	.15
470	Ben Davis	.15
471	Bubba Trammell	.15
472	Jay Witasick	.15
473	Eric Owens	.15
474	Damian Jackson	.15
475	Adam Eaton	.15
476	Mike Darr	.15
477	Phil Nevin, Trevor Hoffman	.15
478	Scott Rolen	.25
479	Robert Person	.15
480	Mike Lieberthal	.15
481	Reggie Taylor	.15
482	Paul Byrd	.15
483	Bruce Chen	.15
484	Pat Burrell	.25
485	Kevin Jordan	.15
486	Bobby Abreu	.15
487	Randy Wolf	.15
488	Kevin Sefcik	.15
489	Brian Hunter	.15
490	Doug Glanville	.15
491	Kent Bottenfield	.15
492	Travis Lee	.15
493	Jeff Brantley	.15
494	Omar Daal	.15
495	Bobby Abreu, Randy Wolf	.15
496	Jason Kendall	.15
497	Adrian Brown	.15
498	Warren Morris	.15
499	Brian Giles	.20
500	Jimmy Anderson	.15
501	John Vander Wal	.15
502	Mike Williams	.15
503	Aramis Ramirez	.15
504	Pat Meares	.15
505	Jason Schmidt	.15
506	Todd Ritchie	.15
507	Abraham Nunez	.15
508	Jose Silva	.15
509	Francisco Cordova	.15
510	Kevin Young	.15
511	Derek Bell	.15
512	Kris Benson	.15
513	Brian Giles, Jose Silva	.15
514	Ken Griffey Jr.	1.00
515	Scott Williamson	.15
516	Dmitri Young	.15
517	Sean Casey	.20
518	Barry Larkin	.25
519	Juan Castro	.15
520	Danny Graves	.15
521	Aaron Boone	.15
522	Pokey Reese	.15
523	Elmer Dessens	.15
524	Michael Tucker	.15
525	Benito Santiago	.15
526	Pete Harnisch	.15
527	Alex Ochoa	.15
528	Gookie Dawkins	.15
529	Seth Etherton	.15
530	Rob Bell	.15
531	Ken Griffey Jr., Steve Parris	.50
532	Todd Helton	.50
533	Jose Jimenez	.15
534	Todd Walker	.15
535	Ron Gant	.15
536	Neifi Perez	.15
537	Butch Huskey	.15
538	Pedro Astacio	.15
539	Juan Pierre	.15
540	Jeff Cirillo	.15
541	Ben Petrick	.15
542	Brian Bohanon	.15
543	Larry Walker	.25
544	Masato Yoshii	.15
545	Denny Neagle	.15
546	Brent Mayne	.15
547	Mike Hampton	.20
548	Todd Hollandsworth	.15
549	Brian Rose	.15
550	Todd Helton, Pedro Astacio	.20
551	Jason Hart	.15
552	Joe Crede	.15
553	Timoniel Perez	.15
554	Brady Clark	.15
555	Adam Pettyjohn **RC**	.15
556	Jason Grilli	.15
557	Paxton Crawford	.15
558	Jay Spurgeon	.15
559	Hector Ortiz	.15
560	Vernon Wells	.15
561	Aubrey Huff	.15
562	Xavier Nady	.25
563	Billy McMillon	.15
564	Ichiro Suzuki **RC**	8.00
565	Tomas de la Rosa	.15
566	Matt Ginter	.15
567	Sun-Woo Kim	.15
568	Nick Johnson	.15
569	Pablo Ozuna	.15
570	Tike Redman	.15
571	Brian Cole	.15
572	Ross Gload	.15
573	Dee Brown	.15
574	Tony McKnight	.15
575	Allen Levrault	.15
576	Lesli Brea	.15
577	Adam Bernero	.15
578	Tom Davey	.15
579	Morgan Burkhart	.15
580	Britt Reames	.15
581	Dave Coggin	.15
582	Trey Moore	.15
583	Matt Kinney	.15
584	Pedro Feliz	.15
585	Brandon Inge	.15
586	Alex Hernandez	.15
587	Toby Hall	.15
588	Grant Roberts	.15
589	Brian Sikorski	.15
590	Aaron Myette	.15
591	Derek Jeter (Big Play Makers)	1.00
592	Ivan Rodriguez (Big Play Makers)	.40
593	Alex Rodriguez (Big Play Makers)	.75
594	Carlos Delgado (Big Play Makers)	.30
595	Mark McGwire (Big Play Makers)	.75
596	Troy Glaus (Big Play Makers)	.40
597	Sammy Sosa (Big Play Makers)	.75
598	Vladimir Guerrero (Big Play Makers)	.50
599	Manny Ramirez (Big Play Makers)	.40
600	Pedro J. Martinez (Big Play Makers)	.50
601	Chipper Jones (Big Play Makers)	.75
602	Jason Giambi (Big Play Makers)	.20
603	Frank Thomas (Big Play Makers)	.50
604	Ken Griffey Jr. (Big Play Makers)	.75
605	Nomar Garciaparra (Big Play Makers)	.75
606	Randy Johnson (Big Play Makers)	.40
607	Mike Piazza (Big Play Makers)	.75
608	Barry Bonds (Big Play Makers)	.50
609	Todd Helton (Big Play Makers)	.40
610	Jeff Bagwell (Big Play Makers)	.40
611	Ken Griffey Jr. (Victory's Best)	.75
612	Carlos Delgado (Victory's Best)	.40
613	Jeff Bagwell (Victory's Best)	.40
614	Jason Giambi (Victory's Best)	.20
615	Cal Ripken Jr. (Victory's Best)	1.00
616	Brian Giles (Victory's Best)	.15
617	Bernie Williams (Victory's Best)	.30
618	Greg Maddux (Victory's Best)	.75
619	Troy Glaus (Victory's Best)	.40
620	Greg Vaughn (Victory's Best)	.15
621	Sammy Sosa (Victory's Best)	.75
622	Pat Burrell (Victory's Best)	.20
623	Ivan Rodriguez (Victory's Best)	.40
624	Chipper Jones (Victory's Best)	.75
625	Barry Bonds (Victory's Best)	.50
626	Roger Clemens (Victory's Best)	.50
627	Jim Edmonds (Victory's Best)	.15
628	Nomar Garciaparra (Victory's Best)	.75
629	Frank Thomas (Victory's Best)	.50
630	Mike Piazza (Victory's Best)	.75
631	Randy Johnson (Victory's Best)	.40
632	Andruw Jones (Victory's Best)	.30
633	David Wells (Victory's Best)	.15
634	Manny Ramirez (Victory's Best)	.40
635	Preston Wilson (Victory's Best)	.15
636	Todd Helton (Victory's Best)	.40
637	Kerry Wood (Victory's Best)	.15
638	Albert Belle (Victory's Best)	.15
639	Juan Gonzalez (Victory's Best)	.40
640	Vladimir Guerrero (Victory's Best)	.50
641	Gary Sheffield (Victory's Best)	.15
642	Larry Walker (Victory's Best)	.15
643	Magglio Ordonez (Victory's Best)	.15
644	Jermaine Dye (Victory's Best)	.15
645	Scott Rolen (Victory's Best)	.20
646	Tony Gwynn (Victory's Best)	.50
647	Shawn Green (Victory's Best)	.15
648	Roberto Alomar (Victory's Best)	.30
649	Eric Milton (Victory's Best)	.15
650	Mark McGwire (Victory's Best)	.75
651	Tim Hudson (Victory's Best)	.15
652	Jose Canseco (Victory's Best)	.20
653	Tom Glavine (Victory's Best)	.20
654	Derek Jeter (Victory's Best)	1.00
655	Alex Rodriguez (Victory's Best)	.75
656	Darin Erstad (Victory's Best)	.15
657	Jason Kendall (Victory's Best)	.15
658	Pedro Martinez (Victory's Best)	.50
659	Richie Sexson (Victory's Best)	.15
660	Rafael Palmeiro (Victory's Best)	.20

2001 Upper Deck Vintage Sample

Styled shamelessly after the 1963 Topps set, this retro-look UD issue was previewed with a sample card. Virtually identical in format to the issued version, the promo has stats on back only through 1999 and is overprinted with a large diagonal "SAMPLE."

#	Player	NM/M
30	Ken Griffey Jr.	4.00

2001 Upper Deck Vintage

	NM/M
Complete Set (400):	30.00
Common Player:	.10
Pack (10):	2.00
Box (24):	40.00

#	Player	Price
1	Darin Erstad	.25
2	Seth Etherton	.10
3	Troy Glaus	.50
4	Bengie Molina	.10
5	Mo Vaughn	.20
6	Tim Salmon	.25
7	Ramon Ortiz	.10
8	Adam Kennedy	.10
9	Garret Anderson	.25
10	Troy Percival	.10
11	2000 Angels Lineup	.10
12	Jason Giambi	.50
13	Tim Hudson	.25
14	Adam Piatt	.10
15	Miguel Tejada	.25
16	Mark Mulder	.25
17	Eric Chavez	.25
18	Ramon Hernandez	.10
19	Terrence Long	.10
20	Jason Isringhausen	.10
21	Barry Zito	.50
22	Ben Grieve	.10
23	2000 Athletics Lineup	.10
24	David Wells	.10
25	Raul Mondesi	.20
26	Darrin Fletcher	.10
27	Shannon Stewart	.10
28	Kelvim Escobar	.10
29	Tony Batista	.10
30	Carlos Delgado	.50
31	Brad Fullmer	.10
32	Billy Koch	.10
33	Jose Cruz Jr.	.10
34	2000 Blue Jays Lineup	.10
35	Greg Vaughn	.10
36	Roberto Hernandez	.10
37	Vinny Castilla	.10
38	Gerald Williams	.10
39	Aubrey Huff	.10
40	Bryan Rekar	.10
41	Albie Lopez	.10
42	Fred McGriff	.25
43	Miguel Cairo	.10
44	Ryan Rupe	.10
45	2000 Devil Rays Lineup	.10
46	Jim Thome	.50
47	Roberto Alomar	.50
48	Bartolo Colon	.25
49	Omar Vizquel	.20
50	Travis Fryman	.20
51	Manny Ramirez	.50
52	Dave Burba	.10
53	Chuck Finley	.10
54	Russ Branyan	.10
55	Kenny Lofton	.25
56	2000 Indians Lineup	.10
57	Alex Rodriguez	1.50
58	Jay Buhner	.10
59	Aaron Sele	.10
60	Kazuhiro Sasaki	.20
61	Edgar Martinez	.20
62	John Halama	.10
63	Mike Cameron	.10
64	Fred Garcia	.10
65	John Olerud	.20
66	Jamie Moyer	.10
67	Gil Meche	.10
68	2000 Mariners Lineup	.10
69	Cal Ripken Jr.	2.00
70	Sidney Ponson	.10
71	Chris Richard	.10
72	Jose Mercedes	.10
73	Albert Belle	.15
74	Mike Mussina	.50
75	Brady Anderson	.15
76	Delino DeShields	.10
77	Melvin Mora	.10
78	Luis Matos	.10
79	Brook Fordyce	.10
80	2000 Orioles Lineup	.10
81	Rafael Palmeiro	.50
82	Rick Helling	.10
83	Ruben Mateo	.10
84	Rusty Greer	.10
85	Ivan Rodriguez	.50
86	Doug Davis	.10
87	Gabe Kapler	.15
88	Mike Lamb	.10
89	Alex Rodriguez	1.50
90	Kenny Rogers	.10
91	2000 Rangers Lineup	.10
92	Nomar Garciaparra	1.50
93	Trot Nixon	.10
94	Tomokazu Ohka	.10
95	Pedro Martinez	.75
96	Dante Bichette	.10
97	Jason Varitek	.10
98	Rolando Arrojo	.10
99	Carl Everett	.10
100	Derek Lowe	.10
101	Troy O'Leary	.10
102	Tim Wakefield	.10
103	2000 Red Sox Lineup	.10
104	Mike Sweeney	.10
105	Carlos Febles	.10
106	Joe Randa	.10
107	Jeff Suppan	.10
108	Mac Suzuki	.10
109	Jermaine Dye	.10
110	Carlos Beltran	.25
111	Mark Quinn	.10
112	Johnny Damon	.20
113	2000 Royals Lineup	.10
114	Tony Clark	.10
115	Dean Palmer	.10
116	Brian Moehler	.10
117	Brad Ausmus	.10
118	Juan Gonzalez	.50
119	Juan Encarnacion	.10
120	Jeff Weaver	.10
121	Bobby Higginson	.10
122	Todd Jones	.10
123	Deivi Cruz	.10
124	2000 Tigers Lineup	.10
125	Corey Koskie	.10
126	Matt Lawton	.10
127	Mark Redman	.10
128	David Ortiz	.10
129	Jay Canizaro	.10
130	Eric Milton	.10
131	Jacque Jones	.10
132	J.C. Romero	.10
133	Ron Coomer	.10
134	Brad Radke	.10
135	2000 Twins Lineup	.10
136	Carlos Lee	.10
137	Frank Thomas	.75
138	Mike Sirotka	.10
139	Charles Johnson	.10
140	James Baldwin	.10
141	Magglio Ordonez	.25
142	Jon Garland	.10
143	Paul Konerko	.10
144	Ray Durham	.10
145	Keith Foulke	.10
146	Chris Singleton	.10
147	2000 White Sox Lineup	.10
148	Bernie Williams	.50
149	Orlando Hernandez	.15
150	David Justice	.25
151	Andy Pettitte	.25
152	Mariano Rivera	.25
153	Derek Jeter	2.00
154	Jorge Posada	.25
155	Jose Canseco	.50
156	Glenallen Hill	.10
157	Paul O'Neill	.25
158	Denny Neagle	.10
159	Chuck Knoblauch	.10
160	Roger Clemens	1.50
161	2000 Yankees Lineup	.10
162	Jeff Bagwell	.50
163	Moises Alou	.20
164	Lance Berkman	.40
165	Shane Reynolds	.10
166	Ken Caminiti	.10
167	Craig Biggio	.25
168	Jose Lima	.10
169	Octavio Dotel	.10
170	Richard Hidalgo	.20
171	Scott Elarton	.10
172	2000 Astros Lineup	.10
173	Rafael Furcal	.25
174	Greg Maddux	1.00
175	Quilvio Veras	.10
176	Chipper Jones	1.00
177	Andres Galarraga	.25
178	Brian Jordan	.10
179	Tom Glavine	.25
180	Kevin Millwood	.25
181	Javier Lopez	.25
182	B.J. Surhoff	.10
183	Andruw Jones	.50
184	Andy Ashby	.10
185	2000 Braves Lineup	.10
186	Richie Sexson	.40
187	Jeff D'Amico	.10
188	Ron Belliard	.10
189	Jeromy Burnitz	.10
190	Jimmy Haynes	.10
191	Marquis Grissom	.10
192	Jose Hernandez	.10
193	Geoff Jenkins	.20
194	Jamey Wright	.10
195	Mark Loretta	.10
196	2000 Brewers Lineup	.10
197	Rick Ankiel	.10
198	Mark McGwire	1.50
199	Fernando Vina	.10
200	David Renteria	.10
201	Darryl Kile	.10
202	Jim Edmonds	.25
203	Ray Lankford	.10
204	Garrett Stephenson	.10
205	Fernando Tatis	.10
206	Will Clark	.40
207	J.D. Drew	.15
208	2000 Cardinals Lineup	.10
209	Mark Grace	.25
210	Eric Young	.10
211	Sammy Sosa	1.50
212	Jon Lieber	.10
213	Joe Girardi	.10
214	Kevin Tapani	.10
215	Ricky Gutierrez	.10
216	Kerry Wood	.50
217	Rondell White	.20
218	Damon Buford	.10
219	2000 Cubs Lineup	.10
220	Luis Gonzalez	.25
221	Randy Johnson	.75
222	Jay Bell	.10
223	Erubiel Durazo	.10
224	Matt Williams	.25
225	Steve Finley	.10
226	Curt Schilling	.40
227	Todd Stottlemyre	.10
228	Tony Womack	.10
229	Brian Anderson	.10
230	2000 Diamondbacks Lineup	.10
231	Gary Sheffield	.40
232	Adrian Beltre	.25
233	Todd Hundley	.10
234	Chan Ho Park	.10
235	Shawn Green	.25
236	Kevin Brown	.25
237	Tom Goodwin	.10
238	Mark Grudzielanek	.10
239	Ismael Valdes	.10
240	Eric Karros	.10
241	2000 Dodgers Lineup	.10
242	Jose Vidro	.10
243	Javier Vazquez	.20
244	Orlando Cabrera	.10
245	Peter Bergeron	.10
246	Vladimir Guerrero	.75
247	Dustin Hermanson	.10
248	Tony Armas Jr.	.10
249	Lee Stevens	.10
250	Milton Bradley	.10
251	Carl Pavano	.10
252	2000 Expos Lineup	.10
253	Ellis Burks	.10
254	Robb Nen	.10
255	J.T. Snow	.10
256	Barry Bonds	2.00
257	Shawn Estes	.10
258	Jeff Kent	.20
259	Kirk Rueter	.10
260	Bill Mueller	.10
261	Livan Hernandez	.10
262	Rich Aurilia	.10
263	2000 Giants Lineup	.10
264	Ryan Dempster	.10
265	Cliff Floyd	.10
266	Mike Lowell	.10
267	A.J. Burnett	.10
268	Preston Wilson	.10
269	Luis Castillo	.10
270	Henry Rodriguez	.10
271	Antonio Alfonseca	.10
272	Derek Lee	.10
273	Mark Kotsay	.10
274	Brad Penny	.10
275	2000 Marlins Lineup	.10
276	Mike Piazza	1.00
277	Jay Payton	.10
278	Al Leiter	.15
279	Mike Bordick	.10
280	Armando Benitez	.10
281	Todd Zeile	.10
282	Mike Hampton	.20
283	Edgardo Alfonzo	.10
284	Derek Bell	.10
285	Robin Ventura	.20
286	2000 Mets Lineup	.10
287	Tony Gwynn	.75
288	Trevor Hoffman	.10
289	Ryan Klesko	.20
290	Phil Nevin	.10
291	Matt Clement	.10
292	Ben Davis	.10
293	Ruben Rivera	.10
294	Bret Boone	.25
295	Adam Eaton	.10
296	Eric Owens	.10
297	2000 Padres Lineup	.10
298	Bob Abreu	.20
299	Mike Lieberthal	.10
300	Robert Person	.10
301	Scott Rolen	.50
302	Randy Wolf	.10
303	Bruce Chen	.10
304	Travis Lee	.10
305	Kent Bottenfield	.10
306	Pat Burrell	.50
307	Doug Glanville	.10
308	2000 Phillies Lineup	.10
309	Brian Giles	.25
310	Todd Ritchie	.10
311	Warren Morris	.10
312	John Vander Wal	.10
313	Kris Benson	.10
314	Jason Kendall	.10

315 Kevin Young .10
316 Francisco Cordova .10
317 Jimmy Anderson .10
318 2000 Pirates Lineup .10
319 Ken Griffey Jr. 1.00
320 Pokey Reese .10
321 Chris Stynes .10
322 Barry Larkin .40
323 Steve Parris .10
324 Michael Tucker .10
325 Dmitri Young .10
326 Pete Harnisch .10
327 Adam Graves .10
328 Aaron Boone .10
329 Sean Casey .10
330 2000 Reds Lineup .10
331 Todd Helton .50
332 Pedro Astacio .10
333 Larry Walker .25
334 Ben Petrick .10
335 Brian Bohanon .10
336 Juan Pierre .10
337 Jeffrey Hammonds .10
338 Jeff Cirillo .10
339 Todd Hollandsworth .10
340 2000 Rockies Lineup .10
341 Matt Wise, Keith Luuloa, Derrick Turnbow (Vintage Rookies) .10
342 Jason Hart, Jose Ortiz, Mario Encarnacion (Vintage Rookies) .10
343 Vernon Wells, Pascual Coco, Josh Phelps (Vintage Rookies) .25
344 Travis Harper, Kenny Kelley, Toby Hall (Vintage Rookies) .10
345 Danys Baez, Tim Drew, Martin Vargas **RC** (Vintage Rookies) .10
346 Ichiro Suzuki **RC**, Ryan Franklin, Ryan Christianson (Vintage Rookies) 10.00
347 Jay Spurgeon, Lesli Brea, Carlos Casimiro (Vintage Rookies) .10
348 B.J. Waszgis, Brian Sikorski, Joaquin Benoit (Vintage Rookies) .10
349 Sun-Woo Kim, Paxton Crawford, Steve Lomasney (Vintage Rookies) .10
350 Kris Wilson, Orber Moreno, Dee Brown (Vintage Rookies) .10
351 Mark Johnson, Brandon Inge, Adam Bernero (Vintage Rookies) .10
352 Danny Ardoin, Matt Kinney, Jason Ryan (Vintage Rookies) .10
353 Rocky Biddle, Joe Crede, Aaron Myette (Vintage Rookies) .10
354 Nick Johnson, D'Angelo Jimenez, Willi Mo Pena (Vintage Rookies) .10
355 Tony McKnight, Aaron McNeal, Keith Ginter (Vintage Rookies) .10
356 Mark DeRosa, Jason Marquis, Wes Helms (Vintage Rookies) .10
357 Allen Levrault, Horacio Estrada, Santiago Perez (Vintage Rookies) .10
358 Luis Saturria, Gene Stechschulte, Britt Reames (Vintage Rookies) .10
359 Joey Nation, Corey Patterson, Cole Liniak (Vintage Rookies) .25
360 Alex Cabrera, Geraldo Guzman, Nelson Figueroa (Vintage Rookies) .10
361 Hiram Bocachica, Mike Judd, Luke Prokopec (Vintage Rookies) .10
362 Tomas de la Rosa, Yohanny Valera, Talmadge Nunnari (Vintage Rookies) .10
363 Ryan Vogelsong, Juan Melo, Chad Zerbe (Vintage Rookies) .10
364 Jason Grilli, Pablo Ozuna, Ramon Castro (Vintage Rookies) .10
365 Timoniel Perez, Grant Roberts, Brian Cole (Vintage Rookies) .10
366 Tom Davey, Xavier Nady, Dave Maurer (Vintage Rookies) .50
367 Jimmy Rollins, Mark Brownson, Reggie Taylor (Vintage Rookies) .25
368 Alex Hernandez, Adam Hyzdu, Tike Redman (Vintage Rookies) .10
369 Brady Clark, John Riedling, Mike Bell (Vintage Rookies) .10
370 Giovanni Carrara, Josh Kalinowski, Elvis Pena (Vintage Rookies) .10
371 Jim Edmonds (Postseason Scrapbook) .10
372 Edgar Martinez (Postseason Scrapbook) .10
373 Rickey Henderson (Postseason Scrapbook) .10
374 Barry Zito (Postseason Scrapbook) .25
375 Tino Martinez (Postseason Scrapbook) .10
376 J.T. Snow (Postseason Scrapbook) .10
377 Bobby Jones (Postseason Scrapbook) .10
378 Alex Rodriguez (Postseason Scrapbook) 1.00
379 Mike Hampton (Postseason Scrapbook) .10
380 Roger Clemens (Postseason Scrapbook) .50
381 Jay Payton (Postseason Scrapbook) .10
382 John Olerud (Postseason Scrapbook) .10
383 David Justice (Postseason Scrapbook) .25
384 Mike Hampton (Postseason Scrapbook) .10
385 Yankees Celebrate (Postseason Scrapbook) .75
386 Jose Vizcaino (Postseason Scrapbook) .10
387 Roger Clemens (Postseason Scrapbook) .75
388 Todd Zeile (Postseason Scrapbook) .10
389 Derek Jeter (Postseason Scrapbook) 1.25
390 Yankees Celebrate (Postseason Scrapbook) .50
391 Nomar Garciaparra - AL Batting (Big League Leaders) .75
392 Todd Helton - NL Batting (Big League Leaders) .25
393 Troy Glaus - AL HR (Big League Leaders) .25
394 Sammy Sosa - NL HR (Big League Leaders) .50
395 Edgar Martinez - AL RBI (Big League Leaders) .10
396 Todd Helton - NL RBI (Big League Leaders) .25
397 Pedro Martinez - AL ERA (Big League Leaders) .40
398 Kevin Brown - NL ERA (Big League Leaders) .10
399 David Wells, Tim Hudson - AL Wins (Big League Leaders) .10
400 Tom Glavine - NL Wins (Big League Leaders) .10

All-Star Tributes

NM/M
Complete Set (10): 20.00
Common Player: 1.00
Inserted 1:23
1 Derek Jeter 4.00
2 Mike Piazza 2.00
3 Carlos Delgado 1.00
4 Pedro Martinez 1.50
5 Vladimir Guerrero 1.50
6 Mark McGwire 3.00
7 Alex Rodriguez 3.00
8 Barry Bonds 4.00
9 Chipper Jones 2.00
10 Sammy Sosa 2.50

Fantasy Outfield Combo Jersey

NM/M
Production 25 Cards
FO-CJ Joe DiMaggio, Mickey Mantle, Ken Griffey Jr. 1,000

Glory Days

NM/M
Complete Set (15): 15.00
Common Player: .50
Inserted 1:15
1 Jermaine Dye .50
2 Chipper Jones 2.00
3 Todd Helton 1.00
4 Magglio Ordonez .75
5 Tony Gwynn 1.50
6 Jim Edmonds .75
7 Rafael Palmeiro 1.00
8 Barry Bonds 4.00
9 Carl Everett .50
10 Mike Piazza 2.00
11 Brian Giles .50
12 Tony Batista .50
13 Jeff Bagwell 1.00
14 Ken Griffey Jr. 2.00
15 Troy Glaus 1.00

Mantle Pinstripes Exclusive

NM/M
Complete Set (56): 75.00
Common Mantle: 2.00
One Pack/Box

Mantle Pinstripes Memorabilia

NM/M
Print runs listed:
MMB Mickey Mantle/Bat/100 100.00
MMCJ Mickey Mantle, Roger Maris/Jsy/50 300.00
MMJ Mickey Mantle/Jsy/100 125.00

Matinee Idols

NM/M
Complete Set (20): 10.00
Common Player: .50
Inserted 1:4
1 Ken Griffey Jr. 1.00
2 Derek Jeter 2.00
3 Barry Bonds 2.00
4 Chipper Jones 1.00
5 Mike Piazza 1.00
6 Todd Helton .50
7 Randy Johnson .75
8 Alex Rodriguez 1.50
9 Sammy Sosa 1.50
10 Cal Ripken Jr. 2.00
11 Nomar Garciaparra 1.50
12 Carlos Delgado .50
13 Jason Giambi .50
14 Ivan Rodriguez .50
15 Vladimir Guerrero .75
16 Gary Sheffield .50
17 Frank Thomas .50
18 Jeff Bagwell .50
19 Pedro Martinez .75
20 Mark McGwire 1.50

Retro Rules

NM/M
Complete Set (15): 20.00
Common Player: .50
Inserted 1:15
1 Nomar Garciaparra 3.00
2 Frank Thomas 1.00
3 Jeff Bagwell 1.00
4 Sammy Sosa 2.50
5 Derek Jeter 4.00
6 David Wells .50
7 Vladimir Guerrero 1.50
8 Jim Thome 1.00
9 Mark McGwire 3.00
10 Todd Helton 1.00
11 Tony Gwynn 1.50
12 Bernie Williams .75
13 Cal Ripken Jr. 4.00
14 Brian Giles .75
15 Jason Giambi 1.50

Timeless Teams Bat

NM/M
Common Player: 8.00
Inserted 1:72
NYY-JD Joe DiMaggio 150.00
NYY-TH Tommy Henrich 8.00
NYY-CK Charlie Keller 8.00
NYY-BD Bill Dickey 20.00
BK-JR Jackie Robinson 90.00
BK-RC Roy Campanella 50.00
BK-GH Gil Hodges 25.00
BK-DN Don Newcombe 8.00
LA-SG Steve Garvey 8.00
LA-RC Ron Cey 8.00
LA-BR Bill Russell 8.00
LA-DB Dusty Baker 8.00
BA-BP Boog Powell 8.00
BA-BR Brooks Robinson 25.00
BA-FR Frank Robinson 20.00
BA-MB Mark Belanger 8.00
PI-RC Roberto Clemente 100.00
PI-WS Willie Stargell 20.00
PI-MS Manny Sanguillen 8.00
PI-AO Al Oliver 8.00
OA-RJ Reggie Jackson 20.00
OA-SB Sal Bando 8.00
OA-GT Gene Tenace 8.00
OA-JR Joe Rudi 8.00
CI2-JB Johnny Bench 25.00
CI2-TP Tony Perez 15.00
CI2-JM Joe Morgan 8.00
CI2-KG Ken Griffey Sr. 8.00
NYM-NR Nolan Ryan 40.00
NYM-RS Ron Swoboda 8.00
NYM-EK Ed Kranepool 8.00
NYM-TA Tommie Agee 8.00

Timeless Teams Combo Bat

NM/M
Common Card: 75.00
Production 100 Sets
NYY41 Joe DiMaggio, Tommy Henrich, Bill Dickey, Charlie Keller 200.00
BKN55 Jackie Robinson, Roy Campanella, Gil Hodges, Don Newcombe 175.00
BAL70 Frank Robinson, Brooks Robinson, Mark Belanger, Boog Powell 120.00
LA81 Steve Garvey, Ron Cey, Dusty Baker, Bill Russell 75.00
PIT71 Roberto Clemente, Willie Stargell, Bill Mazeroski, Al Oliver 200.00
OAK72 Reggie Jackson, Sal Bando, Gene Tenace, Joe Rudi 80.00
CIN75 Johnny Bench, Tony Perez, Joe Morgan, Ken Griffey Sr. 120.00
NYM69 Nolan Ryan, Ron Swoboda, Ed Kranepool, Tommie Agee 200.00

Timeless Teams Jersey

NM/M
Common Player: 15.00
Inserted 1:288
NYY-MM Mickey Mantle 160.00
NYY-RM Roger Maris 50.00
NYY-BR Bobby Richardson 15.00
CI-DC Dave Concepcion 15.00
CI-TP Tony Perez 20.00
CI-KG Ken Griffey Sr. 15.00
CI-JM Joe Morgan 20.00

Timeless Teams Combo Jersey

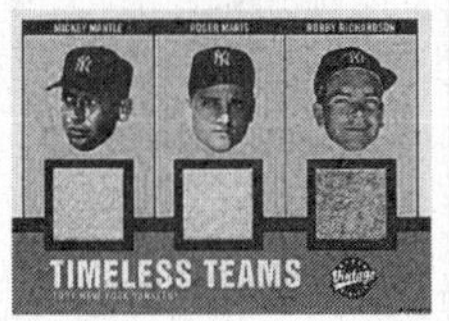

NM/M
Production 100 Sets
NYY61 Mickey Mantle, Roger Maris, Bobby Richardson 250.00
CIN75 Dave Concepcion, Tony Perez, Ken Griffey Sr. 120.00

Coca-Cola Cal Ripken, Jr. Tribute

To commemorate his final season Upper Deck produced for Coca-Cola a set of eight cards featuring highlights from the Iron Man's career. Cards #1-4 were given away in a cello pack to fans at the September 21 and October 1 O's games at Camden Yards. Cards #5-8 were given away at games on September 22-23 and October 2-3. Also in each cello pack was a Coke coupon card. Fronts have borderless color photos with an UD logo and Ripken's name in gold foil. A special Ripken Tribute logo appears at lower-left. Backs repeat the front photo, have a large uniform number 8 in the background and present various sets of stats. The Coke logo appears among those on back.

NM/M
Complete Set (8): 10.00
Common Card: 1.50
1 Cal Ripken, Jr. (Rookie of the Year) 1.50
2 Cal Ripken, Jr. (1991 AL MVP) 1.50
3 Cal Ripken, Jr. (1991 Gold Glove) 1.50
4 Cal Ripken, Jr. (The "Iron Man") 1.50
5 Cal Ripken, Jr. (400th HR) 1.50
6 Cal Ripken, Jr. (3,000 Hit) 1.50
7 Cal Ripken, Jr. (2001 All-Star MVP) 1.50
8 Cal Ripken, Jr. (Retirement Announcement) 1.50
Coupon Card .25

Ritz-Oreo

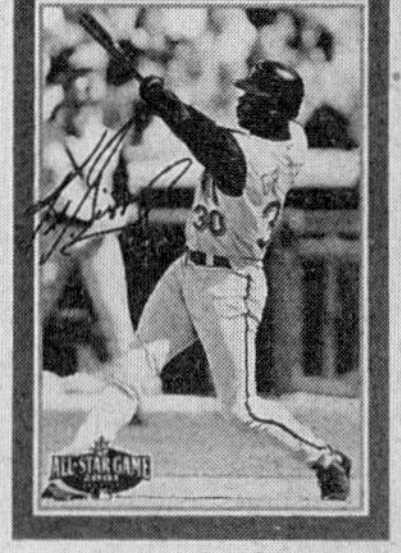

In conjunction with its sponsorship of the 2001 All-Star Game in Seattle, Ritz-Oreo issued a pair of cards distributed in product packages. In standard 2-1/2" x 3-1/2" format, one card is bordered in red and pictures Griffey batting; a blue bordered card has a picture of him throwing. Backs have biographical data - "Height: 150 Oreos / Weight: 27,060 Ritz," recent stats, a quote and logos of all parties involved. The cards were also available with a pair of Fleer Derek Jeter cards in a mail-in offer.

NM/M
Complete Set (2): 3.00
(1) Ken Griffey Jr./Btg 2.00
(2) Ken Griffey Jr./Throwing 2.00

Twizzlers Big League Challenge

Each specially marked 16-oz. package of Twizzlers candy contained one card from this set. The 2-1/2" x 3-1/2" cards have on front a photo from the Big League Challenge event, with UD and Twizzlers logos and the player's 2000 home run total. Backs repeat the Big League Challenge logo and have career highlights.

NM/M
Complete Set (10): 7.50
Common Player: .50
1 Jason Giambi 1.00
2 Carlos Delgado .50
3 Troy Glaus 1.00

4 Jim Edmonds .50
5 Richard Hidalgo .50
6 Gary Sheffield .50
7 Todd Helton .75
8 Jose Canseco .75
9 Frank Thomas 1.00
10 Barry Bonds 2.00

2002 Upper Deck

NM/M
Complete Set (745): 150.00
Complete Series I (500): 100.00
Complete Series II (245): 50.00
Common Player: .15
Series 1 Hobby Pack (8): 4.00
Series 1 Hobby Box (24): 75.00
Series 2 Hobby Pack (8): 1.25
Series 2 Hobby Box (24): 25.00
1 Mark Prior/SR 4.00
2 Mark Teixeira/SR 1.50
3 Brian Roberts/SR .25
4 Jason Romano/SR .25
5 Dennis Stark/SR **RC** .50
6 Oscar Salazar/SR .50
7 John Patterson/SR .25
8 Shane Loux/SR .25
9 Marcus Giles/SR .40
10 Juan Cruz/SR .25
11 Jorge Julio/SR .25
12 Adam Dunn/SR .50
13 Delvin James/SR .25
14 Jeremy Affeldt/SR .25
15 Tim Raines Jr./SR .25
16 Luke Hudson/SR .25
17 Todd Sears/SR .25
18 George Perez/SR .25
19 Wilmy Caceres/SR .25
20 Abraham Nunez/SR .25
21 Mike Amrhein/SR .25
22 Carlos Hernandez/SR .25
23 Scott Hodges/SR .25
24 Brandon Knight/SR .25
25 Geoff Goetz/SR .25
26 Carlos Garcia/SR .25
27 Luis Pineda/SR .25
28 Chris Gissell/SR .25
29 Jae Weong/SR .25
30 Paul Phillips/SR .25
31 Cory Aldridge/SR .25
32 Aaron Cook/SR **RC** .50
33 Rendy Espina/SR .25
34 Jason Phillips/SR .25
35 Carlos Silva/SR .25
36 Ryan Mills/SR .25
37 Pedro Santana/SR .25
38 John Grabow/SR .25
39 Cody Ransom/SR .15
40 Orlando Woodlands/SR .25
41 Bud Smith/SR .25
42 Junior Guerrero/SR .25
43 David Brous/SR .25
44 Steve Green/SR .25
45 Brian Rogers/SR .25
46 Juan Figueroa/SR .25
47 Nick Punto/SR .25
48 Junior Herndon/SR .25
49 Justin Kaye/SR .25
50 Jason Karnuth/SR .25
51 Troy Glaus .40
52 Bengie Molina .15
53 Ramon Ortiz .15
54 Adam Kennedy .15
55 Jarrod Washburn .15
56 Troy Percival .15
57 David Eckstein .15
58 Ben Weber .15
59 Larry Barnes .15
60 Ismael Valdes .15
61 Benji Gil .15
62 Scott Schoeneweis .15
63 Pat Rapp .15
64 Jason Giambi .50
65 Mark Mulder .25
66 Ron Gant .15
67 Johnny Damon .25
68 Adam Piatt .15
69 Jermaine Dye .25
70 Jason Hart .15
71 Eric Chavez .40
72 Jim Mecir .15
73 Barry Zito .40
74 Jason Isringhausen .15
75 Jeremy Giambi .15
76 Olmedo Saenz .15
77 Terrence Long .15
78 Ramon Hernandez .15
79 Chris Carpenter .15
80 Raul Mondesi .15
81 Carlos Delgado .50
82 Billy Koch .15
83 Vernon Wells .25
84 Darrin Fletcher .15
85 Homer Bush .15
86 Pasqual Coco .15
87 Shannon Stewart .15
88 Chris Woodward .15
89 Joe Lawrence .15
90 Esteban Loaiza .15
91 Cesar Izturis .15
92 Kelvim Escobar .15
93 Greg Vaughn .15
94 Brent Abernathy .15
95 Tanyon Sturtze .15
96 Steve Cox .15
97 Aubrey Huff .15
98 Jesus Colome .15
99 Ben Grieve .15
100 Esteban Yan .15
101 Joe Kennedy .15
102 Felix Martinez .15
103 Nick Bierbrodt .15
104 Damian Rolls .15
105 Russ Johnson .15
106 Toby Hall .15
107 Roberto Alomar .40
108 Bartolo Colon .25
109 John Rocker .15
110 Juan Gonzalez .50
111 Einar Diaz .15
112 Chuck Finley .15
113 Kenny Lofton .25
114 Danys Baez .25
115 Travis Fryman .25
116 C.C. Sabathia .25
117 Paul Shuey .15
118 Marty Cordova .15
119 Ellis Burks .15
120 Bob Wickman .15
121 Edgar Martinez .25
122 Freddy Garcia .15
123 Ichiro Suzuki 1.50
124 John Olerud .25
125 Gil Meche .15
126 Dan Wilson .15
127 Aaron Sele .15
128 Kazuhiro Sasaki .15
129 Mark McLemore .15
130 Carlos Guillen .15
131 Al Martin .15
132 David Bell .15
133 Jay Buhner .15
134 Stan Javier .15
135 Tony Batista .15
136 Jason Johnson .15
137 Brook Fordyce .15
138 Mike Kinkade .15
139 Willis Roberts .15
140 David Segui .15
141 Josh Towers .15
142 Jeff Conine .15
143 Chris Richard .15
144 Pat Hentgen .15
145 Melvin Mora .15
146 Jerry Hairston Jr. .15
147 Calvin Maduro .15
148 Brady Anderson .15
149 Alex Rodriguez 1.50
150 Kenny Rogers .15
151 Chad Curtis .15
152 Ricky Ledee .15
153 Rafael Palmeiro .50
154 Rob Bell .15
155 Rick Helling .15
156 Doug Davis .15
157 Mike Lamb .15
158 Gabe Kapler .15
159 Jeff Zimmerman .15
160 Bill Haselman .15
161 Tim Crabtree .15
162 Carlos Pena .15
163 Nomar Garciaparra 1.00
164 Shea Hillenbrand .15
165 Hideo Nomo .40
166 Manny Ramirez .50
167 Jose Offerman .15
168 Scott Hatteberg .15
169 Trot Nixon .25
170 Darren Lewis .15
171 Derek Lowe .25
172 Troy O'Leary .15
173 Tim Wakefield .15
174 Chris Stynes .15
175 John Valentin .15
176 David Cone .15
177 Neifi Perez .15
178 Brent Mayne .15
179 Dan Reichert .15
180 A.J. Hinch .15
181 Chris George .15
182 Mike Sweeney .15
183 Jeff Suppan .15
184 Roberto Hernandez .15
185 Joe Randa .15
186 Paul Byrd .15
187 Luis Ordaz .15
188 Kris Wilson .15
189 Dee Brown .15
190 Tony Clark .15
191 Matt Anderson .15
192 Robert Fick .15
193 Juan Encarnacion .15
194 Dean Palmer .15
195 Victor Santos .15
196 Damion Easley .15
197 Jose Lima .15
198 Deivi Cruz .15
199 Roger Cedeno .15
200 Jose Macias .15
201 Jeff Weaver .15
202 Brandon Inge .15
203 Brian Moehler .15
204 Brad Radke .15
205 Doug Mientkiewicz .15
206 Cristian Guzman .15
207 Corey Koskie .15
208 LaTroy Hawkins .15
209 J.C. Romero .15
210 Chad Allen .15
211 Torii Hunter .25
212 Travis Miller .15
213 Joe Mays .15
214 Todd Jones .15
215 David Ortiz .40
216 Brian Buchanan .15
217 A.J. Pierzynski .15
218 Carlos Lee .15
219 Gary Glover .15
220 Jose Valentin .15
221 Aaron Rowand .15
222 Sandy Alomar Jr. .15
223 Herbert Perry .15
224 Jon Garland .15
225 Mark Buehrle .15
226 Chris Singleton .15
227 Kip Wells .15
228 Ray Durham .15
229 Joe Crede .15
230 Keith Foulke .15
231 Royce Clayton .15
232 Andy Pettitte .40
233 Derek Jeter 2.00
234 Jorge Posada .40
235 Roger Clemens 1.50
236 Paul O'Neill .25
237 Nick Johnson .15
238 Gerald Williams .15
239 Mariano Rivera .25
240 Alfonso Soriano .50
241 Ramiro Mendoza .15
242 Mike Mussina .50
243 Luis Sojo .15
244 Scott Brosius .15
245 David Justice .25
246 Wade Miller .15
247 Brad Ausmus .15
248 Jeff Bagwell .50
249 Daryle Ward .15
250 Shane Reynolds .15
251 Chris Truby .15
252 Billy Wagner .15
253 Craig Biggio .25
254 Moises Alou .25
255 Vinny Castilla .15
256 Tim Redding .15
257 Roy Oswalt .40
258 Julio Lugo .15
259 Chipper Jones .75
260 Greg Maddux 1.00
261 Ken Caminiti .15
262 Kevin Millwood .25
263 Keith Lockhart .15
264 Rey Sanchez .15
265 Jason Marquis .15
266 Brian Jordan .15
267 Steve Karsay .15
268 Wes Helms .15
269 B.J. Surhoff .15
270 Wilson Betemit .15
271 John Smoltz .25
272 Rafael Furcal .25
273 Jeromy Burnitz .15
274 Jimmy Haynes .15
275 Mark Loretta .15
276 Jose Hernandez .15
277 Paul Rigdon .15
278 Alex Sanchez .15
279 Chad Fox .15
280 Devon White .15
281 Tyler Houston .15
282 Ronnie Belliard .15
283 Luis Lopez .15
284 Ben Sheets .40
285 Curtis Leskanic .15
286 Henry Blanco .15
287 Mark McGwire 2.00
288 Edgar Renteria .25
289 Matt Morris .25
290 Gene Stechschulte .15
291 Dustin Hermanson .15
292 Eli Marrero .15
293 Albert Pujols 1.50
294 Luis Saturria .15
295 Bobby Bonilla .15
296 Garrett Stephenson .15
297 Jim Edmonds .40
298 Rick Ankiel .15
299 Placido Polanco .15
300 Dave Veres .15
301 Sammy Sosa 1.50
302 Eric Young .15
303 Kerry Wood .75
304 Jon Lieber .15
305 Joe Girardi .15
306 Fred McGriff .25
307 Jeff Fassero .15
308 Julio Zuleta .15
309 Kevin Tapani .15
310 Rondell White .15
311 Julian Tavarez .15
312 Tom Gordon .15
313 Corey Patterson .25
314 Bill Mueller .15
315 Randy Johnson .75
316 Chad Moeller .15
317 Tony Womack .15
318 Erubiel Durazo .15
319 Luis Gonzalez .25
320 Brian Anderson .15
321 Reggie Sanders .15
322 Greg Colbrunn .15
323 Robert Ellis .15
324 Jack Cust .15
325 Bret Prinz .15
326 Steve Finley .15
327 Byung-Hyun Kim .15
328 Albie Lopez .15
329 Gary Sheffield .40
330 Mark Grudzielanek .15
331 Paul LoDuca .15
332 Tom Goodwin .15
333 Andy Ashby .15
334 Hiram Bocachica .15
335 Dave Hansen .15
336 Kevin Brown .25
337 Marquis Grissom .15
338 Terry Adams .15
339 Chan Ho Park .15
340 Adrian Beltre .25
341 Luke Prokopec .15
342 Jeff Shaw .15
343 Vladimir Guerrero .75
344 Orlando Cabrera .15
345 Tony Armas Jr. .15
346 Michael Barrett .15
347 Geoff Blum .15
348 Ryan Minor .15
349 Peter Bergeron .15
350 Graeme Lloyd .15
351 Jose Vidro .15
352 Javier Vazquez .15
353 Matt Blank .15
354 Masato Yoshii .15
355 Carl Pavano .15
356 Barry Bonds 2.00
357 Shawon Dunston .15
358 Livan Hernandez .15
359 Felix Rodriguez .15
360 Pedro Feliz .15
361 Calvin Murray .15
362 Robb Nen .15
363 Marvin Benard .15
364 Russ Ortiz .15
365 Jason Schmidt .25
366 Rich Aurilia .15
367 John Vander Wal .15
368 Benito Santiago .15
369 Ryan Dempster .15
370 Charles Johnson .15
371 Alex Gonzalez .15
372 Luis Castillo .15
373 Mike Lowell .25
374 Antonio Alfonseca .15
375 A.J. Burnett .15
376 Brad Penny .15
377 Jason Grilli .15
378 Derrek Lee .25
379 Matt Clement .15
380 Eric Owens .15
381 Vladimir Nunez .15
382 Cliff Floyd .15
383 Mike Piazza 1.25
384 Lenny Harris .15
385 Glendon Rusch .15
386 Todd Zeile .15
387 Al Leiter .25
388 Armando Benitez .15
389 Alex Escobar .15
390 Kevin Appier .15
391 Matt Lawton .15
392 Bruce Chen .15
393 John Franco .15
394 Tsuyoshi Shinjo .15
395 Rey Ordonez .15
396 Joe McEwing .15
397 Ryan Klesko .15
398 Brian Lawrence .15
399 Kevin Walker .15
400 Phil Nevin .15
401 Bubba Trammell .15
402 Wiki Gonzalez .15
403 D'Angelo Jimenez .15
404 Rickey Henderson .40
405 Mike Darr .15
406 Trevor Hoffman .15
407 Damian Jackson .15
408 Santiago Perez .15
409 Cesar Crespo .15
410 Robert Person .15
411 Travis Lee .15
412 Scott Rolen .75
413 Turk Wendell .15
414 Randy Wolf .15
415 Kevin Jordan .15
416 Jose Mesa .15
417 Mike Lieberthal .15
418 Bobby Abreu .25
419 Tomas Perez .15
420 Doug Glanville .15
421 Reggie Taylor .15
422 Jimmy Rollins .40
423 Brian Giles .25
424 Rob Mackowiak .15
425 Bronson Arroyo .15
426 Kevin Young .15
427 Jack Wilson .15
428 Adam Brown .15
429 Chad Hermansen .15
430 Jimmy Anderson .15
431 Aramis Ramirez .25
432 Todd Ritchie .15
433 Pat Meares .15
434 Warren Morris .15
435 Derek Bell .15
436 Ken Griffey Jr. 1.00
437 Elmer Dessens .15
438 Ruben Rivera .15
439 Jason LaRue .15
440 Sean Casey .25
441 Pete Harnisch .15
442 Danny Graves .15
443 Aaron Boone .15
444 Dmitri Young .15
445 Brandon Larson .15
446 Pokey Reese .15
447 Todd Walker .15
448 Juan Castro .15
449 Todd Helton .50
450 Ben Petrick .15
451 Juan Pierre .15
452 Jeff Cirillo .15
453 Juan Uribe .15
454 Brian Bohanon .15
455 Terry Shumpert .15
456 Mike Hampton .15
457 Shawn Chacon .15
458 Adam Melhuse .15
459 Greg Norton .15
460 Gabe White .15
461 Ichiro Suzuki (World Stage) 1.50
462 Carlos Delgado (World Stage) .40
463 Manny Ramirez (World Stage) .50
464 Miguel Tejada (World Stage) .25
465 Tsuyoshi Shinjo (World Stage) .15
466 Bernie Williams (World Stage) .40
467 Juan Gonzalez (World Stage) .50
468 Andruw Jones (World Stage) .40
469 Ivan Rodriguez (World Stage) .50
470 Larry Walker (World Stage) .25
471 Hideo Nomo (World Stage) .25
472 Albert Pujols (World Stage) 1.00
473 Pedro Martinez (World Stage) .75
474 Vladimir Guerrero (World Stage) .75
475 Tony Batista (World Stage) .15
476 Kazuhiro Sasaki (World Stage) .15
477 Richard Hidalgo (World Stage) .15
478 Carlos Lee (World Stage) .15
479 Roberto Alomar (World Stage) .40
480 Rafael Palmeiro (World Stage) .50
481 Ken Griffey Jr. (Griffey Gallery) .50
482 Ken Griffey Jr. (Griffey Gallery) .50
483 Ken Griffey Jr. (Griffey Gallery) .50
484 Ken Griffey Jr. (Griffey Gallery) .50
485 Ken Griffey Jr. (Griffey Gallery) .50
486 Ken Griffey Jr. (Griffey Gallery) .50
487 Ken Griffey Jr. (Griffey Gallery) .50
488 Ken Griffey Jr. (Griffey Gallery) .50
489 Ken Griffey Jr. (Griffey Gallery) .50
490 Ken Griffey Jr. (Griffey Gallery) .50
491 Barry Bonds (Season Highlights Checklist) .75
492 Hideo Nomo (Season Highlights Checklist) .15
493 Ichiro Suzuki (Season Highlights Checklist) .50
494 Cal Ripken Jr. (Season Highlights Checklist) .75
495 Tony Gwynn (Season Highlights Checklist) .40
496 Randy Johnson (Season Highlights Checklist) .40
497 A.J. Burnett (Season Highlights Checklist) .15
498 Rickey Henderson (Season Highlights Checklist) .15
499 Albert Pujols (Season Highlights Checklist) .75
500 Luis Gonzalez (Season Highlights Checklist) .25
501 Brandon Puffer **RC** .50
502 Rodrigo Rosario **RC** .50
503 Tom Shearn **RC** .50
504 Reed Johnson **RC** .50
505 Chris Baker **RC** .50
506 John Ennis **RC** .50
507 Luis Martinez **RC** .50
508 So Taguchi **RC** .75
509 Scotty Layfield **RC** .50
510 Francis Beltran **RC** .50
511 Brandon Backe **RC** .50
512 Doug DeVore **RC** .50
513 Jeremy Ward **RC** .50
514 Jose Vaverde **RC** .50
515 P.J. Bevis **RC** .50
516 Victor Alvarez **RC** .50
517 Kazuhisa Ishii **RC** 2.00
518 Jorge Nunez **RC** .50
519 Eric Good **RC** .50
520 Ron Calloway **RC** .50
521 Valentino Pasucci .25
522 Nelson Castro **RC** .50
523 Deivis Santos .25
524 Luis Ugueto **RC** .50
525 Matt Thornton .25
526 Hansel Izquierdo **RC** .75
527 Tyler Yates **RC** .50
528 Mark Corey **RC** .50
529 Jaime Cerda **RC** .50
530 Satoru Komiyama **RC** .50
531 Steve Bechler **RC** .50
532 Ben Howard **RC** .50
533 Anderson Machado **RC** .50
534 Jorge Padilla **RC** .50
535 Eric Junge **RC** .50
536 Adrian Burnside **RC** .50
537 Mike Gonzalez **RC** .50
538 Josh Hancock **RC** .50
539 Colin Young **RC** .50
540 Rene Reyes **RC** .50
541 Cam Esslinger **RC** .50
542 Tim Kalita **RC** .50
543 Kevin Frederick **RC** .50
544 Kyle Kane **RC** .50
545 Edwin Almonte **RC** .50
546 Aaron Sele .15
547 Garret Anderson .40
548 Darin Erstad .25
549 Brad Fullmer .15
550 Kevin Appier .15
551 Tim Salmon .25
552 David Justice .25
553 Billy Koch .15
554 Scott Hatteberg .15
555 Tim Hudson .25
556 Miguel Tejada .25
557 Carlos Pena .15
558 Mike Sirotka .15
559 Jose Cruz Jr. .15
560 Josh Phelps .15
561 Brandon Lyon .15
562 Luke Prokopec .15
563 Felipe Lopez .15
564 Jason Standridge .15
565 Chris Gomez .15
566 John Flaherty .15
567 Jason Tyner .15
568 Bobby Smith .15
569 Wilson Alvarez .15
570 Matt Lawton .15
571 Omar Vizquel .25
572 Jim Thome .75
573 Brady Anderson .15
574 Alex Escobar .15
575 Russell Branyan .15
576 Bret Boone .25
577 Ben Davis .15
578 Mike Cameron .15
579 Jamie Moyer .15
580 Ruben Sierra .15
581 Jeff Cirillo .15
582 Marty Cordova .15
583 Mike Bordick .15
584 Brian Roberts .15
585 Luis Matos .15
586 Geronimo Gil .15
587 Jay Gibbons .15
588 Carl Everett .15
589 Ivan Rodriguez .50
590 Chan Ho Park .15
591 Juan Gonzalez .50
592 Hank Blalock .40
593 Todd Van Poppel .15
594 Pedro J. Martinez .75
595 Jason Varitek .15
596 Tony Clark .15
597 Johnny Damon .25
598 Dustin Hermanson .15
599 John Burkett .15
600 Carlos Beltran .40
601 Mark Quinn .15
602 Chuck Knoblauch .15
603 Michael Tucker .15
604 Carlos Febles .15
605 Jose Rosado .15
606 Dmitri Young .15
607 Bobby Higginson .15
608 Craig Paquette .15
609 Mitch Meluskey .15
610 Wendell Magee .15
611 Mike Rivera .15
612 Jacque Jones .15
613 Luis Rivas .15
614 Eric Milton .15
615 Eddie Guardado .15
616 Matt LeCroy .15
617 Mike Jackson .15
618 Magglio Ordonez .25
619 Frank Thomas .50
620 Rocky Biddle .15
621 Paul Konerko .25
622 Todd Ritchie .15
623 Jon Rauch .15
624 John Vander Wal .15
625 Rondell White .15
626 Jason Giambi .50
627 Robin Ventura .25
628 David Wells .15
629 Bernie Williams .50

630 Lance Berkman .25
631 Richard Hidalgo .15
632 Gregg Zaun .15
633 Jose Vizcaino .15
634 Octavio Dotel .15
635 Morgan Ensberg .15
636 Andruw Jones .50
637 Tom Glavine .40
638 Gary Sheffield .40
639 Vinny Castilla .15
640 Javy Lopez .25
641 Albie Lopez .15
642 Geoff Jenkins .25
643 Jeffrey Hammonds .15
644 Alex Ochoa .15
645 Richie Sexson .40
646 Eric Young .15
647 Glendon Rusch .15
648 Tino Martinez .25
649 Fernando Vina .15
650 J.D. Drew .25
651 Woody Williams .15
652 Darryl Kile .15
653 Jason Isringhausen .15
654 Moises Alou .25
655 Alex Gonzalez .15
656 Delino DeShields .15
657 Todd Hundley .15
658 Chris Stynes .15
659 Jason Bere .15
660 Curt Schilling .40
661 Craig Counsell .15
662 Mark Grace .40
663 Matt Williams .25
664 Jay Bell .15
665 Rick Helling .15
666 Shawn Green .40
667 Eric Karros .15
668 Hideo Nomo .40
669 Omar Daal .15
670 Brian Jordan .15
671 Cesar Izturis .15
672 Fernando Tatis .15
673 Lee Stevens .15
674 Tomokazu Ohka .15
675 Brian Schneider .15
676 Brad Wilkerson .15
677 Bruce Chen .15
678 Tsuyoshi Shinjo .15
679 Jeff Kent .25
680 Kirk Rueter .15
681 J.T. Snow .15
682 David Bell .15
683 Reggie Sanders .15
684 Preston Wilson .15
685 Vic Darensbourg .15
686 Josh Beckett .40
687 Pablo Ozuna .15
688 Mike Redmond .15
689 Scott Strickland .15
690 Mo Vaughn .25
691 Roberto Alomar .50
692 Edgardo Alfonzo .15
693 Shawn Estes .15
694 Roger Cedeno .15
695 Jeromy Burnitz .15
696 Ray Lankford .15
697 Mark Kotsay .15
698 Kevin Jarvis .15
699 Bobby Jones .15
700 Sean Burroughs .15
701 Ramon Vazquez .15
702 Pat Burrell .40
703 Marlon Byrd .15
704 Brandon Duckworth .15
705 Marlon Anderson .15
706 Vicente Padilla .15
707 Kip Wells .15
708 Jason Kendall .15
709 Pokey Reese .15
710 Pat Meares .15
711 Kris Benson .15
712 Armando Rios .15
713 Mike Williams .15
714 Barry Larkin .40
715 Adam Dunn .40
716 Juan Encarnacion .15
717 Scott Williamson .15
718 Wilton Guerrero .15
719 Chris Reitsma .15
720 Larry Walker .25
721 Denny Neagle .15
722 Todd Zeile .15
723 Jose Ortiz .15
724 Jason Jennings .15
725 Tony Eusebio .15
726 Ichiro Suzuki 1.00
727 Barry Bonds 1.50
728 Randy Johnson .50
729 Albert Pujols 1.00
730 Roger Clemens .50
731 Sammy Sosa .50
732 Alex Rodriguez .50
733 Chipper Jones .40
734 Rickey Henderson .25
735 Marioners Team Photo .15
736 Luis Gonzalez .25
737 Derek Jeter 1.50
738 Ichiro Suzuki 1.00
739 Barry Bonds 1.50
740 Curt Schilling .25
741 Shawn Green .25
742 Jason Giambi .50
743 Roberto Alomar .25
744 Larry Walker .15
745 Mark McGwire .75

AL Centennial Bats

NM/M
Inserted 1:144
JD Joe DiMaggio 125.00
MM Mickey Mantle 150.00
BR Babe Ruth 150.00

AL Centennial Jerseys

NM/M
Common Player: 10.00
Inserted 1:144
PM Pedro Martinez 10.00
CR Cal Ripken Jr. 40.00
AR Alex Rodriguez 15.00
IR Ivan Rodriguez 10.00
NR Nolan Ryan 40.00
FT Frank Thomas 10.00

AL Centennial G-U Jerseys Autograph

No Pricing
Production 25 Sets

All-Star Salute Game Jerseys

NM/M
Common Player: 10.00
Inserted 1:288
SA Sparky Anderson 10.00
LB Lou Boudreau 10.00
DE Dennis Eckersley 10.00
NF Nellie Fox 15.00
KG Ken Griffey Jr. 25.00
AR Alex Rodriguez 25.00
DS Don Sutton 10.00
IS Ichiro Suzuki 40.00

Big Fly Zone

NM/M
Complete Set (10): 15.00
Common Player: .50
Inserted 1:14
Z1 Mark McGwire 4.00
Z2 Ken Griffey Jr. 3.00
Z3 Manny Ramirez 1.00
Z4 Sammy Sosa 3.00
Z5 Todd Helton 1.00
Z6 Barry Bonds 4.00
Z7 Luis Gonzalez .50
Z8 Alex Rodriguez 4.00
Z9 Carlos Delgado 1.00
Z10 Chipper Jones 1.50

Breakout Performers

NM/M
Complete Set (10): 10.00
Common Player: .50
Inserted 1:14
BP1 Ichiro Suzuki 3.00
BP2 Albert Pujols 4.00
BP3 Doug Mientkiewicz .50
BP4 Lance Berkman 1.00
BP5 Tsuyoshi Shinjo .50
BP6 Ben Sheets 1.00
BP7 Jimmy Rollins .75
BP8 J.D. Drew .75
BP9 Bret Boone .50
BP10 Alfonso Soriano 1.00

Championship Caliber

NM/M
Complete Set (6): 10.00
Common Player: 1.00
Inserted 1:23
CC1 Derek Jeter 5.00
CC2 Roberto Alomar 1.00
CC3 Chipper Jones 2.00

CC4 Gary Sheffield 1.00
CC5 Roger Clemens 3.00
CC6 Greg Maddux 2.50

Championship Caliber Swatches

NM/M
Common Player: 8.00
Inserted 1:288
RA Roberto Alomar/SP 20.00
KB Kevin Brown/SP 10.00
CF Cliff Floyd 10.00
ChJ Charles Johnson 8.00
RJ Randy Johnson 10.00
CJo Chipper Jones/SP 25.00
BL Barry Larkin 10.00
GM Greg Maddux/SP 40.00
TM Tino Martinez 8.00
JO John Olerud 8.00
AP Andy Pettitte 10.00
JP Jorge Posada 10.00
CS Curt Schilling 10.00
BW Bernie Williams 10.00

Chasing History

NM/M
Complete Set (15): 12.00
Common Player: .50
Inserted 1:11
CH1 Sammy Sosa 2.00
CH2 Ken Griffey Jr. 1.50
CH3 Roger Clemens 2.00
CH4 Barry Bonds 3.00
CH5 Rafael Palmeiro 1.00
CH6 Andres Galarraga .50
CH7 Juan Gonzalez 1.00
CH8 Roberto Alomar 1.00
CH9 Randy Johnson 1.00
CH10 Jeff Bagwell 1.00
CH11 Fred McGriff .50
CH12 Matt Williams .50
CH13 Greg Maddux 1.50
CH14 Robb Nen .50
CH15 Kenny Lofton .50

Combo Bat

NM/M
Inserted 1:288
CB-RG Alex Rodriguez, Ken Griffey Jr. 30.00
CB-DM Joe DiMaggio, Mickey Mantle 200.00

Combo Jersey

NM/M
Common Duo: 10.00
Inserted 1:288
RS Alex Rodriguez, Sammy Sosa 30.00
RM Nolan Ryan, Pedro Martinez 40.00
RC Nolan Ryan, Roger Clemens 50.00
BS Barry Bonds, Sammy Sosa 40.00
HK Shigetoshi Hasegawa, Byung-Hun Kim 10.00

First Timers Jerseys

NM/M
Common Player: 8.00
Inserted 1:288
RB Russell Branyan 8.00
OD Omar Daal 8.00
FG Freddy Garcia 8.00
ML Matt Lawton 8.00
JM Joe Mays 8.00
EM Eric Milton 8.00
CP Corey Patterson 10.00
AP Albert Pujols 50.00
SS Shannon Stewart 8.00

First Timers Jerseys Autograph

No Pricing
Production 25 Sets

Game Jerseys

NM/M
Common Player: 8.00
Production 350 Sets
Golds: .75-1.5X
Production 100
TB Tony Batista 8.00
AB Adrian Beltre 8.00
JC Jeff Cirillo 8.00
KG Ken Griffey Jr. 20.00
TH Tim Hudson 10.00
MP Mike Piazza 15.00
SR Scott Rolen 15.00
CS Curt Schilling 15.00
SS Sammy Sosa 25.00
FT Frank Thomas 12.00
PW Preston Wilson 8.00

Game Jersey Autograph

NM/M
Common Player: 20.00
Production 200 Sets
BB Barry Bonds 200.00
CD Carlos Delgado 25.00
RF Rafael Furcal 20.00
JGi Jason Giambi 35.00
KG Ken Griffey Jr. 125.00
AJ Andruw Jones 35.00
AP Albert Pujols 125.00
CR Cal Ripken Jr. 200.00
NR Nolan Ryan 140.00
GS Gary Sheffield 20.00
IS Ichiro Suzuki 300.00
PW Preston Wilson 20.00

Game-Used Base

NM/M
Common Player: 5.00
Inserted 1:288
BB Barry Bonds 20.00
RC Roger Clemens 20.00
CD Carlos Delgado 5.00
JG Jason Giambi 10.00
TG Troy Glaus 8.00
JG Juan Gonzalez 10.00
LG Luis Gonzalez 5.00
SG Shawn Green 5.00
KG Ken Griffey Jr. 15.00
DJ Derek Jeter 25.00
AJ Andruw Jones 8.00
CJ Chipper Jones 10.00
MM Mark McGwire 40.00
MP Mike Piazza 15.00
CR Cal Ripken Jr. 40.00
AR Alex Rodriguez 15.00
IR Ivan Rodriguez 8.00
KS Kazuhiro Sasaki 5.00
SS Sammy Sosa 20.00
IS Ichiro Suzuki 50.00

Game-Used Base Autograph

Complete Set (1):
Production 25

Game-Used Base Combo

NM/M
Common Combo: 40.00
Inserted 1:288
RG Alex Rodriguez, Ken Griffey Jr. 40.00
MJ Mark McGwire, Derek Jeter 60.00

Game-Worn Gems

NM/M
Common Player: 5.00
Inserted 1:48
Golds: 1-2X
Production 100 Sets
RA Roberto Alomar 8.00
EC Eric Chavez 6.00
CD Carlos Delgado 8.00
DE Darin Erstad/SP 10.00
FG Freddy Garcia/SP 8.00
TG Tom Glavine 8.00
JG Juan Gonzalez 8.00
LG Luis Gonzalez/SP 10.00
MH Mike Hampton/SP 8.00
CJ Chipper Jones 10.00
JK Jason Kendall 5.00
RK Ryan Klesko/SP 8.00
GM Greg Maddux 15.00
EM Edgar Martinez 8.00
PM Pedro Martinez/SP 15.00
TM Tino Martinez 8.00
JM Joe Mays 5.00
EM Eric Milton 5.00
PN Phil Nevin 5.00
HN Hideo Nomo/SP 30.00
JO John Olerud/SP 8.00
RP Robert Person 5.00
CR Cal Ripken Jr. 40.00
IR Ivan Rodriguez 10.00
SR Scott Rolen 15.00
CS Curt Schilling 10.00
AS Aaron Sele 5.00
GS Gary Sheffield/SP 8.00
FT Frank Thomas 10.00
OV Omar Vizquel/SP 10.00
RY Robin Yount 15.00

Double Game-Worn Gems

NM/M
Common Card: 8.00
Production 450 Sets
Golds: 1-2X
Production 100 Sets
NK Phil Nevin, Ryan Klesko 8.00
VB Omar Vizquel, Russell Branyan 10.00
DH Jermaine Dye, Tim Hudson 10.00
TO Frank Thomas, Magglio Ordonez 15.00
MI Edgar Martinez, Ichiro Suzuki/150 80.00
GS Luis Gonzalez, Curt Schilling 15.00
AP Roberto Alomar, Mike Piazza 20.00
PL Robert Person, Mike Lieberthal 8.00
MM Kevin Millwood, Greg Maddux 20.00
KG Jason Kendall, Brian Giles 10.00
DF Carlos Delgado, Shannon Stewart 10.00
PN Chan Ho Park, Hideo Nomo 30.00

Global Swatch Jerseys

NM/M
Common Player: 5.00
Inserted 1:144
CD Carlos Delgado 8.00
SH Shigetoshi Hasegawa 5.00
BK Byung-Hun Kim 5.00
HN Hideo Nomo 35.00
CP Chan Ho Park 5.00
MR Manny Ramirez 10.00
KS Kazuhiro Sasaki 5.00
TS Tsuyoshi Shinjo 5.00
IS Ichiro Suzuki 50.00
MY Masato Yoshii 5.00

Global Swatch Jerseys Autograph

No Pricing
Production 25 Sets

McGwire Memorabilia

NM/M
Common Card:
AM-J Mark McGwire/ Jsy/70 75.00
AM-B Mark McGwire/ Bat/70 75.00
MMc Mark McGwire/500 HR Club Bat/350 300.00
MM-SS Mark McGwire, Sammy Sosa/25 (Combo Jersey) 200.00
MM-KG Mark McGwire, Ken Griffey Jr./25 (Combo Jersey) 250.00
MM-JG Mark McGwire, Jason Giambi/25 (Combo Jersey) 200.00

Patch Numbers

Complete Set (3):
Common Player:

Return of the Ace

NM/M
Complete Set (15): 15.00
Common Player: 1.00
Inserted 1:11
RA1 Randy Johnson 2.00
RA2 Greg Maddux 3.00
RA3 Pedro Martinez 2.00
RA4 Freddy Garcia 1.00
RA5 Matt Morris 1.00
RA6 Mark Mulder 1.00
RA7 Wade Miller 1.00
RA8 Kevin Brown 1.00
RA9 Roger Clemens 4.00
RA10 Jon Lieber 1.00
RA11 C.C. Sabathia 1.00
RA12 Tim Hudson 1.50
RA13 Curt Schilling 2.00
RA14 Al Leiter 1.00
RA15 Mike Mussina 1.50

Sons of Summer Game Jerseys

NM/M
Common Player: 10.00
Inserted 1:288
RA Roberto Alomar 10.00
JB Jeff Bagwell 10.00
RC Roger Clemens 15.00
JG Juan Gonzalez 10.00
GM Greg Maddux 15.00
PM Pedro Martinez/SP 15.00
MP Mike Piazza 15.00
AR Alex Rodriguez 15.00

Superstar Summit

NM/M
Complete Set (6): 15.00
Common Player: 1.50
Inserted 1:23
SS1 Sammy Sosa 3.00
SS2 Alex Rodriguez 4.00
SS3 Mark McGwire 4.00
SS4 Barry Bonds 4.00
SS5 Mike Piazza 3.00
SS6 Ken Griffey Jr. 2.50

Superstar Summit II

NM/M
Complete Set (15): 25.00
Common Player: 1.00
Inserted 1:11
SS1 Alex Rodriguez 4.00
SS2 Jason Giambi 1.00
SS3 Vladimir Guerrero 1.50
SS4 Randy Johnson 1.50
SS5 Chipper Jones 1.50
SS6 Ichiro Suzuki 3.00
SS7 Sammy Sosa 2.50
SS8 Greg Maddux 2.00
SS9 Ken Griffey Jr. 2.50
SS10 Todd Helton 1.00
SS11 Barry Bonds 4.00
SS12 Derek Jeter 4.00
SS13 Mike Piazza 3.00
SS14 Ivan Rodriguez 1.00
SS15 Frank Thomas 1.00

The People's Choice Game Jerseys

NM/M
Common Player: 5.00
Inserted 1:24
Golds: 1-2X
Production 100 Sets
JBa Jeff Bagwell 10.00
EB Ellis Burks/SP 10.00
JBu Jeromy Burnitz 5.00
OD Omar Daal 5.00
CD Carlos Delgado 8.00
RF Rafael Furcal 6.00

AG	Andres Galarraga/SP	10.00
BG	Brian Giles	5.00
JG	Juan Gonzalez	10.00
KG	Ken Griffey Jr.	20.00
TG	Tony Gwynn	12.00
SH	Sterling Hitchcock	5.00
HI	Hideki Irabu	5.00
CJ	Charles Johnson	5.00
DL	Derek Lowe	8.00
GM	Greg Maddux	15.00
TM	Tino Martinez	10.00
JN	Jeff Nelson	5.00
RO	Rey Ordonez	5.00
RP	Rafael Palmeiro/SP	15.00
RP	Robert Person/SP	10.00
AP	Andy Pettitte	10.00
MP	Mike Piazza	15.00
TR	Tim Raines	5.00
MRa	Manny Ramirez	10.00
MRi	Mariano Rivera	8.00
AR	Alex Rodriguez	15.00
TS	Tim Salmon	6.00
CS	Curt Schilling	10.00
TSh	Tsuyoshi Shinjo	5.00
JS	J.T. Snow	5.00
SS	Sammy Sosa	20.00
MS	Mike Stanton	5.00
FT	Frank Thomas	10.00
RV	Robin Ventura	6.00
OV	Omar Vizquel	6.00
DW	David Wells	6.00
BW	Bernie Williams	8.00
MW	Matt Williams/SP	10.00

UD Patch Logo

		NM/M
Common Player:		60.00
Inserted 1:2,500		
Prices for Stripes & Numbers identical.		
BB	Barry Bonds	125.00
JG	Jason Giambi	60.00
KG	Ken Griffey Jr.	100.00
PM	Pedro Martinez	80.00
CR	Cal Ripken Jr.	150.00
AR	Alex Rodriguez	125.00
SS	Sammy Sosa	100.00

UD Patch Numbers

Complete Set (7):
Common Player:

UD Patch Stripes

Complete Set (7):
Common Player:

Patch Stripes Autograph

Complete Set (2):
Common Player:

Yankees Dynasty Combo Base

		NM/M
Common Combo:		50.00
JW	Derek Jeter, Bernie Williams	60.00
CJ	Roger Clemens, Derek Jeter	75.00

Yankees Dynasty Jerseys

		NM/M
Common Combo:		20.00
Inserted 1:288		
PR	Andy Pettitte, Mariano Rivera	25.00
BT	Wade Boggs, Joe Torre	25.00
CP	Roger Clemens, Jorge Posada	50.00
DM	Joe DiMaggio, Mickey Mantle	300.00
RK	Willie Randolph, Chuck Knoblauch	20.00
BJ	Scott Brosius, David Justice	20.00
OM	Paul O'Neill, Tino Martinez	25.00
WO	Bernie Williams, Paul O'Neill	25.00
WG	David Wells, Dwight Gooden	25.00
GC	Joe Girardi, David Cone	25.00
KR	Chuck Knoblauch, Tim Raines	25.00

2001 All-Star HR Derby Jerseys

		NM/M
Common Player:		10.00
Inserted 1:288		
BrB	Bret Boone	10.00
JG	Jason Giambi	15.00
TH	Todd Helton	15.00
AR	Alex Rodriguez	20.00
SS	Sammy Sosa	25.00

2001's Greatest Hits

		NM/M
Complete Set (10):		20.00
Common Player:		1.00
Inserted 1:14		
GH1	Barry Bonds	4.00
GH2	Ichiro Suzuki	3.00
GH3	Albert Pujols	3.00
GH4	Mike Piazza	2.50
GH5	Alex Rodriguez	3.00
GH6	Mark McGwire	3.00
GH7	Manny Ramirez	1.00
GH8	Ken Griffey Jr.	2.00
GH9	Sammy Sosa	3.00
GH10	Derek Jeter	4.00

2002 UD Authentics

		NM/M
Complete Set (200):		50.00
Common Player:		.25
Reversed Negatives:		1-2.5X
Inserted 1:9		
Pack (5):		2.50
Box (18):		35.00
1	Brad Fullmer	.25
2	Garret Anderson	.40
3	Darin Erstad	.40
4	Jarrod Washburn	.25
5	Troy Glaus	.50
6	Barry Zito	.40
7	David Justice	.40
8	Eric Chavez	.40
9	Tim Hudson	.40
10	Miguel Tejada	.40
11	Jermaine Dye	.25
12	Mark Mulder	.40
13	Carlos Delgado	.50
14	Jose Cruz Jr.	.25
16	Shannon Stewart	.25
17	Raul Mondesi	.25
18	Tanyon Sturtze	.25
19	Toby Hall	.25
20	Greg Vaughn	.25
21	Aubrey Huff	.25
22	Ben Grieve	.25
23	Brent Abernathy	.25
24	Jim Thome	.75
25	C.C. Sabathia	.25
26	Matt Lawton	.25
27	Omar Vizquel	.25
28	Ellis Burks	.25
29	Russ Branyan	.25
30	Bartolo Colon	.40
31	Ichiro Suzuki	1.50
32	John Olerud	.40
33	Freddy Garcia	.25
34	Mike Cameron	.25
35	Jeff Cirillo	.25
36	Kazuhiro Sasaki	.25
37	Edgar Martinez	.40
38	Bret Boone	.25
39	Jeff Conine	.25
40	Melvin Mora	.25
41	Jason Johnson	.25
42	Chris Richard	.25
43	Tony Batista	.25
44	Ivan Rodriguez	.50
45	Gabe Kapler	.25
46	Rafael Palmeiro	.50
47	Alex Rodriguez	1.50
48	Juan Gonzalez	.50
49	Carl Everett	.25
50	Nomar Garciaparra	1.50
51	Trot Nixon	.25
52	Manny Ramirez	.50
53	Pedro J. Martinez	.75
54	Johnny Damon	.40
55	Shea Hillenbrand	.25
56	Mike Sweeney	.25
57	Mark Quinn	.25
58	Joe Randa	.25
59	Carlos Beltran	.40
60	Chuck Knoblauch	.25
61	Robert Fick	.25
62	Jeff Weaver	.25
63	Bobby Higginson	.25
64	Dean Palmer	.25
65	Dmitri Young	.25
66	Corey Koskie	.25
67	Doug Mientkiewicz	.25
68	Joe Mays	.25
69	Torii Hunter	.40
70	Cristian Guzman	.25
71	Jacque Jones	.25
72	Magglio Ordonez	.40
73	Paul Konerko	.25
74	Carlos Lee	.25
75	Mark Buehrle	.25
76	Jose Canseco	.50
77	Frank Thomas	.50
78	Roger Clemens	1.50
79	Derek Jeter	2.00
80	Jason Giambi	.50
81	Rondell White	.25
82	Bernie Williams	.50
83	Jorge Posada	.50
84	Mike Mussina	.50
85	Alfonso Soriano	.75
86	Wade Miller	.25
87	Jeff Bagwell	.50
88	Craig Biggio	.40
89	Roy Oswalt	.40
90	Lance Berkman	.40
91	Daryle Ward	.25
92	Chipper Jones	.75
93	Greg Maddux	1.00
94	Marcus Giles	.25
95	Gary Sheffield	.50
96	Tom Glavine	.50
97	Andruw Jones	.50
98	Rafael Furcal	.25
99	Richie Sexson	.40
100	Ben Sheets	.40
101	Jose Hernandez	.25
102	Geoff Jenkins	.40
103	Jeffrey Hammonds	.25
104	Edgar Renteria	.40
105	Matt Morris	.40
106	Tino Martinez	.25
107	Jim Edmonds	.40
108	Albert Pujols	1.50
109	J.D. Drew	.40
110	Fernando Vina	.25
111	Darryl Kile	.25
112	Sammy Sosa	1.50
113	Fred McGriff	.40
114	Kerry Wood	.75
115	Moises Alou	.40
116	Jon Lieber	.25
117	Mark Grace	.50
118	Randy Johnson	.75
119	Curt Schilling	.50
120	Luis Gonzalez	.40
121	Steve Finley	.25
122	Matt Williams	.40
123	Shawn Green	.40
124	Kevin Brown	.40
125	Adrian Beltre	.40
126	Paul LoDuca	.25
127	Hideo Nomo	.50
128	Brian Jordan	.25
129	Vladimir Guerrero	.75
130	Javier Vazquez	.25
131	Jose Vidro	.25
132	Orlando Cabrera	.25
133	Jeff Kent	.25
134	Rich Aurilia	.25
135	Russ Ortiz	.25
136	Barry Bonds	2.00
137	Preston Wilson	.25
138	Ryan Dempster	.25
139	Cliff Floyd	.25
140	Josh Beckett	.40
141	Mike Lowell	.40
142	Mike Piazza	1.00
143	Roberto Alomar	.50
144	Al Leiter	.40
145	Edgardo Alfonzo	.25
146	Roger Cedeno	.25
147	Jeromy Burnitz	.25
148	Phil Nevin	.25
149	Mark Kotsay	.25
150	Ryan Klesko	.25
151	Trevor Hoffman	.25
152	Bobby Abreu	.40
153	Scott Rolen	.75
154	Jimmy Rollins	.40
155	Robert Person	.25
156	Pat Burrell	.40
157	Randy Wolf	.25
158	Brian Giles	.40
159	Aramis Ramirez	.50
160	Kris Benson	.25
161	Jason Kendall	.25
162	Ken Griffey Jr.	1.00
163	Sean Casey	.40
164	Adam Dunn	.50
165	Barry Larkin	.50
166	Todd Helton	.50
167	Mike Hampton	.25
168	Larry Walker	.40
169	Juan Pierre	.25
170	Juan Uribe	.25
171	So Taguchi **RC**	2.00
172	Brendan Donnelly **RC**	.75
173	Chris Baker **RC**	.50
174	John Ennis **RC**	.75
175	Francis Beltran **RC**	.75
176	Danny Wright	.50
177	Brandon Backe **RC**	.75
178	Mark Corey **RC**	.75
179	Kazuhisa Ishii **RC**	3.00
180	Ron Calloway **RC**	.50
181	Kevin Frederick **RC**	.75
182	Jaime Cerda **RC**	.75
183	Doug DeVore **RC**	.50
184	Brandon Puffer **RC**	.75
185	Andy Pratt **RC**	.50
186	Adrian Burnside **RC**	.50
187	Josh Hancock **RC**	.75
188	Jorge Nunez **RC**	.50
189	Tyler Yates **RC**	1.00
190	Kyle Kane **RC**	.75
191	Jose Valverde **RC**	1.00
192	Matt Thornton	.50
193	Ben Howard **RC**	.50
194	Reed Johnson **RC**	1.50
195	Rene Reyes **RC**	.50
196	Jeremy Ward **RC**	.50
197	Steve Bechler **RC**	.50
198	Cam Esslinger **RC**	.50
199	Michael Crudale **RC**	.50
200	Todd Donovan **RC**	.50

Retro UD Jerseys

		NM/M
Common Player:		5.00
Inserted 1:16		
Golds:		1-2X
Production 275 Sets		
Reverse Neg.:		1-2X
Production 350 Sets		
JB	Jeff Bagwell	15.00
KB	Kevin Brown	8.00
EC	Eric Chavez	5.00
RC	Roger Clemens/SP	25.00
CD	Carlos Delgado	8.00
JD	J.D. Drew	10.00
JE	Jim Edmonds	8.00
DE	Darin Erstad	5.00
RF	Rafael Furcal	5.00
JG	Jason Giambi	10.00
TG	Tom Glavine	10.00
LG	Luis Gonzalez	5.00
KG	Ken Griffey Jr.	20.00
TH	Todd Helton	12.00
RJ	Randy Johnson	12.00
AJ	Andruw Jones	8.00
CJ	Chipper Jones	15.00
GM	Greg Maddux	15.00
MP	Mike Piazza	15.00
MR	Manny Ramirez	10.00
AR	Alex Rodriguez	15.00
IR	Ivan Rodriguez	10.00
SS	Sammy Sosa/SP	20.00
MS	Mike Sweeney	5.00
FT	Frank Thomas	10.00
BW	Bernie Williams	10.00
BZ	Barry Zito	8.00

UD Heroes of Baseball

		NM/M
Complete Set (30):		150.00
Ichiro:		8.00
Griffey Jr.:		6.00
Alex Rodriguez:		8.00
Production 1,989 Sets		
HB-I1-10	Ichiro Suzuki	8.00
HB-G1-10	Ken Griffey Jr.	6.00
HB-R1-10	Alex Rodriguez	8.00

Signed UD Heroes of Baseball

		NM/M
Random Inserts:		
G	Ken Griffey Jr./185	125.00
R	Alex Rodriguez/185	90.00
I	Ichiro Suzuki/125	400.00

Retro UD Star Rookie Jerseys

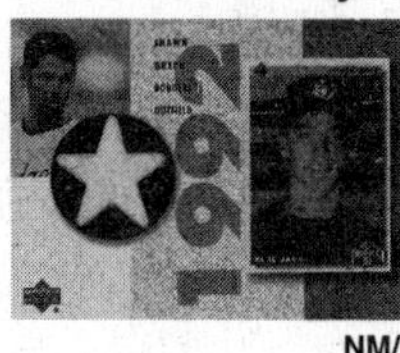

		NM/M
Common Player:		5.00
Inserted 1:16		
Golds:		1-2X
Production 275 Sets		
CB	Craig Biggio	8.00
PB	Pat Burrell	8.00
BG	Brian Giles	5.00
JG	Juan Gonzalez	8.00
LG	Luis Gonzalez	8.00
SG	Shawn Green	8.00
KG	Ken Griffey Jr.	20.00
RJ	Randy Johnson	10.00
CJ	Chipper Jones	10.00
DJ	David Justice	5.00
RK	Ryan Klesko	5.00
KL	Kenny Lofton	5.00
PM	Pedro J. Martinez	15.00
HN	Hideo Nomo	15.00
JO	John Olerud	5.00
MO	Magglio Ordonez	8.00
RP	Robert Person	5.00
AP	Albert Pujols	20.00
MR	Manny Ramirez/SP	15.00
AR	Alex Rodriguez	20.00
IR	Ivan Rodriguez	10.00
KS	Kazuhiro Sasaki	5.00
GS	Gary Sheffield	8.00
SS	Sammy Sosa/SP	20.00
I	Ichiro Suzuki	40.00
JT	Jim Thome	12.00
LW	Larry Walker	5.00

Signed Retro UD Star Rookie Jerseys

		NM/M
Production 40 Sets		
KG	Ken Griffey Jr.	100.00
AR	Alex Rodriguez	150.00
JT	Jim Thome	75.00

Reverse Negative Retro UD Jerseys

Complete Set (29):
Common Player:

Stars of '89 Jerseys

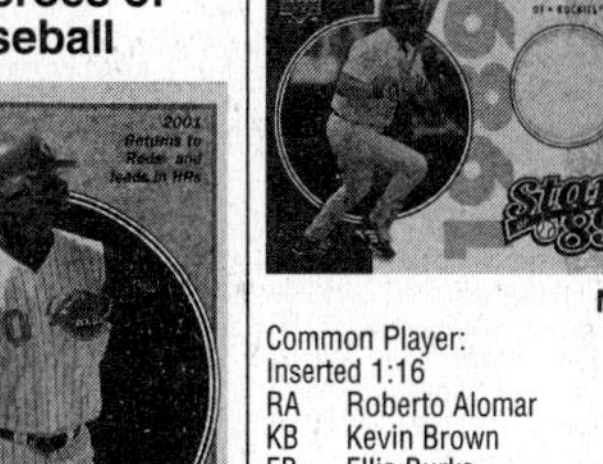

		NM/M
Common Player:		5.00
Inserted 1:16		
RA	Roberto Alomar	8.00
KB	Kevin Brown	8.00
EB	Ellis Burks	5.00
JC	Jose Canseco	8.00
RC	Roger Clemens	15.00
DC	David Cone	5.00
AG	Andres Galarraga	5.00
TG	Tom Glavine	10.00
JG	Juan Gonzalez	10.00
MG	Mark Grace	8.00
KG	Ken Griffey Jr.	20.00
RH	Rickey Henderson	10.00
RJ	Randy Johnson	10.00
DJ	David Justice	5.00
BL	Barry Larkin/SP	15.00
AL	Al Leiter	5.00
GM	Greg Maddux	15.00
EM	Edgar Martinez	8.00
FM	Fred McGriff	5.00
JO	John Olerud	5.00
PO	Paul O'Neill	8.00
RP	Rafael Palmeiro	8.00
CS	Curt Schilling	8.00
GS	Gary Sheffield	8.00
SS	Sammy Sosa	15.00
RV	Robin Ventura	5.00
LW	Larry Walker	5.00
MW	Matt Williams	5.00

1989 Flashbacks

		NM/M
Complete Set (12):		30.00
Common Player:		1.50
Production 4,225 Sets		
F1	Ken Griffey Jr.	8.00
F2	Gary Sheffield	1.50
F3	Randy Johnson	3.00
F4	Roger Clemens	4.00
F5	Greg Maddux	5.00
F6	Mark Grace	2.00
F7	Barry Bonds	5.00
F8	Roberto Alomar	2.00
F9	Sammy Sosa	5.00
F10	Rafael Palmeiro	2.00
F11	Edgar Martinez	1.50
F12	Jose Canseco	2.00

2002 Upper Deck Ballpark Idols

		NM/M
Complete Set (245):		125.00
Common Player:		.15
Common (201-245):		3.00
Production 1,750		
Pack (5):		2.00
Box (24 + Bobber):		50.00
1	Troy Glaus	.40
2	Kevin Appier	.15
3	Darin Erstad	.25
4	Garret Anderson	.25
5	Brad Fullmer	.15
6	Tim Salmon	.25
7	Eric Chavez	.25
8	Tim Hudson	.25
9	David Justice	.25
10	Barry Zito	.25
11	Miguel Tejada	.40
12	Mark Mulder	.40
13	Jermaine Dye	.15
14	Carlos Delgado	.40
15	Jose Cruz Jr.	.15
16	Brandon Lyon	.15
17	Shannon Stewart	.15
18	Eric Hinske	.25
19	Chris Carpenter	.15
20	Greg Vaughn	.15
21	Tanyon Sturtze	.15
22	Jason Tyner	.15
23	Toby Hall	.15
24	Ben Grieve	.15
25	Jim Thome	.75
26	Omar Vizquel	.25
27	Ricky Gutierrez	.15
28	C.C. Sabathia	.15
29	Ellis Burks	.15
30	Matt Lawton	.15
31	Milton Bradley	.15
32	Edgar Martinez	.25
33	Ichiro Suzuki	1.50
34	Bret Boone	.25
35	Freddy Garcia	.25
36	Mike Cameron	.15
37	John Olerud	.25
38	Kazuhiro Sasaki	.15
39	Jeff Cirillo	.15
40	Jeff Conine	.15
41	Marty Cordova	.15
42	Tony Batista	.15
43	Jerry Hairston Jr.	.15
44	Jason Johnson	.15
45	David Segui	.15
46	Alex Rodriguez	2.00
47	Rafael Palmeiro	.50
48	Carl Everett	.15
49	Chan Ho Park	.15
50	Ivan Rodriguez	.50
51	Juan Gonzalez	.50
52	Hank Blalock	.50
53	Manny Ramirez	.50
54	Pedro J. Martinez	.75
55	Tony Clark	.15
56	Nomar Garciaparra	1.25
57	Johnny Damon	.25
58	Trot Nixon	.25
59	Rickey Henderson	.50

60 Mike Sweeney .15
61 Neifi Perez .15
62 Joe Randa .15
63 Carlos Beltran .25
64 Chuck Knoblauch .15
65 Michael Tucker .15
66 Dean Palmer .15
67 Bobby Higginson .15
68 Dmitri Young .15
69 Randall Simon .15
70 Mitch Meluskey .15
71 Damion Easley .15
72 Joe Mays .15
73 Doug Mientkiewicz .15
74 Corey Koskie .15
75 Brad Radke .15
76 Cristian Guzman .15
77 Torii Hunter .25
78 Eric Milton .15
79 Frank Thomas .50
80 Paul Konerko .25
81 Mark Buehrle .15
82 Magglio Ordonez .25
83 Carlos Lee .15
84 Joe Crede .15
85 Derek Jeter 2.00
86 Bernie Williams .50
87 Mike Mussina .50
88 Jorge Posada .40
89 Roger Clemens 1.50
90 Jason Giambi .50
91 Alfonso Soriano .75
92 Rondell White .15
93 Jeff Bagwell .50
94 Lance Berkman .40
95 Roy Oswalt .25
96 Richard Hidalgo .15
97 Wade Miller .15
98 Craig Biggio .25
99 Greg Maddux 1.00
100 Chipper Jones .75
101 Gary Sheffield .40
102 Rafael Furcal .15
103 Andruw Jones .50
104 Vinny Castilla .15
105 Marcus Giles .15
106 Tom Glavine .40
107 Richie Sexson .40
108 Geoff Jenkins .15
109 Glendon Rusch .15
110 Eric Young .15
111 Ben Sheets .25
112 Alex Sanchez .15
113 Albert Pujols 1.50
114 J.D. Drew .25
115 Matt Morris .25
116 Jim Edmonds .40
117 Tino Martinez .15
118 Scott Rolen .75
119 Edgar Renteria .25
120 Sammy Sosa 1.50
121 Kerry Wood .75
122 Moises Alou .25
123 Jon Lieber .15
124 Fred McGriff .25
125 Juan Cruz .15
126 Alex Gonzalez .15
127 Corey Patterson .25
128 Randy Johnson .75
129 Luis Gonzalez .25
130 Steve Finley .15
131 Matt Williams .15
132 Curt Schilling .50
133 Mark Grace .40
134 Craig Counsell .15
135 Shawn Green .25
136 Kevin Brown .25
137 Hideo Nomo .40
138 Paul LoDuca .15
139 Brian Jordan .15
140 Eric Karros .15
141 Adrian Beltre .25
142 Vladimir Guerrero .75
143 Fernando Tatis .15
144 Javier Vazquez .15
145 Orlando Cabrera .15
146 Tony Armas Jr. .15
147 Jose Vidro .15
148 Barry Bonds 2.00
149 Rich Aurilia .15
150 Tsuyoshi Shinjo .15
151 Jeff Kent .25
152 Russ Ortiz .15
153 Jason Schmidt .25
154 Reggie Sanders .15
155 Preston Wilson .15
156 Luis Castillo .15
157 Charles Johnson .15
158 Josh Beckett .40
159 Derrek Lee .25
160 Mike Lowell .25
161 Mike Piazza 1.00
162 Roberto Alomar .40
163 Al Leiter .25
164 Mo Vaughn .25
165 Jeromy Burnitz .15
166 Edgardo Alfonzo .15
167 Roger Cedeno .15
168 Ryan Klesko .25
169 Brian Lawrence .15
170 Sean Burroughs .15
171 Phil Nevin .15
172 Ramon Vazquez .15
173 Mark Kotsay .15
174 Marlon Anderson .15
175 Mike Lieberthal .15
176 Bobby Abreu .25
177 Pat Burrell .40
178 Robert Person .15
179 Brandon Duckworth .15
180 Jimmy Rollins .25
181 Brian Giles .25
182 Pokey Reese .15
183 Kris Benson .15
184 Aramis Ramirez .25
185 Jason Kendall .15
186 Kip Wells .15
187 Ken Griffey Jr. 1.00
188 Adam Dunn .50
189 Barry Larkin .40
190 Sean Casey .25
191 Austin Kearns .25
192 Aaron Boone .15
193 Todd Helton .50
194 Juan Pierre .15
195 Mike Hampton .15
196 Jose Ortiz .15
197 Larry Walker .25
198 Juan Uribe .15
199 Ichiro Suzuki (Checklist) .75
200 Jason Giambi (Checklist) .25
201 Franklyn German **RC** 3.00
202 Rodrigo Rosario **RC** 3.00
203 Brandon Puffer **RC** 3.00
204 Kirk Saarloos 3.00
205 Chris Baker **RC** 3.00
206 John Ennis **RC** 3.00
207 Luis Martinez **RC** 3.00
208 So Taguchi **RC** 6.00
209 Michael Crudale **RC** 3.00
210 Francis Beltran **RC** 3.00
211 Brandon Backe **RC** 3.00
212 Felix Escalona **RC** 3.00
213 Jose Valverde **RC** 4.00
214 Doug DeVore **RC** 3.00
215 Kazuhisa Ishii **RC** 6.00
216 Victor Alvarez **RC** 3.00
217 Ron Calloway **RC** 3.00
218 Eric Good **RC** 3.00
219 Jorge Nunez 3.00
220 Deivis Santos 3.00
221 Nelson Castro **RC** 3.00
222 Matt Thornton 3.00
223 Jason Simontacchi **RC** 3.00
224 Hansel Izquierdo **RC** 3.00
225 Tyler Yates **RC** 4.00
226 Jaime Cerda **RC** 3.00
227 Satoru Komiyama **RC** 3.00
228 Steve Bechler **RC** 3.00
229 Ben Howard **RC** 3.00
230 Todd Donovan **RC** 3.00
231 Jorge Padilla **RC** 3.00
232 Eric Junge **RC** 3.00
233 Anderson Machado **RC** 3.00
234 Adrian Burnside **RC** 3.00
235 Mike Gonzalez **RC** 3.00
236 Josh Hancock **RC** 3.00
237 Anastacio Martinez **RC** 3.00
238 Chris Booker **RC** 3.00
239 Rene Reyes **RC** 3.00
240 Cam Esslinger **RC** 3.00
241 Oliver Perez **RC** 10.00
242 Tim Kalita **RC** 3.00
243 Kevin Frederick **RC** 3.00
244 Mitch Wylie **RC** 3.00
245 Edwin Almonte **RC** 3.00

Bronze

Stars (1-200): 5-10X
SP's (201-245): .75-1.5X
Production 100 Sets

Gold

No pricing due to scarcity.
Production 25 Sets

Bobbers

NM/M
Inserted 1:Box
Roberto Alomar 10.00
Jeff Bagwell 15.00
Josh Beckett 10.00
Barry Bonds 30.00
Sean Burroughs 8.00
Roger Clemens 20.00
Joe DiMaggio/555/Away 40.00
Joe DiMaggio/361/Home 50.00
Nomar Garciaparra 20.00
Jason Giambi 10.00
Luis Gonzalez 8.00
Ken Griffey Jr. 20.00
Vladimir Guerrero 15.00
Kazuhisa Ishii 10.00
Derek Jeter/SP/Away 40.00
Randy Johnson/D'backs 15.00
Randy Johnson/Expos 15.00
Chipper Jones 15.00
Greg Maddux 20.00
Mickey Mantle/777/Away 50.00
Mickey Mantle/536/Home 60.00
Mark McGwire/Cards 35.00
Mike Piazza/Mets 20.00
Mark Prior 15.00
Albert Pujols 25.00
Alex Rodriguez 20.00
Ivan Rodriguez 10.00
Curt Schilling/D'backs 10.00
Sammy Sosa/Cubs/Away 25.00
Ichiro Suzuki/SP/Away 30.00
Frank Thomas 10.00
Jim Thome 15.00

Bobbers Autograph

NM/M
Common Autograph
Inserted 1:14 Boxes
Josh Beckett 60.00

Bobbers Gold

NM/M
Amount produced listed
Joe DiMaggio/56/Away 100.00
Joe DiMaggio/41/Home 125.00
Mickey Mantle/77/Away 140.00
Mickey Mantle/61/Home 125.00

Field Garb Jerseys

NM/M
Common Player: 4.00
Inserted 1:72
TB Tony Batista 4.00
BG Brian Giles 4.00
RJ Randy Johnson 10.00
JK Jeff Kent 4.00
TM Tino Martinez 4.00
JO John Olerud 4.00
AR Alex Rodriguez 12.00
IR Ivan Rodriguez 6.00
MS Mike Sweeney 4.00
RV Robin Ventura 4.00
LW Larry Walker 4.00
BZ Barry Zito 6.00

Figure Heads

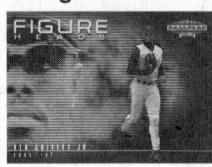

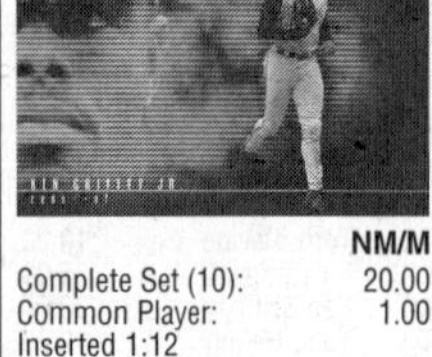

NM/M
Complete Set (10): 20.00
Common Player: 1.00
Inserted 1:12
F1 Ichiro Suzuki 3.00
F2 Sammy Sosa 2.50
F3 Alex Rodriguez 4.00
F4 Jason Giambi 1.00
F5 Barry Bonds 4.00
F6 Chipper Jones 1.50
F7 Mike Piazza 2.00
F8 Derek Jeter 4.00
F9 Nomar Garciaparra 2.50
F10 Ken Griffey Jr. 2.00

Player's Club Jerseys

NM/M
Common Player: 6.00
Inserted 1:72
KB Kevin Brown 6.00
DE Darin Erstad 8.00
RF Rafael Furcal 6.00
TH Tim Hudson 6.00
AJ Andruw Jones 8.00
JK Jason Kendall 6.00
MM Mark McGwire/SP 70.00
PN Phil Nevin 6.00
HN Hideo Nomo 20.00
MO Magglio Ordonez 6.00
CS Curt Schilling 8.00
IS Ichiro Suzuki/SP 40.00
JT Jim Thome 12.00

Playmakers 2002

NM/M
Complete Set (20): 25.00
Common Player: .75
Inserted 1:6
P1 Ken Griffey Jr. 2.00
P2 Alex Rodriguez 4.00
P3 Sammy Sosa 2.50
P4 Derek Jeter 4.00
P5 Mike Piazza 2.00
P6 Jason Giambi 1.00
P7 Barry Bonds 4.00
P8 Frank Thomas 1.00
P9 Randy Johnson 1.50
P10 Chipper Jones 1.50
P11 Jeff Bagwell 1.00
P12 Vladimir Guerrero 1.50
P13 Albert Pujols 3.00
P14 Nomar Garciaparra 2.50
P15 Ichiro Suzuki 3.00
P16 Troy Glaus 1.00
P17 Ivan Rodriguez 1.00
P18 Carlos Delgado .75
P19 Greg Maddux 2.00
P20 Todd Helton 1.00

Uniform Sluggers

NM/M
Common Player: 5.00
Inserted 1:72
JB Jeff Bagwell 8.00
JGi Jason Giambi 8.00
JGo Juan Gonzalez 8.00
SG Shawn Green 5.00
KG Ken Griffey Jr./SP 25.00
TH Todd Helton 8.00
CJ Chipper Jones 10.00
MM Mickey Mantle/SP 100.00
MP Mike Piazza 15.00
AR Alex Rodriguez 12.00
BW Bernie Williams 8.00

2002 Upper Deck Collectors Club

As one of the membership benefits of its Collector's Club, persons opting for the MLB option received an exclusive 20-card set. Typical UD quality with UV coating on front and back, silver-foil highlights on front and a hologram on back, the cards are standard 2-1/2" x 3-1/2". Fronts have game-action photos bordered in blue. Backs have a portrait photo, biographical data, career highlights and recent stats. Cards are numbered with an "MLB" prefix.

NM/M
Complete Set (20): 15.00
Common Player: .25
1 Alex Rodriguez 2.00
2 Barry Bonds 1.00
3 Ken Griffey Jr. 2.00
4 Sammy Sosa 1.00
5 Jason Giambi .50
6 Ichiro 3.00
7 Chipper Jones 1.50
8 Derek Jeter 1.50
9 Nomar Garciaparra 1.00
10 Greg Maddux .75
11 Mike Piazza 1.50
12 Frank Thomas 1.00
13 Albert Pujols 1.50
14 Randy Johnson .50
15 Pedro Martinez .50
16 Todd Helton .25
17 Vladimir Guerrero .60
18 Jeff Bagwell .60
19 Roger Clemens .75
20 Shawn Green .25

Memorabilia

Besides the 20-card base set benefit of joining Upper Deck's Collectors Club, one of six game-used memorabilia cards was also included. The cards are horizontal in format with a color action photo on front. Backs have a statement of authenticity.

NM/M
Complete Set (6): 50.00
Common Player: 10.00
AR-B Alex Rodriguez/Bat 10.00
AR-J Alex Rodriguez/Jsy 10.00
JR-B Ken Griffey Jr./Bat 10.00
JR-J Ken Griffey Jr./Jsy 10.00
SS-B Sammy Sosa/Bat 15.00
SS-J Sammy Sosa/Jsy 15.00

2002 Upper Deck Diamond Connection

NM/M
Complete Set (550):
Common Player: .15
Common Rk (91-200): 4.00
Production 1,500
Common Jersey (201-270): 4.00
Production 775
Common Jersey (271-320): 5.00
Production 200
Common Jersey (321-353): 5.00
Production 150
Common Jersey (354-368): 6.00
Production 100
Common Bat (369-438): 5.00
Production 775
Common Bat (439-488): 5.00
Production 200
Common Bat (489-521): 5.00
Production 150
Common Bat (522-536): 10.00
Production 100
Pack (5): 4.00
Box (14): 50.00
1 Troy Glaus .50
2 Darin Erstad .40
3 Barry Zito .40
4 Eric Chavez .40
5 Tim Hudson .40
6 Miguel Tejada .40
7 Carlos Delgado .40
8 Shannon Stewart .15
9 Greg Vaughn .15
10 Jim Thome .75
11 C.C. Sabathia .15
12 Ichiro Suzuki 1.50
13 Edgar Martinez .25
14 Bret Boone .25
15 Freddy Garcia .15
16 Jeff Conine .15
17 Alex Rodriguez 2.00
18 Rafael Palmeiro .50
19 Ivan Rodriguez .50
20 Juan Gonzalez .50
21 Pedro J. Martinez .75
22 Nomar Garciaparra 1.50
23 Manny Ramirez .50
24 Carlos Beltran .25
25 Mike Sweeney .15
26 Dmitri Young .15
27 Bobby Higginson .15
28 Corey Koskie .15
29 Cristian Guzman .15
30 Doug Mientkiewicz .15
31 Torii Hunter .25
32 Frank Thomas .50
33 Mark Buehrle .15
34 Carlos Lee .15
35 Magglio Ordonez .40
36 Roger Clemens 1.50
37 Bernie Williams .50
38 Jason Giambi .75
39 Derek Jeter 2.00
40 Mike Mussina .50
41 Jeff Bagwell .50
42 Richard Hidalgo .15
43 Lance Berkman .40
44 Roy Oswalt .40
45 Chipper Jones .75
46 Gary Sheffield .40
47 Andruw Jones .50
48 Greg Maddux 1.00
49 Geoff Jenkins .15
50 Ben Sheets .25
51 Richie Sexson .40
52 Albert Pujols 1.50
53 Matt Morris .25
54 J.D. Drew .40
55 Tino Martinez .25
56 Sammy Sosa 1.50
57 Kerry Wood .75
58 Moises Alou .25
59 Fred McGriff .25
60 Randy Johnson .75
61 Luis Gonzalez .25
62 Curt Schilling .50
63 Kevin Brown .25
64 Shawn Green .40
65 Paul LoDuca .15
66 Vladimir Guerrero .75
67 Jose Vidro .15
68 Barry Bonds 2.00
69 Jeff Kent .25
70 Rich Aurilia .15
71 Preston Wilson .15
72 Josh Beckett .40
73 Cliff Floyd .25
74 Mike Piazza 1.00
75 Mo Vaughn .25
76 Roberto Alomar .40
77 Jeromy Burnitz .15
78 Phil Nevin .15
79 Sean Burroughs .15
80 Scott Rolen .75
81 Bobby Abreu .25
82 Pat Burrell .40
83 Brian Giles .40
84 Jason Kendall .15
85 Ken Griffey Jr. 1.00
86 Adam Dunn .50
87 Aaron Boone .15
88 Larry Walker .25
89 Todd Helton .50
90 Mike Hampton .15
91 Brandon Puffer **RC** 4.00
92 Rodrigo Rosario **RC** 4.00
93 Tom Shearn **RC** 4.00
94 Morgan Ensberg 4.00
95 Jason Lane 4.00
96 Franklyn German **RC** 4.00
97 Carlos Pena 4.00
98 Joe Orloski **RC** 4.00
99 Reed Johnson **RC** 6.00
100 Chris Baker **RC** 4.00
101 Corey Thurman **RC** 4.00
102 Gustavo Chacin **RC** 4.00
103 Eric Hinske 4.00
104 John Foster **RC** 4.00
105 John Ennis **RC** 4.00
106 Kevin Gryboski **RC** 4.00
107 Jung Bong 4.00
108 Travis Wilson 4.00
109 Luis Martinez **RC** 4.00
110 Brian Mallette **RC** 4.00
111 Takahito Nomura **RC** 4.00
112 Bill Hall 4.00
113 Jeff Deardorff **RC** 4.00
114 Cristian Guerrero 4.00
115 Scotty Layfield **RC** 4.00
116 Michael Crudale **RC** 4.00
117 So Taguchi **RC** 6.00
118 Jeremy Lambert **RC** 4.00
119 Jimmy Journell 4.00
120 Francis Beltran **RC** 4.00
121 Mark Prior 6.00
122 Ben Christensen 4.00
123 Jorge Sosa **RC** 4.00
124 Brandon Backe **RC** 4.00
125 Steve Kent **RC** 4.00
126 Felix Escalona **RC** 4.00
127 P.J. Bevis **RC** 4.00
128 Jose Valverde **RC** 4.00
129 Doug DeVore **RC** 4.00
130 Jeremy Ward **RC** 4.00
131 Mike Koplove 4.00
132 Luis Terrero 4.00
133 John Patterson 4.00
134 Victor Alvarez **RC** 4.00
135 Kirk Saarloos 4.00
136 Kazuhisa Ishii **RC** 8.00
137 Steve Colyer 4.00
138 Cesar Izturis 4.00
139 Ron Calloway **RC** 4.00
140 Eric Good **RC** 4.00
141 Jorge Nunez **RC** 4.00
142 Ron Chiavacci 4.00
143 Donnie Bridges 4.00
144 Nelson Castro **RC** 4.00
145 Deivis Santos 4.00
146 Kurt Ainsworth 4.00
147 Arturo McDowell 4.00
148 Allan Simpson **RC** 4.00
149 Matt Thornton 4.00
150 Luis Ugueto **RC** 4.00
151 J.J. Putz **RC** 4.00
152 Hansel Izquierdo **RC** 4.00
153 Oliver Perez **RC** 4.00
154 Jaime Cerda **RC** 4.00
155 Mark Corey **RC** 4.00
156 Tyler Yates **RC** 6.00
157 Satoru Komiyama **RC** 4.00
158 Adam Walker **RC** 4.00
159 Steve Bechler **RC** 6.00
160 Erik Bedard 4.00
161 Todd Donovan **RC** 4.00
162 Clifford Bartosh **RC** 4.00
163 Ben Howard **RC** 8.00
164 Andy Shibilo **RC** 4.00
165 Dennis Tankersley 4.00
166 Mike Bynum 4.00
167 Anderson Machado **RC** 4.00
168 Peter Zamora **RC** 5.00
169 Eric Junge **RC** 4.00
170 Elio Serrano **RC** 4.00
171 Jorge Padilla **RC** 4.00
172 Marlon Byrd 4.00
173 Adrian Burnside **RC** 4.00
174 Mike Gonzalez **RC** 4.00
175 J.R. House 4.00
176 Hank Blalock 6.00
177 Travis Hughes **RC** 4.00
178 Mark Teixeira 6.00
179 Josh Hancock **RC** 4.00
180 Anastacio Martinez **RC** 4.00

181	Jorge de la Rosa **RC**	4.00
182	Ben Broussard	4.00
183	Austin Kearns	4.00
184	Corky Miller	4.00
185	Colin Young **RC**	4.00
186	Cam Esslinger **RC**	4.00
187	Rene Reyes **RC**	4.00
188	Aaron Cook **RC**	4.00
189	Alexis Gomez	4.00
190	Nate Field **RC**	4.00
191	Miguel Asencio **RC**	4.00
192	Brandon Berger	4.00
193	Fernando Rodney	4.00
194	Andy Van Hekken	4.00
195	Kevin Frederick **RC**	4.00
196	Todd Sears	4.00
197	Edwin Almonte **RC**	4.00
198	Kyle Kane **RC**	4.00
199	Mitch Wylie **RC**	4.00
200	Mike Porzio	4.00
201	Darin Erstad	6.00
202	Tim Salmon	6.00
203	Jeff Bagwell	10.00
204	Lance Berkman	6.00
205	Eric Chavez	6.00
206	Tim Hudson	6.00
207	Carlos Delgado	6.00
208	Chipper Jones	10.00
209	Gary Sheffield	6.00
210	Greg Maddux	15.00
211	Tom Glavine	6.00
212	Mike Mussina	10.00
213	J.D. Drew	6.00
214	Rick Ankiel	4.00
215	Sammy Sosa	15.00
216	Mike Lieberthal	6.00
217	Fred McGriff	8.00
218	David Wells	4.00
219	Curt Schilling	10.00
220	Luis Gonzalez	6.00
221	Mark Grace	10.00
222	Kevin Brown	4.00
223	Hideo Nomo	20.00
224	Jose Vidro	4.00
225	Jeff Kent	4.00
226	Rich Aurilia	4.00
227	Kenny Lofton	4.00
228	C.C. Sabathia	4.00
229	Edgar Martinez	8.00
230	Freddy Garcia	4.00
231	Cliff Floyd	4.00
232	Preston Wilson	4.00
233	Mike Piazza	10.00
234	Roberto Alomar	8.00
235	Trevor Hoffman	4.00
236	Ryan Klesko	5.00
237	Sean Burroughs	4.00
238	Scott Rolen	10.00
239	Pat Burrell	8.00
240	Edgardo Alfonzo	4.00
241	Brian Giles	8.00
242	Jason Kendall	5.00
243	Alex Rodriguez	15.00
244	Juan Gonzalez	8.00
245	Ivan Rodriguez	8.00
246	Rafael Palmeiro	8.00
247	Ken Griffey Jr.	12.00
248	Adam Dunn	15.00
249	Barry Larkin	5.00
250	Manny Ramirez	10.00
251	Pedro Martinez	10.00
252	Todd Helton	8.00
253	Larry Walker	6.00
254	Randy Johnson	10.00
255	Mike Sweeney	4.00
256	Carlos Beltran	6.00
257	Dmitri Young	4.00
258	Joe Mays	4.00
259	Doug Mientkiewicz	4.00
260	Corey Koskie	4.00
261	Magglio Ordonez	8.00
262	Frank Thomas	8.00
263	Ray Durham	4.00
264	Jason Giambi	10.00
265	Bernie Williams	8.00
266	Roger Clemens	15.00
267	Mariano Rivera	6.00
268	Robin Ventura	6.00
269	Andy Pettitte	10.00
270	Jorge Posada	8.00
271	Mike Piazza	15.00
272	Alex Rodriguez	15.00
273	Ken Griffey Jr.	15.00
274	Jason Giambi	10.00
275	Frank Thomas	8.00
276	Greg Maddux	15.00
277	Sammy Sosa	15.00
278	Roger Clemens	15.00
279	Jeff Bagwell	10.00
280	Todd Helton	8.00
281	Ichiro Suzuki	40.00
282	Randy Johnson	10.00
283	Jim Thome	15.00
284	Ivan Rodriguez	8.00
285	Darin Erstad	6.00
286	Eric Chavez	8.00
287	Barry Zito	10.00
288	Carlos Delgado	8.00
289	Omar Vizquel	6.00
290	Edgar Martinez	8.00
291	Manny Ramirez	10.00
292	Mike Sweeney	6.00
293	Tom Glavine	8.00
294	Joe Mays	6.00
295	Eric Milton	6.00
296	Magglio Ordonez	8.00
297	Bernie Williams	8.00
298	Trevor Hoffman	6.00
299	Andruw Jones	8.00
300	Aubrey Huff	5.00
301	Jim Edmonds	8.00
302	Kerry Wood	10.00
303	Luis Gonzalez	8.00
304	Shawn Green	6.00
305	Jose Vidro	5.00
306	Jeff Kent	5.00
307	Edgardo Alfonzo	5.00
308	Preston Wilson	5.00
309	Roberto Alomar	10.00
310	Jeromy Burnitz	5.00
311	Phil Nevin	5.00
312	Ryan Klesko	5.00
313	Bobby Abreu	6.00
314	Scott Rolen	12.00
315	Kazuhiro Sasaki	5.00
316	Jason Kendall	5.00
317	Sean Casey	5.00
318	Larry Walker	5.00
319	Mike Hampton	5.00
320	Juan Gonzalez	8.00
321	Darin Erstad	8.00
322	Tim Hudson	8.00
323	Carlos Delgado	8.00
324	Greg Vaughn	5.00
325	Jim Thome	15.00
326	Ichiro Suzuki	40.00
327	Rafael Palmeiro	8.00
328	Alex Rodriguez	15.00
329	Juan Gonzalez	8.00
330	Manny Ramirez	10.00
331	Carlos Beltran	6.00
332	Eric Milton	4.00
333	Frank Thomas	8.00
334	Roger Clemens	15.00
335	Jason Giambi	10.00
336	Lance Berkman	8.00
337	Greg Maddux	15.00
338	Chipper Jones	10.00
339	Sean Casey	8.00
340	Jim Edmonds	8.00
341	Kerry Wood	10.00
342	Sammy Sosa	15.00
343	Luis Gonzalez	8.00
344	Shawn Green	6.00
345	Jeff Kent	6.00
346	Preston Wilson	5.00
347	Roberto Alomar	10.00
348	Phil Nevin	5.00
349	Scott Rolen	12.00
350	Mike Sweeney	5.00
351	Ken Griffey Jr.	15.00
352	Todd Helton	8.00
353	Larry Walker	5.00
354	Alex Rodriguez	15.00
355	Pedro J. Martinez	10.00
356	Frank Thomas	10.00
357	Jason Giambi	10.00
358	Bernie Williams	10.00
359	Jeff Bagwell	10.00
360	Chipper Jones	10.00
361	Sammy Sosa	20.00
362	Randy Johnson	10.00
363	Shawn Green	6.00
364	Mike Piazza	15.00
365	Ichiro Suzuki	50.00
366	Ken Griffey Jr.	15.00
367	Larry Walker	8.00
368	Jim Edmonds	8.00
369	Darin Erstad	8.00
370	Tim Salmon	8.00
371	Mark Kotsay	5.00
372	Craig Biggio	8.00
373	Eric Chavez	10.00
374	David Justice	8.00
375	Carlos Delgado	8.00
376	Chipper Jones	15.00
377	Gary Sheffield	6.00
378	Greg Maddux	10.00
379	Eric Karros	5.00
380	Fred McGriff	8.00
381	J.D. Drew	8.00
382	Rick Ankiel	5.00
383	Sammy Sosa	15.00
384	Moises Alou	5.00
385	Ben Grieve	5.00
386	Greg Vaughn	5.00
387	Jay Payton	5.00
388	Luis Gonzalez	6.00
389	Ray Durham	5.00
390	Shawn Green	8.00
391	Hideo Nomo	20.00
392	Jose Vidro	5.00
393	Jeff Kent	5.00
394	Adrian Beltre	5.00
395	Jim Thome	15.00
396	Bobby Abreu	5.00
397	Edgar Martinez	10.00
398	Carl Everett	5.00
399	Luis Castillo	5.00
400	Preston Wilson	5.00
401	Jermaine Dye	8.00
402	Roberto Alomar	8.00
403	Todd Hundley	5.00
404	Ryan Klesko	5.00
405	Phil Nevin	5.00
406	Scott Rolen	10.00
407	Rafael Furcal	5.00
408	Miguel Tejada	8.00
409	Brian Giles	6.00
410	Jason Kendall	5.00
411	Alex Rodriguez	15.00
412	Juan Gonzalez	8.00
413	Ivan Rodriguez	8.00
414	Rafael Palmeiro	8.00
415	Ken Griffey Jr.	15.00
416	Edgardo Alfonzo	5.00
417	Barry Larkin	8.00
418	Manny Ramirez	8.00
419	Pedro J. Martinez	12.00
420	Todd Helton	8.00
421	Larry Walker	8.00
422	Garret Anderson	6.00
423	Mike Sweeney	5.00
424	Carlos Beltran	5.00
425	Javier Lopez	5.00
426	J.T. Snow	5.00
427	Doug Mientkiewicz	5.00
428	John Olerud	5.00
429	Magglio Ordonez	6.00
430	Frank Thomas	10.00
431	Kenny Lofton	5.00
432	Al Leiter	5.00
433	Bernie Williams	8.00
434	Roger Clemens	15.00
435	Tom Glavine	8.00
436	Robin Ventura	6.00
437	Chan Ho Park	5.00
438	Jorge Posada	8.00
439	Charles Johnson	5.00
440	Alex Rodriguez	20.00
441	Ken Griffey Jr.	15.00
442	Mark Kotsay	5.00
443	Frank Thomas	10.00
444	Greg Maddux	20.00
445	Sammy Sosa	20.00
446	Tom Glavine	10.00
447	Chipper Jones	15.00
448	Todd Helton	10.00
449	Jeff Cirillo	5.00
450	Steve Finley	8.00
451	Jim Thome	15.00
452	Ivan Rodriguez	8.00
453	Darin Erstad	8.00
454	Eric Chavez	8.00
455	Miguel Tejada	8.00
456	Carlos Delgado	8.00
457	Omar Vizquel	5.00
458	Edgar Martinez	10.00
459	Johnny Damon	8.00
460	Russell Branyan	5.00
461	Kenny Lofton	5.00
462	Jermaine Dye	5.00
463	Ellis Burks	5.00
464	Magglio Ordonez	8.00
465	Bernie Williams	10.00
466	Tim Salmon	5.00
467	Andruw Jones	8.00
468	Jeffrey Hammonds	5.00
469	Jim Edmonds	10.00
470	Kerry Wood	15.00
471	Luis Gonzalez	8.00
472	Shawn Green	8.00
473	Jose Vidro	5.00
474	Jeff Kent	6.00
475	Javier Lopez	5.00
476	Preston Wilson	5.00
477	Roberto Alomar	10.00
478	Robin Ventura	6.00
479	Phil Nevin	5.00
480	Ryan Klesko	8.00
481	Bobby Abreu	6.00
482	Scott Rolen	10.00
483	Brian Giles	8.00
484	Jason Kendall	5.00
485	Tsuyoshi Shinjo	5.00
486	Larry Walker	6.00
487	Mike Lieberthal	5.00
488	Juan Gonzalez	8.00
489	Darin Erstad	6.00
490	Tom Glavine	10.00
491	Carlos Delgado	6.00
492	Greg Vaughn	5.00
493	Jim Thome	15.00
494	Mark Grace	15.00
495	Rafael Palmeiro	8.00
496	Alex Rodriguez	20.00
497	Juan Gonzalez	8.00
498	Miguel Tejada	8.00
499	Carlos Beltran	5.00
500	Andruw Jones	8.00
501	Frank Thomas	10.00
502	Andres Galarraga	5.00
503	Gary Sheffield	8.00
504	Craig Biggio	8.00
505	Greg Maddux	20.00
506	Chipper Jones	20.00
507	Pat Burrell	10.00
508	Jim Edmonds	10.00
509	Kerry Wood	15.00
510	Sammy Sosa	20.00
511	Luis Gonzalez	8.00
512	Shawn Green	8.00
513	Edgardo Alfonzo	5.00
514	Preston Wilson	5.00
515	Roberto Alomar	10.00
516	Phil Nevin	5.00
517	Scott Rolen	15.00
518	Brian Giles	8.00
519	Jorge Posada	10.00
520	Todd Helton	12.00
521	Larry Walker	8.00
522	Alex Rodriguez	25.00
523	Pedro J. Martinez	20.00
524	Frank Thomas	12.00
525	Jason Giambi	15.00
526	Bernie Williams	10.00
527	J.D. Drew	10.00
528	Chipper Jones	20.00
529	Sammy Sosa	25.00
530	Randy Johnson	15.00
531	Shawn Green	10.00
532	Kevin Brown	10.00
533	Brian Giles	10.00
534	Ken Griffey Jr.	20.00
535	Larry Walker	10.00
536	Jim Edmonds	10.00
537	Sean Casey/Jsy/775	8.00
538	Ichiro Suzuki/Jsy/775	40.00
539	Pat Burrell/Jsy/200	10.00
540	Adam Dunn/Jsy/200	20.00
541	Lance Berkman/Jsy/200	10.00
542	Cliff Floyd/Jsy/150	8.00
543	Roger Clemens/Jsy/100	20.00
544	Kerry Wood/Bat/775	15.00
545	Andruw Jones/Bat/775	8.00
546	Manny Ramirez/Bat/200	10.00
547	Jorge Posada/Bat/200	10.00
548	Fred McGriff/Bat/200	8.00
549	Mike Sweeney/Bat/150	6.00
550	Todd Helton/Bat/100	12.00

Great Connections

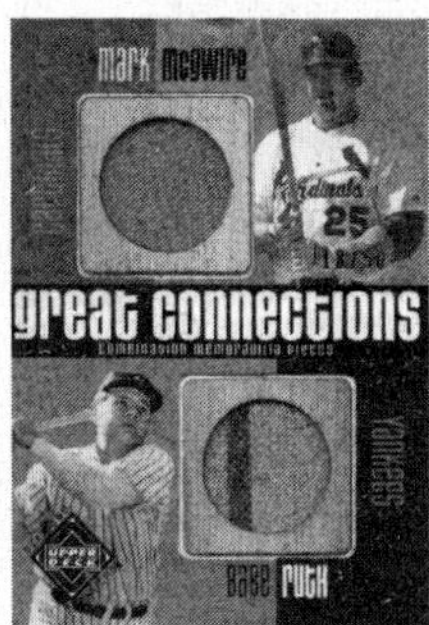

NM/M

Production 50 Sets

GC-GR	Jason Giambi, Babe Ruth	350.00
GC-MD	Mickey Mantle, Joe DiMaggio	350.00
GC-MR	Mark McGwire, Babe Ruth	350.00
GC-MS	Mark McGwire, Sammy Sosa	200.00
GC-RR	Alex Rodriguez, Nolan Ryan	150.00
GC-IG	Ichiro Suzuki, Ken Griffey Jr.	150.00

Mem. Signatures Bat

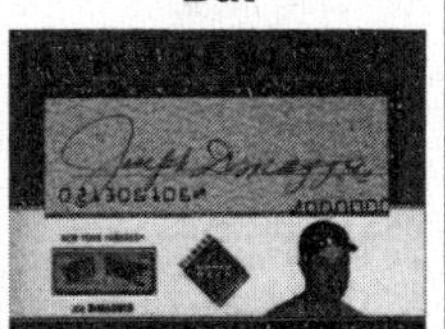

NM/M

Varying quantities produced

JD	Joe DiMaggio/20	600.00
JG	Jason Giambi/49	60.00
KG	Ken Griffey Jr./49	150.00
MMc	Mark McGwire/49	300.00
JM	Joe Morgan/99	35.00
KP	Kirby Puckett/145	75.00
CR	Cal Ripken Jr/145	150.00
AR	Alex Rodriguez/145	100.00
NR	Nolan Ryan/99	150.00
SS	Sammy Sosa/99	150.00
IS	Ichiro Suzuki/99	250.00

Mem. Signatures Jsy

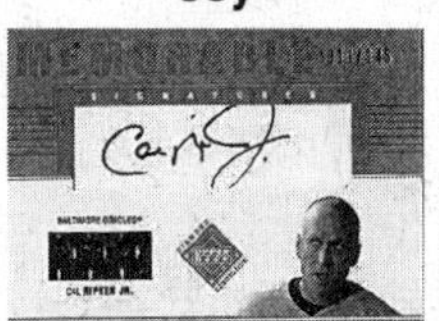

NM/M

Varying quantities produced

Gold: .75-1X

Production 150

EB	Ernie Banks/150	80.00
JD	Joe DiMaggio/20	550.00
KG	Ken Griffey Jr./49	150.00
SK	Sandy Koufax/150	300.00
MMc	Mark McGwire/49	300.00
JM	Joe Morgan/99	35.00
CR	Cal Ripken Jr/145	150.00
AR	Alex Rodriguez/145	100.00
NR	Nolan Ryan/99	150.00
SS	Sammy Sosa/99	200.00
IS	Ichiro Suzuki/99	250.00

Employees Mark McGwire Jersey-Bat Card

To thank its employees for "dedication and commitment to excellence," UD created this special game-used jersey-bat card in an edition of 350 serially numbered pieces. The 3-1/2" x 2-1/2" horizontal cards have action and portrait photos of Big Mac on front. Near the center is a laser-cut Cardinals logo cut from a McGwire bat, superimposed on a swatch of jersey. The serial number is in gold foil below. Back has another portrait photo and a message from UD CEO Richard McWilliam.

NM/M

UDC-MM Mark McGwire 165.00

2002 Upper Deck Honor Roll

NM/M

Complete Set (100):		25.00
Common Player:		.15
Pack (5):		2.00
Box (24):		30.00
1	Randy Johnson	.50
2	Mike Piazza	.75
3	Albert Pujols	1.00
4	Roberto Alomar	.25
5	Chipper Jones	.50
6	Rich Aurilia	.15
7	Barry Bonds	1.00
8	Ken Griffey Jr.	.75
9	Sammy Sosa	.75
10	Roger Clemens	.75
11	Ivan Rodriguez	.40
12	Jason Giambi	.40
13	Bret Boone	.15
14	Troy Glaus	.25
15	Alex Rodriguez	.75
16	Manny Ramirez	.40
17	Bernie Williams	.40
18	Ichiro Suzuki	.75
19	Matt Thornton	.25
20	Chris Baker **RC**	.25
21	Tyler Yates **RC**	.50
22	Jorge Nunez **RC**	.50
23	Rene Reyes **RC**	.50
24	Ben Howard **RC**	.50
25	Ron Calloway **RC**	.40
26	Danny Wright	.15
27	Reed Johnson **RC**	.50
28-31	Randy Johnson	.25
32-35	Mike Piazza	.50
36-39	Albert Pujols	.75
40-43	Roberto Alomar	.20
44-47	Chipper Jones	.50
48-51	Rich Aurilia	.15
52-55	Barry Bonds	1.00
56-59	Ken Griffey Jr.	.75
60-63	Sammy Sosa	.50
64-67	Roger Clemens	.75
68-71	Ivan Rodriguez	.25
72-75	Jason Giambi	.25
76-79	Bret Boone	.15
80-83	Troy Glaus	.20
84-87	Alex Rodriguez	.75
88-91	Manny Ramirez	.25
92-95	Bernie Williams	.20
96-99	Ichiro Suzuki	1.00
100	Checklist (Original nine players.) (Nine team names.)	.25

Silver

Stars: 4-8X

Production 100 Sets

Batting Glove

NM/M

Numbered to 250

BB	Bret Boone/89	20.00
JG	Jason Giambi	20.00
KG	Ken Griffey Jr.	40.00
AR	Alex Rodriguez	25.00
IR1	Ivan Rodriguez	20.00
IR2	Ivan Rodriguez	20.00
SS	Sammy Sosa	30.00
I	Ichiro Suzuki/46	150.00

Game Jersey

NM/M

Common Player: 10.00

Inserted 1:90

Golds: 2-3X

Production 99 Sets

Each player has multiple versions.

BB	Bret Boone/SP/45	10.00
RC	Roger Clemens	20.00
JG	Jason Giambi/SP	15.00
KG	Ken Griffey Jr.	25.00
CJ	Chipper Jones	15.00
AR	Alex Rodriguez	15.00
IR	Ivan Rodriguez	10.00
SS	Sammy Sosa/SP	25.00
I	Ichiro Suzuki/SP	40.00

Star Swatches Game Jersey

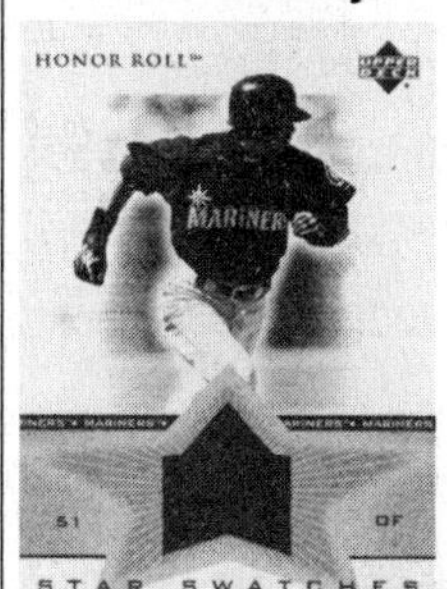

NM/M

Common Player: 10.00

Inserted 1:90

Golds: 2-5X

Production 24

BB	Bret Boone/45	10.00
RC	Roger Clemens/29	40.00
JG	Jason Giambi	10.00
KG	Ken Griffey Jr./SP	25.00
CJ	Chipper Jones	15.00
AR	Alex Rodriguez	15.00
IR	Ivan Rodriguez	10.00
SS	Sammy Sosa	20.00
I	Ichiro Suzuki/SP	40.00

Time Capsule Game Jersey

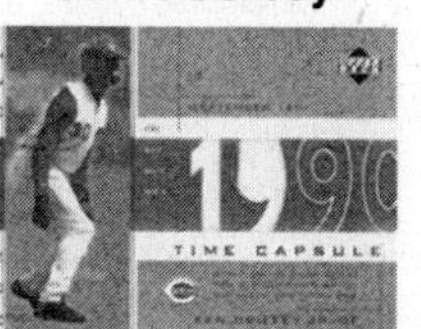

NM/M

Common Player: 8.00

Inserted 1:90

Golds: 2-3X

Production 99 Sets

BB	Bret Boone	8.00
RC	Roger Clemens	20.00
JG	Jason Giambi/52	15.00
CJ	Chipper Jones	10.00
AR	Alex Rodriguez	15.00
IR	Ivan Rodriguez/SP	15.00
SS	Sammy Sosa	20.00
I	Ichiro Suzuki	40.00

Stitch of Nine Game Jersey

NM/M
Common Player: 10.00
Inserted 1:90
Golds: 2-5X
Production 24 Sets
BB Bret Boone/45 10.00
RC Roger Clemens 20.00
JG Jason Giambi/SP 10.00
KG Ken Griffey Jr. 15.00
CJ Chipper Jones 10.00
AR Alex Rodriguez 15.00
IR Ivan Rodriguez 10.00
SS Sammy Sosa 20.00
I Ichiro Suzuki/85 40.00

Game-Used Bat

NM/M
Common Player: 10.00
Numbered to 99.
Each player has multiple versions.
BB Bret Boone 10.00
RC Roger Clemens 30.00
JG Jason Giambi 15.00
KG Ken Griffey Jr. 40.00
CJ Chipper Jones 20.00
AR Alex Rodriguez 20.00
IR Ivan Rodriguez 15.00
SS Sammy Sosa 30.00
I Ichiro Suzuki 40.00

2002 Upper Deck MVP

NM/M
Complete Set (300): 20.00
Common Player: .10
Pack (8): 1.50
Box (24): 25.00
1 Darin Erstad .20
2 Ramon Ortiz .10
3 Garret Anderson .20
4 Jarrod Washburn .10
5 Troy Glaus .20
6 Brendan Donnelly **RC** .10
7 Troy Percival .10
8 Tim Salmon .15
9 Aaron Sele .10
10 Brad Fullmer .10
11 Scott Hatteberg .10
12 Barry Zito .20
13 Tim Hudson .20
14 Miguel Tejada .25
15 Jermaine Dye .10
16 Mark Mulder .20
17 Eric Chavez .15
18 Terrence Long .10
19 Carlos Pena .10
20 David Justice .20
21 Jeremy Giambi .10
22 Shannon Stewart .10
23 Raul Mondesi .15
24 Chris Carpenter .10
25 Carlos Delgado .20
26 Mike Sirotka .10
27 Reed Johnson **RC** .15
28 Darrin Fletcher .10
29 Jose Cruz Jr. .10
30 Vernon Wells .10
31 Tanyon Sturtze .10
32 Toby Hall .10
33 Brent Abernathy .10
34 Ben Grieve .10
35 Joe Kennedy .10
36 Dewon Brazelton .10
37 Aubrey Huff .10
38 Steve Cox .10
39 Greg Vaughn .10
40 Brady Anderson .10
41 Chuck Finley .10
42 Jim Thome .40
43 Russell Branyan .10
44 C.C. Sabathia .10
45 Matt Lawton .10
46 Omar Vizquel .10
47 Bartolo Colon .15
48 Alex Escobar .10
49 Ellis Burks .10
50 Bret Boone .10
51 John Olerud .20
52 Jeff Cirillo .10
53 Ichiro Suzuki 1.00
54 Kazuhiro Sasaki .10
55 Freddy Garcia .10
56 Edgar Martinez .15
57 Matt Thornton .10
58 Mike Cameron .10
59 Carlos Guillen .10
60 Jeff Conine .10
61 Tony Batista .10
62 Jason Johnson .10
63 Melvin Mora .10
64 Brian Roberts .10
65 Josh Towers .10
66 Steve Bechler **RC** .10
67 Jerry Hairston Jr. .10
68 Chris Richard .10
69 Alex Rodriguez 1.00
70 Chan Ho Park .10
71 Ivan Rodriguez .25
72 Jeff Zimmerman .10
73 Mark Teixeira .20
74 Gabe Kapler .10
75 Frank Catalanotto .10
76 Rafael Palmeiro .25
77 Doug Davis .10
78 Carl Everett .10
79 Pedro J. Martinez .40
80 Nomar Garciaparra .75
81 Tony Clark .10
82 Trot Nixon .10
83 Manny Ramirez .25
84 Josh Hancock **RC** .10
85 Johnny Damon .20
86 Jose Offerman .10
87 Rich Garces .10
88 Shea Hillenbrand .10
89 Carlos Beltran .20
90 Mike Sweeney .10
91 Jeff Suppan .10
92 Joe Randa .10
93 Chuck Knoblauch .10
94 Mark Quinn .10
95 Neifi Perez .10
96 Carlos Febles .10
97 Miguel Asencio **RC** .10
98 Michael Tucker .10
99 Dean Palmer .10
100 Jose Lima .10
101 Craig Paquette .10
102 Dmitri Young .10
103 Bobby Higginson .10
104 Jeff Weaver .10
105 Matt Anderson .10
106 Damion Easley .10
107 Eric Milton .10
108 Doug Mientkiewicz .10
109 Cristian Guzman .10
110 Brad Radke .10
111 Torii Hunter .20
112 Corey Koskie .10
113 Joe Mays .10
114 Jacque Jones .10
115 David Ortiz .20
116 Kevin Frederick **RC** .20
117 Magglio Ordonez .20
118 Ray Durham .10
119 Mark Buehrle .10
120 Jon Garland .10
121 Paul Konerko .10
122 Todd Ritchie .10
123 Frank Thomas .25
124 Edwin Almonte **RC** .10
125 Carlos Lee .10
126 Kenny Lofton .15
127 Roger Clemens .75
128 Derek Jeter 1.00
129 Jorge Posada .20
130 Bernie Williams .25
131 Mike Mussina .25
132 Alfonso Soriano .40
133 Robin Ventura .15
134 John Vander Wal .10
135 Jason Giambi .25
136 Mariano Rivera .20
137 Rondell White .10
138 Jeff Bagwell .25
139 Wade Miller .10
140 Richard Hidalgo .10
141 Julio Lugo .10
142 Roy Oswalt .20
143 Rodrigo Rosario **RC** .10
144 Lance Berkman .20
145 Craig Biggio .20
146 Shane Reynolds .10
147 John Smoltz .20
148 Chipper Jones .40
149 Gary Sheffield .20
150 Rafael Furcal .10
151 Greg Maddux .50
152 Tom Glavine .20
153 Andruw Jones .25
154 John Ennis **RC** .20
155 Vinny Castilla .10
156 Marcus Giles .10
157 Javy Lopez .10
158 Richie Sexson .20
159 Geoff Jenkins .20
160 Jeffrey Hammonds .10
161 Alex Ochoa .10
162 Ben Sheets .20
163 Jose Hernandez .10
164 Eric Young .10
165 Luis Montanez .10
166 Albert Pujols .75
167 Darryl Kile .10
168 So Taguchi **RC** .50
169 Jim Edmonds .20
170 Fernando Vina .10
171 Matt Morris .10
172 J.D. Drew .20
173 Bud Smith .10
174 Edgar Renteria .20
175 Placido Polanco .10
176 Tino Martinez .10
177 Sammy Sosa .75
178 Moises Alou .20
179 Kerry Wood .40
180 Delino DeShields .10
181 Alex Gonzalez .10
182 Jon Lieber .10
183 Fred McGriff .15
184 Corey Patterson .15
185 Mark Prior .50
186 Tom Gordon .10
187 Francis Beltran **RC** .10
188 Randy Johnson .40
189 Luis Gonzalez .10
190 Matt Williams .15
191 Mark Grace .25
192 Curt Schilling .25
193 Doug DeVore **RC** .20
194 Erubiel Durazo .10
195 Steve Finley .15
196 Craig Counsell .10
197 Shawn Green .25
198 Kevin Brown .20
199 Paul LoDuca .10
200 Brian Jordan .15
201 Andy Ashby .10
202 Darren Dreifort .10
203 Adrian Beltre .15
204 Victor Alvarez **RC** .10
205 Eric Karros .10
206 Hideo Nomo .25
207 Vladimir Guerrero .40
208 Javier Vazquez .10
209 Michael Barrett .10
210 Jose Vidro .10
211 Brad Wilkerson .10
212 Tony Armas Jr. .10
213 Eric Good **RC** .10
214 Orlando Cabrera .10
215 Lee Stevens .10
216 Jeff Kent .10
217 Rich Aurilia .10
218 Robb Nen .10
219 Calvin Murray .10
220 Russ Ortiz .10
221 Deivis Santos .10
222 Marvin Benard .10
223 Jason Schmidt .10
224 Reggie Sanders .10
225 Barry Bonds 1.00
226 Brad Penny .10
227 Cliff Floyd .10
228 Mike Lowell .20
229 Derrek Lee .10
230 Ryan Dempster .10
231 Josh Beckett .20
232 Hansel Izquierdo **RC** .10
233 Preston Wilson .10
234 A.J. Burnett .10
235 Charles Johnson .10
236 Mike Piazza .50
237 Al Leiter .20
238 Jay Payton .10
239 Roger Cedeno .10
240 Jeromy Burnitz .10
241 Roberto Alomar .20
242 Mo Vaughn .20
243 Shawn Estes .10
244 Armando Benitez .10
245 Tyler Yates **RC** .10
246 Phil Nevin .10
247 D'Angelo Jimenez .10
248 Ramon Vazquez .10
249 Bubba Trammell .10
250 Trevor Hoffman .10
251 Ben Howard **RC** .20
252 Mark Kotsay .10
253 Ray Lankford .10
254 Ryan Klesko .10
255 Scott Rolen .40
256 Robert Person .10
257 Jimmy Rollins .25
258 Pat Burrell .20
259 Anderson Machado **RC** .10
260 Randy Wolf .10
261 Travis Lee .10
262 Mike Lieberthal .10
263 Doug Glanville .10
264 Bobby Abreu .10
265 Brian Giles .15
266 Kris Benson .10
267 Aramis Ramirez .10
268 Kevin Young .10
269 Jack Wilson .10
270 Mike Williams .10
271 Jimmy Anderson .10
272 Jason Kendall .10
273 Pokey Reese .10
274 Robert Mackowiak .10
275 Sean Casey .20
276 Juan Encarnacion .10
277 Austin Kearns .20
278 Danny Graves .10
279 Ken Griffey Jr. .50
280 Barry Larkin .20
281 Todd Walker .10
282 Elmer Dessens .10
283 Aaron Boone .10
284 Adam Dunn .40
285 Larry Walker .15
286 Rene Reyes **RC** .20
287 Juan Uribe .10
288 Mike Hampton .10
289 Todd Helton .40
290 Juan Pierre .10
291 Denny Neagle .10
292 Jose Ortiz .10
293 Todd Zeile .10
294 Ben Petrick .10
295 Checklist 1-50 (Ken Griffey Jr.) .25
296 Checklist 51-100 (Derek Jeter) .50
297 Checklist 101-150 (Sammy Sosa) .30
298 Checklist 151-200 (Ichiro Suzuki) .50
299 Checklist 201-250 (Barry Bonds) .50
300 Checklist 251-300 (Alex Rodriguez) .40

Silver

Stars: 5-10X
Production 100 Sets

Gold

No Pricing
Production 25 Sets

Ichiro - A Season to Remember

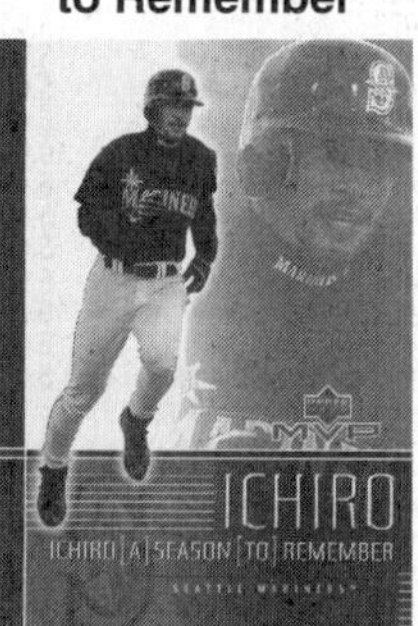

NM/M
Complete Set (10): 15.00
Ichiro's (1-10): 2.00
Inserted 1:10
I1-10 Ichiro Suzuki 2.50

Ichiro - A Season to Remember Bat

No Pricing
Production 25

Ichiro - A Season to Remember Jersey

Complete Set (1):

Souvenirs Bats

NM/M
Common Player: 8.00
Inserted 1:144
RA Roberto Alomar 20.00
CD Carlos Delgado 8.00
BG Brian Giles 8.00
LG Luis Gonzalez 8.00
SG Shawn Green 8.00
KG Ken Griffey Jr. 25.00
TH Todd Helton 15.00
DJ David Justice 8.00
JK Jeff Kent 8.00
RK Ryan Klesko 8.00
GM Greg Maddux 20.00
EM Edgar Martinez 10.00
DM Doug Mientkiewicz 8.00
MO Magglio Ordonez 8.00
RP Rafael Palmeiro/97 18.00
MP Mike Piazza/97 25.00
AR Alex Rodriguez 15.00
IR Ivan Rodriguez 10.00
SR Scott Rolen 10.00
GS Gary Sheffield 8.00
SS Sammy Sosa 20.00
MS Mike Sweeney 8.00
FT Frank Thomas/97 25.00
JT Jim Thome 10.00
GV Greg Vaughn 8.00
LW Larry Walker 8.00
BW Bernie Williams 10.00

Souvenirs Jerseys

NM/M
Common Player: 5.00
Inserted 1:48
RA Roberto Alomar 10.00
GA Garret Anderson 10.00
JB Jeff Bagwell 10.00
AB Adrian Beltre 8.00
JB Jeromy Burnitz 5.00
RC Roger Clemens 15.00
CD Carlos Delgado 8.00
DE Darin Erstad 8.00
RF Rafael Furcal 8.00
JG Juan Gonzalez 10.00
THo Trevor Hoffman 5.00
THu Tim Hudson 8.00
JK Jeff Kent 8.00
PK Paul Konerko/SP 10.00
MK Mark Kotsay 5.00
KL Kenny Lofton 8.00
EM Edgar Martinez 10.00
JP Jay Payton/SP 10.00
MP Mike Piazza 15.00
AR Alex Rodriguez 15.00
IR Ivan Rodriguez 10.00
SR Scott Rolen 10.00
TS Tim Salmon 10.00
FT Frank Thomas 15.00
JT Jim Thome/SP 15.00
RV Robin Ventura 5.00
OV Omar Vizquel 8.00
PW Preston Wilson 5.00
TZ Todd Zeile 5.00

Souvenirs Bat/Jersey Combos

NM/M
Common Card: 10.00
Inserted 1:144
Gold: No Pricing
Production 25 Sets
EA Edgardo Alfonzo 10.00
RA Roberto Alomar 15.00
JB Jeff Bagwell 20.00
AB Adrian Beltre 15.00
CD Carlos Delgado 15.00
DE Darin Erstad 20.00
JG Jason Giambi 20.00
BG Brian Giles 15.00
LG Luis Gonzalez 15.00
SG Shawn Green 15.00
KG Ken Griffey Jr. 40.00
TH Todd Helton 20.00
RJ Randy Johnson 25.00
CJ Chipper Jones 20.00
JK Jeff Kent 15.00
MO Magglio Ordonez 15.00
RP Rafael Palmeiro 20.00
MP Mike Piazza 15.00
AR Alex Rodriguez 25.00
IR Ivan Rodriguez 15.00
SR Scott Rolen 15.00
SS Sammy Sosa 15.00
JT Jim Thome 25.00
RV Robin Ventura 10.00
OV Omar Vizquel/97 20.00
BW Bernie Williams/97 25.00
TZ Todd Zeile 10.00

National Convention

A multi-sport set of 15 cards was specially produced as a give-away for attendees at the 2002 National Sports Collectors Convention in Chicago. VIP admissions received the complete set, regular show-goers received a three-card cello pack. The baseball cards follow the format of UD's regular 2002 issue and feature a distinguishing line of type on front and special numbering on back. Only the baseball players from the set are listed here.

NM/M
Complete Baseball Set (5): 10.00
Common Player: 2.00
N1 Mark McGwire 3.00
N2 Sammy Sosa 3.00
N3 Jason Giambi 2.00
N4 Ichiro 3.00
N5 Ken Griffey Jr. 3.00

2002 Upper Deck Ovation

NM/M
Complete Set (120): 120.00
Common Player: .25
Common (61-89, 120): 3.00
Production 2,002
Pack (5): 1.50
Box (24): 30.00
1 Troy Glaus .40
2 David Justice .40
3 Tim Hudson .40
4 Jermaine Dye .25
5 Carlos Delgado .40
6 Greg Vaughn .25
7 Jim Thome .75
8 C.C. Sabathia .25
9 Ichiro Suzuki 1.50
10 Edgar Martinez .40
11 Chris Richard .25
12 Rafael Palmeiro .50
13 Alex Rodriguez 2.00
14 Ivan Rodriguez .50
15 Nomar Garciaparra 1.50
16 Manny Ramirez .50
17 Pedro J. Martinez .75
18 Mike Sweeney .25
19 Dmitri Young .25
20 Doug Mientkiewicz .25
21 Brad Radke .25
22 Cristian Guzman .25
23 Frank Thomas .50
24 Magglio Ordonez .40
25 Bernie Williams .50
26 Derek Jeter 2.00
27 Jason Giambi .50
28 Roger Clemens 1.50
29 Jeff Bagwell .50
30 Lance Berkman .40
31 Chipper Jones .75
32 Gary Sheffield .40
33 Greg Maddux 1.00
34 Richie Sexson .40
35 Albert Pujols 1.60
36 Tino Martinez .25
37 J.D. Drew .40
38 Sammy Sosa 1.50
39 Moises Alou .40
40 Randy Johnson .75
41 Luis Gonzalez .40
42 Shawn Green .40
43 Kevin Brown .25
44 Vladimir Guerrero .75
45 Barry Bonds 2.00
46 Jeff Kent .40
47 Cliff Floyd .25
48 Josh Beckett .50
49 Mike Piazza 1.00
50 Mo Vaughn .25
51 Jeromy Burnitz .25
52 Roberto Alomar .40
53 Phil Nevin .25
54 Scott Rolen .75
55 Jimmy Rollins .50
56 Brian Giles .40
57 Ken Griffey Jr. 1.00
58 Sean Casey .40
59 Larry Walker .40
60 Todd Helton .50
61 Rodrigo Rosario **RC** 5.00
62 Reed Johnson **RC** 8.00
63 John Ennis **RC** 3.00
64 Luis Martinez **RC** 3.00
65 So Taguchi **RC** 6.00
66 Brandon Backe **RC** 3.00
67 Doug DeVore **RC** 3.00
68 Victor Alvarez **RC** 3.00
69 Kazuhisa Ishii **RC** 8.00
70 Eric Good **RC** 3.00
71 Deivis Santos 3.00
72 Matt Thornton 3.00
73 Hansel Izquierdo **RC** 3.00
74 Tyler Yates **RC** 6.00

75 Jaime Cerda **RC** 3.00
76 Satoru Komiyama **RC** 3.00
77 Steve Bechler **RC** 3.00
78 Ben Howard **RC** 3.00
79 Jorge Padilla **RC** 3.00
80 Eric Junge **RC** 3.00
81 Anderson Machado **RC** 3.00
82 Adrian Burnside **RC** 3.00
83 Josh Hancock **RC** 3.00
84 Anastacio Martinez **RC** 3.00
85 Rene Reyes **RC** 3.00
86 Nate Field **RC** 3.00
87 Tim Kalita **RC** 3.00
88 Kevin Frederick **RC** 3.00
89 Edwin Almonte **RC** 3.00
90-94 Ichiro Suzuki .75
95-99 Ken Griffey Jr. .75
100-104 Jason Giambi .40
105-109 Sammy Sosa .75
110-114 Alex Rodriguez .75
115-119 Mark McGwire .75
120 Alex Rodriguez, Ken Griffey Jr., Mark McGwire, Sammy Sosa, Jason Giambi, Ichiro Suzuki 15.00

Silver

(1-60): 1-30X
(61-89, 120): .5-1X
(90-119): 2-4X

Gold

(1-60) Print Run 25-50: 8-15X
(1-60) P/R 51-75: 4-8X
(1-60) P/R 76-90: 3-5X
(61-120) 25 of each produced
Print runs based on stats.

Authentic McGwire

NM/M
Varying quantities produced
AM-B Mark McGwire/ Bat/70 100.00
AM-BG Mark McGwire/ Bat/50 100.00
AM-J Mark McGwire/ Jsy/70 100.00
AM-JG Mark McGwire/ Jsy/50 100.00

Diamond Futures Jersey

NM/M
Common Player: 5.00
Inserted 1:72
Golds production 25: No Pricing
LB Lance Berkman 8.00
RB Russell Branyan 5.00
PB Pat Burrell 8.00
FG Freddy Garcia 5.00
TH Tim Hudson 6.00
JK Jason Kendall 5.00
JP Jorge Posada 10.00
IR Ivan Rodriguez 10.00
JR Jimmy Rollins 5.00
KS Kazuhiro Sasaki 5.00
JV Jose Vidro 5.00
BZ Barry Zito 8.00

Lead Performer Jersey

NM/M
Common Player: 5.00
Inserted 1:72
Golds: No Pricng
Production 25 Sets
JB Jeff Bagwell 8.00
CD Carlos Delgado 6.00
JGi Jason Giambi 10.00
JG Juan Gonzalez 8.00
LG Luis Gonzalez 5.00
KG Ken Griffey Jr./SP 20.00
MP Mike Piazza 15.00
AR Alex Rodriguez 15.00
IR Ivan Rodriguez 8.00
SS Sammy Sosa/SP 15.00
IS Ichiro Suzuki 40.00
FT Frank Thomas 8.00

Spokesman Spotlight

No Pricng
Production 25 Sets

Swatches Jersey

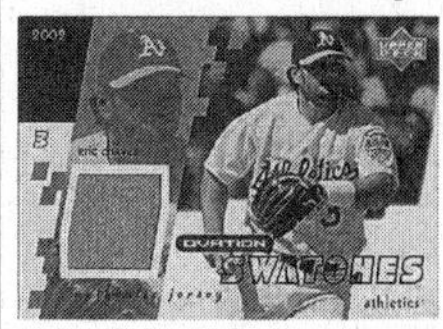

NM/M
Common Player: 5.00
Inserted 1:72
Golds: 25 sets produced, No Pricing.
RA Roberto Alomar/SP 20.00
EB Ellis Burks 5.00
JB Jeromy Burnitz 5.00
EC Eric Chavez 6.00
CD Carlos Delgado 6.00
DE Darin Erstad 5.00
MG Mark Grace 10.00
CJ Chipper Jones 12.00
GM Greg Maddux 15.00
PM Pedro J. Martinez 10.00
AR Alex Rodriguez 15.00
BW Bernie Williams 10.00

2002 Upper Deck Piece of History

NM/M
Complete Set (132): 200.00
Common Player: .15
Common SP (91-132): 5.00
Production 625
Pack (5): 2.00
Box (24): 40.00
1 Troy Glaus .40
2 Darin Erstad .25
3 Reggie Jackson .50
4 Miguel Tejada .40
5 Tim Hudson .25
6 Jim "Catfish" Hunter .25
7 Joe Carter .15
8 Carlos Delgado .40
9 Greg Vaughn .15
10 Early Wynn .15
11 Omar Vizquel .15
12 Jim Thome .75
13 Ichiro Suzuki 1.50
14 Edgar Martinez .25
15 Freddy Garcia .15
16 Cal Ripken Jr/SP 15.00
17 Jeff Conine .15
18 Juan Gonzalez .50
19 Nolan Ryan/SP 15.00
20 Alex Rodriguez/SP 10.00
21 Rafael Palmeiro .50
22 Ivan Rodriguez .50
23 Carlton Fisk .25
24 Wade Boggs .30
25 Pedro J. Martinez .75
26 Nomar Garciaparra 1.50
27 Manny Ramirez .50
28 Mike Sweeney .15
29 Bobby Higginson .15
30 Kirby Puckett .75
31 Doug Mientkiewicz .15
32 Corey Koskie .15
33 Joe Mays .15
34 Frank Thomas .50
35 Magglio Ordonez .25
36 Jason Giambi/SP 5.00
37 Derek Jeter/SP 10.00
38 Mickey Mantle/SP 15.00
39 Joe DiMaggio 2.00
40 Roger Maris 1.00
41 Roger Clemens 1.50
42 Bernie Williams .50
43 Jeff Bagwell .50
44 Lance Berkman .25
45 Eddie Mathews .50
46 Andruw Jones .40
47 Phil Niekro .15
48 Gary Sheffield .25
49 Chipper Jones .75
50 Greg Maddux 1.00
51 Robin Yount .50
52 Richie Sexson .25
53 Jim Edmonds .25
54 J.D. Drew .25
55 Albert Pujols 1.50
56 Andre Dawson .25
57 Billy Williams .15
58 Ernie Banks .50
59 Sammy Sosa/SP 10.00
60 Randy Johnson .50
61 Curt Schilling .50
62 Luis Gonzalez .25
63 Kirk Gibson .25
64 Steve Garvey .15
65 Sandy Koufax/SP 15.00
66 Shawn Green .25
67 Hideo Nomo .25
68 Kevin Brown .15
69 Vladimir Guerrero .75
70 Tim Raines .15
71 Gaylord Perry .15
72 Mel Ott .25
73 Willie McCovey .15
74 Barry Bonds/SP 10.00
75 Jeff Kent .15
76 Cliff Floyd .15
77 Dwight Gooden .15
78 Tom Seaver .50
79 Mike Piazza 1.00
80 Roberto Alomar .50
81 Dave Winfield .25
82 Tony Gwynn .75
83 Scott Rolen .75
84 Bill Mazeroski .15
85 Willie Stargell .25
86 Brian Giles .25
87 Ken Griffey Jr./SP 10.00
88 Sean Casey .25
89 Todd Helton .50
90 Larry Walker .25
91 Brendan Donnelly **RC** 5.00
92 Tom Shearn **RC** 5.00
93 Brandon Puffer **RC** 5.00
94 Corey Thurman **RC** 5.00
95 Reed Johnson **RC** 8.00
96 Gustavo Chacin **RC** 5.00
97 Chris Baker **RC** 5.00
98 John Ennis **RC** 5.00
99 So Taguchi **RC** 8.00
100 Michael Crudale **RC** 5.00
101 Francis Beltran **RC** 5.00
102 Jose Valverde **RC** 8.00
103 Doug DeVore **RC** 5.00
104 Jeremy Ward **RC** 5.00
105 P.J. Bevis **RC** 5.00
106 Steve Kent **RC** 5.00
107 Brandon Backe **RC** 5.00
108 Jorge Nunez **RC** 5.00
109 Kazuhisa Ishii **RC** 10.00
110 Ron Calloway **RC** 5.00
111 Valentino Pasucci 5.00
112 J.J. Putz **RC** 5.00
113 Matt Thornton 5.00
114 Allan Simpson **RC** 5.00
115 Jaime Cerda **RC** 5.00
116 Mark Corey **RC** 5.00
117 Tyler Yates **RC** 8.00
118 Steve Bechler **RC** 5.00
119 Ben Howard **RC** 5.00
120 Clifford Bartosh **RC** 5.00
121 Todd Donovan **RC** 5.00
122 Eric Junge **RC** 5.00
123 Adrian Burnside **RC** 5.00
124 Andy Pratt **RC** 5.00
125 Josh Hancock **RC** 5.00
126 Rene Reyes **RC** 5.00
127 Cam Esslinger **RC** 5.00
128 Colin Young **RC** 5.00
129 Kevin Frederick **RC** 5.00
130 Kyle Kane **RC** 5.00
131 Mitch Wylie **RC** 5.00
132 Danny Wright 5.00

Batting Champs

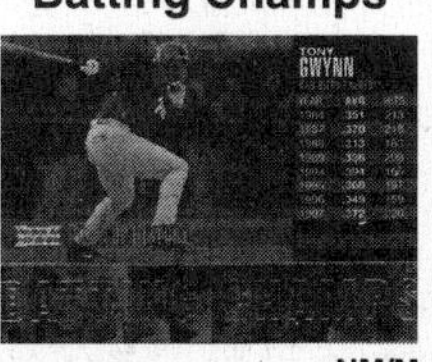

NM/M
Complete Set (10): 18.00
Common Player: 1.50
Inserted 1:30
B1 Tony Gwynn 2.00
B2 Frank Thomas 2.00
B3 Billy Williams 1.50
B4 Edgar Martinez 1.50
B5 Bernie Williams 1.50
B6 Mickey Mantle 6.00
B7 Larry Walker 1.50
B8 Gary Sheffield 1.50
B9 Wade Boggs 1.50
B10 Alex Rodriguez 4.00

Batting Champ Jerseys

NM/M
Common Player: 5.00
Inserted 1:96
WB Wade Boggs 10.00
AG Andres Galarraga 5.00
TG Tony Gwynn 15.00
MM Mickey Mantle/50 200.00
EM Edgar Martinez 10.00
JO John Olerud 8.00
PO Paul O'Neil 10.00
TR Tim Raines 10.00
AR Alex Rodriguez 15.00
GS Gary Sheffield/SP 8.00
FT Frank Thomas 8.00
LW Larry Walker/SP 8.00
BeW Bernie Williams 10.00

Batting Champ Jerseys Auto.

Complete Set (5):
Common Player:

ERA Leaders

NM/M
Complete Set (10): 18.00
Common Player: 1.00
Inserted 1:30
E1 Greg Maddux 3.00
E2 Pedro J. Martinez 2.00
E3 Freddy Garcia 1.00
E4 Randy Johnson 2.00
E5 Tom Seaver 2.00
E6 Early Wynn 1.00
E7 Dwight Gooden 1.00
E8 Kevin Brown 1.00
E9 Roger Clemens 3.00
E10 Nolan Ryan 6.00

POH ERA Leaders Jerseys

NM/M
Common Player: 8.00
Inserted 1:96
KB Kevin Brown 8.00
RC Roger Clemens 15.00
FG Freddy Garcia 8.00
DG Dwight Gooden 8.00
CH "Catfish" Hunter/SP 15.00
RJ Randy Johnson 15.00
SK Sandy Koufax/SP 100.00
GM Greg Maddux 15.00
PM Pedro Martinez 15.00
PN Phil Niekro 8.00
NR Nolan Ryan/SP 50.00
TS Tom Seaver 15.00

ERA Leaders Jerseys Autographs

NM/M
Production 24 Sets
RC Roger Clemens 200.00
SK Sandy Koufax 750.00

Hitting for the Cycle

NM/M
Complete Set (20): 35.00
Common Player: 1.00
Inserted 1:15
H1 Alex Rodriguez 4.00
H2 Andre Dawson 1.00
H3 Cal Ripken Jr. 6.00
H4 Carlton Fisk 1.50
H5 Dante Bichette 1.00
H6 Dave Winfield 1.50
H7 Eric Chavez 1.00
H8 Robin Yount 2.00
H9 Jason Kendall 1.00
H10 Jay Buhner 1.00
H11 Jeff Kent 1.00
H12 Joe DiMaggio 6.00
H13 John Olerud 1.00
H14 Kirby Puckett 3.00
H15 Luis Gonzalez 1.50
H16 Mark Grace 1.50
H17 Mickey Mantle 6.00
H18 Miguel Tejada 1.00
H19 Rondell White 1.00
H20 Todd Helton 2.00

Hitting for the Cycle Bats

NM/M
Inserted 1:576
DB Dante Bichette 10.00
JB Jay Buhner 10.00
EC Eric Chavez 10.00
AD Andre Dawson 10.00
CF Carlton Fisk 25.00
LG Luis Gonzalez 10.00
MM Mickey Mantle/50 200.00
CR Cal Ripken Jr/SP 75.00
AR Alex Rodriguez 25.00
DW Dave Winfield 15.00

Hitting for the Cycle Bats Aut

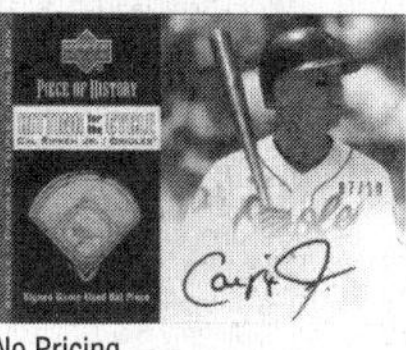

No Pricing
Production 10 Sets

Tape Measure Heroes

NM/M
Complete Set (30): 50.00
Common Player: 1.00
Inserted 1:10
TM1 Joe Carter 1.00
TM2 Cal Ripken Jr. 6.00
TM3 Mike Piazza 4.00
TM4 Shawn Green 1.25
TM5 Mark McGwire 5.00
TM6 Reggie Jackson 1.50
TM7 Mickey Mantle 6.00
TM8 Manny Ramirez 2.00
TM9 Mo Vaughn 1.00
TM10 Jeff Bagwell 2.00
TM11 Sammy Sosa 3.00
TM12 Tony Gwynn 2.00
TM13 Bill Mazeroski 1.00
TM14 Jose Canseco 1.50
TM15 Brian Giles 1.00
TM16 Kirk Gibson 1.00
TM17 Kirby Puckett 3.00
TM18 Wade Boggs 1.50
TM19 Albert Pujols 3.00
TM20 David Justice 1.00
TM21 Steve Garvey 1.00
TM22 Luis Gonzalez 1.50
TM23 Derek Jeter 6.00
TM24 Robin Yount 2.00
TM25 Barry Bonds 3.00
TM26 Alex Rodriguez 4.00
TM27 Willie Stargell 1.50
TM28 Carlton Fisk 1.50
TM29 Carlos Delgado 1.50
TM30 Ken Griffey Jr. 5.00

Tape Measure Heroes Jerseys

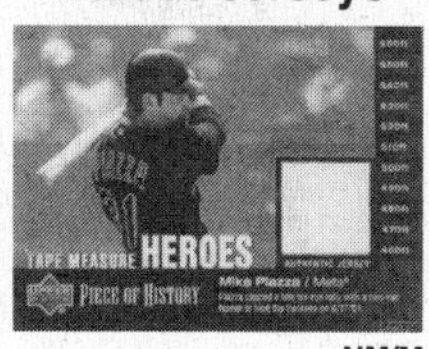

NM/M
Common Player: 5.00
Inserted 1:96
JB Jeff Bagwell 12.00
WB Wade Boggs 15.00
JCa Jose Canseco 10.00
JoC Joe Carter 5.00
CD Carlos Delgado 8.00
CF Carlton Fisk 10.00
SGa Steve Garvey 5.00
KGi Kirk Gibson 8.00
BG Brian Giles 5.00
SGr Shawn Green 8.00
KGr Ken Griffey Jr./90 40.00
MMa Mickey Mantle/50 200.00
RM Roger Maris/50 100.00
BM Bill Mazeroski 10.00
MP Mike Piazza 15.00
MR Manny Ramirez 10.00
CR Cal Ripken Jr. 30.00
AR Alex Rodriguez 15.00
SS Sammy Sosa 15.00
WS Willie Stargell 15.00
RY Robin Yount/SP 25.00

The MVP Club

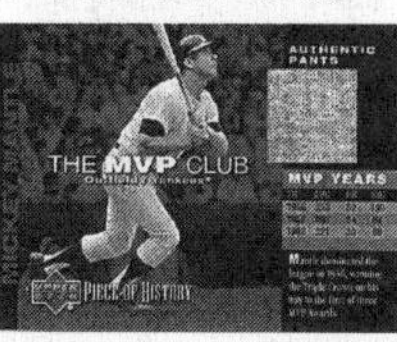

NM/M
Complete Set (14): 30.00
Common Player: 1.00
Inserted 1:22
M1 Jason Giambi 2.00
M2 Sammy Sosa 3.00
M3 Cal Ripken Jr. 6.00
M4 Robin Yount 2.00
M5 Ken Griffey Jr. 5.00
M6 Kirk Gibson 1.00
M7 Mickey Mantle 6.00
M8 Barry Bonds 3.00
M9 Frank Thomas 2.00
M10 Reggie Jackson 2.00
M11 Jeff Bagwell 2.00
M12 Roger Clemens 3.00
M13 Steve Garvey 1.00
M14 Chipper Jones 3.00

MVP Club Jerseys

NM/M
Common Player: 8.00
Inserted 1:96
JB Jeff Bagwell 10.00
RC Roger Clemens 15.00
SG Steve Garvey 8.00
JGi Jason Giambi 10.00
KGi Kirk Gibson 10.00
JGo Juan Gonzalez 10.00
KGr Ken Griffey Jr. 15.00
RJ Reggie Jackson 15.00
CJ Chipper Jones 15.00
JK Jeff Kent 8.00
BL Barry Larkin/SP 25.00
MM Mickey Mantle/50 200.00
RM Roger Maris/50 100.00
CR Cal Ripken Jr. 35.00
IR Ivan Rodriguez 10.00
SS Sammy Sosa 15.00
FT Frank Thomas 10.00
RY Robin Yount/SP 25.00

MVP Club Jerseys Auto.

No Pricing
Production 10 Sets

The 500 Home Run Club

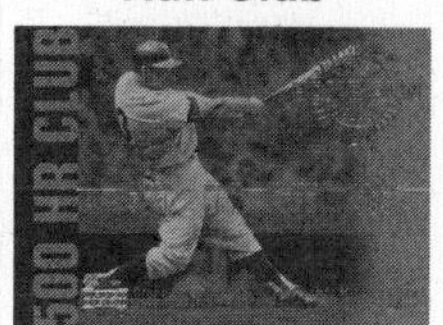

NM/M
Complete Set (9): 25.00
Common Player: 1.50
Inserted 1:9
HR1 Harmon Killebrew 3.00
HR2 Jimmie Foxx 3.00
HR3 Reggie Jackson 3.00
HR4 Mickey Mantle 8.00
HR5 Ernie Banks 3.00
HR6 Eddie Mathews 3.00
HR7 Mark McGwire 6.00
HR8 Willie McCovey 1.50
HR9 Mel Ott 3.00

POH 500 HR Club Jerseys

NM/M
Inserted 1:336
HA Hank Aaron 40.00
EB Ernie Banks/SP 40.00
JF Jimmie Foxx 40.00
RJ Reggie Jackson 25.00
MM Mickey Mantle/50 200.00
EM Eddie Mathews 30.00
WM Willie McCovey 20.00
MO Mel Ott 40.00

500 HR Club Jerseys Auto.

No Pricing
Production 10 Sets

300 Game Winners

NM/M
Complete Set (6): 12.00
Common Player: 1.00
Inserted 1:50
GW1 Nolan Ryan 6.00
GW2 Tom Seaver 3.00
GW3 Cy Young 3.00
GW4 Gaylord Perry 1.00
GW5 Early Wynn 1.00
GW6 Phil Niekro 1.00

300 Game Winners Jerseys

NM/M
Common Player: 15.00
Inserted 1:576
PN Phil Niekro 10.00
GP Gaylord Perry 10.00

NR Nolan Ryan/SP 50.00
TS Tom Seaver/SP 20.00

2002 Upper Deck Prospect Premieres

NM/M
Complete Set (109):
Common Player (1-60): .40
Common (61-85): 5.00
Inserted 1:18
Common (86-97): 10.00
Inserted 1:18
Pack (4): 8.00
Box (18): 120.00
1 Josh Rupe **RC** .40
2 Blair Johnson **RC** .40
3 Jason Pridie **RC** .75
4 Tim Gilhooly **RC** .40
5 Kennard Jones **RC** .40
6 Darrell Rasner **RC** .40
7 Adam Donachie **RC** .75
8 Josh Murray **RC** .40
9 Brian Dopirak **RC** 1.00
10 Jason Cooper **RC** .50
11 Zach Hammes **RC** .40
12 Jon Lester **RC** 15.00
13 Kevin Jepsen **RC** .40
14 Curtis Granderson **RC** 4.00
15 David Bush **RC** .75
16 Joel Guzman **RC** .50
17a Matt Pender **RC** (Black, photo is Curtis Granderson.) .40
17b Matt Pender (White, correct photo.) 2.00
18 Derick Grigsby **RC** .40
19 Jeremy Reed **RC** 3.00
20 Jonathan Broxton **RC** 1.00
21 Jesse Crain **RC** .40
22 Justin Jones **RC** 1.00
23 Brian Slocum **RC** .50
24 Brian McCann **RC** 5.00
25 Francisco Liriano **RC** 8.00
26 Fred Lewis **RC** 1.00
27 Steve Stanley **RC** .40
28 Chris Snyder **RC** .40
29 Daniel Cevette **RC** .40
30 Kiel Fisher **RC** .40
31 Brandon Wheeder **RC** .40
32 Pat Osborn **RC** .40
33 Taber Lee **RC** .40
34 Dan Ortmeyer **RC** .75
35 Josh Johnson **RC** 2.00
36 Val Majewski **RC** .75
37 Larry Broadway **RC** .50
38 Joey Gomes **RC** 1.00
39 Eric Thomas **RC** .40
40 James Loney **RC** 4.00
41 Charlie Morton **RC** .40
42 Mark McLemore .40
43 Matt Craig **RC** .40
44 Ryan Rodriguez **RC** .40
45 Rich Hill **RC** 2.00
46 Bob Malek **RC** .40
47 Justin Maureau **RC** .40
48 Randy Braun **RC** .40
49 Brian Grant **RC** .50
50 Tyler Davidson **RC** .50
51 Travis Hanson **RC** .50
52 Kyle Boyer **RC** .40
53 James Holcomb **RC** .40
54 Ryan Williams **RC** .40
55 Ben Crockett **RC** .40
56 Adam Greenberg **RC** .75
57 John Baker **RC** .40
58 Matt Carson **RC** .40
59 Jonathan George **RC** .40
60 David Jensen **RC** .40
61 Nick Swisher **RC** 15.00
62 Brent Cleven **RC** 8.00
63 Royce Ring **RC** 8.00
64 Mike Nixon **RC** 5.00
65 Ricky Barrett **RC** 5.00
66 Russ Adams **RC** 8.00
67 Joe Mauer **RC** 30.00
68 Jeff Francoeur **RC** 40.00
69 Joseph Blanton **RC** 10.00
70 Micah Schilling **RC** 8.00
71 John McCurdy **RC** 5.00
72 Sergio Santos **RC** 8.00
73 Josh Womack **RC** 5.00
74 Jared Doyle **RC** 5.00
75 Ben Fritz **RC** 5.00
76 Greg Miller 10.00
77 Luke Hagerty **RC** 8.00
78 Matt Whitney **RC** 10.00
79 Dan Meyer **RC** 5.00
80 Bill Murphy **RC** 5.00
81 Zach Segovia **RC** 8.00
82 Steve Obenchain **RC** 8.00
83 Matt Clanton **RC** 8.00
84 Mark Teahen **RC** 10.00
85 Kyle Pawelczyk **RC** 8.00
86 Khalil Greene/Auto. **RC** 50.00
87 Joe Saunders/Auto. **RC** 10.00
88 Jeremy Hermida/Auto. **RC** 40.00
89 Drew Meyer/Auto. **RC** 10.00
90 Jeff Francis/Auto. **RC** 30.00
91 Scott Moore/Auto. **RC** 10.00
92 Prince Fielder/Auto. **RC** 250.00
93 Zack Greinke/Auto. **RC** 40.00
94 Chris Gruler/Auto. **RC** 10.00
95 Scott Kazmir/Auto. **RC** 80.00
96 B.J. Upton/Auto. **RC** 75.00
97 Clint Everts/Auto. **RC** 15.00
98 Cal Ripken Jr. 1.00
99 Cal Ripken Jr. 1.00
100-104 Mark McGwire 1.00
105-109 Joe DiMaggio 1.00

UD Heroes of Baseball

Ripken caps off 1983 season by winning MVP

NM/M
Complete Ripken Set (10): 15.00
Common Ripken: 2.00
Complete Morgan Set (10): 4.00
Common Morgan: .50
Complete Stargell Set (10): 5.00
Common Stargell: .50
Complete Seaver Set (10): 10.00
Common Seaver: 1.25
Complete Mantle Set (10): 15.00
Common Mantle: 2.00
Complete DiMaggio Set (10): 12.00
Common DiMaggio: 1.50
Complete Gwynn Set (10): 10.00
Common Gwynn: 1.25
Complete McGwire Set (10): 12.00
Common McGwire: 1.50
Complete Ozzie Smith (10): 8.00
Common Ozzie: 1.00
Sets include Headers
Inserted 1:1

Heroes of Baseball Quads

NM/M
Common Quad: 10.00
Production 85 Sets
1 Joe DiMaggio, Tony Gwynn 15.00
2 Joe DiMaggio, Tony Gwynn, Cal Ripken Jr. 20.00
3 Joe DiMaggio, Mickey Mantle, Willie Stargell 20.00
4 Tony Gwynn, Ozzie Smith, Willie Stargell 10.00
5 Tony Gwynn, Willie Stargell, Joe DiMaggio, Joe Morgan 15.00
6 Tony Gwynn, Willie Stargell, Cal Ripken Jr., Ozzie Smith 15.00
7 Mickey Mantle, Mark McGwire, Joe Morgan, Tom Seaver 20.00
8 Mickey Mantle, Tom Seaver 20.00
9 Mark McGwire, Joe Morgan 20.00
10 Mark McGwire, Cal Ripken Jr., Tony Gwynn, Joe DiMaggio 25.00
11 Mark McGwire, Tom Seaver, Joe Morgan, Ozzie Smith 15.00
12 Joe Morgan, Tony Gwynn 10.00
13 Joe Morgan, Joe DiMaggio, Mickey Mantle, Cal Ripken Jr. 25.00
14 Joe Morgan, Joe DiMaggio, Willie Stargell, Tony Gwynn 15.00
15 Ozzie Smith, Joe DiMaggio, Ozzie Smith, Willie Stargell 15.00
16 Ozzie Smith, Mark McGwire, Willie Stargell, Tony Gwynn 15.00
17 Ozzie Smith, Tom Seaver, Mark McGwire 15.00
18 Cal Ripken Jr., Mickey Mantle, Joe DiMaggio, Joe Morgan 20.00
19 Cal Ripken Jr., Mark McGwire, Cal Ripken Jr. 20.00
20 Tom Seaver, Joe DiMaggio, Tom Seaver, Joe DiMaggio 15.00
21 Willie Stargell, Tom Seaver, Joe Morgan, Ozzie Smith 10.00
22 Tom Seaver, Cal Ripken Jr., Mark McGwire, Mickey Mantle 20.00
23 Willie Stargell, Ozzie Smith 10.00
24 Willie Stargell, Ozzie Smith, Tom Seaver, Joe Morgan 10.00

Future Gems Quads

NM/M
Common Card: 4.00
Inserted 1:Box
1 David Bush, Matt Craig, Blair Johnson, Brian McCann 4.00
2 Jason Cooper, Jonathan George, Larry Broadway, Joel Guzman 4.00
3 Matt Craig, Josh Murray, Brian McCann, Jason Pridie 4.00
4 Jesse Crain, Brian Grant, Curtis Granderson, Joey Gomes 4.00
5 Tyler Davidson, Val Majewski, Kennard Jones, Daniel Cevette 4.00
6 Joe DiMaggio, Jon Lester, Mac, Mark McLemore 4.00
7 Jonathan George, Jeremy Reed, Adam Donachie, Matt Carson 4.00
8 Jonathan George, Eric Thomas, Joel Guzman, Kiel Fisher 4.00
9 Tim Gilhooly, Brandon Wheeder, Brian Slocum, Brian Dopirak 4.00
10 Brian Grant, Rich Hill, Joey Gomes, Joe DiMaggio 4.00
11 Derick Grigsby, Bob Malek, James Loney, Fred Lewis 4.00
12 Zach Hammes, James Holcomb, Cal Ripken Jr., Kennard Jones 4.00
13 Rich Hill, Mark McGwire, Brian Grant, Matt Carson 4.00
14 James Holcomb, David Jensen, Kennard Jones, Ryan Williams 4.00
15 David Jensen, Francisco Liriano, Ryan Williams, Travis Hanson 4.00
16 Blair Johnson, Jesse Crain, Adam Greenberg, Curtis Granderson 4.00
17 Jon Lester, Jonathan George, Adam Donachie, Mark McLemore 4.00
18 Francisco Liriano, Mark McGwire, Travis Hanson, Taber Lee 4.00
19 Val Majewski, Charlie Morton, Daniel Cevette, Joey Gomes 4.00
20 Bob Malek, Zach Hammes, Fred Lewis, Cal Ripken Jr. 4.00
21 Justin Maureau, Joe DiMaggio, Chris Snyder, Mark McGwire 4.00
22 Mark McGwire, Bob Malek, Joe DiMaggio, Kyle Boyer 4.00
23 Charlie Morton, David Bush, Joey Gomes, Blair Johnson 4.00
24 Josh Murray, Mark McGwire, Jason Pridie, Joe DiMaggio 4.00
25 Matt Pender, Mark McGwire, Mark McLemore, Ryan Rodriguez 4.00
26 Jason Pridie, Josh Murray, Matt Craig, Brian McCann 4.00
27 Jeremy Reed, Blair Johnson, Matt Carson, Adam Greenberg 4.00
28 Cal Ripken Jr., Jason Cooper, Matt Carson, Larry Broadway 4.00
29 Ryan Rodriguez, Eric Thomas, Pat Osborn, Randy Braun 4.00
30 Josh Rupe, Tyler Davidson, John Baker, Kennard Jones 4.00
31 Eric Thomas, Derick Grigsby, Randy Braun, James Loney 4.00
32 Eric Thomas, Matt Pender, Kiel Fisher, Mark McLemore 4.00
33 Brandon Wheeder, Rich Hill, Brian Dopirak, Brian Grant 4.00

2002 Upper Deck Rookie Debut

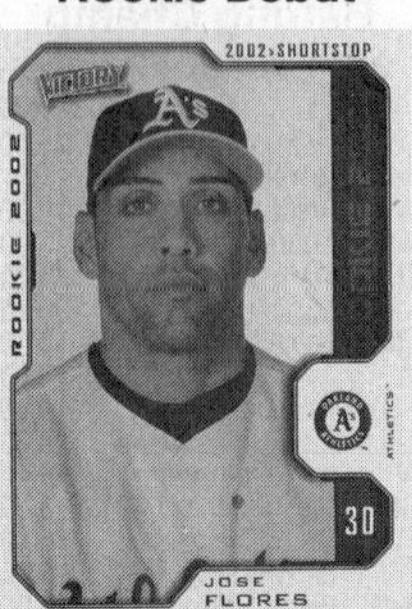

NM/M
Common Player: .10
Pack (5): 1.50
Box (24): 30.00
Honor Roll
Common Honor Roll Rk (131-190): .25
Golds (131-190): 5-10X
Production 50
101 Curt Schilling .40
102 Geronimo Gil .10
103 Cliff Floyd .10
104 Derek Lowe .10
105 Hee Seop Choi .10
106 Mark Prior .50
107 Joe Borchard .10
108 Austin Kearns .40
109 Adam Dunn .50
110 Brandon Phillips .10
111 Carlos Pena .10
112 Andy Van Hekken .10
113 Juan Encarnacion .10
114 Lance Berkman .25
115 Torii Hunter .25
116 Bartolo Colon .10
117 Raul Mondesi .20
118 Alfonso Soriano .75
119 Miguel Tejada .40
120 Ray Durham .10
121 Eric Chavez .20
122 Brett Myers .10
123 Marlon Byrd .10
124 Sean Burroughs .10
125 Kenny Lofton .10
126 Scott Rolen .50
127 Carl Crawford .10
128 Josh Phelps .10
129 Eric Hinske .10
130 Orlando Hudson .10
131 Barry Wesson .40
132 Jose Valverde **RC** .25
133 Kevin Gryboski **RC** .25
134 Trey Hodges **RC** .25
135 Howie Clark **RC** .25
136 Josh Hancock **RC** .25
137 Freddy Sanchez **RC** .25
138 Francis Beltran **RC** .10
139 Mike Mahoney .10
140 Brian Tallet .10
141 Jason Davis **RC** .50
142 Carl Sadler **RC** .25
143 Jason Beverlin **RC** .25
144 Josh Bard **RC** .25
145 Aaron Cook **RC** .25
146 Eric Eckenstahler **RC** .25
147 Tim Kalita **RC** .25
148 Franklyn German **RC** .25
149 Hansel Izquierdo **RC** .25
150 Brandon Puffer **RC** .25
151 Rodrigo Rosario **RC** .25
152 Kirk Saarloos .10
153 Jeriome Robertson **RC** .25
154 Jeremy Hill **RC** .25
155 Wes Obermueller **RC** .25
156 Aaron Guiel **RC** .25
157 Kazuhisa Ishii **RC** 1.00
158 David Ross .10
159 Jayson Durocher **RC** .25
160 Luis Martinez **RC** .25
161 Shane Nance **RC** .25
162 Eric Good **RC** .25
163 Jamey Carroll **RC** .25
164 Jaime Cerda **RC** .25
165 Satoru Komiyama **RC** .25
166 Adam Walker **RC** .25
167 Nate Field **RC** .25
168 Cody McKay **RC** .25
169 Jose Flores **RC** .25
170 Eric Junge **RC** .25
171 Jorge Padilla **RC** .25
172 Oliver Perez **RC** 1.00
173 Julius Matos **RC** .25
174 Wilbert Nieves **RC** .25
175 Clay Condrey **RC** .25
176 Mike Crudale **RC** .25
177 Jason Simontacchi **RC** .50
178 So Taguchi **RC** .50
179 Jose Rodriguez .10
180 Jorge Sosa **RC** .25
181 Felix Escalona **RC** .25
182 Lance Carter **RC** .25
183 Travis Hughes .10
184 Reynaldo Garcia **RC** .25
185 Mike Smith .10
186 Corey Thurman **RC** .25
187 Ken Huckaby **RC** .50
188 Reed Johnson **RC** .50
189 Kevin Cash **RC** .25
190 Scott Wiggins **RC** .25

Ovation
Common SP (151-180): 3.00
Production 2,002
Golds (151-180): 2-4X
Production 50
121 Curt Schilling .50
122 Cliff Floyd .15
123 Derek Lowe .15
124 Hee Seop Choi .25
125 Mark Prior .75
126 Joe Borchard .15
127 Austin Kearns .50
128 Adam Dunn .75
129 Jay Payton .15
130 Carlos Pena .15
131 Andy Van Hekken .15
132 Andres Torres .15
133 Ben Diggins .15
134 Torii Hunter .40
135 Bartolo Colon .25
136 Raul Mondesi .25
137 Alfonso Soriano 1.00
138 Miguel Tejada .75
139 Ray Durham .15
140 Eric Chavez .40
141 Marlon Byrd .15
142 Brett Myers .15
143 Sean Burroughs .15
144 Kenny Lofton .15
145 Scott Rolen .75
146 Carl Crawford .15
147 Jayson Werth .15
148 Josh Phelps .15
149 Eric Hinske .15
150 Orlando Hudson .15
151 Jose Valverde **RC** 5.00
152 Trey Hodges **RC** 3.00
153 Joey Dawley 3.00
154 Travis Driskill **RC** 3.00
155 Howie Clark 3.00
156 Jorge De La Rosa **RC** 3.00
157 Freddy Sanchez 3.00
158 Earl Snyder **RC** 5.00
159 Cliff Lee **RC** 8.00
160 Josh Bard **RC** 3.00
161 Aaron Cook **RC** 3.00
162 Franklyn German **RC** 3.00
163 Brandon Puffer **RC** 3.00
164 Kirk Saarloos 3.00
165 Jeriome Robertson **RC** 3.00
166 Miguel Asencio **RC** 3.00
167 Shawn Sedlacek 3.00
168 Jayson Durocher **RC** 3.00
169 Shane Nance **RC** 3.00
170 Jamey Carroll **RC** 8.00
171 Oliver Perez **RC** 10.00
172 Wilbert Nieves 3.00
173 Clay Condrey **RC** 3.00
174 Chris Snelling **RC** 5.00
175 Mike Crudale **RC** 3.00
176 Jason Simontacchi **RC** 3.00
177 Felix Escalona **RC** 3.00
178 Lance Carter **RC** 3.00
179 Scott Wiggins **RC** 3.00
180 Kevin Cash **RC** 3.00

Victory
Common Rk (606-660): .20
551 John Lackey .25
552 Francisco Rodriguez .50
553 Cliff Floyd .10
554 Derek Lowe .10
555 Mark Bellhorn .10
556 Matt Clement .10
557 Hee Seop Choi .25
558 Joe Borchard .10
559 Ryan Dempster .10
560 Russell Branyan .10
561 Brandon Larson .10
562 Coco Crisp .10
563 Karim Garcia .10
564 Brandon Phillips .10
565 Jay Payton .10
566 Gabe Kapler .10
567 Carlos Pena .10
568 George Lombard .10
569 Andy Van Hekken .10
570 Andres Torres .10
571 Justin Wayne .10
572 Juan Encarnacion .10
573 Abraham Nunez .10
574 Peter Munro .10
575 Jason Lane .10
576 Dave Roberts .10
577 Eric Gagne .10
578 Alex Sanchez .10
579 Jim Rushford **RC** .10
580 Ben Diggins .10
581 Eddie Guardado .10
582 Bartolo Colon .20
583 Endy Chavez .10
584 Raul Mondesi .20
585 Jeff Weaver .10
586 Marcus Thames .10
587 Ted Lilly .10
588 Ray Durham .10
589 Jeremy Giambi .10
590 Vicente Padilla .10
591 Brett Myers .10
592 Josh Fogg .10
593 Tony Alvarez .10
594 Jake Peavy .10
595 Dennis Tankersley .10
596 Sean Burroughs .10
597 Kenny Lofton .10
598 Scott Rolen .50
599 Chuck Finley .10
600 Carl Crawford .10
601 Kevin Mench .10
602 Juan Gonzalez .50
603 Jayson Werth .10
604 Eric Hinske .10
605 Josh Phelps .10
606 Jose Valverde **RC** .20
607 John Ennis **RC** .20
608 Trey Hodges **RC** .20
609 Kevin Gryboski **RC** .20
610 Travis Driskill **RC** .20
611 Howie Clark **RC** .20
612 Freddy Sanchez **RC** .20
613 Josh Hancock **RC** .20
614 Jorge De La Rosa **RC** .20
615 Mike Mahoney .20
616 Jason Davis **RC** .20
617 Josh Bard **RC** .20
618 Jason Beverlin **RC** .20
619 Carl Sadler **RC** .20

620 Earl Snyder **RC** .50
621 Aaron Cook **RC** .20
622 Eric Eckenstahler **RC** .20
623 Franklyn German **RC** .20
624 Kirk Saarloos .50
625 Rodrigo Rosario **RC** .20
626 Jeriome Robertson **RC** .20
627 Brandon Puffer **RC** .20
628 Miguel Asencio **RC** .20
629 Aaron Guiel **RC** .30
630 Ryan Bukvich **RC** .20
631 Jeremy Hill **RC** .20
632 Kazuhisa Ishii **RC** .75
633 Jayson Durocher **RC** .20
634 Shane Nance **RC** .20
635 Eric Good **RC** .20
636 Jamey Carroll **RC** .50
637 Jaime Cerda **RC** .20
638 Nate Field **RC** .20
639 Cody McKay **RC** .20
640 Jose Flores **RC** .20
641 Jorge Padilla **RC** .20
642 Anderson Machado **RC** .20
643 Eric Junge **RC** .20
644 Oliver Perez **RC** .75
645 Julius Matos **RC** .20
646 Ben Howard **RC** .20
647 Julio Mateo **RC** .20
648 Matt Thornton .10
649 Chris Snelling **RC** .50
650 Jason Simontacchi **RC** .50
651 So Taguchi **RC** .40
652 Mike Crudale **RC** .20
653 Mike Coolbaugh .10
654 Felix Escalona **RC** .20
655 Jorge Sosa **RC** .20
656 Lance Carter **RC** .20
657 Reynaldo Garcia **RC** .20
658 Kevin Cash **RC** .40
659 Ken Huckaby **RC** .20
660 Scott Wiggins **RC** .20

Climbing the Ladder

Common Player:
Production 25 Sets, Not Priced

Elite Company

Common Player:
Production 25, Not Priced

Making Their Marks

Common Player:
Production 25 Sets, Not Priced

Solid Contact

NM/M
Common Player: 4.00
Inserted 1:24
BA Bobby Abreu 4.00
EA Edgardo Alfonzo 4.00
RA Roberto Alomar 10.00
MA Moises Alou 6.00
JC Jose Cruz Jr. 6.00
CD Carlos Delgado/SP 8.00
JE Jim Edmonds 6.00
CE Carl Everett 4.00
JG Jason Giambi/50 15.00
BG Brian Giles 6.00
KG Ken Griffey Jr. 15.00
TH Todd Helton 8.00
JK Jason Kendall 4.00
BL Barry Larkin 10.00
EM Edgar Martinez 8.00
FM Fred McGriff 8.00
DM Doug Mientkiewicz 6.00
JO John Olerud 6.00
MO Magglio Ordonez 6.00
JP Jorge Posada 10.00
AR Alex Rodriguez 15.00
IR Ivan Rodriguez 6.00
GS Gary Sheffield 6.00
SS Sammy Sosa 15.00
TA Fernando Tatis 4.00
FT Frank Thomas 8.00
JT Jim Thome 12.00
OV Omar Vizquel 6.00
BW Bernie Williams 8.00
MW Matt Williams 4.00

2002 Upper Deck Rookie Update

NM/M
Common Player: .25
Pack (5): 3.00
Box (15): 35.00
SP Authentic
Common SP (201-230): 5.00
Production 1,999
171 Erubiel Durazo .25
172 Junior Spivey .25
173 Geronimo Gil .25
174 Cliff Floyd .25

175 Brandon Larsen .25
176 Aaron Boone .25
177 Shawn Estes .25
178 Austin Kearns .75
179 Joe Borchard .25
180 Russell Branyan .25
181 Jay Payton .25
182 Andres Torres .25
183 Andy Van Hekken .25
184 Alex Sanchez .25
185 Endy Chavez .25
186 Bartolo Colon .25
187 Raul Mondesi .40
188 Robin Ventura .25
189 Mike Mussina .75
190 Jorge Posada .75
191 Ted Lilly .25
192 Ray Durham .25
193 Brett Myers .25
194 Marlon Byrd .25
195 Vicente Padilla .25
196 Josh Fogg .25
197 Kenny Lofton .25
198 Scott Rolen 1.00
199 Jason Lane .25
200 Josh Phelps .25
201 Travis Driskill **RC** 5.00
202 Howie Clark **RC** 5.00
203 Mike Mahoney 5.00
204 Brian Tallet 5.00
205 Kirk Saarloos 5.00
206 Barry Wesson 5.00
207 Aaron Guiel **RC** 5.00
208 Shawn Sedlacek 5.00
209 Jose Diaz 5.00
210 Jorge Nunez 5.00
211 Danny Mota 5.00
212 David Ross 5.00
213 Jayson Durocher **RC** 5.00
214 Shane Nance **RC** 5.00
215 Wilbert Nieves **RC** 5.00
216 Freddy Sanchez **RC** 5.00
217 Alex Pelaez 5.00
218 Jamey Carroll **RC** 5.00
219 J.J. Trujillo 5.00
220 Kevin Pickford 5.00
221 Clay Condrey **RC** 5.00
222 Chris Snelling **RC** 5.00
223 Cliff Lee **RC** 8.00
224 Jeremy Hill **RC** 5.00
225 Jose Rodriguez 5.00
226 Lance Carter **RC** 5.00
227 Ken Huckaby **RC** 5.00
228 Scott Wiggins **RC** 5.00
229 Corey Thurman **RC** 5.00
230 Kevin Cash **RC** 5.00
SPx
Common SPx Auto. (221-250): 10.00
Production 825
191 Tom Glavine .75
192 Cliff Floyd .25
193 Mark Prior 1.50
194 Corey Patterson .50
195 Paul Konerko .50
196 Adam Dunn 1.00
197 Joe Borchard .25
198 Carlos Pena .25
199 Juan Encarnacion .25
200 Luis Castillo .25
201 Torii Hunter .50
202 Hee Seop Choi .50
203 Bartolo Colon .40
204 Raul Mondesi .40
205 Jeff Weaver .25
206 Eric Munson .25
207 Alfonso Soriano 1.00
208 Ray Durham .25
209 Eric Chavez .50
210 Brett Myers .25
211 Jeremy Giambi .25
212 Vicente Padilla .25
213 Felipe Lopez .25
214 Sean Burroughs .25
215 Kenny Lofton .25
216 Scott Rolen 1.00
217 Carl Crawford .25
218 Juan Gonzalez .75
219 Orlando Hudson .25
220 Eric Hinske .25
221 Adam Walker **RC** 10.00
222 Aaron Cook **RC** 10.00
223 Cam Esslinger **RC** 10.00
224 Kirk Saarloos 10.00
225 Jose Diaz 10.00
226 David Ross 10.00
227 Jayson Durocher **RC** 10.00
228 Brian Mallette 10.00
229 Aaron Guiel **RC** 10.00
230 Jorge Nunez 10.00
231 Satoru Komiyama **RC** 15.00
232 Tyler Yates **RC** 15.00
233 Peter Zamora **RC** 10.00
234 Mike Gonzalez **RC** 10.00
235 Oliver Perez **RC** 30.00
236 Julius Matos **RC** 10.00
237 Andy Shibilo 10.00
238 Jason Simontacchi **RC** 10.00
239 Ron Chiavacci 10.00
240 Deivis Santos 10.00
241 Travis Driskill **RC** 10.00
242 Jorge De La Rosa **RC** 10.00
243 Anastacio Martinez **RC** 10.00
244 Earl Snyder **RC** 10.00
245 Freddy Sanchez **RC** 10.00
246 Miguel Asencio **RC** 10.00
247 Juan Brito 10.00
248 Franklyn German **RC** 10.00
249 Chris Snelling **RC** 10.00
250 Ken Huckaby **RC** 10.00
Diamond Connection
Common SP (601-630): 4.00
Production 1,999
571 Erubiel Durazo .25
572 Geronimo Gil .25
573 Shea Hillenbrand .50
574 Cliff Floyd .25
575 Corey Patterson .50
576 Joe Borchard .25
577 Austin Kearns .75
578 Ryan Dempster .25
579 Brandon Larsen .25
580 Luis Castillo .25
581 Juan Encarnacion .25
582 Chin-Feng Chen .25
583 Hideo Nomo .75
584 Bartolo Colon .40
585 Raul Mondesi .40
586 Eric Munson .25
587 Alfonso Soriano 1.00
588 Ted Lilly .25
589 Ray Durham .25
590 Brett Myers .25
591 Brandon Phillips .25
592 Kenny Lofton .25
593 Scott Rolen 1.00
594 Jim Edmonds .50
595 Carl Crawford .25
596 Hank Blalock .50
597 Kevin Mench .25
598 Josh Phelps .25
599 Orlando Hudson .25
600 Eric Hinske .25
601 Mike Mahoney 4.00
602 Jason Davis **RC** 8.00
603 Trey Hodges **RC** 4.00
604 Josh Bard **RC** 4.00
605 Jeriome Robertson **RC** 4.00
606 Jose Diaz 4.00
607 Jorge Nunez 4.00
608 Danny Mota 4.00
609 David Ross 4.00
610 Jayson Durocher **RC** 4.00
611 Freddy Sanchez **RC** 4.00
612 Julius Matos **RC** 4.00
613 Wilbert Nieves **RC** 4.00
614 Brian Kozlowski 4.00
615 Jason Simontacchi **RC** 4.00
616 Mike Coolbaugh 4.00
617 Travis Driskill **RC** 4.00
618 Howie Clark **RC** 4.00
619 Earl Snyder **RC** 6.00
620 Carl Sadler **RC** 4.00
621 Jason Beverlin **RC** 4.00
622 Terry Pearson 4.00
623 Eric Eckenstahler **RC** 4.00
624 Shawn Sedlacek 4.00
625 Aaron Guiel **RC** 5.00
626 Ryan Bukvich **RC** 4.00
627 Julio Mateo **RC** 4.00
628 Chris Snelling **RC** 6.00
629 Lance Carter **RC** 4.00
630 Scott Wiggins **RC** 4.00

Star Tributes

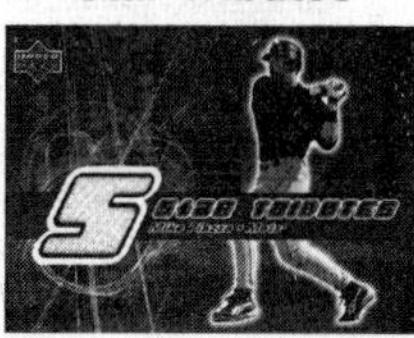

NM/M
Common Player: 5.00
Inserted 1:15
JB Josh Beckett 8.00
LB Lance Berkman 6.00
RC Roger Clemens 15.00
CD Carlos Delgado 5.00
JD Joe DiMaggio/SP 75.00
AD Adam Dunn 8.00
JG Jason Giambi 10.00
TG Tom Glavine 8.00
LG Luis Gonzalez/SP 8.00
SG Shawn Green 5.00
KG Ken Griffey Jr. 12.00
KI Kazuhisa Ishii 8.00
RJ Randy Johnson 10.00
CJ Chipper Jones 10.00
PM Pedro J. Martinez 8.00
MM Mark McGwire/SP 50.00
RP Rafael Palmeiro 8.00
MPi Mike Piazza 10.00
MPr Mark Prior 5.00
AR Alex Rodriguez 10.00
IR Ivan Rodriguez 8.00
KS Kazuhiro Sasaki 5.00
CS Curt Schilling 8.00
TS Tsuyoshi Shinjo 5.00
AS Alfonso Soriano 10.00
SS Sammy Sosa 12.00
MS Mike Sweeney 5.00
FT Frank Thomas 8.00

Signed Star Tributes

NM/M
Production 50 Sets
Copper & Silver: No Pricing
Production 25
Gold: No Pricing
Production 5
SS-MM Mark McGwire 350.00

USA Future Watch Swatches

NM/M
Common Player: 5.00
Inserted 1:15
Red: 1.5-2X
Production 50
Copper: No Pricing
Production 25
Gold: No Pricing
Production 5
AA Abe Alvarez 5.00
MA Michael Aubrey 10.00
KB Kyle Bakker 8.00
CC Chad Cordero 5.00
SC Shane Costa 5.00
SF Sam Fuld 8.00
AH Aaron Hill 8.00
PH Philip Humber 8.00
CJ Conor Jackson 5.00
GJ Grant Johnson 5.00
MJ Mark Jurich 5.00
WL Wes Littleton 8.00
EP Eric Patterson 5.00
DP Dustin Pedroia 5.00
LP Landon Powell 5.00
CQ Carlos Quentin 8.00
CS Clint Sammons 5.00
KS Kyle Sleeth 10.00
HS Huston Street 5.00
BS Brad Sullivan 8.00
RW Rickie Weeks 15.00
BZ Bob Zimmermann 5.00

2002 Upper Deck Sweet Spot

NM/M
Complete Set (175):
Common Player: .25
Common (91-130): 4.00
Production 1,300
Common Auto. (131-145): 15.00
Production 750 or 100
Common Game Faces (146-175): 3.00
Inserted 1:24
Parallel (146-175): 1.5X-3X
Production 100
Pack (4): 8.00
Box (12): 90.00
1 Troy Glaus .50
2 Darin Erstad .50
3 Tim Hudson .50
4 Eric Chavez .50
5 Barry Zito .50
6 Miguel Tejada .50
7 Carlos Delgado .50
8 Eric Hinske .25
9 Ben Grieve .25
10 Jim Thome 1.00
11 C.C. Sabathia .25
12 Omar Vizquel .40
13 Ichiro Suzuki 2.00
14 Edgar Martinez .40
15 Bret Boone .40
16 Freddy Garcia .25
17 Tony Batista .25
18 Geronimo Gil .25
19 Alex Rodriguez 2.50
20 Rafael Palmeiro .75
21 Ivan Rodriguez .75
22 Hank Blalock .50
23 Juan Gonzalez .75
24 Nomar Garciaparra 2.00
25 Pedro J. Martinez 1.00
26 Manny Ramirez 1.00
27 Mike Sweeney .25
28 Carlos Beltran .50
29 Dmitri Young .25
30 Torii Hunter .50
31 Eric Milton .25
32 Corey Koskie .25
33 Frank Thomas .75
34 Mark Buehrle .25
35 Magglio Ordonez .50
36 Roger Clemens 2.00
37 Derek Jeter 3.00
38 Jason Giambi .75
39 Alfonso Soriano 1.00
40 Bernie Williams .50
41 Jeff Bagwell .75
42 Roy Oswalt .50
43 Lance Berkman .50
44 Greg Maddux 1.50
45 Chipper Jones 1.00
46 Gary Sheffield .50
47 Andruw Jones .75
48 Richie Sexson .50
49 Ben Sheets .50
50 Albert Pujols 2.00
51 Matt Morris .40
52 J.D. Drew .50
53 Sammy Sosa 2.00
54 Kerry Wood 1.00
55 Mark Prior 1.00
56 Moises Alou .50
57 Corey Patterson .50
58 Randy Johnson 1.00
59 Luis Gonzalez .40
60 Curt Schilling .75
61 Shawn Green .50
62 Kevin Brown .40
63 Paul LoDuca .25
64 Adrian Beltre .50
65 Vladimir Guerrero 1.00
66 Jose Vidro .25
67 Javier Vazquez .25
68 Barry Bonds 3.00
69 Jeff Kent .40
70 Rich Aurilia .25
71 Mike Lowell .40
72 Josh Beckett .50
73 Brad Penny .25
74 Roberto Alomar .50
75 Mike Piazza 1.50
76 Jeromy Burnitz .25
77 Mo Vaughn .25
78 Phil Nevin .25
79 Sean Burroughs .25
80 Jeremy Giambi .25
81 Bobby Abreu .50
82 Jimmy Rollins .50
83 Pat Burrell .50
84 Brian Giles .50
85 Aramis Ramirez .50
86 Ken Griffey Jr. 1.50
87 Adam Dunn .75
88 Austin Kearns .50
89 Todd Helton .75
90 Larry Walker .50
91 Earl Snyder **RC** 6.00
92 Jorge Padilla **RC** 4.00
93 Felix Escalona **RC** 4.00
94 John Foster **RC** 4.00
95 Brandon Puffer **RC** 4.00
96 Steve Bechler **RC** 4.00
97 Hansel Izquierdo **RC** 4.00
98 Chris Baker **RC** 4.00
99 Jeremy Ward **RC** 4.00
100 Kevin Frederick **RC** 4.00
101 Josh Hancock **RC** 4.00
102 Allan Simpson **RC** 4.00
103 Mitch Wylie **RC** 4.00
104 Mark Corey **RC** 4.00
105 Victor Alvarez **RC** 4.00
106 Todd Donovan **RC** 4.00
107 Nelson Castro **RC** 4.00
108 Chris Booker **RC** 4.00
109 Corey Thurman **RC** 4.00
110 Kirk Saarloos 4.00
111 Michael Crudale **RC** 4.00
112 Jason Simontacchi **RC** 4.00
113 Ron Calloway **RC** 4.00
114 Brandon Backe **RC** 4.00
115 Tom Shearn **RC** 4.00
116 Oliver Perez **RC** 6.00
117 Kyle Kane **RC** 4.00
118 Francis Beltran **RC** 4.00
119 So Taguchi **RC** 8.00
120 Doug DeVore **RC** 4.00
121 Juan Brito **RC** 4.00
122 Clifford Bartosh **RC** 4.00
123 Eric Junge **RC** 4.00
124 Joe Orloski **RC** 4.00
125 Scotty Layfield **RC** 4.00
126 Jorge Sosa **RC** 4.00
127 Satoru Komiyama **RC** 4.00
128 Edwin Almonte **RC** 4.00
129 Takahito Nomura **RC** 4.00
130 John Ennis **RC** 4.00
131 Kazuhisa Ishii/ Auto./100 **RC** 90.00
132 Ben Howard/ Auto./100 **RC** 20.00
133 Aaron Cook/ Auto./750 **RC** 15.00
134 Anderson Machado/ Auto./750 **RC** 15.00
135 Luis Ugueto/ Auto./750 **RC** 15.00
136 Tyler Yates/ Auto./750 **RC** 20.00
137 Rodrigo Rosario/ Auto./750 **RC** 15.00
138 Jaime Cerda/ Auto./750 **RC** 15.00
139 Luis Martinez/ Auto./750 **RC** 15.00
140 Rene Reyes/ Auto./750 **RC** 15.00
141 Eric Good/ Auto./750 **RC** 15.00
142 Matt Thornton/ Auto./100 25.00
143 Steve Kent/ Auto./750 **RC** 15.00
144 Jose Valverde/ Auto./750 **RC** 15.00
145 Adrian Burnside/ Auto./750 **RC** 15.00
146 Barry Bonds 15.00
147 Ken Griffey Jr. 10.00
148 Alex Rodriguez 12.00
149 Jason Giambi 4.00
150 Chipper Jones 5.00
151 Nomar Garciaparra 10.00
152 Mike Piazza 10.00
153 Sammy Sosa 10.00
154 Derek Jeter 15.00
155 Jeff Bagwell 4.00
156 Albert Pujols 10.00
157 Ichiro Suzuki 10.00
158 Randy Johnson 5.00
159 Frank Thomas 4.00
160 Greg Maddux 8.00
161 Jim Thome 5.00
162 Scott Rolen 6.00
163 Shawn Green 3.00
164 Vladimir Guerrero 6.00
165 Troy Glaus 3.00
166 Carlos Delgado 4.00
167 Luis Gonzalez 3.00
168 Roger Clemens 10.00
169 Todd Helton 4.00
170 Eric Chavez 3.00
171 Rafael Palmeiro 4.00
172 Pedro J. Martinez 5.00
173 Lance Berkman 3.00
174 Josh Beckett 4.00
175 Sean Burroughs 3.00

Bat Barrels

Common Player:
100 Total Produced

Legendary Signatures

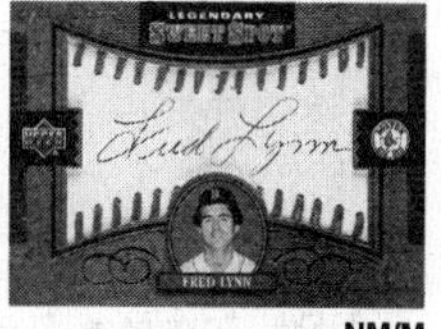

NM/M
Common Autograph: 20.00
Inserted 1:72
LA Luis Aparicio/485 25.00
RF Rollie Fingers/866 20.00
SG Steve Garvey/871 20.00
KH Keith Hernandez/906 20.00
FJ Ferguson Jenkins/ 857 20.00
AK Al Kaline/835 40.00
SK Sandy Koufax/485 200.00
FL Fred Lynn/853 20.00
MM Mark McGwire/90 575.00
PM Paul Molitor/852 30.00
GP Gaylord Perry/921 25.00
BP Boog Powell/944 20.00
CR Cal Ripken Jr./194 175.00
BR Brooks Robinson 35.00
AT Alan Trammell/843 25.00

McGwire Priority Signing Auto

NM/M
100 Redemptions Produced
MM Mark McGwire 350.00

Signatures

NM/M
Common Autograph: 20.00
Inserted 1:72
LB Lance Berkman/291 35.00
HB Hank Blalock/291 40.00
BB Barry Bonds/380 200.00
JB Jeromy Burnitz/291 20.00
SB Sean Burroughs/291 20.00
RC Roger Clemens/194 150.00
CD Carlos Delgado/291 25.00
AD Adam Dunn/291 40.00
FG Freddy Garcia/145 25.00
JG Jason Giambi/291 40.00
BG Brian Giles/291 25.00
TG Tom Glavine/291 40.00
LG Luis Gonzalez/291 20.00
KG Ken Griffey Jr./291 125.00
AJ Andruw Jones/291 25.00
RO Roy Oswalt/291 20.00
MPr Mark Prior/291 60.00
AR Alex Rodriguez/291 160.00
SR Scott Rolen/291 40.00
SS Sammy Sosa/145 200.00
MS Mike Sweeney/291 20.00
IS Ichiro Suzuki/145 400.00
FT Frank Thomas/291 60.00
JT Jim Thome/291 50.00
BZ Barry Zito/291 30.00

Sweet Swatches

NM/M
Common Player: 5.00
Inserted 1:12
JBa Jeff Bagwell 8.00
JBe Josh Beckett 6.00
SB Sean Burroughs 5.00
EC Eric Chavez 6.00
JE Jim Edmonds 8.00
DE Darin Erstad 5.00
JGi Jason Giambi 8.00
BG Brian Giles 5.00
JGo Juan Gonzalez 6.00
LG Luis Gonzalez 5.00
SG Shawn Green 5.00
KG Ken Griffey Jr. 15.00
KI Kazuhisa Ishii 10.00
CJ Chipper Jones 10.00
GM Greg Maddux 12.00
PM Pedro J. Martinez 10.00
MP Mike Piazza 15.00
AR Alex Rodriguez 15.00
IR Ivan Rodriguez 8.00
SR Scott Rolen 8.00
SS Sammy Sosa 15.00
IS Ichiro Suzuki 40.00
FT Frank Thomas 8.00
OV Omar Vizquel 5.00
BW Bernie Williams 8.00

USA Jerseys

NM/M
Common Player: 5.00
Inserted 1:12
BA Brent Abernathy 5.00
TB Taggert Bozied 8.00
DB Dewon Brazelton 5.00
AE Adam Everett 5.00
DG Danny Graves 5.00
JG Jake Gautreau 5.00
JK Josh Karp 5.00
AK Adam Kennedy 8.00
JM Joe Mauer 20.00
DM Doug Mientkiewicz 6.00
EM Eric Munson 5.00
XN Xavier Nady 5.00
RO Roy Oswalt 8.00
MP Mark Prior 10.00
JR Jon Rauch 5.00
MT Mark Teixeira 8.00
JW Justin Wayne 5.00

2002 Upper Deck Sweet Spot Classics

NM/M
Complete Set (90): 40.00
Common Player: .40
Pack (4): 20.00
Box (12): 200.00
1 Mickey Mantle 4.00
2 Joe DiMaggio 3.00
3 Babe Ruth 3.00
4 Ty Cobb 1.50
5 Nolan Ryan 3.00
6 Sandy Koufax 2.00
7 Cy Young 1.00
8 Roberto Clemente 2.00
9 Lefty Grove .50
10 Lou Gehrig 2.50
11 Walter Johnson 1.00
12 Honus Wagner 1.00
13 Christy Mathewson .75
14 Jackie Robinson 1.50
15 Joe Morgan .50
16 Reggie Jackson .75
17 Eddie Collins .40
18 Cal Ripken Jr. 3.00
19 Hank Greenberg .40
20 Harmon Killebrew .75
21 Johnny Bench 1.00
22 Ernie Banks 1.00
23 Willie McCovey .40
24 Mel Ott .40
25 Tom Seaver 1.00
26 Tony Gwynn .75
27 Dave Winfield .50
28 Willie Stargell .40
29 Mark McGwire 2.00
30 Al Kaline .75
31 Jimmie Foxx .75
32 Satchel Paige 1.50
33 Eddie Murray .40
34 Lou Boudreau .40
35 "Shoeless" Joe Jackson 1.50
36 Luke Appling .40
37 Ralph Kiner .40
38 Robin Yount .75
39 Paul Molitor .75
40 Juan Marichal .40
41 Brooks Robinson .75
42 Wade Boggs .50
43 Kirby Puckett 1.00
44 Yogi Berra 1.00
45 George Sisler .40
46 Buck Leonard .40
47 Billy Williams .40
48 Duke Snider .75
49 Don Drysdale .60
50 Bill Mazeroski .40
51 Tony Oliva .40
52 Luis Aparicio .40
53 Carlton Fisk .40
54 Kirk Gibson .40
55 Jim "Catfish" Hunter .40
56 Joe Carter .40
57 Gaylord Perry .40
58 Don Mattingly 2.00
59 Eddie Mathews 1.25
60 Ferguson Jenkins .40
61 Roy Campanella 1.00
62 Orlando Cepeda .40
63 Tony Perez .40
64 Dave Parker .40
65 Richie Ashburn .40
66 Andre Dawson .40
67 Dwight Evans .40
68 Rollie Fingers .40
69 Dale Murphy .40
70 Ron Santo .40
71 Steve Garvey .40
72 Monte Irvin .40
73 Alan Trammell .40
74 Ryne Sandberg 1.00
75 Gary Carter .40
76 Fred Lynn .40
77 Maury Wills .40
78 Ozzie Smith 1.00
79 Bobby Bonds .60
80 Mickey Cochrane .60
81 Dizzy Dean .60
82 Graig Nettles .60
83 Keith Hernandez .40
84 Boog Powell .40
85 Jack Clark .40
86 Dave Stewart .40
87 Tommy Lasorda .40
88 Dennis Eckersley .40
89 Ken Griffey Sr. .40
90 Bucky Dent .40

Bat Barrels

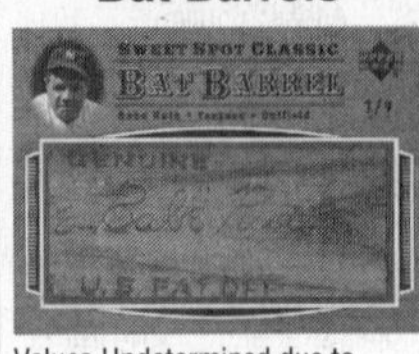

Values Undetermined due to scarcity.

Game Jersey

NM/M
Common Player: 5.00
Inserted 1:8
WB Wade Boggs 12.00
GC Gary Carter 10.00
JC Joe Carter 5.00
JD Joe DiMaggio/53 180.00
RF Rollie Fingers 5.00
SG Steve Garvey 5.00
TG Tony Gwynn 15.00
RJ Reggie Jackson 15.00
SK Sandy Koufax/SP 125.00
BM Bill Madlock 5.00
MM Mickey Mantle/53 250.00
JMa Juan Marichal 10.00
DM Don Mattingly 25.00
PM Paul Molitor 15.00
EM Eddie Murray 10.00
GN Graig Nettles 8.00
DP Dave Parker 5.00
CR Cal Ripken Jr. 25.00
NR Nolan Ryan 40.00
RS Ryne Sandberg 15.00
TS Tom Seaver 15.00
OS Ozzie Smith 15.00
DSn Duke Snider/53 80.00
WS Willie Stargell 10.00
DSt Dave Stewart 5.00
BW Billy Williams 8.00
RY Robin Yount 15.00

Game Jersey Gold

The game-jersey cards in Sweet Spot Classics were paralleled in a special Gold Edition, with each player's swatch cards numbered within an edition of 25 each.

No Pricing
Production 25 Sets

Game-Used Bats

NM/M
Common Player: 5.00
Inserted 1:8
JB Johnny Bench 15.00
YB Yogi Berra 15.00
WB Wade Boggs 12.00
BBo Bob Boone 5.00
BBu Bill Buckner 5.00
GC Gary Carter 10.00
RC Roberto Clemente 50.00
BD Bucky Dent 8.00
JD Joe DiMaggio/40 180.00
DE Dwight Evans 8.00
SG Steve Garvey 8.00
HG Hank Greenberg/SP 50.00
KG Ken Griffey Sr. 5.00
TG Tony Gwynn 15.00
RJ Reggie Jackson 10.00
FJ Ferguson Jenkins 10.00
AK Al Kaline 15.00
FL Fred Lynn 5.00
BM Bill Madlock 5.00
DM Don Mattingly 25.00
PM Paul Molitor 15.00
TM Thurman Munson 35.00
GN Graig Nettles 8.00
DP Dave Parker 5.00
KP Kirby Puckett 15.00
CR Cal Ripken Jr. 25.00
BR Brooks Robinson 15.00
NR Nolan Ryan 40.00
BW Billy Williams 8.00
DW Dave Winfield 10.00

Game-Used Bats Gold

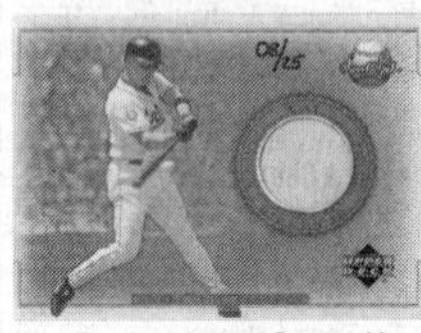

Each of the Game-Used Bats cards in Sweet Spot Classics can also be found in a Gold Edition, numbered to just 25 for each player.

NM/M
Common Player: 25.00
JB Johnny Bench 100.00
YB Yogi Berra 125.00
WB Wade Boggs 100.00
BBo Bob Boone 40.00
BBu Bill Buckner 35.00
GC Gary Carter 40.00
RC Roberto Clemente 250.00
BD Bucky Dent 25.00
JD Joe DiMaggio 250.00
DE Dwight Evans 25.00
SG Steve Garvey 35.00
HG Hank Greenberg 125.00
KG Ken Griffey Sr. 25.00
TG Tony Gwynn 150.00
RJ Reggie Jackson 150.00
FJ Ferguson Jenkins 45.00
AK Al Kaline 75.00
FL Fred Lynn 25.00
BM Bill Madlock 25.00
DM Don Mattingly 125.00
PM Paul Molitor 40.00
TM Thurman Munson 150.00
GN Graig Nettles 25.00
DP Dave Parker 25.00
KP Kirby Puckett 125.00
CR Cal Ripken Jr. 225.00
BR Brooks Robinson 75.00
NR Nolan Ryan 175.00
BW Billy Williams 45.00
DW Dave Winfield 45.00

Sweet Spot Signatures

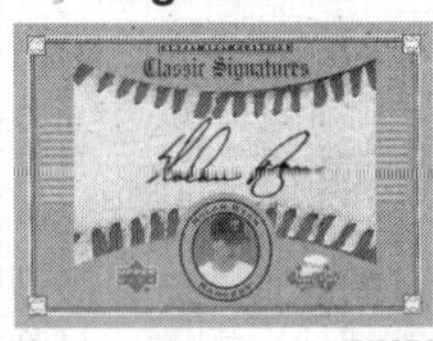

NM/M
Common Autograph: 20.00
Inserted 1:24
EB Ernie Banks 60.00
JB Johnny Bench 60.00
YB Yogi Berra/100 150.00
AD Andre Dawson/100 100.00
BD Bucky Dent 20.00
DeE Dennis Eckersley 40.00
RF Rollie Fingers 25.00
CF Carlton Fisk/100 125.00
SG Steve Garvey 25.00
KG Kirk Gibson/SP 50.00
KH Keith Hernandez 30.00
RJ Reggie Jackson/SP 100.00
FJ Ferguson Jenkins 25.00
AK Al Kaline 40.00
SK Sandy Koufax/SP 250.00
TL Tommy Lasorda 35.00
FL Fred Lynn 25.00
DoM Don Mattingly 100.00
BM Bill Mazeroski 40.00
WM Willie McCovey/SP 75.00
PM Paul Molitor 40.00
JM Joe Morgan 25.00
DaM Dale Murphy 50.00
GP Gaylord Perry 25.00
BP Boog Powell 25.00
KP Kirby Puckett 180.00
CR Cal Ripken Jr. 180.00
BR Brooks Robinson 50.00
NR Nolan Ryan/74 300.00
TS Tom Seaver 50.00
OS Ozzie Smith/137 200.00
DaS Dave Stewart 25.00
AT Alan Trammell 30.00
DW Dave Winfield/70 125.00

Sweet Spot Signatures Gold

Each of the Sweet Spot Signatures autographed ball-panel cards was also made in a Gold Edition numbered to just 25 of each player.

No Pricing
Production 25 Sets

Classic Signatures - Hawaii

As part of its participation in the Hawaii hobby trade conference in March, 2002, Upper Deck foil-packed 400 specially marked pieces of its Classic Signatures insert card for distribution to retailers. The ultra-thick cards with an actual autographed piece of baseball displayed are overprinted "HAWAII XVII" in the lower-right corner. Numbers in parentheses are the reported production for that player.

NM/M
Common Player: 50.00
AD Andre Dawson/10 200.00
AK Al Kaline/25 80.00
AT Alan Trammell/25 60.00
BD Bucky Dent/25 50.00
BP Boog Powell/25 60.00
BR Brooks Robinson/25 150.00
CF Carlton Fisk/10 200.00
CR Cal Ripken Jr./10 600.00
DaM Dale Murphy/10 400.00
DaS Dave Stewart/25 50.00
DeE Dennis Eckersley/25 75.00
EB Ernie Banks/10 150.00
FJ Ferguson Jenkins/25 50.00
FL Fred Lynn/25 75.00
GP Gaylord Perry/25 75.00
KH Keith Hernandez/20 65.00
PM Paul Molitor/25 75.00
RF Rollie Fingersv 60.00
SG Steve Garvey/25 75.00
SK Sandy Koufax/5 800.00

2002 Upper Deck UD-Plus

NM/M
Common Player: 2.00
Production 1,125 Sets
1 two-card pack per Series 2 H pack
Comp. Set can be exchanged for Jsy cards
Redemption Deadline 5-16-03
UD1 Darin Erstad 3.00
UD2 Troy Glaus 3.00
UD3 Tim Hudson 3.00
UD4 Jermaine Dye 2.00
UD5 Barry Zito 2.00
UD6 Carlos Delgado 3.00
UD7 Shannon Stewart 2.00
UD8 Greg Vaughn 2.00
UD9 Jim Thome 5.00
UD10 C.C. Sabathia 2.00
UD11 Ichiro Suzuki 10.00
UD12 Edgar Martinez 2.00
UD13 Bret Boone 2.00
UD14 Freddy Garcia 2.00
UD15 Matt Thornton 2.00
UD16 Jeff Conine 2.00
UD17 Steve Bechler 2.00
UD18 Rafael Palmeiro 4.00
UD19 Juan Gonzalez 4.00
UD20 Alex Rodriguez 10.00
UD21 Ivan Rodriguez 4.00
UD22 Carl Everett 2.00
UD23 Manny Ramirez 4.00
UD24 Nomar Garciaparra 10.00
UD25 Pedro J. Martinez 4.00
UD26 Mike Sweeney 2.00
UD27 Chuck Knoblauch 2.00
UD28 Dmitri Young 2.00
UD29 Bobby Higginson 2.00
UD30 Dean Palmer 2.00
UD31 Doug Mientkiewicz 2.00
UD32 Corey Koskie 2.00
UD33 Brad Radke 2.00
UD34 Cristian Guzman 2.00
UD35 Frank Thomas 4.00
UD36 Magglio Ordonez 3.00
UD37 Carlos Lee 2.00
UD38 Roger Clemens 10.00
UD39 Bernie Williams 3.00
UD40 Derek Jeter 15.00
UD41 Jason Giambi 4.00
UD42 Mike Mussina 3.00
UD43 Jeff Bagwell 4.00
UD44 Lance Berkman 3.00
UD45 Wade Miller 2.00
UD46 Greg Maddux 8.00
UD47 Chipper Jones 5.00
UD48 Andruw Jones 4.00
UD49 Gary Sheffield 3.00
UD50 Richie Sexson 3.00
UD51 Albert Pujols 10.00
UD52 J.D. Drew 3.00
UD53 Matt Morris 2.00
UD54 Jim Edmonds 3.00
UD55 So Taguchi 2.00
UD56 Sammy Sosa 10.00
UD57 Fred McGriff 3.00
UD58 Kerry Wood 5.00
UD59 Moises Alou 3.00
UD60 Randy Johnson 5.00
UD61 Luis Gonzalez 3.00
UD62 Mark Grace 3.00
UD63 Curt Schilling 4.00
UD64 Matt Williams 2.00
UD65 Kevin Brown 3.00
UD66 Brian Jordan 2.00
UD67 Shawn Green 3.00
UD68 Hideo Nomo 3.00
UD69 Kazuhisa Ishii 4.00
UD70 Vladimir Guerrero 4.00
UD71 Jose Vidro 2.00
UD72 Eric Good 2.00
UD73 Barry Bonds 15.00
UD74 Jeff Kent 3.00
UD75 Rich Aurilia 2.00
UD76 Deivis Santos 2.00
UD77 Preston Wilson 2.00
UD78 Cliff Floyd 2.00
UD79 Josh Beckett 4.00
UD80 Hansel Izquierdo 2.00
UD81 Mike Piazza 10.00
UD82 Roberto Alomar 3.00
UD83 Mo Vaughn 3.00
UD84 Jeromy Burnitz 2.00
UD85 Phil Nevin 2.00
UD86 Ryan Klesko 2.00
UD87 Bobby Abreu 3.00
UD88 Scott Rolen 5.00
UD89 Jimmy Rollins 2.50
UD90 Jason Kendall 2.00
UD91 Brian Giles 3.00
UD92 Aramis Ramirez 3.00
UD93 Ken Griffey Jr. 10.00
UD94 Sean Casey 2.00
UD95 Barry Larkin 3.00
UD96 Adam Dunn 4.00
UD97 Todd Helton 4.00
UD98 Larry Walker 3.00
UD99 Mike Hampton 2.00
UD100 Rene Reyes 2.00

Memorabila Moments Jerseys

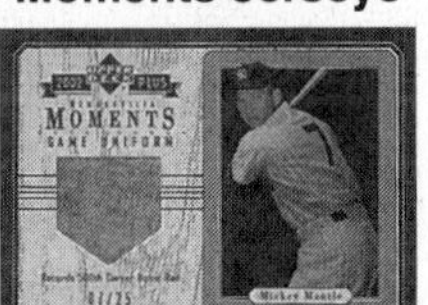

NM/M
Common DiMaggio (1-5): 125.00
Common Mantle: (1-5): 200.00
MM-JD1 Joe DiMaggio 125.00
MM-JD2 Joe DiMaggio 125.00
MM-JD3 Joe DiMaggio 125.00
MM-JD4 Joe DiMaggio 125.00
MM-JD5 Joe DiMaggio 125.00
MM-MM1 Mickey Mantle/25 (Pants) 200.00
MM-MM2 Mickey Mantle 200.00

MM-MM3 Mickey Mantle 200.00
MM-MM4 Mickey Mantle 200.00
MM-MM5 Mickey Mantle 200.00

Pinstripe Immortals

Complete Set (10):
Common Player:

2002 Upper Deck Ultimate Collection

NM/M
Complete Set (120):
Common Player (1-60): 2.00
Production 799
Common Player (61-110, 114-120): 10.00
Production 550
Common (111-113): 25.00
Production 330
Pack (4): 100.00
Box (4): 350.00
1 Troy Glaus 2.50
2 Luis Gonzalez 2.00
3 Curt Schilling 2.50
4 Randy Johnson 4.00
5 Andruw Jones 2.50
6 Greg Maddux 6.00
7 Chipper Jones 5.00
8 Gary Sheffield 2.00
9 Cal Ripken Jr. 12.00
10 Manny Ramirez 3.00
11 Pedro J. Martinez 4.00
12 Nomar Garciaparra 8.00
13 Sammy Sosa 6.00
14 Kerry Wood 4.00
15 Mark Prior 4.00
16 Magglio Ordonez 2.00
17 Frank Thomas 3.00
18 Adam Dunn 3.00
19 Ken Griffey Jr. 8.00
20 Jim Thome 4.00
21 Larry Walker 2.00
22 Todd Helton 3.00
23 Nolan Ryan 12.00
24 Jeff Bagwell 3.00
25 Roy Oswalt 2.00
26 Lance Berkman 2.00
27 Mike Sweeney 2.00
28 Shawn Green 2.00
29 Hideo Nomo 2.00
30 Torii Hunter 2.00
31 Vladimir Guerrero 5.00
32 Tom Seaver 4.00
33 Mike Piazza 8.00
34 Roberto Alomar 2.00
35 Derek Jeter 12.00
36 Alfonso Soriano 5.00
37 Jason Giambi 4.00
38 Roger Clemens 8.00
39 Mike Mussina 2.50
40 Bernie Williams 2.50
41 Joe DiMaggio 10.00
42 Mickey Mantle 15.00
43 Miguel Tejada 3.00
44 Eric Chavez 2.00
45 Barry Zito 2.00
46 Pat Burrell 2.50
47 Jason Kendall 2.00
48 Brian Giles 2.00
49 Barry Bonds 15.00
50 Ichiro Suzuki 8.00
51 Stan Musial 8.00
52 J.D. Drew 2.00
53 Scott Rolen 5.00
54 Albert Pujols 10.00
55 Mark McGwire 10.00
56 Alex Rodriguez 10.00
57 Ivan Rodriguez 3.00
58 Juan Gonzalez 2.50
59 Rafael Palmeiro 3.00
60 Carlos Delgado 2.50
61 Jose Valverde **RC** 10.00
62 Doug DeVore **RC** 10.00
63 John Ennis **RC** 10.00
64 Joey Dawley 10.00
65 Trey Hodges **RC** 10.00
66 Mike Mahoney 10.00
67 Aaron Cook **RC** 10.00
68 Rene Reyes **RC** 10.00
69 Mark Corey 10.00
70 Hansel Izquierdo **RC** 10.00
71 Brandon Puffer **RC** 10.00
72 Jeriome Robertson **RC** 10.00
73 Jose Diaz 10.00
74 David Ross 10.00
75 Jayson Durocher **RC** 10.00
76 Eric Good **RC** 10.00
77 Satoru Komiyama **RC** 10.00
78 Tyler Yates **RC** 10.00
79 Eric Junge **RC** 10.00
80 Anderson Machado **RC** 10.00
81 Adrian Burnside **RC** 10.00
82 Ben Howard **RC** 10.00
83 Clay Condrey **RC** 10.00
84 Nelson Castro **RC** 10.00
85 So Taguchi **RC** 15.00
86 Mike Crudale **RC** 10.00
87 Scotty Layfield **RC** 10.00
88 Steve Bechler **RC** 10.00
89 Travis Driskill **RC** 10.00
90 Howie Clark **RC** 10.00
91 Josh Hancock **RC** 10.00
92 Jorge De La Rosa **RC** 10.00
93 Anastacio Martinez **RC** 10.00
94 Brian Tallet 10.00
95 Carl Sadler **RC** 10.00
96 Cliff Lee **RC** 15.00
97 Josh Bard **RC** 10.00
98 Wes Obermueller **RC** 10.00
99 Juan Brito 10.00
100 Aaron Guiel **RC** 10.00
101 Jeremy Hill **RC** 10.00
102 Kevin Frederick **RC** 10.00
103 Nate Field **RC** 10.00
104 Julio Mateo **RC** 10.00
105 Chris Snelling **RC** 15.00
106 Felix Escalona **RC** 10.00
107 Reynaldo Garcia **RC** 10.00
108 Mike Smith **RC** 10.00
109 Ken Huckaby **RC** 10.00
110 Kevin Cash **RC** 10.00
111 Kazuhisa Ishii/ Auto. **RC** 40.00
112 Freddy Sanchez/ Auto. **RC** 25.00
113 Jason Simontacchi/ Auto. **RC** 25.00
114 Jorge Padilla/ Auto. **RC** 15.00
115 Kirk Saarloos/Auto. 15.00
116 Rodrigo Rosario/ Auto. **RC** 15.00
117 Oliver Perez/ Auto. **RC** 50.00
118 Miguel Asencio/ Auto. **RC** 15.00
119 Franklyn German/ Auto. **RC** 15.00
120 Jaime Cerda/ Auto. **RC** 15.00

Double Barrel

NM/M
Quantity produced listed
DB-RI Ivan Rodriguez, Alex Rodriguez/5 2,225
DB-RR Cal Ripken Jr., Alex Rodriguez/9 1,625
DB-TO Magglio Ordonez, Frank Thomas/4 950.00

Jerseys Tier 1

NM/M
Common Player: 10.00
Production 99 Sets
Golds: .75-1.5X
Production 50 Sets
RC Roger Clemens 20.00
JD Joe DiMaggio 100.00
AD Adam Dunn 15.00
JG Jason Giambi 15.00
KG Ken Griffey Jr. 20.00
KI Kazuhisa Ishii 10.00
RJ Randy Johnson 15.00
AJ Andruw Jones 10.00
CJ Chipper Jones 15.00
MM Mickey Mantle 125.00
PM Pedro J. Martinez 15.00
MC Mark McGwire 60.00
MP Mike Piazza 15.00
PR Mark Prior 15.00
MR Manny Ramirez 10.00
CR Cal Ripken Jr. 40.00
AR Alex Rodriguez 25.00
IR Ivan Rodriguez 15.00
AS Alfonso Soriano 20.00
SS Sammy Sosa 25.00
IS Ichiro Suzuki 45.00

Jerseys Tier 2

NM/M
Same price as Tier 1.
Production 99 Sets
Golds: 1.5-2X
Production 25 Sets
JF-RC Roger Clemens 20.00
JF-JD Joe DiMaggio 100.00
JF-AD Adam Dunn 15.00
JF-JG Jason Giambi 15.00
JF-KG Ken Griffey Jr. 20.00
JF-KI Kazuhisa Ishii 10.00
JF-RJ Randy Johnson 15.00
JF-AJ Andruw Jones 10.00
JF-CJ Chipper Jones 15.00
JF-MM Mickey Mantle 125.00
JF-PM Pedro J. Martinez 15.00
JF-MC Mark McGwire 60.00
JF-MP Mike Piazza 15.00
JF-PR Mark Prior 20.00
JF-MR Manny Ramirez 10.00
JF-CR Cal Ripken Jr. 40.00
JF-AR Alex Rodriguez 25.00
JF-IR Ivan Rodriguez 15.00
JF-AS Alfonso Soriano 20.00
JF-SS Sammy Sosa 25.00
JF-IS Ichiro Suzuki 45.00

Jerseys Tier 3

NM/M
Common Player: 8.00
Stars: .4-.6X Tier 1 Price
Production 199 Sets
JP-RC Roger Clemens 15.00
JP-AD Adam Dunn 10.00
JP-JG Jason Giambi 10.00
JP-KG Ken Griffey Jr. 15.00
JP-KI Kazuhisa Ishii 8.00
JP-RJ Randy Johnson 12.00
JP-AJ Andruw Jones 8.00
JP-CJ Chipper Jones 12.00
JP-MM Mickey Mantle 75.00
JP-PM Pedro J. Martinez 10.00
JP-MC Mark McGwire 40.00
JP-MP Mike Piazza 15.00
JP-PR Mark Prior 10.00
JP-MR Manny Ramirez 8.00
JP-CR Cal Ripken Jr. 30.00
JP-AR Alex Rodriguez 15.00
JP-IR Ivan Rodriguez 8.00
JP-AS Alfonso Soriano 12.00
JP-SS Sammy Sosa 20.00
JP-IS Ichiro Suzuki 30.00
JP-BW Bernie Williams 8.00

Jerseys Tier 4

NM/M
Common Player: 8.00
Stars: .4-.6X Tier 1 Price
Production 199 Sets
JR-RC Roger Clemens 15.00
JR-AD Adam Dunn 10.00
JR-JG Jason Giambi 10.00
JR-KG Ken Griffey Jr. 15.00
JR-KI Kazuhisa Ishii 8.00
JR-RJ Randy Johnson 10.00
JR-AJ Andruw Jones 8.00
JR-CJ Chipper Jones 10.00
JR-MM Mickey Mantle 75.00
JR-PM Pedro J. Martinez 10.00
JR-MC Mark McGwire 40.00
JR-MP Mike Piazza 15.00
JR-PR Mark Prior 10.00
JR-MR Manny Ramirez 8.00
JR-CR Cal Ripken Jr. 25.00
JR-AR Alex Rodriguez 15.00
JR-IR Ivan Rodriguez 8.00
JR-AS Alfonso Soriano 15.00
JR-SS Sammy Sosa 20.00
JR-IS Ichiro Suzuki 30.00
JR-BW Bernie Williams 8.00

Mark McGwire Signing Redem.

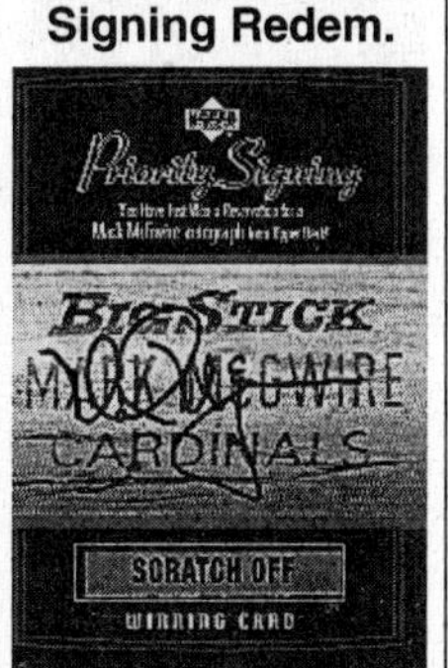

NM/M
Exchange Card 1:500 Packs:
1-MM Mark McGwire 600.00

Signatures Tier 1

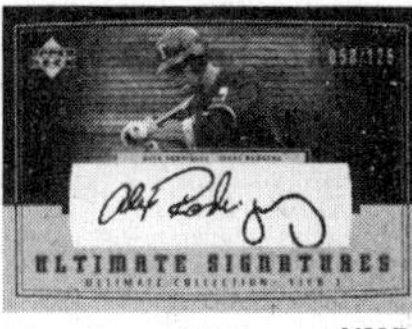

NM/M
Common Autograph: 20.00
Quantity produced listed
Golds: No Pricing
Production 25 Sets
RA1 Roberto Alomar/155 45.00
LB1 Lance Berkman/179 25.00
PB1 Pat Burrell/95 25.00
RC1 Roger Clemens/320 80.00
CD1 Carlos Delgado/95 25.00
JD1 J.D. Drew/220 25.00
AD1 Adam Dunn/125 45.00
JG1 Jason Giambi/295 25.00
BG1 Brian Giles/220 20.00
LG1 Luis Gonzalez/199 20.00
KG1 Ken Griffey Jr./195 100.00
JK1 Jason Kendall/220 20.00
MP1 Mark Prior/160 40.00
CR1 Cal Ripken Jr./75 165.00
AR1 Alex Rodriguez/329 100.00
SR1 Scott Rolen/160 30.00
GS1 Gary Sheffield/95 20.00
JT1 Jim Thome/95 60.00
BZ1 Barry Zito/199 25.00

Signatures Tier 2

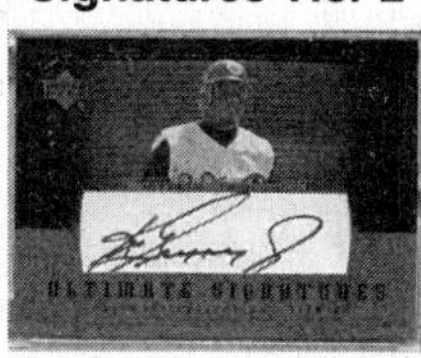

NM/M
Quantity produced listed
Golds: No Pricing
Production 10 Sets
JB2 Jeff Bagwell/51 55.00
LB2 Lance Berkman/85 40.00
JG2 Jason Giambi/50 60.00
LG2 Luis Gonzalez/70 25.00
KG2 Ken Griffey Jr./30 150.00
TG2 Tony Gwynn/51 75.00
TH2 Todd Helton/51 60.00
AJ2 Andruw Jones/51 50.00
MP2 Mark Prior/60 60.00
KP2 Kirby Puckett/75 60.00
AR2 Alex Rodriguez/75 100.00
SR2 Scott Rolen/60 50.00
DS2 Duke Snider/51 60.00
FT2 Frank Thomas/51 65.00
KW2 Kerry Wood/51 75.00
BZ2 Barry Zito/70 40.00

Signed Excellence

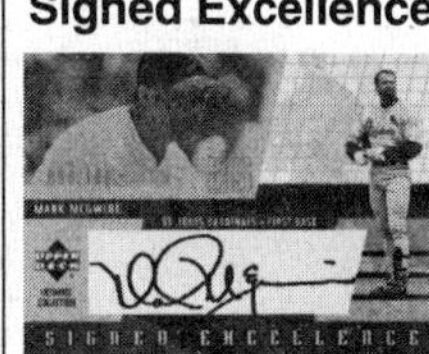

NM/M
Quantity produced listed
Golds: No Pricing
Production One Set
I1 Ichiro Suzuki/56 375.00
I2 Ichiro Suzuki/51 375.00
I5 Ichiro Suzuki/Btg 250.00
I6 Ichiro Suzuki/ Throwing 250.00
MM1 Mark McGwire/70 275.00
MM2 Mark McGwire/65 275.00
MM3 Mark McGwire/49 300.00
MM5 Mark McGwire/ Standing 220.00
MM6 Mark McGwire/ Waving 220.00
MM7 Mark McGwire/Fldg 220.00
SS1 Sammy Sosa/66 175.00
SS2 Sammy Sosa/64 175.00
SS3 Sammy Sosa/54 175.00
SS5 Sammy Sosa/ Running 150.00
SS6 Sammy Sosa/ Holding Bat 150.00
SS7 Sammy Sosa/150 150.00

Signed Excellence Gold

Complete Set (5):
Common Player:

Patch

NM/M
Common Player: 25.00
Production 100 Sets
LG Luis Gonzalez 25.00
SG Shawn Green 25.00
TH Todd Helton 40.00
KI Kazuhisa Ishii 40.00
CJ Chipper Jones 40.00
MM Mark McGwire 125.00
MP Mark Prior 30.00
IR Ivan Rodriguez 40.00
SS Sammy Sosa 65.00
IS Ichiro Suzuki 150.00

Double Patches

NM/M
Production 100 Sets
Golds: .75-1.5X
Production 50 Sets
DE J.D. Drew, Jim Edmonds 60.00
GC Jason Giambi, Roger Clemens 80.00
IG Ken Griffey Jr., Ichiro Suzuki 125.00
JS Randy Johnson, Curt Schilling 60.00
MG Tom Glavine, Greg Maddux 75.00
MS Sammy Sosa, Mark McGwire 150.00
PA Mike Piazza, Roberto Alomar 80.00
RG Alex Rodriguez, Juan Gonzalez 80.00
RM Manny Ramirez, Pedro J. Martinez 50.00

2002 Upper Deck Victory

NM/M
Complete Set (550): 40.00
Common Player: .10
Pack (10): 1.00
Box (36): 25.00
1 Troy Glaus .30
2 Tim Salmon .20
3 Troy Percival .10
4 Darin Erstad .25
5 Adam Kennedy .10
6 Scott Spiezio .10
7 Ramon Ortiz .10
8 Ismael Valdes .10
9 Jarrod Washburn .10
10 Garret Anderson .10
11 David Eckstein .10
12 Mo Vaughn .25
13 Benji Gil .10
14 Bengie Molina .10
15 Scott Schoeneweis .10
16 Troy Glaus, Ramon Ortiz .20
17 David Justice .20
18 Jermaine Dye .10
19 Eric Chavez .25
20 Jeremy Giambi .10
21 Terrence Long .10
22 Miguel Tejada .20
23 Johnny Damon .10
24 Jason Hart .10
25 Adam Piatt .10
26 Billy Koch .10
27 Ramon Hernandez .10
28 Eric Byrnes .10
29 Olmedo Saenz .10
30 Barry Zito .20
31 Tim Hudson .25
32 Mark Mulder .20
33 Jason Giambi, Mark Mulder .25
34 Carlos Delgado .40
35 Shannon Stewart .10
36 Vernon Wells .10
37 Homer Bush .10
38 Brad Fullmer .10
39 Jose Cruz .10
40 Felipe Lopez .10
41 Raul Mondesi .20
42 Esteban Loaiza .10
43 Darrin Fletcher .10
44 Mike Sirotka .10
45 Luke Prokopec .10
46 Chris Carpenter .10
47 Roy Halladay .10
48 Kelvim Escobar .10
49 Carlos Delgado, Billy Koch .20
50 Nick Bierbrodt .10
51 Greg Vaughn .10
52 Ben Grieve .10
53 Damian Rolls .10
54 Russ Johnson .10
55 Brent Abernathy .10
56 Steve Cox .10
57 Aubrey Huff .10
58 Randy Winn .10
59 Jason Tyner .10
60 Tanyon Sturtze .10
61 Joe Kennedy .10
62 Jared Sandberg .10
63 Esteban Yan .10
64 Ryan Rupe .10
65 Toby Hall .10
66 Greg Vaughn, Tanyon Sturtze .10
67 Matt Lawton .10
68 Juan Gonzalez .40
69 Jim Thome .25
70 Einar Diaz .10
71 Ellis Burks .10
72 Kenny Lofton .10
73 Omar Vizquel .10
74 Russell Branyan .10
75 Brady Anderson .10
76 John Rocker .10
77 Travis Fryman .10
78 Wil Cordero .10
79 Chuck Finley .10
80 C.C. Sabathia .10
81 Bartolo Colon .10
82 Bob Wickman .10
83 Roberto Alomar, C.C. Sabathia .20
84 Ichiro Suzuki 1.50
85 Edgar Martinez .10
86 Aaron Sele .10
87 Carlos Guillen .10
88 Bret Boone .10
89 John Olerud .20
90 Jamie Moyer .10
91 Ben Davis .10
92 Dan Wilson .10
93 Jeff Cirillo .10
94 John Halama .10
95 Freddy Garcia .10
96 Kazuhiro Sasaki .10
97 Mike Cameron .10
98 Paul Abbott .10
99 Mark McLemore .10
100 Ichiro Suzuki, Freddy Garcia .50
101 Jeff Conine .10
102 David Segui .10
103 Marty Cordova .10
104 Tony Batista .10
105 Chris Richard .10
106 Willis Roberts .10
107 Melvin Mora .10
108 Mike Bordick .10
109 Jay Gibbons .10
110 Mike Kinkade .10
111 Brian Roberts .10
112 Jerry Hairston Jr. .10
113 Jason Johnson .10
114 Josh Towers .10
115 Calvin Maduro .10
116 Sidney Ponson .10
117 Jeff Conine, Jason Johnson .10
118 Alex Rodriguez 1.00
119 Ivan Rodriguez .40
120 Frank Catalanotto .10
121 Mike Lamb .10
122 Ruben Sierra .10
123 Rusty Greer .10
124 Rafael Palmeiro .20
125 Gabe Kapler .15
126 Aaron Myette .10
127 Kenny Rogers .10
128 Carl Everett .10
129 Rick Helling .10
130 Ricky Ledee .10
131 Michael Young .10
132 Doug Davis .10
133 Jeff Zimmerman .10
134 Alex Rodriguez, Rick Helling .40
135 Manny Ramirez .40
136 Nomar Garciaparra 1.00
137 Jason Varitek .10
138 Dante Bichette .10
139 Tony Clark .10
140 Scott Hatteberg .10

141 Trot Nixon .10
142 Hideo Nomo .25
143 Dustin Hermanson .10
144 Chris Stynes .10
145 Jose Offerman .10
146 Pedro Martinez .50
147 Shea Hillenbrand .10
148 Tim Wakefield .10
149 Troy O'Leary .10
150 Ugueth Urbina .10
151 Manny Ramirez, Hideo Nomo .25
152 Carlos Beltran .10
153 Dee Brown .10
154 Mike Sweeney .10
155 Luis Alicea .10
156 Raul Ibanez .10
157 Mark Quinn .10
158 Joe Randa .10
159 Roberto Hernandez .10
160 Neifi Perez .10
161 Carlos Febles .10
162 Jeff Suppan .10
163 Dave McCarty .10
164 Blake Stein .10
165 Chad Durbin .10
166 Paul Byrd .10
167 Carlos Beltran, Jeff Suppan .10
168 Craig Paquette .10
169 Dean Palmer .10
170 Shane Halter .10
171 Bobby Higginson .10
172 Robert Fick .10
173 Jose Macias .10
174 Deivi Cruz .10
175 Damion Easley .10
176 Brandon Inge .10
177 Mark Redman .10
178 Dmitri Young .10
179 Steve Sparks .10
180 Jeff Weaver .10
181 Victor Santos .10
182 Jose Lima .10
183 Matt Anderson .10
184 Roger Cedeno, Steve Sparks .10
185 Doug Mientkiewicz .10
186 Cristian Guzman .10
187 Torii Hunter .10
188 Matt LeCroy .10
189 Corey Koskie .10
190 Jacque Jones .10
191 Luis Rivas .10
192 David Ortiz .10
193 A.J. Pierzynski .10
194 Brian Buchanan .10
195 Joe Mays .10
196 Brad Radke .10
197 Denny Hocking .10
198 Eric Milton .10
199 LaTroy Hawkins .10
200 Doug Mientkiewicz, Joe Mays .10
201 Magglio Ordonez .20
202 Jose Valentin .10
203 Chris Singleton .10
204 Aaron Rowand .10
205 Paul Konerko .10
206 Carlos Lee .10
207 Ray Durham .10
208 Keith Foulke .10
209 Todd Ritchie .10
210 Royce Clayton .10
211 Jose Canseco .20
212 Frank Thomas .40
213 David Wells .10
214 Mark Buehrle .10
215 Jon Garland .10
216 Magglio Ordonez, Mark Buehrle .15
217 Derek Jeter 1.50
218 Bernie Williams .30
219 Rondell White .10
220 Jorge Posada .20
221 Alfonso Soriano .50
222 Ramiro Mendoza .10
223 Jason Giambi .75
224 John Vander Wal .10
225 Steve Karsay .10
226 Nick Johnson .10
227 Mariano Rivera .20
228 Orlando Hernandez .10
229 Andy Pettitte .20
230 Robin Ventura .10
231 Roger Clemens .60
232 Mike Mussina .40
233 Derek Jeter, Roger Clemens .50
234 Moises Alou .20
235 Lance Berkman .20
236 Craig Biggio .20
237 Octavio Dotel .10
238 Jeff Bagwell .40
239 Richard Hidalgo .10
240 Morgan Ensberg .10
241 Julio Lugo .10
242 Daryle Ward .10
243 Roy Oswalt .20
244 Billy Wagner .10
245 Brad Ausmus .10
246 Jose Vizcaino .10
247 Wade Miller .10
248 Shane Reynolds .10
249 Jeff Bagwell, Wade Miller .20
250 Chipper Jones .75
251 Brian Jordan .10
252 B.J. Surhoff .10
253 Rafael Furcal .10
254 Julio Franco .10
255 Javy Lopez .10
256 John Burkett .10
257 Andruw Jones .20
258 Marcus Giles .10
259 Wes Helms .10
260 Greg Maddux .75
261 John Smoltz .10
262 Tom Glavine .20
263 Vinny Castilla .10
264 Kevin Millwood .10
265 Jason Marquis .10
266 Chipper Jones, Greg Maddux .40
267 Tyler Houston .10
268 Mark Loretta .10
269 Richie Sexson .20
270 Jeromy Burnitz .10
271 Jimmy Haynes .10
272 Geoff Jenkins .20
273 Ron Belliard .10
274 Jose Hernandez .10
275 Jeffrey Hammonds .10
276 Curtis Leskanic .10
277 Devon White .10
278 Ben Sheets .20
279 Henry Blanco .10
280 Jamey Wright .10
281 Allen Levrault .10
282 Jeff D'Amico .10
283 Richie Sexson, Jimmy Haynes .10
284 Albert Pujols .75
285 Jason Isringhausen .10
286 J.D. Drew .25
287 Placido Polanco .10
288 Jim Edmonds .20
289 Fernando Vina .10
290 Edgar Renteria .10
291 Mike Matheny .10
292 Bud Smith .10
293 Mike Defelice .10
294 Woody Williams .10
295 Eli Marrero .10
296 Matt Morris .10
297 Darryl Kile .10
298 Kerry Robinson .10
299 Luis Saturria .10
300 Albert Pujols, Matt Morris .40
301 Sammy Sosa .75
302 Michael Tucker .10
303 Bill Mueller .10
304 Ricky Gutierrez .10
305 Fred McGriff .20
306 Eric Young .10
307 Corey Patterson .10
308 Alex Gonzalez .10
309 Ron Coomer .10
310 Kerry Wood .20
311 Delino DeShields .10
312 Jon Lieber .10
313 Tom Gordon .10
314 Todd Hundley .10
315 Jason Bere .10
316 Kevin Tapani .10
317 Sammy Sosa, Jon Lieber .40
318 Steve Finley .10
319 Luis Gonzalez .25
320 Mark Grace .25
321 Craig Counsell .10
322 Matt Williams .20
323 Tony Womack .10
324 Junior Spivey .10
325 David Dellucci .10
326 Jay Bell .10
327 Curt Schilling .25
328 Randy Johnson .40
329 Danny Bautista .10
330 Miguel Batista .10
331 Erubiel Durazo .10
332 Brian Anderson .10
333 Byung-Hyun Kim .10
334 Luis Gonzalez, Curt Schilling .20
335 Paul LoDuca .10
336 Gary Sheffield .20
337 Shawn Green .25
338 Adrian Beltre .20
339 Darren Dreifort .10
340 Mark Grudzielanek .10
341 Eric Karros .10
342 Cesar Izturis .10
343 Tom Goodwin .10
344 Marquis Grissom .10
345 Kevin Brown .20
346 James Baldwin .10
347 Terry Adams .10
348 Alex Cora .10
349 Andy Ashby .10
350 Chan Ho Park .20
351 Shawn Green, Chan Ho Park .20
352 Jose Vidro .10
353 Vladimir Guerrero .40
354 Orlando Cabrera .10
355 Fernando Tatis .10
356 Michael Barrett .10
357 Lee Stevens .10
358 Geoff Blum .10
359 Brad Wilkerson .10
360 Peter Bergeron .10
361 Javier Vazquez .10
362 Tony Armas Jr. .10
363 Tomokazu Ohka .10
364 Scott Strickland .10
365 Vladimir Guerrero, Javier Vazquez .20
366 Barry Bonds .75
367 Rich Aurilia .10
368 Jeff Kent .10
369 Andres Galarraga .20
370 Desi Relaford .10
371 Shawon Dunston .10
372 Benito Santiago .10
373 Tsuyoshi Shinjo .10
374 Calvin Murray .10
375 Marvin Benard .10
376 J.T. Snow .10
377 Livan Hernandez .10
378 Russ Ortiz .10
379 Robb Nen .10
380 Jason Schmidt .10
381 Barry Bonds, Russ Ortiz .30
382 Cliff Floyd .10
383 Antonio Alfonseca .10
384 Mike Redmond .10
385 Mike Lowell .10
386 Derrek Lee .10
387 Preston Wilson .10
388 Luis Castillo .10
389 Charles Johnson .10
390 Eric Owens .10
391 Alex Gonzalez .10
392 Josh Beckett .10
393 Brad Penny .10
394 Ryan Dempster .10
395 Matt Clement .10
396 A.J. Burnett .10
397 Cliff Floyd, Ryan Dempster .10
398 Mike Piazza 1.00
399 Joe McEwing .10
400 Todd Zeile .10
401 Jay Payton .10
402 Roger Cedeno .10
403 Rey Ordonez .10
404 Edgardo Alfonzo .10
405 Roberto Alomar .30
406 Glendon Rusch .10
407 Timo Perez .10
408 Al Leiter .15
409 Lenny Harris .10
410 Shawn Estes .10
411 Armando Benitez .10
412 Kevin Appier .10
413 Bruce Chen .10
414 Mike Piazza, Al Leiter .40
415 Phil Nevin .10
416 Ryan Klesko .10
417 Mark Kotsay .10
418 Ray Lankford .10
419 Mike Darr .10
420 D'Angelo Jimenez .10
421 Bubba Trammell .10
422 Adam Eaton .10
423 Ramon Vazquez .10
424 Cesar Crespo .10
425 Trevor Hoffman .10
426 Kevin Jarvis .10
427 Wiki Gonzalez .10
428 Damian Jackson .10
429 Brian Lawrence .10
430 Phil Nevin, Trevor Hoffman .10
431 Scott Rolen .25
432 Marlon Anderson .10
433 Bobby Abreu .10
434 Jimmy Rollins .20
435 Doug Glanville .10
436 Travis Lee .10
437 Brandon Duckworth .10
438 Pat Burrell .25
439 Kevin Jordan .10
440 Robert Person .10
441 Johnny Estrada .10
442 Randy Wolf .10
443 Jose Mesa .10
444 Mike Lieberthal .10
445 Bobby Abreu, Robert Person .10
446 Brian Giles .20
447 Jason Kendall .10
448 Aramis Ramirez .10
449 Rob Mackowiak .10
450 Abraham Nunez .10
451 Pat Meares .10
452 Craig Wilson .10
453 Jack Wilson .10
454 Gary Matthews Jr. .10
455 Kevin Young .10
456 Derek Bell .10
457 Kip Wells .10
458 Jimmy Anderson .10
459 Kris Benson .10
460 Brian Giles, Todd Ritchie .10
461 Sean Casey .20
462 Wilton Guerrero .10
463 Jason LaRue .10
464 Juan Encarnacion .10
465 Todd Walker .10
466 Aaron Boone .10
467 Pete Harnisch .10
468 Ken Griffey Jr. 1.00
469 Adam Dunn .40
470 Barry Larkin .20
471 Kelly Stinnett .10
472 Pokey Reese .10
473 Brady Clark .10
474 Scott Williamson .10
475 Danny Graves .10
476 Ken Griffey Jr., Elmer Dessens .10
477 Larry Walker .25
478 Todd Helton .40
479 Juan Pierre .10
480 Juan Uribe .10
481 Mario Encarnacion .10
482 Jose Ortiz .10
483 Todd Hollandsworth .10
484 Alex Ochoa .10
485 Mike Hampton .10
486 Terry Shumpert .10
487 Denny Neagle .10
488 Jose Jimenez .10
489 Jason Jennings .10
490 Todd Helton, Mike Hampton .20
491 Tim Redding .10
492 Mark Teixeira 2.00
493 Alex Cintron .10
494 Tim Raines Jr. .10
495 Juan Cruz .20
496 Joe Crede .10
497 Steve Green .10
498 Mike Rivera .10
499 Mark Prior 1.00
500 Ken Harvey .10
501 Tim Spooneybarger .10
502 Adam Everett .10
503 Jason Standridge .10
504 Nick Neugebauer .10
505 Adam Johnson .10
506 Sean Douglass .10
507 Brandon Berger .10
508 Alex Escobar .10
509 Doug Nickle .10
510 Jason Middlebrook .10
511 Dewon Brazelton .10
512 Yorvit Torrealba .10
513 Henry Mateo .10
514 Dennis Tankersley .10
515 Marlon Byrd .75
516 Andy Barkett .10
517 Orlando Hudson .10
518 Josh Fogg .10
519 Ryan Drese .10
520 Mike MacDougal .10
521 Luis Pineda .10
522 Jack Cust .10
523 Kurt Ainsworth .10
524 Bart Miadich .10
525 Dernell Stenson .10
526 Carlos Zambrano .10
527 Austin Kearns .50
528 Larry Barnes .10
529 Mike Cuddyer .10
530 Carlos Pena .75
531 Derek Jeter 1.00
532 Ken Griffey Jr. .75
533 Manny Ramirez .25
534 Luis Gonzalez .20
535 Sammy Sosa .50
536 Roger Clemens .40
537 Phil Nevin .10
538 Mike Piazza .75
539 Alex Rodriguez .75
540 Jason Giambi .50
541 Randy Johnson .25
542 Albert Pujols .50
543 Jeff Bagwell .25
544 Shawn Green .15
545 Carlos Delgado .15
546 Pedro Martinez .25
547 Todd Helton .25
548 Roberto Alomar .20
549 Barry Bonds .40
550 Ichiro Suzuki 1.00

Gold

Stars: 3-6X
Inserted 1:2

2002 Upper Deck Vintage

	NM/M
Complete Set (300):	30.00
Common Player:	.10
Pack (10):	2.00
Box (24):	35.00

1 Darin Erstad .20
2 Mo Vaughn .20
3 Ramon Ortiz .10
4 Garret Anderson .25
5 Troy Glaus .40
6 Troy Percival .10
7 Tim Salmon .20
8 Wilmy Caceres, Elpidio Guzman .10
9 2001 Anaheim Angels .10
10 Jason Giambi .50
11 Mark Mulder .25
12 Jermaine Dye .10
13 Miguel Tejada .40
14 Tim Hudson .25
15 Eric Chavez .25
16 Barry Zito .25
17 Oscar Salazar, Juan Pena .10
18 2001 Oakland Athletics .10
19 Carlos Delgado .40
20 Raul Mondesi .15
21 Chris Carpenter .10
22 Jose Cruz Jr. .10
23 Alex Gonzalez .10
24 Brad Fullmer .10
25 Shannon Stewart .10
26 Brandon Lyon, Vernon Wells .10
27 2001 Toronto Blue Jays .10
28 Greg Vaughn .10
29 Toby Hall .10
30 Ben Grieve .10
31 Aubrey Huff .10
32 Tanyon Sturtze .10
33 Brent Abernathy .10
34 Dewon Brazelton, Delvin James .10
35 2001 Tampa Bay Devil Rays .10
36 Roberto Alomar .40
37 Juan Gonzalez .50
38 Bartolo Colon .25
39 C.C. Sabathia .10
40 Jim Thome .75
41 Omar Vizquel .20
42 Russell Branyan .10
43 Ryan Drese, Roy Smith .10
44 2001 Cleveland Indians .10
45 Edgar Martinez .20
46 Bret Boone .20
47 Freddy Garcia .10
48 John Olerud .25
49 Kazuhiro Sasaki .10
50 Ichiro Suzuki 1.50
51 Mike Cameron .10
52 Rafael Soriano, Dennis Stark .10
53 2001 Seattle Mariners .10
54 Tony Batista .10
55 Jeff Conine .10
56 Jason Johnson .10
57 Jay Gibbons .10
58 Chris Richard .10
59 Josh Towers .10
60 Jerry Hairston Jr. .10
61 Sean Douglass, Tim Raines Jr. .10
62 2001 Baltimore Orioles .10
63 Alex Rodriguez 1.50
64 Ruben Sierra .10
65 Ivan Rodriguez .50
66 Gabe Kapler .20
67 Rafael Palmeiro .50
68 Frank Catalanotto .10
69 Mark Teixeira, Carlos Pena .40
70 2001 Texas Rangers .10
71 Nomar Garciaparra 1.00
72 Pedro Martinez .75
73 Trot Nixon .10
74 Dante Bichette .10
75 Manny Ramirez .50
76 Carl Everett .10
77 Hideo Nomo .40
78 Dernell Stenson, Juan Diaz .10
79 2001 Boston Red Sox .10
80 Mike Sweeney .10
81 Carlos Febles .10
82 Dee Brown .10
83 Neifi Perez .10
84 Mark Quinn .10
85 Carlos Beltran .25
86 Joe Randa .10
87 Ken Harvey, Mike MacDougal .10
88 2001 Kansas City Royals .10
89 Dean Palmer .10
90 Jeff Weaver .10
91 Jose Lima .10
92 Tony Clark .10
93 Damion Easley .10
94 Bobby Higginson .10
95 Robert Fick .10
96 Pedro Santana, Mike Rivera .10
97 2001 Detroit Tigers .10
98 Doug Mientkiewicz .10
99 David Ortiz .25
100 Joe Mays .10
101 Corey Koskie .10
102 Eric Milton .10
103 Cristian Guzman .10
104 Brad Radke .10
105 Juan Rincon, Adam Johnson .10
106 2001 Minnesota Twins .10
107 Frank Thomas .50
108 Carlos Lee .10
109 Mark Buehrle .10
110 Jose Canseco .25
111 Magglio Ordonez .25
112 Jon Garland .10
113 Ray Durham .10
114 Joe Crede, Josh Fogg .10
115 2001 Chicago White Sox .10
116 Derek Jeter 2.00
117 Roger Clemens 1.50
118 Alfonso Soriano .75
119 Paul O'Neill .25
120 Jorge Posada .25
121 Bernie Williams .40
122 Mariano Rivera .25
123 Tino Martinez .20
124 Mike Mussina .50
125 Nick Johnson, Erick Almonte .10
126 2001 New York Yankees .10
127 Jeff Bagwell .50
128 Wade Miller .10
129 Lance Berkman .25
130 Moises Alou .25
131 Craig Biggio .20
132 Roy Oswalt .20
133 Richard Hidalgo .15
134 Morgan Ensberg, Tim Redding .10
135 2001 Houston Astros .10
136 Greg Maddux 1.00
137 Chipper Jones .75
138 Brian Jordan .10
139 Marcus Giles .10
140 Andruw Jones .40
141 Tom Glavine .40
142 Rafael Furcal .25
143 Wilson Betemit, Horacio Ramirez .10
144 2001 Atlanta Braves .10
145 Jeromy Burnitz .10
146 Ben Sheets .25
147 Geoff Jenkins .20
148 Devon White .10
149 Jimmy Haynes .15
150 Richie Sexson .40
151 Jose Hernandez .10
152 Jose Mieses, Alex Sanchez .10
153 2001 Milwaukee Brewers .10
154 Mark McGwire 2.00
155 Albert Pujols 1.50
156 Matt Morris .20
157 J.D. Drew .25
158 Jim Edmonds .25
159 Bud Smith .10
160 Darryl Kile .10
161 William Ortega, Luis Saturria .10
162 2001 St. Louis Cardinals .10
163 Sammy Sosa 1.00
164 Jon Lieber .10
165 Eric Young .10
166 Kerry Wood .75
167 Fred McGriff .25
168 Corey Patterson .25
169 Rondell White .15
170 Juan Cruz, Mark Prior 1.00
171 2001 Chicago Cubs .10
172 Luis Gonzalez .25
173 Randy Johnson .75
174 Matt Williams .20
175 Mark Grace .25
176 Steve Finley .10
177 Reggie Sanders .10
178 Curt Schilling .40
179 Alex Cintron, Jack Cust .10
180 2001 Arizona Diamondbacks .10
181 Gary Sheffield .25
182 Paul LoDuca .10
183 Chan Ho Park .10
184 Shawn Green .25
185 Eric Karros .15
186 Adrian Beltre .25
187 Kevin Brown .25
188 Ricardo Rodriguez, Carlos Garcia .10
189 2001 Los Angeles Dodgers .10
190 Vladimir Guerrero .75
191 Javier Vazquez .10
192 Jose Vidro .10
193 Fernando Tatis .10
194 Orlando Cabrera .10
195 Lee Stevens .10
196 Tony Armas Jr. .10
197 Donnie Bridges, Henry Mateo .10

198 2001 Montreal Expos .10
199 Barry Bonds 2.00
200 Rich Aurilia .10
201 Russ Ortiz .10
202 Jeff Kent .20
203 Jason Schmidt .25
204 John Vander Wal .10
205 Robb Nen .10
206 Yorvit Torrealba, Kurt Ainsworth .10
207 2001 San Francisco Giants .10
208 Preston Wilson .10
209 Brad Penny .10
210 Cliff Floyd .10
211 Luis Castillo .10
212 Ryan Dempster .10
213 Charles Johnson .10
214 A.J. Burnett .10
215 Abraham Nunez, Josh Beckett .20
216 2001 Florida Marlins .10
217 Mike Piazza 1.00
218 Al Leiter .20
219 Edgardo Alfonzo .10
220 Tsuyoshi Shinjo .10
221 Matt Lawton .10
222 Robin Ventura .15
223 Jay Payton .10
224 Alex Escobar, Jae Weong Seo .10
225 2001 New York Mets .10
226 Ryan Klesko .20
227 D'Angelo Jimenez .10
228 Trevor Hoffman .10
229 Phil Nevin .10
230 Mark Kotsay .10
231 Brian Lawrence .10
232 Bubba Trammell .10
233 Jason Middlebrook, Xavier Nady .10
234 2001 San Diego Padres .10
235 Scott Rolen .75
236 Jimmy Rollins .25
237 Mike Lieberthal .10
238 Bobby Abreu .25
239 Brandon Duckworth .10
240 Robert Person .10
241 Pat Burrell .20
242 Nick Punto, Carlos Silva .10
243 2001 Philadelphia Phillies .10
244 Brian Giles .20
245 Jack Wilson .10
246 Kris Benson .10
247 Jason Kendall .20
248 Aramis Ramirez .25
249 Todd Ritchie .10
250 Robert Mackowiak .10
251 John Grabow, Humberto Cota .10
252 2001 Pittsburgh Pirates .10
253 Ken Griffey Jr. 1.00
254 Barry Larkin .25
255 Sean Casey .25
256 Aaron Boone .10
257 Dmitri Young .10
258 Pokey Reese .10
259 Adam Dunn .50
260 David Espinosa, Dane Sardinha .10
261 2001 Cincinnati Reds .10
262 Todd Helton .50
263 Mike Hampton .20
264 Juan Pierre .10
265 Larry Walker .25
266 Juan Uribe .10
267 Jose Ortiz .10
268 Jeff Cirillo .10
269 Jason Jennings, Luke Hudson .10
270 2001 Colorado Rockies .10
271 Ichiro Suzuki, Jason Giambi, Roberto Alomar (League Leaders) .75
272 Larry Walker, Todd Helton, Moises Alou (League Leaders) .10
273 Alex Rodriguez, Jim Thome, Rafael Palmeiro (League Leaders) .75
274a Barry Bonds, Sammy Sosa, Juan Gonzalez (League Leaders) (No player names.) 1.00
274b Barry Bonds, Sammy Sosa, Juan Gonzalez (League Leaders)(Player names added.) 3.00
275 Roger Clemens, Mark Mulder, Jamie Moyer (League Leaders) .50
276 Curt Schilling, Matt Morris, Randy Johnson (League Leaders) .10
277 Freddy Garcia, Mike Mussina, Joe Mays (League Leaders) .10
278 Randy Johnson, Curt Schilling, John Burkett (League Leaders) .10
279 Mariano Rivera, Kazuhiro Sasaki, Keith Foulke (League Leaders) .10
280 Robb Nen, Armando Benitez, Trevor Hoffman (League Leaders) .10
281 Jason Giambi .25
282 Jorge Posada .15
283 Jim Thome .25
284 Edgar Martinez .10
285 Andruw Jones .20
286 Chipper Jones .50
287 Matt Williams .15
288 Curt Schilling .20
289 Derek Jeter 1.00
290 Mike Mussina .25
291 Bret Boone .10
292 Alfonso Soriano .40
293 Randy Johnson .25
294 Tom Glavine .20
295 Curt Schilling .25
296 Randy Johnson .40
297 Derek Jeter 1.00
298 Tino Martinez .10
299 Curt Schilling .20
300 Luis Gonzalez .20

Day at the Park

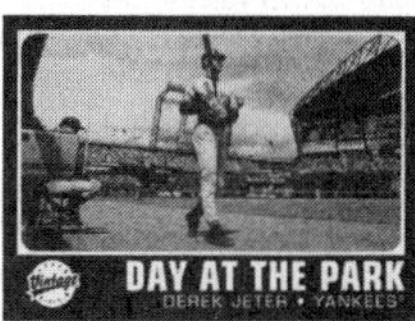

NM/M
Complete Set (6): 15.00
Inserted 1:23
DP1 Ichiro Suzuki 3.00
DP2 Derek Jeter 5.00
DP3 Alex Rodriguez 4.00
DP4 Mark McGwire 4.00
DP5 Barry Bonds 5.00
DP6 Sammy Sosa 3.00

Night-Gamers

NM/M
Complete Set (12): 10.00
Common Player: .50
Inserted 1:11
NG1 Todd Helton .75
NG2 Manny Ramirez .75
NG3 Ivan Rodriguez .50
NG4 Albert Pujols 2.50
NG5 Greg Maddux 1.50
NG6 Carlos Delgado .50
NG7 Frank Thomas .75
NG8 Derek Jeter 3.00
NG9 Troy Glaus .50
NG10 Jeff Bagwell .75
NG11 Juan Gonzalez .75
NG12 Randy Johnson 1.00

Sandlot Stars

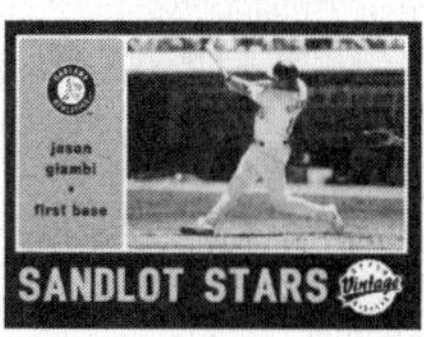

NM/M
Complete Set (12): 15.00
Common Player: .75
Inserted 1:11
SS1 Ken Griffey Jr. 1.50
SS2 Derek Jeter 3.00
SS3 Ichiro Suzuki 2.00
SS4 Nomar Garciaparra 2.00
SS5 Sammy Sosa 2.00
SS6 Chipper Jones 1.00
SS7 Jason Giambi .75
SS8 Alex Rodriguez 2.50
SS9 Mark McGwire 2.50
SS10 Barry Bonds 3.00
SS11 Mike Piazza 2.00
SS12 Vladimir Guerrero 1.00

Special Collection Jerseys

NM/M
Common Player: 8.00
Inserted 1:144
StB Stan Bahnsen 8.00
SaB Sal Bando 10.00
BC Bert Campaneris 10.00
AD Andre Dawson 15.00
RF Rollie Fingers 15.00
MG Mark Grace 15.00
MH Mike Hegan 8.00
CH "Catfish" Hunter 20.00
RJ Reggie Jackson 15.00
FJ Ferguson Jenkins 15.00
PL Paul Linblad 8.00
JR Joe Rudi 10.00
RS Ryne Sandberg 50.00
SS Sammy Sosa 25.00
BW Billy Williams 10.00

Timeless Teams Bat

NM/M
Inserted 1:288
SEA Ichiro Suzuki, Edgar Martinez, John Olerud, Bret Boone 75.00
NYY Mariano Rivera, Bernie Williams, Paul O'Neill, Jorge Posada 40.00
ATL Tom Glavine, Greg Maddux, Chipper Jones, Andruw Jones 40.00
CLE Juan Gonzalez, Jim Thome, Roberto Alomar, Kenny Lofton 30.00
OAK Jose Canseco, Ricky Henderson, Dave Parker, Don Baylor 30.00
OF Mickey Mantle, Joe DiMaggio, Reggie Jackson, Babe Ruth 300.00
1B Willie McCovey, Frank Thomas, Hank Greenberg, Eddie Murray 30.00
OF Ken Griffey Jr., Barry Bonds, Ricky Henderson, Tony Gwynn 50.00

Timeless Teams Combos

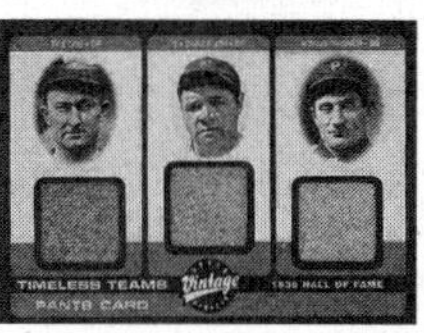

NM/M
Inserted 1:288
NYY00 Roger Clemens, Mariano Rivera, Bernie Williams 40.00
ATL96 Greg Maddux, Chipper Jones, Andruw Jones 40.00
OAK74 Rollie Fingers, Jim "Catfish" Hunter, Reggie Jackson 40.00
HOF36 Ty Cobb, Babe Ruth, Honus Wagner/ Pants 1,500

Timeless Teams Jerseys

NM/M
Common Player: 10.00
Inserted 1:144
JB Johnny Bench 20.00
DE Dwight Evans 15.00
RF Rollie Fingers 15.00
CH "Catfish" Hunter 15.00
RJ Reggie Jackson 15.00
AJ Andruw Jones 15.00
CJ Chipper Jones 15.00
FL Fred Lynn 15.00
EMa Edgar Martinez 15.00
WM Willie McCovey 15.00
EMu Eddie Murray 15.00
KS Kazuhiro Sasaki 10.00

Vintage Aces Jerseys

NM/M
Common Player: 8.00
Inserted 1:144
JD John Denny 8.00
TH Tim Hudson 10.00
FJ Ferguson Jenkins 10.00
RJ Randy Johnson 20.00
GM Greg Maddux 25.00
JM Juan Marichal 15.00
MMa Mike Marshall 8.00
PM Pedro Martinez 20.00
MMu Mike Mussina 25.00
HN Hideo Nomo 20.00
NR Nolan Ryan 100.00
JS Johnny Sain 20.00
MT Mike Torrez 8.00

Vintage Signature Combos

NM/M
Production 100 Sets
FB Carlton Fisk, Johnny Bench 100.00
JM Reggie Jackson, Willie McCovey 80.00
SD Ryne Sandberg, Andre Dawson 100.00
BR Sal Bando, Joe Rudi 40.00
EL Dwight Evans, Fred Lynn 60.00
AT Roberto Alomar, Jim Thome 75.00
BB Yogi Berra, Johnny Bench 100.00
GR Ken Griffey Jr., Alex Rodriguez 300.00
JO Edgar Martinez, John Olerud 60.00

2002 Upper Deck World Series Heroes

NM/M
Complete Set (180): 20.00
Common Player: .15
Common RC (91-135): 1.50
Common (136-180): 1.00
Inserted 1:10
Pack (5): 2.00
Box (24): 40.00
1 Jim "Catfish" Hunter .15
2 Jimmie Foxx .50
3 Mark McGwire 2.00
4 Rollie Fingers .25
5 Rickey Henderson .40
6 Joe Carter .15
7 John Olerud .15
8 Roberto Alomar .50
9 Pat Hentgen .15
10 Devon White .15
11 Eddie Mathews .50
12 Greg Maddux 1.00
13 Chipper Jones .75
14 Tom Glavine .25
15 Andruw Jones .50
16 David Justice .25
17 Fred McGriff .15
18 Ryan Klesko .15
19 John Smoltz .25
20 Javy Lopez .25
21 Marquis Grissom .15
22 Robin Yount .75
23 Ozzie Smith .75
24 Frankie Frisch .15
25 Stan Musial 1.00
26 Randy Johnson .75
27 Luis Gonzalez .25
28 Matt Williams .15
29 Steve Finley .15
30 Sandy Koufax 1.50
31 Duke Snider .50
32 Kirk Gibson .15
33 Steve Garvey .15
34 Jackie Robinson 1.50
35 Don Drysdale .50
36 Juan Marichal .50
37 Mel Ott .50
38 Orlando Cepeda .15
39 Jim Thome .75
40 Manny Ramirez .50
41 Omar Vizquel .15
42 Lou Boudreau .15
43 Gary Sheffield .25
44 Moises Alou .25
45 Livan Hernandez .15
46 Edgar Renteria .25
47 Al Leiter .15
48 Tom Seaver .75
49 Gary Carter .15
50 Mike Piazza 1.00
51 Nolan Ryan 2.00
52 Robin Ventura .15
53 Mike Hampton .15
54 Jesse Orosco .15
55 Cal Ripken Jr. 2.00
56 Brooks Robinson .75
57 Tony Gwynn .75
58 Kevin Brown .15
59 Curt Schilling .50
60 Cy Young .50
61 Honus Wagner .75
62 Willie Stargell .40
63 Wade Boggs .40
64 Carlton Fisk .40
65 Ken Griffey Sr. .15
66 Joe Morgan .15
67 Johnny Bench 1.00
68 Barry Larkin .40
69 Jose Rijo .15
70 Ty Cobb 1.50
71 Kirby Puckett 1.00
72 Chuck Knoblauch .15
73 Harmon Killebrew .50
74 Mickey Mantle 2.50
75 Joe DiMaggio 2.00
76 Don Larsen .40
77 Thurman Munson .75
78 Roger Maris 1.50
79 Phil Rizzuto .50
80 Babe Ruth 2.50
81 Lou Gehrig 2.00
82 Billy Martin .40
83 Derek Jeter 2.00
84 Roger Clemens 1.50
85 Tino Martinez .15
86 Bernie Williams .50
87 Mariano Rivera .25
88 Andy Pettitte .40
89 David Wells .15
90 Jorge Posada .25
91 Rodrigo Rosario **RC** 1.50
92 Brandon Puffer **RC** 1.50
93 Franklyn German **RC** 1.50
94 Reed Johnson **RC** 1.50
95 Chris Baker **RC** 1.50
96 John Ennis **RC** 1.50
97 Luis Martinez **RC** 1.50
98 Takaki Nomura **RC** 1.50
99 So Taguchi **RC** 4.00
100 Michael Crudale **RC** 1.50
101 Francis Beltran **RC** 1.50
102 Steve Kent **RC** 1.50
103 Jorge Sosa **RC** 1.50
104 Felix Escalona **RC** 1.50
105 Jose Valverde **RC** 1.50
106 Doug DeVore **RC** 1.50
107 Kazuhisa Ishii **RC** 4.00
108 Victor Alvarez **RC** 1.50
109 Eric Good **RC** 1.50
110 Jorge Nunez **RC** 1.50
111 Ron Calloway **RC** 1.50
112 Nelson Castro **RC** 1.50
113 Matt Thornton 1.50
114 Luis Ugueto **RC** 1.50
115 Hansel Izquierdo **RC** 1.50
116 Jaime Cerda **RC** 1.50
117 Mark Corey **RC** 1.50
118 Tyler Yates **RC** 2.50
119 Satoru Komiyama **RC** 1.50
120 Steve Bechler **RC** 1.50
121 Ben Howard **RC** 1.50
122 Anderson Machado **RC** 1.50
123 Jorge Padilla **RC** 1.50
124 Eric Junge **RC** 1.50
125 Adrian Burnside **RC** 1.50
126 Mike Gonzalez **RC** 1.50
127 Anastacio Martinez **RC** 1.50
128 Josh Hancock **RC** 1.50
129 Rene Reyes **RC** 1.50
130 Aaron Cook **RC** 1.50
131 Cam Esslinger **RC** 1.50
132 Juan Brito **RC** 1.50
133 Miguel Ascencio **RC** 1.50
134 Kevin Frederick **RC** 1.50
135 Edwin Almonte **RC** 1.50
136 Troy Glaus 1.00
137 Darin Erstad 1.00
138 Jeff Bagwell 1.00
139 Lance Berkman 1.50
140 Tim Hudson 1.25
141 Eric Chavez 1.25
142 Barry Zito 1.50
143 Carlos Delgado 1.00
144 Richie Sexson 1.50
145 Albert Pujols 4.00
146 Sammy Sosa 4.00
147 Kerry Wood 2.00
148 Greg Vaughn 1.00
149 Shawn Green 1.00
150 Vladimir Guerrero 2.50
151 Barry Bonds 6.00
152 C.C. Sabathia 1.00
153 Ichiro Suzuki 5.00
154 Freddy Garcia 1.00
155 Edgar Martinez 1.00
156 Josh Beckett 1.00
157 Cliff Floyd 1.00
158 Mo Vaughn 1.00
159 Jeromy Burnitz 1.00
160 Sean Burroughs 1.00
161 Phil Nevin 1.00
162 Scott Rolen 2.00
163 Brian Giles 1.25
164 Alex Rodriguez 5.00
165 Ivan Rodriguez 1.50
166 Juan Gonzalez 1.25
167 Rafael Palmeiro 1.50
168 Nomar Garciaparra 4.00
169 Pedro J. Martinez 2.00
170 Ken Griffey Jr. 4.00
171 Adam Dunn 1.50
172 Todd Helton 1.50
173 Mike Sweeney 1.00
174 Carlos Beltran 1.00
175 Dmitri Young 1.00
176 Doug Mientkiewicz 1.00
177 Torii Hunter 1.00
178 Frank Thomas 1.50
179 Magglio Ordonez 1.00
180 Jason Giambi 1.50

Base

NM/M
Complete Set (1):
DJ Derek Jeter 35.00

Bats

NM/M
Common Player: 15.00
Inserted 1:288
JD Joe DiMaggio/SP 100.00
MM Mickey Mantle 125.00
KP Kirby Puckett 25.00
ES Enos Slaughter 15.00

Jerseys

NM/M
Common Player: 10.00
Inserted 1:288
JC Joe Carter 10.00
CF Carlton Fisk 15.00
DL Don Larsen 20.00
BM Bill Mazeroski 15.00

Jerseys Autograph

No Pricing
Production 25 Sets

Match-Ups Memorabilia

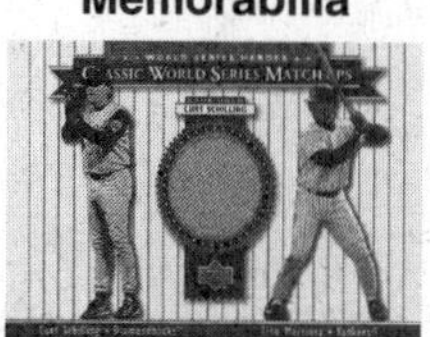

NM/M
Common Card: 8.00
Inserted 1:24
MU00 Mike Piazza, Roger Clemens 15.00
MU00a Andy Pettitte, Mike Piazza 15.00
MU00b Al Leiter, Derek Jeter 10.00
MU00d Edgardo Alfonzo, Mariano Rivera 8.00
MU00e John Franco, Derek Jeter 10.00
MU00c Robin Ventura, Roger Clemens 8.00
MU01 Mariano Rivera, Luis Gonzalez 8.00
MU01a Paul O'Neill, Curt Schilling 8.00
MU01b Bernie Williams, Randy Johnson 8.00
MU01c David Justice, Curt Schilling 8.00
MU01d Randy Johnson, Bernie Williams 8.00
MU01e Curt Schilling, Tino Martinez 8.00
MU01f Roger Clemens, Luis Gonzalez 15.00
MU01g Paul O'Neill, Byung-Hyun Kim 10.00
MU01h Luis Gonzalez, Mariano Rivera/97 12.00
MU03 Honus Wagner, Cy Young 100.00
MU09 Ty Cobb, Honus Wagner/SP 125.00
MU30 Jimmie Foxx 25.00
MU36 Joe DiMaggio, Mel Ott/SP 80.00
MU49 Duke Snider, Joe DiMaggio 25.00
MU53 Jackie Robinson, Billy Martin 25.00
MU55 Mickey Mantle, Jackie Robinson 110.00
MU56 Don Larsen, Duke Snider 25.00
MU56a Don Larsen, Jackie Robinson 20.00
MU57 Eddie Mathews, Yogi Berra 15.00
MU58 Yogi Berra, Eddie Mathews 15.00
MU62 Roger Maris, Juan Marichal 40.00
MU63 Sandy Koufax, Mickey Mantle 100.00
MU66 Don Drysdale, Brooks Robinson/SP 40.00

MU69 Nolan Ryan, Brooks Robinson 50.00
MU72 Joe Morgan, Jim "Catfish" Hunter 8.00
MU72a Rollie Fingers, Johnny Bench 10.00
MU73 Tom Seaver, "Catfish" Hunter 15.00
MU74 Jim "Catfish" Hunter, Steve Garvey 8.00
MU74a Davey Lopes, Jim "Catfish" Hunter 8.00
MU76 Ken Griffey Sr., Thurman Munson 12.00
MU76a Thurman Munson, Johnny Bench 20.00
MU78 Thurman Munson, Steve Garvey 15.00
MU78a Bill Russell, Thurman Munson 12.00
MU81 Steve Garvey, Dave Winfield 8.00
MU82 Robin Yount, Ozzie Smith 15.00
MU83 Cal Ripken Jr., Joe Morgan 25.00
MU84 Jack Morris, Tony Gwynn 12.00
MU86 Jesse Orosco, Roger Clemens 15.00
MU87 Ozzie Smith, Kirby Puckett 15.00
MU88 Mark McGwire, Kirk Gibson/SP 60.00
MU90 Barry Larkin, Mark McGwire/SP 20.00
MU91 Tom Glavine, Kirby Puckett 15.00
MU93 Joe Carter, Curt Schilling 8.00
MU95 Dennis Martinez, David Justice 8.00
MU96 Andruw Jones, Andy Pettitte 8.00
MU96a Tim Raines, Tom Glavine 10.00
MU96b Kenny Rogers, Chipper Jones 8.00
MU95a Kenny Lofton, John Smoltz 8.00
MU97 Jim Thome, Kevin Brown 10.00
MU98 Tony Gwynn, Bernie Williams 10.00
MU98a Trevor Hoffman, Bernie Williams/SP 8.00
MU99 Jorge Posada, Greg Maddux 15.00
MU99a Greg Maddux, Derek Jeter 15.00
MU99b Paul O'Neill, John Smoltz 8.00
MU99c Chipper Jones, Mariano Rivera 15.00

Patch Collection

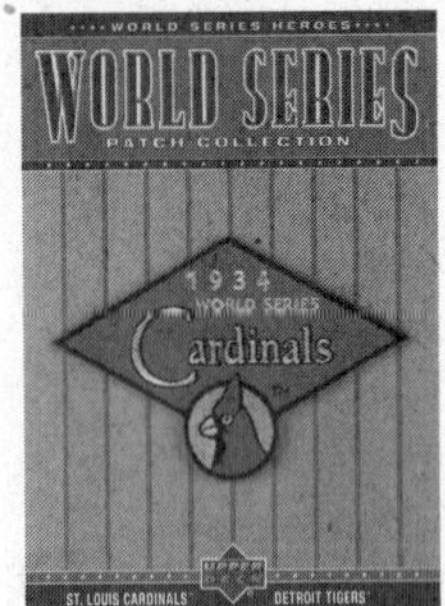

NM/M
Common Patch: 15.00
Inserted 1:Hobby Box
WS03 1903 World Series 25.00
WS05 1905 World Series 25.00
WS06 1906 World Series 20.00
WS07 1907 World Series 20.00
WS08 1908 World Series 25.00
WS09 1909 World Series 20.00
WS10 1910 World Series 20.00
WS11 1911 World Series 20.00
WS12 1912 World Series 30.00
WS13 1913 World Series 20.00
WS14 1914 World Series 25.00
WS15 1915 World Series 20.00
WS16 1916 World Series 25.00
WS17 1917 World Series 20.00
WS18 1918 World Series 30.00
WS19 1919 World Series 25.00
WS20 1920 World Series 20.00
WS21 1921 World Series 15.00
WS22 1922 World Series 20.00
WS23 1923 World Series 20.00
WS24 1924 World Series 20.00
WS25 1925 World Series 25.00
WS26 1926 World Series 20.00
WS27 1927 World Series 30.00
WS28 1928 World Series 25.00
WS29 1929 World Series 20.00
WS30 1930 World Series 20.00
WS31 1931 World Series 25.00
WS32 1932 World Series 30.00
WS33 1933 World Series 20.00
WS34 1934 World Series 20.00
WS35 1935 World Series 20.00
WS36 1936 World Series 20.00
WS37 1937 World Series 20.00
WS38 1938 World Series 25.00
WS39 1939 World Series 20.00
WS40 1940 World Series 20.00
WS41 1941 World Series 20.00
WS42 1942 World Series 20.00
WS43 1943 World Series 20.00
WS44 1944 World Series 30.00
WS45 1945 World Series 20.00
WS46 1946 World Series 25.00
WS47 1947 World Series 25.00
WS48 1948 World Series 30.00
WS49 1949 World Series 25.00
WS50 1950 World Series 25.00
WS51 1951 World Series 25.00
WS52 1952 World Series 20.00
WS53 1953 World Series 25.00
WS54 1954 World Series 15.00
WS55 1955 World Series 25.00
WS56 1956 World Series 25.00
WS57 1957 World Series 25.00
WS58 1958 World Series 20.00
WS59 1959 World Series 20.00
WS60 1960 World Series 20.00
WS61 1961 World Series 35.00
WS62 1962 World Series 20.00
WS63 1963 World Series 20.00
WS64 1964 World Series 20.00
WS65 1965 World Series 20.00
WS66 1966 World Series 20.00
WS67 1967 World Series 20.00
WS68 1968 World Series 20.00
WS69 1969 World Series 35.00
WS70 1970 World Series 20.00
WS71 1971 World Series 20.00
WS72 1972 World Series 20.00
WS73 1973 World Series 20.00
WS74 1974 World Series 20.00
WS75 1975 World Series 30.00
WS76 1976 World Series 30.00
WS77 1977 World Series 20.00
WS78 1978 World Series 20.00
WS79 1979 World Series 20.00
WS80 1980 World Series 20.00
WS81 1981 World Series 20.00
WS82 1982 World Series 25.00
WS83 1983 World Series 25.00
WS84 1984 World Series 20.00
WS85 1985 World Series 20.00
WS86 1986 World Series 20.00
WS87 1987 World Series 20.00
WS88 1988 World Series 20.00
WS89 1989 World Series 20.00
WS90 1990 World Series 20.00
WS91 1991 World Series 20.00
WS92 1992 World Series 20.00
WS93 1993 World Series 20.00
WS95 1995 World Series 20.00
WS96 1996 World Series 20.00
WS97 1997 World Series 20.00
WS98 1998 World Series 15.00
WS99 1999 World Series 20.00
WS01 2001 World Series 20.00

Patch Collection Autographs

NM/M
Inserted 1:336
WS93 Joe Carter 40.00
WS99 Roger Clemens 100.00
WS74 Rollie Fingers 30.00
WS75 Carlton Fisk 60.00
WS81 Steve Garvey 35.00
WS65 Sandy Koufax 250.00
WS56 Don Larsen 60.00
WS89 Mark McGwire 275.00
WS76 Joe Morgan 40.00
WS91 Kirby Puckett 60.00
WS83 Cal Ripken Jr. 175.00
WS70 Brooks Robinson 80.00
WS69 Nolan Ryan 200.00
WS73 Tom Seaver 60.00
WS55 Duke Snider 75.00
WS82 Ozzie Smith 90.00

2002 Upper Deck 40-Man

NM/M
Complete Set (1182): 200.00
Common Player: .15
Silvers: 1-30X
Inserted 1:4
Rainbows: 5-10X
Production 40 Sets
Hobby Pack (10): 1.75
Hobby Box (24): 30.00
1 Darin Erstad .40
2 Kevin Appier .15
3 Scott Schoeneweis .15
4 Bengie Molina .15
5 Troy Glaus .50
6 Adam Kennedy .15
7 Aaron Sele .15
8 Garret Anderson .25
9 Ramon Ortiz .15
10 Dennis Cook .15
11 Scott Spiezio .15
12 Orlando Palmeiro .15
13 Troy Percival .15
14 David Eckstein .15
15 Jarrod Washburn .40
16 Nathan Haynes .15
17 Benji Gil .15
18 Alfredo Amezega .15
19 Ben Weber .15
20 Al Levine .15
21 Brad Fullmer .15
22 Elpidio Guzman .15
23 Tim Salmon .25
24 Jose Nieves .15
25 Shawn Wooten .15
26 Lou Pote .15
27 Mickey Callaway .15
28 Steve Green .15
29 John Lackey .15
30 Mark Lukasiewicz .15
31 Jorge Fabregas .15
32 Jeff Da Vanon .15
33 Elvin Nina .15
34 Donne Wall .15
35 Eric Chavez .50
36 Jermaine Dye .15
37 Scott Hatteberg .15
38 Mark Mulder .50
39 Ramon Hernandez .15
40 Jim Mecir .15
41 Barry Zito .50
42 Greg Myers .15
43 David Justice .50
44 Mike Magnante .15
45 Terrence Long .15
46 Tim Hudson .50
47 Olmedo Saenz .15
48 Billy Koch .15
49 Carlos Pena .50
50 Mike Venafro .15
51 Mark Ellis .15
52 Randy Velarde .15
53 Jeremy Giambi .15
54 Mike Colagelo .15
55 Mike Holtz .15
56 Chad Bradford .15
57 Miguel Tejada .50
58 Mike Fyhrie .15
59 Eric Hiljus .15
60 Juan Pena .15
61 Mario Valdez .15
62 Franklyn German **RC** .50
63 Carlos Delgado .50
64 Orlando Hudson .15
65 Chris Carpenter .15
66 Kelvim Escobar .15
67 Felipe Lopez .15
68 Brandon Lyon .15
69 Jose Cruz Jr. .15
70 Luke Prokopec .15
71 Darrin Fletcher .15
72 Bob File .15
73 Felix Heredia .15
74 Mike Sirotka .15
75 Shannon Stewart .15
76 Joe Lawrence .15
77 Chris Woodward .15
78 Dan Plesac .15
79 Pedro Borbon .15
80 Roy Halladay .40
81 Raul Mondesi .40
82 Steve Parris .15
83 Homer Bush .15
84 Esteban Loaiza .15
85 Vernon Wells .15
86 Justin Miller .15
87 Scott Eyre .15
88 Dave Berg .15
89 Gustavo Chacin **RC** .15
90 Joe Orloski **RC** .40
91 Corey Thurman **RC** .15
92 Tom Wilson .15
93 Eric Hinske .50
94 Chris Baker **RC** .40
95 Reed Johnson **RC** .40
96 Greg Vaughn .15
97 Toby Hall .15
98 Brent Abernathy .15
99 Bobby Smith .15
100 Tanyon Sturtze .15
101 Chris Gomez .15
102 Joe Kennedy .15
103 Ben Grieve .15
104 Aubrey Huff .15
105 Jesus Colome .15
106 Felix Escalona **RC** .40
107 Paul Wilson .15
108 Ryan Rupe .15
109 Jason Tyner .15
110 Esteban Yan .15
111 Russ Johnson .15
112 Randy Winn .15
113 Wilson Alvarez .15
114 Wilmy Caceres .15
115 Steve Cox .15
116 Dewon Brazelton .15
117 Doug Creek .15
118 Jason Conti .15
119 John Flaherty .15
120 Delvin James .15
121 Steve Kent **RC** .15
122 Kevin McGlinchy .15
123 Travis Phelps .15
124 Bobby Seay .15
125 Travis Harper .15
126 Victor Zambrano .15
127 Jace Brewer .15
128 Jason Smith .15
129 Ramon Soler .15
130 Brandon Backe **RC** .50
131 Jorge Sosa **RC** .25
132 Jim Thome .75
133 Brady Anderson .15
134 C.C. Sabathia .15
135 Einar Diaz .15
136 Ricky Gutierrez .15
137 Danys Baez .15
138 Bob Wickman .15
139 Milton Bradley .15
140 Bartolo Colon .40
141 Jolbert Cabrera .15
142 Eddie Taubensee .15
143 Ellis Burks .15
144 Omar Vizquel .40
145 Eddie Perez .15
146 Jaret Wright .15
147 Chuck Finley .15
148 Paul Shuey .15
149 Travis Fryman .15
150 Wil Cordero .15
151 Ricardo Rincon .15
152 Victor Martinez .15
153 Charles Nagy .15
154 Alex Escobar .15
155 Russell Branyan .15
156 Matt Lawton .15
157 Ryan Drese .15
158 Jerrod Riggan .15
159 David Riske .15
160 Jake Westbrook .15
161 Mark Wohlers .15
162 John McDonald .15
163 Ichiro Suzuki 1.50
164 Freddy Garcia .15
165 Edgar Martinez .15
166 Ben Davis .15
167 Shigetoshi Hasegawa .15
168 Carlos Guillen .15
169 Ruben Sierra .15
170 Joel Pineiro .15
171 Norm Charlton .15
172 Bret Boone .15
173 Jamie Moyer .15
174 Jeff Nelson .15
175 Kazuhiro Sasaki .50
176 Jeff Cirillo .15
177 Mark McLemore .15
178 Paul Abbott .15
179 Mike Cameron .15
180 Dan Wilson .15
181 John Olerud .50
182 Arthur Rhodes .15
183 Desi Relaford .15
184 John Halama .15
185 Antonio Perez .15
186 Ryan Anderson .15
187 James Baldwin .15
188 Ryan Franklin .15
189 Justin Kaye .15
190 J.J. Putz **RC** .40
191 Allan Simpson **RC** .40
192 Matt Thornton .15
193 Luis Ugueto **RC** .40
194 Chris Richard .15
195 Sidney Ponson .15
196 Brook Fordyce .15
197 Luis Matos .15
198 Josh Towers .15
199 David Segui .15
200 Chris Brock .15
201 Tony Batista .15
202 Erik Bedard .15
203 Marty Cordova .15
204 Jerry Hairston Jr. .15
205 Jason Johnson .15
206 Buddy Groom .15
207 Mike Bordick .15
208 Melvin Mora .15
209 Calvin Maduro .15
210 Jeff Conine .15
211 Luis Rivera .15
212 Jay Gibbons .15
213 B.J. Ryan .15
214 Sean Douglass .15
215 Rodrigo Lopez .15
216 Rick Bauer .15
217 Scott Erickson .15
218 Jorge Julio .15
219 Willis Roberts .15
220 John Stephens .15
221 Geronimo Gil .15
222 Chris Singleton .15
223 Mike Paradis .15
224 John Parrish .15
225 Steve Bechler **RC** .50
226 Mike Moriarty **RC** .15
227 Luis Garcia .15
228 Alex Rodriguez 1.50
229 Mark Teixeira .50
230 Chan Ho Park .15
231 Todd Van Poppel .15
232 Mike Young .15
233 Kenny Rogers .15
234 Rusty Greer .15
235 Rafael Palmeiro .50
236 Francisco Cordero .15
237 John Rocker .15
238 Dave Burba .15
239 Travis Hafner .15
240 Kevin Mench .15
241 Carl Everett .15
242 Ivan Rodriguez .50
243 Jeff Zimmerman .15
244 Juan Gonzalez .50
245 Herbert Perry .15
246 Rob Bell .15
247 Doug Davis .15
248 Frank Catalanotto .15
249 Jay Powell .15
250 Gabe Kapler .15
251 Joaquin Benoit .15
252 Jovanny Cedeno .15
253 Hideki Irabu .15
254 Dan Miceli .15
255 Danny Kolb .15
256 Colby Lewis .15
257 Rich Rodriguez .15
258 Ismael Valdes .15
259 Bill Haselman .15
260 Jason Hart .15
261 Rudy Seanez .15
262 Travis Hughes **RC** .40
263 Hank Blalock .50
264 Steve Woodard .15
265 Nomar Garciaparra 1.50
266 Pedro J. Martinez .75
267 Frank Castillo .15
268 Johnny Damon .15
269 Doug Mirabelli .15
270 Derek Lowe .40
271 Shea Hillenbrand .50
272 Paxton Crawford .15
273 Tony Clark .15
274 Dustin Hermanson .15
275 Trot Nixon .15
276 John Burkett .15
277 Rich Garces .15
278 Josh Hancock **RC** .15
279 Michael Coleman .15
280 Darren Oliver .15
281 Jason Varitek .15
282 Jose Offerman .15
283 Tim Wakefield .15
284 Rolando Arrojo .15
285 Rickey Henderson .50
286 Ugueth Urbina .15
287 Casey Fossum .15
288 Manny Ramirez .50
289 Sun-Woo Kim .15
290 Juan Diaz .15
291 Willie Banks .15
292 Jorge De La Rosa **RC** .50
293 Juan Pena .15
294 Jeff Wallace .15
295 Calvin Pickering .15
296 Anastacio Martinez **RC** .40
297 Carlos Baerga .15
298 Rey Sanchez .15
299 Mike Sweeney .15
300 Jeff Suppan .15
301 Brent Mayne .15
302 Chad Durbin .15
303 Dan Reichert .15
304 Raul Ibanez .15
305 Joe Randa .15
306 Chris George .15
307 Michael Tucker .15
308 Paul Byrd .15
309 Kris Wilson .15
310 Luis Alicea .15
311 Neifi Perez .15
312 Brian Shouse .15
313 Chuck Knoblauch .15
314 Dave McCarty .15
315 Blake Stein .15
316 Alexis Gomez .15
317 Mark Quinn .15
318 A.J. Hinch .15
319 Carlos Febles .15
320 Roberto Hernandez .15
321 Brandon Berger .15
322 Jeff Austin **RC** .15
323 Corey Bailey .15
324 Tony Cogan .15
325 Nate Field **RC** .40
326 Jason Grimsley .15
327 Darrell May .15
328 Donnie Sadler .15
329 Carlos Beltran .15
330 Miguel Asencio **RC** .40
331 Jeff Weaver .15
332 Bobby Higginson .15
333 Mike Rivera .15
334 Matt Anderson .15
335 Craig Paquette .15
336 Jose Lima .15
337 Juan Acevedo .15
338 Danny Patterson .15
339 Andres Torres .15
340 Dean Palmer .15
341 Randall Simon .15
342 Craig Monroe .15
343 Damion Easley .15
344 Robert Fick .15
345 Steve Sparks .15
346 Dmitri Young .15
347 Nate Cornejo .15
348 Matt Miller .15
349 Wendell Magee .15
350 Shane Halter .15
351 Brian Moehler .15
352 Mitch Meluskey .15
353 Jose Macias .15
354 Mark Redman .15
355 Jeff Farnsworth .15
356 Kris Keller .15
357 Adam Pettyjohn .15
358 Fernando Rodney .15
359 Andy Van Hekken .15
360 Damian Jackson .15
361 Jose Paniagua .15
362 Jacob Cruz .15
363 Doug Mientkiewicz .15
364 Torii Hunter .15
365 Brad Radke .15
366 Denny Hocking .15
367 Mike Jackson .15
368 Eddie Guardado .15
369 Jacque Jones .15
370 Joe Mays .15
371 Matt Kinney .15
372 Kyle Lohse .15
373 David Ortiz .15
374 Luis Rivas .15
375 Jay Canizaro .15
376 Dustan Mohr .15
377 LaTroy Hawkins .15
378 Warren Morris .15
379 A.J. Pierzynski .15
380 Eric Milton .15
381 Bob Wells .15
382 Cristian Guzman .15
383 Brian Buchanan .15
384 Bobby Kielty .15
385 Corey Koskie .15
386 J.C. Romero .15
387 Jack Cressend .15
388 Mike Duvall .15
389 Tony Fiore .15
390 Tom Prince .15
391 Todd Sears .15
392 Kevin Frederick **RC** .40
393 Frank Thomas .50
394 Mark Buehrle .15
395 Jon Garland .15
396 Jeff Liefer .15
397 Magglio Ordonez .50
398 Rocky Biddle .15
399 Lorenzo Barcelo .15
400 Ray Durham .15
401 Bob Howry .15
402 Aaron Rowand .15
403 Keith Foulke .15
404 Paul Konerko .50
405 Sandy Alomar Jr. .15
406 Mark Johnson .15
407 Carlos Lee .15
408 Jose Valentin .15
409 Jon Rauch .15
410 Royce Clayton .15
411 Kenny Lofton .40
412 Tony Graffanino .15
413 Todd Ritchie .15
414 Antonio Osuna .15
415 Gary Glover .15
416 Mike Porzio .15
417 Danny Wright .15
418 Kelly Wunsch .15
419 Miguel Olivo .15
420 Edwin Almonte **RC** .15
421 Kyle Kane **RC** .50
422 Mitch Wylie **RC** .15
423 Derek Jeter 2.00
424 Jason Giambi .50
425 Roger Clemens 1.50
426 Enrique Wilson .15
427 David Wells .15
428 Mike Mussina .50
429 Bernie Williams .50
430 Mike Stanton .15
431 Sterling Hitchcock .15
432 Alex Graman .15
433 Robin Ventura .50
434 Mariano Rivera .50
435 Jay Tessmer .15
436 Andy Pettitte .50
437 John Vander Wal .15
438 Adrian Hernandez .15
439 Alberto Castillo .15
440 Steve Karsay .15
441 Alfonso Soriano .75
442 Rondell White .15
443 Nick Johnson .50
444 Jorge Posada .50
445 Ramiro Mendoza .15
446 Gerald Williams .15
447 Orlando Hernandez .15
448 Randy Choate .15
449 Randy Keisler .15
450 Ted Lilly .15
451 Christian Parker .15
452 Ron Coomer .15
453 Marcus Thames .15
454 Drew Henson .50
455 Jeff Bagwell .50
456 Wade Miller .15
457 Lance Berkman .50
458 Julio Lugo .15
459 Roy Oswalt .40
460 Nelson Cruz .15
461 Morgan Ensberg .15
462 Geoff Blum .15
463 Ryan Jamison **RC** .50
464 Billy Wagner .15
465 Dave Mlicki .15
466 Brad Ausmus .15
467 Jose Vizcaino .15

468 Craig Biggio .50
469 Shane Reynolds .15
470 Gregg Zaun .15
471 Octavio Dotel .15
472 Carlos Hernandez .15
473 Richard Hidalgo .15
474 Daryle Ward .15
475 Orlando Merced .15
476 John Buck .15
477 Adam Everett .15
478 Doug Brocail .15
479 Brad Lidge .15
480 Scott Linebrink .15
481 T.J. Mathews .15
482 Greg Miller .15
483 Hipolito Pichardo .15
484 Brandon Puffer **RC** .15
485 Ricky Stone .15
486 Jason Lane .15
487 Brian L. Hunter .15
488 Rodrigo Rosario **RC** .50
489 Tom Shearn **RC** .50
490 Gary Sheffield .40
491 Tom Glavine .40
492 Mike Remlinger .15
493 Henry Blanco .15
494 Vinny Castilla .15
495 Chris Hammond .15
496 Kevin Millwood .50
497 Darren Holmes .15
498 Cory Aldridge .15
499 Tim Spooneybarger .15
500 Rafael Furcal .50
501 Albie Lopez .15
502 Javy Lopez .40
503 Greg Maddux 1.00
504 Andruw Jones .50
505 Steve Torrealba .15
506 George Lombard .15
507 B.J. Surhoff .15
508 Marcus Giles .15
509 Derrick Lewis .15
510 Wes Helms .15
511 John Smoltz .50
512 Chipper Jones .75
513 Jason Marquis .15
514 Mark DeRosa .15
515 Jung Bong .15
516 Kevin Gryboski **RC** .15
517 Damian Moss .15
518 Horacio Ramirez .15
519 Scott Sobkowiak .15
520 Billy Sylvester .15
521 Nick Green .15
522 Travis Wilson .15
523 Ryan Langerhans .15
524 John Ennis **RC** .50
525 John Foster **RC** .15
526 Keith Lockhart .15
527 Julio Franco .15
528 Richie Sexson .50
529 Jeffrey Hammonds .15
530 Ben Sheets .50
531 Mike DeJean .15
532 Mark Loretta .15
533 Alex Ochoa .15
534 Jamey Wright .15
535 Jose Hernandez .15
536 Glendon Rusch .15
537 Geoff Jenkins .50
538 Luis S. Lopez .15
539 Curtis Leskanic .15
540 Chad Fox .15
541 Tyler Houston .15
542 Nick Neugebauer .15
543 Matt Stairs .15
544 Paul Rigdon .15
545 Bill Hall .15
546 Luis Vizcaino .15
547 Lenny Harris .15
548 Alex Sanchez .15
549 Raul Casanova .15
550 Eric Young .15
551 Jeff Deardorff **RC** .15
552 Nelson Figueroa .15
553 Ron Belliard .15
554 Mike Buddie .15
555 Jose Cabrera .15
556 J.M. Gold .15
557 Ray King .15
558 Jose Mieses .15
559 Takahito Nomura **RC** .50
560 Ruben Quevedo .15
561 Jackson Melian .15
562 Cristian Guerrero .15
563 Paul Bako .15
564 Luis Martinez **RC** .50
565 Brian Mallette **RC** .50
566 Matt Morris .50
567 Tino Martinez .40
568 Fernando Vina .15
569 Gene Stechschulte .15
570 Andy Benes .15
571 Placido Polanco .15
572 Luis Garcia .15
573 Jim Edmonds .50
574 Bud Smith .15
575 Mike Matheny .15
576 Garrett Stephenson .15
577 Miguel Cairo .15
578 Darryl Kile .15
579 Mike Timlin .15
580 Rick Ankiel .15
581 Jason Isringhausen .15
582 Albert Pujols 1.50
583 Eli Marrero .15
584 Steve Kline .15
585 J.D. Drew .50
586 Mike DiFelice .15
587 Dave Veres .15
588 Kerry Robinson .15
589 Edgar Renteria .15
590 Woody Williams .15
591 Chance Caple .15
592 Michael Crudale **RC** .15
593 Luther Hackman .15
594 Josh Pearce .15
595 Kevin Joseph .15
596 Jimmy Journell .15
597 Jeremy Lambert **RC** .40
598 Mike Matthews .15
599 Les Walrond .15
600 Keith McDonald .15
601 William Ortega .15
602 Scotty Layfield **RC** .50
603 So Taguchi **RC** 1.00
604 Eduardo Perez .15
605 Sammy Sosa 1.50
606 Kerry Wood .75
607 Kyle Farnsworth .15
608 Alex Gonzalez .15
609 Tom Gordon .15
610 Carlos Zambrano .15
611 Roosevelt Brown .15
612 Bill Mueller .15
613 Mark Prior 1.50
614 Darren Lewis .15
615 Joe Girardi .15
616 Fred McGriff .50
617 Jon Lieber .15
618 Robert Machado .15
619 Corey Patterson .50
620 Joe Borowski .15
621 Todd Hundley .15
622 Jason Bere .15
623 Moises Alou .40
624 Jeff Fassero .15
625 Jesus Sanchez .15
626 Chris Stynes .15
627 Delino DeShields .15
628 Augie Ojeda .15
629 Juan Cruz .15
630 Ben Christensen .15
631 Mike Meyers .15
632 Will Ohman .15
633 Steve Smyth .15
634 Mark Bellhorn .15
635 Nate Frese .15
636 David Kelton .15
637 Francis Beltran **RC** .40
638 Antonio Alfonseca .15
639 Donovan Osborne .15
640 Shawn Sonnier .15
641 Matt Clement .15
642 Luis Gonzalez .25
643 Brian Anderson .15
644 Randy Johnson .75
645 Mark Grace .50
646 Danny Bautista .15
647 Junior Spivey .15
648 Jay Bell .15
649 Miguel Batista .15
650 Tony Womack .15
651 Byung-Hyun Kim .15
652 Steve Finley .40
653 Rick Helling .15
654 Curt Schilling .50
655 Erubiel Durazo .15
656 Chris Donnels .15
657 Greg Colbrunn .15
658 Mike Morgan .15
659 Jose Guillen .15
660 Matt Williams .50
661 Craig Counsell .15
662 Greg Swindell .15
663 Rod Barajas .15
664 David Dellucci .15
665 Todd Stottlemyre .15
666 P.J. Bevis **RC** .15
667 Mike Koplove .15
668 Mike Myers .15
669 John Patterson .15
670 Bret Prinz .15
671 Jeremy Ward **RC** .50
672 Danny Klassen .15
673 Luis Terrero .15
674 Jose Valverde **RC** .50
675 Doug DeVore **RC** .50
676 Quinton McCracken .15
677 Paul LoDuca .15
678 Mark Grudzielanek .15
679 Kevin Brown .50
680 Paul Quantrill .15
681 Shawn Green .50
682 Hideo Nomo .50
683 Eric Gagne .15
684 Giovanni Carrara .15
685 Marquis Grissom .15
686 Hiram Bocachica .15
687 Guillermo Mota .15
688 Alex Cora .15
689 Odalis Perez .15
690 Brian Jordan .15
691 Andy Ashby .15
692 Eric Karros .40
693 Chad Krueter .15
694 Dave Roberts .15
695 Omar Daal .15
696 Dave Hansen .15
697 Adrian Beltre .50
698 Terry Mulholland .15
699 Cesar Izturis .15
700 Steve Colyer .15
701 Carlos Garcia .15
702 Ricardo Rodriguez .15
703 Darren Dreifort .15
704 Jeff Reboulet .15
705 Victor Alvarez **RC** .50
706 Kazuhisa Ishii **RC** 2.00
707 Jose Vidro .15
708 Henry Mateo .15
709 Tony Armas Jr. .15
710 Carl Pavano .15
711 Peter Bergeron .15
712 Bruce Chen .15
713 Orlando Cabrera .15
714 Britt Reames .15
715 Masato Yoshii .15
716 Fernando Tatis .15
717 Graeme Lloyd .15
718 Scott Stewart .15
719 Lou Collier .15
720 Michael Barrett .15
721 Vladimir Guerrero .75
722 Troy Mattes .15
723 Brian Schneider .15
724 Lee Stevens .15
725 Javier Vazquez .15
726 Brad Wilkerson .15
727 Zach Day .15
728 Ed Vosberg .15
729 Tomokazu Ohka .15
730 Mike Mordecai .15
731 Donnie Bridges .15
732 Ron Chiavacci .15
733 T.J. Tucker .15
734 Scott Hodges .15
735 Valentino Pascucci .15
736 Andres Galarraga .15
737 Scott Downs .15
738 Eric Good **RC** .15
739 Ron Calloway **RC** .50
740 Jorge Nunez **RC** .15
741 Henry Rodriguez .15
742 Jeff Kent .15
743 Russ Ortiz .15
744 Felix Rodriguez .15
745 Benito Santiago .15
746 Tsuyoshi Shinjo .50
747 Tim Worrell .15
748 Marvin Benard .15
749 Kurt Ainsworth .15
750 Edwards Guzman .15
751 J.T. Snow .15
752 Jason Christiansen .15
753 Robb Nen .15
754 Barry Bonds 2.00
755 Shawon Dunston .15
756 Chad Zerbe .15
757 Ramon E. Martinez .15
758 Calvin Murray .15
759 Pedro Feliz .15
760 Jason Schmidt .15
761 Damon Minor .15
762 Reggie Sanders .15
763 Rich Aurilia .15
764 Kirk Rueter .15
765 David Bell .15
766 Yorvit Torrealba .15
767 Livan Hernandez .15
768 Felix Diaz .15
769 Aaron Fultz .15
770 Ryan Jensen .15
771 Arturo McDowell .15
772 Carlos Valderrama .15
773 Nelson Castro **RC** .50
774 Jay Witasick .15
775 Deivis Santos .15
776 Josh Beckett .15
777 Charles Johnson .15
778 Derrek Lee .15
779 A.J. Burnett .15
780 Vic Darensbourg .15
781 Cliff Floyd .50
782 Jose Cueto .15
783 Nate Teut .15
784 Alex Gonzalez .15
785 Brad Penny .15
786 Kevin Olsen .15
787 Mike Lowell .15
788 Mike Redmond .15
789 Braden Looper .15
790 Eric Owens .15
791 Andy Fox .15
792 Vladimir Nunez .15
793 Luis Castillo .15
794 Ryan Dempster .15
795 Armando Almanza .15
796 Preston Wilson .15
797 Pablo Ozuna .15
798 Gary Knotts .15
799 Ramon Castro .15
800 Benito Baez .15
801 Michael Tejera .15
802 Claudio Vargas .15
803 Chip Ambres .15
804 Hansel Izquierdo **RC** .50
805 Tim Raines .15
806 Marty Malloy .15
807 Julian Tavarez .15
808 Roberto Alomar .50
809 Al Leiter .50
810 Jeromy Burnitz .15
811 John Franco .15
812 Edgardo Alfonzo .15
813 Mike Piazza 1.00
814 Shawn Estes .15
815 Joe McEwing .15
816 David Weathers .15
817 Pedro Astacio .15
818 Timoniel Perez .15
819 Grant Roberts .15
820 Rey Ordonez .15
821 Steve Trachsel .15
822 Roger Cedeno .15
823 Mark Johnson .15
824 Armando Benitez .15
825 Vance Wilson .15
826 Jay Payton .15
827 Mo Vaughn .50
828 Scott Strickland .15
829 Mark Guthrie .15
830 Jeff D'Amico .15
831 Mark Corey **RC** .50
832 Kane Davis .15
833 Jae Weong Seo .15
834 Pat Strange .15
835 Adam Walker **RC** .15
836 Tyler Walker .15
837 Gary Matthews Jr. .15
838 Jaime Cerda **RC** .25
839 Satoru Komiyama **RC** .50
840 Tyler Yates **RC** .50
841 John Valentin .15
842 Ryan Klesko .40
843 Wiki Gonzalez .15
844 Trevor Hoffman .15
845 Sean Burroughs .40
846 Alan Embree .15
847 Dennis Tankersley .15
848 D'Angelo Jimenez .15
849 Kevin Jarvis .15
850 Mark Kotsay .15
851 Phil Nevin .25
852 Jeremy Fikac .15
853 Brett Tomko .15
854 Brian Lawrence .15
855 Steve Reed .15
856 Bubba Trammell .15
857 Tom Davey .15
858 Ramon Vazquez .15
859 Tom Lampkin .15
860 Bobby Jones .15
861 Ray Lankford .15
862 Mark Sweeney .15
863 Adam Eaton .15
864 Trenidad Hubbard .15
865 Jason Boyd .15
866 Javier Cardona .15
867 Clifford Bartosh **RC** .50
868 Mike Bynum .15
869 Eric Cyr **RC** .50
870 Jose Nunez .15
871 Ron Gant .15
872 Deivi Cruz .15
873 Ben Howard **RC** .50
874 Todd Donovan **RC** .25
875 Andy Shibilo **RC** .15
876 Scott Rolen .75
877 Jose Mesa .15
878 Rheal Cormier .15
879 Travis Lee .15
880 Mike Lieberthal .15
881 Brandon Duckworth .15
882 David Coggin .15
883 Bobby Abreu .50
884 Turk Wendell .15
885 Marlon Byrd .15
886 Jason Michaels .15
887 Robert Person .15
888 Tomas Perez .15
889 Jimmy Rollins .50
890 Vicente Padilla .15
891 Pat Burrell .50
892 Dave Hollins .15
893 Randy Wolf .15
894 Jose Santiago .15
895 Doug Glanville .15
896 Cliff Politte .15
897 Marlon Anderson .15
898 Ricky Bottalico .15
899 Terry Adams .15
900 Brad Baisley .15
901 Hector Mercado .15
902 Elio Serrano **RC** .50
903 Todd Pratt .15
904 Peter Zamora **RC** .50
905 Nick Punto .15
906 Ricky Ledee .15
907 Eric Junge **RC** .15
908 Anderson Machado **RC** .50
909 Jorge Padilla **RC** .50
910 John Mabry .15
911 Brian Giles .50
912 Jason Kendall .40
913 Jack Wilson .15
914 Kris Benson .15
915 Aramis Ramirez .15
916 Mike Fetters .15
917 Adrian Brown .15
918 Pokey Reese .15
919 Dave Williams .15
920 Mike Benjamin .15
921 Kip Wells .15
922 Mike Williams .15
923 Pat Meares .15
924 Ron Villone .15
925 Armando Rios .15
926 Jimmy Anderson .15
927 Robert Mackowiak .15
928 Kevin Young .15
929 Brian Boehringer .15
930 Joe Beimel .15
931 Chad Hermansen .15
932 Scott Sauerbeck .15
933 Josh Fogg .15
934 Mike Gonzalez **RC** .15
935 Mike Lincoln .15
936 Sean Lowe .15
937 Matt Guerrier .15
938 Ryan Vogelsong .15
939 J.R. House .15
940 Craig Wilson .15
941 Tony Alvarez .15
942 J.J. Davis .15
943 Abraham Nunez .15
944 Adrian Burnside **RC** .50
945 Ken Griffey Jr. 1.00
946 Jimmy Haynes .15
947 Juan Castro .15
948 Jose Rijo .15
949 Corky Miller .15
950 Elmer Dessens .15
951 Aaron Boone .15
952 Juan Encarnacion .15
953 Chris Reitsma .15
954 Wilton Guerrero .15
955 Danny Graves .15
956 Jim Brower .15
957 Barry Larkin .50
958 Todd Walker .15
959 Gabe White .15
960 Adam Dunn .50
961 Jason LaRue .15
962 Reggie Taylor .15
963 Sean Casey .40
964 Scott Williamson .15
965 Austin Kearns .50
966 Kelly Stinnett .15
967 Jose Acevedo .15
968 Gookie Dawkins .15
969 Brady Clark .15
970 Scott Sullivan .15
971 Ricardo Aramboles .15
972 Lance Davis .15
973 Seth Etherton .15
974 Luke Hudson .15
975 Joey Hamilton .15
976 Luis Pineda .15
977 John Riedling .15
978 Jose Silva .15
979 Dane Sardinha .15
980 Ben Broussard .15
981 David Espinosa .15
982 Ruben Mateo .15
983 Larry Walker .50
984 Juan Uribe .15
985 Mike Hampton .15
986 Aaron Cook **RC** .15
987 Jose Ortiz .15
988 Todd Jones .15
989 Todd Helton .50
990 Shawn Chacon .15
991 Jason Jennings .15
992 Todd Zeile .15
993 Ben Petrick .15
994 Denny Neagle .15
995 Jose Jimenez .15
996 Juan Pierre .15
997 Todd Hollandsworth .15
998 Kent Mercker .15
999 Greg Norton .15
1000 Terry Shumpert .15
1001 Mark Little .15
1002 Gary Bennett .15
1003 Dennys Reyes .15
1004 Justin Speier .15
1005 John Thomson .15
1006 Rick White .15
1007 Colin Young **RC** .40
1008 Cam Esslinger **RC** .50
1009 Rene Reyes **RC** .50
1010 Mike James .15
1011 Morgan Ensberg .15
1012 Adam Everett .15
1013 Rodrigo Rosario .15
1014 Carlos Pena .15
1015 Eric Hinske .50
1016 Orlando Hudson .15
1017 Reed Johnson .15
1018 Jung Bong .15
1019 Bill Hall .15
1020 Mark Prior 1.50
1021 Francis Beltran .15
1022 David Kelton .15
1023 Felix Escalona .15
1024 Jorge Sosa .15
1025 Dewon Brazelton .15
1026 Jose Valverde .15
1027 Luis Terrero .15
1028 Kazuhisa Ishii 1.00
1029 Cesar Izturis .15
1030 Ryan Jensen .15
1031 Matt Thornton .15
1032 Hansel Izquierdo .15
1033 Jaime Cerda .15
1034 Erik Bedard .15
1035 Sean Burroughs .15
1036 Ben Howard .15
1037 Ramon Vazquez .15
1038 Marlon Byrd .15
1039 Josh Fogg .15
1040 Hank Blalock .50
1041 Mark Teixeira .50
1042 Kevin Mench .15
1043 Dane Sardinha .15
1044 Austin Kearns .50
1045 Anastacio Martinez .15
1046 Eric Munson .15
1047 Jon Rauch .15
1048 Nick Johnson .50
1049 Alex Graman .15
1050 Drew Henson .50
1051 Darin Erstad .50
1052 Garret Anderson .15
1053 Craig Biggio .50
1054 Lance Berkman .50
1055 Jeff Bagwell .50
1056 Shannon Stewart .15
1057 Chipper Jones .75
1058 J.D. Drew .50
1059 Moises Alou .15
1060 Mark Grace .50
1061 Jose Vidro Expos .15
1062 Vladimir Guerrero .75
1063 Matt Lawton .15
1064 Ichiro Suzuki 1.50
1065 Edgar Martinez .15
1066 John Olerud .50
1067 Jeff Cirillo .15
1068 Mike Lowell .15
1069 Mike Piazza 1.00
1070 Roberto Alomar .50
1071 Bobby Abreu .15
1072 Jason Kendall .15
1073 Brian Giles .50
1074 Rafael Palmeiro .50
1075 Ivan Rodriguez .50
1076 Alex Rodriguez 1.50
1077 Juan Gonzalez .50
1078 Nomar Garciaparra 1.50
1079 Manny Ramirez .50
1080 Sean Casey .25
1081 Barry Larkin .25
1082 Larry Walker .40
1083 Carlos Beltran .15
1084 Corey Koskie .15
1085 Magglio Ordonez .25
1086 Frank Thomas .50
1087 Kenny Lofton .25
1088 Derek Jeter 2.00
1089 Bernie Williams .50
1090 Jason Giambi .50
1091 Troy Glaus .50
1092 Jeff Bagwell .50
1093 Lance Berkman .50
1094 David Justice .25
1095 Eric Chavez .25
1096 Carlos Delgado .40
1097 Gary Sheffield .40
1098 Chipper Jones .75
1099 Andruw Jones .50
1100 Richie Sexson .40
1101 Albert Pujols 1.50
1102 Sammy Sosa 1.50
1103 Fred McGriff .40
1104 Greg Vaughn .15
1105 Matt Williams .25
1106 Luis Gonzalez .40
1107 Shawn Green .40
1108 Andres Galarraga .15
1109 Vladimir Guerrero .75
1110 Barry Bonds 2.00
1111 Rich Aurilia .15
1112 Ellis Burks .15
1113 Jim Thome .50
1114 Bret Boone .15
1115 Cliff Floyd .15
1116 Mike Piazza 1.00
1117 Jeromy Burnitz .15
1118 Phil Nevin .15
1119 Brian Giles .50
1120 Rafael Palmeiro .50
1121 Juan Gonzalez .50
1122 Alex Rodriguez 1.50
1123 Manny Ramirez .50
1124 Ken Griffey Jr. 1.00
1125 Larry Walker .40
1126 Todd Helton .50
1127 Mike Sweeney .15
1128 Frank Thomas .50
1129 Paul Konerko .40
1130 Jason Giambi .50
1131 Aaron Sele .15
1132 Roy Oswalt .40
1133 Wade Miller .15
1134 Tim Hudson .40
1135 Barry Zito .40
1136 Mark Mulder .25
1137 Greg Maddux 1.00
1138 Tom Glavine .40
1139 Ben Sheets .40
1140 Darryl Kile .15
1141 Matt Morris .15
1142 Kerry Wood .40
1143 Jon Lieber .15
1144 Juan Cruz .15
1145 Randy Johnson .75
1146 Curt Schilling .50
1147 Kevin Brown .15
1148 Javier Vazquez .15
1149 Russ Ortiz .15
1150 C.C. Sabathia .15
1151 Bartolo Colon .15
1152 Freddy Garcia .15
1153 Jamie Moyer .15
1154 Josh Beckett .50
1155 Brad Penny .15
1156 Al Leiter .40
1157 Brandon Duckworth .15
1158 Robert Person .15
1159 Kris Benson .15
1160 Chan Ho Park .15
1161 Pedro J. Martinez .75
1162 Mike Hampton .15
1163 Jeff Weaver .15
1164 Joe Mays .15
1165 Brad Radke .15
1166 Eric Milton .15
1167 Roger Clemens 1.00
1168 Mike Mussina .50
1169 Andy Pettitte .50
1170 David Wells .15
1171 Ken Griffey Jr. 1.00
1172 Ichiro Suzuki 1.00
1173 Jason Giambi .50
1174 Alex Rodriguez 1.00
1175 Sammy Sosa .75

1176	Nomar Garciaparra	1.00
1177	Barry Bonds	1.00
1178	Mike Piazza	.75
1179	Derek Jeter	1.50
1180	Randy Johnson	.40
1181	Jeff Bagwell	.40
1182	Albert Pujols	1.00

Gargantuan Gear

		NM/M
Common Player:		3.00
Gold:		2X
Production 100 Sets		
G-JB	James Baldwin	3.00
G-BC	Bruce Chen	3.00
G-JD	Jermaine Dye/SP	5.00
G-JG	Juan Gonzalez	6.00
G-BG	Ben Grieve	3.00
G-KG	Ken Griffey Jr.	10.00
G-TH	Tim Hudson	6.00
G-AJ	Andruw Jones	6.00
G-JK	Jeff Kent	3.00
G-ML	Mike Lieberthal	3.00
G-TM	Tino Martinez	3.00
G-JO	John Olerud	3.00
G-MO	Magglio Ordonez	5.00
G-MP	Mike Piazza	15.00
G-JP	Jorge Posada	8.00
G-AP	Andy Pettitte	6.00
G-BR	Brad Radke	3.00
G-AR	Alex Rodriguez	10.00
G-SR	Scott Rolen	10.00
G-CS	Curt Schilling	8.00
G-AS	Aaron Sele	3.00
G-IS	Ichiro Suzuki/SP	30.00
G-BW	Bernie Williams	8.00
G-DY	Dmitri Young	3.00
G-TZ	Todd Zeile	3.00

Looming Large Jerseys

		NM/M
Common Player:		8.00
Production 250 Sets		
Gold:		2X
Production 40 Sets		
LBa	Jeff Bagwell	10.00
LB	Lance Berkman	10.00
JBu	John Burkett	8.00
SC	Sean Casey	10.00
TC	Tony Clark	8.00
RC	Roger Clemens	20.00
JC	Jeff Cirillo	8.00
JD	J.D. Drew	10.00
CE	Carl Everett	8.00
CF	Chuck Finley	8.00
TF	Travis Fryman	8.00
JGi	Jason Giambi	10.00
BG	Brian Giles	10.00
TG	Tom Glavine	10.00
JGo	Juan Gonzalez	10.00
KG	Ken Griffey Jr.	20.00
TH	Todd Helton	15.00
RJ	Randy Johnson	15.00
DK	Darryl Kile	8.00
AL	Al Leiter	8.00
ML	Mike Lieberthal	8.00
KL	Kenny Lofton	8.00
GM	Greg Maddux	15.00
EM	Edgar Martinez	10.00
FM	Fred McGriff	10.00
MO	Maggilo Ordonez	8.00
HN	Hideo Nomo	50.00
RP	Rafael Palmeiro	10.00
JP	Jorge Posada	10.00
SR	Shane Reynolds	8.00
AR	Alex Rodriguez	15.00
JR	Jimmy Rollins	8.00
KS	Kazuhiro Sasaki	8.00
CS	Curt Schilling	10.00
JS	J.T. Snow	8.00
SS	Sammy Sosa	20.00
FT	Frank Thomas	10.00
IV	Ismael Valdes	8.00
RV	Randy Velarde	8.00
RV	Ron Villone	8.00
BZ	Barry Zito	10.00

Lumber Yard

		NM/M
Common Player:		10.00
Inserted 1:168		
LY1	Chipper Jones	15.00
LY2	Joe DiMaggio	40.00
LY3	Albert Pujols	20.00
LY4	Mark McGwire	30.00
LY5	Sammy Sosa	15.00
LY6	Vladimir Guerrero	15.00
LY7	Barry Bonds	25.00
LY8	Mickey Mantle	50.00
LY9	Mike Piazza	15.00
LY10	Alex Rodriguez	15.00
LY11	Nomar Garciaparra	15.00
LY12	Ken Griffey Jr.	20.00
LY13	Frank Thomas	10.00
LY14	Jason Giambi	15.00
LY15	Derek Jeter	25.00
LY16	Luis Gonzalez	10.00
LY17	Jeff Bagwell	10.00
LY18	Todd Helton	10.00

Mark McGwire Flashbacks

	NM/M
Complete Set (40):	120.00
Common McGwire:	4.00
Inserted 1:24	
MM1-MM40 Mark McGwire	4.00

Mark McGwire Flashbacks

Super Swatches

		NM/M
Common Player:		5.00
Production 250 Sets		
Gold:		1-2X
Production 40 Sets		
EA	Edgardo Alfonzo	5.00
RA	Rich Aurilia	5.00
JB	Jeff Bagwell	15.00
SC	Sean Casey	8.00
CD	Carlos Delgado	8.00
RD	Ray Durham	5.00
DE	Darin Erstad	8.00
JG	Juan Gonzalez	8.00
MG	Mark Grace	8.00
SG	Shawn Green	8.00
KG	Ken Griffey Jr.	20.00
TG	Tony Gwynn	15.00
MH	Mike Hampton	5.00
TH	Trevor Hoffman	5.00
CJ	Chipper Jones	10.00
DJ	David Justice	8.00
KL	Kenny Lofton	5.00
JM	Joe Mays	5.00
EM	Eric Milton	5.00
MM	Matt Morris	5.00
HN	Hideo Nomo	50.00
JP	Jorge Posada	10.00
MR	Manny Ramirez	12.00
MR	Mariano Rivera	10.00
AR	Alex Rodriguez	15.00
IR	Ivan Rodriguez	10.00
KS	Kazuhiro Sasaki	5.00
CS	Curt Schilling	10.00
BS	Ben Sheets	8.00
SS	Sammy Sosa	20.00
IS	Ichiro Suzuki	40.00
MS	Mike Sweeney	5.00
FT	Frank Thomas	10.00
GV	Greg Vaughn	5.00
JV	Jose Vidro	5.00
DW	David Wells	5.00
MY	Masato Yoshii	5.00

Twizzlers

Specially marked packages of Twizzlers candy contained one of 10 cards in a set comprised of portrait and action cards of each of five athletes. Only a single baseball player was included in the set and listed here. Fronts are bordered in white with vignetted photos. Blue-bordered backs have a few sentences about the player along with Twizzlers and UD logos.

		NM/M
3	Nomar Garciaparra/ Action	2.00
4	Nomar Garciaparra/ Portrait	2.00

2003 Upper Deck

		NM/M
Complete Set (540):		75.00
Common Player:		.15
Common RC (501-529):		.50

Series 1 or 2 Pack (8):		2.50
Series 1 or 2 Box (24):		45.00
1	John Lackey	.15
2	Alex Cintron	.15
3	Jose Leon	.15
4	Bobby Hill	.15
5	Brandon Larson	.15
6	Raul Gonzalez	.15
7	Ben Broussard	.15
8	Earl Snyder	.15
9	Ramon Santiago	.15
10	Jason Lane	.15
11	Keith Ginter	.15
12	Kirk Saarloos	.15
13	Juan Brito	.15
14	Runelvys Hernandez	.15
15	Shawn Sedlacek	.15
16	Jayson Durocher	.15
17	Kevin Frederick	.15
18	Zach Day	.15
20	Marcus Thames	.15
21	Esteban German	.15
22	Brett Myers	.15
23	Oliver Perez	.25
24	Dennis Tankersley	.15
25	Julius Matos	.15
26	Jake Peavy	.15
27	Eric Cyr	.15
28	Mike Crudale	.15
29	Josh Pearce	.15
30	Carl Crawford	.15
31	Tim Salmon	.25
32	Troy Glaus	.50
33	Adam Kennedy	.15
34	David Eckstein	.15
35	Bengie Molina	.15
36	Jarrod Washburn	.15
37	Ramon Ortiz	.15
38	Eric Chavez	.40
39	Miguel Tejada	.50
40	Adam Piatt	.15
41	Jermaine Dye	.15
42	Olmedo Saenz	.15
43	Tim Hudson	.25
44	Barry Zito	.25
45	Billy Koch	.15
46	Shannon Stewart	.15
47	Kelvim Escobar	.15
48	Jose Cruz Jr.	.15
49	Vernon Wells	.15
50	Roy Halladay	.15
51	Esteban Loaiza	.15
52	Eric Hinske	.15
53	Steve Cox	.15
54	Brent Abernathy	.15
55	Ben Grieve	.15
56	Aubrey Huff	.15
57	Jared Sandberg	.15
58	Paul Wilson	.15
59	Tanyon Sturtze	.15
60	Jim Thome	.60
61	Omar Vizquel	.25
62	C.C. Sabathia	.15
63	Chris Magruder	.15
64	Ricky Gutierrez	.15
65	Einar Diaz	.15
66	Danys Baez	.15
67	Ichiro Suzuki	2.00
68	Ruben Sierra	.15
69	Carlos Guillen	.15
70	Mark McLemore	.15
71	Dan Wilson	.15
72	Jamie Moyer	.15
73	Joel Pineiro	.15
74	Edgar Martinez	.25
75	Tony Batista	.15
76	Jay Gibbons	.15
77	Chris Singleton	.15
78	Melvin Mora	.15
79	Geronimo Gil	.15
80	Rodrigo Lopez	.15
81	Jorge Julio	.15
82	Rafael Palmeiro	.50
83	Juan Gonzalez	.50
84	Mike Young	.15
85	Hideki Irabu	.15
86	Chan Ho Park	.15
87	Kevin Mench	.15
88	Doug Davis	.15
89	Pedro Martinez	.75
90	Shea Hillenbrand	.15
91	Derek Lowe	.15
92	Jason Varitek	.25
93	Tony Clark	.15
94	John Burkett	.15
95	Frank Castillo	.15
96	Nomar Garciaparra	2.00
97	Rickey Henderson	.40
98	Mike Sweeney	.15
99	Carlos Febles	.15
100	Mark Quinn	.15
101	Raul Ibanez	.15
102	A.J. Hinch	.15
103	Paul Byrd	.15
104	Chuck Knoblauch	.15
105	Dmitri Young	.15
106	Randall Simon	.15
107	Brandon Inge	.15
108	Damion Easley	.15
109	Carlos Pena	.15
110	George Lombard	.15
111	Juan Acevedo	.15
112	Torii Hunter	.25
113	Doug Mientkiewicz	.15
114	David Ortiz	.50
115	Eric Milton	.15
116	Eddie Guardado	.15
117	Cristian Guzman	.15
118	Corey Koskie	.15
119	Magglio Ordonez	.25
120	Mark Buehrle	.15
121	Todd Ritchie	.15
122	Jose Valentin	.15
123	Paul Konerko	.25
124	Carlos Lee	.15
125	Jon Garland	.15
126	Jason Giambi	.40
127	Derek Jeter	2.00
128	Roger Clemens	1.50
129	Raul Mondesi	.15
130	Jorge Posada	.25
131	Rondell White	.15
132	Robin Ventura	.25
133	Mike Mussina	.50
134	Jeff Bagwell	.50
135	Craig Biggio	.25
136	Morgan Ensberg	.15
137	Richard Hidalgo	.15
138	Brad Ausmus	.15
139	Roy Oswalt	.25
140	Carlos Hernandez	.15
141	Shane Reynolds	.15
142	Gary Sheffield	.25
143	Andruw Jones	.50
144	Tom Glavine	.40
145	Rafael Furcal	.25
146	Javy Lopez	.25
147	Vinny Castilla	.15
148	Marcus Giles	.15
149	Kevin Millwood	.15
150	Jason Marquis	.15
151	Ruben Quevedo	.15
152	Ben Sheets	.25
153	Geoff Jenkins	.15
154	Jose Hernandez	.15
155	Glendon Rusch	.15
156	Jeffrey Hammonds	.15
157	Alex Sanchez	.15
158	Jim Edmonds	.25
159	Tino Martinez	.25
160	Albert Pujols	1.50
161	Eli Marrero	.15
162	Woody Williams	.15
163	Fernando Vina	.15
164	Jason Isringhausen	.15
165	Jason Simontacchi	.15
166	Kerry Robinson	.15
167	Sammy Sosa	1.25
168	Juan Cruz	.15
169	Fred McGriff	.25
170	Antonio Alfonseca	.15
171	Jon Lieber	.15
172	Mark Prior	.50
173	Moises Alou	.25
174	Matt Clement	.15
175	Mark Bellhorn	.15
176	Randy Johnson	.75
177	Luis Gonzalez	.25
178	Tony Womack	.15
179	Mark Grace	.30
180	Junior Spivey	.15
181	Byung-Hyun Kim	.15
182	Danny Bautista	.15
183	Brian Anderson	.15
184	Shawn Green	.25
185	Brian Jordan	.15
186	Eric Karros	.15
187	Andy Ashby	.15
188	Cesar Izturis	.15
189	Dave Roberts	.15
190	Eric Gagne	.40
191	Kazuhisa Ishii	.15
192	Adrian Beltre	.25
193	Vladimir Guerrero	.75
194	Tony Armas Jr.	.15
195	Bartolo Colon	.15
196	Troy O'Leary	.15
197	Tomokazu Ohka	.15
198	Brad Wilkerson	.15
199	Orlando Cabrera	.15
200	Barry Bonds	2.00
201	David Bell	.15
202	Tsuyoshi Shinjo	.15
203	Benito Santiago	.15
204	Livan Hernandez	.15
205	Jason Schmidt	.40
206	Kirk Reuter	.15
207	Ramon E. Martinez	.15
208	Mike Lowell	.25
209	Luis Castillo	.15
210	Derrek Lee	.25
211	Andy Fox	.15
212	Eric Owens	.15
213	Charles Johnson	.15
214	Brad Penny	.15
215	A.J. Burnett	.15
216	Edgardo Alfonzo	.15
217	Roberto Alomar	.50
218	Rey Ordonez	.15
219	Al Leiter	.15
220	Roger Cedeno	.15
221	Timoniel Perez	.15
222	Jeromy Burnitz	.15
223	Pedro Astacio	.15
224	Joe McEwing	.15
225	Ryan Klesko	.15
226	Ramon Vazquez	.15
227	Mark Kotsay	.15
228	Bubba Trammell	.15
229	Wiki Gonzalez	.15
230	Trevor Hoffman	.15
231	Ron Gant	.15
232	Bobby Abreu	.25
233	Marlon Anderson	.15
234	Jeremy Giambi	.15
235	Jimmy Rollins	.25
236	Mike Lieberthal	.15
237	Vicente Padilla	.15
238	Randy Wolf	.15
239	Pokey Reese	.15
240	Brian Giles	.25
241	Jack Wilson	.15
242	Mike Williams	.15
243	Kip Wells	.15
244	Robert Mackowiak	.15
245	Craig Wilson	.15
246	Adam Dunn	.60
247	Sean Casey	.25
248	Todd Walker	.15
249	Corky Miller	.15
250	Ryan Dempster	.15
251	Reggie Taylor	.15
252	Aaron Boone	.15
253	Larry Walker	.30
254	Jose Ortiz	.15
255	Todd Zeile	.15
256	Bobby Estalella	.15
257	Juan Pierre	.15
258	Terry Shumpert	.15
259	Mike Hampton	.15
260	Denny Stark	.15
261	Shawn Green	.25
262	Derek Lowe	.15
263	Barry Bonds	1.00
264	Mike Cameron	.15
265	Luis Castillo	.15
266	Vladimir Guerrero	.40
267	Jason Giambi	.25
268	Eric Gagne	.25
269	Magglio Ordonez	.20
270	Jim Thome	.40
271	Garret Anderson	.40
272	Tony Percival	.15
273	Brad Fullmer	.15
274	Scott Spezio	.15
275	Darin Erstad	.40
276	Francisco Rodriguez	.15
277	Kevin Appier	.15
278	Shawn Wooten	.15
279	Eric Owens	.15
280	Scott Hatteberg	.15
281	Terrence Long	.15
282	Mark Mulder	.25
283	Ramon Hernandez	.15
284	Ted Lilly	.15
285	Erubiel Durazo	.15
286	Mark Ellis	.15
287	Carlos Delgado	.50
288	Orlando Hudson	.15
289	Chris Woodward	.15
290	Mark Hendrickson	.15
291	Josh Phelps	.15
292	Ken Huckaby	.15
293	Justin Miller	.15
294	Travis Lee	.15
295	Jorge Sosa	.15
296	Joe Kennedy	.15
297	Carl Crawford	.15
298	Toby Hall	.15
299	Rey Ordonez	.15
300	Brandon Phillips	.15
301	Matt Lawton	.15
302	Ellis Burks	.15
303	Bill Selby	.15
304	Travis Hafner	.15
305	Milton Bradley	.15
306	Karim Garcia	.15
307	Cliff Lee	.15
308	Jeff Cirillo	.15
309	John Olerud	.25
310	Kazuhiro Sasaki	.15
311	Freddy Garcia	.15
312	Bret Boone	.25
313	Mike Cameron	.15
314	Ben Davis	.15
315	Randy Winn	.15
316	Gary Matthews Jr.	.15
317	Jeff Conine	.15
318	Sidney Ponson	.15
319	Jerry Hairston	.15
320	David Segui	.15
321	Scott Erickson	.15
322	Marty Cordova	.15
323	Hank Blalock	.50
324	Herbert Perry	.15
325	Alex Rodriguez	2.00
326	Carl Everett	.15
327	Einar Diaz	.15
328	Ugueth Urbina	.15
329	Mark Teixeira	.40
330	Manny Ramirez	.75
331	Johnny Damon	.50
332	Trot Nixon	.25
333	Tim Wakefield	.15
334	Casey Fossum	.15
335	Todd Walker	.15
336	Jeremy Giambi	.15
337	Bill Mueller	.15
338	Ramiro Mendoza	.15
339	Carlos Beltran	.50
340	Jason Grimsley	.15
341	Brent Mayne	.15
342	Angel Berroa	.15
343	Albie Lopez	.15
344	Michael Tucker	.15
345	Bobby Higginson	.15
346	Shane Halter	.15
347	Jeremy Bonderman	2.00
348	Eric Munson	.15
349	Andy Van Hekken	.15
350	Matt Anderson	.15
351	Jacque Jones	.15
352	A.J. Pierzynski	.15
353	Joe Mays	.15
354	Brad Radke	.15
355	Dustan Mohr	.15
356	Bobby Kielty	.15
357	Michael Cuddyer	.15
358	Luis Rivas	.15
359	Frank Thomas	.75
360	Joe Borchard	.15
361	D'Angelo Jimenez	.15
362	Bartolo Colon	.25
363	Joe Crede	.15
364	Miguel Olivo	.15
365	Billy Koch	.15
366	Bernie Williams	.50
367	Nick Johnson	.15
368	Andy Pettitte	.40
369	Mariano Rivera	.25
370	Alfonso Soriano	.75
371	David Wells	.15
372	Drew Henson	.15
373	Juan Rivera	.15
374	Steve Karsay	.15
375	Jeff Kent	.25
376	Lance Berkman	.50
377	Octavio Dotel	.15
378	Julio Lugo	.15
379	Jason Lane	.15
380	Wade Miller	.15
381	Billy Wagner	.15
382	Brad Ausmus	.15
383	Mike Hampton	.15
384	Chipper Jones	.75
385	John Smoltz	.25
386	Greg Maddux	1.25
387	Javy Lopez	.25
388	Robert Fick	.15
389	Mark DeRosa	.15
390	Russ Ortiz	.15
391	Julio Franco	.15
392	Richie Sexson	.50
393	Eric Young	.15
394	Robert Machado	.15
395	Mike DeJean	.15
396	Todd Ritchie	.15
397	Royce Clayton	.15
398	Nick Neugebauer	.15
399	J.D. Drew	.25
400	Edgar Renteria	.25
401	Scott Rolen	.75
402	Matt Morris	.25
403	Garrett Stephenson	.15
404	Eduardo Perez	.15
405	Mike Matheny	.15
406	Miguel Cairo	.15
407	Brett Tomko	.15
408	Bobby Hill	.15
409	Troy O'Leary	.15
410	Corey Patterson	.40
411	Kerry Wood	.75
412	Eric Karros	.15
413	Hee Seop Choi	.15
414	Alex Gonzalez	.15
415	Matt Clement	.15
416	Mark Grudzielanek	.15
417	Curt Schilling	.50
418	Steve Finley	.15
419	Craig Counsell	.15
420	Matt Williams	.15
421	Quinton McCracken	.15
422	Chad Moeller	.15
423	Lyle Overbay	.15
424	Miguel Batista	.15
425	Paul LoDuca	.15
426	Kevin Brown	.25
427	Hideo Nomo	.40
428	Fred McGriff	.25
429	Joe Thurston	.15
430	Odalis Perez	.15
431	Darren Dreifort	.15
432	Todd Hundley	.15
433	Dave Roberts	.15
434	Jose Vidro	.15
435	Javier Vazquez	.15
436	Michael Barrett	.15
437	Fernando Tatis	.15
438	Peter Bergeron	.15
439	Endy Chavez	.15
440	Orlando Hernandez	.15
441	Marvin Bernard	.15
442	Rich Aurilia	.15
443	Pedro Feliz	.15
444	Robb Nen	.15
445	Ray Durham	.15
446	Marquis Grissom	.15
447	Damian Moss	.15
448	Edgardo Alfonzo	.15
449	Juan Pierre	.15
450	Braden Looper	.15
451	Alex Gonzalez	.15

452 Justin Wayne .15
453 Josh Beckett .25
454 Juan Encarnacion .15
455 Ivan Rodriguez .50
456 Todd Hollandsworth .15
457 Cliff Floyd .15
458 Rey Sanchez .15
459 Mike Piazza 1.50
460 Mo Vaughn .15
461 Armando Benitez .15
462 Tsuyoshi Shinjo .15
463 Tom Glavine .40
464 David Cone .15
465 Phil Nevin .15
466 Sean Burroughs .15
467 Jake Peavy .15
468 Brian Lawrence .15
469 Mark Loretta .15
470 Dennis Tankersley .15
471 Jesse Orosco .15
472 Jim Thome .75
473 Kevin Millwood .40
474 David Bell .15
475 Pat Burrell .40
476 Brandon Duckworth .15
477 Jose Mesa .15
478 Marlon Byrd .15
479 Reggie Sanders .15
480 Jason Kendall .25
481 Aramis Ramirez .40
482 Kris Benson .15
483 Matt Stairs .15
484 Kevin Young .15
485 Kenny Lofton .25
486 Austin Kearns .40
487 Barry Larkin .25
488 Jason LaRue .15
489 Ken Griffey Jr. 1.25
490 Danny Graves .15
491 Russell Branyan .15
492 Reggie Taylor .15
493 Jimmy Haynes .15
494 Charles Johnson .15
495 Todd Helton .75
496 Juan Uribe .15
497 Preston Wilson .15
498 Chris Stynes .15
499 Jason Jennings .15
500 Jay Payton .15
501 Hideki Matsui **RC** 5.00
502 Jose Contreras **RC** 2.00
503 Brandon Webb **RC** 2.00
504 Robby Hammock **RC** .50
505 Matt Kata **RC** .50
506 Tim Olson **RC** .50
507 Michael Hessman **RC** .50
508 Jon Leicester **RC** .50
509 Todd Wellemeyer **RC** .50
510 David Sanders **RC** .50
511 Josh Stewart **RC** .50
512 Luis Ayala **RC** .50
513 Clint Barmes **RC** 2.00
514 Josh Willingham **RC** .50
515 Alejandro Machado **RC** .50
516 Felix Sanchez **RC** .50
517 Willie Eyre **RC** .50
518 Brent Hoard **RC** .50
519 Lew Ford **RC** 1.50
520 Terrmel Sledge **RC** .50
521 Jeremy Griffiths .15
522 Phil Seibel **RC** .50
523 Craig Brazell **RC** .50
524 Prentice Redman **RC** .50
525 Jeff Duncan **RC** .50
526 Shane Bazzell **RC** .75
527 Bernie Castro **RC** .50
528 Rett Johnson **RC** .50
529 Bobby Madritsch **RC** 3.00
530 Rocco Baldelli .40
531 Alex Rodriguez 1.00
532 Eric Chavez .25
533 Miguel Tejada .25
534 Ichiro Suzuki .75
535 Sammy Sosa .75
536 Barry Zito .25
537 Darin Erstad .25
538 Alfonso Soriano .50
539 Troy Glaus .25
540 Nomar Garciaparra .75

Gold

Gold (541-600): 2-3X
One gold set per hobby case.

AL All-Star Swatch

NM/M
Common Player: 5.00
Inserted 1:144 Retail
MC Mike Cameron 5.00
RD Ray Durham 5.00
CE Carl Everett 5.00
CF Chuck Finley 5.00
TF Travis Fryman 6.00
JG Juan Gonzalez 8.00
JM Joe Mays 5.00
MO Magglio Ordonez 8.00
AP Andy Pettitte 8.00
JP Jorge Posada 8.00
MR Mariano Rivera 10.00
AS Aaron Sele 5.00
MS Mike Sweeney 5.00

Big League Breakdown

NM/M
Complete Set (15): 20.00

Common Player: .50
Inserted 1:8
BL1 Troy Glaus .75
BL2 Miguel Tejada .75
BL3 Chipper Jones 1.50
BL4 Torii Hunter .50
BL5 Nomar Garciaparra 3.00
BL6 Sammy Sosa 2.50
BL7 Todd Helton 1.00
BL8 Lance Berkman .75
BL9 Shawn Green .50
BL10 Vladimir Guerrero 1.50
BL11 Jason Giambi .50
BL12 Derek Jeter 4.00
BL13 Barry Bonds 4.00
BL14 Ichiro Suzuki 3.00
BL15 Alex Rodriguez 4.00

Game Jersey Autograph

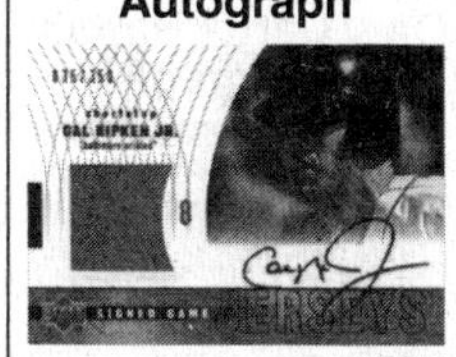

NM/M
Golds: 1.5-2X
Production 25 or 75
RC Roger Clemens/350 100.00
JG Jason Giambi/350 40.00
KG Ken Griffey Jr./350 110.00
MM Mark McGwire/150 350.00
CR Cal Ripken Jr/350 140.00
AR Alex Rodriguez/350 120.00
SS Sammy Sosa/150 140.00

Game Swatches Hobby

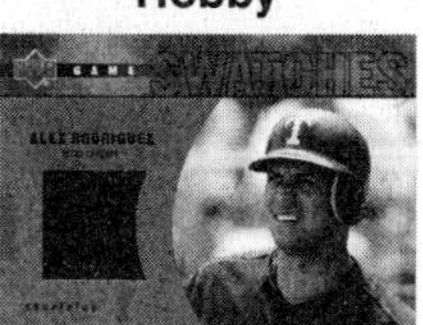

NM/M
Common Player: 5.00
Inserted 1:72
SB Sean Burroughs/SP 8.00
CD Carlos Delgado/SP 8.00
GM Greg Maddux 15.00
MM Mike Mussina 10.00
MO Magglio Ordonez 5.00
CP Carlos Pena 5.00
MP Mike Piazza/SP 15.00
AR Alex Rodriguez 15.00
CC C.C. Sabathia 5.00
CS Curt Schilling/100 10.00
SS Sammy Sosa 15.00
BW Bernie Williams 10.00

Game Swatches Retail

NM/M
Common Player: 5.00
Inserted 1:72
RC Roger Clemens 15.00
JD J.D. Drew 5.00
AD Adam Dunn 8.00
JE Jim Edmonds 8.00
DE Darin Erstad 8.00
JG Jason Giambi 8.00
KG Ken Griffey Jr. 12.00
TH Tim Hudson 6.00
RJ Randy Johnson 8.00
JK Jeff Kent 5.00
EM Edgar Martinez 6.00
IR Ivan Rodriguez 6.00
FT Frank Thomas 8.00

Leading Swatches

NM/M
Common Player: 4.00
Inserted 1:24
Golds: 1-2X
Production 100 Sets
BA Bobby Abreu 6.00
GA Garret Anderson 6.00
JB Jeff Bagwell 6.00
JB1 Jeff Bagwell 6.00
TB Tony Batista 4.00
AB Adrian Beltre 6.00
LB Lance Berkman 4.00
PB Pat Burrell 6.00
PB1 Pat Burrell 6.00
EC Eric Chavez 6.00
RC Roger Clemens 10.00
RC1 Roger Clemens 10.00
CD Carlos Delgado 6.00
JD J.D. Drew 4.00
AD Adam Dunn 8.00
AD1 Adam Dunn 8.00
JE Jim Edmonds 4.00
JG Jason Giambi 6.00
JG1 Jason Giambi 6.00
BG Brian Giles 4.00
TG Troy Glaus 4.00
GO Juan Gonzalez 6.00
LG Luis Gonzalez 4.00
SG Shawn Green 4.00
SG1 Shawn Green 4.00
KG Ken Griffey Jr. 12.00
KG1 Ken Griffey Jr. 12.00
VG Vladimir Guerrero 8.00
THe Todd Helton 6.00
THu Tim Hudson 4.00
TH1 Tim Hudson 4.00
KI Kazuhisa Ishii 4.00
RJ Randy Johnson 8.00
RJ1 Randy Johnson 8.00
AJ Andruw Jones 6.00
AJ1 Andruw Jones 6.00
CJ Chipper Jones 8.00
KE Jason Kendall 4.00
JL Javy Lopez 4.00
GM Greg Maddux 10.00
GM1 Greg Maddux 10.00
PM Pedro J. Martinez 8.00
HM Hideki Matsui 40.00
HM1 Hideki Matsui 50.00
HN Hideo Nomo 8.00
RO Roy Oswalt 4.00
RO1 Roy Oswalt 4.00
RP Rafael Palmeiro 6.00
RP1 Rafael Palmeiro 6.00
CP Corey Patterson 6.00
JP Jay Payton 4.00
TP Troy Percival 4.00
AP Andy Pettitte 6.00
MP Mike Piazza 10.00
MP1 Mike Piazza 10.00
MR Manny Ramirez 8.00
AR Alex Rodriguez 10.00
AR1 Alex Rodriguez 10.00
IR Ivan Rodriguez 6.00
SR Scott Rolen 8.00
KS Kazuhiro Sasaki 4.00
CS Curt Schilling 8.00
AS Aaron Sele 4.00
JS J.T. Snow 4.00
AS Alfonso Soriano 8.00
AS1 Alfonso Soriano 8.00
SS Sammy Sosa 12.00
SS1 Sammy Sosa 12.00
MS Mike Stanton 4.00
IS Ichiro Suzuki 25.00
IS1 Ichiro Suzuki 25.00
MS Mike Sweeney 4.00
MT Miguel Tejada 6.00
MT1 Miguel Tejada 6.00
JT Jim Thome 8.00
JT1 Jim Thome 8.00
OV Omar Vizquel 4.00
LW Larry Walker 4.00
BW Bernie Williams 6.00
BW1 Bernie Williams 6.00
KW Kerry Wood 8.00
BZ Barry Zito 6.00

Lineup Time Jerseys

NM/M
Common Player: 6.00
Inserted 1:96
RC Roger Clemens/SP 20.00
CD Carlos Delgado 8.00
JD J.D. Drew 6.00
SG Shawn Green 8.00
TH Todd Helton 8.00
RJ Randy Johnson/SP 15.00
GM Greg Maddux 10.00
IS Ichiro Suzuki 40.00
JT Jim Thome 10.00
BW Bernie Williams 10.00

Magical Performances

NM/M
Common Player: 8.00
Inserted 1:96
Golds: 1-2X
Production 50 Sets
MP1 Hideki Matsui 20.00
MP2 Ken Griffey Jr. 15.00
MP3 Ichiro Suzuki 15.00
MP4 Ken Griffey Jr. 15.00
MP5 Hideo Nomo 8.00
MP6 Mickey Mantle 40.00
MP7 Ken Griffey Jr. 15.00
MP8 Barry Bonds 20.00
MP9 Mickey Mantle 40.00
MP10 Tom Seaver 8.00
MP11 Mike Piazza 15.00
MP12 Roger Clemens 12.00
MP13 Nolan Ryan 30.00
MP14 Nomar Garciaparra 15.00
MP15 Ernie Banks 15.00
MP16 Stan Musial 25.00
MP17 Mickey Mantle 40.00
MP18 Nolan Ryan 30.00
MP19 Nolan Ryan 30.00
MP20 Mickey Mantle 40.00
MP21 Ichiro Suzuki 15.00
MP22 Nolan Ryan 30.00
MP23 Tom Seaver 8.00
MP24 Ken Griffey Jr. 15.00
MP25 Hideo Nomo 8.00
MP26 Ken Griffey Jr. 15.00
MP27 Mark McGwire 30.00
MP28 Barry Bonds 20.00
MP29 Alex Rodriguez 20.00
MP30 Nolan Ryan 30.00
MP31 Mark McGwire 30.00
MP32 Nolan Ryan 30.00
MP33 Sammy Sosa 15.00
MP34 Ichiro Suzuki 15.00
MP35 Barry Bonds 20.00
MP36 Derek Jeter 20.00
MP37 Roger Clemens 15.00
MP38 Jason Giambi 8.00
MP39 Mickey Mantle 40.00
MP40 Ted Williams 40.00
MP41 Ted Williams 40.00
MP42 Ted Williams 40.00

Mark of Greatness

NM/M
400 Total cards produced
MoG Mark McGwire 350.00
MoG Mark McGwire/Silver/70 400.00

Masters with the Leather

NM/M
Complete Set (12): 20.00
Common Player: .75
Inserted 1:12
L1 Darin Erstad .75
L2 Andruw Jones 1.50
L3 Greg Maddux 3.00
L4 Nomar Garciaparra 3.00
L5 Torii Hunter 1.00
L6 Roberto Alomar 1.00
L7 Derek Jeter 5.00
L8 Eric Chavez 1.00
L9 Ichiro Suzuki 3.00
L10 Jim Edmonds 1.00
L11 Scott Rolen 1.50
L12 Alex Rodriguez 4.00

Matsui Mania

Complete Set (18):
Common Player:

Mid-Summer Stars

NM/M
Common Player: 5.00
Inserted 1:72
RC Roger Clemens 12.00
CD Carlos Delgado 8.00
JE Jim Edmonds 8.00
DE Darin Erstad 8.00
FG Freddy Garcia 5.00
TG Tom Glavine 8.00
JG Juan Gonzalez 8.00
SG Shawn Green/SP 8.00
RJ Randy Johnson 10.00
AJ Andruw Jones 6.00
EM Edgar Martinez 8.00
HN Hideo Nomo 20.00
MP Mike Piazza 15.00
MR Manny Ramirez 8.00
AR Alex Rodriguez 15.00
KS Kazuhiro Sasaki 8.00
CS Curt Schilling 10.00
SS Sammy Sosa 15.00
IS Ichiro Suzuki/SP 40.00
FT Frank Thomas 8.00
RV Robin Ventura 8.00
DW David Wells 5.00
BZ Barry Zito 8.00

National Pride

NM/M
Common Player: 3.00
Inserted 1:24
AA Abe Alvarez 3.00
MA Michael Aubrey 15.00
KB Kyle Bakker 3.00
SB Sean Burroughs 5.00
CC Chad Cordero 3.00
SC Shane Costa 3.00
RF Robert Fick 3.00
SF Sam Fuld 3.00
AH Aaron Hill 8.00
BH Bobby Hill 3.00
BH1 Bobby Hill 3.00
AJ A.J. Hinch 3.00
PH Philip Humber 5.00
CJ Conor Jackson 3.00
JJe Jason Jennings 3.00
GJ Grant Johnson 3.00
JJ Jacque Jones 8.00
JJ1 Jacque Jones 8.00
MJ Mark Jurich 3.00
AK Austin Kearns 12.00
AK1 Austin Kearns 12.00
WL Wes Littleton 3.00
EM Eric Milton 5.00
EM1 Eric Milton 5.00
RO Roy Oswalt 6.00
RO1 Roy Oswalt 6.00
EP Eric Patterson 3.00
DP Dustin Pedroia 3.00
LP Landon Powell 3.00
MP Mark Prior 15.00
MP1 Mark Prior 15.00
CQ Carlos Quentin 3.00
KSa Kirk Saarloos 3.00
KSa1 Kirk Saarloos 3.00
CS Clint Sammons 5.00
KSl Kyle Sleeth 5.00
HS Huston Street 5.00
BS Brad Sullivan 3.00
BS1 Brad Sullivan 3.00
RW Rickie Weeks 15.00
RW1 Rickie Weeks 15.00
BZ Bob Zimmermann 3.00

NL All-Star Swatch

NM/M
Common Player: 5.00
Inserted 1:72
SC Sean Casey 5.00
CF Cliff Floyd 5.00
TGl Tom Glavine 8.00
TGw Tony Gwynn 12.00
MH Mike Hampton 5.00
TH Trevor Hoffman 5.00
RK Ryan Klesko 5.00
AL Al Leiter 5.00
FM Fred McGriff 5.00
MM Matt Morris 8.00
CS Curt Schilling 8.00
JV Jose Vidro 5.00

Patch Logo

NM/M
Quantity produced listed
JB Jeff Bagwell/41 60.00
KG Ken Griffey Jr./50 100.00
TH Todd Helton/41 50.00
KI Kazuhisa Ishii/54 40.00
RJ Randy Johnson/50 75.00
CJ Chipper Jones/52 80.00
GM Greg Maddux/50 100.00
MP Mike Piazza/61 120.00
SS Sammy Sosa/60 100.00
FT Frank Thomas/52 60.00
BW Bernie Williams/42 40.00

2003 Upper Deck Patch Number

NM/M
Quantity produced listed
JG Jason Giambi/68 40.00
KG Ken Griffey Jr./97 70.00
KI Kazuhisa Ishii/63 40.00
RJ Randy Johnson/90 75.00
MG Mark McGwire/60 180.00
AR Alex Rodriguez/56 90.00
SS Sammy Sosa/100 80.00
FT Frank Thomas/91 60.00
BW Bernie Williams/66 50.00

Patch Stripes

NM/M
Quantity produced listed
JB Jeff Bagwell/73 60.00
JG Jason Giambi/66 40.00
KG Ken Griffey Jr./63 75.00
KI Kazuhisa Ishii/58 40.00
RJ Randy Johnson/58 65.00
CJ Chipper Jones/58 60.00
MG Mark McGwire/63 180.00
AR Alex Rodriguez/63 80.00
SS Sammy Sosa/63 100.00
IS Ichiro Suzuki/63 180.00
FT Frank Thomas/58 60.00
BW Bernie Williams/58 50.00

Piece of the Action

NM/M
Common Player: 5.00
Inserted 1:288
Cards are not serial numbered.
Print runs provided by Upper Deck.
BA Bobby Abreu/125 5.00
GA Garret Anderson/150 5.00
AB Adrian Beltre/100 10.00
BB Barry Bonds/125 30.00
KB Kevin Brown/100 5.00
PB Pat Burrell/150 8.00
DE Darin Erstad/125 5.00
FG Freddy Garcia/100 5.00
BG Brian Giles/100 5.00
TG Troy Glaus/150 6.00
JG Juan Gonzalez/100 8.00
LG Luis Gonzalez/100 5.00
SG Shawn Green/175 5.00
VG Vladimir Guerrero/50 15.00
THe Todd Helton/100 10.00
THo Trevor Hoffman/150 5.00
DJ Derek Jeter/65 40.00
RJ Randy Johnson/100 10.00
CJ Chipper Jones/62 15.00
JK Jason Kendall/100 5.00
KE Jeff Kent/150 5.00
RK Ryan Klesko/75 6.00
EM Edgar Martinez/125 5.00
PM Pedro Martinez/150 10.00
PN Phil Nevin/75 5.00
HN Hideo Nomo/100 20.00
RP Rafael Palmeiro/150 10.00
Ara Aramis Ramirez/100 8.00
MP Mike Piazza/150 15.00
ARo Alex Rodriguez/100 15.00
KS Kazuhiro Sasaki/100 5.00
CS Curt Schilling/100 10.00
RS Richie Sexson/160 8.00
GS Gary Sheffield/100 6.00
SS Sammy Sosa/85 20.00
FT Frank Thomas/150 8.00
JT Jim Thome/125 10.00
JV Jose Vidro/100 5.00
LW Larry Walker/150 5.00
BW Bernie Williams/125 6.00

Slammin' Sammy Tribute Jersey

NM/M
384 Total produced
SST Sammy Sosa 175.00
SST Sammy Sosa/Gold/25 290.00
SST Sammy Sosa/Silver/66 240.00

Star-Spangled Swatches

NM/M
Common Player: 4.00
Inserted 1:72
MA Michael Aubrey 8.00
KB Kyle Bakker 4.00
CC Chad Cordero 4.00
SC Shane Costa 6.00
AH Aaron Hill 4.00
PH Philip Humber 6.00
CJ Conor Jackson 8.00
GJ Grant Johnson 4.00
EP Eric Patterson 8.00
DP Dustin Pedroia 10.00
LP Landon Powell 6.00
CQ Carlos Quentin 8.00
KS Kyle Sleeth 6.00
HS Huston Street 10.00
BS Brad Sullivan 4.00
RW Rickie Weeks 15.00

Superior Sluggers

NM/M
Complete Set (18): 30.00
Common Player: 1.00
Inserted 1:8
S1 Troy Glaus 1.00
S2 Chipper Jones 1.50
S3 Manny Ramirez 1.50
S4 Ken Griffey Jr. 2.50
S5 Jim Thome 1.50
S6 Todd Helton 1.00
S7 Lance Berkman 1.00
S8 Derek Jeter 4.00
S9 Vladimir Guerrero 1.50
S10 Mike Piazza 2.50
S11 Hideki Matsui 3.00
S12 Barry Bonds 4.00
S13 Mickey Mantle 5.00
S14 Alex Rodriguez 3.00
S15 Ted Williams 3.00
S16 Carlos Delgado 1.00
S17 Frank Thomas 1.00
S18 Adam Dunn 1.50

Super Patch Logos

Common Player:
Inserted 1:7,500
No Pricing

Super Patch Numbers

Common Player:
Inserted 1:7,500
No Pricing

Super Patch Stripes

Common Player:
Inserted 1:7,500
No Pricing

Superstar Scrapbooks

No pricing due to scarcity.
Production 24 Sets
Silvers: No Pricing
Production Six Sets
Golds: No Pricing
Production One Set

Superstar Slam Jerseys

NM/M
Common Player: 4.00
Inserted 1:48
JB Jeff Bagwell 8.00
JG Jason Giambi 6.00
JGo Juan Gonzalez 6.00
LG Luis Gonzalez 4.00
KG Ken Griffey Jr. 15.00
CJ Chipper Jones 10.00
MP Mike Piazza 10.00
AR Alex Rodriguez 15.00
SS Sammy Sosa 15.00
FT Frank Thomas 8.00

The Chase for 755

NM/M
Complete Set (15): 15.00
Common Player: .75
Inserted 1:8
C1 Troy Glaus .75
C2 Andruw Jones 1.00
C3 Manny Ramirez 1.25
C4 Sammy Sosa 2.50
C5 Ken Griffey Jr. 3.00
C6 Adam Dunn 1.25
C7 Todd Helton 1.00
C8 Lance Berkman .75
C9 Jeff Bagwell 1.00
C10 Shawn Green .75
C11 Vladimir Guerrero 1.50
C12 Barry Bonds 4.00
C13 Alex Rodriguez 3.00
C14 Juan Gonzalez .75
C15 Carlos Delgado .75

Triple Game Jersey

NM/M
Quantity produced listed
Golds: 1.5-2X
Production 50, 25 or 10
ARZ Randy Johnson, Curt Schilling, Luis Gonzalez/150 40.00
CIN Ken Griffey Jr., Sean Casey, Adam Dunn/150 40.00
HOU Jeff Bagwell, Lance Berkman, Craig Biggio/150 40.00
TEX Rafael Palmeiro, Alex Rodriguez, Juan Gonzalez/150 40.00
ATL Chipper Jones, Greg Maddux, Gary Sheffield/75 65.00
CHC Sammy Sosa, Moises Alou, Kerry Wood/75 50.00
NYM Mike Piazza, Roberto Alomar, Mo Vaughn/75 40.00
SEA Ichiro Suzuki, Freddy Garcia, Bret Boone/75 80.00

500 HR Club

NM/M
Production 350 Cards
SS Sammy Sosa/350 150.00
SS Sammy Sosa/ Auto./21 2,300

2003 UD Authentics

NM/M
Complete Set (130):
Common Player: .25
Common Rk Hype (101-130): 4.00
Production 999
Pack (4): 10.00
Box (10 + Framed Auto.): 170.00
1 Pee Wee Reese .25
2 Richie Ashburn .25
3 Derek Jeter 2.50
4 Alex Rodriguez 2.00
5 Jose Vidro .25
6 Miguel Tejada .50
7 Nomar Garciaparra 2.00
8 Pat Burrell .50
9 Albert Pujols 2.00
10 Jeff Bagwell .75
11 Stan Musial 1.00
12 Mickey Mantle 3.00
13 J.D. Drew .25
14 Ivan Rodriguez .75
15 Joe Morgan .25
16 Ted Williams 2.00
17 Travis Hafner .25
18 Chipper Jones 1.50
19 Hideo Nomo .50
20 Gary Sheffield .50
21 Jacque Jones .25
22 Alfonso Soriano 1.50
23 Roberto Alomar .50
24 Jeff Kent .40
25 Omar Vizquel .40
26 Ernie Banks 1.00
27 Shawn Green .50
28 Tim Hudson .50
29 Jim Edmonds .50
30 Brandon Larson .25
31 Doug Mientkiewicz .25
32 Darin Erstad .50
33 Bobby Hill .25
34 Todd Helton .75
35 Kazuhisa Ishii .25
36 Lance Berkman .50
37 Eric Hinske .25
38 Jason Kendall .25
39 Bob Feller .50
40 Luis Gonzalez .40
41 Sammy Sosa 2.00
42 Mike Piazza 1.50
43 Roger Clemens 2.00
44 Jose Cruz Jr. .25
45 Mark Prior 1.50
46 Mark Teixeira .40
47 Phil Nevin .25
48 Lyle Overbay .25
49 Manny Ramirez .75
50 Brian Giles .40
51 Preston Wilson .25
52 Jermaine Dye .25
53 Troy Glaus .50
54 Frank Thomas .75
55 Jim Thome .75
56 Barry Bonds 2.50
57 Carlos Delgado .75
58 Jason Giambi 1.00
59 Joe Mays .25
60 Andruw Jones .75
61 Billy Williams .25
62 Vladimir Guerrero .75
63 Scott Rolen .75
64 Juan Marichal .25
65 Austin Kearns .50
66 Kerry Wood .75
67 Bret Boone .25
68 Shea Hillenbrand .25
69 Mike Sweeney .25
70 Rocco Baldelli .25
71 Ken Griffey Jr. 1.50
72 Cliff Floyd .25
73 Greg Maddux 1.50
74 Mike Hampton .25
75 Larry Walker .40
76 Nolan Ryan 3.00
77 Rollie Fingers .25
78 Mike Mussina .75
79 Matt Morris .25
80 Robin Roberts .25
81 Barry Zito .50
82 Curt Schilling .50
83 Ken Harvey .25
84 Troy Percival .25
85 Tom Seaver 1.00
86 Mariano Rivera .40
87 Raul Mondesi .25
88 Adam Dunn .50
89 Roy Oswalt .25
90 Pedro J. Martinez 1.00
91 Andy Pettitte .50
92 Tom Glavine .50
93 Torii Hunter .50
94 Joe Thurston .25
95 Runelvys Hernandez .25
96 Randy Johnson 1.00
97 Bernie Williams .75
98 Ichiro Suzuki 1.50
99 C.C. Sabathia .25
100 Bobby Abreu .40
101 Jose Contreras **RC** 6.00
102 Hideki Matsui **RC** 15.00
103 Chris Capuano **RC** 6.00
104 Willie Eyre **RC** 4.00
105 Lew Ford **RC** 6.00
106 Shane Bazzell **RC** 4.00
107 Guillermo Quiroz **RC** 6.00
108 Fernando Cabrera **RC** 4.00
109 Francisco Cruceta **RC** 4.00
110 Jhonny Peralta 4.00
111 Bobby Madritsch **RC** 8.00
112 Diegomar Markwell **RC** 4.00
113 Matt Bruback **RC** 4.00
114 Matt Kata **RC** 6.00
115 Rob Hammock **RC** 4.00
116 Brandon Webb **RC** 10.00
117 Jon Leicester **RC** 4.00
118 Josh Willingham **RC** 6.00
119 Prentice Redman **RC** 4.00
120 Jeff Duncan **RC** 4.00
121 Craig Brazell **RC** 6.00
122 Jeremy Griffiths 4.00
123 Phil Seibel **RC** 4.00
124 Luis Ayala **RC** 4.00
125 Miguel Ojeda **RC** 6.00
126 Jeremy Wedel **RC** 4.00
127 Josh Hall **RC** 6.00
128 Oscar Villarreal **RC** 4.00
129 Clint Barmes **RC** 8.00
130 Nook Logan **RC** 4.00

Rookie Hype Gold

Cards (101-130): 1-2X
Production 50

Cut Signatures

Common Player:

Framed Autograph

NM/M
Common Framed Autograph: 40.00
Inserted 1:Box
Lance Berkman/150 40.00
Lance Berkman/50 60.00
Hank Blalock/325 45.00
Hank Blalock/300 45.00
Hank Blalock/200 45.00
Hank Blalock/175 45.00
Pat Burrell/330 40.00
Pat Burrell/240 40.00
Pat Burrell/150 40.00
Gary Carter/225 50.00
Gary Carter/75 60.00
Jose Contreras/350 50.00
Jose Contreras/120 50.00
Carlton Fisk/250 50.00
Carlton Fisk/125 75.00
Carlton Fisk/70 80.00
Nomar Garciaparra/250 100.00
Nomar Garciaparra/150 100.00
Nomar Garciaparra/75 120.00
Jason Giambi/350 40.00
Jason Giambi/300 40.00
Jason Giambi/200 40.00
Jason Giambi/150 40.00
Jason Giambi/100 40.00
Jason Giambi/75 40.00
Bob Gibson/200 60.00
Bob Gibson/50 120.00
Bob Gibson/45 120.00
Troy Glaus/350 40.00
Troy Glaus/200 40.00
Troy Glaus/100 50.00
Tom Glavine/275 50.00
Tom Glavine/150 50.00
Tom Glavine/47 75.00
Ken Griffey Jr/325 90.00
Ken Griffey Jr./200 90.00
Ken Griffey Jr/75 100.00
Ken Griffey Jr./30 120.00
Vladimir Guerrero/150 60.00
Vladimir Guerrero/27 125.00
Drew Henson/350 40.00
Drew Henson/300 40.00
Drew Henson/250 40.00
Drew Henson/100 40.00
Chipper Jones/350 70.00
Chipper Jones/200 70.00
Chipper Jones/100 85.00
Austin Kearns/325 40.00
Austin Kearns/300 40.00
Austin Kearns/200 40.00
Austin Kearns/175 40.00
Austin Kearns/28 80.00
Hideki Matsui/75 300.00
Hideki Matsui/55 300.00
Mark Prior/300 60.00
Mark Prior/250 60.00
Mark Prior/175 60.00
Mark Prior/100 60.00
Cal Ripken Jr/125 175.00
Cal Ripken Jr./50 200.00
Phil Rizzuto/350 50.00
Phil Rizzuto/200 60.00
Phil Rizzuto/100 75.00
Scott Rolen/300 50.00
Scott Rolen/100 65.00
Scott Rolen/27 120.00
Nolan Ryan/150 125.00
Nolan Ryan/100 180.00
Nolan Ryan/50 200.00
Nolan Ryan/34 240.00
Tom Seaver/100 75.00
Tom Seaver/50 100.00
Tom Seaver/41 100.00
Ozzie Smith/150 85.00
Ozzie Smith/50 120.00
Duke Snider/150 60.00
Duke Snider/50 100.00
Ichiro Suzuki/75 300.00
Ichiro Suzuki/51 350.00
Mark Teixeira/325 60.00
Mark Teixeira/200 60.00
Mark Teixeira/175 60.00
Mark Teixeira/150 60.00

Star Quality

NM/M
Common Player: 4.00
Production 350 unless noted.
Golds: 1-2X
Production 50, 25 or 10
No Pricing for #'d to 25 or less.
RA Roberto Alomar 6.00
JB Jeff Bagwell 8.00
JO Josh Beckett 4.00
LB Lance Berkman 5.00
RC Roger Clemens 15.00
RC1 Roger Clemens 15.00
CD Carlos Delgado 5.00
JD J.D. Drew 4.00
AD Adam Dunn 6.00
JG Jason Giambi 4.00
TR Troy Glaus 5.00
TG Tom Glavine 4.00
SG Shawn Green 4.00
KG Ken Griffey Jr./250 12.00
VG Vladimir Guerrero 6.00
TH Todd Helton 6.00
EH Eric Hinske 4.00
CJ Chipper Jones 8.00
AK Austin Kearns 8.00
JK Jeff Kent 4.00
MM Mickey Mantle/250 100.00
HM Hideki Matsui/250 25.00
PM Paul Molitor/250 8.00
MU Mike Mussina 6.00
HN Hideo Nomo 8.00
RO Roy Oswalt 4.00
RP Rafael Palmeiro 6.00
MP Mark Prior 10.00
AP Albert Pujols 20.00
AP1 Albert Pujols 20.00
CR Cal Ripken Jr./250 25.00
NR Nolan Ryan/130 50.00
TS Tom Seaver 8.00
GS Gary Sheffield 4.00
AS Alfonso Soriano 10.00
SS Sammy Sosa/250 12.00
CS Casey Stengel 15.00
JT Jim Thome 8.00
BW Bernie Williams 8.00
TW Ted Williams/250 65.00
KW Kerry Wood 8.00

Threads of Time

NM/M
Common Player: 4.00
Production 350, unless noted.
Golds: 1-2X
Production 50, 25 or 10
No Pricing for #'d to 25 or less.
JB Johnny Bench 10.00
GC Gary Carter 4.00
RC Roger Clemens 15.00
TC Ty Cobb 100.00
DD Don Drysdale 15.00
DE Dennis Eckersley 4.00
RF Rollie Fingers 4.00
LG Lou Gehrig/250 140.00
JG Jason Giambi/250 6.00
JU Juan Gonzalez 5.00
KG Ken Griffey Jr./250 12.00
VG Vladimir Guerrero 6.00
RJ Randy Johnson 8.00
CJ Chipper Jones 8.00
HK Harmon Killebrew 12.00
GM Greg Maddux 8.00
MM Mickey Mantle/250 100.00
RM Roger Maris 40.00
PM Pedro J. Martinez 8.00
DM Don Mattingly 20.00
HN Hideo Nomo 8.00
AP Andy Pettitte 6.00
MP Mike Piazza 10.00
AP Albert Pujols 20.00
CR Cal Ripken Jr. 25.00
FR Frank Robinson 8.00
AR Alex Rodriguez 12.00
IR Ivan Rodriguez 5.00
NR Nolan Ryan 30.00
RS Ryne Sandberg 12.00
TS Tom Seaver 8.00
OS Ozzie Smith 10.00
SS Sammy Sosa/250 12.00
IS Ichiro Suzuki/250 30.00
FT Frank Thomas 6.00
JT Jim Thome 8.00
HW Honus Wagner 75.00
TW Ted Williams/250 65.00
MW Maury Wills 4.00
DW Dave Winfield/250 6.00

Gary Carter Hawaii Autograph

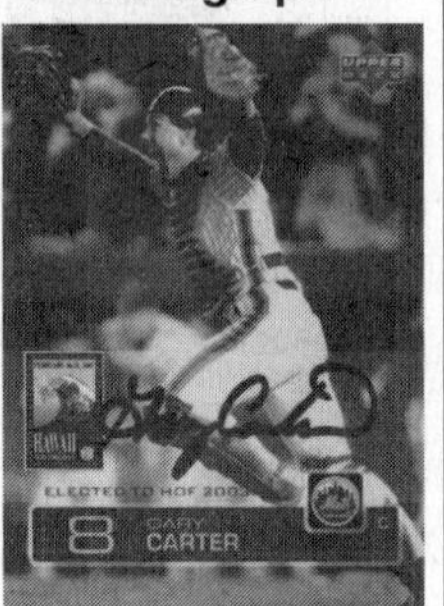

Participants in the card company's golf outing at the SCD Hawaii Trade Conference received this specially produced card of Gary Carter, long known for his refusal to sign cards except for specific charitable causes. The card has the Hawaii show logo on front, along with a gold-foil notation of his Hall of Fame election. Back has a statement of authenticity.

NM/M
GC Gary Carter 25.00

2003 Upper Deck Classic Portraits

NM/M
Complete Set (232):
Common Player: .15
Common SP (101-145): 2.00
Inserted 1:4
Common SP (145-190): 3.00
Production 2,003
Common Royalty (191-232): 2.00
Production 1,200
Pack (5): 3.00
Box (18 + Bust): 75.00
1 Ken Griffey Jr. 1.50
2 Randy Johnson 1.00
3 Rafael Furcal .25
4 Omar Vizquel .25
5 Shawn Green .40
6 Roy Oswalt .40
7 Hideo Nomo .40
8 Jason Giambi .40
9 Barry Bonds 2.50
10 Mike Piazza 1.50
11 Ichiro Suzuki 2.00
12 Carlos Delgado .40
13 Preston Wilson .15
14 Lance Berkman .25
15 Magglio Ordonez .25
16 Kerry Wood .75
17 Ivan Rodriguez .75
18 Chipper Jones 1.00
19 Adam Dunn .75
20 C.C. Sabathia .15
21 Mike MacDougal .15
22 Torii Hunter .40
23 Jim Thome .75
24 Hank Blalock .40
25 Johnny Damon .50
26 Troy Glaus .40
27 Manny Ramirez .75
28 Mark Prior 1.00
29 Brent Mayne .15
30 Derek Jeter 2.50
31 Tim Hudson .40
32 Mike Cameron .15
33 Mark Teixeira .40
34 Shannon Stewart .15
35 Tim Salmon .25
36 Luis Gonzalez .25
37 Jason Johnson .15
38 Shea Hillenbrand .15
39 Bartolo Colon .25
40 Austin Kearns .40
41 Vladimir Guerrero 1.00
42 Tom Glavine .40
43 Andres Galarraga .25
44 Kazuhiro Sasaki .15
45 Juan Gonzalez .75
46 Vernon Wells .25
47 Jeff Bagwell .75
48 Mike Sweeney .15
49 Carlos Beltran .50
50 Dave Roberts .15
51 Todd Helton .75
52 Carlos Pena .15
53 Darin Erstad .25
54 Gary Sheffield .40
55 Lyle Overbay .15
56 Sammy Sosa 1.50
57 Mike Mussina .50
58 Matt Morris .25
59 Roberto Alomar .50
60 Larry Walker .25
61 Jacque Jones .15
62 Josh Beckett .40
63 Richie Sexson .50
64 Derek Lowe .15
65 Pedro J. Martinez 1.00
66 Moises Alou .25
67 Craig Biggio .25
68 Curt Schilling .75
69 Jesse Foppert .15
70 Nomar Garciaparra 1.50
71 Barry Zito .40
72 Alfonso Soriano .75
73 Miguel Tejada .50
74 Rafael Palmeiro .50
75 Albert Pujols 2.00
76 Mariano Rivera .25
77 Bobby Abreu .25
78 Alex Rodriguez 2.00
79 Andruw Jones .50
80 Frank Thomas .75
81 Greg Maddux 1.50
82 Jim Edmonds .40
83 Bernie Williams .50
84 Roger Clemens 2.00
85 Eric Chavez .25
86 Scott Rolen 1.00
87 Jorge Posada .50
88 Bret Boone .25
89 Ben Sheets .25
90 John Olerud .15
91 J.D. Drew .25
92 Aaron Boone .15
93 Corey Koskie .15
94 Sean Casey .25
95 Jose Cruz Jr. .15
96 Pat Burrell .40
97 Jose Guillen .15
98 Mark Mulder .25
99 Garret Anderson .25
100 Kazuhisa Ishii .15
101 Dave Matranga **RC** 2.00
102 Colin Porter **RC** 2.00
103 Jason Gilfillan **RC** 2.00
104 Carlos Mendez **RC** 2.00
105 Jason Shiell **RC** 2.00
106 Kevin Tolar **RC** 2.00
107 Termel Sledge **RC** 3.00
108 Craig Brazell **RC** 4.00
109 Bernie Castro **RC** 2.00
110 Tim Olson **RC** 3.00
111 Kevin Ohme **RC** 2.00
112 Pedro Liriano 2.00
113 Joe Borowski 2.00
114 Edgar Gonzalez **RC** 3.00
115 Joe Thurston 2.00
116 Bobby Hill 2.00
117 Michel Hernandez **RC** 2.00
118 Arnie Munoz **RC** 2.00
119 David Sanders **RC** 2.00
120 Willie Eyre **RC** 3.00
121 Brent Hoard **RC** 2.00
122 Lew Ford **RC** 4.00
123 Beau Kemp **RC** 2.00
124 Jonathan Pridie **RC** 2.00
125 Mike Ryan **RC** 4.00
126 Richard Fischer **RC** 2.00
127 Luis Ayala **RC** 2.00
128 Mike Neu **RC** 2.00
129 Joe Valentine **RC** 2.00
130 Nate Bland **RC** 2.00
131 Shane Bazzell **RC** 2.00
132 Jason Roach **RC** 2.00
133 Diegomar Markwell **RC** 2.00
134 Francisco Rosario **RC** 2.00

135 Guillermo Quiroz **RC** 4.00
136 Jerome Williams 2.00
137 Fernando Cabrera **RC** 2.00
138 Francisco Cruceta **RC** 2.00
139 Jhonny Peralta 4.00
140 Rett Johnson **RC** 2.00
141 Aaron Looper **RC** 2.00
142 Bobby Madritsch **RC** 6.00
143 Dan Haren 3.00
144 Jose Castillo 2.00
145 Chris Waters **RC** 3.00
146 Hideki Matsui **RC** 10.00
147 Jose Contreras **RC** 4.00
148 Felix Sanchez **RC** 3.00
149 Jon Leicester **RC** 3.00
150 Todd Wellemeyer **RC** 3.00
151 Matt Bruback **RC** 3.00
152 Chris Capuano **RC** 5.00
153 Oscar Villarreal **RC** 3.00
154 Matt Kata **RC** 3.00
155 Robby Hammock **RC** 3.00
156 Gerald Laird 3.00
157 Brandon Webb **RC** 6.00
158 Tommy Whiteman **RC** 3.00
159 Andrew Brown **RC** 3.00
160 Alfredo Gonzalez **RC** 3.00
161 Carlos Rivera 3.00
162 Rick Roberts **RC** 3.00
163 Dontrelle Willis 3.00
164 Josh Willingham **RC** 4.00
165 Prentice Redman **RC** 3.00
166 Jeff Duncan **RC** 4.00
167 Jose Reyes 3.00
168 Jeremy Griffiths 3.00
169 Phil Seibel **RC** 3.00
170 Heath Bell **RC** 3.00
171 Anthony Ferrari **RC** 3.00
172 Mike Nicolas **RC** 3.00
173 Cory Stewart **RC** 3.00
174 Miguel Ojeda **RC** 5.00
175 Rickie Weeks **RC** 10.00
176 Delmon Young **RC** 10.00
177 Tommy Phelps 3.00
178 Josh Hall **RC** 4.00
179 Ryan Cameron **RC** 3.00
180 Garrett Atkins 3.00
181 Clint Barmes **RC** 6.00
182 Michael Hessman **RC** 3.00
183 Chin-Hui Tsao 3.00
184 Rocco Baldelli 3.00
185 Bo Hart **RC** 3.00
186 Wilfredo Ledezma **RC** 3.00
187 Miguel Cabrera 5.00
188 Ian Ferguson **RC** 3.00
189 Micheal Nakamura **RC** 3.00
190 Alejandro Machado **RC** 3.00
191 Mickey Mantle 12.00
192 Ted Williams 10.00
193 Mark Prior 6.00
194 Stan Musial 6.00
195 Phil Rizzuto 3.00
196 Nolan Ryan 12.00
197 Tom Seaver 4.00
198 Robin Yount 5.00
199 Yogi Berra 3.00
200 Ernie Banks 8.00
201 Willie McCovey 3.00
202 Ralph Kiner 3.00
203 Ken Griffey Jr. 4.00
204 Sammy Sosa 5.00
205 Derek Jeter 8.00
206 Nomar Garciaparra 6.00
207 Alex Rodriguez 6.00
208 Ichiro Suzuki 4.00
209 Mike Piazza 4.00
210 Jackie Robinson 6.00
211 Roberto Clemente 8.00
212 Babe Ruth 12.00
213 Duke Snider 3.00
214 Greg Maddux 4.00
215 Juan Marichal 3.00
216 Joe Morgan 2.00
217 Rollie Fingers 2.00
218 Warren Spahn 4.00
219 Pee Wee Reese 2.00
220 Troy Glaus 2.00
221 Jason Giambi 2.00
222 Roger Clemens 6.00
223 Pedro J. Martinez 3.00
224 Chipper Jones 4.00
225 Randy Johnson 3.00
226 Jim Thome 3.00
227 Barry Bonds 8.00
228 Hideo Nomo 2.00
229 Whitey Ford 3.00
230 Bob Gibson 4.00
231 Alfonso Soriano 4.00
232 Richie Ashburn 3.00

Gold

No pricing due to scarcity.
Production 25 Sets

Bust Signature

NM/M
Complete Set (17):
Common Player:
NG Nomar Garciaparra 80.00
HM Hideki Matsui 180.00

Classic Stitches Jersey

NM/M
Common Player: 4.00
Production 299 Sets
Golds: No Pricing
Production 25 Sets
JB Jeff Bagwell 6.00
RB Rocco Baldelli 4.00
HB Hank Blalock 6.00
HC Hee Seop Choi 4.00
RC Roger Clemens 15.00
JD J.D. Drew 4.00
AD Adam Dunn 8.00
JE Jim Edmonds 6.00
RF Rafael Furcal 4.00
JG Jason Giambi 6.00
TG Troy Glaus 6.00
SG Shawn Green 4.00
KG Ken Griffey Jr. 10.00
VG Vladimir Guerrero 8.00
TH Torii Hunter 6.00
RJ Randy Johnson 8.00
AJ Andruw Jones 6.00
CJ Chipper Jones 8.00
JK Jeff Kent 4.00
ML Mike Lowell 4.00
GM Greg Maddux 10.00
PM Pedro J. Martinez 8.00
HM Hideki Matsui 40.00
MM Matt Morris 6.00
HN Hideo Nomo 8.00
MO Magglio Ordonez 4.00
RO Roy Oswalt 4.00
CP Corey Patterson 6.00
AP Andy Pettitte 6.00
MI Mike Piazza 8.00
MP Mark Prior 8.00
AL Albert Pujols 15.00
AR Alex Rodriguez 10.00
IR Ivan Rodriguez 6.00
CS Curt Schilling 8.00
GS Gary Sheffield 6.00
AS Alfonso Soriano 8.00
SS Sammy Sosa 15.00
IS Ichiro Suzuki 25.00
JT Jim Thome 8.00
DW Dontrelle Willis 8.00
KW Kerry Wood 8.00

Classic Stitches Patch

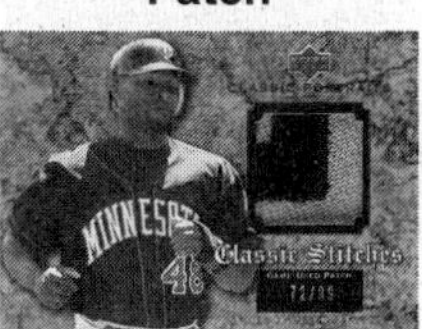

NM/M
Common Player: 15.00
Production 99 Sets
Golds: No Pricing
Production 10 Sets
JB Jeff Bagwell 25.00
RB Rocco Baldelli 25.00
HB Hank Blalock 25.00
HC Hee Seop Choi 15.00
RC Roger Clemens 40.00
JD J.D. Drew 15.00
AD Adam Dunn 15.00
JE Jim Edmonds 20.00
RF Rafael Furcal 15.00
JG Jason Giambi 15.00
TG Troy Glaus 15.00
SG Shawn Green 15.00
KG Ken Griffey Jr. 50.00
VG Vladimir Guerrero 25.00
TH Torii Hunter 15.00
RJ Randy Johnson 30.00
AJ Andruw Jones 15.00
CJ Chipper Jones 25.00
JK Jeff Kent 15.00
ML Mike Lowell 15.00
GM Greg Maddux 35.00
PM Pedro J. Martinez 25.00
HM Hideki Matsui 85.00
MM Matt Morris 15.00
HN Hideo Nomo 40.00
MO Magglio Ordonez 15.00
RO Roy Oswalt 15.00
CP Corey Patterson 20.00
AP Andy Pettitte 20.00
MI Mike Piazza 40.00
MP Mark Prior 15.00
AL Albert Pujols 40.00
AR Alex Rodriguez 50.00
IR Ivan Rodriguez 20.00
CS Curt Schilling 20.00
GS Gary Sheffield 15.00
AS Alfonso Soriano 20.00
SS Sammy Sosa 35.00
IS Ichiro Suzuki 120.00
JT Jim Thome 20.00
DW Dontrelle Willis 20.00
KW Kerry Wood 25.00

Signs of Success

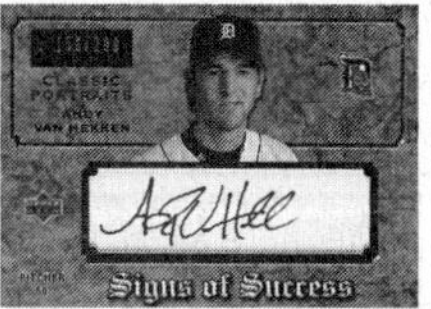

NM/M
Common Player: 6.00
MI Milton Bradley/220 10.00
DB Dewon Brazelton/299 6.00
JB John Buck/98 8.00
MB Mark Buehrle/220 10.00
BR Brandon Claussen/121 6.00
BC Brad Cresse/121 10.00
JD Johnny Damon/297 30.00
BD Ben Diggins/299 6.00
AG Alex Graman/215 10.00
KG Ken Griffey Jr./299 90.00
TG Tony Gwynn/49 80.00
DH Drew Henson/246 15.00
BH Ben Howard/299 6.00
HI Hansel Izquierdo/299 8.00
JJ Jimmy Journell/98 8.00
DK David Kelton/102 8.00
KL Kenny Lofton/296 15.00
CM Corwin Malone/103 8.00
BP Brandon Phillips/131 10.00
SR Scott Rolen/100 20.00
CC C.C. Sabathia/106 15.00
MT Mark Teixeira/280 25.00
TH Matt Thornton/298 6.00
AH Andy Van Hekken/299 8.00
JU Justin Wayne/299 8.00
JW Jayson Werth/299 8.00
JE Jerome Williams/103 15.00

Bronze Bust

NM/M
Common Player:
YB Yogi Berra 25.00
RC Roberto Clemente 60.00
NG Nomar Garciaparra 40.00
JG Jason Giambi 25.00
BG Bob Gibson 25.00
KG Ken Griffey Jr./300 40.00
MM Mickey Mantle 70.00
HM Hideki Matsui 30.00
SM Stan Musial 40.00
BRS Babe Ruth/Sox/300 60.00
BRY Babe Ruth/Yanks 60.00
NRA Nolan Ryan/Astros 50.00
NRA Nolan Ryan/Astros/300 50.00
NRM Nolan Ryan/Mets 50.00
TSM Tom Seaver/Mets 25.00
TSR Tom Seaver/Reds/300 25.00
TSR Tom Seaver/Reds 25.00
DS Duke Snider 25.00
SS Sammy Sosa/300 40.00
IS Ichiro Suzuki/300 40.00
TW Ted Williams 50.00

Bronze Bust Autograph

NM/M
Some not priced due to scarcity.
YB Yogi Berra 100.00
NG Nomar Garciaparra/106 125.00
BG Bob Gibson 60.00
KG Ken Griffey Jr. 100.00
HM Hideki Matsui 250.00
SM Stan Musial/62 120.00
DS Duke Snider 90.00
IS Ichiro Suzuki/62 275.00

Marble Bust

NM/M
Common Player:
YB Yogi Berra/125 40.00
YB Yogi Berra/250 25.00
RC Roberto Clemente/250 70.00
NG Nomar Garciaparra/250 40.00
JG Jason Giambi 25.00
BG Bob Gibson/125 30.00
BG Bob Gibson/250 25.00
KG Ken Griffey Jr./250 40.00
MM Mickey Mantle/80 80.00
MM Mickey Mantle/125 80.00
HM Hideki Matsui/250 60.00
SM Stan Musial/250 50.00
BRS Babe Ruth Sox/250 60.00
BRY Babe Ruth/Yanks/125 75.00
BRY Babe Ruth/Yanks/250 65.00
NRA Nolan Ryan/Astros/125 60.00
NRA Nolan Ryan/Astros/250 50.00
NRM Nolan Ryan/Mets/125 60.00
NRM Nolan Ryan/Mets/250 50.00
TSM Tom Seaver/Mets/125 40.00
TSM Tom Seaver/Mets/250 30.00
TSR Tom Seaver/Reds/125 40.00
TSR Tom Seaver/Reds/250 30.00
DS Duke Snider/100 40.00
DS Duke Snider/250 40.00
SS Sammy Sosa/250 40.00
IS Ichiro Suzuki/250 50.00
TW Ted Williams/125 65.00
TW Ted Williams/250 50.00

Marble Autograph

No pricing due to scarcity.

Pewter Bust

NM/M
Common Player:
YB Yogi Berra/75 40.00
YB Yogi Berra/100 40.00
RC Roberto Clemente/100 100.00
NG Nomar Garciaparra/100 60.00
JG Jason Giambi/100 40.00
BG Bob Gibson/75 40.00
BG Bob Gibson/100 40.00
KG Ken Griffey Jr./100 70.00
MM Mickey Mantle/75 125.00
MM Mickey Mantle/100 125.00
HM Hideki Matsui/100 50.00
SM Stan Musial/100 60.00
BRS Babe Ruth/Sox/100 80.00
BRY Babe Ruth/Yanks/75 90.00
BRY Babe Ruth/Yanks/100 90.00
NRA Nolan Ryan/Astros/75 80.00
NRA Nolan Ryan/Astros/100 80.00
NRM Nolan Ryan/Mets/75 80.00
NRM Nolan Ryan/Mets/100 80.00
TSM Tom Seaver/Mets/75 40.00
TSM Tom Seaver/Mets/100 40.00
TSR Tom Seaver/Reds/100 40.00
TSR Tom Seaver/Reds/75 40.00
DS Duke Snider/75 40.00
DS Duke Snider/100 40.00
SS Sammy Sosa/100 60.00
IS Ichiro Suzuki/100 65.00
TW Ted Williams/75 100.00
TW Ted Williams/100 100.00

Pewter Autograph Bust

No pricing due to scarcity.

Roger Clemens 300 Wins

To commemorate The Rocket's milestone, fans at Yankee Stadium on August 28 received this cello-wrapped set. Backs repeat the front format and have a line of stats and a career highlight.

NM/M
Complete Set (6): 15.00
Common Card: 3.00
1 Roger Clemens (1999 post-season wins) 3.00
2 Roger Clemens (2000 post-season wins) 3.00
3 Roger Clemens (Sixth Cy Young) 3.00
4 Roger Clemens (4,000 Ks) 3.00
5 Roger Clemens (300th win) 3.00
-- Header Card 3.00

2003 Upper Deck Finite

NM/M
Complete Set (380):
Common Player (1-100): 1.00
Production 1,999
Common (101-150): 1.00
Production 1,599
Common (151-180): 2.00
Production 499
Common (181-200): 2.50
Production 299
Common (201-300): 1.50
Production 1,299
Common (301-330): 3.00
Production 599
Common (331-360): 3.00
Production 299
Common (361-380): 5.00
Production 150
Pack (3): 9.00
Box (10): 80.00
1 Darin Erstad 1.00
2 Garret Anderson 1.50
3 Tim Salmon 1.00
4 Troy Glaus 1.50
5 Luis Gonzalez 1.00
6 Randy Johnson 2.00
7 Curt Schilling 1.50
8 Andruw Jones 1.50
9 Gary Sheffield 1.50
10 Rafael Furcal 1.00
11 Greg Maddux 3.00
12 Chipper Jones 2.50
13 Tony Batista 1.00
14 Jay Gibbons 1.00
15 Johnny Damon 1.00
16 Derek Lowe 1.00
17 Nomar Garciaparra 3.00
18 Pedro J. Martinez 2.00
19 Manny Ramirez 1.50
20 Mark Prior 2.00
21 Kerry Wood 1.50
22 Corey Patterson 1.00
23 Sammy Sosa 3.00
24 Moises Alou 1.00
25 Magglio Ordonez 1.00
26 Frank Thomas 1.50
27 Paul Konerko 1.00
28 Bartolo Colon 1.00
29 Adam Dunn 1.00
30 Austin Kearns 1.00
31 Aaron Boone 1.00
32 Ken Griffey Jr. 2.50
33 Omar Vizquel 1.00
34 C.C. Sabathia 1.00
35 Brandon Phillips 1.00
36 Larry Walker 1.00
37 Preston Wilson 1.00
38 Todd Helton 1.50
39 Eric Munson 1.00
40 Ivan Rodriguez 1.50
41 Josh Beckett 1.50
42 Roy Oswalt 1.00
43 Craig Biggio 1.00
44 Jeff Bagwell 1.50
45 Dontrelle Willis 1.00
46 Carlos Beltran 1.00
47 Brent Mayne 1.00
48 Hideo Nomo 1.00
49 Rickey Henderson 1.00
50 Adrian Beltre 1.00
51 Miguel Cabrera 2.00
52 Kazuhisa Ishii 1.00
53 Richie Sexson 1.00
54 Torii Hunter 1.00
55 Jacque Jones 1.00
56 A.J. Pierzynski 1.00
57 Jose Vidro 1.00
58 Vladimir Guerrero 2.00
59 Tom Glavine 1.00
60 Jose Reyes 1.00
61 Mike Piazza 2.50
62 Jorge Posada 1.50
63 Mike Mussina 1.50
64 Robin Ventura 1.00
65 Mariano Rivera 1.00
66 Roger Clemens 3.00
67 Jason Giambi 2.00
68 Bernie Williams 1.50
69 Alfonso Soriano 2.00
70 Derek Jeter 5.00
71 Miguel Tejada 1.50
72 Eric Chavez 1.00
73 Tim Hudson 1.00
74 Barry Zito 1.50
75 Pat Burrell 1.00
76 Jim Thome 2.00
77 Bobby Abreu 1.00
78 Brian Giles 1.00
79 Reggie Sanders 1.00
80 Ryan Klesko 1.00
81 Edgardo Alfonzo 1.00
82 Rich Aurilia 1.00
83 Barry Bonds 5.00
84 Mike Cameron 1.00
85 Kazuhiro Sasaki 1.00
86 Bret Boone 1.00
87 Ichiro Suzuki 3.00
88 J.D. Drew 1.00
89 Jim Edmonds 1.00
90 Scott Rolen 2.00
91 Matt Morris 1.00
92 Tino Martinez 1.00
93 Albert Pujols 3.00
94 Rocco Baldelli 1.00
95 Hank Blalock 1.50
96 Alex Rodriguez 3.00
97 Rafael Palmeiro 1.50
98 Eric Hinske 1.00
99 Orlando Hudson 1.00
100 Carlos Delgado 1.50
101 Albert Pujols 3.00
102 Alex Rodriguez 3.00
103 Alfonso Soriano 2.00
104 Andruw Jones 1.50
105 Barry Zito 1.50
106 Bernie Williams 1.50
107 Carlos Delgado 1.50
108 Chipper Jones 2.50
109 Curt Schilling 1.50
110 Doug Mientkiewicz 1.00
111 Frank Thomas 1.50
112 Garret Anderson 1.50
113 Gary Sheffield 1.50
114 Greg Maddux 3.00
115 Hank Blalock 1.00
116 Hideki Matsui 4.00
117 Hideo Nomo 1.50
118 Ichiro Suzuki 3.00
119 Ivan Rodriguez 1.50
120 Jason Giambi 2.00
121 Jeff Bagwell 1.50
122 Jeff Kent 1.00
123 Jerome Williams 1.00
124 Jeromy Burnitz 1.00
125 Jim Thome 2.00
126 Jose Cruz Jr. 1.00
127 Ken Griffey Jr. 2.50
128 Kerry Wood 1.50
129 Lance Berkman 1.00
130 Luis Gonzalez 1.00
131 Manny Ramirez 1.50
132 Mark Prior 2.00
133 Miguel Cabrera 2.00
134 Miguel Tejada 1.50
135 Mike Piazza 2.50
136 Pat Burrell 1.00
137 Pedro J. Martinez 2.00
138 Rafael Furcal 1.00
139 Randy Johnson 2.00
140 Rich Harden 1.00
141 Rickey Henderson 1.50
142 Roberto Alomar 1.50
143 Roger Clemens 3.00
144 Sammy Sosa 3.00
145 Shawn Green 1.00
146 Todd Helton 1.50
147 Tom Glavine 1.00
148 Torii Hunter 1.00
149 Troy Glaus 1.00
150 Vladimir Guerrero 2.00
151 Adam Dunn 2.00
152 Albert Pujols 6.00

153 Alex Rodriguez 6.00
154 Alfonso Soriano 3.00
155 Andruw Jones 2.50
156 Barry Bonds 8.00
157 Carlos Delgado 2.50
158 Chipper Jones 3.00
159 Derek Jeter 8.00
160 Gary Sheffield 2.50
161 Hank Blalock 2.50
162 Hideki Matsui 6.00
163 Ichiro Suzuki 4.00
164 J.D. Drew 2.00
165 Jason Giambi 3.00
166 Jeff Bagwell 3.00
167 Jeff Kent 2.00
168 Jim Edmonds 2.00
169 Jim Thome 3.00
170 Ken Griffey Jr. 5.00
171 Luis Gonzalez 2.00
172 Magglio Ordonez 2.00
173 Manny Ramirez 2.50
174 Mike Lowell 2.00
175 Mike Piazza 4.00
176 Nomar Garciaparra 6.00
177 Rafael Palmeiro 2.50
178 Shawn Green 2.00
179 Troy Glaus 2.00
180 Vladimir Guerrero 3.00
181 Albert Pujols 8.00
182 Alex Rodriguez 8.00
183 Alfonso Soriano 4.00
184 Bernie Williams 2.50
185 Chipper Jones 4.00
186 Derek Jeter 10.00
187 Hideki Matsui 8.00
188 Ichiro Suzuki 6.00
189 Jim Thome 3.00
190 Joe DiMaggio 8.00
191 Ken Griffey Jr. 6.00
192 Mickey Mantle 12.00
193 Mike Piazza 5.00
194 Pedro J. Martinez 4.00
195 Randy Johnson 4.00
196 Roger Clemens 6.00
197 Sammy Sosa 6.00
198 Ted Williams 8.00
199 Troy Glaus 2.50
200 Vladimir Guerrero 3.00
201 Aaron Looper **RC** 2.00
202 Alejandro Machado 1.50
203 Alfredo Gonzalez **RC** 2.00
204 Andrew Brown **RC** 2.00
205 Anthony Ferrari 1.50
206 Aquilino Lopez **RC** 2.00
207 Beau Kemp **RC** 2.00
208 Bernie Castro 1.50
209 Bobby Madritsch **RC** 8.00
210 Brandon Villafuerte 1.50
211 Brent Hoard **RC** 2.00
212 Brian Stokes 1.50
213 Carlos Mendez 1.50
214 Chris Capuano **RC** 4.00
215 Chris Waters 1.50
216 Clint Barmes **RC** 5.00
217 Colin Porter **RC** 1.50
218 Cory Stewart 1.50
219 Craig Brazell **RC** 3.00
220 D.J. Carrasco **RC** 1.50
221 Daniel Cabrera **RC** 1.50
222 Dave Matranga **RC** 2.00
223 David Sanders 1.50
224 Diegomar Markwell 1.50
225 Edgar Gonzalez **RC** 2.00
226 Felix Sanchez 1.50
227 Fernando Cabrera **RC** 2.00
228 Francisco Cruceta **RC** 2.00
229 Francisco Rosario **RC** 2.00
230 Garrett Atkins 1.50
231 Gerald Laird 1.50
232 Guillermo Quiroz **RC** 4.00
233 Heath Bell **RC** 2.00
234 Delmon Young **RC** 10.00
235 Jason Shiell **RC** 2.00
236 Jeremy Bonderman 10.00
237 Jeremy Griffiths 1.50
238 Jeremy Guthrie 1.50
239 Jeremy Wedel **RC** 2.00
240 Carlos Rivera 1.50
241 Joe Valentine 1.50
242 Jon Leicester 1.50
243 Jonathan Pridie 1.50
244 Jorge Cordova 1.50
245 Jose Castillo 1.50
246 Josh Hall **RC** 2.00
247 Josh Stewart **RC** 1.50
248 Josh Willingham **RC** 3.00
249 Julio Manon **RC** 1.50
250 Kevin Correia **RC** 1.50
251 Kevin Ohme **RC** 2.00
252 Kevin Tolar 1.50
253 Luis De Los Santos 1.50
254 Jermaine Clark 1.50
255 Mark Malaska **RC** 2.00
256 Juan Dominguez 1.50
257 Michael Hessman **RC** 1.50
258 Micheal Nakamura **RC** 2.00
259 Miguel Ojeda **RC** 1.50
260 Mike Gallo 1.50
261 Edwin Jackson **RC** 6.00
262 Mike Ryan **RC** 1.50
263 Nate Bland **RC** 1.50
264 Nate Robertson 3.00
265 Nook Logan **RC** 2.00
266 Phil Seibel **RC** 1.50
267 Prentice Redman **RC** 2.00
268 Rafael Betancourt 1.50
269 Rett Johnson **RC** 2.00
270 Richard Fischer 1.50
271 Rick Roberts **RC** 2.00
272 Roger Deago 1.50
273 Ryan Cameron **RC** 1.50
274 Shane Bazzell 2.00
275 Erasmo Ramirez 1.50
276 Terrmel Sledge **RC** 2.00
277 Tim Olson **RC** 3.00
278 Tommy Phelps 1.50
279 Tommy Whiteman 1.50
280 Willie Eyre **RC** 2.00
281 Alex Prieto **RC** 2.00
282 Michel Hernandez **RC** 1.50
283 Greg Jones **RC** 1.50
284 Victor Martinez 1.50
285 Tom Gregorio **RC** 2.00
286 Marcus Thames 1.50
287 Jorge DePaula **RC** 1.50
288 Aaron Miles **RC** 3.00
289 Reynaldo Garcia 1.50
290 Brian Sweeney **RC** 1.50
291 Pete LaForest **RC** 2.00
292 Pete Zoccolilo **RC** 1.50
293 Danny Garcia **RC** 1.50
294 Jonny Gomes 1.50
295 Rosman Garcia **RC** 1.50
296 Mike Edwards 1.50
297 Marlon Byrd 1.50
298 Khalil Greene 4.00
299 Jose Valverde 1.50
300 Drew Henson 1.50
301 Chris Bootcheck 3.00
302 Matt Belisle 3.00
303 Kevin Gregg 3.00
304 Bobby Jenks 3.00
305 Jason Young 3.00
306 Laynce Nix 3.00
307 Robb Quinlan 3.00
308 Chase Utley 3.00
309 Humberto Quintero **RC** 4.00
310 Tim Raines Jr. 3.00
311 Stephen Smitherman 3.00
312 Jason Anderson 3.00
313 Joe Dawley 3.00
314 Chad Cordero **RC** 3.00
315 Victor Alvarez 3.00
316 Jimmy Gobble 3.00
317 Jared Fernandez 3.00
318 Eric Bruntlett 3.00
319 Neal Cotts 3.00
320 Ryan Madson 3.00
321 Rocco Baldelli 3.00
322 Graham Koonce **RC** 3.00
323 Bobby Crosby 3.00
324 Mike Wood 3.00
325 Jesse Garcia 3.00
326 Noah Lowry 6.00
327 Edwin Almonte 3.00
328 Justin Morneau 3.00
329 Steve Colyer 3.00
330 Vinnie Chulk 3.00
331 Brian Schmack 3.00
332 Stephen Randolph **RC** 3.00
333 Pedro Feliciano 3.00
334 Koyie Hill 3.00
335 Geoff Geary **RC** 3.00
336 Jon Switzer 3.00
337 Xavier Nady 3.00
338 Rich Harden 3.00
339 Dontrelle Willis 4.00
340 Angel Berroa 3.00
341 Jerome Williams 3.00
342 Brandon Claussen 3.00
343 Kurt Ainsworth 3.00
344 Horacio Ramirez 3.00
345 Hee Seop Choi 3.00
346 Billy Traber 3.00
347 Brandon Phillips 3.00
348 Jody Gerut 3.00
349 Mark Teixeira 4.00
350 Javier Lopez 3.00
351 Miguel Cabrera 5.00
352 Brad Lidge 3.00
353 Mike MacDougal 3.00
354 Ken Harvey 3.00
355 Chien-Ming Wang **RC** 40.00
356 Aaron Heilman 3.00
357 Jason Phillips 3.00
358 Jason Bay 3.00
359 Arnie Munoz 3.00
360 Ian Ferguson **RC** 3.00
361 Ryan Wagner **RC** 8.00
362 Rickie Weeks **RC** 30.00
363 Chad Gaudin **RC** 8.00
364 Jason Gilfillan **RC** 5.00
365 Jason Roach 5.00
366 Jhonny Peralta 6.00
367 Mike Neu **RC** 5.00
368 Jose Contreras **RC** 10.00
369 Wilfredo Ledezma **RC** 5.00
370 Lew Ford **RC** 8.00
371 Luis Ayala **RC** 5.00
372 Bo Hart **RC** 5.00
373 Brandon Webb **RC** 15.00
374 Dan Haren 15.00
375 Hideki Matsui **RC** 50.00
376 Jeff Duncan **RC** 8.00
377 Matt Kata **RC** 5.00
378 Oscar Villarreal **RC** 5.00
379 Rob Hammock **RC** 5.00
380 Todd Wellemeyer **RC** 5.00

Game Face (193-217):
Common Rookie: 5.00
Production 299
193 Aaron Looper **RC** 5.00
194 Alex Prieto **RC** 5.00
195 Bo Hart **RC** 5.00
196 Chad Gaudin **RC** 5.00
197 Colin Porter **RC** 5.00
198 D.J. Carrasco **RC** 5.00
199 Dan Haren 10.00
200 Delmon Young **RC** 25.00
201 Dontrelle Willis 5.00
202 Jon Switzer 5.00
203 Edwin Jackson **RC** 8.00
204 Fernando Cabrera **RC** 5.00
205 Garrett Atkins 8.00
206 Jeremy Bonderman 12.00
207 Kevin Ohme **RC** 5.00
208 Khalil Greene 10.00
209 Luis Ayala **RC** 5.00
210 Matt Kata **RC** 5.00
211 Noah Lowry 10.00
212 Rich Harden 5.00
213 Rickie Weeks **RC** 15.00
214 Rosman Garcia **RC** 5.00
215 Ryan Wagner **RC** 5.00
216 Tom Gregorio **RC** 5.00
217 Wilfredo Ledezma **RC** 5.00

SP Authentic (190-239):
Common SP Authentic Rookie: 4.00
Production 699
190 Aaron Looper 4.00
191 Alex Prieto 4.00
192 Alfredo Gonzalez **RC** 4.00
193 Andrew Brown **RC** 4.00
194 Anthony Ferrari 4.00
195 Aquilino Lopez **RC** 4.00
196 Beau Kemp **RC** 4.00
197 Bo Hart **RC** 4.00
198 Chad Gaudin **RC** 10.00
199 Colin Porter **RC** 4.00
200 D.J. Carrasco **RC** 4.00
201 Dan Haren 20.00
202 Danny Garcia **RC** 4.00
203 Jon Switzer 4.00
204 Edwin Jackson **RC** 4.00
205 Fernando Cabrera **RC** 4.00
206 Garrett Atkins 6.00
207 Gerald Laird 4.00
208 Greg Jones **RC** 4.00
209 Ian Ferguson **RC** 4.00
210 Jason Roach 4.00
211 Jason Shiell **RC** 4.00
212 Jeremy Bonderman 15.00
213 Jeremy Wedel **RC** 4.00
214 Jhonny Peralta 4.00
215 Delmon Young **RC** 35.00
216 Jorge DePaula **RC** 4.00
217 Josh Hall **RC** 4.00
218 Julio Manon **RC** 4.00
219 Kevin Correia **RC** 4.00
220 Kevin Ohme **RC** 4.00
221 Kevin Tolar 4.00
222 Luis Ayala **RC** 4.00
223 Luis De Los Santos 4.00
224 Chad Cordero **RC** 4.00
225 Mark Malaska **RC** 4.00
226 Khalil Greene 10.00
227 Micheal Nakamura **RC** 4.00
228 Michel Hernandez **RC** 4.00
229 Miguel Ojeda **RC** 4.00
230 Mike Neu **RC** 4.00
231 Nate Bland **RC** 4.00
232 Pete LaForest **RC** 4.00
233 Rickie Weeks **RC** 20.00
234 Rosman Garcia **RC** 4.00
235 Ryan Wagner **RC** 4.00
236 Lance Niekro 4.00
237 Tom Gregorio **RC** 4.00
238 Tommy Phelps 4.00
239 Wilfredo Ledezma **RC** 4.00

SPX (179-193, 381-387):
179 Chad Gaudin/150 **RC** 15.00
180 Chris Capuano/150 **RC** 15.00
181 Danny Garcia/150 **RC** 8.00
182 Delmon Young/150 **RC** 50.00
183 Edwin Jackson/150 **RC** 20.00
184 Greg Jones/150 **RC** 8.00
185 Jeremy Bonderman/150 25.00
186 Jorge DePaula/150 **RC** 8.00
187 Khalil Greene/150 25.00
188 Chad Cordero/150 **RC** 8.00
189 Miguel Cabrera/150 10.00
190 Rich Harden/150 10.00
191 Rickie Weeks/150 **RC** 30.00
192 Rosman Garcia/150 **RC** 8.00
193 Tom Gregorio/150 **RC** 8.00
381 Andrew Brown/Jsy/Auto./355 **RC** 15.00
382 Delmon Young/Jsy/Auto./355 **RC** 400.00
383 Colin Porter/Jsy/Auto./355 **RC** 15.00
385 Rickie Weeks/Jsy/Auto./355 **RC** 200.00
386 Dave Matranga/Jsy/Auto./355 **RC** 15.00
387 Bo Hart/Jsy/Auto./355 **RC** 15.00

UD Authentics (131-140):
Common UD Authentics: 5.00
Production 150
131 Dan Haren 10.00
132 Delmon Young **RC** 25.00
133 Dontrelle Willis 6.00
134 Edwin Jackson **RC** 5.00
135 Jeremy Bonderman 15.00
136 Khalil Greene 10.00
137 Rich Harden 5.00
138 Rickie Weeks **RC** 20.00
139 Rosman Garcia **RC** 5.00
140 Ryan Wagner **RC** 5.00

Gold

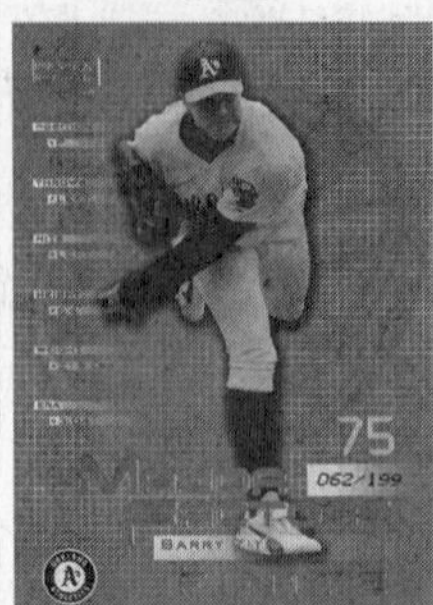

Gold (1-150): 1-2X
Gold (151-180): 1X
Production 199
Gold (181-200): 1-2X
Production 99

Elements Jersey

NM/M
Common Player: 4.00
JB Jeff Bagwell 8.00
RB Rocco Baldelli 6.00
HB Hank Blalock 6.00
HC Hee Seop Choi 4.00
JD J.D. Drew 4.00
AD Adam Dunn 6.00
JE Jim Edmonds 5.00
SG Shawn Green 5.00
KG Ken Griffey Jr./SP 15.00
TH Torii Hunter 6.00
CJ Chipper Jones 6.00
JK Jeff Kent 4.00
ML Mike Lowell 4.00
GM Greg Maddux 8.00
HM Hideki Matsui 25.00
MM Matt Morris 5.00
RO Roy Oswalt 5.00
CP Corey Patterson 5.00
AP Andy Pettitte 6.00
MI Mike Piazza 8.00
MP Mark Prior 10.00
AL Albert Pujols 15.00
AR Alex Rodriguez 10.00
AS Alfonso Soriano 6.00
IS Ichiro Suzuki 15.00
JT Jim Thome 10.00
RW Rickie Weeks/SP 15.00
DW Dontrelle Willis 6.00
KW Kerry Wood 8.00
DY Delmon Young/SP 20.00

Elements Patch

No pricing due to scarcity.
Production 25 Sets
Patch Gold: No Pricing
Production 10 Sets

First Class Jersey

NM/M
Common Player: 4.00
RC Roger Clemens 10.00
JD Joe DiMaggio/SP 80.00

TG Troy Glaus 5.00
LG Luis Gonzalez 4.00
KG Ken Griffey Jr. 12.00
VG Vladimir Guerrero 8.00
RJ Randy Johnson 8.00
CJ Chipper Jones 6.00
MM Mickey Mantle/SP 100.00
PM Pedro J. Martinez 8.00
HM Hideki Matsui 25.00
MP Mike Piazza 8.00
AP Albert Pujols 20.00
AR Alex Rodriguez 10.00
AS Alfonso Soriano 6.00
SS Sammy Sosa 10.00
IS Ichiro Suzuki 15.00
JT Jim Thome 10.00
BW Bernie Williams 6.00
TW Ted Williams/SP 75.00

Signatures

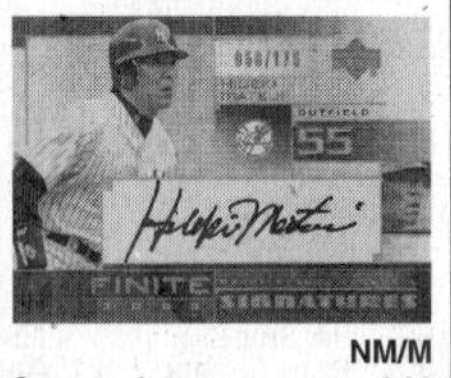

NM/M
Common Auto: 6.00
Varying quantities produced
EA Erick Almonte/355 6.00
SZ Shane Bazzell/250 6.00
MC Miguel Cabrera/100 50.00
RC Roger Clemens/50 150.00
WE Willie Eyre/200 6.00
NG Nomar Garciaparra/50 80.00
RK Rob Hammock/200 6.00
RN Rich Harden/150 25.00
BH Bo Hart/150 8.00
HM Hideki Matsui/99 250.00
MP Mark Prior/75 40.00
JR Jose Reyes/100 40.00
SR Scott Rolen/100 40.00
CS C.C. Sabathia/50 15.00
DS David Sanders/150 6.00
PS Phil Seibel/200 6.00
IS Ichiro Suzuki/25 350.00
MT Mark Teixeira/200 25.00
BW Brandon Webb/150 25.00
JW Jerome Williams/150 15.00
DW Dontrelle Willis/50 40.00
DY Delmon Young/50 80.00

SPX Jersey Autograph

NM/M
Production 355
DW Dontrelle Willis 40.00
KG Khalil Greene 60.00
RH Rich Harden 35.00

Stars and Stripes

NM/M
Common Player: 2.00
Production 299 Sets
USA-1 Justin Orenduff 2.00
USA-2 Micah Owings 2.00
USA-3 Steven Register 2.00
USA-4 Huston Street 6.00
USA-5 Justin Verlander 8.00
USA-6 Jered Weaver 8.00
USA-7 Matt Campbell 4.00
USA-8 Stephen Head 2.00
USA-9 Mark Romanczuk 2.00
USA-10 Jeff Clement 10.00
USA-11 Mike Nickeas 2.00
USA-12 Tyler Greene 2.00
USA-13 Paul Janish 2.00
USA-14 Jeff Larish 2.00
USA-15 Eric Patterson 2.00
USA-16 Dustin Pedroia 6.00
USA-17 Michael Griffin 2.00
USA-18 Brent Lillibridge 2.00
USA-19 Danny Putnam 5.00
USA-20 Seth Smith 5.00

Stars and Stripes Jersey

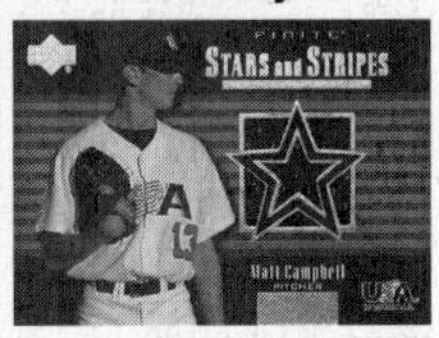

NM/M
Common Player: 4.00
J1 Justin Orenduff 4.00
J2 Micah Owings 4.00
J3 Steven Register 4.00
J4 Huston Street 8.00
J5 Justin Verlander 8.00
J6 Jered Weaver 8.00
J7 Matt Campbell 6.00
J8 Stephen Head 4.00
J9 Mark Romanczuk 4.00
J10 Jeff Clement 10.00
J11 Mike Nickeas 4.00
J12 Tyler Greene 4.00
J13 Paul Janish 4.00
J14 Jeff Larish 4.00
J15 Eric Patterson 4.00
J16 Dustin Pedroia 8.00
J17 Michael Griffin 4.00
J18 Brent Lillibridge 4.00
J19 Danny Putnam 6.00
J20 Seth Smith 6.00

2003 Upper Deck First Pitch

NM/M
Complete Set (300): 50.00
Common Player: .10
Common SP (271-300): 1.00
Inserted 1:4
Pack (5): 1.00
Box (36): 25.00
1 John Lackey .10
2 Alex Cintron .10
3 Jose Leon .10
4 Bobby Hill .10
5 Brandon Larson .10
6 Raul Gonzalez .10
7 Ben Broussard .10
8 Earl Snyder .10
9 Ramon Santiago .10
10 Jason Lane .10
11 Rob Hammock **RC** .50
12 Kirk Saarloos .10
13 Juan Brito .10
14 Runelvys Hernandez .10
15 Shawn Sedlacek .10
16 Jayson Durocher .10
17 Kevin Frederick .10
18 Zach Day .10
19 Marco Scutaro .10
20 Marcus Thames .10
21 Esteban German .10
22 Brett Myers .10
23 Oliver Perez .10
24 Dennis Tankersley .10
25 Julius Matos .10
26 Jake Peavy .10
27 Eric Cyr .10
28 Mike Crudale .10
29 Josh Pearce .10
30 Carl Crawford .10
31 Tim Salmon .25
32 Troy Glaus .50
33 Adam Kennedy .10
34 David Eckstein .10
35 Bengie Molina .10
36 Jarrod Washburn .10
37 Ramon Ortiz .10
38 Eric Chavez .25
39 Miguel Tejada .25
40 Adam Piatt .10
41 Jermaine Dye .10
42 Olmedo Saenz .10
43 Tim Hudson .20
44 Barry Zito .25
45 Billy Koch .10
46 Shannon Stewart .10
47 Kelvim Escobar .10
48 Jose Cruz Jr. .10
49 Vernon Wells .10
50 Roy Halladay .10
51 Esteban Loaiza .10

52 Eric Hinske .10
53 Steve Cox .10
54 Brent Abernathy .10
55 Ben Grieve .10
56 Aubrey Huff .10
57 Jared Sandberg .10
58 Paul Wilson .10
59 Tanyon Sturtze .10
60 Jim Thome .50
61 Omar Vizquel .20
62 C.C. Sabathia .10
63 Chris Magruder .10
64 Ricky Gutierrez .10
65 Einar Diaz .10
66 Danys Baez .10
67 Ichiro Suzuki .75
68 Ruben Sierra .10
69 Carlos Guillen .10
70 Mark McLemore .10
71 Dan Wilson .10
72 Jamie Moyer .10
73 Joel Pineiro .10
74 Edgar Martinez .10
75 Tony Batista .10
76 Jay Gibbons .10
77 Chris Singleton .10
78 Melvin Mora .10
79 Geronimo Gil .10
80 Rodrigo Lopez .10
81 Jorge Julio .10
82 Rafael Palmeiro .40
83 Juan Gonzalez .40
84 Mike Young .10
85 Hideki Irabu .10
86 Chan Ho Park .10
87 Kevin Mench .10
88 Doug Davis .10
89 Pedro J. Martinez .75
90 Shea Hillenbrand .10
91 Derek Lowe .10
92 Jason Varitek .10
93 Tony Clark .10
94 John Burkett .10
95 Frank Castillo .10
96 Nomar Garciaparra 1.00
97 Rickey Henderson .25
98 Mike Sweeney .10
99 Carlos Febles .10
100 Mark Quinn .10
101 Raul Ibanez .10
102 A.J. Hinch .10
103 Paul Byrd .10
104 Chuck Knoblauch .10
105 Dmitri Young .10
106 Randall Simon .10
107 Brandon Inge .10
108 Damion Easley .10
109 Carlos Pena .10
110 George Lombard .10
111 Juan Acevedo .10
112 Torii Hunter .25
113 Doug Mientkiewicz .10
114 David Ortiz .10
115 Eric Milton .10
116 Eddie Guardado .10
117 Cristian Guzman .10
118 Corey Koskie .10
119 Magglio Ordonez .25
120 Mark Buehrle .10
121 Todd Ritchie .10
122 Jose Valentin .10
123 Paul Konerko .10
124 Carlos Lee .10
125 Jon Garland .10
126 Jason Giambi .75
127 Derek Jeter 1.50
128 Roger Clemens 1.00
129 Raul Mondesi .25
130 Jorge Posada .25
131 Rondell White .10
132 Robin Ventura .20
133 Mike Mussina .40
134 Jeff Bagwell .50
135 Craig Biggio .20
136 Morgan Ensberg .10
137 Richard Hidalgo .10
138 Brad Ausmus .10
139 Roy Oswalt .20
140 Carlos Hernandez .10
141 Shane Reynolds .10
142 Gary Sheffield .25
143 Andruw Jones .25
144 Tom Glavine .25
145 Rafael Furcal .20
146 Javy Lopez .10
147 Vinny Castilla .10
148 Marcus Giles .10
149 Kevin Millwood .20
150 Jason Marquis .10
151 Ruben Quevedo .10
152 Ben Sheets .10
153 Geoff Jenkins .10
154 Jose Hernandez .10
155 Glendon Rusch .10
156 Jeffrey Hammonds .10
157 Alex Sanchez .10
158 Jim Edmonds .25
159 Tino Martinez .10
160 Albert Pujols .75
161 Eli Marrero .10
162 Woody Williams .10
163 Fernando Vina .10
164 Jason Isringhausen .10
165 Jason Simontacchi .10
166 Kerry Robinson .10
167 Sammy Sosa .75
168 Juan Cruz .10
169 Fred McGriff .20
170 Antonio Alfonseca .10
171 Jon Lieber .10
172 Mark Prior .50
173 Moises Alou .20
174 Matt Clement .10
175 Mark Bellhorn .10
176 Randy Johnson .50
177 Luis Gonzalez .20
178 Tony Womack .10
179 Mark Grace .25
180 Junior Spivey .10
181 Byung-Hyun Kim .10
182 Danny Bautista .10
183 Brian Anderson .10
184 Shawn Green .25
185 Brian Jordan .10
186 Eric Karros .10
187 Andy Ashby .10
188 Cesar Izturis .10
189 Dave Roberts .10
190 Eric Gagne .10
191 Kazuhisa Ishii .10
192 Adrian Beltre .10
193 Vladimir Guerrero .50
194 Tony Armas Jr. .10
195 Bartolo Colon .10
196 Troy O'Leary .10
197 Tomokazu Ohka .10
198 Brad Wilkerson .10
199 Orlando Cabrera .10
200 Barry Bonds 1.50
201 David Bell .10
202 Tsuyoshi Shinjo .10
203 Benito Santiago .10
204 Livan Hernandez .10
205 Jason Schmidt .10
206 Kirk Rueter .10
207 Ramon E. Martinez .10
208 Mike Lowell .10
209 Luis Castillo .10
210 Derek Lee .10
211 Andy Fox .10
212 Eric Owens .10
213 Charles Johnson .10
214 Brad Penny .10
215 A.J. Burnett .10
216 Edgardo Alfonzo .10
217 Roberto Alomar .40
218 Rey Ordonez .10
219 Al Leiter .10
220 Roger Cedeno .10
221 Timoniel Perez .10
222 Jeromy Burnitz .10
223 Pedro Astacio .10
224 Joe McEwing .10
225 Ryan Klesko .20
226 Ramon Vazquez .10
227 Mark Kotsay .10
228 Bubba Trammell .10
229 Wiki Gonzalez .10
230 Trevor Hoffman .10
231 Ron Gant .10
232 Bobby Abreu .20
233 Marlon Anderson .10
234 Jeremy Giambi .10
235 Jimmy Rollins .20
236 Mike Lieberthal .10
237 Vicente Padilla .10
238 Randy Wolf .10
239 Pokey Reese .10
240 Brian Giles .25
241 Jack Wilson .10
242 Mike Williams .10
243 Kip Wells .10
244 Robert Mackowiak .10
245 Craig Wilson .10
246 Adam Dunn .50
247 Sean Casey .10
248 Todd Walker .10
249 Corky Miller .10
250 Ryan Dempster .10
251 Reggie Taylor .10
252 Aaron Boone .10
253 Larry Walker .10
254 Jose Ortiz .10
255 Todd Zeile .10
256 Bobby Estalella .10
257 Juan Pierre .10
258 Terry Shumpert .10
259 Mike Hampton .10
260 Denny Stark .10
261 Shawn Green .20
262 Derek Lowe .10
263 Barry Bonds .50
264 Mike Cameron .10
265 Luis Castillo .10
266 Vladimir Guerrero .40
267 Jason Giambi .40
268 Eric Gagne .10
269 Magglio Ordonez .20
270 Jim Thome .25
271 Hideki Matsui **RC** 20.00
272 Jose Contreras **RC** 4.00
273 Robert Madritsch 1.00
274 Shane Bazzell **RC** 1.50
275 Felix Sanchez **RC** 2.00
276 Todd Wellemeyer **RC** 2.00
277 Lew Ford **RC** 2.00
278 Jeremy Griffiths 1.00
279 Oscar Villarreal **RC** 1.00
280 Brandon Webb **RC** 3.00
281 Delvis Lantigua 3.00
282 Josh Willingham **RC** 1.00
283 Mike Nicolas **RC** 1.00
284 Mike Hampton 1.00
285 Jim Thome 2.00
286 Bartolo Colon 1.00
287 Orlando Hernandez 1.00
288 Jeremy Giambi 1.00
289 Jeff Kent 1.50
290 Tom Glavine 1.50
291 Cliff Floyd 1.00
292 Tsuyoshi Shinjo 1.00
293 Jose Cruz Jr. 1.00
294 Edgardo Alfonzo 1.00
295 Andres Galarraga 1.00
296 Troy O'Leary 1.00
297 Eric Karros 1.00
298 Ivan Rodriguez 1.50
299 Fred McGriff 1.50
300 Preston Wilson 1.00

Signature Stars

NM/M

Print runs listed:
NM Nomar Garciaparra/100 100.00
JG Jason Giambi/100 30.00
KG Ken Griffey Jr./100 75.00
KGS Ken Griffey Sr./800 6.00
SS Sammy Sosa/50 175.00
IS Ichiro Suzuki/50 375.00

2003 Upper Deck Game Face Promo

This card introduces UD's Game Face brand for '03. Back has a large diagonal "SAMPLE" overprint.

NM/M

30 Ken Griffey Jr. 2.00

2003 Upper Deck Game Face

NM/M

Complete Set (192):
Common Player: .25
Common Base SP: 1.00
Inserted 1:4
Common SP (121-150): 2.00
Inserted 1:8
Common SP (151-192): 3.00
Inserted 1:16
Pack (4): 4.00
Box (24): 75.00
1 Darin Erstad .50
2 Garret Anderson .50
3 Tim Salmon .50
4 Jarrod Washburn .25
5 Troy Glaus/SP 1.50
6 Luis Gonzalez .50
7 Junior Spivey .25
8 Randy Johnson/SP 2.00
9 Curt Schilling/SP 1.50
10 Andruw Jones .75
11 Gary Sheffield .50
12 Rafael Furcal .25
13 Greg Maddux/SP 3.00
14 Chipper Jones/SP 3.00
15 Tony Batista .25
16 Rodrigo Lopez .25
17 Jay Gibbons .25
18 Shea Hillenbrand .25
19 Johnny Damon .25
20 Derek Lowe .25
21 Nomar Garciaparra 2.50
22 Pedro J. Martinez/SP 2.00
23 Manny Ramirez/SP 1.50
24 Mark Prior 1.00
25 Kerry Wood .75
26 Corey Patterson .25
27 Sammy Sosa 2.00
28 Magglio Ordonez .50
29 Frank Thomas 1.00
30 Paul Konerko .25
31 Adam Dunn 1.00
32 Austin Kearns 1.00
33 Aaron Boone .25
34 Ken Griffey Jr./SP 3.00
35 Omar Vizquel .40
36 C.C. Sabathia .25
37 Karim Garcia/SP 1.00
38 Larry Walker .40
39 Preston Wilson .25
40 Jay Payton .25
41 Todd Helton/SP 1.50
42 Carlos Pena .25
43 Eric Munson .25
44 Mike Lowell .25
45 Josh Beckett .25
46 A.J. Burnett .25
47 Roy Oswalt .50
48 Craig Biggio .50
49 Jeff Bagwell/SP 1.50
50 Lance Berkman/SP 1.25
51 Mike Sweeney .25
52 Carlos Beltran .25
53 Hideo Nomo .75
54 Odalis Perez .25
55 Adrian Beltre .25
56 Shawn Green/SP 1.00
57 Kazuhisa Ishii/SP 1.00
58 Ben Sheets .50
59 Richie Sexson .50
60 Torii Hunter .50
61 Jacque Jones .25
62 Eric Milton .25
63 Corey Koskie .25
64 A.J. Pierzynski .25
65 Jose Vidro .25
66 Bartolo Colon .25
67 Vladimir Guerrero/SP 1.50
68 Tom Glavine .50
69 Mike Piazza/SP 3.00
70 Roberto Alomar/SP 1.50
71 Jorge Posada .75
72 Mike Mussina .75
73 Robin Ventura .25
74 Raul Mondesi .50
75 Roger Clemens/SP 3.00
76 Jason Giambi/SP 2.00
77 Bernie Williams/SP 1.50
78 Alfonso Soriano/SP 2.00
79 Derek Jeter/SP 6.00
80 Miguel Tejada .75
81 Eric Chavez .50
82 Tim Hudson .50
83 Barry Zito .50
84 Mark Mulder .50
85 Pat Burrell 1.00
86 Jim Thome 1.00
87 Bobby Abreu .50
88 Brian Giles .50
89 Jason Kendall .40
90 Aramis Ramirez .25
91 Ryan Klesko .25
92 Phil Nevin .25
93 Sean Burroughs .25
94 J.T. Snow .25
95 Rich Aurilia .25
96 Benito Santiago .25
97 Barry Bonds/SP 6.00
98 Edgar Martinez .25
99 John Olerud .50
100 Bret Boone .25
101 Ichiro Suzuki/SP 3.00
102 J.D. Drew .50
103 Jim Edmonds .50
104 Scott Rolen 1.00
105 Matt Morris .50
106 Tino Martinez .25
107 Albert Pujols/SP 2.00
108 Aubrey Huff .25
109 Carl Crawford .25
110 Rafael Palmeiro .75
111 Hank Blalock .50
112 Alex Rodriguez/SP 5.00
113 Kevin Mench/SP 1.00
114 Juan Gonzalez/SP 1.50
115 Shannon Stewart .25
116 Vernon Wells .25
117 Josh Phelps .25
118 Eric Hinske .25
119 Orlando Hudson .25
120 Carlos Delgado/SP 1.00
121 David Sanders **RC** 2.00
122 Rob Hammock **RC** 2.00
123 Rett Johnson **RC** 2.00
124 Mike Nicolas **RC** 2.00
125 Terrmel Sledge **RC** 3.00
126 Ryan Cameron **RC** 4.00
127 Prentice Redman **RC** 2.00
128 Clint Barmes **RC** 6.00
129 Brent Hoard **RC** 2.00
130 Willie Eyre **RC** 2.00
131 Phil Seibel **RC** 2.00
132 Chris Capuano **RC** 5.00
133 Bobby Madritsch **RC** 8.00
134 Shane Bazzell **RC** 2.00
135 Jeremy Griffiths 3.00
136 Jon Leicester **RC** 3.00
137 Brandon Webb **RC** 5.00
138 Todd Wellemeyer **RC** 2.00
139 Jose Contreras **RC** 5.00
140 Felix Sanchez **RC** 2.00
141 Arnie Munoz **RC** 2.00
142 Delvis Lantigua **RC** 2.00
143 Francisco Cruceta **RC** 2.00
144 Josh Willingham **RC** 3.00
145 Oscar Villarreal **RC** 2.00
146 Ian Ferguson **RC** 2.00
147 Pedro Liriano 2.00
148 Lew Ford **RC** 5.00
149 Jeff Duncan **RC** 2.00
150 Richard Fischer **RC** 2.00
151 Troy Glaus 3.00
152 Randy Johnson 5.00
153 Hideki Matsui **RC** 15.00
154 Chipper Jones 6.00
155 Nomar Garciaparra 10.00
156 Pedro J. Martinez 5.00
157 Ted Williams 15.00
158 Sammy Sosa 8.00
159 Ken Griffey Jr. 8.00
160 Vladimir Guerrero 5.00
161 Mike Piazza 8.00
162 Mickey Mantle 30.00
163 Alfonso Soriano 6.00
164 Derek Jeter 15.00
165 Roger Clemens 8.00
166 Jason Giambi 4.00
167 Barry Bonds 15.00
168 Ichiro Suzuki 8.00
169 Albert Pujols 8.00
170 Mark McGwire 15.00
171 Alex Rodriguez 10.00
172 Ken Griffey Jr., Roy Oswalt 6.00
173 Barry Zito, Troy Glaus 3.00
174 Tim Hudson, Ichiro Suzuki 8.00
175 Alex Rodriguez, Mark Mulder 10.00
176 Tom Glavine, Vladimir Guerrero 4.00
177 Mike Piazza, Greg Maddux 6.00
178 Mark McGwire, Sammy Sosa 10.00
179 Lance Berkman, Mark Prior 4.00
180 Albert Pujols, Kerry Wood 6.00
181 Randy Johnson, Jeff Bagwell 4.00
182 Derek Jeter, Curt Schilling 10.00
183 Barry Bonds, Hideo Nomo 10.00
184 Todd Helton, Kazuhisa Ishii 4.00
185 Freddy Garcia, Eric Chavez 3.00
186 Al Leiter, Chipper Jones 6.00
187 Ted Williams, Nomar Garciaparra 10.00
188 Pedro J. Martinez, Hideki Matsui 15.00
189 Derek Lowe, Bernie Williams 3.00
190 Roger Clemens, Mike Piazza 10.00
191 Mike Mussina, Manny Ramirez 4.00
192 Jason Giambi, Mickey Mantle 20.00

Autograph

NM/M

Common Player:
Inserted 1:576
Golds: No Pricing
Production 25
LB Lance Berkman/SP 50.00
JG Jason Giambi 40.00
KG Ken Griffey Jr. 125.00
TH Todd Helton/SP 45.00
HM Hideki Matsui/SP 250.00
MM Mark McGwire/SP 350.00
MP Mark Prior/SP 40.00
SS Sammy Sosa 120.00
IS Ichiro Suzuki/SP 300.00
BZ Barry Zito 40.00

Gear

NM/M

Common Player: 4.00
Inserted 1:8
Patches: 3-5X
Production 100 Sets
BA Bobby Abreu 4.00
EA Edgardo Alfonzo 4.00
JB Jeff Bagwell 8.00
CB Carlos Beltran 6.00
LB Lance Berkman 6.00
AB Aaron Boone/SP 8.00
PB Pat Burrell 6.00
EC Eric Chavez 4.00
RC Roger Clemens 15.00
CD Carlos Delgado 4.00
DR J.D. Drew 4.00
DR2 J.D. Drew 4.00
AD Adam Dunn 8.00
JE Jim Edmonds 6.00
DE Darin Erstad 4.00
DE2 Darin Erstad 4.00
JG Jason Giambi 6.00
BG Brian Giles 4.00
TG Tom Glavine 6.00
GO Juan Gonzalez 6.00
LG Luis Gonzalez 4.00
LG2 Luis Gonzalez 4.00
SG Shawn Green 4.00
TH Todd Helton/SP 8.00
TI Tim Hudson 4.00
HU Torii Hunter 4.00
KI Kazuhisa Ishii 4.00
RJ Randy Johnson 8.00
AJ Andruw Jones 6.00
CJ Chipper Jones 8.00
JJ Jacque Jones 4.00
AK Austin Kearns 4.00
JK Jason Kendall 4.00
KE Jeff Kent 6.00
RK Ryan Klesko 4.00
ML Mike Lowell 4.00
GM Greg Maddux 10.00
GM2 Greg Maddux 10.00
EM Edgar Martinez 6.00
PM Pedro J. Martinez 8.00
MM Mike Mussina 8.00
HN Hideo Nomo 8.00
MO Magglio Ordonez 4.00
RO Roy Oswalt 4.00
RP Rafael Palmeiro 8.00
MiP Mike Piazza 10.00
JP Jorge Posada 8.00
MaP Mark Prior 8.00
MR Manny Ramirez 8.00
AR Alex Rodriguez 10.00
AR2 Alex Rodriguez 10.00
IR Ivan Rodriguez 8.00
SR Scott Rolen 8.00
CS Curt Schilling 8.00
RS Richie Sexson 6.00
AS Alfonso Soriano 8.00
SS Sammy Sosa 10.00
IS Ichiro Suzuki/SP 50.00
MS Mike Sweeney 4.00
MT Miguel Tejada 6.00
FT Frank Thomas 8.00
JT Jim Thome 8.00
JV Jose Vidro 4.00
OV Omar Vizquel 4.00
LW Larry Walker 4.00
BW Bernie Williams 6.00
PW Preston Wilson 4.00
KW Kerry Wood 8.00
BZ Barry Zito 4.00
BZ2 Barry Zito 4.00

Patch

Common Player:
Production 100 Sets

2003 Upper Deck Honor Roll

NM/M

Complete Set (161):
Common Player: .20
Common Even # SP (2-60): 1.00
Inserted 1:6
Common SP (131-161): 3.00
Production 2,500
Pack (5): 1.50
Box (24): 30.00
1 Derek Jeter 2.00
2 Derek Jeter/SP 5.00
3 Alex Rodriguez 1.50
4 Alex Rodriguez/SP 5.00
5 Roger Clemens 1.50

6	Roger Clemens/SP	4.00
7	Mike Piazza	1.00
8	Mike Piazza/SP	3.00
9	Jeff Bagwell	.50
10	Jeff Bagwell/SP	1.50
11	Vladimir Guerrero	.75
12	Vladimir Guerrero/SP	2.00
13	Ken Griffey Jr.	1.00
14	Ken Griffey Jr./SP	3.00
15	Greg Maddux	1.00
16	Greg Maddux/SP	3.00
17	Chipper Jones	.75
18	Chipper Jones/SP	2.00
19	Randy Johnson	.75
20	Randy Johnson/SP	2.00
21	Miguel Tejada	.50
22	Miguel Tejada/SP	1.50
23	Nomar Garciaparra	1.50
24	Nomar Garciaparra/SP	4.00
25	Ichiro Suzuki	1.50
26	Ichiro Suzuki/SP	4.00
27	Sammy Sosa	1.00
28	Sammy Sosa/SP	3.00
29	Albert Pujols	2.00
30	Albert Pujols/SP	5.00
31	Alfonso Soriano	.75
32	Alfonso Soriano/SP	2.00
33	Barry Bonds	2.00
34	Barry Bonds/SP	6.00
35	Jeff Kent	.30
36	Jeff Kent/SP	1.00
37	Jim Thome	.50
38	Jim Thome/SP	1.50
39	Pedro J. Martinez	.75
40	Pedro J. Martinez/SP	2.00
41	Todd Helton	.50
42	Todd Helton/SP	1.50
43	Troy Glaus	.50
44	Troy Glaus/SP	1.50
45	Mark Prior	.75
46	Mark Prior/SP	2.00
47	Tom Glavine	.40
48	Tom Glavine/SP	1.00
49	Pat Burrell	.40
50	Pat Burrell/SP	1.00
51	Barry Zito	.40
52	Barry Zito/SP	1.00
53	Bernie Williams	.50
54	Bernie Williams/SP	1.50
55	Curt Schilling	.50
56	Curt Schilling/SP	1.50
57	Darin Erstad	.30
58	Darin Erstad/SP	1.00
59	Carlos Delgado	.50
60	Carlos Delgado/SP	1.50
61	Gary Sheffield	.40
62	Gary Sheffield	.40
63	Frank Thomas	.50
64	Frank Thomas	.50
65	Lance Berkman	.40
66	Lance Berkman	.40
67	Shawn Green	.40
68	Shawn Green	.40
69	Hideo Nomo	.40
70	Hideo Nomo	.40
71	Torii Hunter	.40
72	Torii Hunter	.40
73	Roberto Alomar	.50
74	Roberto Alomar	.50
75	Andruw Jones	.50
76	Andruw Jones	.50
77	Scott Rolen	.75
78	Scott Rolen	.75
79	Eric Chavez	.40
80	Eric Chavez	.40
81	Rafael Palmeiro	.50
82	Rafael Palmeiro	.50
83	Bobby Abreu	.20
84	Bobby Abreu	.20
85	Craig Biggio	.20
86	Craig Biggio	.20
87	Rafael Furcal	.20
88	Rafael Furcal	.20
89	Jose Vidro	.20
90	Jose Vidro	.20
91	Luis Gonzalez	.20
92	Luis Gonzalez	.20
93	Roy Oswalt	.20
94	Roy Oswalt	.20
95	Cliff Floyd	.20
96	Cliff Floyd	.20
97	Larry Walker	.20
98	Larry Walker	.20
99	Jim Edmonds	.30
100	Jim Edmonds	.30
101	Adam Dunn	.40
102	Adam Dunn	.40
103	J.D. Drew	.20
104	J.D. Drew	.20
105	Josh Beckett	.20
106	Josh Beckett	.20
107	Brian Giles	.20
108	Brian Giles	.20
109	Magglio Ordonez	.40
110	Magglio Ordonez	.40
111	Edgardo Alfonzo	.20
112	Edgardo Alfonzo	.20
113	Bartolo Colon	.20
114	Bartolo Colon	.20
115	Roy Halladay	.20
116	Roy Halladay	.20
117	Joe Thurston	.20
118	Joe Thurston	.20
119	Brandon Phillips	.20
120	Brandon Phillips	.20
121	Kazuhisa Ishii	.20
122	Kazuhisa Ishii	.20
123	Mike Mussina	.40
124	Mike Mussina	.40
125	Tim Hudson	.40
126	Tim Hudson	.40
127	Mariano Rivera	.20
128	Mariano Rivera	.20
129	Travis Hafner	.20
130	Travis Hafner	.20
131	Hideki Matsui **RC**	20.00
132	Jose Contreras **RC**	5.00
133	Jason Anderson	3.00
134	Willie Eyre **RC**	3.00
135	Shane Bazzell **RC**	3.00
136	Guillermo Quiroz **RC**	5.00
137	Francisco Cruceta **RC**	3.00
138	Jhonny Peralta	4.00
139	Aaron Looper **RC**	3.00
140	Bobby Madritsch **RC**	6.00
141	Michael Hessman **RC**	3.00
142	Todd Wellemeyer **RC**	3.00
143	Matt Bruback **RC**	3.00
144	Chris Capuano **RC**	5.00
145	Oscar Villarreal **RC**	3.00
146	Prentice Redman **RC**	3.00
147	Jeff Duncan **RC**	5.00
148	Phil Seibel **RC**	3.00
149	Arnaldo Munoz	3.00
150	David Sanders **RC**	3.00
151	Rick Roberts **RC**	3.00
152	Terrmel Sledge **RC**	4.00
153	Franklin Perez	3.00
154	Jeremy Wedel **RC**	3.00
155	Ian Ferguson **RC**	3.00
156	Josh Hall **RC**	4.00
157	Rocco Baldelli	3.00
158	Alejandro Machado **RC**	3.00
159	Jorge Cordova **RC**	3.00
160	Wilfredo Ledezma **RC**	3.00
161	Luis Ayala **RC**	3.00

Silver

Even # SP's (2-60):	1-2X
Non-SP's (1-130):	4-8X
SP's (132-161):	.5-1X
Production 150 Sets	

Gold

Production 25 Sets:
No pricing due to scarcity.

Dean's List

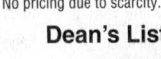

		NM/M
Common Player:		4.00
Inserted 1:24		
RC	Roger Clemens	10.00
RC1	Roger Clemens	10.00
JG1	Jason Giambi	4.00
JG1	Jason Giambi	4.00
TG	Troy Glaus	4.00
TG1	Troy Glaus	4.00
NG	Shawn Green	4.00
NG1	Shawn Green	4.00
VG	Vladimir Guerrero	6.00
VG	Vladimir Guerrero	6.00
KG	Ken Griffey Jr.	10.00
KG1	Ken Griffey Jr.	10.00
CJ	Chipper Jones	8.00
CJ1	Chipper Jones	8.00
HM	Hideki Matsui	20.00
HM1	Hideki Matsui	20.00
HN	Hideo Nomo	10.00
HN1	Hideo Nomo	10.00
MP	Mike Piazza	10.00
MP1	Mike Piazza	10.00
MA	Mark Prior	8.00
MA1	Mark Prior	8.00
AP	Albert Pujols	15.00
AP1	Albert Pujols	15.00
AR	Alex Rodriguez	10.00
AR1	Alex Rodriguez	10.00
SS	Sammy Sosa	10.00
IS	Ichiro Suzuki	20.00
IS1	Ichiro Suzuki	20.00

Grade A Batting Gloves

		NM/M
Most not priced due to scarcity.		
Inserted 1:960		
RA	Roberto Alomar/65	20.00
CD	Carlos Delgado/65	15.00
TG	Troy Glaus/60	15.00
JG	Juan Gonzalez/65	15.00
RM	Raul Mondesi/65	10.00
RP	Rafael Palmeiro/65	20.00
MR	Manny Ramirez/69	20.00
AR	Alex Rodriguez/67	25.00
IR	Ivan Rodriguez/70	20.00
MT	Miguel Tejada/70	10.00
FT	Frank Thomas/70	20.00

Leather of Distinction

		NM/M
Most not priced due to scarcity.		
Inserted 1:960		
KG	Ken Griffey Jr./70	30.00
RP	Rafael Palmeiro/70	20.00
MP	Mike Piazza/50	40.00
MR	Manny Ramirez/70	20.00
AR	Alex Rodriguez/70	25.00
IR	Ivan Rodriguez/69	20.00
TS	Tim Salmon/70	10.00
GS	Gary Sheffield/70	10.00
FT	Frank Thomas/70	20.00
OV	Omar Vizquel/65	10.00

Magazine

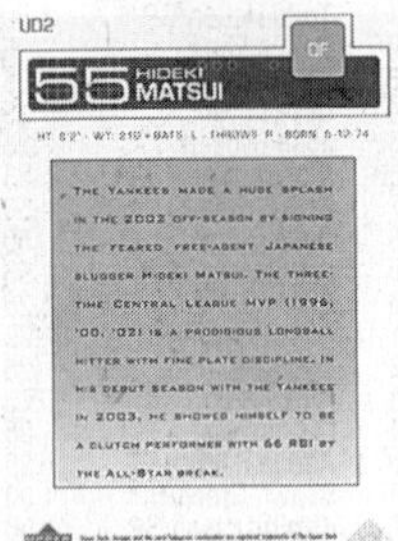

Three baseball players were included in a nine-card sheet inserted into a special-edition collectors' magazine produced by Upper Deck in November 2003. Cards are in standard 2-1/2" x 3-1/2" format perforated on two, three, or four sides, depending on their placement on the panel. Fronts have game-action photos with player name, position and uniform number. Backs have personal data and a career summary. Only the baseball players are listed here.

		NM/M
Complete Magazine:		12.00
Common Player:		1.00
UD2	Hideki Matsui	1.00
UD4	Ichiro	1.50
UD7	Mickey Mantle	2.00

Hideki Matsui Hawaii

The first licensed card of Yankees Japanese import slugger Hideki Matsui was distributed to attendees at the 2003 Hawaii Trade Conference. The card features silver-foil accents on front.

		NM/M
HM	Hideki Matsui	75.00

2003 Upper Deck MVP

		NM/M
Complete Set (220):		20.00
Complete Factory Set (330):		30.00
Common Player:		.10
Pack (8):		1.50
Box (24):		25.00
1	Troy Glaus	.40
2	Darin Erstad	.25
3	Jarrod Washburn	.10
4	Francisco Rodriguez	.10
5	Garret Anderson	.20
6	Tim Salmon	.20
7	Adam Kennedy	.10
8	Randy Johnson	.50
9	Luis Gonzalez	.20
10	Curt Schilling	.50
11	Junior Spivey	.10
12	Craig Counsell	.10
13	Mark Grace	.25
14	Steve Finley	.10
15	Javy Lopez	.10
16	Rafael Furcal	.10
17	John Smoltz	.15
18	Greg Maddux	.75
19	Chipper Jones	.50
20	Gary Sheffield	.20
21	Andruw Jones	.20
22	Tony Batista	.10
23	Geronimo Gil	.10
24	Jay Gibbons	.10
25	Rodrigo Lopez	.10
26	Chris Singleton	.10
27	Melvin Mora	.10
28	Jeff Conine	.10
29	Nomar Garciaparra	1.00
30	Pedro J. Martinez	.50
31	Manny Ramirez	.50
32	Shea Hillenbrand	.10
33	Johnny Damon	.40
34	Jason Varitek	.25
35	Derek Lowe	.10
36	Trot Nixon	.10
37	Sammy Sosa	.75
38	Kerry Wood	.50
39	Mark Prior	.50
40	Moises Alou	.20
41	Corey Patterson	.25
42	Hee Seop Choi	.10
43	Mark Bellhorn	.10
44	Frank Thomas	.40
45	Mark Buehrle	.20
46	Magglio Ordonez	.20
47	Carlos Lee	.20
48	Paul Konerko	.20
49	Joe Borchard	.10
50	Joe Crede	.10
51	Ken Griffey Jr.	.75
52	Adam Dunn	.40
53	Austin Kearns	.40
54	Aaron Boone	.10
55	Sean Casey	.10
56	Danny Graves	.10
57	Russell Branyan	.10
58	Matt Lawton	.10
59	C.C. Sabathia	.10
60	Omar Vizquel	.20
61	Brandon Phillips	.10
62	Karim Garcia	.10
63	Ellis Burks	.10
64	Cliff Lee	.10
65	Todd Helton	.40
66	Larry Walker	.20
67	Jay Payton	.10
68	Brent Butler	.10
69	Juan Uribe	.10
70	Jason Jennings	.10
71	Denny Stark	.10
72	Dmitri Young	.10
73	Carlos Pena	.10
74	Andres Torres	.10
75	Andy Van Hekken	.10
76	George Lombard	.10
77	Eric Munson	.10
78	Bobby Higginson	.10
79	Luis Castillo	.10
80	A.J. Burnett	.10
81	Juan Encarnacion	.10
82	Ivan Rodriguez	.40
83	Mike Lowell	.10
84	Josh Beckett	.25
85	Brad Penny	.10
86	Craig Biggio	.25
87	Jeff Kent	.20
88	Morgan Ensberg	.10
89	Daryle Ward	.10
90	Jeff Bagwell	.40
91	Roy Oswalt	.20
92	Lance Berkman	.25
93	Mike Sweeney	.10
94	Carlos Beltran	.40
95	Raul Ibanez	.10
96	Carlos Febles	.10
97	Joe Randa	.10
98	Shawn Green	.25
99	Kevin Brown	.15
100	Paul LoDuca	.10
101	Adrian Beltre	.25
102	Eric Gagne	.20
103	Kazuhisa Ishii	.10
104	Odalis Perez	.10
105	Brian Jordan	.10
106	Geoff Jenkins	.10
107	Richie Sexson	.25
108	Ben Sheets	.20
109	Alex Sanchez	.10
110	Eric Young	.10
111	Jose Hernandez	.10
112	Torii Hunter	.25
113	Eric Milton	.10
114	Corey Koskie	.10
115	Doug Mientkiewicz	.10
116	A.J. Pierzynski	.10
117	Jacque Jones	.10
118	Cristian Guzman	.10
119	Bartolo Colon	.10
120	Brad Wilkerson	.10
121	Michael Barrett	.10
122	Vladimir Guerrero	.50
123	Jose Vidro	.10
124	Javier Vazquez	.10
125	Endy Chavez	.10
126	Roberto Alomar	.25
127	Mike Piazza	1.00
128	Jeromy Burnitz	.10
129	Mo Vaughn	.15
130	Tom Glavine	.25
131	Al Leiter	.15
132	Armando Benitez	.10
133	Timoniel Perez	.10
134	Roger Clemens	1.00
135	Derek Jeter	1.50
136	Jason Giambi	.25
137	Alfonso Soriano	.50
138	Bernie Williams	.25
139	Mike Mussina	.25
140	Jorge Posada	.20
141	Hideki Matsui **RC**	4.00
142	Robin Ventura	.10
143	David Wells	.10
144	Nick Johnson	.10
145	Tim Hudson	.20
146	Eric Chavez	.20
147	Barry Zito	.25
148	Miguel Tejada	.40
149	Jermaine Dye	.10
150	Mark Mulder	.20
151	Terrence Long	.10
152	Scott Hatteberg	.10
153	Marlon Byrd	.10
154	Jim Thome	.40
155	Marlon Anderson	.10
156	Vicente Padilla	.10
157	Bobby Abreu	.20
158	Jimmy Rollins	.25
159	Pat Burrell	.40
160	Brian Giles	.20
161	Aramis Ramirez	.20
162	Jason Kendall	.20
163	Josh Fogg	.10
164	Kip Wells	.10
165	Pokey Reese	.10
166	Kris Benson	.10
167	Ryan Klesko	.20
168	Brian Lawrence	.10
169	Mark Kotsay	.10
170	Jake Peavy	.20
171	Phil Nevin	.10
172	Sean Burroughs	.10
173	Trevor Hoffman	.10
174	Jason Schmidt	.20
175	Kirk Rueter	.10
176	Barry Bonds	1.50
177	Pedro Feliz	.10
178	Rich Aurilia	.10
179	Benito Santiago	.10
180	J.T. Snow	.10
181	Robb Nen	.10
182	Ichiro Suzuki	1.00
183	Edgar Martinez	.10
184	Bret Boone	.10
185	Freddy Garcia	.10
186	John Olerud	.20
187	Mike Cameron	.10
188	Joel Pineiro	.10
189	Albert Pujols	1.25
190	Matt Morris	.20
191	J.D. Drew	.20
192	Scott Rolen	.50
193	Tino Martinez	.20
194	Jim Edmonds	.20
195	Edgar Renteria	.20
196	Fernando Vina	.10
197	Jason Isringhausen	.10
198	Ben Grieve	.10
199	Carl Crawford	.10
200	Dewon Brazelton	.10
201	Aubrey Huff	.10
202	Jared Sandberg	.10
203	Steve Cox	.10
204	Carl Everett	.10
205	Kevin Mench	.10
206	Alex Rodriguez	1.00
207	Rafael Palmeiro	.40
208	Michael Young	.10
209	Hank Blalock	.40
210	Juan Gonzalez	.25
211	Carlos Delgado	.20
212	Eric Hinske	.20
213	Josh Phelps	.10
214	Mark Hendrickson	.10
215	Roy Halladay	.10
216	Orlando Hudson	.10
217	Shannon Stewart	.10
218	Vernon Wells	.10
219	Ichiro Suzuki	.40
220	Jason Giambi	.25
221	Scott Spiezio	.10
222	Rich Fischer	.10
223	Bengie Molina	.10
224	David Eckstein	.10
225	Brandon Webb **RC**	1.50
226	Oscar Villarreal	.10
227	Rob Hammock **RC**	.40
228	Matt Kata **RC**	.40
229	Lyle Overbay	.10
230	Chris Capuano **RC**	.50
231	Horacio Ramirez	.10
232	Shane Reynolds	.10
233	Russ Ortiz	.10
234	Mike Hampton	.10
235	Mike Hessman	.10
236	Byung-Hyun Kim	.10
237	Freddy Sanchez	.10
238	Jason Shiell	.10
239	Ryan Cameron	.10
240	Todd Wellemeyer **RC**	.40
241	Joe Borowski	.10
242	Alex Gonzalez	.10
243	Jon Leicester	.10
244	David Sanders	.10
245	Roberto Alomar	.25
246	Barry Larkin	.25
247	Jhonny Peralta	.10
248	Zach Sorensen	.10
249	Jason Davis	.10
250	Coco Crisp	.10
251	Greg Vaughn	.10
252	Preston Wilson	.10
253	Denny Neagle	.10
254	Clint Barmes **RC**	1.00
255	Jeremy Bonderman	1.00
256	Wilfredo Ledezma **RC**	.10
257	Dontrelle Willis	.25
258	Alex Gonzalez	.10
259	Tommy Phelps	.10
260	Kirk Saarloos	.10
261	Colin Porter **RC**	.10
262	Nate Bland	.10
263	Jason Gilfillan	.10
264	Mike MacDougal	.10
265	Ken Harvey	.10
266	Brent Mayne	.10
267	Miguel Cabrera	.40
268	Hideo Nomo	.25
269	Dave Roberts	.10
270	Fred McGriff	.20
271	Joe Thurston	.10
272	Royce Clayton	.10
273	Micheal Nakamura	.10
274	Brad Radke	.10
275	Joe Mays	.10
276	Lew Ford **RC**	1.00
277	Michael Cuddyer	.10
278	Luis Ayala	.10
279	Julio Manon	.10
280	Anthony Ferrari	.10
281	Livan Hernandez	.10
282	Jae Weong Seo	.10
283	Jose Reyes	.40
284	Tony Clark	.10
285	Ty Wigginton	.10
286	Cliff Floyd	.10
287	Jeremy Griffiths	.10
288	Jason Roach	.10
289	Jeff Duncan	.10
290	Phil Seibel	.10
291	Prentice Redman **RC**	.25
292	Jose Contreras **RC**	1.00
293	Ruben Sierra	.10
294	Andy Pettitte	.25
295	Aaron Boone	.10
296	Mariano Rivera	.20
297	Michel Hernandez	.10
298	Mike Neu	.10
299	Erubiel Durazo	.10
300	Billy McMillon	.10
301	Rich Harden	.10
302	David Bell	.10
303	Kevin Millwood	.20
304	Mike Lieberthal	.10
305	Jeremy Wedel	.10
306	Kenny Lofton	.10
307	Reggie Sanders	.10
308	Randall Simon	.10
309	Xavier Nady	.10
310	Rod Beck	.10
311	Miguel Ojeda	.10
312	Mark Loretta	.10
313	Edgardo Alfonzo	.10
314	Andres Galarraga	.10
315	Jose Cruz Jr.	.10
316	Jesse Foppert	.10
317	Kurt Ainsworth	.10
318	Dan Wilson	.10
319	Ben Davis	.10
320	Rocco Baldelli	.25
321	Al Martin	.10
322	Runelvys Hernandez	.10
323	Dan Haren	.50
324	Bo Hart **RC**	.25
325	Einar Diaz	.10
326	Mike Lamb	.10
327	Aquilino Lopez	.10
328	Reed Johnson	.10
329	Diegomar Markwell	.10
330	Hideki Matsui	.75

Gold

Stars (1-220):	6-12X
Production 150 Sets	
Black Stars:	10-20X
Production 50 Sets	

Silver Stars: 1-2X
Inserted 1:2

Base-to-Base

NM/M
Inserted 1:488
CP Roger Clemens, Mike Piazza 25.00
IG Ichiro Suzuki, Ken Griffey Jr. 40.00
IJ Ichiro Suzuki, Derek Jeter 45.00
JW Derek Jeter, Bernie Williams 25.00
MB Mark McGwire, Barry Bonds 60.00
RJ Alex Rodriguez, Derek Jeter 40.00

Covering the Bases

NM/M
Common Player: 4.00
Inserted 1:125
BB Barry Bonds 15.00
CD Carlos Delgado 4.00
JD J.D. Drew 4.00
DE Darin Erstad 6.00
TG Troy Glaus 6.00
LG Luis Gonzalez 4.00
SG Shawn Green 6.00
DJ Derek Jeter 15.00
MP Mike Piazza 12.00
AR Alex Rodriguez 12.00
IR Ivan Rodriguez 4.00
IS Ichiro Suzuki 15.00
MT Miguel Tejada 6.00
FT Frank Thomas 8.00
JT Jim Thome 10.00

Covering the Plate Bat

NM/M
Common Player: 6.00
Inserted 1:160
RA Roberto Alomar 15.00
RF Rafael Furcal 8.00
VG Vladimir Guerrero 8.00
FM Fred McGriff 6.00
MM Mark McGwire 60.00
JT Jim Thome 12.00

Dual Aces

NM/M
Common Card: 8.00
Inserted 1:488
BS Kevin Brown, Curt Schilling 10.00
CJ Roger Clemens, Randy Johnson 20.00
CL Roger Clemens, Al Leiter 15.00
ML Matt Morris, Al Leiter 8.00
SJ Curt Schilling, Randy Johnson 12.00
SM Curt Schilling, Andy Pettitte 10.00

Express Delivery

NM/M
Complete Set (15): 10.00
Common Player: .50
Inserted 1:12
ED1 Randy Johnson 2.00
ED2 Curt Schilling 1.00
ED3 Pedro J. Martinez 2.00
ED4 Kerry Wood 1.00
ED5 Mark Prior 1.50
ED6 A.J. Burnett .50
ED7 Josh Beckett .50
ED8 Roy Oswalt .75
ED9 Hideo Nomo .75
ED10 Ben Sheets .50
ED11 Bartolo Colon .50
ED12 Roger Clemens 2.50
ED13 Mike Mussina .75
ED14 Tim Hudson .75
ED15 Matt Morris .50

MVP Celebration

NM/M
Common Player: 1.50
#'d to yr. MVP was won
MVP1 Yogi Berra 4.00
MVP2 Mickey Mantle 15.00
MVP3 Mickey Mantle 15.00
MVP4 Mickey Mantle 15.00
MVP5 Roger Clemens 5.00
MVP6 Rickey Henderson 4.00
MVP7 Frank Thomas 4.00
MVP8 Mo Vaughn 1.50
MVP9 Juan Gonzalez 3.00
MVP10 Ken Griffey Jr. 6.00
MVP11 Juan Gonzalez 3.00
MVP12 Ivan Rodriguez 2.00
MVP13 Jason Giambi 4.00
MVP14 Ichiro Suzuki 6.00
MVP15 Miguel Tejada 2.00
MVP16 Barry Bonds 8.00
MVP17 Barry Bonds 8.00
MVP18 Barry Bonds 8.00
MVP19 Jeff Bagwell 4.00
MVP20 Barry Larkin 1.50
MVP21 Larry Walker 1.50
MVP22 Sammy Sosa 6.00
MVP23 Chipper Jones 5.00
MVP24 Jeff Kent 1.50
MVP25 Barry Bonds 8.00
MVP26 Barry Bonds 8.00
MVP27 Ken Griffey Sr. 1.50
MVP28 Roger Clemens 5.00
MVP29 Ken Griffey Jr. 6.00
MVP30 Fred McGriff 1.50
MVP31 Jeff Conine 1.50
MVP32 Mike Piazza 6.00
MVP33 Sandy Alomar Jr. 1.50
MVP34 Roberto Alomar 2.50
MVP35 Pedro J. Martinez 4.00
MVP36 Derek Jeter 8.00
MVP37 Rickey Henderson 4.00
MVP38 Roberto Alomar 2.50
MVP39 Bernie Williams 3.00
MVP40 Marquis Grissom 1.50
MVP41 David Wells 1.50
MVP42 Orlando Hernandez 1.50
MVP43 David Justice 1.50
MVP44 Andy Pettitte 2.00
MVP45 Adam Kennedy 1.50
MVP46 John Smoltz 1.50
MVP47 Curt Schilling 2.00
MVP48 Javy Lopez 1.50
MVP49 Livan Hernandez 1.50
MVP50 Sterling Hitchcock 1.50
MVP51 Mike Hampton 1.50
MVP52 Craig Counsell 1.50
MVP53 Benito Santiago 1.50
MVP54 Tom Glavine 2.00
MVP55 Livan Hernandez 1.50
MVP56 Mariano Rivera 1.50
MVP57 Derek Jeter 8.00
MVP58 Randy Johnson 4.00
MVP59 Curt Schilling 2.50
MVP60 Troy Glaus 3.00
MVP61 Yogi Berra 4.00
MVP62 Yogi Berra 4.00
MVP63 Mickey Mantle 15.00
MVP64 Mickey Mantle 15.00
MVP65 Ken Griffey Sr. 1.50
MVP66 Rickey Henderson 4.00
MVP67 Roberto Alomar 2.50
MVP68 Bernie Williams 3.00
MVP69 Livan Hernandez 1.50
MVP70 Sammy Sosa 6.00
MVP71 Sterling Hitchcock 1.50
MVP72 David Wells 1.50
MVP73 Mariano Rivera 1.50
MVP74 Chipper Jones 5.00
MVP75 Ivan Rodriguez 2.00
MVP76 Derek Jeter 8.00
MVP77 Jason Giambi 4.00
MVP78 Jeff Kent 1.50
MVP79 Mike Hampton 1.50
MVP80 Randy Johnson 4.00
MVP81 Curt Schilling 2.50
MVP82 Barry Bonds 8.00
MVP83 Ichiro Suzuki 6.00
MVP84 Ichiro Suzuki 6.00
MVP85 Adam Kennedy 1.50
MVP86 Benito Santiago 1.50
MVP87 Troy Glaus 3.00
MVP88 Troy Glaus 3.00
MVP89 Miguel Tejada 2.00
MVP90 Barry Bonds 8.00

Prosign

Common Autograph:
Production 25 Sets
No Pricing

Pro View

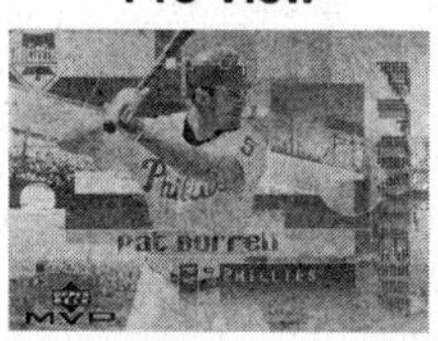

NM/M
Complete Set (45): 65.00
Common Player: .75
Inserted 2:Box
Golds: 2-3X
PV1 Troy Glaus 1.50
PV2 Darin Erstad 1.00
PV3 Randy Johnson 2.00
PV4 Curt Schilling 1.50
PV5 Luis Gonzalez .75
PV6 Chipper Jones 2.00
PV7 Andruw Jones 1.00
PV8 Greg Maddux 3.00
PV9 Pedro J. Martinez 2.00
PV10 Manny Ramirez 2.00
PV11 Sammy Sosa 3.00
PV12 Mark Prior 1.50
PV13 Magglio Ordonez 1.00
PV14 Frank Thomas 1.50
PV15 Ken Griffey Jr. 3.00
PV16 Adam Dunn 1.50
PV17 Jim Thome 1.50
PV18 Todd Helton 1.00
PV19 Jeff Bagwell 1.50
PV20 Lance Berkman 1.00
PV21 Shawn Green .75
PV22 Hideo Nomo 1.00
PV23 Vladimir Guerrero 2.00
PV24 Roberto Alomar 1.00
PV25 Mike Piazza 4.00
PV26 Jason Giambi 1.00
PV27 Roger Clemens 3.00
PV28 Alfonso Soriano 2.00
PV29 Derek Jeter 6.00
PV30 Miguel Tejada 1.50
PV31 Eric Chavez .75
PV32 Barry Zito 1.00
PV33 Pat Burrell 1.50
PV34 Brian Giles .75
PV35 Barry Bonds 6.00
PV36 Ichiro Suzuki 4.00
PV37 Albert Pujols 5.00
PV38 Scott Rolen 1.50
PV39 J.D. Drew .75
PV40 Mark McGwire 5.00
PV41 Alex Rodriguez 5.00
PV42 Rafael Palmeiro 1.00
PV43 Juan Gonzalez 1.00
PV44 Eric Hinske .75
PV45 Carlos Delgado .75

SportsNut Fantasy

NM/M
Complete Set (90): 45.00
Common Player: .40
Inserted 1:3
Prices for unscratched cards.
SN1 Troy Glaus 1.00
SN2 Darin Erstad .50
SN3 Luis Gonzalez .50
SN4 Andruw Jones .75
SN5 Chipper Jones 2.00
SN6 Gary Sheffield .50
SN7 Jay Gibbons .40
SN8 Manny Ramirez 1.00
SN9 Shea Hillenbrand .40
SN10 Johnny Damon .40
SN11 Nomar Garciaparra 2.50
SN12 Sammy Sosa 2.00
SN13 Magglio Ordonez .75
SN14 Frank Thomas .75
SN15 Ken Griffey Jr. 1.50
SN16 Adam Dunn 1.00
SN17 Matt Lawton .40
SN18 Larry Walker .40
SN19 Todd Helton .75
SN20 Carlos Pena .40
SN21 Mike Lowell .40
SN22 Jeff Bagwell 1.00
SN23 Lance Berkman .75
SN24 Mike Sweeney .50
SN25 Carlos Beltran .40
SN26 Shawn Green .75
SN27 Richie Sexson .50
SN28 Torii Hunter .40
SN29 Jacque Jones .40
SN30 Vladimir Guerrero 1.50
SN31 Jose Vidro .40
SN32 Roberto Alomar .50
SN33 Mike Piazza 2.00
SN34 Alfonso Soriano 1.50
SN35 Derek Jeter 3.00
SN36 Jason Giambi 2.00
SN37 Bernie Williams .75
SN38 Eric Chavez .75
SN39 Miguel Tejada .75
SN40 Jim Thome 1.00
SN41 Pat Burrell 1.00
SN42 Bobby Abreu .50
SN43 Brian Giles .50
SN44 Jason Kendall .40
SN45 Ryan Klesko .40
SN46 Phil Nevin .40
SN47 Barry Bonds 4.00
SN48 Rich Aurilia .40
SN49 Ichiro Suzuki 2.00
SN50 Bret Boone .40
SN51 J.D. Drew .40
SN52 Jim Edmonds .75
SN53 Albert Pujols 1.50
SN54 Scott Rolen 1.00
SN55 Ben Grieve .40
SN56 Alex Rodriguez 3.00
SN57 Rafael Palmeiro .75
SN58 Juan Gonzalez .50
SN59 Carlos Delgado .40
SN60 Josh Phelps .40
SN61 Jarrod Washburn .40
SN62 Randy Johnson 1.00
SN63 Curt Schilling .75
SN64 Greg Maddux 1.50
SN65 Mike Hampton .40
SN66 Rodrigo Lopez .40
SN67 Pedro J. Martinez 1.50
SN68 Derek Lowe .40
SN69 Mark Prior 1.00
SN70 Kerry Wood .75
SN71 Mark Buehrle .40
SN72 Roy Oswalt .50
SN73 Wade Miller .40
SN74 Odalis Perez .40
SN75 Hideo Nomo .50
SN76 Ben Sheets .40
SN77 Eric Milton .40
SN78 Bartolo Colon .40
SN79 Tom Glavine .40
SN80 Al Leiter .40
SN81 Roger Clemens 2.00
SN82 Mike Mussina .75
SN83 Tim Hudson .75
SN84 Barry Zito .75
SN85 Mark Mulder .50
SN86 Vicente Padilla .40
SN87 Jason Schmidt .40
SN88 Freddy Garcia .40
SN89 Matt Morris .40
SN90 Roy Halladay .40

Talk of the Town

NM/M
Complete Set (15): 20.00
Common Player: .75
Inserted 1:12
TT1 Hideki Matsui 3.00
TT2 Chipper Jones 1.00
TT3 Manny Ramirez 1.50
TT4 Sammy Sosa 2.00
TT5 Ken Griffey Jr. 2.00
TT6 Lance Berkman .75
TT7 Shawn Green .75
TT8 Vladimir Guerrero 1.50
TT9 Mike Piazza 2.50
TT10 Jason Giambi .75
TT11 Alfonso Soriano 1.50
TT12 Ichiro Suzuki 2.50
TT13 Albert Pujols 3.00
TT14 Alex Rodriguez 3.00
TT15 Eric Hinske .75

Three Bagger

NM/M
Inserted 1:488
BMP Barry Bonds, Mark McGwire, Mike Piazza 80.00
GIB Ken Griffey Jr., Ichiro Suzuki, Barry Bonds 60.00
GTD Troy Glaus, Frank Thomas, Carlos Delgado 10.00
IBJ Ichiro Suzuki, Barry Bonds, Derek Jeter 80.00
JWP Derek Jeter, Bernie Williams, Jorge Posada 35.00
SCB Curt Schilling, Roger Clemens, Kevin Brown 20.00

Total Bases

NM/M
Production 150 Sets
BB Barry Bonds 20.00
RC Roger Clemens 20.00
TG Troy Glaus 8.00
KG Ken Griffey Jr. 15.00
DJ Derek Jeter 20.00
MM Mark McGwire 25.00
MP Mike Piazza 15.00
AR Alex Rodriguez 15.00
IS Ichiro Suzuki 30.00

2003 Upper Deck Patch Collection Promo

NM/M
SAMPLEIchiro 6.00

2003 Upper Deck Patch Collection

NM/M
Complete Set (161):
Common Player: .25
Common SP Patch (121-161): 4.00
All-Star & HOF Patches (121-150):
Inserted 1:40
Rookie Patches (151-161):
Inserted 1:20
Pack (5): 4.75
Box (20): 80.00
1 Darin Erstad .40
2 Troy Glaus .75
3 Robby Hammock **RC** .25
4 Luis Gonzalez .50
5 Randy Johnson/SP 3.00
6 Curt Schilling/SP 2.50
7 Oscar Villarreal **RC** .25
8 Gary Sheffield .50
9 Mike Hampton .25
10 Greg Maddux 1.50
11 Chipper Jones 1.50
12 Tony Batista .25
13 Rodrigo Lopez .25
14 Jay Gibbons .25
15 Shea Hillenbrand .25
16 Johnny Damon .25
17 Derek Lowe .25
18 Nomar Garciaparra 2.00
19 Pedro J. Martinez 1.00
20 Manny Ramirez .75
21 Mark Prior .75
22 Kerry Wood .50
23 Corey Patterson .25
24 Sammy Sosa 1.50
25 Troy O'Leary .25
26 Frank Thomas .75
27 Magglio Ordonez .40
28 Bartolo Colon .25
29 Austin Kearns .75
30 Aaron Boone .25
31 Ken Griffey Jr. 1.50
32 Adam Dunn .75
33 C.C. Sabathia .25
34 Karim Garcia .25
35 Larry Walker .40
36 Preston Wilson .40
37 Jason Jennings .25
38 Todd Helton .75
39 Carlos Pena .25
40 Eric Munson .25
41 Ivan Rodriguez .50
42 Josh Beckett .25
43 A.J. Burnett .25
44 Roy Oswalt .25
45 Craig Biggio .40
46 Jeff Bagwell .75
47 Lance Berkman .50
48 Jeff Kent .40
49 Carlos Beltran .25
50 Mike Sweeney .25
51 Hideo Nomo .50
52 Adrian Beltre .25
53 Shawn Green .50
54 Kazuhisa Ishii .25
55 Ben Sheets .25
56 Richie Sexson .50
57 Torii Hunter .50
58 Doug Mientkiewicz .25
59 Eric Milton .25
60 Corey Koskie .25
61 Joe Mays .25
62 Jose Vidro .25
63 Vladimir Guerrero .75
64 Luis Ayala **RC** .25
65 Cliff Floyd .25
66 Tom Glavine .50
67 Mike Piazza 2.00
68 Roberto Alomar .50
69 Al Leiter .25
70 Mike Mussina .50
71 Mariano Rivera .40
72 Drew Henson .25
73 Roger Clemens 1.50
74 Jason Giambi 1.00
75 Bernie Williams .50
76 Alfonso Soriano 1.50
77 Derek Jeter 3.00
78 Miguel Tejada .50
79 Jermaine Dye .25
80 Tim Hudson .50
81 Barry Zito .50
82 Mark Mulder .40
83 Pat Burrell .50
84 Jim Thome .75
85 Bobby Abreu .40
86 Kevin Millwood .40
87 Jason Kendall .40
88 Brian Giles .40
89 Phil Nevin .25
90 Sean Burroughs .25
91 Oliver Perez .25
92 Jose Cruz Jr. .25
93 Rich Aurilia .25
94 Edgardo Alfonzo .25
95 Barry Bonds 3.00
96 J.T. Snow .25
97 Mike Cameron .25
98 John Olerud .50
99 Bret Boone .25
100 Ichiro Suzuki 1.50
101 J.D. Drew .40
102 Jim Edmonds .50
103 Scott Rolen .75
104 Matt Morris .40
105 Tino Martinez .40
106 Albert Pujols 1.50
107 Rocco Baldelli .25
108 Carl Crawford .25
109 Mark Teixeira .50
110 Rafael Palmeiro .50
111 Hank Blalock .50
112 Alex Rodriguez 2.50
113 Kevin Mench .25
114 Juan Gonzalez .75
115 Shannon Stewart .25
116 Vernon Wells .40
117 Josh Phelps .25
118 Eric Hinske .25
119 Orlando Hudson .25
120 Carlos Delgado .50
121 Alex Rodriguez 10.00
122 Nomar Garciaparra 10.00
123 Miguel Tejada 4.00
124 Jim Thome 8.00
125 Alfonso Soriano 6.00
126 Vladimir Guerrero 6.00
127 Derek Jeter 15.00
128 Mike Piazza 8.00
129 Ichiro Suzuki 12.00
130 Pedro J. Martinez 8.00
131 Luis Gonzalez 4.00
132 Adam Dunn 6.00
133 Shawn Green 4.00
134 Barry Zito 4.00
135 Torii Hunter 5.00
136 Ted Williams 20.00
137 Mickey Mantle 25.00

138 Ernie Banks 10.00
139 Yogi Berra 8.00
140 Rollie Fingers 4.00
141 Jim "Catfish" Hunter 4.00
142 Juan Marichal 8.00
143 Eddie Mathews 10.00
144 Willie McCovey 10.00
145 Joe Morgan 5.00
146 Stan Musial 12.00
147 Pee Wee Reese 10.00
148 Phil Rizzuto 6.00
149 Nolan Ryan 20.00
150 Tom Seaver 8.00
151 Hideki Matsui **RC** 15.00
152 Jose Contreras **RC** 5.00
153 Lew Ford **RC** 5.00
154 Jeremy Griffiths 4.00
155 Guillermo Quiroz **RC** 4.00
156 Ryan Cameron **RC** 4.00
157 Jon Leicester **RC** 4.00
158 Josh Willingham **RC** 4.00
159 Shane Bazzell **RC** 4.00
160 Willie Eyre **RC** 4.00
161 Prentice Redman **RC** 4.00

All-Star Game History Patches

NM/M
Common Patch: 8.00
Inserted 2:Box
1 1933 All-Star Game 12.00
2 1934 All-Star Game 15.00
3 1935 All-Star Game 15.00
4 1936 All-Star Game 10.00
5 1937 All-Star Game 10.00
6 1938 All-Star Game 10.00
7 1939 All-Star Game 15.00
8 1940 All-Star Game 15.00
9 1941 All-Star Game 10.00
10 1942 All-Star Game 15.00
11 1943 All-Star Game 12.00
12 1944 All-Star Game 12.00
13 1946 All-Star Game 15.00
14 1947 All-Star Game 15.00
15 1948 All-Star Game 15.00
16 1949 All-Star Game 15.00
17 1950 All-Star Game 12.00
18 1951 All-Star Game 12.00
19 1952 All-Star Game 15.00
20 1953 All-Star Game 12.00
21 1954 All-Star Game 12.00
22 1955 All-Star Game 10.00
23 1956 All-Star Game 12.00
24 1957 All-Star Game 15.00
25 1958 All-Star Game 12.00
26 1959 All-Star Game 15.00
27 1959 All-Star Game 15.00
28 1960 All-Star Game 10.00
29 1960 All-Star Game 15.00
30 1961 All-Star Game 10.00
31 1961 All-Star Game 15.00
32 1962 All-Star Game 8.00
33 1962 All-Star Game 12.00
34 1963 All-Star Game 10.00
35 1964 All-Star Game 15.00
36 1965 All-Star Game 10.00
37 1966 All-Star Game 15.00
38 1967 All-Star Game 12.00
39 1968 All-Star Game 8.00
40 1969 All-Star Game 10.00
41 1970 All-Star Game 15.00
42 1971 All-Star Game 10.00
43 1972 All-Star Game 10.00
44 1973 All-Star Game 10.00
45 1974 All-Star Game 10.00
46 1975 All-Star Game 10.00
47 1976 All-Star Game 15.00
48 1977 All-Star Game 12.00
49 1978 All-Star Game 10.00
50 1979 All-Star Game 8.00
51 1980 All-Star Game 8.00
52 1981 All-Star Game 10.00
53 1982 All-Star Game 8.00
54 1983 All-Star Game 10.00
55 1984 All-Star Game 10.00
56 1985 All-Star Game 10.00
57 1986 All-Star Game 10.00
58 1987 All-Star Game 8.00
59 1988 All-Star Game 10.00
60 1989 All-Star Game 8.00
61 1990 All-Star Game 15.00
62 1991 All-Star Game 8.00
63 1992 All-Star Game 8.00
64 1993 All-Star Game 10.00
65 1994 All-Star Game 15.00
66 1995 All-Star Game 8.00
67 1996 All-Star Game 12.00
68 1997 All-Star Game 10.00
69 1998 All-Star Game 8.00
70 1999 All-Star Game 15.00
71 2000 All-Star Game 10.00
72 2001 All-Star Game 10.00
73 2002 All-Star Game 12.00

MVPs Patches

NM/M
Common Player: 5.00
Inserted 1:20
1 Derek Jeter 15.00
2 Randy Johnson 8.00
3 Curt Schilling 6.00
4 Troy Glaus 5.00
5 Ted Williams 15.00
6 Ted Williams 15.00
7 Mickey Mantle 20.00
8 Mickey Mantle 20.00
9 Phil Rizzuto 5.00
10 Roger Clemens 10.00
11 Ken Griffey Jr. 10.00
12 Jason Giambi 5.00
13 Ichiro Suzuki 15.00
14 Roger Clemens 10.00
15 Yogi Berra 6.00
16 Sammy Sosa 10.00
17 Derek Jeter 15.00
18 Mike Piazza 10.00
19 Barry Bonds 15.00
20 Stan Musial 12.00
21 Joe Morgan 5.00

Signature Patches

NM/M
Common Autograph: 25.00
Inserted 1:320
JB Jeff Bagwell 50.00
LB Lance Berkman 50.00
RC Roger Clemens 160.00
AD Adam Dunn 60.00
FG Freddy Garcia 30.00
JG Jason Giambi 40.00
LG Luis Gonzalez 40.00
KG Ken Griffey Jr. 100.00
DH Drew Henson 40.00
EH Eric Hinske 25.00
TP Troy Percival 25.00
SR Scott Rolen 50.00
CS Curt Schilling 50.00
GS Gary Sheffield 50.00
IS Ichiro Suzuki 300.00
MT Miguel Tejada 50.00
BZ Barry Zito 40.00

2003 Upper Deck Play Ball Promos

Each April 2003 newsstand issue of Tuff Stuff magazine included a Play Ball promo card inside its poly bag. The cards differ from the issued version only in the appearance on front of a silver-foil "UD PROMO" notation. It is not known how many different players cards were used in the promotion.

NM/M
Common Player: .25
Stars: 1.5-2.5X

2003 Upper Deck Play Ball Sample

This promo card differs from the issued version in its card number and in the appearance on back of a large overprinted typewriter-style "SAMPLE."

NM/M
1 Mark McGwire 2.00

2003 Upper Deck Play Ball

NM/M
Complete Set (104):
Common Player: .25
Common Summer of '41 (74-88): 4.00
Inserted 1:24
Common Ted Williams (89-103): 10.00
Inserted 1:24
Pack (5): 2.50
Box (24): 40.00
1 Troy Glaus .40
2 Darin Erstad .25
3 Randy Johnson .75
4 Luis Gonzalez .40
5 Curt Schilling .75
6 Tom Glavine .40
7 Chipper Jones .75
8 Greg Maddux 1.00
9 Andruw Jones .40
10 Pedro J. Martinez .75
11 Manny Ramirez .75
12 Nomar Garciaparra 1.00
13 Billy Williams .25
14 Sammy Sosa 1.00
15 Kerry Wood .75
16 Mark Prior .75
17 Ernie Banks 1.00
18 Frank Thomas .75
19 Joe Morgan .25
20 Ken Griffey Jr. 1.25
21 Adam Dunn .75
22 Jim Thome .50
23 Todd Helton .50
24 Larry Walker .40
25 Lance Berkman .40
26 Roy Oswalt .40
27 Jeff Bagwell .50
28 Nolan Ryan 2.00
29 Mike Sweeney .25
30 Shawn Green .40
31 Hideo Nomo .40
32 Kazuhisa Ishii .25
33 Richie Sexson .40
34 Robin Yount .75
35 Harmon Killebrew .75
36 Torii Hunter .25
37 Vladimir Guerrero .75
38 Roberto Alomar .50
39 Mike Piazza 1.00
40 Tom Seaver .75
41 Phil Rizzuto .50
42 Yogi Berra .75
43 Mike Mussina .50
44 Roger Clemens 1.50
45 Derek Jeter 2.00
46 Jason Giambi .25
47 Bernie Williams .25
48 Alfonso Soriano .75
49 Jim "Catfish" Hunter .25
50 Barry Zito .40
51 Eric Chavez .40
52 Tim Hudson .40
53 Rollie Fingers .25
54 Miguel Tejada .50
55 Pat Burrell .40
56 Brian Giles .40
57 Willie Stargell .50
58 Phil Nevin .25
59 Orlando Cepeda .25
60 Barry Bonds 2.00
61 Jeff Kent .40
62 Willie McCovey .25
63 Ichiro Suzuki 1.50
64 Stan Musial 1.50
65 Albert Pujols 2.00
66 J.D. Drew .40
67 Scott Rolen .75
68 Mark McGwire 1.00
69 Alex Rodriguez 1.00
70 Juan Gonzalez .40
71 Ivan Rodriguez .50
72 Rafael Palmeiro .50
73 Carlos Delgado .40
74 Ted Williams 15.00
75 Hank Greenberg 6.00
76 Joe DiMaggio 15.00
77 Lefty Gomez 6.00
78 Tommy Henrich 4.00
79 Pee Wee Reese 5.00
80 Mel Ott 6.00
81 Carl Hubbell 6.00
82 Jimmie Foxx 8.00
83 Joe Cronin 4.00
84 Charlie Gehringer 5.00
85 Frank Hayes 5.00
86 Babe Dahlgren 4.00
87 Dolph Camilli 4.00
88 Johnny Vander Meer 4.00
89-103 Ted Williams 10.00
104 Hideki Matsui **RC** 5.00

Red Back

NM/M
Stars (1-73): 1.5-2X
SP's (74-103): 1-1.5X
Matsui Red #104: 10.00
Inserted 1:2

BuyBacks

No Pricing

Game-Used Memorabilia Tier 1

NM/M
Common Player: 5.00
Inserted 1:82
Golds: Not Priced
Production 25 Sets
RC1 Roger Clemens 20.00
CD1 Carlos Delgado 5.00
DR1 J.D. Drew 5.00
AD1 Adam Dunn 10.00
JG1 Jason Giambi 5.00
LG1 Luis Gonzalez 5.00
KG1 Ken Griffey Jr. 15.00
TH1 Tommy Henrich 5.00
KI1 Kazuhisa Ishii 5.00
CJ1 Chipper Jones 10.00
MM1 Mark McGwire 50.00
RP1 Rafael Palmeiro 8.00
MP1 Mike Piazza 10.00
PR1 Mark Prior 8.00
IR1 Ivan Rodriguez 8.00
CS1 Curt Schilling 8.00
AS1 Alfonso Soriano 8.00
SS1 Sammy Sosa 10.00
IS1 Ichiro Suzuki 30.00
MS1 Mike Sweeney 5.00
BW1 Bernie Williams 5.00

Game-Used Memorabilia Tier 2

NM/M
Common Player: 5.00
Production 150 Sets
JB2 Jeff Bagwell 10.00
LB2 Lance Berkman 5.00
JD2 Joe DiMaggio 100.00
DE2 Darin Erstad 5.00
JG2 Jason Giambi 5.00
SG2 Shawn Green 5.00
KG2 Ken Griffey Jr. 15.00
RJ2 Randy Johnson 10.00
AJ2 Andruw Jones 8.00
CJ2 Chipper Jones 10.00
GM2 Greg Maddux 15.00
PM2 Pedro J. Martinez 10.00
MM2 Mark McGwire 60.00
MP2 Mike Piazza 10.00
MR2 Manny Ramirez 10.00
AR2 Alex Rodriguez 15.00
CS2 Curt Schilling 10.00
SS2 Sammy Sosa 15.00
IS2 Ichiro Suzuki 50.00
JT2 Jim Thome 10.00
KW2 Kerry Wood 10.00

Game-Used Memorabilia Auto.

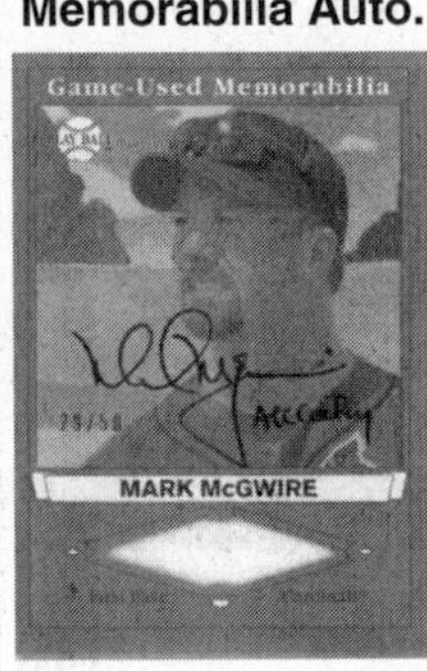

NM/M
Production 50 except A-Rod.
JB2 Jeff Bagwell 75.00
LB2 Lance Berkman 75.00
JG2 Jason Giambi 50.00
KG2 Ken Griffey Jr. 125.00
AJ2 Andruw Jones 50.00
MM2 Mark McGwire 350.00
AR2 Alex Rodriguez/285 100.00
CS2 Curt Schilling 75.00
SS2 Sammy Sosa 180.00
IS2 Ichiro Suzuki 375.00
JT2 Jim Thome 75.00
KW2 Kerry Wood 75.00

Mini

NM/M
Complete Set (73): 40.00
Common Player: .50
Inserted 1:2
1 Troy Glaus .50
2 Darin Erstad .50
3 Randy Johnson 1.00
4 Luis Gonzalez .50
5 Curt Schilling .75
6 Tom Glavine .50
7 Chipper Jones 1.00
8 Greg Maddux 1.50
9 Andruw Jones .75
10 Pedro J. Martinez 1.00
11 Manny Ramirez 1.00
12 Nomar Garciaparra 2.00
13 Billy Williams .50
14 Sammy Sosa 2.00
15 Kerry Wood 1.00
16 Mark Prior 1.00
17 Ernie Banks 1.50
18 Frank Thomas 1.00
19 Joe Morgan .50
20 Ken Griffey Jr. 2.00
21 Adam Dunn 1.00
22 Jim Thome 1.00
23 Todd Helton .75
24 Larry Walker .50
25 Lance Berkman .75
26 Roy Oswalt .50
27 Jeff Bagwell 1.00
28 Nolan Ryan 3.00
29 Mike Sweeney .50
30 Shawn Green .50
31 Hideo Nomo .75
32 Kazuhisa Ishii .50
33 Richie Sexson .50
34 Robin Yount 1.00
35 Harmon Killebrew 1.00
36 Torii Hunter .75
37 Vladimir Guerrero 1.00
38 Roberto Alomar .75
39 Mike Piazza 2.00
40 Tom Seaver 1.00
41 Phil Rizzuto .75
42 Yogi Berra 1.50
43 Mike Mussina .75
44 Roger Clemens 2.00
45 Derek Jeter 3.00
46 Jason Giambi .50
47 Bernie Williams .75
48 Alfonso Soriano 1.00
49 Jim "Catfish" Hunter .50
50 Barry Zito .50
51 Eric Chavez .50
52 Tim Hudson .50
53 Rollie Fingers .50
54 Miguel Tejada 1.00
55 Pat Burrell 1.00
56 Brian Giles .50
57 Willie Stargell .75
58 Phil Nevin .50
59 Orlando Cepeda .50
60 Barry Bonds 3.00
61 Jeff Kent .50
62 Willie McCovey .50
63 Ichiro Suzuki 2.50
64 Stan Musial 2.00
65 Albert Pujols 3.00
66 J.D. Drew .50
67 Scott Rolen 1.00
68 Mark McGwire 2.00
69 Alex Rodriguez 2.50
70 Juan Gonzalez 1.00
71 Ivan Rodriguez 1.00
72 Rafael Palmeiro .75
73 Carlos Delgado .50

Original Artwork Redemption

89 Total Redemption Cards

Reprint Series Original 1941

NM/M
Complete Set (25): 15.00
Common Player: .75
Inserted 1:2
R1 Ted Williams 2.50
R2 Hank Greenberg .75
R3 Joe DiMaggio 2.50
R4 Lefty Gomez .75
R5 Tommy Henrich .75
R6 Pee Wee Reese .75
R7 Mel Ott 1.00
R8 Carl Hubbell .75
R9 Jimmie Foxx 1.00
R10 Joe Cronin .75
R11 Charley Gehringer .75
R12 Frank Hayes .75
R13 Babe Dahlgren .75
R14 Dolph Camilli .75
R15 Johnny Vander Meer .75
R16 Bucky Walters .75
R17 Red Ruffing .75
R18 Charlie Keller .75
R19 Bob Johnson .75
R20 Emil "Dutch" Leonard .75
R21 Barney McCosky .75
R22 Soupy Campbell .75
R23 Roy Weatherly .75
R24 Bobby Doerr .75
R25 Bill Dickey .75

The Yankee Clipper: 1941 Streak

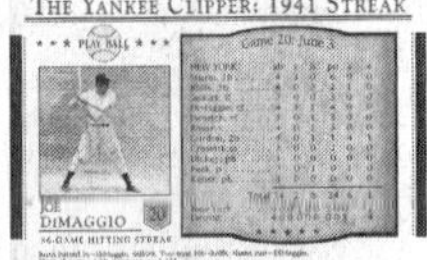

NM/M
Complete Set (56): 250.00
Common DiMaggio (1-41): 5.00
Inserted 1:12
Common DiMaggio (42-56): 8.00
Inserted 1:24
S-1-41 Joe DiMaggio 5.00
S-42-56 Joe DiMaggio 8.00

Play Ball Hawaii

To introduce its retro-styled Play Ball brand, Upper Deck created a special promo set for the SCD Hawaii Trade Conference. Each of the special cards has a whimsical tropical artwork background and the trade show logo on front. Three of the cards, with appropriate authentication on back, were seeded in the promo packs in an autographed version, with the McGwire card reported as much scarcer than the Sosa and Giambi autographs.

		NM/M
Complete Set (10):		30.00
Common Player:		2.00
KY1	"Slammin'" Sammy Sosa	5.00
SS	"Slammin'" Sammy Sosa/Auto.	125.00
KY2	Ken "The Kid" Griffey Jr.	6.00
KY3	Jason Giambi	3.00
JG	Jason Giambi/Auto.	35.00
KY4	Ichiro	10.00
KY5	Mark "Big Mac" McGwire	7.50
MM	Mark "Big Mac" McGwire/Auto.	250.00
KY6	Troy Glaus	2.00
KY7	Derek Jeter	7.50
KY8	Barry Bonds	6.50
KY9	Alex "A-Rod" Rodriguez	5.00
KY10	Nomar Garciaparra	6.00

2003 Upper Deck Prospect Premieres

		NM/M
Complete Set (90):		30.00
Common Player:		.25
Pack (4):		7.00
Box (18):		100.00
1	Bryan Opdyke **RC**	.25
2	Gabriel Sosa **RC**	.25
3	Tila Reynolds **RC**	.25
4	Aaron Hill **RC**	1.00
5	Aaron Marsden **RC**	.25
6	Abe Alvarez **RC**	.75
7	Adam Jones **RC**	3.00
8	Adam Miller **RC**	2.50
9	Andre Ethier **RC**	3.00
10	Tony Gwynn Jr. **RC**	.75
11	Brad Snyder **RC**	1.00
12	Brad Sullivan **RC**	.75
13	Brian Anderson **RC**	1.50
14	Brian Buscher **RC**	.25
15	Brian Snyder **RC**	.75
16	Carlos Quentin **RC**	3.00
17	Chad Billingsley **RC**	3.00
18	Fraser Dizard **RC**	.50
19	Chris Durbin **RC**	.50
20	Chris Ray **RC**	.50
21	Conor Jackson **RC**	2.00
22	Kory Casto **RC**	.50
23	Craig Whitaker **RC**	.75
24	Daniel Moore **RC**	.25
25	Daric Barton **RC**	2.00
26	Darin Downs **RC**	.75
27	David Murphy **RC**	1.00
28	Dustin Majewski **RC**	.50
29	Edgardo Baez **RC**	.25
30	Jake Fox **RC**	.75
31	Jake Stevens **RC**	.50
32	Jamie D'Antona **RC**	1.00
33	James Houser **RC**	.50
34	Jarrod Saltalamacchia **RC**	2.00
35	Jason Hirsh **RC**	2.00
36	Javi Herrera **RC**	1.00
37	Jeff Allison **RC**	.75
38	John Hudgins **RC**	.50
39	Jo Jo Reyes **RC**	.50
40	Justin James **RC**	.50
41	Kurt Isenberg **RC**	.50
42	Kyle Boyer	.75
43	Lastings Milledge **RC**	5.00
44	Luis Atilano **RC**	.50
45	Matt Murton **RC**	1.50
46	Matt Moses **RC**	1.00
47	Matt Harrison **RC**	.50
48	Michael Bourn **RC**	.50
49	Miguel Vega **RC**	.50
50	Mitch Maier **RC**	1.00
51	Omar Quintanilla **RC**	.50
52	Ryan Sweeney **RC**	1.50
53	Scott Baker **RC**	.75
54	Sean Rodriguez **RC**	.75
55	Steve Lerud **RC**	.25
56	Thomas Pauly **RC**	.25
57	Tom Gorzelanny **RC**	1.00
58	Tim Moss **RC**	.25
59	Robbie Wooley **RC**	.50
60	Trey Webb **RC**	.25
61	Wes Littleton **RC**	.50
62	Beau Vaughan **RC**	.25
63	Willy Jo Ronda **RC**	.50
64	Chris Lubanski **RC**	1.50
65	Ian Stewart **RC**	4.00
66	John Danks **RC**	1.00
67	Kyle Sleeth **RC**	1.00
68	Michael Aubrey **RC**	1.50
69	Kevin Kouzmanoff **RC**	3.00
70	Ryan Harvey **RC**	1.50
71	Tim Stauffer **RC**	1.00
72	Tony Richie **RC**	.25
73	Brandon Wood **RC**	8.00
74	David Aardsma **RC**	.75
75	David Shinskie **RC**	.50
76	Dennis Dove **RC**	.25
77	Eric Sultemeier **RC**	.25
78	Jay Sborz **RC**	.25
79	Jimmy Barthmaier **RC**	.50
80	Josh Whitesell **RC**	.25
81	Josh Anderson **RC**	.25
82	Kenny Lewis **RC**	.50
83	Mateo Miramontes **RC**	.50
84	Nicholas Markakis **RC**	4.00
85	Paul Bacot **RC**	.50
86	Peter Stonard **RC**	.25
87	Reggie Willits **RC**	3.00
88	Shane Costa **RC**	.50
89	Billy Sadler **RC**	.25
90	Delmon Young **RC**	8.00

Star Rookie Signature

		NM/M
Common Autograph:		5.00
Inserted 1:9		
P1	Bryan Opdyke	10.00
P2	Gabriel Sosa	8.00
P3	Tila Reynolds	5.00
P4	Aaron Hill	15.00
P5	Aaron Marsden	10.00
P6	Abe Alvarez	15.00
P7	Adam Jones	90.00
P8	Adam Miller	75.00
P9	Andre Ethier	60.00
P10	Tony Gwynn Jr.	20.00
P11	Brad Snyder	25.00
P12	Brad Sullivan	15.00
P13	Brian Anderson	20.00
P14	Brian Buscher	8.00
P15	Brian Snyder	10.00
P16	Carlos Quentin	40.00
P17	Chad Billingsley	40.00
P19	Chris Durbin	10.00
P20	Chris Ray	8.00
P21	Conor Jackson	30.00
P22	Kory Casto	8.00
P23	Craig Whitaker	10.00
P24	Daniel Moore	10.00
P25	Daric Barton	60.00
P26	Darin Downs	15.00
P27	David Murphy	30.00
P29	Edgardo Baez	12.00
P30	Jake Fox	15.00
P31	Jake Stevens	20.00
P32	Jamie D'Antona	25.00
P33	James Houser	15.00
P34	Jarrod Saltalamacchia	60.00
P35	Jason Hirsh	35.00
P36	Javi Herrera	10.00
P37	Jeff Allison	25.00
P38	John Hudgins	10.00
P39	Jo Jo Reyes	10.00
P40	Justin James	10.00
P41	Kurt Isenberg	10.00
P42	Kyle Boyer	12.00
P43	Lastings Milledge	60.00
P44	Luis Atilano	8.00
P45	Matt Murton	25.00
P46	Matt Moses	35.00
P48	Michael Bourn	15.00
P49	Miguel Vega	15.00
P50	Mitch Maier	25.00
P51	Omar Quintanilla	15.00
P52	Ryan Sweeney	40.00
P53	Scott Baker	15.00
P55	Steve Lerud	15.00
P56	Thomas Pauly	10.00
P57	Tom Gorzelanny	30.00
P58	Tim Moss	10.00
P60	Trey Webb	10.00
P61	Wes Littleton	15.00
P62	Beau Vaughan	10.00
P63	Willy Jo Ronda	10.00
P64	Chris Lubanski	25.00
P65	Ian Stewart	80.00
P66	John Danks	50.00
P67	Kyle Sleeth	20.00
P68	Michael Aubrey	40.00
P70	Ryan Harvey	30.00
P71	Tim Stauffer	30.00

Star Rookie Jersey

		NM/M
Common Player:		4.00
Inserted 1:18		
P72	Tony Richie	4.00
P73	Brandon Wood	15.00
P74	David Aardsma	5.00
P75	David Shinskie	4.00
P76	Dennis Dove	6.00
P77	Eric Sultemeier	4.00
P78	Jay Sborz	4.00
P79	Jimmy Barthmaier	4.00
P80	Josh Whitesell	4.00
P81	Josh Anderson	8.00
P82	Kenny Lewis	8.00
P83	Mateo Miramontes	8.00
P84	Nicholas Markakis	25.00
P85	Paul Bacot	4.00
P86	Peter Stonard	4.00
P87	Reggie Willits	30.00
P88	Shane Costa	4.00
P89	Billy Sadler	4.00
P91	Kyle Sleeth	8.00
P92	Ian Stewart	25.00
P93	Fraser Dizard	6.00
P94	Abe Alvarez	6.00
P95	Adam Jones	15.00
P96	Brian Anderson	8.00
P97	Chris Durbin	4.00
P98	Craig Whitaker	8.00
P99	Jake Fox	4.00
P100	Kurt Isenberg	4.00
P101	Luis Atilano	4.00
P102	Miguel Vega	4.00
P103	Mitch Maier	8.00
P104	Ryan Sweeney	10.00
P105	Scott Baker	4.00
P106	Sean Rodriguez	8.00
P108	Trey Webb	4.00
P109	Willy Jo Ronda	6.00
P110	John Danks	8.00
P111	Michael Aubrey	10.00
P112	Lastings Milledge	30.00
P113	Chris Lubanski	10.00

SportsFest Star Rookies

Persons who opened a box of Upper Deck product at the company's booth during the June 27-29 show in Chicago received this cellophane wrapped set of six Star Rookies.

		NM/M
Complete Set (6):		6.00
Common Player:		.25
AM	Alejandro Machado	.25
HB	Hank Blalock	.50
HC	Hee Seop Choi	.25
HM	Hideki Matsui	5.00
RB	Rocco Baldelli	1.50
RH	Runelvys Hernandez	.25

2003 Upper Deck Standing O!

		NM/M
Complete Set (126):		30.00
Common Player:		.15
Common SP (85-126):		.75
Inserted 1:4		
Pack (4):		1.50
Box (24):		25.00
1	Darin Erstad	.25
2	Troy Glaus	.40
3	Tim Salmon	.25
4	Luis Gonzalez	.25
5	Randy Johnson	.50
6	Curt Schilling	.25
7	Andruw Jones	.25
8	Greg Maddux	.75
9	Chipper Jones	.75
10	Gary Sheffield	.25
11	Rodrigo Lopez	.15
12	Geronimo Gil	.15
13	Nomar Garciaparra	1.00
14	Pedro J. Martinez	.50
15	Manny Ramirez	.40
16	Mark Prior	.50
17	Kerry Wood	.25
18	Sammy Sosa	.75
19	Magglio Ordonez	.25
20	Frank Thomas	.40
21	Adam Dunn	.40
22	Ken Griffey Jr.	.75
23	Sean Casey	.15
24	Omar Vizquel	.15
25	C.C. Sabathia	.15
26	Larry Walker	.25
27	Todd Helton	.40
28	Ivan Rodriguez	.40
29	Josh Beckett	.15
30	Roy Oswalt	.25
31	Jeff Kent	.25
32	Jeff Bagwell	.40
33	Lance Berkman	.25
34	Mike Sweeney	.15
35	Carlos Beltran	.15
36	Hideo Nomo	.40
37	Shawn Green	.25
38	Kazuhisa Ishii	.15
39	Geoff Jenkins	.25
40	Richie Sexson	.25
41	Torii Hunter	.25
42	Jacque Jones	.15
43	Jose Vidro	.15
44	Vladimir Guerrero	.50
45	Cliff Floyd	.15
46	Al Leiter	.15
47	Mike Piazza	1.00
48	Tom Glavine	.25
49	Roberto Alomar	.25
50	Roger Clemens	.75
51	Jason Giambi	.50
52	Bernie Williams	.40
53	Alfonso Soriano	1.00
54	Derek Jeter	1.50
55	Miguel Tejada	.25
56	Eric Chavez	.25
57	Barry Zito	.25
58	Pat Burrell	.25
59	Jim Thome	.40
60	Brian Giles	.25
61	Jason Kendall	.25
62	Ryan Klesko	.25
63	Phil Nevin	.15
64	Sean Burroughs	.15
65	Jason Schmidt	.15
66	Rich Aurilia	.15
67	Barry Bonds	1.50
68	Randy Winn	.15
69	Freddy Garcia	.15
70	Ichiro Suzuki	.75
71	J.D. Drew	.15
72	Jim Edmonds	.25
73	Scott Rolen	.40
74	Matt Morris	.25
75	Albert Pujols	.75
76	Tino Martinez	.15
77	Rey Ordonez	.15
78	Carl Crawford	.15
79	Rafael Palmeiro	.25
80	Kevin Mench	.15
81	Alex Rodriguez	1.25
82	Juan Gonzalez	.40
83	Carlos Delgado	.25
84	Eric Hinske	.15
85	Richard Fischer **RC**	.75
86	Brandon Webb **RC**	1.50
87	Rob Hammock **RC**	.75
88	Matt Kata **RC**	1.00
89	Tim Olson **RC**	.75
90	Oscar Villarreal **RC**	.75
91	Michael Hessman **RC**	.75
92	Daniel Cabrera **RC**	.75
93	Jon Leicester **RC**	.75
94	Todd Wellemeyer **RC**	1.00
95	Felix Sanchez **RC**	.75
96	David Sanders **RC**	.75
97	Josh Stewart **RC**	.75
98	Arnie Munoz **RC**	.75
99	Ryan Cameron **RC**	.75
100	Clint Barmes **RC**	1.50
101	Josh Willingham **RC**	.75
103	Willie Eyre **RC**	.75
104	Brent Hoard **RC**	.75
105	Terrmel Sledge **RC**	1.00
106	Phil Seibel **RC**	.75
107	Craig Brazell **RC**	2.00
108	Jeff Duncan **RC**	.75
110	Bernie Castro **RC**	.75
111	Mike Nicolas **RC**	.75
112	Rett Johnson **RC**	.75
113	Bobby Madritsch **RC**	.75
114	Luis Ayala **RC**	.75
115	Hideki Matsui **RC**	10.00
116	Jose Contreras **RC**	1.50
117	Lew Ford **RC**	1.50
118	Jeremy Griffiths	.75
119	Guillermo Quiroz **RC**	1.00
120	Alejandro Machado **RC**	1.00
121	Francisco Cruceta **RC**	.75
122	Prentice Redman **RC**	1.00
123	Shane Bazzell **RC**	1.50
124	Jason Anderson	.75
125	Ian Ferguson **RC**	.75
126	Nook Logan **RC**	1.00

Die-Cut Disc

Stars (1-84):	1-2X
Inserted 1:1	
SP's (85-126):	1.5-3X
Inserted 1:48	

Starring Role Jersey

		NM/M
Not Priced yet, not enough market info.		
Inserted 1:240		
SR-RC	Roger Clemens	20.00
SR-JG	Jason Giambi	10.00
SR-LG	Luis Gonzalez	8.00
SR-SG	Shawn Green	5.00
SR-RJ	Randy Johnson	10.00
SR-MC	Mark McGwire/SP	40.00
SR-AR	Alex Rodriguez	20.00

2003 Upper Deck Sweet Spot

		NM/M
Complete Set (232):		
Common Player:		.25
Common SP:		1.00
Inserted 1:4		
Common SP (131-190):		3.00
Production 2,003		
Common SP (191-232):		4.00
Production 1,430 unless noted.		
Pack (4):		9.00
Box (12):		90.00
1	Darin Erstad	.50
2	Garret Anderson	.50
3	Tim Salmon	.50
4	Troy Glaus	.75
5	Luis Gonzalez	.50
6	Randy Johnson	1.00
7	Curt Schilling	.50
8	Lyle Overbay	.25
9	Andruw Jones/SP	2.00
10	Gary Sheffield/SP	1.50
11	Rafael Furcal/SP	1.00
12	Greg Maddux/SP	4.00
13	Chipper Jones/SP	4.00
14	Tony Batista	.25
15	Rodrigo Lopez	.25
16	Jay Gibbons	.25
17	Jason Johnson	.25
18	Byung-Hyun Kim/SP	1.00
19	Johnny Damon/SP	2.50
20	Derek Lowe/SP	1.00
21	Nomar Garciaparra/SP	5.00
22	Pedro Martinez/SP	3.00
23	Manny Ramirez/SP	2.50
24	Mark Prior	1.00
25	Kerry Wood	1.00
26	Corey Patterson	.50
27	Sammy Sosa	2.00
28	Moises Alou	.40
29	Magglio Ordonez	.40
30	Frank Thomas	.75
31	Paul Konerko	.25
32	Roberto Alomar	.50
33	Adam Dunn	.75
34	Austin Kearns	.50
35	Ryan Wagner **RC**	.25
36	Ken Griffey Jr.	1.50
37	Sean Casey	.25
38	Omar Vizquel	.40
39	C.C. Sabathia	.25
40	Jason Davis	.25
41	Travis Hafner	.25
42	Brandon Phillips	.25
43	Larry Walker	.40
44	Preston Wilson	.25
45	Jay Payton	.25
46	Todd Helton	.75
47	Carlos Pena	.25
48	Eric Munson	.25
49	Ivan Rodriguez	.75
50	Josh Beckett	.50
51	Alex Gonzalez	.25
52	Roy Oswalt	.40
53	Craig Biggio	.40
54	Jeff Bagwell	.75
55	Lance Berkman	.50
56	Mike Sweeney	.25
57	Carlos Beltran	.75
58	Brent Mayne	.25
59	Mike MacDougal	.25
60	Hideo Nomo	.50
61	Dave Roberts	.25
62	Adrian Beltre	.50
63	Shawn Green	.50
64	Kazuhisa Ishii	.25
65	Rickey Henderson	.50
66	Richie Sexson	.50
67	Torii Hunter	.50
68	Jacque Jones	.25
69	Joe Mays	.25
70	Corey Koskie	.25
71	A.J. Pierzynski	.25
72	Jose Vidro	.25
73	Vladimir Guerrero	.75
74	Tom Glavine	.50
75	Mike Piazza	1.50
76	Jose Reyes	.50
77	Jae Weong Seo	.25
78	Jorge Posada/SP	2.00
79	Mike Mussina/SP	2.00
80	Robin Ventura/SP	1.00
81	Mariano Rivera/SP	1.50
82	Roger Clemens/SP	6.00
83	Jason Giambi/SP	1.50
84	Bernie Williams/SP	2.00
85	Alfonso Soriano/SP	3.00
86	Derek Jeter	2.50
87	Miguel Tejada	.75
88	Eric Chavez	.50
89	Tim Hudson	.50
90	Barry Zito	.50
91	Mark Mulder	.50
92	Erubiel Durazo	.25
93	Pat Burrell	.50
94	Jim Thome	.75
95	Bobby Abreu	.50
96	Brian Giles	.40
97	Reggie Sanders	.25
98	Jose Hernandez	.25
99	Ryan Klesko	.25
100	Sean Burroughs	.25
101	Edgardo Alfonzo/SP	1.00
102	Rich Aurilia/SP	1.00
103	Jose Cruz Jr./SP	1.00
104	Barry Bonds/SP	6.00
105	Andres Galarraga/SP	1.00
106	Mike Cameron	.25
107	Kazuhiro Sasaki	.25
108	Bret Boone	.40
109	Ichiro Suzuki	2.00
110	John Olerud	.40
111	J.D. Drew/SP	1.50
112	Jim Edmonds/SP	2.00
113	Scott Rolen/SP	3.00
114	Matt Morris/SP	1.00
115	Tino Martinez/SP	1.00
116	Albert Pujols/SP	6.00
117	Jared Sandberg	.25
118	Carl Crawford	.25
119	Rafael Palmeiro	.50
120	Hank Blalock	.50
121	Alex Rodriguez	2.50
122	Kevin Mench	.25
123	Juan Gonzalez	.75
124	Mark Teixeira	.50
125	Shannon Stewart	.25
126	Vernon Wells	.50
127	Josh Phelps	.25
128	Eric Hinske	.25
129	Orlando Hudson	.25

130 Carlos Delgado .75
131 Jason Shiell **RC** 3.00
132 Kevin Tolar **RC** 3.00
133 Nate Bland **RC** 3.00
134 Brent Hoard **RC** 3.00
135 Jonathan Pridie **RC** 3.00
136 Mike Ryan **RC** 4.00
137 Francisco Rosario **RC** 3.00
138 Runelvys Hernandez 3.00
139 Guillermo Quiroz **RC** 4.00
140 Chin-Hui Tsao 3.00
141 Rett Johnson **RC** 3.00
142 Colin Porter **RC** 3.00
143 Jose Castillo 3.00
144 Chris Waters **RC** 3.00
145 Jeremy Guthrie 3.00
146 Pedro Liriano 3.00
147 Joe Borowski 3.00
148 Felix Sanchez **RC** 3.00
149 Todd Wellemeyer **RC** 3.00
150 Gerald Laird 3.00
151 Brandon Webb **RC** 8.00
152 Tommy Whiteman **RC** 3.00
153 Carlos Rivera 3.00
154 Rick Roberts **RC** 3.00
155 Terrmel Sledge **RC** 3.00
156 Jeff Duncan **RC** 3.00
157 Craig Brazell **RC** 3.00
158 Bernie Castro **RC** 3.00
159 Cory Stewart **RC** 3.00
160 Brandon Villafuerte **RC** 3.00
161 Tommy Phelps 3.00
162 Josh Hall **RC** 3.00
163 Ryan Cameron **RC** 3.00
164 Garrett Atkins 3.00
165 Brian Stokes **RC** 3.00
166 Rafael Betancourt **RC** 3.00
167 Jaime Cerda 3.00
168 Danny Carrasco **RC** 3.00
169 Ian Ferguson **RC** 3.00
170 Jorge Cordova **RC** 3.00
171 Eric Munson 3.00
172 Nook Logan **RC** 3.00
173 Jeremy Bonderman 10.00
174 Kyle Snyder 3.00
175 Rich Harden 5.00
176 Kevin Ohme **RC** 3.00
177 Roger Deago **RC** 3.00
178 Marlon Byrd 3.00
179 Dontrelle Willis 5.00
180 Bobby Hill 3.00
181 Jesse Foppert 3.00
182 Andrew Good 3.00
183 Chase Utley 3.00
184 Bo Hart **RC** 3.00
185 Dan Haren 4.00
186 Tim Olson **RC** 3.00
187 Joe Thurston 3.00
188 Jason Anderson 3.00
189 Jason Gilfillan **RC** 3.00
190 Rickie Weeks **RC** 12.00
191 Hideki Matsui/500 **RC** 25.00
192 Jose Contreras **RC** 8.00
193 Willie Eyre **RC** 4.00
194 Matt Bruback **RC** 4.00
195 Heath Bell **RC** 4.00
196 Lew Ford **RC** 8.00
197 Jeremy Griffiths 5.00
198 Oscar Villarreal/ 500 **RC** 5.00
199 Francisco Cruceta **RC** 5.00
200 Fernando Cabrera **RC** 5.00
201 Jhonny Peralta 4.00
202 Shane Bazzell **RC** 4.00
203 Bobby Madritsch/ 500 **RC** 15.00
204 Phil Seibel **RC** 4.00
205 Josh Willingham **RC** 6.00
206 Robby Hammock/ 500 **RC** 5.00
207 Alejandro Machado **RC** 5.00
208 David Sanders **RC** 4.00
209 Mike Neu/500 **RC** 5.00
210 Andrew Brown **RC** 4.00
211 Nathan Robertson **RC** 6.00
212 Miguel Ojeda **RC** 4.00
213 Beau Kemp **RC** 4.00
214 Aaron Looper **RC** 4.00
215 Alfredo Gonzalez **RC** 4.00
216 Richard Fischer/ 500 **RC** 5.00
218 Jeremy Wedel **RC** 6.00
219 Prentice Redman **RC** 4.00
220 Michel Hernandez **RC** 6.00
221 Rocco Baldelli/500 5.00
222 Luis Ayala **RC** 5.00
223 Arnie Munoz **RC** 4.00
224 Wilfredo Ledezma **RC** 4.00
225 Chris Capuano **RC** 8.00
226 Aquilino Lopez **RC** 4.00
227 Joe Valentine/500 **RC** 5.00
228 Matt Kata/1,200 **RC** 5.00
229 Diegomar Markwell/ 1,200 **RC** 4.00
230 Clint Barmes/ 1,200 **RC** 15.00
231 Mike Nicolas/500 **RC** 5.00
232 Jon Leicester/ 1,200 **RC** 5.00

Autographs Black Ink

NM/M

Common Player:
Red & Blue Ink variations exist.
Reds not priced due to scarcity.

Mirror Parallel: No Pricing
Production 25
HB Hank Blalock 30.00
HB Hank Blalock/Blue/40 40.00
PB Pat Burrell 30.00
PB Pat Burrell/Blue/40 40.00
RC Roger Clemens/73 125.00
RC Roger Clemens/ Blue/40 150.00
JC Jose Contreras 40.00
JC Jose Contreras/ Blue/40 50.00
AD Adam Dunn 30.00
AD Adam Dunn/Blue/40 50.00
NG Nomar Garciaparra 75.00
NG Nomar Garciaparra/ Blue/40 100.00
JG Jason Giambi 20.00
JG Jason Giambi/ Blue/40 30.00
TR Troy Glaus 35.00
TR Troy Glaus/Blue/40 50.00
GL Tom Glavine 30.00
GL Tom Glavine/Blue/40 50.00
KG Ken Griffey Jr. 75.00
KG Ken Griffey Jr./ Blue/40 100.00
KGs Ken Griffey Sr. 15.00
KGs Ken Griffey Sr./ Blue/40 20.00
VG Vladimir Guerrero 50.00
VG Vladimir Guerrero/ Blue/40 65.00
TG Tony Gwynn 40.00
HA Travis Hafner 15.00
HA Travis Hafner/Blue/40 25.00
BH Bo Hart 10.00
BH Bo Hart/Blue/40 15.00
TH Todd Helton/45 75.00
TH Todd Helton/Blue/40 75.00
DH Drew Henson 25.00
DH Drew Henson/ Blue/40 40.00
KI Kazuhisa Ishii 35.00
KI Kazuhisa Ishii/ Blue/40 50.00
AK Austin Kearns 20.00
AK Austin Kearns/ Blue/40 25.00
HM Hideki Matsui 300.00
HM Hideki Matsui/ Blue/40 375.00
RO Roy Oswalt 25.00
RO Roy Oswalt/Blue/40 35.00
LO Lyle Overbay 15.00
LO Lyle Overbay/Blue/40 20.00
BP Brandon Phillips 10.00
BP Brandon Phillips/ Blue/40 15.00
MP Mark Prior 30.00
MP Mark Prior/Blue/40 40.00
JR Jose Reyes 40.00
JR Jose Reyes/Blue/40 60.00
CR Cal Ripken Jr. 165.00
CR Cal Ripken Jr./ Blue/40 220.00
NR Nolan Ryan 120.00
NR Nolan Ryan/Blue/40 165.00
TS Tim Salmon 25.00
TS Tim Salmon/Blue/40 35.00
CS Curt Schilling 40.00
CS Curt Schilling/ Blue/40 75.00
GS Gary Sheffield 30.00
GS Gary Sheffield/ Blue/40 40.00
SS Sammy Sosa/ Blue/40 150.00
IS Ichiro Suzuki/ Blue/40 400.00
IS Ichiro Suzuki/ Red/35 400.00
MT Mark Teixeira 40.00
MT Mark Teixeira/ Blue/40 50.00
JT Jim Thome 40.00
JT Jim Thome/Blue/40 60.00
BW Brandon Webb 40.00
BW Brandon Webb/ Blue/40 60.00
RW Rickie Weeks 70.00
JW Jerome Williams 25.00
JW Jerome Williams/ Blue/40 35.00
DW Dontrelle Willis 45.00
DW Dontrelle Willis/ Blue/40 75.00

Game-Used Barrel

NM/M

Quantity produced listed
No Pricing due to scarcity.

KW-BB Kerry Wood/2 (2/04 Auction) 1,000

Barrel Autographs

NM/M

Quantity produced listed
HB Hank Blalock/420 35.00
PB Pat Burrell/345 35.00
RC Roger Clemens/49 220.00
AD Adam Dunn/345 40.00
TR Troy Glaus/345 40.00
TG Tom Glavine/345 45.00
KG Ken Griffey Jr./295 125.00
HM Hideki Matsui/124 400.00
CR Cal Ripken Jr./149 180.00
NR Nolan Ryan/445 150.00
JT Jim Thome/345 65.00

Patch

NM/M

Common Player: 4.00
Inserted 1:6
Logo Patch Parallel: 1-2X
Production 75 Sets
JB1 Jeff Bagwell 6.00
LB1 Lance Berkman 5.00
BB1 Barry Bonds 15.00
PB1 Pat Burrell 5.00
RC1 Roger Clemens 12.00
CD1 Carlos Delgado 4.00
AD1 Adam Dunn 5.00
JE1 Jim Edmonds 4.00
DE1 Darin Erstad 4.00
NG1 Nomar Garciaparra 10.00
JG1 Jason Giambi 4.00
TG1 Troy Glaus 5.00
TO1 Tom Glavine 5.00
LG1 Luis Gonzalez 4.00
SG1 Shawn Green 5.00
KG1 Ken Griffey Jr. 8.00
VG1 Vladimir Guerrero 6.00
TH1 Torii Hunter 5.00
KI1 Kazuhisa Ishii 4.00
DJ1 Derek Jeter 15.00
RJ1 Randy Johnson 6.00
AJ1 Andruw Jones 5.00
CJ1 Chipper Jones 10.00
JK1 Jeff Kent 4.00
GM1 Greg Maddux 10.00
PM1 Pedro J. Martinez 6.00
HN1 Hideo Nomo 5.00
MO1 Magglio Ordonez 4.00
CP1 Corey Patterson 6.00
MP1 Mike Piazza 10.00
MA1 Mark Prior 8.00
AP1 Albert Pujols 15.00
AR1 Alex Rodriguez 10.00
CS1 Curt Schilling 6.00
GS1 Gary Sheffield 6.00
AS1 Alfonso Soriano 8.00
SS1 Sammy Sosa 10.00
IS1 Ichiro Suzuki 10.00
MT1 Miguel Tejada 6.00
JT1 Jim Thome 6.00
BW1 Bernie Williams 5.00
BZ1 Barry Zito 4.00

Game-Used Patch

Production 25 or 10
No pricing due to scarcity.

Swatches

NM/M

Common Player: 4.00
Inserted 1:24

Tier 2: 1-2X
Production 75
RA Roberto Alomar 4.00
PB Pat Burrell 6.00
RC Roger Clemens 10.00
NM Nomar Garciaparra 15.00
NG1 Nomar Garciaparra 4.00
JG Jason Giambi 8.00
TG Troy Glaus 4.00
TG1 Troy Glaus 5.00
TO Tom Glavine 4.00
LG Luis Gonzalez 4.00
KG Ken Griffey Jr. 10.00
VG Vladimir Guerrero 6.00
TH Torii Hunter 5.00
RJ Randy Johnson 6.00
AJ Andruw Jones 5.00
CJ Chipper Jones 8.00
AK Austin Kearns 6.00
GM Greg Maddux 10.00
MM Mickey Mantle 120.00
HM Hideki Matsui 45.00
HM1 Hideki Matsui 4.00
RO Roy Oswalt 4.00
RO1 Roy Oswalt 4.00
MP Mike Piazza 10.00
MA Mark Prior 3.00
AP Albert Pujols 15.00
AR Alex Rodriguez 10.00
CS Curt Schilling 5.00
GS Gary Sheffield 4.00
AS Alfonso Soriano 10.00
AS1 Alfonso Soriano 4.00
SS Sammy Sosa 12.00
IS Ichiro Suzuki 20.00
MT Miguel Tejada 4.00
FT Frank Thomas 6.00
JT Jim Thome 8.00
BW Bernie Williams 4.00
TW Ted Williams 60.00
BZ Barry Zito 4.00

2003 Upper Deck Sweet Spot Classic

NM/M

Complete Set (150):
Common Player: .40
Common Ted Williams (91-120): 5.00
Production 1,941
Common Yankee Heritage (121-150): 2.00
Production 1,500
Pack (4): 12.00
Box (12): 120.00
1 Al Hrabosky .40
2 Al Lopez .40
3 Andre Dawson .75
4 Bill Buckner .40
5 Billy Williams .50
6 Bob Feller .75
7 Bob Lemon .40
8 Bobby Doerr .40
9 Cecil Cooper .40
10 Cal Ripken Jr. 2.50
11 Carlton Fisk .60
12 Jim "Catfish" Hunter .40
13 Chris Chambliss .40
14 Dale Murphy .75
15 Gaylord Perry .40
16 Dave Kingman .40
17 Dave Parker .40
18 Dave Stewart .40
19 David Cone .40
20 Dennis Eckersley .60
21 Don Baylor .40
22 Don Sutton .40
23 Duke Snider 1.00
24 Dwight Evans .40
25 Dwight Gooden .40
26 Earl Weaver .40
27 Early Wynn .40
28 Eddie Mathews 1.50
29 Enos Slaughter .40
30 Ernie Banks 1.50
31 Fred Lynn .40
32 Fred Stanley .40
33 Gary Carter .75
34 George Foster .40
35 Hal Newhouser .40
36 George Kell .40
37 Harmon Killebrew 1.50
38 Hoyt Wilhelm .40
39 Jack Morris .40
40 Jim Bunning .40
41 Jim Gilliam .40
42 Jim Leyritz .40
43 Jimmy Key .40
44 Joe Carter .40
45 Joe Morgan .40
46 John Montefusco .40
47 Johnny Bench 2.00
48 Johnny Podres .40
49 Jose Canseco .75
50 Juan Marichal .40
51 Keith Hernandez .40
52 Ken Griffey Sr. .40
53 Kirby Puckett 1.50
54 Kirk Gibson .40
55 Larry Doby .40
56 Lee May .40
57 Lee Mazzilli .40
58 Lou Boudreau .40
59 Mark McGwire 3.00
60 Maury Wills .40
61 Mike Pagliarulo .40
62 Monte Irvin .75
63 Nolan Ryan 3.00
64 Orlando Cepeda .40
65 Ozzie Smith 1.50
66 Paul O'Neill .40
67 Pee Wee Reese .40
68 Phil Niekro .40
69 Ralph Kiner .40
70 Red Schoendienst .40
71 Richie Ashburn .40
72 Rick Ferrell .40
73 Robin Roberts .40
74 Robin Yount 1.50
75 Hideki Matsui/ 1,999 **RC** 20.00
75 Hideki Matsui/ Red/500 25.00
75 Hideki Matsui/ Blue/250 30.00
75 Hideki Matsui/ Silver/25 200.00
76 Rollie Fingers .40
77 Ron Cey .40
78 Tom Seaver 1.00
79 Sparky Anderson .40
80 Stan Musial 2.00
81 Steve Garvey .40
82 Ted Williams 3.00
83 Tommy Lasorda .40
84 Tony Gwynn 1.00
85 Tony Perez .40
86 Vida Blue .40
87 Warren Spahn .75
88 Bob Gibson 1.00
89 Willie McCovey .40
90 Willie Stargell .75
91-120 Ted Williams 5.00
121 Babe Ruth 8.00
122 Bucky Dent 2.00
123 Casey Stengel 3.00
124 Dave Righetti 2.00
125 Dave Winfield 3.00
126 Dick Tidrow 2.00
127 Dock Ellis 2.00
128 Don Mattingly 8.00
129 Hank Bauer 2.00
130 Jim Bouton 2.00
131 Jim Kaat 2.00
132 Joe DiMaggio 6.00
133 Joe Torre 3.00
134 Lou Piniella 2.00
135 Mel Stottlemyre 2.00
136 Mickey Mantle 15.00
137 Mickey Rivers 2.00
138 Phil Rizzuto 4.00
139 Ralph Branca 2.00
140 Ralph Houk 2.00
141 Roger Maris 6.00
142 Ron Guidry 2.00
143 Ruben Amaro Jr. 2.00
144 Sparky Lyle 2.00
145 Thurman Munson 5.00
146 Tommy Henrich 2.00
147 Tommy John 2.00
148 Tony Kubek 2.00
149 Whitey Ford 4.00
150 Yogi Berra 4.00

Game Jersey

NM/M

Common Player: 5.00
Inserted 1:16
EB Ernie Banks 15.00
JB Johnny Bench 15.00
JC Jose Canseco 6.00
GC Gary Carter 6.00
RC Ron Cey 5.00

CC Cecil Cooper 6.00
AD Andre Dawson 6.00
RF Rollie Fingers 5.00
CF Carlton Fisk 8.00
GF George Foster 5.00
SG Steve Garvey 5.00
JG Jim Gilliam 6.00
TG Tony Gwynn 8.00
HK Harmon Killebrew 12.00
FL Fred Lynn 5.00
LM Lee May 5.00
MM Mark McGwire 30.00
JM Joe Morgan 6.00
DM Dale Murphy 10.00
SM Stan Musial 25.00
DP Dave Parker 5.00
JP Johnny Podres 5.00
KP Kirby Puckett 12.00
CR Cal Ripken Jr. 20.00
NR Nolan Ryan 30.00
OS Ozzie Smith 10.00
DS Duke Snider 12.00
WS Willie Stargell/SP 15.00
TW Ted Williams/SP 100.00
RY Robin Yount 10.00

Greats Autograph

NM/M

Common Autograph:
Blue, Black and Red ink variations exist.
Listings without notations are blue ink.
EB Ernie Banks/Black/73 80.00
DB Don Baylor 25.00
DB Don Baylor/Black/50 35.00
JB Johnny Bench/ Black/73 100.00
BB Bill Buckner 20.00
BB Bill Buckner/Black/85 25.00
GC Gary Carter/ Black/173 40.00
JC Joe Carter/Black/173 35.00
OC Orlando Cepeda 20.00
OC Orlando Cepeda/ Black/34 35.00
AD Andre Dawson 20.00
AD Andre Dawson/ Black/75 30.00
DEc Dennis Eckersley 25.00
DE Dwight Evans 20.00
DE Dwight Evans/ Black/100 30.00
RF Rollie Fingers/ Black/73 30.00
RF Rollie Fingers/Red/25 90.00
CF Carlton Fisk 50.00
GF George Foster/ Black/173 35.00
SG Steve Garvey/ Black/174 30.00
GI Kirk Gibson/ Black/173 30.00
KG Ken Griffey Sr. 20.00
KG Ken Griffey Sr./ Black/100 25.00
TG Tony Gwynn 45.00
TG Tony Gwynn/ Black/101 60.00
KH Keith Hernandez/ Black/173 40.00
KH Keith Hernandez/ Red/25 110.00
AH Al Hrabosky 25.00
AH Al Hrabosky/ Black/100 35.00
HK Harmon Killebrew/ Black/73 80.00
MM Mark McGwire/ Black/73 425.00
JoM Joe Morgan/ Black/169 40.00
JMo Jack Morris/ Black/123 40.00
DM Dale Murphy 30.00
PN Phil Niekro/Black/173 30.00
PN Phil Niekro/Red/25 75.00

DP Dave Parker/ Black/113 30.00
TP Tony Perez/Black/51 65.00
JP Johnny Podres/ Black/173 30.00
JP Johnny Podres/ Red/25 80.00
KP Kirby Puckett 45.00
KP Kirby Puckett/ Black/174 60.00
CR Cal Ripken Jr. 150.00
CR Cal Ripken Jr/ Black/38 250.00
RR Robin Roberts/ Black/173 40.00
TS Tom Seaver/Black/74 80.00
TS Tom Seaver/Red/25 135.00
SN Duke Snider 40.00
SN Duke Snider/ Black/100 50.00
DSt Dave Stewart 15.00
DSu Don Sutton/ Black/123 30.00
AT Alan Trammell/ Black/173 35.00
BW Billy Williams/ Black/173 35.00
TW Ted Williams/9 3,650
MW Maury Wills/ Black/173 30.00
RY Robin Yount/ Black/73 100.00
RY Robin Yount/Red/25 200.00

Patch Logo

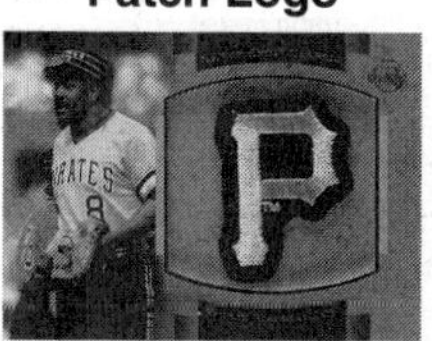

NM/M
Common Player: 5.00
Note: some are actual game-used patches.
EB1 Ernie Banks 12.00
JB1 Johnny Bench 12.00
JB2 Johnny Bench/150 50.00
JB3 Johnny Bench/150 35.00
YB1 Yogi Berra 12.00
YB2 Yogi Berra/350 25.00
YB3 Yogi Berra/150 35.00
JD1 Joe DiMaggio 20.00
JD2 Joe DiMaggio/50 85.00
JD3 Joe DiMaggio/350 30.00
JD4 Joe DiMaggio/150 40.00
CF1 Carlton Fisk 8.00
CF2 Carlton Fisk/150 10.00
GF1 George Foster/350 10.00
GF2 George Foster 5.00
SG1 Steve Garvey 5.00
SG2 Steve Garvey/350 10.00
SG3 Steve Garvey/150 30.00
SG4 Steve Garvey/50 25.00
SG5 Steve Garvey/50 25.00
KG1 Kirk Gibson 5.00
KG2 Kirk Gibson/350 12.00
TG1 Tony Gwynn 8.00
TG2 Tony Gwynn/150 50.00
TG3 Tony Gwynn/350 25.00
CH1 Catfish Hunter/350 10.00
CH2 Catfish Hunter 5.00
CH4 Catfish Hunter/50 30.00
FL1 Fred Lynn 5.00
FL2 Fred Lynn/350 10.00
FL3 Fred Lynn/150 15.00
FL4 Fred Lynn/50 20.00
MM1 Mickey Mantle 35.00
MM2 Mickey Mantle/150 85.00
MM3 Mickey Mantle/150 85.00
MM4 Mickey Mantle/150 75.00
RM1 Roger Maris 15.00
RM2 Roger Maris/350 25.00
RM3 Roger Maris/150 40.00
RM4 Roger Maris/50 60.00
HM1 Hideki Matsui 25.00
MC1 Mark McGwire 20.00
MC2 Mark McGwire/350 50.00
JM1 Joe Morgan 6.00
JM2 Joe Morgan/350 8.00
JM3 Joe Morgan/150 15.00
JM4 Joe Morgan/150 30.00
JM5 Joe Morgan/100 15.00
KP1 Kirby Puckett 10.00
KP2 Kirby Puckett/40 100.00
CR1 Cal Ripken Jr. 25.00
CR2 Cal Ripken Jr/75 100.00
CR3 Cal Ripken Jr./150 50.00
BR1 Babe Ruth/350 40.00
BR2 Babe Ruth 30.00
BR3 Babe Ruth/150 50.00
NR1 Nolan Ryan 25.00
NR2 Nolan Ryan/350 40.00
NR3 Nolan Ryan/150 50.00
NR4 Nolan Ryan/105 100.00
OS1 Ozzie Smith 10.00
OS2 Ozzie Smith/350 20.00
OS3 Ozzie Smith/150 60.00
OS4 Ozzie Smith/100 40.00
OS5 Ozzie Smith/100 35.00
DS1 Duke Snider 8.00
DS2 Duke Snider/150 25.00
DS3 Duke Snider/350 15.00
DS5 Duke Snider/150 20.00
DS6 Duke Snider/150 20.00
WS1 Willie Stargell 5.00
WS2 Willie Stargell/137 50.00
WS3 Willie Stargell/150 25.00
WS4 Willie Stargell/50 40.00
BW1 Billy Williams 6.00
TW1 Ted Williams 20.00
TW2 Ted Williams/350 40.00
RY1 Robin Yount 8.00
RY2 Robin Yount/150 40.00
RY3 Robin Yount/350 20.00

Pinstripes

NM/M
Common Player: 5.00
Inserted 1:40
YB Yogi Berra 15.00
JB Jim Bouton 5.00
DE Bucky Dent 8.00
JD Joe DiMaggio 100.00
DG Dwight Gooden 5.00
MM Mickey Mantle 140.00
DM Don Mattingly 25.00
TM Thurman Munson 30.00
DR Dave Righetti 5.00
PR Phil Rizzuto 15.00
BR Babe Ruth 250.00
CS Casey Stengel 12.00

Yankee Greats Auto.

NM/M
Common Autograph:
RA Ruben Amaro Sr. 25.00
RA Ruben Amaro Sr./ Black/100 30.00
RA Ruben Amaro Sr./ Red/25 60.00
HB Hank Bauer 30.00
HB Hank Bauer/Black/75 40.00
YB Yogi Berra/Black/73 100.00
JB Jim Bouton 25.00
JB Jim Bouton/ Black/100 30.00
RB Ralph Branca 25.00
RB Ralph Branca/ Black/100 30.00
JC Jose Canseco/ Black/73 90.00
JC Jose Canseco/ Red/25 150.00
CC Chris Chambliss 30.00
CC Chris Chambliss/ Black/101 35.00
CC Chris Chambliss/ Red/25 75.00
DC David Cone/Black/74 75.00
DC David Cone/Red/25 110.00
BD Bucky Dent 20.00
JD Joe DiMaggio/5 2,325
DE Dock Ellis/Black/174 25.00
DE Dock Ellis/Red/25 65.00
DG Dwight Gooden/ Black/74 70.00
GU Ron Guidry 35.00
GU Ron Guidry/ Black/100 45.00
TH Tommy Henrich 35.00
TH Tommy Henrich/ Black/100 40.00
TH Tommy Henrich/ Red/25 125.00
RH Ralph Houk 25.00
RH Ralph Houk/ Black/100 30.00
TJ Tommy John 30.00
TJ Tommy John/ Black/100 35.00
JKa Jim Kaat 20.00
JKa Jim Kaat/Black/25 25.00
JKe Jimmy Key 40.00
JKe Jimmy Key/Black/100 50.00
DK Dave Kingman 25.00
DK Dave Kingman/ Black/100 30.00
TK Tony Kubek/ Black/123 15.00
JL Jim Leyritz 25.00
JL Jim Leyritz/Black/100 35.00
JL Jim Leyritz/Red/25 65.00
SL Sparky Lyle 30.00
SL Sparky Lyle/ Black/100 40.00
MM Mickey Mantle/Blue/7 2,850
DM Don Mattingly/ Black/74 100.00
DM Don Mattingly/ Red/25 340.00
LM Lee Mazzilli 30.00
JM John Montefusco 20.00
JM John Montefusco/ Black/100 25.00
JM John Montefusco/ Red/25 50.00
PO Paul O'Neill 50.00
PO Paul O'Neill/ Black/100 65.00
PO Paul O'Neill/Red/25 100.00
MP Mike Pagliarulo 20.00
MP Mike Pagliarulo/ Black/99 25.00
MP Mike Pagliarulo/ Red/25 60.00
LP Lou Piniella 40.00
LP Lou Piniella/ Black/100 45.00
DR Dave Righetti/ Black/173 40.00
DR Dave Righetti/Red/25 85.00
MR Mickey Rivers/ Black/73 40.00
PR Phil Rizzuto/ Black/173 55.00
FS Fred Stanley 25.00
FS Fred Stanley/ Black/101 25.00
MS Mel Stottlemyre/ Black/73 85.00
DT Dick Tidrow 20.00
DT Dick Tidrow/ Black/101 25.00
DT Dick Tidrow/Red/25 70.00
JT Joe Torre/Black/73 60.00
JT Joe Torre/Red/25 140.00
DW Dave Winfield/ Black/25 165.00

2003 Upper Deck Ultimate Collection

NM/M
Complete Set (181):
Common Player (1-84): 2.00
Production 850
Common (85-117): 3.00
Production 625
Common (118-140): 3.00
Production 399
Common (141-158): 4.00
Production 250
Common (159-168): 6.00
Production 100
Common (169-174): 25.00
Common (175-180): 10.00
169-180 Production 250
Pack (4): 90.00
Box (4): 300.00
1 Ichiro Suzuki 8.00
2 Ken Griffey Jr. 6.00
3 Sammy Sosa 6.00
4 Jason Giambi 2.00
5 Mike Piazza 5.00
6 Derek Jeter 10.00
7 Randy Johnson 4.00
8 Barry Bonds 10.00
9 Carlos Delgado 3.00
10 Mark Prior 3.00
11 Vladimir Guerrero 4.00
12 Alfonso Soriano 4.00
13 Jim Thome 4.00
14 Pedro J. Martinez 4.00
15 Nomar Garciaparra 5.00
16 Chipper Jones 4.00
17 Rocco Baldelli 2.00
18 Dontrelle Willis 2.00
19 Garret Anderson 2.00
20 Jeff Bagwell 2.00
21 Jim Edmonds 2.50
22 Rickey Henderson 3.00
23 Torii Hunter 2.50
24 Tom Glavine 2.50
25 Hideo Nomo 2.50
26 Luis Gonzalez 2.50
27 Alex Rodriguez 8.00
28 Albert Pujols 10.00
29 Manny Ramirez 4.00
30 Rafael Palmeiro 3.00
31 Bernie Williams 3.00
32 Curt Schilling 3.00
33 Roger Clemens 8.00
34 Andruw Jones 2.00
35 J.D. Drew 2.00
36 Kerry Wood 3.00
37 Scott Rolen 3.00
38 Darin Erstad 2.00
39 Joe DiMaggio 8.00
40 Magglio Ordonez 2.00
41 Todd Helton 3.00
42 Barry Zito 2.00
43 Mickey Mantle 10.00
44 Miguel Tejada 3.00
45 Troy Glaus 2.00
46 Kazuhisa Ishii 2.00
47 Adam Dunn 3.00
48 Ted Williams 8.00
49 Mike Mussina 3.00
50 Ivan Rodriguez 3.00
51 Jacque Jones 2.00
52 Stan Musial 6.00
53 Mariano Rivera 2.50
54 Larry Walker 2.50
55 Aaron Boone 2.00
56 Hank Blalock 2.50
57 Rich Harden 2.00
58 Lance Berkman 2.00
59 Eric Chavez 2.00
60 Carlos Beltran 3.00
61 Roy Oswalt 2.00
62 Moises Alou 2.00
63 Nolan Ryan 10.00
64 Jeff Kent 2.00
65 Roberto Alomar 2.00
66 Runelvys Hernandez 2.00
67 Roy Halladay 3.00
68 Tim Hudson 2.50
69 Tom Seaver 4.00
70 Edgardo Alfonzo 2.00
71 Andy Pettitte 2.00
72 Preston Wilson 2.00
73 Frank Thomas 3.00
74 Jerome Williams 2.00
75 Shawn Green 2.50
76 David Wells 2.00
77 John Smoltz 2.00
78 Jorge Posada 3.00
79 Marlon Byrd 2.00
80 Austin Kearns 2.00
81 Bret Boone 2.00
82 Rafael Furcal 2.50
83 Jay Gibbons 2.00
84 Shane Reynolds 2.00
85 Nate Bland **RC** 3.00
86 Willie Eyre **RC** 3.00
87 Jeremy Guthrie 3.00
88 Jeremy Wedel **RC** 3.00
89 Jhonny Peralta 6.00
90 Luis Ayala **RC** 3.00
91 Michael Hessman **RC** 3.00
92 Micheal Nakamura **RC** 3.00
93 Nook Logan **RC** 3.00
94 Rett Johnson **RC** 5.00
95 Josh Hall **RC** 4.00
96 Julio Manon **RC** 3.00
97 Heath Bell **RC** 3.00
98 Ian Ferguson **RC** 3.00
99 Jason Gilfillan **RC** 3.00
100 Jason Roach 3.00
101 Jason Shiell **RC** 3.00
102 Terrmel Sledge **RC** 5.00
103 Phil Seibel **RC** 3.00
104 Jeff Duncan **RC** 6.00
105 Mike Neu **RC** 3.00
106 Colin Porter **RC** 3.00
107 Dave Matranga **RC** 3.00
108 Aaron Looper **RC** 3.00
109 Jeremy Bonderman 20.00
110 Miguel Ojeda **RC** 3.00
111 Chad Cordero **RC** 3.00
112 Shane Bazell **RC** 4.00
113 Tim Olson **RC** 5.00
114 Michel Hernandez **RC** 3.00
115 Chien-Ming Wang **RC** 50.00
116 Josh Stewart **RC** 3.00
117 Clint Barmes **RC** 10.00
118 Craig Brazell **RC** 5.00
119 Josh Willingham **RC** 8.00
120 Brent Hoard **RC** 3.00
121 Francisco Rosario **RC** 3.00
122 Rick Roberts **RC** 3.00
123 Geoff Geary **RC** 3.00
124 Edgar Gonzalez **RC** 3.00
125 Kevin Correia **RC** 3.00
126 Ryan Cameron **RC** 3.00
127 Beau Kemp **RC** 3.00
128 Tommy Phelps 3.00
129 Mark Malaska **RC** 3.00
130 Kevin Ohme **RC** 3.00
131 Humberto Quintero **RC** 3.00
132 Aquilino Lopez **RC** 3.00
133 Andrew Brown **RC** 3.00
134 Wilfredo Ledezma **RC** 3.00
135 Luis De Los Santos 3.00
136 Garrett Atkins 3.00
137 Fernando Cabrera **RC** 3.00
138 D.J. Carrasco **RC** 3.00
139 Alfredo Gonzalez **RC** 3.00
140 Alex Prieto **RC** 3.00
141 Matt Kata **RC** 5.00
142 Chris Capuano **RC** 15.00
143 Bobby Madritsch **RC** 20.00
144 Greg Jones **RC** 4.00
145 Pete Zoccolillo **RC** 4.00
146 Chad Gaudin **RC** 10.00
147 Rosman Garcia **RC** 4.00
148 Gerald Laird 4.00
149 Danny Garcia **RC** 4.00
150 Stephen Randolph **RC** 4.00
151 Pete LaForest **RC** 8.00
152 Brian Sweeney **RC** 4.00
153 Aaron Miles **RC** 4.00
154 Jorge DePaula **RC** 4.00
155 Graham Koonce **RC** 10.00
156 Tom Gregorio **RC** 4.00
157 Javier Lopez 4.00
158 Oscar Villarreal **RC** 4.00
159 Prentice Redman **RC** 6.00
160 Francisco Cruceta **RC** 6.00
161 Guillermo Quiroz **RC** 20.00
162 Jeremy Griffiths 10.00
163 Lew Ford **RC** 20.00
164 Rob Hammock **RC** 10.00
165 Todd Wellemeyer **RC** 10.00
166 Ryan Wagner **RC** 10.00
167 Edwin Jackson **RC** 20.00
168 Dan Haren 20.00
169 Hideki Matsui/ Auto. **RC** 275.00
170 Jose Contreras/Auto. 30.00
171 Delmon Young/ Auto. **RC** 275.00
172 Rickie Weeks/ Auto. **RC** 100.00
173 Brandon Webb/ Auto. **RC** 120.00
174 Bo Hart/Auto. **RC** 10.00
175 Rocco Baldelli/Auto. 25.00
176 Jose Reyes/Auto. 30.00
177 Dontrelle Willis/Auto. 40.00
178 Bobby Hill/Auto. 10.00
179 Jae Weong Seo/Auto. 20.00
180 Jesse Foppert/Auto. 20.00
CL Checklist 2.00

Gold

Stars (1-184): 1.5-3X
(85-117): 1-2X
Production 50
(118-140): 1-2X
Production 35
(141-158): 1-2X
Production 25
(159-168): No Pricing
Production 10
(169-180): No Pricing
Production 25

Buybacks

NM/M
Production 1-75
Hank Blalock/35 40.00
Hank Blalock 03 40M/25 40.00
Hank Blalock 03 GF/25 40.00
Hank Blalock 03 Patch/25 40.00
Hank Blalock 03 SPA/20 40.00
Hank Blalock 03 SPA/25 40.00
Hank Blalock 03 VIN/25 40.00
Luis Gonzalez 03 40M HR/25 40.00
Luis Gonzalez 03 SPA/25 40.00
Luis Gonzalez 03 VIN/25 40.00
Ken Griffey Jr. 02-3 SUP/75 80.00
Ken Griffey Jr. 02-3 SUP Spok/50 80.00
Ken Griffey Jr. 03 40M/50 80.00
Ken Griffey Jr. 03 40M/50 80.00
Ken Griffey Jr. 03 40M/50 80.00
Ken Griffey Jr. 03 40M/50 80.00
Ken Griffey Jr. 03 40M T40/50 80.00
Ken Griffey Jr. 03 GF/50 80.00
Ken Griffey Jr. 03 HON/50 80.00
Ken Griffey Jr. 03 HON SP/30 100.00
Ken Griffey Jr. 03 Patch/75 80.00
Ken Griffey Jr. 03 PB/75 80.00
Ken Griffey Jr. 03 SPA/50 80.00
Ken Griffey Jr. 03 SPA/75 80.00
Ken Griffey Jr. 03 SPx/75 80.00
Ken Griffey Jr. 03 SWS/75 80.00
Ken Griffey Jr. 03 UDA/75 80.00
Ken Griffey Jr. 03 VIN/50 80.00
Torii Hunter 03 Patch/25 40.00
Torii Hunter 03 PB/50 30.00
Torii Hunter 03 VIN/25 40.00
Austin Kearns 03 40M/33 30.00
Hideki Matsui 03 40M/20 250.00
Hideki Matsui 03 40M Flag/20 250.00
Hideki Matsui 03 GF/18 250.00
Hideki Matsui 03 PB/17 250.00
Hideki Matsui 03 UD/25 250.00
Hideki Matsui 03 VIN/25 250.00
Stan Musial 02 SPLC/30 75.00
Stan Musial 02 WSH/25 75.00
Stan Musial 03 PB/50 60.00
Stan Musial 03 SWSC/37 75.00
Stan Musial 03 VIN/50 60.00
Sammy Sosa 02-3 SUP/25 120.00
Sammy Sosa 03 PB/25 120.00
Sammy Sosa 03 SPA/25 120.00
Sammy Sosa 03 VIN/25 120.00
Mark Teixeira 03 40M/50 40.00
Mark Teixeira 03 Patch/50 40.00
Mark Teixeira 03 SPA RA/25 50.00
Mark Teixeira 03 SWS/23 50.00
Mark Teixeira 03 UD/25 50.00
Mark Teixeira 03 VIN/25 50.00

Double Barrel

NM/M
No pricing due to scarcity.
DB-AE Darin Erstad, Garret Anderson/3 (3/04 Auction) 645.00
DB-GS Tom Seaver, Tom Glavine/2 (3/04 Auction) 700.00

Game Jersey Tier 1

NM/M
Common Player: 8.00
Production 99 Sets
Copper: No Pricing
Production 10 Sets
Gold: .75-2X
No pricing production of 20 or less.
RB Rocco Baldelli 8.00
PB Pat Burrell 8.00
RC Roger Clemens 20.00
CD Carlos Delgado 10.00
AD Adam Dunn 10.00
JE Jim Edmonds 8.00
RF Rafael Furcal 8.00
JG Jason Giambi 8.00
TR Troy Glaus 10.00
TG Tom Glavine 10.00
SG Shawn Green 8.00
KG Ken Griffey Jr. 20.00
VG Vladimir Guerrero 10.00
TH Torii Hunter 8.00
KI Kazuhisa Ishii 8.00
RJ Randy Johnson 12.00
AJ Andruw Jones 10.00
CJ Chipper Jones 15.00
GM Greg Maddux 15.00
HM Hideki Matsui 50.00
MM Mike Mussina 8.00
HN Hideo Nomo 15.00
MI Mike Piazza 15.00
MP Mark Prior 15.00
AP Albert Pujols 25.00
MR Manny Ramirez 12.00
JR Jose Reyes 10.00
AR Alex Rodriguez 15.00
CS Curt Schilling 10.00
GS Gary Sheffield 8.00
AS Alfonso Soriano 10.00
SS Sammy Sosa 25.00
IS Ichiro Suzuki 50.00
MT Miguel Tejada 10.00
FT Frank Thomas 10.00
JT Jim Thome 10.00
RW Rickie Weeks 15.00
BW Bernie Williams 10.00
DW Dontrelle Willis 10.00
KW Kerry Wood 10.00
DY Delmon Young 15.00
BZ Barry Zito 8.00

Game Jersey Tier 2

Tier 2: 1X Tier 1 Price
Production 75 Sets

Dual Jersey

NM/M

Common Duo: 10.00
Production 50 Sets
Gold: 1-1.25X
Production 25 Sets
AH Alfonso Soriano, Hideki Matsui 40.00
AI Albert Pujols, Ichiro Suzuki 50.00
BK Jeff Kent, Jeff Bagwell 15.00
CA Chipper Jones, Andruw Jones 15.00
CJ Carlos Delgado, Jason Giambi 15.00
DE Jim Edmonds, J.D. Drew 10.00
DG Carlos Delgado, Vladimir Guerrero 15.00
DM Mickey Mantle, Joe DiMaggio 250.00
DP Carlos Delgado, Rafael Palmeiro 15.00
DW Joe DiMaggio, Ted Williams 150.00
GB Shawn Green, Kevin Brown 10.00
GD Adam Dunn, Ken Griffey Jr. 25.00
GE Darin Erstad, Troy Glaus 10.00
GP Rafael Palmeiro, Ken Griffey Jr. 25.00
GR Alex Rodriguez, Nomar Garciaparra 25.00
GS Vladimir Guerrero, Sammy Sosa 25.00
HJ Torii Hunter, Jacque Jones 10.00
HZ Roy Halladay, Barry Zito 10.00
IG Ken Griffey Jr., Ichiro Suzuki 50.00
IN Ichiro Suzuki, Hideo Nomo 50.00
IS Sammy Sosa, Ichiro Suzuki 45.00
JF Andruw Jones, Rafael Furcal 15.00
JM Mike Piazza, Jorge Posada 20.00
MC Greg Maddux, Roger Clemens 30.00
MW Ted Williams, Mickey Mantle 250.00
NI Hideo Nomo, Kazuhisa Ishii 30.00
NM Hideki Matsui, Hideo Nomo 60.00
PC Roger Clemens, Pedro J. Martinez 25.00
PM Mike Mussina, Andy Pettitte 15.00
PS Sammy Sosa, Mark Prior 30.00
RM Pedro J. Martinez, Manny Ramirez 15.00
RP Rafael Palmeiro, Alex Rodriguez 20.00
SA Albert Pujols, Scott Rolen 40.00
SB Alfonso Soriano, Bernie Williams 15.00
SJ Randy Johnson, Curt Schilling 20.00
SM Greg Maddux, John Smoltz 25.00
TB Mark Teixeira, Hank Blalock 15.00
TH Todd Helton, Jim Thome 15.00
TR Alex Rodriguez, Miguel Tejada 20.00
WL Mike Lowell, Dontrelle Willis 15.00
YW Delmon Young, Rickie Weeks 35.00

Game Used Patch

NM/M

Common Player: 15.00
Production 99 Sets
Copper: 1-1.5X
Production 35 Sets
Gold: 1-1.5X
Production 25 Sets
RB Rocco Baldelli 20.00
PB Pat Burrell 20.00
RC Roger Clemens 50.00
CD Carlos Delgado 15.00
AD Adam Dunn 20.00
JE Jim Edmonds 20.00
RF Rafael Furcal 15.00
JG Jason Giambi 20.00
TR Troy Glaus 25.00
TG Tom Glavine 25.00
SG Shawn Green 15.00
KG Ken Griffey Jr. 45.00
VG Vladimir Guerrero 30.00
RH Roy Halladay 20.00
TH Torii Hunter 20.00
KI Kazuhisa Ishii 20.00
RJ Randy Johnson 25.00
AJ Andruw Jones 25.00
CJ Chipper Jones 30.00
GM Greg Maddux 40.00
HM Hideki Matsui 85.00
MM Mike Mussina 25.00
HN Hideo Nomo 40.00
MI Mike Piazza 35.00
MP Mark Prior 30.00
AP Albert Pujols 50.00
MR Manny Ramirez 30.00
JR Jose Reyes 30.00
AR Alex Rodriguez 50.00
CS Curt Schilling 25.00
AS Alfonso Soriano/42 25.00
SS Sammy Sosa 35.00
IS Ichiro Suzuki 75.00
MT Miguel Tejada 25.00
FT Frank Thomas 25.00
JT Jim Thome 30.00
RW Rickie Weeks 25.00
BW Bernie Williams 20.00
DW Dontrelle Willis 30.00
KW Kerry Wood 40.00
DY Delmon Young 35.00
BZ Barry Zito 20.00

Dual Patch

NM/M

Common Duo: 20.00
Production 99 unless noted.
Gold: .75-1.25X
Production 35
AI Ichiro Suzuki, Albert Pujols 100.00
AM Andy Pettitte, Mike Mussina 25.00
BK Jeff Bagwell, Jeff Kent 25.00
CA Andruw Jones, Chipper Jones 30.00
CV Carlos Delgado, Vladimir Guerrero 35.00
DE Jim Edmonds, J.D. Drew 25.00
DG Carlos Delgado, Jason Giambi 25.00
DP Carlos Delgado, Rafael Palmeiro/35 40.00
GB Shawn Green, Kevin Brown 20.00
GD Adam Dunn, Ken Griffey Jr. 45.00
GE Darin Erstad, Troy Glaus 30.00
GP Ken Griffey Jr., Rafael Palmeiro/35 50.00
GR Alex Rodriguez, Nomar Garciaparra 75.00
GS Vladimir Guerrero, Sammy Sosa 40.00
HJ Torii Hunter, Jacque Jones/83 20.00
HZ Roy Halladay, Barry Zito 35.00
IG Ken Griffey Jr., Ichiro Suzuki 90.00
IN Ichiro Suzuki, Hideo Nomo 140.00
IS Sammy Sosa, Ichiro Suzuki 90.00
JF Rafael Furcal, Andruw Jones 25.00
JG John Smoltz, Greg Maddux 40.00
MC Greg Maddux, Roger Clemens/75 60.00
NI Hideo Nomo, Kazuhisa Ishii/63 65.00
NM Hideki Matsui, Hideo Nomo/35 180.00
PM Mike Piazza, Jorge Posada/73 35.00
PR Roger Clemens, Pedro Martinez/35 60.00
PS Sammy Sosa, Mark Prior 40.00
RM Pedro J. Martinez, Manny Ramirez 40.00
RP Rafael Palmeiro, Alex Rodriguez/35 40.00
SA Albert Pujols, Scott Rolen 75.00
SJ Randy Johnson, Curt Schilling 40.00
SM Alfonso Soriano, Hideki Matsui 80.00
TB Mark Teixeira, Hank Blalock 40.00
TH Jim Thome, Todd Helton 35.00
TR Alex Rodriguez, Miguel Tejada 50.00
WL Mike Lowell, Dontrelle Willis/85 35.00
YW Delmon Young, Rickie Weeks/28 75.00

Ultimate Signature Tier 1

NM/M

Common Player: 20.00
AP1 Albert Pujols/40 200.00
AP2 Albert Pujols/35 200.00
AR1 Alex Rodriguez/ 75 EXCH 125.00
AR2 Alex Rodriguez/ 60 EXCH 125.00
BG1 Bob Gibson/299 20.00
BG2 Bob Gibson/199 20.00
CD1 Carlos Delgado/150 20.00
CR1 Cal Ripken Jr./85 150.00
CR2 Cal Ripken Jr./85 150.00
CY1 Carl Yastrzemski/199 65.00
DY1 Delmon Young/300 60.00
DY2 Delmon Young/300 60.00
EG1 Eric Gagne/350 25.00
GC1 Gary Carter/199 20.00
GM1 Greg Maddux/250 60.00
GM2 Greg Maddux/140 80.00
HM1 Hideki Matsui/250 250.00
HM2 Hideki Matsui/240 250.00
IS1 Ichiro Suzuki/199 300.00
IS2 Ichiro Suzuki/99 350.00
JG1 Jason Giambi/35 40.00
JG2 Jason Giambi/35 40.00
KG1 Ken Griffey Jr./350 75.00
KG2 Ken Griffey Jr./350 75.00
KW1 Kerry Wood/170 40.00
KW2 Kerry Wood/85 40.00
MP1 Mark Prior/299 40.00
MP2 Mark Prior/225 40.00
NG1 Nomar Garciaparra/ 125 EXCH 80.00
NG2 Nomar Garciaparra/ 180 80.00
NR1 Nolan Ryan/85 100.00
NR2 Nolan Ryan/75 100.00
OS1 Ozzie Smith/199 50.00
RC1 Roger Clemens/70 125.00
RC2 Roger Clemens/30 150.00
RJ1 Randy Johnson/75 75.00
RJ2 Randy Johnson/50 85.00
RS1 Ryne Sandberg/240 50.00
RS2 Ryne Sandberg/200 50.00
RW1 Rickie Weeks/300 40.00
RW2 Rickie Weeks/300 40.00
TS1 Tom Seaver/75 50.00
TS2 Tom Seaver/60 50.00
VG1 Vladimir Guerrero/75 50.00
VG2 Vladimir Guerrero/50 50.00

Ultimate Signatures Tier 2

NM/M

Production 25 Sets 40.00
GC Gary Carter 50.00
RC Roger Clemens 200.00
CD Carlos Delgado 40.00
EG Eric Gagne 75.00
NG Nomar Garciaparra 120.00
JG Jason Giambi 50.00
BG Bob Gibson 60.00
KG Ken Griffey Jr. 120.00
VG Vladimir Guerrero 90.00
RJ Randy Johnson 100.00
GM Greg Maddux 200.00
HM Hideki Matsui 380.00
MP Mark Prior 80.00
AP Albert Pujols 250.00
CR Cal Ripken Jr. 250.00
AR Alex Rodriguez 200.00
NR Nolan Ryan 165.00
RS Ryne Sandberg 120.00
TS Tom Seaver 65.00
OS Ozzie Smith 100.00
IS Ichiro Suzuki 400.00
RW Rickie Weeks 100.00
KW Kerry Wood 75.00
CY Carl Yastrzemski 125.00
DY Delmon Young 125.00

2003 Upper Deck Victory

NM/M

Complete Set (200): 40.00
Common Player (1-100): .10
Common (101-200): .40
Cards (101-128): Inserted 1:4
(129-168): 1:5
(169-188): 1:10
(189-200): 1:20
Pack (6): .75
Box (36): 20.00

1 Troy Glaus .40
2 Garret Anderson .20
3 Tim Salmon .20
4 Darin Erstad .20
5 Luis Gonzalez .20
6 Curt Schilling .25
7 Randy Johnson .50
8 Junior Spivey .10
9 Andruw Jones .25
10 Greg Maddux .75
11 Chipper Jones .75
12 Gary Sheffield .20
13 John Smoltz .10
14 Geronimo Gil .10
15 Tony Batista .10
16 Trot Nixon .10
17 Manny Ramirez .40
18 Pedro J. Martinez .50
19 Nomar Garciaparra 1.00
20 Derek Lowe .10
21 Shea Hillenbrand .10
22 Sammy Sosa .75
23 Kerry Wood .25
24 Mark Prior .40
25 Magglio Ordonez .20
26 Frank Thomas .40
27 Mark Buehrle .10
28 Paul Konerko .10
29 Adam Dunn .40
30 Ken Griffey Jr. .75
31 Austin Kearns .25
32 Matt Lawton .10
33 Larry Walker .20
34 Todd Helton .25
35 Jeff Bagwell .40
36 Roy Oswalt .20
37 Lance Berkman .25
38 Mike Sweeney .10
39 Carlos Beltran .10
40 Kazuhisa Ishii .10
41 Shawn Green .20
42 Hideo Nomo .25
43 Adrian Beltre .20
44 Richie Sexson .25
45 Ben Sheets .20
46 Torii Hunter .25
47 Jacque Jones .10
48 Corey Koskie .10
49 Vladimir Guerrero .50
50 Jose Vidro .10
51 Mo Vaughn .20
52 Mike Piazza 1.00
53 Roberto Alomar .25
54 Derek Jeter 1.50
55 Alfonso Soriano .75
56 Jason Giambi .75
57 Roger Clemens .75
58 Mike Mussina .25
59 Bernie Williams .25
60 Jorge Posada .20
61 Nick Johnson .10
62 Hideki Matsui **RC** 4.00
63 Eric Chavez .20
64 Barry Zito .20
65 Miguel Tejada .25
66 Tim Hudson .20
67 Pat Burrell .40
68 Bobby Abreu .20
69 Jimmy Rollins .20
70 Brett Myers .10
71 Jim Thome .40
72 Jason Kendall .20
73 Brian Giles .20
74 Aramis Ramirez .10
75 Sean Burroughs .10
76 Ryan Klesko .20
77 Phil Nevin .10
78 Barry Bonds 1.50
79 J.T. Snow .10
80 Rich Aurilia .10
81 Ichiro Suzuki 1.00
82 Edgar Martinez .10
83 Freddy Garcia .10
84 Jim Edmonds .20
85 J.D. Drew .10
86 Scott Rolen .40
87 Albert Pujols .50
88 Mark McGwire 1.25
89 Matt Morris .20
90 Ben Grieve .10
91 Carl Crawford .10
92 Alex Rodriguez 1.25
93 Carl Everett .10
94 Juan Gonzalez .25
95 Rafael Palmeiro .20
96 Hank Blalock .20
97 Carlos Delgado .20
98 Josh Phelps .10
99 Eric Hinske .10
100 Shannon Stewart .10
101 Albert Pujols 1.00
102 Alex Rodriguez 2.50
103 Alfonso Soriano 1.00
104 Barry Bonds 3.00
105 Bernie Williams .50
106 Brian Giles .50
107 Chipper Jones .75
108 Darin Erstad .50
109 Derek Jeter 3.00
110 Eric Chavez .50
111 Miguel Tejada .50
112 Ichiro Suzuki 1.50
113 Rafael Palmeiro .40
114 Jason Giambi 1.50
115 Jeff Bagwell .75
116 Jim Thome .75
117 Ken Griffey Jr. 1.50
118 Lance Berkman .50
119 Luis Gonzalez .40
120 Manny Ramirez .75
121 Mike Piazza 2.00
122 J.D. Drew .40
123 Sammy Sosa 1.50
124 Scott Rolen .75
125 Shawn Green .50
126 Todd Helton .50
127 Troy Glaus .75
128 Vladimir Guerrero 1.00
129 Albert Pujols 1.00
130 Brian Giles .50
131 Carlos Delgado .50
132 Curt Schilling .50
133 Derek Jeter 3.00
134 Frank Thomas .75
135 Greg Maddux 1.50
136 Jeff Bagwell .75
137 Jim Thome .75
138 Jorge Posada .50
139 Kazuhisa Ishii .40
140 Larry Walker .40
141 Luis Gonzalez .40
142 Miguel Tejada .50
143 Pat Burrell .75
144 Pedro J. Martinez 1.00
145 Rafael Palmeiro .50
146 Roger Clemens 1.50
147 Tim Hudson .50
148 Troy Glaus .75
149 Alfonso Soriano 1.00
150 Andruw Jones .50
151 Barry Zito .50
152 Darin Erstad .50
153 Eric Chavez .50
154 Alex Rodriguez 2.50
155 J.D. Drew .40
156 Jason Giambi 1.50
157 Jason Kendall .40
158 Ken Griffey Jr. 1.50
159 Lance Berkman .50
160 Mike Mussina .50
161 Mike Piazza 2.00
162 Nomar Garciaparra 2.00
163 Randy Johnson 1.00
164 Roberto Alomar .50
165 Scott Rolen .75
166 Shawn Green .50
167 Torii Hunter .50
168 Vladimir Guerrero 1.00
169 Alex Rodriguez 2.50
170 Andruw Jones .50
171 Bernie Williams .50
172 Ichiro Suzuki 1.50
173 Miguel Tejada .50
174 Nomar Garciaparra 2.00
175 Pedro J. Martinez 1.00
176 Randy Johnson 1.00
177 Todd Helton .50
178 Vladimir Guerrero 1.00
179 Barry Bonds 3.00
180 Carlos Delgado .50
181 Chipper Jones 1.50
182 Frank Thomas .75
183 Lance Berkman .50
184 Larry Walker .40
185 Manny Ramirez .75
186 Mike Piazza 2.00
187 Sammy Sosa 1.50
188 Shawn Green .50
189 Chipper Jones 1.50
190 Curt Schilling .50
191 Derek Jeter 3.00
192 Ken Griffey Jr. 1.50
193 Sammy Sosa 1.50
194 Vladimir Guerrero 1.00
195 Alex Rodriguez 2.50
196 Barry Bonds 3.00
197 Greg Maddux 1.50
198 Ichiro Suzuki 1.50
199 Jason Giambi 1.50
200 Mike Piazza 2.00

Parallels

Tier 1 Green: 1-2X
Inserted 1:1
Tier 2 Orange: 2-4X
Inserted 1:8
Tier 3 Blue: 3-6X
Production 650
Tier 4 Purple: 10-25X
Production 50 Sets
Tier 5 Red: No Pricing
Production 25 Sets

2003 Upper Deck Vintage

NM/M

Complete Set (280):
Common Player: .15
Common SP (223-232): 1.50
Inserted 1:7
Common SP (233-247): .50
Inserted 1:5
Common 3D SP (248-277): 6.00
Inserted 1:48
Pack (8): 2.00
Box (24): 45.00
1 Troy Glaus .25
2 Darin Erstad .25
3 Garret Anderson .25
4 Jarrod Washburn .15
5 Nolan Ryan 2.00
6 Tim Salmon .25
7 Troy Percival .15
8 Alex Ochoa/SP 4.00
9 Daryle Ward .15
10 Jeff Bagwell .50
11 Roy Oswalt .25
12 Lance Berkman .40
13 Craig Biggio .25
14 Richard Hidalgo .15
15 Tim Hudson .25
16 Eric Chavez .25
17 Barry Zito .25
18 Miguel Tejada .50
19 Mark Mulder .25
20 Rollie Fingers .15
21 Jim "Catfish" Hunter .25
22 Jermaine Dye .15
23 Ray Durham/SP 4.00
24 Carlos Delgado .25
25 Eric Hinske .15
26 Josh Phelps .15
27 Shannon Stewart .15
28 Vernon Wells .15
29 John Smoltz .25
30 Greg Maddux 1.00
31 Chipper Jones .75
32 Gary Sheffield .25
33 Andruw Jones .40
34 Tom Glavine .25
35 Rafael Furcal .15
36 Phil Niekro .15
37 Eddie Mathews .50
38 Robin Yount .75
39 Richie Sexson .25
40 Ben Sheets .15
41 Geoff Jenkins .15
42 Alex Sanchez .15
43 Jason Isringhausen .15
44 Albert Pujols 1.50
45 Matt Morris .15
46 J.D. Drew .25
47 Jim Edmonds .25
48 Stan Musial 1.00
49 Red Schoendienst .15
50 Edgar Renteria .25
51 Mark McGwire/SP 10.00
52 Scott Rolen/SP 5.00
53 Mark Bellhorn .15
54 Kerry Wood .50
55 Mark Prior .50
56 Moises Alou .25
57 Corey Patterson .25
58 Ernie Banks .75
59 Hee Seop Choi .15
60 Billy Williams .15
61 Sammy Sosa/SP 8.00
62 Ben Grieve .15
63 Jared Sandberg .15
64 Carl Crawford .15
65 Randy Johnson .75
66 Luis Gonzalez .25
67 Steve Finley .15
68 Junior Spivey .15
69 Erubiel Durazo .15
70 Curt Schilling/SP 8.00
71 Al Lopez .15
72 Pee Wee Reese .25
73 Eric Gagne .25
74 Shawn Green .25
75 Kevin Brown .15
76 Paul LoDuca .15
77 Adrian Beltre .25
78 Hideo Nomo .40
79 Eric Karros .15
80 Odalis Perez .15
81 Kazuhisa Ishii/SP 5.00
82 Tommy Lasorda .15
83 Fernando Tatis .15
84 Vladimir Guerrero .75

85 Jose Vidro .15
86 Javier Vazquez .15
87 Brad Wilkerson .15
88 Bartolo Colon/SP 4.00
89 Monte Irvin .15
90 Robb Nen .15
91 Reggie Sanders .15
92 Jeff Kent .25
93 Rich Aurilia .15
94 Orlando Cepeda .15
95 Juan Marichal .25
96 Willie McCovey .25
97 David Bell .15
98 Barry Bonds/SP 10.00
99 Kenny Lofton/SP 4.00
100 Jim Thome .50
101 C.C. Sabathia .15
102 Omar Vizquel .25
103 Lou Boudreau .15
104 Larry Doby .25
105 Bob Lemon .15
106 John Olerud .25
107 Edgar Martinez .15
108 Bret Boone .15
109 Freddy Garcia .15
110 Mike Cameron .15
111 Kazuhiro Sasaki .15
112 Ichiro Suzuki/SP 8.00
113 Mike Lowell .15
114 Josh Beckett .25
115 A.J. Burnett .15
116 Juan Pierre .15
117 Derrek Lee .25
118 Luis Castillo .15
119 Juan Encarnacion/SP 4.00
120 Roberto Alomar .40
121 Edgardo Alfonzo .15
122 Jeromy Burnitz .15
123 Mo Vaughn .25
124 Tom Seaver .50
125 Al Leiter .15
126 Mike Piazza/SP 8.00
127 Tony Batista .15
128 Geronimo Gil .15
129 Chris Singleton .15
130 Rodrigo Lopez .15
131 Jay Gibbons .15
132 Melvin Mora .15
133 Earl Weaver .15
134 Trevor Hoffman .15
135 Phil Nevin .15
136 Sean Burroughs .15
137 Ryan Klesko .15
138 Mark Kotsay .15
139 Mike Lieberthal .15
140 Bobby Abreu .25
141 Jimmy Rollins .25
142 Pat Burrell .40
143 Vicente Padilla .15
144 Richie Ashburn .15
145 Jeremy Giambi/SP 4.00
146 Josh Fogg .15
147 Brian Giles .25
148 Aramis Ramirez .25
149 Jason Kendall .15
150 Ralph Kiner .15
151 Willie Stargell .25
152 Kevin Mench .15
153 Rafael Palmeiro .25
154 Ivan Rodriguez .40
155 Hank Blalock .25
156 Juan Gonzalez .40
157 Carl Everett .15
158 Alex Rodriguez/SP 10.00
159 Nomar Garciaparra 1.25
160 Derek Lowe .15
161 Manny Ramirez .50
162 Shea Hillenbrand .25
163 Bobby Doerr .15
164 Johnny Damon .40
165 Jason Varitek .25
166 Pedro Martinez/SP 8.00
167 Cliff Floyd/SP 4.00
168 Ken Griffey Jr. 1.25
169 Adam Dunn .50
170 Austin Kearns .25
171 Aaron Boone .15
172 Joe Morgan .25
173 Sean Casey .15
174 Todd Walker .15
175 Ryan Dempster/SP 4.00
176 Shawn Estes/SP 4.00
177 Gabe Kapler/SP 4.00
178 Jason Jennings .15
179 Todd Helton .40
180 Larry Walker .25
181 Preston Wilson .15
182 Jay Payton/SP 4.00
183 Mike Sweeney .15
184 Carlos Beltran .50
185 Paul Byrd .15
186 Raul Ibanez .15
187 Rick Ferrell .15
188 Early Wynn .15
189 Dmitri Young .15
190 Jim Bunning .15
191 George Kell .15
192 Hal Newhouser .15
193 Bobby Higginson .15
194 Carlos Pena/SP 4.00
195 Sparky Anderson .25
196 Torii Hunter .25
197 Eric Milton .15
198 Corey Koskie .15
199 Jacque Jones .15
200 Harmon Killebrew .50
201 Doug Mientkiewicz .15
202 Frank Thomas .50
203 Mark Buehrle .15
204 Magglio Ordonez .25
205 Paul Konerko .25
206 Joe Borchard .15
207 Hoyt Wilhelm .15
208 Carlos Lee .15
209 Roger Clemens 1.50
210 Nick Johnson .15
211 Jason Giambi .25
212 Alfonso Soriano .75
213 Bernie Williams .40
214 Robin Ventura .15
215 Jorge Posada .25
216 Mike Mussina .40
217 Yogi Berra .75
218 Phil Rizzuto .40
219 Mariano Rivera .25
220 Derek Jeter/SP 12.00
221 Jeff Weaver/SP 4.00
222 Raul Mondesi/SP 4.00
223 Freddy Sanchez, Josh Hancock 2.00
224 Joe Borchard, Miguel Olivo 2.00
225 Brandon Phillips, Josh Bard 1.50
226 Andy Van Hekken, Andres Torres 1.50
227 Jason Lane, Jeriome Robertson 1.50
228 Chin-Feng Chen, Joe Thurston 1.50
229 Endy Chavez, Jamey Carroll 1.50
230 Drew Henson, Alex Graman 2.50
231 Dewon Brazelton, Lance Carter 1.50
232 Jayson Werth, Kevin Cash 1.50
233 Randy Johnson, Curt Schilling, Barry Zito 1.00
234 Pedro J. Martinez, Randy Johnson, Derek Lowe 1.00
235 Randy Johnson, Curt Schilling, Pedro J. Martinez 1.00
236 John Smoltz, Eric Gagne, Mike Williams .50
237 Randy Johnson, Bartolo Colon, A.J. Burnett 1.00
238 Alfonso Soriano, Ichiro Suzuki, Vladimir Guerrero 1.50
239 Alex Rodriguez, Jim Thome, Sammy Sosa 2.00
240 Barry Bonds, Manny Ramirez, Mike Sweeney 2.00
241 Alfonso Soriano, Alex Rodriguez, Derek Jeter 2.00
242 Alex Rodriguez, Magglio Ordonez, Miguel Tejada 2.00
243 Luis Castillo, Juan Pierre, Dave Roberts .50
244 Nomar Garciaparra, Garret Anderson, Alfonso Soriano 1.00
245 Johnny Damon, Jimmy Rollins, Kenny Lofton .50
246 Barry Bonds, Jim Thome, Manny Ramirez 2.00
247 Barry Bonds, Brian Giles, Manny Ramirez 2.00
248 Troy Glaus 10.00
249 Luis Gonzalez 6.00
250 Chipper Jones 15.00
251 Nomar Garciaparra 15.00
252 Manny Ramirez 10.00
253 Sammy Sosa 15.00
254 Frank Thomas 10.00
255 Magglio Ordonez 6.00
256 Adam Dunn 10.00
257 Ken Griffey Jr. 15.00
258 Jim Thome 10.00
259 Todd Helton 8.00
260 Larry Walker 6.00
261 Lance Berkman 6.00
262 Jeff Bagwell 10.00
263 Mike Sweeney 6.00
264 Shawn Green 6.00
265 Vladimir Guerrero 12.00
266 Mike Piazza 15.00
267 Jason Giambi 15.00
268 Pat Burrell 20.00
269 Barry Bonds 15.00
270 Mark McGwire 20.00
271 Alex Rodriguez 15.00
272 Carlos Delgado 6.00
273 Richie Sexson 6.00
274 Andruw Jones 8.00
275 Derek Jeter 20.00
276 Juan Gonzalez 8.00
277 Albert Pujols 12.00
278 Jason Giambi/CL .75
279 Sammy Sosa/CL .75
280 Ichiro Suzuki/CL .75

All Caps

NM/M
Common Player: 8.00
Production 250 Sets
JB Jeff Bagwell 15.00
LB Lance Berkman 8.00
DE Darin Erstad 8.00
RF Rafael Furcal 8.00
JG Juan Gonzalez 10.00
LG Luis Gonzalez 8.00
TG Tony Gwynn 25.00
TH Tim Hudson 10.00
GM Greg Maddux 30.00
RP Rafael Palmeiro 10.00
CP Chan Ho Park 8.00
MP Mike Piazza 35.00
KS Kazuhiro Sasaki 8.00
MV Mo Vaughn 8.00
RV Robin Ventura 8.00

Capping the Action

NM/M
Common Player: 10.00
Quantity produced listed
RA Roberto Alomar/101 20.00
CD Carlos Delgado/91 10.00
JG Juan Gonzalez/99 20.00
SG Shawn Green/125 20.00
KG Ken Griffey Jr./102 40.00
TH Todd Helton/99 20.00
PM Pedro Martinez/125 25.00
MM Mike Mussina/109 40.00
HM Hideo Nomo/117 45.00
RP Rafael Palmeiro/125 20.00
AR Alex Rodriguez/110 25.00
IR Ivan Rodriguez/125 15.00
SR Scott Rolen/109 25.00
AS Alfonso Soriano/109 20.00
SS Sammy Sosa/125 40.00

Crackin the Lumber

NM/M
Production 25
Golds: No Pricing
Production 5
JG Jason Giambi 25.00
IS Ichiro Suzuki 125.00

Crowning Glory

No pricing due to scarcity.
Production 25 Sets

Dropping the Hammer

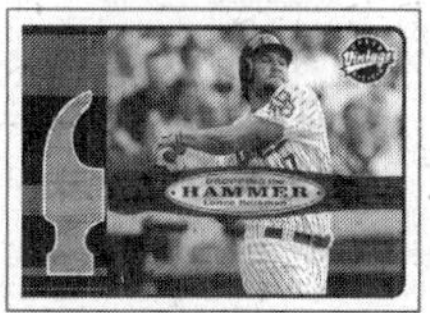

NM/M
Common Player: 6.00
Inserted 1:130
Golds: 1.5-2X
Production 100 Sets
BA Bobby Abreu 8.00
RA Roberto Alomar 10.00
LB Lance Berkman 8.00
RF Rafael Furcal 6.00
JG Jason Giambi 6.00
SG Shawn Green 6.00
KG Ken Griffey Jr. 15.00
TH Todd Helton 8.00
AJ Andruw Jones 8.00
DJ David Justice 8.00
KL Kenny Lofton 6.00
FM Fred McGriff 8.00
MO Magglio Ordonez 6.00
RP Rafael Palmeiro 8.00
MP Mike Piazza 15.00
AR Alex Rodriguez 15.00
SS Sammy Sosa 20.00
TA Fernando Tatis 6.00
MT Miguel Tejada 8.00
FT Frank Thomas 10.00
JT Jim Thome 10.00
RV Robin Ventura 6.00
OV Omar Vizquel 6.00
LW Larry Walker 8.00
PW Preston Wilson 6.00

Men with Hats

NM/M
Common Player: 8.00
Inserted 1:285
VC Vinny Castilla 8.00
EC Eric Chavez 10.00
JD Johnny Damon 15.00
AD Adam Dunn 15.00
JG Jason Giambi 8.00
TH Todd Helton 10.00
HU Tim Hudson 10.00
AJ Andruw Jones 10.00
JK Jason Kendall 8.00
KL Kenny Lofton 8.00
AR Alex Rodriguez 20.00
MT Miguel Tejada 12.00
FT Frank Thomas 12.00
TW Todd Walker 8.00
BW Bernie Williams 10.00

Slugfest

NM/M
Common Player: 8.00
Production 200 Sets
Golds: 1.5-2.5X
Production 50 Sets
CD Carlos Delgado 8.00
SG Shawn Green 8.00
AJ Andruw Jones 8.00
RP Rafael Palmeiro 8.00
MP Mike Piazza 20.00
AR Alex Rodriguez 15.00
FT Frank Thomas 10.00
JT Jim Thome 10.00
LW Larry Walker 8.00
BW Bernie Williams 10.00

Timeless Teams Bat

NM/M
Common Card: 20.00
Production 175 Sets
BLAR Pat Burrell, Mike Lieberthal, Bobby Abreu, Jimmy Rollins 25.00
CTDJ Eric Chavez, Miguel Tejada, Jermaine Dye, David Justice 25.00
DEMR J.D. Drew, Jim Edmonds, Tino Martinez, Scott Rolen 40.00
DGCL Adam Dunn, Ken Griffey Jr., Sean Casey, Barry Larkin 40.00
GNBL Shawn Green, Hideo Nomo, Adrian Beltre, Paul LoDuca 40.00
GPMS Jason Giambi, Jorge Posada, Raul Mondesi, Alfonso Soriano 30.00
GWVS Jason Giambi, Bernie Williams, Robin Ventura, Alfonso Soriano 40.00
HWPZ Todd Helton, Larry Walker, Juan Pierre, Todd Zeile 25.00
IMBC Ichiro Suzuki, Edgar Martinez, Bret Boone, Mike Cameron 90.00
JGSW Randy Johnson, Luis Gonzalez, Curt Schilling, Matt Williams 40.00
JJSF Chipper Jones, Andruw Jones, Gary Sheffield, Rafael Furcal 40.00
KNKB Ryan Klesko, Phil Nevin, Mark Kotsay, Sean Burroughs 20.00
MGLJ Greg Maddux, Tom Glavine, Javy Lopez, Chipper Jones 40.00
OTLK Magglio Ordonez, Frank Thomas, Carlos Lee, Paul Konerko 30.00
PVAA Mike Piazza, Mo Vaughn, Roberto Alomar, Edgardo Alfonzo 40.00
RGRP Alex Rodriguez, Juan Gonzalez, Ivan Rodriguez, Rafael Palmeiro 40.00
RMHN Manny Ramirez, Pedro J. Martinez, Shea Hillenbrand, Trot Nixon 30.00
SMAP Sammy Sosa, Fred McGriff, Moises Alou, Corey Patterson 40.00

UD Giants

NM/M
Complete Set (42): 45.00
Common Player: .75
Inserted 1:Box
RA Roberto Alomar 1.00
JB Jeff Bagwell 1.00
LB Lance Berkman 1.00
BB Barry Bonds 4.00
PB Pat Burrell 1.00
RC Roger Clemens 4.00
CD Carlos Delgado .75
JD J.D. Drew .75
AD Adam Dunn 1.50
NG Nomar Garciaparra 3.00
JG Jason Giambi .75
BG Brian Giles .75
GO Juan Gonzalez 1.00
LG Luis Gonzalez .75
SG Shawn Green .75
KG Ken Griffey Jr. 3.00
VG Vladimir Guerrero 1.50
TH Todd Helton 1.00
KI Kazuhisa Ishii .75
RJ Randy Johnson 1.50
AJ Andruw Jones 1.00
CJ Chipper Jones 2.50
GM Greg Maddux 2.50
PM Pedro J. Martinez 1.50
MM Mike Mussina 1.00
HN Hideo Nomo 1.00
MO Magglio Ordonez .75
RP Rafael Palmeiro 1.00
MP Mike Piazza 3.00
PR Mark Prior 1.00
AP Albert Pujols 4.00
MR Manny Ramirez 1.50
AR Alex Rodriguez 4.00
IR Ivan Rodriguez 1.50
SR Scott Rolen 1.50
CS Curt Schilling 1.50
SS Sammy Sosa 2.50
IS Ichiro Suzuki 3.00
FT Frank Thomas 1.00
JT Jim Thome 1.50
BW Bernie Williams 1.00
KW Kerry Wood 1.50

Vintage Hitmen

NM/M
Production 150 Sets
Golds: Not Priced
Production 10 Sets
JG Jason Giambi 10.00
KG Ken Griffey Jr. 30.00
MM Mark McGwire 60.00
IS Ichiro Suzuki 60.00

Vintage Hitmen Double Signed

NM/M
Production 75
Gold: Not Priced
Production 5
MS Mark McGwire, Sammy Sosa 600.00

2003 UD Yankees Signature Series

NM/M
Complete Set (90): 65.00
Common Player: .50
Pack (3): 17.00
Box (10): 140.00
1 Al Downing .50
2 Allen Gettel .50
3 Art Ditmar .50
4 Babe Ruth 6.00
5 Bill Virdon .50
6 Billy Martin 2.00
7 Bob Cerv .50
8 Bob Turley .50
9 Bobby Cox .75
10 Bobby Richardson 1.00
11 Bobby Shantz .50
12 Bucky Dent .75
13 Bud Metheny .50
14 Casey Stengel 2.00
15 Charlie Hayes .50
16 Charlie Silvera .50
17 Chris Chambliss .50
18 Danny Cater .50
19 Dave Kingman .75
20 Dave Righetti .75
21 Dave Winfield 2.00
22 David Cone .75
23 Dick Tidrow .50
24 Doc Medich .50
25 Dock Ellis .50
26 Don Gullett .50
27 Don Mattingly 5.00
28 Dwight Gooden .75
29 Eddie Robinson .50
30 Felipe Alou .50
31 Fred Sanford .50
32 Fred Stanley .50
33 Gene Michael .50
34 Hank Bauer .50
35 Hector Lopez .50
36 Horace Clarke .50
37 Jake Gibbs .50
38 Jerry Coleman .50
39 Jerry Lumpe .50
40 Jim Bouton .50
41 Jim Kaat 1.00
42 Jim Mason .50
43 Jimmy Key .50
44 Joe DiMaggio 5.00
45 Joe Torre 1.00
46 John Montefusco .50
47 Johnny Blanchard .50
48 Johnny Callison .50
49 Lew Burdette .50
50 Johnny Kucks .50
51 Steve Balboni .50
52 Ken Singleton .50
53 Lee Mazzilli .50
54 Lou Gehrig 5.00
55 Lou Piniella 1.00
56 Luis Tiant .50
57 Marius Russo .50
58 Mel Stottlemyre .75
59 Mickey Mantle 6.00
60 Mike Pagliarulo .50
61 Mike Torrez .50
62 Miller Huggins .50
63 Norm Siebern .50
64 Paul O'Neill .75
65 Phil Niekro .50
66 Phil Rizzuto 3.00
67 Ralph Branca .50
68 Ralph Houk .50
69 Ralph Terry .50
70 Randy Gumpert .50
71 Roger Maris 5.00
72 Ron Blomberg .50
73 Ron Guidry 1.00
74 Ruben Amaro .50
75 Ryne Duren .50
76 Sam McDowell .50
77 Sparky Lyle .50
78 Thurman Munson 3.00
79 Tom Sturdivant .50
80 Tom Tresh .50
81 Tommy Byrne .50
82 Tommy Henrich .50
83 Tommy John .75
84 Tony Kubek .75
85 Tony Lazzeri .50
86 Virgil Trucks .50
87 Wade Boggs 1.00
88 Whitey Ford 3.00
89 Willie Randolph .75
90 Yogi Berra 3.00

Monumental Cuts

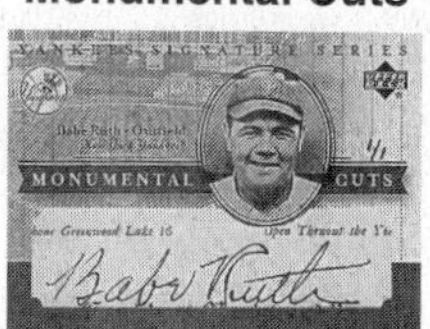

NM/M
30 total cards produced:
MC-LG Lou Gehrig/1 (6/03 Auction) 17,600
MC-MM Mickey Mantle/1 (1/04 Auction) 10,000
MC-BM Billy Martin/9 825.00
MC-TM Thurman Munson/1 (3/04 Auction) 2,605
MC-BR Babe Ruth/1 (4/04 Auction) 12,600

Pinstripe Excell. Dual

NM/M

Common Dual Autograph: 20.00
Production 125 Sets

AA	Felipe Alou, Ruben Amaro	50.00
BA	Hank Bauer, Felipe Alou	50.00
BP	Wade Boggs, Mike Pagliarulo	60.00
BT	Jim Bouton, Ralph Terry	50.00
CK	Chris Chambliss, Dave Kingman	60.00
DC	Bucky Dent, Chris Chambliss	50.00
DR	Bucky Dent, Willie Randolph	80.00
DS	Ryne Duren, Tom Sturdivant	35.00
FB	Whitey Ford, Yogi Berra	150.00
GB	Jake Gibbs, Johnny Blanchard	40.00
GM	Ron Guidry, John Montefusco	80.00
GR	Ron Guidry, Willie Randolph	80.00
JK	Tommy John, Jim Kaat	60.00
LG	Sparky Lyle, Ron Guidry	75.00
LM	Jerry Lumpe, Jim Mason	25.00
MC	John Montefusco, Chris Chambliss	60.00
MK	Gene Michael, Tony Kubek	60.00
ML	Sam McDowell, Sparky Lyle	50.00
MR	Don Mattingly, Dave Righetti	150.00
NT	Phil Niekro, Luis Tiant	50.00
RB	Bobby Richardson, Hank Bauer	75.00
RC	Bobby Richardson, Jerry Coleman	50.00
SC	Ken Singleton, Jerry Coleman	60.00
ST	Tom Sturdivant, Bob Turley	40.00
TK	Luis Tiant, Jim Kaat	60.00
TM	Mike Torrez, Lee Mazzilli	50.00
BRi	Hank Bauer, Phil Rizzuto	75.00
BRu	Tommy Byrne, Marius Russo	30.00

Pride of New York Auto.

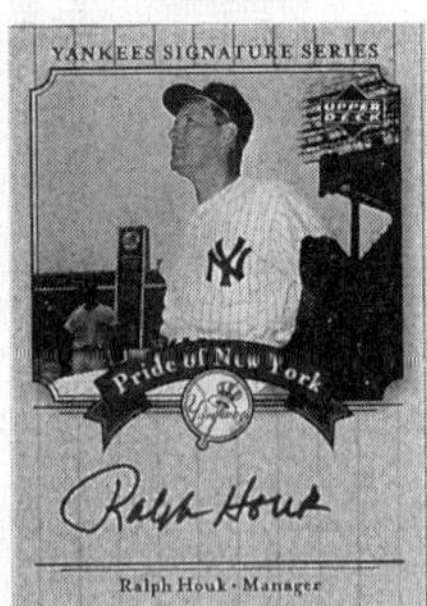

NM/M

Common Autograph: 8.00
Inserted 1:1

JA	Jason Alexander/SP	600.00
FA	Felipe Alou	15.00
RA	Ruben Amaro	8.00
SB	Steve Balboni	8.00
HB	Hank Bauer	10.00
YB	Yogi Berra	85.00
JB	Johnny Blanchard	15.00
RBl	Ron Blomberg	10.00
WB	Wade Boggs	40.00
JB	Jim Bouton	10.00
RBr	Ralph Branca	8.00
LB	Lew Burdette	10.00
TB	Tommy Byrne	10.00
CAS	Johnny Callison	8.00
TC	Tom Carroll	8.00
CAL	Brian Cashman/SP	250.00
DC	Danny Cater	8.00
CE	Bob Cerv	8.00
CC	Chris Chambliss	12.00
HC	Horace Clarke	10.00
JC	Jerry Coleman	10.00
CO	David Cone	25.00
CX	Bobby Cox	12.00
DE	Bucky Dent	12.00
DI	Art Ditmar	10.00
AD	Al Downing	8.00
BD	Brian Doyle	8.00
RD	Ryne Duren	10.00
EL	Dock Ellis	10.00
WF	Whitey Ford	50.00
AG	Allen Gettel	8.00
JG	Jake Gibbs	8.00
GO	Dwight Gooden	15.00
JO	John Goodman	300.00
RaG	Ron Guidry	15.00
DG	Don Gullett	8.00
RoG	Randy Gumpert	8.00
CH	Charlie Hayes	10.00
TH	Tommy Henrich	30.00
RH	Ralph Houk	12.00
TJ	Tommy John	10.00
JK	Jim Kaat	15.00
KE	Jimmy Key	15.00
DK	Dave Kingman	15.00
TK	Tony Kubek	25.00
KU	Johnny Kucks	10.00
HL	Hector Lopez	10.00
JL	Jerry Lumpe	8.00
SL	Sparky Lyle	10.00
JM	Jim Mason	8.00
MA	Don Mattingly	80.00
LM	Lee Mazzilli	10.00
SM	Sam McDowell	8.00
DM	Doc Medich	8.00
GM	Gene Michael	10.00
MO	John Montefusco	8.00
PN	Phil Niekro	15.00
PO	Paul O'Neill/SP	25.00
MP	Mike Pagliarulo	8.00
LP	Lou Piniella/SP	20.00
WR	Willie Randolph/SP	15.00
HR	Hal Reniff	10.00
BR	Bobby Richardson	15.00
DR	Dave Righetti	15.00
PR	Phil Rizzuto	40.00
ER	Eddie Robinson	8.00
MR	Marius Russo	10.00
FS	Fred Sanford	8.00
BS	Bobby Shantz	10.00
NS	Norm Siebern	8.00
CS	Charlie Silvera	10.00
KS	Ken Singleton	10.00
ST	Fred Stanley	8.00
MS	Mel Stottlemyre	15.00
TS	Tom Sturdivant	8.00
RT	Ralph Terry	10.00
LT	Luis Tiant	10.00
DT	Dick Tidrow	10.00
JT	Joe Torre	35.00
MT	Mike Torrez	8.00
TT	Tom Tresh	15.00
VT	Virgil Trucks	10.00
BT	Bob Turley	12.00
BV	Bill Virdon	8.00
DW	Dave Winfield/SP	75.00
JW	Jim Wynn	8.00
DZ	Don Zimmer	40.00

Yankees Forever Triple

NM/M

Common Triple Auto.:
Production 50 Sets

ALB	Felipe Alou, Hector Lopez, Hank Bauer	120.00
AOM	Felipe Alou, Paul O'Neill, Lee Mazzilli	150.00
BSB	Yogi Berra, Bobby Shantz, Hank Bauer	200.00
DFB	Al Downing, Whitey Ford, Yogi Berra	240.00
DRC	Bucky Dent, Willie Randolph, Chris Chambliss	125.00
EMG	Dock Ellis, Doc Medich, Don Gullett	125.00
FKB	Whitey Ford, Johnny Kucks, Jim Bouton	150.00
GCK	Dwight Gooden, David Cone, Jimmy Key	150.00
GRJ	Ron Guidry, Dave Righetti, Tommy John	150.00
HMC	Ralph Houk, Gene Michael, Bobby Cox	120.00
HRB	Tommy Henrich, Phil Rizzuto, Ralph Branca	150.00
JKL	Tommy John, Jim Kaat, Sparky Lyle	120.00
KCC	Dave Kingman, Chris Chambliss, Danny Cater	120.00
KGT	Jim Kaat, Don Gullett, Mike Torrez	120.00
KJB	Jim Kaat, Tommy John, Jim Bouton	120.00
MTT	John Montefusco, Mike Torrez, Dick Tidrow	120.00
OBK	Paul O'Neill, Wade Boggs, Jimmy Key	175.00
PTV	Lou Piniella, Joe Torre, Bill Virdon	150.00
RBC	Phil Rizzuto, Yogi Berra, Jerry Coleman	220.00
RKD	Phil Rizzuto, Tony Kubek, Bucky Dent	150.00
RRC	Bobby Richardson, Willie Randolph, Jerry Coleman	150.00
RSB	Marius Russo, Tom Sturdivant, Tommy Byrne	120.00
SSB	Fred Stanley, Charlie Silvera, Johnny Blanchard	120.00
STE	Mel Stottlemyre, Luis Tiant, Dock Ellis	120.00
TCO	Joe Torre, David Cone, Paul O'Neill	175.00
TLN	Luis Tiant, Sparky Lyle, Phil Niekro	120.00
TMT	Luis Tiant, Sam McDowell, Ralph Terry	120.00
WHM	Dave Winfield, Tommy Henrich, Lee Mazzilli	160.00
WMG	Dave Winfield, Don Mattingly, Ron Guidry	300.00
WPC	Dave Winfield, Lou Piniella, Chris Chambliss	100.00

Yankees 100th Anniversary

NM/M

Complete Set (30): 15.00
Common Player: .50

1	Babe Ruth	2.00
2	Tony Lazzeri	.50
3	Lou Gehrig	1.50
4	Lou Gehrig	1.50
5	Red Rolfe	.50
6	Lou Gehrig	1.50
7	Bill Dickey	.50
8	Joe DiMaggio	1.50
9	Charlie Keller	.50
10	Frank Crosetti	.50
11	Phil Rizzuto	.50
12	Joe DiMaggio	1.50
13	Joe DiMaggio	1.50
14	Phil Rizzuto	.50
15	Mickey Mantle	2.00
16	Yogi Berra	.75
17	Yogi Berra	.75
18	Mickey Mantle	2.00
19	Whitey Ford	.50
20	Mickey Mantle	2.00
21	Thurman Munson	.75
22	Thurman Munson	.75
23	Bernie Williams	.50
24	Jorge Posada	.50
25	Mariano Rivera	.50
26	Derek Jeter	1.50
27	Hideki Matsui	1.00
28	Hideki Matsui	1.00
29	Roger Clemens	1.50
30	Yankee Stadium	.50

2003 Upper Deck 40-Man Sample

A different front photo and a large black "SAMPLE" on back distinguish the promo card for UD's large set.

NM/M

KG	Ken Griffey Jr.	3.00

2003 Upper Deck 40-Man

NM/M

Complete Set (990): 200.00
Common Player: .25
Common Rk (877-960): .40
Pack (10): 2.00
Box (24): 35.00

1	Troy Glaus	.50
2	Darin Erstad	.40
3	Garret Anderson	.50
4	Aaron Sele	.25
5	Adam Kennedy	.25
6	Scott Spiezio	.25
7	Troy Percival	.25
8	David Eckstein	.25
9	Ramon Ortiz	.25
10	Bengie Molina	.25
11	Tim Salmon	.50
12	John Lackey	.25
13	Brad Fullmer	.25
14	Jarrod Washburn	.25
15	Shawn Wooten	.25
16	Kevin Appier	.25
17	Ben Weber	.25
18	Eric Owens	.25
19	Matt Wise	.25
20	Francisco Rodriguez	.25
21	Scot Shields	.25
22	Jose Molina	.25
23	Scott Schoeneweis	.25
24	Derrick Turnbow	.25
25	Benji Gil	.25
26	Julio Ramirez	.25
27	Mickey Callaway	.25
28	Barry Zito	.50
29	Tim Hudson	.50
30	Mark Mulder	.40
31	Eric Chavez	.40
32	Miguel Tejada	.50
33	Terrence Long	.25
34	Jermaine Dye	.25
35	Erubiel Durazo	.25
36	Scott Hatteberg	.25
37	Chris Singleton	.25
38	Keith Foulke	.25
39	John Halama	.25
40	Mark Ellis	.25
41	Ted Lilly	.25
42	Jim Mecir	.25
43	Adam Piatt	.25
44	Freddie Bynum	.25
45	Adam Morrissey	.25
46	Jeremy Fikac	.25
47	Ricardo Rincon	.25
48	Ramon Hernandez	.25
49	Micah Bowie	.25
50	Chad Bradford	.25
51	Eric Byrnes	.25
52	Ron Gant	.25
53	Jose Flores	.25
54	Mark Johnson	.25
55	Carlos Delgado	.75
56	Orlando Hudson	.25
57	Kelvim Escobar	.25
58	Eric Hinske	.25
59	Doug Creek	.25
60	Josh Phelps	.25
61	Shannon Stewart	.40
62	Roy Halladay	.40
63	Vernon Wells	.40
64	Mark Henrickson	.25
65	Mike Bordick	.25
66	Jayson Werth	.25
67	Chris Woodward	.25
68	Ken Huckaby	.25
69	Frank Catalanotto	.25
70	Jason Kershner	.25
71	Greg Myers	.25
72	Tanyon Sturtze	.25
73	Trever Miller	.25
74	Pete Walker	.25
75	Alexis Rios	.25
76	Tom Wilson	.25
77	Dave Berg	.25
78	Doug Linton	.25
79	Cliff Politte	.25
80	Damion Easley	.25
81	Toby Hall	.25
82	George Lombard	.25
83	Ben Grieve	.25
84	Aubrey Huff	.25
85	Jesus Colome	.25
86	Dewon Brazelton	.25
87	Rey Ordonez	.25
88	Al Martin	.25
89	Carl Crawford	.25
90	Travis Lee	.25
91	Marlon Anderson	.25
92	Javier Valentin	.25
93	Joe Kennedy	.25
94	Jorge Sosa	.25
95	Travis Harper	.25
96	Bobby Seay	.25
97	Seth McClung	.25
98	Delvin James	.25
99	Victor Zambrano	.25
100	Terry Shumpert	.25
101	Josh Hamilton	.50
102	Jared Sandberg	.25
103	Steve Parris	.25
104	C.C. Sabathia	.25
105	Omar Vizquel	.40
106	Milton Bradley	.25
107	Ellis Burks	.25
108	Danys Baez	.25
109	Jason Davis	.25
110	Terry Mulholland	.25
111	Matt Lawton	.25
112	Alex Escobar	.25
113	Mark Wohlers	.25
114	Josh Bard	.25
115	Bill Selby	.25
116	Brandon Phillips	.25
117	Jason Bere	.25
118	Casey Blake	.25
119	Travis Hafner	.25
120	Brian Anderson	.25
121	David Riske	.25
122	Karim Garcia	.25
123	Ricardo Rodriguez	.25
124	Carl Sadler	.25
125	Jose Santiago	.25
126	Tim Laker	.25
127	John McDonald	.25
128	Jake Westbrook	.25
129	Ichiro Suzuki	1.00
130	Freddy Garcia	.25
131	Edgar Martinez	.40
132	Ben Davis	.25
133	Shigetoshi Hasegawa	.25
134	Carlos Guillen	.25
135	Randy Winn	.25
136	John Mabry	.25
137	Matt Thornton	.25
138	Bret Boone	.40
139	Jamie Moyer	.25
140	Giovanni Carrara	.25
141	Kazuhiro Sasaki	.25
142	Jeff Cirillo	.25
143	Mark McLemore	.25
144	Pat Borders	.25
145	Mike Cameron	.25
146	Dan Wilson	.25
147	John Olerud	.40
148	Arthur Rhodes	.25
149	Rafael Soriano	.25
150	Greg Colbrunn	.25
151	Ryan Franklin	.25
152	Joel Pineiro	.25
153	Jeff Nelson	.25
154	Jerry Hairston	.25
155	Rick Helling	.25
156	Gary Matthews Jr.	.25
157	Jeff Conine	.25
158	Sidney Ponson	.25
159	Tony Batista	.25
160	Jay Gibbons	.40
161	Marty Cordova	.25
162	Geronimo Gil	.25
163	Deivi Cruz	.25
164	B.J. Ryan	.25
165	Jason Johnson	.25
166	Buddy Groom	.25
167	Pat Hentgen	.25
168	Omar Daal	.25
169	Willis Roberts	.25
170	Scott Erickson	.25
171	David Segui	.25
172	Brook Fordyce	.25
173	Rodrigo Lopez	.25
174	Jose Leon	.25
175	Jose Morban	.25
176	Melvin Mora	.25
177	B.J. Surhoff	.25
178	Jorge Julio	.25
179	Alex Rodriguez	2.00
180	Mark Teixeira	.40
181	Chan Ho Park	.25
182	Todd Van Poppel	.25
183	Todd Greene	.25
184	Ismael Valdes	.25
185	Rusty Greer	.25
186	Rafael Palmeiro	.50
187	Francisco Cordero	.25
188	Einar Diaz	.25
189	Doug Glanville	.25
190	Michael Young	.25
191	Kevin Mench	.25
192	Carl Everett	.25
193	Herbert Perry	.25
194	Jeff Zimmerman	.25
195	Juan Gonzalez	.50
196	Ugueth Urbina	.25
197	Jermaine Clark	.25
198	John Thomson	.25
199	Hank Blalock	.50
200	Jay Powell	.25
201	Mike Lamb	.25
202	Aaron Fultz	.25
203	Esteban Yan	.25
204	Nomar Garciaparra	2.00
205	Pedro J. Martinez	.75
206	John Burkett	.25
207	Johnny Damon	.40
208	Doug Mirabelli	.25
209	Derek Lowe	.25
210	Shea Hillenbrand	.25
211	Brandon Lyon	.25
212	Trot Nixon	.25
213	Jason Varitek	.25
214	Tim Wakefield	.25
215	Manny Ramirez	.75
216	Todd Walker	.25
217	Jeremy Giambi	.25
218	Ramiro Mendoza	.25
219	Bill Mueller	.25
220	David Ortiz	.25
221	Mike Timlin	.25
222	Alan Embree	.25
223	Bob Howry	.25
224	Chad Fox	.25
225	Damian Jackson	.25
226	Casey Fossum	.25
227	Steve Woodard	.25
228	Freddy Sanchez	.25
229	Mike Sweeney	.25
230	Desi Relaford	.25
231	Brent Mayne	.25
232	Angel Berroa	.25
233	Albie Lopez	.25
234	Raul Ibanez	.25
235	Joe Randa	.25
236	Chris George	.25
237	Michael Tucker	.25
238	Mendy Lopez	.25
239	Kris Wilson	.25
240	Jason Grimsley	.25
241	Carlos Febles	.25
242	Runelvys Hernandez	.25
243	Mike MacDougal	.25
244	Carlos Beltran	.40
245	Brandon Berger	.25
246	Darrell May	.25
247	Miguel Asencio	.25
248	Ryan Bukvich	.25
249	Dee Brown	.25
250	Jeremy Hill	.25
251	Jeremy Affeldt	.25
252	Ken Harvey	.25
253	Bobby Higginson	.25
254	Matt Anderson	.25
255	Dmitri Young	.25
256	Gene Kingsdale	.25
257	Craig Paquette	.25
258	Adam Bernero	.25
259	Andres Torres	.25
260	Carlos Pena	.25
261	Dean Palmer	.25
262	Eric Munson	.25
263	Omar Infante	.25
264	Shane Halter	.25
265	Jeremy Bonderman	2.00
266	Steve Sparks	.25
267	Gary Knotts	.25
268	Mike Maroth	.25
269	Nate Cornejo	.25
270	Matt Roney	.25
271	Franklyn German	.25
272	Matt Walbeck	.25
273	Brandon Inge	.25
274	Hiram Bocachica	.25
275	Chris Spurling	.25
276	Craig Monroe	.25
277	Ramon Santiago	.25
278	Doug Mientkiewicz	.25
279	Torii Hunter	.50
280	Brad Radke	.25
281	Denny Hocking	.25
282	Tom Prince	.25
283	Eddie Guardado	.25
284	Jacque Jones	.25
285	Joe Mays	.25
286	Mike Fetters	.25
287	LaTroy Hawkins	.25
288	A.J. Pierzynski	.25
289	Eric Milton	.25
290	Cristian Guzman	.25
291	Bobby Kielty	.25
292	Corey Koskie	.25
293	J.C. Romero	.25
294	Mike Cuddyer	.25
295	Luis Rivas	.25
296	Matt LeCroy	.25
297	Tony Fiore	.25
298	Dustan Mohr	.25
299	Chris Gomez	.25
300	Johan Santana	.25
301	Kyle Lohse	.25
302	Frank Thomas	.75
303	Mark Buehrle	.25
304	Jon Garland	.25
305	Magglio Ordonez	.50
306	Paul Konerko	.25
307	Sandy Alomar Jr.	.25
308	Carlos Lee	.25
309	Jon Rauch	.25
310	Esteban Loaiza	.25
311	Gary Glover	.25
312	Kelly Wunsch	.25
313	Tony Graffanino	.25
314	Aaron Rowand	.25
315	Armando Rios	.25
316	Jose Valentin	.25
317	D'Angelo Jimenez	.25
318	Joe Crede	.25
319	Miguel Olivo	.25
320	Rick White	.25
321	Billy Koch	.25
322	Tom Gordon	.25
323	Bartolo Colon	.40
324	Josh Paul	.25
325	Joe Borchard	.25
326	Damaso Marte	.25
327	Derek Jeter	2.00
328	Jason Giambi	.75
329	Roger Clemens	2.00
330	Enrique Wilson	.25
331	Dave Wells	.25
332	Mike Mussina	.50
333	Bernie Williams	.50
334	Todd Zeile	.25
335	Sterling Hitchcock	.25
336	Juan Acevedo	.25
337	Robin Ventura	.25
338	Mariano Rivera	.40
339	John Flaherty	.25
340	Andy Pettitte	.50
341	Antonio Osuna	.25
342	Erick Almonte	.25
343	Chris Hammond	.25
344	Steve Karsay	.25
345	Alfonso Soriano	1.00
346	Bubba Trammell	.25
347	Nick Johnson	.25
348	Jorge Posada	.50
349	Jeff Weaver	.25
350	Raul Mondesi	.25
351	Randy Choate	.25
352	Drew Henson	.25
353	Jeff Bagwell	.75
354	Wade Miller	.25
355	Lance Berkman	.40

356 Julio Lugo .25
357 Roy Oswalt .40
358 Bruce Chen .25
359 Morgan Ensberg .25
360 Geoff Blum .25
361 Brian Moehler .25
362 Billy Wagner .40
363 Peter Munro .25
364 Brad Ausmus .25
365 Jose Vizcaino .25
366 Craig Biggio .40
367 Tim Redding .25
368 Gregg Zaun .25
369 Octavio Dotel .25
370 Carlos Hernandez .25
371 Richard Hidalgo .25
372 Jeriome Robertson .25
373 Orlando Merced .25
374 John Buck .25
375 Adam Everett .25
376 Raul Chavez .25
377 Brad Lidge .25
378 Jeff Kent .40
379 Scott Linebrink .25
380 Greg Miller .25
381 Kirk Saarloos .25
382 Brandon Puffer .25
383 Ricky Stone .25
384 Jason Lane .25
385 Brian L. Hunter .25
386 Rodrigo Rosario .25
387 Horacio Ramirez .25
388 Gary Sheffield .50
389 Mike Hampton .25
390 Robert Fick .25
391 Henry Blanco .25
392 Vinny Castilla .25
393 Joe Dawley .25
394 Jung Bong .25
395 Rafael Furcal .40
396 Javy Lopez .40
397 Greg Maddux 1.25
398 Andruw Jones .50
399 John Smoltz .40
400 Chipper Jones 1.00
401 Mark DeRosa .25
402 Shane Reynolds .25
403 Kevin Gryboski .25
404 Russ Ortiz .25
405 Roberto Hernandez .25
406 Ray King .25
407 Matt Franco .25
408 Marcus Giles .25
409 Trey Hodges .25
410 Darren Holmes .25
411 Julio Franco .25
412 Darren Bragg .25
413 Richie Sexson .50
414 Jeffrey Hammonds .25
415 Ben Sheets .25
416 Mike DeJean .25
417 Royce Clayton .25
418 Wes Helms .25
419 Valerio de los Santos .25
420 Brady Clark .25
421 Glendon Rusch .25
422 Geoff Jenkins .40
423 John Foster .25
424 Curtis Leskanic .25
425 Todd Ritchie .25
426 Enrique Cruz .25
427 Wayne Franklin .25
428 Matt Ford .25
429 Matt Kinney .25
430 Scott Podsednik 2.00
431 Luis Vizcaino .25
432 Shane Nance .25
433 Alex Sanchez .25
434 John Vander Wal .25
435 Eric Young .25
436 Eddie Perez .25
437 Jason Conti .25
438 Matt Morris .25
439 Tino Martinez .25
440 Fernando Vina .25
441 Kiko Calero .25
442 Cal Eldred .25
443 Jimmy Journell .25
444 Jim Edmonds .40
445 Jeff Fassero .25
446 Mike Matheny .25
447 Garrett Stephenson .25
448 Brett Tomko .25
449 So Taguchi .25
450 Eduardo Perez .25
451 Lance Painter .25
452 Jason Isringhausen .25
453 Albert Pujols 2.00
454 Eli Marrero .25
455 Jason Simontacchi .25
456 J.D. Drew .25
457 Scott Rolen .75
458 Orlando Palmeiro .25
459 Dustin Hermanson .25
460 Edgar Renteria .25
461 Woody Williams .25
462 Chris Carpenter .25
463 Sammy Sosa 1.50
464 Kerry Wood .75
465 Kyle Farnsworth .25
466 Alex Gonzalez .25
467 Eric Karros .25
468 Troy O'Leary .25
469 Mark Grudzielanek .25
470 Alan Benes .25
471 Mark Prior 1.50
472 Paul Bako .25
473 Shawn Estes .25
474 Matt Clement .25
475 Ramon Martinez .25
476 Tom Goodwin .25
477 Corey Patterson .25
478 Moises Alou .40
479 Juan Cruz .25
480 Bobby Hill .25
481 Mark Bellhorn .25
482 Mark Guthrie .25
483 Mike Remlinger .25
484 Lenny Harris .25
485 Antonio Alfonseca .25
486 Dave Veres .25
487 Hee Seop Choi .25
488 Luis Gonzalez .40
489 Lyle Overbay .25
490 Randy Johnson .75
491 Mark Grace .50
492 Danny Bautista .25
493 Junior Spivey .25
494 Matt Williams .25
495 Miguel Batista .25
496 Tony Womack .25
497 Byung-Hyun Kim .25
498 Steve Finley .25
499 Craig Counsell .25
500 Curt Schilling .50
501 Elmer Dessens .25
502 Rod Barajas .25
503 David Dellucci .25
504 Mike Koplove .25
505 Mike Myers .25
506 Matt Mantei .25
507 Stephen Randolph **RC** .40
508 Chad Moeller .25
509 Carlos Baerga .25
510 Andrew Good .25
511 Quinton McCracken .25
512 Jason Romano .25
513 Jolbert Cabrera .25
514 Darren Dreifort .25
515 Kevin Brown .40
516 Paul Quantrill .25
517 Shawn Green .40
518 Hideo Nomo .40
519 Eric Gagne .25
520 Troy Brohawn .25
521 Kazuhisa Ishii .25
522 Guillermo Mota .25
523 Alex Cora .25
524 Odalis Perez .25
525 Brian Jordan .25
526 Andy Ashby .25
527 Fred McGriff .40
528 Adrian Beltre .40
529 Daryle Ward .25
530 Todd Hundley .25
531 David Ross .25
532 Paul Shuey .25
533 Paul LoDuca .25
534 Dave Roberts .25
535 Mike Kinkade .25
536 Cesar Izturis .25
537 Ron Coomer .25
538 Jose Vidro .25
539 Henry Mateo .25
540 Tony Armas Jr. .25
541 Joey Eischen .25
542 Orlando Cabrera .25
543 Jose Macias .25
544 Fernando Tatis .25
545 Jeff Liefer .25
546 Michael Barrett .25
547 Vladimir Guerrero .75
548 Javier Vazquez .25
549 Brad Wilkerson .25
550 Zach Day .25
551 Tomokazu Ohka .25
552 Livan Hernandez .25
553 Endy Chavez .25
554 Dan Smith .25
555 Scott Stewart .25
556 T.J. Tucker .25
557 Jamey Carroll .25
558 Ron Calloway .25
559 Brian Schneider .25
560 Orlando Hernandez .25
561 Wil Cordero .25
562 Rocky Biddle .25
563 Edgardo Alfonzo .25
564 Andres Galarraga .25
565 Felix Rodriguez .25
566 Benito Santiago .25
567 Jose Cruz .25
568 Tim Worrell .25
569 Marvin Benard .25
570 Kurt Ainsworth .25
571 Jim Brower .25
572 J.T. Snow .25
573 Scott Eyre .25
574 Robb Nen .25
575 Barry Bonds 2.50
576 Ray Durham .25
577 Marquis Grissom .25
578 Pedro Feliz .25
579 Jason Schmidt .25
580 Rich Aurilia .25
581 Kirk Rueter .25
582 Chad Zerbe .25
583 Damian Moss .25
584 Neifi Perez .25
585 Joe Nathan .25
586 Ruben Rivera .25
587 Yorvit Torrealba .25
588 Josh Beckett .50
589 Todd Hollandsworth .25
590 Derrek Lee .25
591 A.J. Burnett .25
592 Juan Pierre .25
593 Mark Redman .25
594 Blaine Neal .25
595 Mike Mordecai .25
596 Alex Gonzalez .25
597 Brad Penny .25
598 Tim Spooneybarger .25
599 Mike Lowell .25
600 Mike Redmond .25
601 Braden Looper .25
602 Ivan Rodriguez .50
603 Andy Fox .25
604 Vladimir Nunez .25
605 Luis Castillo .25
606 Juan Encarnacion .25
607 Armando Almanza .25
608 Gerald Williams .25
609 Carl Pavano .25
610 Michael Tejera .25
611 Ramon Castro .25
612 Brian Banks .25
613 Roberto Alomar .50
614 Al Leiter .25
615 Jeromy Burnitz .25
616 John Franco .25
617 Tom Glavine .40
618 Mike Piazza 1.00
619 Cliff Floyd .25
620 Joe McEwing .25
621 David Weathers .25
622 Pedro Astacio .25
623 Timoniel Perez .25
624 Jason Phillips .25
625 Ty Wigginton .25
626 Steve Trachsel .25
627 Roger Cedeno .25
628 Tsuyoshi Shinjo .25
629 Armando Benitez .25
630 Vance Wilson .25
631 Mike Stanton .25
632 Mo Vaughn .25
633 Scott Strickland .25
634 Rey Sanchez .25
635 Jay Bell .25
636 David Cone .25
637 Jae Weong So .25
638 Ryan Klesko .40
639 Wiki Gonzalez .25
640 Trevor Hoffman .25
641 Sean Burroughs .25
642 Mike Bynum .25
643 Clay Condrey .25
644 Gary Bennett .25
645 Kevin Jarvis .25
646 Mark Kotsay .25
647 Phil Nevin .25
648 Dave Hansen .25
649 Keith Lockhart .25
650 Brian Lawrence .25
651 Jay Witasick .25
652 Rondell White .25
653 Jaret Wright .25
654 Luther Hackman .25
655 Jake Peavy .25
656 Brian Buchanan .25
657 Mark Loretta .25
658 Oliver Perez .25
659 Adam Eaton .25
660 Xavier Nady .25
661 Jesse Orosco .25
662 Ramon Vazquez .25
663 Jim Thome .75
664 Jose Mesa .25
665 Rheal Cormier .25
666 David Bell .25
667 Mike Lieberthal .25
668 Brandon Duckworth .25
669 David Coggin .25
670 Bobby Abreu .40
671 Turk Wendell .25
672 Marlon Byrd .25
673 Jason Michaels .25
674 Kevin Millwood .40
675 Tomas Perez .25
676 Jimmy Rollins .50
677 Vicente Padilla .25
678 Pat Burrell .50
679 Tyler Houston .25
680 Hector Mercado .25
681 Carlos Silva .25
682 Nick Punto .25
683 Ricky Ledee .25
684 Randy Wolf .25
685 Todd Pratt .25
686 Placido Polanco .25
687 Chase Utley .25
688 Brian Giles .25
689 Jason Kendall .40
690 Matt Stairs .25
691 Kris Benson .25
692 Julian Tavarez .25
693 Reggie Sanders .25
694 Jeff D'Amico .25
695 Pokey Reese .25
696 Kenny Lofton .25
697 Mike Williams .25
698 David Williams .25
699 Kevin Young .25
700 Brian Boehringer .25
701 Scott Sauerbeck .25
702 Josh Fogg .25
703 Joe Beimel .25
704 Dennys Reyes .25
705 Jeff Suppan .25
706 Solomon Torres .25
707 Kip Wells .25
708 Craig Wilson .25
709 Jack Wilson .25
710 Robert Mackowiak .25
711 Abraham Nunez .25
712 Randall Simon .25
713 Josias Manzanillo .25
714 Ken Griffey Jr. 1.00
715 Jimmy Haynes .25
716 Felipe Lopez .25
717 Jimmy Anderson .25
718 Ryan Dempster .25
719 Russell Branyan .25
720 Aaron Boone .25
721 Luke Prokopec .25
722 Felix Heredia .25
723 Scott Sullivan .25
724 Danny Graves .25
725 Kent Mercker .25
726 Barry Larkin .40
727 Jason LaRue .25
728 Gabe White .25
729 Adam Dunn .50
730 Brandon Larson .25
731 Reggie Taylor .25
732 Sean Casey .25
733 Scott Williamson .25
734 Austin Kearns .50
735 Kelly Stinnett .25
736 Ruben Mateo .25
737 Wily Mo Pena .25
738 Larry Walker .40
439 Juan Uribe .25
740 Denny Neagle .25
741 Darren Oliver .25
742 Charles Johnson .25
743 Todd Jones .25
744 Todd Helton .75
745 Shawn Chacon .25
746 Jason Jennings .25
747 Preston Wilson .25
748 Chris Richard .25
749 Chris Stynes .25
750 Jose Jimenez .25
751 Gabe Kapler .25
752 Jay Payton .25
753 Aaron Cook .25
754 Greg Norton .25
755 Scott Elarton .25
756 Brian Fuentes .25
757 Jose Hernandez .25
758 Nelson Cruz .25
759 Justin Speier .25
760 Javier Lopez .40
761 Garret Anderson .40
762 Tony Batista .25
763 Mark Buehrle .25
764 Johnny Damon .40
765 Freddy Garcia .25
766 Nomar Garciaparra .75
767 Jason Giambi .50
768 Roy Halladay .25
769 Shea Hillenbrand .25
770 Torii Hunter .40
771 Derek Jeter 1.00
772 Paul Konerko .25
773 Derek Lowe .25
774 Pedro J. Martinez .50
775 A.J. Pierzynski .25
776 Jorge Posada .40
777 Manny Ramirez .40
778 Mariano Rivera .25
779 Alex Rodriguez 1.00
780 Kazuhiro Sasaki .25
781 Alfonso Soriano .50
782 Ichiro Suzuki .50
783 Mike Sweeney .25
784 Miguel Tejada .40
785 Ugueth Urbina .25
786 Robin Ventura .25
787 Omar Vizquel .25
788 Randy Winn .25
789 Barry Zito .40
790 Lance Berkman .25
791 Barry Bonds 1.00
792 Adam Dunn .40
793 Tom Glavine .25
794 Luis Gonzalez .25
795 Shawn Green .25
796 Vladimir Guerrero .40
797 Todd Helton .40
798 Trevor Hoffman .25
799 Randy Johnson .50
800 Andruw Jones .40
801 Byung-Hyun Kim .25
802 Mike Lowell .25
803 Eric Gagne .25
804 Matt Morris .25
805 Robb Nen .25
806 Vicente Padilla .25
807 Odalis Perez .25
808 Mike Piazza .50
809 Mike Remlinger .25
810 Scott Rolen .40
811 Jimmy Rollins .50
812 Benito Santiago .25
813 Curt Schilling .40
814 Richie Sexson .40
815 John Smoltz .25
816 Sammy Sosa .75
817 Junior Spivey .25
818 Jose Vidro .25
819 Mike Williams .25
820 Luis Castillo .25
821 Jason Giambi .40
822 Luis Gonzalez .25
823 Sammy Sosa .75
824 Ken Griffey Jr. .75
825 Ken Griffey Jr. .75
826 Tino Martinez .25
827 Barry Bonds 1.00
828 Frank Thomas .40
829 Ken Griffey Jr. .75
830 Barry Bonds 1.00
831 Tim Salmon .25
832 Troy Glaus .25
833 Robb Nen .25
834 Jeff Kent .25
835 Scott Spiezio .25
836 Darin Erstad .25
837 Randy Johnson .50
838 Chipper Jones .50
839 Greg Maddux .75
840 Nomar Garciaparra .75
841 Manny Ramirez .40
842 Pedro J. Martinez .50
843 Sammy Sosa .75
844 Ken Griffey Jr. .75
845 Jim Thome .40
846 Vladimir Guerrero .50
847 Mike Piazza .50
848 Derek Jeter 1.00
849 Jason Giambi .40
850 Roger Clemens 1.00
851 Alfonso Soriano .50
852 Hideki Matsui 4.00
853 Barry Bonds 1.00
854 Ichiro Suzuki .50
855 Albert Pujols .75
856 Alex Rodriguez .75
857 Darin Erstad .25
858 Troy Glaus .25
859 Curt Schilling .25
860 Luis Gonzalez .25
861 Tom Glavine .25
862 Andruw Jones .40
863 Gary Sheffield .25
864 Frank Thomas .40
865 Mark Prior 1.00
866 Ivan Rodriguez .40
867 Jeff Bagwell .40
868 Lance Berkman .25
869 Shawn Green .25
870 Hideo Nomo .40
871 Torii Hunter .25
872 Bernie Williams .25
873 Barry Zito .25
874 Pat Burrell .25
875 Carlos Delgado .25
876 Miguel Tejada .25
877 Hideki Matsui **RC** 4.00
878 Jose Contreras **RC** 2.00
879 Jason Anderson .40
880 Jason Shiell **RC** .40
881 Kevin Tolar **RC** .40
882 Michel Hernandez **RC** .40
883 Arnie Munoz **RC** .40
884 David Sanders **RC** .40
885 Willie Eyre **RC** .40
886 Brent Hoard **RC** .40
887 Lew Ford **RC** 2.00
888 Beau Kemp **RC** .75
889 Jonathan Pridie **RC** .40
890 Mike Ryan **RC** .40
891 Richard Fischer **RC** .40
892 Luis Ayala **RC** .40
893 Mike Neu **RC** .40
894 Joe Valentine **RC** .40
895 Nate Bland **RC** .40
896 Shane Bazzell **RC** .75
897 Aquilino Lopez **RC** .40
898 Diegomar Markwell **RC** .40
899 Francisco Rosario **RC** .40
900 Guillermo Quiroz **RC** .75
901 Luis De Los Santos .40
902 Fernando Cabrera **RC** .40
903 Francisco Cruceta **RC** .40
904 Jhonny Peralta .50
905 Rett Johnson **RC** .50
906 Aaron Looper **RC** .40
907 Bobby Madritsch **RC** .40
908 Luis Matos .25
909 Jose Castillo .25
910 Chris Waters **RC** .40
911 Jeremy Guthrie .25
912 Pedro Liriano .25
913 Joe Borowski .25
914 Felix Sanchez **RC** .40
915 Jon Leicester **RC** .40
916 Todd Wellemeyer **RC** .75
917 Matt Bruback **RC** .25
918 Chris Capuano **RC** 1.50
919 Oscar Villarreal **RC** .25
920 Matt Kata **RC** .75
921 Robby Hammock **RC** .75
922 Gerald Laird .25
923 Brandon Webb **RC** 3.00
924 Tommy Whiteman **RC** .40
925 Andrew Brown **RC** .40
926 Alfredo Gonzalez **RC** .40
927 Carlos Rivera .25
928 Rick Roberts **RC** .40
929 Terrmel Sledge **RC** .40
930 Josh Willingham **RC** .40
931 Prentice Redman **RC** .50
932 Jeff Duncan **RC** 1.50
933 Craig Brazell **RC** 1.00
934 Jeremy Griffiths .25
935 Phil Seibel **RC** .40
936 Heath Bell **RC** .40
937 Bernie Castro **RC** .40
938 Mike Nicolas **RC** .40
939 Cory Stewart **RC** .40
940 Shane Victorino **RC** .40
941 Brandon Villafuerte **RC** .40
942 Jeremy Wedel **RC** .40
943 Tommy Phelps .25
944 Josh Hall **RC** .75
945 Ryan Cameron **RC** .40
946 Garrett Atkins .25
947 Clint Barmes **RC** .75
948 Michael Hessman **RC** .40
949 Brian Stokes **RC** .40
950 Rocco Baldelli 1.00
951 Hector Luna .25
952 Jaime Cerda .25
953 D.J. Carrasco **RC** .40
954 Ian Ferguson **RC** .40
955 Tim Olson **RC** .75
956 Alejandro Machado **RC** .40
957 Jorge Cordova **RC** .40
958 Wilfredo Ledezma **RC** .40
959 Nathan Robertson **RC** .40
960 Nook Logan **RC** .40
961 Anaheim Angels .25
962 Baltimore Orioles .25
963 Boston Red Sox .25
964 Chicago White Sox .25
965 Cleveland Indians .25
966 Detroit Tigers .25
967 Kansas City Royals .25
968 Minnesota Twins .25
969 New York Yankees .25
970 Oakland Athletics .25
971 Seattle Mariners .25
972 Tampa Bay Devil Rays .25
973 Texas Rangers .25
974 Toronto Blue Jays .25
975 Arizona Diamondbacks .25
976 Atlanta Braves .25
977 Chicago Cubs .25
978 Cincinnati Reds .25
979 Colorado Rockies .25
980 Florida Marlins .25
981 Houston Astros .25
982 Los Angeles Dodgers .25
983 Milwaukee Brewers .25
984 Montreal Expos .25
985 New York Mets .25
986 Philadelphia Phillies .25
987 Pittsburgh Pirates .25
988 San Diego Padres .25
989 San Francisco Giants .25
990 St. Louis Cardinals .25

Rainbow

Stars (1-990): 10-20X
Rookies: 4-8X
Production 40 Sets

Red, White & Blue

Stars (1-990): 1-30X
Rookies: 1-2X
#'s 1-752 Inserted 1:6
#'s 877-960 1:36

Endorsements

NM/M

Inserted 1:500
Some not priced due to scarcity.
RA Rick Ankiel 20.00
DB Dewon Brazelton/50 15.00
BD Ben Diggins 15.00
AG Alex Graman/50 15.00
KGS Ken Griffey Sr. 15.00
HI Hansel Izquierdo/50 15.00
JL Jon Lieber 15.00
CM Corwin Malone/50 15.00
TO Tomokazu Ohka 20.00

Vintage Update

NM/M

Complete Set (61): 15.00
Common Player: .40
Inserted 1:Pack
281 Tom Glavine 1.00
282 Josh Stewart .40
283 Aquilino Lopez .40
284 Horacio Ramirez .40
285 Brandon Phillips .40
286 Kirk Saarloos .40
287 Runelvys Hernandez .40
288 Hideki Matsui 5.00
289 Jeremy Bonderman 3.00
290 Russ Ortiz .40
291 Ken Harvey .40
292 Edgardo Alfonzo .40
293 Oscar Villarreal .40
294 Marlon Byrd .40
295 Josh Bard .40
296 David Cone .40
297 Mike Neu .40
298 Cliff Floyd .40
299 Travis Lee .40
300 Jeff Kent .50
301 Ron Calloway .40
302 Bartolo Colon .40
303 Jose Contreras 1.50
304 Mark Teixeira 1.00
305 Ivan Rodriguez 1.00
306 Jim Thome 1.00
307 Shane Reynolds .40
308 Luis Ayala .40
309 Lyle Overbay .40
310 Travis Hafner .40
311 Wilfredo Ledezma .40
312 Rocco Baldelli 1.50
313 Jason Anderson .40
314 Kenny Lofton .75
315 Brandon Larson .40
316 Ty Wigginton .40
317 Fred McGriff .40
318 Antonio Osuna .40
319 Corey Patterson .40
320 Erubiel Durazo .40

321 Mike MacDougal .40
322 Sammy Sosa 2.00
323 Mike Hampton .40
324 Ramiro Mendoza .40
325 Kevin Millwood .75
326 Dave Roberts .40
327 Todd Zeile .40
328 Reggie Sanders .40
329 Billy Koch .40
330 Mike Stanton .40
331 Orlando Hernandez .40
332 Tony Clark .40
333 Chris Hammond .40
334 Michael Cuddyer .40
335 Sandy Alomar .40
336 Jose Cruz Jr. .40
337 Omar Daal .40
338 Robert Fick .40
339 Daryle Ward .40
340 David Bell .40
341 Checklist .40

Post MVP Action

Half a dozen former MVPs are featured in this cereal-box insert set. Cards have 3-D game-action sequences on front. Backs have another (regular) player photo along with personal data and stats. The cards were issued two per cello pack in special two-box packages of Post cereals.

NM/M
Complete Set (6): 4.00
Common Player: .50
1 Barry Bonds .75
2 Miguel Tejada .50
3 Ichiro 1.00
4 Ken Griffey Jr. .75
5 Jason Giambi .50
6 Sammy Sosa .75

Post Redemption

This set of 31 cards was only available via a mail-in redemption offer. Collectors who assembled all six CD-Roms six CD-Roms from Post cereal boxes could find a coded number to order the set. Fronts are white-bordered with an action photo and player name, position and team logo. Backs have a portrait photo, uniform number, personal data, 2002 and career stats, a UD hologram and logos of the sponsors and licensors. Cards are printed on extra-thick stock.

NM/M
Complete Set (31): 15.00
Common Player: .50
1 Troy Percival .50
2 Curt Schilling .65
3 John Smoltz .50
4 Tony Batista .50
5 Pedro Martinez .75
6 Sammy Sosa 1.00
7 Paul Konerko .50
8 Ken Griffey Jr. 1.00
9 Jim Thome .50
10 Larry Walker .50
11 Bobby Higginson .50
12 Luis Castillo .50
13 Craig Biggio .50
14 Mike Sweeney .50
15 Shawn Green .60
16 Richie Sexson .50
17 Torii Hunter .00
18 Vladimir Guerrero .75
19 Mike Piazza 1.50
20 Jason Giambi .60
21 Miguel Tejada .60
22 Pat Burrell .50
23 Brian Giles .50
24 Trevor Hoffman .50
25 Barry Bonds 2.00
26 Ichiro 2.00
27 Albert Pujols 2.00
28 Randy Winn .50
29 Alex Rodriguez 1.50
30 Carlos Delgado .50
31 Troy Glaus .75

SSS Puerto Rico

To commemorate the historic "home" games of the Montreal Expos at San Juan, P.R., the SSS Group health care plan sponsored an uncut sheet featuring Latin players from the Expos and among the five teams which visited the island during the season. Sheets measure 7-1/2" x 10-1/2". Individual cards are UV-coated, silver-foil highlighted and feature color poses or action photos. Back of the sheet has a ghost-image action photo of Jose Vidro overprinted with advertising for the sponsor. Licensor logos also appear.

NM/M
Uncut Sheet: 10.00
Complete Set (9): 10.00
Common Player: 1.00
(1) Roberto Alomar 1.00
(2) Juan Gonzalez 1.50
(3) Alex Rodriguez 3.00
(4) Ivan Rodriguez 1.50
(5) Sammy Sosa 3.00
(6) Jose Vidro 1.00
(7) Javier Vazquez 1.00
(8) Javy Lopez 1.00
(9) Sponsor's Logo .10

2004 Upper Deck

NM/M
Complete Set (540): 75.00
Common Player: .15
Hobby Pack (8): 2.00
Hobby Box (24): 40.00
1 Dontrelle Willis .40
2 Edgar Gonzalez .15
3 Jose Reyes .50
4 Jae Weong Seo .15
5 Miguel Cabrera .25
6 Jesse Foppert .15
7 Mike Neu .15
8 Micheal Nakamura .15
9 Luis Ayala .15
10 Jared Sandberg .15
11 Jhonny Peralta .15
12 Wilfredo Ledezma .15
13 Jason Roach .15
14 Kirk Saarloos .15
15 Cliff Lee .15
16 Bobby Hill .15
17 Lyle Overbay .15
18 Josh Hall .15
19 Joe Thurston .15
20 Matt Kata .15
21 Jeremy Bonderman .15
22 Julio Manon .15
23 Rodrigo Rosario .15
24 Robby Hammock .15
25 David Sanders .15
26 Miguel Ojeda .15
27 Mark Teixeira .25
28 Franklyn German .15
29 Ken Harvey .15
30 Xavier Nady .15
31 Tim Salmon .25
32 Troy Glaus .40
33 Adam Kennedy .15
34 David Eckstein .15
35 Bengie Molina .15
36 Jarrod Washburn .15
37 Ramon Ortiz .15
38 Eric Chavez .25
39 Miguel Tejada .25
40 Chris Singleton .15
41 Jermaine Dye .15
42 John Halama .15
43 Tim Hudson .40
44 Barry Zito .40
45 Ted Lilly .15
46 Bobby Kielty .15
47 Kelvim Escobar .15
48 Josh Phelps .15
49 Vernon Wells .25
50 Roy Halladay .25
51 Orlando Hudson .15
52 Eric Hinske .15
53 Brandon Backe .15
54 Dewon Brazelton .15
55 Ben Grieve .15
56 Aubrey Huff .15
57 Toby Hall .15
58 Rocco Baldelli .40
59 Al Martin .15
60 Brandon Phillips .15
61 Omar Vizquel .25
62 C.C. Sabathia .15
63 Milton Bradley .15
64 Ricky Gutierrez .15
65 Matt Lawton .15
66 Danys Baez .15
67 Ichiro Suzuki 1.00
68 Randy Winn .15
69 Carlos Guillen .15
70 Mark McLemore .15
71 Dan Wilson .15
72 Jamie Moyer .15
73 Joel Pineiro .15
74 Edgar Martinez .25
75 Tony Batista .15
76 Jay Gibbons .15
77 Jeff Conine .15
78 Melvin Mora .15
79 Geronimo Gil .15
80 Rodrigo Lopez .15
81 Jorge Julio .15
82 Rafael Palmeiro .50
83 Juan Gonzalez .40
84 Mike Young .15
85 Alex Rodriguez 1.50
86 Einar Diaz .15
87 Kevin Mench .15
88 Hank Blalock .40
89 Pedro J. Martinez .75
90 Byung-Hyun Kim .15
91 Derek Lowe .25
92 Jason Varitek .15
93 Manny Ramirez .50
94 John Burkett .15
95 Todd Walker .15
96 Nomar Garciaparra 1.50
97 Trot Nixon .15
98 Mike Sweeney .15
99 Carlos Febles .15
100 Mike MacDougal .15
101 Raul Ibanez .15
102 Jason Grimsley .15
103 Chris George .15
104 Brent Mayne .15
105 Dmitri Young .15
106 Eric Munson .15
107 A.J. Hinch .15
108 Andres Torres .15
109 Bobby Higginson .15
110 Shane Halter .15
111 Matt Walbeck .15
112 Torii Hunter .40
113 Doug Mientkiewicz .15
114 Lew Ford .15
115 Eric Milton .15
116 Eddie Guardado .15
117 Cristian Guzman .15
118 Corey Koskie .15
119 Magglio Ordonez .40
120 Mark Buehrle .15
121 Billy Koch .15
122 Jose Valentin .15
123 Paul Konerko .15
124 Carlos Lee .15
125 Jon Garland .15
126 Jason Giambi .75
127 Derek Jeter 1.50
128 Roger Clemens 1.50
129 Andy Pettitte .40
130 Jorge Posada .40
131 David Wells .15
132 Hideki Matsui 1.50
133 Mike Mussina .50
134 Jeff Bagwell .50
135 Craig Biggio .25
136 Morgan Ensberg .15
137 Richard Hidalgo .15
138 Brad Ausmus .15
139 Roy Oswalt .25
140 Billy Wagner .15
141 Octavio Dotel .15
142 Gary Sheffield .40
143 Andruw Jones .40
144 John Smoltz .25
145 Rafael Furcal .25
146 Javy Lopez .25
147 Shane Reynolds .15
148 Horacio Ramirez .15
149 Mike Hampton .15
150 Jung Bong .15
151 Ruben Quevedo .15
152 Ben Sheets .15
153 Geoff Jenkins .25
154 Royce Clayton .15
155 Glendon Rusch .15
156 John Vander Wal .15
157 Scott Podsednik .40
158 Jim Edmonds .40
159 Tino Martinez .15
160 Albert Pujols 1.50
161 Matt Morris .15
162 Woody Williams .15
163 Edgar Renteria .15
164 Jason Isringhausen .15
165 Jason Simontacchi .15
166 Kerry Robinson .15
167 Sammy Sosa 1.25
168 Joe Borowski .15
169 Tony Womack .15
170 Antonio Alfonseca .15
171 Corey Patterson .15
172 Mark Prior 1.00
173 Moises Alou .25
174 Matt Clement .15
175 Randall Simon .15
176 Randy Johnson .75
177 Luis Gonzalez .25
178 Craig Counsell .15
179 Miguel Batista .15
180 Steve Finley .15
181 Brandon Webb .15
182 Danny Bautista .15
183 Oscar Villarreal .15
184 Shawn Green .25
185 Brian Jordan .15
186 Fred McGriff .25
187 Andy Ashby .15
188 Rickey Henderson .50
189 Dave Roberts .15
190 Eric Gagne .15
191 Kazuhisa Ishii .15
192 Adrian Beltre .15
193 Vladimir Guerrero .75
194 Livan Hernandez .15
195 Ron Calloway .15
196 Sun-Woo Kim .15
197 Wil Cordero .15
198 Brad Wilkerson .15
199 Orlando Cabrera .15
200 Barry Bonds 2.00
201 Ray Durham .15
202 Andres Galarraga .15
203 Benito Santiago .15
204 Jose Cruz Jr. .15
205 Jason Schmidt .15
206 Kirk Rueter .15
207 Felix Rodriguez .15
208 Mike Lowell .15
209 Luis Castillo .15
210 Derrek Lee .25
211 Andy Fox .15
212 Tommy Phelps .15
213 Todd Hollandsworth .15
214 Brad Penny .15
215 Juan Pierre .15
216 Mike Piazza 1.00
217 Jae Weong Seo .15
218 Ty Wigginton .15
219 Al Leiter .15
220 Roger Cedeno .15
221 Timoniel Perez .15
222 Aaron Heilman .15
223 Pedro Astacio .15
224 Joe McEwing .15
225 Ryan Klesko .15
226 Brian Giles .25
227 Mark Kotsay .15
228 Brian Lawrence .15
229 Rod Beck .15
230 Trevor Hoffman .15
231 Sean Burroughs .15
232 Bobby Abreu .25
233 Jim Thome .50
234 David Bell .15
235 Jimmy Rollins .25
236 Mike Lieberthal .15
237 Vicente Padilla .15
238 Randy Wolf .15
239 Reggie Sanders .15
240 Jason Kendall .15
241 Jack Wilson .15
242 Jose Hernandez .15
243 Kip Wells .15
244 Carlos Rivera .15
245 Craig Wilson .15
246 Adam Dunn .40
247 Sean Casey .15
248 Danny Graves .15
249 Ryan Dempster .15
250 Barry Larkin .40
251 Reggie Taylor .15
252 Wily Mo Pena .15
253 Larry Walker .25
254 Mark Sweeney .15
255 Preston Wilson .15
256 Jason Jennings .15
257 Charles Johnson .15
258 Jay Payton .15
259 Chris Stynes .15
260 Juan Uribe .15
261 Hideki Matsui 1.00
262 Barry Bonds 1.00
263 Dontrelle Willis .25
264 Kevin Millwood .15
265 Billy Wagner .15
266 Rocco Baldelli .25
267 Roger Clemens .75
268 Rafael Palmeiro .25
269 Miguel Cabrera .25
270 Jose Contreras .15
271 Aaron Sele .15
272 Bartolo Colon .25
273 Darin Erstad .25
274 Francisco Rodriguez .15
275 Garret Anderson .40
276 Jose Guillen .15
277 Troy Percival .15
278 Alex Cintron .15
279 Casey Fossum .15
280 Elmer Dessens .15
281 Jose Valverde .15
282 Matt Mantei .15
283 Richie Sexson .40
284 Roberto Alomar .40
285 Shea Hillenbrand .15
286 Chipper Jones .75
287 Greg Maddux 1.00
288 J.D. Drew .25
289 Marcus Giles .15
290 Mike Hessman .15
291 John Thomson .15
292 Russ Ortiz .15
293 Adam Loewen .15
294 Jack Cust .15
295 Jerry Hairston .15
296 Kurt Ainsworth .15
297 Luis Matos .15
298 Marty Cordova .15
299 Sidney Ponson .15
300 Bill Mueller .15
301 Curt Schilling .50
302 David Ortiz .50
303 Johnny Damon .25
304 Keith Foulke .15
305 Pokey Reese .15
306 Scott Williamson .15
307 Tim Wakefield .15
308 Alex Gonzalez .15
309 Aramis Ramirez .40
310 Carlos Zambrano .40
311 Juan Cruz .15
312 Kerry Wood .75
313 Kyle Farnsworth .15
314 Aaron Rowand .15
315 Esteban Loaiza .15
316 Frank Thomas .50
317 Joe Borchard .15
318 Joe Crede .15
319 Miguel Olivo .15
320 Willie Harris .15
321 Aaron Harang .15
322 Austin Kearns .25
323 Brandon Claussen .15
324 Brandon Larson .15
325 Ryan Freel .15
326 Ken Griffey Jr. 1.00
327 Ryan Wagner .15
328 Alex Escobar .15
329 Coco Crisp .15
330 David Riske .15
331 Jody Gerut .15
332 Josh Bard .15
333 Travis Hafner .25
334 Chin-Hui Tsao .15
335 Denny Stark .15
336 Jeromy Burnitz .15
337 Shawn Chacon .15
338 Todd Helton .50
339 Vinny Castilla .15
340 Alex Sanchez .15
341 Carlos Pena .15
342 Fernando Vina .15
343 Jason Johnson .15
344 Matt Anderson .15
345 Mike Maroth .15
346 Rondell White .15
347 A.J. Burnett .15
348 Alex Gonzalez .15
349 Armando Benitez .15
350 Carl Pavano .15
351 Hee Seop Choi .15
352 Ivan Rodriguez .50
353 Josh Beckett .50
354 Josh Willingham .15
355 Adam Everett .15
356 Brandon Duckworth .15
357 Jason Lane .15
358 Jeff Kent .25
359 Jeriome Robertson .15
360 Lance Berkman .25
361 Wade Miller .15
362 Aaron Guiel .15
363 Angel Berroa .15
364 Carlos Beltran .50
365 David DeJesus .15
366 Desi Relaford .15
367 Joe Randa .15
368 Runelvys Hernandez .15
369 Edwin Jackson .15
370 Hideo Nomo .40
371 Jeff Weaver .15
372 Juan Encarnacion .15
373 Odalis Perez .15
374 Paul LoDuca .15
375 Robin Ventura .15
376 Bill Hall .15
377 Chad Moeller .15
378 Chris Capuano .15
379 Junior Spivey .15
380 Rickie Weeks .25
381 Wes Helms .15
382 Brad Radke .15
383 Jacque Jones .15
384 Joe Mays .15
385 Joe Nathan .15
386 Johan Santana .15
387 Nick Punto .15
388 Shannon Stewart .15
389 Carl Everett .15
390 Claudio Vargas .15
391 Jose Vidro .15
392 Nick Johnson .15
393 Rocky Biddle .15
394 Tony Armas .15
395 Braden Looper .15
396 Cliff Floyd .15
397 Jason Phillips .15
398 Mike Cameron .15
399 Tom Glavine .40
400 Kenny Lofton .25
401 Alfonso Soriano .50
402 Bernie Williams .40
403 Javier Vazquez .15
404 Jon Lieber .15
405 Jose Contreras .15
406 Kevin Brown .25
407 Mariano Rivera .25
408 Arthur Rhodes .15
409 Eric Byrnes .15
410 Erubiel Durazo .15
411 Graham Koonce .15
412 Marco Scutaro .15
413 Mark Mulder .15
414 Mark Redman .15
415 Rich Harden .15
416 Brett Myers .15
417 Chase Utley .15
418 Kevin Millwood .25
419 Marlon Byrd .15
420 Pat Burrell .25
421 Placido Polanco .15
422 Tim Worrell .15
423 Jason Bay .15
424 Josh Fogg .15
425 Kris Benson .15
426 Mike Gonzalez .15
427 Oliver Perez .15
428 Tike Redman .15
429 Adam Eaton .15
430 Ismael Valdez .15
431 Jake Peavy .15
432 Khalil Greene .15
433 Mark Loretta .15
434 Phil Nevin .15
435 Ramon Hernandez .15
436 A.J. Pierzynski .15
437 Edgardo Alfonzo .15
438 J.T. Snow .15
439 Jerome Williams .15
440 Marquis Grissom .15
441 Robb Nen .15
442 Bret Boone .25
443 Freddy Garcia .15
444 Gil Meche .15
445 John Olerud .25
446 Rich Aurilia .15
447 Shigetoshi Hasegawa .15
448 Bo Hart .15
449 Dan Haren .15
450 Jason Marquis .15
451 Marlon Anderson .15
452 Scott Rolen .75
453 So Taguchi .15
454 Carl Crawford .15
455 Delmon Young .25
456 Geoff Blum .15
457 Jesus Colome .15
458 Jonny Gomes .15
459 Lance Carter .15
460 Robert Fick .15
461 Chan Ho Park .15
462 Francisco Cordero .15
463 Jeff Nelson .15
464 Jeff Zimmerman .15
465 Kenny Rogers .15
466 Aquilino Lopez .15
467 Carlos Delgado .50
468 Frank Catalanotto .15
469 Reed Johnson .15
470 Pat Hentgen .15
471 Curt Schilling .25
472 Gary Sheffield .25
473 Javier Vazquez .15
474 Kazuo Matsui 1.00
475 Kevin Brown .25
476 Rafael Palmeiro .25
477 Richie Sexson .25
478 Roger Clemens .75
479 Vladimir Guerrero .50
480 Alex Rodriguez 1.00
481 Jake Woods .25
482 Tim Bittner .25
483 Brandon Medders .50
484 Casey Daigle .25
485 Jerry Gil .25
486 Mike Gosling .25
487 Jose Capellan 1.00
488 Onil Joseph .25
489 Roman Colon .25
490 David Crouthers .25
491 Eddy Rodriguez .25
492 Franklyn Gracesqui .50
493 Jamie Brown .25
494 Jerome Gamble .25
495 Tim Hamulack .25
496 Chris Vasquez .25
497 Renyel Pinto .50
498 Ronny Cedeno .25
499 Enemencio Pacheco .25
500 Ryan Meaux .25
501 Ryan Wing .25

502 Shingo Takatsu 1.00
503 William Bergolla .25
504 Ivan Ochoa .25
505 Mariano Gomez .25
506 Justin Hampson .25
507 Justin Huisman .25
508 Scott Dohmann .25
509 Donnie Kelly .50
510 Chris Aguila .25
511 Lincoln Holdzkom **RC** .25
512 Freddy Guzman .25
513 Hector Gimenez .25
514 Jorge Vasquez .25
515 Jason Frasor .25
516 Chris Saenz .50
517 Dennis Sarfate .25
518 Colby Miller .25
519 Jason Bartlett .25
520 Chad Bentz .25
521 Josh Labandeira .25
522 Shawn Hill .25
523 Kazuo Matsui **RC** 3.00
524 Carlos Hines .25
525 Michael Vento 2.00
526 Scott Proctor .50
527 Sean Henn .50
528 David Aardsma .25
529 Ian Snell .50
530 Mike Johnson .25
531 Akinori Otsuka .75
532 Rusty Tucker .25
533 Justin Knoedler .25
534 Merkin Valdez 1.00
535 Greg Dobbs .25
536 Justin Leone .25
537 Shawn Camp .25
538 Edwin Moreno .25
539 Angel Chavez .25
540 Jesse Harper .25
Reflections Update Set (50): 30.00
341 Shingo Takatsu 3.00
342 Franklyn Gracesqui .75
343 Angel Chavez .75
344 Jorge Sequea .75
345 David Aardsma .75
346 Ramon Ramirez **RC** .75
347 Lino Urdaneta .75
348 Orlando Rodriguez .75
349 Jason Szuminski .75
350 Luis Gonzalez .75
351 John Gall 1.00
352 Kevin Cave .75
353 Chris Oxspring .75
354 Freddy Guzman .75
355 Jeff Bennett .75
356 Jorge Vasquez .75
357 Merkin Valdez 2.00
358 Tim Hamulack .75
359 Hector Gimenez .75
360 Jerry Gil .75
361 Ryan Wing .75
362 Shawn Hill .75
363 Jason Bartlett .75
364 Renyel Pinto .75
365 Carlos Vasquez .75
366 Mike Vento 1.50
367 Casey Daigle .75
368 Chad Bentz 1.00
369 Chris Saenz .75
370 Shawn Camp .75
371 Carlos Hines .75
372 Edwin Moreno .75
373 Mike Wuertz .75
374 Aarom Baldiris **RC** 1.50
375 Ronny Cedeno .75
376 Akinori Otsuka 1.50
377 Jose Capellan 2.00
378 Justin Germano .75
379 Justin Knoedler .75
380 Mariano Gomez .75
381 Fernando Nieve 1.50
382 Scott Proctor .75
383 Roman Colon .75
384 Onil Joseph .75
385 Eddy Rodriguez .75
386 Enemencio Pacheco .75
387 William Bergolla .75
388 Ivan Ochoa .75
389 Rusty Tucker .75
390 Roberto Novoa .75
SPGU Patch Edition Update Set (50): 85.00
121 Richie Sexson 3.00
122 Javier Vazquez 2.00
123 Alex Rodriguez 8.00
124 Javy Lopez 3.00
125 Miguel Tejada 3.00
126 Bartolo Colon 2.00
127 Ivan Rodriguez 4.00
128 Rafael Palmeiro 3.00
129 Kevin Brown 3.00
130 Gary Sheffield 3.00
131 Greg Maddux 5.00
132 Curt Schilling 4.00
133 Roger Clemens 8.00
134 Alfonso Soriano 3.00
135 Vladimir Guerrero 4.00
136 Carlos Vasquez 2.00
137 Roman Colon 2.00
138 William Bergolla 2.00
139 Jason Bartlett 2.00
140 Casey Daigle 2.00
141 Ryan Wing 2.00
142 Chris Saenz 2.00
143 Edwin Moreno 2.00
144 Shawn Hill 2.00
145 Eddy Rodriguez 2.00
146 Justin Knoedler 2.00
147 Renyel Pinto 2.00
148 Kevin Cave 2.00
149 Carlos Hines 2.00
150 Merkin Valdez **RC** 4.00
151 Tim Hamulack **RC** 2.00
152 Hector Gimenez **RC** 2.00
153 Mike Vento **RC** 5.00
154 Scott Proctor **RC** 3.00
155 Rusty Tucker **RC** 2.00
156 Akinori Otsuka **RC** 4.00
157 Ronny Cedeno **RC** 2.00
158 Jose Capellan **RC** 6.00
159 Justin Germano 2.00
160 Shingo Takatsu **RC** 5.00
161 Fernando Nieve 2.00
162 Mike Wuertz 2.00
163 Jerry Gil 2.00
164 Jorge Vasquez 2.00
165 Chad Bentz 4.00
166 Luis Gonzalez 2.00
167 Ivan Ochoa 2.00
168 Onil Joseph 2.00
169 Enemencio Pacheco 2.00
170 Kazuo Matsui **RC** 8.00
Play Ball Update Set (50): 20.00
183 Kazuo Matsui **RC** 3.00
184 Jerry Gil .50
185 Jose Capellan **RC** 2.00
186 Tim Hamulack .50
187 Renyel Pinto .50
188 Carlos Vasquez .50
189 Enemencio Pacheco .50
190 Ronny Cedeno .50
191 Mariano Gomez .50
192 Carlos Hines .50
193 Michael Vento .50
194 David Aardsma .50
195 Hector Gimenez .50
196 Fernando Nieve .50
197 Chris Saenz .50
198 Shawn Hill .50
199 Angel Chavez .50
200 Scott Proctor .50
201 William Bergolla .50
202 Justin Germano .50
203 Onil Joseph .50
204 Rusty Tucker .50
205 Justin Knoedler .50
206 Casey Daigle .50
207 Edwin Moreno .50
208 Chad Bentz .50
209 Ryan Wing .50
210 Shawn Camp .50
211 Eddy Rodriguez .50
212 Roman Colon .50
213 Jason Bartlett .50
214 Jorge Vasquez .50
215 Ivan Ochoa .50
216 Akinori Otsuka .50
217 Merkin Valdez **RC** 2.00
218 Shingo Takatsu **RC** 2.00
219 Chris Oxspring .50
220 Kevin Cave .50
221 Ramon Ramirez .50
222 Orlando Rodriguez .50
223 Lino Urdaneta .50
224 Franklyn Gracesqui .50
225 Mike Wuertz .50
226 Jorge Sequea .50
227 Luis Gonzalez .50
228 Jason Szuminski .50
229 John Gall .50
230 Freddy Guzman .50
231 Jeff Bennett .50
232 Roberto Novoa .50
Vintage Update Set (50): 10.00
451 Alex Rodriguez 1.50
452 Javy Lopez .40
453 Alfonso Soriano .50
454 Vladimir Guerrero .50
455 Rafael Palmeiro .50
456 Gary Sheffield .50
457 Curt Schilling .50
458 Miguel Tejada .50
459 Kevin Brown .40
460 Richie Sexson .50
461 Roger Clemens 1.50
462 Javier Vazquez .25
463 Bartolo Colon .25
464 Ivan Rodriguez .50
465 Greg Maddux 1.00
466 Jamie Brown .25
467 David Crouthers .25
468 Jason Frasor .25
469 Greg Dobbs .25
470 Jesse Harper .25
471 Nick Regilio **RC** .25
472 Ryan Wing .25
473 Akinori Otsuka **RC** 1.00
474 Shingo Takatsu **RC** 1.50
475 Kazuo Matsui **RC** 3.00
476 Michael Vento **RC** 1.00
477 Mike Gosling .25
478 Justin Huisman .25
479 Justin Hampson .25
480 Dennis Sarfate .25
481 Ian Snell **RC** 1.50
482 Tim Bausher **RC** .25
483 Donnie Kelly .25
484 Jerome Gamble .25
485 Mike Rouse .50
486 Merkin Valdez **RC** .75
487 Lincoln Holdzkom **RC** .25
488 Justin Leone **RC** .25
489 Sean Henn .25
490 Brandon Medders **RC** .25
491 Mike Johnston **RC** .25
492 Tim Bittner .25
493 Mike Wuertz .25
494 Chad Bentz .50
495 Ryan Meaux **RC** .25
496 Chris Aguila **RC** .25
497 Jake Woods **RC** .25
498 Scott Dohmann **RC** .25
499 Colby Miller .25
500 Josh Labandeira .25

Glossy

NM/M
Complete Factory Set (590): 85.00
Glossy: 1-2X
Issued only in factory sets.

Authentic Stars Jersey

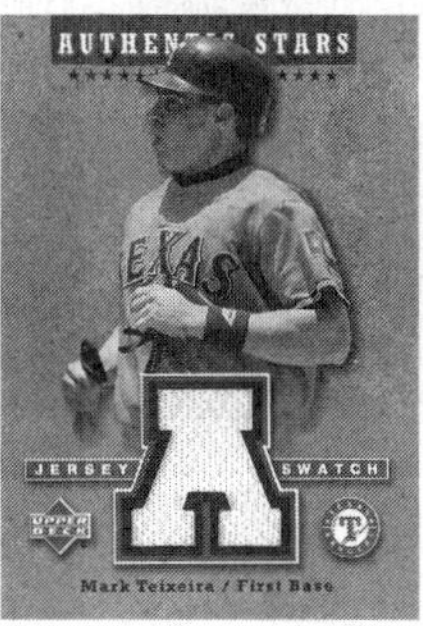

NM/M
Common Player: 4.00
Inserted 1:48
Golds: 1-2X
Production 100 Sets
BA Bobby Abreu 6.00
RO Roberto Alomar 6.00
JB Jeff Bagwell 6.00
RB Rocco Baldelli 10.00
JH Josh Beckett 5.00
HB Hank Blalock 5.00
EC Eric Chavez 4.00
RC Roger Clemens 15.00
CD Carlos Delgado 5.00
JD J.D. Drew 4.00
DE Darin Erstad 4.00
JG Jason Giambi 8.00
TG Troy Glaus 5.00
TL Tom Glavine 6.00
VG Vladimir Guerrero 8.00
SG Shawn Green 5.00
KG Ken Griffey Jr. 15.00
TH Todd Helton 8.00
TO Torii Hunter 6.00
RJ Randy Johnson 8.00
AJ Andruw Jones 6.00
CJ Chipper Jones 8.00
JK Jeff Kent 4.00
GM Greg Maddux 10.00
PM Pedro J. Martinez 8.00
TM Tino Martinez 4.00
HM Hideki Matsui 35.00
PN Phil Nevin 4.00
MI Mike Piazza 10.00
MP Mark Prior 10.00
AP Albert Pujols 15.00
AR Alex Rodriguez 12.00
IR Ivan Rodriguez 8.00
CS Curt Schilling 5.00
AS Alfonso Soriano 10.00
SS Sammy Sosa 12.00
IS Ichiro Suzuki 30.00
MT Mark Teixeira 8.00
FT Frank Thomas 8.00
LW Larry Walker 4.00
BW Bernie Williams 6.00
BZ Barry Zito 6.00

Awesome Honors

NM/M
Complete Set (10): 15.00
1 Albert Pujols 5.00
2 Alex Rodriguez 5.00
3 Angel Berroa 5.00
4 Dontrelle Willis 1.00
5 Eric Gagne 1.50
6 Garret Anderson 1.00
7 Ivan Rodriguez 1.50
8 Josh Beckett 1.50
9 Mariano Rivera 1.00
10 Roy Halladay .75

Awesome Honors Jersey

NM/M
Golds: 1.5-2X
Production 165
GA Garret Anderson 5.00
JB Josh Beckett 6.00
BB Bret Boone 5.00
MC Mike Cameron 4.00
LC Luis Castillo 4.00
EC Eric Chavez 5.00
JE Jim Edmonds 6.00
EG Eric Gagne 12.00
EG1 Eric Gagne 12.00
JG Jason Giambi 8.00

VG Vladimir Guerrero 8.00
RH Roy Halladay 6.00
MH Mike Hampton 4.00
TH Todd Helton 6.00
HU Torii Hunter 5.00
AJ Andruw Jones 6.00
DL Derrek Lee 5.00
EM Edgar Martinez 5.00
BM Bengie Molina 4.00
JM Jamie Moyer 4.00
MU Mike Mussina 8.00
JO John Olerud 5.00
MO Magglio Ordonez 5.00
AP Albert Pujols 10.00
AP2 Albert Pujols 10.00
MR Mariano Rivera 5.00
AR Alex Rodriguez 10.00
AR3 Alex Rodriguez 10.00
IR Ivan Rodriguez 8.00
SR Scott Rolen 8.00
JS John Smoltz 5.00
AS Alfonso Soriano 8.00
IS Ichiro Suzuki 20.00
JT Jim Thome 8.00
DW Dontrelle Willis 6.00

Famous Quotes

NM/M
Complete Set (20): 30.00
Q-1 Al Lopez .75
Q-2 Bob Feller 1.00
Q-3 Bob Gibson 1.50
Q-4 Brooks Robinson 1.50
Q-5 Cal Ripken Jr. 5.00
Q-6 Carl Yastrzemski 2.00
Q-7 Earl Weaver .75
Q-8 Eddie Mathews 2.00
Q-9 Ernie Banks 2.00
Q-10 Greg Maddux 2.00
Q-11 Joe DiMaggio 4.00
Q-12 Mickey Mantle 6.00
Q-13 Nolan Ryan 6.00
Q-14 Stan Musial 4.00
Q-15 Ted Williams 5.00
Q-16 Tom Seaver 2.00
Q-17 Tommy Lasorda .75
Q-18 Warren Spahn 2.00
Q-19 Whitey Ford 1.50
Q-20 Yogi Berra 2.00

First Pitch

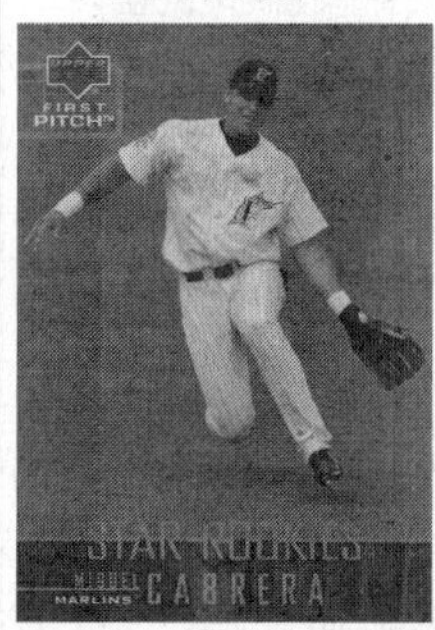

NM/M
Common Player: 5.00
Inserted 1:72
SP7 LeBron James 20.00
SP8 Mr. Hockey 10.00
SP10 Ernie Banks 10.00
SP11 General Tommy Franks 5.00
SP12 Ben Affleck 10.00
SP13 Halle Berry 10.00
SP14 George H.W. Bush 5.00
SP15 George W. Bush 5.00

Game Winners

NM/M
Common Player: 5.00
Golds: 1-1.5X
Production 50 Sets
GW-BA Bobby Abreu 8.00
GW-JB Jeff Bagwell 8.00
GW-HB Hank Blalock 8.00
GW-MC Miguel Cabrera 8.00
GW-JE Jim Edmonds 5.00
GW-DE Darin Erstad 5.00
GW-RF Rafael Furcal (Gold parallel only.) 5.00
GW-JG Jason Giambi 8.00
GW-TG Troy Glaus 5.00
GW-AG Alex Gonzalez 5.00
GW-SG Shawn Green 5.00
GW-VG Vladimir Guerrero 10.00
GW-TH Todd Helton 8.00
GW-RH Ramon Hernandez 5.00
GW-HU Torii Hunter 5.00
GW-DJ Derek Jeter 25.00
GW-AJ Andruw Jones 8.00
GW-CJ Chipper Jones 8.00
GW-RK Ryan Klesko 5.00
GW-ML Mike Lowell 5.00
GW-HM Hideki Matsui 25.00
GW-TN Trot Nixon (Gold parallel only.) 10.00
GW-MO Magglio Ordonez 5.00
GW-CP Corey Patterson 5.00
GW-MP Mike Piazza 10.00
GW-JP Jorge Posada 8.00
GW-AP Albert Pujols 15.00
GW-IR Ivan Rodriguez 8.00
GW-SR Scott Rolen 10.00
GW-GS Gary Sheffield 5.00
GW-AS Alfonso Soriano 8.00
GW-MT Mark Teixeira 5.00
GW-TE Miguel Tejada 5.00
GW-JT Jim Thome 10.00
GW-BW Bernie Williams 8.00

Going Deep Bat

NM/M
Common Player: 6.00
Inserted 1:288
Some not priced yet due to scarcity.
Golds: 1-2X
Production 50 Sets
BA Bobby Abreu/SP/110 6.00
RO Roberto Alomar 8.00
SC Sandy Alomar Jr./SP/95 6.00
GA Garret Anderson 8.00
RA Rich Aurilia/SP/102 6.00
JB Jeff Bagwell/SP/92 10.00
RB Rocco Baldelli/SP 15.00
CB Craig Biggio/SP/89 6.00
JE Jim Edmonds/SP 8.00
DE Darin Erstad 6.00
RF Rafael Furcal/SP 6.00
TG Troy Glaus/SP/113 8.00
SG Shawn Green/SP/100 8.00
KG Ken Griffey Jr./SP 30.00
RH Rickey Henderson/SP/77 10.00
TH Torii Hunter/SP/115 8.00
CJ Chipper Jones/SP/69 15.00
JL Javy Lopez/SP/77 8.00
HM Hideki Matsui/SP/70 45.00
DM Doug Mientkiewicz/SP/123 6.00
HN Hideo Nomo 15.00
MO Magglio Ordonez 6.00
PO Jay Payton/SP/100 6.00
MP Mike Piazza 15.00
JP Jorge Posada 8.00
AP Albert Pujols 20.00
SR Scott Rolen/SP/77 10.00
CS Curt Schilling/SP/57 10.00
AS Alfonso Soriano/SP/53 10.00
JT Jim Thome 10.00
OV Omar Vizquel/SP/115 6.00
BW Bernie Williams/SP/56 8.00
KW Kerry Wood/SP/108 10.00

Headliners Jersey

NM/M
Common Player: 4.00
Inserted 1:48
Golds: 1-2X
Production 100 Sets
TB Tony Batista 4.00
JB Josh Beckett 8.00
LB Lance Berkman 4.00
MB Mark Buehrle 4.00
LC Luis Castillo 4.00

JD Joe DiMaggio/SP/153 90.00
AD Adam Dunn 6.00
JE Jim Edmonds 6.00
RF Robert Fick 4.00
TG Tom Glavine 6.00
LG Luis Gonzalez 4.00
SG Shawn Green 4.00
KG Ken Griffey Jr. 15.00
VG Vladimir Guerrero/SP/153 10.00
RH Roy Halladay 4.00
JH Jose Hernandez 4.00
TH Trevor Hoffman 4.00
BK Byung-Hyun Kim 4.00
RK Ryan Klesko 4.00
PK Paul Konerko 4.00
ML Mike Lowell 4.00
GM Greg Maddux 12.00
MM Mickey Mantle/SP/97 125.00
PM Pedro J. Martinez 8.00
HM Hideki Matsui 35.00
MY Matt Morris 4.00
MU Mike Mussina 8.00
MO Magglio Ordonez 4.00
RO Roy Oswalt 4.00
MR Manny Ramirez 6.00
MA Mariano Rivera 6.00
JR Jimmy Rollins 6.00
BS Benito Santiago 4.00
CS Curt Schilling 6.00
JS Junior Spivey 4.00
IS Ichiro Suzuki/SP/153 30.00
MS Mike Sweeney 4.00
MT Miguel Tejada 6.00
JT Jim Thome 8.00
JV Jose Vidro 4.00
TW Ted Williams/SP/153 75.00

Magical Performances

NM/M
Common Player: 6.00
Inserted 1:96
Golds: 1-1.5X
Production 50 Sets
MP1 Mickey Mantle 35.00
MP2 Mickey Mantle 35.00
MP3 Joe DiMaggio 25.00
MP4 Joe DiMaggio 25.00
MP5 Derek Jeter 25.00
MP6 Derek Jeter 25.00
MP7 Roger Clemens 20.00
MP8 Roger Clemens 20.00
MP9 Alfonso Soriano 10.00
MP10 Andy Pettitte 8.00
MP11 Hideki Matsui 30.00
MP12 Mike Mussina 10.00
MP13 Jorge Posada 10.00
MP14 Jason Giambi 10.00
MP15 David Wells 6.00
MP16 Mariano Rivera 10.00
MP17 Yogi Berra 15.00
MP18 Phil Rizzuto 10.00
MP19 Whitey Ford 10.00
MP20 Jose Contreras 8.00
MP21 Jim "Catfish" Hunter 6.00
MP22 Mickey Mantle 35.00
MP23 Mickey Mantle 35.00
MP24 Joe DiMaggio 25.00
MP25 Joe DiMaggio 25.00
MP26 Derek Jeter 25.00
MP27 Derek Jeter 25.00
MP28 Roger Clemens 20.00
MP29 Roger Clemens 20.00
MP30 Alfonso Soriano 10.00
MP31 Andy Pettitte 8.00
MP32 Hideki Matsui 30.00
MP33 Mike Mussina 10.00
MP34 Jorge Posada 10.00
MP35 Jason Giambi 10.00
MP36 David Wells 6.00
MP37 Mariano Rivera 10.00
MP38 Yogi Berra 15.00
MP39 Phil Rizzuto 10.00

MP40 Whitey Ford 10.00
MP41 Jose Contreras 10.00
MP42 Jim "Catfish" Hunter 6.00

Matsui Chronicles

NM/M
Complete Set (60): 35.00
Common Matsui: 1.00
HM1-HM60 Hideki Matsui 1.00

National Pride

NM/M
Complete Set (20): 25.00
Common Player: 1.00
Inserted 1:6
USA1 Justin Orenduff 1.00
USA2 Micah Owings 2.00
USA3 Steven Register 2.00
USA4 Huston Street 1.00
USA5 Justin Verlander 2.00
USA6 Jered Weaver 1.00
USA7 Matt Campbell 1.00
USA8 Stephen Head 1.00
USA9 Mark Romanczuk 1.00
USA10 Jeff Clement 6.00
USA11 Mike Nickeas 2.00
USA12 Tyler Greene 1.00
USA13 Paul Janish 2.00
USA14 Jeff Larish 1.00
USA15 Eric Patterson 1.00
USA16 Dustin Pedroia 1.00
USA17 Michael Griffin 1.00
USA18 Brent Lillibridge 1.00
USA19 Danny Putnam 1.00
USA20 Seth Smith 1.00

National Pride Jersey

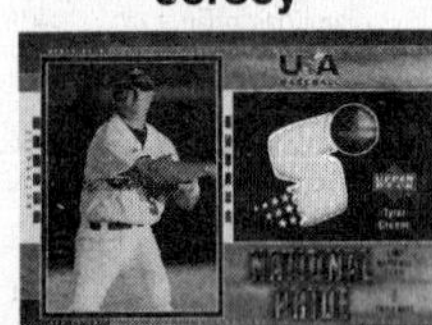

NM/M
Common Player: 4.00
Inserted 1:24
USA1 Justin Orenduff 4.00
USA2 Micah Owings 4.00
USA3 Steven Register 4.00
USA4 Huston Street 4.00
USA5 Justin Verlander 10.00
USA6 Jered Weaver 6.00
USA7 Matt Campbell 8.00
USA8 Stephen Head 4.00
USA9 Mark Romanczuk 4.00
USA10 Jeff Clement 15.00
USA11 Mike Nickeas 4.00
USA12 Tyler Greene 4.00
USA13 Paul Janish 4.00
USA14 Jeff Larish 6.00
USA15 Eric Patterson 4.00
USA16 Dustin Pedroia 10.00
USA17 Michael Griffin 4.00
USA18 Brent Lillibridge 6.00
USA19 Danny Putnam 4.00
USA20 Seth Smith 6.00
USA21 Justin Orenduff 4.00
USA22 Micah Owings 4.00
USA23 Steven Register 4.00
USA24 Huston Street 4.00
USA25 Justin Verlander 10.00
USA26 Jered Weaver 6.00
USA27 Matt Campbell 8.00
USA28 Stephen Head 4.00
USA29 Mark Romanczuk 4.00
USA30 Jeff Clement 15.00
USA31 Mike Nickeas 4.00
USA32 Tyler Greene 4.00
USA33 Paul Janish 4.00
USA34 Jeff Larish 6.00
USA35 Eric Patterson 4.00
USA36 Dustin Pedroia 10.00
USA37 Michael Griffin 4.00
USA38 Brent Lillibridge 6.00
USA39 Danny Putnam 4.00
USA40 Seth Smith 6.00
USA41 Delmon Young 35.00
USA42 Rickie Weeks 12.00
Series 2
TB Thad Bosley 4.00
BB Brian Bruney 6.00
CB Chris Burke 9.00
JC Jesse Crain 8.00
DU Justin Duchscherer 6.00
JD J.D. Durbin 4.00
JG John Grabow 6.00
GG Gabe Gross 4.00
JH J.J. Hardy 6.00
GK Graham Koonce 6.00
GL Gerald Laird 6.00
ML Mike Lamb 4.00
JL Justin Leone 8.00
JM Joe Mauer 15.00
HR Horacio Ramirez 8.00
JR Jeremy Reed 10.00
RR Royce Ring 6.00
ER Eddie Rodriguez 5.00
MR Mike Rouse 8.00
GS Grady Sizemore 10.00
JS Jason Stanford 6.00
JB John Van Benschoten 8.00
TW Todd Williams 4.00
EY Ernie Young 4.00

National Pride Pants

NM/M
CB Chris Burke 9.00
JC Jesse Crain 4.00
DU Justin Duchscherer 6.00
GK Graham Koonce 6.00
JL Justin Leone 8.00
RM Ryan Madson 6.00
JM Joe Mauer 15.00
HR Horacio Ramirez 8.00
RR Royce Ring 6.00
ER Eddie Rodriguez 5.00
MR Mike Rouse 8.00
GS Grady Sizemore 10.00
JS Jason Stanford 6.00
JB John Van Benschoten 8.00

Peak Performers

NM/M
Golds: 1.5X-2X
Production 165
PP-JB Jeff Bagwell 8.00
PP-BE Josh Beckett 6.00
PP-LB Lance Berkman 5.00
PP-CB Craig Biggio 5.00
PP-HB Hank Blalock 8.00
PP-PB Pat Burrell 6.00
PP-LC Luis Castillo 4.00
PP-CD Carlos Delgado 6.00
PP-RF Rafael Furcal 4.00
PP-EG Eric Gagne 12.00
PP-SG Shawn Green 5.00
PP-KG Ken Griffey Jr. 15.00
PP-VG Vladimir Guerrero 8.00
PP-TH Todd Helton 8.00
PP-PL Paul LoDuca 4.00
PP-PM Pedro J. Martinez 8.00
PP-HM Hideki Matsui 25.00
PP-MM Mike Mussina 8.00
PP-HN Hideo Nomo 8.00
PP-MO Magglio Ordonez 5.00
PP-RP Rafael Palmeiro 6.00
PP-PE Andy Pettitte 6.00
PP-BP Brandon Phillips 4.00
PP-MP Mark Prior 10.00
PP-AP Albert Pujols 10.00
PP-JR Jose Reyes 5.00
PP-IR Ivan Rodriguez 8.00
PP-SR Scott Rolen 8.00
PP-SA C.C. Sabathia 4.00
PP-CS Curt Schilling 8.00
PP-AS Alfonso Soriano 8.00
PP-IS Ichiro Suzuki 20.00
PP-MT Miguel Tejada 5.00
PP-FT Frank Thomas 8.00
PP-JT Jim Thome 8.00
PP-DV Omar Vizquel 4.00
PP-VW Vernon Wells 4.00
PP-KW Kerry Wood 10.00

Signature Stars Black Ink

NM/M
Some not priced due to lack of info.
Inserted 1:288
RA Rich Aurilia/479 8.00
AG Andres Galarraga/248 10.00
NG Nomar Garciaparra/69 75.00
VG Vladimir Guerrero/68 40.00
RH Rich Harden/163 8.00
AH Aaron Heilman/49 15.00
TH Torii Hunter/374 10.00
KI Kazuhisa Ishii/58 15.00
BK Billy Koch/429 8.00
HM Hideki Matsui/25 325.00
MU Mike Mussina/68 50.00
MO Magglio Ordonez/377 20.00
JRa Joe Randa/271 10.00
CR Cal Ripken Jr./69 200.00
DR Dave Roberts/278 8.00
NR Nolan Ryan/69 120.00
Series 2
BB Bret Boone/43 15.00
DB Dewon Brazelton/96 5.00
JC Jose Canseco/160 25.00
EC Eric Chavez/60 15.00
EG Eric Gagne/160 20.00
KG Ken Griffey Jr./450 90.00
RH Rich Harden/65 15.00
DR Dave Roberts/450 5.00
NR Nolan Ryan/95 100.00
DS Darryl Strawberry/160 10.00
MT Mark Teixeira/200 25.00
JV Javier Vazquez/60 15.00
BW Brandon Webb/60 15.00
RW Rickie Weeks/65 15.00
DW Dontrelle Willis/160 15.00

Signature Stars Gold Ink

Gold Ink: 1-2X Black Ink
Production 99 Sets

Signature Stars Blue Ink

NM/M
No Pricing
Production 25 Sets
Matsui #'d to 324.
HM Hideki Matsui/324 180.00

Signature Stars Red Ink

No Pricing
Production 10 Sets
Series 2

SPGU Patch Edition Update Patch

NM/M
Production 20 unless noted.
BA Bobby Abreu 40.00
GA Garret Anderson 40.00
RB Rocco Baldelli 30.00
LB Lance Berkman 40.00
HB Hank Blalock 40.00
BB Bret Boone 30.00
BC Bartolo Colon 25.00
JE Jim Edmonds 35.00
EG Eric Gagne 75.00
TG Troy Glaus 35.00
VG Vladimir Guerrero 50.00
TH Torii Hunter 25.00
JJ Jacque Jones 25.00
AK Austin Kearns 30.00
JK Jeff Kent 25.00
RK Ryan Klesko 25.00
EM Edgar Martinez 50.00
KM Kevin Millwood 30.00
MM Mark Mulder 40.00
HN Hideo Nomo 40.00
RO Roy Oswalt 35.00
CP Corey Patterson 30.00
JR Jose Reyes 30.00
RS Richie Sexson 40.00
MS Mike Sweeney 25.00
BW Brandon Webb 25.00
VW Vernon Wells/21 25.00
KW Kerry Wood 50.00

Super Patches Logos

No pricing due to scarcity.
Inserted 1:7,500
Series 2

Super Patches Numbers

No pricing due to scarcity.
Inserted 1:7,500
Series 2

Super Patches Stripes

No pricing due to scarcity.
Inserted 1:7,500
Series 2

Super Sluggers

NM/M
Complete Set (30): 15.00
Common Player: .50
Inserted 1:1 Retail
SL-1 Albert Pujols 2.00
SL-2 Alex Rodriguez 2.00
SL-3 Alfonso Soriano .75
SL-4 Andruw Jones .75
SL-5 Bret Boone .50
SL-6 Carlos Delgado .50
SL-7 Edgar Renteria .50
SL-8 Eric Chavez .50
SL-9 Frank Thomas .75
SL-10 Garret Anderson .50
SL-11 Gary Sheffield .50
SL-12 Jason Giambi .75
SL-13 Javy Lopez .50
SL-14 Jeff Bagwell .75
SL-15 Jim Edmonds .50
SL-16 Jim Thome 1.00
SL-17 Jorge Posada .50
SL-18 Lance Berkman .50
SL-19 Magglio Ordonez .50
SL-20 Manny Ramirez .75
SL-21 Mike Lowell .50
SL-22 Nomar Garciaparra 1.50
SL-23 Preston Wilson .50
SL-24 Rafael Palmeiro .75
SL-25 Richie Sexson .50
SL-26 Sammy Sosa 2.00
SL-27 Shawn Green .50
SL-28 Todd Helton .75
SL-29 Vernon Wells .50
SL-30 Vladimir Guerrero 1.00

Twenty-Five Salute

NM/M
Common Player: 6.00
Inserted 1:12
S1 Barry Bonds 3.00
S2 Troy Glaus .75
S3 Andruw Jones .75
S4 Jay Gibbons .75
S5 Jeremy Giambi .75
S6 Jason Giambi 1.00
S7 Jim Thome 1.00
S8 Rafael Palmeiro 1.00
S9 Carlos Delgado 1.00
S10 Dmitri Young .75

500 HR Club

NM/M
Production 350
RP Rafael Palmeiro 180.00

2003 Update

NM/M
Complete Set (60): 18.00
Common Player: .15
One set per hobby box.
541 Bo Hart 1.50
542 Dan Haren .50
543 Ryan Wagner 1.00
544 Rich Harden .50
545 Dontrelle Willis .75
546 Jerome Williams .25
547 Bobby Crosby 1.00
548 Greg Jones .25
549 Todd Linden .25
550 Byung-Hyun Kim .25
551 Rickie Weeks 4.00
552 Jason Roach .25
553 Oscar Villarreal .25
554 Justin Duchscherer .15
555 Chris Capuano .15
556 Josh Hall .50
557 Luis Matos .15
558 Miguel Ojeda .15
559 Kevin Ohme .15
560 Julio Manon .15
561 Kevin Correia .15
562 Delmon Young 5.00
563 Aaron Boone .15
564 Aaron Looper .15
565 Mike Neu .15
566 Aquilino Lopez .15
567 Jhonny Peralta .15
568 Duaner Sanchez .15
569 Stephen Randolph .15
570 Nate Bland .15
571 Chin-Hui Tsao .15
572 Michel Hernandez .15
573 Rocco Baldelli 1.00
574 Robb Quinlan .15
575 Aaron Heilman .15
576 Jae Weong Seo .15
577 Joe Borowski .15
578 Chris Bootcheck .15
579 Michael Ryan .15
580 Mark Malaska .15
581 Jose Guillen .15
582 Josh Towers .15
583 Tom Gregorio .15
584 Edwin Jackson .15
585 Jason Anderson .15
586 Jose Reyes .50
587 Miguel Cabrera 1.00
588 Nate Bump .15
589 Jeromy Burnitz .15
590 David Ross .15
591 Chase Utley .15
592 Brandon Webb 1.00
593 Masao Kida .15
594 Jimmy Journell .15
595 Eric Young .15
596 Tony Womack .15
597 Amaury Telemaco .15
598 Rickey Henderson .50
599 Esteban Loaiza .15
600 Sidney Ponson .15

2004 Upper Deck Diamond Collection

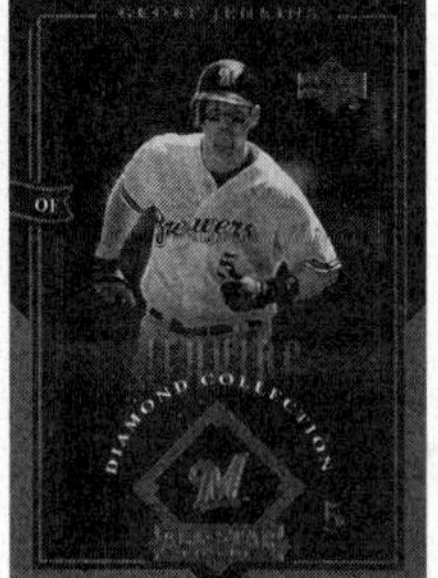

NM/M
Complete Set (120): 70.00
Common Player: .15
Common (91-120): 2.00
Inserted 1:6
Pack (6): 2.00
Box (24): 40.00
1 Garret Anderson .25
2 Darin Erstad .25
3 Troy Glaus .40
4 Curt Schilling .50
5 Brandon Webb .15
6 Randy Johnson .75
7 Andruw Jones .50
8 Chipper Jones .75
9 Gary Sheffield .40
10 Jay Gibbons .25
11 Miguel Tejada .40
12 Tony Batista .15
13 Nomar Garciaparra 1.25
14 Manny Ramirez .50
15 Pedro J. Martinez .75
16 Mark Prior 1.00
17 Kerry Wood .75
18 Sammy Sosa 1.25
19 Bartolo Colon .25
20 Magglio Ordonez .25
21 Frank Thomas .50
22 Adam Dunn .40
23 Austin Kearns .25
24 Ken Griffey Jr. 1.00
25 Brandon Phillips .15
26 Milton Bradley .15
27 Jody Gerut .15
28 Todd Helton .50
29 Larry Walker .25
30 Preston Wilson .25
31 Jeremy Bonderman .15
32 Carlos Pena .15
33 Dmitri Young .15
34 Dontrelle Willis .40
35 Miguel Cabrera .50
36 Mike Lowell .25
37 Jeff Bagwell .50
38 Roy Oswalt .25
39 Lance Berkman .25
40 Carlos Beltran .40
41 Mike Sweeney .15
42 Rondell White .15
43 Hideo Nomo .40
44 Kevin Brown .25
45 Shawn Green .25
46 Ben Sheets .25
47 Geoff Jenkins .25
48 Richie Sexson .40
49 Jacque Jones .15
50 Johan Santana .15
51 Torii Hunter .25
52 Javier Vazquez .25
53 Jose Vidro .15
54 Vladimir Guerrero .75
55 Cliff Floyd .15
56 Mike Piazza 1.00
57 Jose Reyes .50
58 Derek Jeter 2.00
59 Jason Giambi .50
60 Alfonso Soriano .50
61 Eric Chavez .25
62 Barry Zito .25
63 Tim Hudson .25
64 Bobby Abreu .25
65 Jim Thome .75
66 Kevin Millwood .25
67 Roger Clemens 1.50
68 Jason Kendall .15
69 Reggie Sanders .15
70 Phil Nevin .15
71 Ryan Klesko .25
72 Brian Giles .25
73 A.J. Pierzynski .15
74 Jason Schmidt .25
75 Sidney Ponson .15
76 Edgar Martinez .25
77 Ichiro Suzuki 1.00
78 Bret Boone .25
79 Albert Pujols 1.50
80 Scott Rolen .75
81 Jim Edmonds .25
82 Aubrey Huff .15
83 Delmon Young .40
84 Rocco Baldelli .40
85 Alex Rodriguez 1.50
86 Mark Teixeira .25
87 Rafael Palmeiro .50
88 Carlos Delgado .50
89 Vernon Wells .25
90 Roy Halladay .25
91 Brandon Medders **RC** 2.00
92 Colby Miller **RC** 2.00
93 David Crouthers 2.00
94 Dennis Sarfate **RC** 3.00
95 Donald Kelly **RC** 2.00
96 Alec Zumwalt **RC** 2.00
97 Frank Brooks **RC** 2.00
98 Greg Dobbs **RC** 2.00
99 Ian Snell **RC** 3.00
100 Jake Woods 2.00
101 Jamie Brown **RC** 2.00
102 Jason Frasor **RC** 2.00
103 Jerome Gamble **RC** 2.00
104 Jesse Harper **RC** 2.00
105 Josh Labandeira **RC** 2.00
106 Justin Hampson **RC** 2.00
107 Justin Huisman **RC** 2.00
108 Justin Leone **RC** 2.00
109 Chris Aguila **RC** 2.00
110 Lincoln Holdzkom **RC** 2.00
111 Mike Bumatay **RC** 2.00
112 Mike Gosling 2.00
113 Mike Johnston **RC** 2.00
114 Mike Rouse 2.00
115 Nick Regilio **RC** 2.00
116 Ryan Meaux **RC** 2.00
117 Scott Dohmann **RC** 2.00
118 Sean Henn 2.00
119 Tim Bausher **RC** 2.00
120 Tim Bittner **RC** 2.00

Silver Honors

Silver (1-90): 2-4X
Silver (91-120): .75-1X
1-90 inserted 1:6
91-120 inserted 1:48

Gold Honors

Gold (1-90): 5-10X
Gold (91-120): 1-2X
Production 50 Sets

All-Star Promo e-Card

NM/M
Common Player: 1.00
Inserted 1:12
CD Carlos Delgado 1.00
NG Nomar Garciaparra 2.50
VG Vladimir Guerrero 1.50
TH Todd Helton 1.00
AP Albert Pujols 3.00
AS Alfonso Soriano 1.00
SS Sammy Sosa 2.50
IS Ichiro Suzuki 2.50
AR Alex Rodriguez 3.00

Class of 2004 Autograph

NM/M
Quantity produced listed
MC Miguel Cabrera/50 40.00
KG Ken Griffey Jr./100 75.00
VG Vladimir Guerrero/100 40.00
RH Rich Harden/100 15.00
HM Hideki Matsui/100 250.00
MP Mark Prior/100 40.00
JR Jose Reyes/100 30.00
DW Dontrelle Willis/100 40.00
BZ Barry Zito/100 25.00

Dean's List Jersey

NM/M
Common Player: 4.00
Inserted 1:72
BA Jeff Bagwell 8.00
HB Hank Blalock 6.00
JG Jason Giambi 6.00
GL Troy Glaus 6.00
LG Luis Gonzalez 4.00
SG Shawn Green 4.00
KG Ken Griffey Jr. 10.00
VG Vladimir Guerrero 8.00
GM Greg Maddux 10.00
HM Hideki Matsui 20.00
HN Hideo Nomo 8.00
PI Mike Piazza 8.00
MP Mark Prior 8.00
AP Albert Pujols 15.00
AR Alex Rodriguez 10.00
AS Alfonso Soriano 8.00
SS Sammy Sosa 10.00
IS Ichiro Suzuki 20.00
JT Jim Thome 8.00
DW Dontrelle Willis 6.00

Future Gems Jersey

NM/M
Common Player: 4.00
Inserted 1:72
BA Josh Bard 4.00
JB Josh Beckett 8.00
SB Sean Burroughs 6.00
MC Mike Cameron 4.00
AE Adam Eaton 4.00
WE Willie Eyre 4.00
LF Lew Ford 4.00
GU Jeremy Guthrie 4.00
TH Travis Hafner 6.00
RH Roy Halladay 4.00
AH Aaron Heilman 4.00
IS Kazuhisa Ishii 4.00
JJ Jason Jennings 4.00
KA Matt Kata 4.00
MK Mark Kotsay 4.00
JL Jon Leicester 4.00
EM Eric Milton 4.00
JR Jose Reyes 8.00
RR Rick Roberts 4.00
PS Phil Seibel 4.00
BS Ben Sheets 6.00
MT Mark Teixeira 6.00
TW Todd Wellemeyer 6.00
WI Josh Willingham 4.00

Pick the All Star MVP

NM/M
Common Player: .50
Inserted 1:1
BA Bobby Abreu .50
GA Garret Anderson .50
JB Jeff Bagwell .50
BE Josh Beckett .50
CB Carlos Beltran .50
HB Hank Blalock .50
BO Bret Boone .50
OC Orlando Cabrera .50
EC Eric Chavez .50
BC Bartolo Colon .50
JD Johnny Damon .50
CD Carlos Delgado .50
AD Adam Dunn .50
JE Jim Edmonds .50
RF Rafael Furcal .50
NG Nomar Garciaparra 1.50
JG Jason Giambi .75
MG Marcus Giles .50
TG Troy Glaus .50
SG Shawn Green .50
KG Ken Griffey Jr. 1.00
VG Vladimir Guerrero .75
RH Roy Halladay .50
TH Todd Helton .75
HU Tim Hudson .50
TH Torii Hunter .50
DJ Derek Jeter 2.50
RJ Randy Johnson .75
AJ Andruw Jones .50
CJ Chipper Jones .75
JJ Jacque Jones .50
AK Austin Kearns .50
JK Jeff Kent .50
JL Javy Lopez .50
ML Mike Lowell .50
PM Pedro J. Martinez .75
HM Hideki Matsui 1.50
MM Mark Mulder .50
MU Mike Mussina .50
MO Magglio Ordonez .50
RP Rafael Palmeiro .75
PI Mike Piazza 1.00
JP Jorge Posada .50
MP Mark Prior 1.00
AP Albert Pujols 2.00
MR Manny Ramirez .75
ER Edgar Renteria .50
AR Alex Rodriguez 2.00
IR Ivan Rodriguez .75
SR Scott Rolen .75
CS Curt Schilling .75
JS Jason Schmidt .50
RS Richie Sexson .50
GS Gary Sheffield .50
AS Alfonso Soriano .75
SS Sammy Sosa 1.50
IS Ichiro Suzuki 1.50
MS Mike Sweeney .50
MT Mark Teixeira .50
TE Miguel Tejada .50
FT Frank Thomas .75
JT Jim Thome .75
JV Jason Varitek .50
VI Jose Vidro .50
VW Vernon Wells .50
DW Dontrelle Willis .50
PW Preston Wilson .50
KW Kerry Wood 1.00
BZ Barry Zito .50

Premium Stars

Complete Set (15):
Common Player:

Pro Sigs

NM/M
Complete Set (1-240):
Common Player (1-90): .15
Common SP (91-150): 2.00
Inserted 1:6
Common Auto. (151-240): 5.00
Inserted 1:24
Pack (6): 2.00
Box (24): 40.00
1 Alfonso Soriano .50
2 Josh Beckett .50
3 Kerry Wood .75
4 Brandon Webb .15
5 Shannon Stewart .15
6 Larry Walker .25
7 Tim Hudson .25
8 Carlos Lee .25
9 Austin Kearns .25
10 Vernon Wells .25
11 Jeff Bagwell .50
12 Hideo Nomo .50
13 Jerome Williams .15
14 Kevin Brown .25
15 Jose Vidro .15
16 Rocco Baldelli .25
17 Frank Thomas .50
18 Albert Pujols 1.50
19 Bartolo Colon .25
20 C.C. Sabathia .15
21 Andruw Jones .50
22 Reggie Sanders .15
23 Carlos Beltran .50
24 Curt Schilling .50
25 Miguel Tejada .40
26 Barry Zito .50
27 Pedro Martinez .75
28 Sean Burroughs .15
29 Sammy Sosa 1.50
30 Eric Chavez .25
31 Roy Halladay .25
32 Todd Helton .50
33 Mark Prior 1.00
34 Mike Mussina .50
35 Alex Rodriguez 2.00
36 Ivan Rodriguez .50
37 Mike Piazza 1.00
38 Angel Berroa .15
39 Orlando Cabrera .25
40 Jim Thome .75
41 Brian Giles .25
42 Ichiro Suzuki 1.00
43 Edgar Renteria .25
44 Eric Gagne .25
45 Gary Sheffield .40
46 Torii Hunter .25
47 Roger Clemens 1.50
48 Scott Rolen .75
49 Johan Santana .15
50 Jacque Jones .15
51 Hank Blalock .40
52 Rafael Palmeiro .50
53 Dmitri Young .15
54 Ryan Klesko .25
55 Mark Teixeira .25
56 Nomar Garciaparra 1.50
57 Jose Reyes .25
58 Vladimir Guerrero .75
59 Mike Sweeney .15
60 Jorge Posada .40
61 Derek Jeter 2.00
62 Milton Bradley .15
63 Bobby Abreu .25
64 Greg Maddux 1.00
65 Adam Dunn .50
66 Troy Glaus .40
67 Luis Gonzalez .25
68 Shawn Green .25
69 Bret Boone .25
70 Mark Mulder .25
71 Lance Berkman .25
72 Preston Wilson .15
73 Phil Nevin .15
74 Chipper Jones .75
75 Garret Anderson .40
76 Jason Giambi .75
77 Magglio Ordonez .25
78 Jeff Kent .25
79 Richie Sexson .40
80 Mike Lowell .25
81 Ben Sheets .25
82 Randy Johnson .75
83 Dontrelle Willis .25
84 Javier Vazquez .25
85 Geoff Jenkins .25
86 Manny Ramirez .50
87 Jim Edmonds .40
88 Roy Oswalt .25
89 Edgar Martinez .25
90 Carlos Delgado .40
91 Chris Saenz **RC** 5.00
92 Justin Leone **RC** 2.00
93 Shawn Hill **RC** 4.00
94 Chad Bentz **RC** 4.00
95 Jesse Harper **RC** 2.00
96 David Crouthers 2.00
97 Justin Germano **RC** 2.00
98 Tim Bausher **RC** 2.00
99 Greg Dobbs **RC** 5.00
100 Enemencio Pacheco **RC** 8.00
101 Dennis Sarfate **RC** 2.00
102 Edwin Moreno **RC** 4.00
103 Colby Miller **RC** 2.00
104 Mike Rouse 2.00
105 Fernando Nieve **RC** 2.00
106 Tim Hamulack **RC** 6.00
107 Jason Frasor **RC** 2.00
108 Jose Capellan **RC** 5.00
109 Jamie Brown **RC** 3.00
110 Mariano Gomez **RC** 2.00
111 Mike Vento 8.00
112 Josh Labandeira **RC** 3.00
113 Mike Gosling 2.00
114 Shingo Takatsu **RC** 8.00
115 Justin Hampson **RC** 2.00
116 Tim Bittner **RC** 2.00
117 Jerry Gil **RC** 2.00
118 Carlos Vasquez **RC** 5.00
119 Lincoln Holdzkom **RC** 2.00
120 Mike Johnston **RC** 4.00
121 William Bergolla **RC** 2.00
122 Luis Gonzalez 2.00
123 Ivan Ochoa **RC** 4.00
124 Roman Colon **RC** 2.00
125 Renyel Pinto **RC** 6.00
126 Donnie Kelly **RC** 4.00
127 Chris Oxspring **RC** 2.00
128 Sean Henn 5.00
129 Ryan Meaux **RC** 2.00
130 Shawn Camp **RC** 2.00
131 Brandon Medders **RC** 2.00
132 Rusty Tucker **RC** 2.00
133 Kazuo Matsui **RC** 10.00
134 Jorge Sequea **RC** 2.00
135 Hector Gimenez **RC** 4.00
136 Casey Daigle **RC** 2.00
137 Ian Snell **RC** 3.00
138 Scott Dohmann **RC** 2.00
139 Ronny Cedeno **RC** 2.00
140 Jorge Vasquez **RC** 4.00
141 David Aardsma 4.00
142 Carlos Hines **RC** 2.00
143 Scott Proctor **RC** 3.00
144 Jerome Gamble **RC** 5.00
145 Jason Bartlett **RC** 6.00
146 Akinori Otsuka **RC** 8.00
147 Merkin Valdez **RC** 2.00
148 Jake Woods 4.00
149 Chris Aguila **RC** 2.00
150 John Gall **RC** 2.00
151 Aaron Miles 10.00
152 Aquilino Lopez 10.00
153 Bill Hall 10.00
154 Billy Traber 15.00
155 Brad Lidge 12.00
156 Brady Clark 10.00
157 Brandon Duckworth 8.00
158 Brett Tomko 6.00
159 Brian Fuentes 6.00
161 Brooks Kieschnick 8.00
162 Carlos Rivera 6.00
163 Chad Cordero 6.00
164 Chad Tracy 10.00
165 Claudio Vargas 5.00
166 D.J. Carrasco 5.00
167 Damian Rolls 6.00
168 David Sanders 5.00
170 Derrick Turnbow 5.00
171 Desi Relaford 5.00
172 Doug Davis 8.00
173 Dustan Mohr 6.00
176 Frank Catalanotto 8.00
178 Franklyn German 5.00
179 Ron Belliard 5.00
180 Geoff Geary 15.00
181 Greg Colbrunn 5.00
182 Henry Mateo 5.00
183 Brent Mayne 5.00
184 Horacio Ramirez 15.00
185 J.C. Romero 5.00
186 J.J. Putz 8.00
187 Ferdin Tejeda 8.00
188 Jaime Cerda 8.00
189 Jason Michaels 10.00
190 Jason Simontacchi 8.00
191 Jay Witasick 5.00
192 Joe Valentine 8.00
193 Joey Eischen 5.00
194 Johnny Estrada 8.00
195 Jon Garland 5.00
196 Jon Switzer 5.00
197 Jorge Julio 5.00
198 Jorge Sosa 8.00
199 Jose Castillo 5.00
200 Jose Macias 8.00
201 Josh Bard 5.00
202 Juan Cruz 5.00
203 Juan Rivera 5.00
204 Ken Griffey Jr. 150.00
205 Kevin Hooper 5.00
206 Kiko Calero **RC** 15.00
207 Chad Gaudin 5.00
208 Luis Rivas 5.00
209 Mark Corey 5.00
210 Matt Ford 8.00
211 Matt Herges 8.00
212 Miguel Cairo 15.00
213 Fernando Cabrera 5.00
214 Mike MacDougal 5.00
215 Mike Neu 8.00
216 Lew Ford 15.00
217 Mike Wood 8.00
218 Nate Robertson 5.00
219 Nick Punto 5.00
221 Oscar Villarreal 5.00
222 Ramon Vazquez 10.00
223 Randall Simon 5.00
225 Ricky Stone 5.00
229 Ryan Drese 5.00
230 Ryan Ludwick 8.00
231 Scot Shields 5.00
232 Shane Nance 5.00
233 Steve Colyer 5.00
234 Tony Armas 5.00
235 Robby Hammock 5.00
236 Travis Hafner 8.00
237 Victor Martinez 8.00
238 Wilfredo Ledezma 5.00
239 Willie Bloomquist 5.00
240 Yorvit Torrealba 8.00

Pro Sigs Silver

Silver (1-90): 2-3X
Overall odds for parallel 1:6.

Pro Sigs Gold

Gold (1-90): 3-6X
Overall odds for parallel 1:6.

Pro Sigs Blue Ink Autograph

No Pricing
Production 25 Sets

Pro Sigs Red Signature

No Pricing
Production 10 Sets

Pro Sigs Hall of Famers

(No Pricing)

2004 Upper Deck Etchings

NM/M
Complete Set (150):
Common Player: .15
Common SP (91-120): 4.00
Production 2,004
Common SP Black Auto (121-150): 8.00
Production 700
Blue Auto (121-150): .75-1.5X
Production 200
Red Auto (121-150): No Pricing
Production 25

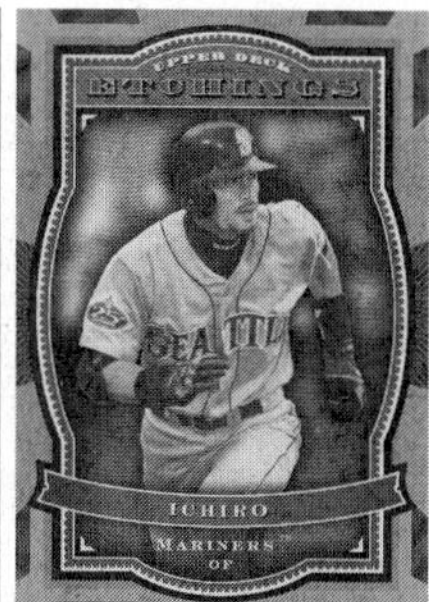

Pack (5): 12.00
Box (12): 120.00
1 Albert Pujols 1.50
2 Torii Hunter .40
3 Jim Edmonds .40
4 Alex Rodriguez 1.50
5 Rafael Palmeiro .50
6 Ken Griffey Jr. 1.00
7 Adam Dunn .50
8 Andruw Jones .50
9 Carlos Lee .15
10 Mike Piazza 1.00
11 Jeff Bagwell .50
12 Hideki Matsui 1.50
13 Gary Sheffield .40
14 Edgar Renteria .40
15 Shawn Green .25
16 Kerry Wood .75
17 Ivan Rodriguez .50
18 Josh Beckett .40
19 Scott Rolen .75
20 Brian Giles .25
21 Derrek Lee .25
22 Mike Lowell .25
23 Mike Mussina .40
24 Sammy Sosa 1.50
25 Brandon Webb .15
26 Jacque Jones .15
27 Randy Johnson 1.00
28 Luis Gonzalez .25
29 Eric Chavez .25
30 Carlos Delgado .40
31 Phil Nevin .15
32 Ichiro Suzuki 1.50
33 Roy Oswalt .25
34 Tim Hudson .25
35 Juan Gonzalez .50
36 Frank Thomas .50
37 Mark Mulder .40
38 Mark Teixeira .40
39 Miguel Tejada .40
40 Jeff Kent .25
41 Andy Pettitte .25
42 Barry Zito .40
43 Roy Halladay .25
44 Rocco Baldelli .25
45 Derek Jeter 2.00
46 Corey Patterson .40
47 Javy Lopez .40
48 A.J. Burnett .15
49 Chipper Jones .75
50 Curt Schilling .50
51 Todd Helton .50
52 Pedro J. Martinez .75
53 Hideo Nomo .40
54 Jose Reyes .50
55 Vernon Wells .15
56 Geoff Jenkins .15
57 Troy Glaus .25
58 Greg Maddux 1.00
59 Jason Schmidt .40
60 Preston Wilson .15
61 Miguel Cabrera .75
62 Hank Blalock .50
63 Rafael Furcal .15
64 Vladimir Guerrero .75
65 Lance Berkman .15
66 Javier Vazquez .15
67 Bret Boone .15
68 Mark Prior 1.00
69 Magglio Ordonez .15
70 Dontrelle Willis .25
71 Richie Sexson .25
72 Alfonso Soriano .75
73 Edwin Jackson .15
74 Jose Vidro .15
75 Jason Giambi .50
76 Kevin Brown .25
77 Orlando Cabrera .15
78 Nomar Garciaparra 1.00
79 Bobby Abreu .25
80 Manny Ramirez .50
81 J.D. Drew .15
82 Roger Clemens 1.50
83 Pat Burrell .15
84 Ryan Klesko .15
85 Garret Anderson .40
86 Johan Santana .15
87 Kevin Millwood .15
88 Austin Kearns .25
89 Jim Thome .75
90 Carlos Beltran .40
91 Kazuo Matsui **RC** 15.00
92 Jamie Brown **RC** 4.00
93 Brandon Medders **RC** 4.00
94 Carlos Vasquez **RC** 4.00
95 Chris Aguila **RC** 4.00
96 David Aardsma 4.00
97 Justin Leone **RC** 4.00
98 Mike Johnston **RC** 4.00
99 Tim Bittner **RC** 4.00
100 Mike Rouse 4.00
101 Dennis Sarfate **RC** 4.00
102 Jason Frasor **RC** 4.00
103 Jorge Vasquez **RC** 4.00
104 Mike Gosling 4.00
105 Jake Woods 4.00
106 Akinori Otsuka **RC** 8.00
107 Lincoln Holdzkom **RC** 4.00
108 Jesse Harper **RC** 4.00
109 Edwin Moreno **RC** 4.00
110 Shingo Takatsu **RC** 6.00
111 Ryan Meaux **RC** 4.00
112 Donnie Kelly **RC** 4.00
113 Jerome Gamble **RC** 4.00
114 Josh Labandeira **RC** 4.00
115 Ian Snell **RC** 8.00
116 Mike Wuertz **RC** 4.00
117 Greg Dobbs **RC** 4.00
118 Sean Henn 4.00
119 David Crouthers 4.00
120 Hector Gimenez **RC** 4.00
121 Renyel Pinto **RC** 10.00
122 Tim Hamulack **RC** 8.00
123 Chris Saenz **RC** 8.00
124 Carlos Hines **RC** 8.00
125 Justin Knoedler **RC** 10.00
126 Onil Joseph **RC** 10.00
127 Ryan Wing 8.00
128 Scott Proctor **RC** 10.00
129 Rusty Tucker **RC** 8.00
130 Fernando Nieve **RC** 8.00
131 Chad Bentz **RC** 10.00
132 Jerry Gil **RC** 8.00
133 Mariano Gomez **RC** 10.00
134 Justin Germano **RC** 10.00
135 Jason Bartlett **RC** 10.00
136 Ronald Belisario **RC** 8.00
137 Enemencio Pacheco 8.00
138 Justin Hampson **RC** 8.00
139 Michael Vento 8.00
140 Merkin Valdez **RC** 10.00
141 Casey Daigle **RC** 8.00
142 Eddy Rodriguez 8.00
143 William Bergolla **RC** 15.00
144 Jose Capellan **RC** 8.00
145 Ronny Cedeno **RC** 8.00
146 Franklyn Gracesqui **RC** 8.00
147 Roman Colon **RC** 10.00
148 Roberto Novoa **RC** 8.00
149 Ivan Ochoa **RC** 10.00
150 Shawn Hill **RC** 8.00

Combo Etchings

NM/M
Production 5-115
Gold Foil: .75-1.5X
Production 1-50
Silver Foil: .75-1X
Production 4-50
No Pricing 15 or less.
JB Josh Beckett/25 60.00
MC Miguel Cabrera/23 50.00
KG Ken Griffey Jr./100 90.00
KG1 Ken Griffey Jr./90 90.00
KG2 Ken Griffey Jr./90 90.00
VG Vladimir Guerrero/60 65.00
DJ1 Derek Jeter/25 200.00
MR Manny Ramirez/60 65.00
MR1 Manny Ramirez/60 65.00
CR Cal Ripken Jr./15 250.00
CR1 Cal Ripken Jr./15 250.00
AR Alex Rodriguez/15 200.00
AR1 Alex Rodriguez/15 200.00
AR2 Alex Rodriguez/115 150.00
KW Kerry Wood/20 65.00
KW1 Kerry Wood/20 65.00
KW2 Kerry Wood/30 50.00

Dual Etchings

NM/M
Production 150 Sets
RJ Alex Rodriguez, Derek Jeter 60.00
WP Kerry Wood, Mark Prior 25.00
RP Jose Reyes, Mike Piazza 30.00
PG Albert Pujols, Vladimir Guerrero 30.00
MM Hideki Matsui, Kazuo Matsui 40.00
MW Mickey Mantle, Ted Williams 180.00

Master Etchings

No Pricing
Production One Set

Star Etchings

NM/M
Quantity produced listed
BA Bobby Abreu/50 20.00
GA Garret Anderson/50 15.00
JB Josh Beckett/50 25.00
CB Carlos Beltran/50 40.00
HB Hank Blalock/50 15.00
BB Bret Boone/50 10.00
MC Miguel Cabrera/50 30.00
EC Eric Chavez/50 15.00
JD J.D. Drew/50 15.00
AD Adam Dunn/50 25.00
NG Nomar Garciaparra/15 60.00

KG	Ken Griffey Jr./50	85.00
KG1	Ken Griffey Jr./50	85.00
VG	Vladimir Guerrero/15	80.00
RH	Roy Halladay/50	15.00
TH	Tim Hudson/50	25.00
GJ	Geoff Jenkins/50	10.00
DL	Derrek Lee/50	25.00
JL	Javy Lopez/50	10.00
ML	Mike Lowell/50	15.00
MU	Mark Mulder/50	15.00
MO	Magglio Ordonez/50	15.00
RO	Roy Oswalt/50	25.00
PR	Mark Prior/50	25.00
JS	Jason Schmidt/50	15.00
MT	Mark Teixeira/50	30.00
TE	Miguel Tejada/50	25.00
BW	Brandon Webb/50	15.00
VW	Vernon Wells/50	15.00
DW	Dontrelle Willis/50	15.00
KW	Kerry Wood/50	20.00

Triple Etchings

NM/M

Production 50 Sets

RJM	Alex Rodriguez, Derek Jeter, Hideki Matsui	125.00
PER	Albert Pujols, Jim Edmonds, Scott Rolen	90.00
SRG	Curt Schilling, Manny Ramirez, Nomar Garciaparra	40.00
SBT	Alfonso Soriano, Hank Blalock, Mark Teixeira	40.00
WPS	Kerry Wood, Mark Prior, Sammy Sosa	50.00
DMW	Joe DiMaggio, Mickey Mantle, Ted Williams	400.00

Etched in Time Black Ink

NM/M

Quantity produced listed

Common Autograph: 6.00

AA	Alfredo Amezaga/375	6.00
SA	Sparky Anderson/375	15.00
TA	Tony Armas/325	6.00
BA	Dusty Baker/150	15.00
JB	Jason Bay/375	15.00
BE	Carlos Beltran/150	30.00
AB	Angel Berroa/1,325	6.00
HB	Hank Blalock/375	15.00
GB	Geoff Blum/375	6.00
BB	Bert Blyleven/375	8.00
CB	Chris Bootcheck/375	8.00
DB	Dewon Brazelton/375	8.00
MB	Marlon Byrd/1,025	8.00
EB	Eric Byrnes/Redemp.	8.00
MC	Miguel Cabrera/1,025	15.00
CA	Chris Capuano/375	8.00
EC	Eric Chavez/375	15.00
AC	Alex Cintron/375	8.00
WC	Will Clark/150	20.00
CL	Brandon Claussen/375	8.00
CC	Chad Cordero/375	6.00
BC	Bobby Crosby/1,325	10.00
AD	Andre Dawson/375	10.00
BD	Brandon Duckworth/375	8.00
ME	Morgan Ensberg/1,325	8.00
DE	Dwight Evans/375	15.00
AE	Adam Everett/325	6.00
WE	Willie Eyre/375	6.00
KF	Kyle Farnsworth/1,325	8.00
PF	Pedro Feliz/325	8.00
RF	Rollie Fingers/375	10.00
JF	Josh Fogg/325	8.00
LF	Lew Ford/375	10.00
NG	Nomar Garciaparra/100	50.00
CG	Chad Gaudin/375	6.00
BG	Brian Giles/375	10.00
MG	Marcus Giles/325	10.00
GO	Jonny Gomes/325	6.00
AG	Adrian Gonzalez/325	8.00
DG	Dwight Gooden/375	10.00
KG	Ken Griffey Jr./1,625	60.00
GR	Ken Griffey Sr./375	8.00
TG	Tony Gwynn/150	40.00
SH	Scott Hairston/375	8.00
RH	Rob Hammock/325	8.00
AH	Aaron Harang/375	12.00
HA	Rich Harden/325	10.00
HE	Ramon Hernandez/325	8.00
RI	Raul Ibanez/325	8.00
EJ	Edwin Jackson/325	8.00
DJ	Derek Jeter	100.00
JJ	Jacque Jones/375	10.00
KA	Al Kaline/375	25.00
MK	Matt Kata/325	8.00
AK	Adam Kennedy/375	6.00
DK	Bobby Kielty/1,325	6.00
HK	Harmon Killebrew/Redemp.	35.00
DK	Dave Kingman/375	8.00
GK	Graham Koonce/375	8.00
LA	Adam LaRoche/1,325	8.00
CS	Carlos Lee/325	10.00
LE	Cliff Lee/1,325	8.00
TL	Ted Lilly/325	8.00
AL	Adam Loewen/375	6.00
ML	Mike Lowell/375	10.00
LM	Luis Matos/325	8.00
DM	Don Mattingly/150	50.00
MA	Joe Mauer/375	25.00
JM	Justin Miller/325	8.00
MO	Jack Morris/375	10.00
MM	Mark Mulder/375	10.00
MU	Dale Murphy/375	20.00
MN	Mike Neu/325	6.00
LN	Laynce Nix/Redemp.	10.00
RO	Roy Oswalt/375	12.00
LO	Lyle Overbay/1,325	8.00
PA	Jim Palmer/375	15.00
CP	Corey Patterson/375	10.00
BP	Brad Penny/375	8.00
JP	Jason Phillips/375	8.00
PO	Boog Powell/375	15.00
MP	Mark Prior/150	30.00
JR	Jose Reyes/325	25.00
JI	Jim Rice/375	10.00
CR	Cal Ripken Jr./100	120.00
BR	Brooks Robinson/375	25.00
RS	Ryne Sandberg/150	50.00
SO	Ron Santo/375	25.00
SS	Steve Sax/375	10.00
MS	Mike Scioscia/375	10.00
BS	Ben Sheets/375	15.00
TS	Terrmel Sledge/325	6.00
DS	Darryl Strawberry/150	15.00
MT	Mark Teixeira/325	20.00
LT	Luis Tiant/375	10.00
AT	Alan Trammell/375	15.00
CU	Chase Utley/375	25.00
RW	Ryan Wagner/1,325	8.00
WK	Rickie Weeks/Redemp.	15.00
JW	Jerome Williams/1,325	8.00
WI	Josh Willingham/1,325	6.00
RA	Randy Winn/375	8.00
KW	Kerry Wood/150	15.00
DY	Delmon Young/375	20.00
MY	Michael Young/1,325	15.00
CZ	Carlos Zambrano/375	25.00

Etched in Time Red Ink

No Pricing

Production 25 Sets

Etched in Time Blue Ink

NM/M

Quantity produced listed

Common Autograph: 6.00

AA	Alfredo Amezaga/100	8.00
SA	Sparky Anderson/250	15.00
TA	Tony Armas/150	6.00
JB	Jason Bay/250	15.00
AB	Angel Berroa/150	8.00
HB	Hank Blalock/250	15.00
GB	Geoff Blum/250	6.00
BB	Bert Blyleven/250	8.00
CB	Chris Bootcheck/100	8.00
DB	Dewon Brazelton/250	8.00
MB	Marlon Byrd/150	8.00
EB	Eric Byrnes/Redemp.	8.00
MC	Miguel Cabrera/150	25.00
CA	Chris Capuano/100	8.00
EC	Eric Chavez/250	15.00
AC	Alex Cintron/100	8.00
WC	Will Clark/50	20.00
CL	Brandon Claussen/100	8.00
CC	Chad Cordero/100	6.00
BC	Bobby Crosby/150	10.00
AD	Andre Dawson/250	10.00
BD	Brandon Duckworth/100	8.00
ME	Morgan Ensberg/150	8.00
DE	Dwight Evans/250	15.00
AE	Adam Everett/150	8.00
WE	Willie Eyre/100	8.00
KF	Kyle Farnsworth/150	8.00
PF	Pedro Feliz/150	8.00
RF	Rollie Fingers/250	10.00
JF	Josh Fogg/150	8.00
LF	Lew Ford/200	10.00
NG	Nomar Garciaparra/50	85.00
CG	Chad Gaudin/100	8.00
BG	Brian Giles/250	10.00
MG	Marcus Giles/150	10.00
GO	Jonny Gomes/150	6.00
AG	Adrian Gonzalez/150	6.00
DG	Dwight Gooden/250	10.00
KG	Ken Griffey Jr./150	75.00
GR	Ken Griffey Sr./250	8.00
VG	Vladimir Guerrero/50	50.00
TG	Tony Gwynn/50	50.00
SH	Scott Hairston/100	8.00
RH	Rob Hammock/150	8.00
AH	Aaron Harang/100	15.00
HA	Rich Harden/150	10.00
HE	Ramon Hernandez/150	8.00
RI	Raul Ibanez/150	8.00
EJ	Edwin Jackson/100	8.00
DJ	Derek Jeter/50	120.00
JJ	Jacque Jones/250	10.00
KA	Al Kaline/250	25.00
MK	Matt Kata/150	8.00
AK	Adam Kennedy/100	8.00
BK	Bobby Kielty/150	8.00
DK	Dave Kingman/250	8.00
GK	Graham Koonce/250	8.00
LA	Adam LaRoche/150	10.00
LE	Cliff Lee/150	10.00
TL	Ted Lilly/150	8.00
ML	Mike Lowell/250	10.00
LM	Luis Matos/150	8.00
DM	Don Mattingly/50	60.00
MA	Joe Mauer/250	25.00
JM	Justin Miller/150	8.00
MO	Jack Morris/250	10.00
MM	Mark Mulder/250	10.00
MU	Dale Murphy/250	25.00
MN	Mike Neu/150	6.00
RO	Roy Oswalt/250	15.00
LO	Lyle Overbay/150	10.00
PA	Jim Palmer/250	15.00
CP	Corey Patterson/250	15.00
BP	Brad Penny/100	8.00
JP	Jason Phillips/250	8.00
LP	Lou Piniella/50	15.00
PO	Boog Powell/250	15.00
MP	Mark Prior/50	20.00
JR	Jose Reyes/150	30.00
JI	Jim Rice/250	10.00
CR	Cal Ripken Jr./50	150.00
BR	Brooks Robinson/250	25.00
RS	Ryne Sandberg/50	60.00
SO	Ron Santo/250	25.00
SS	Steve Sax/250	10.00
MS	Mike Scioscia/250	10.00
BS	Ben Sheets/250	15.00
TS	Terrmel Sledge/150	6.00
MT	Mark Teixeira/150	25.00
LT	Luis Tiant/250	10.00
AT	Alan Trammell/250	15.00
CU	Chase Utley/100	25.00
RW	Ryan Wagner/150	10.00
JW	Jerome Williams/150	10.00
WI	Josh Willingham/150	6.00
RA	Randy Winn/100	10.00
KW	Kerry Wood/50	20.00
DY	Delmon Young/250	20.00
MY	Michael Young/150	15.00
CZ	Carlos Zambrano/250	25.00

Game Bat Blue

NM/M

Common Player:

Purple: 1X

Production 250

Red: 1X

Production 150

Green: 1-2X

Production 50

BA	Bobby Abreu	6.00
RA	Roberto Alomar	6.00
GA	Garret Anderson	6.00
CB	Carlos Beltran	6.00
AB	Adrian Beltre	6.00
LB	Lance Berkman	4.00
HB	Hank Blalock	6.00
BB	Bret Boone	4.00
SC	Sean Casey	4.00
EC	Eric Chavez	6.00
JC	Jose Cruz Jr.	4.00
CD	Carlos Delgado	6.00
JD	J.D. Drew	4.00
AD	Adam Dunn	8.00
JE	Jim Edmonds	4.00
CF	Cliff Floyd	4.00
RF	Rafael Furcal	4.00
NG	Nomar Garciaparra	10.00
JG	Jason Giambi	6.00
BG	Brian Giles	6.00
TG	Troy Glaus	6.00
LG	Luis Gonzalez	4.00
SG	Shawn Green	6.00
KG	Ken Griffey Jr.	12.00
VG	Vladimir Guerrero	10.00
TH	Todd Helton	8.00
HU	Torii Hunter	6.00
GJ	Geoff Jenkins	4.00
DJ	Derek Jeter	20.00
RJ	Randy Johnson	8.00
AJ	Andruw Jones	8.00
CJ	Chipper Jones	8.00
JL	Javy Lopez	6.00
ML	Mike Lowell	6.00
KM	Kazuo Matsui	10.00
MO	Magglio Ordonez	4.00
RP	Rafael Palmeiro	8.00
JP	Jay Payton	4.00
PI	Mike Piazza	10.00
AP	Albert Pujols	15.00
MR	Manny Ramirez	8.00
JR	Jose Reyes	6.00
AR	Alex Rodriguez	15.00
IR	Ivan Rodriguez	8.00
SR	Scott Rolen	15.00
TS	Tim Salmon	6.00
CS	Curt Schilling	6.00
GS	Gary Sheffield	6.00
AS	Alfonso Soriano	8.00
SS	Sammy Sosa	10.00
IS	Ichiro Suzuki	15.00
MT	Mark Teixeira	6.00
TE	Miguel Tejada	6.00
FT	Frank Thomas	8.00
JT	Jim Thome	8.00
OV	Omar Vizquel	4.00
LW	Larry Walker	4.00
VW	Vernon Wells	4.00
BW	Bernie Williams	8.00
KW	Kerry Wood	8.00

2004 Upper Deck First Pitch

NM/M

Complete Set (300): 40.00

Common Player: .10

Common SP (271-300): 1.00

Inserted 1:4

Pack (5): 1.00

Box (36): 25.00

1	Dontrelle Willis	.50
2	Edgar Gonzalez	.25
3	Jose Reyes	.50
4	Jae Weong Seo	.25
5	Miguel Cabrera	.75
6	Jesse Foppert	.25
7	Mike Neu	.25
8	Micheal Nakamura	.25
9	Luis Ayala	.25
10	Jared Sandberg	.25
11	Jhonny Peralta	.25
12	Wilfredo Ledezma	.25
13	Jason Roach	.25
14	Kirk Saarloos	.25
15	Cliff Lee	.25
16	Bobby Hill	.25
17	Lyle Overbay	.25
18	Josh Hall	.25
19	Joe Thurston	.25
20	Matt Kata	.25
21	Jeremy Bonderman	.25
22	Julio Manon	.25
23	Rodrigo Rosario	.25
24	Robby Hammock	.25
25	David Sanders	.25
26	Miguel Ojeda	.25
27	Mark Teixeira	.50
28	Franklyn German	.25
29	Ken Harvey	.25
30	Xavier Nady	.25
31	Tim Salmon	.25
32	Troy Glaus	.25
33	Adam Kennedy	.10
34	David Eckstein	.10
35	Bengie Molina	.10
36	Jarrod Washburn	.10
37	Ramon Ortiz	.10
38	Eric Chavez	.25
39	Miguel Tejada	.25
40	Chris Singleton	.10
41	Jermaine Dye	.10
42	John Halama	.10
43	Tim Hudson	.25
44	Barry Zito	.25
45	Ted Lilly	.10
46	Bobby Kielty	.10
47	Kelvim Escobar	.10
48	Josh Phelps	.10
49	Vernon Wells	.20
50	Roy Halladay	.20
51	Orlando Hudson	.10
52	Eric Hinske	.10
53	Brandon Backe	.10
54	Dewon Brazelton	.10
55	Ben Grieve	.10
56	Aubrey Huff	.10
57	Toby Hall	.10
58	Rocco Baldelli	.50
59	Al Martin	.10
60	Brandon Phillips	.10
61	Omar Vizquel	.10
62	C.C. Sabathia	.10
63	Milton Bradley	.10
64	Ricky Gutierrez	.10
65	Matt Lawton	.10
66	Danys Baez	.10
67	Ichiro Suzuki	1.00
68	Randy Winn	.10
69	Carlos Guillen	.10
70	Mark McLemore	.10
71	Dan Wilson	.10
72	Jamie Moyer	.10
73	Joel Pineiro	.10
74	Edgar Martinez	.20
75	Tony Batista	.10
76	Jay Gibbons	.10
77	Jeff Conine	.10
78	Melvin Mora	.10
79	Geronimo Gil	.10
80	Rodrigo Lopez	.10
81	Jorge Julio	.10
82	Rafael Palmeiro	.40
83	Juan Gonzalez	.40
84	Mike Young	.10
85	Alex Rodriguez	1.00
86	Einar Diaz	.10
87	Kevin Mench	.10
88	Hank Blalock	.25
89	Pedro J. Martinez	.50
90	Byung-Hyun Kim	.10
91	Derek Lowe	.20
92	Jason Varitek	.10
93	Manny Ramirez	.40
94	John Burkett	.10
95	Todd Walker	.10
96	Nomar Garciaparra	1.00
97	Trot Nixon	.10
98	Mike Sweeney	.10
99	Carlos Febles	.10
100	Mike MacDougal	.10
101	Raul Ibanez	.10
102	Jason Grimsley	.10
103	Chris George	.10
104	Brent Mayne	.10
105	Dmitri Young	.10
106	Eric Munson	.10
107	A.J. Hinch	.10
108	Andres Torres	.10
109	Bobby Higginson	.10
110	Shane Halter	.10
111	Matt Walbeck	.10
112	Torii Hunter	.25
113	Doug Mientkiewicz	.10
114	Lew Ford	.10
115	Eric Milton	.10
116	Eddie Guardado	.10
117	Cristian Guzman	.10
118	Corey Koskie	.10
119	Magglio Ordonez	.25
120	Mark Buehrle	.10
121	Billy Koch	.10
122	Jose Valentin	.10
123	Paul Konerko	.10
124	Carlos Lee	.10
125	Jon Garland	.10
126	Jason Giambi	.50
127	Derek Jeter	1.50
128	Roger Clemens	1.00
129	Andy Pettitte	.25
130	Jorge Posada	.25
131	David Wells	.10
132	Hideki Matsui	1.25
133	Mike Mussina	.40
134	Jeff Bagwell	.40
135	Craig Biggio	.20
136	Morgan Ensberg	.10
137	Richard Hidalgo	.10
138	Brad Ausmus	.10
139	Roy Oswalt	.25
140	Billy Wagner	.20
141	Octavio Dotel	.10
142	Gary Sheffield	.25
143	Andruw Jones	.40
144	John Smoltz	.20
145	Rafael Furcal	.20
146	Javy Lopez	.25
147	Shane Reynolds	.10
148	Horacio Ramirez	.10
149	Mike Hampton	.10
150	Jung Bong	.10
151	Ruben Quevedo	.10
152	Ben Sheets	.20
153	Geoff Jenkins	.20
154	Royce Clayton	.10
155	Glendon Rusch	.10
156	John Vander Wal	.10
157	Scott Podsednik	.25
158	Jim Edmonds	.25
159	Tino Martinez	.20
160	Albert Pujols	1.00
161	Matt Morris	.10
162	Woody Williams	.10
163	Edgar Renteria	.10
164	Jason Isringhausen	.10
165	Jason Simontacchi	.10
166	Kerry Robinson	.10
167	Sammy Sosa	1.00
168	Joe Borowski	.10
169	Tony Womack	.10
170	Antonio Alfonseca	.10
171	Corey Patterson	.10
172	Mark Prior	.75
173	Moises Alou	.20
174	Matt Clement	.10
175	Randall Simon	.10
176	Randy Johnson	.50
177	Luis Gonzalez	.20
178	Craig Counsell	.10
179	Miguel Batista	.10
180	Steve Finley	.10
181	Brandon Webb	.10
182	Danny Bautista	.10
183	Oscar Villarreal	.10
184	Shawn Green	.25
185	Brian Jordan	.10
186	Fred McGriff	.20
187	Andy Ashby	.10
188	Rickey Henderson	.25
189	Dave Roberts	.10
190	Eric Gagne	.20
191	Kazuhisa Ishii	.10
192	Adrian Beltre	.10
193	Vladimir Guerrero	.50
194	Livan Hernandez	.10
195	Ron Calloway	.10
196	Sun-Woo Kim	.10
197	Wil Cordero	.10
198	Brad Wilkerson	.10
199	Orlando Cabrera	.10
200	Sidney Ponson	.10
201	Ray Durham	.10
202	Andres Galarraga	.10
203	Benito Santiago	.10
204	Jose Cruz Jr.	.10
205	Jason Schmidt	.10
206	Kirk Rueter	.10
207	Felix Rodriguez	.10
208	Mike Lowell	.10
209	Luis Castillo	.10
210	Derrek Lee	.10
211	Andy Fox	.10
212	Tommy Phelps	.10
213	Todd Hollandsworth	.10
214	Brad Penny	.10
215	Juan Pierre	.10
216	Mike Piazza	.75
217	Jae Weong Seo	.10
218	Ty Wigginton	.10
219	Al Leiter	.10
220	Roger Cedeno	.10
221	Timoniel Perez	.10
222	Aaron Heilman	.10
223	Pedro Astacio	.10
224	Joe McEwing	.10
225	Ryan Klesko	.20
226	Brian Giles	.20
227	Mark Kotsay	.10
228	Brian Lawrence	.10
229	Rod Beck	.10
230	Trevor Hoffman	.10
231	Sean Burroughs	.10
232	Bobby Abreu	.20
233	Jim Thome	.50
234	David Bell	.10
235	Jimmy Rollins	.20
236	Mike Lieberthal	.10
237	Vicente Padilla	.10
238	Randy Wolf	.10
239	Reggie Sanders	.10
240	Jason Kendall	.10
241	Jack Wilson	.10
242	Jose Hernandez	.10
243	Kip Wells	.10
244	Carlos Rivera	.10
245	Craig Wilson	.10
246	Adam Dunn	.25
247	Sean Casey	.10
248	Danny Graves	.10
249	Ryan Dempster	.10
250	Barry Larkin	.25
251	Reggie Taylor	.10
252	Wily Mo Pena	.10
253	Larry Walker	.20
254	Mark Sweeney	.10
255	Preston Wilson	.10
256	Jason Jennings	.10
257	Charles Johnson	.10
258	Jay Payton	.10
259	Chris Stynes	.10
260	Juan Uribe	.10
261	Hideki Matsui/CL	.10
262	Josh Beckett/CL	.20
263	Dontrelle Willis/CL	.20
264	Kevin Millwood/CL	.20
265	Billy Wagner/CL	.10
266	Rocco Baldelli/CL	.25
267	Roger Clemens/CL	.50
268	Rafael Palmeiro/CL	.20
269	Miguel Cabrera/CL	.25
270	Jose Contreras/CL	.10
271	Rickie Weeks	3.00
272	Delmon Young	4.00
273	Chien-Ming Wang	1.00
274	Rich Harden	1.00
275	Edwin Jackson	1.50
276	Dan Haren	1.00
277	Todd Wellemeyer	1.00
278	Prentice Redman	1.00
279	Ryan Wagner	1.50
280	Aaron Looper	1.00
281	Rick Roberts	1.00
282	Josh Willingham	1.00
283	David Crouthers	1.00
284	Chris Capuano	1.00
285	Mike Gosling	1.00

286 Brian Sweeney 1.00
287 Donald Kelly **RC** 1.00
288 Ryan Meaux **RC** 1.50
289 Colin Porter 1.00
290 Jerome Gamble **RC** 1.50
291 Colby Miller **RC** 1.50
292 Ian Ferguson 1.00
293 Tim Bittner **RC** 1.00
294 Jason Frasor **RC** 1.00
295 Brandon Medders **RC** 1.00
296 Mike Johnston **RC** 1.00
297 Tim Bausher **RC** 1.00
298 Justin Leone **RC** 1.00
299 Sean Henn 1.00
300 Michel Hernandez 1.00

First and Foremost

NM/M
Complete Set (14): 40.00
Common Player: 3.00
Inserted 1:Blaster Box
EB Ernie Banks 5.00
GH George H.W. Bush 5.00
GW George W. Bush 5.00
JC Jose Contreras 3.00
WF Whitey Ford 4.00
RH Rich Harden 3.00
DH Dan Haren 3.00
HR Horacio Ramirez 3.00
MS Mike Schmidt 5.00
LT Luis Tiant 3.00
RW Ryan Wagner 3.00
BW Brandon Webb 3.00
JW Jerome Williams 3.00
DW Dontrelle Willis 3.00

Holiday Greeting Card

Continuing its tradition of producing a hobby-related greeting card for its customers, UD in 2004 issued a post-card-sized (6-1/4" x 4-5/8") card featuring a composite black-and-white photo of Yankees greats. The red-and-green design on front includes a replica of the 1939 Baseball Centennial stamp and a Cooperstown postmark.

NM/M
HH04 Babe Ruth, Lou Gehrig, Joe DiMaggio, Mickey Mantle, Derek Jeter 4.00

Japan Series Souvenir Sheet

It was reported that 200,000 of these 7-1/2" x 10-1/2" souvenir sheets were produced to commemorate the 2004 season opening series in Japan between the Yankees and Devil Rays. Sheets were distributed at the exhibition games played between the MLB and Japanese teams. Some were reportedly given to youngsters at the ESPN Zone in New York City as well. Fronts picture three Yankees, three Devil Rays and a pair of Japanese players. On back is a large ghosted image of Hideki Matsui over which is printed in Japanese addresses and phone numbers of UD outlets. The sheets are not perforated.

NM/M
Uncut Sheet: 15.00

2004 UD Legends Timeless Teams

NM/M
Complete Set (300): 40.00
Common Player: .15
Pack (5): 5.00
Box (18): 75.00
1 Bob Gibson .50
2 Lou Brock .50
3 Ray Washburn .15
4 Tim McCarver .15
5 Harmon Killebrew 1.00
6 Jim Kaat .25
7 Jim Perry .15
8 Jim "Mudcat" Grant .15
9 Boog Powell .15
10 Brooks Robinson .50
11 Frank Robinson .50
12 Jim Palmer .25
13 Carl Yastrzemski 1.00
14 Jim Lonborg .15
15 George Scott .15
16 Sparky Lyle .15
17 Rico Petrocelli .15
18 Bob Gibson .50
19 Julian Javier .15
20 Lou Brock .50
21 Orlando Cepeda .15
22 Ray Washburn .15
23 Steve Carlton .50
24 Tim McCarver .15
25 Al Kaline .50
26 Bill Freehan .15
27 Denny McLain .15
28 Dick McAuliffe .15
29 Jim Northrup .15
30 John Hiller .15
31 Mickey Lolich .15
32 Mickey Stanley .15
33 Willie Horton .15
34 Bob Gibson .50
35 Julian Javier .15
36 Lou Brock .50
37 Orlando Cepeda .25
38 Steve Carlton .50
39 Boog Powell .15
40 Brooks Robinson .50
41 Davey Johnson .15
42 Merv Rettenmund .15
43 Eddie Watt .15
44 Frank Robinson .50
45 Jim Palmer .25
46 Mike Cuellar .15
47 Paul Blair .15
48 Pete Richert .15
49 Ellie Hendricks .15
50 Billy Williams .25
51 Randy Hundley .15
52 Ernie Banks 1.00
53 Fergie Jenkins .25
54 Jim Hickman .15
55 Ken Holtzman .15
56 Ron Santo .25
57 Ed Kranepool .15
58 Jerry Koosman .15
59 Nolan Ryan 2.00
60 Tom Seaver .50
61 Boog Powell .15
62 Brooks Robinson .50
63 Davey Johnson .15
64 Merv Rettenmund .15
65 Eddie Watt .15
66 Frank Robinson .50
67 Jim Palmer .25
68 Mike Cuellar .15
69 Paul Blair .15
70 Pete Richert .15
71 Ellie Hendricks .15
72 Al Kaline .50
73 Bill Freehan .15
74 Dick McAuliffe .15
75 Jim Northrup .15
76 John Hiller .15
77 Mickey Lolich .15
78 Mickey Stanley .15
79 Willie Horton .15
80 Bert Campaneris .15
81 Blue Moon Odom .15
82 Sal Bando .15
83 Joe Rudi .15
84 Ken Holtzman .15
85 Bill North .15
86 Blue Moon Odom .15
87 Gene Tenace .15
88 Manny Trillo .15
89 Dick Green .15
90 Rollie Fingers .25
91 Sal Bando .15
92 Vida Blue .15
93 Bill Buckner .15
94 Davey Lopes .15
95 Don Sutton .25
96 Al Downing .15
97 Ron Cey .15
98 Steve Garvey .15
99 Tommy John .15
100 Bert Campaneris .15
101 Bill North .15
102 Joe Rudi .15
103 Sal Bando .15
104 Vida Blue .15
105 Carl Yastrzemski .75
106 Carlton Fisk .25
107 Cecil Cooper .15
108 Dwight Evans .15
109 Fred Lynn .15
110 Jim Rice .25
111 Luis Tiant .15
112 Rick Burleson .15
113 Rico Petrocelli .15
114 Pedro Borbon .15
115 Dave Concepcion .15
116 Don Gullett .15
117 George Foster .15
118 Joe Morgan .25
119 Johnny Bench .50
120 Rawly Eastwick .15
121 Sparky Anderson .15
122 Tony Perez .25
123 Billy Williams .25
124 Gene Tenace .15
125 Jim Perry .15
126 Vida Blue .15
127 Pedro Borbon .15
128 Dave Concepcion .15
129 Don Gullett .15
130 George Foster .15
131 Joe Morgan .25
132 Johnny Bench .50
133 Ken Griffey Sr. .15
134 Rawly Eastwick .15
135 Tony Perez .25
136 Bill Russell .15
137 Burt Hooton .15
138 Davey Lopes .15
139 Don Sutton .25
140 Dusty Baker .15
141 Steve Yeager .15
142 Ron Cey .15
143 Steve Garvey .15
144 Tommy John .15
145 Bucky Dent .15
146 Chris Chambliss .15
147 Ed Figueroa .15
148 Graig Nettles .15
149 Lou Piniella .25
150 Roy White .15
151 Don Gullett .15
152 Sparky Lyle .15
153 Brian Doyle .15
154 Bucky Dent .15
155 Chris Chambliss .15
156 Ed Figueroa .15
157 Graig Nettles .15
158 Lou Piniella .25
159 Roy White .15
160 Rich "Goose" Gossage .15
161 Sparky Lyle .15
162 Bobby Grich .15
163 Brian Downing .15
164 Dan Ford .15
165 Nolan Ryan 2.00
166 Dave Concepcion .15
167 George Foster .15
168 Johnny Bench .50
169 Ray Knight .15
170 Tom Seaver .50
171 Bert Blyleven .15
172 Bill Madlock .15
173 Dave Parker .25
174 Phil Garner .15
175 Bill Russell .15
176 Steve Yeager .15
177 Don Sutton .25
178 Dusty Baker .25
179 Jerry Reuss .15
180 Mickey Hatcher .15
181 Pedro Guerrero .15
182 Ron Cey .15
183 Steve Garvey .15
184 Rudy May .15
185 Brian Doyle .15
186 Bucky Dent .15
187 Jim Kaat .15
188 Lou Piniella .15
189 Luis Tiant .15
190 Tommy John .15
191 Bake McBride .15
192 Bob Boone .15
193 Dickie Noles .15
194 Manny Trillo .15
195 Mike Schmidt 1.00
196 Sparky Lyle .15
197 Steve Carlton .50
198 Steve Yeager .15
199 Burt Hooton .15
200 Dusty Baker .15
201 Jerry Reuss .15
202 Mike Scioscia .15
203 Pedro Guerrero .15
204 Ron Cey .15
205 Steve Garvey .15
206 Alejandro Pena .15
207 Steve Sax .15
208 Cecil Cooper .15
209 Gorman Thomas .15
210 Paul Molitor .50
211 Robin Yount 1.00
212 Rollie Fingers .25
213 Don Money .15
214 Rudy May .15
215 Bucky Dent .15
216 Dave Winfield .50
217 Lou Piniella .25
218 Rich "Goose" Gossage .15
219 Tommy John .15
220 Cecil Cooper .15
221 Gorman Thomas .15
222 Paul Molitor .50
223 Robin Yount 1.00
224 Don Money .15
225 Cal Ripken Jr. 2.00
226 Dan Ford .15
227 Jim Palmer .25
228 John Shelby .15
229 Alan Trammell .25
230 Chet Lemon .15
231 Howard Johnson .15
232 Jack Morris .15
233 Kirk Gibson .25
234 Lou Whitaker .15
235 Sparky Anderson .15
236 Dave Winfield .50
237 Don Mattingly 1.00
238 Ken Griffey Sr. .15
239 Phil Niekro .15
240 Yogi Berra .75
241 Bill Buckner .15
242 Bruce Hurst .15
243 Dave Henderson .15
244 Dwight Evans .15
245 Jim Rice .15
246 Tom Seaver .50
247 Wade Boggs .50
248 Bob Boone .15
249 Bobby Grich .15
250 Brian Downing .15
251 Don Sutton .25
252 Terry Forster .15
253 Rick Burleson .15
254 Wally Joyner .15
255 Darryl Strawberry .15
256 Dwight Gooden .15
257 Gary Carter .15
258 Jesse Orosco .15
259 Keith Hernandez .15
260 Lenny Dykstra .15
261 Mookie Wilson .15
262 Ray Knight .15
263 Wally Backman .15
264 Sid Fernandez .15
265 Alan Trammell .25
266 Dan Petry .15
267 Chet Lemon .15
268 Sparky Anderson .15
269 Jack Morris .15
270 Kirk Gibson .15
271 Lou Whitaker .15
272 Bert Blyleven .15
273 Kent Hrbek .15
274 Kirby Puckett .75
275 Alejandro Pena .15
276 Jesse Orosco .15
277 John Shelby .15
278 Kirk Gibson .15
279 Mickey Hatcher .15
280 Mike Scioscia .15
281 Steve Sax .15
282 Darryl Strawberry .15
283 Dwight Gooden .15
284 Gary Carter .15
285 Howard Johnson .15
286 Keith Hernandez .15
287 Lenny Dykstra .15
288 Mookie Wilson .15
289 Wally Backman .15
290 Sid Fernandez .15
291 Jack Morris .15
292 Kent Hrbek .15
293 Kirby Puckett .75
294 Dave Winfield .50
295 Jack Morris .15
296 Joe Carter .15
297 Don Mattingly 1.00
298 Paul O'Neill .15
299 Jack McDowell .15
300 Wade Boggs .50

Gold

No Pricing
Production Five Sets

Autographs

NM/M
Common Autograph: 10.00
Golds: No Pricing
Production Five Sets
Platinum: No Pricing
Production One Set
2 Lou Brock MM/SP/75 20.00
3 Ray Washburn 10.00
4 Tim McCarver 15.00
5 Harmon Killebrew 40.00
6 Jim Kaat 10.00
7 Jim Perry 12.00
9 Boog Powell 10.00
10 Brooks Robinson 35.00
12 Jim Palmer/SP/50 20.00
13 Carl Yastrzemski/SP/25 80.00
14 Jim Lonborg 10.00
15 George Scott 10.00
16 Sparky Lyle 10.00
17 Rico Petrocelli 10.00
18 Bob Gibson/SP/35 40.00
19 Julian Javier 10.00
20 Lou Brock/SP/60 20.00
21 Orlando Cepeda/SP/50 20.00
22 Ray Washburn 10.00
24 Tim McCarver 12.00
25 Al Kaline 25.00
26 Bill Freehan 10.00
27 Denny McLain 20.00
28 Dick McAuliffe 10.00
29 Jim Northrup 15.00
30 John Hiller 10.00
31 Mickey Lolich 15.00
32 Mickey Stanley 10.00
33 Willie Horton 10.00
35 Julian Javier 10.00
36 Lou Brock/SP/50 20.00
38 Steve Carlton/SP/35 30.00
39 Boog Powell 10.00
40 Brooks Robinson/SP/100 40.00
41 Davey Johnson 10.00
42 Merv Rettenmund 10.00
43 Eddie Watt 10.00
46 Mike Cuellar 10.00
47 Paul Blair 10.00
48 Pete Richert 10.00
49 Ellie Hendricks 10.00
50 Billy Williams/SP/75 25.00
51 Randy Hundley 10.00
53 Fergie Jenkins 15.00
54 Jim Hickman 20.00
55 Ken Holtzman 15.00
56 Ron Santo 25.00
57 Ed Kranepool 10.00
58 Jerry Koosman 15.00
59 Nolan Ryan/SP/50 175.00
60 Tom Seaver/SP/50 50.00
61 Boog Powell 12.00
62 Brooks Robinson/SP/35 50.00
63 Davey Johnson 10.00
64 Merv Rettenmund 10.00
65 Eddie Watt 10.00
66 Frank Robinson/SP/50 30.00
67 Jim Palmer/SP/75 20.00
68 Mike Cuellar 12.00
69 Paul Blair 10.00
70 Pete Richert 10.00
71 Ellie Hendricks 10.00
72 Al Kaline 25.00
73 Bill Freehan 10.00
74 Dick McAuliffe 15.00
75 Jim Northrup 15.00
76 John Hiller 10.00
77 Mickey Lolich 15.00
78 Mickey Stanley 10.00
79 Willie Horton 12.00
80 Bert Campaneris 10.00
81 Blue Moon Odom 15.00
82 Sal Bando/Exch 10.00
83 Joe Rudi 10.00
84 Ken Holtzman 10.00
85 Bill North 10.00
86 Blue Moon Odom 15.00
87 Gene Tenace 10.00
88 Manny Trillo 15.00
89 Dick Green 10.00
90 Rollie Fingers 15.00
91 Sal Bando 10.00
92 Vida Blue 15.00
93 Bill Buckner 15.00
94 Davey Lopes 10.00
95 Don Sutton 15.00
96 Al Downing MM 10.00
100 Bert Campaneris 10.00
101 Bill North 10.00
102 Joe Rudi 10.00
103 Sal Bando 10.00
104 Vida Blue/SP/100 15.00
105 Carl Yastrzemski/SP/50 60.00
106 Carlton Fisk/SP/100 30.00
107 Cecil Cooper/SP/75 15.00
108 Dwight Evans/SP/75 10.00
109 Fred Lynn 10.00
110 Jim Rice/SP/100 Exch 20.00
111 Luis Tiant Exch 10.00
112 Rick Burleson 10.00
113 Rico Petrocelli 10.00
114 Pedro Borbon 10.00
115 Dave Concepcion/Exch 10.00
116 Don Gullett 15.00
117 George Foster/SP/50 15.00
119 Johnny Bench/SP/85 50.00
120 Rawly Eastwick 10.00
121 Sparky Anderson 10.00
122 Tony Perez 30.00
123 Billy Williams/SP/50 20.00
124 Gene Tenace 10.00
125 Jim Perry 10.00
126 Vida Blue/SP/75 20.00
127 Pedro Borbon 10.00
128 Dave Concepcion/Exch 10.00
129 Don Gullett 15.00
133 Ken Griffey Sr. 10.00
134 Rawly Eastwick 10.00
135 Tony Perez 30.00
136 Bill Russell 10.00
137 Burt Hooton 10.00
138 Davey Lopes 10.00
139 Don Sutton 15.00
140 Dusty Baker Exch 15.00
141 Steve Yeager/SP/75 Exch 10.00
144 Tommy John/SP/35 15.00
145 Bucky Dent/SP/75 15.00
146 Chris Chambliss 15.00
147 Ed Figueroa 10.00
148 Graig Nettles 15.00
150 Roy White 10.00
151 Don Gullett 15.00
152 Sparky Lyle 10.00
153 Brian Doyle 10.00
155 Chris Chambliss 15.00
156 Ed Figueroa 10.00
157 Graig Nettles 15.00
159 Roy White 10.00
160 Rich "Goose" Gossage 15.00
161 Sparky Lyle 10.00
162 Bobby Grich 10.00
163 Brian Downing 10.00
164 Dan Ford 10.00
166 Dave Concepcion/SP/75 Exch 10.00
169 Ray Knight 10.00
171 Bert Blyleven 15.00
172 Bill Madlock 10.00
173 Dave Parker 12.00
174 Phil Garner 10.00
175 Bill Russell 10.00
176 Steve Yeager 10.00
177 Don Sutton/SP/50 20.00
178 Dusty Baker 15.00
179 Jerry Reuss 10.00
180 Mickey Hatcher 10.00
181 Pedro Guerrero 10.00
182 Ron Cey/SP/50 15.00
183 Steve Garvey/SP/50 15.00
184 Rudy May 10.00
185 Brian Doyle 10.00
186 Bucky Dent/SP/60 15.00
187 Jim Kaat 10.00
188 Lou Piniella/SP/50 15.00
189 Luis Tiant 10.00
190 Tommy John/SP/50 15.00
191 Bake McBride 15.00
192 Bob Boone 10.00
193 Dickie Noles 10.00
194 Manny Trillo 15.00
195 Mike Schmidt/SP/50 75.00
196 Sparky Lyle 10.00
197 Steve Carlton/SP/50 20.00
198 Steve Yeager 10.00
199 Burt Hooton 10.00
200 Dusty Baker/Exch 15.00
201 Jerry Reuss 10.00
202 Mike Scioscia 10.00
203 Pedro Guerrero 10.00
204 Ron Cey/SP/75 10.00
205 Steve Garvey/SP/75 15.00
206 Alejandro Pena 10.00
207 Steve Sax/SP/100 10.00
208 Cecil Cooper/SP/85 15.00
209 Gorman Thomas/Exch 10.00
212 Rollie Fingers 15.00
213 Don Money 10.00
214 Rudy May 10.00
216 Dave Winfield/SP/50 30.00
217 Lou Piniella/SP/75 15.00
218 Rich "Goose" Gossage 15.00
219 Tommy John/SP/75 10.00
220 Cecil Cooper 15.00
221 Gorman Thomas/Exch 10.00
222 Paul Molitor/SP/50 45.00
223 Robin Yount/SP/50 75.00
224 Don Money 10.00
225 Cal Ripken Jr./SP/50 180.00
226 Dan Ford 10.00
228 John Shelby 10.00
229 Alan Trammell 15.00
230 Chet Lemon 10.00
231 Howard Johnson 15.00
232 Jack Morris/SP/35 15.00
233 Kirk Gibson 15.00
234 Lou Whitaker/SP/100 15.00

235 Sparky Anderson 10.00
237 Don Mattingly/SP/50 60.00
238 Ken Griffey Sr. 10.00
239 Phil Niekro 15.00
240 Yogi Berra/SP/47 50.00
241 Bill Buckner 15.00
242 Bruce Hurst 15.00
243 Dave Henderson 10.00
245 Jim Rice/SP/75 Exch 20.00
247 Wade Boggs/SP/50 30.00
248 Bob Boone 10.00
249 Bobby Grich 10.00
250 Brian Downing 10.00
251 Don Sutton/SP/75 15.00
252 Terry Forster 10.00
253 Rick Burleson 10.00
254 Wally Joyner 15.00
255 Darryl Strawberry 15.00
256 Dwight Gooden 15.00
257 Gary Carter/SP/75 20.00
258 Jesse Orosco 10.00
259 Keith Hernandez 15.00
260 Lenny Dykstra 10.00
261 Mookie Wilson 10.00
262 Ray Knight 10.00
263 Wally Backman 10.00
264 Sid Fernandez/Exch 10.00
265 Alan Trammell 15.00
266 Dan Petry 10.00
267 Chet Lemon 10.00
268 Sparky Anderson 10.00
270 Kirk Gibson 15.00
271 Lou Whitaker/SP/50 20.00
272 Bert Blyleven 10.00
273 Kent Hrbek 15.00
275 Alejandro Pena 10.00
276 Jesse Orosco 10.00
277 John Shelby 10.00
278 Kirk Gibson/SP/50 20.00
279 Mickey Hatcher 10.00
280 Mike Scioscia 10.00
281 Steve Sax 10.00
282 Darryl Strawberry 15.00
283 Dwight Gooden 15.00
284 Gary Carter/SP/50 20.00
285 Howard Johnson 10.00
286 Keith Hernandez 15.00
287 Lenny Dykstra 10.00
288 Mookie Wilson 10.00
289 Wally Backman 10.00
290 Sid Fernandez/Exch 10.00
291 Jack Morris/SP/50 15.00
292 Kent Hrbek 15.00
293 Kirby Puckett/SP/50 50.00
294 Dave Winfield/SP/35 35.00
295 Jack Morris/SP/75 15.00
298 Paul O'Neill 40.00
299 Jack McDowell 10.00
300 Wade Boggs/SP/75 25.00

Legendary Combo Signs.

No Pricing

Legendary Combo Cuts

No Pricing

Legendary Sign. Dual

NM/M

Quantity produced listed
BC Lou Brock, Orlando Cepeda/75 40.00
BJ Lou Brock, Julian Javier/150 25.00
BM Wade Boggs, Don Mattingly/50 140.00
BO Vida Blue, Blue Moon Odom/150 25.00
BW Ernie Banks, Billy Williams/25 100.00
CB Steve Carlton, Bret Boone/150 50.00
CG Ron Cey, Steve Garvey/150 40.00
CH Gary Carter, Keith Hernandez/150 30.00
CM Dave Concepcion, Joe Morgan/75 Exch 35.00
DD Bucky Dent, Brian Doyle/150 25.00
FR Fred Lynn, Jim Rice/150 40.00
GA Kirk Gibson, Sparky Anderson/150 40.00
GB Bob Gibson, Lou Brock/50 75.00
GC Dwight Gooden, Gary Carter/150 30.00
GL Rich "Goose" Gossage, Sparky Lyle/150 Exch 25.00
HJ Ken Holtzman, Fergie Jenkins/150 40.00
HK Keith Hernandez, Ray Knight/150 30.00
JH Fergie Jenkins, Randy Hundley/150 40.00
JS Tommy John, Don Sutton/150 25.00
KH Al Kaline, Willie Horton/150 40.00
KK Harmon Killebrew, Jim Kaat/150 50.00
LM Mickey Lolich, Denny McLain/75 60.00
MB Joe Morgan, Johnny Bench/25 80.00
MF Denny McLain, Bill Freehan/150 40.00
NC Graig Nettles, Chris Chambliss/150 30.00
OM Paul O'Neill, Don Mattingly/75 140.00
PC Jim Palmer, Mike Cuellar/150 30.00
PF Tony Perez, George Foster/150 40.00
PH Kirby Puckett, Kent Hrbek/50 65.00
PN Lou Piniella, Graig Nettles/150 30.00
PR Jim Palmer, Merv Rettenmund/150 35.00
RL Bill Russell, Davey Lopes/150 30.00
RR Brooks Robinson, Frank Robinson/50 70.00
RS Nolan Ryan, Tom Seaver/25 250.00
SD Steve Garvey, Davey Lopes/150 25.00
SG Darryl Strawberry, Dwight Gooden/150 40.00
SY Don Sutton, Steve Yeager/150 30.00
TF Luis Tiant, Carlton Fisk/50 45.00
TM Gorman Thomas, Paul Molitor/150 Exch 35.00
WB Mookie Wilson, Bill Buckner/150 30.00
WT Lou Whitaker, Alan Trammell/75 75.00
YM Robin Yount, Paul Molitor/50 120.00
YP Carl Yastrzemski, Rico Petrocelli/50 75.00

Legendary Sign. Triple

NM/M

Quantity produced listed
BCM Johnny Bench, Dave Concepcion, Joe Morgan/25 Exch 100.00
BOM Wade Boggs, Paul O'Neill, Don Mattingly/50 150.00
BRB Sal Bando, Joe Rudi, Vida Blue/75 50.00
BSW Ernie Banks, Ron Santo, Billy Williams/25 140.00
CDK Gary Carter, Lenny Dykstra, Ray Knight/50 75.00
CND Chris Chambliss, Graig Nettles, Bucky Dent/50 50.00
ERL Dwight Evans, Jim Rice, Fred Lynn/50 125.00
GBC Steve Garvey, Dusty Baker, Ron Cey/50 75.00
GBM Bob Gibson, Lou Brock, Tim McCarver/25 100.00
GDR Bobby Grich, Al Downing, Nolan Ryan/25 175.00
GHS Kirk Gibson, Mickey Hatcher, Mike Scioscia/75 85.00
GMP Phil Garner, Bill Madlock, Dave Parker/50 75.00
HHS Jim Hickman, Ken Holtzman, Ron Santo/75 60.00
HSJ Burt Hooton, Don Sutton, Tommy John/50 50.00
JHH Fergie Jenkins, Randy Hundley, Ken Holtzman/75 50.00
KKP Harmon Killebrew, Jim Kaat, Jim Perry/50 65.00
KPG Jim Kaat, Jim Perry, Jim "Mudcat" Grant/75 Exch 40.00
KSR Jerry Koosman, Tom Seaver, Nolan Ryan/25 250.00
MHP Jack Morris, Kent Hrbek, Kirby Puckett/50 100.00
MLF Denny McLain, Mickey Lolich, Bill Freehan/50 60.00
NKH Jim Northrup, Al Kaline, Willie Horton/75 65.00
PBH Kirby Puckett, Bert Blyleven, Kent Hrbek/50 90.00
PCR Jim Palmer, Mike Cuellar, Pete Richert/75 45.00
PPW Jim Palmer, Boog Powell, Earl Weaver/75 60.00
RPR Frank Robinson, Boog Powell, Brooks Robinson/50 80.00
RWP Cal Ripken Jr., Earl Weaver, Jim Palmer/25 250.00
SCB Mike Schmidt, Steve Carlton, Bob Boone/50 125.00
SGS Steve Sax, Pedro Guerrero, Mike Scioscia/75 60.00
TWA Alan Trammell, Lou Whitaker, Sparky Anderson/50 75.00
YCT Robin Yount, Cecil Cooper, Gorman Thomas/50 Exch 120.00
YFT Carl Yastrzemski, Carlton Fisk, Luis Tiant/25 140.00
YMT Robin Yount, Paul Molitor, Gorman Thomas/75 Exch 140.00

Team Terrific GU Brand Logo

NM/M

Quantity produced listed
BO Baltimore Orioles/35 90.00
BR Boston Red Sox/35 80.00
CR Cincinnati Reds/35 80.00
LD Los Angeles Dodgers/35 60.00
MB Milwaukee Brewers/41 50.00
NM New York Mets/35 50.00
OA Oakland A's/39 40.00
SC St. Louis Cardinals/35 75.00

Team Terrific GU Hat Logo

NM/M

Quantity produced listed
BO Baltimore Orioles/50 90.00
BR Boston Red Sox/50 80.00
CR Cincinnati Reds/50 80.00
LD Los Angeles Dodgers/50 60.00
MB Milwaukee Brewers/82 40.00
NM New York Mets/50 50.00
OA Oakland A's/50 40.00
SC St. Louis Cardinals/50 75.00

Team Terrific GU League

No Pricing
Production 15 Sets

Team Terrific GU Stats

No Pricing
Production 1-5

Team Terrific GU Team Logo

NM/M

Quantity produced listed
BO Baltimore Orioles/85 60.00
BR Boston Red Sox/85 50.00
CR Cincinnati Reds/85 75.00
LD Los Angeles Dodgers/85 50.00
MB Milwaukee Brewers/100 30.00
NM New York Mets/85 30.00
OA Oakland A's/100 30.00
SC St. Louis Cardinals/100 50.00

National Trading Card Day

As part of its participation in NTCD on April 3, Upper Deck issued a 15-card foil pack with four baseball player cards, two each football and hockey, three basketball and four golf, plus a header. Only the baseball players are listed here. Fronts have action photos on a ghosted background; backs have recent stats, a photo detail and biographical data. The NTCD logo appears on front in silver foil.

NM/M

Unopened Pack: 4.00
Common Player: .25
UD-2 Hideki Matsui .50
UD-3 Ichiro .50
UD-5 Ken Griffey Jr. .25
UD-12 Sammy Sosa .25

National VIP

Persons purchasing a VIP admission package at the 2004 National Sports Collectors Convention in Cleveland received a cello-wrapped pack of five UV-coated cards with silver-foil stamping on front. Only one baseball player was included.

NM/M

Complete Set (5): 12.00
VIP3 Derek Jeter 3.00

2004 Upper Deck Play Ball Promos

Each July 2004 newsstand issue of Tuff Stuff magazine included a Play Ball promo card inside its poly bag. The cards differ from the issued version only in the appearance on front of a silver-foil "UD PROMO" notation. It is not known how many different plauers cards were used in the promotion.

Common Player:
Stars: 1.5-2.5X

2004 Upper Deck Play Ball

NM/M

Complete Set (183):
Common Player: .15
Common SP (133-162): 3.00
Production 2,004
Common Classic Combo (163-183): 2.00
Production 1,999
Pack (5): 3.00
Box (24): 65.00
1 Hideo Nomo .25
2 Curt Schilling .50
3 Barry Zito .40
4 Nomar Garciaparra 1.50
5 Yogi Berra .50
6 Randy Johnson .75
7 Jason Giambi .75
8 Sammy Sosa 1.25
9 David Ortiz .40
10 Derek Jeter 2.00
11 Warren Spahn .50
12 Mark Prior 1.00
13 Roger Clemens 1.50
14 Mike Piazza 1.00
15 Nolan Ryan 2.00
16 Joe DiMaggio 1.50
17 Alfonso Soriano .75
18 Brandon Webb .25
19 Shawn Green .25
20 Bob Feller .25
21 Mike Schmidt .75
22 Mark Teixeira .25
23 Pedro J. Martinez .75
24 Vladimir Guerrero .75
25 Rafael Furcal .25
26 Derrek Lee .25
27 Carlos Delgado .50
28 Mickey Mantle 3.00
29 Dontrelle Willis .25
30 Ted Williams 1.50
31 Vernon Wells .25
32 Alex Rodriguez 1.50
33 Brooks Robinson .50
34 Tom Seaver .50
35 Ernie Banks .50
36 Bob Gibson .50
37 Jim Thome .75
38 Mike Mussina .50
39 Eric Chavez .25
40 Roy Halladay .25
41 Eric Gagne .40
42 Jose Reyes .40
43 Jeff Bagwell .50
44 Rich Harden .15
45 Jeff Kent .25
46 Lance Berkman .25
47 Adam Dunn .40
48 Richie Sexson .40
49 Andruw Jones .50
50 Ichiro Suzuki 1.25
51 Edgar Renteria .25
52 Rocco Baldelli .25
53 Jim Edmonds .25
54 Magglio Ordonez .25
55 Austin Kearns .25
56 Garret Anderson .40
57 Manny Ramirez .50
58 Roy Oswalt .25
59 Gary Sheffield .40
60 Mark Mulder .25
61 Ben Sheets .25
62 Scott Rolen .75
63 Greg Maddux 1.00
64 Jose Contreras .15
65 Miguel Cabrera .50
66 Hank Blalock .40
67 Miguel Tejada .40
68 Albert Pujols 1.50
69 Hideki Matsui 1.50
70 Mike Lowell .25
71 Tim Hudson .25
72 Bret Boone .25
73 Ivan Rodriguez .50
74 Josh Beckett .50
75 Todd Helton .50
76 Brian Giles .25
77 Orlando Cabrera .15
78 Carlos Beltran .40
79 Jason Schmidt .25
80 Kerry Wood .75
81 Preston Wilson .15
82 Troy Glaus .40
83 Kevin Brown .25
84 Rafael Palmeiro .50
85 Chipper Jones 1.00
86 Reggie Sanders .15
87 Cliff Floyd .15
88 Corey Patterson .25
89 Kevin Millwood .25
90 Aaron Boone .15
91 Darin Erstad .25
92 Richard Hidalgo .15
93 Dmitri Young .15
94 Jeremy Bonderman .15
95 Larry Walker .25
96 Edgar Martinez .25
97 Jerome Williams .15
98 Luis Gonzalez .25
99 Roberto Alomar .40
100 Jerry Hairston Jr. .15
101 Luis Matos .15
102 Andy Pettitte .40
103 Frank Thomas .50
104 Rondell White .25
105 Jody Gerut .15
106 Bartolo Colon .25
107 Johnny Damon .25
108 Ryan Klesko .25
109 Geoff Jenkins .25
110 Jorge Posada .40
111 Melvin Mora .15
112 Bernie Williams .40
113 Shannon Stewart .15
114 Bobby Abreu .25
115 Jose Guillen .25
116 Brandon Phillips .15
117 Jose Vidro .15
118 Mike Sweeney .15
119 Jacque Jones .15
120 Josh Phelps .15
121 Milton Bradley .15
122 Torii Hunter .25
123 Carl Crawford .15
124 Javier Vazquez .25
125 Juan Gonzalez .50
126 Travis Hafner .15
127 Ken Griffey Jr. 1.00
128 Phil Nevin .15
129 Trot Nixon .15
130 Carlos Lee .15
131 Javy Lopez .25
132 Jay Gibbons .15
133 Brandon Medders **RC** 3.00
134 Colby Miller **RC** 3.00
135 David Crouthers 3.00
136 Dennis Sarfate **RC** 5.00
137 Donald Kelly **RC** 3.00
138 Frank Brooks **RC** 5.00
139 Chris Aguila **RC** 3.00
140 Greg Dobbs **RC** 3.00
141 Ian Snell **RC** 5.00
142 Jake Woods 3.00
143 Jamie Brown **RC** 3.00
144 Jason Frasor **RC** 4.00
145 Jerome Gamble **RC** 4.00
146 Jesse Harper **RC** 5.00
147 Josh Labandeira **RC** 4.00
148 Justin Hampson **RC** 4.00
149 Justin Huisman **RC** 4.00
150 Justin Leone **RC** 5.00
151 Lincoln Holdzkom **RC** 3.00
152 Mike Bumatay **RC** 5.00
153 Mike Gosling 5.00
154 Mike Johnston **RC** 3.00
155 Mike Rouse 3.00
156 Nick Regilio **RC** 3.00
157 Ryan Meaux **RC** 3.00
158 Scott Dohmann **RC** 3.00
159 Sean Henn 6.00
160 Tim Bausher **RC** 3.00
161 Tim Bittner **RC** 3.00
162 Alec Zumwalt **RC** 3.00
163 Aaron Boone, Bret Boone, Geoff Jenkins, Mark Prior, Barry Zito 3.00
164 Albert Pujols, Edgar Renteria, Alex Rodriguez 5.00
165 Alfonso Soriano, Sammy Sosa 4.00
166 Bobby Abreu, Jim Thome 2.00
167 Bret Boone, John Olerud, Ichiro Suzuki 4.00
168 Derek Jeter, Alfonso Soriano 6.00
169 Eric Chavez, Miguel Tejada 2.00
170 Garret Anderson, Jim Edmonds, Troy Glaus 2.00
171 Hank Blalock, Alex Rodriguez 5.00
172 Alex Rodriguez, Mark Teixeira, Michael Young, Rafael Palmeiro 5.00
173 Ivan Rodriguez, Dontrelle Willis 2.00
174 Jason Giambi, Derek Jeter 6.00
175 Joe DiMaggio, Mickey Mantle 8.00
176 Joe DiMaggio, Mickey Mantle, Ted Williams 8.00
177 Joe DiMaggio, Ted Williams 6.00
178 Nomar Garciaparra, Alfonso Soriano 4.00
179 Nomar Garciaparra, Jason Giambi 4.00
180 Paul LoDuca, Hideo Nomo 2.00
181 Rafael Palmeiro, Alex Rodriguez, Michael Young 4.00
182 Ralph Kiner, Ted Williams 5.00
183 Aaron Boone, Derek Jeter 6.00

Blue

Blue (1-132): 2-3X
Inserted 1:6

Die-Cut

Die-Cut (1-132): 3-6X
Production 175

Green

No Pricing
Production 15 Sets

Purple

No Pricing
Production One Set

Apparel Collection

NM/M

Common Player: 4.00
Inserted 1:24

JB Jeff Bagwell 6.00
RB Rocco Baldelli 8.00
BE Josh Beckett 6.00
LB Lance Berkman 4.00
CD Carlos Delgado 5.00
JD Joe DiMaggio/ SP/150 75.00
AD Adam Dunn 6.00
RF Rafael Furcal 5.00
JG Jason Giambi 6.00
TG Troy Glaus 6.00
KG Ken Griffey Jr. 15.00
HA Roy Halladay 5.00
RH Rich Harden/SP 8.00
BH Bo Hart 4.00
TH Torii Hunter 4.00
DJ Derek Jeter 15.00
RJ Randy Johnson 8.00
CJ Chipper Jones 8.00
ML Mike Lowell 5.00
MM Mickey Mantle/ SP/150 100.00
PM Pedro J. Martinez 8.00
HM Hideki Matsui 20.00
MU Mike Mussina 6.00
HN Hideo Nomo 6.00
RO Roy Oswalt 4.00
RP Rafael Palmeiro 6.00
PI Mike Piazza 10.00
JP Jorge Posada 8.00
MP Mark Prior 8.00
AP Albert Pujols 10.00
MR Manny Ramirez 6.00
AR Alex Rodriguez 8.00
CS Curt Schilling 6.00
AS Alfonso Soriano 6.00
SS Sammy Sosa 10.00
IS Ichiro Suzuki 15.00
JT Jim Thome 8.00
BW Bernie Williams 5.00
TW Ted Williams/SP/150 70.00
DW Dontrelle Willis 5.00
KW Kerry Wood 8.00
BZ Barry Zito 5.00

Artist's Touch

NM/M
Common Player: 4.00
Production 250
Parallel: 1-2X
Production 50
RB Rocco Baldelli 8.00
JB Josh Beckett 8.00
LB Lance Berkman 5.00
CD Carlos Delgado 6.00
RF Rafael Furcal 5.00
JG Jason Giambi 8.00
TG Troy Glaus 6.00
KG Ken Griffey Jr. 15.00
HA Roy Halladay 5.00
BH Bo Hart 4.00
TH Torii Hunter 5.00
DJ Derek Jeter 15.00
RJ Randy Johnson 8.00
CJ Chipper Jones 8.00
PM Pedro J. Martinez 8.00
HM Hideki Matsui 20.00
MM Mike Mussina 8.00
HN Hideo Nomo 8.00
RO Roy Oswalt 4.00
RP Rafael Palmeiro 8.00
PI Mike Piazza 10.00
JP Jorge Posada 8.00
MP Mark Prior 10.00
AP Albert Pujols 10.00
MR Manny Ramirez/50 10.00
AR Alex Rodriguez 10.00
AS Alfonso Soriano 15.00
SS Sammy Sosa 15.00
IS Ichiro Suzuki 20.00
JT Jim Thome 10.00
BW Bernie Williams 6.00
DW Dontrelle Willis 5.00
KW Kerry Wood 8.00
BZ Barry Zito 6.00

Home Run Heroics

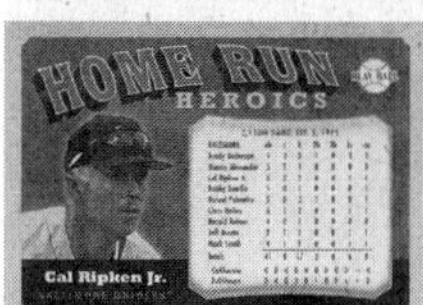

NM/M
Common Player: 2.00
Inserted 1:24
EB Ernie Banks 4.00
HB Hank Blalock 3.00
AB Aaron Boone 2.00
MC Miguel Cabrera 4.00
CD Carlos Delgado 3.00
JD Joe DiMaggio 8.00
JD1 Joe DiMaggio 8.00
JG Jason Giambi 3.00
SG Shawn Green 2.00
KG Ken Griffey Jr. 6.00
KG1 Ken Griffey Jr. 6.00
RH Rickey Henderson 2.00
RJ Randy Johnson 3.00
HK Harmon Killebrew 4.00
MM Mickey Mantle 15.00
MM1 Mickey Mantle 15.00
MM2 Mickey Mantle 15.00
EM Eddie Mathews 4.00
HM Hideki Matsui 6.00
HM1 Hideki Matsui 6.00
WM Willie McCovey 2.00
BM Bill Mueller 2.00
SM Stan Musial 5.00
RP Rafael Palmeiro 3.00
CR Cal Ripken Jr. 10.00
CR1 Cal Ripken Jr. 10.00
AR Alex Rodriguez 6.00
AR1 Alex Rodriguez 6.00
FR Frank Robinson 3.00
MS Mike Schmidt 5.00
RS Red Schoendienst 2.00
AS Alfonso Soriano 4.00
SS Sammy Sosa 6.00
SS1 Sammy Sosa 6.00
SS2 Sammy Sosa 6.00
SS3 Sammy Sosa 6.00
TW Ted Williams 10.00
TW1 Ted Williams 10.00
TW2 Ted Williams 10.00
TW3 Ted Williams 10.00

Rookie Signature Portfolio

NM/M
Common Player: 5.00
Inserted 1:30
CA Chris Aguila 6.00
TB Tim Bausher 8.00
BI Tim Bittner 8.00
FB Frank Brooks 8.00
JB Jamie Brown 5.00
MB Mike Bumatay 8.00
DC David Crouthers 8.00
GD Greg Dobbs 6.00
SD Scott Dohmann 8.00
JF Jason Frasor 8.00
JG Jerome Gamble 8.00
MG Mike Gosling 8.00
HA Justin Hampson 6.00
JH Jesse Harper 8.00
SH Sean Henn 15.00
LH Lincoln Holdzkom 5.00
HU Justin Huisman 5.00
MJ Mike Johnston 10.00
DK Donald Kelly 5.00
JL Josh Labandeira 8.00
LE Justin Leone 10.00
RM Ryan Meaux 5.00
BM Brandon Medders 5.00
CM Colby Miller 5.00
NR Nick Regilio 5.00
MR Mike Rouse 6.00
DS Dennis Sarfate 8.00
IS Ian Snell 20.00
JW Jake Woods 5.00
AZ Alec Zumwalt 8.00

Signature Portfolio

NM/M
Production 100
Parallel: No Pricing
Production 25 or 10
KG Ken Griffey Jr. 100.00
HM Hideki Matsui 250.00
CR Cal Ripken Jr. 120.00
TS Tom Seaver 40.00
CY Carl Yastrzemski 50.00
BZ Barry Zito 30.00

Tools of the Stars

NM/M
Common Player: 6.00
Inserted 1:48
Level 1 Parallel: 1-1.5X
Production 250
Level 2 Parallel: No Pricing
Production 25
JB Josh Beckett 6.00
CD Carlos Delgado 6.00
KG Ken Griffey Jr./SP 15.00
DJ Derek Jeter 15.00
CJ Chipper Jones 8.00
HM Hideki Matsui 15.00
HN Hideo Nomo 6.00
PI Mike Piazza 10.00
AP Albert Pujols 15.00
AR Alex Rodriguez 10.00
AS Alfonso Soriano 6.00
IS Ichiro Suzuki 15.00
JT Jim Thome 8.00
KW Kerry Wood 8.00

2004 Upper Deck Power Up

NM/M
Complete Set (100): 20.00
Common Player: .15
Pack (9): 1.50
Box (24): 25.00
1 Austin Kearns .25
2 Rafael Furcal .25
3 Larry Walker .25
4 Jeremy Bonderman .15
5 Scott Rolen .50
6 Nomar Garciaparra 1.00
7 Jody Gerut .15
8 Troy Glaus .25
9 Roy Halladay .25
10 Barry Zito .40
11 Gary Sheffield .40
12 Ichiro Suzuki 1.00
13 Juan Gonzalez .25
14 Jim Edmonds .25
15 Hank Blalock .40
16 Roy Oswalt .25
17 Magglio Ordonez .25
18 Garret Anderson .40
19 Mark Teixeira .25
20 Mike Sweeney .15
21 Reggie Sanders .15
22 Rafael Palmeiro .40
23 Orlando Cabrera .15
24 Edgar Renteria .25
25 Ryan Klesko .25
26 Torii Hunter .25
27 Bret Boone .25
28 Roberto Alomar .25
29 Frank Thomas .50
30 Chipper Jones .50
31 Eric Chavez .25
32 Miguel Tejada .40
33 Carlos Beltran .40
34 Geoff Jenkins .25
35 Hideki Matsui 1.00
36 Jason Kendall .15
37 Adam Dunn .40
38 Jay Gibbons .15
39 Ivan Rodriguez .50
40 Sidney Ponson .15
41 Albert Pujols 1.00
42 Bartolo Colon .25
43 Lance Berkman .25
44 Brandon Webb .15
45 Shannon Stewart .15
46 Josh Beckett .50
47 Jason Schmidt .25
48 Luis Gonzalez .25
49 Jacque Jones .15
50 Andruw Jones .40
51 Todd Helton .50
52 Javier Vazquez .25
53 Alfonso Soriano .50
54 Manny Ramirez .50
55 Bobby Abreu .25
56 Rocco Baldelli .25
57 Kerry Wood .50
58 Derek Jeter 1.50
59 Phil Nevin .15
60 Jeff Bagwell .40
61 Sammy Sosa 1.00
62 Tom Glavine .25
63 Miguel Cabrera .50
64 Shawn Green .25
65 Mark Prior 1.00
66 Jose Reyes .25
67 Curt Schilling .40
68 Hideo Nomo .25
69 Mike Lowell .25
70 Randy Johnson .50
71 Edgar Martinez .25
72 Dontrelle Willis .25
73 Milton Bradley .15
74 Preston Wilson .15
75 Mike Piazza .75
76 Mike Mussina .40
77 Darin Erstad .25
78 Greg Maddux .75
79 Tim Hudson .25
80 Kevin Millwood .25
81 Dmitri Young .15
82 Ben Sheets .25
83 Alex Rodriguez 1.00
84 Johan Santana .15
85 Jeff Kent .25
86 Pedro Martinez .50
87 Carlos Delgado .40
88 Jim Thome .50
89 Aubrey Huff .15
90 Ken Griffey Jr. 1.00
91 Kevin Brown .25
92 Tony Batista .15
93 Richie Sexson .25
94 Cliff Floyd .15
95 Jose Vidro .15
96 Brian Giles .25
97 Jorge Posada .40
98 Vernon Wells .25
99 Vladimir Guerrero .50
100 Jason Giambi .50

Rare

Stars: 3-4X
Inserted 1:6

Super Rare

Stars: 5-10X
Inserted 1:96

Ultra Rare

Stars: 4-6X
Inserted 1:24

Mega Rare

No Pricing
Inserted 1:240

Shining Through

NM/M
1 Hideo Nomo .25
2 Mark Prior 1.00
3 Scott Rolen .75
4 Luis Gonzalez .25
5 Miguel Tejada .40
6 Richie Sexson .40
7 Jim Edmonds .40
8 Carlos Beltran .40
9 Manny Ramirez .50
10 Torii Hunter .40
11 Garret Anderson .40
12 Eric Chavez .40
13 Juan Gonzalez .40
14 Albert Pujols 1.50
15 Tim Hudson .40
16 Roy Halladay .40
17 Roy Oswalt .25
18 Andruw Jones .50
19 Gary Sheffield .40
20 Magglio Ordonez .40
21 Jason Giambi .75
22 Brian Giles .40
23 Barry Zito .40
24 Todd Helton .50
25 Randy Johnson .50
26 Pedro Martinez .75
27 Vernon Wells .25
28 Lance Berkman .40
29 Mike Mussina .50
30 Carlos Delgado .40
31 Ivan Rodriguez .50
32 Kevin Brown .40
33 Kerry Wood .75
34 Mark Teixeira .40
35 Hideki Matsui 1.50
36 Troy Glaus .40
37 Mike Piazza 1.00
38 Nomar Garciaparra 1.50
39 Vladimir Guerrero .75
40 Derek Jeter 2.00
41 Jason Schmidt .40
42 Alex Rodriguez/Yanks 1.50
43 Jeff Bagwell .50
44 Shawn Green .40
45 Sammy Sosa 1.50
46 Josh Beckett .75
47 Bret Boone .40
48 Ichiro Suzuki 1.00
49 Jeff Kent .40
50 Rafael Palmeiro .50
51 Curt Schilling .50
52 Greg Maddux 1.00
53 Mike Lowell .40
54 Dontrelle Willis .40
55 Alfonso Soriano .50
56 Preston Wilson .25
57 Jorge Posada .40
58 Frank Thomas .50
59 Jim Thome .75
60 Ken Griffey Jr. 1.00
61 Rocco Baldelli .40
62 Jose Vidro .25
63 Austin Kearns .25
64 Cliff Floyd .25
65 Phil Nevin .25
66 Darin Erstad .15
67 Johan Santana .25
68 Chipper Jones .75
69 Brandon Webb .25
70 Hank Blalock .40
71 Adam Dunn .40
72 Javier Vazquez .25
73 Jacque Jones .25
74 Bobby Abreu .40
75 Edgar Renteria .40
76 Roger Clemens 1.50
77 Rafael Furcal .40
78 Mike Sweeney .25
79 Geoff Jenkins .25
80 Orlando Cabrera .25
81 Ben Sheets .40
82 Shannon Stewart .25
83 Ryan Klesko .40
84 Edgar Martinez .40
85 Kevin Millwood .40
86 Bartolo Colon .40
87 Larry Walker .25
88 Tom Glavine .40
89 Miguel Cabrera .75
90 Jose Reyes .40

Stickers

NM/M
1 Hideo Nomo .50
2 Mark Prior 2.00
3 Scott Rolen 1.50
4 Luis Gonzalez .50
5 Miguel Tejada .75
6 Richie Sexson .75
7 Jim Edmonds .75
8 Carlos Beltran .75
9 Manny Ramirez 1.00
10 Torii Hunter .75
11 Garret Anderson .75
12 Eric Chavez .75
13 Juan Gonzalez .75
14 Albert Pujols 3.00
15 Tim Hudson .75
16 Roy Halladay .75
17 Roy Oswalt .50
18 Andruw Jones 1.00
19 Gary Sheffield .75
20 Magglio Ordonez .75
21 Jason Giambi 1.50
22 Brian Giles .75
23 Barry Zito .75
24 Todd Helton 1.00
25 Randy Johnson 1.50
26 Pedro Martinez 1.50
27 Vernon Wells .50
28 Lance Berkman .75
29 Mike Mussina .75
30 Carlos Delgado .75
31 Ivan Rodriguez 1.00
32 Kevin Brown .75
33 Kerry Wood 1.50
34 Mark Teixeira .75
35 Hideki Matsui 2.50
36 Troy Glaus .75
37 Mike Piazza 2.00
38 Nomar Garciaparra 3.00
39 Vladimir Guerrero 1.50
40 Derek Jeter 4.00
41 Jason Schmidt .50
42 Alex Rodriguez 3.00
43 Jeff Bagwell 1.00
44 Shawn Green .75
45 Sammy Sosa 2.50
46 Josh Beckett 1.00
47 Bret Boone .50
48 Ichiro Suzuki 2.00
49 Jeff Kent .75
50 Rafael Palmeiro 1.00
51 Curt Schilling 1.00
52 Greg Maddux 2.00
53 Mike Lowell .75
54 Dontrelle Willis .75
55 Alfonso Soriano 1.00
56 Preston Wilson .50
57 Jorge Posada .75
58 Frank Thomas 1.00
59 Jim Thome 1.50
60 Ken Griffey Jr. 2.00
61 Rocco Baldelli .75
62 Jose Vidro .50
63 Austin Kearns .50
64 Phil Nevin .50
65 Darin Erstad .50
66 Johan Santana .50
67 Chipper Jones 1.50
68 Brandon Webb .50
69 Hank Blalock .75
70 Adam Dunn .75
71 Javier Vazquez .75
72 Jacque Jones .50
73 Bobby Abreu .75
74 Edgar Renteria .75
75 Rafael Furcal .75
76 Mike Sweeney .50
77 Geoff Jenkins .50
78 Shannon Stewart .50
79 Ryan Klesko .75
80 Edgar Martinez .75
81 Kevin Millwood .75
82 Bartolo Colon .75
83 Tom Glavine .75
84 Miguel Cabrera 1.50
85 Jose Reyes .75
86 Padres/Astros/A's/ Angels/Cubs/D-Rays .50
87 Pirates/M's/Expos/Twins/ Reds/Phils .50
88 Royals/O's/W.Sox/ Dodgers/Marlins/Yanks .50
89 Giants/Mets/Cards/ Indians/Braves/Rangers .50
90 Tigers/R.Sox/Rockies/ D-Backs/Brewers/Jay .50

2004 Upper Deck R Class

NM/M
Complete Set (180): 50.00
Common Player: .10
Pack (6): 2.50
Box (24): 50.00
1 Adam Dunn .50
2 Jose Vidro .10
3 Vladimir Guerrero .75
4 Hideo Nomo .25
5 Eric Chavez .25
6 Carlos Delgado .40
7 Javy Lopez .25
8 Javier Vazquez .25
9 Miguel Cabrera .75
10 Manny Ramirez .50
11 Scott Rolen .75
12 Rafael Furcal .10
13 Jim Thome .75
14 Edgar Renteria .25
15 Jason Kendall .10
16 Alfonso Soriano .75
17 Troy Glaus .40
18 Vernon Wells .10
19 Todd Helton .50
20 Mark Mulder .25
21 Albert Pujols 2.00
22 Andy Pettitte .25
23 Kevin Millwood .10
24 Bret Boone .10
25 Ken Griffey Jr. 1.00
26 Kevin Brown .20
27 J.D. Drew .25
28 Corey Patterson .40
29 Jason Giambi .40
30 Jason Schmidt .25
31 Jose Reyes .25
32 Torii Hunter .25
33 Brian Giles .25
34 Garret Anderson .25
35 Mark Teixeira .40
36 Sammy Sosa 1.50
37 Rocco Baldelli .25
38 Jeff Bagwell .50
39 Rafael Palmeiro .50
40 Derrek Lee .25
41 Randy Johnson .75
42 Roger Clemens 1.50
43 Austin Kearns .25
44 Dontrelle Willis .10
45 Lance Berkman .25
46 Juan Gonzalez .40
47 Ichiro Suzuki 1.50
48 Pat Burrell .25
49 Miguel Tejada .40
50 Mike Piazza 1.00
51 Mark Prior .75
52 C.C. Sabathia .10
53 Jacque Jones .10

54	Carlos Beltran	.75
55	Mike Mussina	.40
56	Mike Lowell	.25
57	Phil Nevin	.10
58	Andruw Jones	.40
59	Barry Zito	.25
60	Magglio Ordonez	.25
61	Carlos Lee	.20
62	Nomar Garciaparra	1.00
63	Kerry Wood	.75
64	Luis Gonzalez	.20
65	Derek Jeter	2.00
66	Preston Wilson	.10
67	Greg Maddux	1.00
68	Pedro J. Martinez	.75
69	Richie Sexson	.25
70	Hank Blalock	.50
71	Chipper Jones	.75
72	Ivan Rodriguez	.50
73	Roy Halladay	.25
74	Tim Hudson	.25
75	Ryan Klesko	.10
76	Hideki Matsui	1.50
77	Josh Beckett	.40
78	Brandon Webb	.10
79	Alex Rodriguez	2.00
80	Jim Edmonds	.40
81	Jeff Kent	.10
82	Bobby Abreu	.25
83	Curt Schilling	.75
84	Roy Oswalt	.25
85	Orlando Cabrera	.75
86	Johan Santana	.50
87	Geoff Jenkins	.10
88	Gary Sheffield	.40
89	Shawn Green	.25
90	Frank Thomas	.50
91	Tim Hamulack **RC**	.25
92	Shingo Takatsu **RC**	.50
93	Justin Huisman	.25
94	Sean Henn	.50
95	Jamie Brown	.25
96	Dennis Sarfate **RC**	.25
97	Lincoln Holdzkom **RC**	.25
98	Roman Colon **RC**	.25
99	Scott Dohmann **RC**	.25
100	Ivan Ochoa	.25
101	Akinori Otsuka **RC**	.50
102	Fernando Nieve **RC**	.25
103	Mike Johnston **RC**	.25
104	Mariano Gomez **RC**	.25
105	Justin Leone **RC**	.25
106	Evan Rust **RC**	.25
107	Mike Rouse	.25
108	Ian Snell **RC**	.50
109	Jason Bartlett	.25
110	Ryan Wing	.25
111	Nick Regilio **RC**	.25
112	Merkin Valdez **RC**	.50
113	Josh Labandeira **RC**	.25
114	David Aardsma	.75
115	Justin Knoedler **RC**	.25
116	Shawn Hill **RC**	.25
117	Casey Daigle **RC**	.25
118	Donnie Kelly **RC**	.25
119	Justin Germano **RC**	.25
120	Eddy Rodriguez	.25
121	Onil Joseph **RC**	.25
122	Mike Wuertz	.50
123	Roberto Novoa **RC**	.25
124	Jerome Gamble **RC**	.50
125	Justin Hampson **RC**	.25
126	Ronald Belisario **RC**	.25
127	Tim Bausher **RC**	.25
128	Chris Saenz **RC**	.25
129	Hector Gimenez **RC**	.25
130	Ronny Cedeno **RC**	.25
131	Jason Frasor **RC**	.25
132	Kazuo Matsui **RC**	2.00
133	Mike Gosling	.25
134	Jerry Gil **RC**	.25
135	Orlando Rodriguez **RC**	.25
136	Jorge Vasquez **RC**	.50
137	Chris Aguila **RC**	.25
138	Tim Bittner **RC**	.25
139	Jake Woods	.25
140	Enemencio Pacheco	.25
141	David Crouthers	.25
142	Jose Capellan **RC**	1.00
143	Chad Bentz **RC**	.25
144	Michael Vento	.75
145	Scott Proctor **RC**	.50
146	Edwin Moreno **RC**	.25
147	Brandon Medders **RC**	.25
148	Renyel Pinto **RC**	.25
149	Rusty Tucker **RC**	.25
150	Ryan Meaux **RC**	.25
151	William Bergolla	.25
152	Angel Chavez	.25
153	Colby Miller **RC**	.25
154	John Gall **RC**	.25
155	Carlos Hines **RC**	.25
156	Carlos Vasquez **RC**	.50
157	Justin Lehr **RC**	.25
158	Kevin Cave **RC**	.25
159	Jeff Bennett **RC**	.25
160	Greg Dobbs **RC**	.25
161	Jorge Sequea **RC**	.25
162	Chris Oxspring **RC**	.25
163	Franklyn Gracesqui **RC**	.25
164	Shawn Camp **RC**	.25
165	Lino Urdaneta	.25
166	Luis Gonzalez	.25
167	Ramon Ramirez **RC**	.50
168	Freddy Guzman **RC**	.25
169	Chris Shelton **RC**	1.50
170	Andres Blanco	.25
171	Aarom Baldiris **RC**	.25
172	Kazuhito Tadano **RC**	.50
173	Brian Dallimore **RC**	.25
174	Eduardo Villacis	.25
175	Frank Francisco **RC**	.25
176	Edwin Jackson	.25
177	Bobby Crosby	.50
178	Joe Mauer	.50
179	Rickie Weeks	.50
180	Delmon Young	.50

First Class Black Ink Auto

		NM/M
Inserted 1:2,880		
SA	Sandy Alomar	20.00
PB	Pat Burrell	30.00
MC	Miguel Cabrera	40.00
CD	Carlos Delgado	30.00
EG	Eric Gagne	50.00
KG	Ken Griffey Jr.	80.00
TH	Trevor Hoffman	30.00
BL	Barry Larkin	40.00
PL	Paul LoDuca	30.00
EM	Edgar Martinez	40.00
MP	Mark Prior	40.00
HR	Horacio Ramirez	20.00
DW	Dontrelle Willis	30.00

First Class Blue Ink Auto

No Pricing
Production Three Sets

Jersey

		NM/M
Common Player:		4.00
Inserted 1:12		
RA	Roberto Alomar	6.00
BA	Jeff Bagwell	8.00
RB	Rocco Baldelli	4.00
JB	Josh Beckett	4.00
HB	Hank Blalock	8.00
BB	Bret Boone	4.00
KB	Kevin Brown	4.00
EC	Eric Chavez	4.00
RC	Roger Clemens	12.00
CD	Carlos Delgado	4.00
JG	Jason Giambi	6.00
GL	Troy Glaus	4.00
TG	Tom Glavine	6.00
KG	Ken Griffey Jr.	12.00
VG	Vladimir Guerrero	8.00
TH	Todd Helton	8.00
HU	Torii Hunter	4.00
DJ	Derek Jeter	15.00
RJ	Randy Johnson	8.00
AJ	Andruw Jones	6.00
CJ	Chipper Jones	8.00
EM	Edgar Martinez	4.00
PM	Pedro J. Martinez	8.00
HM	Hideki Matsui	20.00
KM	Kazuo Matsui	10.00
HN	Hideo Nomo	8.00
PI	Mike Piazza	10.00
MP	Mark Prior	6.00
AP	Albert Pujols	15.00
MR	Manny Ramirez	8.00
RI	Mariano Rivera	8.00
IR	Ivan Rodriguez	8.00
SR	Scott Rolen	8.00
CS	Curt Schilling	8.00
GS	Gary Sheffield	6.00
AS	Alfonso Soriano	8.00
SS	Sammy Sosa	10.00
IS	Ichiro Suzuki	25.00
MT	Miguel Tejada	6.00
BW	Bernie Williams	6.00
DW	Dontrelle Willis	4.00
KW	Kerry Wood	8.00

Taking Over!

		NM/M
Common Player:		3.00
1-20 production 650		
21-30 production 150		
TO-1	Richie Sexson, Lyle Overbay	3.00
TO-2	Jason Phillips, Mike Piazza	6.00
TO-3	Barry Larkin, William Bergolla	4.00
TO-4	Jason Dubois, Moises Alou	3.00
TO-5	Nook Logan, Alex Sanchez	3.00
TO-6	Merkin Valdez, Robb Nen	4.00
TO-7	Troy Percival, Francisco Rodriguez	3.00
TO-8	Carlos Beltran, David DeJesus	4.00
TO-9	Alex Rodriguez, Michael Young	6.00
TO-10	Alexis Rios, Vernon Wells	3.00
TO-11	Matt Lawton, Grady Sizemore	3.00
TO-12	Danny Graves, Ryan Wagner	3.00
TO-13	Miguel Cabrera, Jeff Conine	4.00
TO-14	Josh Willingham, Ramon Castro	3.00
TO-15	Junior Spivey, Rickie Weeks	3.00
TO-16	Guillermo Quiroz, Greg Myers	3.00
TO-17	Scott Hatteberg, Graham Koonce	3.00
TO-18	Rene Reyes, Larry Walker	4.00
TO-19	Khalil Greene, Ramon Vazquez	4.00
TO-20	Billy Wagner, Octavio Dotel	3.00
TO-21	Joe Mauer, A.J. Pierzynski	8.00
TO-22	Javier Vazquez, Roger Clemens	10.00
TO-23	Curt Schilling, Brandon Webb	3.00
TO-24	Delmon Young, Cirilo Cruz Jr.	8.00
TO-25	Vladimir Guerrero, Tim Salmon	8.00
TO-26	Gary Sheffield, J.D. Drew	3.00
TO-27	Miguel Tejada, Bobby Crosby	8.00
TO-28	Edwin Jackson, Kevin Brown	3.00
TO-29	Kazuo Matsui, Jose Reyes	10.00
TO-30	Wily Mo Pena, Ken Griffey Jr.	10.00

2004 Upper Deck Reflections Sample

		NM/M
S38	Ichiro	3.00

2004 Upper Deck Reflections

		NM/M
Complete Set (340):		
Common (1-100):		.50
Common SP (101-130):		4.00
Production 1,250		
Common Jersey (131-214):		4.00
Common Jersey (215-298):		4.00
Production 100 (215-298):		
Common Auto. (299-340):		15.00
Production 35		
Pack (4):		8.00
Box (8):		50.00
1	Adam Dunn	1.00
2	Albert Pujols	3.00
3	Alex Rodriguez	3.00
4	Alfonso Soriano	1.00
5	Andruw Jones	1.00
6	Austin Kearns	.50
7	Rafael Furcal	.50
8	Barry Zito	.75
9	Bartolo Colon	.50
10	Ben Sheets	.50
11	Bernie Williams	.75
12	Bobby Abreu	.50
13	Brandon Webb	.50
14	Bret Boone	.50
15	Brian Giles	.50
16	Carlos Beltran	.50
17	Carlos Delgado	.75
18	Carlos Lee	.50
19	Chipper Jones	1.50
20	Corey Patterson	.50
21	Curt Schilling	.75
22	Delmon Young	.50
23	Derek Jeter	4.00
24	Dmitri Young	.50
25	Dontrelle Willis	.50
26	Edgar Martinez	.50
27	Edgar Renteria	.50
28	Eric Chavez	.50
29	Eric Gagne	.75
30	Frank Thomas	1.50
31	Garret Anderson	.50
32	Gary Sheffield	.50
33	Geoff Jenkins	.50
34	Greg Maddux	2.00
35	Hank Blalock	.75
36	Hideki Matsui	3.00
37	Hideo Nomo	.75
38	Ichiro Suzuki	2.50
39	Ivan Rodriguez	1.00
40	Jacque Jones	.50
41	Jason Giambi	1.50
42	Jason Schmidt	.75
43	Javy Lopez	.75
44	Jay Gibbons	.50
45	Jeff Bagwell	1.00
46	Jeff Kent	.50
47	Jeremy Bonderman	.50
48	Jim Edmonds	.75
49	Jim Thome	1.50
50	Johnny Damon	.75
51	Jorge Posada	.75
52	Jose Contreras	.50
53	Jose Reyes	.75
54	Jose Vidro	.50
55	Josh Beckett	1.00
56	Juan Gonzalez	1.00
57	Ken Griffey Jr.	2.50
58	Kerry Wood	1.50
59	Kevin Brown	.50
60	Kevin Millwood	.50
61	Lance Berkman	.50
62	Larry Walker	.50
63	Luis Gonzalez	.50
64	Magglio Ordonez	.50
65	Manny Ramirez	1.00
66	Mark Mulder	.50
67	Mark Prior	2.00
68	Mark Teixeira	.50
69	Miguel Cabrera	1.50
70	Miguel Tejada	.75
71	Mike Lowell	.75
72	Mike Mussina	.75
73	Mike Piazza	2.00
74	Mike Sweeney	.50
75	Milton Bradley	.50
76	Nomar Garciaparra	2.00
77	Orlando Cabrera	.50
78	Pedro Martinez	1.50
79	Phil Nevin	.50
80	Preston Wilson	.50
81	Rafael Palmeiro	1.00
82	Randy Johnson	1.50
83	Rich Harden	.50
84	Richie Sexson	.75
85	Rickie Weeks	.50
86	Rocco Baldelli	.75
87	Roy Halladay	.75
88	Roy Oswalt	.75
89	Ryan Klesko	.50
90	Sammy Sosa	2.50
91	Scott Rolen	1.50
92	Shannon Stewart	.50
93	Shawn Green	.50
94	Tim Hudson	.75
95	Todd Helton	1.00
96	Torii Hunter	.75
97	Trot Nixon	.50
98	Troy Glaus	.75
99	Vernon Wells	.50
100	Vladimir Guerrero	1.50
101	Brandon Medders **RC**	4.00
102	Colby Miller **RC**	4.00
103	David Crouthers	4.00
104	Dennis Sarfate **RC**	4.00
105	Donnie Kelly **RC**	4.00
106	Alec Zumwalt **RC**	4.00
107	Chris Aguila **RC**	4.00
108	Greg Dobbs **RC**	4.00
109	Ian Snell **RC**	8.00
110	Jake Woods	4.00
111	Jamie Brown **RC**	4.00
112	Jason Frasor **RC**	4.00
113	Jerome Gamble **RC**	4.00
114	Jesse Harper **RC**	4.00
115	Josh Labandeira **RC**	5.00
116	Justin Hampson **RC**	4.00
117	Justin Huisman **RC**	4.00
118	Justin Leone **RC**	8.00
119	Kazuo Matsui **RC**	15.00
120	Lincoln Holdzkom **RC**	4.00
121	Mike Bumatay **RC**	4.00
122	Mike Gosling	4.00
123	Mike Johnston **RC**	4.00
124	Mike Rouse	4.00
125	Nick Regilio **RC**	4.00
126	Ryan Meaux **RC**	4.00
127	Scott Dohmann **RC**	4.00
128	Sean Henn	6.00
129	Tim Bausher **RC**	4.00
130	Tim Bittner **RC**	4.00
131	Adam Dunn	6.00
132	Andruw Jones	6.00
133	Austin Kearns	4.00
134	Bartolo Colon	4.00
135	Ben Sheets	5.00
136	Bernie Williams	5.00
137	Bobby Abreu	4.00
138	Brian Giles	4.00
139	Carlos Lee	4.00
140	Chipper Jones	8.00
141	Corey Patterson	4.00
142	Darin Erstad	4.00
143	Edgar Martinez	4.00
144	Vladimir Guerrero	8.00
145	Eric Gagne	4.00
146	Frank Thomas	8.00
147	Garret Anderson	4.00
148	Roger Clemens	12.00
149	Greg Maddux	8.00
150	Jacque Jones	4.00
151	Randy Johnson	8.00
152	Javy Lopez	4.00
153	Mike Piazza	8.00
154	Albert Pujols	15.00
155	Jim Edmonds	4.00
156	Eric Milton	4.00
157	Jorge Posada	6.00
158	J.D. Drew	4.00
159	Jose Vidro	4.00
160	Kevin Millwood	4.00
161	Larry Walker	4.00
162	Luis Gonzalez	4.00
163	Mike Sweeney	4.00
164	Kerry Wood	4.00
165	Mike Cameron	4.00
166	Phil Nevin	4.00
167	Rocco Baldelli	4.00
168	Ryan Klesko	4.00
169	Shannon Stewart	4.00
170	Torii Hunter	6.00
171	Trot Nixon	4.00
172	Vernon Wells	4.00
173	Alfonso Soriano	6.00
174	Andruw Jones	6.00
175	Barry Zito	4.00
176	Brandon Webb	4.00
177	Bret Boone	4.00
178	Scott Rolen	6.00
179	Carlos Delgado	4.00
180	Curt Schilling	8.00
181	Dontrelle Willis	4.00
182	Eric Chavez	4.00
183	Frank Thomas	8.00
184	Gary Sheffield	6.00
185	Greg Maddux	8.00
186	Hank Blalock	4.00
187	Hideki Matsui	15.00
188	Hideo Nomo	8.00
189	Ichiro Suzuki	15.00
190	Ivan Rodriguez	6.00
191	Jason Giambi	6.00
192	Rafael Furcal	4.00
193	Jeff Bagwell	6.00
194	Jeff Kent	4.00
195	Jim Thome	6.00
196	Jose Reyes	8.00
197	Josh Beckett	6.00
198	Juan Gonzalez	4.00
199	Ken Griffey Jr.	15.00
200	Kevin Brown	4.00
201	Lance Berkman	6.00
202	Magglio Ordonez	5.00
203	Mark Mulder	4.00
204	Mark Teixeira	6.00
205	Miguel Tejada	6.00
206	Mike Mussina	6.00
207	Preston Wilson	4.00
208	Rafael Palmeiro	6.00
209	Alex Rodriguez	15.00
210	Richie Sexson	4.00
211	Roy Halladay	6.00
212	Roy Oswalt	5.00
213	Tim Hudson	5.00
214	Troy Glaus	4.00
215	Adam Dunn	8.00
216	Austin Kearns	4.00
217	Bartolo Colon	4.00
218	Ben Sheets	5.00
219	Bernie Williams	6.00
220	Bobby Abreu	5.00
221	Bret Boone	4.00
222	Todd Helton	6.00
223	Chipper Jones	8.00
224	Corey Patterson	6.00
225	Darin Erstad	4.00
226	Dontrelle Willis	4.00
227	Edgar Martinez	4.00
228	Eric Gagne	4.00
229	Garret Anderson	4.00
230	Roger Clemens	20.00
231	Hank Blalock	4.00
232	Jacque Jones	4.00
233	Jeff Bagwell	8.00
234	Jeff Kent	4.00
235	Jeremy Bonderman	4.00
236	Jim Edmonds	4.00
237	Jorge Posada	8.00
238	J.D. Drew	4.00
239	Jose Reyes	10.00
240	Jose Vidro	4.00
241	Kevin Millwood	4.00
242	Luis Gonzalez	4.00
243	Mike Sweeney	4.00
244	Jason Giambi	6.00
245	Manny Ramirez	8.00
246	Phil Nevin	4.00
247	Preston Wilson	4.00
248	Alex Rodriguez	20.00
249	Richie Sexson	4.00
250	Rocco Baldelli	4.00
251	Ryan Klesko	4.00
252	Sammy Sosa	8.00
253	Torii Hunter	4.00
254	Mike Lowell	6.00
255	Troy Glaus	4.00
256	Vernon Wells	6.00
257	Albert Pujols	20.00
258	Alex Rodriguez	20.00
259	Alfonso Soriano	8.00
260	Roger Clemens	20.00
261	Barry Zito	4.00
262	Brandon Webb	6.00
263	Carlos Delgado	6.00
264	Curt Schilling	8.00
265	Derek Jeter	25.00
266	Eric Chavez	4.00
267	Gary Sheffield	8.00
268	Hideki Matsui	25.00
269	Hideo Nomo	10.00
270	Ichiro Suzuki	25.00
271	Ivan Rodriguez	8.00
272	Jason Giambi	6.00
273	Jim Thome	8.00
274	Josh Beckett	10.00
275	Juan Gonzalez	8.00
276	Ken Griffey Jr.	20.00
277	Kerry Wood	4.00
278	Kevin Brown	4.00
279	Lance Berkman	6.00
280	Magglio Ordonez	8.00
281	Manny Ramirez	8.00
282	Mark Mulder	4.00
283	Mark Prior	6.00
284	Mark Teixeira	6.00
285	Miguel Tejada	6.00
286	Mike Mussina	8.00
287	Mike Piazza	10.00
288	Pedro Martinez	10.00
289	Rafael Palmeiro	8.00
290	Randy Johnson	10.00
291	Roy Halladay	6.00
292	Roy Oswalt	6.00
293	Sammy Sosa	10.00
294	Scott Rolen	8.00
295	Shawn Green	6.00
296	Tim Hudson	6.00
297	Todd Helton	6.00
298	Vladimir Guerrero	10.00
299	Bret Boone	10.00
300	Alex Rodriguez	200.00
301	Dontrelle Willis	30.00
302	Barry Larkin	30.00
303	Barry Zito	25.00
304	Eric Chavez	20.00
305	Bernie Williams	85.00
306	Brandon Webb	20.00
307	Cal Ripken Jr.	175.00
308	Carl Yastrzemski	65.00
309	Carlos Delgado	25.00
310	Shawn Green	25.00
311	Eric Gagne	15.00
312	Frank Thomas	40.00
313	Carlos Lee	20.00
314	Garret Anderson	20.00
315	Hideki Matsui	300.00
316	Jim Edmonds	40.00
317	Jeff Bagwell	40.00
318	Luis Gonzalez	20.00
319	Mike Mussina	40.00
320	John Smoltz	60.00
321	Jose Reyes	40.00
322	Josh Beckett	50.00
323	Juan Gonzalez	25.00
324	Ken Griffey Jr.	140.00
325	Rich Harden	20.00
326	Pat Burrell	25.00
327	Mark Teixeira	25.00
328	Roy Oswalt	30.00
329	Miguel Tejada	40.00
330	Mike Hampton	15.00
331	Mike Piazza	175.00
332	Nolan Ryan	120.00
333	Orlando Hernandez	25.00
334	Paul Lo Duca	25.00
335	Roberto Alomar	40.00
336	Rocco Baldelli	20.00
337	Trevor Hoffman	25.00
338	Tom Glavine	50.00
339	Tom Seaver	60.00
340	Mark Prior	25.00

Black

Black (1-100):	No Pricing
Production One Set	
Black Auto. (101-130):	No Pricing
Production One Set	
Black Jersey (173-214):	No Pricing
Production One Set	
Black Jersey (257-298):	No Pricing
Production One Set	
Black Jsy Auto. (299-340):	No Pricing
Production One Set	

Blue

Blue (1-100):	2-4X
Production 250	

Blue (215-256): 1-2X
Production 15

Gold

Gold (1-100): 5-10X
Production 15
Gold Auto. (101-130): 2X
Production 250
Gold Auto. parallel (101-130): 2X
Production 125
Gold Jersey (131-172): 1.5-3X
Production 15
Gold Jersey (257-298): No Pricing
Production 5
Gold Jsy Auto. (299-340): 1X
Production 15

Red

Red (1-100): 4-6X
Production 50
Red Jersey (131-214): 1.5-2X
Production 50
Red Jersey (215-256): 1-1.5X
Production 50

2004 Upper Deck Rivals: Yankees vs Red Sox

NM/M
Complete Sealed Set (32): 25.00
Common Player (1-30): .50
1 Alex Rodriguez 2.00
2 Bobby Doerr .75
3 Don Mattingly 1.50
4 Dwight Evans .50
5 Fred Lynn .50
6 Jason Giambi .50
7 Jim Rice .50
8 Lou Gehrig 2.00
9 Luis Tiant .50
10 Manny Ramirez 1.00
11 Mike Mussina .75
12 Pedro Martinez 1.00
13 Phil Rizzuto .75
14 Whitey Ford .75
15 Yogi Berra 1.00
16 Tim Wakefield .50
17 Billy Martin .75
18 Mike Torrez, Bucky Dent .50
19 Nomar Garciaparra, Derek Jeter 2.00
20 Gary Sheffield, Curt Schilling 1.00
21 Joe DiMaggio, Dick Newsome 1.50
22 Joe DiMaggio, Lefty Grove 1.50
23 Joe DiMaggio, Ted Williams 1.50
24 Jorge Posada, Jason Varitek .50
25 Mickey Mantle, Carl Yastrzemski 2.00
26 Tracy Stallard, Roger Maris 1.00
27 Carlton Fisk, Thurman Munson 1.00
28 Babe Ruth 2.00
29 Roger Clemens 1.50
30 Wade Boggs .50

Commemorative

NM/M
Complete Set (5): 10.00

One oversized card per set.
Babe Ruth 4.00
Ted Williams 3.00
Derek Jeter 3.00
Nomar Garciaparra 2.00
Mickey Mantle 5.00

"What If"

NM/M
Common Player: 4.00
Production 2,150 Sets
1 Aaron Boone 4.00
2 Alex Rodriguez 10.00
3 Babe Ruth 10.00
4 Babe Ruth 10.00
5 Billy Martin 4.00
6 Bucky Dent 4.00
7 Carl Yastrzemski 8.00
8 Carlton Fisk 5.00
9 Derek Jeter 10.00
10 Hideki Matsui 8.00
11 Joe DiMaggio 8.00
12 Joe Torre 4.00
13 Mickey Mantle 15.00
14 Pedro Martinez 6.00
15 Pee Wee Reese 4.00
16 Roger Clemens 8.00
17 Roger Maris 8.00
18 Ted Williams 8.00
19 Ted Williams 8.00
20 Carl Yastrzemski 8.00

What If Auto

No Pricing

SportsNut

Complete Set (90):
Common Player:

2004 Upper Deck Sweet Spot

NM/M
Complete Set (262):
Common Player: .25
Common (91-170): 3.00
Production 799
Common SP (171-230): 1.50
Production 399
Common SP (231-250): 1.50
Production 299
Common SP (251-260): 3.00
Production 199
Pack (4): 10.00
Box (12): 100.00
1 Albert Pujols 3.00
2 Alex Rodriguez 3.00
3 Alfonso Soriano 1.00
4 Andruw Jones .50
5 Andy Pettitte .25
6 Aubrey Huff .25
7 Austin Kearns .50
8 Barry Zito .50
9 Bobby Abreu .50
10 Brandon Webb .25
11 Bret Boone .25
12 Brian Giles .25
13 C.C. Sabathia .25
14 Carlos Beltran 1.00
15 Carlos Delgado .50
16 Chipper Jones 1.00
17 Cliff Floyd .25
18 Curt Schilling 1.00
19 Delmon Young .50
20 Derek Jeter 3.00
21 Dontrelle Willis .25
22 Edgar Martinez .50
23 Edgar Renteria .50
24 Eric Chavez .50
25 Eric Gagne .50
26 Frank Thomas .75
27 Garret Anderson .50
28 Gary Sheffield .75
29 Geoff Jenkins .25
30 Greg Maddux 1.50
31 Hank Blalock .75
32 Hideo Nomo .50
33 Ichiro Suzuki 2.00
34 Ivan Rodriguez .75
35 Jacque Jones .25
36 Jason Giambi .50
37 Jason Schmidt .50
38 Javier Vazquez .25
39 Javy Lopez .50
40 Jeff Bagwell .75
41 Jim Edmonds .50
42 Jim Thome .75
43 Joe Mauer .50
44 John Smoltz .50
45 Jose Cruz Jr. .25
46 Jose Reyes .50
47 Jose Vidro .25
48 Josh Beckett .50
49 Ken Griffey Jr. 1.50
50 Kerry Wood 1.00
51 Kevin Brown .25
52 Larry Walker .50
53 Magglio Ordonez .25
54 Manny Ramirez .75
55 Mark Mulder .50
56 Mark Prior 1.00
57 Mark Teixeira .50
58 Miguel Cabrera 1.00
59 Miguel Tejada .50
60 Mike Lowell .40
61 Mike Mussina .75
62 Mike Piazza 1.50
63 Nomar Garciaparra 1.50
64 Orlando Cabrera .40
65 Pat Burrell .25
66 Pedro J. Martinez 1.00
67 Phil Nevin .25
68 Preston Wilson .25
69 Rafael Furcal .25
70 Rafael Palmeiro .75
71 Randy Johnson 1.00
72 Craig Wilson .25
73 Rich Harden .25
74 Richie Sexson .50
75 Rickie Weeks .50
76 Rocco Baldelli .50
77 Roger Clemens 2.50
78 Roy Halladay .25
79 Roy Oswalt .50
80 Ryan Klesko .25
81 Sammy Sosa 2.00
82 Scott Podsednik .25
83 Scott Rolen 1.00
84 Shawn Green .40
85 Tim Hudson .40
86 Todd Helton .75
87 Torii Hunter .40
88 Troy Glaus .25
89 Vernon Wells .25
90 Vladimir Guerrero 1.00
91 Aarom Baldiris **RC** 3.00
92 Akinori Otsuka **RC** 8.00
93 Andres Blanco **RC** 5.00
94 Angel Chavez **RC** 3.00
95 Brian Dallimore **RC** 8.00
96 Carlos Hines **RC** 5.00
97 Carlos Vasquez **RC** 5.00
98 Casey Daigle **RC** 3.00
99 Chad Bentz **RC** 3.00
100 Chris Aguila **RC** 3.00
101 Chris Oxspring **RC** 5.00
102 Chris Saenz **RC** 3.00
103 Chris Shelton **RC** 10.00
104 Colby Miller **RC** 5.00
105 David Crouthers 3.00
106 David Aardsma **RC** 5.00
107 Dennis Sarfate **RC** 3.00
108 Donnie Kelly **RC** 3.00
109 Eddy Rodriguez **RC** 3.00
110 Eduardo Villacis **RC** 3.00
111 Edwin Moreno **RC** 5.00
112 Enemencio Pacheco **RC** 5.00
113 Fernando Nieve **RC** 3.00
114 Franklyn Gracesqui **RC** 3.00
115 Freddy Guzman **RC** 3.00
116 Greg Dobbs **RC** 3.00
117 Hector Gimenez **RC** 3.00
118 Ian Snell **RC** 5.00
119 Ivan Ochoa **RC** 5.00
120 Jake Woods 5.00
121 Jamie Brown **RC** 5.00
122 Jason Bartlett **RC** 3.00
123 Jason Frasor **RC** 3.00
124 Jeff Bennett **RC** 3.00
125 Jerome Gamble **RC** 5.00
126 Jerry Gil **RC** 3.00
127 Brandon Medders **RC** 3.00
128 Ryan Meaux **RC** 3.00
129 John Gall **RC** 3.00
130 Jorge Sequea **RC** 3.00
131 Jorge Vasquez **RC** 5.00
132 Jose Capellan **RC** 8.00
133 Josh Labandeira **RC** 3.00
134 Justin Germano **RC** 8.00
135 Justin Hampson **RC** 5.00
136 Justin Huisman **RC** 5.00
137 Justin Knoedler **RC** 5.00
138 Justin Leone **RC** 5.00
139 Kazuhito Tadano **RC** 5.00
140 Kazuo Matsui **RC** 10.00
141 Kevin Cave **RC** 5.00
142 Lincoln Holdzkom **RC** 3.00
143 Lino Urdaneta **RC** 3.00
144 Luis A. Gonzalez **RC** 5.00
145 Mariano Gomez **RC** 5.00
146 Merkin Valdez **RC** 5.00
147 Michael Vento **RC** 8.00
148 Mike Wuertz **RC** 5.00
149 Mike Gosling 5.00
150 Mike Johnston **RC** 3.00
151 Mike Rouse 5.00
152 Nick Regilio **RC** 5.00
153 Onil Joseph **RC** 3.00
154 Orlando Rodriguez **RC** 5.00
155 Ramon Ramirez **RC** 5.00
156 Renyel Pinto **RC** 5.00
157 Roberto Novoa **RC** 5.00
158 Roman Colon **RC** 3.00
159 Ronald Belisario **RC** 5.00
160 Ronny Cedeno **RC** 8.00
161 Rusty Tucker **RC** 5.00
162 Ryan Wing 3.00
163 Scott Dohmann **RC** 3.00
164 Scott Proctor **RC** 5.00
165 Sean Henn 5.00
166 Shawn Camp **RC** 5.00
167 Shawn Hill **RC** 3.00
168 Shingo Takatsu **RC** 8.00
169 Tim Hamulack **RC** 3.00
170 William Bergolla **RC** 3.00
171 Adam Dunn 2.00
172 Albert Pujols 8.00
173 Alex Rodriguez 8.00
174 Alfonso Soriano 3.00
175 Andruw Jones 2.00
176 Bret Boone 1.50
177 Brian Giles 1.50
178 Carlos Delgado 2.00
179 Derrek Lee 2.00
180 Eric Chavez 1.50
181 Frank Thomas 2.00
182 Garret Anderson 1.50
183 Gary Sheffield 2.00
184 Hank Blalock 2.00
185 Jason Giambi 1.50
186 Javy Lopez 1.50
187 Jeff Bagwell 2.00
188 Jim Edmonds 2.00
189 Jim Thome 2.00
190 Ken Griffey Jr. 4.00
191 Lance Berkman 1.50
192 Magglio Ordonez 1.50
193 Manny Ramirez 3.00
194 Mike Lowell 1.50
195 Mike Piazza 5.00
196 Preston Wilson 1.50
197 Rafael Palmeiro 2.00
198 Richie Sexson 1.50
199 Sammy Sosa 5.00
200 Scott Rolen 4.00
201 Shawn Green 1.50
202 Todd Helton 2.00
203 Troy Glaus 1.50
204 Vernon Wells 1.50
205 Vladimir Guerrero 3.00
206 Garret Anderson, Vladimir Guerrero 3.00
207 Luis Gonzalez, Richie Sexson 2.00
208 Andruw Jones, Chipper Jones 3.00
209 Javy Lopez, Miguel Tejada 2.00
210 Manny Ramirez, David Ortiz 5.00
211 Derrek Lee, Sammy Sosa 5.00
212 Frank Thomas, Magglio Ordonez 2.00
213 Austin Kearns, Ken Griffey Jr. 4.00
214 Preston Wilson, Todd Helton 2.00
215 Delmon Young, Ivan Rodriguez 2.00
216 Miguel Cabrera, Mike Lowell 3.00
217 Jeff Bagwell, Lance Berkman 2.00
218 Lyle Overbay, Geoff Jenkins 1.50
219 Adrian Beltre, Shawn Green 2.00
220 Jacque Jones, Torii Hunter 1.50
221 Jose Vidro, N. Johnson 1.50
222 Kazuo Matsui, Mike Piazza 5.00
223 Alex Rodriguez, Jason Giambi 6.00
224 Eric Chavez, Jermaine Dye 1.50
225 Jim Thome, Pat Burrell 2.50
226 Brian Giles, Phil Nevin 1.50
227 Bret Boone, Ichiro Suzuki 6.00
228 Albert Pujols, Scott Rolen 8.00
229 Hank Blalock, Mark Teixeira 3.00
230 Carlos Delgado, Vernon Wells 2.00
231 Albert Pujols 8.00
232 Alex Rodriguez 8.00
233 Chipper Jones 3.00
234 Craig Biggio 1.50
235 Curt Schilling 2.00
236 Derek Jeter 8.00
237 Ivan Rodriguez 2.00
238 Jeff Bagwell 2.00
239 Jim Edmonds 2.00
240 Jim Thome 2.00
241 Josh Beckett 2.00
242 Kerry Wood 3.00
243 Kevin Brown 1.50
244 Mark Prior 2.00
245 Miguel Tejada 2.00
246 Mike Mussina 2.00
247 Nomar Garciaparra 4.00
248 Pedro J. Martinez 3.00
249 Randy Johnson 3.00
250 Roger Clemens 6.00
251 Alex Rodriguez, Derek Jeter 12.00
252 Alfonso Soriano, Hank Blalock 4.00
253 Bobby Abreu, Pat Burrell 3.00
254 Edgar Renteria, Scott Rolen 4.00
255 Garret Anderson, Vladimir Guerrero 4.00
256 Jeff Bagwell, Jeff Kent 3.00
257 Jose Reyes, Kazuo Matsui 4.00
258 K. Greene, S. Burroughs 4.00
259 Marcus Giles, Rafael Furcal 3.00
260 Manny Ramirez, Johnny Damon 6.00
261 Tim Bausher **RC** 3.00
262 Tim Bittner **RC** 5.00

Limited

No Pricing
Production 10 Sets

Sweet Impressions Plates

No Pricing
Production One Set

Wood

Stars (1-90): 3-6X
SP's (91-262): .75-1.5X
Production 99 Sets

Diamond Champs Jersey

NM/M
Common Player: 5.00
Production 150 Sets
GA Garret Anderson 5.00
JB Josh Beckett 8.00
RC Roger Clemens 12.00
EG Eric Gagne 8.00
KG Ken Griffey Jr. 12.00
RH Roy Halladay 5.00
DJ Derek Jeter 20.00
RJ Randy Johnson 10.00
CJ Chipper Jones 8.00
GM Greg Maddux 10.00
PM Pedro J. Martinez 8.00
PE Andy Pettitte 5.00
MP Mike Piazza 10.00
AP Albert Pujols 20.00
AR Alex Rodriguez/Yanks 15.00
IR Ivan Rodriguez 8.00
CS Curt Schilling 8.00
IS Ichiro Suzuki 30.00
MT Miguel Tejada 6.00
BZ Barry Zito 5.00

Home Run Heroes Jersey

NM/M
Common Player: 5.00
Production 199 Sets
GA Garret Anderson 5.00
JB Jeff Bagwell 8.00
CB Carlos Beltran 8.00
AB Adrian Beltre 8.00
LB Lance Berkman 5.00
HB Hank Blalock 8.00
BB Bret Boone 5.00
PB Pat Burrell 5.00
MC Miguel Cabrera 10.00
EC Eric Chavez 5.00
CD Carlos Delgado 5.00
JD J.D. Drew 5.00
AD Adam Dunn 8.00
JE Jim Edmonds 8.00
JG Jason Giambi 5.00
BG Brian Giles 5.00
TG Troy Glaus 5.00
LG Luis Gonzalez 5.00
SG Shawn Green 5.00
KG Ken Griffey Jr./Bat Up 12.00
KG1 Ken Griffey Jr./Swing 12.00
VG Vladimir Guerrero 10.00
HA Travis Hafner 5.00
TH Todd Helton 8.00
DJ Derek Jeter 20.00
AJ Andruw Jones 6.00
CJ Chipper Jones 8.00
JK Jeff Kent 5.00
DL Derrek Lee 5.00
ML Mike Lowell 5.00
HM Hideki Matsui 25.00
JM Joe Mauer 8.00
FM Fred McGriff 5.00
MO Magglio Ordonez 5.00
DO David Ortiz 15.00
RP Rafael Palmeiro 8.00
MP Mike Piazza 10.00
JP Jorge Posada 5.00
AP Albert Pujols 20.00
MR Manny Ramirez 8.00
AR Alex Rodriguez/Yanks/Bat Up 15.00
AR1 Alex Rodriguez/Yanks/Swing 15.00
IR Ivan Rodriguez 8.00
SR Scott Rolen 10.00
RS Richie Sexson 5.00
GS Gary Sheffield 8.00
AS Alfonso Soriano 8.00
SS Sammy Sosa 12.00
MT Mark Teixeira 6.00
TE Miguel Tejada 6.00
FT Frank Thomas 8.00
JT Jim Thome 10.00
VW Vernon Wells 5.00
BW Bernie Williams 8.00
PW Preston Wilson 5.00

Marquee Attractions Jersey

NM/M
Common Player: 5.00
Production 199 Sets
HB Hank Blalock 8.00
MC Miguel Cabrera 10.00
EC Eric Chavez 5.00
RC Roger Clemens 12.00
CD Carlos Delgado 5.00
EG Eric Gagne 8.00
BG Brian Giles 5.00
KG Ken Griffey Jr. 12.00
VG Vladimir Guerrero 10.00
TH Todd Helton 8.00
HU Torii Hunter 5.00
DJ Derek Jeter 20.00
RJ Randy Johnson 10.00
AJ Andruw Jones 5.00
PI Mike Piazza 10.00
MP Mark Prior 8.00
AP Albert Pujols 20.00
AR Alex Rodriguez 15.00
IR Ivan Rodriguez 8.00
CS Curt Schilling 10.00
JS Jason Schmidt 8.00
BS Ben Sheets 8.00
IS Ichiro Suzuki 30.00
MS Mike Sweeney 5.00
MT Miguel Tejada 8.00
FT Frank Thomas 8.00
JT Jim Thome 10.00

Signatures

NM/M
Common Player: 10.00
Black Stitch: No Pricing
Production One Set
GA Garret Anderson 20.00
RB Rocco Baldelli 20.00
BE Josh Beckett 40.00
CB Carlos Beltran 25.00
AB Angel Berroa 10.00
HB Hank Blalock 15.00
BB Bret Boone 10.00
PB Pat Burrell 15.00
SB Sean Burroughs 10.00
MC Miguel Cabrera 40.00
EC Eric Chavez 20.00
WC Will Clark 25.00
RC Roger Clemens 150.00
JD J.D. Drew 15.00
AD Adam Dunn 20.00
NG Nomar Garciaparra 50.00
BG Brian Giles 10.00
MG Marcus Giles 10.00
GL Tom Glavine 40.00
JG Juan Gonzalez 20.00
LG Luis Gonzalez 15.00
KG Ken Griffey Jr. 75.00
VG Vladimir Guerrero 50.00
TG Tony Gwynn 40.00
HA Roy Halladay 20.00
RH Rich Harden 15.00
TH Todd Helton 40.00
HI Richard Hidalgo 10.00
HO Trevor Hoffman 20.00

TI Tim Hudson 20.00
HU Torii Hunter 20.00
GJ Geoff Jenkins 10.00
DJ Derek Jeter 160.00
JJ Jacque Jones 10.00
AK Austin Kearns 15.00
RK Ryan Klesko 10.00
CL Carlos Lee 15.00
DL Derrek Lee 20.00
ML Mike Lieberthal 10.00
EL Esteban Loaiza 10.00
LO Mike Lowell 20.00
MA Mike Marshall/SP/34 40.00
EM Edgar Martinez 50.00
DM Don Mattingly 60.00
JM Joe Mauer 25.00
MU Mark Mulder 20.00
MM Mike Mussina 40.00
RO Roy Oswalt 20.00
CP Corey Patterson 15.00
OP Odalis Perez 10.00
PI Mike Piazza 150.00
SP Scott Podsednik 15.00
MP Mark Prior 20.00
AP Albert Pujols 220.00
MR Manny Ramirez 60.00
JR Jose Reyes 40.00
CR Cal Ripken Jr. 180.00
IR Ivan Rodriguez 50.00
SR Scott Rolen 30.00
NR Nolan Ryan 150.00
RS Ryne Sandberg 75.00
SA Johan Santana 20.00
JS Jason Schmidt 15.00
TS Tom Seaver 50.00
BS Ben Sheets 20.00
GS Gary Sheffield 35.00
SM John Smoltz 50.00
IS Ichiro Suzuki 250.00
MT Mark Teixeira 25.00
TE Miguel Tejada 25.00
FT Frank Thomas 50.00
JV Javier Vazquez 15.00
WA Billy Wagner 15.00
BW Brandon Webb 15.00
WE Rickie Weeks 15.00
VW Vernon Wells/30 25.00
DW Dontrelle Willis 20.00
RW Randy Wolf 15.00
KW Kerry Wood 20.00
DY Delmon Young 20.00
CZ Carlos Zambrano 40.00

Signatures Red-Blue Stitch

NM/M
Quantity produced listed
GA Garret Anderson/45 25.00
RB Rocco Baldelli/35 25.00
BE Josh Beckett/45 40.00
CB Carlos Beltran/45 40.00
AB Angel Berroa/45 20.00
HB Hank Blalock/45 25.00
BB Bret Boone/45 20.00
PB Pat Burrell/35 25.00
SB Sean Burroughs/45 15.00
MC Miguel Cabrera/45 40.00
EC Eric Chavez/45 25.00
WC Will Clark/45 25.00
RC Roger Clemens/30 175.00
JD J.D. Drew/40 25.00
AD Adam Dunn/45 25.00
NG Nomar Garciaparra/45 60.00
BG Brian Giles/45 15.00
MG Marcus Giles/45 20.00
GL Tom Glavine/45 60.00
JG Juan Gonzalez/45 25.00
LG Luis Gonzalez/45 25.00
KG Ken Griffey Jr./44 100.00
VG Vladimir Guerrero/45 75.00
TG Tony Gwynn/45 60.00
HA Roy Halladay/35 25.00
RH Rich Harden/45 25.00
TH Todd Helton/45 50.00
HI Richard Hidalgo/45 15.00
HO Trevor Hoffman/45 25.00
TI Tim Hudson/45 25.00
HU Torii Hunter/45 25.00
EJ Edwin Jackson/45 15.00
GJ Geoff Jenkins/45 15.00
DJ Derek Jeter/35 275.00
JJ Jacque Jones/45 20.00
AK Austin Kearns/45 25.00
RK Ryan Klesko/45 15.00
CL Carlos Lee/45 20.00
DL Derrek Lee/45 35.00
ML Mike Lieberthal/45 25.00
EL Esteban Loaiza/45 15.00
LO Mike Lowell/35 30.00
EM Edgar Martinez/30 50.00
DM Don Mattingly/45 85.00
JM Joe Mauer/45 35.00
MU Mark Mulder/45 20.00
RO Roy Oswalt/45 25.00
CP Corey Patterson/45 25.00
OP Odalis Perez/45 20.00
SP Scott Podsednik/45 20.00
MP Mark Prior/45 25.00
AP Albert Pujols/45 250.00
MR Manny Ramirez/40 80.00
JR Jose Reyes/45 50.00
CR Cal Ripken Jr./35 250.00
IR Ivan Rodriguez/45 50.00
NR Nolan Ryan/40 170.00
RS Ryne Sandberg/40 80.00
SA Johan Santana/45 65.00
JS Jason Schmidt/45 25.00
TS Tom Seaver/35 75.00
BS Ben Sheets/55 25.00
GS Gary Sheffield/45 50.00
SM John Smoltz/40 80.00
IS Ichiro Suzuki/25 500.00
MT Mark Teixeira/45 40.00
TE Miguel Tejada/25 50.00
FT Frank Thomas/25 75.00
JV Javier Vazquez/45 20.00
WA Billy Wagner/45 20.00
BW Brandon Webb/45 20.00
WE Rickie Weeks/45 25.00
VW Vernon Wells/29 25.00
DW Dontrelle Willis/45 25.00
RW Randy Wolf/45 20.00
KW Kerry Wood/45 25.00
DY Delmon Young/45 25.00
CZ Carlos Zambrano/30 50.00

Signatures Barrel

NM/M
Cards not serial numbered, quantity produced provided by Upper Deck.
GA Garret Anderson/74 20.00
RB Rocco Baldelli/19 25.00
BE Josh Beckett/65 50.00
CB Carlos Beltran/55 40.00
AB Angel Berroa/64 15.00
HB Hank Blalock/74 25.00
BB Bret Boone/64 15.00
SB Sean Burroughs/64 15.00
MC Miguel Cabrera/64 40.00
EC Eric Chavez/74 25.00
AD Adam Dunn/74 30.00
NG Nomar Garciaparra/38 75.00
BG Brian Giles/64 15.00
MG Marcus Giles/64 15.00
GL Tom Glavine/64 50.00
KG Ken Griffey Jr./64 125.00
VG Vladimir Guerrero/38 60.00
HA Roy Halladay/64 30.00
RH Rich Harden/64 20.00
TH Todd Helton/38 60.00
HI Richard Hidalgo/64 15.00
HO Trevor Hoffman/68 25.00
TI Tim Hudson/64 30.00
HU Torii Hunter/64 30.00
EJ Edwin Jackson/64 Exch 15.00
GJ Geoff Jenkins/64 15.00
DJ Derek Jeter/53 275.00
JJ Jacque Jones/64 15.00
AK Austin Kearns/64 20.00
RK Ryan Klesko/64 15.00
CL Carlos Lee/64 25.00
DL Derrek Lee/64 50.00
ML Mike Lieberthal/64 15.00
EL Esteban Loaiza/64 15.00
LO Mike Lowell/64 30.00
EM Edgar Martinez/64 40.00
DM Don Mattingly/38 125.00
JM Joe Mauer/72 50.00
MU Mark Mulder/64 20.00
MM Mike Mussina/64 50.00
RO Roy Oswalt/64 40.00
CP Corey Patterson/74 Exch 25.00
OP Odalis Perez/64 15.00
PI Mike Piazza/38 150.00
SP Scott Podsednik/64 25.00
MP Mark Prior/64 25.00
AP Albert Pujols/64 250.00
MR Manny Ramirez/63 75.00
JR Jose Reyes/49 50.00
CR Cal Ripken Jr./38 220.00
AR Alex Rodriguez/28 300.00
IR Ivan Rodriguez/64 50.00
NR Nolan Ryan/38 180.00
SA Johan Santana/64 60.00
JS Jason Schmidt/64 25.00
TS Tom Seaver/38 75.00
BS Ben Sheets/64 25.00
GS Gary Sheffield/38 60.00
IS Ichiro Suzuki/64 500.00
MT Mark Teixeira/64 50.00
TE Miguel Tejada/64 50.00
JV Javier Vazquez/64 20.00
WA Billy Wagner/64 20.00
BW Brandon Webb/64 30.00
WE Rickie Weeks/64 25.00
VW Vernon Wells/33 20.00
DW Dontrelle Willis/64 25.00
RW Randy Wolf/64 15.00
KW Kerry Wood/64 25.00
DY Delmon Young/74 50.00
CZ Carlos Zambrano/38 40.00

Signatures Dual

No Pricing
Production 10 Sets

Signatures Glove

NM/M
Production 5-25
GA Garret Anderson/25 40.00
RB Rocco Baldelli/25 40.00
BE Josh Beckett/25 75.00
CB Carlos Beltran/25 50.00
AB Angel Berroa/25 25.00
HB Hank Blalock/25 40.00
BB Bret Boone/25 25.00
PB Pat Burrell/15 40.00
SB Sean Burroughs/25 25.00
MC Miguel Cabrera/25 100.00
EC Eric Chavez/25 50.00
WC Will Clark/25 100.00
AD Adam Dunn/25 60.00
NG Nomar Garciaparra/25 100.00
BG Brian Giles/25 35.00
MG Marcus Giles/25 30.00
GL Tom Glavine/25 65.00
JG Juan Gonzalez/25 50.00
LG Luis Gonzalez/25 40.00
KG Ken Griffey Jr./25 200.00
VG Vladimir Guerrero/25 100.00
TG Tony Gwynn/25 100.00
HA Roy Halladay/24 50.00
RH Rich Harden/25 40.00
TH Todd Helton/25 80.00
HI Richard Hidalgo/15 25.00
HO Trevor Hoffman/15 50.00
TI Tim Hudson/25 65.00
HU Torii Hunter/25 40.00
EJ Edwin Jackson/25 20.00
GJ Geoff Jenkins/25 30.00
JJ Jacque Jones/25 20.00
AK Austin Kearns/25 40.00
CL Carlos Lee/25 50.00
DL Derrek Lee/25 60.00
ML Mike Lieberthal/25 30.00
EL Esteban Loaiza/25 30.00
MA Mike Marshall/25 50.00
EM Edgar Martinez/25 75.00
DM Don Mattingly/25 180.00
JM Joe Mauer/25 50.00
MU Mark Mulder/25 40.00
MM Mike Mussina/25 75.00
RO Roy Oswalt/25 65.00
CP Corey Patterson/25 40.00
OP Odalis Perez/25 40.00
SP Scott Podsednik/25 40.00
MP Mark Prior/25 50.00
AP Albert Pujols/25 300.00
MR Manny Ramirez/25 120.00
JR Jose Reyes/25 75.00
CR Cal Ripken Jr./25 275.00
IR Ivan Rodriguez/25 75.00
NR Nolan Ryan/25 250.00
RS Ryne Sandberg/20 125.00
SA Johan Santana/25 75.00
JS Jason Schmidt/25 40.00
BS Ben Sheets/25 50.00
GS Gary Sheffield/20 75.00
MT Mark Teixeira/25 75.00
TE Miguel Tejada/25 60.00
JV Javier Vazquez/25 40.00
WA Billy Wagner/25 40.00
BW Brandon Webb/25 40.00
WE Rickie Weeks/25 30.00
DW Dontrelle Willis/25 50.00
KW Kerry Wood/25 50.00
DY Delmon Young/25 50.00

Signatures Historical Ball

No Pricing
Production One Set

Sweet Sticks

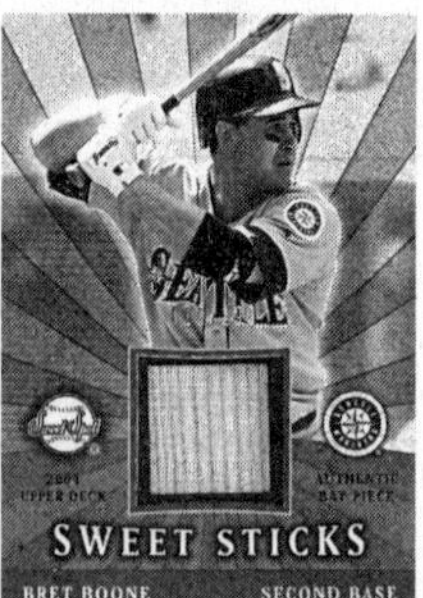

NM/M
Common Player: 4.00
Production 199 Sets
BA Bobby Abreu 6.00
MA Moises Alou 6.00
GA Garret Anderson 4.00
JB Jeff Bagwell 8.00
BE Carlos Beltran 8.00
AB Adrian Beltre 4.00
LB Lance Berkman 4.00
CB Craig Biggio 4.00
HB Hank Blalock 8.00
BB Bret Boone 4.00
PB Pat Burrell 4.00
MC Miguel Cabrera 8.00
EC Eric Chavez 6.00
RC Roger Clemens 15.00
CD Carlos Delgado 6.00
JD J.D. Drew 6.00
AD Adam Dunn 8.00
JE Jim Edmonds 6.00
RF Rafael Furcal 4.00
NG Nomar Garciaparra 12.00
JG Jason Giambi 6.00
BG Brian Giles 4.00
MG Marcus Giles 4.00
TG Troy Glaus 4.00
GL Tom Glavine 6.00
LG Luis Gonzalez 4.00
SG Shawn Green 4.00
KG Ken Griffey Jr. 15.00
VG Vladimir Guerrero 8.00
TH Todd Helton 8.00
DJ Derek Jeter 25.00
RJ Randy Johnson 8.00
CJ Chipper Jones 10.00
AJ Andruw Jones 6.00
JK Jeff Kent 4.00
DL Derrek Lee 4.00
ML Mike Lowell 4.00
GM Greg Maddux 10.00
HM Hideki Matsui 35.00
KM Kazuo Matsui 15.00
MO Magglio Ordonez 4.00
RP Rafael Palmeiro 8.00
MP Mike Piazza 10.00
PR Mark Prior 6.00
AP Albert Pujols 20.00
MR Manny Ramirez 8.00
ER Edgar Renteria 6.00
JR Jose Reyes 6.00
CR Cal Ripken Jr. 30.00
AR Alex Rodriguez 15.00
IR Ivan Rodriguez 8.00
SR Scott Rolen 10.00
CS Curt Schilling 6.00
RS Richie Sexson 6.00
GS Gary Sheffield 8.00
AS Alfonso Soriano 8.00
SS Sammy Sosa 10.00
IS Ichiro Suzuki 40.00
MT Mark Teixeira 6.00
TE Miguel Tejada 6.00
FT Frank Thomas 8.00
JT Jim Thome 8.00
LW Larry Walker 6.00
TW Ted Williams 60.00
PW Preston Wilson 4.00

Sweet Sticks Dual

NM/M
Common Duo: 10.00
Production 100 Sets
BT Hank Blalock, Mark Teixeira 10.00
CL Miguel Cabrera, Mike Lowell 10.00
JC Randy Johnson, Roger Clemens 25.00
JG Derek Jeter, Nomar Garciaparra 25.00
JM Jose Reyes, Kazuo Matsui 25.00
MM Hideki Matsui, Kazuo Matsui 40.00
PR Albert Pujols, Scott Rolen 40.00
RG Manny Ramirez, Nomar Garciaparra 15.00
RJ Alex Rodriguez, Derek Jeter 50.00
RP Ivan Rodriguez, Mike Piazza 15.00
TB Jim Thome, Pat Burrell 20.00
WP Kerry Wood, Mark Prior 12.00

Sweet Sticks Triple

NM/M
Production 50 Sets
GPS Ken Griffey Jr., Rafael Palmeiro, Sammy Sosa 40.00
JJD Andruw Jones, Chipper Jones, J.D. Drew 25.00
JSG Derek Jeter, Ichiro Suzuki, Ken Griffey Jr. 120.00
MWP Greg Maddux, Kerry Wood, Mark Prior 35.00
RJG Alex Rodriguez, Derek Jeter, Jason Giambi 65.00

Sweet Sticks Quad

NM/M
Production 25 Sets
PRSG Albert Pujols, Alex Rodriguez, Ichiro Suzuki, Ken Griffey Jr. 125.00
RGDM Babe Ruth, Lou Gehrig, Joe DiMaggio, Mickey Mantle 1,200

Sweet Threads

NM/M
Common Player: 4.00
Patch: 1.5-2.5X
Production 85 Sets
JB Jeff Bagwell 8.00
CB Carlos Beltran 8.00
LB Lance Berkman 4.00
HB Hank Blalock 8.00
BB Bret Boone 4.00
MC Miguel Cabrera 8.00
EC Eric Chavez 4.00
BC Bartolo Colon 4.00
CD Carlos Delgado 4.00
JG Jason Giambi 6.00
BG Brian Giles 4.00
TG Troy Glaus 4.00
SG Shawn Green 4.00

VG Vladimir Guerrero 8.00
RH Rich Harden 4.00
HE Todd Helton 8.00
TH Tim Hudson 4.00
ML Mike Lowell 4.00
EM Edgar Martinez 4.00
KM Kazuo Matsui/SP 15.00
JM Joe Mauer 8.00
MM Mark Mulder 4.00
HN Hideo Nomo 8.00
MO Magglio Ordonez 4.00
RO Roy Oswalt 4.00
MP Mark Prior 6.00
MR Manny Ramirez 8.00
JR Jose Reyes 4.00
SS Sammy Sosa 10.00
JS Jason Schmidt 6.00
RS Richie Sexson 4.00
GS Gary Sheffield 6.00
AS Alfonso Soriano 8.00
MT Mark Teixeira 6.00
FT Frank Thomas 8.00
JT Jim Thome 8.00
RW Rickie Weeks 4.00
VW Vernon Wells 4.00
DW Dontrelle Willis 4.00
PW Preston Wilson 4.00
KW Kerry Wood 8.00
DY Delmon Young 8.00

Sweet Threads Dual

NM/M
Common Duo: 5.00
Production 150 Sets
Patch: 1.5-2X
Production 60 Sets
BP Angel Berroa, Scott Podsednik 4.00
BT Hank Blalock, Mark Teixeira 10.00
CK Curt Schilling, Kevin Brown 10.00
CS Roger Clemens, Sammy Sosa 20.00
DT Carlos Delgado, Jim Thome 8.00
GH Eric Gagne, Roy Halladay 8.00
HG Tim Hudson, Vladimir Guerrero 10.00
JC Randy Johnson, Roger Clemens 25.00
JH Andruw Jones, Torii Hunter 8.00
JJ Andruw Jones, Chipper Jones 10.00
MM Hideki Matsui, Kazuo Matsui 50.00
MP Joe Mauer, Mark Prior 10.00
PC Andy Pettitte, Roger Clemens 20.00
PP Jorge Posada, Mike Piazza 15.00
PS Albert Pujols, Ichiro Suzuki 50.00
PW Albert Pujols, Kerry Wood 15.00
RJ Alex Rodriguez, Derek Jeter 50.00
RM Jose Reyes, Kazuo Matsui 15.00
SB Alfonso Soriano, Bret Boone 8.00
SM Gary Sheffield, Pedro J. Martinez 12.00
WP Kerry Wood, Mark Prior 10.00
YW Delmon Young, Rickie Weeks 10.00

Sweet Threads Triple

NM/M
Common Trio: 10.00
Production 99 Sets
Triple Patch: 2X
No pricing 15 or less.
AGG Garret Anderson, Troy Glaus, Vladimir Guerrero 20.00
BKE Jeff Bagwell, Jeff Kent, Morgan Ensberg 15.00
BLR Adrian Beltre, Mike Lowell, Scott Rolen 20.00
BMS Bret Boone, Edgar Martinez, Ichiro Suzuki 50.00
BWC Josh Beckett, Kerry Wood, Roger Clemens 30.00
CMM Bobby Crosby, Joe Mauer, Kazuo Matsui 30.00
DHW Carlos Delgado, Roy Halladay, Vernon Wells 15.00
DKG Adam Dunn, Austin Kearns, Ken Griffey Jr. 20.00
DMJ Joe DiMaggio, Mickey Mantle, Derek Jeter 220.00
DMW Joe DiMaggio, Mickey Mantle, Ted Williams 250.00
DRN Johnny Damon, Manny Ramirez, Trot Nixon 40.00
FRP Keith Foulke, Mariano Rivera, Troy Percival 25.00
GPS Ken Griffey Jr., Rafael Palmeiro, Sammy Sosa 35.00
JJD Andruw Jones, Chipper Jones, J.D. Drew 20.00
JTG Derek Jeter, Miguel Tejada, Nomar Garciaparra 40.00
JWH Edwin Jackson, Jerome Williams, Rich Harden 10.00
KVG Jeff Kent, Jose Vidro, Marcus Giles 10.00
LTO Carlos Lee, Frank Thomas, Magglio Ordonez 20.00
LTP Javy Lopez, Miguel Tejada, Rafael Palmeiro 20.00
MCF Kazuo Matsui, Miguel Cabrera, Rafael Furcal 20.00
MMH Mike Mussina, Pedro J. Martinez, Tim Hudson 25.00
MSH Joe Mauer, Johan Santana, Torii Hunter 35.00
MWP Greg Maddux, Kerry Wood, Mark Prior 25.00
PAS Corey Patterson, Moises Alou, Sammy Sosa 30.00
PCO Andy Pettitte, Roger Clemens, Roy Oswalt 25.00
PRR Albert Pujols, Edgar Renteria, Scott Rolen 40.00
PTH Albert Pujols, Jim Thome, Todd Helton 30.00
RCB Alex Rodriguez, Eric Chavez, Hank Blalock 30.00
RGJ Alex Rodriguez, Ken Griffey Jr., Randy Johnson 35.00
RGW Jose Reyes, Khalil Greene, Rickie Weeks 30.00
RJG Alex Rodriguez, Derek Jeter, Jason Giambi 60.00
RMP Jose Reyes, Kazuo Matsui, Mike Piazza 25.00
SBK Alfonso Soriano, Bret Boone, Jeff Kent 20.00
SBP Jason Schmidt, Josh Beckett, Mark Prior 15.00
SBT Alfonso Soriano, Hank Blalock, Mark Teixeira 20.00
SLM Curt Schilling, Derek Lowe, Pedro J. Martinez 40.00
VBM Javier Vazquez, Kevin Brown, Mike Mussina 20.00
WBP Brandon Webb, Josh Beckett, Mark Prior 15.00
WGS Billy Wagner, Eric Gagne, John Smoltz 20.00
WRC Kerry Wood, Nolan Ryan, Roger Clemens 60.00
YCW Delmon Young, Miguel Cabrera, Rickie Weeks 20.00
ZMH Barry Zito, Mark Mulder, Tim Hudson 10.00

Sweet Threads Quad

NM/M
Common Quad: 20.00
Production 99 Sets
Quad Patch: No Pricing

Production 1-15
BADH Carlos Beltran, Garret Anderson, Johnny Damon, Torii Hunter 30.00
BBGS Angel Berroa, Carlos Beltran, Alex Gonzalez, Mike Sweeney 20.00
BPJC Josh Beckett, Mark Prior, Randy Johnson, Roger Clemens 30.00
BWRC Josh Beckett, Kerry Wood, Nolan Ryan, Roger Clemens 50.00
CAGG Bartolo Colon, Garret Anderson, Troy Glaus, Vladimir Guerrero 25.00
DHHW Carlos Delgado, Eric Hinske, Roy Halladay, Vernon Wells 20.00
DOGP Carlos Delgado, David Ortiz, Jason Giambi, Rafael Palmeiro 25.00
GNKB Brian Giles, Phil Nevin, Ryan Klesko, Sean Burroughs 25.00
GNLG Eric Gagne, Hideo Nomo, Paul LoDuca, Shawn Green 30.00
JBGB Chipper Jones, Lance Berkman, Luis Gonzalez, Pat Burrell 25.00
JEGW Andruw Jones, Jim Edmonds, Ken Griffey Jr., Preston Wilson 35.00
JJDF Andruw Jones, Chipper Jones, J.D. Drew, Rafael Furcal 25.00
JMSH Jacque Jones, Joe Mauer, Shannon Stewart, Torii Hunter 35.00
JRMT Derek Jeter, Edgar Renteria, Kazuo Matsui, Miguel Tejada 40.00
KGCS Austin Kearns, Brian Giles, Miguel Cabrera, Sammy Sosa 25.00
LMRS Carlos Lee, Hideki Matsui, Manny Ramirez, Shannon Stewart 75.00
LTOK Carlos Lee, Frank Thomas, Magglio Ordonez, Paul Konerko 25.00
LTPP Javy Lopez, Miguel Tejada, Raffy, Sidney Ponson 25.00
MMMH Mark Mulder, Mike Mussina, Pedro J. Martinez, Roy Halladay 25.00
MTTS Edgar Martinez, Jim Thome, Mark Teixeira, Mike Sweeney 20.00
NSGH Phil Nevin, Richie Sexson, Shawn Green, Todd Helton 20.00
PBBC Andy Pettitte, Craig Biggio, Jeff Bagwell, Roger Clemens 40.00
PLBT Albert Pujols, Lee, Jeff Bagwell, Jim Thome 40.00
PRER Albert Pujols, Edgar Renteria, Jim Edmonds, Scott Rolen 70.00
PWPS Corey Patterson, Kerry Wood, Mark Prior, Sammy Sosa 40.00
RCBG Alex Rodriguez, Eric Chavez, Hank Blalock, Troy Glaus 30.00
RJDM Alex Rodriguez, Derek Jeter, Joe DiMaggio, Mickey Mantle 275.00
RLPM Ivan Rodriguez, Javy Lopez, Jorge Posada, Joe Mauer 40.00
RMPG Jose Reyes, Kazuo Matsui, Mike Piazza, Tom Glavine 30.00
SBKV Alfonso Soriano, Bret Boone, Jeff Kent, Jose Vidro 20.00
SBMM Curt Schilling, Kevin Brown, Mike Mussina, Pedro J. Martinez 40.00
SDRM Curt Schilling, Johnny Damon, Manny Ramirez, Pedro J. Martinez 60.00
SSOG Gary Sheffield, Ichiro Suzuki, Magglio Ordonez, Vladimir Guerrero 50.00
VCBM Javier Vazquez, Jose Contreras, Kevin Brown, Mike Mussina 25.00
WATM Billy Wagner, Bobby Abreu, Jim Thome, Kevin Millwood 30.00
WBCL Dontrelle Willis, Josh Beckett, Miguel Cabrera, Mike Lowell 20.00
WGJS Brandon Webb, Luis Gonzalez, Randy Johnson, Richie Sexson 25.00
ZMHH Barry Zito, Mark Mulder, Rich Harden, Tim Hudson 35.00

2004 Upper Deck Sweet Spot Classic

NM/M
Complete Set (161):
Common Player (1-90): .40
Common (91-161): 2.00
Production 1,910-1,999
Pack (4): 15.00
Box (12): 150.00
1 Al Kaline 1.00
2 Andre Dawson .40
3 Bert Blyleven .40
4 Bill Dickey .40
5 Bill Mazeroski .40
6 Billy Martin .40
7 Bob Feller .50
8 Bob Gibson 1.00
9 Bob Lemon .40
10 George Kell .40
11 Bobby Doerr .40
12 Brooks Robinson 1.00
13 Cal Ripken Jr. 4.00
14 Carl Hubbell .40
15 Carl Yastrzemski 1.50
16 Charlie Keller .40
17 Chuck Dressen .40
18 Cy Young 1.00
19 Dave Winfield .75
20 Dizzy Dean .75
21 Don Drysdale .75
22 Don Larsen .75
23 Don Mattingly 2.50
24 Don Newcombe .40
25 Duke Snider .75
26 Early Wynn .40
27 Eddie Mathews 1.00
28 Elston Howard .40
29 Frank Robinson .75
30 Gary Carter .40
31 Gil Hodges .40
32 Gil McDougald .40
33 Hank Greenberg .75
34 Harmon Killebrew 1.50
35 Harry Caray .40
36 Honus Wagner 1.00
37 Hoyt Wilhelm .40
38 Jackie Robinson 2.00
39 Jim Bunning .40
40 Jim Palmer .75
41 Jimmie Foxx 1.00
42 Jimmy Wynn .40
43 Joe DiMaggio 3.00
44 Joe Torre .40
45 Johnny Mize .40
46 Juan Marichal .75
47 Larry Doby .40
48 Lefty Gomez .40
49 Lefty Grove .40
50 Leo Durocher .40
51 Lou Boudreau .40
52 Lou Brock .50
53 Lou Gehrig 3.00
54 Luis Aparicio .40
55 Maury Wills .40
56 Mel Allen .40
57 Mel Ott .40
58 Mickey Cochrane .40
59 Mickey Mantle 4.00
60 Mike Schmidt 2.00
61 Monte Irvin .40
62 Nolan Ryan 4.00
63 Pee Wee Reese .50
64 Phil Rizzuto .50
65 Ralph Kiner .40
66 Richie Ashburn .40
67 Rick Ferrell .40
68 Roberto Clemente 2.50
69 Robin Roberts .40
70 Robin Yount 1.00
71 Rogers Hornsby .75
72 Rollie Fingers .40
73 Roy Campanella .75
74 Ryne Sandberg 1.50
75 Tony Gwynn 1.00
76 Satchel Paige .75
77 Shoeless Joe Jackson 2.00
78 Stan Musial 2.00
79 Ted Williams 3.00
80 Thurman Munson .75
81 Tom Seaver 1.50
82 Tommy Henrich .40
83 Tony Perez .40
84 Tris Speaker .40
85 Vida Blue .40
86 Wade Boggs .50
87 Walter Johnson .75
88 Warren Spahn 1.00
89 Whitey Ford .75
90 Willie McCovey .40
91 Andre Dawson 2.50
92 Andre Dawson 2.50
93 Ernie Banks 4.00
94 Bob Lemon 2.00
95 Cal Ripken Jr. 8.00
96 Cal Ripken Jr. 8.00
97 Carl Yastrzemski 3.00
98 Carlton Fisk 2.50
99 Cy Young 4.00
100 Don Larsen 2.50
101 Don Newcombe 2.00
102 Don Newcombe 2.00
103 Dwight Evans 2.00
104 Elston Howard 2.50
105 Frank Robinson 3.00
106 Frank Robinson 3.00
107 Frank Robinson 3.00
108 Gil McDougald 2.00
109 Hank Greenberg 4.00
110 Harmon Killebrew 4.00
111 Hoyt Wilhelm 2.00
112 Hoyt Wilhelm 2.00
113 Jackie Robinson 5.00
114 Jackie Robinson 5.00
115 Jackie Robinson 5.00
116 Jackie Robinson 5.00
117 Jim Bunning 2.00
118 Joe DiMaggio 6.00
119 Joe Morgan 2.00
120 Johnny Mize 2.50
121 Johnny Mize 2.50
122 Juan Marichal 3.00
123 Ken Griffey Sr. 2.00
124 Larry Doby 2.50
125 Lefty Gomez 2.00
126 Lou Boudreau 2.00
127 Lou Gehrig 6.00
128 Lou Gehrig 6.00
129 Mark McGwire 6.00
130 Mark McGwire 6.00
131 Maury Wills 2.00
132 Mel Ott 3.00
133 Mike Schmidt 5.00
134 Nolan Ryan 8.00
135 Nolan Ryan 8.00
136 Pee Wee Reese 2.00
137 Nolan Ryan 8.00
138 Richie Ashburn 2.50
139 Roberto Clemente 8.00
140 Roberto Clemente 8.00
141 Robin Roberts 2.00
142 Robin Yount 3.00
143 Roger Clemens 2.00
144 Rollie Fingers 2.00
145 Rollie Fingers 2.00
146 Roy Campanella 3.00
147 Ryne Sandberg 4.00
149 Satchel Paige 4.00
150 Stan Musial 5.00
151 Stan Musial 5.00
152 Stan Musial 5.00
153 Ted Williams 6.00
154 Ted Williams 6.00
155 Tom Seaver 3.00
156 Tom Seaver 3.00
157 Wade Boggs 2.50
158 Warren Spahn 3.00
159 Warren Spahn 3.00
160 Joe DiMaggio 6.00
161 Yogi Berra 4.00

Game Used Patch

NM/M
Some not priced due to scarcity.
Holofoil: No Pricing
Production 10
BB Bert Blyleven/113 25.00
WB Wade Boggs/90 30.00
AD Andre Dawson/100 20.00
TG Tony Gwynn/100 35.00
CK Charlie Keller/55 30.00
ML Mickey Lolich/115 15.00
DM Don Mattingly/176 40.00
GM Gil McDougald/31 25.00
TM Thurman Munson/100 30.00
FR Frank Robinson/50 30.00
NR Nolan Ryan/96 65.00
TS Tom Seaver/94 30.00
MW Maury Wills/78 25.00
CY Carl Yastrzemski/20 65.00
RY Robin Yount/100 30.00

Jersey

NM/M
Common Player: 5.00
Production 275 Sets
Holofoils: 1.5-2X

Production 50
SA Sparky Anderson 6.00
SB Sal Bando 5.00
RB Ron Blomberg 5.00
BB Bert Blyleven 5.00
WB Wade Boggs 8.00
WB1 Wade Boggs 8.00
JB Jim Bunning 5.00
GC Gary Carter 6.00
RC Roberto Clemente 65.00
AD Andre Dawson 5.00
AD1 Andre Dawson 5.00
JD Joe DiMaggio 70.00
CD Chuck Dressen 5.00
KG Ken Griffey Sr. 5.00
TG Tony Gwynn 10.00
EH Elston Howard 8.00
CK Charlie Keller 15.00
ML Mickey Lolich 6.00
MM Mickey Mantle 125.00
JM Juan Marichal 8.00
RM Roger Maris 45.00
BM Billy Martin 8.00
EM Eddie Mathews 10.00
DM Don Mattingly 20.00
GM Gil McDougald 8.00
JO Johnny Mize 10.00
TM Thurman Munson 20.00
SM Stan Musial 25.00
JP Jim Palmer 8.00
CR Cal Ripken Jr. 20.00
PR Phil Rizzuto 15.00
FR Frank Robinson 8.00
JR Jackie Robinson 40.00
NR Nolan Ryan 25.00
TS Tom Seaver 15.00
OS Ozzie Smith 10.00
JT Joe Torre 8.00
TW Ted Williams 70.00
MW Maury Wills 5.00
CY Carl Yastrzemski 15.00
RY Robin Yount 10.00

Logo Patch

NM/M
Common Level 1: 5.00
Production 300
Level 2: 1X
Production 230
Level 3: 1X
Production 200
Level 4: 1-1.5X
Production 150
Level 5: 1-1.5X
Production 125
Level 6: 1-2X
Production 75
Level 7: 1.5-2.5X
Production 50
Level 8: No Pricing
Production 25
AL Mel Allen 5.00
LA Luis Aparicio 5.00
RA Richie Ashburn 6.00
WB Wade Boggs 8.00
LB Lou Boudreau 5.00
BR Lou Brock 8.00
JB Jim Bunning 5.00
CA Roy Campanella 8.00
GC Gary Carter 5.00
HC Harry Caray 10.00
RC Roberto Clemente 25.00
TC Ty Cobb 12.00
CO Mickey Cochrane 5.00
AD Andre Dawson 8.00
DD Dizzy Dean 8.00
BD Bill Dickey 5.00
JD Joe DiMaggio 15.00
LD Larry Doby 6.00
DO Bobby Doerr 6.00
DR Don Drysdale 6.00
DU Leo Durocher 5.00
BF Bob Feller 8.00
RF Rick Ferrell 6.00
FI Rollie Fingers 6.00
WF Whitey Ford 6.00
JF Jimmie Foxx 8.00
FF Frankie Frisch 5.00
GE Lou Gehrig 15.00
CG Charlie Gehringer 8.00
BG Bob Gibson 8.00
LG Lefty Gomez 5.00
HG Hank Greenberg 10.00
GR Lefty Grove 6.00
TH Tommy Henrich 5.00
GH Gil Hodges 8.00
RH Rogers Hornsby 8.00
CH Carl Hubbell 5.00
IR Monte Irvin 5.00
JJ Shoeless Joe Jackson 20.00
FJ Ferguson Jenkins 6.00
WJ Walter Johnson 8.00
AK Al Kaline 15.00
HK Harmon Killebrew 15.00
RK Ralph Kiner 8.00
DL Don Larsen 6.00
TL Tommy Lasorda 5.00
BL Bob Lemon 5.00
ML Mickey Lolich 5.00
MI Mickey Mantle 40.00
MA Juan Marichal 6.00
BM Billy Martin 8.00
EM Eddie Mathews 8.00
CM Christy Mathewson 10.00
DM Don Mattingly 20.00
WM Willie McCovey 8.00
JM Johnny Mize 6.00
TM Thurman Munson 10.00
SM Stan Musial 10.00
DN Don Newcombe 5.00
MO Mel Ott 6.00
SP Satchel Paige 10.00
JP Jim Palmer 8.00
TP Tony Perez 5.00
GP Gaylord Perry 5.00
PR Pee Wee Reese 6.00
CR Cal Ripken Jr. 30.00
RI Phil Rizzuto 8.00
RR Robin Roberts 6.00
RO Brooks Robinson 12.00
FR Frank Robinson 8.00
JR Jackie Robinson 12.00
RU Babe Ruth 20.00
NR Nolan Ryan 25.00
RS Ryne Sandberg 20.00
MS Mike Schmidt 15.00
TS Tom Seaver 10.00
SK Bill "Moose" Skowron 5.00
ES Enos Slaughter 5.00
DS Duke Snider 8.00
WS Warren Spahn 10.00
TR Tris Speaker 8.00
JT Joe Torre 5.00
HW Honus Wagner 10.00
WI Hoyt Wilhelm 5.00
TW Ted Williams 20.00
MW Maury Wills 5.00
DW Dave Winfield 6.00
EW Early Wynn 5.00
YA Carl Yastrzemski 12.00
CY Cy Young 10.00

Signature Black Ink

NM/M
Common Autograph: 15.00
2 Preacher Roe/225 25.00
4 Bob Feller/65 45.00
5 Bob Gibson/50 50.00
6 Harry Kalas/100 45.00
7 Bobby Doerr/100 25.00
8 Cal Ripken Jr./50 165.00
9 Carl Yastrzemski/35 110.00
10 Carlton Fisk/100 45.00
11 Chuck Tanner/150 15.00
12 Cito Gaston/150 15.00
13 Danny Ozark/150 15.00
14 Dave Winfield/80 50.00
15 Davey Johnson/175 15.00
16 Ernie Harwell/100 50.00
17 Dick Williams/150 15.00
18 Don Mattingly/40 100.00
19 Don Newcombe/40 35.00
20 Duke Snider/35 60.00
21 Steve Carlton/150 35.00
22 Felipe Alou/175 20.00
23 Frank Robinson/65 40.00
24 Gary Carter/100 35.00
25 Gene Mauch/225 15.00
26 George Bamberger/225 15.00
28 Gus Suhr/100 30.00
30 Harmon Killebrew/50 70.00
31 Jack McKeon/225 20.00
32 Jim Bunning/100 25.00
33 Jimmy Piersall/212 20.00
35 Johnny Bench/50 75.00
36 Juan Marichal/50 40.00
37 Lou Brock/50 50.00
38 George Kell/40 50.00
39 Maury Wills/40 30.00
41 Mike Schmidt/40 100.00
42 Nolan Ryan/50 135.00
43 Ozzie Smith/65 75.00
44 Eddie Mayo/140 15.00
45 Phil Rizzuto/50 50.00
46 Ralph Kiner/40 45.00
47 Lonny Frey/114 15.00
48 Bill Mazeroski/50 40.00
49 Robin Roberts/40 40.00
50 Robin Yount/40 75.00
52 Roger Craig/175 15.00
55 Tony Perez/40 70.00
56 Sparky Anderson/175 20.00
57 Stan Musial/40 100.00
58 Ted Radcliffe/225 25.00
60 Tom Seaver/25 70.00
61 Tony Gwynn/65 75.00
62 Tony LaRussa/275 15.00
63 Tony Oliva/150 20.00
64 Tony Pena/150 15.00
66 Whitey Ford/45 65.00
67 Yogi Berra/65 75.00

Signature Blue Ink

NM/M
Common Autograph: 15.00
Some not priced due to scarcity.
2 Preacher Roe/150 25.00
4 Bob Feller/50 45.00
5 Bob Gibson/25 60.00
6 Harry Kalas/50 50.00
7 Bobby Doerr/50 30.00
8 Cal Ripken Jr./25 200.00
10 Carlton Fisk/50 50.00
11 Chuck Tanner/125 15.00
12 Cito Gaston/125 15.00
13 Danny Ozark/125 15.00
14 Dave Winfield/35 60.00
15 Davey Johnson/150 15.00
16 Ernie Harwell/50 50.00
17 Dick Williams/125 15.00
21 Steve Carlton/100 35.00
22 Felipe Alou/125 20.00
23 Frank Robinson/50 40.00
24 Gary Carter/75 35.00
25 Gene Mauch/150 15.00
26 George Bamberger/150 15.00
28 Gus Suhr/85 30.00
31 Jack McKeon/150 25.00
32 Jim Bunning/65 60.00
33 Jimmy Piersall/150 25.00
35 Johnny Bench/25 90.00
38 George Kell/25 50.00
39 Maury Wills/25 40.00
41 Mike Schmidt/25 80.00
42 Nolan Ryan/25 175.00
43 Ozzie Smith/50 75.00
44 Eddie Mayo/50 20.00
45 Phil Rizzuto/25 60.00
47 Lonny Frey/75 15.00
48 Bill Mazeroski/25 40.00
49 Robin Roberts/25 40.00
50 Robin Yount/25 75.00
52 Roger Craig/150 15.00
56 Sparky Anderson/150 25.00
57 Stan Musial/25 120.00
58 Ted Radcliffe/150 50.00
62 Tony LaRussa/145 15.00
63 Tony Oliva/125 25.00
64 Tony Pena/115 15.00
67 Yogi Berra/50 70.00

Signature Holofoil

NM/M
Many not priced due to scarcity.
SSA-4 Bob Feller/25 70.00
SSA-5 Bob Gibson/25 60.00
SSA-11 Chuck Tanner/100 15.00
SSA-12 Cito Gaston/100 15.00
SSA-13 Danny Ozark/100 15.00
SSA-15 Davey Johnson/50 20.00
SSA-17 Dick Williams/100 15.00
SSA-22 Felipe Alou/50 30.00
SSA-24 Gary Carter/50 45.00
SSA-45 Phil Rizzuto/25 60.00
SSA-49 Robin Roberts/25 40.00
SSA-50 Robin Yount/25 75.00
SSA-52 Roger Craig/50 20.00
SSA-56 Sparky Anderson/50 30.00
SSA-57 Stan Musial/25 120.00
SSA-62 Tony LaRussa/50 20.00
SSA-63 Tony Oliva/100 25.00
SSA-64 Tony Pena/100 15.00

Signature Red Ink

NM/M
Many not priced due to scarcity.
SSA-14 Dave Winfield/25 65.00
SSA-25 Gene Mauch/25 25.00
SSA-26 George Bamberger/25 30.00

Wood Barrel Auto.

NM/M
Varying quantities produced
Some not priced due to scarcity.
HB Harold Baines/200 35.00
JB Johnny Bench/50 120.00
WB Wade Boggs/200 60.00
SM Stan Musial/25 185.00
CR Cal Ripken Jr./25 300.00
NR Nolan Ryan/25 200.00
RS Ron Santo/203 45.00
TS Tom Seaver/25 140.00
BW Billy Williams/200 35.00

2004 Upper Deck Ultimate Collection

NM/M
Complete Set (222):
Common Player (1-126): 2.00
Production 675
Common (127-168): 4.00
Production 525
Common (169-194): 6.00
Production 299
Common (195-209, 222) 8.00
Production 199
Common (210-221): 15.00
Production 75
Pack (4): 80.00
Box (4): 275.00
1 Al Kaline 4.00
2 Billy Williams 2.00
3 Bob Feller 2.00
4 Bob Gibson 4.00
5 Bob Lemon 2.00
6 Bobby Doerr 2.00
7 Brooks Robinson 3.00
8 Cal Ripken Jr. 10.00
9 Jim "Catfish" Hunter 2.00
10 Eddie Mathews 4.00
11 Enos Slaughter 2.00
12 Ernie Banks 4.00
13 Fergie Jenkins 2.00
14 Gaylord Perry 2.00
15 Harmon Killebrew 4.00
16 Jim Bunning 2.00
17 Joe DiMaggio 6.00
18 Joe Morgan 2.00
19 Juan Marichal 2.00
20 Lou Brock 2.00
21 Luis Aparicio 2.00
22 Mickey Mantle 12.00
23 Mike Schmidt 6.00
24 Monte Irvin 2.00
25 Nolan Ryan 8.00
26 Pee Wee Reese 2.00
27 Phil Niekro 2.00
28 Phil Rizzuto 3.00
29 Ralph Kiner 3.00
30 Richie Ashburn 2.00
31 Robin Roberts 3.00
32 Robin Yount 5.00
33 Rod Carew 2.00
34 Rollie Fingers 2.00
35 Stan Musial 6.00
36 Ted Williams 8.00
37 Tom Seaver 4.00
38 Warren Spahn 4.00
39 Whitey Ford 3.00
40 Willie McCovey 3.00
41 Willie Stargell 3.00
42 Yogi Berra 4.00
43 Adrian Beltre 2.00
44 Albert Pujols 8.00
45 Alex Rodriguez 6.00
46 Alfonso Soriano 3.00
47 Andruw Jones 2.00
48 Andy Pettitte 2.00
49 Aubrey Huff 2.00
50 Barry Larkin 2.00
51 Ben Sheets 2.00
52 Bernie Williams 2.00
53 Bobby Abreu 2.00
54 Brad Penny 2.00
55 Bret Boone 2.00
56 Brian Giles 2.00
57 Carlos Beltran 3.00
58 Carlos Delgado 2.00
59 Carlos Guillen 2.00
60 Carlos Lee 2.00
61 Carlos Zambrano 2.00
62 Chipper Jones 4.00
63 Craig Biggio 2.00
64 Craig Wilson 2.00
65 Curt Schilling 4.00
66 David Ortiz 4.00
67 Derek Jeter 10.00
68 Eric Chavez 2.00
69 Eric Gagne 3.00
70 Frank Thomas 3.00
71 Garret Anderson 2.00
72 Gary Sheffield 3.00
73 Greg Maddux 5.00
74 Hank Blalock 3.00
75 Hideki Matsui 6.00
76 Ichiro Suzuki 6.00
77 Ivan Rodriguez 3.00
78 J.D. Drew 2.00
79 Jake Peavy 2.00
80 Jason Schmidt 2.00
81 Jeff Bagwell 3.00
82 Jeff Kent 2.00
83 Jim Thome 4.00
84 Joe Mauer 2.00
85 Johan Santana 3.00
86 Jose Reyes 3.00
87 Jose Vidro 2.00
88 Ken Griffey Jr. 5.00
89 Kerry Wood 4.00
90 Larry Walker 2.00
91 Luis Gonzalez 2.00
92 Lyle Overbay 2.00
93 Magglio Ordonez 2.00
94 Manny Ramirez 4.00
95 Mark Mulder 2.00
96 Mark Prior 3.00
97 Mark Teixeira 2.00
98 Melvin Mora 2.00
99 Michael Young 2.00
100 Miguel Cabrera 4.00
101 Miguel Tejada 3.00
102 Mike Lowell 2.00
103 Mike Piazza 6.00
104 Mike Sweeney 2.00
105 Nomar Garciaparra 6.00
106 Oliver Perez 2.00
107 Pedro J. Martinez 4.00
108 Preston Wilson 2.00
109 Rafael Palmeiro 4.00
110 Randy Johnson 4.00
111 Roger Clemens 10.00
112 Roy Halladay 2.00
113 Roy Oswalt 2.00
114 Sammy Sosa 6.00
115 Scott Podsednik 2.00
116 Scott Rolen 4.00
117 Shawn Green 2.00
118 Tim Hudson 2.00
119 Todd Helton 3.00
120 Tom Glavine 3.00
121 Torii Hunter 2.00
122 Travis Hafner 2.00
123 Troy Glaus 2.00
124 Vernon Wells 2.00
125 Victor Martinez 2.00
126 Vladimir Guerrero 4.00
127 Aarom Baldiris **RC** 8.00
128 Alfredo Simon **RC** 4.00
129 Andres Blanco **RC** 4.00
130 Jeff Bajenaru **RC** 4.00
131 Bartolome Fortunato **RC** 4.00
132 Brandon Medders **RC** 4.00
133 Brian Dallimore **RC** 4.00
134 Carlos Hines **RC** 4.00
135 Carlos Vasquez **RC** 8.00
136 Casey Daigle **RC** 4.00
137 Chad Bentz **RC** 4.00
138 Chris Aguila **RC** 4.00
139 Chris Saenz **RC** 4.00
140 Chris Shelton **RC** 10.00
141 Colby Miller **RC** 4.00
142 David Crouthers 4.00
143 David Aardsma **RC** 4.00
144 Dennis Sarfate **RC** 4.00
145 Donnie Kelly **RC** 4.00
146 Eddy Rodriguez **RC** 8.00
147 Eduardo Villacis **RC** 4.00
148 Edwardo Sierra **RC** 6.00
149 Edwin Moreno **RC** 6.00
150 Kyle Denney **RC** 4.00
151 Evan Rust **RC** 4.00
152 Fernando Nieve **RC** 4.00
153 Frank Francisco **RC** 4.00
154 Franklyn Gracesqui **RC** 4.00
155 Freddy Guzman **RC** 4.00
156 Greg Dobbs **RC** 4.00
157 Hector Gimenez **RC** 4.00
158 Jason Alfaro **RC** 4.00
159 Jake Woods **RC** 4.00
160 Andy Green **RC** 4.00
161 Jason Bartlett **RC** 8.00
162 Jason Frasor **RC** 4.00
163 Jeff Bennett **RC** 4.00
164 Jerome Gamble **RC** 4.00
165 Jerry Gil **RC** 4.00
166 Joe Hietpas **RC** 4.00
167 Jorge Sequea **RC** 4.00
168 Jorge Vasquez **RC** 6.00
169 Josh Labandeira **RC** 6.00
170 Justin Germano **RC** 6.00
171 Justin Hampson **RC** 6.00
172 Chris Young **RC** 30.00
173 Justin Knoedler **RC** 6.00
174 Justin Lehr **RC** 6.00
175 Justin Leone **RC** 10.00
176 Kazuhito Tadano **RC** 8.00
177 Kevin Cave **RC** 6.00
178 Lincoln Holdzkom **RC** 6.00
179 Mike Rose **RC** 6.00
180 Luis Gonzalez **RC** 6.00
181 Mariano Gomez **RC** 6.00
182 Rene Rivera **RC** 6.00
183 Mike Wuertz **RC** 8.00
184 Mike Gosling 6.00
185 Mike Johnston **RC** 6.00
186 Mike Rouse 6.00
187 Nick Regilio **RC** 6.00
188 Onil Joseph **RC** 6.00
189 Orlando Rodriguez **RC** 6.00
190 Phil Stockman **RC** 6.00
191 Renyel Pinto **RC** 10.00
192 Roberto Novoa **RC** 12.00
193 Roman Colon **RC** 6.00
194 Ronald Belisario **RC** 6.00
195 Ronny Cedeno **RC** 8.00
196 Ryan Meaux **RC** 8.00
197 Ryan Wing 8.00
198 Scott Dohmann **RC** 8.00
199 Joey Gathright **RC** 10.00
200 Shawn Camp **RC** 8.00
201 Shawn Hill **RC** 8.00
202 Steve Andrade **RC** 8.00
203 Tim Bausher **RC** 8.00
204 Tim Bittner **RC** 8.00
205 Brad Halsey **RC** 10.00
206 William Bergolla **RC** 8.00
207 Kameron Loe **RC** 8.00
208 Jesse Crain **RC** 10.00
209 Scott Kazmir 25.00
210 Akinori Otsuka/Auto. **RC** 60.00
211 Chris Oxspring/Auto. **RC** 15.00
212 Ian Snell/Auto. **RC** 30.00
213 John Gall/Auto. **RC** 20.00
214 Jose Capellan/Auto. **RC** 20.00
215 Yadier Molina/Auto. **RC** 40.00
216 Merkin Valdez/Auto. **RC** 25.00
217 Ramon Ramirez/Auto. **RC** 15.00
218 Rusty Tucker/Auto. **RC** 20.00
219 Scott Proctor/Auto. **RC** 25.00
220 Sean Henn/Auto. 15.00
221 Shingo Takatsu/Auto. **RC** 75.00
222 Kazuo Matsui **RC** 30.00

Gold

Gold (1-194): 1-2X
Production 50
Gold (195-222): No Pricing
Production 25
Gold 210-221 Production 15

Platinum

Platinum (1-126): No Pricing
Production 10
Platinum (210-221): No Pricing
Production One

Rainbow

Rainbows: No Pricing
Production One Set

Achievement Material

NM/M
Common Player:
EB Ernie Banks/58 25.00
JB Johnny Bench/68 15.00
YB Yogi Berra/51 20.00
GB George Brett/80 25.00
CA Roy Campanella/51 25.00
RO Rod Carew/77 15.00
SC Steve Carlton/72 10.00
OC Orlando Cepeda/58 10.00
CL Roger Clemens/86 25.00
RC Roberto Clemente/66 100.00
JD Joe DiMaggio/39 100.00
DD Don Drysdale/62 15.00
BG Bob Gibson/68 15.00
KG Ken Griffey Jr./97 25.00
DJ Derek Jeter/96 40.00
RJ Randy Johnson/99 15.00
HK Harmon Killebrew/69 15.00
GM Greg Maddux/92 20.00
MA Mickey Mantle/56 200.00
RM Roger Maris/61 80.00
PM Pedro J. Martinez/99 15.00
DM Don Mattingly/85 20.00
MC Willie McCovey/59 15.00
TM Thurman Munson/70 15.00
EM Eddie Murray/77 15.00
JP Jim Palmer/73 10.00
MP Mike Piazza/93 20.00
CR Cal Ripken Jr./82 50.00
BR Brooks Robinson/64 15.00
FR Frank Robinson/66 10.00
JR Jackie Robinson/47 65.00
RS Ryne Sandberg/84 40.00
MS Mike Schmidt/80 25.00
TS Tom Seaver/69 15.00
SS Sammy Sosa/98 20.00
TW Ted Williams/42 100.00
CY Carl Yastrzemski/67 25.00
RY Robin Yount/82 25.00

All-Stars Signatures

NM/M
Most not priced.
RC Rod Carew/18 40.00
SM Stan Musial/24 75.00
BR Brooks Robinson/15 60.00
CY Carl Yastrzemski/18 80.00

Bat Barrel Signatures

No Pricing
Production 1-5

Dual Legendary Materials

NM/M
Common Player:
Production 50 Sets
BM Willie McCovey, Ernie Banks 40.00
BR Roger Maris, Babe Ruth 300.00
CB Yogi Berra, Roy Campanella 35.00
CM Roberto Clemente, Thurman Munson 100.00
CS Duke Snider, Roy Campanella 40.00
DM Mickey Mantle, Joe DiMaggio 200.00
DW Joe DiMaggio, Ted Williams 150.00
FD Don Drysdale, Bob Feller 25.00
MB Yogi Berra, Thurman Munson 50.00
MC Mickey Mantle, Roberto Clemente 180.00
MM Mickey Mantle, Roger Maris 220.00
MW Mickey Mantle, Ted Williams 200.00
RB Ernie Banks, Jackie Robinson 75.00
RC Jackie Robinson, Roy Campanella 75.00
RD Joe DiMaggio, Babe Ruth 275.00
RM Babe Ruth, Mickey Mantle 400.00
RP Jackie Robinson, Satchel Paige 100.00
RW Roberto Clemente, Willie McCovey 100.00
WM Eddie Mathews, Ted Williams 125.00

Dual Materials

NM/M
Common Player:
Production 60 Sets
BC Brooks Robinson, Cal Ripken Jr. 50.00
BM Yogi Berra, Thurman Munson 40.00
BP Johnny Bench, Mike Piazza 25.00
BS Mike Schmidt, George Brett 40.00
CK Harmon Killebrew, Rod Carew 30.00
CM Willie McCovey, Will Clark 30.00
ER Ryne Sandberg, Ernie Banks 60.00
GS Sammy Sosa, Ken Griffey Jr. 40.00
JC Randy Johnson, Roger Clemens 40.00
JM Derek Jeter, Don Mattingly 60.00
MB Johnny Bench, Thurman Munson 40.00
MC Don Mattingly, Will Clark 40.00
MP Mark Prior, Joe Mauer 25.00
MR Bill Mazeroski, Jackie Robinson 60.00
MT Kazuo Matsui, Shingo Takatsu 30.00
MY Robin Yount, Paul Molitor 40.00
PR Manny Ramirez, Albert Pujols 50.00
RC Nolan Ryan, Roger Clemens 60.00
RP Mike Piazza, Ivan Rodriguez 20.00
RR Brooks Robinson, Frank Robinson 25.00
RT Thurman Munson, Roy Campanella 30.00
SG Ken Griffey Jr., Ichiro Suzuki 60.00
SP Mark Prior, Ben Sheets 10.00
SR Duke Snider, Pee Wee Reese 30.00
SS Sammy Sosa, Ryne Sandberg 50.00
TS Jim Thome, Mike Schmidt 35.00
WM Don Mattingly, Dave Winfield 40.00
WP Mark Prior, Kerry Wood 20.00
WR Kerry Wood, Nolan Ryan 50.00
YR Manny Ramirez, Carl Yastrzemski 35.00

Dual Materials Signature

NM/M
Production 25 Sets
AB Luis Aparicio, Ernie Banks 100.00
BB Wade Boggs, Hank Blalock 80.00
BC Brooks Robinson, Cal Ripken Jr. 250.00
BF Carlton Fisk, Johnny Bench 100.00
BG Carlos Beltran, Ken Griffey Jr. 150.00
BJ Derek Jeter, Yogi Berra 200.00
BM Brian Giles, Marcus Giles 35.00
BP Johnny Bench, Mike Piazza 160.00
BR Jim Bunning, Robin Roberts 40.00
BT Hank Blalock, Mark Teixeira 60.00
CB Hank Blalock, Eric Chavez 50.00
CC Steve Carlton, Roger Clemens 150.00
CJ Roger Clemens, Randy Johnson 300.00
CK Harmon Killebrew, Rod Carew 80.00
CL Miguel Cabrera, Mike Lowell 75.00
CM Miguel Cabrera, Carlos Beltran 125.00
DD Derek Jeter, Don Mattingly 300.00
DG Gaylord Perry, Don Sutton 50.00
DJ Jim Rice, Dave Parker 80.00
DS Ryne Sandberg, Andre Dawson 125.00
DW Andre Dawson, Billy Williams 50.00
ER Ryne Sandberg, Ernie Banks 160.00
FC Bob Feller, Rocky Colavito 75.00
FR Bob Feller, Nolan Ryan 180.00
GB Brooks Robinson, George Brett 140.00
GC Ron Guidry, Steve Carlton 50.00
GG Ken Griffey Sr., Ken Griffey Jr. 150.00
GM Mike Schmidt, George Brett 150.00
GP Rafael Palmeiro, Ken Griffey Jr. 150.00
GR Greg Maddux, Roger Clemens 300.00
GS John Smoltz, Eric Gagne 75.00
IV Ivan Rodriguez, Victor Martinez 65.00
JB Ernie Banks, Fergie Jenkins 100.00
JC Randy Johnson, Steve Carlton 125.00
JD Johnny Podres, Don Sutton 50.00
JG Randy Johnson, Ken Griffey Jr. 200.00
JM Chipper Jones, Dale Murphy 150.00
JP Jim Palmer, Fergie Jenkins 50.00
JR Cal Ripken Jr., Derek Jeter 500.00
KG Ken Griffey Jr., Harmon Killebrew 150.00
KN Kerry Wood, Nolan Ryan 175.00
KT Scott Kazmir, Shingo Takatsu 75.00
LB Yogi Berra, Don Larsen 180.00
MB Johnny Bench, Joe Morgan 80.00
MC Don Mattingly, Will Clark 125.00
MH Mark Mulder, Tim Hudson 50.00
MP Mark Prior, Joe Mauer 80.00
MS Bill Mazeroski, Ryne Sandberg 150.00
MW Will Clark, Mark Grace 75.00
MY Robin Yount, Paul Molitor 150.00
NR Roger Clemens, Nolan Ryan 300.00
OR Manny Ramirez, David Ortiz 200.00
OS Stan Musial, Ozzie Smith 150.00
PC Will Clark, Rafael Palmeiro 100.00
PN Phil Niekro, Gaylord Perry 50.00
PS Johnny Podres, Duke Snider 60.00
RB Rod Carew, Bill Mazeroski 75.00
RC Eric Chavez, Brooks Robinson 60.00
RM Eddie Murray, Cal Ripken Jr. 275.00
RP Brooks Robinson, Jim Palmer 65.00
RR Brooks Robinson, Frank Robinson 75.00
RS Robin Roberts, Steve Carlton 60.00
RT Miguel Tejada, Cal Ripken Jr. 200.00
SC Mike Schmidt, Steve Carlton 150.00
SF Ben Sheets, Bob Feller 50.00
SG Eric Gagne, Bruce Sutter 75.00
SO Ben Sheets, Roy Oswalt 50.00
SP Mark Prior, Ben Sheets 80.00
SR Brooks Robinson, Mike Schmidt 150.00
SS Tom Seaver, Ben Sheets 75.00
TB Tony Gwynn, Brian Giles 75.00
TC Mark Teixeira, Miguel Cabrera 75.00
WM Dave Winfield, Don Mattingly 150.00
WO Orlando Cepeda, Willie McCovey 75.00
WW Will Clark, Willie McCovey 75.00
YR Carl Yastrzemski, Manny Ramirez 160.00

Game Materials

NM/M
Common Player: 8.00
Production 99 Sets
EB Ernie Banks 15.00
JB Johnny Bench 10.00
WB Wade Boggs 8.00
GB George Brett 20.00
LB Lou Brock 8.00
RC Rod Carew 8.00
SC Steve Carlton 8.00
WC Will Clark 8.00
CL Roger Clemens 20.00
TC Ty Cobb 100.00
DD Don Drysdale 8.00
BF Bob Feller 8.00
CF Carlton Fisk 10.00
BG Bob Gibson 10.00
KG Ken Griffey Jr. 20.00
TG Tony Gwynn 10.00
DJ Derek Jeter 30.00
RJ Randy Johnson 15.00
AK Al Kaline 15.00
HK Harmon Killebrew 10.00
MA Juan Marichal 8.00
RM Roger Maris 50.00
ED Eddie Mathews 15.00
DM Don Mattingly 25.00
BM Bill Mazeroski 8.00
WM Willie McCovey 8.00
PM Paul Molitor 10.00
TM Thurman Munson 15.00
EM Eddie Murray 15.00
SM Stan Musial 25.00
JP Jim Palmer 8.00
PI Mike Piazza 15.00
MP Mark Prior 10.00
AP Albert Pujols 25.00
CR Cal Ripken Jr. 40.00
BR Brooks Robinson 10.00
FR Frank Robinson 8.00
JR Jackie Robinson 40.00
RS Ryne Sandberg 25.00
MS Mike Schmidt 15.00
TS Tom Seaver 10.00
OS Ozzie Smith 15.00
DS Duke Snider 10.00
WS Warren Spahn 15.00
WSt Willie Stargell 8.00
IS Ichiro Suzuki 60.00
DW Dave Winfield 8.00
KW Kerry Wood 10.00
CY Carl Yastrzemski 20.00
RY Robin Yount 20.00

Game Patch

NM/M
Common Player:
Production 75 unless noted.
5 Color +: 1.5X
BA Jeff Bagwell 25.00
BE Josh Beckett 15.00
CB Carlos Beltran 25.00
JB Johnny Bench 50.00
YB Yogi Berra 50.00
HB Hank Blalock 15.00
WB Wade Boggs 20.00
GB George Brett 50.00
LB Lou Brock 40.00
BU Jim Bunning/66 30.00
CA Miguel Cabrera 30.00
RC Rod Carew 30.00
RO Rod Carew 30.00
GC Gary Carter 30.00
EC Eric Chavez 15.00
WC Will Clark 30.00
WC1 Will Clark 30.00
RC Roger Clemens 40.00
RB Roberto Clemente 200.00
CO1 Rocky Colavito 80.00
JD Joe DiMaggio 180.00
BF Bob Feller 40.00
NF Nellie Fox/55 125.00
GL Troy Glaus 20.00
KG Ken Griffey Jr. 50.00
VG Vladimir Guerrero 30.00
RG Ron Guidry 30.00
TG Tony Gwynn 30.00
TH Todd Helton 25.00
CH Jim "Catfish" Hunter 30.00

DJ Derek Jeter 40.00
RJ Randy Johnson 25.00
RJ1 Randy Johnson 25.00
CJ Chipper Jones 25.00
HK Harmon Killebrew 40.00
GM Greg Maddux 35.00
GM1 Greg Maddux 35.00
MA Juan Marichal 25.00
PE Pedro J. Martinez 25.00
HM Hideki Matsui/44 100.00
KM Kazuo Matsui 50.00
DM Don Mattingly 40.00
JM Joe Mauer 30.00
BM Bill Mazeroski/55 60.00
WM Willie McCovey 35.00
PM Paul Molitor 30.00
MO Joe Morgan 20.00
TM Thurman Munson 40.00
MU Eddie Murray 40.00
SM Stan Musial 75.00
RP Rafael Palmeiro 25.00
JP Jim Palmer 25.00
PI Mike Piazza 30.00
PO Johnny Podres 30.00
MP Mark Prior 20.00
AP Albert Pujols 50.00
MR Manny Ramirez 25.00
CR Cal Ripken Jr. 60.00
BR Brooks Robinson 40.00
IR Ivan Rodriguez 25.00
SR Scott Rolen 25.00
NR Nolan Ryan/51 50.00
NR1 Nolan Ryan 50.00
NR2 Nolan Ryan 50.00
RS Ryne Sandberg 50.00
CS Curt Schilling 25.00
MS Mike Schmidt 40.00
TS Tom Seaver 20.00
BS Ben Sheets 25.00
GS Gary Sheffield 20.00
OS Ozzie Smith 40.00
AS Alfonso Soriano 25.00
SS Sammy Sosa 35.00
SP Warren Spahn/62 60.00
WS Willie Stargell 30.00
IS Ichiro Suzuki 120.00
MT Mark Teixeira 15.00
TE Miguel Tejada 25.00
JT Jim Thome 35.00
BW Bernie Williams 20.00
WI Billy Williams 20.00
DW Dave Winfield 35.00
KW Kerry Wood 25.00
CY Carl Yastrzemski 50.00
RY Robin Yount 40.00

Dual Game Patch

NM/M

Production 25 Sets
BB Carlos Beltran, Jeff Bagwell 40.00
BC Josh Beckett, Miguel Cabrera 40.00
BG Lou Brock, Tony Gwynn 75.00
BS Mike Schmidt, George Brett 100.00
BT Hank Blalock, Mark Teixeira 40.00
CG Rod Carew, Tony Gwynn 50.00
CP Mike Piazza, Gary Carter 50.00
CR Eric Chavez, Scott Rolen 50.00
FB Johnny Bench, Carlton Fisk 50.00
FR Nolan Ryan, Bob Feller 100.00
GC Will Clark, Mark Grace 40.00
GG Ken Griffey Sr., Ken Griffey Jr. 75.00
GM Stan Musial, Bob Gibson 60.00
GS Mark Grace, Ryne Sandberg 100.00
HF Rollie Fingers, Jim "Catfish" Hunter 30.00
JC Roger Clemens, Randy Johnson 75.00
JJ Chipper Jones, Andruw Jones 40.00
JM Derek Jeter, Hideki Matsui 125.00
KC Rod Carew, Harmon Killebrew 60.00
KM Willie McCovey, Harmon Killebrew 50.00
KS Sammy Sosa, Ken Griffey Jr. 75.00
LS Fred Lynn, Ichiro Suzuki 100.00
MG Greg Maddux, Tom Glavine 50.00
MJ Chipper Jones, Eddie Mathews 75.00
MM Kazuo Matsui, Hideki Matsui 120.00
MY Robin Yount, Paul Molitor 60.00
PC Will Clark, Rafael Palmeiro 40.00
PR Scott Rolen, Albert Pujols 100.00
RC Nolan Ryan, Roger Clemens 100.00

RM Cal Ripken Jr., Eddie Murray 150.00
RP Cal Ripken Jr., Jim Palmer 125.00
RR Jackie Robinson, Pee Wee Reese 150.00
RS Nolan Ryan, Tom Seaver 100.00
RT Cal Ripken Jr., Miguel Tejada 75.00
SB Jim Bunning, Mike Schmidt 75.00
SM Pedro J. Martinez, Curt Schilling 60.00
ST Mike Schmidt, Jim Thome 75.00
WM Don Mattingly, Dave Winfield 75.00
WP Mark Prior, Kerry Wood 50.00
WS Billy Williams, Sammy Sosa 60.00
YR Carl Yastrzemski, Jim Rice 75.00

Game Patch Signatures

NM/M

Common Player:
Production 30 Sets
EB Ernie Banks 75.00
CB Carlos Beltran 65.00
JB Johnny Bench 65.00
HB Hank Blalock 50.00
WB Wade Boggs 65.00
GB George Brett 100.00
MC Miguel Cabrera 65.00
RC Rod Carew 50.00
EC Eric Chavez 40.00
WC Will Clark 60.00
AD Andre Dawson 40.00
BG Bob Gibson 50.00
KG Ken Griffey Jr. 125.00
TG Tony Gwynn 65.00
DJ Derek Jeter 200.00
RJ Randy Johnson 125.00
AK Al Kaline 75.00
HK Harmon Killebrew 75.00
GM Greg Maddux 150.00
MA Juan Marichal 50.00
DM Don Mattingly 100.00
JM Joe Mauer 60.00
WM Willie McCovey 50.00
PM Paul Molitor 60.00
MU Mark Mulder 40.00
EM Eddie Murray 80.00
SM Stan Musial 120.00
RO Roy Oswalt 50.00
JP Jim Palmer 50.00
PI Mike Piazza 125.00
MP Mark Prior 60.00
JR Jim Rice 50.00
CR Cal Ripken Jr. 200.00
BR Brooks Robinson 60.00
FR Frank Robinson 50.00
NR Nolan Ryan 150.00
RS Ryne Sandberg 150.00
MS Mike Schmidt 125.00
SC Red Schoendienst 40.00
TS Tom Seaver 75.00
BS Ben Sheets 50.00
OS Ozzie Smith 50.00
MT Mark Teixeira 50.00
KW Kerry Wood 75.00
CY Carl Yastrzemski 100.00
RY Robin Yount 80.00

Stat Patch

NM/M

Quantity produced listed
5+ Color Patch: 1.5X
JB Jeff Bagwell/47 25.00
CB Carlos Beltran/29 35.00
CB1 Carlos Beltran/41 30.00
BE Johnny Bench/45 50.00
HB Hank Blalock/29 20.00
GB George Brett/20 80.00
GB1 George Brett/30 75.00
WC Will Clark/35 50.00
CL1 Roger Clemens/24 50.00
DD Don Drysdale/25 50.00
EG Eric Gagne/55 25.00
VG Vladimir Guerrero/44 25.00
VG1 Vladimir Guerrero/40 25.00
TG Tony Gwynn/56 40.00
TG1 Tony Gwynn/25 50.00
DJ Derek Jeter/32 60.00
DJ1 Derek Jeter/24 60.00
RJ Randy Johnson/20 40.00
CJ Chipper Jones/45 25.00
HK Harmon Killebrew/49 50.00
GM1 Greg Maddux/20 40.00
GM2 Greg Maddux/17 40.00
JM Juan Marichal/26 30.00
MA Pedro Martinez/23 35.00
HM Hideki Matsui/31 120.00
DM Don Mattingly/35 75.00
PM Paul Molitor/39 40.00
TM Thurman Munson/20 75.00
PN Phil Niekro/23 30.00
PN1 Phil Niekro/23 30.00
RP Rafael Palmeiro/47 25.00
JP1 Jim Palmer/23 30.00
PI Mike Piazza/40 40.00
AP Albert Pujols/43 60.00
AP1 Albert Pujols/51 50.00

MR Manny Ramirez/45 25.00
JR1 Jim Rice/46 25.00
CR Cal Ripken Jr./34 100.00
CR1 Cal Ripken Jr./47 75.00
IR Ivan Rodriguez/35 30.00
IR1 Ivan Rodriguez/25 30.00
SR Scott Rolen/31 30.00
RS Ryne Sandberg/40 65.00
RS1 Ryne Sandberg/19 100.00
MS Mike Schmidt/48 65.00
TS Tom Seaver/25 50.00
JS John Smoltz/24 30.00
JS1 John Smoltz/55 25.00
AS Alfonso Soriano/39 20.00
AS1 Alfonso Soriano/43 20.00
SS1 Sammy Sosa/66 30.00
WS Willie Stargell/48 50.00
IS Ichiro Suzuki/56 120.00
MT Miguel Tejada/34 25.00
JT Jim Thome/52 25.00
CY Carl Yastrzemski/44 50.00
RY Robin Yount/49 50.00
DW Dave Winfield/37 25.00

Super Patch

No Pricing
Production 4-20

Gold Glove Sign. Materials

No Pricing
Production 1-16

Legendary Materials

NM/M

Common Player: 10.00
Production 50 Sets
EB Ernie Banks 20.00
YB Yogi Berra 20.00
CA Roy Campanella 15.00
RC Roberto Clemente 100.00
TC Ty Cobb 100.00
JD Joe DiMaggio 100.00
DD Don Drysdale 15.00
BF Bob Feller 10.00
MM Mickey Mantle 200.00
RM Roger Maris 60.00
EM Eddie Mathews 20.00
WM Willie McCovey 15.00
TM Thurman Munson 25.00
SM Stan Musial 40.00
SP Satchel Paige 50.00
JR Jackie Robinson 60.00
BR Babe Ruth 250.00
DS Duke Snider 15.00
TW Ted Williams 80.00

Logo Patch Signatures

No Pricing
Production One Set

Loyalty Game Jersey Sign.

NM/M

Quantity produced listed
EB Ernie Banks/19 85.00
GB George Brett/21 100.00
TG Tony Gwynn/20 70.00
HK Harmon Killebrew/21 75.00
CR Cal Ripken Jr./21 200.00
BR Brooks Robinson/23 50.00
MS Mike Schmidt/18 100.00
CY Carl Yastrzemski/23 85.00
RY Robin Yount/20 85.00

Materials Signatures

NM/M

Production 50 Sets
BA Bobby Abreu 25.00
JE Jeff Bagwell 50.00
EB Ernie Banks 75.00
BE Josh Beckett 25.00
CB Carlos Beltran 60.00
JB Johnny Bench 60.00
HB Hank Blalock 30.00
WB Wade Boggs 50.00
WB1 Wade Boggs 50.00
GB George Brett 80.00
LB Lou Brock 40.00
LB1 Lou Brock 40.00
BU Jim Bunning 30.00
CA Miguel Cabrera 40.00
RC Rod Carew 40.00
RC1 Rod Carew 40.00
SC Steve Carlton 35.00
SC1 Steve Carlton 35.00
GC Gary Carter 30.00
GC1 Gary Carter 30.00
JC Joe Carter 30.00
OC Orlando Cepeda 35.00
OC1 Orlando Cepeda 35.00
EC Eric Chavez 30.00
WC Will Clark 40.00
WC1 Will Clark 40.00
WC2 Will Clark 40.00
WC3 Will Clark 40.00
CL Roger Clemens 125.00
CL1 Roger Clemens 125.00
CL2 Roger Clemens 125.00
CO Rocky Colavito 75.00

CO1 Rocky Colavito 75.00
AD Andre Dawson 30.00
AD1 Andre Dawson 30.00
DE Dennis Eckersley 30.00
DE1 Dennis Eckersley 30.00
BF Bob Feller 30.00
RF Rollie Fingers 30.00
RF1 Rollie Fingers 30.00
CF Carlton Fisk 40.00
CF1 Carlton Fisk 40.00
EG Eric Gagne 50.00
NG Nomar Garciaparra 125.00
NG1 Nomar Garciaparra 125.00
BG Bob Gibson 40.00
MG Mark Grace 40.00
KG Ken Griffey Jr. 100.00
KG1 Ken Griffey Jr. 100.00
VG Vladimir Guerrero 65.00
RG Ron Guidry 40.00
TG Tony Gwynn 50.00
HE Todd Helton 40.00
TH Tim Hudson 30.00
FJ Fergie Jenkins 30.00
DJ Derek Jeter 150.00
RJ Randy Johnson 100.00
RJ1 Randy Johnson 100.00
CJ Chipper Jones 50.00
AK Al Kaline 50.00
HK Harmon Killebrew 60.00
DL Don Larsen 50.00
ML Mike Lowell 20.00
GM Greg Maddux 100.00
GM1 Greg Maddux 100.00
JU Juan Marichal 30.00
DO Don Mattingly 80.00
JM Joe Mauer 40.00
JM1 Joe Mauer 40.00
BM Bill Mazeroski 40.00
MC Willie McCovey 40.00
PM Paul Molitor 50.00
PM1 Paul Molitor 50.00
PM2 Paul Molitor 50.00
MO Joe Morgan 30.00
MU Mark Mulder 30.00
DM Dale Murphy 40.00
EM Eddie Murray 80.00
EM1 Eddie Murray 80.00
RO Roy Oswalt 25.00
RP Rafael Palmeiro 50.00
JP Jim Palmer 30.00
TP Tony Perez 30.00
GP Gaylord Perry 25.00
GP1 Gaylord Perry 25.00
PI Mike Piazza 100.00
PI1 Mike Piazza 100.00
PO Johnny Podres 30.00
MP Mark Prior 60.00
MP1 Mark Prior 60.00
MR Manny Ramirez 75.00
JR Jim Rice 30.00
CR Cal Ripken Jr. 180.00
RR Robin Roberts 30.00
BR Brooks Robinson 40.00
FR Frank Robinson 35.00
FR1 Frank Robinson 35.00
IR Ivan Rodriguez 50.00
SR Scott Rolen 50.00
NR Nolan Ryan 120.00
NR1 Nolan Ryan 120.00
NR2 Nolan Ryan 120.00
NR3 Nolan Ryan 120.00
SA Ryne Sandberg 100.00
MS Mike Schmidt 75.00
RS Red Schoendienst 30.00
TS Tom Seaver 50.00
TS1 Tom Seaver 50.00
BS Ben Sheets 30.00
BS1 Ben Sheets 30.00
OS Ozzie Smith 60.00
JS John Smoltz 50.00
SN Duke Snider 40.00
SN1 Duke Snider 40.00
AS Alfonso Soriano 40.00
DS Don Sutton 30.00
MT Mark Teixeira 40.00
TE Miguel Tejada 40.00
TE1 Miguel Tejada/34 40.00
FT Frank Thomas 60.00
RW Rickie Weeks 30.00
RW1 Rickie Weeks 30.00
BW Billy Williams 30.00
DW Dave Winfield 40.00
DW1 Dave Winfield 40.00
KW Kerry Wood 50.00
CY Carl Yastrzemski 75.00
DY Delmon Young 40.00
DY1 Delmon Young 40.00
RY Robin Yount 60.00

Quadruple Materials

No Pricing
Production 15 Sets

Signature Numbers Patch

NM/M

Quantity produced listed
WB Wade Boggs/26 65.00
LB Lou Brock/20 50.00
MC Miguel Cabrera/24 60.00
BF Bob Feller/19 50.00
EG Eric Gagne/38 50.00
KG Ken Griffey Jr./30 120.00
VG Vladimir Guerrero/27 80.00
DM Don Mattingly/23 100.00

WM Willie McCovey/44 60.00
RO Roy Oswalt/44 30.00
PI Mike Piazza/31 120.00
MP Mark Prior/22 60.00
RS Ryne Sandberg/23 125.00
MS Mike Schmidt/20 100.00
MT Mark Teixeira/23 40.00
BW Billy Williams/26 40.00
DW Dave Winfield/31 50.00
RY Robin Yount/19 100.00

Signatures

NM/M

Common Player: 20.00
Production 25 unless noted.
Gold: 1-1.5X
Production 10-25
No pricing 20 or less.
Platinum: No Pricing
Production One Set
LA1 Luis Aparicio 20.00
BE Johnny Bench 50.00
YB Yogi Berra 50.00
WB Wade Boggs 50.00
MC1 Miguel Cabrera 50.00
CW Rod Carew 40.00
CA1 Steve Carlton 30.00
CL Roger Clemens 125.00
BF1 Bob Feller 35.00
RF1 Rollie Fingers 25.00
WF Whitey Ford 50.00
NG Nomar Garciaparra 100.00
GI Bob Gibson 40.00
VG Vladimir Guerrero 50.00
RJ Randy Johnson 100.00
AK1 Al Kaline 50.00
HK1 Harmon Killebrew 60.00
RK1 Ralph Kiner 40.00
GM Greg Maddux 80.00
WI Willie McCovey 40.00
MO Joe Morgan 25.00
EM Eddie Murray 75.00
MU Stan Musial 75.00
JP1 Jim Palmer 30.00
PI Mike Piazza 100.00
MP Mark Prior 40.00
KP Kirby Puckett 65.00
CR Cal Ripken Jr. 160.00
RR1 Robin Roberts 30.00
BR1 Brooks Robinson 50.00
RY Ryne Sandberg 75.00
TS Tom Seaver 50.00
OS Ozzie Smith 60.00
SN Duke Snider 40.00
DW Dave Winfield 35.00
CY Carl Yastrzemski 75.00

Signatures Tier B

NM/M

Common Player:
BA Bobby Abreu/25 30.00
LA Luis Aparicio/25 25.00
CB Carlos Beltran/25 50.00
BI Craig Biggio/25 40.00
HB Hank Blalock/25 35.00
BL Bert Blyleven/99 20.00
JB Jim Bunning/99 20.00
MC Miguel Cabrera/99 30.00
SC Sean Casey/99 20.00
OC Orlando Cepeda/25 25.00
EC Eric Chavez/25 30.00
WC Will Clark/25 40.00
RC Rocky Colavito/99 50.00
DC David Cone/99 20.00
CC Carl Crawford/99 10.00
AD Andre Dawson/25 25.00
BD Bobby Doerr/99 25.00
DE Dennis Eckersley/25 35.00
BF Bob Feller/25 30.00
RF Rollie Fingers/25 25.00
GF George Foster/25 20.00
EG Eric Gagne/25 50.00
BG Brian Giles/99 10.00
MG Marcus Giles/99 10.00
DG Dwight Gooden/99 20.00
GG Rich "Goose" Gossage/99 10.00
GR Mark Grace/99 30.00
KG Ken Griffey Sr./69 15.00
RG Ron Guidry/25 40.00
TH Travis Hafner/99 20.00
KH Keith Hernandez/99 15.00
FH Frank Howard/99 15.00
MI Monte Irvin/25 25.00
JK Jim Kaat/99 20.00
AK Al Kaline/25 60.00
GK George Kell/99 20.00
HK Harmon Killebrew/25 60.00
RK Ralph Kiner/25 40.00
ML Mike Lowell/99 10.00
SL Sparky Lyle/99 10.00
FL Fred Lynn/25 20.00
VM Victor Martinez/99 20.00
JM Joe Mauer/99 25.00
BM Bill Mazeroski/25 50.00
MM Mark Mulder/99 20.00
DM Dale Murphy/99 30.00
GN Graig Nettles/99 15.00
DN Don Newcombe/25 25.00
RO Roy Oswalt/99 20.00
AO Akinori Otsuka/99 40.00
JP Jim Palmer/99 20.00
DP Dave Parker/25 25.00
CP Corey Patterson/99 20.00
TP Tony Perez/25 35.00
GP Gaylord Perry/25 20.00
PO Johnny Podres/99 25.00

RR Robin Roberts/25 30.00
BR Brooks Robinson/25 50.00
AR Al Rosen/99 20.00
SA Ron Santo/99 25.00
JS Jason Schmidt/99 25.00
RS Red Schoendienst/25 30.00
BS Ben Sheets/99 25.00
SM John Smoltz/25 50.00
SU Bruce Sutter/99 25.00
ST Shingo Takatsu/99 40.00
MT Mark Teixeira/25 40.00
LT Luis Tiant/99 10.00
RW Rickie Weeks/99 20.00
BW Billy Williams/25 30.00
MW Maury Wills/25 20.00
DY Delmon Young/99 25.00

Signatures Duals

NM/M

Production 25 Sets
BB Wade Boggs, Hank Blalock 80.00
BC Miguel Cabrera, Carlos Beltran 120.00
BG Carlos Beltran, Ken Griffey Jr. 175.00
BR Jim Bunning, Robin Roberts 75.00
BS George Brett, Mike Schmidt 150.00
BT Hank Blalock, Mark Teixeira 70.00
CB Hank Blalock, Eric Chavez 50.00
CJ Roger Clemens, Randy Johnson 300.00
CL Mike Lowell, Miguel Cabrera 50.00
CR Eric Chavez, Brooks Robinson 65.00
DW Billy Williams, Andre Dawson 40.00
EF Rollie Fingers, Dennis Eckersley 50.00
FR Bob Feller, Nolan Ryan 160.00
GC Will Clark, Mark Grace 65.00
GG Marcus Giles, Brian Giles 40.00
GK Ken Griffey Jr., Harmon Killebrew 150.00
GS John Smoltz, Eric Gagne 85.00
IC Monte Irvin, Orlando Cepeda 50.00
JC Steve Carlton, Randy Johnson 125.00
JM Derek Jeter, Don Mattingly 300.00
JP Jim Palmer, Fergie Jenkins 50.00
JT Fergie Jenkins, Luis Tiant 50.00
KG Ken Griffey Sr., Ken Griffey Jr. 175.00
KK Al Kaline, Harmon Killebrew 80.00
MC Don Mattingly, Will Clark 125.00
MH Mark Mulder, Tim Hudson 40.00
MP Joe Mauer, Mark Prior 60.00
NR Roger Clemens, Nolan Ryan 400.00
NS Don Sutton, Don Newcombe 40.00
PC Rafael Palmeiro, Will Clark 120.00
PN Phil Niekro, Gaylord Perry 40.00
PR Jim Rice, Dave Parker 60.00
PS Ben Sheets, Mark Prior 60.00
RC Steve Carlton, Robin Roberts 40.00
RJ Derek Jeter, Cal Ripken Jr. 500.00
RP Brooks Robinson, Jim Palmer 75.00
SF Ben Sheets, Bob Feller 40.00
SG Eric Gagne, Bruce Sutter 60.00
SO Ben Sheets, Roy Oswalt 40.00
SP Don Sutton, Gaylord Perry 40.00
TC Mark Teixeira, Miguel Cabrera 80.00
VM Miguel Cabrera, Vladimir Guerrero 100.00
WS Billy Williams, Ron Santo 60.00

Signatures Triple

No Pricing
Production 20 Sets

Quadruple

No Pricing
Production 10 Sets

Signatures Six

No Pricing
Production Five Sets

Signatures Eight

No Pricing
Production One Set

2004 Upper Deck USA

		NM/M
Complete Factory Set (204):		50.00
Complete Set (200):		25.00
Common Player:		.15
1	Jim Abbott	.25
2	Brent Abernathy	.15
3	Kurt Ainsworth	.15
4	Abe Alvarez	.15
5	Matt Anderson	.15
6	Jeff Austin	.15
7	Justin Wayne	.15
8	Scott Bankhead	.15
9	Josh Bard	.15
10	Michael Barrett	.15
11	Mark Bellhorn	.25
12	Buddy Bell	.15
13	Andy Benes	.25
14	Kris Benson	.25
15	Peter Bergeron	.15
16	Rocky Biddle	.15
17	Casey Blake	.15
18	Willie Bloomquist	.25
19	Jeremy Bonderman	.25
20	Jeff Weaver	.25
21	Joe Borchard	.15
22	Rickie Weeks	.50
23	Rob Bowen	.15
24	Milton Bradley	.25
25	Dan Wheeler	.15
26	Ben Broussard	.15
27	Brian Bruney	.15
28	Mark Budzinski	.15
29	Kirk Bullinger	.15
30	Chris Burke	.25
31	Sean Burnett	.15
32	Jeromy Burnitz	.25
33	Pat Burrell	.50
34	Sean Burroughs	.50
35	Paul Byrd	.25
36	Chris Capuano	.15
37	Scott Cassidy	.15
38	Will Clark	.75
39	Chad Cordero	.15
40	Carl Crawford	.25
41	Bobby Crosby	.75
42	Brad Wilkerson	.15
43	Michael Cuddyer	.25
44	Ben Davis	.15
45	Gookie Dawkins	.15
46	Rod Dedeaux	.15
47	R.A. Dickey	.15
48	Ben Diggins	.15
49	Lenny DiNardo	.15
50	Ryan Drese	.15
51	Tim Drew	.15
52	Todd Williams	.15
53	Justin Duchscherer	.15
54	J.D. Durbin	.15
55	Scott Elarton	.15
56	Adam Everett	.15
57	Dan Wilson	.15
58	Steve Finley	.25
59	Casey Fossum	.15
60	Terry Francona	.15
61	Ryan Franklin	.15
62	Ryan Freel	.15
63	John Van Benschoten	.15
64	Nomar Garciaparra	1.00
65	Chris George	.15
66	Jody Gerut	.15
67	Jason Giambi	.40
68	Matt Ginter	.15
69	Troy Glaus	.50
70	Tom Goodwin	.15
71	Mike Gosling	.15
72	Danny Graves	.15
73	Shawn Green	.50
74	Khalil Greene	.75
75	Todd Greene	.15
76	Seth Greisinger	.15
77	Gabe Gross	.15
78	Jeffrey Hammonds	.25
79	Aaron Heilman	.15
80	Paul Wilson	.15
81	Todd Helton	.75
82	Dustin Hermanson	.15
83	Bobby Hill	.15
84	Koyie Hill	.15
85	A.J. Hinch	.15
86	Matt Holliday	.50
87	Ted Wood	.15
88	Ken Huckaby	.15
89	Orlando Hudson	.15
90	Ernie Young	.15
91	Jason Jennings	.25
92	Charles Johnson	.25
93	Jacque Jones	.15
94	Matt Kata	.15
95	Austin Kearns	.25
96	Adam Kennedy	.25
97	Brooks Kieschnick	.25
98	Jesse Crain	.15
99	Scott Kazmir	1.50
100	Billy Koch	.25
101	Paul Konerko	.25
102	Graham Koonce	.15
103	Casey Kotchman	.50
104	Chris Snyder	.15
105	Nick Swisher	.50
106	Gerald Laird	.15
107	Barry Larkin	.50
108	Mike Lamb	.15
109	Tommy Lasorda	.25
110	Matt LeCroy	.15
111	Travis Lee	.25
112	Justin Leone	.15
113	John Vander Wal	.15
114	Braden Looper	.15
115	Shane Loux	.15
116	Ryan Ludwick	.25
117	Jason Varitek	.40
118	Ryan Madson	.15
119	Dave Magadan	.15
120	Tino Martinez	.25
121	Joe Mauer	.50
122	David McCarty	.15
123	Robin Ventura	.25
124	Jack McDowell	.25
125	Todd Walker	.25
126	Mark McGwire	1.50
127	Gil Meche	.15
128	Doug Mientkiewicz	.25
129	Matt Morris	.25
130	Warren Morris	.15
131	Mark Mulder	.50
132	Calvin Murray	.15
133	Eric Munson	.25
134	Mike Mussina	.50
135	Xavier Nady	.15
136	Shane Nance	.15
137	Mike Neill	.15
138	Augie Ojeda	.15
139	John Olerud	.25
140	Gregg Olson	.15
141	Roy Oswalt	.50
142	Jim Parque	.15
143	John Patterson	.15
144	Brad Penny	.15
145	Jay Powell	.15
146	Mark Prior	.75
147	Horacio Ramirez	.15
148	Jon Rauch	.15
149	Jeremy Reed	.25
150	Bob Watson	.15
151	Matt Riley	.15
152	Brian Roberts	.15
153	Dave Roberts	.15
154	Frank Robinson	.50
155	J.C. Romero	.15
156	David Ross	.15
157	Cory Vance	.15
158	Kirk Saarloos	.15
159	Anthony Sanders	.15
160	Dane Sardinha	.15
161	Bobby Seay	.15
162	Phil Seibel	.15
163	Aaron Sele	.15
164	Ben Sheets	.50
165	Paul Shuey	.15
166	Grady Sizemore	.50
167	Reggie Smith	.15
168	John Smoltz	.50
169	Zach Sorensen	.15
170	Scott Spiezio	.25
171	Ed Sprague	.15
172	Jason Stanford	.15
173	Dave Stewart	.15
174	Scott Stewart	.15
175	B.J. Surhoff	.15
176	Bill Swift	.15
177	Mike Tonis	.15
178	Jason Tyner	.15
179	Michael Tucker	.15
180	B.J. Upton	.75
181	Eric Valent	.15
182	Ron Villone	.15
183	2000: Team USA Shocks Cuba	.15
184	1984: Abbott halts Japan	.15
185	1996: Berman's Boys Take Third	.15
186	1984: Team USA Takes Second	.15
187	2000: Home Run Heroics	.15
188	1999: Neill's Hit Boosts Team USA	.15
189	1996: High Five for Team USA	.15
190	1992: Garciaparra Makes the Roster	.50
191	2003: USA Rolls to Record	.15
192	1995: Juniors Are Golden In Boston	.15
193	1999: The Streak Goes On	.15
194	1998: Perfect Finish in St. Louis	.15
195	1999: McGwire's Number Retired	1.00
196	2000: Filled with Firsts	.15
197	Red, White and Blue Cardinal	.15
198	2000: Quick Start for Neill	.15
199	1999: Jensen Goes Deep vs. Cuba	.15
200	2000: Mauer on the Mark	.25

Team USA Jersey

		NM/M
Common Player:		4.00
Inserted 1:Factory Set		
KA	Kurt Ainsworth	4.00
BB	Brian Bruney	4.00
CB	Chris Burke	4.00
SB	Sean Burroughs	4.00
JD	Justin Duchscherer	4.00
AE	Adam Everett	4.00
JG	Jason Giambi	6.00
GG	Gabe Gross	4.00
DH	Dustin Hermanson	4.00
MH	Matt Holliday	15.00
GK	Graham Koonce	4.00
GL	Gerald Laird	4.00
JL	Justin Leone	6.00
JM	Joe Mauer	10.00
DM	Doug Mientkiewicz	6.00
EM	Eric Munson	8.00
XN	Xavier Nady	4.00
RO	Roy Oswalt	6.00
MP	Mark Prior	8.00
HR	Horacio Ramirez	4.00
JR	Jon Rauch	4.00
RE	Jeremy Reed	5.00
FR	Frank Robinson	8.00
MR	Mike Rouse	4.00
BS	Ben Sheets	8.00
GS	Grady Sizemore	10.00
DS	Dave Stewart	6.00
JV	John Van Benschoten	4.00
JW	Jeff Weaver	4.00
BW	Brad Wilkerson	4.00

Team USA Signature Black Ink

		NM/M
Common Autograph:		5.00
Signatures Inserted 3:Factory Set		
ABB	Jim Abbott/180	20.00
ABE	Brent Abernathy/360	5.00
AIN	Kurt Ainsworth/360	8.00
ALV	Abe Alvarez/360	10.00
AND	Matt Anderson/360	5.00
AUS	Jeff Austin/360	5.00
BANK	Scott Bankhead/360	5.00
BARD	Josh Bard/350	5.00
BARR	Michael Barrett/360	10.00
BELL	Buddy Bell/81	25.00
BEN	Andy Benes/350	10.00
BENS	Kris Benson/180	15.00
BERG	Peter Bergeron/360	5.00
BLA	Casey Blake/180	10.00
BLO	Willie Bloomquist/175	15.00
BON	Jeremy Bonderman/150	10.00
BOR	Joe Borchard/350	10.00
BRAD	Milton Bradley/360	15.00
BRO	Ben Broussard/210	5.00
BRU	Brian Bruney/160	5.00
BUD	Mark Budzinski/360	5.00
BULL	Kirk Bullinger/360	5.00
BURK	Chris Burke/350	8.00
BU	Sean Burnett/180	5.00
BURN	Jeromy Burnitz/360	15.00
BUR	Pat Burrell/360	15.00
BURR	Sean Burroughs/360	10.00
BYRD	Paul Byrd/360	10.00
CAP	Chris Capuano/150	8.00
CASS	Scott Cassidy/360	5.00
CLA	Will Clark/60	75.00
COR	Chad Cordero/360	5.00
CR	Jesse Crain/180	10.00
CRA	Carl Crawford/60	35.00
CUD	Michael Cuddyer/370	8.00
DAV	Ben Davis/344	5.00
DED	Rod Dedeaux/29	40.00
DIC	R.A. Dickey/180	5.00
DIG	Ben Diggins/180	8.00
DIN	Lenny DiNardo/150	5.00
DRE	Ryan Drese/180	8.00
DREW	Tim Drew/360	5.00
DUCH	Justin Duchscherer/210	8.00
DUR	J.D. Durbin/180	5.00
ELAR	Scott Elarton/180	8.00
EVER	Adam Everett/360	8.00
FIN	Steve Finley/360	10.00
FOSS	Casey Fossum/320	8.00
FRAN	Terry Francona/150	40.00
FRA	Ryan Franklin/360	5.00
FRE	Ryan Freel/360	5.00
GEO	Chris George/360	5.00
GER	Jody Gerut/350	5.00
GIAM	Jason Giambi/60	50.00
GIN	Matt Ginter/179	8.00
GLA	Troy Glaus/120	35.00
GOS	Mike Gosling/150	8.00
DRA	Danny Graves/360	8.00
GR	Shawn Green/150	40.00
GRE	Khalil Greene/180	40.00
GREE	Todd Greene/120	10.00
GREI	Seth Greisinger/360	5.00
GRO	Gabe Gross/150	5.00
HAM	Jeffrey Hammonds/150	10.00
HEIL	Aaron Heilman/350	5.00
HELT	Todd Helton/71	50.00
HERM	Dustin Hermanson/150	10.00
HI	Bobby Hill/360	5.00
HILL	Koyie Hill/150	5.00
HIN	A.J. Hinch/360	5.00
HUCK	Ken Huckaby/360	5.00
HUD	Orlando Hudson/360	10.00
JENN	Jason Jennings/350	8.00
JON	Jacque Jones/150	10.00
KATA	Matt Kata/350	8.00
KAZ	Scott Kazmir/360	30.00
KENN	Adam Kennedy/150	8.00
KIES	Brooks Kieschnick/360	8.00
KOCH	Billy Koch/71	20.00
KON	Paul Konerko/179	15.00
KOO	Graham Koonce/360	8.00
KOTC	Casey Kotchman/150	20.00
LAMB	Mike Lamb/360	5.00
LAR	Barry Larkin/60	75.00
LEC	Matt LeCroy/360	5.00
LEE	Travis Lee/360	8.00
LEO	Justin Leone/150	10.00
LOO	Braden Looper/360	5.00
LOUX	Shane Loux/360	5.00
MAD	Ryan Madson/360	8.00
MAG	Dave Magadan/360	8.00
MART	Tino Martinez/360	20.00
MAU	Joe Mauer/360	35.00
MCC	David McCarty/360	10.00
MCDO	Jack McDowell/60	20.00
MEC	Gil Meche/360	5.00
MIE	Doug Mientkiewicz/300	10.00
MOR	Matt Morris/150	10.00
MORR	Warren Morris/360	5.00
MUL	Mark Mulder/180	10.00
MUN	Eric Munson/510	8.00
MURR	Calvin Murray/360	5.00
MUSS	Mike Mussina/60	50.00
NADY	Xavier Nady/360	5.00
NAN	Shane Nance/150	5.00
NEI	Mike Neill/360	5.00
OJE	Augie Ojeda/360	5.00
OLE	John Olerud/360	20.00
OLS	Gregg Olson/180	5.00
OSW	Roy Oswalt/350	15.00
PARQ	Jim Parque/360	5.00
PATT	John Patterson/210	5.00
PEN	Brad Penny/360	8.00
POW	Jay Powell/180	5.00
PRI	Mark Prior/350	40.00
RAM	Horacio Ramirez/150	10.00
RAU	Jon Rauch/359	5.00
REED	Jeremy Reed/180	10.00
RIL	Matt Riley/60	15.00
ROB	Brian Roberts/60	20.00
ROBE	Dave Roberts/360	10.00
ROM	J.C. Romero/360	5.00
ROSS	David Ross/360	5.00
SAAR	Kirk Saarloos/360	5.00
SAND	Anthony Sanders/360	5.00
SAR	Dane Sardinha/360	5.00
SEAY	Bobby Seay/360	5.00
SEI	Phil Seibel/150	8.00
SELE	Aaron Sele/360	10.00
SHE	Ben Sheets/143	25.00
SHU	Paul Shuey/360	5.00
SIZE	Grady Sizemore/160	35.00
SMI	Reggie Smith/360	10.00
SMO	John Smoltz/360	35.00
SNY	Chris Snyder/360	5.00
SPI	Scott Spiezio/360	10.00
SPR	Ed Sprague/360	10.00
STE	Dave Stewart/180	15.00
STEW	Scott Stewart/360	5.00
SUR	B.J. Surhoff/60	30.00
SWIF	Bill Swift/360	5.00
SWI	Nick Swisher/360	10.00
TON	Mike Tonis/350	5.00
TUCK	Michael Tucker/150	10.00
TYN	Jason Tyner/360	8.00
VAL	Eric Valent/360	8.00
VANB	John Van Benschoten/180	10.00
VAN	Cory Vance/360	5.00
VAND	John Vander Wal/360	10.00
VAR	Jason Varitek/360	40.00
VENT	Robin Ventura/360	15.00
VILL	Ron Villone/359	5.00
WALK	Todd Walker/60	20.00
WAT	Bob Watson/150	8.00
WAY	Justin Wayne/150	8.00
WEA	Jeff Weaver/360	10.00
WEEK	Rickie Weeks/360	15.00
WHEE	Dan Wheeler/360	5.00
WILL	Todd Williams/360	5.00
WI	Dan Wilson/360	10.00
WIL	Paul Wilson/360	5.00
WOOD	Ted Wood/330	5.00
YOUN	Ernie Young/350	8.00

Team USA Signature Blue Ink

		NM/M
Common Autograph:		8.00
ABB	Jim Abbott/60	30.00
ABE	Brent Abernathy/120	8.00
AIN	Kurt Ainsworth/120	8.00
ALV	Abe Alvarez/120	10.00
AND	Matt Anderson/110	8.00
AUS	Jeff Austin/120	8.00
BANK	Scott Bankhead/120	8.00
BARD	Josh Bard/100	8.00
BARR	Michael Barrett/120	8.00
BELL	Buddy Bell/29	25.00
BEN	Andy Benes/100	10.00
BENS	Kris Benson/60	25.00
BERG	Peter Bergeron/120	8.00
BLA	Casey Blake/60	20.00
BLO	Willie Bloomquist/51	20.00
BON	Jeremy Bonderman/90	10.00
BOR	Joe Borchard/100	8.00
BOW	Rob Bowen/510	8.00
BRAD	Milton Bradley/120	15.00
BRO	Ben Broussard/150	8.00
BRU	Brian Bruney/60	10.00
BUD	Mark Budzinski/120	8.00
BULL	Kirk Bullinger/120	8.00
BURK	Chris Burke/110	8.00
BU	Sean Burnett/60	10.00
BURN	Jeromy Burnitz/120	15.00
BUR	Pat Burrell/80	15.00
BURR	Sean Burroughs/142	8.00
BYRD	Paul Byrd/120	8.00
CAP	Chris Capuano/90	8.00
CASS	Scott Cassidy/120	8.00
CLA	Will Clark/30	80.00
COR	Chad Cordero/120	8.00
CR	Jesse Crain/60	15.00
CUD	Michael Cuddyer/89	8.00
DAV	Ben Davis/100	8.00
DED	Rod Dedeaux/25	30.00
DIC	R.A. Dickey/60	10.00
DIG	Ben Diggins/30	15.00
DIN	Lenny DiNardo/60	10.00
DRE	Ryan Drese/60	10.00
DREW	Tim Drew/120	8.00
DUCH	Justin Duchscherer/110	8.00
DUR	J.D. Durbin/60	10.00
ELAR	Scott Elarton/60	10.00
EVER	Adam Everett/120	8.00
FIN	Steve Finley/120	15.00
FOSS	Casey Fossum/100	8.00
FRAN	Terry Francona/40	40.00
FRA	Ryan Franklin/120	8.00
FRE	Ryan Freel/110	8.00
GAR	Nomar Garciaparra/60	75.00
GEO	Chris George/120	8.00
GER	Jody Gerut/100	8.00
GIAM	Jason Giambi/30	50.00
GIN	Matt Ginter/42	10.00
GLA	Troy Glaus/60	30.00
GOS	Mike Gosling/60	10.00
DRA	Danny Graves/120	8.00
GR	Shawn Green/90	30.00
GRE	Khalil Greene/60	50.00
GREE	Todd Greene/60	10.00
GREI	Seth Greisinger/120	8.00
GRO	Gabe Gross/90	8.00
HAM	Jeffrey Hammonds/90	10.00
HEIL	Aaron Heilman/100	8.00
HELT	Todd Helton/20	65.00
HERM	Dustin Hermanson/90	10.00
HI	Bobby Hill/120	8.00
HILL	Koyie Hill/90	8.00
HIN	A.J. Hinch/120	8.00
HUCK	Ken Huckaby/120	8.00
HUD	Orlando Hudson/110	15.00
JENN	Jason Jennings/100	8.00
JON	Jacque Jones/60	20.00
KATA	Matt Kata/100	8.00
KAZ	Scott Kazmir/110	35.00
KEAR	Austin Kearns/110	20.00
KENN	Adam Kennedy/90	8.00
KIES	Brooks Kieschnick/120	8.00
KOCH	Billy Koch/18	25.00
KON	Paul Konerko/52	20.00
KOO	Graham Koonce/120	8.00
KOTC	Casey Kotchman/60	30.00
LAMB	Mike Lamb/120	8.00
LAR	Barry Larkin/20	80.00
LAS	Tommy Lasorda/30	60.00
LEC	Matt LeCroy/120	8.00
LEE	Travis Lee/120	8.00
LEO	Justin Leone/60	15.00
LOO	Braden Looper/120	8.00
LOUX	Shane Loux/110	8.00
LUD	Ryan Ludwick/450	8.00
MAD	Ryan Madson/110	8.00
MAG	Dave Magadan/120	8.00
MART	Tino Martinez/120	20.00
MAU	Joe Mauer/120	35.00
MCC	David McCarty/120	10.00
MCDO	Jack McDowell/30	20.00
MEC	Gil Meche/120	8.00
MIE	Doug Mientkiewicz/120	10.00
MOR	Matt Morris/90	15.00
MORR	Warren Morris/120	8.00
MUL	Mark Mulder/110	15.00
MURR	Calvin Murray/120	8.00
MUSS	Mike Mussina/30	50.00
NADY	Xavier Nady/120	8.00
NAN	Shane Nance/60	10.00
NEI	Mike Neill/110	8.00
OJE	Augie Ojeda/119	8.00
OLE	John Olerud/120	20.00
OLS	Gregg Olson/60	10.00
OSW	Roy Oswalt/100	15.00
PARQ	Jim Parque/120	8.00
PATT	John Patterson/120	8.00
PEN	Brad Penny/110	8.00
POW	Jay Powell/60	10.00
PRI	Mark Prior/108	40.00
RAM	Horacio Ramirez/90	8.00
RAU	Jon Rauch/100	8.00
REED	Jeremy Reed/45	20.00
ROBE	Dave Roberts/120	8.00
ROBI	Frank Robinson/30	90.00
ROM	J.C. Romero/120	8.00
ROSS	David Ross/120	8.00
SAAR	Kirk Saarloos/120	8.00
SAND	Anthony Sanders/120	8.00
SAR	Dane Sardinha/110	8.00
SEAY	Bobby Seay/120	8.00
SEI	Phil Seibel/90	8.00
SELE	Aaron Sele/120	10.00
SHU	Paul Shuey/120	8.00
SIZE	Grady Sizemore/60	35.00
SMI	Reggie Smith/120	10.00
SMO	John Smoltz/120	40.00
SNY	Chris Snyder/120	8.00
SOR	Zach Sorensen/450	8.00
SPI	Scott Spiezio/120	8.00
SPR	Ed Sprague/120	8.00
STAN	Jason Stanford/450	8.00
STE	Dave Stewart/90	10.00
STEW	Scott Stewart/119	8.00
SWIF	Bill Swift/120	8.00
SWI	Nick Swisher/110	20.00
TON	Mike Tonis/100	8.00
TUCK	Michael Tucker/90	10.00
TYN	Jason Tyner/120	8.00
UPT	B.J. Upton/120	30.00
VAL	Eric Valent/120	8.00
VANB	John Van Benschoten/60	20.00
VAN	Cory Vance/120	8.00
VAND	John Vander Wal/120	8.00
VAR	Jason Varitek/100	40.00
VENT	Robin Ventura/120	15.00
VILL	Ron Villone/120	8.00
WAT	Bob Watson/60	10.00
WAY	Justin Wayne/60	10.00
WEA	Jeff Weaver/120	8.00
WEEK	Rickie Weeks/120	15.00
WHEE	Dan Wheeler/120	8.00
WILL	Todd Williams/90	8.00
WI	Dan Wilson/120	10.00
WIL	Paul Wilson/110	8.00
WOOD	Ted Wood/120	8.00
YOUN	Ernie Young/130	10.00

Team USA Signature Red Ink

		NM/M
Common Autograph:		10.00
Some not priced due to scarcity.		
ABE	Brent Abernathy/20	15.00
AIN	Kurt Ainsworth/20	15.00
AND	Matt Anderson/30	15.00
AUS	Jeff Austin/20	15.00
BARD	Josh Bard/50	10.00
BARR	Michael Barrett/20	20.00
BEN	Andy Benes/50	15.00
BLO	Willie Bloomquist/25	25.00
BOR	Joe Borchard/50	10.00
BRAD	Milton Bradley/20	25.00
BRO	Ben Broussard/40	15.00
BRU	Brian Bruney/30	15.00
BURK	Chris Burke/50	10.00
BURN	Jeromy Burnitz/20	25.00
BUR	Pat Burrell/29	25.00
BYRD	Paul Byrd/20	20.00
CRO	Bobby Crosby/60	50.00
CUD	Michael Cuddyer/40	10.00
DAV	Ben Davis/50	10.00
DIN	Lenny DiNardo/40	10.00
EVER	Adam Everett/20	15.00
FIN	Steve Finley/20	25.00
FOSS	Casey Fossum/42	10.00
FRE	Ryan Freel/30	15.00
GAR	Nomar Garciaparra/30	125.00
GER	Jody Gerut/50	10.00
GLA	Troy Glaus/20	60.00
GOS	Mike Gosling/40	10.00
HEIL	Aaron Heilman/50	10.00
HIN	A.J. Hinch/20	15.00
HUD	Orlando Hudson/30	25.00
JENN	Jason Jennings/50	15.00
JON	Jacque Jones/40	20.00
KATA	Matt Kata/50	15.00
KAZ	Scott Kazmir/30	75.00
KEAR	Austin Kearns/30	35.00
KON	Paul Konerko/23	25.00
KOO	Graham Koonce/20	15.00
KOTC	Casey Kotchman/40	35.00
LEC	Matt LeCroy/20	15.00
LEE	Travis Lee/20	15.00
LEO	Justin Leone/40	20.00
LOUX	Shane Loux/30	15.00
LUD	Ryan Ludwick/50	10.00
MAD	Ryan Madson/30	15.00
MART	Tino Martinez/20	40.00
MAU	Joe Mauer/20	65.00
MCC	David McCarty/20	25.00
MIE	Doug Mientkiewicz/20	25.00
NADY	Xavier Nady/20	15.00
NAN	Shane Nance/40	10.00
NEI	Mike Neill/30	15.00
OSW	Roy Oswalt/50	20.00
PARQ	Jim Parque/20	15.00
PATT	John Patterson/20	15.00
PEN	Brad Penny/30	15.00
PRI	Mark Prior/48	60.00
RAU	Jon Rauch/53	10.00
REED	Jeremy Reed/25	25.00
ROM	J.C. Romero/20	15.00
SAR	Dane Sardinha/30	15.00
SIZE	Grady Sizemore/30	40.00
SMO	John Smoltz/20	65.00
SOR	Zach Sorensen/50	10.00
SPR	Ed Sprague/20	15.00
STAN	Jason Stanford/50	10.00
STE	Dave Stewart/30	25.00
SWI	Nick Swisher/30	40.00
TON	Mike Tonis/50	10.00
UPT	B.J. Upton/20	40.00

VAR Jason Varitek/30 70.00
VENT Robin Ventura/20 25.00
WAT Bob Watson/30 15.00
WAY Justin Wayne/40 10.00
WEA Jeff Weaver/20 25.00
WEEK Rickie Weeks/20 25.00
WILL Todd Williams/50 10.00
WIL Paul Wilson/30 15.00
WOOD Ted Wood/30 15.00
YOUN Ernie Young/50 10.00

Team USA Signature Green Ink

No Pricing
Production 1-3

2004 Upper Deck Vintage

NM/M
Complete Set (450):
Common Player: .15
Common SP (301-315): .50
Inserted 1:5
Common SP (316-325): .40
Inserted 1:7
Common SP (326-350): .40
Inserted 1:5
Common 3D SP (351-440): 2.00
Inserted 1:12
Old Judge (441-450) found in bonus packs.
Pack (8): 2.50
Box (24 + 1 Bonus Pack): 50.00

1 Albert Pujols 1.50
2 Carlos Delgado .50
3 Todd Helton .50
4 Nomar Garciaparra 1.50
5 Vladimir Guerrero .75
6 Alfonso Soriano .75
7 Alex Rodriguez 1.50
8 Jason Giambi .75
9 Derek Jeter 2.00
10 Pedro J. Martinez .75
11 Ivan Rodriguez .50
12 Mark Prior 1.00
13 Marquis Grissom .15
14 Barry Zito .25
15 Alex Cintron .15
16 Wade Miller .15
17 Eric Chavez .25
18 Matt Clement .15
19 Orlando Cabrera .15
20 Odalis Perez .15
21 Lance Berkman .25
22 Keith Foulke .15
23 Shawn Green .25
24 Byung-Hyun Kim .15
25 Geoff Jenkins .25
26 Torii Hunter .40
27 Richard Hidalgo .15
28 Edgar Martinez .25
29 Placido Polanco .15
30 Brad Lidge .15
31 Alex Escobar .15
32 Garret Anderson .25
33 Larry Walker .25
34 Ken Griffey Jr. 1.00
35 Junior Spivey .15
36 Carlos Beltran .25
37 Bartolo Colon .25
38 Ichiro Suzuki 1.00
39 Ramon Ortiz .15
40 Roy Oswalt .25
41 Mike Piazza 1.00
42 Benito Santiago .15
43 Mike Mussina .50
44 Jeff Kent .25
45 Curt Schilling .50
46 Adam Dunn .40
47 Mike Sweeney .15
48 Chipper Jones 1.00
49 Frank Thomas .50
50 Kerry Wood .50
51 Rod Beck .15
52 Brian Giles .25
53 Hank Blalock .25
54 Andruw Jones .50
55 Dmitri Young .15
56 Juan Pierre .15
57 Jacque Jones .15
58 Phil Nevin .15
59 Rocco Baldelli .25
60 Greg Maddux 1.00
61 Eric Gagne .15
62 Tim Hudson .25
63 Brian Lawrence .15
64 Sammy Sosa 1.00
65 Corey Koskie .15
66 Bobby Abreu .25
67 Preston Wilson .15
68 Jay Gibbons .15
69 Dontrelle Willis .25
70 Richie Sexson .40
71 Kevin Millwood .25
72 Randy Johnson .75
73 Jack Cust .15
74 Randy Wolf .15
75 Johan Santana .15
76 Magglio Ordonez .25
77 Sean Casey .15
78 Billy Wagner .25
79 Javier Vazquez .15
80 Jorge Posada .40
81 Jason Schmidt .15
82 Bret Boone .25
83 Jeff Bagwell .50
84 Rickie Weeks .25
85 Troy Percival .15
86 Jose Vidro .15
87 Freddy Garcia .15
88 Manny Ramirez .50
89 John Smoltz .25
90 Moises Alou .25
91 Ugueth Urbina .15
92 Bobby Hill .15
93 Marcus Giles .15
94 Aramis Ramirez .25
95 Brad Wilkerson .15
96 Ray Durham .15
97 David Wells .15
98 Paul LoDuca .15
99 Danny Graves .15
100 Jason Kendall .25
101 Carlos Lee .25
102 Rafael Furcal .25
103 Mike Lowell .15
104 Kevin Brown .25
105 Vicente Padilla .15
106 Miguel Tejada .40
107 Bernie Williams .40
108 Octavio Dotel .15
109 Steve Finley .15
110 Lyle Overbay .15
111 Delmon Young .25
112 Bo Hart .15
113 Jason Lane .15
114 Matt Roney .15
115 Brian Roberts .15
116 Tom Glavine .25
117 Rich Aurilia .15
118 Adam Kennedy .15
119 Hee Seop Choi .15
120 Trot Nixon .15
121 Gary Sheffield .40
122 Jay Payton .15
123 Brad Penny .15
124 Garrett Atkins .15
125 Aubrey Huff .15
126 Juan Gonzalez .40
127 Jason Jennings .15
128 Luis Gonzalez .25
129 Vinny Castilla .15
130 Esteban Loaiza .15
131 Erubiel Durazo .15
132 Eric Hinske .15
133 Scott Rolen .75
134 Craig Biggio .25
135 Tim Wakefield .15
136 Darin Erstad .25
137 Denny Stark .15
138 Ben Sheets .25
139 Hideo Nomo .40
140 Derrek Lee .25
141 Matt Mantei .15
142 Reggie Sanders .15
143 Jose Guillen .15
144 Joe Mays .15
145 Jimmy Rollins .25
146 Juan Encarnacion .15
147 Joe Crede .15
148 Aaron Guiel .15
149 Mark Mulder .25
150 Travis Lee .15
151 Josh Phelps .15
152 Michael Young .15
153 Paul Konerko .15
154 John Lackey .15
155 Damian Moss .15
156 Javy Lopez .25
157 Joe Borowski .15
158 Jose Cruz Jr. .15
159 Ramon Hernandez .15
160 Raul Ibanez .15
161 Adrian Beltre .15
162 Bobby Higginson .15
163 Jorge Julio .15
164 Miguel Batista .15
165 Luis Castillo .15
166 Aaron Harang .15
167 Ken Harvey .15
168 Rocky Biddle .15
169 Mariano Rivera .25
170 Matt Morris .15
171 Laynce Nix .15
172 Mike Maroth .15
173 Francisco Rodriguez .15
174 Livan Hernandez .15
175 Aaron Heilman .15
176 Nick Johnson .15
177 Woody Williams .15
178 Joe Kennedy .15
179 Jesse Foppert .15
180 Ryan Franklin .15
181 Endy Chavez .15
182 Chin-Hui Tsao .15
183 Todd Walker .15
184 Edgardo Alfonzo .15
185 Edgar Renteria .15
186 Matt LeCroy .15
187 Carl Everett .15
188 Jeff Conine .15
189 Jason Varitek .15
190 Russ Ortiz .15
191 Melvin Mora .15
192 Mark Buehrle .15
193 Bill Mueller .15
194 Miguel Cabrera .25
195 Carlos Zambrano .15
196 Jose Valverde .15
197 Danys Baez .15
198 Mike MacDougal .15
199 Zach Day .15
200 Roy Halladay .25
201 Jerome Williams .15
202 Josh Fogg .15
203 Mark Kotsay .15
204 Pat Burrell .40
205 A.J. Pierzynski .15
206 Fred McGriff .25
207 Brandon Larson .15
208 Robb Quinlan .15
209 David Ortiz .15
210 A.J. Burnett .15
211 John Vander Wal .15
212 Jim Thome .75
213 Matt Kata .15
214 Kip Wells .15
215 Scott Podsednik .40
216 Rickey Henderson .25
217 Travis Hafner .15
218 Tony Batista .15
219 Robert Fick .15
220 Derek Lowe .25
221 Ryan Klesko .25
222 Joe Beimel .15
223 Doug Mientkiewicz .15
224 Angel Berroa .15
225 Adam Eaton .15
226 C.C. Sabathia .15
227 Wilfredo Ledezma .15
228 Jason Johnson .15
229 Ryan Wagner .15
230 Al Leiter .15
231 Joel Pineiro .15
232 Jason Isringhausen .15
233 John Olerud .25
234 Ron Calloway .15
235 Jose Reyes .40
236 J.D. Drew .15
237 Jared Sandberg .15
238 Gil Meche .15
239 Jose Contreras .15
240 Eric Milton .15
241 Jason L. Phillips .15
242 Luis Ayala .15
243 Bobby Kielty .15
244 Jose Lima .15
245 Brooks Kieschnick .15
246 Xavier Nady .15
247 Dan Haren .15
248 Victor Zambrano .15
249 Kelvim Escobar .15
250 Oliver Perez .15
251 Jamie Moyer .15
252 Orlando Hudson .15
253 Danny Kolb .15
254 Jake Peavy .15
255 Kris Benson .15
256 Roger Clemens 1.50
257 Jim Edmonds .40
258 Rafael Palmeiro .50
259 Jae Weong Seo .15
260 Chase Utley .15
261 Rich Harden .15
262 Mark Teixeira .25
263 Johnny Damon .25
264 Luis Matos .15
265 Shigetoshi Hasegawa .15
266 Alfredo Amezaga .15
267 Tim Worrell .15
268 Kazuhisa Ishii .15
269 Miguel Ojeda .15
270 Kazuhiro Sasaki .15
271 Hideki Matsui 2.00
272 Troy Glaus .40
273 Michael Tucker .15
274 Lew Ford .15
275 Brian Jordan .15
276 David Eckstein .15
277 Robby Hammock .15
278 Corey Patterson .25
279 Wes Helms .15
280 Jermaine Dye .15
281 Cliff Floyd .15
282 Dustan Mohr .15
283 Kevin Mench .15
284 Ellis Burks .15
285 Jerry Hairston Jr. .15
286 Tim Salmon .25
287 Omar Vizquel .25
288 Andy Pettitte .40
289 Guillermo Mota .15
290 Tino Martinez .15
291 Lance Carter .15
292 Francisco Cordero .15
293 Robb Nen .15
294 Mike Cameron .15
295 Jhonny Peralta .15
296 Braden Looper .15
297 Jarrod Washburn .15
298 Mark Prior .50
299 Alfonso Soriano .25
300 Rocco Baldelli .25
301 Pedro J. Martinez 1.50
302 Mark Prior 2.00
303 Barry Zito .75
304 Roger Clemens 2.50
305 Randy Johnson 1.50
306 Roy Halladay .50
307 Hideo Nomo .75
308 Roy Oswalt .50
309 Kerry Wood 1.00
310 Dontrelle Willis .75
311 Mark Mulder .50
312 Brandon Webb .50
313 Mike Mussina .75
314 Curt Schilling .75
315 Tim Hudson .75
316 Dontrelle Willis .75
317 Juan Pierre .40
318 Hideki Matsui 4.00
319 Andy Pettitte .75
320 Mike Mussina .75
321 Roger Clemens 2.50
322 Alex Gonzalez .40
323 Brad Penny .40
324 Ivan Rodriguez .75
325 Josh Beckett 1.00
326 Aaron Boone .40
327 Jeff Suppan .40
328 Shea Hillenbrand .40
329 Jeromy Burnitz .40
330 Sidney Ponson .40
331 Rondell White .50
332 Shannon Stewart .40
333 Armando Benitez .40
334 Roberto Alomar 1.00
335 Raul Mondesi .50
336 Morgan Ensberg .40
337 Milton Bradley .40
338 Brandon Webb .50
339 Marlon Byrd .40
340 Carlos Pena .40
341 Brandon Phillips .40
342 Josh Beckett 1.00
343 Eric Munson .40
344 Brett Myers .40
345 Austin Kearns 1.00
346 Jody Gerut .40
347 Vernon Wells .50
348 Jeff Duncan .40
349 Sean Burroughs .40
350 Jeremy Bonderman .40
351 Hideki Matsui 15.00
352 Jason Giambi 8.00
353 Alfonso Soriano 6.00
354 Derek Jeter 15.00
355 Aaron Boone 3.00
356 Jorge Posada 5.00
357 Bernie Williams 5.00
358 Manny Ramirez 5.00
359 Nomar Garciaparra 12.00
360 Johnny Damon 3.00
361 Jason Varitek 2.50
362 Carlos Delgado 5.00
363 Vernon Wells 4.00
364 Jay Gibbons 4.00
365 Tony Batista 2.00
366 Rocco Baldelli 5.00
367 Aubrey Huff 2.00
368 Carlos Beltran 4.00
369 Mike Sweeney 3.00
370 Magglio Ordonez 4.00
371 Frank Thomas 6.00
372 Carlos Lee 2.00
373 Roberto Alomar 4.00
374 Jacque Jones 2.00
375 Torii Hunter 4.00
376 Milton Bradley 2.00
377 Travis Hafner 2.00
378 Jody Gerut 2.00
379 Dmitri Young 2.00
380 Carlos Pena 2.00
381 Ichiro Suzuki 10.00
382 Bret Boone 3.00
383 Edgar Martinez 3.00
384 Eric Chavez 3.00
385 Miguel Tejada 3.00
386 Erubiel Durazo 2.00
387 Jose Guillen 2.00
388 Garret Anderson 3.00
389 Troy Glaus 4.00
390 Alex Rodriguez 10.00
391 Rafael Palmeiro 5.00
392 Hank Blalock 4.00
393 Mark Teixeira 4.00
394 Gary Sheffield 4.00
395 Andruw Jones 5.00
396 Chipper Jones 8.00
397 Javy Lopez 3.00
398 Marcus Giles 2.00
399 Rafael Furcal 3.00
400 Jim Thome 5.00
401 Bobby Abreu 3.00
402 Pat Burrell 3.00
403 Mike Lowell 3.00
404 Ivan Rodriguez 5.00
405 Derrek Lee 3.00
406 Miguel Cabrera 5.00
407 Vladimir Guerrero 6.00
408 Orlando Cabrera 2.00
409 Jose Vidro 2.00
410 Mike Piazza 8.00
411 Cliff Floyd 3.00
412 Albert Pujols 15.00
413 Scott Rolen 6.00
414 Jim Edmonds 4.00
415 Edgar Renteria 3.00
416 Lance Berkman 3.00
417 Jeff Bagwell 5.00
418 Jeff Kent 3.00
419 Richard Hidalgo 2.00
420 Morgan Ensberg 2.00
421 Sammy Sosa 10.00
422 Moises Alou 3.00
423 Ken Griffey Jr. 10.00
424 Adam Dunn 4.00
425 Austin Kearns 4.00
426 Richie Sexson 4.00
427 Geoff Jenkins 3.00
428 Brian Giles 3.00
429 Reggie Sanders 2.00
430 Rich Aurilia 2.00
431 Jose Cruz Jr. 2.00
432 Shawn Green 3.00
433 Jeromy Burnitz 2.00
434 Luis Gonzalez 3.00
435 Todd Helton 5.00
436 Preston Wilson 2.00
437 Larry Walker 3.00
438 Ryan Klesko 3.00
439 Phil Nevin 2.00
440 Sean Burroughs 2.00
441 Sammy Sosa 3.00
442 Albert Pujols 4.00
443 Magglio Ordonez .50
444 Vladimir Guerrero 1.50
445 Todd Helton 1.00
446 Jason Giambi 1.50
447 Ichiro Suzuki 3.00
448 Alex Rodriguez 3.00
449 Carlos Delgado .75
450 Manny Ramirez 1.00

Black & White

Cards (1-300): 1-2X
Inserted 1:6
SP's (301-325): 1-2X
Inserted 1:24
SP's (326-350): 1-2X
Inserted 1:20
B/W Color Variations: 6-10X
Inserted 1:48

Old Judge

NM/M
Complete Set (20): 15.00
Common Player: .40
Inserted 3:bonus pack.
Blue Back: 1-2X
Inserted 1:4 bonus packs.
Red Back: 2-3X
Inserted 1:12 bonus packs.

11 Randy Johnson 1.50
12 Pedro J. Martinez 1.50
13 Mark Prior 2.00
14 Barry Zito .50
15 Roy Oswalt .40
16 Roy Halladay .50
17 Curt Schilling .75
18 Mike Mussina .75
19 Kevin Brown .40
20 Roger Clemens 2.50
21 Eric Gagne .50
22 Mariano Rivera .50
23 Mike Piazza 2.00
24 Jorge Posada .75
25 Jeff Kent .50
26 Alfonso Soriano 1.00
27 Scott Rolen 1.00
28 Eric Chavez .50
29 Edgar Renteria .40
30 Hideki Matsui 4.00

Stellar Signatures

NM/M
Inserted 1:600
HM Hideki Matsui 300.00
MP Mike Piazza 150.00
AR Alex Rodriguez 100.00
TS Tom Seaver 50.00
IS Ichiro Suzuki 200.00
CY C. Yastrzemski/125 75.00
BZ Barry Zito 40.00

Stellar Stat Men

NM/M
Common Player: 4.00
Inserted 1:24

1 Jose Reyes 6.00
2 Bo Hart 8.00
3 Hideki Matsui 30.00
4 Dontrelle Willis 6.00
5 Rocco Baldelli 6.00

6 Ichiro Suzuki 20.00
7 Mike Lowell 6.00
8 Derek Jeter 20.00
9 Ken Griffey Jr. 15.00
10 Sammy Sosa 12.00
11 Kerry Wood 10.00
12 Chipper Jones 6.00
13 Alfonso Soriano 8.00
14 Khalil Greene 6.00
15 Jim Thome 8.00
16 Rafael Furcal 5.00
17 Andrew Brown 4.00
18 Mark Prior 10.00
19 Barry Zito 6.00
20 Al Leiter 4.00
21 Carlos Delgado 6.00
22 Pedro J. Martinez 8.00
23 Alex Rodriguez 10.00
24 Lance Berkman 5.00
25 Jeff Bagwell 6.00
26 Bernie Williams 6.00
27 Hideo Nomo 8.00
28 Randy Johnson 8.00
29 Curt Schilling 8.00
30 Mike Piazza 10.00
31 Albert Pujols 12.00
32 Joe DiMaggio 100.00
33 Ted Williams 60.00
34 Mickey Mantle 100.00
35 Mike Mussina 8.00
36 Rich Harden 5.00
37 Roy Oswalt 4.00
38 Torii Hunter 8.00
39 Jorge Posada 6.00
40 Troy Glaus 6.00
41 Manny Ramirez 6.00
42 Roy Halladay 5.00

Timeless Teams

NM/M
Common Quad: 15.00
Inserted 1:400
Production 175 Sets

1 Derek Jeter, Jason Giambi, Alfonso Soriano, Hideki Matsui 90.00
2 Randy Johnson, Luis Gonzalez, Steve Finley, Curt Schilling 20.00
4 Johnny Damon, Manny Ramirez, Nomar Garciaparra, Trot Nixon 35.00
5 Alex Rodriguez, Rafael Palmeiro, Mark Teixeira, Hank Blalock 35.00
6 Roberto Alomar, Frank Thomas, Magglio Ordonez, Carl Everett 20.00
7 Shannon Stewart, Torii Hunter, Jacque Jones, Doug Mientkiewicz 15.00
8 Jim Edmonds, Scott Rolen, J.D. Drew, Albert Pujols 40.00
9 Bret Boone, John Olerud, Mike Cameron, Ichiro Suzuki 45.00
10 Jeff Bagwell, Craig Biggio, Jeff Kent, Lance Berkman 20.00
11 Tim Salmon, Garret Anderson, Darin Erstad, Troy Glaus 15.00
12 Bernie Williams, Alfonso Soriano, Jorge Posada, Hideki Matsui 85.00
13 Carlos Beltran, Michael Tucker, Mike Sweeney, Brent Mayne 15.00
14 Jim Thome, Mike Lieberthal, Bobby Abreu, Marlon Byrd 30.00
15 Ivan Rodriguez, Juan Encarnacion, Mike Lowell, Miguel Cabrera 25.00
16 Sammy Sosa, Kerry Wood, Moises Alou, Corey Patterson 50.00
17 Andres Galarraga, Edgardo Alfonzo, Jose Cruz Jr., Rich Aurilia 15.00
18 Derek Jeter, Bernie Williams, Alfonso Soriano, Hideki Matsui 90.00

2004 Upper Deck Yankees Classics Promos

Each of the cards in Yankees Classics was issued in a foil-overprinted version with "UD PROMO" across the front. Cards were inserted into specially marked card shop and newsstand issues of Tuff Stuff magazine.

	NM/M
Common Player:	.50
Stars:	1.5X

2004 Upper Deck Yankees Classics

		NM/M
Complete Set (90):		20.00
Common Player:		.25
Pack (5):		6.00
Box (24):		120.00
1	Bill "Moose" Skowron	.50
2	Bob Cerv	.50
3	Bobby Murcer	.50
4	Bobby Richardson	.25
5	Brian Doyle	.25
6	Bucky Dent	.25
7	Chris Chambliss	.25
8	Clete Boyer	.25
9	Dave Kingman	.25
10	Dave Righetti	.25
11	Dave Winfield	.50
12	David Cone	.25
13	Red Ruffing	.25
14	Dock Ellis	.25
15	Don Baylor	.25
16	Don Larsen	.75
17	Don Mattingly	1.50
18	Dwight Gooden	.40
19	Ed Figueroa	.25
20	Joe Torre	.50
21	Darryl Strawberry	.40
22	Horace Clarke	.25
23	Gaylord Perry	.25
24	Phil Linz	.25
25	Gil McDougald	.25
26	Rich "Goose" Gossage	.25
27	Graig Nettles	.25
28	Hank Bauer	.25
29	Jack Clark	.25
30	Don Gullett	.25
31	Jim Abbott	.25
32	Jim Bouton	.25
33	Jim Kaat	.40
34	Jim Leyritz	.25
35	Jim Wynn	.25
36	Jimmy Key	.25
37	Joe Niekro	.25
38	Joe Pepitone	.25
39	John Wetteland	.25
40	Ken Griffey Sr.	.25
41	Felipe Alou	.25
42	Kevin Maas	.25
43	Lindy McDaniel	.25
44	Lou Piniella	.50
45	Luis Tiant	.25
46	Mel Stottlemyre	.25
47	Mickey Rivers	.25
48	Oscar Gamble	.25
49	Pat Dobson	.25
50	Paul O'Neill	.50
51	Phil Niekro	.25
52	Phil Rizzuto	.75
53	Doc Medich	.25
54	Rick Cerone	.25
55	Ron Blomberg	.25
56	Ron Guidry	.50
57	Roy White	.25
58	Rudy May	.25
59	Sam McDowell	.25
60	Sparky Lyle	.25
61	Steve Balboni	.25
62	Steve Sax	.25
63	Jerry Coleman	.25
64	Tom Tresh	.25
65	Tommy John	.25
66	Tony Kubek	.50
67	Wade Boggs	.50
68	Whitey Ford	.75
69	Willie Randolph	.25
70	Yogi Berra	1.00
71	Babe Ruth	3.00
72	Bill Dickey	.50
73	Billy Martin	.50
74	Bob Meusel	.25
75	Casey Stengel	.50
76	Elston Howard	.25
77	Jim "Catfish" Hunter	.50
78	Joe DiMaggio	2.00
79	Lefty Gomez	.50
80	Lou Gehrig	2.00
81	Mickey Mantle	3.00
82	Miller Huggins	.25
83	Roger Maris	1.50
84	Thurman Munson	.75
85	Tony Lazzeri	.50
86	Yankee Stadium	.75
87	Times Square	.50
88	Central Park	.50
89	Empire State Building	.50
90	Statue of Liberty	.50

Bronze

Bronze: 4-8X
Production 99 Sets

Silver

Silver: No Pricing

Gold

Gold: 8-15X
Production 30 Sets

Classic Cuts

No Pricing
Production One Set

Classic Scripts Single Auto

		NM/M
Common Autograph:		10.00
Inserted 1:8		
AU-1	Bill "Moose" Skowron	15.00
AU-2	Bob Cerv	10.00
AU-3	Bobby Murcer/SP	60.00
AU-4	Bobby Richardson	15.00
AU-5	Brian Doyle	10.00
AU-6	Bucky Dent	10.00
AU-7	Chris Chambliss	12.00
AU-8	Clete Boyer	15.00
AU-9	Dave Kingman	10.00
AU-10	Dave Righetti	10.00
AU-11	Dave Winfield/SP	60.00
AU-12	David Cone	10.00
AU-14	Dock Ellis	10.00
AU-15	Don Baylor/SP	25.00
AU-16	Don Larsen/SP	40.00
AU-17	Don Mattingly/SP	85.00
AU-18	Dwight Gooden	15.00
AU-19	Ed Figueroa	10.00
AU-20	Joe Torre/SP	125.00
AU-21	Darryl Strawberry	20.00
AU-23	Gaylord Perry	20.00
AU-24	Phil Linz	10.00
AU-25	Gil McDougald	15.00
AU-26	Rich "Goose" Gossage	20.00
AU-27	Graig Nettles	15.00
AU-28	Hank Bauer	15.00
AU-29	Jack Clark	15.00
AU-31	Jim Abbott	15.00
AU-32	Jim Bouton	15.00
AU-33	Jim Kaat	15.00
AU-34	Jim Leyritz/SP	25.00
AU-35	Jim Wynn	10.00
AU-36	Jimmy Key	10.00
AU-37	Joe Niekro	10.00
AU-38	Joe Pepitone	15.00
AU-39	John Wetteland/SP	20.00
AU-40	Ken Griffey Sr.	12.00
AU-42	Kevin Maas	10.00
AU-43	Lindy McDaniel	10.00
AU-44	Lou Piniella/SP	35.00
AU-45	Luis Tiant	20.00
AU-46	Mel Stottlemyre	15.00
AU-47	Mickey Rivers	15.00
AU-48	Oscar Gamble	15.00
AU-49	Pat Dobson	15.00
AU-50	Paul O'Neill/SP	40.00
AU-51	Phil Niekro	15.00
AU-52	Phil Rizzuto/SP	75.00
AU-53	Doc Medich	10.00
AU-54	Rick Cerone	15.00
AU-55	Ron Blomberg	10.00
AU-56	Ron Guidry	25.00
AU-57	Roy White	12.00
AU-58	Rudy May	10.00
AU-59	Sam McDowell	10.00
AU-60	Sparky Lyle	12.00
AU-61	Steve Balboni	10.00
AU-62	Steve Sax	10.00
AU-63	Jerry Coleman	15.00
AU-64	Tom Tresh	15.00
AU-65	Tommy John	15.00
AU-66	Tony Kubek/SP	400.00
AU-67	Wade Boggs/SP	60.00
AU-68	Whitey Ford/SP	60.00
AU-69	Willie Randolph/SP	25.00
AU-70	Yogi Berra/SP	75.00

Classic Scripts Dual Auto

		NM/M
Production 100 Sets		
SC	Bill "Moose" Skowron, Bob Cerv	50.00
MP	Bobby Murcer, Lou Piniella	65.00
CB	Chris Chambliss, Ron Blomberg	50.00
BN	Clete Boyer, Graig Nettles	50.00
RC	Dave Righetti, Rick Cerone	60.00
ED	Dock Ellis, Pat Dobson	70.00
BG	Don Baylor, Ken Griffey Sr.	65.00
MW	Don Mattingly, Dave Winfield	150.00
FG	Ed Figueroa, Ron Guidry	60.00
MB	Bobby Murcer, Hank Bauer	75.00
GL	Rich "Goose" Gossage, Sparky Lyle	50.00
NB	Graig Nettles, Wade Boggs	80.00
KJ	Jim Kaat, Tommy John	60.00
KA	Jimmy Key, Jim Abbott	50.00
PS	Joe Pepitone, Bill "Moose" Skowron	50.00
MM	Kevin Maas, Don Mattingly	100.00
RW	Mickey Rivers, Roy White	50.00
OL	Paul O'Neil, Jim Leyritz	75.00
RM	Phil Rizzuto, Gil McDougald	100.00
SD	Steve Sax, Brian Doyle	40.00
KR	Tony Kubek, Bobby Richardson	100.00
FL	Whitey Ford, Don Larsen	125.00
BL	Yogi Berra, Don Larsen	150.00
BH	Yogi Berra, Joe Torre	100.00
BF	Yogi Berra, Whitey Ford	150.00
WM	Bobby Murcer, Roy White	75.00
DN	Bucky Dent, Graig Nettles	50.00
CN	Chris Chambliss, Graig Nettles	50.00
CL	David Cone, Don Larsen	100.00
MC	Don Mattingly, Jack Clark	85.00
BM	Don Mattingly, Wade Boggs	150.00
SG	Darryl Strawberry, Dwight Gooden	75.00
CG	David Cone, Dwight Gooden	70.00

Classic Scripts Triple Auto

No Pricing
Production 20 Sets

Classic Scripts Single Auto

		NM/M
Common Autograph:		10.00
Inserted 1:8		
AU-1	Bill "Moose" Skowron	15.00
AU-2	Bob Cerv	10.00
AU-3	Bobby Murcer/SP	60.00
AU-4	Bobby Richardson	15.00
AU-5	Brian Doyle	10.00
AU-6	Bucky Dent	10.00
AU-7	Chris Chambliss	12.00
AU-8	Clete Boyer	15.00
AU-9	Dave Kingman	10.00
AU-10	Dave Righetti	10.00
AU-11	Dave Winfield/SP	60.00
AU-12	David Cone	10.00
AU-14	Dock Ellis	10.00
AU-15	Don Baylor/SP	25.00
AU-16	Don Larsen/SP	40.00
AU-17	Don Mattingly/SP	85.00
AU-18	Dwight Gooden	15.00
AU-19	Ed Figueroa	10.00
AU-20	Joe Torre/SP	125.00
AU-21	Darryl Strawberry	20.00
AU-23	Gaylord Perry	20.00
AU-24	Phil Linz	10.00
AU-25	Gil McDougald	15.00
AU-26	Rich "Goose" Gossage	20.00
AU-27	Graig Nettles	15.00
AU-28	Hank Bauer	15.00
AU-29	Jack Clark	15.00
AU-31	Jim Abbott	15.00
AU-32	Jim Bouton	15.00
AU-33	Jim Kaat	15.00
AU-34	Jim Leyritz/SP	25.00
AU-35	Jim Wynn	10.00
AU-36	Jimmy Key	10.00
AU-37	Joe Niekro	10.00
AU-38	Joe Pepitone	15.00
AU-39	John Wetteland/SP	20.00
AU-40	Ken Griffey Sr.	12.00
AU-42	Kevin Maas	10.00
AU-43	Lindy McDaniel	10.00
AU-44	Lou Piniella/SP	35.00
AU-45	Luis Tiant	20.00
AU-46	Mel Stottlemyre	15.00
AU-47	Mickey Rivers	15.00
AU-48	Oscar Gamble	15.00
AU-49	Pat Dobson	15.00
AU-50	Paul O'Neill/SP	40.00
AU-51	Phil Niekro	15.00
AU-52	Phil Rizzuto/SP	75.00
AU-53	Doc Medich	10.00
AU-54	Rick Cerone	15.00
AU-55	Ron Blomberg	10.00
AU-56	Ron Guidry	25.00
AU-57	Roy White	12.00
AU-58	Rudy May	10.00
AU-59	Sam McDowell	10.00
AU-60	Sparky Lyle	12.00
AU-61	Steve Balboni	10.00
AU-62	Steve Sax	10.00
AU-63	Jerry Coleman	15.00
AU-64	Tom Tresh	15.00
AU-65	Tommy John	15.00
AU-66	Tony Kubek/SP	400.00
AU-67	Wade Boggs/SP	60.00
AU-68	Whitey Ford/SP	60.00
AU-69	Willie Randolph/SP	25.00
AU-70	Yogi Berra/SP	75.00

Classic Scripts Dual Auto

		NM/M
Production 100 Sets		
SC	Bill "Moose" Skowron, Bob Cerv	50.00
MP	Bobby Murcer, Lou Piniella	65.00
CB	Chris Chambliss, Ron Blomberg	50.00
BN	Clete Boyer, Graig Nettles	50.00
RC	Dave Righetti, Rick Cerone	60.00
ED	Dock Ellis, Pat Dobson	70.00
BG	Don Baylor, Ken Griffey Sr.	65.00
MW	Don Mattingly, Dave Winfield	150.00
FG	Ed Figueroa, Ron Guidry	60.00
MB	Bobby Murcer, Hank Bauer	75.00
GL	Rich "Goose" Gossage, Sparky Lyle	50.00
NB	Graig Nettles, Wade Boggs	80.00
KJ	Jim Kaat, Tommy John	60.00
KA	Jimmy Key, Jim Abbott	50.00
PS	Joe Pepitone, Bill "Moose" Skowron	50.00
MM	Kevin Maas, Don Mattingly	100.00
RW	Mickey Rivers, Roy White	50.00
OL	Paul O'Neil, Jim Leyritz	75.00
RM	Phil Rizzuto, Gil McDougald	100.00
SD	Steve Sax, Brian Doyle	40.00
KR	Tony Kubek, Bobby Richardson	100.00
FL	Whitey Ford, Don Larsen	125.00
BL	Yogi Berra, Don Larsen	150.00
BH	Yogi Berra, Joe Torre	100.00
BF	Yogi Berra, Whitey Ford	150.00
WM	Bobby Murcer, Roy White	75.00
DN	Bucky Dent, Graig Nettles	50.00
CN	Chris Chambliss, Graig Nettles	50.00
CL	David Cone, Don Larsen	100.00
MC	Don Mattingly, Jack Clark	85.00
BM	Don Mattingly, Wade Boggs	150.00
SG	Darryl Strawberry, Dwight Gooden	75.00
CG	David Cone, Dwight Gooden	70.00

Classic Scripts Triple Auto

No Pricing
Production 20 Sets

Classic Scripts Quad Auto

No Pricing
Production 10 Sets

Mitchell & Ness Pennant

		NM/M
Inserted 1:Box		
Cards:		.3X
P2	1927 World Series/96	25.00
P3	1928 World Series/96	25.00
P4	1932 World Series/96	25.00
P6	1937 World Series/96	25.00
P8	1939 World Series/96	25.00
P10	1943 World Series/97	25.00
P11	1947 World Series/97	25.00
P13	1950 World Series/97	25.00
P15	1952 World Series/97	25.00
P17	1956 World Series/97	25.00
P18	1958 World Series/97	25.00
P23	1996 World Series/99	25.00
P24	1998 World Series/99	25.00
P25	1999 World Series/99	25.00
P26	2000 World Series/100	25.00
MM57	Mickey Mantle - 1957 MVP/97	30.00
MM62	Mickey Mantle - 1962 MVP/98	30.00

Mitchell & Ness Pennant Card

		NM/M
Inserted 1:Box		
P2	1927 World Series/1,927	5.00
P3	1928 World Series/1,928	5.00
P4	1932 World Series/1,932	5.00
P5	1936 World Series/36	10.00
P6	1937 World Series/1,937	5.00
P7	1938 World Series/38	10.00
P8	1939 World Series/1,939	5.00
P9	1941 World Series/41	10.00
P10	1943 World Series/1,943	5.00
P11	1947 World Series/1,947	5.00
P12	1949 World Series/49	10.00
P13	1950 World Series/1,950	5.00
P14	1951 World Series/51	10.00
P15	1952 World Series/1,952	5.00
P16	1953 World Series/53	10.00
P17	1956 World Series/1,956	5.00
P18	1958 World Series/1,958	5.00
P19	1961 World Series/61	10.00
P20	1962 World Series/62	10.00
P21	1977 World Series/77	8.00
P22	1978 World Series/78	8.00
P23	1996 World Series/1,996	5.00
P24	1998 World Series/1,998	5.00
P25	1999 World Series/1,999	5.00
P26	2000 World Series/2,000	5.00
MM57	Mickey Mantle - 1957 MVP/1,957	8.00
MM62	Mickey Mantle - 1962 MVP/1,962	8.00

Mitchell & Ness Jersey Redempt

		NM/M
Inserted 1:384		
Production 40-99		
MNJ1	Babe Ruth/40	350.00
MNJ2	Bill Dickey/75	120.00
MNJ3	Billy Martin/99	150.00
MNJ4	Bobby Murcer/99	100.00
MNJ5	Bucky Dent/92	100.00
MNJ6	Casey Stengel/65	120.00
MNJ7	"Catfish" Hunter/92	120.00
MNJ8	Chris Chambliss/99	80.00
MNJ9	Don Larsen/75	120.00
MNJ10	Don Mattingly/92	150.00
MNJ11	Elston Howard/88	100.00
MNJ12	Rich "Goose" Gossage/92	100.00
MNJ13	Graig Nettles/99	100.00
MNJ14	Joe DiMaggio/55	200.00
MNJ15	Lefty Gomez/81	120.00
MNJ16	Lou Gehrig/40	200.00
MNJ17	Lou Piniella/92	120.00
MNJ18	Mickey Mantle/50	275.00
MNJ19	Bill "Moose" Skowron/85	125.00
MNJ20	Phil Rizzuto/40	150.00
MNJ21	Roy White/50	100.00
MNJ22	Roger Maris/92	200.00
MNJ23	Ron Guidry/99	100.00
MNJ24	Sparky Lyle/99	100.00
MNJ25	Thurman Munson/91	200.00
MNJ26	Tony Kubek/75	150.00
MNJ27	Tony Lazzeri/79	120.00
MNJ28	Whitey Ford/43	180.00
MNJ29	Willie Randolph/92	100.00
MNJ30	Yogi Berra/50	200.00

Gravity Games Cleveland Indians

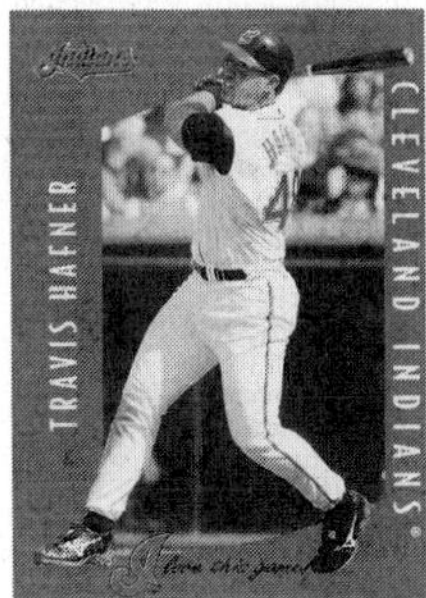

In conjunction with the Gravity Games held September 15-19 in Cleveland, Upper Deck created this team set. Cards were distributed in team-logoed foil packs containing four player cards and a header card. Fronts are bordered in red with game action photos. Backs have a close-up from the front photo, personal data, career highlights, 2003 and lifetime stats.

		NM/M
Complete Set (12):		7.50
Common Player:		.50
1	C.C. Sabathia	.65
2	Travis Hafner	.75
3	Casey Blake	.75
4	Matt Lawton	.50
5	Jason Davis	.50
6	Ben Broussard	.50
7	Omar Vizquel	.50
8	Cliff Lee	.50
9	Ronnie Belliard	.50
10	Jody Gerut	.75
11	Victor Martinez	1.00
12	Coco Crisp	1.00
---	Header Card	.05

Sunkist

Photos of six former major leaguers in their Little League days are featured on this set. Five million of the cards were inserted into bags of oranges to help promote the fruit company's sponsorship of the youth program.

		NM/M
Complete Set (6):		6.00
Common Player:		.50
1	Rollie Fingers	1.00
2	Gary Carter	2.00
3	Mark McGwire	3.00
4	Mickey Morandini	.50
5	Paul O'Neill	.50
6	Dave Steib	.50

2005 Upper Deck

		NM/M
Complete Set (500):		75.00
Common Player:		.15
Common (211-250):		.50
Hobby Pack (8):		3.00
Hobby Box (24):		65.00
1	Casey Kotchman	.15
2	Chone Figgins	.15
3	David Eckstein	.15
4	Jarrod Washburn	.15
5	Robb Quinlan	.15
6	Troy Glaus	.25
7	Vladimir Guerrero	.75
8	Brandon Webb	.15
9	Danny Bautista	.15
10	Luis Gonzalez	.15
11	Matt Kata	.15
12	Randy Johnson	.75
13	Robby Hammock	.15
14	Shea Hillenbrand	.15
15	Adam LaRoche	.15
16	Andruw Jones	.25
17	Horacio Ramirez	.15
18	John Smoltz	.25
19	Johnny Estrada	.15
20	Mike Hampton	.15
21	Rafael Furcal	.15
22	Brian Roberts	.15
23	Javy Lopez	.25
24	Jay Gibbons	.15
25	Jorge Julio	.15
26	Melvin Mora	.15
27	Miguel Tejada	.25
28	Rafael Palmeiro	.50
29	Derek Lowe	.25
30	Jason Varitek	.25
31	Kevin Youkilis	.15
32	Manny Ramirez	.75
33	Curt Schilling	.75
34	Pedro Martinez	.75
35	Trot Nixon	.15
36	Corey Patterson	.25
37	Derrek Lee	.25
38	LaTroy Hawkins	.15
39	Mark Prior	.75
40	Matt Clement	.15
41	Moises Alou	.25
42	Sammy Sosa	1.50
43	Aaron Rowand	.15
44	Carlos Lee	.15
45	Jose Valentin	.15
46	Juan Uribe	.15
47	Magglio Ordonez	.25
48	Mark Buehrle	.15
49	Paul Konerko	.25
50	Adam Dunn	.50
51	Barry Larkin	.25
52	D'Angelo Jimenez	.15
53	Danny Graves	.15
54	Paul Wilson	.15
55	Sean Casey	.25
56	Wily Mo Pena	.25
57	Ben Broussard	.15
58	C.C. Sabathia	.15
59	Casey Blake	.15
60	Cliff Lee	.15
61	Matt Lawton	.15
62	Omar Vizquel	.15
63	Victor Martinez	.15
64	Charles Johnson	.15
65	Joe Kennedy	.15
66	Jeromy Burnitz	.15
67	Matt Holliday	.50
68	Preston Wilson	.15
69	Royce Clayton	.15
70	Shawn Estes	.15
71	Bobby Higginson	.15
72	Brandon Inge	.15
73	Carlos Guillen	.15
74	Dmitri Young	.15
75	Eric Munson	.15
76	Jeremy Bonderman	.15
77	Ugueth Urbina	.15
78	Josh Beckett	.40
79	Dontrelle Willis	.15
80	Jeff Conine	.15
81	Juan Pierre	.15
82	Luis Castillo	.15
83	Miguel Cabrera	.75
84	Mike Lowell	.25
85	Andy Pettitte	.25
86	Brad Lidge	.15
87	Carlos Beltran	.50
88	Craig Biggio	.25
89	Jeff Bagwell	.50
90	Roger Clemens	1.50
91	Roy Oswalt	.25
92	Benito Santiago	.15
93	Jeremy Affeldt	.15
94	Juan Gonzalez	.25
95	Ken Harvey	.15
96	Mike MacDougal	.15
97	Mike Sweeney	.15
98	Zack Greinke	.15
99	Adrian Beltre	.40
100	Alex Cora	.15
101	Cesar Izturis	.15
102	Eric Gagne	.40
103	Kazuhisa Ishii	.15
104	Milton Bradley	.15
105	Shawn Green	.25
106	Danny Kolb	.15
107	Ben Sheets	.25
108	Brooks Kieschnick	.15
109	Craig Counsell	.15
110	Geoff Jenkins	.15
111	Lyle Overbay	.15
112	Scott Podsednik	.15
113	Corey Koskie	.15
114	Johan Santana	.40
115	Joe Mauer	.25
116	Justin Morneau	.25
117	Lew Ford	.15
118	Matt LeCroy	.15
119	Torii Hunter	.25
120	Brad Wilkerson	.15
121	Chad Cordero	.15
122	Livan Hernandez	.15
123	Jose Vidro	.15
124	Termel Sledge	.15
125	Tony Batista	.15
126	Zach Day	.15
127	Al Leiter	.25
128	Jae Weong Seo	.15
129	Jose Reyes	.40
130	Kazuo Matsui	.15
131	Mike Piazza	1.00
132	Todd Zeile	.15
133	Cliff Floyd	.15
134	Alex Rodriguez	2.00
135	Derek Jeter	2.00
136	Gary Sheffield	.40
137	Hideki Matsui	1.50
138	Jason Giambi	.25
139	Jorge Posada	.25
140	Mike Mussina	.40
141	Barry Zito	.25
142	Bobby Crosby	.25
143	Octavio Dotel	.15
144	Eric Chavez	.25
145	Jermaine Dye	.15
146	Mark Kotsay	.15
147	Tim Hudson	.25
148	Billy Wagner	.15
149	Bobby Abreu	.25
150	David Bell	.15
151	Jim Thome	.50
152	Jimmy Rollins	.25
153	Mike Lieberthal	.15
154	Randy Wolf	.15
155	Craig Wilson	.15
156	Daryle Ward	.15
157	Jack Wilson	.15
158	Jason Kendall	.15
159	Kip Wells	.15
160	Oliver Perez	.15
161	Robert Mackowiak	.15
162	Brian Giles	.25
163	Brian Lawrence	.15
164	David Wells	.15
165	Jay Payton	.15
166	Ryan Klesko	.15
167	Sean Burroughs	.15
168	Trevor Hoffman	.15
169	Brett Tomko	.15
170	J.T. Snow	.15
171	Jason Schmidt	.25
172	Kirk Rueter	.15
173	A.J. Pierzynski	.15
174	Pedro Feliz	.15
175	Ray Durham	.15
176	Eddie Guardado	.15
177	Edgar Martinez	.15
178	Ichiro Suzuki	1.50
179	Jamie Moyer	.15
180	Joel Pineiro	.15
181	Randy Winn	.15
182	Raul Ibanez	.15
183	Albert Pujols	2.00
184	Edgar Renteria	.25
185	Jason Isringhausen	.15
186	Jim Edmonds	.40
187	Matt Morris	.15
188	Reggie Sanders	.15
189	Tony Womack	.15
190	Aubrey Huff	.15
191	Danys Baez	.15
192	Carl Crawford	.15
193	Jose Cruz Jr.	.15
194	Rocco Baldelli	.15
195	Tino Martinez	.15
196	Dewon Brazelton	.15
197	Alfonso Soriano	.75
198	Brad Fullmer	.15
199	Gerald Laird	.15
200	Hank Blalock	.50
201	Laynce Nix	.15
202	Mark Teixeira	.25
203	Mike Young	.15
204	Alexis Rios	.15
205	Eric Hinske	.15
206	Miguel Batista	.15
207	Orlando Hudson	.15
208	Roy Halladay	.15
209	Ted Lilly	.15
210	Vernon Wells	.15
211	Aarom Baldiris	.50
212	B.J. Upton	1.00
213	Dallas McPherson	.50
214	Brian Dallimore	.50
215	Chris Oxspring	.50
216	Chris Shelton	.50
217	David Wright	1.50
218	Edwardo Sierra	.50
219	Fernando Nieve	.50
220	Frank Francisco	.50
221	Jeff Bennett	.50
222	Justin Lehr	.50
223	John Gall	.50
224	Jorge Sequea	.50
225	Justin Germano	.50
226	Kazuhito Tadano	.50
227	Kevin Cave	.50
228	Joe Blanton	.50
229	Luis Gonzalez	.50
230	Mike Wuertz	.50
231	Mike Rouse	.50
232	Nick Regilio	.50
233	Orlando Rodriguez	.50
234	Phil Stockman	.50
235	Ramon Ramirez	.50
236	Roberto Novoa	.50
237	Dioner Navarro	.50
238	Tim Bausher	.50
239	Logan Kensing	.50
240	Andy Green	.50
241	Brad Halsey	.50
242	Charles Thomas	.50
243	George Sherrill	.50
244	Jesse Crain	.50
245	Jimmy Serrano	.50
246	Joe Horgan	.50
247	Chris Young **RC**	1.50
248	Joey Gathright	.50
249	Gavin Floyd	.50
250	Ryan Howard	1.00
251	Lance Cormier	.15
252	Matt Treanor	.15
253	Jeff Francis	.15
254	Nick Swisher	.15
255	Scott Atchison	.15
256	Travis Blackley	.15
257	Travis Smith	.15
258	Yadier Molina	.15
259	Jeff Keppinger	.15
260	Scott Kazmir	1.00
261	Garret Anderson, Vladimir Guerrero	.40
262	Luis Gonzalez, Randy Johnson	.40
263	Andruw Jones, Chipper Jones	.40
264	Miguel Tejada, Rafael Palmeiro	.40
265	Curt Schilling, Manny Ramirez	.50
266	Mark Prior, Sammy Sosa	.75
267	Frank Thomas, Magglio Ordonez	.25
268	Barry Larkin, Ken Griffey Jr.	.75
269	C.C. Sabathia, Victor Martinez	.15
270	Jeromy Burnitz, Todd Helton	.25
271	Dmitri Young, Ivan Rodriguez	.40
272	Josh Beckett, Miguel Cabrera	.25
273	Jeff Bagwell, Roger Clemens	.75
274	Ken Harvey, Mike Sweeney	.15
275	Adrian Beltre, Eric Gagne	.25
276	Ben Sheets, Geoff Jenkins	.15
277	Joe Mauer, Torii Hunter	.15
278	Jose Vidro, Livan Hernandez	.15
279	Kazuo Matsui, Mike Piazza	.50
280	Alex Rodriguez, Derek Jeter	1.00
281	Eric Chavez, Tim Hudson	.15
282	Bobby Abreu, Jim Thome	.40
283	Craig Wilson, Jason Kendall	.15
284	Brian Giles, Phil Nevin	.15
285	A.J. Pierzynski, Jason Schmidt	.15
286	Bret Boone, Ichiro Suzuki	.75
287	Albert Pujols, Scott Rolen	.75
288	Aubrey Huff, Tino Martinez	.15
289	Hank Blalock, Mark Teixeira	.15
290	Carlos Delgado, Roy Halladay	.15
291	Vladimir Guerrero	.40
292	Curt Schilling	.25
293	Mark Prior	.40
294	Josh Beckett	.15
295	Roger Clemens	.75
296	Derek Jeter	.75
297	Eric Chavez	.15
298	Jim Thome	.25
299	Albert Pujols	.75
300	Hank Blalock	.25
301	Bartolo Colon	.25
302	Darin Erstad	.15
303	Garret Anderson	.25
304	Orlando Cabrera	.15
305	Steve Finley	.15
306	Javier Vazquez	.15
307	Russ Ortiz	.15
308	Chipper Jones	.75
309	Marcus Giles	.15
310	Raul Mondesi	.15
311	B.J. Ryan	.15
312	Luis Matos	.15
313	Sidney Ponson	.15
314	Bill Mueller	.15
315	David Ortiz	.75
316	Johnny Damon	.75
317	Keith Foulke	.15
318	Mark Bellhorn	.15
319	Wade Miller	.15
320	Aramis Ramirez	.40
321	Carlos Zambrano	.40
322	Greg Maddux	1.25
323	Kerry Wood	.50
324	Nomar Garciaparra	1.00
325	Todd Walker	.15
326	Frank Thomas	.50
327	Freddy Garcia	.15
328	Joe Crede	.15
329	Jose Contreras	.15
330	Orlando Hernandez	.15
331	Shingo Takatsu	.15
332	Austin Kearns	.15
333	Eric Milton	.15
334	Ken Griffey Jr.	1.00
335	Aaron Boone	.15
336	David Riske	.15
337	Jake Westbrook	.15
338	Kevin Millwood	.15
339	Travis Hafner	.25
340	Aaron Miles	.15
341	Jeff Baker	.15
342	Todd Helton	.50
343	Garrett Atkins	.15
344	Carlos Pena	.15
345	Ivan Rodriguez	.50
346	Rondell White	.15
347	Troy Percival	.15
348	A.J. Burnett	.25
349	Carlos Delgado	.40
350	Guillermo Mota	.15
351	Paul LoDuca	.15
352	Jason Lane	.15
353	Lance Berkman	.25
354	Angel Berroa	.15
355	David DeJesus	.15
356	Ruben Gotay	.15
357	Jose Lima	.15
358	Brad Penny	.15
359	J.D. Drew	.25
360	Jayson Werth	.15
361	Jeff Kent	.25
362	Odalis Perez	.15
363	Brady Clark	.15
364	Junior Spivey	.15
365	Rickie Weeks	.25
366	Jacque Jones	.15
367	Joe Nathan	.15
368	Nick Punto	.15
369	Shannon Stewart	.15
370	Doug Mientkiewicz	.15
371	Kris Benson	.15
372	Tom Glavine	.25
373	Victor Zambrano	.15
374	Bernie Williams	.40
375	Carl Pavano	.15
376	Jaret Wright	.15
377	Kevin Brown	.25
378	Mariano Rivera	.25
379	Dan Haren	.15
380	Eric Byrnes	.15
381	Erubiel Durazo	.15
382	Rich Harden	.25
383	Brett Myers	.15
384	Chase Utley	.25
385	Marlon Byrd	.15
386	Pat Burrell	.25
387	Placido Polanco	.15
388	Freddy Sanchez	.15
389	Jason Bay	.25
390	Josh Fogg	.15
391	Adam Eaton	.15
392	Jake Peavy	.40
393	Khalil Greene	.40
394	Mark Loretta	.15
395	Phil Nevin	.15
396	Ramon Hernandez	.15
397	Woody Williams	.15
398	Armando Benitez	.15
399	Edgardo Alfonzo	.15
400	Marquis Grissom	.15
401	Mike Matheny	.15
402	Richie Sexson	.40
403	Bret Boone	.15
404	Gil Meche	.15
405	Chris Carpenter	.40
406	Jeff Suppan	.15
407	Larry Walker	.40
408	Mark Grudzielanek	.15
409	Mark Mulder	.25
410	Scott Rolen	.75
411	Josh Phelps	.15
412	Jonny Gomes	.15
413	Francisco Cordero	.15
414	Kenny Rogers	.15
415	Richard Hidalgo	.15
416	David Bush	.15
417	Frank Catalanotto	.15
418	Gabe Gross	.15
419	Guillermo Quiroz	.15
420	Reed Johnson	.15
421	Cristian Guzman	.15
422	Esteban Loaiza	.15
423	Jose Guillen	.25
424	Nick Johnson	.25
425	Vinny Castilla	.15
426	Peter Orr **RC**	.50
427	Tadahito Iguchi **RC**	4.00
428	Jeff Baker	.15
429	Marcos Caryajal **RC**	.50
430	Justin Verlander **RC**	3.00
431	Luke Scott **RC**	1.00
432	Willy Taveras	.15
433	Ambiorix Burgos **RC**	.50
434	Andy Sisco	.15
435	Denny Bautista	.15
436	Mark Teahen	.15
437	Ervin Santana	.15
438	Dennis Houlton **RC**	.50
439	Philip Humber **RC**	1.00
440	Steve Schmoll **RC**	.50
441	J.J. Hardy	.15
442	Ambiorix Concepcion **RC**	.50
443	Dae-Sung Koo **RC**	.50
444	Andy Phillips	.15
445	Dan Meyer	.15
446	Huston Street	.15
447	Keiichi Yabu **RC**	.50
448	Jeff Niemann **RC**	1.00
449	Jeremy Reed	.15
450	Tony Blanco	.15
451	Albert Pujols	.75
452	Alex Rodriguez	.75
453	Curt Schilling	.40
454	Derek Jeter	.75
455	Greg Maddux	.50
456	Ichiro Suzuki	.50
457	Ivan Rodriguez	.25
458	Jeff Bagwell	.25
459	Jim Thome	.25
460	Ken Griffey Jr.	.50
461	Manny Ramirez	.40
462	Mike Mussina	.25
463	Mike Piazza	.40
464	Pedro Martinez	.40
465	Rafael Palmeiro	.25
466	Randy Johnson	.40
467	Roger Clemens	.75
468	Sammy Sosa	.50
469	Todd Helton	.25
470	Vladimir Guerrero	.40
471	Vladimir Guerrero	.25
472	Shawn Green	.15
473	John Smoltz	.15
474	Miguel Tejada	.25
475	Curt Schilling	.25
476	Mark Prior	.40
477	Frank Thomas	.25
478	Ken Griffey Jr.	.50
479	C.C. Sabathia	.15
480	Todd Helton	.25
481	Ivan Rodriguez	.25
482	Miguel Cabrera	.40
483	Roger Clemens	.50
484	Mike Sweeney	.15
485	Eric Gagne	.15
486	Ben Sheets	.15
487	Johan Santana	.25
488	Mike Piazza	.40
489	Derek Jeter	.50
490	Eric Chavez	.15
491	Jim Thome	.25
492	Craig Wilson	.15
493	Jake Peavy	.15
494	Jason Schmidt	.15
495	Ichiro Suzuki	.50
496	Albert Pujols	.50
497	Carl Crawford	.15
498	Mark Teixeira	.25
499	Vernon Wells	.15
500	Jose Vidro	.15

Emerald

Stars (301-500): 10-20X
Production 25 Sets
Exclusive to Series 2.

Blue

Stars (301-500): 4-6X
Production 150 Sets
Exclusive to Series 2.

Gold

Stars (301-500): 4-8X
Production 99 Sets
Exclusive to Series 2.

Platinum

No Pricing
Production Five Sets
Exclusive to Series 2.

American Flag

No Pricing
Production 15 Sets

Retro

Retro: 2-3X
One retro box per hobby case.

Lasting Impressions

No Pricing
Production One Set
One press plate per color.

Plates

No Pricing
Production one set per color.

Diamond Images - Wingfield Collection

		NM/M
Complete Set (20):		45.00
Common Player:		2.00
Inserted 1:9		
DI-1	Eddie Mathews	3.00
DI-2	Ernie Banks	4.00
DI-3	Joe DiMaggio	6.00

DI-4 Mickey Mantle 8.00
DI-5 Pee Wee Reese 2.00
DI-6 Phil Rizzuto 2.00
DI-7 Stan Musial 4.00
DI-8 Ted Williams 6.00
DI-9 Bob Feller 2.00
DI-10 Whitey Ford 2.00
DI-11 Willie Stargell 2.00
DI-12 Yogi Berra 2.00
DI-13 Roy Campanella 2.00
DI-14 Franklin D. Roosevelt 2.00
DI-15 Harry S. Truman 2.00
DI-16 Dwight D. Eisenhower 2.00
DI-17 John F. Kennedy 2.00
DI-18 Lyndon B. Johnson 2.00
DI-19 Richard Nixon 2.00
DI-20 Thurman Munson 3.00

Hall of Fame Plaques

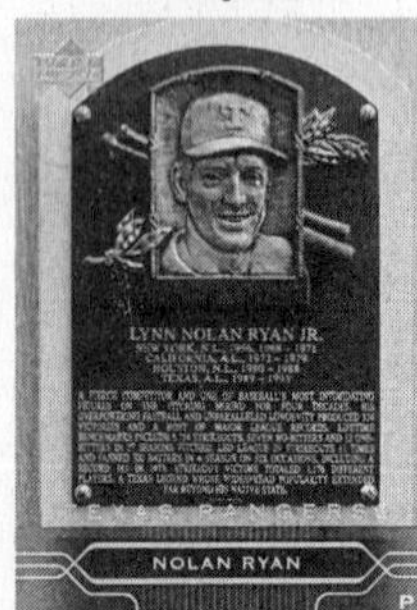

NM/M
Complete Set (10): 40.00
Common Player: 3.00
Inserted 1:36
SP-16 Ernie Banks 4.00
SP-17 Yogi Berra 4.00
SP-18 Whitey Ford 3.00
SP-19 Bob Gibson 3.00
SP-20 Willie McCovey 3.00
SP-21 Stan Musial 6.00
SP-22 Nolan Ryan 12.00
SP-23 Mike Schmidt 8.00
SP-24 Tom Seaver 4.00
SP-25 Robin Yount 4.00

Game Jersey

NM/M
Common Jersey: 5.00
Inserted 1:8
JB Jeff Bagwell/SP 8.00
CB Carlos Beltran/SP 8.00
AB Adrian Beltre 5.00
LB Lance Berkman 5.00
HB Hank Blalock 5.00
MC Miguel Cabrera 8.00
EC Eric Chavez 5.00
EG Eric Gagne 5.00
TG Troy Glaus 5.00
KG Ken Griffey Jr./SP 15.00
VG Vladimir Guerrero 8.00
HE Todd Helton 8.00
TH Tim Hudson 5.00
HU Torii Hunter 5.00
DJ Derek Jeter 25.00
RJ Randy Johnson/SP 10.00
CJ Chipper Jones 8.00
JK Jeff Kent 5.00
GM Greg Maddux/SP 10.00
PM Pedro Martinez 8.00
MM Mark Mulder 5.00
DO David Ortiz/SP 10.00
PI Mike Piazza 8.00
MP Mark Prior 8.00
AP Albert Pujols 20.00
MR Manny Ramirez/SP 10.00
IR Ivan Rodriguez 8.00
SR Scott Rolen 8.00
JS Johan Santana/SP 10.00
CS Curt Schilling 8.00
SM John Smoltz 8.00
AS Alfonso Soriano 8.00
SS Sammy Sosa 10.00
MT Mark Teixeira/SP 8.00
TE Miguel Tejada 8.00
FT Frank Thomas 8.00
JT Jim Thome/SP 8.00

KW Kerry Wood 8.00
DW David Wright 10.00

Game Patch

NM/M
Inserted 1:288
DJ Derek Jeter 75.00
CR Cal Ripken Jr. 75.00

Marquee Attractions

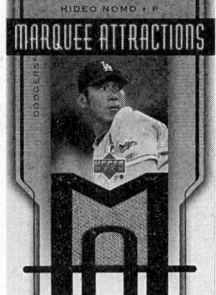

NM/M
Common Player: 4.00
Inserted 1:12
GA Garret Anderson 4.00
JB Jeff Bagwell 8.00
BE Josh Beckett 4.00
KB Kevin Brown 4.00
MC Miguel Cabrera 8.00
RC Roger Clemens 15.00
CD Carlos Delgado 4.00
AD Adam Dunn 8.00
EG Eric Gagne 6.00
JG Jason Giambi 4.00
BG Brian Giles 4.00
SG Shawn Green 4.00
KG Ken Griffey Jr. 12.00
VG Vladimir Guerrero 8.00
TH Todd Helton 8.00
HO Trevor Hoffman 4.00
DJ Derek Jeter 20.00
RJ Randy Johnson 10.00
AJ Andruw Jones 6.00
CJ Chipper Jones 8.00
GM Greg Maddux 10.00
PM Pedro Martinez 10.00
HM Hideki Matsui 30.00
KM Kazuo Matsui 8.00
JM Joe Mauer 8.00
HN Hideo Nomo 10.00
RO Roy Oswalt 4.00
PE Andy Pettitte 6.00
PI Mike Piazza 10.00
MP Mark Prior 6.00
AP Albert Pujols 15.00
IR Ivan Rodriguez 8.00
CS Curt Schilling 8.00
JS Jason Schmidt 6.00
SS Sammy Sosa 12.00
IS Ichiro Suzuki 25.00
MT Miguel Tejada 6.00
JT Jim Thome 8.00
BW Billy Wagner 4.00
DW Dontrelle Willis 4.00
PW Preston Wilson 4.00
KW Kerry Wood 8.00

Matinee Idols

NM/M
Common Player: 4.00
Inserted 1:12 Hobby
JB Jeff Bagwell 8.00
RB Rocco Baldelli 4.00
BE Josh Beckett 6.00
HB Hank Blalock 6.00
BB Bret Boone/SP 6.00
PB Pat Burrell 6.00
SB Sean Burroughs 4.00
EC Eric Chavez 6.00
RC Roger Clemens 15.00
CD Carlos Delgado 4.00
JE Jim Edmonds 6.00
JG Jason Giambi 4.00
TG Troy Glaus 4.00
KG Ken Griffey Jr. 12.00
VG Vladimir Guerrero 8.00
RH Roy Halladay 4.00
TH Todd Helton 8.00
HU Torii Hunter 4.00
DJ Derek Jeter 20.00
RJ Randy Johnson 8.00
CJ Chipper Jones 8.00
ML Mike Lowell 4.00
MM Mike Mussina 6.00
PI Mike Piazza 10.00

MP Mark Prior 6.00
CR Cal Ripken Jr. 25.00
SR Scott Rolen 8.00
NR Nolan Ryan 25.00
CS Curt Schilling 8.00
TS Tom Seaver 8.00
GS Gary Sheffield 6.00
SS Sammy Sosa 12.00
MT Mark Teixeira 6.00
JT Jim Thome 8.00
BW Billy Wagner 4.00
RW Rickie Weeks 4.00
VW Vernon Wells 4.00
DW Dontrelle Willis 4.00
KW Kerry Wood 8.00
BZ Barry Zito 4.00

Milestone Materials

NM/M
Common Jersey: 5.00
BA Jeff Bagwell 8.00
JB Jason Bay 5.00
CB Carlos Beltran 8.00
BC Bobby Crosby 5.00
EG Eric Gagne 5.00
KG Ken Griffey Jr. 15.00
VG Vladimir Guerrero 8.00
RJ Randy Johnson 8.00
GM Greg Maddux 10.00
DO David Ortiz 8.00
RP Rafael Palmeiro 8.00
JP Jake Peavy 8.00
AP Albert Pujols 20.00
MR Manny Ramirez 8.00
JS Johan Santana 8.00
CS Curt Schilling 8.00
MT Mark Teixeira 5.00
TE Miguel Tejada 8.00
JT Jim Thome 8.00

Origins

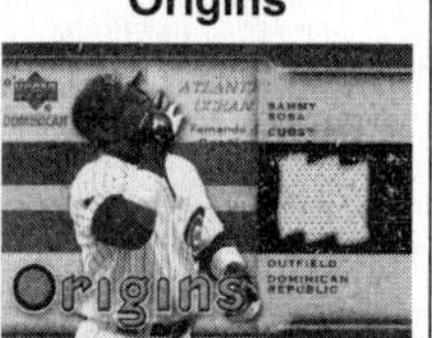

NM/M
Common Player: 4.00
Inserted 1:12 Hobby
Inserted 1:24 Retail
GA Garret Anderson 4.00
CB Carlos Beltran 10.00
AB Adrian Beltre 6.00
LB Lance Berkman 4.00
MC Miguel Cabrera 8.00
RF Rafael Furcal 4.00
EG Eric Gagne 6.00
BG Brian Giles 4.00
JG Juan Gonzalez 8.00
LG Luis Gonzalez 4.00
VG Vladimir Guerrero 8.00
TH Tim Hudson 4.00
AJ Andruw Jones 6.00
JK Jeff Kent 4.00
JL Javy Lopez 4.00
GM Greg Maddux 10.00
PM Pedro Martinez 10.00
HM Hideki Matsui 30.00
KM Kazuo Matsui 8.00
MM Mark Mulder 4.00
HN Hideo Nomo 10.00
MO Magglio Ordonez 4.00
RP Rafael Palmeiro 8.00
PE Jake Peavy 4.00
JP Jorge Posada 4.00
AP Albert Pujols 15.00
MR Manny Ramirez 8.00
JR Jose Reyes 4.00
IR Ivan Rodriguez 8.00
JS Jason Schmidt 4.00
RS Richie Sexson 4.00
AS Alfonso Soriano 8.00
SS Sammy Sosa 12.00
IS Ichiro Suzuki 25.00
MT Miguel Tejada 6.00
BU B.J. Upton 8.00
JV Javier Vazquez 4.00
PW Preston Wilson 4.00

Rewind to 1997 Jersey

NM/M
Common Jersey:
Inserted 1:288
JB Jeff Bagwell 25.00
WC Will Clark 20.00
KG Ken Griffey Jr. 40.00
VG Vladimir Guerrero 25.00
TG Tony Gwynn 30.00
DJ Derek Jeter 40.00
RJ Randy Johnson 25.00
AJ Andruw Jones 20.00
CJ Chipper Jones 30.00
GM Greg Maddux 40.00
PM Pedro Martinez 25.00
MP Mike Piazza 30.00
MR Manny Ramirez 30.00
CR Cal Ripken Jr. 40.00
IR Ivan Rodriguez 20.00
SR Scott Rolen 25.00
CS Curt Schilling 20.00
JS John Smoltz 25.00
FT Frank Thomas 25.00
JT Jim Thome 25.00

Signature Sensations

No Pricing
Production 15 Sets
Die-Cut: No Pricing
Production 10 Sets

Signature Stars

NM/M
Common Player:
Inserted 1:288 Hobby
CB Carlos Beltran/SP 40.00
HB Hank Blalock 25.00
MC Miguel Cabrera 35.00
BC Bobby Crosby 30.00
LF Lew Ford 10.00
KG Ken Griffey Jr. 80.00
JL Javy Lopez 15.00
JM Joe Mauer 20.00
OP Odalis Perez 20.00
CR Cal Ripken Jr./SP 180.00
BS Ben Sheets 15.00
DW Dontrelle Willis 20.00
KW Kerry Wood 25.00
DY Delmon Young 25.00

Signature Stars Retail

Inserted 1:480 Retail

Super Patch - Names

No Pricing
Cards are not serial numbered.

Super Patch - Numbers

No Pricing
Cards are not serial numbered.

Super Patch - Logos

No Pricing
Cards are not serial numbered.

World Series Heroes

NM/M
Complete Set (45): 20.00
Common Player: .25
Inserted 1:1 Retail
WS-1 Garret Anderson .50
WS-2 Troy Glaus .50
WS-3 Vladimir Guerrero 1.00
WS-4 Andruw Jones .50
WS-5 Chipper Jones 1.00
WS-6 Curt Schilling 1.00
WS-7 Keith Foulke .25
WS-8 Manny Ramirez .75
WS-9 Nomar Garciaparra 1.50
WS-10 Pedro Martinez 1.00
WS-11 Kerry Wood 1.00
WS-12 Mark Prior 1.00
WS-13 Sammy Sosa 2.00
WS-14 Frank Thomas .75
WS-15 Magglio Ordonez .25
WS-16 Dontrelle Willis .25
WS-17 Josh Beckett .50
WS-18 Miguel Cabrera .75
WS-19 Jeff Bagwell .75
WS-20 Lance Berkman .25
WS-21 Roger Clemens 2.00
WS-22 Eric Gagne .50
WS-23 Torii Hunter .50
WS-24 Mike Piazza 1.50
WS-25 Alex Rodriguez 2.00
WS-26 Derek Jeter 2.00
WS-27 Gary Sheffield .50
WS-28 Hideki Matsui 1.50
WS-29 Jason Giambi .50
WS-30 Jorge Posada .50
WS-31 Kevin Brown .25
WS-32 Mariano Rivera .50
WS-33 Mike Mussina .50
WS-34 Eric Chavez .25
WS-35 Mark Mulder .25
WS-36 Tim Hudson .25
WS-37 Billy Wagner .25
WS-38 Jim Thome .75
WS-39 Brian Giles .25
WS-40 Jason Schmidt .25
WS-41 Albert Pujols 2.00
WS-42 Scott Rolen .75
WS-43 Alfonso Soriano .75
WS-44 Hank Blalock .75
WS-45 Mark Teixeira .50

2004 Update Set

NM/M
Complete Set (50): 10.00
Common Player: .15
Inserted 1:Hobby Box
541 Alex Rodriguez 1.50
542 Roger Clemens 1.50
543 Andy Pettitte .25
544 Vladimir Guerrero .75
545 David Wells .15
546 Derek Lee .25
547 Carlos Beltran .50
548 Orlando Cabrera .25
549 Paul LoDuca .15
550 Dave Roberts .15
551 Guillermo Mota .15
552 Steve Finley .15
553 Juan Encarnacion .15
554 Larry Walker .50
555 Ty Wigginton .15
556 Doug Mientkiewicz .15
557 Roberto Alomar .40
558 B.J. Upton .50
559 Brad Penny .15
560 Hee Seop Choi .15
561 David Wright 1.00
562 Nomar Garciaparra 1.00
563 Felix Rodriguez .15
564 Victor Zambrano .15
565 Kris Benson .15
566 Aarom Baldiris .15
567 Joey Gathright .15
568 Charles Thomas .15
569 Brian Dallimore .15
570 Chris Oxspring .15
571 Chris Shelton .15
572 Dioner Navarro .25
573 Edwardo Sierra .15
574 Fernando Nieve .15
575 Frank Francisco .15
576 Jeff Bennett .15
577 Justin Lehr .15
578 John Gall .15
579 Jorge Sequea .15
580 Justin Germano .15
581 Kazuhito Tadano .15
582 Kevin Cave .15
583 Jesse Crain .15
584 Luis Gonzalez .15
585 Mike Wuertz .15
586 Orlando Rodriguez .15
587 Phil Stockman .15
588 Ramon Ramirez .15
589 Roberto Novoa .15
590 Scott Kazmir 1.50

2004 Update - Authentic Stars

NM/M
Common Player: 8.00
1:12 '04 Update Sets
Production 75 Sets
CB Carlos Beltran 15.00
LB Lance Berkman 8.00
JE Jim Edmonds 8.00
RF Rafael Furcal 8.00
HA Roy Halladay 8.00
RH Rich Harden 8.00
HU Tim Hudson 8.00
DJ Derek Jeter 35.00
AK Austin Kearns 8.00
HN Hideo Nomo 20.00
MO Magglio Ordonez 8.00
OS Roy Oswalt 8.00
RP Rafael Palmeiro 12.00
MR Manny Ramirez 15.00
JR Jose Reyes 8.00
SR Scott Rolen 15.00
TE Miguel Tejada 8.00
JT Jim Thome 12.00
WE Brandon Webb 8.00
VW Vernon Wells 8.00
PW Preston Wilson 8.00
KW Kerry Wood 8.00

2004 Update - Awesome Honors

NM/M
Common Player: 8.00
1:12 '04 Update Set
Production 75 Sets
BE Adrian Beltre 10.00
AB Angel Berroa 8.00
KB Kevin Brown 8.00
MC Miguel Cabrera 15.00
RC Roger Clemens 20.00
EG Eric Gagne 12.00
BG Brian Giles 8.00
DL Derrek Lee 8.00
KM Kazuo Matsui 20.00
JM Joe Mauer 10.00
PE Andy Pettitte 10.00
SP Scott Podsednik 8.00
AP Albert Pujols 25.00
IR Ivan Rodriguez 12.00
SC Curt Schilling 12.00
RS Richie Sexson 8.00
GS Gary Sheffield 8.00
AS Alfonso Soriano 15.00
VA Javier Vazquez 8.00

4,000 Strikeout Autographs

Production 50 Sets
Quad Signature: No Pricing
Production 10

4,000-Strikeout Commemorative

NM/M
Production 4,000
Steve Carlton, Nolan Ryan, Roger Clemens, Randy Johnson 12.00

2005 UD All-Star Classics

NM/M
Complete Set (100): 25.00
Common Player: .15
Pack (8): 3.00
Box (24): 60.00
1 Albert Pujols 2.00
2 Alex Rodriguez 1.50
3 Alfonso Soriano .75
4 Barry Zito .25
5 Bobby Abreu .40
6 Carlos Beltran .50
7 Carlos Delgado .40
8 Chipper Jones .75
9 Curt Schilling .75
10 David Ortiz .75
11 Derek Jeter 2.00
12 Edgar Renteria .25
13 Eric Gagne .25
14 Frank Thomas .50
15 Gary Sheffield .40
16 Greg Maddux 1.00
17 Hank Blalock .40
18 Hideki Matsui 1.50
19 Ichiro Suzuki 1.50
20 Ivan Rodriguez .50
21 Jason Schmidt .25
22 Jason Varitek .25
23 Jeff Kent .25
24 Jim Thome .75
25 Jorge Posada .25
26 Ken Griffey Jr. 1.00

27 Kerry Wood .75
28 Lance Berkman .25
29 Manny Ramirez .75
30 Mariano Rivera .40
31 Mark Mulder .25
32 Mark Prior .75
33 Miguel Cabrera .75
34 Miguel Tejada .50
35 Mike Piazza 1.00
36 Nomar Garciaparra 1.00
37 Pedro Martinez .75
38 Randy Johnson .75
39 Richie Sexson .25
40 Roger Clemens 2.00
41 Roy Halladay .25
42 Sammy Sosa 1.50
43 Scott Rolen .75
44 Sean Casey .25
45 Tim Hudson .25
46 Todd Helton .50
47 Tom Glavine .40
48 Torii Hunter .25
49 Troy Glaus .25
50 Vladimir Guerrero .75
51 Adrian Beltre .25
52 Alexis Rios .15
53 Aubrey Huff .15
54 Brandon Webb .25
55 Dallas McPherson .25
56 David Wright .75
57 Edwin Jackson .15
58 Grady Sizemore .40
59 Tadahito Iguchi **RC** 3.00
60 Jake Peavy .40
61 Jake Westbrook .15
62 Jason Bay .25
63 Jeff Francis .15
64 Jeremy Reed .15
65 Joe Mauer .40
66 Johan Santana .50
67 Jose Capellan .15
68 Jose Reyes .25
69 Justin Morneau .40
70 Mark Teixeira .40
71 Oliver Perez .25
72 Rich Harden .25
73 Rickie Weeks .25
74 Ryan Howard .25
75 Scott Kazmir .15
76 Al Kaline .75
77 Bill Mazeroski .25
78 Bob Feller .50
79 Bob Gibson .50
80 Brooks Robinson .75
81 Cal Ripken Jr. 3.00
82 Carlton Fisk .25
83 Eddie Murray .50
84 Gaylord Perry .25
85 Harmon Killebrew .75
86 Jim Palmer .50
87 Joe DiMaggio 1.50
88 Joe Morgan .25
89 Johnny Bench .75
90 Juan Marichal .25
91 Lou Brock .25
92 Mike Schmidt 1.00
93 Nolan Ryan 2.00
94 Ozzie Smith .75
95 Phil Niekro .25
96 Robin Yount .50
97 Rollie Fingers .25
98 Tom Seaver .50
99 Willie McCovey .50
100 Yogi Berra .75

Gold

Stars (1-100): 4-8X
Production 499 Sets

Box Scores

NM/M
Complete Set (20): 50.00
Common Player: 1.50
Inserted 1:24
1 Juan Marichal 2.00
2 Brooks Robinson 3.00
3 Tony Perez 1.50
4 Willie McCovey 2.00
5 Harmon Killebrew 3.00
6 Johnny Bench 3.00
7 Joe Morgan 1.50
8 Lou Brock 1.50
9 Jim Palmer 1.50
10 Mike Schmidt 5.00
11 Ozzie Smith 4.00
12 Roger Clemens 6.00
13 Cal Ripken Jr. 8.00
14 Ken Griffey Jr. 4.00
15 Greg Maddux 4.00
16 Alex Rodriguez 5.00
17 Derek Jeter 6.00
18 Johnny Damon 3.00
19 Garret Anderson 1.50
20 Alfonso Soriano 2.00

Matchups

NM/M
Complete Set (20): 40.00
Common Player: 1.50
Inserted 1:24
1 Hank Blalock 2.00
2 Curt Schilling 3.00
3 Manny Ramirez 3.00
4 Ken Griffey Jr. 4.00
5 Brooks Robinson 3.00
6 Harmon Killebrew 3.00
7 Carl Yastrzemski 4.00
8 Cal Ripken Jr. 8.00
9 Trevor Hoffman 1.50
10 Eric Gagne 2.00
11 Alfonso Soriano 2.00
12 David Ortiz 3.00
13 Andruw Jones 1.50
14 Garret Anderson 1.50
15 Magglio Ordonez 1.50
16 Derek Jeter 6.00
17 Chipper Jones 3.00
18 Roberto Alomar 2.00
19 Mike Piazza 3.00
20 Alex Rodriguez 5.00

Midsummer Classics

NM/M
Complete Set (20): 40.00
Common Player: 1.50
Inserted 1:24
1 Derek Jeter 6.00
2 Pedro Martinez 2.00
3 Mike Piazza 3.00
4 Randy Johnson 2.00
5 Gary Sheffield 2.00
6 Albert Pujols 6.00
7 David Ortiz 3.00
8 Manny Ramirez 3.00
9 Garret Anderson 1.50
10 Andruw Jones 1.50
11 Todd Helton 2.00
12 Paul Konerko 1.50
13 Alfonso Soriano 2.00
14 Magglio Ordonez 1.50
15 Cal Ripken Jr. 8.00
16 Ken Griffey Jr. 3.00
17 Harmon Killebrew 3.00
18 Mike Schmidt 5.00
19 Frank Thomas 2.00
20 Alex Rodriguez 5.00

Midsummer Swatches

NM/M
Common Player: 4.00
Inserted 1:12
Patches: No Pricing
Production 25 Sets
MA Moises Alou/Jsy 6.00
JB Jeff Bagwell/Jsy 6.00
CB Carlos Beltran/Jsy 8.00
CI Craig Biggio/Jsy 6.00
BB Bret Boone/Jsy 4.00
CD Carlos Delgado/Jsy 6.00
JE Jim Edmonds/Jsy 6.00
KF Keith Foulke/Jsy 6.00
RF Rafael Furcal/Jsy 4.00
EG Eric Gagne/Jsy 8.00
SG Shawn Green/Jsy 4.00
KG Ken Griffey Jr./Jsy 25.00
TH Todd Helton/Jsy 8.00
TI Torii Hunter/Jsy 6.00
AJ Andruw Jones/Pants 6.00
CJ Chipper Jones/Jsy 8.00
JK Jeff Kent/Jsy 4.00
RK Ryan Klesko 4.00
ML Matt Lawton/Jsy 4.00
PL Paul LoDuca/Jsy 4.00
JL Javy Lopez/Jsy 4.00
PM Pedro Martinez/Jsy 8.00
VM Victor Martinez/Jsy 4.00
DO David Ortiz/Pants 8.00
RP Rafael Palmeiro/Jsy 8.00
MP Mike Piazza/Jsy 15.00
ER Edgar Renteria/Jsy 6.00
CR Cal Ripken Jr./Pants 35.00
CC C.C. Sabathia/Jsy 4.00
SC Jason Schmidt/Jsy 4.00
BS Ben Sheets/Jsy 6.00
GS Gary Sheffield/Jsy 8.00
JS John Smoltz/Jsy 10.00
SS Sammy Sosa/Jsy 10.00
IS Ichiro Suzuki/Jsy 30.00
MS Mike Sweeney/Jsy 4.00
MT Miguel Tejada/Jsy 8.00
FT Frank Thomas/Jsy 8.00
JT Jim Thome/Jsy 8.00
OM Omar Vizquel/Jsy 6.00
WE David Wells/Jsy 4.00
DW Dontrelle Willis/Jsy 8.00

MVP's

NM/M
Complete Set (20): 45.00
Common Player: 1.00
Inserted 1:24
1 Alfonso Soriano 2.00
2 Ken Griffey Sr. 4.00
3 Brooks Robinson 3.00
4 Cal Ripken Jr. 8.00
5 Cal Ripken Jr. 8.00
6 Derek Jeter 6.00
7 Carl Yastrzemski 4.00
8 Garret Anderson 1.50
9 Jeff Conine 1.00
10 Joe Morgan 1.50
11 Juan Marichal 2.00
12 Julio Franco 1.00
13 Ken Griffey Jr. 4.00
14 Mike Piazza 3.00
15 Pedro Martinez 3.00
16 Roberto Alomar 2.00
17 Roger Clemens 6.00
18 Sandy Alomar Jr. 1.00
19 Tony Perez 1.50
20 Willie McCovey 2.00

Perennial All-Stars

NM/M
Complete Set (20): 40.00
Common Player: 2.00
Inserted 1:24
1 Albert Pujols 6.00
2 Alex Rodriguez 5.00
3 Alfonso Soriano 2.00
4 Curt Schilling 3.00
5 Derek Jeter 6.00
6 Eric Gagne 2.00
7 Greg Maddux 4.00
8 Ichiro Suzuki 5.00
9 Ivan Rodriguez 2.00
10 Jim Thome 2.00
11 Ken Griffey Jr. 4.00
12 Mariano Rivera 2.00
13 Miguel Tejada 2.00
14 Mike Piazza 3.00
15 Randy Johnson 2.00
16 Roger Clemens 6.00
17 Sammy Sosa 4.00
18 Scott Rolen 3.00
19 Todd Helton 2.00
20 Vladimir Guerrero 2.00

2005 Upper Deck Artifacts Promos

Each of the first 100 cards in Upper Deck Artifacts was issued in a foil-overprinted version with "UD PROMO" across the front. Cards were inserted into specially marked card shop and newsstand issues of Tuff Stuff magazine.

NM/M
Common Player: .50
Stars: 1.5X

2005 Upper Deck Artifacts

NM/M
Complete Set (200):
Common Player (1-100): .25
Common (101-150): 2.00
Production 1,350
Common (151-200): 2.00
Production 1,999
Pack (4): 10.00
Box (10): 90.00
1 Adam Dunn .75
2 Adrian Beltre .75
3 Albert Pujols 3.00
4 Alex Rodriguez 2.50
5 Alfonso Soriano 1.00
6 Andruw Jones .50
7 Andy Pettitte .50
8 Aramis Ramirez .50
9 Aubrey Huff .25
10 Barry Larkin .50
11 Ben Sheets .50
12 Bernie Williams .50
13 Bobby Abreu .50
14 Brad Penny .25
15 Bret Boone .25
16 Brian Giles .25
17 Carl Crawford .25
18 Carl Pavano .50
19 Carlos Beltran .75
20 Carlos Delgado .75
21 Carlos Guillen .25
22 Carlos Lee .50
23 Carlos Zambrano .50
24 Chipper Jones 1.00
25 Craig Biggio .50
26 Craig Wilson .25
27 Curt Schilling 1.00
28 David Ortiz 1.00
29 Derek Jeter 3.00
30 Eric Chavez .50
31 Eric Gagne .50
32 Frank Thomas .75
33 Garret Anderson .50
34 Gary Sheffield .50
35 Greg Maddux 1.50
36 Hank Blalock .75
37 Hideki Matsui 2.00
38 Ichiro Suzuki 2.50
39 Ivan Rodriguez .75
40 J.D. Drew .50
41 Jake Peavy .50
42 Jason Kendall .25
43 Jason Schmidt .50
44 Jeff Bagwell .75
45 Jeff Kent .50
46 Jim Edmonds .50
47 Jim Thome 1.00
48 Joe Mauer .75
49 Johan Santana .75
50 John Smoltz .50
51 Jose Reyes .50
52 Jose Vidro .25
53 Josh Beckett .50
54 Ken Griffey Jr. 1.50
55 Kerry Wood 1.00
56 Kevin Brown .25
57 Lance Berkman .50
58 Larry Walker .50
59 Livan Hernandez .25
60 Luis Gonzalez .25
61 Lyle Overbay .25
62 Magglio Ordonez .25
63 Manny Ramirez 1.00
64 Mark Mulder .50
65 Mark Prior 1.00
66 Mark Teixeira .50
67 Melvin Mora .25
68 Michael Young .25
69 Miguel Cabrera 1.00
70 Miguel Tejada .75
71 Mike Lowell .25
72 Mike Mussina .50
73 Mike Piazza 1.50
74 Mike Sweeney .25
75 Nomar Garciaparra 2.00
76 Oliver Perez .25
77 Paul Konerko .25
78 Pedro Martinez 1.00
79 Preston Wilson .25
80 Rafael Furcal .25
81 Rafael Palmeiro .75
82 Randy Johnson 1.00
83 Richie Sexson .50
84 Roger Clemens 3.00
85 Roy Halladay .50
86 Roy Oswalt .50
87 Sammy Sosa 2.00
88 Scott Podsednik .25
89 Scott Rolen 1.00
90 Shawn Green .25
91 Steve Finley .25
92 Tim Hudson .50
93 Todd Helton .75
94 Tom Glavine .50
95 Torii Hunter .25
96 Travis Hafner .25
97 Troy Glaus .50
98 Vernon Wells .25
99 Victor Martinez .50
100 Vladimir Guerrero 1.00
101 Aaron Rowand 2.00
102 Adam LaRoche 2.00
103 Adrian Gonzalez 2.00
104 Alexis Rios 2.00
105 Angel Guzman 2.00
106 B.J. Upton 3.00
107 Bobby Crosby 3.00
108 Bobby Madritsch 2.00
109 Brandon Claussen 2.00
110 Bucky Jacobsen 2.00
111 Casey Kotchman 2.00
112 Chad Cordero 2.00
113 Chase Utley 2.00
114 Chris Burke 2.00
115 Dallas McPherson 4.00
116 Daniel Cabrera 2.00
117 David DeJesus 2.00
118 David Wright 6.00
119 Eddy Rodriguez 2.00
120 Edwin Jackson 2.00
121 Gabe Gross 2.00
122 Garrett Atkins 2.00
123 Gavin Floyd 2.00
124 Gerald Laird 2.00
125 Guillermo Quiroz 2.00
126 J.D. Closser 2.00
127 Jason Bay 4.00
128 Jason Dubois 2.00
129 Jason Lane 2.00
130 Jayson Werth 2.00
131 Jeff Francis 2.00
132 Jesse Crain 2.00
133 Joe Blanton 2.00
134 Joe Mauer 4.00
135 Jose Capellan 2.00
136 Kevin Youkilis 2.00
137 Khalil Greene 3.00
138 Laynce Nix 2.00
139 Nick Swisher 2.00
140 Oliver Perez 2.00
141 Rickie Weeks 2.00
142 Robb Quinlan 2.00
143 Roman Colon 2.00
144 Ryan Howard 4.00
145 Ryan Wagner 2.00
146 Scott Kazmir 4.00
147 Scott Proctor 2.00
148 Wily Mo Pena 2.00
149 Yhency Brazoban 2.00
150 Zack Greinke 2.00
151 Al Kaline 5.00
152 Babe Ruth 8.00
153 Billy Williams 2.00
154 Bob Feller 3.00
155 Bob Gibson 4.00
156 Bob Lemon 2.00
157 Bobby Doerr 2.00
158 Brooks Robinson 4.00
159 Cal Ripken Jr. 10.00
160 Christy Mathewson 4.00
161 Cy Young 5.00
162 Dizzy Dean 5.00
163 Don Drysdale 2.00
164 Eddie Mathews 4.00
165 Enos Slaughter 2.00
166 Ernie Banks 5.00
167 Fergie Jenkins 2.00
168 George Sisler 2.00
169 Harmon Killebrew 4.00
170 Honus Wagner 5.00
171 Jackie Robinson 5.00
172 Jimmie Foxx 4.00
173 Joe DiMaggio 6.00
174 Joe Morgan 2.00
175 Juan Marichal 2.00
176 Lou Brock 2.00
177 Lou Gehrig 6.00
178 Luis Aparicio 2.00
179 Mel Ott 4.00
180 Mickey Cochrane 2.00
181 Mickey Mantle 10.00
182 Mike Schmidt 6.00
183 Nolan Ryan 8.00
184 Pee Wee Reese 2.00
185 Phil Rizzuto 2.00
186 Ralph Kiner 2.00
187 Rogers Hornsby 3.00
188 Roy Campanella 3.00
189 Satchel Paige 4.00
190 Stan Musial 5.00
191 Rick Ferrell 2.00
192 Thurman Munson 5.00
193 Tom Seaver 4.00
194 Ty Cobb 6.00
195 Walter Johnson 5.00
196 Warren Spahn 4.00
197 Whitey Ford 4.00
198 Willie McCovey 3.00
199 Willie Stargell 3.00
200 Yogi Berra 4.00

Rainbow Blue

Blue (1-100): 3-5X
Blue (101-200): 1-2X
Production 100 Sets

Rainbow Gold

Gold (1-100): 6-10X
Gold (101-200): 2-3X
Production 25 Sets

Rainbow Platinum

No Pricing
Production One Set

Rainbow Red

Red (1-100): 4-8X
Red (101-200): 1.5-3X
Production 50 Sets

AL/NL Artifacts

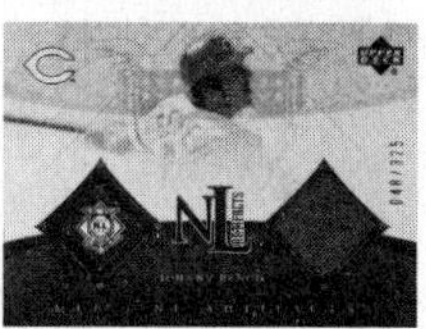

NM/M
Common Player: 4.00
Production 325 unless noted.
Rainbow: .75-1.5X
Production 99 Sets
BA Bobby Abreu/Jsy 6.00
JB Jason Bay/Jsy 6.00
CB Carlos Beltran/Jsy 8.00
AB Adrian Beltre/Jsy 6.00
BE Johnny Bench/Jsy 10.00
YB Yogi Berra/Pants 15.00
HB Hank Blalock/Jsy 8.00
BB Bert Blyleven/Jsy 6.00
WB Wade Boggs/Jsy 8.00
GB George Brett/Jsy 15.00
MC Miguel Cabrera/Jsy 10.00
RCA Rod Carew/Jsy 8.00
CA Steve Carlton/Jsy 6.00
SC Sean Casey/Jsy 4.00
OC Orlando Cepeda/Jsy/185 8.00
EC Eric Chavez/Jsy 4.00
WC Will Clark/Jsy/100 10.00
CN Roger Clemens/Jsy 15.00
BC Bobby Crosby/Jsy 6.00
AD Andre Dawson/Jsy 6.00
BD Bobby Doerr/Bat 6.00
BF Bob Feller/Pants 10.00
EG Eric Gagne/Jsy 8.00
BG Bob Gibson/Pants 10.00
GI Brian Giles/Jsy 4.00
MG Marcus Giles/Jsy 4.00
DG Dwight Gooden/Pants 6.00
MK Mark Grace/Jsy/175 8.00
KG Ken Griffey Jr./Jsy 15.00
GR Ken Griffey Sr./Jsy 4.00
TG Tony Gwynn/Jsy 10.00
TH Travis Hafner/Jsy 4.00
RH Rich Harden/Jsy 8.00
KHN Keith Hernandez/Bat 4.00
KHA Kent Hrbek/Jsy 4.00
AH Aubrey Huff/Jsy 4.00
DJ Derek Jeter/Jsy 20.00
RJ Randy Johnson/Jsy 10.00
JK Jim Kaat/Jsy 6.00
AK Al Kaline/Jsy 10.00
GK George Kell/Bat 6.00
HK Harmon Killebrew/Jsy 10.00
RK Ralph Kiner/Bat 6.00
DK Dave Kingman/Bat 4.00
CK Casey Kotchman/Jsy 4.00
DL Derrek Lee/Jsy 6.00
ML Mike Lowell/Jsy 4.00
SL Sparky Lyle/Pants 4.00
FL Fred Lynn/Bat 4.00

GM Greg Maddux/ Jsy/275 12.00
VM Victor Martinez/Jsy 6.00
MA Don Mattingly/Jsy 20.00
JM Joe Mauer/Jsy 10.00
WM Willie McCovey/Jsy 8.00
DMA Dallas McPherson/Jsy 8.00
PM Paul Molitor/Jsy 8.00
MM Mark Mulder/Jsy 6.00
DMN Dale Murphy/Jsy/150 8.00
GN Graig Nettles/Jsy 4.00
PN Phil Niekro/Jsy 4.00
LN Laynce Nix/Jsy 4.00
DO David Ortiz/Jsy 10.00
RO Roy Oswalt/Jsy 4.00
AO Akinori Otsuka/Jsy 4.00
JPA Jim Palmer/Jsy 8.00
CP Corey Patterson/Jsy 6.00
JPN Jake Peavy/Jsy 6.00
BPN Brad Penny/Jsy 4.00
RP Rico Petrocelli/Pants 8.00
SP Scott Podsednik/Jsy 4.00
BPA Boog Powell/Jsy 6.00
MP Mark Prior/Jsy 8.00
AP Albert Pujols/Jsy 25.00
JRN Jose Reyes/Jsy/250 8.00
JRA Jim Rice/Jsy 8.00
CR Cal Ripken Jr./Jsy 25.00
BR Brooks Robinson/Jsy 8.00
FR Frank Robinson/Jsy 8.00
SR Scott Rolen/Jsy 10.00
NR Nolan Ryan/Jsy 25.00
JSA Johan Santana/Jsy 10.00
JSN Jason Schmidt/Jsy 6.00
MS Mike Schmidt/Jsy 15.00
TS Tom Seaver/Jsy 8.00
BS Ben Sheets/Jsy 6.00
SM John Smoltz/Jsy 8.00
SU Bruce Sutter/Jsy 6.00
ST Shingo Takatsu/Jsy 6.00
MT Mark Teixeira/Jsy 8.00
BU B.J. Upton/Jsy 6.00
RW Rickie Weeks/Jsy 6.00
MW Maury Wills/Jsy 6.00
KW Kerry Wood/Jsy 8.00
DW David Wright/Jsy 10.00
CY Carl Yastrzemski/Jsy 15.00
MY Michael Young/Jsy 6.00
RY Robin Yount/Jsy 15.00
CZ Carlos Zambrano/Jsy 6.00

AL/NL Artifacts Signatures

NM/M
Production 30 Sets
Rare Artifacts: No Pricing
Production One Set
BA Bobby Abreu/ Jsy/Redemp. 20.00
JB Jason Bay/Jsy 30.00
CB Carlos Beltran/ Jsy/Redemp. 25.00
AB Adrian Beltre/Jsy 30.00
BE Johnny Bench/Jsy 65.00
YB Yogi Berra/Pants 60.00
HB Hank Blalock/Jsy 25.00
BB Bert Blyleven/Jsy 30.00
WB Wade Boggs/Jsy 50.00
GB George Brett/Jsy 120.00
MC Miguel Cabrera/Jsy 40.00
RCA Rod Carew/Jsy 40.00
SC Sean Casey/Jsy 30.00
CA Steve Carlton/Jsy 40.00
OC Orlando Cepeda/Jsy 35.00
EC Eric Chavez/Jsy 30.00
WC Will Clark/Jsy 50.00
RCN Roger Clemens/ Jsy/Redemp. 100.00
BC Bobby Crosby/ Jsy/Redemp. 20.00
AD Andre Dawson/Jsy 30.00
BD Bobby Doerr/Bat 35.00
BF Bob Feller/Pants 40.00
EG Eric Gagne/ Jsy/Redemp. 50.00
BG Bob Gibson/Pants 50.00
GI Brian Giles/Jsy 20.00
MG Marcus Giles/Jsy 20.00
DG Dwight Gooden/ Pants 30.00
MK Mark Grace/Jsy 50.00
KL Khalil Greene/Jsy 50.00
KG Ken Griffey Jr./Jsy 120.00
GR Ken Griffey Sr./Jsy 25.00
TG Tony Gwynn/Jsy 90.00
TH Travis Hafner/Jsy 20.00
RH Rich Harden/Jsy 40.00
KHN Keith Hernandez/Bat 20.00
KHA Kent Hrbek/Jsy 50.00
AH Aubrey Huff/Jsy 25.00
DJ Derek Jeter/Jsy 200.00
JK Jim Kaat/Jsy 25.00
AK Al Kaline/Jsy 50.00
GK George Kell/Bat 30.00
HK Harmon Killebrew/ Jsy 60.00
RK Ralph Kiner/Bat 50.00
DK Dave Kingman/Bat 25.00
CK Casey Kotchman/Jsy 25.00
DL Derrek Lee/Jsy 40.00
ML Mike Lowell/Jsy 20.00
SL Sparky Lyle/Pants 20.00
FL Fred Lynn/Bat 25.00
GM Greg Maddux/ Jsy/Redemp. 150.00
VM Victor Martinez/Jsy 30.00
MA Don Mattingly/Jsy 100.00
JM Joe Mauer/Jsy/ Redemp. 35.00
BM Bill Mazeroski/ Jsy/Redemp. 30.00
WM Willie McCovey/Jsy 50.00
DMA Dallas McPherson/ Jsy/Redemp. 30.00
PM Paul Molitor/Jsy 40.00
MM Mark Mulder/Jsy 25.00
DMN Dale Murphy/Jsy 35.00
GN Graig Nettles/Jsy 35.00
PN Phil Niekro/Jsy 25.00
LN Laynce Nix/Jsy 20.00
DO David Ortiz/Jsy 50.00
RO Roy Oswalt/Jsy 25.00
AO Akinori Otsuka/Jsy 40.00
JPA Jim Palmer/Jsy 40.00
CP Corey Patterson/ Jsy/Redemp. 30.00
JPN Jake Peavy/Jsy 50.00
BPN Brad Penny/Jsy 20.00
RP Rico Petrocelli/Pants 25.00
SP Scott Podsednik/Jsy 25.00
MP Mark Prior/Jsy 50.00
AP Albert Pujols/ Jsy/Redemp. 220.00
JRN Jose Reyes/ Jsy/Redemp. 40.00
JRA Jim Rice/Jsy 40.00
CR Cal Ripken Jr./Jsy 200.00
BR Brooks Robinson/Jsy 50.00
FR Frank Robinson/Jsy 40.00
SR Scott Rolen/ Jsy/Redemp. 75.00
NR Nolan Ryan/Jsy 125.00
JSA Johan Santana/ Jsy/Redemp. 65.00
JSN Jason Schmidt/Jsy 50.00
MS Mike Schmidt/Jsy 60.00
TS Tom Seaver/Jsy 50.00
BS Ben Sheets/ Jsy/Redemp. 30.00
SM John Smoltz/ Jsy/Redemp. 75.00
SU Bruce Sutter/Jsy 20.00
ST Shingo Takatsu/Jsy 50.00
MT Mark Teixeira/Jsy 45.00
BU B.J. Upton/Jsy 25.00
RW Rickie Weeks/Jsy 25.00
MW Maury Wills/Jsy 25.00
KW Kerry Wood/Jsy 50.00
DW David Wright/Jsy 65.00
CY Carl Yastrzemski/Jsy 85.00
MY Michael Young/ Jsy/Redemp. 25.00
RY Robin Yount/Jsy 75.00
CZ Carlos Zambrano/Jsy 35.00

Autofacts

NM/M
Production 15-699
Rainbow: No Pricing
Production One Set
JB Jason Bay/599 15.00
AB Adrian Beltre/ 75 Redemp. 25.00
BE Johnny Bench/15 75.00
HB Hank Blalock/25 35.00
GB George Brett/15 140.00
MI Miguel Cabrera/25 40.00
OC Orlando Cepeda/25 35.00
EC Eric Chavez/25 30.00
RC Rocky Colavito/75 75.00
BC Bobby Crosby/ 350 Redemp. 15.00
AD Andre Dawson/25 30.00
BF Bob Feller/25 40.00
SF Sid Fernandez/599 10.00
LD1 Lenny Dykstra/ Mets/599 10.00
LD2 Lenny Dykstra/ Phils/599 10.00
FR Bill Freehan/ 599 Redemp. 10.00
GI Marcus Giles/350 12.00
DG1 Dwight Gooden/ Mets/350 15.00
DG2 Dwight Gooden/ Yanks/350 15.00
GR Khalil Greene/599 25.00
JR Ken Griffey Jr./699 75.00
KG1 Ken Griffey Sr./ Reds/699 10.00
KG2 Ken Griffey Sr./ Yanks/699 10.00
TH Travis Hafner/599 12.00
RH Rich Harden/599 20.00
KH1 Keith Hernandez/ Mets/350 15.00
KH2 Keith Hernandez/ Cards/350 15.00
HO Ken Holtzman/599 10.00
BH Burt Hooton/599 8.00
HR Kent Hrbek/599 15.00
AH Aubrey Huff/350 8.00
DJ Derek Jeter/350 150.00
JK1 Jim Kaat Cards/458 15.00
JK2 Jim Kaat Twins/458 15.00
AK Al Kaline/15 80.00
DK Dave Kingman/75 25.00
CK Casey Kotchman/599 10.00
EK Ed Kranepool 12.00
JL Jim Lonborg/599 15.00
ML Mike Lowell/75 15.00
SL1 Sparky Lyle/Sox/599 8.00
SL2 Sparky Lyle/ Yanks/599 8.00
FL Fred Lynn/25 25.00
VM Victor Martinez/599 15.00
JM Joe Mauer/ 25 Redemp. 30.00
MC Dallas McPherson/ 599 Redemp. 20.00
DM Dale Murphy/75 25.00
GN Graig Nettles/75 25.00
PN1 Phil Niekro/Braves/75 20.00
PN2 Phil Niekro/Yanks/75 20.00
LN Laynce Nix/599 10.00
RO Roy Oswalt/350 15.00
AO Akinori Otsuka/599 25.00
JP Jim Palmer/25 35.00
CP Corey Patterson/ 75 Redemp. 25.00
JA Jake Peavy/75 30.00
BP Brad Penny/599 15.00
OP Oliver Perez/350 20.00
PE Jim Perry/599 10.00
RP Rico Petrocelli/599 15.00
SP Scott Podsednik/75 15.00
PO Boog Powell/350 15.00
MP Mark Prior/15 50.00
CR Cal Ripken Jr./15 200.00
BR Brooks Robinson/25 50.00
NR Nolan Ryan/15 175.00
JS Johan Santana/ 350 Redemp. 40.00
BS Ben Sheets/ 75 Redemp. 20.00
SU Bruce Sutter/350 12.00
ST Shingo Takatsu/599 20.00
MT Mark Teixeira/25 40.00
LT Luis Tiant/75 20.00
BU B.J. Upton/599 15.00
RW Rickie Weeks/75 15.00
KW Kerry Wood/15 50.00
DW David Wright/599 50.00
MY Michael Young/ 599 Redemp. 12.00

Dual Artifacts

NM/M
Production 99 Sets
Rainbow: 1-2X
Production 25 Sets
AB Bobby Abreu/Jsy, Carlos Beltran/Jsy 15.00
AD Adrian Beltre/Jsy, Dallas McPherson/ Jsy 15.00
AG Bobby Abreu/Jsy, Ken Griffey Jr./Jsy 15.00
BB George Brett/Jsy, Wade Boggs/Jsy 20.00
BC Adrian Beltre/Jsy, Eric Chavez/Jsy 8.00
BD Bob Gibson/Pants, Dwight Gooden/Pants 8.00
BE Bobby Crosby/Jsy, Eric Chavez/Jsy 10.00
BJ Brooks Robinson/Jsy, Jim Palmer/Jsy 20.00
BK Jason Bay/Jsy, Ralph Kiner/Bat 10.00
BM Brian Giles/Jsy, Marcus Giles/Jsy 8.00
BN Hank Blalock/Jsy, Laynce Nix/Jsy 8.00
BP Carlos Beltran/Jsy, Corey Patterson/Jsy 12.00
BR Ernie Banks/Pants, Frank Robinson/Jsy 20.00
BS Ben Sheets/Jsy, Scott Podsednik/Jsy 8.00
BY Hank Blalock/Jsy, Michael Young/Jsy 8.00
CB Jason Bay/Jsy, Bobby Crosby/Jsy 8.00
CC Miguel Cabrera/Jsy, Orlando Cepeda/Jsy 12.00
CG Dwight Gooden/Pants, Gary Carter/Jsy 10.00
CH Sean Casey/Jsy, Travis Hafner/Jsy 8.00
CK Harmon Killebrew/Jsy, Rod Carew/Jsy 25.00
CL Miguel Cabrera/Jsy, Mike Lowell/Jsy 10.00
CM Will Clark/Jsy, Willie McCovey/ Jsy/56 25.00
CN Eric Chavez/Jsy, Graig Nettles/Jsy 8.00
CO Roger Clemens/Jsy, Roy Oswalt/Jsy 15.00
CR Bobby Crosby/Jsy, Cal Ripken Jr./Jsy 40.00
DC Andre Dawson/Jsy, Orlando Cepeda/Jsy 10.00
DK Bobby Doerr/Bat, George Kell/Bat 10.00
FB Carlton Fisk/Jsy, Johnny Bench/Jsy 20.00
FW Bob Feller/Pants, Kerry Wood/Jsy 15.00
GB Brian Giles/Jsy, Jason Bay/Jsy 8.00
GC Ken Griffey Jr./Jsy, Sean Casey/Jsy 15.00
GG Ken Griffey Sr./Jsy, Ken Griffey Jr./Jsy 15.00
GK Ken Griffey Jr./Jsy, Ralph Kiner/Bat 20.00
GL Eric Gagne/Jsy, Sparky Lyle/Pants 10.00
GS Dwight Gooden/Pants, Tom Seaver/Jsy 15.00
HC Bobby Crosby/Jsy, Rich Harden/Jsy 8.00
HG Keith Hernandez/Bat, Mark Grace/Jsy 10.00
HH Aubrey Huff/Jsy, Travis Hafner/Jsy 8.00
HM Travis Hafner/Jsy, Victor Martinez/Jsy 8.00
HU Aubrey Huff/Jsy, B.J. Upton/Jsy 10.00
HW Harmon Killebrew/Jsy, Willie McCovey/ Jsy/44 25.00
JG Derek Jeter/Jsy, Khalil Greene/Jsy 35.00
JJ Joe Mauer/Jsy, Johan Santana/Jsy 15.00
JR Jim Rice/Jsy, Rico Petrocelli/Pants 8.00
JW Derek Jeter/Jsy, Maury Wills/Jsy 35.00
JY Johnny Bench/Jsy, Yogi Berra/Pants 25.00
KB Jim Kaat/Jsy, Bert Blyleven/Jsy 10.00
KC Jim Kaat/Jsy, Steve Carlton/Jsy 10.00
KD Keith Hernandez/Bat, Don Mattingly/Jsy 20.00
KK Al Kaline/Jsy, Ralph Kiner/Bat 15.00
KM Al Kaline/Jsy, Dale Murphy/Jsy 15.00
KN Jim Kaat/Jsy, Phil Niekro/Jsy 10.00
LC Derrek Lee/Jsy, Sean Casey/Jsy 10.00
LG Derrek Lee/Jsy, Mark Grace/Jsy 10.00
LP Fred Lynn/Bat, Rico Petrocelli/Pants 10.00
LR Fred Lynn/Bat, Jim Rice/Jsy 10.00
MC Don Mattingly/Jsy, Will Clark/Jsy 20.00
MD Bill Mazeroski/Jsy, Bobby Doerr/Bat 10.00
MH Mark Mulder/Jsy, Rich Harden/Jsy 10.00
MK Bill Mazeroski/Jsy, Ralph Kiner/Bat 20.00
MM Joe Mauer/Jsy, Victor Martinez/Jsy 8.00
MS Dale Murphy/Jsy, Mike Schmidt/Jsy 20.00
MW Paul Molitor/Jsy, Rickie Weeks/Jsy 15.00
NL Graig Nettles/Jsy, Sparky Lyle/Pants 15.00
NT Laynce Nix/Jsy, Mark Teixeira/Jsy 10.00
NY Laynce Nix/Jsy, Michael Young/Jsy 10.00
OF David Ortiz/Jsy, Carlton Fisk/Jsy 20.00
OG Akinori Otsuka/Jsy, Khalil Greene/Jsy 15.00
OP Akinori Otsuka/Jsy, Jake Peavy/Jsy 15.00
OT Akinori Otsuka/Jsy, Shingo Takatsu/Jsy 20.00
PD Andre Dawson/Jsy, Corey Patterson/Jsy 15.00
PG Brad Penny/Jsy, Eric Gagne/Jsy 10.00
PH Jake Peavy/Jsy, Rich Harden/Jsy 12.00
PP Boog Powell/Jsy, Jim Palmer/Jsy 15.00
PR Boog Powell/Jsy, Brooks Robinson/Jsy 20.00
PS Brad Penny/Jsy, Jason Schmidt/Jsy 8.00
RB Ernie Banks/Pants, Cal Ripken Jr./Jsy 40.00
RC Nolan Ryan/Jsy, Steve Carlton/Jsy 30.00
RJ Jose Reyes/Jsy, Rickie Weeks/Jsy 10.00
RP Frank Robinson/Jsy, Boog Powell/Jsy 25.00
RR Frank Robinson/Jsy, Brooks Robinson/Jsy 25.00
RW David Wright/Jsy, Scott Rolen/Jsy 15.00
SB Bert Blyleven/Jsy, Johan Santana/Jsy 15.00
SC Johan Santana/Jsy, Roger Clemens/Jsy 20.00
SF Ben Sheets/Jsy, Bob Feller/Pants 15.00
SG Bruce Sutter/Jsy, Eric Gagne/Jsy 15.00
SM Jason Schmidt/Jsy, Mark Mulder/Jsy 10.00
SO Ben Sheets/Jsy, Roy Oswalt/Jsy 10.00
SP Ben Sheets/Jsy, Brad Penny/Jsy 10.00
TH Mark Teixeira/Jsy, Travis Hafner/Jsy 10.00
TL Shingo Takatsu/Jsy, Sparky Lyle/Pants 10.00
TY Mark Teixeira/Jsy, Michael Young/Jsy 10.00
UJ B.J. Upton/Jsy, Derek Jeter/Jsy 30.00
WL David Wright/Jsy, Mike Lowell/Jsy 10.00
WR David Wright/Jsy, Jose Reyes/Jsy 10.00
YM Robin Yount/Jsy, Paul Molitor/Jsy 25.00
YP Carl Yastrzemski/Jsy, Rico Petrocelli/Pants 15.00
ZM Carlos Zambrano/Jsy, Greg Maddux/Jsy 15.00
ZP Carlos Zambrano/Jsy, Mark Prior/Jsy 10.00
ZW Carlos Zambrano/Jsy, Kerry Wood/Jsy 20.00

Dual Artifacts Bat

NM/M
Production 25 Sets
BC Josh Beckett, Miguel Cabrera 20.00
BW Josh Beckett, Kerry Wood 20.00
DR Carlos Delgado, Manny Ramirez 20.00
GC Ken Griffey Jr., Miguel Cabrera 30.00
GS Ken Griffey Sr., Ichiro Suzuki 80.00
JP Derek Jeter, Mike Piazza 50.00
JR Derek Jeter, Manny Ramirez 50.00
RG Manny Ramirez, Vladimir Guerrero 20.00
RJ Cal Ripken Jr., Derek Jeter 100.00
RT Cal Ripken Jr., Miguel Tejada 60.00
SG Ichiro Suzuki, Vladimir Guerrero 60.00
WP Kerry Wood, Mark Prior 25.00

Dual Artifacts Signatures

No Pricing
Production 10 Sets

MLB Apparel

NM/M
Production 325 unless noted.
Rainbow: 1-2X
Production 99 Sets
BA Bobby Abreu/Jsy 6.00
GA Garret Anderson/Jsy 6.00
JB Jason Bay/Jsy 6.00
CB Carlos Beltran/Jsy 8.00
AB Adrian Beltre/Jsy 6.00
BE Johnny Bench/Jsy 10.00
YB Yogi Berra/Pants 15.00
HB Hank Blalock/Jsy 8.00
BB Bert Blyleven/Jsy/150 8.00
WB Wade Boggs/Jsy 8.00
BO Bret Boone/Jsy 4.00
GB George Brett/Jsy 15.00
MI Miguel Cabrera/Jsy 10.00
RC Rod Carew/Jsy 8.00
CA Steve Carlton/Jsy 6.00
GC Gary Carter/Jsy 8.00
SC Sean Casey/Jsy 4.00
OC Orlando Cepeda/Jsy 8.00
EC Eric Chavez/Jsy 4.00
WC Will Clark/Jsy/100 10.00
CL Roger Clemens/Jsy 15.00
BC Bobby Crosby/Jsy 6.00
AD Andre Dawson/Jsy 6.00
BF Bob Feller/Pants 10.00
CF Carlton Fisk/R. Sox/ Jsy/175 10.00
CF1 Carlton Fisk/ W. Sox/Jsy/175 10.00
EG Eric Gagne/Jsy 8.00
BG Bob Gibson/Pants 10.00
GI Brian Giles/Jsy 4.00
GS Marcus Giles/Jsy 4.00
DG Dwight Gooden/Pants 6.00
MK Mark Grace/Jsy/175 8.00
KL Khalil Greene/Jsy 8.00
KG Ken Griffey Jr./Jsy 15.00
GR Ken Griffey Sr./Jsy 4.00
TG Tony Gwynn/Jsy 10.00
TH Travis Hafner/Jsy 4.00
RH Rich Harden/Jsy 8.00
KH Kent Hrbek/Jsy 4.00
HU Tim Hudson/Jsy 6.00
AH Aubrey Huff/Jsy 4.00
TO Torii Hunter/Jsy 4.00
DJ Derek Jeter/Jsy 20.00
JJ Jacque Jones/Jsy 4.00
JK Jim Kaat/Jsy 6.00
AK Al Kaline/Jsy 10.00
HK Harmon Killebrew/ Jsy 10.00
CK Casey Kotchman/Jsy 4.00
DL Derrek Lee/Jsy 6.00
ML Mike Lowell/Jsy 4.00
SL Sparky Lyle/Pants 4.00
VM Victor Martinez/Jsy 6.00
MA Don Mattingly/Jsy 20.00
JM Joe Mauer/Jsy 10.00
BM Bill Mazeroski/ Jsy/100 12.00
WM Willie McCovey/Jsy 8.00
MC Dallas McPherson/Jsy 8.00
PM Paul Molitor/Jsy 8.00
MM Mark Mulder/Jsy 6.00
DM Dale Murphy/Jsy/150 8.00
GN Graig Nettles/Jsy 4.00
PN Phil Niekro/Jsy 4.00
LN Laynce Nix/Jsy 4.00
DO David Ortiz/Jsy 10.00
RO Roy Oswalt/Jsy 4.00
AO Akinori Otsuka/Jsy 4.00
PA Jim Palmer/Jsy 8.00
CP Corey Patterson/Jsy 6.00
JP Jake Peavy/Jsy 6.00
PE Brad Penny/Jsy 4.00
RP Rico Petrocelli/Pants 8.00
SP Scott Podsednik/Jsy 4.00
BP Boog Powell/Jsy 6.00
MP Mark Prior/Jsy 8.00
RE Jose Reyes/Jsy 8.00
JR Jim Rice/Jsy 8.00
CR Cal Ripken Jr./Jsy 25.00
BR Brooks Robinson/Jsy 8.00
FR Frank Robinson/Jsy 8.00
SR Scott Rolen/Jsy 10.00
NR Nolan Ryan/Jsy 25.00
SA Johan Santana/Jsy 10.00
JS Jason Schmidt/Jsy 6.00
MS Mike Schmidt/Jsy 15.00
TS Tom Seaver/Jsy/300 8.00
BS Ben Sheets/Jsy 6.00
SM John Smoltz/Jsy 8.00
SU Bruce Sutter/Jsy 6.00
ST Shingo Takatsu/Jsy 6.00
MT Mark Teixeira/Jsy 8.00
BU B.J. Upton/Jsy 6.00
JV Jose Vidro/Jsy 4.00
RW Rickie Weeks/Jsy 6.00
MW Maury Wills/Jsy 6.00
KW Kerry Wood/Jsy 8.00
DW David Wright/Jsy 10.00
CY Carl Yastrzemski/Jsy 15.00
MY Michael Young/Jsy 6.00
RY Robin Yount/Jsy 15.00
CZ Carlos Zambrano/Jsy 6.00

MLB Apparel Autographs

NM/M
Production 30 Sets
Rare: No Pricing
Production One Set
BA Bobby Abreu/ Jsy/Redemp. 25.00
GA Garret Anderson/Jsy 20.00
JB Jason Bay/Jsy 30.00
CB Carlos Beltran/ Jsy/Redemp. 25.00
AB Adrian Beltre/Jsy 25.00
BE Johnny Bench/Jsy 65.00
YB Yogi Berra/Pants 60.00
HB Hank Blalock/Jsy 25.00
BB Bert Blyleven/Jsy 30.00
WB Wade Boggs/Jsy 50.00
BO Bret Boone/Jsy 20.00
GB George Brett/Jsy 100.00
MI Miguel Cabrera/Jsy 40.00
RC Rod Carew/Jsy 40.00
CA Steve Carlton/Jsy 30.00
GC Gary Carter/Jsy 30.00
SC Sean Casey/Jsy 30.00
OC Orlando Cepeda/Jsy 35.00
EC Eric Chavez/ Jsy/Redemp. 30.00
WC Will Clark/Jsy 50.00
CL Roger Clemens/ Jsy/Redemp. 120.00
BC Bobby Crosby/ Jsy/Redemp. 20.00
AD Andre Dawson/Jsy 30.00
BF Bob Feller/Pants 40.00
CF Carlton Fisk R. Sox/ Jsy 40.00
CF1 Carlton Fisk W. Sox/ Jsy 40.00
EG Eric Gagne/Jsy 30.00
BG Bob Gibson/Pants 50.00
GI Brian Giles/Jsy 20.00
GS Marcus Giles/Jsy 20.00

DG Dwight Gooden/Pants 30.00
MK Mark Grace/Jsy 40.00
KL Khalil Greene/Jsy 30.00
KG Ken Griffey Jr./Jsy 120.00
GR Ken Griffey Sr./Jsy 25.00
TG Tony Gwynn/Jsy 80.00
TH Travis Hafner/Jsy 25.00
RH Rich Harden/Jsy 30.00
KH Kent Hrbek/Jsy 50.00
HU Tim Hudson/Jsy 40.00
AH Aubrey Huff/Jsy 25.00
TO Torii Hunter/Jsy 25.00
DJ Derek Jeter/Jsy 200.00
JJ Jacque Jones/Jsy 20.00
JK Jim Kaat/Jsy 25.00
AK Al Kaline/Jsy 50.00
HK Harmon Killebrew/Jsy 60.00
CK Casey Kotchman/Jsy 25.00
DL Derrek Lee/Jsy 40.00
ML Mike Lowell/Jsy 20.00
SL Sparky Lyle/Pants 20.00
VM Victor Martinez/Jsy 25.00
MA Don Mattingly/Jsy 100.00
JM Joe Mauer/Jsy/Redemp. 35.00
BM Bill Mazeroski/Jsy 30.00
WM Willie McCovey/Jsy 50.00
MC Dallas McPherson/Jsy/Redemp. 20.00
PM Paul Molitor/Jsy 40.00
MM Mark Mulder/Jsy 20.00
DM Dale Murphy/Jsy 35.00
GN Graig Nettles/Jsy 35.00
PN Phil Niekro/Jsy 25.00
LN Laynce Nix/Jsy 20.00
DO David Ortiz/Jsy 50.00
RO Roy Oswalt/Jsy 25.00
AO Akinori Otsuka/Jsy 40.00
PA Jim Palmer/Jsy 40.00
CP Corey Patterson/Jsy/Redemp. 30.00
JP Jake Peavy/Jsy 40.00
PE Brad Penny/Jsy 20.00
RP Rico Petrocelli/Pants 25.00
SP Scott Podsednik/Jsy 25.00
BP Boog Powell/Jsy 25.00
MP Mark Prior/Jsy 35.00
RE Jose Reyes/Jsy/Redemp. 40.00
JR Jim Rice/Jsy 30.00
CR Cal Ripken Jr./Jsy 200.00
BR Brooks Robinson/Jsy 50.00
FR Frank Robinson/Jsy 40.00
SR Scott Rolen/Jsy/Redemp. 75.00
NR Nolan Ryan/Jsy 125.00
SA Johan Santana/Jsy/Redemp. 50.00
JS Jason Schmidt/Jsy 30.00
MS Mike Schmidt/Jsy 60.00
TS Tom Seaver/Jsy 50.00
BS Ben Sheets/Jsy/Redemp. 25.00
SM John Smoltz/Jsy/Redemp. 75.00
SU Bruce Sutter/Jsy 20.00
ST Shingo Takatsu/Jsy 25.00
MT Mark Teixeira/Jsy 40.00
BU B.J. Upton/Jsy 25.00
JV Jose Vidro/Jsy 20.00
RW Rickie Weeks/Jsy 25.00
MW Maury Wills/Jsy 25.00
KW Kerry Wood/Jsy 30.00
DW David Wright/Jsy 80.00
CY Carl Yastrzemski/Jsy 85.00
MY Michael Young/Jsy/Redemp. 25.00
RY Robin Yount 75.00
CZ Carlos Zambrano/Jsy 35.00

Patches

NM/M
Production 50 unless noted.
BA Bobby Abreu 15.00
GA Garret Anderson 15.00
JB Jason Bay 20.00
CB Carlos Beltran 20.00
AB Adrian Beltre 20.00
BE Johnny Bench 25.00
HB Hank Blalock 20.00
BB Bert Blyleven 20.00
WB Wade Boggs 20.00
BO Bret Boone 12.00
GB George Brett 40.00
MI Miguel Cabrera 25.00
RC Rod Carew 25.00
CA Steve Carlton/30 25.00
GC Gary Carter 30.00
SC Sean Casey 12.00
EC Eric Chavez 15.00
WC Will Clark/20 50.00
CL Roger Clemens 30.00
BC Bobby Crosby 20.00
AD Andre Dawson 20.00
EG Eric Gagne 20.00
GI Brian Giles 12.00
GS Marcus Giles 12.00
DG Dwight Gooden 20.00
MK Mark Grace 35.00
KL Khalil Greene 25.00
KG Ken Griffey Jr. 40.00
GR Ken Griffey Sr. 12.00
TG Tony Gwynn 25.00
TH Travis Hafner 15.00
RH Rich Harden 20.00
KH Kent Hrbek 35.00
HU Tim Hudson 20.00
AH Aubrey Huff 12.00
TO Torii Hunter 15.00
DJ Derek Jeter 65.00
RJ Randy Johnson 25.00
JJ Jacque Jones 15.00
JK Jim Kaat 20.00
HK Harmon Killebrew 40.00
CK Casey Kotchman 20.00
DL Derrek Lee 15.00
ML Mike Lowell 12.00
GM Greg Maddux 35.00
VM Victor Martinez 15.00
MA Don Mattingly 40.00
JM Joe Mauer 30.00
WM Willie McCovey 25.00
MC Dallas McPherson 20.00
MM Mark Mulder 20.00
DM Dale Murphy 25.00
GN Graig Nettles 20.00
PN Phil Niekro 20.00
LN Laynce Nix 12.00
DO David Ortiz 25.00
RO Roy Oswalt 15.00
AO Akinori Otsuka 25.00
PA Jim Palmer 20.00
CP Corey Patterson 25.00
JP Jake Peavy 20.00
PE Brad Penny 12.00
SP Scott Podsednik 12.00
BP Boog Powell 20.00
MP Mark Prior 20.00
RE Jose Reyes 20.00
CR Cal Ripken Jr. 60.00
BR Brooks Robinson/35 40.00
FR Frank Robinson 20.00
SR Scott Rolen 25.00
NR Nolan Ryan 50.00
SA Johan Santana 25.00
JS Jason Schmidt 25.00
MS Mike Schmidt 30.00
BS Ben Sheets 20.00
SM John Smoltz 30.00
SU Bruce Sutter 15.00
ST Shingo Takatsu 20.00
MT Mark Teixeira 20.00
BU B.J. Upton 20.00
JV Jose Vidro 12.00
RW Rickie Weeks 20.00
MW Maury Wills/20 20.00
KW Kerry Wood 25.00
DW David Wright 35.00
CY Carl Yastrzemski 40.00
MY Michael Young 15.00
RY Robin Yount 30.00
CZ Carlos Zambrano 25.00

Signature Patches

No Pricing
Production 10 unless noted.

2005 Upper Deck Baseball Heroes

NM/M
Complete Set (200):
Common (1-100): 2.00
Common (101-200): 2.00
Production 575
Tin (8): 50.00
1-5 Bob Feller 3.00
6-10 Brooks Robinson 3.00
11-15 Cal Ripken Jr. 8.00
16-20 Carl Yastrzemski 5.00
21-25 Don Mattingly 6.00
26-30 Tom Seaver 3.00
31-35 Harmon Killebrew 3.00
36-40 Jim Palmer 2.00
41-45 Mike Schmidt 6.00
46-50 Ozzie Smith 4.00
51-55 Paul Molitor 3.00
56-60 Al Kaline 3.00
61-65 Robin Yount 4.00
66-70 Ryne Sandberg 4.00
71-75 Stan Musial 5.00
76-80 Steve Carlton 2.00
81-85 Tony Gwynn 3.00
86-90 Wade Boggs 3.00
91-95 Will Clark 3.00
96-100 Yogi Berra 4.00
101-105 Babe Ruth 8.00
106-110 Roger Maris 6.00
111-115 Don Drysdale 2.00
116-120 Eddie Mathews 4.00
121-125 Honus Wagner 6.00
126-130 Jackie Robinson 5.00
131-135 Jimmie Foxx 5.00
136-140 Joe DiMaggio 6.00
141-145 Johnny Mize 4.00
146-150 Lefty Grove 3.00
151-155 Lou Gehrig 6.00
156-160 Mel Ott 4.00
161-165 Mickey Mantle 12.00
166-170 Roberto Clemente 8.00
171-175 Rogers Hornsby 6.00
176-180 Roy Campanella 3.00
181-185 Satchel Paige 6.00
186-190 Ted Williams 8.00
191-195 Thurman Munson 5.00
196-200 Ty Cobb 5.00

Emerald

Emerald (1-100): 1-1.5X
Emerald (101-200): 1-1.5X
Production 199 Sets

Red

Red (1-200): 1-2X
Production 75 Sets

Blue

No Pricing
Production 10 Sets

Gold

No Pricing
Production One Set

Jeter Jersey

Common Jeter:
Production 75 Sets

Jeter

NM/M
Complete Set (9): 25.00
Common Jeter: 3.00
Inserted 1:6
91-99 Derek Jeter 3.00

Jeter Jersey

Common Jeter:
Production 75 Sets

Jeter Signature

No Pricing
Production Two Sets

Memorabilia

No Pricing
Production 10 Sets

Memorabilia Emerald

NM/M
Production 99 Sets
Blue: 1X
Production 99 Sets
Bronze: 1-1.5X
Production 50 Sets
Gold: No Pricing
Production One Set
Red: 1X
Production 99 Sets
Silver: No Pricing
Production 15 Sets
1-5 Bob Feller 10.0
6-10 Brooks Robinson 10.00
11-15 Cal Ripken Jr. 25.00
16-20 Carl Yastrzemski 15.00
21-25 Don Mattingly 20.00
26-30 Tom Seaver 10.00
31-35 Harmon Killebrew 10.00
36-40 Jim Palmer 8.00
41-45 Mike Schmidt 20.00
46-50 Ozzie Smith 20.00
51-55 Paul Molitor 10.00
56-60 Al Kaline 12.00
61-65 Robin Yount 15.00
66-70 Ryne Sandberg 15.00
71-75 Stan Musial 20.00
76-80 Steve Carlton 10.00
81-85 Tony Gwynn 20.00
86-90 Wade Boggs 10.00
91-95 Will Clark 10.00
96-100 Yogi Berra 15.00

Signature Cuts

No Pricing
Production 1-10

Signature Emerald

NM/M
Production 99 Sets
Blue: 1-1.5X
Production 20 Sets
Red: 1X
Production 49 Sets
Gold: No Pricing
Production One Set
Patches: No Pricing
Production Five Sets
1-5 Bob Feller 35.00
6-10 Brooks Robinson 35.00
11-15 Cal Ripken Jr. 125.00
16-20 Carl Yastrzemski 65.00
21-25 Don Mattingly 60.00
26-30 Tom Seaver 50.00
31-35 Harmon Killebrew 40.00
36-40 Jim Palmer 25.00
41-45 Mike Schmidt 50.00
46-50 Ozzie Smith 50.00
51-55 Paul Molitor 30.00
56-60 Al Kaline 40.00
61-65 Robin Yount 40.00
66-70 Ryne Sandberg 50.00
71-75 Stan Musial 75.00
76-80 Steve Carlton 25.00
81-85 Tony Gwynn 40.00
86-90 Wade Boggs 35.00
91-95 Will Clark 30.00
96-100 Yogi Berra 60.00

Signature Memorabilia

No Pricing
Production 15 Sets

2005 Upper Deck Classics Promos

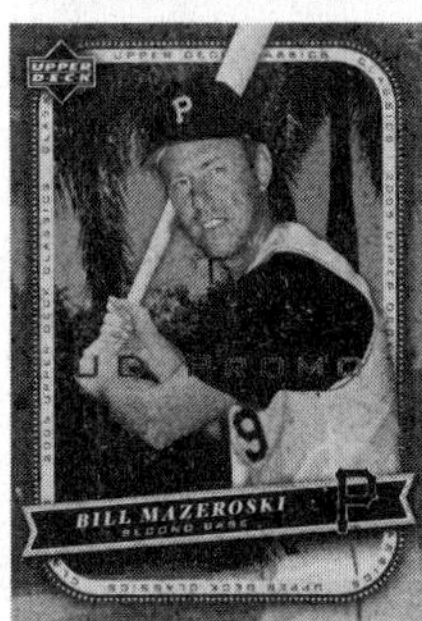

Each of the first 100 cards in Upper Deck Classics was issued in a silver foil-overprinted version with "UD PROMO" across the front. Cards were inserted into specially marked card shop and newsstand issues of Tuff Stuff magazine.

Common Player:
Stars: 1.5X

2005 Upper Deck Classics

NM/M
Complete Set (130): 50.00
Common Player: .15
Common SP (101-130): 1.00
Inserted 1:4
Pack (8): 3.00
Hobby Box (28): 60.00
1 Al Kaline .50
2 Al Lopez .15
3 Allie Reynolds .15
4 Babe Herman .15
5 Bill Mazeroski .15
6 Bill Russell .15
7 Billy Herman .15
8 Billy Williams .25
9 Bob Feller .50
10 Bob Gibson .75
11 Bob Lemon .15
12 Bobby Doerr .15
13 Boog Powell .15
14 Ken Hubbs .15
15 Brooks Robinson .75
16 Buck Leonard .15
17 Cal Ripken Jr. 2.00
18 Carl Hubbell .15
19 Jim "Catfish" Hunter .25
20 Johnny Hopp .15
21 Charlie Gehringer .15
22 Curt Flood .15
23 Jimmie Foxx .75
24 Dave McNally .15
25 Davey Lopes .15
26 Don Drysdale .50
27 Don Sutton .50
28 Earl Weaver .15
29 Early Wynn .15
30 Edd Roush .15
31 Eddie Mathews .75
32 Enos Slaughter .15
33 Fergie Jenkins .50
34 Frank Howard .15
35 Leon Wagner .15
36 Frank Crosetti .15
37 Gaylord Perry .15
38 George Bell .15
39 George Kell .15
40 Graig Nettles .15
41 Hal Newhouser .15
42 Harmon Killebrew .75
43 Harvey Kuenn .15
44 Howard Johnson .15
45 Hoyt Wilhelm .15
46 Jack Clark .15
47 Jack Morris .15
48 Jim Bunning .15
49 Jim Palmer .50
50 Joe Adcock .15
51 Joe Carter .15
52 Casey Stengel .50
53 Joe Morgan .50
54 Joe Sewell .15
55 "Smoky" Joe Wood .15
56 Johnny Bench .75
57 Johnny Mize .15
58 Jose Canseco .50
59 Juan Marichal .50
60 Keith Hernandez .15
61 Ken Griffey Sr. .15
62 Kent Hrbek .15
63 Kevin Mitchell .15
64 Kirk Gibson .25
65 Larry Doby .15
66 Lou Boudreau .15
67 Lou Brock .50
68 Luis Aparicio .15
69 Luke Appling .15
70 Monte Irvin .50
71 Nellie Fox .15
72 Norm Cash .15
73 Orlando Cepeda .25
74 Pedro Guerrero .15
75 Pee Wee Reese .15
76 Phil Niekro .15
77 Phil Rizzuto .50
78 Ralph Kiner .15
79 Ray Dandridge .15
80 Red Schoendienst .15
81 Richie Ashburn .15
82 Rick Ferrell .15
83 Robin Roberts .50
84 Rollie Fingers .15
85 Ron Cey .15
86 Sparky Anderson .15
87 Stan Coveleski .15
88 Ted Kluszewski .15
89 Ted Lyons .15
90 Tom Seaver .50
91 Tommie Agee .15
92 Tommy Lasorda .15
93 Tony Perez .25
94 Vada Pinson .15
95 Waite Hoyt .15
96 Warren Spahn .75
97 Willie McCovey .50
98 Lyman Bostock .15
99 Willie Stargell .50
100 Yogi Berra .75
101 Andre Dawson 1.00
102 Andy Van Slyke 1.00
103 Bret Saberhagen 1.00
104 Carl Yastrzemski 2.50
105 Carlton Fisk 1.50
106 Dale Murphy 1.50
107 Darryl Strawberry 1.00
108 David Cone 1.00
109 Dennis Eckersley 1.50
110 Don Mattingly 2.50
111 Dwight Gooden 1.00
112 Eddie Murray 1.50
113 Eric Davis 1.00
114 Fred Lynn 1.00
115 George Brett 3.00
116 Jim Rice 1.00
117 John Kruk 1.50
118 Lenny Dykstra 1.00
119 Mickey Mantle 4.00
120 Mike Schmidt 3.00
121 Nolan Ryan 3.00
122 Ozzie Smith 2.00
123 Paul Molitor 2.00
124 Robin Yount 2.00
125 Ryne Sandberg 2.00
126 Steve Carlton 1.50
127 Ted Williams 3.00
128 Tony Gwynn 2.00
129 Wade Boggs 2.00
130 Will Clark 2.00

Silver

Silver (1-100): 2-3X
Silver (101-130): 1-2X
Production 399 Sets

Gold

Gold (1-100): 2-4X
Gold (101-130): 1-2X
Production 199 Sets

Platinum

Platinum (1-100): 5-10X
Platinum (101-130): 3-5X
Production 25 Sets

Classic Counterparts

NM/M
Common Duo: 2.00
Production 1,999 Sets
CC Will Clark, Jack Clark 2.00
CG David Cone, Dwight Gooden 2.00
DS Darryl Strawberry, Lenny Dykstra 2.00
GB Wade Boggs, Tony Gwynn 4.00
GP Ken Griffey Sr., Tony Perez 2.00
KD John Kruk, Lenny Dykstra 2.00
KH John Kruk, Kent Hrbek 2.00
LR Jim Rice, Fred Lynn 2.00
MC Kevin Mitchell, Will Clark 2.00
MH Don Mattingly, Keith Hernandez 6.00
MY Robin Yount, Paul Molitor 5.00
NC Ron Cey, Graig Nettles 2.00
PH Boog Powell, Frank Howard 2.00
RC Steve Carlton, Nolan Ryan 8.00
RL Bill Russell, Davey Lopes 2.00
RS Tom Seaver, Nolan Ryan 8.00
SD Darryl Strawberry, Eric Davis 2.00
SG Dwight Gooden, Darryl Strawberry 2.00
SR Cal Ripken Jr., Mike Schmidt 10.00
VC Andy Van Slyke, Jack Clark 2.00

Classic Counterparts Materials

NM/M
CC Jack Clark, Will Clark 8.00
CG David Cone, Dwight Gooden 8.00
DS Darryl Strawberry, Lenny Dykstra 8.00
GB Wade Boggs, Tony Gwynn 20.00
GP Ken Griffey Sr., Tony Perez 8.00
KD John Kruk, Lenny Dykstra 15.00
KH John Kruk, Kent Hrbek 8.00
LR Jim Rice, Fred Lynn 8.00
MC Kevin Mitchell, Will Clark 8.00
MH Don Mattingly, Keith Hernandez 15.00
MY Robin Yount, Paul Molitor 15.00
NC Graig Nettles, Ron Cey 8.00
PH Boog Powell, Frank Howard 10.00
RC Steve Carlton, Nolan Ryan 40.00
RL Bill Russell, Davey Lopes 8.00
RS Tom Seaver, Nolan Ryan 50.00
SD Darryl Strawberry, Eric Davis 10.00
SG Dwight Gooden, Darryl Strawberry 8.00
SR Cal Ripken Jr., Mike Schmidt 50.00
VC Andy Van Slyke, Jack Clark 10.00

Classic Counterparts Signature

NM/M
DS Darryl Strawberry, Lenny Dykstra 20.00
GP Ken Griffey Sr., Tony Perez 30.00
KD John Kruk, Lenny Dykstra 40.00
KH John Kruk, Kent Hrbek 40.00
LR Jim Rice, Fred Lynn 40.00

NC	Graig Nettles, Ron Cey	35.00
RL	Bill Russell, Davey Lopes	25.00

Classic Cuts

		NM/M
Quantity produced listed		
FC	Frankie Crosetti/84	100.00
BH	Babe Herman/50	150.00
CH	Carl Hubbell/25	150.00
TL	Ted Lyons/83	120.00

Classic Fantasy Team

No Pricing
Inserted 1:448

Classic Materials

		NM/M
Common Player:		5.00
WB	Wade Boggs	10.00
GB	George Brett	10.00
CA	Jose Canseco	10.00
JO	Joe Carter	5.00
RC	Ron Cey	5.00
JC	Jack Clark	5.00
WC	Will Clark	8.00
DC	David Cone	8.00
ED	Eric Davis	10.00
AD	Andre Dawson	8.00
AD1	Andre Dawson	8.00
LD	Lenny Dykstra	5.00
DE	Dennis Eckersley	5.00
FI	Carlton Fisk	8.00
GI	Kirk Gibson	5.00
DG	Dwight Gooden	5.00
GG	Rich "Goose" Gossage	5.00
KG	Ken Griffey Jr.	5.00
PG	Pedro Guerrero	5.00
TG	Tony Gwynn	10.00
KH	Keith Hernandez	5.00
FH	Frank Howard	8.00
HR	Kent Hrbek	8.00
DL	Davey Lopes	5.00
FL	Fred Lynn	5.00
MA	Don Mattingly	15.00
PM	Paul Molitor	10.00
PM1	Paul Molitor SP	10.00
JM	Jack Morris	5.00
DM	Dale Murphy	8.00
GN	Graig Nettles	10.00
BP	Boog Powell SP	8.00
JR	Jim Rice	5.00
CR	Cal Ripken Jr.	25.00
BR	Bill Russell	5.00
NR	Nolan Ryan	20.00
RS	Ryne Sandberg	15.00
MS	Mike Schmidt	15.00
DS	Darryl Strawberry	5.00
AV	Andy Van Slyke	20.00
CY	Carl Yastrzemski	20.00
RY	Robin Yount	10.00

Classic Moments

		NM/M
Common Player:		2.00
Production 1,999 Sets		
WB	Wade Boggs	4.00
SC	Steve Carlton	2.00
CA	Joe Carter	2.00
JC	Jack Clark	2.00
LD	Lenny Dykstra	2.00
FI	Carlton Fisk	3.00
KG	Kirk Gibson	2.00
TG	Tony Gwynn	4.00
WJ	Wally Joyner	2.00
KM	Kevin Mitchell	2.00
PM	Paul Molitor	4.00
JM	Jack Morris	2.00
GP	Gaylord Perry	2.00
CR	Cal Ripken Jr.	10.00
NR	Nolan Ryan	8.00
BS	Bret Saberhagen	2.00
RS	Ryne Sandberg	5.00
MS	Mike Schmidt	6.00
DS	Don Sutton	2.00
RY	Robin Yount	5.00

Classic Moments Materials

		NM/M
Common Player:		5.00
WB	Wade Boggs	10.00
SC	Steve Carlton	8.00
CA	Joe Carter	5.00
JC	Jack Clark	5.00
LD	Lenny Dykstra	5.00
FI	Carlton Fisk	8.00
KG	Kirk Gibson	5.00
TG	Tony Gwynn	10.00
WJ	Wally Joyner	5.00
KM	Kevin Mitchell	5.00
PM	Paul Molitor	10.00
JM	Jack Morris	5.00
GP	Gaylord Perry	5.00
CR	Cal Ripken Jr.	25.00
NR	Nolan Ryan	20.00
RS	Ryne Sandberg	15.00
MS	Mike Schmidt	15.00
DS	Don Sutton	5.00
RY	Robin Yount	12.00

Classic Moments Signatures

		NM/M
Common Autograph:		10.00
SC	Steve Carlton	20.00
JC	Jack Clark	15.00
LD	Lenny Dykstra	15.00
FI	Carlton Fisk	40.00
KG	Kirk Gibson	25.00
TG	Tony Gwynn	40.00
WJ	Wally Joyner	20.00
KM	Kevin Mitchell	10.00
PM	Paul Molitor	25.00
JM	Jack Morris	20.00
GP	Gaylord Perry	15.00
BS	Bret Saberhagen	15.00
MS	Mike Schmidt	60.00
DS	Don Sutton	15.00
RY	Robin Yount	40.00

Classic Seasons

		NM/M
Common Player:		2.00
Production 1,999 Sets		
BE	George Bell	2.00
JC	Jose Canseco	3.00
CL	Jack Clark	2.00
WC	Will Clark	3.00
DC	David Cone	2.00
ED	Eric Davis	2.00
AD	Andre Dawson	2.00
KG	Kirk Gibson	2.00
DG	Dwight Gooden	2.00
FL	Fred Lynn	2.00
MA	Don Mattingly	6.00
KM	Kevin Mitchell	2.00
DM	Dale Murphy	3.00
JR	Jim Rice	2.00
CR	Cal Ripken Jr.	10.00
NR	Nolan Ryan	8.00
BS	Bret Saberhagen	2.00
RS	Ryne Sandberg	5.00
MS	Mike Schmidt	6.00
CY	Carl Yastrzemski	6.00

Classic Seasons Materials

		NM/M
Common Player:		5.00
BE	George Bell	5.00
JC	Jose Canseco	10.00
CL	Jack Clark	5.00
WC	Will Clark	8.00
DC	David Cone	5.00
ED	Eric Davis SP	8.00
AD	Andre Dawson	8.00
KG	Kirk Gibson	5.00
DG	Dwight Gooden	5.00
FL	Fred Lynn	5.00
MA	Don Mattingly	15.00
KM	Kevin Mitchell	5.00
DM	Dale Murphy	8.00
JR	Jim Rice	5.00
CR	Cal Ripken Jr.	25.00
NR	Nolan Ryan	20.00
RS	Ryne Sandberg	15.00
MS	Mike Schmidt	15.00
CY	Carl Yastrzemski	20.00

Classic Seasons Signatures

		NM/M
Common Auto.:		10.00
BE	George Bell	15.00
JC	Jose Canseco	40.00
CL	Jack Clark	15.00
WC	Will Clark	40.00
DC	David Cone	15.00
ED	Eric Davis	20.00
AD	Andre Dawson	20.00
KG	Kirk Gibson	25.00
DG	Dwight Gooden	12.00
FL	Fred Lynn	15.00
MA	Don Mattingly	60.00
KM	Kevin Mitchell	10.00
DM	Dale Murphy	20.00
BS	Bret Saberhagen	15.00
MS	Mike Schmidt	60.00

League Leaders

		NM/M
Common Player:		2.00
Production 999 Sets		
GB	George Bell	2.00
WB	Wade Boggs	4.00
JC	Jack Clark	2.00
WC	Will Clark	3.00
AD	Andre Dawson	3.00
LD	Lenny Dykstra	2.00
DE	Dennis Eckersley	3.00
DG	Dwight Gooden	2.00
GG	Rich "Goose" Gossage	2.00
PG	Pedro Guerrero	2.00
TG	Tony Gwynn	4.00
KH	Keith Hernandez	2.00
FH	Frank Howard	2.00
HJ	Howard Johnson	2.00
MA	Don Mattingly	8.00
KM	Kevin Mitchell	2.00
PM	Paul Molitor	4.00
DM	Dale Murphy	3.00
JR	Jim Rice	2.00
AV	Andy Van Slyke	2.00

League Leaders Materials

		NM/M
Common Player:		5.00
GB	George Bell	5.00
WB	Wade Boggs	10.00
JC	Jack Clark	5.00
WC	Will Clark	8.00
AD	Andre Dawson	8.00
LD	Lenny Dykstra	5.00
DE	Dennis Eckersley	8.00
DG	Dwight Gooden	5.00
GG	Rich "Goose" Gossage	5.00
PG	Pedro Guerrero	5.00
TG	Tony Gwynn SP	10.00
KH	Keith Hernandez	5.00
FH	Frank Howard	8.00
HJ	Howard Johnson	5.00
MA	Don Mattingly	15.00
KM	Kevin Mitchell	5.00
PM	Paul Molitor	10.00
DM	Dale Murphy	8.00
JR	Jim Rice	5.00
AV	Andy Van Slyke	20.00

League Leaders Signatures

		NM/M
Common Auto.:		10.00
GB	George Bell	10.00
JC	Jack Clark	15.00
WC	Will Clark	40.00
AD	Andre Dawson	20.00
LD	Lenny Dykstra	15.00
DE	Dennis Eckersley	15.00
DG	Dwight Gooden	15.00
GG	Rich "Goose" Gossage	15.00
PG	Pedro Guerrero	10.00
KH	Keith Hernandez	15.00
FH	Frank Howard	15.00
HJ	Howard Johnson	15.00
MA	Don Mattingly	60.00
KM	Kevin Mitchell	10.00
PM	Paul Molitor	25.00
DM	Dale Murphy	20.00
JR	Jim Rice	15.00

Post Season Performers

		NM/M
Common Player:		2.00
Production 999 Sets		
JO	Jose Canseco	3.00
CA	Joe Carter	2.00
JC	Jack Clark	2.00
WC	Will Clark	3.00
DC	David Cone	2.00
ED	Eric Davis	2.00
LD	Lenny Dykstra	2.00
CF	Carlton Fisk	3.00
DG	Dwight Gooden	2.00
PG	Pedro Guerrero	2.00
KH	Kent Hrbek	2.00
JK	John Kruk	3.00
KM	Kevin Mitchell	2.00
PM	Paul Molitor	4.00
JM	Jack Morris	2.00
CR	Cal Ripken Jr.	10.00
BR	Brooks Robinson	4.00
BS	Bret Saberhagen	2.00
MS	Mike Schmidt	6.00
DS	Darryl Strawberry	2.00

Post Season Performers Materials

		NM/M
Common Player:		5.00
JO	Jose Canseco	10.00
CA	Joe Carter	5.00
JC	Jack Clark/SP	5.00
WC	Will Clark	8.00
DC	David Cone	8.00
ED	Eric Davis/SP	10.00
LD	Lenny Dykstra/SP	5.00
CF	Carlton Fisk	8.00
DG	Dwight Gooden	5.00
PG	Pedro Guerrero	5.00
KH	Kent Hrbek	8.00
JK	John Kruk/SP	15.00
KM	Kevin Mitchell	5.00
PM	Paul Molitor/SP	10.00
JM	Jack Morris	5.00
CR	Cal Ripken Jr./SP	25.00
BR	Brooks Robinson	10.00
MS	Mike Schmidt	15.00
DS	Darryl Strawberry	5.00

Post Season Performers Signatures

		NM/M
Common Auto.:		10.00
JO	Jose Canseco	40.00
JC	Jack Clark	15.00
WC	Will Clark	40.00
DC	David Cone	15.00
ED	Eric Davis	20.00
LD	Lenny Dykstra	15.00
CF	Carlton Fisk	40.00
DG	Dwight Gooden	12.00
PG	Pedro Guerrero	10.00
KH	Kent Hrbek	20.00
JK	John Kruk	30.00
KM	Kevin Mitchell	10.00
PM	Paul Molitor	25.00
JM	Jack Morris	20.00
BR	Brooks Robinson	25.00
BS	Bret Saberhagen	15.00
MS	Mike Schmidt	60.00
SS	Darryl Strawberry	20.00

Pirates All-Stars

An All-Star Game logo was added to UD Classics cards of seven Pirates All-Stars and the cards were given away at PNC

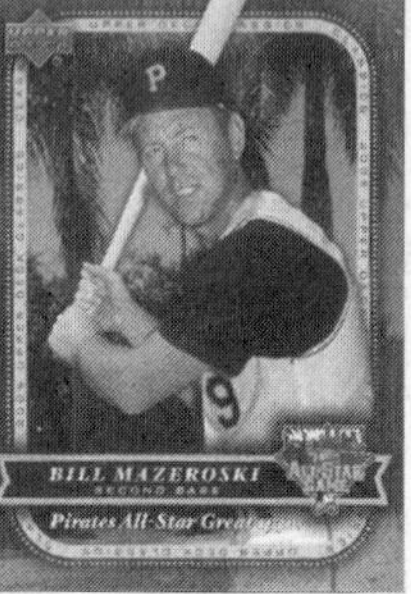

Park one per game between September 19-22 and September 30-October 2.

		NM/M
Complete Set (7):		20.00
Common Player:		2.00
PP1	Ralph Kiner	4.00
PP2	Bill Mazeroski	5.00
PP3	Roberto Clemente	7.50
PP4	Willie Stargell	4.00
PP5	Tony Pena	2.00
PP6	Andy Van Slyke	2.00
PP7	Jason Bay	2.00

2005 Upper Deck ESPN

		NM/M
Complete Set (90):		20.00
Common Player:		.15
Pack (9):		3.00
Box (24):		60.00
1	Garret Anderson	.25
2	Troy Glaus	.25
3	Vladimir Guerrero	.75
4	Luis Gonzalez	.25
5	Randy Johnson	.75
6	Andruw Jones	.40
7	Chipper Jones	.75
8	J.D. Drew	.25
9	John Smoltz	.25
10	Miguel Tejada	.50
11	Rafael Palmeiro	.50
12	Curt Schilling	.75
13	David Ortiz	.75
14	Manny Ramirez	.75
15	Pedro J. Martinez	.75
16	Carlos Zambrano	.25
17	Greg Maddux	1.00
18	Kerry Wood	.75
19	Mark Prior	.75
20	Nomar Garciaparra	1.50
21	Sammy Sosa	1.50
22	Carlos Lee	.25
23	Frank Thomas	.50
24	Magglio Ordonez	.25
25	Paul Konerko	.25
26	Adam Dunn	.50
27	Ken Griffey Jr.	1.00
28	Travis Hafner	.15
29	Victor Martinez	.25
30	Todd Helton	.50
31	Ivan Rodriguez	.50
32	Carl Pavano	.15
33	Josh Beckett	.25
34	Miguel Cabrera	.75
35	Mike Lowell	.15
36	Carlos Beltran	.50
37	Craig Biggio	.25
38	Jeff Bagwell	.50
39	Lance Berkman	.25
40	Roger Clemens	2.00
41	Roy Oswalt	.25
42	Mike Sweeney	.15
43	Adrian Beltre	.25
44	Brad Penny	.15
45	Eric Gagne	.40
46	Shawn Green	.25
47	Steve Finley	.15
48	Ben Sheets	.25
49	Scott Podsednik	.15
50	Joe Mauer	.25
51	Johan Santana	.50
52	Torii Hunter	.25
53	Jose Vidro	.15
54	Livan Hernandez	.15
55	Jose Reyes	.25
56	Mike Piazza	1.00
57	Tom Glavine	.25
58	Alex Rodriguez	1.50
59	Bernie Williams	.25
60	Derek Jeter	2.00
61	Gary Sheffield	.50
62	Hideki Matsui	1.50
63	Kevin Brown	.15
64	Mike Mussina	.25
65	Eric Chavez	.25
66	Mark Mulder	.25
67	Tim Hudson	.25
68	Bobby Abreu	.25
69	Jim Thome	.75
70	Craig Wilson	.15
71	Jason Kendall	.15
72	Oliver Perez	.15
73	Brian Giles	.15
74	Jake Peavy	.15
75	Jason Schmidt	.25
76	Bret Boone	.15
77	Ichiro Suzuki	1.50
78	Albert Pujols	2.00
79	Jim Edmonds	.25
80	Larry Walker	.40
81	Scott Rolen	.75
82	Aubrey Huff	.15
83	Carl Crawford	.15
84	Alfonso Soriano	.75
85	Hank Blalock	.50
86	Mark Teixeira	.50
87	Michael Young	.25
88	Carlos Delgado	.40
89	Roy Halladay	.25
90	Vernon Wells	.25

Award Winners

		NM/M
Inserted 1:5		
25th Anniv.:		4X-8X
Production 25 Sets		
AW-1	Gary Sheffield	1.00
AW-2	Greg Maddux	2.00
AW-3	Mike Piazza	2.00
AW-4	Jeff Bagwell	1.00
AW-5	Kenny Rogers	.50
AW-6	Cal Ripken Jr.	4.00
AW-7	Greg Maddux	2.00
AW-8	Hideo Nomo	.75
AW-9	Javier Lopez	.50
AW-10	Jim Edmonds	.75
AW-11	Ken Griffey Jr.	2.00
AW-12	Larry Walker	.75
AW-13	Nomar Garciaparra	2.50
AW-14	Roger Clemens	4.00
AW-15	David Wells	.50
AW-16	Sammy Sosa	2.50
AW-17	Pedro J. Martinez	1.50
AW-18	Andres Galarraga	.50
AW-19	Derek Jeter	4.00
AW-20	Alfonso Soriano	1.50

Ink

Inserted 1:480

Sports Center Swatches

		NM/M
Common Player:		4.00
Inserted 1:12		
GA	Garret Anderson	4.00
RB	Rocco Baldelli	4.00
CB	Carlos Beltran	8.00
AB	Adrian Beltre	8.00
LB	Lance Berkman	4.00
BI	Craig Biggio	4.00
HB	Hank Blalock	8.00
BB	Bret Boone	4.00
MG	Miguel Cabrera	8.00
EC	Eric Chavez	4.00
BC	Bartolo Colon	4.00
CC	Carl Crawford	4.00
JD	J.D. Drew	4.00
AD	Adam Dunn	8.00
JE	Jim Edmonds	6.00

EG Eric Gagne 6.00
TG Troy Glaus 6.00
KG Ken Griffey Jr. 15.00
TH Tim Hudson 4.00
AH Aubrey Huff 4.00
DJ Derek Jeter 20.00
JK Jeff Kent 4.00
PK Paul Konerko 4.00
DL Derrek Lee 4.00
LO Derek Lowe 4.00
MM Mark Mulder 4.00
CP Corey Patterson 6.00
AP Albert Pujols 20.00
IR Ivan Rodriguez 8.00
SA Johan Santana 8.00
JS Jason Schmidt 6.00
BS Ben Sheets 4.00
AS Alfonso Soriano 8.00
IS Ichiro Suzuki 25.00
MS Mike Sweeney 4.00
MT Mark Teixeira 6.00
JT Jim Thome 10.00
BU B.J. Upton 6.00
VW Vernon Wells 4.00
DW David Wright/SP 15.00
MY Mike Young/SP 10.00

Sports Century

NM/M
Inserted 1:5
25th Anniv.: 4-8X
Production 25 Sets
SC-1 Babe Ruth 4.00
SC-2 Jackie Robinson 2.00
SC-4 Ty Cobb 2.00
SC-5 Joe DiMaggio 3.00
SC-6 Lou Gehrig 3.00
SC-7 Mickey Mantle 5.00
SC-8 Walter Johnson 1.00
SC-9 Stan Musial 2.00
SC-10 Satchel Paige 1.00
SC-11 Bob Gibson 1.00
SC-12 Roberto Clemente 3.00
SC-13 Cy Young 1.00
SC-14 Honus Wagner 2.00
SC-15 Rogers Hornsby 1.00

Sports Century Signatures

Inserted 1:480

The Magazine Covers

NM/M
Inserted 1:5
25th Anniv.: 4-8X
Production 25 Sets
MC-1 Roger Clemens 4.00
MC-2 Derek Jeter 4.00
MC-3 Randy Johnson, Pedro J. Martinez 1.50
MC-4 Nomar Garciaparra 2.50
MC-5 Manny Ramirez 1.50
MC-6 Ken Griffey Jr. 2.00
MC-7 Mike Piazza 2.00
MC-8 Ichiro Suzuki 3.00
MC-9 Vladimir Guerrero 1.50
MC-10 Randy Johnson 1.50
MC-11 A.J. Pierzynski, Doug Mientkiewicz, Jacque Jones, Torii Hunter .50
MC-12 Jason Giambi .50
MC-13 Jeff Kent .50
MC-14 Albert Pujols 4.00
MC-15 Kazuo Matsui .50
MC-16 Miguel Cabrera 1.50
MC-17 Alex Rodriguez 3.00
MC-18 Ivan Rodriguez 1.00
MC-19 Eric Gagne 1.00
MC-20 Jim Edmonds, Albert Pujols, Scott Rolen .75

This Day in Baseball History

NM/M
Inserted 1:5
25th Anniv.: 4-8X
Production 25 Sets
BH-1 Cal Ripken Jr. 4.00
BH-2 Nolan Ryan 4.00
BH-3 Nolan Ryan 4.00
BH-4 Roger Clemens 4.00
BH-5 Thurman Munson 2.00
BH-6 Mickey Mantle 5.00
BH-7 Ernie Banks 2.00
BH-8 Roy Campanella 1.00
BH-9 Yogi Berra 2.00
BH-10 Mickey Mantle 5.00
BH-11 Jackie Robinson 3.00
BH-12 Joe DiMaggio 3.00
BH-13 Bob Feller 1.00
BH-14 Lou Gehrig 3.00
BH-15 Ty Cobb 2.00
BH-16 Babe Ruth 4.00
BH-17 Walter Johnson 1.00
BH-18 Rogers Hornsby 1.00
BH-19 George Sisler 1.00
BH-20 Cy Young 1.00

Web Gems

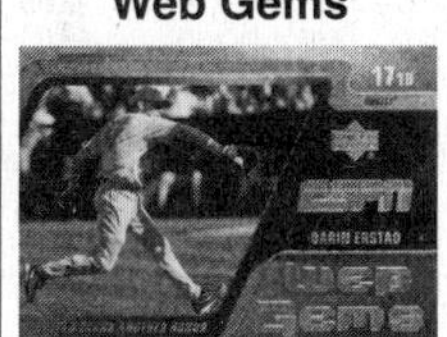

NM/M
Inserted 1:5
25th Anniv.: 4-8X
Production 25 Sets
WG-1 Adrian Beltre .75
WG-2 Alex Rodriguez 3.00
WG-3 Andruw Jones .75
WG-4 Bernie Williams .75
WG-5 Bret Boone .50
WG-6 Cesar Izturis .50
WG-7 Darin Erstad .50
WG-8 Derek Jeter 4.00
WG-9 Derrek Lee .75
WG-10 Eric Chavez .75
WG-11 Greg Maddux 2.00
WG-12 Ichiro Suzuki 3.00
WG-13 Ivan Rodriguez 1.00
WG-14 Jim Edmonds .75
WG-15 Ken Griffey Jr. 2.00
WG-16 Larry Walker .75
WG-17 Miguel Tejada .75
WG-18 Mike Mussina .75
WG-19 Nomar Garciaparra 2.50
WG-20 Scott Rolen 1.50
WG-21 Steve Finley .50
WG-22 Todd Helton 1.00
WG-23 Torii Hunter .50
WG-24 Vernon Wells .50
WG-25 Vladimir Guerrero 1.50

2005 Upper Deck First Pitch

NM/M
Complete Set (330):
Common (1-330): .10
Common (301-330): 1.00
Inserted 1:4
Common (321-330): 2.00
Inserted 1:36
Pack (5): 1.00
Box (36): 30.00
1 Casey Kotchman .10
2 Chone Figgins .10
3 David Eckstein .10
4 Jarrod Washburn .10
5 Robb Quinlan .10
6 Troy Glaus .25
7 Vladimir Guerrero .50
8 Brandon Webb .10
9 Danny Bautista .10
10 Luis Gonzalez .25
11 Matt Kata .10
12 Randy Johnson .50
13 Robby Hammock .10
14 Shea Hillenbrand .10
15 Adam LaRoche .10
16 Andruw Jones .40
17 Horacio Ramirez .10
18 John Smoltz .25
19 Johnny Estrada .10
20 Mike Hampton .10
21 Rafael Furcal .10
22 Brian Roberts .10
23 Javy Lopez .25
24 Jay Gibbons .10
25 Jorge Julio .10
26 Melvin Mora .10
27 Miguel Tejada .40
28 Rafael Palmeiro .40
29 Derek Lowe .10
30 Jason Varitek .25
31 Kevin Youkilis .10
32 Manny Ramirez .50
33 Curt Schilling .50
34 Pedro J. Martinez .50
35 Trot Nixon .10
36 Corey Patterson .25
37 Derrek Lee .25
38 LaTroy Hawkins .10
39 Mark Prior .50
40 Matt Clement .10
41 Moises Alou .25
42 Sammy Sosa 1.00
43 Aaron Rowand .10
44 Carlos Lee .10
45 Jose Valentin .10
46 Juan Uribe .10
47 Magglio Ordonez .10
48 Mark Buehrle .10
49 Paul Konerko .10
50 Adam Dunn .40
51 Barry Larkin .25
52 D'Angelo Jimenez .10
53 Danny Graves .10
54 Paul Wilson .10
55 Sean Casey .10
56 Wily Mo Pena .10
57 Ben Broussard .10
58 C.C. Sabathia .10
59 Casey Blake .10
60 Cliff Lee .10
61 Matt Lawton .10
62 Omar Vizquel .10
63 Victor Martinez .25
64 Charles Johnson .10
65 Joe Kennedy .10
66 Jeromy Burnitz .10
67 Matt Holliday .25
68 Preston Wilson .10
69 Royce Clayton .10
70 Shawn Estes .10
71 Bobby Higginson .10
72 Brandon Inge .10
73 Carlos Guillen .10
74 Dmitri Young .10
75 Eric Munson .10
76 Jeremy Bonderman .10
77 Ugueth Urbina .10
78 Josh Beckett .25
79 Dontrelle Willis .25
80 Jeff Conine .10
81 Juan Pierre .10
82 Luis Castillo .10
83 Miguel Cabrera .50
84 Mike Lowell .10
85 Andy Pettitte .25
86 Brad Lidge .10
87 Carlos Beltran .40
88 Craig Biggio .25
89 Jeff Bagwell .40
90 Roger Clemens 1.50
91 Roy Oswalt .25
92 Benito Santiago .10
93 Jeremy Affeldt .10
94 Juan Gonzalez .25
95 Ken Harvey .10
96 Mike MacDougal .10
97 Mike Sweeney .10
98 Zack Greinke .10
99 Adrian Beltre .25
100 Alex Cora .10
101 Cesar Izturis .10
102 Eric Gagne .25
103 Kazuhisa Ishii .10
104 Milton Bradley .10
105 Shawn Green .25
106 Danny Kolb .10
107 Ben Sheets .25
108 Brooks Kieschnick .10
109 Craig Counsell .10
110 Geoff Jenkins .10
111 Lyle Overbay .10
112 Scott Podsednik .10
113 Corey Koskie .10
114 Johan Santana .50
115 Joe Mauer .25
116 Justin Morneau .25
117 Lew Ford .10
118 Matt LeCroy .10
119 Torii Hunter .10
120 Brad Wilkerson .10
121 Chad Cordero .10
122 Livan Hernandez .10
123 Jose Vidro .10
124 Terrmel Sledge .10
125 Tony Batista .10
126 Zach Day .10
127 Al Leiter .10
128 Jae Weong Seo .10
129 Jose Reyes .25
130 Kazuo Matsui .10
131 Mike Piazza .75
132 Todd Zeile .10
133 Cliff Floyd .10
134 Alex Rodriguez 1.50
135 Derek Jeter 1.50
136 Gary Sheffield .40
137 Hideki Matsui 1.00
138 Jason Giambi .25
139 Jorge Posada .25
140 Mike Mussina .25
141 Barry Zito .25
142 Bobby Crosby .25
143 Octavio Dotel .10
144 Eric Chavez .25
145 Jermaine Dye .10
146 Mark Kotsay .10
147 Tim Hudson .25
148 Billy Wagner .10
149 Bobby Abreu .25
150 David Bell .10
151 Jim Thome .50
152 Jimmy Rollins .20
153 Mike Lieberthal .10
154 Randy Wolf .10
155 Craig Wilson .10
156 Daryle Ward .10
157 Jack Wilson .10
158 Jason Kendall .10
159 Kip Wells .10
160 Oliver Perez .25
161 Robert Mackowiak .10
162 Brian Giles .10
163 Brian Lawrence .10
164 David Wells .10
165 Jay Payton .10
166 Ryan Klesko .10
167 Sean Burroughs .10
168 Trevor Hoffman .10
169 Brett Tomko .10
170 J.T. Snow .10
171 Jason Schmidt .25
172 Kirk Rueter .10
173 A.J. Pierzynski .10
174 Pedro Feliz .10
175 Ray Durham .10
176 Eddie Guardado .10
177 Edgar Martinez .10
178 Ichiro Suzuki 1.00
179 Jamie Moyer .10
180 Joel Pineiro .10
181 Randy Winn .10
182 Raul Ibanez .10
183 Albert Pujols 1.50
184 Edgar Renteria .25
185 Jason Isringhausen .10
186 Jim Edmonds .25
187 Matt Morris .10
188 Reggie Sanders .10
189 Tony Womack .10
190 Aubrey Huff .10
191 Danys Baez .10
192 Carl Crawford .10
193 Jose Cruz Jr. .10
194 Rocco Baldelli .10
195 Tino Martinez .10
196 Dewon Brazelton .10
197 Alfonso Soriano .50
198 Brad Fullmer .10
199 Gerald Laird .10
200 Hank Blalock .50
201 Laynce Nix .10
202 Mark Teixeira .40
203 Mike Young .25
204 Alexis Rios .10
205 Eric Hinske .10
206 Miguel Batista .10
207 Orlando Hudson .10
208 Roy Halladay .10
209 Ted Lilly .10
210 Vernon Wells .10
211 Aarom Baldiris .10
212 B.J. Upton .25
213 Dallas McPherson .25
214 Brian Dallimore .10
215 Chris Oxspring .10
216 Chris Shelton .10
217 David Wright .75
218 Edwardo Sierra .10
219 Fernando Nieve .10
220 Frank Francisco .10
221 Jeff Bennett .10
222 Justin Lehr .10
223 John Gall .10
224 Jorge Sequea .10
225 Justin Germano .10
226 Kazuhito Tadano .10
227 Kevin Cave .10
228 Joe Blanton .10
229 Luis Gonzalez .10
230 Mike Wuertz .10
231 Mike Rouse .10
232 Nick Regilio .10
233 Orlando Rodriguez .10
235 Ramon Ramirez .10
236 Roberto Novoa .10
237 Dioner Navarro .10
238 Tim Bausher .10
239 Logan Kensing .10
240 Andy Green .10
241 Brad Halsey .10
242 Charles Thomas .10
243 George Sherrill .10
244 Jesse Crain .10
245 Jimmy Serrano .10
246 Joe Horgan .10
247 Chris Young .10
248 Joey Gathright .10
249 Gavin Floyd .10
250 Ryan Howard .50
251 Lance Cormier .10
252 Matt Treanor .10
253 Jeff Francis .10
254 Nick Swisher .10
255 Scott Atchison .10
256 Travis Blackley .10
257 Travis Smith .10
258 Yadier Molina .10
259 Jeff Keppinger .10
260 Scott Kazmir .50
261 Garret Anderson, Vladimir Guerrero .25
262 Luis Gonzalez, Randy Johnson .25
263 Chipper Jones, Andruw Jones .25
264 Miguel Tejada, Rafael Palmeiro .25
265 Manny Ramirez, Curt Schilling .25
266 Mark Prior, Sammy Sosa .50
267 Frank Thomas, Magglio Ordonez .25
268 Barry Larkin, Ken Griffey Jr. .50
269 C.C. Sabathia, Victor Martinez .10
270 Jeromy Burnitz, Todd Helton .25
271 Ivan Rodriguez, Dmitri Young .25
272 Josh Beckett, Miguel Cabrera .25
273 Jeff Bagwell, Roger Clemens .50
274 Mike Sweeney, Ken Harvey .10
275 Eric Gagne, Adrian Beltre .25
276 Ben Sheets, Geoff Jenkins .10
277 Torii Hunter, Joe Mauer .10
278 Jose Vidro, Livan Hernandez .10
279 Mike Piazza, Kazuo Matsui .25
280 Alex Rodriguez, Derek Jeter .75
281 Eric Chavez, Tim Hudson .10
282 Bobby Abreu, Jim Thome .25
283 Jason Kendall, Craig Wilson .10
284 Phil Nevin, Brian Giles .10
285 Jason Schmidt, A.J. Pierzynski .10
286 Bret Boone, Ichiro Suzuki .50
287 Albert Pujols, Scott Rolen .75
288 Aubrey Huff, Tino Martinez .10
289 Hank Blalock, Mark Teixeira .25
290 Roy Halladay, Carlos Delgado .10
291 Vladimir Guerrero .50
292 Curt Schilling .50
293 Mark Prior .50
294 Josh Beckett .25
295 Roger Clemens 1.00
296 Derek Jeter 1.00
297 Eric Chavez .10
298 Jim Thome .50
299 Albert Pujols 1.00
300 Hank Blalock .25
301 Guillermo Quiroz 1.00
302 Jeff Bajenaru 1.00
303 Bartolome Fortunato 1.00
304 Jason Alfaro 1.00
305 Mike Rose 1.00
306 Joe Hietpas 1.00
307 Kyle Denney 1.00
308 Rene Rivera 1.00
309 Kameron Loe 1.00
310 Rickie Weeks 1.50
311 Gustavo Chacin 1.00
312 Chris Burke 1.00
313 Yhency Brazoban 1.00
314 Brandon League 1.00
315 Jose Capellan 1.00
316 Russ Adams 1.00
317 Adrian Gonzalez 1.00
318 Jason Dubois 1.00
319 Abe Alvarez 1.00
320 Eric Crozier 1.00
321 Bengie Molina, Bartolo Colon 2.00
322 C.C. Sabathia, Victor Martinez 2.00
323 Jake Peavy, Ramon Hernandez 2.00
324 A.J. Pierzynski, Jason Schmidt 3.00
325 Joe Mauer, Johan Santana 3.00
326 Mark Prior, Michael Barrett 3.00
327 Jorge Posada, Mike Mussina 3.00
328 Roger Clemens, Brad Ausmus 4.00
329 Roy Halladay, Guillermo Quiroz 2.00
330 Mike Piazza, Tom Glavine 3.00

Fabric

NM/M
Common Player:
Inserted 1:180
JB Jeff Bagwell 8.00
BE Josh Beckett 5.00
BB Bret Boone 5.00
EC Eric Chavez 5.00
JE Jim Edmonds 5.00
EG Eric Gagne 8.00
TG Troy Glaus 5.00
KG Ken Griffey Jr./SP 20.00
TH Torii Hunter 5.00
DJ Derek Jeter 20.00
AJ Andruw Jones 5.00
CJ Chipper Jones 8.00
MM Mark Mulder 5.00
MO Magglio Ordonez 5.00
SR Scott Rolen 8.00
CS Curt Schilling 8.00
GS Gary Sheffield/SP 8.00
AS Alfonso Soriano 8.00
SS Sammy Sosa 10.00
IS Ichiro Suzuki/SP 25.00

Jumbos

NM/M
Common Player: 1.00
FP-1 Shingo Takatsu 1.00
FP-2 Jeff Francis 1.00
FP-3 Jesse Crain 1.00
FP-4 Jose Capellan 1.00
FP-5 Zack Greinke 1.00
FP-6 Scott Proctor 1.00
FP-7 Scott Kazmir 3.00
FP-8 Gavin Floyd 1.00
FP-9 Joe Blanton 1.00
FP-10 Akinori Otsuka 1.00

Signature Stars

Inserted 1:720

2005 UD Hall of Fame

NM/M
Complete Set (100):
Common Player: 3.00
Production 550 Sets
Tin (4): 125.00
1 Al Kaline 4.00
2 Al Lopez 3.00
3 Bill Mazeroski 3.00
4 Billy Williams 3.00
5 Bob Feller 4.00
6 Bob Gibson 4.00
7 Bob Lemon 3.00
8 Bobby Doerr 3.00
9 Brooks Robinson 5.00
10 Buck Leonard 3.00
11 Carl Yastrzemski 5.00
12 Carlton Fisk 4.00
13 Casey Stengel 4.00
14 Jim "Catfish" Hunter 3.00
15 Dave Winfield 4.00
16 Dennis Eckersley 3.00
17 Dizzy Dean 4.00
18 Don Drysdale 4.00
19 Don Sutton 3.00
20 Duke Snider 4.00
21 Early Wynn 3.00
22 Eddie Mathews 5.00

23 Eddie Murray 4.00
24 Enos Slaughter 3.00
25 Ernie Banks 5.00
26 Fergie Jenkins 3.00
27 Frank Robinson 4.00
28 Gary Carter 3.00
29 Gaylord Perry 3.00
30 George Brett 8.00
31 George Kell 3.00
32 George Sisler 3.00
33 Hal Newhouser 3.00
34 Harmon Killebrew 5.00
35 Hoyt Wilhelm 3.00
36 Jackie Robinson 5.00
37 Jim Bunning 3.00
38 Jim Palmer 3.00
39 Jimmie Foxx 5.00
40 Joe Morgan 3.00
41 Johnny Bench 5.00
42 Johnny Mize 3.00
43 Juan Marichal 3.00
44 Kirby Puckett 4.00
45 Larry Doby 3.00
46 Lefty Grove 3.00
47 Lou Boudreau 3.00
48 Lou Brock 4.00
49 Luis Aparicio 3.00
50 Mel Ott 4.00
51 Mickey Cochrane 4.00
52 Monte Irvin 3.00
53 Orlando Cepeda 3.00
54 Ozzie Smith 5.00
55 Paul Molitor 4.00
56 Pee Wee Reese 3.00
57 Phil Niekro 3.00
58 Phil Rizzuto 3.00
59 Pie Traynor 3.00
60 Ralph Kiner 3.00
61 Red Schoendienst 3.00
62 Richie Ashburn 3.00
63 Rick Ferrell 3.00
64 Robin Roberts 3.00
65 Robin Yount 5.00
66 Rod Carew 3.00
67 Rogers Hornsby 4.00
68 Rollie Fingers 3.00
69 Roy Campanella 4.00
70 Steve Carlton 3.00
71 Tony Perez 3.00
72 Warren Spahn 5.00
73 Whitey Ford 4.00
74 Willie McCovey 4.00
75 Willie Stargell 4.00
76 Yogi Berra 5.00
77 Babe Ruth 8.00
78 Honus Wagner 4.00
79 Lou Gehrig 6.00
80 Mickey Mantle 15.00
81 Ty Cobb 6.00
82 Ryne Sandberg 5.00
83 Satchel Paige 5.00
84 Wade Boggs 4.00
85 Reggie Jackson 4.00
86 Babe Ruth 8.00
87 Christy Mathewson 4.00
88 Cy Young 4.00
89 Honus Wagner 5.00
90 Joe DiMaggio 6.00
91 Lou Gehrig 6.00
92 Mickey Mantle 15.00
93 Mike Schmidt 6.00
94 Nolan Ryan 8.00
95 Satchel Paige 5.00
96 Stan Musial 5.00
97 Ted Williams 6.00
98 Tom Seaver 4.00
99 Ty Cobb 6.00
100 Walter Johnson 4.00

Green

Green (1-100): 1X
Production 200 Sets

Silver

Silver (1-100): 1-1.5X
Production 99 Sets

Gold

Gold (1-100): 1.5-2X
Production 25 Sets

Rainbow

No Pricing
Production One Set

Class of Cooperstown

NM/M

Production 50 Sets
Gold: No Pricing
Production Five Sets
Silver: No Pricing
Production 15 Sets
Rainbow: No Pricing
Production One Set
LA1 Luis Aparicio 4.00
LA2 Luis Aparicio 4.00
EB1 Ernie Banks 6.00
EB2 Ernie Banks 6.00
BE1 Johnny Bench 6.00
BE2 Johnny Bench 6.00
YB1 Yogi Berra 5.00
YB2 Yogi Berra 5.00
GB1 George Brett 10.00
GB2 George Brett 10.00
GB3 George Brett 10.00
LB1 Lou Brock 4.00
JB1 Jim Bunning 4.00
JB2 Jim Bunning 4.00
RC1 Rod Carew 4.00
RC2 Rod Carew 4.00
SC1 Steve Carlton 4.00
SC2 Steve Carlton 4.00
SC3 Steve Carlton 4.00
SC4 Steve Carlton 4.00
GC1 Gary Carter 4.00
GC2 Gary Carter 4.00
OC1 Orlando Cepeda 4.00
BD1 Bobby Doerr 4.00
BD2 Bobby Doerr 4.00
DE1 Dennis Eckersley 4.00
BF1 Bob Feller 4.00
BF2 Bob Feller 4.00
RF1 Rollie Fingers 4.00
CF1 Carlton Fisk 4.00
CF2 Carlton Fisk 4.00
WF1 Whitey Ford 5.00
WF2 Whitey Ford 5.00
BG1 Bob Gibson 5.00
BG2 Bob Gibson 5.00
MI1 Monte Irvin 4.00
MI2 Monte Irvin 4.00
RJ1 Reggie Jackson 5.00
RJ2 Reggie Jackson 5.00
RJ3 Reggie Jackson 5.00
FJ1 Fergie Jenkins 4.00
AK1 Al Kaline 6.00
AK2 Al Kaline 6.00
AK3 Al Kaline 6.00
GK1 George Kell 4.00
HK1 Harmon Killebrew 6.00
HK2 Harmon Killebrew 6.00
HK3 Harmon Killebrew 6.00
HK4 Harmon Killebrew 6.00
RK1 Ralph Kiner 4.00
RK2 Ralph Kiner 4.00
MA1 Juan Marichal 4.00
MA2 Juan Marichal 4.00
BM1 Bill Mazeroski 4.00
WM1 Willie McCovey 5.00
WM2 Willie McCovey 5.00
PM1 Paul Molitor 5.00
PM2 Paul Molitor 5.00
PM3 Paul Molitor 5.00
JM1 Joe Morgan 4.00
JM2 Joe Morgan 4.00
EM1 Eddie Murray 4.00
SM1 Stan Musial 6.00
SM2 Stan Musial 6.00
PN1 Phil Niekro 4.00
JP1 Jim Palmer 4.00
JP2 Jim Palmer 4.00
TP1 Tony Perez 4.00
GP1 Gaylord Perry 4.00
GP2 Gaylord Perry 4.00
KP1 Kirby Puckett 5.00
RR1 Robin Roberts 4.00
BR1 Brooks Robinson 5.00
BR2 Brooks Robinson 5.00
BR3 Brooks Robinson 5.00
FR1 Frank Robinson 5.00
FR2 Frank Robinson 5.00
NR1 Nolan Ryan 10.00
NR2 Nolan Ryan 10.00
NR3 Nolan Ryan 10.00
NR4 Nolan Ryan 10.00
MS1 Mike Schmidt 6.00
MS2 Mike Schmidt 6.00
MS3 Mike Schmidt 6.00
RS1 Red Schoendienst 4.00
TS1 Tom Seaver 5.00
TS2 Tom Seaver 5.00
OS1 Ozzie Smith 6.00
OS2 Ozzie Smith 6.00
SN1 Duke Snider 5.00
DS1 Don Sutton 4.00
BW1 Billy Williams 4.00
BW2 Billy Williams 4.00
BW3 Billy Williams 4.00
DW1 Dave Winfield 4.00
DW2 Dave Winfield 4.00
CY1 Carl Yastrzemski 6.00
CY2 Carl Yastrzemski 6.00
RY1 Robin Yount 6.00
RY2 Robin Yount 6.00

Class of Cooperstown Autograph

NM/M

Production 25 Sets
Gold: No Pricing
Production Five Sets
Silver: No Pricing
Production 15 Sets
Rainbow: No Pricing
Material Gold: No Pricing
Production Five Sets
Material Silver: No Pricing
Production 15 Sets
Patch Gold: No Pricing
Production Five Sets
Patch Silver: No Pricing
Production 10 Sets
LA1 Luis Aparicio 20.00
LA2 Luis Aparicio 20.00
EB1 Ernie Banks 50.00
EB2 Ernie Banks 50.00
BE1 Johnny Bench 40.00
BE2 Johnny Bench 40.00
YB1 Yogi Berra 60.00
YB2 Yogi Berra 60.00
GB1 George Brett 60.00
GB2 George Brett 60.00
GB3 George Brett 60.00
LB1 Lou Brock 35.00
JB1 Jim Bunning 25.00
JB2 Jim Bunning 25.00
RC1 Rod Carew 30.00
RC2 Rod Carew 30.00
SC1 Steve Carlton 20.00
SC2 Steve Carlton 20.00
SC3 Steve Carlton 20.00
SC4 Steve Carlton 20.00
GC1 Gary Carter 25.00
GC2 Gary Carter 25.00
OC1 Orlando Cepeda 25.00
BD1 Bobby Doerr 15.00
BD2 Bobby Doerr 15.00
DE1 Dennis Eckersley 20.00
BF1 Bob Feller 30.00
BF2 Bob Feller 30.00
RF1 Rollie Fingers 20.00
CF1 Carlton Fisk 30.00
CF2 Carlton Fisk 30.00
WF1 Whitey Ford 50.00
WF2 Whitey Ford 50.00
BG1 Bob Gibson 35.00
BG2 Bob Gibson 35.00
MI1 Monte Irvin 25.00
MI2 Monte Irvin 25.00
RJ1 Reggie Jackson 40.00
RJ2 Reggie Jackson 40.00
RJ3 Reggie Jackson 40.00
FJ1 Fergie Jenkins 20.00
AK1 Al Kaline 40.00
AK2 Al Kaline 40.00
AK3 Al Kaline 40.00
GK1 George Kell 20.00
HK1 Harmon Killebrew 40.00
HK2 Harmon Killebrew 40.00
HK3 Harmon Killebrew 40.00
HK4 Harmon Killebrew 40.00
RK1 Ralph Kiner 40.00
RK2 Ralph Kiner 40.00
MA1 Juan Marichal 25.00
MA2 Juan Marichal 25.00
BM1 Bill Mazeroski 40.00
WM1 Willie McCovey 40.00
WM2 Willie McCovey 40.00
PM1 Paul Molitor 30.00
PM2 Paul Molitor 30.00
PM3 Paul Molitor 30.00
JM1 Joe Morgan 25.00
JM2 Joe Morgan 25.00
EM1 Eddie Murray 50.00
SM1 Stan Musial 60.00
SM2 Stan Musial 60.00
PN1 Phil Niekro 20.00
JP1 Jim Palmer 20.00
JP2 Jim Palmer 20.00
TP1 Tony Perez 20.00
GP1 Gaylord Perry 20.00
GP2 Gaylord Perry 20.00
KP1 Kirby Puckett 40.00
RR1 Robin Roberts 25.00
BR1 Brooks Robinson 30.00
BR2 Brooks Robinson 30.00
BR3 Brooks Robinson 30.00
FR1 Frank Robinson 20.00
FR2 Frank Robinson 20.00
NR1 Nolan Ryan 90.00
NR2 Nolan Ryan 90.00
NR3 Nolan Ryan 90.00
NR4 Nolan Ryan 90.00
MS1 Mike Schmidt 50.00
MS2 Mike Schmidt 50.00
MS3 Mike Schmidt 50.00
RS1 Red Schoendienst 35.00
TS1 Tom Seaver 40.00
TS2 Tom Seaver 40.00
OS1 Ozzie Smith 40.00
OS2 Ozzie Smith 40.00
SN1 Duke Snider 40.00
DS1 Don Sutton 20.00
BW1 Billy Williams 20.00
BW2 Billy Williams 20.00
BW3 Billy Williams 20.00
DW1 Dave Winfield 30.00
DW2 Dave Winfield 30.00
CY1 Carl Yastrzemski 50.00
CY2 Carl Yastrzemski 50.00
RY1 Robin Yount 40.00
RY2 Robin Yount 40.00

Class of Cooperstown Calling

NM/M

Production 50 Sets
Gold: No Pricing
Production Five Sets
Green: .75-1.5X
Production 25 Sets
Silver: No Pricing
Production 15 Sets
Rainbow: No Pricing
Production One Set
LA1 Luis Aparicio 4.00
LA2 Luis Aparicio 4.00
EB1 Ernie Banks 6.00
BE1 Johnny Bench 6.00
YB1 Yogi Berra 5.00
WB1 Wade Boggs 5.00
WB2 Wade Boggs 5.00
WB3 Wade Boggs 5.00
GB1 George Brett 10.00
GB2 George Brett 10.00
LB1 Lou Brock 4.00
LB2 Lou Brock 4.00
JB1 Jim Bunning 4.00
RC1 Rod Carew 4.00
RC2 Rod Carew 4.00
SC1 Steve Carlton 4.00
SC2 Steve Carlton 4.00
GC1 Gary Carter 4.00
GC2 Gary Carter 4.00
GC3 Gary Carter 4.00
OC1 Orlando Cepeda 4.00
OC2 Orlando Cepeda 4.00
BD1 Bobby Doerr 4.00
BD2 Bobby Doerr 4.00
DE1 Dennis Eckersley 4.00
DE2 Dennis Eckersley 4.00
BF1 Bob Feller 4.00
BF2 Bob Feller 4.00
RF1 Rollie Fingers 4.00
RF2 Rollie Fingers 4.00
CF1 Carlton Fisk 4.00
CF2 Carlton Fisk 4.00
WF1 Whitey Ford 5.00
BG1 Bob Gibson 5.00
MI1 Monte Irvin 4.00
RJ1 Reggie Jackson 5.00
RJ2 Reggie Jackson 5.00
RJ3 Reggie Jackson 5.00
FJ1 Fergie Jenkins 4.00
FJ2 Fergie Jenkins 4.00
AK1 Al Kaline 6.00
AK2 Al Kaline 6.00
GK1 George Kell 4.00
HK1 Harmon Killebrew 6.00
HK2 Harmon Killebrew 6.00
RK1 Ralph Kiner 4.00
JM1 Juan Marichal 4.00
BM1 Bill Mazeroski 4.00
WM1 Willie McCovey 5.00
PM1 Paul Molitor 5.00
PM2 Paul Molitor 5.00
PM3 Paul Molitor 5.00
MO1 Joe Morgan 4.00
MO2 Joe Morgan 4.00
EM1 Eddie Murray 4.00
EM2 Eddie Murray 4.00
SM1 Stan Musial 6.00
SM2 Stan Musial 6.00
PN1 Phil Niekro 4.00
PN2 Phil Niekro 4.00
JP1 Jim Palmer 4.00
JP2 Jim Palmer 4.00
TP1 Tony Perez 4.00
TP2 Tony Perez 4.00
GP1 Gaylord Perry 4.00
GP2 Gaylord Perry 4.00
KP1 Kirby Puckett 5.00
KP2 Kirby Puckett 5.00
RR1 Robin Roberts 4.00
BR1 Brooks Robinson 5.00
BR2 Brooks Robinson 5.00
BR3 Brooks Robinson 5.00
FR1 Frank Robinson 5.00
NR1 Nolan Ryan 10.00
NR2 Nolan Ryan 10.00
NR3 Nolan Ryan 10.00
NR4 Nolan Ryan 10.00
SA1 Ryne Sandberg 6.00
SA2 Ryne Sandberg 6.00
SA3 Ryne Sandberg 6.00
MS1 Mike Schmidt 6.00
MS2 Mike Schmidt 6.00
MS3 Mike Schmidt 6.00
RS1 Red Schoendienst 4.00
TS1 Tom Seaver 5.00
OS1 Ozzie Smith 6.00
OS2 Ozzie Smith 6.00
OS3 Ozzie Smith 6.00
SN1 Duke Snider 5.00
DS1 Don Sutton 4.00
DS2 Don Sutton 4.00
DS3 Don Sutton 4.00
BW1 Billy Williams 4.00
BW2 Billy Williams 4.00
DW1 Dave Winfield 4.00
CY1 Carl Yastrzemski 6.00
CY2 Carl Yastrzemski 6.00
RY1 Robin Yount 6.00
RY2 Robin Yount 6.00
RY3 Robin Yount 6.00

Class of Cooperstown Calling Auto.

NM/M

Production 25 Sets
Gold: No Pricing
Production Five Sets
Silver: No Pricing
Production 15 Sets
Rainbow: No Pricing
Production One Set
Material Gold: No Pricing
Production Five Sets
Material Silver: No Pricing
Production 15 Sets
Patch Gold: No Pricing
Production Two Sets
Patch Silver: No Pricing
Production 10 Sets
LA1 Luis Aparicio 20.00
LA2 Luis Aparicio 20.00
EB1 Ernie Banks 50.00
BE1 Johnny Bench 40.00
YB1 Yogi Berra 60.00
WB1 Wade Boggs 35.00
WB2 Wade Boggs 35.00
WB3 Wade Boggs 35.00
GB1 George Brett 60.00
GB2 George Brett 60.00
LB1 Lou Brock 35.00
LB2 Lou Brock 35.00
JB1 Jim Bunning 25.00
RC1 Rod Carew 30.00
RC2 Rod Carew 30.00
SC1 Steve Carlton 20.00
SC2 Steve Carlton 20.00
GC1 Gary Carter 25.00
GC2 Gary Carter 25.00
GC3 Gary Carter 25.00
OC1 Orlando Cepeda 25.00
OC2 Orlando Cepeda 25.00
BD1 Bobby Doerr 15.00
BD2 Bobby Doerr 15.00
DE1 Dennis Eckersley 20.00
DE2 Dennis Eckersley 20.00
BF1 Bob Feller 30.00
BF2 Bob Feller 30.00
RF1 Rollie Fingers 20.00
RF2 Rollie Fingers 20.00
CF1 Carlton Fisk 30.00
CF2 Carlton Fisk 30.00
WF1 Whitey Ford 50.00
BG1 Bob Gibson 35.00
MI1 Monte Irvin 25.00
RJ1 Reggie Jackson 40.00
RJ2 Reggie Jackson 40.00
RJ3 Reggie Jackson 40.00
FJ1 Fergie Jenkins 20.00
FJ2 Fergie Jenkins 20.00
AK1 Al Kaline 40.00
AK2 Al Kaline 40.00
GK1 George Kell 20.00
HK1 Harmon Killebrew 40.00
HK2 Harmon Killebrew 40.00
RK1 Ralph Kiner 40.00
JM1 Juan Marichal 25.00
BM1 Bill Mazeroski 40.00
WM1 Willie McCovey 40.00
PM1 Paul Molitor 30.00
PM2 Paul Molitor 30.00
PM3 Paul Molitor 30.00
MO1 Joe Morgan 25.00
MO2 Joe Morgan 25.00
EM1 Eddie Murray 50.00
EM2 Eddie Murray 50.00
SM1 Stan Musial 60.00
SM2 Stan Musial 60.00
PN1 Phil Niekro 20.00
PN2 Phil Niekro 20.00
JP1 Jim Palmer 20.00
JP2 Jim Palmer 20.00
TP1 Tony Perez 20.00
TP2 Tony Perez 20.00
GP1 Gaylord Perry 20.00
GP2 Gaylord Perry 20.00
KP1 Kirby Puckett 40.00
KP2 Kirby Puckett 40.00
RR1 Robin Roberts 40.00
BR1 Brooks Robinson 30.00
BR2 Brooks Robinson 30.00
BR3 Brooks Robinson 30.00
FR1 Frank Robinson 20.00
NR1 Nolan Ryan 90.00
NR2 Nolan Ryan 90.00
NR3 Nolan Ryan 90.00
NR4 Nolan Ryan 90.00
SA1 Ryne Sandberg 60.00
SA2 Ryne Sandberg 60.00
SA3 Ryne Sandberg 60.00
MS1 Mike Schmidt 50.00
MS2 Mike Schmidt 50.00
MS3 Mike Schmidt 50.00
RS1 Red Schoendienst 35.00
TS1 Tom Seaver 40.00
OS1 Ozzie Smith 40.00
OS2 Ozzie Smith 40.00
OS3 Ozzie Smith 40.00
SN1 Duke Snider 40.00
DS1 Don Sutton 20.00
DS2 Don Sutton 20.00
DS3 Don Sutton 20.00
BW1 Billy Williams 20.00
BW2 Billy Williams 20.00
DW1 Dave Winfield 30.00
CY1 Carl Yastrzemski 50.00
CY2 Carl Yastrzemski 50.00
RY1 Robin Yount 40.00
RY2 Robin Yount 40.00
RY3 Robin Yount 40.00

Cooperstown Cuts

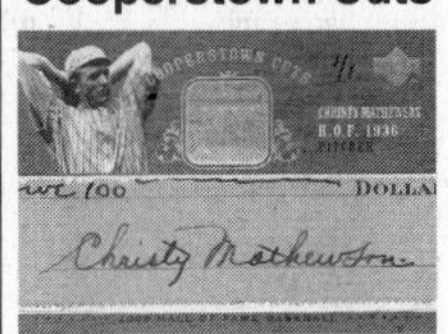

NM/M

Production 1-20
JM Johnny Mize/20 180.00

Cooperstown Cuts Memorabilia

No Pricing
Production 1-20

Essential Enshrinement

NM/M

Production 50 Sets
Gold: No Pricing
Production Five Sets
Silver: No Pricing
Production 15 Sets
Rainbow: No Pricing
Production One Set
LA1 Luis Aparicio 4.00
EB1 Ernie Banks 6.00
BE1 Johnny Bench 6.00
BE2 Johnny Bench 6.00
YB1 Yogi Berra 5.00
YB2 Yogi Berra 5.00
WB1 Wade Boggs 5.00
WB2 Wade Boggs 5.00
WB3 Wade Boggs 5.00
GB1 George Brett 10.00
GB2 George Brett 10.00
GB3 George Brett 10.00
LB1 Lou Brock 4.00
LB2 Lou Brock 4.00
JB1 Jim Bunning 4.00
RC1 Rod Carew 4.00
RC2 Rod Carew 4.00
SC1 Steve Carlton 4.00
SC2 Steve Carlton 4.00
GC1 Gary Carter 4.00
GC2 Gary Carter 4.00
OC1 Orlando Cepeda 4.00
BD1 Bobby Doerr 4.00
BD2 Bobby Doerr 4.00
DE1 Dennis Eckersley 4.00
BF1 Bob Feller 4.00
BF2 Bob Feller 4.00
RF1 Rollie Fingers 4.00
CF1 Carlton Fisk 4.00
CF2 Carlton Fisk 4.00
WF1 Whitey Ford 5.00
WF2 Whitey Ford 5.00
BG1 Bob Gibson 5.00
BG2 Bob Gibson 5.00
MI1 Monte Irvin 4.00
RJ1 Reggie Jackson 5.00
RJ2 Reggie Jackson 5.00
RJ3 Reggie Jackson 5.00
FJ1 Fergie Jenkins 4.00
FJ2 Fergie Jenkins 4.00
AK1 Al Kaline 6.00
AK2 Al Kaline 6.00
GK1 George Kell 4.00
HK1 Harmon Killebrew 6.00
HK2 Harmon Killebrew 6.00
RK1 Ralph Kiner 4.00
JM1 Juan Marichal 4.00
BM1 Bill Mazeroski 4.00
WM1 Willie McCovey 5.00
PM1 Paul Molitor 5.00
PM2 Paul Molitor 5.00
PM3 Paul Molitor 5.00
MO1 Joe Morgan 4.00
MO2 Joe Morgan 4.00
MO3 Joe Morgan 4.00
EM1 Eddie Murray 4.00
EM2 Eddie Murray 4.00
SM1 Stan Musial 6.00
SM2 Stan Musial 6.00
PN1 Phil Niekro 4.00
PN2 Phil Niekro 4.00
JP1 Jim Palmer 4.00
JP2 Jim Palmer 4.00
TP1 Tony Perez 4.00
GP1 Gaylord Perry 4.00
GP2 Gaylord Perry 4.00
KP1 Kirby Puckett 5.00
KP2 Kirby Puckett 5.00
RR1 Robin Roberts 4.00
BR1 Brooks Robinson 5.00
BR2 Brooks Robinson 5.00
BR3 Brooks Robinson 5.00
FR1 Frank Robinson 5.00
FR2 Frank Robinson 5.00
NR1 Nolan Ryan 10.00
NR2 Nolan Ryan 10.00
NR3 Nolan Ryan 10.00
NR4 Nolan Ryan 10.00
SA1 Ryne Sandberg 6.00
SA2 Ryne Sandberg 6.00
SA3 Ryne Sandberg 6.00

MS1 Mike Schmidt 6.00
MS2 Mike Schmidt 6.00
RS1 Red Schoendienst 4.00
TS1 Tom Seaver 5.00
OS1 Ozzie Smith 6.00
OS2 Ozzie Smith 6.00
SN1 Duke Snider 5.00
SN2 Duke Snider 5.00
DS1 Don Sutton 4.00
DS2 Don Sutton 4.00
BW1 Billy Williams 4.00
BW2 Billy Williams 4.00
DW1 Dave Winfield 4.00
CY1 Carl Yastrzemski 6.00
CY2 Carl Yastrzemski 6.00
CY3 Carl Yastrzemski 6.00
RY1 Robin Yount 6.00
RY2 Robin Yount 6.00
RY3 Robin Yount 6.00

Essential Enshrinement Autograph

NM/M
Production 25 Sets
Gold: No Pricing
Production Five Sets
Silver: No Pricing
Production 15 Sets
Rainbow: No Pricing
Production One Set
Material Gold: No Pricing
Production Five Sets
Material Silver: No Pricing
Production 15 Sets
Patch Gold: No Pricing
Production Five Sets
Patch Silver: No Pricing
Production 10 Sets
LA1 Luis Aparicio 20.00
EB1 Ernie Banks 50.00
BE1 Johnny Bench 40.00
BE2 Johnny Bench 40.00
YB1 Yogi Berra 60.00
YB2 Yogi Berra 60.00
WB1 Wade Boggs 35.00
WB2 Wade Boggs 35.00
WB3 Wade Boggs 35.00
GB1 George Brett 60.00
GB2 George Brett 60.00
GB3 George Brett 60.00
LB1 Lou Brock 35.00
LB2 Lou Brock 35.00
JB1 Jim Bunning 25.00
RC1 Rod Carew 30.00
RC2 Rod Carew 30.00
SC1 Steve Carlton 20.00
SC2 Steve Carlton 20.00
GC1 Gary Carter 25.00
GC2 Gary Carter 25.00
OC1 Orlando Cepeda 25.00
BD1 Bobby Doerr 15.00
BD2 Bobby Doerr 15.00
DE1 Dennis Eckersley 20.00
BF1 Bob Feller 30.00
BF2 Bob Feller 30.00
RF1 Rollie Fingers 20.00
CF1 Carlton Fisk 30.00
CF2 Carlton Fisk 30.00
WF1 Whitey Ford 50.00
WF2 Whitey Ford 50.00
BG1 Bob Gibson 35.00
BG2 Bob Gibson 35.00
MI1 Monte Irvin 25.00
RJ1 Reggie Jackson 40.00
RJ2 Reggie Jackson 40.00
RJ3 Reggie Jackson 40.00
FJ1 Fergie Jenkins 20.00
FJ2 Fergie Jenkins 20.00
AK1 Al Kaline 40.00
AK2 Al Kaline 40.00
GK1 George Kell 20.00
HK1 Harmon Killebrew 40.00
HK2 Harmon Killebrew 40.00
RK1 Ralph Kiner 40.00
JM1 Juan Marichal 25.00
BM1 Bill Mazeroski 40.00
WM1 Willie McCovey 40.00
PM1 Paul Molitor 30.00
PM2 Paul Molitor 30.00
PM3 Paul Molitor 30.00
MO1 Joe Morgan 25.00
MO2 Joe Morgan 25.00
MO3 Joe Morgan 25.00
EM1 Eddie Murray 50.00
EM2 Eddie Murray 50.00
SM1 Stan Musial 60.00
SM2 Stan Musial 60.00
PN1 Phil Niekro 20.00
PN2 Phil Niekro 20.00
JP1 Jim Palmer 20.00
JP2 Jim Palmer 20.00
TP1 Tony Perez 20.00
GP1 Gaylord Perry 20.00
GP2 Gaylord Perry 20.00
KP1 Kirby Puckett 40.00
KP2 Kirby Puckett 40.00
RR1 Robin Roberts 25.00
BR1 Brooks Robinson 30.00
BR2 Brooks Robinson 30.00
BR3 Brooks Robinson 30.00
FR1 Frank Robinson 20.00
FR2 Frank Robinson 20.00
NR1 Nolan Ryan 90.00
NR2 Nolan Ryan 90.00
NR3 Nolan Ryan 90.00
NR4 Nolan Ryan 90.00
SA1 Ryne Sandberg 60.00
SA2 Ryne Sandberg 60.00
SA3 Ryne Sandberg 60.00
MS1 Mike Schmidt 50.00
MS2 Mike Schmidt 50.00
RS1 Red Schoendienst 35.00
TS1 Tom Seaver 40.00
OS1 Ozzie Smith 40.00
OS2 Ozzie Smith 40.00
SN1 Duke Snider 40.00
SN2 Duke Snider 40.00
DS1 Don Sutton 20.00
DS2 Don Sutton 20.00
BW1 Billy Williams 20.00
BW2 Billy Williams 20.00
DW1 Dave Winfield 30.00
CY1 Carl Yastrzemski 50.00
CY2 Carl Yastrzemski 50.00
CY3 Carl Yastrzemski 50.00
RY1 Robin Yount 40.00
RY2 Robin Yount 40.00
RY3 Robin Yount 40.00

Hall of Fame Materials

NM/M
Production 25 Sets
Gold: No Pricing
Production Five Sets
Silver: No Pricing
Production 15 Sets
Rainbow: No Pricing
Production One Set
Green: No Pricing
Production 10 Sets
RC1 Roberto Clemente 120.00
RC2 Roberto Clemente 120.00
RC3 Roberto Clemente 120.00
TC1 Ty Cobb 100.00
TC2 Ty Cobb 100.00
TC3 Ty Cobb 100.00
MC1 Mickey Cochrane 40.00
DD1 Dizzy Dean 80.00
DD2 Dizzy Dean 80.00
JD1 Joe DiMaggio 90.00
JD2 Joe DiMaggio 90.00
JD3 Joe DiMaggio 90.00
JF1 Jimmie Foxx 60.00
JF2 Jimmie Foxx 60.00
LG1 Lou Gehrig 180.00
LG2 Lou Gehrig 180.00
LG3 Lou Gehrig 180.00
RH1 Rogers Hornsby 80.00
MM1 Mickey Mantle 250.00
MM2 Mickey Mantle 250.00
MM3 Mickey Mantle 250.00
JM1 Johnny Mize 30.00
JM2 Johnny Mize 30.00
JM3 Johnny Mize 30.00
MO1 Mel Ott 40.00
MO2 Mel Ott 40.00
SP1 Satchel Paige 50.00
SP2 Satchel Paige 50.00
SP3 Satchel Paige 50.00
JR1 Jackie Robinson 60.00
JR2 Jackie Robinson 60.00
JR3 Jackie Robinson 60.00
BR1 Babe Ruth 250.00
BR2 Babe Ruth 250.00
BR3 Babe Ruth 250.00
GS1 George Sisler 40.00
GS2 George Sisler 40.00
TW1 Ted Williams 85.00
TW2 Ted Williams 85.00
TW3 Ted Williams 85.00

Hall of Fame Seasons

NM/M
Production 50 Sets
Gold: No Pricing
Production Five Sets
Silver: No Pricing
Production 15 Sets
Rainbow: No Pricing
Production One Set
LA1 Luis Aparicio 4.00
EB1 Ernie Banks 6.00
BE1 Johnny Bench 6.00
BE2 Johnny Bench 6.00
YB1 Yogi Berra 5.00
YB2 Yogi Berra 5.00
WB1 Wade Boggs 5.00
WB2 Wade Boggs 5.00
WB3 Wade Boggs 5.00
GB1 George Brett 10.00
GB2 George Brett 10.00
LB1 Lou Brock 4.00
LB2 Lou Brock 4.00
JB1 Jim Bunning 4.00
RC1 Rod Carew 4.00
RC2 Rod Carew 4.00
GC1 Gary Carter 4.00
SC1 Steve Carlton 4.00
SC2 Steve Carlton 4.00
SC3 Steve Carlton 4.00
OC1 Orlando Cepeda 4.00
BD1 Bobby Doerr 4.00
DE1 Dennis Eckersley 4.00
DE2 Dennis Eckersley 4.00
DE3 Dennis Eckersley 4.00
BF1 Bob Feller 4.00
BF2 Bob Feller 4.00
RF1 Rollie Fingers 4.00
CF1 Carlton Fisk 4.00
CF2 Carlton Fisk 4.00
WF1 Whitey Ford 5.00
WF2 Whitey Ford 5.00
BG1 Bob Gibson 5.00
BG2 Bob Gibson 5.00
MI1 Monte Irvin 4.00
RJ1 Reggie Jackson 5.00
RJ2 Reggie Jackson 5.00
RJ3 Reggie Jackson 5.00
FJ1 Fergie Jenkins 4.00
FJ2 Fergie Jenkins 4.00
AK1 Al Kaline 6.00
AK2 Al Kaline 6.00
AK3 Al Kaline 6.00
GK1 George Kell 4.00
HK1 Harmon Killebrew 6.00
HK2 Harmon Killebrew 6.00
HK3 Harmon Killebrew 6.00
RK1 Ralph Kiner 4.00
JM1 Juan Marichal 4.00
BM1 Bill Mazeroski 4.00
WM1 Willie McCovey 5.00
PM1 Paul Molitor 5.00
PM2 Paul Molitor 5.00
PM3 Paul Molitor 5.00
MO1 Joe Morgan 4.00
MO2 Joe Morgan 4.00
EM1 Eddie Murray 4.00
EM2 Eddie Murray 4.00
SM1 Stan Musial 6.00
SM2 Stan Musial 6.00
PN1 Phil Niekro 4.00
PN2 Phil Niekro 4.00
JP1 Jim Palmer 4.00
JP2 Jim Palmer 4.00
JP3 Jim Palmer 4.00
TP1 Tony Perez 4.00
GP1 Gaylord Perry 4.00
GP2 Gaylord Perry 4.00
KP1 Kirby Puckett 5.00
KP2 Kirby Puckett 5.00
RR1 Robin Roberts 4.00
BR1 Brooks Robinson 5.00
BR2 Brooks Robinson 5.00
BR3 Brooks Robinson 5.00
FR1 Frank Robinson 5.00
FR2 Frank Robinson 5.00
NR1 Nolan Ryan 10.00
NR2 Nolan Ryan 10.00
NR3 Nolan Ryan 10.00
NR4 Nolan Ryan 10.00
SA1 Ryne Sandberg 6.00
SA2 Ryne Sandberg 6.00
MS1 Mike Schmidt 6.00
MS2 Mike Schmidt 6.00
MS3 Mike Schmidt 6.00
RS1 Red Schoendienst 4.00
TS1 Tom Seaver 5.00
TS2 Tom Seaver 5.00
OS1 Ozzie Smith 6.00
OS2 Ozzie Smith 6.00
SN1 Duke Snider 5.00
DS1 Don Sutton 4.00
DS2 Don Sutton 4.00
BW1 Billy Williams 4.00
BW2 Billy Williams 4.00
DW1 Dave Winfield 4.00
CY1 Carl Yastrzemski 6.00
CY2 Carl Yastrzemski 6.00
RY1 Robin Yount 6.00
RY2 Robin Yount 6.00

Hall of Fame Seasons Autograph

NM/M
Production 25 Sets
Gold: No Pricing
Production Five Sets
Silver: No Pricing
Production 15 Sets
Rainbow: No Pricing
Production One Set
Material Gold: No Pricing
Production Five Sets
Material Silver: No Pricing
Production 15 Sets
Patch Gold: No Pricing
Production Five Sets
Patch Silver: No Pricing
Production 10 Sets
LA1 Luis Aparicio 20.00
EB1 Ernie Banks 50.00
BE1 Johnny Bench 40.00
BE2 Johnny Bench 40.00
YB1 Yogi Berra 60.00
YB2 Yogi Berra 60.00
WB1 Wade Boggs 35.00
WB2 Wade Boggs 35.00
WB3 Wade Boggs 35.00
GB1 George Brett 60.00
GB2 George Brett 60.00
LB1 Lou Brock 35.00
LB2 Lou Brock 35.00
JB1 Jim Bunning 25.00
RC1 Rod Carew 30.00
RC2 Rod Carew 30.00
GC1 Gary Carter 25.00
SC1 Steve Carlton 20.00
SC2 Steve Carlton 20.00
SC3 Steve Carlton 20.00
OC1 Orlando Cepeda 25.00
BD1 Bobby Doerr 15.00
DE1 Dennis Eckersley 20.00
DE2 Dennis Eckersley 20.00
DE3 Dennis Eckersley 20.00
BF1 Bob Feller 30.00
BF2 Bob Feller 30.00
RF1 Rollie Fingers 20.00
CF1 Carlton Fisk 30.00
CF2 Carlton Fisk 30.00
WF1 Whitey Ford 50.00
WF2 Whitey Ford 50.00
BG1 Bob Gibson 35.00
BG2 Bob Gibson 35.00
MI1 Monte Irvin 25.00
RJ1 Reggie Jackson 40.00
RJ2 Reggie Jackson 40.00
RJ3 Reggie Jackson 40.00
FJ1 Fergie Jenkins 20.00
FJ2 Fergie Jenkins 20.00
AK1 Al Kaline 40.00
AK2 Al Kaline 40.00
AK3 Al Kaline 40.00
GK1 George Kell 20.00
HK1 Harmon Killebrew 40.00
HK2 Harmon Killebrew 40.00
HK3 Harmon Killebrew 40.00
RK1 Ralph Kiner 40.00
JM1 Juan Marichal 25.00
BM1 Bill Mazeroski 40.00
WM1 Willie McCovey 40.00
PM1 Paul Molitor 30.00
PM2 Paul Molitor 30.00
PM3 Paul Molitor 30.00
MO1 Joe Morgan 25.00
MO2 Joe Morgan 25.00
EM1 Eddie Murray 50.00
EM2 Eddie Murray 50.00
SM1 Stan Musial 60.00
SM2 Stan Musial 60.00
PN1 Phil Niekro 20.00
PN2 Phil Niekro 20.00
JP1 Jim Palmer 20.00
JP2 Jim Palmer 20.00
JP3 Jim Palmer 20.00
TP1 Tony Perez 20.00
GP1 Gaylord Perry 20.00
GP2 Gaylord Perry 20.00
KP1 Kirby Puckett 40.00
KP2 Kirby Puckett 40.00
RR1 Robin Roberts 25.00
BR1 Brooks Robinson 30.00
BR2 Brooks Robinson 30.00
BR3 Brooks Robinson 30.00
FR1 Frank Robinson 20.00
FR2 Frank Robinson 20.00
NR1 Nolan Ryan 90.00
NR2 Nolan Ryan 90.00
NR3 Nolan Ryan 90.00
NR4 Nolan Ryan 90.00
SA1 Ryne Sandberg 60.00
SA2 Ryne Sandberg 60.00
MS1 Mike Schmidt 50.00
MS2 Mike Schmidt 50.00
MS3 Mike Schmidt 50.00
RS1 Red Schoendienst 35.00
TS1 Tom Seaver 40.00
TS2 Tom Seaver 40.00
OS1 Ozzie Smith 40.00
OS2 Ozzie Smith 40.00
SN1 Duke Snider 40.00
DS1 Don Sutton 20.00
DS2 Don Sutton 20.00
BW1 Billy Williams 20.00
BW2 Billy Williams 20.00
DW1 Dave Winfield 30.00
CY1 Carl Yastrzemski 50.00
CY2 Carl Yastrzemski 50.00
RY1 Robin Yount 40.00
RY2 Robin Yount 40.00

Hall Worthy

NM/M
Production 50 Sets
Gold: No Pricing
Production Five Sets
Silver: No Pricing
Production 15 Sets
Rainbow: No Pricing
Production One Set
LA1 Luis Aparicio 4.00
EB1 Ernie Banks 6.00
BE1 Johnny Bench 6.00
BE2 Johnny Bench 6.00
YB1 Yogi Berra 5.00
WB1 Wade Boggs 5.00
WB2 Wade Boggs 5.00
WB3 Wade Boggs 5.00
GB1 George Brett 10.00
GB2 George Brett 10.00
GB3 George Brett 10.00
LB1 Lou Brock 4.00
LB2 Lou Brock 4.00
JB1 Jim Bunning 4.00
RC1 Rod Carew 4.00
RC2 Rod Carew 4.00
SC1 Steve Carlton 4.00
SC2 Steve Carlton 4.00
GC1 Gary Carter 4.00
GC2 Gary Carter 4.00
OC1 Orlando Cepeda 4.00
OC2 Orlando Cepeda 4.00
BD1 Bobby Doerr 4.00
DE1 Dennis Eckersley 4.00
DE2 Dennis Eckersley 4.00
DE3 Dennis Eckersley 4.00
DE4 Dennis Eckersley 4.00
BF1 Bob Feller 4.00
BF2 Bob Feller 4.00
RF1 Rollie Fingers 4.00
RF2 Rollie Fingers 4.00
CF1 Carlton Fisk 4.00
CF2 Carlton Fisk 4.00
WF1 Whitey Ford 5.00
BG1 Bob Gibson 5.00
MI1 Monte Irvin 4.00
RJ1 Reggie Jackson 5.00
RJ2 Reggie Jackson 5.00
RJ3 Reggie Jackson 5.00
RJ4 Reggie Jackson 5.00
FJ1 Fergie Jenkins 4.00
FJ2 Fergie Jenkins 4.00
FJ3 Fergie Jenkins 4.00
AK1 Al Kaline 4.00
AK2 Al Kaline 4.00
GK1 George Kell 4.00
HK1 Harmon Killebrew 6.00
HK2 Harmon Killebrew 6.00
RK1 Ralph Kiner 4.00
JM1 Juan Marichal 4.00
BM1 Bill Mazeroski 4.00
WM1 Willie McCovey 5.00
PM1 Paul Molitor 5.00
PM2 Paul Molitor 5.00
MO1 Joe Morgan 4.00
MO2 Joe Morgan 4.00
EM1 Eddie Murray 4.00
EM2 Eddie Murray 4.00
EM3 Eddie Murray 4.00
SM1 Stan Musial 6.00
PN1 Phil Niekro 4.00
PN2 Phil Niekro 4.00
JP1 Jim Palmer 4.00
JP2 Jim Palmer 4.00
TP1 Tony Perez 4.00
TP2 Tony Perez 4.00
GP1 Gaylord Perry 4.00
GP2 Gaylord Perry 4.00
KP1 Kirby Puckett 5.00
RR1 Robin Roberts 4.00
BR1 Brooks Robinson 5.00
BR2 Brooks Robinson 5.00
FR1 Frank Robinson 5.00
FR2 Frank Robinson 5.00
NR1 Nolan Ryan 10.00
NR2 Nolan Ryan 10.00
NR3 Nolan Ryan 10.00
NR4 Nolan Ryan 10.00
SA1 Ryne Sandberg 6.00
SA2 Ryne Sandberg 6.00
SA3 Ryne Sandberg 6.00
MS1 Mike Schmidt 6.00
MS2 Mike Schmidt 6.00
MS3 Mike Schmidt 6.00
RS1 Red Schoendienst 4.00
TS1 Tom Seaver 5.00
TS2 Tom Seaver 5.00
OS1 Ozzie Smith 6.00
OS2 Ozzie Smith 6.00
SN1 Duke Snider 5.00
SN2 Duke Snider 5.00
DS1 Don Sutton 4.00
DS2 Don Sutton 4.00
DS3 Don Sutton 4.00
BW1 Billy Williams 4.00
DW1 Dave Winfield 4.00
CY1 Carl Yastrzemski 6.00
CY2 Carl Yastrzemski 6.00
RY1 Robin Yount 6.00
RY2 Robin Yount 6.00

Hall Worthy Autograph

NM/M
Production 25 Sets
Gold: No Pricing
Production Five Sets
Silver: No Pricing
Production 15 Sets
Rainbow: No Pricing
Production One Set
Material Gold: No Pricing
Production Five Sets
Material Silver: No Pricing
Production 15 Sets
Patch Gold: No Pricing
Production Five Sets
Patch Silver: No Pricing
Production 10 Sets
LA1 Luis Aparicio 20.00
EB1 Ernie Banks 50.00
BE1 Johnny Bench 40.00
BE2 Johnny Bench 40.00
YB1 Yogi Berra 60.00
WB1 Wade Boggs 35.00
WB2 Wade Boggs 35.00
WB3 Wade Boggs 35.00
GB1 George Brett 60.00
GB2 George Brett 60.00
GB3 George Brett 60.00
LB1 Lou Brock 35.00
LB2 Lou Brock 35.00
JB1 Jim Bunning 25.00
RC1 Rod Carew 30.00
RC2 Rod Carew 30.00
SC1 Steve Carlton 20.00
SC2 Steve Carlton 20.00
GC1 Gary Carter 25.00
GC2 Gary Carter 25.00
OC1 Orlando Cepeda 25.00
OC2 Orlando Cepeda 25.00
BD1 Bobby Doerr 15.00
DE1 Dennis Eckersley 20.00
DE2 Dennis Eckersley 20.00
DE3 Dennis Eckersley 20.00
DE4 Dennis Eckersley 20.00
BF1 Bob Feller 30.00
BF2 Bob Feller 30.00
RF1 Rollie Fingers 20.00
RF2 Rollie Fingers 20.00
CF1 Carlton Fisk 30.00
CF2 Carlton Fisk 30.00
WF1 Whitey Ford 50.00
BG1 Bob Gibson 35.00
MI1 Monte Irvin 25.00
RJ1 Reggie Jackson 40.00
RJ2 Reggie Jackson 40.00
RJ3 Reggie Jackson 40.00
RJ4 Reggie Jackson 40.00
FJ1 Fergie Jenkins 20.00
FJ2 Fergie Jenkins 20.00
FJ3 Fergie Jenkins 20.00
AK1 Al Kaline 40.00
AK2 Al Kaline 40.00
GK1 George Kell 20.00
HK1 Harmon Killebrew 40.00
HK2 Harmon Killebrew 40.00
RK1 Ralph Kiner 40.00
JM1 Juan Marichal 25.00
BM1 Bill Mazeroski 40.00
WM1 Willie McCovey 40.00
PM1 Paul Molitor 30.00
PM2 Paul Molitor 30.00
MO1 Joe Morgan 25.00
MO2 Joe Morgan 25.00
EM1 Eddie Murray 50.00
EM2 Eddie Murray 50.00
EM3 Eddie Murray 50.00
SM1 Stan Musial 60.00
PN1 Phil Niekro 20.00
PN2 Phil Niekro 20.00
JP1 Jim Palmer 20.00
JP2 Jim Palmer 20.00
TP1 Tony Perez 20.00
TP2 Tony Perez 20.00
GP1 Gaylord Perry 20.00
GP2 Gaylord Perry 20.00
KP1 Kirby Puckett 40.00
RR1 Robin Roberts 25.00
BR1 Brooks Robinson 30.00
BR2 Brooks Robinson 30.00
FR1 Frank Robinson 20.00
FR2 Frank Robinson 20.00
NR1 Nolan Ryan 90.00
NR2 Nolan Ryan 90.00
NR3 Nolan Ryan 90.00
NR4 Nolan Ryan 90.00
SA1 Ryne Sandberg 60.00
SA2 Ryne Sandberg 60.00
SA3 Ryne Sandberg 60.00
MS1 Mike Schmidt 50.00
MS2 Mike Schmidt 50.00
MS3 Mike Schmidt 50.00
RS1 Red Schoendienst 35.00
TS1 Tom Seaver 40.00
TS2 Tom Seaver 40.00
OS1 Ozzie Smith 40.00
OS2 Ozzie Smith 40.00
SN1 Duke Snider 40.00
SN2 Duke Snider 40.00
DS1 Don Sutton 20.00
DS2 Don Sutton 20.00
DS3 Don Sutton 20.00
BW1 Billy Williams 20.00
DW1 Dave Winfield 30.00
CY1 Carl Yastrzemski 50.00
CY2 Carl Yastrzemski 50.00
RY1 Robin Yount 40.00
RY2 Robin Yount 40.00

Signs of Cooperstown Duals

NM/M
Production 50 Sets
Gold: No Pricing
Production Five Sets
Silver: No Pricing
Production 15 Sets
Rainbow: No Pricing
Production One Set
AB Ernie Banks, Luis Aparicio 6.00
AS Luis Aparicio, Ozzie Smith 8.00
BC Steve Carlton, Jim Bunning 4.00
BF Frank Robinson, Brooks Robinson 5.00
BG George Brett, Brooks Robinson 10.00
BM Lou Brock, Stan Musial 8.00
BR Jim Bunning, Robin Roberts 4.00
BS Ernie Banks, Ryne Sandberg 10.00
CM Orlando Cepeda, Willie McCovey 4.00
CS Tom Seaver, Gary Carter 4.00
DB Wade Boggs, Bobby Doerr 4.00
EF Dennis Eckersley, Rollie Fingers 4.00
FB Johnny Bench, Carlton Fisk 6.00
FC Bob Feller, Steve Carlton 4.00
FP Bob Feller, Gaylord Perry 4.00
GC Bob Gibson, Steve Carlton 5.00
GF Bob Gibson, Whitey Ford 5.00

IM	Monte Irvin, Willie McCovey	5.00
JJ	Joe Morgan, Johnny Bench	6.00
JM	Reggie Jackson, Willie McCovey	5.00
JW	Reggie Jackson, Dave Winfield	5.00
JY	Yogi Berra, Johnny Bench	6.00
KK	Al Kaline, George Kell	6.00
KP	Kirby Puckett, Harmon Killebrew	6.00
LO	Lou Brock, Ozzie Smith	8.00
MK	Bill Mazeroski, Ralph Kiner	5.00
MP	Joe Morgan, Tony Perez	4.00
MY	Robin Yount, Paul Molitor	6.00
NS	Steve Carlton, Nolan Ryan	10.00
PM	Gaylord Perry, Juan Marichal	4.00
PN	Gaylord Perry, Phil Niekro	4.00
PR	Rod Carew, Paul Molitor	5.00
RC	Rod Carew, Nolan Ryan	10.00
RP	Jim Palmer, Brooks Robinson	5.00
RS	Tom Seaver, Nolan Ryan	10.00
RW	Ryne Sandberg, Wade Boggs	10.00
SB	George Brett, Mike Schmidt	10.00
SC	Mike Schmidt, Steve Carlton	10.00
SK	Ralph Kiner, Duke Snider	5.00
SM	Ozzie Smith, Stan Musial	8.00
SP	Gaylord Perry, Don Sutton	4.00
SR	Mike Schmidt, Brooks Robinson	10.00
SS	Red Schoendienst, Ozzie Smith	8.00
SW	Billy Williams, Ryne Sandberg	10.00
WB	Billy Williams, Ernie Banks	6.00
WJ	Billy Williams, Fergie Jenkins	4.00
WS	Ozzie Smith, Dave Winfield	6.00
WY	Yogi Berra, Whitey Ford	6.00
YF	Carlton Fisk, Carl Yastrzemski	6.00
YJ	Reggie Jackson, Carl Yastrzemski	6.00

Signs of Cooperstown Duals Auto.

NM/M

Production 20 Sets
Gold: No Pricing
Production Five Sets
Silver: No Pricing
Production 10 Sets
Rainbow: No Pricing
Production One Set

AB	Ernie Banks, Luis Aparicio	80.00
AS	Luis Aparicio, Ozzie Smith	60.00
BC	Steve Carlton, Jim Bunning	35.00
BF	Frank Robinson, Brooks Robinson	60.00
BG	George Brett, Brooks Robinson	90.00
BM	Lou Brock, Stan Musial	100.00
BR	Jim Bunning, Robin Roberts	60.00
BS	Ernie Banks, Ryne Sandberg	120.00
CM	Orlando Cepeda, Willie McCovey	50.00
CS	Tom Seaver, Gary Carter	80.00
DB	Wade Boggs, Bobby Doerr	50.00
EF	Dennis Eckersley, Rollie Fingers	35.00
FB	Johnny Bench, Carlton Fisk	75.00
FC	Bob Feller, Steve Carlton	40.00
FP	Bob Feller, Gaylord Perry	40.00
GC	Bob Gibson, Steve Carlton	60.00
GF	Bob Gibson, Whitey Ford	75.00
IM	Monte Irvin, Willie McCovey	60.00
JJ	Joe Morgan, Johnny Bench	80.00
JM	Reggie Jackson, Willie McCovey	100.00
JW	Reggie Jackson, Dave Winfield	80.00
JY	Yogi Berra, Johnny Bench	150.00
KK	Al Kaline, George Kell	85.00
KP	Kirby Puckett, Harmon Killebrew	80.00
LO	Lou Brock, Ozzie Smith	65.00
MK	Bill Mazeroski, Ralph Kiner	75.00
MP	Joe Morgan, Tony Perez	50.00
MY	Robin Yount, Paul Molitor	85.00
NS	Steve Carlton, Nolan Ryan	150.00
PM	Gaylord Perry, Juan Marichal	40.00
PN	Gaylord Perry, Phil Niekro	40.00
PR	Rod Carew, Paul Molitor	50.00
RC	Rod Carew, Nolan Ryan	150.00
RP	Jim Palmer, Brooks Robinson	50.00
RS	Tom Seaver, Nolan Ryan	180.00
RW	Ryne Sandberg, Wade Boggs	100.00
SB	George Brett, Mike Schmidt	140.00
SC	Mike Schmidt, Steve Carlton	85.00
SK	Ralph Kiner, Duke Snider	65.00
SM	Ozzie Smith, Stan Musial	120.00
SP	Gaylord Perry, Don Sutton	40.00
SR	Mike Schmidt, Brooks Robinson	75.00
SS	Red Schoendienst, Ozzie Smith	65.00
SW	Billy Williams, Ryne Sandberg	90.00
WB	Billy Williams, Ernie Banks	90.00
WJ	Billy Williams, Fergie Jenkins	50.00
WS	Ozzie Smith, Dave Winfield	75.00
WY	Yogi Berra, Whitey Ford	100.00
YF	Carlton Fisk, Carl Yastrzemski	100.00
YJ	Reggie Jackson, Carl Yastrzemski	100.00

Signs of Cooperstown Triples

NM/M

Production 50 Sets
Gold: No Pricing
Production Five Sets
Silver: No Pricing
Production 15 Sets
Rainbow: No Pricing
Production One Set

ASY	Robin Yount, Luis Aparicio, Ozzie Smith	8.00
BFJ	Jim Palmer, Frank Robinson, Brooks Robinson	5.00
BSB	George Brett, Mike Schmidt, Wade Boggs	10.00
BSY	Ernie Banks, Robin Yount, Ozzie Smith	8.00
CMI	Monte Irvin, Orlando Cepeda, Willie McCovey	5.00
DFY	Carlton Fisk, Carl Yastrzemski, Bobby Doerr	8.00
DYB	Carl Yastrzemski, Wade Boggs, Bobby Doerr	8.00
FPE	Bob Feller, Dennis Eckersley, Gaylord Perry	4.00
FRC	Bob Feller, Steve Carlton, Nolan Ryan	10.00
FSE	Dennis Eckersley, Rollie Fingers, Don Sutton	4.00
GCE	Bob Gibson, Dennis Eckersley, Steve Carlton	4.00
GSM	Bob Gibson, Stan Musial, Ozzie Smith	8.00
JFB	Yogi Berra, Reggie Jackson, Whitey Ford	8.00
JPR	Nolan Ryan, Gaylord Perry, Fergie Jenkins	10.00
KKB	Al Kaline, George Kell, Jim Bunning	6.00
KPC	Rod Carew, Kirby Puckett, Harmon Killebrew	6.00
KSR	Ralph Kiner, Duke Snider, Frank Robinson	5.00
KWR	Al Kaline, Frank Robinson, Dave Winfield	6.00
MBP	Johnny Bench, Tony Perez, Joe Morgan	6.00
MCM	Orlando Cepeda, Willie McCovey, Juan Marichal	5.00
MMS	Joe Morgan, Red Schoendienst, Bill Mazeroski	4.00
MRJ	Eddie Murray, Reggie Jackson, Frank Robinson	5.00
MSC	Rod Carew, Joe Morgan, Ryne Sandberg	6.00
MYF	Robin Yount, Paul Molitor, Rollie Fingers	6.00
PMC	Rod Carew, Kirby Puckett, Paul Molitor	6.00
RAP	Jim Palmer, Luis Aparicio, Brooks Robinson	5.00
RBC	Steve Carlton, Jim Bunning, Robin Roberts	4.00
RBS	George Brett, Mike Schmidt, Brooks Robinson	10.00
RSR	Robin Roberts, Don Sutton, Nolan Ryan	10.00
SRC	Mike Schmidt, Steve Carlton, Robin Roberts	8.00
WBI	Billy Williams, Monte Irvin, Lou Brock	4.00
WBJ	Billy Williams, Ernie Banks, Fergie Jenkins	6.00
WJB	Reggie Jackson, Wade Boggs, Dave Winfield	6.00
WSP	Dave Winfield, Ozzie Smith, Gaylord Perry	6.00
YKM	Ralph Kiner, Carl Yastrzemski, Stan Musial	8.00

Signs of Cooperstown Triple Auto.

NM/M

Production 20 Sets 75.00
Gold: No Pricing
Production Five Sets
Silver: No Pricing
Production 10 Sets
Rainbow: No Pricing
Production One Set

ASY	Robin Yount, Luis Aparicio, Ozzie Smith	140.00
BFJ	Jim Palmer, Frank Robinson, Brooks Robinson	80.00
BSB	George Brett, Mike Schmidt, Wade Boggs	185.00
BSY	Ernie Banks, Robin Yount, Ozzie Smith	150.00
CMI	Monte Irvin, Orlando Cepeda, Willie McCovey	75.00
DFY	Carlton Fisk, Carl Yastrzemski, Bobby Doerr	125.00
DYB	Carl Yastrzemski, Wade Boggs, Bobby Doerr	125.00
FRC	Bob Feller, Steve Carlton, Nolan Ryan	200.00
GSM	Bob Gibson, Ozzie Smith, Stan Musial	185.00
JFB	Yogi Berra, Reggie Jackson, Whitey Ford	185.00
JPR	Nolan Ryan, Gaylord Perry, Fergie Jenkins	150.00
KPC	Rod Carew, Kirby Puckett, Harmon Killebrew	120.00
KSR	Ralph Kiner, Duke Snider, Frank Robinson	120.00
MBP	Joe Morgan, Tony Perez, Johnny Bench	160.00
MCM	Orlando Cepeda, Willie McCovey, Juan Marichal	100.00
MSC	Joe Morgan, Rod Carew, Ryne Sandberg	125.00
MYF	Robin Yount, Paul Molitor, Rollie Fingers	125.00
PMC	Rod Carew, Kirby Puckett, Paul Molitor	100.00
RAP	Jim Palmer, Luis Aparicio, Brooks Robinson	80.00
RBC	Steve Carlton, Jim Bunning, Robin Roberts	85.00
RBS	George Brett, Mike Schmidt, Brooks Robinson	200.00
SRC	Mike Schmidt, Steve Carlton, Robin Roberts	150.00
WJB	Reggie Jackson, Wade Boggs, Dave Winfield	120.00
WSP	Dave Winfield, Ozzie Smith, Gaylord Perry	120.00
YKM	Ralph Kiner, Carl Yastrzemski, Stan Musial	140.00

Signs of Cooperstown Quads

NM/M

Production 50 Sets
Gold: No Pricing
Production Five Sets
Silver: No Pricing
Production 15 Sets
Rainbow: No Pricing
Production One Set

BMYC	George Brett, Rod Carew, Robin Yount, Paul Molitor	10.00
BSAY	Ernie Banks, Robin Yount, Luis Aparicio, Ozzie Smith	8.00
FCBB	Yogi Berra, Johnny Bench, Carlton Fisk, Gary Carter	6.00
FGRC	Bob Feller, Bob Gibson, Steve Carlton, Nolan Ryan	10.00
KCPM	Tony Perez, Orlando Cepeda, Harmon Killebrew, Willie McCovey	6.00
KYBM	Al Kaline, Lou Brock, Carl Yastrzemski, Stan Musial	8.00
MBKM	Ernie Banks, Eddie Murray, Harmon Killebrew, Willie McCovey	8.00
MDMC	Bill Mazeroski, Rod Carew, Joe Morgan, Bobby Doerr	5.00
MRKS	Eddie Murray, Mike Schmidt, Frank Robinson, Harmon Killebrew	10.00
RBKS	George Brett, Mike Schmidt, Brooks Robinson, George Kell	10.00
SPNS	Tom Seaver, Phil Niekro, Don Sutton, Gaylord Perry	6.00
SPSF	Tom Seaver, Jim Palmer, Whitey Ford, Don Sutton	6.00
SRCS	Tom Seaver, Steve Carlton, Don Sutton, Nolan Ryan	10.00
WYKM	Billy Williams, Ralph Kiner, Carl Yastrzemski, Stan Musial	8.00
YWMM	Eddie Murray, Carl Yastrzemski, Stan Musial, Dave Winfield	8.00

Signs of Cooperstown Quads Auto

No pricing
Production 10 Sets
Gold: No Pricing
Production Five Sets
Rainbow: No Pricing
Production One Set

2005 UD Mini Jersey Collection

NM/M

Complete Set (100): 15.00
Common Player: .15
Pack (3 + mini jersey): 6.00
Box (18): 90.00

1	Garret Anderson	.25
2	Vladimir Guerrero	.75
3	Luis Gonzalez	.15
4	Shawn Green	.25
5	Troy Glaus	.25
6	Andruw Jones	.50
7	Chipper Jones	.75
8	John Smoltz	.40
9	Tim Hudson	.40
10	Miguel Tejada	.50
11	Sammy Sosa	1.00
12	Curt Schilling	.75
13	David Ortiz	.75
14	Johnny Damon	.75
15	Manny Ramirez	.75
16	Greg Maddux	1.00
17	Kerry Wood	.50
18	Mark Prior	.75
19	Nomar Garciaparra	1.00
20	Frank Thomas	.50
21	Adam Dunn	.50
22	Ken Griffey Jr.	1.50
23	Travis Hafner	.25
24	Victor Martinez	.15
25	Todd Helton	.50
26	Ivan Rodriguez	.50
27	Magglio Ordonez	.15
28	Carlos Delgado	.40
29	Miguel Cabrera	.75
30	Jeff Bagwell	.50
31	Lance Berkman	.25
32	Roger Clemens	2.00
33	Roy Oswalt	.25
34	Mike Sweeney	.15
35	Eric Gagne	.15
36	J.D. Drew	.15
37	Ben Sheets	.40
38	Johan Santana	.50
39	Torii Hunter	.15
40	Carlos Beltran	.50
41	Mike Piazza	1.00
42	Pedro Martinez	.75
43	Alex Rodriguez	1.50
44	Derek Jeter	2.00
45	Hideki Matsui	1.50
46	Mike Mussina	.40
47	Randy Johnson	.75
48	Bobby Crosby	.40
49	Eric Chavez	.40
50	Bobby Abreu	.40
51	Jim Thome	.50
52	Jason Bay	.15
53	Oliver Perez	.15
54	Jake Peavy	.40
55	Khalil Greene	.40
56	Jason Schmidt	.15
57	Moises Alou	.40
58	Adrian Beltre	.40
59	Ichiro Suzuki	1.50
60	Albert Pujols	2.00
61	Jim Edmonds	.40
62	Mark Mulder	.40
63	Scott Rolen	.75
64	Aubrey Huff	.15
65	Alfonso Soriano	.50
66	Hank Blalock	.40
67	Mark Teixeira	.50
68	Roy Halladay	.40
69	Jose Vidro	.15
70	Livan Hernandez	.15
71	Atlanta Braves	.15
72	Chicago Cubs	.15
73	Chicago White Sox	.15
74	Cincinnati Reds	.15
75	Cleveland Indians	.15
76	Houston Astros	.15
77	L.A. Angels of Anaheim	.15
78	Los Angeles Dodgers	.15
79	New York Yankees	.15
80	Oakland Athletics	.15
81	Philadelphia Phillies	.15
82	Pittsburgh Pirates	.15
83	San Diego Padres	.15
84	San Francisco Giants	.15
85	Texas Rangers	.15
86	Cal Ripken Jr.	2.00
87	Derek Jeter	2.00
88	Hank Blalock	.40
89	Hideo Nomo	.40
90	Joe DiMaggio	1.00
91	Joe Morgan	.50
92	Ken Griffey Jr.	1.50
93	Larry Doby	.50
94	Pedro J. Martinez	.75
95	Randy Johnson	.75
96	Rick Ferrell	.15
97	Roger Clemens	2.00
98	Stan Musial	1.00
99	Ted Williams	1.50
100	Torii Hunter	.15

Mini Jerseys

NM/M

1	Vladimir Guerrero	5.00
2	Chipper Jones	5.00
3	Curt Schilling	5.00
4	Johnny Damon	5.00
5	Manny Ramirez	5.00
6	Kerry Wood	5.00
7	Nomar Garciaparra	5.00
8	Ken Griffey Jr.	5.00
9	Miguel Cabrera	5.00
10	Roger Clemens	10.00
11	Eric Gagne	5.00
12	Johan Santana	5.00
13	Carlos Beltran	5.00
14	Mike Piazza	5.00
15	Pedro Martinez	5.00
16	Alex Rodriguez	5.00
17	Derek Jeter	15.00
18	Hideki Matsui	8.00
19	Randy Johnson	5.00
20	Jim Thome	5.00
21	Ichiro Suzuki	8.00
22	Albert Pujols	10.00

Mini Jersey Autograph

NM/M

Inserted 1:480

1	Ken Griffey Jr.	150.00
2	David Wright	50.00
5	Adrian Beltre	50.00

Mini Replica Flannel Jerseys

NM/M

Inserted 1:18

1	Ted Williams	20.00
2	Jackie Robinson	15.00
3	Satchel Paige	15.00
4	Ty Cobb	15.00
5	Babe Ruth	30.00
6	Joe DiMaggio	20.00
7	Lou Gehrig	25.00
8	Mickey Mantle	30.00
9	Roberto Clemente	20.00

2005 Upper Deck MVP

NM/M

Complete Set (90): 20.00
Common Player: .10
Pack (6): 1.50
Box (24): 30.00

1	Adam Dunn	.40
2	Adrian Beltre	.40
3	Albert Pujols	1.50
4	Alex Rodriguez	1.50
5	Alfonso Soriano	.50
6	Andruw Jones	.40
7	Aubrey Huff	.10
8	Barry Zito	.25
9	Ben Sheets	.25
10	Bobby Abreu	.25
11	Bobby Crosby	.25
12	Bret Boone	.10
13	Brian Giles	.10
14	Carlos Beltran	.40
15	Carlos Delgado	.25
16	Carlos Lee	.25
17	Chipper Jones	.50
18	Craig Biggio	.25
19	Curt Schilling	.40
20	Dallas McPherson	.10
21	David Ortiz	.50
22	David Wright	.50
23	Derek Jeter	1.50
24	Derek Lowe	.10
25	Eric Chavez	.25
26	Eric Gagne	.25
27	Frank Thomas	.40
28	Garret Anderson	.25
29	Gary Sheffield	.40
30	Greg Maddux	1.00
31	Hank Blalock	.25
32	Hideki Matsui	1.00
33	Ichiro Suzuki	1.00
34	Ivan Rodriguez	.40
35	J.D. Drew	.10
36	Jake Peavy	.25
37	Jason Bay	.10
38	Jason Giambi	.25
39	Jason Schmidt	.25
40	Jeff Bagwell	.40
41	Jeff Kent	.25
42	Jim Edmonds	.25
43	Jim Thome	.40
44	Joe Mauer	.25
45	Johan Santana	.50
46	John Smoltz	.25
47	Johnny Damon	.50
48	Jorge Posada	.25
49	Jose Vidro	.10
50	Josh Beckett	.25
51	Kazuo Matsui	.10
52	Ken Griffey Jr.	1.00
53	Kerry Wood	.25
54	Khalil Greene	.25
55	Lance Berkman	.25
56	Livan Hernandez	.10
57	Luis Gonzalez	.10
58	Magglio Ordonez	.10
59	Manny Ramirez	.50
60	Mark Mulder	.25
61	Mark Prior	.50
62	Mark Teixeira	.40
63	Miguel Cabrera	.50
64	Miguel Tejada	.40
65	Mike Mussina	.25
66	Mike Piazza	1.00
67	Mike Sweeney	.10

68 Moises Alou .25
69 Nomar Garciaparra .75
70 Oliver Perez .10
71 Paul Konerko .25
72 Pedro Martinez .50
73 Rafael Palmeiro .25
74 Randy Johnson .50
75 Richie Sexson .25
76 Roger Clemens 1.50
77 Roy Halladay .25
78 Roy Oswalt .25
79 Sammy Sosa .75
80 Scott Rolen .50
81 Shawn Green .10
82 Steve Finley .10
83 Tim Hudson .25
84 Todd Helton .40
85 Tom Glavine .25
86 Torii Hunter .25
87 Travis Hafner .10
88 Troy Glaus .25
89 Victor Martinez .25
90 Vladimir Guerrero .50

All-Star Signatures

No Pricing
Inserted 1:480

Batter Up!

NM/M
Common Player: .25
Inserted 1:1
BU-1 Al Kaline .50
BU-2 Bill Mazeroski .25
BU-3 Billy Williams .25
BU-4 Bob Feller .50
BU-5 Bob Gibson .50
BU-6 Bob Lemon .25
BU-7 Brooks Robinson .50
BU-8 Carlton Fisk .50
BU-9 Jim "Catfish" Hunter .25
BU-10 Dennis Eckersley .25
BU-11 Eddie Mathews .75
BU-12 Eddie Murray .50
BU-13 Fergie Jenkins .25
BU-14 Gaylord Perry .25
BU-15 Harmon Killebrew .75
BU-16 Jim Bunning .25
BU-17 Jim Palmer .50
BU-18 Joe DiMaggio 1.50
BU-19 Joe Morgan .25
BU-20 Johnny Bench .75
BU-21 Juan Marichal .50
BU-22 Lou Brock .50
BU-23 Luis Aparicio .25
BU-24 Mike Schmidt 1.50
BU-25 Monte Irvin .50
BU-26 Nolan Ryan 2.00
BU-27 Orlando Cepeda .25
BU-28 Ozzie Smith .75
BU-29 Pee Wee Reese .25
BU-30 Phil Niekro .25
BU-31 Phil Rizzuto .50
BU-32 Ralph Kiner .25
BU-33 Richie Ashburn .25
BU-34 Robin Roberts .25
BU-35 Robin Yount .75
BU-36 Rollie Fingers .25
BU-37 Tom Seaver .75
BU-38 Tony Perez .25
BU-39 Warren Spahn .75
BU-40 Willie McCovey .50
BU-41 Willie Stargell .50
BU-42 Yogi Berra .75

Jersey

NM/M
Common Jersey: 4.00
Inserted 1:24
CB Carlos Beltran 6.00
AB Adrian Beltre 4.00
HB Hank Blalock 4.00
SB Sean Burroughs 4.00
MC Miguel Cabrera 6.00
EC Eric Chavez 4.00
EG Eric Gagne 4.00
KG Ken Griffey Jr. 10.00
VG Vladimir Guerrero 6.00
TH Todd Helton 6.00
DJ Derek Jeter 15.00
RJ Randy Johnson 6.00
CJ Chipper Jones 6.00
GM Greg Maddux 8.00
PI Mike Piazza 8.00
MP Mark Prior 6.00
AP Albert Pujols 15.00
MR Manny Ramirez 6.00
IR Ivan Rodriguez 6.00
SR Scott Rolen 6.00
JS Johan Santana 6.00
CS Curt Schilling 6.00
AS Alfonso Soriano 6.00
SS Sammy Sosa 8.00
MT Mark Teixeira 6.00
TE Miguel Tejada 6.00
JT Jim Thome 6.00
KW Kerry Wood 4.00

2005 UD Origins Promos

Each of the cards in UD Origins was issued in a foil-overprinted version with "UD PROMO" across the front. Cards were inserted into specially marked card shop and newsstand issues of Tuff Stuff magazine.

NM/M
Common Player: .50
Stars: 1.5X

2005 UD Origins

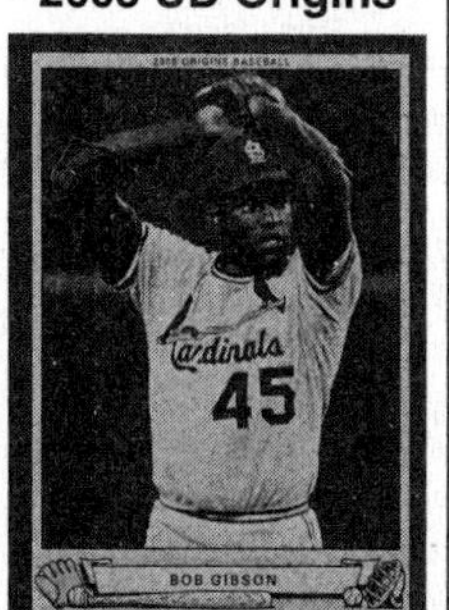

NM/M
Complete Set (200):
Common Player: .50
Tin (20): 50.00
1 Jim Edmonds .75
2 Jason Schmidt .75
3 J.D. Drew .75
4 Luis Gonzalez .50
5 Nomar Garciaparra 2.00
6 Jake Peavy .75
7 Rafael Furcal .50
8 Craig Biggio .75
9 Ken Griffey Jr. 3.00
10 Mike Piazza 2.00
11 Jose Vidro .50
12 Ivan Rodriguez 1.00
13 Carl Crawford .50
14 Roger Clemens 4.00
15 Kerry Wood 1.00
16 Vernon Wells .50
17 Carlos Guillen .50
18 Tim Hudson .75
19 Carl Pavano .50
20 Carlos Beltran 1.00
21 Pedro Martinez 1.50
22 Hideki Matsui 3.00
23 Frank Thomas 1.00
24 Curt Schilling 1.50
25 Manny Ramirez 1.50
26 Alex Rodriguez 4.00
27 Aubrey Huff .50
28 David Ortiz 1.50
29 Mark Prior 1.00
30 Albert Pujols 4.00
31 Miguel Cabrera 1.50
32 Brad Penny .50
33 Carlos Delgado .75
34 Aramis Ramirez 1.00
35 Josh Beckett .75
36 Rafael Palmeiro 1.00
37 Bret Boone .50
38 Lance Berkman .75
39 Carlos Zambrano .75
40 Adam Dunn 1.00
41 Livan Hernandez .75
42 Mike Mussina .75
43 Ben Sheets .75
44 Derek Jeter 4.00
45 Kazuo Matsui .50
46 Bobby Abreu .75
47 Jeff Bagwell 1.00
48 Travis Hafner .50
49 Torii Hunter .75
50 Kevin Brown .50
51 Alfonso Soriano 1.50
52 Jim Thome 1.00
53 John Smoltz .75
54 Mike Sweeney .75
55 Andy Pettitte .75
56 Chipper Jones 1.50
57 Randy Johnson 1.50
58 Steve Finley .50
59 Larry Walker .75
60 Troy Glaus .75
61 Greg Maddux 2.50
62 Shawn Green .50
63 Roy Halladay .75
64 Jeff Kent .50
65 Scott Podsednik .50
66 Miguel Tejada 1.00
67 Lyle Overbay .50
68 Bernie Williams .75
69 Todd Helton 1.00
70 Melvin Mora .50
71 Magglio Ordonez .50
72 Carlos Lee .75
73 Roy Oswalt .75
74 Victor Martinez .50
75 Scott Rolen 1.50
76 Eric Chavez .75
77 Paul Konerko .75
78 Jose Reyes .50
79 Barry Larkin .75
80 Johnny Damon 1.00
81 Eric Gagne .75
82 Andruw Jones 1.00
83 Gary Sheffield 1.00
84 Richie Sexson .75
85 Sammy Sosa 2.50
86 Mark Teixeira 1.00
87 Vladimir Guerrero 1.50
88 Michael Young .50
89 Johan Santana 1.00
90 Adrian Beltre .75
91 Tom Glavine .75
92 Hank Blalock .75
93 Preston Wilson .50
94 Jason Kendall .50
95 Mike Lowell .50
96 Craig Wilson .50
97 Ichiro Suzuki 3.00
98 Mark Mulder .75
99 Garret Anderson .75
100 Brian Giles .50
101 Robin Yount 3.00
102 Ernie Banks 3.00
103 Mike Schmidt 5.00
104 Enos Slaughter 1.00
105 Red Schoendienst 1.00
106 Hoyt Wilhelm 1.00
107 Lou Brock 2.00
108 Rollie Fingers 1.00
109 Gaylord Perry 1.00
110 Bobby Doerr 1.00
111 Larry Doby 1.00
112 Al Lopez 1.00
113 Joe Morgan 1.50
114 Luis Aparicio 1.00
115 Willie McCovey 2.00
116 Bob Lemon 1.00
117 Early Wynn 1.00
118 Bob Feller 2.00
119 Cal Ripken Jr. 8.00
120 George Kell 1.00
121 Juan Marichal 1.50
122 Monte Irvin 1.50
123 Harmon Killebrew 3.00
124 Lou Boudreau 1.00
125 Mickey Mantle 8.00
126 Richie Ashburn 1.00
127 Pee Wee Reese 1.50
128 Whitey Ford 2.00
129 Tom Seaver 2.00
130 Phil Rizzuto 2.00
131 Yogi Berra 3.00
132 Warren Spahn 2.00
133 Billy Williams 1.50
134 Jim Bunning 1.00
135 Ralph Kiner 1.00
136 Ted Williams 6.00
137 Rick Ferrell 1.00
138 Robin Roberts 1.00
139 Brooks Robinson 3.00
140 Hal Newhouser 1.00
141 Jim "Catfish" Hunter 1.00
142 Phil Niekro 1.00
143 Fergie Jenkins 1.00
144 Al Kaline 3.00
145 Stan Musial 4.00
146 Joe DiMaggio 6.00
147 Willie Stargell 2.00
148 Nolan Ryan 6.00
149 Babe Ruth 6.00
150 Bob Gibson 2.00
151 David DeJesus .50
152 Chris Burke .50
153 Chad Cordero .50
154 Kevin Youkilis .50
155 Bucky Jacobsen .50
156 B.J. Upton .50
157 Aaron Rowand .50
158 Jose Capellan .50
159 David Wright 2.00
160 Jason Bay .50
161 Edwin Jackson .50
162 Scott Kazmir .50
163 J.D. Closser .50
164 Chase Utley 1.00
165 Nick Swisher .50
166 Casey Kotchman .50
167 Bobby Crosby .50
168 Zack Greinke .50
169 Gavin Floyd .50
170 Jeff Francis .50
171 Dallas McPherson .50
172 Gabe Gross .50
173 Brandon Claussen .50
174 Wily Mo Pena .50
175 Robb Quinlan .50
176 Oliver Perez .50
177 Guillermo Quiroz .50
178 Ryan Howard 1.00
179 Gerald Laird .50
180 Jayson Werth .50
181 Bobby Madritsch .50
182 Laynce Nix .50
183 Eddy Rodriguez .50
184 Rickie Weeks 1.00
185 Scott Proctor .50
186 Adam LaRoche .50
187 Yhency Brazoban .50
188 Adrian Gonzalez .50
189 Jason Lane .50
190 Ryan Wagner .50
191 Roman Colon .50
192 Alexis Rios .50
193 Joe Mauer 1.00
194 Garrett Atkins .50
195 Daniel Cabrera .50
196 Khalil Greene 2.00
197 Joe Blanton .50
198 Jason Dubois .50
199 Angel Guzman .50
200 Jesse Crain .50

Black

No Pricing
Production One Set

Blue

Stars (1-200): 2-4X
Production 50 Sets

Gold

No Pricing
Production 20 Sets

Red

Stars (1-200): 2-3X
Production 99 Sets

Origins Materials Jersey

NM/M
Inserted 2:Tin
Old Judge: 1X
JB Jeff Bagwell 8.00
CB Carlos Beltran 8.00
AB Adrian Beltre 5.00
LB Lance Berkman 5.00
HB Hank Blalock 5.00
MC Miguel Cabrera 8.00
EC Eric Chavez 5.00
JD J.D. Drew 5.00
GL Troy Glaus 5.00
KG Ken Griffey Jr. 10.00
VG Vladimir Guerrero 8.00
TG Tony Gwynn/SP 10.00
HE Todd Helton 5.00
TH Tim Hudson 5.00
HU Torii Hunter 5.00
DJ Derek Jeter 15.00
RJ Randy Johnson 8.00
AJ Andruw Jones 5.00
CJ Chipper Jones 8.00
GM Greg Maddux 10.00
HM Hideki Matsui 15.00
KM Hideki Matsui 5.00
DO David Ortiz 8.00
PI Mike Piazza 8.00
MP Mark Prior 8.00
AP Albert Pujols 15.00
MR Manny Ramirez 8.00
CR Cal Ripken Jr./SP 25.00
IR Ivan Rodriguez 8.00
SR Scott Rolen 8.00
NR Nolan Ryan/SP 30.00
CS Curt Schilling 8.00
BS Ben Sheets 5.00
GS Gary Sheffield 5.00
AS Alfonso Soriano 8.00
SS Sammy Sosa 8.00
IS Ichiro Suzuki 20.00
MT Mark Teixeira 5.00
TE Miguel Tejada 8.00
FT Frank Thomas 8.00
JT Jim Thome 8.00
KW Kerry Wood 8.00

Origins Nostalgic Signs

NM/M
One sign per tin.
CB Carlos Beltran 8.00
AB Adrian Beltre 5.00
HB Hank Blalock 5.00
MC Miguel Cabrera 8.00
EC Eric Chavez 5.00
RC Roger Clemens 15.00
TC Ty Cobb 20.00
JD Joe DiMaggio 20.00
LG Lou Gehrig 15.00
KG Ken Griffey Jr. 12.00
VG Vladimir Guerrero 8.00
TH Todd Helton 8.00
DJ Derek Jeter 15.00
RJ Randy Johnson 8.00
WJ Walter Johnson 15.00
CJ Chipper Jones 8.00
PM Pedro Martinez 8.00
HM Hideki Matsui 20.00
DO David Ortiz 8.00
SP Satchel Paige 12.00
MP Mike Piazza 10.00
MPR Mark Prior 8.00
AP Albert Pujols 20.00
MR Manny Ramirez 8.00
CR Cal Ripken Jr. 25.00
JR Jackie Robinson 12.00
AR Alex Rodriguez 12.00
IR Ivan Rodriguez 8.00
SR Scott Rolen 8.00
BR Babe Ruth 20.00
NR Nolan Ryan 20.00
JS Johan Santana 8.00
CS Curt Schilling 10.00
AS Alfonso Soriano 8.00
SS Sammy Sosa 10.00
IS Ichiro Suzuki 12.00
MT Miguel Tejada 8.00
FT Frank Thomas 8.00
JT Jim Thome 8.00
HW Honus Wagner 10.00
TW Ted Williams 25.00

Origins Old Judge

NM/M
Common Player: .50
Blue: 2-3X
Red: 1-2X
Gold: No Pricing
1 Jake Peavy 1.00
2 Derek Jeter 5.00
3 Adrian Beltre 1.00
4 Hank Blalock 1.00
5 Preston Wilson .50
6 Randy Johnson 2.00
7 Pedro Martinez 2.00
8 Michael Young 1.00
9 Steve Finley .50
10 Shawn Green .75
11 Carlos Beltran 1.50
12 Bernie Williams 1.00
13 Brian Giles .50
14 Kevin Brown .50
15 Barry Larkin 1.00
16 Troy Glaus 1.00
17 Bret Boone .50
18 Jason Kendall .50
19 Johnny Damon 1.50
20 Josh Beckett 1.00
21 Carl Pavano .50
22 Chipper Jones 2.00
23 Ivan Rodriguez 1.50
24 Kerry Wood 1.50
25 Ken Griffey Jr. 3.00
26 Greg Maddux 3.00
27 Kazuo Matsui .50
28 Albert Pujols 5.00
29 Victor Martinez .50
30 Johan Santana 1.50
31 Bobby Abreu .75
32 Paul Konerko .75
33 Gary Sheffield 1.00
34 Jose Vidro .50
35 Alex Rodriguez 4.00
36 Alfonso Soriano 1.50
37 Mark Teixeira 1.50
38 Nomar Garciaparra 2.50
39 Sammy Sosa 3.00
40 Garret Anderson 1.00
41 Eric Chavez 1.00
42 Magglio Ordonez .50
43 Larry Walker 1.00
44 Brad Penny .50
45 Jeff Bagwell 1.50
46 Craig Biggio .75
47 Torii Hunter .75
48 Mike Lowell .50
49 Ben Sheets 1.00
50 Miguel Tejada 1.50
51 Jim Edmonds 1.00
52 Mark Mulder 1.00
53 Curt Schilling 1.50
54 Roger Clemens 5.00
55 Jason Schmidt .50
56 Rafael Furcal .50
57 Scott Rolen 2.00
58 Carlos Zambrano .75
59 Mike Sweeney .50
60 Vladimir Guerrero 2.00
61 Miguel Cabrera 2.00
62 Lance Berkman .50
63 Lyle Overbay .50
64 Livan Hernandez .50
65 Aramis Ramirez 1.00
66 Ichiro Suzuki 4.00
67 Roy Oswalt .50
68 Carl Crawford .50
69 Craig Wilson .50
70 Carlos Lee .75
71 J.D. Drew .50
72 Rafael Palmeiro 1.50
73 Jeff Kent .50
74 Adam Dunn 1.50
75 Andy Pettitte 1.00
76 Luis Gonzalez .50
77 Frank Thomas 1.50
78 John Smoltz 1.00
79 Hideki Matsui 3.00
80 Tom Glavine .50
81 Jose Reyes .50
82 Jim Thome 1.50
83 Mark Prior 2.00
84 Roy Halladay .75
85 Carlos Delgado 1.00
86 Melvin Mora .50
87 David Ortiz 2.00
88 Travis Hafner .50
89 Carlos Guillen .50
90 Tim Hudson .50
91 Vernon Wells .50
92 Andruw Jones 1.50
93 Mike Mussina 1.00
94 Mike Piazza 3.00
95 Richie Sexson 1.00
96 Aubrey Huff .50
97 Scott Podsednik .50
98 Eric Gagne .50
99 Manny Ramirez 2.00
100 Todd Helton 1.50
101 Joe Morgan 1.00
102 Billy Williams 1.00
103 Pee Wee Reese 1.00
104 Lou Boudreau 1.00
105 Richie Ashburn 1.00
106 Jim Bunning 1.00
107 Hal Newhouser 1.00
108 Rick Ferrell 1.00
109 Ted Williams 5.00
110 Ralph Kiner 1.00
111 Warren Spahn 2.50
112 George Kell .50
113 Willie Stargell 2.00
114 Jim "Catfish" Hunter .50
115 Tom Seaver 2.00
116 Cal Ripken Jr. 8.00
117 Al Lopez .50
118 Ernie Banks 3.00
119 Lou Brock 2.00
120 Robin Yount 3.00
121 Nolan Ryan 6.00
122 Larry Doby 1.00
123 Al Kaline 2.00
124 Willie McCovey 2.00
125 Stan Musial 3.00
126 Phil Niekro 1.00
127 Babe Ruth 6.00
128 Rollie Fingers 1.00
129 Juan Marichal 1.00
130 Early Wynn 1.00
131 Luis Aparicio 1.00
132 Brooks Robinson 3.00
133 Mike Schmidt 5.00
134 Gaylord Perry 1.00
135 Bob Lemon 1.00
136 Monte Irvin 1.50
137 Mickey Mantle 8.00
138 Phil Rizzuto 1.50
139 Robin Roberts 1.50
140 Bobby Doerr 1.00
141 Bob Gibson 2.00
142 Enos Slaughter 1.00
143 Yogi Berra 3.00
144 Whitey Ford 2.00
145 Red Schoendienst 1.00
146 Joe DiMaggio 5.00
147 Harmon Killebrew 2.00
148 Hoyt Wilhelm 1.00
149 Fergie Jenkins 1.00
150 Bob Feller 1.50
151 Scott Proctor .50
152 Adam LaRoche .50
153 Ryan Howard 1.00
154 Laynce Nix .50
155 Garrett Atkins .50
156 Chris Burke .50
157 Oliver Perez .50
158 Wily Mo Pena .50
159 B.J. Upton .50
160 Gavin Floyd .50
161 Jesse Crain .50
162 Khalil Greene 3.00
163 Eddy Rodriguez .50
164 Edwin Jackson .50
165 Scott Kazmir .50
166 Ryan Wagner .50
167 Nick Swisher .50
168 Joe Blanton .50
169 Alexis Rios .50
170 Chad Cordero .50
171 Jason Dubois .50
172 Chase Utley 1.00
173 David DeJesus .50
174 Zack Greinke .50
175 Bobby Crosby 1.00
176 Angel Guzman .50
177 Adrian Gonzalez .50
178 Guillermo Quiroz .50
179 Gerald Laird .50
180 Rickie Weeks 1.00
181 Jayson Werth .50
182 Buck Jacobsen .50
183 J.D. Closser .50
184 Jason Bay .50
185 Roman Colon .50
186 Casey Kotchman .50
187 Yhency Brazoban .50
188 Bobby Madritsch .50
189 Gabe Gross .50
190 Brandon Claussen .50
191 Aaron Rowand .50
192 Jeff Francis .50
193 David Wright 2.00
194 Jose Capellan .50

195 Jason Lane .50
196 Daniel Cabrera .50
197 Joe Mauer 1.00
198 Kevin Youkilis .50
199 Dallas McPherson .50
200 Robb Quinlan .50

Origins Old Judge Autographs

NM/M
Common Auto.: 12.00
Bronze: No Pricing
JB Jason Bay 15.00
AB Adrian Beltre 12.00
MC Miguel Cabrera 25.00
CC Carl Crawford Exch 12.00
BC Bobby Crosby Exch 15.00
BD Bobby Doerr 15.00
BF Bob Feller 25.00
MG Marcus Giles Exch 15.00
DG Dwight Gooden 15.00
GR Khalil Greene 20.00
KG Ken Griffey Jr. 75.00
RG Ron Guidry 15.00
TG Tony Gwynn 50.00
TH Travis Hafner 15.00
RH Rich Harden 15.00
KH Keith Hernandez 15.00
FH Frank Howard 20.00
HO Ryan Howard 75.00
AH Aubrey Huff 8.00
DJ Derek Jeter 150.00
SK Scott Kazmir 20.00
DK Dave Kingman 15.00
CK Casey Kotchman 15.00
SL Sparky Lyle 12.00
VM Victor Martinez 15.00
MA Don Mattingly 65.00
DM Dallas McPherson 12.00
PM Paul Molitor 40.00
OS Roy Oswalt 15.00
AO Akinori Otsuka 15.00
JP Jim Palmer 15.00
PE Jake Peavy 25.00
OP Oliver Perez 15.00
CR Cal Ripken Jr./25 180.00
BR Brooks Robinson 30.00
RO Al Rosen 15.00
JS Johan Santana/Exch 35.00
RS Ron Santo 25.00
MS Mike Schmidt 75.00
BS Ben Sheets 12.00
ST Shingo Takatsu 15.00
MT Mark Teixeira 25.00
BU B.J. Upton 15.00
CU Chase Utley 25.00
RW Rickie Weeks 15.00
DW David Wright 60.00
RY Robin Yount 50.00
CZ Carlos Zambrano 20.00

Origins Old Judge Materials Jersey

NM/M
Common Jersey: 5.00
JB Jeff Bagwell 8.00
CB Carlos Beltran 8.00
AB Adrian Beltre 5.00
LB Lance Berkman 5.00
HB Hank Blalock 5.00
MC Miguel Cabrera 8.00
EC Eric Chavez 5.00
JD J.D. Drew 5.00
GL Troy Glaus 5.00
KG Ken Griffey Jr. 10.00
VG Vladimir Guerrero 8.00
TG Tony Gwynn/SP 10.00
HE Todd Helton 5.00
TH Tim Hudson 5.00
HU Torii Hunter 5.00
DJ Derek Jeter 15.00
RJ Randy Johnson 8.00
AJ Andruw Jones 5.00
CJ Chipper Jones 8.00
GM Greg Maddux 10.00
HM Hideki Matsui 15.00
KM Kazuo Matsui 5.00
DO David Ortiz 8.00
PI Mike Piazza 8.00
MP Mark Prior 8.00
AP Albert Pujols 15.00
MR Manny Ramirez 8.00
CR Cal Ripken Jr./SP 25.00
SR Scott Rolen 8.00
NR Nolan Ryan/SP 30.00
CS Curt Schilling 8.00
BS Ben Sheets 5.00
GS Gary Sheffield 5.00
AS Alfonso Soriano 8.00
SS Sammy Sosa 8.00
IS Ichiro Suzuki 20.00
MT Mark Teixeira 5.00
TE Miguel Tejada 8.00
FT Frank Thomas 8.00
JT Jim Thome 8.00
KW Kerry Wood 8.00

Origins Signatures

NM/M
Common Auto.: 12.00
Bronze: No Pricing
Production Five Sets
JB1 Jason Bay 15.00
AB1 Adrian Beltre 12.00
MC1 Miguel Cabrera 25.00
CC1 Carl Crawford/Exch 12.00
BC1 Bobby Crosby/Exch 15.00
BD1 Bobby Doerr 15.00
BF1 Bob Feller 25.00
MG1 Marcus Giles 15.00
DG1 Dwight Gooden 15.00
GR1 Khalil Greene 20.00
KG1 Ken Griffey Jr. 75.00
RG1 Ron Guidry 15.00
TG1 Tony Gwynn 50.00
TH1 Travis Hafner 15.00
RH1 Rich Harden 15.00
KH1 Keith Hernandez 15.00
FH1 Frank Howard 20.00
HO1 Ryan Howard 75.00
AH1 Aubrey Huff 8.00
DJ1 Derek Jeter 150.00
SK1 Scott Kazmir 20.00
DK1 Dave Kingman 15.00
CK1 Casey Kotchman 15.00
SL1 Sparky Lyle 12.00
VM1 Victor Martinez 15.00
MA1 Don Mattingly 65.00
DM1 Dallas McPherson 12.00
PM1 Paul Molitor 40.00
OS1 Roy Oswalt 15.00
AO1 Akinori Otsuka 15.00
JP1 Jim Palmer 15.00
PE1 Jake Peavy 25.00
OP1 Oliver Perez 15.00
CR1 Cal Ripken Jr./25 180.00
BR1 Brooks Robinson 30.00
RO1 Al Rosen 15.00
JS1 Johan Santana/Exch 35.00
RS1 Ron Santo 25.00
MS1 Mike Schmidt 75.00
BS1 Ben Sheets 12.00
ST1 Shingo Takatsu 15.00
MT1 Mark Teixeira 25.00
BU1 B.J. Upton 15.00
CU1 Chase Utley 25.00
RW1 Rickie Weeks 15.00
DW1 David Wright 60.00
RY1 Robin Yount 50.00
CZ1 Carlos Zambrano 20.00

Origins Tins

NM/M
Common Tin: 5.00
TC Ty Cobb 5.00
DJ Derek Jeter 10.00
WJ Walter Johnson 5.00
HW Honus Wagner 5.00

2005 UD Past Time Pennants

NM/M
Complete Set (90): 20.00
Common Player: .20
Pack (5): 4.00
Box (20): 70.00
1 Al Kaline .50
2 Al Rosen .20
3 Bert Blyleven .20
4 Bill Mazeroski .20
5 Billy Williams .20
6 Bob Feller .50
7 Bob Gibson .75
8 Bob Lemon .20
9 Bobby Doerr .40
10 Brooks Robinson .75
11 Bruce Sutter .30
12 Bucky Dent .20
13 Cal Ripken Jr. 2.00
14 Carl Yastrzemski .75
15 Carlton Fisk .40
16 Jim "Catfish" Hunter .20
17 Dale Murphy .40
18 Dave Parker .20
19 Don Larsen .50
20 Don Mattingly 1.00
21 Don Newcombe .20
22 Duke Snider .50
23 Early Wynn .20
24 Eddie Matthews .75
25 Eddie Murray .50
26 Enos Slaughter .20
27 Ernie Banks .75
28 Fergie Jenkins .20
29 Frank Howard .20
30 Frank Robinson .50
31 Fred Lynn .20
32 Gary Carter .20
33 Gaylord Perry .20
34 George Brett 1.50
35 George Kell .20
36 Rich "Goose" Gossage .20
37 Graig Nettles .20
38 Harmon Killebrew .75
39 Jack Morris .20
40 Jim Bunning .20
41 Felipe Alou .20
42 Jim Palmer .40
43 Jim Rice .20
44 Joe DiMaggio 1.50
45 Joe Morgan .20
46 Johnny Bench .75
47 Johnny Podres .20
48 Juan Marichal .20
49 Keith Hernandez .20
50 Kirby Puckett .75
51 Larry Doby .20
52 Lou Brock .40
53 Luis Aparicio .20
54 Luis Tiant .20
55 Maury 4illis .20
56 Mickey Mantle 2.00
57 Mike Schmidt 1.50
58 Monte Irvin .20
59 Nolan Ryan 1.50
60 Orlando Cepeda .20
61 Ozzie Smith .75
62 Paul Molitor .50
63 Pee Wee Reese .20
64 Phil Niekro .20
65 Phil Rizzuto .50
66 Ralph Kiner .20
67 Richie Ashburn .20
68 Rico Petrocelli .20
69 Robin Roberts .20
70 Robin Yount .75
71 Rocky Colavito .20
72 Rod Carew .40
73 Rollie Fingers .20
74 Ron Guidry .20
75 Ron Santo .20
76 Tony Gwynn .75
77 Sparky Lyle .20
78 Stan Musial 1.00
79 Steve Carlton .40
80 Rick Ferrell .20
81 Tom Seaver .75
82 Tommy John .20
83 Tony Perez .20
84 Wade Boggs .50
85 Warren Spahn .75
86 Whitey Ford .40
87 Will Clark .50
88 Willie McCovey .50
89 Willie Stargell .40
90 Yogi Berra .75

Silver

Gold: 3-5X
Production 100 Sets

Gold

Gold: 4-8X
Production 50 Sets

Mitchell & Ness Jersey Redem

Total Production
Per Player 36-37

Mitchell & Ness Pennants

NM/M
Common Pennant: 15.00
Inserted 1:Hobby Box
1903 1903 Boston Americans/100 20.00
1905 1095 New York Giants/100 20.00
1906 1906 Chicago White Sox/100 20.00
1907 1907 Detroit Tigers/100 20.00
1908 1908 Chicago Cubs/105 25.00
1909 1909 Pittsburgh Pirates/125 20.00
1910 1910 Philadelphia A's/125 20.00
1912 1912 Boston Red Sox/125 20.00
1914 1914 Boston Braves/125 20.00
1915 1915 Philadelphia Phillies/125 20.00
1916 1916 Brooklyn Robins/200 20.00
1917 1917 New York Giants/200 20.00
1918 1918 Boston Red Sox/200 20.00
1919 1919 Chicago White Sox/200 20.00
1920 1920 Cleveland Indians/200 15.00
1921 1921 New York Yankees/200 25.00
1922 1922 New York Giants/200 20.00
1924 1924 Washington Senators/200 20.00
1925 1925 Pittsburgh Pirates/200 15.00
1926 1926 Saint Louis Cardinals/200 20.00
1927 1927 New York Yankees/500 25.00
1928 1928 New York Yankees/500 25.00
1929 1929 Chicago Cubs/337 20.00
1930 1930 Philadelphia A's/337 15.00
1931 1931 Saint Louis Cardinals/337 20.00
1932 1932 Chicago Cubs/337 20.00
1934 1934 Detroit Tigers/337 15.00
1935 1935 Chicago Cubs/337 20.00
1936 1936 New York Yankees/337 25.00
1937 1937 New York Giants/337 20.00
1938 1938 New York Yankees/337 25.00
1939 1939 Cincinnati Reds/337 15.00
1940 1940 Cincinnati Reds/337 15.00
1941 1941 Brooklyn Dodgers/337 25.00
1942 1942 Saint Louis Cardinals/337 20.00
1943 1943 New York Yankees/500 25.00
1944 1944 Saint Louis Browns/337 15.00
1945 1945 Chicago Cubs/337 20.00
1946 1946 Boston Red Sox/337 20.00
1947 1947 Brooklyn Dodgers/337 25.00
1948 1948 Boston Braves/337 15.00
1949 1949 New York Yankees/337 25.00
1950 1950 Philadelphia Phillies/337 15.00
1951 1951 New York Giants/337 15.00
1952 1952 Brooklyn Dodgers/500 20.00
1953 1953 New York Yankees/337 25.00
1954 1954 Cleveland Indians/337 15.00
1955 1955 Brooklyn Dodgers/337 25.00
1956 1956 Brooklyn Dodgers/500 25.00
1957 1957 Milwaukee Braves/337 20.00
1958 1958 New York Yankees/500 25.00
1959 1959 Los Angeles Dodgers/337 20.00
1960 1960 Pittsburgh Pirates/337 15.00
1961 1961 Cincinnati Reds/337 15.00
1962 1962 San Francisco Giants/337 20.00
1963 1963 Los Angeles Dodgers/337 20.00
1964 1964 Saint Louis Cardinals/337 20.00
1965 1965 Minnesota Twins/337 15.00
1966 1966 Baltimore Orioles/337 20.00
1967 1967 Boston Red Sox/337 20.00
1968 1968 Detroit Tigers/337 15.00
1969 1969 New York Mets/337 20.00
1970 1970 Baltimore Orioles/337 20.00
1971 1971 Pittsburgh Pirates/337 15.00
1972 1972 Oakland A's/337 20.00
1973 1973 Oakland A's/337 20.00
1974 1974 Los Angeles Dodgers/337 20.00
1977 1977 New York Yankees/337 25.00
1978 1978 Los Angeles Dodgers/337 20.00
1979 1979 Pittsburgh Pirates/337 15.00
1980 1980 Philadelphia Phillies/337 20.00
1981 1981 Los Angeles Dodgers/337 20.00
1982 1982 Milwaukee Brewers/337 20.00
1983 1983 Baltimore Orioles/337 20.00
1984 1984 San Diego Padres/337 15.00
1985 1985 Kansas City Royals/337 15.00
1986 1986 Boston Red Sox/337 25.00
1988 1988 Los Angeles Dodgers/337 20.00
1975B 1975 Boston Red Sox/337 25.00
1975C 1975 Cincinnati Reds/337 20.00

Mitchell & Ness Penn Autograph

NM/M
Production 86-87
JB Johnny Bench/87 80.00
SC Steve Carlton/87 60.00
RF Rollie Fingers/87 40.00
CF Carlton Fisk/87 60.00
SG Steve Garvey/40 40.00
AK Al Kaline/87 75.00
PM Paul Molitor/87 75.00
GN Graig Nettles/87 50.00
DN Don Newcombe/87 40.00
BR Brooks Robinson/87 75.00
TS Tom Seaver/87 80.00
CY Carl Yastrzemski/86 80.00

Signatures Bronze

NM/M
SP's Production 3-25
FA Felipe Alou 15.00
RB Rick Burleson 10.00
DC David Cone 10.00
LD Lenny Dykstra 12.00
SF Sid Fernandez 10.00
BF Bill Freehan 10.00
DG Dwight Gooden 15.00
KG Ken Griffey Sr. 10.00
GU Don Gullett 8.00
PG Pedro Guerrero 10.00
HO Ken Holtzman 10.00
BH Burt Hooton 10.00
WH Willie Horton/EXCH 12.00
FH Frank Howard 15.00
HR Kent Hrbek 15.00
RH Randy Hundley 10.00
TJ Tommy John 15.00
WJ Wally Joyner 15.00
DK Dave Kingman 10.00
KN Ray Knight 10.00
SL Sparky Lyle 10.00
BM Bill Madlock 10.00
BO Bobby Murcer 15.00
RP Rico Petrocelli 12.00
BP Boog Powell 25.00
AR Al Rosen 15.00
SS Steve Sax 10.00
SC Mike Scioscia/EXCH 15.00
WI Mookie Wilson 15.00

Signatures Silver

NM/M
FA Felipe Alou 10.00
LA Luis Aparicio 20.00
BB Bert Blyleven 15.00
BR Lou Brock 30.00
JB Jim Bunning/EXCH 15.00
RB Rick Burleson 10.00
ST Steve Carlton 35.00
GC Gary Carter 20.00
OC Orlando Cepeda 20.00
CC Chris Chambliss 15.00
WC Will Clark 40.00
RC Rocky Colavito 65.00
DC David Cone 15.00
DE Bucky Dent 12.00
BD Bobby Doerr 15.00
LD Lenny Dykstra 10.00
CE Carl Erskine/EXCH 12.00
EV Dwight Evans 30.00
FE Bob Feller 30.00
SF Sid Fernandez 10.00
RF Rollie Fingers 20.00
BF Bill Freehan 10.00
DG Dwight Gooden 15.00
GG Rich "Goose" Gossage 15.00
KG Ken Griffey Sr. 10.00
GU Don Gullett 8.00
PG Pedro Guerrero 10.00
KH Keith Hernandez 15.00
HO Ken Holtzman 10.00
BH Burt Hooton 10.00
WH Willie Horton/EXCH 10.00
FH Frank Howard 15.00
HR Kent Hrbek 15.00
RH Randy Hundley 10.00
MI Monte Irvin 25.00
FJ Fergie Jenkins 20.00
TJ Tommy Jones 15.00
WJ Wally Joyner 15.00
AK Al Kaline 50.00
GK George Kell 15.00
HK Harmon Killebrew 50.00
RK Ralph Kiner 40.00
DK Dave Kingman 10.00
KN Ray Knight 10.00
DL Don Larsen/EXCH 30.00
SL Sparky Lyle 10.00
FL Fred Lynn 15.00
BM Bill Madlock 10.00
JU Juan Marichal/EXCH 20.00
MA Bill Mazeroski 30.00
PM Paul Molitor 40.00
MO Joe Morgan 20.00
JM Jack Morris 15.00
BO Bobby Murcer 20.00
MU Dale Murphy 25.00
GN Graig Nettles 20.00
DN Don Newcombe 15.00
JP Jim Palmer 30.00
DP Dave Parker 20.00
TP Tony Perez/EXCH 40.00
GP Gaylord Perry 15.00
RP Rico Petrocelli 15.00
PO Johnny Podres 25.00
BP Boog Powell 20.00
JR Jim Rice 20.00
RO Brooks Robinson 60.00
AR Al Rosen 15.00
RS Ron Santo 25.00
SS Steve Sax 10.00
SC Mike Scioscia/EXCH 20.00
BS Bill "Moose" Skowron 15.00
SU Bruce Sutter 15.00
LT Luis Tiant 15.00
BW Billy Williams/EXCH 15.00
MW Maury Wills 20.00

Signatures Gold

NM/M
Many not priced due to scarcity.
FA Felipe Alou 20.00
RB Rick Burleson 15.00
LD Lenny Dykstra 20.00
SF Sid Fernandez 15.00
BF Bill Freehan 15.00
KG Ken Griffey Sr. 15.00
PG Pedro Guerrero 15.00
GU Don Gullett 10.00
HO Ken Holtzman 15.00
BH Burt Hooton 15.00
WH Willie Horton/EXCH 15.00
HR Kent Hrbek 20.00
RH Randy Hundley 10.00
DK Dave Kingman 15.00
KN Ray Knight 15.00
SL Sparky Lyle 15.00
BM Bill Madlock 15.00
BO Bobby Murcer 25.00
RP Rico Petrocelli 15.00

Signatures Dual

Production 15-24

2005 Upper Deck Portraits

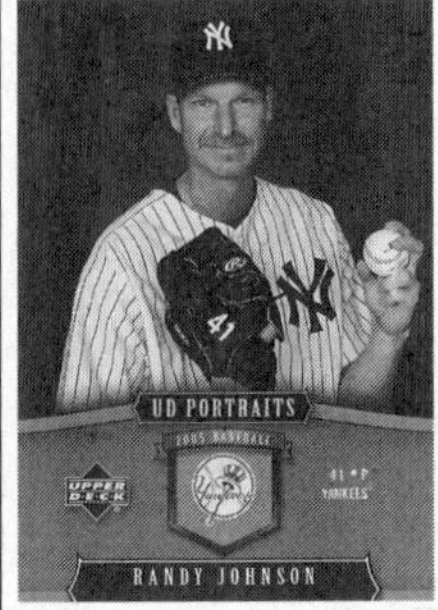

NM/M
Complete Set (100): 25.00
Common Player: .25
Box (7 Cards + 8x10): 100.00
1 Dallas McPherson .25
2 Steve Finley .25
3 Vladimir Guerrero .75
4 Troy Glaus .25
5 Andruw Jones .50
6 Chipper Jones .75
7 John Smoltz .50
8 Marcus Giles .25

9 Tim Hudson .50
10 Cal Ripken Jr. 3.00
11 Miguel Tejada .50
12 Curt Schilling .75
13 David Ortiz .75
14 Edgar Renteria .25
15 Jason Varitek .50
16 Jim Rice .50
17 Johnny Damon .75
18 Matt Clement .25
19 Wade Boggs .75
20 Aramis Ramirez .50
21 Carlos Zambrano .50
22 Corey Patterson .25
23 Fergie Jenkins .25
24 Greg Maddux 1.50
25 Kerry Wood .50
26 Mark Prior .75
27 Nomar Garciaparra .75
28 Ryne Sandberg 1.50
29 Frank Thomas .50
30 Adam Dunn .50
31 Barry Larkin .50
32 Ken Griffey Jr. 1.50
33 Sean Casey .25
34 Travis Hafner .25
35 Victor Martinez .25
36 Todd Helton .50
37 Ivan Rodriguez .50
38 Magglio Ordonez .25
39 Josh Beckett .25
40 Miguel Cabrera .75
41 Mike Lowell .25
42 Craig Biggio .50
43 Jeff Bagwell .50
44 Roger Clemens 2.00
45 Roy Oswalt .25
46 Bo Jackson .50
47 Prince Fielder 5.00
48 Eric Gagne .25
49 J.D. Drew .25
50 Ben Sheets .50
51 Robin Yount .75
52 Jacque Jones .25
53 Joe Mauer .50
54 Johan Santana .75
55 Justin Morneau .25
56 Torii Hunter .25
57 Dontrelle Willis .50
58 David Wright 1.00
59 Gary Carter .25
60 Jose Reyes .40
61 Keith Hernandez .25
62 Mike Piazza 1.00
63 Pedro Martinez .75
64 Tom Glavine .50
65 Carl Pavano .25
66 Derek Jeter 2.00
67 Don Mattingly 1.00
68 Mike Mussina .50
69 Randy Johnson .75
70 Bobby Crosby .25
71 Eric Chavez .25
72 Rich Harden .25
73 Bobby Abreu .50
74 Mike Schmidt 1.00
75 Jason Bay .25
76 Oliver Perez .25
77 Brian Giles .25
78 Jake Peavy .50
79 Khalil Greene .25
80 Tony Gwynn .75
81 Jason Schmidt .25
82 Will Clark .50
83 Adrian Beltre .25
84 Justin Verlander 2.00
85 Albert Pujols 2.00
86 Jim Edmonds .50
87 Mark Mulder .50
88 Scott Rolen .75
89 Aubrey Huff .25
90 B.J. Upton .25
91 Carl Crawford .25
92 Tadahito Iguchi 4.00
93 Scott Kazmir .25
94 Alfonso Soriano .75
95 Hank Blalock .25
96 Mark Teixeira .50
97 Michael Young .25
98 Nolan Ryan 2.00
99 Roy Halladay .50
100 Jose Vidro .25

Emerald Jersey

NM/M

Common Player: 4.00
Production 99 Sets
Blue: 1-1.5X
Production 25 Sets
Gold: 1-2X
Production 15 Sets
1 Dallas McPherson 4.00
2 Steve Finley 4.00
3 Vladimir Guerrero 8.00
4 Troy Glaus 4.00
5 Andruw Jones 6.00
6 Chipper Jones 8.00
7 John Smoltz 6.00
8 Marcus Giles 4.00
9 Tim Hudson 6.00
10 Cal Ripken Jr. 25.00
11 Miguel Tejada 8.00
12 Curt Schilling 8.00
13 David Ortiz 8.00
14 Edgar Renteria 4.00
15 Jason Varitek 6.00
16 Jim Rice 6.00
17 Johnny Damon 8.00
18 Matt Clement 4.00
19 Wade Boggs 8.00
20 Aramis Ramirez 6.00
21 Carlos Zambrano 6.00
22 Corey Patterson 4.00
23 Fergie Jenkins 6.00
24 Greg Maddux 10.00
25 Kerry Wood 6.00
26 Mark Prior 8.00
27 Nomar Garciaparra 8.00
28 Ryne Sandberg 12.00
29 Frank Thomas 6.00
30 Adam Dunn 6.00
31 Barry Larkin 6.00
32 Ken Griffey Jr. 15.00
33 Sean Casey 4.00
34 Travis Hafner 6.00
35 Victor Martinez 4.00
36 Todd Helton 6.00
37 Ivan Rodriguez 6.00
38 Magglio Ordonez 4.00
39 Josh Beckett 6.00
40 Miguel Cabrera 8.00
41 Mike Lowell 4.00
42 Craig Biggio 6.00
43 Jeff Bagwell 8.00
44 Roger Clemens 15.00
45 Roy Oswalt 6.00
46 Bo Jackson 10.00
48 Eric Gagne 6.00
49 J.D. Drew 4.00
50 Ben Sheets 4.00
51 Robin Yount 15.00
52 Jacque Jones 4.00
53 Joe Mauer 6.00
54 Johan Santana 6.00
55 Justin Morneau 4.00
56 Torii Hunter 4.00
57 Dontrelle Willis 6.00
58 David Wright 10.00
59 Gary Carter 6.00
60 Jose Reyes 6.00
61 Keith Hernandez 4.00
62 Mike Piazza 8.00
63 Pedro Martinez 8.00
64 Tom Glavine 6.00
65 Carl Pavano 4.00
66 Derek Jeter 15.00
67 Don Mattingly 15.00
68 Mike Mussina 6.00
69 Randy Johnson 8.00
70 Bobby Crosby 4.00
71 Eric Chavez 4.00
72 Rich Harden 4.00
73 Bobby Abreu 6.00
74 Mike Schmidt 10.00
75 Jason Bay 4.00
76 Oliver Perez 4.00
77 Brian Giles 4.00
78 Jake Peavy 6.00
79 Khalil Greene 6.00
80 Tony Gwynn 8.00
81 Jason Schmidt 4.00
82 Will Clark 8.00
83 Adrian Beltre 4.00
85 Albert Pujols 15.00
86 Jim Edmonds 6.00
87 Mark Mulder 6.00
88 Scott Rolen 6.00
89 Aubrey Huff 4.00
90 B.J. Upton 4.00
91 Carl Crawford 4.00
92 Tadahito Iguchi 15.00
93 Scott Kazmir 4.00
94 Alfonso Soriano 6.00
95 Hank Blalock 6.00
96 Mark Teixeira 6.00
97 Michael Young 6.00
98 Nolan Ryan 15.00
99 Roy Halladay 6.00
100 Jose Vidro 4.00

Jersey Auto. Platinum

No Pricing
Production 10 Sets

Scrapbook Materials

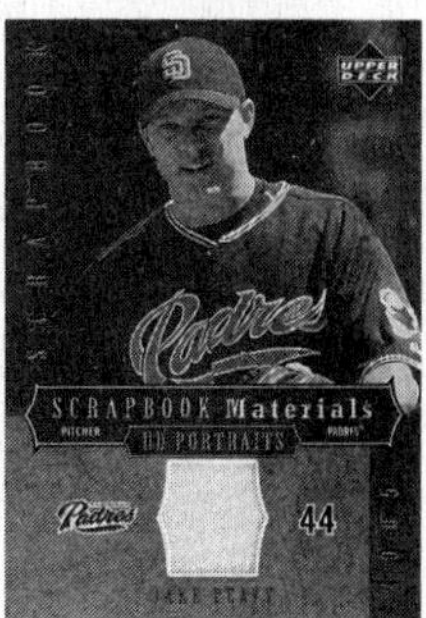

NM/M

Complete Set (59):
Common Player:
BA Bobby Abreu 4.00
JB Jeff Bagwell 6.00
BE Josh Beckett 4.00
AB Adrian Beltre 4.00
BI Craig Biggio 6.00
CA Miguel Cabrera 8.00
WC Will Clark 6.00
CL Matt Clement 4.00
BC Bobby Crosby 4.00
JE Jim Edmonds 6.00
SF Steve Finley 4.00
BG Brian Giles 4.00
GR Khalil Greene 6.00
KG Ken Griffey Jr. 15.00
TG Tony Gwynn 8.00
RH Roy Halladay 4.00
TH Todd Helton 6.00
KH Keith Hernandez 4.00
HU Torii Hunter 4.00
BJ Bo Jackson 10.00
DJ Derek Jeter 20.00
AJ Andruw Jones 6.00
CJ Chipper Jones 8.00
JJ Jacque Jones 4.00
SK Scott Kazmir 4.00
BL Barry Larkin 6.00
ML Mike Lowell 4.00
VM Victor Martinez 4.00
MA Don Mattingly 15.00
JM Joe Mauer 6.00
MC Dallas McPherson 4.00
MO Justin Morneau 4.00
DM Dale Murphy 6.00
MM Mike Mussina 6.00
OR Magglio Ordonez 4.00
DO David Ortiz 8.00
PA Corey Patterson 4.00
CP Carl Pavano 4.00
JP Jake Peavy 6.00
OP Oliver Perez 4.00
MP Mark Prior 6.00
AP Albert Pujols 15.00
JR Jim Rice 6.00
CR Cal Ripken Jr. 20.00
NR Nolan Ryan 15.00
RS Ryne Sandberg 10.00
SA Johan Santana 6.00
JS Jason Schmidt 4.00
MS Mike Schmidt 10.00
SM John Smoltz 6.00
MT Mark Teixeira 6.00
FT Frank Thomas 6.00
BU B.J. Upton 4.00
JV Jose Vidro 4.00
WI Dontrelle Willis 6.00
DW David Wright 10.00
CZ Carlos Zambrano 6.00

Scrapbook Moments

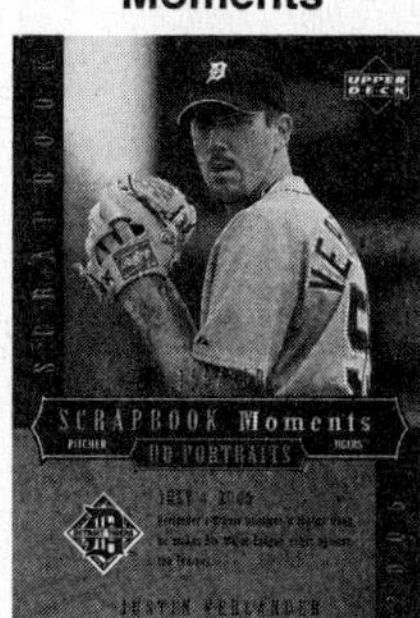

NM/M

Common Player: 1.00
Production 250 Sets
BA Bobby Abreu 1.50
JB Jeff Bagwell 1.50
BE Josh Beckett 1.50
AB Adrian Beltre 1.50
BI Craig Biggio 1.50
CA Miguel Cabrera 2.00
WC Will Clark 1.50
RC Roger Clemens 6.00
CL Matt Clement 1.00
BC Bobby Crosby 1.00
JE Jim Edmonds 1.50
PF Prince Fielder 6.00
SF Steve Finley 1.00
BG Brian Giles 1.00
GR Khalil Greene 1.50
KG Ken Griffey Jr. 4.00
TG Tony Gwynn 2.00
RH Roy Halladay 1.00
TH Todd Helton 1.50
KH Keith Hernandez 1.00
HU Torii Hunter 1.00
BJ Bo Jackson 2.00
DJ Derek Jeter 6.00
AJ Andruw Jones 1.50
CJ Chipper Jones 2.00
JJ Jacque Jones 1.00
SK Scott Kazmir 1.00
BL Barry Larkin 1.50
ML Mike Lowell 1.00
VM Victor Martinez 1.00
MA Don Mattingly 4.00
JM Joe Mauer 1.50
MC Dallas McPherson 1.00
MO Justin Morneau 1.00
DM Dale Murphy 2.00
MM Mike Mussina 1.50
OR Magglio Ordonez 1.00
DO David Ortiz 2.00
PA Corey Patterson 1.00
CP Carl Pavano 1.00
JP Jake Peavy 1.50
OP Oliver Perez 1.00
MP Mark Prior 2.00
AP Albert Pujols 6.00
JR Jim Rice 1.50
CR Cal Ripken Jr. 8.00
NR Nolan Ryan 6.00
RS Ryne Sandberg 4.00
SA Johan Santana 2.00
JS Jason Schmidt 1.00
MS Mike Schmidt 4.00
SM John Smoltz 1.50
MT Mark Teixeira 1.50
FT Frank Thomas 1.50
BU B.J. Upton 1.00
VE Justin Verlander 2.00
JV Jose Vidro 1.00
WI Dontrelle Willis 1.50
DW David Wright 3.00
CZ Carlos Zambrano 1.50

Scrapbook Signatures

No Pricing
Production 20 Sets

Signature Portraits 8x10

NM/M

Common Player:
DB Dusty Baker 100 25.00
JB Jason Bay 25.00
HB Hank Blalock 25.00
WB Wade Boggs 40 50.00
CA Miguel Cabrera 40.00
JD Johnny Damon 99 50.00
GR Khalil Greene 35.00
VG Vladimir Guerrero 40 75.00
KH Keith Hernandez 20.00
DJ Derek Jeter 150 200.00
SK Scott Kazmir 25.00
VM Victor Martinez 25.00
MA Don Mattingly 65.00
JM Joe Mauer 30.00
DM Dale Murphy 30.00
SM Stan Musial 40 80.00
JN Jeff Niemann 25.00
RO Roy Oswalt 30.00
PI Mike Piazza 35 125.00
MP Mark Prior 50 40.00
CR Cal Ripken Jr. 50 160.00
BR Brooks Robinson 50.00
NR Nolan Ryan 25 140.00
RS Ryne Sandberg 99 100.00
MS Mike Schmidt 50.00
BS Ben Sheets 25.00
OS Ozzie Smith 50.00
DS Duke Snider 150 60.00
MT Mark Teixeira 35.00
BU B.J. Upton 20.00
VE Justin Verlander 40.00
DW David Wright 80.00

Sig. Portraits Cuts 8x10 Card

No Pricing
Production 1-25

Signature Portraits Dual 8x10

NM/M

Production 25-99
BT Mark Teixeira, Hank Blalock 99 50.00
HS Rich Harden, Ben Sheets 99 40.00
NV Justin Verlander, Jeff Niemann 99 50.00
SH Tim Hudson, John Smoltz 75 75.00
WP Kerry Wood, Mark Prior 99 85.00
WR David Wright, Jose Reyes 99 140.00

Sig. Portraits Dual Cuts 8x10

No Pricing
Production 1-2

Sign. Portraits Triple 8x10

No Pricing
Production 15 Sets

Signature Portraits Quad 8x10

No Pricing
Production Five Sets

2005 Upper Deck Pros & Prospects

NM/M

Complete Set (200):
Common Player (1-100): .15
Common SP (101-150): 3.00
Production 999

Common SP (151-175): 4.00
Production 499
Common SP (176-200): 5.00
Production 199
Pack (6): 2.75
Box (24): 60.00
1 Adam Dunn .40
2 Aramis Ramirez .40
3 Bobby Abreu .25
4 Mike Lowell .15
5 Josh Beckett .25
6 Derek Jeter 1.50
7 Alex Rodriguez 1.25
8 Andruw Jones .25
9 Brian Giles .15
10 Ivan Rodriguez .40
11 Aubrey Huff .15
12 Jake Peavy .25
13 Hank Blalock .25
14 Curt Schilling .50
15 Carlos Zambrano .40
16 Mike Mussina .40
17 Travis Hafner .15
18 Scott Rolen .50
19 Luis Gonzalez .25
20 Torii Hunter .25
21 Greg Maddux 1.00
22 J.D. Drew .25
23 Kevin Brown .15
24 Carl Pavano .25
25 David Ortiz .50
26 Jose Reyes .40
27 Johan Santana .50
28 Todd Helton .40
29 Jason Kendall .15
30 Pedro Martinez .50
31 Chipper Jones .50
32 Ben Sheets .25
33 Garret Anderson .25
34 Carl Crawford .15
35 Jason Schmidt .25
36 Johnny Damon .50
37 Richie Sexson .25
38 Brad Penny .15
39 Carlos Delgado .40
40 Gary Sheffield .40
41 John Smoltz .25
42 Eric Chavez .25
43 Carlos Guillen .15
44 Jeff Kent .25
45 Miguel Tejada .40
46 Shawn Green .25
47 Vernon Wells .15
48 Albert Pujols 1.50
49 Alfonso Soriano .50
50 Eric Gagne .40
51 Mark Prior .50
52 Rafael Furcal .25
53 Preston Wilson .15
54 Barry Larkin .25
55 Randy Johnson .50
56 Craig Wilson .15
57 Victor Martinez .15
58 Jim Thome .50
59 Paul Konerko .15
60 Jeff Bagwell .40
61 Lyle Overbay .15
62 Miguel Cabrera .50
63 Melvin Mora .15
64 Scott Podsednik .25
65 Mark Mulder .25
66 Mark Teixeira .40
67 Tom Glavine .25
68 Frank Thomas .40
69 Livan Hernandez .15
70 Kazuo Matsui .15
71 Jose Vidro .15
72 Ichiro Suzuki 1.25
73 Roger Clemens 1.50
74 Manny Ramirez .50
75 Michael Young .15
76 Rafael Palmeiro .40
77 Steve Finley .15
78 Andy Pettitte .25
79 Lance Berkman .25
80 Adrian Beltre .25
81 Carlos Lee .25
82 Bret Boone .15
83 Magglio Ordonez .15
84 Sammy Sosa 1.00
85 Tim Hudson .25
86 Vladimir Guerrero .50
87 Carlos Beltran .40
88 Kerry Wood .50
89 Jim Edmonds .25
90 Mike Sweeney .15
91 Nomar Garciaparra 1.00
92 Mike Piazza 1.00
93 Roy Halladay .25
94 Troy Glaus .25
95 Bernie Williams .25
96 Larry Walker .25
97 Craig Biggio .25
98 Roy Oswalt .25
99 Ken Griffey Jr. 1.00
100 Hideki Matsui 1.00
101 Bucky Jacobsen 3.00
102 J.D. Closser 3.00
103 Antonio Perez 3.00
104 Chris Shelton 3.00
105 David Aardsma 3.00
106 Jake Woods 3.00
107 Jung Bong 3.00
108 Kazuhito Tadano 3.00
109 John Van Benschoten 3.00
110 Jesse Foppert 3.00
111 Joe Borchard 3.00
112 Brandon Phillips 3.00
113 J.D. Durbin 3.00
114 Brandon Claussen 3.00
115 Robb Quinlan 3.00
116 Aaron Harang 3.00
117 Chris Burke 3.00
118 Sergio Mitre 3.00
119 David DeJesus 3.00
120 Gustavo Chacin 3.00
121 Xavier Nady 3.00
122 Garrett Atkins 3.00
123 Jimmy Gobble 3.00
124 Yhency Brazoban 3.00
125 David Kelton 3.00
126 Dewon Brazelton 3.00
127 Koyie Hill 3.00
128 Roman Colon 3.00
129 Daniel Cabrera 3.00
130 Chris Bootcheck 3.00
131 Brad Halsey 3.00
132 Bobby Madritsch 3.00
133 Grady Sizemore 3.00
134 Akinori Otsuka 3.00
135 Wilfredo Ledezma 3.00
136 Russ Adams 3.00
137 Joe Crede 3.00
138 Chad Cordero 3.00
139 Willie Harris 3.00
140 Joey Gathright 3.00
141 Logan Kensing 3.00
142 Jon Leicester 3.00
143 Freddy Guzman 3.00
144 Jonny Gomes 3.00
145 Jeff Bajenaru 3.00
146 Andres Blanco 3.00
147 Jhonny Peralta 3.00
148 Jayson Werth 3.00
149 Bill Hall 3.00
150 Jason Davis 3.00
151 Gabe Gross 4.00
152 Abe Alvarez 4.00
153 Josh Willingham 4.00
154 Merkin Valdez 4.00
155 Jeff Niemann **RC** 8.00
156 Yadier Molina 4.00
157 Guillermo Quiroz 4.00
158 Ian Snell 4.00
159 Dan Meyer 4.00
160 Jason Lane 4.00
161 Adrian Gonzalez 4.00
162 Eddy Rodriguez 4.00
163 Jason Dubois 4.00
164 Juan Rincon 4.00
165 Ryan Wagner 4.00
166 Nick Swisher 4.00
167 Chad Tracy 4.00
168 Dioner Navarro 4.00
169 Gerald Laird 4.00
170 Alexis Rios 4.00
171 Aaron Rowand 4.00
172 Adam LaRoche 4.00
173 Kevin Youkilis 4.00
174 Philip Humber **RC** 6.00
175 Chin-Hui Tsao 4.00
176 Jeff Francis 5.00
177 Chase Utley 5.00
178 Gavin Floyd 5.00
179 David Wright 10.00
180 B.J. Upton 5.00
181 Laynce Nix 5.00
182 Joe Mauer 8.00
183 Justin Morneau 5.00
184 Zack Greinke 5.00
185 Jose Capellan 5.00
186 Khalil Greene 5.00
187 Oliver Perez 5.00
188 Joe Blanton 5.00
189 Wily Mo Pena 5.00
190 Dallas McPherson 6.00
191 Edwin Jackson 5.00
192 Casey Kotchman 5.00
193 Jesse Crain 5.00
194 Ryan Howard 6.00
195 Bobby Crosby 5.00
196 Jason Bay 5.00
197 Rickie Weeks 5.00
198 Scott Proctor 5.00
199 Dan Haren 5.00
200 Scott Kazmir 5.00

Gold

Gold (1-100): 4-8X
Production 125
Gold (101-150): 1X
Production 150
Gold (151-175): 1X
Production 99
Gold (176-200): No Pricing
Production 25

Future Fabrics

NM/M
Common Player: 4.00
Gold: 1-2X
Production 75 Sets
MC Miguel Cabrera 8.00
BC Bobby Crosby 6.00
KG Khalil Greene 6.00
RH Rich Harden 4.00
EH Eric Hinske 4.00
JJ Jacque Jones 4.00
KE Austin Kearns 4.00
AK Adam Kennedy 4.00
CK Casey Kotchman 4.00
VM Victor Martinez 4.00
KM Kazuo Matsui 4.00
JM Joe Mauer 8.00
DM Dallas McPherson 6.00
TN Trot Nixon 4.00
SP Sidney Ponson 4.00
JR Jose Reyes 4.00
CS C.C. Sabathia 4.00
SS Shannon Stewart 4.00
BU B.J. Upton 4.00
JW Jayson Werth 4.00
DW David Wright 15.00

Pro Material

NM/M
Common Player: 6.00
Gold: 1-2X
Production 50 Sets
JB Jeff Bagwell 6.00
CB Carlos Beltran 8.00
AB Adrian Beltre 6.00
HB Hank Blalock 6.00
EC Eric Chavez 6.00
KG Ken Griffey Jr. 10.00
VG Vladimir Guerrero 8.00
TH Todd Helton 8.00
DJ Derek Jeter 20.00
RJ Randy Johnson 8.00
CJ Chipper Jones 8.00
PI Mike Piazza 8.00
MP Mark Prior 6.00
AP Albert Pujols 15.00
MR Manny Ramirez 8.00
SR Scott Rolen 8.00
CS Curt Schilling 8.00
SS Sammy Sosa 8.00
IS Ichiro Suzuki 25.00
MT Miguel Tejada 8.00
JT Jim Thome 8.00

Signs of Stardom

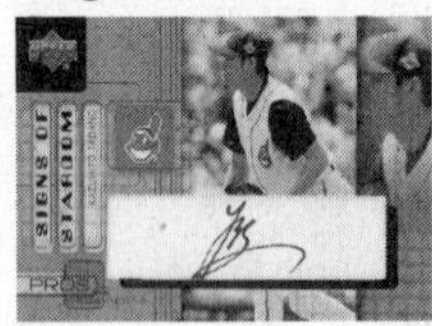

NM/M
Common Autograph: 8.00
RB Rocco Baldelli 15.00
JB Josh Beckett 15.00
AB Angel Berroa 8.00
HB Hank Blalock 20.00
SB Sean Burroughs 8.00
MC Miguel Cabrera 30.00
CC Chad Cordero 8.00
BC Bobby Crosby 15.00
AE Adam Eaton 12.00
FF Frank Francisco 8.00
JF Jason Frasor 8.00
GA John Gall 8.00
MG Marcus Giles 15.00
GR Khalil Greene 25.00
RH Rich Harden 20.00
MJ Mike Johnston 8.00
SK Scott Kazmir 20.00
JK Jeff Keppinger 8.00
CK Casey Kotchman 15.00
CL Cliff Lee 8.00
JL Justin Leone 8.00
MA Joe Mauer 25.00
AO Akinori Otsuka 20.00
LO Lyle Overbay 10.00
CP Corey Patterson 15.00
PE Jake Peavy 30.00
OP Oliver Perez 20.00
SP Scott Podsednik 15.00
HR Horacio Ramirez 8.00
JR Jose Reyes 30.00
MR Mike Rouse 8.00
BS Ben Sheets 15.00
TS Terrmel Sledge 10.00
KT Kazuhito Tadano 20.00
ST Shingo Takatsu 25.00
MT Mark Teixeira 30.00
WA Ryan Wagner 10.00
WE Brandon Webb 10.00
RW Rickie Weeks 15.00
JW Jerome Williams 8.00
DW Dontrelle Willis 25.00

Stardom Signatures

NM/M
EB Ernie Banks/240 50.00
BE Josh Beckett/50 20.00
BL Hank Blalock/50 20.00
JG Jason Giambi/100 15.00
KG Ken Griffey Jr./198 75.00
AK Al Kaline/99 50.00
JM Joe Morgan/194 25.00
KP Kirby Puckett/156 50.00

2005 Upper Deck Pro Sigs

NM/M
Complete Set (132): 25.00
Common Player: .10
Common Rookie (91-132): .25
Inserted 1:1
Pack (6): 2.00
Box (24): 40.00
1 Dallas McPherson .10
2 Garret Anderson .25
3 Steve Finley .10
4 Vladimir Guerrero .50
5 Luis Gonzalez .10
6 Shawn Green .10
7 Troy Glaus .25
8 Andruw Jones .40
9 Chipper Jones .50
10 John Smoltz .25
11 Tim Hudson .40
12 Miguel Tejada .40
13 Rafael Palmeiro .25
14 Sammy Sosa .75
15 Curt Schilling .50
16 David Ortiz .50
17 Johnny Damon .50
18 Manny Ramirez .50
19 Greg Maddux 1.00
20 Kerry Wood .25
21 Mark Prior .50
22 Nomar Garciaparra .50
23 Frank Thomas .40
24 Paul Konerko .25
25 Adam Dunn .40
26 Ken Griffey Jr. 1.00
27 Travis Hafner .10
28 Victor Martinez .10
29 Todd Helton .40
30 Ivan Rodriguez .40
31 Magglio Ordonez .10
32 Carlos Delgado .25
33 Josh Beckett .25
34 Miguel Cabrera .50
35 Craig Biggio .25
36 Jeff Bagwell .40
37 Lance Berkman .25
38 Roger Clemens 1.50
39 Roy Oswalt .25
40 Mike Sweeney .10
41 Derek Lowe .10
42 Eric Gagne .25
43 J.D. Drew .10
44 Jeff Kent .10
45 Ben Sheets .25
46 Carlos Lee .25
47 Joe Mauer .25
48 Johan Santana .50
49 Torii Hunter .25
50 Carlos Beltran .40
51 David Wright 1.00
52 Kazuo Matsui .10
53 Mike Piazza .75
54 Pedro Martinez .50
55 Tom Glavine .25
56 Alex Rodriguez 1.50
57 Derek Jeter 1.50
58 Gary Sheffield .40
59 Hideki Matsui 1.00
60 Jason Giambi .25
61 Jorge Posada .25
62 Mike Mussina .25
63 Randy Johnson .50
64 Barry Zito .25
65 Bobby Crosby .25
66 Eric Chavez .25
67 Bobby Abreu .25
68 Jim Thome .40
69 Jason Bay .25
70 Oliver Perez .10
71 Brian Giles .10
72 Jake Peavy .25
73 Khalil Greene .25
74 Jason Schmidt .10
75 Moises Alou .25
76 Adrian Beltre .25
77 Bret Boone .10
78 Ichiro Suzuki 1.00
79 Richie Sexson .25
80 Albert Pujols 1.50
81 Jim Edmonds .25
82 Mark Mulder .25
83 Scott Rolen .50
84 Aubrey Huff .10
85 Alfonso Soriano .50
86 Hank Blalock .25
87 Mark Teixeira .25
88 Roy Halladay .25
89 Jose Vidro .10
90 Livan Hernandez .10
91 Tony Pena **RC** .25
92 Luis Hernandez **RC** .25
93 Peter Orr **RC** .25
94 Anibal Sanchez **RC** .75
95 Luis Mendoza **RC** .25
96 Stephen Drew **RC** 6.00
97 Russel Rohlicek **RC** .25
98 Casey Rogowski **RC** .25
99 Pedro Lopez **RC** .25
100 Tadahito Iguchi **RC** 2.00
101 Daylan Childress **RC** .25
102 John Morillo **RC** .50
103 Marcos Carvajal **RC** .25
104 Ubaldo Jimenez **RC** .25
105 Justin Verlander **RC** 2.00
106 Chris Resop **RC** .25
107 Yorman Bazardo **RC** .25
108 Jared Gothreaux **RC** .25
109 Luke Scott **RC** 1.00
110 Ambiorix Burgos **RC** .50
111 Prince Fielder 4.00
112 Dennis Houlton **RC** .25
113 Franquelis Osoria **RC** .25
114 Norihiro Nakamura **RC** 1.00
115 Oscar Robles **RC** .25
116 Steve Schmoll **RC** .25
117 Luis Pena **RC** .25
118 David Gassner **RC** .25
119 Ambiorix Concepcion **RC** .50
120 Dae-Sung Koo **RC** .25
121 Matt Lindstrom **RC** .25
122 Colter Bean **RC** .25
123 Keiichi Yabu **RC** .25
124 Philip Humber **RC** 1.00
125 Wladimir Balentien **RC** 1.00
126 Tony Giarratano **RC** .25
127 Shane Costa **RC** .25
128 Jeff Niemann **RC** 1.00
129 Nick Masset **RC** .25
130 Ismael Ramirez **RC** .25
131 John Hattig Jr. **RC** .25
132 Brandon McCarthy **RC** 1.50

Silver

Silver: 1-30X
Inserted 1:5

Gold

Gold: 2-4X
Production 350 Sets

Signature Sensations

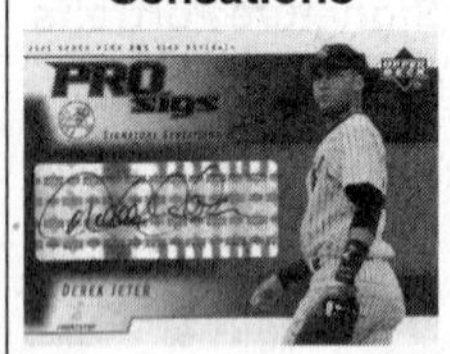

NM/M
Inserted 1:24
Silver: 1-2X
Production 50 Sets
Gold: No Pricing
Production Five Sets
AA Abe Alvarez 10.00
BA Bronson Arroyo 25.00
GA Garrett Atkins 8.00
DB Denny Bautista 5.00
RB Russell Branyan 5.00
MC Miguel Cabrera 35.00
KC Kiko Calero 5.00
CC Chad Cordero 10.00
JC Juan Cruz 5.00
BD Brandon Duckworth 5.00
JE Johnny Estrada 8.00
LF Lew Ford/SP 10.00
TH Travis Hafner 15.00
KH Keith Hernandez/SP 20.00
OH Orlando Hernandez 75.00
OI Omar Infante 5.00
DJ Derek Jeter/SP 150.00
JJ Jorge Julio 5.00
AM Aaron Miles 5.00
YM Yadier Molina 15.00
RN Roberto Novoa 5.00
NP Nick Punto 5.00
HR Horacio Ramirez/SP 10.00
AR Aaron Rowand 25.00
CS Cory Sullivan 8.00
JS Jeff Suppan 10.00
BT Brett Tomko 5.00
MV Merkin Valdez 5.00
DW David Wright 70.00

2005 Upper Deck Reflections Promos

Each of the first 100 cards in Upper Deck Reflections was issued in a foil-overprinted version with "UD PROMO" across the front. Cards were inserted into specially marked card shop and newsstand issues of Tuff Stuff magazine.

NM/M
Common Player: .50
Stars: 1.5X

2005 Upper Deck Reflections

NM/M
Complete Set (200):
Common (1-100): .50
Common SP (101-150): 1.00
Inserted 1:2
Common SP (151-200): 2.00
Inserted 1:2
Pack (4): 8.00
Box (12): 80.00
1 Corey Patterson .50
2 Curt Schilling 1.00
3 Todd Helton .75
4 Johnny Damon 1.00
5 Alex Rodriguez 2.50
6 Vladimir Guerrero 1.00
7 John Smoltz .50
8 Ivan Rodriguez .75
9 Roy Halladay .50
10 Carlos Beltran .75
11 Ichiro Suzuki 2.00
12 Jim Edmonds .50
13 Andruw Jones .50
14 Scott Podsednik .50
15 Troy Glaus .50
16 Miguel Cabrera 1.00
17 Adrian Beltre .50
18 Ben Sheets .50
19 Alfonso Soriano 1.00
20 Brian Giles .50
21 Carl Crawford .50
22 Frank Thomas .75
23 Jeff Kent .50
24 Eric Gagne .50
25 Shawn Green .50
26 Sammy Sosa 2.00
27 Carlos Lee .50
28 Ken Griffey Jr. 2.00
29 Mike Lowell .50
30 Magglio Ordonez .50
31 Aubrey Huff .50
32 Travis Hafner .50
33 Albert Pujols 3.00
34 Vernon Wells .50
35 Roy Oswalt .50
36 Jose Guillen .50
37 Jim Thome .75
38 Bobby Abreu .50
39 Bret Boone .50
40 Mark Teixeira .50
41 Garret Anderson .50
42 Jose Reyes .75
43 Bernie Williams .50
44 Greg Maddux 1.50
45 Gary Sheffield .50
46 Josh Beckett .50
47 Chipper Jones 1.00
48 Hank Blalock .50
49 C.C. Sabathia .50
50 Manny Ramirez 1.00
51 Pedro Martinez 1.00
52 Michael Young .50
53 Jacque Jones .50
54 Marcus Giles .50
55 Steve Finley .50
56 Miguel Tejada .75
57 Mike Sweeney .50
58 Lance Berkman .50
59 J.D. Drew .50
60 Jeromy Burnitz .50
61 Johan Santana .75
62 Victor Martinez .50
63 Carl Pavano .50
64 Roger Clemens 3.00
65 Richie Sexson .50
66 Tim Hudson .50
67 Melvin Mora .50
68 Angel Berroa .50
69 Rafael Palmeiro .75
70 Randy Johnson 1.00
71 Torii Hunter .50
72 Luis Gonzalez .50
73 Kazuo Matsui .50
74 Hideki Matsui 2.00
75 Mark Prior 1.00
76 Jeff Bagwell .75
77 Eric Chavez .50
78 Mark Loretta .50
79 Adam Dunn .75
80 Kerry Wood 1.00
81 Jose Vidro .50
82 Jason Schmidt .50
83 Carlos Delgado .50
84 Scott Rolen 1.00
85 David Ortiz 1.00
86 Edgar Renteria 1.00
87 Nomar Garciaparra 1.50
88 Mike Piazza 1.50
89 Mark Mulder .50
90 Tom Glavine .50
91 Paul Konerko .50
92 Larry Walker .50
93 Derek Jeter 3.00
94 Jake Peavy .50
95 Carlos Zambrano .50
96 Russ Ortiz .50
97 Barry Zito .50
98 Austin Kearns .50
99 Pedro Feliz .50
100 Rich Harden .50
101 Adam LaRoche 1.00
102 Brandon Claussen 1.00
103 Gavin Floyd 1.00
104 Daniel Cabrera 1.00
105 Joe Mauer 2.00
106 Khalil Greene 2.00
107 David Wright 3.00
108 Rickie Weeks 2.00
109 Robb Quinlan 1.00
110 Bucky Jacobsen 1.00
111 Ryan Howard 2.00
112 Jeff Francis 1.00
113 Jason Lane 1.00
114 Alexis Rios 1.00
115 Bobby Madritsch 1.00
116 Jesse Crain 1.00
117 Oliver Perez 1.00
118 Garrett Atkins 1.00
119 Casey Kotchman 2.00
120 B.J. Upton 1.00
121 Laynce Nix 1.00
122 Adrian Gonzalez 1.00
123 Joe Blanton 1.00
124 Gabe Gross 1.00
125 Scott Kazmir 2.00
126 Zack Greinke 1.00
127 Edwin Jackson 1.00
128 Jason Bay 1.00
129 J.D. Closser 1.00
130 Jason Dubois 1.00
131 Dallas McPherson 2.00
132 Chad Cordero 1.00
133 Angel Guzman 1.00
134 Jayson Werth 1.00
135 Ryan Wagner 1.00
136 Guillermo Quiroz 1.00
137 Scott Proctor 1.00
138 Chris Burke 1.00
139 Nick Swisher 1.00
140 David DeJesus 1.00
141 Yhency Brazoban 1.00
142 Bobby Crosby 1.00
143 Chase Utley 1.00
144 Wily Mo Pena 1.00
145 Roman Colon 1.00
146 Eddy Rodriguez 1.00
147 Gerald Laird 1.00
148 Jose Capellan 1.00
149 Aaron Rowand 1.00
150 Kevin Youkilis 1.00
151 Bob Feller 2.00
152 Robin Yount 4.00
153 Willie Stargell 2.00
154 Cal Ripken Jr. 8.00
155 Monte Irvin 2.00
156 Nolan Ryan 6.00
157 Bob Lemon 2.00
158 Richie Ashburn 2.00
159 Billy Williams 2.00
160 Luis Aparicio 2.00
161 Phil Niekro 2.00
162 Bobby Doerr 2.00
163 Mike Schmidt 6.00
164 Stan Musial 4.00
165 George Kell 2.00
166 Joe Morgan 2.00
167 Whitey Ford 3.00
168 Rick Ferrell 2.00
169 Jim "Catfish" Hunter 2.00
170 Red Schoendienst 2.00
171 Tom Seaver 4.00
172 Pee Wee Reese 2.00
173 Lou Boudreau 2.00
174 Hal Newhouser 2.00
175 Harmon Killebrew 3.00
176 Jim Bunning 2.00
177 Willie McCovey 3.00
178 Bob Gibson 3.00
179 Juan Marichal 2.00
180 Robin Roberts 2.00
181 Gaylord Perry 2.00
182 Brooks Robinson 4.00
183 Al Lopez 2.00
184 Joe DiMaggio 6.00
185 Al Kaline 3.00
186 Rollie Fingers 2.00
187 Mickey Mantle 10.00
188 Enos Slaughter 2.00
189 Ernie Banks 4.00
190 Eddie Mathews 3.00
191 Tommy Lasorda 2.00
192 Fergie Jenkins 2.00
193 Lou Brock 2.00
194 Larry Doby 2.00
195 Phil Rizzuto 3.00
196 Warren Spahn 4.00
197 Ralph Kiner 2.00
198 Hoyt Wilhelm 2.00
199 Early Wynn 2.00
200 Yogi Berra 4.00

Blue

Blue (1-100): 2-4X
Blue (101-200): 1-2.5X
Production 75 Sets

Emerald

Emerald (1-100): 4-8X
Emerald (101-200): 3-5X
Production 25 Sets

Platinum

Platinum (1-200): No Pricing
Production One Set

Purple

Purple (1-100): 2-4X
Purple (101-200): 1-2.5X
Production 99 Sets

Red

Red (1-100): 2-4X
Red (101-200): 1-2.5X
Production 99 Sets

Turquoise

Turquoise (1-100): 3-5X
Turquoise (101-200): 1.5-3X
Production 50 Sets

Cut From the Same Cloth

NM/M
Common Duo: 8.00
Production 225 Sets
Red: 1-1.5X
Production 99 Sets
Blue: 1-2X
Production 50 Sets
Platinum: No Pricing
Production One Set
AA Albert Pujols, Adrian Beltre 20.00
AB Carlos Beltran, Bobby Abreu 10.00
AG Garret Anderson, Vladimir Guerrero 10.00
AH Alfonso Soriano, Hank Blalock 10.00
AJ Albert Pujols, Jim Thome 20.00
AM Adrian Beltre, Miguel Cabrera 10.00
AT Jim Thome, Bobby Abreu 10.00
AW Albert Pujols, Will Clark 20.00
BB Jeff Bagwell, Craig Biggio 10.00
BG Carlos Beltran, Ken Griffey Jr. 15.00
BM Paul Molitor, George Brett 20.00
BO Josh Beckett, Roy Oswalt 8.00
BP Johnny Bench, Mike Piazza 15.00
BR Adrian Beltre, Scott Rolen 10.00
BS George Brett, Mike Schmidt 25.00
BT Mark Teixeira, Hank Blalock 10.00
BW Hank Blalock, David Wright 15.00
CB Bobby Crosby, Jason Bay 8.00

CC	Bobby Crosby, Eric Chavez	8.00
CG	Bobby Crosby, Khalil Greene	8.00
CL	Miguel Cabrera, Mike Lowell	10.00
CP	Carl Crawford, Scott Podsednik	8.00
CR	Scott Rolen, Eric Chavez	10.00
CT	Miguel Tejada, Bobby Crosby	10.00
DM	Mike Schmidt, Dale Murphy	15.00
DR	Manny Ramirez, Johnny Damon	15.00
GI	Brian Giles, Marcus Giles	8.00
GS	Sammy Sosa, Ken Griffey Jr.	20.00
GV	Jose Guillen, Jose Vidro	8.00
HH	Tim Hudson, Rich Harden	8.00
HK	Kent Hrbek, Harmon Killebrew	20.00
JD	J.D. Drew, Chipper Jones	10.00
JH	Torii Hunter, Jacque Jones	8.00
JJ	Chipper Jones, Andruw Jones	10.00
JM	Don Mattingly, Derek Jeter	30.00
JR	Randy Johnson, Nolan Ryan	30.00
JS	Steve Carlton, Johan Santana	10.00
JT	Miguel Tejada, Derek Jeter	25.00
KH	Jason Kendall, Tim Hudson	8.00
KM	Dallas McPherson, Casey Kotchman	10.00
MB	Wade Boggs, Don Mattingly	20.00
MC	Don Mattingly, Will Clark	20.00
MH	Mark Mulder, Tim Hudson	8.00
MJ	Dale Murphy, Chipper Jones	15.00
MK	Harmon Killebrew, Justin Morneau	15.00
MM	Kazuo Matsui, Hideki Matsui	30.00
MS	Johan Santana, Joe Mauer	12.00
MW	Dallas McPherson, David Wright	20.00
MY	Robin Yount, Paul Molitor	20.00
OD	Johnny Damon, David Ortiz	15.00
OT	Shingo Takatsu, Akinori Otsuka	15.00
PB	Jim Bunning, Jim Palmer	10.00
PC	Miguel Cabrera, Albert Pujols	20.00
PG	Albert Pujols, Vladimir Guerrero	25.00
PP	Mike Piazza, Jorge Posada	15.00
PR	Albert Pujols, Scott Rolen	25.00
PS	Tom Seaver, Mark Prior	10.00
PT	Mark Teixeira, Albert Pujols	20.00
RJ	Cal Ripken Jr., Derek Jeter	40.00
RM	Ivan Rodriguez, Victor Martinez	8.00
RO	Manny Ramirez, David Ortiz	20.00
RP	Ivan Rodriguez, Mike Piazza	15.00
RR	Cal Ripken Jr., Brooks Robinson	35.00
RT	Miguel Tejada, Cal Ripken Jr.	30.00
RW	Scott Rolen, David Wright	15.00
SB	Ryne Sandberg, Wade Boggs	25.00
SM	Pedro J. Martinez, Curt Schilling	15.00
SO	Curt Schilling, David Ortiz	15.00
SP	Ben Sheets, Mark Prior	10.00
SR	Scott Rolen, Mike Schmidt	15.00
ST	Alfonso Soriano, Mark Teixeira	15.00
TC	Mark Teixeira, Miguel Cabrera	15.00
TH	Todd Helton, Jim Thome	10.00
TP	Rafael Palmeiro, Miguel Tejada	10.00
TR	Manny Ramirez, Jim Thome	12.00
TS	Jim Thome, Mike Schmidt	15.00
UJ	Derek Jeter, B.J. Upton	25.00
UK	B.J. Upton, Scott Kazmir	8.00
UW	B.J. Upton, David Wright	15.00
VJ	Jose Vidro, Nick Johnson	8.00
WB	Bernie Williams, Carlos Beltran	10.00
WJ	Bernie Williams, Derek Jeter	25.00
WM	Bernie Williams, Hideki Matsui	30.00
WP	Mark Prior, Kerry Wood	10.00
WR	Kerry Wood, Nolan Ryan	30.00
YR	Manny Ramirez, Carl Yastrzemski	20.00
ZM	Mark Mulder, Barry Zito	8.00
BD1	Carlos Beltran, Johnny Damon	10.00
BD2	Johnny Damon, Carlos Beltran	10.00
GG1	Ken Griffey Jr., Ken Griffey Sr.	15.00
GG2	Ken Griffey Sr., Ken Griffey Jr.	15.00

Cut From Same Cloth Patch

		NM/M
Production 99 Sets		
AM	Adrian Beltre, Miguel Cabrera	25.00
BR	Adrian Beltre, Scott Rolen	25.00
BS	George Brett, Mike Schmidt	40.00
BT	Mark Teixeira, Hank Blalock	20.00
CB	Jason Bay, Bobby Crosby	20.00
CG	Bobby Crosby, Khalil Greene	20.00
CP	Gary Carter, Mike Piazza	35.00
CR	Eric Chavez, Scott Rolen	25.00
DG	Ken Griffey Jr., Adam Dunn	40.00
GC	Miguel Cabrera, Ken Griffey Jr.	40.00
GI	Brian Giles, Marcus Giles	15.00
JM	Derek Jeter, Don Mattingly	60.00
JR	Cal Ripken Jr., Derek Jeter	80.00
KM	Dallas McPherson, Casey Kotchman	25.00
MJ	Chipper Jones, Dale Murphy	30.00
MP	Mike Piazza, Joe Mauer	30.00
MW	Dallas McPherson, David Wright	30.00
MY	Robin Yount, Paul Molitor	40.00
OB	Wade Boggs, David Ortiz	30.00
OT	Shingo Takatsu, Akinori Otsuka	30.00
PB	Albert Pujols, Adrian Beltre	40.00
PC	Albert Pujols, Miguel Cabrera	40.00
PR	Albert Pujols, Scott Rolen	40.00
RJ	Randy Johnson, Nolan Ryan	40.00
RP	Ivan Rodriguez, Mike Piazza	30.00
RR	Cal Ripken Jr., Brooks Robinson	50.00
RW	Nolan Ryan, Kerry Wood	40.00
SB	Ryne Sandberg, Wade Boggs	50.00
SP	Ben Sheets, Mark Prior	20.00
TC	Mark Teixeira, Miguel Cabrera	30.00
TO	Mark Teixeira, David Ortiz	25.00
UJ	Derek Jeter, B.J. Upton	40.00
UW	B.J. Upton, David Wright	25.00
WB	David Wright, Hank Blalock	30.00
WP	Mark Prior, Kerry Wood	30.00
WR	David Wright, Scott Rolen	30.00
YO	David Ortiz, Carl Yastrzemski	50.00
GG1	Ken Griffey Sr., Ken Griffey Jr.	40.00
GG2	Ken Griffey Jr., Ken Griffey Sr.	40.00

Cut From the Same Cloth Auto Patch

		NM/M
Production 25 Sets		
BT	Mark Teixeira, Hank Blalock	120.00
DG	Ken Griffey Jr., Adam Dunn	240.00
GC	Miguel Cabrera, Ken Griffey Jr.	240.00
JR	Derek Jeter, Cal Ripken Jr.	500.00
MJ	Chipper Jones, Dale Murphy	140.00
PC	Albert Pujols, Miguel Cabrera	350.00
RP	Mike Piazza, Ivan Rodriguez	140.00
SB	Ryne Sandberg, Wade Boggs	160.00
TO	Mark Teixeira, David Ortiz	100.00
WB	David Wright, Hank Blalock	100.00
WR	David Wright, Scott Rolen	100.00

Dual Signature

		NM/M
Red:		1-1.5X
Production 99 Sets		
Blue:		1.5-2X
Production 35 Sets		
Platinum:		No Pricing
Production One Set		
ABAR	Al Rosen, Adrian Beltre	30.00
ABDM	Adrian Beltre, Dallas McPherson	30.00
ABDW	David Wright, Adrian Beltre	40.00
ABEC	Adrian Beltre, Eric Chavez	30.00
ABJL	Adrian Beltre, Justin Leone	30.00
ABSR	Adrian Beltre, Scott Rolen	30.00
AHBU	Aubrey Huff, B.J. Upton	25.00
AHCC	Carl Crawford, Aubrey Huff	25.00
AKDM	Al Kaline, Dale Murphy	50.00
AOST	Akinori Otsuka, Shingo Takatsu	40.00
ARCC	Alexis Rios, Carl Crawford	20.00
ARKG	Alexis Rios, Ken Griffey Jr.	65.00
ARTH	Al Rosen, Travis Hafner	25.00
BAKY	Kevin Youkilis, Bronson Arroyo	50.00
BCCR	Bobby Crosby, Cal Ripken Jr.	160.00
BCDJ	Derek Jeter, Bobby Crosby	125.00
BCEC	Bobby Crosby, Eric Chavez	25.00
BCJB	Bobby Crosby, Jason Bay	35.00
BCKG	Khalil Greene, Bobby Crosby	35.00
BDWB	Bobby Doerr, Wade Boggs	50.00
BGMG	Brian Giles, Marcus Giles	25.00
BPFH	Frank Howard, Boog Powell	30.00
BRRS	Brooks Robinson, Ron Santo	40.00
BSJC	Ben Sheets, Jose Capellan	20.00
BSRW	Rickie Weeks, Ben Sheets	35.00
BSSK	Ben Sheets, Scott Kazmir	20.00
BUDJ	B.J. Upton, Derek Jeter	125.00
BURW	B.J. Upton, Rickie Weeks	30.00
BUSK	B.J. Upton, Scott Kazmir	25.00
BWKG	Billy Williams, Ken Griffey Jr.	80.00
CCNJ	Nick Johnson, Chad Cordero	25.00
CKDM	Casey Kotchman, Dallas McPherson	35.00
CKKH	Keith Hernandez, Casey Kotchman	20.00
CKMT	Casey Kotchman, Mark Teixeira	35.00
CTDM	Charles Thomas, Dale Murphy	30.00
CTJC	Charles Thomas, Jose Capellan	15.00
CTRH	Charles Thomas, Ryan Howard	50.00
CZJS	Johan Santana, Carlos Zambrano	60.00
CZLT	Carlos Zambrano, Luis Tiant	20.00
DGDB	Dwight Gooden, Dewon Brazelton	20.00
DGJB	Jim Bouton, Dwight Gooden	20.00
DGJS	Dwight Gooden, Johan Santana	50.00
DJDM	Derek Jeter, Don Mattingly	200.00
DJKG	Derek Jeter, Khalil Greene	140.00
DKFH	Frank Howard, Dave Kingman	25.00
DMDW	David Wright, Dallas McPherson	50.00
DMJB	Dale Murphy, Jason Bay	40.00
DMJL	Justin Leone, Dallas McPherson	20.00
DMKY	Dallas McPherson, Kevin Youkilis	20.00
DMMS	Dallas McPherson, Mike Schmidt	75.00
DMRH	Dallas McPherson, Ryan Howard	50.00
DOKY	David Ortiz, Kevin Youkilis	60.00
DWJL	Justin Leone, David Wright	40.00
DWKH	David Wright, Keith Hernandez	65.00
DWKY	David Wright, Kevin Youkilis	40.00
DWMS	David Wright, Mike Schmidt	100.00
DWSR	David Wright, Scott Rolen	65.00
ECSR	Scott Rolen, Eric Chavez	50.00
FHMT	Mark Teixeira, Frank Howard	40.00
FHNJ	Frank Howard, Nick Johnson	25.00
GPJP	Gaylord Perry, Jake Peavy	30.00
ISJC	Jose Capellan, Ian Snell	15.00
ISMV	Ian Snell, Merkin Valdez	15.00
ISSK	Ian Snell, Scott Kazmir	20.00
JBIS	Ian Snell, Joe Blanton	20.00
JBJP	Jim Bunning, Jim Palmer	30.00
JBMV	Merkin Valdez, Joe Blanton	15.00
JBRH	Joe Blanton, Rich Harden	20.00
JBSK	Scott Kazmir, Joe Blanton	20.00
JCMV	Merkin Valdez, Jose Capellan	15.00
JLRH	Justin Leone, Ryan Howard	50.00
JPJB	Jake Peavy, Joe Blanton	25.00
JPKG	Jake Peavy, Khalil Greene	50.00
JPRH	Jake Peavy, Rich Harden	40.00
JPSK	Jake Peavy, Scott Kazmir	30.00
JRDW	Jose Reyes, David Wright	75.00
JSMP	Johan Santana, Mark Prior	100.00
JSSC	Johan Santana, Steve Carlton	50.00
JSSK	Johan Santana, Scott Kazmir	40.00
JVMG	Marcus Giles, Jose Vidro	20.00
KGKG	Ken Griffey Sr., Ken Griffey Jr.	100.00
KGMC	Ken Griffey Jr., Miguel Cabrera	100.00
KYWB	Kevin Youkilis, Wade Boggs	50.00
MCRH	Ryan Howard, Miguel Cabrera	80.00
MGRW	Rickie Weeks, Marcus Giles	35.00
MTHB	Hank Blalock, Mark Teixeira	50.00
MTMC	Miguel Cabrera, Mark Teixeira	60.00
MTRH	Mark Teixeira, Ryan Howard	80.00
MVRH	Merkin Valdez, Rich Harden	20.00
PBKG	Pat Burrell, Ken Griffey Jr.	85.00
PBMC	Pat Burrell, Miguel Cabrera	40.00
RHDO	Ryan Howard, David Ortiz	80.00
RHRO	Roy Oswalt, Rich Harden	30.00
RHSK	Rich Harden, Scott Kazmir	25.00
THVM	Victor Martinez, Travis Hafner	20.00
TOKH	Kent Hrbek, Tony Oliva	30.00
VMYM	Victor Martinez, Yadier Molina	20.00

Fabric Jersey

		NM/M
Common Player:		
Inserted 1:12		
CB	Carlos Beltran	8.00
AB	Adrian Beltre	6.00
HB	Hank Blalock	6.00
WB	Wade Boggs/SP	10.00
GB	George Brett/SP	15.00
MC	Miguel Cabrera	8.00
EC	Eric Chavez	4.00
WC	Will Clark/SP	10.00
JD	Johnny Damon	10.00
KG	Ken Griffey Jr.	15.00
VG	Vladimir Guerrero	8.00
TH	Todd Helton	6.00
DJ	Derek Jeter/SP	20.00
RJ	Randy Johnson	8.00
CJ	Chipper Jones	8.00
GM	Greg Maddux	10.00
HM	Hideki Matsui	20.00
DM	Don Mattingly/SP	20.00
PM	Paul Molito/ SP	8.00
DO	David Ortiz	8.00
PI	Mike Piazza	10.00
MP	Mark Prior	6.00
AP	Albert Pujols	15.00
MR	Manny Ramirez	8.00
CR	Cal Ripken Jr./SP	25.00
IR	Ivan Rodriguez	8.00
SR	Scott Rolen	8.00
NR	Nolan Ryan/SP	25.00
JS	Johan Santana	8.00
CS	Curt Schilling	8.00
MS	Mike Schmidt/SP	15.00
AS	Alfonso Soriano	8.00
MT	Mark Teixeira	6.00
TE	Miguel Tejada	8.00
JT	Jim Thome	8.00
BW	Bernie Williams	6.00
KW	Kerry Wood	8.00
DW	David Wright	10.00
CY	Carl Yastrzemski/SP	25.00
RY	Robin Yount/SP	10.00

Fabric Reflections Patch

		NM/M
Production 99 Sets		
JB	Jason Bay	15.00
AB	Adrian Beltre	10.00
HB	Hank Blalock	15.00
WB	Wade Boggs	20.00
GB	George Brett	50.00
PB	Pat Burrell	15.00
CA	Miguel Cabrera	20.00
EC	Eric Chavez	10.00
BC	Bobby Crosby	10.00
MG	Marcus Giles	10.00
DG	Dwight Gooden	15.00
GR	Khalil Greene	15.00
KG	Ken Griffey Jr.	40.00
RH	Rich Harden	15.00
DJ	Derek Jeter	50.00
RJ	Randy Johnson	20.00
AJ	Andruw Jones	15.00
SK	Scott Kazmir	10.00
MA	Don Mattingly	30.00
MC	Dallas McPherson	10.00
PM	Paul Molitor	20.00
DM	Dale Murphy	15.00
DO	David Ortiz	20.00
RO	Roy Oswalt	10.00
JP	Jake Peavy	15.00
GP	Gaylord Perry	10.00
PI	Mike Piazza	20.00
MP	Mark Prior	15.00
AP	Albert Pujols	50.00
CR	Cal Ripken Jr.	60.00
SR	Scott Rolen	20.00
NR	Nolan Ryan	40.00
JS	Johan Santana	20.00
MS	Mike Schmidt	25.00
BS	Ben Sheets	15.00
ST	Shingo Takatsu	15.00
MT	Mark Teixeira	15.00
BU	B.J. Upton	10.00
DW	David Wright	20.00
RY	Robin Yount	30.00
CZ	Carlos Zambrano	15.00

Fabric Reflections Auto Patch

		NM/M
Production 50 Sets		
JB	Jason Bay	50.00
AB	Adrian Beltre	30.00
HB	Hank Blalock	40.00
WB	Wade Boggs	60.00
PB	Pat Burrell	35.00
CA	Miguel Cabrera	40.00
EC	Eric Chavez	30.00
BC	Bobby Crosby	30.00
DG	Dwight Gooden	40.00
GR	Khalil Greene	50.00
KG	Ken Griffey Jr.	125.00
RH	Rich Harden	35.00
DJ	Derek Jeter	275.00
RJ	Randy Johnson	100.00
AJ	Andruw Jones	75.00
SK	Scott Kazmir	40.00
MA	Don Mattingly	125.00
MC	Dallas McPherson	30.00
PM	Paul Molitor	50.00
DM	Dale Murphy	40.00
DO	David Ortiz	75.00
RO	Roy Oswalt	50.00
JP	Jake Peavy	40.00
GP	Gaylord Perry	30.00
PI	Mike Piazza	120.00
MP	Mark Prior	50.00
AP	Albert Pujols	300.00
CR	Cal Ripken Jr.	225.00
SR	Scott Rolen	50.00
NR	Nolan Ryan	150.00
JS	Johan Santana	50.00
MS	Mike Schmidt	100.00
BS	Ben Sheets	30.00
ST	Shingo Takatsu	40.00
MT	Mark Teixeira	50.00
BU	B.J. Upton	35.00
DW	David Wright	100.00
RY	Robin Yount	75.00
CZ	Carlos Zambrano	40.00

Super Swatch

		NM/M
Production 50 Sets		
Red:		1-1.5X
Production 25 Sets		
Blue:		No Pricing
Production 10 Sets		
BO	Bobby Abreu	15.00
RA	Roberto Alomar	15.00
MA	Moises Alou	10.00
GA	Garret Anderson	10.00
BA	Jeff Bagwell	15.00
RB	Rocco Baldelli	10.00
JB	Jason Bay	15.00
BE	Josh Beckett	10.00
CB	Carlos Beltran	15.00
AB	Adrian Beltre	8.00
LB	Lance Berkman	10.00
BI	Craig Biggio	10.00
HB	Hank Blalock	10.00
BB	Bret Boone	8.00
KB	Kevin Brown	8.00
MC	Miguel Cabrera	15.00
EC	Eric Chavez	10.00
CC	Carl Crawford	10.00
BC	Bobby Crosby	10.00
DA	Johnny Damon	20.00
CD	Carlos Delgado	15.00
JD	J.D. Drew	10.00
AD	Adam Dunn	15.00
JE	Jim Edmonds	15.00
KF	Keith Foulke	10.00
EG	Eric Gagne	10.00
JG	Jason Giambi	10.00
BG	Brian Giles	8.00
MG	Marcus Giles	8.00
TG	Tom Glavine	10.00
LG	Luis Gonzalez	10.00
SG	Shawn Green	10.00
GR	Khalil Greene	12.00
KG	Ken Griffey Jr.	40.00
VG	Vladimir Guerrero	15.00
HA	Roy Halladay	10.00
RH	Rich Harden	10.00
HE	Todd Helton	10.00
HO	Trevor Hoffman	10.00
TH	Tim Hudson	12.00
AH	Aubrey Huff	8.00
HU	Torii Hunter	10.00
DJ	Derek Jeter	40.00
RJ	Randy Johnson	15.00
AJ	Andruw Jones	15.00
CJ	Chipper Jones	15.00
JJ	Jacque Jones	8.00
SK	Scott Kazmir	8.00
JK	Jason Kendall	8.00
ML	Mike Lowell	8.00
GM	Greg Maddux	30.00
PM	Pedro Martinez	15.00
VM	Victor Martinez	8.00
HM	Hideki Matsui	50.00
KM	Kazuo Matsui	15.00
DM	Dallas McPherson	12.00
JM	Justin Morneau	20.00
MM	Mark Mulder	10.00
MU	Mike Mussina	15.00
HN	Hideo Nomo	40.00
MO	Magglio Ordonez	8.00
DO	David Ortiz	15.00
RO	Roy Oswalt	10.00
AO	Akinori Otsuka	15.00
RP	Rafael Palmeiro	15.00
CP	Corey Patterson	10.00
PI	Mike Piazza	20.00
SP	Scott Podsednik	10.00
JP	Jorge Posada	15.00
MP	Mark Prior	15.00
AP	Albert Pujols	40.00
MR	Manny Ramirez	20.00
ER	Edgar Renteria	10.00
JR	Jose Reyes	12.00
IR	Ivan Rodriguez	12.00
SR	Scott Rolen	15.00
CS	C.C. Sabathia	8.00
SA	Johan Santana	15.00
SC	Curt Schilling	15.00
JS	Jason Schmidt	12.00
RS	Richie Sexson	10.00
BS	Ben Sheets	10.00
GS	Gary Sheffield	15.00
AS	Alfonso Soriano	15.00
SS	Sammy Sosa	20.00
MS	Mike Sweeney	8.00
ST	Shingo Takatsu	15.00
MT	Mark Teixeira	15.00
TE	Miguel Tejada	15.00
JT	Jim Thome	15.00

JV Jose Vidro 8.00
WA Billy Wagner 10.00
VW Vernon Wells 8.00
BW Bernie Williams 10.00
KW Kerry Wood 15.00
DW David Wright 25.00
BZ Barry Zito 10.00

San Diego Padres

This cello-wrapped team set was a stadium giveaway at a promotional game.

NM/M
Complete Set (33): 7.00
Common Player: .25
1 Rod Beck .25
2 Adam Eaton .25
3 Trevor Hoffman .40
4 Brian Lawrence .25
5 Scott Linebrink .25
6 Blaine Neal .25
7 Akinori Otsuka .50
8 Jake Peavy .25
9 Ricky Stone .25
10 David Wells .25
11 Jay Witasick .25
12 Ramon Hernandez .25
13 Miguel Ojeda .25
14 Rich Aurilia .25
15 Sean Burroughs .35
16 Brian Buchanan .25
17 Khalil Greene .40
18 Dave Hansen .25
19 Mark Loretta .25
20 Phil Nevin .25
21 Brian Giles .35
22 Ryan Klesko .25
23 Terrence Long .25
24 Xavier Nady .25
25 Jay Payton .25
26 Sterling Hitchcock .25
27 Bruce Bochy .25
28 Rob Picciolo .25
29 Swinging Friar (Mascot) .25
30 Davey Lopes .25
31 Dave Magadan .25
32 Tony Muser .25
33 Darren Balsley .25

SportsFest Redemption

Six-card cello packs with individual cards serially numbered on front from an edition of 750 were available to persons redeeming wrappers from Upper Deck products purchased at SportsFest 2005 in Chicago.

NM/M
Complete Set (6): 5.00
Common Player: .50
MLB1 Ken Griffey Jr. 1.50
MLB2 Mark Prior .75
MLB3 Derek Jeter 2.00
MLB4 Carlos Beltran 1.00
MLB5 Albert Pujols 2.00
MLB6 Curt Schilling .50

2005 Upper Deck Sweet Spot

NM/M
Complete Set (90): 20.00
Common Player: .25

Pack (5): 12.00
Box (12): 120.00
1 Magglio Ordonez .25
2 Craig Biggio .50
3 Hank Blalock .40
4 Nomar Garciaparra .75
5 Ken Griffey Jr. 1.50
6 Khalil Greene .40
7 Andruw Jones .50
8 Ichiro Suzuki 1.50
9 Philip Humber **RC** 1.50
10 Vladimir Guerrero .75
11 Carlos Delgado .40
12 Jeff Niemann **RC** 1.50
13 Chipper Jones .75
14 Jose Vidro .25
15 Miguel Cabrera .75
16 Albert Pujols 2.00
17 Tadahito Iguchi **RC** 2.50
18 Norihiro Nakamura **RC** 1.50
19 Jeff Bagwell .50
20 Troy Glaus .40
21 Scott Rolen .75
22 Derek Lowe .25
23 Mark Prior .75
24 Bobby Abreu .40
25 David Wright 1.00
26 Barry Zito .40
27 Livan Hernandez .25
28 Mark Teixeira .50
29 Manny Ramirez .75
30 Paul Konerko .40
31 Victor Martinez .25
32 Greg Maddux 1.50
33 Jim Thome .50
34 Miguel Tejada .50
35 Ivan Rodriguez .50
36 Carlos Beltran .50
37 Steve Finley .25
38 Torii Hunter .25
39 Bobby Crosby .25
40 Jorge Posada .40
41 Ben Sheets .40
42 Mike Piazza 1.00
43 Luis Gonzalez .25
44 Joe Mauer .50
45 Shawn Green .25
46 Eric Gagne .40
47 Kerry Wood .40
48 Derek Jeter 2.00
49 Josh Beckett .25
50 Alex Rodriguez 1.50
51 Aubrey Huff .25
52 Eric Chavez .40
53 Sammy Sosa 1.00
54 Roger Clemens 2.00
55 Mike Mussina .50
56 Mike Sweeney .25
57 Oliver Perez .25
58 Tim Hudson .40
59 Justin Verlander **RC** 2.00
60 Johan Santana .50
61 Hideki Matsui 1.50
62 Mark Mulder .40
63 Jake Peavy .40
64 Adam Dunn .50
65 Dallas McPherson .25
66 Jeff Kent .25
67 Pedro Martinez .75
68 J.D. Drew .25
69 Frank Thomas .50
70 Kazuo Matsui .25
71 Travis Hafner .40
72 John Smoltz .40
73 Jason Schmidt .25
74 Carlos Lee .25
75 Todd Helton .50
76 David Ortiz .75
77 Roy Oswalt .40
78 Brian Giles .25
79 Gary Sheffield .50
80 Jason Bay .40
81 Alfonso Soriano .75
82 Randy Johnson .75
83 Tom Glavine .40
84 Richie Sexson .40
85 Curt Schilling .75
86 Adrian Beltre .40
87 Jim Edmonds .40
88 Roy Halladay .40
89 Johnny Damon .75
90 Lance Berkman .40

Gold

Gold (1-90): 1-2X
Production 599 Sets

Platinum

Platinum (1-90): 2-4X
Production 99 Sets

Plutonium

No Pricing
Production One Set

Majestic Materials

NM/M
Common Player: 4.00
Gold: 1-1.5X
Production 75 Sets
Platinum: No Pricing
Production 10 Sets
Plutonium: No Pricing
Production One Set
Patch: 2-3X
Production 35 Sets
BA Bobby Abreu 4.00
MA Moises Alou 4.00
JB Jason Bay 4.00
BE Josh Beckett 4.00
LB Lance Berkman 4.00
CB Craig Biggio 6.00
BB Bret Boone 4.00
BC Bobby Crosby 4.00
CD Carlos Delgado 4.00
JD J.D. Drew 4.00
AD Adam Dunn 6.00
JE Jim Edmonds 6.00
JG Jason Giambi 6.00
BG Brian Giles 4.00
TG Troy Glaus 4.00
LG Luis Gonzalez 4.00
SG Shawn Green 4.00
KG Khalil Greene 6.00
HA Travis Hafner 4.00
RH Roy Halladay 4.00
TH Tim Hudson 4.00
HU Torii Hunter 4.00
TI Tadahito Iguchi 5.00
AJ Andruw Jones 6.00
SK Scott Kazmir 4.00
JK Jeff Kent 4.00
VM Victor Martinez 4.00
KM Kazuo Matsui 4.00
JM Joe Mauer 6.00
DM Dallas McPherson 4.00
MM Mark Mulder 4.00
MU Mike Mussina 6.00
MO Magglio Ordonez 4.00
RO Roy Oswalt 4.00
JP Jake Peavy 6.00
OP Oliver Perez 4.00
AP Andy Pettitte 6.00
PO Jorge Posada 6.00
ER Edgar Renteria 4.00
JR Jose Reyes 4.00
JS Jason Schmidt 4.00
RS Richie Sexson 6.00
BS Ben Sheets 4.00
GS Gary Sheffield 6.00
ST Shingo Takatsu 4.00
BU B.J. Upton 4.00
JV Jose Vidro 4.00
VW Vernon Wells 4.00
DW David Wright 10.00
BZ Barry Zito 4.00

Majestic Materials Dual

NM/M
Production 25 Sets
Gold: No Pricing
Production Five Sets
Plutonium: No Pricing
Production One Set
Patch: No Pricing
Production Five Sets
BB Craig Biggio, Jeff Bagwell 15.00
BP Jason Bay, Oliver Perez 10.00
BS Adrian Beltre, Richie Sexson 10.00
BT Hank Blalock, Mark Teixeira 12.00
CC Bobby Crosby, Eric Chavez 10.00
DG Adam Dunn, Ken Griffey Jr. 25.00
DK J.D. Drew, Jeff Kent 10.00
DR Johnny Damon, Manny Ramirez 15.00
GG Shawn Green, Troy Glaus 10.00
GR Eric Gagne, Mariano Rivera 15.00
HM Travis Hafner, Victor Martinez 10.00
JJ Andruw Jones, Chipper Jones 15.00
MC Don Mattingly, Will Clark 25.00
MW Dallas McPherson, David Wright 15.00
PC Albert Pujols, Miguel Cabrera 25.00
PG Jake Peavy, Khalil Greene 12.00
PL Albert Pujols, Derrek Lee 25.00
RM Jose Reyes, Kazuo Matsui 10.00
RO Ivan Rodriguez, Magglio Ordonez 10.00
RT Brian Roberts, Miguel Tejada 15.00
SH John Smoltz, Tim Hudson 12.00
SM Joe Mauer, Johan Santana 15.00
TI Shingo Takatsu, Tadahito Iguchi 20.00
UK B.J. Upton, Scott Kazmir 10.00
WC David Wright, Miguel Cabrera 15.00

Majestic Materials Triple

NM/M
Production 25 Sets
Gold: No Pricing
Production Five Sets
Plutonium: No Pricing
Production One Set
Patch: No Pricing
Production Five Sets
BPO Josh Beckett, Mark Prior, Roy Oswalt 15.00
BSB George Brett, Mike Schmidt, Wade Boggs 30.00
BTH Jeff Bagwell, Jim Thome, Todd Helton 20.00
HRG Torii Hunter, Manny Ramirez, Vladimir Guerrero 20.00
JCG Andruw Jones, Miguel Cabrera, Vladimir Guerrero 15.00
JRT Derek Jeter, Edgar Renteria, Miguel Tejada 25.00
MMP Greg Maddux, Pedro Martinez, Jake Peavy 25.00
MSG Greg Maddux, John Smoltz, Tom Glavine 40.00
OGP David Ortiz, Jason Giambi, Rafael Palmeiro 20.00
PBC Albert Pujols, Carlos Beltran, Miguel Cabrera 40.00
RBW Nolan Ryan, Josh Beckett, Kerry Wood 40.00
RGB Cal Ripken Jr., Tony Gwynn, Wade Boggs 50.00
SSJ Curt Schilling, Johan Santana, Randy Johnson 25.00
VPP Jason Varitek, Jorge Posada, Mike Piazza 20.00
WRG David Wright, Scott Rolen, Troy Glaus 25.00

Majestic Materials Quad

NM/M
Production 25 Sets
Gold: No Pricing
Production Five Sets
Plutonium: No Pricing
Production One Set
Patch: No Pricing
Production Five Sets
JJSH Andruw Jones, Chipper Jones, John Smoltz, Tim Hudson 25.00
JSJP Derek Jeter, Gary Sheffield, Randy Johnson, Jorge Posada 60.00
OVDR David Ortiz, Jason Varitek, Johnny Damon, Manny Ramirez 40.00
PEWR Albert Pujols, Jim Edmonds, Larry Walker, Scott Rolen 50.00
ZMWP Carlos Zambrano, Greg Maddux, Kerry Wood, Mark Prior 30.00

Signatures Game Used Ball

No Pricing
Production One Set

Sign. Black Stitch Black Ink

No Pricing
Production One Set
Blue Ink: No Pricing
Production One Set
Red Ink: No Pricing
Production One Set

Sign. Red Stitch Black Ink

NM/M
Production 58-350
JB Jason Bay/350 20.00
HB Hank Blalock/175 20.00
WB Wade Boggs/175 40.00
CA Miguel Cabrera/175 40.00
SC Steve Carlton/58 25.00
SE Sean Casey/350 15.00
WC Will Clark/175 25.00
RC Roger Clemens/175 120.00
CC Carl Crawford/350 15.00
BC Bobby Crosby/350 20.00
DA Andre Dawson/175 20.00
AD Adam Dunn/175 25.00
GF Gavin Floyd/350 15.00
NG Nomar Garciaparra/175 60.00
MG Marcus Giles/350 15.00
GR Khalil Greene/350 20.00
KG Ken Griffey Jr./175 75.00
RH Rich Harden/350 15.00
KH Keith Hernandez/350 15.00
HO Ryan Howard/350 75.00
AH Aubrey Huff/350 15.00
PH Philip Humber/350 15.00
BJ Bo Jackson/175 70.00
DJ Derek Jeter/175 150.00
RJ Randy Johnson/175 75.00
AJ Andruw Jones/175 40.00
SK Scott Kazmir/350 15.00
BL Barry Larkin/175 25.00
EM Edgar Martinez/175 30.00
MA Don Mattingly/175 60.00
PM Paul Molitor/175 25.00
MO Justin Morneau/350 25.00
MM Mark Mulder/350 20.00
JN Jeff Niemann/350 15.00
RO Roy Oswalt/350 25.00
LO Lyle Overbay/350 12.00
JP Jake Peavy/350 20.00
PI Mike Piazza/175 80.00
MP Mark Prior/175 40.00
AP Albert Pujols/175 160.00
AR Aramis Ramirez/350 25.00
RE Jose Reyes/350 35.00
CR Cal Ripken Jr./175 120.00
NR Nolan Ryan/175 80.00
RS Ryne Sandberg/175 65.00
MS Mike Schmidt/175 50.00
MT Mark Teixeira/175 40.00
BU B.J. Upton/350 15.00
JV Justin Verlander/350 35.00
DW David Wright/350 60.00
RY Robin Yount/175 50.00
CZ Carlos Zambrano/350 20.00

Sign. Red Stitch Blue Ink

NM/M
Production 75-135
JB Jason Bay 25.00
HB Hank Blalock/75 20.00
WB Wade Boggs/75 40.00
CA Miguel Cabrera/75 40.00
SE Sean Casey/135 15.00
WC Will Clark/75 25.00
RC Roger Clemens/75 120.00
CC Carl Crawford/135 15.00
BC Bobby Crosby/135 20.00
DA Andre Dawson/75 20.00
AD Adam Dunn/75 30.00
GF Gavin Floyd/135 15.00
NG Nomar Garciaparra/75 65.00
MG Marcus Giles/135 15.00
GL Tom Glavine/135 25.00
GR Khalil Greene/135 25.00
KG Ken Griffey Jr./75 80.00
HA Travis Hafner/135 20.00
RH Rich Harden/135 15.00
KH Keith Hernandez/135 15.00
HO Ryan Howard/135 75.00
AH Aubrey Huff/135 15.00
PH Philip Humber/135 15.00
BJ Bo Jackson/75 75.00
DJ Derek Jeter/75 150.00
RJ Randy Johnson/75 85.00
AJ Andruw Jones/75 40.00
SK Scott Kazmir/135 15.00
BL Barry Larkin/75 30.00
EM Edgar Martinez/75 35.00
MA Don Mattingly/75 70.00
PM Paul Molitor/75 25.00
MO Justin Morneau/135 30.00
MM Mark Mulder/135 25.00
JN Jeff Niemann/135 15.00
RO Roy Oswalt/135 25.00
LO Lyle Overbay/135 12.00
CP Corey Patterson/135 15.00
JP Jake Peavy/135 25.00
PI Mike Piazza/75 80.00
MP Mark Prior/75 50.00
AP Albert Pujols/75 160.00
AR Aramis Ramirez/135 25.00
RE Jose Reyes/135 35.00
CR Cal Ripken Jr./75 120.00
NR Nolan Ryan/75 80.00
RS Ryne Sandberg/75 65.00
MS Mike Schmidt/75 50.00
MT Mark Teixeira/75 40.00
BU B.J. Upton/135 15.00
JV Justin Verlander/135 35.00
DW David Wright/135 60.00
RY Robin Yount/75 50.00
CZ Carlos Zambrano/135 20.00

Sign. Red Stitch Red Ink

NM/M
Production 15-35
JB Jason Bay/35 25.00
SE Sean Casey/35 25.00
CC Carl Crawford/35 20.00
BC Bobby Crosby 35.00
AD Adam Dunn/15 60.00
GF Gavin Floyd/35 25.00
MG Marcus Giles/35 15.00
GL Tom Glavine/35 40.00
GR Khalil Greene/35 40.00
HA Travis Hafner/35 30.00
RH Rich Harden/35 30.00
KH Keith Hernandez/35 25.00
HO Ryan Howard/35 90.00
AH Aubrey Huff/35 20.00
PH Philip Humber/35 30.00
SK Scott Kazmir/35 20.00
MO Justin Morneau/35 30.00
MM Mark Mulder/35 30.00
JN Jeff Niemann/35 25.00
RO Roy Oswalt/35 40.00
LO Lyle Overbay/35 15.00
CP Corey Patterson/35 20.00
JP Jake Peavy/35 30.00
AP Albert Pujols/15 250.00
AR Aramis Ramirez/35 40.00
RE Jose Reyes/35 40.00
BU B.J. Upton/35 25.00
JV Justin Verlander/35 50.00
DW David Wright/35 100.00
CZ Carlos Zambrano/35 35.00

Signatures Dual Red Stitch

NM/M
Production 25 Sets
BJ Bobby Crosby, Jason Bay 40.00
BW Adrian Beltre, David Wright 90.00
CG Bobby Crosby, Khalil Greene 50.00
DC Adam Dunn, Sean Casey 50.00
FH Gavin Floyd, Ryan Howard 120.00
GC Ken Griffey Jr., Miguel Cabrera 120.00
GL Khalil Greene, Mark Loretta 60.00
JC Randy Johnson, Roger Clemens 240.00
JG Andruw Jones, Ken Griffey Jr. 150.00
JM Derek Jeter, Don Mattingly 300.00
LG Barry Larkin, Ken Griffey Jr. 120.00
LR Barry Larkin, Cal Ripken Jr. 160.00
MG Greg Maddux, Tom Glavine 150.00
MJ Pedro Martinez, Randy Johnson 125.00
NH Jeff Niemann, Philip Humber 50.00
PB Jason Bay, Oliver Perez 40.00
PC Albert Pujols, Miguel Cabrera 300.00
PO Jake Peavy, Roy Oswalt 75.00
RJ Cal Ripken Jr., Derek Jeter 300.00
SB Ryne Sandberg, Wade Boggs 125.00
SG Nomar Garciaparra, Ryne Sandberg 150.00
SP Ben Sheets, Jake Peavy 50.00
WC David Wright, Miguel Cabrera 120.00
WR David Wright, Jose Reyes 180.00

Sign. Red-Blue Stitch Black Ink

NM/M
Production 25-50
JB Jason Bay/50 25.00
HB Hank Blalock/25 25.00
WB Wade Boggs/25 50.00
CA Miguel Cabrera/25 65.00
SC Steve Carlton/25 25.00

SE Sean Casey/50 20.00
WC Will Clark/25 35.00
RC Roger Clemens/25 160.00
CC Carl Crawford/50 15.00
BC Bobby Crosby/50 35.00
DA Andre Dawson/25 25.00
AD Adam Dunn/25 40.00
GF Gavin Floyd/50 15.00
NG Nomar Garciaparra/25 65.00
MG Marcus Giles/50 15.00
GR Khalil Greene/50 30.00
KG Ken Griffey Jr./25 120.00
RH Rich Harden/50 20.00
KG Keith Hernandez/50 20.00
HO Ryan Howard/50 85.00
AH Aubrey Huff/50 20.00
PH Philip Humber/50 20.00
BJ Bo Jackson/25 90.00
DJ Derek Jeter/25 250.00
RJ Randy Johnson/25 120.00
AJ Andruw Jones/25 50.00
SK Scott Kazmir/50 20.00
BL Barry Larkin/25 40.00
EM Edgar Martinez/25 40.00
MA Don Mattingly/25 90.00
PM Paul Molitor/25 40.00
MO Justin Morneau/50 25.00
MM Mark Mulder/50 25.00
JN Jeff Niemann/50 20.00
RO Roy Oswalt/50 35.00
LO Lyle Overbay/50 12.00
JP Jake Peavy/50 20.00
PI Mike Piazza/25 100.00
MP Mark Prior/25 60.00
AP Albert Pujols/25 220.00
RE Jose Reyes/50 40.00
CR Cal Ripken Jr./25 165.00
NR Nolan Ryan/25 100.00
RS Ryne Sandberg/25 80.00
JS Johan Santana/25 55.00
MS Mike Schmidt/25 75.00
MT Mark Teixeira/25 50.00
BU B.J. Upton/50 20.00
JV Justin Verlander/50 40.00
DW David Wright/50 120.00
RY Robin Yount/25 65.00
CZ Carlos Zambrano/50 30.00

Sign. Red-Blue Stitch Blue Ink

NM/M
Production 15-30
Red Ink: No Pricing
Production 5-10
JB Jason Bay/30 25.00
SE Sean Casey/30 25.00
CC Carl Crawford/30 20.00
BC Bobby Crosby/30 35.00
GF Gavin Floyd/30 25.00
MG Marcus Giles/30 15.00
GL Tom Glavine/30 40.00
GR Khalil Greene/30 40.00
HA Travis Hafner/30 30.00
RH Rich Harden/30 25.00
KH Keith Hernandez/30 25.00
HO Ryan Howard/30 90.00
PH Philip Humber/30 30.00
SK Scott Kazmir/30 20.00
MO Justin Morneau/30 30.00
MM Mark Mulder/30 30.00
JN Jeff Niemann/30 25.00
RO Roy Oswalt/30 40.00
LO Lyle Overbay/30 15.00
CP Corey Patterson/30 20.00
JP Jake Peavy/30 30.00
AR Aramis Ramirez/30 40.00
RE Jose Reyes/30 45.00
BU B.J. Upton/30 25.00
JV Justin Verlander/30 50.00
DW David Wright/30 120.00
CZ Carlos Zambrano/30 35.00

Signature Game Used Barrel

No Pricing
Production 1-10

Signatures Barrel Black Ink

NM/M
Production 25-50
JB Jason Bay/50 20.00
HB Hank Blalock/25 25.00
CA Miguel Cabrera/25 70.00
SC Steve Carlton/25 25.00
SE Sean Casey/50 20.00
WC Will Clark/25 25.00
CC Carl Crawford/50 15.00
BC Bobby Crosby/50 30.00
DA Andre Dawson/25 25.00
AD Adam Dunn/25 40.00
GF Gavin Floyd/50 20.00
NG Nomar Garciaparra/25 80.00
MG Marcus Giles/50 15.00
GL Tom Glavine/50 30.00
GR Khalil Greene/50 35.00
KG Ken Griffey Jr./25 85.00
HA Travis Hafner/50 25.00
RH Rich Harden/50 20.00
KH Keith Hernandez/50 20.00
HO Ryan Howard/50 90.00
AH Aubrey Huff/50 15.00
PH Philip Humber/50 25.00
BJ Bo Jackson/25 75.00
DJ Derek Jeter/25 250.00
RJ Randy Johnson/25 125.00
AJ Andruw Jones/25 50.00
SK Scott Kazmir/50 20.00
BL Barry Larkin/25 40.00
EM Edgar Martinez/50 40.00
MA Don Mattingly/25 85.00
PM Paul Molitor/25 40.00
MO Justin Morneau/50 25.00
MM Mark Mulder/50 25.00
JN Jeff Niemann/50 20.00
RO Roy Oswalt/50 35.00
LO Lyle Overbay/50 15.00
JP Jake Peavy/50 25.00
PI Mike Piazza/25 100.00
MP Mark Prior/25 50.00
AP Albert Pujols/25 220.00
AR Aramis Ramirez/50 30.00
CR Cal Ripken Jr./25 180.00
NR Nolan Ryan/25 100.00
RS Ryne Sandberg/25 75.00
MS Mike Schmidt/25 70.00
MT Mark Teixeira/25 40.00
BU B.J. Upton/50 20.00
JV Justin Verlander/50 40.00
DW David Wright/50 100.00
RY Robin Yount/25 90.00
CZ Carlos Zambrano/50 30.00

Signatures Barrel Blue Ink

NM/M
Production 15-30
JB Jason Bay/30 25.00
SE Sean Casey/30 25.00
CC Carl Crawford/30 20.00
BC Bobby Crosby/30 35.00
AD Adam Dunn/15 60.00
GF Gavin Floyd/30 25.00
MG Marcus Giles/30 15.00
GL Tom Glavine/30 40.00
GR Khalil Greene/30 40.00
HA Travis Hafner/30 30.00
RH Rich Harden/30 25.00
KH Keith Hernandez/30 25.00
HO Ryan Howard/30 90.00
AH Aubrey Huff/30 20.00
PH Philip Humber/30 30.00
SK Scott Kazmir/30 20.00
MO Justin Morneau/30 30.00
MM Mark Mulder/30 30.00
JN Jeff Niemann/30 25.00
RO Roy Oswalt/30 40.00
LO Lyle Overbay/30 15.00
CP Corey Patterson/30 20.00
JP Jake Peavy/30 30.00
AP Albert Pujols/15 250.00
AR Aramis Ramirez/30 40.00
BU B.J. Upton/30 25.00
JV Justin Verlander/30 50.00
DW David Wright/30 100.00
CZ Carlos Zambrano/30 35.00

Signatures Barrel Red Ink

No Pricing
Production 5-10

Signatures Dual Barrel

No Pricing
Production 15 Sets

Signatures Game Used Glove

No Pricing
Production 9-10

Signatures Glove Black Ink

NM/M
Production 15-30
JB Jason Bay/30 40.00
SE Sean Casey/30 35.00
CC Carl Crawford/30 30.00
BC Bobby Crosby/30 40.00
GF Gavin Floyd/30 30.00
MG Marcus Giles/30 25.00
GL Tom Glavine/30 50.00
GR Khalil Greene/30 50.00
HA Travis Hafner/30 40.00
RH Rich Harden/30 35.00
KH Keith Hernandez/30 30.00
HO Ryan Howard/30 100.00
AH Aubrey Huff/30 25.00
PH Philip Humber/30 40.00
SK Scott Kazmir/30 30.00
MO Justin Morneau/30 40.00
MM Mark Mulder/30 40.00
JN Jeff Niemann/30 30.00
RO Roy Oswalt/30 50.00
LO Lyle Overbay/30 20.00
CP Corey Patterson/30 25.00
JP Jake Peavy/30 40.00
AR Aramis Ramirez/30 50.00
BU B.J. Upton/30 35.00
JV Justin Verlander/30 50.00
DW David Wright/30 100.00
CZ Carlos Zambrano/30 40.00

Signatures Glove Blue Ink

No Pricing
Production 5-10
Red Ink: No Pricing
Production 2-5

Signatures Dual Glove

No Pricing
Production 10 Sets

Sweet Threads

NM/M
Common Player: 4.00
Gold: 1-1.5X
Production 75 Sets
Platinum: No Pricing
Production 10 Sets
Plutonium: No Pricing
Production One Set
Patch: 2-4X
Production 35 Sets
JB Jeff Bagwell 6.00
CB Carlos Beltran 6.00
AB Adrian Beltre 4.00
HB Hank Blalock 4.00
WB Wade Boggs 8.00
GB George Brett 10.00
MC Miguel Cabrera 8.00
EC Eric Chavez 4.00
WC Will Clark 6.00
BC Bartolo Colon 4.00
JD Johnny Damon 6.00
EG Eric Gagne 4.00
TG Tom Glavine 6.00
KG Ken Griffey Jr. 12.00
VG Vladimir Guerrero 8.00
GW Tony Gwynn 8.00
TH Todd Helton 6.00
HO Trevor Hoffman 4.00
BJ Bo Jackson 8.00
DJ Derek Jeter 20.00
RJ Randy Johnson 8.00
CJ Chipper Jones 8.00
CL Carlos Lee 4.00
GM Greg Maddux 10.00
PM Pedro Martinez 8.00
DM Don Mattingly 10.00
DO David Ortiz 8.00
RP Rafael Palmeiro 6.00
PI Mike Piazza 8.00
MP Mark Prior 6.00
AP Albert Pujols 15.00
MR Manny Ramirez 8.00
CR Cal Ripken Jr. 20.00
IR Ivan Rodriguez 6.00
SR Scott Rolen 6.00
NR Nolan Ryan 12.00
RS Ryne Sandberg 8.00
JS Johan Santana 6.00
CS Curt Schilling 6.00
MS Mike Schmidt 10.00
SM John Smoltz 6.00
AS Alfonso Soriano 6.00
SS Sammy Sosa 8.00
MT Mark Teixeira 6.00
TE Miguel Tejada 6.00
FT Frank Thomas 6.00
JT Jim Thome 6.00
JV Jason Varitek 10.00
BW Bernie Williams 6.00
KW Kerry Wood 4.00

Sweet Threads Dual

NM/M
Production 25 Sets
Gold: No Pricing
Production Five Sets
Patch: No Pricing
Production Five Sets
Plutonium: No Pricing
Production One Set
BG Carlos Beltran, Ken Griffey Jr. 25.00
BM Carlos Beltran, Pedro Martinez 15.00
DC Carlos Delgado, Miguel Cabrera 15.00
GC Ken Griffey Jr., Miguel Cabrera 25.00
GM Dallas McPherson, Vladimir Guerrero 15.00
JB Bo Jackson, George Brett 25.00
JJ Randy Johnson, Derek Jeter 40.00
JM Derek Jeter, Don Mattingly 50.00
JS Jim Thome, Mike Schmidt 30.00
MG Greg Maddux, Tom Glavine 25.00
MJ Mike Mussina, Randy Johnson 20.00
MP Greg Maddux, Mark Prior 25.00
OR David Ortiz, Manny Ramirez 20.00
PO Andy Pettitte, Roy Oswalt 10.00
PR Pedro Martinez, Randy Johnson 20.00
PS Rafael Palmeiro, Sammy Sosa 20.00
PW David Wright, Mike Piazza 30.00
RJ Cal Ripken Jr., Derek Jeter 70.00
RP Albert Pujols, Scott Rolen 30.00
RT Cal Ripken Jr., Miguel Tejada 40.00
SB Ryne Sandberg, Wade Boggs 30.00
SJ Curt Schilling, Randy Johnson 20.00
SV Curt Schilling, Jason Varitek 20.00
WP Kerry Wood, Mark Prior 15.00

Sweet Threads Triple

NM/M
Production 25 Sets
Gold: No Pricing
Production Five Sets
Plutonium: No Pricing
Production One Set
Patch: No Pricing
Production Five Sets
BBB Craig Biggio, Jeff Bagwell, Lance Berkman 20.00
BWP Carlos Beltran, David Wright, Mike Piazza 25.00
GGG Luis Gonzalez, Shawn Green, Troy Glaus 10.00
JMB Randy Johnson, Mike Mussina, Kevin Brown 25.00
JWS Derek Jeter, Bernie Williams, Gary Sheffield 50.00
KGD Austin Kearns, Ken Griffey Jr., Adam Dunn 30.00
LOP Brad Lidge, Roy Oswalt, Andy Pettitte 15.00
ODR David Ortiz, Johnny Damon, Manny Ramirez 25.00
PER Albert Pujols, Jim Edmonds, Scott Rolen 40.00
PWM Mark Prior, Kerry Wood, Greg Maddux 30.00
RDN Manny Ramirez, Johnny Damon, Trot Nixon 30.00
SBT Alfonso Soriano, Hank Blalock, Mark Teixeira 20.00
SMJ Curt Schilling, Pedro Martinez, Randy Johnson 25.00
TPS Miguel Tejada, Rafael Palmeiro, Sammy Sosa 20.00

Sweet Threads Quad

NM/M
Production 25 Sets
Gold: No Pricing
Production Five Sets
Plutonium: No Pricing
Production One Set
Patch: No Pricing
Production Five Sets
BMCB Adrian Beltre, Dallas McPherson, Eric Chavez, Hank Blalock 25.00
BRGG Carlos Beltran, Manny Ramirez, Ken Griffey Jr., Vladimir Guerrero 40.00
POTH Albert Pujols, David Ortiz, Jim Thome, Todd Helton 40.00
RBGB Cal Ripken Jr., Brett George, Tony Gwynn, Wade Boggs 90.00
RVMP Ivan Rodriguez, Jason Varitek, Joe Mauer, Jorge Posada 30.00

2005 Upper Deck Sweet Spot Classic

NM/M
Complete Set (100): 30.00
Common Player: .40
Pack (4): 12.00
Box (12): 120.00
1 Al Kaline 1.00
2 Al Rosen .40
3 Babe Ruth 4.00
4 Bill Mazeroski .40
5 Billy Williams .40
6 Bob Feller .75
7 Bob Gibson 1.00
8 Bobby Doerr .40
9 Brooks Robinson 1.00
10 Cal Ripken Jr. 4.00
11 Carl Yastrzemski 2.00
12 Carlton Fisk .40
13 Casey Stengel .40
14 Christy Mathewson 2.00
15 Cy Young 1.50
16 Dale Murphy .75
17 Dave Winfield .75
18 Dennis Eckersley .40
19 Dizzy Dean 1.00
20 Don Drysdale .75
21 Don Mattingly 3.00
22 Don Newcombe .40
23 Don Sutton .40
24 Duke Snider 1.00
25 Dwight Evans .40
26 Eddie Mathews 1.50
27 Eddie Murray 1.00
28 Enos Slaughter .40
29 Ernie Banks 2.00
30 Frank Howard .40
31 Frank Robinson .75
32 Gary Carter .40
33 Gaylord Perry .40
34 George Brett 3.00
35 George Kell .40
36 George Sisler .40
37 Larry Doby .40
38 Harmon Killebrew 1.50
39 Honus Wagner 2.00
40 Jackie Robinson 2.00
41 Jim Bunning .40
42 Jim Palmer .75
43 Jim Rice .40
44 Jimmie Foxx .40
45 Joe DiMaggio 3.00
46 Joe Morgan .40
47 Johnny Bench 2.00
48 Johnny Mize .40
49 Johnny Podres .40
50 Juan Marichal .40
51 Keith Hernandez .40
52 Kirby Puckett 1.00
53 Lefty Grove .40
54 Lou Brock .75
55 Lou Gehrig 4.00
56 Luis Aparicio .40
57 Fergie Jenkins .40
58 Maury Wills .40
59 Mel Ott 1.50
60 Mickey Cochrane 1.00
61 Mickey Mantle 4.00
62 Mike Schmidt 3.00
63 Monte Irvin .75
64 Nolan Ryan 4.00
65 Orlando Cepeda .40
66 Ozzie Smith 1.50
67 Paul Molitor 1.00
68 Pee Wee Reese .40
69 Phil Niekro .40
70 Phil Rizzuto 1.00
71 Ralph Kiner .40
72 Richie Ashburn .40
73 Roberto Clemente 4.00
74 Robin Roberts .40
75 Robin Yount 2.00
76 Rocky Colavito 1.00
77 Rod Carew .75
78 Rogers Hornsby 1.00
79 Rollie Fingers .40
80 Roy Campanella 1.00
81 Bob Lemon .40
82 Red Schoendienst .40
83 Satchel Paige 2.00
84 Stan Musial 2.50
85 Steve Carlton .75
86 Ted Williams 3.00
87 Thurman Munson 1.50
88 Tom Seaver 1.00
89 Tony Gwynn 1.50
90 Tony Perez .40
91 Ty Cobb 2.00
92 Wade Boggs 1.00
93 Walter Johnson 1.00
94 Warren Spahn 1.50
95 Whitey Ford 1.00
96 Will Clark .75
97 Jim "Catfish" Hunter .40
98 Willie McCovey .75
99 Willie Stargell 1.00
100 Yogi Berra 1.50

Silver

Cards (1-100): 2-4X
Production 100 Sets

Gold

Cards (1-100): 4-8X
Production 50 Sets

Classic Materials

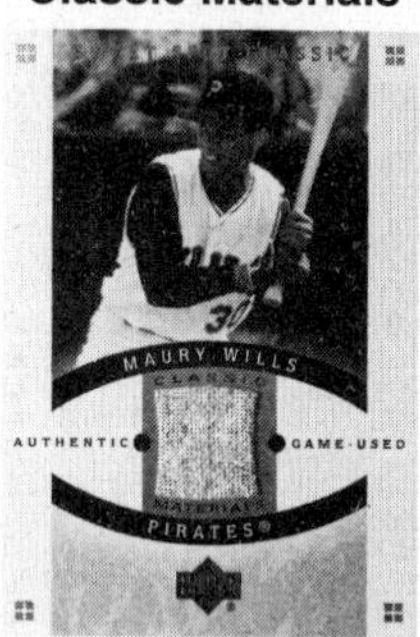

NM/M
Common Player: 6.00
BE Johnny Bench 15.00
YB Yogi Berra 20.00
WB Wade Boggs 10.00
GB George Brett 10.00
GB1 George Brett 10.00
LB Lou Brock 8.00
JB Jim Bunning 10.00
CP Roy Campanella 12.00
CA Rod Carew 8.00
SC Steve Carlton 8.00
GC Gary Carter 6.00
OC Orlando Cepeda 8.00
WC Will Clark 10.00
WC1 Will Clark 10.00
RC Roberto Clemente 60.00
TC Ty Cobb/SP 100.00
CO Rocky Colavito 25.00
DC David Cone 6.00
AD Andre Dawson 6.00
JD Joe DiMaggio 80.00
DD Don Drysdale 10.00
BF Bob Feller 12.00
CF Carlton Fisk 8.00
LG Lou Gehrig/SP 160.00
BG Bob Gibson 10.00
MG Mark Grace 8.00
RG Ron Guidry 8.00
TG Tony Gwynn 12.00
CH Jim "Catfish" Hunter 8.00
FJ Fergie Jenkins 8.00
AK Al Kaline 10.00
HK Harmon Killebrew 12.00
MM Mickey Mantle/SP 120.00
MA Juan Marichal 8.00
EM Eddie Mathews 10.00
DM Don Mattingly 15.00
DM1 Don Mattingly 15.00
BM Bill Mazeroski 10.00
WI Willie McCovey 10.00
PM Paul Molitor 10.00
JM Joe Morgan 6.00
JM1 Joe Morgan 6.00
TM Thurman Munson/SP 25.00
MU Dale Murphy 10.00
ED Eddie Murray 8.00
ED1 Eddie Murray 8.00
SM Stan Musial/SP 20.00
PN Phil Niekro 6.00
SP Satchel Paige/SP 50.00
JP Jim Palmer 8.00
TP Tony Perez 8.00
GP Gaylord Perry 6.00
RE Pee Wee Reese/SP 15.00

RI Jim Rice 8.00
CR Cal Ripken Jr. 20.00
CR1 Cal Ripken Jr. 20.00
PR Phil Rizzuto 15.00
RR Robin Roberts 10.00
RO Brooks Robinson 10.00
FR Frank Robinson 8.00
JR Jackie Robinson 50.00
BR Babe Ruth/SP 275.00
NR Nolan Ryan 25.00
NR1 Nolan Ryan 25.00
MS Mike Schmidt 15.00
MS1 Mike Schmidt 15.00
SD Red Schoendienst 8.00
TS Tom Seaver 10.00
OS Ozzie Smith/SP 15.00
SN Duke Snider 10.00
WS Warren Spahn 15.00
DS Don Sutton 6.00
DS1 Don Sutton 6.00
FV Fernando Valenzuela 6.00
TW Ted Williams/SP 75.00
MW Maury Wills 6.00
MW1 Maury Wills 6.00
DW Dave Winfield 6.00
DW1 Dave Winfield 6.00
EW Early Wynn 10.00
CY Carl Yastrzemski 15.00
RY Robin Yount 12.00

Dual Signatures

No Pricing
Production 15 Sets

Patch

NM/M
Some not priced due to scarcity.
LA Luis Aparicio/19 150.00
BE Johnny Bench/32 100.00
WB Wade Boggs/25 60.00
WB1 Wade Boggs/34 60.00
GB George Brett/38 80.00
GB1 George Brett/50 80.00
LB Lou Brock/34 90.00
SC Steve Carlton/50 60.00
GC Gary Carter/47 50.00
GC1 Gary Carter/34 50.00
OC Orlando Cepeda/40 50.00
DC David Cone/39 50.00
JD Joe DiMaggio/38 250.00
CF1 Carlton Fisk/50 70.00
RG Ron Guidry/30 40.00
TG Tony Gwynn/34 80.00
TG1 Tony Gwynn/30 80.00
FH Frank Howard/34 85.00
FJ Fergie Jenkins/34 60.00
WI Willie McCovey/50 60.00
JM Joe Morgan/50 60.00
MU Dale Murphy/34 80.00
ED Eddie Murray/34 70.00
ED1 Eddie Murray/50 70.00
PN Phil Niekro/44 50.00
TP Tony Perez/34 75.00
GP Gaylord Perry/34 50.00
PO Johnny Podres/50 60.00
RI Jim Rice/34 50.00
CR Cal Ripken Jr./34 150.00
CR1 Cal Ripken Jr./34 150.00
RO Brooks Robinson/50 85.00
RO1 Brooks Robinson/43 85.00
FR Frank Robinson/34 80.00
JR Jackie Robinson/12 250.00
SD Red Schoendienst/42 60.00
TS Tom Seaver/50 50.00
TS1 Tom Seaver/50 50.00
OS Ozzie Smith/34 100.00
ST Willie Stargell/50 65.00
BS Bruce Sutter/50 50.00
DS Don Sutton/34 40.00
DS1 Don Sutton/50 40.00
MW Maury Wills/50 60.00
MW1 Maury Wills/47 60.00
DW1 Dave Winfield/50 75.00
CY Carl Yastrzemski/35 100.00
RY Robin Yount/34 75.00

Sweet Leather Signatures

No Pricing
Production 25 Sets

Sweet Spot Signatures

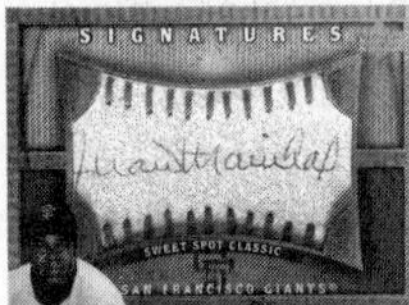

NM/M
Common Autograph: 20.00
Inserted 1:12
Blue/Red Stitch: 1.5-2X
Production 40 Sets
Black Stitch: No Pricing
Production One Set
LA Luis Aparicio 25.00
HB Harold Baines 20.00
EB Ernie Banks 75.00
BE Johnny Bench 60.00
YB Yogi Berra SP 60.00
WB Wade Boggs 50.00
GB George Brett 85.00
JB Jim Bunning 20.00
JC Jose Canseco 40.00
CA Rod Carew 50.00
SC Steve Carlton 40.00
GC Gary Carter 25.00
OC Orlando Cepeda 25.00
WC Will Clark 30.00
RC Rocky Colavito/SP 85.00
DC David Cone 20.00
AD Andre Dawson 20.00
BD Bobby Doerr 25.00
DE Dennis Eckersley 25.00
EV Dwight Evans 20.00
BF Bob Feller 40.00
RF Rollie Fingers 20.00
CF Carlton Fisk 40.00
WF Whitey Ford 60.00
BG Bob Gibson 40.00
MG Mark Grace 40.00
TG Tony Gwynn 50.00
EH Ernie Harwell/SP 40.00
KH Keith Hernandez 20.00
FH Frank Howard 25.00
MI Monte Irvin 25.00
BJ Bo Jackson 50.00
DJ David Justice 20.00
KA Harry Kalas 25.00
AK Al Kaline 40.00
GK George Kell 25.00
HK Harmon Killebrew 50.00
RK Ralph Kiner/SP 50.00
MA Juan Marichal 25.00
DM Don Mattingly 80.00
BM Bill Mazeroski 40.00
MC Willie McCovey/SP 60.00
PM Paul Molitor 40.00
JM Joe Morgan/SP 35.00
MU Dale Murphy 25.00
SM Stan Musial 100.00
DN Don Newcombe 25.00
PN Phil Niekro 25.00
JP Jim Palmer 25.00
TP Tony Perez 25.00
GP Gaylord Perry 25.00
PO Johnny Podres 20.00
KP Kirby Puckett/SP 50.00
JR Jim Rice 25.00
CR Cal Ripken Jr. 160.00
PR Phil Rizzuto 50.00
RR Robin Roberts 30.00
BR Brooks Robinson 40.00
FR Frank Robinson 40.00
AR Al Rosen 20.00
NR Nolan Ryan 125.00
RS Ron Santo 35.00
MS Mike Schmidt 80.00
RE Red Schoendienst 30.00
TS Tom Seaver 60.00
OS Ozzie Smith 60.00
SN Duke Snider 40.00
ST Rusty Staub 20.00
SU Bruce Sutter 20.00
DS Don Sutton 20.00
LT Luis Tiant 20.00
FV Fernando Valenzuela 30.00
BW Billy Williams 25.00
MW Matt Williams 20.00
WI Maury Wills 20.00
CY Carl Yastrzemski 100.00
RY Robin Yount/SP 85.00

Sweet Sticks Signatures

NM/M
Production 35 Sets
LA Luis Aparicio 50.00
HB Harold Baines 40.00
EB Ernie Banks 125.00
BE Johnny Bench 75.00
YB Yogi Berra 80.00
WB Wade Boggs 75.00
GB George Brett 140.00
JB Jim Bunning 40.00
JC Jose Canseco 75.00
CA Rod Carew 75.00
SC Steve Carlton 50.00
GC Gary Carter 40.00
OC Orlando Cepeda 50.00
WC Will Clark 65.00
RC Rocky Colavito 120.00
DC David Cone 50.00
AD Andre Dawson 50.00
BD Bobby Doerr 50.00
DE Dennis Eckersley 50.00
EV Dwight Evans 60.00
BF Bob Feller 75.00
RF Rollie Fingers 45.00
CF Carlton Fisk 75.00
WF Whitey Ford 85.00
BG Bob Gibson 65.00
MG Mark Grace 75.00
TG Tony Gwynn 85.00
EH Ernie Harwell 50.00
KH Keith Hernandez 40.00
FH Frank Howard 50.00
MI Monte Irvin 50.00
BJ Bo Jackson 140.00
DJ David Justice 40.00
AK Al Kaline 80.00
GK George Kell 40.00
HK Harmon Killebrew 80.00
RK Ralph Kiner 75.00
MA Juan Marichal 50.00
DM Don Mattingly 125.00
BM Bill Mazeroski 90.00
MC Willie McCovey 85.00
PM Paul Molitor 60.00
JM Joe Morgan 50.00
MU Dale Murphy 50.00
SM Stan Musial 140.00
DN Don Newcombe 50.00
PN Phil Niekro 40.00
JP Jim Palmer 50.00
TP Tony Perez 50.00
GP Gaylord Perry 40.00
PO Johnny Podres 40.00
KP Kirby Puckett 100.00
JR Jim Rice 50.00
CR Cal Ripken Jr. 240.00
PR Phil Rizzuto 75.00
RR Robin Roberts 50.00
BR Brooks Robinson 65.00
FR Frank Robinson 60.00
AR Al Rosen 50.00
NR Nolan Ryan 150.00
RS Ron Santo 65.00
MS Mike Schmidt 125.00
RE Red Schoendienst 50.00
TS Tom Seaver 85.00
OS Ozzie Smith 90.00
SN Duke Snider 75.00
ST Rusty Staub 40.00
SU Bruce Sutter 30.00
DS Don Sutton 40.00
LT Luis Tiant 40.00
BW Billy Williams 40.00
MW Matt Williams 50.00
WI Maury Wills 40.00
CY Carl Yastrzemski 120.00
RY Robin Yount 100.00

Wingfield Classic Collection

NM/M
Common Player: 4.00
Inserted 1:Box
1 Al Kaline 4.00
2 Pee Wee Reese 4.00
3 Stan Musial, Ted Williams 6.00
4 Bill Dickey 4.00
5 Frank Robinson 5.00
6 Billy Martin 4.00
7 Casey Stengel, Joe DiMaggio 6.00
8 Bob Feller, Dwight D. Eisenhower 4.00
9 Duke Snider 5.00
10 Carl Yastrzemski 8.00
11 Honus Wagner 6.00
12 Dwight D. Eisenhower, Clark Griffith 4.00
13 Mickey Mantle, Joe DiMaggio 15.00
14 Don Drysdale 4.00
15 Ted Williams 8.00
16 Al Kaline, Mickey Mantle 15.00
17 Ernie Banks 6.00
18 Lou Boudreau 4.00
19 George Sisler, Harmon Killebrew 6.00
20 Gil Hodges 4.00
21 Rogers Hornsby 6.00
22 Luis Aparicio 4.00
23 Jackie Robinson 10.00
24 Joe Morgan 4.00
25 Enos Slaughter 4.00
26 Joe DiMaggio 8.00
27 Mickey Mantle, Ted Kluszewski 15.00
28 John F. Kennedy 6.00
29 Johnny Bench 8.00
30 Juan Marichal 4.00
31 Larry Doby 4.00
32 Don Newcombe, Elston Howard 4.00
33 Harmon Killebrew, Dwight D. Eisenhower 6.00
34 Roger Maris, Mickey Mantle 20.00
35 Mickey Mantle, Stan Musial 15.00
36 Ted Williams, Mickey Mantle, Yogi Berra 15.00
37 Nellie Fox 6.00
38 Richie Asburn 4.00
39 Roberto Clemente 15.00
40 Stan Musial, Robin Roberts 8.00
41 Tommy Heinrich, Joe DiMaggio 8.00
42 Roy Campanella 6.00
43 Rocky Colavito, Harmon Killebrew 6.00
44 Steve Carlton 4.00
45 Thurman Munson 6.00
46 Luis Aparicio, Ernie Banks 6.00
47 Gil Hodges, Yogi Berra, Dwight D. Eisenhower 6.00
48 Whitey Ford 6.00
49 Mickey Mantle, Yogi Berra, Joe DiMaggio 15.00
50 Yogi Berra 8.00

The National Chicago Legends

These gold-foil enhanced cards were only available as an Upper Deck wrapper redemption on July 31 during the National Sports Collectors Convention in Chicago. On front cards have a serial number from within an edition of 750 each. Two of the six cards in the set were former Cubs.

NM/M
CL1 Ernie Banks 3.00
CL2 Ryne Sandberg 3.00

The National Cubs/White Sox

These gold-foil enhanced cards were only available as an Upper Deck wrapper redemption on July 30 during the National Sports Collectors Convention in Chicago. On front cards have a serial number from within an edition of 750 each. Special autographed versions of each card, serially numbered to five each, were randomly distributed.

NM/M
Complete Set (6): 12.50
Common Player: 2.00
MLB1 Mark Prior 3.00
MLB2 Greg Maddux 4.00
MLB3 Derrek Lee 4.00
MLB4 Kerry Wood 3.00
MLB5 Tadahito Iguchi 2.00
MLB6 Paul Konerko 2.00

2005 UD Ultimate Collection

NM/M
Common (1-100): 1.50
Production 475
Common (101-237): 3.00
Production 275
Common (238-242): 50.00
Production 99
Pack (4): 85.00
Box (4): 300.00
1 A.J. Burnett 1.50
2 Adam Dunn 2.00
3 Adrian Beltre 2.00
4 Albert Pujols 8.00
5 Alex Rodriguez 8.00
6 Alfonso Soriano 3.00
7 Andruw Jones 3.00
8 Andy Pettitte 2.00
9 Aramis Ramirez 2.00
10 Aubrey Huff 1.50
11 Ben Sheets 2.00
12 Bobby Abreu 2.00
13 Bobby Crosby 1.50
14 Chris Carpenter 2.00
15 Brian Giles 1.50
16 Brian Roberts 1.50
17 Carl Crawford 2.00
18 Carlos Beltran 3.00
19 Carlos Delgado 2.00
20 Carlos Zambrano 2.00
21 Chipper Jones 3.00
22 Corey Patterson 1.50
23 Craig Biggio 1.50
24 Curt Schilling 3.00
25 Dallas McPherson 1.50
26 David Ortiz 3.00
27 David Wright 5.00
28 Delmon Young 2.00
29 Derek Jeter 8.00
30 Derrek Lee 3.00
31 Dontrelle Willis 2.00
32 Eric Chavez 2.00
33 Eric Gagne 2.00
34 Francisco Rodriguez 1.50
35 Gary Sheffield 2.00
36 Greg Maddux 5.00
37 Hank Blalock 1.50
38 Hideki Matsui 5.00
39 Ichiro Suzuki 5.00
40 Ivan Rodriguez 3.00
41 J.D. Drew 1.50
42 Jake Peavy 2.00
43 Jason Bay 2.00
44 Jason Schmidt 2.00
45 Jeff Bagwell 2.00
46 Jeff Kent 2.00
47 Jeremy Bonderman 2.00
48 Jim Edmonds 2.00
49 Jim Thome 2.00
50 Joe Mauer 2.00
51 Johan Santana 3.00
52 John Smoltz 2.00
53 Johnny Damon 3.00
54 Jose Reyes 3.00
55 Jose Vidro 1.50
56 Josh Beckett 1.50
57 Justin Morneau 2.00
58 Ken Griffey Jr. 5.00
59 Kerry Wood 2.00
60 Khalil Greene 1.50
61 Lance Berkman 2.00
62 Larry Walker 2.00
63 Luis Gonzalez 1.50
64 Manny Ramirez 3.00
65 Mark Buehrle 2.00
66 Mark Mulder 2.00
67 Mark Prior 3.00
68 Mark Teixeira 3.00
69 Michael Young 2.00
70 Miguel Cabrera 3.00
71 Miguel Tejada 3.00
72 Mike Mussina 2.00
73 Mike Piazza 4.00
74 Moises Alou 2.00
75 Nomar Garciaparra 3.00
76 Oliver Perez 1.50
77 Pat Burrell 2.00
78 Paul Konerko 2.00
79 Pedro Feliz 1.50
80 Pedro Martinez 3.00
81 Randy Johnson 3.00
82 Richie Sexson 2.00
83 Rickie Weeks 2.00
84 Roger Clemens 8.00
85 Roy Halladay 2.00
86 Roy Oswalt 2.00
87 Sammy Sosa 3.00
88 Scott Kazmir 1.50
89 Scott Rolen 3.00
90 Shawn Green 2.00
91 Tim Hudson 2.00
92 Todd Helton 2.00
93 Tom Glavine 2.00
94 Torii Hunter 2.00
95 Travis Hafner 2.00
96 Troy Glaus 2.00
97 Vernon Wells 1.50
98 Victor Martinez 1.50
99 Vladimir Guerrero 3.00
100 Zack Greinke 1.50
101 Al Kaline 4.00
102 Babe Ruth 10.00
103 Bo Jackson 4.00
104 Bob Gibson 5.00
105 Brooks Robinson 5.00
106 Cal Ripken Jr. 12.00
107 Carl Yastrzemski 5.00
108 Carlton Fisk 3.00
109 Jim "Catfish" Hunter 3.00
110 Christy Mathewson 5.00
111 Cy Young 5.00
112 Don Mattingly 6.00
113 Eddie Mathews 5.00
114 Eddie Murray 4.00
115 Gary Carter 3.00
116 Harmon Killebrew 4.00
117 Jim Palmer 3.00
118 Jimmie Foxx 4.00
119 Joe DiMaggio 8.00
120 Johnny Bench 4.00
121 Lefty Grove 3.00
122 Lou Gehrig 8.00
123 Mel Ott 3.00
124 Reggie Jackson 4.00
125 Mike Schmidt 5.00
126 Nolan Ryan 8.00
127 Ozzie Smith 5.00
128 Paul Molitor 4.00
129 Pee Wee Reese 3.00
130 Robin Yount 5.00
131 Ryne Sandberg 6.00
132 Ted Williams 8.00
133 Thurman Munson 4.00
134 Tom Seaver 4.00
135 Tony Gwynn 4.00
136 Wade Boggs 3.00
137 Walter Johnson 4.00
138 Warren Spahn 4.00
139 Will Clark 3.00
140 Willie McCovey 3.00
141 Willie Stargell 4.00
142 Yogi Berra 5.00
143 Ambiorix Burgos **RC** 4.00
144 Ambiorix Concepcion **RC** 4.00
145 Anibal Sanchez **RC** 15.00
146 Bill McCarthy **RC** 4.00
147 Brian Burres **RC** 4.00
148 Carlos Ruiz **RC** 4.00
149 Casey Rogowski **RC** 6.00
150 Chris Resop **RC** 4.00
151 Chris Roberson **RC** 4.00
152 Chris Seddon **RC** 4.00
153 Colter Bean **RC** 4.00
154 Dae-Sung Koo **RC** 4.00
155 Danny Rueckel **RC** 4.00
156 David Gassner **RC** 4.00
157 Ryan Howard 8.00
158 D.J. Houlton **RC** 4.00
159 Derek Wathan **RC** 4.00
160 Devon Lowery **RC** 4.00
161 Enrique Gonzalez **RC** 4.00
162 Erick Threets **RC** 4.00
163 Eude Brito **RC** 4.00
164 Francisco Butto **RC** 4.00
165 Franquelis Osoria **RC** 4.00
166 Garrett Jones **RC** 4.00
167 Geovany Soto **RC** 6.00
168 Ismael Ramirez **RC** 4.00
169 Jared Gothreaux **RC** 4.00
170 Jason Hammel **RC** 4.00
171 Jeff Housman **RC** 4.00
172 Jeff Miller **RC** 4.00
173 Jeff Francoeur 10.00
174 John Hattig Jr. **RC** 4.00
175 Jorge Campillo **RC** 4.00
176 Juan Morillo **RC** 4.00
177 Justin Wechsler **RC** 4.00
178 Keiichi Yabu **RC** 4.00
179 Kendry Morales **RC** 15.00
180 Luis Hernandez **RC** 4.00
181 Luis Mendoza **RC** 4.00
182 Luis Pena **RC** 4.00
183 Luis Rodriguez **RC** 4.00
184 Luke Scott **RC** 10.00
185 Marcos Carvajal **RC** 4.00
186 Mark Woodyard **RC** 4.00
187 Matt Smith **RC** 4.00
188 Matt Lindstrom **RC** 4.00
189 Miguel Negron **RC** 6.00
190 Mike Morse **RC** 4.00
191 Nate McLouth **RC** 4.00
192 Nick Masset **RC** 4.00
193 Paulino Reynoso **RC** 4.00
194 Pedro Lopez **RC** 4.00
195 Peter Orr **RC** 4.00
196 Randy Messenger **RC** 4.00
197 Randy Williams **RC** 4.00
198 Raul Tablado **RC** 4.00
199 Ronny Paulino **RC** 8.00
200 Russel Rohlicek **RC** 4.00
201 Russell Martin **RC** 15.00
202 Scott Baker **RC** 6.00
203 Scott Munter **RC** 4.00
204 Sean Thompson **RC** 4.00
205 Sean Tracey **RC** 4.00
206 Steve Schmoll **RC** 4.00
207 Tony Pena **RC** 4.00
208 Travis Bowyer **RC** 4.00
209 Ubaldo Jimenez **RC** 4.00
210 Wladimir Balentien **RC** 10.00
211 Yorman Bazardo **RC** 4.00
212 Yuniesky Betancourt **RC** 8.00
213 Adam Shabala **RC** 4.00
214 Brandon McCarthy **RC** 10.00
215 Chad Orvella **RC** 4.00
216 Jermaine Van Buren 4.00
217 Anthony Reyes **RC** 30.00
218 Dana Eveland **RC** 8.00
219 Brian Anderson 10.00
220 Hayden Penn **RC** 8.00
221 Chris Denorfia **RC** 6.00
222 Joel Peralta **RC** 4.00
223 Ryan Garko **RC** 10.00
224 Felix Hernandez 15.00
225 Mark McLemore **RC** 4.00
226 Melky Cabrera **RC** 15.00
227 Nelson Cruz **RC** 8.00
228 Norihiro Nakamura 8.00
229 Oscar Robles **RC** 4.00
230 Rick Short **RC** 4.00
231 Ryan Zimmerman **RC** 35.00
232 Ryan Speier **RC** 4.00
233 Ryan Spilborghs **RC** 6.00
234 Shane Costa **RC** 4.00
235 Zachary Duke 6.00
236 Tony Giarratano **RC** 4.00
237 Jeff Niemann **RC** 10.00
238 Stephen Drew/Auto. **RC** 180.00
239 Justin Verlander/Auto. **RC** 250.00
240 Prince Fielder/Auto. 500.00
241 Philip Humber/Auto. **RC** 85.00
242 Tadahito Iguchi/Auto. **RC** 100.00

Silver

Silver (101-237): 1X-2X
Production 50 Sets

2005 UD Ultimate Signature Edition

NM/M
Complete Set (110):

Common (1-100): 2.00
Production 825
Common (101-110): 8.00
Production 225
Tin (3): 85.00
1 Al Kaline 4.00
2 Babe Ruth 10.00
3 Billy Williams 2.00
4 Bob Feller 2.00
5 Bob Gibson 3.00
6 Brooks Robinson 3.00
7 Carlton Fisk 2.00
8 Cy Young 3.00
9 Dizzy Dean 3.00
10 Don Drysdale 2.00
11 Eddie Mathews 4.00
12 Enos Slaughter 2.00
13 Ernie Banks 5.00
14 Fergie Jenkins 2.00
15 Eddie Murray 3.00
16 Harmon Killebrew 4.00
17 Honus Wagner 3.00
18 Jackie Robinson 5.00
19 Jimmie Foxx 4.00
20 Joe DiMaggio 6.00
21 Joe Morgan 2.00
22 Juan Marichal 2.00
23 Larry Doby 2.00
24 Jim Palmer 2.00
25 Johnny Bench 4.00
26 Lou Brock 2.00
27 Lou Gehrig 6.00
28 Mel Ott 3.00
29 Mickey Cochrane 2.00
30 Mickey Mantle 12.00
31 Mike Schmidt 5.00
32 Nolan Ryan 8.00
33 Pee Wee Reese 2.00
34 Phil Rizzuto 3.00
35 Ralph Kiner 2.00
36 Robin Yount 3.00
37 Ozzie Smith 4.00
38 Roy Campanella 3.00
39 Satchel Paige 4.00
40 Stan Musial 5.00
41 Ted Williams 8.00
42 Thurman Munson 4.00
43 Tom Seaver 3.00
44 Ty Cobb 4.00
45 Walter Johnson 3.00
46 Warren Spahn 4.00
47 Whitey Ford 3.00
48 Willie McCovey 3.00
49 Willie Stargell 3.00
50 Yogi Berra 4.00
51 Adrian Beltre 8.00
52 Albert Pujols 6.00
53 Alex Rodriguez 3.00
54 Alfonso Soriano 2.00
55 Andruw Jones 2.00
56 B.J. Upton 2.00
57 Ben Sheets 2.00
58 Bret Boone 2.00
59 Brian Giles 2.00
60 Carlos Beltran 3.00
61 Carlos Delgado 2.00
62 Chipper Jones 4.00
63 Curt Schilling 4.00
64 David Ortiz 4.00
65 Derek Jeter 8.00
66 Eric Chavez 2.00
67 Frank Thomas 3.00
68 Gary Sheffield 2.00
69 Greg Maddux 5.00
70 Hank Blalock 2.00
71 Hideki Matsui 6.00
72 Ichiro Suzuki 6.00
73 Ivan Rodriguez 3.00
74 Jason Schmidt 2.00
75 Jeff Bagwell 2.00
76 Jim Thome 3.00
77 Johnny Damon 4.00
78 Jose Vidro 2.00
79 Ken Griffey Jr. 5.00
80 Kerry Wood 3.00
81 Manny Ramirez 4.00
82 Mark Prior 2.00
83 Mark Teixeira 2.00
84 Miguel Cabrera 3.00
85 Miguel Tejada 3.00
86 Mike Mussina 2.00
87 Mike Piazza 4.00
88 Mike Sweeney 2.00
89 Oliver Perez 2.00
90 Pedro Martinez 4.00
91 Rafael Palmeiro 3.00
92 Randy Johnson 4.00
93 Roger Clemens 8.00
94 Sammy Sosa 5.00
95 Scott Rolen 3.00
96 Tim Hudson 2.00
97 Todd Helton 2.00
98 Torii Hunter 2.00
99 Victor Martinez 2.00
100 Vladimir Guerrero 4.00
101 Adrian Gonzalez 8.00
102 Ambiorix Burgos **RC** 25.00
103 Ambiorix Concepcion **RC** 20.00
104 Dan Meyer 15.00
105 Ervin Santana 25.00
106 Gavin Floyd 20.00
107 Joe Blanton 20.00
108 Eric Crozier 10.00
109 Mark Teahen 25.00
110 Ryan Howard 50.00

Platinum

Cards (101-110):
Production One Set

Immortal Inscriptions

NM/M

Production 10-99
Platinum: No Pricing
Production One Set
WB Wade Boggs/75 80.00
JB Jim Bunning/99 60.00
SC Steve Carlton/99 40.00
WC Will Clark/99 60.00
EG Eric Gagne/99 80.00
KG Ken Griffey Jr./99 200.00
TG Tony Gwynn/50 140.00
DM Don Mattingly/75 150.00
BR Brooks Robinson/99 50.00
TS Tom Seaver/25 90.00
OS Ozzie Smith/75 80.00
FT Frank Thomas/50 100.00

Signature Cuts

Production One Set

Signature Cy Young

NM/M

Production 1-250
CM David Cone, Greg Maddux/35 150.00
EG Eric Gagne, Dennis Eckersley/200 50.00
ES Dennis Eckersley, Bruce Sutter/250 30.00
GF Ron Guidry, Whitey Ford/250 65.00
GM Bob Gibson, Denny McLain/175 40.00
LC Sparky Lyle, Steve Carlton/250 30.00
MS Tom Seaver, Denny McLain 50.00
NF Don Newcombe, Whitey Ford 60.00
PC Gaylord Perry, Steve Carlton/250 40.00
PS Jim Palmer, Tom Seaver/100 75.00

Signature Decades

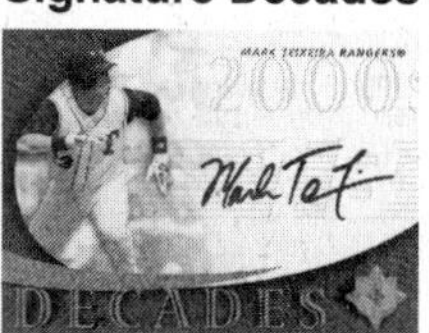

NM/M

Some not priced due to scarcity.
Platinum: No Pricing
Production One Set
LA Luis Aparicio 20.00
LA1 Luis Aparicio 20.00
CB Carlos Beltran/99 35.00
YB Yogi Berra/25 80.00
WB Wade Boggs/25 65.00
WB1 Wade Boggs/25 65.00
LB Lou Brock/50 35.00
JB Jim Bunning 20.00
MC Miguel Cabrera 30.00
JC Jose Canseco/99 40.00
SC Steve Carlton 20.00
SC1 Steve Carlton 20.00
GC Gary Carter/50 25.00
OC Orlando Cepeda 15.00
WC Will Clark/99 40.00
RC Rocky Colavito 50.00
RC1 Rocky Colavito 50.00
AD Andre Dawson 15.00
BD Bobby Doerr 15.00
DE Dennis Eckersley 25.00
BF Bob Feller 25.00
RF Rollie Fingers 15.00
KG Ken Griffey Jr. 65.00
RG Ron Guidry 25.00
KH Keith Hernandez 10.00
KH1 Keith Hernandez 10.00
MI Monte Irvin 20.00
BJ Bo Jackson/50 60.00
FJ Fergie Jenkins/50 20.00
DJ Derek Jeter/99 160.00
AK Al Kaline/99 30.00
GK George Kell 15.00
HK Harmon Killebrew/99 40.00
RK Ralph Kiner/99 30.00
DL Don Larsen/99 25.00
FL Fred Lynn 15.00
JM Juan Marichal/99 25.00
DM Don Mattingly/25 85.00
BM Bill Mazeroski/99 40.00
PM Paul Molitor/99 25.00
MO Joe Morgan/50 25.00
MU Dale Murphy 25.00
DN Don Newcombe/99 20.00
PN Phil Niekro 20.00
DO David Ortiz 40.00
RO Roy Oswalt 15.00
JP Jim Palmer 20.00
TP Tony Perez 25.00
GP Gaylord Perry 15.00
GP1 Gaylord Perry 15.00
JR Jim Rice 20.00
BR Brooks Robinson 30.00
FR Frank Robinson/25 40.00
AR Al Rosen 15.00
JS Johan Santana 40.00
RS Ron Santo 25.00
BS Ben Sheets 15.00
SU Don Sutton 15.00
MT Mark Teixeira 25.00
LT Luis Tiant 15.00
LT1 Luis Tiant 15.00
BU B.J. Upton 15.00
RW Rickie Weeks 20.00
BW Billy Williams 20.00
MW Maury Wills 15.00
RY Robin Yount/25 70.00

Signature Hits

NM/M

Production 1-125
BM Stan Musial, Lou Brock/35 125.00
MY Robin Yount, Paul Molitor/125 75.00
WG Dave Winfield, Tony Gwynn/35 90.00
YB Wade Boggs, Carl Yastrzemski/35 100.00

Signature HRs

NM/M

Production 1-250
BS Mike Schmidt, Ernie Banks/25 180.00
GM Ken Griffey Jr., Willie McCovey/250 100.00
KM Willie McCovey, Harmon Killebrew/35 75.00
RG Frank Robinson, Ken Griffey Jr./250 85.00

Signature MVPs

NM/M

Production 1-250
BM Don Mattingly, Yogi Berra/175 100.00
BS Ernie Banks, Ryne Sandberg/25 200.00
CM Stan Musial, Orlando Cepeda/100 75.00
DS Ryne Sandberg, Andre Dawson/175 80.00
EF Dennis Eckersley, Rollie Fingers/250 30.00
FC George Foster, Rod Carew/125 40.00
GM Joe Morgan, Ken Griffey Jr./250 75.00
HY Robin Yount, Keith Hernandez/200 50.00
JR Ivan Rodriguez, Chipper Jones/35 125.00
KC Harmon Killebrew, Rod Carew/100 80.00
KM Harmon Killebrew, Willie McCovey/35 80.00
LM Fred Lynn, Joe Morgan/200 30.00
LW Maury Wills, Barry Larkin/250 35.00
MB Joe Morgan, Johnny Bench/100 60.00
MG Denny McLain, Bob Gibson/175 40.00
MY Robin Yount, Dale Murphy/175 60.00
PR Dave Parker, Jim Rice/250 40.00
SF Mike Schmidt, Rollie Fingers/175 60.00
SS Mike Schmidt, Ryne Sandberg/75 140.00
TB Frank Thomas, Jeff Bagwell/50 90.00
YC Orlando Cepeda, Carl Yastrzemski/100 65.00
YS Carl Yastrzemski, Jim Rice/100 75.00

Signature No-Hitters

NM/M

Production 1-250
BG Bob Gibson, Jim Bunning/125 60.00
CL Don Larsen, David Cone/250 40.00
FR Nolan Ryan, Bob Feller/25 150.00
GP Bob Gibson, Jim Palmer/125 50.00

Signature Numbers

NM/M

Production 1-49
Platinum: No Pricing
Production One Set
WB Wade Boggs/26 40.00
MC Miguel Cabrera/24 50.00
JC Jose Canseco/33 50.00
CA Rod Carew/29 35.00
SC Steve Carlton/32 25.00
OC Orlando Cepeda/30 25.00
WC Will Clark/22 60.00
CL Roger Clemens/22 200.00
RF Rollie Fingers/34 20.00
CF Carlton Fisk/27 40.00
EG Eric Gagne/38 40.00
BG Bob Gibson/45 25.00
GL Tom Glavine/47 40.00
KG Ken Griffey Jr./30 125.00
VG Vladimir Guerrero/27 50.00
RG Ron Guidry/49 60.00
TG Tony Gwynn/19 80.00
MI Monte Irvin/20 30.00
FJ Fergie Jenkins/31 20.00
RJ Randy Johnson/41 75.00
MA Juan Marichal/27 40.00
DM Don Mattingly/23 125.00
WM Willie McCovey/44 40.00
EM Eddie Murray/33 120.00
DO David Ortiz/34 50.00
RO Roy Oswalt/44 25.00
JP Jim Palmer/22 30.00
PI Mike Piazza/31 100.00
MP Mark Prior/22 60.00
KP Kirby Puckett/34 85.00
FR Frank Robinson/20 50.00
SR Scott Rolen/27 40.00
NR Nolan Ryan/34 120.00
TS Tom Seaver/41 75.00
JS John Smoltz/29 60.00
FT Frank Thomas/35 80.00
BW Billy Williams/26 30.00
DW Dave Winfield/31 35.00
KW Kerry Wood/34 40.00
RY Robin Yount/19 75.00

Signature ROYs

NM/M

Production 1-250
CM Willie McCovey, Orlando Cepeda/75 65.00
CS Rod Carew, Tom Seaver/25 100.00
DM Andre Dawson, Eddie Murray/25 70.00
FB Carlton Fisk, Johnny Bench/35 80.00
FL Fred Lynn/125, Carlton Fisk/125 60.00
GR Nomar Garciaparra, Scott Rolen/200 85.00
GS Dwight Gooden, Tom Seaver/100 60.00
JG Derek Jeter, Nomar Garciaparra/75 185.00
RA Frank Robinson, Luis Aparicio/125 50.00
RJ Derek Jeter, Cal Ripken Jr./75 300.00
SG Dwight Gooden, Darryl Strawberry/250 40.00
WD Andre Dawson, Billy Williams/250 30.00

Signature Supremacy

NM/M

Production 15-99
LA Luis Aparicio/50 40.00
JB Jeff Bagwell 75.00
CB Carlos Beltran/50 30.00
BE Johnny Bench/25 60.00
YB Yogi Berra/25 60.00
HB Hank Blalock/50 25.00
WB Wade Boggs/25 60.00
LB Lou Brock/25 40.00
BU Jim Bunning/99 25.00
MC Miguel Cabrera/99 40.00
JC Jose Canseco/25 60.00
CA Rod Carew/25 35.00
SC Steve Carlton/99 25.00
OC Orlando Cepeda/99 20.00
EC Eric Chavez/99 15.00
WC Will Clark/50 40.00
AD Andre Dawson/99 20.00
BD Bobby Doerr/99 20.00
BF Bob Feller/99 25.00
RF Rollie Fingers/99 15.00
CF Carlton Fisk/25 40.00
EG Eric Gagne/50 25.00
KG Ken Griffey Jr./99 80.00
RG Ron Guidry/99 20.00
TH Tim Hudson/50 25.00
MI Monte Irvin/99 20.00
DJ Derek Jeter/50 200.00
AK Al Kaline/50 60.00
GK George Kell/99 25.00
HK Harmon Killebrew/50 40.00
RK Ralph Kiner/25 40.00
JU Juan Marichal/25 50.00
MA Don Mattingly/25 80.00
BM Bill Mazeroski/50 40.00
PM Paul Molitor/50 40.00
JM Joe Morgan/25 30.00
MM Mark Mulder/99 15.00
DM Dale Murphy/99 25.00
MU Stan Musial/25 125.00
DN Don Newcombe/99 20.00
DO David Ortiz/99 40.00
RO Roy Oswalt/99 15.00
JP Jim Palmer/99 25.00
TP Tony Perez/99 25.00
MP Mark Prior/25 60.00
JR Jim Rice/99 15.00
RR Robin Roberts/99 30.00
BR Brooks Robinson/99 30.00
FR Frank Robinson/25 40.00
SR Scott Rolen/25 50.00
AR Al Rosen/99 25.00
SA Ryne Sandberg/25 85.00
JS Johan Santana/99 40.00
RS Ron Santo 25.00
MS Mike Schmidt/25 100.00
TS Tom Seaver/25 50.00
BS Ben Sheets/99 20.00
OS Ozzie Smith/25 50.00
SM John Smoltz/50 50.00
AS Alfonso Soriano/25 40.00
MT Mark Teixeira/99 25.00
FT Frank Thomas/25 80.00
BW Billy Williams/99 25.00
DW Dave Winfield/25 40.00
CY Carl Yastrzemski/25 100.00
RY Robin Yount/25 75.00

Signs of October

NM/M

Production 1-250
BW Mookie Wilson, Bill Buckner/250 40.00
CS John Smoltz, Joe Carter/250 50.00
EG Kirk Gibson, Dennis Eckersley/200 40.00
FM Carlton Fisk, Joe Morgan/100 50.00
GB Bob Gibson, Lou Brock/100 70.00
GG Ron Guidry, Steve Garvey/250 30.00
GL Mickey Lolich, Bob Gibson/100 40.00
JG Derek Jeter, Tony Gwynn/250 185.00
LB Yogi Berra, Don Larsen/250 85.00
MP Jack Morris, Kirby Puckett/100 85.00
PS Ozzie Smith, Kirby Puckett/35 125.00
RR Frank Robinson, Brooks Robinson/250 65.00
SB George Brett, Ozzie Smith 150.00
SY Ozzie Smith, Robin Yount/100 85.00
TG Kirk Gibson, Alan Trammell/250 40.00

2005 Upper Deck Trilogy

NM/M

Complete Set (100): 40.00
Common Player: .50
Pack (5): 20.00
Box (9): 170.00
1 A.J. Burnett .50
2 Adam Dunn 1.00
3 Adrian Beltre .50
4 Albert Pujols 4.00
5 Alex Rodriguez 3.00
6 Alfonso Soriano 1.00
7 Andruw Jones 1.00
8 Aramis Ramirez .50
9 Ben Sheets .75
10 Bobby Abreu .75
11 Bobby Crosby .50
12 Ryan Zimmerman **RC** 15.00
13 Brian Giles .50
14 Brian Roberts .50
15 Carl Crawford .50
16 Carlos Beltran 1.00
17 Carlos Delgado .75
18 Carlos Zambrano .75
19 Chipper Jones 1.00
20 Corey Patterson .50
21 Craig Biggio .50
22 Curt Schilling 1.50
23 Dallas McPherson .50
24 David Ortiz 1.50
25 David Wright 1.50
26 Delmon Young 1.00
27 Derek Jeter 4.00
28 Derrek Lee 1.00
29 Dontrelle Willis 1.00
30 Eric Chavez .50
31 Eric Gagne .50
32 Francisco Rodriguez .50
33 Gary Sheffield 1.00
34 Greg Maddux 2.00
35 Hank Blalock .50
36 Hideki Matsui 2.50
37 Ichiro Suzuki 3.00
38 Ivan Rodriguez 1.00
39 J.D. Drew .50
40 Jake Peavy .75
41 Jason Bay .50
42 Jason Schmidt .50
43 Jeff Bagwell 1.00
44 Jeff Kent .50
45 Jeff Niemann **RC** 2.00
46 Jeremy Bonderman .50
47 Jim Edmonds .75
48 Jim Thome 1.00
49 Joe Mauer .75
50 Johan Santana 1.00
51 John Smoltz .75
52 Johnny Damon 1.00
53 Jose Reyes .75
54 Jose Vidro .50
55 Josh Beckett .50
56 Justin Morneau .50
57 Justin Verlander **RC** 4.00
58 Ken Griffey Jr. 3.00
59 Kendry Morales **RC** 6.00
60 Kerry Wood .75
61 Khalil Greene .75
62 Lance Berkman .75
63 Luis Gonzalez .50
64 Manny Ramirez 1.50
65 Mark Buehrle .75
66 Mark Mulder .50
67 Mark Prior 1.00
68 Mark Teixeira 1.00
69 Michael Young .50
70 Miguel Cabrera 1.50
71 Miguel Tejada 1.00
72 Mike Mussina 1.00
73 Mike Piazza 1.50
74 Nomar Garciaparra 1.00
75 Pat Burrell .50
76 Paul Konerko .75
77 Pedro Martinez 1.50
78 Philip Humber **RC** 2.00
79 Prince Fielder 8.00
80 Randy Johnson 1.50
81 Richie Sexson .75
82 Rickie Weeks .75
83 Roger Clemens 4.00
84 Roy Halladay .75
85 Roy Oswalt .75
86 Sammy Sosa 1.50
87 Scott Kazmir .50
88 Scott Rolen 1.00
89 Stephen Drew **RC** 8.00
90 Tadahito Iguchi **RC** 4.00
91 Tim Hudson .75
92 Todd Helton 1.00
93 Tom Glavine .75
94 Torii Hunter .75
95 Travis Hafner .75
96 Troy Glaus .75
97 Vernon Wells .50
98 Victor Martinez .50
99 Vladimir Guerrero 1.50
100 Zack Greinke .50

Generations

Complete Set (6):
Common Player:

Generation Future Lumber Silver

NM/M

Production 100 Sets
Gold: 1X
Production 60 Sets
RC Robinson Cano 20.00
CA Jorge Cantu 6.00
GF Gavin Floyd 4.00
BH Brad Halsey 4.00
JJ J.J. Hardy 4.00
RH Ryan Howard 50.00
LN Laynce Nix 4.00
JP Jhonny Peralta 6.00
JR Jeremy Reed 4.00
AR Alexis Rios 6.00
RI Juan Rivera 4.00
BJ B.J. Upton 6.00
JW Jayson Werth 4.00
YO Kevin Youkilis 6.00

Generation Future Materials Silver

NM/M

Common Player: 4.00
Production 120 Sets

Gold: 1X
Production 75 Sets
BA Bronson Arroyo 6.00
GA Garrett Atkins 4.00
JE Jeff Baker 4.00
CL Clint Barmes 6.00
JB Jason Bartlett 4.00
BL Joe Blanton 4.00
DB Dewon Brazelton 4.00
YB Yhency Brazoban 4.00
CB Chris Burke 6.00
DC Daniel Cabrera 4.00
RC Robinson Cano 20.00
CA Jorge Cantu 6.00
GC Gustavo Chacin 4.00
JD J.D. Closser 4.00
DD David DeJesus 4.00
DU Jason Dubois 4.00
GF Gavin Floyd 4.00
JF Jeff Francis 4.00
AG Adrian Gonzalez 4.00
BH Brad Halsey 4.00
JJ J.J. Hardy 4.00
DH Danny Haren 4.00
AH Aaron Hill 4.00
HO Dennis Houlton 4.00
RH Ryan Howard 20.00
TI Tadahito Iguchi 15.00
EJ Edwin Jackson 4.00
DK Dae-Sung Koo 4.00
KO Casey Kotchman 4.00
JL Jason Lane 4.00
DM Dallas McPherson 6.00
AM Aaron Miles 4.00
YM Yadier Molina 4.00
MY Brett Myers 4.00
XN Xavier Nady 4.00
LN Laynce Nix 4.00
JP Jhonny Peralta 6.00
RQ Robb Quinlan 4.00
JR Jeremy Reed 4.00
AR Alexis Rios 6.00
RI Juan Rivera 4.00
ES Ervin Santana 6.00
SS Steve Schmoll 4.00
LS Luke Scott 4.00
SI Grady Sizemore 10.00
HS Huston Street 10.00
NS Nick Swisher 8.00
WT Willy Taveras 8.00
MT Mark Teahen 4.00
TH Charles Thomas 4.00
CT Chad Tracy 4.00
BJ B.J. Upton 4.00
CU Chase Utley 10.00
WA Ryan Wagner 4.00
RW Rickie Weeks 8.00
JW Jayson Werth 4.00
KY Keiichi Yabu 4.00
YO Kevin Youkilis 6.00

Generations Future Sig. Silver

NM/M
Common Player: 8.00
Production 50-199
Bronze: 1-1.5X
Production 35 Sets
Gold: No Pricing
Production 15 Sets
GA Garrett Atkins/199 10.00
JB Jason Bartlett/199 8.00
BE Colter Bean/199 8.00
BL Joe Blanton/99 10.00
YB Yhency Brazoban/199 10.00
AB Ambiorix Burgos/199 8.00
CB Chris Burke/199 15.00
DC Daniel Cabrera/199 15.00
JO Jose Capellan/199 10.00
JD J.D. Closser/99 10.00
AC Ambiorix Concepcion/199 8.00
DD David DeJesus/99 12.00
SD Stephen Drew/75 100.00
DU Jason Dubois/99 10.00
PF Prince Fielder/75 100.00
GF Gavin Floyd/99 10.00
JF Jeff Francis/99 12.00
AG Adrian Gonzalez/99 15.00
JG Jared Gothreaux/199 8.00
GG Gabe Gross/99 10.00
JJ J.J. Hardy/199 25.00
JH John Hattig Jr./199 10.00
FH Felix Hernandez/60 80.00
HO Dennis Houlton/199 10.00
RH Ryan Howard/99 40.00
PH Philip Humber/75 20.00
TI Tadahito Iguchi/75 150.00
EJ Edwin Jackson/99 8.00
KO Casey Kotchman/99 10.00
JL Jason Lane/99 10.00
ML Matt Lindstrom/199 8.00
PL Pedro Lopez/189 10.00
RM Russell Martin/199 20.00
KM Kendry Morales/199 30.00
JN Jeff Niemann/75 40.00
PO Peter Orr/199 15.00
TP Tony Pena/199 8.00
RQ Robb Quinlan/199 8.00
AR Alexis Rios/99 15.00
CR Casey Rogowski/199 10.00
RR Russel Rohlicek/199 8.00
SS Steve Schmoll/199 8.00
LS Luke Scott/199 10.00
TS Tim Stauffer/199 8.00
NS Nick Swisher/99 15.00
MT Mark Teahen/199 8.00
TH Charles Thomas/199 12.00
BJ B.J. Upton/50 20.00
CU Chase Utley/50 20.00
JV Justin Verlander/75 60.00
RW Rickie Weeks/50 25.00
JW Jayson Werth/99 15.00
KY Keiichi Yabu/199 25.00
YO Kevin Youkilis/99 25.00
DY Delmon Young/50 40.00
RZ Ryan Zimmerman/150 125.00

Generations of Lumber Triple

NM/M
Production 85 Sets 10.00
ARU B.J. Upton, Jimmy Rollins, Luis Aparicio 15.00
BCU Wade Boggs, B.J. Upton, Carl Crawford 15.00
BHH Travis Hafner, Ryan Howard, Harold Baines 15.00
BMY Bill Mueller, Wade Boggs, Kevin Youkilis 15.00
CCC Will Clark, Jack Clark, Orlando Cepeda 12.00
DAR Bobby Abreu, Eric Davis, Alex Rios 10.00
EDY Kevin Youkilis, Dwight Evans, Johnny Damon 20.00
GDP Ken Griffey Jr., Wily Mo Pena, Adam Dunn 25.00
GGC Miguel Cabrera, Ken Griffey Jr., Tony Gwynn 25.00
HDH Ryan Howard, Adam Dunn, Frank Howard 15.00
HOH Frank Howard, Ryan Howard, David Ortiz 20.00
JGU Bo Jackson, Ken Griffey Jr., B.J. Upton 25.00
JHR Alex Rios, Bo Jackson, Torii Hunter 15.00
JSP Bo Jackson, Gary Sheffield, Wily Mo Pena 15.00
KBH Pat Burrell, John Kruk, Ryan Howard 15.00
LJU Barry Larkin, Derek Jeter, B.J. Upton 30.00
LYU B.J. Upton, Barry Larkin, Michael Young 12.00
MDW Jayson Werth, Dale Murphy, Adam Dunn 15.00
MMJ Don Mattingly, Derek Jeter, Bobby Murcer 50.00
MOH Ryan Howard, David Ortiz, Eddie Murray 20.00
NBW Adrian Beltre, David Wright, Graig Nettles 15.00
OAR Bobby Abreu, Tony Oliva, Alex Rios 10.00
PDP Wily Mo Pena, Eric Davis, Tony Perez 10.00
PGP Tony Perez, Ken Griffey Jr., Wily Mo Pena 25.00
RJC Cal Ripken Jr., Derek Jeter, Bobby Crosby 50.00
ROY David Ortiz, Jim Rice, Kevin Youkilis 20.00
RRT Brooks Robinson, Cal Ripken Jr., Miguel Tejada 40.00
SBW Mike Schmidt, Adrian Beltre, David Wright 20.00
SDW Duke Snider, Jayson Werth, J.D. Drew 20.00
SMR Aramis Ramirez, Bill Madlock, Ron Santo 20.00
SSP Ron Santo, Ryne Sandberg, Corey Patterson 35.00

Generations of Materials Triple

NM/M
Common Trio: 10.00
Production 50 Sets
AAD Aramis Ramirez, Al Rosen, Dallas McPherson 15.00
AFB Luis Aparicio, Rafael Furcal, Jason Bartlett 15.00
API Tadahito Iguchi, Scott Podsednik, Luis Aparicio 25.00
ARU Jimmy Rollins, Luis Aparicio, B.J. Upton 15.00
BCU B.J. Upton, Carl Crawford, Wade Boggs 15.00
BHH Ryan Howard, Harold Baines, Travis Hafner 15.00
BLS Craig Biggio, Jason Lane, Luke Scott 15.00
BMY Kevin Youkilis, Wade Boggs, Bill Mueller 15.00
CCC Will Clark, Jack Clark, Orlando Cepeda 15.00
CCK Sean Casey, Will Clark, Casey Kotchman 15.00
CMG Justin Morneau, Adrian Gonzalez, Will Clark 15.00
CTG Will Clark, Adrian Gonzalez, Mark Teixeira 15.00
DAR Alex Rios, Eric Davis, Bobby Abreu 10.00
DBS Lenny Dykstra, Jason Bay, Nick Swisher 10.00
DGL Jason Lane, Ken Griffey Jr., Andre Dawson 25.00
DHL Lenny Dykstra, Torii Hunter, Jason Lane 10.00
DPD Jason Dubois, Corey Patterson, Andre Dawson 10.00
DPT Lenny Dykstra, Scott Podsednik, Willy Taveras 15.00
EDY Kevin Youkilis, Johnny Damon, Dwight Evans 20.00
GAS Bobby Abreu, Tony Gwynn, Nick Swisher 25.00
GDP Wily Mo Pena, Adam Dunn, Ken Griffey Jr. 25.00
GGC Ken Griffey Jr., Tony Gwynn, Miguel Cabrera 25.00
GMY Kevin Youkilis, Mike Greenwell, Bill Mueller 15.00
GWJ Dwight Gooden, Dontrelle Willis, Edwin Jackson 15.00
HDH Frank Howard, Adam Dunn, Ryan Howard 15.00
HOH Ryan Howard, David Ortiz, Frank Howard 20.00
JGU B.J. Upton, Bo Jackson, Ken Griffey Jr. 25.00
JHR Bo Jackson, Torii Hunter, Alex Rios 20.00
JMK Casey Kotchman, Wally Joyner, Dallas McPherson 10.00
JSP Bo Jackson, Gary Sheffield, Wily Mo Pena 15.00
KBH Pat Burrell, John Kruk, Ryan Howard 15.00
KBU John Kruk, Pat Burrell, Chase Utley 25.00
LJU B.J. Upton, Barry Larkin, Derek Jeter 35.00
LYU Barry Larkin, Michael Young, B.J. Upton 35.00
MBS Nick Swisher, Pat Burrell, Dale Murphy 20.00
MCG Don Mattingly, Sean Casey, Adrian Gonzalez 30.00
MDW Adam Dunn, Jayson Werth, Dale Murphy 20.00
MMJ Don Mattingly, Derek Jeter, Bobby Murcer 60.00
MOH David Ortiz, Ryan Howard, Eddie Murray 20.00
NBW Adrian Beltre, David Wright, Graig Nettles 20.00
OAR Bobby Abreu, Tony Oliva, Alex Rios 10.00
PDP Wily Mo Pena, Eric Davis, Tony Perez 10.00
PGD Tony Perez, Brian Giles, Jason Dubois 10.00
PGP Wily Mo Pena, Ken Griffey Jr., Tony Perez 30.00
RBT Brooks Robinson, Adrian Beltre, Mark Teahen 20.00
RCD Carl Crawford, David DeJesus, Tim Raines 10.00
RJC Derek Jeter, Cal Ripken Jr., Bobby Crosby 50.00
ROY Jim Rice, David Ortiz, Kevin Youkilis 25.00
RRM Brooks Robinson, Cal Ripken Jr., Melvin Mora 50.00
RRT Miguel Tejada, Cal Ripken Jr., Brooks Robinson 50.00
SBM Dallas McPherson, Adrian Beltre, Mike Schmidt 20.00
SBW Mike Schmidt, Adrian Beltre, David Wright 20.00
SDW Duke Snider, Jayson Werth, J.D. Drew 20.00
SGU Ryne Sandberg, Chase Utley, Marcus Giles 35.00
SRU Chase Utley, Mike Schmidt, Jimmy Rollins 40.00
SRW Ryne Sandberg, Brian Roberts, Rickie Weeks 25.00
VGB Jason Bay, Brian Giles, Andy Van Slyke 10.00
VPD Andy Van Slyke, Corey Patterson, David DeJesus 10.00
WBI Tadahito Iguchi, Frank White, Craig Biggio 20.00
WCT Willie Wilson, Willy Taveras, Carl Crawford 15.00

Generations of Signatures

NM/M
Production 35 Sets
AYU B.J. Upton, Luis Aparicio, Michael Young 40.00
BPN Jake Peavy, Jeff Niemann, Jim Bunning 50.00
CTG Will Clark, Mark Teixeira, Adrian Gonzalez 60.00
DBU Chase Utley, Craig Biggio, Bobby Doerr 50.00
DGL Ken Griffey Jr., Andre Dawson, Jason Lane 100.00
DGU Marcus Giles, Chase Utley, Bobby Doerr 50.00
DLB Bobby Doerr, Mark Loretta, Chris Burke 30.00
FPH Rich Harden, Mark Prior, Bob Feller 50.00
GDP Ken Griffey Jr., Adam Dunn, Wily Mo Pena 100.00
HDG Adam Dunn, Frank Howard, Gabe Gross 40.00
JHR Torii Hunter, Bo Jackson, Alex Rios 85.00
JKM Casey Kotchman, Kendry Morales, Wally Joyner 50.00
LJU Barry Larkin, Derek Jeter, B.J. Upton 250.00
MBV Justin Verlander, Jack Morris, Jeremy Bonderman 90.00
MMJ Derek Jeter, Don Mattingly, Bobby Murcer 260.00
NBW David Wright, Graig Nettles, Adrian Beltre 75.00
OHM Tony Oliva, Kent Hrbek, Justin Morneau 50.00
PBF Gaylord Perry, Jeremy Bonderman, Gavin Floyd 35.00
PGP Tony Perez, Ken Griffey Jr., Wily Mo Pena 100.00
PPH Philip Humber, Jim Palmer, Jake Peavy 50.00
PPS Jake Peavy, Tim Stauffer, Gaylord Perry 40.00
RCD Tim Raines, David DeJesus, Carl Crawford 40.00
RJC Bobby Crosby, Cal Ripken Jr., Derek Jeter 400.00
RRM Cal Ripken Jr., Melvin Mora, Brooks Robinson 180.00
RSH Nolan Ryan, John Smoltz, Philip Humber 165.00
SBT Mark Teahen, Adrian Beltre, Ron Santo 50.00
SBW Adrian Beltre, Mike Schmidt, David Wright 100.00
SGH J.J. Hardy, Ozzie Smith, Khalil Greene 70.00
SMR Ron Santo, Bill Madlock, Aramis Ramirez 50.00
SRW Brian Roberts, Ryne Sandberg, Rickie Weeks 85.00
VGB Jason Bay, Brian Giles, Andy Van Slyke 65.00

Generations Past Lumber

NM/M
Common Player: 4.00
Production 115 unless noted.
Gold: 1-1.5X
Production 25-75
LA Luis Aparicio 8.00
HB Harold Baines 4.00
DB Dusty Baker 6.00
JB Johnny Bench 10.00
WB Wade Boggs 8.00
BB Bill Buckner 6.00
CA Rod Carew 8.00
SC Steve Carlton 6.00
GC Gary Carter 6.00
OC Orlando Cepeda 6.00
CY Ron Cey 4.00
JC Jack Clark 4.00
WC Will Clark 8.00
TC Ty Cobb/99 100.00
MC Mickey Cochrane/99 25.00
ED Eric Davis 8.00
AD Andre Dawson 6.00
JD Joe DiMaggio/99 65.00
BD Bobby Doerr 8.00
LD Lenny Dykstra 4.00
DE Dwight Evans 6.00
CF Carlton Fisk 6.00
GF George Foster 4.00
JF Jimmie Foxx/99 50.00
FR Bill Freehan 4.00
LG Lou Gehrig/99 140.00
DG Dwight Gooden 4.00
GR Lefty Grove/99 40.00
TG Tony Gwynn 10.00
KH Keith Hernandez 6.00
RH Rogers Hornsby/99 40.00
FH Frank Howard 6.00
BJ Bo Jackson 10.00
RJ Reggie Jackson 10.00
JO Wally Joyner 4.00
GK George Kell 8.00
JK John Kruk 4.00
BL Barry Larkin 6.00
DL Davey Lopes 4.00
BM Bill Madlock 4.00
MA Don Mattingly 25.00
FM Fred McGriff 6.00
JM Johnny Mize 4.00
TM Thurman Munson 20.00
MU Bobby Murcer 4.00
DM Dale Murphy 8.00
MY Eddie Murray 8.00
SM Stan Musial 20.00
GN Graig Nettles 6.00
TO Tony Oliva 6.00
MO Mel Ott 25.00
TP Tony Perez 6.00
GP Gaylord Perry 6.00
RP Rico Petrocelli 6.00
BP Boog Powell 6.00
TR Tim Raines 4.00
RI Jim Rice 6.00
CR Cal Ripken Jr. 25.00
RO Brooks Robinson 8.00
JR Jackie Robinson 20.00
AR Al Rosen 10.00
BR Babe Ruth/99 140.00
NR Nolan Ryan 25.00
SA Ryne Sandberg 15.00
RS Ron Santo 10.00
MS Mike Schmidt 15.00
SI George Sisler 20.00
SK Bill "Moose" Skowron 6.00
OS Ozzie Smith 20.00
SN Duke Snider 10.00
DS Darryl Strawberry 6.00
AT Alan Trammell 8.00
AV Andy Van Slyke 8.00
FW Frank White 4.00
WW Willie Wilson 4.00
YA Carl Yastrzemski 25.00

Generation Past Material Silver

NM/M
Common Player: 4.00
Production 99 unless noted.
Gold: 1-1.5X
Production 25 Sets
LA Luis Aparicio 8.00
HB Harold Baines 4.00
DB Dusty Baker 6.00
JB Johnny Bench 10.00
WB Wade Boggs 8.00
BU Jim Bunning 6.00
RC Roy Campanella 20.00
CA Rod Carew 8.00
SC Steve Carlton 6.00
GC Gary Carter 6.00
OC Orlando Cepeda 6.00
CY Ron Cey 4.00
JC Jack Clark 4.00
WC Will Clark 8.00
DC David Cone 4.00
ED Eric Davis 8.00
AD Andre Dawson 6.00
DD Dizzy Dean/75 40.00
JD Joe DiMaggio/75 85.00
DR Don Drysdale 10.00
LD Lenny Dykstra 4.00
BF Bob Feller 10.00
CF Carlton Fisk 8.00
LG Lou Gehrig/75 150.00
DG Dwight Gooden 4.00
RG Ron Guidry 8.00
TG Tony Gwynn 10.00
KH Keith Hernandez 6.00
RH Rogers Hornsby/75 65.00
FH Frank Howard 6.00
HR Kent Hrbek 8.00
BJ Bo Jackson 10.00
RJ Reggie Jackson 10.00
JO Wally Joyner 6.00
JK John Kruk 8.00
BL Barry Larkin 6.00
DL Davey Lopes 4.00
BM Bill Madlock 4.00
EM Eddie Mathews/75 20.00
CM Christy Mathewson/75 80.00
MA Don Mattingly 25.00
JM Johnny Mize 15.00
JA Jack Morris 4.00
TM Thurman Munson 20.00
MU Bobby Murcer 8.00
DM Dale Murphy 8.00
MY Eddie Murray 8.00
SM Stan Musial 20.00
GN Graig Nettles 6.00
TO Tony Oliva 6.00
MO Mel Ott/75 30.00
SP Satchel Paige/75 50.00
JP Jim Palmer 6.00
TP Tony Perez 6.00
GP Gaylord Perry 6.00
RP Rico Petrocelli 6.00
BP Boog Powell 4.00
TR Tim Raines 4.00
RI Jim Rice 6.00
CR Cal Ripken Jr. 25.00
RO Brooks Robinson 10.00
AR Al Rosen 10.00
NR Nolan Ryan 25.00
SA Ryne Sandberg 15.00
MS Mike Schmidt 15.00
AV Andy Van Slyke 8.00
OS Ozzie Smith 15.00
SN Duke Snider 10.00
DS Darryl Strawberry 6.00
FW Frank White 4.00
WW Willie Wilson 4.00
YA Carl Yastrzemski 15.00

Generations Past Auto. Silver

NM/M
Common Player: 10.00
Production 24-99.
Bronze: 1-1.5X
Production 10 or 35.
No pricing for prod. of 10.
Gold: No Pricing
Production 5-15
LA Luis Aparicio/50 20.00
HB Harold Baines/199 15.00
DB Dusty Baker/25 20.00
WB Wade Boggs/50 35.00
BB Bill Buckner/50 15.00
BU Jim Bunning/99 20.00
CA Rod Carew/25 35.00
SC Steve Carlton/25 20.00
CY Ron Cey/199 15.00
JC Jack Clark/199 10.00
WC Will Clark/25 40.00
DC David Cone/99 15.00
ED Eric Davis/199 15.00
AD Andre Dawson/99 20.00
BD Bobby Doerr/199 15.00
LD Lenny Dykstra/199 15.00
DE Dwight Evans/50 20.00
BF Bob Feller/99 25.00
GF George Foster/199 10.00
FR Bill Freehan/199 15.00
RG Ron Guidry/199 15.00
KH Keith Hernandez/199 15.00
FH Frank Howard/199 15.00
HR Kent Hrbek/199 15.00
BJ Bo Jackson/50 50.00
RJ Reggie Jackson/25 50.00
JO Wally Joyner/199 15.00
GK George Kell/199 15.00
JK John Kruk/199 20.00
BL Barry Larkin/99 25.00
DL Davey Lopes/199 10.00
BM Bill Madlock/199 10.00
MA Don Mattingly/25 75.00
FM Fred McGriff/199 25.00
JA Jack Morris/199 15.00
MU Bobby Murcer/199 25.00
DM Dale Murphy/99 25.00

SM Stan Musial/25 80.00
GN Graig Nettles/199 15.00
TO Tony Oliva/99 15.00
JP Jim Palmer/50 20.00
TP Tony Perez/25 30.00
GP Gaylord Perry/199 15.00
BP Boog Powell/199 15.00
TR Tim Raines/199 15.00
RI Jim Rice/99 15.00
RO Brooks Robinson/50 30.00
AR Al Rosen/199 15.00
NR Nolan Ryan/25 100.00
SA Ryne Sandberg/50 60.00
RS Ron Santo/199 30.00
MS Mike Schmidt/25 60.00
SK Bill Skowron/199 15.00
OS Ozzie Smith/25 50.00
DS Darryl Strawberry/99 15.00
AT Alan Trammell/50 20.00
AV Andy Van Slyke/199 20.00
FW Frank White/199 15.00
WW Willie Wilson/199 15.00

Generation Present Lumber Silver

NM/M
Common Player: 4.00
Production 115 Sets
Gold: 1X
Production 75 Sets
BA Bobby Abreu 4.00
GA Garret Anderson 4.00
JE Jeff Bagwell 6.00
CB Carlos Beltran 6.00
AB Adrian Beltre 4.00
LB Lance Berkman 4.00
BI Craig Biggio 6.00
HB Hank Blalock 4.00
BO Jeremy Bonderman 4.00
PB Pat Burrell 4.00
AJ A.J. Burnett 4.00
MC Miguel Cabrera 8.00
SC Sean Casey 4.00
EC Eric Chavez 4.00
RC Roger Clemens 12.00
CC Carl Crawford 4.00
BC Bobby Crosby 4.00
DA Johnny Damon 8.00
CD Carlos Delgado 4.00
JD J.D. Drew 4.00
AD Adam Dunn 6.00
RF Rafael Furcal 4.00
JG Jason Giambi 6.00
BG Brian Giles 4.00
MG Marcus Giles 4.00
TG Troy Glaus 4.00
GR Khalil Greene 6.00
KG1 Ken Griffey Jr. 20.00
KG2 Ken Griffey Jr. 20.00
KG3 Ken Griffey Jr. 20.00
VG Vladimir Guerrero 8.00
HA Travis Hafner 4.00
TH Todd Helton 4.00
AH Aubrey Huff 6.00
HU Torii Hunter 4.00
DJ Derek Jeter 20.00
RJ Randy Johnson 8.00
JO Andruw Jones 6.00
CJ Chipper Jones 8.00
JK Jeff Kent 4.00
DL Derrek Lee 8.00
ML Mark Loretta 4.00
GM Greg Maddux 15.00
PM Pedro Martinez 8.00
VM Victor Martinez 4.00
JM Joe Mauer 6.00
BM Bill Mueller 4.00
DO David Ortiz 8.00
PA Corey Patterson 4.00
WM Wily Mo Pena 4.00
PI Mike Piazza 8.00
SP Scott Podsednik 4.00
MP Mark Prior 6.00
AP Albert Pujols 20.00
AR Aramis Ramirez 4.00
MR Manny Ramirez 8.00
RE Jose Reyes 4.00
BR Brian Roberts 4.00
IR Ivan Rodriguez 6.00
SR Scott Rolen 6.00
JR Jimmy Rollins 4.00
CS Curt Schilling 8.00
GS Gary Sheffield 6.00
SM John Smoltz 6.00
AS Alfonso Soriano 6.00
SS Sammy Sosa 8.00
MT Mark Teixeira 8.00
TE Miguel Tejada 6.00
FT Frank Thomas 6.00
JT Jim Thome 6.00
JV Jason Varitek 8.00
VI Jose Vidro 4.00
BW Bernie Williams 6.00
WI Dontrelle Willis 6.00
KW Kerry Wood 4.00
DW David Wright 20.00
MY Michael Young 4.00
CZ Carlos Zambrano 4.00

Generations Present Materials Silver

NM/M
Common Player: 4.00
Production 99 Sets
Gold: 1-1.5X
Production 25 Sets
BA Bobby Abreu 4.00
GA Garret Anderson 4.00
JE Jeff Bagwell 6.00
JB Jason Bay 4.00
CB Carlos Beltran 6.00
AB Adrian Beltre 4.00
LB Lance Berkman 4.00
BI Craig Biggio 6.00
HB Hank Blalock 4.00
BO Jeremy Bonderman 4.00
PB Pat Burrell 4.00
AJ A.J. Burnett 4.00
MC Miguel Cabrera 8.00
SC Sean Casey 4.00
EC Eric Chavez 4.00
RC Roger Clemens 12.00
CC Carl Crawford 4.00
BC Bobby Crosby 4.00
DA Johnny Damon 8.00
CD Carlos Delgado 4.00
JD J.D. Drew 4.00
AD Adam Dunn 6.00
RF Rafael Furcal 4.00
JG Jason Giambi 6.00
BG Brian Giles 4.00
MG Marcus Giles 4.00
TG Troy Glaus 4.00
GR Khalil Greene 6.00
ZG Zack Greinke 4.00
KG1 Ken Griffey Jr. 20.00
KG2 Ken Griffey Jr. 20.00
KG3 Ken Griffey Jr. 20.00
VG Vladimir Guerrero 8.00
HA Travis Hafner 4.00
RH Rich Harden 4.00
TH Todd Helton 6.00
AH Aubrey Huff 4.00
HU Torii Hunter 4.00
DJ Derek Jeter 20.00
RJ Randy Johnson 8.00
JO Andruw Jones 6.00
CJ Chipper Jones 8.00
SK Scott Kazmir 4.00
JK Jeff Kent 4.00
DL Derrek Lee 8.00
BL Brad Lidge 4.00
ML Mark Loretta 4.00
GM Greg Maddux 15.00
PM Pedro Martinez 8.00
VM Victor Martinez 4.00
JM Joe Mauer 6.00
ME Melvin Mora 4.00
MO Justin Morneau 4.00
BM Bill Mueller 4.00
MM Mark Mulder 4.00
DO David Ortiz 8.00
RO Roy Oswalt 4.00
PA Corey Patterson 4.00
JP Jake Peavy 4.00
WM Wily Mo Pena 4.00
PI Mike Piazza 8.00
SP Scott Podsednik 6.00
MP Mark Prior 6.00
AP Albert Pujols 20.00
AR Aramis Ramirez 4.00
MR Manny Ramirez 8.00
RE Jose Reyes 4.00
BR Brian Roberts 4.00
IR Ivan Rodriguez 6.00
SR Scott Rolen 6.00
JR Jimmy Rollins 4.00
JS Johan Santana 6.00
CS Curt Schilling 8.00
BS Ben Sheets 4.00
GS Gary Sheffield 6.00
SM John Smoltz 6.00
AS Alfonso Soriano 6.00
SS Sammy Sosa 8.00
MT Mark Teixeira 8.00
TE Miguel Tejada 6.00
FT Frank Thomas 6.00
JT Jim Thome 6.00
JV Jason Varitek 8.00
VI Jose Vidro 4.00
BW Bernie Williams 6.00
WI Dontrelle Willis 6.00
KW Kerry Wood 4.00
DW David Wright 20.00
MY Michael Young 4.00
CZ Carlos Zambrano 4.00

Generations Present Signatures

NM/M
Common Player: 10.00
Production 25-199.
Bronze: 1-1.5X
Production 10 or 35.
No pricing for prod. of 10.
Gold: No Pricing
Production 5-15.
GA Garret Anderson/25 20.00
JB Jason Bay/199 15.00
BI Craig Biggio/25 35.00
BO Jeremy Bonderman/199 15.00
MC Miguel Cabrera/25 40.00
SC Sean Casey/50 15.00
CC Carl Crawford/99 15.00
BC Bobby Crosby/99 15.00
AD Adam Dunn/95 25.00
RF Rafael Furcal/99 15.00
BG Brian Giles/99 12.00
MG Marcus Giles/199 10.00
GR Khalil Greene/135 25.00
ZG Zack Greinke/199 15.00
KG1 Ken Griffey Jr./199 75.00
KG2 Ken Griffey Jr./199 75.00
KG3 Ken Griffey Jr./199 75.00
HA Travis Hafner/199 15.00
RH Rich Harden/199 15.00
AH Aubrey Huff/199 15.00
HU Torii Hunter/25 25.00
DJ Derek Jeter/99 150.00
DL Derrek Lee/25 40.00
BL Brad Lidge/99 25.00
ML Mark Loretta/99 15.00
VM Victor Martinez/99 15.00
JM Joe Mauer/25 25.00
ME Melvin Mora/199 10.00
MO Justin Morneau/99 20.00
MM Mark Mulder/99 15.00
DO David Ortiz/25 50.00
RO Roy Oswalt/25 30.00
JP Jake Peavy/99 15.00
WM Wily Mo Pena/199 15.00
SP Scott Podsednik/99 20.00
MP Mark Prior/25 40.00
AR Aramis Ramirez/99 15.00
BR Brian Roberts/99 15.00
BS Ben Sheets/99 15.00
GS Gary Sheffield/25 35.00
SM John Smoltz/25 50.00
MT Mark Teixeira/25 50.00
TE Miguel Tejada/25 40.00
FT Frank Thomas/25 50.00
VI Jose Vidro/99 10.00
WI Dontrelle Willis/25 30.00
DW David Wright/135 50.00
MY Michael Young/199 15.00

Signature Dual Material

NM/M
Common Player: 20.00
Production 75 Sets
HB Harold Baines 25.00
AB Adrian Beltre 25.00
BI Craig Biggio 40.00
WB Wade Boggs 50.00
MC Miguel Cabrera 50.00
SC Sean Casey 25.00
OC Orlando Cepeda 40.00
CL Jack Clark 20.00
WC Will Clark 50.00
CC Carl Crawford 20.00
BC Bobby Crosby 30.00
ED Eric Davis 35.00
AD Andre Dawson 30.00
DU Adam Dunn 40.00
LD Lenny Dykstra 20.00
BG Brian Giles 20.00
GI Marcus Giles 20.00
KG Ken Griffey Jr. 150.00
TG Tony Gwynn 60.00
TH Travis Hafner 30.00
FH Frank Howard 30.00
RH Ryan Howard 75.00
AH Aubrey Huff 20.00
HU Torii Hunter 30.00
DJ Derek Jeter 300.00
WJ Wally Joyner 40.00
BL Barry Larkin 40.00
MA Bill Madlock 25.00
VM Victor Martinez 25.00
DM Don Mattingly 90.00
BM Bobby Murcer 35.00
GN Graig Nettles 30.00
TO Tony Oliva 25.00
DO David Ortiz 75.00
CP Corey Patterson 20.00
WP Wily Mo Pena 25.00
TP Tony Perez 40.00
SP Scott Podsednik 50.00
AP Albert Pujols 250.00
TR Tim Raines 30.00
RA Aramis Ramirez 35.00
RE Jose Reyes 40.00
RI Jim Rice 35.00
CR Cal Ripken Jr. 150.00
BR Brooks Robinson 50.00
RS Ryne Sandberg 80.00
MS Mike Schmidt 75.00
MT Mark Teixeira 60.00
MI Miguel Tejada 50.00
BU B.J. Upton 25.00
AV Andy Van Slyke 30.00
JV Jose Vidro 20.00
JW Jayson Werth 20.00
DW David Wright 80.00
KY Kevin Youkilis 20.00

2005 Upper Deck Update

NM/M
Complete Update Set (186):
Common Player (1-100): .15
Common Rookie (101-177): 3.00
Production 599
Common Rk Auto. (178-186): 10.00
Production 75
Pack (5): 5.00
Box (24): 110.00
1 A.J. Burnett .15
2 Adam Dunn .50
3 Adrian Beltre .25
4 Albert Pujols 2.00
5 Alex Rodriguez 2.00
6 Alfonso Soriano .50
7 Andruw Jones .50
8 Aramis Ramirez .25
9 Barry Zito .25
10 Bartolo Colon .25
11 Ben Sheets .25
12 Bobby Abreu .25
13 Bobby Crosby .25
14 Michael Cuddyer .15
15 Brian Giles .15
16 Brian Roberts .15
17 Carl Crawford .15
18 Carlos Beltran .50
19 Carlos Delgado .40
20 Carlos Lee .15
21 Carlos Zambrano .25
22 Chase Utley .25
23 Chipper Jones .75
24 Chris Carpenter .25
25 Craig Biggio .25
26 Curt Schilling .75
27 David Ortiz .75
28 David Wright 1.00
29 Derek Jeter 2.00
30 Derrek Lee .50
31 Dontrelle Willis .25
32 Eric Chavez .25
33 Eric Gagne .25
34 Francisco Rodriguez .15
35 Gary Sheffield .40
36 Greg Maddux 1.00
37 Hank Blalock .25
38 Hideki Matsui 1.50
39 Ichiro Suzuki 1.50
40 Ivan Rodriguez .50
41 J.D. Drew .15
42 Jake Peavy .25
43 Jason Bay .25
44 Jason Schmidt .15
45 Jeff Bagwell .40
46 Jeff Kent .25
47 Jeremy Bonderman .15
48 Jim Edmonds .40
49 Jim Thome .50
50 Joe Mauer .25
51 Johan Santana .50
52 John Smoltz .25
53 Johnny Damon .75
54 Jose Reyes .25
55 Jose Vidro .15
56 Josh Beckett .25
57 Justin Morneau .15
58 Ken Griffey Jr. 1.50
59 Kenny Rogers .15
60 Kerry Wood .25
61 Khalil Greene .25
62 Lance Berkman .25
63 Livan Hernandez .15
64 Luis Gonzalez .15
65 Manny Ramirez .75
66 Mark Buehrle .25
67 Mark Mulder .25
68 Mark Prior .50
69 Mark Teixeira .50
70 Michael Young .25
71 Miguel Cabrera .75
72 Miguel Tejada .50
73 Mike Mussina .40
74 Mike Piazza .75
75 Moises Alou .25
76 Morgan Ensberg .25
77 Nomar Garciaparra .50
78 Pat Burrell .25
79 Paul Konerko .75
80 Pedro Martinez .75
81 Randy Johnson .75
82 Rich Harden .25
83 Richie Sexson .25
84 Rickie Weeks .25
85 Robinson Cano .25
86 Roger Clemens 2.00
87 Roy Halladay .25
88 Roy Oswalt .25
89 Sammy Sosa .75
90 Scott Kazmir .15
91 Scott Rolen .75
92 Shawn Green .25
93 Tim Hudson .25
94 Todd Helton .50
95 Tom Glavine .25
96 Torii Hunter .25
.25 Travis Hafner .15
.25 Troy Glaus .15
99 Vernon Wells .15
100 Vladimir Guerrero .75
101 Adam Shabala **RC** 3.00
102 Ambiorix Burgos **RC** 3.00
103 Anibal Sanchez **RC** 10.00
104 Bill McCarthy **RC** 3.00
105 Brandon McCarthy **RC** 6.00
106 Brian Burres **RC** 3.00
107 Carlos Ruiz **RC** 4.00
108 Casey Rogowski **RC** 3.00
109 Chad Orvella **RC** 3.00
110 Chris Resop **RC** 5.00
111 Chris Roberson **RC** 3.00
112 Chris Seddon **RC** 3.00
113 Colter Bean **RC** 3.00
114 Dae-Sung Koo **RC** 3.00
115 David Gassner **RC** 3.00
116 Brian Anderson 5.00
117 D.J. Houlton **RC** 3.00
118 Derek Wathan **RC** 3.00
119 Devon Lowery **RC** 3.00
120 Enrique Gonzalez **RC** 3.00
121 Eude Brito **RC** 3.00
122 Francisco Butto **RC** 3.00
123 Franquelis Osoria **RC** 5.00
124 Garrett Jones **RC** 3.00
125 Geovany Soto **RC** 4.00
126 Hayden Penn **RC** 5.00
127 Ismael Ramirez **RC** 3.00
128 Jared Gothreaux **RC** 3.00
129 Jason Hammel **RC** 3.00
130 Jeff Miller **RC** 3.00
131 Joel Peralta **RC** 3.00
132 John Hattig Jr. **RC** 3.00
133 Jorge Campillo **RC** 3.00
134 Juan Morillo **RC** 3.00
135 Ryan Garko **RC** 6.00
136 Keiichi Yabu **RC** 6.00
137 Luis Hernandez **RC** 5.00
138 Luis Pena **RC** 3.00
139 Luis Rodriguez **RC** 3.00
140 Luke Scott **RC** 5.00
141 Marcos Carvajal **RC** 3.00
142 Mark Woodyard **RC** 3.00
143 Matt Smith **RC** 3.00
144 Matt Lindstrom **RC** 5.00
145 Miguel Negron **RC** 3.00
146 Mike Morse **RC** 5.00
147 Nate McLouth **RC** 3.00
148 Nelson Cruz **RC** 5.00
149 Nick Masset **RC** 3.00
150 Oscar Robles **RC** 3.00
151 Paulino Reynoso **RC** 3.00
152 Pedro Lopez **RC** 3.00
153 Peter Orr **RC** 3.00
154 Randy Messenger **RC** 3.00
155 Randy Williams **RC** 3.00
156 Raul Tablado **RC** 3.00
157 Ronny Paulino **RC** 4.00
158 Russel Rohlicek **RC** 4.00
159 Russell Martin **RC** 12.00
160 Scott Baker **RC** 5.00
161 Scott Munter **RC** 4.00
162 Sean Thompson **RC** 4.00
163 Sean Tracey **RC** 3.00
164 Shane Costa **RC** 3.00
165 Steve Schmoll **RC** 3.00
166 Tony Giarratano **RC** 5.00
167 Tony Pena **RC** 3.00
168 Travis Bowyer **RC** 5.00
169 Ubaldo Jimenez **RC** 3.00
170 Wladimir Balentien **RC** 8.00
171 Yorman Bazardo **RC** 3.00
172 Yuniesky Betancourt **RC** 5.00
173 Chris Denorfia **RC** 5.00
174 Dana Eveland **RC** 5.00
175 Jermaine Van Buren **RC** 3.00
176 Mark McLemore **RC** 3.00
177 Ryan Spilborghs **RC** 3.00
178 Ambiorix Concepcion **RC** 10.00
179 Jeff Niemann **RC** 25.00
180 Justin Verlander **RC** 80.00
181 Kendry Morales **RC** 30.00
182 Philip Humber **RC** 25.00
183 Prince Fielder 250.00
184 Stephen Drew **RC** 75.00
185 Tadahito Iguchi **RC** 80.00
186 Ryan Zimmerman **RC** 140.00
Common Artifacts RC (201-285): 3.00
Production 799
201 Adam Shabala **RC** 3.00
202 Ambiorix Burgos **RC** 3.00
203 Ambiorix Concepcion **RC** 3.00
204 Anibal Sanchez **RC** 10.00
205 Bill McCarthy **RC** 3.00
206 Brandon McCarthy **RC** 5.00
207 Brian Burres **RC** 3.00
208 Carlos Ruiz **RC** 4.00
209 Casey Rogowski **RC** 3.00
210 Chad Orvella **RC** 3.00
211 Chris Resop **RC** 3.00
212 Chris Roberson **RC** 3.00
213 Chris Seddon **RC** 3.00
214 Colter Bean **RC** 3.00
215 Dae-Sung Koo **RC** 3.00
216 David Gassner **RC** 3.00
217 Brian Anderson 4.00
218 D.J. Houlton **RC** 3.00
219 Derek Wathan **RC** 3.00
220 Devon Lowery **RC** 3.00
221 Enrique Gonzalez **RC** 3.00
222 Eude Brito **RC** 3.00
223 Francisco Butto **RC** 3.00
224 Franquelis Osoria **RC** 5.00
225 Garrett Jones **RC** 3.00
226 Geovany Soto **RC** 4.00
227 Hayden Penn **RC** 3.00
228 Ismael Ramirez **RC** 3.00
229 Jared Gothreaux **RC** 3.00
230 Jason Hammel **RC** 3.00
231 Jeff Miller **RC** 3.00
232 Jeff Niemann **RC** 5.00
233 Joel Peralta **RC** 3.00
234 John Hattig Jr. **RC** 3.00
235 Jorge Campillo **RC** 3.00
236 Juan Morillo **RC** 3.00
237 Justin Verlander **RC** 15.00
238 Ryan Garko **RC** 5.00
239 Keiichi Yabu **RC** 5.00
240 Kendry Morales **RC** 5.00
241 Luis Hernandez **RC** 3.00
242 Luis Pena **RC** 3.00
243 Luis Rodriguez **RC** 3.00
244 Luke Scott **RC** 5.00
245 Marcos Carvajal **RC** 3.00
246 Mark Woodyard **RC** 3.00
247 Matt Smith **RC** 3.00
248 Matt Lindstrom **RC** 3.00
249 Miguel Negron **RC** 3.00
250 Mike Morse **RC** 3.00
251 Nate McLouth **RC** 4.00
252 Nelson Cruz **RC** 5.00
253 Nick Masset **RC** 3.00
254 Oscar Robles **RC** 3.00
255 Paulino Reynoso **RC** 3.00
256 Pedro Lopez **RC** 3.00
257 Peter Orr **RC** 3.00
258 Philip Humber **RC** 5.00
259 Prince Fielder 20.00
260 Randy Messenger **RC** 3.00
261 Randy Williams **RC** 3.00
262 Raul Tablado **RC** 3.00
263 Ronny Paulino **RC** 4.00
264 Russel Rohlicek **RC** 3.00
265 Russell Martin **RC** 8.00
266 Scott Baker **RC** 5.00
267 Scott Munter **RC** 3.00
268 Sean Thompson **RC** 3.00
269 Sean Tracey **RC** 3.00
270 Shane Costa **RC** 3.00
271 Stephen Drew **RC** 10.00
272 Steve Schmoll **RC** 5.00
273 Tadahito Iguchi **RC** 6.00
274 Tony Giarratano **RC** 4.00
275 Tony Pena **RC** 3.00
276 Travis Bowyer **RC** 5.00
277 Ubaldo Jimenez **RC** 3.00
278 Wladimir Balentien **RC** 5.00
279 Yorman Bazardo **RC** 4.00
280 Yuniesky Betancourt 5.00
281 Ryan Zimmerman **RC** 15.00
282 Chris Denorfia **RC** 5.00
283 Dana Eveland **RC** 5.00
284 Jermaine Van Buren **RC** 3.00
285 Mark McLemore **RC** 3.00
Common Reflections RC (201-286): 1.00
201 Adam Shabala **RC** 1.00
202 Ambiorix Burgos **RC** 1.00
203 Ambiorix Concepcion **RC** 1.00
204 Anibal Sanchez **RC** 3.00
205 Bill McCarthy **RC** 1.00
206 Brandon McCarthy **RC** 2.00
207 Brian Burres **RC** 1.00
208 Carlos Ruiz **RC** 1.00
209 Casey Rogowski **RC** 1.00
210 Chad Orvella **RC** 1.00
211 Chris Resop **RC** 1.50
212 Chris Roberson **RC** 1.00
213 Chris Seddon **RC** 1.00
214 Colter Bean **RC** 1.00
215 Dae-Sung Koo **RC** 1.00
216 Yuniesky Betancourt **RC** 2.00
217 David Gassner **RC** 1.00
218 Brian Anderson 1.50
219 Dennis Houlton **RC** 1.00
220 Derek Wathan **RC** 1.00
221 Devon Lowery **RC** 1.00
222 Enrique Gonzalez **RC** 1.00
223 Ryan Zimmerman **RC** 8.00
224 Eude Brito **RC** 1.00
225 Francisco Butto **RC** 1.00
226 Franquelis Osoria **RC** 1.00
227 Garrett Jones **RC** 1.00
228 Geovany Soto **RC** 1.50
229 Hayden Penn **RC** 1.50
230 Ismael Ramirez **RC** 1.50
231 Jared Gothreaux **RC** 1.00
232 Jason Hammel **RC** 1.00
233 Chris Denorfia **RC** 1.50
234 Jeff Miller **RC** 1.00
235 Jeff Niemann **RC** 2.00
236 Dana Eveland **RC** 2.00
237 Joel Peralta **RC** 1.00
238 John Hattig Jr. **RC** 1.00
239 Jorge Campillo **RC** 1.00
240 Juan Morillo **RC** 1.00
241 Justin Verlander **RC** 5.00
242 Ryan Garko **RC** 2.50
243 Keiichi Yabu **RC** 1.00
244 Kendry Morales **RC** 2.00
245 Luis Hernandez **RC** 1.00
246 Jermaine Van Buren **RC** 1.00
247 Luis Pena **RC** 1.00
248 Luis Rodriguez **RC** 1.00
249 Luke Scott **RC** 1.50
250 Marcos Carvajal **RC** 1.00
251 Mark Woodyard **RC** 1.00
252 Matt Smith **RC** 1.00
253 Matt Lindstrom **RC** 1.00
254 Miguel Negron **RC** 1.00
255 Mike Morse **RC** 1.00
256 Nate McLouth **RC** 1.00
257 Nelson Cruz **RC** 2.00
258 Nick Masset **RC** 1.00
259 Mark McLemore **RC** 1.00
260 Oscar Robles **RC** 1.00
261 Paulino Reynoso **RC** 1.00
262 Pedro Lopez **RC** 1.00
263 Peter Orr **RC** 1.00
264 Philip Humber **RC** 2.00
265 Prince Fielder 10.00
266 Randy Messenger **RC** 1.00
267 Randy Williams **RC** 1.00
268 Raul Tablado **RC** 1.00
269 Ronny Paulino **RC** 1.50
270 Russel Rohlicek **RC** 1.00
271 Russell Martin **RC** 2.00
272 Scott Baker **RC** 1.00
273 Scott Munter **RC** 1.00

274 Sean Thompson **RC** 1.00
275 Sean Tracey **RC** 1.00
276 Shane Costa **RC** 1.00
277 Stephen Drew **RC** 5.00
278 Steve Schmoll **RC** 1.00
279 Ryan Spilborghs **RC** 1.50
280 Tadahito Iguchi **RC** 2.00
281 Tony Giarratano **RC** 1.00
282 Tony Pena **RC** 1.00
283 Travis Bowyer **RC** 1.50
284 Ubaldo Jimenez **RC** 1.00
285 Wladimir Balentien **RC** 2.50
286 Yorman Bazardo **RC** 1.00
Common Origins RC (201-286): .75
201 Adam Shabala **RC** .75
202 Ambiorix Burgos **RC** .75
203 Ambiorix Concepcion **RC** .75
204 Anibal Sanchez **RC** 2.00
205 Bill McCarthy **RC** .75
206 Brandon McCarthy **RC** 2.00
207 Brian Burres **RC** .75
208 Carlos Ruiz **RC** 1.00
209 Casey Rogowski **RC** 1.00
210 Chad Orvella **RC** .75
211 Chris Resop **RC** 1.00
212 Chris Roberson **RC** 1.00
213 Chris Seddon **RC** .75
214 Colter Bean **RC** 1.00
215 Dae-Sung Koo **RC** .75
216 Yuniesky Betancourt **RC** 1.50
217 David Gassner **RC** .75
218 Brian Anderson **RC** 1.00
219 Dennis Houlton **RC** .75
220 Derek Wathan **RC** .75
221 Devon Lowery **RC** .75
222 Enrique Gonzalez **RC** .75
223 Ryan Zimmerman **RC** 5.00
224 Eude Brito **RC** .75
225 Francisco Butto **RC** 1.00
226 Franquelis Osoria **RC** 1.00
227 Garrett Jones **RC** 1.00
228 Geovany Soto **RC** 1.00
229 Hayden Penn **RC** 1.00
230 Ismael Ramirez **RC** 1.00
231 Jared Gothreaux **RC** .75
232 Jason Hammel **RC** .75
233 Chris Denorfia **RC** 1.00
234 Jeff Miller **RC** .75
235 Jeff Niemann **RC** 1.50
236 Dana Eveland **RC** 1.00
237 Joel Peralta **RC** .75
238 John Hattig Jr. **RC** 1.00
239 Jorge Campillo **RC** 1.00
240 Juan Morillo **RC** 1.00
241 Justin Verlander **RC** 5.00
242 Ryan Garko **RC** 2.00
243 Keiichi Yabu **RC** 1.00
244 Kendry Morales **RC** 2.00
245 Luis Hernandez **RC** .75
246 Jermaine Van Buren **RC** .75
247 Luis Pena **RC** .75
248 Luis Rodriguez **RC** .75
249 Luke Scott **RC** 1.50
250 Marcos Carvajal **RC** 1.00
251 Mark Woodyard **RC** 1.00
252 Matt Smith **RC** 1.00
253 Matt Lindstrom **RC** 1.00
254 Miguel Negron **RC** 1.50
255 Mike Morse **RC** 1.50
256 Nate McLouth **RC** 1.00
257 Nelson Cruz **RC** 1.50
258 Nick Masset **RC** .75
259 Mark McLemore **RC** 1.00
260 Oscar Robles **RC** .75
261 Paulino Reynoso **RC** .75
262 Pedro Lopez **RC** 1.00
263 Peter Orr **RC** 1.00
264 Philip Humber **RC** 1.50
265 Prince Fielder 8.00
266 Randy Messenger **RC** .75
267 Randy Williams **RC** 1.00
268 Raul Tablado **RC** .75
269 Ronny Paulino **RC** 1.50
270 Russel Rohlicek **RC** .75
271 Russell Martin **RC** 1.50
272 Scott Baker **RC** 1.50
273 Ryan Spilborghs **RC** 1.00
274 Scott Munter **RC** .75
275 Sean Thompson **RC** 1.00
276 Sean Tracey **RC** 1.00
277 Shane Costa **RC** 1.00
278 Stephen Drew **RC** 4.00
279 Steve Schmoll **RC** 1.00
280 Tadahito Iguchi **RC** 2.00
281 Tony Giarratano **RC** .75
282 Tony Pena **RC** .75
283 Travis Bowyer **RC** 1.00
284 Ubaldo Jimenez **RC** 1.00
285 Wladimir Balentien **RC** 2.00
286 Yorman Bazardo **RC** 1.00
Common SP Authentic Auto. (101-186): 8.00
Production 185
101 Adam Shabala **RC** 10.00
102 Ambiorix Burgos **RC** 10.00
103 Ambiorix Concepcion **RC** 10.00
104 Anibal Sanchez **RC** 25.00
106 Brandon McCarthy **RC** 25.00
107 Brian Burres **RC** 10.00
108 Carlos Ruiz **RC** 15.00
109 Casey Rogowski **RC** 10.00
110 Chad Orvella **RC** 10.00
111 Chris Resop **RC** 12.00
112 Chris Roberson **RC** 10.00
113 Chris Seddon **RC** 10.00
114 Colter Bean **RC** 15.00
116 David Gassner **RC** 10.00
117 Brian Anderson 25.00
120 Devon Lowery **RC** 10.00
121 Enrique Gonzalez **RC** 10.00
122 Eude Brito **RC** 8.00
123 Francisco Butto **RC** 10.00
124 Franquelis Osoria **RC** 15.00
125 Garrett Jones **RC** 10.00
126 Geovany Soto **RC** 30.00
127 Hayden Penn **RC** 15.00
128 Ismael Ramirez **RC** 8.00
129 Jared Gothreaux **RC** 10.00
130 Jason Hammel **RC** 10.00
131 Jeff Miller **RC** 8.00
132 Jeff Niemann **RC** 40.00
133 Joel Peralta **RC** 10.00
134 John Hattig Jr. **RC** 15.00
135 Jorge Campillo **RC** 8.00
136 Juan Morillo **RC** 10.00
137 Justin Verlander **RC** 185.00
138 Ryan Garko **RC** 50.00
139 Keiichi Yabu **RC** 15.00
140 Kendry Morales **RC** 60.00
141 Luis Hernandez **RC** 10.00
143 Luis Rodriguez **RC** 10.00
144 Luke Scott **RC** 50.00
145 Marcos Carvajal **RC** 10.00
146 Mark Woodyard **RC** 10.00
147 Matt Smith **RC** 8.00
148 Matt Lindstrom **RC** 10.00
149 Miguel Negron **RC** 15.00
150 Mike Morse **RC** 20.00
151 Nate McLouth **RC** 20.00
152 Nelson Cruz **RC** 30.00
153 Nick Masset **RC** 10.00
155 Paulino Reynoso **RC** 10.00
156 Pedro Lopez **RC** 15.00
157 Peter Orr **RC** 10.00
158 Philip Humber **RC** 20.00
159 Prince Fielder 250.00
160 Randy Messenger **RC** 8.00
162 Raul Tablado **RC** 10.00
163 Ronny Paulino **RC** 20.00
164 Russel Rohlicek **RC** 10.00
165 Russell Martin **RC** 125.00
166 Scott Baker **RC** 20.00
167 Scott Munter **RC** 10.00
168 Sean Thompson **RC** 10.00
169 Sean Tracey **RC** 15.00
170 Shane Costa **RC** 10.00
171 Stephen Drew **RC** 80.00
172 Steve Schmoll **RC** 10.00
173 Tadahito Iguchi **RC** 75.00
174 Tony Giarratano **RC** 15.00
175 Tony Pena **RC** 8.00
176 Travis Bowyer **RC** 10.00
177 Ubaldo Jimenez **RC** 15.00
178 Wladimir Balentien **RC** 75.00
179 Yorman Bazardo **RC** 15.00
181 Ryan Zimmerman **RC** 180.00
182 Chris Denorfia **RC** 15.00
184 Jermaine Van Buren **RC** 15.00
185 Mark McLemore **RC** 10.00
Common SPx Auto. (101-179): 8.00
Production 185
101 Adam Shabala **RC** 10.00
102 Ambiorix Burgos **RC** 10.00
103 Ambiorix Concepcion **RC** 10.00
104 Anibal Sanchez **RC** 25.00
106 Brandon McCarthy **RC** 25.00
107 Brian Burres **RC** 10.00
108 Carlos Ruiz **RC** 15.00
109 Casey Rogowski **RC** 15.00
110 Chad Orvella **RC** 10.00
111 Chris Resop **RC** 15.00
112 Chris Roberson **RC** 15.00
113 Chris Seddon **RC** 10.00
114 Colter Bean **RC** 15.00
115 David Gassner **RC** 10.00
116 Brian Anderson **RC** 15.00
118 Devon Lowery **RC** 8.00
119 Enrique Gonzalez **RC** 10.00
120 Eude Brito **RC** 10.00
121 Francisco Butto **RC** 10.00
122 Franquelis Osoria **RC** 10.00
123 Garrett Jones **RC** 10.00
124 Geovany Soto **RC** 30.00
125 Hayden Penn **RC** 15.00
126 Ismael Ramirez **RC** 8.00
127 Jared Gothreaux **RC** 10.00
128 Jason Hammel **RC** 10.00
129 Jeff Miller **RC** 8.00
130 Jeff Niemann **RC** 30.00
131 Joel Peralta **RC** 10.00
132 John Hattig Jr. **RC** 10.00
133 Jorge Campillo **RC** 8.00
134 Juan Morillo **RC** 8.00
135 Justin Verlander **RC** 160.00
136 Ryan Garko **RC** 40.00
137 Kendry Morales **RC** 50.00
138 Luis Hernandez **RC** 10.00
140 Luis Rodriguez **RC** 10.00
141 Mark Woodyard **RC** 10.00
142 Matt Smith **RC** 8.00
143 Matt Lindstrom **RC** 10.00
144 Miguel Negron **RC** 15.00
145 Mike Morse **RC** 20.00
146 Nate McLouth **RC** 20.00
147 Nelson Cruz **RC** 25.00
148 Nick Masset **RC** 8.00
150 Paulino Reynoso **RC** 10.00
151 Pedro Lopez **RC** 15.00
152 Philip Humber **RC** 20.00
153 Prince Fielder 250.00
154 Randy Messenger **RC** 8.00
156 Raul Tablado **RC** 10.00
157 Ronny Paulino **RC** 15.00
158 Russel Rohlicek **RC** 10.00
159 Russell Martin **RC** 125.00
160 Scott Baker **RC** 20.00
161 Scott Munter **RC** 10.00
162 Sean Thompson **RC** 10.00
163 Sean Tracey **RC** 10.00
164 Shane Costa **RC** 10.00
165 Stephen Drew **RC** 75.00
166 Tony Giarratano **RC** 15.00
167 Tony Pena **RC** 8.00
168 Travis Bowyer **RC** 10.00
169 Ubaldo Jimenez **RC** 15.00
170 Wladimir Balentien **RC** 75.00
171 Yorman Bazardo **RC** 10.00
173 Ryan Zimmerman **RC** 120.00
174 Chris Denorfia **RC** 15.00
176 Jermaine Van Buren **RC** 10.00
177 Mark McLemore **RC** 8.00
179 Ryan Speier **RC** 10.00
Common Sweet Spot RC (91-174): .75
91 Adam Shabala **RC** .75
92 Ambiorix Burgos **RC** .75
93 Ambiorix Concepcion **RC** 1.00
94 Anibal Sanchez **RC** 2.00
95 Bill McCarthy **RC** .75
96 Brandon McCarthy **RC** 2.00
97 Brian Burres **RC** .75
98 Carlos Ruiz **RC** 1.00
99 Casey Rogowski **RC** 1.00
100 Chad Orvella **RC** .75
101 Chris Resop **RC** 1.00
102 Chris Roberson **RC** 1.00
103 Chris Seddon **RC** .75
104 Colter Bean **RC** 1.00
105 Dae-Sung Koo **RC** .75
106 Ryan Zimmerman **RC** 6.00
107 David Gassner **RC** .75
108 Brian Anderson 1.50
109 D.J. Houlton **RC** 1.00
110 Derek Wathan **RC** .75
111 Devon Lowery **RC** .75
112 Enrique Gonzalez **RC** .75
113 Chris Denorfia **RC** 1.00
114 Eude Brito **RC** .75
115 Francisco Butto **RC** 1.00
116 Franquelis Osoria **RC** 1.00
117 Garrett Jones **RC** .75
118 Geovany Soto **RC** 1.00
119 Hayden Penn **RC** 1.00
120 Ismael Ramirez **RC** .75
121 Jared Gothreaux **RC** .75
122 Jason Hammel **RC** .75
123 Dana Eveland **RC** 1.50
124 Jeff Miller **RC** .75
125 Jermaine Van Buren **RC** 1.00
126 Joel Peralta **RC** .75
127 John Hattig Jr. **RC** 1.00
128 Jorge Campillo **RC** .75
129 Juan Morillo **RC** .75
130 Ryan Garko **RC** 2.00
131 Keiichi Yabu **RC** 1.00
132 Kendry Morales **RC** 2.00
133 Luis Hernandez **RC** .75
134 Mark McLemore **RC** 1.00
135 Luis Pena **RC** .75
136 Luis Rodriguez **RC** .75
137 Luke Scott **RC** 1.50
138 Marcos Carvajal **RC** 1.00
139 Mark Woodyard **RC** 1.00
140 Matt Smith **RC** .75
141 Matt Lindstrom **RC** 1.00
142 Miguel Negron **RC** 1.00
143 Mike Morse **RC** 1.00
144 Nate McLouth **RC** 1.00
145 Nelson Cruz **RC** 1.50
146 Nick Masset **RC** .75
147 Ryan Spilborghs **RC** 1.00
148 Oscar Robles **RC** .75
149 Paulino Reynoso **RC** .75
150 Pedro Lopez **RC** 1.00
151 Peter Orr **RC** .75
152 Prince Fielder 8.00
153 Randy Messenger **RC** .75
154 Randy Williams **RC** 1.00
155 Raul Tablado **RC** .75
156 Ronny Paulino **RC** 1.50
157 Russel Rohlicek **RC** .75
158 Russell Martin **RC** 2.50
159 Scott Baker **RC** 1.50
160 Scott Munter **RC** .75
161 Sean Thompson **RC** 1.00
162 Sean Tracey **RC** 1.00
163 Shane Costa **RC** 1.00
164 Stephen Drew **RC** 4.00
165 Steve Schmoll **RC** .75
166 Ryan Speier **RC** 1.00
167 Tadahito Iguchi **RC** 2.00
168 Tony Giarratano **RC** 1.00
169 Tony Pena **RC** .75
170 Travis Bowyer **RC** .75
171 Ubaldo Jimenez **RC** 1.00
172 Wladimir Balentien **RC** 1.50
173 Yorman Bazardo **RC** .75
174 Yuniesky Betancourt **RC** 1.50
Common Ultimate Signature Ed.(111-193): 8.00
Production 125
111 Adam Shabala **RC** 10.00
112 Anibal Sanchez **RC** 25.00
114 Brandon McCarthy **RC** 25.00
115 Brian Burres **RC** 10.00
116 Carlos Ruiz **RC** 15.00
117 Casey Rogowski **RC** 10.00
118 Chad Orvella **RC** 10.00
119 Chris Resop **RC** 12.00
120 Chris Roberson **RC** 12.00
121 Chris Seddon **RC** 12.00
122 Colter Bean **RC** 15.00
124 David Gassner **RC** 10.00
125 Brian Anderson 15.00
128 Devon Lowery **RC** 10.00
129 Enrique Gonzalez **RC** 15.00
130 Eude Brito **RC** 8.00
131 Francisco Butto **RC** 10.00
132 Franquelis Osoria **RC** 10.00
133 Garrett Jones **RC** 10.00
134 Geovany Soto **RC** 30.00
135 Hayden Penn **RC** 15.00
136 Ismael Ramirez **RC** 8.00
137 Jared Gothreaux **RC** 10.00
138 Jason Hammel **RC** 10.00
139 Jeff Miller **RC** 10.00
140 Jeff Niemann **RC** 30.00
141 Joel Peralta **RC** 10.00
142 John Hattig Jr. **RC** 15.00
143 Jorge Campillo **RC** 10.00
144 Juan Morillo **RC** 10.00
145 Justin Verlander **RC** 125.00
146 Ryan Garko **RC** 40.00
147 Keiichi Yabu **RC** 15.00
148 Kendry Morales **RC** 20.00
149 Luis Hernandez **RC** 10.00
151 Luis Rodriguez **RC** 10.00
152 Luke Scott **RC** 30.00
153 Marcos Carvajal **RC** 10.00
154 Mark Woodyard **RC** 10.00
155 Matt Smith **RC** 10.00
156 Matt Lindstrom **RC** 10.00
157 Miguel Negron **RC** 15.00
158 Mike Morse **RC** 15.00
159 Nate McLouth **RC** 20.00
160 Nelson Cruz **RC** 20.00
161 Nick Masset **RC** 8.00
162 Mark McLemore **RC** 10.00
164 Paulino Reynoso **RC** 10.00
165 Pedro Lopez **RC** 10.00
166 Peter Orr **RC** 10.00
167 Philip Humber **RC** 20.00
168 Prince Fielder 200.00
169 Randy Messenger **RC** 10.00
171 Raul Tablado **RC** 10.00
172 Ronny Paulino **RC** 15.00
173 Russel Rohlicek **RC** 8.00
174 Russell Martin **RC** 75.00
175 Scott Baker **RC** 20.00
176 Scott Munter **RC** 10.00
177 Sean Thompson **RC** 10.00
178 Sean Tracey **RC** 10.00
179 Shane Costa **RC** 10.00
180 Stephen Drew **RC** 60.00
181 Steve Schmoll **RC** 10.00
182 Tadahito Iguchi **RC** 50.00
183 Tony Giarratano **RC** 10.00
184 Tony Pena **RC** 10.00
185 Travis Bowyer **RC** 10.00
186 Ubaldo Jimenez **RC** 15.00
187 Wladimir Balentien **RC** 50.00
188 Yorman Bazardo **RC** 10.00
190 Ryan Zimmerman **RC** 100.00
191 Chris Denorfia **RC** 10.00
192 Ryan Speier **RC** 10.00
193 Jermaine Van Buren **RC** 10.00

Silver

Silver (101-177): 1X
Production 450
Silver (178-186): No Pricing
Production 25 Sets

Gold

Gold (101-177): 1-1.5X
Production 150
Gold (178-186): No Pricing
Production 10 Sets

Platinum

Platinum (101-177): No Pricing
Production 25
Platinum (178-186): No Pricing
Production One Set

Artifacts Blue

Blue (201-285): 1-1.5X
Production 100

Artifacts Gold

Gold (201-285): No Pricing
Production 25 Sets

Artifacts Red

Red (201-285): 1-2X
Production 50

Artifacts Platinum

No Pricing
Production One Set

Draft Generations Triple Signatures

No Pricing
Production 10 Sets

Link to Future Dual Autographs

NM/M
Common Duo: 15.00
Production 35 Sets
BR Wladimir Balentien, Jeremy Reed 20.00
BW Dontrelle Willis, Yorman Bazardo 40.00
CD David DeJesus, Shane Costa 15.00
DD J.D. Drew, Stephen Drew 125.00
DJ Stephen Drew, Derek Jeter 275.00
FO Prince Fielder, Lyle Overbay 75.00
FT Prince Fielder, Mark Teixeira 100.00
FW Prince Fielder, Rickie Weeks 100.00
GO Roy Oswalt, Jared Gothreaux 25.00
HF Luis Hernandez, Rafael Furcal 20.00
HG Tom Glavine, Philip Humber 50.00
MB Jason Bay, Nate McLouth 30.00
MK Casey Kotchman, Kendry Morales 40.00
NK Scott Kazmir, Jeff Niemann 40.00
NW Vernon Wells, Miguel Negron 25.00
OB Yhency Brazoban, Franquelis Osoria 20.00
OG Peter Orr, Marcus Giles 25.00
PV Javier Vazquez, Tony Pena 15.00
RH Roy Halladay, Ismael Ramirez 30.00
SK Chris Seddon, Scott Kazmir 30.00
SL Jason Lane, Luke Scott 40.00
VB Justin Verlander, Jeremy Bonderman 100.00
VC Roger Clemens, Justin Verlander 175.00
ZC Ryan Zimmerman, Chad Cordero 100.00

Link to the Past Dual Autographs

NM/M
Common Duo: 20.00
Production 25 Sets
BC Steve Carlton, Eude Brito 30.00
BM Juan Marichal, Brian Burres 30.00
CS Darryl Strawberry, Ambiorix Concepcion 25.00
GT Alan Trammell, Tony Giarratano 30.00
HG Dwight Gooden, Philip Humber 40.00
HS Philip Humber, Tom Seaver 50.00
IA Luis Aparicio, Tadahito Iguchi 125.00
IC Tadahito Iguchi, Rod Carew 125.00
JH Kent Hrbek, Garrett Jones 40.00
JJ Jack Morris, Justin Verlander 75.00
MC Rod Carew, Kendry Morales 40.00
MJ Kendry Morales, Wally Joyner 40.00
MV Andy Van Slyke, Nate McLouth 40.00
NB Miguel Negron, George Bell 40.00
NR Nolan Ryan, Jeff Niemann 150.00
PP Jim Palmer, Hayden Penn 40.00
RD Lenny Dykstra, Chris Roberson 30.00
TP Gaylord Perry, Sean Thompson 20.00
VM Justin Verlander, Denny McLain 75.00

Origins Blue

Blue (201-286): 2-4X
Production 50 Sets

Origins Gold

Gold (201-286): No Pricing
Production 20 Sets

Origins Black

No Pricing
Production One Set

Origins Red

Red (201-286): 2-3X
Production 99 Sets

Origins Old Judge

Old Judge (201-286): 1X
Inserted 1:2
Blue: 2-3X
Production 50 Sets
Red: 1-2X
Production 99 Sets
Gold: No Pricing
Production 20 Sets
Black: No Pricing
Production One Set

Quad Signatures

No Pricing
Production Five Sets

Reflections Blue

Blue (201-286): 2-4X
Production 75 Sets

Reflections Emerald

Emerald (201-286): 3-6X
Production 25 Sets

Reflections Purple

Purple (201-286): 1.5-3X
Production 99 Sets

Reflections Platinum

No Pricing
Production One Set

Reflections Red

Red (201-286): 1.5-3X
Production 99 Sets

Reflections Turquoise

Turquoise (201-286): 2-4X
Production 50 Sets

SP Authentic Gold

Gold (101-186): No Pricing
Production 10

SPx Silver

Silver (101-179): No Pricing
Production 10

Sweet Spot Gold

Gold (91-174): 1.5-2X
Production 399

Sweet Spot Platinum

Platinum (91-174): 2-3X
Production 99

Sweet Spot Plutonium

No Pricing
Production One Set

Ultimate Signature Ed. Platinum

No Pricing
Production One Set

2006 Upper Deck

NM/M
Complete Series 1 (500): 150.00
Complete Series 2 (500): 100.00
Complete Update (250):
Common Player: .15
Common Update SP: 4.00
Inserted 1:2 Update
Series 1 Pack (8): 3.50
Series 1 Box (24): 70.00
Series 2 Pack (6): 3.50

Series 2 Box (24): 75.00
Update Pack (8): 3.00
Update Box (24): 60.00
1 Adam Kennedy .15
2 Bartolo Colon .25
3 Bengie Molina .15
4 Casey Kotchman .15
5 Chone Figgins .15
6 Dallas McPherson .15
7 Darin Erstad .25
8 Ervin Santana .25
9 Francisco Rodriguez .15
10 Garret Anderson .25
11 Jarrod Washburn .15
12 John Lackey .15
13 Juan Rivera .15
14 Orlando Cabrera .15
15 Paul Byrd .15
16 Steve Finley .15
17 Vladimir Guerrero .75
18 Alex Cintron .15
19 Brandon Lyon .15
20 Brandon Webb .15
21 Chad Tracy .15
22 Chris Snyder .15
23 Claudio Vargas .15
24 Conor Jackson **(RC)** .15
25 Craig Counsell .15
26 Javier Vazquez .15
27 Jose Valverde .15
28 Luis Gonzalez .15
29 Royce Clayton .15
30 Russ Ortiz .15
31 Shawn Green .15
32 Dustin Nippert **(RC)** .15
33 Tony Clark .15
34 Troy Glaus .25
35 Adam LaRoche .15
36 Andruw Jones .50
37 Craig Hansen **RC** 3.00
38 Chipper Jones .75
39 Horacio Ramirez .15
40 Jeff Francoeur .25
41 John Smoltz .25
42 Joey Devine **RC** .50
43 Johnny Estrada .15
44 Anthony Lerew **(RC)** .15
45 Julio Franco .15
46 Kyle Farnsworth .15
47 Marcus Giles .15
48 Mike Hampton .15
49 Rafael Furcal .25
50 Chuck James **(RC)** .25
51 Tim Hudson .40
52 B.J. Ryan .15
53 Bernie Castro .15
54 Brian Roberts .25
55 Walter Young .15
56 Daniel Cabrera .15
57 Eric Byrnes .15
58 Alejandro Freire **RC** .50
59 Erik Bedard .15
60 Javy Lopez .25
61 Jay Gibbons .15
62 Jorge Julio .15
63 Luis Matos .15
64 Melvin Mora .15
65 Miguel Tejada .40
66 Rafael Palmeiro .25
67 Rodrigo Lopez .15
68 Sammy Sosa .75
69 Alejandro Machado .15
70 Bill Mueller .15
71 Bronson Arroyo .15
72 Curt Schilling .75
73 David Ortiz .75
74 David Wells .15
75 Edgar Renteria .25
76 Ryan Jorgensen **RC** .25
77 Jason Varitek .50
78 Johnny Damon .75
79 Keith Foulke .15
80 Kevin Youkilis .15
81 Manny Ramirez .75
82 Matt Clement .15
83 Hanley Ramirez **(RC)** .50
84 Tim Wakefield .15
85 Trot Nixon .15
86 Wade Miller .15
87 Aramis Ramirez .40
88 Carlos Zambrano .25
89 Corey Patterson .15
90 Derrek Lee .50
91 Geovany Soto **(RC)** .15
92 Greg Maddux 1.00
93 Jeromy Burnitz .15
94 Jerry Hairston .15
95 Kerry Wood .25
96 Mark Prior .50
97 Matt Murton .15
98 Michael Barrett .15
99 Neifi Perez .15
100 Nomar Garciaparra .50
101 Rich Hill .15
102 Ryan Dempster .15
103 Todd Walker .15
104 A.J. Pierzynski .15
105 Aaron Rowand .15
106 Bobby Jenks .15
107 Carl Everett .15
108 Dustin Hermanson .15
109 Frank Thomas .40
110 Freddy Garcia .15
111 Jermaine Dye .15
112 Joe Crede .15
113 Jon Garland .15
114 Jose Contreras .25
115 Juan Uribe .15
116 Mark Buehrle .25
117 Orlando Hernandez .15
118 Paul Konerko .40
119 Scott Podsednik .15
120 Tadahito Iguchi .25
121 Aaron Harang .15
122 Adam Dunn .50
123 Austin Kearns .25
124 Brandon Claussen .15
125 Chris Denorfia **(RC)** .15
126 Edwin Encarnacion .15
127 Miguel Perez **(RC)** .15
128 Felipe Lopez .15
129 Jason LaRue .15
130 Ken Griffey Jr. 1.50
131 Chris Booker .15
132 Luke Hudson .15
133 Jason Bergmann **RC** .50
134 Ryan Freel .15
135 Sean Casey .15
136 Wily Mo Pena .15
137 Aaron Boone .15
138 Ben Broussard .15
139 Ryan Garko **(RC)** .15
140 C.C. Sabathia .15
141 Casey Blake .15
142 Cliff Lee .15
143 Coco Crisp .15
144 David Riske .15
145 Grady Sizemore .40
146 Jake Westbrook .15
147 Jhonny Peralta .25
148 Josh Bard .15
149 Kevin Millwood .25
150 Ronnie Belliard .15
151 Scott Elarton .15
152 Travis Hafner .40
153 Victor Martinez .25
154 Aaron Cook .15
155 Aaron Miles .15
156 Brad Hawpe .15
157 Mike Esposito .15
158 Chin-Hui Tsao .15
159 Clint Barmes .15
160 Cory Sullivan .15
161 Garrett Atkins .15
162 J.D. Closser .15
163 Jason Jennings .15
164 Jeff Baker .15
165 Jeff Francis .15
166 Luis Gonzalez .15
167 Matt Holliday .50
168 Todd Helton .50
169 Brandon Inge .15
170 Carlos Guillen .25
171 Carlos Pena .15
172 Chris Shelton .15
173 Craig Monroe .15
174 Curtis Granderson .15
175 Dmitri Young .15
176 Ivan Rodriguez .40
177 Jason Johnson .15
178 Jeremy Bonderman .15
179 Magglio Ordonez .15
180 Mark Woodyard **(RC)** .15
181 Nook Logan .15
182 Omar Infante .15
183 Placido Polanco .15
184 Chris Heintz **RC** .50
185 A.J. Burnett .15
186 Alex Gonzalez .15
187 Josh Johnson **(RC)** .15
188 Carlos Delgado .40
189 Dontrelle Willis .25
190 Josh Wilson **(RC)** .15
191 Jason Vargas .15
192 Jeff Conine .15
193 Jeremy Hermida **(RC)** .15
194 Josh Beckett .25
195 Juan Encarnacion .15
196 Juan Pierre .15
197 Luis Castillo .15
198 Miguel Cabrera .75
199 Mike Lowell .15
200 Paul LoDuca .15
201 Todd Jones .15
202 Adam Everett .15
203 Andy Pettitte .40
204 Brad Ausmus .15
205 Brad Lidge .15
206 Brandon Backe .15
207 Charlton Jimerson .15
208 Chris Burke .15
209 Craig Biggio .25
210 Daniel Wheeler .15
211 Jason Lane .15
212 Jeff Bagwell .50
213 Lance Berkman .40
214 Luke Scott .15
215 Morgan Ensberg .25
216 Roger Clemens 2.00
217 Roy Oswalt .25
218 Willy Taveras .15
219 Andres Blanco .15
220 Angel Berroa .15
221 Ruben Gotay .15
222 David DeJesus .15
223 Emil Brown .15
224 J.P. Howell .15
225 Jeremy Affeldt .15
226 Jimmy Gobble .15
227 John Buck .15
228 Jose Lima .15
229 Mark Teahen .15
230 Matt Stairs .15
231 Mike MacDougal .15
232 Mike Sweeney .15
233 Runelvys Hernandez .15
234 Terrence Long .15
235 Zack Greinke .15
236 Ron Flores **RC** .50
237 Brad Penny .15
238 Cesar Izturis .15
239 D.J. Houlton .15
240 Derek Lowe .15
241 Eric Gagne .25
242 Hee Seop Choi .15
243 J.D. Drew .25
244 Jason Phillips .15
245 Jason Repko .15
246 Jayson Werth .15
247 Jeff Kent .25
248 Jeff Weaver .15
249 Milton Bradley .15
250 Odalis Perez .15
251 Hong-Chih Kuo .15
252 Oscar Robles .15
253 Ben Sheets .25
254 Bill Hall .15
255 Brady Clark .15
256 Carlos Lee .25
257 Chris Capuano .15
258 Nelson Cruz **(RC)** .15
259 Derrick Turnbow .15
260 Doug Davis .15
261 Geoff Jenkins .15
262 J.J. Hardy .15
263 Lyle Overbay .15
264 Prince Fielder **(RC)** .75
265 Rickie Weeks .25
266 Russell Branyan .15
267 Tomokazu Ohka .15
268 Jonah Bayliss **RC** .75
269 Brad Radke .15
270 Carlos Silva .15
271 Francisco Liriano **(RC)** .50
272 Jacque Jones .15
273 Joe Mauer .25
274 Travis Bower .15
275 Joe Nathan .15
276 Johan Santana .50
277 Justin Morneau .15
278 Kyle Lohse .15
279 Lew Ford .15
280 Matthew LeCroy .15
281 Michael Cuddyer .15
282 Nick Punto .15
283 Scott Baker .15
284 Shannon Stewart .15
285 Torii Hunter .25
286 Braden Looper .15
287 Carlos Beltran .50
288 Cliff Floyd .15
289 David Wright .75
290 Doug Mientkiewicz .15
291 Anderson Hernandez **(RC)** .15
292 Jose Reyes .50
293 Kazuo Matsui .15
294 Kris Benson .15
295 Miguel Cairo .15
296 Mike Cameron .15
297 Robert Andino **RC** .50
298 Mike Piazza .75
299 Pedro Martinez .75
300 Tom Glavine .25
301 Victor Diaz .15
302 Tim Hamulack .15
303 Alex Rodriguez 2.00
304 Bernie Williams .25
305 Carl Pavano .15
306 Chien-Ming Wang .40
307 Derek Jeter 2.00
308 Gary Sheffield .40
309 Hideki Matsui 1.00
310 Jason Giambi .40
311 Jorge Posada .25
312 Kevin Brown .15
313 Mariano Rivera .25
314 Matt Lawton .15
315 Mike Mussina .25
316 Randy Johnson .75
317 Robinson Cano .25
318 Michael Vento .15
319 Tino Martinez .25
320 Tony Womack .15
321 Barry Zito .25
322 Bobby Crosby .15
323 Bobby Kielty .15
324 Dan Johnson .15
325 Danny Haren .15
326 Eric Chavez .25
327 Erubiel Durazo .15
328 Huston Street .25
329 Jason Kendall .15
330 Jay Payton .15
331 Joe Blanton .15
332 Joe Kennedy .15
333 Kirk Saarloos .15
334 Mark Kotsay .15
335 Nick Swisher .15
336 Rich Harden .25
337 Scott Hatteberg .15
338 Billy Wagner .25
339 Bobby Abreu .50
340 Brett Myers .15
341 Chase Utley .40
342 Danny Sandoval **RC** .50
343 David Bell .15
344 Gavin Floyd .15
345 Jim Thome .50
346 Jimmy Rollins .40
347 Jon Lieber .15
348 Kenny Lofton .15
349 Mike Lieberthal .15
350 Pat Burrell .25
351 Randy Wolf .15
352 Ryan Howard .75
353 Vicente Padilla .15
354 Bryan Bullington .15
355 J.J. Furmaniak **(RC)** .15
356 Craig Wilson .15
357 Matt Capps **(RC)** .15
358 Tom Gorzelanny **(RC)** .15
359 Jack Wilson .15
360 Jason Bay .25
361 Jose Mesa .15
362 Josh Fogg .15
363 Kip Wells .15
364 Steve Stemle **RC** .50
365 Oliver Perez .15
366 Robert Mackowiak .15
367 Ronny Paulino **(RC)** .15
368 Tike Redman .15
369 Zachary Duke .15
370 Adam Eaton .15
371 Scott Feldman **RC** .50
372 Brian Giles .25
373 Brian Lawrence .15
374 Damian Jackson .15
375 Dave Roberts .15
376 Jake Peavy .25
377 Joe Randa .15
378 Khalil Greene .15
379 Mark Loretta .25
380 Ramon Hernandez .15
381 Robert Fick .15
382 Ryan Klesko .15
383 Trevor Hoffman .15
384 Woody Williams .15
385 Xavier Nady .15
386 Armando Benitez .15
387 Brad Hennessey .15
388 Brian Myrow **RC** .50
389 Edgardo Alfonzo .15
390 J.T. Snow .15
391 Jeremy Accardo **RC** .15
392 Jason Schmidt .25
393 Lance Niekro .15
394 Matt Cain **(RC)** .25
395 Daniel Ortmeier **(RC)** .15
396 Moises Alou .25
397 Doug Clark .15
398 Omar Vizquel .15
399 Pedro Feliz .15
400 Randy Winn .15
401 Ray Durham .15
402 Adrian Beltre .15
403 Eddie Guardado .15
404 Felix Hernandez .50
405 Gil Meche .15
406 Ichiro Suzuki 1.50
407 Jamie Moyer .15
408 Jeff Nelson .15
409 Jeremy Reed .15
410 Joel Pineiro .15
411 Jaime Bubela **(RC)** .15
412 Raul Ibanez .15
413 Richie Sexson .40
414 Ryan Franklin .15
415 Willie Bloomquist .15
416 Yorvit Torrealba .15
417 Yuniesky Betancourt .15
418 Jeff Harris **RC** .25
419 Albert Pujols 2.00
420 Chris Carpenter .25
421 David Eckstein .15
422 Jason Isringhausen .15
423 Jason Marquis .15
424 Adam Wainwright **(RC)** .15
425 Jim Edmonds .25
426 Ryan Theriot **(RC)** 1.00
427 Chris Duncan .15
428 Mark Grudzielanek .15
429 Mark Mulder .25
430 Matt Morris .25
431 Reggie Sanders .15
432 Scott Rolen .50
433 Tyler Johnson **(RC)** .15
434 Yadier Molina .15
435 Alex Gonzalez .15
436 Aubrey Huff .15
437 Tim Corcoran **RC** .40
438 Carl Crawford .25
439 Casey Fossum .15
440 Danys Baez .15
441 Edwin Jackson .15
442 Joey Gathright .15
443 Jonny Gomes .25
444 Jorge Cantu .15
445 Julio Lugo .15
446 Nick Green .15
447 Rocco Baldelli .15
448 Scott Kazmir .15
449 Seth McClung .15
450 Toby Hall .15
451 Travis Lee .15
452 Craig Breslow **RC** .25
453 Alfonso Soriano .50
454 Chris Young .15
455 David Dellucci .15
456 Francisco Cordero .15
457 Gary Matthews .15
458 Hank Blalock .25
459 Juan Dominguez .15
460 Josh Rupe .15
461 Kenny Rogers .15
462 Kevin Mench .15
463 Laynce Nix .15
464 Mark Teixeira .50
465 Michael Young .25
466 Richard Hidalgo .15
467 Jason Botts **(RC)** .15
468 Aaron Hill .15
469 Alex Rios .15
470 Corey Koskie .15
471 Chris Demaria **RC** .50
472 Eric Hinske .15
473 Frank Catalanotto .15
474 John-Ford Griffin **(RC)** .15
475 Gustavo Chacin .15
476 Josh Towers .15
477 Miguel Batista .15
478 Orlando Hudson .15
479 Reed Johnson .15
480 Roy Halladay .40
481 Shaun Marcum **(RC)** .15
482 Shea Hillenbrand .15
483 Ted Lilly .15
484 Vernon Wells .25
485 Brad Wilkerson .15
486 Darrell Rasner **(RC)** .15
487 Chad Cordero .15
488 Cristian Guzman .15
489 Esteban Loaiza .15
490 John Patterson .15
491 Jose Guillen .15
492 Jose Vidro .15
493 Livan Hernandez .15
494 Marlon Byrd .15
495 Nick Johnson .15
496 Preston Wilson .15
497 Ryan Church .15
498 Ryan Zimmerman **(RC)** .50
499 Tony Armas .15
500 Vinny Castilla .15
501 Andy Green .15
502 Damion Easley .15
503 Eric Byrnes .15
504 Jason Grimsley .15
505 Jeff DaVanon .15
506 Johnny Estrada .15
507 Luis Vizcaino .15
508 Miguel Batista .15
509 Orlando Hernandez .15
510 Orlando Hudson .15
511 Terry Mulholland .15
512 Chris Reitsma .15
513 Edgar Renteria .25
514 John Thomson .15
515 Jorge Sosa .15
516 Oscar Villarreal .15
517 Peter Orr .15
518 Ryan Langerhans .15
519 Todd Pratt .15
520 Wilson Betemit .15
521 Brian Jordan .15
522 Lance Cormier .15
523 Matt Diaz .15
524 Mike Remlinger .15
525 Bruce Chen .15
526 Chris Gomez .15
527 Chris Ray .15
528 Corey Patterson .15
529 David Newhan .15
530 Ed Rogers **(RC)** .25
531 John Halama .15
532 Kris Benson .15
533 LaTroy Hawkins .15
534 Raul Chavez .15
535 Alex Cora .15
536 Alex Gonzalez .15
537 Coco Crisp .15
538 David Riske .15
539 Doug Mirabelli .15
540 Josh Beckett .25
541 J.T. Snow .15
542 Mike Timlin .15
543 Julian Tavarez .15
544 Rudy Seanez .15
545 Wily Mo Pena .15
546 Bob Howry .15
547 Glendon Rusch .15
548 Henry Blanco .15
549 Jacque Jones .15
550 Jerome Williams .15
551 John Mabry .15
552 Juan Pierre .25
553 Scott Eyre .15
554 Scott Williamson .15
555 Wade Miller .15
556 Will Ohman .15
557 Alex Cintron .15
558 Robert Mackowiak .15
559 Brandon McCarthy .15
560 Chris Widger .15
561 Cliff Politte .15
562 Javier Vazquez .15
563 Jim Thome .75
564 Matt Thornton .15
565 Neal Cotts .15
566 Pablo Ozuna .15
567 Ross Gload .15
568 Brandon Phillips .15
569 Bronson Arroyo .15
570 Dave Williams .15
571 David Ross .15
572 David Weathers .15
573 Eric Milton .15
574 Javier Valentin .15
575 Kent Mercker .15
576 Matt Belisle .15
577 Paul Wilson .15
578 Rich Aurilia .15
579 Rick White .15
580 Scott Hatteberg .15
581 Todd Coffey .15
582 Bob Wickman .15
583 Danny Graves .15
584 Eduardo Perez .15
585 Guillermo Mota .15
586 Jason Davis .15
587 Jason Johnson .15
588 Jason Michaels .15
589 Rafael Betancourt .15
590 Ramon Vazquez .15
591 Scott Sauerbeck .15
592 Todd Hollandsworth .15
593 Brian Fuentes .15
594 Danny Ardoin .15
595 David Cortes .15
596 Eli Marrero .15
597 Jamey Carroll .15
598 Jason Smith .15
599 Josh Fogg .15
600 Miguel Ojeda .15
601 Mike DeJean .15
602 Ray King .15
603 Omar Quintanilla **(RC)** .25
604 Zach Day .15
605 Fernando Rodney .15
606 Kenny Rogers .15
607 Mike Maroth .15
608 Nate Robertson .15
609 Todd Jones .15
610 Vance Wilson .15
611 Bobby Seay .15
612 Chris Spurling .15
613 Raul Colon .15
614 Jason Grilli .15
615 Marcus Thames .15
616 Ramon Santiago .15
617 Alfredo Amezaga .15
618 Brian Moehler .15
619 Chris Aguila .15
620 Franklyn German .15
621 Joe Borowski .15
622 Logan Kensing **(RC)** .25
623 Matt Treanor .15
624 Miguel Olivo .15
625 Sergio Mitre .15
626 Todd Wellemeyer .15
627 Wes Helms .15
628 Chad Qualls .15
629 Eric Bruntlett .15
630 Mike Gallo .15
631 Mike Lamb .15
632 Orlando Palmeiro .15
633 Russ Springer .15
634 Dan Wheeler .15
635 Eric Munson .15
.15
637 Trever Miller .15
638 Ambiorix Burgos .15
639 Andrew Sisco .15
640 Denny Bautista .15
641 Doug Mientkiewicz .15
642 Elmer Dessens .15
643 Esteban German .15
644 Joe Nelson **(RC)** .25
645 Mark Grudzielanek .15
646 Mark Redman .15
647 Mike Wood .15
648 Paul Bako .15
649 Reggie Sanders .15
650 Scott Elarton .15
651 Shane Costa .15
652 Tony Graffanino .15
653 Jason Bulger **(RC)** .25
654 Chris Bootcheck **(RC)** .25
655 Esteban Yan .15
656 Hector Carrasco .15
657 J.C. Romero .15
658 Jeff Weaver .15
659 Jose Molina .15
660 Kelvim Escobar .15
661 Maicer Izturis .15
662 Robb Quinlan .15
663 Scot Shields .15
664 Tim Salmon .15
665 Bill Mueller .15
666 Brett Tomko .15
667 Dioner Navarro .15
668 Jae Weong Seo .15
669 Jose Cruz .15
670 Kenny Lofton .15
671 Lance Carter .15
672 Nomar Garciaparra .75
673 Olmedo Saenz .15
674 Rafael Furcal .15
675 Ramon Martinez .15
676 Ricky Ledee .15
677 Sandy Alomar .15
678 Yhency Brazoban .15
679 Corey Koskie .15
680 Dan Kolb .15
681 Gabe Gross .15
682 Jeff Cirillo .15
683 Matt Wise .15
684 Rick Helling .15
685 Chad Moeller .15
686 David Bush .15
687 Jorge De La Rosa .15
688 Justin Lehr .15
689 Jason Bartlett .15
690 Jesse Crain .15
691 Juan Rincon .15
692 Luis Castillo .15
693 Mike Redmond .15
694 Rondell White .15
695 Tony Batista .15
696 Juan Castro .15
697 Luis Rodriguez .15
698 Matt Guerrier .15
699 Willie Eyre **(RC)** .25
700 Aaron Heilman .15
701 Billy Wagner .25

702 Carlos Delgado .50
703 Chad Bradford .15
704 Chris Woodward .15
705 Darren Oliver .15
706 Duaner Sanchez .15
707 Endy Chavez .15
708 Jorge Julio .15
709 Jose Valentin .15
710 Julio Franco .15
711 Paul LoDuca .15
712 Ramon Castro .15
713 Steve Trachsel .15
714 Victor Zambrano .15
715 Xavier Nady .15
716 Andy Phillips .15
717 Bubba Crosby .15
718 Jaret Wright .15
719 Kelly Stinnett .15
720 Kyle Farnsworth .15
721 Mike Meyers .15
722 Octavio Dotel .15
723 Ron Villone .15
724 Scott Proctor .15
725 Shawn Chacon .15
726 Tanyon Sturtze .15
727 Adam Melhuse .15
728 Brad Halsey .15
729 Esteban Loaiza .15
730 Frank Thomas .50
731 Jay Witasick .15
732 Justin Duchscherer .15
733 Kiko Calero .15
734 Marco Scutaro .15
735 Mark Ellis .15
736 Milton Bradley .15
737 Aaron Fultz .15
738 Aaron Rowand .15
739 Geoff Geary .15
740 Arthur Rhodes .15
741 Chris Coste **RC** .40
742 Rheal Cormier .15
743 Ryan Franklin .15
744 Ryan Madson .15
745 Sal Fasano .15
746 Tom Gordon .15
747 Abraham Nunez .15
748 David Dellucci .15
749 Julio Santana .15
750 Shane Victorino .15
751 Damaso Marte .15
752 Freddy Sanchez .15
753 Humberto Cota .15
754 Jeromy Burnitz .15
755 Joe Randa .15
756 Jose Castillo .15
757 Mike Gonzalez .15
758 Ryan Doumit .15
759 Sean Burnett .15
760 Sean Casey .15
761 Ian Snell .15
762 John Grabow .15
763 Jose Hernandez .15
764 Roberto Hernandez .15
765 Ryan Vogelsong .15
766 Victor Sanchez .15
767 Adrian Gonzalez .15
768 Alan Embree .15
769 Brian Sweeney **(RC)** .25
770 Chan Ho Park .15
771 Clay Hensley .15
772 Dewon Brazelton .15
773 Doug Brocail .15
774 Eric Young .15
775 Geoff Blum .15
776 Josh Bard .15
777 Mark Bellhorn .15
778 Mike Cameron .15
779 Mike Piazza .75
780 Rob Bowen .15
781 Scott Cassidy .15
782 Scott Linebrink .15
783 Shawn Estes .15
784 Terrmel Sledge .15
785 Vinny Castilla .15
786 Jeff Fassero .15
787 Jose Vizcaino .15
788 Mark Sweeney .15
789 Matt Morris .15
790 Steve Finley .15
791 Tim Worrell .15
792 Jamey Wright .15
793 Jason Ellison .15
794 Noah Lowry .15
795 Steve Kline .15
796 Todd Greene .15
797 Carl Everett .15
798 George Sherrill .15
799 J.J. Putz .15
800 Jake Woods .15
801 Jose Lopez .15
802 Julio Mateo .15
803 Mike Morse .15
804 Rafael Soriano .15
805 Roberto Petagine .15
806 Aaron Miles .15
807 Braden Looper .15
808 Gary Bennett .15
809 Hector Luna .15
810 Jeff Suppan .15
811 John Rodriguez .15
812 Josh Hancock .15
813 Juan Encarnacion .15
814 Larry Bigbie .15
815 Scott Spiezio .15
816 Sidney Ponson .15
817 So Taguchi .15
818 Brian Meadows .15
819 Damon Hollins .15
820 Dan Miceli .15
821 Doug Waechter .15
822 Jason Childers .25
823 Josh Paul .15
824 Julio Lugo .15
825 Mark Hendrickson .15
826 Sean Burroughs .15
827 Shawn Camp .15
828 Travis Harper .15
829 Ty Wigginton .15
830 Adam Eaton .15
831 Adrian Brown .15
832 Akinori Otsuka .15
833 Antonio Alfonseca .15
834 Brad Wilkerson .15
835 D'Angelo Jimenez .15
836 Gerald Laird .15
837 Joaquin Benoit .15
838 Kameron Loe .15
839 Kevin Millwood .15
840 Mark DeRosa .15
841 Phil Nevin .15
842 Rod Barajas .15
843 Vicente Padilla .15
844 A.J. Burnett .15
845 Bengie Molina .15
846 Gregg Zaun .15
847 John McDonald .15
848 Lyle Overbay .15
849 Russ Adams .15
850 Troy Glaus .15
851 Vinnie Chulk .15
852 B.J. Ryan .15
853 Justin Speier .15
854 Pete Walker .15
855 Scott Downs .15
856 Scott Schoeneweis .15
857 Alfonso Soriano .75
858 Brian Schneider .15
859 Daryle Ward .15
860 Felix Rodriguez .15
861 Gary Majewski .15
862 Joey Eischen .15
863 Jon Rauch .15
864 Marlon Anderson .15
865 Matthew LeCroy .15
866 Mike Stanton .15
867 Ramon Ortiz .15
868 Robert Fick .15
869 Royce Clayton .15
870 Ryan Drese .15
871 Vladimir Guerrero .40
872 Craig Biggio .15
873 Barry Zito .15
874 Vernon Wells .15
875 Chipper Jones .40
876 Prince Fielder .75
877 Albert Pujols 1.00
878 Greg Maddux .75
879 Carl Crawford .15
880 Brandon Webb .15
881 J.D. Drew .15
882 Jason Schmidt .15
883 Victor Martinez .15
884 Ichiro Suzuki .75
885 Miguel Cabrera .40
886 David Wright .75
887 Alfonso Soriano .40
888 Miguel Tejada .40
889 Khalil Greene .15
890 Ryan Howard 1.00
891 Jason Bay .15
892 Mark Teixeira .25
893 Manny Ramirez .40
894 Ken Griffey Jr. .75
895 Todd Helton .25
896 Angel Berroa .15
897 Ivan Rodriguez .25
898 Johan Santana .25
899 Paul Konerko .25
900 Derek Jeter 1.00
901 Macay McBride **(RC)** .25
902 Tony Pena **(RC)** .25
903 Peter Moylan **RC** .50
904 Aaron Rakers **(RC)** .25
905 Chris Britton **RC** .50
906 Nicholas Markakis **(RC)** .50
907 Sendy Rleal **RC** .50
908 Val Majewski **(RC)** .25
909 Jermaine Van Buren **(RC)** .25
910 Jonathan Papelbon **(RC)** 4.00
911 Angel Pagan **(RC)** .50
912 David Aardsma **(RC)** .25
913 Sean Marshall **(RC)** .25
914 Brian Anderson **(RC)** .25
915 Freddie Bynum **(RC)** .25
916 Fausto Carmona **(RC)** .25
917 Kelly Stoppach **(RC)** .25
918 Choo Freeman **(RC)** .25
919 Ryan Shealy **(RC)** .25
920 Joel Zumaya **(RC)** 6.00
921 Jordan Tata **RC** 1.00
922 Justin Verlander **(RC)** 1.00
923 Carlos Martinez **RC** .50
924 Chris Resop **(RC)** .25
925 Dan Uggla **(RC)** .50
926 Eric Reed **(RC)** .25
927 Hanley Ramirez **(RC)** .75
928 Yusmeiro Petit **(RC)** .25
929 Josh Willingham **(RC)** .25
930 Mike Jacobs **(RC)** .25
931 Reggie Abercrombie **(RC)** .25
932 Ricky Nolasco **(RC)** .25
933 Scott Olsen **(RC)** .25
934 Fernando Nieve **(RC)** .25
935 Taylor Buchholz **(RC)** .25
936 Cody Ross **(RC)** .25
937 James Loney **(RC)** .25
938 Takashi Saito **RC** 2.00
939 Tim Hamulack **(RC)** .25
940 Chris Demaria **RC** .50
941 Jose Capellan **(RC)** .25
942 David Gassner **(RC)** .25
943 Jason Kubel **(RC)** .25
944 Brian Bannister **(RC)** .25
945 Mike Thompson **RC** .50
946 Cole Hamels **(RC)** 5.00
947 Paul Maholm **(RC)** .25
948 John Van Benschoten **(RC)** .25
949 Nate McLouth **(RC)** .25
950 Ben Johnson **(RC)** .25
951 Josh Barfield **(RC)** .25
952 Travis Ishikawa **(RC)** .25
953 Jack Taschner **(RC)** .25
954 Kenji Johjima **RC** 5.00
955 Skip Schumaker **(RC)** .25
956 Ruddy Lugo **(RC)** .25
957 Jason Hammel **(RC)** .25
958 Chris Roberson **(RC)** .25
959 Fabio Castro **RC** .50
960 Ian Kinsler **(RC)** .50
961 John Koronka **(RC)** .25
962 Brandon Watson **(RC)** .25
963 Jon Lester **(RC)** 5.00
964 Ben Hendrickson **(RC)** .25
965 Martin Prado **(RC)** .25
966 Erick Aybar **(RC)** .25
967 Bobby Livingston **(RC)** .25
968 Ryan Spilborghs **(RC)** .25
969 Tommy Murphy **(RC)** .25
970 Howie Kendrick **(RC)** 5.00
971 Casey Janssen **RC** 1.00
972 Michael O'Connor **RC** .50
973 Conor Jackson **(RC)** .25
974 Jeremy Hermida **(RC)** .25
975 Renyel Pinto **(RC)** .25
976 Prince Fielder **(RC)** 1.50
977 Kevin Frandsen **(RC)** .25
978 Ty Taubenheim **RC** .50
979 Rich Hill **(RC)** .25
980 Jonathan Broxton **(RC)** .25
981 Jamie Shields **RC** .50
982 Carlos Villanueva **RC** .50
983 Boone Logan **RC** 1.00
984 Brian Wilson **RC** .50
985 Andre Ethier **(RC)** 3.00
986 Michael Napoli **RC** 1.50
987 Agustin Montero **(RC)** .25
988 Jack Hannahan **RC** .50
989 Boof Bonser **(RC)** .25
990 Carlos Ruiz **(RC)** .25
991 Jason Botts **(RC)** .25
992 Kendry Morales **(RC)** .50
993 Alay Soler **RC** 3.00
994 Santiago Ramirez **(RC)** .25
995 Saul Rivera **(RC)** .25
996 Anthony Reyes **(RC)** .25
997 Matthew Kemp **(RC)** .50
998 Jae-Kuk Ryu **RC** .50
999 Lastings Milledge **(RC)** 1.00
1000 Jered Weaver **(RC)** 4.00
1001 Stephen Drew **(RC)** 1.00
1002 Carlos Quentin **(RC)** .50
1003 Livan Hernandez .15
1004 Chris Young **(RC)** .50
1005 Alberto Callaspo/SP **(RC)** 6.00
1006 Enrique Gonzalez **(RC)** .25
1007 Tony Pena **(RC)** .25
1008 Bob Melvin .15
1009 Fernando Tatis .15
1010 Willy Aybar **(RC)** .25
1011 Ken Ray **(RC)** .25
1012 Scott Thorman **(RC)** .50
1013 Eric Hinske/SP 4.00
1014 Kevin Barry **(RC)** .50
1015 Bobby Cox .15
1016 Phil Stockman **(RC)** .25
1017 Brayan Pena **(RC)** .25
1018 Adam Loewen **(RC)** .25
1019 Brandon Fahey **RC** .50
1020 Jim Hoey **RC** .50
1021 Kurt Birkins/SP **RC** 8.00
1022 Jim Johnson **RC** .75
1023 Sam Perlozzo .15
1024 Cory Morris **RC** .50
1025 Hayden Penn **(RC)** .25
1026 Javy Lopez .15
1027 Dustin Pedroia **(RC)** .50
1028 Kason Gabbard **(RC)** .50
1029 David Pauley **(RC)** .25
1030 Kyle Snyder .15
1031 Terry Francona .15
1032 Craig Breslow **RC** .50
1033 Bryan Corey **(RC)** .25
1034 Manny Delcarmen **(RC)** 1.00
1035 Carlos Marmol **RC** .50
1036 Buck Coats **(RC)** .50
1037 Ryan O'Malley/SP **RC** 10.00
1038 Angel Guzman **(RC)** .25
1039 Ronny Cedeno .15
1040 Juan Mateo **RC** .50
1041 Cesar Izturis .15
1042 Les Walrond **(RC)** .50
1043 Geovany Soto **(RC)** .50
1044 Sean Tracey **(RC)** .25
1045 Ozzie Guillen/SP 6.00
1046 Royce Clayton .15
1047 Norris Hopper **RC** .50
1048 Bill Bray **(RC)** .25
1049 Jerry Narron .15
1050 Brendan Harris **(RC)** .25
1051 Brian Shackelford .15
1052 Jeremy Sowers **(RC)** .50
1053 Joe Inglett **RC** 1.50
1054 Brian Slocum **(RC)** .25
1055 Andrew Brown **(RC)** .25
1056 Rafael Perez **RC** .50
1057 Edward Mujica **RC** .50
1058 Andy Marte **(RC)** .25
1059 Shin-Soo Choo **(RC)** .50
1060 Jeremy Guthrie **(RC)** .25
1061 Franklin Gutierrez/SP **(RC)** 6.00
1062 Kazuo Matsui .15
1063 Chris Iannetta **RC** .50
1064 Manny Corpas **RC** .50
1065 Clint Hurdle .15
1066 Ramon Ramirez **(RC)** .25
1067 Sean Casey .15
1068 Zach Miner **(RC)** .25
1069 Brent Clevlen/SP **(RC)** 8.00
1070 Bob Wickman .15
1071 Jim Leyland .15
1072 Alexis Gomez **(RC)** .25
1073 Anibal Sanchez **(RC)** .50
1074 Taylor Tankersley **(RC)** .25
1075 Eric Wedge .15
1076 Jonah Bayliss **RC** .50
1077 Paul Hoover/SP **(RC)** 8.00
1078 Eddie Guardado .15
1079 Cody Ross **(RC)** .25
1080 Aubrey Huff .15
1081 Jason Hirsh **(RC)** .25
1082 Brandon League .15
1083 Matt Albers **(RC)** .25
1084 Chris Sampson **RC** 1.50
1085 Phil Garner .15
1086 J.R. House **(RC)** .25
1087 Ryan Shealy **(RC)** .25
1088 Stephen Andrade **(RC)** .25
1089 Bob Keppel **(RC)** .25
1090 Buddy Bell .15
1091 Justin Huber **(RC)** .25
1092 Paul Phillips **(RC)** .25
1093 Greg Jones/SP **(RC)** 8.00
1094 Jeff Mathis **(RC)** .50
1095 Dustin Moseley **(RC)** .50
1096 Joe Saunders **(RC)** .25
1097 Reggie Willits **(RC)** 1.50
1098 Mike Scioscia .15
1099 Greg Maddux 1.50
1100 Wilson Betemit .15
1101 Chad Billingsley/SP **(RC)** 8.00
1102 Russell Martin **(RC)** .25
1103 Grady Little .15
1104 David Bell .15
1105 Kevin Mench .15
1106 Laynce Nix .15
1107 Chris Barnwell **RC** .50
1108 Tony Gwynn Jr. **(RC)** .50
1109 Corey Hart **(RC)** .25
1110 Zach Jackson **(RC)** .25
1111 Francisco Cordero .15
1112 Joe Winklesas **(RC)** .25
1113 Ned Yost .15
1114 Matt Garza **(RC)** .50
1115 Chris Heintz .15
1116 Pat Neshek **RC** 4.00
1117 Josh Rabe/SP **RC** 15.00
1118 Mike Rivera .15
1119 Ron Gardenhire .15
1120 Shawn Green .15
1121 Oliver Perez .15
1122 Heath Bell .15
1123 Bartolome Fortunato **(RC)** .25
1124 Anderson Garcia **RC** .75
1125 John Maine/SP **(RC)** 10.00
1126 Henry Owens **RC** .50
1127 Mike Pelfrey **RC** 3.00
1128 Royce Ring **(RC)** .25
1129 Willie Randolph .15
1130 Bobby Abreu .50
1131 Craig Wilson .15
1132 T.J. Beam **(RC)** .25
1133 Colter Bean/SP **(RC)** 8.00
1134 Melky Cabrera **(RC)** .50
1135 Mitch Jones **(RC)** .50
1136 Jeffrey Karstens **RC** 1.00
1137 Wilbert Nieves **(RC)** .25
1138 Kevin Reese **(RC)** .50
1139 Kevin Thompson **(RC)** .50
1140 Jose Veras **RC** .15
1141 Joe Torre .50
1142 Jeremy Brown **(RC)** .25
1143 Santiago Casilla **(RC)** .25
1144 Shane Komine **RC** 1.00
1145 Mike Rouse **(RC)** .25
1146 Jason Windsor **(RC)** .75
1147 Ken Macha .15
1148 Jamie Moyer .15
1149 Phil Nevin/SP 8.00
1150 Eude Brito **(RC)** .50
1151 Fabio Castro .15
1152 Jeff Conine .15
1153 Scott Mathieson **(RC)** .25
1154 Brian Sanches **(RC)** .25
1155 Matt Smith **RC** .50
1156 Joe Thurston **(RC)** .25
1157 Marlon Anderson/SP 8.00
1158 Xavier Nady .15
1159 Shawn Chacon .15
1160 Rajai Davis **(RC)** .25
1161 Yurendell de Caster **(RC)** .50
1162 Marty McLeary **(RC)** .25
1163 Chris Duffy .15
1164 Joshua Sharpless **RC** 1.00
1165 Jim Tracy .15
1166 David Wells .15
1167 Russell Branyan .15
1168 Todd Walker .15
1169 Paul McAnulty **(RC)** .25
1170 Bruce Bochy .15
1171 Shea Hillenbrand .15
1172 Eliezer Alfonzo **RC** .50
1173 Justin Knoedler/SP **(RC)** 8.00
1174 Jonathan Sanchez **(RC)** .25
1175 Travis Smith **(RC)** .25
1176 Cha Sueng Baek .15
1177 T.J. Bohn **(RC)** .25
1178 Emiliano Fruto **RC** .50
1179 Sean Green **RC** .50
1180 Jon Huber **RC** .50
1181 Adam Jones/SP **(RC)** 8.00
1182 Mark Lowe **(RC)** .25
1183 Eric O'Flaherty **RC** .50
1184 Preston Wilson .15
1185 Mike Hargrove .15
1186 Jeff Weaver .15
1187 Ronnie Belliard .15
1188 John Gall **(RC)** .25
1189 Josh Kinney/SP **RC** 10.00
1190 Tony LaRussa .15
1191 Scott Dunn **(RC)** .25
1192 B.J. Upton .15
1193 Jon Switzer **(RC)** .25
1194 Benjamin Zobrist **(RC)** .50
1195 Joe Maddon .15
1196 Carlos Lee .15
1197 Matt Stairs .15
1198 Nick Massett **(RC)** .25
1199 Nelson Cruz **(RC)** .25
1200 Francisco Rosario **(RC)** .25
1201 Wes Littleton **(RC)** .25
1202 Drew Meyer **(RC)** .25
1203 John Rheinecker **(RC)** .25
1204 Robinson Tejeda .15
1205 Jeremy Accardo/SP 8.00
1206 Luis Figueroa **RC** .50
1207 John Hattig Jr. **(RC)** .25
1208 Dustin McGowan **(RC)** .25
1209 Ryan Roberts **RC** .50
1210 Davis Romero **(RC)** .25
1211 Ty Taubenheim .15
1212 John Gibbons .15
1213 Shawn Hill/SP **(RC)** 8.00
1214 Brandon Harper **RC** .25
1215 Travis Hughes **(RC)** .25
1216 Chris Schroder **RC** .50
1217 Austin Kearns .15
1218 Felipe Lopez .15
1219 Roy Corcoran **RC** .25
1220 Melvin Dorta **RC** .50
1221 Brandon Webb/SP 4.00
1222 Andruw Jones/SP 6.00
1223 Miguel Tejada/SP 6.00
1224 David Ortiz/SP 8.00
1225 Derrek Lee/SP 6.00
1226 Jim Thome/SP 6.00
1227 Ken Griffey Jr./SP 8.00
1228 Travis Hafner/SP 6.00
1229 Todd Helton/SP 6.00
1230 Magglio Ordonez/SP 4.00
1231 Miguel Cabrera/SP 8.00
1232 Lance Berkman/SP 6.00
1233 Mike Sweeney/SP 4.00
1234 Vladimir Guerrero/SP 8.00
1235 Nomar Garciaparra/SP 8.00
1236 Prince Fielder/SP 8.00
1237 Johan Santana/SP 8.00
1238 Pedro Martinez/SP 6.00
1239 Derek Jeter/SP 10.00
1240 Barry Zito/SP 6.00
1241 Ryan Howard/SP 10.00
1242 Jason Bay/SP 6.00
1243 Trevor Hoffman/SP 4.00
1244 Jason Schmidt/SP 6.00
1245 Ichiro Suzuki/SP 8.00
1246 Albert Pujols/SP 10.00
1247 Carl Crawford/SP 4.00
1248 Mark Teixeira/SP 6.00
1249 Vernon Wells/SP 6.00
1250 Alfonso Soriano/SP 8.00

Blue

Blue: 2-4X
Production 299 Sets

Gold

Gold: 2-4X
Production 299 Sets

All-Upper Deck Team

No Pricing

Amazing Greats

NM/M
Complete Set: 25.00
Common Player: .50
BA Bobby Abreu .75
JB Jeff Bagwell .75
CB Carlos Beltran 1.00
AB Adrian Beltre .50
MC Miguel Cabrera 1.00
RC Roger Clemens 3.00
CC Carl Crawford .50
JD Johnny Damon 1.00
JE Jim Edmonds .50
RF Rafael Furcal .50
EG Eric Gagne .50
JG Jason Giambi .75
TG Tom Glavine .50
KG Ken Griffey Jr. 2.00
HE Todd Helton .75
TH Tim Hudson .50
DJ Derek Jeter 3.00
RJ Randy Johnson 1.00
AJ Andruw Jones 1.00
CJ Chipper Jones 1.00
JJ Jacque Jones .50
PK Paul Konerko .75
CL Carlos Lee .50
JL Javy Lopez .50
GM Greg Maddux 2.00
PM Pedro Martinez 1.00
DO David Ortiz 1.00
RO Roy Oswalt .50
RP Rafael Palmeiro .75
CP Corey Patterson .50
MP Mike Piazza 1.00
PR Mark Prior .75
AP Albert Pujols 3.00
MR Manny Ramirez 1.00
JR Jose Reyes .75
IR Ivan Rodriguez .75
SR Scott Rolen 1.00
JS Johan Santana 1.00
CS Curt Schilling 1.00
GS Gary Sheffield .75
SM John Smoltz .50
AS Alfonso Soriano .75
SS Sammy Sosa 1.00
MT Mark Teixeira .75
TE Miguel Tejada .75
FT Frank Thomas .75
JT Jim Thome .75
DW Dontrelle Willis .50
KW Kerry Wood .50
WR David Wright 1.50

Amazing Greats Materials

NM/M
Complete Set:
Common Player:
BA Bobby Abreu 6.00
JB Jeff Bagwell 6.00
CB Carlos Beltran 6.00
AB Adrian Beltre 4.00
MC Miguel Cabrera 8.00
RC Roger Clemens 15.00
CC Carl Crawford 6.00
JD Johnny Damon 10.00
JE Jim Edmonds 6.00
RF Rafael Furcal 4.00
EG Eric Gagne 4.00
JG Jason Giambi 6.00
TG Tom Glavine 6.00
KG Ken Griffey Jr. 20.00
HE Todd Helton 6.00
TH Tim Hudson 4.00
DJ Derek Jeter 20.00
RJ Randy Johnson 8.00
AJ Andruw Jones 8.00
CJ Chipper Jones 8.00
JJ Jacque Jones 4.00
PK Paul Konerko 6.00
CL Carlos Lee 4.00
JL Javy Lopez 4.00
GM Greg Maddux 12.00
PM Pedro Martinez 8.00

DO	David Ortiz	8.00
RO	Roy Oswalt	6.00
RP	Rafael Palmeiro	6.00
CP	Corey Patterson	4.00
MP	Mike Piazza	10.00
PR	Mark Prior	6.00
AP	Albert Pujols	20.00
MR	Manny Ramirez	8.00
JR	Jose Reyes	8.00
IR	Ivan Rodriguez	6.00
SR	Scott Rolen	8.00
JS	Johan Santana	8.00
CS	Curt Schilling	8.00
GS	Gary Sheffield	6.00
SM	John Smoltz	8.00
AS	Alfonso Soriano	6.00
SS	Sammy Sosa	10.00
MT	Mark Teixeira	8.00
TE	Miguel Tejada	10.00
FT	Frank Thomas	6.00
JT	Jim Thome	8.00
DW	Dontrelle Willis	6.00
KW	Kerry Wood	4.00
WR	David Wright	15.00

Diamond Collection Materials

		NM/M
Common Player:		4.00
AL	Moises Alou	6.00
JB	Jeff Bagwell	6.00
RB	Rocco Baldelli	4.00
OC	Orlando Cabrera	4.00
MC	Mike Cameron	4.00
EC	Eric Chavez	6.00
CO	Jose Contreras	4.00
JC	Jesse Crain	4.00
BC	Bobby Crosby	4.00
JD	Johnny Damon	10.00
AE	Adam Eaton	4.00
JE	Jim Edmonds	6.00
SF	Steve Finley	4.00
FG	Freddy Garcia	4.00
GO	Juan Gonzalez	4.00
KG	Ken Griffey Jr.	20.00
JG	Jose Guillen	4.00
MH	Mike Hampton	4.00
AH	Aubrey Huff	4.00
EJ	Edwin Jackson	4.00
DJ	Derek Jeter	20.00
NJ	Nick Johnson	4.00
RJ	Randy Johnson	8.00
JJ	Jacque Jones	4.00
SK	Scott Kazmir	4.00
KE	Austin Kearns	4.00
JK	Jason Kendall	4.00
AK	Adam Kennedy	4.00
CK	Casey Kotchman	4.00
LA	Matt Lawton	4.00
ML	Mike Lieberthal	4.00
PL	Paul LoDuca	4.00
KL	Kenny Lofton	4.00
LO	Mike Lowell	4.00
GM	Greg Maddux	12.00
MA	Kazuo Matsui	4.00
KM	Kevin Millwood	4.00
DO	David Ortiz	8.00
AO	Akinori Otsuka	4.00
CP	Carl Pavano	4.00
JP	Jorge Posada	6.00
BR	Brad Radke	4.00
IR	Ivan Rodriguez	6.00
CC	C.C. Sabathia	4.00
CS	Chris Shelton	10.00
JS	John Smoltz	8.00
SS	Shannon Stewart	4.00
JT	Jim Thome	8.00
JW	Jayson Werth	4.00
PW	Preston Wilson	4.00

Diamond Debut

NM/M
Common Player: 1.00
#'s 1-40 found in Series 1 packs
#'s 41-82 found in Series 2 packs
Inserted 1:4 Walmart packs.
Series 2 Common Player: .50

1	Tadahito Iguchi	1.00
2	Huston Street	.50
3	Norihiro Nakamura	.50
4	Chien-Ming Wang	1.00
5	Pedro Lopez	.50
6	Robinson Cano	2.00
7	Tim Stauffer	.50
8	Ervin Santana	.50
9	Brandon McCarthy	.50
10	Hayden Penn	.50
11	Mike Morse	.50
12	Chad Orvella	.50
13	Prince Fielder	3.00
14	Edwin Encarnacion	.50
15	Scott Olsen	.50
16	Chris Resop	.50
17	Justin Verlander	2.00
18	Melky Cabrera	.50
19	Jeff Francoeur	.50
20	Yuniesky Betancourt	.50
21	Conor Jackson	.50
22	Felix Hernandez	1.00
23	Anthony Reyes	.50
24	John-Ford Griffin	.50
25	Adam Wainwright	.50
26	Ryan Garko	.50
27	Chuck James	.50
28	Tom Seaver	2.00
29	Johnny Bench	2.00
30	Reggie Jackson	2.00
31	Rod Carew	2.00
32	Nolan Ryan	4.00
33	Richie Ashburn	.50
34	Yogi Berra	2.00
35	Lou Brock	1.50
36	Carlton Fisk	1.50
37	Joe Morgan	.50
38	Bob Gibson	2.00
39	Willie McCovey	2.00
40	Harmon Killebrew	2.00
41	Takashi Saito	2.00
42	Kenji Johjima	5.00
43	Joel Zumaya	1.50
44	Dan Uggla	1.00
45	Taylor Buchholz	1.00
46	Josh Barfield	1.00
47	Brian Bannister	1.00
48	Nicholas Markakis	1.00
49	Carlos Martinez	1.00
50	Macay McBride	1.00
51	Brian Anderson	1.00
52	Freddie Bynum	1.00
53	Kelly Stoppach	1.00
54	Choo Freeman	1.00
55	Ryan Shealy	1.00
56	Chris Resop	1.00
57	Hanley Ramirez	1.50
58	Mike Jacobs	1.00
59	Cody Ross	1.00
60	Jose Capellan	1.00
61	David Gassner	1.00
62	Jason Kubel	1.00
63	Jered Weaver	4.00
64	Paul Maholm	1.00
65	Nate McLouth	1.00
66	Ben Johnson	1.00
67	Jack Taschner	1.00
68	Skip Schumaker	1.00
69	Brandon Watson	1.00
70	David Wright	3.00
71	David Ortiz	2.50
72	Alex Rodriguez	4.00
73	Johan Santana	2.00
74	Greg Maddux	3.00
75	Ichiro Suzuki	3.00
76	Albert Pujols	4.00
77	Hideki Matsui	3.00
78	Vladimir Guerrero	2.00
79	Pedro Martinez	2.00
80	Mike Schmidt	2.00
81	Al Kaline	2.00
82	Robin Yount	2.00

Derek Jeter Promo

No Pricing

First Class Cuts

No Pricing
Production One Set

First Class Legends

NM/M
Gold: 1-2X
Production 699 Sets
Platinum: 2-3X
Production 99 Sets
Spectrum: No Pricing
Production One Set

1-20	Babe Ruth	3.00
21-40	Ty Cobb	2.00
41-60	Honus Wagner	2.00
61-80	Christy Mathewson	1.00
81-100	Walter Johnson	1.00

Signature Sensations

		NM/M
Inserted 1:288 Hobby		
BA	Bronson Arroyo	20.00
GA	Garrett Atkins	10.00
SB	Scott Baker	15.00
KC	Kiko Calero	5.00
JE	Johnny Estrada	8.00
KG	Ken Griffey Jr.	100.00
TR	Travis Hafner	25.00
BH	Bobby Hill	5.00
JJ	Josh Johnson	10.00
AL	Al Leiter	15.00
AM	Aaron Miles	15.00
YM	Yadier Molina	20.00
NP	Nick Punto	8.00
AR	Aaron Rowand	15.00
CS	Cory Sullivan	10.00
JS	Jeff Suppan	15.00
JV	Joe Valentine	10.00
DY	Delmon Young	25.00

Star Attractions

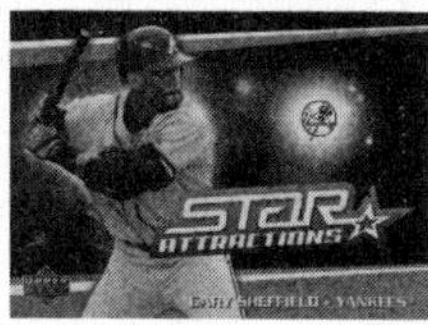

		NM/M
Gold:		1X-2X
Production 699 Sets		
BA	Bobby Abreu	.75
GA	Garret Anderson	.50
JB	Josh Beckett	.50
CB	Carlos Beltran	.75
AB	Adrian Beltre	.50
LB	Lance Berkman	.50
JC	Jose Contreras	.50
JD	Johnny Damon	1.00
CD	Carlos Delgado	.75
JE	Jim Edmonds	.75
EG	Eric Gagne	.50
JG	Jason Giambi	.75
SG	Shawn Green	.50
GR	Khalil Greene	.50
KG	Ken Griffey Jr.	2.00
GU	Jose Guillen	.50
RH	Rich Harden	.50
AH	Aubrey Huff	.50
TH	Torii Hunter	.50
TI	Tadahito Iguchi	.50
DJ	Derek Jeter	3.00
AJ	Andruw Jones	1.00
CJ	Chipper Jones	1.00
JJ	Jacque Jones	.50
CL	Carlos Lee	.50
DL	Derrek Lee	1.00
JL	Javy Lopez	.50
GM	Greg Maddux	2.00
PM	Pedro Martinez	1.00
JM	Joe Mauer	.50
MM	Mark Mulder	.50
MO	Magglio Ordonez	.50
DO	David Ortiz	1.00
AP	Andy Pettitte	.75
JP	Jorge Posada	.75
MP	Mark Prior	.75
PU	Albert Pujols	3.00
MR	Manny Ramirez	1.00
JR	Jose Reyes	.75
CS	Curt Schilling	1.00
JS	Jason Schmidt	.50
GS	Gary Sheffield	.75
SM	John Smoltz	.75
AS	Alfonso Soriano	.75
MT	Mark Teixeira	.75
FT	Frank Thomas	.75
DW	Dontrelle Willis	.50
KW	Kerry Wood	.50
WR	David Wright	1.50
BZ	Barry Zito	.50

Star Attractions Swatches

		NM/M
Common Player:		4.00
BA	Bobby Abreu	6.00
GA	Garret Anderson	4.00
JB	Josh Beckett	4.00
CB	Carlos Beltran	6.00
AB	Adrian Beltre	4.00
LB	Lance Berkman	6.00
JC	Jose Contreras	4.00
JD	Johnny Damon	10.00
CD	Carlos Delgado	6.00
JE	Jim Edmonds	6.00
EG	Eric Gagne	4.00
JG	Jason Giambi	6.00
SG	Shawn Green	4.00
GR	Khalil Greene	4.00
KG	Ken Griffey Jr.	20.00
GU	Jose Guillen	4.00
RH	Rich Harden	6.00
AH	Aubrey Huff	4.00
TH	Torii Hunter	4.00
TI	Tadahito Iguchi	10.00
DJ	Derek Jeter	20.00
AJ	Andruw Jones	8.00
CJ	Chipper Jones	8.00
JJ	Jacque Jones	4.00
CL	Carlos Lee	4.00
DL	Derrek Lee	8.00
JL	Javy Lopez	4.00
GM	Greg Maddux	12.00
PM	Pedro Martinez	8.00
JM	Joe Mauer	4.00
MM	Mark Mulder	4.00
MO	Magglio Ordonez	4.00
DO	David Ortiz	8.00
AP	Andy Pettitte	6.00
JP	Jorge Posada	6.00
MP	Mark Prior	6.00
PU	Albert Pujols	20.00
MR	Manny Ramirez	8.00
JR	Jose Reyes	8.00
CS	Curt Schilling	8.00
JS	Jason Schmidt	4.00
GS	Gary Sheffield	6.00
SM	John Smoltz	8.00
AS	Alfonso Soriano	6.00
MT	Mark Teixeira	6.00
FT	Frank Thomas	6.00
DW	Dontrelle Willis	6.00
KW	Kerry Wood	4.00
WR	David Wright	15.00
BZ	Barry Zito	4.00

Team Pride

		NM/M
Gold:		1X-2X
Production 699 Sets		
BA	Bobby Abreu	.75
GA	Garret Anderson	.50
JB	Jeff Bagwell	.75
RB	Rocco Baldelli	.50
SC	Sean Casey	.50
LC	Luis Castillo	.50
EC	Eric Chavez	.50
JD	Johnny Damon	1.00
CD	Carlos Delgado	.75
JE	Jim Edmonds	.75
ME	Morgan Ensberg	.50
KF	Keith Foulke	.50
EG	Eric Gagne	.50
LG	Luis Gonzalez	.50
GR	Khalil Greene	.50
KG	Ken Griffey Jr.	2.00
RH	Rich Harden	.50
TH	Trevor Hoffman	.50
AH	Aubrey Huff	.50
DJ	Derek Jeter	3.00
NJ	Nick Johnson	.50
AJ	Andruw Jones	1.00
CJ	Chipper Jones	1.00
RK	Ryan Klesko	.50
CK	Casey Kotchman	.50
ML	Mike Lieberthal	.50
LO	Mike Lowell	.50
GM	Greg Maddux	2.00
MA	Joe Mauer	.50
JM	Jamie Moyer	.50
DO	David Ortiz	1.00
PE	Andy Pettitte	.75
JP	Jorge Posada	.50
MP	Mark Prior	.75
AP	Albert Pujols	3.00
JR	Jose Reyes	.50
IR	Ivan Rodriguez	.75
CC	C.C. Sabathia	.50
CS	Curt Schilling	1.00
JS	John Smoltz	.75
MS	Mike Sweeney	.50
FT	Frank Thomas	.75
JT	Jim Thome	.75
VA	Jason Varitek	.75
JV	Jose Vidro	.50
BW	Bernie Williams	.50
DW	Dontrelle Willis	.50
KW	Kerry Wood	.50
MY	Michael Young	.50

Diamond Collection

		NM/M
Gold:		1-2X
Production 699 Sets		
AL	Moises Alou	.50
JB	Jeff Bagwell	.75
RB	Rocco Baldelli	.50
OC	Orlando Cabrera	.50
MC	Mike Cameron	.50
EC	Eric Chavez	.50
CO	Jose Contreras	.50
JC	Jesse Crain	.50
BC	Bobby Crosby	.50
JD	Johnny Damon	1.00
AE	Adam Eaton	.50
JE	Jim Edmonds	.50
SF	Steve Finley	.50
FG	Freddy Garcia	.50
GO	Juan Gonzalez	.50
KG	Ken Griffey Jr.	2.00
JG	Jose Guillen	.50
MH	Mike Hampton	.50
AH	Aubrey Huff	.50
EJ	Edwin Jackson	.50
DJ	Derek Jeter	3.00
NJ	Nick Johnson	.50
RJ	Randy Johnson	1.00
JJ	Jacque Jones	.50
SK	Scott Kazmir	.50
KE	Austin Kearns	.50
JK	Jason Kendall	.50
AK	Adam Kennedy	.50
CK	Casey Kotchman	.50
LA	Matt Lawton	.50
ML	Mike Lieberthal	.50
PL	Paul LoDuca	.50
KL	Kenny Lofton	.50
LO	Mike Lowell	.50
GM	Greg Maddux	2.00
MA	Kazuo Matsui	.50
KM	Kevin Millwood	.50
DO	David Ortiz	1.00
AO	Akinori Otsuka	.50
CP	Carl Pavano	.50
JP	Jorge Posada	.50
BR	Brad Radke	.50
IR	Ivan Rodriguez	.75
CC	C.C. Sabathia	.50
CS	Chris Shelton	.50
JS	John Smoltz	.75
SS	Shannon Stewart	.50
JT	Jim Thome	.75
JW	Jayson Werth	.50
PW	Preston Wilson	.50

Game Jersey

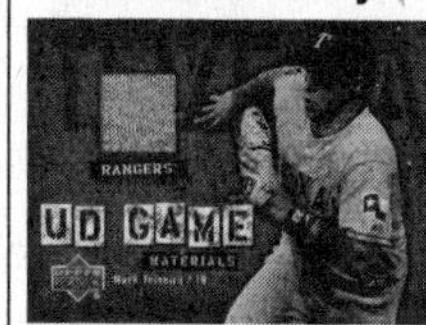

		NM/M
Common Player:		4.00
JB	Jeff Bagwell	6.00
MC	Miguel Cabrera	8.00
EC	Eric Chavez	4.00
RC	Roger Clemens	15.00
JD	Johnny Damon	10.00
JE	Jim Edmonds	6.00
RF	Rafael Furcal	4.00
EG	Eric Gagne	4.00
JG	Jason Giambi	6.00
KG	Ken Griffey Jr.	20.00
VG	Vladimir Guerrero	8.00
RH	Roy Halladay	4.00
DJ	Derek Jeter	20.00
RJ	Randy Johnson	8.00
AJ	Andruw Jones	8.00
CJ	Chipper Jones	8.00
JJ	Jacque Jones	4.00
DL	Derrek Lee	8.00
GM	Greg Maddux	12.00
PM	Pedro Martinez	8.00
DO	David Ortiz	8.00
RP	Rafael Palmeiro	6.00
CP	Corey Patterson	4.00
JP	Jake Peavy	6.00
MP	Mike Piazza	8.00
PO	Jorge Posada	6.00
PR	Mark Prior	6.00
AP	Albert Pujols	20.00
MR	Manny Ramirez	8.00
BR	Brian Roberts	8.00
IR	Ivan Rodriguez	6.00
SR	Scott Rolen	8.00
JS	Johan Santana	8.00
CS	Curt Schilling	8.00
SM	John Smoltz	8.00
AS	Alfonso Soriano	6.00
MT	Mark Teixeira	8.00
TE	Miguel Tejada	8.00
FT	Frank Thomas	8.00
JT	Jim Thome	8.00
DW	Dontrelle Willis	6.00
WR	David Wright	15.00
Series 2		
BA	Bobby Abreu	6.00
GA	Garrett Atkins	4.00
JB	Josh Beckett	4.00
CB	Carlos Beltran	8.00
AB	Adrian Beltre	4.00
BI	Craig Biggio	6.00
HB	Hank Blalock	4.00
SC	Sean Casey	4.00
JD	Johnny Damon	10.00
CD	Carlos Delgado	6.00
AD	Adam Dunn	6.00
PF	Prince Fielder	15.00
TG	Tom Glavine	6.00
GR	Khalil Greene	4.00
KG	Ken Griffey Jr.	20.00
HA	Travis Hafner	6.00
TH	Todd Helton	6.00
RH	Ryan Howard	20.00
TI	Tadahito Iguchi	8.00
DJ	Derek Jeter	20.00
PK	Paul Konerko	6.00
CL	Carlos Lee	6.00
JL	Javy Lopez	4.00
VM	Victor Martinez	6.00
JM	Joe Mauer	8.00
MM	Mike Mussina	6.00
MO	Magglio Ordonez	4.00
RO	Roy Oswalt	6.00
AP	Andy Pettitte	6.00
MP	Mike Piazza	8.00
JR	Jose Reyes	8.00
GS	Gary Sheffield	6.00
SI	Grady Sizemore	10.00
JV	Jason Varitek	8.00
CW	Chien-Ming Wang	15.00
RW	Rickie Weeks	6.00
KW	Kerry Wood	4.00
MY	Michael Young	4.00
RZ	Ryan Zimmerman	15.00
BZ	Barry Zito	6.00

Team Pride Materials

		NM/M
Common Player:		4.00
BA	Bobby Abreu	6.00
GA	Garret Anderson	4.00
JB	Jeff Bagwell	6.00
RB	Rocco Baldelli	4.00
SC	Sean Casey	4.00
LC	Luis Castillo	4.00
EC	Eric Chavez	4.00
JD	Johnny Damon	10.00
CD	Carlos Delgado	6.00
JE	Jim Edmonds	6.00
ME	Morgan Ensberg	4.00
KF	Keith Foulke	4.00
EG	Eric Gagne	4.00
LG	Luis Gonzalez	4.00
GR	Khalil Greene	4.00
KG	Ken Griffey Jr.	20.00
RH	Rich Harden	4.00
TH	Trevor Hoffman	4.00
AH	Aubrey Huff	4.00
DJ	Derek Jeter	20.00
NJ	Nick Johnson	4.00
AJ	Andruw Jones	8.00
CJ	Chipper Jones	8.00
RK	Ryan Klesko	4.00
CK	Casey Kotchman	4.00
ML	Mike Lieberthal	4.00
LO	Mike Lowell	4.00
GM	Greg Maddux	12.00
MA	Joe Mauer	4.00
JM	Jamie Moyer	4.00
DO	David Ortiz	8.00
PE	Andy Pettitte	6.00
JP	Jorge Posada	6.00
MP	Mark Prior	6.00
AP	Albert Pujols	20.00
JR	Jose Reyes	8.00
IR	Ivan Rodriguez	6.00
CC	C.C. Sabathia	4.00
CS	Curt Schilling	8.00
JS	John Smoltz	8.00
MS	Mike Sweeney	4.00
FT	Frank Thomas	6.00
JT	Jim Thome	8.00
VA	Jason Varitek	6.00
JV	Jose Vidro	4.00
BW	Bernie Williams	6.00
DW	Dontrelle Willis	6.00
KW	Kerry Wood	4.00
MY	Michael Young	4.00
BZ	Barry Zito	4.00

Game Patch

		NM/M
Inserted 1:288		
JB	Jeff Bagwell	20.00
MC	Miguel Cabrera	25.00
RC	Roger Clemens	30.00
JD	Johnny Damon	25.00
JE	Jim Edmonds	20.00
RF	Rafael Furcal	15.00
KG	Ken Griffey Jr.	40.00
VG	Vladimir Guerrero	25.00
RH	Roy Halladay	15.00
DJ	Derek Jeter	50.00
RJ	Randy Johnson	25.00
AJ	Andruw Jones	20.00
DL	Derrek Lee	20.00
GM	Greg Maddux	25.00
PM	Pedro Martinez	25.00
RP	Rafael Palmeiro	15.00
JP	Jake Peavy	20.00
MP	Mike Piazza	20.00
PR	Mark Prior	20.00
AP	Albert Pujols	50.00
MR	Manny Ramirez	25.00
BR	Brian Roberts	15.00
SR	Scott Rolen	20.00
JS	Johan Santana	20.00
SM	John Smoltz	25.00
TE	Miguel Tejada	25.00
FT	Frank Thomas	20.00
JT	Jim Thome	20.00
DW	Dontrelle Willis	20.00
WR	David Wright	40.00
Series 2:		No Pricing

Silver Spectrum

No Pricing
Production 25 Sets

Printing Plates

No Pricing
Production one set per color.

Rookie Foil Gold

Gold: 4X-8X
Production 99 Sets
Platinum: No Pricing
Production 15 Sets

Rookie Foil Silver

Silver: 2-4X
Production 399 Sets

Inaugural Images

		NM/M
Common Player:		.50
II-1	Sung-Heon Hong	.50
II-2	Yulieski Gourriel	.50
II-3	Tsuyoshi Nishioka	1.00
II-4	Miguel Cabrera	1.50
II-5	Yung-Chi Chen	.50
II-6	Omari Romero	.50
II-7	Ken Griffey Jr.	2.00
II-8	Bernie Williams	.75
II-9	Daniel Cabrera	.50
II-10	David Ortiz	1.50
II-11	Alex Rodriguez	3.00
II-12	Frederich Cepeda	.50
II-13	Derek Jeter	3.00
II-14	Jorge Cantu	.50
II-15	Alexi Ramirez	.50
II-16	Yoandy Garlobo	.50
II-17	Koji Uehara	.50
II-18	Nobuhiko Matsunaka	.50
II-19	Tomoya Satozaki	.50
II-20	Seung-Yeop Lee	.50
II-21	Yulieski Gourriel	.50
II-22	Adrian Beltre	.50
II-23	Ken Griffey Jr.	2.00
II-24	Jong Beom Lee	.50
II-25	Ichiro Suzuki	2.00
II-26	Yoandy Garlobo	.50
II-27	Daisuke Matsuzaka	15.00
II-28	Yadel Marti	.50
II-29	Chan Ho Park	.50
II-30	Daisuke Matsuzaka	15.00

INKredible

		NM/M
Inserted 1:288		
JB	Joe Blanton	10.00
CA	Miguel Cabrera	40.00
CO	Chad Cordero	20.00
JC	Jesse Crain	10.00
CC	Carl Crawford	20.00
NG	Nomar Garciaparra	60.00
KG	Ken Griffey Jr.	120.00
TH	Travis Hafner	30.00
JH	J.J. Hardy	20.00
TI	Tadahito Iguchi/SP 91	50.00
DJ	Derek Jeter	200.00
SK	Scott Kazmir	20.00
CK	Casey Kotchman	10.00
VM	Victor Martinez	20.00
JM	Joe Mauer/SP 91	40.00
MO	Justin Morneau	25.00
BM	Brett Myers/SP 72	15.00
LO	Lyle Overbay/SP 91	25.00
JR	Jeremy Reed	15.00
RE	Jose Reyes/SP 91	40.00
AR	Alexis Rios	20.00
BR	Brian Roberts	20.00
MT	Mark Teixeira	25.00
JV	Justin Verlander/SP 91	40.00
WI	Dontrelle Willis	20.00
DW	David Wright/SP 91	60.00
KY	Kevin Youkilis	25.00
RZ	Ryan Zimmerman/SP 91	50.00

Player Highlights

		NM/M
Common Player:		.50
PH-1	Andruw Jones	1.00
PH-2	Manny Ramirez	1.00
PH-3	Travis Hafner	1.00
PH-4	Johnny Damon	1.00
PH-5	Miguel Cabrera	1.00
PH-6	Chris Carpenter	.75
PH-7	Derrek Lee	1.00
PH-8	Jason Bay	.75
PH-9	Jason Varitek	1.00
PH-10	Ryan Howard	2.00
PH-11	Mark Teixeira	.75
PH-12	Carlos Delgado	.75
PH-13	Bartolo Colon	.50
PH-14	David Wright	2.00
PH-15	Miguel Tejada	.75
PH-16	Mike Piazza	1.00
PH-17	Paul Konerko	.75
PH-18	Jermaine Dye	.75
PH-19	Ichiro Suzuki	2.00
PH-20	Brad Wilkerson	.50
PH-21	Hideki Matsui	2.00
PH-22	Albert Pujols	3.00
PH-23	Chris Burke	.50
PH-24	Derek Jeter	3.00
PH-25	Brian Roberts	.75
PH-26	David Ortiz	1.50
PH-27	Alex Rodriguez	3.00
PH-28	Ken Griffey Jr.	2.00
PH-29	Prince Fielder	2.00
PH-30	Bobby Abreu	.75
PH-31	Vladimir Guerrero	1.00
PH-32	Tadahito Iguchi	1.00
PH-33	Jose Reyes	1.00
PH-34	Scott Podsednik	.75
PH-35	Gary Sheffield	.75

Run Producers

		NM/M
Common Player:		
RP-1	Ty Cobb	2.00
RP-2	Derrek Lee	1.00
RP-3	Andruw Jones	1.00
RP-4	David Ortiz	1.50
RP-5	Lou Gehrig	3.00
RP-6	Ken Griffey Jr.	2.00
RP-7	Albert Pujols	3.00
RP-8	Derek Jeter	3.00
RP-9	Manny Ramirez	1.00
RP-10	Alex Rodriguez	3.00
RP-11	Gary Sheffield	.75
RP-12	Miguel Cabrera	1.00
RP-13	Hideki Matsui	2.00
RP-14	Vladimir Guerrero	1.00
RP-15	David Wright	2.00
RP-16	Mike Schmidt	2.00
RP-17	Mark Teixeira	.75
RP-18	Babe Ruth	4.00
RP-19	Jimmie Foxx	2.00
RP-20	Honus Wagner	2.00

Speed to Burn

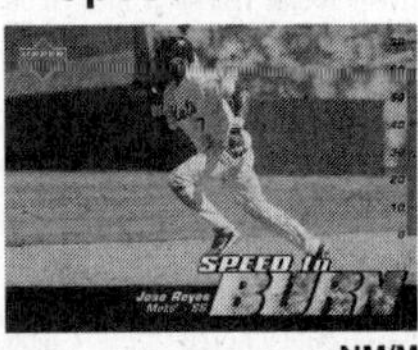

		NM/M
Common Player:		.50
SB-1	Lou Brock	1.00
SB-3	Alfonso Soriano	1.50
SB-4	Carl Crawford	.75
SB-5	Chone Figgins	.50
SB-6	Ichiro Suzuki	2.00
SB-7	Jose Reyes	1.00
SB-8	Juan Pierre	.50
SB-9	Scott Podsednik	.75
SB-11	Alex Rodriguez	3.00
SB-12	David Wright	2.00
SB-14	Bobby Abreu	.75
SB-15	Brian Roberts	.75

All-Time Legends

		NM/M
Common Player:		1.00
AT-1	Ty Cobb	3.00
AT-2	Lou Gehrig	4.00
AT-3	Babe Ruth	5.00
AT-4	Jimmie Foxx	3.00
AT-5	Honus Wagner	3.00
AT-6	Lou Brock	2.00
AT-8	Christy Mathewson	2.00
AT-9	Walter Johnson	2.00
AT-10	Mike Schmidt	3.00
AT-11	Al Kaline	2.00
AT-12	Robin Yount	2.00
AT-13	Johnny Bench	2.00
AT-14	Yogi Berra	2.00
AT-15	Rod Carew	1.00
AT-16	Bob Feller	1.00
AT-17	Carlton Fisk	1.00
AT-18	Bob Gibson	2.00
AT-19	Cy Young	2.00
AT-21	Jackie Robinson	3.00
AT-22	Harmon Killebrew	2.00
AT-23	Mickey Cochrane	1.00
AT-24	Eddie Mathews	2.00
AT-25	Bill Mazeroski	1.00
AT-26	Willie McCovey	2.00
AT-27	Eddie Murray	2.00
AT-28	Lefty Grove	1.00
AT-29	Jim Palmer	1.00
AT-30	Pee Wee Reese	1.00
AT-31	Phil Rizzuto	2.00
AT-32	Brooks Robinson	2.00
AT-33	Nolan Ryan	4.00
AT-34	Tom Seaver	2.00
AT-35	Ozzie Smith	2.00
AT-36	Roy Campanella	2.00
AT-37	Thurman Munson	3.00
AT-38	Mel Ott	2.00
AT-39	Satchel Paige	2.00
AT-40	Rogers Hornsby	2.00

World Baseball Classic Jersey

		NM/M
Inserted 1:24		
Patch:		No Pricing
Production Eight Sets		
JB	Jason Bay	10.00
EB	Erik Bedard	4.00
CB	Carlos Beltran	15.00
MC	Miguel Cabrera	15.00
VC	Vinny Castilla	4.00
FC	Frederich Cepeda	15.00
TC	Tai-San Chang	200.00
RC	Roger Clemens	30.00
JD	Johnny Damon	15.00
CD	Carlos Delgado	10.00
ME	Michel Enriquez	20.00
MF	Maikel Folch	20.00
JF	Jeff Francis	4.00
FR	Jeff Francoeur	15.00
FG	Freddy Garcia	4.00
YG	Yulieski Gourriel	25.00
KG	Ken Griffey Jr.	25.00
JG	Jason Grilli	4.00
HS	Chia-Hsien Hseih	125.00
CH	Chin-Lung Hu	75.00
JH	Justin Huber	4.00
AI	Akinori Iwamura	50.00
AJ	Andruw Jones	15.00
MK	Munenori Kawasaki	50.00
PL	Pedro Lazo	20.00
CL	Carlos Lee	4.00
DL	Derrek Lee	10.00
JL	Jong Beom Lee	8.00
WL	Wei-Chu Lin	180.00
GL	Guangbiao Liu	10.00
VM	Victor Martinez	10.00
NM	Nobuhiko Matsunaka	60.00
DM	Daisuke Matsuzaka	350.00
YM	Yunieski Maya	15.00
JM	Justin Morneau	10.00
TN	Tsuyoshi Nishioka	60.00
MO	Michihiro Ogasawara	60.00
DO	David Ortiz	20.00
WP	Wei-Lun Pan	80.00
EP	Eduardo Paret	20.00
JP	Jin Man Park	15.00
OP	Oliver Perez	4.00
PE	Ariel Pestano	20.00
MP	Mike Piazza	25.00
AP	Albert Pujols	30.00
AR	Alex Rodriguez	25.00
IR	Ivan Rodriguez	10.00
JS	Johan Santana	15.00
MS	Min Han Son	10.00
AS	Alfonso Soriano	15.00
I	Ichiro Suzuki	220.00
HT	Hitoshi Tamura	50.00
MT	Mark Teixeira	10.00
TE	Miguel Tejada	15.00
KU	Koji Uehara	100.00
JV	Jason Varitek	20.00
TW	Tsuyoshi Wada	60.00
WW	Wei Wang	20.00
SW	Shunsuke Watanabe	50.00
GY	Guogang Yang	10.00

Update Gold

Gold (1001-1250): 4-8X
Gold SP's: .5-1X
Production 99 Sets

Update Inkredible

		NM/M
Inserted 1:24 Retail		
EA	Erick Aybar	10.00
BA	Brandon Backe	10.00
CB	Colter Bean	10.00
YB	Yuniesky Betancourt	10.00
EB	Eude Brito	15.00
BB	Ben Broussard	15.00
AB	Ambiorix Burgos	15.00
GC	Gustavo Chacin	8.00
BC	Brandon Claussen	10.00
CO	Chad Cordero/SP	15.00
CA	Carl Crawford	15.00
CC	Coco Crisp	15.00
CD	Chris Duffy	10.00
JD	Jermaine Dye	15.00
GF	Gavin Floyd	5.00
RF	Ryan Freel	15.00
RG	Ryan Garko	15.00
KG	Ken Griffey Jr./SP	125.00
AH	Aaron Harang	10.00
JH	John Hattig Jr.	10.00
MH	Matt Holliday	20.00
TI	Tadahito Iguchi/SP	30.00
CI	Cesar Izturis	5.00
DJ	Derek Jeter/SP	200.00
AJ	Adam Jones	25.00
JO	Jacque Jones	15.00
JJ	Jorge Julio/SP	10.00
CK	Casey Kotchman	10.00
CL	Cliff Lee	10.00
NL	Noah Lowry	15.00
BM	Brandon McCarthy/SP	15.00
ZM	Zach Miner	10.00
YM	Yadier Molina	15.00
MM	Matt Murton	20.00
LN	Leo Nunez	8.00
AP	Angel Pagan	10.00
PA	John Patterson	5.00
RP	Ronny Paulino	15.00
JP	Jhonny Peralta	15.00
PE	Joel Peralta	8.00
PI	Joel Pineiro	8.00
DR	Darrell Rasner	10.00
KR	Ken Ray	8.00
AR	Alex Rios/SP	30.00
JR	Juan Rivera/SP	20.00
BR	Brian Roberts	15.00
MR	Mike Rouse	10.00
RS	Ryan Shealy	15.00
NS	Nick Swisher	15.00
MT	Mark Teahen	15.00
MV	Michael Vento	8.00
BW	Brian Wilson	8.00
CW	C.J. Wilson	5.00
KY	Kevin Youkilis	15.00

Update Star Attractions

		NM/M
Inserted 1:2 Retail		
Silver:		2-3X
Production 99 Sets		
BR	Brian Anderson	.50
EA	Erick Aybar	.50
WA	Willy Aybar	.50
JO	Josh Barfield	.50
BI	Chad Billingsley	.75
MC	Matt Cain	.75
RC	Ronny Cedeno	.50
SD	Stephen Drew	1.50
AE	Andre Ethier	1.00
PF	Prince Fielder	1.50
TG	Tony Gwynn Jr.	.50
CH	Cole Hamels	1.00
HI	Jason Hirsh	.50
HU	Justin Huber	.50
CO	Conor Jackson	.50
JA	Chuck James	.50
KJ	Kenji Johjima	1.50
JJ	Josh Johnson	.50
AJ	Adam Jones	.50
MK	Matthew Kemp	.50
HK	Howie Kendrick	1.00
JK	Jason Kubel	.50
LE	Jon Lester	1.50
FL	Francisco Liriano	1.00
AL	Adam Loewen	.50
NM	Nicholas Markakis	.75
AM	Andy Marte	.50
RM	Russell Martin	.50
MA	Jeff Mathis	.50
DM	Dustin McGowan	.50
LM	Lastings Milledge	1.00
KM	Kendry Morales	.50
SO	Scott Olsen	.50
PA	Jonathan Papelbon	1.00
DP	Dustin Pedroia	.50
PE	Mike Pelfrey	1.50
HP	Hayden Penn	.50
CQ	Carlos Quentin	.50
HR	Hanley Ramirez	1.00
AR	Anthony Reyes	.50
AN	Anibal Sanchez	.50
SW	Jeremy Sowers	.50
DU	Dan Uggla	.50
JV	Justin Verlander	2.00
CY	Chris Young	.50
AW	Adam Wainwright	.50
JW	Jered Weaver	1.00
RZ	Ryan Zimmerman	1.50
JZ	Joel Zumaya	1.00

World Baseball Classic

		NM/M
Complete Set (50):		20.00
Common Player:		.25
1	Derek Jeter	1.50
2	Ken Griffey Jr.	1.00
3	Derrek Lee	.50
4	Dontrelle Willis	.25
5	Alex Rodriguez	1.50
6	Jeff Francoeur	.25
7	Roger Clemens	1.50
8	Johnny Damon	.50
9	Chipper Jones	.50
10	Mark Teixeira	.50
11	Chase Utley	.50
12	Jake Peavy	.50
13	Michael Collins	.25
14	Justin Huber	.25
15	Jason Bay	.50
16	Jeff Francis	.25
17	Justin Morneau	.25
18	Guogang Yang	.25
19	Wei Wang	.25
20	Chia-Hsien Hseih	.25
21	Chin-Lung Hu	.25
22	Wei-Lun Pan	.25
23	Yung-Chi Chen	.25
24	Mike Piazza	.50
25	Albert Pujols	1.50
26	David Ortiz	.50
27	Jose Reyes	.50
28	Miguel Tejada	.50
29	Ichiro Suzuki	1.00
30	Nobuhiko Matsunaka	.25
31	Toshiaki Imae	.25
32	Kazuhiro Wada	.25
33	Shunsuke Watanabe	.25
34	Jong Bong	.25
35	Jong Beom Lee	.25
36	Seung-Yeop Lee	.25
37	Vinny Castilla	.25
38	Oliver Perez	.50
39	Jorge Cantu	.25
40	Andruw Jones	.50
41	Carlos Lee	.50
42	Carlos Beltran	.50
43	Carlos Delgado	.50
44	Ivan Rodriguez	.50
45	Bernie Williams	.50
46	Bobby Abreu	.50
47	Miguel Cabrera	.50
48	Johan Santana	.50
49	Victor Martinez	.50
50	Omar Vizquel	.25

2006 Upper Deck Artifacts

		NM/M
Complete Set (100):		35.00
Common Player:		.25
Pack (4):		10.00
Box (10):		90.00
1	Luis Gonzalez	.25
2	Conor Jackson **(RC)**	.25
3	Joey Devine **RC**	1.00
4	Andruw Jones	.75
5	Chipper Jones	1.00
6	John Smoltz	.50
7	Jeff Francoeur	.50
8	Brian Roberts	.25
9	Miguel Tejada	.75
10	Nicholas Markakis **(RC)**	.25
11	Curt Schilling	1.00
12	David Ortiz	1.00
13	Johnny Damon	1.00
14	Manny Ramirez	1.00
15	Jonathan Papelbon **(RC)**	6.00
16	Aramis Ramirez	.50
17	Carlos Zambrano	.50
18	Derrek Lee	.75
19	Greg Maddux	2.00
20	Mark Prior	.75
21	Mark Buehrle	.50
22	Paul Konerko	.50
23	Adam Dunn	.75
24	Ken Griffey Jr.	2.00
25	Travis Hafner	.50
26	Victor Martinez	.50
27	Todd Helton	.75
28	Ivan Rodriguez	.75
29	Jeremy Bonderman	.25
30	Jeremy Hermida **(RC)**	.25
31	Carlos Delgado	.50
32	Dontrelle Willis	.50
33	Josh Beckett	.50
34	Miguel Cabrera	1.00
35	Craig Biggio	.50
36	Lance Berkman	.50
37	Roger Clemens	3.00
38	Roy Oswalt	.50
39	Josh Willingham **(RC)**	.25
40	Hanley Ramirez **(RC)**	.50
41	Prince Fielder **(RC)**	2.00
42	Zack Greinke	.25
43	Francisco Rodriguez	.25
44	Vladimir Guerrero	1.00
45	Tim Hamulack **(RC)**	.25
46	Jeff Kent	.50
47	Ben Sheets	.50
48	Rickie Weeks	.50
49	Francisco Liriano **(RC)**	4.00
50	Joe Mauer	.75
51	Johan Santana	.75
52	Justin Morneau	.50
53	Torii Hunter	.50
54	Carlos Beltran	.75
55	David Wright	2.00
56	Jose Reyes	.75
57	Mike Piazza	1.00
58	Pedro Martinez	1.00
59	Alex Rodriguez	3.00
60	Derek Jeter	3.00
61	Hideki Matsui	2.00
62	Randy Johnson	1.00
63	Justin Verlander **(RC)**	1.00
64	Bobby Crosby	.25
65	Eric Chavez	.50
66	Brian Anderson **(RC)**	.25
67	Bobby Abreu	.50
68	Pat Burrell	.50
69	Jason Bay	.50
70	Oliver Perez	.25
71	Chuck James **(RC)**	.25
72	Brian Giles	.25
73	Jake Peavy	.25
74	Khalil Greene	.25
75	Jason Schmidt	.50
76	Kenji Johjima **RC**	4.00
77	Jeremy Accardo **RC**	.50
78	Adrian Beltre	.25
79	Ichiro Suzuki	2.00
80	Jeff Harris **RC**	.50
81	Felix Hernandez	.75
82	Albert Pujols	3.00
83	Chris Carpenter	.75
84	Jim Edmonds	.50
85	Scott Rolen	.75
86	Mike Jacobs **(RC)**	.25
87	Carl Crawford	.50
88	Anderson Hernandez **(RC)**	.25
89	Scott Kazmir	.50
90	Josh Rupe **(RC)**	.25
91	Scott Feldman **RC**	.25
92	Alfonso Soriano	.75
93	Hank Blalock	.50
94	Mark Teixeira	.75
95	Michael Young	.50
96	Roy Halladay	.50
97	Vernon Wells	.50
98	Jason Bergmann **RC**	.50
99	Ryan Zimmerman **(RC)**	4.00
100	Jose Vidro	.25

AL/NL Artifacts

		NM/M
Common Player:		4.00
Production 325 Sets		
Red:		.75-1.5X
Production 100-250		
Green:		.75-1.5X
Production 150 Sets		
GA	Garrett Atkins	4.00
JB	Jeff Bagwell	8.00
SB	Scott Baker	4.00
RB	Rocco Baldelli	4.00
CL	Clint Barmes	4.00
JA	Jason Bay	8.00
HB	Hank Blalock	4.00
BL	Joe Blanton	4.00

JB Jeremy Bonderman 6.00
BB Ben Broussard 4.00
MB Mark Buehrle 6.00
CB Chris Burke 4.00
MC Miguel Cabrera 8.00
MA Matt Cain 6.00
JC Jorge Cantu 4.00
CA Chris Capuano 4.00
CC Chris Carpenter 10.00
GC Gustavo Chacin 4.00
EC Eric Chavez 4.00
RC Ryan Church 4.00
CH Chad Cordero 4.00
CC Carl Crawford 6.00
CR Joe Crede 4.00
CO Coco Crisp 6.00
ZD Zachary Duke 4.00
AD Adam Dunn/250 8.00
JE Jim Edmonds 6.00
ME Morgan Ensberg 4.00
PF Prince Fielder 15.00
JF Jeff Francoeur 6.00
EG Eric Gagne 4.00
GA Jon Garland 4.00
MG Marcus Giles 4.00
JG Jonny Gomes 6.00
KG Ken Griffey Jr. 15.00
VG Vladimir Guerrero 8.00
TH Travis Hafner 8.00
BH Bill Hall/235 4.00
AH Aaron Harang 4.00
DH Danny Haren 4.00
TH Todd Helton 6.00
FH Felix Hernandez 6.00
RH Ramon Hernandez 4.00
TR Trevor Hoffman 4.00
MH Matt Holliday 6.00
RY Ryan Howard 15.00
TI Tadahito Iguchi 8.00
CO Conor Jackson 4.00
DJ Derek Jeter 25.00
DA Dan Johnson 4.00
NJ Nick Johnson 4.00
RJ Randy Johnson/235 8.00
CJ Chipper Jones 8.00
SK Scott Kazmir 6.00
LE Carlos Lee 6.00
CL Cliff Lee 4.00
DL Derrek Lee 8.00
BL Brad Lidge 4.00
FL Felipe Lopez 4.00
ML Mark Loretta 4.00
NL Noah Lowry 4.00
PM Pedro Martinez 8.00
VM Victor Martinez 6.00
JM Joe Mauer 10.00
BM Brian McCann 8.00
BM Brandon McCarthy 4.00
YM Yadier Molina 4.00
JU Justin Morneau 6.00
JN Joe Nathan 4.00
DO David Ortiz 10.00
RO Roy Oswalt 6.00
JP Jake Peavy 6.00
PE Jhonny Peralta 4.00
JP Joel Pineiro 4.00
SP Scott Podsednik 6.00
MP Mark Prior 6.00
AP Albert Pujols/250 20.00
MR Manny Ramirez 8.00
JR Jose Reyes 8.00
IR Ivan Rodriguez 6.00
ES Ervin Santana 4.00
CS Chris Shelton 4.00
GS Grady Sizemore 10.00
JS John Smoltz/250 250.00
AS Alfonso Soriano 8.00
HS Huston Street 4.00
NS Nick Swisher 4.00
MT Miguel Tejada 6.00
CU Chase Utley 10.00
JV Jason Varitek 8.00
RW Rickie Weeks 6.00
JW Jake Westbrook 4.00
DW Dontrelle Willis 8.00
JW Jack Wilson/200 4.00
WR David Wright 20.00
DY Dmitri Young 4.00
MY Michael Young 4.00
RZ Ryan Zimmerman 15.00

Awesome Artifacts

NM/M
Common Player: 10.00
Production 45 unless noted.
BA Jeff Bagwell 12.00
HB Harold Baines 10.00
SB Scott Baker 10.00
RB Rocco Baldelli 10.00
CB Clint Barmes 10.00
JB Jason Bay 12.00
HA Hank Blalock 10.00
BL Joe Blanton 10.00
MB Mark Buehrle 10.00
BU Chris Burke 10.00
MC Miguel Cabrera 15.00
CA Matt Cain 10.00
CH Chris Carpenter 15.00
GC Gustavo Chacin 10.00
EC Eric Chavez 10.00
WC Will Clark 12.00
CC Carl Crawford 12.00
DD Don Drysdale/25 25.00
ZD Zachary Duke 10.00
AD Adam Dunn 15.00
JE Jim Edmonds 12.00
ME Morgan Ensberg 10.00
PF Prince Fielder 20.00
CF Carlton Fisk 15.00
FG Gavin Floyd 10.00
JF Jeff Francoeur 12.00
EG Eric Gagne 10.00
FG Freddy Garcia/21 10.00
GA Jon Garland 10.00
SG Steve Garvey 10.00
JG Jonny Gomes 10.00
KG Ken Griffey Jr. 30.00
VG Vladimir Guerrero 15.00
BH Bill Hall 10.00
AH Aaron Harang 10.00
DH Danny Haren 10.00
TH Todd Helton 10.00
FH Felix Hernandez 15.00
TR Trevor Hoffman 10.00
RH Rogers Hornsby/25 100.00
RY Ryan Howard 25.00
BO Bo Jackson 15.00
CO Conor Jackson 10.00
DJ Derek Jeter 40.00
DA Dan Johnson 10.00
NJ Nick Johnson 10.00
RA Randy Johnson 15.00
CJ Chipper Jones 15.00
JL Jason Lane 10.00
DL Don Larsen/25 25.00
CL Cliff Lee 10.00
DE Derrek Lee 15.00
NL Noah Lowry 10.00
PM Pedro Martinez 15.00
EM Eddie Mathews 15.00
BR Brian McCann 15.00
BM Brandon McCarthy 10.00
JM Johnny Mize/25 20.00
YM Yadier Molina 10.00
JU Justin Morneau 12.00
DO David Ortiz 25.00
RO Roy Oswalt 10.00
SP Satchel Paige 100.00
DP Dave Parker 10.00
JP Jake Peavy 10.00
PE Jhonny Peralta 10.00
GP Gaylord Perry 10.00
JO Joel Pineiro 10.00
MP Mark Prior 10.00
AP Albert Pujols 40.00
MR Manny Ramirez 15.00
CR Cal Ripken Jr. 40.00
IR Ivan Rodriguez 10.00
AR Aaron Rowand 10.00
ES Ervin Santana 10.00
RS Ron Santo 10.00
JA Jason Schmidt 10.00
CS Chris Shelton 10.00
GS Grady Sizemore 15.00
JS John Smoltz 15.00
AS Alfonso Soriano 15.00
HS Huston Street 10.00
NS Nick Swisher 10.00
MI Miguel Tejada 10.00
FT Frank Thomas 15.00
CU Chase Utley 20.00
AV Andy Van Slyke 10.00
JV Jason Varitek 20.00
RW Rickie Weeks 10.00
DW David Wells 10.00
WE Jake Westbrook 10.00
WI Dontrelle Willis 12.00
JW Jack Wilson 10.00
WR David Wright 30.00
CY Carl Yastrzemski/25 40.00
RZ Ryan Zimmerman 25.00

Apparel

NM/M
Common Player:
Production 325 Sets
Gold: .75-1.5X
Production 150 Sets
Silver: 1X
Production 250 Sets
Rare Apparel: No Pricing
Production One Set
AT Garrett Atkins 4.00
HB Harold Baines 4.00
SB Scott Baker 6.00
RB Rocco Baldelli 4.00
BA Clint Barmes 4.00
BY Jason Bay 8.00
YB Yuniesky Betancourt 4.00
JO Joe Blanton 4.00
JE Jeremy Bonderman 4.00
BB Ben Broussard 4.00
CB Chris Burke 4.00
MC Miguel Cabrera 8.00
MA Matt Cain 6.00
JU Jorge Cantu 6.00
CS Chris Capuano 4.00
CH Chris Carpenter 10.00
GC Gustavo Chacin 4.00
RC Ryan Church 4.00
WC Will Clark 8.00
CD Chad Cordero 4.00
CA Carl Crawford 6.00
CO Coco Crisp 6.00
PF Prince Fielder 15.00
CF Carlton Fisk 8.00
GF Gavin Floyd 4.00
GA Jon Garland 6.00
SG Steve Garvey 8.00
MG Marcus Giles 4.00
JG Jonny Gomes 4.00
GO Adrian Gonzalez 4.00
GG Rich "Goose" Gossage 4.00
KG Ken Griffey Jr. 15.00
AH Aaron Harang 4.00
DH Danny Haren 4.00
JH Jeremy Hermida 4.00
FH Felix Hernandez 8.00
RH Ramon Hernandez 4.00
MH Matt Holliday 8.00
HO Ryan Howard 15.00
TI Tadahito Iguchi 8.00
BO Bo Jackson 10.00
CJ Conor Jackson 4.00
DJ Derek Jeter 25.00
DA Dan Johnson 4.00
SK Scott Kazmir 8.00
KE Jason Kendall 4.00
CK Casey Kotchman 4.00
JK John Kruk 8.00
JL Jason Lane 4.00
DO Don Larsen 15.00
LE Carlos Lee 6.00
CL Cliff Lee 4.00
DL Derrek Lee 8.00
BL Brad Lidge 4.00
FL Felipe Lopez 4.00
ML Mark Loretta 4.00
NL Noah Lowry 4.00
BI Bill Madlock 4.00
JM Joe Mauer 10.00
BC Brian McCann 8.00
BM Brandon McCarthy 4.00
FM Fred McGriff 8.00
YM Yadier Molina 4.00
MO Justin Morneau 8.00
JN Joe Nathan 4.00
GN Graig Nettles 4.00
OR Magglio Ordonez 4.00
RO Roy Oswalt 6.00
PE Jake Peavy 6.00
JP Jhonny Peralta 4.00
GP Gaylord Perry 6.00
PI Joel Pineiro 4.00
SP Scott Podsednik 6.00
BP Boog Powell 4.00
JY Jeremy Reed 4.00
HR Jose Reyes 8.00
CR Cal Ripken Jr. 20.00
BR Brian Roberts 4.00
AR Aaron Rowand 4.00
ES Ervin Santana 4.00
RS Ron Santo 15.00
MS Mike Schmidt 10.00
SH Chris Shelton 4.00
GS Grady Sizemore 10.00
HS Huston Street 4.00
NS Nick Swisher 8.00
ST So Taguchi 6.00
CU Chase Utley 10.00
AV Andy Van Slyke 4.00
RW Rickie Weeks 6.00
JW Jake Westbrook 4.00
DW Dontrelle Willis 6.00
WR David Wright 20.00
CY Carl Yastrzemski 15.00
DY Dmitri Young 4.00
MY Michael Young 4.00
RZ Ryan Zimmerman 15.00

Apparel Autographs

NM/M
Production 30 Sets
Patch Auto.: No Pricing
Production 10 Sets
AT Garrett Atkins 20.00
HB Harold Baines 20.00
SB Scott Baker 15.00
BA Clint Barmes 15.00
BY Jason Bay 30.00
YB Yuniesky Betancourt 20.00
JO Joe Blanton 20.00
JE Jeremy Bonderman 30.00
BB Ben Broussard 15.00
CB Chris Burke 15.00
MC Miguel Cabrera 40.00
MA Matt Cain 40.00
CS Chris Capuano 20.00
CH Chris Carpenter 50.00
GC Gustavo Chacin 15.00
RC Ryan Church 20.00
WC Will Clark 40.00
CD Chad Cordero 20.00
CA Carl Crawford 25.00
CO Coco Crisp 40.00
JD Jermaine Dye 20.00
PF Prince Fielder 75.00
CF Carlton Fisk 40.00
SG Steve Garvey 25.00
MG Marcus Giles 25.00
JG Jonny Gomes 25.00
GO Adrian Gonzalez 20.00
GG Rich "Goose" Gossage 35.00
KG Ken Griffey Jr. 100.00
AH Aaron Harang 15.00
DH Danny Haren 20.00
JH Jeremy Hermida 25.00
FH Felix Hernandez 50.00
RH Ramon Hernandez 15.00
HO Ryan Howard/23 85.00
TI Tadahito Iguchi 50.00
BO Bo Jackson 100.00
CJ Conor Jackson 40.00
DJ Derek Jeter 200.00
DA Dan Johnson 20.00
SK Scott Kazmir 40.00
CK Casey Kotchman 25.00
JK John Kruk 30.00
DO Don Larsen 25.00
LE Carlos Lee 25.00
CL Cliff Lee 15.00
DL Derrek Lee 40.00
BL Brad Lidge 20.00
FL Felipe Lopez 25.00
NL Noah Lowry 40.00
BI Bill Madlock 15.00
JM Joe Mauer 50.00
BM Brandon McCarthy 15.00
YM Yadier Molina 40.00
MO Justin Morneau 30.00
JN Joe Nathan 25.00
GN Graig Nettles 30.00
OR Magglio Ordonez 35.00
RO Roy Oswalt 25.00
PE Jake Peavy 40.00
JP Jhonny Peralta 15.00
GP Gaylord Perry 25.00
PI Joel Pineiro 25.00
SP Scott Podsednik 30.00
BP Boog Powell 25.00
JR Jose Reyes 40.00
CR Cal Ripken Jr. 180.00
AR Aaron Rowand 20.00
RS Ron Santo 75.00
MS Mike Schmidt 60.00
SH Chris Shelton 15.00
HS Huston Street 20.00
NS Nick Swisher 25.00
CU Chase Utley 75.00
AV Andy Van Slyke 25.00
RW Rickie Weeks 25.00
JW Jake Westbrook 20.00
DW Dontrelle Willis 35.00
WR David Wright 85.00
CY Carl Yastrzemski 65.00
DY Dmitri Young 15.00
MY Michael Young 25.00
RZ Ryan Zimmerman 75.00

Autofacts

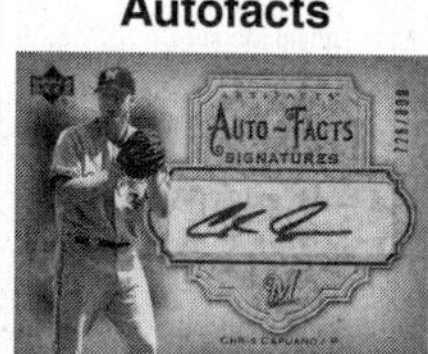

NM/M
Production 5-800
JA Jeremy Accardo/800 15.00
LA Luis Aparicio/250 15.00
GA Garrett Atkins/800 15.00
CB Clint Barmes/800 10.00
JB Jason Bay/200 20.00
GB George Bell/715 20.00
BE Jason Bergmann/800 10.00
BY Clete Boyer/485 15.00
MC Miguel Cabrera/250 30.00
MA Matt Cain/700 20.00
CP Jose Capellan/800 10.00
CA Chris Capuano/800 15.00
CH Chris Carpenter/51 40.00
JC Joe Carter/400 15.00
GC Gustavo Chacin/800 10.00
CC Chris Chambliss/400 15.00
RC Ryan Church/800 10.00
CK Jack Clark/800 10.00
CO Coco Crisp/600 25.00
ED Eric Davis/487 15.00
AD Andre Dawson/300 20.00
CD Chris Demaria/800 10.00
DA Chris Denorfia/659 10.00
DE Joey Devine/150 10.00
JD Jermaine Dye/652 15.00
LD Lenny Dykstra/412 15.00
SF Scott Feldman/800 10.00
PF Prince Fielder/200 50.00
GF George Foster/300 10.00
SG Steve Garvey/300 15.00
MG Marcus Giles/350 15.00
GO Jonny Gomes/700 10.00
GG Rich "Goose" Gossage/300 20.00
KG Ken Griffey Jr./800 60.00
TH Travis Hafner/400 20.00
TM Tim Hamulack/742 10.00
AH Aaron Harang/800 10.00
DH Danny Haren/800 15.00
JE Jeff Harris/800 10.00
FH Felix Hernandez/300 30.00
KH Kent Hrbek/239 15.00
TI Tadahito Iguchi/700 30.00
BO Bo Jackson/250 50.00
CJ Conor Jackson/800 15.00
RJ Reggie Jackson/200 50.00
DJ Derek Jeter/100 150.00
AJ Andruw Jones/150 50.00
IK Ian Kinsler/800 20.00
JK Jason Kubel/400 10.00
JL Jason Lane/800 10.00
BL Barry Larkin/300 35.00
CL Cliff Lee/600 10.00
DL Derrek Lee/300 30.00
BI Bill Madlock/300 15.00
PM Pedro Martinez/100 60.00
JM Joe Mauer/400 35.00
AM Aaron Miles/494 10.00
YM Yadier Molina/800 20.00
JN Joe Nathan/800 15.00
GN Graig Nettles/300 20.00
TO Tony Oliva/300 15.00
MO Magglio Ordonez/437 25.00
JP Jhonny Peralta/700 15.00
TP Tony Perez/251 25.00
HR Hanley Ramirez/500 20.00
RE Chris Resop/800 10.00
JR Jim Rice/200 20.00
CR Cal Ripken Jr./100 100.00
BR Brian Roberts/200 15.00
AR Aaron Rowand/520 15.00
JS Johan Santana/150 50.00
CS Chris Shelton/350 15.00
HS Huston Street/500 15.00
NS Nick Swisher/700 20.00
WT Willy Taveras/500 10.00
CU Chase Utley/200 50.00
AV Andy Van Slyke/800 20.00
JV Justin Verlander/700 40.00
RW Rickie Weeks/91 25.00
JW Jake Westbrook/650 10.00
WI Dontrelle Willis/50 20.00
MW Maury Wills/150 15.00
DW David Wright/300 65.00
CY Chris Young/700 15.00
DY Dmitri Young/300 10.00
MY Michael Young/600 20.00
CZ Carlos Zambrano/200 25.00
RZ Ryan Zimmerman/800 40.00

2006 Upper Deck Cardinals World Series

NM/M
Complete Set (25): 25.00
Complete Factory Set: 40.00
Common player: .50
1 Ronnie Belliard .50
2 Gary Bennett .50
3 Chris Carpenter 3.00
4 Chris Duncan 1.00
5 David Eckstein 3.00
6 Jim Edmonds 3.00
7 Juan Encarnacion 1.00
8 Randy Flores .50
9 Josh Hancock .50
10 Tyler Johnson .50
11 Josh Kinney .50
12 Braden Looper .50
13 Aaron Miles .50
14 Yadier Molina 1.00
15 Albert Pujols 5.00
16 Anthony Reyes 1.50
17 John Rodriguez .50
18 Scott Rolen 3.00
19 Jeff Suppan 1.00
20 Scott Spiezio .50
21 So Taguchi .50
22 Brad Thompson .50
23 Adam Wainwright 2.00
24 Jeff Weaver .50
25 Preston Wilson .50

Jumbo

NM/M
Jumbo Team Photo: 2.00

Memorable Moment

NM/M
Complete Set (9): 5.00
1 Albert Pujols 2.00
2 Juan Encarnacion .50
3 So Taguchi .50
4 Jeff Suppan .50
5 Albert Pujols 2.00
6 Yadier Molina .50
7 Anthony Reyes .50
8 David Eckstein 1.00
9 Jeff Weaver .50

Season Highlight

NM/M
Complete Set (15): 5.00
1 Scott Rolen 1.00
2 Mark Mulder .50
3 Albert Pujols 2.00
4 Albert Pujols 2.00
5 Chris Carpenter 1.00
6 Juan Encarnacion .50
7 Adam Wainwright .50
8 Yadier Molina .50
9 So Taguchi .50
10 Jeff Suppan .50
11 Jim Edmonds 1.00
12 Chris Duncan .50
13 Scott Spiezio .50
14 Scott Rolen 1.00
15 Ronnie Belliard .50

2006 Upper Deck Epic

NM/M
Complete Set (300):
Common Player: 2.00
Production 450 Sets
Pack (3): 35.00
Box (5): 150.00
1 Conor Jackson **(RC)** 2.00
2 Brandon Webb 3.00
3 Craig Counsell 2.00
4 Luis Gonzalez 2.00
5 Miguel Batista 2.00
6 Orlando Hudson 2.00
7 Russ Ortiz 2.00
8 Shawn Green 2.00
9 Andruw Jones 4.00
10 Chipper Jones 5.00
11 Edgar Renteria 3.00
12 Jeff Francoeur 2.00
13 John Smoltz 3.00
14 Marcus Giles 2.00
15 Mike Hampton 2.00
16 Tim Hudson 3.00
17 Erik Bedard 2.00
18 Brian Roberts 2.00
19 Javy Lopez 2.00
20 Jay Gibbons 2.00
21 Jeff Conine 2.00
22 Melvin Mora 2.00
23 Miguel Tejada 4.00
24 Daniel Cabrera 2.00
25 Rodrigo Lopez 2.00
26 Ramon Hernandez 2.00
27 Bronson Arroyo 2.00
28 Curt Schilling 5.00
29 David Ortiz 5.00
30 David Wells 2.00
31 Jason Varitek 4.00
32 Josh Beckett 3.00
33 Kevin Youkilis 3.00
34 Manny Ramirez 5.00
35 Matt Clement 2.00
36 Mike Lowell 2.00
37 Tim Wakefield 2.00
38 Trot Nixon 2.00
39 Aramis Ramirez 3.00
40 Carlos Zambrano 3.00
41 Derrek Lee 4.00
42 Greg Maddux 10.00
43 Juan Pierre 2.00
44 Kerry Wood 2.00
45 Mark Prior 4.00
46 Michael Barrett 2.00
47 Ryan Dempster 2.00
48 Todd Walker 2.00
49 Wade Miller 2.00
50 A.J. Pierzynski 2.00
51 Brian Anderson **(RC)** 2.00
52 Frank Thomas 4.00
53 Javier Vazquez 2.00
54 Jim Thome 4.00
55 Joe Crede 2.00
56 Jon Garland 2.00
57 Juan Uribe 2.00
58 Mark Buehrle 3.00
59 Paul Konerko 3.00
60 Scott Podsednik 2.00
61 Tadahito Iguchi 3.00
62 Aaron Harang 2.00
63 Adam Dunn 4.00
64 Austin Kearns 3.00
65 Edwin Encarnacion 2.00
66 Eric Milton 2.00
67 Felipe Lopez 2.00
68 Jason LaRue 2.00
69 Ken Griffey Jr. 10.00
70 Wily Mo Pena 2.00
71 Aaron Boone 2.00
72 Ben Broussard 2.00
73 C.C. Sabathia 2.00
74 Casey Blake 2.00
75 Cliff Lee 2.00
76 Grady Sizemore 3.00
77 Jake Westbrook 2.00
78 Josh Bard 2.00
79 Travis Hafner 4.00
80 Victor Martinez 2.00
81 Chin-Hui Tsao 2.00
82 Clint Barmes 2.00
83 Garrett Atkins 2.00
84 Josh Wilson **(RC)** 2.00
85 Luis Gonzalez 2.00
86 Matt Holliday 2.00
87 Todd Helton 4.00
88 Brandon Inge 2.00
89 Carlos Guillen 2.00
90 Chris Shelton 2.00
91 Craig Monroe 2.00
92 Dmitri Young 2.00
93 Ivan Rodriguez 4.00
94 Jeremy Bonderman 3.00
95 Magglio Ordonez 2.00

96 Alberto Gonzalez **RC** 2.00
97 Brian Moehler 2.00
98 Dontrelle Willis 3.00
99 Jeremy Hermida **(RC)** 3.00
100 Jason Vargas 2.00
101 Miguel Cabrera 5.00
102 Adam Everett 2.00
103 Andy Pettitte 3.00
104 Brad Ausmus 2.00
105 Brad Lidge 2.00
106 Craig Biggio 3.00
107 Dan Wheeler 2.00
108 Jeff Bagwell 4.00
109 Lance Berkman 3.00
110 Morgan Ensberg 2.00
111 Preston Wilson 2.00
112 Roger Clemens 10.00
113 Roy Oswalt 3.00
114 David Gassner **(RC)** 2.00
115 Angel Berroa 2.00
116 Doug Mientkiewicz 2.00
117 Joe Mays 2.00
118 Mark Grudzielanek 2.00
119 Mike Sweeney 2.00
120 Reggie Sanders 2.00
121 Runelvys Hernandez 2.00
122 Scott Elarton 2.00
123 Brandon Watson **(RC)** 2.00
124 Zack Greinke 2.00
125 Brad Penny 2.00
126 Derek Lowe 2.00
127 Eric Gagne 2.00
128 J.D. Drew 3.00
129 Jayson Werth 2.00
130 Jeff Kent 3.00
131 Nomar Garciaparra 4.00
132 Olmedo Saenz 2.00
133 Rafael Furcal 3.00
134 Ben Sheets 3.00
135 Bill Hall 2.00
136 Carlos Lee 3.00
137 Geoff Jenkins 2.00
138 Prince Fielder **(RC)** 10.00
139 Rickie Weeks 3.00
140 Jose Capellan **(RC)** 2.00
141 Brad Radke 2.00
142 Joe Mauer 6.00
143 Joe Nathan 2.00
144 Johan Santana 5.00
145 Justin Morneau 3.00
146 Kyle Lohse 2.00
147 Lew Ford 2.00
148 Luis Castillo 2.00
149 Matthew LeCroy 2.00
150 Michael Cuddyer 2.00
151 Shannon Stewart 2.00
152 Torii Hunter 3.00
153 Billy Wagner 2.00
154 Carlos Beltran 5.00
155 Carlos Delgado 4.00
156 Cliff Floyd 2.00
157 David Wright 10.00
158 Jose Reyes 8.00
159 Kazuo Matsui 2.00
160 Mike Piazza 6.00
161 Paul LoDuca 2.00
162 Pedro Martinez 5.00
163 Tom Glavine 3.00
164 Victor Diaz 2.00
165 Alex Rodriguez 15.00
166 Bernie Williams 3.00
167 Carl Pavano 2.00
168 Chien-Ming Wang 5.00
169 Derek Jeter 15.00
170 Gary Sheffield 4.00
171 Hideki Matsui 8.00
172 Jason Giambi 4.00
173 Johnny Damon 5.00
174 Jorge Posada 4.00
175 Robinson Cano 5.00
176 Mariano Rivera 4.00
177 Mike Mussina 4.00
178 Randy Johnson 5.00
179 Miguel Cairo 2.00
180 Barry Zito 3.00
181 Bobby Crosby 2.00
182 Bobby Kielty 2.00
183 Eric Chavez 3.00
184 Josh Barfield **(RC)** 2.00
185 Esteban Loaiza 2.00
186 Huston Street 3.00
187 Jason Kendall 2.00
188 Nick Swisher 3.00
189 Aaron Rowand 2.00
190 Bobby Abreu 3.00
191 Chase Utley 5.00
192 Gavin Floyd 2.00
193 Jimmy Rollins 4.00
194 Mike Lieberthal 2.00
195 Pat Burrell 3.00
196 Ryan Howard 8.00
197 Craig Wilson 2.00
198 Jack Wilson 2.00
199 Jason Bay 4.00
200 Joe Randa 2.00
201 Josh Fogg 2.00
202 Kip Wells 2.00
203 Sean Casey 2.00
204 Zachary Duke 2.00
205 Brian Giles 3.00
206 Dave Roberts 2.00
207 Jake Peavy 4.00
208 Khalil Greene 2.00
209 Mike Cameron 2.00
210 Ryan Klesko 2.00
211 Trevor Hoffman 2.00
212 Vinny Castilla 2.00
213 Armando Benitez 2.00
214 Jason Schmidt 3.00
215 Matt Morris 2.00
216 Moises Alou 3.00
217 Omar Vizquel 2.00
218 Ray Durham 2.00
219 Adrian Beltre 2.00
220 Carl Everett 2.00
221 Kenji Johjima **RC** 15.00
222 Felix Hernandez 4.00
223 Ichiro Suzuki 10.00
224 Jamie Moyer 2.00
225 Jeremy Reed 2.00
226 Joel Pineiro 2.00
227 Raul Ibanez 2.00
228 Rickie Sexson 3.00
229 Albert Pujols 15.00
230 Chris Carpenter 5.00
231 David Eckstein 2.00
232 Jason Marquis 2.00
233 Jeff Suppan 2.00
234 Jim Edmonds 4.00
235 Yadier Molina 2.00
236 Mark Mulder 3.00
237 Scott Rolen 5.00
238 Alex Gonzalez 2.00
239 Aubrey Huff 2.00
240 Carl Crawford 3.00
241 Casey Fossum 2.00
242 Joey Gathright 2.00
243 Scott Kazmir 3.00
244 Toby Hall 2.00
245 Travis Lee 2.00
246 Adam Eaton 2.00
247 Francisco Cordero 2.00
248 Hank Blalock 3.00
249 Kevin Mench 2.00
250 Kevin Millwood 2.00
251 Laynce Nix 2.00
252 Mark Teixeira 4.00
253 Michael Young 2.00
254 A.J. Burnett 2.00
255 Alex Rios 3.00
256 B.J. Ryan 2.00
257 Corey Koskie 2.00
258 Josh Towers 2.00
259 Lyle Overbay 2.00
260 Reed Johnson 2.00
261 Roy Halladay 3.00
262 Russ Adams 2.00
263 Troy Glaus 3.00
264 Vernon Wells 3.00
265 Alfonso Soriano 4.00
266 John Patterson 2.00
267 Damian Jackson 2.00
268 Jose Guillen 2.00
269 Jose Vidro 2.00
270 Livan Hernandez 2.00
271 Adam Kennedy 2.00
272 Bartolo Colon 2.00
273 Bengie Molina 2.00
274 Casey Kotchman 2.00
275 Chone Figgins 2.00
276 Matt Cain **(RC)** 5.00
277 Darin Erstad 2.00
278 Edgardo Alfonzo 2.00
279 Francisco Rodriguez 2.00
280 Garret Anderson 3.00
281 Vladimir Guerrero 5.00
282 Chris Denorfia **(RC)** 2.00
283 Joey Devine **RC** 4.00
284 Justin Verlander **(RC)** 10.00
285 Scott Feldman **RC** 5.00
286 Jason Bergmann **RC** 4.00
287 Jeremy Accardo **RC** 4.00
288 Adam Wainwright **(RC)** 8.00
289 Hanley Ramirez **(RC)** 5.00
290 Josh Johnson **(RC)** 3.00
291 Ryan Zimmerman **(RC)** 20.00
292 Anderson Hernandez **(RC)** 4.00
293 Francisco Liriano **(RC)** 20.00
294 Josh Willingham **(RC)** 3.00
295 Hong-Chih Kuo **(RC)** 8.00
296 Steve Stemle **RC** 4.00
297 Jeff Harris **RC** 4.00
298 John Van Benschoten **(RC)** 4.00
299 Jonathan Papelbon **(RC)** 25.00
300 Jason Kubel **(RC)** 4.00

Awesome 8 Materials

Production 1-10

Epic Endorsements

NM/M

Production 10-45
JB Jason Bay/45 30.00
CB Craig Biggio/30 60.00
WB Wade Boggs/30 75.00
LB Lou Brock/30 75.00
JI Jim Bunning/30 30.00
MC1 Miguel Cabrera/30 50.00
MC2 Miguel Cabrera/30 50.00
RC Rod Carew/30 50.00
SC1 Steve Carlton/27 35.00
SC2 Steve Carlton/27 35.00
EC Eric Chavez/30 30.00
WC Will Clark/23 50.00
AD Adam Dunn/45 40.00
BF1 Bob Feller/45 40.00
BF2 Bob Feller/45 40.00
PF Prince Fielder/45 75.00
CF Carlton Fisk/30 50.00
SG Steve Garvey/45 30.00
BG Bob Gibson/30 60.00
KG1 Ken Griffey Jr./30 150.00
KG2 Ken Griffey Jr./30 150.00
KG3 Ken Griffey Jr./30 150.00
TG Tony Gwynn/30 50.00
JH1 Jeremy Hermida/45 30.00
JH2 Jeremy Hermida/45 30.00
FH1 Felix Hernandez/30 50.00
FH2 Felix Hernandez/30 50.00
RH Ryan Howard/45 100.00
BO Bo Jackson/30 85.00
DJ1 Derek Jeter/30 200.00
DJ2 Derek Jeter/30 200.00
DJ3 Derek Jeter/30 200.00
AJ Andruw Jones/30 40.00
LA Don Larsen/30 40.00
FL Fred Lynn/45 25.00
BM Bill Mazeroski/30 60.00
PM1 Paul Molitor/30 40.00
PM2 Paul Molitor/30 40.00
TO Tony Oliva/45 30.00
DO David Ortiz/30 85.00
RO1 Roy Oswalt/45 40.00
RO2 Roy Oswalt/45 40.00
JP1 Jim Palmer/30 40.00
JP2 Jim Palmer/30 40.00
JA Jake Peavy/45 25.00
TP Tony Perez/45 40.00
AP Albert Pujols/15 400.00
CR Cal Ripken Jr./15 280.00
BN Brian Roberts/45 30.00
BR1 Brooks Robinson/30 75.00
BR2 Brooks Robinson/30 75.00
FR Frank Robinson/30 40.00
RS1 Ryne Sandberg/45 100.00
CS Curt Schilling/15 75.00
TS Tom Seaver/30 60.00
OS Ozzie Smith/30 75.00
SM John Smoltz/30 150.00
AS Alfonso Soriano/30 40.00
DS Don Sutton/30 30.00
CU Chase Utley/45 50.00
BW Billy Williams/45 25.00
DW1 Dontrelle Willis/30 40.00
DW2 Dontrelle Willis/30 40.00
MW Maury Wills/45 25.00
WR David Wright/25 100.00
RZ1 Ryan Zimmerman/30 100.00
RZ2 Ryan Zimmerman/30 100.00

Epic Events

NM/M

Common Player: 2.00
Production 675 Sets
EE1 Ryan Howard 4.00
EE2 Tadahito Iguchi 2.00
EE3 Paul Konerko 2.00
EE4 Craig Biggio 2.00
EE5 Alex Rodriguez 6.00
EE6 Ichiro Suzuki 5.00
EE7 David Ortiz 4.00
EE8 Miguel Cabrera 3.00
EE9 Dontrelle Willis 2.00
EE10 Mark Teixeira 3.00
EE11 Hideki Matsui 5.00
EE12 Albert Pujols 8.00
EE13 Albert Pujols 8.00
EE14 Greg Maddux 5.00
EE15 Greg Maddux 5.00
EE16 Manny Ramirez 3.00
EE17 Mark Teixeira 3.00
EE18 Alex Rodriguez 6.00
EE19 Manny Ramirez 3.00
EE20 Randy Johnson 3.00
EE21 Jason Varitek 3.00
EE22 Vladimir Guerrero 3.00
EE23 Roger Clemens 8.00
EE24 Manny Ramirez 3.00
EE25 Curt Schilling 3.00
EE26 Johnny Damon 3.00
EE27 David Ortiz 4.00
EE28 David Wright 6.00
EE29 Ichiro Suzuki 5.00
EE30 Ichiro Suzuki 5.00
EE31 Adam Dunn 3.00
EE32 Adrian Beltre 2.00
EE33 Javy Lopez 2.00
EE34 Greg Maddux 5.00
EE35 Randy Johnson 3.00
EE36 Jim Thome 3.00
EE37 Adam Dunn 3.00
EE38 Bobby Abreu 2.00
EE39 Felix Hernandez 3.00
EE40 Greg Maddux 5.00
EE41 Ken Griffey Jr. 6.00
EE42 Randy Johnson 3.00
EE43 Johan Santana 3.00
EE44 Magglio Ordonez 2.00
EE45 Josh Beckett 2.00
EE46 Ivan Rodriguez 3.00
EE47 Alfonso Soriano 3.00
EE48 Eric Gagne 2.00
EE49 Hank Blalock 2.00
EE50 Roger Clemens 8.00
EE51 Derek Jeter 8.00
EE52 Derek Jeter 8.00
EE53 Barry Zito 2.00
EE54 Alex Rodriguez 6.00
EE55 Nomar Garciaparra 3.00
EE56 Torii Hunter 2.00
EE57 Ichiro Suzuki 5.00
EE58 Randy Johnson 3.00
EE59 Ichiro Suzuki 5.00
EE60 Albert Pujols 8.00
EE61 Albert Pujols 8.00
EE62 Ichiro Suzuki 5.00
EE63 Derek Jeter 8.00
EE64 Pedro Martinez 3.00
EE65 Chris Shelton 2.00
EE66 Ivan Rodriguez 3.00
EE67 Chipper Jones 3.00
EE68 Pedro Martinez 3.00
EE69 Ken Griffey Jr. 6.00
EE70 Jeff Bagwell 3.00
EE71 Nomar Garciaparra 3.00
EE72 Mark Prior 3.00
EE73 Kerry Wood 2.00
EE74 Andruw Jones 3.00
EE75 Derek Jeter 8.00
EE76 Cal Ripken Jr. 10.00
EE77 Ken Griffey Jr. 6.00
EE78 Ken Griffey Jr. 6.00
EE79 Mike Piazza 4.00
EE80 Nolan Ryan 6.00
EE81 Greg Maddux 5.00
EE82 Greg Maddux 5.00
EE83 Roger Clemens 8.00
EE84 Ozzie Smith 4.00
EE85 Tom Seaver 4.00
EE86 Thurman Munson 4.00
EE87 Reggie Jackson 3.00
EE88 Johnny Bench 4.00
EE89 Mike Schmidt 4.00
EE90 Carlton Fisk 2.00
EE91 Eddie Mathews 3.00
EE92 Roy Campanella 4.00
EE93 Jackie Robinson 6.00
EE94 Joe DiMaggio 6.00
EE95 Jimmie Foxx 5.00
EE96 Lou Gehrig 10.00
EE97 Babe Ruth 10.00
EE98 Ty Cobb 6.00
EE99 Honus Wagner 5.00
EE100 Cy Young 5.00

Four Barrel

No Pricing
Production One Set

Foursome Fabrics

NM/M

Production 5-50
CMBF Carlton Fisk, Thurman Munson, Johnny Bench, Gary Carter/25 70.00
GRSM Tom Seaver, Nolan Ryan, Juan Marichal, Bob Gibson/50 60.00
MBSP Albert Pujols, Lou Brock, Stan Musial, Ozzie Smith/30 100.00
PJGG Ken Griffey Jr., Derek Jeter, Vladimir Guerrero, Albert Pujols/50 100.00
RCJP Mark Prior, Nolan Ryan, Roger Clemens, Randy Johnson/50 50.00
WRRJ Pee Wee Reese, Honus Wagner, Cal Ripken Jr., Derek Jeter/20 300.00
WYBS Ted Williams, Wade Boggs, Curt Schilling, Carl Yastrzemski/50 85.00

2006 Upper Deck Epic Materials

NM/M

Production 10-185
No pricing production 15 or less.
Orange: .75-1.5X
Production 5-185
Red: .75-1.5X
Production 10-185
Light Purple: .75-1.5X
Production 4-185
Dark Purple: .75-1.5X
Production 3-185
Blue: .75-1.5X
Production 3-99
Teal: .75-1.5X
Production 5-99
Green: 1-1.5X
Production 3-75
Dark Green: 1-2X
Production 3-50
Grey: 1-2X
Production 3-40
Gold: 1-1.25X
Production 1-25
EB Ernie Banks/155 15.00
JB1 Johnny Bench/155 10.00
JB2 Johnny Bench/155 10.00
WB1 Wade Boggs/185 10.00
WB2 Wade Boggs/185 10.00
LD1 Lou Brock/48 10.00
LB2 Lou Brock/48 10.00
RC1 Roger Clemens/155 20.00
RC2 Roger Clemens/155 20.00
RC3 Roger Clemens/155 20.00
CL1 Roberto Clemente/50 75.00
JD1 Joe DiMaggio/185 65.00
JD2 Joe DiMaggio/173 65.00
JD3 Joe DiMaggio/99 75.00
CF Carlton Fisk/169 10.00
CF2 Carlton Fisk/185 10.00
WF Whitey Ford/155 15.00
LG1 Lou Gehrig/15 165.00
LG2 Lou Gehrig/15 165.00
LG3 Lou Gehrig/15 165.00
BG Bob Gibson/155 10.00
BG2 Bob Gibson/155 15.00
HG Hank Greenberg/50 40.00
KG1 Ken Griffey Jr./175 15.00
KG2 Ken Griffey Jr./175 15.00
KG3 Ken Griffey Jr./175 15.00
VG Vladimir Guerrero/145 8.00
VG2 Vladimir Guerrero/145 8.00
GH Gil Hodges/39 15.00
RH Rogers Hornsby/50 75.00
RE1 Reggie Jackson/52 12.00
RE2 Reggie Jackson/52 12.00
RE3 Reggie Jackson/52 12.00
DJ1 Derek Jeter/185 25.00
DJ2 Derek Jeter/185 25.00
DJ3 Derek Jeter/185 25.00
RJ1 Randy Johnson/145 10.00
RJ2 Randy Johnson/145 10.00
HK Harmon Killebrew/155 15.00
JM Juan Marichal/155 8.00
ED Eddie Mathews/75 10.00
DM1 Don Mattingly/185 15.00
DM2 Don Mattingly/185 15.00
WM Willie McCovey/155 15.00
WM2 Willie McCovey/155 15.00
WM3 Willie McCovey/155 15.00
PM1 Paul Molitor/155 10.00
PM2 Paul Molitor/155 10.00
JO Joe Morgan/145 8.00
JO2 Joe Morgan/155 8.00
TH1 Thurman Munson/35 30.00
TH2 Thurman Munson/35 30.00
EM1 Eddie Murray/185 8.00
EM2 Eddie Murray/165 8.00
EM3 Eddie Murray/155 8.00
SM1 Stan Musial/50 25.00
SM2 Stan Musial/75 25.00
MP1 Mike Piazza/145 12.00
MP2 Mike Piazza/145 12.00
MA Mark Prior/185 8.00
MA2 Mark Prior/185 8.00
KP1 Kirby Puckett/155 15.00
KP2 Kirby Puckett/155 15.00
AP1 Albert Pujols/185 20.00
AP2 Albert Pujols/185 20.00
AP3 Albert Pujols/185 20.00
PR1 Pee Wee Reese/145 15.00
PR2 Pee Wee Reese/145 15.00
CR1 Cal Ripken Jr./185 25.00
CR2 Cal Ripken Jr./177 25.00
CR3 Cal Ripken Jr./155 25.00
RO Brooks Robinson/49 15.00
RO2 Brooks Robinson/99 15.00
FR1 Frank Robinson/130 10.00
FR2 Frank Robinson/130 10.00
BR1 Babe Ruth/15 250.00
BR2 Babe Ruth/15 250.00
NR1 Nolan Ryan/155 20.00
NR2 Nolan Ryan/155 20.00
NR3 Nolan Ryan/155 20.00
RS1 Ryne Sandberg/155 15.00
RS2 Ryne Sandberg/155 15.00
RS3 Ryne Sandberg/155 15.00
MS1 Mike Schmidt/185 15.00
MS2 Mike Schmidt/185 15.00
MS3 Mike Schmidt/185 15.00
TS Tom Seaver/155 15.00
TS2 Tom Seaver/155 15.00
OS1 Ozzie Smith/155 15.00
OS2 Ozzie Smith/155 15.00
HW Honus Wagner/16 200.00
TW1 Ted Williams/125 50.00
TW2 Ted Williams/125 50.00
CY1 Carl Yastrzemski/185 15.00
CY2 Carl Yastrzemski/185 15.00
CY3 Carl Yastrzemski/185 15.00
RY1 Robin Yount/155 10.00
RY2 Robin Yount/155 10.00

Blue

No Pricing

Dark Green

No Pricing

Dark Purple

No Pricing

Green

No Pricing

Grey

No Pricing

Gold

No Pricing

Light Purple

No Pricing

Orange

No Pricing

Red

No Pricing

Signatures

No Pricing
Production Five Sets

Teal

(No Pricing)

Swatch

NM/M

Common Player: 10.00
Production 50 Sets
JB Jason Bay 15.00
EC Eric Chavez 10.00
RC Roger Clemens 30.00
CF Carlton Fisk 15.00
KG1 Ken Griffey Jr. 30.00
KG2 Ken Griffey Jr. 30.00
VG Vladimir Guerrero 15.00
TG Tony Gwynn 25.00
DJ1 Derek Jeter 50.00
DJ2 Derek Jeter 50.00
RJ Randy Johnson 20.00
PM Pedro J. Martinez 15.00
JM Joe Morgan 10.00
DO David Ortiz 25.00
RO Roy Oswalt 10.00
JP Jake Peavy 10.00
MP Mark Prior 10.00
AP Albert Pujols 40.00
MR Manny Ramirez 15.00
JR Jose Reyes 15.00
CR Cal Ripken Jr. 40.00
IR Ivan Rodriguez 12.00
SR Scott Rolen 20.00
JS Johan Santana 10.00
CS Curt Schilling 15.00
MT Mark Teixeira 12.00
MI Miguel Tejada 10.00
DW Dontrelle Willis 10.00
CY Carl Yastrzemski 20.00
RZ Ryan Zimmerman 30.00

Triple Materials

NM/M

Production 3-99
BER Eddie Murray, Brooks Robinson, Johnny Bench/60 35.00
BMR Brooks Robinson, Wade Boggs, Paul Molitor/99 30.00
BSP Ryne Sandberg, Ernie Banks, Mark Prior/99 40.00
CDG Ken Griffey Jr., Ty Cobb, Joe DiMaggio/15 300.00
FJJ Whitey Ford, Reggie Jackson, Derek Jeter/99 60.00
FMJ Don Mattingly, Reggie Jackson, Whitey Ford/51 40.00
GJC Randy Johnson, Roger Clemens, Bob Gibson/99 40.00
GMG Eddie Murray, Hank Greenberg, Lou Gehrig/25 150.00
GPS Tom Seaver, Bob Gibson, Mark Prior/99 30.00
GRM Ken Griffey Jr., Willie McCovey, Frank Robinson/99 40.00
JGK Vladimir Guerrero, Reggie Jackson, Harmon Killebrew/99 40.00
JKR Harmon Killebrew, Frank Robinson, Reggie Jackson/99 40.00
JMM Derek Jeter, Don Mattingly, Thurman Munson/25 125.00
JPG Albert Pujols, Ken Griffey Jr., Derek Jeter/99 100.00
MBF Carlton Fisk, Thurman Munson, Johnny Bench/99 40.00
MBG Johnny Bench, Joe Morgan, Ken Griffey Jr./99 50.00
MBP Albert Pujols, Lou Brock, Stan Musial/24 90.00
MFM Carlton Fisk, Eddie Murray, Thurman Munson/99 30.00
MMG Steve Garvey, Eddie Murray, Don Mattingly/49 40.00
MPS Tom Seaver, Mike Piazza, Eddie Murray/99 30.00
MSY Ozzie Smith, Paul Molitor, Robin Yount/49 40.00
RBS Cal Ripken Jr., Wade Boggs, Mike Schmidt/99 50.00
RCJ Nolan Ryan, Roger Clemens, Randy Johnson/75 50.00
RJD Reggie Jackson, Joe DiMaggio, Babe Ruth/99 300.00
RRM Jackie Robinson, Frank Robinson, Willie McCovey/50 50.00
SMH Ryne Sandberg, Rogers Hornsby, Joe Morgan/25 80.00
WSR Honus Wagner, Pee Wee Reese, Ozzie Smith/99 100.00

YRJ Cal Ripken Jr., Derek Jeter, Robin Yount/99 60.00
YWB Ted Williams, Wade Boggs, Carl Yastrzemski/25 140.00

Pairings

NM/M

Production 5-99
BB Wade Boggs, Brooks Robinson/99 25.00
BM Johnny Bench, Joe Morgan/99 20.00
BR Bob Gibson, Nolan Ryan/99 30.00
BS Lou Brock, Ozzie Smith/99 30.00
BS2 Wade Boggs, Ryne Sandberg/99 25.00
CJ Roger Clemens, Randy Johnson/99 25.00
CR Roger Clemens, Nolan Ryan/99 40.00
DG Joe DiMaggio, Lou Gehrig/25 220.00
FB Carlton Fisk, Johnny Bench/99 20.00
FP Carlton Fisk, Mike Piazza/99 20.00
GB Bob Gibson, Lou Brock/99 25.00
GC Hank Greenberg, Ty Cobb/25 150.00
GG Ken Griffey Jr., Vladimir Guerrero/99 40.00
GP Ken Griffey Jr., Kirby Puckett/99 35.00
GR Lou Gehrig, Cal Ripken Jr./45 180.00
JD Derek Jeter, Joe DiMaggio/99 125.00
JG Derek Jeter, Ken Griffey Jr./99 75.00
JJ Reggie Jackson, Derek Jeter/99 40.00
JK Reggie Jackson, Harmon Killebrew/99 30.00
JM Derek Jeter, Don Mattingly/99 80.00
JS Reggie Jackson, Mike Schmidt/99 30.00
KP Harmon Killebrew, Kirby Puckett/99 30.00
MB Thurman Munson, Johnny Bench/30 40.00
MM Juan Marichal, Willie McCovey/99 25.00
MM2 Don Mattingly, Thurman Munson/30 75.00
MR Eddie Mathews, Brooks Robinson/50 50.00
MS Eddie Mathews, Mike Schmidt/50 40.00
MY Paul Molitor, Robin Yount/99 25.00
PH Albert Pujols, Rogers Hornsby/99 75.00
PM Albert Pujols, Stan Musial/99 60.00
RJ Pee Wee Reese, Derek Jeter/99 35.00
RM Cal Ripken Jr., Eddie Murray/99 40.00
RR2 Brooks Robinson, Frank Robinson/99 25.00
RY Frank Robinson, Carl Yastrzemski/99 40.00
SB Ryne Sandberg, Ernie Banks/99 40.00
SM Ryne Sandberg, Joe Morgan/99 30.00
SR Tom Seaver, Nolan Ryan/99 40.00
SS Ryne Sandberg, Ozzie Smith/99 35.00
WC Honus Wagner, Roberto Clemente/25 225.00
WD Ted Williams, Joe DiMaggio/45 200.00
WM Ted Williams, Stan Musial/45 75.00
YW Carl Yastrzemski, Ted Williams/50 100.00

2006 Upper Deck First Pitch

NM/M

Complete Set (220): 35.00
Common Player: .10
Pack (5): 1.50
Box (36): 40.00
1 Chad Tracy .10
2 Conor Jackson **(RC)** .10
3 Craig Counsell .10
4 Javier Vazquez .10
5 Luis Gonzalez .10
6 Shawn Green .25
7 Troy Glaus .25
8 Joey Devine **RC** 1.00
9 Andruw Jones .40
10 Chipper Jones .50
11 John Smoltz .25
12 Marcus Giles .10
13 Jeff Francoeur .25
14 Tim Hudson .25
15 Brian Roberts .10
16 Erik Bedard .10
17 Javy Lopez .10
18 Melvin Mora .10
19 Miguel Tejada .40
20 Alejandro Freire **RC** 1.00
21 Sammy Sosa .75
22 Craig Hansen **RC** 3.00
23 Curt Schilling .50
24 David Ortiz .50
25 Edgar Renteria .25
26 Johnny Damon .50
27 Manny Ramirez .50
28 Matt Clement .10
29 Trot Nixon .10
30 Aramis Ramirez .25
31 Carlos Zambrano .25
32 Derrek Lee .50
33 Greg Maddux 1.00
34 Jeromy Burnitz .10
35 Kerry Wood .25
36 Mark Prior .40
37 Nomar Garciaparra .50
38 Aaron Rowand .10
39 Chris Demaria **RC** .25
40 Jon Garland .10
41 Mark Buehrle .25
42 Paul Konerko .25
43 Scott Podsednik .25
44 Tadahito Iguchi .25
45 Adam Dunn .40
46 Austin Kearns .10
47 Felipe Lopez .10
48 Ken Griffey Jr. 1.00
49 Ryan Freel .10
50 Sean Casey .10
51 Wily Mo Pena .10
52 C.C. Sabathia .10
53 Cliff Lee .10
54 Coco Crisp .10
55 Grady Sizemore .25
56 Jake Westbrook .10
57 Travis Hafner .25
58 Victor Martinez .25
59 Aaron Miles .10
60 Clint Barmes .10
61 Garrett Atkins .10
62 Jeff Baker .10
63 Jeff Francis .10
64 Matt Holliday .25
65 Todd Helton .40
66 Carlos Guillen .10
67 Chris Shelton .10
68 Dmitri Young .10
69 Ivan Rodriguez .40
70 Jeremy Bonderman .10
71 Magglio Ordonez .25
72 Placido Polanco .10
73 A.J. Burnett .10
74 Carlos Delgado .40
75 Dontrelle Willis .25
76 Josh Beckett .25
77 Juan Pierre .10
78 Ryan Jorgensen **RC** .50
79 Miguel Cabrera .40
80 Robert Andino **RC** .50
81 Andy Pettitte .25
82 Brad Lidge .10
83 Craig Biggio .25
84 Jeff Bagwell .40
85 Lance Berkman .25
86 Morgan Ensberg .25
87 Roger Clemens 1.50
88 Roy Oswalt .25
89 Angel Berroa .10
90 David DeJesus .10
91 Steve Stemle **RC** 1.00
92 Jonah Bayliss **RC** 2.00
93 Mike Sweeney .10
94 Ryan Theriot **(RC)** 1.00
95 Zack Greinke .10
96 Brad Penny .10
97 Cesar Izturis .10
98 Brian Myrow **RC** 1.00
99 Eric Gagne .25
100 J.D. Drew .10
101 Jeff Kent .25
102 Milton Bradley .10
103 Odalis Perez .10
104 Ben Sheets .25
105 Brady Clark .10
106 Carlos Lee .25
107 Geoff Jenkins .10
108 Lyle Overbay .10
109 Prince Fielder **(RC)** .50
110 Rickie Weeks .25
111 Jacque Jones .10
112 Joe Mauer .25
113 Joe Nathan .10
114 Johan Santana .50
115 Justin Morneau .20
116 Chris Heintz **RC** 1.00
117 Torii Hunter .25
118 Carlos Beltran .40
119 Cliff Floyd .10
120 David Wright .75
121 Jose Reyes .40
122 Mike Cameron .10
123 Mike Piazza .50
124 Pedro Martinez .50
125 Tom Glavine .25
126 Alex Rodriguez 1.50
127 Derek Jeter 1.50
128 Gary Sheffield .40
129 Hideki Matsui .75
130 Jason Giambi .25
131 Jorge Posada .25
132 Mariano Rivera .25
133 Mike Mussina .25
134 Randy Johnson .50
135 Barry Zito .25
136 Bobby Crosby .10
137 Danny Haren .10
138 Eric Chavez .25
139 Huston Street .10
140 Ron Flores **RC** .50
141 Nick Swisher .10
142 Rich Harden .25
143 Bobby Abreu .25
144 Danny Sandoval **RC** .50
145 Chase Utley .25
146 Jim Thome .40
147 Jimmy Rollins .25
148 Pat Burrell .25
149 Ryan Howard .50
150 Craig Wilson .10
151 Jack Wilson .10
152 Jason Bay .25
153 Matt Lawton .10
154 Oliver Perez .10
155 Robert Mackowiak .10
156 Zachary Duke .10
157 Brian Giles .25
158 Jake Peavy .25
159 Craig Breslow **RC** 1.00
160 Khalil Greene .10
161 Mark Loretta .10
162 Ryan Klesko .10
163 Trevor Hoffman .10
164 J.T. Snow .10
165 Jason Schmidt .25
166 Marquis Grissom .10
167 Moises Alou .25
168 Omar Vizquel .10
169 Pedro Feliz .10
170 Jeremy Accardo **RC** .50
171 Adrian Beltre .25
172 Ichiro Suzuki 1.00
173 Felix Hernandez .50
174 Jeff Harris **RC** .25
175 Randy Winn .10
176 Raul Ibanez .10
177 Richie Sexson .25
178 Albert Pujols 1.50
179 Chris Carpenter .25
180 David Eckstein .10
181 Jim Edmonds .25
182 Larry Walker .25
183 Matt Morris .10
184 Reggie Sanders .10
185 Scott Rolen .40
186 Aubrey Huff .10
187 Jonny Gomes .10
188 Carl Crawford .25
189 Tim Corcoran **RC** 1.00
190 Julio Lugo .10
191 Rocco Baldelli .10
192 Scott Kazmir .10
193 Alfonso Soriano .40
194 Hank Blalock .25
195 Kenny Rogers .10
196 Scott Feldman **RC** 1.00
197 Laynce Nix .10
198 Mark Teixeira .50
199 Michael Young .10
200 Aaron Hill .10
201 Alex Rios .10
202 Eric Hinske .10
203 Gustavo Chacin .10
204 Roy Halladay .25
205 Shea Hillenbrand .10
206 Vernon Wells .25
207 Brad Wilkerson .10
208 Chad Cordero .10
209 Jose Guillen .10
210 Jose Vidro .10
211 Livan Hernandez .10
212 Preston Wilson .10
213 Jason Bergmann **RC** 1.00
214 Bartolo Colon .25
215 Chone Figgins .10
216 Darin Erstad .25
217 Francisco Rodriguez .10
218 Garret Anderson .25
219 Steve Finley .10
220 Vladimir Guerrero .50

Diamond Stars

NM/M

Complete Set (35): 30.00
Common Player: .50
Inserted 1:3
1 Luis Gonzalez .50
2 Andruw Jones 1.00
3 John Smoltz .75
4 Miguel Tejada 1.00
5 Johnny Damon 1.50
6 Manny Ramirez 1.50
7 Derrek Lee 1.50
8 Mark Prior 1.00
9 Mark Buehrle .50
10 Ken Griffey Jr. 3.00
11 Travis Hafner .75
12 Todd Helton 1.00
13 Ivan Rodriguez .75
14 Miguel Cabrera 1.50
15 Roger Clemens 4.00
16 Mike Sweeney .50
17 Jeff Kent .75
18 Carlos Lee .50
19 Johan Santana 1.50
20 Torii Hunter .50
21 Pedro Martinez 1.50
22 Alex Rodriguez 4.00
23 Derek Jeter 4.00
24 Eric Chavez .75
25 Bobby Abreu .75
26 Jason Bay .75
27 Jake Peavy .75
28 Moises Alou .50
29 Ichiro Suzuki 3.00
30 Albert Pujols 4.00
31 Carl Crawford .75
32 Mark Teixeira 1.50
33 Roy Halladay .50
34 Jose Guillen .50
35 Vladimir Guerrero 1.50

Goin' Deep

NM/M

Complete Set (35): 20.00
Common Player: .50
Inserted 1:3
1 Adam Dunn 1.00
2 Albert Pujols 4.00
3 Alex Rodriguez 4.00
4 Alfonso Soriano 1.00
5 Andruw Jones 1.00
6 Aramis Ramirez .75
7 Bobby Abreu .75
8 Brian Giles .50
9 Carlos Delgado .75
10 Carlos Lee .50
11 Chipper Jones 1.50
12 David Ortiz 1.50
13 David Wright 2.00
14 Derrek Lee 1.00
15 Eric Chavez .50
16 Gary Sheffield .75
17 Hideki Matsui 2.50
18 Jeff Kent .75
19 Jim Edmonds .75
20 Ken Griffey Jr. 3.00
21 Luis Gonzalez .50
22 Manny Ramirez 1.50
23 Mark Teixeira 1.00
24 Miguel Cabrera 1.50
25 Miguel Tejada 1.00
26 Moises Alou .50
27 Pat Burrell .75
28 Paul Konerko .75
29 Rafael Palmeiro .75
30 Richie Sexson .75
31 Todd Helton 1.00
32 Torii Hunter .50
33 Travis Hafner .75
34 Vernon Wells .50
35 Vladimir Guerrero 1.50

Hot Stove Headlines

NM/M

Complete Set (20): 15.00
Common Player: .50
Inserted 1:3
1 Alex Rodriguez 3.00
2 Carlos Beltran .75
3 Carlos Delgado .50
4 Curt Schilling 1.00
5 Derrek Lee .75
6 Greg Maddux 2.00
7 Hideki Matsui 2.00
8 Ichiro Suzuki 2.00
9 Ivan Rodriguez .50
10 Jim Thome .50
11 Johnny Damon 1.00
12 Ken Griffey Jr. 2.00
13 Manny Ramirez 1.00
14 Miguel Tejada .75
15 Nomar Garciaparra .75
16 Pedro Martinez 1.00
17 Randy Johnson 1.00
18 Roger Clemens 3.00
19 Scott Rolen .75
20 Vladimir Guerrero 1.00

Signature Stars

NM/M

Common Player:
DR J.D. Drew 25.00
JE Johnny Estrada 10.00
RH Rich Harden 15.00
PL Paul LoDuca 15.00
VM Victor Martinez 15.00
YM Yadier Molina 10.00
GQ Guillermo Quiroz 10.00
RI Juan Rivera 15.00
IS Ian Snell 10.00
RW Ryan Wagner 10.00

Frito Lay

NM/M

Complete Set (30): 25.00
Common player: 1.00
1 Luis Gonzalez 1.00
2 Miguel Tejada 1.50
3 Chipper Jones 2.00
4 David Ortiz 2.00
5 Mark Prior 1.00
6 Paul Konerko 1.00
7 Ken Griffey Jr. 3.00
8 Travis Hafner 1.00
9 Todd Helton 1.50
10 Ivan Rodriguez 1.50
11 Dontrelle Willis 1.00
12 Mike Sweeney 1.00
13 Lance Berkman 1.00
14 Vladimir Guerrero 2.00
15 Jeff Kent 1.00
16 Ben Sheets 1.00
17 Torii Hunter 1.00
18 Pedro Martinez 2.00
19 Alex Rodriguez 4.00
20 Bobby Abreu 1.00
21 Eric Chavez 1.00
22 Jason Bay 1.00
23 Ichiro Suzuki 2.50
24 Jake Peavy 1.50
25 Carl Crawford 1.00
26 Omar Vizquel 1.00
27 Mark Teixeira 2.00
28 Albert Pujols 4.00
29 Roy Halladay 1.00
30 Ryan Zimmerman 1.50

2006 Upper Deck Future Stars

NM/M

Complete Set (159):
Common Player (1-75): .25
Common Autograph (76-159): 5.00
Some SP Auto's not priced yet.
Pack (4): 4.00
Box (24): 80.00
1 Miguel Tejada .75
2 Brian Roberts .25
3 Brandon Webb .25
4 Luis Gonzalez .25
5 Andruw Jones .75
6 Chipper Jones 1.00
7 John Smoltz .75
8 Curt Schilling 1.00
9 Josh Beckett .25
10 David Ortiz 1.00
11 Manny Ramirez 1.00
12 Jim Thome 1.00
13 Paul Konerko .75
14 Jermaine Dye .25
15 Derrek Lee .75
16 Greg Maddux 2.00
17 Ken Griffey Jr. 2.00
18 Adam Dunn .75
19 Felipe Lopez .25
20 Travis Hafner .75
21 Victor Martinez .25
22 Grady Sizemore .75
23 Todd Helton .75
24 Matt Holliday .50
25 Jeremy Bonderman .25
26 Ivan Rodriguez .75
27 Miguel Cabrera 1.00
28 Dontrelle Willis .25
29 Roger Clemens 2.00
30 Roy Oswalt .25
31 Lance Berkman .75
32 Reggie Sanders .25
33 Vladimir Guerrero 1.00
34 Chone Figgins .25
35 Jeff Kent .25
36 Eric Gagne .25
37 Carlos Lee .25
38 Rickie Weeks .25
39 Johan Santana 1.00
40 Torii Hunter .25
41 Alex Rodriguez 2.00
42 Derek Jeter 2.50
43 Randy Johnson 1.00
44 Hideki Matsui 1.50
45 Johnny Damon 1.00
46 Pedro Martinez 1.00
47 David Wright 2.00
48 Carlos Beltran .75
49 Rich Harden .25
50 Eric Chavez .25
51 Huston Street .25
52 Ryan Howard 2.00
53 Bobby Abreu .75
54 Chase Utley .75
55 Jason Bay .75
56 Jake Peavy .75
57 Brian Giles .25
58 Trevor Hoffman .25
59 Jason Schmidt .25
60 Randy Winn .25
61 Kenji Johjima .75
62 Ichiro Suzuki 1.50
63 Felix Hernandez .75
64 Albert Pujols 2.50
65 Chris Carpenter .75
66 Jim Edmonds .25
67 Carl Crawford .25
68 Scott Kazmir .25
69 Jonny Gomes .25
70 Mark Teixeira .75
71 Michael Young .25
72 Vernon Wells .75
73 Roy Halladay .25
74 Nick Johnson .25
75 Alfonso Soriano .75
76 Adam Wainwright **(RC)** 20.00
77 Anderson Hernandez **(RC)** 5.00
78 Andre Ethier/SP **(RC)** 40.00
79 Colter Bean/SP **(RC)** 10.00
80 Ben Johnson **(RC)** 5.00
81 Boof Bonser/SP **(RC)** 20.00
82 Boone Logan **RC** 8.00
83 Brian Anderson **(RC)** 5.00
84 Brian Bannister **(RC)** 8.00
85 Chris Denorfia/SP **(RC)** 8.00
86 Chad Billingsley/SP **(RC)** 25.00
87 Cody Ross **(RC)** 5.00
88 Cole Hamels/SP **(RC)** 50.00
89 Conor Jackson **(RC)** 15.00
91 Dave Gassner/SP **(RC)** 8.00
92 Jordan Tata **RC** 10.00
93 Eric Reed **(RC)** 8.00
94 Fausto Carmona **(RC)** 15.00
96 Francisco Liriano/SP **(RC)** 35.00
97 Freddie Bynum **(RC)** 5.00
98 Hanley Ramirez/SP **(RC)** 30.00
99 Hong-Chih Kuo/SP **(RC)** 50.00
100 Ian Kinsler **(RC)** 20.00
101 Nelson Cruz SP **(RC)** 15.00
102 Ruddy Lugo **(RC)** 5.00
103 Jason Kubel **(RC)** 15.00
104 Jeff Harris **RC** 5.00
105 Santiago Ramirez **(RC)** 5.00
107 Jeremy Accardo/SP **RC** 15.00
108 Jeremy Hermida/SP **(RC)** 20.00
109 Joel Zumaya SP **(RC)** 40.00
110 Joey Devine 8.00
111 John Koronka **(RC)** 5.00
112 Jonathan Papelbon **(RC)** 40.00
113 Jose Capellan **(RC)** 5.00
114 Josh Johnson **(RC)** 10.00
115 Josh Rupe/SP **(RC)** 10.00
116 Josh Willingham/SP **(RC)** 15.00
117 Josh Wilson **(RC)** 8.00
119 Kelly Shoppach **(RC)** 8.00
120 Kendry Morales **(RC)** 15.00
121 Sean Tracey **(RC)** 8.00
122 Macay McBride **(RC)** 8.00
124 Matt Cain **(RC)** 20.00
125 Russell Martin **(RC)** 20.00
126 Tim Hamulack/SP **(RC)** 8.00
127 Mike Jacobs **(RC)** 8.00
128 Ben Hendrickson **(RC)** 5.00
129 Jack Taschner **(RC)** 5.00
130 Nate McLouth **(RC)** 10.00
131 Jeremy Sowers/SP **(RC)** 15.00
132 Paul Maholm **(RC)** 5.00
134 Jason Bergmann **RC** 10.00
135 Rich Hill/SP **(RC)** 25.00
137 Scott Dunn **(RC)** 5.00
138 Ryan Zimmerman **(RC)** 40.00
139 Anibal Sanchez **(RC)** 15.00
140 Sean Marshall **(RC)** 10.00
141 Takashi Saito/SP **RC** 40.00
142 Taylor Buchholz **(RC)** 10.00
143 Carlos Quentin/SP **(RC)** 15.00
144 Matt Garza **(RC)** 20.00
145 Wilbert Nieves **(RC)** 8.00
146 Jamie Shields **RC** 10.00
149 Aaron Rakers **(RC)** 5.00
150 Bobby Livingston **(RC)** 8.00
151 Brendan Harris **(RC)** 5.00
153 Chris Britton **RC** 10.00
154 Howie Kendrick/SP **(RC)** 40.00
155 Jermaine Van Buren **(RC)** 8.00
157 Matt Capps **(RC)** 10.00
158 Peter Moylan **RC** 5.00
159 Ty Taubenheim **RC** 15.00

Black

Black (1-75): 8-15X
Production 50 Sets

Blue

Blue (1-75): 4-8X
Production 99 Sets

Gold

Gold (1-75): 15-25X
Production 25 Sets

Green

Green (1-75): 2-4X
Production 499 Sets

Purple

Purple (1-75): 1-2X
Production 1,799 Sets

Red

Red (1-75): 3-5X
Production 299 Sets

Rookie Signatures Red Ink

Red Ink (76-159): 1.5-2X
Production 35 Sets

Future Stars

NM/M

Common Player: 1.00

Black: 8-15X
Production 50 Sets
Blue: 4-8X
Production 99 Sets
Gold: 15-25X
Production 25 Sets
Green: 2-4X
Production 499 Sets
Purple: 1-2X
Production 1,799 Sets
Red: 3-5X
Production 299 Sets
1 Adam Loewen 1.00
2 Nan Wang 2.00
3 Yi Feng 1.50
4 Chien-Ming Chang 2.00
5 Yung-Chi Chen 2.00
6 Chin-Lung Hu 1.50
7 Yadel Marti 1.00
8 Frederich Cepeda 1.00
9 Pedro Luis Lazo 1.00
10 Osmany Urrutia 1.00
11 Yoandy Garlobo 1.00
12 Nobuhiko Matsunaka 2.00
13 Daisuke Matsuzaka 5.00
14 Tsuyoshi Nishioka 2.00
15 Tomoya Satozaki 1.00
16 Koji Uehara 1.00
17 Shunsuke Watanabe 2.00
18 Jong Beom Lee 1.00
19 Sidney de Jong 1.00
20 Shairon Martis 1.00
21 Len Pecota 1.00
22 Dicky Gonzalez 1.00
23 Nicholas Dempsey 1.00
24 Jason Kubel 1.00
25 Chase Utley 2.00

Clear Patch to History Triple Sign

NM/M

BSJ Andruw Jones, Alfonso Soriano, Jason Bay 40.00
CUK Carl Crawford, Scott Kazmir, B.J. Upton 50.00
DRR Jose Reyes, Stephen Drew, Hanley Ramirez 75.00
GEH Andre Ethier, Jeremy Hermida, Tony Gwynn Jr. 40.00
MML Justin Morneau, Joe Mauer, Francisco Liriano 75.00
MOH Travis Hafner, Justin Morneau, Lyle Overbay 60.00
NHP Trevor Hoffman, Joe Nathan, Jonathan Papelbon 60.00
PSO Ben Sheets, Roy Oswalt, Jake Peavy 50.00
PVW Justin Verlander, Jonathan Papelbon, Jered Weaver 100.00
SBH Chad Billingsley, Alay Soler, Cole Hamels 40.00
SHL Francisco Liriano, Jeremy Sowers, Cole Hamels 60.00
TZU Ryan Zimmerman, B.J. Upton, Troy Tulowitzki 60.00
VBZ Jeremy Bonderman, Justin Verlander, Joel Zumaya 100.00

2006 Upper Deck Ovation

NM/M

Complete Set (126):
Common (1-84): .25
Common SP (85-126): 5.00
Production 999
Pack (5): 5.00
Box (18): 75.00
1 Vladimir Guerrero .75
2 Bartolo Colon .25
3 Chone Figgins .25
4 Lance Berkman .40
5 Roy Oswalt .40
6 Craig Biggio .40
7 Rich Harden .25
8 Eric Chavez .40
9 Huston Street .25
10 Vernon Wells .40
11 Roy Halladay .50
12 Troy Glaus .40
13 Andruw Jones .50
14 Chipper Jones .75
15 John Smoltz .40
16 Carlos Lee .40
17 Rickie Weeks .40
18 J.J. Hardy .25
19 Albert Pujols 2.00
20 Chris Carpenter .50
21 Scott Rolen .75
22 Derrek Lee .50
23 Mark Prior .50
24 Aramis Ramirez .40
25 Carl Crawford .40
26 Scott Kazmir .40
27 Luis Gonzalez .25
28 Brandon Webb .25
29 Chad Tracy .25
30 Jeff Kent .40
31 J.D. Drew .40
32 Jason Schmidt .40
33 Randy Winn .25
34 Travis Hafner .50
35 Victor Martinez .40
36 Grady Sizemore .40
37 Ichiro Suzuki 1.50
38 Felix Hernandez .40
39 Adrian Beltre .25
40 Miguel Cabrera .75
41 Dontrelle Willis .40
42 David Wright 1.50
43 Jose Reyes .50
44 Pedro Martinez .75
45 Carlos Beltran .50
46 Alfonso Soriano .75
47 Livan Hernandez .25
48 Jose Guillen .25
49 Miguel Tejada .50
50 Brian Roberts .25
51 Melvin Mora .25
52 Jake Peavy .40
53 Brian Giles .25
54 Khalil Greene .25
55 Bobby Abreu .40
56 Ryan Howard 1.00
57 Chase Utley .50
58 Jason Bay .40
59 Sean Casey .25
60 Mark Teixeira .50
61 Michael Young .40
62 Hank Blalock .40
63 Manny Ramirez .75
64 David Ortiz .75
65 Josh Beckett .40
66 Jason Varitek .50
67 Ken Griffey Jr. 1.50
68 Adam Dunn .50
69 Todd Helton .50
70 Garrett Atkins .25
71 Reggie Sanders .25
72 Mike Sweeney .25
73 Chris Shelton .25
74 Ivan Rodriguez .50
75 Johan Santana .75
76 Torii Hunter .40
77 Justin Morneau .50
78 Jim Thome .50
79 Paul Konerko .40
80 Scott Podsednik .40
81 Derek Jeter 2.00
82 Hideki Matsui 1.50
83 Johnny Damon .75
84 Alex Rodriguez 2.00
85 Conor Jackson **(RC)** 8.00
86 Joey Devine **RC** 5.00
87 Jonathan Papelbon **(RC)** 20.00
88 Freddie Bynum **(RC)** 5.00
89 Chris Denorfia **(RC)** 8.00
90 Ryan Shealy **(RC)** 5.00
91 Josh Wilson **(RC)** 5.00
92 Brian Anderson **(RC)** 5.00
93 Justin Verlander **(RC)** 15.00
94 Jeremy Hermida **(RC)** 5.00
95 Mike Jacobs **(RC)** 5.00
96 Josh Johnson **(RC)** 8.00
97 Hanley Ramirez **(RC)** 8.00
98 Josh Willingham **(RC)** 8.00
99 Cole Hamels **(RC)** 10.00
100 Hong-Chih Kuo **(RC)** 15.00
101 Cody Ross **(RC)** 8.00
102 Jose Capellan **(RC)** 5.00
103 Prince Fielder **(RC)** 15.00
104 Dave Gassner **(RC)** 5.00
105 Jason Kubel **(RC)** 5.00
106 Francisco Liriano **(RC)** 10.00
107 Anderson Hernandez **(RC)** 5.00
108 Boof Bonser **(RC)** 8.00
109 Jered Weaver **(RC)** 10.00
110 Ben Johnson **(RC)** 5.00
111 Jeff Harris **RC** 5.00
112 Stephen Drew **(RC)** 10.00
113 Matt Cain **(RC)** 8.00
114 Skip Schumaker **(RC)** 5.00
115 Adam Wainwright **(RC)** 8.00
116 Jeremy Sowers **(RC)** 5.00
117 Jason Bergmann **RC** 5.00
118 Chad Billingsley **(RC)** 10.00
119 Ryan Zimmerman **(RC)** 15.00
120 Macay McBride **(RC)** 5.00
121 Aaron Rakers **(RC)** 5.00
122 Alay Soler **RC** 5.00
123 Melky Cabrera **(RC)** 15.00
124 Tim Hamulack **(RC)** 5.00
125 Andre Ethier **(RC)** 15.00
126 Kenji Johjima **RC** 15.00

Gold

Gold (1-84): 4-8X
Production 499 Sets

Gold Autographs

NM/M

Production 99 Sets
85 Conor Jackson 25.00
86 Joey Devine 15.00
87 Jonathan Papelbon 75.00
88 Freddie Bynum 10.00
89 Chris Denorfia 10.00
90 Ryan Shealy 20.00
92 Brian Anderson 10.00
93 Justin Verlander 50.00
94 Jeremy Hermida 20.00
95 Mike Jacobs 10.00
96 Josh Johnson 20.00
97 Hanley Ramirez 25.00
98 Josh Willingham 25.00
99 Cole Hamels 60.00
101 Cody Ross 20.00
102 Jose Capellan 15.00
105 Jason Kubel 15.00
106 Francisco Liriano 50.00
107 Anderson Hernandez 10.00
108 Boof Bonser 15.00
109 Jered Weaver 40.00
110 Ben Johnson 15.00
111 Jeff Harris 15.00
113 Matt Cain 25.00
114 Skip Schumaker 15.00
115 Adam Wainwright 25.00
116 Jeremy Sowers 15.00
117 Jason Bergmann 10.00
118 Chad Billingsley 25.00
119 Ryan Zimmerman 90.00
120 Macay McBride 10.00
121 Aaron Rakers 10.00
122 Alay Soler 10.00
123 Melky Cabrera 50.00
124 Tim Hamulack 20.00
125 Andre Ethier 70.00

Apparel

NM/M

Common Player: 4.00
BA Jason Bay 8.00
LB Lance Berkman 8.00
JB Jeremy Bonderman 8.00
AB A.J. Burnett 6.00
EC Eric Chavez 6.00
CC Carl Crawford 6.00
JE Jim Edmonds 8.00
PF Prince Fielder 10.00
CF Chone Figgins 6.00
JF Jeff Francoeur 10.00
JG Jonny Gomes 6.00
KG Khalil Greene 8.00
GR Ken Griffey Jr. 20.00
VG Vladimir Guerrero 8.00
HA Travis Hafner 8.00
JH J.J. Hardy 4.00
HE Todd Helton 8.00
FH Felix Hernandez 8.00
TH Trevor Hoffman 8.00
RH Ryan Howard 20.00
HU Torii Hunter 6.00
DJ Derek Jeter 25.00
JK Jeff Kent 6.00
RK Ryan Klesko 4.00
CL Carlos Lee 6.00
VM Victor Martinez 8.00
JM Joe Mauer 8.00
TN Trot Nixon 6.00
DO David Ortiz 15.00
RO Roy Oswalt 8.00
AO Akinori Otsuka 6.00
MP Mark Prior 6.00
AP Albert Pujols 25.00
MR Manny Ramirez 10.00
SR Scott Rolen 8.00
CS Chris Shelton 4.00
GS Grady Sizemore 8.00
HS Huston Street 6.00
MT Mark Teixeira 8.00
VW Vernon Wells 8.00
DW David Wright 15.00
RZ Ryan Zimmerman/SP 25.00

Center Stage

NM/M

Common Player: 1.00
JB Josh Beckett 1.00
DC Daniel Cabrera 1.00
CA Miguel Cabrera 3.00
JC Jose Contreras 1.00
AC Aaron Cook 1.00
BC Bobby Crosby 1.00
MC Michael Cuddyer 1.00
DD David DeJesus 1.00
SD Stephen Drew 2.00
JF Jason Frasor 1.00
KG Ken Griffey Jr. 5.00
VG Vladimir Guerrero 3.00
FH Felix Hernandez 2.00
RH Runelvys Hernandez 1.00
DJ Derek Jeter 8.00
DL Derrek Lee 2.00
YM Yadier Molina 1.00
MP Mark Prior 2.00
AP Albert Pujols 8.00
FS Freddy Sanchez 1.00
CS Chris Shelton 1.00
IS Ian Snell 1.00
MT Mark Teixeira 2.00
CW Chien-Ming Wang 10.00
DW David Wright 4.00

Center Stage Signatures

No Pricing
Production 25 Sets

Curtain Calls

NM/M

Common Player: 1.00
DC Daniel Cabrera 1.00
EC Eric Chavez 1.00
JC Jose Contreras 1.00
BC Bobby Crosby 1.00
DD David DeJesus 1.00
KG1 Ken Griffey Jr. 4.00
KG2 Ken Griffey Jr. 4.00
RH Rich Harden 1.00
HE Runelvys Hernandez 1.00
YM Yadier Molina 1.00
TO Tomokazu Ohka 1.00
MP Mark Prior 2.00
HR Horacio Ramirez 1.00
FS Freddy Sanchez 1.00
CS Chris Shelton 1.00
MT Miguel Tejada 2.00
CW Chien-Ming Wang 10.00
JE Jered Weaver 2.00
JW Josh Willingham 1.00
MY Michael Young 1.00

Curtain Calls Signatures

No Pricing
Production 25 Sets

Ovation Nation

NM/M

Common Player: 2.00
JB Jason Bay 3.00
DC Daniel Cabrera 2.00
MC Miguel Cabrera 4.00
FC Frederich Cepeda 2.00
YG Yoandy Garlobo 2.00
KG Ken Griffey Jr. 8.00
DJ Derek Jeter 8.00
AJ Andruw Jones 3.00
SL Seung-Yeop Lee 4.00
DM Daisuke Matsuzaka 15.00
NM Nobuhiko Matsunaka 4.00
AP Albert Pujols 8.00
JS Johan Santana 3.00
JA Jae Weong Seo 2.00
MT Miguel Tejada 3.00

Ovation Nation Signatures

No Pricing
Production 25 Sets

Spotlight Signatures

NM/M

Common Autograph: 10.00
JB Josh Beckett/SP 40.00
DC Daniel Cabrera 15.00
CA Miguel Cabrera 25.00
SC Shawn Camp 10.00
EC Eric Chavez/SP 15.00
JC Jose Contreras 30.00
AC Aaron Cook 6.00
LC Lance Cormier 10.00
BC Bobby Crosby 10.00
MC Michael Cuddyer/SP 15.00
DD David DeJesus 15.00
JD Jorge De La Rosa 10.00
JF Jason Frasor 15.00
FG Franklyn German 10.00
MG Mike Gonzalez 10.00
AG Andy Green 6.00
KG1 Ken Griffey Jr. 85.00
KG2 Ken Griffey Jr. 85.00
HA Rich Harden/SP 15.00
RH Runelvys Hernandez 10.00
EJ Edwin Jackson 10.00
YM Yadier Molina 25.00
FN Fernando Nieve 10.00
TO Tomokazu Ohka 30.00
MP Mark Prior 25.00
HR Horacio Ramirez/SP 10.00
DR David Ross 20.00
KS Kirk Saarloos 10.00
FS Freddy Sanchez 25.00
CS1 Chris Shelton 10.00
CS2 Chris Shelton 10.00
TE Miguel Tejada/SP 25.00
MT Matt Thornton 10.00
TR Matt Treanor 20.00
RW Ryan Wagner 10.00
CW Chien-Ming Wang 200.00
JW Josh Willingham/SP 15.00
MW Mike Wuertz 15.00
MY Michael Young 15.00

Superstar Theatre

NM/M

Common Player: 1.00
BA Jason Bay 2.00
JB Josh Beckett 1.00
DC Daniel Cabrera 1.00
MC Miguel Cabrera 3.00
CC Chris Carpenter 2.00
JC Jose Contreras 1.00
BC Bobby Crosby 1.00
DD David DeJesus 1.00
KG1 Ken Griffey Jr. 6.00
KG2 Ken Griffey Jr. 6.00
TH Travis Hafner 2.00
RH Rich Harden 1.00
DJ Derek Jeter 8.00
AJ Andruw Jones 2.00
DL Derrek Lee 3.00
PM Pedro Martinez 3.00
HM Hideki Matsui 4.00
YM Yadier Molina 1.00
TO Tomokazu Ohka 1.00
DO David Ortiz 3.00
MP Mark Prior 2.00
AP Albert Pujols 8.00
MR Manny Ramirez 3.00
AR Alex Rodriguez 6.00
CS Chris Shelton 1.00
IS Ichiro Suzuki 6.00
TE Mark Teixeira 2.00
MT Miguel Tejada 2.00
CW Chien-Ming Wang 10.00
MY Michael Young 2.00

Superstar Theatre Signatures

No Pricing
Production 25 Sets

2006 Upper Deck Special FX

NM/M

Complete Set (1025):
Common Player: .25
Common RC (901-1025): .50
Pack (4): 5.00
Box (16): 75.00
1 Adam Kennedy .25
2 Bartolo Colon .25
3 Bengie Molina .25
4 Casey Kotchman .25
5 Chone Figgins .25
6 Dallas McPherson .25
7 Darin Erstad .25
8 Ervin Santana .50
9 Francisco Rodriguez .25
10 Garret Anderson .25
11 Jarrod Washburn .25
12 John Lackey .25
13 Juan Rivera .25
14 Orlando Cabrera .25
15 Paul Byrd .25
16 Steve Finley .25
17 Vladimir Guerrero 1.00
18 Alex Cintron .25
19 Brandon Lyon .25
20 Brandon Webb .50
21 Chad Tracy .25
22 Chris Snyder .25
23 Claudio Vargas .25
24 Conor Jackson .50
25 Craig Counsell .25
26 Javier Vazquez .25
27 Jose Valverde .25
28 Luis Gonzalez .25
29 Royce Clayton .25
30 Russ Ortiz .25
31 Shawn Green .25
32 Dustin Nippert .25
33 Tony Clark .25
34 Troy Glaus .50
35 Adam LaRoche .25
36 Andruw Jones 1.00
37 Craig Hansen .50
38 Chipper Jones 1.00
39 Horacio Ramirez .25
40 Jeff Francoeur .50
41 John Smoltz .50
42 Joey Devine .25
43 Johnny Estrada .25
44 Anthony Lerew .25
45 Julio Franco .25
46 Kyle Farnsworth .25
47 Marcus Giles .25
48 Mike Hampton .25
49 Rafael Furcal .50
50 Chuck James .25
51 Tim Hudson .50
52 B.J. Ryan .25
53 Bernie Castro .25
54 Brian Roberts .25
55 Walter Young .25
56 Daniel Cabrera .25
57 Eric Byrnes .25
58 Alejandro Freire .25
59 Erik Bedard .50
60 Javy Lopez .25
61 Jay Gibbons .25
62 Jorge Julio .25
63 Luis Matos .25
64 Melvin Mora .25
65 Miguel Tejada .75
66 Rafael Palmeiro .75
67 Rodrigo Lopez .25
68 Sammy Sosa 1.00
69 Alejandro Machado .25
70 Bill Mueller .25
71 Bronson Arroyo .25
72 Curt Schilling .75
73 David Ortiz 1.00
74 David Wells .25
75 Edgar Renteria .25
76 Ryan Jorgensen .25
77 Jason Varitek .75
78 Johnny Damon 1.00
79 Keith Foulke .25
80 Kevin Youkilis .50
81 Manny Ramirez 1.00
82 Matt Clement .25
83 Hanley Ramirez .50
84 Tim Wakefield .25
85 Trot Nixon .25
86 Wade Miller .25
87 Aramis Ramirez .50
88 Carlos Zambrano .50
89 Corey Patterson .25
90 Derrek Lee .75
91 Geovany Soto .25
92 Greg Maddux 2.00
93 Jeromy Burnitz .25
94 Jerry Hairston Jr. .25
95 Kerry Wood .50
96 Mark Prior .75
97 Matt Murton .25
98 Michael Barrett .25
99 Neifi Perez .25
100 Nomar Garciaparra 1.00
101 Rich Hill .25
102 Ryan Dempster .25
103 Todd Walker .25
104 A.J. Pierzynski .25
105 Aaron Rowand .25
106 Bobby Jenks .25
107 Carl Everett .25
108 Dustin Hermanson .25
109 Frank Thomas 1.00
110 Freddy Garcia .25
111 Jermaine Dye .25
112 Joe Crede .50
113 Jon Garland .25
114 Jose Contreras .25
115 Juan Uribe .25
116 Mark Buehrle .25
117 Orlando Hernandez .25
118 Paul Konerko .75
119 Scott Podsednik .25
120 Tadahito Iguchi .25
121 Aaron Harang .25
122 Adam Dunn .75
123 Austin Kearns .25
124 Brandon Claussen .25
125 Chris Denorfia .25
126 Edwin Encarnacion .25
127 Miguel Perez .25
128 Felipe Lopez .25
129 Jason LaRue .25
130 Ken Griffey Jr. 2.00
131 Chris Booker .25
132 Luke Hudson .25
133 Jason Bergmann .25
134 Ryan Freel .25
135 Sean Casey .25
136 Wily Mo Pena .25
137 Aaron Boone .25
138 Ben Broussard .25
139 Ryan Garko .25
140 C.C. Sabathia .25
141 Casey Blake .25
142 Cliff Lee .25
143 Coco Crisp .25
144 David Riske .25
145 Grady Sizemore .50
146 Jake Westbrook .25
147 Jhonny Peralta .25
148 Josh Bard .25
149 Kevin Millwood .25
150 Ronnie Belliard .25
151 Scott Elarton .25
152 Travis Hafner .50
153 Victor Martinez .25
154 Aaron Cook .25
155 Aaron Miles .25
156 Brad Hawpe .25
157 Mike Esposito .25
158 Chin-Hui Tsao .25
159 Clint Barmes .25
160 Cory Sullivan .25
161 Garrett Atkins .25
162 J.D. Closser .25
163 Jason Jennings .25
164 Jeff Baker .25
165 Jeff Francis .25
166 Luis Gonzalez .25
167 Matt Holliday .50
168 Todd Helton .75
169 Brandon Inge .25
170 Carlos Guillen .25
171 Carlos Pena .25
172 Chris Shelton .25
173 Craig Monroe .25
174 Curtis Granderson .25
175 Dmitri Young .25
176 Ivan Rodriguez .75
177 Jason Johnson .25
178 Jeremy Bonderman .50
179 Magglio Ordonez .25
180 Mark Woodyard .25
181 Nook Logan .25
182 Omar Infante .25
183 Placido Polanco .25
184 Chris Heintz .25
185 A.J. Burnett .25
186 Alex Gonzalez .25
187 Josh Johnson .25
188 Carlos Delgado .75
189 Dontrelle Willis .50
190 Josh Wilson .25

191 Jason Vargas .25
192 Jeff Conine .25
193 Jeremy Hermida .50
194 Josh Beckett .50
195 Juan Encarnacion .25
196 Juan Pierre .25
197 Luis Castillo .25
198 Miguel Cabrera 1.00
199 Mike Lowell .25
200 Paul LoDuca .25
201 Todd Jones .25
202 Adam Everett .25
203 Andy Pettitte .50
204 Brad Ausmus .25
205 Brad Lidge .25
206 Brandon Backe .25
207 Charlton Jimerson .25
208 Chris Burke .25
209 Craig Biggio .50
210 Dan Wheeler .25
211 Jason Lane .25
212 Jeff Bagwell .50
213 Lance Berkman .50
214 Luke Scott .25
215 Morgan Ensberg .25
216 Roger Clemens 2.50
217 Roy Oswalt .50
218 Willy Taveras .25
219 Andres Blanco .25
220 Angel Berroa .25
221 Ruben Gotay .25
222 David DeJesus .25
223 Emil Brown .25
224 J.P. Howell .25
225 Jeremy Affeldt .25
226 Jimmy Gobble .25
227 John Buck .25
228 Jose Lima .25
229 Mark Teahen .25
230 Matt Stairs .25
231 Mike MacDougal .25
232 Mike Sweeney .25
233 Runelvys Hernandez .25
234 Terrence Long .25
235 Zack Greinke .25
236 Ron Flores .25
237 Brad Penny .25
238 Cesar Izturis .25
239 D.J. Houlton .25
240 Derek Lowe .25
241 Eric Gagne .25
242 Hee Seop Choi .25
243 J.D. Drew .50
244 Jason Phillips .25
245 Jason Repko .25
246 Jayson Werth .25
247 Jeff Kent .50
248 Jeff Weaver .25
249 Milton Bradley .25
250 Odalis Perez .25
251 Hong-Chih Kuo .25
252 Oscar Robles .25
253 Ben Sheets .50
254 Bill Hall .25
255 Brady Clark .25
256 Carlos Lee .50
257 Chris Capuano .25
258 Nelson Cruz .25
259 Derrick Turnbow .25
260 Doug Davis .25
261 Geoff Jenkins .25
262 J.J. Hardy .25
263 Lyle Overbay .25
264 Prince Fielder .75
265 Rickie Weeks .50
266 Russell Branyan .25
267 Tomokazu Ohka .25
268 Jonah Bayliss .25
269 Brad Radke .25
270 Carlos Silva .25
271 Francisco Liriano .50
272 Jacque Jones .25
273 Joe Mauer .50
274 Travis Bowyer .25
275 Joe Nathan .25
276 Johan Santana 1.00
277 Justin Morneau .75
278 Kyle Lohse .25
279 Lew Ford .25
280 Matthew LeCroy .25
281 Michael Cuddyer .25
282 Nick Punto .25
283 Scott Baker .25
284 Shannon Stewart .25
285 Torii Hunter .50
286 Braden Looper .25
287 Carlos Beltran .75
288 Cliff Floyd .25
289 David Wright 1.50
290 Doug Mientkiewicz .25
291 Anderson Hernandez .25
292 Jose Reyes 1.00
293 Kazuo Matsui .25
294 Kris Benson .25
295 Miguel Cairo .25
296 Mike Cameron .25
297 Robert Andino .25
298 Mike Piazza 1.00
299 Pedro Martinez 1.00
300 Tom Glavine .50
301 Victor Diaz .25
302 Tim Hamulack .25
303 Alex Rodriguez 2.50
304 Bernie Williams .50
305 Carl Pavano .25
306 Chien-Ming Wang 1.00
307 Derek Jeter 2.50
308 Gary Sheffield .50
309 Hideki Matsui 1.50
310 Jason Giambi .75
311 Jorge Posada .50
312 Kevin Brown .25
313 Mariano Rivera .50
314 Matt Lawton .25
315 Mike Mussina .50
316 Randy Johnson 1.00
317 Robinson Cano .50
318 Michael Vento .25
319 Tino Martinez .25
320 Tony Womack .25
321 Barry Zito .50
322 Bobby Crosby .25
323 Bobby Kielty .25
324 Dan Johnson .25
325 Danny Haren .25
326 Eric Chavez .50
327 Erubiel Durazo .25
328 Huston Street .25
329 Jason Kendall .25
330 Jay Payton .25
331 Joe Blanton .25
332 Joe Kennedy .25
333 Kirk Saarloos .25
334 Mark Kotsay .25
335 Nick Swisher .50
336 Rich Harden .25
337 Scott Hatteberg .25
338 Billy Wagner .25
339 Bobby Abreu .50
340 Brett Myers .25
341 Chase Utley 1.00
342 Danny Sandoval .25
343 David Bell .25
344 Gavin Floyd .25
345 Jim Thome .75
346 Jimmy Rollins .50
347 Jon Lieber .25
348 Kenny Lofton .25
349 Mike Lieberthal .25
350 Pat Burrell .50
351 Randy Wolf .25
352 Ryan Howard 1.50
353 Vicente Padilla .25
354 Bryan Bullington .25
355 J.J. Furmaniak .25
356 Craig Wilson .25
357 Matt Capps .25
358 Tom Gorzelanny .25
359 Jack Wilson .25
360 Jason Bay .50
361 Jose Mesa .25
362 Josh Fogg .25
363 Kip Wells .25
364 Steve Stemle .25
365 Oliver Perez .25
366 Robert Mackowiak .25
367 Ronny Paulino .25
368 Tike Redman .25
369 Zachary Duke .25
370 Adam Eaton .25
371 Scott Feldman .25
372 Brian Giles .25
373 Brian Lawrence .25
374 Damian Jackson .25
375 Dave Roberts .25
376 Jake Peavy .50
377 Joe Randa .25
378 Khalil Greene .25
379 Mark Loretta .25
380 Ramon Hernandez .25
381 Robert Fick .25
382 Ryan Klesko .25
383 Trevor Hoffman .25
384 Woody Williams .25
385 Xavier Nady .25
386 Armando Benitez .25
387 Brad Hennessey .25
388 Brian Myrow .25
389 Edgardo Alfonzo .25
390 J.T. Snow .25
391 Jeremy Accardo .25
392 Jason Schmidt .50
393 Lance Niekro .25
394 Matt Cain .25
395 Daniel Ortmeier .25
396 Moises Alou .50
397 Doug Clark .25
398 Omar Vizquel .25
399 Pedro Feliz .25
400 Randy Winn .25
401 Ray Durham .25
402 Adrian Beltre .50
403 Eddie Guardado .25
404 Felix Hernandez .50
405 Gil Meche .25
406 Ichiro Suzuki 1.50
407 Jamie Moyer .25
408 Jeff Nelson .25
409 Jeremy Reed .25
410 Joel Pineiro .25
411 Jaime Bubela .25
412 Raul Ibanez .25
413 Richie Sexson .50
414 Ryan Franklin .25
415 Willie Bloomquist .25
416 Yorvit Torrealba .25
417 Yuniesky Betancourt .25
418 Jeff Harris .25
419 Albert Pujols 2.50
420 Chris Carpenter .75
421 David Eckstein .50
422 Jason Isringhausen .25
423 Jason Marquis .25
424 Adam Wainwright .50
425 Jim Edmonds .50
426 Ryan Theriot .50
427 Tim Duncan .25
428 Mark Grudzielanek .25
429 Mark Mulder .50
430 Matt Morris .25
431 Reggie Sanders .25
432 Scott Rolen 1.00
433 Tyler Johnson .25
434 Yadier Molina .25
435 Alex Gonzalez .25
436 Aubrey Huff .25
437 Tim Corcoran .25
438 Carl Crawford .50
439 Casey Fossum .25
440 Danys Baez .25
441 Edwin Jackson .25
442 Joey Gathright .25
443 Jonny Gomes .25
444 Jorge Cantu .25
445 Julio Lugo .25
446 Nick Green .25
447 Rocco Baldelli .25
448 Scott Kazmir .50
449 Seth McClung .25
450 Toby Hall .25
451 Travis Lee .25
452 Craig Breslow .25
453 Alfonso Soriano 1.00
454 Chris Young .25
455 David Dellucci .25
456 Francisco Cordero .25
457 Gary Matthews .25
458 Hank Blalock .50
459 Juan Dominguez .25
460 Josh Rupe .25
461 Kenny Rogers .25
462 Kevin Mench .25
463 Laynce Nix .25
464 Mark Teixeira .75
465 Michael Young .25
466 Richard Hidalgo .25
467 Jason Botts .25
468 Aaron Hill .25
469 Alex Rios .25
470 Corey Koskie .25
471 Chris Demaria .25
472 Eric Hinske .25
473 Frank Catalanotto .25
474 John-Ford Griffin .25
475 Gustavo Chacin .25
476 Josh Towers .25
477 Miguel Batista .25
478 Orlando Hudson .25
479 Reed Johnson .25
480 Roy Halladay .50
481 Shaun Marcum .25
482 Shea Hillenbrand .25
483 Ted Lilly .25
484 Vernon Wells .50
485 Brad Wilkerson .25
486 Darrell Rasner .25
487 Chad Cordero .25
488 Cristian Guzman .25
489 Esteban Loaiza .25
490 John Patterson .25
491 Jose Guillen .25
492 Jose Vidro .25
493 Livan Hernandez .25
494 Marlon Byrd .25
495 Nick Johnson .25
496 Preston Wilson .25
497 Ryan Church .25
498 Ryan Zimmerman .50
499 Tony Armas .25
500 Vinny Castilla .25
501 Andy Green .25
502 Damion Easley .25
503 Eric Byrnes .25
504 Jason Grimsley .25
505 Jeff DaVanon .25
506 Johnny Estrada .25
507 Luis Vizcaino .25
508 Miguel Batista .25
509 Orlando Hernandez .25
510 Orlando Hudson .25
511 Terry Mulholland .25
512 Chris Reitsma .25
513 Edgar Renteria .25
514 John Thomson .25
515 Jorge Sosa .25
516 Oscar Villarreal .25
517 Peter Orr .25
518 Ryan Langerhans .25
519 Todd Pratt .25
520 Wilson Betemit .25
521 Brian Jordan .25
522 Lance Cormier .25
523 Matt Diaz .25
524 Mike Remlinger .25
525 Bruce Chen .25
526 Chris Gomez .25
527 Chris Ray .25
528 Corey Patterson .25
529 David Newhan .25
530 Ed Rogers .25
531 John Halama .25
532 Kris Benson .25
533 LaTroy Hawkins .25
534 Raul Chavez .25
535 Alex Cora .25
536 Alex Gonzalez .25
537 Coco Crisp .25
538 David Riske .25
539 Doug Mirabelli .25
540 Josh Beckett .50
541 J.T. Snow .25
542 Mike Timlin .25
543 Julian Tavarez .25
544 Rudy Seanez .25
545 Wily Mo Pena .25
546 Bob Howry .25
547 Glendon Rusch .25
548 Henry Blanco .25
549 Jacque Jones .25
550 Jerome Williams .25
551 John Mabry .25
552 Juan Pierre .25
553 Scott Eyre .25
554 Scott Williamson .25
555 Wade Miller .25
556 Will Ohman .25
557 Alex Cintron .25
558 Robert Mackowiak .25
559 Brandon McCarthy .25
560 Chris Widger .25
561 Cliff Politte .25
562 Javier Vazquez .25
563 Jim Thome .75
564 Matt Thornton .25
565 Neal Cotts .25
566 Pablo Ozuna .25
567 Ross Gload .25
568 Brandon Phillips .25
569 Bronson Arroyo .25
570 Dave Williams .25
571 David Ross .25
572 David Weathers .25
573 Eric Milton .25
574 Javier Valentin .25
575 Kent Mercker .25
576 Matt Belisle .25
577 Paul Wilson .25
578 Rich Aurilia .25
579 Rick White .25
580 Scott Hatteberg .25
581 Todd Coffey .25
582 Bob Wickman .25
583 Danny Graves .25
584 Eduardo Perez .25
585 Guillermo Mota .25
586 Jason Davis .25
587 Jason Johnson .25
588 Jason Michaels .25
589 Rafael Betancourt .25
590 Ramon Vazquez .25
591 Scott Sauerbeck .25
592 Todd Hollandsworth .25
593 Brian Fuentes .25
594 Danny Ardoin .25
595 David Cortes .25
596 Eli Marrero .25
597 Jamey Carroll .25
598 Jason Smith .25
599 Josh Fogg .25
600 Miguel Ojeda .25
601 Mike DeJean .25
602 Ray King .25
603 Omar Quintanilla .25
604 Zach Day .25
605 Fernando Rodney .25
606 Kenny Rogers .25
607 Mike Maroth .25
608 Nate Robertson .25
609 Todd Jones .25
610 Vance Wilson .25
611 Bobby Seay .25
612 Chris Spurling .25
613 Ramon Colon .25
614 Jason Grilli .25
615 Marcus Thames .25
616 Ramon Santiago .25
617 Alfredo Amezaga .25
618 Brian Moehler .25
619 Chris Aguila .25
620 Franklyn German .25
621 Joe Borowski .25
622 Logan Kensing .25
623 Matt Treanor .25
624 Miguel Olivo .25
625 Sergio Mitre .25
626 Todd Wellemeyer .25
627 Wes Helms .25
628 Chad Qualls .25
629 Eric Bruntlett .25
630 Mike Gallo .25
631 Mike Lamb .25
632 Orlando Palmeiro .25
633 Russ Springer .25
634 Dan Wheeler .25
635 Eric Munson .25
636 Preston Wilson .25
637 Trever Miller .25
638 Ambiorix Burgos .25
639 Andrew Sisco .25
640 Denny Bautista .25
641 Doug Mientkiewicz .25
642 Elmer Dessens .25
643 Esteban German .25
644 Joe Nelson .25
645 Mark Grudzielanek .25
646 Mark Redman .25
647 Mike Wood .25
648 Paul Bako .25
649 Reggie Sanders .25
650 Scott Elarton .25
651 Shane Costa .25
652 Tony Graffanino .25
653 Jason Bulger .25
654 Chris Bootcheck .25
655 Esteban Yan .25
656 Hector Carrasco .25
657 J.C. Romero .25
658 Jeff Weaver .25
659 Jose Molina .25
660 Kelvim Escobar .25
661 Maicer Izturis .25
662 Robb Quinlan .25
663 Scot Shields .25
664 Tim Salmon .25
665 Bill Mueller .25
666 Brett Tomko .25
667 Dioner Navarro .25
668 Jae Weong Seo .25
669 Jose Cruz .25
670 Kenny Lofton .25
671 Lance Carter .25
672 Nomar Garciaparra 1.00
673 Olmedo Saenz .25
674 Rafael Furcal .25
675 Ramon Martinez .25
676 Ricky Ledee .25
677 Sandy Alomar .25
678 Yhency Brazoban .25
679 Corey Koskie .25
680 Danny Kolb .25
681 Gabe Gross .25
682 Jeff Cirillo .25
683 Matt Wise .25
684 Rick Helling .25
685 Chad Moeller .25
686 David Bush .25
687 Jorge De La Rosa .25
688 Justin Lehr .25
689 Jason Bartlett .25
690 Jesse Crain .25
691 Juan Rincon .25
692 Luis Castillo .25
693 Mike Redmond .25
694 Rondell White .25
695 Tony Batista .25
696 Juan Castro .25
697 Luis Rodriguez .25
698 Matt Guerrier .25
699 Willie Eyre .25
700 Aaron Heilman .25
701 Billy Wagner .25
702 Carlos Delgado .75
703 Chad Bradford .25
704 Chris Woodward .25
705 Darren Oliver .25
706 Duaner Sanchez .25
707 Endy Chavez .25
708 Jorge Julio .25
709 Jose Valentin .25
710 Julio Franco .25
711 Paul LoDuca .25
712 Ramon Castro .25
713 Steve Trachsel .25
714 Victor Zambrano .25
715 Xavier Nady .25
716 Andy Phillips .25
717 Bubba Crosby .25
718 Jaret Wright .25
719 Kelly Stinnett .25
720 Kyle Farnsworth .25
721 Mike Meyers .25
722 Octavio Dotel .25
723 Ron Villone .25
724 Scott Proctor .25
725 Shawn Chacon .25
726 Tanyon Sturtze .25
727 Adam Melhuse .25
728 Brad Halsey .25
729 Esteban Loaiza .25
730 Frank Thomas 1.00
731 Jay Witasick .25
732 Justin Duchscherer .25
733 Kiko Calero .25
734 Marco Scutaro .25
735 Mark Ellis .25
736 Milton Bradley .25
737 Aaron Fultz .25
738 Aaron Rowand .25
739 Geoff Geary .25
740 Arthur Rhodes .25
741 Chris Coste .25
742 Rheal Cormier .25
743 Ryan Franklin .25
744 Ryan Madson .25
745 Sal Fasano .25
746 Tom Gordon .25
747 Abraham Nunez .25
748 David Dellucci .25
749 Julio Santana .25
750 Shane Victorino .25
751 Damaso Marte .25
752 Freddy Sanchez .25
753 Humberto Cota .25
754 Jeromy Burnitz .25
755 Joe Randa .25
756 Jose Castillo .25
757 Mike Gonzalez .25
758 Ryan Doumit .25
759 Sean Burnett .25
760 Sean Casey .25
761 Ian Snell .25
762 John Grabow .25
763 Jose Hernandez .25
764 Roberto Hernandez .25
765 Ryan Vogelsong .25
766 Victor Sanchez .25
767 Adrian Gonzalez .25
768 Alan Embree .25
769 Brian Sweeney .25
770 Chan Ho Park .25
771 Clay Hensley .25
772 Dewon Brazelton .25
773 Doug Brocail .25
774 Eric Young .25
775 Geoff Blum .25
776 Josh Bard .25
777 Mark Bellhorn .25
778 Mike Cameron .25
779 Mike Piazza 1.00
780 Rob Bowen .25
781 Scott Cassidy .25
782 Scott Linebrink .25
783 Shawn Estes .25
784 Terrmel Sledge .25
785 Vinny Castilla .25
786 Jeff Fassero .25
787 Jose Vizcaino .25
788 Mark Sweeney .25
789 Matt Morris .25
790 Steve Finley .25
791 Tim Worrell .25
792 Jamey Wright .25
793 Jason Ellison .25
794 Noah Lowry .25
795 Steve Kline .25
796 Todd Greene .25
797 Carl Everett .25
798 George Sherrill .25
799 J.J. Putz .25
800 Jake Woods .25
801 Jose Lopez .25
802 Julio Mateo .25
803 Mike Morse .25
804 Rafael Soriano .25
805 Roberto Petagine .25
806 Aaron Miles .25
807 Braden Looper .25
808 Gary Bennett .25
809 Hector Luna .25
810 Jeff Suppan .25
811 John Rodriguez .25
812 Josh Hancock .25
813 Juan Encarnacion .25
814 Larry Bigbie .25
815 Scott Spiezio .25
816 Sidney Ponson .25
817 So Taguchi .25
818 Brian Meadows .25
819 Damon Hollins .25
820 Dan Miceli .25
821 Doug Waechter .25
822 Jason Childers .25
823 Josh Paul .25
824 Julio Lugo .25
825 Mark Hendrickson .25
826 Sean Burroughs .25
827 Shawn Camp .25
828 Travis Harper .25
829 Ty Wigginton .25
830 Adam Eaton .25
831 Adrian Brown .25
832 Akinori Otsuka .25
833 Antonio Alfonseca .25
834 Brad Wilkerson .25
835 D'Angelo Jimenez .25
836 Gerald Laird .25
837 Joaquin Benoit .25
838 Kameron Loe .25
839 Kevin Millwood .25
840 Mark DeRosa .25
841 Phil Nevin .25
842 Rod Barajas .25
843 Vicente Padilla .25
844 A.J. Burnett .25
845 Bengie Molina .25
846 Gregg Zaun .25
847 John McDonald .25
848 Lyle Overbay .25
849 Russ Adams .25
850 Troy Glaus .50
851 Vinnie Chulk .25
852 B.J. Ryan .25
853 Justin Speier .25
854 Pete Walker .25
855 Scott Downs .25
856 Scott Schoeneweis .25
857 Alfonso Soriano 1.00
858 Brian Schneider .25
859 Daryle Ward .25
860 Felix Rodriguez .25
861 Gary Majewski .25
862 Joey Eischen .25
863 Jon Rauch .25
864 Marlon Anderson .25
865 Matthew LeCroy .25
866 Mike Stanton .25
867 Ramon Ortiz .25
868 Robert Fick .25
869 Royce Clayton .25
870 Ryan Drese .25
871 Vladimir Guerrero .50
872 Craig Biggio .25
873 Barry Zito .25
874 Vernon Wells .25
875 Chipper Jones .50
876 Prince Fielder .50
877 Albert Pujols 1.50
878 Greg Maddux 1.00
879 Carl Crawford .25
880 Brandon Webb .25
881 J.D. Drew .25
882 Jason Schmidt .25
883 Victor Martinez .25
884 Ichiro Suzuki .75
885 Miguel Cabrera .50
886 David Wright .75
887 Alfonso Soriano .50
888 Miguel Tejada .25
889 Khalil Greene .25
890 Ryan Howard 1.00
891 Jason Bay .25
892 Mark Teixeira .50
893 Manny Ramirez .75
894 Ken Griffey Jr. 1.00
895 Todd Helton .50
896 Angel Berroa .25
897 Ivan Rodriguez .50
898 Johan Santana .50

899 Paul Konerko .50
900 Derek Jeter 1.50
901 Macay McBride (RC) .50
902 Tony Pena (RC) .50
903 Peter Moylan RC .75
904 Aaron Rakers (RC) .50
905 Chris Britton RC .75
906 Nicholas Markakis (RC) 1.00
907 Sendy Rleal RC .50
908 Val Majewski (RC) .50
909 Jermaine Van Buren (RC) .50
910 Jonathan Papelbon (RC) 3.00
911 Angel Pagan (RC) .50
912 David Aardsma (RC) .50
913 Sean Marshall (RC) .50
914 Brian Anderson (RC) .50
915 Freddie Bynum (RC) .50
916 Fausto Carmona (RC) .50
917 Kelly Shoppach (RC) .50
918 Choo Freeman (RC) .50
919 Ryan Shealy (RC) .50
920 Joel Zumaya (RC) 2.00
921 Jordan Tata RC 1.00
922 Justin Verlander (RC) 2.00
923 Carlos Martinez RC .50
924 Chris Resop (RC) .50
925 Dan Uggla (RC) .50
926 Eric Reed (RC) .50
927 Hanley Ramirez (RC) 1.00
928 Yusmeiro Petit (RC) .50
929 Josh Willingham (RC) .50
930 Mike Jacobs (RC) .50
931 Reggie Abercrombie (RC) .50
932 Ricky Nolasco (RC) .50
933 Scott Olsen (RC) .50
934 Fernando Nieve (RC) .50
935 Taylor Buchholz (RC) .50
936 Cody Ross (RC) .50
937 James Loney (RC) .50
938 Takashi Saito RC 1.00
939 Tim Hamulack (RC) .50
940 Chris Demaria RC .50
941 Jose Capellan (RC) .50
942 Dave Gassner (RC) .50
943 Jason Kubel (RC) .50
944 Brian Bannister (RC) .50
945 Mike Thompson RC .50
946 Cole Hamels (RC) 2.00
947 Paul Maholm (RC) .50
948 John Van Benschoten (RC) .50
949 Nate McLouth (RC) .50
950 Ben Johnson (RC) .50
951 Josh Barfield (RC) .50
952 Travis Ishikawa (RC) .50
953 Jack Taschner (RC) .50
954 Kenji Johjima RC 3.00
955 Skip Schumaker (RC) .50
956 Ruddy Lugo (RC) .50
957 Jason Hammel (RC) .50
958 Chris Roberson (RC) .50
959 Fabio Castro RC .50
960 Ian Kinsler (RC) .50
961 John Koronka (RC) .50
962 Brandon Watson (RC) .50
963 Jon Lester RC 3.00
964 Ben Hendrickson (RC) .50
965 Martin Prado (RC) .50
966 Erick Aybar (RC) .50
967 Bobby Livingston (RC) .50
968 Ryan Spilborghs (RC) .50
969 Tommy Murphy (RC) .50
970 Howie Kendrick (RC) 1.50
971 Casey Janssen RC .50
972 Michael O'Connor RC .50
973 Conor Jackson (RC) 1.00
974 Jeremy Hermida (RC) .50
975 Renyel Pinto (RC) .50
976 Prince Fielder (RC) 2.00
977 Kevin Frandsen (RC) .50
978 Ty Taubenheim RC .50
979 Rich Hill (RC) .50
980 Jonathan Broxton (RC) .50
981 Jamie Shields RC .50
982 Carlos Villanueva RC 1.00
983 Boone Logan RC .50
984 Brian Wilson RC .50
985 Andre Ethier (RC) 2.00
986 Michael Napoli RC 1.00
987 Agustin Montero (RC) .50
988 Jack Hannahan RC .50
989 Boof Bonser (RC) .50
990 Carlos Ruiz (RC) .50
991 Jason Botts (RC) .50
992 Kendry Morales (RC) .50
993 Alay Soler RC .50
994 Santiago Ramirez (RC) .50
995 Saul Rivera (RC) .50
996 Anthony Reyes (RC) 1.00
997 Matthew Kemp (RC) 1.00
998 Jae-Kuk Ryu RC 1.50
999 Lastings Milledge (RC) 1.00
1000 Jered Weaver (RC) 2.00
1001 Jeremy Sowers (RC) 1.00
1002 Chad Billingsley (RC) 1.00
1003 Stephen Drew (RC) 2.00
1004 Tony Gwynn (RC) .50
1005 Melky Cabrera (RC) 1.00
1006 Eliezer Alfonzo RC .50
1007 Dana Eveland (RC) .50
1008 Luis Figueroa RC .50
1009 Emiliano Fruto RC .50
1010 Clay Hensley (RC) .50
1011 Zach Jackson (RC) .50
1012 Bobby Keppel (RC) .50
1013 Carlos Marmol RC 1.00
1014 Russell Martin (RC) 1.00
1015 Leo Nunez (RC) .50
1016 Ken Ray (RC) .50
1017 Mike Rouse (RC) .50
1018 Kevin Thompson (RC) .50
1019 C.J. Wilson (RC) .50
1020 Steve Andrade (RC) .50
1021 Ed Rogers (RC) .50
1022 Joe Nelson (RC) .50
1023 Omar Quintanilla (RC) .50
1024 Chris Bootcheck (RC) .50
1025 Jason Childers RC .50

FX Blue

Blue (1-900): 1-1.5X
Blue RC: 1X
Inserted 1:4

Green

Green (1-900): 2-3X
Green RC: 1-2X
Production 99 Sets

Purple

Purple (1-900): 2-3X
Purple RC: 1-2X
Production 150 Sets

Red

Red (1-900): 3-4X
Red RC: 2-3X
Production 50 Sets

Materials

NM/M
Common Player: 5.00
JB Jason Bay 8.00
LB Lance Berkman 5.00
MC Miguel Cabrera 10.00
MA Matt Cain 10.00
CA Chris Carpenter 8.00
CC Carl Crawford 5.00
CR Coco Crisp 8.00
AD Adam Dunn 8.00
PF Prince Fielder 15.00
RF Rafael Furcal 5.00
JG Jason Giambi 8.00
TG Troy Glaus 5.00
KG Ken Griffey Jr. 15.00
VG Vladimir Guerrero 8.00
TH Travis Hafner 8.00
HA Roy Halladay 8.00
CH Cole Hamels 15.00
JH Jeremy Hermida 5.00
FH Felix Hernandez 10.00
RH Ryan Howard 20.00
DJ Derek Jeter 20.00
KJ Kenji Johjima 15.00
AJ Andruw Jones 8.00
SK Scott Kazmir 5.00
IK Ian Kinsler 8.00
DL Derrek Lee 10.00
FL Francisco Liriano 10.00
PM Pedro Martinez 8.00
VM Victor Martinez 5.00
JM Joe Mauer 10.00
LM Lastings Milledge 10.00
KM Kendry Morales 5.00
DO David Ortiz 15.00
JP Jonathan Papelbon 15.00
AP Albert Pujols 20.00
HR Hanley Ramirez 10.00
JR Jose Reyes 15.00
JS Johan Santana 10.00
GS Grady Sizemore 10.00
AS Alfonso Soriano 8.00
MT Mark Teixeira 8.00
TE Miguel Tejada 8.00
JT Jim Thome 10.00
CU Chase Utley 15.00
JV Justin Verlander 15.00
WE Jered Weaver 10.00
RW Rickie Weeks 8.00
JW Josh Willingham 5.00
RZ Ryan Zimmerman 15.00

Player Highlights

NM/M
Common Player: .50
1 Andruw Jones 1.00
2 Manny Ramirez 1.00
3 Travis Hafner .75
4 Johnny Damon 1.00
5 Miguel Cabrera 1.00
6 Chris Carpenter 1.00
7 Derrek Lee 1.00
8 Jason Bay .75
9 Jason Varitek 1.00
10 Ryan Howard 3.00
11 Mark Teixeira 1.00
12 Carlos Delgado .75
13 Bartolo Colon .50
14 David Wright 2.00
15 Miguel Tejada .75
16 Mike Piazza 1.50
17 Paul Konerko .75
18 Jermaine Dye .50
19 Ichiro Suzuki 2.00
20 Brad Wilkerson .50
21 Hideki Matsui 2.00
22 Albert Pujols 3.00
23 Chris Burke .50
24 Derek Jeter 3.00
25 Brian Roberts .50
26 David Ortiz 1.00
27 Alex Rodriguez 2.00
28 Ken Griffey Jr. 2.00
29 Prince Fielder .75
30 Bobby Abreu .75
31 Vladimir Guerrero 1.00
32 Tadahito Iguchi .50
33 Jose Reyes .75
34 Scott Podsednik .50
35 Gary Sheffield .75

Run Producers

NM/M
Common Player: 1.00
1 Ty Cobb 3.00
2 Derrek Lee 1.50
3 Andruw Jones 1.50
4 David Ortiz 1.50
5 Lou Gehrig 4.00
6 Ken Griffey Jr. 4.00
7 Albert Pujols 5.00
8 Derek Jeter 5.00
9 Manny Ramirez 1.50
10 Alex Rodriguez 5.00
11 Gary Sheffield 1.00
12 Miguel Cabrera 1.50
13 Hideki Matsui 3.00
14 Vladimir Guerrero 1.50
15 David Wright 3.00
16 Mike Schmidt 1.50
17 Mark Teixeira 1.00
18 Babe Ruth 5.00
19 Jimmie Foxx 3.00
20 Honus Wagner 3.00

Special Endorsements

NM/M
Common Player: 5.00
Inserted 1:16
RA Reggie Abercrombie 5.00
AC Jeremy Accardo 5.00
BA Brian Anderson 5.00
AN Robert Andino 5.00
BR Brian Bannister 8.00
JB Jason Bay 20.00
BW Craig Breslow 8.00
CB Chris Britton 5.00
TB Taylor Buchholz 10.00
FB Freddie Bynum 8.00
MI Miguel Cabrera 20.00
MC Matt Cain 20.00
JC Jose Capellan/SP 8.00
CM Matt Capps 5.00
FC Fausto Carmona 8.00
TC Tim Corcoran 5.00
DE Chris Denorfia 8.00
JD Joey Devine 8.00
AE Andre Ethier 20.00
EV Dana Eveland 10.00
RF Ron Flores 5.00
KF Kevin Frandsen 8.00
DG Dave Gassner 8.00
KG Ken Griffey Jr. 60.00
TH Travis Hafner 15.00
CH Cole Hamels 40.00
BH Brendan Harris 5.00
HA Jeff Harris 5.00
HG Keith Hattig 8.00
HE Jeremy Hermida 15.00
AH Anderson Hernandez/SP 5.00
JU Justin Huber 8.00
JA Conor Jackson 15.00
MJ Mike Jacobs 8.00
DJ Derek Jeter 200.00
BJ Ben Johnson 8.00
JJ Josh Johnson 10.00
KE Howie Kendrick 20.00
IK Ian Kinsler 15.00
KO John Koronka 8.00
JK Jason Kubel 8.00
HK Hong-Chih Kuo 40.00
FL Francisco Liriano 20.00
BL Boone Logan 5.00
RL Ruddy Lugo 6.00
PM Paul Maholm 8.00
SM Sean Marshall 10.00
NI Nick Massett 8.00
MM Macay McBride 8.00
NM Nate McLouth 8.00
KM Kendry Morales 10.00
PE Peter Moylan 8.00
FN Fernando Nieve 5.00
WN Wilbert Nieves 8.00
JP Jonathan Papelbon 30.00
AA Aaron Rakers 5.00
HR Hanley Ramirez 20.00
RE Chris Resop 5.00
RB Chris Roberson 8.00
CR Cody Ross 8.00
RC Carlos Ruiz 10.00
RU Josh Rupe 8.00
TS Takashi Saito 25.00
RS Ryan Shealy 10.00
JS James Shields 20.00
KS Kelly Shoppach 8.00
MS Matt Smith 8.00
GS Geovany Soto 8.00
DU Dan Uggla 15.00
CU Chase Utley 30.00
JV John Van Benschoten 15.00
VE Justin Verlander/SP 30.00
AW Adam Wainwright 20.00
JW Jered Weaver 20.00
RW Rickie Weeks 15.00
WI Josh Willingham 15.00
DW Dontrelle Willis 15.00
JO Josh Wilson 8.00
RZ Ryan Zimmerman/SP 40.00
JZ Joel Zumaya 15.00

Star Attractions

NM/M
Common Player: .50
Inserted 1:8
BA Bobby Abreu .75
JB Josh Beckett .50
CB Carlos Beltran 1.00
LB Lance Berkman .75
JC Jose Contreras .50
JD Johnny Damon 1.50
CD Carlos Delgado .75
JE Jim Edmonds .75
JG Jason Giambi 1.00
KG Ken Griffey Jr. 3.00
RH Rich Harden .50
DJ Derek Jeter 4.00
AJ Andruw Jones 1.00
CJ Chipper Jones 1.50
DL Derrek Lee 1.50
GM Greg Maddux 3.00
PM Pedro Martinez 1.50
JM Joe Mauer 1.00
MO Magglio Ordonez .50
DO David Ortiz 1.50
PU Albert Pujols 4.00
MR Manny Ramirez 1.50
JR Jose Reyes 1.50
CS Curt Schilling 1.50
JS Jason Schmidt .50
SM John Smoltz .75
AS Alfonso Soriano 1.50
MT Mark Teixeira 1.00
DW Dontrelle Willis .50
WR David Wright 2.50

WBC Counterparts

NM/M
Common Duo: 1.00
Inserted 1:6
1 Yulieski Gourriel, Daisuke Matsuzaka 5.00
2 Ken Griffey Jr., Yoandy Garlobo 3.00
3 Ken Griffey Jr., Ichiro Suzuki 3.00
4 Derek Jeter, Chin-Lung Hu 4.00
5 Frederich Cepeda, Jong Beom Lee 1.00
6 Nobuhiko Matsunaka, Seung-Yeop Lee 2.00
7 Tsuyoshi Nishioka, Guangbiao Liu 1.00
8 Ichiro Suzuki, Osmany Urrutia 2.50
9 Daisuke Matsuzaka, Roger Clemens 8.00
10 Yadel Marti, Chan Ho Park 1.00
11 Koji Uehara, Jae Weong Seo 1.00
12 Shunsuke Watanabe, Bartolo Colon 2.00
13 Daisuke Matsuzaka, Johan Santana 5.00
14 Pedro Luis Lazo, Freddy Garcia 1.00
15 Koji Uehara, Roger Clemens 3.00

2006 Upper Deck Sweet Spot

NM/M
Complete Set (184):
Common Player: .25
Common Auto. (101-184): 15.00
Production 45-275
Pack (5): 10.00
Box (12): 110.00

1 Bartolo Colon .25
2 Garret Anderson .25
3 Francisco Rodriguez .25
4 Dallas McPherson .25
5 Andy Pettitte .40
6 Lance Berkman .50
7 Willy Taveras .25
8 Bobby Crosby .25
9 Danny Haren .25
10 Nick Swisher .25
11 Vernon Wells .50
12 Orlando Hudson .25
13 Roy Halladay .50
14 Andruw Jones .75
15 Chipper Jones .75
16 Jeff Francoeur .40
17 John Smoltz .50
18 Carlos Lee .40
19 Rickie Weeks .40
20 Bill Hall .25
21 Jim Edmonds .40
22 David Eckstein .25
23 Mark Mulder .40
24 Aramis Ramirez .50
25 Greg Maddux 1.50
26 Nomar Garciaparra .75
27 Carlos Zambrano .40
28 Scott Kazmir .40
29 Jorge Cantu .25
30 Carl Crawford .40
31 Luis Gonzalez .25
32 Troy Glaus .40
33 Shawn Green .25
34 Jeff Kent .40
35 Milton Bradley .25
36 Cesar Izturis .25
37 Omar Vizquel .25
38 Moises Alou .40
39 Randy Winn .25
40 Jason Schmidt .40
41 Coco Crisp .25
42 C.C. Sabathia .40
43 Cliff Lee .25
44 Ichiro Suzuki 1.50
45 Richie Sexson .50
46 Jeremy Reed .25
47 Carlos Delgado .50
48 Miguel Cabrera .75
49 Luis Castillo .25
50 Carlos Beltran .50
51 Tom Glavine .50
52 David Wright 1.50
53 Cliff Floyd .25
54 Chad Cordero .25
55 Jose Vidro .25
56 Jose Guillen .25
57 Nick Johnson .25
58 Miguel Tejada .50
59 Melvin Mora .25
60 Javy Lopez .25
61 Khalil Greene .25
62 Brian Giles .25
63 Trevor Hoffman .25
64 Bobby Abreu .40
65 Jimmy Rollins .50
66 Pat Burrell .40
67 Billy Wagner .25
68 Jack Wilson .25
69 Zachary Duke .25
70 Craig Wilson .25
71 Mark Teixeira .50
72 Hank Blalock .40
73 David Dellucci .25
74 Manny Ramirez .75
75 Johnny Damon .75
76 Jason Varitek .50
77 Trot Nixon .25
78 Adam Dunn .50
79 Felipe Lopez .25
80 Brandon Claussen .25
81 Sean Casey .25
82 Todd Helton .50
83 Clint Barmes .25
84 Matt Holliday .50
85 Mike Sweeney .25
86 Zack Greinke .25
87 David DeJesus .25
88 Ivan Rodriguez .50
89 Jeremy Bonderman .25
90 Magglio Ordonez .25
91 Torii Hunter .40
92 Joe Nathan .25
93 Michael Cuddyer .25
94 Paul Konerko .50
95 Jermaine Dye .25
96 Jon Garland .25
97 Alex Rodriguez 2.00
98 Hideki Matsui 1.50
99 Jason Giambi .50
100 Mariano Rivera .40
101 Adrian Beltre/99 25.00
102 Matt Cain/275 (RC) 30.00
103 Craig Biggio/99 35.00
104 Eric Chavez/99 25.00
105 J.D. Drew/99 25.00
106 Eric Gagne/99 50.00
107 Tim Hudson/99 40.00
108 Tom Glavine/275 40.00
109 David Ortiz/99 85.00
110 Scott Rolen/275 40.00
111 Johan Santana/99 50.00
112 Curt Schilling/96 75.00
113 John Smoltz/99 75.00
114 Alfonso Soriano/99 75.00
115 Kerry Wood/99 25.00
116 Edwin Jackson/99 20.00
117 Felix Hernandez/125 50.00
118 Prince Fielder/99 (RC) 100.00
119 Vladimir Guerrero/86 50.00
120 Roger Clemens/99 140.00
121 Albert Pujols/45 250.00
122 Chris Carpenter/99 50.00
123 Derrek Lee/99 40.00
124 Dontrelle Willis/99 30.00
125 Roy Oswalt/99 35.00
126 Ryan Garko/275 (RC) 25.00
127 Tadahito Iguchi/275 60.00
128 Mark Loretta/275 25.00
129 Joe Mauer/275 40.00
130 Victor Martinez/275 30.00
131 Wily Mo Pena/275 30.00
132 Oliver Perez/274 15.00
133 Corey Patterson/275 25.00
134 Ben Sheets/275 20.00
135 Michael Young/275 25.00
136 Jonny Gomes/275 25.00
137 Derek Jeter/99 175.00
138 Ken Griffey Jr./275 100.00
139 Ryan Zimmerman/275 (RC) 60.00
140 Scott Baker/275 (RC) 20.00
141 Huston Street/275 30.00
142 Jason Bay/275 30.00
143 Ryan Howard/275 75.00
145 Travis Hafner/275 35.00
146 Brian Myrow/275 RC 20.00
147 Scott Podsednik/275 35.00
148 Brian Roberts/275 25.00
149 Grady Sizemore/135 45.00
150 Chris Demaria/275 RC 15.00
151 Jonah Bayliss/275 RC 20.00
152 Geovany Soto/275 (RC) 20.00
153 Lyle Overbay/275 20.00
154 Joey Devine/275 RC 20.00
155 Alejandro Freire/275 RC 15.00
156 Conor Jackson/275 (RC) 35.00
157 Danny Sandoval/275 RC 15.00
158 Chase Utley/275 50.00
159 Jeff Harris/275 RC 20.00
160 Ron Flores/275 RC 20.00
161 Scott Feldman/275 RC 20.00
162 Yadier Molina/275 30.00
163 Tim Corcoran/275 RC 20.00
164 Craig Hansen/275 RC 40.00
165 Jason Bergmann/275 RC 25.00
166 Craig Breslow/275 RC 25.00
167 Jhonny Peralta/275 30.00
168 Jeremy Hermida/275 (RC) 30.00
169 Scott Kazmir/275 25.00
170 Bobby Crosby/99 25.00
171 Rich Harden/275 25.00
172 Casey Kotchman/275 15.00
173 Tim Hamulack/275 (RC) 15.00
174 Justin Morneau/275 30.00
175 Jake Peavy/275 30.00
176 Yuniesky Betancourt/275 30.00
177 Jeremy Accardo/275 RC 25.00
178 Jorge Cantu/200 25.00
179 Marlon Byrd/275 20.00
180 Ryan Jorgensen/275 RC 20.00
181 Chris Denorfia/275 (RC) 20.00
182 Steve Stemle/275 15.00
183 Robert Andino/275 RC 20.00
184 Chris Heintz/275 RC 15.00

Sign. Bat Barrel Black Ink

NM/M
Production 13-25
107 Tim Hudson/25 50.00
110 Scott Rolen/25 50.00
111 Johan Santana/25 60.00
115 Kerry Wood/25 30.00
117 Felix Hernandez/25 100.00
118 Prince Fielder/25 100.00
119 Vladimir Guerrero/25 75.00
121 Albert Pujols/25 275.00
125 Roy Oswalt/25 40.00
127 Tadahito Iguchi/25 90.00
131 Wily Mo Pena/25 40.00
139 Ryan Zimmerman/25 100.00
143 Ryan Howard/25 90.00
151 Jonah Bayliss/25 30.00
153 Lyle Overbay/25 30.00
154 Joey Devine/25 30.00
160 Ron Flores/25 30.00

167 Jhonny Peralta/25 40.00
174 Justin Morneau/25 50.00
178 Jorge Cantu/25 40.00
182 Steve Stemle/25 25.00

Sign. Bat Barrel Blue Ink

No Pricing
Production Three to Five Sets

Sign. Black Stitch Black Ink

No Pricing
Production One Set
Blue Ink: No Pricing
Production One Set

Sig. Glove Leather Black Ink

No Pricing
Production 5-15
Blue Ink: No Pricing
Production 5-15

Sign. Red Stitch Blue Ink

NM/M
Production 15-150
101 Adrian Beltre/25 35.00
102 Matt Cain/150 40.00
103 Craig Biggio/25 50.00
106 Eric Gagne/25 60.00
107 Tim Hudson/25 40.00
109 David Ortiz/25 120.00
110 Scott Rolen/150 40.00
111 Johan Santana/25 60.00
112 Curt Schilling/25 100.00
113 John Smoltz/25 90.00
116 Edwin Jackson/150 20.00
118 Prince Fielder/25 100.00
119 Vladimir Guerrero/25 80.00
122 Chris Carpenter/25 60.00
123 Derrek Lee/25 50.00
124 Dontrelle Willis/25 40.00
125 Roy Oswalt/25 40.00
126 Ryan Garko/150 25.00
127 Tadahito Iguchi/150 75.00
128 Mark Loretta/114 35.00
129 Joe Mauer/150 40.00
130 Victor Martinez/150 35.00
131 Wily Mo Pena/150 30.00
132 Oliver Perez/135 15.00
133 Corey Patterson/150 30.00
134 Ben Sheets/150 25.00
135 Michael Young/150 30.00
136 Jonny Gomes/150 40.00
137 Derek Jeter/25 200.00
138 Ken Griffey Jr./150 100.00
139 Ryan Zimmerman/150 60.00
140 Scott Baker/150 20.00
141 Huston Street/150 40.00
142 Jason Bay/150 35.00
143 Ryan Howard/150 75.00
144 Mike Piazza/100 100.00
145 Travis Hafner/150 40.00
146 Brian Myrow/150 20.00
147 Scott Podsednik/150 40.00
148 Brian Roberts/150 25.00
149 Grady Sizemore/75 50.00
150 Chris Demaria/150 20.00
151 Jonah Bayliss/150 20.00
152 Geovany Soto/150 20.00
153 Lyle Overbay/150 20.00
154 Joey Devine/150 20.00
155 Alejandro Freire/150 20.00
156 Conor Jackson/150 40.00
157 Danny Sandoval/150 20.00
158 Chase Utley/150 50.00
159 Jeff Harris/150 20.00
160 Ron Flores/150 20.00
161 Scott Feldman/150 20.00
162 Yadier Molina/135 30.00
163 Tim Corcoran/150 20.00
164 Craig Hansen/150 40.00
165 Jason Bergmann/150 20.00
166 Craig Breslow/150 25.00
167 Jhonny Peralta/120 30.00
168 Jeremy Hermida/150 35.00
169 Scott Kazmir/150 35.00
170 Bobby Crosby/25 35.00
171 Rich Harden/150 25.00
172 Casey Kotchman/150 20.00
173 Tim Hamulack/150 20.00
174 Justin Morneau/150 35.00
175 Jake Peavy/150 30.00
176 Yuniesky Betancourt/150 30.00
177 Jeremy Accardo/150 25.00
178 Jorge Cantu/25 40.00
179 Marlon Byrd/40 30.00
180 Ryan Jorgensen/150 20.00
181 Chris Denorfia/150 25.00
182 Steve Stemle/150 15.00
183 Robert Andino/150 25.00
184 Chris Heintz/150 20.00

Sign. Red-Blue Stitch Black Ink

NM/M
Production 25-99
101 Adrian Beltre/50 30.00
102 Matt Cain/99 40.00
103 Craig Biggio/50 50.00
105 J.D. Drew/50 30.00
106 Eric Gagne/50 50.00
107 Tim Hudson/50 40.00
108 Tom Glavine/99 50.00
109 David Ortiz/50 85.00
110 Scott Rolen/99 40.00
111 Johan Santana/50 50.00
112 Curt Schilling/45 80.00
113 John Smoltz/50 80.00
114 Alfonso Soriano/50 80.00
115 Kerry Wood/49 30.00
116 Edwin Jackson/50 20.00
117 Felix Hernandez/60 65.00
118 Prince Fielder/50 100.00
119 Vladimir Guerrero/50 50.00
120 Roger Clemens/50 150.00
121 Albert Pujols/25 250.00
122 Chris Carpenter/50 50.00
123 Derrek Lee/50 40.00
124 Dontrelle Willis/50 30.00
125 Roy Oswalt/50 40.00
126 Ryan Garko/99 30.00
127 Tadahito Iguchi/99 75.00
128 Mark Loretta/99 35.00
129 Joe Mauer/99 40.00
130 Victor Martinez/99 35.00
131 Wily Mo Pena/99 30.00
132 Oliver Perez/99 15.00
133 Corey Patterson/99 30.00
134 Ben Sheets/99 25.00
135 Michael Young/99 30.00
136 Jonny Gomes/99 40.00
137 Derek Jeter/50 175.00
138 Ken Griffey Jr./99 100.00
139 Ryan Zimmerman/99 75.00
140 Scott Baker/99 20.00
141 Huston Street/99 40.00
142 Jason Bay/99 35.00
143 Ryan Howard/99 75.00
145 Travis Hafner/99 40.00
146 Brian Myrow/99 20.00
147 Scott Podsednik/99 40.00
148 Brian Roberts/99 25.00
149 Grady Sizemore/50 50.00
150 Chris Demaria/99 20.00
151 Jonah Bayliss/99 20.00
152 Geovany Soto/99 20.00
153 Lyle Overbay/99 20.00
154 Joey Devine/99 20.00
155 Alejandro Freire/99 20.00
156 Conor Jackson/99 40.00
157 Danny Sandoval/99 20.00
158 Chase Utley/99 50.00
159 Jeff Harris/99 20.00
160 Ron Flores/99 20.00
161 Scott Feldman/99 20.00
162 Yadier Molina/99 30.00
163 Tim Corcoran/99 20.00
164 Craig Hansen/99 40.00
165 Jason Bergmann/99 20.00
166 Craig Breslow/99 25.00
167 Jhonny Peralta/90 30.00
168 Jeremy Hermida/99 35.00
169 Scott Kazmir/99 35.00
170 Bobby Crosby/50 25.00
171 Rich Harden/99 25.00
172 Casey Kotchman/99 20.00
173 Tim Hamulack/99 20.00
174 Justin Morneau/99 35.00
175 Jake Peavy/99 30.00
176 Yuniesky Betancourt/99 30.00
177 Jeremy Accardo/99 25.00
178 Jorge Cantu/50 30.00
179 Marlon Byrd/99 25.00
180 Ryan Jorgensen/99 20.00
181 Chris Denorfia/99 25.00
182 Steve Stemle/99 15.00
183 Robert Andino/91 25.00
184 Chris Heintz/99 20.00

Sign. Red-Blue Stitch Blue Ink

NM/M
Production 10-50
102 Matt Cain/40 40.00
110 Scott Rolen/50 40.00
116 Edwin Jackson/50 20.00
127 Tadahito Iguchi/50 75.00
128 Mark Loretta/50 40.00
129 Joe Mauer/50 40.00
130 Victor Martinez/50 35.00
131 Wily Mo Pena/50 35.00
132 Oliver Perez/30 20.00
133 Corey Patterson/50 30.00
134 Ben Sheets/50 25.00
136 Jonny Gomes/50 30.00
138 Ken Griffey Jr./50 125.00
139 Ryan Zimmerman/50 75.00
140 Scott Baker/50 20.00
141 Huston Street/50 40.00
142 Jason Bay/50 40.00
143 Ryan Howard/50 75.00
144 Mike Piazza/50 140.00
145 Travis Hafner/50 50.00
146 Brian Myrow/50 20.00
147 Scott Podsednik/50 40.00
148 Brian Roberts/50 30.00
149 Grady Sizemore/25 60.00
150 Chris Demaria/50 20.00
151 Jonah Bayliss/50 20.00
152 Geovany Soto/50 20.00
153 Lyle Overbay/50 20.00
154 Joey Devine/50 20.00
155 Alejandro Freire/50 20.00
156 Conor Jackson/50 40.00
157 Danny Sandoval/50 20.00
158 Chase Utley/50 60.00
159 Jeff Harris/50 20.00
160 Ron Flores/50 20.00
161 Scott Feldman/50 20.00
162 Yadier Molina/30 40.00
163 Tim Corcoran/50 20.00
164 Craig Hansen/50 50.00
165 Jason Bergmann/50 20.00
166 Craig Breslow/50 25.00
167 Jhonny Peralta/50 35.00
168 Jeremy Hermida/50 40.00
170 Bobby Crosby/50 25.00
171 Rich Harden/50 25.00
172 Casey Kotchman/50 20.00
173 Tim Hamulack/50 20.00
174 Justin Morneau/50 35.00
175 Jake Peavy/49 30.00
177 Jeremy Accardo/50 25.00
180 Ryan Jorgensen/50 20.00
181 Chris Denorfia/50 25.00
182 Steve Stemle/50 15.00
183 Robert Andino/50 25.00
184 Chris Heintz/50 20.00

Super Sweet Swatch

NM/M
Production 299 Sets
Gold: 1-2X
Production 75 Sets
Platinum: 1.5-3X
Production 45 Sets
BA Bobby Abreu 8.00
GA Garret Anderson 5.00
AT Garrett Atkins 5.00
JL Jeff Bagwell 10.00
RB Rocco Baldelli 8.00
JB Jason Bay 10.00
BE Josh Beckett 5.00
LB Lance Berkman 10.00
CB Craig Biggio 6.00
HB Hank Blalock 6.00
MI Miguel Cabrera 12.00
MA Matt Cain 10.00
EC Eric Chavez 5.00
BC Brandon Claussen 5.00
MC Matt Clement 5.00
CR Bobby Crosby/136 5.00
CD Carlos Delgado 8.00
ZD Zachary Duke 5.00
AD Adam Dunn 8.00
DY Jermaine Dye 5.00
AE Adam Eaton 5.00
ED Jim Edmonds 8.00
JE Johnny Estrada 5.00
PF Prince Fielder 20.00
FR Jeff Francoeur 10.00
EG Eric Gagne 5.00
FG Freddy Garcia 5.00
JG Jason Giambi 10.00
BG Brian Giles 5.00
MG Marcus Giles 5.00
TG Troy Glaus/160 8.00
GL Tom Glavine 8.00
KG Ken Griffey Jr. 30.00
VG Vladimir Guerrero 12.00
HA Travis Hafner 10.00
HY Roy Halladay 8.00
TO Todd Helton/232 10.00
FH Felix Hernandez 10.00
HE Ramon Hernandez 5.00
HO Trevor Hoffman 5.00
RH Ryan Howard 20.00
TH Tim Hudson 8.00
HU Torii Hunter 6.00
DJ Derek Jeter 30.00
NJ Nick Johnson 5.00
AJ Andruw Jones 10.00
CJ Chipper Jones 10.00
JJ Jacque Jones 5.00
SK Scott Kazmir 8.00
RK Ryan Klesko 5.00
KO Paul Konerko 10.00
DL Derrek Lee 10.00
ML Mark Loretta 6.00
NL Noah Lowry 5.00
PM Pedro Martinez 15.00
VM Victor Martinez 8.00
JM Joe Mauer 12.00
JU Justin Morneau 8.00
MM Mark Mulder 5.00
TN Trot Nixon 8.00
DO David Ortiz 12.00
RO Roy Oswalt 8.00
JA Jay Payton 5.00
PE Jake Peavy 8.00
AN Andy Pettitte 8.00
PI Mike Piazza 15.00
JP Jorge Posada 12.00
MP Mark Prior 10.00
AP Albert Pujols 30.00
MR Manny Ramirez 12.00
JR Jose Reyes 8.00
IR Ivan Rodriguez/193 10.00
SR Scott Rolen 10.00
SA Johan Santana 10.00
CS Curt Schilling 10.00
JS Jason Schmidt 8.00
RS Richie Sexson 10.00
BS Ben Sheets 5.00
GS Gary Sheffield 10.00
GR Grady Sizemore 20.00
JO John Smoltz 10.00
ST Huston Street 8.00
MS Mike Sweeney 5.00
NS Nick Swisher 10.00
TX Mark Teixeira 10.00
MT Miguel Tejada 10.00
FT Frank Thomas 10.00
JV Jason Varitek 15.00
RW Rickie Weeks 10.00
WE David Wells 5.00
VW Vernon Wells 10.00
BW Bernie Williams 8.00
DW Dontrelle Willis 8.00
JW Jack Wilson 5.00
KW Kerry Wood 5.00
RZ Ryan Zimmerman 15.00
BZ Barry Zito 6.00

2006 UD Sweet Spot Update

NM/M
Complete Set (182):
Common Player (1-100): .25
Common Auto. (101-184): 10.00
Production 98-499
Pack (5): 10.00
Box (12): 110.00
1 Luis Gonzalez .25
2 Chad Tracy .25
3 Brandon Webb .50
4 Andruw Jones 1.00
5 Chipper Jones 1.00
6 John Smoltz .50
7 Tim Hudson .50
8 Miguel Tejada .50
9 Brian Roberts .25
10 Ramon Hernandez .25
11 Curt Schilling .75
12 David Ortiz 1.00
13 Manny Ramirez 1.00
14 Jason Varitek 1.00
15 Josh Beckett .50
16 Greg Maddux 2.00
17 Derrek Lee .75
18 Mark Prior .75
19 Aramis Ramirez .50
20 Jim Thome .75
21 Paul Konerko .75
22 Scott Podsednik .50
23 Jose Contreras .25
24 Ken Griffey Jr. 2.00
25 Adam Dunn .75
26 Felipe Lopez .25
27 Travis Hafner .50
28 Victor Martinez .25
29 Grady Sizemore .75
30 Jhonny Peralta .25
31 Todd Helton .75
32 Garrett Atkins .25
33 Clint Barmes .25
34 Ivan Rodriguez .75
35 Chris Shelton .25
36 Jeremy Bonderman .50
37 Miguel Cabrera 1.00
38 Dontrelle Willis .50
39 Lance Berkman .50
40 Morgan Ensberg .25
41 Roy Oswalt .50
42 Reggie Sanders .25
43 Mike Sweeney .25
44 Vladimir Guerrero 1.00
45 Bartolo Colon .50
46 Chone Figgins .25
47 Nomar Garciaparra 1.00
48 Jeff Kent .50
49 J.D. Drew .50
50 Carlos Lee .50
51 Ben Sheets .50
52 Rickie Weeks .50
53 Johan Santana 1.00
54 Torii Hunter .50
55 Joe Mauer .75
56 Pedro Martinez 1.00
57 David Wright 2.00
58 Carlos Beltran .75
59 Carlos Delgado .75
60 Jose Reyes .75
61 Derek Jeter 3.00
62 Alex Rodriguez 2.50
63 Randy Johnson 1.00
64 Hideki Matsui 2.00
65 Gary Sheffield .75
66 Rich Harden .50
67 Eric Chavez .50
68 Huston Street .25
69 Bobby Crosby .25
70 Bobby Abreu .50
71 Ryan Howard 2.00
72 Chase Utley 1.00
73 Pat Burrell .50
74 Jason Bay .50
75 Sean Casey .25
76 Mike Piazza 1.50
77 Jake Peavy .50
78 Brian Giles .25
79 Milton Bradley .25
80 Omar Vizquel .25
81 Jason Schmidt .50
82 Ichiro Suzuki 2.00
83 Felix Hernandez .50
84 Kenji Johjima .50
85 Albert Pujols 3.00
86 Chris Carpenter .75
87 Scott Rolen 1.00
88 Jim Edmonds .50
89 Carl Crawford .50
90 Jonny Gomes .25
91 Scott Kazmir .50
92 Mark Teixeira .75
93 Michael Young .50
94 Phil Nevin .25
95 Vernon Wells .50
96 Roy Halladay .50
97 Troy Glaus .50
98 Alfonso Soriano 1.00
99 Nick Johnson .25
100 Jose Vidro .25
101 Adam Wainwright/100 **(RC)** 40.00
102 Anderson Hernandez/100 **(RC)** 15.00
103 Andre Ethier/150 **(RC)** 35.00
104 Jason Botts/100 **(RC)** 15.00
105 Ben Johnson/400 **(RC)** 10.00
106 Boof Bonser/100 **(RC)** 20.00
107 Boone Logan/200 **RC** 10.00
108 Brian Anderson/200 **(RC)** 10.00
109 Brian Bannister/100 **(RC)** 15.00
110 Chris Denorfia/100 **(RC)** 10.00
111 Agustin Montero/100 **(RC)** 15.00
112 Cody Ross/100 **(RC)** 10.00
113 Cole Hamels/399 **(RC)** 35.00
114 Conor Jackson/400 **(RC)** 10.00
115 Dan Uggla/125 **(RC)** 25.00
116 Dave Gassner/100 **(RC)** 10.00
117 C.J. Wilson/150 **(RC)** 10.00
118 Eric Reed/150 **(RC)** 10.00
119 Fausto Carmona/99 **(RC)** 10.00
120 Fernando Nieve/100 **(RC)** 10.00
121 Francisco Liriano/499 **(RC)** 25.00
122 Freddie Bynum/100 **(RC)** 10.00
123 Hanley Ramirez/100 **(RC)** 30.00
124 Hong-Chih Kuo/100 **(RC)** 125.00
125 Ian Kinsler/100 **(RC)** 40.00
126 Carlos Marmol/100 **RC** 15.00
127 Bobby Keppel/200 **(RC)** 10.00
128 Jason Kubel/100 **(RC)** 15.00
129 Jeff Harris/100 **RC** 10.00
130 Alay Soler/100 **RC** 15.00
131 Jered Weaver/100 **(RC)** 30.00
132 Carlos Quentin/100 **(RC)** 30.00
133 Jeremy Hermida/100 **(RC)** 20.00
134 Joel Zumaya/100 **(RC)** 50.00
135 Joey Devine/100 **RC** 15.00
136 John Koronka/98 **(RC)** 10.00
137 Jonathan Papelbon/399 **(RC)** 40.00
138 Jose Capellan/240 **(RC)** 10.00
139 Josh Johnson/100 **(RC)** 20.00
140 Josh Rupe/100 **(RC)** 10.00
141 Josh Willingham/100 **(RC)** 20.00
143 Justin Verlander/100 **(RC)** 40.00
144 Kelly Shoppach/100 **(RC)** 10.00
145 Kendry Morales/100 **(RC)** 20.00
146 Kevin Thompson/100 **(RC)** 10.00
147 Macay McBride/100 **(RC)** 15.00
148 Martin Prado/100 **(RC)** 10.00
149 Matt Cain/150 **(RC)** 25.00
150 Clay Hensley/100 **(RC)** 10.00
151 Ty Taubenheim/100 **RC** 30.00
152 Mike Jacobs/200 **(RC)** 15.00
153 Saul Rivera/100 **(RC)** 15.00
154 Mike Thompson/100 **RC** 15.00
155 Nate McLouth/100 **(RC)** 15.00
156 Michael Vento/100 **(RC)** 15.00
157 Paul Maholm/200 **(RC)** 10.00
159 Reggie Abercrombie/100 **(RC)** 15.00
160 Mike Rouse/100 **(RC)** 10.00
161 Ken Ray/100 **(RC)** 15.00
162 Ron Flores/100 **RC** 10.00
163 Ryan Zimmerman/100 **(RC)** 50.00
164 Erick Aybar/100 **(RC)** 20.00
165 Sean Marshall/150 **(RC)** 20.00
166 Takashi Saito/100 **RC** 40.00
167 Taylor Buchholz/100 **(RC)** 15.00
168 Matt Murton/100 **(RC)** 30.00
169 Luis Figueroa/100 **RC** 15.00
170 Wilbert Nieves/100 **(RC)** 15.00
171 James Shields/100 **RC** 20.00
172 Jon Lester/399 **(RC)** 30.00
173 Craig Hansen/100 **RC** 30.00
174 Aaron Rakers/100 **(RC)** 10.00
175 Bobby Livingston/100 **(RC)** 15.00
176 Brendan Harris/100 **(RC)** 10.00
177 Zach Jackson/100 **(RC)** 15.00
178 Chris Britton/100 **RC** 10.00
179 Howie Kendrick/399 **(RC)** 25.00
180 Zach Miner/100 **(RC)** 15.00
181 Kevin Frandsen/100 **(RC)** 10.00
182 Matt Capps/100 **(RC)** 10.00
183 Peter Moylan/100 **RC** 15.00
184 Melky Cabrera/100 **(RC)** 50.00

Sig. Red/Blue Stitch Red Ink

NM/M
Production 40-225
101 Adam Wainwright/50 40.00
103 Andre Ethier/50 40.00
105 Ben Johnson/100 10.00
106 Boof Bonser/50 20.00
107 Boone Logan/50 15.00
108 Brian Anderson/100 10.00
109 Brian Bannister/100 15.00
110 Chris Denorfia/50 10.00
112 Cody Ross/50 10.00
113 Cole Hamels/225 40.00
114 Conor Jackson/100 10.00
115 Dan Uggla/50 30.00
116 Dave Gassner/50 10.00
117 C.J. Wilson/50 10.00
118 Eric Reed/100 10.00
119 Fausto Carmona/50 10.00
120 Fernando Nieve/50 10.00
121 Francisco Liriano/175 30.00
122 Freddie Bynum/100 10.00
123 Hanley Ramirez/50 40.00
124 Hong-Chih Kuo/50 200.00
125 Ian Kinsler/45 50.00
126 Carlos Marmol/50 20.00
127 Bobby Keppel/100 10.00
128 Jason Kubel/50 20.00
130 Alay Soler/50 20.00
131 Jered Weaver/50 40.00
132 Carlos Quentin/50 30.00
133 Jeremy Hermida/50 20.00
134 Joel Zumaya/50 50.00
135 Joey Devine/50 20.00
136 John Koronka/50 10.00
137 Jonathan Papelbon/175 50.00
138 Jose Capellan/50 10.00
139 Josh Johnson/100 20.00
140 Josh Rupe/50 10.00
141 Josh Willingham/50 20.00
143 Justin Verlander/50 50.00
144 Kelly Shoppach/50 15.00
146 Kevin Thompson/50 10.00
147 Macay McBride/50 15.00
150 Clay Hensley/49 10.00
151 Ty Taubenheim/50 35.00
152 Mike Jacobs/100 15.00
153 Saul Rivera/50 15.00
154 Mike Thompson/50 15.00
155 Nate McLouth/50 15.00
156 Michael Vento/50 15.00
159 Reggie Abercrombie/50 15.00
160 Mike Rouse/50 10.00
161 Ken Ray/50 15.00
162 Ron Flores/50 10.00
163 Ryan Zimmerman/50 60.00
164 Erick Aybar/50 20.00
165 Sean Marshall/50 30.00
167 Taylor Buchholz/50 15.00
168 Matt Murton/50 40.00
169 Luis Figueroa/50 20.00
170 Wilbert Nieves/50 20.00
171 James Shields/50 20.00
172 Jon Lester/175 40.00
174 Aaron Rakers/50 10.00

175 Bobby Livingston/50 20.00
176 Brendan Harris/50 10.00
177 Zach Jackson/50 20.00
178 Chris Britton/50 10.00
179 Howie Kendrick/175 30.00
181 Kevin Frandsen/50 10.00
182 Matt Capps/50 10.00
183 Peter Moylan/50 15.00

Veteran Red Stitch Blue Ink

NM/M

Production 30-525
AG Tony Gwynn Jr./425 20.00
AH Aaron Harang/425 20.00
AP Albert Pujols/30 250.00
AZ Aramis Ramirez/225 25.00
BJ B.J. Upton/193 15.00
BR Brian Roberts/300 15.00
CC Carl Crawford/425 15.00
CU Chase Utley/425 40.00
DJ Derek Jeter/75 200.00
DW Dontrelle Willis/125 25.00
HS Huston Street/200 15.00
JB Jason Bay/425 20.00
JM Joe Mauer/57 40.00
JN Joe Nathan/200 20.00
JS Jeremy Sowers/425 20.00
JT Jim Thome/75 50.00
KG Ken Griffey Jr./359 80.00
KG2 Ken Griffey Jr./358 80.00
KY Kevin Youkilis/425 25.00
LO Lyle Overbay/525 15.00
MC Miguel Cabrera/525 25.00
MO Justin Morneau/425 25.00
RC Roger Clemens/30 150.00
SD Stephen Drew/525 25.00
SK Scott Kazmir/522 20.00
SM John Smoltz/507 35.00
SP Scott Podsednik/247 15.00
SS Mark Mulder/300 15.00
TH Travis Hafner/525 25.00
TI Tadahito Iguchi/425 30.00
VM Victor Martinez/71 20.00

Veteran Red/Blue Stitch Red Ink

NM/M

Production 10-299
AG Tony Gwynn Jr./299 25.00
AH Aaron Harang/299 20.00
AZ Aramis Ramirez/99 30.00
BJ B.J. Upton/100 20.00
BR Brian Roberts/100 20.00
CC Carl Crawford/299 20.00
CU Chase Utley/299 40.00
DW Dontrelle Willis/35 35.00
HS Huston Street/100 20.00
JB Jason Bay/299 25.00
JN Joe Nathan/100 20.00
JS Jeremy Sowers/299 20.00
KG Ken Griffey Jr./38 120.00
KG2 Ken Griffey Jr./37 120.00
KY Kevin Youkilis/299 30.00
LO Lyle Overbay/299 15.00
MC Miguel Cabrera/299 30.00
MO Justin Morneau/299 30.00
SD Stephen Drew/299 30.00
SK Scott Kazmir/296 25.00
SP Scott Podsednik/199 15.00
SS Mark Mulder/298 15.00
TH Travis Hafner/299 25.00
TI Tadahito Iguchi/299 40.00
VM Victor Martinez/61 20.00

Signatures Black Stitch/Ink

No Pricing
Production One Set

Sweet Beginnings Swatches

NM/M

Common Player: 5.00
AB Adrian Beltre 5.00
AI Akinori Iwamura 30.00
AJ Andruw Jones 10.00
AP Ariel Pestano 5.00
AR Alex Rios 8.00
AS Alfonso Soriano 10.00
BA Bobby Abreu 5.00
BB Brian Bannister 5.00
BI Chad Billingsley 10.00
BW Bernie Williams 10.00
CA Miguel Cabrera 10.00
CB Carlos Beltran 10.00
CD Carlos Delgado 8.00
CH Chin-Lung Hu 50.00
CJ Conor Jackson 8.00
CL Carlos Lee 5.00
CM Matt Cain 10.00
CU Chris Duncan 10.00
CZ Carlos Zambrano 8.00
DL Derrek Lee 8.00
DO David Ortiz 15.00
EB Erik Bedard 10.00
EP Eduardo Paret 8.00
FA Fausto Carmona 5.00
FC Frederich Cepeda 8.00
FL Francisco Liriano/SP 35.00
GY Guogang Yang 5.00
HA Cole Hamels 15.00
HC Hee Seop Choi 5.00
HT Hitoshi Tamura 30.00
IK Ian Kinsler 10.00
IR Ivan Rodriguez 10.00
IS Ichiro Suzuki 150.00
JB Jason Bay 10.00
JD Johnny Damon 10.00
JF Jeff Francis 5.00
JH Jeremy Hermida 8.00
JL Jong Beom Lee 8.00
JM Justin Morneau 15.00
JP Jin Man Park 8.00
JS Johan Santana 15.00
JV Jason Varitek 20.00
JZ Joel Zumaya 15.00
KE Matthew Kemp 10.00
KG Ken Griffey Jr. 20.00
KJ Kenji Johjima/SP 35.00
KU Koji Uehara 30.00
LO Javy Lopez 8.00
MA Moises Alou 8.00
MC Michael Collins 8.00
ME Michel Enriquez 8.00
MF Maikel Folch 5.00
MJ Mike Jacobs 8.00
MK Munenori Kawasaki 40.00
MN Michael Napoli 8.00
MO Michihiro Ogasawara 30.00
MP Mike Piazza 15.00
MS Min Han Son 10.00
MT Miguel Tejada 8.00
NM Nobuhiko Matsunaka 30.00
NS Naoyuki Shimizu 25.00
OU Osmany Urrutia 10.00
PF Prince Fielder SP 25.00
PL Pedro Luis Lazo 5.00
PU Albert Pujols 25.00
RO Alex Rodriguez 20.00
SH Jamie Shields 10.00
SW Shunsuke Watanabe 30.00
TN Tsuyoshi Nishioka 30.00
TW Tsuyoshi Wada 30.00
VE Justin Verlander 20.00
VM Victor Martinez 8.00
VO Vicyohandry Odelin 5.00
WI Josh Willingham 8.00
WL Wei-Chu Lin 50.00
YG Yulieski Gourriel 10.00
YM Yuneiski Maya 10.00

Dual Signatures

NM/M

Production 1-55
BN Taylor Buchholz, Fernando Nieve/55 30.00
CK Scott Kazmir, Carl Crawford/55 40.00
CU Carl Crawford, B.J. Upton/45 40.00
CW Chris Carpenter, Dontrelle Willis/35 50.00
CZ Miguel Cabrera, Ryan Zimmerman/35 75.00
EG Andre Ethier, Tony Gwynn Jr./35 40.00
GG Vladimir Guerrero, Ken Griffey Jr./35 150.00
GT Ken Griffey Jr., Jim Thome/35 150.00
HD Dan Uggla, Howie Kendrick/55 40.00
HK Jeremy Hermida, Jason Kubel/55 30.00
HW Jeremy Hermida, Josh Willingham/55 30.00
KR Brian Roberts, Howie Kendrick/35 40.00
KU B.J. Upton, Scott Kazmir/55 35.00
KW Scott Kazmir, Dontrelle Willis/35 35.00
LN Francisco Liriano, Joe Nathan/35 50.00
MM Joe Mauer, Justin Morneau/35 60.00
MO Justin Morneau, Lyle Overbay/35 40.00
PO Jake Peavy, Roy Oswalt/35 40.00
PZ Jonathan Papelbon, Joel Zumaya/35 90.00
RO Alex Rios, Lyle Overbay/35 30.00
RR Jose Reyes, Hanley Ramirez/35 60.00
SN Huston Street, Joe Nathan/35 30.00
TI Jim Thome, Tadahito Iguchi/35 100.00
TJ Jeremy Sowers, Travis Hafner/35 40.00
UD Stephen Drew, B.J. Upton/35 75.00
UH Cole Hamels, Chase Utley/35 90.00
UU Chase Utley, Dan Uggla/35 50.00
UW Dan Uggla, Josh Willingham/55 30.00
ZU Ryan Zimmerman, B.J. Upton/35 60.00

Spokesmen Signatures

No Pricing
Production Five Sets

Sweet Beginnings Patch

NM/M

Common Player:
AB Adrian Beltre 30.00
AE Andre Ethier 50.00
AJ Andruw Jones 40.00
AP Ariel Pestano 30.00
AS Alfonso Soriano 75.00
BA Bobby Abreu 60.00
BB Brian Bannister 40.00
BI Chad Billingsley 40.00
BW Bernie Williams 80.00
CA Miguel Cabrera 60.00
CB Carlos Beltran 60.00
CD Carlos Delgado 50.00
CJ Conor Jackson 60.00
CL Carlos Lee 40.00
CM Matt Cain 75.00
CU Chris Duncan 50.00
CZ Carlos Zambrano 50.00
DL Derrek Lee 60.00
DO David Ortiz 75.00
DU Dan Uggla 35.00
EB Erik Bedard 40.00
EP Eduardo Paret 30.00
FA Fausto Carmona 40.00
FC Frederich Cepeda 40.00
FL Francisco Liriano 50.00
HA Cole Hamels 50.00
HK Hong-Chih Kuo 200.00
JB Jason Bay 50.00
JD Johnny Damon 50.00
JF Jeff Francis 40.00
JH Jeremy Hermida 40.00
JJ Josh Johnson 40.00
JO Josh Barfield 40.00
JS Johan Santana 80.00
JV Jason Varitek 50.00
JZ Joel Zumaya 50.00
KE Matthew Kemp 50.00
KJ Kenji Johjima 150.00
KU Koji Uehara 200.00
LE Jon Lester 50.00
LO Javy Lopez 50.00
MC Michael Collins 40.00
ME Michel Enriquez 50.00
MF Maikel Folch 40.00
MJ Mike Jacobs 40.00
MK Munenori Kawasaki 250.00
MN Michael Napoli 40.00
MO Michihiro Ogasawara 200.00
MP Mike Piazza 85.00
MS Min Han Son SP 140.00
NI Nicholas Markakis 60.00
NM Nobuhiko Matsunaka 75.00
NS Naoyuki Shimizu 120.00
OU Osmany Urrutia 50.00
PA Jonathan Papelbon 85.00
PE Mike Pelfrey 75.00
PL Pedro Luis Lazo 40.00
PU Albert Pujols 150.00
RN Ricky Nolasco 40.00
RZ Ryan Zimmerman 60.00
TW Tsuyoshi Wada 250.00
VE Justin Verlander 60.00
VM Victor Martinez 50.00
VO Vicyohandry Odelin 30.00
WE Jered Weaver 50.00
WI Josh Willingham 40.00
YG Yulieski Gourriel 75.00
YM Yuneiski Maya 35.00
RM Russell Martin 60.00

Signatures Barrels Black Ink

NM/M

Production 34-70
Blue Ink: No Pricing
Production 9-20
Silver Ink: No Pricing
Production One Set
101 Adam Wainwright/35 50.00
103 Andre Ethier/35 50.00
105 Ben Johnson/35 20.00
106 Boof Bonser/35 25.00
107 Boone Logan/35 20.00
108 Brian Anderson/35 20.00
109 Brian Bannister/35 25.00
110 Chris Denorfia/35 20.00
112 Cody Ross/35 20.00
113 Cole Hamels/70 50.00
114 Conor Jackson/35 25.00
115 Dan Uggla/35 35.00
116 Dave Gassner/35 20.00
117 C.J. Wilson/35 15.00
118 Eric Reed/35 20.00
119 Fausto Carmona/35 20.00
120 Fernando Nieve/35 15.00
121 Francisco Liriano/70 40.00
122 Freddie Bynum/35 15.00
123 Hanley Ramirez/35 50.00
124 Hong-Chih Kuo/35 200.00
125 Ian Kinsler/35 60.00
126 Carlos Marmol/35 25.00
127 Bobby Keppel/35 15.00
128 Jason Kubel/35 20.00
130 Alay Soler/35 25.00
132 Carlos Quentin/35 30.00
133 Jeremy Hermida/35 25.00
134 Joel Zumaya/35 65.00
135 Joey Devine/35 20.00
136 John Koronka/35 15.00
137 Jonathan Papelbon/70 60.00
138 Jose Capellan/35 20.00
139 Josh Johnson/35 20.00
141 Josh Willingham/35 20.00
143 Justin Verlander/35 50.00
144 Kelly Shoppach/35 20.00
146 Kevin Thompson/35 25.00
147 Macay McBride/35 15.00
149 Matt Cain/35 40.00
150 Clay Hensley/35 20.00
151 Ty Taubenheim/35 35.00
152 Mike Jacobs/35 20.00
153 Saul Rivera/35 15.00
154 Mike Thompson/35 20.00
155 Nate McLouth/35 20.00
156 Michael Vento/35 20.00
157 Paul Maholm/35 25.00
159 Reggie Abercrombie/35 20.00
160 Mike Rouse/35 15.00
161 Ken Ray/35 15.00
162 Ron Flores/35 15.00
163 Ryan Zimmerman/35 65.00
164 Erick Aybar/35 25.00
165 Sean Marshall/35 25.00
167 Taylor Buchholz/35 15.00
168 Matt Murton/35 50.00
169 Luis Figueroa/34 20.00
170 Wilbert Nieves/30 25.00
171 Jamie Shields/35 35.00
172 Jon Lester/70 50.00
174 Aaron Rakers/35 15.00
175 Bobby Livingston/35 20.00
176 Brendan Harris/35 15.00
177 Zach Jackson/35 20.00
178 Chris Britton/35 20.00
179 Howie Kendrick/70 40.00
181 Kevin Frandsen/35 15.00
182 Matt Capps/35 15.00
183 Peter Moylan/35 20.00

Signatures Leather Black Ink

NM/M

Production 20-40
Blue Ink: No Pricing
Production 5-10
Silver Ink: No Pricing
Production One Set
113 Cole Hamels/40 60.00
121 Francisco Liriano/40 60.00
137 Jonathan Papelbon/40 75.00
172 Jon Lester/40 60.00
179 Howie Kendrick/40 50.00

Sign.-Veterans Barrels Black Ink

NM/M

Production 10-35
Blue Ink: No Pricing
Production 1-20
Silver Ink: No Pricing
Production One Set
AG Tony Gwynn Jr./35 30.00
AH Aaron Harang/35 35.00
AZ Aramis Ramirez/35 30.00
BJ B.J. Upton/35 35.00
BR Brian Roberts/35 25.00
CC Carl Crawford/35 30.00
CU Chase Utley/35 70.00
HS Huston Street/35 30.00
JB Jason Bay/35 30.00
JN Joe Nathan/35 30.00
JS Jeremy Sowers/35 35.00
KG Ken Griffey Jr./28 100.00
KG2 Ken Griffey Jr./27 100.00
KY Kevin Youkilis/35 40.00
LO Lyle Overbay/35 25.00
MC Miguel Cabrera/35 50.00
MO Justin Morneau/35 35.00
SD Stephen Drew/35 60.00
SK Scott Kazmir/33 30.00
SM John Smoltz/35 60.00
SO Scott Podsednik/35 25.00
SS Mark Mulder/35 25.00
TH Travis Hafner/35 40.00
TI Tadahito Iguchi/35 60.00
VM Victor Martinez/35 30.00

Sign.-Veteran Leather Black Ink

Production 5-20
Blue Ink: No Pricing
Production 1-5
Silver Ink: No Pricing
Production One Set

2006 UD Ultimate Collection

NM/M

Complete Set (290):
Common Player (1-100): 1.50
Common RC Auto. (101-175): 10.00
Production 180 unless noted.
Common (191-290): 2.00
Production 799
Pack (4): 80.00
Box (4): 300.00
1 Babe Ruth 8.00
2 Chad Tracy 1.50
3 Brandon Webb 1.50
4 Andruw Jones 3.00
5 Chipper Jones 4.00
6 John Smoltz 2.00
7 Eddie Mathews 4.00
8 Miguel Tejada 3.00
9 Brian Roberts 1.50
10 Mickey Cochrane 2.00
11 Curt Schilling 3.00
12 David Ortiz 4.00
13 Manny Ramirez 4.00
14 Johnny Bench 4.00
15 Cy Young 2.00
16 Greg Maddux 5.00
17 Derrek Lee 3.00
18 Yogi Berra 4.00
19 Walter Johnson 2.00
20 Jim Thome 3.00
21 Paul Konerko 2.00
22 Lou Gehrig 6.00
23 Jose Contreras 1.50
24 Ken Griffey Jr. 5.00
25 Adam Dunn 3.00
26 Reggie Jackson 3.00
27 Travis Hafner 2.00
28 Victor Martinez 1.50
29 Grady Sizemore 3.00
30 Casey Stengel 3.00
31 Todd Helton 3.00
32 Nolan Ryan 8.00
33 Clint Barmes 1.50
34 Ivan Rodriguez 3.00
35 Chris Shelton 1.50
36 Ty Cobb 5.00
37 Miguel Cabrera 4.00
38 Dontrelle Willis 2.00
39 Lance Berkman 2.00
40 Tom Seaver 4.00
41 Roy Oswalt 2.00
42 Christy Mathewson 3.00
43 Luis Aparicio 1.50
44 Vladimir Guerrero 4.00
45 Bartolo Colon 1.50
46 Roy Campanella 2.00
47 George Sisler 1.50
48 Jeff Kent 1.50
49 J.D. Drew 1.50
50 Carlos Lee 1.50
51 Willie Stargell 3.00
52 Rickie Weeks 1.50
53 Johan Santana 4.00
54 Torii Hunter 1.50
55 Joe Mauer 2.00
56 Pedro Martinez 4.00
57 David Wright 5.00
58 Carlos Beltran 3.00
59 Jimmie Foxx 3.00
60 Jose Reyes 3.00
61 Derek Jeter 8.00
62 Alex Rodriguez 6.00
63 Randy Johnson 4.00
64 Hideki Matsui 5.00
65 Thurman Munson 4.00
66 Rich Harden 1.50
67 Eric Chavez 2.00
68 Don Drysdale 3.00
69 Bobby Crosby 1.50
70 Pee Wee Reese 1.50
71 Ryan Howard 6.00
72 Chase Utley 4.00
73 Jackie Robinson 5.00
74 Jason Bay 3.00
75 Honus Wagner 4.00
76 Lefty Grove 3.00
77 Jake Peavy 3.00
78 Brian Giles 1.50
79 Eddie Murray 3.00
80 Omar Vizquel 1.50
81 Jason Schmidt 2.00
82 Ichiro Suzuki 5.00
83 Felix Hernandez 3.00
84 Kenji Johjima 8.00
85 Albert Pujols 8.00
86 Chris Carpenter 3.00
87 Brooks Robinson 3.00
88 Dizzy Dean 3.00
89 Carl Crawford 2.00
90 Rogers Hornsby 3.00
91 Scott Kazmir 2.00
92 Mark Teixeira 3.00
93 Michael Young 2.00
94 Johnny Mize 1.50
95 Vernon Wells 3.00
96 Roy Halladay 2.00
97 Mel Ott 1.50
98 Alfonso Soriano 4.00
99 Joe Morgan 3.00
100 Satchel Paige 4.00
101 Adam Wainwright **(RC)** 30.00
102 Anderson Hernandez **(RC)** 10.00
103 Andre Ethier **(RC)** 35.00
104 Ben Johnson **(RC)** 15.00
105 Boof Bonser **(RC)** 20.00
106 Boone Logan **RC** 10.00
107 Brian Anderson **(RC)** 10.00
108 Brian Bannister **(RC)** 15.00
109 Chris Demaria **RC** 10.00
110 Chris Denorfia **(RC)** 10.00
111 Cody Ross **(RC)** 10.00
112 Cole Hamels **(RC)** 50.00
113 Conor Jackson **(RC)** 20.00
114 Dan Uggla **(RC)** 25.00
115 Dave Gassner **(RC)** 10.00
116 Eric Reed **(RC)** 10.00
117 Fausto Carmona **(RC)** 10.00
118 Fernando Nieve **(RC)** 10.00
119 Francisco Liriano **(RC)** 50.00
120 Freddie Bynum **(RC)** 10.00
121 Hanley Ramirez **(RC)** 25.00
122 Hong-Chih Kuo **(RC)** 85.00
123 Ian Kinsler **(RC)** 50.00
124 Jason Hammel **(RC)** 10.00
125 Jason Kubel **(RC)** 10.00
126 Jeff Harris **RC** 10.00
127 Jered Weaver/150 **(RC)** 60.00
128 Jeremy Accardo **(RC)** 10.00
129 Jeremy Hermida **(RC)** 20.00
130 Joel Zumaya **(RC)** 30.00
131 Joey Devine **RC** 10.00
132 John Koronka **(RC)** 15.00
133 John Van Benschoten **(RC)** 10.00
134 Jonathan Papelbon **(RC)** 50.00
135 Jose Capellan **(RC)** 10.00
136 Josh Johnson **(RC)** 15.00
137 Josh Rupe **(RC)** 10.00
138 Josh Willingham **(RC)** 15.00
139 Josh Wilson **(RC)** 10.00
140 Justin Verlander **(RC)** 60.00
141 Kelly Shoppach **(RC)** 10.00
142 Kendry Morales **(RC)** 15.00
143 Macay McBride **(RC)** 10.00
144 Martin Prado **(RC)** 10.00
145 Matt Cain **(RC)** 30.00
146 Mike Jacobs **(RC)** 10.00
147 Mike Thompson **RC** 10.00
148 Nate McLouth **(RC)** 10.00
149 Paul Maholm **(RC)** 10.00
150 Prince Fielder **(RC)** 50.00
151 Reggie Abercrombie **(RC)** 10.00
152 Rich Hill **(RC)** 40.00
153 Ron Flores **RC** 15.00
154 Ruddy Lugo **(RC)** 10.00
155 Ryan Zimmerman **(RC)** 60.00
156 Sean Marshall **(RC)** 20.00
157 Takashi Saito **RC** 30.00
158 Taylor Buchholz **(RC)** 15.00
159 Tony Pena **(RC)** 10.00
160 Wilbert Nieves **(RC)** 10.00
161 Jamie Shields **RC** 20.00
162 Jon Lester **(RC)** 40.00
163 Craig Hansen **RC** 40.00
164 Aaron Rakers **(RC)** 10.00
165 Yusmeiro Petit **(RC)** 10.00
166 Bobby Livingston **(RC)** 10.00
167 Brendan Harris **(RC)** 10.00
169 Carlos Ruiz **(RC)** 15.00
170 Chris Britton **RC** 10.00
171 Howie Kendrick **(RC)** 40.00
172 Jermaine Van Buren 10.00
173 Kevin Frandsen **(RC)** 20.00
174 Matt Capps **(RC)** 10.00
175 Peter Moylan **RC** 10.00
191 Richie Ashburn/799 3.00
192 Lou Brock 4.00
193 Lou Boudreau 2.00
194 Orlando Cepeda 2.00
195 Bobby Doerr 2.00
196 Dennis Eckersley 2.00
197 Bob Feller 3.00
198 Rollie Fingers 2.00
199 Carlton Fisk 4.00
200 Bob Gibson 4.00
201 Jim "Catfish" Hunter 3.00
202 Fergie Jenkins 3.00
203 Al Kaline 5.00
204 Harmon Killebrew 5.00
205 Ralph Kiner 3.00
206 Buck Leonard 3.00
207 Juan Marichal 2.00
208 Bill Mazeroski 4.00
209 Willie McCovey 4.00
210 Jim Palmer 2.00
211 Tony Perez 2.00
212 Gaylord Perry 2.00
213 Phil Rizzuto 4.00
214 Robin Roberts 2.00
215 Mike Schmidt 6.00
216 Enos Slaughter 2.00
217 Ozzie Smith 5.00
218 Billy Williams 2.00
219 Robin Yount 5.00
220 Carlos Quentin **(RC)** 4.00
221 Jeff Francoeur 2.00
222 Brian McCann 2.00
223 Nicholas Markakis **(RC)** 6.00
224 Josh Beckett 2.00
225 Jason Varitek 4.00
226 Mark Prior 4.00
227 Aramis Ramirez 3.00
228 Jermaine Dye 2.00
229 Tadahito Iguchi 2.00
230 Bobby Jenks 2.00
231 C.C. Sabathia 2.00
232 Jeff Francis 2.00
233 Matt Holliday 2.00
234 Magglio Ordonez 2.00
235 Kenny Rogers 2.00
236 Roger Clemens 8.00
237 Andy Pettitte 3.00
238 Craig Biggio 3.00
239 Chone Figgins 2.00
240 John Lackey 2.00
241 Nomar Garciaparra 4.00
242 Prince Fielder **(RC)** 6.00
243 Ben Sheets 3.00

244 Bill Hall 2.00
245 Justin Morneau 4.00
246 Joe Nathan 2.00
247 Carlos Delgado 3.00
248 Shawn Green 2.00
249 Billy Wagner 2.00
250 Jason Giambi 4.00
251 Mike Mussina 4.00
252 Mariano Rivera 4.00
253 Robinson Cano 4.00
254 Bobby Abreu 3.00
255 Huston Street 2.00
256 Frank Thomas 4.00
257 Danny Haren 2.00
258 Jason Kendall 2.00
259 Nick Swisher 3.00
260 Pat Burrell 3.00
261 Tom Gordon 2.00
262 Freddy Sanchez 2.00
263 Trevor Hoffman 2.00
264 Khalil Greene 2.00
265 Adrian Gonzalez 2.00
266 Moises Alou 2.00
267 Matt Morris 2.00
268 Pedro Feliz 2.00
269 Richie Sexson 3.00
270 Hoyt Wilhelm 2.00
271 Adrian Beltre 2.00
272 Jim Edmonds 3.00
273 Scott Rolen 4.00
274 Jason Isringhausen 2.00
275 Jorge Cantu 2.00
276 Hank Blalock 2.00
277 Kevin Millwood 2.00
278 Alex Rios 2.00
279 Troy Glaus 3.00
280 B.J. Ryan 2.00
281 Nick Johnson 2.00
282 Chad Cordero 2.00
283 Austin Kearns 2.00
284 Ricky Nolasco **(RC)** 2.00
285 Travis Ishikawa **(RC)** 2.00
286 Lastings Milledge **(RC)** 4.00
287 James Loney **(RC)** 4.00
288 Red Schoendienst 3.00
289 Warren Spahn 4.00
290 Early Wynn **(RC)** 2.00

Printing Plates

No Pricing
Production one set per color.

Ensemble Materials 3

Production 25 Sets
Patch: No Pricing
Production 20 Sets

Ensemble Materials 4

Production 20 Sets
Patch: No Pricing
Production 15 Sets

Ensemble Signature 3

NM/M
Production 50 Sets
Triple 15: No Pricing
Production 15 Sets
Triple 1 of 1: No Pricing

AHW Josh Willingham, Reggie Abercrombie, Jeremy Hermida 40.00
BBB Jeff Bagwell, Craig Biggio, Lance Berkman 100.00
BBW Taylor Buchholz, Adam Wainwright, Brian Bannister 50.00
BDD George Bell, Eric Davis, Andre Dawson 50.00
BHR Roy Halladay, A.J. Burnett, Alex Rios 40.00
BKM Ralph Kiner, Bill Mazeroski, Jason Bay 85.00
BNO Taylor Buchholz, Roy Oswalt, Fernando Nieve 30.00
BSH A.J. Burnett, Rich Harden, Ben Sheets 40.00
BUK Craig Biggio, Chase Utley, Ian Kinsler 75.00
BWC Matt Cain, Brian Bannister, Adam Wainwright 40.00
BWV Justin Verlander, Boof Bonser, Jered Weaver 85.00
CBP Oliver Perez, Jason Bay, Sean Casey 30.00
CBS Ron Cey, Dusty Baker, Don Sutton 50.00
CBZ Boof Bonser, Joel Zumaya, Matt Cain 50.00
CDV Jack Clark, Eric Davis, Andy Van Slyke 50.00
CHK Jason Kubel, Melky Cabrera, Jeremy Hermida 50.00
CHO Chris Carpenter, Roy Oswalt, Rich Harden 60.00
CKH Rich Harden, Bobby Crosby, Jason Kendall 40.00
CKS Carl Crawford, Scott Kazmir, Jamie Shields 50.00
CLH Cole Hamels, Fausto Carmona, Francisco Liriano 80.00
CMH Victor Martinez, Travis Hafner, Fausto Carmona 60.00
CNS Graig Nettles, Ron Cey, Ron Santo 50.00
CPC Carl Crawford, Coco Crisp, Scott Podsednik 40.00
CSS John Smoltz, Roger Clemens, Curt Schilling 200.00
CWW Josh Willingham, Dontrelle Willis, Miguel Cabrera 50.00
CZC Miguel Cabrera, Eric Chavez, Ryan Zimmerman 80.00
DJH Hanley Ramirez, Derek Jeter, Jose Reyes 200.00
DPA Scott Podsednik, Jermaine Dye, Brian Anderson 40.00
DPI Jermaine Dye, Scott Podsednik, Tadahito Iguchi 60.00
FGC David Cone, Dwight Gooden, Sid Fernandez 75.00
FJM Prince Fielder, Conor Jackson, Kendry Morales 50.00
FWL Rickie Weeks, Prince Fielder, Carlos Lee 60.00
GCN Graig Nettles, Rich "Goose" Gossage, Chris Chambliss 50.00
GCS Bret Saberhagen, Dwight Gooden, David Cone 30.00
GJB Derek Jeter, Ken Griffey Jr., Jason Bay 250.00
GJP Derek Jeter, Albert Pujols, Ken Griffey Jr. 500.00
GLK Dave Gassner, Jason Kubel, Francisco Liriano 50.00
GPN Joe Nathan, Eric Gagne, Jonathan Papelbon 50.00
GRS Alex Rios, Alfonso Soriano, Vladimir Guerrero 90.00
HBS Rich Harden, Nick Swisher, Joe Blanton 50.00
HKP Boog Powell, John Kruk, Kent Hrbek 40.00
HMK Mark Mulder, Scott Kazmir, Cole Hamels 60.00
HNP Jonathan Papelbon, Trevor Hoffman, Joe Nathan 75.00
HOT David Ortiz, Travis Hafner, Mark Teixeira 100.00
HWU Josh Willingham, Jeremy Hermida, Dan Uggla 30.00
IKU Dan Uggla, Ian Kinsler, Tadahito Iguchi 85.00
JCN Melky Cabrera, Wilbert Nieves, Derek Jeter 150.00
JGS Ken Griffey Jr., Andruw Jones, Alfonso Soriano 120.00
JRR Derek Jeter, Jose Reyes, Hanley Ramirez 200.00
JWV Jered Weaver, Justin Verlander, Josh Johnson 75.00
KGJ John Kruk, Mark Grace, Wally Joyner 80.00
KLB Francisco Liriano, Boof Bonser, Jason Kubel 50.00
KUU Ian Kinsler, Dan Uggla, Chase Utley 65.00
KWM Josh Willingham, Victor Martinez, Jason Kendall 30.00
LGB Francisco Liriano, Boof Bonser, Dave Gassner 40.00
LHC Felix Hernandez, Fausto Carmona, Francisco Liriano 50.00
LPO Derrek Lee, David Ortiz, Albert Pujols 250.00
MCN Ron Cey, Graig Nettles, Bill Madlock 50.00
MMK Jason Kendall, Joe Mauer, Victor Martinez 40.00
MNL Joe Mauer, Francisco Liriano, Joe Nathan 50.00
MWC Chris Carpenter, Mark Mulder, Adam Wainwright 75.00
MWP Josh Willingham, Russell Martin, Ronny Paulino 30.00
NLP Jonathan Papelbon, Brad Lidge, Joe Nathan 50.00
OBL Brad Lidge, Roy Oswalt, Taylor Buchholz 40.00
PCL Oliver Perez, Francisco Liriano, Fausto Carmona 50.00
PHL Cole Hamels, Francisco Liriano, Oliver Perez 65.00
PSO Roy Oswalt, Jake Peavy, Ben Sheets 40.00
PVW Justin Verlander, Jered Weaver, Jonathan Papelbon 90.00
RHW Jeremy Hermida, Josh Willingham, Cody Ross 30.00
RMM Victor Martinez, Joe Mauer, Ivan Rodriguez 65.00
RRB Jose Reyes, Yuniesky Betancourt, Hanley Ramirez 60.00
SGM Greg Maddux, John Smoltz, Tom Glavine 180.00
SJF Chris Shelton, Prince Fielder, Mike Jacobs 40.00
SKM Russell Martin, Takashi Saito, Hong-Chih Kuo 200.00
SWB Taylor Buchholz, Jamie Shields, Jered Weaver 60.00
TGB Frank Thomas, Ken Griffey Jr., Jeff Bagwell 150.00
TKY Michael Young, Mark Teixeira, Ian Kinsler 75.00
UHC Jeremy Hermida, Dan Uggla, Miguel Cabrera 75.00
URC Miguel Cabrera, Dan Uggla, Hanley Ramirez 40.00
URW Hanley Ramirez, Dan Uggla, Josh Willingham 35.00
VBZ Justin Verlander, Jeremy Bonderman, Joel Zumaya 120.00
VWL Jered Weaver, Francisco Liriano, Justin Verlander 120.00
WJC Josh Johnson, Jered Weaver, Matt Cain 70.00
WJO Scott Olsen, Josh Johnson, Dontrelle Willis 40.00
WSV Justin Verlander, Jered Weaver, Jamie Shields 65.00
ZBC Joel Zumaya, Matt Cain, Boof Bonser 60.00
ZHZ Carlos Zambrano, Felix Hernandez, Joel Zumaya 60.00

Ensemble Signatures 4

No Pricing
Production 25 Sets

Ensemble Signatures 5

No Pricing
Production 15 Sets

Ensemble Signatures 6

No Pricing
Production 10 Sets

Ensemble Signatures 8

Production One Set

Game Materials

NM/M
Common Player: 8.00
Production 50 Sets

AB A.J. Burnett 8.00
AD Adam Dunn 10.00
AJ Andruw Jones 12.00
AP Albert Pujols 30.00
AR Alex Rios 8.00
AS Alfonso Soriano 10.00
BA Brian Bannister 8.00
BG Brian Giles 8.00
BM Bill Mazeroski 15.00
BO Jeremy Bonderman 10.00
BR Brian Roberts 8.00
CA Melky Cabrera 15.00
CC Carl Crawford 10.00
CH Chris Carpenter 15.00
CJ Conor Jackson 10.00
CL Carlos Lee 10.00
CR Coco Crisp 10.00
CS Chris Shelton 8.00
CU Chase Utley 20.00
CZ Carlos Zambrano 10.00
DJ Derek Jeter 30.00
DJ2 Derek Jeter 30.00
DL Derrek Lee 30.00
DU Dan Uggla 10.00
DW Dontrelle Willis 10.00
FH Felix Hernandez 12.00
FL Francisco Liriano 15.00
GA Garrett Atkins 8.00
GP Gaylord Perry 10.00
HA Cole Hamels 15.00
HB Hank Blalock 10.00
HC Craig Hansen 15.00
HO Trevor Hoffman 10.00
HR Hanley Ramirez 15.00
HT Tim Hudson 10.00
HU Torii Hunter 10.00
HY Roy Halladay 10.00
IK Ian Kinsler 10.00
IR Ivan Rodriguez 10.00
JB Jason Bay 12.00
JD Jermaine Dye 10.00
JH Jeremy Hermida 8.00
JJ Josh Johnson 8.00
JK Jason Kendall 8.00
JM Joe Mauer 10.00
JN Joe Nathan 10.00
JP Jake Peavy 10.00
JR Jose Reyes 15.00
JS Johan Santana 12.00
JV Justin Verlander 15.00
JW Jered Weaver 15.00
JZ Joel Zumaya 15.00
KG Ken Griffey Jr. 25.00
KG2 Ken Griffey Jr. 25.00
KH Khalil Greene 8.00
KJ Kenji Johjima 20.00
KM Kendry Morales 8.00
KU Jason Kubel 8.00
KY Kevin Youkilis 10.00
LA Luis Aparicio 10.00
LM Lastings Milledge 10.00
LY Fred Lynn 8.00
MA Matt Cain 15.00
MC Miguel Cabrera 15.00
MG Marcus Giles 8.00
MH Matt Holliday 15.00
ML Mark Loretta 8.00
MM Melvin Mora 8.00
MO Justin Morneau 12.00
MS Mike Schmidt 20.00
MT Mark Teixeira 12.00
MU Mark Mulder 10.00
MY Michael Young 10.00
NS Nick Swisher 10.00
PA Jonathan Papelbon 20.00
PF Prince Fielder 15.00
PM Paul Molitor 15.00
RC Cal Ripken Jr. 40.00
RH Rich Harden 10.00
RI Jim Rice 15.00
RO Roy Oswalt 10.00
RW Rickie Weeks 10.00
RZ Ryan Zimmerman 20.00
SK Scott Kazmir 10.00
SP Scott Podsednik 10.00
TE Miguel Tejada 12.00
TG Tony Gwynn 15.00
TH Travis Hafner 10.00
TI Tadahito Iguchi 10.00
TP Tony Perez 10.00
VM Victor Martinez 10.00
WC Will Clark 15.00
WI Josh Willingham 8.00
YB Yuniesky Betancourt 8.00

Legendary Materials

NM/M
Production 5-55

AR Al Rosen/55 15.00
BD Bill Dickey/55 30.00
BD2 Bill Dickey/55 30.00
BG Bob Gibson/25 20.00
BM Bill Mazeroski/25 20.00
BO Bo Jackson/55 20.00
BO2 Bo Jackson/55 20.00
CF Carlton Fisk/55 10.00
CF2 Carlton Fisk/55 10.00
CW Rod Carew/55 10.00
CW2 Rod Carew/55 10.00
CY Carl Yastrzemski/25 20.00
CY2 Carl Yastrzemski/25 20.00
GP Gaylord Perry/55 10.00
GP2 Gaylord Perry/55 10.00
JB Johnny Bench/55 20.00
JO Joe Morgan/55 10.00
JO2 Joe Morgan/55 10.00
JU Juan Marichal/55 10.00
KI Kirk Gibson/55 10.00
KP Kirby Puckett/55 20.00
KP2 Kirby Puckett/55 20.00
MA Don Mattingly/55 25.00
MA2 Don Mattingly/55 25.00
MW Maury Wills/41 10.00
NR Nolan Ryan/55 35.00
NR2 Nolan Ryan/25 40.00
NR3 Nolan Ryan/25 40.00
OS Ozzie Smith/55 20.00
OS2 Ozzie Smith/55 20.00
PM Paul Molitor/55 10.00
PM2 Paul Molitor/55 10.00
PN Phil Niekro/55 10.00
PN2 Phil Niekro/55 10.00
RJ Reggie Jackson/25 20.00
RJ2 Reggie Jackson/35 15.00
RK Ralph Kiner/25 20.00
RO Brooks Robinson/35 15.00
RO2 Brooks Robinson/35 15.00
RS Ryne Sandberg/35 25.00
RY Robin Yount/25 15.00
RY2 Robin Yount/25 15.00
SC Steve Carlton/55 10.00
SC2 Steve Carlton/47 10.00
SU Don Sutton/55 10.00
SU2 Don Sutton/55 10.00
TG Tony Gwynn/55 20.00
TG2 Tony Gwynn/55 20.00
TP Tony Perez/55 15.00
TP2 Tony Perez/55 15.00
WB Wade Boggs/55 15.00
WB2 Wade Boggs/55 15.00
WC Will Clark/45 15.00
WC2 Will Clark/45 15.00

Legendary Ensemble Signatures

No Pricing
Production 25 Sets

Maximum Materials

Production 25 Sets
Patch: No Pricing
Production 15 Sets

Numbers Materials

NM/M
Production 35 Sets

AB A.J. Burnett 10.00
AD Adam Dunn 12.00
AJ Andruw Jones 15.00
AP Albert Pujols 40.00
AR Alex Rios 10.00
AS Alfonso Soriano 15.00
BA Brian Bannister 10.00
BG Brian Giles 10.00
BM Bill Mazeroski 15.00
BO Jeremy Bonderman 15.00
BR Brian Roberts 10.00
CA Melky Cabrera 15.00
CC Carl Crawford 10.00
CH Chris Carpenter 15.00
CJ Conor Jackson 15.00
CL Carlos Lee 10.00
CR Coco Crisp 10.00
CS Chris Shelton 10.00
CU Chase Utley 20.00
CZ Carlos Zambrano 15.00
DJ Derek Jeter 40.00
DJ2 Derek Jeter 40.00
DL Derrek Lee 15.00
DU Dan Uggla 15.00
DW Dontrelle Willis 15.00
FH Felix Hernandez 15.00
FL Francisco Liriano 20.00
GA Garrett Atkins 10.00
GP Gaylord Perry 15.00
HA Cole Hamels 25.00
HB Hank Blalock 10.00
HC Craig Hansen 20.00
HO Trevor Hoffman 10.00
HR Hanley Ramirez 20.00
HT Tim Hudson 10.00
HU Torii Hunter 10.00
HY Roy Halladay 10.00
IK Ian Kinsler 10.00
IR Ivan Rodriguez 15.00
JB Jason Bay 15.00
JD Jermaine Dye 10.00
JH Jeremy Hermida 10.00
JJ Josh Johnson 12.00
JK Jason Kendall 10.00
JM Joe Mauer 15.00
JN Joe Nathan 10.00
JP Jake Peavy 10.00
JR Jose Reyes 20.00
JS Johan Santana 20.00
JV Justin Verlander 20.00
JW Jered Weaver 20.00
JZ Joel Zumaya 20.00
KG Ken Griffey Jr. 35.00
KG2 Ken Griffey Jr. 35.00
KH Khalil Greene 10.00
KJ Kenji Johjima 30.00
KM Kendry Morales 10.00
KU Jason Kubel 10.00
KY Kevin Youkilis 15.00
LA Luis Aparicio 10.00
LM Lastings Milledge 15.00
LY Fred Lynn 10.00
MA Matt Cain 15.00
MC Miguel Cabrera 15.00
MG Marcus Giles 10.00
MH Matt Holliday 10.00
ML Mark Loretta 10.00
MM Melvin Mora 10.00
MO Justin Morneau 15.00
MS Mike Schmidt 25.00
MT Mark Teixeira 15.00
MU Mark Mulder 10.00
MY Michael Young 10.00
NS Nick Swisher 10.00
PA Jonathan Papelbon 25.00
PF Prince Fielder 20.00
PM Paul Molitor 15.00
RC Cal Ripken Jr. 75.00
RH Rich Harden 10.00
RI Jim Rice 15.00
RO Roy Oswalt 15.00
RW Rickie Weeks 10.00
RZ Ryan Zimmerman 25.00
SK Scott Kazmir 10.00
SP Scott Podsednik 10.00
TE Miguel Tejada 15.00
TG Tony Gwynn 20.00
TH Travis Hafner 15.00
TI Tadahito Iguchi 15.00
TP Tony Perez 15.00
VM Victor Martinez 10.00
WC Will Clark 15.00
WI Josh Willingham 10.00
YB Yuniesky Betancourt 10.00

Ultimate Patch

NM/M
Production 50 unless noted.
Patch Signature: No Pricing
Production 10 Sets

AB A.J. Burnett 15.00
AD Adam Dunn 20.00
AJ Andruw Jones 20.00
AP Albert Pujols 60.00
AR Alex Rios 15.00
AS Alfonso Soriano 25.00
BA Brian Bannister 15.00
BG Brian Giles 15.00
BO Jeremy Bonderman 25.00
BR Brian Roberts 15.00
CA Melky Cabrera 25.00
CC Carl Crawford 15.00
CH Chris Carpenter 20.00
CJ Conor Jackson 15.00
CL Carlos Lee 15.00
CR Coco Crisp 20.00
CS Chris Shelton 15.00
CU Chase Utley 35.00
CZ Carlos Zambrano 20.00
DJ Derek Jeter 50.00
DJ2 Derek Jeter 50.00
DL Derrek Lee 20.00
DU Dan Uggla 20.00
DW Dontrelle Willis 15.00
FH Felix Hernandez 20.00
FL Francisco Liriano 25.00
GA Garrett Atkins 15.00
GP Gaylord Perry/27 20.00
HA Cole Hamels 25.00
HB Hank Blalock 15.00
HO Trevor Hoffman 15.00
HR Hanley Ramirez 25.00
HT Tim Hudson 15.00
HU Torii Hunter 15.00
HY Roy Halladay 15.00
IR Ivan Rodriguez 20.00
JB Jason Bay 20.00
JD Jermaine Dye 15.00
JH Jeremy Hermida 20.00
JJ Josh Johnson 20.00
JK Jason Kendall 15.00
JM Joe Mauer 25.00
JN Joe Nathan 15.00
JP Jake Peavy 15.00
JR Jose Reyes 30.00
JS Johan Santana 25.00
JV Justin Verlander 40.00
JW Jered Weaver 25.00
JZ Joel Zumaya/47 30.00
KG Ken Griffey Jr. 50.00
KG2 Ken Griffey Jr. 50.00
KH Khalil Greene 15.00
KJ Kenji Johjima 35.00
KM Kendry Morales 20.00
KU Jason Kubel 15.00
LA Luis Aparicio 20.00
LM Lastings Milledge 30.00
LY Fred Lynn 15.00
MA Matt Cain 25.00
MC Miguel Cabrera 25.00
MG Marcus Giles 15.00
MH Matt Holliday 30.00
ML Mark Loretta/40 15.00
MM Melvin Mora 15.00
MO Justin Morneau 30.00
MS Mike Schmidt 30.00
MT Mark Teixeira 20.00
MU Mark Mulder 15.00
MY Michael Young 20.00
NS Nick Swisher 20.00
PF Prince Fielder 25.00
PM Paul Molitor 20.00
RC Cal Ripken Jr. 75.00
RH Rich Harden 20.00
RI Jim Rice/31 20.00
RO Roy Oswalt 25.00
RW Rickie Weeks 20.00
RZ Ryan Zimmerman 50.00
SK Scott Kazmir 20.00
SP Scott Podsednik 15.00
TE Miguel Tejada 20.00
TG Tony Gwynn 30.00
TH Travis Hafner 20.00
TI Tadahito Iguchi 30.00
VM Victor Martinez 15.00
WC Will Clark 20.00
WI Josh Willingham 15.00
YB Yuniesky Betancourt 15.00

Tandem Materials

NM/M
Production 25 Sets
Signature: No Pricing
Production 15 Sets
Signature Patch: No Pricing
Production Five Sets
Signature Logo: No Pricing
Production One Set

AA Alfonso Soriano, Alex Rios 20.00
AH Garrett Atkins, Matt Holliday 10.00
BH Felix Hernandez, Yuniesky Betancourt 20.00

BM Brian Bannister, Lastings Milledge 20.00
BR Yuniesky Betancourt, Hanley Ramirez 25.00
BV Justin Verlander, Jeremy Bonderman 40.00
CL Coco Crisp, Mark Loretta 20.00
CP Carl Crawford, Scott Podsednik 15.00
CS Cole Hamels, Scott Kazmir 25.00
CW Dontrelle Willis, Chris Carpenter 15.00
CZ Miguel Cabrera, Ryan Zimmerman 25.00
FP Tony Perez, Prince Fielder 20.00
FW Prince Fielder, Rickie Weeks 20.00
GP Ken Griffey Jr., Albert Pujols 50.00
HB Matt Holliday, Jason Bay 15.00
HF Prince Fielder, Travis Hafner 20.00
HG Trevor Hoffman, Brian Giles 10.00
HJ Andruw Jones, Torii Hunter 15.00
HK Jeremy Hermida, Jason Kubel 10.00
HM Travis Hafner, Victor Martinez 10.00
HN Trevor Hoffman, Joe Nathan 10.00
HO Roy Oswalt, Rich Harden 15.00
HP Trevor Hoffman, Jonathan Papelbon 25.00
HR Hanley Ramirez, Jeremy Hermida 15.00
HW Jeremy Hermida, Josh Willingham 10.00
ID Jermaine Dye, Tadahito Iguchi 15.00
JB Bill Mazeroski, Jason Bay 20.00
JG Derek Jeter, Ken Griffey Jr. 40.00
JR Derek Jeter, Cal Ripken Jr. 60.00
KB Brian Giles, Khalil Greene 10.00
KM Joe Mauer, Jason Kendall 15.00
KU Ian Kinsler, Dan Uggla 10.00
KY Ian Kinsler, Michael Young 10.00
LF Prince Fielder, Carlos Lee 20.00
MH Livan Hernandez, Kendry Morales 10.00
MM Joe Mauer, Victor Martinez 20.00
MP Tony Perez, Kendry Morales 15.00
MR Melvin Mora, Brian Roberts 10.00
MW Rickie Weeks, Paul Molitor 20.00
NJ Joe Mauer, Joe Nathan 20.00
NM Joe Mauer, Joe Nathan 15.00
PO Roy Oswalt, Jake Peavy 15.00
PP Jake Peavy, Gaylord Perry 15.00
SH Rich Harden, Nick Swisher 15.00
TY Michael Young, Mark Teixeira 15.00
VM Justin Verlander, Jack Morris 20.00
WM Josh Willingham, Joe Mauer 20.00
YL Kevin Youkilis, Mark Loretta 15.00
ZJ Josh Johnson, Joel Zumaya 20.00
ZZ Joel Zumaya, Carlos Zambrano 20.00

Tri-Marks Signatures

No Pricing
Production 15 Sets

Game Materials Signatures

NM/M

Production 35 Sets
AB A.J. Burnett 25.00
AD Adam Dunn 25.00
AJ Andruw Jones 50.00
AP Albert Pujols 250.00
AR Alex Rios 25.00
AS Alfonso Soriano 60.00
BA Brian Bannister 25.00
BG Brian Giles 25.00
BM Bill Mazeroski 40.00
BO Jeremy Bonderman 50.00
BR Brian Roberts 25.00
CA Melky Cabrera 40.00
CC Carl Crawford 25.00
CH Chris Carpenter 30.00
CJ Conor Jackson 35.00
CL Carlos Lee 25.00
CR Coco Crisp 30.00
CS Chris Shelton 25.00
CU Chase Utley 60.00
CZ Carlos Zambrano 40.00
DJ Derek Jeter 250.00
DJ2 Derek Jeter 250.00
DL Derrek Lee 35.00
DU Dan Uggla 40.00
DW Dontrelle Willis 30.00
FH Felix Hernandez 40.00
FL Francisco Liriano 50.00
GA Garrett Atkins 25.00
GP Gaylord Perry 25.00
HA Cole Hamels 60.00
HB Hank Blalock 25.00
HC Craig Hansen 40.00
HO Trevor Hoffman 30.00
HR Hanley Ramirez 60.00
HT Tim Hudson 30.00
HU Torii Hunter 25.00
HY Roy Halladay 25.00
IK Ian Kinsler 30.00
IR Ivan Rodriguez 35.00
JB Jason Bay 30.00
JD Jermaine Dye 25.00
JH Jeremy Hermida 25.00
JJ Josh Johnson 35.00
JK Jason Kendall 25.00
JM Joe Mauer 40.00
JN Joe Nathan 25.00
JP Jake Peavy 30.00
JR Jose Reyes 40.00
JS Johan Santana 50.00
JV Justin Verlander 60.00
JW Jered Weaver 40.00
JZ Joel Zumaya 60.00
KG Ken Griffey Jr. 120.00
KG2 Ken Griffey Jr. 120.00
KH Khalil Greene 35.00
KM Kendry Morales 30.00
KU Jason Kubel 25.00
KY Kevin Youkilis 25.00
LA Luis Aparicio 25.00
LY Fred Lynn 25.00
MA Matt Cain 40.00
MC Miguel Cabrera 50.00
MG Marcus Giles 25.00
MH Matt Holliday 30.00
ML Mark Loretta 25.00
MM Melvin Mora 25.00
MO Justin Morneau 40.00
MS Mike Schmidt 50.00
MU Mark Mulder 25.00
MY Michael Young 25.00
NS Nick Swisher 25.00
PA Jonathan Papelbon 60.00
PM Paul Molitor 35.00
RC Cal Ripken Jr. 150.00
RH Rich Harden 30.00
RI Jim Rice 30.00
RO Roy Oswalt 30.00
RW Rickie Weeks 25.00
RZ Ryan Zimmerman 65.00
SK Scott Kazmir 30.00
SP Scott Podsednik 25.00
TE Miguel Tejada 30.00
TG Tony Gwynn 60.00
TH Travis Hafner 30.00
TI Tadahito Iguchi 40.00
TP Tony Perez 30.00
VM Victor Martinez 30.00
WC Will Clark 35.00
WI Josh Willingham 25.00
YB Yuniesky Betancourt 25.00

Numbers Patch

NM/M

Production 35 unless noted
AB A.J. Burnett 20.00
AD Adam Dunn 25.00
AJ Andruw Jones 25.00
AP Albert Pujols 80.00
AR Alex Rios 20.00
AS Alfonso Soriano 25.00
BA Brian Bannister 15.00
BG Brian Giles 20.00
BO Jeremy Bonderman 25.00
BR Brian Roberts 20.00
CC Carl Crawford 20.00
CH Chris Carpenter 25.00
CJ Conor Jackson 20.00
CL Carlos Lee 20.00
CR Coco Crisp 20.00
CS Chris Shelton 15.00
CU Chase Utley 40.00
CZ Carlos Zambrano 25.00
DJ Derek Jeter 65.00
DJ2 Derek Jeter 65.00
DL Derrek Lee 25.00
DU Dan Uggla 20.00
DW Dontrelle Willis 25.00
FH Felix Hernandez 25.00
FL Francisco Liriano 30.00
GA Garrett Atkins 20.00
HA Cole Hamels 40.00
HB Hank Blalock 20.00
HO Trevor Hoffman 20.00
HR Hanley Ramirez 30.00
HT Tim Hudson 20.00
HU Torii Hunter 20.00
HY Roy Halladay 20.00
IK Ian Kinsler 20.00
IR Ivan Rodriguez 25.00
JB Jason Bay 25.00
JD Jermaine Dye 20.00
JH Jeremy Hermida 20.00
JJ Josh Johnson 20.00
JK Jason Kendall 20.00
JM Joe Mauer 40.00
JN Joe Nathan 20.00
JP Jake Peavy 20.00
JR Jose Reyes 40.00
JS Johan Santana 30.00
JV Justin Verlander 40.00
JW Jered Weaver 30.00
JZ Joel Zumaya 35.00
KG Ken Griffey Jr. 50.00
KG2 Ken Griffey Jr. 50.00
KH Khalil Greene 20.00
KJ Kenji Johjima 50.00
KM Kendry Morales 20.00
KU Jason Kubel 20.00
KY Kevin Youkilis 20.00
LA Luis Aparicio 20.00
LM Lastings Milledge 20.00
LY Fred Lynn 20.00
MA Matt Cain 30.00
MC Miguel Cabrera 25.00
MG Marcus Giles 20.00
MH Matt Holliday 20.00
ML Mark Loretta 20.00
MM Melvin Mora 20.00
MO Justin Morneau 25.00
MS Mike Schmidt 50.00
MT Mark Teixeira 25.00
MU Mark Mulder 20.00
MY Michael Young 20.00
NS Nick Swisher 20.00
PF Prince Fielder 30.00
PM Paul Molitor 30.00
RC Cal Ripken Jr. 100.00
RH Rich Harden 20.00
RI Jim Rice 25.00
RO Roy Oswalt 20.00
RW Rickie Weeks 20.00
RZ Ryan Zimmerman 35.00
SK Scott Kazmir 20.00
SP Scott Podsednik 20.00
TE Miguel Tejada 25.00
TG Tony Gwynn 30.00
TH Travis Hafner 25.00
TI Tadahito Iguchi 25.00
VM Victor Martinez 20.00
WC Will Clark 25.00
WI Josh Willingham 20.00
YB Yuniesky Betancourt 15.00

Signature Patch

No Pricing
Production 10 Sets

Tandem Patch

NM/M

Production 35 Sets
AA Alfonso Soriano, Alex Rios 15.00
AH Garrett Atkins, Matt Holliday 15.00
AJ Luis Aparicio, Derek Jeter 40.00
BH Felix Hernandez, Yuniesky Betancourt 20.00
BM Brian Bannister, Lastings Milledge 15.00
BR Yuniesky Betancourt, Hanley Ramirez 20.00
BV Justin Verlander, Jeremy Bonderman 40.00
CH Melky Cabrera, Jeremy Hermida 20.00
CL Coco Crisp, Mark Loretta 15.00
CM Lastings Milledge, Melky Cabrera 25.00
CO Roy Oswalt, Roger Clemens 50.00
CP Carl Crawford, Scott Podsednik 15.00
CR Miguel Cabrera, Hanley Ramirez 20.00
CS Cole Hamels, Scott Kazmir 50.00
CV Justin Verlander, Matt Cain 40.00
CW Dontrelle Willis, Chris Carpenter 30.00
CZ Miguel Cabrera, Ryan Zimmerman 30.00
DH Hanley Ramirez, Derek Jeter 60.00
FW Prince Fielder, Rickie Weeks 30.00
GD Adam Dunn, Ken Griffey Jr. 40.00
GG Tony Gwynn, Brian Giles 30.00
GP Ken Griffey Jr., Albert Pujols 80.00
GR Ken Griffey Jr., Alex Rios 40.00
GT Ken Griffey Jr., Frank Thomas 50.00
HB Matt Holliday, Jason Bay 20.00
HF Prince Fielder, Travis Hafner 30.00
HG Trevor Hoffman, Brian Giles 15.00
HJ Andruw Jones, Torii Hunter 25.00
HK Jeremy Hermida, Jason Kubel 15.00
HM Travis Hafner, Victor Martinez 15.00
HN Trevor Hoffman, Joe Nathan 15.00
HO Roy Oswalt, Rich Harden 20.00
HP Trevor Hoffman, Jonathan Papelbon 30.00
HR Hanley Ramirez, Jeremy Hermida 25.00
HW Jeremy Hermida, Josh Willingham 15.00
ID Jermaine Dye, Tadahito Iguchi 25.00
JC Derek Jeter, Melky Cabrera 65.00
JG Derek Jeter, Ken Griffey Jr. 80.00
JJ Derek Jeter, Reggie Jackson 60.00
JK Kendry Morales, Jered Weaver 30.00
JM Kenji Johjima, Victor Martinez 30.00
JR Derek Jeter, Cal Ripken Jr. 100.00
KB Brian Giles, Khalil Greene 20.00
KC Scott Kazmir, Carl Crawford 15.00
KM Joe Mauer, Jason Kendall 25.00
KU Ian Kinsler, Dan Uggla 20.00
KY Ian Kinsler, Michael Young 15.00
LC Fred Lynn, Coco Crisp 20.00
LF Prince Fielder, Carlos Lee 20.00
LH Francisco Liriano, Cole Hamels 40.00
MF Kendry Morales, Prince Fielder 25.00
MH Livan Hernandez, Kendry Morales 15.00
ML Francisco Liriano, Joe Mauer 35.00
MM Joe Mauer, Victor Martinez 25.00
MR Melvin Mora, Brian Roberts 15.00
MW Rickie Weeks, Paul Molitor 20.00
NJ Joe Mauer, Joe Nathan 20.00
NL Joe Nathan, Francisco Liriano 30.00
NM Joe Mauer, Joe Nathan 30.00
NP Joe Nathan, Jonathan Papelbon 30.00
PC Matt Cain, Gaylord Perry 30.00
PH Jonathan Papelbon, Craig Hansen 50.00
PO Roy Oswalt, Jake Peavy 20.00
PP Jake Peavy, Gaylord Perry 15.00
RC Coco Crisp, Alex Rios 15.00
RM Lastings Milledge, Jose Reyes 30.00
RR Jose Reyes, Hanley Ramirez 40.00
RS Mike Schmidt, Cal Ripken Jr. 75.00
RU Hanley Ramirez, Dan Uggla 25.00
RV Ivan Rodriguez, Justin Verlander 35.00
SH Rich Harden, Nick Swisher 15.00
SJ Conor Jackson, Chris Shelton 25.00
SZ Ryan Zimmerman, Mike Schmidt 40.00
TY Michael Young, Mark Teixeira 20.00
UK Chase Utley, Ian Kinsler 40.00
UM Chase Utley, Joe Morgan 40.00
UR Brian Roberts, Dan Uggla 15.00
VM Justin Verlander, Jack Morris 40.00
VZ Justin Verlander, Joel Zumaya 40.00
WM Josh Willingham, Joe Mauer 25.00
WR Hanley Ramirez, Josh Willingham 25.00
WV Justin Verlander, Jered Weaver 40.00
YL Kevin Youkilis, Mark Loretta 20.00
ZA Garrett Atkins, Ryan Zimmerman 40.00
ZC Ryan Zimmerman, Miguel Cabrera 40.00
ZJ Josh Johnson, Joel Zumaya 20.00
ZZ Joel Zumaya, Carlos Zambrano 30.00

2007 Upper Deck

NM/M

Complete Set (1020):
Common Player: .15
Rookie Redemption: 75.00
Hobby Pack (15): 5.00
Hobby Box (16): 70.00
1 Doug Slaten **RC** .50
2 Miguel Montero **(RC)** .25
3 Brian Burres **(RC)** .25
4 Devern Hansack **RC** 2.00
5 David Murphy **(RC)** .25
6 Jose Reyes **RC** .50
7 Scott Moore **(RC)** .25
8 Josh Fields **(RC)** .50
9 Chris Stewart **RC** .50
10 Jerry Owens **(RC)** .25
11 Ryan Sweeney **(RC)** .25
12 Kevin Kouzmanoff **(RC)** .50
13 Jeff Baker **(RC)** .25
14 Justin Hampson **(RC)** .25
15 Jeff Salazar **(RC)** .25
16 Alvin Colina **RC** .50
17 Troy Tulowitzki **(RC)** .50
18 Andrew Miller **RC** 4.00
19 Mike Rabelo **RC** 1.00
20 Jose Diaz **(RC)** .25
21 Angel Sanchez **RC** .50
22 Ryan Braun **(RC)** 1.00
23 Delwyn Young **(RC)** .25
24 Drew Anderson **(RC)** .25
25 Dennis Sarfate **(RC)** .25
26 Vinny Rottino **(RC)** .25
27 Glen Perkins **(RC)** .25
28 Alexi Casilla **RC** 1.00
29 Philip Humber **(RC)** .50
30 Andy Cannizaro **RC** .50
31 Jeremy Brown .25
32 Sean Henn **(RC)** .25
33 Brian Rogers .15
34 Carlos Maldonado **(RC)** .25
35 Juan Morillo **(RC)** .25
36 Fred Lewis **(RC)** .25
37 Patrick Misch **(RC)** .25
38 Billy Sadler **(RC)** .25
39 Ryan Feierabend **(RC)** .25
40 Cesar Jimenez **RC** .75
41 Oswaldo Navarro **RC** .50
42 Travis Chick **(RC)** .25
43 Delmon Young **(RC)** 1.00
44 Shawn Riggans **(RC)** .25
45 Brian Stokes **(RC)** .25
46 Juan Salas **(RC)** .25
47 Joaquin Arias **(RC)** .25
48 Adam Lind **(RC)** .50
49 Beltran Perez **(RC)** .25
50 Brett Campbell **RC** .50
51 Brian Roberts .25
52 Miguel Tejada .50
53 Brandon Fahey .15
54 Jay Gibbons .15
55 Corey Patterson .15
56 Nicholas Markakis .25
57 Ramon Hernandez .15
58 Kris Benson .15
59 Adam Loewen .15
60 Erik Bedard .25
61 Chris Ray .15
62 Chris Britton .15
63 Daniel Cabrera .15
64 Sendy Rleal .15
65 Manny Ramirez .75
66 David Ortiz .75
67 Gabe Kapler .15
68 Alex Cora .15
69 Dustin Pedroia .15
70 Trot Nixon .15
71 Doug Mirabelli .15
72 Mark Loretta .15
73 Curt Schilling .75
74 Jonathan Papelbon .50
75 Tim Wakefield .15
76 Jon Lester .25
77 Craig Hansen .15
78 Keith Foulke .15
79 Jermaine Dye .15
80 Jim Thome .50
81 Tadahito Iguchi .15
82 Robert Mackowiak .15
83 Brian Anderson .15
84 Juan Uribe .15
85 A.J. Pierzynski .15
86 Alex Cintron .15
87 Jon Garland .15
88 Jose Contreras .15
89 Neal Cotts .15
90 Bobby Jenks .15
91 Mike MacDougal .15
92 Javier Vazquez .15
93 Travis Hafner .40
94 Jhonny Peralta .25
95 Ryan Garko .15
96 Victor Martinez .25
97 Hector Luna .15
98 Casey Blake .15
99 Jason Michaels .15
100 Shin-Soo Choo .15
101 C.C. Sabathia .25
102 Paul Byrd .15
103 Jeremy Sowers .15
104 Cliff Lee .15
105 Rafael Betancourt .15
106 Francisco Cruceta .15
107 Sean Casey .15
108 Brandon Inge .15
109 Placido Polanco .15
110 Omar Infante .15
111 Ivan Rodriguez .50
112 Magglio Ordonez .25
113 Craig Monroe .15
114 Marcus Thames .15
115 Justin Verlander .50
116 Todd Jones .15
117 Kenny Rogers .15
118 Joel Zumaya .25
119 Jeremy Bonderman .50
120 Nate Robertson .15
121 Mark Teahen .15
122 Ryan Shealy .25
123 Mitch Maier **(RC)** .25
124 Doug Mientkiewicz .15
125 Mark Grudzielanek .15
126 Shane Costa .15
127 John Buck .15
128 Reggie Sanders .15
129 Mike Sweeney .15
130 Mark Redman .15
131 Todd Wellemeyer .15
132 Scott Elarton .15
133 Ambiorix Burgos .15
134 Joe Nelson .15
135 Howie Kendrick .40
136 Chone Figgins .15
137 Orlando Cabrera .25
138 Maicer Izturis .15
139 Jose Molina .15
140 Vladimir Guerrero .75
141 Darin Erstad .15
142 Juan Rivera .15
143 Jered Weaver .40
144 John Lackey .25
145 Joe Saunders .15
146 Bartolo Colon .15
147 Scot Shields .15
148 Francisco Rodriguez .25
149 Justin Morneau .50
150 Jason Bartlett .15
151 Luis Castillo .15
152 Nick Punto .15
153 Shannon Stewart .15
154 Michael Cuddyer .15
155 Jason Kubel .15
156 Joe Mauer .50
157 Francisco Liriano .25
158 Joe Nathan .25
159 Dennys Reyes .15
160 Brad Radke .15
161 Boof Bonser .15
162 Juan Rincon .15
163 Derek Jeter 2.00
164 Jason Giambi .50
165 Robinson Cano .50
166 Andy Phillips .15
167 Bobby Abreu .40
168 Gary Sheffield .50
169 Bernie Williams .40
170 Melky Cabrera .25
171 Mike Mussina .50
172 Chien-Ming Wang .50
173 Mariano Rivera .50
174 Scott Proctor .15
175 Jaret Wright .15
176 Kyle Farnsworth .15
177 Eric Chavez .25
178 Bobby Crosby .15
179 Frank Thomas .50
180 Dan Johnson .15
181 Marco Scutaro .15
182 Nick Swisher .40
183 Milton Bradley .25
184 Jay Payton .15
185 Joe Blanton .15
186 Barry Zito .40
187 Rich Harden .25
188 Esteban Loaiza .15
189 Huston Street .25
190 Chad Gaudin .15
191 Richie Sexson .40
192 Yuniesky Betancourt .15
193 Willie Bloomquist .15
194 Ben Broussard .15
195 Kenji Johjima .25
196 Ichiro Suzuki 1.00
197 Raul Ibanez .15
198 Chris Snelling/SP .15
199 Felix Hernandez .50
200 Cha Sueng Baek .15
201 Joel Pineiro .15
202 Julio Mateo .15
203 J.J. Putz .15
204 Rafael Soriano .15
205 Jorge Cantu .15
206 B.J. Upton .25
207 Ty Wigginton .15
208 Greg Norton .15
209 Dioner Navarro .15
210 Carl Crawford .40
211 Jonny Gomes .15
212 Damon Hollins .15
213 Scott Kazmir .25
214 Casey Fossum .15
215 Ruddy Lugo .15
216 James Shields .15
217 Tyler Walker .15
218 Shawn Camp .15
219 Mark Teixeira .50
220 Hank Blalock .25
221 Ian Kinsler .25
222 Jerry Hairston Jr. .15
223 Gerald Laird .15
224 Carlos Lee .40
225 Gary Matthews .15
226 Mark DeRosa .15
227 Kip Wells .15
228 Akinori Otsuka .15

229 Vicente Padilla .15
230 John Koronka .15
231 Kevin Millwood .25
232 Wes Littleton .15
233 Troy Glaus .40
234 Lyle Overbay .25
235 Aaron Hill .15
236 John McDonald .15
237 Bengie Molina .15
238 Vernon Wells .25
239 Reed Johnson .15
240 Frank Catalanotto .15
241 Roy Halladay .40
242 B.J. Ryan .15
243 Gustavo Chacin .15
244 Scott Downs .15
245 Casey Janssen .15
246 Justin Speier .15
247 Stephen Drew .40
248 Conor Jackson .25
249 Orlando Hudson .15
250 Chad Tracy .15
251 Johnny Estrada .15
252 Luis Gonzalez .15
253 Eric Byrnes .15
254 Carlos Quentin .15
255 Brandon Webb .25
256 Claudio Vargas .15
257 Juan Cruz .15
258 Jorge Julio .15
259 Luis Vizcaino .15
260 Livan Hernandez .15
261 Chipper Jones .75
262 Edgar Renteria .25
263 Adam LaRoche .25
264 Willy Aybar .15
265 Brian McCann .40
266 Ryan Langerhans .15
267 Jeff Francoeur .40
268 Matt Diaz .15
269 Tim Hudson .25
270 John Smoltz .40
271 Oscar Villarreal .15
272 Horacio Ramirez .15
273 Bob Wickman .15
274 Chad Paronto .15
275 Derrek Lee .50
276 Ryan Theriot .15
277 Cesar Izturis .15
278 Ronny Cedeno .15
279 Michael Barrett .25
280 Juan Pierre .15
281 Jacque Jones .15
282 Matt Murton .25
283 Carlos Zambrano .25
284 Mark Prior .25
285 Rich Hill .40
286 Sean Marshall .15
287 Ryan Dempster .15
288 Ryan O'Malley .15
289 Scott Hatteberg .15
290 Brandon Phillips .15
291 Edwin Encarnacion .15
292 Rich Aurilia .15
293 David Ross .15
294 Ken Griffey Jr. 1.00
295 Ryan Freel .15
296 Chris Denorfia .15
297 Bronson Arroyo .15
298 Aaron Harang .15
299 Brandon Claussen .15
300 Todd Coffey .15
301 David Weathers .15
302 Eric Milton .15
303 Todd Helton .50
304 Clint Barmes .15
305 Kazuo Matsui .15
306 Jamey Carroll .15
307 Yorvit Torrealba .15
308 Matt Holliday .50
309 Choo Freeman .15
310 Brad Hawpe .25
311 Jason Jennings .15
312 Jeff Francis .25
313 Josh Fogg .15
314 Aaron Cook .15
315 Ubaldo Jimenez .15
316 Manny Corpas .15
317 Miguel Cabrera .75
318 Dan Uggla .15
319 Hanley Ramirez .50
320 Wes Helms .15
321 Miguel Olivo .15
322 Jeremy Hermida .15
323 Cody Ross .15
324 Josh Willingham .15
325 Dontrelle Willis .25
326 Anibal Sanchez .15
327 Josh Johnson .15
328 Jose Garcia .15
329 Joe Borowski .15
330 Taylor Tankersley .15
331 Lance Berkman .50
332 Craig Biggio .40
333 Aubrey Huff .15
334 Adam Everett .15
335 Brad Ausmus .15
336 Willy Taveras .25
337 Luke Scott .15
338 Chris Burke .15
339 Roger Clemens 1.50
340 Andy Pettitte .40
341 Brandon Backe .15
342 Hector Gimenez .15
343 Brad Lidge .15
344 Dan Wheeler .15
345 Nomar Garciaparra .75
346 Rafael Furcal .25

347 Wilson Betemit .15
348 Julio Lugo .15
349 Russell Martin .25
350 Andre Ethier .25
351 Matthew Kemp .25
352 Kenny Lofton .15
353 Brad Penny .15
354 Derek Lowe .25
355 Chad Billingsley .25
356 Greg Maddux 1.00
357 Takashi Saito .15
358 Jonathan Broxton .25
359 Prince Fielder 1.00
360 Rickie Weeks .40
361 Bill Hall .25
362 J.J. Hardy .15
363 Jeff Cirillo .15
364 Tony Gwynn Jr. .15
365 Corey Hart .15
366 Laynce Nix .15
367 Doug Davis .15
368 Ben Sheets .40
369 Chris Capuano .15
370 David Bush .15
371 Derrick Turnbow .15
372 Francisco Cordero .15
373 Jose Reyes 1.00
374 Carlos Delgado .50
375 Julio Franco .15
376 Jose Valentin .15
377 Paul LoDuca .15
378 Carlos Beltran .50
379 Shawn Green .15
380 Lastings Milledge .25
381 Endy Chavez .15
382 Pedro Martinez .75
383 John Maine .15
384 Orlando Hernandez .15
385 Steve Trachsel .15
386 Billy Wagner .15
387 Ryan Howard 1.50
388 Chase Utley .75
389 Jimmy Rollins .50
390 Chris Coste .15
391 Jeff Conine .15
392 Aaron Rowand .15
393 Shane Victorino .15
394 David Dellucci .15
395 Cole Hamels .40
396 Jamie Moyer .15
397 Ryan Madson .15
398 Brett Myers .25
399 Tom Gordon .15
400 Geoff Geary .15
401 Freddy Sanchez .15
402 Xavier Nady .15
403 Jose Castillo .15
404 Joe Randa .15
405 Jason Bay .40
406 Chris Duffy .15
407 Jose Bautista .15
408 Ronny Paulino .15
409 Ian Snell .25
410 Zachary Duke .15
411 Tom Gorzelanny .15
412 Shane Youman .15
413 Mike Gonzalez .15
414 Matt Capps .15
415 Adrian Gonzalez .25
416 Josh Barfield .25
417 Todd Walker .15
418 Khalil Greene .15
419 Mike Piazza .75
420 Dave Roberts .15
421 Mike Cameron .15
422 Geoff Blum .15
423 Jake Peavy .40
424 Chris Young .25
425 Woody Williams .15
426 Clay Hensley .15
427 Cla Meredith .15
428 Trevor Hoffman .15
429 Shea Hillenbrand .15
430 Pedro Feliz .15
431 Ray Durham .15
432 Mark Sweeney .15
433 Eliezer Alfonzo .15
434 Moises Alou .25
435 Steve Finley .15
436 Todd Linden .15
437 Jason Schmidt .25
438 Matt Cain .25
439 Noah Lowry .15
440 Brad Hennessey .15
441 Armando Benitez .15
442 Jonathan Sanchez .15
443 Albert Pujols 2.00
444 Ronnie Belliard .15
445 David Eckstein .15
446 Aaron Miles .15
447 Yadier Molina .15
448 Jim Edmonds .25
449 Chris Duncan .15
450 Juan Encarnacion .15
451 Chris Carpenter .50
452 Jeff Suppan .15
453 Jason Marquis .15
454 Jeff Weaver .15
455 Jason Isringhausen .15
456 Braden Looper .15
457 Ryan Zimmerman .40
458 Nick Johnson .15
459 Felipe Lopez .25
460 Brian Schneider .15
461 Alfonso Soriano .75
462 Austin Kearns .15
463 Ryan Church .15
464 Alex Escobar .15

465 Ramon Ortiz .15
466 Tony Armas .15
467 Michael O'Connor .15
468 Chad Cordero .15
469 Jon Rauch .15
470 Pedro Astacio .15
471 Miguel Tejada .25
472 David Ortiz .50
473 Jermaine Dye .25
474 Travis Hafner .25
475 Magglio Ordonez .25
476 Mark Teahen .15
477 Vladimir Guerrero .50
478 Justin Morneau .50
479 Derek Jeter 1.00
480 Nick Swisher .25
481 Ichiro Suzuki .50
482 Scott Kazmir .25
483 Mark Teixeira .25
484 Vernon Wells .25
485 Brandon Webb .25
486 Andruw Jones .40
487 Carlos Zambrano .25
488 Adam Dunn .25
489 Matt Holliday .50
490 Miguel Cabrera .50
491 Lance Berkman .25
492 Nomar Garciaparra .50
493 Prince Fielder 1.00
494 Carlos Beltran .40
495 Ryan Howard 1.00
496 Jason Bay .25
497 Adrian Gonzalez .25
498 Matt Cain .25
499 Albert Pujols 1.00
500 Ryan Zimmerman .25
501 Daisuke Matsuzaka
Suit **RC** 30.00
502 Kei Igawa **RC** 5.00
503 Akinori Iwamura **RC** 6.00
521 Randy Johnson .75
522 Brandon Lyon .15
523 Robby Hammock .15
524 Micah Owings **(RC)** .15
525 Doug Davis .15
526 Brian Barden **RC** .50
527 Alberto Callaspo .15
528 Stephen Drew .25
529 Chris Young .25
530 Edgar Gonzalez .15
531 Brandon Medders .15
532 Tony Pena .15
533 Jose Valverde .15
534 Chris Snyder .15
535 Tony Clark .15
536 Scott Hairston .15
537 Jeff DaVanon .15
538 Randy Johnson .40
539 Mark Redman .15
540 Andruw Jones .50
541 Rafael Soriano .15
542 Scott Thorman .15
543 Chipper Jones .75
544 Mike Gonzalez .15
545 Lance Cormier .15
546 Kyle Davies .15
547 Mike Hampton .15
548 Chuck James .15
549 Macay McBride .15
550 Tanyon Sturtze .15
551 Tyler Yates .15
552 Peter Orr .15
553 Craig Wilson .15
554 Chris Woodward .15
556 Chipper Jones .40
557 Chad Bradford .15
558 John Parrish .15
559 Jeremy Guthrie .15
560 Steve Trachsel .15
561 Scott Williamson .15
562 Jaret Wright .15
563 Paul Bako .15
564 Chris Gomez .15
565 Melvin Mora .15
566 Freddie Bynum .15
567 Aubrey Huff .15
568 Jay Payton .15
569 Miguel Tejada .50
570 Kurt Birkins .15
571 Danys Baez .15
572 Brian Roberts .25
573 Josh Beckett .50
574 Matt Clement .15
575 Hideki Okajima **RC** 5.00
576 Javier Lopez .15
577 Joel Pineiro .15
578 J.C. Romero .15
579 Kyle Snyder .15
580 Julian Tavarez .15
581 Mike Timlin .15
582 Jason Varitek .50
583 Mike Lowell .25
584 Kevin Youkilis .25
585 Coco Crisp .15
586 J.D. Drew .25
587 Eric Hinske .15
588 Wily Mo Pena .15
589 Julio Lugo .15
590 David Ortiz .75
591 Manny Ramirez .75
592 Daisuke Matsuzaka 5.00
593 Scott Eyre .15
594 Angel Guzman .15
595 Bob Howry .15
596 Ted Lilly .15
597 Juan Mateo .15
598 Wade Miller .15
599 Carlos Zambrano .25

600 Will Ohman .15
601 Mike Wuertz .15
602 Henry Blanco .15
603 Aramis Ramirez .40
604 Cliff Floyd .15
605 Kerry Wood .25
606 Alfonso Soriano .75
607 Daryle Ward .15
608 Jason Marquis .15
609 Mark DeRosa .15
610 Neal Cotts .15
611 Derrek Lee .50
612 Aramis Ramirez .25
613 David Aardsma .15
614 Mark Buehrle .25
615 Nick Massett .15
616 Andrew Sisco .15
617 Matt Thornton .15
618 Toby Hall .15
619 Joe Crede .15
620 Paul Konerko .25
621 Darin Erstad .15
622 Pablo Ozuna .15
623 Scott Podsednik .15
624 Jim Thome .50
625 Jermaine Dye .15
626 Jim Thome .25
627 Adam Dunn .50
628 Bill Bray .15
629 Alex Gonzalez .15
630 Josh Hamilton **(RC)** 1.00
631 Matt Belisle .15
632 Rheal Cormier .15
633 Kyle Lohse .15
634 Eric Milton .15
635 Kirk Saarloos .15
636 Mike Stanton .15
637 Javier Valentin .15
638 Juan Castro .15
639 Jeff Conine .15
640 Jon Coutlangus **(RC)** .50
641 Ken Griffey Jr. 1.50
642 Ken Griffey Jr. .75
643 Fernando Cabrera .15
644 Fausto Carmona .15
645 Jason Davis .15
646 Aaron Fultz .15
647 Roberto Hernandez .15
648 Jake Westbrook .15
649 Kelly Stoppach .15
650 Josh Barfield .25
651 Andy Marte .15
652 Joe Inglett .15
653 David Dellucci .15
654 Joe Borowski .15
655 Franklin Gutierrez .15
656 Trot Nixon .15
657 Grady Sizemore .50
658 Mike Rouse .15
659 Travis Hafner .40
660 Victor Martinez .40
661 C.C. Sabathia .40
662 Grady Sizemore .25
663 Jeremy Affeldt .15
664 Taylor Buchholz .15
665 Brian Fuentes .15
666 LaTroy Hawkins .15
667 Byung-Hyun Kim .15
668 Brian Lawrence .15
669 Rodrigo Lopez .15
670 Jeff Francis .15
671 Chris Iannetta .15
672 Garrett Atkins .25
673 Todd Helton .50
674 Steve Finley .15
675 John Mabry .15
676 Willy Taveras .15
677 Jason Hirsh .15
678 Ramon Ramirez .15
679 Matt Holliday .75
680 Todd Helton .25
681 Roman Colon .15
682 Chad Durbin .15
683 Jason Grilli .15
684 Wilfredo Ledezma .15
685 Mike Maroth .15
686 Jose Mesa .15
687 Justin Verlander .50
688 Fernando Rodney .15
689 Vance Wilson .15
690 Carlos Guillen .15
691 Neifi Perez .15
692 Curtis Granderson .15
693 Gary Sheffield .50
694 Justin Verlander .25
695 Kevin Gregg .15
696 Logan Kensing .15
697 Randy Messenger .15
698 Sergio Mitre .15
699 Ricky Nolasco .15
700 Scott Olsen .25
701 Renyel Pinto .15
702 Matt Treanor .15
703 Alfredo Amezaga .15
704 Aaron Boone .15
705 Mike Jacobs .15
706 Miguel Cabrera .75
707 Joe Borchard .15
708 Jorge Julio .15
709 Rick Vanden Hurk **RC** 2.00
710 Lee Gardner **(RC)** .50
711 Matt Lindstrom **(RC)** .50
712 Henry Owens .15
713 Hanley Ramirez .50
714 Alejandro De Aza **RC** .50
715 Hanley Ramirez .25
716 Dave Borkowski .15
717 Jason Jennings .15

718 Trever Miller .15
719 Roy Oswalt .40
720 Wandy Rodriguez .15
721 Humberto Quintero .15
722 Morgan Ensberg .15
723 Mike Lamb .15
724 Mark Loretta .15
725 Jason Lane .15
726 Carlos Lee .40
727 Orlando Palmeiro .15
728 Woody Williams .15
729 Chad Qualls .15
730 Lance Berkman .40
731 Rick White .15
732 Chris Sampson .15
733 Carlos Lee .15
734 Jorge De La Rosa .15
735 Octavio Dotel .15
736 Jimmy Gobble .15
737 Zack Greinke .15
738 Luke Hudson .15
739 Gil Meche .15
740 Joel Peralta .15
741 Odalis Perez .15
742 David Riske .15
743 Jason LaRue .15
744 Tony Pena .15
745 Esteban German .15
746 Ross Gload .15
747 Emil Brown .15
748 David DeJesus .15
749 Brandon Duckworth .15
750 Alex Gordon **RC** 3.00
751 Jered Weaver .50
752 Vladimir Guerrero .75
753 Hector Carrasco .15
754 Kelvim Escobar .15
755 Darren Oliver .15
756 Dustin Moseley .15
757 Ervin Santana .15
758 Mike Napoli .15
759 Shea Hillenbrand .15
760 Casey Kotchman .15
761 Reggie Willits .15
762 Robb Quinlan .15
763 Garret Anderson .15
764 Gary Mathews .15
765 Justin Speier .15
766 Jered Weaver .25
767 Joe Beimel .15
768 Yhency Brazoban .15
769 Elmer Dessens .15
770 Mark Hendrickson .15
771 Hong-Chih Kuo .25
772 Jason Schmidt .25
773 Brett Tomko .15
774 Randy Wolf .15
775 Mike Lieberthal .15
776 Marlon Anderson .15
777 Jeff Kent .25
778 Ramon Martinez .15
779 Olmedo Saenz .15
780 Luis Gonzalez .25
781 Juan Pierre .25
782 Jason Repko .15
783 Nomar Garciaparra .75
784 Wilson Valdez .15
785 Jason Schmidt .15
786 Greg Aquino .15
787 Brian Shouse .15
788 Jeff Suppan .15
789 Carlos Villanueva .15
790 Matt Wise .15
791 Johnny Estrada .15
792 Craig Counsell .15
793 Tony Graffanino .15
794 Corey Koskie .15
795 Claudio Vargas .15
796 Brady Clark .15
797 Gabe Gross .15
798 Geoff Jenkins .15
799 Kevin Mench .15
800 Bill Hall .25
801 Sidney Ponson .15
802 Jesse Crain .15
803 Matt Guerrier .15
804 Pat Neshek .15
805 Ramon Ortiz .15
806 Johan Santana .75
807 Carlos Silva .15
808 Mike Redmond .15
809 Jeff Cirillo .15
810 Luis Rodriguez .15
811 Lew Ford .15
812 Torii Hunter .40
813 Jason Tyner .15
814 Rondell White .15
815 Justin Morneau .50
816 Joe Mauer .40
817 Johan Santana .40
818 David Newhan .15
819 Aaron Sele .15
820 Ambiorix Burgos .15
821 Pedro Feliciano .15
822 Tom Glavine .50
823 Aaron Heilman .15
824 Guillermo Mota .15
825 Jose Reyes 1.00
826 Oliver Perez .15
827 Duaner Sanchez .15
828 Scott Schoeneweis .15
829 Ramon Castro .15
830 Damion Easley .15
831 David Wright 1.50
832 Moises Alou .25
833 Carlos Beltran .50
834 Dave Williams .15
835 David Wright .75

836 Brian Bruney .15
837 Mike Myers .15
838 Carl Pavano .15
839 Andy Pettitte .40
840 Luis Vizcaino .15
841 Jorge Posada .40
842 Miguel Cairo .15
843 Doug Mientkiewicz .15
844 Derek Jeter 2.00
845 Alex Rodriguez 2.00
846 Johnny Damon .75
847 Hideki Matsui 1.00
848 Josh Phelps .15
849 Phil Hughes **(RC)** 4.00
850 Roger Clemens 2.00
851 Jason Giambi .25
852 Kiko Calero .15
853 Justin Duchscherer .15
854 Alan Embree .15
855 Todd Walker .15
856 Rich Harden .15
857 Danny Haren .40
858 Joe Kennedy .15
859 Jason Kendall .15
860 Adam Melhuse .15
861 Mark Ellis .15
863 Mark Kotsay .15
864 Shannon Stewart .15
865 Mike Piazza .75
866 Mike Piazza .40
867 Antonio Alfonseca .15
868 Carlos Ruiz .15
869 Adam Eaton .15
870 Freddy Garcia .15
871 Jon Lieber .15
872 Matt Smith .15
873 Rod Barajas .15
874 Wes Helms .15
875 Abraham Nunez .15
876 Pat Burrell .25
877 Jayson Werth .15
878 Greg Dobbs .15
879 Joseph Bisenius **RC** .50
880 Michael Bourn **(RC)** .50
881 Chase Utley .75
882 Ryan Howard 1.50
883 Chase Utley .40
884 Tony Armas .15
885 Shawn Chacon .15
886 John Grabow .15
887 Paul Maholm .15
888 Damaso Marte .15
889 Salomon Torres .15
890 Humberto Cota .15
891 Ryan Doumit .15
892 Adam LaRoche .25
893 Jack Wilson .15
894 Nate McLouth .15
895 Brad Eldred .15
896 Jonah Bayliss .15
897 Juan Perez **RC** .50
898 Jason Bay .40
899 Adam LaRoche .15
900 Doug Brocail .15
901 Scott Cassidy .15
902 Scott Linebrink .15
903 Greg Maddux 1.50
904 Jake Peavy .40
905 Mike Thompson .15
906 David Wells .15
907 Josh Bard .15
908 Rob Bowen .15
909 Marcus Giles .15
910 Russell Branyan .15
911 Jose Cruz .15
912 Terrmel Sledge .15
913 Trevor Hoffman .25
914 Brian Giles .25
915 Trevor Hoffman .25
916 Vinnie Chulk .15
917 Kevin Correia .15
918 Tim Lincecum **RC** 25.00
919 Matt Morris .15
920 Russ Ortiz .15
921 Barry Zito .25
922 Bengie Molina .15
923 Rich Aurilia .15
924 Omar Vizquel .25
925 Jason Ellison .15
926 Ryan Klesko .15
927 Dave Roberts .15
928 Randy Winn .15
929 Barry Zito .25
930 Miguel Batista .15
931 Horacio Ramirez .15
932 Chris Reitsma .15
933 George Sherrill .15
934 Jarrod Washburn .15
935 Jeff Weaver .15
936 Jake Woods .15
937 Adrian Beltre .25
938 Jose Lopez .15
939 Ichiro Suzuki 1.50
940 Jose Vidro .15
941 Jose Guillen .15
942 Sean White **RC** .50
943 Brandon Morrow **RC** 4.00
944 Felix Hernandez .50
945 Felix Hernandez .25
946 Randy Flores .15
947 Ryan Franklin .15
948 Kelvin Jimenez **RC** .50
949 Tyler Johnson .15
950 Mark Mulder .15
951 Anthony Reyes .15
952 Russ Springer .15
953 Brad Thompson .15
954 Adam Wainwright .15

955 Kip Wells .15
956 Gary Bennett .15
957 Adam Kennedy .15
958 Scott Rolen .75
959 Scott Spiezio .15
960 So Taguchi .15
961 Preston Wilson .15
962 Skip Schumaker .15
963 Albert Pujols 2.00
964 Chris Carpenter .50
965 Chris Carpenter .25
966 Edwin Jackson .15
967 Jae-Kuk Ryu .15
968 Jae Weong Seo .15
969 Jon Switzer .15
970 Josh Paul .15
971 Benjamin Zobrist .15
972 Rocco Baldelli .15
973 Scott Kazmir .25
974 Carl Crawford .25
975 Delmon Young .50
976 Bruce Chen .15
977 Joaquin Benoit .15
978 Scott Feldman .15
979 Eric Gagne .15
980 Kameron Loe .15
981 Brandon McCarthy .15
982 Robinson Tejeda .15
983 C.J. Wilson .15
984 Mark Teixeira .50
985 Michael Young .25
986 Kenny Lofton .25
987 Brad Wilkerson .15
988 Nelson Cruz .15
989 Sammy Sosa .75
990 Michael Young .25
991 Vernon Wells .40
992 Matt Stairs .15
993 Jeremy Accardo .15
994 A.J. Burnett .15
995 Jason Frasor .15
996 Roy Halladay .40
997 Shaun Marcum .15
998 Tomokazu Ohka .15
999 Josh Towers .15
1000 Gregg Zaun .15
1001 Royce Clayton .15
1002 Jason Smith .15
1003 Alex Rios .25
1004 Frank Thomas .75
1005 Roy Halladay .25
1006 Jesus Flores **RC** .50
1007 Dmitri Young .15
1008 Ray King .15
1009 Micah Bowie .15
1010 Shawn Hill .15
1011 John Patterson .15
1012 Levale Speigner **RC** .50
1013 Ryan Wagner .15
1014 Jerome Williams .15
1015 Ryan Zimmerman .50
1016 Cristian Guzman .15
1017 Nook Logan .15
1018 Chris Snelling .15
1019 Ronnie Belliard .15
1020 Nick Johnson .15

Gold

Gold: 8-15X
Production 75 Sets

Printing Plates

No Pricing
Production one set per color.

First Edition

NM/M
Complete Set (300): 35.00
Common Player: .10
Pack (10): 1.00
Box (36): 30.00
1 Doug Slaten **RC** .25
2 Miguel Montero **(RC)** .25
3 Brian Burres **(RC)** .25
4 Devern Hansack **RC** 1.00
5 David Murphy **(RC)** .25
6 Jose Reyes **RC** .25
7 Scott Moore **(RC)** .25
8 Josh Fields **(RC)** .25
9 Chris Stewart **RC** .25
10 Jerry Owens **(RC)** .25
11 Ryan Sweeney **(RC)** .25
12 Kevin Kouzmanoff **(RC)** .40
13 Jeff Baker **(RC)** .25
14 Justin Hampson **(RC)** .25
15 Jeff Salazar **(RC)** .25
16 Alvin Colina **RC** .25
17 Troy Tulowitzki **(RC)** .50
18 Andrew Miller **RC** 3.00
19 Mike Rabelo **RC** .25
20 Jose Diaz **(RC)** .25
21 Angel Sanchez **RC** .25
22 Ryan Braun **(RC)** .25
23 Delwyn Young **(RC)** .25
24 Drew Anderson **(RC)** .25
25 Dennis Sartate **(RC)** .25
26 Vinny Rottino **(RC)** .25
27 Glen Perkins **(RC)** .25
28 Alexi Casilla **RC** .25
29 Philip Humber **(RC)** .25
30 Andy Cannizaro **RC** .25
31 Jeremy Brown .10
32 Sean Henn **(RC)** .25
33 Brian Rogers **(RC)** .25
34 Carlos Maldonado **(RC)** .25
35 Juan Morillo **(RC)** .25
36 Fred Lewis **(RC)** .25
37 Patrick Misch **(RC)** .25
38 Billy Sadler **(RC)** .25
39 Ryan Feierabend **(RC)** .25
40 Cesar Jimenez **RC** .25
41 Oswaldo Navarro **RC** .25
42 Travis Chick **(RC)** .25
43 Delmon Young **(RC)** .50
44 Shawn Riggans **(RC)** .25
45 Brian Stokes **(RC)** .25
46 Juan Salas **(RC)** .25
47 Joaquin Arias **(RC)** .25
48 Adam Lind **(RC)** .50
49 Beltran Perez **(RC)** .25
50 Brett Campbell **RC** .25
51 Miguel Tejada .40
52 Brandon Fahey .10
53 Jay Gibbons .10
54 Nicholas Markakis .25
55 Kris Benson .10
56 Erik Bedard .25
57 Chris Ray .10
58 Chris Britton .10
59 Manny Ramirez .50
60 David Ortiz .50
61 Alex Cora .10
62 Trot Nixon .10
63 Doug Mirabelli .10
64 Curt Schilling .50
65 Jonathan Papelbon .50
66 Craig Hansen .10
67 Jermaine Dye .25
68 Jim Thome .40
69 Robert Mackowiak .10
70 Brian Anderson .10
71 A.J. Pierzynski .10
72 Alex Cintron .10
73 Jose Contreras .10
74 Bobby Jenks .10
75 Mike MacDougal .10
76 Travis Hafner .40
77 Ryan Garko .10
78 Victor Martinez .25
79 Casey Blake .10
80 Shin-Soo Choo .10
81 Paul Byrd .10
82 Jeremy Sowers .10
83 Cliff Lee .10
84 Sean Casey .10
85 Brandon Inge .10
86 Omar Infante .10
87 Magglio Ordonez .10
88 Marcus Thames .10
89 Justin Verlander .50
90 Todd Jones .10
91 Joel Zumaya .25
92 Nate Robertson .10
93 Mark Teahen .25
94 Ryan Shealy .10
95 Mark Grudzielanek .10
96 Shane Costa .10
97 Reggie Sanders .10
98 Mark Redman .10
99 Todd Wellemeyer .10
100 Ambiorix Burgos .10
101 Joe Nelson .10
102 Orlando Cabrera .25
103 Maicer Izturis .10
104 Vladimir Guerrero .50
105 Juan Rivera .10
106 Jered Weaver .40
107 Joe Saunders .10
108 Bartolo Colon .10
109 Francisco Rodriguez .25
110 Justin Morneau .50
111 Luis Castillo .10
112 Michael Cuddyer .10
113 Joe Mauer .40
114 Francisco Liriano .25
115 Joe Nathan .25
116 Brad Radke .10
117 Juan Rincon .10
118 Derek Jeter 1.50
119 Jason Giambi .40
120 Bobby Abreu .40
121 Gary Sheffield .40
122 Melky Cabrera .25
123 Chien-Ming Wang .50
124 Mariano Rivera .40
125 Jaret Wright .10
126 Kyle Farnsworth .10
127 Frank Thomas .50
128 Dan Johnson .10
129 Marco Scutaro .10
130 Jay Payton .10
131 Joe Blanton .10
132 Rich Harden .25
133 Esteban Loaiza .10
134 Chad Gaudin .10
135 Yuniesky Betancourt .10
136 Willie Bloomquist .10
137 Ichiro Suzuki 1.00
138 Raul Ibanez .10
139 Chris Snelling .10
140 Cha Sueng Baek .10
141 Julio Mateo .10
142 Rafael Soriano .10
143 Jorge Cantu .10
144 B.J. Upton .10
145 Dioner Navarro .10
146 Carl Crawford .40
147 Damon Hollins .10
148 Casey Fossum .10
149 Ruddy Lugo .10
150 Tyler Walker .10
151 Shawn Camp .10
152 Ian Kinsler .25
153 Jerry Hairston Jr. .10
154 Gerald Laird .10
155 Mark DeRosa .10
156 Kip Wells .10
157 Vicente Padilla .10
158 John Koronka .10
159 Wes Littleton .10
160 Lyle Overbay .10
161 Aaron Hill .10
162 John McDonald .10
163 Vernon Wells .10
164 Frank Catalanotto .10
165 Roy Halladay .25
166 B.J. Ryan .10
167 Casey Janssen .10
168 Stephen Drew .50
169 Conor Jackson .10
170 Chad Tracy .10
171 Johnny Estrada .10
172 Eric Byrnes .10
173 Carlos Quentin .10
174 Brandon Webb .25
175 Jorge Julio .10
176 Luis Vizcaino .10
177 Chipper Jones .50
178 Adam LaRoche .25
179 Brian McCann .25
180 Ryan Langerhans .10
181 Matt Diaz .10
182 John Smoltz .25
183 Oscar Villarreal .10
184 Chad Paronto .10
185 Derrek Lee .40
186 Ryan Theriot .10
187 Ronny Cedeno .10
188 Juan Pierre .10
189 Matt Murton .10
190 Carlos Zambrano .25
191 Mark Prior .25
192 Ryan Dempster .10
193 Ryan O'Malley .10
194 Brandon Phillips .10
195 Rich Aurilia .10
196 Ken Griffey Jr. 1.00
197 Ryan Freel .10
198 Aaron Harang .10
199 Brandon Claussen .10
200 David Weathers .10
201 Eric Milton .10
202 Kazuo Matsui .10
203 Jamey Carroll .10
204 Matt Holliday .25
205 Brad Hawpe .10
206 Jason Jennings .10
207 Josh Fogg .10
208 Aaron Cook .10
209 Miguel Cabrera .50
210 Dan Uggla .10
211 Hanley Ramirez .40
212 Jeremy Hermida .10
213 Cody Ross .10
214 Josh Willingham .10
215 Anibal Sanchez .10
216 Jose Garcia .10
217 Taylor Tankersley .10
218 Lance Berkman .40
219 Craig Biggio .25
220 Brad Ausmus .10
221 Willy Taveras .10
222 Chris Burke .10
223 Roger Clemens 1.00
224 Brandon Backe .10
225 Brad Lidge .10
226 Dan Wheeler .10
227 Wilson Betemit .10
228 Julio Lugo .10
229 Russell Martin .25
230 Kenny Lofton .10
231 Brad Penny .10
232 Chad Billingsley .10
233 Greg Maddux 1.00
234 Jonathan Broxton .10
235 Rickie Weeks .25
236 Bill Hall .25
237 Tony Gwynn Jr. .10
238 Corey Hart .10
239 Laynce Nix .10
240 Ben Sheets .25
241 David Bush .10
242 Francisco Cordero .10
243 Jose Reyes .50
244 Carlos Delgado .40
245 Paul LoDuca .10
246 Carlos Beltran .40
247 Lastings Milledge .25
248 Pedro Martinez .50
249 John Maine .10
250 Steve Trachsel .10
251 Ryan Howard 1.00
252 Jimmy Rollins .25
253 Chris Coste .10
254 Jeff Conine .10
255 David Dellucci .10
256 Cole Hamels .25
257 Ryan Madson .10
258 Brett Myers .25
259 Freddy Sanchez .10
260 Xavier Nady .10
261 Jose Castillo .10
262 Jason Bay .25
263 Jose Bautista .10
264 Ronny Paulino .10
265 Zachary Duke .10
266 Shane Youman .10
267 Matt Capps .10
268 Adrian Gonzalez .25
269 Josh Barfield .10
270 Mike Piazza .75
271 Dave Roberts .10
272 Geoff Blum .10
273 Chris Young .10
274 Woody Williams .10
275 Cla Meredith .10
276 Trevor Hoffman .25
277 Ray Durham .10
278 Mark Sweeney .10
279 Eliezer Alfonzo .10
280 Todd Linden .10
281 Jason Schmidt .25
282 Noah Lowry .10
283 Brad Hennessey .10
284 Jonathan Sanchez .10
285 Albert Pujols 1.50
286 David Eckstein .10
287 Jim Edmonds .25
288 Chris Duncan .10
289 Juan Encarnacion .10
290 Jeff Suppan .10
291 Jeff Weaver .10
292 Braden Looper .10
293 Ryan Zimmerman .25
294 Nick Johnson .10
295 Alfonso Soriano .50
296 Austin Kearns .10
297 Alex Escobar .10
298 Tony Armas .10
299 Chad Cordero .10
300 Jon Rauch .10

First Edition Printing Plates

No Pricing
Production one set per color.

1989 Reprints

NM/M
Common Player: 1.00
AK Al Kaline 2.00
BF Bob Feller 1.00
BR Babe Ruth 5.00
CA Rod Carew 1.00
CF Carlton Fisk 1.00
CM Christy Mathewson 1.00
CS Casey Stengel 1.00
CY Cy Young 1.00
DR Don Drysdale 1.00
FR Frank Robinson 1.00
GE Lou Gehrig 3.00
HW Honus Wagner 2.00
JB Johnny Bench 1.50
JF Jimmie Foxx 2.00
JR Jackie Robinson 2.00
LG Lefty Grove 1.00
LJ LeBron James 3.00
MJ Michael Jordan 5.00
MO Mel Ott 1.00
RB Reggie Bush 3.00
RC Roy Campanella 1.00
RH Rogers Hornsby 1.00
RJ Reggie Jackson 1.50
RO Brooks Robinson 1.50
SC Sidney Crosby 4.00
SM Stan Musial 1.50
SP Satchel Paige 2.00
TC Ty Cobb 3.00
TM Thurman Munson 3.00
WJ Walter Johnson 2.00

Cal Ripken Jr. and Tony Gwynn Road to the Hall

No Pricing

Cal Ripken Jr. Chronicles

NM/M
Common Ripken: 8.00
1-50 Cal Ripken Jr. 8.00

Cal Ripken Jr./Lou Gehrig Iron Man

NM/M
Common Ripken/Gehrig: 20.00
Autograph: No Pricing
Production One
1 Cal Ripken Jr., Lou Gehrig 20.00
2 Lou Gehrig, Cal Ripken Jr. 20.00
3 Cal Ripken Jr., Lou Gehrig 20.00
4 Lou Gehrig, Cal Ripken Jr. 20.00
5 Cal Ripken Jr., Lou Gehrig 20.00
6 Lou Gehrig, Cal Ripken Jr. 20.00
7 Cal Ripken Jr., Lou Gehrig 20.00
8 Lou Gehrig, Cal Ripken Jr. 20.00
9 Cal Ripken Jr., Lou Gehrig 20.00
10 Lou Gehrig, Cal Ripken Jr. 20.00
11 Cal Ripken Jr., Lou Gehrig 20.00
12 Lou Gehrig, Cal Ripken Jr. 20.00
13 Cal Ripken Jr., Lou Gehrig 20.00
14 Lou Gehrig, Stephen Drew 20.00
15 Cal Ripken Jr., Lou Gehrig 20.00
16 Lou Gehrig, Cal Ripken Jr. 20.00
17 Cal Ripken Jr., Lou Gehrig 20.00
18 Lou Gehrig, Cal Ripken Jr. 20.00
19 Cal Ripken Jr., Lou Gehrig 20.00
20 Lou Gehrig, Cal Ripken Jr. 20.00
21 Cal Ripken Jr., Lou Gehrig 20.00
22 Lou Gehrig, Cal Ripken Jr. 20.00
23 Cal Ripken Jr., Lou Gehrig 20.00
24 Lou Gehrig, Cal Ripken Jr. 20.00
25 Cal Ripken Jr., Lou Gehrig 20.00
26 Lou Gehrig, Cal Ripken Jr. 20.00
27 Cal Ripken Jr., Lou Gehrig 20.00
28 Lou Gehrig, Cal Ripken Jr. 20.00
29 Cal Ripken Jr., Lou Gehrig 20.00
30 Lou Gehrig, Cal Ripken Jr. 20.00
31 Cal Ripken Jr., Lou Gehrig 20.00
32 Lou Gehrig, Cal Ripken Jr. 20.00
33 Cal Ripken Jr., Lou Gehrig 20.00
34 Lou Gehrig, Cal Ripken Jr. 20.00
35 Cal Ripken Jr., Lou Gehrig 20.00
36 Lou Gehrig, Cal Ripken Jr. 20.00
37 Cal Ripken Jr., Lou Gehrig 20.00
38 Lou Gehrig, Cal Ripken Jr. 20.00
39 Cal Ripken Jr., Lou Gehrig 20.00
40 Lou Gehrig, Cal Ripken Jr. 20.00
41 Cal Ripken Jr., Lou Gehrig 20.00
42 Lou Gehrig, Cal Ripken Jr. 20.00
43 Cal Ripken Jr., Lou Gehrig 20.00
44 Lou Gehrig, Cal Ripken Jr. 20.00
45 Cal Ripken Jr., Lou Gehrig 20.00
46 Lou Gehrig, Cal Ripken Jr. 20.00
47 Cal Ripken Jr., Lou Gehrig 20.00
48 Lou Gehrig, Cal Ripken Jr. 20.00
49 Cal Ripken Jr., Lou Gehrig 20.00
50 Lou Gehrig, Cal Ripken Jr. 20.00

Ken Griffey Jr. Chronicles

NM/M
Common Griffey: 5.00
1-50 Ken Griffey Jr. 5.00

MVP Predictors

NM/M
Common Predictor: 3.00
1 Miguel Tejada 4.00
2 David Ortiz 8.00
3 Manny Ramirez 8.00
4 Jermaine Dye 4.00
5 Jim Thome 6.00
6 Paul Konerko 5.00
7 Travis Hafner 6.00
8 Grady Sizemore 6.00
9 Victor Martinez 4.00
10 Magglio Ordonez 3.00
11 Justin Verlander 4.00
12 Vladimir Guerrero 8.00
13 Jered Weaver 4.00
14 Justin Morneau 6.00
15 Joe Mauer 6.00
16 Johan Santana 8.00
17 Alex Rodriguez 25.00
18 Derek Jeter 15.00
19 Jason Giambi 5.00
20 Johnny Damon 6.00
21 Bobby Abreu 4.00
23 Frank Thomas 5.00
24 Eric Chavez 3.00
25 Ichiro Suzuki 8.00
26 Adrian Beltre 3.00
27 Carl Crawford 5.00
28 Scott Kazmir 4.00
29 Mark Teixeira 6.00
30 Michael Young 5.00
31 Carlos Lee 4.00
32 Vernon Wells 5.00
33 Roy Halladay 4.00
34 Troy Glaus 4.00
35 Stephen Drew 3.00
36 Chipper Jones 5.00
37 Andruw Jones 5.00
38 Adam LaRoche 4.00
39 Derrek Lee 8.00
40 Aramis Ramirez 6.00
41 Adam Dunn 4.00
42 Ken Griffey Jr. 10.00
43 Matt Holliday 8.00
44 Garrett Atkins 5.00
45 Miguel Cabrera 6.00
46 Hanley Ramirez 4.00
47 Dan Uggla 3.00
48 Lance Berkman 5.00
49 Roy Oswalt 4.00
50 Nomar Garciaparra 4.00
51 J.D. Drew 4.00
52 Rafael Furcal 4.00
53 Prince Fielder 15.00
54 Bill Hall 5.00
55 Jose Reyes 8.00
56 Carlos Beltran 8.00
57 Carlos Delgado 5.00
58 David Wright 10.00
60 Chase Utley 8.00
61 Ryan Howard 10.00
62 Jimmy Rollins 15.00
63 Jason Bay 5.00
64 Freddy Sanchez 3.00
65 Adrian Gonzalez 4.00
66 Albert Pujols 15.00
67 Scott Rolen 6.00
68 Chris Carpenter 5.00
69 Alfonso Soriano 8.00
70 Ryan Zimmerman 5.00

Playoff Predictors

NM/M
Common Predictor: 3.00
1 Arizona Diamondbacks 5.00
2 Atlanta Braves 5.00
3 Baltimore Orioles 3.00
4 Boston Red Sox 25.00
5 Chicago Cubs 5.00
6 Chicago White Sox 5.00
7 Cincinnati Reds 3.00
8 Cleveland Indians 5.00
9 Colorado Rockies 5.00
10 Detroit Tigers 5.00
11 Florida Marlins 3.00
12 Houston Astros 5.00
13 Kansas City Royals 3.00
14 Los Angeles Angels 5.00
15 Los Angeles Dodgers 5.00
16 Milwaukee Brewers 5.00
17 Minnesota Twins 5.00
18 New York Mets 5.00
19 New York Yankees 15.00
20 Oakland Athletics 5.00
21 Philadelphia Phillies 5.00
22 Pittsburgh Pirates 3.00
23 San Diego Padres 5.00
24 San Francisco Giants 5.00
25 Seattle Mariners 5.00
26 St. Louis Cardinals 5.00
27 Tampa Bay Devil Rays 3.00
28 Texas Rangers 5.00
29 Toronto Blue Jays 5.00
30 Washington Nationals 3.00

Star Power

NM/M
Inserted 2:1 Fat Packs
AJ Andruw Jones 1.50
AP Albert Pujols 5.00
AR Alex Rodriguez 5.00
BR Brian Roberts 1.00
BZ Barry Zito .75
CA Chris Carpenter 1.50
CB Carlos Beltran 1.50
CC Carl Crawford 1.00
CJ Chipper Jones 2.00
CS Curt Schilling 1.50
CU Chase Utley 1.50
CZ Carlos Zambrano 1.00
DA Johnny Damon 1.50
DJ Derek Jeter 5.00
DO David Ortiz 2.00
DW Dontrelle Willis .75
FS Freddy Sanchez .75
FT Frank Thomas 1.50
HA Roy Halladay 1.00
HO Trevor Hoffman .75
IS Ichiro Suzuki 3.00
JB Jason Bay 1.00
JD Jermaine Dye .75
JM Joe Mauer 1.00
JP Jake Peavy 1.00
JR Jose Reyes 2.00
JS Johan Santana 1.50
JT Jim Thome 1.50
JU Justin Morneau 1.50
JV Justin Verlander 1.50
KG Ken Griffey Jr. 4.00
KR Kenny Rogers .75
LB Lance Berkman 1.00
MA Matt Cain 1.00
MC Miguel Cabrera 2.00
MH Matt Holliday 1.00
MO Magglio Ordonez .75
MR Manny Ramirez 1.50
MT Mark Teixeira 1.00
MY Michael Young 1.00
NG Nomar Garciaparra 1.50
NS Nick Swisher 1.00
PF Prince Fielder 1.50

RH Ryan Howard 3.00
RO Roy Oswalt 1.00
RZ Ryan Zimmerman 1.00
SM John Smoltz 1.00
TH Travis Hafner 1.00
VG Vladimir Guerrero 1.50
WR David Wright 2.00

Star Signings

NM/M
Common Auto.: 5.00
AB Ambiorix Burgos 8.00
AC Aaron Cook 5.00
AH Aubrey Huff/SP 15.00
AR Alex Rios 20.00
BA Bobby Abreu 35.00
BL Joe Blanton 8.00
BO Jeremy Bonderman 30.00
BR Brandon Backe 8.00
CJ Conor Jackson 15.00
CO Chad Cordero 10.00
CP Corey Patterson 10.00
CS Chris Shelton 8.00
CY Chris Young/SP 20.00
DH Danny Haren 10.00
DJ Derek Jeter 150.00
DU Chris Duffy 10.00
GA Garrett Atkins 10.00
GC Gustavo Chacin 8.00
HS Huston Street 15.00
HU Torii Hunter 15.00
IS Ian Snell SP 20.00
JA Jeremy Accardo 8.00
JB Jason Bergmann/SP 8.00
JD Joey Devine 8.00
JG Jonny Gomes 8.00
JJ Jorge Julio 8.00
JK Jason Kubel 8.00
JM Justin Morneau 25.00
JN Joe Nathan 15.00
JS Jason Bay 15.00
KW Jake Westbrook 10.00
KF Keith Foulke 10.00
KG Ken Griffey Jr. 75.00
KM Kevin Mench 10.00
KS Kirk Saarloos 8.00
KY Kevin Youkilis 20.00
LN Laynce Nix/SP 8.00
LO Lyle Overbay 10.00
MH Matt Holliday 25.00
MK Mark Kotsay 10.00
MM Melvin Mora 15.00
NM Nate McLouth/SP 15.00
RC Ryan Church 15.00
RG Ryan Garko 15.00
RI Juan Rivera/SP 8.00
RJ Reed Johnson 15.00
RU Carlos Ruiz 10.00
SC Sean Casey/SP 10.00
SD Stephen Drew 25.00
SP Scott Podsednik/SP 20.00
TI Tadahito Iguchi 25.00
VE Justin Verlander 30.00
WM Wily Mo Pena 15.00
XN Xavier Nady 15.00
YB Yuniesky Betancourt 20.00
Common Player: 10.00
AC Alberto Callaspo 10.00
AG Alex Gordon 40.00
AI Akinori Iwamura/SP 30.00
AS Angel Sanchez 10.00
BA Jeff Baker 10.00
BB Brian Burres 10.00
BE Josh Beckett/SP 40.00
BO Ben Broussard 10.00
BU B.J. Upton/SP 40.00
CB Craig Biggio/SP 40.00
CC Carl Crawford/SP 20.00
CR Cal Ripken Jr./SP 125.00
DJ Derek Jeter 140.00
DY Delmon Young/SP 20.00
ED Elijah Dukes 15.00
FH Felix Hernandez 30.00
IK Ian Kinsler/SP 15.00
IS Ian Snell 15.00
JD J.D. Drew/SP 15.00
KG Ken Griffey Jr./SP 75.00
KI Kei Igawa/SP 50.00
NC Nelson Cruz 10.00
OP Oliver Perez/SP 20.00
RA Chris Ray 15.00
SA Juan Salas 10.00
SH Sean Henn 10.00
YO Chris Young 20.00
ZS Zack Segovia 15.00

Game Materials

NM/M
Common Player: 4.00
Patch: 2-4X
AJ Andruw Jones 8.00
AP Albert Pujols 20.00
BE Josh Beckett 6.00
BR Brian Roberts 6.00
BS Ben Sheets 6.00
CA Chris Carpenter 8.00
CB Carlos Beltran 10.00
CC Carl Crawford 6.00
CD Carlos Delgado 8.00
CL Carlos Lee 6.00
CP Corey Patterson 4.00
CS C.C. Sabathia 6.00
DJ Derek Jeter 20.00
DO David Ortiz 10.00
DW Dontrelle Willis 6.00
EC Eric Chavez 4.00
FH Felix Hernandez 8.00
HU Torii Hunter 6.00
IR Ivan Rodriguez 8.00
JB Jason Bay 8.00
JG Jason Giambi 8.00
JM Joe Mauer 8.00
JR Jose Reyes 10.00
JS Johan Santana 8.00
JU Juan Uribe 4.00
JV Justin Verlander 15.00
KG Ken Griffey Jr. 15.00
MC Miguel Cabrera 8.00
MH Matt Holliday 8.00
MM Melvin Mora 4.00
MO Justin Morneau 10.00
MR Manny Ramirez 8.00
MS Mike Sweeney 4.00
MT Miguel Tejada 6.00
MU Mike Mussina 8.00
OR Magglio Ordonez 4.00
PF Prince Fielder 15.00
RH Roy Halladay 6.00
RZ Ryan Zimmerman 8.00
SR Scott Rolen 8.00
TH Tim Hudson 4.00
VM Victor Martinez 6.00
Series 2: 5.00
AB A.J. Burnett 4.00
AP Albert Pujols 20.00
AR Alex Rios 4.00
BA Bobby Abreu 5.00
BC Bartolo Colon 4.00
BJ Bobby Jenks 4.00
CC Carl Crawford 5.00
CJ Chipper Jones 10.00
CS Curt Schilling 8.00
CU Chase Utley 10.00
DJ Derek Jeter 20.00
EB Erik Bedard 12.00
EN Juan Encarnacion 4.00
FR Jeff Francoeur/SP 10.00
GS Gary Sheffield 8.00
HB Hank Blalock 4.00
HO Trevor Hoffman 4.00
JD Johnny Damon 8.00
JE Jim Edmonds 5.00
JF Jeff Francis 4.00
JS John Smoltz 10.00
JT Jim Thome 8.00
JV Jose Vidro 4.00
KG Ken Griffey Jr. 15.00
LB Lance Berkman 4.00
LG Luis Gonzalez 4.00
MR Manny Ramirez 8.00
MT Mark Teixeira 8.00
RB Rocco Baldelli 4.00
RJ Randy Johnson 8.00
RN Ricky Nolasco 4.00
RO Roy Oswalt 8.00
RW Rickie Weeks 4.00
SD Stephen Drew 4.00
SK Scott Kazmir 4.00
SR Scott Rolen 8.00
TG Tom Glavine 8.00
TH Todd Helton 8.00
TN Trot Nixon 4.00
VG Vladimir Guerrero 8.00
ZD Zachary Duke 4.00

First Edition Aces

NM/M
Common Player: .50
Inserted 1:4
BW Brandon Webb .50
CC Chris Carpenter .75
CS Curt Schilling .75
CZ Carlos Zambrano .50
DW Dontrelle Willis .50
FH Felix Hernandez .50
JS Johan Santana .75
JV Justin Verlander .75
PM Pedro Martinez .75
RC Roger Clemens 2.00
RH Roy Halladay .50
SA C.C. Sabathia .50
SM John Smoltz .50
RJ Randy Johnson .75
SK Scott Kazmir .50

First Edition Foundations

NM/M
Common Player: .50
Inserted 1:6
AL Adam Lind 1.00
AM Andrew Miller 3.00
DM David Murphy .50
DY Delmon Young 1.00
FL Fred Lewis .50
GP Glen Perkins .50
JA Joaquin Arias .50
JF Josh Fields .50
JO Jerry Owens .50
JS Jeff Salazar .50
MM Mitch Maier .50
MO Miguel Montero .50
PH Philip Humber .50
RB Ryan Braun .50
RS Ryan Sweeney .50
SM Scott Moore .50
SR Shawn Riggans .50
TC Travis Chick .50
TT Troy Tulowitzki 1.00
UJ Ubaldo Jimenez .50

First Edition Leading Off

NM/M
Common Player: .50
Inserted 1:6
AS Alfonso Soriano 1.00
BR Brian Roberts .50
CF Chone Figgins .50
DR Dave Roberts .50
FR Ryan Freel .50
GS Grady Sizemore 1.00
HR Hanley Ramirez 1.00
IS Ichiro Suzuki 2.00
JD Johnny Damon 1.00
JP Juan Pierre .50
JR Jose Reyes 2.00
RF Rafael Furcal .50
RO Jimmy Rollins .75
SP Scott Podsednik .50
WT Willy Taveras .50

First Edition Momentum Swing

NM/M
Common Player: .50
Inserted 1:6
AD Adam Dunn .75
AJ Andruw Jones 1.00
AP Albert Pujols 2.50
AR Alex Rodriguez 2.50
AS Alfonso Soriano 1.00
CB Carlos Beltran 1.00
CD Carlos Delgado .75
DL Derrek Lee .75
DO David Ortiz 1.00
JB Jason Bay .75
JD Jermaine Dye .50
JG Jason Giambi .75
JM Justin Morneau 1.00
JT Jim Thome .75
LB Lance Berkman .75
MC Miguel Cabrera 1.00
MT Mark Teixeira .75
RH Ryan Howard 2.00
TH Travis Hafner .75
VG Vladimir Guerrero 1.00

First Edition Pennant Chasers

NM/M
Common Player: .25
Inserted 1:4
AR Aramis Ramirez .75
CC Carl Crawford .75
CG Carlos Guillen .25
CJ Chipper Jones 1.00
CU Chase Utley 1.00
DA Johnny Damon 1.00
DU Dan Uggla .25
DW David Wright 1.50
FS Freddy Sanchez .25
JM Joe Mauer .75
JR Juan Rivera .25
KG Ken Griffey Jr. 2.00
MH Matt Holliday .50
MR Manny Ramirez 1.00
MT Miguel Tejada .50
MY Michael Young .50
NG Nomar Garciaparra .75
NS Nick Swisher .50
OH Orlando Hudson .25
PF Prince Fielder .75
PK Paul Konerko .50
RD Ray Durham .25
RI Raul Ibanez .25
RO Roy Oswalt .50
RZ Ryan Zimmerman .75
SR Scott Rolen .75
TE Mark Teahen .25
TH Trevor Hoffman .50
VM Victor Martinez .50
VW Vernon Wells .50

Cal Ripken Box Set

NM/M
Complete Set (45): 35.00
Common Ripken: 1.00
1-45 Cal Ripken Jr. 1.00

2007 Upper Deck Spectrum

NM/M
Complete Set (149):
Common Player (1-100): .25
Common Auto. (101-149): 10.00
Pack (5): 6.00
Box (20): 110.00
1 Miguel Tejada .50
2 Brian Roberts .40
3 Melvin Mora .25
4 David Ortiz 1.00
5 Manny Ramirez .75
6 Jason Varitek .50
7 Curt Schilling .75
8 Jim Thome .50
9 Paul Konerko .40
10 Jermaine Dye .40
11 Travis Hafner .50
12 Victor Martinez .40
13 Grady Sizemore .50
14 C.C. Sabathia .40
15 Ivan Rodriguez .50
16 Magglio Ordonez .25
17 Carlos Guillen .25
18 Justin Verlander .50
19 Shane Costa .25
20 Emil Brown .25
21 Mark Teahen .25
22 Vladimir Guerrero .75
23 Jered Weaver .50
24 Juan Rivera .25
25 Justin Morneau .75
26 Joe Mauer .50
27 Torii Hunter .40
28 Johan Santana .75
29 Derek Jeter 2.00
30 Alex Rodriguez 2.00
31 Johnny Damon .75
32 Jason Giambi .50
33 Frank Thomas .50
34 Nick Swisher .40
35 Eric Chavez .40
36 Ichiro Suzuki 1.50
37 Raul Ibanez .25
38 Richie Sexson .40
39 Carl Crawford .40
40 Rocco Baldelli .40
41 Scott Kazmir .40
42 Michael Young .40
43 Mark Teixeira .50
44 Carlos Lee .50
45 Gary Matthews .25
46 Vernon Wells .40
47 Roy Halladay .50
48 Lyle Overbay .25
49 Brandon Webb .50
50 Conor Jackson .25
51 Stephen Drew .50
52 Chipper Jones .75
53 Andruw Jones .50
54 Adam LaRoche .25
55 John Smoltz .50
56 Derrek Lee .50
57 Aramis Ramirez .50
58 Carlos Zambrano .50
59 Ken Griffey Jr. 1.50
60 Adam Dunn .50
61 Aaron Harang .40
62 Todd Helton .50
63 Matt Holliday .50
64 Garrett Atkins .40
65 Miguel Cabrera .75
66 Hanley Ramirez .50
67 Dontrelle Willis .50
68 Lance Berkman .50
69 Roy Oswalt .50
70 Roger Clemens 1.50
71 J.D. Drew .40
72 Nomar Garciaparra .75
73 Rafael Furcal .40
74 Jeff Kent .40
75 Prince Fielder 1.00
76 Bill Hall .40
77 Rickie Weeks .40
78 Jose Reyes .75
79 David Wright 1.00
80 Carlos Delgado .50
81 Carlos Beltran .50
82 Ryan Howard 1.50
83 Chase Utley .75
84 Jimmy Rollins .50
85 Jason Bay .40
86 Freddy Sanchez .25
87 Zachary Duke .25
88 Trevor Hoffman .25
89 Adrian Gonzalez .25
90 Mike Piazza .75
91 Ray Durham .25
92 Omar Vizquel .25
93 Jason Schmidt .40
94 Albert Pujols 2.00
95 Scott Rolen .75
96 Jim Edmonds .40
97 Chris Carpenter .50
98 Alfonso Soriano .75
99 Ryan Zimmerman .50
100 Nick Johnson .25
101 Adam Lind **(RC)** 15.00
102 Alexi Casilla/SP **RC** 40.00
103 Andrew Miller **RC** 50.00
104 Andy Cannizaro **RC** 15.00
105 Angel Sanchez/SP **RC** 20.00
106 Brian Stokes **(RC)** 10.00
107 Carlos Maldonado **(RC)** 15.00
108 Cesar Jimenez **RC** 10.00
109 Chris Stewart **RC** 10.00
111 David Murphy **(RC)** 10.00
112 Delmon Young/SP **(RC)** 30.00
113 Delwyn Young **(RC)** 15.00
114 Dennis Sarfate/SP **(RC)** 10.00
116 Drew Anderson **(RC)** 10.00
117 Fred Lewis **(RC)** 10.00
118 Glen Perkins **(RC)** 15.00
119 Hector Gimenez/SP **(RC)** 10.00
120 Jeff Baker **(RC)** 10.00
121 Jeff Fiorentino **(RC)** 10.00
122 Jeff Salazar **(RC)** 10.00
124 Joaquin Arias/SP **(RC)** 15.00
125 Jon Knott/SP **(RC)** 15.00
128 Juan Morillo **RC** 10.00
129 Juan Perez/SP **RC** 15.00
130 Juan Salas **(RC)** 10.00
131 Justin Hampson **(RC)** 10.00
132 Kevin Hooper/SP **(RC)** 25.00
133 Kevin Kouzmanoff **(RC)** 15.00
134 Michael Bourn **(RC)** 15.00
135 Miguel Montero/SP **(RC)** 15.00
136 Mike Rabelo/SP **RC** 25.00
137 Mitch Maier **(RC)** 15.00
138 Oswaldo Navarro/SP **RC** 15.00
139 Patrick Misch **(RC)** 10.00
140 Philip Humber **(RC)** 20.00
141 Ryan Braun **(RC)** 15.00
143 Ryan Sweeney **(RC)** 10.00
144 Scott Moore **(RC)** 10.00
145 Sean Henn/SP **(RC)** 20.00
146 Shawn Riggans/SP **(RC)** 20.00
148 Troy Tulowitzki **(RC)** 25.00
149 Ubaldo Jimenez **(RC)** 10.00

Gold

Stars (1-100): 5-10X
Production 99 Sets

Red

Stars (1-100): 5-10X
Production 99 Sets

Jersey Number

Jersey # (25-57): 5-10X
No pricing production 1-24.
Cards are #'d to jersey number.

Grand Slamarama

NM/M
Common Player: 10.00
AD Adam Dunn 15.00
AP Albert Pujols 50.00
AR Alex Rodriguez 40.00
BA Bobby Abreu 15.00
BG Brian Giles 10.00
CD Carlos Delgado 20.00
CJ Chipper Jones 30.00
DA Johnny Damon 25.00
DO David Ortiz 30.00
DW David Wright 40.00
HA Travis Hafner 15.00
JD Jermaine Dye 15.00
JM Justin Morneau 20.00
JT Jim Thome 25.00
KG Ken Griffey Jr. 40.00
MR Manny Ramirez 25.00
NG Nomar Garciaparra 15.00
RH Ryan Howard 40.00
RS Richie Sexson 20.00
VG Vladimir Guerrero 20.00

Ripken Road to the Hall

NM/M
Common Ripken: 8.00
Production 99 Sets
Autographs: No Pricing
Production Five Sets
CR1-CR100 Cal Ripken Jr. 8.00

Rookie Retrospectrum

NM/M
Common Player: .50
Red: 2-4X
Production 99 Sets
AE Andre Ethier .50
AW Adam Wainwright 1.00
BA Josh Barfield .50
BB Boof Bonser .50
BO Jason Botts .50
CA Matt Capps .50
CB Chad Billingsley .50
CD Chris Demaria .50
CF Choo Freeman .50
CH Clay Hensley .50
CQ Carlos Quentin .50
DE Chris Denorfia .50
DU Dan Uggla .50
FC Fausto Carmona .50
FL Francisco Liriano 1.00
HA Cole Hamels 1.00
HK Howie Kendrick 1.00
HR Hanley Ramirez 1.00
JA Jeremy Accardo .50
JB Jason Bergmann .50
JC Jose Capellan .50
JD Joey Devine .50
JH Jeremy Hermida .50
JK Jason Kubel .50
JL Jon Lester 1.00
JP Jonathan Papelbon 1.00
JV Justin Verlander 1.00
JW Jered Weaver 1.00
JZ Joel Zumaya 1.00
KM Kendry Morales .50
LM Lastings Milledge 1.00
MA Nicholas Markakis 1.00
MC Matt Cain 1.00
ME Melky Cabrera .50
MG Matt Garza 1.00
MJ Mike Jacobs .50
MM Matt Murton .50
NM Nate McLouth .50
PF Prince Fielder 1.00
RA Reggie Abercrombie .50
RG Ryan Garko .50
RM Russell Martin .50
RP Ronny Paulino .50
RS Ryan Shealy .50
RZ Ryan Zimmerman 1.00
SD Stephen Drew 1.00
TB Taylor Buchholz .50
TG Tony Gwynn Jr. .50
TS Takashi Saito .50
WI Josh Willingham .50

2007 Upper Deck Spectrum Season Retrospectrum

NM/M
Common Player: .50
Red: 2-4X
Production 99 Sets
AH Aaron Harang .50
AP Albert Pujols 4.00
AR Aramis Ramirez 1.00
AS Alfonso Soriano 1.50
BA Bobby Abreu .50
BH Bill Hall .50
BL Joe Blanton .50
CA Miguel Cabrera 1.50
CB Carlos Beltran 1.00
CC Chris Carpenter 1.00
CD Carlos Delgado 1.00
CO Jose Contreras .50
CU Chase Utley 1.50
CW Chien-Ming Wang 1.50
CY Chris Young .50
CZ Carlos Zambrano 1.00
DJ Derek Jeter 4.00
DO David Ortiz 1.50
FS Freddy Sanchez .50
FT Frank Thomas 1.00
GM Greg Maddux 2.50
GS Grady Sizemore 1.50
HO Trevor Hoffman .50
HR Hanley Ramirez 1.00
JB Jason Bay 1.00
JC Joe Crede .50
JD Johnny Damon 1.50
JM Joe Mauer 1.00
JR Jose Reyes 1.50
JS Jeff Suppan 1.50
JT Jim Thome 1.00
KG Ken Griffey Jr. 3.00
MC Michael Cuddyer .50
MH Matt Holliday 1.00
ML Mark Loretta .50
MO Justin Morneau 1.50
MY Michael Young 1.00
NG Nomar Garciaparra 1.50
OR Magglio Ordonez .50
OV Omar Vizquel .50
RC Roger Clemens 3.00
RF Rafael Furcal .50
RH Ryan Howard 3.00
SA Johan Santana 1.50
SK Scott Kazmir .50
TH Travis Hafner 1.00
TI Tadahito Iguchi .50
VG Vladimir Guerrero 1.50
VW Vernon Wells .50
WT Willy Taveras .50

Shining Star Signatures

NM/M
Production 15-99
AD Adam Dunn/99 25.00
AG Adrian Gonzalez/99 20.00
AR Alex Rios/99 20.00
BH Bill Hall/99 20.00
CZ Carlos Zambrano/99 30.00
DJ Derek Jeter/54 200.00
DL Derrek Lee/99 30.00
DO David Ortiz/99 60.00
GA Garrett Atkins/99 15.00
HR Hanley Ramirez/99 25.00
JB Jason Bay/99 25.00
JM Joe Mauer/99 25.00
JR Jose Reyes/99 30.00
JS Johan Santana/99 50.00
KG Ken Griffey Jr./99 70.00
KY Kevin Youkilis/99 20.00
MH Matt Holliday/99 25.00
MO Justin Morneau/99 30.00
RI Juan Rivera/99 15.00
TH Travis Hafner/72 30.00

Aligning the Stars

NM/M
Production 99 Sets

BPO David Ortiz, Lance Berkman, Albert Pujols 30.00
CJM Roger Clemens, Greg Maddux, Randy Johnson 30.00
CRR Scott Rolen, Aramis Ramirez, Miguel Cabrera 25.00
DBF Lance Berkman, Prince Fielder, Carlos Delgado 20.00
GRS Manny Ramirez, Gary Sheffield, Ken Griffey Jr. 35.00
HRW Trevor Hoffman, Mariano Rivera, Billy Wagner 20.00
HTT Travis Hafner, Frank Thomas, Jim Thome 20.00
JDB Andruw Jones, Carlos Beltran, Adam Dunn 25.00
JGC Jason Giambi, Derek Jeter, Robinson Cano 60.00
JTY Derek Jeter, Miguel Tejada, Michael Young 30.00
LHP Albert Pujols, Derrek Lee, Todd Helton 30.00
LVP Francisco Liriano, Justin Verlander, Jonathan Papelbon 30.00
MKT Mark Teixeira, Justin Morneau, Paul Konerko 20.00
MOW Pedro Martinez, Roy Oswalt, Dontrelle Willis 20.00
RFR Jose Reyes, Jimmy Rollins, Rafael Furcal 20.00
RMM Ivan Rodriguez, Victor Martinez, Joe Mauer 20.00
RSV Jason Varitek, Curt Schilling, Manny Ramirez 30.00
SBA Carlos Beltran, Alfonso Soriano, Bobby Abreu 25.00
SCF Carl Crawford, Grady Sizemore, Chone Figgins 20.00
SHS Johan Santana, Roy Halladay, C.C. Sabathia 20.00
WGD Vladimir Guerrero, Vernon Wells, Johnny Damon 20.00

2007 Upper Deck Spectrum Super Swatches

NM/M
Production 50 Sets
AD Adam Dunn 10.00
AJ Andruw Jones 15.00
AP Albert Pujols 35.00
AR Aramis Ramirez 10.00
BA Bobby Abreu 10.00
BC Bobby Crosby 10.00
BE Josh Beckett 10.00
BU B.J. Upton 15.00
BZ Barry Zito 10.00
CB Carlos Beltran 20.00
CC Carl Crawford 10.00
CD Carlos Delgado 15.00
CJ Chipper Jones 15.00
CL Roger Clemens 25.00
CS Curt Schilling 15.00
CU Chase Utley 20.00
DA Johnny Damon 15.00
DJ Derek Jeter 35.00
DL Derrek Lee 15.00
DO David Ortiz 25.00
FT Frank Thomas 15.00
GS Gary Sheffield 15.00
HA Travis Hafner 10.00
HR Hanley Ramirez 10.00
JB Jeremy Bonderman 15.00
JD J.D. Drew 10.00
JR Jose Reyes 25.00
JS Johan Santana 15.00
JT Jim Thome 15.00
JV Jason Varitek 15.00
JW Jered Weaver 15.00
KG Ken Griffey Jr. 30.00
KJ Kenji Johjima 15.00
LB Lance Berkman 10.00
MT Miguel Tejada 10.00
PE Andy Pettitte 10.00
PF Prince Fielder 15.00
PK Paul Konerko 10.00
RB Rocco Baldelli 10.00
RC Robinson Cano 20.00
RH Roy Halladay 10.00
RJ Randy Johnson 15.00
RS Richie Sexson 10.00
SR Scott Rolen 15.00
TH Todd Helton 10.00
VE Justin Verlander 15.00
VG Vladimir Guerrero 15.00
VW Vernon Wells 10.00

Spectrum Swatches

NM/M
Production 199 Sets
Gold: 1X
Production 75 Sets
Patch: 2-3X
Production 50 Sets
AB Adrian Beltre 4.00
AG Adrian Gonzalez 6.00
AH Aaron Hill 4.00
AK Austin Kearns 4.00
AP Albert Pujols 25.00
AR Aaron Rowand 4.00
AS Alfonso Soriano 10.00
BA Bobby Abreu 6.00
BC Bartolo Colon 4.00
BG Brian Giles 4.00
BI Brandon Inge 4.00
BJ B.J. Upton 6.00
BL Joe Blanton 4.00
BR B.J. Ryan 4.00
BS Ben Sheets 6.00
BW Billy Wagner 6.00
CA Jorge Cantu 4.00
CB Clint Barmes 4.00
CC Chad Cordero 4.00
CD Chris Duffy 4.00
CG Carlos Guillen 4.00
CK Casey Kotchman 4.00
CO Coco Crisp 6.00
CR Bobby Crosby 4.00
CS C.C. Sabathia 6.00
CU Chase Utley 15.00
CY Chris Young 6.00
CZ Carlos Zambrano 8.00
DA Johnny Damon 10.00
DC Daniel Cabrera 6.00
DH Danny Haren 6.00
DJ Derek Jeter 25.00
DL Derrek Lee 8.00
DM Dallas McPherson 4.00
DO David Ortiz 15.00
DU Dan Uggla 6.00
DW Dontrelle Willis 6.00
ES Johnny Estrada 6.00
FG Freddy Garcia 4.00
FL Francisco Liriano 10.00
FS Freddy Sanchez 4.00
GA Garrett Atkins 8.00
GC Gustavo Chacin 4.00
GR Curtis Granderson 8.00
GS Grady Sizemore 10.00
HR Hanley Ramirez 8.00
HS Huston Street 6.00
HU Aubrey Huff 4.00
IS Ian Snell 8.00
JB Jeremy Bonderman 10.00
JC Joe Crede 6.00
JD J.D. Drew 8.00
JE Jermaine Dye 6.00
JF Jeff Francoeur 8.00
JH J.J. Hardy 6.00
JM Joe Mauer 10.00
JN Joe Nathan 6.00
JP Jake Peavy 8.00
JR Jose Reyes 15.00
JT Jim Thome 8.00
JU Justin Duchscherer 4.00
JW Jake Westbrook 4.00
KG Ken Griffey Jr. 25.00
KH Khalil Greene 6.00
LN Laynce Nix 4.00
MA Matt Cain 8.00
MB Mark Buehrle 4.00
MC Mike Cameron 4.00
ME Morgan Ensberg 4.00
MH Matt Holliday 8.00
MI Michael Cuddyer 6.00
MM Melvin Mora 4.00
MO Justin Morneau 10.00
MT Miguel Tejada 8.00
NL Noah Lowry 4.00
NS Nick Swisher 6.00
OR Magglio Ordonez 6.00
PA Jonathan Papelbon 15.00
PE Jhonny Peralta 6.00
PF Prince Fielder 10.00
PL Paul LoDuca 6.00
RA Aramis Ramirez 8.00
RF Rafael Furcal 8.00
RH Rich Harden 8.00
RJ Reed Johnson 4.00
RO Brian Roberts 8.00
RQ Robb Quinlan 4.00
RW Rickie Weeks 8.00
RZ Ryan Zimmerman 8.00
SC Sean Casey 4.00
SK Scott Kazmir 8.00
TH Torii Hunter 8.00
TI Tadahito Iguchi 6.00
TN Trot Nixon 6.00
VM Victor Martinez 6.00
WT Willy Taveras 6.00
YM Yadier Molina 8.00
ZD Zachary Duke 8.00
ZG Zack Greinke 6.00

Rookie Retrospectrum Signatures

NM/M
Production 199 unless noted.
BB Boof Bonser 15.00
BO Jason Botts 10.00
CA Matt Capps/134 10.00
CD Chris Demaria 8.00
CF Choo Freeman 8.00
CH Clay Hensley 10.00
CQ Carlos Quentin 25.00
DU Dan Uggla 15.00
FC Fausto Carmona/158 10.00
FL Francisco Liriano 25.00
HA Cole Hamels/90 35.00
HK Howie Kendrick 20.00
HR Hanley Ramirez 25.00
JA Jeremy Accardo/32 20.00
JC Jose Capellan 6.00
JD Joey Devine 8.00
JH Jeremy Hermida 10.00
JK Jason Kubel 10.00
JL Jon Lester 20.00
JP Jonathan Papelbon 40.00
JW Jered Weaver/99 40.00
JZ Joel Zumaya 20.00
KM Kendry Morales 15.00
MG Matt Garza 20.00
MJ Mike Jacobs 20.00
MM Matt Murton 20.00
RA Reggie Abercrombie 8.00
RG Ryan Garko 15.00
RM Russell Martin 25.00
RS Ryan Shealy 15.00
RZ Ryan Zimmerman 40.00
SD Stephen Drew 25.00
TB Taylor Buchholz 10.00
TS Takashi Saito 30.00
WI Josh Willingham 15.00

2007 UD Spectrum Season Retrospectrum Signatures

NM/M
Production 25 unless noted
AS Alfonso Soriano 75.00
BA Bobby Abreu 40.00
BH Bill Hall 20.00
BL Joe Blanton 15.00
CA Miguel Cabrera 50.00
CU Chase Utley 65.00
CZ Carlos Zambrano 35.00
DJ Derek Jeter 180.00
DO David Ortiz 80.00
FT Frank Thomas 75.00
GM Greg Maddux 150.00
HO Trevor Hoffman 30.00
HR Hanley Ramirez 25.00
JB Jason Bay 30.00
JM Joe Mauer 30.00
KG Ken Griffey Jr. 120.00
MH Matt Holliday 35.00
ML Mark Loretta 15.00
MO Justin Morneau 30.00
RC Roger Clemens 120.00
RF Rafael Furcal 30.00
SA Johan Santana 50.00
SK Scott Kazmir 25.00
TH Travis Hafner 40.00
TI Tadahito Iguchi 40.00
VG Vladimir Guerrero 60.00

2007 Upper Deck Spectrum Rookie Signatures Gold Die-cut

NM/M
Production 50 Sets
101 Adam Lind 40.00
103 Andrew Miller 100.00
104 Andy Cannizaro 25.00
105 Angel Sanchez 30.00
106 Brian Stokes 15.00
109 Chris Stewart 15.00
111 David Murphy 20.00
112 Delmon Young 40.00
113 Delwyn Young 25.00
114 Dennis Sarfate 20.00
116 Drew Anderson 15.00
117 Fred Lewis 20.00
118 Glen Perkins 20.00
120 Jeff Baker 20.00
121 Jeff Fiorentino 15.00
122 Jeff Salazar 15.00
125 Jon Knott 25.00
128 Juan Morillo 15.00
131 Justin Hampson 15.00
132 Kevin Hooper 40.00
133 Kevin Kouzmanoff 25.00
134 Michael Bourn 15.00
137 Mitch Maier 25.00
139 Patrick Misch 15.00
140 Philip Humber 30.00
141 Ryan Braun 20.00
143 Ryan Sweeney 20.00
144 Scott Moore 15.00
145 Sean Henn 30.00
146 Shawn Riggans 30.00
148 Troy Tulowitzki 35.00
149 Ubaldo Jimenez 15.00

Signature Patch

NM/M
Production 6-25
AG Adrian Gonzalez/25 40.00
AS Alfonso Soriano/25 65.00
BA Bobby Abreu/25 50.00
BJ B.J. Upton/25 30.00
BS Ben Sheets/25 35.00
CR Bobby Crosby/25 25.00
CZ Carlos Zambrano/25 40.00
DJ Derek Jeter/25 200.00
DL Derrek Lee/25 40.00
DO David Ortiz/25 100.00
DU Dan Uggla/25 35.00
DW Dontrelle Willis/25 40.00
GA Garrett Atkins/25 30.00

2007 Upper Deck Premier

NM/M
Common Player (1-200): 4.00
Production 99 Sets
Common RC (201-244): 4.00
Production 199 Sets
Box (1): 300.00
1 Roy Campanella 10.00
2 Ty Cobb 12.00
3 Mickey Cochrane 4.00
4 Dizzy Dean 8.00
5 Don Drysdale 8.00
6 Jimmie Foxx 10.00
7 Lou Gehrig 15.00
8 Lefty Grove 4.00
9 Rogers Hornsby 10.00
10 Walter Johnson 10.00
11 Eddie Mathews 10.00
12 Christy Mathewson 10.00
13 Johnny Mize 8.00
14 Thurman Munson 10.00
15 Mel Ott 8.00
16 Satchel Paige 10.00
17 Jackie Robinson 10.00
18 Babe Ruth 20.00
19 George Sisler 4.00
20 Honus Wagner 10.00
21 Cy Young 10.00
22 Luis Aparicio 4.00
23 Johnny Bench 10.00
24 Yogi Berra 10.00
25 Rod Carew 4.00
26 Orlando Cepeda 6.00
27 Bob Feller 8.00
28 Carlton Fisk 8.00
29 Bob Gibson 8.00
30 Jim "Catfish" Hunter 4.00
31 Reggie Jackson 8.00
32 Al Kaline 8.00
33 Harmon Killebrew 8.00
34 Buck Leonard 4.00
35 Juan Marichal 4.00
36 Bill Mazeroski 6.00
37 Willie McCovey 6.00
38 Joe Morgan 6.00
39 Eddie Murray 6.00
40 Jim Palmer 6.00
41 Tony Perez 6.00
42 Pee Wee Reese 4.00
43 Brooks Robinson 8.00
44 Nolan Ryan 20.00
45 Mike Schmidt 10.00
46 Tom Seaver 8.00
47 Enos Slaughter 4.00
48 Willie Stargell 8.00
49 Early Wynn 4.00
50 Robin Yount 8.00
51 Tony Gwynn 8.00
52 Cal Ripken Jr. 20.00
53 Ernie Banks 10.00
54 Wade Boggs 8.00
55 Steve Carlton 6.00
56 Will Clark 8.00
57 Fergie Jenkins 4.00
58 Bo Jackson 10.00
59 Don Mattingly 15.00
60 Stan Musial 10.00
61 Frank Robinson 8.00
62 Ryne Sandberg 10.00
63 Ozzie Smith 8.00
64 Carl Yastrzemski 10.00
65 Dave Winfield 8.00
66 Paul Molitor 8.00
67 Jason Bay 6.00
68 Freddy Sanchez 4.00
69 Josh Beckett 6.00
70 Carlos Beltran 8.00
71 Craig Biggio 6.00
72 Matt Holliday 6.00
73 A.J. Burnett 4.00
74 Miguel Cabrera 8.00
75 Dontrelle Willis 6.00
76 Chris Carpenter 8.00
77 Roger Clemens 15.00
78 Johnny Damon 8.00
79 Jermaine Dye 4.00
80 Jim Thome 8.00
81 Vladimir Guerrero 8.00
82 Travis Hafner 6.00
83 Victor Martinez 6.00
84 Trevor Hoffman 6.00
85 Derek Jeter 20.00
86 Ken Griffey Jr. 15.00
87 Randy Johnson 8.00
88 Andruw Jones 8.00
89 Derrek Lee 8.00
90 Greg Maddux 10.00
91 Magglio Ordonez 4.00
92 David Ortiz 10.00
93 Jake Peavy 6.00
94 Roy Oswalt 6.00
95 Mike Piazza 10.00
96 Jose Reyes 15.00
97 Ivan Rodriguez 8.00
98 Johan Santana 8.00
99 Scott Rolen 8.00
100 Curt Schilling 8.00
101 John Smoltz 6.00
102 Alfonso Soriano 8.00
103 Miguel Tejada 6.00
104 Frank Thomas 8.00
105 Chase Utley 10.00
106 Joe Mauer 8.00
107 Alex Rodriguez 20.00
108 Alex Rios 6.00
109 Justin Verlander 8.00
110 Ryan Howard 15.00
111 Jered Weaver 6.00
112 Francisco Liriano 6.00
113 David Wright 10.00
114 Felix Hernandez 8.00
115 Jeremy Sowers 4.00
116 Cole Hamels 8.00
117 B.J. Upton 6.00
118 Chien-Ming Wang 35.00
119 Justin Morneau 8.00
120 Jonny Gomes 4.00
121 Adrian Gonzalez 6.00
122 Bill Hall 6.00
123 Rich Harden 4.00
124 Rich Hill 4.00
125 Tadahito Iguchi 4.00
126 Scott Kazmir 4.00
127 Howie Kendrick 6.00
128 Dan Uggla 4.00
129 Hanley Ramirez 8.00
130 Josh Willingham 4.00
131 Nicholas Markakis 6.00
132 Grady Sizemore 8.00
133 Ian Kinsler 6.00
134 Jonathan Papelbon 8.00
135 Ryan Zimmerman 8.00
136 Stephen Drew 8.00
137 Adam Wainwright 4.00
138 Joel Zumaya 6.00
139 Prince Fielder 10.00
140 Carl Crawford 6.00
141 Huston Street 4.00
142 Matt Cain 8.00
143 Andre Ethier 6.00
144 Brian McCann 4.00
145 Josh Barfield 4.00
146 Anibal Sanchez 4.00
147 Brian Roberts 6.00
148 Brandon Webb 6.00
149 Chipper Jones 10.00
150 Tim Hudson 4.00
151 Adam LaRoche 4.00
152 Jeff Francoeur 8.00
153 Marcus Giles 4.00
154 Jason Varitek 8.00
155 Coco Crisp 4.00
156 Manny Ramirez 8.00
157 Trot Nixon 4.00
158 Carlos Zambrano 6.00
159 Mark Prior 6.00
160 Aramis Ramirez 6.00
161 Mark Buehrle 4.00
162 Paul Konerko 6.00
163 Adam Dunn 8.00
164 C.C. Sabathia 6.00
165 Todd Helton 8.00
166 Garrett Atkins 4.00
167 Jeremy Bonderman 6.00
168 Curtis Granderson 4.00
169 Sean Casey 4.00
170 Lance Berkman 6.00
171 Brad Lidge 4.00
172 Reggie Sanders 4.00
173 Brad Penny 4.00
174 Nomar Garciaparra 8.00
175 Jeff Kent 4.00
176 Chone Figgins 4.00
177 Ben Sheets 6.00
178 Rickie Weeks 6.00
179 Joe Nathan 4.00
180 Torii Hunter 6.00
181 Carlos Delgado 8.00
182 Tom Glavine 6.00
183 Paul LoDuca 4.00
184 Mariano Rivera 8.00
185 Robinson Cano 8.00
186 Bobby Abreu 6.00
187 Hideki Matsui 10.00
188 Barry Zito 6.00
189 Eric Chavez 4.00
190 Jimmy Rollins 6.00
191 Khalil Greene 4.00
192 Brian Giles 4.00
193 Jason Schmidt 4.00
194 Ichiro Suzuki 30.00
195 David Eckstein 4.00
196 Jim Edmonds 6.00
197 Mark Teixeira 6.00
198 Michael Young 6.00
199 Vernon Wells 6.00
200 Roy Halladay 6.00
201 Delmon Young **(RC)** 8.00
202 Andrew Miller **RC** 20.00
203 Troy Tulowitzki **(RC)** 20.00
204 Jeff Fiorentino **(RC)** 4.00
205 David Murphy **(RC)** 4.00
206 Jeff Baker **(RC)** 4.00
207 Kevin Hooper **(RC)** 4.00
208 Kevin Kouzmanoff **(RC)** 6.00
209 Adam Lind **(RC)** 6.00
210 Mike Rabelo **RC** 6.00
212 Mitch Maier **RC** 6.00
213 Ryan Braun **(RC)** 4.00
214 Vinny Rottino **(RC)** 4.00
215 Drew Anderson **(RC)** 4.00
216 Alexi Casilla **RC** 6.00
217 Glen Perkins **(RC)** 4.00
218 Cesar Jimenez **RC** 4.00
219 Tim Gradoville **RC** 4.00
220 Shane Youman **RC** 4.00
221 Billy Sadler **(RC)** 4.00
222 Patrick Misch **(RC)** 4.00
223 Juan Salas **(RC)** 4.00
224 Beltran Perez **(RC)** 4.00
225 Hector Gimenez **(RC)** 4.00
226 Philip Humber **(RC)** 4.00
227 Eric Stults **RC** 8.00
228 Dennis Sarfate **(RC)** 4.00
229 Andy Cannizaro **RC** 4.00
230 Juan Morillo **(RC)** 6.00
231 Fred Lewis **(RC)** 4.00
232 Ryan Sweeney **(RC)** 4.00
233 Chris Narveson **(RC)** 4.00
234 Michael Bourn **(RC)** 4.00
235 Joaquin Arias **(RC)** 4.00
236 Carlos Maldonado **(RC)** 4.00
237 Alvin Colina **RC** 4.00
238 Jon Knott **(RC)** 4.00
239 Justin Hampson **(RC)** 4.00
240 Jeff Salazar **(RC)** 4.00
241 Josh Fields **(RC)** 4.00
242 Delwyn Young **(RC)** 4.00
243 Daisuke Matsuzaka **RC** 75.00
244 Kei Igawa **RC** 15.00

Bronze

Bronze (201-244): 1X
Production 75 Sets

Printing Plates

Production one set per color.

Gold

Gold (201-244): 1-1.5X
Production 49 Sets

Platinum

Production One Set

Silver

Silver (201-244): 1X
Production 99 Sets

Autograph Parallel

No Pricing
Production 25 Sets

Emerging Stars Dual Auto

NM/M
Production 50 Sets
Bronze: 1-1.5X
Production 25 Sets
Gold: No Pricing
Production 10 Sets
Platinum: No Pricing
Production One Set
BU Josh Barfield, Dan Uggla 25.00
BV Jeremy Bonderman, Justin Verlander 50.00
CA Carlos Rios, Carl Crawford 30.00
FJ Felix Hernandez, Jered Weaver 50.00
GB Josh Barfield, Adrian Gonzalez 25.00
GC Carl Crawford, Jonny Gomes 25.00
HP Philip Humber, Mike Pelfrey 35.00
HS Huston Street, Rich Harden 30.00
HV Rich Harden, Justin Verlander 40.00
IK Tadahito Iguchi, Ian Kinsler 25.00
KL Francisco Liriano, Scott Kazmir 35.00
KS Scott Kazmir, Jeremy Sowers 25.00
LH Jon Lester, Craig Hansen 40.00
MB Jeremy Brown, Joe Mauer 35.00
MG Justin Morneau, Adrian Gonzalez 40.00
MH Andrew Miller, Cole Hamels 65.00
MZ Andrew Miller, Joel Zumaya 50.00
PH Jonathan Papelbon, Craig Hansen 50.00
PW Jonathan Papelbon, Adam Wainwright 50.00
QD Carlos Quentin, Stephen Drew 30.00
RB Rickie Weeks, Bill Hall 40.00
RD Jose Reyes, Stephen Drew 60.00
RR Hanley Ramirez, Jose Reyes 75.00
RY Alex Rios, Delmon Young 40.00
SH Jeremy Sowers, Cole Hamels 25.00
SJ Anibal Sanchez, Josh Johnson 20.00

SW Adam Wainwright, Huston Street 30.00
TD Stephen Drew, Troy Tulowitzki 30.00
TR Troy Tulowitzki, Hanley Ramirez 30.00
UG Jonny Gomes, B.J. Upton 25.00
UR Dan Uggla, Hanley Ramirez 30.00
UU Chase Utley, Dan Uggla 50.00
VH Felix Hernandez, Justin Verlander 75.00
VM Justin Verlander, Andrew Miller 75.00
WE Josh Willingham, Andre Ethier 25.00
WK Jered Weaver, Howie Kendrick 40.00
WL Jered Weaver, Francisco Liriano 50.00
YT Delmon Young, Troy Tulowitzki 40.00
ZW Joel Zumaya, Adam Wainwright 30.00

Emerging Stars Triple Auto

NM/M
Production 50 Sets
Bronze: 1-1.5X
Production 25 Sets
Gold: No Pricing
Production 10 Sets
Platinum: No Pricing
Production One Set
ELS James Loney, Andre Ethier, Takashi Saito 50.00
HHL Cole Hamels, Rich Hill, Francisco Liriano 75.00
HQE Carlos Quentin, Matt Holliday, Andre Ethier 40.00
KUK Howie Kendrick, Dan Uggla, Ian Kinsler 40.00
LBG Matt Garza, Francisco Liriano, Boof Bonser 50.00
MHL Francisco Liriano, Cole Hamels, Andrew Miller 80.00
MKL Jason Kubel, Francisco Liriano, Justin Morneau 40.00
MSK Scott Kazmir, Jeremy Sowers, Andrew Miller 40.00
MVB Andrew Miller, Justin Verlander, Jeremy Bonderman 100.00
MYE Andre Ethier, Nicholas Markakis, Delmon Young 70.00
PSW Adam Wainwright, Huston Street, Jonathan Papelbon 50.00
QEY Carlos Quentin, Delmon Young, Andre Ethier 40.00
RRD Hanley Ramirez, Stephen Drew, Jose Reyes 75.00
SHK Scott Kazmir, Jeremy Sowers, Cole Hamels 50.00
TDR Troy Tulowitzki, Stephen Drew, Hanley Ramirez 50.00
THA Matt Holliday, Garrett Atkins, Troy Tulowitzki 50.00
UKW Howie Kendrick, Chase Utley, Rickie Weeks 60.00
UUW Rickie Weeks, Chase Utley, Dan Uggla 50.00
UYK B.J. Upton, Scott Kazmir, Delmon Young 50.00
VMZ Justin Verlander, Joel Zumaya, Andrew Miller 80.00
WHV Jered Weaver, Justin Verlander, Felix Hernandez 85.00
WZS Adam Wainwright, Joel Zumaya, Takashi Saito 40.00
YER Alex Rios, Delmon Young, Andre Ethier 40.00

Hallmarks Autographs

NM/M
Production 5-57
Gold: No Pricing
Production 25 Sets
Platinum: No Pricing
Production One Set
LA Luis Aparicio/57 25.00
MS Mike Schmidt/48 40.00
OS Ozzie Smith/57 50.00
PM Paul Molitor/39 25.00
RJ Reggie Jackson/47 50.00
RS Ryne Sandberg/40 60.00
RY Robin Yount/46 40.00
SC Steve Carlton/27 35.00
WF Whitey Ford/25 50.00
WM Willie McCovey/45 30.00

Insignias Autographs

NM/M
Production 50 Sets
Gold: 1-1.5X
Production 25 Sets
Platinum: No Pricing
Production One Set
AK Al Kaline 35.00
AM Andrew Miller 60.00
BU B.J. Upton 25.00
CR Cal Ripken Jr. 100.00
DJ Derek Jeter 150.00
DL Derrek Lee 30.00
DM Don Mattingly 60.00
DY Delmon Young 30.00
EB Ernie Banks 50.00
FH Felix Hernandez 50.00
JM Joe Mauer 40.00
JP Jake Peavy 30.00
JR Jose Reyes 80.00
JT Jim Thome 50.00
JW Jered Weaver 30.00
KG Ken Griffey Jr. 90.00
MO Justin Morneau 30.00
OS Ozzie Smith 50.00
PA Jim Palmer 20.00
TG Tony Gwynn 40.00
TT Troy Tulowitzki 25.00
WC Will Clark 25.00

Noteworthy Autographs

NM/M
Production 1-86 15.00
Gold: No Pricing
Production 25 Sets
Platinum: No Pricing
Production One Set
AD Andre Dawson/50 50.00
AK Al Kaline/50 50.00
AS Alfonso Soriano/35 35.00
BA Jeff Bagwell/75 75.00
BE Josh Beckett/50 40.00
BJ Bo Jackson/35 75.00
BR Brooks Robinson/35 40.00
CB Craig Biggio/65 40.00
CC Chris Carpenter/50 40.00
DB Dusty Baker/25 30.00
DE Dennis Eckersley/75 15.00
DS Don Sutton/50 15.00
FJ Fergie Jenkins/74 15.00
FR Frank Robinson/31 40.00
GS Gary Sheffield/86 30.00
JB Jim Bunning/54 30.00
JC Jack Clark/75 15.00
JM Juan Marichal/65 25.00
JP Jim Palmer/65 20.00
JS Johan Santana/65 50.00
KW Kerry Wood/35 20.00
LA Luis Aparicio/35 15.00
MM Mark Mulder/35 15.00
MO Justin Morneau/50 30.00
MT Miguel Tejada/50 25.00
PE Jake Peavy/55 30.00
PM Paul Molitor/40 25.00
RS Ryne Sandberg/45 50.00
TG Tom Glavine/47 60.00
TH Torii Hunter/26 30.00
WB Wade Boggs/45 25.00
AP Albert Pujols/49 200.00
BF Bob Feller/62 30.00
CF Carlton Fisk/37 40.00
CR Cal Ripken Jr./34 125.00
DJ Derek Jeter/44 150.00
DM Don Mattingly/35 75.00
HR Hanley Ramirez/51 30.00
JB Johnny Bench/45 50.00
JM Joe Mauer/36 40.00
JT Jim Thome/52 40.00
JZ Joel Zumaya/62 15.00
KG Ken Griffey Jr./56 75.00
RY Robin Yount/29 50.00
TG Tony Gwynn/56 40.00

Preeminence

NM/M
Production 50 Sets
Gold: 1-1.5X
Production 25 Sets
Platinum: No Pricing
Production One Set
AP Albert Pujols 200.00
BJ Bo Jackson 60.00
BR Brooks Robinson 25.00
CC Chris Carpenter 25.00
CR Cal Ripken Jr. 120.00
CY Carl Yastrzemski 50.00
DJ Derek Jeter 150.00
GM Greg Maddux 100.00
JB Johnny Bench 50.00
JM Joe Mauer 40.00
JT Jim Thome 40.00
JV Justin Verlander 50.00
KG Ken Griffey Jr. 75.00
MS Mike Schmidt 50.00
NR Nolan Ryan 90.00
RC Roger Clemens 100.00
RJ Reggie Jackson 50.00
RS Ryne Sandberg 60.00
SM Stan Musial 60.00
TG Tony Gwynn 40.00
VG Vladimir Guerrero 50.00

Foursomes

No Pricing
Production 15 Sets

Octographs

No Pricing
Production Five Sets

Pairings

NM/M
Production 25 Sets
AK Andruw Jones, Ken Griffey Jr. 125.00
BD Dave Winfield, Bo Jackson 75.00
BF Johnny Bench, Carlton Fisk 75.00
BJ Yogi Berra, Derek Jeter 250.00
BM Don Mattingly, Wade Boggs 120.00
BU Chase Utley, Craig Biggio 75.00
CG Chris Carpenter, Bob Gibson 50.00
CO Chris Carpenter, Roy Oswalt 60.00
CR Craig Biggio, Ryne Sandberg 100.00
ER Ernie Banks, Ryne Sandberg 150.00
FO Bob Feller, Roy Oswalt 125.00
GF Bob Feller, Bob Gibson 50.00
GR Cal Ripken Jr., Ken Griffey Jr. 250.00
JG Ken Griffey Jr., Derek Jeter 250.00
JW Dave Winfield, Reggie Jackson 75.00
MC Don Mattingly, Will Clark 80.00
MG Tony Gwynn, Stan Musial 125.00
MM Joe Mauer, Victor Martinez 50.00
MR Frank Robinson, Eddie Murray 75.00
OY Carl Yastrzemski, David Ortiz 125.00
PG Albert Pujols, Ken Griffey Jr. 250.00
RG Tony Gwynn, Cal Ripken Jr. 200.00
RJ Cal Ripken Jr., Derek Jeter 250.00
RN Roger Clemens, Nolan Ryan 275.00
RP Ivan Rodriguez, Mike Piazza 75.00
RR Cal Ripken Jr., Brooks Robinson 180.00
SA Luis Aparicio, Ozzie Smith 75.00
SB Brooks Robinson, Scott Rolen 60.00
SG Alfonso Soriano, Vladimir Guerrero 80.00
SM Ryne Sandberg, Joe Morgan 75.00
TM Willie McCovey, Jim Thome 60.00
WC Dontrelle Willis, Miguel Cabrera 50.00
YM Paul Molitor, Robin Yount 80.00

Patches Dual

NM/M
Production 75 unless noted.
Platinum: No Pricing
Production 5-10
Masterpiece: No Pricing
Production One Set
Gold: .75-1X
Production 6-58
No pricing prod. 25 or less.
AD Adam Dunn 20.00
AP Albert Pujols 60.00
AS Alfonso Soriano 20.00
BU B.J. Upton 20.00
CH Cole Hamels 25.00
CR Cal Ripken Jr. 50.00
CU Chase Utley 25.00
DJ Derek Jeter 40.00
DJ2 Derek Jeter 40.00
DM Don Mattingly 35.00
ED Jim Edmonds 20.00
FL Francisco Liriano 15.00
GM Greg Maddux 30.00
IR Ivan Rodriguez 20.00
JB Johnny Bench 25.00
JG Jason Giambi 15.00
JM Joe Mauer 20.00
JO Randy Johnson 20.00
JP Jake Peavy 15.00
JR Jose Reyes 40.00
JT Jim Thome 20.00
JT2 Jim Thome 20.00
JV Justin Verlander/42 25.00
JW Jered Weaver 20.00
KG Ken Griffey Jr. 40.00
KG2 Ken Griffey Jr. 40.00
KM Kendry Morales 15.00
LB Lance Berkman 15.00
MC Miguel Cabrera 30.00
MR Manny Ramirez 25.00
MS Mike Schmidt 30.00
MT Mark Teixeira 20.00
NR Nolan Ryan 50.00
PF Prince Fielder 40.00
PM Pedro Martinez 30.00
RJ Reggie Jackson 25.00
RS Ryne Sandberg 40.00
RZ Ryan Zimmerman 35.00
SA Johan Santana 25.00
TE Miguel Tejada 20.00
TG Tony Gwynn 25.00
TO Tom Glavine 30.00
VG Vladimir Guerrero 25.00
VG2 Vladimir Guerrero 25.00

Patches Triple

NM/M
Production 1-99
Gold: .75-1X
Production 1-57
No pricing prod. 25 or less.
Platinum: No Pricing
Production Five Sets
Masterpiece: No Pricing
Production One Set
AJ Andruw Jones/97 30.00
CC Chris Carpenter/97 30.00
CD Carlos Delgado/94 25.00
CJ Chipper Jones/95 40.00
CL Carlos Lee/99 20.00
CR Cal Ripken Jr./82 60.00
CS Curt Schilling/90 30.00
EM Eddie Murray/77 30.00
FR Frank Robinson/56 25.00
FT Frank Thomas/90 30.00
GM Greg Maddux/87 40.00
JT Jim Thome/91 20.00
KG Ken Griffey Jr./89 50.00
MR Manny Ramirez/94 30.00
OS Ozzie Smith/78 50.00
RJ Randy Johnson/89 30.00
RO Roy Halladay/99 25.00
TE Miguel Tejada/98 20.00
TG Tony Gwynn/82 40.00
TS Tom Seaver/67 35.00
VG Vladimir Guerrero/97 30.00
WB Wade Boggs/82 30.00
JT2 Jim Thome/91 20.00
KG2 Ken Griffey Jr./89 50.00

Penmanship Autographs

NM/M
Production 1-98
Masterpiece: No Pricing
Production One Set
AK Al Kaline/53 30.00
BF Bob Feller/36 25.00
BJ Bo Jackson/86 40.00
BR Brooks Robinson/57 30.00
CB Craig Biggio/88 50.00
CC Chris Carpenter/97 40.00
CF Carlton Fisk/72 25.00
CR Cal Ripken Jr./82 100.00
CR2 Cal Ripken Jr./82 100.00
CY Carl Yastrzemski/61 60.00
DJ Derek Jeter/96 150.00
DJ2 Derek Jeter/96 150.00
DL Derrek Lee/97 25.00
DM Don Mattingly/83 50.00
DM2 Don Mattingly/83 50.00
EB Ernie Banks/54 60.00
GM Greg Maddux/87 80.00
IR Ivan Rodriguez/91 40.00
JB Johnny Bench/68 50.00
JI Jim Palmer/65 25.00
JS John Smoltz/88 75.00
JT Jim Thome/91 40.00
KG Ken Griffey Jr./89 75.00
KG2 Ken Griffey Jr./89 75.00
LA Luis Aparicio/56 25.00
MS Mike Schmidt/73 50.00
NR Nolan Ryan/68 100.00
OZ Ozzie Smith/78 50.00
PM Paul Molitor/78 35.00
PM2 Paul Molitor/78 35.00
RA Randy Johnson/89 50.00
RC Roger Clemens/84 100.00
RJ Reggie Jackson/68 65.00
RS Ryne Sandberg/82 50.00
RY Robin Yount/74 40.00
SC Steve Carlton/67 25.00
SM Stan Musial/42 60.00
SR Scott Rolen/97 35.00
TE Miguel Tejada/98 25.00
TG Tony Gwynn/82 40.00
TG2 Tony Gwynn 40.00
TP Tony Perez/65 30.00
VG Vladimir Guerrero/97 60.00
WB Wade Boggs/82 35.00
WC Will Clark/86 25.00
WF Whitey Ford/50 50.00
WM Willie McCovey/59 40.00
YB Yogi Berra/47 50.00

Remnants Triple

NM/M
Production 75 Sets
Gold: .75-1.5X
Production 6-60
No pricing prod. 25 or less.
Platinum: No Pricing
Production 10 Sets
Masterpiece: No Pricing
Production One Set
AP Albert Pujols 30.00
AP2 Albert Pujols 30.00
AS Alfonso Soriano 15.00
BM Bill Mazeroski 20.00
BR Babe Ruth 400.00
CA Roy Campanella 35.00
CF Carlton Fisk 15.00
CJ Chipper Jones 25.00
CL Roger Clemens 25.00
CR Cal Ripken Jr. 30.00
CS Curt Schilling 15.00
CU Chase Utley 25.00
CY Carl Yastrzemski 25.00
DJ Derek Jeter 30.00
DJ2 Derek Jeter 30.00
DM Don Mattingly 40.00
DO David Ortiz 25.00
EM Eddie Mathews 30.00
FR Frank Robinson 20.00
HO Rogers Hornsby 80.00
JB Johnny Bench 20.00
JD Joe DiMaggio 125.00
JO Jose Reyes 30.00
JR Jackie Robinson 75.00
JT Jim Thome 15.00
KG Ken Griffey Jr. 25.00
KG2 Ken Griffey Jr. 25.00
MO Mel Ott 50.00
MR Manny Ramirez 15.00
MS Mike Schmidt 25.00
NR Nolan Ryan 40.00
PM Paul Molitor 15.00
PR Pee Wee Reese 25.00
RC Roberto Clemente 75.00
RJ Reggie Jackson 30.00
RO Brooks Robinson 15.00
RS Ryne Sandberg 25.00
RY Robin Yount 25.00
SM Stan Musial 30.00
TG Tony Gwynn 20.00
TM Thurman Munson 35.00
VG Vladimir Guerrero 15.00

Remnants Quad

NM/M
Production 1-96
Gold: .75-1.5X
Production 2-57
No pricing prod. 25 or less.
Platinum: No Pricing
Production Five Sets
Masterpiece: No Pricing
Production One Set
AK Al Kaline/53 35.00
BM Bill Mazeroski/56 30.00
CL Roberto Clemente/55 120.00
CR Cal Ripken Jr./82 50.00
CY Carl Yastrzemski/61 30.00
DJ Derek Jeter/96 50.00
DM Don Mattingly/83 35.00
EM Eddie Mathews/52 40.00
HK Harmon Killebrew/55 40.00
JB Johnny Bench/68 25.00
JD Joe DiMaggio/36 125.00
JF Jimmie Foxx/27 100.00
JR Jackie Robinson/47 100.00
JT Jim Thome/91 15.00
KG Ken Griffey Jr./89 30.00
LG Lou Gehrig/25 400.00
MI Johnny Mize/36 40.00
MS Mike Schmidt/73 30.00
NR Nolan Ryan/68 60.00
RC Roger Clemens/84 30.00
RJ Reggie Jackson/68 25.00
RN Brooks Robinson/57 25.00
RO Roy Campanella/48 25.00
SM Stan Musial/42 50.00
TM Thurman Munson/70 40.00

Six

Production 10 Sets

Stitchings

NM/M
Production 50 Sets
Stitchings 35: 1X
Production 35 Sets
1 Babe Ruth 40.00
2 Babe Ruth 40.00
3 Babe Ruth 40.00
4 Ty Cobb 25.00
5 Ty Cobb 25.00
6 Lou Gehrig 30.00
7 Lou Gehrig 30.00
8 Joe DiMaggio 30.00
9 Joe DiMaggio 30.00
12 Roberto Clemente 30.00
13 Roberto Clemente 30.00
14 Jackie Robinson 30.00
15 Jackie Robinson 30.00
16 Cy Young 15.00
17 Cy Young 15.00
18 Nolan Ryan 30.00
19 Nolan Ryan 30.00
20 Reggie Jackson 15.00
21 Reggie Jackson 15.00
22 Ken Griffey Jr. 25.00
23 Ken Griffey Jr. 25.00
24 Derek Jeter 30.00
25 Derek Jeter 30.00
26 Jimmie Foxx 20.00
27 Jimmie Foxx 20.00
28 Rogers Hornsby 25.00
30 Walter Johnson 25.00
31 Walter Johnson 25.00
32 Ernie Banks 25.00
33 Ernie Banks 25.00
34 Christy Mathewson 15.00
35 Johnny Mize 15.00
36 Thurman Munson 25.00
37 Thurman Munson 25.00
38 Mel Ott 15.00
39 Satchel Paige 20.00
40 George Sisler 15.00
41 Casey Stengel 15.00
42 Honus Wagner 25.00
43 Honus Wagner 25.00
44 Roy Campanella 20.00
45 Mickey Cochrane 15.00
46 Dizzy Dean 15.00
47 Don Drysdale 15.00
48 Lefty Grove 15.00
49 Roger Clemens 25.00
50 Roger Clemens 25.00
51 Cal Ripken Jr. 40.00
52 Cal Ripken Jr. 40.00
53 Tony Gwynn 20.00
54 Tony Gwynn 20.00
55 Johnny Bench 20.00
56 Yogi Berra 20.00
57 Carlton Fisk 15.00
58 Joe Morgan 15.00
59 Brooks Robinson 15.00
60 Mike Schmidt 25.00
61 Willie Stargell 20.00
62 Tom Seaver 20.00
63 Ozzie Smith 25.00
64 Albert Pujols 30.00
65 Albert Pujols 30.00
66 Ryan Howard 20.00
67 David Ortiz 20.00
68 Randy Johnson 25.00
69 Greg Maddux 20.00
70 Greg Maddux 20.00
71 Johan Santana 15.00
72 Al Kaline 15.00
73 Ryne Sandberg 20.00
74 Robin Yount 20.00
75 Frank Robinson 15.00
76 Frank Robinson 15.00
78 Stan Musial 30.00
79 Carl Yastrzemski 20.00
80 Don Mattingly 30.00
81 Ichiro Suzuki 30.00
82 Yogi Berra 15.00
83 Carlton Fisk, Johnny Bench 20.00
84 Johnny Bench, Thurman Munson 25.00
85 Babe Ruth, Lou Gehrig 30.00
86 Yogi Berra, Whitey Ford 20.00
87 Yogi Berra, Don Larsen 20.00
88 Dennis Eckersley, Kirk Gibson 15.00
90 Pee Wee Reese, Jackie Robinson 20.00
91 Jackie Robinson, Satchel Paige 25.00
92 Lou Gehrig, Cal Ripken Jr. 30.00
93 George Sisler, Ichiro Suzuki 30.00
94 Steve Carlton, Roger Clemens, Randy Johnson, Nolan Ryan 40.00
95 Dave Concepcion, Tony Perez, Johnny Bench, Joe Morgan 25.00
96 Babe Ruth, Jimmie Foxx, Mel Ott, Eddie Mathews 40.00
97 Roger Clemens, Greg Maddux, Tom Seaver, Nolan Ryan 40.00
98 Roberto Clemente, Tony Gwynn, Stan Musial, Cal Ripken Jr. 40.00
DM Daisuke Matsuzaka 60.00
KI Kei Igawa 25.00
MI Daisuke Matsuzaka, Kei Igawa 50.00

Stitchings Cuts

Production One Set

Trios Autographs

No Pricing
Production 20 Sets

Rare Patches Dual

NM/M
Production 50 Sets
Gold: 1-1.5X
Production 25 Sets
Platinum: No Pricing
Production 10 Sets
Masterpiece: No Pricing
Production One Set
BM Joe Mauer, Johnny Bench 40.00
BR Brian Roberts, Robinson Cano 25.00

BS Anibal Sanchez, A.J. Burnett 20.00
CP Jake Peavy, Chris Carpenter 30.00
CW Miguel Cabrera, Dontrelle Willis 30.00
DB Carlos Beltran, Carlos Delgado 30.00
DT Miguel Tejada, Stephen Drew 25.00
ER Scott Rolen, Jim Edmonds 40.00
FM Justin Morneau, Prince Fielder 35.00
FW Prince Fielder, Rickie Weeks 40.00
GP Albert Pujols, Ken Griffey Jr. 75.00
HR Trevor Hoffman, Mariano Rivera 40.00
HS Jeremy Sowers, Cole Hamels 30.00
JG Ken Griffey Jr., Derek Jeter 75.00
JJ Andruw Jones, Chipper Jones 40.00
MG Tom Glavine, Greg Maddux 70.00
MH Travis Hafner, Victor Martinez 25.00
MJ Derek Jeter, Don Mattingly 80.00
OT Jim Thome, David Ortiz 35.00
PO Roy Oswalt, Jake Peavy 25.00
PS Curt Schilling, Jonathan Papelbon 50.00
RC Roger Clemens, Nolan Ryan 80.00
RD Derek Jeter, Reggie Jackson 50.00
RG Cal Ripken Jr., Tony Gwynn 75.00
RJ Roy Halladay, Johan Santana 40.00
RU Jimmy Rollins, Chase Utley 50.00
SG Alfonso Soriano, Vladimir Guerrero 40.00
SH Johan Santana, Felix Hernandez 40.00
SM Joe Morgan, Ryne Sandberg 50.00
TR Miguel Tejada, Jose Reyes 40.00
TT Jim Thome, Frank Thomas 40.00
UC Carl Crawford, B.J. Upton 40.00
WJ Josh Johnson, Dontrelle Willis 20.00
WL Francisco Liriano, Jered Weaver 30.00
YM Robin Yount, Paul Molitor 40.00
ZU Ryan Zimmerman, B.J. Upton 40.00

Rare Patches Triple

NM/M
Production 25 Sets
Gold: No Pricing
Production 10 Sets
Platinum: No Pricing
Production Five Sets
Masterpiece: No Pricing
Production One Set
CRM Nolan Ryan, Greg Maddux, Roger Clemens 125.00
MRM Ivan Rodriguez, Victor Martinez, Joe Mauer 40.00
POG Albert Pujols, David Ortiz, Vladimir Guerrero 80.00
RGM Cal Ripken Jr., Tony Gwynn, Paul Molitor 100.00
SHK Scott Kazmir, Jeremy Sowers, Cole Hamels 30.00
UWR Chase Utley, Rickie Weeks, Brian Roberts 40.00
WLV Francisco Liriano, Justin Verlander, Jered Weaver 50.00

Premier Rare Remnants Quad

No Pricing
Production 25 Sets
Gold: No Pricing
Production 10 Sets
Platinum: No Pricing
Production Five Sets
Masterpiece: No Pricing
Production One Set

Rare Remnants Triple

NM/M
Production 50 Sets
Gold: 1-1.5X
Production 25 Sets
Platinum: No Pricing
Production 10 Sets
Masterpiece: No Pricing
Production One Set
BMP Tony Perez, Joe Morgan, Johnny Bench 30.00
BZV Jeremy Bonderman, Justin Verlander, Joel Zumaya 40.00
CBF Brooks Robinson, Frank Robinson, Cal Ripken Jr. 50.00
CFY Jimmie Foxx, Joe Cronin, Carl Yastrzemski 60.00
CMK Ralph Kiner, Bill Mazeroski, Roberto Clemente 100.00
CPR Chris Carpenter, Albert Pujols, Scott Rolen 40.00
DMP Jorge Posada, Thurman Munson, Bill Dickey 50.00
DMR Pedro Martinez, Carlos Delgado, Jose Reyes 40.00
DRB Jose Reyes, Carlos Delgado, Carlos Beltran 40.00
FBM Carlton Fisk, Thurman Munson, Johnny Bench 35.00
FGG Hank Greenberg, Lou Gehrig, Jimmie Foxx 180.00
FMT Justin Morneau, Mark Teixeira, Prince Fielder 30.00
GGJ Andruw Jones, Ken Griffey Jr., Vladimir Guerrero 40.00
JCM Greg Maddux, Randy Johnson, Roger Clemens 40.00
JJR Derek Jeter, Randy Johnson, Mariano Rivera 50.00
JMM Thurman Munson, Don Mattingly, Reggie Jackson 75.00
KUC B.J. Upton, Carl Crawford, Scott Kazmir 25.00
KVJ Joe Mauer, Victor Martinez, Kenji Johjima 25.00
LMS Joe Mauer, Francisco Liriano, Johan Santana 25.00
LSH Francisco Liriano, Jeremy Sowers, Cole Hamels 25.00
OPS Jake Peavy, Roy Oswalt, Ben Sheets 20.00
OTB Lance Berkman, David Ortiz, Jim Thome 25.00
PJG Derek Jeter, Ken Griffey Jr., Albert Pujols 50.00
PMH Albert Pujols, Stan Musial, Rogers Hornsby 80.00
RCD Nolan Ryan, Don Drysdale, Roger Clemens 50.00
RDG Lou Gehrig, Joe DiMaggio, Babe Ruth 475.00
RFS Bruce Sutter, Rollie Fingers, Mariano Rivera 25.00
RRR Nolan Ryan 60.00
RWH Nolan Ryan, Felix Hernandez, Jered Weaver 30.00
RYS Robin Yount, Cal Ripken Jr., Ozzie Smith 40.00
SGA Vladimir Guerrero, Bobby Abreu, Alfonso Soriano 25.00
SHM Joe Morgan, Rogers Hornsby, Ryne Sandberg 50.00
SJZ Randy Johnson, Barry Zito, Johan Santana 25.00
SRB Brooks Robinson, Wade Boggs, Mike Schmidt 40.00
TJY Miguel Tejada, Derek Jeter, Michael Young 30.00
TTH Mark Teixeira, Jim Thome, Todd Helton 20.00
VWJ Josh Johnson, Justin Verlander, Jered Weaver 25.00
YBM Paul Molitor, Wade Boggs, Robin Yount 25.00

World Series Ticket

Production One

Patches Dual Auto.

NM/M
Production 25 Sets
AD Adam Dunn 40.00
BR Brooks Robinson 50.00
BU B.J. Upton 40.00
CH Cole Hamels 50.00
CR Cal Ripken Jr. 180.00
DJ Derek Jeter 200.00
DM Don Mattingly 140.00
FL Francisco Liriano 40.00
IR Ivan Rodriguez 50.00
JB Johnny Bench 60.00
KM Kendry Morales 30.00
NR Nolan Ryan 150.00
RJ Reggie Jackson 75.00
RS Ryne Sandberg 75.00

Patches Triple Auto.

No Pricing
Production 15 Sets

Penmanship Auto. Jersey Number

NM/M
Production 1-58
AM Andrew Miller/50 60.00
CF Carlton Fisk/27 40.00
CH Cole Hamels/35 50.00
CZ Carlos Zambrano/38 25.00
DL Derrek Lee/25 35.00
DW Dontrelle Willis/35 25.00
DY Delmon Young/35 30.00
FH Felix Hernandez/34 50.00
FL Francisco Liriano/47 30.00
GM Greg Maddux/36 100.00
JG Jonny Gomes/31 20.00
JP Jake Peavy/44 40.00
JS John Smoltz/29 65.00
JV Justin Verlander/35 50.00
JW Jered Weaver/56 25.00
JZ Joel Zumaya/54 30.00
MO Justin Morneau/33 30.00
NR Nolan Ryan/34 100.00
NS Nick Swisher/33 30.00
PA Jonathan Papelbon/58 50.00
PH Philip Humber/49 20.00
RA Randy Johnson/41 60.00
RO Roy Oswalt/45 25.00
SA Johan Santana/57 40.00
SC Steve Carlton/32 25.00
SR Scott Rolen/27 40.00
VG Vladimir Guerrero/27 50.00
VM Victor Martinez/41 25.00
WB Wade Boggs/26 40.00
WM Willie McCovey/44 40.00

Remnants Triple Autograph

No Pricing
Production 25 Sets

Remnants Quad Autograph

Production 15 Sets

Stitchings Autograph

No Pricing
Production 25 Sets

1989 Rookie Reprint Signatures

No Pricing
Production Five Sets

1989 Rookie Reprints

NM/M
Common Player: 1.00
AG Alex Gordon 3.00
AI Akinori Iwamura 3.00
AS Angel Sanchez 1.00
BN Jared Burton 1.00
BU Jamie Burke 1.00
CJ Cesar Jimenez 1.00
CS Chris Stewart 1.00
DK Donald Kelly 1.00
DM Daisuke Matsuzaka 20.00
DY Delmon Young 2.00
ED Elijah Dukes 1.00
GM Gustavo Molina 1.00
HG Hector Gimenez 1.00
JA Joaquin Arias 1.00
JB Jeff Baker 1.00
JD John Danks 1.00
JF Jesus Flores 1.00
JG Jose Garcia 1.00
JH Josh Hamilton 2.00
JM Jay Marshall 1.00
JP Juan Perez 1.00
KC Kevin Cameron 1.00
KI Kei Igawa 2.00
KK Kevin Kouzmanoff 2.00
KO Kory Casto 1.00
MB Michael Bourn 1.00
MC Matt Chico 1.00
MM Miguel Montero 1.00
MO Micah Owings 1.00
MR Mike Rabelo 1.00
RB Ryan Braun 1.00
SA Juan Salas 1.00
SH Sean Henn 1.00
SL Doug Slaten 1.00
SO Joakim Soria 1.00
ST Brian Stokes 1.00
TB Travis Buck 1.00
TT Troy Tulowitzki 2.00
ZS Zack Segovia 1.00

Cooperstown Calling

NM/M
Common Player: 1.00
AJ Andruw Jones 1.50
AP Albert Pujols 5.00
AR Alex Rodriguez 5.00
AS Alfonso Soriano 2.00
BI Craig Biggio 1.00
BW Billy Wagner 1.00
CA Chris Carpenter 1.50
CB Carlos Beltran 2.00
CC Carl Crawford 1.00
CD Carlos Delgado 1.50
CJ Chipper Jones 2.00
CR Cal Ripken Jr. 5.00
CS Curt Schilling 2.00
DJ Derek Jeter 5.00
DO David Ortiz 2.00
FT Frank Thomas 1.50
GM Greg Maddux 3.00
GS Gary Sheffield 1.50
HA Travis Hafner 1.00
HE Todd Helton 1.50
HO Ryan Howard 4.00
IR Ivan Rodriguez 1.50
IS Ichiro Suzuki 3.00
JD Johnny Damon 2.00
JG Jason Giambi 1.50
JK Jeff Kent 1.00
JM Justin Morneau 2.00
JS Johan Santana 2.00
JT Jim Thome 1.50
KG Ken Griffey Jr. 4.00
MC Miguel Cabrera 2.00
MM Mike Mussina 1.50
MP Mike Piazza 3.00
MR Manny Ramirez 2.00
MT Mark Teixeira 1.50
OV Omar Vizquel 1.00
PE Andy Pettitte 1.00
PM Pedro Martinez 2.00
RH Roy Halladay 1.00
RI Mariano Rivera 1.50
RJ Randy Johnson 2.00
RO Roy Oswalt 1.00
SI Grady Sizemore 2.00
SM John Smoltz 1.50
SR Scott Rolen 1.50
SS Sammy Sosa 2.00
TE Miguel Tejada 1.50
TG Tom Glavine 1.00
TH Trevor Hoffman 1.00
VG Vladimir Guerrero 2.00

MVP Potential

NM/M
Common Player: 1.00
1 Stephen Drew 1.00
2 Brian McCann 1.00
3 Adam LaRoche 1.00
4 Brian Roberts 1.00
5 Manny Ramirez 2.00
6 David Ortiz 2.00
7 J.D. Drew 1.00
8 Alfonso Soriano 2.00
9 Aramis Ramirez 1.50
10 Derrek Lee 1.50
11 Jermaine Dye 1.00
12 Paul Konerko 1.00
13 Jim Thome 1.50
14 Adam Dunn 1.50
15 Travis Hafner 1.00
16 Victor Martinez 1.00
17 Grady Sizemore 2.00
18 Garrett Atkins 1.00
19 Matt Holliday 1.00
20 Magglio Ordonez 1.00
21 Miguel Cabrera 2.00
22 Hanley Ramirez 2.00
23 Dan Uggla 1.00
24 Lance Berkman 1.50
25 Carlos Lee 1.50
26 Jered Weaver 1.50
27 Nomar Garciaparra 2.00
28 Rafael Furcal 1.00
29 Prince Fielder 3.00
30 Joe Mauer 1.50
31 Johan Santana 2.00
32 David Wright 3.00
33 Jose Reyes 3.00
34 Carlos Beltran 2.00
35 Robinson Cano 1.50
36 Derek Jeter 5.00
37 Bobby Abreu 1.00
38 Johnny Damon 2.00
39 Nick Swisher 1.00
40 Chase Utley 2.00
41 Jason Bay 1.00
42 Adrian Gonzalez 1.00
43 Adrian Beltre 1.00
44 Scott Rolen 1.50
45 Carl Crawford 1.00
46 Mark Teixeira 1.50
47 Michael Young 1.00
48 Vernon Wells 1.00
49 Roy Halladay 1.00
50 Ryan Zimmerman 2.00

Rookie of the Year Predictor

NM/M
Common Player: 3.00
1 Doug Slaten 3.00
2 Miguel Montero 3.00
4 Kory Casto 3.00
5 Jesus Flores 3.00
6 John Danks 3.00
7 Daisuke Matsuzaka 60.00
9 Chris Stewart 3.00
10 Kevin Cameron 3.00
13 Kevin Kouzmanoff 5.00
14 Jeff Baker 3.00
15 Donald Kelly 3.00
16 Troy Tulowitzki 8.00
18 Cesar Jimenez 3.00
20 Jose Garcia 3.00
21 Micah Owings 3.00
22 Josh Hamilton 6.00
24 Jamie Burke 3.00
25 Mike Rabelo 3.00
26 Elijah Dukes 3.00
27 Travis Buck 3.00
28 Kei Igawa 5.00
29 Sean Henn 3.00
32 Michael Bourn 3.00
33 Alex Gordon 20.00
35 Matt Chico 3.00
38 Gustavo Molina 3.00
39 Jared Burton 3.00
40 Jay Marshall 3.00
42 Akinori Iwamura 20.00
43 Delmon Young 8.00
44 Juan Salas 3.00
45 Zack Segovia 3.00
46 Brian Stokes 3.00
47 Joaquin Arias 3.00
48 Hector Gimenez 3.00
49 Ryan Braun 3.00
50 Juan Perez 3.00

Ticket to Stardom

NM/M
Common Player: 2.00
AG Alex Gordon 8.00
AI Akinori Iwamura 4.00
AS Angel Sanchez 2.00
BN Jared Burton 2.00
BU Jamie Burke 2.00
CH Matt Chico 2.00
CJ Cesar Jimenez 2.00
CS Chris Stewart 2.00
DA John Danks 2.00
DK Donald Kelly 2.00
DM Daisuke Matsuzaka 2.00
DS Doug Slaten 2.00
DY Delmon Young 4.00
ED Elijah Dukes 2.00
GM Gustavo Molina 2.00
HG Hector Gimenez 2.00
JA Joaquin Arias 2.00
JB Jeff Baker 2.00
JF Jesus Flores 2.00
JG Jose Garcia 2.00
JH Josh Hamilton 4.00
JM Jay Marshall 2.00
JP Juan Perez 2.00
KC Kevin Cameron 2.00
KI Kei Igawa 4.00
KK Kevin Kouzmanoff 3.00
KO Kory Casto 2.00
MB Michael Bourn 2.00
MM Miguel Montero 2.00
MO Micah Owings 2.00
MR Mike Rabelo 2.00
RB Ryan Braun 2.00
SA Juan Salas 2.00
SH Sean Henn 2.00
SO Joakim Soria 2.00
ST Brian Stokes 2.00
TB Travis Buck 2.00
TT Troy Tulowitzki 4.00
ZS Zack Segovia 2.00

Cooperstown Calling Autograph

No Pricing

Ticket to Stardom Autograph

No Pricing

2007 Upper Deck Artifacts

NM/M
Complete Set (100): 35.00
Common Player: .25
Pack (4): 10.00
Box (10): 90.00
1 Miguel Tejada .50
2 David Ortiz 1.00
3 Manny Ramirez 1.00
4 Curt Schilling .75
5 Jim Thome .75
6 Paul Konerko .50
7 Jermaine Dye .50
8 Travis Hafner .50
9 Victor Martinez .50
10 Grady Sizemore .50
11 Ivan Rodriguez .75
12 Magglio Ordonez .50
13 Justin Verlander .75
14 Mark Teahen .25
15 Vladimir Guerrero 1.00
16 Jered Weaver .50
17 Justin Morneau .75
18 Joe Mauer .50
19 Torii Hunter .50
20 Johan Santana 1.00
21 Derek Jeter 3.00
22 Alex Rodriguez 3.00
23 Johnny Damon .75
24 Huston Street .25
25 Nick Swisher .50
26 Ichiro Suzuki 2.00
27 Richie Sexson .50
28 Carl Crawford .50
29 Scott Kazmir .50
30 Michael Young .50
31 Mark Teixeira .75
32 Vernon Wells .50
33 Roy Halladay .50
34 Brandon Webb .50
35 Stephen Drew .50
36 Chipper Jones 1.00
37 Andruw Jones .75
38 Derrek Lee .75
39 Aramis Ramirez .75
40 Ken Griffey Jr. 2.00
41 Adam Dunn .50
42 Todd Helton .75
43 Matt Holliday .50
44 Miguel Cabrera 1.00
45 Hanley Ramirez 1.00
46 Dontrelle Willis .50
47 Lance Berkman .50
48 Roy Oswalt .50
49 Craig Biggio .50
50 Nomar Garciaparra 1.00
51 Derek Lowe .25
52 Prince Fielder 1.00
53 Rickie Weeks .25
54 Jose Reyes 2.00
55 David Wright 2.00
56 Carlos Beltran .75
57 Ryan Howard 2.00
58 Chase Utley 1.00
59 Jimmy Rollins .75
60 Jason Bay .50
61 Freddy Sanchez .25
62 Trevor Hoffman .50
63 Adrian Gonzalez .50
64 Omar Vizquel .25
65 Matt Cain .50
66 Albert Pujols 3.00
67 Jim Edmonds .50
68 Chris Carpenter .75
69 David Eckstein .25
70 Ryan Zimmerman .50
71 Alexi Casilla **RC** .50
72 Andrew Miller **RC** 5.00
73 Andy Cannizaro **RC** 1.00
74 Brian Stokes **(RC)** .50
75 Carlos Maldonado **(RC)** .50
76 Cesar Jimenez **RC** 1.00
77 Daisuke Matsuzaka **RC** 8.00
78 Delmon Young **(RC)** 1.00
79 Delwyn Young **(RC)** .50
80 Fred Lewis **(RC)** 1.00
81 Glen Perkins **(RC)** .50
82 Jeff Baker **(RC)** .50
83 Jeff Fiorentino **(RC)** .50
84 Jeff Salazar **(RC)** .50
85 Jerry Owens **(RC)** .50
86 Josh Fields **(RC)** .50
87 Juan Perez **RC** .50
88 Juan Salas **(RC)** .50
89 Justin Hampson **(RC)** .50
90 Kevin Kouzmanoff **(RC)** .50
91 Michael Bourn **(RC)** .50
92 Miguel Montero **(RC)** .50
93 Mike Rabelo **RC** .50
94 Oswaldo Navarro **RC** .50
95 Philip Humber **(RC)** .50
96 Ryan Braun **RC** .50
97 Ryan Sweeney **(RC)** .50
98 Sean Henn **(RC)** .50
99 Jose Reyes **RC** 1.00
100 Troy Tulowitzki **(RC)** 1.00

Antiquity Artifacts

NM/M
Production 199 Sets
Patch: 1.5-3X
Production 50 Sets
AB Adrian Beltre 6.00
AJ Andruw Jones 6.00
AL Adam LaRoche 4.00
AP Albert Pujols 20.00
AR Aramis Ramirez 6.00
AT Garrett Atkins 4.00
BA Bobby Abreu 6.00
BC Bartolo Colon 4.00
BE Carlos Beltran 8.00
BG Brian Giles 4.00
BO Jeremy Bonderman 6.00
BR Brian Roberts 4.00
BU B.J. Upton 6.00
BW Billy Wagner 4.00
BZ Barry Zito 4.00
CA Miguel Cabrera 8.00
CB Craig Biggio 6.00
CC Carl Crawford 6.00
CF Chone Figgins 4.00
CH Chris Carpenter 8.00
CJ Chipper Jones 8.00
CL Carlos Lee 6.00
CR Cal Ripken Jr. 25.00
CS Curt Schilling 8.00
CU Chase Utley 10.00
DJ Derek Jeter 20.00
DO David Ortiz 10.00
DR J.D. Drew 4.00
DU Dan Uggla 4.00
DW Dontrelle Willis 4.00
EC Eric Chavez 4.00

ED	Jim Edmonds	6.00
FG	Freddy Garcia	4.00
FH	Felix Hernandez	6.00
FL	Francisco Liriano	6.00
FT	Frank Thomas	8.00
GA	Garret Anderson	4.00
GJ	Geoff Jenkins	4.00
GM	Greg Maddux	10.00
GR	Ken Griffey Jr.	20.00
GS	Grady Sizemore	8.00
HA	Rich Harden	4.00
HB	Hank Blalock	4.00
HO	Trevor Hoffman	6.00
HR	Hanley Ramirez	8.00
HS	Huston Street	4.00
HU	Torii Hunter	6.00
IR	Ivan Rodriguez	8.00
JA	Jason Bay	6.00
JC	Jorge Cantu	4.00
JD	Jermaine Dye	4.00
JE	Johnny Estrada	4.00
JF	Jeff Francoeur	8.00
JG	Jason Giambi	6.00
JJ	Josh Johnson	4.00
JK	Jeff Kent	6.00
JM	Joe Mauer	8.00
JP	Jake Peavy	8.00
JR	Jimmy Rollins	8.00
JS	Jason Schmidt	4.00
JT	Jim Thome	8.00
JV	Justin Verlander	8.00
JZ	Joel Zumaya	6.00
KG	Khalil Greene	4.00
LB	Lance Berkman	6.00
LG	Luis Gonzalez	4.00
MO	Justin Morneau	8.00
MR	Manny Ramirez	8.00
MT	Mark Teixeira	6.00
MY	Michael Young	6.00
NS	Nick Swisher	4.00
OR	Magglio Ordonez	4.00
PA	Jonathan Papelbon	10.00
PB	Pat Burrell	4.00
PE	Jhonny Peralta	4.00
PF	Prince Fielder	10.00
PK	Paul Konerko	6.00
PM	Pedro Martinez	8.00
PO	Jorge Posada	8.00
RC	Roger Clemens	10.00
RE	Jose Reyes	10.00
RH	Roy Halladay	6.00
RJ	Randy Johnson	8.00
RO	Roy Oswalt	6.00
RW	Rickie Weeks	4.00
RZ	Ryan Zimmerman	6.00
SA	Johan Santana	8.00
SK	Scott Kazmir	4.00
SM	John Smoltz	6.00
SR	Scott Rolen	6.00
TE	Miguel Tejada	6.00
TG	Tom Glavine	6.00
TH	Todd Helton	8.00
TI	Tim Hudson	4.00
VA	Jason Varitek	6.00
VG	Vladimir Guerrero	8.00
VM	Victor Martinez	6.00
VW	Vernon Wells	4.00

Bat Knobs

Production One Set

Autofacts

		NM/M
Common Auto.:		10.00
AD	Adam Dunn	20.00
AK	Austin Kearns	10.00
AL	Adam LaRoche	10.00
AM	Andrew Miller	40.00
AS	Angel Sanchez	10.00
BC	Bobby Crosby	10.00
BE	Josh Beckett	25.00
BO	Jeremy Bonderman/SP	35.00
BT	Jason Bartlett	10.00
BU	Ambiorix Burgos/SP	10.00
CJ	Cesar Jimenez	10.00
CL	Carlos Lee/SP	15.00
CR	Cal Ripken Jr.	125.00
CY	Chris Young	20.00
CZ	Carlos Zambrano	30.00
DJ	Derek Jeter	140.00
DO	David Ortiz/SP	50.00
DW	Dontrelle Willis	15.00
DY	Delmon Young/SP	15.00
EC	Eric Chavez	15.00
GA	Garrett Atkins	10.00
HA	Rich Harden	15.00
HG	Hector Gimenez	10.00
HK	Hong-Chih Kuo	30.00
HR	Hanley Ramirez	20.00
IK	Ian Kinsler	15.00
JA	Joaquin Arias	10.00
JB	Jason Bay	15.00
JC	Jesse Crain	15.00
JE	Johnny Estrada	15.00
JG	Jonny Gomes	10.00
JJ	Josh Johnson	10.00
JW	Jered Weaver	15.00
JZ	Joel Zumaya/SP	20.00
KE	Howie Kendrick	15.00
KG	Ken Griffey Jr.	75.00
KM	Kendry Morales	10.00
KN	Jon Knott	10.00
KW	Kerry Wood	15.00
MJ	Mike Jacobs	10.00
MM	Miguel Montero	10.00
PA	Jonathan Papelbon	25.00
PE	Jhonny Peralta	15.00
PH	Philip Humber	10.00
RA	Chris Ray	10.00
RC	Roger Clemens	100.00
RH	Rich Hill	15.00
RW	Rickie Weeks	15.00
SB	Scott Baker	10.00
SD	Stephen Drew	15.00
SK	Scott Kazmir	15.00
SR	Scott Rolen/SP	20.00
TI	Tadahito Iguchi	20.00
TT	Troy Tulowitzki	20.00
UP	B.J. Upton	15.00
VE	Justin Verlander	20.00
VG	Vladimir Guerrero/SP	40.00
VM	Victor Martinez	15.00
WI	Josh Willingham	10.00
YB	Yuniesky Betancourt	15.00
ZG	Zack Greinke	10.00
ZS	Zack Segovia	15.00

Awesome Artifacts

		NM/M
Production 50 Sets		
AD	Adam Dunn	15.00
AG	Adrian Gonzalez	15.00
AP	Albert Pujols	40.00
AR	Aramis Ramirez	15.00
AS	Alfonso Soriano	20.00
BA	Bobby Abreu	15.00
BC	Bartolo Colon	10.00
BG	Brian Giles	10.00
BI	Craig Biggio	15.00
BR	Brian Roberts	15.00
BW	Billy Wagner	15.00
BZ	Barry Zito	15.00
CA	Carl Crawford	15.00
CB	Carlos Beltran	20.00
CC	Carl Crawford	15.00
CD	Carlos Delgado	15.00
CF	Chone Figgins	15.00
CJ	Chipper Jones	20.00
CL	Carlos Lee	15.00
CR	Cal Ripken Jr.	40.00
CS	Curt Schilling	15.00
CU	Chase Utley	20.00
DJ	Derek Jeter	40.00
DO	David Ortiz	20.00
DU	Dan Uggla	15.00
DW	Dontrelle Willis	15.00
EC	Eric Chavez	15.00
FG	Freddy Garcia	10.00
FH	Felix Hernandez	15.00
FL	Francisco Liriano	15.00
FT	Frank Thomas	20.00
GA	Garret Anderson	15.00
GM	Greg Maddux	20.00
GR	Khalil Greene	15.00
GS	Grady Sizemore	20.00
HA	Roy Halladay	15.00
HB	Hank Blalock	15.00
HE	Todd Helton	15.00
HR	Hanley Ramirez	20.00
HS	Huston Street	15.00
HU	Torii Hunter	15.00
IK	Ian Kinsler	15.00
IR	Ivan Rodriguez	15.00
JA	Jason Bay	15.00
JB	Jeremy Bonderman	20.00
JC	Jorge Cantu	10.00
JD	Jermaine Dye	10.00
JE	Jim Edmonds	15.00
JF	Jeff Francoeur	20.00
JG	Jason Giambi	15.00
JH	Johnny Damon	20.00
JJ	Josh Johnson	10.00
JK	Jeff Kent	15.00
JM	Joe Mauer	15.00
JO	Josh Barfield	15.00
JP	Jake Peavy	15.00
JR	Jimmy Rollins	15.00
JS	Jason Schmidt	15.00
JT	Jim Thome	15.00
JV	Justin Verlander	20.00
JW	Jered Weaver	15.00
JZ	Joel Zumaya	15.00
KG	Ken Griffey Jr.	30.00
KM	Kendry Morales	15.00
MC	Miguel Cabrera	20.00
MO	Justin Morneau	15.00
MR	Manny Ramirez	20.00
MT	Mark Teixeira	15.00
MY	Michael Young	15.00
OR	Magglio Ordonez	15.00
OS	Roy Oswalt	15.00
PA	Jonathan Papelbon	20.00
PB	Pat Burrell	15.00
PE	Jhonny Peralta	15.00
PF	Prince Fielder	20.00
PO	Jorge Posada	20.00
RC	Robinson Cano	20.00
RE	Jose Reyes	30.00
RF	Rafael Furcal	15.00
RH	Rich Harden	15.00
RJ	Randy Johnson	20.00
RO	Roger Clemens	25.00
RW	Rickie Weeks	15.00
RZ	Ryan Zimmerman	20.00
SK	Scott Kazmir	15.00
SM	John Smoltz	15.00
SR	Scott Rolen	20.00
TG	Tom Glavine	20.00
TH	Trevor Hoffman	15.00
TI	Tim Hudson	15.00
TR	Travis Hafner	15.00
VA	Jason Varitek	20.00
VG	Vladimir Guerrero	15.00
VM	Victor Martinez	15.00
VW	Vernon Wells	15.00

Divisional Artifacts

		NM/M
Common Player:		
Production 199 Sets		
Gold:		1X
Production 130 Sets		
AA	Aaron Rowand	6.00
AD	Adam Dunn	6.00
AJ	Andruw Jones	8.00
AL	Adam LaRoche	6.00
AR	Aramis Ramirez	10.00
BA	Bobby Abreu	6.00
BC	Bartolo Colon	4.00
BE	Carlos Beltran	8.00
BG	Brian Giles	4.00
BO	Jeremy Bonderman	10.00
BR	Brian Roberts	6.00
BW	Billy Wagner	6.00
BZ	Barry Zito	6.00
CA	Robinson Cano	10.00
CB	Craig Biggio	6.00
CC	Carl Crawford	6.00
CD	Carlos Delgado/178	6.00
CH	Chris Carpenter	8.00
CJ	Chipper Jones	8.00
CL	Carlos Lee	6.00
CR	Cal Ripken Jr.	25.00
CS	Curt Schilling	8.00
CU	Chase Utley	10.00
DJ	Derek Jeter	25.00
DO	David Ortiz	15.00
DU	Dan Uggla	6.00
DW	Dontrelle Willis	6.00
EC	Eric Chavez	6.00
FG	Freddy Garcia	4.00
FH	Felix Hernandez	6.00
FL	Francisco Liriano	8.00
FT	Frank Thomas	8.00
GA	Garret Anderson	4.00
GM	Greg Maddux	10.00
GR	Ken Griffey Jr.	20.00
GS	Grady Sizemore	10.00
HA	Rich Harden	4.00
HB	Hank Blalock	4.00
HO	Trevor Hoffman	6.00
HR	Hanley Ramirez	8.00
HU	Torii Hunter	6.00
IK	Ian Kinsler	6.00
IR	Ivan Rodriguez	8.00
JA	Jason Bay	6.00
JC	Jorge Cantu	4.00
JD	Jermaine Dye	6.00
JE	Jim Edmonds	6.00
JF	Jeff Francoeur	10.00
JG	Jason Giambi	8.00
JJ	Josh Johnson	4.00
JK	Jeff Kent	6.00
JM	Joe Mauer	8.00
JN	Joe Nathan	6.00
JO	Josh Barfield	4.00
JP	Jake Peavy	6.00
JR	Jimmy Rollins	10.00
JS	Jason Schmidt	4.00
JT	Jim Thome	8.00
JV	Justin Verlander	10.00
JW	Jered Weaver	8.00
JZ	Joel Zumaya	8.00
KG	Khalil Greene	8.00
KM	Kendry Morales	4.00
LB	Lance Berkman	6.00
MC	Miguel Cabrera	8.00
ME	Melky Cabrera	8.00
MO	Justin Morneau	8.00
MR	Manny Ramirez	8.00
MT	Mark Teixeira	8.00
MY	Michael Young	8.00
NS	Nick Swisher	6.00
OR	Magglio Ordonez	8.00
PA	Jonathan Papelbon	15.00
PB	Pat Burrell	6.00
PE	Jhonny Peralta	6.00
PF	Prince Fielder	15.00
PK	Paul Konerko	8.00
PO	Jorge Posada	8.00
RC	Roger Clemens	15.00
RE	Jose Reyes	15.00
RH	Roy Halladay	8.00
RJ	Randy Johnson	8.00
RO	Roy Oswalt	6.00
RW	Rickie Weeks	8.00
RZ	Ryan Zimmerman	10.00
SK	Scott Kazmir	6.00
SM	John Smoltz	8.00
SR	Scott Rolen	8.00
TG	Tom Glavine	8.00
TH	Todd Helton	8.00
TI	Tim Hudson	6.00
TR	Travis Hafner/117	6.00
VA	Jason Varitek	10.00
VG	Vladimir Guerrero	8.00
VM	Victor Martinez	8.00
VW	Vernon Wells	6.00

Apparel

		NM/M
Production 199 unless noted.		
Rare Apparel:		No Pricing
Production One Set		
Gold:		1X
Production 130 Sets		
AB	Adrian Beltre	6.00
AD	Adam Dunn	8.00
AJ	Andruw Jones/25	10.00
AL	Adam LaRoche	6.00
AP	Albert Pujols	20.00
AR	Aramis Ramirez	10.00
AT	Garrett Atkins	6.00
BA	Bobby Abreu	6.00
BC	Bartolo Colon	4.00
BG	Brian Giles	4.00
BI	Craig Biggio	6.00
BO	Jeremy Bonderman	10.00
BR	Brian Roberts	6.00
BU	B.J. Upton	8.00
BW	Billy Wagner	6.00
BZ	Barry Zito	6.00
CB	Carlos Beltran	8.00
CC	Carl Crawford	6.00
CH	Cole Hamels	10.00
CJ	Chipper Jones	8.00
CL	Carlos Lee	6.00
CR	Cal Ripken Jr.	25.00
CS	Curt Schilling	8.00
CU	Chase Utley	10.00
DJ	Derek Jeter	25.00
DO	David Ortiz	15.00
DU	Dan Uggla	6.00
DW	Dontrelle Willis	6.00
DY	Jermaine Dye	4.00
EC	Eric Chavez	6.00
ES	Johnny Estrada	8.00
FG	Freddy Garcia	4.00
FH	Felix Hernandez	6.00
FL	Francisco Liriano	8.00
FT	Frank Thomas	8.00
GA	Garret Anderson	4.00
GJ	Geoff Jenkins	4.00
GM	Greg Maddux	10.00
GR	Khalil Greene	8.00
GS	Grady Sizemore	10.00
HA	Roy Halladay	6.00
HB	Hank Blalock	8.00
HE	Todd Helton	8.00
HO	Trevor Hoffman	6.00
HR	Hanley Ramirez	8.00
HU	Torii Hunter	6.00
IR	Ivan Rodriguez	8.00
JB	Jason Bay	6.00
JC	Jorge Cantu	4.00
JD	J.D. Drew	6.00
JE	Jim Edmonds	6.00
JF	Jeff Francoeur	10.00
JG	Jason Giambi	8.00
JJ	Josh Johnson	4.00
JK	Jeff Kent	6.00
JM	Joe Mauer	8.00
JN	Joe Nathan	6.00
JO	Johnny Damon	8.00
JP	Jake Peavy	6.00
JR	Jimmy Rollins	10.00
JS	Jason Schmidt	4.00
JT	Jim Thome	8.00
JV	Justin Verlander	10.00
JZ	Joel Zumaya	8.00
KG	Ken Griffey Jr.	20.00
LB	Lance Berkman	6.00
LG	Luis Gonzalez	4.00
MC	Miguel Cabrera/67	10.00
MO	Justin Morneau	8.00
MR	Manny Ramirez	8.00
MT	Mark Teixeira	8.00
MY	Michael Young	8.00
OR	Magglio Ordonez	8.00
PA	Jonathan Papelbon	15.00
PB	Pat Burrell	6.00
PE	Jhonny Peralta	6.00
PF	Prince Fielder	15.00
PM	Pedro Martinez	10.00
PO	Jorge Posada	8.00
RC	Roger Clemens	15.00
RE	Jose Reyes	15.00
RH	Rich Harden	4.00
RI	Mariano Rivera	10.00
RJ	Randy Johnson	8.00
RO	Roy Oswalt	6.00
RW	Rickie Weeks	8.00
RZ	Ryan Zimmerman	10.00
SA	Johan Santana	8.00
SK	Scott Kazmir/31	6.00
SM	John Smoltz	8.00
SR	Scott Rolen	8.00
TG	Tom Glavine	8.00
TH	Tim Hudson	6.00
TR	Travis Hafner	6.00
VA	Jason Varitek	10.00
VG	Vladimir Guerrero/99	8.00
VM	Victor Martinez	8.00
VW	Vernon Wells	6.00

Divisional Artifacts Auto.

		NM/M
Production 25 unless noted.		
BO	Jeremy Bonderman	50.00
BR	Brian Roberts	40.00
CB	Craig Biggio	40.00
CC	Carl Crawford/55	20.00
CL	Carlos Lee	25.00
CR	Cal Ripken Jr.	180.00
CS	Curt Schilling	50.00
DO	David Ortiz	60.00
DW	Dontrelle Willis/55	20.00
EC	Eric Chavez	20.00
FH	Felix Hernandez/55	50.00
FT	Frank Thomas	75.00
GA	Garret Anderson/55	20.00
HA	Rich Harden	20.00
HR	Hanley Ramirez/55	25.00
IK	Ian Kinsler	20.00
JA	Jason Bay	20.00
JD	Jermaine Dye	20.00
JJ	Josh Johnson/55	15.00
JM	Joe Mauer	40.00
JP	Jake Peavy	30.00
JT	Jim Thome	50.00
JZ	Joel Zumaya	25.00
KG	Khalil Greene	25.00
KM	Kendry Morales/55	15.00
MC	Miguel Cabrera	35.00
MO	Justin Morneau	40.00
MY	Michael Young	20.00
PA	Jonathan Papelbon	30.00
PE	Jhonny Peralta	20.00
PM	Pedro Martinez	80.00
RC	Roger Clemens	120.00
RH	Roy Halladay	35.00
RW	Rickie Weeks	20.00
SK	Scott Kazmir	25.00
TI	Tim Hudson	30.00
VG	Vladimir Guerrero	50.00
VM	Victor Martinez	30.00

Apparel Autograph

		NM/M
Production 25 unless noted.		
AL	Adam LaRoche	20.00
AT	Garrett Atkins/55	15.00
BI	Craig Biggio	40.00
BO	Jeremy Bonderman	50.00
BR	Brian Roberts	40.00
BU	B.J. Upton	25.00
CC	Carl Crawford/55	20.00
CH	Cole Hamels	40.00
CL	Carlos Lee	25.00
CR	Cal Ripken Jr.	180.00
CS	Curt Schilling	50.00
DO	David Ortiz	60.00
DW	Dontrelle Willis	20.00
EC	Eric Chavez	20.00
ES	Johnny Estrada	20.00
FH	Felix Hernandez/23	50.00
FT	Frank Thomas	75.00
GA	Garret Anderson/55	20.00
GR	Khalil Greene/55	25.00
HA	Roy Halladay	35.00
HR	Hanley Ramirez	25.00
JB	Jason Bay/55	20.00
JJ	Josh Johnson	15.00
JP	Jake Peavy	30.00
JT	Jim Thome	50.00
JZ	Joel Zumaya	25.00
MC	Miguel Cabrera	35.00
MO	Justin Morneau	40.00
PA	Jonathan Papelbon	30.00
PE	Jhonny Peralta	20.00
PM	Pedro Martinez	80.00
RC	Roger Clemens	120.00
RH	Rich Harden	20.00
OW	Rickie Weeks	20.00
SK	Scott Kazmir	25.00
VG	Vladimir Guerrero	50.00
VW	Victor Martinez	30.00

2007 Upper Deck Elements

		NM/M
Complete Set (252):		.50
Common player (1-126):		.25
Common RC (127-252):		5.00
Production 550		
Pack (3):		10.00
Box (15):		125.00
1	Stephen Drew	.50
2	Andruw Jones	1.00
3	Chipper Jones	1.00
4	Miguel Tejada	.75
5	David Ortiz	1.00
6	Manny Ramirez	1.00
7	Derrek Lee	.75
8	Alfonso Soriano	1.00
9	Jermaine Dye	.50
10	Jim Thome	.75
11	Ken Griffey Jr.	2.00
12	Adam Dunn	.75
13	Travis Hafner	.50
14	Grady Sizemore	1.00
15	Todd Helton	.75
16	Gary Sheffield	.75
17	Miguel Cabrera	1.00
18	Lance Berkman	.50
19	Mark Teahen	.25
20	Vladimir Guerrero	1.00
21	Jered Weaver	.50
22	Rafael Furcal	.50
23	Prince Fielder	1.00
24	Justin Morneau	.75
25	Johan Santana	1.00
26	David Wright	2.00
27	Jose Reyes	2.00
28	Derek Jeter	3.00
29	Alex Rodriguez	3.00
30	Nick Swisher	.50
31	Ryan Howard	2.00
32	Jason Bay	.50
33	Adrian Gonzalez	.50
34	Ray Durham	.25
35	Ichiro Suzuki	2.00
36	Albert Pujols	3.00
37	Scott Rolen	.75
38	Carl Crawford	.75
39	Mark Teixeira	.75
40	Michael Young	.50
41	Vernon Wells	.50
42	Ryan Zimmerman	.50
43	Stephen Drew	.50
44	Andruw Jones	1.00
45	Chipper Jones	1.00
46	Miguel Tejada	.75
47	David Ortiz	1.00
48	Manny Ramirez	1.00
49	Derrek Lee	.75
50	Alfonso Soriano	1.00
51	Jermaine Dye	.50
52	Jim Thome	.75
53	Ken Griffey Jr.	2.00
54	Adam Dunn	.75
55	Travis Hafner	.50
56	Grady Sizemore	1.00
57	Todd Helton	.75
58	Gary Sheffield	.75
59	Miguel Cabrera	1.00
60	Lance Berkman	.50
61	Mark Teahen	.25
62	Vladimir Guerrero	1.00
63	Jered Weaver	.50
64	Rafael Furcal	.50
65	Prince Fielder	1.00
66	Justin Morneau	.75
67	Johan Santana	1.00
68	David Wright	2.00
69	Jose Reyes	2.00
70	Derek Jeter	3.00
71	Alex Rodriguez	3.00
72	Nick Swisher	.50
73	Ryan Howard	2.00
74	Jason Bay	.50
75	Adrian Gonzalez	.50
76	Ray Durham	.25
77	Ichiro Suzuki	2.00
78	Albert Pujols	3.00
79	Scott Rolen	.75
80	Carl Crawford	.50
81	Mark Teixeira	.75
82	Michael Young	.50
83	Vernon Wells	.50
84	Ryan Zimmerman	.50
85	Stephen Drew	.50
86	Andruw Jones	1.00
87	Chipper Jones	1.00
88	Miguel Tejada	.75
89	David Ortiz	1.00
90	Manny Ramirez	1.00
91	Derrek Lee	.75
92	Alfonso Soriano	1.00
93	Jermaine Dye	.50
94	Jim Thome	.75
95	Ken Griffey Jr.	2.00
96	Adam Dunn	.75
97	Travis Hafner	.50
98	Grady Sizemore	1.00
99	Todd Helton	.75
100	Gary Sheffield	.75
101	Miguel Cabrera	1.00
102	Lance Berkman	.50
103	Mark Teahen	.25
104	Vladimir Guerrero	1.00
105	Jered Weaver	.50
106	Rafael Furcal	.50
107	Prince Fielder	1.00
108	Justin Morneau	.75
109	Johan Santana	1.00
110	David Wright	2.00
111	Jose Reyes	2.00
112	Derek Jeter	3.00
113	Alex Rodriguez	3.00
114	Nick Swisher	.50
115	Ryan Howard	2.00
116	Jason Bay	.50
117	Adrian Gonzalez	.50
118	Ray Durham	.25
119	Ichiro Suzuki	2.00
120	Albert Pujols	3.00
121	Scott Rolen	.75
122	Carl Crawford	.50
123	Mark Teixeira	.75
124	Michael Young	.50
125	Vernon Wells	.50
126	Ryan Zimmerman	.50
127	Miguel Montero **(RC)**	5.00
128	Doug Slaten **RC**	5.00
129	Hunter Pence **(RC)**	30.00
130	Brian Burres **(RC)**	5.00
131	Daisuke Matsuzaka **RC**	25.00
132	Hideki Okajima **RC**	10.00
133	Devern Hansack **RC**	5.00
134	Felix Pie **(RC)**	8.00
135	Ryan Sweeney **(RC)**	5.00
136	Chris Stewart **RC**	5.00
137	Jarrod Saltalamacchia **(RC)**	8.00
138	John Danks **(RC)**	8.00
139	Travis Buck **(RC)**	5.00
140	Troy Tulowitzki **(RC)**	8.00
141	Chase Wright **RC**	8.00
142	Matt DeSalvo **(RC)**	5.00
143	Micah Owings **(RC)**	5.00
144	Jeff Baker **(RC)**	5.00
145	Andy LaRoche **(RC)**	10.00
146	Billy Butler **(RC)**	10.00
147	Jose Garcia **RC**	5.00
148	Angel Sanchez **RC**	5.00
149	Alex Gordon **RC**	25.00
150	Glen Perkins **(RC)**	5.00
151	Alexi Casilla **RC**	8.00
152	Joe Smith **RC**	5.00
153	Kei Igawa **RC**	15.00
154	Sean Henn **(RC)**	5.00
155	Phil Hughes **(RC)**	20.00
156	Michael Bourn **(RC)**	5.00
157	Josh Hamilton **(RC)**	10.00
158	Kevin Kouzmanoff **(RC)**	5.00

159 Tim Lincecum **RC** 50.00
160 Brandon Morrow **RC** 10.00
161 Brandon Wood **(RC)** 8.00
162 Akinori Iwamura **RC** 10.00
163 Delmon Young **(RC)** 8.00
164 Juan Salas **(RC)** 5.00
165 Elijah Dukes **RC** 8.00
166 Joaquin Arias **(RC)** 5.00
167 Adam Lind **(RC)** 5.00
168 Matt Chico **(RC)** 5.00
169 Miguel Montero **(RC)** 5.00
170 Doug Slaten **RC** 5.00
171 Hunter Pence **(RC)** 30.00
172 Brian Burres **(RC)** 5.00
173 Daisuke Matsuzaka **RC** 25.00
174 Hideki Okajima **RC** 10.00
175 Devern Hansack **RC** 5.00
176 Felix Pie **(RC)** 8.00
177 Ryan Sweeney **(RC)** 5.00
178 Chris Stewart **RC** 5.00
179 Jarrod Saltalamacchia **(RC)** 8.00
180 John Danks **(RC)** 8.00
181 Travis Buck **(RC)** 5.00
182 Troy Tulowitzki **(RC)** 8.00
183 Chase Wright **RC** 8.00
184 Matt DeSalvo **(RC)** 5.00
185 Micah Owings **(RC)** 5.00
186 Jeff Baker **(RC)** 5.00
187 Andy LaRoche **(RC)** 10.00
188 Billy Butler **(RC)** 10.00
189 Jose Garcia **RC** 5.00
190 Angel Sanchez **RC** 5.00
191 Alex Gordon **RC** 25.00
192 Glen Perkins **(RC)** 5.00
193 Alexi Casilla **RC** 8.00
194 Joe Smith **RC** 5.00
195 Kei Igawa **RC** 15.00
196 Sean Henn **(RC)** 5.00
197 Phil Hughes **(RC)** 20.00
198 Michael Bourn **(RC)** 5.00
199 Josh Hamilton **(RC)** 10.00
200 Kevin Kouzmanoff **(RC)** 5.00
201 Tim Lincecum **RC** 50.00
202 Brandon Morrow **RC** 10.00
203 Brandon Wood **(RC)** 8.00
204 Akinori Iwamura **RC** 10.00
205 Delmon Young **(RC)** 8.00
206 Juan Salas **(RC)** 5.00
207 Elijah Dukes **RC** 8.00
208 Joaquin Arias **(RC)** 5.00
209 Adam Lind **(RC)** 5.00
210 Matt Chico **(RC)** 5.00
211 Miguel Montero **(RC)** 5.00
212 Doug Slaten **RC** 5.00
213 Hunter Pence **(RC)** 30.00
214 Brian Burres **(RC)** 5.00
215 Daisuke Matsuzaka **RC** 25.00
216 Hideki Okajima **RC** 10.00
217 Devern Hansack **RC** 5.00
218 Felix Pie **(RC)** 8.00
219 Ryan Sweeney **(RC)** 5.00
220 Chris Stewart **RC** 5.00
221 Jarrod Saltalamacchia **(RC)** 8.00
222 John Danks **(RC)** 8.00
223 Travis Buck **(RC)** 5.00
224 Troy Tulowitzki **(RC)** 8.00
225 Chase Wright **RC** 8.00
226 Matt DeSalvo **(RC)** 5.00
227 Micah Owings **(RC)** 5.00
228 Jeff Baker **(RC)** 5.00
229 Andy LaRoche **(RC)** 10.00
230 Billy Butler **(RC)** 10.00
231 Jose Garcia **RC** 5.00
232 Angel Sanchez **RC** 5.00
233 Alex Gordon **RC** 25.00
234 Glen Perkins **(RC)** 5.00
235 Alexi Casilla **RC** 8.00
236 Joe Smith **RC** 5.00
237 Kei Igawa **RC** 15.00
238 Sean Henn **(RC)** 5.00
239 Phil Hughes **(RC)** 20.00
240 Michael Bourn **(RC)** 5.00
241 Josh Hamilton **(RC)** 10.00
242 Kevin Kouzmanoff **(RC)** 5.00
243 Tim Lincecum **RC** 50.00
244 Brandon Morrow **RC** 10.00
245 Brandon Wood **(RC)** 8.00
246 Akinori Iwamura **RC** 10.00
247 Delmon Young **(RC)** 8.00
248 Juan Salas **(RC)** 5.00
249 Elijah Dukes **RC** 8.00
250 Joaquin Arias **(RC)** 5.00
251 Adam Lind **(RC)** 5.00
252 Matt Chico **(RC)** 5.00

Printing Plates

Production one set per color.

Clear-Cut Elements

NM/M
Production 350 unless noted.
Gold: 1X
Production 49-199 Sets
Silver: 1.5X
Production 13-99 Sets
AH Aaron Harang 20.00
AK Austin Kearns/234 15.00
AS Alfonso Soriano 40.00
BB Brian Bannister 15.00
BR Brian Roberts 20.00
CA Matt Cain 20.00
CC Chris Carpenter 20.00
CP Corey Patterson 15.00
CR Cal Ripken Jr. 100.00
CR Carl Crawford 20.00
DJ Derek Jeter 200.00
DW Dontrelle Willis 15.00
FL Francisco Liriano 25.00
GR Ken Griffey Jr. 75.00
HR Hanley Ramirez 25.00
JB Jason Bay 20.00
JG Jonny Gomes 10.00
JH Jeremy Hermida 15.00
JP Jake Peavy 20.00
JT Jim Thome 30.00
JV Justin Verlander 30.00
JZ Joel Zumaya 20.00
KG Khalil Greene 15.00
KW Kerry Wood 15.00
MC Miguel Cabrera 30.00
MG Marcus Giles 10.00
MH Matt Holliday 20.00
ML Mark Loretta 10.00
MM Melvin Mora 10.00
MT Miguel Tejada 25.00
RH Rich Harden 10.00
RJ Reed Johnson 10.00
RZ Ryan Zimmerman 25.00
SA Johan Santana 30.00
SK Scott Kazmir 20.00
SR Scott Rolen 25.00
TH Travis Hafner 20.00
VM Victor Martinez 20.00

Dual Elements

NM/M
Production 50 unless noted.
BB Craig Biggio 15.00
BB Lance Berkman 15.00
BM Josh Beckett 60.00
BM Daisuke Matsuzaka 60.00
BS Freddy Sanchez 15.00
BS Jason Bay 15.00
CA Carlos Beltran 20.00
CA Alfonso Soriano 20.00
CB Carl Crawford 10.00
CB Rocco Baldelli 10.00
CM Mark Mulder 15.00
CM Chris Carpenter 15.00
DB Carlos Delgado 20.00
DB Carlos Beltran 20.00
DG Ken Griffey Jr. /29 25.00
DG Adam Dunn 25.00
DJ Derek Jeter 40.00
DJ Johnny Damon 40.00
GG Brian Giles 10.00
GG Marcus Giles 10.00
GJ Ken Griffey Jr. 50.00
GJ Derek Jeter 50.00
GM Tom Glavine 25.00
GM Pedro Martinez 25.00
GS Vladimir Guerrero 20.00
GS Alfonso Soriano 20.00
GT Ken Griffey Jr. 30.00
GT Frank Thomas 30.00
HB Roy Halladay 15.00
HB A.J. Burnett 15.00
HU Chase Utley 25.00
HU Cole Hamels 25.00
JJ Andruw Jones 25.00
JJ Chipper Jones 25.00
JR Derek Jeter 50.00
JR Jose Reyes 50.00
JT Derek Jeter 30.00
JT Miguel Tejada 30.00
LP Jon Lester 30.00
LP Jonathan Papelbon 30.00
MM Victor Martinez 15.00
MM Joe Mauer 15.00
MS Greg Maddux 30.00
MS John Smoltz 30.00
MT Justin Morneau 20.00
MT Joe Mauer 20.00
OR Manny Ramirez 30.00
OR David Ortiz 30.00
PG Ken Griffey Jr. 50.00
PG Albert Pujols 50.00
PZ Jonathan Papelbon 25.00
PZ Joel Zumaya 25.00
RH Mariano Rivera 15.00
RH Trevor Hoffman 15.00
RR Jose Reyes 30.00
RR Hanley Ramirez 30.00
RW Vernon Wells 15.00
RW Alex Rios 15.00
SB Curt Schilling 30.00
SB Josh Beckett 30.00
SH Travis Hafner 25.00
SH Grady Sizemore 25.00
SZ Barry Zito 20.00
SZ Johan Santana 20.00
TH Jim Thome 20.00
TH Travis Hafner 20.00
TK Jim Thome 20.00
TK Paul Konerko 20.00
TM Mark Teixeira 20.00
TM Justin Morneau 20.00
TR Miguel Tejada 20.00
TR Brian Roberts 20.00
TY Michael Young 20.00
TY Mark Teixeira 20.00
UU Chase Utley 20.00
UU Dan Uggla 20.00
VB Jeremy Bonderman 20.00
VB Justin Verlander 20.00
WH Vernon Wells 15.00
WH Torii Hunter 15.00
WJ Randy Johnson 20.00
WJ Brandon Webb 20.00
WS Johan Santana 25.00
WS Brandon Webb 25.00
ZR Scott Rolen 25.00
ZR Ryan Zimmerman 25.00

Elemental Autographs

NM/M
Common Autograph: 10.00
AI Akinori Iwamura 30.00
AL Adam LaRoche 15.00
BA Bronson Arroyo 20.00
BH Bill Hall 15.00
BL Joe Blanton 10.00
BN Brendan Harris 10.00
BO Jeremy Bonderman 20.00
BR Jared Burton 20.00
BT Jason Bartlett 10.00
BU Brian Burres 10.00
BW Brandon Wood 15.00
CB Cha Sueng Baek 20.00
CO Jon Coutlangus 20.00
CR Cal Ripken Jr. 100.00
CU Chase Utley 20.00
CW Chase Wright 20.00
DB Denny Bautista 10.00
DC Daniel Cabrera 15.00
DJ Derek Jeter 200.00
DU Dan Uggla 15.00
DW Dontrelle Willis 15.00
FP Felix Pie 15.00
GA Garrett Atkins 10.00
GC Gustavo Chacin 15.00
GO Alex Gordon 40.00
GP Glen Perkins 10.00
HA Rich Harden 10.00
HE Sean Henn 10.00
HR Hanley Ramirez 25.00
IK Ian Kinsler 15.00
JA Joaquin Arias 10.00
JB Jason Bay 20.00
JC Jesse Crain 10.00
JG Jonny Gomes 10.00
JH Josh Hamilton 25.00
JK Jon Knott 10.00
JO Josh Willingham 10.00
JP Jake Peavy 20.00
JV Justin Verlander 25.00
JW Jayson Werth 15.00
KE Howie Kendrick 15.00
KI Kei Igawa 30.00
KM Kendry Morales 10.00
KY Kevin Youkilis 20.00
LA Andy LaRoche 15.00
LI Bobby Livingston 15.00
LS Luke Scott 15.00
PA Jonathan Papelbon 25.00
PE Jhonny Peralta 15.00
RC Roger Clemens 80.00
RH Rich Hill 15.00
RL Ruddy Lugo 10.00
RO Scott Rolen 20.00
RT Ryan Theriot 35.00
SD Stephen Drew 20.00
SH James Shields 15.00
SK Scott Kazmir 15.00
SO Jeremy Sowers 10.00
SS Skip Schumaker 15.00
ST Scott Thorman 10.00
TB Travis Buck 15.00
TH Travis Hafner 15.00
TI Tadahito Iguchi 20.00
VM Victor Martinez 20.00
WO Jason Wood 10.00

Elemental Autographs Dual

Production 15 Sets

Elemental Autographs Triple

Production Five Sets

Elemental Autographs Quad

Production One Set

Essential Elements

NM/M
Common Player: 5.00
Patches: 2-4x
AB Adrian Beltre 5.00
AD Adam Dunn 8.00
AJ Andruw Jones 8.00
AP Andy Pettitte 8.00
AR Aramis Ramirez 8.00
AS Alfonso Soriano 8.00
BA Bobby Abreu 5.00
BC Bobby Crosby 5.00
BE Carlos Beltran 8.00
BG Brian Giles 5.00
BO Jeremy Bonderman 15.00
BR Brian Roberts 8.00
BU B.J. Upton 5.00
BW Billy Wagner 5.00
BZ Barry Zito 5.00
CA Miguel Cabrera 10.00
CB Craig Biggio 8.00
CC Carl Crawford 8.00
CH Cole Hamels 20.00
CJ Chipper Jones 10.00
CS Curt Schilling 8.00
CU Chase Utley 20.00
DA Johnny Damon 10.00
DM Daisuke Matsuzaka 60.00
DO David Ortiz 15.00
DR J.D. Drew 5.00
DU Dan Uggla 8.00
DW Dontrelle Willis 5.00
EC Eric Chavez 5.00
ED Jim Edmonds 5.00
FG Freddy Garcia 5.00
FH Felix Hernandez 8.00
FL Francisco Liriano 8.00
FT Frank Thomas 15.00
GA Garret Anderson 5.00
GJ Geoff Jenkins 5.00
GM Greg Maddux 20.00
GS Grady Sizemore 20.00
HA Rich Harden 5.00
HB Hank Blalock 5.00
HO Trevor Hoffman 8.00
HS Huston Street 5.00
HU Torii Hunter 8.00
IR Ivan Rodriguez 8.00
JA Jason Bay 8.00
JB Josh Beckett 8.00
JC Jorge Cantu 5.00
JD Jermaine Dye 8.00
JE Johnny Estrada 5.00
JF Jeff Francoeur 15.00
JG Jason Giambi 8.00
JJ Josh Johnson 5.00
JK Jeff Kent 5.00
JM Joe Mauer 8.00
JP Jake Peavy 8.00
JR Jimmy Rollins 8.00
JS Johan Santana 10.00
JT Jim Thome 8.00
JV Justin Verlander 10.00
KG Khalil Greene 8.00
LB Lance Berkman 8.00
LG Luis Gonzalez 5.00
MM Mike Mussina 10.00
MO Justin Morneau 10.00
MP Mike Piazza 20.00
MR Manny Ramirez 10.00
MT Mark Teixeira 10.00
MY Michael Young 8.00
OR Magglio Ordonez 10.00
PA Jonathan Papelbon 15.00
PB Pat Burrell 8.00
PE Jhonny Peralta 8.00
PO Jorge Posada 10.00
PU Albert Pujols 25.00
RE Jose Reyes 15.00
RH Roy Halladay 10.00
RI Mariano Rivera 10.00
RJ Randy Johnson 15.00
RO Roy Oswalt 10.00
RW Rickie Weeks 8.00
RZ Ryan Zimmerman 15.00
SK Scott Kazmir 8.00
SM John Smoltz 10.00
SR Scott Rolen 10.00
TE Miguel Tejada 8.00
TH Todd Helton 10.00
TI Tim Hudson 10.00
TR Travis Hafner 8.00
VG Vladimir Guerrero 10.00
VM Victor Martinez 8.00

Quad Elements

No Pricing Production 10 Sets

Triple Elements

Production 25 Sets

2007 UD Sweet Spot Classic

NM/M
Common Player: 2.00
Production 575 Sets
Tin (5): 100.00
1 Phil Niekro 2.00
2 Fred McGriff 3.00
3 Bob Horner 2.00
4 Earl Weaver 2.00
5 Boog Powell 2.00
6 Eddie Murray 4.00
7 Fred Lynn 2.00
8 Dwight Evans 2.00
9 Jim Rice 3.00
10 Carlton Fisk 4.00
11 Luis Tiant 2.00
12 Robin Yount 4.00
13 Bobby Doerr 2.00
14 Ryne Sandberg 5.00
15 Billy Williams 3.00
16 Andre Dawson 3.00
17 Mark Grace 3.00
18 Ron Santo 3.00
19 Shawon Dunston 2.00
20 Harold Baines 2.00
21 Carlton Fisk 4.00
22 Sparky Anderson 2.00
23 George Foster 2.00
24 Dave Parker 2.00
25 Ken Griffey Jr. 2.00
26 Dave Concepcion 2.00
27 Rafael Palmeiro 3.00
28 Al Rosen 2.00
29 Kirk Gibson 2.00
30 Alan Trammell 3.00
31 Jack Morris 2.00
32 Willie Horton 2.00
33 J.R. Richard 2.00
34 Jose Cruz 2.00
36 Willie Wilson 2.00
37 Bo Jackson 4.00
38 Nolan Ryan 8.00
39 Don Baylor 2.00
40 Maury Wills 2.00
41 Tommy John 2.00
42 Ron Cey 2.00
43 Davey Lopes 2.00
44 Tommy Lasorda 2.00
45 Burt Hooton 2.00
46 Reggie Smith 2.00
47 Rollie Fingers 2.00
48 Cecil Cooper 2.00
49 Paul Molitor 4.00
50 Vern Stephens 2.00
51 Tony Oliva 2.00
52 Andres Galarraga 2.00
53 Tim Raines 2.00
54 Dennis Martinez 2.00
55 Lee Mazzilli 2.00
56 Rusty Staub 2.00
57 David Cone 2.00
58 Reggie Jackson 4.00
59 Ron Guidry 2.00
60 Tino Martinez 3.00
61 Don Mattingly 6.00
62 Chris Chambliss 2.00
63 Sparky Lyle 2.00
64 Rich "Goose" Gossage 2.00
65 Dave Righetti 2.00
66 Phil Garner 2.00
67 Bill Madlock 2.00
68 Kent Hrbek 2.00
69 Al Oliver 2.00
70 John Kruk 2.00
71 Greg Luzinski 2.00
72 Dick Allen 2.00
73 Richie Ashburn 3.00
74 Gary Matthews 2.00
76 Mike Schmidt 5.00
77 Waite Hoyt 2.00
78 Bruce Sutter 2.00
79 Roger Maris 6.00
80 Joe Torre 3.00
81 Kevin Mitchell 2.00
82 John Montefusco 2.00
83 Rick Reuschel 2.00
84 Will Clark 3.00
85 Jack Clark 2.00
86 Matt Williams 2.00
87 Steve Garvey 3.00
88 Dave Winfield 3.00
89 Jay Buhner 2.00
90 Edgar Martinez 2.00
91 Carney Lansford 2.00
92 Sal Bando 2.00
93 Dave Stewart 2.00
94 Dennis Eckersley 3.00
95 Jose Canseco 3.00
96 Dennis Eckersley 3.00
97 Roberto Alomar 3.00
98 George Bell 2.00
99 Joe Carter 2.00
100 Frank Howard 2.00
101 Brooks Robinson 4.00
102 Frank Robinson 4.00
103 Jim Palmer 3.00
104 Cal Ripken Jr. 8.00
105 Warren Spahn 4.00
106 Cy Young 4.00
107 Waite Hoyt 2.00
108 Carl Yastrzemski 4.00
109 Johnny Pesky 3.00
110 Wade Boggs 3.00
111 Jackie Robinson 4.00
112 Roy Campanella 4.00
113 Pee Wee Reese 2.00
114 Don Newcombe 2.00
115 Rod Carew 4.00
116 Ernie Banks 4.00
117 Fergie Jenkins 2.00
118 Al Lopez 2.00
119 Luis Aparicio 2.00
120 Toby Harrah 2.00
121 Joe Morgan 3.00
122 Johnny Bench 4.00
123 Tony Perez 3.00
124 Ted Kluszewski 2.00
125 Bob Feller 3.00
126 Bob Lemon 2.00
127 Larry Doby 3.00
128 Lou Boudreau 2.00
129 George Kell 2.00
130 Hal Newhouser 2.00
131 Al Kaline 4.00
132 Ty Cobb 5.00
133 Denny McLain 3.00
134 Buck Leonard 3.00
135 Dean Chance 2.00
136 Don Drysdale 3.00
137 Don Sutton 3.00
138 Eddie Mathews 4.00
139 Paul Molitor 4.00
140 Kirby Puckett 5.00
141 Rod Carew 3.00
142 Harmon Killebrew 4.00
143 Monte Irvin 3.00
144 Mel Ott 3.00
145 Christy Mathewson 4.00
146 Hoyt Wilhelm 2.00
147 Tom Seaver 4.00
148 Joe McCarthy 2.00
149 Joe DiMaggio 6.00
150 Lou Gehrig 6.00
151 Babe Ruth 8.00
152 Casey Stengel 3.00
153 Phil Rizzuto 4.00
154 Thurman Munson 5.00
155 Johnny Mize 2.00
156 Yogi Berra 4.00
157 Roger Maris 5.00
158 Don Larsen 3.00
159 Bill "Moose" Skowron 2.00
160 Lou Piniella 3.00
161 Joe Pepitone 2.00
162 Ray Dandridge 2.00
163 Rollie Fingers 2.00
165 Reggie Jackson 4.00
166 Mickey Cochrane 3.00
167 Jimmie Foxx 4.00
168 Lefty Grove 3.00
169 Gus Zernial 2.00
170 Jim Bunning 2.00
171 Steve Carlton 3.00
172 Robin Roberts 3.00
173 Ralph Kiner 3.00
174 Willie Stargell 4.00
175 Roberto Clemente 6.00
176 Bill Mazeroski 2.00
177 Honus Wagner 5.00
178 Pie Traynor 3.00
179 Elroy Face 2.00
180 Dick Groat 2.00
181 Tony Gwynn 4.00
182 Willie McCovey 3.00
183 Gaylord Perry 2.00
184 Juan Marichal 3.00
185 Orlando Cepeda 3.00
186 Satchel Paige 4.00
187 George Sisler 3.00
188 Rogers Hornsby 4.00
189 Stan Musial 4.00
190 Dizzy Dean 3.00
191 Bob Gibson 4.00
192 Red Schoendienst 2.00
193 Lou Brock 3.00
194 Enos Slaughter 2.00
195 Nolan Ryan 8.00
196 Mickey Vernon 2.00
197 Walter Johnson 4.00
198 Rick Ferrell 2.00
199 Roy Sievers 2.00
200 Judy Johnson 2.00

Ripken Immortal Membership

Production One Set

Classic Memorabilia

NM/M
Common Player: 5.00
Patch: 2-4X
Production 55 Sets
AD Andre Dawson 8.00
AK Al Kaline 10.00
AO Al Oliver 8.00
BE Johnny Bench 15.00
BJ Bo Jackson 15.00
BM Bill Madlock 5.00
BO Wade Boggs 8.00
BR Babe Ruth/SP 200.00
BS Bruce Sutter 5.00
CL Roberto Clemente 40.00
CM Christy Mathewson/SP 125.00
CR Cal Ripken Jr. 20.00
CS Casey Stengel 10.00
CY Carl Yastrzemski 10.00
DD Dizzy Dean 30.00
DE Dennis Eckersley 5.00
DM Don Mattingly 15.00
DP Dave Parker 5.00
DR Don Drysdale 10.00
DS Don Sutton 5.00
DW Dave Winfield 10.00
ED Eddie Murray 8.00
EM Eddie Mathews 15.00
EV Dwight Evans 5.00
EW Early Wynn 8.00
FG Fred McGriff 5.00
FI Rollie Fingers 5.00
FR Frank Robinson 10.00
GF George Foster 5.00
GG Rich "Goose" Gossage 8.00
GI Kirk Gibson 5.00
GP Gaylord Perry 5.00
GW Tony Gwynn 10.00
HB Harold Baines/SP 8.00
HK Harmon Killebrew/SP 10.00

JB Jim Bunning 8.00
JD Joe DiMaggio 60.00
JI Jim Rice 8.00
JM Jack Morris 5.00
JP Jim Palmer 8.00
JU Juan Marichal 8.00
KG Ken Griffey Jr. 5.00
KH Kent Hrbek 5.00
KP Kirby Puckett 15.00
LA Luis Aparicio 5.00
LB Lou Brock 8.00
LG Lou Gehrig 150.00
MA Don Mattingly 15.00
ME Eddie Murray 8.00
MG Mark Grace 8.00
MO Mel Ott 20.00
MP Paul Molitor 10.00
MR Edgar Martinez 5.00
MS Mike Schmidt 15.00
MW Maury Wills 5.00
NR Nolan Ryan 20.00
PA Dave Parker 5.00
PE Tony Perez 5.00
PM Paul Molitor 10.00
PN Phil Niekro 5.00
PR Pee Wee Reese/SP 25.00
RF Rollie Fingers 5.00
RG Ron Guidry 10.00
RH Rogers Hornsby 25.00
RK Ralph Kiner 10.00
RM Roger Maris 30.00
RO Roy Campanella 15.00
RS Ron Santo 10.00
RY Nolan Ryan 20.00
SC Red Schoendienst 8.00
SG Steve Garvey 5.00
ST Steve Carlton 8.00
SU Bruce Sutter 5.00
TG Tony Gwynn 10.00
TM Thurman Munson 20.00
TO Tony Oliva 8.00
TP Tony Perez 5.00
TR Tim Raines 5.00
WB Wade Boggs 8.00
WC Will Clark 5.00
WM Willie McCovey 8.00
WS Willie Stargell 8.00
YO Robin Yount 10.00
CF1 Carlton Fisk 8.00
CF2 Carlton Fisk 8.00
FR1 Frank Robinson 10.00
MI1 Johnny Mize 10.00
MI2 Johnny Mize 10.00
RC1 Rod Carew 8.00
RC2 Rod Carew 8.00
RJ1 Reggie Jackson 10.00
RJ2 Reggie Jackson 10.00
RJ3 Reggie Jackson 10.00

Legendary Lettermen

NM/M
Represents total cards produced
LL1 Babe Ruth/100 150.00
LL2 Ty Cobb/100 75.00
LL3 Christy Mathewson/90 50.00
LL4 Jackie Robinson/80 60.00
LL5 Roy Campanella/100 50.00
LL6 Lou Gehrig/90 150.00
LL7 Mel Ott/75 25.00
LL8 Jimmie Foxx/100 50.00
LL9 Satchel Paige/125 40.00
LL10 Don Drysdale/200 30.00
LL11 Rogers Hornsby/175 60.00
LL12 Honus Wagner/150 50.00
LL13 Babe Ruth/105 150.00
LL14 Dizzy Dean/100 50.00
LL15 Ty Cobb/60 75.00
LL16 Walter Johnson/105 50.00
LL17 Walter Johnson/80 50.00
LL18 Cal Ripken Jr./200 100.00
LL19 Sandy Koufax/150 250.00
LL20 Thurman Munson/150 40.00
LL21 Thurman Munson/70 40.00
LL22 Cal Ripken Jr./175 100.00
LL23 Tony Gwynn/125 50.00
LL24 Nolan Ryan/80 50.00
LL25 Nolan Ryan/165 50.00
LL26 Jackie Robinson/70 60.00
LL27 Carlton Fisk/80 40.00
LL28 Carl Yastrzemski/165 60.00
LL29 Johnny Bench/125 50.00
LL30 Ryne Sandberg/200 100.00
LL31 Don Mattingly/135 75.00
LL32 Ernie Banks/165 40.00
LL33 Bill Mazeroski/135 50.00
LL34 Ernie Banks/125 40.00
LL35 Bob Gibson/150 40.00
LL36 Mike Schmidt/175 60.00
LL37 Al Kaline/150 40.00
LL38 Reggie Jackson/175 50.00
LL39 Stan Musial/150 50.00
LL40 Bo Jackson/175 50.00
LL41 Bo Jackson/105 50.00
LL42 Stan Musial/150 50.00

Dual Sig Red Stitch-Blue Ink

NM/M
Production 50 Sets
Black Stitch Red Ink: No Pricing
Production One Set
Gold Stitch Black Ink: No Pricing
Production 15 Sets
AG Luis Aparicio, Ozzie Guillen 30.00
BF Carlton Fisk, Johnny Bench 75.00
BG Harold Baines, Ozzie Guillen 50.00
BR Robin Roberts, Jim Bunning 60.00
CG Tony Gwynn, Rod Carew 90.00
CO Tony Oliva, Rod Carew 40.00
FE Dennis Eckersley, Rollie Fingers 50.00
FG Elroy Face, Dick Groat 50.00
FM Mike Schmidt, Frank Robinson 80.00
FR Carlton Fisk, Jim Rice 50.00
GR Bob Gibson, J.R. Richard 50.00
GS Steve Garvey, Reggie Smith 30.00
GW Tony Gwynn, Dave Winfield 80.00
HK Al Kaline, Willie Horton 80.00
JS Reggie Smith, Reggie Jackson 50.00
KM Ralph Kiner, Bill Mazeroski 75.00
LT Tim Raines, Lou Brock 40.00
MC Jack Clark, Willie McCovey 75.00
MG Juan Marichal, Bob Gibson 60.00
MK Stan Musial, Al Kaline 125.00
MM Don Mattingly, Tino Martinez 80.00
MR Edgar Martinez, Harold Reynolds 50.00
OH Tony Oliva, Kent Hrbek 40.00
RR Nolan Ryan, J.R. Richard 150.00
RS Cal Ripken Jr., Mike Schmidt 180.00
SB Ron Santo, Ernie Banks 125.00
SC Mike Schmidt, Steve Carlton 80.00
SD Ryne Sandberg, Shawon Dunston 80.00
SF Rollie Fingers, Bruce Sutter 60.00
SS Ron Santo, Ryne Sandberg 125.00
SV Mickey Vernon, Roy Sievers 30.00
YP Carl Yastrzemski, Johnny Pesky 100.00

Immortal Signatures

Common Player

Signatures Sepia Black Ink

NM/M
Production 16-199
Red Ink: No Pricing
Production 15 Sets
CF Carlton Fisk/124 30.00
CY Carl Yastrzemski/124 50.00
DM Don Mattingly/124 50.00
DS Duke Snider/30 75.00
JM Juan Marichal/124 30.00
JR Jim Rice/85 30.00
MU Dale Murphy/183 25.00
NR Nolan Ryan/123 80.00
OS Ozzie Smith/183 50.00
RS Ryne Sandberg/199 50.00
TG Tony Gwynn/199 50.00

Signatures Sepia Blue Ink

NM/M
Production 15-199
AK Al Kaline/199 30.00
BW Billy Williams/199 20.00
CF Carlton Fisk/78 30.00
CY Carl Yastrzemski/90 60.00
DM Don Mattingly/78 60.00
DS Duke Snider/199 40.00
EM Edgar Martinez/74 40.00
JM Juan Marichal/84 25.00
JR Jim Rice/75 25.00
LM Lee Mazzilli/199 15.00
MU Dale Murphy/75 50.00
NR Nolan Ryan/80 80.00
OS Ozzie Smith/75 60.00
RC Rocky Colavito/199 50.00
TG Tony Gwynn/199 50.00
WC Will Clark/199 25.00

Signatures Black Ink

NM/M
Common Signature: 15.00
Production 175 unless noted.
AG Andres Galarraga 20.00
AK Al Kaline 30.00
AO Al Oliver 15.00
BJ Bo Jackson 50.00
BM Bill Mazeroski 40.00
BO Wade Boggs/75 40.00
BS Bruce Sutter/75 20.00
CF Carlton Fisk/75 35.00
DA Dick Allen 20.00
DL Don Larsen 30.00
DM Don Mattingly/75 60.00
EC Dennis Eckersley 20.00
EM Edgar Martinez 30.00
FM Fred McGriff 25.00
GP Gaylord Perry 20.00
HB Harold Baines 15.00
JB Johnny Bench/75 60.00
JK John Kruk 20.00
MO Jack Morris 20.00
MS Mike Schmidt/75 50.00
NR Nolan Ryan/75 80.00
OG Ozzie Guillen 20.00
RA Roberto Alomar 25.00
RI Jim Rice 20.00
RJ Reggie Jackson/75 60.00
RS Ryne Sandberg/75 60.00
SA Ron Santo 30.00
SM Reggie Smith 20.00
TG Tony Gwynn/75 50.00
TM Tino Martinez 35.00
TP Tony Perez 25.00
TR Tim Raines 20.00
WB Wade Boggs/75 40.00
WD Willie Davis/75 20.00
WM Willie McCovey/75 50.00
YB Yogi Berra/75 80.00
BR Brooks Robinson 30.00
BW Billy Williams 30.00
CL Carney Lansford 20.00
CO Dave Concepcion 25.00
CY Carl Yastrzemski 50.00
DG Dick Groat 30.00
DS Don Sutton 20.00
DW Dave Winfield 25.00
EB Ernie Banks 60.00
EF Elroy Face 20.00
EV Dwight Evans 20.00
FL Fred Lynn 15.00
FR Frank Robinson/35 50.00
GI Bob Gibson 40.00
JI Jim Bunning 20.00
JP Johnny Pesky 30.00
JR Jim Rice 20.00
KG Ken Griffey Sr. 15.00
KO Sandy Koufax 350.00
LA Luis Aparicio 25.00
LB Lou Brock/75 40.00
MA Juan Marichal 25.00
MG Mark Grace 30.00
MU Stan Musial/75 80.00
MV Mickey Vernon 20.00
OS Ozzie Smith/75 60.00
PN Phil Niekro 20.00
RC Rod Carew 30.00
RF Rollie Fingers 20.00
RK Ralph Kiner/75 40.00
RR Robin Roberts 30.00
RY Robin Yount 40.00
SC Steve Carlton 30.00
SD Shawon Dunston 25.00
SG Steve Garvey 25.00
SK Bill "Moose" Skowron 20.00
TH Toby Harrah 15.00
TO Tony Oliva 20.00
WH Willie Horton 20.00

2007 Upper Deck Goudey

NM/M
Complete Set (288):
Common Player (1-200): .15
Common SP (201-240): 1.50
Inserted 1:6
Common Heads Up (241-288): 2.00
Inserted 1:10
Hobby Pack (8): 5.00
Hobby Box (24): 100.00
1 A.J. Burnett .25
2 Aaron Boone .15
3 Aaron Rowand .25
4 Adam Dunn .50
5 Adrian Beltre .25
6 Albert Pujols 2.00
7 Ivan Rodriguez .50
8 Alfonso Soriano .75
9 Andruw Jones .50
10 Andy Pettitte .50
11 Aramis Ramirez .40
12 B.J. Upton .25
13 Barry Zito .25
14 Bartolo Colon .15
15 Ben Sheets .25
16 Bobby Abreu .25
17 Bobby Crosby .15
18 Brian Giles .15
19 Brian Roberts .25
20 C.C. Sabathia .40
21 Carlos Beltran .75
22 Carlos Delgado .50
23 Carlos Lee .25
24 Carlos Zambrano .25
25 Chad Cordero .15
26 Chad Tracy .15
27 Chipper Jones .75
28 Craig Biggio .25
29 Curt Schilling .50
30 Danny Haren .25
31 Darin Erstad .15
32 David Ortiz .75
33 Billy Wagner .15
34 Derek Jeter 2.00
35 Derek Lee .50
36 Dontrelle Willis .25
37 Edgar Renteria .25
38 Eric Chavez .25
39 Felix Hernandez .25
40 Garret Anderson .25
41 Garrett Atkins .25
42 Gary Sheffield .50
43 Grady Sizemore .75
44 Greg Maddux 1.50
45 Hank Blalock .25
46 Hanley Ramirez .75
47 J.D. Drew .25
48 Jacque Jones .15
49 Jake Peavy .40
50 Jake Westbrook .15
51 Jason Bay .25
52 Jason Giambi .50
53 Jason Schmidt .25
54 Jason Varitek .40
55 Troy Tulowitzki .40
56 Jeff Francoeur .40
57 Jeff Kent .25
58 Jeremy Bonderman .25
59 Jim Edmonds .25
60 Jim Thome .50
61 Jimmy Rollins .50
62 Joe Mauer .25
63 Johan Santana .75
64 John Smoltz .40
65 Johnny Damon .75
66 Jose Reyes .75
67 Josh Beckett .40
68 Justin Morneau .50
69 Ken Griffey Jr. 1.50
70 Kerry Wood .15
71 Khalil Greene .25
72 Lance Berkman .25
73 Livan Hernandez .15
74 Manny Ramirez .75
75 Mark Mulder .25
76 Chase Utley .75
77 Mark Teixeira .50
78 Miguel Tejada .40
79 Miguel Cabrera .75
80 Mike Piazza .75
81 Pat Burrell .25
82 Paul LoDuca .15
83 Pedro Martinez .75
84 Prince Fielder 1.00
85 Rafael Furcal .25
86 Randy Johnson .75
87 Richie Sexson .25
88 Robinson Cano .75
89 Roy Halladay .40
90 Roy Oswalt .40
91 Scott Rolen .50
92 Tim Hudson .25
93 Todd Helton .50
94 Tom Glavine .50
95 Torii Hunter .40
96 Travis Hafner .40
97 Trevor Hoffman .25
98 Vernon Wells .40
99 Vladimir Guerrero .75
100 Zachary Duke .15
101 Alex Rodriguez 2.00
102 Ryan Howard 1.00
103 Michael Barrett .15
104 Ichiro Suzuki 1.50
105 Hideki Matsui 1.50
106 Jered Weaver .40
107 Dan Uggla .25
108 Ryan Freel .15
109 Bill Hall .25
110 Ray Durham .15
111 Morgan Ensberg .15
112 Shawn Green .25
113 Brandon Webb .40
114 Frank Thomas .75
115 Corey Patterson .15
116 Edwin Encarnacion .15
117 Mike Cameron .15
118 Matt Holliday .40
119 Jhonny Peralta .25
120 Nick Swisher .25
121 Brad Penny .15
122 Kenji Johjima .25
123 Francisco Rodriguez .15
124 Mark Teahen .15
125 Jonathan Papelbon .50
126 Carlos Guillen .15
127 Freddy Sanchez .15
128 Chien-Ming Wang .75
129 Andre Ethier .15
130 Matt Cain .25
131 Austin Kearns .15
132 Ramon Hernandez .15
133 Chris Carpenter .40
134 Michael Cuddyer .15
135 Stephen Drew .25
136 David Wright .75
137 David DeJesus .15
138 Gary Matthews .15
139 Brandon Phillips .15
140 Josh Barfield .15
141 Alex Gordon 1.00
142 Scott Kazmir .15
143 Luis Gonzalez .15
144 Mike Sweeney .15
145 Luis Castillo .15
146 Huston Street .15
147 Phil Hughes 1.00
148 Adrian Gonzalez .25
149 Raul Ibanez .15
150 Joe Crede .15
151 Mark Loretta .15
152 Adam LaRoche .25
153 Troy Glaus .40
154 Conor Jackson .15
155 Michael Young .25
156 Scott Podsednik .15
157 David Eckstein .15
158 Mike Jacobs .15
159 Nomar Garciaparra .75
160 Mariano Rivera .50
161 Pedro Feliz .15
162 Josh Hamilton .15
163 Ryan Langerhans .15
164 Willy Taveras .15
165 Carl Crawford .25
166 Melvin Mora .15
167 Francisco Liriano .25
168 Orlando Cabrera .25
169 Chris Duncan .15
170 Johnny Estrada .15
171 Ryan Zimmerman .50
172 Rickie Weeks .25
173 Paul Konerko .40
174 Jack Wilson .15
175 Jorge Posada .40
176 Magglio Ordonez .25
177 Nick Johnson .15
178 Geoff Jenkins .15
179 Reggie Sanders .15
180 Moises Alou .25
181 Glen Perkins .15
182 Brad Lidge .15
183 Kevin Kouzmanoff .15
184 Jorge Cantu .15
185 Carlos Quentin .15
186 Rich Harden .15
187 Jose Vidro .15
188 Aaron Harang .15
189 Noah Lowry .15
190 Jermaine Dye .25
191 Victor Martinez .25
192 Chone Figgins .25
193 Aubrey Huff .15
194 Jason Isringhausen .15
195 Brian McCann .40
196 Juan Pierre .15
197 Delmon Young .50
198 Felipe Lopez .15
199 Brad Hawpe .15
200 Justin Verlander .40
201 Mike Schmidt 3.00
202 Nolan Ryan 4.00
203 Cal Ripken Jr. 4.00
204 Harmon Killebrew 3.00
205 Reggie Jackson 2.00
206 Johnny Bench 2.00
207 Carlton Fisk 2.00
208 Yogi Berra 3.00
209 Al Kaline 3.00
210 Alan Trammell 1.50
211 Bill Mazeroski 2.00
212 Bob Gibson 2.00
213 Brooks Robinson 3.00
214 Carl Yastrzemski 3.00
215 Don Mattingly 3.00
216 Fergie Jenkins 1.50
217 Jim Rice 1.50
218 Lou Brock 2.00
219 Rod Carew 2.00
220 Stan Musial 3.00
221 Tom Seaver 3.00
222 Tony Gwynn 3.00
223 Wade Boggs 2.00
224 Alex Rodriguez 4.00
225 David Wright 3.00
226 Ryan Howard 3.00
227 Ichiro Suzuki 3.00
228 Ken Griffey Jr. 3.00
229 Daisuke Matsuzaka 4.00
230 Kei Igawa 1.50
231 Akinori Iwamura 2.00
232 Derek Jeter 4.00
233 Albert Pujols 4.00
234 Greg Maddux 3.00
235 David Ortiz 3.00
236 Manny Ramirez 2.00
237 Johan Santana 2.00
238 Pedro Martinez 2.00
239 Roger Clemens 4.00
240 Vladimir Guerrero 2.00
241 Ken Griffey Jr. 4.00
242 Derek Jeter 5.00
243 Ichiro Suzuki 4.00
244 Cal Ripken Jr. 5.00
245 Daisuke Matsuzaka 5.00
246 Kei Igawa 2.00
247 Joe Mauer 2.00
248 Babe Ruth 5.00
249 Johnny Bench 3.00
250 Reggie Jackson 3.00
251 Carlton Fisk 3.00
252 Albert Pujols 5.00
253 Nolan Ryan 5.00
254 Ryan Howard 4.00
255 Mike Schmidt 4.00
256 Brooks Robinson 4.00
257 Harmon Killebrew 4.00
258 Alex Rodriguez 5.00
259 David Ortiz 4.00
260 David Wright 4.00
261 Al Kaline 4.00
262 Justin Verlander 3.00
263 Chase Utley 4.00
264 Justin Morneau 3.00
265 Ken Griffey Jr. 4.00
266 Derek Jeter 5.00
267 Ichiro Suzuki 4.00
268 Cal Ripken Jr. 5.00
269 Daisuke Matsuzaka 5.00
270 Kei Igawa 2.00
271 Joe Mauer 2.00
272 Babe Ruth 5.00
273 Johnny Bench 3.00
274 Reggie Jackson 3.00
275 Carlton Fisk 3.00
276 Albert Pujols 5.00
277 Nolan Ryan 5.00
278 Ryan Howard 4.00
279 Mike Schmidt 4.00
280 Brooks Robinson 4.00
281 Harmon Killebrew 4.00
282 Alex Rodriguez 5.00
283 David Ortiz 4.00
284 David Wright 4.00
285 Al Kaline 4.00
286 Justin Verlander 3.00
287 Chase Utley 4.00
288 Justin Morneau 3.00

1933 Goudey Originals

Inserted 2:Case
See 1933 Goudey Pricing

Signatures Blue Ink

NM/M
Common Signature: 20.00
Production 125 unless noted.
AG Andres Galarraga 20.00
AK Al Kaline 30.00
AO Al Oliver 20.00
BJ Bo Jackson 50.00
BM Bill Mazeroski 40.00
BO Wade Boggs/35 50.00
BS Bruce Sutter/35 25.00
CF Carlton Fisk/35 40.00
DA Dick Allen 20.00
DL Don Larsen 30.00
DM Don Mattingly/35 60.00
EC Dennis Eckersley 20.00
EM Edgar Martinez 30.00
FM Fred McGriff 30.00
GP Gaylord Perry 20.00
HB Harold Baines 20.00
JB Johnny Bench/35 60.00
JK John Kruk 20.00
MO Jack Morris 20.00
MS Mike Schmidt/35 75.00
NR Nolan Ryan/35 120.00
OG Ozzie Guillen 20.00
RA Roberto Alomar 25.00
RI Jim Rice 20.00
RJ Reggie Jackson/35 60.00
RS Ryne Sandberg/35 60.00
SA Ron Santo 30.00
SM Reggie Smith 20.00
TG Tony Gwynn/35 60.00
TM Tino Martinez 40.00
TP Tony Perez 25.00
TR Tim Raines 20.00
WB Wade Boggs/35 50.00
WD Willie Davis/35 20.00
WM Willie McCovey/35 60.00
YB Yogi Berra/35 80.00
BR Brooks Robinson 30.00
BW Billy Williams 20.00
CL Carney Lansford 15.00
CO Dave Concepcion 15.00
CY Carl Yastrzemski 60.00
DG Dick Groat 25.00
DS Don Sutton 20.00
DW Dave Winfield 25.00
EB Ernie Banks 60.00
EF Elroy Face 30.00
EV Dwight Evans 20.00
FL Fred Lynn 15.00
FR Frank Robinson/75 40.00
GI Bob Gibson 30.00
JI Jim Bunning 20.00
JP Johnny Pesky 25.00
JR Jim Rice 20.00
KG Ken Griffey Sr. 20.00
KO Sandy Koufax 300.00
LA Luis Aparicio 20.00
LB Lou Brock/35 40.00
MA Juan Marichal 30.00
MG Mark Grace 25.00
MU Stan Musial/35 80.00
MV Mickey Vernon 20.00
OS Ozzie Smith/35 60.00
PN Phil Niekro 15.00
RC Rod Carew 30.00
RF Rollie Fingers 20.00
RK Ralph Kiner/35 40.00
RR Robin Roberts 20.00
RY Robin Yount 40.00
SC Steve Carlton 25.00
SD Shawon Dunston 25.00
SG Steve Garvey 20.00
SK Bill "Moose" Skowron 20.00
TH Toby Harrah 15.00
TO Tony Oliva 20.00
WH Willie Horton 25.00

Signatures Barrel Black Ink

NM/M
Production 50 or 15

Barrel Blue Ink: 1X
Production 25 or 75
No pricing for production 15 or 25.
AG Andres Galarraga/50 25.00
AK Al Kaline/50 50.00
AO Al Oliver/50 30.00
BJ Bo Jackson/50 60.00
BM Bill Mazeroski/50 50.00
DL Don Larsen/50 50.00
EC Dennis Eckersley/50 30.00
EM Edgar Martinez/50 40.00
FM Fred McGriff/50 30.00
GP Gaylord Perry/50 30.00
HB Harold Baines/50 25.00
JK John Kruk/50 30.00
MO Jack Morris/50 20.00
OG Ozzie Guillen/50 25.00
RA Roberto Alomar/50 40.00
RI Jim Rice/50 30.00
SA Ron Santo/50 50.00
SM Reggie Smith/50 25.00
TM Tino Martinez/50 50.00
TP Tony Perez/50 30.00
TR Tim Raines/50 30.00
EV Dwight Evans/50 20.00
JI Jim Bunning/50 25.00
KG Ken Griffey Sr./50 20.00
LA Luis Aparicio/50 20.00
MA Juan Marichal/50 30.00
WH Willie Horton/50 30.00

Sig. Black Barrel Silver Ink

NM/M
Production 3-47
Gold Ink: No pricing
Production one set
EC Dennis Eckersley/43 30.00
FM Fred McGriff/27 40.00
GP Gaylord Perry/36 25.00
JK John Kruk/29 30.00
MO Jack Morris/47 25.00
TM Tino Martinez/24 50.00
TP Tony Perez/24 40.00
TR Tim Raines/30 40.00
EV Dwight Evans/24 35.00
KG Ken Griffey Sr./30 25.00
WH Willie Horton/23 35.00

Sig Black Leather Silver Ink

NM/M
Production 3-47
Green Ink: No Pricing
Production One Set
BS Bruce Sutter/42 30.00
CF Carlton Fisk/27 40.00
EC Dennis Eckersley/43 30.00
FM Fred McGriff/27 40.00
GP Gaylord Perry/36 25.00
JK John Kruk/29 30.00
MO Jack Morris/47 25.00
NR Nolan Ryan/30 140.00
RJ Reggie Jackson/44 60.00
TM Tino Martinez/24 50.00
TP Tony Perez/24 40.00
TR Tim Raines/30 40.00
WM Willie McCovey/44 60.00
BW Billy Williams/26 25.00
DG Dick Groat/24 50.00
DW Dave Winfield/31 30.00
EF Elroy Face/26 30.00
EV Dwight Evans/24 35.00
GI Bob Gibson/45 50.00
KG Ken Griffey Sr./30 25.00
KO Sandy Koufax/32 350.00
MA Juan Marichal/27 35.00
PN Phil Niekro/35 35.00
RC Rod Carew/29 30.00
RF Rollie Fingers/34 20.00
RR Robin Roberts/36 40.00
SC Steve Carlton/32 30.00
WH Willie Horton/23 35.00

Sig. Gold Stitch Black Ink

NM/M
Production 25 or 99
Blue Ink: 1-1.5X
Production 15 or 50
AG Andres Galarraga/99 20.00
AK Al Kaline/99 40.00
AO Al Oliver/99 15.00
BJ Bo Jackson/99 60.00
BM Bill Mazeroski/99 40.00
BO Wade Boggs/25 40.00
CF Carlton Fisk/25 40.00
DA Dick Allen/99 20.00
DL Don Larsen/99 30.00
DM Don Mattingly/25 75.00
EC Dennis Eckersley/99 30.00
EM Edgar Martinez/99 40.00
FM Fred McGriff/99 40.00
GP Gaylord Perry/99 20.00
HB Harold Baines/99 20.00
JK John Kruk/99 25.00
MO Jack Morris/99 15.00
MS Mike Schmidt/25 80.00
OG Ozzie Guillen/99 20.00
RA Roberto Alomar/99 30.00
RI Jim Rice/99 20.00
RS Ryne Sandberg/25 80.00
SA Ron Santo/99 40.00
SM Reggie Smith/99 20.00
TG Tony Gwynn/25 75.00
TM Tino Martinez/99 30.00
TP Tony Perez/99 20.00
TR Tim Raines/99 15.00
WB Wade Boggs/25 40.00
WD Willie Davis/25 30.00
WM Willie McCovey/25 60.00
YB Yogi Berra/25 80.00
BR Brooks Robinson/99 35.00
BW Billy Williams/99 25.00
CL Carney Lansford/99 20.00
CO Dave Concepcion/99 25.00
CY Carl Yastrzemski/99 65.00
DG Dick Groat/99 30.00
DS Don Sutton/99 20.00
DW Dave Winfield/99 30.00
EB Ernie Banks/99 65.00
EF Elroy Face/99 25.00
EV Dwight Evans/99 20.00
FL Fred Lynn/99 20.00
FR Frank Robinson/25 40.00
GI Bob Gibson/99 40.00
JI Jim Bunning/99 25.00
JP Johnny Pesky/99 30.00
JR Jim Rice/99 25.00
KG Ken Griffey Sr./99 20.00
KO Sandy Koufax/99 300.00
LA Luis Aparicio/99 20.00
LB Lou Brock/25 40.00
MA Juan Marichal/99 30.00
MG Mark Grace/99 30.00
MU Stan Musial/25 100.00
MV Mickey Vernon/99 25.00
OS Ozzie Smith/25 75.00
PN Phil Niekro/99 20.00
RC Rod Carew/99 35.00
RF Rollie Fingers/99 20.00
RK Ralph Kiner/25 60.00
RR Robin Roberts/99 30.00
RY Robin Yount/99 40.00
SC Steve Carlton/99 30.00
SD Shawon Dunston/99 20.00
SG Steve Garvey/99 20.00
SK "Moose" Skowron/99 20.00
TH Toby Harrah/99 15.00
TO Tony Oliva/99 20.00
WH Willie Horton/99 20.00

Signatures Leather Blue Ink

NM/M
Production 75 unless noted
Gold Ink: 1-1.5X
Production 15 or 50
AG Andres Galarraga 25.00
AK Al Kaline 50.00
AO Al Oliver 25.00
BJ Bo Jackson 75.00
BM Bill Mazeroski 50.00
BO Wade Boggs/25 40.00
CF Carlton Fisk/25 40.00
DA Dick Allen 20.00
DL Don Larsen 40.00
DM Don Mattingly/25 75.00
EC Dennis Eckersley 30.00
EM Edgar Martinez 50.00
FM Fred McGriff 40.00
GP Gaylord Perry 20.00
HB Harold Baines 20.00
JK John Kruk 20.00
MO Jack Morris 20.00
MS Mike Schmidt/25 80.00
OG Ozzie Guillen 20.00
RA Roberto Alomar 50.00
RI Jim Rice 25.00
RS Ryne Sandberg/25 80.00
SA Ron Santo 50.00
SM Reggie Smith 20.00
TG Tony Gwynn/25 75.00
TM Tino Martinez 30.00
TP Tony Perez 30.00
TR Tim Raines 20.00
WB Wade Boggs/25 40.00
WD Willie Davis/25 30.00
WM Willie McCovey/25 60.00
YB Yogi Berra/25 80.00
BR Brooks Robinson/25 60.00
CL Carney Lansford/25 20.00
CO Dave Concepcion/25 20.00
CY Carl Yastrzemski/25 80.00
DG Dick Groat/25 25.00
DS Don Sutton/25 20.00
DW Dave Winfield/25 40.00
EB Ernie Banks/25 80.00
EF Elroy Face/25 30.00
EV Dwight Evans 25.00
FL Fred Lynn/25 20.00
FR Frank Robinson/25 50.00
JI Jim Bunning 25.00
JP Johnny Pesky/25 35.00
JR Jim Rice/25 25.00
KG Ken Griffey Sr. 15.00
KO Sandy Koufax/25 350.00
LA Luis Aparicio 30.00
LB Lou Brock/25 40.00
MA Juan Marichal 35.00
MG Mark Grace/25 40.00
MU Stan Musial/25 100.00
MV Mickey Vernon/25 30.00
OS Ozzie Smith/25 80.00
PN Phil Niekro/25 25.00
RC Rod Carew/25 50.00
RF Rollie Fingers/25 30.00
RK Ralph Kiner/25 50.00
RR Robin Roberts/25 40.00
RY Robin Yount/25 60.00
SC Steve Carlton/25 25.00
SD Shawon Dunston/25 25.00
SG Steve Garvey/25 30.00
SK "Moose" Skowron/25 30.00
TH Toby Harrah/25 20.00
TO Tony Oliva/25 30.00
WH Willie Horton/25 30.00

Sig. Silver Stitch Blue Ink

NM/M
Production 3-47
Black Ink: No pricing
Production 15 or 25
BS Bruce Sutter/42 25.00
CF Carlton Fisk/27 40.00
EC Dennis Eckersley/43 30.00
FM Fred McGriff/27 40.00
GP Gaylord Perry/36 25.00
JK John Kruk/29 30.00
MO Jack Morris/47 25.00
NR Nolan Ryan/30 140.00
RJ Reggie Jackson/44 60.00
TM Tino Martinez/24 50.00
TP Tony Perez/24 40.00
TR Tim Raines/30 40.00
WB Wade Boggs/26 50.00
WM Willie McCovey/44 60.00
BW Billy Williams/26 25.00
DG Dick Groat/24 50.00
DW Dave Winfield/31 40.00
EF Elroy Face/26 30.00
EV Dwight Evans/24 35.00
GI Bob Gibson/45 50.00
KG Ken Griffey Sr./30 25.00
KO Sandy Koufax/32 350.00
MA Juan Marichal/27 40.00
PN Phil Niekro/35 35.00
RC Rod Carew/29 40.00
RF Rollie Fingers/34 20.00
RR Robin Roberts/36 40.00
SC Steve Carlton/32 30.00
WH Willie Horton/23 35.00

2007 UD SP Rookie Edition

NM/M
Complete Set (284):
Common player (1-100): .25
Common RC (101-142): .50
Common SP (143-234): 1.00
Inserted 1:2
Common (235-284): .25
Pack (8): 5.00
Box (14): 65.00
1 Chipper Jones .75
2 Andruw Jones .50
3 Jeff Francoeur .75
4 Stephen Drew .25
5 Randy Johnson .75
6 Brandon Webb .50
7 Alfonso Soriano .75
8 Derrek Lee .50
9 Aramis Ramirez .50
10 Carlos Zambrano .40
11 Ken Griffey Jr. 1.50
12 Adam Dunn .50
13 Bronson Arroyo .25
14 Todd Helton .50
15 Jeff Francis .25
16 Matt Holliday .50
17 Hanley Ramirez .75
18 Dontrelle Willis .25
19 Miguel Cabrera .75
20 Lance Berkman .40
21 Roy Oswalt .50
22 Carlos Lee .50
23 Nomar Garciaparra .75
24 Jason Schmidt .25
25 Juan Pierre .40
26 Rafael Furcal .40
27 Rickie Weeks .25
28 Prince Fielder .75
29 Ben Sheets .40
30 David Wright 1.00
31 Jose Reyes .75
32 Pedro Martinez .75
33 Carlos Beltran .50
34 Cole Hamels .50
35 Jimmy Rollins .50
36 Ryan Howard 1.00
37 Jason Bay .40
38 Freddy Sanchez .25
39 Zachary Duke .25
40 Jake Peavy .40
41 Greg Maddux 1.50
42 Trevor Hoffman .25
43 Matt Cain .25
44 Barry Zito .25
45 Omar Vizquel .25
46 Albert Pujols 2.00
47 Chris Carpenter .50
48 Jim Edmonds .40
49 Scott Rolen .50
50 Ryan Zimmerman .50
51 Felipe Lopez .25
52 Austin Kearns .25
53 Miguel Tejada .40
54 Erik Bedard .40
55 Chris Ray .25
56 David Ortiz .75
57 Curt Schilling .50
58 Manny Ramirez .50
59 Jonathan Papelbon .50
60 Jim Thome .50
61 Paul Konerko .40
62 Bobby Jenks .25
63 Grady Sizemore .75
64 Victor Martinez .40
65 C.C. Sabathia .40
66 Ivan Rodriguez .50
67 Justin Verlander .50
68 Joel Zumaya .25
69 Jeremy Bonderman .40
70 Gil Meche .25
71 Mike Sweeney .25
72 Mark Teahen .25
73 Vladimir Guerrero .75
74 Howie Kendrick .25
75 Francisco Rodriguez .25
76 Johan Santana .75
77 Justin Morneau .50
78 Joe Mauer .50
79 Joe Nathan .25
80 Alex Rodriguez 2.00
81 Derek Jeter 2.00
82 Johnny Damon .75
83 Mariano Rivera .50
84 Rich Harden .25
85 Mike Piazza .75
86 Nick Swisher .40
87 Ichiro Suzuki 1.50
88 Felix Hernandez .50
89 Kenji Johjima .40
90 Richie Sexson .40
91 Carl Crawford .40
92 Scott Kazmir .40
93 B.J. Upton .40
94 Michael Young .40
95 Mark Teixeira .50
96 Eric Gagne .25
97 Hank Blalock .25
98 Vernon Wells .40
99 Roy Halladay .40
100 Frank Thomas .75
101 Joaquin Arias **(RC)** .50
102 Jeff Baker **(RC)** .50
103 Brian Barden **RC** .50
104 Michael Bourn **(RC)** .50
105 Kevin Slowey **(RC)** 1.50
106 Chase Wright **RC** 1.00
107 Kory Casto **(RC)** .50
108 Matt Chico **(RC)** .50
109 Matt DeSalvo **(RC)** 1.00
110 Homer Bailey **(RC)** 1.00
111 Ryan Braun **(RC)** 3.00
112 Felix Pie **(RC)** 1.00
113 Jesus Flores **RC** .50
114 Ryan Sweeney **(RC)** .50
115 Ryan Braun **RC** .50
116 Alex Gordon **RC** 1.50
117 Josh Hamilton **(RC)** 1.50
118 Sean Henn **(RC)** .50
119 Kei Igawa **RC** 1.00
120 Akinori Iwamura **RC** 1.50
121 Andy LaRoche **(RC)** 1.50
122 Kevin Kouzmanoff **(RC)** 1.50
123 Matt Lindstrom **(RC)** .50
124 Tim Lincecum **RC** 4.00
125 Daisuke Matsuzaka **RC** 4.00
126 Gustavo Molina **RC** .50
127 Miguel Montero **(RC)** .50
128 Brandon Morrow **RC** 1.50
129 Hideki Okajima **RC** 1.50
130 Adam Lind **(RC)** .50
131 Mike Rabelo **RC** .50
132 Micah Owings **(RC)** .50
133 Brandon Wood **(RC)** .50
134 Alexi Casilla **RC** 1.00
135 Joe Smith **RC** .50
136 Hunter Pence **(RC)** 3.00
137 Glen Perkins **(RC)** .50
138 Chris Stewart **RC** .50
139 Troy Tulowitzki **(RC)** 2.00
140 Billy Butler **(RC)** 1.00
141 Delmon Young **(RC)** 1.00
142 Phil Hughes **(RC)** 2.00
143 Joaquin Arias 1.00
144 Jeff Baker 1.00
145 Brian Barden 1.00
146 Michael Bourn 1.00
147 Kevin Slowey 2.00
148 Chase Wright 2.00
149 Kory Casto 1.00
150 Matt Chico 1.00
151 Shawn Riggans 1.00
152 Juan Salas 1.00
153 Ryan Braun 5.00
154 Felix Pie 1.00
155 Jesus Flores 1.00
156 Ryan Sweeney 1.00
157 Ryan Braun 1.00
158 Alex Gordon 4.00
159 Josh Hamilton 2.00
160 Sean Henn 1.00
161 Kei Igawa 2.00
162 Akinori Iwamura 2.00
163 Andy LaRoche 1.00
164 Kevin Kouzmanoff 1.00
165 Matt Lindstrom 1.00
166 Tim Lincecum 6.00
167 Daisuke Matsuzaka 6.00
168 Gustavo Molina 1.00
169 Miguel Montero 1.00
170 Brandon Morrow 1.00
171 Hideki Okajima 3.00
172 Adam Lind 1.00
173 Mike Rabelo 1.00
174 Micah Owings 1.00
175 Brandon Wood 1.00
176 Alexi Casilla 2.00
177 Joe Smith 1.00
178 Hunter Pence 5.00
179 Glen Perkins 1.00
180 Chris Stewart 1.00
181 Troy Tulowitzki 3.00
182 Billy Butler 2.00
183 Delmon Young 2.00
184 Phil Hughes 3.00
185 Joaquin Arias 1.00
186 Jeff Baker 1.00
187 Mark Reynolds 1.50
188 Joseph Bisenius 1.00
189 Michael Bourn 1.00
190 Zack Segovia 1.00
191 Kevin Slowey 2.00
192 Chase Wright 2.00
193 Rocky Cherry 1.00
194 Danny Putnam 1.50
195 Kory Casto 1.00
196 Matt Chico 1.00
197 John Danks 1.00
198 Homer Bailey 1.50
199 Ryan Braun 5.00
200 Felix Pie 1.00
201 Jesus Flores 1.00
202 Andy Gonzalez 1.00
203 Ryan Sweeney 1.00
204 Jarrod Saltalamacchia 1.50
205 Alex Gordon 4.00
206 Josh Hamilton 2.00
207 Sean Henn 1.00
208 Kei Igawa 2.00
209 Akinori Iwamura 2.00
210 Andy LaRoche 1.00
211 Rick Vanden Hurk 1.00
212 Kevin Kouzmanoff 1.00
213 Matt Lindstrom 1.00
214 Tim Lincecum 6.00
215 Daisuke Matsuzaka 6.00
216 Gustavo Molina 1.00
217 Miguel Montero 1.00
218 Brandon Morrow 2.00
219 Hideki Okajima 3.00
220 Adam Lind 1.00
221 Mike Rabelo 1.00
222 Brian Burres 1.00
223 Micah Owings 1.00
224 Brandon Wood 1.00
225 Alexi Casilla 2.00
226 Joe Smith 1.00
227 Hunter Pence 5.00
228 Glen Perkins 1.00
229 Chris Stewart 1.00
230 Ben Francisco 1.00
231 Troy Tulowitzki 3.00
232 Billy Butler 2.00
233 Delmon Young 2.00
234 Phil Hughes 3.00
235 Joaquin Arias .50
236 Jeff Baker .50
237 Mark Reynolds 1.00
238 Joseph Bisenius .50
239 Michael Bourn .50
240 Zack Segovia .50
241 Travis Buck .50
242 Chase Wright 1.00
243 Rocky Cherry 1.00
244 Danny Putnam .50
245 Kory Casto .50
246 Matt Chico .50
247 John Danks .50
248 Juan Salas .50
249 Ryan Braun 3.00
250 Felix Pie 1.00
251 Jesus Flores .50
252 Andy Gonzalez .50
253 Ryan Sweeney .50
254 Jarrod Saltalamacchia 1.00
255 Alex Gordon 1.50
256 Josh Hamilton 1.50
257 Sean Henn .50
258 Kei Igawa 1.00
259 Akinori Iwamura 1.50
260 Andy LaRoche 1.50
261 Rick Vanden Hurk .50
262 Kevin Kouzmanoff 1.50
263 Matt Lindstrom .50
264 Tim Lincecum 4.00
265 Daisuke Matsuzaka 4.00
266 Gustavo Molina .50
267 Miguel Montero .50
268 Brandon Morrow 1.50
269 Hideki Okajima 1.50
270 Adam Lind .50
271 Mike Rabelo .50
272 Brian Burres .50
273 Micah Owings .50
274 Brandon Wood .50
275 Alexi Casilla 1.00
276 Joe Smith .50
277 Hunter Pence 3.00
278 Glen Perkins .50
279 Chris Stewart .50
280 Ben Francisco .50
281 Troy Tulowitzki 2.00
282 Billy Butler 1.00
283 Delmon Young 1.00
284 Phil Hughes 2.00

Autographs

NM/M
Common Autograph: 8.00
101 Joaquin Arias 8.00
102 Jeff Baker 8.00
103 Brian Barden 8.00
104 Michael Bourn 10.00
105 Kevin Slowey 15.00
106 Chase Wright 15.00
107 Kory Casto 8.00
108 Matt Chico 8.00
109 Matt DeSalvo 15.00
110 Homer Bailey 20.00
111 Ryan Braun 75.00
112 Felix Pie 15.00
113 Jesus Flores 15.00
114 Ryan Sweeney 8.00
115 Ryan Braun 10.00
116 Alex Gordon/SP 60.00
117 Josh Hamilton 20.00
118 Sean Henn 8.00
121 Andy LaRoche 15.00
122 Kevin Kouzmanoff 15.00
123 Matt Lindstrom 8.00
124 Tim Lincecum/SP 100.00
125 Daisuke Matsuzaka/SP 275.00
126 Gustavo Molina 15.00
127 Miguel Montero 8.00
128 Brandon Morrow 15.00
130 Adam Lind 10.00
131 Mike Rabelo 10.00
132 Micah Owings 15.00
133 Brandon Wood 15.00
134 Alexi Casilla 10.00
135 Joe Smith 10.00
136 Hunter Pence/SP 50.00
137 Glen Perkins 8.00
138 Chris Stewart 8.00
139 Troy Tulowitzki/SP 30.00
140 Billy Butler 25.00
142 Phil Hughes/SP 80.00
143 Joaquin Arias 8.00
144 Jeff Baker 8.00
145 Brian Barden 8.00
146 Michael Bourn 10.00
147 Kevin Slowey 15.00
148 Chase Wright 15.00
149 Kory Casto 8.00
150 Matt Chico 8.00
151 Shawn Riggans 8.00
152 Juan Salas 8.00
153 Ryan Braun 75.00
154 Felix Pie 15.00
155 Jesus Flores 15.00
156 Ryan Sweeney 8.00
157 Ryan Braun 10.00
158 Alex Gordon/SP 60.00
159 Josh Hamilton 20.00
160 Sean Henn 8.00
163 Andy LaRoche 15.00
164 Kevin Kouzmanoff 15.00
165 Matt Lindstrom 8.00
166 Tim Lincecum/SP 100.00
167 Daisuke Matsuzaka/SP 275.00
168 Gustavo Molina 15.00
169 Miguel Montero 8.00
170 Brandon Morrow 15.00
172 Adam Lind 10.00
173 Mike Rabelo 10.00
174 Micah Owings 15.00
175 Brandon Wood 15.00
176 Alexi Casilla 10.00
177 Joe Smith 10.00
178 Hunter Pence 50.00
179 Glen Perkins 8.00
180 Chris Stewart 8.00
181 Troy Tulowitzki 30.00
182 Billy Butler 25.00
184 Phil Hughes/SP 80.00
185 Joaquin Arias 8.00
186 Jeff Baker 8.00
188 Joseph Bisenius 8.00
189 Michael Bourn 8.00
190 Zack Segovia 8.00
191 Kevin Slowey 15.00
192 Chase Wright 15.00
193 Rocky Cherry 20.00
194 Danny Putnam 20.00
195 Kory Casto 8.00
196 Matt Chico 8.00
197 John Danks 8.00
198 Homer Bailey 20.00
199 Ryan Braun 75.00
200 Felix Pie 15.00
201 Jesus Flores 15.00
202 Andy Gonzalez 10.00
203 Ryan Sweeney/SP 10.00
204 Jarrod Saltalamacchia 15.00
205 Alex Gordon/SP 60.00
206 Josh Hamilton/SP 20.00
207 Sean Henn 8.00
210 Andy LaRoche 15.00
211 Rick Vanden Hurk 8.00
212 Kevin Kouzmanoff 15.00
213 Matt Lindstrom 8.00
214 Tim Lincecum/SP 100.00
215 Daisuke Matsuzaka/SP 275.00
216 Gustavo Molina 15.00
217 Miguel Montero 8.00
218 Brandon Morrow 15.00
220 Adam Lind 10.00
221 Mike Rabelo 10.00
222 Brian Burres 8.00
223 Micah Owings 15.00
224 Brandon Wood/SP 15.00
225 Alexi Casilla 10.00
226 Joe Smith 10.00
227 Hunter Pence/SP 50.00
228 Glen Perkins 8.00
229 Chris Stewart 8.00
230 Ben Francisco 8.00
231 Troy Tulowitzki/SP 30.00
232 Billy Butler/SP 25.00
234 Phil Hughes/SP 80.00
235 Joaquin Arias 8.00
236 Jeff Baker 8.00

238 Joseph Bisenius 8.00
239 Michael Bourn 10.00
240 Zack Segovia 10.00
242 Chase Wright 15.00
243 Rocky Cherry 20.00
244 Danny Putnam 20.00
245 Kory Casto 8.00
246 Matt Chico 8.00
247 John Danks 8.00
248 Juan Salas 8.00
249 Ryan Braun/SP 75.00
250 Felix Pie 15.00
251 Jesus Flores 15.00
252 Andy Gonzalez 8.00
253 Ryan Sweeney 8.00
254 Jarrod Saltalamacchia/SP 15.00
255 Alex Gordon/SP 60.00
256 Josh Hamilton 20.00
257 Sean Henn 8.00
260 Andy LaRoche 15.00
261 Rick Vanden Hurk 8.00
262 Kevin Kouzmanoff 15.00
263 Matt Lindstrom 8.00
264 Tim Lincecum/SP 100.00
265 Daisuke Matsuzaka/SP 275.00
266 Gustavo Molina 15.00
267 Miguel Montero 8.00
268 Brandon Morrow 15.00
270 Adam Lind 10.00
271 Mike Rabelo 10.00
272 Brian Burres 8.00
273 Micah Owings 15.00
274 Brandon Wood 15.00
275 Alexi Casilla 10.00
276 Joe Smith 10.00
277 Hunter Pence/SP 50.00
278 Glen Perkins 8.00
279 Chris Stewart 8.00
280 Ben Francisco 8.00
281 Troy Tulowitzki/SP 30.00
282 Billy Butler/SP 25.00
284 Phil Hughes/SP 80.00

1934-36 Diamond Stars

No Pricing
Production 15 Sets
Autographs: No Pricing
Production One Set

1941 Double Play

No Pricing
Production 15 Sets
Autographs: No Pricing
Production One Set

Graphs

NM/M
Common Autograph: 5.00
AC Alberto Callaspo 10.00
AH Aaron Harang 20.00
AK Al Kaline SP 150.00
AM Andy Marte 8.00
AR Aaron Rowand 20.00
BA Brian Anderson 5.00
BB Brian Bannister 15.00
BE Johnny Bench/SP 150.00
BO Boof Bonser 10.00
BU B.J. Upton 20.00
CC Carl Crawford 10.00
CF Carlton Fisk SP 50.00
CL Cliff Lee 8.00
CO Coco Crisp 20.00
CR Cal Ripken Jr./SP 160.00
CY Chris Young 15.00
DJ Derek Jeter 150.00
FH Felix Hernandez 30.00
GA Garrett Atkins 10.00
GP Glen Perkins 5.00
HA Bill Hall 10.00
HI Rich Hill 15.00
HR Hanley Ramirez 25.00
JB Jason Bay 10.00
JW Jered Weaver 15.00
JZ Joel Zumaya 15.00
KG Ken Griffey Jr./SP 100.00
KJ Kelly Johnson 15.00
KK Kevin Kouzmanoff 15.00
LS Luke Scott 8.00
MO Justin Morneau 25.00
MS Mike Schmidt/SP 80.00
RA Reggie Abercrombie 8.00
RT Ryan Theriot 25.00
RZ Ryan Zimmerman 30.00
SA Anibal Sanchez 5.00
SK Scott Kazmir 15.00
TB Taylor Buchholz 8.00
VM Victor Martinez 15.00
YB Yogi Berra/SP 75.00

Sports Royalty

NM/M
Common Card: 2.00
AI Akinori Iwamura 2.00
AP Albert Pujols 8.00
AS Alfonso Soriano 3.50
CC Chris Carpenter 2.00
CR Cal Ripken Jr. 15.00
DJ Derek Jeter 8.00
DM Daisuke Matsuzaka 8.00
DO David Ortiz 4.00
DS Dean Smith 3.00
ES Emmitt Smith 5.00
GH Gordie Howe 10.00
GM Greg Maddux 5.00
HI Martina Hingis 4.00
HR Hanley Ramirez 3.00
JM Justin Morneau 3.00
JN Joe Namath 5.00
JV Justin Verlander 2.00
JW John Wooden 2.00
KB Kobe Bryant 4.00
KD Kevin Durant 8.00
KG Ken Griffey Jr. 8.00
KH Katie Hoff 2.00
KI Kei Igawa 2.00
LE Jeanette Lee 2.00
LJ LeBron James 10.00
LT LaDainian Tomlinson 8.00
MH Mia Hamm 5.00
MJ Michael Jordan 15.00
NR Nolan Ryan 15.00
PI Mike Piazza 4.00
PM Peyton Manning 8.00
RH Roy Halladay 2.00
RJ Randy Johnson 3.00
RL Ryan Lochte 2.00
SA Johan Santana 3.00
SC Sidney Crosby 15.00
TH Trevor Hoffman 2.00
TW Tiger Woods 20.00
VG Vladimir Guerrero 3.00

Immortals Memorabilia

Inserted 1:288

Sports Royalty Auto.

NM/M
Common Autograph: 25.00
AI Akinori Iwamura 25.00
CR Cal Ripken Jr. 180.00
DJ Derek Jeter 140.00
DM Daisuke Matsuzaka 250.00
DO David Ortiz 75.00
GH Gordie Howe 100.00
GM Greg Maddux 160.00
HI Martina Hingis 100.00
HR Hanley Ramirez 25.00
JM Justin Morneau 25.00
JV Justin Verlander 60.00
JW John Wooden 125.00
KG Ken Griffey Jr. 100.00
KH Katie Hoff 75.00
KI Kei Igawa 30.00
LE Jeanette Lee 150.00
LJ LeBron James 300.00
LT LaDainian Tomlinson 150.00
MH Mia Hamm 125.00
RH Roy Halladay 30.00
RL Ryan Lochte 65.00
SC Sidney Crosby 200.00

Memorabilia

NM/M
Common Player: 4.00
1 A.J. Burnett 4.00
3 Aaron Rowand 4.00
4 Adam Dunn 8.00
5 Adrian Beltre 6.00
6 Albert Pujols 20.00
7 Ivan Rodriguez 8.00
8 Alfonso Soriano 15.00
9 Andruw Jones 6.00
10 Andy Pettitte 8.00
11 Aramis Ramirez 8.00
12 B.J. Upton 6.00
13 Barry Zito 6.00
14 Bartolo Colon SP 6.00
15 Ben Sheets 6.00
16 Bobby Abreu SP 6.00
17 Bobby Crosby 4.00
18 Brian Giles 4.00
19 Brian Roberts 6.00
20 C.C. Sabathia 8.00
21 Carlos Beltran 8.00
22 Carlos Delgado 6.00
23 Carlos Lee 6.00
24 Carlos Zambrano 6.00
26 Chad Tracy 4.00
27 Chipper Jones 8.00
28 Craig Biggio 6.00
29 Curt Schilling 8.00
31 Darin Erstad 4.00
32 David Ortiz 10.00
33 Billy Wagner 6.00
34 Derek Jeter 20.00
35 Derrek Lee 8.00
36 Dontrelle Willis 6.00
37 Edgar Renteria 4.00
38 Eric Chavez 4.00
39 Felix Hernandez 8.00
40 Garret Anderson 4.00
41 Garrett Atkins 4.00
42 Gary Sheffield 8.00
43 Grady Sizemore 8.00
44 Greg Maddux 15.00
45 Hank Blalock 4.00
46 Hanley Ramirez 10.00
47 J.D. Drew 4.00
49 Jake Peavy 6.00
50 Jake Westbrook 4.00
51 Jason Bay 8.00
52 Jason Giambi 8.00
54 Jason Varitek 10.00
56 Jeff Francoeur 10.00
57 Jeff Kent 6.00
58 Jeremy Bonderman 6.00
59 Jim Edmonds 6.00
60 Jim Thome 6.00
61 Jimmy Rollins 8.00
62 Joe Mauer 6.00
63 Johan Santana 8.00
64 John Smoltz 8.00
66 Jose Reyes 20.00
67 Josh Beckett 8.00
68 Justin Morneau 8.00
69 Ken Griffey Jr. 15.00
70 Kerry Wood 6.00
71 Khalil Greene 6.00
72 Lance Berkman 6.00
73 Livan Hernandez 4.00
74 Manny Ramirez 8.00
75 Mark Mulder 4.00
76 Chase Utley 15.00
77 Mark Teixeira 8.00
78 Miguel Tejada 6.00
79 Miguel Cabrera 8.00
80 Mike Piazza 10.00
81 Pat Burrell 6.00
82 Paul LoDuca 4.00
83 Pedro Martinez 8.00
84 Prince Fielder 15.00
85 Rafael Furcal 6.00
86 Randy Johnson 8.00
87 Richie Sexson 6.00
88 Robinson Cano 8.00
89 Roy Halladay 8.00
90 Roy Oswalt 8.00
91 Scott Rolen 6.00
92 Tim Hudson 6.00
93 Todd Helton 8.00
94 Tom Glavine 8.00
95 Torii Hunter 6.00
96 Travis Hafner 8.00
97 Trevor Hoffman 6.00
98 Vernon Wells 6.00
99 Vladimir Guerrero 8.00
100 Zachary Duke 4.00

2007 Upper Deck Future Stars

NM/M
Common Player (1-100): .25
Common RC Auto. (101-189): 8.00
Pack (4): 4.00
Box (24): 90.00
1 Brandon Webb .40
2 Conor Jackson .25
3 Stephen Drew .40
4 Chipper Jones .75
5 Andruw Jones .40
6 Jeff Francoeur .75
7 John Smoltz .40
8 Miguel Tejada .50
9 Nicholas Markakis .50
10 Brian Roberts .25
11 David Ortiz .75
12 Manny Ramirez .75
13 Josh Beckett .50
14 Curt Schilling .75
15 Derrek Lee .50
16 Aramis Ramirez .50
17 Carlos Zambrano .50
18 Alfonso Soriano .75
19 Jim Thome .50
20 Paul Konerko .50
21 Jon Garland .25
22 Ken Griffey Jr. 1.50
23 Adam Dunn .50
24 Aaron Harang .25
25 Travis Hafner .40
26 Victor Martinez .50
27 Grady Sizemore .75
28 C.C. Sabathia .50
29 Todd Helton .50
30 Matt Holliday .50
31 Garrett Atkins .40
32 Ivan Rodriguez .50
33 Magglio Ordonez .40
34 Gary Sheffield .50
35 Justin Verlander .50
36 Miguel Cabrera .75
37 Hanley Ramirez .75
38 Dontrelle Willis .25
39 Lance Berkman .50
40 Roy Oswalt .50
41 Carlos Lee .50
42 Gil Meche .25
43 Emil Brown .25
44 Mark Teahen .25
45 Vladimir Guerrero .75
46 Jered Weaver .40
47 Howie Kendrick .25
48 Juan Pierre .40
49 Nomar Garciaparra .75
50 Rafael Furcal .40
51 Jeff Kent .40
52 Prince Fielder 1.00
53 Ben Sheets .40
54 Rickie Weeks .25
55 Justin Morneau .50
56 Joe Mauer .50
57 Torii Hunter .40
58 Johan Santana .75
59 Jose Reyes .75
60 David Wright .75
61 Carlos Delgado .50
62 Carlos Beltran .50
63 Derek Jeter 2.00
64 Alex Rodriguez 2.00
65 Johnny Damon .50
66 Jason Giambi .50
67 Bobby Abreu .50
68 Mike Piazza .75
69 Nick Swisher .40
70 Eric Chavez .25
71 Ryan Howard 1.00
72 Chase Utley .75
73 Jimmy Rollins .50
74 Jason Bay .40
75 Freddy Sanchez .25
76 Zachary Duke .25
77 Greg Maddux 1.00
78 Adrian Gonzalez .25
79 Jake Peavy .40
80 Ray Durham .25
81 Barry Zito .25
82 Matt Cain .25
83 Ichiro Suzuki 1.50
84 Felix Hernandez .50
85 Richie Sexson .40
86 Albert Pujols 2.00
87 Scott Rolen .75
88 Chris Carpenter .50
89 Chris Duncan .25
90 Carl Crawford .40
91 Rocco Baldelli .25
92 Scott Kazmir .25
93 Michael Young .25
94 Mark Teixeira .50
95 Ian Kinsler .25
96 Troy Glaus .40
97 Vernon Wells .40
98 Roy Halladay .40
99 Ryan Zimmerman .50
100 Nick Johnson .25
101 Zack Segovia **(RC)** 8.00
102 Joaquin Arias **(RC)** 8.00
104 Travis Buck **(RC)** 10.00
105 Mike Schultz **RC** 8.00
107 Sean Henn **(RC)** 8.00
108 Ryan Braun **RC** 10.00
109 Rick Vanden Hurk **RC** 10.00
110 Carlos Gomez/SP **RC** 35.00
111 Mike Rabelo **RC** 10.00
112 Felix Pie **(RC)** 15.00
113 Miguel Montero **(RC)** 8.00
114 Michael Bourn **(RC)** 15.00
115 Micah Owings/SP **(RC)** 15.00
116 Matt Lindstrom **(RC)** 8.00
117 Matt Chico **(RC)** 8.00
118 Levale Speigner **RC** 8.00
119 Lee Gardner **(RC)** 8.00
120 Kory Casto **(RC)** 8.00
121 Kevin Kouzmanoff **(RC)** 15.00
122 Kevin Cameron **RC** 8.00
124 Tyler Clippard **(RC)** 15.00
125 Juan Perez **RC** 10.00
126 Josh Hamilton/SP **(RC)** 20.00
127 Joseph Bisenius **RC** 10.00
128 Jose Garcia **RC** 8.00
129 Jon Knott **RC** 8.00
130 Jon Coutlangus **(RC)** 10.00
131 John Danks **(RC)** 8.00
132 Joe Smith **RC** 10.00
133 Matt Brown **RC** 10.00
134 Joakim Soria **RC** 20.00
135 Jesus Flores **RC** 10.00
136 Jeff Baker **(RC)** 8.00
137 Jay Marshall **RC** 10.00
138 Jared Burton **RC** 10.00
139 Jamie Vermilyea **RC** 8.00
140 Jamie Burke **(RC)** 8.00
141 Ryan Rowland-Smith **RC** 10.00
142 Connor Robertson **RC** 8.00
143 Hector Gimenez **(RC)** 8.00
144 Gustavo Molina **RC** 8.00
145 Glen Perkins **(RC)** 8.00
146 Joba Chamberlain/SP **RC** 250.00
147 Doug Slaten **RC** 8.00
148 Ryan Braun **(RC)** 60.00
149 Delmon Young/SP **(RC)** 40.00
150 Garrett Jones **(RC)** 8.00
152 Cesar Jimenez **RC** 8.00
153 Brian Stokes **(RC)** 8.00
154 Brian Burres **(RC)** 15.00
155 Brian Barden/SP **RC** 15.00
156 Kyle Kendrick **RC** 25.00
157 Andrew Miller **RC** 20.00
158 Alexi Casilla **RC** 10.00
159 Alex Gordon/SP **RC** 60.00
159 A.J. Murray **RC** 8.00
162 Adam Lind **(RC)** 8.00
163 Chase Wright **RC** 15.00
164 Dallas Braden **RC** 8.00
165 Rocky Cherry **RC** 15.00
166 Andy Gonzalez **RC** 8.00
167 Neal Musser **RC** 10.00
168 Mark Reynolds **RC** 20.00
169 Dennis Dove **(RC)** 10.00
170 Justin Hampson **(RC)** 8.00
171 Phil Hughes/SP **(RC)** 60.00
172 Kelvin Jimenez **RC** 8.00
173 Hunter Pence/SP **(RC)** 50.00
174 Brad Salmon **RC** 10.00
175 Ryan Sweeney **(RC)** 10.00
176 Brandon Wood **(RC)** 15.00
177 Billy Butler/SP **(RC)** 40.00
178 Ben Francisco **(RC)** 8.00
180 Yoel Hernandez **RC** 8.00
181 Tim Lincecum/SP **RC** 60.00
182 Danny Putnam **(RC)** 8.00
183 Jarrod Saltalamacchia/SP **(RC)** 15.00
184 Andy LaRoche/SP **(RC)** 20.00
185 Matt DeSalvo **(RC)** 10.00
186 Fred Lewis **(RC)** 10.00
187 Anthony Lerew **(RC)** 8.00
188 Jesse Litsch **RC** 10.00
189 Daisuke Matsuzaka/SP **RC** 250.00

Gold

Gold (1-100, 189): 3-6X
Production 99 Sets

Red

Red (1-100, 189): 2-4X
Production 199 Sets

2007 UD Masterpieces

NM/M
Complete Set (90): 50.00
Common player (1-90): .50
Pack (4): 8.00
Box (18): 120.00
1 Babe Ruth 4.00
2 Babe Ruth 4.00
3 Bobby Thomson .50
4 Bill Mazeroski 1.00
5 Carlton Fisk 1.00
6 Kirk Gibson 1.00
7 Don Larsen 2.00
8 Lou Gehrig 4.00
9 Roger Maris 3.00
10 Cal Ripken Jr. 4.00
11 Bucky Dent .50
12 Ryan Howard 3.00
13 Brooks Robinson 2.00
14 David Ortiz 2.00
15 Hideki Matsui 3.00
16 Roger Clemens 4.00
17 Sandy Koufax 5.00
18 Reggie Jackson 2.00
19 Ozzie Smith 3.00
20 Ty Cobb 3.00
21 Walter Johnson 2.00
22 Babe Ruth 4.00
23 Roy Campanella 2.00
24 Jackie Robinson 3.00
25 Carl Yastrzemski 3.00
26 Sandy Koufax 5.00
27 Daisuke Matsuzaka **RC** 8.00
28 Kei Igawa **RC** 1.00
29 Ken Griffey Jr. 3.00
30 Derek Jeter 4.00
31 David Ortiz 2.00
32 Vladimir Guerrero 2.00
33 Chase Utley 2.00
34 Troy Tulowitzki **(RC)** 2.00
35 Joe Mauer 1.00
36 Travis Hafner 1.00
37 Miguel Cabrera 2.00
38 Albert Pujols 4.00
39 Frank Thomas 2.00
40 Mike Piazza 2.00
41 Josh Hamilton .50
42 Cal Ripken Jr., Tony Gwynn 3.00
43 Ichiro Suzuki 3.00
44 Hideki Matsui 3.00
45 Ken Griffey Jr. 3.00
46 Michael Jordan 4.00
47 John F. Kennedy 2.00
48 Randy Johnson 2.00
49 Albert Pujols 4.00
50 Carlos Beltran 1.50
51 Delmon Young **(RC)** 1.00
52 Johan Santana 2.00
53 Cal Ripken Jr. 4.00
54 Yogi Berra, Jackie Robinson 3.00
55 Cal Ripken Jr. 3.00
56 Hanley Ramirez 2.00
57 Victor Martinez 1.00
58 Cole Hamels 2.00
59 Bobby Doerr 1.00
60 Bruce Sutter .50
61 Jason Bay 1.00
62 Luis Aparicio .50
63 Stephen Drew 1.00
64 Jered Weaver 1.00
65 Alex Gordon **RC** 5.00
66 Howie Kendrick .50
67 Ryan Zimmerman 1.00
68 Akinori Iwamura **RC** 1.00
69 Chien-Ming Wang 2.00
70 David Wright 2.00
71 Ryan Howard 3.00
72 Alex Rodriguez 4.00
73 Justin Morneau 1.50
74 Andrew Miller **RC** 3.00
75 Richard Nixon 1.00
76 Bill Clinton 1.00
77 Phil Hughes **(RC)** 3.00
78 Tom Glavine 1.00
79 Chipper Jones 2.00
80 Craig Biggio 1.00
81 Chris Chambliss .50
82 Tim Lincecum **RC** 5.00
83 Billy Butler **(RC)** 1.00
84 Andy LaRoche **(RC)** 1.00
85 1969 New York Mets 2.00
86 2004 Boston Red Sox 2.00
87 Roberto Clemente 3.00
88 Chase Utley 2.00
89 Reggie Jackson 2.00
90 Curt Schilling 2.00

Printing Plates

No Pricing
Production one set per color.

Artist's Proof

Production One Set

Black Linen

Black Linen (1-90): 4-6X
Production 99 Sets

Blue Steel

Blue Steel (1-90): 4-8X
Production 50 Sets

Bronze

Production One Set

Celestial Blue

Production One Set

Deep Blue

Black Linen (1-90): 4-6X
Production 75 Sets

Green Linen

Green (1-90): 2-3X

Hades

Hades (1-90): 4-8X
Production 50 Sets

Ionised

Production One Set

Persian Blue Linen

Production One Set

Pinot Red

Pinot Red (1-90): 4-6X
Production 75 Sets

Red Linen

Production One Set

Rusted

Rusted (1-90): 4-8X
Production 50 Sets

Black

Black (1-90): 4-6X
Production 99 Sets

Urban Gray

Production One Set

5x7 Box Topper

NM/M
Common Player: 5.00
Inserted 1:Box
1 Cal Ripken Jr. 15.00
2 Ken Griffey Jr. 10.00
3 Derek Jeter 15.00
4 Sandy Koufax 15.00
5 Babe Ruth 15.00
6 Lou Gehrig 15.00
7 Travis Hafner 5.00
8 Victor Martinez 5.00
9 Jered Weaver 5.00
10 Phil Hughes 8.00
11 Bobby Doerr 5.00
12 Billy Butler 5.00
13 Andy LaRoche 5.00
14 Josh Hamilton 5.00
15 Reggie Jackson 8.00
16 Hanley Ramirez 8.00
17 Don Larsen 8.00
18 Ken Griffey Jr. 10.00
19 Jason Bay 5.00
20 Daisuke Matsuzaka 15.00

5x7 Box Topper Autograph

NM/M
Inserted 1:Case
2 Ken Griffey Jr. 85.00
3 Derek Jeter 150.00
7 Travis Hafner 35.00
8 Victor Martinez 25.00
9 Jered Weaver 30.00
10 Phil Hughes 60.00
11 Bobby Doerr 50.00
12 Billy Butler 50.00
13 Andy LaRoche 20.00
14 Josh Hamilton 25.00
15 Reggie Jackson 50.00
16 Hanley Ramirez 35.00
17 Don Larsen 65.00
18 Ken Griffey Jr. 85.00
19 Jason Bay 20.00
20 Daisuke Matsuzaka 275.00

Captured on Canvas

NM/M
Common Player: 4.00
Bronze: No Pricing

Forest Green: No Pricing
Production One Set
AB Adrian Beltre 4.00
AD Adam Dunn 8.00
AI Akinori Iwamura 15.00
AJ Andruw Jones 6.00
AP Albert Pujols 25.00
BA Bobby Abreu 6.00
BC Bobby Crosby 4.00
BE Carlos Beltran 8.00
BG Brian Giles 4.00
BL Brad Lidge 4.00
BO Jeremy Bonderman 6.00
BR Brian Roberts 6.00
BS Ben Sheets 6.00
CA Chris Carpenter 8.00
CB Craig Biggio 6.00
CC Carl Crawford 6.00
CF Carlton Fisk 8.00
CJ Chipper Jones 10.00
CL Carlos Lee 6.00
CR Coco Crisp 4.00
CS C.C. Sabathia 6.00
CU Chase Utley 15.00
CY Carl Yastrzemski 10.00
DJ Derek Jeter 25.00
DL Derrek Lee 8.00
DM Don Mattingly 20.00
DO David Ortiz 10.00
DR J.D. Drew 4.00
DW Dontrelle Willis 4.00
EB Erik Bedard 6.00
EC Eric Chavez 6.00
EG Eric Gagne 4.00
FH Felix Hernandez 8.00
FL Francisco Liriano 6.00
GA Garrett Atkins 6.00
GL Tom Glavine 8.00
GR Khalil Greene 6.00
GS Grady Sizemore 10.00
HA Roy Halladay 6.00
HB Hank Blalock 6.00
HE Todd Helton 8.00
HR Hanley Ramirez 10.00
HS Huston Street 4.00
IR Ivan Rodriguez 8.00
JA Jason Bay 6.00
JB Josh Beckett 8.00
JH J.J. Hardy 6.00
JK Jason Kendall 4.00
JM Joe Mauer 6.00
JN Joe Nathan 6.00
JP Jake Peavy 8.00
JR Jose Reyes 15.00
JS John Smoltz 8.00
JV Jason Varitek 8.00
JW Jered Weaver 6.00
KG Ken Griffey Jr. 20.00
LB Lance Berkman 6.00
MA Daisuke Matsuzaka 50.00
MC Miguel Cabrera 8.00
MG Marcus Giles 4.00
MH Matt Holliday 8.00
MO Magglio Ordonez 6.00
MR Mariano Rivera 8.00
MT Miguel Tejada 8.00
MY Michael Young 6.00
PA Jonathan Papelbon 15.00
RA Manny Ramirez 8.00
RB Rocco Baldelli 6.00
RC Roger Clemens 15.00
RH Rich Harden 4.00
RI Cal Ripken Jr. 20.00
RJ Randy Johnson 8.00
RO Roy Oswalt 8.00
RW Rickie Weeks 6.00
RZ Ryan Zimmerman 10.00
SA Johan Santana 10.00
SC Curt Schilling 10.00
SH Gary Sheffield 8.00
SK Scott Kazmir 6.00
SR Scott Rolen 8.00
TE Mark Teixeira 8.00
TG Tony Gwynn 15.00
TH Tim Hudson 6.00
TR Travis Hafner 6.00
VG Vladimir Guerrero 8.00
VM Victor Martinez 8.00
WC Will Clark 8.00

Stroke of Genius Signatures

NM/M
Common Autograph: 10.00
Parallel: No Pricing
Production One Set
AG Adrian Gonzalez 15.00
AL Andy LaRoche 15.00
BA Bronson Arroyo 25.00
BB Billy Butler 30.00
BO Boof Bonser 10.00
BR Brooks Robinson 40.00
BS Ben Sheets 15.00
BU B.J. Upton 15.00
CD Chris Duffy 10.00
CF Chone Figgins 15.00
CH Cole Hamels 40.00
CQ Carlos Quentin 15.00
CR Cal Ripken Jr. 125.00
DH Danny Haren 15.00
DJ Derek Jeter 150.00
DO David Ortiz 50.00
DU Dan Uggla 15.00
DW Dontrelle Willis 15.00
EC Eric Chavez 10.00
GO Alex Gordon 40.00
GP Glen Perkins 10.00
HA Justin Hampson 10.00
HI Rich Hill 15.00
HK Howard Kendrick 15.00
HP Hunter Pence 50.00
HR Hanley Ramirez 25.00
HS Huston Street 10.00
HU Torii Hunter 20.00
IK Ian Kinsler 15.00
JA Jason Bay 15.00
JB Jeff Baker 10.00
JH Josh Hamilton 20.00
JP Jonathan Papelbon 35.00
JT Jim Thome 35.00
JU Justin Morneau 25.00
JV Justin Verlander 30.00
JW Jered Weaver 20.00
JZ Joel Zumaya 15.00
KE Austin Kearns 10.00
KG Ken Griffey Jr. 80.00
KK Kevin Kouzmanoff 15.00
LE Cliff Lee 10.00
LI Adam Lind 10.00
MB Michael Bourn 15.00
MC Matt Cain 15.00
MO Micah Owings 20.00
MS Mike Schmidt 50.00
PS Phil Hughes 75.00
RA Aramis Ramirez 20.00
RC Roger Clemens 100.00
RH Rich Harden 10.00
RO Roy Oswalt 20.00
RZ Ryan Zimmerman 30.00
SD Stephen Drew 15.00
SH Sean Henn 10.00
SO Jeremy Sowers 10.00
TL Tim Lincecum 50.00
TR Travis Hafner 15.00
TT Troy Tulowitzki 40.00
VM Victor Martinez 20.00
XN Xavier Nady 15.00

All-Star Futures

NM/M
Common player: 2.00
Production 500 sets
AD Alejandro De Aza 2.00
AG Alex Gordon 8.00
AI Akinori Iwamura 3.00
AL Adam Lind 2.00
AM Andrew Miller 4.00
BA Jeff Baker 2.00
BI Billy Butler 5.00
BM Brandon Morrow 3.00
BU B.J. Upton 3.00
BW Brandon Wood 3.00
CA Alexi Casilla 2.00
CG Carlos Gomez 3.00
CW Chase Wright 2.00
CY Chris Young 3.00
DM Daisuke Matsuzaka 15.00
DP Danny Putnam 2.00
DY Delmon Young 4.00
FL Fred Lewis 2.00
FP Felix Pie 3.00
GP Glen Perkins 2.00
HA Josh Hamilton 2.00
HK Howie Kendrick 3.00
HP Hunter Pence 8.00
IK Ian Kinsler 3.00
JA Joaquin Arias 2.00
JD John Danks 2.00
JS Jarrod Saltalamacchia 2.00
JV Justin Verlander 3.00
KC Kory Casto 2.00
KI Kei Igawa 2.00
KK Kevin Kouzmanoff 2.00
LA Andy LaRoche 3.00
MA Matt Chico 3.00
MB Michael Bourn 2.00
MC Matt Cain 2.00
MI Miguel Montero 2.00
ML Matt Lindstrom 2.00
MO Micah Owings 2.00
PF Prince Fielder 4.00
PH Phil Hughes 6.00
RB Ryan Braun 10.00
RS Ryan Sweeney 2.00
RZ Ryan Zimmerman 4.00
SD Stephen Drew 3.00
SM Joe Smith 2.00
SO Joakim Soria 2.00
TB Travis Buck 2.00
TL Tim Lincecum 8.00
TP Tony Pena 2.00
TT Troy Tulowitzki 4.00

Clear Path to History Triple Auto.

NM/M
Some not priced due to scarcity.
CCH Eric Chavez, Bobby Crosby, Rich Harden 20.00
CWR Miguel Cabrera, Dontrelle Willis, Hanley Ramirez 60.00
DMY Chris Young, Stephen Drew, Miguel Montero 30.00
FEG Luis Gonzalez, Andre Ethier, Rafael Furcal 40.00
GKW Vladimir Guerrero, Howie Kendrick, Jered Weaver SP 100.00
GPC Vladimir Guerrero, Albert Pujols, Miguel Cabrera SP 200.00
HAT Garrett Atkins, Matt Holliday, Troy Tulowitzki 100.00
HMS Travis Hafner, Victor Martinez, Jeremy Sowers 50.00
KUC Carl Crawford, Scott Kazmir, B.J. Upton 60.00
KUK Ian Kinsler, Dan Uggla, Howie Kendrick 25.00
MPM Melvin Mora, Corey Patterson, Nick Markakis 25.00
VZR Justin Verlander, Ryan Zimmerman, Hanley Ramirez 50.00

Cy Young Futures

NM/M
Common Player: 2.00
Production 500 Sets
AL Anthony Lerew 2.00
AM Andrew Miller 4.00
BM Brandon Morrow 3.00
CH Cole Hamels 4.00
CW Chase Wright 2.00
DM Daisuke Matsuzaka 15.00
GP Glen Perkins 2.00
JD John Danks 2.00
JG Jose Garcia 2.00
JL Jon Lester 4.00
JS Jeremy Sowers 2.00
JV Justin Verlander 3.00
JZ Joel Zumaya 2.00
KI Kei Igawa 3.00
MA Matt Chico 2.00
MC Matt Cain 2.00
MO Micah Owings 2.00
PH Phil Hughes 6.00
RV Rick Vanden Hurk 2.00
SH Sean Henn 2.00
SK Scott Kazmir 3.00
SM Joe Smith 2.00
TC Tyler Clippard 2.00
TL Tim Lincecum 8.00
ZS Zack Segovia 2.00

MVP Futures

NM/M
Common Player: 2.00
Production 500 Sets
AD Alejandro De Aza 2.00
AG Alex Gordon 8.00
AI Akinori Iwamura 3.00
AL Adam Lind 2.00
DM Daisuke Matsuzaka 15.00
DY Delmon Young 4.00
FP Felix Pie 3.00
HP Hunter Pence 8.00
IK Ian Kinsler 3.00
JA Joaquin Arias 2.00
JB Jeff Baker 2.00
JH Josh Hamilton 2.00
JS Jarrod Saltalamacchia 2.00
JV Justin Verlander 3.00
KI Kei Igawa 2.00
KK Kevin Kouzmanoff 2.00
LA Andy LaRoche 3.00
MB Michael Bourn 2.00
MM Miguel Montero 2.00
PF Prince Fielder 4.00
RB Ryan Braun 10.00
RS Ryan Sweeney 2.00
RZ Ryan Zimmerman 4.00
TB Travis Buck 2.00
TT Troy Tulowitzki 4.00

Rookie Dated Debuts

NM/M
Common player: 2.00
Production 999 Sets
Autographs: No pricing
Production 10 Sets
AC Alexi Casilla 2.00
AD Alejandro De Aza 2.00
AG Alex Gordon 5.00
AI Akinori Iwamura 2.00
AL Adam Lind 2.00
BA Jeff Baker 2.00
BB Brian Barden 2.00
BI Joseph Bisenius 2.00
BM Brandon Morrow 2.00
BW Brandon Wood 2.00
CA Kory Casto 2.00
CG Carlos Gomez 3.00
CR Cal Ripken Jr. 10.00
CW Chase Wright 2.00
DA John Danks 2.00
DJ Derek Jeter 10.00
DM Daisuke Matsuzaka 10.00
DY Delmon Young 3.00
ED Elijah Dukes 2.00
FL Fred Lewis 2.00
FP Felix Pie 2.00
GM Gustavo Molina 2.00
GP Glen Perkins 2.00
HO Hideki Okajima 3.00
HP Hunter Pence 6.00
JA Joaquin Arias 2.00
JC Jon Coutlangus 2.00
JF Jesus Flores 2.00
JH Josh Hamilton 2.00
JM Jay Marshall 2.00
JP Juan Perez 2.00
JS Joakim Soria 2.00
KC Kevin Cameron 2.00
KG Ken Griffey Jr. 8.00
KI Kei Igawa 2.00
KK Kevin Kouzmanoff 2.00
LA Andy LaRoche 3.00
LG Lee Gardner 2.00
MB Michael Bourn 2.00
MC Matt Chico 2.00
MM Miguel Montero 2.00
MO Micah Owings 2.00
MR Mike Rabelo 2.00
PH Phil Hughes 5.00
RS Ryan Sweeney 2.00
SA Jarrod Saltalamacchia 2.00
SM Joe Smith 2.00
TB Travis Buck 2.00
TL Tim Lincecum 5.00
TT Troy Tulowitzki 4.00

Two for the Bigs

NM/M
Common Duo: 2.00
Production 999 Sets
Autographs: No Pricing
Production 10 Sets
AS Joaquin Arias, Chris Stewart 2.00
BB Michael Bourn, Joseph Bisenius 2.00
BD Travis Buck, Elijah Dukes 2.00
BG Ryan Braun, Alex Gordon 8.00
BS Ryan Braun, Joakim Soria 2.00
BT Jeff Baker, Troy Tulowitzki 4.00
CF Kory Casto, Jesus Flores 2.00
CL Matt Chico, Tim Lincecum 4.00
CP Alexi Casilla, Glen Perkins 2.00
CS Matt Chico, Levale Speigner 2.00
DG Alejandro De Aza, Lee Gardner 2.00
DK Daisuke Matsuzaka, Kei Igawa 6.00
DM John Danks, Gustavo Molina 2.00
DT Stephen Drew, Troy Tulowitzki 4.00
DV Alejandro De Aza, Rick Vanden Hurk 2.00
DW Chase Wright, Matt DeSalvo 2.00
DY Chris Young, Stephen Drew 3.00
GB Alex Gordon, Billy Butler 5.00
GF Hector Gimenez, Jesus Flores 2.00
GI Alex Gordon, Akinori Iwamura 5.00
GL Alex Gordon, Andy LaRoche 5.00
GM Alex Gordon, Daisuke Matsuzaka 8.00
GP Hector Gimenez, Hunter Pence 4.00
HB Josh Hamilton, Jared Burton 2.00
HD Josh Hamilton, Alejandro De Aza 2.00
HL Phil Hughes, Tim Lincecum 8.00
HP Josh Hamilton, Hunter Pence 4.00
II Akinori Iwamura, Kei Igawa 3.00
KC Kevin Kouzmanoff, Kevin Cameron 2.00
LG Matt Lindstrom, Lee Gardner 2.00
LV Adam Lind 2.00
MG Hector Gimenez, Miguel Montero 2.00
MI Daisuke Matsuzaka, Akinori Iwamura 5.00
MO Daisuke Matsuzaka, Hideki Okajima 5.00
MR Gustavo Molina, Mike Rabelo 2.00
MW Brandon Morrow, Sean White 2.00
OL Micah Owings, Tim Lincecum 4.00
OM Micah Owings, Miguel Montero 2.00
PB Danny Putnam, Travis Buck 2.00
PD Hunter Pence, Alejandro De Aza 4.00
PH Josh Hamilton, Felix Pie 2.00
PP Felix Pie, Hunter Pence 4.00
RS Mike Rabelo, Chris Stewart 2.00
SM Jarrod Saltalamacchia, Miguel Montero 2.00
ST Jarrod Saltalamacchia, Troy Tulowitzki 4.00
SW Joe Smith, Chase Wright 2.00
TB Travis Buck, Billy Butler 3.00
WH Chase Wright, Phil Hughes 4.00
YD Delmon Young, Elijah Dukes 2.00
YM Delmon Young, Daisuke Matsuzaka 5.00

All-Star Futures Auto.

NM/M
Common Auto.: 8.00
AG Alex Gordon/SP 60.00
AI Akinori Iwamura/SP 8.00
AL Adam Lind 8.00
AM Andrew Miller 20.00
BA Jeff Baker 8.00
BI Billy Butler 40.00
BU B.J. Upton 8.00
BW Brandon Wood 15.00
CA Alexi Casilla 8.00
CG Carlos Gomez 35.00
CW Chase Wright 15.00
CY Chris Young 15.00
DM Daisuke Matsuzaka/SP 250.00
DP Danny Putnam 8.00
DY Delmon Young/SP 8.00
FL Fred Lewis 10.00
FP Felix Pie 15.00
GP Glen Perkins 8.00
HA Josh Hamilton 20.00
HK Howie Kendrick 25.00
HP Hunter Pence 50.00
IK Ian Kinsler 15.00
JA Joaquin Arias 8.00
JD John Danks 8.00
JS Jarrod Saltalamacchia 15.00
JV Justin Verlander/SP 8.00
KC Kory Casto 8.00
KI Kei Igawa/SP 8.00
KK Kevin Kouzmanoff 10.00
LA Andy LaRoche 15.00
MA Matt Chico 8.00
MC Matt Cain 15.00
MI Miguel Montero 8.00
ML Matt Lindstrom 8.00
MO Micah Owings 15.00
PF Prince Fielder/SP 60.00
PH Phil Hughes/SP 60.00
RB Ryan Braun 60.00
RS Ryan Sweeney 10.00
RZ Ryan Zimmerman/SP 8.00
SD Stephen Drew/SP 8.00
SM Joe Smith 10.00
SO Joakim Soria 15.00
TB Travis Buck 10.00
TL Tim Lincecum 60.00
TP Tony Pena 8.00
TT Troy Tulowitzki 30.00

Cy Young Futures Auto.

NM/M
Common Auto.: 8.00
AL Anthony Lerew 8.00
AM Andrew Miller 20.00
CW Chase Wright 15.00
DM Daisuke Matsuzaka SP 250.00
GP Glen Perkins 8.00
JD John Danks 8.00
JG Jose Garcia 8.00
JZ Joel Zumaya 15.00
MA Matt Chico 8.00
MC Matt Cain 15.00
MO Micah Owings 15.00
PH Phil Hughes SP 60.00
RV Rick Vanden Hurk 10.00
SH Sean Henn 8.00
SM Joe Smith 10.00
TC Tyler Clippard 15.00
TL Tim Lincecum 60.00
ZS Zack Segovia 8.00

MVP Futures Auto.

NM/M
Common Auto.: 8.00
AG Alex Gordon/SP 60.00
AL Adam Lind 8.00
DM Daisuke Matsuzaka/SP 250.00
FP Felix Pie 15.00
HP Hunter Pence 50.00
IK Ian Kinsler 15.00
JA Joaquin Arias 8.00
JB Jeff Baker 8.00
JH Josh Hamilton 20.00
JS Jarrod Saltalamacchia 15.00
KK Kevin Kouzmanoff 10.00
LA Andy LaRoche 20.00
MB Michael Bourn 15.00
MM Miguel Montero 8.00
PF Prince Fielder 60.00
RB Ryan Braun 60.00
RS Ryan Sweeney 10.00
TB Travis Buck 10.00

2007 UD Ultimate Collection

NM/M
Common Player (1-100): 1.50
Production 450
Common RC Auto. (101-141): 10.00
Production 289-299
Pack (4): 75.00
Box (4): 250.00
1 Chipper Jones 4.00
2 Andruw Jones 2.00
3 Tim Hudson 2.00
4 Stephen Drew 2.00
5 Randy Johnson 3.00
6 Brandon Webb 2.00
7 Alfonso Soriano 3.00
8 Derrek Lee 2.00
9 Aramis Ramirez 2.00
10 Carlos Zambrano 2.00
11 Ken Griffey Jr. 6.00
12 Adam Dunn 2.00
13 Ryan Freel 1.50
14 Todd Helton 2.00
15 Garrett Atkins 1.50
16 Matt Holliday 2.00
17 Hanley Ramirez 3.00
18 Dontrelle Willis 1.50
19 Miguel Cabrera 3.00
20 Lance Berkman 2.00
21 Roy Oswalt 2.00
22 Carlos Lee 2.00
23 Nomar Garciaparra 3.00
24 Jason Schmidt 1.50
25 Juan Pierre 1.50
26 Russell Martin 2.00
27 Rickie Weeks 1.50
28 Prince Fielder 4.00
29 Ben Sheets 1.50
30 David Wright 5.00
31 Jose Reyes 4.00
32 Pedro Martinez 3.00
33 Carlos Beltran 2.00
34 Brett Myers 1.50
35 Jimmy Rollins 3.00
36 Ryan Howard 6.00
37 Jason Bay 2.00
38 Freddy Sanchez 1.50
39 Ian Snell 1.50
40 Jake Peavy 2.00
41 Greg Maddux 5.00
42 Brian Giles 1.50
43 Matt Cain 2.00
44 Barry Zito 1.50
45 Ray Durham 1.50
46 Albert Pujols 8.00
47 Chris Carpenter 2.00
48 Chris Duncan 1.50
49 Scott Rolen 2.00
50 Ryan Zimmerman 2.00
51 Chad Cordero 1.50
52 Ryan Church 1.50
53 Miguel Tejada 2.00
54 Erik Bedard 2.00
55 Brian Roberts 1.50
56 David Ortiz 4.00
57 Josh Beckett 3.00
58 Manny Ramirez 3.00
59 Daisuke Matsuzaka RC 25.00
60 Jim Thome 2.00
61 Paul Konerko 2.00
62 Jermaine Dye 1.50
63 Grady Sizemore 3.00
64 Victor Martinez 2.00
65 C.C. Sabathia 2.00
66 Ivan Rodriguez 2.00
67 Justin Verlander 2.00
68 Gary Sheffield 2.00
69 Jeremy Bonderman 2.00
70 Gil Meche 1.50
71 Mike Sweeney 1.50
72 Mark Teahen 1.50
73 Vladimir Guerrero 3.00
74 Howie Kendrick 1.50
75 Francisco Rodriguez 1.50
76 Johan Santana 3.00
77 Justin Morneau 2.00
78 Joe Mauer 2.00
79 Michael Cuddyer 1.50
80 Alex Rodriguez 8.00
81 Derek Jeter 8.00
82 Johnny Damon 3.00
83 Roger Clemens 6.00
84 Rich Harden 1.50
85 Mike Piazza 3.00
86 Huston Street 1.50
87 Ichiro Suzuki 6.00

88 Felix Hernandez 2.00
89 Kenji Johjima 1.50
90 Adrian Beltre 1.50
91 Carl Crawford 1.50
92 Scott Kazmir 1.50
93 B.J. Upton 1.50
94 Michael Young 1.50
95 Mark Teixeira 2.00
96 Sammy Sosa 3.00
97 Hank Blalock 1.50
98 Vernon Wells 2.00
99 Roy Halladay 2.00
100 Frank Thomas 3.00
101 Adam Lind **(RC)** 10.00
102 Akinori Iwamura **RC** 30.00
103 Andrew Miller **RC** 40.00
104 Michael Bourn **(RC)** 10.00
105 Kory Casto **(RC)** 10.00
106 Ryan Braun **(RC)** 75.00
107 Sean Gallagher **(RC)** 10.00
108 Billy Butler **(RC)** 30.00
109 Alexi Casilla **RC** 10.00
110 Chris Stewart **RC** 10.00
111 Matt DeSalvo **(RC)** 15.00
112 Chase Headley **(RC)** 15.00
113 Delmon Young **(RC)** 25.00
114 Homer Bailey **(RC)** 20.00
115 Kurt Suzuki **(RC)** 15.00
116 Alex Gordon **RC** 50.00
117 Josh Hamilton **(RC)** 20.00
118 Fred Lewis **(RC)** 10.00
119 Glen Perkins **(RC)** 10.00
120 Hector Gimenez **(RC)** 10.00
121 Phil Hughes **(RC)** 70.00
122 Jeff Baker **(RC)** 10.00
123 Adam LaRoche **(RC)** 15.00
124 Tim Lincecum **RC** 100.00
125 Joaquin Arias **(RC)** 10.00
126 Daisuke Matsuzaka **RC** 300.00
127 Micah Owings **(RC)** 20.00
128 Hunter Pence **(RC)** 50.00
129 Matt Chico **(RC)** 10.00
130 Kei Igawa **RC** 30.00
131 Kevin Kouzmanoff **(RC)** 15.00
132 Miguel Montero **(RC)** 10.00
133 Mike Rabelo **RC** 10.00
134 Felix Pie **(RC)** 20.00
135 Curtis Thigpen **(RC)** 10.00
136 Ryan Braun **RC** 10.00
137 Ryan Sweeney **(RC)** 10.00
138 Brandon Wood **(RC)** 20.00
139 Troy Tulowitzki **(RC)** 40.00
140 Justin Upton **RC** 80.00
141 Joba Chamberlain **(RC)** 220.00

2007 UD Sweet Spot

NM/M

Common Player (1-100): 2.00
Production 850
Common RC Auto. (101-142): 10.00
Tin (6): 100.00
1 Adam Dunn 3.00
2 Adrian Beltre 3.00
3 Albert Pujols 10.00
4 Alex Rios 2.00
5 Alex Rodriguez 10.00
6 Alfonso Soriano 4.00
7 Andruw Jones 3.00
8 Aramis Ramirez 3.00
9 B.J. Upton 2.00
10 Barry Zito 2.00
11 Bartolo Colon 2.00
12 Ben Sheets 2.00
13 Bill Hall 2.00
14 Brad Penny 2.00
15 Brandon Webb 3.00
16 C.C. Sabathia 3.00
17 Carl Crawford 2.00
18 Carlos Beltran 3.00
19 Carlos Guillen 2.00
20 Carlos Lee 2.00
21 Chase Utley 5.00
22 Chien-Ming Wang 6.00
23 Chipper Jones 4.00
24 Chris Carpenter 3.00
25 Cole Hamels 4.00
26 Craig Biggio 3.00
27 Curt Schilling 4.00
28 Danny Haren 3.00
29 David Ortiz 5.00
30 David Wright 5.00
31 Delmon Young 2.00
32 Derek Jeter 10.00
33 Derrek Lee 3.00
34 Dontrelle Willis 2.00
35 Felix Hernandez 4.00
36 Frank Thomas 4.00
37 Gil Meche 2.00
38 Grady Sizemore 5.00
39 Greg Maddux 6.00
40 Ian Kinsler 2.00
41 Ichiro Suzuki 6.00
42 Ivan Rodriguez 3.00
43 Jake Peavy 3.00
44 Jason Bay 3.00
45 Jason Varitek 3.00
46 Jeff Kent 3.00
47 Jermaine Dye 2.00
48 Jim Edmonds 2.00
49 Jim Thome 3.00
50 Jimmy Rollins 5.00
51 Joe Mauer 3.00
52 Johan Santana 4.00
53 John Smoltz 3.00
54 Jonathan Papelbon 4.00
55 Jorge Posada 3.00
56 Jose Reyes 4.00
57 Josh Beckett 4.00
58 Justin Morneau 3.00
59 Justin Verlander 3.00
60 Ken Griffey Jr. 8.00
61 Kenji Johjima 2.00
62 Lance Berkman 3.00
63 Magglio Ordonez 3.00
64 Manny Ramirez 4.00
65 Mariano Rivera 3.00
66 Mark Buehrle 2.00
67 Mark Teixeira 3.00
68 Matt Holliday 3.00
69 Matt Morris 2.00
70 Melvin Mora 2.00
71 Michael Young 2.00
72 Miguel Cabrera 4.00
73 Miguel Tejada 3.00
74 Mike Lowell 2.00
75 Mike Mussina 3.00
76 Mike Piazza 4.00
77 Nick Swisher 2.00
78 Orlando Hudson 2.00
79 Paul Konerko 3.00
80 Paul LoDuca 2.00
81 Pedro Martinez 4.00
82 Prince Fielder 5.00
83 Randy Johnson 4.00
84 Rickie Weeks 2.00
85 Roger Clemens 8.00
86 Roy Halladay 3.00
87 Roy Oswalt 3.00
88 Russell Martin 3.00
89 Ryan Howard 6.00
90 Ryan Zimmerman 3.00
91 Sammy Sosa 3.00
92 Scott Rolen 3.00
93 Shawn Green 2.00
94 Todd Helton 3.00
95 Tom Glavine 3.00
96 Torii Hunter 2.00
97 Travis Hafner 3.00
98 Vernon Wells 2.00
99 Victor Martinez 3.00
100 Vladimir Guerrero 4.00
101 Adam Lind **(RC)** 15.00
102 Akinori Iwamura/SP **RC** 40.00
103 Alex Gordon **RC** 50.00
104 Alexi Casilla **RC** 15.00
105 Andy LaRoche **(RC)** 15.00
106 Billy Butler **(RC)** 25.00
107 Ryan Rowland-Smith **RC** 15.00
108 Brandon Wood **(RC)** 15.00
109 Brian Burres **(RC)** 10.00
110 Chase Wright **RC** 15.00
111 Chris Stewart **RC** 10.00
112 Daisuke Matsuzaka/SP **RC** 300.00
113 Delmon Young/SP **(RC)** 30.00
114 Andrew Sonnanstine **RC** 15.00
115 Andrew Miller **RC** 30.00
116 Fred Lewis **(RC)** 15.00
117 Glen Perkins/SP **(RC)** 15.00
118 David Murphy **(RC)** 15.00
119 Hunter Pence **(RC)** 50.00
120 Jarrod Saltalamacchia **(RC)** 20.00
121 Jeff Baker/SP **(RC)** 20.00
122 Jesus Flores/SP **RC** 20.00
124 Joe Smith **RC** 15.00
125 Jon Knott **(RC)** 10.00
126 Josh Hamilton **(RC)** 25.00
127 Justin Hampson **(RC)** 15.00
128 Kei Igawa/SP **RC** 30.00
129 Kevin Cameron **RC** 10.00
130 Matt Chico **(RC)** 10.00
131 Matt DeSalvo **(RC)** 15.00
132 Micah Owings/SP **(RC)** 40.00
133 Michael Bourn **(RC)** 10.00
134 Miguel Montero **(RC)** 15.00
135 Phil Hughes/SP **(RC)** 60.00
136 Rick Vanden Hurk **RC** 15.00
138 Tim Lincecum **RC** 100.00
139 Travis Buck **(RC)** 20.00
140 Troy Tulowitzki/SP **(RC)** 60.00
141 Sean Henn **(RC)** 15.00
142 Zack Segovia **(RC)** 15.00
MB Michael Buysner/SP 30.00

Dual Signatures Red Stitch Blue Ink

No Pricing
Production 5-15

Signatures Red Stitch Blue Ink

NM/M

Common Auto.: 10.00
AG Adrian Gonzalez/350 15.00
AK Austin Kearns/299 10.00
AL Adam LaRoche/350 15.00
BB Boof Bonser/299 10.00
BR Brian Bruney/299 10.00
BW Brandon Wood/350 15.00
CB Chad Billingsley/299 25.00
CC Chris Capuano/299 10.00
CJ Conor Jackson/299 15.00
CL Cliff Lee/299 10.00
CQ Carlos Quentin/299 10.00
CY Chris Young/350 15.00
DC Daniel Cabrera/299 10.00
DH Danny Haren/299 20.00
DR Darrell Rasner/299 10.00
EA Erick Aybar/299 15.00
GP Glen Perkins/350 10.00
HK Howie Kendrick/350 15.00
HP Hunter Pence/350 35.00
JH Josh Hamilton/350 25.00
JK Jason Kubel/299 10.00
JN Joe Nathan/299 15.00
JW Josh Willingham/299 10.00
KA Jeff Karstens/299 10.00
KS Kurt Suzuki/299 15.00
LI Adam Lind/299 10.00
LO Lyle Overbay/299 10.00
MC Matt Cain/299 15.00
RH Rich Hill/299 15.00
RM Russell Martin/299 25.00
SE Sergio Mitre/299 10.00
TB Travis Buck/299 20.00
YG Chris B. Young/299 20.00
AD Adam Dunn/99 20.00
AI Akinori Iwamura/99 35.00
AM Andrew Miller/99 30.00
AX Alex Gordon/99 50.00
BP Brandon Phillips/99 20.00
CA Carl Crawford/99 15.00
CH Cole Hamels/99 30.00
CK Casey Kotchman/99 15.00
DY Delmon Young/99 25.00
FH Felix Hernandez/99 35.00
FP Felix Pie/99 20.00
HA Travis Hafner/99 25.00
HS Huston Street/99 15.00
JL Jon Lester/99 25.00
JP Jonathan Papelbon/99 50.00
JS Jeremy Sowers/99 15.00
JV Jason Varitek/99 50.00
MH Matt Holliday/99 40.00
MM Melvin Mora/99 10.00
PH Phil Hughes/99 60.00
PK Paul Konerko/99 30.00
RC Roger Clemens/99 80.00
RI Rich Harden/99 10.00
RW Rickie Weeks/99 15.00
RZ Ryan Zimmerman/99 25.00
SK Scott Kazmir/99 20.00
TG Tom Glavine/99 40.00
TH Torii Hunter/99 15.00
TL Tim Lincecum/99 60.00
VE Justin Verlander/99 40.00
VM Victor Martinez/99 20.00

Sweet Swatch Memorabilia

NM/M

Common Player: 4.00
Patch: 2-4X
Production 25 Sets
AD Adam Dunn 8.00
AJ Andruw Jones 6.00
AP Albert Pujols 15.00
AS Alfonso Soriano 8.00
AT Garrett Atkins 4.00
BA Bobby Abreu 6.00
BE Josh Beckett 10.00
BG Brian Giles 4.00
BI Craig Biggio 6.00
BO Jeremy Bonderman 6.00
BR Brian Roberts 6.00
BU B.J. Upton 6.00
BW Billy Wagner 4.00
CA Chris Carpenter 6.00
CB Carlos Beltran 8.00
CC Carl Crawford 4.00
CH Cole Hamels 8.00
CJ Chipper Jones 8.00
CL Carlos Lee 6.00
CS Curt Schilling 8.00
CU Chase Utley 15.00
DJ Derek Jeter 20.00
DM 4.00
DM Daisuke Matsuzaka 30.00
DO David Ortiz 10.00
DW Dontrelle Willis 4.00
EB Erik Bedard 6.00
EC Eric Chavez 4.00
FG Freddy Garcia 4.00
FH Felix Hernandez 8.00
FL Francisco Liriano 6.00
FT Frank Thomas 8.00
GA Garret Anderson 4.00
GM Greg Maddux 8.00
GR Khalil Greene 6.00
GS Grady Sizemore 15.00
HA Roy Halladay 6.00
HB Hank Blalock 4.00
HE Todd Helton 6.00
HO Trevor Hoffman 4.00
HR Hanley Ramirez 8.00
HS Huston Street 4.00
HU Torii Hunter 6.00
IK Ian Kinsler 4.00
IR Ivan Rodriguez 6.00
JB Jason Bay 6.00
JD Jermaine Dye 4.00
JE Jim Edmonds 4.00
JF Jeff Francoeur 8.00
JG Jason Giambi 6.00
JK Jeff Kent 4.00
JM Joe Mauer 6.00
JN Joe Nathan 4.00
JP Jake Peavy 6.00
JR Jimmy Rollins 10.00
JS Jason Schmidt 4.00
JT Jim Thome 8.00
JV Jason Varitek 8.00
JW Jered Weaver 6.00
JZ Joel Zumaya 4.00
KG Ken Griffey Jr. 15.00
KM Kendry Morales 4.00
LB Lance Berkman 6.00
LG Luis Gonzalez 4.00
MC Miguel Cabrera 8.00
MM Mike Mussina 6.00
MO Justin Morneau 8.00
MR Manny Ramirez 8.00
MT Mark Teixeira 6.00
MY Michael Young 6.00
OR Magglio Ordonez 6.00
OS Roy Oswalt 6.00
PA Jonathan Papelbon 10.00
PB Pat Burrell 4.00
PE Jhonny Peralta 4.00
PF Prince Fielder 10.00
PM Pedro Martinez 8.00
PO Jorge Posada 8.00
RC Robinson Cano 10.00
RE Jose Reyes 10.00
RH Rich Harden 4.00
RI Mariano Rivera 8.00
RJ Randy Johnson 8.00
RO Roger Clemens 10.00
RW Rickie Weeks 4.00
RZ Ryan Zimmerman 6.00
SA Johan Santana 8.00
SD Stephen Drew 6.00
SK Scott Kazmir 4.00
SM John Smoltz 6.00
SR Scott Rolen 6.00
TE Miguel Tejada 6.00
TG Tom Glavine 8.00
TH Tim Hudson 6.00
TR Travis Hafner 6.00
VE Justin Verlander 8.00
VG Vladimir Guerrero 8.00
VM Victor Martinez 6.00
VW Vernon Wells 4.00

Dual Signatures Black Glove Gold Ink

No Pricing
Production 5-10
Silver Ink: No Pricing
Production One Set
Leather Black Ink: No Pricing
Production 5-15

Dual Signatures Gold Stitch Gold Ink

No Pricing
Production 5-10
Silver Ink: No Pricing
Production Five Sets

Signatures Bat Barrel Blue Ink

NM/M

Production 1-99
Silver Ink: 1-1.5X
Production 25 or 15
Gold Ink: No Pricing
Production One Set
Red Ink: No Pricing
Production Five Sets
No pricing production under 25.
AK Austin Kearns/25 15.00
AL Adam LaRoche/25 20.00
BB Boof Bonser/26 20.00
BR Brian Bruney/29 20.00
CB Chad Billingsley/58 30.00
CC Chris Capuano/39 15.00
CL Cliff Lee/31 15.00
CY Chris Young/32 20.00
DC Daniel Cabrera/35 15.00
DR Darrell Rasner/27 20.00
EA Erick Aybar/23 20.00
GP Glen Perkins/60 10.00
HK Howie Kendrick/47 25.00
JH Josh Hamilton/33 25.00
JN Joe Nathan/36 20.00
KS Kurt Suzuki/99 20.00
LI Adam Lind/99 15.00
RH Rich Hill/51 25.00
RM Russell Martin/55 40.00
SE Sergio Mitre/99 15.00
AD Adam Dunn/44 25.00
AM Andrew Miller/48 30.00
BP Brandon Phillips/99 20.00
CH Cole Hamels/35 35.00
CK Casey Kotchman/99 15.00
FH Felix Hernandez/34 50.00
FP Felix Pie/99 20.00
HA Travis Hafner/48 25.00
JL Jon Lester/31 40.00
JP Jonathan Papelbon/58 40.00
JS Jeremy Sowers/45 20.00
JV Jason Varitek/33 50.00
PH Phil Hughes/65 60.00
PK Paul Konerko/99 30.00
RI Rich Harden/40 15.00
TG Tom Glavine/47 40.00
TH Torii Hunter/48 20.00
TL Tim Lincecum/55 75.00
VE Justin Verlander/35 50.00
VM Victor Martinez/41 30.00

Sign. Black Bat Barrel Silver Ink

Production 10 or 15
Gold Ink: No Pricing
Production One Set
Red Ink: No Pricing
Production Five Sets

Signatures Glove Black Ink

NM/M

Production 25 or 75
Silver Ink: 1-1.5X
Production 25 or 10
Green Ink: No Pricing
Production One Set
No pricing product. under 25.
AG Adrian Gonzalez/75 20.00
AK Austin Kearns/75 20.00
AL Adam LaRoche/75 20.00
BB Boof Bonser/75 15.00
BR Brian Bruney/75 20.00
BW Brandon Wood/75 20.00
CB Chad Billingsley/75 30.00
CC Chris Capuano/75 15.00
CJ Conor Jackson/75 20.00
CL Cliff Lee/75 20.00
CQ Carlos Quentin/75 15.00
CY Chris Young/75 20.00
DC Daniel Cabrera/75 15.00
DH Dan Haren/75 30.00
DR Darrell Rasner/75 15.00
EA Erick Aybar/75 20.00
GP Glen Perkins/75 15.00
HK Howie Kendrick/75 20.00
HP Hunter Pence/75 65.00
JH Josh Hamilton/75 40.00
JK Jason Kubel/75 20.00
JN Joe Nathan/75 20.00
JW Josh Willingham/75 20.00
KA Jeff Karstens/75 15.00
KS Kurt Suzuki/75 20.00
LO Lyle Overbay/75 15.00
MC Matt Cain/75 25.00
RH Rich Hill/75 25.00
RM Russell Martin/75 30.00
SE Sergio Mitre/75 15.00
TB Travis Buck/75 25.00
YG Chris B. Young/75 25.00
AD Adam Dunn/25 30.00
AI Akinori Iwamura/25 40.00
AM Andrew Miller/25 35.00
AX Alex Gordon/25 75.00
BP Brandon Phillips/25 30.00
CA Carl Crawford/25 25.00
CH Cole Hamels/25 40.00
CK Casey Kotchman/25 20.00
DY Delmon Young/25 30.00
FH Felix Hernandez/25 50.00
FP Felix Pie/25 30.00
HA Travis Hafner/25 30.00
HS Huston Street/25 20.00
JL Jon Lester/25 50.00
JP Jonathan Papelbon/25 50.00
JS Jeremy Sowers/25 20.00
JV Jason Varitek/25 60.00
MH Matt Holliday/25 50.00
MM Melvin Mora/25 15.00
PH Phil Hughes/25 90.00
PK Paul Konerko/25 40.00
RC Roger Clemens/25 100.00
RI Rich Harden/25 20.00
RW Rickie Weeks/25 20.00
RZ Ryan Zimmerman/25 40.00
SK Scott Kazmir/25 30.00
TG Tom Glavine/25 50.00
TH Torii Hunter/25 25.00
TL Tim Lincecum/25 100.00
VE Justin Verlander/25 50.00
VM Victor Martinez/25 35.00

Signatures Gold Stitch Gold Ink

NM/M

Production 25 or 99
Red/Blue Stitch Red Ink: No Pricing
Production 5 or 15
AG Adrian Gonzalez/99 20.00
AK Austin Kearns/99 20.00
AL Adam LaRoche/99 20.00
BB Boof Bonser/99 15.00
BR Brian Bruney/99 20.00
BW Brandon Wood/99 20.00
CB Chad Billingsley/99 30.00
CC Chris Capuano/99 15.00
CJ Conor Jackson/99 20.00
CL Cliff Lee/99 20.00
CQ Carlos Quentin/99 15.00
CY Chris Young/99 20.00
DC Daniel Cabrera/99 15.00
DH Danny Haren/99 30.00
DR Darrell Rasner/99 15.00
EA Erick Aybar/99 20.00
GP Glen Perkins/99 15.00
HK Howie Kendrick/99 20.00
HP Hunter Pence/99 65.00
JH Josh Hamilton/99 40.00
JK Jason Kubel/99 20.00
JN Joe Nathan/99 20.00
JW Josh Willingham/99 20.00
KA Jeff Karstens/99 15.00
KS Kurt Suzuki/99 20.00
LI Adam Lind/99 15.00
LO Lyle Overbay/99 15.00
MC Matt Cain/99 25.00
RH Rich Hill/99 25.00
RM Russell Martin/99 30.00
SE Sergio Mitre/99 15.00
TB Travis Buck/99 25.00
YG Chris B. Young/99 25.00
AD Adam Dunn/25 30.00
AI Akinori Iwamura/25 40.00
AM Andrew Miller/25 35.00
AX Alex Gordon/25 75.00
BP Brandon Phillips/25 30.00
CA Carl Crawford/25 25.00
CH Cole Hamels/25 40.00
CK Casey Kotchman/25 20.00
DY Delmon Young/25 30.00
FH Felix Hernandez/25 50.00
FP Felix Pie/25 30.00
HA Travis Hafner/25 30.00
HS Huston Street/25 20.00
JL Jon Lester/25 50.00
JP Jonathan Papelbon/25 50.00
JS Jeremy Sowers/25 20.00
JV Jason Varitek/25 60.00
MH Matt Holliday/25 50.00
MM Melvin Mora/25 15.00
PH Phil Hughes/25 90.00
PK Paul Konerko/25 40.00
RC Roger Clemens/25 100.00
RI Rich Harden/25 20.00
RW Rickie Weeks/25 20.00
RZ Ryan Zimmerman/25 40.00
SK Scott Kazmir/25 30.00
TG Tom Glavine/25 50.00
TH Torii Hunter/25 25.00
TL Tim Lincecum/25 100.00
VE Justin Verlander/25 50.00
VM Victor Martinez/25 35.00

Signatures Silver Stitch Silver Ink

NM/M

Production 1-99
No pricing product. under 25.
AK Austin Kearns/25 20.00
AL Adam LaRoche/25 25.00
BB Boof Bonser/26 20.00
BR Brian Bruney/25 20.00
CB Chad Billingsley/58 30.00
CC Chris Capuano/39 15.00
CL Cliff Lee/31 20.00
CY Chris Young/32 20.00
DC Daniel Cabrera/35 15.00
DR Darrell Rasner/27 20.00
EA Erick Aybar/32 25.00
GP Glen Perkins/60 15.00
HK Howie Kendrick/47 20.00
JH Josh Hamilton/33 40.00
JN Joe Nathan/36 20.00
KS Kurt Suzuki/99 20.00
AI Adam Lind/99 15.00
RH Rich Hill/51 25.00
RM Russell Martin/55 30.00
SE Sergio Mitre/99 15.00
YG Chris B. Young/24 30.00
AD Adam Dunn/44 25.00
AM Andrew Miller/48 30.00
BP Brandon Phillips/99 20.00
CH Cole Hamels/35 35.00
CK Casey Kotchman/99 15.00
FH Felix Hernandez/34 50.00
FP Felix Pie/99 20.00
HA Travis Hafner/48 25.00
JL Jon Lester/31 40.00
JP Jonathan Papelbon/58 40.00
JS Jeremy Sowers/45 20.00
JV Jason Varitek/33 50.00
PH Phil Hughes/65 60.00
PK Paul Konerko/99 30.00
RI Rich Harden/40 15.00
TG Tom Glavine/47 40.00
TH Torii Hunter/48 20.00
TL Tim Lincecum/55 75.00
VE Justin Verlander/35 50.00
VM Victor Martinez/41 30.00

Signatures Black Glove Silver Ink

NM/M

Production 10 or 25
Gold Ink: No Pricing
Production Five Sets
Metallic Blue Ink: No Pricing
Production One Set
No pricing prod. under 25.
AG Adrian Gonzalez/25 25.00
AK Austin Kearns/25 20.00
AL Adam LaRoche/25 20.00
BB Boof Bonser/25 15.00
BR Brian Bruney/25 20.00
BW Brandon Wood/25 25.00
CB Chad Billingsley/25 35.00
CC Chris Capuano/25 15.00
CJ Conor Jackson/25 20.00
CL Cliff Lee/25 20.00
CQ Carlos Quentin/25 15.00
CY Chris Young/25 20.00
DC Daniel Cabrera/25 15.00

DH	Danny Haren/25	35.00
DR	Darrell Rasner/25	15.00
EA	Erick Aybar/25	20.00
GP	Glen Perkins/25	15.00
HP	Hunter Pence/25	75.00
JH	Josh Hamilton/25	50.00
JK	Jason Kubel/25	20.00
JN	Joe Nathan/25	20.00
JW	Josh Willingham/25	20.00
KA	Jeff Karstens/25	15.00
KS	Kurt Suzuki/25	20.00
LO	Lyle Overbay/25	15.00
MC	Matt Cain/25	30.00
RH	Rich Hill/25	30.00
RM	Russell Martin/25	50.00
SE	Sergio Mitre/25	15.00
TB	Travis Buck/25	25.00
YG	Chris B. Young/25	30.00

America's Pastime Signature

		NM/M
AD	Adam Dunn	15.00
AE	Andre Ethier	10.00
AG	Adrian Gonzalez	10.00
AJ	A.J. Burnett	10.00
AK	Al Kaline	30.00
AL	Adam LaRoche	10.00
AP	Albert Pujols	150.00
AV	Andy Van Slyke	15.00
BB	Boof Bonser	10.00
BE	Johnny Bench	30.00
BJ	B.J. Upton	15.00
BM	Bill Mazeroski	25.00
CB	Chad Billingsley	15.00
CC	Chad Cordero	10.00
CH	Cole Hamels	30.00
CK	Casey Kotchman	10.00
CQ	Carlos Quentin	10.00
CR	Craig Biggio	50.00
CT	Curtis Thigpen	10.00
CW	Chien-Ming Wang	100.00
CY	Chris Young	10.00
DH	Danny Haren	15.00
DJ	Derek Jeter	125.00
DM	Don Mattingly	50.00
DS	Don Sutton	15.00
DU	Dan Uggla	15.00
DY	Delmon Young	15.00
EB	Ernie Banks	50.00
FH	Felix Hernandez	25.00
FR	Frank Robinson	25.00
GA	Garrett Atkins	10.00
GP	Gaylord Perry	15.00
GR	Khalil Greene	15.00
GW	Tony Gwynn	50.00
HA	Travis Hafner	15.00
HB	Homer Bailey	15.00
HE	Chase Headley	10.00
HO	Howie Kendrick	10.00
HR	Hanley Ramirez	20.00
HS	Huston Street	10.00
HU	Torii Hunter	15.00
IK	Ian Kinsler	10.00
JB	Jason Bay	15.00
JE	Jeremy Bonderman	15.00
JI	Jim Rice	20.00
JL	James Loney	20.00
JM	Jack Morris	10.00
JN	Joe Nathan	20.00
JO	Joe Blanton	10.00
JT	Jim Thome	30.00
JV	Justin Verlander	30.00
JZ	Joel Zumaya	15.00
KI	Kei Igawa	25.00
KJ	Kelly Johnson	10.00
KM	Kendry Morales	10.00
LA	Andy LaRoche	15.00
LE	Jon Lester	20.00
LY	John Lackey	10.00
MA	Daisuke Matsuzaka	250.00
MB	Matt Brown	10.00
MC	Matt Cain	15.00
MH	Matt Holliday	30.00
MM	Melvin Mora	10.00
MS	Mike Schmidt	40.00
MT	Mark Teixeira	20.00
NM	Nicholas Markakis	20.00
NW	Nick Swisher	10.00
OS	Ozzie Smith	50.00
PA	Jim Palmer	15.00
PB	Jonathan Papelbon	30.00
PK	Paul Konerko	15.00
RA	Aramis Ramirez	20.00
RB	Ryan Braun	50.00
RF	Rafael Furcal	15.00
RG	Ryan Garko	10.00
RH	Rich Harden	10.00
RI	Rich Hill	10.00
RT	Ryan Theriot	15.00
RW	Rickie Weeks	10.00
RZ	Ryan Zimmerman	25.00
SD	Stephen Drew	20.00
SG	Sean Gallagher	10.00
SK	Scott Kazmir	15.00
SM	Stan Musial	75.00
SO	Joakim Soria	10.00
TG	Tom Glavine	50.00
TP	Tony Perez	15.00
TR	Tim Raines	10.00
TT	Troy Tulowitzki	40.00
VM	Victor Martinez	15.00
VW	Vernon Wells	15.00
WC	Will Clark	15.00
WI	Josh Willingham	10.00
WM	Willie McCovey	60.00
XN	Xavier Nady	10.00

America's Ultimate Pastime Materials

NM/M

Production 75 unless noted
Patch: 2X
Production 5-50
No pricing 25 or less
Gold: No Pricing
Production 25 Sets

AB	Adrian Beltre	8.00
AJ	Andruw Jones	10.00
AP	Andy Pettitte	10.00
AS	Alfonso Soriano	10.00
BA	Bobby Abreu	8.00
BE	Josh Beckett	10.00
BG	Brian Giles	5.00
BJ	Jeff Bagwell	8.00
BR	Brian Roberts	10.00
BS	Ben Sheets	8.00
BW	Brandon Webb	8.00
CA	Chris Carpenter	8.00
CB	Carlos Beltran	10.00
CC	Carl Crawford	5.00
CF	Carlton Fisk	10.00
CJ	Chipper Jones	10.00
CL	Carlos Lee	8.00
CR	Cal Ripken Jr.	25.00
CS	Curt Schilling	10.00
CU	Chase Utley	15.00
DJ	Derek Jeter	25.00
DL	Derrek Lee	10.00
DO	David Ortiz	15.00
DW	Dontrelle Willis	5.00
FH	Felix Hernandez	10.00
FL	Francisco Liriano	10.00
FR	Francisco Rodriguez/64	5.00
GA	Garrett Atkins	5.00
GM	Greg Maddux	15.00
GS	Gary Sheffield	10.00
GW	Tony Gwynn	15.00
HA	Rich Harden	5.00
HB	Hank Blalock	5.00
HR	Hanley Ramirez	10.00
JA	Jason Bay	8.00
JB	Jeremy Bonderman	8.00
JE	Jim Edmonds	8.00
JG	Jason Giambi	8.00
JM	Justin Morneau	10.00
JN	Joe Nathan	8.00
JO	Randy Johnson	10.00
JP	Jonathan Papelbon	10.00
JR	Jim Rice	8.00
JS	Johan Santana	10.00
JT	Jim Thome	10.00
JV	Justin Verlander	10.00
JW	Josh Willingham	5.00
KG	Ken Griffey Jr.	15.00
KP	Kirby Puckett	25.00
KY	Kevin Youkilis	8.00
LB	Lance Berkman	8.00
LO	Lou Brock/25	15.00
MA	Joe Mauer	8.00
MC	Matt Cain	8.00
MH	Matt Holliday	10.00
MI	Miguel Cabrera	10.00
MM	Mike Mussina	10.00
MR	Manny Ramirez	10.00
MS	Mike Schmidt	20.00
MT	Miguel Tejada	10.00
MY	Michael Young	8.00
MZ	Pedro Martinez	10.00
NR	Nolan Ryan	25.00
OR	Magglio Ordonez	8.00
OS	Ozzie Smith	15.00
PE	Jake Peavy	10.00
PF	Prince Fielder	15.00
PM	Paul Molitor	10.00
PU	Albert Pujols	25.00
RB	Rocco Baldelli	5.00
RC	Roger Clemens	15.00
RE	Jose Reyes	15.00
RH	Roy Halladay	8.00
RJ	Reggie Jackson	15.00
RO	Roy Oswalt	8.00
RS	Ryne Sandberg	15.00
RW	Rickie Weeks	8.00
RZ	Ryan Zimmerman	8.00
SC	Steve Carlton	8.00
SE	Richie Sexson	8.00
SI	Grady Sizemore	15.00
SK	Scott Kazmir	8.00
SM	John Smoltz	10.00
TE	Mark Teixeira	10.00
TG	Troy Glaus	8.00
TH	Todd Helton	8.00
TR	Travis Hafner	8.00
VA	Jason Varitek	10.00
VG	Vladimir Guerrero	10.00
VM	Victor Martinez	8.00
WC	Will Clark	8.00
CF2	Carlton Fisk	10.00
GW2	Tony Gwynn	15.00
MR2	Manny Ramirez	10.00
RE2	Jose Reyes	15.00
SI2	Grady Sizemore	15.00
TR2	Travis Hafner	8.00
VG2	Vladimir Guerrero	10.00

The Ultimate Card

Production One Set

The Ultimate Iron Man Signature

Production Eight Sets

The Ultimate Logo

Production One Set

The Ultimate Patch

Production 25 unless noted.

The Ultimate Six Signatures

Production 10 Sets

Ultimate Champions Signatures

Production 4-10

Ultimate Ensemble Dual Patches

No Pricing
Production 25 Sets

Ultimate Ensemble Triple Patch

Production 15 Sets

Ultimate Ensemble Quad Patch

Production 10 Sets

Ultimate Ensemble Dual Swatch

NM/M

Production 75 sets unless noted.

BD	J.D. Drew, Jason Bay	10.00
BH	Jeremy Bonderman, Rich Harden	10.00
BZ	Wade Boggs, Ryan Zimmerman	10.00
CG	Vladimir Guerrero, Miguel Cabrera	15.00
CJ	Curt Schilling, Josh Beckett	15.00
CR	Roger Clemens, Nolan Ryan	25.00
CW	Matt Cain, Jered Weaver	10.00
FT	Mark Teixeira, Prince Fielder	15.00
GD	Ken Griffey Jr., Adam Dunn	20.00
GM	Tom Glavine, Pedro Martinez	10.00
GP	Tony Gwynn, Jake Peavy	15.00
GR	Tony Gwynn, Cal Ripken Jr.	30.00
HH	Todd Helton, Matt Holliday	10.00
HJ	Felix Hernandez, Kenji Johjima	10.00
HR	J.J. Hardy, Jose Reyes	10.00
HW	Vernon Wells, Roy Halladay	10.00
IK	Paul Konerko, Tadahito Iguchi	10.00
JJ	Andruw Jones, Chipper Jones	10.00
JR	Derek Jeter, Mariano Rivera	25.00
JV	Victor Martinez, Joe Mauer	10.00
KY	Scott Kazmir, Delmon Young	10.00
LS	Derrek Lee, Alfonso Soriano	10.00
MB	Mike Schmidt, Brooks Robinson	25.00
MC	Michael Cuddyer, Justin Morneau	10.00
MM	Justin Morneau, Joe Mauer	10.00
NR	Mariano Rivera, Joe Nathan	10.00
OB	Lance Berkman, Roy Oswalt	10.00
PC	Chris Carpenter, Albert Pujols	20.00
PO	David Ortiz, Albert Pujols	20.00
RB	Ivan Rodriguez, Johnny Bench	15.00
SB	Carlos Beltran, Grady Sizemore	15.00
SC	Alfonso Soriano, Carl Crawford/52	10.00
SL	Johan Santana, Francisco Liriano	10.00
SP	John Smoltz, Jake Peavy	10.00
SR	Cal Ripken Jr., Ryne Sandberg/63	50.00
SW	Johan Santana, Brandon Webb	10.00
TR	Cal Ripken Jr., Miguel Tejada	20.00
WU	Rickie Weeks, Chase Utley	15.00
YR	Michael Young, Jose Reyes	15.00

Ultimate Ensemble Triple Swatch

NM/M

Production 50 Sets

BCG	Troy Glaus, Eric Chavez, Hank Blalock	15.00
CBG	Tony Gwynn, Will Clark, Wade Boggs	20.00
CRS	Nolan Ryan, Don Sutton, Steve Carlton	25.00
CSK	Johan Santana, Scott Kazmir, Steve Carlton	15.00
FHS	Ben Sheets, J.J. Hardy, Prince Fielder	15.00
GRR	Khalil Greene, Jose Reyes, Hanley Ramirez	25.00
HTP	Mike Piazza, Frank Thomas, Travis Hafner	15.00
LPD	Barry Larkin, Tony Perez, Adam Dunn	15.00
LRS	Ozzie Smith, Barry Larkin, Cal Ripken Jr.	25.00
MCS	Roger Clemens, Pedro Martinez, Don Sutton	25.00
MJG	Ken Griffey Jr., Chipper Jones, Joe Mauer	25.00
MMP	Jorge Posada, Victor Martinez, Joe Mauer	15.00
MSB	Curt Schilling, Josh Beckett, Daisuke Matsuzaka	65.00
MSU	Ryne Sandberg, Bill Mazeroski, Chase Utley	25.00
OCZ	Chris Carpenter, Roy Oswalt, Carlos Zambrano	15.00
ODH	Jermaine Dye, Travis Hafner, David Ortiz	15.00
OMT	David Ortiz, Mark Teixeira, Justin Morneau	15.00
OPR	David Ortiz, Albert Pujols, Jose Reyes	25.00
PJL	Andruw Jones, Derrek Lee, Albert Pujols	25.00
RDB	Carlos Delgado, Carlos Beltran, Ivan Rodriguez	15.00
RJG	Ken Griffey Jr., Cal Ripken Jr., Derek Jeter	50.00
RPJ	Kirby Puckett, Jim Rice, Reggie Jackson	60.00
RPS	Manny Ramirez, Alfonso Soriano, Albert Pujols	25.00
RSB	Wade Boggs, Mike Schmidt, Brooks Robinson	40.00
SHS	Roy Halladay, Josh Beckett, Johan Santana	15.00
UWG	Marcus Giles, Rickie Weeks, Chase Utley	20.00
YBO	Wade Boggs, David Ortiz, Carl Yastrzemski	25.00
YJT	Derek Jeter, Miguel Tejada, Michael Young	25.00
YTS	Sammy Sosa, Michael Young, Mark Teixeira	20.00
ZAJ	Chipper Jones, Garrett Atkins, Ryan Zimmerman	15.00

Ultimate Ensemble Quad Swatch

No Pricing
Production 25 unless noted.

Ultimate Futures Signatures

Production 25 unless noted.

Ultimate Legendary Signatures

Production 25 Sets

Ultimate Numbers Match Signature

NM/M

Production 2-48

AR	Garrett Atkins, Mark Reynolds/27	15.00
BW	Jeremy Bonderman, Chase Wright/38	15.00
DZ	Carlos Zambrano, Jason Bay/38	25.00
FG	Vladimir Guerrero, Carlton Fisk/27	75.00
HH	Travis Hafner, Torii Hunter/48	25.00
HR	Nolan Ryan, Felix Hernandez/34	100.00
HV	Justin Verlander, Cole Hamels/35	50.00
HW	Chien-Ming Wang, Rich Harden/40	180.00
JD	Adam Dunn, Reggie Jackson/44	50.00
WH	Dontrelle Willis, Cole Hamels/35	50.00

Ultimate Numbers Materials

NM/M

Production 1-75
No pricing 25 or less

AB	A.J. Burnett/34	8.00
AD	Adam Dunn/44	10.00
AJ	Andruw Jones/25	10.00
AN	Andy Pettitte/46	10.00
BA	Bobby Abreu/53	10.00
BE	Adrian Beltre/29	10.00
BZ	Barry Zito/75	8.00
CC	Chris Carpenter/29	10.00
CF	Carlton Fisk/27	10.00
CL	Carlos Lee/45	8.00
CS	Curt Schilling/38	10.00
CU	Chase Utley/26	15.00
DL	Derrek Lee/25	10.00
DO	David Ortiz/34	15.00
DY	Delmon Young/26	10.00
FH	Felix Hernandez/34	10.00
FL	Francisco Liriano/47	10.00
GA	Garrett Atkins/27	8.00
GL	Troy Glaus/25	8.00
GP	Gaylord Perry/36	10.00
HA	Roy Halladay/32	8.00
HF	Travis Hafner/48	8.00
HU	Torii Hunter/48	8.00
JE	Jeremy Bonderman/38	8.00
JH	Josh Hamilton/33	15.00
JS	Johan Santana/57	10.00
JT	Jim Thome/25	10.00
JV	Jason Varitek/33	20.00
MO	Maggio Ordonez/30	8.00
NR	Nolan Ryan/34	40.00
OS	Roy Oswalt/44	10.00
PF	Prince Fielder/28	15.00
RC	Rod Carew/29	10.00
RH	Rich Harden/40	8.00
RJ	Randy Johnson/51	10.00
SA	C.C. Sabathia/52	8.00
SC	Steve Carlton/32	10.00
SR	Scott Rolen/27	10.00
TG	Tom Glavine/47	15.00
TR	Tim Raines/30	8.00
TV	Trevor Hoffman/51	8.00
VG	Vladimir Guerrero/27	10.00
VM	Victor Martinez/41	10.00
WI	Dontrelle Willis/35	8.00
CF2	Carlton Fisk/72	10.00
DL2	Derrek Le/25	10.00
DO2	David Ortiz/25	15.00

Ultimate Star Materials

NM/M

Common Player: 5.00
Patch Autograph: No Pricing
Production Five Sets
Autographs: No Pricing
Production 15 Sets

AD	Adam Dunn	8.00
AG	Alex Gordon	15.00
AK	Austin Kearns	5.00
AP	Albert Pujols	20.00
BG	Brian Giles	5.00
BI	Craig Biggio	8.00
BO	Jeremy Bonderman	8.00
BS	Ben Sheets	5.00
BU	B.J. Upton	8.00
CA	Chris Carpenter	8.00
CF	Carlton Fisk	8.00
CL	Carlos Lee	8.00
CR	Cal Ripken Jr.	20.00
CY	Carl Yastrzemski	15.00
CZ	Carlos Zambrano	8.00
DH	Danny Haren	8.00
DJ	Derek Jeter	20.00
DL	Derrek Lee	8.00
DM	Don Mattingly	15.00
DO	David Ortiz	15.00
DW	Dontrelle Willis	5.00
EC	Eric Chavez	5.00
FH	Felix Hernandez	8.00
FL	Francisco Liriano	8.00
FR	Francisco Rodriguez	5.00
FT	Frank Thomas	10.00
GA	Garrett Atkins	5.00
GR	Khalil Greene	8.00
GW	Tony Gwynn	10.00
HA	Roy Halladay	8.00
HP	Hunter Pence	15.00
HR	Hanley Ramirez	10.00
HS	Huston Street	5.00
HU	Torii Hunter	10.00
JA	Jason Bay	8.00
JB	Josh Beckett	10.00
JH	Jeremy Hermida	5.00
JL	John Lackey	5.00
JM	Joe Mauer	8.00
JN	Joe Nathan	5.00
JP	Jonathan Papelbon	15.00
JR	Jim Rice	8.00
JS	John Smoltz	8.00
JT	Jim Thome	8.00
JU	Justin Morneau	8.00
KG	Ken Griffey Jr.	15.00
MA	Matt Cain	8.00
MC	Miguel Cabrera	10.00
MH	Matt Holliday	10.00
MS	Mike Schmidt	15.00
MT	Mark Teixeira	8.00
MY	Michael Young	5.00
NM	Nicholas Markakis	8.00
NR	Nolan Ryan	20.00
NS	Nick Swisher	5.00
OR	Roy Oswalt	8.00
OS	Ozzie Smith	15.00
PA	Jim Palmer	8.00
PE	Jake Peavy	8.00
PF	Prince Fielder	10.00
PK	Paul Konerko	8.00
PM	Paul Molitor	8.00
RA	Roberto Alomar	8.00
RC	Roger Clemens	15.00
RF	Rollie Fingers	8.00
RH	Rich Harden	5.00
RJ	Randy Johnson	10.00
RO	Rod Carew	10.00
RW	Rickie Weeks	8.00
RY	Robin Yount	10.00
RZ	Ryan Zimmerman	10.00
SK	Scott Kazmir	8.00
TG	Tom Glavine	10.00
TH	Travis Hafner	8.00
TI	Tim Hudson	8.00
TT	Troy Tulowitzki	15.00
VM	Victor Martinez	8.00
VW	Vernon Wells	5.00
WB	Wade Boggs	10.00
WI	Josh Willingham	5.00
AG2	Alex Gordon	15.00
AK2	Austin Kearns	5.00
CL2	Carlos Lee	8.00
CR2	Cal Ripken Jr.	20.00
DJ2	Derek Jeter	20.00
DW2	Dontrelle Willis	5.00
FH2	Felix Hernandez	8.00
GA2	Garrett Atkins	5.00
JT2	Jim Thome	8.00
JU2	Justin Morneau	8.00
MA2	Matt Cain	8.00
MH2	Matt Holliday	10.00
MT2	Mark Teixeira	8.00
MY2	Michael Young	5.00
PE2	Jake Peavy	8.00
PM2	Paul Molitor	8.00
RZ2	Ryan Zimmerman	10.00
TH2	Travis Hafner	8.00

Ultimate Team Marks

NM/M

Production 60 sets unless noted.

CL	Carlos Lee/57	20.00
CY	Carl Yastrzemski/58	50.00
DJ	Derek Jeter	140.00
DL	Derrek Lee/58	25.00
DO	David Ortiz	65.00
DW	Dontrelle Willis/56	10.00
FH	Felix Hernandez	30.00
JM	Joe Mauer	25.00
MO	Justin Morneau	25.00
MT	Mark Teixeira	15.00
PF	Prince Fielder	50.00
VM	Victor Martinez	15.00
VW	Vernon Wells	10.00

Ultimate Team Materials

NM/M

Production 50 unless noted.
Patch: No Pricing
Production 19-25
Autographs: No Pricing
Production 1-10

AD	Adam Dunn	8.00
AK	Austin Kearns	5.00
AN	Garret Anderson	5.00
AP	Albert Pujols	20.00
BE	Josh Beckett	10.00
BG	Brian Giles	5.00
BS	Ben Sheets	8.00
BU	B.J. Upton	8.00
CA	Rod Carew	10.00
CF	Carlton Fisk	8.00
CH	Chris Carpenter	8.00
CL	Carlos Lee	8.00
CR	Bobby Crosby	5.00
CY	Carl Yastrzemski	15.00
DH	Danny Haren	8.00
DJ	Derek Jeter	25.00
DL	Derrek Lee	8.00
DM	Don Mattingly	15.00
DO	David Ortiz	10.00
DW	Dontrelle Willis	5.00
EC	Eric Chavez	5.00
FH	Felix Hernandez	8.00
FJ	Fergie Jenkins	8.00
FL	Francisco Liriano	10.00
FR	Francisco Rodriguez	5.00
FT	Frank Thomas	10.00
GA	Garrett Atkins	5.00
GR	Khalil Greene	8.00
GW	Tony Gwynn	10.00
HA	Rich Harden	5.00
HP	Hunter Pence	15.00
HR	Hanley Ramirez	10.00
HS	Huston Street	5.00
HU	Tim Hudson	8.00
JA	Jason Bay	8.00
JE	Jeremy Bonderman	8.00
JG	Jonny Gomes	5.00
JH	Jeremy Hermida	5.00
JI	Jim Palmer	8.00

JL John Lackey 5.00
JM Joe Mauer 8.00
JN Joe Nathan 5.00
JP Jake Peavy 8.00
JR Jim Rice 8.00
JS John Smoltz 8.00
JT Jim Thome 8.00
KG Ken Griffey Jr. 15.00
KM Kendry Morales 5.00
MA Daisuke Matsuzaka 60.00
MC Matt Cain 8.00
MH Matt Holliday 10.00
MI Miguel Cabrera 10.00
MO Justin Morneau 8.00
MS Mike Schmidt 10.00
MT Mark Teixeira 8.00
MY Michael Young 5.00
NM Nicholas Markakis 10.00
NR Nolan Ryan 25.00
OS Ozzie Smith 15.00
PA Jonathan Papelbon 10.00
PF Prince Fielder 15.00
PK Paul Konerko 8.00
PM Paul Molitor 10.00
PN Phil Niekro 8.00
RA Roberto Alomar 8.00
RC Roger Clemens 15.00
RF Rollie Fingers 8.00
RH Roy Halladay 8.00
RI Cal Ripken Jr. 30.00
RJ Randy Johnson 10.00
RO Roy Oswalt 8.00
RS Ryne Sandberg 15.00
RW Rickie Weeks 8.00
RY Robin Yount/25 15.00
RZ Ryan Zimmerman 8.00
SK Scott Kazmir 8.00
TG Tom Glavine 10.00
TH Torii Hunter 8.00
TR Travis Hafner 8.00
TT Troy Tulowitzki 10.00
VM Victor Martinez 8.00
WI Josh Willingham 5.00
DW2 Dontrelle Willis 5.00
EC2 Eric Chavez 5.00
GA2 Garrett Atkins 5.00
HS2 Huston Street 5.00
KG2 Ken Griffey Jr. 15.00
MH2 Matt Holliday 10.00
MI2 Miguel Cabrera 10.00
MO2 Justin Morneau 8.00
OS2 Ozzie Smith 15.00
RI2 Cal Ripken Jr. 30.00
RZ2 Ryan Zimmerman 8.00
SK2 Scott Kazmir 8.00
TR2 Travis Hafner 8.00
WI2 Josh Willingham 5.00

Ultimate Write of Passage

NM/M

Production 60 Sets
BH Jeff Baker/Auto., Matt Holliday 10.00
BR Ryan Braun/Auto., Scott Rolen 75.00
GR Alex Gordon/Auto., Alex Rodriguez 50.00
HS Cole Hamels/Auto., Johan Santana 40.00
IC Kei Igawa/Auto. 25.00
IR Akinori Iwamura/Auto., Aramis Ramirez 30.00
KB Howie Kendrick/Auto., Craig Biggio 10.00
KJ Kevin Kouzmanoff/Auto., Chipper Jones 10.00
LZ Tim Lincecum/Auto., Barry Zito 60.00
MS Andrew Miller/Auto., C.C. Sabathia 25.00
PG Hunter Pence/Auto., Ken Griffey Jr. 50.00
PK Glen Perkins/Auto., Scott Kazmir 10.00
QC Carlos Quentin/Auto., Carl Crawford 10.00
RF Hanley Ramirez/Auto., Rafael Furcal 25.00
SD Ryan Sweeney/Auto., Jermaine Dye 10.00
SS Jeremy Sowers/Auto., C.C. Sabathia 10.00
TD Curtis Thigpen/Auto., Carlos Delgado 10.00
TJ Troy Tulowitzki/Auto., Derek Jeter 40.00
UU B.J. Upton/Auto., Chase Utley 15.00
YG Delmon Young/Auto., Vladimir Guerrero 15.00

Ultimate Collection Jersey Parallel

NM/M

Production 50 Sets
Patch: No Pricing
Production 25 Sets
1 Chipper Jones 10.00
2 Andruw Jones 8.00
3 Tim Hudson 8.00
4 Stephen Drew 8.00
5 Randy Johnson 10.00
6 Brandon Webb 8.00
7 Alfonso Soriano 10.00
8 Derrek Lee 8.00
9 Aramis Ramirez 8.00
10 Carlos Zambrano 10.00
11 Ken Griffey Jr. 15.00
12 Adam Dunn 8.00
13 Ryan Freel 5.00
14 Todd Helton 8.00
15 Garrett Atkins 5.00
16 Matt Holliday 10.00
17 Hanley Ramirez 10.00
18 Dontrelle Willis 5.00
19 Miguel Cabrera 10.00
20 Lance Berkman 8.00
21 Roy Oswalt 8.00
22 Carlos Lee 8.00
24 Jason Schmidt 5.00
25 Juan Pierre 5.00
26 Russell Martin 8.00
27 Rickie Weeks 5.00
28 Prince Fielder 15.00
29 Ben Sheets 8.00
31 Jose Reyes 10.00
32 Pedro 1artinez 10.00
33 Carlos Beltran 10.00
34 Brett Myers 5.00
35 Jimmy Rollins 15.00
37 Jason Bay 8.00
38 Freddy Sanchez 5.00
39 Ian Snell 5.00
40 Jake Peavy 10.00
41 Greg Maddux 15.00
42 Brian Giles 5.00
43 Matt Cain 8.00
44 Barry Zito 8.00
45 Ray Durham 5.00
46 Albert Pujols 20.00
47 Chris Carpenter 8.00
48 Chris Duncan 5.00
49 Scott Rolen 8.00
50 Ryan Zimmerman 8.00
51 Chad Cordero 5.00
52 Ryan Church 5.00
53 Miguel Tejada 8.00
54 Erik Bedard 15.00
55 Brian Roberts 8.00
56 David Ortiz 15.00
57 Josh Beckett 10.00
58 Manny Ramirez 10.00
59 Daisuke Matsuzaka 60.00
60 Jim Thome 8.00
61 Paul Konerko 8.00
62 Jermaine Dye 8.00
63 Grady Sizemore 15.00
64 Victor Martinez 8.00
65 C.C. Sabathia 8.00
66 Ivan Rodriguez 8.00
67 Justin Verlander 10.00
68 Gary Sheffield 8.00
69 Jeremy Bonderman 8.00
70 Gil Meche 5.00
71 Mike Sweeney 5.00
72 Mark Teahen 5.00
73 Vladimir Guerrero 10.00
74 Howie Kendrick 8.00
75 Francisco Rodriguez 5.00
76 Johan Santana 10.00
77 Justin Morneau 8.00
78 Joe Mauer 8.00
79 Michael Cuddyer 5.00
81 Derek Jeter 25.00
83 Roger Clemens 15.00
84 Rich Harden 5.00
85 Mike Piazza 15.00
86 Huston Street 5.00
88 Felix Hernandez 10.00
89 Kenji Johjima 8.00
90 Adrian Beltre 8.00
91 Carl Crawford 8.00
92 Scott Kazmir 8.00
93 B.J. Upton 8.00
94 Michael Young 5.00
95 Mark Teixeira 8.00
97 Hank Blalock 5.00
98 Vernon Wells 5.00
99 Vernon Wells 8.00
100 Frank Thomas 10.00

2007 UD Black

NM/M

Common Jersey Auto. (1-42): 15.00
Production 16-75
Common RC Auto. (43-72): 25.00
Production 99
Pack (1): 80.00
Box (2): 150.00
1 Brandon Webb/75 25.00
2 Tim Hudson/75 30.00
3 Cal Ripken Jr./75 150.00
4 Nicholas Markakis/35 40.00
5 David Ortiz/52 100.00
6 Jonathan Papelbon/75 40.00
7 Coco Crisp/43 30.00
8 Derrek Lee/62 30.00
10 Adam Dunn/75 40.00
11 Ken Griffey Jr./75 80.00
12 Travis Hafner/52 60.00
13 Victor Martinez/75 40.00
14 Garrett Atkins/75 20.00
15 Justin Verlander/75 40.00
16 Jeremy Bonderman/75 25.00
17 Curtis Granderson/75 40.00
18 Hanley Ramirez/75 40.00
19 Dan Uggla/74 15.00
20 Lance Berkman/75 30.00
21 Mark Teahen/75 15.00
22 John Lackey/75 20.00
23 Howie Kendrick/75 30.00
25 Prince Fielder/75 75.00
26 Torii Hunter/75 25.00
27 Justin Morneau/75 40.00
28 John Maine/75 40.00
30 Danny Haren/75 25.00
31 Eric Chavez/64 25.00
32 Cole Hamels/75 30.00
33 Jason Bay/75 25.00
34 Adrian Gonzalez/75 20.00
35 Chris Young/75 30.00
36 Matt Cain/75 30.00
37 Felix Hernandez/75 60.00
38 Chris Duncan/75 30.00
39 B.J. Upton/75 30.00
40 Ian Kinsler/75 40.00
41 Roy Halladay/75 25.00
42 Chad Cordero/72 25.00
43 Adam Lind **(RC)** 25.00
44 Akinori Iwamura **RC** 100.00
45 Alex Gordon **RC** 120.00
46 Andy LaRoche **(RC)** 30.00
47 Billy Butler **(RC)** 50.00
48 David Murphy **(RC)** 30.00
49 Brandon Wood **(RC)** 40.00
50 Carlos Gomez **RC** 60.00
51 Chase Headley **(RC)** 25.00
52 Curtis Thigpen **(RC)** 25.00
53 Joba Chamberlain **RC** 300.00
54 Delmon Young **(RC)** 40.00
55 Felix Pie **(RC)** 40.00
56 Homer Bailey **(RC)** 40.00
57 Hunter Pence **(RC)** 100.00
58 Josh Hamilton **(RC)** 40.00
59 Kei Igawa **RC** 60.00
60 Kevin Slowey **(RC)** 30.00
61 Kurt Suzuki **(RC)** 40.00
62 Mark Reynolds **RC** 50.00
63 Daisuke Matsuzaka **RC** 450.00
64 Justin Upton **RC** 75.00
65 Phil Hughes **(RC)** 75.00
66 Ryan Braun **(RC)** 100.00
67 Ryan Sweeney **(RC)** 25.00
68 Sean Gallagher **(RC)** 25.00
69 Tim Lincecum **RC** 140.00
70 Travis Buck **(RC)** 25.00
71 Troy Tulowitzki **(RC)** 100.00
72 Yovani Gallardo **(RC)** 60.00

Printing Plates

No Pricing
Production one set per color.

Natural Pearl

No Pricing
Production One Set

Gold

No Pricing
Production 10 Sets

Pure White Pack Autographs

Production One Set

Rookie Signatures

NM/M

Common Player (1-100): 4.00
Production 99
Common RC Auto. (101-191): 15.00
Production 125-235
Box (6 Cards): 250.00
1 Ichiro Suzuki 15.00
2 Alex Rodriguez 20.00
3 David Wright 15.00
4 Ryan Howard 15.00
5 Ken Griffey Jr. 15.00
6 Derek Jeter 20.00
7 Vladimir Guerrero 8.00
8 Roger Clemens 10.00
9 Greg Maddux 10.00
10 Johan Santana 8.00
11 Nomar Garciaparra 4.00
12 Carlos Beltran 6.00
13 Carlos Delgado 5.00
14 Manny Ramirez 6.00
15 John Lackey 4.00
16 David Ortiz 8.00
17 Curt Schilling 6.00
18 Cal Ripken Jr. 20.00
19 Albert Pujols 20.00
20 Frank Thomas 5.00
21 Chris Carpenter 4.00
22 Prince Fielder 8.00
23 Justin Morneau 6.00
24 Joe Mauer 5.00
25 Torii Hunter 5.00
26 Jake Peavy 6.00
27 Roy Oswalt 5.00
28 Craig Biggio 4.00
29 Lance Berkman 4.00
30 Carlos Zambrano 4.00
31 Derrek Lee 5.00
32 Aramis Ramirez 5.00
33 Noah Lowry 4.00
34 Magglio Ordonez 4.00
35 Ivan Rodriguez 4.00
36 Johnny Damon 5.00
37 Justin Verlander 5.00
38 John Smoltz 5.00
39 Chipper Jones 8.00
40 Jeff Francoeur 5.00
41 Hanley Ramirez 8.00
42 Miguel Cabrera 8.00
43 Josh Beckett 8.00
44 Cole Hamels 6.00
45 Chase Utley 6.00
46 Grady Sizemore 8.00
47 Travis Hafner 5.00
48 Victor Martinez 5.00
49 Russell Martin 5.00
50 Jason Varitek 4.00
51 Hideki Matsui 10.00
52 Carl Crawford 5.00
53 Scott Kazmir 5.00
54 Miguel Tejada 5.00
55 Erik Bedard 5.00
56 Carlos Lee 5.00
57 Sammy Sosa 5.00
58 Mark Teixeira 6.00
59 Michael Young 4.00
60 Jim Thome 6.00
61 Paul Konerko 5.00
62 Jermaine Dye 4.00
63 Mark Teahen 4.00
64 Felix Hernandez 6.00
65 Andruw Jones 5.00
66 Pedro Martinez 8.00
67 Randy Johnson 6.00
68 Ryan Zimmerman 6.00
69 Matt Holliday 8.00
70 Todd Helton 5.00
71 Brian Bannister 4.00
72 Jeremy Bonderman 5.00
73 Adam Dunn 5.00
74 Aaron Harang 4.00
75 Jason Bay 5.00
76 Adam LaRoche 5.00
77 Freddy Sanchez 4.00
78 Dan Uggla 4.00
79 Joe Nathan 4.00
80 Brad Penny 4.00
81 Takashi Saito 4.00
82 Jimmy Rollins 8.00
83 Jose Reyes 10.00
84 Jered Weaver 6.00
85 Chien-Ming Wang 10.00
86 Jonathan Papelbon 8.00
87 Mariano Rivera 6.00
88 Eric Byrnes 5.00
89 Nicholas Markakis 6.00
90 Brian Roberts 4.00
91 Omar Vizquel 4.00
92 Vernon Wells 5.00
93 Danny Haren 5.00
94 Ben Sheets 4.00
95 B.J. Upton 6.00
96 Adrian Gonzalez 5.00
97 J.J. Hardy 4.00
98 Mike Piazza 8.00
99 Roy Halladay 5.00
100 Alfonso Soriano 8.00
101 Sean Henn/Auto./235 **(RC)** 15.00
102 Sean White/Auto./235 **RC** 15.00
103 Mike Schultz/Auto./235 **RC** 15.00
104 Michael Bourn/Auto./235 **(RC)** 20.00
105 Matt Chico/Auto./235 **(RC)** 15.00
106 Matt Lindstrom/Auto./235 **(RC)** 15.00
107 Connor Robertson/Auto./235 **RC** 15.00
108 Jay Marshall/Auto./235 **RC** 15.00
109 Jared Burton/Auto./235 **RC** 15.00
110 Juan Perez/Auto./235 **RC** 15.00
111 Scott Moore/Auto./235 **(RC)** 15.00
112 Brad Salmon/Auto./235 **RC** 15.00
113 Danny Putnam/Auto./235 **(RC)** 15.00
114 Kelvin Jimenez/Auto./235 **RC** 15.00
115 Dennis Dove/Auto./235 **(RC)** 15.00
116 Yoel Hernandez/Auto./235 **RC** 20.00
117 Devern Hansack/Auto./235 **RC** 15.00
118 Mike Rabelo/Auto./235 **(RC)** 15.00
119 Miguel Montero/Auto./235 **(RC)** 15.00
120 Kevin Cameron/Auto./235 **(RC)** 15.00
121 Joseph Bisenius/Auto./235 **RC** 15.00
122 Ryan Z. Braun/Auto./235 **RC** 15.00
123 Levale Speigner/Auto./235 **RC** 15.00
124 Lee Gardner/Auto./235 **(RC)** 15.00
125 Ryan Rowland-Smith/Auto./235 **RC** 15.00
126 Zack Segovia/Auto./235 **(RC)** 15.00
127 Rick Vanden Hurk/Auto./235 **RC** 15.00
128 Dallas Braden/Auto./235 **RC** 15.00
129 Rocky Cherry/Auto./235 **RC** 15.00
130 Andy Gonzalez/Auto./235 **(RC)** 15.00
131 Neal Musser/Auto./235 **RC** 15.00
132 Garrett Jones/Auto./235 **(RC)** 15.00
133 Ben Francisco/Auto./235 **(RC)** 15.00
134 Jon Coutlangus/Auto./235 **(RC)** 15.00
135 A.J. Murray/Auto./235 **RC** 15.00
136 Brett Carroll/Auto./235 **RC** 15.00
137 John Danks/Auto./235 **RC** 20.00
138 Kyle Kendrick/Auto./235 **(RC)** 25.00
139 Joaquin Arias/Auto./235 **(RC)** 15.00
140 Matt Brown/Auto./235 **RC** 15.00
141 Kurt Suzuki/Auto./150 **(RC)** 25.00
142 Curtis Thigpen/Auto./150 **(RC)** 20.00
143 Jerry Owens/Auto./150 **(RC)** 15.00
144 Billy Butler/Auto./150 **(RC)** 35.00
145 Kei Igawa/Auto./150 **RC** 40.00
146 Mike Fontenot/Auto./150 **(RC)** 20.00
147 Brandon Wood/Auto./150 **(RC)** 30.00
148 Alexi Casilla/Auto./150 **RC** 15.00
149 Jeff Baker/Auto./150 **(RC)** 15.00
150 Brian Barden/Auto./150 **RC** 20.00
151 Chris Stewart/Auto./150 **RC** 15.00
152 Jon Knott/Auto./150 **(RC)** 15.00
153 Chase Wright/Auto./150 **RC** 15.00
154 Chase Headley/Auto./150 **(RC)** 30.00
155 Jesse Litsch/Jsy/Auto./199 **RC** 20.00
156 Tyler Clippard/Auto./150 **(RC)** 15.00
157 Matt DeSalvo/Auto./150 **(RC)** 15.00
158 Kory Casto/Auto./150 **(RC)** 15.00
159 Jarrod Saltalamacchia/Jsy Auto/199 **(RC)** 25.00
160 Glen Perkins/Auto./150 **(RC)** 15.00
161 Ryan Braun/Jsy/Auto./199 **(RC)** 75.00
162 Justin Upton/Jsy/Auto./199 **RC** 60.00
163 Tim Lincecum/Jsy/Auto./199 **RC** 120.00
164 Fred Lewis/Auto./150 **(RC)** 15.00
165 Alex Gordon/Jsy/Auto./199 **RC** 60.00
166 Akinori Iwamura/Jsy/Auto./199 **RC** 30.00
167 Delmon Young/Jsy/Auto./199 **(RC)** 40.00
168 Troy Tulowitzki/Jsy/Auto./199 **(RC)** 60.00
169 Daisuke Matsuzaka/Jsy/Auto./199 **RC** 450.00
170 Josh Hamilton/Jsy/Auto./199 **(RC)** 30.00
171 Kevin Kouzmanoff/Jsy/Auto./199 **(RC)** 25.00
172 Hunter Pence/Jsy/Auto./199 **(RC)** 60.00
173 Felix Pie/Jsy/Auto./199 **(RC)** 30.00
174 Andrew Miller/Jsy/Auto./199 **RC** 40.00
175 Yovani Gallardo/Jsy/Auto./199 **(RC)** 50.00
176 Ryan Sweeney/Jsy/Auto./199 **(RC)** 15.00
177 Josh Fields/Jsy/Auto./199 **(RC)** 30.00
178 Mark Reynolds/Jsy/Auto./199 **RC** 30.00
180 Homer Bailey/Auto./150 **(RC)** 25.00
182 Joba Chamberlain/Auto./150 **RC** 375.00
184 Travis Metcalf/Jsy/Auto./125 **RC** 15.00
185 Kevin Slowey/Jsy/Auto./199 **(RC)** 25.00
186 Phil Hughes/Auto./150 **(RC)** 80.00
187 Micah Owings/Auto./150 **(RC)** 25.00
188 Joe Smith/Auto./150 **RC** 15.00
189 Joakim Soria/Jsy/Auto./199 **RC** 15.00
190 Adam Lind/Jsy/Auto./199 **(RC)** 20.00
191 Andy LaRoche/Jsy/Auto./199 **(RC)** 25.00
192 Brandon Morrow/Jsy/175 **RC** 25.00
193 Carlos Gomez/Jsy/Auto./125 **RC** 40.00
194 Yunel Escobar/Auto./150 **(RC)** 50.00

August - Auto. Patch

NM/M

Production 25 unless noted.
Gold: No Pricing
Production Five Sets
Pearl: No Pricing
Production One Set
BS Ben Sheets 30.00
BU B.J. Upton 40.00
CC Carl Crawford 40.00
CD Chris Duncan 40.00
CG Curtis Granderson 60.00
CH Cole Hamels 40.00
CO Chad Cordero 30.00
DL Derrek Lee 50.00
DW Dontrelle Willis 30.00
FH Felix Hernandez 80.00
FT Frank Thomas 125.00
GA Garrett Atkins 30.00
GR Khalil Greene 40.00
HR Hanley Ramirez 75.00
JM Justin Morneau 50.00
MH Matt Holliday 60.00
PK Paul Konerko 50.00
RH Roy Halladay 60.00
TH Travis Hafner 75.00
VM Victor Martinez 40.00

Exclusive - Eight Autos.

Production Three Sets
Gold: No Pricing
Production Two Sets

Game Day - Box Score Autos.

NM/M

Production 50 Sets
Gold: No Pricing
Production 10 Sets
AE Andre Ethier 25.00
AG Adrian Gonzalez 25.00
AH Aaron Harang 20.00
AI Akinori Iwamura 35.00
AL Adam LaRoche 15.00
AM Andrew Miller 30.00
AR Aaron Rowand 20.00
BA Bronson Arroyo 15.00
BB Billy Butler 30.00
BP Brandon Phillips 20.00
BS Ben Sheets 20.00
CC Coco Crisp 20.00
CG Curtis Granderson 40.00
CH Cole Hamels 30.00
DH Danny Haren 20.00
DW Dontrelle Willis 20.00
FC Fausto Carmona 25.00
FL Fred Lewis 15.00
GO Alex Gordon 40.00
JB Joe Blanton 15.00
JM John Maine 20.00
JN Joe Nathan 15.00
JV Justin Verlander 35.00
KG Ken Griffey Jr. 80.00
KI Kei Igawa 30.00
KJ Kelly Johnson 15.00
LI Francisco Liriano 25.00
MC Matt Cain 20.00
MM Melvin Mora 15.00
PH Phil Hughes 60.00
RB Ryan Braun 50.00
RZ Ryan Zimmerman 30.00
TB Travis Buck 15.00
TH Tim Hudson 30.00

2007 UD Black Game Day - Lineup Card Autos

NM/M

Production 50 Sets
Gold: No Pricing
Production 10 Sets
AE Andre Ethier 25.00
AG Alberto Gonzalez 25.00
AH Aaron Harang 20.00
AI Akinori Iwamura 35.00
AL Adam LaRoche 15.00
AM Andre Miller 30.00
AR Aaron Rowand 20.00
BA Bronson Arroyo 15.00
BB Billy Butler 30.00
BP Brandon Phillips 20.00
BS Ben Sheets 20.00
CC Coco Crisp 20.00
CG Curtis Granderson 40.00
CH Cole Hamels 30.00
DH Danny Haren 20.00
20 Dontrelle Willis 20.00
FC Fausto Carmona 25.00
FL Fred Lewis 15.00
GO Alex Gordon 40.00
JB Joe Blanton 15.00
JM John Maine 20.00

JN Joe Nathan 15.00
JV Justin Verlander 35.00
KG Ken Griffey Jr. 80.00
KI Kei Igawa 30.00
KJ Kelly Johnson 15.00
LI Francisco Liriano 25.00
MC Matt Cain 20.00
MM Melvin Mora 15.00
PH Phil Hughes 60.00
RB Ryan Braun 50.00
RZ Ryan Zimmerman 30.00
TB Travis Buck 15.00
TH Tim Hudson 30.00

Game Day - Ticket Autos.

NM/M
Production 50 unless noted.
Gold: No Pricing
Production 10 Sets
AE Andre Ethier 25.00
AG Alberto Gonzalez 25.00
AH Aaron Harang 20.00
AI Akinori Iwamura 35.00
AL Adam LaRoche 15.00
AM Andre Miller 30.00
AR Aaron Rowand 20.00
BA Bronson Arroyo 15.00
BB Billy Butler 30.00
BP Brandon Phillips 20.00
BS Ben Sheets 20.00
CC Coco Crisp 20.00
CG Curtis Granderson 40.00
CH Cole Hamels 30.00
DH Danny Haren 20.00
20 Dontrelle Willis 20.00
FC Fausto Carmona 25.00
FL Fred Lewis 15.00
GO Alex Gordon 40.00
JB Joe Blanton 15.00
JN Joe Nathan 15.00
JV Justin Verlander 35.00
KG Ken Griffey Jr./15 80.00
KI Kei Igawa 30.00
KJ Kelly Johnson 15.00
LI Francisco Liriano 25.00
MC Matt Cain 20.00
MM Melvin Mora 15.00
PH Phil Hughes 60.00
RB Ryan Braun 50.00
RZ Ryan Zimmerman 30.00
TB Travis Buck 15.00
TH Tim Hudson 30.00

Illustrious - Dual Autos.

NM/M
Production 25 unless noted
Gold: No Pricing
Production 15 Sets
BB Joe Blanton, Dallas Braden 20.00
BH Chase Headley, Ryan Braun 50.00
CK Austin Kearns, Chad Cordero 25.00
CL Matt Cain, Tim Lincecum 75.00
GB Alex Gordon, Billy Butler 50.00
GL Adam LaRoche, Tom Gorzelanny 20.00
HB Matt Holliday, Jeff Baker 25.00
HC Aaron Harang, Jon Coutlangus 25.00
HG Rich Hill, Sean Gallagher 25.00
HP Josh Hamilton, Brandon Phillips 20.00
KW Howie Kendrick, Brandon Wood 20.00
LL Adam LaRoche, Andy LaRoche 25.00
MF Victor Martinez, Ben Francisco 20.00
MM Melvin Mora, Nicholas Markakis 40.00
PS Kevin Slowey, Cal Ripken Jr. 25.00
SM John Maine, Ben Sheets 25.00
YI Delmon Young, Akinori Iwamura 35.00

Illustrious - Dual Materials Auto.

NM/M
Production 50 unless noted
Patch: No Pricing
Production 15 Sets
CI Akinori Iwamura, Eric Chavez 30.00
CK Carl Crawford, Scott Kazmir 30.00
CP Coco Crisp, Jonathan Papelbon 40.00
GB Alex Gordon, Ryan Braun 180.00
GC Coco Crisp, Curtis Granderson 40.00
GY Adrian Gonzalez, Chris Young 25.00
HH Danny Haren, Rich Harden 25.00
HM John Maine, Aaron Harang 25.00
HW Dontrelle Willis, Jeremy Hermida 20.00
LC Matt Cain, Tim Lincecum 75.00
LK John Lackey, Howie Kendrick 30.00
LP Carlos Lee, Hunter Pence 60.00
MM Victor Martinez, Russell Martin 40.00
NH Torii Hunter, Joe Nathan 25.00
NM Melvin Mora, Nicholas Markakis 30.00
RG Brian Giles, Aaron Rowand 25.00
SB Huston Street, Joe Blanton 20.00
UW Josh Willingham, Dan Uggla 20.00
UY B.J. Upton, Delmon Young 30.00
ZB Jeremy Bonderman, Joel Zumaya 30.00

Lustrous - Autos.

NM/M
Production 50 unless noted.
Gold: No Pricing
Production 10 Sets
AG Alex Gordon 40.00
BB Billy Butler 30.00
BU B.J. Upton 20.00
CC Carl Crawford 20.00
CH Cole Hamels 30.00
DL Derrek Lee 25.00
DU Dan Uggla 20.00
DW Dontrelle Willis 20.00
GA Garrett Atkins 20.00
GR Khalil Greene 20.00
HA Josh Hamilton 30.00
HP Hunter Pence 40.00
HR Hanley Ramirez 30.00
HS Huston Street 20.00
IK Ian Kinsler 20.00
JB Jason Bay 25.00
JH Jeremy Hermida 15.00
JL Jon Lester 30.00
JN Joe Nathan 20.00
JV Justin Verlander 40.00
KE Howie Kendrick 20.00
KG Ken Griffey Jr. 80.00
KI Kei Igawa 30.00
MO Justin Morneau 25.00
PA Jonathan Papelbon 35.00
PF Prince Fielder 75.00
PH Phil Hughes 60.00
PK Paul Konerko 30.00
RO Roy Oswalt 30.00
RT Ryan Theriot 25.00
RZ Ryan Zimmerman 30.00
TH Torii Hunter 20.00
JW Vernon Wells 20.00

2007 UD Black Lustrous - Materials Auto.

NM/M
Production 32-50
Gold: No Pricing
Production 10 Sets
AD Adam Dunn/35 25.00
AE Andre Ethier/50 20.00
BO Jeremy Bonderman/46 30.00
BU B.J. Upton/48 20.00
CC Carl Crawford/43 20.00
CL Carlos Lee/46 20.00
CR Cal Ripken Jr./50 140.00
DH Danny Haren/50 20.00
DJ Derek Jeter/50 150.00
DL Derrek Lee/46 25.00
DU Dan Uggla/46 20.00
DW Dontrelle Willis/45 20.00
FH Felix Hernandez/32 40.00
GR Khalil Greene/37 20.00
HR Hanley Ramirez/33 30.00
HS Huston Street/32 20.00
IK Ian Kinsler/50 20.00
JB Jason Bay/48 25.00
JH Jeremy Hermida/49 15.00
JM Joe Mauer/50 25.00
JN Joe Nathan/34 20.00
JV Justin Verlander/37 40.00
KE Howie Kendrick/41 20.00
KG Ken Griffey Jr./50 80.00
KM Kendry Morales/50 15.00
MC Matt Cain/50 15.00
MM Melvin Mora/46 15.00
NM Nicholas Markakis/50 30.00
PA Jonathan Papelbon/48 35.00
PF Prince Fielder/49 75.00
RZ Ryan Zimmerman/44 30.00
SD Stephen Drew/45 25.00
TH Torii Hunter/50 20.00
VW Vernon Wells/50 20.00

Bat Barrels - Auto.

NM/M
Production 50 Sets
Gold: No Pricing
Production 10 Sets
AD Adam Dunn 50.00
AE Andre Ethier 25.00
AI Akinori Iwamura 50.00
AL Andy LaRoche 30.00
BO Jeremy Bonderman 30.00
BU B.J. Upton 20.00
CC Carl Crawford 20.00
CL Carlos Lee 25.00
DY Delmon Young 25.00
GA Garrett Atkins 25.00
HK Howie Kendrick 25.00
HR Hanley Ramirez 40.00
HU Torii Hunter 25.00
IK Ian Kinsler 20.00
JB Jason Bay 25.00
JH Josh Hamilton 25.00
JM Joe Mauer 25.00
KG Ken Griffey Jr. 75.00
KJ Kelly Johnson 20.00
MO Justin Morneau 35.00
MT Mark Teixeira 30.00
RB Ryan Braun 75.00
TH Travis Hafner 35.00
TT Troy Tulowitzki 75.00

Pride of a Nation

NM/M
Production 75 Sets
Gold: No Pricing
Production 10 Sets
AH Aaron Harang 20.00
AR Aaron Rowand 20.00
BO Jeremy Bonderman 30.00
BP Brandon Phillips 30.00
CA Carl Crawford 25.00
CC Coco Crisp 25.00
CG Curtis Granderson 40.00
CL Carlos Lee 35.00
DH Danny Haren 20.00
DL Derrek Lee 30.00
DU Dan Uggla 25.00
DW Dontrelle Willis 25.00
EC Eric Chavez 25.00
FH Felix Hernandez 75.00
FT Frank Thomas 60.00
HR Hanley Ramirez 40.00
JB Jason Bay 30.00
JL John Lackey 25.00
JM John Maine 20.00
LB Lance Berkman 40.00
MM Melvin Mora 25.00
MO Justin Morneau 40.00
PF Prince Fielder 60.00
RO Roy Oswalt 50.00
SK Scott Kazmir 25.00
VM Victor Martinez 30.00

2007 UD Black Prodigious - Materials Auto.

NM/M
Production 50 Sets unless noted
Gold: No Pricing
Production 10 Sets
AD Adam Dunn 40.00
AE Andre Ethier 25.00
AR Aaron Rowand 20.00
BO Jeremy Bonderman 30.00
BP Brandon Phillips 25.00
BU B.J. Upton 20.00
CC Coco Crisp 20.00
CD Chris Duncan 25.00
CH Cole Hamels 30.00
CL Cliff Lee 15.00
CR Carl Crawford 20.00
CY Chris Young 25.00
DH Danny Haren 20.00
DU Dan Uggla 20.00
DW Dontrelle Willis 20.00
FH Felix Hernandez 50.00
GA Garrett Atkins 20.00
HA Josh Hamilton 25.00
HK Hong-Chih Kuo 60.00
HR Hanley Ramirez 40.00
HS Huston Street 25.00
IK Ian Kinsler 20.00
JB Joe Blanton 20.00
JH Jeremy Hermida 15.00
JL Jon Lester 25.00
JN Joe Nathan 20.00
JS Johan Santana 50.00
JV Justin Verlander 35.00
JZ Joel Zumaya 20.00
KE Howie Kendrick 25.00
KW Kerry Wood 20.00
MO Justin Morneau 35.00
MT Mark Teixeira 30.00
PA Jonathan Papelbon 40.00
RI Cal Ripken Jr. 125.00
RW Rickie Weeks 20.00
SK Scott Kazmir 25.00
SR Scott Rolen 25.00
TG Tom Glavine 50.00
VW Vernon Wells 20.00

Prodigious Autos.

NM/M
Production 75 unless noted.
Gold: 1-1.5X
Production 25 Sets
AE Andre Ethier 25.00
AG Adrian Gonzalez 25.00
AH Aaron Harang 20.00
AI Akinori Iwamura 50.00
AR Aaron Rowand/50 20.00
BB Billy Butler 25.00
BP Brandon Phillips/50 25.00
BS Ben Sheets/50 20.00
BU B.J. Upton 20.00
CA Carl Crawford 20.00
CC Coco Crisp/50 20.00
CG Curtis Granderson/50 40.00
CH Cole Hamels/50 30.00
CO Chad Cordero/50 20.00
CR Cal Ripken Jr. 150.00
CY Chris Young/50 25.00
DH Danny Haren 20.00
DU Dan Uggla 20.00
DY Delmon Young 25.00
FP Felix Pie 25.00
GA Garrett Atkins 20.00
GO Alex Gordon 40.00
GP Glen Perkins 15.00
HB Homer Bailey 35.00
HK Howie Kendrick/50 25.00
HP Hunter Pence 40.00
HS Huston Street/50 25.00
JB Jeremy Bonderman 25.00
JE Johnny Estrada 15.00
JH Josh Hamilton/50 25.00
JL John Lackey/50 20.00
JM John Maine/50 20.00
JP Jonathan Papelbon 40.00
JS Joakim Soria 15.00
JV Justin Verlander/50 35.00
JW Josh Willingham/50 20.00
KI Kei Igawa 35.00
KJ Kelly Johnson/50 20.00
LE Jon Lester 25.00
MC Matt Cain 25.00
MH Matt Holliday 30.00
MM Melvin Mora/50 15.00
MO Justin Morneau 35.00
NM Nicholas Markakis 25.00
NS Nick Swisher 25.00
PK Paul Konerko/50 30.00
RB Ryan Braun 50.00
RH Rich Harden/50 15.00
RZ Ryan Zimmerman 40.00
SK Scott Kazmir 25.00
TH Tim Hudson 30.00
TL Tim Lincecum 65.00
VM Victor Martinez/50 30.00
YG Yovani Gallardo/50 30.00

Prominent Numbers Autos.

NM/M
Production 1-58
Gold: No Pricing
Production 10 Sets
AH Aaron Harang/39 25.00
BL Joe Blanton/55 15.00
CG Curtis Granderson/28 40.00
CH Cole Hamels/35 30.00
CY Chris Young/32 25.00
DY Delmon Young/26 20.00
FH Felix Hernandez/34 40.00
GA Garrett Atkins/27 25.00
HK Howie Kendrick/47 25.00
JB Jason Bay/38 20.00
JE Johnny Estrada/33 15.00
JN Joe Nathan/36 20.00
JP Jonathan Papelbon/58 40.00
JV Justin Verlander/35 40.00
JZ Joel Zumaya/54 20.00
MA John Maine/33 25.00
MB Michael Bourn/45 20.00
RH Rich Harden/40 20.00

Triptych - Triple Autos.

No Pricing
Production 15 Sets
Gold: No Pricing
Production Five Sets

Triptych - Triple Materials Auto.

NM/M
Production 25 Sets
DU Dan Uggla 30.00
PF Prince Fielder 60.00
TH Torii Hunter 25.00

Upper Echelon - Quad Autos.

No Pricing
Production Five Sets
Gold: No Pricing
Production Three Sets

Upper Echelon - Quad Materials Auto.

Production 2-5
Patch: No Pricing
Production One Set

Gold

Gold (1-100): 1-1.5X
Production 75
Gold RC (101-191): 1-1.5X
Production 25-99

Gold Spectrum Patch

Production One Set

Silver Spectrum

Production One Set

2008 Upper Deck

NM/M
Complete Series One Set (400): 50.00
Common Player: .15
Hobby Pack (20): 5.00
Hobby Box (16): 70.00
1 Joe Saunders .15
2 Kelvim Escobar .15
3 Jered Weaver .25
4 Justin Speier .15
5 Scot Shields .15
6 Mike Napoli .15
7 Orlando Cabrera .25
8 Casey Kotchman .15
9 Vladimir Guerrero .75
10 Garret Anderson .15
11 Roy Oswalt .50
12 Wandy Rodriguez .15
13 Woody Williams .15
14 Chad Qualls .15
15 Brian Moehler .15
16 Mark Loretta .15
17 Brad Ausmus .15
18 Ty Wigginton .15
19 Carlos Lee .50
20 Hunter Pence .50
21 Danny Haren .25
22 Lenny DiNardo .15
23 Chad Gaudin .15
24 Huston Street .15
25 Andrew Brown .15
26 Mike Piazza .50
27 Jack Cust .15
28 Mark Ellis .15
29 Shannon Stewart .15
30 Travis Buck .15
31 Shaun Marcum .15
32 A.J. Burnett .25
33 Jesse Litsch .15
34 Casey Janssen .15
35 Jeremy Accardo .15
36 Gregg Zaun .15
37 Aaron Hill .15
38 Frank Thomas .50
39 Matt Stairs .15
40 Vernon Wells .25
41 Tim Hudson .25
42 Chuck James .15
43 Buddy Carlyle .15
44 Rafael Soriano .15
45 Peter Moylan .15
46 Brian McCann .25
47 Edgar Renteria .25
48 Mark Teixeira .50
49 Willie Harris .15
50 Andruw Jones .50
51 Ben Sheets .25
52 David Bush .15
53 Yovani Gallardo .50
54 Francisco Cordero .15
55 Matt Wise .15
56 Johnny Estrada .15
57 Prince Fielder 1.00
58 J.J. Hardy .15
59 Corey Hart .25
60 Geoff Jenkins .15
61 Adam Wainwright .25
62 Joel Pineiro .15
63 Brad Thompson .15
64 Jason Isringhausen .15
65 Troy Percival .15
66 Yadier Molina .15
67 Albert Pujols 2.00
68 David Eckstein .15
69 Jim Edmonds .25
70 Rick Ankiel .25
71 Ted Lilly .15
72 Rich Hill .25
73 Jason Marquis .15
74 Carlos Marmol .15
75 Ryan Dempster .15
76 Jason Kendall .15
77 Aramis Ramirez .50
78 Ryan Theriot .15
79 Alfonso Soriano .50
80 Jacque Jones .15
81 James Shields .25
82 Andrew Sonnanstine .15
83 Scott Dohmann .15
84 Al Reyes .15
85 Dioner Navarro .15
86 B.J. Upton .50
87 Carlos Pena .15
88 Brendan Harris .15
89 Josh Wilson .15
90 Jonny Gomes .15
91 Brandon Webb .25
92 Micah Owings .15
93 Livan Hernandez .15
94 Doug Slaten .15
95 Brandon Lyon .15
96 Miguel Montero .15
97 Stephen Drew .25
98 Mark Reynolds .15
99 Conor Jackson .25
100 Chris B. Young .25
101 Chad Billingsley .25
102 Derek Lowe .15
103 Mark Hendrickson .15
104 Takashi Saito .15
105 Rudy Seanez .15
106 Russell Martin .50
107 Jeff Kent .25
108 Nomar Garciaparra .25
109 Matthew Kemp .50
110 Juan Pierre .25
111 Matt Cain .25
112 Barry Zito .15
113 Kevin Correia .15
114 Brad Hennessey .15
115 Jack Taschner .15
116 Bengie Molina .15
117 Ryan Klesko .15
118 Omar Vizquel .15
119 Dave Roberts .15
120 Rajai Davis .15
121 Fausto Carmona .25
122 Jake Westbrook .15
123 Cliff Lee .15
124 Rafael Betancourt .15
125 Joe Borowski .15
126 Victor Martinez .25
127 Travis Hafner .25
128 Ryan Garko .25
129 Kenny Lofton .15
130 Franklin Gutierrez .15
131 Felix Hernandez .50
132 Jeff Weaver .15
133 J.J. Putz .15
134 Brandon Morrow .15
135 Sean Green .15
136 Kenji Johjima .15
137 Jose Vidro .15
138 Richie Sexson .25
139 Ichiro Suzuki 1.50
140 Ben Broussard .15
141 Sergio Mitre .15
142 Scott Olsen .15
143 Rick Vanden Hurk .15
144 Justin Miller .15
145 Lee Gardner .15
146 Miguel Olivo .15
147 Hanley Ramirez .75
148 Mike Jacobs .15
149 Josh Willingham .15
150 Alfredo Amezaga .15
151 John Maine .25
152 Tom Glavine .50
153 Orlando Hernandez .15
154 Billy Wagner .15
155 Aaron Heilman .15
156 David Wright 1.00
157 Luis Castillo .15
158 Shawn Green .15
159 Damion Easley .15
160 Carlos Delgado .50
161 Shawn Hill .15
162 Mike Bacsik .15
163 John Lannan .15
164 Chad Cordero .15
165 Jon Rauch .15
166 Jesus Flores .15
167 Dmitri Young .15
168 Cristian Guzman .15
169 Austin Kearns .15
170 Nook Logan .15
171 Erik Bedard .25
172 Daniel Cabrera .15
173 Chris Ray .15
174 Danys Baez .15
175 Chad Bradford .15
176 Ramon Hernandez .15
177 Miguel Tejada .50
178 Freddie Bynum .15
179 Corey Patterson .15
180 Aubrey Huff .15
181 Chris Young .25
182 Greg Maddux 1.50
183 Clay Hensley .15
184 Kevin Cameron .15
185 Doug Brocail .15
186 Josh Bard .15
187 Kevin Kouzmanoff .25
188 Geoff Blum .15
189 Milton Bradley .15
190 Brian Giles .15
191 Jamie Moyer .15
192 Kyle Kendrick .15
193 Kyle Lohse .15
194 Antonio Alfonseca .15
195 Ryan Madson .15
196 Chris Coste .15
197 Chase Utley .75
198 Tadahito Iguchi .15
199 Aaron Rowand .15
200 Shane Victorino .25
201 Paul Maholm .15
202 Ian Snell .25
203 Shane Youman .15
204 Damaso Marte .15
205 Shawn Chacon .15
206 Ronny Paulino .15
207 Jack Wilson .15
208 Adam LaRoche .25
209 Ryan Doumit .15
210 Xavier Nady .15
211 Kevin Millwood .15
212 Brandon McCarthy .15
213 Joaquin Benoit .15
214 Wes Littleton .15
215 Mike Wood .15
216 Gerald Laird .15
217 Hank Blalock .15
218 Ian Kinsler .25
219 Marlon Byrd .15
220 Brad Wilkerson .15

221	Tim Wakefield	.15
222	Daisuke Matsuzaka	1.00
223	Julian Tavarez	.15
224	Hideki Okajima	.25
225	Manny Delcarmen	.15
226	Doug Mirabelli	.15
227	Dustin Pedroia	.25
228	Mike Lowell	.15
229	Manny Ramirez	.75
230	Coco Crisp	.15
231	Bronson Arroyo	.15
232	Matt Belisle	.15
233	Jared Burton	.15
234	David Weathers	.15
235	Mike Gosling	.15
236	David Ross	.15
237	Jeff Keppinger	.15
238	Edwin Encarnacion	.25
239	Ken Griffey Jr.	1.50
240	Adam Dunn	.50
241	Jeff Francis	.25
242	Jason Hirsh	.15
243	Josh Fogg	.15
244	Manny Corpas	.15
245	Jeremy Affeldt	.15
246	Yorvit Torrealba	.15
247	Todd Helton	.50
248	Kazuo Matsui	.15
249	Brad Hawpe	.25
250	Willy Taveras	.15
251	Brian Bannister	.15
252	Zack Greinke	.15
253	Kyle Davies	.15
254	David Riske	.15
255	Joel Peralta	.15
256	Joe Buck	.15
257	Mark Grudzielanek	.15
258	Ross Gload	.15
259	Billy Butler	.25
260	David DeJesus	.15
261	Jeremy Bonderman	.25
262	Chad Durbin	.15
263	Andrew Miller	.25
264	Bobby Seay	.15
265	Todd Jones	.15
266	Brandon Inge	.15
267	Sean Casey	.15
268	Placido Polanco	.15
269	Gary Sheffield	.50
270	Magglio Ordonez	.25
271	Matt Garza	.25
272	Boof Bonser	.25
273	Scott Baker	.15
274	Joe Nathan	.15
275	Dennys Reyes	.15
276	Joe Mauer	.50
277	Michael Cuddyer	.15
278	Jason Bartlett	.15
279	Torii Hunter	.50
280	Jason Tyner	.15
281	Mark Buehrle	.15
282	Jon Garland	.15
283	Jose Contreras	.15
284	Matt Thornton	.15
285	Ryan Bukvich	.15
286	Juan Uribe	.15
287	Jim Thome	.50
288	Scott Podsednik	.15
289	Jerry Owens	.15
290	Jermaine Dye	.25
291	Andy Pettitte	.25
292	Phil Hughes	.50
293	Mike Mussina	.25
294	Joba Chamberlain	.50
295	Brian Bruney	.15
296	Jorge Posada	.25
297	Derek Jeter	2.00
298	Jason Giambi	.25
299	Johnny Damon	.50
300	Melky Cabrera	.25
301	Jonathan Albaladejo **RC**	.50
302	Josh Anderson **RC**	.25
303	Wladimir Balentien **RC**	.25
304	Josh Banks **RC**	.25
305	Daric Barton **RC**	.25
306	Jerry Blevins **RC**	.50
307	Emilio Bonifacio **RC**	.50
308	Lance Broadway **RC**	.50
309	Clay Buchholz **RC**	.50
310	Billy Buckner **RC**	.25
311	Jeff Clement **RC**	.50
312	Willie Collazo **RC**	.50
313	Ross Detwiler **RC**	.50
314	Sam Fuld **RC**	1.00
315	Harvey Garcia **RC**	.25
316	Alberto Gonzalez **RC**	.50
317	Ryan Hanigan **RC**	.50
318	Kevin Hart **RC**	.50
319	Luke Hochevar **RC**	2.00
320	Chin-Lung Hu **RC**	.50
321	Rob Johnson **RC**	.25
322	Radhames Liz **RC**	.50
323	Ian Kennedy **RC**	4.00
324	Joe Koshansky **RC**	.50
325	Donny Lucy **RC**	.50
326	Justin Maxwell **RC**	.50
327	Jonathan Meloan **RC**	.50
328	Luis 1endoza **RC**	.25
329	Jose Morales **RC**	.25
330	Nyjer Morgan **RC**	.50
331	Carlos Muniz **RC**	.50
332	Bill Murphy **RC**	.25
333	Josh Newman **RC**	.50
334	Ross Ohlendorf **RC**	1.00
335	Troy Patton **RC**	.50
336	Felipe Paulino **RC**	.50
337	Steve Pearce **RC**	2.00
338	Heath Phillips **RC**	.50
339	Justin Ruggiano **RC**	.50
340	Clint Sammons **RC**	.50
341	Bronson Sardinha **RC**	.50
342	Chris Seddon **RC**	.25
343	Seth Smith **RC**	.50
344	Mitch Stetter **RC**	.50
345	David Davidson **RC**	.50
346	Rich Thompson **RC**	.25
347	J.R. Towles **RC**	2.50
348	Eugenio Velez **RC**	1.00
349	Joey Votto **RC**	1.00
350	Bill White **RC**	.50
351	Vladimir Guerrero	.75
352	Lance Berkman	.50
353	Danny Haren	.25
354	Frank Thomas	.50
355	Chipper Jones	.75
356	Prince Fielder	1.00
357	Albert Pujols	2.00
358	Alfonso Soriano	.75
359	B.J. Upton	.50
360	Eric Byrnes	.25
361	Russell Martin	.50
362	Tim Lincecum	.50
363	Grady Sizemore	.50
364	Ichiro Suzuki	1.50
365	Hanley Ramirez	.75
366	David Wright	1.00
367	Ryan Zimmerman	.50
368	Nicholas Markakis	.50
369	Jake Peavy	.50
370	Ryan Howard	1.00
371	Freddy Sanchez	.15
372	Michael Young	.25
373	David Ortiz	.75
374	Ken Griffey Jr.	1.50
375	Matt Holliday	.50
376	Brian Bannister	.15
377	Magglio Ordonez	.25
378	Johan Santana	.75
379	Jim Thome	.50
380	Alex Rodriguez	2.00
381	Alex Rodriguez	2.00
382	Brandon Webb	.50
383	Chone Figgins	.25
384	Clay Buchholz	.50
385	Curtis Granderson	.50
386	Frank Thomas	.50
387	Fred Lewis	.15
388	Garret Anderson	.15
389	J.R. Towles	.25
390	Jake Peavy	.50
391	Jim Thome	.50
392	Jimmy Rollins	.75
393	Johan Santana	.75
394	Justin Verlander	.50
395	Mark Buehrle	.15
396	Matt Holliday	.50
397	Jarrod Saltalamacchia	.15
398	Sammy Sosa	.50
399	Tom Glavine	.50
400	Trevor Hoffman	.15

1969 O Pee Chee Reprints

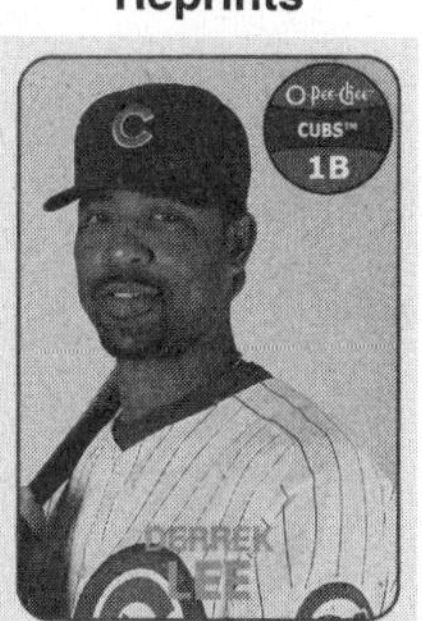

		NM/M
AG	Alex Gordon	.50
AP	Albert Pujols	2.00
AR	Alex Rodriguez	2.00
BP	Brad Penny	.25
BR	Babe Ruth	2.00
BU	B.J. Upton	.50
BW	Brandon Webb	.50
CD	Chris Duncan	.25
CJ	Chipper Jones	1.00
CL	Carlos Lee	.50
CP	Carlos Pena	.50
CU	Chase Utley	.75
CY	Chris Young	.25
DH	Danny Haren	.25
DJ	Derek Jeter	2.00
DL	Derrek Lee	.50
DM	Daisuke Matsuzaka	1.00
DO	David Ortiz	1.00
DW	David Wright	1.00
EB	Erik Bedard	.50
ER	Edgar Renteria	.25
GS	Gary Sheffield	.50
HP	Hunter Pence	.50
HR	Hanley Ramirez	.75
IS	Ichiro Suzuki	1.50
JB	Jason Bay	.50
JJ	J.J. Putz	.25
JM	Justin Morneau	.50
JP	Jake Peavy	.50
JR	Jose Reyes	.75
JS	Johan Santana	.75
JT	Jim Thome	.75
JW	Jered Weaver	.50
KG	Ken Griffey Jr.	1.50
MC	Miguel Cabrera	.75
MH	Matt Holliday	.50
MO	Magglio Ordonez	.50
MR	Manny Ramirez	.75
MT	Mark Teixeira	.50
NL	Noah Lowry	.25
PF	Prince Fielder	1.00
PH	Brandon Phillips	.50
RA	Aramis Ramirez	.50
RB	Ryan Braun	.75
RH	Ryan Howard	1.00
RM	Russell Martin	.50
RZ	Ryan Zimmerman	.50
TH	Todd Helton	.50
VG	Vladimir Guerrero	.75
VW	Vernon Wells	.25

1997 UD Jersey

		NM/M
Common Jersey:		4.00
Patch:		2-4X
AP	Albert Pujols	15.00
BC	Bobby Crosby	4.00
BG	Brian Giles	4.00
BR	B.J. Ryan	4.00
BS	Ben Sheets	6.00
CS	Curt Schilling	8.00
DL	Derek Lowe	4.00
DO	David Ortiz	10.00
GJ	Geoff Jenkins	4.00
HK	Hong-Chih Kuo	6.00
IR	Ivan Rodriguez	6.00
JB	Joe Blanton	4.00
JC	Joe Crede	4.00
JJ	Josh Johnson	4.00
JS	James Shields	6.00
JW	Jake Westbrook	4.00
LM	Lastings Milledge	6.00
MC	Miguel Cabrera	8.00
MO	Magglio Ordonez	6.00
NM	Nicholas Markakis	8.00
PE	Andy Pettitte	6.00
RB	Rocco Baldelli	4.00
TH	Todd Helton	8.00
VM	Victor Martinez	6.00
XN	Xavier Nady	4.00

1998 UD Jersey

		NM/M
Common Jersey:		4.00
Patch:		2-4X
BH	Bill Hall	4.00
BS	Ben Sheets	6.00
CF	Chone Figgins	6.00
CZ	Carlos Zambrano	6.00
EG	Eric Gagne	4.00
FC	Fausto Carmona	6.00
FH	Felix Hernandez	8.00
GS	Grady Sizemore	8.00
HB	Hank Blalock	6.00
IS	Ian Snell	6.00
JE	Johnny Estrada	4.00
JJ	Jacque Jones	4.00
JK	Jason Kendall	4.00
JS	Johan Santana	8.00
KM	Kevin Millwood	4.00
MB	Mark Buehrle	4.00
MG	Marcus Giles	4.00
NM	Nicholas Markakis	8.00
PK	Paul Konerko	6.00
VM	Victor Martinez	8.00

1999 UD Jersey

		NM/M
Common Jersey:		4.00
Patch:		2-4X
BR	Brian Roberts	6.00
CD	Chris Duffy	4.00
CJ	Chipper Jones	10.00
CS	C.C. Sabathia	8.00
DL	Derrek Lee	8.00
DW	David Wells	4.00
EB	Erik Bedard	8.00
FS	Freddy Sanchez	4.00
JB	Jason Bay	6.00
JD	Johnny Damon	4.00
JG	Jeremy Guthrie	4.00
JH	J.J. Hardy	4.00
JK	Jason Kubel	4.00
JP	Jorge Posada	6.00
KJ	Kenji Johjima	4.00
KM	Kendry Morales	4.00
MT	Mark Teixeira	8.00
RW	Rickie Weeks	6.00
TE	Miguel Tejada	6.00
TH	Travis Hafner	6.00

500 Home Run Club Bat

		NM/M
FT	Frank Thomas	80.00
JT	Jim Thome	50.00

All Rookie Team Signatures

		NM/M
Common Auto.:		10.00
AI	Akinori Iwamura	30.00
AL	Adam Lind	10.00
AM	Andrew Miller	25.00
BB	Billy Butler	15.00
BU	Brian Burres	10.00
DM	Daisuke Matsuzaka	300.00
HA	Justin Hampson	10.00
KC	Kevin Cameron	10.00
KK	Kyle Kendrick	20.00
MB	Michael Bourn	10.00
MF	Mike Fontenot	15.00
MO	Micah Owings	15.00
RB	Ryan Braun	40.00
SO	Joakim Soria	10.00

Derek Jeter Chronicles

		NM/M
Common Jeter:		10.00
1-20	Derek Jeter	10.00

Derek Jeter OPC Reprints

		NM/M
Common Jeter:		8.00
1-15	Derek Jeter	8.00

Hot Commodities

		NM/M
Common Player:		.75
1	Miguel Tejada	.75
2	Daisuke Matsuzaka	3.00
3	David Ortiz	1.50
4	Manny Ramirez	1.00
5	Alex Rodriguez	3.00
6	Derek Jeter	3.00
7	Carl Crawford	.50
8	Alex Rios	.50
9	Jim Thome	.50
10	Grady Sizemore	1.00
11	Travis Hafner	.50
12	Victor Martinez	.50
13	Justin Verlander	1.00
14	Magglio Ordonez	.50
15	Gary Sheffield	.75
16	Alex Gordon	.75
17	Justin Morneau	.75
18	Johan Santana	1.00
19	Vladimir Guerrero	1.00
20	Danny Haren	.50
21	Ichiro Suzuki	2.00
22	Mark Teixeira	1.00
23	Chipper Jones	1.00
24	John Smoltz	.50
25	Miguel Cabrera	1.00
26	Hanley Ramirez	1.00
27	Jose Reyes	1.00
28	David Wright	2.00
29	Carlos Beltran	1.00
30	Ryan Howard	2.00
31	Chase Utley	1.00
32	Ryan Zimmerman	1.00
33	Aramis Ramirez	.75
34	Derrek Lee	.75
35	Alfonso Soriano	1.00
36	Ken Griffey Jr.	2.00
37	Adam Dunn	1.00
38	Carlos Lee	.75
39	Lance Berkman	.75
40	Prince Fielder	1.50
41	Ryan Braun	1.50
42	Jason Bay	.50
43	Albert Pujols	3.00
44	Brandon Webb	.75
45	Matt Holliday	.75
46	Brad Penny	.50
47	Russell Martin	.75
48	Trevor Hoffman	.50
49	Jake Peavy	.75
50	Tim Lincecum	1.00

Inkredible

		NM/M
Common Auto.:		10.00
AL	Adam Lind	10.00
CP	Corey Patterson	10.00
CR	Cody Ross	10.00
DL	Derrek Lee	25.00
EA	Erick Aybar	10.00
JB	Josh Barfield	10.00
JH	Jason Hammel	10.00
JS	James Shields	15.00
LS	Luke Scott	10.00
MJ	Mike Jacobs	10.00
RC	Ryan Church	15.00
RL	Ruddy Lugo	10.00
RS	Ryan Shealy	10.00
SO	Jorge Sosa	15.00
TB	Taylor Buchholz	10.00

Milestone Memorabilia

		NM/M
Common Player:		8.00
GS	Gary Sheffield	10.00
KG	Ken Griffey Jr.	25.00
TG	Tom Glavine	15.00
TH	Trevor Hoffman	8.00

Mr. November

		NM/M
Common Jeter:		10.00
1-15	Derek Jeter	10.00

Presidential Predictors

		NM/M
Common Predictor:		4.00
1	Rudolph Giuliani	8.00
2	John Edwards	8.00
3	John McCain	10.00
4	Barack Obama	10.00
5	Mitt Romney	4.00
6	Fred Thompson	4.00
8	Al Gore	4.00
9	Wild Card	4.00

Season Highlights Signatures

		NM/M
Common Auto.:		10.00
BB	Brian Bannister	15.00
BF	Ben Francisco	10.00
CS	Curt Schilling	30.00
FL	Fred Lewis	10.00
FT	Frank Thomas	100.00
JS	Jarrod Saltalamacchia	15.00
JW	Josh Willingham	8.00
KK	Kevin Kouzmanoff	10.00
MO	Micah Owings	15.00
MR	Mark Reynolds	8.00
MT	Miguel Tejada	20.00
PF	Prince Fielder	50.00
RS	Ryan Spilborghs	10.00

Signature Sensations

		NM/M
Common Auto.:		8.00
AM	Aaron Miles	20.00
BH	Brendan Harris	8.00
CB	Cha Sueng Baek	15.00
DL	Derrek Lee	25.00
JP	Joel Peralta	8.00
JS	James Shields	10.00
JV	John Van Benschoten	8.00
LS	Luke Scott	10.00
MC	Matt Cain	15.00
RA	Reggie Abercrombie	10.00
SM	Sean Marshall	15.00

Star Quest

		NM/M
Common Player:		.75
Blue:		1X
Rainbow:		2-3X
Red:		
1	Ichiro Suzuki	3.00
2	Ryan Braun	2.00
3	Prince Fielder	2.00
4	Ken Griffey Jr.	3.00
5	Vladimir Guerrero	1.50
6	Travis Hafner	.75
7	Matt Holliday	1.00
8	Ryan Howard	2.50
9	Derek Jeter	4.00
10	Chipper Jones	1.50
11	Carlos Lee	.75
12	Justin Morneau	1.00
13	Magglio Ordonez	1.00
14	David Ortiz	2.00
15	Jake Peavy	1.00
16	Albert Pujols	4.00
17	Hanley Ramirez	1.50
18	Manny Ramirez	1.50
19	Jose Reyes	2.00
20	Alex Rodriguez	4.00
21	Johan Santana	1.50
22	Grady Sizemore	1.50
23	Alfonso Soriano	1.50
24	Mark Teixeira	1.00
25	Frank Thomas	1.00
26	Jim Thome	1.00
27	Chase Utley	1.50
28	Brandon Webb	1.00
29	David Wright	2.50
30	Michael Young	.75

The House that Ruth Built

		NM/M
Complete Set (25):		50.00
Common Ruth:		3.00
1-25	Babe Ruth	3.00

Game Jersey

		NM/M
Common Jersey:		4.00
Patch:		2-4X
BR	Brian Roberts	6.00
CB	Carlos Beltran	10.00
CC	Coco Crisp	4.00
CG	Carlos Guillen	6.00
DC	Daniel Cabrera	4.00
DJ	Derek Jeter	20.00
DO	David Ortiz	10.00
DW	Dontrelle Willis	4.00
EG	Eric Gagne	4.00
GC	Gustavo Chacin	4.00
GJ	Geoff Jenkins	4.00
JB	Jason Bay	6.00
JD	Justin Duchscherer	4.00
JP	Jake Peavy	8.00
JS	Jeremy Sowers	4.00
JV	Jason Varitek	10.00
KM	Kazuo Matsui	6.00
ME	Morgan Ensberg	4.00
MM	Melvin Mora	4.00
MS	Mike Sweeney	4.00
MY	Michael Young	6.00
PA	Jonathan Papelbon	15.00
RH	Roy Halladay	6.00
TS	Takashi Saito	6.00

Autographs

		NM/M
Common Auto:		8.00
CD	Chris Duffy	8.00
CS	Curt Schilling	25.00
JP	Joel Peralta	8.00
JS	Jorge Sosa	15.00
JV	John Van Benschoten	8.00
LS	Luke Scott	8.00
RH	Ramon Hernandez	15.00
SA	Kirk Saarloos	10.00
SF	Scott Feldman	10.00
SH	James Shields	10.00
SR	Saul Rivera	10.00
SS	Skip Schumaker	15.00
ZG	Zack Greinke	10.00

2008 Upper Deck Superstar

		NM/M
Common Player:		1.00
Retail Jumbo Exclusive		
Cards have bronze foil		
Autograph:		No Pricing
Production 5 Sets		
9	Vladimir Guerrero	2.00
48	Mark Teixeira	2.00
57	Prince Fielder	3.00
67	Albert Pujols	4.00
139	Ichiro Suzuki	3.00
147	Hanley Ramirez	2.00
156	David Wright	3.00
239	Ken Griffey Jr.	3.00
270	Magglio Ordonez	1.00
297	Derek Jeter	4.00

1993 USA Rice

To promote rice consumption and raise money for the pictured athletes' favorite charities, the USA Rice Council issued this multi-sport card set and made it available by mail for a $2 donation. All players are pictured in civilian clothes with either a blue or red border around. Backs of most cards have rice recipes and indicate the charity to which the athlete is donating their portion of the proceeds. Cards are standard 2-1/2" x 3-1/2".

		NM/M
Complete Set (10):		10.00
Common Card:		.50
1	Steve Sax (Cooking)	1.00
2	Troy Aikman (Football)	3.00
3	Roger Clemens	7.50
4	Zina Garrison (Tennis)	.50
5	Warren Moon (Football)	2.00
6	Summer Sanders (Swimming)	.50
7	Steve Sax (Lifting weights.)	1.00
8	Brian Shimer (Bobsledder)	.50
9	Food Guide Pyramid	.25
10	Healthy Eating Tips	.25

1999 U.S. Cellular Milwaukee Brewers

The four Milwaukee Brewers who have had their uniform numbers retired by the team, plus Jackie Robinson, whose #42 was retired by MLB edict, are honored on this foldout promotion given to fans October 2 at County Stadium. Five 4" x 6" cards make up the panel, which is perfo-

rated between the cards for ease of separation. Cards have player action photos on front (color except for Robinson) on a muted blue-green stadium photo background. At lower-right is a gold-foil seal with the player's name and number. At top is a sponsor logo and part of the legend "COMMEMORATING GREATNESS" which runs contiguously across the panel. Backs have a black-and-white photo, career data and highlights.

		NM/M
Complete Set, Panel:		12.00
Complete Set, Singles (5):		8.00
Common Player:		1.00
4	Paul Molitor	4.00
19	Robin Yount	4.00
34	Rollie Fingers	1.00
42	Jackie Robinson	3.00
44	Hank Aaron	5.00

1993 U.S. Department of Transportation Safety Set

This six-card set (issued in three-card panels) was sponsored by the U.S. Department of Transportation and distributed at the Little League World Series. Standard size cards have red and blue borders on front, along with the Little League logo. Backs are printed in red and blue and include a highway safety message and sponsors/licensors logos.

		NM/M
Complete Set (6):		11.00
Common Player:		1.50
Panel 1		4.00
1	Orel Hershiser	.50
2	Don Mattingly	3.00
3	Mike Mussina	1.00
Panel 2		6.00
(4)	Mike Piazza	2.50
(5)	Cal Ripken Jr.	4.00
(6)	Mo Vaughn	.50

1987 U.S. Forestry Service Smokey Bear's Team

The U.S. Forestry Service and Major League Baseball united in an effort to promote National Smokey the Bear Day. Two perforated sheets of baseball cards, one each for the American and National Leagues, were produced. The sheet of American Leaguers measures 18" x 24" and con-

tains 16 full-color cards. The National League sheet measures 20" x 18" and contains 15 cards. Each individual card is 4" x 6" and contains a fire prevention tip on the back. An average number of 25,000 sets was sent to all teams.

		NM/M
Complete Set (31):		12.00
Complete A.L. Sheet:		7.00
Complete N.L. Sheet:		7.00
Common Player:		.25
1A	Jose Canseco	.75
1N	Steve Sax	.25
2A	Dennis "Oil Can" Boyd	.25
2Na	Dale Murphy (Shirttail out.)	5.00
2Nb	Dale Murphy (Shirttail in.)	.90
3A	John Candelaria	.25
3Na	Jody Davis (Standing)	3.00
3Nb	Jody Davis (Kneeling)	.25
4A	Harold Baines	.25
4N	Bill Gullickson	.25
5A	Joe Carter	.25
5N	Mike Scott	.25
6A	Jack Morris	.25
6N	Roger McDowell	.25
7A	Buddy Biancalana	.25
7N	Steve Bedrosian	.25
8A	Kirby Puckett	3.00
8N	Johnny Ray	.25
9A	Mike Pagliarulo	.25
9N	Ozzie Smith	3.00
10A	Larry Sheets	.25
10N	Steve Garvey	.50
11A	Mike Moore	.25
11N	Smokey Bear Logo Card	.05
12A	Charlie Hough	.25
12N	Mike Krukow	.25
13A	Smokey Bear Logo Card	.05
13N	Smokey Bear	.05
14A	Tom Henke	.25
14N	Mike Fitzgerald	.25
15A	Jim Gantner	.25
15N	National League Logo Card	.05
16A	American League Logo Card	.05

1990 U.S. Playing Card All-Stars

Sold as a boxed set, these cards are the standard 2-1/2" x 3-1/2" format but feature rounded corners. Each card features a color player photo with the upper-left and lower-right corners inset to provide for playing card designations. A team logo appears in the lower-left corner. On American League players' cards (Clubs and Spades) the player's name and position appear in white in a blue box beneath the photo. On National Leaguers' cards (Hearts and Diamonds) the box is red and the printing black. Card backs are identical, with blue borders and a multi-colored "1990 Baseball Major League All-Stars" logo on a pinstriped white center panel. A premium version with the cards' edges silvered was also issued. These cards have a small diagonal "nip" at each rounded corner.

		NM/M
Complete Set (56):		5.00
Common Player:		.05
HEARTS		
J	Bobby Bonilla	.05
Q	Kevin Mitchell	.05
K	Darryl Strawberry	.05
A	Ramon Martinez	.05
2	Mike Scioscia	.05
3	Jeff Brantley	.05
4	Ryne Sandberg	.75
5	Chris Sabo	.05
6	Ozzie Smith	.75
7	John Franco	.05
8	Matt Williams	.05
9	Andre Dawson	.25
10	Benito Santiago	.05
CLUBS		
J	Wade Boggs	.75
Q	George Bell	.05
K	Rickey Henderson	.50
A	Bob Welch	.05
2	Lance Parrish	.05
3	Bret Saberhagen	.05
4	Gregg Olson	.05
5	Brook Jacoby	.05
6	Ozzie Guillen	.05
7	Ellis Burks	.05
8	Dennis Eckersley	.40
9	Bobby Thigpen	.05
10	Dave Stieb	.05
DIAMONDS		
J	Tony Gwynn	.75
Q	Will Clark	.05
K	Barry Bonds	1.50
A	Frank Viola	.05
2	Greg Olson	.05
3	Dennis Martinez	.05
4	Roberto Alomar	.20
5	Tim Wallach	.05
6	Barry Larkin	.05
7	Neal Heaton	.05
8	Dave Smith	.05
9	Lenny Dykstra	.05
10	Shawon Dunston	.05
SPADES		
J	Ken Griffey Jr.	1.00
Q	Dave Parker	.05
K	Cecil Fielder	.05
A	Roger Clemens	.85
2	Sandy Alomar	.05
3	Randy Johnson	.50
4	Steve Sax	.05
5	Kelly Gruber	.05
6	Chuck Finley	.05
7	Doug Jones	.05
8	Kirby Puckett	.75
9	Cal Ripken, Jr.	1.50
10	Alan Trammell	.05
WILD CARDS/JOKERS		
---	Jack Armstrong (Joker)	.05
---	Julio Franco (Joker)	.05
---	Rob Dibble, Randy Myers (Wild Card)	.05
---	Mark McGwire, Jose Canseco (Wild Card)	1.00

1991 U.S. Playing Card All-Stars

In standard 2-1/2" x 3-1/2" format, though with rounded corners, this 56-card set was produced by the country's leading maker of playing cards and sold as a boxed set. Fronts have a color player photo with the top-left and bottom-right corners inset to include playing card designations. A team logo appears in the upper-right corner. On American Leaguers' cards (Hearts and Diamonds), the player's name and position appear in white in a green stripe beneath the photo. National League players (Clubs and Spades) have a yellow stripe with black printing. Backs are red-bordered with a colorful "1991 Baseball Major League All-Stars" logo on a pinstriped white center panel. A silver-edged premium version was also issued. These cards have a diagonal "nip" at each rounded corner. A Canadian version, with the imprint of International Playing Card, also exists.

		NM/M
Complete Set (56):		4.00
Common Player:		.05
HEARTS		
J	Rickey Henderson	.50
Q	Roberto Alomar	.20
K	Dave Henderson	.05
A	Jack Morris	.05
2	Ozzie Guillen	.05
3	Jack McDowell	.05
4	Joe Carter	.05
5	Mark Langston	.05
6	Julio Franco	.05
7	Rick Aguilera	.05
8	Paul Molitor	.50
9	Ruben Sierra	.05
10	Roger Clemens	.85
CLUBS		
J	Andre Dawson	.25
Q	Chris Sabo	.05
K	Ivan Calderon	.05
A	Tony Gwynn	.75
2	Paul O'Neill	.05
3	John Smiley	.05
4	Howard Johnson	.05
5	Mike Morgan	.05
6	Barry Larkin	.05
7	Frank Viola	.05
8	Juan Samuel	.05
9	Craig Biggio	.05
10	Lee Smith	.05
DIAMONDS		
J	Sandy Alomar	.05
Q	Cecil Fielder	.05
K	Cal Ripken, Jr.	1.50
A	Ken Griffey Jr.	1.00
2	Carlton Fisk	.50
3	Scott Sanderson	.05
4	Kirby Puckett	.75
5	Jeff Reardon	.05
6	Rafael Palmeiro	.40
7	Bryan Harvey	.05
8	Jimmy Key	.05
9	Harold Baines	.05
10	Dennis Eckersley	.40
SPADES		
J	Benito Santiago	.05
Q	Ryne Sandberg	.75
K	Ozzie Smith	.75
A	Tom Glavine	.10
2	Eddie Murray	.60
3	Pete Harnisch	.05
4	John Kruk	.05
5	Tom Browning	.05
6	George Bell	.05
7	Dennis Martinez	.05
8	Brett Butler	.05
9	Terry Pendleton	.05
10	Rob Dibble	.05
WILD CARDS/JOKERS		
---	Bobby Bonilla (Joker)	.05
---	Danny Tartabull	.05
---	Wade Boggs (Wild Card)	.75
---	Will Clark (Wild Card)	.05

1992 U.S. Playing Card Aces

This 56-card boxed set features 13 top players in each of four major statistical categories, ranked by performance. Hearts feature RBI leaders, Clubs depict home run hitters, batting average leaders are featured on Diamonds and Spades have pitchers with lowest ERAs. Card fronts feature full-bleed color photos, with the playing card suit and rank overprinted in opposing corners. A team logo is in the lower-left, along with a black box containing the player's name and position in gold. Backs have a red, white and gold "Major League Baseball 1992 Aces" against a black background. The 2-1/2" x 3-1/2" cards have rounded corners.

		NM/M
Complete Set (56):		4.00
Common Player:		.05
HEARTS		
J	Will Clark	.05
Q	Howard Johnson	.05
K	Jose Canseco	.35
A	Cecil Fielder	.05
2	Juan Gonzalez	.25
3	Andre Dawson	.25
4	Ron Gant	.05
5	Fred McGriff	.05
6	Joe Carter	.05
7	Frank Thomas	.50
8	Cal Ripkin (Ripken)	1.50
9	Ruben Sierra	.05
10	Barry Bonds	1.50
CLUBS		
J	Cal Ripkin (Ripken)	1.50
Q	Howard Johnson	.05
K	Cecil Fielder	.05
A	Jose Canseco	.40
2	Chili Davis	.05
3	Mickey Tettleton	.05
4	Danny Tartabull	.05
5	Fred McGriff	.05
6	Andre Dawson	.25
7	Frank Thomas	.75
8	Ron Gant	.05
9	Cal Ripkin (Ripken)	1.50
10	Matt Williams	.05
DIAMONDS		
J	Ken Griffey Jr.	1.00
Q	Willie Randolph	.05
K	Wade Boggs	.75
A	Julio Franco	.05
2	Danny Tartabull	.05
3	Tony Gwynn	.75
4	Frank Thomas	.60
5	Hal Morris	.05
6	Kirby Puckett	.75
7	Terry Pendleton	.05
8	Rafael Palmeiro	.50
9	Cal Ripkin (Ripken)	1.50
10	Paul Molitor	.60
SPADES		
J	Tim Belcher	.05
Q	Tom Glavine	.15
K	Jose Rijo	.05
A	Dennis Martinez	.05
2	Mike Moore	.05
3	Nolan Ryan	1.50
4	Jim Abbott	.05
5	Bill Wegman	.05
6	Mike Morgan	.05
7	Jose DeLeon	.05
8	Pete Harnisch	.05
9	Tom Candiotti	.05
10	Roger Clemens	.85
JOKERS		
---	Roger Clemens (Joker)	.85
---	Tom Glavine (Joker)	.15
---	Home Run Rummy Game Instructions	.05
---	Header Card	.05

All-Stars

Players from the 1992 All-Star Game are featured in this set of 56 playing cards. In playing card format of 2-1/2" x 3-1/2" with rounded corners, the cards have a photo on front with a team logo in the upper-right corner. Traditional playing card suits and values are in the upper-left and lower-right corners. Player names are in a yellow (American League) or red (National League) box beneath the photo. Backs have a large product logo on a white background with a dark blue-green border. Appropriate licensor and manufacturer logos appear at bottom. The set was sold in a box featuring miniature representations of some of the cards.

		NM/M
Complete Set (56):		5.00
Common Player:		.05
AC	Roberto Alomar	.20
2C	Joe Carter	.05
3C	Juan Guzman	.05
4C	Charles Nagy	.05
5C	Robin Ventura	.05
6C	Chuck Knoblauch	.05
7C	Ruben Sierra	.05
8C	Paul Molitor	.60
9C	Carlos Baerga	.05
10C	Edgar Martinez	.05
JC	Sandy Alomar Jr.	.05
QC	Mark McGwire	1.25
KC	Wade Boggs	.75
AS	Ken Griffey Jr.	1.00
2S	Ivan Rodriguez	.50
3S	Roberto Kelly	.05
4S	Brady Anderson	.05
5S	Travis Fryman	.05
6S	Jeff Montgomery	.05
7S	Jack McDowell	.05
8S	Rick Aguilera	.05
9S	Kevin Brown	.05
10S	Roger Clemens	.85
JS	Jose Canseco	.35
QS	Cal Ripken Jr.	1.50
KS	Kirby Puckett	.75
AH	Andy Van Slyke	.05
2H	Greg Maddux	.75
3H	Larry Walker	.05
4H	Tom Pagnozzi	.05
5H	David Cone	.05
6H	Tony Fernandez	.05
7H	Will Clark	.05
8H	Gary Sheffield	.30
9H	Mike Sharperson	.05
10H	John Kruk	.05
JH	Ryne Sandberg	.75
QH	Ozzie Smith	.75
KH	Fred McGriff	.05
AD	Tony Gwynn	.75
2D	Bob Tewksbury	.05
3D	Ron Gant	.05
4D	Doug Jones	.05
5D	Craig Biggio	.05
6D	Bip Roberts	.05
7D	Norm Charlton	.05
8D	John Smoltz	.05
9D	Lee Smith	.05
10D	Tom Glavine	.25
JD	Benito Santiago	.05
QD	Terry Pendleton	.05
KD	Barry Bonds	1.50
WILD	Dennis Eckersley	.50
JOKER	Mike Mussina, Mark Langston	.15
JOKER	Darren Daulton, Dennis Martinez	.05
---	Advertising Card	.05

Team Sets

Besides two All-Star sets, the U.S. Playing Card Co. in 1992 issued playing card team sets for five teams. All were issued as 56-card boxed sets in a similar format. Cards are 2-1/2" x 3-1/2" with rounded corners. Fronts feature player photos with insets at the upper-left and lower-right corners displaying card suit designations and rankings. The player's name and position appear in a colored strip beneath the photo. Backs feature a large color team logo set on a gray background with either dark blue or red pinstriping and heavy vertical side bars. A silver-edged World Series premium version of the Braves and Twins sets were also issued; on these cards each rounded corner has a diagonal "nip."

Atlanta Braves

		NM/M
Complete Set (56):		5.00
Common Player:		.10
HEARTS		
J	Dave Justice	.10
Q	Juan Berenguer	.10
K	Ron Gant	.10
A	Otis Nixon	.10
2	Deion Sanders	.20
3	Mike Stanton	.10
4	Sid Bream	.10
5	Armando Reynoso	.10
6	Brian Hunter	.10
7	Kent Mercker	.10

8	Lonnie Smith	.10
9	Jeff Treadway	.10
10	Tom Glavine	.35
CLUBS		
J	Pete Smith	.10
Q	Jeff Blauser	.10
K	Charlie Leibrandt	.10
A	Terry Pendleton	.10
2	Mark Lemke	.10
3	Armando Reynoso	.10
4	Kent Mercker	.10
5	Marvin Freeman	.10
6	Rico Rossy	.10
7	Dave Justice	.10
8	Juan Berenguer	.10
9	Ron Gant	.10
10	Otis Nixon	.10
DIAMONDS		
J	Brian Hunter	.10
Q	Rafael Belliard	.10
K	Greg Olson	.10
A	Steve Avery	.10
2	Marvin Freeman	.10
3	Pete Smith	.10
4	Mike Heath	.10
5	Jeff Blauser	.10
6	Jim Clancy	.10
7	Rico Rossy	.10
8	John Smoltz	.10
9	Charlie Leibrandt	.10
10	Terry Pendleton	.10
SPADES		
J	John Smoltz	.10
Q	Lonnie Smith	.10
K	Jeff Treadway	.10
A	Tom Glavine	.35
2	Jim Clancy	.10
3	Deion Sanders	.20
4	Mark Lemke	.10
5	Mike Heath	.10
6	Mike Stanton	.10
7	Sid Bream	.10
8	Rafael Belliard	.10
9	Greg Olson	.10
10	Steve Avery	.10
JOKERS		
---	N.L. Logo (Joker)	.05
---	N.L. Logo (Joker)	.05
---	'92 Braves Home Schedule	.05
---	Atlanta Braves History	.05

World Series - Braves

		NM/M
Complete Set (56):		5.00
Common Player:		.05
AC	Charlie Leibrandt	.10
2C	Vinny Castilla	.10
3C	Alejandro Pena	.10
4C	Mark Lemke	.10
5C	Marvin Freeman	.10
6C	Dave Justice	.10
7C	Mike Stanton	.10
8C	Terry Pendleton	.10
9C	Jeff Treadway	.10
10C	Brian Hunter	.10
JC	Steve Avery	.10
QC	Jeff Blauser	.10
KC	Ron Gant	.10
AS	Terry Pendleton	.10
2S	Ryan Klesko	.10
3S	Jeff Treadway	.10
4S	Pete Smith	.10
5S	Ron Gant	.10
6S	Sid Bream	.10
7S	Deion Sanders	.15
8S	Tom Glavine	.35
9S	Kent Mercker	.10
10S	Lonnie Smith	.10
JS	Damon Berryhill	.10
QS	Marvin Freeman	.10
KS	John Smoltz	.10
AH	Dave Justice	.10
2H	Kent Mercker	.10
3H	Lonnie Smith	.10
4H	Greg Olson	.10
5H	Jeff Reardon	.10
6H	Steve Avery	.10
7H	Otis Nixon	.10
8H	Juan Berenguer	.10
9H	Greg Olson	.10
10H	Mike Bielecki	.10
JH	Mike Stanton	.10
QH	Deion Sanders	.15
KH	Pete Smith	.10
AD	Otis Nixon	.10
2D	Juan Berenguer	.10
3D	Francisco Cabrera	.10
4D	Damon Berryhill	.10
5D	Brian Hunter	.10
6D	Charlie Leibrandt	.10
7D	Jeff Blauser	.10
8D	John Smoltz	.10
9D	Alejandro Pena	.10
10D	Mark Lemke	.10
JD	Jeff Reardon	.10
QD	Sid Bream	.10
KD	Tom Glavine	.35
WILD	Mike Bielecki	.10
WILD	David Nied	.10
WILD	Mark Wohlers	.10
JOKER	Checklist	.05

Boston Red Sox

		NM/M
Complete Set (56):		5.00
Common Player:		.10
HEARTS		
J	Jack Clark	.10
Q	Jeff Gray	.10
K	Greg Harris	.10
A	Roger Clemens	1.00
2	Matt Young	.10
3	John Marzano	.10
4	Dennis Lamp	.10
5	Danny Darwin	.10
6	Jeff Reardon	.10
7	Phil Plantier	.10
8	Tony Fossas	.10
9	Carlos Quintana	.10
10	Wade Boggs	.75
CLUBS		
J	Luis Rivera	.10
Q	John Marzano	.10
K	Jody Reed	.10
A	Mike Greenwell	.10
2	Danny Darwin	.10
3	Dan Petry	.10
4	Dana Kiecker	.10
5	Greg Harris	.10
6	Tony Pena	.10
7	Dan Petry	.10
8	Jeff Gray	.10
9	Jack Clark	.10
10	Roger Clemens	1.00
DIAMONDS		
J	Tom Brunansky	.10
Q	Mo Vaughn	.25
K	Ellis Burks	.10
A	Joe Hesketh	.10
2	Steve Lyons	.10
3	Dana Kiecker	.10
4	Tony Fossas	.10
5	Matt Young	.10
6	Luis Rivera	.10
7	Tom Bolton	.10
8	Kevin Morton	.10
9	Jody Reed	.10
10	Mike Greenwell	.10
SPADES		
J	Tony Pena	.10
Q	Phil Plantier	.10
K	Carlos Quintana	.10
A	Wade Boggs	.75
2	Tom Bolton	.10
3	Mo Vaughn	.25
4	Kevin Morton	.10
5	Steve Lyons	.10
6	Tom Brunansky	.10
7	Dennis Lamp	.10
8	Joe Hesketh	.10
9	Ellis Burks	.10
10	Jeff Reardon	.10
JOKERS		
---	A.L. Logo (Joker)	.10
---	A.L. Logo (Joker) (Joker)	.10
---	'92 Red Sox Home Schedule	.10
---	Boston Red Sox Team History	.10

Chicago Cubs

		NM/M
Complete Set (56):		5.00
Common Player:		.10
HEARTS		
J	Jerome Walton	.10
Q	Chico Walker	.10
K	Chuck McElroy	.10
A	Andre Dawson	.30
2	Dwight Smith	.10
3	Rick Wilkins	.10
4	Doug Dascenzo	.10
5	Bob Scanlan	.10
6	Chico Walker	.10
7	Paul Assenmacher	.10
8	Mark Grace	.25
9	Ryne Sandberg	1.00
10	Danny Jackson	.10
CLUBS		
J	Hector Villanueva	.10
Q	Doug Dascenzo	.10
K	Shawon Dunston	.10
A	George Bell	.10
2	Greg Scott	.10
3	Jose Vizcaino	.10
4	Heathcliff Slocumb	.10
5	Danny Jackson	.10
6	Shawn Boskie	.10
7	Luis Salazar	.10
8	Chuck McElroy	.10
9	Andre Dawson	.30
10	Dave Smith	.10
DIAMONDS		
J	Frank Castillo	.10
Q	Les Lancaster	.10
K	Paul Assenmacher	.10
A	Greg Maddux	1.00
2	Shawn Boskie	.10
3	Ced Landrum	.10
4	Gary Scott	.10
5	Ced Landrum	.10
6	Jose Vizcaino	.10
7	Mike Harkey	.10
8	Jerome Walton	.10
9	George Bell	.10
10	Frank Castillo	.10
SPADES		
J	Bob Scanlan	.10
Q	Luis Salazar	.10
K	Mark Grace	.25
A	Ryne Sandberg	1.00
2	Frank Castillo	.10
3	Mike Harkey	.10
4	Dave Smith	.10
5	Les Lancaster	.10
6	Hector Villanueva	.10
7	Shawon Dunston	.10
8	Heathcliff Slocumb	.10
9	Greg Maddux	1.00
10	Dwight Smith	.10
JOKERS		
---	N.L. logo (Joker)	.10
---	N.L. logo (Joker)	.10
---	'92 Cubs Home Schedule	.10
---	Chicago Cubs Team History	.10

1992 U.S. Playing Card Detroit Tigers

		NM/M
Complete Set (56):		5.00
Common Player:		.10
HEARTS		
J	Lloyd Moseby	.10
Q	Walt Terrell	.10
K	Mickey Tettleton	.10
A	Cecil Fielder	.10
2	Andy Allanson	.10
3	Dave Bergman	.10
4	Steve Searcy	.10
5	Dan Galeker	.10
6	Jerry Don Gleaton	.10
7	Paul Gibson	.10
8	Alan Trammell	.25
9	Frank Tanana	.10
10	John Cerutti	.10
CLUBS		
J	Rob Deer	.10
Q	Skeeter Barnes	.10
K	Pete Incaviglia	.10
A	Tony Phillips	.10
2	Dan Galeker	.10
3	Walt Terrell	.10
4	David Haas	.10
5	Pete Incaviglia	.10
6	Travis Fryman	.10
7	Scott Aldred	.10
8	Skeeter Barnes	.10
9	Mickey Tettleton	.10
10	Cecil Fielder	.10
DIAMONDS		
J	Milt Cuyler	.10
Q	Travis Fryman	.10
K	Lou Whitaker	.10
A	Bill Gullickson	.10
2	John Cerutti	.10
3	Steve Searcy	.10
4	David Haas	.10
5	Lloyd Moseby	.10
6	Scott Livingstone	.10
7	John Shelby	.10
8	Mike Henneman	.10
9	Dave Bergman	.10
10	Tony Phillips	.10
SPADES		
J	Alan Trammell	.25
Q	Jerry Don Gleaton	.10
K	Mike Henneman	.10
A	Frank Tanana	.10
2	Scott Aldred	.10
3	Scott Livingstone	.10
4	John Shelby	.10
5	Rob Deer	.10
6	Milt Cuyler	.10
7	Andy Allanson	.10
8	Paul Gibson	.10
9	Lou Whitaker	.10
10	Bill Gullickson	.10
JOKERS		
---	A.L. Logo (Joker)	.10
---	A.L. Logo (Joker)	.10
---	'92 Tigers Home Schedule	.10
---	Detroit Tigers Team History	.10

Minnesota Twins

		NM/M
Complete Set (56):		5.00
Common Player:		.10
HEARTS		
J	Scott Leius	.10
Q	Rick Aguilera	.10
K	Jack Morris	.10
A	Kirby Puckett	.75
2	Junior Ortiz	.10
3	Paul Abbott	.10
4	Steve Bedrosian	.10
5	Pedro Munoz	.10
6	Mike Pagliarulo	.10
7	Greg Gagne	.10
8	Chuck Knoblauch	.10
9	Kevin Tapani	.10
10	Scott Erickson	.10
CLUBS		
J	Carl Willis	.10
Q	Dan Gladden	.10
K	Kent Hrbek	.10
A	Shane Mack	.10
2	Allan Anderson	.10
3	Al Newman	.10
4	Junior Ortiz	.10
5	Mike Pagliarulo	.10
6	Terry Leach	.10
7	Scott Leius	.10
8	Rick Aguilera	.10
9	Jack Morris	.10
10	Kirby Puckett	.75
DIAMONDS		
J	Gene Larkin	.10
Q	Randy Bush	.10
K	Chili Davis	.10
A	Brian Harper	.10
2	Al Newman	.10
3	Allan Anderson	.10
4	David West	.10
5	Terry Leach	.10
6	Mark Guthrie	.10
7	Carl Willis	.10
8	Dan Gladden	.10
9	Kent Hrbek	.10
10	Shane Mack	.10
SPADES		
J	Greg Gagne	.10
Q	Chuck Knoblauch	.10
K	Kevin Tapani	.10
A	Scott Erickson	.10
2	Paul Abbott	.10
3	David West	.10
4	Steve Bedrosian	.10
5	Mark Guthrie	.10
6	Pedro Munoz	.10
7	Gene Larkin	.10
8	Randy Bush	.10
9	Chili Davis	.10
10	Brian Harper	.10
JOKERS		
---	A.L. Logo (Joker)	.10
---	A.L. Logo (Joker)	.10
---	'92 Twins Home Schedule	.10
----	Minnesota Twins Team History	.10

1993 U.S. Playing Card Aces

Major league superstars with the top 1992 statistical performance in four major categories are featured in this set of playing cards. Spades feature the 13 lowest ERAs; Hearts depict the baker's dozen stolen base leaders; the 13 players with highest home run totals and batting average are featured on clubs and diamonds, respectively. The 2-1/2" x 3-1/2" cards have rounded corners and traditional trading card suits and values in the upper-left and lower-right corners. Borderless color player photos are featured on front, with color team logos at lower-left. Player names and positions are printed in a black box at bottom. Backs have a red background with a large product logo and smaller licensor and manufacturer logos at bottom. The box in which the cards were sold is enhanced with gold foil and features miniature representations of some of the cards.

		NM/M
Complete Set (56):		4.00
Common Player:		.05
AC	Juan Gonzalez	.15
2C	Dave Hollins	.05
3C	Darren Daulton	.05
4C	Ken Griffey Jr.	.75
5C	Rob Deer	.05
6C	Mickey Tettleton	.05
7C	Gary Sheffield	.25
8C	Joe Carter	.05
9C	Albert Belle	.05
10C	Barry Bonds	1.50
JC	Fred McGriff	.05
QC	Cecil Fielder	.05
KC	Mark McGwire	1.00
AS	Bill Swift	.05
2S	Tom Glavine	.35
3S	Sid Fernandez	.05
4S	Greg Swindell	.05
5S	Juan Guzman	.05
6S	Jose Rijo	.05
7S	Mike Morgan	.05
8S	Mike Mussina	.35
9S	Dennis Martinez	.05
10S	Kevin Appier	.05
JS	Roger Clemens	.65
QS	Curt Schilling	.35
KS	Greg Maddux	.60
AH	Marquis Grissom	.05
2H	Chad Curtis	.05
3H	Ozzie Smith	.60
4H	Bip Roberts	.05
5H	Steve Finley	.05
6H	Tim Raines	.05
7H	Delino DeShields	.05
8H	Rickey Henderson	.50
9H	Roberto Alomar	.10
10H	Luis Polonia	.05
JH	Brady Anderson	.05
QH	Pat Listach	.05
KH	Kenny Lofton	.05
AD	Edgar Martinez	.05
2D	Roberto Alomar	.10
3D	Terry Pendleton	.05
4D	Carlos Baerga	.05
5D	Shane Mack	.05
6D	Tony Gwynn	.60
7D	Paul Molitor	.50
8D	Frank Thomas	.50
9D	Bip Roberts	.05
10D	John Kruk	.05
JD	Andy Van Slyke	.05
QD	Kirby Puckett	.60
KD	Gary Sheffield	.25
WILD	Cal Ripken Jr.	1.50
JOKER	National League Logo	.05
JOKER	American League Logo	.05
---	Advertising Card	.05

1992 Rookies

Top rookies of the 1992 season are featured in full-color on the fronts of these playing cards. Player name and position are printed in white in a green stripe beneath the photo. A team logo is in the upper-right corner. Backs are printed in dark green with gold pinstripes and a large gold, red and purple logo.

		NM/M
Complete Boxed Set (56):		4.00
Common Player:		.10
AC	Kenny Lofton	.10
2C	Eric Fox	.10
3C	Mark Wohlers	.10
4C	John Patterson	.10
5C	Eric Young	.10
6C	Arthur Rhodes	.10
7C	Jeff Frye	.10
8C	Scott Servais	.10
9C	Ruben Amaro Jr.	.10
10C	Reggie Sanders	.10
JC	Alan Mills	.10
QC	Bob Zupcic	.10
KC	Cal Eldred	.10
AS	Eric Karros	.10
2S	Butch Henry	.10
3S	Wil Cordero	.10
4S	Pedro Astacio	.10
5S	Derek Bell	.10
6S	David Nied	.10
7S	Jeff Kent	.35
8S	David Haas	.10
9S	Ed Taubensee	.10
10S	Royce Clayton	.10
JS	Moises Alou	.10
QS	Rusty Meacham	.10
KS	Chad Curtis	.10
AH	Pat Listach	.10
2H	Pat Mahomes	.10
3H	Greg Colbrunn	.10
4H	Dan Walters	.10
5H	John Vander Wal	.10
6H	Jeff Branson	.10
7H	Monty Fariss	.10
8H	Rey Sanchez	.10
9H	Robert Wickman	.10
10H	Derrick May	.10
JH	Donovan Osborne	.10
QH	Scott Livingstone	.10
KH	Gary DiSarcina	.10
AD	Dave Fleming	.10
2D	Reggie Jefferson	.10
3D	Anthony Young	.10
4D	Kevin Koslofski	.10
5D	Brian Williams	.10
6D	Brian Jordan	.10
7D	John Doherty	.10
8D	Lenny Webster	.10
9D	Roberto Hernandez	.10
10D	Frank Seminara	.10
JD	Scott Cooper	.10
QD	Andy Stankiewicz	.10
KD	Tim Wakefield	.10
JOKER	Eric Karros (N.L. ROY)	.10
JOKER	Pat Listach (A.L. ROY)	.10
---	Rookie Qualification Rules	.10
---	Checklist	.10

Team Sets

For a second year the leading U.S. manufacturer of playing cards produced several team sets depicting ballplayers. Each was sold as a 56-card set in standard 2-1/2" x 3-1/2" round-corner playing card format in a colorful flip-top box. Backs of each team set carry a team logo. Fronts have portrait or action photo and playing card suits and values. Most players are represented twice in each team set in different photos.

Cincinnati Reds

		NM/M
Complete Set (56):		4.00
Common Player:		.10
AC	Tim Belcher	.10
2C	Jacob Brumfield	.10
3C	Rob Dibble	.10
4C	Jose Rijo	.10
5C	Dan Wilson	.10
6C	Cecil Espy	.10
7C	Tom Browning	.10
8C	Steve Foster	.10
9C	Jacob Brumfield	.10
10C	Jeff Branson	.10
JC	Greg Cadaret	.10
QC	Hal Morris	.10
KC	Joe Oliver	.10
AS	Bip Roberts	.10
2S	Cesar Hernandez	.10
3S	Chris Hammond	.10
4S	Scott Ruskin	.10
5S	John Smiley	.10
6S	Roberto Kelly	.10

7S	Barry Larkin	.25
8S	Gary Varsho	.10
9S	Hal Morris	.10
10S	Dwayne Henry	.10
JS	Tommy Gregg	.10
QS	Kevin Mitchell	.10
KS	Rob Dibble	.10
AH	Barry Larkin	.25
2H	Willie Greene	.10
3H	Steve Foster	.10
4H	Greg Cadaret	.10
5H	Chris Sabo	.10
6H	Joe Oliver	.10
7H	Milton Hill	.10
8H	Tim Belcher	.10
9H	Scott Ruskin	.10
10H	Cecil Espy	.10
JH	Roberto Kelly	.10
QH	Tom Browning	.10
KH	Reggie Sanders	.10
AD	Jose Rijo	.10
2D	Dwayne Henry	.10
3D	Jeff Branson	.10
4D	Milton Hill	.10
5D	Tim Costo	.10
6D	Bip Roberts	.10
7D	Kevin Mitchell	.10
8D	Tim Pugh	.10
9D	Reggie Sanders	.10
10D	Chris Hammond	.10
JD	Gary Varsho	.10
QD	John Smiley	.10
KD	Chris Sabo	.10
WILD	Tony Perez	.50
JOKER	Riverfront Stadium	.10
	Reds Schedule	.10
	Checklist	.10

Colorado Rockies

		NM/M
Complete Set (56):		4.00
Common Player:		.10
AC	Jim Tatum	.10
2C	Charlie Hayes	.10
3C	Dale Murphy	.50
4C	Scott Aldred	.10
5C	Braulio Castillo	.10
6C	Danny Sheaffer	.10
7C	Jerald Clark	.10
8C	Willie Blair	.10
9C	Daryl Boston	.10
10C	Andy Ashby	.10
JC	Butch Henry	.10
QC	Alex Cole	.10
KC	Vinny Castilla	.10
AS	David Nied	.10
2S	Andres Galarraga	.10
3S	Gary Wayne	.10
4S	Freddie Benavides	.10
5S	Butch Henry	.10
6S	Gerald Young	.10
7S	Jeff Parrett	.10
8S	Braulio Castillo	.10
9S	Darren Holmes	.10
10S	Dale Murphy	.50
JS	Eric Young	.10
QS	Bruce Ruffin	.10
KS	Joe Girardi	.10
AH	Charlie Hayes	.10
2H	Jim Tatum	.10
3H	Andy Ashby	.10
4H	Vinny Castilla	.10
5H	Steve Reed	.10
6H	Daryl Boston	.10
7H	Alex Cole	.10
8H	Bryn Smith	.10
9H	Danny Sheaffer	.10
10H	Willie Blair	.10
JH	Dante Bichette	.10
QH	Jerald Clark	.10
DH	Scott Aldred	.10
AD	Andres Galarraga	.10
2D	David Nied	.10
3D	Dante Bichette	.10
4D	Joe Girardi	.10
5D	Bryn Smith	.10
6D	Darren Holmes	.10
7D	Bruce Ruffin	.10
8D	Eric Young	.10
9D	Gerald Young	.10
10D	Gary Wayne	.10
JD	Steve Reed	.10
QD	Jeff Parrett	.10
KD	Freddie Benavides	.10

Florida Marlins

		NM/M
Complete Set (56):		4.00
Common Player:		.10
AC	Walt Weiss	.10
2C	Dave Magadan	.10
3C	Chris Carpenter	.10
4C	Dave Magadan	.10
5C	Bob McClure	.10
6C	Junior Felix	.10
7C	Walt Weiss	.10
8C	Steve Decker	.10
9C	Jeff Conine	.15
10C	Bryan Harvey	.10
JC	Orestes Destrade	.10
QC	Chris Hammond	.10
KC	Monty Fariss	.10
AS	Alex Arias	.10
2S	Benito Santiago	.10
3S	Ryan Bowen	.10
4S	Steve Decker	.10
5S	Jeff Conine	.15
6S	Bret Barberie	.10
7S	Orestes Destrade	.10
8S	Greg Briley	.10
9S	Charlie Hough	.10
10S	Bob Natal	.10
JS	Jack Armstrong	.10
QS	Junior Felix	.10
KS	Richie Lewis	.10
AH	Benito Santiago	.10
2H	Walt Weiss	.10
3H	Monty Fariss	.10
4H	Chris Hammond	.10
5H	Joe Klink	.10
6H	Chuck Carr	.10
7H	Alex Arias	.10
8H	Charlie Hough	.10
9H	Junior Felix	.10
10H	Jim Corsi	.10
JH	Jeff Conine	.15
QH	Trevor Hoffman	.10
KH	Rich Renteria	.10
AD	Dave Magadan	.10
2D	Jack Armstrong	.10
3D	Bryan Harvey	.10
4D	Richie Lewis	.10
5D	Scott Pose	.10
6D	Rich Renteria	.10
7D	Trevor Hoffman	.10
8D	Jim Corsi	.10
9D	Ryan Bowen	.10
10D	Orestes Destrade	.10
JD	Bret Barberie	.10
QD	Chuck Carr	.10
KD	Chris Carpenter	.10
JOKER	N.L. Logo	.10
JOKER	N.L. Logo	.10
---	Opening Day Roster	.10
---	Marlins Schedule	.10

1994 U.S. Playing Card Aces

Statistical leaders from the 1993 season are featured in this deck of playing cards. Pitchers with the lowest ERAs are shown on the spades; stolen base leaders are featured on the hearts; home run hitters are depicted on the clubs, and diamonds host the batting average leaders. Cards are 2-1/2" x 3-1/2" with rounded corners. Fronts have full-bleed photos with the suit and value of the playing card in the upper-left and lower-right corners. The player's name, position and team logo are at lower-left. Backs are printed in dark blue with vertical silver stripes at each side and a red, white and blue "Baseball Aces" logo at top. Licensing logos appear at the bottom. Besides the 52 player cards in the boxed set, there is a checklist card, A.L. and N.L. logo cards and a U.S. Playing Card Co. advertising card.

		NM/M
Complete Set (56):		6.00
Common Player:		.10
AC	Barry Bonds	1.50
2C	Phil Plantier	.10
3C	Bobby Bonilla	.10
4C	Mike Piazza	1.00
5C	Ron Gant	.10
6C	Rafael Palmeiro	.50
7C	Fred McGriff	.10
8C	Matt Williams	.10
9C	Albert Belle	.10
10C	Dave Justice	.10
JC	Frank Thomas	.60
QC	Ken Griffey Jr.	1.00
KC	Juan Gonzalez	.30
AS	Greg Maddux	.75
2S	Tom Candiotti	.10
3S	Jimmy Key	.10
4S	Jack McDowell	.10
5S	John Burkett	.10
6S	Tom Glavine	.25
7S	Pete Harnisch	.10
8S	Wilson Alvarez	.10
9S	Steve Avery	.10
10S	Bill Swift	.10
JS	Mark Portugal	.10
QS	Kevin Appier	.10
KS	Jose Rijo	.10
AH	Kenny Lofton	.10
2H	Brett Butler	.10
3H	Eric Young	.10
4H	Delino DeShields	.10
5H	Darren Lewis	.10
6H	Gregg Jefferies	.10
7H	Otis Nixon	.10
8H	Chad Curtis	.10
9H	Rickey Henderson	.60
10H	Marquis Grissom	.10
JH	Luis Polonia	.10
QH	Roberto Alomar	.20
KH	Chuck Carr	.10
AD	Andres Galarraga	.10
2D	John Kruk	.10
3D	Frank Thomas	.60
4D	Mike Piazza	1.00
5D	Jeff Bagwell	.60
6D	Carlos Baerga	.10
7D	Mark Grace	.10
8D	Kenny Lofton	.10
9D	Roberto Alomar	.20
10D	Paul Molitor	.60
JD	Barry Bonds	1.50
QD	Gregg Jefferies	.10
KD	John Olerud	.10
Joker	National League Logo	.05
Joker	American League Logo	.05
---	Checklist	.05
---	Advertising Card	.05

Atlanta Braves

The most popular Braves are pictured on up to three of the cards in this deck. In 2-1/2" x 3-1/2" round-cornered format, the large color photos on the card fronts have their upper-left and lower-right corners clipped to display traditional playing card suits and values. The player name and position are printed in black in a gold strip below the photo. Backs have the Braves logo on a dark blue background with red stripes on the left and right edges. Brand and licensor logos are at bottom. The cards were sold in a colorful box.

		NM/M
Complete Set (56):		4.00
Common Player:		.10
AC	Ron Gant	.10
2C	Chipper Jones	1.00
3C	Terry Pendleton	.10
4C	Mark Wohlers	.10
5C	Pedro Borbon	.10
6C	Steve Avery	.10
7C	Deion Sanders	.15
8C	Dave Justice	.10
9C	Dave Gallagher	.10
10C	Rafael Belliard	.10
JC	Greg McMichael	.10
QC	John Smoltz	.10
KC	Fred McGriff	.10
AS	Jeff Blauser	.10
2S	Mike Stanton	.10
3S	Ryan Klesko	.10
4S	Mike Potts	.10
5S	Charlie O'Brien	.10
6S	Steve Bedrosian	.10
7S	Javier Lopez	.10
8S	Greg Maddux	.75
9S	Deion Sanders	.15
10S	Ramon Caraballo	.10
JS	Kent Mercker	.10
QS	Mark Wohlers	.10
KS	Tom Glavine	.25
AH	Dave Justice	.10
2H	Mark Lemke	.10
3H	Javier Lopez	.10
4H	Rafael Belliard	.10
5H	Bill Pecota	.10
6H	Tom Glavine	.25
7H	Milt Hill	.10
8H	Jeff Blauser	.10
9H	Ryan Klesko	.10
10H	Terry Pendleton	.10
JH	Mike Stanton	.10
QH	Steve Avery	.10
KH	Deion Sanders	.15
AD	Greg Maddux	.75
2D	Ron Gant	.10
3D	Kent Mercker	.10
4D	Greg McMichael	.10
5D	Tony Tarasco	.10
6D	John Smoltz	.10
7D	Fred McGriff	.10
8D	Ron Gant	.10
9D	Mike Kelly	.10
10D	Steve Bedrosian	.10
JD	Bill Pecota	.10
QD	Mark Lemke	.10
KD	Terry Pendleton	.10
Joker	Atlanta Braves Logo	.10
Joker	National League Logo	.10
---	Checklist	.10
---	'94 Braves Home Schedule	.10

Baltimore Orioles

The 1994 Baltimore Orioles are featured in this deck of playing cards. Color photos of the players have clipped corners to display traditional playing card suits and values in the upper-left and lower-right corners. Beneath the photo is an orange strip with the player's name and position in white. Backs have a large Orioles logo on a pinstriped background. Company and licensor logos are at the bottom. Cards measure 2-1/2" x 3-1/2" with rounded corners. The set was sold in a colorful cardboard box.

		NM/M
Complete Set (56):		4.00
Common Player:		.10
AC	Chris Hoiles	.10
2C	Mike Cook	.10
3C	Paul Carey	.10
4C	Jeff Tackett	.10
5C	Arthur Rhodes	.10
6C	Damon Buford	.10
7C	David Segui	.10
8C	Ben McDonald	.10
9C	Cal Ripken Jr.	1.00
10C	Brad Pennington	.10
JC	Jack Voigt	.10
QC	Jeffrey Hammonds	.10
KC	Rafael Palmeiro	.60
AS	Mark McLemore	.10
2S	Manny Alexander	.10
3S	Kevin McGehee	.10
4S	Jim Poole	.10
5S	Leo Gomez	.10
6S	Tim Hulett	.10
7S	Mike Devereaux	.10
8S	Brady Anderson	.10
9S	Mike Mussina	.40
10S	Sherman Obando	.10
JS	Alan Mills	.10
QS	Jamie Moyer	.10
KS	Harold Baines	.10
AH	Cal Ripken Jr.	1.00
2H	Harold Baines	.10
3H	John O'Donoghue	.10
4H	Sid Fernandez	.10
5H	Alan Mills	.10
6H	Jamie Moyer	.10
7H	Harold Baines	.10
8H	Mark McLemore	.10
9H	Jeff Tackett	.10
10H	Arthur Rhodes	.10
JH	Damon Buford	.10
QH	David Segui	.10
KH	Ben McDonald	.10
AD	Mike Mussina	.40
2D	Mike Oquist	.10
3D	Brad Pennington	.10
4D	Jeffrey Hammonds	.10
5D	Jack Voigt	.10
6D	Chris Sabo	.10
7D	Rafael Palmeiro	.60
8D	Chris Hoiles	.10
9D	Jim Poole	.10
10D	Leo Gomez	.10
JD	Tim Hulett	.10
QD	Mike Devereaux	.10
KD	Brady Anderson	.10
Joker	Baltimore Orioles Logo	.10
Joker	American League Logo	.10
---	Checklist	.10
---	'94 Orioles Home Schedule	.10

Philadelphia Phillies

Veterans and rookies on the roster of the '94 Phils are featured in this deck of playing cards; the most popular players appear on up to three cards each. In standard 2-1/2" x 3-1/2" round-cornered format, the large color photos have their top-left and bottom-right corners clipped to display traditional playing card suits and values. The player's name and position are printed in black on a red strip beneath the photo. Backs have a large Phillies logo on a gray pinstriped background. Company and licensor logos are at bottom. The cards were sold in a decorative box.

		NM/M
Complete Set (56):		4.00
Common Player:		.10
AC	Pete Incaviglia	.10
2C	Lenny Dykstra	.10
3C	Milt Thompson	.10
4C	Mickey Morandini	.10
5C	Kevin Stocker	.10
6C	Terry Mulholland	.10
7C	Curt Schilling	.35
8C	Darren Daulton	.10
9C	Terry Mulholland	.10
10C	Roger Mason	.10
JC	Mariano Duncan	.10
QC	Ben Rivera	.10
KC	John Kruk	.10
AS	Dave Hollins	.10
2S	Danny Jackson	.10
3S	Todd Pratt	.10
4S	David West	.10
5S	Lenny Dykstra	.10
6S	Wes Chamberlain	.10
7S	Tommy Greene	.10
8S	Tony Longmire	.10
9S	Brad Brink	.10
10S	Ricky Jordan	.10
JS	Kim Batiste	.10
QS	Tyler Green	.10
KS	Jim Eisenreich	.10
AH	Lenny Dykstra	.10
2H	Tony Longmire	.10
3H	Kim Batiste	.10
4H	Pete Incaviglia	.10
5H	Ben Rivera	.10
6H	Ricky Jordan	.10
7H	Dave Hollins	.10
8H	Kevin Foster	.10
9H	Kevin Stocker	.10
10H	Mike Williams	.10
JH	Milt Thompson	.10
QH	Curt Schilling	.10
KH	Darren Daulton	.10
AD	Terry Mulholland	.10
2D	Brad Brink	.10
3D	Roger Mason	.10
4D	Mariano Duncan	.10
5D	Danny Jackson	.10
6D	Jim Eisenreich	.10
7D	John Kruk	.10
8D	David West	.10
9D	Todd Pratt	.10
10D	Wes Chamberlain	.10
JD	Jim Eisenreich	.10
QD	Mickey Morandini	.10
KD	Tommy Greene	.10
Joker	Phillies Logo	.10
Joker	National League Logo	.10
---	Checklist	.10
---	'94 Phillies Home Schedule	.10

S.F. Giants

Veterans and rookies on the roster of the '94 Giants are featured in this deck of playing cards; the most popular players appear on up to three cards each. In standard 2-1/2" x 3-1/2" round-cornered format, the large color photos have their top-left and bottom-right corners clipped to display traditional playing card suits and values. The player's name and position are printed in white on an orange strip beneath the photo. Backs have a large Giants logo on a gray pinstriped background. Company and licensor logos are at bottom. The cards were sold in a decorative box.

		NM/M
Complete Set (56):		4.00
Common Player:		.10
AC	Matt Williams	.10
2C	John Patterson	.10
3C	Steve Hosey	.10
4C	Jeff Reed	.10
5C	Mike Jackson	.10
6C	Kirt Manwaring	.10
7C	Royce Clayton	.10
8C	Robby Thompson	.10
9C	Luis Mercedes	.10
10C	Mike Benjamin	.10
JC	Mark Carreon	.10
QC	Dave Burba	.10
KC	John Burkett	.10
AS	Barry Bonds	1.00
2S	Salomon Torres	.10
3S	Kevin Rogers	.10
4S	Todd Benzinger	.10
5S	Dave Martinez	.10
6S	Darren Lewis	.10
7S	Willie McGee	.10
8S	Bill Swift	.10
9S	Paul Faries	.10
10S	Trevor Wilson	.10
JS	Steve Scarsone	.10
QS	Bryan Hickerson	.10
KS	Rod Beck	.10
AH	Robby Thompson	.10
2H	Paul Faries	.10
3H	Trevor Wilson	.10
4H	Steve Scarsone	.10
5H	Bryan Hickerson	.10
6H	Rod Beck	.10
7H	Barry Bonds	1.00
8H	John Patterson	.10
9H	J.R. Phillips	.10
10H	Jeff Reed	.10
JH	Mike Jackson	.10
QH	Kirt Manwaring	.10
KH	Royce Clayton	.10
AD	Bill Swift	.10
2D	Luis Mercedes	.10
3D	Mike Benjamin	.10
4D	Mark Carreon	.10
5D	Dave Burba	.10
6D	John Burkett	.10
7D	Matt Williams	.10
8D	Salomon Torres	.10
9D	Kevin Rogers	.10
10D	Todd Benzinger	.10
JD	Dave Martinez	.10
QD	Darren Lewis	.10
KD	Willie McGee	.10
JOKER	Giants Home Schedule	.10
JOKER	Checklist	.10
---	N.L. Logo	.10
---	Giants Logo	.10

1993 Rookies

The top rookies from the 1993 season are featured on this deck of playing cards; several players appear on more than one card in the deck. Fronts have color player photos at center, with traditional playing card suits and values in the upper-left and lower-right borders. A team logo is at upper-right. The player's name and position appear in white in a purple strip at lower-left. Backs are purple with a large product logo at top-center and licensor/licensee logos at bottom. Cards measure 2-1/2" x 3-1/2" with rounded corners and were sold in a specially decorated cardboard box.

		NM/M
Complete Set (56):		4.00
Common Player:		.10
AC	Mike Piazza	1.00
2C	Vinny Castilla	.10
3C	Wil Cordero	.10
4C	Ryan Thompson	.10
5C	Craig Paquette	.10
6C	Carlos Garcia	.10
7C	Jeff Conine	.10
8C	Bret Boone	.10
9C	Jeromy Burnitz	.10
10C	J.T. Snow	.10
JC	Al Martin	.10
QC	Troy Neel	.10
KC	Tim Salmon	.10
AS	Greg McMichael	.10
2S	Paul Quantrill	.10
3S	Steve Reed	.10
4S	Trevor Hoffman	.10
5S	Tim Pugh	.10
6S	Angel Miranda	.10
7S	Steve Cooke	.10
8S	Aaron Sele	.10
9S	Kirk Rueter	.10
10S	Rene Arocha	.10
JS	Pedro Martinez	.75
QS	Armadno Reynoso	.10
KS	Jason Bere	.10
AH	Kevin Stocker	.10
2H	Alex Arias	.10
3H	Carlos Garcia	.10
4H	Erik Pappas	.10
5H	Al Martin	.10
6H	Tim Salmon	.10
7H	Mike Lansing	.10
8H	Rich Amaral	.10
9H	Brent Gates	.10
10H	David Hulse	.10
JH	Troy Neel	.10
QH	Jeff Conine	.10
KH	Mike Piazza	1.00
AD	Chuck Carr	.10
2D	Jeff McNeeley	.10
3D	Joe Kmak	.10
4D	Phil Hiatt	.10
5D	Brent Gates	.10
6D	Wil Cordero	.10
7D	Al Martin	.10
8D	Wayne Kirby	.10
9D	Lou Frazier	.10
10D	Carlos Garcia	.10
JD	Rich Amaral	.10
QD	Mike Lansing	.10
KD	David Hulse	.10
Joker	Tim Salmon (Rookie of the Year)	.10
Joker	Mike Piazza (Rookie of the Year)	.75
--	Checklist	.10
--	Rookie Qualification Rules	.10

1995 U.S. Playing Card Aces

Baseball's 1994 statistical leaders in home runs (clubs), ERA (spades), stolen bases (hearts) and batting average (diamonds) are featured in this deck of playing cards. Measuring a standard 2-1/2" x 3-1/2" with rounded corners, cards have borderless action photos on front with traditional playing card suits and denominations in the upper-left and lower-right corners. The player's color team logo, name and position appear in the lower-left corner. Backs are silver with black side stripes and a red-and-black Aces logo at center. Sets were sold in a colorful cardboard box.

		NM/M
Complete Set (56):		5.00
Common Player:		.10
AC	Matt Williams	.10
2C	Joe Carter	.10
3C	Dante Bichette	.10
4C	Cecil Fielder	.10
5C	Kevin Mitchell	.10
6C	Andres Galarraga	.10
7C	Jose Canseco	.35
8C	Fred McGriff	.10
9C	Albert Belle	.10
10C	Barry Bonds	1.00
JC	Frank Thomas	.50
QC	Jeff Bagwell	.50
KC	Ken Griffey Jr.	.75
AS	Greg Maddux	.60
2S	Steve Trachsel	.10
3S	Randy Johnson	.50
4S	Bobby Jones	.10
5S	Jose Rijo	.10
6S	Mike Mussina	.30
7S	Shane Reynolds	.10
8S	Jeff Fassero	.10
9S	David Cone	.10
10S	Roger Clemens	.65
JS	Doug Drabek	.10
QS	Bret Saberhagen	.10
KS	Steve Ontiveros	.10
AH	Kenny Lofton	.10
2H	Brian McRae	.10
3H	Alex Cole	.10
4H	Barry Bonds	1.00
5H	Darren Lewis	.10
6H	Brady Anderson	.10
7H	Chuck Carr	.10
8H	Chuck Knoblauch	.10
9H	Marquis Grissom	.10
10H	Deion Sanders	.15
JH	Craig Biggio	.10
QH	Otis Nixon	.10
KH	Vince Coleman	.10
AD	Tony Gwynn	.60
2D	Gregg Jefferies	.10
3D	Kevin Mitchell	.10
4D	Will Clark	.10
5D	Hal Morris	.10
6D	Moises Alou	.10
7D	Paul Molitor	.50
8D	Wade Boggs	.60
9D	Kenny Lofton	.10
10D	Frank Thomas	.50
JD	Albert Belle	.10
QD	Paul O'Neill	.10
KD	Jeff Bagwell	.50
Joker	American League logo	.05
Joker	National League logo	.05
---	Checklist	.05
---	MicroMini Team card order form	.05

2000 U.S. Playing Card All Century Baseball Team

Fifty-two members of baseball's All Century team are featured on this deck of playing cards. On round-cornered playing card stock in 2-1/2" x 3-1/2" format, cards have black-and-white photos vignetted on front with the player name at bottom. In opposite corners are a color baseball with the card's value at center and the suit printed in red or black below. Backs are predominantly blue with gold borders and pinstriping. The cards were issued with four All Century team logos in a cardboard box within an embossed lithographed steel case.

		NM/M
Complete Boxed Set (56):		6.00
Common Player:		.10
AC	"Wee" Willie Keeler	.10
2C	Bob Feller	.10
3C	Luke Appling	.10
4C	Jerome "Dizzy" Dean	.15
5C	Johnny Bench	.25
6C	Lou Brock	.10
7C	Joe Cronin	.10
8C	Mickey Cochrane	.10
9C	Rod Carew	.10
10C	Bill Dickey	.10
JC	Josh Gibson	.10
QC	Lou Gehrig	.75
KC	Jackie Robinson	.75
AS	Babe Ruth	1.00
2S	Leroy "Satchel" Paige	.40
3S	Willie McCovey	.10
4S	Joe Morgan	.10
5S	Mel Ott	.10
6S	Jim Palmer	.10
7S	Frank Robinson	.10
8S	Mike Schmidt	.40
9S	George Sisler	.10
10S	Al Simmons	.10
JS	Denton "Cy" Young	.10
QS	Ozzie Smith	.25
KS	Tris Speaker	.10
AH	Bob Gibson	.10
2H	Whitey Ford	.10
3H	Christy Mathewson	.15
4H	Ralph Kiner	.10
5H	Juan Marichal	.10
6H	Bob "Lefty" Grove	.10
7H	Carl Hubbell	.10
8H	Al Kaline	.15
9H	Rogers Hornsby	.10
10H	Harmon Killebrew	.10
JH	Walter Johnson	.10
QH	Jimmie Foxx	.10
KH	Carlton Fisk	.10
AD	Eddie Collins	.10
2D	Robin Roberts	.10
3D	Honus Wagner	.20
4D	Warren Spahn	.10
5D	Mickey Mantle	1.50
6D	Brooks Robinson	.10
7D	Hank Aaron	.75
8D	Rollie Fingers	.10
9D	Dennis Eckersley	.10
10D	Ty Cobb	.75
JD	Joe Medwick	.10
QD	Ernie Banks	.15
KD	Grover Cleveland Alexander	.10

1989 U.S. Postal Service Legends

In 1989 the U.S. Postal Service offered to collectors a Legends set for $7.95. The set consists of a heavily illustrated 24-page "Baseball Scrapbook and Stamp Album," a set of the four U.S. postage stamps which had been issued to that time honoring individual players, and a set of cards matching the stamps. The 2-1/2" x 3-1/2" cards have color reproductions of the stamps on front, bordered in white with red and blue striping. Backs are in red, black and orange and feature player data and major league stats.

		NM/M
Complete Set, Album, Stamps, Cards:		24.00
Card Set (4):		15.00
3	Babe Ruth	4.00
4	Lou Gehrig	3.00
21	Roberto Clemente	5.00
42	Jackie Robinson	3.00

2000 U.S. Postal Service Legends of Baseball Stamps

Twenty of the players nominated to baseball's All-Century team are featured on this souvenir sheet of 33-cent stamps issued by the USPS during ceremonies in Atlanta for the 2000 All-Star Game. The players chosen to appear were all Hall of Famers and, as per post office rules, had been deceased at least 10 years prior to the stamps' issue. Many of the pastel paintings by Joseph Saffold are familiar to card collectors because the illustrations are based on earlier photos which have been seen on vintage cards. A total of 225 million of the self-adhesive 1-1/4" x 1-9/16" stamps was produced, with the 7-1/8" x 7-13/16" souvenir panel originally retailing at face value - $6.60. It was reported that 11,250,000 sheets were printed.

		NM/M
Complete Sheet:		8.00
Common Player:		.35
(1)	Roberto Clemente	.60
(2)	Ty Cobb	.45
(3)	Mickey Cochrane	.35
(4)	Eddie Collins	.35
(5)	Dizzy Dean	.35
(6)	Jimmie Foxx	.35
(7)	Lou Gehrig	.50
(8)	Josh Gibson	.35
(9)	Lefty Grove	.35
(10)	Rogers Hornsby	.35
(11)	Walter Johnson	.35
(12)	Christy Mathewson	.35
(13)	Satchel Paige	.45
(14)	Jackie Robinson	.60
(15)	Babe Ruth	.60
(16)	George Sisler	.35
(17)	Tris Speaker	.35
(18)	Pie Traynor	.35
(19)	Honus Wagner	.35
(20)	Cy Young	.35

2000 USPS Legends of Baseball Post Cards

In conjunction with the issue of a souvenir sheet of 33-cent stamps, the USPS also issued a boxed set of "Legends of Baseball" post cards. The 5" x 7" cards have a large reproduction of each stamp on front against a beige background. Postcard-style backs have color logos of the USPS and MLB's All-Century Team, along with address lines and a stamp box. At upper-left is a summary of the player's career. The cards were issued in a colorful folder with an All-Century Team hologram. The boxed sets sold for $5.95. Production was reported as 62,500 sets.

		NM/M
Complete Boxed Set (20):		9.00
Common Player:		.75
(1)	Roberto Clemente	1.50
(2)	Ty Cobb	1.25
(3)	Mickey Cochrane	.75
(4)	Eddie Collins	.75
(5)	Dizzy Dean	.75
(6)	Jimmie Foxx	.75
(7)	Lou Gehrig	1.25
(8)	Josh Gibson	.75
(9)	Lefty Grove	.75
(10)	Rogers Hornsby	.75
(11)	Walter Johnson	.75
(12)	Christy Mathewson	.75
(13)	Satchel Paige	1.25
(14)	Jackie Robinson	1.50
(15)	Babe Ruth	1.50
(16)	George Sisler	.75
(17)	Tris Speaker	.75
(18)	Pie Traynor	.75
(19)	Honus Wagner	.75
(20)	Cy Young	.75

2000 USPS Legends of Baseball Postal Card Booklet

In conjunction with the issue of a souvenir sheet of 33-cent stamps, the USPS also issued a bound booklet of "Legends of Baseball" postal cards. By definition, postal cards have the "stamp" pre-printed. The 4-1/4" x 6-1/16" cards have borderless color artwork on front, pastel paintings which reproduce the stamps' artwork. On the divided back a 20-cent "stamp" version of the player picture is printed at top-right. There is a short biography at top-left. The cards were perforated with an 11/16" stub attaching it to the bound book. With a $4 face value, the booklets were originally sold for $8.95 at the post office. Production was reported as 105,000 sets.

		NM/M
Complete Booklet (20):		12.50
Common Player:		.75
(1)	Roberto Clemente	1.50
(2)	Ty Cobb	1.25
(3)	Mickey Cochrane	.75
(4)	Eddie Collins	.75
(5)	Dizzy Dean	.75
(6)	Jimmie Foxx	.75
(7)	Lou Gehrig	1.25
(8)	Josh Gibson	.75
(9)	Lefty Grove	.75
(10)	Rogers Hornsby	.75
(11)	Walter Johnson	.75
(12)	Christy Mathewson	.75
(13)	Satchel Paige	1.25
(14)	Jackie Robinson	1.50
(15)	Babe Ruth	1.50
(16)	George Sisler	.75
(17)	Tris Speaker	.75
(18)	Pie Traynor	.75
(19)	Honus Wagner	.75
(20)	Cy Young	.75

2000 Verizon Tampa Bay Devil Rays

This team set was a stadium giveaway at a promotional date. Fronts of the 2-1/2" x 3-1/2" cards have game-action photos on which a silver dollar-size portion remains in natural color while the balance of the picture is a purple duo-tone. Backs are in gray with a purple box for complete pro stats, capped by a dime-size color player portrait. The set is listed here according to uniform numbers which appear on back.

		NM/M
Complete Set (28):		7.50
Common Player:		.25
1	Miguel Cairo	.25
2	Randy Winn	.25
4	Gerald Williams	.25
6	John Flaherty	.25
8	Mike DiFelice	.25
9	Vinny Castilla	.25
10	Russ Johnson	.25
11	Larry Rothschild	.25
13	Ozzie Guillen	.25
16	Felix Martinez	.25
21	Bubba Trammell	.25
23	Greg Vaughn	.25
28	Steve Cox	.25
29	Fred McGriff	.50
30	Jose Guillen	.25
32	Albie Lopez	.25
33	Jose Canseco	2.50
35	Bryan Rekar	.25
39	Roberto Hernandez	.25
40	Wilson Alvarez	.25
43	Esteban Yan	.25
46	Steve Trachsel	.25
51	Rick White	.25
57	Juan Guzman	.25
---	Coaches (Orlando Gomez, Billy Hatcher, Bill Russell, Jose Cardenal, Bill Fischer, Leon Roberts)	.25
00	Raymond (Mascot)	.25
---	Wade Boggs (Literacy Champion)	3.50
---	A's for the Rays	.10

1989 Very Fine Pirates

This 30-card set Pirates set was sponsored by Veryfine fruit juices and issued in the form of two uncut, perforated panels, each containing 15 standard-size cards. A third panel featured color action photographs. The panels were distributed in a promotion to fans attending the April 23 game at Three Rivers Stadium. The cards display the Pirates' traditional black and gold color scheme. The backs include player data and complete stats.

		NM/M
Complete Three-Panel Set:		15.00
Complete Singles Set (30):		13.50
Common Player:		.25
0	Junior Ortiz	.25

2	Gary Redus	.25
3	Jay Bell	.25
5	Sid Bream	.25
6	Rafael Belliard	.25
10	Jim Leyland	.25
11	Glenn Wilson	.25
12	Mike La Valliere	.25
13	Jose Lind	.25
14	Ken Oberkfell	.25
15	Doug Drabek	.25
16	Bob Kipper	.25
17	Bob Walk	.25
18	Andy Van Slyke	.25
23	R.J. Reynolds	.25
24	Barry Bonds	12.00
25	Bobby Bonilla	.25
26	Neal Heaton	.25
30	Benny Distefano	.25
35	Jim Gott	.25
41	Mike Dunne	.25
43	Bill Landrum	.25
44	John Cangelosi	.25
49	Jeff Robinson	.25
52	Dorn Taylor	.25
54	Brian Fisher	.25
57	John Smiley	.25
31/37	Ray Miller, Tommy Sandt	.25
32/36	Bruce Kimm, Gene Lamont	.25
39/45	Milt May, Rich Donnelly	.25
---	Rich Donnelly (39-45)	.25

2002 Viagra Rafael Palmeiro

Spokesman Rafael Palmeiro is featured on five of the nine cards in this set issued to promote the drug Viagra. (Models are pictured on the other four cards.) Sets were issued in a cello-wrapped pack with a detailed information sheet on the drug. Evidently distributed to medical professionals, the exact manner and range of the cards' distribution is unknown. In standard 2-1/2" x 3-1/2" format, cards are printed on rather thin stock which is UV coated on each side. Except for one card which has a Palmeiro portrait photo on back along with personal data and stats, the backs have information on the drug.

		NM/M
Complete Set (9):		4.50
Common Card:		.05
(1)	Rafael Palmeiro (Game-action photo.)	1.25
(2)	Rafael Palmeiro (Bat at ready pose.)	1.25
(3)	Rafael Palmeiro (Batting follow-through.)	1.25
(4)	Rafael Palmeiro (Jersey close-up.)	1.25
(5)	Rafael Palmeiro/ Portrait	1.25
(6)	Communication	.05
(7)	Diabetes	.05
(8)	Hyperlipidemia	.05
(9)	Hypertension	.05

1991 Vine Line Chicago Cubs

This set was produced in conjunction with the official fan magazine of the Chicago Cubs, "Vine Line." Issued in nine-card panels for insertion into issues of the magazine, the panels were apparently also offered as a complete set via a mail-in offer. Cards measure the standard 2-1/2" x 3-1/2" and will be perforated on two, three or four sides, depending on their placement on the panel. Fronts are bordered in black with white typography that has

the player name, position and uniform number. The player photo is in color with the background in stippled black-and-white. Backs have a black-and-white player portrait, biographical data, career highlights, 1990 and career stats and a brown and green background. The cards are listed here by uniform number.

		NM/M
Complete Singles Set (36):		6.00
Complete Panel Set (4):		7.50
Common Card:		.25
3	Jose Martinez	.25
4	Don Zimmer	.25
5	Chuck Cottier	.25
6	Joe Altobelli	.25
7	Joe Girardi	.25
8	Andre Dawson	.45
9	Damon Berryhill	.25
10	Luis Salazar	.25
11	George Bell	.25
12	Shawon Dunston	.25
16	Jose Vizcaino	.25
17	Mark Grace	.50
18	Dwight Smith	.25
19	Hector Villanueva	.25
20	Jerome Walton	.25
22	Mike Harkey	.25
23	Ryne Sandberg	2.00
24	Chico Walker	.25
25	Gary Scott	.25
29	Doug Dascenzo	.25
31	Greg Maddux	2.00
32	Danny Jackson	.25
34	Dick Pole	.25
35	Chuck McElroy	.25
36	Mike Bielecki	.25
37	Erik Pappas	.25
40	Rick Sutcliffe	.25
42	Dave Smith	.25
44	Steve Wilson	.25
45	Paul Assenmacher	.25
47	Shawn Boskie	.25
48	Phil Roof	.25
50	Les Lancaster	.25
51	Heathcliff Slocumb	.25
31	Fergie Jenkins (Hall of Fame)	.50
---	Most Valuable Players (Ryne Sandberg, Andre Dawson, George Bell)	.40

1994 Vine Line Chicago Cubs Postcards

Chicago Cubs Vine Line, the team's official monthly paper, produced this set of promotional postcards. The 4" x 5-1/2" cards have black-and-white or color pictures with maroon borders. Backs are in color with a description of the front photo. The unnumbered cards are checklisted here in chronological order.

		NM/M
Complete Set (10):		10.00
Common Card:		1.00
(1)	Wrigley Field 1914-1994/ 1935	1.00
(2)	Wrigley Field 1914-1994/ 1988	1.00
(3)	Harry Caray 50 Seasons (7th inning stretch)	1.00
(4)	Harry Caray 50 Seasons (1989 w/Stan Musial)	1.00
(5)	1969 (team composite)	2.50
(6)	1969 (Ken Holtzman (No-hitter.))	1.50
(7)	1984 (Clinching NL East)	1.00
(8)	1969 (Final game celebration)	1.00
(9)	1989 (Boys of Zimmer)	1.00
(10)	1989 (Clinching NL East)	1.00

1998 Virginia Lottery Baseball Legends Cards

This set of cards was one of several consolation prizes available in the commonwealth's scratch-off lottery game featuring Hall of Famers who had played in Virginia. The 2-1/2" x 3-1/2" cards have larger versions of the player photos found on the tickets. Borders are in red, white, blue, and black. Black-and-white backs have career highlights and stats. Cards can be found in either signed or autographed versions.

		NM/M
Complete Set (4):		4.00
Autographed Set (4):		25.00
Common Player:		1.00
Common Autograph:		8.00
(1)	Yogi Berra	2.00
(1)	Yogi Berra/Auto.	15.00
(2)	Willie McCovey	1.00
(2)	Willie McCovey/Auto.	10.00
(3)	Phil Niekro	1.00
(3)	Phil Niekro/Auto.	8.00
(4)	Duke Snider	1.50
(4)	Duke Snider/Auto.	12.00

W

1986 Wallich Enterprises Padres Sports Cards

This set of artwork postcards was designed to be the first in a series which never materialized. The cards feature color artwork on front with a wide border and player name beneath.

		NM/M
Complete Set (15):		35.00
Common Player:		3.00
(1)	Kurt Bevacqua	3.00
(2)	Dave Dravecky	4.00
(3)	Tim Flannery, Jerry Royster	3.00
(4)	Steve Garvey	6.00
(5)	Rich Gossage	4.00
(6)	Tony Gwynn	9.00
(7)	Andy Hawkins	3.00
(8)	LaMarr Hoyt	3.00
(9)	Terry Kennedy	3.00
(10)	Carmelo Martinez	3.00
(11)	Kevin McReynolds	4.00
(12)	Graig Nettles	4.00
(13)	Eric Show	3.00
(14)	Garry Templeton	4.00
(15)	Player composite	3.00

1998 Washington Senators 1969 Reunion

In conjunction with a card-show reunion of the '69 Nats, this set of cards was issued in uncut sheet form at the reunion breakfast. Featuring original artwork portraits atop cartoon bodies in the style of 1938 Goudey Heads-Up cards, the 2-1/2" x 2-7/8" cards have a reunion logo in an upper-corner. Backs have a team logo, player personal data, 1969 and career stats, and a quote about the player by Washington sports talk radio personality Phil Wood. Cards are listed here alphabetically.

		NM/M
Complete Set, Uncut Sheet:		15.00
Complete Set, Singles (28):		12.00
Common Player:		.25
(1)	Bernie Allen	.25
(2)	Hank Allen	.25
(3)	Frank Bertaina	.25
(4)	Dick Billings	.25
(5)	Dick Bosman	.25
(6)	Ed Brinkman	.25
(7)	Joe Camacho	.25
(8)	Casey Cox	.25
(9)	Tim Cullen	.25
(10)	Mike Epstein	.40
(11)	Jim French	.25
(12)	Jim Hannan	.25
(13)	Dennis Higgins	.25
(14)	Johnny Holliday (Announcer)	.25
(15)	Frank Howard	.50
(16)	Sid Hudson	.25
(17)	Bob Humphreys	.25
(18)	Frank Kreutzer	.25
(19)	Lee Maye	.25
(20)	Ken McMullen	.25
(21)	Ron Menchine (Announcer)	.25
(22)	Ed Stroud	.25
(23)	Wayne Terwilliger	.25
(24)	Del Unser	.25
(25)	Fred Valentine	.25
(26)	Shelby Whitfield (Announcer)	.25
(27)	Ted Williams	6.00
(28)	Checklist	.25

1988 Weis Winners Super Stars Discs

(See 1988 Super Stars Discs for checklist and price guide.)

1985 Wendy's Tigers

This set contains 22 cards measuring 2-1/2" x 3-1/2", which carry both Wendy's Hamburgers and Coca-Cola logos and were produced by Topps. The cards feature a color photo with the player's identification underneath the picture. Backs are identical to 1985 Topps cards except they have different card numbers and are done in a red and black color scheme. Cards were distributed three to a pack along with a "Header"

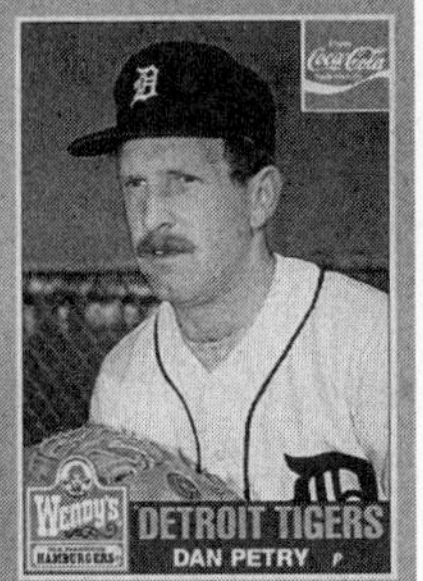

checklist in a cellophane package at selected Wendy's outlets in Michigan only.

		NM/M
Complete Set (22):		5.00
Common Player:		.25
1	Sparky Anderson	.50
2	Doug Bair	.25
3	Juan Berenguer	.25
4	Dave Bergman	.25
5	Tom Brookens	.25
6	Marty Castillo	.25
7	Darrell Evans	.40
8	Barbaro Garbey	.25
9	Kirk Gibson	.65
10	Johnny Grubb	.25
11	Willie Hernandez	.25
12	Larry Herndon	.25
13	Rusty Kuntz	.25
14	Chet Lemon	.25
15	Aurelio Lopez	.25
16	Jack Morris	.35
17	Lance Parrish	.65
18	Dan Petry	.25
19	Bill Scherrer	.25
20	Alan Trammell	1.00
21	Lou Whitaker	.50
22	Milt Wilcox	.25

1994 Wendy's Roberto Clemente Hologram

This single-card set was issued by the restaurant chain in a stated edition of 90,000. The front has a black-bordered hologram picturing Clemente at bat, with the number 3,000 in a box at upper-right. The back has a couple of color photos of the Pirates' star along with biographical data and a career summary.

		NM/M
(1)	Roberto Clemente	6.00

1993 Whataburger Nolan Ryan

Issued in two-card cello packs at Whataburger restaurants, this set honors the career of Nolan Ryan. Cards have action photos set against colorized backgrounds and overlayed with ribbed plastic to create a 3-D effect. A card title is printed in white in the lower-left corner, with the logo of Triad (the card's maker) in the lower-right. In the upper-left corner is a red "Nolan Ryan's Recollections" logo. Backs have color logos of the hamburger chain, Triad, Coca-Cola and Major League Baseball, along with a quote from Ryan about the career highlight and a facsimile autograph. The cards are unnumbered.

		NM/M
Complete Set (10):		6.00
Common Card:		1.00
(1)	Nolan Ryan (1st No-hitter)	1.00
(2)	Nolan Ryan (2nd No-Hitter)	1.00
(3)	Nolan Ryan (3rd No-hitter)	1.00
(4)	Nolan Ryan (4th No-hitter)	1.00
(5)	Nolan Ryan (5th No-hitter)	1.00
(6)	Nolan Ryan (6th No-hitter)	1.00
(7)	Nolan Ryan (7th No-hitter)	1.00
(8)	Nolan Ryan (5,000th Strikeout)	1.00
(9)	Nolan Ryan (300th Win)	1.00
(10)	Nolan Ryan (On horse.)	1.00

1982 Wheaties Indians

These 2-13/16" x 4-1/8" cards were given out ten at a time during three special promotional games; later the complete set was placed on sale at the Indians' gift shop. The cards represented the first time in 30 years that Wheaties had been associated with a baseball card set. Fronts feature color photos surrounded by a wide white border with the player's name and position below the picture. The Indians logo is in the lower-left corner while the Wheaties logo is in the lower-right. Card backs have a Wheaties ad.

		NM/M
Complete Set (30):		7.50
Common Player:		.25
(1)	Chris Bando	.25
(2)	Alan Bannister	.25
(3)	Len Barker	.25
(4)	Bert Blyleven	.75
(5)	Tom Brennan	.25
(6)	Joe Charboneau	1.00
(7)	Rodney Craig	.25
(8)	John Denny	.25
(9)	Miguel Dilone	.25
(10)	Jerry Dybzinski	.25
(11)	Mike Fischlin	.25
(12)	Dave Garcia	.25
(13)	Johnny Goryl	.25
(14)	Mike Hargrove	.50
(15)	Toby Harrah	.50
(16)	Ron Hassey	.25
(17)	Von Hayes	.25
(18)	Dennis Lewallyn	.25
(19)	Rick Manning	.25
(20)	Bake McBride	.25
(21)	Tommy McCraw	.25
(22)	Jack Perconte	.25
(23)	Mel Queen	.25
(24)	Dennis Sommers	.25
(25)	Lary Sorensen	.25
(26)	Dan Spillner	.25
(27)	Rick Sutcliffe	.75
(28)	Andre Thornton	.50
(29)	Rick Waits	.25
(30)	Eddie Whitson	.25

1983 Wheaties Indians

A 32-card set marked the second year of Wheaties involvement with the Indians. Distribution of the 2-13/16" x 4-1/8" cards changed slightly in that the entire set was given away on the day of the special promotional game. As happened in 1982, the set was then placed on sale at the team's gift shop. The set includes 27 players, four coaches and the manager. The format of the cards remained basically the same on the front although the backs of player cards were changed to include complete major and minor league statistics.

		NM/M
Complete Set (32):		5.00
Common Player:		.25
(1)	Bud Anderson	.25
(2)	Jay Baller	.25
(3)	Chris Bando	.25
(4)	Alan Bannister	.25
(5)	Len Barker	.25
(6)	Bert Blyleven	.50
(7)	Wil Culmer	.25
(8)	Miguel Dilone	.25
(9)	Juan Eichelberger	.25
(10)	Jim Essian	.25
(11)	Mike Ferraro	.25
(12)	Mike Fischlin	.25
(13)	Julio Franco	.35
(14)	Ed Glynn	.25
(15)	Johnny Goryl	.25
(16)	Mike Hargrove	.35
(17)	Toby Harrah	.35
(18)	Ron Hassey	.25
(19)	Neal Heaton	.25
(20)	Rick Manning	.25
(21)	Bake McBride	.25
(22)	Don McMahon	.25
(23)	Ed Napoleon	.25
(24)	Broderick Perkins	.25
(25)	Dennis Sommers	.25
(26)	Lary Sorensen	.25
(27)	Dan Spillner	.25
(28)	Rick Sutcliffe	.35
(29)	Andre Thornton	.35
(30)	Manny Trillo	.25
(31)	George Vukovich	.25
(32)	Rick Waits	.25

1984 Wheaties Indians

The 2-13/16" x 4-1/8" cards again were given out at Municipal Stadium as part of a promotion involving Wheaties and the Indians on July 22. The set was down from 32 cards in 1983 to 29. There are 26 players as well as cards for the manager, coaches and team mascot. Design of the cards is virtually identical to prior years. The 1984 set is numbered by uniform number. A total of 15,000 sets were printed and any left over from the promotion were placed on sale in the team's gift shop.

		NM/M
Complete Set (29):		9.00
Common Player:		.50
2	Brett Butler	.75
4	Tony Bernazard	.50
8	Carmelo Castillo	.50
10	Pat Tabler	.50
13	Ernie Camacho	.50
14	Julio Franco	.75
15	Broderick Perkins	.50
16	Jerry Willard	.50
18	Pat Corrales	.50
21	Mike Hargrove	.75
22	Mike Fischlin	.50
23	Chris Bando	.50
24	George Vukovich	.50
26	Brook Jacoby	.50
27	Steve Farr	.50
28	Bert Blyleven	1.00
29	Andre Thornton	.75
30	Joe Carter	1.50
31	Steve Comer	.50
33	Roy Smith	.50
34	Mel Hall	.50
36	Jamie Easterly	.50
37	Don Schulze	.50
38	Luis Aponte	.50
44	Neal Heaton	.50
46	Mike Jeffcoat	.50
54	Tom Waddell	.50
---	Coaching Staff (Bobby Bonds, John Goryl, Don McMahon, Ed Napoleon, Dennis Sommers)	.50
---	Tom-E-Hawk (Mascot)	.50

1997 Wheaties All-Stars

Forty-five years after it last printed baseball cards on its cereal boxes, Wheaties issued a cross-brand set of 30 cards in 1997. Top players are generally grouped by positions in groups of six on the box backs. Boxes also feature three player photos on front and an ad for obtaining a player photoball. The three series of cards found on 18 oz. boxes of Wheaties carry a Topps logo in upper-right corner. The top of the cards' fronts have action photos. A blue box below the photo has the player name and career highlights in white. A green, blue or orange border surrounds the card, which is separated from the rest of the box back by a black dotted line. Backs, printed inside the box, have limited personal data and full major league stats. Perfectly cut cards from these boxes measure about 2-1/2" x 3-13/16". Somewhat smaller at 2-1/16" x 3-3/8", though identical in format, are the cards found on the backs of Honey Frosted Wheaties and Crispy Wheaties 'n Raisins. Cards on the former carry a Pinnacle logo; the latter are marked Upper Deck. Both have orange borders surrounding the cards.

		NM/M
Complete Set, Boxes (5):		12.00
Complete Set, Singles (30):		15.00
Common Player:		.25
All Star Players Complete Box:		3.50
(1)	Ken Griffey Jr.	.75
(2)	Greg Maddux	.65
(3)	Paul Molitor	.50
(4)	Cal Ripken Jr.	1.50
(5)	Frank Thomas	.50
(6)	Mo Vaughn	.25
All Star Players Complete Box:		3.00
(7)	Barry Bonds	1.50
(8)	Ken Caminiti	.25
(9)	Ken Griffey Jr.	.75
(10)	Chipper Jones	.65
(11)	Chuck Knoblauch	.25
(12)	Alex Rodriguez	1.00
All Star Infielders Complete Box:		2.50
(13)	Jeff Bagwell	.50
(14)	Mark McGwire	1.00
(15)	Mike Piazza	.75
(16)	Cal Ripken Jr.	1.50
(17)	Ryne Sandberg	.65
(18)	Frank Thomas	.50
All Star Outfielders Complete Box:		2.50
(19)	Barry Bonds	1.50
(20)	Ellis Burks	.25
(21)	Juan Gonzalez	.35
(22)	Ken Griffey Jr.	.75
(23)	Tony Gwynn	.65
(24)	Bernie Williams	.25
All Star Pitchers Complete Box:		2.00
(25)	Andy Benes	.25
(26)	David Cone	.25
(27)	Greg Maddux	.65
(28)	Mike Mussina	.35
(29)	Hideo Nomo	.35
(30)	John Smoltz	.25

1995 Wienerschnitzel L.A. Dodgers POGs

The Dodger Stadium hot dog concessionaire sponsored this promotion which was given away to youngsters attending a May 13 Dodgers game. The issue consists of 14 POGs die cut from an 8-1/2" x 10-3/4" cardboard sheet. The POGs picture the team's winners of the Rookie of the Year Award from Jackie Robinson in 1947 through Raul Mondesi in 1994. The individual POGs measure 1-5/8" in diameter. Fronts have a sepia or color player portrait at center, with a blue border of lighter blue stars. Backs are printed in red and blue on white and have a bit of player information plus the logos of the team, sponsor and World POG Federation.

		NM/M
Complete Set, Panel:		8.00
Complete Set, Singles (14):		7.00
Common Player:		.25
1	Jackie Robinson	3.00
2	Don Newcombe	.50
3	Joe Black	.50
4	Jim Gilliam	.35
5	Frank Howard	.35
6	Jim Lefebvre	.25
7	Ted Sizemore	.25
8	Rick Sutcliffe	.25
9	Steve Howe	.25
10	Fernando Valenzuela	.35
11	Steve Sax	.25
12	Eric Karros	.25
13	Mike Piazza	2.00
14	Raul Mondesi	.25

1993 Ted Williams Co. Promos

Though they are unmarked as sample cards, the promos issued for the debut Ted Williams Card Co. set are easily distinguished from the regularly issued versions. The #1 Williams card has different front photos and his name in green, rather than orange, and the Paige and Gonzalez cards have text backs in the promo version, rather than checklists.

		NM/M
Complete Set (3):		10.00
Common Player:		2.00
1	Ted Williams	5.00
115	Satchel Paige	3.00
160	Juan Gonzalez	2.00

1993 Ted Williams Card Company

Without a license from the players' union, the premiere issue of the Ted Williams Card Company relied on innovative subsets to create interest in its "old-timers" set. The first 96 cards in the set comprise the base issue. Those cards feature a black-and-white or color action photo set against a background of a second ghost-image photo. The player's name is at bottom with the card company logo conspicuous at top. Backs have some biographical detail, a career summary, the player's five best seasons' and career stats. Subsets numbered contiguously with the base set include a 19-card Negro Leagues series highlighted with green-foil; five cards featuring the All-American Girls Professional Baseball League; a 10-card "Ted's Greatest Hitters" series; 10 "Barrier Breakers" cards featuring Negro Leagues veterans who later played in the majors; a 10-card "Goin' North" subset featuring major league stars of the 1940s-1970s in minor league photos, and, a pair of five-card "Dawning of a Legacy" series featuring Juan Gonzalez and Jeff Bagwell. There were also several insert card series which are listed separately. The cards were packaged with a pair of die-cut player or team logo POGs.

		NM/M
Complete Set (160):		12.00
Common Player:		.05
Wax Pack (12):		.75
Wax Box (36):		20.00
1	Ted Williams	3.00
2	Rick Ferrell	.05
3	Jim Lonborg	.05
4	Mel Parnell	.05
5	Jim Piersall	.05
6	Luis Tiant	.05
7	Carl Yastrzemski	.50
8	Ralph Branca	.05
9	Roy Campanella	.50
10	Ron Cey	.05
11	Tommy Davis	.05
12	Don Drysdale	.35
13	Carl Erskine	.10
14	Steve Garvey	.10
15	Don Newcombe	.10
16	Duke Snider	.50
17	Maury Wills	.05
18	Jim Fregosi	.05
19	Bobby Grich	.05
20	Bill Buckner	.05
21	Billy Herman	.05
22	Ferguson Jenkins	.10
23	Ron Santo	.15
24	Billy Williams	.10
25	Luis Aparicio	.10
26	Luke Appling	.10
27	Minnie Minoso	.15
28	Johnny Bench	.50
29	George Foster	.05
30	Joe Morgan	.15
31	Buddy Bell	.05
32	Lou Boudreau	.10
33	Rocky Colavito	.25
34	Jim "Mudcat" Grant	.05
35	Tris Speaker	.10
36	Ray Boone	.05
37	Darrell Evans	.05
38	Al Kaline	.35
39	George Kell	.10
40	Mickey Lolich	.05
41	Cesar Cedeno	.05
42	Sal Bando	.05
43	Vida Blue	.05
44	Bert Campaneris	.05
45	Ken Holtzman	.05
46	Lew Burdette	.05
47	Bob Horner	.05
48	Warren Spahn	.10
49	Cecil Cooper	.05
50	Tony Oliva	.10
51	Bobby Bonds	.10
52	Alvin Dark	.05
53	Dave Dravecky	.05
54	Monte Irvin	.10
55	Willie Mays	1.00
56	Bud Harrelson	.05
57	Dave Kingman	.05
58	Yogi Berra	.50
59	Don Baylor	.05
60	Jim Bouton	.05
61	Bobby Brown	.05
62	Whitey Ford	.40
63	Lou Gehrig	1.50
64	Charlie Keller	.05
65	Eddie Lopat	.05
66	Johnny Mize	.10
67	Bobby Murcer	.05
68	Graig Nettles	.05
69	Bobby Shantz	.05
70	Richie Ashburn	.10
71	Larry Bowa	.05
72	Steve Carlton	.40
73	Robin Roberts	.10
74	Matty Alou	.05
75	Harvey Haddix	.05
76	Ralph Kiner	.10
77	Bill Madlock	.05
78	Bill Mazeroski	.35
79	Al Oliver	.05
80	Manny Sanguillen	.05
81	Willie Stargell	.10
82	Al Brumbry	.05
83	Davey Johnson	.05
84	Boog Powell	.10
85	Earl Weaver	.10
86	Lou Brock	.10
87	Orlando Cepeda	.10
88	Curt Flood	.05
89	Joe Garagiola	.35
90	Bob Gibson	.10
91	Rogers Hornsby	.20
92	Enos Slaughter	.10
93	Joe Torre	.20
94	Gaylord Perry	.10
95	Checklist 1-49	.05
96	Checklist 50-96	.05
97	Cool Papa Bell	.10
98	Garnett Blair	.05
99	Gene Benson	.05
100	Lyman Bostock, Sr.	.10
101	Marlin Carter	.05
102	Oscar Charleston	.10
103	Ray Dandridge	.10
104	Mahlon Duckett	.05
105	Josh Gibson	.20
106	Cowan Hyde	.05
107	"Judy" Johnson	.10
108	Buck Leonard	.10
109	Pop Lloyd	.10
110	Lester Lockett	.05
111	Max Manning	.05
112	Satchel Paige	.50
113	Armando Vazquez	.05
114	Smokey Joe Williams	.10
115	Negro Leagues Checklist (Satchel Paige)	.05
116	Alice Hohlmeyer	.05
117	Dotty Kamenshek	.05
118	Pepper Davis	.05
119	Marge Wenzell	.05
120	AAGPBA Checklist	.05
121	The Babe (Babe Ruth)	1.50
122	The Iron Horse (Lou Gehrig)	.75
123	Double X (Jimmie Foxx)	.20
124	Rajah (Rogers Hornsby)	.10
125	The Georgia Peach (Ty Cobb)	.75
126	The Say Hey Kid (Willie Mays)	.50
127	Ralph (Ralph Kiner)	.10
128	The Grey Eagle (Tris Speaker)	.10
129	The Big Cat (Johnny Mize)	.10
130	Ted's Greatest Hitters Checklist	.05
131	Satchel Paige	.25
132	Joe Black	.10
133	Roy Campanella	.25
134	Larry Doby	.10
135	Jim Gilliam	.05
136	Monte Irvin	.10
137	Sam Jethroe	.05
138	Willie Mays	.50
139	Don Newcombe	.05
140	Barrier Breakers Checklist	.05
141	Roy Campanella	.25
142	Bob Gibson	.10
143	Boog Powell	.10
144	Willie Mays	.50
145	Johnny Mize	.10
146	Monte Irvin	.10
147	Earl Weaver	.10
148	Ted Williams	1.50
149	Jim Gilliam	.05
150	Goin' North Checklist	.05
151	Juan Gonzalez (Footsteps to Greatness)	.25
151a	Juan Gonzalez (Autographed, edition of 43.)	60.00
152	Juan Gonzalez (Sign 'em Up)	.25
152a	Juan Gonzalez (Autographed, edition of 43.)	60.00
153	Juan Gonzalez (The Road to Success)	.25
153a	Juan Gonzalez (Autographed, edition of 43.)	60.00
154	Juan Gonzalez (Looking Ahead)	.25
154a	Juan Gonzalez (Autographed, edition of 43.)	60.00
155	"Dawning of a Legacy" Checklist	.05
156	Jeff Bagwell (Born with Red Sox Blood)	.50
157	Jeff Bagwell (Movin' Up, Then Out)	.50
158	Jeff Bagwell (Year 1)	.50
159	Jeff Bagwell (Year 2)	.50
160	"Dawning of a Legacy" Checklist (Juan Gonzalez)	.05

Etched in Stone

This 10-card insert set documents the career of Roberto Clemente, using sepia-toned and color photographs on the card front, highlighted by a gold-foil embossed "Tribute '93" logo in the lower-left corner and an "Etched in Stone" logo at upper-right. Backs have a detailed biography. Cards are numbered ES1 through ES10.

		NM/M
Complete Set (10):		12.00
Common Player:		2.00
1	Youth (Roberto Clemente)	2.00
2	Sign Up (Roberto Clemente)	2.00
3	Try-Out (Roberto Clemente)	2.00
4	Playing Mad (Roberto Clemente)	2.00
5	Minor Leagues (Roberto Clemente)	2.00
6	1955-1959 (Roberto Clemente)	2.00
7	1960 (Roberto Clemente)	2.00
8	1963 (Roberto Clemente)	2.00
9	1970 (Roberto Clemente)	2.00
10	Etched in Stone Checklist	2.00

Locklear Collection

The paintings of former major leaguer Gene Locklear are featured in this 10-card insert set. The central image of the player is set against a background of multiple player images in orange, red and purple tones. The player's name is in dark blue on the left edge and a "Gene Locklear Collection" logo is in lower-right. On back is a commentary on the player, a card number with an "LC" suffix and, at bottom center, a serial number. The cards of Ted

Williams can be found in an autographed insert version numbered on back from within an edition of 406.

NM/M
Complete Set (10): 12.00
Common Player: .75
Ted Williams Autographed: 500.00
1 Yogi Berra 1.00
2 Lou Brock .75
3 Willie Mays 2.00
4 Johnny Mize .75
5 Satchel Paige 1.50
6 Babe Ruth 3.00
7 Enos Slaughter .75
8 Carl Yastrzemski 1.00
9 Ted Williams 2.50
10 Locklear Collection Checklist .10

Memories

Four historical World Series of the 1950s-1970s are featured in five-card runs within the "Memories" insert set. Fronts have black-and-white or color player photos. In the lower-left corner is a vintage press camera with "Memories" and the year emanating from the flashbulb. The Ted Williams Card Co. logo is at upper-right. The player's name is in white at bottom-center. Cards are numbered with an "M" prefix on back and feature a headline announcing the team's World Series victory and a summary of the featured player's performance in that Fall Classic.

NM/M
Complete Set (20): 45.00
Common Player: 1.00
1955 BROOKLYN DODGERS
1 Roy Campanella 3.50
2 Jim Gilliam 2.00
3 Gil Hodges 3.50
4 Duke Snider 3.50
5 1955 Dodgers Checklist .60
1963 L.A. DODGERS
6 Don Drysdale 3.50
7 Tommy Davis 2.25
8 Johnny Podres 2.25
9 Maury Wills 3.50
10 1963 Dodgers Checklist .60
1971 PITTSBURGH PIRATES
11 Roberto Clemente 9.00
12 Al Oliver 1.00
13 Manny Sanguillen 1.00
14 Willie Stargell 2.00
15 1971 Pirates Checklist .60
1975 CINCINNATI REDS
16 Johnny Bench 4.50
17 George Foster 1.25
18 Joe Morgan 3.00
19 Tony Perez 2.00
20 1975 Red Checklist .60

POGs

These 26 cards featuring two die-cut POGs on each were issued as inserts in 1993 Ted Williams packs. Fronts of the extra-thick cardboard cards have a black background with the logos of the card company and the Cooperstown Collection. Two 1-5/8" diameter POGs appear on each card, picturing either players or team logos. Backs are blank. The unnumbered POG cards are listed here alphabetically, with player POGs listed first.

NM/M
Complete Set (26): 4.00
Common Player: .25
(1) Yogi Berra, Roy Campanella 1.00
(2) Brooklyn Dodgers (Roy Campanella) .50
(3) Tommy Davis, George Foster .25
(4) Lou Gehrig, Ted Williams 2.00
(5) New York Yankees (Lou Gehrig) 1.50
(6) Ted Williams, #9 patch .75
(7) 1993 World Series patch .25
(8) Baltimore Elite Giants .25
(9) New York Mets .25
(10) New York Cuban Stars .25
(11) Minnesota Twins .25
(12) St. Louis Browns .25
(13) Detroit Tigers .25
(14) Kansas City Royals .25
(15) Detroit Stars .25
(16) Kansas City Athletics .25
(17) Florida Marlins .25
(18) New York Black Yankees .25
(19) New York Yankees .25
(20) New York Harlem Stars .25
(21) Philadelphia Stars .25
(22) New York Giants .25
(23) San Diego Padres .25
(24) Negro Leagues Classic Teams .25
(25) #21 (Clemente) patch .25
(26) St. Louis Cardinals .25

Brooks Robinson

This 10-card insert set, numbered BR1 through BR10, traces the baseball career of Hall of Fame Orioles third baseman Brooks Robinson. Card fronts feature sepia-toned or color photos highlighted by the player's name in gold foil down the left side and a "Brooks Robinson Collection" diamond logo at lower-right. Backs include a career summary or batting or fielding stats. Autographed versions were a random retail packaging insert.

NM/M
Complete Set (10): 7.50
Common Player: 1.00
Autographed: 20.00
1BR Salad Days (Brooks Robinson) 1.00
2BR Career Batting Stats (Brooks Robinson) 1.00
3BR '66 World Series (Brooks Robinson) 1.00
4BR Career Fielding Stats (Brooks Robinson) 1.00
5BR '70 Series #2 (Brooks Robinson) 1.00
6BR '70 Series #1 (Brooks Robinson) 1.00
7BR Comin' Up (Brooks Robinson) 1.00
8BR All Star Games (Brooks Robinson) 1.00
9BR 1964 (Brooks Robinson) 1.00
10BR Brooks Robinson Collection Checklist 1.00

1994 Ted Williams Card Company

Lack of a players' association license again limited the company to using two major leaguers in its second annual card set, but it spiced up its 1994 edition with hot prospects in the minor leagues, more high-tech production values and innovative subsets and chase cards. The base set for 1994 includes 162 cards. The first 92 feature retired or deceased players. Those cards feature a color or colorized photo set against a background of a second ghost-image photo or the actual photo background. Vertically at right is a stone image on which the player's name is printed in extremely difficult to read gold letters. The edge of the stone and the card company logo are embossed. Backs have biographical and career details, and stats for the player's five top seasons. Subsets numbered consecutively with the base cards include a seven-card "Women of Baseball" series; 18 Negro Leaguers, 18 current minor leaguers in a series titled "The Campaign;" 10 "Goin' North" cards of former superstars as minor leaguers; nine "Swingin' for the Fences" cards of home run hitters, and, a nine-card "Dawning of a Legacy" series featuring Cliff Floyd and Tim Salmon. The several insert card series are listed separately. Autographed cards of Leon Day were random pack inserts.

NM/M
Complete Set (162): 15.00
Common Player: .10
Wax Pack (12): 1.00
Wax Box (36): 30.00
Jumbo Pack(20): 2.00
Jumbo Box (24): 35.00
1 Ted Williams 4.00
P1 Ted Williams (Promo card.) 2.50
2 Bernie Carbo .10
3 Bobby Doerr .10
4 Fred Lynn .10
5 Johnny Pesky .10
6 Rico Petrocelli .10
7 Cy Young .25
8 Paul Blair .10
9 Andy Etchebarren .10
10 Brooks Robinson .20
11 Gil Hodges .20
12 Tommy John .15
13 Rick Monday .10
14 Dean Chance .10
15 Doug DeCinces .10
16 Gabby Hartnett .10
17 Don Kessinger .10
18 Bruce Sutter .20
19 Eddie Collins .10
20 Nellie Fox .20
21 Carlos May .10
22 Ted Kluszewski .25
23 Vada Pinson .10
24 Johnny Vander Meer .10
25 Bob Feller .20
26 Mike Garcia .10
27 Sam McDowell .10
28 Al Rosen .10
29 Norm Cash .15
30 Ty Cobb 1.50
31 Mark Fidrych .20
32 Hank Greenberg .25
33 Denny McLain .10
34 Virgil Trucks .10
35 Enos Cabell .10
36 Mike Scott .10
37 Bob Watson .10
38 Amos Otis .10
39 Frank White .10
40 Joe Adcock .10
41 Rico Carty .10
42 Ralph Garr .10
43 Eddie Mathews .20
44 Ben Oglivie .10
45 Gorman Thomas .10
46 Earl Battey .10
47 Rod Carew .20
48 Jim Kaat .10
49 Harmon Killebrew .20
50 Gary Carter .25
51 Steve Rogers .10
52 Rusty Staub .10
53 Sal Maglie .10
54 Juan Marichal .20
55 Mel Ott .10
56 Bobby Thomson .10
57 Tommie Agee .10
58 Tug McGraw .10
59 Elston Howard .15
60 Sparky Lyle .10
61 Billy Martin .15
62 Thurman Munson .25
63 Bobby Richardson .15
64 Bill Skowron .15
65 Mickey Cochrane .10
66 Rollie Fingers .10
67 Lefty Grove .10
68 Catfish Hunter .10
69 Connie Mack .10
70 Al Simmons .10
71 Dick Allen .15
72 Bob Boone .10
73 Del Ennis .10
74 Chuck Klein .10
75 Mike Schmidt .50
76 Dock Ellis .10
77 Elroy Face .10
78 Phil Garner .10
79 Bill Mazeroski .20
80 Pie Traynor .10
81 Honus Wagner .25
82 Dizzy Dean .25
83 Red Schoendienst .10
84 Randy Jones .10
85 Nate Colbert .10
86 Jeff Burroughs .10
87 Jim Sundberg .10
88 Frank Howard .10
89 Walter Johnson .20
90 Eddie Yost .10
91 Checklist 1-46 .10
92 Checklist 47-92 .10
93 Faye Dancer .10
94 Snookie Doyle .10
95 Maddy English .10
96 Nickie Fox .10
97 Sophie Kurys .10
98 Alma Ziegler .10
99 Women of Baseball Checklist .10
100 Newton Allen .10
101 Willard Brown .10
102 Larry Brown .10
103 Leon Day .10
103a Leon Day/Auto. 20.00
104 John Donaldson .10
105 Rube Foster .10
106 Bud Fowler .10
107 Vic Harris .10
108 Webster McDonald .10
109 John "Buck" O'Neil .10
110 Ted "Double Duty" Radcliffe .10
111 Wilber "Bullet" Rogan .10
112 Toni Stone .10
113 Jim Taylor .10
114 Moses "Fleetwood" Walker .15
115 George Wilson .10
116 Judson Wilson .10
117 Negro Leagues Checklist .10
118 Howard Battle .10
119 John Burke .10
120 Brian Dubose .10
121 Alex Gonzalez .15
122 Jose Herrera .10
123 Jason Giambi 1.00
124 Derek Jeter 4.50
125 Charles Johnson .25
126 Daron Kirkreit .10
127 Jason Moler .10
128 Vince Moore .10
129 Chad Mottola .10
130 Jose Silva .10
131 Makato Suzuki (Makoto) .10
132 Brien Taylor .10
133 Michael Tucker .10
134 Billy Wagner .25
135 The Campaign Checklist .10
136 Gary Carter .10
137 Tony Conigliaro .10
138 Sparky Lyle .10
139 Roger Maris .45
140 Vada Pinson .10
141 Mike Schmidt .50
142 Frank White .10
143 Ted Williams 2.50
144 Goin' North Checklist .10
145 Joe Adcock .10
146 Rocky Colavito .25
147 Lou Gehrig 2.00
148 Gil Hodges .25
149 Bob Horner .10
150 Willie Mays 1.50
151 Mike Schmidt .50
152 Pat Seery .10
153 Swingin' for the Fences Checklist .10
154 Cliff Floyd (The Honors Begin) .15
155 Cliff Floyd (The Top Polecat) .15
156 Cliff Floyd (Minor League Team of the Year) .15
157 Cliff Floyd (Major League Debut) .15
158 Tim Salmon (Award Winner) .15
159 Tim Salmon (Early Professional Career) .15
160 Tim Salmon (An MVP Season) .15
161 Tim Salmon (Rookie of the Year) .15
162 Dawning of a Legacy Checklist .10

Etched in Stone

A metallized effect highlights the front design of this insert series commemorating the career of Roger Maris. Color (or colorized) photos appear to have been revealed by chiseling away a rock face which forms much of the front border. Backs have career write-ups overprinted on a design which forms a large "Etched in Stone" design when the cards are laid together in order. Cards have an "ES" prefix to the card number. Cards can be found with either brown or red "rock" borders. The red version is valued at double the brown.

NM/M
Complete Set (9): 7.50
Common Player: 1.00
1 Roger Maris (Scouting Report) 1.00
2 Roger Maris (Traded) 1.00
3 Roger Maris (Career Year) 1.00
4 Roger Maris (1961) 1.00
5 Roger Maris (Silent Accomplishments) 1.00
6 Roger Maris (Team Player) 1.00
7 Roger Maris (Reborn) 1.00
8 Roger Maris (Hero's Welcome) 1.00
9 Checklist (Roger Maris) .20

Dan Gardiner

Sports artist Dan Gardiner was commissioned to produce a series of nine insert cards depicting hot minor league prospects for this insert set. Players are depicted in posed portraits on front and in action paintings on the back. Cards carry a "DG" prefix to the card number and each card is serially numbered in the upper-left corner.

NM/M
Complete Set (9): 6.00
Common Player: .25
1 Michael Jordan 2.50
2 Michael Tucker .25
3 Derek Jeter 3.50
4 Charles Johnson .25
5 Howard Battle .25
6 Quilvio Vergas (Veras) .25
7 Brian Hunter .25
8 Brien Taylor .25
9 Checklist .05

Locklear Collection

Paintings of eight Hall of Famers plus a checklist are featured in this insert set. The art is the work of former major leaguer Gene Locklear. The cards are numbered with an "LC" suffix.

NM/M
Complete Set (9): 7.50
Common Player: 1.00
11 Ty Cobb 2.00
12 Bob Feller 1.00
13 Lou Gehrig 2.00
14 Josh Gibson 1.00
15 Walter Johnson 1.00
16 Casey Stengel 1.00
17 Honus Wagner 1.00
18 Cy Young 1.00
19 Checklist .05

LP Cards

Two premium insert cards in the 1994 Ted Williams Co. set carry an "LP" card number prefix. One depicts basketball superstar Larry Bird playing baseball during his college days at Indiana State University. The other card depicts Ted Williams speaking at the opening of the

Ted Williams Museum. Fronts use a metallized technology. Backs describe the action. A few genuinely autographed Bird cards are known, featuring an embossed seal of authenticity.

		NM/M
Complete Set (2):		8.00
1	Larry Bird	5.00
1a	Larry Bird/Auto.	200.00
2	Ted Williams	5.00

Memories

Continuing the card numbers from the 1993 Memories insert set, the 1994 version features highlights of the 1954, 1961, 1968 and 1975 World Series. Card fronts feature metallized images in a snapshot format. The year is noted in large pink numbers at lower-left. Backs describe each player's participation in that particular World Series and are numbered with an "M" prefix.

		NM/M
Complete Set (20):		11.00
Common Player:		.50
21	Monte Irvin	.50
22	Sal Maglie	.50
23	Dusty Rhodes	.50
24	Hank Thompson	.50
25	Yogi Berra	1.25
26	Elston Howard	.75
27	Roger Maris	1.50
28	Bobby Richardson	.75
29	Norm Cash	.75
30	Al Kaline	1.00
31	Mickey Lolich	.50
32	Denny McLain	.50
33	Bernie Carbo	.50
34	Fred Lynn	.50
35	Rico Petrocelli	.50
36	Luis Tiant	.50
37	Checklist	.05

Mike Schmidt Collection

This nine-card insert set honors the career of Hall of Fame Phillies third baseman Mike Schmidt. Fronts feature full-bleed metallized color photos. Backs have a Phillies flag design with a career biography. Cards are numbered with an "MS" prefix.

		NM/M
Complete Set (9):		7.50
Common Player:		1.00
1	Mike Schmidt (Mike)	1.00
2	Mike Schmidt (The White House)	1.00
3	Mike Schmidt (Soaping Up)	1.00
4	Mike Schmidt (The Promised Land)	1.00
5	Mike Schmidt (Who's Who)	1.00
6	Mike Schmidt (The Call)	1.00
7	Mike Schmidt (Leading the Way)	1.00
8	Mike Schmidt (Award Winner)	1.00
9	Checklist	.35

The 500 Club

Major leaguers with 500 or more career home runs are featured in this nine-card insert set. Fronts have full-bleed metallized photos, some in color and some which have been colorized. A logo picturing a hanging "The 500 Club" sign appears at lower-left, with the player's name in gold. Backs have a basic design that looks for all the world like a toilet seat, in which the player's home run prowess is recalled. Cards are numbered with a "5C" prefix. Two versions of each card exist, one has brown graphic highlights on front, one has red. The red highlighted cards are worth about 25 percent more than the brown.

		NM/M
Complete Set (9):		7.50
Common Player:		.75
1	Hank Aaron	1.50
2	Reggie Jackson	1.25
3	Harmon Killebrew	.75
4	Mickey Mantle	2.25
5	Jimmie Foxx	.75
6	Babe Ruth	2.00
7	Mike Schmidt	1.25
8	Ted Williams	1.50
9	Checklist	.05

Trade for Babe

This nine-card set was available to persons who found a randomly packaged "Trade for Babe" redemption card in packs of Ted Williams Co. cards. A $4.50 postage/handling fee was necessary for redemption and a reported 9,999 trade sets were available. Card fronts feature colorized photos of Ruth while backs have text concerning the front theme. Cards are numbered with a "TB" prefix.

		NM/M
Complete Set (9):		15.00
Common Player:		2.00
----	Babe Ruth (Redemption card, expired Nov. 30, 1994.)	2.00
1	Babe Ruth (George Herman Ruth)	2.00
2	Babe Ruth (King of the Hill)	2.00
3	Babe Ruth (On to New York)	2.00
4	Babe Ruth (Called Shot?)	2.00
5	Babe Ruth (The Bambino and the Iron Horse)	2.00
6	Babe Ruth (Larger Than Life)	2.00
7	Babe Ruth (Always a Yankee)	2.00
8	Babe Ruth (The Babe)	2.00
9	Babe Ruth (Checklist)	2.00

1990 Windwalker Discs

The origins of this disc set, even its name, are not recorded. The set is comprised on nine dual-headed 3-7/8" discs. Each disc features two players from the 1990 American League All-Star team. No similar issue is known for the National League. Each side has a color action photo and a facsimile autograph. The unnumbered discs are checklisted here alphabetically.

		NM/M
Complete Set (9):		15.00
Common Disc:		.70
(1)	Sandy Alomar Jr., Dave Parker	.75
(2)	George Bell, Julio Franco	.75
(3)	Wade Boggs, Kirby Puckett	3.00
(4)	Jose Canseco, Rickey Henderson	2.50
(5)	Roger Clemens, Bob Welch	3.50
(6)	Cecil Fielder, Bret Saberhagen	.75
(7)	Chuck Finley, Kelly Gruber	.75
(8)	Ken Griffey Jr., Steve Sax	4.00
(9)	Ozzie Guillen, Cal Ripken Jr.	5.00

1991 Wiz Mets

This 450-card issue was one of several sponsored by the East Coast WIZ home entertainment stores in the early 1990s. Virtually every player in Mets history is included in the set. Each of three series of 15-card perforated sheets was co-sponsored by a large electronics manufacturer: AT&T, Fisher or Maxell. Sheets measure 10" x 9", with individual cards measuring 2" x 3". Card fronts have a black-and-white photo at center with the player's name at left and position at right. A color Mets logo is above and a WIZ logo below. Blue corner decorations complete the front design. Backs are printed in black-and-white, have Mets and sponsors' logos, years the player appeared with the Mets and his Mets career stats. Single cards from this set are seldom available.

		NM/M
Complete Set (450):		45.00
Common Player:		.10
1	Don Aase	.10
2	Tommie Agee	.30
3	Rick Aguilera	.20
4	Jack Aker	.10
5	Neil Allen	.10
6	Bill Almon	.10
7	Sandy Alomar	.10
8	Jesus Alou	.10
9	George Altman	.10
10	Luis Alvarado	.10
11	Craig Anderson	.10
12	Rick Anderson	.10
13	Bob Apodaca	.10
14	Gerry Arrigo	.10
15	Richie Ashburn	6.00
16	Tucker Ashford	.10
17	Bob Aspromonte	.10
18	Benny Ayala	.10
19	Wally Backman	.10
20	Kevin Baez	.10
21	Bob Bailor	.10
22	Rick Baldwin	.10
23	Billy Baldwin	.10
24	Lute Barnes	.10
25	Ed Bauta	.10
26	Billy Beane	.10
27	Larry Bearnarth	.10
28	Blaine Beatty	.10
29	Jim Beauchamp	.10
30	Gus Bell	.30
31	Dennis Bennett	.10
32	Butch Benton	.10
33	Juan Berenguer	.10
34	Bruce Berenyi	.10
35	Dwight Bernard	.10
36	Yogi Berra	6.00
37	Jim Bethke	.10
38	Mike Bishop	.10
39	Terry Blocker	.10
40	Bruce Bochy	.10
41	Bruce Boisclair	.10
42	Dan Boitano	.10
43	Mark Bomback	.10
44	Don Bosch	.10
45	Daryl Boston	.10
46	Ken Boswell	.10
47	Ed Bouchee	.10
48	Larry Bowa	.20
49	Ken Boyer	.50
50	Mark Bradley	.10
51	Eddie Bressoud	.10
52	Hubie Brooks	.30
53	Kevin Brown	.10
54	Leon Brown	.10
55	Mike Bruhert	.10
56	Jerry Buchek	.10
57	Larry Burright	.10
58	Ray Burris	.10
59	John Candelaria	.10
60	Chris Cannizzarro	.10
61	Buzz Capra	.10
62	Jose Cardenal	.10
63	Don Cardwell	.10
64	Duke Carmel	.10
65	Chuck Carr	.10
66	Mark Carreon	.10
67	Gary Carter	4.00
68	Elio Chacon	.10
69	Dean Chance	.10
70	Kelvin Chapman	.10
71	Ed Charles	.40
72	Rich Chiles	.10
73	Harry Chiti	.10
74	John Christensen	.10
75	Joe Christopher	.10
76	Galen Cisco	.10
77	Donn Clendenon	.40
78	Gene Clines	.10
79	Choo Choo Coleman	.40
80	Kevin Collins	.10
81	David Cone	.75
82	Bill Connors	.10
83	Cliff Cook	.10
84	Tim Corcoran	.10
85	Mardie Cornejo	.10
86	Billy Cowan	.10
87	Roger Craig	.10
88	Jerry Cram	.10
89	Mike Cubbage	.10
90	Ron Darling	.20
91	Ray Daviault	.10
92	Tommie Davis	.10
93	John DeMerit	.10
94	Bill Denehy	.10
95	Jack DiLauro	.10
96	Carlos Diaz	.10
97	Mario Diaz	.10
98	Steve Dillon	.10
99	Sammy Drake	.10
100	Jim Dwyer	.10
101	Duffy Dyer	.10
102	Len Dykstra	.50
103	Tom Edens	.10
104	Dave Eilers	.10
105	Larry Elliot	.10
106	Dock Ellis	.10
107	Kevin Elster	.20
108	Nino Espinosa	.10
109	Chuck Estrada	.10
110	Francisco Estrada	.10
111	Pete Falcone	.10
112	Sid Fernandez	.20
113	Chico Fernandez	.10
114	Sergio Ferrer	.10
115	Jack Fisher	.10
116	Mike Fitzgerald	.10
117	Shaun Fitzmaurice	.10
118	Gil Flores	.10
119	Doug Flynn	.10
120	Tim Foli	.10
121	Rich Folkers	.10
122	Larry Foss	.10
123	George Foster	.30
124	Leo Foster	.10
125	Joe Foy	.10
126	John Franco	.30
127	Jim Fregosi	.20
128	Bob Friend	.10
129	Danny Frisella	.10
130	Brent Gaff	.10
131	Bob Gallagher	.10
132	Ron Gardenhire	.10
133	Rob Gardner	.10
134	Wes Gardner	.10
135	Wayne Garrett	.10
136	Rod Gaspar	.10
137	Gary Gentry	.10
138	Jim Gibbons	.10
139	Bob Gibson	.10
140	Brian Giles	.10
141	Joe Ginsberg	.10
142	Ed Glynn	.10
143	Jesse Gonder	.30
144	Dwight Gooden	1.00
145	Greg Goossen	.10
146	Tom Gorman	.10
147	Jim Gosger	.10
148	Bill Graham	.10
149	Wayne Graham	.10
150	Dallas Green	.30
151	Pumpsie Green	.10
152	Tom Grieve	.10
153	Jerry Grote	.20
154	Joe Grzenda	.10
155	Don Hahn	.10
156	Tom Hall	.10
157	Jack Hamilton	.10
158	Ike Hampton	.10
159	Tim Harkness	.10
160	Bud Harrelson	.40
161	Greg Harris	.10
162	Greg Harts	.10
163	Andy Hassler	.10
164	Tom Hausman	.10
165	Ed Hearn	.10
166	Richie Hebner	.30
167	Danny Heep	.10
168	Jack Heidemann	.10
169	Bob Heise	.10
170	Ken Henderson	.10
171	Steve Henderson	.10
172	Bob Hendley	.10
173	Phil Hennigan	.10
174	Bill Hepler	.10
175	Ron Herbel	.10
176	Manny Hernandez	.10
177	Keith Hernandez	.50
178	Tommy Herr	.10
179	Rick Herrscher	.10
180	Jim Hickman	.10
181	Joe Hicks	.10
182	Chuck Hiller	.10
183	Dave Hillman	.10
184	Jerry Hinsley	.10
185	Gil Hodges	2.00
186	Ron Hodges	.10
187	Scott Holman	.10
188	Jay Hook	.10
189	Mike Howard	.10
190	Jesse Hudson	.10
191	Keith Hughes	.10
192	Todd Hundley	.30
193	Ron Hunt	.10
194	Willard Hunter	.10
195	Clint Hurdle	.10
196	Jeff Innis	.10
197	Al Jackson	.10
198	Roy Lee Jackson	.10
199	Gregg Jefferies	1.00
200	Stan Jefferson	.10
201	Chris Jelic	.10
202	Bob Johnson	.10
203	Howard Johnson	.75
204	Bob W. Johnson	.10
205	Randy Jones	.10
206	Sherman Jones	.10
207	Cleon Jones	.30
208	Ross Jones	.10
209	Mike Jorgensen	.10
210	Rod Kanehl	.10
211	Dave Kingman	.50
212	Bobby Klaus	.10
213	Jay Kleven	.10
214	Lou Klimchock	.10
215	Ray Knight	.30
216	Kevin Kobel	.10
217	Gary Kolb	.10
218	Cal Koonce	.10
219	Jerry Koosman	.30
220	Ed Kranepool	.30
221	Gary Kroll	.10
222	Clem Labine	.30
223	Jack Lamabe	.10
224	Hobie Landrith	.10
225	Frank Lary	.10
226	Bill Latham	.10
227	Terry Leach	.10
228	Tim Leary	.10
229	John Lewis	.10
230	David Liddell	.10
231	Phil Linz	.10
232	Ron Locke	.10
233	Skip Lockwood	.10
234	Mickey Lolich	.30
235	Phil Lombardi	.10
236	Al Luplow	.10
237	Ed Lynch	.10
238	Barry Lyons	.10
239	Ken MacKenzie	.10
240	Julio Machado	.10
241	Elliot Maddox	.10
243	Dave Magadan	.10
244	Phil Mankowski	.10
245	Felix Mantilla	.10
246	Mike Marshall	.10
247	Dave Marshall	.10
248	Jim Marshall	.10
249	Mike A. Marshall	.10
250	J.C. Martin	.10
251	Jerry Martin	.10
252	Teddy Martinez	.10
253	Jon Matlack	.20
254	Jerry May	.10
255	Willie Mays	15.00
256	Lee Mazzilli	.20
257	Jim McAndrew	.10
258	Bob McClure	.10
259	Roger McDowell	.30
260	Tug McGraw	.40
261	Jeff McKnight	.10
262	Roy McMillan	.10
263	Kevin McReynolds	.30
264	George Medich	.20
265	Orlando Mercado	.10
266	Butch Metzger	.10
267	Felix Millan	.10
268	Bob G. Miller	.10
269	Bob L. Miller	.10
270	Dyar Miller	.10
271	Larry Miller	.10
272	Keith Miller	.10
273	Randy Milligan	.10
274	John Milner	.10
275	John Mitchell	.10
276	Kevin Mitchell	.30
277	Wilmer Mizell	.10
278	Herb Moford	.10
279	Willie Montanez	.10
280	Joe Moock	.10
281	Tommy Moore	.10
282	Bob Moorhead	.10
283	Jerry Morales	.10
284	Al Moran	.10
285	Jose Moreno	.10
286	Bill Murphy	.10
287	Dale Murray	.10
288	Dennis Musgraves	.10
289	Jeff Musselman	.10
290	Randy Myers	.30
291	Bob Myrick	.10
292	Danny Napoleon	.10
293	Charlie Neal	.10
294	Randy Niemann	.10
295	Joe Nolan	.10
296	Dan Norman	.10
297	Ed Nunez	.10
298	Charlie O'Brien	.10
299	Tom O'Malley	.10
300	Bob Ojeda	.30
301	Jose Oquendo	.10
302	Jesse Orosco	.10
303	Junior Ortiz	.10
304	Brian Ostrosser	.10
305	Amos Otis	.30
306	Rick Ownbey	.10
307	John Pacella	.10
308	Tom Paciorek	.10
309	Harry Parker	.10
310	Tom Parsons	.10
311	Al Pedrique	.10
312	Brock Pemberton	.10
313	Alejandro Pena	.10
314	Bobby Pfeil	.10
315	Mike Phillips	.10
316	Jim Piersall	.30
317	Joe Pignatano	.10
318	Grover Powell	.10
319	Rich Puig	.10
320	Charlie Puleo	.10
321	Gary Rajsich	.10
322	Mario Ramirez	.10
323	Lenny Randle	.10
324	Bob Rauch	.10
325	Jeff Reardon	.30
326	Darren Reed	.10
327	Hal Reniff	.10
328	Ronn Reynolds	.10
329	Tom Reynolds	.10
330	Dennis Ribant	.10
331	Gordie Richardson	.10
332	Dave Roberts	.10
333	Les Rohr	.10
334	Luis Rosado	.10
335	Don Rose	.10
336	Don Rowe	.10
337	Dick Rusteck	.10
338	Nolan Ryan	15.00
339	Ray Sadecki	.10
340	Joe Sambito	.10
341	Amado Samuel	.10
342	Juan Samuel	.10
343	Ken Sanders	.10
344	Rafael Santana	.10
345	Mackey Sasser	.10
346	Mac Scarce	.10
347	Jim Schaffer	.10

348 Dan Schatzeder .10
349 Calvin Schiraldi .10
350 Al Schmelz .10
351 Dave Schneck .10
352 Ted Schreiber .10
353 Don Schulze .10
354 Mike Scott .30
355 Ray Searage .10
356 Tom Seaver 10.00
357 Dick Selma .10
358 Art Shamsky .30
359 Bob Shaw .10
360 Don Shaw .10
361 Norm Sherry .10
362 Craig Shipley .10
363 Bart Shirley .10
364 Bill Short .10
365 Paul Siebert .10
366 Ken Singleton .30
367 Doug Sisk .10
368 Bobby Gene Smith .10
369 Charley Smith .10
370 Dick Smith .10
371 Duke Snider 10.00
372 Warren Spahn 4.00
373 Larry Stahl .10
374 Roy Staiger .10
375 Tracy Stallard .10
376 Leroy Stanton .10
377 Rusty Staub 1.00
378 John Stearns .10
379 John Stephenson .10
380 Randy Sterling .10
381 George Stone .10
382 Darryl Strawberry 1.00
383 John Strohmayer .10
384 Brent Strom .10
385 Dick Stuart .30
386 Tom Sturdivant .10
387 Bill Sudakis .10
388 John Sullivan .10
389 Darrell Sutherland .10
390 Ron Swoboda .30
391 Craig Swan .10
392 Rick Sweet .10
393 Pat Tabler .10
394 Kevin Tapani .10
395 Randy Tate .10
396 Frank Taveras .10
397 Chuck Taylor .10
398 Ron Taylor .10
399 Bob Taylor .10
400 Sammy Taylor .10
401 Walt Terrell .10
402 Ralph Terry .10
403 Tim Teufel .30
404 George Theodore .10
405 Frank Thomas .20
406 Lou Thornton .10
407 Marv Throneberry .50
408 Dick Tidrow .10
409 Rusty Tillman .10
410 Jackson Todd .10
411 Joe Torre 1.50
412 Mike Torrez .10
413 Kelvin Torve .10
414 Alex Trevino .10
415 Wayne Twitchell .10
416 Del Unser .10
417 Mike Vail .10
418 Bobby Valentine .40
419 Ellis Valentine .10
420 Julio Valera .10
421 Tom Veryzer .10
422 Frank Viola .30
423 Bill Wakefield .10
424 Gene Walter .10
425 Claudell Washington .10
426 Hank Webb .10
427 Al Weis .20
428 Dave West .10
429 Wally Whitehurst .10
430 Carl Willey .10
431 Nick Willhite .10
432 Charlie Williams .10
433 Mookie Wilson .60
434 Herm Winningham .10
435 Gene Woodling .30
436 Billy Wynne .10
437 Joel Youngblood .10
438 Pat Zachry .10
439 Don Zimmer .30
(440) Checklist 1-40 .10
(441) Checklist 41-80 .10
(442) Checklist 81-120 .10
(443) Checklist 121-160 .10
(444) Checklist 161-200 .10
(445) Checklist 201-240 .10
(446) Checklist 241-280 .10
(447) Checklist 281-320 .10
(448) Checklist 321-360 .10
(449) Checklist 361-400 .10
(450) Checklist 401-439 .10

1991 Wiz Yankees of the '50's

Yankees players from the 1950s dynasty are featured in this set distributed in several series at various promotional games. The cards were produced in a perforated sheet format, the 2" x 3" individual cards can be separated with ease. Fronts feature blue-and-white duo-tone photos with the familiar Yankee Stadium facade in blue at top and the player name in black below. Backs are printed in blue on white. The series name is printed beneath the top name bar, along with a line indicating the player's years with the Yankees and a few career stats. At bottom of all cards are Wiz Home Entertainment Centers and AT&T logos, along with a Yankees Classics logo. The unnumbered cards are checklisted here alphabetically.

NM/M
Complete Set, Panels (9): 20.00
Complete Set, Singles (125): 20.00
Common Player: .25
(1) Loren Babe .25
(2) Hank Bauer .40
(3) Zeke Bella .25
(4) Lou Berberet .25
(5) Yogi Berra 2.00
(6) Ewell Blackwell .35
(7) Johnny Blanchard .35
(8) Gary Blaylock .25
(9) Don Bollweg .25
(10) Clete Boyer .35
(11) Ralph Branca .25
(12) Fritzie Brickell .25
(13) Jim Brideweser .25
(14) Jim Bronstad .50
(15) Bobby Brown .35
(16) Lew Burdette .35
(17) Harry Byrd .25
(18) Tommy Byrne .25
(19) Andy Carey .25
(20) Tommy Carroll .25
(21) Bob Cerv .35
(22) Al Cicotte .25
(23) Jim Coates .25
(24) Jerry Coleman .25
(25) Rip Coleman .25
(26) Joe Collins .25
(27) Clint Courtney .25
(28) Bobby Del Greco .25
(29) Jim Delsing .25
(30) Murry Dickson .25
(31) Joe DiMaggio 6.00
(32) Art Ditmar .25
(33) Sonny Dixon .25
(34) Ryne Duren .35
(35) Tom Ferrick .25
(36) Whitey Ford 2.00
(37) Mark Freeman .25
(38) Tom Gorman .25
(39) Ted Gray .25
(40) Eli Grba .25
(41) Bob Grim .25
(42) Woodie Held .25
(43) Tommy Henrich .35
(44) Johnny Hopp .25
(45) Ralph Houk .35
(46) Elston Howard .50
(47) Ken Hunt .25
(48) Billy Hunter .25
(49) Johnny James .25
(50) Jackie Jensen .45
(51) Billy Johnson .25
(52) Darrell Johnson .25
(53) Charlie Keller .35
(54) Jim Konstanty .25
(55) Steve Kraly .25
(56) Jack Kramer .25
(57) Tony Kubek .50
(58) Johnny Kucks .25
(59) Bob Kuzava .25
(60) Don Larsen 1.00
(61) Frank Leja .25
(62) Johnny Lindell .25
(63) Ed Lopat .40
(64) Hector Lopez .25
(65) Jerry Lumpe .25
(66) Duke Maas .25
(67) Dave Madison .25
(68) Sal Maglie .35
(69) Mickey Mantle 12.00
(70) Cliff Mapes .25
(71) Billy Martin 1.50
(72) Mickey McDermott .25
(73) Jim McDonald .25
(74) Gil McDougald .45
(75) Bill Miller .25
(76) Willie Miranda .25
(77) Johnny Mize .75
(78) Zack Monroe .25
(79) Tom Morgan .25
(80) Bob Muncrief .25
(81) Ernie Nevel .50
(82) Irv Noren .25
(83) Joe Ostrowski .25
(84) Stubby Overmire .25
(85) Joe Page .25
(86) Duane Pillette .25
(87) Jim Pisoni .25
(88) Bob Porterfield .25
(89) Vic Raschi .50
(90) Bill Renna .25
(91) Allie Reynolds .50
(92) Bobby Richardson .75
(93) Phil Rizzuto 2.00
(94) Eddie Robinson .25
(95) Johnny Sain .50
(96) Fred Sanford .25
(97) Ray Scarborough .25
(98) Harry Schaeffer .25
(99) Art Schallok (Schallock) .50
(100) Johnny Schmitz .25
(101) Art Schults .50
(102) Kal Segrist .25
(103) Bobby Shantz .35
(104) Spec Shea .25
(105) Norm Siebern .25
(106) Charlie Silvera .25
(107) Harry Simpson .35
(108) Lou Skizas .25
(109) Bill Skowron .75
(110) Enos Slaughter 1.00
(111) Gerry Staley .25
(112) Snuffy Stirnweiss .25
(113) Marlin Stuart .25
(114) Tom Sturdivant .25
(115) Bill Terry .25
(116) Dick Tettelbach .50
(117) Marv Throneberry .35
(118) Gus Triandos .35
(119) Virgil Trucks .35
(120) Bob Turley .50
(121) Frank Verdi .25
(122) Dick Wakefield .25
(123) Bob Wiesler .25
(124) Archie Wilson .25
(125) George Wilson .25

1992 Wiz Yankees Classics

More than 600 different Yankees players from the turn of the century through the 1980s are featured in this set. Produced and distributed in five series at various promotional games, the cards share a common design and theme. Originally in a 10" x 9" perforated sheet format, the 2" x 3" individual cards can be separated with ease. Fronts feature blue-and-white duo-tone photos with the familiar Yankee Stadium facade in blue at top and the player name in black below. Backs are printed in blue on white. The series name is printed beneath the top name bar, along with a line indicating the player's years with the Yankees and a few career stats. At bottom of all cards are the Yankees Classics and Wiz Home Entertainment Centers logos, along with the logo of the co-sponsor. The Yankees of the '60s and All-Star series were co-sponsored by American Express; the '70s series by Fisher; the '80s by Minolta and the Hall of Famers by Aiwa. The unnumbered cards are checklisted here alphabetically within series.

NM/M
Complete Set (638): 95.00
Common Player: .20

Complete Series, Yankees of the '60s: 25.00
(1) Jack Aker .20
(2) Ruben Amaro .20
(3) Luis Arroyo .20
(4) Stan Bahnsen .20
(5) Steve Barber .20
(6) Ray Barker .20
(7) Rich Beck .20
(8) Yogi Berra 2.00
(9) Johnny Blanchard .50
(10) Gil Blanco .20
(11) Ron Blomberg .20
(12) Len Boehmer .20
(13) Jim Bouton .50
(14) Clete Boyer .50
(15) Jim Brenneman .20
(16) Marshall Bridges .20
(17) Harry Bright .20
(18) Hal Brown .20
(19) Billy Bryan .20
(20) Bill Burbach .20
(21) Andy Carey .20
(22) Duke Carmel .20
(23) Bob Cerv .20
(24) Horace Clarke .20
(25) Tex Clevenger .20
(26) Lu Clinton .20
(27) Jim Coates .20
(28) Rocky Colavito 1.50
(29) Billy Cowan .20
(30) Bobby Cox .50
(31) Jack Cullen .20
(32) John Cumberland .20
(33) Bud Daley .20
(34) Joe DeMaestri .20
(35) Art Ditmar .20
(36) Al Downing .30
(37) Ryne Duren .30
(38) Doc Edwards .20
(39) John Ellis .20
(40) Frank Fernandez .20
(41) Mike Ferraro .20
(42) Whitey Ford 2.00
(43) Bob Friend .20
(44) John Gabler .20
(45) Billy Gardner .20
(46) Jake Gibbs .20
(47) Jesse Gonder .20
(48) Pedro Gonzalez .20
(49) Eli Grba .20
(50) Kent Hadley .20
(51) Bob Hale .20
(52) Jimmie Hall .20
(53) Steve Hamilton .20
(54) Mike Hegan .30
(55) Bill Henry .20
(56) Elston Howard .90
(57) Dick Howser .50
(58) Ken Hunt .20
(59) Johnny James .20
(60) Elvio Jiminez .20
(61) Deron Johnson .30
(62) Ken Johnson .20
(63) Mike Jurewicz .50
(64) Mike Kekich .20
(65) John Kennedy .20
(66) Jerry Kenney .20
(67) Fred Kipp .20
(68) Ron Klimkowski .20
(69) Andy Kosco .20
(70) Tony Kubek .75
(71) Bill Kunkel .20
(72) Phil Linz .20
(73) Dale Long .20
(74) Art Lopez .20
(75) Hector Lopez .20
(76) Jim Lyttle .20
(77) Duke Maas .20
(78) Mickey Mantle 10.00
(79) Roger Maris 4.00
(80) Lindy McDaniel .20
(81) Danny McDevitt .20
(82) Dave McDonald .20
(83) Gil McDougald .50
(84) Tom Metcalf .20
(85) Bob Meyer .20
(86) Gene Michael .30
(87) Pete Mikkelsen .20
(88) John Miller .20
(89) Bill Monbouquette .20
(90) Archie Moore .20
(91) Ross Moschitto .20
(92) Thurman Munson 2.00
(93) Bobby Murcer .75
(94) Don Nottebart .20
(95) Nate Oliver .20
(96) Joe Pepitone .50
(97) Cecil Perkins .20
(98) Fritz Peterson .20
(99) Jim Pisoni .20
(100) Pedro Ramos .20
(101) Jack Reed .20
(102) Hal Reniff .20
(103) Roger Repoz .20
(104) Bobby Richardson .90
(105) Dale Roberts .50
(106) Bill Robinson .20
(107) Ellie Rodriguez .20
(108) Charlie Sands .20
(109) Bob Schmidt .20
(110) Dick Schofield .30
(111) Billy Shantz .20
(112) Bobby Shantz .30
(113) Rollie Sheldon .20
(114) Tom Shopay .20
(115) Bill Short .20
(116) Dick Simpson .20
(117) Bill Skowron .50
(118) Charley Smith .20
(119) Tony Solaita .20
(120) Bill Stafford .20
(121) Mel Stottlemyre .30
(122) Hal Stowe .20
(123) Fred Talbot .20
(124) Frank Tepedino .20
(125) Ralph Terry .20
(126) Lee Thomas .20
(127) Bobby Tiefenauer .20
(128) Bob Tillman .20
(129) Thad Tillotson .20
(130) Earl Torgeson .20
(131) Tom Tresh .50
(132) Bob Turley .40
(133) Elmer Valo .20
(134) Joe Verbanic .20
(135) Steve Whitaker .20
(136) Roy White .40
(137) Stan Williams .20
(138) Dooley Womack .20
(139) Ron Woods .20
(140) John Wyatt .20

Complete Series, Yankees of the '70s 16.00
(1) Jack Aker .20
(2) Doyle Alexander .20
(3) Bernie Allen .20
(4) Sandy Alomar .20
(5) Felipe Alou .25
(6) Matty Alou .20
(7) Dell Alston .20
(8) Rick Anderson .20
(9) Stan Bahnsen .20
(10) Frank Baker .20
(11) Jim Beattie .20
(12) Fred Beene .20
(13) Juan Beniquez .20
(14) Dave Bergman .20
(15) Juan Bernhardt .20
(16) Rick Bladt .20
(17) Paul Blair .20
(18) Wade Blasingame .20
(19) Steve Blateric .20
(20) Curt Blefary .20
(21) Ron Blomberg .20
(22) Len Boehmer .20
(23) Bobby Bonds .30
(24) Ken Brett .20
(25) Ed Brinkman .20
(26) Bobby Brown .20
(27) Bill Burbach .20
(28) Ray Burris .20
(29) Tom Buskey .20
(30) Johnny Callison .20
(31) Danny Cater .20
(32) Chris Chambliss .30
(33) Horace Clarke .20
(34) Ken Clay .20
(35) Al Closter .20
(36) Rich Coggins .20
(37) Loyd Colson .20
(38) Casey Cox .20
(39) John Cumberland .20
(40) Ron Davis .20
(41) Jim Deidel .20
(42) Rick Dempsey .30
(43) Bucky Dent .40
(44) Kerry Dineen .20
(45) Pat Dobson .20
(46) Brian Doyle .20
(47) Rawly Eastwick .20
(48) Dock Ellis .20
(49) John Ellis .20
(50) Ed Figueroa .20
(51) Oscar Gamble .20
(52) Damaso Garcia .20
(53) Rob Gardner .20
(54) Jake Gibbs .20
(55) Fernando Gonzalez .20
(56) Rich Gossage .40
(57) Larry Gowell .20
(58) Wayne Granger .20
(59) Mike Griffin .20
(60) Ron Guidry .75
(61) Brad Gulden .20
(62) Don Gullett .20
(63) Larry Gura .20
(64) Roger Hambright .20
(65) Steve Hamilton .20
(66) Ron Hansen .20
(67) Jim Hardin .20
(68) Jim Ray Hart .20
(69) Fran Healy .20
(70) Mike Heath .20
(71) Mike Hegan .30
(72) Elrod Hendricks .20
(73) Ed Herrmann .20
(74) Rich Hinton .20
(75) Ken Holtzman .20
(76) Don Hood .20
(77) Catfish Hunter 1.00
(78) Grant Jackson .20
(79) Reggie Jackson 2.00
(80) Tommy John .90
(81) Alex Johnson .20
(82) Cliff Johnson .20
(83) Jay Johnstone .30
(84) Darryl Jones .20
(85) Gary Jones .20
(86) Jim Kaat .40
(87) Bob Kammeyer .20
(88) Mike Kekich .20
(89) Jerry Kenney .20
(90) Dave Kingman .50
(91) Ron Klimkowski .20
(92) Steve Kline .20
(93) Mickey Klutts .20
(94) Hal Lanier .20
(95) Eddie Leon .20
(96) Terry Ley .20
(97) Paul Lindblad .20
(98) Gene Locklear .20
(99) Sparky Lyle .40
(100) Jim Lyttle .20
(101) Elliott Maddox .20
(102) Jim Magnuson .20
(103) Tippy Martinez .20
(104) Jim Mason .20
(105) Carlos May .20
(106) Rudy May .20
(107) Larry McCall .20
(108) Mike McCormick .20
(109) Lindy McDaniel .20
(110) Sam McDowell .30
(111) Rich McKinney .20
(112) George Medich .20
(113) Andy Messersmith .30
(114) Gene Michael .20
(115) Paul Mirabella .20
(116) Bobby Mitchell .20
(117) Gerry Moses .20
(118) Thurman Munson 2.00
(119) Bobby Murcer .75
(120) Larry Murray .20
(121) Jerry Narron .20
(122) Graig Nettles .40
(123) Bob Oliver .20
(124) Dave Pagan .20
(125) Gil Patterson .20
(126) Marty Perez .20
(127) Fritz Peterson .20
(128) Lou Piniella .50
(129) Dave Rajsich .20
(130) Domingo Ramos .20
(131) Lenny Randle .20
(132) Willie Randolph .50
(133) Dave Righetti .30
(134) Mickey Rivers .30
(135) Bruce Robinson .20
(136) Jim Roland .20
(137) Celerino Sanchez .20
(138) Rick Sawyer .20
(139) George Scott .30
(140) Duke Sims .20
(141) Roger Slagle .20
(142) Jim Spencer .20
(143) Charlie Spikes .20
(144) Roy Staiger .20
(145) Fred Stanley .30
(146) Bill Sudakis .20
(147) Ron Swoboda .20
(148) Frank Tepedino .20
(149) Stan Thomas .20
(150) Gary Thomasson .20
(151) Luis Tiant .40
(152) Dick Tidrow .20
(153) Rusty Torres .20
(154) Mike Torrez .20
(155) Cesar Tovar .20
(156) Cecil Upshaw .20
(157) Otto Velez .20
(158) Joe Verbanic .20
(159) Mike Wallace .20
(160) Danny Walton .20
(161) Pete Ward .20
(162) Gary Waslewski .20
(163) Dennis Werth .20
(164) Roy White .30
(165) Terry Whitfield .20
(166) Walt Williams .20
(167) Ron Woods .20
(168) Dick Woodson .20
(169) Ken Wright .20
(170) Jimmy Wynn .20
(171) Jim York .20
(172) George Zeber .20

Complete Series, Yankees of the '80s: 17.50
(1) Luis Aguayo .20
(2) Doyle Alexander .20
(3) Neil Allen .20
(4) Mike Armstrong .20
(5) Brad Arnsberg .20
(6) Tucker Ashford .20
(7) Steve Balboni .20
(8) Jesse Barfield .30
(9) Don Baylor .40
(10) Dale Berra .20
(11) Doug Bird .20
(12) Paul Blair .20
(13) Mike Blowers .20
(14) Juan Bonilla .20
(15) Rich Bordi .20
(16) Scott Bradley .20
(17) Marshall Brant .20
(18) Tom Brookens .20
(19) Bob Brower .20
(20) Bobby Brown .20
(21) Curt Brown .20
(22) Jay Buhner .50
(23) Marty Bystrom .20
(24) Greg Cadaret .20
(25) Bert Campaneris .30
(26) John Candelaria .30
(27) Chuck Cary .20
(28) Bill Castro .20
(29) Rick Cerone .30
(30) Chris Chambliss .30
(31) Clay Christiansen .20
(32) Jack Clark .30
(33) Pat Clements .20
(34) Dave Collins .25
(35) Don Cooper .20
(36) Henry Cotto .20
(37) Joe Cowley .20
(38) Jose Cruz .20
(39) Bobby Davidson .20
(40) Ron Davis .20
(41) Brian Dayett .20
(42) Ivan DeJesus .20
(43) Bucky Dent .50
(44) Jim Deshaies .20
(45) Orestes Destrade .20
(46) Brian Dorsett .20
(47) Rich Dotson .20
(48) Brian Doyle .20
(49) Doug Drabek .30
(50) Mike Easler .20
(51) Dave Eiland .20

No.	Player	Price
(52)	Roger Erickson	.20
(53)	Juan Espino	.20
(54)	Alvaro Espinoza	.20
(55)	Barry Evans	.20
(56)	Ed Figueroa	.20
(57)	Pete Filson	.20
(58)	Mike Fischlin	.20
(59)	Brian Fisher	.20
(60)	Tim Foli	.20
(61)	Ray Fontenot	.20
(62)	Barry Foote	.20
(63)	George Frazier	.20
(64)	Bill Fulton	.20
(65)	Oscar Gamble	.20
(66)	Bob Geren	.20
(67)	Rich Gossage	.40
(68)	Mike Griffin	.20
(69)	Ken Griffey	.30
(70)	Cecilio Guante	.20
(71)	Lee Guetterman	.20
(72)	Ron Guidry	.50
(73)	Brad Gulden	.20
(74)	Don Gullett	.20
(75)	Bill Gullickson	.20
(76)	Mel Hall	.20
(77)	Toby Harrah	.25
(78)	Ron Hassey	.20
(79)	Andy Hawkins	.20
(80)	Rickey Henderson	1.50
(81)	Leo Hernandez	.20
(82)	Butch Hobson	.20
(83)	Al Holland	.20
(84)	Roger Holt	.20
(85)	Jay Howell	.25
(86)	Rex Hudler	.20
(87)	Charles Hudson	.20
(88)	Keith Hughes	.20
(89)	Reggie Jackson	2.00
(90)	Stan Javier	.20
(91)	Stan Jefferson	.20
(92)	Tommy John	.50
(93)	Jimmy Jones	.20
(94)	Ruppert Jones	.20
(95)	Jim Kaat	.30
(96)	Curt Kaufman	.20
(97)	Roberto Kelly	.30
(98)	Steve Kemp	.25
(99)	Matt Keough	.20
(100)	Steve Kiefer	.20
(101)	Ron Kittle	.20
(102)	Dave LaPoint	.20
(103)	Marcus Lawton	.20
(104)	Joe Lefebvre	.20
(105)	Al Leiter	.20
(106)	Jim Lewis	.20
(107)	Bryan Little	.20
(108)	Tim Lollar	.20
(109)	Phil Lombardi	.20
(110)	Vic Mata	.20
(111)	Don Mattingly	4.00
(112)	Rudy May	.20
(113)	John Mayberry	.20
(114)	Lee Mazzilli	.25
(115)	Lance McCullers	.20
(116)	Andy McGaffigan	.20
(117)	Lynn McGlothen	.20
(118)	Bobby Meacham	.20
(119)	Hensley Muelens	.30
(120)	Larry Milbourne	.20
(121)	Kevin Mmahat	.20
(122)	Dale Mohorcic	.20
(123)	John Montefusco	.20
(124)	Omar Moreno	.20
(125)	Mike Morgan	.20
(126)	Jeff Moronko	.20
(127)	Hal Morris	.25
(128)	Jerry Mumphrey	.20
(129)	Bobby Murcer	.35
(130)	Dale Murray	.20
(131)	Gene Nelson	.20
(132)	Joe Niekro	.30
(133)	Phil Niekro	.90
(134)	Scott Nielsen	.20
(135)	Otis Nixon	.20
(136)	Johnny Oates	.20
(137)	Mike O'Berry	.20
(138)	Rowland Office	.20
(139)	John Pacella	.20
(140)	Mike Pagliarulo	.30
(141)	Clay Parker	.20
(142)	Dan Pasqua	.20
(143)	Mike Patterson	.20
(144)	Hipolito Pena	.20
(145)	Gaylord Perry	.50
(146)	Ken Phelps	.20
(147)	Lou Piniella	.40
(148)	Eric Plunk	.20
(149)	Luis Polonia	.30
(150)	Alfonso Pulido	.20
(151)	Jamie Quirk	.20
(152)	Bobby Ramos	.20
(153)	Willie Randolph	.40
(154)	Dennis Rasmussen	.20
(155)	Shane Rawley	.20
(156)	Rick Reuschel	.20
(157)	Dave Revering	.20
(158)	Rick Rhoden	.20
(159)	Dave Righetti	.30
(160)	Jose Rijo	.20
(161)	Andre Robertson	.20
(162)	Bruce Robinson	.20
(163)	Aurelio Rodriguez	.20
(164)	Edwin Rodriguez	.20
(165)	Gary Roenicke	.20
(166)	Jerry Royster	.20
(167)	Lenn Sakata	.20
(168)	Mark Salas	.20
(169)	Billy Sample	.20
(170)	Deion Sanders	1.00
(171)	Rafael Santana	.20
(172)	Steve Sax	.30
(173)	Don Schulze	.20
(174)	Rodney Scott	.20
(175)	Rod Scurry	.20
(176)	Dennis Sherrill	.20
(177)	Steve Shields	.20
(178)	Bob Shirley	.20
(179)	Joel Skinner	.20
(180)	Don Slaught	.30
(181)	Roy Smalley	.20
(182)	Keith Smith	.20
(183)	Eric Soderholm	.20
(184)	Jim Spencer	.20
(185)	Fred Stanley	.20
(186)	Dave Stegman	.20
(187)	Tim Stoddard	.20
(188)	Walt Terrell	.20
(189)	Bob Tewksbury	.25
(190)	Luis Tiant	.40
(191)	Wayne Tolleson	.20
(192)	Steve Trout	.20
(193)	Tom Underwood	.20
(194)	Randy Velarde	.30
(195)	Gary Ward	.20
(196)	Claudell Washington	.30
(197)	Bob Watson	.20
(198)	Dave Wehrmeister	.20
(199)	Dennis Werth	.20
(200)	Stefan Wever	.20
(201)	Ed Whitson	.20
(202)	Ted Wilborn	.20
(203)	Dave Winfield	1.00
(204)	Butch Wynegar	.20
(205)	Paul Zuvella	.20
	Complete Series, Yankees All-Stars	17.50
(1)	Luis Arroyo	.20
(2)	Hank Bauer	.35
(3)	Yogi Berra	2.00
(4)	Bobby Bonds	.30
(5)	Ernie Bonham	.20
(6)	Hank Borowy	.20
(7)	Jim Bouton	.20
(8)	Tommy Byrne	.20
(9)	Chris Chambliss	.20
(10)	Spud Chandler	.20
(11)	Ben Chapman	.20
(12)	Jim Coates	.20
(13)	Jerry Coleman	.20
(14)	Frank Crosetti	.20
(15)	Ron Davis	.20
(16)	Bucky Dent	.30
(17)	Bill Dickey	.50
(18)	Joe DiMaggio	6.00
(19)	Al Downing	.20
(20)	Ryne Duren	.30
(21)	Whitey Ford	2.00
(22)	Lou Gehrig	6.00
(23)	Lefty Gomez	.40
(24)	Joe Gordon	.20
(25)	Rich Gossage	.30
(26)	Bob Grim	.20
(27)	Ron Guidry	.30
(28)	Rollie Hemsley	.20
(29)	Rickey Henderson	1.50
(30)	Tommy Henrich	.20
(31)	Elston Howard	.35
(32)	Catfish Hunter	.30
(33)	Reggie Jackson	2.00
(34)	Tommy John	.30
(35)	Billy Johnson	.20
(36)	Charlie Keller	.20
(37)	Tony Kubek	.35
(38)	Johnny Kucks	.20
(39)	Tony Lazzeri	.30
(40)	Johnny Lindell	.20
(41)	Ed Lopat	.30
(42)	Sparky Lyle	.30
(43)	Mickey Mantle	10.00
(44)	Roger Maris	4.00
(45)	Billy Martin	.75
(46)	Don Mattingly	4.00
(47)	Gil McDougald	.30
(48)	George McQuinn	.20
(49)	Johnny Mize	.40
(50)	Thurman Munson	2.00
(51)	Bobby Murcer	.30
(52)	Johnny Murphy	.20
(53)	Graig Nettles	.20
(54)	Phil Niekro	.80
(55)	Irv Noren	.20
(56)	Joe Page	.20
(57)	Monte Pearson	.20
(58)	Joe Pepitone	.30
(59)	Fritz Peterson	.20
(60)	Willie Randolph	.30
(61)	Vic Raschi	.20
(62)	Allie Reynolds	.30
(63)	Bobby Richardson	.35
(64)	Dave Righetti	.20
(65)	Mickey Rivers	.20
(66)	Phil Rizzuto	2.00
(67)	Aaron Robinson	.20
(68)	Red Rolfe	.20
(69)	Buddy Rosar	.20
(70)	Red Ruffing	.20
(71)	Marius Russo	.20
(72)	Babe Ruth	7.50
(73)	Johnny Sain	.40
(74)	Scott Sanderson	.20
(75)	Steve Sax	.20
(76)	George Selkirk	.20
(77)	Bobby Shantz	.20
(78)	Spec Shea	.20
(79)	Bill Skowron	.35
(80)	Snuffy Stirnweiss	.20
(81)	Mel Stottlemyre	.20
(82)	Ralph Terry	.20
(83)	Tom Tresh	.20
(84)	Bob Turley	.20
(85)	Roy White	.30
(86)	Dave Winfield	1.00
	Complete Series, Yankees Hall of Famers	15.00
(1)	Home Run Baker	.50
(2)	Ed Barrow	.20
(3)	Yogi Berra	2.00
(4)	Frank Chance	.50
(5)	Jack Chesbro	.20
(6)	Earle Combs	.20
(7)	Stan Coveleski	.20
(8)	Bill Dickey	.50
(9)	Joe DiMaggio	6.00
(10)	Whitey Ford	2.00
(11)	Lou Gehrig	6.00
(12)	Lefty Gomez	.50
(13)	Clark C. Griffith	.20
(14)	Burleigh Grimes	.20
(15)	Bucky Harris	.20
(16)	Waite Hoyt	.20
(17)	Miller Huggins	.20
(18)	Catfish Hunter	.30
(19)	Willie Keeler	.20
(20)	Tony Lazzeri	.20
(21)	Larry MacPhail	.20
(22)	Mickey Mantle	10.00
(23)	Joe McCarthy	.20
(24)	Johnny Mize	.35
(25)	Herb Pennock	.20
(26)	Gaylord Perry	.20
(27)	Branch Rickey	.20
(28)	Red Ruffing	.20
(29)	Babe Ruth	7.50
(30)	Joe Sewell	.20
(31)	Enos Slaughter	.30
(32)	Casey Stengel	.30
(33)	Dazzy Vance	.20
(34)	Paul Waner	.20
(35)	George M. Weiss	.20

1990 Wonder Stars

The cards were found in specially marked loaves of Wonder Bread, in a special plastic pocket to protect them from product stains (and vice versa). Uncut sheets could also be obtained for $3 and proofs of purchase. Produced by Mike Schechter Associates, the photos at the center of the cards have team logos airbrushed away for lack of a license from MLB; the cards are licensed by the players' union. A red border surrounds the photo on front. Backs are printed in red and blue on white and have up to five years' worth of stats, a few lines of career highlights and a facsimile autograph.

		NM/M
Complete Set (20):		9.00
Common Player:		.25
Uncut Sheet:		12.50
1	Bo Jackson	.30
2	Roger Clemens	1.00
3	Jim Abbott	.25
4	Orel Hershiser	.25
5	Ozzie Smith	.75
6	Don Mattingly	1.00
7	Kevin Mitchell	.25
8	Jerome Walton	.25
9	Kirby Puckett	.75
10	Darryl Strawberry	.25
11	Robin Yount	.60
12	Tony Gwynn	.75
13	Alan Trammell	.25
14	Jose Canseco	.50
15	Greg Swindell	.25
16	Nolan Ryan	2.00
17	Howard Johnson	.25
18	Ken Griffey Jr.	2.00
19	Will Clark	.25
20	Ryne Sandberg	.60

1985 Woolworth

This 44-card boxed set was produced by Topps for the Woolworth's chain stores, though "Woolworth's" does not appear anywhere on the individual cards. Featuring a combination of black-and-white and color photos of baseball record holders from all eras, the set is in the standard 2-1/2" x 3-1/2" format. Backs, printed in blue and orange, give career details and personal data. Because it combined old-timers with current players, the set did not achieve a great deal of collector popularity. The set was reissued in 1987 in a different box at the Boardwalk and Baseball theme park in Florida.

		NM/M
Complete Set (44):		7.50
Common Player:		.10
1	Hank Aaron	.60
2	Grover Alexander	.15
3	Ernie Banks	.30
4	Yogi Berra	.30
5	Lou Brock	.10
6	Steve Carlton	.25
7	Jack Chesbro	.10
8	Ty Cobb	.60
9	Sam Crawford	.10
10	Rollie Fingers	.10
11	Whitey Ford	.30
12	Johnny Frederick	.10
13	Frankie Frisch	.10
14	Lou Gehrig	.75
15	Jim Gentile	.10
16	Dwight Gooden	.10
17	Rickey Henderson	.40
18	Rogers Hornsby	.10
19	Frank Howard	.10
20	Cliff Johnson	.10
21	Walter Johnson	.25
22	Hub Leonard	.10
23	Mickey Mantle	2.00
24	Roger Maris	.50
25	Christy Mathewson	.25
26	Willie Mays	.60
27	Stan Musial	.50
28	Dan Quisenberry	.10
29	Frank Robinson	.25
30	Pete Rose	1.00
31	Babe Ruth	1.50
32	Nolan Ryan	1.50
33	George Sisler	.10
34	Tris Speaker	.10
35	Ed Walsh	.10
36	Lloyd Waner	.10
37	Earl Webb	.10
38	Ted Williams	.75
39	Maury Wills	.10
40	Hack Wilson	.10
41	Owen Wilson	.10
42	Willie Wilson	.10
43	Rudy York	.10
44	Cy Young	.25

1986 Woolworth

Labeled "Topps' Collector Series" in a red band at the top of the front, this set marked the second year of Topps' production of a special boxed set for the Woolworth chain of stores, though Woolworth's name does not appear anywhere on the card. The 2-1/2" x 3-1/2" cards feature a color photo with its lower-right corner rolled up to reveal the words "Super Star" on a bright yellow border. The player's name appears in the lower-left corner.

		NM/M
Complete Set (33):		6.00
Common Player:		.10
1	Tony Armas	.10
2	Don Baylor	.10
3	Wade Boggs	.75
4	George Brett	1.00
5	Bill Buckner	.10
6	Rod Carew	.75
7	Gary Carter	.75
8	Cecil Cooper	.10
9	Darrell Evans	.10
10	Dwight Evans	.10
11	George Foster	.10
12	Bobby Grich	.10
13	Tony Gwynn	.75
14	Keith Hernandez	.10
15	Reggie Jackson	.75
16	Dave Kingman	.10
17	Carney Lansford	.10
18	Fred Lynn	.10
19	Bill Madlock	.10
20	Don Mattingly	1.50
21	Willie McGee	.10
22	Hal McRae	.10
23	Dale Murphy	.35
24	Eddie Murray	.75
25	Ben Oglivie	.10
26	Al Oliver	.10
27	Dave Parker	.10
28	Jim Rice	.35
29	Pete Rose	1.50
30	Mike Schmidt	1.00
31	Gorman Thomas	.10
32	Willie Wilson	.10
33	Dave Winfield	.75

1987 Woolworth

The "Baseball Highlights" boxed set of 33 cards was prepared by Topps for distribution at stores in the Woolworth's chain, although the retailer's name does not appear on the cards. Each card measures 2-1/2" x 3-1/2" in size and features a memorable baseball event that occurred during the 1986 season. The glossy set sold for $1.99.

		NM/M
Complete Set (33):		2.00
Common Player:		.05
1	Steve Carlton	.20
2	Cecil Cooper	.05
3	Rickey Henderson	.20
4	Reggie Jackson	.35
5	Jim Rice	.15
6	Don Sutton	.15
7	Roger Clemens	.40
8	Mike Schmidt	.40
9	Jesse Barfield	.05
10	Wade Boggs	.35
11	Tim Raines	.05
12	Jose Canseco	.25
13	Todd Worrell	.05
14	Dave Righetti	.05
15	Don Mattingly	.40
16	Tony Gwynn	.25
17	Marty Barrett	.05
18	Mike Scott	.05
19	World Series Game #1 (Bruce Hurst)	.05
20	World Series Game #1 (Calvin Schiraldi)	.05
21	World Series Game #2 (Dwight Evans)	.05
22	World Series Game #2 (Dave Henderson)	.05
23	World Series Game #3 (Len Dykstra)	.05
24	World Series Game #3 (Bob Ojeda)	.05
25	World Series Game #4 (Gary Carter)	.05
26	World Series Game #4 (Ron Darling)	.05
27	Jim Rice	.15
28	Bruce Hurst	.05
29	World Series Game #6 (Darryl Strawberry)	.05
30	World Series Game #6 (Ray Knight)	.05
31	World Series Game #6 (Keith Hernandez)	.05
32	World Series Game #7 (Mets Celebrate)	.05
33	Ray Knight	.05

1988 Woolworth

This 33-card boxed set was produced by Topps for exclusive distribution at Woolworth stores. The set includes 18 individual player cards and 15 World Series game-action photo cards. World Series cards include two for each game of the Series, plus a card of 1987 Series MVP Frank Viola. A white-lettered caption beneath the photo consists of either the player's name or a World Series game notation. Card backs are red, white and blue and contain a brief description of the photo on the front.

		NM/M
Complete Set (33):		2.00
Common Player:		.05
1	Don Baylor	.05
2	Vince Coleman	.05
3	Darrell Evans	.05
4	Don Mattingly	.60
5	Eddie Murray	.35
6	Nolan Ryan	.75
7	Mike Schmidt	.60
8	Andre Dawson	.20
9	George Bell	.05
10	Steve Bedrosian	.05
11	Roger Clemens	.60
12	Tony Gwynn	.50
13	Wade Boggs	.50
14	Benny Santiago	.05
15	Mark McGwire	.65
16	Dave Righetti	.05
17	Jeffrey Leonard	.05
18	Gary Gaetti	.05
19	World Series Game #1 (Frank Viola)	.05
20	World Series Game #1 (Dan Gladden)	.05
21	World Series Game #2 (Bert Blyleven)	.05
22	World Series Game #2 (Gary Gaetti)	.05
23	World Series Game #3 (John Tudor)	.05
24	World Series Game #3 (Todd Worrell)	.05
25	World Series Game #4 (Tom Lawless)	.05
26	World Series Game #4 (Willie McGee)	.05
27	World Series Game #5 (Danny Cox)	.05
28	World Series Game #5 (Curt Ford)	.05
29	World Series Game #6 (Don Baylor)	.05
30	World Series Game #6 (Kent Hrbek)	.05
31	World Series Game #7 (Kirby Puckett)	.35
32	World Series Game #7 (Greg Gagne)	.05
33	World Series MVP (Frank Viola)	.05

1989 Woolworth

This 33-card set was produced by Topps for the Woolworth store chain and was sold in a special box with a checklist on the back. The glossy-coated cards commemorate the most memorable moments in baseball from the 1988 season. The backs include a description of the various highlights.

		NM/M
Complete Set (33):		4.00
Common Player:		.05
1	Jose Canseco	.30
2	Kirk Gibson	.05
3	Frank Viola	.05
4	Orel Hershiser	.05
5	Walt Weiss	.05
6	Chris Sabo	.05
7	George Bell	.05
8	Wade Boggs	.65
9	Tom Browning	.05
10	Gary Carter	.50
11	Andre Dawson	.20
12	John Franco	.05
13	Randy Johnson	.50
14	Doug Jones	.05
15	Kevin McReynolds	.05
16	Gene Nelson	.05
17	Jeff Reardon	.05
18	Pat Tabler	.05
19	Tim Belcher	.05
20	Dennis Eckersley	.35
21	Orel Hershiser	.05
22	Gregg Jefferies	.05
23	Jose Canseco	.30
24	Kirk Gibson	.05
25	Orel Hershiser	.05
26	Mike Marshall	.05
27	Mark McGwire	1.00
28	Rick Honeycutt	.05
29	Tim Belcher	.05
30	Jay Howell	.05
31	Mickey Hatcher	.05
32	Mike Davis	.05
33	Orel Hershiser	.05

1990 Woolworth

This 33-card boxed set recalls baseball highlights of 1989. The cards are styled like past Woolworth sets, with game-action or posed photos framed in green. Backs are in blue, white and black with a headline and explanation of the commemoration. The set features award winners and regular and post-season highlights.

		NM/M
Complete Set (33):		2.50
Common Player:		.05
1	Robin Yount	.30
2	Kevin Mitchell	.05
3	Bret Saberhagen	.05
4	Mark Davis	.05
5	Gregg Olson	.05
6	Jerome Walton	.05
7	Bert Blyleven	.05
8	Wade Boggs	.45
9	George Brett	.50
10	Vince Coleman	.05
11	Andre Dawson	.20
12	Dwight Evans	.05
13	Carlton Fisk	.30
14	Rickey Henderson	.30
15	Dale Murphy	.15
16	Eddie Murray	.30
17	Jeff Reardon	.05
18	Rick Reuschel	.05
19	Cal Ripken, Jr.	.75
20	Nolan Ryan	.75
21	Ryne Sandberg	.45
22	Robin Yount	.30
23	Rickey Henderson	.30
24	Will Clark	.05
25	Dave Stewart	.05
26	Walt Weiss	.05
27	Mike Moore	.05
28	Terry Steinbach	.05
29	Dave Henderson	.05
30	Matt Williams	.05
31	Rickey Henderson	.30
32	Kevin Mitchell	.05
33	Dave Stewart	.05

1991 Woolworth

This 33-card boxed set was produced by Topps for distribution at Woolworth stores. Yellow borders are featured on the fronts of the glossy cards. The backs feature baseball highlights from the previous season. Award winners, regular season and World Series highlights are showcased.

		NM/M
Complete Set (33):		3.00
Common Player:		.05
1	Barry Bonds	.75
2	Rickey Henderson	.45
3	Doug Drabek	.05
4	Bob Welch	.05
5	Dave Justice	.10
6	Sandy Alomar, Jr.	.05
7	Bert Blyleven	.05
8	George Brett	.60
9	Andre Dawson	.25
10	Dwight Evans	.05
11	Alex Fernandez	.05
12	Carlton Fisk	.45
13	Kevin Maas	.05
14	Dale Murphy	.20
15	Eddie Murray	.45
16	Dave Parker	.05
17	Jeff Reardon	.05
18	Cal Ripken, Jr.	.75
19	Nolan Ryan	.75
20	Ryne Sandberg	.50
21	Bobby Thigpen	.05
22	Robin Yount	.45
23	Nasty Boys (Rob Dibble, Randy Myers)	.05
24	Dave Stewart	.05
25	Eric Davis	.05
26	Rickey Henderson	.45
27	Billy Hatcher	.05
28	Joe Oliver	.05
29	Chris Sabo	.05
30	Barry Larkin	.05
31	Jose Rijo	.05
32	Reds Celebrate	.05
33	Jose Rijo (World Series MVP)	.05

1986-88 World Wide Sports Conlon Collection

Marketed as complete series through World Wide Sports, five sets of black-and-white cards featuring the game's great players of the 1905-1935 era were made utilizing the photos of Charles Martin Conlon. The 2-1/2" x 3-1/2" cards carry the copyright of "The Sporting News," owner of the Conlon photos. The 60 cards of Series one each feature a Babe Ruth logo in the lower-left corner, the only graphic on the borderless card front. Series two has no front logo. Series 3-5 have a sliding Ty Cobb logo. Backs feature a line of career stats, a few bits of biographical data and a paragraph of highlights written by TSN historian Paul MacFarlane. The first two series were produced in an edition of 12,000 sets each; production of the other series was not announced. Cards in Series 3-5 are not numbered and are checklisted here alphabetically. Series designations are in small print at back-bottom.

		NM/M
Complete Set (211):		100.00
Common Player:		.25
Series 1 - 1986:		18.00
1	Lou Gehrig	1.50
2	Ty Cobb	1.00
3	Grover C. Alexander	.35
4	Walter Johnson	.50
5	Bill Klem	.25
6	Ty Cobb	1.00
7	Gordon S. Cochrane	.25
8	Paul Waner	.25
9	Joe Cronin	.25
10	Jay Hannah Dean	.25
11	Leo Durocher	.25
12	Jimmie Foxx	.25
13	Babe Ruth	2.00
14	Mike Gonzalez, Frank Frisch, Clyde Wares	.25
15	Carl Hubbell	.25
16	Miller Huggins	.25
17	Lou Gehrig	1.50
18	Connie Mack	.25
19	Heinie Manush	.25
20	Babe Ruth	2.00
21	Al Simmons	.25
22	Pepper Martin	.25
23	Christy Mathewson	.50
24	Ty Cobb	1.00
25	Stanley Harris	.25
26	Waite Hoyt	.25
27	Rube Marquard	.25
28	Joe McCarthy	.25
29	John McGraw	.25
30	Tris Speaker	.25
31	Bill Terry	.25
32	Christy Mathewson	.50
33	Casey Stengel	.25
34	Robert W. Meusel	.25
35	George Edward Waddell	.25
36	Mel Ott	.25
37	Roger Peckinpaugh	.25
38	Pie Traynor	.25
39	Chief Bender	.25
40	John W. Coombs	.25
41	Ty Cobb	1.00
42	Harry Heilmann	.25
43	Charlie Gehringer	.25
44	Rogers Hornsby	.25
45	Vernon Gomez	.25
46	Christy Mathewson	.50
47	Robert M. Grove	.25
48	Babe Ruth	2.00
49	Fred Merkle	.25
50	Babe Ruth	2.00
51	Herb Pennock	.25
52	Lou Gehrig	1.50
53	Fred Clarke	.25
54	Babe Ruth	2.00
55	John P. Wagner	.50
56	Hack Wilson	.25
57	Lou Gehrig	1.50
58	Lloyd Waner	.25
59	Charles Martin Conlon	.25
60	Charles & Margie Conlon	.25
---	Header Card	.25
Series 2 - 1987:		15.00
1	Lou Gehrig	1.50
2	Vernon Gomez	.25
3	Christy Mathewson	.50
4	Grover Alexander	.25
5	Ty Cobb	1.00
6	Walter Johnson	.50
7	Charles (Babe) Adams	.25
8	Nick Altrock	.25
9	Al Schacht	.25
10	Hugh Critz	.25
11	Henry Cullop	.25
12	Jake Daubert	.25
13	Bill Donovan	.25
14	Chick Hafey	.25
15	Bill Hallahan	.25
16	Fred Haney	.25
17	Charles Hartnett	.25
18	Walter Henline	.25
19	Ed Rommel	.25
20	Ralph "Babe" Pinelli	.25
21	Bob Meusel	.25
22	Emil Meusel	.25
23	Smead Jolley	.25
24	Ike Boone	.25
25	Earl Webb	.25
26	Charles Comiskey	.25
27	Edward Collins	.25
28	Geroge (Buck) Weaver	.50
29	Eddie Cicotte	.50
30	Sam Crawford	.25
31	Chuck Dressen	.25
32	Arthur Fletcher	.25
33	Hugh Duffy	.25
34	Ira Flagstead	.25
35	Harry Hooper	.25
36	George E. Lewis	.25
37	James Dykes	.25
38	Leon Goslin	.25
39	Henry Gowdy	.25
40	Charles Grimm	.25
41	Mark Koenig	.25
42	James Hogan	.25
43	William Jacobson	.25
44	Fielder Jones	.25
45	George Kelly	.25
46	Adolfo Luque	.40
47	Walter Maranville	.25
48	Carl Mays	.25
49	Eddie Plank	.25
50	Hubert Pruett	.25
51	John (Picus) Quinn	.25
52	Charles (Flint) Rhem	.25
53	Amos Rusie	.25
54	Edd Roush	.25
55	Ray Schalk	.25
56	Ernie Shore	.25
57	Joe Wood	.25
58	George Sisler	.25
59	James Thorpe	3.00
60	Earl Whitehill	.25
Series 3 - 1988:		35.00
(1)	Ace Adams	1.00
(2)	Grover C. Alexander	2.00
(3)	Eldon Auker	1.00
(4)	Jack Barry	1.00
(5)	Wally Berger	1.00
(6)	Ben Chapman	1.00
(7)	Mickey Cochrane	1.00
(8)	Frank Crosetti	1.00
(9)	Paul Dean	1.00
(10)	Leo Durocher	1.00
(11)	Wes Ferrell	1.00
(12)	Hank Gowdy	1.00
(13)	Andy High	1.00
(14)	Rogers Hornsby	2.00
(15)	Carl Hubbell	1.00
(16)	Joe Judge	1.00
(17)	Tony Lazzeri	1.00
(18)	Pepper Martin	1.00
(19)	Lee Meadows	1.00
(20)	Jimmy Murphy	1.00
(21)	Steve O'Neill	1.00
(22)	Ed Plank	1.00
(23)	John P. Quinn	1.00
(24)	Charlie Root	1.00
(25)	Babe Ruth	6.00
(26)	Fred Snodgrass	1.00
(27)	Tris Speaker	2.00
(28)	Bill Terry	1.00
(29)	Jeff Tesreau	1.00
(30)	George Torporcer	1.00
Series 4 - 1988:		30.00
(1)	Dale Alexander	1.00
(2)	Morris "Red" Badgro	1.00
(3)	Dick Bartell	1.00
(4)	Max Bishop	1.00
(5)	Hal Chase	1.50
(6)	Ty Cobb	2.00
(7)	Nick Cullop	1.00
(8)	Dizzy Dean	2.50
(9)	Chuck Dressen	1.00
(10)	Jimmy Dykes	1.00
(11)	Art Fletcher	1.00
(12)	Charlie Grimm	1.00
(13)	Lefty Grove	1.00
(14)	Baby Doll Jacobson	1.00
(15)	Bill Klem	1.00
(16)	Mark Koenig	1.00
(17)	Duffy Lewis	1.00
(18)	Carl Mays	1.00
(19)	Fred Merkle	1.00
(20)	Greasy Neale	1.50
(21)	Mel Ott	1.00
(22)	"Babe" Pinelli	1.00
(23)	Flint Rhem	1.00
(24)	Slim Sallee	1.00
(25)	Al Simmons	1.00
(26)	George Sisler	1.00
(27)	Riggs Stephenson	1.00
(28)	Jim Thorpe	4.00
(29)	Bill Wambsganss	1.00
(30)	Cy Young	2.50
Series 5 - 1988:		30.00
(1)	Nick Altrock	1.00
(2)	Del Baker	1.00
(3)	Moe Berg	4.50
(4)	Zeke Bonura	1.00
(5)	Eddie Collins	1.00
(6)	Hugh Critz	1.00
(7)	George Dauss	1.00
(8)	Joe Dugan	1.00
(9)	Howard Ehmke	1.00
(10)	Jimmie Foxx	2.50
(11)	Frank Frisch	1.00
(12)	Lou Gehrig	6.00
(13)	Charlie Gehringer	1.00
(14)	Kid Gleason	1.00
(15)	Lefty Gomez	1.00
(16)	Babe Herman	1.00
(17)	Bill James	1.00
(18)	Joe Kuhel	1.00
(19)	Dolf Luque	1.50
(20)	John McGraw	1.00
(21)	Stuffy McInnis	1.00
(22)	Bob Meusel	1.00
(23)	Lefty O'Doul	1.00
(24)	Hub Pruett	1.00
(25)	Paul Richards	1.00
(26)	Bob Shawkey	1.00
(27)	Gabby Street	1.00
(28)	Johnny Tobin	1.00
(29)	Rube Waddell	1.00
(30)	Billy Werber	1.00

1988 World Wide Sports 1933 All-Stars

The photos of Charles M. Conlon in The Sporting News' archive are the basis for this collectors' issue depicting the players of the original All-Star Game of 1933. Fronts have sepia photo of the players on a 2-1/2" x 3-1/2" format. The only graphics added to the front are in the upper-right corner designating the league which the player represented. Backs have 1933 and career stats, along with a career summary. The unnumbered cards are checklisted here in alphabetical order within league.

		NM/M
Complete Set (48):		12.00
Common Player:		.25
American League		6.00
(1)	Luke Appling	.25
(2)	Earl Averill	.25
(3)	Tommy Bridges	.25
(4)	Ben Chapman	.25
(5)	Mickey Cochrane	.25
(6)	Joe Cronin	.25
(7)	Alvin Crowder	.25
(8)	Bill Dickey	.35
(9)	Jimmie Foxx	.45
(10)	Lou Gehrig	1.00
(11)	Charlie Gehringer	.35
(12)	Lefty Gomez	.25
(13)	Lefty Grove	.25
(14)	Mel Harder	.25
(15)	Pinky Higgins	.25
(16)	Urban Hodapp	.25
(17)	Roy Johnson	.25
(18)	Joe Kuhel	.25
(19)	Tony Lazzeri	.25
(20)	Heinie Manush	.25
(21)	Babe Ruth	1.50
(22)	Al Simmons	.25
(23)	Evar Swanson	.25
(24)	Earl Whitehill	.25
National League		6.00
(1)	Wally Berger	.25
(2)	Guy Bush	.25
(3)	Ripper Collins	.25
(4)	Spud Davis	.25
(5)	Dizzy Dean	.45
(6)	Johnny Frederick	.25
(7)	Larry French	.25
(8)	Frank Frisch	.25
(9)	Chick Fullis	.25
(10)	Chick Hafey	.25
(11)	Carl Hubbell	.25
(12)	Chuck Klein	.25
(13)	Freddie Lindstrom	.25
(14)	Pepper Martin	.25
(15)	Ducky Medwick	.25
(16)	Tony Piet	.25
(17)	Wes Schulmerich	.25
(18)	Hal Schumacher	.25
(19)	Riggs Stephenson	.25
(20)	Bill Terry	.25
(21)	Paul Traynor	.25
(22)	Arky Vaughan	.25
(23)	Paul Waner	.25
(24)	Lon Warneke	.25

1988 World Wide Sports 1933 Negro All Stars

The photos of Charles M. Conlon in The Sporting News' archive are the basis for this collectors' issue depicting "1933 Negro All Stars. Fronts have borderless sepia photos of the players on a 2-1/2" x 3-1/2" format. The only graphics added to the front are in the upper-right corner designating the All-Star status. Backs have a few personal data along with a career summary. The unnumbered cards are checklisted here in alphabetical order.

		NM/M
Complete Set (12):		7.50
Common Player:		1.00
(1)	Cool Papa Bell	1.00
(2)	Oscar Charleston	1.00
(3)	Martin Dihigo	1.00
(4)	Andrew "Rube" Foster	1.00
(5)	Josh Gibson	2.00
(6)	Judy Johnson	1.00
(7)	Buck Leonard	1.00
(8)	Pop Lloyd	1.00
(9)	Dave Malarcher	1.00
(10)	Satchel Paige	2.50
(11)	Willie Wells	1.00
(12)	Joe Williams	1.00

1989 W/R Associates Mark Grace

This collectors' issue traces the career of Mark Grace on a nine-card panel which includes eight standard 2-1/2" x 3-1/2" cards and a 5" x 7" card on a sheet with overall dimensions of 10-5/8" x 14". Because the issue was licensed only by the player, and not Major League Baseball, all Cubs uniform logos have been removed from the photos. Cards are numbered on front and back with a year identifying the photo. Backs are printed in red, white and blue and include biographical data and career summary. The large-format card offers complete major and minor league stats on back. The cards on the sheet are not perforated and individual cards are rarely encountered. Sheets were offered in either autographed or unautographed form with production limited to 15,000 sheets.

		NM/M
Complete Sheet:		7.50
Complete Sheet, Autographed:		25.00
Complete Set, Cut (9):		7.50
Common Card:		.50
73	Mark Grace (Boyhood photo.)	.50
83	Mark Grace (San Diego State)	.50
86	Mark Grace (Minor League)	.50
87	Mark Grace/Throwing	.50
88a	Mark Grace/Fldg	.50
88b	Mark Grace (Wedding)	.50
89a	Mark Grace, Mark Grace/Btg	.50
89b	Mark Grace/Btg	.50
----	Mark Grace (5" x 7" Portrait, Autographed)	25.00
----	Mark Grace (5" x 7" Portrait, Unsigned)	4.00

1985 WTBS Atlanta Braves

This set of large-format (8-1/4" x 10-3/4") cards was issued by the Braves' TV broadcaster, WTBS. The sets were given to potential sponsors as part of a "kit" inviting them to Florida to attend a spring training game. It was reported that only 600 sets were printed and 150 of them were destroyed. Fronts feature player portraits on brightly colored backgrounds. There is a facsimile autograph and a large star-boxed "AMERICA'S TEAM." Backs are in red and black and have some vital data and stats for the 1982-84 seasons. Cards are numbered according to uniform number.

		NM/M
Complete Set (4):		50.00
Common Player:		7.50
3	Dale Murphy	35.00
7	Brad Komminsk	7.50
15	Claudell Washington	7.50
42	Bruce Sutter	15.00

1991 WWOR N.Y. Mets

This set of 5-1/2" x 7-1/2" cards was issued by WWOR-TV in New York City, which carried the Mets telecasts in 1991. The cards were evidently intended for use as a sales promotion, as the backs detail Neilsen ratings for the games. Fronts have game action photos with green borders in a design not unlike 1991 Donruss.

		NM/M
Complete Set (12):		15.00
Common Player:		2.00
(1)	Darryl Boston	2.00
(2)	Vince Coleman	2.00
(3)	David Cone	2.00
(4)	Kevin Elster	2.00
(5)	Sid Fernandez	2.00
(6)	John Franco	2.00
(7)	Dwight Gooden	2.00
(8)	Jeff Innis	2.00
(9)	Howard Johnson	2.00
(10)	Dave Magadan	2.00
(11)	Mackey Sasser	2.00
(12)	Wally Whitehurst	2.00

1993 Yoo-Hoo

The Yoo-Hoo beverage company, which had a promotional affiliation with Yogi Berra as far back as the 1950's, made Berra the #1 card in a 1993 set of 20 baseball legends that was released in two series. All of the players included in the set are retired, and all but five are Hall of Famers (at this printing). The unnumbered cards feature a yellow border with a color photo on the front; the backs have the player's statistics and biographical information.

		NM/M
Complete Set (20):		7.00
Common Player:		.25
Series 1		
(1)	Yogi Berra	.50
(2)	Joe Morgan	.35
(3)	Duke Snider	.50
(4)	Steve Garvey	.30
(5)	Jim Rice	.35
(6)	Bob Feller	.35
(7)	Pete Rose	1.00
(8)	Rod Carew	.35
(9)	Gaylord Perry	.25
(10)	Graig Nettles	.25
Series 2		
(1)	Johnny Bench	.40
(2)	Lou Brock	.35
(3)	Stan Musial	1.00
(4)	Willie McCovey	.35
(5)	Whitey Ford	.50
(6)	Phil Rizzuto	.50
(7)	Tom Seaver	.50
(8)	Willie Stargell	.35
(9)	Brooks Robinson	.35
(10)	Al Kaline	.45

1994 Yoo-Hoo

Issued in conjunction with Rawling's, sponsor of the Gold Glove Award, this set features past winners. Cards have color photos on which team logos have been airbrushed away. Borders are bright yellow. Backs have career stats and highlights. A limited number of Yaz autographed cards were randomly inserted into the packs in which the cards were distributed.

		NM/M
Complete Set (20):		6.00
Common Player:		.25
Yastrzemski Autograph:		30.00
1	Luis Aparicio	.25
2	Bobby Bonds	.25
3	Bob Boone	.25
4	Steve Carlton	.35
5	Roberto Clemente	2.00
6	Bob Gibson	.25
7	Keith Hernandez	.25
8	Jim Kaat	.25
9	Roger Maris	.60
10	Don Mattingly	1.00
11	Thurman Munson	.60
12	Phil Rizzuto	.50
13	Brooks Robinson	.40
14	Ryne Sandberg	.75
15	Mike Schmidt	1.00
16	Carl Yastrzemski	.60
17	Fact Card	.05
18	Fact Card	.05
19	Fact Card	.05
20	Fact Card	.05

Z

1982 Zellers Expos

Issued by Zellers department stores in Canada, this 60-card set was produced in the form of 20 three-card panels. The cards feature a round photo of the player on a yellow background. A red "Zellers" is above the photo and on either side of it are the words "Baseball Pro Tips" in English on the left and in French on the right. The player's name and the title of the playing tip are under the photo. Backs have the playing tip in both languages. Single cards measure 2-1/2" x 3-1/2" while the whole panel is 7-1/2" x 3-1/2". Although a number of stars are depicted, this set is not terribly popular as collectors do not generally like the playing tips idea. Total panels are worth more than separated cards.

		NM/M
Complete Set (20):		6.00
Common Player:		.25
1	Gary Carter (Catching Position)	1.50
2	Steve Rogers (Pitching Stance)	.25
3	Tim Raines (Sliding)	.50
4	Andre Dawson (Batting Stance)	.60
5	Terry Francona (Contact Hitting)	.25
6	Gary Carter (Fielding Pop Fouls)	1.50
7	Warren Cromartie (Fielding at First Base)	.25
8	Chris Speier (Fielding at Shortstop)	.25
9	Billy DeMars (Signals)	.25
10	Andre Dawson (Batting Stroke)	.60
11	Terry Francona (Outfield Throws)	.25
12	Woodie Fryman (Holding the Runner-Left Handed)	.25
13	Gary Carter (Fielding Low Balls)	1.50
14	Andre Dawson (Playing Centerfield)	.60
15	Bill Gullickson (The Slurve)	.25
16	Gary Carter (Catching Stance)	1.50
17	Scott Sanderson (Fielding as a Pitcher)	.25
18	Warren Cromartie (Handling Bad Throws)	.25
19	Gary Carter (Hitting Stride)	1.50
20	Ray Burris (Holding the Runner-Right Handed)	.25

1995 Zenith Samples

As Pinnacle extended its top-of-the-line brand name into baseball, this nine-card cello-wrapped samples set was sent to dealers to famil-

iarize them with the product. Using the same state of the art all-foil metalized printing on extra heavy 24-point cardboard stock, the samples are virtually identical to the issued version, except for a white "SAMPLE" printed diagonally across front and back.

		NM/M
Complete Set (9):		10.00
Common Player:		.75
12	Cal Ripken Jr.	3.00
20	Dante Bichette	.75
51	Jim Thome	1.00
70	Mark Grace	1.00
97	Ryan Klesko	.75
111	Chipper Jones (Rookie)	2.00
113	Curtis Goodwin (Rookie)	.75
7	Hideo Nomo (Rookie Roll Call)	2.00
---	Header Card	.05

1995 Zenith

At the top of the pyramid of Pinnacle's baseball card lines for 1995 was Zenith, a super-premium brand utilizing all-foil metallized printing technology on double-thick 24-point cardboard stock to emphasize the quality look and feel. Six-card packs carried a retail price of $3.99. Two styles comprise the 150-card base set. The 110 veteran player cards are curiously arranged in alphabetical order according to the player's first names (with the exception of card #48, a special Japanese-language card of Hideo Nomo). These cards have a color player action photo on a black and gold background that is a view of a pyramid from its pinnacle. One the horizontal back, a portrait photo of the player in a partly-cloudy blue sky overlooks a playing field which offers his hit location preferences versus righty and lefty pitching. A scoreboard has his 1994 and career stats. The Pinnacle anti-counterfeiting optical-variable bar is in the lower-right corner. The rookie cards which comprise the final 40 cards in the set have a color photo at center with a gold-tone version of the same picture in the background. A large gold "ROOKIE" is vertically at right. Backs are similar to those on the verterans' cards except they have a scouting report in place of the hit-location chart.

		NM/M
Complete Set (150):		15.00
Common Player:		.10
Pack (6):		1.50
Wax Box (24):		17.50
1	Albert Belle	.10
2	Alex Fernandez	.10
3	Andy Benes	.10
4	Barry Larkin	.10
5	Barry Bonds	2.50
6	Ben McDonald	.10
7	Bernard Gilkey	.10
8	Billy Ashley	.10
9	Bobby Bonilla	.10
10	Bret Saberhagen	.10
11	Brian Jordan	.10
12	Cal Ripken Jr.	2.50
13	Carlos Baerga	.10
14	Carlos Delgado	.35
15	Cecil Fielder	.10
16	Chili Davis	.10
17	Chuck Knoblauch	.10
18	Craig Biggio	.10
19	Danny Tartabull	.10
20	Dante Bichette	.10
21	Darren Daulton	.10
22	Dave Justice	.10
23	Dave Winfield	.75
24	David Cone	.10
25	Dean Palmer	.10
26	Deion Sanders	.20
27	Dennis Eckersley	.65
28	Derek Bell	.10
29	Don Mattingly	1.50
30	Edgar Martinez	.10
31	Eric Karros	.10
32	Erik Hanson	.10
33	Frank Thomas	.75
34	Fred McGriff	.10
35	Gary Sheffield	.45
36	Gary Gaetti	.10
37	Greg Maddux	1.25
38	Gregg Jefferies	.10
39	Ivan Rodriguez	.65
40	Kenny Rogers	.10
41	J.T. Snow	.10
42	Hal Morris	.10
43	Eddie Murray (3,000 hit)	.50
44	Javier Lopez	.10
45	Jay Bell	.10
46	Jeff Conine	.10
47	Jeff Bagwell	.75
48	Hideo Nomo **RC**	2.00
49	Jeff Kent	.10
50	Jeff King	.10
51	Jim Thome	.65
52	Jimmy Key	.10
53	Joe Carter	.10
54	John Valentin	.10
55	John Olerud	.10
56	Jose Canseco	.45
57	Jose Rijo	.10
58	Jose Offerman	.10
59	Juan Gonzalez	.45
60	Ken Caminiti	.10
61	Ken Griffey Jr.	1.75
62	Kenny Lofton	.10
63	Kevin Appier	.10
64	Kevin Seitzer	.10
65	Kirby Puckett	1.25
66	Kirk Gibson	.10
67	Larry Walker	.10
68	Lenny Dykstra	.10
69	Manny Ramirez	.75
70	Mark Grace	.10
71	Mark McGwire	2.00
72	Marquis Grissom	.10
73	Jim Edmonds	.10
74	Matt Williams	.10
75	Mike Mussina	.45
76	Mike Piazza	1.75
77	Mo Vaughn	.10
78	Moises Alou	.10
79	Ozzie Smith	1.25
80	Paul O'Neill	.10
81	Paul Molitor	.75
82	Rafael Palmeiro	.65
83	Randy Johnson	.75
84	Raul Mondesi	.10
85	Ray Lankford	.10
86	Reggie Sanders	.10
87	Rickey Henderson	.75
88	Rico Brogna	.10
89	Roberto Alomar	.25
90	Robin Ventura	.10
91	Roger Clemens	1.50
92	Ron Gant	.10
93	Rondell White	.10
94	Royce Clayton	.10
95	Ruben Sierra	.10
96	Rusty Greer	.10
97	Ryan Klesko	.10
98	Sammy Sosa	1.25
99	Shawon Dunston	.10
100	Steve Ontiveros	.10
101	Tim Naehring	.10
102	Tim Salmon	.10
103	Tino Martinez	.10
104	Tony Gwynn	1.25
105	Travis Fryman	.10
106	Vinny Castilla	.10
107	Wade Boggs	1.25
108	Wally Joyner	.10
109	Wil Cordero	.10
110	Will Clark	.10
111	Chipper Jones	1.25
112	C.J. Nitkowski	.10
113	Curtis Goodwin	.10
114	Tim Unroe	.10
115	Vaughn Eshelman	.10
116	Marty Cordova	.10
117	Dustin Hermanson	.10
118	Rich Becker	.10
119	Ray Durham	.10
120	Shane Andrews	.10
121	Scott Ruffcorn	.10
122	Mark Grudzielanek **RC**	.25
123	James Baldwin	.10
124	Carlos Perez **RC**	.10
125	Julian Tavarez	.10
126	Joe Vitiello	.10
127	Jason Bates	.10
128	Edgardo Alfonzo	.10
129	Juan Acevedo	.10
130	Bill Pulsipher	.10
131	Bob Higginson **RC**	.25
132	Russ Davis	.10
133	Charles Johnson	.10
134	Derek Jeter	2.50
135	Phil Nevin	.10
136	LaTroy Hawkins	.10
137	Brian Hunter	.10
138	Roberto Petagine	.10
139	Jim Pittsley	.10
140	Garret Anderson	.10
141	Ugueth Urbina	.10
142	Antonio Osuna	.10
143	Michael Tucker	.10
144	Benji Gil	.10
145	Jon Nunnally	.10
146	Alex Rodriguez	2.00
147	Todd Hollandworth	.10
148	Alex Gonzalez	.10
149	Hideo Nomo **RC**	2.00
150	Shawn Green	.30
---	Numeric Checklist	.10
---	Chase Program Checklist	.10

All-Star Salute

The most common of the Zenith inserts is a series of 18 All-Star Salute cards. Fronts have action photos printed on foil. Backs have the 1995 All-Star Game logo and a large photo of the player taken at the game, with a few words about his All-Star history. The Salute cards are seeded at the rate of one per six packs, on average.

		NM/M
Complete Set (18):		16.00
Common Player:		.50
1	Cal Ripken Jr.	3.00
2	Frank Thomas	1.00
3	Mike Piazza	2.00
4	Kirby Puckett	1.50
5	Manny Ramirez	1.00
6	Tony Gwynn	1.50
7	Hideo Nomo	.75
8	Matt Williams	.50
9	Randy Johnson	1.00
10	Raul Mondesi	.50
11	Albert Belle	.50
12	Ivan Rodriguez	1.00
13	Barry Bonds	3.00
14	Carlos Baerga	.50
15	Ken Griffey Jr.	2.00
16	Jeff Conine	.50
17	Frank Thomas	1.00
18	Cal Ripken Jr., Barry Bonds	2.00

Rookie Roll Call

Dufex foil printing technology on both front and back is featured on this insert set. Fronts have a large and a small player photo on a green background dominated by a large star. Backs have another photo on a green and gold background. A prestigious black and gold box at left in the hor-

izontally formatted design has a few good words about the prospect. Stated odds of finding a Rookie Roll Call card are one per 24 packs, on average.

		NM/M
Complete Set (18):		17.50
Common Player:		.60
1	Alex Rodriguez	6.00
2	Derek Jeter	7.50
3	Chipper Jones	5.00
4	Shawn Green	1.50
5	Todd Hollandsworth	.60
6	Bill Pulsipher	.60
7	Hideo Nomo	1.50
8	Ray Durham	.60
9	Curtis Goodwin	.60
10	Brian Hunter	.60
11	Julian Tavarez	.60
12	Marty Cordova	.60
13	Michael Tucker	.60
14	Edgardo Alfonzo	.60
15	LaTroy Hawkins	.60
16	Carlos Perez	.60
17	Charles Johnson	.60
18	Benji Gil	.60

Z-Team

The scarcest of the Zenith insert cards are those of 18 "living legends" profiled in the Z-Team series. Found at an average rate of only one per 72 packs, the cards are printed in technology Pinnacle calls 3-D Dufex.

		NM/M
Complete Set (18):		85.00
Common Player:		2.00
1	Cal Ripken Jr.	15.00
2	Ken Griffey Jr.	10.00
3	Frank Thomas	6.00
4	Matt Williams	2.00
5	Mike Piazza	10.00
6	Barry Bonds	15.00
7	Raul Mondesi	2.00
8	Greg Maddux	7.50
9	Jeff Bagwell	6.00
10	Manny Ramirez	6.00
11	Larry Walker	2.00
12	Tony Gwynn	7.50
13	Will Clark	2.00
14	Albert Belle	2.00
15	Kenny Lofton	2.00
16	Rafael Palmeiro	4.50
17	Don Mattingly	9.00
18	Carlos Baerga	2.00

1996 Zenith

Pinnacle's 1996 Zenith set has 150 cards in the regular set, including 30 Rookies, 20 Honor roll and two checklist cards. Each card in the set has a parallel Artist's Proof version (seeded one per every 35 packs). Insert sets include Z Team, Mozaics and two versions of Diamond Club. Normal Dufex versions of Diamond Club appear one every 24 packs; parallel versions, which have an actual diamond chip incorporated into the card design, were seeded one per every 350 packs.

		NM/M
Complete Set (150):		15.00
Common Player:		.10
Common Artist's Proofs:		2.00
Star Artist's Proofs:		12X
Pack (6):		1.50
Wax Box (24):		25.00
1	Ken Griffey Jr.	2.00
2	Ozzie Smith	1.50
3	Greg Maddux	1.50
4	Rondell White	.10
5	Mark McGwire	2.50
6	Jim Thome	.75
7	Ivan Rodriguez	.75
8	Marc Newfield	.10
9	Travis Fryman	.10
10	Fred McGriff	.10
11	Shawn Green	.25
12	Mike Piazza	2.00
13	Dante Bichette	.10
14	Tino Martinez	.10
15	Sterling Hitchcock	.10
16	Ryne Sandberg	1.50
17	Rico Brogna	.10
18	Roberto Alomar	.25
19	Barry Larkin	.10
20	Bernie Williams	.10
21	Gary Sheffield	.50
22	Frank Thomas	1.00
23	Gregg Jefferies	.10
24	Jeff Bagwell	1.00
25	Marty Cordova	.10
26	Jim Edmonds	.10
27	Jay Bell	.10
28	Ben McDonald	.10
29	Barry Bonds	3.00
30	Mo Vaughn	.10
31	Johnny Damon	.35
32	Dean Palmer	.10
33	Ismael Valdes	.10
34	Manny Ramirez	1.00
35	Edgar Martinez	.10
36	Cecil Fielder	.10
37	Ryan Klesko	.10
38	Ray Lankford	.10
39	Tim Salmon	.10
40	Joe Carter	.10
41	Jason Isringhausen	.10
42	Rickey Henderson	1.00
43	Lenny Dykstra	.10
44	Andre Dawson	.25
45	Paul O'Neill	.10
46	Ray Durham	.10
47	Raul Mondesi	.10
48	Jay Buhner	.10
49	Eddie Murray	1.00
50	Henry Rodriguez	.10
51	Hal Morris	.10
52	Mike Mussina	.50
53	Wally Joyner	.10
54	Will Clark	.10
55	Chipper Jones	1.50
56	Brian Jordan	.10
57	Larry Walker	.10
58	Wade Boggs	1.50
59	Melvin Nieves	.10
60	Charles Johnson	.10
61	Juan Gonzalez	.50
62	Carlos Delgado	.35
63	Reggie Sanders	.10
64	Brian Hunter	.10
65	Edgardo Alfonzo	.10
66	Kenny Lofton	.10
67	Paul Molitor	1.00
68	Mike Bordick	.10
69	Garret Anderson	.10
70	Orlando Merced	.10
71	Craig Biggio	.10
72	Chuck Knoblauch	.10
73	Mark Grace	.10
74	Jack McDowell	.10
75	Randy Johnson	1.00
76	Cal Ripken Jr.	3.00
77	Matt Williams	.10
78	Benji Gil	.10
79	Moises Alou	.10
80	Robin Ventura	.10
81	Greg Vaughn	.10
82	Carlos Baerga	.10
83	Roger Clemens	1.75
84	Hideo Nomo	.50
85	Pedro Martinez	1.00
86	John Valentin	.10
87	Andres Galarraga	.10
88	Andy Pettitte	.30
89	Derek Bell	.10
90	Kirby Puckett	1.50
91	Tony Gwynn	1.50
92	Brady Anderson	.10
93	Derek Jeter	3.00
94	Michael Tucker	.10
95	Albert Belle	.10
96	David Cone	.10
97	J.T. Snow	.10
98	Tom Glavine	.35
99	Alex Rodriguez	2.50
100	Sammy Sosa	1.50
101	Karim Garcia	.15
102	Alan Benes	.10
103	Chad Mottola	.10
104	Robin Jennings **RC**	.10
105	Bob Abreu	.10
106	Tony Clark	.10
107	George Arias	.10
108	Jermaine Dye	.10
109	Jeff Suppan	.10
110	Ralph Milliard **RC**	.10
111	Ruben Rivera	.10
112	Billy Wagner	.10
113	Jason Kendall	.10
114	Mike Grace **RC**	.10
115	Edgar Renteria	.10
116	Jason Schmidt	.10
117	Paul Wilson	.10
118	Rey Ordonez	.10
119	Rocky Coppinger **RC**	.10
120	Wilton Guerrero **RC**	.10
121	Brooks Kieschnick	.10
122	Raul Casanova	.10
123	Alex Ochoa	.10
124	Chan Ho Park	.10
125	John Wasdin	.10
126	Eric Owens	.10
127	Justin Thompson	.10
128	Chris Snopek	.10
129	Terrell Wade	.10
130	Darin Erstad **RC**	1.50
131	Albert Belle (Honor Roll)	.10
132	Cal Ripken Jr. (Honor Roll)	1.50
133	Frank Thomas (Honor Roll)	.60
134	Greg Maddux (Honor Roll)	.75
135	Ken Griffey Jr. (Honor Roll)	1.00
136	Mo Vaughn (Honor Roll)	.10
137	Chipper Jones (Honor Roll)	.75
138	Mike Piazza (Honor Roll)	1.00
139	Ryan Klesko (Honor Roll)	.10
140	Hideo Nomo (Honor Roll)	.20
141	Roberto Alomar (Honor Roll)	.10
142	Manny Ramirez (Honor Roll)	.60
143	Gary Sheffield (Honor Roll)	.10
144	Barry Bonds (Honor Roll)	1.50
145	Matt Williams (Honor Roll)	.10
146	Jim Edmonds (Honor Roll)	.10
147	Derek Jeter (Honor Roll)	1.50
148	Sammy Sosa (Honor Roll)	.75
149	Kirby Puckett (Honor Roll)	.75
150	Tony Gwynn (Honor Roll)	.75

Artist's Proofs

Each card in the '96 Zenith base set can also be found in a specially marked Artist's Proof version. The AP cards were found on average of once per 35 packs.

	NM/M
Common Player:	2.00
Stars:	12X

Diamond Club

Twenty different players are featured on these two 1996 Pinnacle Zenith insert cards. Normal Dufex versions are inserted one per every 24 packs. Parallel versions of these cards, containing an ac-

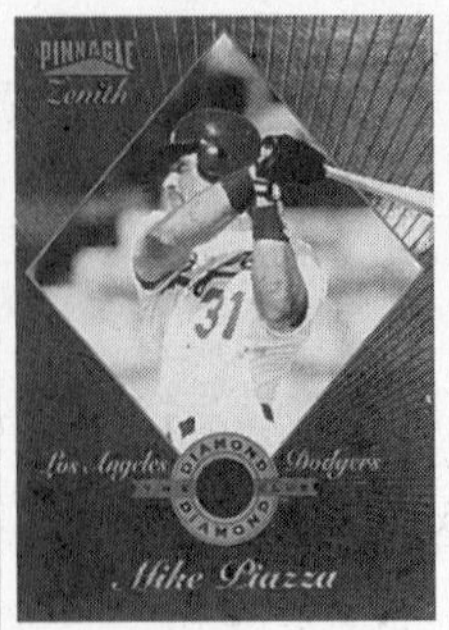

tual diamond chip incorporated into the design, were seeded one per every 350 packs.

		NM/M
Complete Set (20):		17.50
Common Player:		.45
Diamond Versions:		12X
1	Albert Belle	.45
2	Mo Vaughn	.45
3	Ken Griffey Jr.	1.50
4	Mike Piazza	1.50
5	Cal Ripken Jr.	2.50
6	Jermaine Dye	.45
7	Jeff Bagwell	1.00
8	Frank Thomas	1.00
9	Alex Rodriguez	2.00
10	Ryan Klesko	.45
11	Roberto Alomar	.60
12	Sammy Sosa	1.25
13	Matt Williams	.45
14	Gary Sheffield	.75
15	Ruben Rivera	.45
16	Darin Erstad	.60
17	Randy Johnson	1.00
18	Greg Maddux	1.25
19	Karim Garcia	.60
20	Chipper Jones	1.25

Mozaics

Each of these 1996 Pinnacle Zenith cards contains multiple player images for the team represented on the card. The cards were inserted one per every 10 packs.

		NM/M
Complete Set (25):		30.00
Common Card:		.45
1	Greg Maddux, Chipper Jones, Ryan Klesko	3.00
2	Juan Gonzalez, Will Clark, Ivan Rodriguez	1.00
3	Frank Thomas, Robin Ventura, Ray Durham	1.00
4	Matt Williams, Barry Bonds, Osvaldo Fernandez	5.00
5	Ken Griffey Jr., Randy Johnson, Alex Rodriguez	4.00
6	Sammy Sosa, Ryne Sandberg, Mark Grace	4.00
7	Jim Edmonds, Tim Salmon, Garret Anderson	.45
8	Cal Ripken Jr., Roberto Alomar, Mike Mussina	5.00
9	Mo Vaughn, Roger Clemens, John Valentin	3.50
10	Barry Larkin, Reggie Sanders, Hal Morris	.45
11	Ray Lankford, Brian Jordan, Ozzie Smith	1.50
12	Dante Bichette, Larry Walker, Andres Galarraga	.45
13	Mike Piazza, Hideo Nomo, Raul Mondesi	4.00
14	Ben McDonald, Greg Vaughn, Kevin Seitzer	.45
15	Joe Carter, Carlos Delgado, Alex Gonzalez	.60
16	Gary Sheffield, Charles Johnson, Jeff Conine	.45
17	Rondell White, Moises Alou, Henry Rodriguez	.45
18	Albert Belle, Manny Ramirez, Carlos Baerga	1.00
19	Kirby Puckett, Paul Molitor, Chuck Knoblauch	1.50
20	Tony Gwynn, Rickey Henderson, Wally Joyner	2.00
21	Mark McGwire, Mike Bordick, Scott Brosius	4.00
22	Paul O'Neill, Bernie Williams, Wade Boggs	1.50
23	Jay Bell, Orlando Merced, Jason Kendall	.45
24	Rico Brogna, Paul Wilson, Jason Isringhausen	.45
25	Jeff Bagwell, Craig Biggio, Derek Bell	1.00

Z-Team Samples

Each of the first nine micro-etched plastic-printed Z-Team insert cards can also be found in an edition which is overprinted "SAMPLE" on the front. These cards were distributed to hobby dealers.

		NM/M
Complete Set (9):		35.00
Common Player:		3.00
1	Ken Griffey Jr.	4.50
2	Albert Belle	3.00
3	Cal Ripken Jr.	7.50
4	Frank Thomas	3.50
5	Greg Maddux	4.00
6	Mo Vaughn	3.00
7	Chipper Jones	4.00
8	Mike Piazza	4.50
9	Ryan Klesko	3.00

Z-Team

Pinnacle's 1996 Zenith baseball continues the Z-Team insert concept with a new clear plastic treatment that is micro-etched for a see-through design that allows light to shine through etched highlights and a green baseball field background. The 18 cards were seeded one per every 72 packs.

		NM/M
Complete Set (18):		100.00
Common Player:		3.00
1	Ken Griffey Jr.	12.50
2	Albert Belle	3.00
3	Cal Ripken Jr.	20.00
4	Frank Thomas	7.50
5	Greg Maddux	10.00
6	Mo Vaughn	3.00
7	Chipper Jones	10.00
8	Mike Piazza	12.50
9	Ryan Klesko	3.00
10	Hideo Nomo	4.50
11	Roberto Alomar	3.00
12	Manny Ramirez	6.00
13	Gary Sheffield	3.50
14	Barry Bonds	20.00
15	Matt Williams	3.00
16	Jim Edmonds	3.00
17	Kirby Puckett	10.00
18	Sammy Sosa	10.00

1997 Zenith Samples

The extent of the sample-marked version of the standard-size '97 Zenith cards is unknown.

		NM/M
Common Player:		1.50
S1	Ken Griffey Jr.	5.00
S6	Kenny Lofton	1.50

1997 Zenith

This set combines standard size trading cards with cards in an 8" x 10" format. The standard size set consists of 60 cards. Card fronts feature full-bleed photos and the word "Zenith," but no reference to the player's name or team is found on the fronts. Backs have another player photo, a hit location chart and 1996/career stats. There are four inserts in the set, all of which are printed on the larger size format - 8" x 10", 8" x 10" Dufex, 8" x 10" V-2, and Z-Team. Each sale unit contained one pack of five standard-size cards and two larger size cards for a suggested retail price of $9.99.

		NM/M
Complete Set (50):		15.00
Common Player:		.10
Pack (5 cards, 2 8x10):		2.00
Wax Box (12):		25.00
1	Frank Thomas	.75
2	Tony Gwynn	1.00
3	Jeff Bagwell	.75
4	Paul Molitor	.75
5	Roberto Alomar	.20
6	Mike Piazza	1.25
7	Albert Belle	.10
8	Greg Maddux	1.00
9	Barry Larkin	.10
10	Tony Clark	.10
11	Larry Walker	.10
12	Chipper Jones	1.00
13	Juan Gonzalez	.40
14	Barry Bonds	2.00
15	Ivan Rodriguez	.65
16	Sammy Sosa	1.00
17	Derek Jeter	2.00
18	Hideo Nomo	.40
19	Roger Clemens	1.00
20	Ken Griffey Jr.	1.25

21	Andy Pettitte	.25
22	Alex Rodriguez	1.50
23	Tino Martinez	.10
24	Bernie Williams	.10
25	Ken Caminiti	.10
26	John Smoltz	.10
27	Javier Lopez	.10
28	Mark McGwire	1.50
29	Gary Sheffield	.50
30	David Justice	.10
31	Randy Johnson	.75
32	Chuck Knoblauch	.10
33	Mike Mussina	.40
34	Deion Sanders	.20
35	Cal Ripken Jr.	2.00
36	Darin Erstad	.30
37	Kenny Lofton	.10
38	Jay Buhner	.10
39	Brady Anderson	.10
40	Edgar Martinez	.10
41	Mo Vaughn	.10
42	Ryne Sandberg	1.00
43	Andruw Jones	.75
44	Nomar Garciaparra	1.00
45	Hideki Irabu **RC**	.25
46	Wilton Guerrero	.10
47	Jose Cruz Jr. **RC**	.45
48	Vladimir Guerrero	.75
49	Scott Rolen	.65
50	Jose Guillen	.10

V-2

This eight-card die-cut insert utilizes motion technology as well as foil printing to create a very high-tech 8" x 10" card. Cards were inserted 1:47 packs.

		NM/M
Complete Set (8):		45.00
Common Player:		5.00
1	Ken Griffey Jr.	7.50
2	Andruw Jones	5.00
3	Frank Thomas	5.00
4	Mike Piazza	7.50
5	Alex Rodriguez	10.00
6	Cal Ripken Jr.	12.00
7	Derek Jeter	12.00
8	Vladimir Guerrero	5.00

Z-Team

This nine-card 8" x 10" insert is printed on a mirror gold mylar foil stock with each card sequentially numbered to 1,000.

		NM/M
Complete Set (9):		60.00
Common Player:		3.00
1	Ken Griffey Jr.	9.00
2	Larry Walker	3.00
3	Frank Thomas	6.00
4	Alex Rodriguez	10.00
5	Mike Piazza	9.00
6	Cal Ripken Jr.	12.50
7	Derek Jeter	12.50
8	Andruw Jones	6.00
9	Roger Clemens	7.50

8x10 and 8x10 Dufex

This 24-card insert takes select cards from the standard set and blows them up to an 8" x 10" format. Cards were inserted one per pack. A Dufex version of each 8" x 10" insert card was also available at a rate of one per pack (except in packs which contained either a Z-Team or V-2 card).

		NM/M
Complete Set (24):		20.00
Common Player:		.50
Dufex versions:		1X
Samples:		1X
1	Frank Thomas	1.00
2	Tony Gwynn	1.50
3	Jeff Bagwell	1.00
4	Ken Griffey Jr.	2.00
5	Mike Piazza	2.00
6	Greg Maddux	1.50
7	Ken Caminiti	.50
8	Albert Belle	.50
9	Ivan Rodriguez	.75
10	Sammy Sosa	1.50
11	Mark McGwire	2.50
12	Roger Clemens	1.75
13	Alex Rodriguez	2.50
14	Chipper Jones	1.50
15	Juan Gonzalez	.60
16	Barry Bonds	3.00
17	Derek Jeter	3.00
18	Hideo Nomo	.60
19	Cal Ripken Jr.	3.00
20	Hideki Irabu	.50
21	Andruw Jones	1.00
22	Nomar Garciaparra	1.50
23	Vladimir Guerrero	1.00
24	Scott Rolen	.75

1998 Zenith Samples

To introduce its "Dare to Tear" concept, Zenith's promo cards for 1998 included a specially-marked standard-size (2-1/2" x 3-1/2") sample card within a 5" x 7" card. All cards are marked "SAMPLE" on back, but are otherwise identical to the issued versions.

		NM/M
Complete Set, Large (9):		17.50
Common Player, Large:		1.00
Complete Set, Small (6):		12.00
Common Player, Small:		1.00
Z1	Nomar Garciaparra	2.00
Z3	Greg Maddux	2.00
Z4	Frank Thomas	1.50
Z9	Andruw Jones	1.50
Z15	Derek Jeter	4.00
Z21	Mike Piazza	2.50
Z22	Tony Gwynn	2.00
Z35	Ivan Rodriguez	1.00
Z40	Ken Griffey Jr.	2.50
2	Ken Griffey Jr.	2.50
12	Greg Maddux	2.00
14	Mike Piazza	2.50
17	Derek Jeter	4.00
18	Nomar Garciaparra	2.00
19	Ivan Rodriguez	1.00

1998 Zenith

Zenith was part of Pinnacle's "Dare to Tear" program. Sold in three-card packs, the set consists of 5" x 7" cards, each with a standard-size card packaged inside. Collectors had to decide whether to keep the large cards or tear them open to get the smaller card inside. Eighty 5" x 7" cards and 100 regular cards comprise the set. The regular, or Z2, cards were paralleled twice - Z-Silver (1:7) and Z-Gold (numbered to 100). The large cards also had two parallels - Impulse (1:7) and Gold Impulse (numbered to 100).

		NM/M
Complete Set (100):		25.00
Common Player:		.10
Silvers:		2X
Inserted 1:7		
Pack (3):		2.50
Wax Box (18):		35.00
1	Larry Walker	.10
2	Ken Griffey Jr.	1.75
3	Cal Ripken Jr.	2.50
4	Sammy Sosa	1.50
5	Andruw Jones	1.00
6	Frank Thomas	1.00
7	Tony Gwynn	1.50
8	Rafael Palmeiro	.75
9	Tim Salmon	.10
10	Randy Johnson	1.00
11	Juan Gonzalez	.50
12	Greg Maddux	1.50
13	Vladimir Guerrero	1.00
14	Mike Piazza	1.75
15	Andres Galarraga	.10
16	Alex Rodriguez	2.00
17	Derek Jeter	2.50
18	Nomar Garciaparra	1.50
19	Ivan Rodriguez	.75
20	Chipper Jones	1.50
21	Barry Larkin	.10
22	Mo Vaughn	.10
23	Albert Belle	.10
24	Scott Rolen	.65
25	Sandy Alomar Jr.	.10
26	Roberto Alomar	.30
27	Andy Pettitte	.30
28	Chuck Knoblauch	.10
29	Jeff Bagwell	1.00
30	Mike Mussina	.30
31	Fred McGriff	.10
32	Roger Clemens	1.50
33	Rusty Greer	.10
34	Edgar Martinez	.10
35	Paul Molitor	1.00
36	Mark Grace	.10
37	Darin Erstad	.30
38	Kenny Lofton	.10
39	Tom Glavine	.35
40	Javier Lopez	.10
41	Will Clark	.10
42	Tino Martinez	.10
43	Raul Mondesi	.10
44	Brady Anderson	.10
45	Chan Ho Park	.10
46	Jason Giambi	.75
47	Manny Ramirez	1.00
48	Jay Buhner	.10
49	Dante Bichette	.10
50	Jose Cruz Jr.	.10
51	Charles Johnson	.10
52	Bernard Gilkey	.10
53	Johnny Damon	.35
54	David Justice	.10
55	Justin Thompson	.10
56	Bobby Higginson	.10
57	Todd Hundley	.10
58	Gary Sheffield	.50
59	Barry Bonds	2.50
60	Mark McGwire	2.00
61	John Smoltz	.10
62	Tony Clark	.10
63	Brian Jordan	.10
64	Jason Kendall	.10
65	Mariano Rivera	.20
66	Pedro Martinez	1.00
67	Jim Thome	.75
68	Neifi Perez	.10
69	Kevin Brown	.10
70	Hideo Nomo	.50
71	Craig Biggio	.10
72	Bernie Williams	.10
73	Jose Guillen	.10
74	Ken Caminiti	.10
75	Livan Hernandez	.10
76	Ray Lankford	.10
77	Jim Edmonds	.10
78	Matt Williams	.10
79	Mark Kotsay	.10
80	Moises Alou	.10
81	Antone Williamson	.10
82	Jaret Wright	.10
83	Jacob Cruz	.10
84	Abraham Nunez	.10
85	Raul Ibanez	.10
86	Miguel Tejada	.10
87	Derek Lee	.50
88	Juan Encarnacion	.10
89	Todd Helton	.75
90	Travis Lee	.10
91	Ben Grieve	.10
92	Ryan McGuire	.10
93	Richard Hidalgo	.10
94	Paul Konerko	.15
95	Shannon Stewart	.10
96	Homer Bush	.10
97	Lou Collier	.10
98	Jeff Abbott	.10
99	Brett Tomko	.10
100	Fernando Tatis	.10

Z-Silver

This parallel set reprinted all 100 standard sized cards in Zenith on silver foilboard, with

a "Z-Silver" logo across the bottom center. Z-Silvers were inserted one per seven packs.

	NM/M
Common Player:	1.00
Stars/RC's:	2X
Inserted 1:7	

Z-Gold

	NM/M
Common Player:	3.00
Stars/Rookies	12X
Production 100 Sets	

Epix

Epix is a cross-brand insert. The set honors Plays, Games, Seasons and Moments in the careers of top baseball players. Epix consisted of 24 cards in Zenith, inserted 1:11. The cards have orange, purple and emerald versions.

		NM/M
Complete Set (24):		95.00
Common (Orange) Card:		1.50
Purples:		1X
Emeralds:		2X
1	Ken Griffey Jr./S	7.50
2	Juan Gonzalez/S	2.50
3	Jeff Bagwell/S	4.50
4	Ivan Rodriguez/S	4.00
5	Nomar Garciaparra/S	6.00
6	Ryne Sandberg/S	6.00
7	Frank Thomas/M	4.50
8	Derek Jeter/M	12.00
9	Tony Gwynn/M	6.00
10	Albert Belle/M	1.50
11	Scott Rolen/M	3.50
12	Barry Larkin/M	1.50
13	Alex Rodriguez/P	9.00
14	Cal Ripken Jr./P	12.00
15	Chipper Jones/P	6.00
16	Roger Clemens/P	6.50
17	Mo Vaughn/P	1.50
18	Mark McGwire/P	9.00
19	Mike Piazza/G	7.50
20	Andruw Jones/G	4.50
21	Greg Maddux/G	6.00
22	Barry Bonds/G	12.00
23	Paul Molitor/G	4.50
24	Eddie Murray/G	4.50

Raising the Bar

Raising the Bar is a 15-card insert seeded 1:25. The set features players who have set high standards for other players to follow.

		NM/M
Complete Set (15):		25.00
Common Player:		1.25
Inserted 1:25		
1	Ken Griffey Jr.	3.00
2	Frank Thomas	1.50
3	Alex Rodriguez	3.50
4	Tony Gwynn	2.50
5	Mike Piazza	3.00
6	Ivan Rodriguez	1.25
7	Cal Ripken Jr.	4.50
8	Greg Maddux	2.50
9	Hideo Nomo	1.25
10	Mark McGwire	3.50
11	Juan Gonzalez	1.25
12	Andruw Jones	1.50
13	Jeff Bagwell	1.50
14	Chipper Jones	2.50
15	Nomar Garciaparra	2.50

Rookie Thrills

Rookie Thrills is a 15-card insert seeded 1:25. The set features many of the top rookies of 1998 in action photos printed on a silver-foil background. Backs have a few words about the player's career to that point.

		NM/M
Complete Set (15):		20.00
Common Player:		1.50
Inserted 1:25		
1	Travis Lee	1.50
2	Juan Encarnacion	1.50
3	Derrek Lee	1.50
4	Raul Ibanez	1.50
5	Ryan McGuire	1.50
6	Todd Helton	3.00
7	Jacob Cruz	1.50
8	Abraham Nunez	1.50
9	Paul Konerko	2.00
10	Ben Grieve	1.50
11	Jeff Abbott	1.50
12	Richard Hidalgo	1.50
13	Jaret Wright	1.50
14	Lou Collier	1.50
15	Miguel Tejada	2.00

Z-Team

The Z Team insert was created in 5" x 7" and standard-size versions, each inserted at a 1:35 pack rate. The nine Rookie Z Team cards were seeded 1:58 and gold versions of both were found 1:175.

		NM/M
Complete Set (18):		35.00
Common Player:		1.25
Golds:		2X
Inserted 1:175		
1	Frank Thomas	2.50
2	Ken Griffey Jr.	3.50
3	Mike Piazza	3.50
4	Cal Ripken Jr.	6.00
5	Alex Rodriguez	5.00
6	Greg Maddux	3.00
7	Derek Jeter	6.00
8	Chipper Jones	3.00
9	Roger Clemens	3.25
10	Ben Grieve	1.25
11	Derrek Lee	1.75
12	Jose Cruz Jr.	1.25
13	Nomar Garciaparra	3.00
14	Travis Lee	1.50
15	Todd Helton	2.00
16	Paul Konerko	1.75
17	Miguel Tejada	1.25
18	Scott Rolen	2.00

Z-Team 5x7

The 5" x 7" Z-Team insert is a nine-card set seeded one per 35 packs.

		NM/M
Complete Set (9):		40.00
Common Player:		3.00
Inserted 1:35		
1	Frank Thomas	3.00
2	Ken Griffey Jr.	5.00
3	Mike Piazza	5.00
4	Cal Ripken Jr.	7.50
5	Alex Rodriguez	6.00
6	Greg Maddux	4.00
7	Derek Jeter	7.50
8	Chipper Jones	4.00
9	Roger Clemens	4.50

5x7

The 80 Zenith 5" x 7" cards all contained a regular-size card. Collectors could tear open the 5" x 7" to get at the smaller card inside. The set has two parallels: 5" x 7" Impulse (1:7) and 5" x 7" Gold Impulse (1:43).

		NM/M
Complete Set (80):		30.00
Common Player:		.25
Impulse Silvers:		1.5X
Inserted 1:7		
1	Nomar Garciaparra	2.00
2	Andres Galarraga	.25
3	Greg Maddux	2.00
4	Frank Thomas	1.00
5	Mark McGwire	3.00
6	Rafael Palmeiro	.75
7	John Smoltz	.25
8	Jeff Bagwell	1.00
9	Andruw Jones	1.00
10	Rusty Greer	.25
11	Paul Molitor	1.00
12	Bernie Williams	.25
13	Kenny Lofton	.25
14	Alex Rodriguez	3.00
15	Derek Jeter	4.00
15s	Derek Jeter ("SAMPLE" overprint on back.)	4.00
16	Scott Rolen	.65
17	Albert Belle	.25
18	Mo Vaughn	.25
19	Chipper Jones	2.00
20	Chuck Knoblauch	.25
21	Mike Piazza	3.00
22	Tony Gwynn	2.00
22s	Tony Gwynn ("SAMPLE" overprint on back.)	2.00
23	Juan Gonzalez	.50
24	Andy Pettitte	.35
25	Tim Salmon	.25
26	Brady Anderson	.25
27	Mike Mussina	.40
28	Edgar Martinez	.25
29	Jose Guillen	.25
30	Hideo Nomo	.50
31	Jim Thome	.65
32	Mark Grace	.25
33	Darin Erstad	.50
34	Bobby Higginson	.25
35	Ivan Rodriguez	.75
36	Todd Hundley	.25
37	Sandy Alomar Jr.	.25
38	Gary Sheffield	.40
39	David Justice	.25
40	Ken Griffey Jr.	2.50
40s	Ken Griffey Jr. ("SAMPLE" overprint on back.)	2.50
41	Vladimir Guerrero	1.00
42	Larry Walker	.25
43	Barry Bonds	4.00

44	Randy Johnson	1.00
45	Roger Clemens	2.25
46	Raul Mondesi	.25
47	Tino Martinez	.25
48	Jason Giambi	.50
49	Matt Williams	.25
50	Cal Ripken Jr.	4.00
51	Barry Larkin	.25
52	Jim Edmonds	.25
53	Ken Caminiti	.25
54	Sammy Sosa	2.00
55	Tony Clark	.25
56	Manny Ramirez	1.00
57	Bernard Gilkey	.25
58	Jose Cruz Jr.	.25
59	Brian Jordan	.25
60	Kevin Brown	.25
61	Craig Biggio	.25
62	Javier Lopez	.25
63	Jay Buhner	.25
64	Roberto Alomar	.40
65	Justin Thompson	.25
66	Todd Helton	.75
67	Travis Lee	.25
68	Paul Konerko	.35
69	Jaret Wright	.25
70	Ben Grieve	.25
71	Juan Encarnacion	.25
72	Ryan McGuire	.25
73	Derrek Lee	.60
74	Abraham Nunez	.25
75	Richard Hidalgo	.25
76	Miguel Tejada	.25
77	Jacob Cruz	.25
78	Homer Bush	.25
79	Jeff Abbott	.25
80	Lou Collier	.25
	Checklist	.10

5x7 Impulse Silver

These silver parallels reprinted each of the 80 cards in the 5" x 7" set. Cards were called Impulse and carried that logo on the front and were inserted one per seven packs. Since these cards contained other cards inside them, they are condition sensitive and only worth full price if left in mint condition and not cut open.

	NM/M
Common Player:	2.00
Stars/RC's:	1.5X
Inserted 1:7	

5x7 Impulse Gold

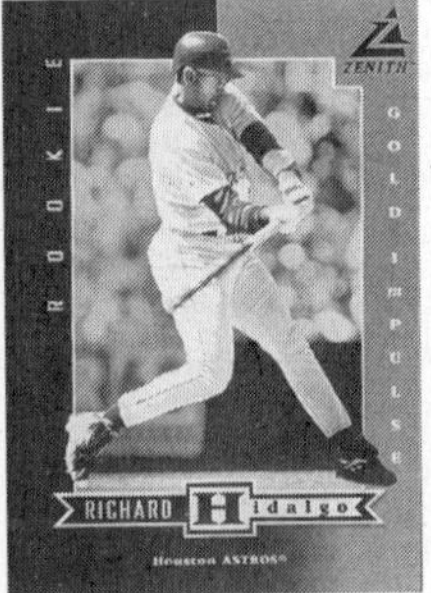

These gold parallels reprint each of the 80 cards in the 5" x 7" set. Cards carry a Gold Impulse logo on front and are serially numbered from within an edition of 100 each on back. Silver or Gold Impulse parallels were inserted one per seven packs. Since these cards contained other cards inside them, they are condition sensitive and only worth full price if left in mint condition and not cut open.

NM/M

Common Player:	5.00
Stars/RC's:	20X
Inserted 1:7	

1992 Ziploc

Dow Brands produced an 11-card set of All-Stars in 1992 that featured mostly Hall of Famers, with the exception only of Nellie Fox. The cards were included in specially-marked Ziploc packages, and also could be purchased by mail.

		NM/M
Complete Set (11):		4.00
Common Player:		.45
1	Warren Spahn	.50
2	Bob Gibson	.50
3	Rollie Fingers	.50
4	Carl Yastrzemski	1.00
5	Brooks Robinson	.50
6	Pee Wee Reese	.75
7	Willie McCovey	.50
8	Willie Mays	2.00
9	Nellie Fox	.50
10	Yogi Berra	.75
11	Hank Aaron	2.00

Abbreviation Key

IS: Interleague Showdown
OPS: Overprinted "Promotional Sample"
ED: Expansion Draft
AS: All-Star
HL: Hit List
RC: Rookie Class
RC or (RC): Rookie Card
UPT: Unlimited Potential/Talent
SF: Star Factor
SP: Short Print
DT: Double Team
GLS: Gold Leaf Stars
CC: Curtain Calls
GLR: Gold Leaf Rookies
TP: Top Performers
FF: Future Foundation
DK: Diamond King
RR: Rated Rookie
DP: Double Print
IA: In Action
PC: Promo Card
SR: Star Rookie

MINOR LEAGUE (1867-1969)

Prior to 1970 virtually all minor league baseball cards were issued as single cards rather than the complete sets. Like contemporary major league cards they were usually intended as premiums given away with the purchase of goos and services.

The listings which follow offer individual card prices in three grades of preservation to allow accurate valuations of superstar and other special interest cards, along with cards that were short-printed or otherwise are scarce.

1959 APCO Meat Packing Co. San Antonio Missions

The extent of this issue, as well as its distribution are not known. The 3-1/2" x 4-1/2" black-and-white cards may have been packaged with meat products and/or given away at the ballpark. The team was Class AA affiliate of the Chicago Cubs.

	NM	EX	VG
Common Player:	50.00	25.00	15.00
(1) Russell Gragg	50.00	25.00	15.00
(2) Mike Lutz (In Corpus Christi uniform.)	50.00	25.00	15.00

1960 Armour Meats Denver Bears

Ten cards from this Class AA farm team of the Detroit Tigers have been checklisted, with others possibly to be discovered. The black-and-white blank-backed cards measure 2-1/2" x 3-1/4" and were issued with a coupon attached to the right side. The unnumbered cards are checklisted here alphabetically.

	NM	EX	VG
Complete Set (10):	650.00	325.00	195.00
Common Player:	75.00	37.00	22.00
(1) George Alusik	75.00	37.00	22.00
(2) Tony Bartirome	75.00	37.00	22.00
(3) Edward J. Donnelly	75.00	37.00	22.00
(4) James R. McDaniel	75.00	37.00	22.00
(5) Charlie Metro	75.00	37.00	22.00
(6) Harry Perkowski	75.00	37.00	22.00
(7) Vernon E. Rapp	75.00	37.00	22.00
(8) James Stump	75.00	37.00	22.00
(9) Ozzie Virgil	75.00	37.00	22.00
(10) Robert Walz	75.00	37.00	22.00

1940 Associated Stations San Francisco Seals

This album and sticker set was created as a premium by a Northern California gas company. Individual stickers were given away each week at participating service stations. The blank-backed, 1-3/4" x 2-5/8" stickers have the player's name in a black strip at the bottom. Pages in the accompanying 3-1/2" x 6" album have space for an autograph and a few career highlights for each player. The checklist is presented in page order of the album.

	NM	EX	VG
Complete Set (26):	500.00	250.00	125.00
Common Player:	20.00	10.00	6.00
Album:	100.00	50.00	30.00
(1) "Lefty" O'Doul	40.00	20.00	12.00
(2) Sam Gibson	20.00	10.00	6.00
(3) Brooks Holder	20.00	10.00	6.00
(4) Ted Norbert	20.00	10.00	6.00
(5) Win Ballou	20.00	10.00	6.00
(6) Al Wright	20.00	10.00	6.00
(7) Al Epperly	20.00	10.00	6.00
(8) Orville Jorgens	20.00	10.00	6.00
(9) Larry Powell	20.00	10.00	6.00
(10) Joe Sprinz	20.00	10.00	6.00
(11) Harvey Storey	20.00	10.00	6.00
(12) Jack Burns	20.00	10.00	6.00
(13) Bob Price	20.00	10.00	6.00
(14) Larry Guay	20.00	10.00	6.00
(15) Frank Dasso	20.00	10.00	6.00
(16) Eddie Stutz	20.00	10.00	6.00
(17) John Barrett	20.00	10.00	6.00
(18) Eddie Botelho	20.00	10.00	6.00
(19) Ferris Fain	30.00	15.00	9.00
(20) Larry Woodall	20.00	10.00	6.00
(21) Ted Jennings	20.00	10.00	6.00
(22) Jack Warner	20.00	10.00	6.00
(23) Wil Leonard	20.00	10.00	6.00
(24) Gene Kiley	20.00	10.00	6.00
(25) Bob Jensen	20.00	10.00	6.00
(26) Wilfrid Le Febvre	20.00	10.00	6.00

1952 Atlanta Crackers Souvenir Pictures Album

Rather than a set of individual baseball cards, the Class AA Southern Association farm club of the Boston Braves issued this souvenir picture album depicting players (including future major leaguers like Chuck Tanner, Art Fowler and Carl Wiley), staff and media. About 8-1/8" x 7-1/2", the album has embossed metallic light blue covers and dark blue graphics. Inside are eight black-and-white pages with three card-like images per page. The pictures are in about the same size and format as Globe Printing's contemporary minor league baseball card team sets.

	NM	EX	VG
Complete Souvenir Book: 1952 Atlanta Crackers	400.00	200.00	120.00

1910 A.W.H./A.W.A. Caramels Virginia League (E222)

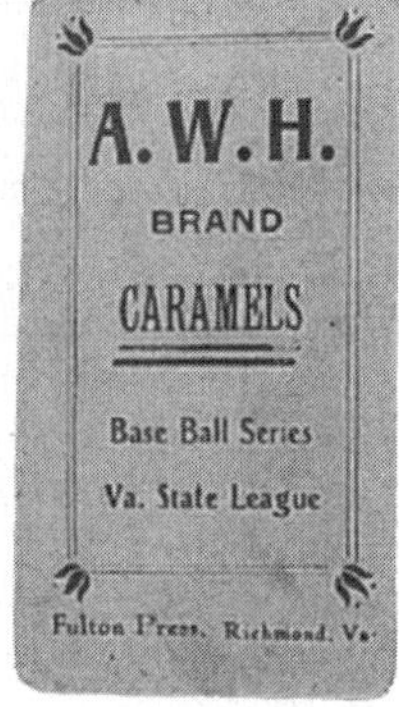

This rare set of cards picturing players from the Virginia League was issued by the A.W.H. (or A.W.A.) Caramel Co. in 1910. The cards measure 1-1/2" x 2-3/4" and feature player portraits in either red, black, brown or blue duotones. Examples of 12 different cards have been found. The front of the card displays the player's last name and team below his photo. The back states "A.W.H. (or A.W.A.) Brand Caramels" in large letters with "Base Ball Series/Va. State League" below. At least four variations in back typography and borders are known.

	NM	EX	VG
Complete Set (12):	100,000	40,000	25,000
Common Player:	9,000	3,600	2,250
(1) Tom Guiheen	9,000	3,600	2,250
(2) Hooker	9,000	3,600	2,250
(3) Ison	9,000	3,600	2,250
(4) Lipe	9,000	3,600	2,250
(5) McCauley	9,000	3,600	2,250
(6) Otey	9,000	3,600	2,250
(7) Revelle	9,000	3,600	2,250
(8) Ryan	9,000	3,600	2,250
(9) Shaugnessy	9,000	3,600	2,250
(10) Sieber	9,000	3,600	2,250
(11) Smith	9,000	3,600	2,250
(12) Titman	9,000	3,600	2,250

B

1910 Baltimore News Orioles

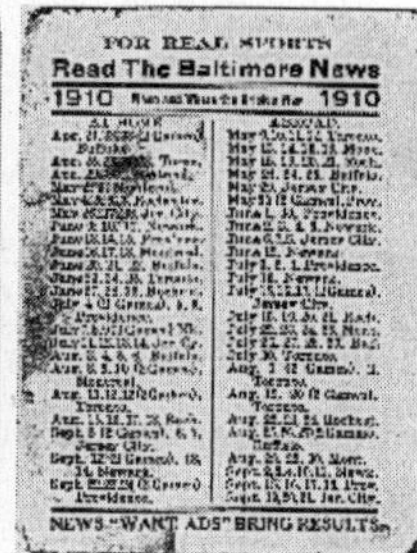
FOR REAL SPORTS
Read The Baltimore News
1910 1910
NEWS "WANT ADS" BRING RESULTS

The Eastern League Baltimore Orioles are featured in this set of schedule cards issued by a local newspaper. Cards measure 2-3/4" x 3-1/2" and feature player photographs on front, with a wide border. Player name, position, team and league are printed at the bottom of the photo. Backs have both the "Home" and "Abroad" schedule for the team, along with ads at top and bottom for the newspaper. All printing on front is in red-and-white; backs are in black-and-white. The checklist here is likely incomplete.

	NM	EX	VG
Common Player:	1,200	600.00	350.00
(1) Byers	1,200	600.00	350.00
(2) Jim Egan	1,200	600.00	350.00
(3) Maisel	1,200	600.00	350.00
(4) Malloy	1,200	600.00	350.00
(5) Jimmy Murray	1,200	600.00	350.00

1914 Baltimore News Orioles

Read The Baltimore News
1914 When and Where the Orioles Play. 1914
AT HOME. ABROAD.
This Card is Given to

The International League Baltimore Orioles are one of two teams featured (along with the city's Federal League team) in this set of newspaper promotional cards. The 2-5/8" x 3-5/8" cards are monochrome printed in either blue or red with wide borders on front framing full-length action poses on which the background has been erased in favor of artificial shadows. Player name, position and league are printed on front. Backs have a "HOME" and "ABROAD" schedule with an ad for the paper at top and a line at bottom which reads,

"This Card is Given to," with space for a signature. At least one card, a Babe Ruth, has been seen with "Compliments Baltimore International League" replacing the newspaper ad at top. Only the minor league Orioles players are listed here, the Terrapins cards are listed in the major league section of this catalog. This checklist is almost certainly incomplete.

		NM	EX	VG
Common Player:		3,000	1,500	900.00
(1)	Neal Ball	3,000	1,500	900.00
(2)	Ensign Cottrell	3,000	1,500	900.00
(3)	Birdie Cree	3,000	1,500	900.00
(4)	Bert Daniels	3,000	1,500	900.00
(5)	Davidson	3,000	1,500	900.00
(6)	Jack Dunn	4,500	2,250	1,350
(8)	Gleichmann	3,000	1,500	900.00
(9)	Allen Russell (Allan)	3,000	1,500	900.00
(10)	Babe Ruth (Blue PSA 4 (VG-EX) card sold in 5/05 auction for $244,000. Red PSA 1 (Poor-Fair) sold in 4/06 auction for $150,800. Upgraded VG sold in 5/07 auction for $517,000)			
(11)	Ernie Shore	3,000	1,500	900.00
(12)	George Twombley (Twombly)	3,000	1,500	900.00

1952 Baltimore Orioles Team Issue

ROY WEATHERLY

While most of the company's issues were for minor league teams in the lower classifications, Globe Printing of San Jose, Calif., also produced a set for the International League Baltimore Orioles. Similar to the company's other issues, the black-and-white cards measure about 2-1/4" x 3-3/8". Reliable reports indicate that individual cards were given away with ice cream purchases at the ballpark. The checklist here is obviously incomplete. In 1952 the O's were the top farm club of the Philadelphia Phillies.

		NM	EX	VG
Common Player:		75.00	37.50	22.50
(1)	Al Cihocki	75.00	37.50	22.50
(2)	Blix Donnelly	75.00	37.50	22.50
(3)	Bob Greenwood	75.00	37.50	22.50
(4)	Don Heffner	75.00	37.50	22.50
(5)	Russ Kerns	75.00	37.50	22.50
(6)	Howie Moss	75.00	37.50	22.50
(7)	Dee Phillips	75.00	37.50	22.50
(8)	Jerry Scala	75.00	37.50	22.50
(9)	Danny Schell	75.00	37.50	22.50
(10)	Paul Stuffel	75.00	37.50	22.50
(11)	Roy Weatherly	75.00	37.50	22.50

1923 Baltimore Shirt Co. Kansas City Blues

LENA BLACKBURNE

This unusual souvenir of the American Association Champion K.C. Blues is in the form of a 48" x 3-5/8" accordian-fold packet. Individual 1-7/8" x 3-1/4" black-and-white photos of the players are glued onto the black backing paper. Because the photos are rather easily removed, they may be encountered as singles. The players are checklisted here as they originally appeared, from left to right, on the foldout. There is no advertising on the individual pictures, just on the outer covers.

		NM	EX	VG
Complete Foldout:		1,000	500.00	300.00
Complete Set, Singles:		750.00	375.00	225.00
Common Player:		50.00	25.00	15.00
(1)	Wilbur Good	50.00	25.00	15.00
(2)	Bill Skiff	50.00	25.00	15.00
(3)	Lew McCarty	50.00	25.00	15.00
(4)	Dudley Branom	50.00	25.00	15.00
(5)	Lena Blackburne	55.00	27.50	16.50
(6)	Walter Hammond	50.00	25.00	15.00
(7)	Glen Wright (Glenn)	60.00	30.00	18.00
(8)	Geo. Armstrong	50.00	25.00	15.00
(9)	Beals Becker	50.00	25.00	15.00
(10)	"Dutch" Zwilling	50.00	25.00	15.00
(11)	Pete Scott	50.00	25.00	15.00
(12)	"Bunny" Brief	50.00	25.00	15.00
(13)	Jimmie Zinn	50.00	25.00	15.00
(14)	Ferd Schupp	50.00	25.00	15.00
(15)	Roy Wilkinson	50.00	25.00	15.00
(16)	Ray Caldwell	50.00	25.00	15.00
(17)	Joe Dawson	50.00	25.00	15.00
(18)	John Saladna	50.00	25.00	15.00
(19)	Herb Thormahlen	50.00	25.00	15.00
(20)	"Nick" Carter	50.00	25.00	15.00
(21)	George Muehlebach (President)	50.00	25.00	15.00

1909 Bastian Gum Pin

It is unknown whether other members of the championship 1909 Rochester Bronchos of the Eastern League were honored on these black-and-white pinback celluloid buttons or only their manager. The pin measures about 1-1/4" in diameter and as originally issued had a paper insert in back crediting it to Bastian Bros. Gum.

	NM	EX	VG
John H. Ganzel	150.00	75.00	45.00

1961 Bee Hive Starch Toronto Maple Leafs

BEE HIVE PLAYER PHOTO
DAVE POPE, outfielder - 1961

This 24-card set features players of the Toronto Maple Leafs, an independent team in the International League which featured future Hall of Fame Manager Sparky Anderson as its second baseman. The black-and-white cards are printed on thin, blank-backed stock and measure approximately 2-1/2" x 3-1/4". As the cards are not numbered, the checklist below is presented alphabetically.

		NM	EX	VG
Complete Set (24):		2,400	1,200	725.00
Common Player:		90.00	45.00	25.00
(1)	George Anderson	450.00	225.00	135.00
(2)	Fritzie Brickell	90.00	45.00	25.00
(3)	Ellis Burton	90.00	45.00	25.00
(4)	Bob Chakales	90.00	45.00	25.00
(5)	Rip Coleman	90.00	45.00	25.00
(6)	Steve Demeter	90.00	45.00	25.00
(7)	Joe Hannah	90.00	45.00	25.00
(8)	Earl Hersh	90.00	45.00	25.00
(9)	Lou Jackson	90.00	45.00	25.00
(10)	Ken Johnson	90.00	45.00	25.00
(11)	Lou Johnson	90.00	45.00	25.00
(12)	John Lipon	90.00	45.00	25.00
(13)	Carl Mathias	90.00	45.00	25.00
(14)	Bill Moran	90.00	45.00	25.00
(15)	Ron Negray	90.00	45.00	25.00
(16)	Herb Plews	90.00	45.00	25.00
(17)	Dave Pope	90.00	45.00	25.00
(18)	Steve Ridzik	90.00	45.00	25.00
(19)	Raul Sanchez	90.00	45.00	25.00
(20)	Pat Scantlebury	90.00	45.00	25.00
(21)	Bill Smith	90.00	45.00	25.00
(22)	Bob Smith	90.00	45.00	25.00
(23)	Chuck Tanner	125.00	65.00	35.00
(24)	Tim Thompson	90.00	45.00	25.00

1911 Big Eater Sacramento Solons

BYRAM
SAC'TO
HE EATS "BIG EATER"

This very rare set was issued circa 1911 and includes only members of the Pacific Coast League Sacramento Solons. The black-and-white cards measure 2-1/8" x 4" and feature action photos. The lower part of the card contains a three-line caption that includes the player's last name, team designation (abbreviated to "Sac'to"), and the promotional line: "He Eats 'Big Eater'." Although the exact origin is undetermined, it is believed that "Big Eaters" were a candy novelty.

		NM	EX	VG
Complete Set (20):		50,000	20,000	12,000
Common Player:		2,750	1,100	700.00
(1)	Frank Arellanes	2,750	1,100	700.00
(2)	Spider Baum	2,750	1,100	700.00
(3)	Herb Byram	2,750	1,100	700.00
(4)	Babe Danzig	2,750	1,100	700.00
(5)	Jack Fitzgerald	2,750	1,100	700.00
(6)	George Gaddy	2,750	1,100	700.00
(7)	Al Heister	2,750	1,100	700.00
(8)	Ben Hunt	2,750	1,100	700.00
(9)	Butch Kerns	2,750	1,100	700.00
(10)	Mickey LaLonge	2,750	1,100	700.00
(11)	Dutch Lerchen	2,750	1,100	700.00
(12)	Jimmy Lewis	2,750	1,100	700.00
(13)	Chris Mahoney	2,750	1,100	700.00
(14)	Dick Nebinger	2,750	1,100	700.00
(15)	Patsy O'Rourke	2,750	1,100	700.00
(16)	Jimmy Shinn	2,750	1,100	700.00
(17)	Chester Thomas	2,750	1,100	700.00
(18)	Fuller Thompson	2,750	1,100	700.00
(19)	Frank Thornton	2,750	1,100	700.00
(20)	Deacon Van Buren	2,750	1,100	700.00

1950 Big League Stars (V362)

Chuck Connors
MONTREAL ROYALS
Infielder
Born at Brooklyn, N.Y., on April 10, 1921. Bats left. Throws left. 6'5". 210 lbs. Hit .319, 20 homers and batted in 108 runs with Royals in 1949.
Champ intérieur
Né à Brooklyn, N.Y., le 10 avril 1921. Frappe de la gauche, lance de la gauche. 6'5". 210 livres. Frappa .319, 20 coups de circuit et participa à 108 buts avec les Royaux en 1949.
BIG LEAGUE STARS — No. 2

International League players are featured in this 48-card set. Measuring 3-1/4" x 2-5/8", the blank-backed cards are printed in blue-on-white with English and French stats and biographical data.

		NM	EX	VG
Complete Set (48):		4,500	2,750	1,200
Common Player:		90.00	40.00	25.00
1	Rocky Bridges	100.00	50.00	30.00
2	Chuck Connors	650.00	325.00	200.00
3	Jake Wade	90.00	40.00	25.00
4	Al Cihocki	90.00	40.00	25.00
5	John Simmons	90.00	40.00	25.00
6	Frank Trechock	90.00	40.00	25.00
7	Steve Lembo	90.00	40.00	25.00
8	Johnny Welaj	90.00	40.00	25.00
9	Seymour Block	90.00	40.00	25.00
10	Pat McGlothlin	90.00	40.00	25.00
11	Bryan Stephens	90.00	40.00	25.00
12	Clarence Podbielan	90.00	40.00	25.00
13	Clem Hausmann	90.00	40.00	25.00
14	Turk Lown	90.00	40.00	25.00
15	Joe Payne	90.00	40.00	25.00
16	Coacker Triplett (Coaker)	90.00	40.00	25.00
17	Nick Strincevich	90.00	40.00	25.00
18	Charlie Thompson	90.00	40.00	25.00

19	Erick Silverman	90.00	40.00	25.00
20	George Schmees	90.00	40.00	25.00
21	George Binks	90.00	40.00	25.00
22	Gino Cimoli	100.00	50.00	30.00
23	Marty Tabacheck	90.00	40.00	25.00
24	Al Gionfriddo	100.00	50.00	30.00
25	Ronnie Lee	90.00	40.00	25.00
26	Clyde King	90.00	40.00	25.00
27	Harry Heslet	90.00	40.00	25.00
28	Jerry Scala	90.00	40.00	25.00
29	Boris Woyt	90.00	40.00	25.00
30	Jack Collum	90.00	40.00	25.00
31	Chet Laabs	90.00	40.00	25.00
32	Carden Gillwater	90.00	40.00	25.00
33	Irving Medlinger	90.00	40.00	25.00
34	Toby Atwell	90.00	40.00	25.00
35	Charlie Marshall	90.00	40.00	25.00
36	Johnny Mayo	90.00	40.00	25.00
37	Gene Markland	90.00	40.00	25.00
38	Russ Kerns	90.00	40.00	25.00
39	Jim Prendergast	90.00	40.00	25.00
40	Lou Welaj	90.00	40.00	25.00
41	Clyde Kluttz	90.00	40.00	25.00
42	Bill Glynn	90.00	40.00	25.00
43	Don Richmond	90.00	40.00	25.00
44	Hank Biasatti	90.00	40.00	25.00
45	Tom Lasorda	600.00	300.00	180.00
46	Al Roberge	90.00	40.00	25.00
47	George Byam	90.00	40.00	25.00
48	Dutch Mele	90.00	40.00	25.00

1910 Bishop & Co. P.C.L. Teams (E221)

A very rare issue, this series of team pictures of clubs in the Pacific Coast League was distributed by Bishop & Co. of Los Angeles in 1910. The team photos were printed on a thin, newsprint-type paper that measures an elongated 10" x 2-3/4". Although there were six teams in the PCL at the time, only five clubs have been found - the sixth team, Sacramento, was apparently never issued. The cards indicate that they were issued with five-cent packages of Bishop's Milk Chocolate and that the photos were taken by the Los Angeles Examiner. The black-and-white team photos are found with red, blue, yellow, purple, or green background.

		NM	EX	VG
Complete Set (5):		32,000	13,000	8,000
Common Team:		6,000	2,700	1,700
(1)	Los Angeles	6,000	2,700	1,700
(2)	Oakland	6,000	2,700	1,700
(3)	Portland	6,000	2,700	1,700
(4)	San Francisco	6,000	2,700	1,700
(5)	Vernon	6,000	2,700	1,700

1910 Bishop & Co. P.C.L. (E99)

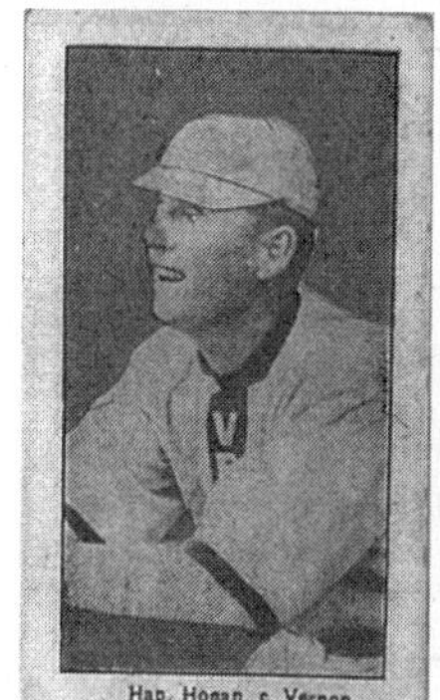
Hap. Hogan, c. Vernon

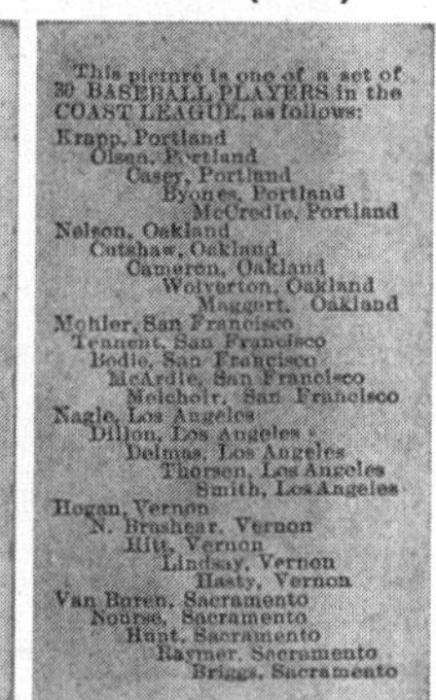
This picture is one of a set of 30 BASEBALL PLAYERS in the COAST LEAGUE, as follows:
Krapp, Portland
Olsen, Portland
Casey, Portland
Byones, Portland
McCredie, Portland
Nelson, Oakland
Cutshaw, Oakland
Cameron, Oakland
Wolverton, Oakland
Maggert, Oakland
Mohler, San Francisco
Tennent, San Francisco
Bodie, San Francisco
McArdle, San Francisco
Melchoir, San Francisco
Nagle, Los Angeles
Dillon, Los Angeles
Delmas, Los Angeles
Thorsen, Los Angeles
Smith, Los Angeles
Hogan, Vernon
N. Brashear, Vernon
Hitt, Vernon
Lindsay, Vernon
Hasty, Vernon
Van Buren, Sacramento
Nourse, Sacramento
Hunt, Sacramento
Raymer, Sacramento
Briggs, Sacramento

The first of two obscure sets produced by the Los Angeles candy maker Bishop & Co., this 30-card set was issued in 1910 and depicts players from the Pacific Coast League, showing five players from each of the six teams. The cards measure approximately 1-1/2" x 2-3/4" and feature black-and-white player photos with colored backgrounds (green, blue, purple, yellow, or rarely, black). The player's last name, position and team appear along the bottom. The backs of the cards contain the complete checklist in groups of five, according to team, with each name indented slightly more than the name above. Cards in the 1910 set do not contain the name "Bishop & Company, California" along the bottom on the back.

		NM	EX	VG
Complete Set (30):		50,000	21,000	13,000
Common Player:		1,750	700.00	435.00
(1)	Bodie	2,000	800.00	500.00
(2)	N. Brashear	1,750	700.00	435.00
(3)	Briggs	1,750	700.00	435.00
(4)	Byones (Byrnes)	1,750	700.00	435.00
(5)	Cameron	1,750	700.00	435.00
(6)	Casey	1,750	700.00	435.00
(7)	Cutshaw	1,750	700.00	435.00
(8)	Delmas	1,750	700.00	435.00
(9)	Dillon	1,750	700.00	435.00
(10)	Hasty	1,750	700.00	435.00
(11)	Hitt	1,750	700.00	435.00
(12)	Hap. Hogan	1,750	700.00	435.00
(13)	Hunt	1,750	700.00	435.00
(14)	Krapp	1,750	700.00	435.00
(15)	John Lindsay	1,750	700.00	435.00
(16)	Maggert	1,750	700.00	435.00
(17)	McArdle	1,750	700.00	435.00
(18)	McCredie (McCreedie)	1,750	700.00	435.00
(19)	Melchior	1,750	700.00	435.00
(20)	Mohler	1,750	700.00	435.00
(21)	Nagle	1,750	700.00	435.00
(22)	Nelson	1,750	700.00	435.00
(23)	Nourse	1,750	700.00	435.00
(24)	Olsen	1,750	700.00	435.00
(25)	Raymer	1,750	700.00	435.00
(26)	Smith	1,750	700.00	435.00
(27)	Tennent (Tennant)	1,750	700.00	435.00
(28)	Thorsen	1,750	700.00	435.00
(29)	Van Buren	1,750	700.00	435.00
(30)	Wolverton	1,750	700.00	435.00

1911 Bishop & Co. P.C.L. Type I (E100)

P. O'Rourke, 2b Sacramento

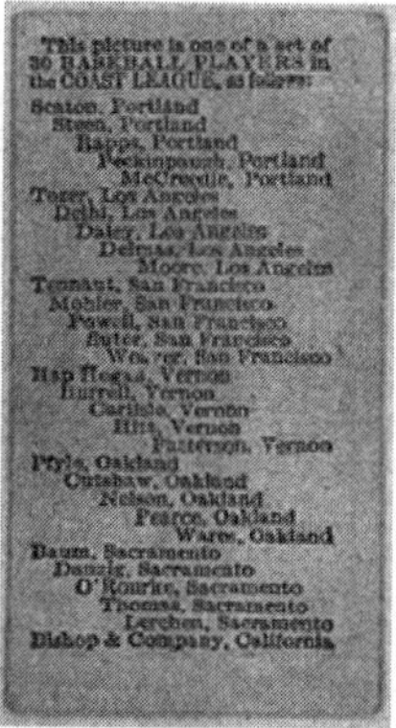
This picture is one of a set of 30 BASEBALL PLAYERS in the COAST LEAGUE, as follows:
Seaton, Portland
Steen, Portland
Rapps, Portland
Peckinpaugh, Portland
McCredie, Portland
Tozer, Los Angeles
Delhi, Los Angeles
Daley, Los Angeles
Delmas, Los Angeles
Moore, Los Angeles
Tennant, San Francisco
Mohler, San Francisco
Powell, San Francisco
Suter, San Francisco
Hap Hogan, Vernon
Burrell, Vernon
Carlisle, Vernon
Hitt, Vernon
Patterson, Vernon
Pfyle, Oakland
Cutshaw, Oakland
Nelson, Oakland
Pearce, Oakland
Wares, Oakland
Baum, Sacramento
Danzig, Sacramento
O'Rourke, Sacramento
Thomas, Sacramento
Lerchen, Sacramento
Bishop & Company, California

This set was issued by the confectioner Bishop & Co. of Los Angeles, which had produced a similar set a year earlier. Both sets showcased star players from the Pacific Coast League. The cards measure approximately 1-1/2" x 2-3/4" and feature black-and-white photos with a background of green, blue, yellow, purple or red. The backs contain the complete checklist of the set, listing the players in groups of five by team, with one line indented slightly more than the previous one. In addition to the checklist, the 1911 set can be differentiated from the previous year because the line "Bishop & Company, California" appears along the bottom.

		NM	EX	VG
Complete Set (30):		55,000	22,000	13,500
Common Player:		1,700	675.00	425.00
(1)	Spider Baum	1,700	675.00	425.00
(2)	Burrell	1,700	675.00	425.00
(3)	Carlisle	1,700	675.00	425.00
(4)	Cutshaw	1,700	675.00	425.00
(5)	Pete Daley	1,700	675.00	425.00
(6)	Danzig	1,700	675.00	425.00
(7)	Delhi	1,700	675.00	425.00
(8)	Delmas	1,700	675.00	425.00
(9)	Hitt	1,700	675.00	425.00
(10)	Hap Hogan (Actually Walter Bray.)	1,700	675.00	425.00
(11)	Lerchen	1,700	675.00	425.00
(12)	McCreddie (McCreedie)	1,700	675.00	425.00
(13)	Mohler	1,700	675.00	425.00
(14)	Moore	1,700	675.00	425.00
(15)	Slim Nelson	1,700	675.00	425.00
(16)	P. O'Rourke	1,700	675.00	425.00
(17)	Patterson	1,700	675.00	425.00
(18)	Bunny Pearce	1,700	675.00	425.00
(19)	Peckinpaugh	1,700	675.00	425.00
(20)	Monte Pfyle (Pfyl)	1,700	675.00	425.00
(21)	Powell	1,700	675.00	425.00
(22)	Rapps	1,700	675.00	425.00
(23)	Seaton	1,700	675.00	425.00
(24)	Steen	1,700	675.00	425.00
(25)	Suter	1,700	675.00	425.00
(26)	Tennant	1,700	675.00	425.00
(27)	Thomas	1,700	675.00	425.00
(28)	Tozer	1,700	675.00	425.00
(29)	Clyde Wares	1,700	675.00	425.00
(30)	Weaver	6,500	2,600	1,625

1911 Bishop & Co. P.C.L. Type II (E100)

Sutor, p., Frisco.

Currently little over half of the checklist of Bishop & Co. (E100) has been found in a second version. These cards have thus far been seen only with green and orange backgrounds, are blank-backed, have larger, reversed negatives, cropping of the photos and have caption differences.

		NM	EX	VG
Common Player:		1,850	750.00	450.00
(1)	Burrell	1,850	750.00	450.00
(2)	Danzig	1,850	750.00	450.00
(3)	Delhi	1,850	750.00	450.00
(4)	Hitt	1,850	750.00	450.00
(5)	Lerchen	1,850	750.00	450.00
(6)	McCreddie (McCreedie)	1,850	750.00	450.00
(7)	Slim Nelson	1,850	750.00	450.00
(8)	P. O'Rourke	1,850	750.00	450.00
(9)	Patterson	1,850	750.00	450.00
(10)	Bunny Pearce	1,850	750.00	450.00
(11)	Monte Pfyle	1,850	750.00	450.00
(12)	Rapps	1,850	750.00	450.00
(13)	Seaton	1,850	750.00	450.00
(14)	Steen	1,850	750.00	450.00
(15)	Suter	1,850	750.00	450.00
(16)	Tennant	1,850	750.00	450.00
(17)	Weaver	6,500	2,600	1,625

1954 Blossom Dairy Charleston Senators

JOE TORPEY
Compliments of Blossom Dairy Company

The Class AAA farm team of the Chicago White Sox is featured in this team set sponsored by a Charleston, W. Va., dairy. The 2-1/4" x 3-3/16" black-and-white cards are either a late issue by Globe Printing (which issued many minor league sets from 1951-52) or were patterned after the Globe issues, right down to the issue of an album to house the cards. A white box is superimposed over the posed action photos and contains the player and sponsor identification. Cards are blank-backed.

		NM	EX	VG
Complete Set (22):		2,200	1,100	650.00
Common Player:		100.00	50.00	30.00
Album:		150.00	75.00	45.00
(1)	Al Baro	100.00	50.00	30.00
(2)	Joe Becker	100.00	50.00	30.00
(3)	Joe Carroll	100.00	50.00	30.00
(4)	Gerald "Red" Fahr	100.00	50.00	30.00
(5)	Dick Fowler	100.00	50.00	30.00
(6)	Alex Garbowski	100.00	50.00	30.00
(7)	Gordon Goldsberry	100.00	50.00	30.00
(8)	Ross Grimsley	100.00	50.00	30.00
(9)	Sam Hairston	125.00	65.00	35.00
(10)	Phil Haugstad	100.00	50.00	30.00
(11)	Tom Hurd	100.00	50.00	30.00
(12)	Bill Killinger	100.00	50.00	30.00
(13)	John Kropf	100.00	50.00	30.00
(14)	Bob Masser	100.00	50.00	30.00
(15)	Danny Menendez	100.00	50.00	30.00
(16)	Bill Paolisso	100.00	50.00	30.00
(17)	Bill Pope	100.00	50.00	30.00
(18)	Lou Sleater	100.00	50.00	30.00
(19)	Dick Strahs	100.00	50.00	30.00
(20)	Joe Torpey	100.00	50.00	30.00
(21)	Bill Voiselle	100.00	50.00	30.00
(22)	Al Ware	100.00	50.00	30.00

1958 Bond Bread Buffalo Bisons

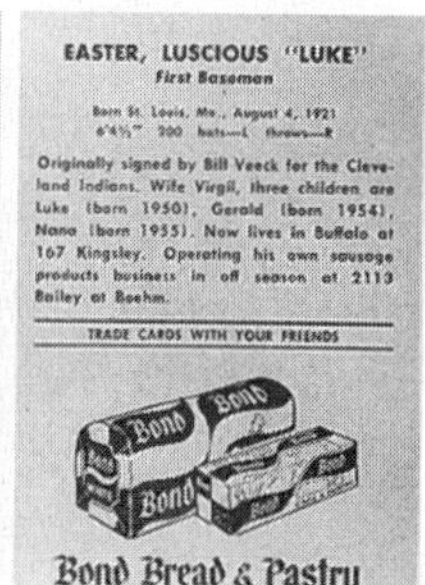

Nine members of the International League affiliate of the Kansas City Athletics are featured in this set. The 2-1/2" x 3-1/2" cards are printed on very thin cardboard. Fronts have a black-

and-white player photo, the player's name and position, and an ad for a TV Western. Card backs are printed in red and blue and include a few biographical details and a career summary, along with an illustrated ad.

		NM	EX	VG
Complete Set (9):		350.00	175.00	100.00
Common Player:		40.00	20.00	12.00
(1)	Al Aber	40.00	20.00	12.00
(2)	Joe Caffie	40.00	20.00	12.00
(3)	Phil Cavaretta	40.00	20.00	12.00
(4)	Rip Coleman	40.00	20.00	12.00
(5)	Luke Easter	60.00	30.00	18.00
(6)	Ken Johnson	40.00	20.00	12.00
(7)	Lou Ortiz	40.00	20.00	12.00
(8)	Jack Phillips	40.00	20.00	12.00
(9)	Jim Small	40.00	20.00	12.00

1949 Bowman Pacific Coast League

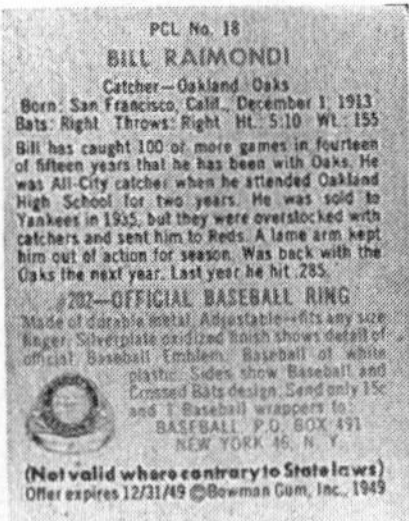

One of the scarcest issues of the postwar period, the 1949 Bowman PCL set was issued only on the West Coast. Like the 1949 Bowman regular issue, the cards contain black-and-white photos overprinted with various pastel colors. Thirty-six cards, which measure 2-1/16" x 2-1/2", make up the set. It is believed that the cards may have been issued only in sheets and not sold in gum packs. Consequently, many cards are found which display evidence of having been cut with a scissors.

		NM	EX	VG
Complete Set (36):		15,000	7,500	4,500
Common Player:		500.00	240.00	145.00
1	Lee Anthony	500.00	240.00	145.00
2	George Metkovich	500.00	240.00	145.00
3	Ralph Hodgin	500.00	240.00	145.00
4	George Woods	500.00	240.00	145.00
5	Xavier Rescigno	500.00	240.00	145.00
6	Mickey Grasso	500.00	240.00	145.00
7	Johnny Rucker	500.00	240.00	145.00
8	Jack Brewer	500.00	240.00	145.00
9	Dom D'Allessandro	500.00	240.00	145.00
10	Charlie Gassaway	500.00	240.00	145.00
11	Tony Freitas	500.00	240.00	145.00
12	Gordon Maltzberger	500.00	240.00	145.00
13	John Jensen	500.00	240.00	145.00
14	Joyner White	500.00	240.00	145.00
15	Harvey Storey	500.00	240.00	145.00
16	Dick Lajeski	500.00	240.00	145.00
17	Albie Glossop	500.00	240.00	145.00
18	Bill Raimondi	500.00	240.00	145.00
19	Ken Holcombe	500.00	240.00	145.00
20	Don Ross	500.00	240.00	145.00
21	Pete Coscarart	500.00	240.00	145.00
22	Tony York	500.00	240.00	145.00
23	Jake Mooty	500.00	240.00	145.00
24	Charles Adams	500.00	240.00	145.00
25	Les Scarsella	500.00	240.00	145.00
26	Joe Marty	500.00	240.00	145.00
27	Frank Kelleher	500.00	240.00	145.00
28	Lee Handley	500.00	240.00	145.00
29	Herman Besse	500.00	240.00	145.00
30	John Lazor	500.00	240.00	145.00
31	Eddie Malone	500.00	240.00	145.00
32	Maurice Van Robays	500.00	240.00	145.00
33	Jim Tabor	500.00	240.00	145.00
34	Gene Handley	500.00	240.00	145.00
35	Tom Seats	500.00	240.00	145.00
36	Ora Burnett	500.00	240.00	145.00

1933 Buffalo Bisons Jigsaw Puzzles

Produced as a stadium promotional giveaway, this set consists of 19 player puzzles and one for Hall of Fame Manager Ray Schalk. Each of the 11" x 14", 200-piece, black-and-white puzzles was produced in an edition of 10,000. Puzzles carried a red serial number, and certain numbers could be redeemed for tickets and other prizes. The known puzzles are checklisted below in alphabetical order.

		NM	EX	VG
Complete Set (15):		5,000	2,500	1,500
Common Player:		335.00	165.00	100.00
(1)	Joe Bartulis	335.00	165.00	100.00
(2)	Joe Bloomer	335.00	165.00	100.00
(3)	Ollie Carnegie	335.00	165.00	100.00
(4)	Clyde "Buck" Crouse	335.00	165.00	100.00
(5)	Harry Danning	335.00	165.00	100.00
(6)	Gilbert English	335.00	165.00	100.00
(7)	Fred Fussell	335.00	165.00	100.00
(8)	Bob Gould	335.00	165.00	100.00
(9)	Len Koenecke	335.00	165.00	100.00
(10)	Ray Lucas	335.00	165.00	100.00
(11)	Clarence Mueller	335.00	165.00	100.00
(12)	Ray Schalk	500.00	250.00	150.00
(13)	Jack Smith	335.00	165.00	100.00
(14)	Roy Tarr	335.00	165.00	100.00
(15)	Johnny Wilson	335.00	165.00	100.00

1934 Buffalo Bisons Team Issue

Apparently a team issue, these 4" x 7-1/16" black-and-white blank-backed cards feature posed action photos with white borders and a facsimile autograph. The player's full name and position are printed in the bottom border, along with a career summary. This checklist is probably incomplete though the exact scope of the issue is unknown.

		NM	EX	VG
Common Player:		200.00	100.00	60.00
(1)	Kenneth L. Ash	200.00	100.00	60.00
(2)	Harold "Ace" Elliott	200.00	100.00	60.00
(3)	Gregory T. Mulleavy	200.00	100.00	60.00
(4)	Irving M. Plummer	200.00	100.00	60.00

1940 Buffalo Bisons Team Issue

Many former and future big leaguers are included in this set of black-and-white, 2" x 3" cards. Fronts picture the players in poses at old Offerman Stadium. The player's name and position are printed in the white border at bottom. Backs have a career summary and highlights. The unnumbered cards are checklisted here alphabetically.

		NM	EX	VG
Complete Set (24):		4,500	2,250	1,350
Common Player:		200.00	100.00	60.00
(1)	Ollie Carnegie	200.00	100.00	60.00
(2)	Dan Carnevale	200.00	100.00	60.00
(3)	Earl Cook	200.00	100.00	60.00
(4)	Les Fleming	200.00	100.00	60.00
(5)	Floyd Giebel	200.00	100.00	60.00
(6)	Jimmy Hutch	200.00	100.00	60.00
(7)	Fred Hutchinson	200.00	100.00	60.00
(8)	Art Jacobs	200.00	100.00	60.00
(9)	John Kroner	200.00	100.00	60.00
(10)	Sal Maglie	300.00	150.00	90.00
(11)	Joe Martin	200.00	100.00	60.00
(12)	Clyde McCullough	200.00	100.00	60.00
(13)	Greg Mulleavy	200.00	100.00	60.00
(14)	Pat Mullin	200.00	100.00	60.00
(15)	Hank Nowak	200.00	100.00	60.00
(16)	Steve O'Neil	200.00	100.00	60.00
(17)	Jimmy Outlaw	200.00	100.00	60.00
(18)	Joe Rogalski	200.00	100.00	60.00
(19)	Les Scarsella	200.00	100.00	60.00
(20)	Mayo Smith	200.00	100.00	60.00
(21)	Floyd Stromme	200.00	100.00	60.00
(22)	Jim Trexler	200.00	100.00	60.00
(23)	Hal White	200.00	100.00	60.00
(24)	Frank Zubik	200.00	100.00	60.00

1947 Buffalo Bisons Team Issue

Despite some anomalies among the players checklisted thus far, this appears to have been a 1947 team-issued set of 8" a 10" black-and-white player photographs. Fronts include player identification in the form of a facsimile autograph. Backs are blank.

		NM	EX	VG
Common Player:		30.00	15.00	9.00
(1)	Johnny Bero	30.00	15.00	9.00
(2)	Hank Biasatti	30.00	15.00	9.00
(3)	Eddie Boland	30.00	15.00	9.00
(4)	Ray Coleman	30.00	15.00	9.00
(5)	Zeb "Red" Eaton	30.00	15.00	9.00
(6)	Lonny Frey	30.00	15.00	9.00
(8)	Freddie Hancock	30.00	15.00	9.00
(9)	Gabby Hartnett	65.00	32.00	19.50
(10)	Clem Hausman	30.00	15.00	9.00
(11)	Manuel Hidalgo	30.00	15.00	9.00
(12)	Chet Laabs	30.00	15.00	9.00
(14)	Johnny McHale	30.00	15.00	9.00
(15)	Edward Mierkowicz	30.00	15.00	9.00
(16)	Eddie Mordarski	30.00	15.00	9.00
(17)	Hank Perry	30.00	15.00	9.00
(18)	Billy Pierce, Ted Gray	45.00	22.00	13.50
(19)	Bill Radulovich	30.00	15.00	9.00
(21)	Earl Rapp, Clint Conatser, Anse Moore, Coaker Triplett	30.00	15.00	9.00
(22)	Vic Wertz	40.00	20.00	12.00

1950 Bush & Hancock/Oak Hall Roanoke Red Sox

These blank-back, black-and-white cards have a portrait photo on front surrounded by a white border. Beneath the photo is a credit line and space for an autograph. Cards exist in 3-1/2" x 5" size with sponsor's credit reading "Compliments of Bush & Hancock," and in 4" x 6" format with sponsor's credit reading, "Compliments of Oak Hall." It is not known whether the checklist presented here is complete. Roanoke was a Class B Piedmont League farm club.

		NM	EX	VG
Common Player:		50.00	25.00	15.00
(1)	Tom Casey	50.00	25.00	15.00
(2)	George Contratto	50.00	25.00	15.00
(3)	Ike Delock	65.00	32.50	20.00
(4)	Red Marion	50.00	25.00	15.00
(5)	Rod Morgan	50.00	25.00	15.00
(6)	Julio Ondani	50.00	25.00	15.00
(7)	Joe Reedy	50.00	25.00	15.00
(8)	Johnny Sehrt	50.00	25.00	15.00
(9)	Sammy White	65.00	32.50	20.00
(10)	Bob Wilson	50.00	25.00	15.00

C

1943 Centennial Flour Seattle Rainiers

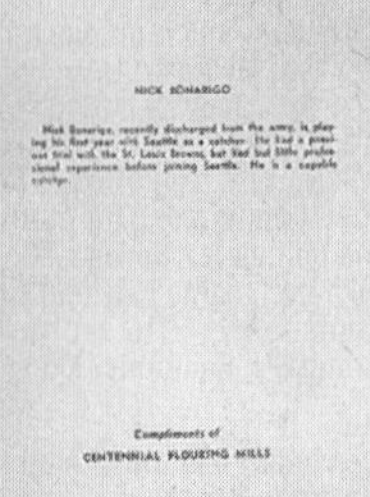

The 25 cards in this 4" x 5" black-and-white set feature players of the Pacific Coast League Seattle Rainiers. Identical in format to the set issued in 1944, the '43s can be identified by the lines of type at the bottom of the card back reading, "Compliments of/CENTENNIAL FLOURING MILLS."

	NM	EX	VG
Complete Set (25):	1,100	550.00	325.00

Common Player:	60.00	30.00	18.00
(1) John Babich	60.00	30.00	18.00
(2) Nick Bonarigo (Buonarigo)	60.00	30.00	18.00
(3) Eddie Carnett	60.00	30.00	18.00
(4) Lloyd Christopher	60.00	30.00	18.00
(5) Joe Demoran	60.00	30.00	18.00
(6) Joe Dobbins	60.00	30.00	18.00
(7) Glenn Elliott	60.00	30.00	18.00
(8) Carl Fischer	60.00	30.00	18.00
(9) Leonard Gabrielson	60.00	30.00	18.00
(10) Stanley Gray	60.00	30.00	18.00
(11) Dick Gyselman	60.00	30.00	18.00
(12) Jim Jewell	60.00	30.00	18.00
(13) Syl Johnson	60.00	30.00	18.00
(14) Pete Jonas	60.00	30.00	18.00
(15) Bill Kats	60.00	30.00	18.00
(16) Lynn King	60.00	30.00	18.00
(17) Bill Lawrence	60.00	30.00	18.00
(18) Clarence Marshall	60.00	30.00	18.00
(19) Bill Matheson	60.00	30.00	18.00
(20) Ford Mullen	60.00	30.00	18.00
(21) Bill Skiff	60.00	30.00	18.00
(22) Byron Speece	60.00	30.00	18.00
(23) Hal Sueme	60.00	30.00	18.00
(24) Hal Turpin	60.00	30.00	18.00
(25) John Yelovic	60.00	30.00	18.00

1944 Centennial Flour Seattle Rainiers

Identical in format to the previous year's issue, the 25 black-and-white 4" x 5" cards issued in 1944 can be differentiated from the 1943 set by the two lines of type at the bottom of each card's back. In the 1944 set, it reads, "Compliments of/CENTENNIAL HOTCAKE AND WAFFLE FLOUR."

	NM	EX	VG
Complete Set (25):	1,350	675.00	400.00
Common Player:	60.00	30.00	18.00
(1) John Babich	60.00	30.00	18.00
(2) Paul Carpenter	60.00	30.00	18.00
(3) Lloyd Christopher	60.00	30.00	18.00
(4) Joe Demoran	60.00	30.00	18.00
(5) Joe Dobbins	60.00	30.00	18.00
(6) Glenn Elliott	60.00	30.00	18.00
(7) Carl Fischer	60.00	30.00	18.00
(8) Bob Garbould (Gorbould)	60.00	30.00	18.00
(9) Stanley Gray	60.00	30.00	18.00
(10) Dick Gyselman	60.00	30.00	18.00
(11) Gene Holt	60.00	30.00	18.00
(12) Roy Johnson	60.00	30.00	18.00
(13) Syl Johnson	60.00	30.00	18.00
(14) Al Libke	60.00	30.00	18.00
(15) Bill Lyman	60.00	30.00	18.00
(16) Bill Matheson	60.00	30.00	18.00
(17) Jack McClure	60.00	30.00	18.00
(18) Jimmy Ripple	60.00	30.00	18.00
(19) Bill Skiff	60.00	30.00	18.00
(20) Byron Speece	60.00	30.00	18.00
(21) Hal Sueme	60.00	30.00	18.00
(22) Frank Tincup	60.00	30.00	18.00
(23) Jack Treece	60.00	30.00	18.00
(24) Hal Turpin	60.00	30.00	18.00
(25) Sicks Stadium	65.00	32.50	20.00

1945 Centennial Flour Seattle Rainiers

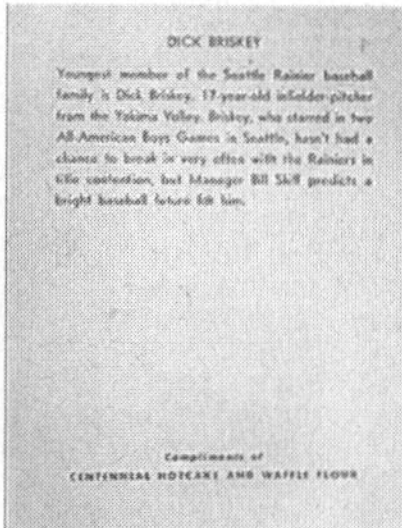

The 27 blue-and-white cards in the third consecutive issue for this Pacific Coast League team are distinguished from the two previous issues by the borderless photo on the front and the fact that the name and team are printed in a black bar at the bottom. The set can be distinguished from the 1947 issue by virtue of the fact that the player biography on back is not surrounded by a frame. The cards measure slightly narrower but longer than the 1943-44 issues, at 3-7/8" x 5-1/8".

	NM	EX	VG
Complete Set (27):	1,500	750.00	450.00
Common Player:	60.00	30.00	18.00
(1) Charley Aleno	60.00	30.00	18.00
(2) Dick Briskey	60.00	30.00	18.00
(3) John Carpenter	60.00	30.00	18.00
(4) Joe Demoran	60.00	30.00	18.00
(5) Joe Dobbins	60.00	30.00	18.00
(6) Glenn Elliott	60.00	30.00	18.00
(7) Bob Finley	60.00	30.00	18.00
(8) Carl Fischer	60.00	30.00	18.00
(9) Keith Frazier	60.00	30.00	18.00
(10) Johnny Gill	60.00	30.00	18.00
(11) Bob Gorbould	60.00	30.00	18.00
(12) Chet Johnson	60.00	30.00	18.00
(13) Syl Johnson	60.00	30.00	18.00
(14) Bill Kats	60.00	30.00	18.00
(15) Billy Lyman	60.00	30.00	18.00
(16) Bill Matheson	60.00	30.00	18.00
(17) George McDonald	60.00	30.00	18.00
(18) Ted Norbert	60.00	30.00	18.00
(19) Alex Palica	60.00	30.00	18.00
(20) Joe Passero	60.00	30.00	18.00
(21) Hal Patchett	60.00	30.00	18.00
(22) Bill Skiff	60.00	30.00	18.00
(23) Byron Speece	60.00	30.00	18.00
(24) Hal Sueme	60.00	30.00	18.00
(25) Eddie Taylor	60.00	30.00	18.00
(26) Hal Turpin	60.00	30.00	18.00
(27) Jack Whipple	60.00	30.00	18.00

1947 Centennial Flour Seattle Rainiers

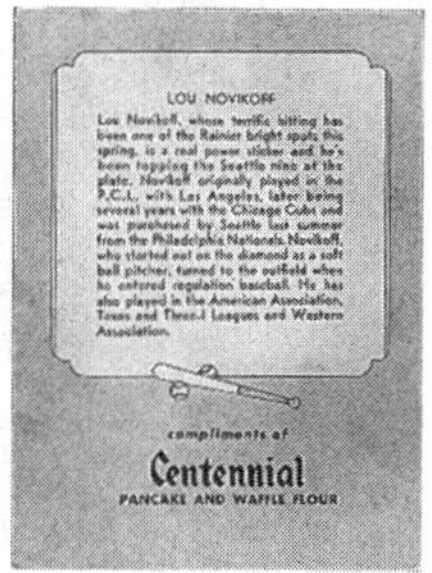

After a lapse of one year, Centennial Flour returned to issue a final black-and-white 32-card set for 1947. Identical in size (3-7/8" x 5-1/8") and front format to the 1945 issue, the '47s can be identified by the white framed box on back containing the player's biography.

	NM	EX	VG
Complete Set (32):	1,100	550.00	325.00
Common Player:	50.00	25.00	15.00
(1) Dick Barrett	50.00	25.00	15.00
(2) Joe Buzas	50.00	25.00	15.00
(3) Paul Carpenter	50.00	25.00	15.00
(4) Rex Cecil	50.00	25.00	15.00
(5) Tony Criscola	50.00	25.00	15.00
(6) Walter Dubiel	50.00	25.00	15.00
(7) Doug Ford	50.00	25.00	15.00
(8) Rollie Hemsley	50.00	25.00	15.00
(9) Jim Hill	50.00	25.00	15.00
(10) Jim Hopper	50.00	25.00	15.00
(11) Sigmund Jakucki	50.00	25.00	15.00
(12) Bob Johnson	60.00	30.00	18.00
(13) Pete Jonas	50.00	25.00	15.00
(14) Joe Kaney	50.00	25.00	15.00
(15) Hillis Layne	50.00	25.00	15.00
(16) Lou Novikoff	50.00	25.00	15.00
(17) Johnny O'Neil	50.00	25.00	15.00
(18) John Orphal	50.00	25.00	15.00
(19) Ike Pearson	50.00	25.00	15.00
(20) Bill Posedel	50.00	25.00	15.00
(21) Don Pulford	50.00	25.00	15.00
(22) Tom Reis	50.00	25.00	15.00
(23) Charley Ripple	50.00	25.00	15.00
(24) Mickey Rocco	50.00	25.00	15.00
(25) Johnny Rucker	50.00	25.00	15.00
(26) Earl Sheely	50.00	25.00	15.00
(27) Bob Stagg	50.00	25.00	15.00
(28) Hal Sueme	50.00	25.00	15.00
(29) Eddie Taylor	50.00	25.00	15.00
(30) Ed Vanni	50.00	25.00	15.00
(31) JoJo White	50.00	25.00	15.00
(32) Tony York	50.00	25.00	15.00

1957-58 Chattanooga Lookouts Team Issue

Based on the known and certainly incomplete checklist seen thus far, this issue of 8" x 10" black-and-white, blank-back player photos can only be generally attributed to year of issue. With a credit line to Moss Photo Service of New York City, the pictures feature action poses of the players taken in historic Engel Stadium. Facsimile autographs are pre-printed on the front. During the late 1950s the Lookouts were the top farm club of the Washington Senators.

	NM	EX	VG
Common Player:	30.00	15.00	9.00
(1) Bobby Brown	30.00	15.00	9.00
(2) Hal Griggs	30.00	15.00	9.00
(2) Harmon Killebrew	200.00	100.00	60.00
(3) Jesse Levan	30.00	15.00	9.00
(3) Ernie Oravetz	30.00	15.00	9.00
(4) Stan Roseboro	30.00	15.00	9.00
(5) Bunky Stewart	30.00	15.00	9.00

1967 Chevron/Uniroyal Vancouver Mounties

These 2" x 3" black-and-white cards were distributed by local gas stations and picture members of the top farm club of the Kansas City A's. Backs are printed in red and black on white.

	NM	EX	VG
Complete Set (27):	4,500	2,250	1,300
Common Player:	200.00	100.00	60.00
(1) Sal Bando	350.00	175.00	105.00
(2) Frank Bastrire (Trainer)	200.00	100.00	60.00
(3) Ossie Chavarria	200.00	100.00	60.00
(4) Jim Dickson	200.00	100.00	60.00
(5) John Donaldson	200.00	100.00	60.00
(6) Jim Driscoll	200.00	100.00	60.00
(7) Bob Duliba	200.00	100.00	60.00
(8) Bill Edgerton	200.00	100.00	60.00
(9) Larry Elliot	200.00	100.00	60.00
(10) Ernie Foli	200.00	100.00	60.00
(11) Joe Gaines	200.00	100.00	60.00
(12) Vern Handrahan	200.00	100.00	60.00
(13) Jim Hughes	200.00	100.00	60.00
(14) Woody Huyke	200.00	100.00	60.00
(15) Rene Lachemann	225.00	110.00	67.00
(16) Bob Meyer	200.00	100.00	60.00
(17) Wayne Norton	200.00	100.00	60.00
(18) Gerry Reimer	200.00	100.00	60.00
(19) Roberto Rodriguez	200.00	100.00	60.00
(20) Ken Sanders	200.00	100.00	60.00
(21) Randy Schwartz	200.00	100.00	60.00
(22) Diego Segui	275.00	135.00	82.00
(23) Paul Seitz	200.00	100.00	60.00
(24) Ron Tompkins	200.00	100.00	60.00
(25) Mickey Vernon	350.00	175.00	105.00
(26) Jim Ward	200.00	100.00	60.00
(27) Don Yingling	200.00	100.00	60.00

1909 Clement Bros. Bread (D380-1)

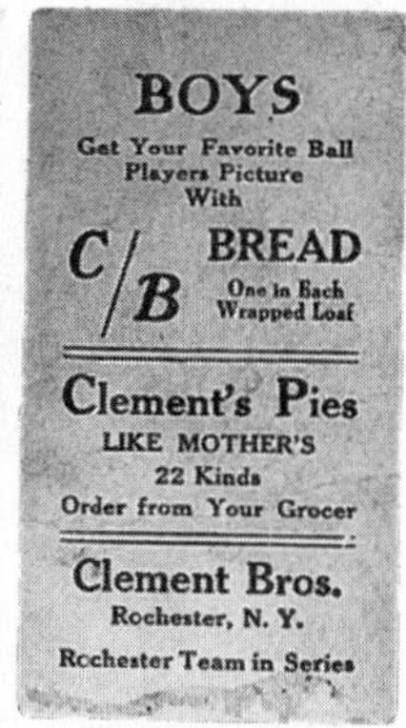

This set features only players of the Rochester team in the Eastern League. According to the bakery ad on back, the cards were distributed one per loaf of bread. The 1-1/2" x 2-3/4" cards feature a player photo on front in an oval frame against a white background. The player's last name, position and "Rochester" are printed beneath.

	NM	EX	VG
Complete Set (8):	25,000	12,500	7,500
Common Player:	5,000	2,500	1,500
(1) Anderson	5,000	2,500	1,500
(2) Heinie Batch	5,000	2,500	1,500
(3) Butler	5,000	2,500	1,500
(4) Ed Holly	5,000	2,500	1,500
(5) Holmes	5,000	2,500	1,500
(6) McConnell	5,000	2,500	1,500
(7) Osborn	5,000	2,500	1,500
(8) Partee	5,000	2,500	1,500

1910 Clement Bros. Bread (D380)

For the second of two annual issues, the bakery added an unknown number of major league players' cards to those of six of the hometeam Rochester club of the Eastern League. While the backs remained identical to the previous issue, featuring advertising for the bakery's bread and pies, the fronts adopted the standard format of the era, black-and-

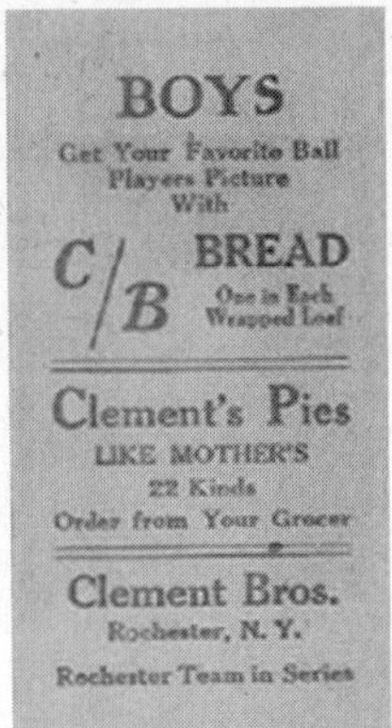

white player photos surrounded by a white border, with the player's last name, position and city printed at bottom. Size remained 1-1/2" x 2-3/4".

	NM	EX	VG
Common Player:	5,750	2,850	1,700
(1) Whitey Alperman	5,750	2,850	1,700
(2) Bailey	5,750	2,850	1,700
(3) Walter Blair	5,750	2,850	1,700
(4) Ty Cobb	40,000	20,000	12,000
(5) Eddie Collins	6,500	3,250	1,950
(6) Roy Hartzell	5,750	2,850	1,700
(7) Harry Howell	5,750	2,850	1,700
(8) Addie Joss	10,000	6,000	3,000
(9) Ditus Lagoe	5,750	2,850	1,700
(10) McConnell	5,750	2,850	1,700
(11) George Mullin	5,750	2,850	1,700
(12) Wilfred Osborn	5,750	2,850	1,700
(13) Harry Patee	5,750	2,850	1,700
(14) Don Carlos Ragan	5,750	2,850	1,700
(15) Oscar Stanage	5,750	2,850	1,700
(16) George Stone	5,750	2,850	1,700
(17) Ed Summers	5,750	2,850	1,700
(18) Joe Tinker	10,000	6,000	3,000
(19) Bert Tooley	5,750	2,850	1,700
(20) Heinie Zimmerman	5,750	2,850	1,700

1953 Coca-Cola Galveston White Caps

This set may have been an issue of the Globe Printing Co., which produced many lower-minors team sets in the years preceding, or it may just share the format. The 2-1/4" x 3-3/8" cards have borderless black-and-white photos on front and blank backs. In a white box near the bottom of the picture is the player name and "Compliments of / Coca-Cola Bottling Co." Galveston was champion of the 1953 Class B Gulf Coast League and not affiliated with any major league team.

	NM	EX	VG
Complete Set (16):	1,000	500.00	300.00
Common Player:	75.00	37.50	22.00
(1) Ed Bohnslav	75.00	37.50	22.00
(2) Mike Conovan	75.00	37.50	22.00
(3) Pop Faucett	75.00	37.50	22.00
(4) Bobby Flis	75.00	37.50	22.00
(5) Stan Goletz	75.00	37.50	22.00
(6) Jerry Kleinsmith	75.00	37.50	22.00
(7) Charlie Lehrmann	75.00	37.50	22.00
(8) Jim Logan	75.00	37.50	22.00
(9) Bob Miller	75.00	37.50	22.00
(10) Tom Moore	75.00	37.50	22.00
(11) Bob Pugatch	75.00	37.50	22.00
(12) Bob Ramsey	75.00	37.50	22.00
(13) Hank Robinson	75.00	37.50	22.00
(14) Charlie Schmidt	75.00	37.50	22.00
(15) Barnie White	75.00	37.50	22.00
(16) Hank Yzquierdo (Izquierdo)	75.00	37.50	22.00

1952 Colorado Springs Sky Sox Team Issue

From the Class A Western League runners-up, this is one of many minor league sets issued in the early 1950s by the Globe Printing Co., of San Jose, Calif. The '52 Sky Sox were a farm team of the Chicago White Sox. Players included former

Negro Leaguers and future major leaguers Connie Johnson and Sam Hairston, plus bonus-baby bust Gus Keriazakos. Cards are about 2-1/4" x 3-1/4", printed in black-and-white with blank backs. An album with die-cut pages to allow the corners of the cards to be slipped in was also available. Cards were likely given away one or two at a time at home games.

	NM	EX	VG
Complete Set (19):	1,200	600.00	360.00
Common Player:	60.00	30.00	18.00
Album:	100.00	50.00	30.00
(1) Jerry Crosby	60.00	30.00	18.00
(2) Vic Fucci	60.00	30.00	18.00
(3) Don Gutteridge	60.00	30.00	18.00
(4) Sam Hairston	90.00	45.00	27.00
(5) Al Jacinto	60.00	30.00	18.00
(6) Connie Johnson	75.00	37.50	22.00
(7) Bob Kellogg	60.00	30.00	18.00
(8) Gus Keriazakos	60.00	30.00	18.00
(9) Ken Landenberger	60.00	30.00	18.00
(10) George Noga	60.00	30.00	18.00
(11) Floyd Penfold	60.00	30.00	18.00
(12) Bill Pope	60.00	30.00	18.00
(13) J.W. Porter	60.00	30.00	18.00
(14) Bill (Red) Rose	60.00	30.00	18.00
(15) Don Rudolph	60.00	30.00	18.00
(16) Andy Skurski	60.00	30.00	18.00
(17) Dick Strahs	60.00	30.00	18.00
(18) Bill Wells	60.00	30.00	18.00
(19) Dick Welteroth	60.00	30.00	18.00

1952 Columbus Cardinals Team Issue

This set of cards was a product of the Globe Printing Co. of San Jose, Calif. The cards were given away at Golden Park during the 1952 season. The cards measure 2-1/8" x 3-3/8" and have black-and-white photos of players with the player's name in a white box in the bottom-left corner of the photograph. The backs are blank. The cards are unnumbered and listed in alphabetical order, although this checklist may not be complete. The team was a Class A South Atlantic League affiliate of the St. Louis Cardinals.

	NM	EX	VG
Complete Set (17):	1,000	500.00	300.00
Common Player:	60.00	30.00	18.00
(1) Chief Bender	60.00	30.00	18.00
(2) Bob Betancourt	60.00	30.00	18.00
(3) Tom Burgess	60.00	30.00	18.00
(4) Jack Byers	60.00	30.00	18.00
(5) Mike Curnan	60.00	30.00	18.00
(6) Gil Daley	60.00	30.00	18.00
(7) Bill Harris	60.00	30.00	18.00
(8) Ev Joyner	60.00	30.00	18.00
(9) Bob Kerce	60.00	30.00	18.00
(10) Ted Lewandowski	60.00	30.00	18.00
(11) John Mackey	60.00	30.00	18.00
(12) Bill Paolisso	60.00	30.00	18.00
(13) Dennis Reeder	60.00	30.00	18.00
(14) Whit Ulrich	60.00	30.00	18.00
(15) Norman Shope	60.00	30.00	18.00
(16) Don Swartz	60.00	30.00	18.00
(17) Len Wile	60.00	30.00	18.00

1955 Columbus Jets Photos

A top farm club of the Kansas City A's in 1955 the Columbus (Ohio) Jets issued these black-and-white glossy photocards. In 3-5/8" x 5-5/8" format, the cards have a facsimile autograph on front. It is possible that the checklist presented here in alphabetical order of the unnumbered cards may be incomplete.

	NM	EX	VG
Complete Set (21):	900.00	450.00	275.00
Common Player:	45.00	22.50	13.50
(1) Hal Bevan	45.00	22.50	13.50
(2) Paul Burris	45.00	22.50	13.50
(3) Ted Del Guercio	45.00	22.50	13.50
(4) Carl Duser	45.00	22.50	13.50
(5) Charlie Haag	45.00	22.50	13.50
(6) Forrest "Spook" Jacobs	60.00	30.00	18.00
(7) Dick Kryhoski	45.00	22.50	13.50
(8) Mike Kume	45.00	22.50	13.50
(9) Al Lakeman	45.00	22.50	13.50
(10) Jackie Mayo	45.00	22.50	13.50
(11) Jim Miller	45.00	22.50	13.50
(12) Al Pinkston	50.00	25.00	15.00
(13) Al Romberger	45.00	22.50	13.50
(14) Bill Stewart	45.00	22.50	13.50
(15) Russ Sullivan	45.00	22.50	13.50
(16) "Jake" Thies	45.00	22.50	13.50
(17) Bob Trice	45.00	22.50	13.50
(18) Ozzie VanBrabant	45.00	22.50	13.50
(19) Frank Verdi	45.00	22.50	13.50
(20) Leroy Wheat	45.00	22.50	13.50
(21) Spider Wilhelm	45.00	22.50	13.50

1957 Columbus Jets Postcards

In 1957, the Columbus (Ohio) Jets began a long association as a top farm team of the Pittsburgh Pirates. That year, the team issued this set of postcards. The black-and-white glossy cards measure 3-9/16" x 5-1/2" and have the player name and position overprinted in black block letters near the bottom of the photo. Backs have postcard indicia and a notice of printing by the Howard Photo Service of New York City. The unnumbered cards are presented here alphabetically but it is unknown whether this checklist is complete at 20.

	NM	EX	VG
Complete Set (20):	900.00	450.00	275.00
Common Player:	45.00	22.50	13.50
(1) Dick Barone	45.00	22.50	13.50
(2) Ron Blackburn	45.00	22.50	13.50
(3) Jackie Brown	45.00	22.50	13.50
(4) Ed Burtschy	45.00	22.50	13.50
(5) Whammy Douglas	50.00	25.00	15.00
(6) Howie Goss	45.00	22.50	13.50
(7) Al Grunwald	45.00	22.50	13.50
(8) Gail Henley	45.00	22.50	13.50
(9) Don Kildoo	45.00	22.50	13.50
(10) Danny Kravitz	45.00	22.50	13.50
(11) Bob Kuzava	45.00	22.50	13.50
(12) Johnny Lipon	45.00	22.50	13.50
(13) Cholly Naranjo	45.00	22.50	13.50
(14) Eddie O'Brien	60.00	30.00	18.00
(15) Frank Oceak	45.00	22.50	13.50
(16) Harding Peterson	60.00	30.00	18.00
(17) John Powers	45.00	22.50	13.50
(18) James Rice	45.00	22.50	13.50
(19) Russ Sullivan	45.00	22.50	13.50
(20) Ken Toothman	45.00	22.50	13.50

1958 Columbus Jets Photos

In format similar to the postcard issue of the previous year, and sharing some of the same pictures, this set of photocards is smaller, at 4" x 5", and is blank-backed. It is unknown whether the alphabetical checklist of the unnumbered cards presented here is complete.

	NM	EX	VG
Complete Set (17):	650.00	325.00	200.00
Common Player:	40.00	20.00	12.00
(1) Gair Allie	40.00	20.00	12.00

(2)	Luis Arroyo	40.00	20.00	12.00
(3)	Tony Bartirome	45.00	22.50	13.50
(4)	Jim Baumer	40.00	20.00	12.00
(5)	Bill Causion	40.00	20.00	12.00
(6)	Whammy Douglas	40.00	20.00	12.00
(7)	Joe Gibbon	40.00	20.00	12.00
(8)	Howie Goss	40.00	20.00	12.00
(9)	Spook Jacobs	50.00	25.00	15.00
(10)	Clyde King	40.00	20.00	12.00
(11)	Cholly Naranjo	40.00	20.00	12.00
(12)	George O'Donnell	40.00	20.00	12.00
(13)	Laurin Pepper	40.00	20.00	12.00
(14)	Dick Rand	40.00	20.00	12.00
(15)	Leo Rodriguez	40.00	20.00	12.00
(16)	Don Rowe	40.00	20.00	12.00
(17)	Art Swanson	40.00	20.00	12.00

1910 Contentnea First Series (T209)

HOFFMAN, RALEIGH

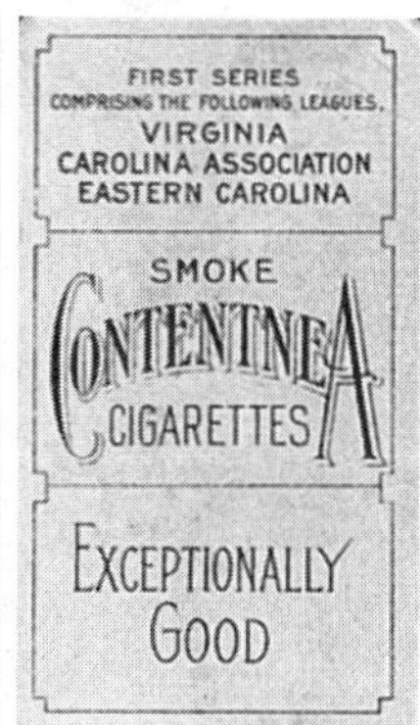

The 1910 Contentnea minor league set actually consists of two distinctively different series, both featuring players from the Virginia League, Carolina Association and Eastern Carolina League. The cards were distributed in packages of Contentnea cigarettes. The first series, featuring color photographs, consists of just 16 cards, each measuring 1-9/16" x 2-11/16". The front of the card has the player's last name and team printed at the bottom, while the back identifies the card as "First Series" and carries an advertisement for Contentnea cigarettes. Many first series cards are also found with rubber-stamped "Factory No. 12, 4th Dist. N.C." on back. The second series, belived to have been issued later in 1910, is a massive 221-card set consisting of black-and-white player photos. The cards in this series are slightly larger, measuring 1-5/8" x 2-3/4". They carry the words "Photo Series" on the back, along with the cigarette advertisement. Only a handful of the players in the Contentnea set ever advanced to the major leagues and the set contains no major stars. Subsequently, it generally holds interest only to collectors who specialize in the old southern minor leagues.

		NM	EX	VG
Complete Set (16):		12,500	6,250	3,725
Common Player:		1,000	600.00	300.00
(1)	Armstrong	1,000	600.00	300.00
(2)	Booles	1,000	600.00	300.00
(3)	Bourquise (Bourquoise)	1,000	600.00	300.00
(4)	Cooper	1,000	600.00	300.00
(5)	Cowell	1,000	600.00	300.00
(6)	Crockett	1,000	600.00	300.00
(7)	Fullenwider	1,000	600.00	300.00
(8)	Gilmore	1,000	600.00	300.00
(9)	Hoffman	1,000	600.00	300.00
(10)	Lane	1,000	600.00	300.00
(11)	Martin	1,000	600.00	300.00
(12)	McGeehan	1,000	600.00	300.00
(13)	Pope	1,200	800.00	400.00
(14)	Sisson	1,000	600.00	300.00
(15)	Stubbe	1,000	600.00	300.00
(16)	Walsh	1,000	600.00	300.00

1910 Contentnea Photo Series (T209)

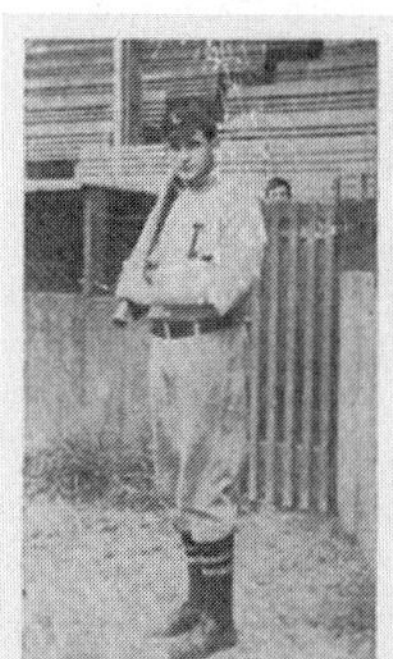
WOOLUMS, LYNCHBURG

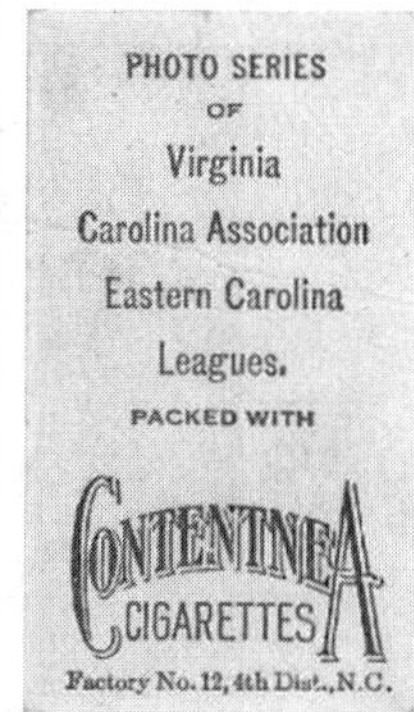

		NM	EX	VG
Common Player:		550.00	275.00	150.00
(1)	Abercrombie	550.00	275.00	150.00
(2)	Andrada	550.00	275.00	150.00
(3)	Armstrong	550.00	275.00	150.00
(4)	Averett	550.00	275.00	150.00
(5)	Baker	550.00	275.00	150.00
(6)	Banner (Bonner)	550.00	275.00	150.00
(7)	Bausewein (Bansewein)	550.00	275.00	150.00
(8)	Beatty	550.00	275.00	150.00
(9)	Bentley	550.00	275.00	150.00
(10)	Beusse	550.00	275.00	150.00
(11)	Biel	550.00	275.00	150.00
(12)	Bigbie (Raleigh)	550.00	275.00	150.00
(13)	Bigbie (Richmond)	550.00	275.00	150.00
(14)	Blackstone	550.00	275.00	150.00
(15)	Bonner	550.00	275.00	150.00
(16)	Bourquin	550.00	275.00	150.00
(17)	Bowen	550.00	275.00	150.00
(18)	Boyle	550.00	275.00	150.00
(19)	Brandon	550.00	275.00	150.00
(20)	Brazelle (Brazell)	550.00	275.00	150.00
(21)	Brent	550.00	275.00	150.00
(22)	Brown	550.00	275.00	150.00
(23)	Busch	550.00	275.00	150.00
(24)	Bussey	550.00	275.00	150.00
(25)	Byrd	550.00	275.00	150.00
(26)	Cafalu (Cefalu)	550.00	275.00	150.00
(27)	Callahan	550.00	275.00	150.00
(28)	Chandler	550.00	275.00	150.00
(29)	Clapp	550.00	275.00	150.00
(30)	Clark (Clarke)	550.00	275.00	150.00
(31)	Clemens	550.00	275.00	150.00
(32)	Clunk	550.00	275.00	150.00
(33)	Cooper	550.00	275.00	150.00
(34)	Corbett	550.00	275.00	150.00
(35)	Cote	550.00	275.00	150.00
(36)	Coutts	550.00	275.00	150.00
(37)	Cowan (Cowen)	550.00	275.00	150.00
(38)	Cowells (Cowell)	550.00	275.00	150.00
(39)	Creagan (Cregan)	550.00	275.00	150.00
(40)	Crockett	550.00	275.00	150.00
(41)	Lave Cross	550.00	275.00	150.00
(42)	Dailey	550.00	275.00	150.00
(43)	C. Derrck (Derrick)	550.00	275.00	150.00
(44)	F. Derrick	550.00	275.00	150.00
(45)	Doak (Greensboro)	550.00	275.00	150.00
(46)	Doak (Wilmington)	550.00	275.00	150.00
(47)	Dobard	550.00	275.00	150.00
(48)	Dobson	550.00	275.00	150.00
(49)	Doyle	550.00	275.00	150.00
(50)	Drumm	550.00	275.00	150.00
(51)	Duvie	550.00	275.00	150.00
(52)	Ebinger	550.00	275.00	150.00
(53)	Eldridge	550.00	275.00	150.00
(54)	Evans	550.00	275.00	150.00
(55)	Fairbanks	550.00	275.00	150.00
(56)	Farmer	550.00	275.00	150.00
(57)	Ferrell	550.00	275.00	150.00
(58)	Fisher	550.00	275.00	150.00
(59)	Flowers	550.00	275.00	150.00
(60)	Fogarty	550.00	275.00	150.00
(61)	Foltz	550.00	275.00	150.00
(62)	Foreman	550.00	275.00	150.00
(63)	Forque	550.00	275.00	150.00
(64)	Francis	550.00	275.00	150.00
(65)	Fulton	550.00	275.00	150.00
(66)	Galvin	550.00	275.00	150.00
(67)	Gardin	550.00	275.00	150.00
(68)	Garman	550.00	275.00	150.00
(69)	Gastmeyer	550.00	275.00	150.00
(70)	Gaston	550.00	275.00	150.00
(71)	Gates	550.00	275.00	150.00
(72)	Gehring	550.00	275.00	150.00
(73)	Gillespie	550.00	275.00	150.00
(74)	Gorham	550.00	275.00	150.00
(75)	Griffin (Danville)	550.00	275.00	150.00
(76)	Griffin (Lynchburg)	550.00	275.00	150.00
(77)	Guiheen	550.00	275.00	150.00
(78)	Gunderson	550.00	275.00	150.00
(79)	Hale	550.00	275.00	150.00
(80)	Halland (Holland)	550.00	275.00	150.00
(81)	Hamilton	550.00	275.00	150.00
(82)	Hammersley	550.00	275.00	150.00
(83)	Handiboe	550.00	275.00	150.00
(84)	Hannifen (Hannifan)	550.00	275.00	150.00
(85)	Hargrave	550.00	275.00	150.00
(86)	Harrington	550.00	275.00	150.00
(87)	Harris	550.00	275.00	150.00
(88)	Hart	550.00	275.00	150.00
(89)	Hartley	550.00	275.00	150.00
(90)	Hawkins	550.00	275.00	150.00
(91)	Hearne (Hearn)	550.00	275.00	150.00
(92)	Hicks	550.00	275.00	150.00
(93)	Hobbs	550.00	275.00	150.00
(94)	Hoffman	550.00	275.00	150.00
(95)	Hooker	550.00	275.00	150.00
(96)	Howard	550.00	275.00	150.00
(97)	Howedel (Howedell)	550.00	275.00	150.00
(98)	Hudson	550.00	275.00	150.00
(99)	Humphrey	550.00	275.00	150.00
(100)	Hyames	600.00	300.00	175.00
(101)	Irvine	550.00	275.00	150.00
(102)	Irving	550.00	275.00	150.00
(103)	Jackson (Greensboro)	550.00	275.00	150.00
(104)	Jackson (Spartanburg)	550.00	275.00	150.00
(105)	Jenkins (Greenville)	550.00	275.00	150.00
(106)	Jenkins (Roanoke)	550.00	275.00	150.00
(107)	Jobson	550.00	275.00	150.00
(108)	Johnson	550.00	275.00	150.00
(109)	Keating	550.00	275.00	150.00
(110)	Kelley	550.00	275.00	150.00
(111)	Kelly (Anderson)	550.00	275.00	150.00
(112)	Kelly (Goldsboro)	550.00	275.00	150.00
(113)	"King" Kelly	550.00	275.00	150.00
(114)	King	550.00	275.00	150.00
(115)	Kite	550.00	275.00	150.00
(116)	Kunkle	550.00	275.00	150.00
(117)	Landgraff	550.00	275.00	150.00
(118)	Lane	550.00	275.00	150.00
(119)	Lathrop	550.00	275.00	150.00
(120)	Lavoia	550.00	275.00	150.00
(121)	Levy	550.00	275.00	150.00
(122)	Lloyd	550.00	275.00	150.00
(123)	Loval	550.00	275.00	150.00
(124)	Lucia	550.00	275.00	150.00
(125)	Luyster	550.00	275.00	150.00
(126)	MacConachie	550.00	275.00	150.00
(127)	Malcolm	550.00	275.00	150.00
(128)	Martin	550.00	275.00	150.00
(129)	Mayberry	550.00	275.00	150.00
(130)	A. McCarthy	550.00	275.00	150.00
(131)	J. McCarthy	550.00	275.00	150.00
(132)	McCormick	550.00	275.00	150.00
(133)	McFarland	550.00	275.00	150.00
(134)	McFarlin	550.00	275.00	150.00
(135)	C. McGeehan	550.00	275.00	150.00
(136)	Dan McGeehan	550.00	275.00	150.00
(137)	McHugh	550.00	275.00	150.00
(138)	McKeavitt (McKevitt)	550.00	275.00	150.00
(139)	Merchant	550.00	275.00	150.00
(140)	Midkiff	550.00	275.00	150.00
(141)	Miller	550.00	275.00	150.00
(142)	Missitt	550.00	275.00	150.00
(143)	Morgan	550.00	275.00	150.00
(144)	Morrissey (Morrisey)	550.00	275.00	150.00
(145)	Mullany (Mullaney)	550.00	275.00	150.00
(146)	Mullinix	550.00	275.00	150.00
(147)	Mundell	600.00	300.00	175.00
(148)	Munsen (Munson)	550.00	275.00	150.00
(149)	Murdock (Murdoch)	550.00	275.00	150.00
(150)	Newton	550.00	275.00	150.00
(151)	Noojin	550.00	275.00	150.00
(152)	Novak	550.00	275.00	150.00
(153)	Ochs	550.00	275.00	150.00
(154)	Painter	550.00	275.00	150.00
(155)	Peloguin	550.00	275.00	150.00
(156)	Phealean (Phelan)	550.00	275.00	150.00
(157)	Phoenix	550.00	275.00	150.00
(158)	Powell	550.00	275.00	150.00
(159)	Presley (Pressley), Pritchard	800.00	400.00	200.00
(160)	Priest	550.00	275.00	150.00
(161)	Prim	550.00	275.00	150.00
(162)	Pritchard	550.00	275.00	150.00
(163)	Rawe (Rowe)	550.00	275.00	150.00
(164)	Redfern (Redfearn)	550.00	275.00	150.00
(165)	Reggy	550.00	275.00	150.00
(166)	Richardson	550.00	275.00	150.00
(167)	Rickard	550.00	275.00	150.00
(168)	Rickert	550.00	275.00	150.00
(169)	Ridgeway (Ridgway)	550.00	275.00	150.00
(170)	Roth	550.00	275.00	150.00
(171)	Salve	550.00	275.00	150.00
(172)	Schmidt	550.00	275.00	150.00
(173)	Schrader	550.00	275.00	150.00
(174)	Schumaker	550.00	275.00	150.00
(175)	Sexton	550.00	275.00	150.00
(176)	Shanghnessy (Shaughnessy)	550.00	275.00	150.00
(177)	Sharp	550.00	275.00	150.00
(178)	Shaw	550.00	275.00	150.00
(179)	Simmons	550.00	275.00	150.00
(180)	A. Smith	550.00	275.00	150.00
(181)	D. Smith	550.00	275.00	150.00
(182)	Smith (Portsmouth)	550.00	275.00	150.00
(183)	Spratt	550.00	275.00	150.00
(184)	Springs	550.00	275.00	150.00
(185)	Stewart	550.00	275.00	150.00
(186)	Stoehr	550.00	275.00	150.00
(187)	Stouch	550.00	275.00	150.00
(188)	Sullivan	550.00	275.00	150.00
(189)	Swindell	550.00	275.00	150.00
(190)	Taxis	550.00	275.00	150.00
(191)	Templin	600.00	300.00	175.00
(192)	Thompson	550.00	275.00	150.00
(193)	B.E. Thompson (Dressed as Uncle Sam.)	2,500	1,250	750.00
(194)	Tiedeman	550.00	275.00	150.00
(195)	Titman	550.00	275.00	150.00
(196)	Toner	550.00	275.00	150.00
(197)	Turner	550.00	275.00	150.00
(198)	Tydeman	550.00	275.00	150.00
(199)	Vail	550.00	275.00	150.00
(200)	Verbout	550.00	275.00	150.00
(201)	Vickery	550.00	275.00	150.00
(202)	Walker (Norfolk)	550.00	275.00	150.00
(203)	Walker (Spartanburg)	550.00	275.00	150.00
(204)	Wallace	550.00	275.00	150.00
(205)	Walsh	550.00	275.00	150.00
(206)	Walters	550.00	275.00	150.00
(207)	Waters	550.00	275.00	150.00
(208)	Waymack	550.00	275.00	150.00
(209)	Webb	550.00	275.00	150.00
(210)	Wehrell	550.00	275.00	150.00
(211)	Weldon	550.00	275.00	150.00
(212)	Welsher	550.00	275.00	150.00
(213)	Westlake	550.00	275.00	150.00
(214)	Williams	550.00	275.00	150.00
(215)	Willis	550.00	275.00	150.00
(216)	Wingo	550.00	275.00	150.00
(217)	Wolf	600.00	300.00	150.00
(218)	Wood	550.00	275.00	150.00
(219)	Woolums	550.00	275.00	150.00
(220)	Workman	550.00	275.00	150.00
(221)	Wright	600.00	300.00	150.00
(222)	Wynne	550.00	275.00	150.00

1924 Crescent Ice Cream Hanbury

Rather than a professional minor league team, this Canadian set features members of an amateur or semi-pro team sponsored by the Hanbury Sawmill in the Vancouver, B.C., Terminal Amateur League. The 2-1/4" x 1-5/8" black-and-white cards have a player portrait photo in an oval on front, with identification and card number below. On back is an identically worded summation of the team's recent seasons' championships, the card number, and an ad for the sponsor.

7—Art Morse
Short Stop

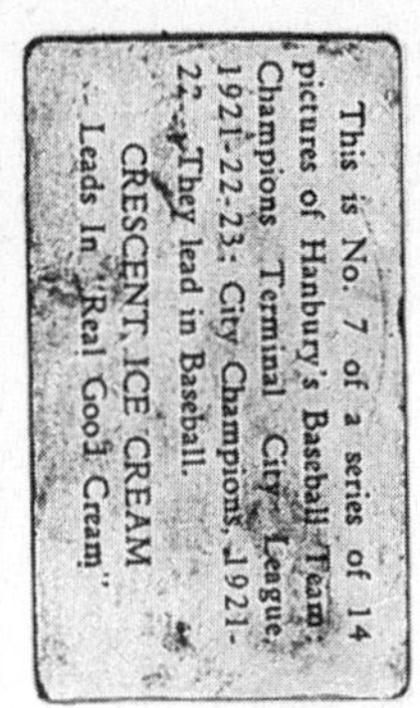
This is No. 7 of a series of 14
pictures of Hanbury's Baseball Team
Champions Terminal City League
1921-22-23; City Champions 1921-
24. They lead in Baseball.
CRESCENT ICE CREAM
Leads In "Real Good Cream"

		NM	EX	VG
Complete Set (14):		4,000	1,350	800.00
Common Player:		300.00	150.00	90.00
1	Jack Lester (Mascot)	300.00	150.00	90.00
2	Frank Coyle	300.00	150.00	90.00
3	Fred Inch	300.00	150.00	90.00
4	Robt. Mills	300.00	150.00	90.00
5	John Daniels (Capt.)	300.00	150.00	90.00
6	Doug. May	300.00	150.00	90.00
7	Art Morse	300.00	150.00	90.00
8	Chas. Stevenson	300.00	150.00	90.00
9	Tom Raftery	300.00	150.00	90.00
10	Frank Williams	300.00	150.00	90.00
11	Unknown	300.00	150.00	90.00
12	Don Stewart	300.00	150.00	90.00
13	Roy Goodall	300.00	150.00	90.00
14	Cecil Kimberley	300.00	150.00	90.00

1940 Crowley's Milk Binghamton Triplets

Members of the Binghamton, N.Y., Eastern League team are known in this set of 3" x 5" cards. Some have been seen with stamped postcard backs. Blue-and-white player photos are framed by a red rendition of a ballpark scene on the front of the unnumbered cards. Each card has a facsimile autograph ostensibly written by the pictured player. It is unknown whether the checklist below is complete. Several of the players later appeared with the N.Y. Yankees and other teams.

		NM	EX	VG
Complete Set (18):		6,000	3,000	1,800
Common Player:		400.00	200.00	120.00
(1)	Jimmy Adlam	400.00	200.00	120.00
(2)	Russ Bergman	400.00	200.00	120.00
(3)	Bruno Betzel	400.00	200.00	120.00
(4)	Bill Bevens	400.00	200.00	120.00
(5)	Johnny Bianco	400.00	200.00	120.00
(6)	Fred Collins	400.00	200.00	120.00
(7)	Vince DeBiassi	400.00	200.00	120.00
(8)	Jack Graham	400.00	200.00	120.00
(9)	Randy Gumpert	400.00	200.00	120.00
(10)	Al Gurske	400.00	200.00	120.00
(11)	Mike Milosevich	400.00	200.00	120.00
(12)	Billie O'Donnell (Trainer)	200.00	100.00	60.00
(13)	Earl Reid	400.00	200.00	120.00
(14)	Aaron Robinson	400.00	200.00	120.00
(15)	Frankie Silvanic	400.00	200.00	120.00
(16)	Pete Suder	400.00	200.00	120.00
(17)	Ray Volps	400.00	200.00	120.00
(18)	Herb White	400.00	200.00	120.00

D

1952 Dallas Eagles Team Issue

A Class AA Texas League farm team of the Cleveland Indians, the Eagles were one of the higher minor league teams chronicled by Globe Printing in its series of 2-1/4" x 3-3/8" blank-back, black-and-white cards sets of the early 1950s. The checklist here is not complete.

		NM	EX	VG
Common Player:		60.00	30.00	18.00
(1)	Dick Aylward	60.00	30.00	18.00
(2)	Jodie Beeler	60.00	30.00	18.00
(3)	Bob Bundy	60.00	30.00	18.00
(4)	Hal Erickson	60.00	30.00	18.00
(5)	Dave Hoskins	60.00	30.00	18.00
(6)	Edward Knoblauch	60.00	30.00	18.00
(7)	Joe Kotrany	60.00	30.00	18.00
(8)	Joe Macko	60.00	30.00	18.00
(9)	Peter Mazar	60.00	30.00	18.00
(10)	Harry Sullivan	60.00	30.00	18.00
(11)	Edward Varhely	60.00	30.00	18.00

1959 Darigold Farms Spokane Indians

TOM DAVIS, Center Field
Compliments of DARIGOLD FARMS

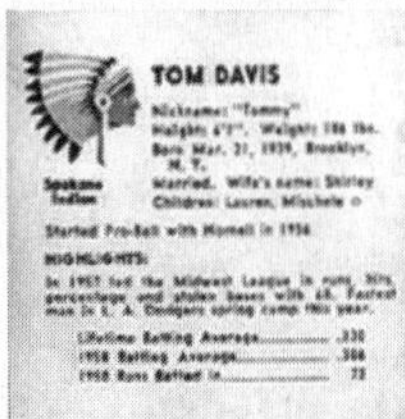
TOM DAVIS
HIGHLIGHTS:

The unnumbered cards in this set were glued to milk cartons by a folded tab at the top of each card. The basic card measures 2-1/2" x 2-3/8", with a 2-1/2" x 2-1/8" tab. Black-and-white player photos are set against colored backgrounds of yellow (1-8), red (9-16) and blue (17-22). Player biographical details and stats are printed in black on the back. Values shown are for cards without the superfluous tabs.

		NM	EX	VG
Complete Set (22):		4,500	2,250	1,350
Common Player:		200.00	100.00	60.00
(1)	Facundo Barragan	200.00	100.00	60.00
(2)	Steve Bilko	225.00	110.00	65.00
(3)	Bobby Bragan	225.00	110.00	65.00
(4)	Chuck Churn	200.00	100.00	60.00
(5)	Tom Davis	450.00	225.00	135.00
(6)	Dom Domenichelli	200.00	100.00	60.00
(7)	Bob Giallombardo	200.00	100.00	60.00
(8)	Connie Grob	200.00	100.00	60.00
(9)	Fred Hatfield	200.00	100.00	60.00
(10)	Bob Lillis	225.00	110.00	65.00
(11)	Lloyd Merritt	200.00	100.00	60.00
(12)	Larry Miller	200.00	100.00	60.00
(13)	Chris Nicolosi	200.00	100.00	60.00
(14)	Allen Norris	200.00	100.00	60.00
(15)	Phil Ortega	200.00	100.00	60.00
(16)	Phillips Paine	200.00	100.00	60.00
(17)	Bill Parsons	200.00	100.00	60.00
(18)	Hisel Patrick	200.00	100.00	60.00
(19)	Tony Roig	200.00	100.00	60.00
(20)	Tom Saffell	200.00	100.00	60.00
(21)	Norm Sherry	250.00	125.00	75.00
(22)	Ben Wade	200.00	100.00	60.00

1960 Darigold Farms Spokane Indians

Compliments of DARIGOLD FARMS

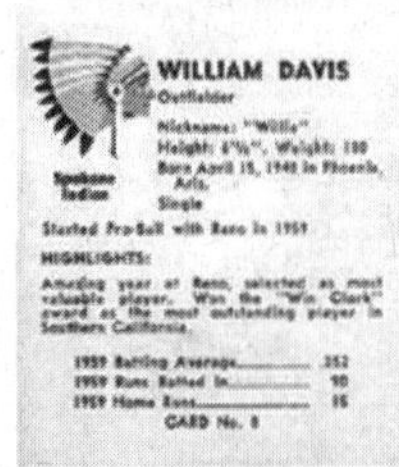
WILLIAM DAVIS
Outfielder
HIGHLIGHTS:

For its second annual baseball card set, the dairy added two cards and numbered the issue on the back. Card fronts were black-and-white photos against colored backgrounds of yellow (1-8), green (9-16) and red (17-24). A facsimile autograph appears on the front as well. The basic card measures 2-3/8" x 2-11/16", with a folded 2-3/8" x 2-1/16" tab at the top, by which the card was glued to a milk carton. Backs are black-and-white. Values shown are for cards without the superfluous tab.

		NM	EX	VG
Complete Set (24):		4,500	2,250	1,350
Common Player:		145.00	75.00	40.00
1	Chris Nicolosi	145.00	75.00	40.00
2	Jim Pagliaroni	145.00	75.00	40.00
3	Roy Smalley	145.00	75.00	40.00
4	Bill Bethel	145.00	75.00	40.00
5	Joe Liscio	145.00	75.00	40.00
6	Curt Roberts	145.00	75.00	40.00
7	Ed Palmquist	145.00	75.00	40.00
8	Willie Davis	300.00	150.00	90.00
9	Bob Giallombardo	145.00	75.00	40.00
10	Pedro Gomez	145.00	75.00	40.00
11	Mel Nelson	145.00	75.00	40.00
12	Charley Smith	145.00	75.00	40.00
13	Clarence Churn	145.00	75.00	40.00
14	Ramon Conde	145.00	75.00	40.00
15	George O'Donnell	145.00	75.00	40.00
16	Tony Roig	145.00	75.00	40.00
17	Frank Howard	450.00	225.00	135.00
18	Billy Harris	145.00	75.00	40.00
19	Mike Brumley	145.00	75.00	40.00
20	Earl Robinson	145.00	75.00	40.00
21	Ron Fairly	400.00	200.00	120.00
22	Joe Frazier	145.00	75.00	40.00
23	Allen Norris	145.00	75.00	40.00
24	Ford Young	145.00	75.00	40.00

E

1928 Pacific Coast League Exhibits

This regional series of 32 cards pictures players from the six California teams in the Pacific Coast League. Like the 1928 major league Exhibits, the PCL cards have a blue tint and are not numbered. They are blank-backed and measure 3-3/8" x 5-3/8". The set includes several misspellings. Cards are occasionally found with a corner clipped, the card corner to be used as a coupon with redemption value.

		NM	EX	VG
Complete Set (32):		17,500	8,750	5,250
Common Player:		500.00	250.00	150.00
1	Buzz Arlett	800.00	400.00	240.00
2	Earl Averill	1,750	875.00	525.00
3	Carl Berger (Walter)	800.00	400.00	240.00
4	"Ping" Bodie	700.00	350.00	210.00
5	Carl Dittmar	500.00	250.00	150.00
6	Jack Fenton	500.00	250.00	150.00
7	Neal "Mickey" Finn (Cornelius)	500.00	250.00	150.00
8	Ray French	500.00	250.00	150.00
9	Tony Governor	500.00	250.00	150.00
10	"Truck" Hannah	500.00	250.00	150.00
11	Mickey Heath	500.00	250.00	150.00
12	Wally Hood	500.00	250.00	150.00
13	"Fuzzy" Hufft	500.00	250.00	150.00
14	Snead Jolly (Smead Jolley)	600.00	300.00	180.00
15	Bobby "Ducky" Jones	500.00	250.00	150.00
16	Rudy Kallio	500.00	250.00	150.00
17	Ray Keating	500.00	250.00	150.00
18	Johnny Kerr	500.00	250.00	150.00
19	Harry Krause	500.00	250.00	150.00
20	Lynford H. Larry (Lary)	500.00	250.00	150.00
21	Dudley Lee	500.00	250.00	150.00
22	Walter "Duster" Mails	500.00	250.00	150.00
23	Jimmy Reese	650.00	325.00	200.00
24	"Dusty" Rhodes	500.00	250.00	150.00
25	Hal Rhyne	500.00	250.00	150.00
26	Hank Severied (Severeid)	500.00	250.00	150.00
27	Earl Sheely	500.00	250.00	150.00
28	Frank Shellenback	500.00	250.00	150.00
29	Gordon Slade	500.00	250.00	150.00
30	Hollis Thurston	500.00	250.00	150.00
31	"Babe" Twombly	500.00	250.00	150.00
32	Earl "Tex" Weathersby	500.00	250.00	150.00

1953 Montreal Royals Exhibits

36
STEVE
LEMBO

Twenty-four Montreal Royals, including many future Brooklyn and L.A. Dodgers and Hall of Fame managers Walt Alston and Tommy Lasorda, were included in a 64-card Canadian issue by Exhibit Supply Co., of Chicago. The cards are slightly smaller, at 3-1/4" x 5-1/4", than standard Exhibits and printed - blank-backed - on gray stock. Numbered on front, cards of the Montreal players can be found in either blue or reddish-brown tint. Only the Royals players from the issue are checklisted here.

		NM	EX	VG
Complete Set (24):		450.00	225.00	135.00
Common Player:		15.00	7.50	4.50
33	Don Hoak	25.00	12.50	7.50
34	Bob Alexander	15.00	7.50	4.50
35	John Simmons	15.00	7.50	4.50
36	Steve Lembo	15.00	7.50	4.50
37	Norm Larker	20.00	10.00	6.00
38	Bob Ludwick	15.00	7.50	4.50
39	Walt Moryn	20.00	10.00	6.00
40	Charlie Thompson	15.00	7.50	4.50
41	Ed Roebuck	20.00	10.00	6.00
42	Russell Rose	15.00	7.50	4.50
43	Edmundo (Sandy) Amoros	25.00	12.50	7.50
44	Bob Milliken	15.00	7.50	4.50
45	Art Fabbro	15.00	7.50	4.50
46	Spook Jacobs	15.00	7.50	4.50
47	Carmen Mauro	15.00	7.50	4.50
48	Walter Fiala	15.00	7.50	4.50
49	Rocky Nelson	15.00	7.50	4.50
50	Tom La Sorda (Lasorda)	60.00	30.00	18.00
51	Ronnie Lee	15.00	7.50	4.50
52	Hampton Coleman	15.00	7.50	4.50
53	Frank Marchio	15.00	7.50	4.50
54	William Sampson	15.00	7.50	4.50
55	Gil Mills	15.00	7.50	4.50
56	Al Ronning	15.00	7.50	4.50
61	Walt Alston	40.00	20.00	12.00

1953 Fargo-Moorhead Twins Team Issue

This set of team-issued cards includes the first of future home-run king Roger Maris (spelled Maras in the traditional family manner). The cards are about 3-1/4" x 5-5/16" with a white border surrounding a black-and-white posed photo. Player identification is in three lines of white type at lower-left. Backs are blank, except some cards which bear a rubber-stamped promotional message from the "Red River Scenes" newspaper. The unnumbered cards are checklisted here in alphabetical order. Three of the players are known in two or more poses.

		NM	EX	VG
Complete Set (21):		3,500	1,750	1,000
Common Player:		60.00	30.00	18.00
(1)	Zeke Bonura	60.00	30.00	18.00
(2)	Bob Borovicka	60.00	30.00	18.00
(3)	Ken Braeseke	60.00	30.00	18.00
(4)	Joe Camacho	60.00	30.00	18.00
(5)	Galen Fiss	60.00	30.00	18.00
(6)	Frank Gravino (Batting follow-through.)	60.00	30.00	18.00
(7)	Frank Gravino (Hands on hips.)	60.00	30.00	18.00
(8)	Frank Gravino (Hands on knees.)	60.00	30.00	18.00
(9)	Santo Luberto/Fldg	60.00	30.00	18.00
(10)	Roger Maras/Fldg	1,250	625.00	375.00
(11)	Roger Maras/Btg	1,250	625.00	375.00
(12)	Jerry Mehlish (Mehlisch)	60.00	30.00	18.00
(13)	Bob Melton	60.00	30.00	18.00
(14)	Ray Mendoza (Stretching at 1B, ball in glove.)	60.00	30.00	18.00
(15)	Ray Mendoza (Stretching at 1B, no ball.)	60.00	30.00	18.00
(16)	John Morse	60.00	30.00	18.00
(17)	Don Nance	60.00	30.00	18.00
(18)	Ray Seif	60.00	30.00	18.00
(19)	Will Sirois	60.00	30.00	18.00
(20)	Dick Wegner	60.00	30.00	18.00
(21)	Don Wolf	60.00	30.00	18.00

1966 Foremost Milk St. Petersburg Cardinals

This 20-card black-and-white set includes players and the manager, Sparky Anderson, of the Florida State League farm club of the St. Louis Cardinals. The unnumbered, blank-backed cards measure 3-1/2" x 5-1/2".

		NM	EX	VG
Complete Set (20):		50.00	25.00	15.00
Common Player:		2.50	1.25	.75
(1)	George "Sparky" Anderson	17.50	8.75	5.25
(2)	Dave Bakenhaster	2.50	1.25	.75
(3)	Leonard Boyer	4.00	2.00	1.25
(4)	Ron Braddock	2.50	1.25	.75
(5)	Thomas "Chip" Coulter	2.50	1.25	.75
(6)	Ernest "Sweet Pea" Davis	2.50	1.25	.75
(7)	Phil Knuckles	2.50	1.25	.75
(8)	Doug Lukens	2.50	1.25	.75
(9)	Terry Milani	2.50	1.25	.75
(10)	Tim Morgan	2.50	1.25	.75
(11)	Harry Parker	2.50	1.25	.75
(12)	Jerry Robertson	2.50	1.25	.75
(13)	Francisco Rodriguez	2.50	1.25	.75
(14)	John "Sonny" Ruberto	2.50	1.25	.75
(15)	Charlie Stewart	2.50	1.25	.75
(16)	Gary L. Stone	2.50	1.25	.75
(17)	Charles "Tim" Thompson	2.50	1.25	.75
(18)	Jose Villar	2.50	1.25	.75
(19)	Archie L. Wade	2.50	1.25	.75
(20)	Jim Williamson	2.50	1.25	.75

1921 Frederick Foto Service

This issue comprises a mix of Pacific Coast League and Major League players. Because Frederick Foto was located in Sacramento, a preponderance of the minor leaguers are Sacramento Senators. The method of the cards' distribution is unknown. The cards are black-and-white glossy photographs glued to a cardboard backing. The photos are bordered in white with top and bottom borders considerably wider than those on the sides. About 1-3/16" x 2-5/8", the cards have blank backs. On front is the player's last name and city, printed in a hand-lettered style. Most cards have a "Freredick / Foto." credit in the same style. Other cards have a banner-and-circle "Foto / Frederick / Service logo." It is likely this checklist is not complete. Gaps have been left in the assigned numbering for future additions.

		NM	EX	VG
Common Player:		300.00	150.00	90.00
(1)	Alexander	300.00	150.00	90.00
(2)	Ike Caveny (Caveney)	300.00	150.00	90.00
(3)	Pete Compton	300.00	150.00	90.00
(4)	Les Cook/Btg	300.00	150.00	90.00
(5)	Les Cook/Fldg	300.00	150.00	90.00
(7)	Carroll Canfield	300.00	150.00	90.00
(8)	Brick Eldred	300.00	150.00	90.00
(9)	Rowdy Elliott	300.00	150.00	90.00
(11)	Tony Faeth	300.00	150.00	90.00
(12)	Paul Fittery	300.00	150.00	90.00
(14)	Griffith	300.00	150.00	90.00
(15)	Charlie Hollocher	300.00	150.00	90.00
(17)	Willie Kamm	300.00	150.00	90.00
(18)	Manny Kopp	300.00	150.00	90.00
(19)	Earl Kuntz (Kunz)	300.00	150.00	90.00
(21)	Duster Mails (Arms at sides.)	300.00	150.00	90.00
(22)	Duster Mails (Hands at chest.)	300.00	150.00	90.00
(23)	Duster Mails (Follow-through.)	300.00	150.00	90.00
(24)	Duster Mails (Wind-up.)	300.00	150.00	90.00
(26)	Patsy McGaffigan	300.00	150.00	90.00
(27)	Roxie Middleton	300.00	150.00	90.00
(28)	Hack Miller	350.00	175.00	105.00
(31)	Dick Niehaus	300.00	150.00	90.00
(32)	Billy Orr (Batting)	300.00	150.00	90.00
(32)	Billy Orr (Hands on knees.)	300.00	150.00	90.00
(33)	Dode Paskert	300.00	150.00	90.00
(34)	Ken Penner (Right foot off ground.)	300.00	150.00	90.00
(35)	Ken Penner (Right foot on ground.)	300.00	150.00	90.00
(36)	Charlie Pick	300.00	150.00	90.00
(37)	Babe Pinelli	400.00	200.00	120.00
(39)	Bill Prough	300.00	150.00	90.00
(41)	Addison Read	300.00	150.00	90.00
(43)	Bill Rodgers	300.00	150.00	90.00
(44)	Pete Rose	300.00	150.00	90.00
(45)	Babe Ruth	20,000	10,000	6,000
(46)	Buddy Ryan (Holding bat, 3/4 length.)	300.00	150.00	90.00
(47)	Buddy Ryan (Holding bat, full-length.)	300.00	150.00	90.00
(48)	Buddy Ryan (Swinging bat.)	300.00	150.00	90.00
(50)	Bobby Schang	300.00	150.00	90.00
(52)	Les Sheehan	300.00	150.00	90.00
(60)	Kettle Wirts (Chicago)	300.00	150.00	90.00
(61)	Kettle Wirts (Dallas)	300.00	150.00	90.00
(62)	Archie Yelle	300.00	150.00	90.00
		300.00	150.00	90.00
	Unidentified player, arms folded.	300.00	150.00	90.00
	Unidentified player, batting follow- through.	300.00	150.00	90.00

1951 Fresno Cardinals Team Issue

These 2-1/4" x 3-3/8" black-and-white, unnumbered, blank-backed cards were one of many minor league team sets issued by Globe Printing of San Jose, Calif., in the early 1950s. Cards were usually given away at the ballpark on a one-per-week or one-per-homestand basis, accounting for the rarity of surviving sets. The team was a California League (Class C) affiliate of the St. Louis Cardinals.

		NM	EX	VG
Complete Set (17):		1,000	500.00	300.00
Common Player:		60.00	30.00	18.00
(1)	Hal Atkinson	60.00	30.00	18.00
(2)	Larry Barton	60.00	30.00	18.00
(3)	Charlie Brooks	60.00	30.00	18.00
(4)	Bill Burton	60.00	30.00	18.00
(5)	Ray Herrera	60.00	30.00	18.00
(6)	Earl Jones	60.00	30.00	18.00
(7)	Jim King	60.00	30.00	18.00
(8)	Whitey Lageman	60.00	30.00	18.00
(9)	Wally Lamers	60.00	30.00	18.00
(10)	John McNamara	75.00	37.00	22.00
(11)	Gerry Mertz	60.00	30.00	18.00
(12)	Frank Olasin	60.00	30.00	18.00
(13)	Howie Phillips	60.00	30.00	18.00
(14)	Jack Ramsey	60.00	30.00	18.00
(15)	Tony Stathos	60.00	30.00	18.00
(16)	Whit Ulrich	60.00	30.00	18.00
(17)	Pete Younie	60.00	30.00	18.00

1952 Frostade

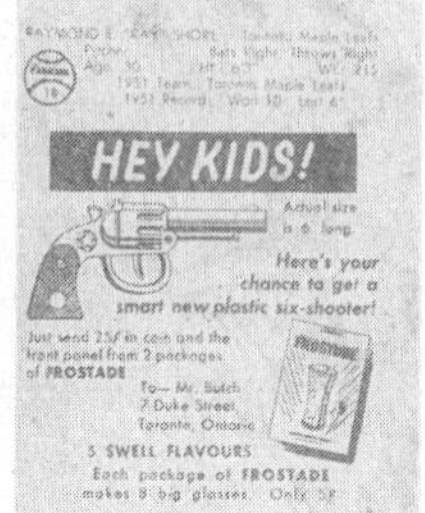

(See 1952 Parkhurst.)

1954 Fruiterie Saint Louis Tommy Lasorda

The date of issue attributed is only a best guess. It is also unknown how many other Montreal Royals players may be found in this issue. Printed in black-and-white on fairly thick 5-1/2" x 7" cardboard, this card features a portrait photo of the Royals' pitcher and future Hall of Fame manager along with a facsimile autograph on the borderless front. Rubber-stamped at top of the otherwise blank back is: "Fruiterie / Saint Louis De Franos / 515 RUE ROY PL. 1729," presumably identification of a Montreal business which distributed the card.

	NM	EX	VG
Tommy Lasorda	100.00	50.00	30.00

1911 Gilmartin Printing Co. S.F. Seals

These extremely scarce cards were issued as a premium by the Gilmartin Printing Co. of San Francisco and feature only members of the city's PCL Seals team. The 5" x 7" cards have full-length posed portraits of the players at center, printed in a blue-green tone and surrounded by a wide white border. The player's name, position team and year are scripted in the lower-left corner of the photo. Backs are blank. This checklist is known to be incomplete. Some cards have the sponsor's imprint below the photo.

		NM	EX	VG
Common Player:		3,000	1,500	900.00
(1)	Claude Berry	3,000	1,500	900.00
(2)	Frank Browning	3,000	1,500	900.00
(6)	Willard Meikle	3,000	1,500	900.00
(7)	Frank Miller	3,000	1,500	900.00
(9)	Harry Sutor	3,000	1,500	900.00
(10)	Tom Tennant	3,000	1,500	900.00
(12)	Geo. Weaver	9,000	4,500	2,700

1956-57 Gil's Drive-Ins Seattle Rainiers

(See 1956-57 Seattle Popcorn for checklist and values.)

1951-1954 Globe Printing

The team-issue card sets and souvenir picture albums listed in previous editions under the heading of Globe Printing are now found alphabetically by team name as per this list:

1951 Fresno Cardinals
1951 San Jose Red Sox
1952 Atlanta Crackers
1952 Baltimore Orioles
1952 Colorado Springs Sky Sox
1952 Columbus Cardinals
1952 Dallas Eagles
1952 Ft. Worth Cats
1952 Great Falls Electrics
1952 Jamestown Falcons
1952 Miami Beach Flamingos
1952 Ogden Reds
1952 Oshkosh Giants
1952 San Diego Padres
1952 Shawnee Hawks
1952-1953 Sioux City Soos
1952 Syracuse Chiefs
1952 Ventura Braves
1954 Sioux City Soos

1943 Golden Quality Ice Cream Wilkes-Barre Barons

This rare war-time minor league issue depicts the Hall of Fame manager, Tony Lazzeri, and players on the Class A Eastern League Barons. The 4" x 5" black-and-white cards have facsimile player autographs. Printed in the bottom border at left are the team and year; at right is "Compliments of Golden Quality Ice Cream Co."

		NM	EX	VG
Complete Set (6):		600.00	300.00	180.00
Common Player:		75.00	37.50	22.50
(1)	Alex Damalitron	75.00	37.50	22.50
(2)	Tony Lazzeri (Bat on shoulder.)	175.00	90.00	55.00
(3)	Tony Lazzeri (Hands on knees.)	175.00	90.00	55.00
(4)	Jim McDonnell	75.00	37.50	22.50
(5)	Joe Pennington	75.00	37.50	22.50
(6)	Ned Tryon	75.00	37.50	22.50

1957 Golden State Dairy S.F. Seals Stickers

There are 23 stickers known in this set, featuring the last minor league team in San Francisco. Virtually every player who appeared in more than 10 games for the Seals that season is included in the set. The stickers measure approximately 2" x 2-1/2", are printed in black-and-white, and blank-backed. A 3-1/2" x 6" album to house the stickers was also issued, with biographical data and space for an autograph on each player's page. The stickers are checklisted here alphabetically, as the stickers are unnumbered.

		NM	EX	VG
Complete Set (23):		550.00	275.00	165.00
Common Player:		25.00	12.50	7.50
Album:		150.00	75.00	45.00
(1)	William "Bill" Abernathie	25.00	12.50	7.50
(2)	Kenneth "Chip" Aspromonte	25.00	12.50	7.50
(3)	Harry "Fritz" Dorish	25.00	12.50	7.50
(4)	Joe "Flash" Gordon	25.00	12.50	7.50
(5)	Grady Hatton Jr.	25.00	12.50	7.50
(6)	Thomas "Tommy" Hurd	25.00	12.50	7.50
(7)	Frank Kellert	25.00	12.50	7.50
(8)	Richard "Marty" Keough	25.00	12.50	7.50
(9)	Leo "Black Cat" Kiely	25.00	12.50	7.50
(10)	Harry William Malmberg	25.00	12.50	7.50
(11)	John McCall	25.00	12.50	7.50
(12)	Albert "Albie" Pearson	40.00	20.00	12.00
(13)	Jack Phillips	25.00	12.50	7.50
(14)	William "Bill" Renna	25.00	12.50	7.50
(15)	Edward "Ed" Sadowski	25.00	12.50	7.50
(16)	Robert W. Smith	25.00	12.50	7.50
(17)	Jack Spring	25.00	12.50	7.50
(18)	Jospeh H. Tanner	25.00	12.50	7.50
(19)	Salvador "Sal" Taormina	25.00	12.50	7.50
(20)	Maynard "Bert" Thiel	25.00	12.50	7.50
(21)	Anthony "Nini" Tornay	25.00	12.50	7.50
(22)	Thomas "Tommy" Umphlett	25.00	12.50	7.50
(23)	Glenn "Cap" Wright	25.00	12.50	7.50

1943 Grand Studio Milwaukee Brewers

It's unknown how these blank-backed, black-and-white, 3-1/2" x 5-1/2" pictures were distributed. The only identification is "PHOTO BY GRAND STUDIO" in the lower-right corner. It's likely the pictures were sold as a set at Borchert Field.

		NM	EX	VG
Complete Set (22):		1,000	500.00	300.00
Common Player:		60.00	30.00	20.00
(1)	Joe Berry	60.00	30.00	20.00
(2)	Bob Bowman	60.00	30.00	20.00
(3)	Earl Caldwell	60.00	30.00	20.00
(4)	Grey Clarke	60.00	30.00	20.00
(5)	Merv Conner	60.00	30.00	20.00
(6)	Paul Erickson	60.00	30.00	20.00
(7)	Charlie Grimm	80.00	40.00	25.00
(8)	Hank Helf	60.00	30.00	20.00
(9)	Don Johnson	60.00	30.00	20.00
(10)	Wes Livengood	60.00	30.00	20.00
(11)	Hershell Martin	60.00	30.00	20.00
(12)	Tommy Nelson	60.00	30.00	20.00
(13)	Ted Norbert	60.00	30.00	20.00
(14)	Bill Norman	60.00	30.00	20.00
(15)	Henry Oana	125.00	65.00	40.00
(16)	Jimmy Pruett	60.00	30.00	20.00
(17)	Bill Sahlin	60.00	30.00	20.00
(18)	Frank Secroy	60.00	30.00	20.00
(19)	Red Smith	60.00	30.00	20.00
(20)	Charles Sproull	60.00	30.00	20.00
(21)	Hugh Todd	60.00	30.00	20.00
(22)	Tony York	60.00	30.00	20.00

1944 Grand Studio Milwaukee Brewers

Future Hall of Fame manager Casey Stengel is featured in the second of three annual team-issued photocard sets. The 3-1/2" x 5-1/2" cards have black-and-white portrait photos with facsimile autographs, bordered in white. Backs are blank.

		NM	EX	VG
Complete Set (26):		900.00	450.00	275.00
Common Player:		50.00	25.00	15.00
(1)	Julio Acosta	50.00	25.00	15.00
(2)	Heinz Becker	50.00	25.00	15.00
(3)	George Binks	50.00	25.00	15.00
(4)	Bob Bowman	50.00	25.00	15.00
(5)	Earl Caldwell	50.00	25.00	15.00
(6)	Dick Culler	50.00	25.00	15.00
(7)	Roy Easterwood	50.00	25.00	15.00
(8)	Jack Farmer	50.00	25.00	15.00
(9)	Charles Gassaway	50.00	25.00	15.00
(10)	Dick Hearn	50.00	25.00	15.00
(11)	Don Hendrickson	50.00	25.00	15.00
(12)	Ed Levy	50.00	25.00	15.00
(13)	Hershel Martin	50.00	25.00	15.00
(14)	Bill Nagel	50.00	25.00	15.00
(15)	Tommy Nelson	50.00	25.00	15.00
(16)	Bill Norman	50.00	25.00	15.00
(17)	Hal Peck	50.00	25.00	15.00
(18)	Jimmy Pruett	50.00	25.00	15.00
(19)	Ken Raddant	50.00	25.00	15.00
(20)	Owen Scheetz	50.00	25.00	15.00
(21)	Eddie Scheive	50.00	25.00	15.00
(22)	Frank Secory	50.00	25.00	15.00
(23)	Red Smith	50.00	25.00	15.00

(24)	Floyd Speer	50.00	25.00	15.00
(25)	Charlie Sproull	50.00	25.00	15.00
(26)	Casey Stengel	300.00	150.00	90.00

1945 Grand Studio Milwaukee Brewers

The format remained unchanged for the last of three annual team-issued photocard sets. The 3-1/2" x 5-1/2" cards have black-and-white portrait photos with facsimile autographs, bordered in white. Backs are blank.

		NM	EX	VG
Complete Set (16):		625.00	300.00	175.00
Common Player:		50.00	25.00	15.00
(1)	Julio Acosta	50.00	25.00	15.00
(2)	Arky Biggs	50.00	25.00	15.00
(3)	Bill Burgo	50.00	25.00	15.00
(4)	Nick Cullop	50.00	25.00	15.00
(5)	Wendell "Peaches" Davis	50.00	25.00	15.00
(6)	Otto Denning	50.00	25.00	15.00
(7)	Lew Flick	50.00	25.00	15.00
(8)	Don Hendrickson	50.00	25.00	15.00
(9)	Ed Kobersky	50.00	25.00	15.00
(10)	Carl Lindquist	50.00	25.00	15.00
(11)	Jack McGillen	50.00	25.00	15.00
(12)	Gene Nance	50.00	25.00	15.00
(13)	Bill Norman	50.00	25.00	15.00
(14)	Joe Rullo	50.00	25.00	15.00
(15)	Owen Scheetz	50.00	25.00	15.00
(16)	Floyd Speer	50.00	25.00	15.00

1952 Great Falls Electrics Team Issue

Formatted like the other known minor league issues from Globe Printing of San Jose, Calif., in the early 1950s, this set chronicles the 1952 version of the Class C (Pioneer League) Great Falls (Montana) Electrics, a farm club of the Brooklyn Dodgers. The blank-backed cards are black-and-white and measure about 2-1/4" x 3-3/8". An album was issued with the cards.

		NM	EX	VG
Complete Set (16):		800.00	400.00	240.00
Common Player:		60.00	30.00	18.00
(1)	Don Bricker	60.00	30.00	18.00
(2)	Larry Hampshire	60.00	30.00	18.00
(3)	Ernie Jordan	60.00	30.00	18.00
(4)	Lou Landini	60.00	30.00	18.00
(5)	Danny Lastres	60.00	30.00	18.00
(6)	Joe Oliffe	60.00	30.00	18.00
(7)	Len Payne	60.00	30.00	18.00
(8)	Lou Rochelli	60.00	30.00	18.00
(9)	Earl Silverthorn	60.00	30.00	18.00
(10)	Eddie Serrano	60.00	30.00	18.00
(11)	Rick Small	60.00	30.00	18.00
(12)	Dick Smith	60.00	30.00	18.00
(13)	Hal Snyder	60.00	30.00	18.00
(14)	Armando Suarez	60.00	30.00	18.00
(15)	Emy Unzicker	60.00	30.00	18.00
Album:		100.00	50.00	30.00

1888 Gypsy Queen California League

Until further specimens are reported, the attributed date of issue is speculative between about 1887-89. Undiscovered until 1998 was the fact that Gypsy Queen, a cigarette manufactured by Goodwin & Co. (Old Judge, etc.) had issued minor league cards, presumably of the relatively new California League. Like some contemporary issues, the card is a stiff piece of cardboard with a sepia-toned player photo glued to it. Size is about 1-1/2" x 2-1/2". As of November 2001, only one card was known from this issue. In Fair to Good condition it was sold at auction for $80,273, then a record price for any 19th Century card.

(1) Jas McDonald

1949 Hage's Dairy

Hage's Dairy of California began a three-year run of regional baseball cards featuring Pacific Coast League players in 1949. The cards were distributed inside popcorn boxes at the concession stand in Lane Field Park, home of the P.C.L. San Diego Padres. The 1949 set, like the following two years, was printed on thin stock measuring on average 2-5/8" x 3-1/8". The checklist includes several different poses for some of the players. Cards were continually being added or withdrawn to reflect roster changes on the minor league clubs. The Hage's sets were dominated by San Diego players, but also included representatives from the seven other P.C.L. teams. The 1949 cards can be found in four different tints: sepia, green, blue, and black-and-white. The unnumbered cards have blank backs or advertising messages on back. The player's name and team appear inside a box on the front of the card, and the 1949 cards can be dated by the large (quarter-inch) type used for the team names, which are sometimes referred to by city and other times by nickname.

		NM	EX	VG
Complete Set (106):		40,000	20,000	10,000
Common Player:		400.00	200.00	100.00
(1)	"Buster" Adams	400.00	200.00	100.00
(2)	"Red" Adams	400.00	200.00	100.00
(3)	Lee Anthony	400.00	200.00	100.00
(4)	Rinaldo Ardizoia	400.00	200.00	100.00
(5)	Del Baker	400.00	200.00	100.00
(6)	Ed Basinski	400.00	200.00	100.00
(7)	Jim Baxes	400.00	200.00	100.00
(8)	H. Becker	400.00	200.00	100.00
(9)	Herman Besse	400.00	200.00	100.00
(10)	Tom Bridges	400.00	200.00	100.00
(11)	Gene Brocker	400.00	200.00	100.00
(12)	Ralph Buxton	400.00	200.00	100.00
(13)	Mickey Burnett	400.00	200.00	100.00
(14)	Dain Clay (Pose)	400.00	200.00	100.00
(15)	Dain Clay (Batting)	400.00	200.00	100.00
(16)	Dain Corriden, Jim Reese	475.00	235.00	120.00
(17)	Pete Coscarart	400.00	200.00	100.00
(18)	Dom Dallessandro	400.00	200.00	100.00
(19)	Con Dempsey	400.00	200.00	100.00
(20)	Vince DiBiasi	400.00	200.00	100.00
(21)	Luke Easter (Batting stance.)	600.00	300.00	150.00
(22)	Luke Easter (Batting follow through.)	600.00	300.00	150.00
(23)	Ed Fernandez	400.00	200.00	100.00
(24)	Les Fleming	400.00	200.00	100.00
(25)	Jess Flores	400.00	200.00	100.00
(26)	Cecil Garriott	400.00	200.00	100.00
(27)	Charles Gassaway	400.00	200.00	100.00
(28)	Mickey Grasso	400.00	200.00	100.00
(29)	Will Hafey/Pitching	400.00	200.00	100.00
(30)	Will Hafey (Pose)	400.00	200.00	100.00
(31)	"Jeep" Handley	400.00	200.00	100.00
(32)	"Bucky" Harris (Pose)	600.00	300.00	150.00
(33)	"Bucky" Harris/Shouting	600.00	300.00	150.00
(34)	Roy Helser	400.00	200.00	100.00
(35)	Lloyd Hittle	400.00	200.00	100.00
(36)	Ralph Hodgin	400.00	200.00	100.00
(37)	Leroy Jarvis	400.00	200.00	100.00
(38)	John Jensen	400.00	200.00	100.00
(39)	Al Jurisich	400.00	200.00	100.00
(40)	Herb Karpel	600.00	300.00	150.00
(41)	Frank Kelleher	400.00	200.00	100.00
(42)	Bill Kelly	400.00	200.00	100.00
(43)	Bob Kelly	400.00	200.00	100.00
(44)	Frank Kerr	400.00	200.00	100.00
(45)	Thomas Kipp	400.00	200.00	100.00
(46)	Al Lien	400.00	200.00	100.00
(47)	Lyman Linde (Pose)	400.00	200.00	100.00
(48)	Lyman Linde/Pitching	400.00	200.00	100.00
(49)	Dennis Luby	400.00	200.00	100.00
(50)	"Red" Lynn	400.00	200.00	100.00
(51)	Pat Malone	400.00	200.00	100.00
(52)	Billy Martin	1,250	625.00	375.00
(53)	Joe Marty	400.00	200.00	100.00
(54)	Cliff Melton	400.00	200.00	100.00
(55)	Steve Mesner	400.00	200.00	100.00
(56)	Leon Mohr	400.00	200.00	100.00
(57)	"Butch" Moran	400.00	200.00	100.00
(58)	Glen Moulder	400.00	200.00	100.00
(59)	Steve Nagy	400.00	200.00	100.00
(60)	Roy Nicely	400.00	200.00	100.00
(61)	Walt Nothe	400.00	200.00	100.00
(62)	John O'Neill	400.00	200.00	100.00
(63)	"Pluto" Oliver	400.00	200.00	100.00
(64)	Al Olsen (Pose)	400.00	200.00	100.00
(65)	Al Olsen/Throwing	400.00	200.00	100.00
(66)	John Ostrowski	400.00	200.00	100.00
(67)	Roy Partee	400.00	200.00	100.00
(68)	Bill Raimondi	400.00	200.00	100.00
(69)	Bill Ramsey	400.00	200.00	100.00
(70)	Len Ratto	400.00	200.00	100.00
(71)	Xavier Rescigno	400.00	200.00	100.00
(72)	John Ritchey/Btg	400.00	200.00	100.00
(73)	John Ritchey/Catching	400.00	200.00	100.00
(74)	Mickey Rocco	400.00	200.00	100.00
(75)	John Rucker	400.00	200.00	100.00
(76)	Clarence Russell	400.00	200.00	100.00
(77)	Jack Salverson	400.00	200.00	100.00
(78)	Charlie Schanz	400.00	200.00	125.00
(79)	Bill Schuster	400.00	200.00	100.00
(80)	Tom Seats	400.00	200.00	100.00
(81)	Neil Sheridan	400.00	200.00	100.00
(82)	Vince Shupe	400.00	200.00	100.00
(83)	Joe Sprinz	400.00	200.00	100.00
(84)	Chuck Stevens	400.00	200.00	100.00
(85)	Harvey Storey	400.00	200.00	100.00
(86)	Jim Tabor (Sacramento)	400.00	200.00	100.00
(87)	Jim Tabor (Seattle)	400.00	200.00	100.00
(88)	"Junior" Thompson	400.00	200.00	100.00
(89)	Arky Vaughn	625.00	310.00	175.00
(90)	Jackie Warner	400.00	200.00	100.00
(91)	Jim Warner	400.00	200.00	100.00
(92)	Dick Wenner	400.00	200.00	100.00
(93)	Max West (Pose)	400.00	200.00	100.00
(94)	Max West (Batting swing.)	400.00	200.00	100.00
(95)	Max West (Batting follow-through.)	400.00	200.00	100.00
(96)	Hank Weyse	400.00	200.00	100.00
(97)	"Fuzzy" White	400.00	200.00	100.00
(98)	Jo Jo White	400.00	200.00	100.00
(99)	Artie Wilson	400.00	200.00	100.00
(100)	Bill Wilson	400.00	200.00	100.00
(101)	Bobbie Wilson (Pose)	400.00	200.00	100.00
(102)	Bobbie Wilson/Pitching	400.00	200.00	100.00
(103)	"Pinky" Woods	400.00	200.00	100.00
(104)	Tony York	400.00	200.00	100.00
(105)	Del Young	400.00	200.00	100.00
(106)	Frank Zak	400.00	200.00	100.00

1950 Hage's Dairy

The 1950 P.C.L. set from Hage's Dairy was similar in design and size (about 2-5/8" x 3-1/8") to the previous year and was again distributed in popcorn boxes at San Diego's Lane Field. The 1950 cards are in black-and-white with a back containing an advertisement for Hage's Milk, Ice Cream or Ice Cream Bars. The advertising backs also contain the player's name and either brief 1949 statistics or career highlights at bottom. Many players were issued in more than one pose. Again, Padres dominate the unnumbered set with lesser representation from the other P.C.L. clubs. For the 1950 edition all team names are referred to by city (no nicknames) and the typeface is smaller. Gaps have been left in the assigned numbering to accommodate future additions to the checklist.

		NM	EX	VG
Complete Set (128):		45,000	22,500	13,500
Common Player:		375.00	185.00	110.00
(1)	"Buster" AdamsKneeling	375.00	185.00	110.00
(2a)	"Buster" Adams (Batting follow-through, with inscription.)	375.00	185.00	110.00
(2b)	"Buster" Adams (Batting follow-through, no inscription.)	375.00	185.00	110.00
(2c)	"Buster" Adams (Batting follow-through, body to left.)	375.00	185.00	110.00
(3a)	"Buster" Adams (Batting stance, caption box touching waist.)	375.00	185.00	110.00
(3b)	"Buster" Adams (Batting stance, caption box not touching waist.)	375.00	185.00	110.00
(4)	"Red" Adams	375.00	185.00	110.00
(5)	Dewey Adkins (Photo actually Albie Glossop.)	375.00	185.00	110.00
(6)	Rinaldo Ardizoia	375.00	185.00	110.00
(7)	Jose Bache	375.00	185.00	110.00
(8a)	Del Baker, Jim Reese (Bat visible at lower right.)	375.00	185.00	110.00
(8b)	Del Baker, Jim Reese (No bat visible.)	375.00	185.00	110.00
(9)	George Bamberger	375.00	185.00	110.00
(10)	Richard Barrett	375.00	185.00	110.00
(11)	Frank Baumholtz	375.00	185.00	110.00
(12)	Henry Behrman	375.00	185.00	110.00
(13)	Bill Bevens	375.00	185.00	110.00
(14)	Ernie Bickhaus	375.00	185.00	110.00
(15)	Bill Burgher (Pose)	375.00	185.00	110.00
(16)	Bill Burgher/Catching	375.00	185.00	110.00
(17)	Mark Christman	375.00	185.00	110.00
(18)	Clint Conatser	375.00	185.00	110.00
(19)	Herb Conyers/Fldg	375.00	185.00	110.00
(20)	Herb Conyers/Btg	375.00	185.00	110.00
(21)	Jim Davis	375.00	185.00	110.00
(22)	Ted Del Guercio	375.00	185.00	110.00
(23)	Vince DiBiasi	375.00	185.00	110.00
(24)	Jess Dobernic	375.00	185.00	110.00
(25)	"Red" Embree (Pose)	375.00	185.00	110.00
(26)	"Red" Embree/Pitching	375.00	185.00	110.00
(27)	Elbie Fletcher	375.00	185.00	110.00
(28)	Guy Fletcher	375.00	185.00	110.00
(30)	Tony Freitas	375.00	185.00	110.00
(31)	Denny Galehouse	375.00	185.00	110.00
(32)	Jack Graham (Pose, looking to left.)	375.00	185.00	110.00
(33)	Jack Graham (Pose, looking straight ahead.)	375.00	185.00	110.00
(34)	Jack Graham (Batting swing.)	375.00	185.00	110.00
(35)	Jack Graham (Batting stance.)	375.00	185.00	110.00
(36)	Orval Grove	375.00	185.00	110.00
(37)	Lee Handley	375.00	185.00	110.00
(38)	Ralph Hodgin	375.00	185.00	110.00
(39)	Don Johnson	375.00	185.00	110.00
(40)	Al Jurisich (Pose)	375.00	185.00	110.00
(41)	Al Jurisich (Pitching wind-up.)	375.00	185.00	110.00
(42)	Al Jurisich (Pitching follow-through.)	375.00	185.00	110.00
(43)	Bill Kelly	375.00	185.00	110.00
(44)	Frank Kerr	375.00	185.00	110.00
(45)	Tom Kipp (Pose)	375.00	185.00	110.00
(46)	Tom Kipp/Pitching	375.00	185.00	110.00
(47)	Mel Knezovich	375.00	185.00	110.00
(48)	Red Kress	375.00	185.00	110.00
(49)	Dario Lodigiani	375.00	185.00	110.00
(50)	Dennis Luby (Pose)	375.00	185.00	110.00
(51)	Dennis Luby/Throwing	375.00	185.00	110.00
(52)	Al Lyons	375.00	185.00	110.00
(53)	Clarence Maddern	375.00	185.00	110.00
(54)	Joe Marty	375.00	185.00	110.00
(55)	Bob McCall	375.00	185.00	110.00
(56)	Cal McIrvin	375.00	185.00	110.00
(57)	Orestes Minoso (Batting follow-through.)	850.00	425.00	250.00
(58)	Orestes Minoso/Bunting	850.00	425.00	250.00
(59)	Leon Mohr	375.00	185.00	110.00
(60)	Dee Moore/Btg	375.00	185.00	110.00
(61)	Dee Moor/Catching	375.00	185.00	110.00
(62)	Jim Moran	375.00	185.00	110.00
(63)	Glen Moulder	375.00	185.00	110.00
(64)	Milt Neilsen (Pose)	375.00	185.00	110.00
(65)	Milt Neilsen/Btg	375.00	185.00	110.00
(66)	Milt Neilsen/Throwing	375.00	185.00	110.00
(67)	Rube Novotney	375.00	185.00	110.00
(68)	Al Olsen	375.00	185.00	110.00
(69)	Manny Perez	375.00	185.00	110.00
(70)	Bill Raemondi (Raimondi)	375.00	185.00	110.00
(71)	Len Ratto	375.00	185.00	110.00
(72)	Mickey Rocco	375.00	185.00	110.00
(73)	Marv Rotblatt	375.00	185.00	110.00
(74)	Lynwood Rowe (Pose)	400.00	200.00	120.00
(75)	Lynwood Rowe/Pitching	400.00	200.00	120.00
(76)	Clarence Russell	375.00	185.00	110.00
(77)	Hal Saltzman (Pitching follow-through.)	375.00	185.00	110.00
(78)	Hal Saltzman (Pitching wind-up.)	375.00	185.00	110.00
(79)	Hal Saltzman (Pitching, leg in air.)	375.00	185.00	110.00
(81)	Mike Sandlock	375.00	185.00	110.00
(82)	Bob Savage (Pose)	375.00	185.00	110.00
(83)	Bob Savage/Pitching	375.00	185.00	110.00
(84)	Charlie Schanz	375.00	185.00	110.00
(85)	Bill Schuster	375.00	185.00	110.00
(86)	Neill Sheridan	375.00	185.00	110.00
(87)	Harry Simpson (Batting swing.)	525.00	260.00	150.00
(88)	Harry Simpson (Batting stance.)	525.00	260.00	150.00
(89)	Harry Simpson (Batting stance, close up.)	525.00	260.00	150.00
(90)	Harry Simpson (Batting follow-through.)	525.00	260.00	150.00
(91)	Elmer Singleton	375.00	185.00	110.00
(92)	Al Smith (Pose)	375.00	185.00	110.00
(93)	Al Smith (Batting stance.)	375.00	185.00	110.00
(94)	Al Smith (Fielding)	375.00	185.00	110.00
(95)	Alphonse Smith (Glove above knee.)	375.00	185.00	110.00
(96)	Alphonse Smith (Glove below knee.)	375.00	185.00	110.00
(97)	Steve Souchock	375.00	185.00	110.00
(98)	Jim Steiner	375.00	185.00	110.00
(99)	Harvey Storey (Batting stance.)	375.00	185.00	110.00
(100)	Harvey Storey (Swinging bat.)	375.00	185.00	110.00
(101)	Harvey Storey/Throwing	375.00	185.00	110.00
(102)	Harvey Storey/Fldg (Ball in glove.)	375.00	185.00	110.00
(103)	Max Surkont	375.00	185.00	110.00
(104)	Jim Tabor	375.00	185.00	110.00
(105)	Forrest Thompson	375.00	185.00	110.00
(106)	Mike Tresh (Pose)	375.00	185.00	110.00
(107)	Mike Tresh/Catching	375.00	185.00	110.00
(108)	Ben Wade	375.00	185.00	110.00
(109)	Kenny Washington	375.00	185.00	110.00
(110)	Bill Waters (Pose)	375.00	185.00	110.00
(111)	Bill Waters/Pitching	375.00	185.00	110.00
(112)	Roy Welmaker (Pose)	375.00	185.00	110.00
(113)	Roy Welmaker/Pitching	375.00	185.00	110.00
(114)	Max West (Pose)	375.00	185.00	110.00
(115)	Max West (Batting stance.)	375.00	185.00	110.00
(116)	Max West/Kneeling	375.00	185.00	110.00
(117)	Max West (Batting follow-through.)	375.00	185.00	110.00
(118)	Al White	375.00	185.00	110.00
(119)	"Whitey" Wietelmann (Pose)	375.00	185.00	110.00
(120)	"Whitey" Wietelmann/Bunting	375.00	185.00	110.00
(121)	"Whitey" Wietelmann (Batting stance.)	375.00	185.00	110.00
(122)	"Whitey" Wietelmann/ Throwing	375.00	185.00	110.00
(123)	Bobbie Wilson	375.00	185.00	110.00
(124)	Bobby Wilson	375.00	185.00	110.00
(125)	Roy Zimmerman	375.00	185.00	110.00
(126)	George Zuverink	375.00	185.00	110.00

1951 Hage's Dairy

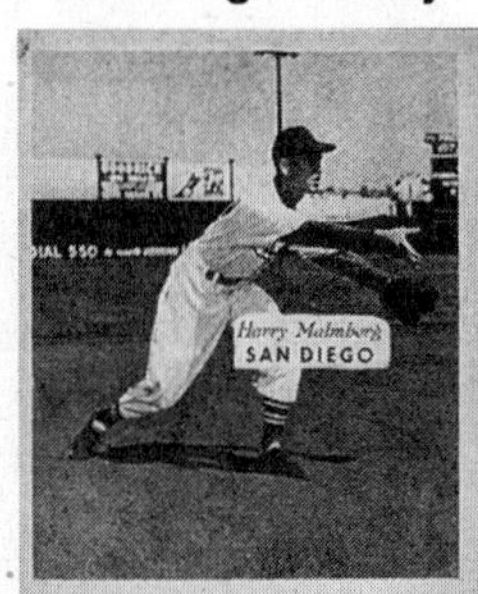

The final year of the Hage's P.C.L. issues saw the set reduced to 53 different unnumbered cards, all but 12 of them Padres. Among them are seven cards of Cleveland Indians players, which were issued during an exhibition series with the major league club, and six cards picturing members of the Hollywood Stars. No other P.C.L. teams are represented. The cards maintained the same size and style of the previous two years but were printed in more color tints, including blue, green, burgundy, gold, gray and sepia (but not black-and-white). The 1951 cards have blank backs and were again distributed in popcorn boxes at the San Diego stadium. The 1951 cards are the most common of the three sets issued by Hage's Dairy. The Indians and Stars players were issued in lesser quantities than the Padres, however, and command a higher value.

		NM	EX	VG
Complete Set (53):		18,000	9,000	5,500
Common Player:		300.00	150.00	90.00
(1)	"Buster" Adams	300.00	150.00	90.00
(2)	Del Baker	300.00	150.00	90.00
(3)	Ray Boone	850.00	425.00	250.00
(4)	Russ Christopher	300.00	150.00	90.00
(5)	Allie Clark	850.00	425.00	250.00
(6)	Herb Conyers	300.00	150.00	90.00
(7)	Luke Easter	450.00	225.00	135.00
(8)	"Red" Embree/Pitching (Foot in air.)	300.00	150.00	90.00
(9)	"Red" Embree/Pitching (Hands up.)	300.00	150.00	90.00
(10)	Jess Flores	850.00	425.00	250.00
(11)	Murray Franklin	300.00	150.00	90.00
(12)	Jack Graham/Portrait	300.00	150.00	90.00
(13)	Jack Graham/Btg	300.00	150.00	90.00
(14)	Gene Handley	300.00	150.00	90.00
(15)	Charles Harris	300.00	150.00	90.00
(16)	Sam Jones/Pitching (Hands back.)	300.00	150.00	90.00
(17)	Sam Jones/Pitching (Hands up.)	300.00	150.00	90.00
(18)	Sam Jones/Pitching (Leg in air.)	300.00	150.00	90.00
(19)	Al Jurisich	300.00	150.00	90.00
(20)	Frank Kerr/Btg	300.00	150.00	90.00
(21)	Frank Kerr/Catching	300.00	150.00	90.00
(22)	Dick Kinaman	300.00	150.00	90.00
(23)	Clarence Maddern/Btg	300.00	150.00	90.00
(24)	Clarence Maddern/Fldg	300.00	150.00	90.00
(25)	Harry Malmberg/Bunting	300.00	150.00	90.00
(26)	Harry Malmberg (Batting follow-through.)	300.00	150.00	90.00
(27)	Harry Malmberg/Fldg	300.00	150.00	90.00
(28)	Gordon Maltzberger	300.00	150.00	90.00
(29)	Al Olsen (Cleveland)	850.00	425.00	250.00
(30)	Al Olsen (San Diego)	300.00	150.00	90.00
(31)	Jimmy Reese (Clapping)	350.00	175.00	100.00
(32)	Jimmy Reese (Hands on knees.)	350.00	175.00	100.00
(33)	Al Rosen	900.00	450.00	270.00
(34)	Joe Rowell	300.00	150.00	90.00
(35)	Mike Sandlock	300.00	150.00	90.00
(36)	George Schmees	300.00	150.00	90.00
(37)	Charlie Sipple	300.00	150.00	90.00
(38)	Harvey Storey (Batting follow-through.)	300.00	150.00	90.00
(39)	Harvey Storey (Batting stance.)	300.00	150.00	90.00
(40)	Harvey Storey/Fldg	300.00	150.00	90.00
(41)	Jack Tobin	300.00	150.00	90.00
(42)	Frank Tornay	300.00	150.00	90.00
(43)	Thurman Tucker	300.00	150.00	90.00
(44)	Ben Wade	300.00	150.00	90.00
(45)	Roy Welmaker	300.00	150.00	90.00
(46)	Leroy Wheat	300.00	150.00	90.00
(47)	Don White	300.00	150.00	90.00
(48)	"Whitey" Wietelman/Btg	300.00	150.00	90.00
(49)	"Whitey" Wietelman/Fldg	300.00	150.00	90.00
(50)	Bobby Wilson/Btg	300.00	150.00	90.00
(51)	Bobby Wilson/Fldg	300.00	150.00	90.00
(52)	Tony York	300.00	150.00	90.00
(53)	George Zuverink	850.00	425.00	250.00

1886 Hancock's Syracuse Stars

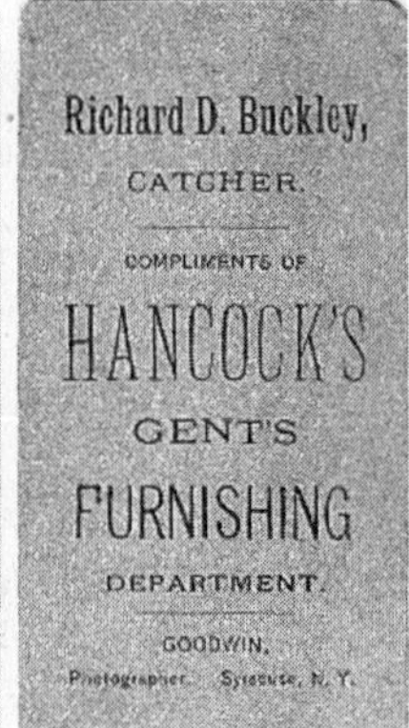

Currently representing the earliest known minor league baseball cards is this issue by a Syracuse department store's menswear department. The 1-5/8" x 3-3/16" cards feature sepia photos glued to a stiff black cardboard backing with a gilt edge. The photos show the players in suits, presumably from the sponsor's racks. Backs have the player name and position printed at top. At center is an ad for Hancock's. At bottom is a credit line to "Goodwin" as photographer. Each card is currently known in only a single example. It is possible other players of the International League Stars may yet be discovered.

Values Undetermined

(1) Richard D. Buckley
(2) Douglas Crothers (SGC-graded Ex., 2005 auction, $18,304.)
(3) Philip H. Tomney

1960 Henry House Wieners Seattle Rainiers

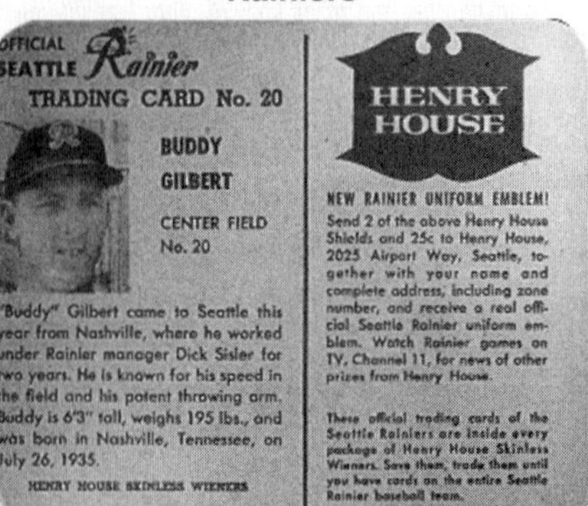

Eighteen different cards are known in this hot dog set; most players played major league baseball prior to their appearance with the Pacific Coast League Seattle Rainiers in 1960. Printed in red, the 4-1/2" x 3-3/4" cards are skip-numbered by player uniform number.

		NM	EX	VG
Complete Set (18):		5,500	2,750	1,600
Common Player:		300.00	150.00	90.00
2	Harry Malmberg	300.00	150.00	90.00
3	Francisco Obregon	300.00	150.00	90.00
4	Johnny O'Brien	375.00	185.00	110.00
5	Gordon Coleman	300.00	150.00	90.00
6	Bill Hain	300.00	150.00	90.00
8	Dick Sisler	300.00	150.00	90.00
9	Jerry Zimmerman	300.00	150.00	90.00
10	Hal Bevan	300.00	150.00	90.00
14	Rudy Regaldo	300.00	150.00	90.00
15	Paul Pettit	300.00	150.00	90.00
20	Buddy Gilbert	300.00	150.00	90.00
21	Erv Palica	300.00	150.00	90.00
22	Joe Taylor	300.00	150.00	90.00
25	Bill Kennedy	300.00	150.00	90.00
26	Dave Stenhouse	300.00	150.00	90.00
28	Ray Ripplemeyer	300.00	150.00	90.00
30	Charlie Beamon	300.00	150.00	90.00
33	Don Rudolph	300.00	150.00	90.00

1888 S.F. Hess California League (N321)

One of several tobacco card sets produced by S.F. Hess & Co. of Rochester, this rare 40-card issue features players from the California League. The cards measure 2-7/8" x 1-1/2" and feature color drawings of players. The player's name and team are printed along the top margin of the card, while the words "S.F. Hess and Co.'s/Creole Cigarettes" appear at the bottom. "California League" is also printed in large capital letters above the player drawing, while the 1888 copyright date appears below. There are 35 players (including one umpire) in the set, and five players are pictured on two cards each, resulting in 40 different cards. One example each of 30 of the cards have been discovered printed on thin paper stock, though the exact nature of that version is undetermined; currently values are about equal to the regular-issue version.

		NM	EX	VG
Common Player:		5,400	3,000	1,800
(1)	Bennett	5,400	3,000	1,800
(2)	Borchers	5,400	3,000	1,800
(3)	Buckley	5,400	3,000	1,800
(4)	Burke/Btg	5,400	3,000	1,800
(5)	Burke (Ready to pitch.)	5,400	3,000	1,800
(6)	Burnett	5,400	3,000	1,800
(7)	Carroll	5,400	3,000	1,800
(8)	Donohue	5,400	3,000	1,800
(9)	Donovan	5,400	3,000	1,800
(10)	Finn	5,400	3,000	1,800
(11)	Gagus	5,400	3,000	1,800
(12)	Hanley	5,400	3,000	1,800
(13)	Hardie (C., wearing mask.)	5,400	3,000	1,800
(14)	Hardie (C.F., with bat.)	5,400	3,000	1,800
(15)	Hayes	5,400	3,000	1,800
(16)	Lawton	5,400	3,000	1,800
(17)	Levy	5,400	3,000	1,800
(18)	Long	5,400	3,000	1,800
(19)	McCord	5,400	3,000	1,800
(20)	Meegan	5,400	3,000	1,800
(21)	Moore	5,400	3,000	1,800
(22)	Mullee	5,400	3,000	1,800
(23)	Newhert	5,400	3,000	1,800
(24)	Noonan	5,400	3,000	1,800
(25)	O'Day	5,400	3,000	1,800
(26)	Perrier	5,400	3,000	1,800
(27)	Powers (1st B., catching)	5,400	3,000	1,800
(28)	Powers (1st B. & Capt., with bat)	5,400	3,000	1,800
(29)	Ryan	5,400	3,000	1,800
(30)	Selna	5,400	3,000	1,800
(31)	Shea	5,400	3,000	1,800
(32)	J. Sheridan (Umpire)	5,400	3,000	1,800
(33)	"Big" Smith	5,400	3,000	1,800
(34)	H. Smith	5,400	3,000	1,800
(35)	J. Smith	5,400	3,000	1,800
(36)	Smett	5,400	3,000	1,800
(37)	Stockwell/Throwing	5,400	3,000	1,800
(38)	Stockwell (With bat.)	5,400	3,000	1,800
(39)	Sweeney	5,400	3,000	1,800
(40)	Whitehead	5,400	3,000	1,800

1888 S.F. Hess California League (N338-1)

This tobacco card set picturing players from the California League is one of the rarest of all 19th Century issues. Issued in the late 1880s by S.F. Hess & Co. of Rochester, these 2-7/8" x 1-1/2" cards are so rare that only several examples are known to exist. Some of the photos in the N338-1 set are identical to the drawings in the N321 set, issued by S.F. Hess in 1888. The N338-1 cards are found with the words "California League" printed in an arc either above or below the player photo. The player's name appears below the photo. At the bottom of the card the words "S.F. Hess & Co.'s Creole Cigarettes" are printed in a rolling style.

		NM	EX	VG
Common Player:		18,000	9,000	5,250
(1)	Borsher	18,000	9,000	5,250
(2)	Buckley	18,000	9,000	5,250
(3)	Carroll	18,000	9,000	5,250
(4)	Ebright	18,000	9,000	5,250
(5)	Gagur (Gagus)	18,000	9,000	5,250
(6)	Incell	18,000	9,000	5,250
(7)	Lawton	18,000	9,000	5,250
(8)	Levy/Throwing	18,000	9,000	5,250
(9)	Levy (With bat.)	18,000	9,000	5,250
(10)	McDonald	18,000	9,000	5,250
(11)	McGinty	20,250	10,125	6,075
(12)	Meegan	18,000	9,000	5,250
(13)	Newhert	18,000	9,000	5,250
(14)	Noonan	18,000	9,000	5,250
(15)	Perrier	18,000	9,000	5,250
(16)	Perrier, H. Smith	18,000	9,000	5,250
(17)	Ryan	18,000	9,000	5,250
(18)	J. Smith, N. Smith	18,000	9,000	5,250
(19)	Sweeney	18,000	9,000	5,250

1888 S.F. Hess Newsboys League (N333)

Although not picturing professional baseball players, these cards issued by S.F. Hess and Co. have a baseball theme. Cards measure 1-1/2" x 2-7/8" and feature pictures of "newsies" from papers in eight different cities (Rochester, Cleveland, Philadelphia, Boston, Albany, Detroit, New York and Syracuse). The boys are pictured in a photographs wearing baseball uniforms, often bearing the name of their newspaper. The boy's name, position and newspaper are printed below, while the words "Newsboys League" appears in capital letters at the top of the card. No identification is provided for the four Philadelphia newsboys, so a photo description is provided in the checklist that follows. Gaps have been left in the assigned numbering for future additions.

		NM	EX	VG
Common Player:		2,400	1,200	725.00
(1)	R.J. Bell	2,400	1,200	725.00
(2)	Bibby (Boston Globe)	2,400	1,200	725.00
(3)	Binden	2,400	1,200	725.00
(4)	Bowen	2,400	1,200	725.00
(5)	Boyle	2,400	1,200	725.00
(6)	Britcher	2,400	1,200	725.00
(7)	Caine	2,400	1,200	725.00
(8)	I. Cohen	2,400	1,200	725.00
(9)	R. Cohen	2,400	1,200	725.00
(10)	Collins (Boston Globe)	2,400	1,200	725.00
(11)	Cross	2,400	1,200	725.00
(12)	F. Cuddy	2,400	1,200	725.00
(13)	E. Daisey	2,400	1,200	725.00
(14)	Davis	2,400	1,200	725.00
(15)	B. Dinsmore	2,400	1,200	725.00
(16)	Donovan	2,400	1,200	725.00
(17)	A. Downer	2,400	1,200	725.00
(18)	Fanelly	2,400	1,200	725.00
(19)	J. Flood	2,400	1,200	725.00
(21)	C. Gallagher	2,400	1,200	725.00
(22)	M.H. Gallagher	2,400	1,200	725.00
(23)	D. Galligher	2,400	1,200	725.00
(24)	J. Galligher	2,400	1,200	725.00
(25)	Haskins	2,400	1,200	725.00
(26)	Herze	2,400	1,200	725.00
(27)	Holmes (Press & Knickerbocker)	2,400	1,200	725.00
(28)	F. Horan	2,400	1,200	725.00
(29)	Hosler	2,400	1,200	725.00
(30)	Hyde	2,400	1,200	725.00
(31)	Keilty	2,400	1,200	725.00
(32)	C. Kellogg	2,400	1,200	725.00
(33)	Mahoney (Rochester Post-Express)	2,400	1,200	725.00
(34)	Mayer	2,400	1,200	725.00
(35)	McCourt (Boston Globe)	2,400	1,200	725.00
(36)	I. McDonald	2,400	1,200	725.00
(37)	McDowell (Rochester)	2,400	1,200	725.00
(38)	McGrady	2,400	1,200	725.00
(39)	O'Brien	2,400	1,200	725.00
(41)	E.C. Murphy	2,400	1,200	725.00
(42)	Sabin	2,400	1,200	725.00
(43)	Shedd	2,400	1,200	725.00
(44)	R. Sheehan	2,400	1,200	725.00
(45)	Smith	2,400	1,200	725.00
(46)	Talbot	2,400	1,200	725.00
(47)	Walsh	2,400	1,200	725.00
(48)	Whitman	2,400	1,200	725.00
(49)	Yeomans	2,400	1,200	725.00
(50)	Cleveland Newsboy (In cap, facing right.)	2,400	1,200	725.00
(51)	Philadelphia Newsboy (Hair parted on right side.)	2,400	1,200	725.00
(52)	Philadelphia Newsboy (Hair parted on left side.)	2,400	1,200	725.00
(53)	Philadelphia Newsboy (No part in hair.)	2,400	1,200	725.00
(54)	Philadelphia Newsboy (Head shaved.)	2,400	1,200	725.00

1949 Hollywood Stars Team Issue

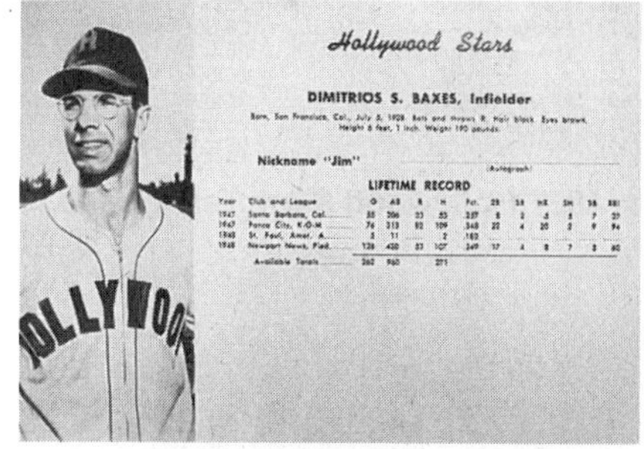

A team issue probably related to similar 1948-49 cards produced by Pacific Coast League cross-town rivals the L.A. Angels, these cards were likely produced by the publisher of the teams' yearbooks and sold at stadium souvenir stands. The cards are blank-backed, printed in black-and-white on thin semi-gloss cardboard, measuring 7-1/16" x 4-7/8". Portrait or posed action photos appear at left with complete major and minor league stats at right. A space for an autograph appears beneath the player's biographical data. The unnumbered cards are checklisted here in alphabetical order.

		NM	EX	VG
Complete Set (24):		500.00	250.00	150.00
Common Player:		25.00	12.50	7.50
(1)	Jim Baxes	25.00	12.50	7.50
(2)	George Fallon	25.00	12.50	7.50
(3)	John Fitzpatrick	25.00	12.50	7.50
(4)	George Genovese	25.00	12.50	7.50
(5)	Herb Gorman	75.00	37.50	22.50
(6)	Gene Handley	25.00	12.50	7.50
(7)	Fred Haney	25.00	12.50	7.50
(8)	Jim Hughes	25.00	12.50	7.50
(9)	Frank Kelleher	25.00	12.50	7.50
(10)	Gordy Maltzberger	25.00	12.50	7.50
(11)	Glen Moulder	25.00	12.50	7.50
(12)	Irv Noren	25.00	12.50	7.50
(13)	Ed Oliver	25.00	12.50	7.50
(14)	Karl Olsen	25.00	12.50	7.50
(15)	John O'Neil	25.00	12.50	7.50
(16)	Jack Paepke	25.00	12.50	7.50
(17)	Willard Ramsdell	25.00	12.50	7.50
(18)	Jack Salveson	25.00	12.50	7.50

(19)	Mike Sandlock	25.00	12.50	7.50
(20)	Art Shallock	25.00	12.50	7.50
(21)	Andy Skurski	25.00	12.50	7.50
(22)	Chuck Stevens	25.00	12.50	7.50
(23)	Al Unser	25.00	12.50	7.50
(24)	George Woods	25.00	12.50	7.50

1950 Hollywood Stars Team Issue

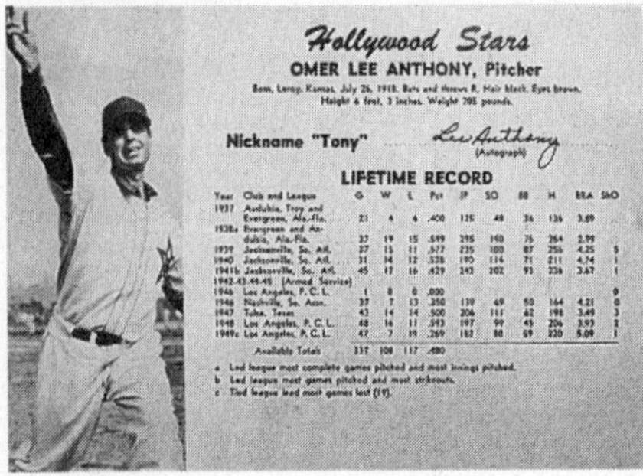

Virtually identical in format to the previous year's issue, the 1950 set differs principally in the inclusion of a facsimile autograph on front. In 1950, the Hollywood Stars were the PCL affiliate of the Brooklyn Dodgers. Both sets were listed in "The American Card Catalog" as W720.

		NM	EX	VG
Complete Set (32):		850.00	425.00	250.00
Common Player:		25.00	12.50	7.50
(1)	Lee Anthony	25.00	12.50	7.50
(2)	Bill Antonello	25.00	12.50	7.50
(3)	Dick Barrett	25.00	12.50	7.50
(4)	Jim Baxes	25.00	12.50	7.50
(5)	Clint Conatser	25.00	12.50	7.50
(6)	Cliff Dapper	25.00	12.50	7.50
(7)	George Fallon	25.00	12.50	7.50
(8)	John Fitzpatrick	25.00	12.50	7.50
(9)	Murray Franklin	25.00	12.50	7.50
(10)	Herb Gorman	75.00	37.50	22.50
(11)	Gene Handley	25.00	12.50	7.50
(12)	Fred Haney	25.00	12.50	7.50
(13)	Clarence Hicks	25.00	12.50	7.50
(14)	Herb Karpel	200.00	100.00	60.00
(15)	Frank Kelleher	25.00	12.50	7.50
(16)	Ken Lehman	25.00	12.50	7.50
(17)	Johnny Lindell	25.00	12.50	7.50
(18)	Gordy Maltzberger	25.00	12.50	7.50
(19)	Dan Menendez	25.00	12.50	7.50
(20)	Pershing Mondroff	25.00	12.50	7.50
(21)	Glen Moulder	25.00	12.50	7.50
(22)	John O'Neil	25.00	12.50	7.50
(23)	Jack Paepke	25.00	12.50	7.50
(24)	Jean Roy	25.00	12.50	7.50
(25)	Jack Salveson	25.00	12.50	7.50
(26)	Mike Sandlock	25.00	12.50	7.50
(27)	Ed Saver	25.00	12.50	7.50
(28)	George Schmees	25.00	12.50	7.50
(29)	Art Shallock	25.00	12.50	7.50
(30)	Chuck Stevens	25.00	12.50	7.50
(31)	Ben Wade	25.00	12.50	7.50
(32)	George Woods	25.00	12.50	7.50

1957 Hollywood Stars Team Issue

Presumably issued by the team, which had a working relationship with the Pittsburgh Pirates, this 23-card set features black-and-white blank-backed photos in a 4-1/8" x 6-3/16" format. Each picture has a facsimile autograph printed in black across the front. The unnumbered cards are checklisted here alphabetically.

		NM	EX	VG
Complete Set (23):		900.00	450.00	275.00
Common Player:		40.00	20.00	12.00
(1)	Jim Baumer	40.00	20.00	12.00
(2)	Carlos Bernier	40.00	20.00	12.00
(3)	Bill Causion	40.00	20.00	12.00
(4)	Chuck Churn	40.00	20.00	12.00
(5)	Bennie Daniels	40.00	20.00	12.00
(6)	Joe Duhem	40.00	20.00	12.00
(7)	John Fitzpatrick	40.00	20.00	12.00
(8)	Bob Garber	40.00	20.00	12.00
(9)	Bill Hall	40.00	20.00	12.00
(10)	Forrest "Spook" Jacobs	50.00	25.00	15.00
(11)	Clyde King	40.00	20.00	12.00
(12)	Nick Koback	40.00	20.00	12.00
(13)	Pete Naton	40.00	20.00	12.00
(14)	George O'Donnell	40.00	20.00	12.00
(15)	Paul Pettit	40.00	20.00	12.00
(16)	Curt Raydon	40.00	20.00	12.00
(17)	Leo Rodriguez	40.00	20.00	12.00
(18)	Don Rowe	40.00	20.00	12.00
(19)	Dick Smith	40.00	20.00	12.00
(20)	R.C. Stevens	40.00	20.00	12.00
(21)	Ben Wade	40.00	20.00	12.00
(22)	Fred Waters	40.00	20.00	12.00
(23)	George Witt	40.00	20.00	12.00

1912 Home Run Kisses (E136)

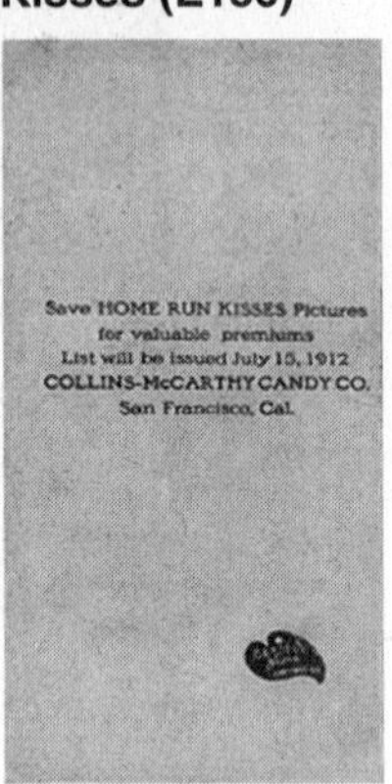

This 90-card set of Pacific Coast League players was produced in 1912 by the San Francisco candy company of Collins-McCarthy. Each card measures about 2-1/4" x 4-3/16" and features sepia-toned player photos surrounded by an ornate frame. The front of the card has the words "Home Run Kisses" above the player's name. Most cards found are blank-backed, but others exist with a back that advises "Save Home Run Kisses Pictures for Valuable Premiums" along with other details of the Collins-McCarthy promotion. A third type of back exists with an advertising logo for "BARDELL / SEPIA/ SAN FRANCISCO." Redeemed cards were punch-cancelled, often with a heart-shaped hole.

		NM	EX	VG
Complete Set (90):		70,000	28,000	16,000
Common Player:		750.00	300.00	185.00
(1)	Ables	750.00	300.00	185.00
(2)	Agnew	750.00	300.00	185.00
(3)	Altman	750.00	300.00	185.00
(4)	Frank Arrelanes (Arellanes)	750.00	300.00	185.00
(5)	Auer	750.00	300.00	185.00
(6)	Bancroft	3,500	1,400	875.00
(7)	Bayless	750.00	300.00	185.00
(8)	Berry	750.00	300.00	185.00
(9)	Boles	750.00	300.00	185.00
(10)	Brashear	750.00	300.00	185.00
(11)	Brooks (Los Angeles)	750.00	300.00	185.00
(12)	Brooks (Oakland)	750.00	300.00	185.00
(13)	Brown	750.00	300.00	185.00
(14)	Burrell	750.00	300.00	185.00
(15)	Butler	750.00	300.00	185.00
(16)	Carlisle	750.00	300.00	185.00
(17)	Carson	750.00	300.00	185.00
(18)	Castleton	750.00	300.00	185.00
(19)	Chadbourne	750.00	300.00	185.00
(20)	Check	750.00	300.00	185.00
(21)	Core	750.00	300.00	185.00
(22)	Corhan	750.00	300.00	185.00
(23)	Coy	750.00	300.00	185.00
(24)	Daley	750.00	300.00	185.00
(25)	Dillon	750.00	300.00	185.00
(26)	Doane	750.00	300.00	185.00
(27)	Driscoll	750.00	300.00	185.00
(28)	Fisher	750.00	300.00	185.00
(29)	Flater	750.00	300.00	185.00
(30)	Gaddy	750.00	300.00	185.00
(31)	Gregg	750.00	300.00	185.00
(32)	Gregory	750.00	300.00	185.00
(33)	Harkness	750.00	300.00	185.00
(34)	Heitmuller	750.00	300.00	185.00
(35)	Henley	750.00	300.00	185.00
(36)	Hiester	750.00	300.00	185.00
(37)	Hoffman	750.00	300.00	185.00
(38)	Hogan	750.00	300.00	185.00
(39)	Hosp	750.00	300.00	185.00
(40)	Howley	750.00	300.00	185.00
(41)	Ireland	750.00	300.00	185.00
(42)	Johnson	750.00	300.00	185.00
(43)	Kane	750.00	300.00	185.00
(44)	Klawitter	750.00	300.00	185.00
(45)	Kreitz	750.00	300.00	185.00
(46)	Krueger	750.00	300.00	185.00
(47)	Leard	750.00	300.00	185.00
(48)	Leverencz	750.00	300.00	185.00
(49)	Lewis	750.00	300.00	185.00
(50)	Bill Lindsay	750.00	300.00	185.00
(51)	Litschi	750.00	300.00	185.00
(52)	Lober	750.00	300.00	185.00
(53)	Malarkey	750.00	300.00	185.00
(54)	Martinoni	750.00	300.00	185.00
(55)	McArdle	750.00	300.00	185.00
(56)	McCorry	750.00	300.00	185.00
(57)	McDowell	750.00	300.00	185.00
(58)	McIver	750.00	300.00	185.00
(59)	Metzger	750.00	300.00	185.00
(60)	Miller	750.00	300.00	185.00
(61)	Mundorf	750.00	300.00	185.00
(62)	Nagle	750.00	300.00	185.00
(63)	Noyes	750.00	300.00	185.00
(64)	Olmstead	750.00	300.00	185.00
(65)	O'Rourke	750.00	300.00	185.00
(66)	Page	750.00	300.00	185.00
(67)	Parkins	750.00	300.00	185.00
(68)	Patterson (Oakland)	750.00	300.00	185.00
(69)	Patterson (Vernon)	750.00	300.00	185.00
(70)	Pernoll	750.00	300.00	185.00
(71)	Powell	750.00	300.00	185.00
(72)	Price	750.00	300.00	185.00
(73)	Raftery	750.00	300.00	185.00
(74)	Raleigh	750.00	300.00	185.00
(75)	Rogers	750.00	300.00	185.00
(76)	Schmidt	750.00	300.00	185.00
(77)	Schwenk	750.00	300.00	185.00
(78)	Sheehan	750.00	300.00	185.00
(79)	Shinn	750.00	300.00	185.00
(80)	Slagle	750.00	300.00	185.00
(81)	Smith	750.00	300.00	185.00
(82)	Stone	750.00	300.00	185.00
(83)	Swain	750.00	300.00	185.00
(84)	Taylor	750.00	300.00	185.00
(85)	Tiedeman	750.00	300.00	185.00
(86)	Toner	750.00	300.00	185.00
(87)	Tozer	750.00	300.00	185.00
(88)	Van Buren	750.00	300.00	185.00
(89)	Williams	750.00	300.00	185.00
(90)	Zacher	750.00	300.00	185.00

1940 Hughes Frozen Confections Sacramento Solons

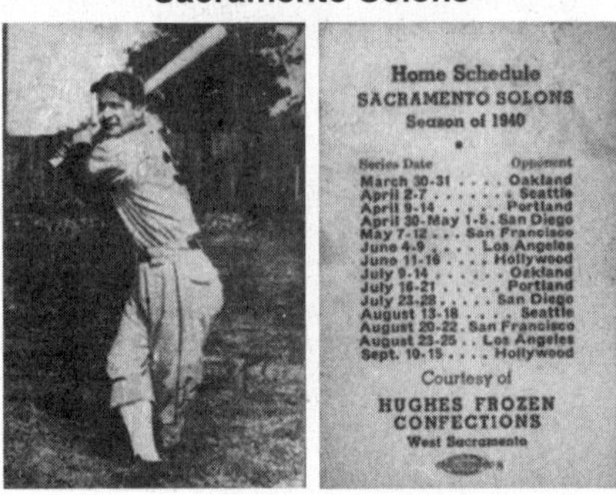

These borderless 2" x 3" black-and-white cards of the Sacramento Solons can be found in two versions, either blank-backed or with the 1940 Solons Pacific Coast League schedule printed on back. Fronts featured action poses with a facsimile autograph.

		NM	EX	VG
Complete Set (20):		7,500	3,750	2,250
Common Player:		400.00	200.00	125.00
(1)	Mel Almada	400.00	200.00	125.00
(2)	Frank Asbell	400.00	200.00	125.00
(3)	Larry Barton	400.00	200.00	125.00
(4)	Robert Blattner	400.00	200.00	125.00
(5)	Bennie Borgmann	400.00	200.00	125.00
(6)	Tony Freitas	400.00	200.00	125.00
(7)	Art Garibaldi	400.00	200.00	125.00
(8)	Jim Grilk	400.00	200.00	125.00
(9)	Gene Handley	400.00	200.00	125.00
(10)	Oscar Judd	400.00	200.00	125.00
(11)	Lynn King	400.00	200.00	125.00
(12)	Norbert Kleinke	400.00	200.00	125.00
(13)	Max Marshall	400.00	200.00	125.00
(14)	William McLaughlin	400.00	200.00	125.00
(15)	Bruce Ogrodowski	400.00	200.00	125.00
(16)	Franich Riel	400.00	200.00	125.00
(17)	Bill Schmidt	400.00	200.00	125.00
(18)	Melvin Wasley	400.00	200.00	125.00
(19)	Chet Wieczorek	400.00	200.00	125.00
(20)	Deb Williams	400.00	200.00	125.00

1957 Hygrade Meats Seattle Rainiers

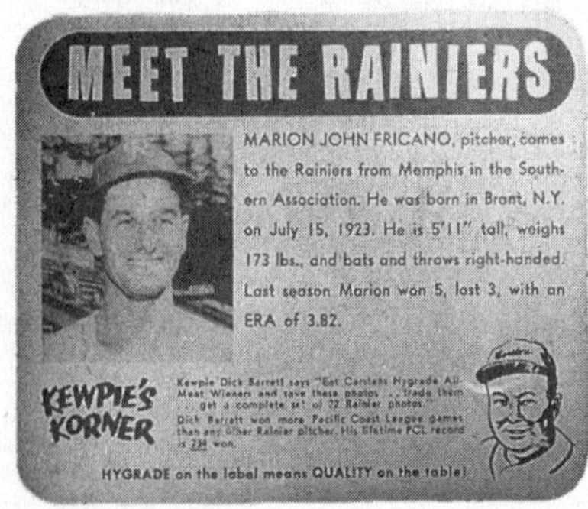

While the front of the cards mentions a complete set of 22 cards, only a dozen have been checklisted to date. The round-cornered cards measure 4-1/2" x 3-3/4" and are printed in red on white. Backs are blank. The cards feature only players of the Pacific Coast League Seattle Rainiers. The cards are unnumbered.

		NM	EX	VG
Common Player:		400.00	200.00	120.00
(1)	Dick Aylward	400.00	200.00	120.00
(2)	Bob Balcena	400.00	200.00	120.00
(3)	Jim Dyck	400.00	200.00	120.00
(4)	Marion Fricano	400.00	200.00	120.00
(5)	Bill Glynn	400.00	200.00	120.00
(6)	Larry Jansen	400.00	200.00	120.00
(7)	Bill Kennedy	400.00	200.00	120.00
(8)	Jack Lohrke	400.00	200.00	120.00
(9)	Frank O'Doul	800.00	400.00	240.00
(10)	Ray Orteig	400.00	200.00	120.00
(11)	Joe Taylor	400.00	200.00	120.00
(12)	Morrie (Maury) Wills	800.00	400.00	240.00

I

1912 Imperial Tobacco (C46)

KELLY
JOSEPH KELLEY
Joseph Kelley, manager Toronto Base Ball Club, of the International League, is one of the best known base ball men in the country. He has been in the game for many years. He was with the Baltimore club when they were three times winners of the National League Championship, playing left field. He was also with Brooklyn when they were pennant winners. He was playing manager of the Boston Club of the National League and also played with Cincinnati.
BASEBALL SERIES. No 27

This minor league set, issued in 1912 by the Imperial Tobacco Co., is the only tobacco baseball set issued in Canada. Designated as C46 in the American Card Catalog, each sepia-toned card measures 1-1/2" x 2-5/8" and features a distinctive card design that pictures the player inside an oval surrounded by a simulated woodgrain background featuring a bat, ball and glove in the borders. The player's last name appears in capital letters in a panel beneath the oval. (An exception is the card of James Murray, whose caption includes both first and last names.) The backs include the player's name and team at the top, followed by a brief biography. The 90 subjects in the set are members of the eight teams in the Eastern League (Rochester, Toronto, Buffalo, Newark, Providence, Baltimore, Montreal and Jersey City), even though the card backs refer to it as the International League. The set contains many players with major league experience, including Hall of Famers Joe Kelley and Joe "Iron Man" McGinnity.

		NM	EX	VG
Complete Set (90):		13,000	6,500	4,000
Common Player:		150.00	75.00	40.00
1	William O'Hara	180.00	90.00	55.00
2	James McGinley	160.00	80.00	50.00
3	"Frenchy" LeClaire	150.00	75.00	40.00
4	John White	150.00	75.00	40.00
5	James Murray	150.00	75.00	40.00
6	Joe Ward	150.00	75.00	40.00
7	Whitey Alperman	150.00	75.00	40.00
8	"Natty" Nattress	150.00	75.00	40.00
9	Fred Sline	150.00	75.00	40.00
10	Royal Rock	150.00	75.00	40.00
11	Ray Demmitt	150.00	75.00	40.00
12	"Butcher Boy" Schmidt	150.00	75.00	40.00
13	Samuel Frock	150.00	75.00	40.00
14	Fred Burchell	150.00	75.00	40.00
15	Jack Kelley	150.00	75.00	40.00
16	Frank Barberich	150.00	75.00	40.00
17	Frank Corridon	150.00	75.00	40.00
18	"Doc" Adkins	150.00	75.00	40.00
19	Jack Dunn	150.00	75.00	40.00
20	James Walsh	150.00	75.00	40.00
21	Charles Hanford	150.00	75.00	40.00
22	Dick Rudolph	150.00	75.00	40.00
23	Curt Elston	150.00	75.00	40.00
24	Phil Silton (Sitton)	150.00	75.00	40.00
25	Charlie French	150.00	75.00	40.00
26	John Ganzel	150.00	75.00	40.00
27	Joe Kelley	750.00	375.00	230.00
28	Benny Meyers	150.00	75.00	40.00
29	George Schirm	150.00	75.00	40.00
30	William Purtell	150.00	75.00	40.00
31	Bayard Sharpe	150.00	75.00	40.00
32	Tony Smith	150.00	75.00	40.00
33	John Lush	150.00	75.00	40.00
34	William Collins	150.00	75.00	40.00
35	Art Phelan	150.00	75.00	40.00
36	Edward Phelps	150.00	75.00	40.00
37	"Rube" Vickers	150.00	75.00	40.00
38	Cy Seymour	150.00	75.00	40.00
39	"Shadow" Carroll	150.00	75.00	40.00
40	Jake Gettman	150.00	75.00	40.00
41	Luther Taylor	300.00	150.00	95.00
42	Walter Justis	150.00	75.00	40.00
43	Robert Fisher	150.00	75.00	40.00
44	Fred Parent	150.00	75.00	40.00
45	James Dygert	150.00	75.00	40.00
46	Johnnie Butler	150.00	75.00	40.00
47	Fred Mitchell	150.00	75.00	40.00
48	Heinie Batch	150.00	75.00	40.00
49	Michael Corcoran	150.00	75.00	40.00
50	Edward Doescher	150.00	75.00	40.00
51	George Wheeler	150.00	75.00	40.00
52	Elijah Jones	150.00	75.00	40.00
53	Fred Truesdale	150.00	75.00	40.00
54	Fred Beebe	150.00	75.00	40.00
55	Louis Brockett	150.00	75.00	40.00
56	Robt. Wells	150.00	75.00	40.00
57	"Lew" McAllister	150.00	75.00	40.00
58	Ralph Stroud	150.00	75.00	40.00
59	James Manser	150.00	75.00	40.00
60	Jim Holmes	150.00	75.00	40.00
61	Rube Dessau	150.00	75.00	40.00
62	Fred Jacklitsch	150.00	75.00	40.00
63	Stanley Graham	150.00	75.00	40.00
64	Noah Henline	150.00	75.00	40.00
65	"Chick" Gandil	775.00	385.00	240.00
66	Tom Hughes	150.00	75.00	40.00
67	Joseph Delehanty	150.00	75.00	40.00
68	Geo. Pierce	150.00	75.00	40.00
69	Bob Gaunt (Gantt)	150.00	75.00	40.00
70	Edward Fitzpatrick	150.00	75.00	40.00
71	Wyatt Lee	150.00	75.00	40.00
72	John Kissinger	150.00	75.00	40.00
73	William Malarkey	150.00	75.00	40.00
74	William Byers	150.00	75.00	40.00
75	George Simmons	150.00	75.00	40.00
76	Daniel Moeller	150.00	75.00	40.00
77	Joseph McGinnity	750.00	375.00	230.00
78	Alex Hardy	150.00	75.00	40.00
79	Bob Holmes	150.00	75.00	40.00
80	William Baxter	150.00	75.00	40.00
81	Edward Spencer	150.00	75.00	40.00
82	Bradley Kocher	150.00	75.00	40.00
83	Robert Shaw	150.00	75.00	40.00
84	Joseph Yeager	150.00	75.00	40.00
85	Anthony Carlo	150.00	75.00	40.00
86	William Abstein	150.00	75.00	40.00
87	Tim Jordan	150.00	75.00	40.00
88	Dick Breen	150.00	75.00	40.00
89	Tom McCarty	150.00	75.00	46.00
90	Ed Curtis	160.00	80.00	50.00

1923 Indianapolis Indians Foldout

Twenty-one players and staff are featured in this black-and-white accordian-fold souvenir. Each of the cards measures about 2" x 3".

	NM	EX	VG
Complete Foldout:	650.00	325.00	195.00
(Checklist not available.)	.00	.00	.00

1950 Indianapolis Indians Team Issue

Action poses are featured in this set of team-issue 8" x 10" black-and-white glossy photos. Players are identified by a facsimile autograph on front. It is unknown whether the checklist is complete. The Indians were the Class AAA American Association affiliate of the Pittsburgh Pirates in 1950.

		NM	EX	VG
Common Player:		30.00	15.00	9.00
(1)	Monty Basgall	30.00	15.00	9.00
(2)	Ted Beard	30.00	15.00	9.00
(3)	Gus Bell	40.00	20.00	12.00
(4)	Eddie Bockman	30.00	15.00	9.00
(5)	Dale Coogan	30.00	15.00	9.00
(6)	"Del" Dallessandro	30.00	15.00	9.00
(7)	Nanny Fernandez	30.00	15.00	9.00
(8)	Eddy Fitz Gerald	30.00	15.00	9.00
(9)	Al Grunwald	30.00	15.00	9.00
(10)	Frank Kalin	30.00	15.00	9.00
(11)	Paul LaPalme	30.00	15.00	9.00
(12)	Royce Lint	30.00	15.00	9.00
(13)	Al Lopez	45.00	22.00	13.50
(14)	Forrest Main	30.00	15.00	9.00
(15)	Danny O'Connell	30.00	15.00	9.00
(16)	Frank Papish	30.00	15.00	9.00
(17)	Eddie Stevens	30.00	15.00	9.00
(18)	Leo Wells	30.00	15.00	9.00

J

1952 Jamestown Falcons Team Issue

This Class D farm club of the Detroit Tigers won the 1952 Pony (Pennsylvania-Ontario-New York) League playoffs. Like other issues of Globe Printing, the roughly 2-1/4" x 3-3/8" cards are black-and-white with blank backs and the player name in a white strip at bottom-front. A light green album slotted to hold the cards is known for this issue.

		NM	EX	VG
Complete Set (18):		800.00	400.00	240.00
Common Player:		60.00	30.00	18.00
Album:		100.00	50.00	30.00
(1)	Dick Barr	60.00	30.00	18.00
(2)	Jerry Davie	60.00	30.00	18.00
(3)	John Fickinger	60.00	30.00	18.00
(4)	Paul Franks	60.00	30.00	18.00
(5)	Red Gookin	60.00	30.00	18.00
(6)	Bill Harbour	60.00	30.00	18.00
(7)	Dick Hatfield	60.00	30.00	18.00
(8)	Charley Lau	90.00	45.00	30.00
(9)	Dick Lisiecki	60.00	30.00	18.00
(10)	Tony Lupien	60.00	30.00	18.00
(11)	Joe Melago	60.00	30.00	18.00
(12)	Claude Mitschele	60.00	30.00	18.00
(13)	Bob Neebling	60.00	30.00	18.00
(14)	Fran Oneto	60.00	30.00	18.00
(15)	George Risley	60.00	30.00	18.00
(16)	Bob Szabo	60.00	30.00	18.00
(17)	Ken Walters	60.00	30.00	18.00
(18)	Gabby Witucki	60.00	30.00	18.00

1909 Walter Johnson "Weiser Wonder" Postcards

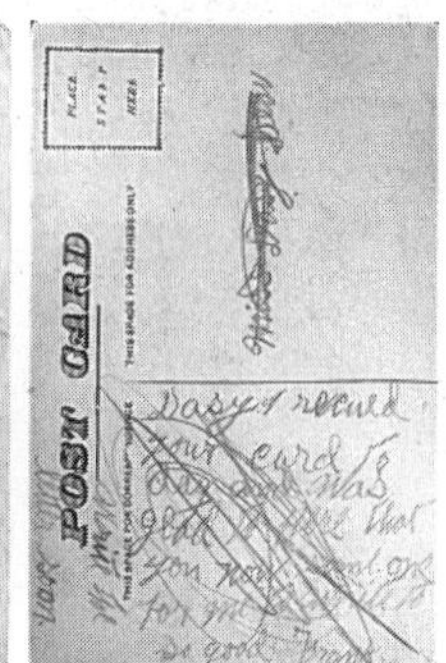

This issue-date(s) on these postcards are conjectural. Two distinct styles are known using versions of the same full-length portrait of Johnson in a studio standing on an ornate rug in front of a curtain depicting drapes, urn, etc. Johnson is wearing the uniform of the Weiser (Idaho) semi-pro team for whom he pitched prior to beginning his Hall of Fame career with the Washington Senators in 1907. The earlier of the cards utilizes the undivided-back postcard format which was current only until 1908. It is printed in sepia tones and identifies Johnson as the "Weiser Wonder" in a line of white type at the bottom. A later version, on a post-1908 divided-back postcard, is printed in bluetone. The card identifies him in a white strip at bottom. It is likely one or both of these cards continued to be produced or at least available after Johnson became a major league star. Both cards are in standard 3-1/2" x 5-1/2" format.

	NM	EX	VG
Walter Johnson (Bluetone)	2,500	1,250	750.00
Walter Johnson (Sepia)	2,500	1,250	750.00

1967 Jones Dairy Buffalo Bison All-Stars

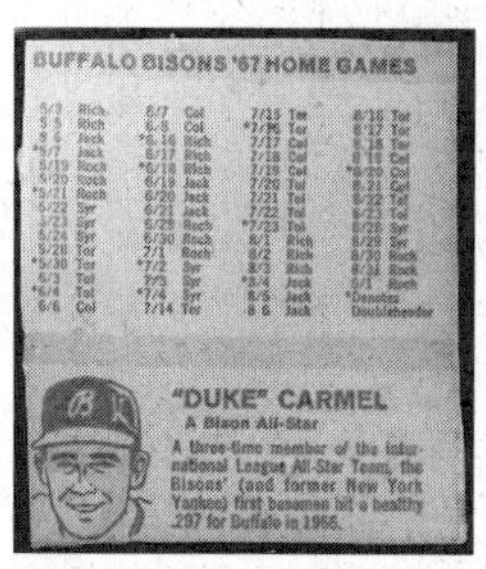

Apparently printed as part of a milk carton, only a single player is known for this issue. Printed in red and yellow, the piece includes a 1967 team home schedule, a player drawing and career highlights in a 2-3/4" x 3-1/8" format. Other players may yet surface.

		NM	EX	VG
(1)	"Duke" Carmel	80.00	40.00	25.00

K

1962 Kahn's Wieners Atlanta Crackers

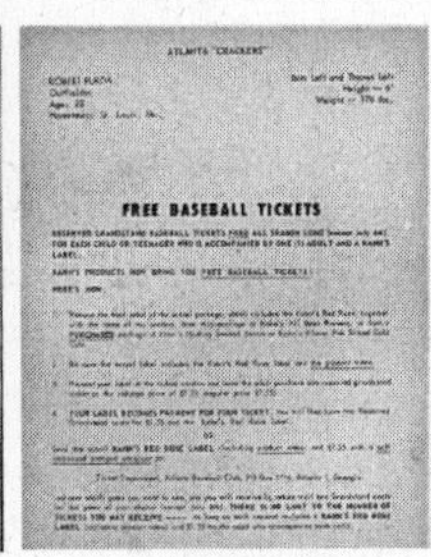
ATLANTA "CRACKERS"

FREE BASEBALL TICKETS

Kahn's made a single foray into the minor league market in 1962 with a separate 24-card set of Atlanta Crackers. The cards feature the same basic format, 3-1/4" x 4", borderless black-and-white photos with a Kahn's ad message in a white panel below the picture, as the major league issue. The backs are slightly different, having a free ticket offer in place of the player stats. Atlanta was the top farm club of the St. Louis Cardinals in 1962. The most famous alumnus in the set is Tim McCarver.

	NM	EX	VG
Complete Set (24):	850.00	425.00	250.00
Common Player:	35.00	17.50	10.00
(1) James (Jimmy) Edward Beauchamp	35.00	17.50	10.00
(2) Gerald Peter Buchek	35.00	17.50	10.00
(3) Robert Burda	35.00	17.50	10.00
(4) Hal Deitz	35.00	17.50	10.00
(5) Robert John Duliba	35.00	17.50	10.00
(6) Harry Michael Fanok	35.00	17.50	10.00
(7) Phil Gagliano	35.00	17.50	10.00
(8) John Glenn	35.00	17.50	10.00
(9) Leroy Gregory	35.00	17.50	10.00
(10) Richard (Dick) Henry Hughes	35.00	17.50	10.00
(11) John Charles Kucks, Jr.	35.00	17.50	10.00
(12) Johnny Joe Lewis	35.00	17.50	10.00
(13) James (Mac - Timmie) Timothy McCarver	75.00	37.50	22.00
(14) Robert F. Milliken	35.00	17.50	10.00
(15) Joe Morgan	35.00	17.50	10.00
(16) Ronald Charles Plaza	35.00	17.50	10.00
(17) Bob Sadowski	35.00	17.50	10.00
(18) Jim Saul	35.00	17.50	10.00
(19) Willard Schmidt	35.00	17.50	10.00
(20) Joe Schultz	35.00	17.50	10.00
(21) Thomas Michael (Mike) Shannon	50.00	25.00	15.00
(22) Paul Louis Toth	35.00	17.50	10.00
(23) Andrew Lou Vickery	35.00	17.50	10.00
(24) Fred Dwight Whitfield	35.00	17.50	10.00

1939 Kimball Automobile Trois-Rivieres Photocards

This set of 18 postcards and an accompanying envelope features the player of the Trois-Rivieres (Three Rivers) club of the Quebec Provincial League. Until 1940, the six-team QPL was not a part of organized baseball's minor league system. Several of the players were either former or future minor leaguers within OB. Paul "Pepper" Martin in the set is not the Pepper Martin of the contemporary, Gas House Gang St. Louis Cardinals. The black-and-white cards are about postcard-size and blank-backed, printed on sturdy card stock.

	NM	EX	VG
Complete Set (18):	1,350	675.00	400.00
Common Player:	90.00	45.00	25.00
(1) George Andrews	90.00	45.00	25.00
(2) Norm Bell	90.00	45.00	25.00
(3) Henry Block	90.00	45.00	25.00
(4) Addie Copple	90.00	45.00	25.00
(5) Phil Corrigan	90.00	45.00	25.00
(6) Joe Dickinson	90.00	45.00	25.00
(7) Bill Hoffner	90.00	45.00	25.00
(8) Jack Leroy	90.00	45.00	25.00
(9) Leo Maloney	90.00	45.00	25.00
(10) Martin	90.00	45.00	25.00
(11) McGurk	90.00	45.00	25.00
(12) Connie O'Leary	90.00	45.00	25.00
(13) James Pickens	90.00	45.00	25.00
(14) Dutch Prather	90.00	45.00	25.00
(15) Jamie Skelton	90.00	45.00	25.00
(16) Byron Speece	90.00	45.00	25.00
(17) Gene Sullivan	90.00	45.00	25.00
(18) Grover Wearshing	90.00	45.00	25.00

1952 Knowles Service Stations Stockton Ports

Contemporary, and sharing a format with the many Globe minor league issues of the early '50s, this set of Stockton Ports (Class C California League) cards carries the advertising of Knowles Service Stations. The blank-backed, black-and-white cards measure 2-1/4" x 3-1/2" and are unnumbered. Among the players is a Japanese national whose card is in strong demand.

	NM	EX	VG
Complete Set (11):	1,000	500.00	300.00
Common Player:	90.00	45.00	25.00
Album:	150.00	75.00	45.00
(1) Wayne Clary	90.00	45.00	25.00
(2) Harry Clements	90.00	45.00	25.00
(3) John Crocco	90.00	45.00	25.00
(4) Tony Freitas	90.00	45.00	25.00
(5) Fibber Hirayama	250.00	125.00	75.00
(6) Dave Mann	90.00	45.00	25.00
(7) Larry Mann	90.00	45.00	25.00
(8) Hank Moreno	90.00	45.00	25.00
(9) Frank Romero	90.00	45.00	25.00
(10) Chuck Thomas	90.00	45.00	25.00
(11) Bud Watkins	90.00	45.00	25.00

1922-23 Kolb's Mothers' Bread Pins (PB4)

Over a two-year period, Kolb's bakery sponsored a series of pins featuring members of the Reading (Pa.) Aces of the International League. The pins are 7/8" in diameter with black-and-white portraits on a white background. The player name (last name only, usually) and position are indicated beneath the photo. Above the photo, in red, is the sponsor's identification. The pins issued in 1922 have "MOTHERS'" in all capital letters; the 1923 pins have "Mothers'" in upper and lower case.

	NM	EX	VG
Complete Set (32):	675.00	350.00	200.00
Common Player:	50.00	25.00	15.00
(1) Spencer Abbott	50.00	25.00	15.00
(2) Charlie Babington	50.00	25.00	15.00
(3) Bill Barrett	50.00	25.00	15.00
(4) R. Bates	50.00	25.00	15.00
(5) Chief Bender	75.00	37.50	22.50
(6) Myrl Brown	50.00	25.00	15.00
(7) Fred Carts	50.00	25.00	15.00
(8) Nig Clarke	50.00	25.00	15.00
(9) Tom Connelly	50.00	25.00	15.00
(10) Gus Getz	50.00	25.00	15.00
(11) Frank Gilhooley	50.00	25.00	15.00
(12) Ray Gordonier	50.00	25.00	15.00
(13) Hinkey Haines	60.00	30.00	18.00
(14) Francis Karpp	50.00	25.00	15.00
(15) Joseph Kelley	50.00	25.00	15.00
(16) Andrew Kotch	50.00	25.00	15.00
(17) William Lightner	50.00	25.00	15.00
(18) Byrd Lynn	50.00	25.00	15.00
(19) Al Mamaux	50.00	25.00	15.00
(20) Martin	50.00	25.00	15.00
(21) Ralph Miller	50.00	25.00	15.00
(22) Otto Pahlman	50.00	25.00	15.00
(23) Sam Post	50.00	25.00	15.00
(24) Al Schact	62.00	31.00	18.50
(25) John Scott	50.00	25.00	15.00
(26) Walt Smallwood	50.00	25.00	15.00
(27) Ross Swartz	50.00	25.00	15.00
(28) Fred Thomas	50.00	25.00	15.00
(29) Myles Thomas	50.00	25.00	15.00
(30) Walt Tragesser	50.00	25.00	15.00
(31) Washburn	50.00	25.00	15.00
(32) Walter Wolfe	50.00	25.00	15.00

L

1952 La Patrie Album Sportif

Ballplayers from Montreal of the International League and several of the teams from the Class C Provincial (Quebec) League were featured in a series of colorized photos printed in the Sunday rotogravure section of "La Patrie" newspaper. The photos are approximately 11" x 15-3/8" with red left and bottom trim and a vertical blue stripe at far left. Player information is printed in black and is in French. A number of the players went on to stardom with the Brooklyn and/or Los Angeles Dodgers.

	NM	EX	VG
Complete Set (20):	700.00	350.00	210.00
Common Player:	25.00	12.50	7.50
(1) Bob Alexander	25.00	12.50	7.50
(2) Herbie Bush	25.00	12.50	7.50
(3) Georges Carpentier	25.00	12.50	7.50
(4) Hampton Coleman	25.00	12.50	7.50
(5) Walter Fiala	25.00	12.50	7.50
(6) Jim Gilliams (Gilliam)	45.00	22.50	13.50
(7) Tom Hackett	25.00	12.50	7.50
(8) Don Hoak	35.00	17.50	10.00
(9) Herbie Lash	25.00	12.50	7.50
(10) Tommy Lasorda	150.00	75.00	45.00
(11) Mal Mallette	25.00	12.50	7.50
(12) Georges Maranda (Aug. 17)	25.00	12.50	7.50
(13) Carmen Mauro	25.00	12.50	7.50
(14) Solly Mohn	25.00	12.50	7.50
(15) Jacques Monette	25.00	12.50	7.50
(16) Johnny Podres	75.00	37.50	22.50
(17) Ed Roebuck	25.00	12.50	7.50
(18) Charlie Thompson	25.00	12.50	7.50
(19) Don Thompson	25.00	12.50	7.50
(20) John Wingo	25.00	12.50	7.50

1928-1932 La Presse Baseball Rotos

Players from Montreal's team in the International League (and occasionally other major and minor league teams' stars) were featured in a series of photos between 1928-32 in the Saturday rotogravure section of Montreal's "La Presse" newspaper. The format remained fairly consistent over the years. Large hand-tinted player photos were featured on the approximately 11" x 17-3/4" pages, with writeup in French below. On back was whatever features and ads happened to appear on the following page. The known baseball player list is presented here in chronological order. Other athletes were also featured in the issue, but are not listed here. Gaps have been left in the numbering to better accommodate future additions to this list.

	NM	EX	VG
Common Player:	60.00	30.00	20.00
1928			
(2) Aldrick Gaudette (May 19)	60.00	30.00	20.00
(4) Robert Shawkey (June 2)	80.00	40.00	24.00
(5) Lachine team photo, portraits of starting nine (June 9)	60.00	30.00	20.00

		NM	EX	VG
(6)	Roy Buckalew, Frank Dunagan, Chester Fowler, Thomas Gulley, Peter Radwan, Richard Smith (June 16)	60.00	30.00	20.00
(7)	Seymour Edward Bailey (June 23)	60.00	30.00	20.00
(8)	Wilson F. Fewster (June 30)	60.00	30.00	20.00
(10)	Tom Daly (July 14)	60.00	30.00	20.00
(14)	Red Holt (Aug. 11)	60.00	30.00	20.00
(17)	George Herman Ruth (Oct. 13)	750.00	375.00	225.00
(20)	Johnny Prud'homme (Nov. 3)	60.00	30.00	20.00
	1929			
(2)	Walter Paul Gautreau (April 13)	60.00	30.00	20.00
(4)	Herb Thormahlen (April 27)	60.00	30.00	20.00
(9)	Elon Hogsett (July 13)	60.00	30.00	20.00
(12)	Robert M. "Lefty" Grove (Oct. 19)	200.00	100.00	60.00
(15)	Philadelphia A's Stars (Mickey Cochrane, Jimmie Foxx, Connie Mack, Al Simmons, Rube Walberg, Bing Miller) (Nov. 16)	90.00	45.00	27.00
	1930			
(3)	Martin Griffin, John Pomorski, Arthur Smith, Herb Thormahlen (May 31)	60.00	30.00	20.00
(4)	James Calleran, Edward Conley, Lee Head, Jimmy Ripple (June 7)	60.00	30.00	20.00
(7)	Del Bissonette (June 28)	60.00	30.00	20.00
(9)	Joe Hauser (July 12)	75.00	37.00	22.00
(14)	Gowell Sylvester Claset (Sept. 13)	60.00	30.00	20.00
(17)	Hack Wilson (Oct. 11)	200.00	100.00	60.00
	1931			
(2)	Chuck Klein (May 30)	175.00	87.00	52.00
(3)	Jocko Conlan (June 6)	100.00	50.00	30.00
(5)	Lee Head (June 20)	60.00	30.00	20.00
(7)	Jimmy Ripple (July 4)	60.00	30.00	20.00
(9)	Sol Mishkin (July 18)	60.00	30.00	20.00
(11)	Walter Brown (Aug. 15)	60.00	30.00	20.00
(15)	Johnny Allen, Frank Barnes, Guy Cantrell, Ken Strong (Nov. 14)	60.00	30.00	20.00
(16)	John Pepper Martin (Nov. 21)	80.00	40.00	24.00
	1932			
(2)	Johnny Grabowski (May 28)	60.00	30.00	20.00
(3)	Charles Sullivan (June 4)	60.00	30.00	20.00
(5)	Walter "Doc" Gautreau (June 18)	60.00	30.00	20.00
(6)	John Clancy (June 25)	60.00	30.00	20.00
(7)	Buck Walters (July 2)	75.00	37.00	22.00
(8)	Bill McAfee (July 9)	60.00	30.00	20.00
(9)	George Puccinelli (July 16)	60.00	30.00	20.00
(11)	Buck Crouse (Aug. 6)	60.00	30.00	20.00
(12)	Ollie Carnegie (Aug. 13)	60.00	30.00	20.00
(13)	Leo Mangum (Aug. 20)	60.00	30.00	20.00
(17)	Roy Parmelee (Nov. 19)	60.00	30.00	20.00
	(Dates of issue not confirmed.)			
	Dan Howley	60.00	30.00	20.00

1952 Laval Dairy Provincial League

This scarce Canadian minor league issue includes only players from the Class C Provincial League, centered in Quebec. The black-and-white cards are blank-backed and measure 1-3/4" x 2-1/2". The player name, position, date and place of birth and card number is in French. Teams represented in the set are Quebec (Braves), St. Jean (Pirates), Three Rivers (Independent), Drummondville (Senators), Granby (Phillies) and Ste. Hyacinthe (Philadelphia A's).

		NM	EX	VG
Complete Set (114):		4,000	2,000	1,200
Common Player:		35.00	17.50	10.00
1	Georges McQuinn	35.00	17.50	10.00
2	Cliff Statham	35.00	17.50	10.00
3	Frank Wilson	35.00	17.50	10.00
4	Frank Neri	35.00	17.50	10.00
5	Georges Maranda	35.00	17.50	10.00
6	Richard "Dick" Cordeiro	35.00	17.50	10.00
7	Roger McCardell	35.00	17.50	10.00
8	Joseph Janiak	35.00	17.50	10.00
9	Herbert Shankman	35.00	17.50	10.00
10	Joe Subbiondo	35.00	17.50	10.00
11	Jack Brenner	35.00	17.50	10.00
12	Donald Buchanan	35.00	17.50	10.00
13	Robert Smith	35.00	17.50	10.00
14	Raymond Lague	35.00	17.50	10.00
15	Mike Fandozzi	35.00	17.50	10.00
16	Dick Moler	35.00	17.50	10.00
17	Edward Bazydio	35.00	17.50	10.00
18	Danny Mazurek	35.00	17.50	10.00
19	Edwin Charles	35.00	17.50	10.00
20	Jack Nullaney	35.00	17.50	10.00
21	Bob Bolan	35.00	17.50	10.00
22	Bob Long	35.00	17.50	10.00
23	Cleo Lewright	35.00	17.50	10.00
24	Herb Taylor	35.00	17.50	10.00
25	Frankie Gaeta	35.00	17.50	10.00
26	Bill Truitt	35.00	17.50	10.00
27	Jean Prats	35.00	17.50	10.00
28	Tex Taylor	35.00	17.50	10.00
29	Ron Delbianco	35.00	17.50	10.00
30	Joe DiLorenzo	35.00	17.50	10.00
31	Johnny Paszek	35.00	17.50	10.00
32	Ken Suess	35.00	17.50	10.00
33	Harry Sims	35.00	17.50	10.00
34	William Jackson	35.00	17.50	10.00
35	Jerry Mayers	35.00	17.50	10.00
36	Gordon Maltzberger	35.00	17.50	10.00
37	Gerry Cabana	35.00	17.50	10.00
38	Gary Rutkey	35.00	17.50	10.00
39	Ken Hatcher	35.00	17.50	10.00
40	Vincent Cosenza	35.00	17.50	10.00
41	Edward Yaeger	35.00	17.50	10.00
42	Jimmy Orr	35.00	17.50	10.00
43	Johnny Di Matino	35.00	17.50	10.00
44	Lenny Wisneski	35.00	17.50	10.00
45	Pete Caniglia	35.00	17.50	10.00
46	Guy Coleman	35.00	17.50	10.00
47	Herb Fleischer	35.00	17.50	10.00
48	Charles Yahrling	35.00	17.50	10.00
49	Roger Bedard	35.00	17.50	10.00
50	Al Barillari	35.00	17.50	10.00
51	Hugh Mulcahy	50.00	25.00	15.00
52	Vincent Canepa	35.00	17.50	10.00
53	Bob Loranger	35.00	17.50	10.00
54	Georges Carpentier	35.00	17.50	10.00
55	Bill Hamilton	35.00	17.50	10.00
56	Hector Lopez	65.00	32.00	19.50
57	Joel Taylor	35.00	17.50	10.00
58	Alonzo Brathwaite	100.00	50.00	30.00
59	Carl McQuillen	35.00	17.50	10.00
60	Robert Trice	35.00	17.50	10.00
61	John Dworak	35.00	17.50	10.00
62	Al Pinkston	50.00	25.00	15.00
63	William Shannon	35.00	17.50	10.00
64	Stanley Wotychowisz	35.00	17.50	10.00
65	Roger Herbert	35.00	17.50	10.00
66	Troy Spencer	35.00	17.50	10.00
67	Johnny Rohan	35.00	17.50	10.00
68	John Sosh	35.00	17.50	10.00
69	Ramon Mason	35.00	17.50	10.00
70	Tom Smith	35.00	17.50	10.00
71	Douglas McBean	35.00	17.50	10.00
72	Bill Babik	35.00	17.50	10.00
73	Dante Cozzi	35.00	17.50	10.00
74	Melville Doxtater	35.00	17.50	10.00
75	William Gilray	35.00	17.50	10.00
76	Armando Diaz	35.00	17.50	10.00
77	Ackroyd Smith	35.00	17.50	10.00
78	Germain Pizarro	35.00	17.50	10.00
79	Jim Heap	35.00	17.50	10.00
80	Herbert Crompton	35.00	17.50	10.00
81	Howard Bodell	35.00	17.50	10.00
82	Andre Schreiser	35.00	17.50	10.00
83	John Wingo	35.00	17.50	10.00
84	Salvatore Arduini	35.00	17.50	10.00
85	Fred Pallito	35.00	17.50	10.00
86	Aaron Osofsky	35.00	17.50	10.00
87	Jack DiGrace	35.00	17.50	10.00
88	Alphonso Chico Girard (Gerrard)	35.00	17.50	10.00
89	Manuel Trabous	35.00	17.50	10.00
90	Tom Barnes	35.00	17.50	10.00
91	Humberto Robinson	35.00	17.50	10.00
92	Jack Bukowatz	35.00	17.50	10.00
93	Marco Mainini	35.00	17.50	10.00
94	Claude St. Vincent	35.00	17.50	10.00
95	Fernand Brosseau	35.00	17.50	10.00
96	John Malangone	35.00	17.50	10.00
97	Pierre Nantel	35.00	17.50	10.00
98	Donald Stevens	35.00	17.50	10.00
99	Jim Prappas	35.00	17.50	10.00
100	Richard Fitzgerald	35.00	17.50	10.00
101	Yves Aubin	35.00	17.50	10.00
102	Frank Novosel	35.00	17.50	10.00
103	Tony Campos	35.00	17.50	10.00
104	Gelso Oviedo	35.00	17.50	10.00
105	Guly Becker	35.00	17.50	10.00
106	Aurelio Ala	35.00	17.50	10.00
107	Orlando Andux	35.00	17.50	10.00
108	Tom Hackett	35.00	17.50	10.00
109	Guillame Vargas	35.00	17.50	10.00
110	Fransisco Salfran	35.00	17.50	10.00
111	Jean-Marc Blais	35.00	17.50	10.00
112	Vince Pizzitola	35.00	17.50	10.00
113	John Olsen	35.00	17.50	10.00
114	Jacques Monette	35.00	17.50	10.00

1948 Los Angeles Angels Team Issue

A team-issued set sold in a paper envelope for $1 at the ballpark, these cards were produced by the same firm which published the team's yearbook, Pacific Coast Sports Publishing Co., of Los Angeles. The blank-backed cards measure 6-3/4" x 4-3/4" and are printed in black-and-white on thin cardboard with a semi-gloss front surface. Cards feature a facsimile player autograph on front, along with a posed action or portrait photo and complete major and minor league stats. The cards are listed in the American Card Catalog, along with the subsequent year's issue, as W725. Many of the players on this Pacific Coast League team were former or future Chicago Cubs. The unnumbered cards are checklisted here alphabetically.

		NM	EX	VG
Complete Set (26):		650.00	325.00	200.00
Common Player:		30.00	15.00	9.00
(1)	Cliff Aberson	30.00	15.00	9.00
(2)	Red Adams	30.00	15.00	9.00
(3)	John Adkins	30.00	15.00	9.00
(4)	Lee Anthony	30.00	15.00	9.00
(5)	Russ Bauers	30.00	15.00	9.00
(6)	Ora Burnett	30.00	15.00	9.00
(7)	Donald Carlsen	30.00	15.00	9.00
(8)	Dom Dallessandro	30.00	15.00	9.00
(9)	Cecil Garriott	30.00	15.00	9.00
(10)	Paul Gillespie	30.00	15.00	9.00
(11)	Al Glossop	30.00	15.00	9.00
(12)	Tom Hafey	30.00	15.00	9.00
(13)	Don Johnson	30.00	15.00	9.00
(14)	Bill Kelly	30.00	15.00	9.00
(15)	Hal Kleine	30.00	15.00	9.00
(16)	Walt Lanfranconi	30.00	15.00	9.00
(17)	Ed Lukon	30.00	15.00	9.00
(18)	Red Lynn	30.00	15.00	9.00
(19)	Eddie Malone	30.00	15.00	9.00
(20)	Len Merullo	30.00	15.00	9.00
(21)	Ralph Novotney	30.00	15.00	9.00
(22)	John Ostrowski	30.00	15.00	9.00
(23)	John Sanford	30.00	15.00	9.00
(24)	Ed Sauer	30.00	15.00	9.00
(25)	Bill Schuster	30.00	15.00	9.00
(26)	John Warner	30.00	15.00	9.00

1949 Los Angeles Angels Team Issue

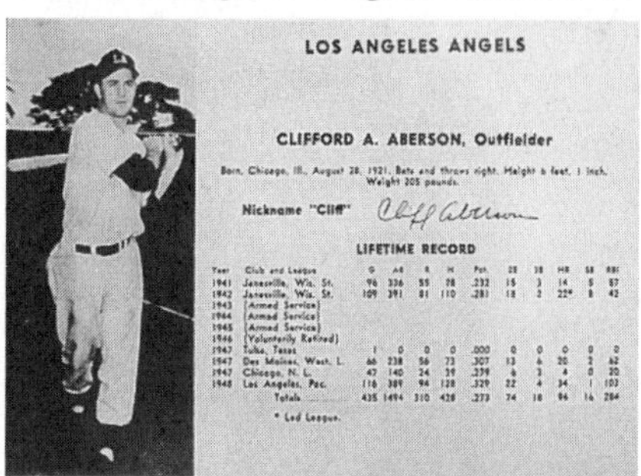

Little changed in the second year of this team issue. Cards remained at 6-3/4" x 4-3/4" in format, printed black-and-white on semi-gloss cardboard with a blank back. Many of the players (and even some of the photos) were repeated from the previous year. The unnumbered cards are checklisted here in alphabetical order.

		NM	EX	VG
Complete Set (39):		1,000	500.00	300.00
Common Player:		30.00	15.00	9.00
(1)	Cliff Aberson	30.00	15.00	9.00
(2)	Donald Alfano	30.00	15.00	9.00
(3)	Quentin Altizer	30.00	15.00	9.00
(4)	Lee Anthony	30.00	15.00	9.00
(5)	Nels Burbrink	30.00	15.00	9.00
(6)	Smoky Burgess	75.00	37.50	22.00
(7)	Don Carlsen	30.00	15.00	9.00
(8)	Joe Damato	30.00	15.00	9.00
(9)	Bill Emmerich	30.00	15.00	9.00
(10)	Ken Gables	30.00	15.00	9.00
(11)	Cecil Garriott	30.00	15.00	9.00
(12)	Al Glossop	30.00	15.00	9.00
(13)	Gordon Goldsberry	30.00	15.00	9.00
(14)	Frank Gustine	30.00	15.00	9.00
(15)	Lee Handley	30.00	15.00	9.00
(16)	Alan Ihde	30.00	15.00	9.00
(17)	Bob Kelley (Announcer)	30.00	15.00	9.00
(18)	Bill Kelly	30.00	15.00	9.00
(19)	Bob Kelly	30.00	15.00	9.00
(20)	Walt Lanfranconi	30.00	15.00	9.00
(21)	Red Lynn	30.00	15.00	9.00
(22)	Clarence Maddern	30.00	15.00	9.00
(23)	Eddie Malone	30.00	15.00	9.00
(24)	Carmen Mauro	30.00	15.00	9.00
(25)	Booker McDaniels	75.00	37.50	22.00
(26)	Cal McLish	50.00	25.00	15.00
(27)	Butch Moran	30.00	15.00	9.00
(28)	Ralph Novotney	30.00	15.00	9.00
(29)	John Ostrowski	30.00	15.00	9.00
(30)	Bobby Rhawn	30.00	15.00	9.00
(31)	Bill Schuster	30.00	15.00	9.00
(32)	Pat Seerey	30.00	15.00	9.00
(33)	Bryan Stephens	30.00	15.00	9.00
(34)	Bob Sturgeon	30.00	15.00	9.00
(35)	Wayne Terwilliger	45.00	22.00	13.50
(36)	Gordon Van Dyke	30.00	15.00	9.00
(37)	John Warner	30.00	15.00	9.00
(38)	Don Watkins	30.00	15.00	9.00

		NM	EX	VG
(39)	Trainers, Bat Boys (Dickie Evans, Joe Liscio, Dave Flores, Billy Lund)	30.00	15.00	9.00

1930-31 Lucke Badge & Button Baltimore Orioles Pins

These 7/8" diameter celluloid pinback buttons were produced by the Baltimore novelty firm of Lucke Badge & Button Co. Issued to honor fan favorites on their "Day," the buttons have black-and-white portrait photos at center, surrounded by a white rim. At top is the player name, at bottom is the team name and year. A paper label inside the back of the button identifies the maker and includes a union label.

	NM	EX	VG
Joe Hauser/1930	300.00	150.00	90.00
Don Heffner/1931	200.00	100.00	60.00

1910 Mascot Gum Pins

Only players from the Eastern League champion Rochester Bronchos are known on these 7/8" diameter pinback buttons. Fronts have a black-and-white player photo on a blue background with the player's last name at left and "ROCHESTER" at right. A paper insert on the reverse advertises "Ball Player's Buttons Free With Mascot Gum." This checklist may not be complete.

		NM	EX	VG
Common Player:		250.00	125.00	80.00
(1)	Anderson	250.00	125.00	80.00
(2)	Heinie Batch	250.00	125.00	80.00
(3)	Blair	250.00	125.00	80.00
(4)	Holmes	250.00	125.00	80.00
(5)	Lafitte	250.00	125.00	80.00
(6)	Manning	250.00	125.00	80.00
(7)	McConnell	250.00	125.00	80.00
(8)	Moeller	250.00	125.00	80.00
(9)	Moran	250.00	125.00	80.00
(10)	Osborn	250.00	125.00	80.00
(11)	Don Carlos Ragan	250.00	125.00	80.00
(12)	Savidge	250.00	125.00	80.00
(13)	Simmons	250.00	125.00	80.00
(14)	Spencer	250.00	125.00	80.00
(15)	Tooley	250.00	125.00	80.00

1952 May Co. Chuck Stevens Premium

The date given is speculative, about midway through the player's term with the Hollywood Stars of the Pacific Coast League. The 4-1/2" x 6" blank-backed black-and-white card features a portrait of what the caption at bottom calls the "popular first baseman." The caption also calls the piece a "MAY CO. 'Back To School' Party Souvenir Photo." The cards are often found bearing the player's autograph, presumably obtained at the event.

	NM	EX	VG
Chuck Stevens	75.00	40.00	25.00

1960s-70s J.D. McCarthy Postcards

For details of J.D. McCarthy's prolific body of black-and-white player postcards, see the introductory material in the vintage major league section.

Common Player: $1-3

SPOKANE INDIANS

(1) Roy Hartsfield

TOLEDO MUD HENS

(1) Loren Babe
(2) Stan Bahnsen
(3) Bill Bethea
(4) Joe Cherry
(5) Horace Clark
(6) Wayne Comer
(7) Jack Cullen (2)
(8) Jack Curtis (2)
(9) Gil Downs
(10) Joe Faraci
(11) Frank Fernandez
(12) Mike Ferraro
(13) Mickey Harrington
(14) Mike Hegan
(15) Jim Horsford (2)
(16) Dick Hughes
(17) Elvio Jiminez (2)
(18) Robert Lasko
(19) Artie Lopez
(20) Roy Majtyka
(21) Tom Martz
(22) Ed Merritt (2)
(23) Archie Moore (2)
(24) Al Moran
(25) Bobby Murcer
(26) Tony Przybycien
(27) Bill Roman
(28) Bob Schmidt (2)
(29) Tom Shafer
(30) Billy Shantz
(31) Shantz-Senger-Babe
(32) Bob Tiefenauer
(33) Paul Toth (2)
(34) Andrew Vickery
(35) Jerry Walker
(36) Don Wallace
(37) Dooley Womack

1954 MD Super Service Sacramento Solons

This issue features only players of the Pacific Coast League Sacramento Solons. The unnumbered cards are printed in black-and-white and carry an ad for a local gas station. The borderless, blank-backed cards measure 2-1/8" x 3-3/8".

		NM	EX	VG
Complete Set (6):		850.00	425.00	250.00
Common Player:		150.00	75.00	45.00
(1)	Joe Brovia	150.00	75.00	45.00
(2)	Al Cicotte	150.00	75.00	45.00
(3)	Nippy Jones	150.00	75.00	45.00
(4)	Richie Meyers	150.00	75.00	45.00
(5)	Hank Schenz	150.00	75.00	45.00
(6)	Bud Sheeley	150.00	75.00	45.00

1952 Miami Beach Flamingos Team Issue

These 2-1/4" x 3-3/8" black-and-white, unnumbered, blank-backed cards were one of many minor league team sets issued by Globe Printing of San Jose, Calif., in the early 1950s. Cards were usually given away at the ballpark on a one-per-week or one-per-homestand basis, accounting for the rarity of surviving sets. An embossed album slotted to accommodate the cards was also issued. The Flamingos were an unaffiliated team in the Class B Florida International League.

		NM	EX	VG
Complete Set (25):		1,000	500.00	300.00
Common Player:		60.00	30.00	18.00
Album:		100.00	50.00	30.00
(1)	Billy Barrett	60.00	30.00	18.00
(2)	Art Bosch	60.00	30.00	18.00
(3)	Jack Caro	60.00	30.00	18.00
(4)	Chuck Ehlman	60.00	30.00	18.00
(5)	Oscar Garmendia	60.00	30.00	18.00
(6)	George Handy	60.00	30.00	18.00
(7)	Clark Henry	60.00	30.00	18.00
(8)	Dario Jiminez	60.00	30.00	18.00
(9)	Jesse Levan	60.00	30.00	18.00
(10)	Bobby Lyons	60.00	30.00	18.00
(11)	Pepper Martin	125.00	62.00	37.00
(12)	Dick McMillin	60.00	30.00	18.00
(13)	Pete Morant	60.00	30.00	18.00
(14)	Chico Morilla	60.00	30.00	18.00
(15)	Ken Munroe	60.00	30.00	18.00
(16)	Walt Nothe	60.00	30.00	18.00
(17)	Marshall O'Coine	60.00	30.00	18.00
(18)	Whitey Platt	60.00	30.00	18.00
(19)	Johnny Podgajny	60.00	30.00	18.00
(20)	Knobby Rosa	60.00	30.00	18.00
(21)	Harry Raulerson	60.00	30.00	18.00
(22)	Mort Smith	60.00	30.00	18.00
(23)	Tommy Venn	60.00	30.00	18.00
(24)	George Wehmeyer	60.00	30.00	18.00
(25)	Ray Williams	60.00	30.00	18.00

1963 Milwaukee Sausage Seattle Rainiers

Inserted into meat packages by a Seattle sausage company, the 11 cards known in this set are all Seattle Rainiers players, several of whom had big league experience. Cards measure approximately 4-1/4"-square and are printed in blue, red and yellow. The unnumbered cards are checklisted in alphabetical order.

		NM	EX	VG
Complete Set (11):		6,000	3,000	1,800
Common Player:		600.00	300.00	180.00
(1)	Dave Hall	600.00	300.00	180.00
(2)	Bill Harrell	600.00	300.00	180.00
(3)	Pete Jernigan	600.00	300.00	180.00
(4)	Bill McLeod	600.00	300.00	180.00
(5)	Mel Parnell	650.00	325.00	200.00
(6)	Elmer Singleton	600.00	300.00	180.00
(7)	Archie Skeen	600.00	300.00	180.00
(8)	Paul Smith	600.00	300.00	180.00
(9)	Pete Smith	600.00	300.00	180.00
(10)	Bill Spanswick	600.00	300.00	180.00
(11)	George Spencer	600.00	300.00	180.00

1909 Minneapolis Tribune/ St. Paul Pioneer Press Mirrors

From the few players known, it is apparent these mirrors were issued in 1909 by two of the Twin Cities' daily newspapers. Each mirror is 2-1/8" diameter with a celluloid back. At center is a black-and-white player photo. All typography is in b/w, as well. A pair of concentric circles around the photo contain the player's name and a short description of his prowess. Olmstead's reads, "Unhittable in the Pinches"; Carisch's reads, "Nails 'em to the Cross Every Time." The outer circle contains an ad for the newspaper. This checklist is probably incomplete.

	NM	EX	VG
Common Player:	200.00	100.00	60.00
(1) Fred Carisch	200.00	100.00	60.00
(2) Michael Kelly	200.00	100.00	60.00
(3) Fred Olmstead	200.00	100.00	60.00

1911 Mono Cigarettes (T217)

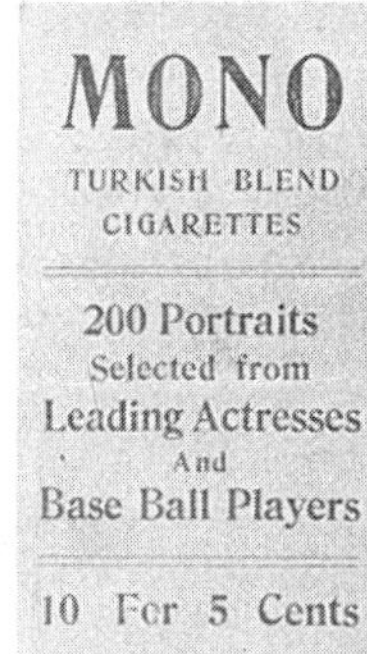

As was common with many tobacco issues of the period, the T217 set - distributed on the West Coast by Mono Cigarettes - feature both baseball players and "Leading Actresses." The 23 baseball players in the Mono set are all from the Pacific Coast League. Two of the players (Delhi and Hughie Smith) are shown in two poses, resulting in a total of 25 different cards. The players are pictured in black-and-white photos on a card that measures approximately 1-1/2" x 2-5/8", the standard size of a tobacco card. The player's name and team appear at the bottom, while the back of the card carries an advertisement for Mono Cigarettes. The Mono set, which can be dated to the 1909-1911 period, is among the rarest of all tobacco cards.

	NM	EX	VG
Complete Set (25):	100,000	50,000	30,000
Common Player:	4,250	2,000	1,100
(1) Aiken	4,250	2,000	1,100
(2) Curtis Bernard	4,250	2,000	1,100
(3) L. Burrell	4,250	2,000	1,100
(4) Chadbourn	4,250	2,000	1,100
(5) R. Couchman	4,250	2,000	1,100
(6) Elmer Criger	4,250	2,000	1,100
(7) Pete Daley	4,250	2,000	1,100
(8) W. Delhi (Glove at chest level.)	4,250	2,000	1,100
(9) W. Delhi (Glove at shoulder level.)	4,250	2,000	1,100
(10) Bert Delmas	4,250	2,000	1,100
(11) Ivan Howard	4,250	2,000	1,100
(12) Kitty Knight	4,250	2,000	1,100
(13) Gene Knapp (Krapp)	4,250	2,000	1,100
(14) Metzger	4,250	2,000	1,100
(15) Carl Mitze	4,250	2,000	1,100
(16) J. O'Rourke	4,250	2,000	1,100
(17) R. Peckinpaugh	4,250	2,000	1,100
(18) Walter Schmidt	4,250	2,000	1,100
(19) Hughie Smith/Btg	4,250	2,000	1,100
(20) Hughie Smith/Fldg	4,250	2,000	1,100
(21) Wm. Stein	4,250	2,000	1,100
(22) Elmer Thorsen	4,250	2,000	1,100
(23) Oscar Vitt	4,250	2,000	1,100
(24) Clyde Wares	4,250	2,000	1,100
(25) Geo. Wheeler	4,250	2,000	1,100

1961 Jeffrey W. Morey Postcards

This set of 3-1/2" x 5-1/2", black-and-white postcards was produced to accomodate fan mail requests by two players each from the Columbus Clippers and Syracuse Chiefs. Fronts have a facsimile autograph. Divided-postcard backs have a credit line to the photographer and standard postcard markings.

	NM	EX	VG
Complete Set (4):	125.00	65.00	37.50
Common Player:	35.00	17.50	10.50
(1) Larry Elliot	35.00	17.50	10.50
(2) Don Rowe	35.00	17.50	10.50
(3) Ted Sadowski	35.00	17.50	10.50
(4) Ron Stillwell	35.00	17.50	10.50

1947 Morley Studios Team Cards

Besides issuing individual player cards of the Tacoma team, Morley Studios also issued postcard-size pictures of the teams in the Class B Western International League of 1947. The 3-1/2" x 5-1/2" cards are blank-backed and carry a "Morley Studios / 1947" imprint on front.

	NM	EX	VG
Complete Set (8):	600.00	300.00	180.00
Common Player:	75.00	37.50	22.50
(1) Bremerton Bluejackets	75.00	37.50	22.50
(2) Salem Senators	75.00	37.50	22.50
(3) Spokane Indians	75.00	37.50	22.50
(4) Tacoma Tigers	75.00	37.50	22.50
(5) Vancouver Capilanos	75.00	37.50	22.50
(6) Victoria Athletics	75.00	37.50	22.50
(7) Yakima Stars	75.00	37.50	22.50
(8) Wenatchee Chiefs	75.00	37.50	22.50

1947 Morley Studios Tacoma Tigers

This set of Tacoma Tigers (Western International League) features borderless black-and-white posed action photos with a facsimile autograph on front. A "Morley Sports Photos" or "Morley Studios" credit line appears at the bottom. Backs of the first seven cards are blank, while the others feature player biographies credited to "Jordan's (bread sponsor) Broadcaster" Clay Huntington and a Series A through F designation (though some cards lack the letter code). The unnumbered cards measure 2-1/2" x 3-1/2".

	NM	EX	VG
Complete Set (28):	3,500	1,750	1,000
Common Player:	125.00	65.00	40.00
Blank-Backed			
(1) Hank Bartolomei	125.00	65.00	40.00
(2) Rod Belcher (Broadcaster)	125.00	65.00	40.00
(3) Tip Berg (Trainer)	125.00	65.00	40.00
(4) Gene Clough	125.00	65.00	40.00
(5) Clay Huntington (Broadcaster)	125.00	65.00	40.00
(6) Donald Mooney (Bat boy.)	125.00	65.00	40.00
(7) Buck Tinsley	125.00	65.00	40.00
Series A			
(8) Richard A. Greco	125.00	65.00	40.00
(9) Cy Greenlaw	125.00	65.00	40.00
(10) Bob Joratz	125.00	65.00	40.00
(11) Earl Kuper	125.00	65.00	40.00
Series B			
(12) Neil Clifford	125.00	65.00	40.00
(13) Red Harvel	125.00	65.00	40.00
(14) Julian Morgan	125.00	65.00	40.00
(15) Pete Tedeschi	125.00	65.00	40.00
Series C			
(16) Stanley Gilson	125.00	65.00	40.00
(17) Harry Nygard	125.00	65.00	40.00
(18) Cleve Ramsey	125.00	65.00	40.00
(19) Pete Sabutis	125.00	65.00	40.00
Series D			
(20) Mitch Chetkovich	125.00	65.00	40.00
(21) Leroy Paton	125.00	65.00	40.00
(22) Carl Shaply	125.00	65.00	40.00
(23) Glenn Stetter	125.00	65.00	40.00
Series E			
(24) Bob Hedington	125.00	65.00	40.00
(25) Ed Keehan	125.00	65.00	40.00
(26) Gordon Walden	125.00	65.00	40.00
Series F			
(27) Maury Donovan	125.00	65.00	40.00
(28) Guy Miller	125.00	65.00	40.00

1952 Mother's Cookies

This is one of the most popular regional minor league sets ever issued. Cards of Pacific Coast League players were included in packages of cookies. Distribution was limited to the West Coast. The 64 cards feature full color photos on a colored background, with player name and team. The cards measure 2-13/16" x 3-1/2", though the cards' rounded corners cause some variation in listed size. Card backs feature a very brief player statistic, card

numbers and an offer for purchasing postage stamps. Five cards (11, 16, 29, 37 and 43) are considered scarce, while card #4 (Chuck Connors) is the most popular.

	NM	EX	VG
Complete Set (64):	4,500	2,100	1,250
Common Player:	60.00	30.00	20.00
1a Johnny Lindell (Regular back.)	80.00	40.00	25.00
1b Johnny Lindell ('52 Hollywood schedule on back)	80.00	40.00	25.00
2 Jim Davis	60.00	30.00	20.00
3 Al Gettle (Gettel)	60.00	30.00	20.00
4 Chuck Connors	600.00	300.00	200.00
5 Joe Grace	60.00	30.00	20.00
6 Eddie Basinski	60.00	30.00	20.00
7a Gene Handley (Regular back.)	60.00	30.00	20.00
7b Gene Handley (Schedule back.)	60.00	30.00	20.00
8 Walt Judnich	60.00	30.00	20.00
9 Jim Marshall	60.00	30.00	20.00
10 Max West	60.00	30.00	20.00
11 Bill MacCawley	120.00	60.00	35.00
12 Moreno Peiretti	60.00	30.00	20.00
13a Fred Haney (Regular back.)	75.00	37.50	22.50
13b Fred Haney ('52 Hollywood schedule on back)	75.00	37.50	22.50
14 Earl Johnson	60.00	30.00	20.00
15 Dave Dahle	60.00	30.00	20.00
16 Bob Talbot	120.00	60.00	35.00
17 Smokey Singleton	60.00	30.00	20.00
18 Frank Austin	60.00	30.00	20.00
19 Joe Gordon	90.00	45.00	27.50
20 Joe Marty	60.00	30.00	20.00
21 Bob Gillespie	60.00	30.00	20.00
22 Red Embree	60.00	30.00	20.00
23a Lefty Olsen (Brown belt.)	60.00	30.00	20.00
23b Lefty Olsen (Black belt.)	90.00	45.00	27.50
24a Whitey Wietelmann (Large photo, much of bat missing.)	60.00	30.00	20.00
24b Whitey Wietelmann (Small photo, more bat shows.)	60.00	30.00	20.00
25 Frank O'Doul	100.00	50.00	30.00
26 Memo Luna	60.00	30.00	20.00
27 John Davis	60.00	30.00	20.00
28 Dick Faber	60.00	30.00	20.00
29 Buddy Peterson	225.00	110.00	67.00
30 Hank Schenz	60.00	30.00	20.00
31 Tookie Gilbert	60.00	30.00	20.00
32 Mel Ott	200.00	100.00	60.00
33 Sam Chapman	60.00	30.00	20.00
34a John Ragni (Outfielder)	60.00	30.00	20.00
34b John Ragni (Pitcher)	100.00	50.00	30.00
35 Dick Cole	60.00	30.00	20.00
36 Tom Saffell	60.00	30.00	20.00
37 Roy Welmaker	120.00	60.00	35.00
38 Lou Stringer	60.00	30.00	20.00
39a Chuck Stevens (Team on back Hollywood.)	60.00	30.00	20.00
39b Chuck Stevens (Team on back Seattle.)	60.00	30.00	20.00
39c Chuck Stevens (No team on back.)	60.00	30.00	20.00
40 Artie Wilson	90.00	45.00	30.00
41 Charlie Schanz	60.00	30.00	20.00
42 Al Lyons	60.00	30.00	20.00
43 Joe Erautt	300.00	150.00	90.00
44 Clarence Maddern	60.00	30.00	20.00
45 Gene Baker	60.00	30.00	20.00
46 Tom Heath	60.00	30.00	20.00
47 Al Lien	60.00	30.00	20.00
48 Bill Reeder	60.00	30.00	20.00
49 Bob Thurman	60.00	30.00	20.00
50 Ray Orteig	60.00	30.00	20.00
51 Joe Brovia	60.00	30.00	20.00
52 Jim Russell	60.00	30.00	20.00
53 Fred Sanford	60.00	30.00	20.00
54 Jim Gladd	60.00	30.00	20.00
55 Clay Hopper	60.00	30.00	20.00
56 Bill Glynn	60.00	30.00	20.00
57 Mike McCormick	60.00	30.00	20.00
58 Richie Myers	60.00	30.00	20.00
59 Vinnie Smith	60.00	30.00	20.00
60a Stan Hack (Brown belt.)	80.00	40.00	25.00
60b Stan Hack (Black belt.)	80.00	40.00	25.00
61 Bob Spicer	60.00	30.00	20.00
62 Jack Hollis	60.00	30.00	20.00
63 Ed Chandler	60.00	30.00	20.00
64 Bill Moisan	85.00	45.00	25.00

1953 Mother's Cookies

The 1953 Mother's Cookies cards are again 2-3/16" x 3-1/2", with rounded corners. There are 63 players from Pacific Coast League teams included. The full-color fronts have facsimile au-

tographs rather than printed player names, and card backs offer a trading card album. Cards are generally more plentiful than in the 1952 set, with 11 of the cards apparently double printed.

		NM	EX	VG
Complete Set (63):		1,725	850.00	525.00
Common Player:		30.00	15.00	9.00
Album:		125.00	65.00	40.00
1	Lee Winter	35.00	17.50	10.00
2	Joe Ostrowski	30.00	15.00	9.00
3	Will Ramsdell	30.00	15.00	9.00
4	Bobby Bragan	40.00	20.00	12.00
5	Fletcher Robbe	30.00	15.00	9.00
6	Aaron Robinson	30.00	15.00	9.00
7	Augie Galan	30.00	15.00	9.00
8	Buddy Peterson	30.00	15.00	9.00
9	Frank Lefty O'Doul	65.00	32.50	20.00
10	Walt Pocekay	30.00	15.00	9.00
11	Nini Tornay	30.00	15.00	9.00
12	Jim Moran	30.00	15.00	9.00
13	George Schmees	30.00	15.00	9.00
14	Al Widmar	30.00	15.00	9.00
15	Ritchie Myers	30.00	15.00	9.00
16	Bill Howerton	30.00	15.00	9.00
17	Chuck Stevens	30.00	15.00	9.00
18	Joe Brovia	30.00	15.00	9.00
19	Max West	30.00	15.00	9.00
20	Eddie Malone	30.00	15.00	9.00
21	Gene Handley	30.00	15.00	9.00
22	William D. McCawley	30.00	15.00	9.00
23	Bill Sweeney	30.00	15.00	9.00
24	Tom Alston	30.00	15.00	9.00
25	George Vico	30.00	15.00	9.00
26	Hank Arft	30.00	15.00	9.00
27	Al Benton	30.00	15.00	9.00
28	"Pete" Milne	30.00	15.00	9.00
29	Jim Gladd	30.00	15.00	9.00
30	Earl Rapp	35.00	17.50	10.00
31	Ray Orteig	30.00	15.00	9.00
32	Eddie Basinski	30.00	15.00	9.00
33	Reno Cheso	30.00	15.00	9.00
34	Clarence Maddern	30.00	15.00	9.00
35	Marino Pieretti	30.00	15.00	9.00
36	Bill Raimondi	30.00	15.00	9.00
37	Frank Kelleher	30.00	15.00	9.00
38	George Bamberger	35.00	17.50	10.00
39	Dick Smith	30.00	15.00	9.00
40	Charley Schanz	30.00	15.00	9.00
41	John Van Cuyk	30.00	15.00	9.00
42	Lloyd Hittle	30.00	15.00	9.00
43	Tommy Heath	30.00	15.00	9.00
44	Frank Kalin	30.00	15.00	9.00
45	Jack Tobin	30.00	15.00	9.00
46	Jim Davis	30.00	15.00	9.00
47	Claude Christie	30.00	15.00	9.00
48	Elvin Tappe	30.00	15.00	9.00
49	Stan Hack	60.00	30.00	18.00
50	Fred Richards	30.00	15.00	9.00
51	Clay Hopper	30.00	15.00	9.00
52	Roy Welmaker	30.00	15.00	9.00
53	Red Adams	30.00	15.00	9.00
54	Piper Davis	60.00	30.00	18.00
55	Spider Jorgensen	30.00	15.00	9.00
56	Lee Walls	30.00	15.00	9.00
57	Jack Phillips	30.00	15.00	9.00
58	Red Lynn	30.00	15.00	9.00
59	Eddie Beckman	30.00	15.00	9.00
60	Gene Desautels	30.00	15.00	9.00
61	Bob Dillinger	30.00	15.00	9.00
62	Al Federoff	55.00	27.50	16.50
63	Bill Boemler	30.00	15.00	9.00

1920 Mrs. Sherlock's Bread Pins

Members of the Toledo Mud Hens of the American Association are featured on this set of pins sponsored by Mrs. Sherlock's Bread. The 7/8" celluloid pins have a player portrait in black-and-white at center, with his name and position indicated below. At top, in either red or black type is, "Mrs. Sherlock's Home Made Bread." Backs credit manufacture to Bastian Bros. of Rochester, N.Y., "Mfr's of ribbon metal and celluloid novelties." The unnumbered pins are checklisted here alphabetically.

		NM	EX	VG
Complete Set (19):		850.00	425.00	250.00
Common Player:		60.00	30.00	18.00
(1)	Brady	60.00	30.00	18.00
(2)	Roger Bresnahan	90.00	45.00	27.00
(3)	Jean Dubuc	60.00	30.00	18.00
(4)	Dyer	60.00	30.00	18.00
(5)	Fox	60.00	30.00	18.00
(6)	Ham Hyatt	60.00	30.00	18.00
(7)	Jones	60.00	30.00	18.00
(8)	Joe Kelly	60.00	30.00	18.00
(9)	M. Kelly	60.00	30.00	18.00
(10)	Art Kores	60.00	30.00	18.00
(11)	McColl	60.00	30.00	18.00
(12)	Norm McNeill (McNeil)	60.00	30.00	18.00
(13)	Middleton	60.00	30.00	18.00
(14)	Murphy	60.00	30.00	18.00
(15)	Nelson	60.00	30.00	18.00
(16)	Dutch Stryker	60.00	30.00	18.00
(17)	Thompson	60.00	30.00	18.00
(18)	Al Wickland	60.00	30.00	18.00
(19)	Joe Wilhoit	60.00	30.00	18.00

1922 Mrs. Sherlock's Bread Pins (PB5)

Members of the Toledo Mud Hens of the American Association are featured on this set of pins sponsored by Mrs. Sherlock's Bread. The 5/8" celluloid pins have a player portrait in brown or green at center, with his name and position indicated below. At top, in either brown or green type is, "Eat Mrs. Sherlock's Bread." The pins are numbered at lower-left.

		NM	EX	VG
Complete Set (21):		900.00	450.00	275.00
Common Player:		60.00	30.00	18.00
1	Roger Bresnahan	90.00	45.00	27.00
2	Brad Kocher	60.00	30.00	18.00
3	Hill	60.00	30.00	18.00
4	Huber	60.00	30.00	18.00
5	Doc Ayers	60.00	30.00	18.00
6	Parks	60.00	30.00	18.00
7	Giard	60.00	30.00	18.00
8	Grimes	60.00	30.00	18.00
9	McCullough	60.00	30.00	18.00
10	Shoup	60.00	30.00	18.00
11	Al Wickland	60.00	30.00	18.00
12	Baker	60.00	30.00	18.00
13	Schauffle	60.00	30.00	18.00
14	Wright	60.00	30.00	18.00
15	Lamar	60.00	30.00	18.00
16	Sallee	60.00	30.00	18.00
17	Fred Luderus	60.00	30.00	18.00
18	Walgomat	60.00	30.00	18.00
19	Ed Konetchy	60.00	30.00	18.00
20	O'Neill	60.00	30.00	18.00
21	Hugh Bedient	60.00	30.00	18.00

1933 Mrs. Sherlock's Bread Pins

Members of the Toledo Mud Hens of the American Association are featured on this set of pins sponsored by Mrs. Sherlock's Bread. The 7/8" celluloid pins have a player portrait in black-and-white at center, with his name and position indicated below. At top, in red type, is "Mrs. Sherlock's Home Made Bread" in two lines. The unnumbered pins are checklisted here alphabetically.

		NM	EX	VG
Complete Set (18):		800.00	400.00	240.00
Common Player:		50.00	25.00	15.00
(1)	LeRoy Bachman	50.00	25.00	15.00
(2)	George Detore	50.00	25.00	15.00
(3)	Frank Doljack	50.00	25.00	15.00
(4)	Milt Galatzer	50.00	25.00	15.00
(5)	Walter Henline	50.00	25.00	15.00
(6)	Roxie Lawson	50.00	25.00	15.00
(7)	Thornton Lee	50.00	25.00	15.00
(8)	Ed Montague	50.00	25.00	15.00
(9)	Steve O'Neill	50.00	25.00	15.00
(10)	Monte Pearson	50.00	25.00	15.00
(11)	Bob Reis	50.00	25.00	15.00
(12)	Scott	50.00	25.00	15.00
(13)	Bill Sweeney	50.00	25.00	15.00
(14)	Hal Trosky	50.00	25.00	15.00
(15)	Pete Turgeon	50.00	25.00	15.00
(16)	Forrest Twogood	50.00	25.00	15.00
(17)	Max West	50.00	25.00	15.00
(18)	Ralph Winegarner	50.00	25.00	15.00

1956 Mutual Savings Dick Stuart

Possibly issued in conjunction with an autograph appearance at the bank, Dick Stuart is pictured on this black-and-white postcard-sized photocard as an outfielder for the Western League Lincoln Chiefs in 1956, the season in which he hit 66 home runs.

	NM	EX	VG
Dick Stuart	100.00	50.00	30.00

1960 National Bank of Washington Tacoma Giants

These 3" x 5" unnumbered cards have color photos on front and are usually found with black-and-white backs with the bank's advertising. Uncut sheets of the cards were sold at Cheney Stadium in Tacoma either blank-backed or with a message from the Tacoma Athletic Commission. Only members of the Pacific Coast League Tacoma Giants are included in the set. The set contains the first card issued of Hall of Fame pitcher Juan Marichal. Unfortunately, fellow Hall of Famer Willie McCovey, who played in 17 games for Tacoma in 1960, is not included in the set.

		NM	EX	VG
Complete Set (21):		1,000	500.00	300.00
Common Player:		30.00	15.00	9.00
(1)	Matty Alou	75.00	37.00	22.00
(2)	Ossie Alvarez	30.00	15.00	9.00
(3)	Don Choate	30.00	15.00	9.00
(4)	Red Davis	30.00	15.00	9.00
(5)	Bob Farley	30.00	15.00	9.00
(6)	Eddie Fisher	30.00	15.00	9.00
(7)	Tom Haller	30.00	15.00	9.00
(8)	Sherman Jones	30.00	15.00	9.00
(9)	Juan Marichal	400.00	200.00	120.00
(10)	Ray Monzant	30.00	15.00	9.00
(11)	Danny O'Connell	30.00	15.00	9.00
(12)	Jose Pagan	30.00	15.00	9.00
(13)	Bob Perry	30.00	15.00	9.00
(14)	Dick Phillips	30.00	15.00	9.00
(15)	Bobby Prescott	30.00	15.00	9.00
(16)	Marshall Renfroe	30.00	15.00	9.00
(17)	Frank Reveira	30.00	15.00	9.00
(18)	Dusty Rhodes	35.00	17.50	10.00
(19)	Sal Taormina	30.00	15.00	9.00
(20)	Verle Tiefenthaler	30.00	15.00	9.00
(21)	Dom Zanni	30.00	15.00	9.00

1961 National Bank of Washington Tacoma Giants

These 3" x 4" cards feature borderless sepia photos on the front. Backs have a sponsor's ad and a few player stats

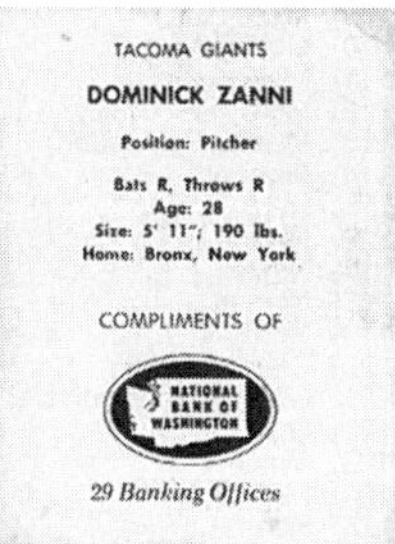

printed in dark blue. The unnumbered cards are checklisted here in alphabetical order.

		NM	EX	VG
Complete Set (21):		800.00	400.00	240.00
Common Player:		30.00	15.00	10.00
(1)	Rafael Alomar	40.00	20.00	12.00
(2)	Ernie Bowman	30.00	15.00	10.00
(3)	Bud Byerly	30.00	15.00	10.00
(4)	Ray Daviault	30.00	15.00	10.00
(5)	Red Davis	30.00	15.00	10.00
(6)	Bob Farley	30.00	15.00	10.00
(7)	Gil Garrido	30.00	15.00	10.00
(8)	John Goetz	30.00	15.00	10.00
(9)	Bill Hain	30.00	15.00	10.00
(10)	Ronald Herbel	30.00	15.00	10.00
(11)	Lynn Lovenguth	30.00	15.00	10.00
(12)	Georges H. Maranda	30.00	15.00	10.00
(13)	Manuel Mota	100.00	50.00	30.00
(14)	John Orsino	30.00	15.00	10.00
(15)	Bob Perry	30.00	15.00	10.00
(16)	Gaylord Perry	175.00	90.00	55.00
(17)	Dick Phillips	30.00	15.00	10.00
(18)	Frank Reveira	30.00	15.00	10.00
(19)	Dusty Rhodes	40.00	20.00	12.00
(20)	Verle Tiefenthaler	30.00	15.00	10.00
(21)	Dom Zanni	30.00	15.00	10.00

1907 Newark Evening World Supplements

The Newark Sailors of the Class A Eastern League are featured in this set of supplements from a local newspaper. The 7-1/2" x 10-15/16" pieces are printed in either sepia or black-and-white. An ornate border surrounds a player pose on a plain background. In a box beneath is player identification. Backs are blank. The unnumbered supplements are checklisted here in alphabetical order, though the list may not yet be complete.

		NM	EX	VG
Common Player:		400.00	200.00	120.00
(1)	William Carrick	400.00	200.00	120.00
(2)	James Cockman	400.00	200.00	120.00
(3)	Clyde Engle	400.00	200.00	120.00
(4)	James Jones	400.00	200.00	120.00
(5)	Paul Krichell	400.00	200.00	120.00
(6)	Henry LaBelle	400.00	200.00	120.00
(7)	William Mahling	400.00	200.00	120.00
(8)	Chas. McCafferty	400.00	200.00	120.00
(9)	Thomas McCarthy	400.00	200.00	120.00
(10)	James Mullen (Mullin)	400.00	200.00	120.00
(11)	Al Pardee	400.00	200.00	120.00
(12)	Bayard Sharpe	400.00	200.00	120.00
(13)	John E. Shea	400.00	200.00	120.00
(14)	Oscar Stanage	400.00	200.00	120.00
(15)	Elmer Zacher	400.00	200.00	120.00

1950 Oak Hall Roanoke Red Sox

(See 1950 Bush & Hancock Roanoke Red Sox.)

1913 Oakland Oaks Team Issue

Stylistically similar to contemporary Zeenuts cards, little is known about this series. The blank-back, approximately 2" x 3-5/8" cards have full-length sepiatone player poses on a sepiatone background. The player's last name and city are printed in all caps in two lines at bottom. It is unknown whether the cards on the list comprise a complete set. Their manner of distribution is likewise unknown, they may have been a strip card issue or a candy insert.

		NM	EX	VG
Common Player:		2,000	1,000	600.00
(1)	Ody Abbott	2,000	1,000	600.00
(2)	Harry Ables	2,000	1,000	600.00
(3)	Jesse Becker	2,000	1,000	600.00
(4)	W.W. Cook	2,000	1,000	600.00
(5)	Bert Coy	2,000	1,000	600.00
(6)	Rube Gardner	2,000	1,000	600.00
(7)	Howard Gregory	2,000	1,000	600.00
(8)	Gus Hetling	2,000	1,000	600.00
(9)	Jack Killilay	2,000	1,000	600.00
(10)	Bill Leard	2,000	1,000	600.00
(11)	John Malarkey	2,000	1,000	600.00
(12)	Carl Mitze	2,000	1,000	600.00
(13)	John Ness	2,000	1,000	600.00
(14)	Henry Olmstead	2,000	1,000	600.00
(15)	Cy Parkin	2,000	1,000	600.00
(16)	W.J. Pearce	2,000	1,000	600.00
(17)	Heine Pernoll	2,000	1,000	600.00
(18)	Ashley Pope	2,000	1,000	600.00
(19)	George Schirm	2,000	1,000	600.00
(20)	Elmer Zacher	2,000	1,000	600.00

1909 Obak (T212)

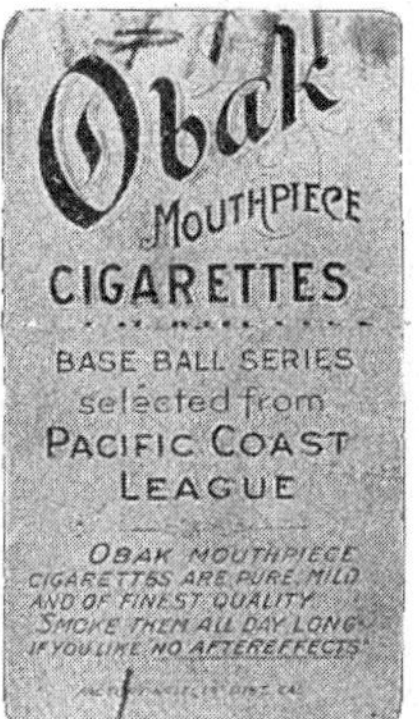

Produced annually from 1909 to 1911, the Obak cards were actually three separate and distinct sets, but they were all grouped together under a single T212 designation in the American Card Catalog. The Obak sets are closely related in style to the more popular T206 "White Border" set issued over the same three-year period, and, in fact, were produced by the California branch of the same American Tobacco Co. conglomerate. The Obaks are the standard tobacco card size, about 1-1/2" x 2-5/8", and feature a colored lithograph, along with the player's name and team, on the front of the card. The year of issue can easily be determined by examing the back. The 1909 issue has blue printing with the name "Obak" appearing in an "Old English" type style. For 1910 the type face was changed to straight block letters; and in 1911 the backs were printed in red and include a brief biography and player statistics. The 1909 edition featured only teams from the Pacific Coast League. Cards can be found with backs that have or do not have a border around the text, though neither version appears to be scarcer than the other. Many 1909 Obaks with the "no-frame" back design show evidence of having been cut by hand from sheets, rather than machine-cut.

		NM	EX	VG
Complete Set (76):		45,000	27,500	11,000
Common Player:		600.00	300.00	140.00
(1)	Baum	600.00	300.00	140.00
(2)	Beall	600.00	300.00	140.00
(3)	Bernard	600.00	300.00	140.00
(4)	Berry	600.00	300.00	140.00
(5)	Bodie	600.00	300.00	140.00
(6)	Boyce	600.00	300.00	140.00
(7)	Brackenridge	600.00	300.00	140.00
(8)	N. Brashear	600.00	300.00	140.00
(9)	Breen	600.00	300.00	140.00
(10)	Brown	600.00	300.00	140.00
(11)	D. Brown	600.00	300.00	140.00
(12)	Browning	600.00	300.00	140.00
(13)	Byrnes	600.00	300.00	140.00
(14)	Cameron	600.00	300.00	140.00
(15)	Carroll	600.00	300.00	140.00
(16)	Carson	600.00	300.00	140.00
(17)	Christian	600.00	300.00	140.00
(18)	Coy	600.00	300.00	140.00
(19)	Delmas	600.00	300.00	140.00
(20)	Dillon	600.00	300.00	140.00
(21)	Eagan	600.00	300.00	140.00
(22)	Easterly (Eastley)	600.00	300.00	140.00
(23)	Ehman	600.00	300.00	140.00
(24)	Fisher	600.00	300.00	140.00
(25)	Fitzgerald	600.00	300.00	140.00
(26)	Flannagan	600.00	300.00	140.00
(27)	Gandil	4,000	2,000	1,500
(28)	Garrett	600.00	300.00	140.00
(29)	Graham	600.00	300.00	140.00
(30)	Graney	600.00	300.00	140.00
(31)	Griffin	600.00	300.00	140.00
(32)	Guyn	600.00	300.00	140.00
(33)	Haley	600.00	300.00	140.00
(34)	Harkins	600.00	300.00	140.00
(35)	Henley	600.00	300.00	140.00
(36)	Hitt	600.00	300.00	140.00
(37)	Hogan	600.00	300.00	140.00
(38)	W. Hogan	600.00	300.00	140.00
(39)	Howard	600.00	300.00	140.00
(40)	Howse	600.00	300.00	140.00
(41)	Jansing	600.00	300.00	140.00
(42)	LaLonge	600.00	300.00	140.00
(43)	C. Lewis	600.00	300.00	140.00
(44)	D. Lewis	600.00	300.00	140.00
(45)	J. Lewis	600.00	300.00	140.00
(46)	Martinke	600.00	300.00	140.00
(47)	McArdle	600.00	300.00	140.00
(48)	McCredie	600.00	300.00	140.00
(49)	McKune	600.00	300.00	140.00
(50)	Melchior	600.00	300.00	140.00
(51)	Mohler	600.00	300.00	140.00
(52)	Mott	600.00	300.00	140.00
(53)	Mundorff	600.00	300.00	140.00
(54)	Murphy	600.00	300.00	140.00
(55)	Nagle	600.00	300.00	140.00
(56)	Nelson	600.00	300.00	140.00
(57)	Olson	600.00	300.00	140.00
(58)	Ornsdorff	600.00	300.00	140.00
(59)	Ort	600.00	300.00	140.00
(60)	Ragan	600.00	300.00	140.00
(61)	Raymer	600.00	300.00	140.00
(62)	Reidy	600.00	300.00	140.00
(63)	Ryan	600.00	300.00	140.00
(64)	Shinn	600.00	300.00	140.00
(65)	Smith	600.00	300.00	140.00
(66)	Speas	600.00	300.00	140.00
(67)	Stoval (Stovall)	600.00	300.00	140.00
(68)	Tennant	600.00	300.00	140.00
(69)	Whalen	600.00	300.00	140.00
(70)	Wheeler	600.00	300.00	140.00
(71)	Wiggs	600.00	300.00	140.00
(72)	Willett	600.00	300.00	140.00
(73)	J. Williams	600.00	300.00	140.00
(74)	R. Williams	600.00	300.00	140.00
(75)	Willis	600.00	300.00	140.00
(76)	Zeider	600.00	300.00	140.00

1910 Obak 150 Subjects (T212)

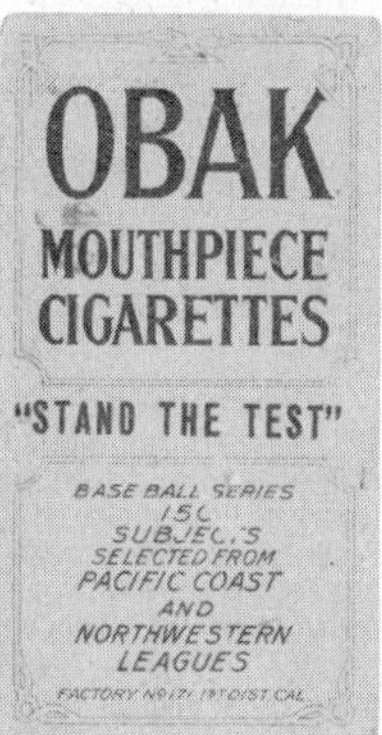

The most common, yet most complex, of the three annual T212 baseball card issues from Obak Cigarettes is the 1910 edition. Besides players from the six Pacific Coast League teams, cards were also issued for the four-team Northwestern League. This change caused the addition of a league abbreviation, along with the player's last name and city on front. Backs are again printed in blue, but utilize a less ornate typography than the 1909 cards. The 1910 Obak set is formatted similar to the more popular T206 "White Border" set issued at the same time "back East," and, in fact, was produced by the California branch of the same American Tobacco Company conglomerate. Obaks are the standard tobacco-card size, about

1-1/2" x 2-5/8", featuring a color lithograph on front. The 1910 issue comprises two major types, one which mentions "150 SUBJECTS," on back, the other specifying "175 SUBJECTS." Forty player cards, all from the PCL, are known to exist in both 150- and 175-subject versions, the former being much scarcer. Many of the 150-subject cards can be found with significant picture variations, such as missing team names on jerseys, plain versus striped caps, different background colors or different picture cropping. Unique to the 1910 Obaks is a selection of 35 different advertising slogans which are found on back between the boxed text elements. How many of the slogans can be found on each player's cards is unknown; some are seen on only a handful of different players' cards while others are found on dozens.

		NM	EX	VG
Complete Set (40):		30,000	16,000	7,000
Common Player:		750.00	400.00	175.00
(1)	Charlie Armbuster (Ambruster)	750.00	400.00	175.00
(2)	Claude Berry	750.00	400.00	175.00
(3)	John Brackenridge	750.00	400.00	175.00
(4)	N. Brashear (Norman)	750.00	400.00	175.00
(5)	Hap Briggs	750.00	400.00	175.00
(6)	Don Cameron	750.00	400.00	175.00
(7)	Bert Coy	750.00	400.00	175.00
(8)	Elmer Criger	750.00	400.00	175.00
(9)	Babe Danzig	750.00	400.00	175.00
(10)	Cap Dillon	750.00	400.00	175.00
(11)	Bill Fisher	750.00	400.00	175.00
(12)	Ed Griffin	750.00	400.00	175.00
(13)	Cack Henley	750.00	400.00	175.00
(14)	Al Hiester	750.00	400.00	175.00
(15)	Happy Hogan	750.00	400.00	175.00
(16)	Ivan Howard	750.00	400.00	175.00
(17)	Gene Krapp	750.00	400.00	175.00
(18)	Mickey LaLonge	750.00	400.00	175.00
(19)	George Manush	750.00	400.00	175.00
(20)	Roy McArdle	750.00	400.00	175.00
(21)	Walt McCredie	750.00	400.00	175.00
(22)	Henry Melchoir	750.00	400.00	175.00
(23)	Kid Mohler	750.00	400.00	175.00
(24)	Walter Moser	750.00	400.00	175.00
(25)	Howard Mundorf	750.00	400.00	175.00
(26)	Howard Murphy	750.00	400.00	175.00
(27)	George Ort	750.00	400.00	175.00
(28)	Hank Perry	750.00	400.00	175.00
(29)	Bill Rapps	750.00	400.00	175.00
(30)	H. Smith (Hugh)	750.00	400.00	175.00
(31)	J. Smith (Jud)	750.00	400.00	175.00
(32)	Bill Steen	750.00	400.00	175.00
(33)	Harry Stewart	750.00	400.00	175.00
(34)	Pinky Swander	750.00	400.00	175.00
(35)	Lefty Tonnesen (Tonneson)	750.00	400.00	175.00
(36)	Jimmy Whalen	750.00	400.00	175.00
(37)	Roy Willett	750.00	400.00	175.00
(38)	Jimmy Williams	750.00	400.00	175.00
(39)	Ralph Willis	750.00	400.00	175.00
(40)	Harry Wolverton	750.00	400.00	175.00

1910 Obak 175 Subjects (T212)

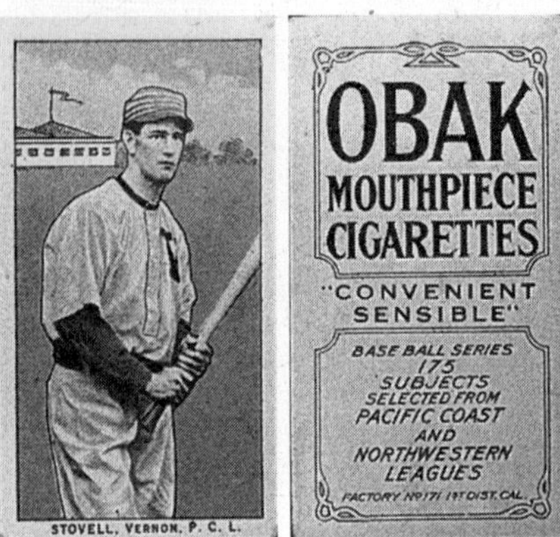

The most common, yet most complex, of the three annual T212 baseball card issues from Obak Cigarettes is the 1910 edition. Besides players from the six Pacific Coast League teams, cards were also issued for the four-team Northwestern League. This change caused the addition of a league abbreviation, along with the player's last name and city on front. Backs are again printed in blue, but utilize a less ornate typography than the 1909 cards. The 1910 Obak set is formatted similar to the more popular T206 "White Border" set issued at the same time "back East," and, in fact, was produced by the California branch of the same American Tobacco Co. conglomerate. Obaks are the standard tobacco-card size, about 1-1/2" x 2-5/8", featuring a color lithograph on front. The 1910 issue comprises two major types, one which mentions "150 SUBJECTS," on back, the other specifying "175 SUBJECTS." Forty player cards, all from the PCL, are known to exist in both 150- and 175-subject versions, the former being much scarcer. Many of the 150-subject cards can be found with significant picture variations, such as missing team names on jerseys, plain versus striped caps, different background colors or different picture cropping. Unique to the 1910 Obaks is a selection of 35 different advertising slogans which are found on back between the boxed text elements. How many of the slogans can be found on each player's cards is unknown; some are seen on only a handful of different players' cards while others are found on dozens.

		NM	EX	VG
Complete Set (175):		40,000	22,500	10,000
Common Player:		300.00	150.00	75.00
(1)	Agnew	300.00	150.00	75.00
(2)	Akin	300.00	150.00	75.00
(3)	Ames	300.00	150.00	75.00
(4)	Annis	300.00	150.00	75.00
(5)	Armbuster (Armbruster)	300.00	150.00	75.00
(6)	Baker	300.00	150.00	75.00
(7)	Bassey	300.00	150.00	75.00
(8)	Baum	300.00	150.00	75.00
	Beall (Now believed not to exist.)			
(9)	Bennett	300.00	150.00	75.00
(10)	Bernard	300.00	150.00	75.00
(11)	Berry	300.00	150.00	75.00
(12)	Blankenship	300.00	150.00	75.00
(13)	Boardman	300.00	150.00	75.00
(14)	Bodie	300.00	150.00	75.00
(15)	Bonner	300.00	150.00	75.00
(16)	Brackenridge	300.00	150.00	75.00
(17)	N. Brashear	300.00	150.00	75.00
(18)	R. Brashear	300.00	150.00	75.00
(19)	Breen	300.00	150.00	75.00
(20)	Briggs	300.00	150.00	75.00
(21)	Brinker	300.00	150.00	75.00
(22)	Briswalter	300.00	150.00	75.00
(23)	Brooks	300.00	150.00	75.00
(24)	Brown (Sacramento)	300.00	150.00	75.00
(25)	Brown (Vernon)	300.00	150.00	75.00
(26)	D. Brown	300.00	150.00	75.00
(27)	Browning	300.00	150.00	75.00
(28)	Burrell	300.00	150.00	75.00
(29)	Byrd	300.00	150.00	75.00
(30)	Byrnes	300.00	150.00	75.00
(31)	Cameron	300.00	150.00	75.00
(32)	Capron	300.00	150.00	75.00
(33)	Carlisle	300.00	150.00	75.00
(34)	Carroll	300.00	150.00	75.00
(35)	Cartwright	300.00	150.00	75.00
(36)	Casey	300.00	150.00	75.00
(37)	Caslleton (Castleton)	400.00	200.00	100.00
(38)	Chenault	300.00	150.00	75.00
(39)	Christian	300.00	150.00	75.00
(40)	Coleman	300.00	150.00	75.00
(41)	Cooney	300.00	150.00	75.00
(42)	Coy	300.00	150.00	75.00
(43)	Criger	300.00	150.00	75.00
(44)	Custer	300.00	150.00	75.00
(45)	Cutshaw	300.00	150.00	75.00
(46)	Daley	300.00	150.00	75.00
(47)	Danzig	300.00	150.00	75.00
(48)	Daringer	300.00	150.00	75.00
(49)	Davis	300.00	150.00	75.00
(50)	Delhi	300.00	150.00	75.00
(51)	Delmas	300.00	150.00	75.00
(52)	Dillon	300.00	150.00	75.00
(53)	Dretchko	300.00	150.00	75.00
(54)	Eastley	300.00	150.00	75.00
(55)	Erickson	300.00	150.00	75.00
(56)	Flannagan	300.00	150.00	75.00
(57)	Fisher (Portland)	300.00	150.00	75.00
(58)	Fisher (Vernon)	300.00	150.00	75.00
(59)	Fitzgerald	300.00	150.00	75.00
(60)	Flood	300.00	150.00	75.00
(61)	Fournier	300.00	150.00	75.00
(62)	Frisk	300.00	150.00	75.00
(63)	Gaddy	300.00	150.00	75.00
(64)	Gardner	300.00	150.00	75.00
(65)	Garrett	300.00	150.00	75.00
(66)	Greggs (Gregg)	300.00	150.00	75.00
(67)	Griffin	300.00	150.00	75.00
(68)	Gurney	300.00	150.00	75.00
(69)	Hall (Seattle)	300.00	150.00	75.00
(70)	Hall (Tacoma)	300.00	150.00	75.00
(71)	Harkins	300.00	150.00	75.00
(72)	Hartman	300.00	150.00	75.00
(73)	Hendrix	300.00	150.00	75.00
(74)	Henley	300.00	150.00	75.00
(75)	Hensling	300.00	150.00	75.00
(76)	Hetling	300.00	150.00	75.00
(77)	Hickey	300.00	150.00	75.00
(78)	Hiester	300.00	150.00	75.00
(79)	Hitt	300.00	150.00	75.00
(80)	Hogan (Oakland)	300.00	150.00	75.00
(81)	Hogan (Vernon)	300.00	150.00	75.00
(82)	Hollis	300.00	150.00	75.00
(83)	Holm	300.00	150.00	75.00
(84)	Howard	300.00	150.00	75.00
(85)	Hunt	300.00	150.00	75.00
(86)	James	300.00	150.00	75.00
(87)	Jansing	300.00	150.00	75.00
(88)	Jensen	300.00	150.00	75.00
(89)	Johnston	300.00	150.00	75.00
(90)	Keener	300.00	150.00	75.00
(91)	Killilay	300.00	150.00	75.00
(92)	Kippert	300.00	150.00	75.00
(93)	Klein	300.00	150.00	75.00
(94)	Krapp	300.00	150.00	75.00
(95)	Kusel	300.00	150.00	75.00
(96)	LaLonge	300.00	150.00	75.00
(97)	Lewis	300.00	150.00	75.00
(98)	J. Lewis	300.00	150.00	75.00
(99)	John Lindsay	300.00	150.00	75.00
(100)	Lively	300.00	150.00	75.00
(101)	Lynch	300.00	150.00	75.00
(102)	Manush	300.00	150.00	75.00
(103)	Martinke	300.00	150.00	75.00
(104)	McArdle	300.00	150.00	75.00
(105)	McCredie	300.00	150.00	75.00
(106)	Melchior	300.00	150.00	75.00
(107)	Miller (San Francisco)	300.00	150.00	75.00
(108)	Miller (Seattle)	300.00	150.00	75.00
(109)	Mitze	300.00	150.00	75.00
(110)	Mohler	300.00	150.00	75.00
(111)	Moser	300.00	150.00	75.00
(112)	Mott	300.00	150.00	75.00
(113)	Mundorff (Mundorf)	300.00	150.00	75.00
(114)	Murphy	300.00	150.00	75.00
(115)	Nagle	300.00	150.00	75.00
(116)	Nelson	300.00	150.00	75.00
(117)	Netzel	300.00	150.00	75.00
(118)	Nourse	300.00	150.00	75.00
(119)	Nordyke	300.00	150.00	75.00
(120)	Olson	300.00	150.00	75.00
(121)	Orendorff (Orsnsdorff)	300.00	150.00	75.00
(122)	Ort	300.00	150.00	75.00
(123)	Ostdiek	300.00	150.00	75.00
(124)	Pennington	300.00	150.00	75.00
(125)	Perrine	300.00	150.00	75.00
(126)	Perry	300.00	150.00	75.00
(127)	Persons	300.00	150.00	75.00
(128)	Rapps	300.00	150.00	75.00
(129)	Raymer	300.00	150.00	75.00
(130)	Raymond	300.00	150.00	75.00
(131)	Rockenfield	300.00	150.00	75.00
(132)	Roth	300.00	150.00	75.00
(133)	D. Ryan	300.00	150.00	75.00
(134)	J. Ryan	300.00	150.00	75.00
(135)	Scharnweber	300.00	150.00	75.00
(136)	Schmutz	300.00	150.00	75.00
(137)	Seaton (Portland)	300.00	150.00	75.00
(138)	Seaton (Seattle)	300.00	150.00	75.00
(139)	Shafer	300.00	150.00	75.00
(140)	Shaw	300.00	150.00	75.00
(141)	Shea	300.00	150.00	75.00
(142)	Shinn	300.00	150.00	75.00
(143)	Smith	300.00	150.00	75.00
(144)	H. Smith	300.00	150.00	75.00
(145)	J. Smith	300.00	150.00	75.00
(146)	Speas	300.00	150.00	75.00
(147)	Spiesman	300.00	150.00	75.00
(148)	Starkell	300.00	150.00	75.00
(149)	Steen	300.00	150.00	75.00
(150)	Stevens	300.00	150.00	75.00
(151)	Stewart	300.00	150.00	75.00
(152)	Stovell (Stovall)	300.00	150.00	75.00
(153)	Streib	300.00	150.00	75.00
(154)	Sugden	300.00	150.00	75.00
(155)	Sutor	300.00	150.00	75.00
(156)	Swain	300.00	150.00	75.00
(157)	Swander	300.00	150.00	75.00
(158)	Tennant	300.00	150.00	75.00
(159)	Thomas	300.00	150.00	75.00
(160)	Thompson	300.00	150.00	75.00
(161)	Thorsen	300.00	150.00	75.00
(162)	Tonnesen (Tonneson)	300.00	150.00	75.00
(163)	Tozer	300.00	150.00	75.00
(164)	Van Buren	300.00	150.00	75.00
(165)	Vitt	300.00	150.00	75.00
(166)	Wares	300.00	150.00	75.00
(167)	Waring	300.00	150.00	75.00
(168)	Warren	300.00	150.00	75.00
(169)	Weed	300.00	150.00	75.00
(170)	Whalen	300.00	150.00	75.00
(171)	Willett	300.00	150.00	75.00
(172)	Williams	300.00	150.00	75.00
(173)	Willis	300.00	150.00	75.00
(174)	Wolverton	300.00	150.00	75.00
(175)	Zackert	300.00	150.00	75.00

1911 Obak (T212)

The last of the three annual T212 baseball card issues from Obak Cigarettes is the 1911 edition, again featuring players from the six Pacific Coast League teams and the four-team Northwestern League. Often using the same chromolithographic picture on front as the 1910 cards, the 1911s are easily distinguished by the use of red, rather than blue, printing on back. Also new to the 1911s was the addition of a sentence or two about the player and, on most cards, recent years' statistics, an innovation also seen on the contemporary T205 cards "back East." In fact the Obaks were produced by the California branch of the same American Tobacco Company conglomerate. Obaks are the standard tobacco card size, about 1-1/2" x 2-5/8".

		NM	EX	VG
Complete Set (175):		60,000	30,000	12,000
Common Player:		350.00	175.00	85.00
(1)	Abbott	350.00	175.00	85.00
(2)	Ables	350.00	175.00	85.00
(3)	Adams	350.00	175.00	85.00

(4)	Agnew	350.00	175.00	85.00
(5)	Akin	350.00	175.00	85.00
(6)	Annis	350.00	175.00	85.00
(7)	Arrelanes (Arellanes)	350.00	175.00	85.00
(8)	Barry	350.00	175.00	85.00
(9)	Bassey	350.00	175.00	85.00
(10)	Baum	350.00	175.00	85.00
(11)	Bennett	350.00	175.00	85.00
(12)	Bernard	350.00	175.00	85.00
(13)	Berry	350.00	175.00	85.00
(14)	Bloomfield	350.00	175.00	85.00
(15)	Bonner	350.00	175.00	85.00
(16)	Brackenridge	350.00	175.00	85.00
(17)	Brashear	350.00	175.00	85.00
(18)	R. Brashear	350.00	175.00	85.00
(19)	Brinker	350.00	175.00	85.00
(20)	Brown	350.00	175.00	85.00
(21)	Browning	350.00	175.00	85.00
(22)	Bues	350.00	175.00	85.00
(23)	Burrell	350.00	175.00	85.00
(24)	Burns	350.00	175.00	85.00
(25)	Butler	350.00	175.00	85.00
(26)	Byram	350.00	175.00	85.00
(27)	Carlisle	350.00	175.00	85.00
(28)	Carson	350.00	175.00	85.00
(29)	Cartwright	350.00	175.00	85.00
(30)	Casey	350.00	175.00	85.00
(31)	Castleton	500.00	250.00	175.00
(32)	Chadbourne	350.00	175.00	85.00
(33)	Christian	350.00	175.00	85.00
(34)	Coleman	350.00	175.00	85.00
(35)	Cooney	350.00	175.00	85.00
(36)	Coy	350.00	175.00	85.00
(37)	Criger	350.00	175.00	85.00
(38)	Crukshank	350.00	175.00	85.00
(39)	Cutshaw	350.00	175.00	85.00
(40)	Daley	350.00	175.00	85.00
(41)	Danzig	350.00	175.00	85.00
(42)	Dashwood	350.00	175.00	85.00
(43)	Davis	350.00	175.00	85.00
(44)	Delhi	350.00	175.00	85.00
(45)	Delmas	350.00	175.00	85.00
(46)	Dillon	350.00	175.00	85.00
(47)	Engel	350.00	175.00	85.00
(48)	Erickson	350.00	175.00	85.00
(49)	Fitzgerald	350.00	175.00	85.00
(50)	Flater	350.00	175.00	85.00
(51)	Frisk	350.00	175.00	85.00
(52)	Fullerton	350.00	175.00	85.00
(53)	Garrett	350.00	175.00	85.00
(54)	Goodman	350.00	175.00	85.00
(55)	Gordon	350.00	175.00	85.00
(56)	Grindle	350.00	175.00	85.00
(57)	Hall	350.00	175.00	85.00
(58)	Harris	350.00	175.00	85.00
(59)	Hasty	350.00	175.00	85.00
(60)	Henderson	350.00	175.00	85.00
(61)	Henley	350.00	175.00	85.00
(62)	Hetling	350.00	175.00	85.00
(63)	Hiester	350.00	175.00	85.00
(64)	Higgins	350.00	175.00	85.00
(65)	Hitt	350.00	175.00	85.00
(66)	Hoffman	350.00	175.00	85.00
(67)	Hogan	350.00	175.00	85.00
(68)	Holm	350.00	175.00	85.00
(69)	Householder	350.00	175.00	85.00
(70)	Hosp	350.00	175.00	85.00
(71)	Howard	350.00	175.00	85.00
(72)	Hunt	350.00	175.00	85.00
(73)	James	350.00	175.00	85.00
(74)	Jensen	350.00	175.00	85.00
(75)	Kading	350.00	175.00	85.00
(76)	Kane	350.00	175.00	85.00
(77)	Kippert	350.00	175.00	85.00
(78)	Knight	350.00	175.00	85.00
(79)	Koestner	350.00	175.00	85.00
(80)	Krueger	350.00	175.00	85.00
(81)	Kuhn	350.00	175.00	85.00
(82)	LaLonge	350.00	175.00	85.00
(83)	Lamline	350.00	175.00	85.00
(84)	Leard	350.00	175.00	85.00
(85)	Lerchen	350.00	175.00	85.00
(86)	Lewis	350.00	175.00	85.00
(87)	Madden	350.00	175.00	85.00
(88)	Maggert	350.00	175.00	85.00
(89)	Mahoney	350.00	175.00	85.00
(90)	McArdle	350.00	175.00	85.00
(91)	McCredie	350.00	175.00	85.00
(92)	McDonnell	350.00	175.00	85.00
(93)	Meikle	350.00	175.00	85.00
(94)	Melchior	350.00	175.00	85.00
(95)	Mensor	650.00	310.00	210.00
(96)	Metzger	350.00	175.00	85.00
(97)	Miller (Oakland)	350.00	175.00	85.00
(98)	Miller (San Francisco)	350.00	175.00	85.00
(99)	Ten Million	3,000	1,500	750.00
(100)	Mitze	350.00	175.00	85.00
(101)	Mohler	350.00	175.00	85.00
(102)	Moore	350.00	175.00	85.00
(103)	Morse	350.00	175.00	85.00
(104)	Moskiman	350.00	175.00	85.00
(105)	Mundorff	350.00	175.00	85.00
(106)	Murray	350.00	175.00	85.00
(107)	Netzel	350.00	175.00	85.00
(108)	Nordyke	350.00	175.00	85.00
(109)	Nourse	350.00	175.00	85.00
(110)	O'Rourke	350.00	175.00	85.00
(111)	Ostdiek	350.00	175.00	85.00
(112)	Patterson	350.00	175.00	85.00
(113)	Pearce	350.00	175.00	85.00
(114)	Peckinpaugh	350.00	175.00	85.00
(115)	Pernoll	350.00	175.00	85.00
(116)	Pfyl	350.00	175.00	85.00
(117)	Powell	350.00	175.00	85.00
(118)	Raleigh	350.00	175.00	85.00
(119)	Rapps	350.00	175.00	85.00
(120)	Raymer	350.00	175.00	85.00
(121)	Raymond	350.00	175.00	85.00
(122)	Reddick	350.00	175.00	85.00
(123)	Roche	350.00	175.00	85.00
(124)	Rockenfield	350.00	175.00	85.00
(125)	Rogers	350.00	175.00	85.00
(126)	Ross	350.00	175.00	85.00
(127)	Ryan	350.00	175.00	85.00
(128)	J. Ryan	350.00	175.00	85.00
(129)	Scharnweber	350.00	175.00	85.00
(130)	Schmidt	350.00	175.00	85.00
(131)	Schmutz	350.00	175.00	85.00
(132)	Seaton (Portland)	350.00	175.00	85.00
(133)	Seaton (Seattle)	350.00	175.00	85.00
(134)	Shaw	350.00	175.00	85.00
(135)	Shea	350.00	175.00	85.00
(136)	Sheehan (Portland)	350.00	175.00	85.00
(137)	Sheehan (Vernon)	350.00	175.00	85.00
(138)	Shinn	350.00	175.00	85.00
(139)	Skeels	350.00	175.00	85.00
(140)	H. Smith	350.00	175.00	85.00
(141)	Speas	350.00	175.00	85.00
(142)	Spencer	350.00	175.00	85.00
(143)	Spiesman	350.00	175.00	85.00
(144)	Starkel	350.00	175.00	85.00
(145)	Steen	350.00	175.00	85.00
(146)	Stewart	350.00	175.00	85.00
(147)	Stinson	350.00	175.00	85.00
(148)	Stovall	350.00	175.00	85.00
(149)	Strand	350.00	175.00	85.00
(150)	Sutor	350.00	175.00	85.00
(151)	Swain	350.00	175.00	85.00
(152)	Tennant	350.00	175.00	85.00
(153)	Thomas (Sacramento)	350.00	175.00	85.00
(154)	Thomas (Victoria)	350.00	175.00	85.00
(155)	Thompson	350.00	175.00	85.00
(156)	Thornton	350.00	175.00	85.00
(157)	Thorsen	350.00	175.00	85.00
(158)	Tiedeman	350.00	175.00	85.00
(159)	Tozer	350.00	175.00	85.00
(160)	Van Buren	350.00	175.00	85.00
(161)	Vitt	350.00	175.00	85.00
(162)	Ward	350.00	175.00	85.00
(163)	Wares	350.00	175.00	85.00
(164)	Warren	350.00	175.00	85.00
(165)	Weaver	7,000	3,500	1,750
(166)	Weed	350.00	175.00	85.00
(167)	Wheeler	350.00	175.00	85.00
(168)	Wiggs	350.00	175.00	85.00
(169)	Willett	350.00	175.00	85.00
(170)	Williams	350.00	175.00	85.00
(171)	Wolverton	350.00	175.00	85.00
(172)	Zacher	350.00	175.00	85.00
(173)	Zackert	350.00	175.00	85.00
(174)	Zamlock	350.00	175.00	85.00
(175)	Zimmerman	350.00	175.00	85.00

1911 Obak Cabinets (T4)

Among the scarcest of all the 20th Century tobacco issues, the T4 Obak Premiums are cabinet-sized cards distributed in conjunction with the better-known Obak T212 card set of players from the Northwestern and Pacific Coast Leagues. The Obak Premiums measure about 5" x 7" and are printed on a cardboard-like paper. The cards featured a black-and-white player photo inside a 3-1/2" x 5" oval. There is no printing on the front of the card to identify the player or indicate the manufacturer. The backs are blank. In most cases the photos used for the premiums are identical to the T212 pictures, except for some cropping differences. Under the Obak mail-in promotion, 50 coupons from cigarette packages were required to obtain just one premium card, which explains their extreme scarcity today. All 175 players pictured in the T212 set were theoretically available as premium cards, but to date many remain undiscovered. Only those cards that have been confirmed to survive are listed with a value here. Most of the Obak premiums that exist in original condition contain a number, written in pencil on the back of the card, that corresponds to the checklist printed on the coupon. A large group of the cabinets, most of which had been cut down to just the oval portrait, was offered in a September 2002 auction.

		NM	EX	VG
	Common Player:	6,750	3,500	2,200
	LOS ANGELES			
1	H. Smith	5,750	2,875	1,725
2	Tozer	5,750	2,875	1,725
3	Howard	5,750	2,875	1,725
4	Daley	5,750	2,875	1,725
5	Bernard			
6	Dillon	5,750	2,875	1,725
7	Delmas			
8	Delhi	5,750	2,875	1,725
9	Criger			
10	Thorsen	5,750	2,875	1,725
11	Agnew			
12	Akin			
13	Metzger			
14	Abbott			
15	Wheeler	5,750	2,875	1,725
16	Moore			
17	Grindle			
	OAKLAND			
18	Wolverton			
19	Mitze	5,750	2,875	1,725
20	Wares			
21	Cutshaw	5,750	2,875	1,725
22	Christian	5,750	2,875	1,725
23	Wiggs			
24	Maggert	5,750	2,875	1,725
25	Pfyl			
26	Pearce			
27	Hetling			
28	Hoffman			
29	Pernoll			
30	Coy			
31	Tiedeman	5,750	2,875	1,725
32	Knight			
33	Flater	5,750	2,875	1,725
34	Zacher	5,750	2,875	1,725
35	Ables	5,750	2,875	1,725
36	Miller			
	PORTLAND (PCL)			
37	Ryan	5,750	2,875	1,725
38	Rapps	5,750	2,875	1,725
39	McCredie			
40	Seaton			
41	Steen			
42	Chadbourne	5,750	2,875	1,725
43	Krueger			
44	Sheehan			
45	Roger Peckinpaugh	5,750	2,875	1,725
46	Bill Rodgers	5,750	2,875	1,725
47	Murray			
48	Fullerton			
49	Kuhn	5,750	2,875	1,725
50	Koestner			
51	Henderson			
52	Barry			
	SACRAMENTO			
53	LaLonge			
54	Heister			
55	Hunt			
56	Van Buren			
57	Fitzgerald	5,750	2,875	1,725
58	Danzig	5,750	2,875	1,725
59	Baum	5,750	2,875	1,725
60	Shinn	5,750	2,875	1,725
61	Nourse			
62	O'Rourke			
63	Lerchen			
64	Thornton			
65	Thomas	5,750	2,875	1,725
66	Thompson			
67	Byram			
68	Frank Arrelanes (Arellanes)			
69	Mahoney			
	SAN FRANCISCO			
70	McArdle			
71	Melchior	5,750	2,875	1,725
72	Vitt	5,750	2,875	1,725
73	Henley			
74	Berry	5,750	2,875	1,725
75	Miller	5,750	2,875	1,725
76	Tennant	5,750	2,875	1,725
77	Mohler	5,750	2,875	1,725
78	Shaw			
79	Sutor	5,750	2,875	1,725
80	Browning	5,750	2,875	1,725
81	Ryan	5,750	2,875	1,725
82	Powell	5,750	2,875	1,725
83	Schmidt	5,750	2,875	1,725
84	Meikle	5,750	2,875	1,725
85	Madden	5,750	2,875	1,725
86	Buck Weaver (VG-EX example auctioned in 2005 for $26,435.)			
87	Moskiman	5,750	2,875	1,725
88	Zamlock	5,750	2,875	1,725
	VERNON			
89	Brown			
90	Hogan			
91	Brashear			
92	Carlisle	5,750	2,875	1,725
93	Burrell	5,750	2,875	1,725
94	Brackenridge	5,750	2,875	1,725
95	Hitt			
96	Willett	5,750	2,875	1,725
97	Stewart	5,750	2,875	1,725
98	Carson	5,750	2,875	1,725
99	Raleigh	5,750	2,875	1,725
100	Ham Patterson	5,750	2,875	1,725
101	Hosp			
102	Sheehan			
103	Castleton			
104	Ross			
105	Stinson	5,750	2,875	1,725
106	McDonnell	5,750	2,875	1,725
107	Kane	5,750	2,875	1,725
	PORTLAND (NWL)			
108	Harris			
109	Garrett			
110	Stovall			
111	Mundorff	5,750	2,875	1,725
112	Lamline			
113	Bloomfield			
114	Williams			
115	Mensor			
116	Casey			
117	Speas			
	SPOKANE			
118	Netzel			

119	Strand			
120	Hasty			
121	Zimmerman			
122	Cooney			
123	Frisk			
124	Nordyke			
125	Kippert			
126	Bonner			
127	Ostdiek			
128	Cartwright			
129	Holm			
	TACOMA			
130	Higgins			
131	Warren			
132	Morse			
133	Burns			
134	Gordon			
135	Bassey			
136	Rockenfield			
137	Coleman			
138	Schmutz			
139	Hall			
140	Annis	5,750	2,875	1,725
	VANCOUVER			
141	Engel			
142	Brashear			
143	Adams			
144	Spiesman			
145	Brinker			
146	Bennett			
147	James			
148	Lewis			
149	Scharnweber			
150	Swain			
151	Jensen			
152	Erickson			
	VICTORIA			
153	Roche			
154	Davis			
155	Goodman			
156	Ward			
157	Reddick			
158	Householder	5,750	2,875	1,725
159	Dashwood	5,750	2,875	1,725
160	Starkel			
161	Thomas			
162	Ten Million			
163	Raymer			
	SEATTLE			
164	Bues			
165	Crukshank			
166	Kading			
167	Spencer	5,750	2,875	1,725
168	Leard			
169	Seaton			
170	Shea			
171	Butler			
172	Skeels			
173	Weed			
174	Raymond	5,750	2,875	1,725
175	Zackert			

1911 Obak Coupon

About 3" x 3", this coupon was found in each box of Obak cigarettes. Printed in green on white, the coupon has a list of the cabinet cards which could be obtained by redeeming 50 of the coupons.

	NM	EX	VG
Obak Coupon	100.00	50.00	30.00

1908 Offerman Buffalo Bisons Postcards

Virtually identical in format to the Major League player postcards issued by American League Publishing Co., Cleveland, these cards carry the imprint of F.J. Offerman and depict Bufalo Bisons players of the Eastern League. The 3-1/2" x 4-1/2" black-and-white cards have a large posed action photo on a white background with a vignetted oval portrait at top. Player information and stats are printed below. The back has typical postcard markings. It is unknown whether this checklist is complete.

		NM	EX	VG
Common Player:		600.00	300.00	180.00
(1)	James Archer	600.00	300.00	180.00
(2)	Larry Hesterfer	600.00	300.00	180.00
(3)	William H. Keister	600.00	300.00	180.00
(4)	Charles Kisinger	600.00	300.00	180.00
(5)	Lewis Knapp	600.00	300.00	180.00
(6)	George McConnell	600.00	300.00	180.00
(7)	William J. Milligan	600.00	300.00	180.00
(8)	William Nattress	600.00	300.00	180.00
(9)	John B. Ryan	600.00	300.00	180.00
(10)	George Schirm	600.00	300.00	180.00
(11)	George Smith	600.00	300.00	180.00
(12)	John White	600.00	300.00	180.00
(13)	Merton Whitney	600.00	300.00	180.00

1952 Ogden Reds Team Issue

These 2-1/4" x 3-3/8" black-and-white, unnumbered, blank-backed cards were one of many minor league team sets issued by Globe Printing of San Jose, Calif., in the early 1950s. Cards were usually given away at the ballpark on a one-per-week or one-per-homestand basis, accounting for the rarity of surviving sets. The O-Reds were a Class C Pioneer League farm club of the Cincinnati Reds.

		NM	EX	VG
Complete Set (18):		800.00	400.00	240.00
Common Player:		60.00	30.00	18.00
Album:		100.00	50.00	30.00
(1)	Ralph Birkofer	60.00	30.00	18.00
(2)	William A. Bowman	60.00	30.00	18.00
(3)	David Bristol	60.00	30.00	18.00
(4)	Vincent E. Capece	60.00	30.00	18.00
(5)	Gerald Davis	60.00	30.00	18.00
(6)	Ralph Dollinger	60.00	30.00	18.00
(7)	Robert E. Durnbaugh	60.00	30.00	18.00
(8)	Raymond Estes	60.00	30.00	18.00
(9)	Robert J. Flowers	60.00	30.00	18.00
(10)	Nunzio Izzo	60.00	30.00	18.00
(11)	Howard E. Leister	60.00	30.00	18.00
(12)	Steve Mesner	60.00	30.00	18.00
(13)	Dee C. Moore	60.00	30.00	18.00
(14)	Augie Navarro (Announcer)	60.00	30.00	18.00
(15)	John Omerza	60.00	30.00	18.00
(16)	James W. St. Claire	60.00	30.00	18.00
(17)	Grady N. Watts	60.00	30.00	18.00
(18)	Carl M. Wells	60.00	30.00	18.00

1955 Old Homestead Franks Des Moines Bruins

A very rare minor league issue, this set features players of the Class A Western League farm team of the Chicago Cubs. Many of the players were future major leaguers. Cards measure about 2-1/2" x 3-3/4" and have black-and-white portrait photos of the players with a facsimile autograph across the jersey. A black strip at the bottom of the card has the player and team name, and the position. Backs have an ad for the issuing hot dog company.

		NM	EX	VG
Complete Set (21):		5,000	2,500	1,500
Common Player:		250.00	125.00	75.00
(1)	Bob Andersoon	250.00	125.00	75.00
(2)	Ray Bellino	250.00	125.00	75.00
(3)	Don Biebel	250.00	125.00	75.00
(4)	Bobby Cooke	250.00	125.00	75.00
(5)	Dave Cunningham	250.00	125.00	75.00
(6)	Bert Flammini	250.00	125.00	75.00
(7)	Gene Fodge	250.00	125.00	75.00
(8)	Eddie Haas	250.00	125.00	75.00
(9)	Paul Hoffmeister	250.00	125.00	75.00
(10)	Pepper Martin	350.00	175.00	100.00
(11)	Jim McDaniel	250.00	125.00	75.00
(12)	Bob McKee	250.00	125.00	75.00
(13)	Paul Menking	250.00	125.00	75.00
(14)	Vern Morgan	250.00	125.00	75.00
(15)	Joe Pearson	250.00	125.00	75.00
(16)	John Pramesa	250.00	125.00	75.00
(17)	Joe Stanka	250.00	125.00	75.00
(18)	Jim Stoddard	250.00	125.00	75.00
(19)	Bob Thorpe	250.00	125.00	75.00
(20)	Burdy Thurlby	250.00	125.00	75.00
(21)	Don Watkins	250.00	125.00	75.00

1959 O'Keefe Ale Montreal Royals

This set of large (3" x 4") player stamps was issued in conjunction with an album as a promotion by O'Keefe Ale in Quebec. The pictures are black-and-white with player identification in the bottom border. Backs are blank and the edges are perforated. Many former Brooklyn Dodgers are included in the issue. The unnumbered stamps are listed here in alphabetical order.

		NM	EX	VG
Complete Set (24):		900.00	450.00	275.00
Common Player:		30.00	15.00	9.00
Album:		200.00	100.00	60.00
(1)	Edmundo Amoros	45.00	22.50	13.50
(2)	Bob Aspromonte	35.00	17.50	10.00
(3)	Batters Records	12.50	6.25	3.75
(4)	Babe Birrer	30.00	15.00	9.00
(5)	Clay Bryant	30.00	15.00	9.00
(6)	Mike Brumley	30.00	15.00	9.00
(7)	Yvon Dunn (Trainer)	20.00	10.00	6.00
(8)	Bill George	30.00	15.00	9.00
(9)	Mike Goliat	30.00	15.00	9.00
(10)	John Gray	30.00	15.00	9.00
(11)	Billy Harris	30.00	15.00	9.00
(12)	Jim Koranda	30.00	15.00	9.00
(13)	Paul LaPalme	30.00	15.00	9.00
(14)	Tom Lasorda	200.00	100.00	60.00
(15)	Bob Lennon	30.00	15.00	9.00
(16)	Clyde Parris	30.00	15.00	9.00
(17)	Pitchers Records	12.50	6.25	3.75
(18)	Ed Rakow	30.00	15.00	9.00
(19)	Curt Roberts	30.00	15.00	9.00
(20)	Freddy Rodriguez	30.00	15.00	9.00
(21)	Harry Schwegman	30.00	15.00	9.00
(22)	Angel Scull	30.00	15.00	9.00
(23)	Dick Teed	30.00	15.00	9.00
(24)	Rene Valdes (Valdez)	30.00	15.00	9.00

1910 Old Mill Cigarettes Series 1 (S. Atlantic League)

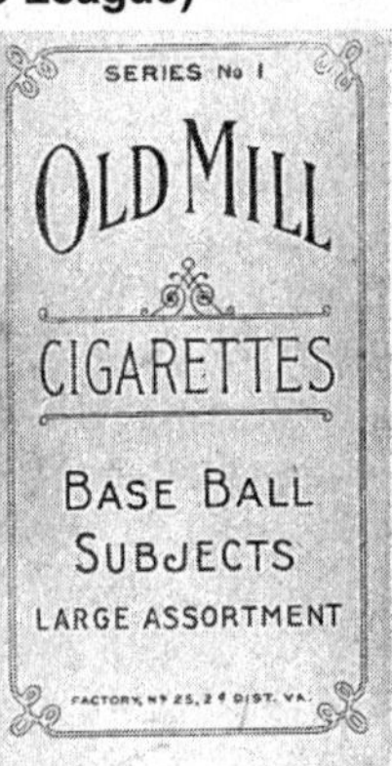

Because of their distinctive red borders, this 1910 minor league tobacco issue is often called the Red Border set by collectors. It's ACC designation is T210. A massive set, it consists of some 640 cards, each measuring 1-1/2" x 2-5/8". Fronts feature a glossy black-and-white photo, while the backs carry an ad for Old Mill Cigarettes. Each of the eight series is devoted to a different minor league. Series 1 features players from the South Atlantic League; Series 2 pictures players from the Virginia League; Series 3 is devoted to the Texas League; Series 4 features the Virginia Valley League; Series 5 pictures players from the Carolina Associations; Series 6 spotlights the Blue Grass League; Series 7 is devoted to the Eastern Carolina League; and Series 8 show players from the Southern Association. The various series are identified by a number along the top on the back of the cards. Collectors generally agree that Series 8 cards, which are often found irregularly sized due to hand-cutting from original sheets, are the scarcest of the series. The relative scarcity of the various series is reflected in the prices listed. Collectors should be aware that some Series 3 cards (Texas League) can be found with orange, rather than red, borders - apparently because not enough red ink was used during part of the print run.

	NM	EX	VG
Common Player:	350.00	150.00	90.00

(1)	Bagwell	350.00	150.00	90.00
(2)	Balenti	360.00	160.00	95.00
(3)	Becker	350.00	150.00	90.00
(4)	Bensen	350.00	150.00	90.00
(5)	Benton	360.00	160.00	95.00
(6)	Bierkortte	350.00	150.00	90.00
(7)	Bierman	350.00	150.00	90.00
(8)	Breitenstein	350.00	150.00	90.00
(9)	Bremmerhof	350.00	150.00	90.00
(10)	Carter	350.00	150.00	90.00
(11)	Cavender	350.00	150.00	90.00
(12)	Collins	350.00	150.00	90.00
(13)	DeFraites	350.00	150.00	90.00
(14)	Dudley	350.00	150.00	90.00
(15)	Dwyer	350.00	150.00	90.00
(16)	Edwards	350.00	150.00	90.00
(17)	Enbanks	360.00	160.00	95.00
(18)	Eubank	350.00	150.00	90.00
(19)	Fox	350.00	150.00	90.00
(20)	Hannifan	350.00	150.00	90.00
(21)	Hartley	350.00	150.00	90.00
(22)	Hauser	350.00	150.00	90.00
(23)	Hille	350.00	150.00	90.00
(24)	Howard	350.00	150.00	90.00
(25)	Hoyt	350.00	150.00	90.00
(26)	Huber	350.00	150.00	90.00
(27)	Ison	350.00	150.00	90.00
(28)	Jones	350.00	150.00	90.00
(29)	Kalkhoff	350.00	150.00	90.00
(30)	Krebs	350.00	150.00	90.00
(31)	Lawrence	350.00	150.00	90.00
(32)	Lee (Jacksonville)	350.00	150.00	90.00
(33)	Lee (Macon)	350.00	150.00	90.00
(34)	Lewis (Columbia)	350.00	150.00	90.00
(35)	Lewis (Columbus)	350.00	150.00	90.00
(36)	Lipe (Batting)	350.00	150.00	90.00
(37)	Lipe (Portrait)	350.00	150.00	90.00
(38)	Long	350.00	150.00	90.00
(39)	Magoon	350.00	150.00	90.00
(40)	Manion	350.00	150.00	90.00
(41)	Marshall	350.00	150.00	90.00
(42)	Martin	350.00	150.00	90.00
(43)	Martina	350.00	150.00	90.00
(44)	Massing	350.00	150.00	90.00
(45)	McLeod	350.00	150.00	90.00
(46)	McMahon	350.00	150.00	90.00
(47)	Morse	350.00	150.00	90.00
(48)	Mullane	350.00	150.00	90.00
(49)	Mulldowney	350.00	150.00	90.00
(50)	Murch	350.00	150.00	90.00
(51)	Norcum	350.00	150.00	90.00
(52)	Pelkey	350.00	150.00	90.00
(53)	Petit	350.00	150.00	90.00
(54)	Pierce	350.00	150.00	90.00
(55)	Pope	350.00	150.00	90.00
(56)	Radebaugh	360.00	160.00	95.00
(57)	Raynolds	350.00	150.00	90.00
(58)	Reagan	350.00	150.00	90.00
(59)	Redfern (Redfearn)	350.00	150.00	90.00
(60)	Reynolds	350.00	150.00	90.00
(61)	Schulz	360.00	160.00	95.00
(62)	Schulze	350.00	150.00	90.00
(63)	Schwietzka	350.00	150.00	90.00
(64)	Shields	360.00	160.00	95.00
(65)	Sisson	350.00	150.00	90.00
(66)	Smith	500.00	200.00	125.00
(67)	Sweeney	350.00	150.00	90.00
(68)	Taffee	350.00	150.00	90.00
(69)	Toren	350.00	150.00	90.00
(70)	Viola	350.00	150.00	90.00
(71)	Wagner	350.00	150.00	90.00
(72)	Wahl	350.00	150.00	90.00
(73)	Weems	350.00	150.00	90.00
(74)	Wells	350.00	150.00	90.00
(75)	Wohlleben	350.00	150.00	90.00

1910 Old Mill Cigarettes Series 2 (Virginia League)

		NM	EX	VG
Common Player:		275.00	135.00	80.00
(1)	Andrada	275.00	135.00	80.00
(2)	Archer	275.00	135.00	80.00
(3)	Baker	275.00	135.00	80.00
(4)	Beham	280.00	140.00	85.00
(5)	Bonner	275.00	135.00	80.00
(6)	Bowen	275.00	135.00	80.00
(7)	Brandon	275.00	135.00	80.00
(8)	Breivogel	275.00	135.00	80.00
(9)	Brooks	275.00	135.00	80.00
(10)	Brown	275.00	135.00	80.00
(11)	Busch	275.00	135.00	80.00
(12)	Bussey	275.00	135.00	80.00
(13)	Cefalu	275.00	135.00	80.00
(14)	Chandler	275.00	135.00	80.00
(15)	Clarke	280.00	140.00	85.00
(16)	Clunk	275.00	135.00	80.00
(17)	Cote	280.00	140.00	85.00
(18)	Cowan	275.00	135.00	80.00
(19)	Decker	275.00	135.00	80.00
(20)	Doyle	275.00	135.00	80.00
(21)	Eddowes	275.00	135.00	80.00
(22)	Fisher	275.00	135.00	80.00
(23)	Fox	275.00	135.00	80.00
(24)	Foxen	275.00	135.00	80.00
(25)	Gaston	275.00	135.00	80.00
(26)	Gehring	275.00	135.00	80.00
(27)	Griffin (Danville)	275.00	135.00	80.00
(28)	Griffin (Lynchburg)	275.00	135.00	80.00
(29)	Hale	275.00	135.00	80.00
(30)	Hamilton	275.00	135.00	80.00
(31)	Hanks	275.00	135.00	80.00
(32)	Hannafin	275.00	135.00	80.00
(33)	Hoffman	280.00	140.00	85.00
(34)	Holland	275.00	135.00	80.00
(35)	Hooker	275.00	135.00	80.00
(36)	Irving	275.00	135.00	80.00
(37)	Jackson (Lynchburg)	280.00	140.00	85.00
(38)	Jackson (Norfolk)	275.00	135.00	80.00
(39)	Jackson (Portsmouth)	275.00	135.00	80.00
(40)	Jackson (Richmond)	275.00	135.00	80.00
(41)	Jenkins	275.00	135.00	80.00
(42)	Keifel	275.00	135.00	80.00
(43)	Kirkpatrick	280.00	140.00	85.00
(44)	Kunkel	275.00	135.00	80.00
(45)	Landgraff	275.00	135.00	80.00
(46)	Larkins	275.00	135.00	80.00
(47)	Laughlin	275.00	135.00	80.00
(48)	Lawlor	275.00	135.00	80.00
(49)	Levy	275.00	135.00	80.00
(50)	Lloyd	275.00	135.00	80.00
(51)	Loos	280.00	140.00	85.00
(52)	Lovell	275.00	135.00	80.00
(53)	Lucia	275.00	135.00	80.00
(54)	MacConachie	275.00	135.00	80.00
(55)	Mayberry	275.00	135.00	80.00
(56)	McFarland	280.00	140.00	85.00
(57)	Messitt	280.00	140.00	85.00
(58)	Michel	275.00	135.00	80.00
(59)	Mullaney	275.00	135.00	80.00
(60)	Munson	275.00	135.00	80.00
(61)	Neuton	275.00	135.00	80.00
(62)	Nimmo	275.00	135.00	80.00
(63)	Norris	275.00	135.00	80.00
(64)	Peterson	275.00	135.00	80.00
(65)	Powell	275.00	135.00	80.00
(66)	Pressly (Pressley)	275.00	135.00	80.00
(67)	Pritchard	275.00	135.00	80.00
(68)	Revelle	275.00	135.00	80.00
(69)	Rowe	275.00	135.00	80.00
(70)	Schmidt	280.00	140.00	85.00
(71)	Schrader	275.00	135.00	80.00
(72)	Sharp	275.00	135.00	80.00
(73)	Shaw	275.00	135.00	80.00
(74)	Smith/Btg (Lynchburg)	275.00	135.00	80.00
(75)	Smith/Catching (Lynchburg)	275.00	135.00	80.00
(76)	Smith (Portsmouth)	280.00	140.00	85.00
(77)	Spicer	275.00	135.00	80.00
(78)	Titman	275.00	135.00	80.00
(79)	Toner	275.00	135.00	80.00
(80)	Tydeman	275.00	135.00	80.00
(81)	Vail	290.00	145.00	90.00
(82)	Verbout	275.00	135.00	80.00
(83)	Walker	275.00	135.00	80.00
(84)	Wallace	275.00	135.00	80.00
(85)	Waymack	275.00	135.00	80.00
(86)	Woolums	275.00	135.00	80.00
(87)	Zimmerman	275.00	135.00	80.00

1910 Old Mill Cigarettes Series 3 (Texas League)

		NM	EX	VG
Common Player:		275.00	125.00	80.00
(1)	Alexander	275.00	125.00	80.00
(2)	Ash	275.00	125.00	80.00
(3)	Bandy	275.00	125.00	80.00
(4)	Barenkemp	275.00	125.00	80.00
(5)	Belew	275.00	125.00	80.00
(6)	Bell	275.00	125.00	80.00
(7)	Bennett	275.00	125.00	80.00
(8)	Berick	275.00	125.00	80.00
(9)	Billiard	275.00	125.00	80.00
(10)	Blanding	275.00	125.00	80.00
(11)	Blue	275.00	125.00	80.00
(12)	Burch	275.00	125.00	80.00
(13)	Burk	275.00	125.00	80.00
(14)	Carlin	275.00	125.00	80.00
(15)	Conaway	275.00	125.00	80.00
(16)	Corkhill	275.00	125.00	80.00
(17)	Cowan	275.00	125.00	80.00
(18)	Coyle	275.00	125.00	80.00
(19)	Crable	275.00	125.00	80.00
(20)	Curry	275.00	125.00	80.00
(21)	Dale	275.00	125.00	80.00
(22)	Davis	275.00	125.00	80.00
(23)	Deardorff	275.00	125.00	80.00
(24)	Donnelley	275.00	125.00	80.00
(25)	Doyle	275.00	125.00	80.00
(26)	Druke	275.00	125.00	80.00
(27)	Dugey	275.00	125.00	80.00
(28)	Ens	275.00	125.00	80.00
(29)	Evans	275.00	125.00	80.00
(30)	Fillman	275.00	125.00	80.00
(31)	Firestine	275.00	125.00	80.00
(32)	Francis	275.00	125.00	80.00
(33)	Galloway	275.00	125.00	80.00
(34)	Gardner	275.00	125.00	80.00
(35)	Gear	275.00	125.00	80.00
(36)	Glawe	275.00	125.00	80.00
(37)	Gordon	275.00	125.00	80.00
(38)	Gowdy	275.00	125.00	80.00
(39)	Harbison	275.00	125.00	80.00
(40)	Harper	275.00	125.00	80.00
(41)	Hicks	275.00	125.00	80.00
(42)	Hill	275.00	125.00	80.00
(43)	Hinninger	275.00	125.00	80.00
(44)	Hirsch	275.00	125.00	80.00
(45)	Hise	275.00	125.00	80.00
(46)	Hooks	275.00	125.00	80.00
(47)	Hornsby	275.00	125.00	80.00
(48)	Howell	275.00	125.00	80.00
(49)	Johnston	275.00	125.00	80.00
(50)	Jolley	275.00	125.00	80.00
(51)	Jones	275.00	125.00	80.00
(52)	Kaphan	275.00	125.00	80.00
(53)	Kipp	275.00	125.00	80.00
(54)	Leidy	275.00	125.00	80.00
(55)	Malloy	275.00	125.00	80.00
(56)	Maloney	275.00	125.00	80.00
(57)	Meagher	275.00	125.00	80.00
(58)	Merritt	275.00	125.00	80.00
(59)	McKay	275.00	125.00	80.00
(60)	Mills	275.00	125.00	80.00
(61)	Morris	275.00	125.00	80.00
(62)	Mullen	275.00	125.00	80.00
(63)	Munsell	275.00	125.00	80.00
(64)	Nagel	275.00	125.00	80.00
(65)	Northen	275.00	125.00	80.00
(66)	Ogle	275.00	125.00	80.00
(67)	Onslow	290.00	140.00	85.00
(68)	Pendleton	275.00	125.00	80.00
(69)	Powell	275.00	125.00	80.00
(70)	Riley	275.00	125.00	80.00
(71)	Robertson	275.00	125.00	80.00
(72)	Rose	275.00	125.00	80.00
(73)	Salazor	275.00	125.00	80.00
(74)	Shindel	275.00	125.00	80.00
(75)	Shontz	275.00	125.00	80.00
(76)	Slaven	275.00	125.00	80.00
(77)	Smith (Bat over shoulder.)	275.00	125.00	80.00
(78)	Smith (Bat at hip level.)	275.00	125.00	80.00
(79)	Spangler	275.00	125.00	80.00
(80)	Stadeli	275.00	125.00	80.00
(81)	Stinson	275.00	125.00	80.00
(82)	Storch	275.00	125.00	80.00
(83)	Stringer	275.00	125.00	80.00
(84)	Tesreau	300.00	150.00	90.00
(85)	Thebo	290.00	140.00	85.00
(86)	Tullas	275.00	125.00	80.00
(87)	Walsh	275.00	125.00	80.00
(88)	Watson	275.00	125.00	80.00
(89)	Weber	275.00	125.00	80.00
(90)	Weeks	275.00	125.00	80.00
(91)	Wertherford	275.00	125.00	80.00
(92)	Wickenhofer	275.00	125.00	80.00
(93)	Williams	275.00	125.00	80.00
(94)	Woodburn	275.00	125.00	80.00
(95)	Yantz	275.00	125.00	80.00

1910 Old Mill Cigarettes Series 4 (Va. Valley League)

		NM	EX	VG
Common Player:		400.00	175.00	100.00
(1)	Aylor	400.00	175.00	100.00
(2)	Benney	400.00	175.00	100.00
(3)	Best	400.00	175.00	100.00
(4)	Bonno	400.00	175.00	100.00
(5)	Brown	400.00	175.00	100.00
(6)	Brumfield	400.00	175.00	100.00
(7)	Campbell	400.00	175.00	100.00
(8)	Canepa	400.00	175.00	100.00
(9)	Carney	400.00	175.00	100.00
(10)	Carter	400.00	175.00	100.00
(11)	Cochrane	400.00	175.00	100.00
(12)	Coller	400.00	175.00	100.00
(13)	Connolly	400.00	175.00	100.00
(14)	Davis	400.00	175.00	100.00
(15)	Connell	400.00	175.00	100.00
(16)	Doshmer	400.00	175.00	100.00
(17)	Dougherty	400.00	175.00	100.00
(18)	Erlewein	400.00	175.00	100.00
(19)	Farrell	400.00	175.00	100.00
(20)	Geary	400.00	175.00	100.00
(21)	Halterman	400.00	175.00	100.00
(22)	Headly	400.00	175.00	100.00
(23)	Hollis	400.00	175.00	100.00
(24)	Hunter	400.00	175.00	100.00
(25)	Johnson	400.00	175.00	100.00
(26)	Kane	400.00	175.00	100.00
(27)	Kuehn	400.00	175.00	100.00
(28)	Leonard	400.00	175.00	100.00
(29)	Lux	400.00	175.00	100.00
(30)	McClain	400.00	175.00	100.00
(31)	Mollenkamp	410.00	180.00	105.00
(32)	Moore	400.00	175.00	100.00
(33)	Moye	400.00	175.00	100.00
(34)	O'Connor	400.00	175.00	100.00
(35)	Orcutt	400.00	175.00	100.00
(36)	Pick	410.00	180.00	105.00
(37)	Pickels	400.00	175.00	100.00
(38)	Schafer	400.00	175.00	100.00
(39)	Seaman	400.00	175.00	100.00
(40)	Spicer	400.00	175.00	100.00
(41)	Stanley	400.00	175.00	100.00
(42)	Stockum	400.00	175.00	100.00
(43)	Titlow	400.00	175.00	100.00
(44)	Waldron	400.00	175.00	100.00
(45)	Wills	400.00	175.00	100.00
(46)	Witter	400.00	175.00	100.00
(47)	Womach	400.00	175.00	100.00
(48)	Young	400.00	175.00	100.00
(49)	Zurlage	400.00	175.00	100.00

1910 Old Mill Cigarettes Series 5 (Carolina Assn.)

	NM	EX	VG
Common Player:	400.00	175.00	100.00
(1) Abercrombie	400.00	175.00	100.00
(2) Averett	400.00	175.00	100.00
(3) Bansewein	400.00	175.00	100.00
(4) Bentley	400.00	175.00	100.00
(5) C.G. Beusse	400.00	175.00	100.00
(6) Fred Beusse	400.00	175.00	100.00
(7) Bigbie	400.00	175.00	100.00
(8) Bivens	400.00	175.00	100.00
(9) Blackstone	400.00	175.00	100.00
(10) Brannon	400.00	175.00	100.00
(11) Brazell	400.00	175.00	100.00
(12) Brent	400.00	175.00	100.00
(13) Bullock	400.00	175.00	100.00
(14) Cashion	425.00	190.00	120.00
(15) Corbett (3/4 length view)	400.00	175.00	100.00
(16) Corbett (Full length view.)	400.00	175.00	100.00
(17) Coutts	400.00	175.00	100.00
(18) Lave Cross	425.00	190.00	120.00
(19) Crouch	400.00	175.00	100.00
(20) C.L. Derrick	410.00	180.00	110.00
(21) F.B. Derrick	400.00	175.00	100.00
(22) Dobard	400.00	175.00	100.00
(23) Drumm	400.00	175.00	100.00
(24) Duvie	400.00	175.00	100.00
(25) Ehrhardt	400.00	175.00	100.00
(26) Eldridge	400.00	175.00	100.00
(27) Fairbanks	400.00	175.00	100.00
(28) Farmer	400.00	175.00	100.00
(29) Ferrell	400.00	175.00	100.00
(30) Finn	400.00	175.00	100.00
(31) Flowers	400.00	175.00	100.00
(32) Fogarty	400.00	175.00	100.00
(33) Francisco	400.00	175.00	100.00
(34) Gardin	400.00	175.00	100.00
(35) Gilmore	400.00	175.00	100.00
(36) Gorham	400.00	175.00	100.00
(37) Gorman	400.00	175.00	100.00
(38) Guss	400.00	175.00	100.00
(39) Hammersley	400.00	175.00	100.00
(40) Hargrave	400.00	175.00	100.00
(41) Harrington	400.00	175.00	100.00
(42) Harris	400.00	175.00	100.00
(43) Hartley	400.00	175.00	100.00
(44) Hayes	400.00	175.00	100.00
(45) Hicks	400.00	175.00	100.00
(46) Humphrey	410.00	180.00	110.00
(47) Jackson	400.00	175.00	100.00
(48) James	400.00	175.00	100.00
(49) Jenkins	400.00	175.00	100.00
(50) Johnston	400.00	175.00	100.00
(51) Kelly	400.00	175.00	100.00
(52) Laval	400.00	175.00	100.00
(53) Lothrop	400.00	175.00	100.00
(54) MacConachie	400.00	175.00	100.00
(55) Mangum	400.00	175.00	100.00
(56) A. McCarthy	400.00	175.00	100.00
(57) J. McCarthy	400.00	175.00	100.00
(58) McEnroe	400.00	175.00	100.00
(59) McFarlin	400.00	175.00	100.00
(60) McHugh	400.00	175.00	100.00
(61) McKevitt	400.00	175.00	100.00
(62) Midkiff	400.00	175.00	100.00
(63) Moore	400.00	175.00	100.00
(64) Noojin	400.00	175.00	100.00
(65) Ochs	400.00	175.00	100.00
(66) Painter	400.00	175.00	100.00
(67) Redfern (Redfearn)	400.00	175.00	100.00
(68) Reis	400.00	175.00	100.00
(69) Rickard	400.00	175.00	100.00
(70) Roth/Btg	400.00	175.00	100.00
(71) Roth/Fldg	400.00	175.00	100.00
(72) Smith	400.00	175.00	100.00
(73) Springs	400.00	175.00	100.00
(74) Stouch	400.00	175.00	100.00
(75) Taxis	400.00	175.00	100.00
(76) Templin	400.00	175.00	100.00
(77) Thrasher	400.00	175.00	100.00
(78) Trammell	400.00	175.00	100.00
(79) Walker	400.00	175.00	100.00
(80) Walters	400.00	175.00	100.00
(81) Wehrell	400.00	175.00	100.00
(82) Weldon	400.00	175.00	100.00
(83) Williams	400.00	175.00	100.00
(84) Wingo	400.00	175.00	100.00
(85) Workman	400.00	175.00	100.00
(86) Wynne	400.00	175.00	100.00
(87) Wysong	400.00	175.00	100.00

1910 Old Mill Cigarettes Series 6 (Blue Grass League)

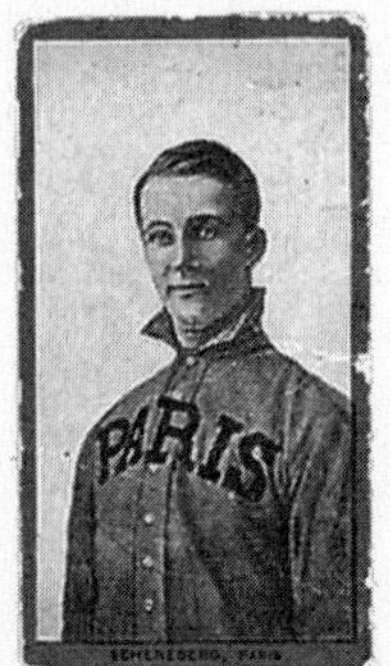

	NM	EX	VG
Common Player:	600.00	250.00	150.00
(1) Angermeier (Fielding)	800.00	400.00	200.00
(2) Angermeir (Portrait)	800.00	400.00	200.00
(3) Atwell	600.00	250.00	150.00
(4) Badger	600.00	250.00	150.00
(5) Barnett	600.00	250.00	150.00
(6) Barney	600.00	250.00	150.00
(7) Beard	600.00	250.00	150.00
(8) Bohannon	600.00	250.00	150.00
(9) Callahan	650.00	275.00	160.00
(10) Chapman	600.00	250.00	150.00
(11) Chase	600.00	250.00	150.00
(12) Coleman	600.00	250.00	150.00
(13) Cornell (Frankfort)	600.00	250.00	150.00
(14) Cornell (Winchester)	600.00	250.00	150.00
(15) Creager	600.00	250.00	150.00
(16) Dailey	600.00	250.00	150.00
(17) Edington	650.00	275.00	160.00
(18) Elgin	600.00	250.00	150.00
(19) Ellis	600.00	250.00	150.00
(20) Everden	600.00	250.00	150.00
(21) Gisler	600.00	250.00	150.00
(22) Goodman	600.00	250.00	150.00
(23) Goostree (Hands behind back.)	600.00	250.00	150.00
(24) Goostree (Leaning on bat.)	800.00	400.00	200.00
(25) Haines	600.00	250.00	150.00
(26) Harold	600.00	250.00	150.00
(27) Heveron	600.00	250.00	150.00
(28) Hicks	600.00	250.00	150.00
(29) Hoffmann	600.00	250.00	150.00
(30) Horn	600.00	250.00	150.00
(31) Kaiser	650.00	275.00	160.00
(32) Keifel	600.00	250.00	150.00
(33) Kimbrough	600.00	250.00	150.00
(34) Kircher (Shelbyville)	600.00	250.00	150.00
(35) Kircher (Winchester)	600.00	250.00	150.00
(36) Kuhlman (3/4 length)	600.00	250.00	150.00
(37) Kuhlmann/Portrait	600.00	250.00	150.00
(38) L'Heureux	600.00	250.00	150.00
(39) McIlvain	600.00	250.00	150.00
(40) McKernan	600.00	250.00	150.00
(41) Meyers	600.00	250.00	150.00
(42) Moloney	650.00	275.00	160.00
(43) Mullin	600.00	250.00	150.00
(44) Olson	600.00	250.00	150.00
(45) Oyler	600.00	250.00	150.00
(46) Reed	600.00	250.00	150.00
(47) Ross	600.00	250.00	150.00
(48) Scheneberg/Fldg	650.00	275.00	160.00
(49) Scheneberg/Portrait	650.00	275.00	160.00
(50) Schultz	600.00	250.00	150.00
(51) Scott	600.00	250.00	150.00
(52) Sinex	600.00	250.00	150.00
(53) Stengel		40,000	20,000
(54) Thoss	600.00	250.00	150.00
(55) Tilford	600.00	250.00	150.00
(56) Toney	650.00	275.00	160.00
(57) Van Landingham (Valladingham) (Lexington)	600.00	250.00	150.00
(58) Van Landingham (Valladingham) (Shelbyville)	600.00	250.00	150.00
(59) Viox	650.00	275.00	160.00
(60) Walden	600.00	250.00	150.00
(61) Whitaker	600.00	250.00	150.00
(62) Wills	600.00	250.00	150.00
(63) Womble	600.00	250.00	150.00
(64) Wright	600.00	250.00	150.00
(65) Yaeger	650.00	275.00	160.00
(66) Yancey	600.00	250.00	150.00

1910 Old Mill Cigarettes Series 7 (E. Carolina League)

	NM	EX	VG
Common Player:	450.00	200.00	125.00
(1) Armstrong	450.00	200.00	125.00
(2) Beatty	450.00	200.00	125.00
(3) Biel	450.00	200.00	125.00
(4) Bonner	450.00	200.00	125.00
(5) Brandt	450.00	200.00	125.00
(6) Brown	450.00	200.00	125.00
(7) Cantwell	450.00	200.00	125.00
(8) Carrol	450.00	200.00	125.00
(9) Cooney	450.00	200.00	125.00
(10) Cooper	450.00	200.00	125.00
(11) Cowell	450.00	200.00	125.00
(12) Creager (Cregan)	450.00	200.00	125.00
(13) Crockett	475.00	220.00	135.00
(14) Dailey	450.00	200.00	125.00
(15) Dobbs	450.00	200.00	125.00
(16) Dussault	450.00	200.00	125.00
(17) Dwyer	450.00	200.00	125.00
(18) Evans	450.00	200.00	125.00
(19) Forgue	450.00	200.00	125.00
(20) Fulton	450.00	200.00	125.00
(21) Galvin	450.00	200.00	125.00
(22) Gastmeyer/Btg	600.00	300.00	150.00
(23) Gastmeyer/Fldg	600.00	300.00	150.00
(24) Gates	450.00	200.00	125.00
(25) Gillespie	450.00	200.00	125.00
(26) Griffin	450.00	200.00	125.00
(27) Gunderson	450.00	200.00	125.00
(28) Ham	450.00	200.00	125.00
(29) Handibe (Handiboe)	475.00	220.00	135.00
(30) Hart	450.00	200.00	125.00
(31) Hartley	450.00	200.00	125.00
(32) Hobbs	450.00	200.00	125.00
(33) Hyames	450.00	200.00	125.00
(34) Irving	450.00	200.00	125.00
(35) Kaiser	450.00	200.00	125.00
(36) Kelley	450.00	200.00	125.00
(37) Kelly	450.00	200.00	125.00
(38) Kelly (Mascot, Goldsboro.)	1,000	600.00	350.00
(39) Luyster	450.00	200.00	125.00
(40) MacDonald	450.00	200.00	125.00
(41) Malcolm	450.00	200.00	125.00
(42) J. Erskine Mayer	475.00	220.00	135.00
(43) McCormac (McCormick)	450.00	200.00	125.00
(44) McGeeham (McGeehan)	475.00	220.00	135.00
(45) Merchant	450.00	200.00	125.00
(46) Mills	450.00	200.00	125.00
(47) Morgan	475.00	220.00	135.00
(48) Morris	450.00	200.00	125.00
(49) Munson	450.00	200.00	125.00
(50) Newman	450.00	200.00	125.00
(51) Noval (Novak)	450.00	200.00	125.00
(52) O'Halloran	450.00	200.00	125.00
(53) Phelan	450.00	200.00	125.00
(54) Prim	450.00	200.00	125.00
(55) Reeves	450.00	200.00	125.00
(56) Richardson	450.00	200.00	125.00
(57) Schumaker	450.00	200.00	125.00
(58) Sharp	450.00	200.00	125.00
(59) Sherrill	450.00	200.00	125.00
(60) Simmons	450.00	200.00	125.00
(61) Steinbach	450.00	200.00	125.00
(62) Stoehr	450.00	200.00	125.00
(63) Taylor	450.00	200.00	125.00
(64) Webb	450.00	200.00	125.00
(65) Whelan	450.00	200.00	125.00
(66) Wolf	450.00	200.00	125.00
(67) Wright	450.00	200.00	125.00

1910 Old Mill Cigarettes Series 8 (Southern Assn.)

	NM	EX	VG
Common Player:	700.00	325.00	200.00
(1) Allen (Memphis)	700.00	325.00	200.00
(2) Allen (Mobile)	750.00	350.00	210.00
(3) Anderson	700.00	325.00	200.00
(4) Babb	750.00	350.00	210.00
(5) Bartley	750.00	350.00	210.00
(6) Bauer	700.00	325.00	200.00
(7) Bay	800.00	400.00	225.00
(8) Bayliss	700.00	325.00	200.00
(9) Berger	750.00	350.00	210.00
(10) Bernhard	700.00	325.00	200.00
(11) Bitroff	700.00	325.00	200.00
(12) Breitenstein	800.00	400.00	225.00
(13) Bronkie	750.00	350.00	210.00
(14) Brooks	700.00	325.00	200.00
(15) Burnett	750.00	350.00	210.00
(16) Cafalu	700.00	325.00	200.00
(17) Carson	700.00	325.00	200.00
(18) Case	750.00	350.00	210.00
(19) Chappelle	750.00	350.00	210.00
(20) Cohen	700.00	325.00	200.00
(21) Collins	700.00	325.00	200.00
(22) Crandall	700.00	325.00	200.00
(23) Cross	700.00	325.00	200.00
(24) Jud. Daly	750.00	350.00	210.00
(25) Davis	700.00	325.00	200.00
(26) Demaree	750.00	350.00	210.00
(27) DeMontreville	700.00	325.00	200.00
(28) E. DeMontreville	750.00	350.00	210.00
(29) Dick	700.00	325.00	200.00
(30) Dobbs	750.00	350.00	210.00
(31) Dudley	700.00	325.00	200.00
(32) Dunn	750.00	350.00	210.00
(33) Elliot	750.00	350.00	210.00
(34) Emery	700.00	325.00	200.00
(35) Erloff	700.00	325.00	200.00
(36) Farrell	700.00	325.00	200.00
(37) Fisher	750.00	350.00	210.00
(38) Fleharty	700.00	325.00	200.00
(39) Flood	750.00	350.00	210.00
(40) Foster	750.00	350.00	210.00
(41) Fritz	800.00	400.00	225.00
(42) Greminger	750.00	350.00	210.00
(43) Gribbon	700.00	325.00	200.00
(44) Griffin	700.00	325.00	200.00
(45) Gygli	700.00	325.00	200.00
(46) Hanks	700.00	325.00	200.00
(47) Hart	800.00	400.00	225.00
(48) Hess	750.00	350.00	210.00
(49) Hickman	750.00	350.00	210.00
(50) Hohnhorst	750.00	350.00	210.00
(51) Huelsman	750.00	350.00	210.00
(52) Jackson			125,000
(53) Jordan	800.00	400.00	225.00
(54) Kane	700.00	325.00	200.00
(55) Kelly	700.00	325.00	200.00
(56) Kerwin	750.00	350.00	210.00

(57)	Keupper	750.00	350.00	210.00
(58)	LaFitte	700.00	325.00	200.00
(59)	Larsen	700.00	325.00	200.00
(60)	Bill Lindsay	750.00	350.00	210.00
(61)	Lynch	700.00	325.00	200.00
(62)	Manuel	750.00	350.00	210.00
(63)	Manush	750.00	350.00	210.00
(64)	Marcan	700.00	325.00	200.00
(65)	Maxwell	750.00	350.00	210.00
(66)	McBride	700.00	325.00	200.00
(67)	McCreery	750.00	350.00	210.00
(68)	McGilvray	750.00	350.00	210.00
(69)	McLaurin	750.00	350.00	210.00
(70)	McTigue	750.00	350.00	210.00
(71)	Miller (Chattanooga)	750.00	350.00	210.00
(72)	Miller (Montgomery)	700.00	325.00	200.00
(73)	Molesworth	750.00	350.00	210.00
(74)	Moran	750.00	350.00	210.00
(75)	Newton	700.00	325.00	200.00
(76)	Nolley	700.00	325.00	200.00
(77)	Osteen	750.00	350.00	210.00
(78)	Owen	700.00	325.00	200.00
(79)	Paige	750.00	350.00	210.00
(80)	Patterson	750.00	350.00	210.00
(81)	Pepe	700.00	325.00	200.00
(82)	Perdue	800.00	400.00	225.00
(83)	Peters	750.00	350.00	210.00
(84)	Phillips	700.00	325.00	200.00
(85)	Pratt	750.00	350.00	210.00
(86)	Rementer	750.00	350.00	210.00
(87)	Rhodes	700.00	325.00	200.00
(88)	Rhoton	700.00	325.00	200.00
(89)	Robertson	700.00	325.00	200.00
(90)	Rogers	700.00	325.00	200.00
(91)	Rohe	750.00	350.00	210.00
(92)	Seabough (Seabaugh)	700.00	325.00	200.00
(93)	Seitz	700.00	325.00	200.00
(94)	Schlitzer	750.00	350.00	210.00
(95)	Schopp	700.00	325.00	200.00
(96)	Siegle	750.00	350.00	210.00
(97)	Smith (Montgomery)	700.00	325.00	200.00
(98)	Sid. Smith (Atlanta)	800.00	400.00	225.00
(99)	Steele	700.00	325.00	200.00
(100)	Swacina	750.00	350.00	210.00
(101)	Sweeney	750.00	350.00	210.00
(102)	Thomas/Fldg	750.00	350.00	210.00
(103)	Thomas/Portrait	750.00	350.00	210.00
(104)	Vinson	700.00	325.00	200.00
(105)	Wagner (Birmingham)	700.00	325.00	200.00
(106)	Wagner (Mobile)	700.00	325.00	200.00
(107)	Walker	700.00	325.00	200.00
(108)	Wanner	750.00	350.00	210.00
(109)	Welf	750.00	350.00	210.00
(110)	Whiteman	750.00	350.00	210.00
(111)	Whitney	700.00	325.00	200.00
(112)	Wilder	700.00	325.00	200.00
(113)	Wiseman	700.00	325.00	200.00
(114)	Yerkes	800.00	400.00	225.00

1910 Old Mill Cabinets (H801-7)

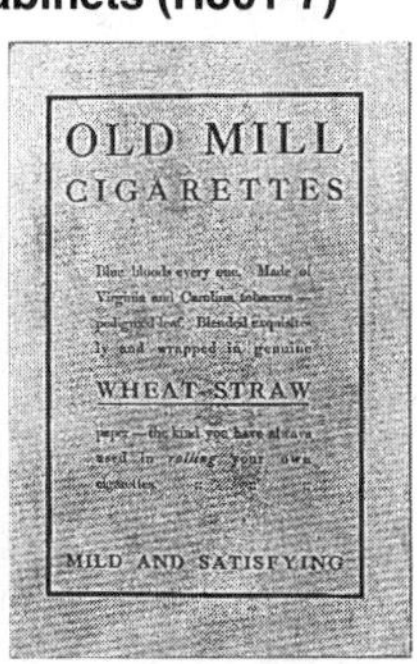

Similar in size and style to the more popular T3 Turkey Red cabinet cards of the same period, the Old Mill cabinets are much scarcer and picture fewer players. Issued in 1910 as a premium by Old Mill Cigarettes, these minor league cards measure approximately 5-3/8" x 7-5/8". Unlike the Turkey Reds, which feature full-color lithographs, the Old Mill cabinet cards picture the players in black-and-white photos surrounded by a wide tan border. The player's last name is printed in black in the lower-left corner, while his team designation appears in the lower-right. Backs carry an advertisement for Old Mill. There are currently 34 known subjects in the set. The Old Mill cabinet cards carry the ACC designation H801-7. Gaps have been left in the numbering to accomodate future additions to this checklist.

		NM	EX	VG
Common Player:		7,500	3,750	2,250
(1)	Armstrong	7,500	3,750	2,250
(2)	Bentley	7,500	3,750	2,250
(3)	Bonner	7,500	3,750	2,250
(4)	Bowen	7,500	3,750	2,250
(5)	Brazille (Brazell)	7,500	3,750	2,250
(6)	Bush (Busch)	7,500	3,750	2,250
(7)	Bussey	7,500	3,750	2,250
(8)	Cross	7,500	3,750	2,250
(9)	Derrick	7,500	3,750	2,250
(10)	Doane	7,500	3,750	2,250
(11)	Doyle	7,500	3,750	2,250
(12)	Fox	7,500	3,750	2,250
(13)	Galvin	7,500	3,750	2,250
(14)	Griffin	7,500	3,750	2,250
(15)	Hearn	7,500	3,750	2,250
(16)	Hobbs	7,500	3,750	2,250
(17)	Hooker	7,500	3,750	2,250
(18)	Kirkpatrick	7,500	3,750	2,250
(19)	Laughlin	7,500	3,750	2,250
(20)	McKevitt	7,500	3,750	2,250
(21)	Munson	7,500	3,750	2,250
(22)	Noojn (Noojin)	7,500	3,750	2,250
(23)	O'Halloran	7,500	3,750	2,250
(24)	Pressly	7,500	3,750	2,250
(25)	Revelle	7,500	3,750	2,250
(26)	Richardson	7,500	3,750	2,250
(27)	Rickard	7,500	3,750	2,250
(28)	Simmons	7,500	3,750	2,250
(29)	A. Smith	7,500	3,750	2,250
(30)	Spratt	7,500	3,750	2,250
(32)	Titman	7,500	3,750	2,250
(33)	Walters	7,500	3,750	2,250
(34)	Wallace	7,500	3,750	2,250
(35)	Weherell (Wehrell)	7,500	3,750	2,250
(36)	Ivey Wingo	7,500	3,750	2,250
(37)	Woolums	7,500	3,750	2,250

1949 Omaha Cardinals Player Picture Book

JIM BARKLEY, Outfield

While not baseball cards, this team booklet served the same purpose - providing fans with pictures of the local Western League (Class A) affiliate of the St. Louis Cardinals. It's also possible that individual player pages of the book have made their way into card collections over the years. The booklet is 5" x 3-1/4" in size, with 20 pages of photos and semi-gloss front and back covers, stapled together at the spine. The front has printed in red: "OMAHA CARDINALS / BASEBALL TEAM / 1949." Each inside page has back-to-back black-and-white photos with identification beneath. The pairings are checklisted here in the order in which they appear in the booklet.

		NM	EX	VG
Complete Booklet:		350.00	175.00	100.00
(1-2)	Ced Durst, Russ Kerns			
(3-4)	Nick Adzick, Bob Rausch			
(5-6)	Ed Nietopski, Fran Haus			
(7-8)	Fritz Marolewski, Bernie Creger			
(9-10)	Vaughn Hazen, Sid Langston			
(11-12)	Bob Reash, Jim Barkley			
(13-14)	Marty Garlock, Hank Williams			
(15-16)	Lou Ciola, Joe Presko			
(17-18)	Dave Thomas, Bob Mahoney			
(19-20)	Stadium Photo (Dick Bokelmann)			

1956 Omaha Cardinals Picture-Pak

Evidently a concession stand souvenir, this "Picture-Pak" is a comb-bound set of 3-1/2" x 4-3/8" black-and-white player portraits. Each picture is printed on semi-gloss cardboard with a white facsimile autograph.

		NM	EX	VG
Complete Book:		300.00	150.00	90.00
(1)	Tom Alston			
(2)	Alberto Baro			
(3)	Nels Burbrink			
(4)	Tom Cheney			
(5)	Ray Coleman			
(6)	Jim Command			
(7)	Chuck Harmon			
(8)	Walt Jamison (?)			
(9)	Stan Jok			
(10)	Gordon Jones			
(11)	Johnny Keane			
(12)	Marty Kutyna			
(13)	Ed Mayer			
(14)	Herb Moford			
(15)	Mo Mozzali			
(16)	Jim Pearce			
(17)	Charlie Peete			
(18)	Danny Schell			
(19)	Dick Schofield			
(20)	Barney Schultz			
(21)	Wally Shannon			
(22)	Glen Stabelfeld			

1957 Omaha Cardinals Picture-Pak

These 3-3/8" x 4-3/8" black-and-white, blank-back photos were sold in a team picture pack. Fronts have a facsimile autograph. The unnumbered cards are checklisted here in alphabetical order.

		NM	EX	VG
Complete Set (25):		800.00	400.00	240.00
Common Player:		35.00	17.50	10.00
(1)	Frank Barnes	35.00	17.50	10.00
(2)	Bill Bergesch	35.00	17.50	10.00
(3)	Dick Brown	35.00	17.50	10.00
(4)	Tom Cheney	35.00	17.50	10.00
(5)	Nels Chittum	35.00	17.50	10.00
(6)	Jim Command	35.00	17.50	10.00
(7)	Chuck Diering	35.00	17.50	10.00
(8)	Sherry Dixon	35.00	17.50	10.00
(9)	Bob Durnbaugh	35.00	17.50	10.00
(10)	Glen Gorbous	35.00	17.50	10.00
(11)	Johnny Keane	35.00	17.50	10.00
(12)	Jim King	35.00	17.50	10.00
(13)	Paul Kippels	35.00	17.50	10.00
(14)	Don Lassetter	35.00	17.50	10.00
(15)	Don Liddle	35.00	17.50	10.00
(16)	Lou Limmer	35.00	17.50	10.00
(17)	Boyd Linker	35.00	17.50	10.00
(18)	Bob Mabe	35.00	17.50	10.00
(19)	Herb Moford	35.00	17.50	10.00
(20)	Rance Pless	35.00	17.50	10.00
(21)	Kelton Russell	35.00	17.50	10.00
(22)	Barney Schultz	35.00	17.50	10.00
(23)	Milt Smith	35.00	17.50	10.00
(24)	Glen Stabelfeld	35.00	17.50	10.00
(25)	Header Card	35.00	17.50	10.00

1958 Omaha Cardinals Picture-Pak

This rare late-1950s minor league issue contains the first card of Hall of Fame pitcher Bob Gibson. Probably sold as a complete set in format similar to major league picture packs of the era, there are 23 player cards and a header card. Cards measure 3-3/8" x 4-3/8", have a black-and-white player picture and facsimile autograph. They are blank-backed. The checklist of the unnumbered cards is printed here in alphabetical order.

		NM	EX	VG
Complete Set (24):		1,500	750.00	450.00
Common Player:		40.00	20.00	12.00
(1)	Tony Alomar	60.00	30.00	18.00
(2)	Dave Benedict	40.00	20.00	12.00
(3)	Bill Bergesch	40.00	20.00	12.00
(4)	Bob Blaylock	40.00	20.00	12.00
(5)	Prentice "Pidge" Browne	40.00	20.00	12.00
(6)	Chris Cannizzaro	40.00	20.00	12.00
(7)	Nels Chittum	40.00	20.00	12.00
(8)	Don Choate	40.00	20.00	12.00
(9)	Phil Clark	40.00	20.00	12.00
(10)	Jim Frey	75.00	37.50	22.50
(11)	Bob Gibson	500.00	250.00	150.00
(12)	Ev Joyner	40.00	20.00	12.00
(13)	Johnny Keane	40.00	20.00	12.00
(14)	Paul Kippels	40.00	20.00	12.00
(15)	Boyd Linker	40.00	20.00	12.00
(16)	Bob Mabe	40.00	20.00	12.00
(17)	Bernard Mateosky	40.00	20.00	12.00

		NM	EX	VG
(18)	Ronnie Plaza	40.00	20.00	12.00
(19)	Bill Queen	40.00	20.00	12.00
(20)	Bill Smith	40.00	20.00	12.00
(21)	Bobby G. Smith	40.00	20.00	12.00
(22)	Lee Tate	40.00	20.00	12.00
(23)	Benny Valenzuela	40.00	20.00	12.00
(24)	Header card	40.00	20.00	12.00

1962 Omaha Dodgers

This unnumbered black-and-white set measures 3-3/8" x 4-1/4" and is blank-backed. It was produced by photographer/collector Mel Bailey in an edition of 1,000 sets, sold for 50 cents by mail and at the stadium concession stand. Cards bear a facsimile autograph.

		NM	EX	VG
Complete Set (22):		175.00	90.00	50.00
Common Player:		12.50	6.25	3.75
(1)	Joe Altobelli	12.50	6.25	3.75
(2)	Jim Barbieri	12.50	6.25	3.75
(3)	Scott Breeden	12.50	6.25	3.75
(4)	Mike Brumley	12.50	6.25	3.75
(5)	Jose Cesar	12.50	6.25	3.75
(6)	Bill Hunter	12.50	6.25	3.75
(7)	Don LeJohn	12.50	6.25	3.75
(8)	Jack Lutz	12.50	6.25	3.75
(9)	Ken McMullen	12.50	6.25	3.75
(10)	Danny Ozark	12.50	6.25	3.75
(11)	Curt Roberts	12.50	6.25	3.75
(12)	Ernie Rodriguez	12.50	6.25	3.75
(13)	Dick Scarbrough	12.50	6.25	3.75
(14)	Bart Shirley	12.50	6.25	3.75
(15)	Dick Smith	12.50	6.25	3.75
(16)	Jack Smith	12.50	6.25	3.75
(17)	Nate Smith	12.50	6.25	3.75
(18)	Gene Snyder	12.50	6.25	3.75
(19)	Burbon Wheeler	12.50	6.25	3.75
(20)	Nick Wilhite (Willhite)	12.50	6.25	3.75
(21)	Jim Williams	12.50	6.25	3.75
(22)	Larry Williams	12.50	6.25	3.75

1952 Oshkosh Giants Team Issue

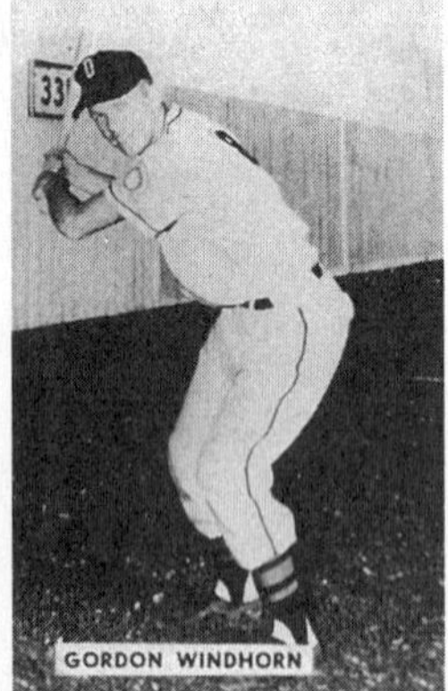

These 2-1/4" x 3-3/8" black-and-white, unnumbered, blank-backed cards were one of many minor league team sets issued by Globe Printing of San Jose, Calif., in the early 1950s. Cards were usually given away at the ballpark on a one-per-week or one-per-homestand basis, accounting for the rarity of surviving sets. The O-Giants were the Wisconsin State League affiliate of the N.Y. Giants. For a Class D team, a surprising number of the Oshkosh players graduated to the major leagues.

		NM	EX	VG
Complete Set (19):		1,000	500.00	300.00
Common Player:		60.00	30.00	18.00
Album:		100.00	50.00	30.00
(1)	Dan Banaszak	60.00	30.00	18.00
(2)	Paul Bentley	60.00	30.00	18.00
(3)	Joe Berke	60.00	30.00	18.00
(4)	Joe DeBellis	60.00	30.00	18.00
(5)	Ron Edwards	60.00	30.00	18.00
(6)	Dave Garcia	60.00	30.00	18.00
(7)	Weldon Grimesley	60.00	30.00	18.00
(8)	Cam Lewis	60.00	30.00	18.00
(9)	Paul McAuley	60.00	30.00	18.00
(10)	Don Mills	60.00	30.00	18.00
(11)	Ed Opich	60.00	30.00	18.00
(12)	John Practico	60.00	30.00	18.00
(13)	Rob R. Schmidt	60.00	30.00	18.00
(14)	Rob W. Schmidt	60.00	30.00	18.00
(15)	Frank Szekula	60.00	30.00	18.00
(16)	Victor Vick	60.00	30.00	18.00
(17)	Donald Wall	60.00	30.00	18.00
(18)	Ken Whitehead	60.00	30.00	18.00
(19)	Gordon Windhorn	60.00	30.00	18.00

P

1911 Pacific Coast Biscuit (D310)

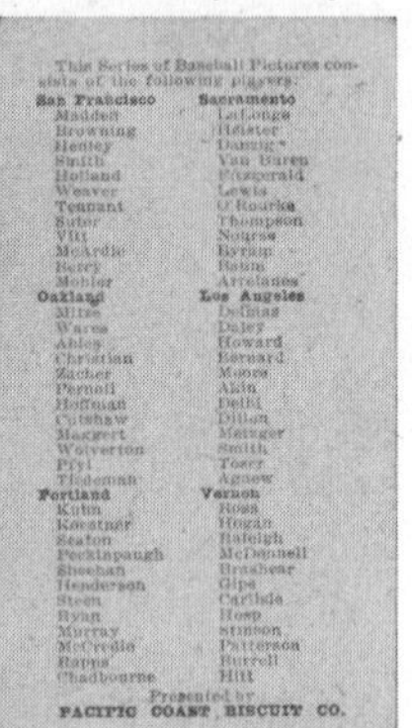

A dozen players each from six Pacific Coast League teams are represented in this set. Cards are about 2-1/2" x 4-1/4" with either black-and-white or sepia pictures on front. Backs have a checklist arranged by team.

		NM	EX	VG
Complete Set (72):		45,000	27,500	13,500
Common Player:		575.00	300.00	175.00
(1)	Ables	575.00	300.00	175.00
(2)	Agnew	575.00	300.00	175.00
(3)	Akin	575.00	300.00	175.00
(4)	Frank Arrelanes (Arellanes)	575.00	300.00	175.00
(5)	Baum	575.00	300.00	175.00
(6)	Bernard	575.00	300.00	175.00
(7)	Berry	575.00	300.00	175.00
(8)	Brashear	575.00	300.00	175.00
(9)	Browning	575.00	300.00	175.00
(10)	Burrell	575.00	300.00	175.00
(11)	Byram	575.00	300.00	175.00
(12)	Carlisle	575.00	300.00	175.00
(13)	Chadbourne	575.00	300.00	175.00
(14)	Christian	575.00	300.00	175.00
(15)	Cutshaw	575.00	300.00	175.00
(16)	Daley	575.00	300.00	175.00
(17)	Danzig	575.00	300.00	175.00
(18)	Delhi	575.00	300.00	175.00
(19)	Delmas	575.00	300.00	175.00
(20)	Dillon	575.00	300.00	175.00
(21)	Fitzgerald	575.00	300.00	175.00
(22)	Gipe	575.00	300.00	175.00
(23)	Heister	575.00	300.00	175.00
(24)	Henderson	575.00	300.00	175.00
(25)	Henley	575.00	300.00	175.00
(26)	Hitt	575.00	300.00	175.00
(27)	Hoffman	575.00	300.00	175.00
(28)	Hogan	575.00	300.00	175.00
(29)	Holland	575.00	300.00	175.00
(30)	Hosp	575.00	300.00	175.00
(31)	Howard	575.00	300.00	175.00
(32)	Kostner	575.00	300.00	175.00
(33)	Kuhn	575.00	300.00	175.00
(34)	LaLonge	575.00	300.00	175.00
(35)	Lewis	575.00	300.00	175.00
(36)	Maddern	575.00	300.00	175.00
(37)	Maggert	575.00	300.00	175.00
(38)	McArdle	575.00	300.00	175.00
(39)	McCredie	575.00	300.00	175.00
(40)	McDonnell	575.00	300.00	175.00
(41)	Metzger	575.00	300.00	175.00
(42)	Mitze	575.00	300.00	175.00
(43)	Mohler	575.00	300.00	175.00
(44)	Moore	575.00	300.00	175.00
(45)	Murray	575.00	300.00	175.00
(46)	Nourse	575.00	300.00	175.00
(47)	O'Rourke	575.00	300.00	175.00
(48)	Patterson	575.00	300.00	175.00
(49)	Peckinpaugh	600.00	300.00	180.00
(50)	Pernoll	575.00	300.00	175.00
(51)	Pfyl	575.00	300.00	175.00
(52)	Raleigh	575.00	300.00	175.00
(53)	Rapps	575.00	300.00	175.00
(54)	Ross	575.00	300.00	175.00
(55)	Ryan	575.00	300.00	175.00
(56)	Seaton	575.00	300.00	175.00
(57)	Sheehan	575.00	300.00	175.00
(58)	A. Smith	575.00	300.00	175.00
(59)	H. Smith	575.00	300.00	175.00
(60)	Steen	575.00	300.00	175.00
(61)	Stinson	575.00	300.00	175.00
(62)	Sutor	575.00	300.00	175.00
(63)	Tennant	575.00	300.00	175.00
(64)	Thompson	575.00	300.00	175.00
(65)	Tiedeman	575.00	300.00	175.00
(66)	Tozer	575.00	300.00	175.00
(67)	Van Buren	575.00	300.00	175.00
(68)	Witt	575.00	300.00	175.00
(69)	Wares	575.00	300.00	175.00
(70)	Weaver	6,000	3,000	1,800
(71)	Wolverton	575.00	300.00	175.00
(72)	Zacher	575.00	300.00	175.00

1911 Pacific Coast Biscuit (D311)

A dozen players each from six Pacific Coast League teams are represented in this set. Cards are about 1-1/2" x 2-5/8" with pastel colored pictures on front. Backs have a checklist arranged by team.

		NM	EX	VG
Complete Set (72):		40,000	20,000	12,000
Common Player:		575.00	300.00	175.00
(1)	Agnew	575.00	300.00	175.00
(2)	Akin	575.00	300.00	175.00
(3)	Frank Arrelanes (Arellanes)	575.00	300.00	175.00
(4)	Baum	575.00	300.00	175.00
(5)	Bernard	575.00	300.00	175.00
(6)	Berry	575.00	300.00	175.00
(7)	Brashear	575.00	300.00	175.00
(8)	Brown	575.00	300.00	175.00
(9)	Browning	575.00	300.00	175.00
(10)	Burrell	575.00	300.00	175.00
(11)	Byram	575.00	300.00	175.00
(12)	Castleton	575.00	300.00	175.00
(13)	Chadbourne	575.00	300.00	175.00
(14)	Christian	575.00	300.00	175.00
(15)	Cutshaw	575.00	300.00	175.00
(16)	Daley	575.00	300.00	175.00
(17)	Danzig	575.00	300.00	175.00
(18)	Delhi	575.00	300.00	175.00
(19)	Delmas	575.00	300.00	175.00
(20)	Dillon	575.00	300.00	175.00
(21)	Fitzgerald	575.00	300.00	175.00
(22)	Gipe	575.00	300.00	175.00
(23)	Gregory	575.00	300.00	175.00
(24)	Harkness	575.00	300.00	175.00
(25)	Heister	575.00	300.00	175.00
(26)	Henderson	575.00	300.00	175.00
(27)	Hoffman	575.00	300.00	175.00
(28)	Hogan	575.00	300.00	175.00
(29)	Holland	575.00	300.00	175.00
(30)	Hosp	575.00	300.00	175.00
(31)	Howard	575.00	300.00	175.00
(32)	Kuhn	575.00	300.00	175.00
(33)	LaLonge	575.00	300.00	175.00
(34)	Lewis	575.00	300.00	175.00
(35)	Maggert	575.00	300.00	175.00
(36)	McArdle	575.00	300.00	175.00
(37)	McCredie	575.00	300.00	175.00
(38)	McDonnell	575.00	300.00	175.00
(39)	Meikle	575.00	300.00	175.00
(40)	Melchior	575.00	300.00	175.00
(41)	Metzger	575.00	300.00	175.00
(42)	Mitze	575.00	300.00	175.00
(43)	Mohler	575.00	300.00	175.00
(44)	Moore	575.00	300.00	175.00
(45)	Murray	575.00	300.00	175.00
(46)	Nourse	575.00	300.00	175.00
(47)	O'Rourke	575.00	300.00	175.00
(48)	Patterson	575.00	300.00	175.00
(49)	Pearce	575.00	300.00	175.00
(50)	Peckinpaugh	600.00	300.00	180.00
(51)	Pernoll	575.00	300.00	175.00
(52)	Pfyl	575.00	300.00	175.00
(53)	Raleigh	575.00	300.00	175.00
(54)	Rapps	575.00	300.00	175.00
(55)	Ryan	575.00	300.00	175.00
(56)	Schmidt	575.00	300.00	175.00
(57)	Seaton	575.00	300.00	175.00
(58)	Sheehan	575.00	300.00	175.00
(59)	A. Smith	575.00	300.00	175.00
(60)	H. Smith	575.00	300.00	175.00
(61)	Stamfield	575.00	300.00	175.00
(62)	Steen	575.00	300.00	175.00
(63)	Stinson	575.00	300.00	175.00
(64)	Sutor	575.00	300.00	175.00
(65)	Tennant	575.00	300.00	175.00
(66)	Thompson	575.00	300.00	175.00
(67)	Tiedeman	575.00	300.00	175.00
(68)	Tozer	575.00	300.00	175.00
(69)	Van Buren	575.00	300.00	175.00
(70)	Vitt	575.00	300.00	175.00
(71)	Wares	575.00	300.00	175.00
(72)	Wolverton	575.00	300.00	175.00

1943-47 Parade Sportive

Over a period of years in the mid-1940s, Montreal sports radio personality Paul Stuart's Parade Sportive program issued a series of baseball player pictures of Montreal Royals and, occasionally, other International League stars. The pictures were issued in 5" x 9-1/2" and 7" x 10" black-and-white, blank-back format. Each picture carries the name of the radio station on which Stuart's program was broadcast, along with an ad at the bottom for one of his sponsors. The unnumbered pictures are listed here alphabetically; it is unknown whether this list constitutes the complete issue.

		NM	EX	VG
Common Player:		30.00	15.00	9.00
(1)	Jack Banta	30.00	15.00	9.00
(2)	Stan Briard	30.00	15.00	9.00
(3)	Les Burge	30.00	15.00	9.00
(4)	Paul Calvert	30.00	15.00	9.00
(5)	Al Campanis	45.00	22.50	13.50
(6)	Red Durrett	30.00	15.00	9.00
(7)	Herman Franks	30.00	15.00	9.00
(8)	John Gabbard	30.00	15.00	9.00
(9)	Roland Gladu	30.00	15.00	9.00
(10)	Ray Hathaway	30.00	15.00	9.00
(11)	Clay Hopper	30.00	15.00	9.00
(12)	John Jorgensen	30.00	15.00	9.00
(13)	Paul "Pepper" Martin	30.00	15.00	9.00
(14)	Steve Nagy	30.00	15.00	9.00
(15)	Roy Portlow (Partlow)	40.00	20.00	12.00
(16)	Marv Rackley	30.00	15.00	9.00
(17)	Jackie Robinson	300.00	150.00	90.00
(18)	Jean-Pierre Roy	30.00	15.00	9.00
(19)	1944 Montreal Royals Team Photo	50.00	25.00	15.00
(20)	1945 Montreal Royals Team Photo (CLUB MONTREAL (ROYAUX) 1945)	60.00	30.00	18.00
(21)	1945 Montreal Royals Team Photo (Les "Royaux" 1945)	60.00	30.00	18.00
(22)	1946 Montreal Royals Team Photo	200.00	100.00	60.00
(23)	Stan Briard, Roland Gladu, Jean-Pierre Roy	30.00	15.00	9.00
(24)	Checklist (Paul Stuart)	30.00	15.00	9.00

1952 Parkhurst

Produced by a Canadian competitor to Kool-Aid, this 100-card set features players from three International League teams, the Toronto Maple Leafs, Montreal Royals and Ottawa Athletics, along with cards featuring baseball playing tips and quizzes. Measuring 2" x 2-1/2", the cards feature black-and-white player photos on front. Backs are printed in red and have a few biographical details, 1951 stats and an ad for Frostade.

		NM	EX	VG
Complete Set (100):		2,400	1,200	725.00
Common Player (1-25, 49-100):		25.00	12.50	7.50
Common Card (26-48):		10.00	5.00	3.00
1	Joe Becker	80.00	35.00	9.00
2	Aaron Silverman	75.00	37.50	22.50
3	Bobby Rhawn	25.00	12.50	7.50
4	Russ Bauers	25.00	12.50	7.50
5	Bill Jennings	25.00	12.50	7.50
6	Grover Bowers	25.00	12.50	7.50
7	Vic Lombardi	25.00	12.50	7.50
8	Billy DeMars	25.00	12.50	7.50
9	Frank Colman	25.00	12.50	7.50
10	Charley Grant	25.00	12.50	7.50
11	Irving Medlinger	25.00	12.50	7.50
12	Burke McLaughlin	25.00	12.50	7.50
13	Lew Morton	25.00	12.50	7.50
14	Red Barrett	25.00	12.50	7.50
15	Leon Foulk	25.00	12.50	7.50
16	Neil Sheridan	25.00	12.50	7.50
17	Ferrell Anderson	25.00	12.50	7.50
18	Roy Shore	25.00	12.50	7.50
19	Duke Markell	75.00	37.50	22.50
20	Bobby Balcena	25.00	12.50	7.50
21	Wilmer Fields	25.00	12.50	7.50
22	Charlie White	25.00	12.50	7.50
23	Red Fahr	25.00	12.50	7.50
24	Jose Bracho	25.00	12.50	7.50
25	Ed Stevens	25.00	12.50	7.50
26	Maple Leaf Stadium	25.00	12.50	7.50
27	Throwing Home	15.00	7.50	4.50
28	Regulation Baseball Diamond	15.00	7.50	4.50
29	Gripping the Bat	15.00	7.50	4.50
30	Hiding the Pitch	15.00	7.50	4.50
31	Catcher's Stance	15.00	7.50	4.50
32	Quiz: "How long does..."	15.00	7.50	4.50
33	Finger and Arm Exercises	15.00	7.50	4.50
34	First Baseman	15.00	7.50	4.50
35	Pitcher's Stance	15.00	7.50	4.50
36	Swinging Bats	15.00	7.50	4.50
37	Quiz: "Can a player advance..."	15.00	7.50	4.50
38	Watch the Ball	15.00	7.50	4.50
39	Quiz: "Can a team..."	15.00	7.50	4.50
40	Quiz: "Can a player put ..."	15.00	7.50	4.50
41	How to Bunt	15.00	7.50	4.50
42	Wrist Snap	15.00	7.50	4.50
43	Pitching Practice	15.00	7.50	4.50
44	Stealing Bases	15.00	7.50	4.50
45	Pitching 1	15.00	7.50	4.50
46	Pitching 2	15.00	7.50	4.50
47	Signals	15.00	7.50	4.50
48	Regulation baseballs	15.00	7.50	4.50
49	Al Ronning	25.00	12.50	7.50
50	Bill Lane	25.00	12.50	7.50
51	Will Sampson	25.00	12.50	7.50
52	Charlie Thompson	25.00	12.50	7.50
53	Ezra McGlothin	25.00	12.50	7.50
54	Spook Jacobs	30.00	15.00	9.00
55	Art Fabbro	25.00	12.50	7.50
56	Jim Hughes	25.00	12.50	7.50
57	Don Hoak	30.00	15.00	9.00
58	Tommy Lasorda	100.00	50.00	30.00
59	Gil Mills	25.00	12.50	7.50
60	Malcolm Mallette	25.00	12.50	7.50
61	Rocky Nelson	25.00	12.50	7.50
62	John Simmons	25.00	12.50	7.50
63	Bob Alexander	25.00	12.50	7.50
64	Dan Bankhead	35.00	17.50	10.00
65	Solomon Coleman	25.00	12.50	7.50
66	Walt Alston	100.00	50.00	30.00
67	Walt Fiala	25.00	12.50	7.50
68	Jim Gilliam	40.00	20.00	12.00
69	Jim Pendleton	25.00	12.50	7.50
70	Gino Cimoli	30.00	15.00	9.00
71	Carmen Mauro	25.00	12.50	7.50
72	Walt Moryn	25.00	12.50	7.50
73	Jim Romano	25.00	12.50	7.50
74	Joe Lutz	25.00	12.50	7.50
75	Ed Roebuck	25.00	12.50	7.50
76	Johnny Podres	40.00	20.00	12.00
77	Walter Novik	25.00	12.50	7.50
78	Lefty Gohl	25.00	12.50	7.50
79	Tom Kirk	25.00	12.50	7.50
80	Bob Betz	25.00	12.50	7.50
81	Bill Hockenbury	25.00	12.50	7.50
82	Al Rubeling	25.00	12.50	7.50
83	Julius Watlington	25.00	12.50	7.50
84	Frank Fanovich	25.00	12.50	7.50
85	Hank Foiles	25.00	12.50	7.50
86	Lou Limmer	25.00	12.50	7.50
87	Ed Hrabcsak	25.00	12.50	7.50
88	Bob Gardner	25.00	12.50	7.50
89	John Metkovich	25.00	12.50	7.50
90	Jean-Pierre Roy	25.00	12.50	7.50
91	Frank Skaff	25.00	12.50	7.50
92	Harry Desert	25.00	12.50	7.50
93	Stan Jok	25.00	12.50	7.50
94	Russ Swingle	25.00	12.50	7.50
95	Bob Wellman	25.00	12.50	7.50
96	John Conway	25.00	12.50	7.50
97	George Maskovich	25.00	12.50	7.50
98	Charlie Bishop	25.00	12.50	7.50
99	Joe Murray	25.00	12.50	7.50
100	Mike Kume	25.00	12.50	7.50

1935 Pebble Beach Clothiers

This series of black-and-white postcards includes only members of the three Bay area Pacific Coast League teams - the Oakland Oaks, Mission Reds and San Francisco Seals. The 3-1/2" x 5-3/8" cards have player identification at left in the bottom white border. The logotype of the clothier which sponsored the issue is at lower-right. The cards - each authentically autographed - were distributed by an area radio station. Backs have typical postcard indicia. This checklist may not be complete.

		NM	EX	VG
Common Player:		750.00	375.00	225.00
(1)	Leroy Anton	750.00	375.00	225.00
(2)	Joe DiMaggio	7,500	3,750	2,250
(3)	Wee Ludolph	750.00	375.00	225.00
(4)	Walter "The Great" Mails	750.00	375.00	225.00
(5)	Lefty O'Doul	3,650	1,825	1,100
(6)	Gabby Street	1,200	600.00	360.00
(7)	Oscar Vitt	900.00	450.00	270.00

1962 Pepsi-Cola Tulsa Oilers

The Texas League farm club of the St. Louis Cardinals is featured in this issue of sepia-colored 2-1/2" x 3-1/2" cards issued regionally by Pepsi. The unnumbered cards are checklisted here alphabetically.

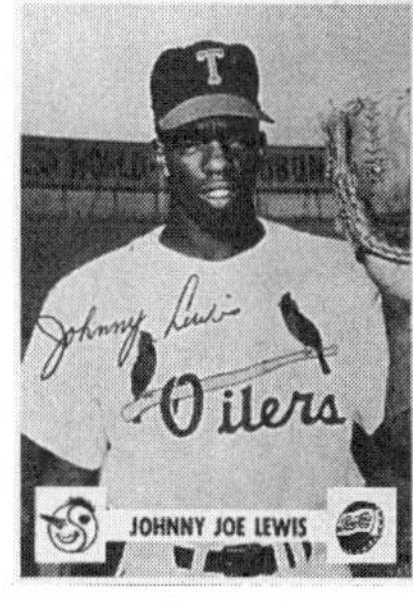

		NM	EX	VG
Complete Set (24):		275.00	135.00	80.00
Common Player:		12.00	6.00	3.50
(1)	Bob Blaylock	12.00	6.00	3.50
(2)	Bud Bloomfield	12.00	6.00	3.50
(3)	Dick Hughes	12.00	6.00	3.50
(4)	Gary Kolb	12.00	6.00	3.50
(5)	Chris Krug	12.00	6.00	3.50
(6)	Hank Kuhlmann	12.00	6.00	3.50
(7)	Whitey Kurowski	12.00	6.00	3.50
(8)	Johnny Joe Lewis	12.00	6.00	3.50
(9)	Elmer Lindsey	12.00	6.00	3.50
(10)	Jeoff Long	12.00	6.00	3.50
(11)	Pepper Martin	15.00	7.50	4.50
(12)	Jerry Marx	12.00	6.00	3.50
(13)	Weldon Maudin	12.00	6.00	3.50
(14)	Dal Maxvill	15.00	7.50	4.50
(15)	Bill McNamee	12.00	6.00	3.50
(16)	Joe Patterson	12.00	6.00	3.50
(17)	Gordon Richardson	12.00	6.00	3.50
(18)	Daryl Robertson	12.00	6.00	3.50
(19)	Tom Schwaner	12.00	6.00	3.50
(20)	Joe Shipley	12.00	6.00	3.50
(21)	Jon Smith	12.00	6.00	3.50
(22)	Clint Stark	12.00	6.00	3.50
(23)	Terry Tucker	12.00	6.00	3.50
(24)	Bill Wakefield	12.00	6.00	3.50

1963 Pepsi-Cola Tulsa Oilers

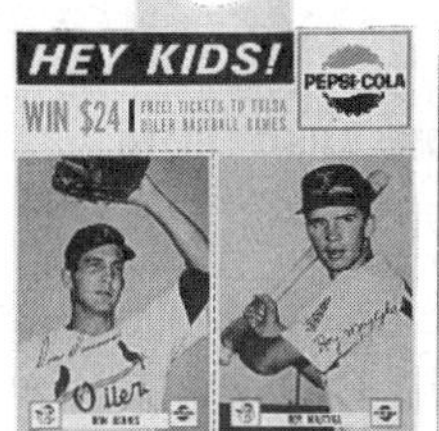

These 2-1/2" x 3-1/2", unnumbered, cards were issued in two-card panels with a holed top panel to hang on bottles. Each player's name could also be found under the cork liner of the bottle caps and when all 24 cards and caps were collected, a $24 prize could be collected. It must be assumed that some player caps were short-printed.

		NM	EX	VG
Complete Set, Singles (24):		75.00	37.50	22.50
Complete Set, Panels (12):		90.00	45.00	27.50
Common Player:		4.00	2.00	1.25
(1)	Dennis Aust	4.00	2.00	1.25
(2)	Jimmy Beauchamp	4.00	2.00	1.25
(3)	"Bud" Bloomfield	4.00	2.00	1.25
(4)	Felix de Leon	4.00	2.00	1.25
(5)	Don Dennis	4.00	2.00	1.25
(6)	Lamar Drummonds	4.00	2.00	1.25
(7)	Tom Hilgendorf	4.00	2.00	1.25
(8)	Gary Kolb	4.00	2.00	1.25
(9)	Chris Krug	4.00	2.00	1.25
(10)	"Bee" Lindsey	4.00	2.00	1.25
(11)	Roy Majtyka	4.00	2.00	1.25
(12)	Pepper Martin	7.50	3.75	2.25
(13)	Jerry Marx	4.00	2.00	1.25
(14)	"Hunkey" Mauldin	4.00	2.00	1.25
(15)	Joe Patterson	4.00	2.00	1.25
(16)	Grover Resinger	4.00	2.00	1.25
(17)	Gordon Richardson	4.00	2.00	1.25
(18)	Jon Smith	4.00	2.00	1.25
(19)	Chuck Taylor	4.00	2.00	1.25
(20)	Terry Tucker (Batboy)	4.00	2.00	1.25
(21)	Lou Vickery	4.00	2.00	1.25
(22)	Bill Wakefield	4.00	2.00	1.25
(23)	Harry Watts	4.00	2.00	1.25
(24)	Jerry Wild	4.00	2.00	1.25

1964 Pepsi-Cola Tulsa Oiler Autograph Cards

These unusual baseball cards - they don't have pictures! - were one of several 1960s issues by Pepsi in conjunction with the Tulsa Oilers. Apparently carton stuffers (they measure 2-3/16" x 9"), the cards provided free children's admission on special Pepsi-Oiler nights. The cards are printed in red, white and blue and have short player biographies under the baseball containing the facsimile autograph. The unnumbered cards are listed here in alphabetical order.

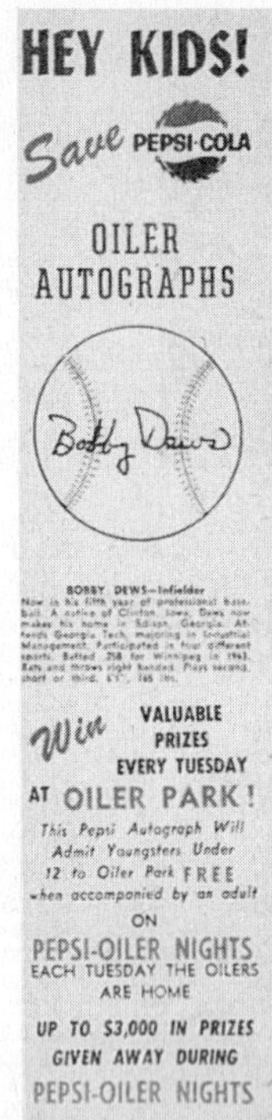

	NM	EX	VG
Complete Set (8):	30.00	15.00	9.00
Common Player:	5.00	2.50	1.50
(1) Bob Blaylock	5.00	2.50	1.50
(2) Nelson Briles	5.00	2.50	1.50
(3) Bobby Dews	5.00	2.50	1.50
(4) Roy Majtyka	5.00	2.50	1.50
(5) Otto Meischner	5.00	2.50	1.50
(6) Rogers Robinson	5.00	2.50	1.50
(7) Jerry Wild	5.00	2.50	1.50
(8) Lou Vickery	5.00	2.50	1.50

1966 Pepsi-Cola Tulsa Oilers

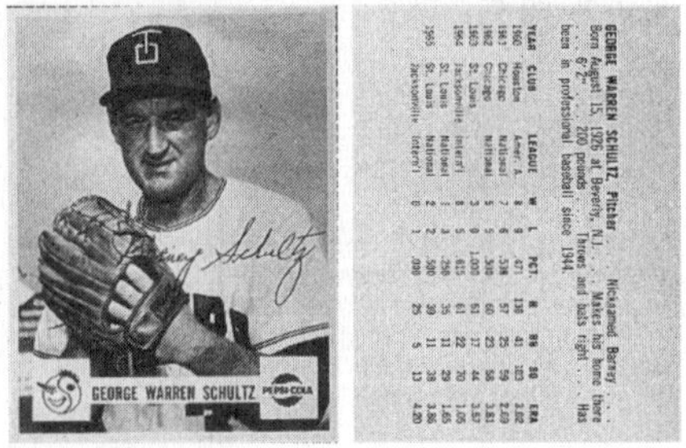

These 2-1/2" x 3-1/2" unnumbered cards were issued in two-card panels. Four cards were double-printed, each appearing on two different panels. Each player's name could also be found under the cork liner of the bottle caps and when all 24 cards and caps were collected, a $24 prize could be collected. It must be assumed that some player cards or caps were short-printed.

	NM	EX	VG
Complete Set (24):	175.00	90.00	55.00
Complete Panel Set (16):	225.00	115.00	70.00
Common Player:	10.00	5.00	3.00
Common Panel:	15.00	7.50	4.50
(1) Florian Ackley	10.00	5.00	3.00
(2) Dennis Aust	10.00	5.00	3.00
(3) Elio Chacon/DP	10.00	5.00	3.00
(4) James Cosman	10.00	5.00	3.00
(5) Mack Creager	10.00	5.00	3.00
(6) Robert Dews/DP	10.00	5.00	3.00
(7) Harold Gilson	10.00	5.00	3.00
(8) Larry Jaster	10.00	5.00	3.00
(9) Alex Johnson	10.00	5.00	3.00
(10) George Kernek/DP	10.00	5.00	3.00
(11) Jose Laboy	10.00	5.00	3.00
(12) Richard LeMay	10.00	5.00	3.00
(13) Charles Metro	10.00	5.00	3.00
(14) David Pavlesic	10.00	5.00	3.00
(15) Robert Pfeil	10.00	5.00	3.00
(16) Ronald Piche	10.00	5.00	3.00
(17) Robert Radovich	10.00	5.00	3.00
(18) David Ricketts/DP	10.00	5.00	3.00
(19) Theodore Savage	10.00	5.00	3.00
(20) George Schultz	10.00	5.00	3.00
(21) Edward Spiezio	10.00	5.00	3.00
(22) Clint Stark	10.00	5.00	3.00
(23) Robert Tolan	10.00	5.00	3.00
(24) Walter Williams	10.00	5.00	3.00

1956 Portland Beaver All-Star Pins

Stars of the Pacific Coast League Portland Beavers, all former and/or future major leaguers, are featured on these 1" black-and-white celluloid pins.

	NM	EX	VG
Complete Set (8):	1,300	650.00	375.00
Common Player:	175.00	90.00	55.00
(1) Jim Baxes	175.00	90.00	55.00
(2) Bob Borkowski	175.00	90.00	55.00
(3) Sam Calderone	175.00	90.00	55.00
(4) Jack Littrell	175.00	90.00	55.00
(5) Luis Marquez	175.00	90.00	55.00
(6) Ed Mickelson	175.00	90.00	55.00
(7) Tom Saffell	175.00	90.00	55.00
(8) Rene Valdez	175.00	90.00	55.00

1958 Ralph's Thriftway Seattle Rainiers

(See 1958 Seattle Popcorn for checklist and values.)

1968 Red Barn Memphis Blues

A regional issue from a Memphis chain of fast-food restaurants, these 2-1/2" x 3-3/4" cards feature members of the New York Mets' Class AA farm team. Cards have a blue-tinted player photo within an orange barn design. Player information is printed below. Backs are blank. The cards are checklisted here by uniform number.

	NM	EX	VG
Complete Set (8):	600.00	300.00	180.00
Common Player:	75.00	37.50	22.50
3 Mike "Spider" Jorgensen	75.00	37.50	22.50
6 Joe Moock	75.00	37.50	22.50
9 Rod Gaspar	75.00	37.50	22.50
16 Barry "Chief" Raziano	75.00	37.50	22.50
17 Curtis "Bubba" Brown	75.00	37.50	22.50
18 Roger Stevens	75.00	37.50	22.50
19 Ron Paul	75.00	37.50	22.50
24 Steve "Teddy" Christopher	75.00	37.50	22.50

1910 Red Sun (T211)

The 1910 minor league tobacco set issued by Red Sun Cigarettes features 75 players from the Southern Association. The Red Sun issue is similar in size and style to the massive 640-card Old Mill set (T210) issued the same year. Cards in both sets measure 1-1/2" x 2-5/8" and feature glossy black-and-white player photos. Unlike the Old Mill set, however, the Red Sun cards have a green border surrounding the photograph and a bright red and white advertisement for Red Sun cigarettes on the back. A line at the bottom promotes the cards as "First Series 1 to 75," implying that additional sets would follow, but apparently none ever did. Each of the 75 subjects in the Red Sun set was also pictured in Series Eight of the Old Mill set. Because of the "Glossy" nature of the photographs, cards in both the Old Mill and Red Sun sets are susceptible to cracking, making condition and proper grading of these cards especially important to collectors.

	NM	EX	VG
Complete Set (75):	65,000	35,000	20,000
Common Player:	1,300	500.00	300.00
(1) Allen	1,300	500.00	300.00
(2) Anderson	1,300	500.00	300.00
(3) Babb	1,300	500.00	300.00
(4) Bartley	1,300	500.00	300.00
(5) Bay	1,300	500.00	300.00
(6) Bayliss	1,300	500.00	300.00
(7) Berger	1,300	500.00	300.00
(8) Bernard	1,300	500.00	300.00
(9) Bitroff	1,300	500.00	300.00
(10) Breitenstein	1,300	500.00	300.00
(11) Bronkie	1,300	500.00	300.00
(12) Brooks	1,300	500.00	300.00
(13) Cafalu	1,300	500.00	300.00
(14) Case	1,300	500.00	300.00
(15) Chappelle	1,300	500.00	300.00
(16) Cohen	1,300	500.00	300.00
(17) Cross	1,300	500.00	300.00
(18) Jud. Daly	1,300	500.00	300.00
(19) Davis	1,300	500.00	300.00
(20) DeMontreville	1,300	500.00	300.00
(21) E. DeMontreville	1,300	500.00	300.00
(22) Dick	1,300	500.00	300.00
(23) Dunn	1,300	500.00	300.00
(24) Erloff	1,300	500.00	300.00
(25) Fisher	1,300	500.00	300.00
(26) Flood	1,300	500.00	300.00
(27) Foster	1,300	500.00	300.00
(28) Fritz	1,300	500.00	300.00
(29) Greminger	1,300	500.00	300.00
(30) Gribbon	1,300	500.00	300.00
(31) Griffin	1,300	500.00	300.00
(32) Gygli	1,300	500.00	300.00
(33) Hanks	1,300	500.00	300.00
(34) Hart	1,300	500.00	300.00
(35) Hess	1,300	500.00	300.00
(36) Hickman	1,300	500.00	300.00
(37) Hohnhorst	1,300	500.00	300.00
(38) Huelsman	1,300	500.00	300.00
(39) Jordan	1,300	500.00	300.00
(40) Kane	1,300	500.00	300.00
(41) Kelly	1,300	500.00	300.00
(42) Kerwin	1,300	500.00	300.00
(43) Keupper	1,300	500.00	300.00
(44) LaFitte	1,300	500.00	300.00
(45) Bill Lindsay	1,300	500.00	300.00
(46) Lynch	1,300	500.00	300.00
(47) Manush	1,300	500.00	300.00
(48) McCreery	1,300	500.00	300.00
(49) Miller	1,300	500.00	300.00
(50) Molesworth	1,300	500.00	300.00
(51) Moran	1,300	500.00	300.00
(52) Nolley	1,300	500.00	300.00
(53) Paige	1,300	500.00	300.00
(54) Pepe	1,300	500.00	300.00
(55) Perdue	1,300	500.00	300.00
(56) Pratt	1,300	500.00	300.00
(57) Rhoton	1,300	500.00	300.00
(58) Robertson	1,300	500.00	300.00
(59) Rogers	1,300	500.00	300.00
(60) Rohe	1,300	500.00	300.00
(61) Seabaugh	1,300	500.00	300.00
(62) Seitz	1,300	500.00	300.00
(63) Siegle	1,300	500.00	300.00
(64) Smith	1,300	500.00	300.00
(65) Sid. Smith	1,300	500.00	300.00
(66) Steele	1,300	500.00	300.00
(67) Swacina	1,300	500.00	300.00
(68) Sweeney	1,300	500.00	300.00
(69) Thomas	1,300	500.00	300.00
(70) Vinson	1,300	500.00	300.00
(71) Wagner	1,300	500.00	300.00
(72) Walker	1,300	500.00	300.00
(73) Welf	1,300	500.00	300.00
(74) Wilder	1,300	500.00	300.00
(75) Wiseman	1,300	500.00	300.00

1945 Remar Bread Oakland Oaks

This 4-7/8" x 3-5/8" card features on front a black-and-white team photo, borderless at the top and sides. In the white strip at bottom, the players are identified. The back is printed in black with red highlights and presents the season stats for batting average and pitchers' won-lost percentage. At right is a picture of a loaf of the sponsor's bread. At present, only two examples of this card are known to exist.

	NM	EX	VG
Oakland Oaks Team Photo	2,500	1,250	750.00

1946 Remar Bread Oakland Oaks

CHARLES (Casey) STENGEL
Oaks Manager 10

Fiery CHAS. (Casey) STENGEL has been in baseball 35 years. During his playing days, STENGEL—a fast, hard-hitting outfielder—was with Brooklyn Dodgers, Boston Braves, New York Giants. Has managed Dodgers, Braves and Milwaukee of American Association. He's noted for his ability to develop young players.

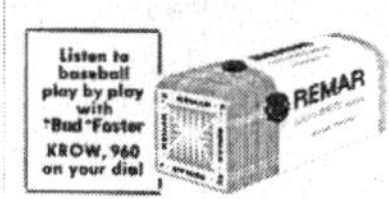

Listen to baseball play by play with "Bud" Foster KROW, 960 on your dial
REMAR

Get the FOUR HOURS FRESHER winner...
REMAR BREAD

Remar Baking Co. issued several baseball card sets in the northern California area from 1946-1950, all picturing members of the Oakland Oaks of the Pacific Coast League. The 1946 set consists of 23 cards (five unnumbered, 18 numbered). Measuring 2" x 3", the cards were printed on heavy paper and feature black and white photos with the player's name, team and position at the bottom. The backs contain a brief write-up plus an ad for Remar Bread printed in red. The cards were distributed one per week. The first five cards were unnumbered. The rest of the set is numbered on the front, but begins with number "5," rather than "6."

		NM	EX	VG
Complete Set (23):		600.00	300.00	180.00
Common Player:		25.00	12.50	7.50
5	Hershell Martin (Herschel)	25.00	12.50	7.50
6	Bill Hart	25.00	12.50	7.50
7	Charlie Gassaway	25.00	12.50	7.50
8	Wally Westlake	25.00	12.50	7.50
9	Mickey Burnett	25.00	12.50	7.50
10	Charles (Casey) Stengel	110.00	55.00	35.00
11	Charlie Metro	25.00	12.50	7.50
12	Tom Hafey	25.00	12.50	7.50
13	Tony Sabol	25.00	12.50	7.50
14	Ed Kearse	25.00	12.50	7.50
15	Bud Foster (Announcer)	25.00	12.50	7.50
16	Johnny Price	25.00	12.50	7.50
17	Gene Bearden	25.00	12.50	7.50
18	Floyd Speer	25.00	12.50	7.50
19	Bryan Stephens	25.00	12.50	7.50
20	Rinaldo (Rugger) Ardizoia	25.00	12.50	7.50
21	Ralph Buxton	25.00	12.50	7.50
22	Ambrose (Bo) Palica	25.00	12.50	7.50
----	Brooks Holder	25.00	12.50	7.50
----	Henry (Cotton) Pippen	25.00	12.50	7.50
----	Billy Raimondi	90.00	45.00	27.50
----	Les Scarsella	25.00	12.50	7.50
----	Glen (Gabby) Stewart	25.00	12.50	7.50

1947 Remar Bread Oakland Oaks

BILLY RAIMONDI
Oaks Catcher 1

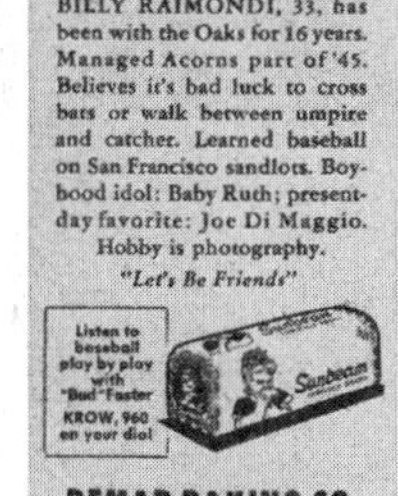

BILLY RAIMONDI, 33, has been with the Oaks for 16 years. Managed Acorns part of '45. Believes it's bad luck to cross bats or walk between umpire and catcher. Learned baseball on San Francisco sandlots. Boyhood idol: Baby Ruth; present-day favorite: Joe Di Maggio. Hobby is photography.
"Let's Be Friends"
Listen to baseball play by play with "Bud" Foster KROW, 960 on your dial
Sunbeam
REMAR BAKING CO.

Remar's second set consisted of 25 numbered cards, again measuring 2" x 3". The cards are nearly identical to the previous year's set, except the loaf of bread on the back is printed in blue, rather than red.

		NM	EX	VG
Complete Set (25):		600.00	300.00	180.00
Common Player:		25.00	12.50	7.50
1	Billy Raimondi	25.00	12.50	7.50
2	Les Scarsella	25.00	12.50	7.50
3	Brooks Holder	25.00	12.50	7.50
4	Charlie Gassaway	25.00	12.50	7.50
5	Mickey Burnett	25.00	12.50	7.50
6	Ralph Buxton	25.00	12.50	7.50
7	Ed Kearse	25.00	12.50	7.50
8	Charles (Casey) Stengel	75.00	37.50	22.50
9	Bud Foster (Announcer)	25.00	12.50	7.50
10	Ambrose (Bo) Palica	25.00	12.50	7.50
11	Tom Hafey	25.00	12.50	7.50
12	Hershel Martin (Herschel)	25.00	12.50	7.50
13	Henry (Cotton) Pippen	25.00	12.50	7.50
14	Floyd Speer	25.00	12.50	7.50
15	Tony Sabol	25.00	12.50	7.50
16	Will Hafey	25.00	12.50	7.50
17	Ray Hamrick	25.00	12.50	7.50
18	Maurice Van Robays	25.00	12.50	7.50
19	Dario Lodigiani	25.00	12.50	7.50
20	Mel (Dizz) Duezabou	25.00	12.50	7.50
21	Damon Hayes	25.00	12.50	7.50
22	Gene Lillard	25.00	12.50	7.50
23	Aldon Wilkie	25.00	12.50	7.50
24	Dewey Soriano	25.00	12.50	7.50
25	Glen Crawford	25.00	12.50	7.50

1948 Remar/Sunbeam Bread Oakland Oaks

1948 Oakland OAKS
Let's Be Friends... REACH FOR SUNBEAM BREAD

One of the great minor league rarities, only two examples of this 3-1/4" x 5-1/2" black-and-white team photo card are known.

	NM	EX	VG
1948 Oakland Oaks Team Photo	2,500	1,250	750.00

1949 Remar Bread Oakland Oaks

BILLY MARTIN
Oaks Infielder

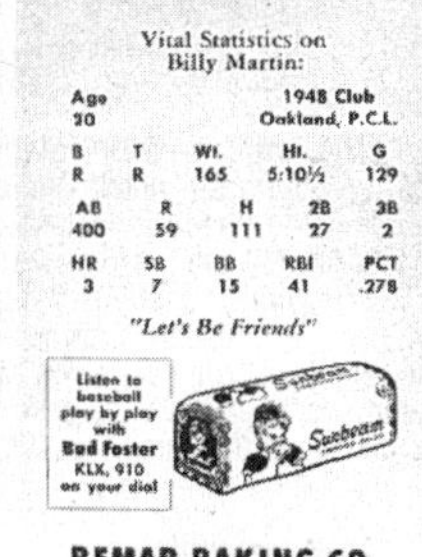

The 1949 Remar Bread issue was increased to 32 cards, again measuring 2" x 3". Unlike the two earlier sets, photos in the 1949 Remar set are surrounded by a thin, white border and are unnumbered. The player's name, team and position appear below the black and white photo. The backs are printed in blue and include the player's 1948 statistics and the distinctive loaf of bread.

		NM	EX	VG
Complete Set (32):		700.00	350.00	210.00
Common Player:		20.00	10.00	6.00
(1)	Ralph Buxton	20.00	10.00	6.00
(2)	Milo Candini	20.00	10.00	6.00
(3)	Rex Cecil	20.00	10.00	6.00
(4)	Loyd Christopher (Lloyd)	20.00	10.00	6.00
(5)	Charles Dressen	20.00	10.00	6.00
(6)	Mel Duezabou	20.00	10.00	6.00
(7)	Bud Foster (Sportscaster)	20.00	10.00	6.00
(8)	Charlie Gassaway	20.00	10.00	6.00
(9)	Ray Hamrick	20.00	10.00	6.00
(10)	Jack Jensen	25.00	12.50	7.50
(11)	Earl Jones	20.00	10.00	6.00
(12)	George Kelly	60.00	30.00	18.00
(13)	Frank Kerr	20.00	10.00	6.00
(14)	Richard Kryhoski	20.00	10.00	6.00
(15)	Harry Lavagetto	20.00	10.00	6.00
(16)	Dario Lodigiani	20.00	10.00	6.00
(17)	Billy Martin	75.00	37.50	22.50
(18)	George Metkovich	20.00	10.00	6.00
(19)	Frank Nelson	20.00	10.00	6.00
(20)	Don Padgett	20.00	10.00	6.00
(21)	Alonzo Perry	40.00	20.00	12.00
(22)	Bill Raimondi	20.00	10.00	6.00
(23)	Earl Rapp	20.00	10.00	6.00
(24)	Eddie Samcoff	20.00	10.00	6.00
(25)	Les Scarsella	20.00	10.00	6.00
(26)	Forest Thompson (Forrest)	20.00	10.00	6.00
(27)	Earl Toolson	20.00	10.00	6.00
(28)	Lou Tost	20.00	10.00	6.00
(29)	Maurice Van Robays	20.00	10.00	6.00
(30)	Jim Wallace	20.00	10.00	6.00
(31)	Arthur Lee Wilson	40.00	20.00	12.00
(32)	Parnell Woods	20.00	10.00	6.00

1950 Remar Bread Oakland Oaks

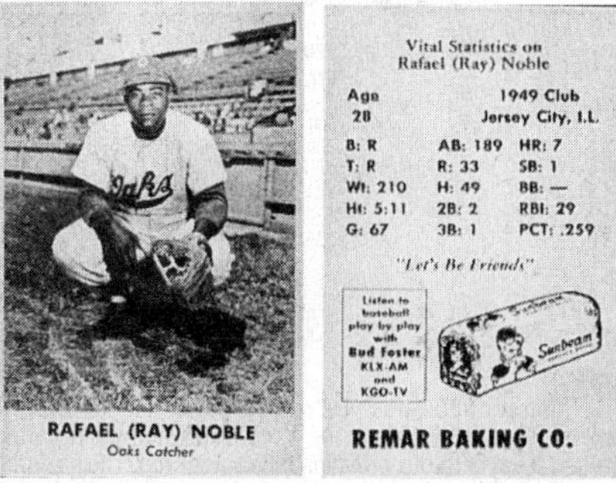

The most common of the Remar Bread issues, the 1950 set contains 27 unnumbered cards, again measuring 2" x 3" and featuring members of the Oakland Oaks. The cards are nearly identical to the previous year's set but can be differentiated by the 1949 statistics on the back.

		NM	EX	VG
Complete Set (27):		500.00	250.00	150.00
Common Player:		20.00	10.00	6.00
(1)	George Bamberger	20.00	10.00	6.00
(2)	Hank Behrman	20.00	10.00	6.00
(3)	Loyd Christopher (Lloyd)	20.00	10.00	6.00
(4)	Chuck Dressen	20.00	10.00	6.00
(5)	Mel Duezabou	20.00	10.00	6.00
(6)	Augie Galan	20.00	10.00	6.00
(7)	Charlie Gassaway	20.00	10.00	6.00
(8)	Allen Gettel	20.00	10.00	6.00
(9)	Ernie W. Groth	20.00	10.00	6.00
(10)	Ray Hamrick	20.00	10.00	6.00
(11)	Earl Harrist	20.00	10.00	6.00
(12)	Billy Herman	60.00	30.00	18.00
(13)	Bob Hofman	20.00	10.00	6.00
(14)	George Kelly	60.00	30.00	18.00
(15)	Harry Lavagetto	20.00	10.00	6.00
(16)	Eddie Malone	20.00	10.00	6.00
(17)	George Metkovich	20.00	10.00	6.00
(18)	Frank Nelson	20.00	10.00	6.00
(19)	Rafael (Ray) Noble	20.00	10.00	6.00
(20)	Don Padgett	20.00	10.00	6.00
(21)	Earl Rapp	20.00	10.00	6.00
(22)	Clyde Shoun	20.00	10.00	6.00
(23)	Forrest Thompson	20.00	10.00	6.00
(24)	Louis Tost	20.00	10.00	6.00
(25)	Dick Wakefield	20.00	10.00	6.00
(26)	Artie Wilson	40.00	20.00	12.00
(27)	Roy Zimmerman	20.00	10.00	6.00

1958 Richmond Virginians Team Issue

This set of black-and-white cards features members of the N.Y. Yankees' top farm club in posed action photos with a stadium background. Issued on a pair of 8-1/2" x 10" sheets, single cards measure about 2-1/8" x 3" including the white borders around the picture. The player name is in a white strip within the photo. Backs have only the player name and a two-line credit at bottom to Galeski Photo Finishing.

		NM	EX	VG
Complete Set (21):		1,200	600.00	360.00
Common Player:		60.00	30.00	18.00
(1)	Billy Bethel	60.00	30.00	18.00
(2)	Cletis Boyer	90.00	45.00	27.50
(3)	Wade Browning	60.00	30.00	18.00
(4)	Bob Chakales	60.00	30.00	18.00
(5)	Jim Coates	60.00	30.00	18.00
(6)	Jim Command	60.00	30.00	18.00
(7)	Bobby Deakin	60.00	30.00	18.00
(8)	Bob Del Greco	60.00	30.00	18.00
(9)	John Jaciuk	60.00	30.00	18.00
(10)	John James	60.00	30.00	18.00
(11)	Deron Johnson	75.00	37.50	22.50
(12)	Len Johnston	60.00	30.00	18.00
(13)	Bob Kline	60.00	30.00	18.00
(14)	Ed Lopat	80.00	40.00	24.00
(15)	Bob Oldis	60.00	30.00	18.00
(16)	Wilson Parsons	60.00	30.00	18.00
(17)	Rance Pless	60.00	30.00	18.00
(18)	Jim Post	60.00	30.00	18.00
(19)	Danny Schell	60.00	30.00	18.00
(20)	Gerry Thomas	60.00	30.00	18.00
(21)	Bob Weisler	60.00	30.00	18.00

1959 Richmond Virginians

Photos of half a dozen local favorites of the International League Richmond Virginians were featured on ticket stubs during the 1959 season. The black-and-white player portions of the stub measure 2" x 3" and are blank-backed. The unnumbered cards are listed here alphabetically. Richmond was a farm club of the N.Y. Yankees.

		NM	EX	VG
Complete Set (6):		1,200	625.00	375.00
Common Player:		90.00	45.00	25.00
(1)	Clete Boyer	300.00	150.00	90.00
(2)	Jim Coates	200.00	100.00	60.00
(3)	Eli Grba	200.00	100.00	60.00
(4)	John James	200.00	100.00	60.00
(5)	Dick Sanders	200.00	100.00	60.00
(6)	Bill Short	200.00	100.00	60.00

1960 Richmond Virginians

In 1960, the Richmond Virginians of the International League continued the practice of using player photos on their game tickets. Black-and-white with a blank-back, the player portions of the tickets can be found in two sizes. Unnumbered cards are checklisted here alphabetically. The Richmond team was a farm club of the N.Y. Yankees.

	NM	EX	VG
Complete Set (6):	1,750	875.00	525.00
Common Player:	300.00	150.00	90.00
SMALL SIZE (2" x 2-3/4")			
(1) Bob Martyn	300.00	150.00	90.00
(2) Jack Reed	300.00	150.00	90.00
LARGE SIZE (2-3/8" x 2-7/8")			
(1) Tony Asaro	300.00	150.00	90.00
(2) Bill Shantz	300.00	150.00	90.00
(3) Jerry Thomas	300.00	150.00	90.00
(4) Bob Weisler	300.00	150.00	90.00

1966 Royal Crown Cola Columbus Yankees

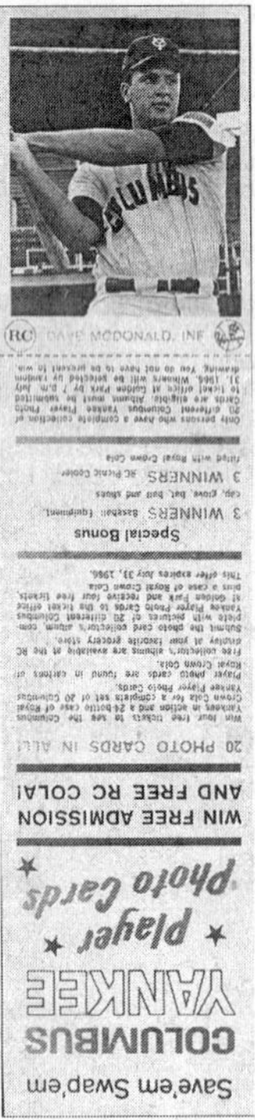

This set of 20 cards was distributed in eight packs of Royal Crown Cola, then based in Columbus, Ga. They were part of a strip measuring 2-1/4" wide. The first 3" of the 9-1/2" strip has a black-and-white photo of the player with his name, position and other biographical data, along with an RC logo in blue and red. The bottom of the strip has a promotion sponsored by the ball club and RC, offering a case of cola for turning in a complete set in an album provided for the cards. Those who turned in the cards were also eligible to win baseball equipment or picnic coolers in a giveaway at a July 31 game that year. Most cards have the advertisement removed. Strips that include the advertisement should be valued at 1.5X of values shown. The cards are unnumbered and listed in alphabetical order.

	NM	EX	VG
Complete Set (20):	800.00	400.00	240.00
Common Player:	40.00	20.00	12.00
Album:	800.00	400.00	240.00
(1) Gil Blanco	40.00	20.00	12.00
(2) Ronnie Boyer	50.00	25.00	15.00
(3) Jim Brenneman	40.00	20.00	12.00
(4) Butch Cretara	40.00	20.00	12.00
(5) Bill Henry	40.00	20.00	12.00
(6) Joe Jeran	40.00	20.00	12.00
(7) Jerry Kenney	40.00	20.00	12.00
(8) Ronnie Kirk	40.00	20.00	12.00
(9) Tom Kowalski	40.00	20.00	12.00
(10) Jim Marrujo	40.00	20.00	12.00
(11) Dave McDonald	40.00	20.00	12.00
(12) Ed Merritt	40.00	20.00	12.00
(13) Jim Palma	40.00	20.00	12.00
(14) Cecil Perkins	40.00	20.00	12.00
(15) Jack Reed	40.00	20.00	12.00
(16) Ellie Rodriguez	60.00	30.00	18.00
(17) John Schroeppel	40.00	20.00	12.00
(18) Dave Truelock	40.00	20.00	12.00
(19) Steve Whitaker	40.00	20.00	12.00
(20) Earl Willoughby	40.00	20.00	12.00

S

1952 San Diego Padres Team Issue

The Padres were one of the highest classification minor league teams for which Globe Printing produced baseball cards in the early 1950s. Like other sets from the San Jose, Calif., printer, the 2-1/8" x 3-3/8" cards are black-and-white, blank-backed and feature the player's name on a white strip on front. Because the Padres are quite often found as a team set, it's likely they were not distributed a card at a time as seems to have been the case with other sets. In 1952, the team was in the Open Classification Pacific Coast League.

	NM	EX	VG
Complete Set (18):	1,000	500.00	300.00
Common Player:	60.00	30.00	18.00
(1) Al Benton	60.00	30.00	18.00
(2) Dain Clay	60.00	30.00	18.00
(3) John Davis	125.00	62.00	37.00
(4) Dick Faber	60.00	30.00	18.00
(5) Ben Flowers	60.00	30.00	18.00
(6) Murray Franklin	60.00	30.00	18.00
(7) Herb Gorman	90.00	45.00	27.50
(8) Jack Graham	60.00	30.00	18.00
(9) Memo Luna	60.00	30.00	18.00
(10) Lefty O'Doul (Seated, light background.)	125.00	62.00	37.00
(11) Lefty O'Doul (Standing, dark background.)	125.00	62.00	37.00
(12) Al Olsen	60.00	30.00	18.00
(13) Jimmie Reese	100.00	50.00	30.00
(14) Al Richter	60.00	30.00	18.00
(15) Jack Salveson	60.00	30.00	18.00
(16) Lou Stringer	60.00	30.00	18.00
(17) Lonnie Summers	60.00	30.00	18.00
(18) Jack Tobin	60.00	30.00	18.00

1950 San Francisco Seals Popcorn

These 3-1/4" x 4-1/2" black-and-white cards were issued with the purchase of caramel corn at Sicks Stadium.

	NM	EX	VG
Complete Set (13):	700.00	350.00	210.00
Common Player:	60.00	30.00	17.50
(1) Dick Briskey	60.00	30.00	17.50
(2) Ralph Buxton	60.00	30.00	17.50
(3) Harry Feldman	60.00	30.00	17.50
(4) Chet Johnson	60.00	30.00	17.50
(5) Al Lien	60.00	30.00	17.50
(6) Dario Lodigiani	60.00	30.00	17.50
(7) Cliff Melton	60.00	30.00	17.50
(8) Roy Nicely	60.00	30.00	17.50
(9) Roy Partee	60.00	30.00	17.50
(10) Manny Perez	60.00	30.00	17.50
(11) Neill Sheridan	60.00	30.00	17.50
(12) Elmer Singleton	60.00	30.00	17.50
(13) Jack Tobin	60.00	30.00	17.50

1953 San Francisco Seals Team Issue

This set of 25 cards was sold at Seals Stadium and by mail for 25 cents. Fronts of the 4" x 5" black-and-white cards contain a player photo with facsimile autograph. The player's name, team and position are printed in the white bottom border. Backs of the unnumbered cards are blank. Melton is a rare short-print which has been reprinted.

	NM	EX	VG
Complete Set (25):	600.00	300.00	180.00
Common Player:	30.00	15.00	9.00
(1) Bill Boemler	30.00	15.00	9.00
(2) Bill Bradford	30.00	15.00	9.00
(3) Reno Cheso	30.00	15.00	9.00
(4) Harlond Clift	30.00	15.00	9.00
(5) Walt Clough	30.00	15.00	9.00
(6) Cliff Coggin	30.00	15.00	9.00
(7) Tommy Heath	30.00	15.00	9.00
(8) Leo Hughes (Trainer)	30.00	15.00	9.00
(9) Frank Kalin	30.00	15.00	9.00
(10) Al Lien	30.00	15.00	9.00
(11) Al Lyons	30.00	15.00	9.00
(12) John McCall	30.00	15.00	9.00
(13) Bill McCawley	30.00	15.00	9.00
(14) Dave Melton/SP	200.00	100.00	60.00
(15) Jim Moran	30.00	15.00	9.00
(16) Bob Muncrief	30.00	15.00	9.00
(17) Leo Righetti	30.00	15.00	9.00
(18) Ted Shandor	30.00	15.00	9.00
(19) Elmer Singleton	30.00	15.00	9.00
(20) Lou Stringer	30.00	15.00	9.00
(21) Sal Taormina	30.00	15.00	9.00
(22) Will Tiesiera	30.00	15.00	9.00
(23) Nini Tornay	30.00	15.00	9.00
(24) George Vico	30.00	15.00	9.00
(25) Jerry Zuvela	30.00	15.00	9.00

1951 San Jose Red Sox Team Issue

These 2-1/4" x 3-3/8" black-and-white, unnumbered, blank-backed cards were one of many minor league team sets issued by Globe Printing of San Jose, Calif., in the early 1950s. Cards were usually given away at the ballpark on a one-per-week or one-per-homestand basis, accounting for the rarity of surviving sets. The team was a Class C farm club for the Boston Red Sox in the California League. An album exists for the set, but curiously, it is dated 1952.

	NM	EX	VG
Complete Set (18):	1,000	500.00	300.00
Common Player:	60.00	30.00	18.00
(1) Ken Aspromonte	75.00	37.00	22.00
(2) Joe Buck	60.00	30.00	18.00
(3) Harold Buckwalter	60.00	30.00	18.00
(4) Al Curtis	60.00	30.00	18.00
(5) Marvin Eyre	60.00	30.00	18.00
(6) Jack Heinen	60.00	30.00	18.00
(7) John Kinney	60.00	30.00	18.00
(8) Walt Lucas	60.00	30.00	18.00
(9) Syl McNinch	60.00	30.00	18.00
(10) Stan McWilliams	60.00	30.00	18.00
(11) Marvin Owen	60.00	30.00	18.00
(12) Dick Piedrotti	60.00	30.00	18.00
(13) Al Schroll	60.00	30.00	18.00
(14) Ed Sobczak	60.00	30.00	18.00
(15) Joe Stephenson	60.00	30.00	18.00
(16) George Storti	60.00	30.00	18.00
(17) Allan Van Alstyne	60.00	30.00	18.00
(18) Floyd Warr	60.00	30.00	18.00

1963 Scheible Press Rochester Red Wings

Stephen Thomas Bilko — First Baseman

Born—Nanticoke, Pa., Nov. 13, 1928

Bats — Right Weight — 242
Throws — Right Height — 6' 1"

Steve began his baseball career with Salisbury in the East Shore League in 1946. No stranger to Rochester fans, Steve played here briefly in 1948, and followed with good years in '49, '50, '51 and '52. His biggest years with the bat came in 1956 and 1957 with Los Angeles of the Pacific Coast League with 55 and 56 homeruns. His lifetime total of homeruns is 381. Steve's last two years were played with the Los Angeles Angels of the American League.

Apparently sold as a stadium concession stand item in a paper and cellophane envelope, the full-color 3-13/16" x 5-7/8" cards are found printed on either a heavy paper stock or thin cardboard stock, each with identical black-and-white back. Two blank-backed cards in slightly larger (4" x 5-7/8") format are checklisted here, although their relationship to the other photos is unknown. The '63 Red Wings were the International League affiliate of the Baltimore Orioles.

		NM	EX	VG
Complete Set (11):		250.00	125.00	75.00
Common Player:		20.00	10.00	6.00
(1)	Joe Altobelli	25.00	12.50	7.50
(2)	Steve Bilko	20.00	10.00	6.00
(3)	Sam E. Bowens	20.00	10.00	6.00
(4)	Don Brummer	20.00	10.00	6.00
(5)	Nelson Chittum (Cardboard only.)	20.00	10.00	6.00
(6a)	Luke Easter (Small format.)	40.00	20.00	12.00
(6b)	Luke Easter (Large format.)	75.00	40.00	25.00
(7)	Darrell Johnson, Chris Krug (Paper only.)	25.00	12.50	7.50
(8)	Ron Kabbes (Large format.)	20.00	10.00	6.00
(9)	Fred Valentine	20.00	10.00	6.00
(10)	Ozzie Virgil	20.00	10.00	6.00
(11)	Ray Youngdahl	20.00	10.00	6.00

1954-1968 Seattle Rainiers/ Angels Popcorn

One of the longest-running minor league baseball card promotions was the 1954-68 Seattle popcorn cards. The principal sponsor was Centennial Mills, which had issued cards in the 1940s. Similar in format throughout their period of issue, the cards are 2" x 3" in size, black-and-white, usually featuring portrait photos on the front with the player's name or name and position below. In some years the cards were printed on semi-glossy stock. Some years' card backs are blank, in other years, backs feature ads for various local businesses; in a few years, cards could be found with both blank and printed backs. Many photo and spelling variations are known throughout the series; most are noted in the appropriate checklists. The unnumbered cards are checklisted alphabetically. It is possible a few stragglers will be added to these checklists in the future. In most years a group of 20 cards was released early in the year, supplemented later in the season as roster changes dictated. The cards were given away with the purchase of a box of popcorn sold at Seattle's Sicks stadium. During the card-issuing era, Seattle was an independent team in the Pacific Coast League in 1954-55. From 1956-60 they were a top farm team in the Reds system. They were a Red Sox affiliate from 1961-64, before tying up with the California Angels in 1965.

(Consult checklists for attribution of blank-back cards.)

1954 Seattle Rainiers Popcorn

BOB HALL
Pitcher

(Blank-back. Most players photographed in dark cap with light "S.")

		NM	EX	VG
Complete Set (26):		2,500	1,250	750.00
Common Player:		110.00	55.00	35.00
(1)	Gene Bearden	110.00	55.00	35.00
(2)	Al Brightman	110.00	55.00	35.00
(3)	Jack Burkowatz	110.00	55.00	35.00
(4)	Tommy Byrne (Photo reversed, backwards "S" on cap.)	110.00	55.00	35.00
(5)	Joe Erautt	110.00	55.00	35.00
(6)	Bill Evans	110.00	55.00	35.00
(7)	Van Fletcher	110.00	55.00	35.00
(8)	Bob Hall	110.00	55.00	35.00
(9)	Pete Hernandez	110.00	55.00	35.00
(10)	Lloyd Jenney	110.00	55.00	35.00
(11)	Joe Joshua	110.00	55.00	35.00
(12)	Vern Kindsfather	110.00	55.00	35.00
(13)	Tom Lovrich	110.00	55.00	35.00
(14)	Clarence Maddern	110.00	55.00	35.00
(15)	Don Mallott	110.00	55.00	35.00
(16)	Loren Meyers	110.00	55.00	35.00
(17)	Steve Nagy	110.00	55.00	35.00
(18)	Ray Orteig	110.00	55.00	35.00
(19)	Gerry Priddy	110.00	55.00	35.00
(20)	George Schmees	110.00	55.00	35.00
(21)	Bill Schuster	110.00	55.00	35.00
(22)	Leo Thomas	110.00	55.00	35.00
(23)	Jack Tobin	110.00	55.00	35.00
(24)	Al Widmer	110.00	55.00	35.00
(25)	Artie Wilson	175.00	85.00	50.00
(26)	Al Zarilla	110.00	55.00	35.00

1955 Seattle Rainiers Popcorn

(Blank-back. All players wearing light caps with "R" logo.)

		NM	EX	VG
Complete Set (22):		2,000	1,000	600.00
Common Player:		110.00	55.00	35.00
(1)	Bob Balcena	110.00	55.00	35.00
(2)	Monty Basgall	110.00	55.00	35.00
(3)	Ewell Blackwell	135.00	65.00	40.00
(4)	Bill Brenner	110.00	55.00	35.00
(5)	Jack Burkowatz	110.00	55.00	35.00
(6)	Van Fletcher	110.00	55.00	35.00
(7)	Joe Ginsberg	110.00	55.00	35.00
(8)	Jehosie Heard	110.00	55.00	35.00
(9)	Fred Hutchinson	110.00	55.00	35.00
(10)	Larry Jansen	110.00	55.00	35.00
(11)	Bob Kelly	110.00	55.00	35.00
(12)	Bill Kennedy	110.00	55.00	35.00
(13)	Lou Kretlow	110.00	55.00	35.00
(14)	Rocco Krsnich	110.00	55.00	35.00
(15)	Carmen Mauro	110.00	55.00	35.00
(16)	John Oldham	110.00	55.00	35.00
(17)	George Schmees	110.00	55.00	35.00
(18)	Elmer Singleton	110.00	55.00	35.00
(19)	Alan Strange	110.00	55.00	35.00
(20)	Gene Verble	110.00	55.00	35.00
(21)	Marv Williams	110.00	55.00	35.00
(22)	Harvey Zernia	110.00	55.00	35.00

1956 Seattle Rainiers Popcorn

JOE TAYLOR
Outfielder

(Blank-back or Gil's Drive-Ins (two locations) ad on back. Players wearing light cap with white "R.")

		NM	EX	VG
Complete Set (27):		2,500	1,250	750.00
Common Player:		110.00	55.00	35.00
(1)	Fred Baczewski	110.00	55.00	35.00
(2)	Bob Balcena	110.00	55.00	35.00
(3)	Bill Brenner	110.00	55.00	35.00
(4)	Sherry Dixon	110.00	55.00	35.00
(5)	Don Fracchia	110.00	55.00	35.00
(6)	Bill Glynn	110.00	55.00	35.00
(7)	Larry Jansen	110.00	55.00	35.00
(8)	Howie Judson	110.00	55.00	35.00
(9)	Bill Kennedy	110.00	55.00	35.00
(10)	Jack Lohrke	110.00	55.00	35.00
(11)	Vic Lombardi	110.00	55.00	35.00
(12)	Carmen Mauro	110.00	55.00	35.00
(13)	Ray Orteig	110.00	55.00	35.00
(14)	Bud Podbielan	110.00	55.00	35.00
(15)	Leo Righetti	110.00	55.00	35.00
(16)	Jim Robertson	110.00	55.00	35.00
(17)	Art Shallock (Schallock)	110.00	55.00	35.00
(18)	Art Schult	110.00	55.00	35.00
(19)	Luke Sewell	135.00	65.00	40.00
(20)	Elmer Singleton	110.00	55.00	35.00
(21a)	Milt Smith (Action)	110.00	55.00	35.00
(21b)	Milt Smith (Portrait)	110.00	55.00	35.00
(22)	Vern Stephens	110.00	55.00	35.00
(23)	Alan Strange	110.00	55.00	35.00
(24)	Joe Taylor	110.00	55.00	35.00
(25)	Artie Wilson	175.00	85.00	50.00
(26)	Harvey Zernia	110.00	55.00	35.00

1957 Seattle Rainiers Popcorn

JIM DYCK
Infielder

By presenting any nine different pictures to either of **GIL'S DRIVE-INS** you will receive **FREE** an 8" x 10" player picture of your choice and you still keep your nine small pictures.

Three locations to serve you

GIL'S DRIVE-IN
4406 Rainier Avenue
1 mile south of Sicks' Stadium
•
3500 Avalon Way
35th S.W. and Avalon Way
West Seattle
•
Burien
1st South and South 152nd

(Blank-back or Gil's Drive-Ins (three locations) ad on back. Players wearing lighter caps with white "R." No base on letter "T" on outfielders or pitchers cards.)

		NM	EX	VG
Complete Set (24):		2,000	1,000	600.00
Common Player:		100.00	50.00	30.00
(1)	Dick Aylward	100.00	50.00	30.00
(2)	Bob Balcena	100.00	50.00	30.00
(3)	Eddie Basinki	100.00	50.00	30.00
(4)	Hal Bevan	100.00	50.00	30.00
(5)	Joe Black	125.00	65.00	35.00
(6)	Juan Delis	100.00	50.00	30.00
(7)	Jim Dyck	100.00	50.00	30.00
(8)	Marion Fricano	100.00	50.00	30.00
(9)	Bill Glynn	100.00	50.00	30.00
(10)	Larry Jansen	100.00	50.00	30.00
(11)	Howie Judson	100.00	50.00	30.00
(12)	Bill Kennedy	100.00	50.00	30.00
(13)	Jack Lohrke	100.00	50.00	30.00
(14)	Carmen Mauro	100.00	50.00	30.00
(15)	George Munger	100.00	50.00	30.00
(16)	Lefty O'Doul	150.00	75.00	45.00
(17)	Ray Orteig	100.00	50.00	30.00
(18)	Duane Pillette	100.00	50.00	30.00
(19)	Bud Podbielan	100.00	50.00	30.00
(20)	Charley Rabe	100.00	50.00	30.00
(21)	Leo Righetti	100.00	50.00	30.00
(22)	Joe Taylor	100.00	50.00	30.00
(23)	Edo Vanni	100.00	50.00	30.00
(24)	Morrie Wills (Maury)	250.00	125.00	75.00

Seattle Rainiers Team Issue

1958 Seattle Rainiers Popcorn

(All cards have Ralph's Thriftway Market ad on back.)

		NM	EX	VG
Complete Set (19):		1,250	625.00	375.00
Common Player:		75.00	35.00	20.00
(1)	Bob Balcena	75.00	35.00	20.00
(2)	Ed Basinki	75.00	35.00	20.00
(3)	Hal Bevan	75.00	35.00	20.00
(4)	Jack Bloomfield	75.00	35.00	20.00
(5)	Juan Delis	75.00	35.00	20.00
(6)	Dutch Dotterer	75.00	35.00	20.00
(7)	Jim Dyck	75.00	35.00	20.00
(8)	Al Federoff	90.00	45.00	27.50
(9)	Art Fowler	75.00	35.00	20.00
(10)	Bill Kennedy	75.00	35.00	20.00
(11)	Marty Kutyna	75.00	35.00	20.00
(12)	Ray Orteig	75.00	35.00	20.00
(13)	Duane Pillette	75.00	35.00	20.00
(14)	Vada Pinson	225.00	110.00	70.00
(15)	Connie Ryan	75.00	35.00	20.00
(16)	Phil Shartzer	75.00	35.00	20.00
(17)	Max Surkont	75.00	35.00	20.00
(18)	Gale Wade	75.00	35.00	20.00
(19)	Ted Wieand	75.00	35.00	20.00

1959 Seattle Rainiers Popcorn

DON RUDOLPH
Pitcher

(Blank-back. First printing cards have players in lighter cap with white "R." Second printing cards have darker caps with shadow around "R.")

		NM	EX	VG
Complete Set (37):		2,500	1,250	750.00
Common Player:		75.00	35.00	20.00
(1)	Bobby Adams	75.00	35.00	20.00
(2)	Frank Amaya	75.00	35.00	20.00
(3)	Hal Bevan	75.00	35.00	20.00

		NM	EX	VG
(4)	Jack Bloomfield	75.00	35.00	20.00
(5)	Clarence Churn	75.00	35.00	20.00
(6)	Jack Dittmer	75.00	35.00	20.00
(7)	Jim Dyck	75.00	35.00	20.00
(8)	Dee Fondy	75.00	35.00	20.00
(9)	Mark Freeman	75.00	35.00	20.00
(10)	Dick Hanlon	75.00	35.00	20.00
(11)	Carroll Hardy	75.00	35.00	20.00
(12)	Bobby Henrich	75.00	35.00	20.00
(13)	Jay Hook	75.00	35.00	20.00
(14)	Fred Hutchinson	75.00	35.00	20.00
(15)	Jake Jenkins	75.00	35.00	20.00
(16)	Eddie Kazak	75.00	35.00	20.00
(17)	Bill Kennedy	75.00	35.00	20.00
(18)	Harry Lowrey	75.00	35.00	20.00
(19a)	Harry Malmbeg (Malmberg)	75.00	35.00	20.00
(19b)	Harry Malmberg	75.00	35.00	20.00
(20)	Bob Mape (Mabe)	75.00	35.00	20.00
(21)	Darrell Martin	75.00	35.00	20.00
(22)	John McCall	75.00	35.00	20.00
(23)	Claude Osteen	75.00	35.00	20.00
(24)	Paul Pettit	75.00	35.00	20.00
(25)	Charley Rabe	75.00	35.00	20.00
(26)	Rudy Regalado	75.00	35.00	20.00
(27)	Eric Rodin	75.00	35.00	20.00
(28)	Don Rudolph	75.00	35.00	20.00
(29)	Lou Skizas	75.00	35.00	20.00
(30)	Dave Stenhouse	75.00	35.00	20.00
(31)	Alan Strange	75.00	35.00	20.00
(32)	Max Surkont	75.00	35.00	20.00
(33)	Ted Tappe	75.00	35.00	20.00
(34)	Elmer Valo	75.00	35.00	20.00
(35)	Gale Wade	75.00	35.00	20.00
(36)	Bill Wight	75.00	35.00	20.00
(37)	Ed Winceniak	75.00	35.00	20.00

1960 Seattle Rainiers Popcorn

(Blank-back. All players posed against outfield fence wearing dark caps with shadowed "R.")

		NM	EX	VG
Complete Set (18):		1,200	600.00	350.00
Common Player:		75.00	35.00	20.00
(1)	Charlie Beamon	75.00	35.00	20.00
(2)	Hal Bevan	75.00	35.00	20.00
(3)	Whammy Douglas	75.00	35.00	20.00
(4)	Buddy Gilbert	75.00	35.00	20.00
(5)	Hal Jeffcoat	75.00	35.00	20.00
(6)	Leigh Lawrence	75.00	35.00	20.00
(7)	Darrell Martin	75.00	35.00	20.00
(8)	Francisco Obregon	75.00	35.00	20.00
(9)	Johnny O'Brien	90.00	45.00	27.50
(10)	Paul Pettitt	75.00	35.00	20.00
(11)	Ray Rippelmeyer (Ripplemeyer)	75.00	35.00	20.00
(12)	Don Rudolph	75.00	35.00	20.00
(13)	Willard Schmidt	75.00	35.00	20.00
(14)	Dick Sisler	75.00	35.00	20.00
(15)	Lou Skizas	75.00	35.00	20.00
(16)	Joe Taylor	75.00	35.00	20.00
(17)	Bob Thurman	75.00	35.00	20.00
(18)	Gerald Zimmerman	75.00	35.00	20.00

1961 Seattle Rainiers Popcorn

(Blank-back. New uniforms: dark cap with stylized "S," "Rainiers" on chest. Many players have both portrait and action poses. Tough to distinguish from 1962 set; names on '61s are more compact, bold than on '62 which has taller, lighter names.)

		NM	EX	VG
Complete Set (29):		2,000	1,000	600.00
Common Player:		75.00	35.00	20.00
(1)	Galen Cisco	75.00	35.00	20.00
(2)	Marlan Coughtry/Btg	75.00	35.00	20.00
(3)	Marlin Coughtry/Portrait	75.00	35.00	20.00
(4)	Pete Cronin	75.00	35.00	20.00
(5)	Arnold Earley	75.00	35.00	20.00
(6)	Bob Heffner/Pitching	75.00	35.00	20.00
(7)	Bob Heffner/Portrait	75.00	35.00	20.00
(8)	Curt Jensen/Action	75.00	35.00	20.00
(9)	Curt Jensen/Portrait	75.00	35.00	20.00
(10)	Harry Malmberg/Coach	75.00	35.00	20.00
(11)	Harry Malmberg (Player-coach.)	75.00	35.00	20.00
(12)	Dave Mann	75.00	35.00	20.00
(13)	Darrell Martin	75.00	35.00	20.00
(14)	Erv Palica/Pitching	75.00	35.00	20.00
(15)	Ervin Palica/Portrait	75.00	35.00	20.00
(16)	Johnny Pesky/Action	90.00	45.00	27.50
(17)	Johnny Pesky/Portrait	90.00	45.00	27.50
(18)	Dick Radatz	100.00	50.00	30.00
(19)	Ted Schreiber/Btg	75.00	35.00	20.00
(20)	Ted Shreiber/Portrait	75.00	35.00	20.00
(21)	Paul Smith/Action	75.00	35.00	20.00
(22)	Paul Smith/Portrait	75.00	35.00	20.00
(23)	John Tillman/Infielder	75.00	35.00	20.00
(24)	Bob Tillman/Catcher	75.00	35.00	20.00
(25)	Bo Toft	75.00	35.00	20.00
(26)	Tom Umphlett/Action	75.00	35.00	20.00
(27)	Tom Umphlett/Portrait	75.00	35.00	20.00
(28)	Earl Wilson	75.00	35.00	20.00
(29)	Ken Wolfe	75.00	35.00	20.00

1962 Seattle Rainiers Popcorn

(Blank-back. Nearly identical to '61s except for player name. On 1961 cards, name is compact and bold; on '62s the name is taller, lighter. Some photos repeated from 1961.)

		NM	EX	VG
Complete Set (19):		1,250	625.00	375.00
Common Player:		75.00	35.00	20.00
(1)	Dave Hall	75.00	35.00	20.00
(2)	Billy Harrell	75.00	35.00	20.00
(3)	Curt Jensen (Jenson)	75.00	35.00	20.00
(4)	Stew MacDonald	75.00	35.00	20.00
(5)	Bill MacLeod	75.00	35.00	20.00
(6)	Dave Mann/Action	75.00	35.00	20.00
(7)	Dave Mann/Portrait	75.00	35.00	20.00
(8)	Dave Morehead	75.00	35.00	20.00
(9)	John Pesky	90.00	45.00	27.50
(10)	Ted Schreiber (Second baseman.)	75.00	35.00	20.00
(11)	Ted Schreiber (Infielder)	75.00	35.00	20.00
(12)	Elmer Singleton	75.00	35.00	20.00
(13)	Archie Skeen	75.00	35.00	20.00
(14)	Pete Smith	75.00	35.00	20.00
(15)	George Spencer	75.00	35.00	20.00
(16)	Bo Toft (1961 photo)	75.00	35.00	20.00
(17)	Bo Toft (New photo.)	75.00	35.00	20.00
(18)	Tom Umphlett	75.00	35.00	20.00
(19)	Ken Wolfe	75.00	35.00	20.00

1963 Seattle Rainiers Popcorn

(Blank-back. No positions stated on cards except for manager and coach. Impossible to differentiate 1963 issue from 1964 except by player selection.)

		NM	EX	VG
Complete Set (15):		800.00	400.00	240.00
Common Player:		60.00	30.00	17.50
(1)	Don Gile	60.00	30.00	17.50
(2)	Dave Hall	60.00	30.00	17.50
(3)	Billy Harrell	60.00	30.00	17.50
(4)	Pete Jernigan	60.00	30.00	17.50
(5)	Stan Johnson	60.00	30.00	17.50
(6)	Dalton Jones	60.00	30.00	17.50
(7)	Mel Parnell	60.00	30.00	17.50
(8)	Joe Pedrazzini	60.00	30.00	17.50
(9)	Elmer Singleton	60.00	30.00	17.50
(10)	Archie Skeen	60.00	30.00	17.50
(11)	Rac Slider	60.00	30.00	17.50
(12)	Pete Smith	60.00	30.00	17.50
(13)	Bill Spanswick	60.00	30.00	17.50
(14)	George Spencer	60.00	30.00	17.50
(15)	Wilbur Wood	90.00	45.00	27.50

1964 Seattle Rainiers Popcorn

(Blank-back. Impossible to differentiate between 1963 and 1964 issues except by player selection.)

		NM	EX	VG
Complete Set (18):		1,000	500.00	300.00
Common Player:		60.00	30.00	17.50
(1)	Earl Averill	60.00	30.00	17.50
(2)	Billy Gardner	60.00	30.00	17.50
(3)	Russ Gibson	60.00	30.00	17.50
(4)	Guido Grilli	60.00	30.00	17.50
(5)	Bob Guindon	60.00	30.00	17.50
(6)	Billy Harrell	60.00	30.00	17.50
(7)	Fred Holmes	60.00	30.00	17.50
(8)	Stan Johnson	60.00	30.00	17.50
(9)	Hal Kolstad	60.00	30.00	17.50
(10)	Felix Maldonado	60.00	30.00	17.50
(11)	Gary Modrell	60.00	30.00	17.50
(12)	Merlin Nippert	60.00	30.00	17.50
(13)	Rico Petrocelli	100.00	50.00	30.00
(14)	Jay Ritchie	60.00	30.00	17.50
(15)	Barry Shetrone	60.00	30.00	17.50
(16)	Pete Smith	60.00	30.00	17.50
(17)	Bill Tuttle	60.00	30.00	17.50
(18)	Edo Vanni	60.00	30.00	17.50

1965 Seattle Angels Popcorn

(Back has cartoon angel batting. Several cards, issued prior to the season, have blank-backs.)

		NM	EX	VG
Complete Set (22):		600.00	300.00	180.00
Common Player:		30.00	15.00	9.00
(1)	Earl Averill	30.00	15.00	9.00
(2)	Tom Burgmeier	30.00	15.00	9.00
(3)	Bob Guindon	30.00	15.00	9.00
(4)	Jack Hernandez	30.00	15.00	9.00
(5)	Fred Holmes	30.00	15.00	9.00
(6)	Ed Kirkpatrick	30.00	15.00	9.00
(7)	Hal Kolstad	30.00	15.00	9.00
(8)	Joe Koppe	30.00	15.00	9.00
(9)	Les Kuhnz	30.00	15.00	9.00
(10)	Bob Lemon	60.00	30.00	17.50
(11)	Bobby Locke	30.00	15.00	9.00
(12)	Jim McGlothlin	30.00	15.00	9.00
(13a)	Bob Radovich (Blank-back.)	30.00	15.00	9.00
(13b)	Bob Radovich (Ad-back.)	30.00	15.00	9.00
(14)	Merritt Ranew	30.00	15.00	9.00
(15)	Jimmie Reese (Blank-back.)	45.00	22.50	13.50
(16a)	Rick Reichardt (Blank-back.)	30.00	15.00	9.00
(16b)	Rick Reichardt (Ad-back.)	30.00	15.00	9.00
(17)	Tom Satriano	30.00	15.00	9.00
(18)	Dick Simpson	30.00	15.00	9.00
(19)	Jack Spring (Blank-back.)	30.00	15.00	9.00
(20)	Ed Sukla	30.00	15.00	9.00
(21)	Jackie Warner	30.00	15.00	9.00
(22)	Stan Williams	30.00	15.00	9.00

1966 Seattle Angels Popcorn

(Cartoon angel pitching on back, first "Presented by" advertiser at bottom is Chevron Dealers.)

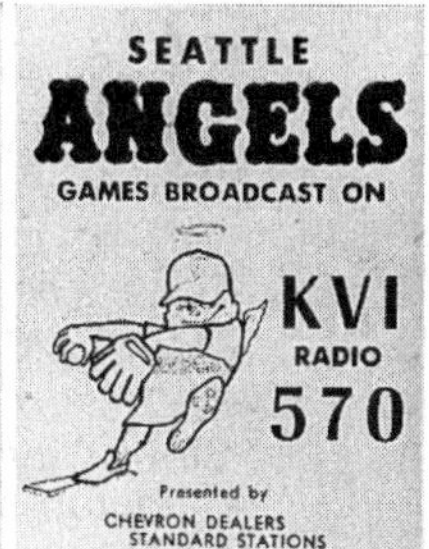

		NM	EX	VG
Complete Set (29):		900.00	450.00	275.00
Common Player:		30.00	15.00	9.00
(1)	Del Bates	30.00	15.00	9.00
(2)	Tom Burgmeier	30.00	15.00	9.00
(3)	Jim Campanis	40.00	20.00	12.00
(4)	Jim Coates	30.00	15.00	9.00
(5)	Tony Cortopassi	30.00	15.00	9.00
(6)	Chuck Estrada	30.00	15.00	9.00
(7)	Ray Hernandez	30.00	15.00	9.00
(8)	Jay Johnstone	50.00	25.00	15.00
(9)	Bill Kelso	30.00	15.00	9.00
(10)	Vic LaRose	30.00	15.00	9.00
(11)	Bobby Locke	30.00	15.00	9.00
(12)	Rudy May	30.00	15.00	9.00
(13)	Andy Messersmith	50.00	25.00	15.00
(14)	Bubba Morton	30.00	15.00	9.00
(15)	Cotton Nash	30.00	15.00	9.00
(16)	John Olerud	50.00	25.00	15.00
(17)	Marty Pattin	30.00	15.00	9.00
(18)	Merritt Ranew	30.00	15.00	9.00
(19)	Minnie Rojas	30.00	15.00	9.00
(20)	George Rubio	30.00	15.00	9.00
(21)	Al Spangler	30.00	15.00	9.00
(22)	Ed Sukla	30.00	15.00	9.00
(23)	Felix Torres	30.00	15.00	9.00
(24)	Hector Torres	30.00	15.00	9.00
(25)	Ken Turner	30.00	15.00	9.00
(26)	Chuck Vinson	30.00	15.00	9.00
(27)	Don Wallace	30.00	15.00	9.00
(28)	Jack D. Warner	30.00	15.00	9.00
(29)	Mike White	30.00	15.00	9.00

1967 Seattle Angels Popcorn

(Cartoon angel pitching on back, first "Presented by" advertiser is Western Airlines.)

		NM	EX	VG
Complete Set (19):		500.00	250.00	150.00
Common Player:		30.00	15.00	9.00
(1)	George Banks	30.00	15.00	9.00
(2)	Tom Burgmeier	30.00	15.00	9.00
(3)	Jim Coates	30.00	15.00	9.00
(4)	Chuck Cottier	30.00	15.00	9.00
(5)	Tony Curry	30.00	15.00	9.00
(6)	Vern Geishert	30.00	15.00	9.00
(7)	Jesse Hickman	30.00	15.00	9.00
(8)	Bill Kelso	30.00	15.00	9.00
(9)	Ed Kirkpatrick	30.00	15.00	9.00
(10)	Chris Krug	30.00	15.00	9.00
(11)	Bobby Locke	30.00	15.00	9.00
(12)	Bill Murphy	30.00	15.00	9.00
(13)	Marty Pattin	30.00	15.00	9.00
(14)	Merritt Ranew	30.00	15.00	9.00
(15)	Bob Sadowski	30.00	15.00	9.00
(16)	Ed Sukla	30.00	15.00	9.00
(17)	Hector Torres	30.00	15.00	9.00
(18)	Chuck Vinson	30.00	15.00	9.00
(19)	Don Wallace	30.00	15.00	9.00

1968 Seattle Angels Popcorn

(Blank-back.)

		NM	EX	VG
Complete Set (18):		500.00	250.00	150.00
Common Player:		30.00	15.00	9.00
(1)	Ethan Blackaby	30.00	15.00	9.00
(2)	Jim Coates	30.00	15.00	9.00
(3)	Tom Egan	30.00	15.00	9.00
(4)	Larry Elliott (Elliot)	30.00	15.00	9.00
(5)	Jim Engelhardt	30.00	15.00	9.00
(6)	Gus Gil	30.00	15.00	9.00
(7)	Bill Harrelson	30.00	15.00	9.00
(8)	Steve Hovley	30.00	15.00	9.00
(9)	Jim Mahoney	30.00	15.00	9.00
(10)	Mickey McGuire	30.00	15.00	9.00
(11)	Joe Overton	30.00	15.00	9.00
(12)	Marty Pattin	30.00	15.00	9.00
(13)	Larry Sherry	30.00	15.00	9.00
(14)	Marv Staehle	30.00	15.00	9.00
(15)	Ed Sukla	30.00	15.00	9.00
(16)	Jarvis Tatum	30.00	15.00	9.00
(17)	Hawk Taylor	30.00	15.00	9.00
(18)	Chuck Vinson	30.00	15.00	9.00

1952 Shawnee Hawks Team Issue

Formatted like the other known minor league issues from Globe Printing of San Jose, Calif., this set chronicles the 1952 version of the Class D (Sooner State League) Shawnee (Okla.) Hawks. The blank-backed cards are black-and-white and measure about 2-1/4" x 3-3/8". The checklist here is incomplete, the set probably having been originally issued with about 18 cards.

		NM	EX	VG
Common Player:		60.00	30.00	18.00
(1)	Russell Bland (Blanco)	60.00	30.00	18.00
(2)	Perry Haddock	60.00	30.00	18.00
(3)	Jim Kenaga	60.00	30.00	18.00
(4)	Hal Long	60.00	30.00	18.00
(5)	Loyd McPherson	60.00	30.00	18.00
(6)	Rolando Olmo	60.00	30.00	18.00
(7)	Dave Rolette	60.00	30.00	18.00
(8)	Hank Salazar	60.00	30.00	18.00

1960 Shopsy's Frankfurters Toronto Maple Leafs

Only the Toronto Maple Leafs of the International League - including many former and future major leaguers - are included in this set. The cards are about 2-1/4" x 3-1/4", blank-back and printed in black-and-white. The unnumbered cards are checklisted here alphabetically.

		NM	EX	VG
Complete Set (23):		2,000	1,000	600.00
Common Player:		90.00	45.00	30.00
Album:		100.00	50.00	30.00
(1)	George Anderson (Sparky)	150.00	75.00	45.00
(2)	Bob Chakales	90.00	45.00	30.00
(3)	Al Cicotte	90.00	45.00	30.00
(4)	Rip Coleman	90.00	45.00	30.00
(5)	Steve Demeter	90.00	45.00	30.00
(6)	Don Dillard	90.00	45.00	30.00
(7)	Frank Funk	90.00	45.00	30.00
(8)	Russ Heman	90.00	45.00	30.00
(9)	Earl Hersh	90.00	45.00	30.00
(10)	Allen Jones	90.00	45.00	30.00
(11)	Jim King	90.00	45.00	30.00
(12)	Jack Kubiszyn	90.00	45.00	30.00
(13)	Mel McGaha	90.00	45.00	30.00
(14)	Bill Moran	90.00	45.00	30.00
(15)	Ron Negray	90.00	45.00	30.00
(16)	Herb Plews	90.00	45.00	30.00
(17)	Steve Ridzik	90.00	45.00	30.00
(18)	Pat Scantlebury	90.00	45.00	30.00
(19)	Bill Smith (Trainer)	90.00	45.00	30.00
(20)	Bob Smith	90.00	45.00	30.00
(21)	Tim Thompson	90.00	45.00	30.00
(22)	Jack Waters	90.00	45.00	30.00
(23)	Archie Wilson	90.00	45.00	30.00

1947 Signal Gasoline Pacific Coast League

Five of the eight PCL teams participated in this baseball card promotion, giving away cards of hometeam players. Because of vagaries of local distribution, some teams, notably Sacramento and Seattle, are scarcer than others, and there are specific player rarities among other teams. The black-and-white cards are 5-9/16" x 3-1/2" and feature on the front a drawing of the player and several personal or career highlights in cartoon form. The artwork was done by former N.Y. Giants pitcher Al Demaree. On the backs are player biographical details, an ad for Signal Gas and an ad for the co-sponsoring radio station in each locale. Cards are unnumbered.

	NM	EX	VG
Complete Set (89):	6,000	3,000	1,800
(Team sets listed below.)	.00	.00	.00

1947 Signal Gasoline Hollywood Stars

		NM	EX	VG
Complete Set (20):		1,200	600.00	350.00
Common Player:		50.00	25.00	15.00
(1)	Ed Albosta	50.00	25.00	15.00
(2)	Carl Cox	50.00	25.00	15.00
(3)	Frank Dasso	50.00	25.00	15.00
(4)	Tod Davis	50.00	25.00	15.00
(5)	Jim Delsing	50.00	25.00	15.00
(6)	Jimmy Dykes	50.00	25.00	15.00
(7)	Paul Gregory	50.00	25.00	15.00
(8)	Fred Haney	50.00	25.00	15.00
(9)	Frank Kelleher	50.00	25.00	15.00
(10)	Joe Krakauskas	50.00	25.00	15.00
(11)	Al Libke	50.00	25.00	15.00
(12)	Tony Lupien	50.00	25.00	15.00
(13)	Xaiver Rescigno	50.00	25.00	15.00
(14)	Jack Sherman	50.00	25.00	15.00
(15)	Andy Skurski	50.00	25.00	15.00
(16)	Glen (Glenn) Stewart	50.00	25.00	15.00
(17)	Al Unser	50.00	25.00	15.00
(18)	Fred Vaughn	50.00	25.00	15.00
(19)	Woody Williams	250.00	125.00	75.00
(20)	Dutch (Gus) Zernial	75.00	37.00	22.00

1947 Signal Gasoline Los Angeles Angels

		NM	EX	VG
Complete Set (18):		700.00	350.00	210.00
Common Player:		40.00	20.00	12.00
(1)	Red Adams	40.00	20.00	12.00
(2)	Larry Barton	40.00	20.00	12.00
(3)	Cliff Chambers	40.00	20.00	12.00
(4)	Lloyd Christopher	40.00	20.00	12.00
(5)	Cece Garriott	40.00	20.00	12.00
(6)	Al Glossop	40.00	20.00	12.00
(7)	Bill Kelly	40.00	20.00	12.00
(8)	Red Lynn	40.00	20.00	12.00
(9)	Eddie Malone	40.00	20.00	12.00
(10)	Dutch McCall	40.00	20.00	12.00
(11)	Don Osborne	40.00	20.00	12.00
(12)	John Ostrowski	40.00	20.00	12.00
(13)	Reggie Otero	40.00	20.00	12.00
(14)	Ray Prim	40.00	20.00	12.00
(15)	Ed Sauer	40.00	20.00	12.00
(16)	Bill Schuster	40.00	20.00	12.00
(17)	Tuck Stainback	40.00	20.00	12.00
(18)	Lou Stringer	40.00	20.00	12.00

1947 Signal Gasoline Oakland Oaks

		NM	EX	VG
Complete Set (19):		800.00	400.00	240.00
Common Player:		40.00	20.00	12.00
(1)	Vic Buccola	40.00	20.00	12.00
(2)	Mickey Burnett	40.00	20.00	12.00
(3)	Ralph Buxton	40.00	20.00	12.00
(4)	Vince DiMaggio	95.00	47.00	28.00
(5)	Dizz Duezabou	40.00	20.00	12.00
(6)	Bud Foster	40.00	20.00	12.00
(7)	Sherriff Gassaway	40.00	20.00	12.00
(8)	Tom Hafey	40.00	20.00	12.00
(9)	Brooks Holder	40.00	20.00	12.00
(10)	Gene Lillard	40.00	20.00	12.00
(11)	Dario Lodigiani	40.00	20.00	12.00
(12)	Hershel Martin	40.00	20.00	12.00
(13)	Cotton Pippen	40.00	20.00	12.00
(14)	Billy Raimondi	40.00	20.00	12.00

		NM	EX	VG
(15)	Tony Sabol	40.00	20.00	12.00
(16)	Les Scarsella	40.00	20.00	12.00
(17)	Floyd Speer	40.00	20.00	12.00
(18)	Casey Stengel	100.00	50.00	30.00
(19)	Maurice Van Robays	40.00	20.00	12.00

1947 Signal Gasoline Sacramento Solons

		NM	EX	VG
Complete Set (16):		2,000	1,000	600.00
Common Player:		60.00	30.00	18.00
(1)	Bud Beasley	60.00	30.00	18.00
(2)	Frank Dasso	60.00	30.00	18.00
(3)	Ed Fitzgerald (Fitz Gerald)	60.00	30.00	18.00
(4)	Guy Fletcher	60.00	30.00	18.00
(5)	Tony Freitas	60.00	30.00	18.00
(6)	Red Mann	60.00	30.00	18.00
(7)	Joe Marty	60.00	30.00	18.00
(8)	Steve Mesner	60.00	30.00	18.00
(9)	Bill Ramsey	60.00	30.00	18.00
(10)	Charley Ripple	250.00	125.00	75.00
(11)	John Rizzo	250.00	125.00	75.00
(12)	Al Smith	250.00	125.00	75.00
(13)	Ronnie Smith	250.00	125.00	75.00
(14)	Tommy Thompson	250.00	125.00	75.00
(15)	Jim Warner	115.00	55.00	35.00
(16)	Ed Zipay	115.00	55.00	35.00

1947 Signal Gasoline Seattle Rainiers

		NM	EX	VG
Complete Set (16):		1,750	875.00	525.00
Common Player:		75.00	37.00	22.00
(1)	Kewpie Barrett	100.00	50.00	30.00
(2)	Herman Besse	100.00	50.00	30.00
(3)	Guy Fletcher	100.00	50.00	30.00
(4)	Jack Jakucki	100.00	50.00	30.00
(5)	Bob Johnson	100.00	50.00	30.00
(6)	Pete Jonas	275.00	135.00	82.00
(7)	Hillis Layne	100.00	50.00	30.00
(8)	Red Mann	100.00	50.00	30.00
(9)	Lou Novikoff	100.00	50.00	30.00
(10)	John O'Neill	100.00	50.00	30.00
(11)	Bill Ramsey	100.00	50.00	30.00
(12)	Mickey Rocco	100.00	50.00	30.00
(13)	George Scharein	100.00	50.00	30.00
(14)	Hal Sueme	100.00	50.00	30.00
(15)	Jo Jo White	100.00	50.00	30.00
(16)	Tony York	100.00	50.00	30.00

1948 Signal Gasoline Oakland Oaks

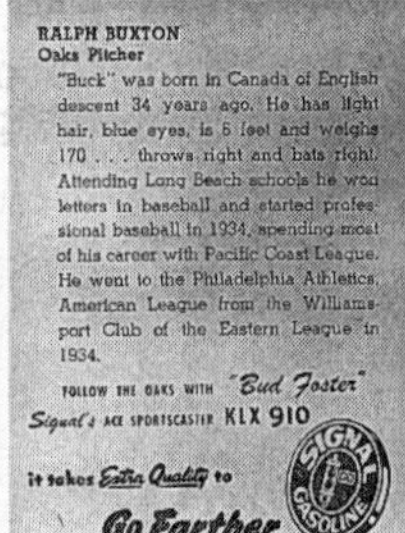

Issued by Signal Oil in the Oakland area in 1948, this 24-card set features members of the Oakland Oaks of the Pacific Coast League. The unnumbered cards, measuring 2-3/8" x 3-1/2", were given away at gas stations. The front consists of a color photo, while the backs (printed in either blue or black) contain a brief player write-up along with a Signal Oil ad and logo.

		NM	EX	VG
Complete Set (24):		900.00	450.00	275.00
Common Player:		40.00	20.00	12.00
(1)	John C. Babich	40.00	20.00	12.00
(2)	Ralph Buxton	40.00	20.00	12.00
(3)	Loyd E. Christopher (Lloyd)	40.00	20.00	12.00
(4)	Merrill Russell Combs	40.00	20.00	12.00
(5)	Melvin E. Deuzabou	40.00	20.00	12.00
(6)	Nicholas ("Nick") Etten	40.00	20.00	12.00
(7)	Bud Foster (Announcer)	40.00	20.00	12.00
(8)	Charles Gassaway	40.00	20.00	12.00
(9)	Will Hafey	40.00	20.00	12.00
(10)	Ray Hamrick	40.00	20.00	12.00
(11)	Brooks Richard Holder	40.00	20.00	12.00
(12)	Earl Jones	40.00	20.00	12.00
(13)	Harry "Cookie" Lavagetto	40.00	20.00	12.00
(14)	Robert E. Lillard	40.00	20.00	12.00
(15)	Dario Lodigiani	40.00	20.00	12.00
(16)	Ernie Lombardi	75.00	37.50	22.50
(17a)	Alfred Manuel Martin (Born 1921.)	65.00	32.50	20.00
(17b)	Alfred Manuel Martin (Born 1928.)	75.00	37.50	22.50
(18)	George Michael Metkovich	40.00	20.00	12.00
(19)	William L. Raimondi	40.00	20.00	12.00
(20)	Les George Scarsella	40.00	20.00	12.00
(21)	Floyd Vernie Speer	40.00	20.00	12.00
(22)	Charles "Casey" Stengel	115.00	57.00	34.00
(23)	Maurice Van Robays	40.00	20.00	12.00
(24)	Aldon Jay Wilkie	40.00	20.00	12.00

1951 Sioux City Soos Postcards

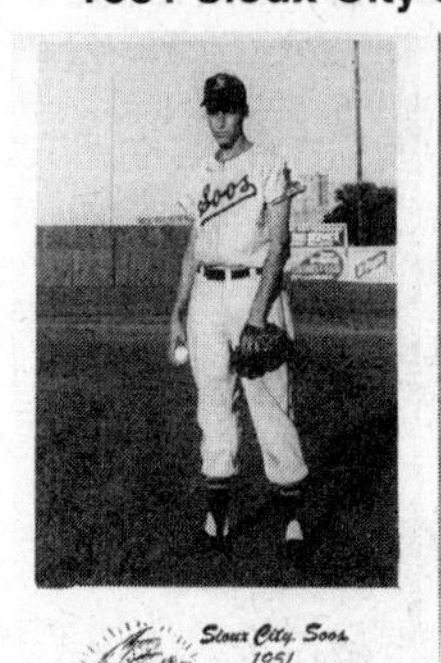

These black-and-white team-issued postcards feature on their fronts posed full-length photos of members of the Class A Western League farm team of the New York Giants. In standard 3-1/2" x 5-1/2" size, the cards have a wide border at bottom which has the team name, the year and a logo featuring an ear of corn. Backs have typical postcard indicia. Players are not identified anywhere on the cards. It is presumed this checklist is incomplete.

		NM	EX	VG
Common Player:		60.00	30.00	18.00
(1)	Ray Berns	60.00	30.00	18.00
(2)	Ed Bressoud	60.00	30.00	18.00
(3)	Mario Picone	60.00	30.00	18.00
(4)	Bob Reid	60.00	30.00	18.00

1952-1953 Sioux City Soos Team Issue

From the Class A Western League, this is one of many minor league team sets issued in the early 1950s by Globe Printing of San Jose, Calif. The early 1950s Soos were a farm team of the New York Giants. Cards are about 2-1/4" x 3-3/8", printed in black-and-white with blank backs. It appears as if the Soos were the only team to have issued cards in both 1952 and 1953, since some cards are known with players unique to each season as well as cards of players who were with Sioux City in both 1952 and 1953.

		NM	EX	VG
Complete Set (29):		1,500	750.00	450.00
Common Player:		60.00	30.00	18.00
Album:		100.00	50.00	30.00
	1952			
(1)	Ray Berns	60.00	30.00	18.00
(2)	Eddie Bressoud	60.00	30.00	18.00
(3)	Irv Burton	60.00	30.00	18.00
(4)	Bob Easterbrook	60.00	30.00	18.00
(5)	George Erath	60.00	30.00	18.00
(6)	Don Fracchia	60.00	30.00	18.00
(7)	Dick Hamlin	60.00	30.00	18.00
(8)	Gail Harris	60.00	30.00	18.00
(9)	Chico Ibanez	60.00	30.00	18.00
(10)	Bob Lee	60.00	30.00	18.00
(11)	Bill McMillan	60.00	30.00	18.00
(12)	Dick Messner	60.00	30.00	18.00
(13)	Roy Pardue	60.00	30.00	18.00
(14)	Mario Picone	60.00	30.00	18.00
(15)	Jim Singleton	60.00	30.00	18.00
(16)	John Uber	60.00	30.00	18.00
(17)	Ernie Yelen	60.00	30.00	18.00
	1952/1953			
(18)	Bob Giddings	60.00	30.00	18.00
(19)	Ray Johnson	60.00	30.00	18.00
(20)	Denny Landry (Bat boy.)	60.00	30.00	18.00
(21)	Vince LaSala	60.00	30.00	18.00
(22)	Ray Mueller	60.00	30.00	18.00
	1953			
(23)	Dick Getter	60.00	30.00	18.00
(24)	Dick Hamlin	60.00	30.00	18.00
(25)	Jake Jenkins	60.00	30.00	18.00
(26)	Jim Jones	60.00	30.00	18.00
(27)	Bob Myers	60.00	30.00	18.00
(28)	Clyde Stevens	60.00	30.00	18.00
(29)	Joe Stupak	60.00	30.00	18.00

1954 Sioux City Soos Souvenir Pictures Album

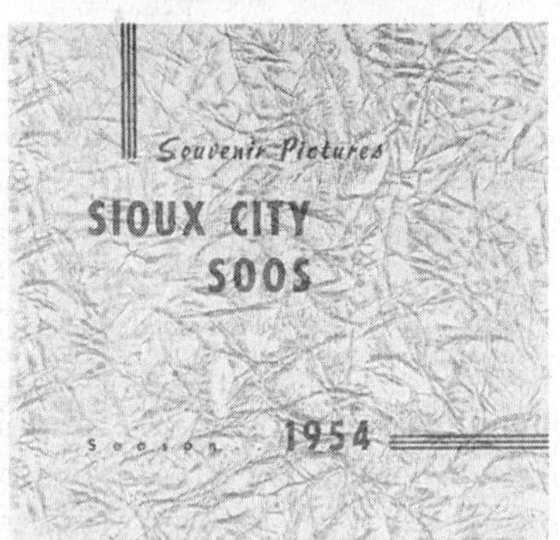

Rather than a set of individual baseball cards, the Class A Western League farm club of the New York Giants issued this souvenir picture album depicting players (including future major league star and N.L. president Bill White), staff and media. About 8-1/8" x 7-1/2", the album has embossed metallic gold covers and orange graphics. Inside are eight black-and-white pages with three card-like images per page. The pictures are in about the same size and format as Globe Printing's contemporary minor league baseball card team sets.

	NM	EX	VG
Complete Souvenir Book: 1954 Sioux City Soos	300.00	150.00	90.00

1947 Smith's Oakland Oaks

Peppery CASEY STENGEL is a baseball veteran of 36 seasons. Stengel, a speedy, hard-hitting outfielder, performed with Brooklyn, New York Giants, Boston Braves. He has managed Dodgers, Braves and Milwaukee. Cagey Casey is noted for his ability to develop young players.

12th and Washington, Oakland

Largest men's and boys' store west of Chicago

This regional set of Oakland Oaks (Pacific Coast League) cards was issued in 1947 by Smith's Clothing stores and is numbered in the lower right corner. The card fronts include a black and white photo with the player's name, team and position below. The backs carry a brief player write-up and an advertisement for Smith's Clothing. The cards measure 2" x 3". The Max Marshall card was apparently short-printed and is much scarcer than the rest of the set.

		NM	EX	VG
Complete Set (25):		800.00	400.00	240.00
Common Player:		25.00	12.50	7.50
1	Charles (Casey) Stengel	125.00	65.00	35.00
2	Billy Raimondi	25.00	12.50	7.50
3	Les Scarsella	25.00	12.50	7.50
4	Brooks Holder	25.00	12.50	7.50
5	Ray Hamrick	25.00	12.50	7.50
6	Gene Lillard	25.00	12.50	7.50
7	Maurice Van Robays	25.00	12.50	7.50
8	Charlie (Sheriff) Gassaway	25.00	12.50	7.50
9	Henry (Cotton) Pippen	25.00	12.50	7.50
10	James Arnold	25.00	12.50	7.50
11	Ralph (Buck) Buxton	25.00	12.50	7.50
12	Ambrose (Bo) Palica	25.00	12.50	7.50
13	Tony Sabol	25.00	12.50	7.50
14	Ed Kearse	25.00	12.50	7.50
15	Bill Hart	25.00	12.50	7.50
16	Donald (Snuffy) Smith	25.00	12.50	7.50
17	Oral (Mickey) Burnett	25.00	12.50	7.50
18	Tom Hafey	25.00	12.50	7.50
19	Will Hafey	25.00	12.50	7.50
20	Paul Gillespie	25.00	12.50	7.50
21	Damon Hayes	25.00	12.50	7.50
22	Max Marshall	350.00	175.00	100.00
23	Mel (Dizz) Duezabou	25.00	12.50	7.50
24	Mel Reeves	25.00	12.50	7.50
25	Joe Faria	25.00	12.50	7.50

1948 Smith's Oakland Oaks

BILLY MARTIN
Oaks Third Baseman 17

Newcomer BILLY MARTIN, 19, comes to the Oaks from Phoenix where he led the league last year with his .393 batting average, 174 R.B.I., 230 base hits and 48 2-base hits. Lives in Berkeley where he was born.

12th and Washington, Oakland
Largest men's and boys' store west of Chicago

The 1948 Smith's Clothing issue was another 25-card regional set featuring members of the Oakland Oaks of the Pacific Coast League. Almost identical to the 1947 Smith's issue, the black and white cards again measure 2" x 3" but were printed on heavier, glossy stock. The player's name, team and position appear below the photo with the card number in the lower right corner. The back has a brief player write-up and an ad for Smith's clothing.

		NM	EX	VG
Complete Set (25):		700.00	350.00	210.00
Common Player:		25.00	12.50	7.50
1	Billy Raimondi	25.00	12.50	7.50
2	Brooks Holder	25.00	12.50	7.50
3	Will Hafey	25.00	12.50	7.50
4	Nick Etten	25.00	12.50	7.50
5	Lloyd Christopher	25.00	12.50	7.50
6	Les Scarsella	25.00	12.50	7.50
7	Ray Hamrick	25.00	12.50	7.50
8	Gene Lillard	25.00	12.50	7.50
9	Maurice Van Robays	25.00	12.50	7.50
10	Charlie Gassaway	25.00	12.50	7.50
11	Ralph (Buck) Buxton	25.00	12.50	7.50
12	Tom Hafey	25.00	12.50	7.50
13	Damon Hayes	25.00	12.50	7.50
14	Mel (Dizz) Duezabou	25.00	12.50	7.50
15	Dario Lodigiani	25.00	12.50	7.50
16	Vic Buccola	25.00	12.50	7.50
17	Billy Martin	90.00	45.00	27.00
18	Floyd Speer	25.00	12.50	7.50
19	Eddie Samcoff	25.00	12.50	7.50
20	Charles (Casey) Stengel	90.00	45.00	27.00
21	Lloyd Hittle	25.00	12.50	7.50
22	Johnny Babich	25.00	12.50	7.50
23	Merrill Combs	25.00	12.50	7.50
24	Eddie Murphy	25.00	12.50	7.50
25	Bob Klinger	25.00	12.50	7.50

1948 Sommer & Kaufmann San Francisco Seals

WILFRED "BILL" LEONARD
Seals Catcher 20

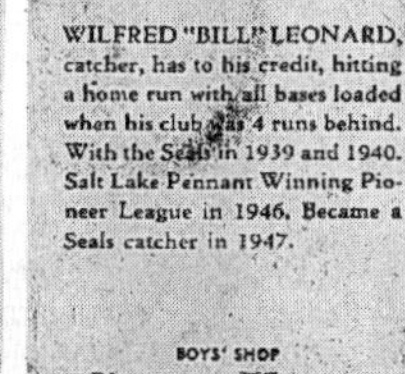
WILFRED "BILL" LEONARD, catcher, has to his credit, hitting a home run with all bases loaded when his club was 4 runs behind. With the Seals in 1939 and 1940. Salt Lake Pennant Winning Pioneer League in 1946. Became a Seals catcher in 1947.
BOYS' SHOP
Sommer & Kaufmann
838 MARKET ST. SAN FRANCISCO 2600 OCEAN AVE. SAN FRANCISCO
35 FOURTH AVE., SAN MATEO

One of the more common of the many Pacific Coast League issues of the late 1940s, this emission from the San Francisco boys' clothier features 30 black-and-white 2" x 3" cards. Fronts have a player photo, name, position and card number. Backs have a few biographical details and stats, along with an ad. The 1948 issue can be differentiated from the 1949 issue by the words "BOYS SHOP" above the company logo on back.

		NM	EX	VG
Complete Set (30):		1,500	750.00	450.00
Common Player:		60.00	30.00	18.50
1	Lefty O'Doul	100.00	50.00	30.00
2	Jack Brewer	60.00	30.00	18.50
3	Con Dempsey	60.00	30.00	18.50
4	Tommy Fine	60.00	30.00	18.50
5	Kenneth Gables	60.00	30.00	18.50
6	Robert Joyce	60.00	30.00	18.50
7	Al Lien	60.00	30.00	18.50
8	Cliff Melton	60.00	30.00	18.50
9	Frank Shofner	60.00	30.00	18.50
10	Don Trower	60.00	30.00	18.50
11	Joe Brovia	60.00	30.00	18.50
12	Dino Paul Restelli	60.00	30.00	18.50
13	Gene Woodling	75.00	37.00	22.00
14	Ben Guintini	60.00	30.00	18.50
15	Felix Mackiewicz	60.00	30.00	18.50
16	John Patrick Tobin	60.00	30.00	18.50
17	Manuel Perez	60.00	30.00	18.50
18	Bill Werle	60.00	30.00	18.50
19	Homer Howell	60.00	30.00	18.50
20	Wilfred Leonard	60.00	30.00	18.50
21	Bruce Ogrodowski	60.00	30.00	18.50
22	Dick Lajeskie	60.00	30.00	18.50
23	Hugh Luby	60.00	30.00	18.50
24	Roy Nicely	60.00	30.00	18.50
25	Ray Orteig	60.00	30.00	18.50
26	Michael Rocco	60.00	30.00	18.50
27	Del Young	60.00	30.00	18.50
28	Joe Sprinz	60.00	30.00	18.50
29	Doc Hughes	60.00	30.00	18.50
30	Batboys (Don Rode, Albert Boro, Charlie Barnes)	60.00	30.00	18.50

1949 Sommer & Kaufmann San Francisco Seals

JACK NICHOLAS BACCIOCCO
Seals Outfielder 19

JACK NICHOLAS BACCIOCCO, outfielder, Born, San Francisco, Feb. 10, 1925. Height 6', weight 185. Throws and bats right. Italian-Swedish descent. With Salt Lake and Reno in 1947. With Salt Lake in 1948. Hit .277.
Sommer & Kaufmann
838 MARKET ST. 2600 OCEAN AVE. SAN FRANCISCO
35 FOURTH AVE., SAN MATEO
Famous for Boys' "Hot Rod" Shoes

Twenty-eight black-and-white cards numbered 1-29 (#24 unknown) make up the second and final card issue of the "Frisco area clothier." Measuring 2" x 3", the cards are nearly identical to the '48 issue. The '49s can be identified by the mention of "Hot Rod" shoes on the back. Fronts feature a borderless player photo with a panel at the bottom giving name, position and card number. Backs have the ad for the boy's shop and a brief biographical player sketch.

		NM	EX	VG
Complete Set (29):		2,000	1,000	600.00
Common Player:		75.00	37.00	22.00
1	Lefty O'Doul	100.00	50.00	30.00
2	Jack Brewer	75.00	37.00	22.00
3	Kenneth Gables	75.00	37.00	22.00
4	Con Dempsey	75.00	37.00	22.00
5	Al Lien	75.00	37.00	22.00
6	Cliff Melton	75.00	37.00	22.00
7	Steve Nagy	75.00	37.00	22.00
8	Manny Perez	75.00	37.00	22.00
9	Roy Jarvis	75.00	37.00	22.00
10	Roy Partee	75.00	37.00	22.00
11	Reno Cheso	75.00	37.00	22.00
12	Dick Lajeskie	75.00	37.00	22.00
13	Roy Nicely	75.00	37.00	22.00
14	Mickey Rocco	75.00	37.00	22.00
15	Frank Shofner	75.00	37.00	22.00
16	Richard Holder	75.00	37.00	22.00
17	Dino Restelli	75.00	37.00	22.00
18	Floyd J. "Arky" Vaughan	150.00	75.00	45.00
19	Jackie Bacciocuu	75.00	37.00	22.00
20	Bob Drilling	75.00	37.00	22.00
21	Del Young	75.00	37.00	22.00
22	Joe Sprinz	75.00	37.00	22.00
23	Doc Hughes	75.00	37.00	22.00
24	Unknown	75.00	37.00	22.00
25	Bert Singleton	75.00	37.00	22.00
26	John Brocker	75.00	37.00	22.00
27	Jack Tobin	75.00	37.00	22.00
28	Walt Judnich	75.00	37.00	22.00
29	Hal Feldman	75.00	37.00	22.00

1909 Spargo Hartford Senators Postcards

E. P. ARBOGAST.

Members on the Connecticut League (Class B) champion Hartford Senators are pictured on these black-and-white postcards. Player portraits are featured in an oval on front with identification below. A photo credit to "Oliver" is provided. The typically formatted back has a credit line for the publisher, A.W. Spargo. It is likely other members of the team exist on cards yet to be reported.

		NM	EX	VG
Common Player:		700.00	350.00	200.00
(1)	C.P. Arbogast	700.00	350.00	200.00
(2)	Tom J. Connery	700.00	350.00	200.00
(3)	Ray L. Fisher	700.00	350.00	200.00
(4)	C.A. Wadleigh	700.00	350.00	200.00

1867 Sterey Photographers Troy Haymakers

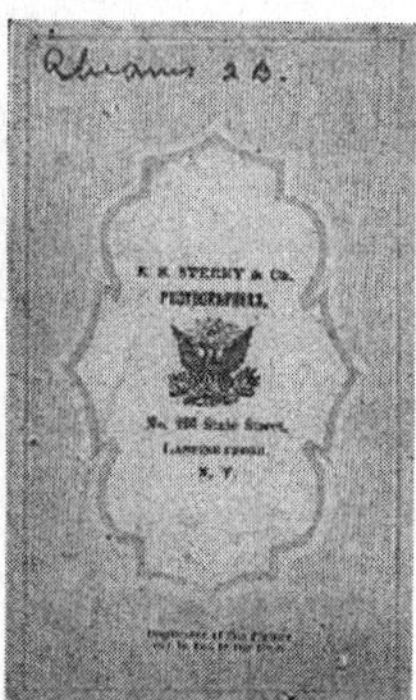

Pre-dating the use of baseball cards as promotional premiums for other products, this issue comprises cartes de visites of members of the Troy Haymakers, one of the powerhouse "amateur" teams in the days prior to the 1871 formation of the National Association, the first professional baseball league. The approximately 2-1/2" x 4" cards have black-and-white player portrait photos glued to a heavy cardboard backing which on its reverse carries in blue the advertising of E.S. Sterey & Co., Photographers, of Lansingburgh, N.Y. The players are not identified on the cards except for the names and, sometimes, positions pencilled on back. While many CDVs of individual players of the era, along with team poses and composites, are known, this issue is important because it represents one of the first efforts to create a "team set." It is likely cards of other Troy players were issued and may surface someday.

		NM	EX	VG
Common Player:		3,000	1,500	900.00
(1)	Abrams	3,000	1,500	900.00
(2)	Bill Craver	4,000	2,000	1,200
(3)	Steve King	4,500	2,250	1,350
(4)	Bub McAtee	4,500	2,250	1,350
(5)	Peter McKeon	3,000	1,500	900.00
(6)	McQuide	3,000	1,500	900.00

1933 St. Paul Daily News

(See 1933 Worch Cigar American Association.)

1946 Sunbeam Bread Sacramento Solons

STEVE MESNER
1946 Solons Third Baseman
Photo by Joe Benetti

STEVE "LITTLE GOLIATH" MESNER, 28, born Los Angeles, Calif.; second season with Solons. Greatest baseball thrill: hitting three home runs in one game. Played in majors with Chicago White Sox, St. Louis Cards, Cincinnati Reds. Hobby: collecting all articles pertaining to baseball.

Listen to Baseball Play by Play With "Tony" Koester KFBK
Sunbeam BREAD

The 21 unnumbered cards in this Pacific Coast League team set are printed with black-and-white fronts containing a borderless player photo with a panel beneath containing name, position and a photo credit. Backs are printed in blue, red and yellow and contain a brief career summary and an ad for the bread brand. Each card can be found with two versions of the ad on back. One has a smaller loaf of bread and the word "Sunbeam" in blue, the other has a larger picture and "Sunbeam" in red. The cards measure approximately 2" x 3". Players are checklisted here in alphabetical order.

		NM	EX	VG
Complete Set (21):		900.00	450.00	240.00
Common Player:		75.00	35.00	20.00
(1)	Bud Beasley	75.00	35.00	20.00
(2)	Jack Calvey	75.00	35.00	20.00
(3)	Gene Corbett	75.00	35.00	20.00
(4)	Bill Conroy	75.00	35.00	20.00
(5)	Guy Fletcher	75.00	35.00	20.00
(6)	Tony Freitas	75.00	35.00	20.00
(7)	Ted Greenhalgh	75.00	35.00	20.00
(8)	Al Jarlett	75.00	35.00	20.00
(9)	Jesse Landrum	75.00	35.00	20.00
(10)	Gene Lillard	75.00	35.00	20.00
(11)	Garth Mann	75.00	35.00	20.00
(12)	Lilo Marcucci	75.00	35.00	20.00
(13)	Joe Marty/SP	225.00	110.00	65.00

		NM	EX	VG
(14)	Steve Mesner	75.00	35.00	20.00
(15)	Herm Pillette	75.00	35.00	20.00
(16)	Earl Sheely	75.00	35.00	20.00
(17)	Al Smith	75.00	35.00	20.00
(18)	Gerald Staley	75.00	35.00	20.00
(19)	Averett Thompson	75.00	35.00	20.00
(20)	Jo Jo White	75.00	35.00	20.00
(21)	Bud Zipay	75.00	35.00	20.00

1947 Sunbeam Bread Sacramento Solons

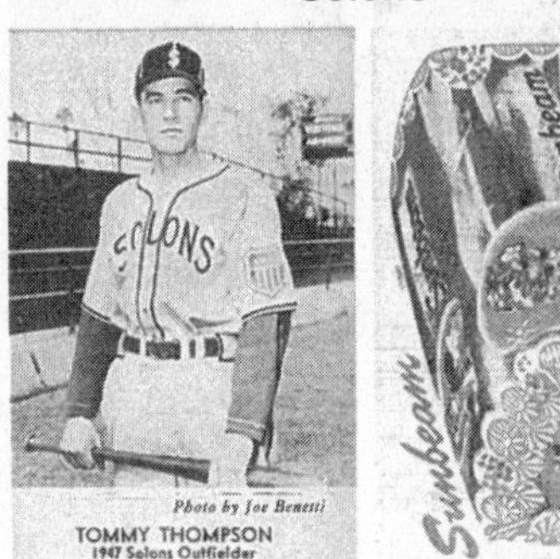

Photo by Joe Bonetti
TOMMY THOMPSON
1947 Solons Outfielder

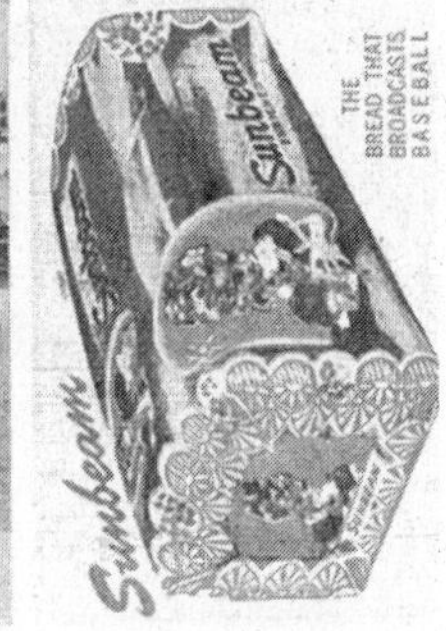

Similar in format to the 1946 issue, the 26 cards in the '47 set again featured black-and-white player photos on front, with a panel beneath giving player name, position and photo credit. Backs of the 2" x 3" cards had a color depiction of a loaf of the sponsoring company's bread. The unnumbered cards are alphabetically checklisted here.

		NM	EX	VG
Complete Set (26):		1,250	625.00	375.00
Common Player:		50.00	25.00	15.00
(1)	Gene Babbit	50.00	25.00	15.00
(2)	Bob Barthelson	50.00	25.00	15.00
(3)	Bud Beasley	50.00	25.00	15.00
(4)	Chuck Cronin	50.00	25.00	15.00
(5)	Eddie Fernandes	50.00	25.00	15.00
(6)	Ed Fitz Gerald	50.00	25.00	15.00
(7)	Guy Fletcher	50.00	25.00	15.00
(8)	Tony Freitas	50.00	25.00	15.00
(9)	Garth Mann	50.00	25.00	15.00
(10)	Joe Marty	50.00	25.00	15.00
(11)	Lou McCollum	50.00	25.00	15.00
(12)	Steve Mesner	50.00	25.00	15.00
(13)	Frank Nelson	50.00	25.00	15.00
(14)	Tommy Nelson	50.00	25.00	15.00
(15)	Joe Orengo	50.00	25.00	15.00
(16)	Hugh Orphan	50.00	25.00	15.00
(17)	Nick Pesut	50.00	25.00	15.00
(18)	Bill Ramsey	50.00	25.00	15.00
(19)	Johnny Rizzo	50.00	25.00	15.00
(20)	Mike Schemer	250.00	125.00	75.00
(21)	Al Smith	50.00	25.00	15.00
(22)	Tommy Thompson	50.00	25.00	15.00
(23)	Jim Warner	50.00	25.00	15.00
(24)	Mel Wasley	50.00	25.00	15.00
(25)	Leo Wells	50.00	25.00	15.00
(26)	Eddie Zipay	50.00	25.00	15.00

1949 Sunbeam/Pureta Sacramento Solons

Players of the Pacific Coast League's Sacramento Solons were featured in this postcard-size (3-1/4" x 5-1/2") set. Fronts featured black-and-white player photos and the logo of the team's radio broadcaster. Backs feature ads for Sunbeam Bread and Pureta meats.

		NM	EX	VG
Complete Set (12):		2,000	1,000	600.00
Common Player:		250.00	125.00	80.00
(1)	Del Baker	250.00	125.00	80.00
(2)	Frankie Dasso	250.00	125.00	80.00
(3)	Walt Dropo	325.00	160.00	100.00
(4)	Bob Gillespie	250.00	125.00	80.00
(5)	Joe Grace	250.00	125.00	80.00
(6)	Ralph Hodgin	250.00	125.00	80.00
(7)	Freddie Marsh	250.00	125.00	80.00
(8)	Joe Marty	250.00	125.00	80.00
(9)	Len Ratto	250.00	125.00	80.00
(10)	Jim Tabor	250.00	125.00	80.00
(11)	Al White	250.00	125.00	80.00
(12)	Bill Wilson	250.00	125.00	80.00

1949 Sunbeam Bread Stockton Ports

SANDY SANDEL
pitcher

PITCHER WARREN HARRY SANDEL is 28, married and has one son. In U.S. Coast Guard three years. Played baseball and basketball in high school. Most interesting experience: shutting out Yankees without a hit in an exhibition game in 1942, pitched three innings. Also chosen for 1949 North All Star Team.
REACH FOR
SUNBEAM
BREAD
PIES
PASTRIES
Gravem-Inglis Baking Co.

These 2" x 3" unnumbered cards can be found printed in either black-and-white or blue tinted. The Ports were the Class C California League farm club of the Chicago White Sox.

		NM	EX	VG
Complete Set (12):		3,000	1,500	900.00
Common Player:		275.00	135.00	85.00
(1)	Nino Bongiovanni	275.00	135.00	85.00
(2)	Lou Bronzan	275.00	135.00	85.00
(3)	Jimmie Brown	275.00	135.00	85.00
(4)	Rocco Cardinale	275.00	135.00	85.00
(5)	Harry Clements	275.00	135.00	85.00
(6)	Norm Grabar	275.00	135.00	85.00
(7)	Bud Guldborg	275.00	135.00	85.00
(8)	Carl Hoberg	275.00	135.00	85.00
(9)	Eddie Murphy	275.00	135.00	85.00
(10)	Sandy Sandel	275.00	135.00	85.00
(11)	Dick Stone	275.00	135.00	85.00
(12)	Matt Zidich	275.00	135.00	85.00

1950 Sunbeam Bread Stockton Ports

ROBERT LOUIS STEVENS
short-stop

SHORT-STOP – ROBERT LOUIS STEVENS, 21, single, native of Stockton. Graduate Edison High, 1947; baseball, football, basketball. Attended Stockton College. Played football. Bats right and throws right. A local boy making good. Signed to first professional contract by Ports, Spring of '49; starting his second season.

Gravem-Inglis Baking Co.

These 2" x 3" unnumbered cards are printed in black-and-white. The Ports were an unaffiliated team in the Class C California League.

		NM	EX	VG
Complete Set (13):		1,800	900.00	550.00
Common Player:		150.00	75.00	45.00
(1)	Richard L. Adams	150.00	75.00	45.00
(2)	James Edward Brown	150.00	75.00	45.00
(3)	Harry Clements	150.00	75.00	45.00
(4)	John Burton Goldborg	150.00	75.00	45.00
(5)	Gerald Lee Haines	150.00	75.00	45.00
(6)	Alfred Michael Heist	150.00	75.00	45.00
(7)	Don Masterson	150.00	75.00	45.00
(8)	Lauren Hugh Monroe	150.00	75.00	45.00
(9)	Frank E. Murray	150.00	75.00	45.00
(10)	Lauren Keith Simon Jr.	150.00	75.00	45.00
(11)	George Anthony Stanich	150.00	75.00	45.00
(12)	Robert Louis Stevens	150.00	75.00	45.00
(13)	Harold Lee Zurcher	150.00	75.00	45.00

1962 Supertest Toronto Maple Leafs

The extent of the checklist for this issue is unknown. It is assumed the cards were given away with gasoline purchases. Printed on thick, porous paper in a 5-1/2" x 8-1/2" format, the cards have a black-and-white photo, facsimile autograph and sponsor's logo on front. Backs are blank.

		NM	EX	VG
Common Player:		60.00	30.00	18.00
(1)	Chuck Dressen	75.00	37.50	22.50
(2)	Russ Heman	60.00	30.00	18.00

1952 Syracuse Chiefs Team Issue

Like the other contemporary issues of Globe Printing, the cards of the '52 Chiefs (International League, unaffiliated) share a blank-back, black-and-white format. Player names are in black in a white strip on front. Cards measure about 2-1/4" x 3-3/8". The checklist here is incomplete.

		NM	EX	VG
Common Player:		60.00	30.00	18.00
(1)	Bruno Betzel	60.00	30.00	18.00
(2)	Johnny Blatnick	60.00	30.00	18.00
(3)	Charles Eisenmann	60.00	30.00	18.00
(4)	Myron Hayworth	60.00	30.00	18.00
(5)	John Welaj	60.00	30.00	18.00

T

1966 Toledo Mud Hens Team Issue

(3-1/4" x 5-1/2") (Unnumbered)

		NM	EX	VG
Complete Set (25):		1,000	500.00	300.00
Common Player:		40.00	20.00	12.00
(1)	Loren Babe	40.00	20.00	12.00
(2)	Stan Bahnsen	40.00	20.00	12.00
(3)	Bill Bethea	40.00	20.00	12.00
(4)	Wayne Comer	40.00	20.00	12.00
(5)	Jack Cullen	40.00	20.00	12.00
(6)	Jack Curtis	40.00	20.00	12.00
(7)	Gil Downs	40.00	20.00	12.00
(8)	Joe Faroci	40.00	20.00	12.00
(9)	Frank Fernandez	40.00	20.00	12.00
(10)	Mike Ferraro	40.00	20.00	12.00
(11)	Doc Foley	40.00	20.00	12.00
(12)	Mike Hegan	40.00	20.00	12.00
(13)	Jim Horsford	40.00	20.00	12.00
(14)	Dick Hughes	40.00	20.00	12.00
(15)	Elvio Jiminez	40.00	20.00	12.00
(16)	Bob Lasko	40.00	20.00	12.00
(17)	Jim Merritt	40.00	20.00	12.00
(18)	Archie Moore	40.00	20.00	12.00
(19)	Bobby Murcer	90.00	45.00	27.00
(20)	Tony Preybycian	40.00	20.00	12.00
(21)	Bob Schmidt	40.00	20.00	12.00
(22)	Charlie Senger, Loren Babe, Bill Shantz	40.00	20.00	12.00
(23)	Bill Shantz	40.00	20.00	12.00
(24)	Paul Toth	40.00	20.00	12.00
(25)	Jerry Walker	40.00	20.00	12.00

1964 True Ade / WGR Buffalo Bisons

Members of the International League Buffalo Bisons, Class AAA farm club of the N.Y. Mets are featured in this set of contest cards. Persons who assembled a complete nine-player set could redeem the cards for ballgame tickets. The cards were found in cartons of Tru Ade beverage. The blank-back cards are printed in red and about 1-1/4" x 6-1/2" overall. At bottom is a player photo with his name and position above, and team below, separated by a dotted line from the upper portion of the card which has contest details and logos of the sponsoring beverage company and WGR radio. The player portion of the card measures about 1-1/4" x 1-1/4". It is evident that at least nine players were issued in the set, possibly with some short-printed; this checklist is, therefore, incomplete. The unnumbered cards are listed here in alphabetical order.

		NM	EX	VG
Common Player:		150.00	75.00	45.00
(1)	Ed Bauta	150.00	75.00	45.00
(2)	Choo Choo Coleman	200.00	100.00	60.00
(3)	Pumpsie Green	300.00	150.00	90.00
(4)	Cleon Jones	200.00	100.00	60.00

1960 Tulsa Oilers Team Issue

This team issue by the St. Louis Cardinals' farm club consists of a dozen black-and-white player photos. Players are identifed by a facsimile autograph on front. Backs of the approximately 4-1/8" x 5" photos are blank.

		NM	EX	VG
Complete Set (18):		350.00	175.00	100.00
Common Player:		20.00	10.00	6.00
(1)	Jim Beauchamp	15.00	7.50	4.50
(2)	Bob Blaylock	20.00	10.00	6.00
(3)	Artie Burnett	20.00	10.00	6.00
(4)	Bill Carpenter	20.00	10.00	6.00
(5)	Julio Gotay	20.00	10.00	6.00
(6)	Jim Hickman	20.00	10.00	6.00
(7)	Ray Katt	20.00	10.00	6.00
(8)	Harry Keister	20.00	10.00	6.00
(9)	Fred Koenig	20.00	10.00	6.00
(10)	Gordon Richardson	20.00	10.00	6.00
(11)	Rich Rogers	20.00	10.00	6.00
(12)	Lynn Rube	20.00	10.00	6.00
(13)	Jim Schaffer	20.00	10.00	6.00
(14)	Clint Stark	20.00	10.00	6.00
(15)	Ted Thiem	20.00	10.00	6.00
(16)	Dixie Walker	20.00	10.00	6.00
(17)	Harry Watts	20.00	10.00	6.00
(18)	Fred Whitfield	20.00	10.00	6.00

1888 Uhlman St. Paul Cabinets

While this cabinet-card issue utilizes the same format (about 4-1/4" x 6-1/2") and the same Goodwin & Co. copyright photos found on contemporary Old Judge cards, they are, according to advertising on the bottom, the product of Uhlman (presumably a studio) in St. Joseph, Mo. All cards known to date depict members of the St. Paul Apostles of the newly formed Western Association.

		NM	EX	VG
Common Player:		900.00	525.00	275.00
(1)	Cal Broughton	900.00	525.00	275.00
(2)	George Treadway	900.00	525.00	275.00
(3)	A.M. Tuckerman	900.00	525.00	275.00

1958 Union Oil Sacramento Solons

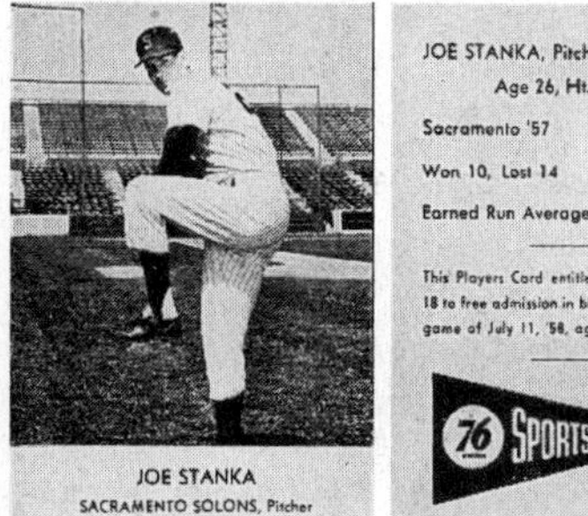

Ten members of the independent Pacific Coast League team were included in a black-and-white card set distributed at Union 76 gas stations in that locale. Fronts feature borderless player photos with a wide white strip at the bottom on which is printed the player, team name and the position. Backs have brief stats, a "76 Sports Club" pennant and information about a specific game for which the card can be exchanged for admission by a child. Cards measure approximately 2-1/2" x 3-1/4".

		NM	EX	VG
Complete Set (10):		500.00	250.00	150.00
Common Player:		50.00	25.00	15.00
(1)	Marshall Bridges	65.00	32.00	19.50
(2)	Dick Cole	50.00	25.00	15.00
(3)	Jim Greengrass	50.00	25.00	15.00
(4)	Al Heist	50.00	25.00	15.00
(5)	Nippy Jones	50.00	25.00	15.00
(6)	Carlos Paula	50.00	25.00	15.00
(7)	Kal Segrist	50.00	25.00	15.00
(8)	Sibbi Sisti	50.00	25.00	15.00
(9)	Joe Stanka	80.00	40.00	24.00
(10)	Bud Watkins	50.00	25.00	15.00

1960 Union Oil Seattle Rainiers

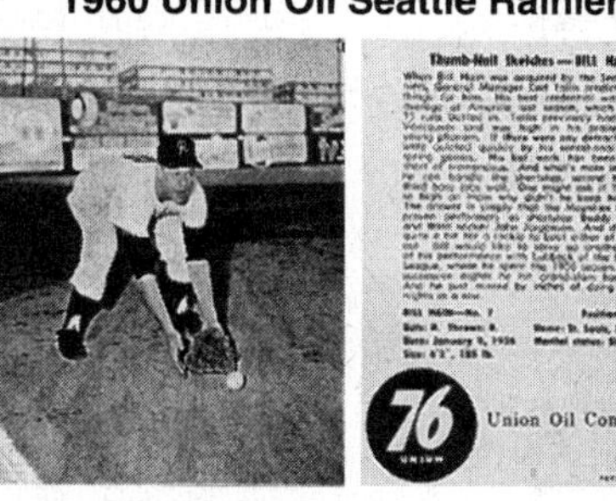

Given away at Union 76 gas stations in the Seattle area, this set of nine full-color cards measure approximately 3-1/8" x 4". Backs have brief biographical data, a career summary and a large Union 76 logo. The cards are skip-numbered.

		NM	EX	VG
Complete Set (9):		200.00	100.00	60.00
Common Player:		12.00	6.00	3.50
4	Francisco Obregon	20.00	10.00	6.00
6	Drew Gilbert	12.00	6.00	3.50
7	Bill Hain	12.00	6.00	3.50
10	Ray Ripplemeyer	100.00	50.00	30.00
13	Joe Taylor	12.00	6.00	3.50
15	Lou Skizas	12.00	6.00	3.50
17	Don Rudolph	12.00	6.00	3.50
19	Gordy Coleman	15.00	7.50	4.50
22	Hal Beven	12.00	6.00	3.50

1961 Union Oil Pacific Coast League

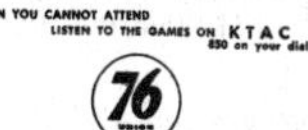

Union Oil Company

The last of three Union Oil PCL issues, the 67 cards in this set feature sepia-toned borderless photos on front in a 3" to 3-1/8" x 4" format. Backs are printed in blue and feature biographical data, a career summary, and ads by the issuing oil company and participating radio station co-sponsors. Six of the eight teams in the '61 PCL are featured, with Salt Lake City and Vancouver not participating in the promotion. Presumably because of smaller print runs, the cards distributed in Hawaii and Spokane bring a premium price. Hall of Fame pitcher Gaylord Perry is featured on his first baseball card in this set. Only the Tacoma cards are numbered and they are skip-numbered.

(Team sets listed below.)

1961 Union Oil Hawaii Islanders

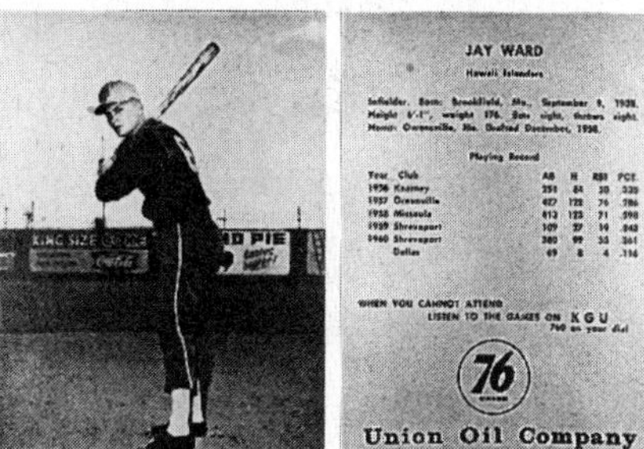

		NM	EX	VG
Complete Set (10):		375.00	185.00	110.00
Common Player:		40.00	20.00	12.00
(1)	Ray Jablonski	40.00	20.00	12.00
(2)	Jim McManus	40.00	20.00	12.00
(3)	George Prescott	75.00	37.50	22.50
(4)	Diego Segui	45.00	22.50	13.50
(5)	Rachel Slider	40.00	20.00	12.00
(6)	Jim Small	40.00	20.00	12.00
(7)	Milt Smith	40.00	20.00	12.00
(8)	Dave Thies	40.00	20.00	12.00
(9)	Jay Ward	40.00	20.00	12.00
(10)	Bill Werle	40.00	20.00	12.00

1961 Union Oil Portland Beavers

		NM	EX	VG
Complete Set (13):		150.00	75.00	45.00
Common Player:		12.00	6.00	3.50
(1)	Ed Bauta	12.00	6.00	3.50
(2)	Vern Benson	12.00	6.00	3.50
(3)	Jerry Buchek	12.00	6.00	3.50
(4)	Bob Burda	12.00	6.00	3.50
(5)	Duke Carmel	12.00	6.00	3.50
(6)	Don Choate	12.00	6.00	3.50
(7)	Phil Gagliano	12.00	6.00	3.50
(8)	Jim Hickman	12.00	6.00	3.50
(9)	Ray Katt	12.00	6.00	3.50
(10)	Mel Nelson	12.00	6.00	3.50
(11)	Jim Shaffer	12.00	6.00	3.50
(12)	Mike Shannon	17.50	8.75	5.25
(13)	Clint Stark	12.00	6.00	3.50

1961 Union Oil San Diego Padres

		NM	EX	VG
Complete Set (12):		175.00	90.00	45.00
Common Player:		12.00	6.00	3.50
(1)	Dick Barone	12.00	6.00	3.50
(2)	Jim Bolger	12.00	6.00	3.50
(3)	Kent Hadley	12.00	6.00	3.50
(4)	Mike Hershberger	15.00	7.50	4.50
(5)	Stan Johnson	12.00	6.00	3.50
(6)	Dick Lines	12.00	6.00	3.50
(7)	Jim Napier	12.00	6.00	3.50
(8)	Tony Roig	12.00	6.00	3.50
(9)	Herb Score	40.00	20.00	12.00
(10)	Harry Simpson	20.00	10.00	6.00
(11)	Joe Taylor	12.00	6.00	3.50
(12)	Ben Wade	12.00	6.00	3.50

1961 Union Oil Seattle Rainiers

		NM	EX	VG
Complete Set (11):		100.00	50.00	30.00
Common Player:		10.00	5.00	3.00
(1)	Galen Cisco	10.00	5.00	3.00
(2)	Lou Clinton	10.00	5.00	3.00
(3)	Marlan Coughtry	10.00	5.00	3.00
(4)	Harry Malmberg	10.00	5.00	3.00
(5)	Dave Mann	10.00	5.00	3.00
(6)	Derrell Martin	10.00	5.00	3.00
(7)	Erv Palica	10.00	5.00	3.00
(8)	John Pesky	15.00	7.50	4.50
(9)	Bob Tillman	10.00	5.00	3.00
(10)	Marv Toft	10.00	5.00	3.00
(11)	Tom Umphlett	10.00	5.00	3.00

1961 Union Oil Spokane Indians

		NM	EX	VG
Complete Set (11):		450.00	225.00	135.00
Common Player:		35.00	17.50	10.00
(1)	Doug Camilli	35.00	17.50	10.00
(2)	Ramon Conde	35.00	17.50	10.00
(3)	Bob Giallombardo	35.00	17.50	10.00
(4)	Mike Goliat	35.00	17.50	10.00
(5)	Preston Gomez/SP	135.00	67.00	40.00
(6)	Rod Graber	35.00	17.50	10.00
(7)	Tim Harkness	35.00	17.50	10.00
(8)	Jim Harwell	35.00	17.50	10.00
(9)	Howie Reed	35.00	17.50	10.00
(10)	Curt Roberts	35.00	17.50	10.00
(11)	Rene Valdes (Valdez)	35.00	17.50	10.00

1961 Union Oil Tacoma Giants

		NM	EX	VG
Complete Set (10):		200.00	100.00	60.00
Common Player:		15.00	7.50	4.50
10	Red Davis	15.00	7.50	4.50
12	Dick Phillips	15.00	7.50	4.50
17	Gil Garrido	15.00	7.50	4.50
20	Georges Maranda	15.00	7.50	4.50
25	John Orsino	15.00	7.50	4.50
26	Dusty Rhodes	20.00	10.00	6.00
28	Ron Herbel	15.00	7.50	4.50
29	Gaylord Perry	60.00	30.00	18.00
30	Rafael Alomar	20.00	10.00	6.00
34	Bob Farley	15.00	7.50	4.50

1961 Union Oil Taiyo Whales

This three-card set was produced in conjunction with an exhibition series played in October 1961, between the Taiyo Whales of Japan's Central League, and the Hawaii Islanders, a Class AAA Pacific Cost League farm club of the K.C. Athletics. The player cards measure just over 3" x 4", while the team photo card is 5" x 3-3/4". Cards are black-and-white and have some player biography and ads for Union

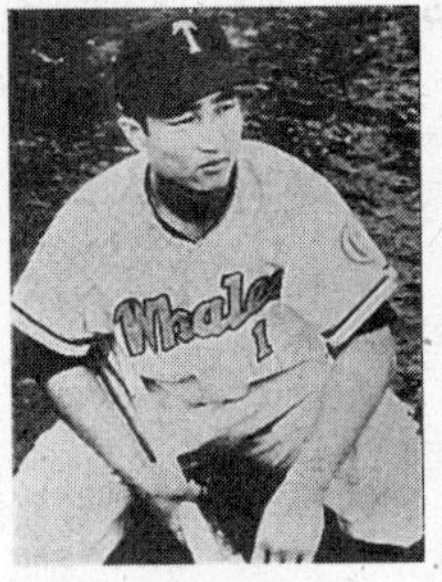

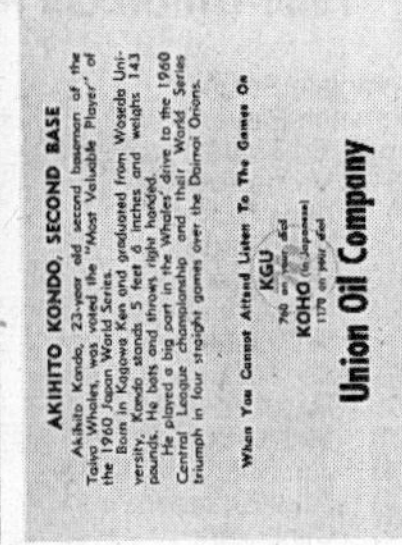

Oil Co., and the English - and Japanese - language radio stations that carried the games.

		NM	EX	VG
Complete Set (3):		175.00	87.00	52.00
(1)	Akihito Kondo	50.00	25.00	15.00
(2)	Gentaro Shimada	50.00	25.00	15.00
(3)	Taiyo Whales Team	90.00	45.00	27.00

1951 Vancouver Capilanos Popcorn Issue

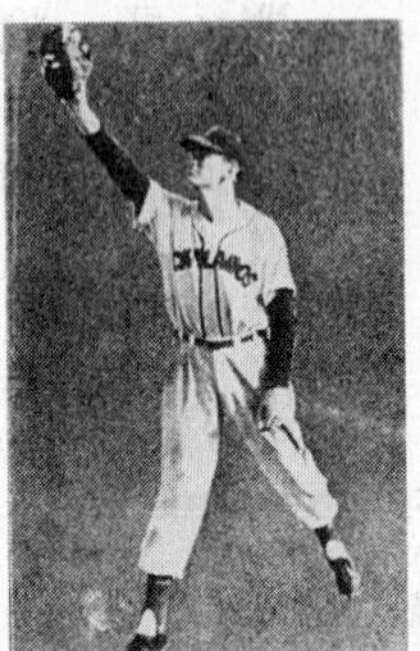

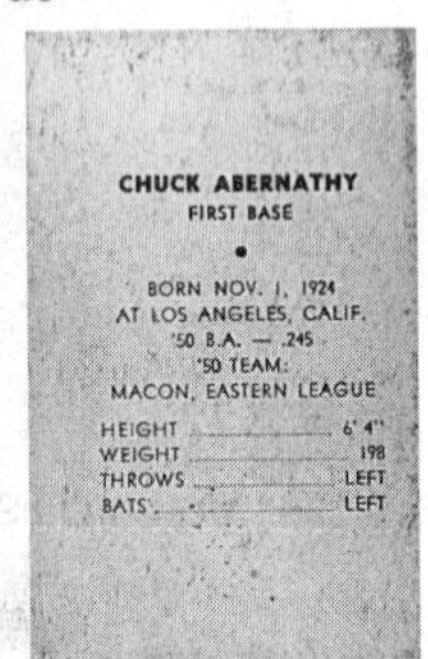

These cards measure 1-7/8" x 2-7/8", are printed in black-and-white and have 1950 stats on back. Names may appear in slightly different form than checklisted here. The Caps played in the Class B Western International League and were not affiliated with any major league club.

		NM	EX	VG
Complete Set (24):		4,000	2,000	1,200
Common Player:		200.00	100.00	60.00
(1)	Chuck Abernathy	200.00	100.00	60.00
(2)	Jerry Barta	200.00	100.00	60.00
(3)	Bud Beasley	200.00	100.00	60.00
(4)	Gordy Brunswick	200.00	100.00	60.00
(5)	Reno Cheso	200.00	100.00	60.00
(6)	Ken Chorlton	200.00	100.00	60.00
(7)	Carl Gunnarson	200.00	100.00	60.00
(8)	Pete Hernandez	200.00	100.00	60.00
(9)	Vern Kindsfather	200.00	100.00	60.00
(10)	Bobby McGuire	200.00	100.00	60.00
(11)	Bob McLean	200.00	100.00	60.00
(12)	Charlie Mead	200.00	100.00	60.00
(13)	Jimmy Moore	200.00	100.00	60.00
(14)	George Nicholas	200.00	100.00	60.00
(15)	John Ritchey	200.00	100.00	60.00
(16)	Sandy Robertson	200.00	100.00	60.00
(17)	Bill Schuster	200.00	100.00	60.00
(18)	Dick Sinovic	200.00	100.00	60.00
(19)	Ron Smith	200.00	100.00	60.00
(20)	Bob Snyder	200.00	100.00	60.00
(21)	Don Tisnerat	200.00	100.00	60.00
(22)	Ray Tran	200.00	100.00	60.00
(23)	Reg Wallis (Trainer)	200.00	100.00	60.00
(24)	Bill Whyte	200.00	100.00	60.00

1952 Vancouver Capilanos Popcorn Issue

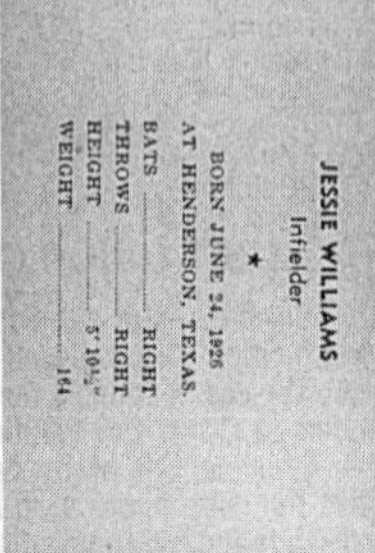

These cards measure 2" x 3-1/8", are printed in black-and-white and have 1951 stats on back. Names may appear in slightly different form than checklisted here. The Caps played in the Class A Western International League and were not affiliated with any major league club.

		NM	EX	VG
Complete Set (20):		3,500	1,750	1,000
Common Player:		200.00	100.00	60.00
(1)	Gordie Brunswick	200.00	100.00	60.00
(2)	Bob Duretto	200.00	100.00	60.00
(3)	Van Fletcher	200.00	100.00	60.00
(4)	John Guldborg	200.00	100.00	60.00
(5)	Paul Jones	200.00	100.00	60.00
(6)	Eddie Locke	200.00	100.00	60.00
(7)	Tom Lovrich	200.00	100.00	60.00
(8)	Jimmy Moore	200.00	100.00	60.00
(9)	George Nicholas	200.00	100.00	60.00
(10a)	John Ritchey	200.00	100.00	60.00
(10b)	Johnny Ritchie	200.00	100.00	60.00
(11)	Bill Schuster	200.00	100.00	60.00
(12)	Bob Snyder	200.00	100.00	60.00
(13)	Len Tran	200.00	100.00	60.00
(14)	Ray Tran	200.00	100.00	60.00
(15)	Edo Vanni	200.00	100.00	60.00
(16)	Jim Wert	200.00	100.00	60.00
(17)	Bill Whyte	200.00	100.00	60.00
(18)	Jessie Williams/Btg	200.00	100.00	60.00
(19)	Jesse Williams/Fldg	200.00	100.00	60.00

1953 Vancouver Capilanos Popcorn Issue

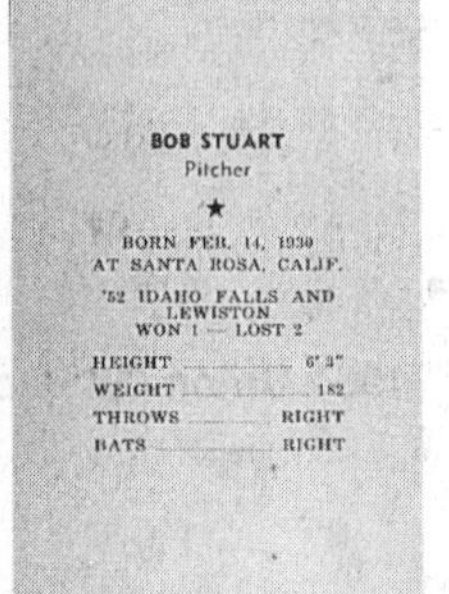

These cards measure 2-3/16" x 3-3/16", are printed in black-and-white and have 1952 stats on back. Names may appear in slightly different form than checklisted here. The Caps played in the Class A Western International League and were not affiliated with any major league club.

		NM	EX	VG
Complete Set (18):		3,000	1,500	900.00
Common Player:		200.00	100.00	60.00
(1)	Dick Briskey	200.00	100.00	60.00
(2)	Jack Bukowatz	200.00	100.00	60.00
(3)	Ken Chorlton	200.00	100.00	60.00
(4)	Van Fletcher	200.00	100.00	60.00
(5)	John Guldborg	200.00	100.00	60.00
(6)	Carl Gunnerson	200.00	100.00	60.00
(7)	Jim Hedgecock	200.00	100.00	60.00
(8)	Gordon Hernandez	200.00	100.00	60.00
(9)	Pete Hernandez	200.00	100.00	60.00
(10)	Jim Leavitt	200.00	100.00	60.00
(11)	Rod MacKay	200.00	100.00	60.00
(12)	Frank Mascaro	200.00	100.00	60.00
(13)	Lonnie Myers	200.00	100.00	60.00
(14)	Rod Owen	200.00	100.00	60.00
(15)	Harvey Storey	200.00	100.00	60.00
(16)	Bob Stuart	200.00	100.00	60.00
(17)	Dale Thomason	200.00	100.00	60.00
(18)	Jim Wert	200.00	100.00	60.00

1954 Vancouver Capilanos Popcorn Issue

These cards measure 2-3/16" x 3-5/16" and are printed in black-and-white. Names may appear in slightly different form than checklisted here. The Caps were the 1954 champs of the Class A Western International League and were not affiliated with any major league club.

		NM	EX	VG
Complete Set (15):		2,500	1,250	750.00
Common Player:		200.00	100.00	60.00
(1)	Bill Brenner	200.00	100.00	60.00
(2)	Ken Chorlton	200.00	100.00	60.00
(3)	Jim Clarke (Clark)	200.00	100.00	60.00
(4)	John Cordell	200.00	100.00	60.00
(5)	Bob Duretto	200.00	100.00	60.00
(6)	Dick Greco	200.00	100.00	60.00
(7)	Arnie Hallgren	200.00	100.00	60.00
(8)	Danny Holden	200.00	100.00	60.00
(9)	Rod McKay	200.00	100.00	60.00
(10)	George Nicholas	200.00	100.00	60.00
(11)	Nick Pesut	200.00	100.00	60.00
(12)	Ken Richardson	200.00	100.00	60.00
(13)	Bob Roberts	200.00	100.00	60.00
(14)	Bob Wellman	200.00	100.00	60.00
(15)	Marvin Williams	200.00	100.00	60.00

1954 Veltex Lewiston Broncs

It is evident from the format of the card and of the accompanying album that this is a product of Globe Printing, which produced many minor league sets in the early 1950s. What makes this set of the 1954 Class A (Western International League) affiliate of the Baltimore Orioles unusual among Globe issues is the mention of a sponsor. The blank-back, black-and-white cards measure 2-3/16" x 3-3/8". The checklist below is obviously incomplete.

		NM	EX	VG
Common player:		60.00	30.00	18.00
Album:		150.00	75.00	45.00
(1)	Larry Barton	60.00	30.00	18.00

1952 Ventura Braves Team Issue

These 2-1/4" x 3-3/8" black-and-white, unnumbered, blank-backed cards were one of many minor league team sets issued by Globe Printing of San Jose, Calif., in the early 1950s. Cards were usually given away at the ballpark on a one-per-week or one-per-homestand basis, accounting for the rarity of surviving complete sets. It is known that 18 V-Braves were issued in this set, though only 14 have been checklisted to date. The team was a Class C California League farm club of the Boston Braves.

		NM	EX	VG
Common Player:		60.00	30.00	18.00
Album:		100.00	50.00	30.00
(1)	Al Aguilar	60.00	30.00	18.00
(2)	Bud Belardi	60.00	30.00	18.00
(3)	Frank Followell	60.00	30.00	18.00
(4)	Glenn Hittner	60.00	30.00	18.00
(5)	Lee Kast	60.00	30.00	18.00
(6)	Richie Morse	60.00	30.00	18.00
(7)	Frank Nubin	60.00	30.00	18.00
(8)	George Owen	60.00	30.00	18.00
(9)	Manny Perez	60.00	30.00	18.00
(10)	Jose Perez	60.00	30.00	18.00
(11)	Harley Resh	60.00	30.00	18.00
(12)	Jack Schlarb	60.00	30.00	18.00
(13)	Bob Sturgeon	60.00	30.00	18.00
(14)	Billy Wells	60.00	30.00	18.00

1911 Western Playground Association

Stars from around the Pacific Coast League are featured on this rare and unusual issue. The 2-1/4" x 3-1/2" cards have a front design similar to contemporary Zeenuts cards: A dark brown border surrounding a sepia posed action picture (which appears to be a heavily retouched photo). Printed in white at left or right are "WESTERN PLAYGROUND ASSOCIATION / P.C. (or sometimes 'P.S.') LEAGUE" and the player's last name. Backs are a "Membership Certificate" indicating the cards could be redeemed for five percent of their seven-cent "face value" toward the purchase of school playground apparatus or supplies. The cards were received with the purchase of "Bank Stock" brand composition books.

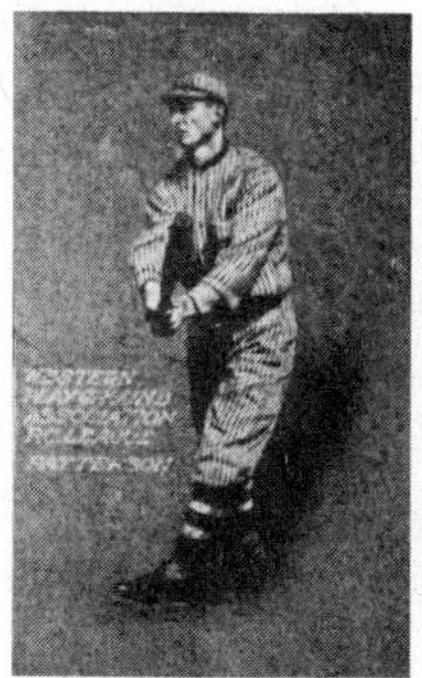

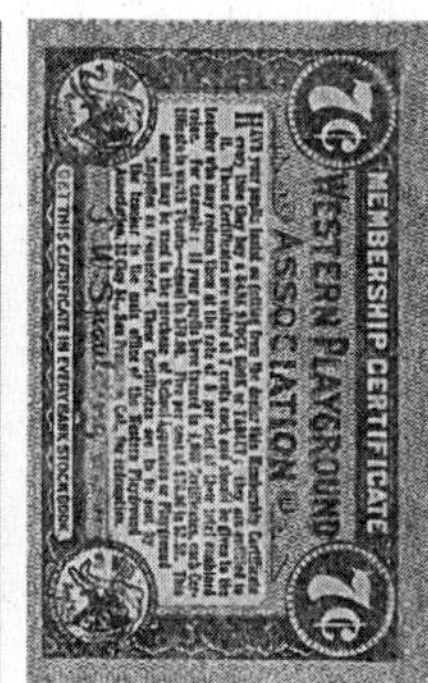

		NM	EX	VG
Common Player:		6,000	3,000	1,800
(1)	Claude Berry	6,000	3,000	1,800
(2)	Roy Brashear	6,000	3,000	1,800
(3)	Herb Byram	6,000	3,000	1,800
(4)	Walt Carlisle	6,000	3,000	1,800
(5)	Roy Caslleton (Castleton)	6,000	3,000	1,800
(6)	Chet Chadborne (Chadbourne)	6,000	3,000	1,800
(7)	Tyler Christian	6,000	3,000	1,800
(8)	Bert Coy	6,000	3,000	1,800
(9)	Pete Daley	6,000	3,000	1,800
(10)	Pop Dillon	6,000	3,000	1,800
(11)	Joe French	6,000	3,000	1,800
(12)	Howie Gregory	6,000	3,000	1,800
(13)	Spec Harkness	6,000	3,000	1,800
(14)	Heinie Heitmuller	6,000	3,000	1,800
(15)	Ben Henderson	6,000	3,000	1,800
(16)	Cack Henley	6,000	3,000	1,800
(17)	Izzy Hoffman	6,000	3,000	1,800
(18)	Happy Hogan	6,000	3,000	1,800
(19)	Johnny Kane	6,000	3,000	1,800
(20)	Jimmy Lewis	6,000	3,000	1,800
(21)	Tom Madden	6,000	3,000	1,800
(22)	Chris Mahoney	6,000	3,000	1,800
(23)	George Metzger	6,000	3,000	1,800
(24)	Fred Miller	6,000	3,000	1,800
(25)	Kid Mohler	6,000	3,000	1,800
(26)	Walter Nagle	6,000	3,000	1,800
(27)	Patsy O'Rourke	6,000	3,000	1,800
(28)	Ham Patterson	6,000	3,000	1,800
(29)	Roger Peckinpaugh	6,000	3,000	1,800
(30)	Bill Rapps	6,000	3,000	1,800
(31)	Bill Rogers (Rodgers)	6,000	3,000	1,800
(32)	Buddy Ryan	6,000	3,000	1,800
(33)	Walter Schmitt (Schmidt)	6,000	3,000	1,800
(34)	Tom Seaton	6,000	3,000	1,800
(35)	Jerry Sheehan	6,000	3,000	1,800
(36)	Harry Stewart	6,000	3,000	1,800
(37)	George Stinson	6,000	3,000	1,800
(38)	Harry Suter (Sutor)	6,000	3,000	1,800
(39)	Harry Wolverton	6,000	3,000	1,800
(40)	Elmer Zacher	6,000	3,000	1,800

1932 Wheaties Minneapolis Millers

Because of their similarity to the 1933 issue which carried Wheaties advertising on the back, these postcard-size photos of the 1932 Millers are believed to also have been issued by the Minneapolis-based cereal company. The 3-7/16" x 5-7/16" cards have black-and-white portraits or posed action photos on front, along with a facsimile autograph. Backs are blank.

		NM	EX	VG
Complete Set (24):		900.00	450.00	275.00
Common Player:		40.00	20.00	12.00
(1)	J.C. "Rube" Benton	40.00	20.00	12.00
(2)	Donie Bush	40.00	20.00	12.00
(3)	Andy Cohen	45.00	22.00	13.50
(4)	"Pea Ridge" Day	40.00	20.00	12.00
(5)	Ray Fitzgerald	40.00	20.00	12.00
(6)	F.P. "Babe" Ganzel	40.00	20.00	12.00
(7)	Wes Griffin	40.00	20.00	12.00
(8)	Spencer Harris	40.00	20.00	12.00
(9)	Joe Hauser	75.00	37.00	22.00
(10)	Frank J. "Dutch" Henry	40.00	20.00	12.00
(11)	Phil Hensick	40.00	20.00	12.00
(12)	Bunker Hill	40.00	20.00	12.00
(13)	Joe Mowry	40.00	20.00	12.00
(14)	Jess Petty	40.00	20.00	12.00
(15)	Paul Richards	45.00	22.00	13.50
(16)	Bill Rodda	40.00	20.00	12.00
(17)	Harry Rose	40.00	20.00	12.00
(18)	Art Ruble	40.00	20.00	12.00
(19)	"Rosy" Ryan	40.00	20.00	12.00
(20)	Al Sheehan	40.00	20.00	12.00
(21)	Ed Sicking	40.00	20.00	12.00
(22)	Ernie Smith	40.00	20.00	12.00
(23)	Hy Van Denberg	40.00	20.00	12.00
(24)	E.R. Vangilder	40.00	20.00	12.00

1933 Wheaties Minneapolis Millers

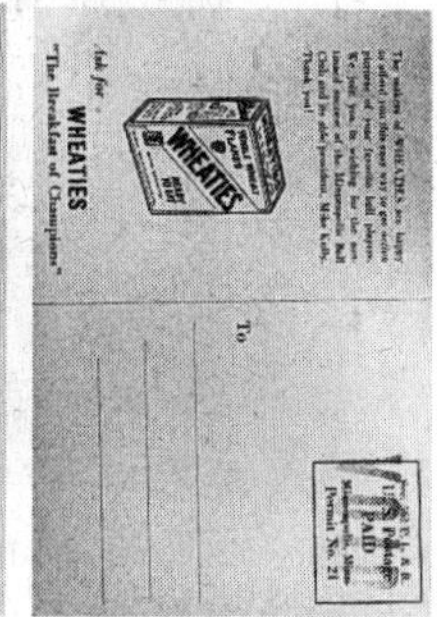

Prior to printing their first major league baseball cards on the backs of cereal boxes in 1935, Wheaties sponsored a minor league set for the hometown Minneapolis Millers in 1933. The 4" x 5-3/4" cards have a sepia-toned posed action photo on front, along with a facsimile autograph. The player's name, position, team and year are printed in the bottom border. The postcard back, printed in black-and-white, has a drawing of a Wheaties box and an ad for the cereal. All unmailed examples seen to date have a purple rubber-stamped "VOID" in the postage box at top. The unnumbered cards are checklisted here alphabetically.

		NM	EX	VG
Complete Set (24):		2,250	1,125	650.00
Common Player:		90.00	45.00	27.00
(1)	Dave Bancroft	150.00	75.00	45.00
(2)	Rube Benton	90.00	45.00	27.00
(3)	Andy Cohen	150.00	75.00	45.00
(4)	Bob Fothergill	90.00	45.00	27.00
(5)	"Babe" Ganzel	90.00	45.00	27.00
(6)	Joe Glenn	90.00	45.00	27.00
(7)	Wes Griffin	90.00	45.00	27.00
(8)	Jack Hallet	90.00	45.00	27.00
(9)	Jerry Harrington (Announcer)	90.00	45.00	27.00
(10)	Spencer Harris	100.00	50.00	30.00
(11)	Joe Hauser	200.00	100.00	60.00
(12)	Butch Henline	90.00	45.00	27.00
(13)	Walter Hilcher	90.00	45.00	27.00
(14)	Dutch Holland	90.00	45.00	27.00
(15)	Harry Holsclaw	90.00	45.00	27.00
(16)	Wes Kingdon	90.00	45.00	27.00
(17)	George Murray	90.00	45.00	27.00
(18)	Leo Norris	90.00	45.00	27.00
(19)	Jess Petty	90.00	45.00	27.00
(20)	Art Ruble	90.00	45.00	27.00
(21)	Al Sheehan (Announcer)	90.00	45.00	27.00
(22)	Ernie Smith	90.00	45.00	27.00
(23)	Wally Tauscher	90.00	45.00	27.00
(24)	Hy VanDenburg	90.00	45.00	27.00

1933 Wheaties Seattle Indians

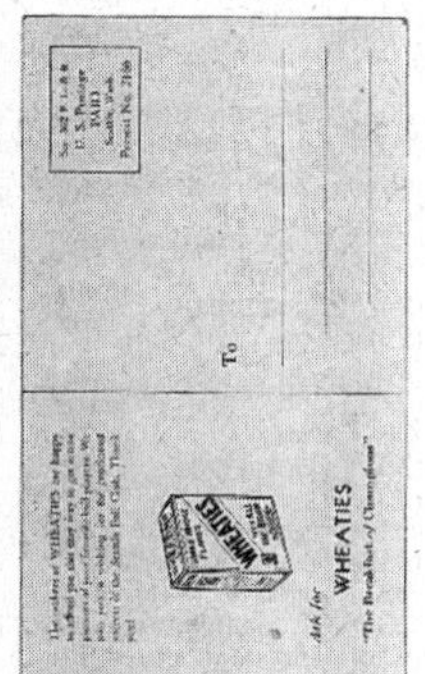

Prior to printing their first major league baseball cards on the backs of cereal boxes in 1935, Wheaties sponsored a minor league set for the Seattle Indians in 1933. The 4-1/8" x 7" cards have a sepia-toned posed portrait or action photo on front, along with a facsimile autograph. The player's name, position, team and year are printed in the bottom border. The postcard back, printed in black-and-white, has a drawing of a Wheaties box and an ad for the cereal. The unnumbered cards are checklisted here alphabetically; it is likely this list is incomplete.

		NM	EX	VG
Common Player:		450.00	225.00	135.00
(1)	George Burns	600.00	300.00	180.00
(2)	Joe Coscarart	450.00	225.00	135.00
(3)	Leo Lassen (Broadcaster)	450.00	225.00	135.00
(4)	Bill Radonits	450.00	225.00	135.00
(5)	"Junk" Walters	450.00	225.00	135.00

1912 Whitehead & Hoag P.C.L. Pins

A paper insert originally in the back of these pins identifies the maker as Whitehead & Hoag of San Francisco. The 7/8" diameter celluloid pins are printed in either black or blue on a white background. A player portrait photo is at center, with his last name below. Above is the city of his team and the Pacific Coast League initials. Listed in the "American Card Catalog" as PM5, the unnumbered pins are checklisted here alphabetically; it's possible additional pins in the issue remain to be reported. All pins seen are Oakland players except McCredie, Shehann, Rapp, and Seaton (Portland) as well as Berry (San Fransisco).

		NM	EX	VG
Complete Set (26):		5,000	2,500	1,500
Common Player:		275.00	135.00	85.00
(1)	Harry Ables	275.00	135.00	85.00
(2)	Claude Berry	275.00	135.00	85.00
(3)	Tyler Christian	275.00	135.00	85.00
(4)	Al Cook	275.00	135.00	85.00
(5)	Bert Coy	275.00	135.00	85.00
(6)	Jack Flater	275.00	135.00	85.00
(7)	Howie Gregory	275.00	135.00	85.00
(8)	Joe Hamilton	275.00	135.00	85.00
(9)	Gus Hetling	275.00	135.00	85.00
(10a)	Hille	275.00	135.00	85.00
(10b)	Mgr. Hille	275.00	135.00	85.00
(11)	Izzy Hoffman	275.00	135.00	85.00
(12)	Bill Leard	275.00	135.00	85.00
(13)	Bill Malarkey	275.00	135.00	85.00
(14)	Elmer Martinoni	275.00	135.00	85.00
(15)	Walter McCredie	275.00	135.00	85.00
(16)	Honus Mitze	275.00	135.00	85.00
(17)	Cy Parkins	275.00	135.00	85.00
(18)	Ashley Pope	275.00	135.00	85.00
(19)	Bill Rapp (Rapps)	275.00	135.00	85.00
(20)	Tom Seaton	275.00	135.00	85.00
(21a)	Bud Sharpe	275.00	135.00	85.00
(21b)	Mgr. Sharpe	275.00	135.00	85.00
(22)	Tommy Sheehan	275.00	135.00	85.00
(23)	Smith	275.00	135.00	85.00
(24)	John Tiedeman (Tiedemann)	275.00	135.00	85.00
(25)	Eddie Wilkinson	275.00	135.00	85.00
(26)	Elmer Zacher	275.00	135.00	85.00

1919 Winkelman's Quaker Bread Pins

This issue of 1-1/4" diameter celluloid pinback buttons features members of the Memphis Chickasaws in black-and-white portraits on a pale yellow background, surrounded by an orange border with the sponsor's advertising. A large turtle is pictured at bottom. Currently only three players are known, though it is likely more were issued.

		NM	EX	VG
Common Player:		1,300	650.00	400.00
(1)	Baerwald	1,300	650.00	400.00
(2)	Carey	1,300	650.00	400.00
(3)	Bob Coulson	1,300	650.00	400.00

1933-34 Worch Cigar American Assoc.

Though the issuer is not identified anywhere on these blank-backed, 3-7/16" x 5-7/16" black-and-white cards (though some are found with a box on front crediting the photo to the St. Paul Daily News), the individual player photos were available as premiums for redemption of cigar bands by the Worch Cigar Co., of St. Paul, Minn. The issue is similar in format to the major league cards of the same era, and indeed the cards were offered together. Most collectors prefer to chase either the major leaguers or the minor leaguers independently, so they are cataloged in that fashion. The set encompasses players from the 1932-35 Minneapolis Millers, the 1933 St. Paul Saints and a handful from the Columbus Redbirds, Kansas City Blues and a few other teams. The unnumbered cards are checklisted below alphabetically. Player

identification is presented in several different styles and may include just the last name or also the first name. Several players are known in more than one pose. The checklist here is likely incomplete.

		NM	EX	VG
Common Player:		45.00	22.50	13.50
(1)	Dave Bancroft	100.00	50.00	30.00
(2)	Clyde Beck	45.00	22.50	13.50
(3)	Rube Benton	45.00	22.50	13.50
(4)	W. Berger	45.00	22.50	13.50
(5)	Brannon	45.00	22.50	13.50
(6)	Spurgeon Chandler	45.00	22.50	13.50
(7)	Tiny Chaplin	45.00	22.50	13.50
(8)	Andy Cohen	45.00	22.50	13.50
(9)	Nick Cullop	45.00	22.50	13.50
(10)	Bob Fenner	45.00	22.50	13.50
(11)	Fischall	45.00	22.50	13.50
(12)	Gaffke	45.00	22.50	13.50
(13a)	Foster Ganzel	45.00	22.50	13.50
(13b)	Foster Ganzel	45.00	22.50	13.50
(14)	Louis Garland	45.00	22.50	13.50
(15)	Joe Glenn	45.00	22.50	13.50
(16)	Angelo Guiliani	45.00	22.50	13.50
(17)	Pinky Hargrave	45.00	22.50	13.50
(18)	Slim Harriss	45.00	22.50	13.50
(19)	Spencer Harris	45.00	22.50	13.50
(20)	Joe Hauser	75.00	37.50	22.50
(21)	Walter Henline	45.00	22.50	13.50
(22)	Phil Hensick	45.00	22.50	13.50
(23)	Walter Hilcher	45.00	22.50	13.50
(24)	Jesse Hill	45.00	22.50	13.50
(25)	Bob Holand	45.00	22.50	13.50
(26)	Harry Holsclaw	45.00	22.50	13.50
(27)	Meredith Hopkins	45.00	22.50	13.50
(28)	Irvine Jeffries	45.00	22.50	13.50
(29)	Monk Joyner	45.00	22.50	13.50
(30)	Fred Koster	45.00	22.50	13.50
(31)	Walter Mails	45.00	22.50	13.50
(32)	Chuck Marrow	45.00	22.50	13.50
(33)	Emmett McCann	45.00	22.50	13.50
(34)	Joe Mowry	45.00	22.50	13.50
(35)	Les Munns	45.00	22.50	13.50
(36)	George Murray	45.00	22.50	13.50
(37)	Floyd Newkirk	45.00	22.50	13.50
(38)	Leo Norris	45.00	22.50	13.50
(39)	Frank Packard	45.00	22.50	13.50
(40)	Ben Paschal	45.00	22.50	13.50
(41a)	Jess Petty/Throwing (Right foot off ground.)	45.00	22.50	13.50
(41b)	Jess Petty	45.00	22.50	13.50
(42)	Ray Radcliff	45.00	22.50	13.50
(43)	Larry Rosenthal	45.00	22.50	13.50
(44a)	Art Ruble	45.00	22.50	13.50
(44b)	Art Ruble	45.00	22.50	13.50
(45)	Art Shires	45.00	22.50	13.50
(46a)	Ernest Smith	45.00	22.50	13.50
(46b)	Ernest Smith	45.00	22.50	13.50
(47)	Ray Starr	45.00	22.50	13.50
(48)	Walter Tauscher	45.00	22.50	13.50
(49)	Myles Thomas	45.00	22.50	13.50
(50)	Phil Todt	45.00	22.50	13.50
(51)	Gene Trow	45.00	22.50	13.50
(52)	Hy Van Denburg	45.00	22.50	13.50
(53)	Elam Van Gilder	45.00	22.50	13.50
(54)	Charles Wilson	45.00	22.50	13.50
(55)	Ab. Wright	45.00	22.50	13.50
(56)	Emil Yde	45.00	22.50	13.50
(57)	Russ Young	45.00	22.50	13.50

1911 Zeenut Pacific Coast League

Produced annually for 28 years, these Pacific Coast League cards were the longest-running and most popular baseball issues ever to appear on the West Coast. Issued by the Collins-McCarthy Candy Co. (later known as the Collins-Hencke Candy Co. and then simply the Collins Candy Co.) of San Francisco, Zeenut cards were inserted in boxes of the company's products: Zeenuts, Ruf-Neks and Home Run Kisses. All Zeenut cards issued from 1913 through 1937 had an approximately half-inch coupon at the bottom that could be redeemed for various prizes. Since most of these coupons were removed (and many not too carefully) Zeenuts are difficult to find in top condition today, and only a very small percentage survived with the coupon intact. (The sizes listed in the following descriptions are for cards without coupons.) Over the 28-year span, it is estimated that nearly 3,700 different cards were issued as part of the Zeenuts series, but new discoveries are still being made, and the checklist continues to grow. It is sometimes difficult to differentiate one year from another after 1930. Because it is so rare to find Zeenuts cards with the coupon still attached, values listed are for cards without the coupon. Cards with the coupon still intact will generally command a significant premium. The first Zeenut cards measure about 2-1/8" x 4" and feature a sepia-toned photo on a brown background surrounded by an off-white border. The backs of the cards are blank. Although the 1911 cards did not include the coupon bottom, some cards have been found with punch holes, indicating they may have also been used for redemptions. A total of 122 different players have been found.

		NM	EX	VG
Common Player:		200.00	85.00	50.00
(1)	Abbott	200.00	85.00	50.00
(2)	Ables	200.00	85.00	50.00
(3a)	Agnew (Large pose.)	200.00	85.00	50.00
(3b)	Agnew (Small pose.)	200.00	85.00	50.00
(4a)	Akin (Large pose.)	200.00	85.00	50.00
(4b)	Akin (Small pose.)	200.00	85.00	50.00
(5)	Frank Arellanes	200.00	85.00	50.00
(6a)	Arlett (Large pose.)	200.00	85.00	50.00
(6b)	Arlett (Middle size pose.)	200.00	85.00	50.00
(6c)	Arlett (Small pose.)	200.00	85.00	50.00
(7)	Barry	200.00	85.00	50.00
(8)	Baum	200.00	85.00	50.00
(9)	Bernard	200.00	85.00	50.00
(10)	Berry	200.00	85.00	50.00
(11)	Bohen	4,500	1,900	1,250
(12)	Brackenridge	200.00	85.00	50.00
(13)	Brashear	200.00	85.00	50.00
(14a)	Brown (Large pose.)	200.00	85.00	50.00
(14b)	Brown (Small pose.)	200.00	85.00	50.00
(15)	Browning	200.00	85.00	50.00
(16a)	Burrell (Large pose.)	200.00	85.00	50.00
(16b)	Burrell (Small pose.)	200.00	85.00	50.00
(17)	Byram	200.00	85.00	50.00
(18)	Carlisle	200.00	85.00	50.00
(19)	Carman	200.00	85.00	50.00
(20a)	Carson (Large pose.)	200.00	85.00	50.00
(20b)	Carson (Middle size pose.)	200.00	85.00	50.00
(20c)	Carson (Small pose.)	200.00	85.00	50.00
(21)	Castleton	200.00	85.00	50.00
(22)	Chadbourne	200.00	85.00	50.00
(23)	Christian	200.00	85.00	50.00
(24)	Couchman	200.00	85.00	50.00
(25)	Coy	200.00	85.00	50.00
(26)	Criger	200.00	85.00	50.00
(27)	Cutshaw	200.00	85.00	50.00
(28)	Daley	200.00	85.00	50.00
(29)	Danzig	200.00	85.00	50.00
(30)	Delhi	200.00	85.00	50.00
(31a)	Delmas (Large pose.)	200.00	85.00	50.00
(31b)	Delmas (Small pose.)	200.00	85.00	50.00
(32)	Dillon	200.00	85.00	50.00
(33a)	Discoll (Name incorrect.)	200.00	85.00	50.00
(33b)	Driscoll (Name correct.)	200.00	85.00	50.00
(34)	Dulin	200.00	85.00	50.00
(35)	Fanning	200.00	85.00	50.00
(36)	Fitzgerald	200.00	85.00	50.00
(37)	Flater	200.00	85.00	50.00
(38)	French	200.00	85.00	50.00
(39)	Fullerton	200.00	85.00	50.00
(40)	Gleason	200.00	85.00	50.00
(41)	Gregory	200.00	85.00	50.00
(42)	Halla	350.00	200.00	100.00
(43)	Harkness	200.00	85.00	50.00
(44a)	Heitmuller (Large pose.)	200.00	85.00	50.00
(44b)	Heitmuller (Small pose.)	200.00	85.00	50.00
(45)	Henley	200.00	85.00	50.00
(46)	Hetling	200.00	85.00	50.00
(47)	Hiester	200.00	85.00	50.00
(48a)	Hitt (Large pose.)	200.00	85.00	50.00
(48b)	Hitt (Small pose.)	200.00	85.00	50.00
(50)	Hoffman	200.00	85.00	50.00
(51)	Hogan	200.00	85.00	50.00
(52a)	Holland (Large pose.)	200.00	85.00	50.00
(52b)	Holland (Small pose.)	200.00	85.00	50.00
(53)	Hosp	200.00	85.00	50.00
(54a)	Howard (Large pose.)	200.00	85.00	50.00
(54b)	Howard (Small pose.)	200.00	85.00	50.00
(55)	Kane	200.00	85.00	50.00
(56)	Kerns	200.00	85.00	50.00
(57)	Kilroy	200.00	85.00	50.00
(58)	Knight	200.00	85.00	50.00
(59)	Koestner	200.00	85.00	50.00
(60)	Krueger	200.00	85.00	50.00
(61)	Kuhn	200.00	85.00	50.00
(62)	LaLonge	200.00	85.00	50.00
(63)	Lerchen	200.00	85.00	50.00
(64)	Leverenz	200.00	85.00	50.00
(65)	Lewis	200.00	85.00	50.00
(66)	Bill Lindsay	200.00	85.00	50.00
(67)	Lober	200.00	85.00	50.00
(68)	Madden	200.00	85.00	50.00
(69)	Maggert	200.00	85.00	50.00
(70)	Mahoney	200.00	85.00	50.00
(71)	Martinoni	200.00	85.00	50.00
(72)	McArdle	200.00	85.00	50.00
(73)	McCredie	200.00	85.00	50.00
(74)	McDonnell	200.00	85.00	50.00
(75a)	McKune (Large pose.)	200.00	85.00	50.00
(75b)	McKune (Middle size pose.)	200.00	85.00	50.00
(75c)	McKune (Small pose.)	200.00	85.00	50.00
(76)	Meikle	200.00	85.00	50.00
(77)	Melchior	200.00	85.00	50.00
(78)	Metzger	200.00	85.00	50.00
(79)	Miller	200.00	85.00	50.00
(80)	Mitze	200.00	85.00	50.00
(81)	Mohler	200.00	85.00	50.00
(82a)	Moore (Large pose.)	200.00	85.00	50.00
(82b)	Moore (Small pose.)	200.00	85.00	50.00
(83a)	Moskiman (Lettering size large.)	200.00	85.00	50.00
(83b)	Moskiman (Lettering size small.)	200.00	85.00	50.00
(84)	Murray	200.00	85.00	50.00
(85)	Naylor	200.00	85.00	50.00
(86)	Nebinger	200.00	85.00	50.00
(87)	Nourse	200.00	85.00	50.00
(88a)	Noyes (Large pose.)	200.00	85.00	50.00
(88b)	Noyes (Small pose.)	200.00	85.00	50.00
(89)	O'Rourke	200.00	85.00	50.00
(90)	Patterson (Oakland)	200.00	85.00	50.00
(91)	Patterson (Vernon)	200.00	85.00	50.00
(92)	Pearce	200.00	85.00	50.00
(93)	Peckinpaugh	250.00	100.00	60.00
(94)	Pernoll	200.00	85.00	50.00
(95)	Pfyl	200.00	85.00	50.00
(96)	Powell	200.00	85.00	50.00
(97a)	Raleigh (Large pose.)	200.00	85.00	50.00
(97b)	Raleigh (Small pose.)	200.00	85.00	50.00
(98)	Rapps	200.00	85.00	50.00
(99)	Rodgers	200.00	85.00	50.00
(100a)	Ryan (Portland, box around name and team.)	300.00	125.00	75.00
(100b)	Ryan (Portland, no box around name and team.)	200.00	85.00	50.00
(101)	Ryan (San Francisco)	200.00	85.00	50.00
(102)	Seaton	200.00	85.00	50.00
(103)	Shaw	200.00	85.00	50.00
(104)	Sheehan	200.00	85.00	50.00
(105)	Shinn	200.00	85.00	50.00
106a	Smith (Los Angeles, large pose.)	200.00	85.00	50.00
(106b)	Smith (Los Angeles, small pose.)	200.00	85.00	50.00
(107a)	Smith (San Francisco, large pose.)	200.00	85.00	50.00
(107b)	Smith (San Francisco, small pose.)	200.00	85.00	50.00
(108)	Steen	200.00	85.00	50.00
(109)	Stewart	200.00	85.00	50.00
(110a)	Stinson (Large pose.)	200.00	85.00	50.00
(110b)	Stinson (Small pose.)	200.00	85.00	50.00
(111)	Sutor	200.00	85.00	50.00
(112)	Tennant	200.00	85.00	50.00
(113)	Thomas	200.00	85.00	50.00
(114)	Thompson	200.00	85.00	50.00
(115)	Thornton	200.00	85.00	50.00
(116)	Tiedeman	200.00	85.00	50.00
(117)	Van Buren	200.00	85.00	50.00
(118)	Vitt	200.00	85.00	50.00
(119)	Wares	200.00	85.00	50.00
(120)	Buck Weaver	14,000	5,500	3,500
(121)	Wolverton	200.00	85.00	50.00
(122)	Zacher	200.00	85.00	50.00
(123)	Zamloch	200.00	85.00	50.00

1912 Zeenut Pacific Coast League

The second series of Zeenut cards measure about 2-1/8" x 4-1/16" and featured sepia-toned photographs on a brown background with no border. Most cards have blank backs, but some have been found with printing advising collectors to "Save Zeenut pictures for valuable premiums," or with one of two sizes of a Bardell logo. The checklist consists of 158 subjects, but more cards are still being discovered. Zeenut cards which were redeemed for prizes will exhibit a hole-punch cancellation, often heart-shaped.

		NM	EX	VG
Common Player:		120.00	60.00	45.00
(1)	Abbott	120.00	60.00	45.00
(2)	Ables	120.00	60.00	45.00
(3)	Agnew	120.00	60.00	45.00
(4)	Altman	120.00	60.00	45.00
(5)	Frank Arellanes	120.00	60.00	45.00
(6)	Auer	120.00	60.00	45.00
(7)	Baker (Horizontal pose.)	120.00	60.00	45.00
(8)	Baker (Vertical pose.)	120.00	60.00	45.00
(9)	Bancroft	1,200	550.00	300.00
(10)	Baum	120.00	60.00	45.00
(11)	Bayless	120.00	60.00	45.00
(12)	Berger	120.00	60.00	45.00
(13)	Berry	120.00	60.00	45.00
(14)	Bohen	120.00	60.00	45.00
(15)	Boles	120.00	60.00	45.00
(16)	Bonner	120.00	60.00	45.00
(17)	Boone	120.00	60.00	45.00
(18)	Brackenridge	120.00	60.00	45.00
(19)	Brashear	120.00	60.00	45.00
(20)	Breen	120.00	60.00	45.00
(21)	Brooks (Los Angeles)	120.00	60.00	45.00
(22)	Brooks (Oakland)	120.00	60.00	45.00
(23)	Brown	120.00	60.00	45.00
(24)	Burch	120.00	60.00	45.00
(25)	Burrell	120.00	60.00	45.00
(26)	Butcher	120.00	60.00	45.00
(27)	Butler	120.00	60.00	45.00
(28)	Byram	120.00	60.00	45.00
(29)	Carlisle	120.00	60.00	45.00
(30)	Carson	120.00	60.00	45.00
(31)	Castleton	120.00	60.00	45.00
(32)	Chadbourne	120.00	60.00	45.00
(33)	Chech	120.00	60.00	45.00
(34)	Cheek	120.00	60.00	45.00
(35)	Christian	120.00	60.00	45.00
(36)	Cook	120.00	60.00	45.00
(37)	Core	120.00	60.00	45.00
(38)	Corhan	120.00	60.00	45.00
(39)	Coy	120.00	60.00	45.00
(40)	Daley	120.00	60.00	45.00
(41)	Delhi	120.00	60.00	45.00
(42)	Dillon	120.00	60.00	45.00
(43)	Doane	120.00	60.00	45.00
(44)	Driscoll	120.00	60.00	45.00
(45)	Durbin	120.00	60.00	45.00
(46)	Fanning	120.00	60.00	45.00
(47)	Felts	120.00	60.00	45.00
(48)	Fisher	120.00	60.00	45.00
(49)	Fitzgerald	120.00	60.00	45.00
(50)	Flater	120.00	60.00	45.00
(51)	Frick	120.00	60.00	45.00
(52)	Gaddy	120.00	60.00	45.00
(53)	Gedeon	120.00	60.00	45.00
(54)	Gilligan	120.00	60.00	45.00
(55)	Girot	120.00	60.00	45.00
(56)	Gray	120.00	60.00	45.00
(57)	Gregg	120.00	60.00	45.00
(58)	Gregory	120.00	60.00	45.00
(59)	Halla	120.00	60.00	45.00
(60)	Hamilton (Oakland)	120.00	60.00	45.00
(61)	Hamilton (San Francisco)	120.00	60.00	45.00
(62)	Harkness	120.00	60.00	45.00
(63)	Hartley	120.00	60.00	45.00
(64)	Heitmuller	120.00	60.00	45.00
(65)	Henley	120.00	60.00	45.00
(66)	Hetling (Glove open.)	120.00	60.00	45.00
(67)	Hetling (Glove closed.)	120.00	60.00	45.00
(68)	Hiester	120.00	60.00	45.00
(69)	Higginbottom	120.00	60.00	45.00
(70)	Hitt	120.00	60.00	45.00
(71)	Hoffman	120.00	60.00	45.00
(72)	Hogan	120.00	60.00	45.00
(73)	Hosp	120.00	60.00	45.00
(74)	Howard	120.00	60.00	45.00
(75)	Howley	120.00	60.00	45.00
(76)	Ireland	120.00	60.00	45.00
(77)	Jackson	120.00	60.00	45.00
(78)	Johnson	120.00	60.00	45.00
(79)	Kane	120.00	60.00	45.00
(80)	Killilay	120.00	60.00	45.00
(81)	Klawitter	120.00	60.00	45.00
(82)	Knight	120.00	60.00	45.00
(83)	Koestner ("P" visible.)	120.00	60.00	45.00
(84)	Koestner (No "P" visible.)	120.00	60.00	45.00
(85)	Kreitz	120.00	60.00	45.00
(86)	Krueger	120.00	60.00	45.00
(87)	LaLonge	120.00	60.00	45.00
(88)	Leard	120.00	60.00	45.00
(89)	Leverenz	120.00	60.00	45.00
(90)	Lewis	120.00	60.00	45.00
(91)	Bill Lindsay	120.00	60.00	45.00
(92)	Litschi	120.00	60.00	45.00
(93)	Lober	120.00	60.00	45.00
(94)	Madden	120.00	60.00	45.00
(95)	Mahoney	120.00	60.00	45.00
(96)	Malarkey	120.00	60.00	45.00
(97)	Martinoni	120.00	60.00	45.00
(98)	McArdle	120.00	60.00	45.00
(99)	McAvoy	120.00	60.00	45.00
(100)	McCorrey	120.00	60.00	45.00
(101)	McCredie	120.00	60.00	45.00
(102)	McDonald	120.00	60.00	45.00
(103)	McDowell	120.00	60.00	45.00
(104)	McIver	120.00	60.00	45.00
(105)	Meikle	120.00	60.00	45.00
(106)	Metzger	120.00	60.00	45.00
(107)	Miller (Sacramento)	120.00	60.00	45.00
(108)	Miller (San Francisco)	120.00	60.00	45.00
(109)	Mitze	120.00	60.00	45.00
(110)	Mohler	120.00	60.00	45.00
(111)	Moore	120.00	60.00	45.00
(112)	Mundorf/Btg	120.00	60.00	45.00
(113)	Mundorf/Fldg	120.00	60.00	45.00
(114)	Nagle	120.00	60.00	45.00
(115)	Noyes	120.00	60.00	45.00
(116)	O'Rourke	120.00	60.00	45.00
(117)	Olmstead	120.00	60.00	45.00
(118)	Orr	120.00	60.00	45.00
(119)	Page	120.00	60.00	45.00
(120)	Parkins	120.00	60.00	45.00
(121)	Patterson (Oakland)	120.00	60.00	45.00
(122)	Patterson (Vernon)	120.00	60.00	45.00
(123)	Pernol	120.00	60.00	45.00
(124)	Pope	120.00	60.00	45.00
(125)	Powell	120.00	60.00	45.00
(126)	Price	120.00	60.00	45.00
(127)	Raftery	120.00	60.00	45.00
(128)	Raleigh	120.00	60.00	45.00
(129)	Rapps ("P" visible.)	120.00	60.00	45.00
(130)	Rapps (No "P" visible.)	120.00	60.00	45.00
(131)	Reidy	120.00	60.00	45.00
(132)	Rodgers	120.00	60.00	45.00
(133)	Rohrer	120.00	60.00	45.00
(134)	Schmidt	120.00	60.00	45.00
(135)	Schwenk	120.00	60.00	45.00
(136)	Sharpe	120.00	60.00	45.00
(137)	Sheehan	120.00	60.00	45.00
(138)	Shinn	120.00	60.00	45.00
(139)	Slagle	120.00	60.00	45.00
(140)	Smith	120.00	60.00	45.00
(141)	Stewart	120.00	60.00	45.00
(142)	Stinson	120.00	60.00	45.00
(143)	Stone	120.00	60.00	45.00
(144)	Sullivan	120.00	60.00	45.00
(145)	Swain	120.00	60.00	45.00
(146)	Taylor	120.00	60.00	45.00
(147)	Temple	120.00	60.00	45.00
(148)	Tiedeman	120.00	60.00	45.00
(149)	Toner	120.00	60.00	45.00
(150)	Tozer	120.00	60.00	45.00
(151)	Van Buren	120.00	60.00	45.00
(152)	Wagner	120.00	60.00	45.00
(153)	Whalen	120.00	60.00	45.00
(154)	Williams (Sacramento)	120.00	60.00	45.00
(155)	Williams (San Francisco)	120.00	60.00	45.00
(156)	Joe Williams	120.00	60.00	45.00
(157)	Wuffli	120.00	60.00	45.00
(158)	Zacher	120.00	60.00	45.00
(159)	Zimmerman	120.00	60.00	45.00

1913 Zeenut Pacific Coast League

The 1913 Zeenut cards measure about 2" x 3-3/4" without the coupon, and feature black-and-white photos on a white, borderless background. To date, 146 different poses have been found. The backs are blank.

		NM	EX	VG
Common Player:		100.00	45.00	25.00
(1)	Abbott	100.00	45.00	25.00
(2)	Ables	100.00	45.00	25.00
(3)	Frank Arelanes (Arellanes)	100.00	45.00	25.00
(4)	Arlett	100.00	45.00	25.00
(5)	Baker	100.00	45.00	25.00
(6)	Baum	100.00	45.00	25.00
(7)	Bayless	100.00	45.00	25.00
(8)	Becker	100.00	45.00	25.00
(9)	Berry	100.00	45.00	25.00
(10)	Bliss	100.00	45.00	25.00
(11)	Boles	100.00	45.00	25.00
(12)	Brackenridge	100.00	45.00	25.00
(13)	Brashear	100.00	45.00	25.00
(14)	Brooks	100.00	45.00	25.00
(15)	Byrnes	100.00	45.00	25.00
(16)	Cadreau	100.00	45.00	25.00
(17)	Carlisle	100.00	45.00	25.00
(18)	Carson	100.00	45.00	25.00
(19)	Cartwright	100.00	45.00	25.00
(20)	Chadbourne	100.00	45.00	25.00
(21)	Charles	100.00	45.00	25.00
(22)	Cheek	100.00	45.00	25.00
(23)	Christian	100.00	45.00	25.00
(24)	Clarke	100.00	45.00	25.00
(25)	Clemons	100.00	45.00	25.00
(26)	Cook	100.00	45.00	25.00
(27)	Corhan	100.00	45.00	25.00
(28)	Coy	100.00	45.00	25.00
(29)	Crabb	100.00	45.00	25.00
(30)	Crisp	100.00	45.00	25.00
(31)	Derrick	100.00	45.00	25.00
(32)	DeCanniere	100.00	45.00	25.00
(33)	Dillon	100.00	45.00	25.00
(34)	Doane	100.00	45.00	25.00
(35)	Douglass	100.00	45.00	25.00
(36)	Downs	100.00	45.00	25.00
(37)	Driscoll	100.00	45.00	25.00
(38)	Drucke	100.00	45.00	25.00
(39)	Elliott	100.00	45.00	25.00
(40)	Ellis	100.00	45.00	25.00
(41)	Fanning	100.00	45.00	25.00
(42)	Fisher	100.00	45.00	25.00
(43)	Fitzgerald	100.00	45.00	25.00
(44)	Gardner	100.00	45.00	25.00
(45)	Gill	100.00	45.00	25.00
(46)	Goodwin	100.00	45.00	25.00
(47a)	Gregory (Large pose.)	100.00	45.00	25.00
(47b)	Gregory (Small pose.)	100.00	45.00	25.00
(48)	Grey	100.00	45.00	25.00
(49)	Guest	100.00	45.00	25.00
(50)	Hagerman	100.00	45.00	25.00
(51)	Halla	100.00	45.00	25.00
(52)	Hallinan	100.00	45.00	25.00
(53)	Harry Heilmann	1,200	550.00	300.00
(54)	Henley	100.00	45.00	25.00
(55)	Hetling	100.00	45.00	25.00
(56)	Higginbotham	100.00	45.00	25.00
(57)	Hitt	100.00	45.00	25.00
(58)	Hoffman	100.00	45.00	25.00
(59)	Hogan (San Francisco)	100.00	45.00	25.00
(60)	Hogan (Vernon)	100.00	45.00	25.00
(61)	Hosp	100.00	45.00	25.00
(62)	Howard (Los Angeles)	100.00	45.00	25.00
(63)	Howard (San Francisco)	100.00	45.00	25.00
(64)	Hughes	100.00	45.00	25.00
(65)	Jackson	100.00	45.00	25.00
(66)	James	100.00	45.00	25.00
(67)	Johnson	100.00	45.00	25.00
(68)	Johnston	100.00	45.00	25.00
(69)	Kane	100.00	45.00	25.00
(70)	Kaylor	100.00	45.00	25.00
(71)	Kenworthy	100.00	45.00	25.00
(72)	Killilay	100.00	45.00	25.00
(73)	Klawitter	100.00	45.00	25.00
(74)	Koestner	100.00	45.00	25.00
(75)	Kores	100.00	45.00	25.00
(76)	Krapp	100.00	45.00	25.00
(77)	Kreitz	100.00	45.00	25.00
(78)	Krause	100.00	45.00	25.00
(79)	Krueger	100.00	45.00	25.00
(80)	Leard	100.00	45.00	25.00
(81)	Leifield	100.00	45.00	25.00
(82)	Lewis	100.00	45.00	25.00
(83)	Bill Lindsay	100.00	45.00	25.00
(84)	Litschi	100.00	45.00	25.00
(85)	Lively	100.00	45.00	25.00
(86)	Lober	100.00	45.00	25.00
(87)	Lohman	100.00	45.00	25.00
(88)	Maggart	100.00	45.00	25.00
(89)	Malarky	100.00	45.00	25.00
(90)	McArdle	100.00	45.00	25.00
(91)	McCarl	100.00	45.00	25.00
(92)	McCormick	100.00	45.00	25.00
(93)	McCorry	100.00	45.00	25.00
(94)	McCredie	100.00	45.00	25.00
(95)	McDonnell	100.00	45.00	25.00
(96)	Meloan	100.00	45.00	25.00
(97)	Metzger	100.00	45.00	25.00
(98)	Miller	100.00	45.00	25.00
(99)	Mitze	100.00	45.00	25.00
(100)	Moore	100.00	45.00	25.00
(101)	Moran	100.00	45.00	25.00
(102)	Mundorf	100.00	45.00	25.00
(103)	Munsell	100.00	45.00	25.00
(104)	Ness	100.00	45.00	25.00
(105)	O'Rourke	100.00	45.00	25.00
(106)	Overall	100.00	45.00	25.00
(107)	Page	100.00	45.00	25.00
(108)	Parkin	100.00	45.00	25.00
(109)	Patterson	100.00	45.00	25.00
(110)	Pearce	100.00	45.00	25.00
(111)	Pernoll	100.00	45.00	25.00
(112)	Perritt	100.00	45.00	25.00
(113)	Pope	100.00	45.00	25.00
(114)	Pruitt	100.00	45.00	25.00
(115)	Raleigh	100.00	45.00	25.00
(116)	Reitmyer	100.00	45.00	25.00
(117)	Riordan	100.00	45.00	25.00
(118)	Rodgers	100.00	45.00	25.00
(119)	Rogers	100.00	45.00	25.00
(120)	Rohrer	100.00	45.00	25.00
(121)	Ryan	100.00	45.00	25.00
(122)	Schaller	100.00	45.00	25.00
(123)	Schirm	100.00	45.00	25.00
(124)	Schmidt	100.00	45.00	25.00
(125)	Schulz	100.00	45.00	25.00
(126)	Sepulveda	100.00	45.00	25.00
(127)	Shinn	100.00	45.00	25.00
(128)	Spenger	100.00	45.00	25.00
(129)	Stanley	100.00	45.00	25.00
(130)	Stanridge	100.00	45.00	25.00
(131)	Stark	100.00	45.00	25.00
(132)	Sterritt	100.00	45.00	25.00
(133)	Stroud	100.00	45.00	25.00
(134)	Tennant	100.00	45.00	25.00
(135)	Thomas	100.00	45.00	25.00
(136)	Todd	100.00	45.00	25.00
(137)	Tonneman	100.00	45.00	25.00
(138)	Tozer	100.00	45.00	25.00
(139)	Van Buren	100.00	45.00	25.00
(140)	Wagner	100.00	45.00	25.00
(141)	West	100.00	45.00	25.00
(142)	Williams	100.00	45.00	25.00
(143)	Wolverton	100.00	45.00	25.00
(144)	Wotell	100.00	45.00	25.00

(145) Wuffli	100.00	45.00	25.00
(146) Young	100.00	45.00	25.00
(147) Zacher	100.00	45.00	25.00
(148) Zimmerman	100.00	45.00	25.00

1914 Zeenut Pacific Coast League

The 1914 Zeenut cards measure about 2" x 4-1/16" without the coupon, and feature black-and-white photos on a gray, borderless background. To date, 146 different poses have been found. The backs are blank.

	NM	EX	VG
Common Player:	75.00	35.00	17.00
(1) Ables	75.00	35.00	17.00
(2) Abstein	75.00	35.00	17.00
(3) Alexander	75.00	35.00	17.00
(4) Arbogast	75.00	35.00	17.00
(5) Arlett	75.00	35.00	17.00
(6) Frank Arrelanes (Arellanes)	75.00	35.00	17.00
(7) Bancroft	450.00	210.00	100.00
(8) Barham	75.00	35.00	17.00
(9) Barrenkamp	75.00	35.00	17.00
(10) Barton	75.00	35.00	17.00
(11) Baum	75.00	35.00	17.00
(12) Bayless	75.00	35.00	17.00
(13a) Bliss (Large pose.)	75.00	35.00	17.00
(13b) Bliss (Small pose.)	75.00	35.00	17.00
(14) Boles	75.00	35.00	17.00
(15) Borton	75.00	35.00	17.00
(16) Brashear	75.00	35.00	17.00
(17) Brenegan	75.00	35.00	17.00
(18) Brooks	75.00	35.00	17.00
(19) Brown	75.00	35.00	17.00
(20) Butler	75.00	35.00	17.00
(21) Jacinto Calvo	350.00	165.00	80.00
(22) Carlisle	75.00	35.00	17.00
(23) Cartwright	75.00	35.00	17.00
(24) Charles	75.00	35.00	17.00
(25) Chech	75.00	35.00	17.00
(26) Christian	75.00	35.00	17.00
(27) Clarke	75.00	35.00	17.00
(28) Colligan	75.00	35.00	17.00
(29) Cook	75.00	35.00	17.00
(31) Coy	75.00	35.00	17.00
(32) Crabb	75.00	35.00	17.00
(33) Davis	75.00	35.00	17.00
(34) Derrick	75.00	35.00	17.00
(35) Devlin	75.00	35.00	17.00
(36) DeCannier	75.00	35.00	17.00
(37) Dillon	75.00	35.00	17.00
(38) Doane	75.00	35.00	17.00
(39) Downs	75.00	35.00	17.00
(40) Ehmke	75.00	35.00	17.00
(41) Ellis	75.00	35.00	17.00
(42) Evans	75.00	35.00	17.00
(43) Fanning	75.00	35.00	17.00
(44) Fisher	75.00	35.00	17.00
(45) Fitzgerald	75.00	35.00	17.00
(46) Fleharty	75.00	35.00	17.00
(47) Frambach	75.00	35.00	17.00
(48) Gardner	75.00	35.00	17.00
(49) Gedeon	75.00	35.00	17.00
(50) Geyer	75.00	35.00	17.00
(51) Gianini	75.00	35.00	17.00
(52) Gregory	75.00	35.00	17.00
(53) Guest	75.00	35.00	17.00
(54) Hallinan	75.00	35.00	17.00
(55) Hannah	75.00	35.00	17.00
(56) Harkness/Btg	75.00	35.00	17.00
(57) Haworth/Btg	75.00	35.00	17.00
(58) Haworth/Catching	75.00	35.00	17.00
(59) Henderson	75.00	35.00	17.00
(60) Henley	75.00	35.00	17.00
(61) Hern	75.00	35.00	17.00
(62) Hettling	75.00	35.00	17.00
(63) Higginbotham	75.00	35.00	17.00
(64) Hitt	75.00	35.00	17.00
(65) Hogan	75.00	35.00	17.00
(66a) Hosp (Large pose.)	75.00	35.00	17.00
(66b) Hosp (Small pose.)	75.00	35.00	17.00
(67) Howard	75.00	35.00	17.00
(68) Hughes (Los Angeles)	75.00	35.00	17.00
(69) Hughes (San Francisco)	75.00	35.00	17.00
(70) Johnson	75.00	35.00	17.00
(71) Kane	75.00	35.00	17.00
(72) Kaylor	75.00	35.00	17.00
(73) Killilay	75.00	35.00	17.00
(74) Klawitter	75.00	35.00	17.00
(75) Klepfler	75.00	35.00	17.00
(76) Kores	75.00	35.00	17.00
(77) Kramer	75.00	35.00	17.00
(78) Krause	75.00	35.00	17.00
(79a) Leard (Large pose.)	75.00	35.00	17.00
(79b) Leard (Small pose.)	75.00	35.00	17.00
(80) Liefeld	75.00	35.00	17.00
(81) Litschi	75.00	35.00	17.00
(82) Lober	75.00	35.00	17.00
(83) Loomis	75.00	35.00	17.00
(84) Love	75.00	35.00	17.00
(85) Lynn	75.00	35.00	17.00
(86) Maggart	75.00	35.00	17.00
(87) Malarkey	75.00	35.00	17.00
(88) Martinoni	75.00	35.00	17.00
(89) McArdle	75.00	35.00	17.00
(90) McCredie	75.00	35.00	17.00
(91) McDonald	75.00	35.00	17.00
(92) Meek	75.00	35.00	17.00
(93) Meloan	75.00	35.00	17.00
(94) Menges	75.00	35.00	17.00
(95) Metzger	75.00	35.00	17.00
(96) Middleton	75.00	35.00	17.00
(97) Mitze	75.00	35.00	17.00
(98) Mohler	75.00	35.00	17.00
(99) Moore	75.00	35.00	17.00
(100) Moran	75.00	35.00	17.00
(101) Mundorf	75.00	35.00	17.00
(102) Murphy	75.00	35.00	17.00
(103) Musser	75.00	35.00	17.00
(104) Ness	75.00	35.00	17.00
(105) O'Leary	75.00	35.00	17.00
(106) Orr	75.00	35.00	17.00
(107) Page	75.00	35.00	17.00
(108) Pape	75.00	35.00	17.00
(109) Parkin	75.00	35.00	17.00
(110a) Peet (Large pose.)	75.00	35.00	17.00
(110b) Peet (Small pose.)	75.00	35.00	17.00
(111) Perkins	75.00	35.00	17.00
(112) Pernoll	75.00	35.00	17.00
(113) Perritt	75.00	35.00	17.00
(114) Powell	75.00	35.00	17.00
(115) Prough	75.00	35.00	17.00
(116) Pruiett	75.00	35.00	17.00
(117) Quinlan	75.00	35.00	17.00
(118a) Raney (Incorrect spelling.)	75.00	35.00	17.00
(118b) Ramey (Correct spelling.)	75.00	35.00	17.00
(119) Rieger	75.00	35.00	17.00
(120) Rodgers	75.00	35.00	17.00
(121) Rogers	75.00	35.00	17.00
(122) Rohrer	75.00	35.00	17.00
(123) Ryan	75.00	35.00	17.00
(124) Ryan	75.00	35.00	17.00
(125) Sawyer	75.00	35.00	17.00
(126) Schaller	75.00	35.00	17.00
(127) Schmidt	75.00	35.00	17.00
(128) Sepulveda	75.00	35.00	17.00
(129) Shinn	75.00	35.00	17.00
(130) Slagle	75.00	35.00	17.00
(131) Speas	75.00	35.00	17.00
(132) Stanridge	75.00	35.00	17.00
(133) Stroud	75.00	35.00	17.00
(134) Tennant	75.00	35.00	17.00
(135) Tobin	75.00	35.00	17.00
(136) Tozer	75.00	35.00	17.00
(137) Van Buren	75.00	35.00	17.00
(138) West	75.00	35.00	17.00
(139) White	75.00	35.00	17.00
(140) Wolter	75.00	35.00	17.00
(141) Wolverton	75.00	35.00	17.00
(142) Yantz	75.00	35.00	17.00
(143) Young	75.00	35.00	17.00
(144) Zacher	75.00	35.00	17.00
(145) Zumwalt	75.00	35.00	17.00

1915 Zeenut Pacific Coast League

The 1915 Zeenut cards are dated on the front, making identification very easy. They measure about 2" x 3-3/4" without the coupon and feature a black-and-white photo on a light background. To date 141 different cards are known to exist. This year is among the toughest of all Zeenuts to find.

	NM	EX	VG
Common Player:	100.00	45.00	25.00
With Coupon:	900.00	400.00	240.00
(1) Ables	100.00	45.00	25.00
(2) Abstein	100.00	45.00	25.00
(3) Alcock	100.00	45.00	25.00
(4) Arbogast	100.00	45.00	25.00
(5) Baerwald	100.00	45.00	25.00
(6) Barbour	100.00	45.00	25.00
(7) Bates	100.00	45.00	25.00
(8) Baum	100.00	45.00	25.00
(9) Bayless	100.00	45.00	25.00
(10) Beatty	100.00	45.00	25.00
(11) Beer	100.00	45.00	25.00
(12) Benham	100.00	45.00	25.00
(13) Berger	100.00	45.00	25.00
(14) Beumiller	100.00	45.00	25.00
(15) Blankenship	100.00	45.00	25.00
(16) Block	100.00	45.00	25.00
(17) Bodie	100.00	45.00	25.00
(18) Boles	100.00	45.00	25.00
(19) Boyd	100.00	45.00	25.00
(20) Bromley	100.00	45.00	25.00
(21) Brown	100.00	45.00	25.00
(22) Burns	300.00	135.00	75.00
(23) Carlisle	100.00	45.00	25.00
(24) Carrisch	100.00	45.00	25.00
(25) Charles	100.00	45.00	25.00
(26) Chech	100.00	45.00	25.00
(27) Christian	100.00	45.00	25.00
(28) Clarke	100.00	45.00	25.00
(29) Couch	100.00	45.00	25.00
(30) Stan Covaleski (Coveleski)	1,200	550.00	300.00
(31) Daniels	100.00	45.00	25.00
(32) Davis	100.00	45.00	25.00
(33) DeCanniere	100.00	45.00	25.00
(34) Dent	100.00	45.00	25.00
(35) Derrick	100.00	45.00	25.00
(36) Dillon	100.00	45.00	25.00
(37) Doane	100.00	45.00	25.00
(38) Downs	100.00	45.00	25.00
(39) Elliott	100.00	45.00	25.00
(40) F. Elliott	100.00	45.00	25.00
(41) Ellis	100.00	45.00	25.00
(42) Evans	100.00	45.00	25.00
(43) Fanning	100.00	45.00	25.00
(44) Faye	100.00	45.00	25.00
(45) Fisher	100.00	45.00	25.00
(46) Fittery	100.00	45.00	25.00
(47) Fitzgerald	100.00	45.00	25.00
(48) Fromme	100.00	45.00	25.00
(49) Gardiner	100.00	45.00	25.00
(50) Gedeon	100.00	45.00	25.00
(51) Gleischmann	100.00	45.00	25.00
(52) Gregory	100.00	45.00	25.00
(53) Guest	100.00	45.00	25.00
(54) Hall	100.00	45.00	25.00
(55) Halla	100.00	45.00	25.00
(56) Hallinan	100.00	45.00	25.00
(57) Hannah	100.00	45.00	25.00
(58) Harper	100.00	45.00	25.00
(59) Harry Heilmann	750.00	335.00	185.00
(60) Henley	100.00	45.00	25.00
(61) Hetling	100.00	45.00	25.00
(62) Higginbotham	100.00	45.00	25.00
(63) Hilliard	100.00	45.00	25.00
(64) Hitt (Winding up.)	100.00	45.00	25.00
(65) Hitt/Throwing	100.00	45.00	25.00
(66) Hogan	100.00	45.00	25.00
(67) Hosp	100.00	45.00	25.00
(68) Howard	100.00	45.00	25.00
(69) Hughes	100.00	45.00	25.00
(70) Johnson	100.00	45.00	25.00
(71) Jones	100.00	45.00	25.00
(72) Kahler	100.00	45.00	25.00
(73) Kane	100.00	45.00	25.00
(74) Karr	100.00	45.00	25.00
(75) Killilay	100.00	45.00	25.00
(76) Klawitter	100.00	45.00	25.00
(77) Koerner	100.00	45.00	25.00
(78) Krause	100.00	45.00	25.00
(79) Kuhn	100.00	45.00	25.00
(80) LaRoy	100.00	45.00	25.00
(81) Leard	100.00	45.00	25.00
(82) Bill Lindsay	100.00	45.00	25.00
(83) Litschi	100.00	45.00	25.00
(84) Lober	100.00	45.00	25.00
(85) Love	100.00	45.00	25.00
(86) Lush	100.00	45.00	25.00
(87) Maggart	100.00	45.00	25.00
(88) Malarkey	100.00	45.00	25.00
(89) Manda	100.00	45.00	25.00
(90) Marcan	100.00	45.00	25.00
(91) Martinoni	100.00	45.00	25.00
(92) McAvoy	100.00	45.00	25.00
(93) McCredie	100.00	45.00	25.00
(94) McDonell	100.00	45.00	25.00
(95) Fred McMullen (McMullin)	7,500	3,500	2,000
(96) Meek	100.00	45.00	25.00
(97) Meloan	100.00	45.00	25.00
(98) Metzger	100.00	45.00	25.00
(99) Middleton	100.00	45.00	25.00
(100) Mitchell	100.00	45.00	25.00
(101) Mitze	100.00	45.00	25.00
(102) Morgan	100.00	45.00	25.00
(103) Mundorff	100.00	45.00	25.00
(104) Murphy	100.00	45.00	25.00
(105) Ness	100.00	45.00	25.00
(106) Nutt	100.00	45.00	25.00
(107) Orr	100.00	45.00	25.00
(108) Pernoll	100.00	45.00	25.00
(109) Perritt	100.00	45.00	25.00
(110) Piercey	100.00	45.00	25.00
(111) Price	100.00	45.00	25.00
(112) Prough	100.00	45.00	25.00
(113) Prueitt	100.00	45.00	25.00
(114) Purtell	100.00	45.00	25.00
(115) Reed	100.00	45.00	25.00
(116) Reisigl	100.00	45.00	25.00
(117) Remneas	100.00	45.00	25.00
(118) Swede Risberg	5,500	2,500	1,500
(119) Rohrer	100.00	45.00	25.00
(120) Russell	100.00	45.00	25.00
(121) Ryan (Los Angeles)	100.00	45.00	25.00
(122) Ryan	100.00	45.00	25.00
(123) Schaller	100.00	45.00	25.00
(124) Schmidt	100.00	45.00	25.00
(125) Scoggins	100.00	45.00	25.00
(126) Sepulveda	100.00	45.00	25.00

(127)	Shinn	100.00	45.00	25.00
(128)	Smith	100.00	45.00	25.00
(129)	Speas	100.00	45.00	25.00
(130)	Spencer	100.00	45.00	25.00
(132)	Tennant	100.00	45.00	25.00
(133)	Terry	100.00	45.00	25.00
(134)	Tobin	100.00	45.00	25.00
(135)	West	100.00	45.00	25.00
(136)	White	100.00	45.00	25.00
(137)	Claude Williams	5,500	2,500	1,500
(138)	Johnny Williams	250.00	110.00	65.00
(139)	Wolter	100.00	45.00	25.00
(140)	Wolverton	100.00	45.00	25.00
(141)	Zacher	100.00	45.00	25.00

1916 Zeenut Pacific Coast League

The 1916 Zeenuts measure about 2" x 3-3/4" without the coupon and are dated on the front (some cards were misdated 1915 however). The card fronts feature black-and-white photos on a blue background. There are 144 known subjects. The 1916 series is among the more difficult.

		NM	EX	VG
Common Player:		75.00	30.00	17.50
(1)	Autrey	75.00	30.00	17.50
(2)	Barbeau	75.00	30.00	17.50
(3)	Barry	75.00	30.00	17.50
(4)	Bassler	75.00	30.00	17.50
(5)	Bates	75.00	30.00	17.50
(6)	Baum	75.00	30.00	17.50
(7)	Bayless	75.00	30.00	17.50
(8)	Beer	75.00	30.00	17.50
(9)	Berg	75.00	30.00	17.50
(10)	Berger	75.00	30.00	17.50
(11)	Blankenship	75.00	30.00	17.50
(12)	Block	75.00	30.00	17.50
(13)	Bodie	150.00	80.00	40.00
(14)	Bohne	250.00	125.00	75.00
(15)	Boles	75.00	30.00	17.50
(16)	Boyd	75.00	30.00	17.50
(17)	Brief	75.00	30.00	17.50
(18)	Brooks	75.00	30.00	17.50
(19)	Brown	75.00	30.00	17.50
(20)	Butler	75.00	30.00	17.50
(21)	Callahan	75.00	30.00	17.50
(22)	Carrisch	75.00	30.00	17.50
(23)	Frank Chance	750.00	375.00	225.00
(24)	Jimmy Claxton	15,000	9,500	7,000
(25)	Coffey	75.00	30.00	17.50
(26)	Cook	75.00	30.00	17.50
(27)	Corbett	75.00	30.00	17.50
(28)	Couch	75.00	30.00	17.50
(29)	Crandall	75.00	30.00	17.50
(30)	Dalton	75.00	30.00	17.50
(31)	Davis	75.00	30.00	17.50
(32)	Derrick	75.00	30.00	17.50
(33)	Doane	75.00	30.00	17.50
(34)	Downs	75.00	30.00	17.50
(35)	Dugan	75.00	30.00	17.50
(36)	Eldred	75.00	30.00	17.50
(37)	F. Elliott	75.00	30.00	17.50
(38)	H. Elliott	75.00	30.00	17.50
(39)	Ellis	75.00	30.00	17.50
(40)	Erickson	75.00	30.00	17.50
(41)	Fanning	75.00	30.00	17.50
(42)	Fisher	75.00	30.00	17.50
(43)	Fittery	75.00	30.00	17.50
(44)	Fitzgerald	75.00	30.00	17.50
(45)	Fromme	75.00	30.00	17.50
(46)	Galloway	75.00	30.00	17.50
(47)	Gardner	75.00	30.00	17.50
(48)	Gay	75.00	30.00	17.50
(49)	Gleischmann	75.00	30.00	17.50
(50)	Griffith	75.00	30.00	17.50
(51)	Griggs	75.00	30.00	17.50
(52)	Guisto	75.00	30.00	17.50
(53)	Hagerman	75.00	30.00	17.50
(54)	Hall	75.00	30.00	17.50
(55)	Hallinan	75.00	30.00	17.50
(56)	Hannah	75.00	30.00	17.50
(57)	Harstadt	75.00	30.00	17.50
(58)	Haworth	75.00	30.00	17.50
(59)	Hess	75.00	30.00	17.50
(60)	Higginbotham	75.00	30.00	17.50
(61)	Hitt	75.00	30.00	17.50
(62)	Hogg	75.00	30.00	17.50
(63)	Hollocher	75.00	30.00	17.50
(64)	Horstman	75.00	30.00	17.50
(65)	Houck	75.00	30.00	17.50
(66)	Howard	75.00	30.00	17.50
(67)	Hughes	75.00	30.00	17.50
(68)	E. Johnston	75.00	30.00	17.50
(69)	G. Johnston	75.00	30.00	17.50
(70)	Jones	75.00	30.00	17.50
(71)	Kahler	75.00	30.00	17.50
(72)	Kane	75.00	30.00	17.50
(73)	Kelly	75.00	30.00	17.50
(74)	Kenworthy	75.00	30.00	17.50
(75)	Klawitter	75.00	30.00	17.50
(76)	Klein	75.00	30.00	17.50
(77)	Koerner	75.00	30.00	17.50
(78)	Krause	75.00	30.00	17.50
(79)	Kuhn	75.00	30.00	17.50
(80)	Lane	75.00	30.00	17.50
(81)	Larsen	75.00	30.00	17.50
(82)	Lush	75.00	30.00	17.50
(83)	Machold	75.00	30.00	17.50
(84)	Maggert	75.00	30.00	17.50
(85)	Manser	75.00	30.00	17.50
(86)	Martin	75.00	30.00	17.50
(87)	Mattick	75.00	30.00	17.50
(88)	McCredie	75.00	30.00	17.50
(89)	McGaffigan	75.00	30.00	17.50
(90)	McLarry	75.00	30.00	17.50
(91)	Menges	75.00	30.00	17.50
(92)	Middleton	75.00	30.00	17.50
(93)	Mitchell	75.00	30.00	17.50
(94)	Mitze	75.00	30.00	17.50
(95)	Munsell	75.00	30.00	17.50
(96)	Murphy	75.00	30.00	17.50
(97)	Nixon	75.00	30.00	17.50
(98)	Noyes	75.00	30.00	17.50
(99)	Nutt	75.00	30.00	17.50
(100)	O'Brien	75.00	30.00	17.50
(101)	Oldham	75.00	30.00	17.50
(102)	Orr	75.00	30.00	17.50
(103)	Patterson	75.00	30.00	17.50
(104)	Perritt	75.00	30.00	17.50
(105)	Prough	75.00	30.00	17.50
(106)	Prueitt	75.00	30.00	17.50
(107)	Quinlan	75.00	30.00	17.50
(108)	Quinn (Portland)	75.00	30.00	17.50
(109)	Quinn (Vernon)	75.00	30.00	17.50
(110)	Rader	75.00	30.00	17.50
(111)	Randall	75.00	30.00	17.50
(112)	Rath	75.00	30.00	17.50
(113)	Reisegl	75.00	30.00	17.50
(114)	Reuther (Ruether)	75.00	30.00	17.50
(115)	Swede Risberg	5,000	2,000	1,250
(116)	Roche	75.00	30.00	17.50
(117)	Ryan	75.00	30.00	17.50
(118)	Ryan	75.00	30.00	17.50
(119)	Scoggins	75.00	30.00	17.50
(120)	Sepulveda	75.00	30.00	17.50
(121)	Schaller	75.00	30.00	17.50
(122)	Sheehan	75.00	30.00	17.50
(123)	Shinn	75.00	30.00	17.50
(124)	Smith	75.00	30.00	17.50
(125)	Sothoron	75.00	30.00	17.50
(126)	Southworth	75.00	30.00	17.50
(127)	Speas	75.00	30.00	17.50
(128)	Spencer	75.00	30.00	17.50
(129)	Standridge	75.00	30.00	17.50
(130)	Steen	75.00	30.00	17.50
(131)	Stumpf	75.00	30.00	17.50
(132)	Vann	75.00	30.00	17.50
(133)	Vaughn	75.00	30.00	17.50
(134)	Ward	75.00	30.00	17.50
(135)	Whalling	75.00	30.00	17.50
(136)	Wilie	75.00	30.00	17.50
(137)	Williams	75.00	30.00	17.50
(138)	Wolverton	75.00	30.00	17.50
(139)	Wuffli	75.00	30.00	17.50
(140)	Zabel	75.00	30.00	17.50
(141)	Zacher	75.00	30.00	17.50
(142)	Zimmerman	75.00	30.00	17.50

1917 Zeenut Pacific Coast League

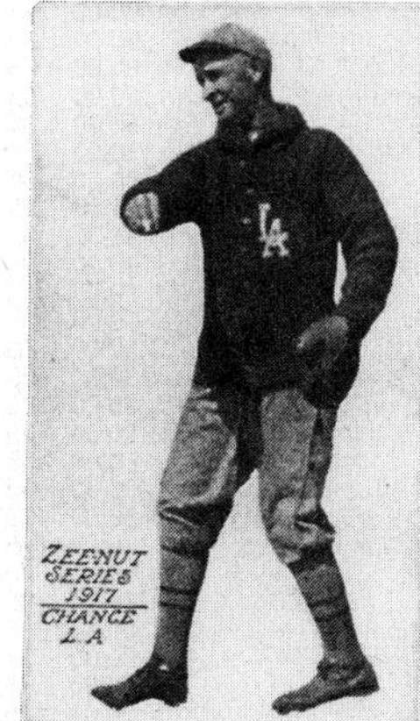

The 1917 Zeenuts measure about 1-3/4" x 3-3/4" and feature black-and-white photos on a light background. They are dated on the front and have blank backs. An advertising poster has been found listing 119 players (two pose variations brings the total to 121), but to date, six players on the list have not been found.

		NM	EX	VG
Common Player:		70.00	35.00	20.00
(1)	Arlett	70.00	35.00	20.00
(2)	Frank Arrelanes (Arellanes)	70.00	35.00	20.00
(3)	Baker/Catching	70.00	35.00	20.00
(4)	Baker/Throwing	70.00	35.00	20.00
(5)	Baldwin	70.00	35.00	20.00
(6)	Bassler	70.00	35.00	20.00
(7)	Baum	70.00	35.00	20.00
(8)	Beer	70.00	35.00	20.00
(9)	Bernhard	70.00	35.00	20.00
(10)	Bliss	70.00	35.00	20.00
(11)	Boles	70.00	35.00	20.00
(12)	Brenton	70.00	35.00	20.00
(13)	Brief	70.00	35.00	20.00
(14)	Brown	70.00	35.00	20.00
(15)	Burns	350.00	200.00	100.00
(16)	Callahan	70.00	35.00	20.00
(17)	Callan	70.00	35.00	20.00
(18)	Jacinto Calvo	375.00	185.00	110.00
(19)	Chadbourne	70.00	35.00	20.00
(20)	Frank Chance	750.00	375.00	225.00
(21)	Coltrin	70.00	35.00	20.00
(22)	Connifer	70.00	35.00	20.00
(23)	Corhan	70.00	35.00	20.00
(24)	Crandall (Los Angeles)	70.00	35.00	20.00
(25)	Crandall (Salt Lake)	70.00	35.00	20.00
(26)	Cress	70.00	35.00	20.00
(27)	Davis	70.00	35.00	20.00
(28)	DeCanniere	70.00	35.00	20.00
(29)	Doane	70.00	35.00	20.00
(30)	Dougan	70.00	35.00	20.00
(31)	Dougherty	70.00	35.00	20.00
(32)	Downs	70.00	35.00	20.00
(33)	Dubuc	70.00	35.00	20.00
(34)	Ellis	70.00	35.00	20.00
(35)	Erickson	70.00	35.00	20.00
(36)	Evans	70.00	35.00	20.00
(37)	Farmer	70.00	35.00	20.00
(38)	Fincher	70.00	35.00	20.00
(39)	Fisher	70.00	35.00	20.00
(40)	Fitzgerald	70.00	35.00	20.00
(41)	Fournier	70.00	35.00	20.00
(42)	Fromme	70.00	35.00	20.00
(43)	Galloway	70.00	35.00	20.00
(44)	Gislason	70.00	35.00	20.00
(45)	Goodbred	70.00	35.00	20.00
(46)	Griggs	70.00	35.00	20.00
(47)	Groehling	70.00	35.00	20.00
(48)	Hall (Los Angeles)	70.00	35.00	20.00
(49)	Hall (San Francisco)	70.00	35.00	20.00
(50)	Hannah	70.00	35.00	20.00
(51)	Harstad	70.00	35.00	20.00
(52)	Helfrich	70.00	35.00	20.00
(53)	Hess	70.00	35.00	20.00
(54)	Hitt	70.00	35.00	20.00
(55)	Hoff	70.00	35.00	20.00
(56)	Hollacher	70.00	35.00	20.00
(57)	Hollywood	70.00	35.00	20.00
(58)	Houck	70.00	35.00	20.00
(59)	Howard	70.00	35.00	20.00
(60)	Hughes	70.00	35.00	20.00
(61)	Johnson	70.00	35.00	20.00
(62)	Kilhullen	70.00	35.00	20.00
(63)	Killiffer (Killefer)	70.00	35.00	20.00
(64)	Koerner	70.00	35.00	20.00
(65)	Krause	70.00	35.00	20.00
(66)	Lane	70.00	35.00	20.00
(67)	Lapan	70.00	35.00	20.00
(68)	Leake	70.00	35.00	20.00
(69)	Lee	70.00	35.00	20.00
(70)	Leverenz	70.00	35.00	20.00
(71)	Maggert	70.00	35.00	20.00
(72)	Maisel	70.00	35.00	20.00
(73)	Mattick	70.00	35.00	20.00
(74)	McCreedie	70.00	35.00	20.00
(75)	McLarry	70.00	35.00	20.00
(76)	Mensor	650.00	325.00	200.00
(77)	Emil "Irish" Meusel	350.00	175.00	100.00
(78)	Middleton	70.00	35.00	20.00
(79)	Miller/Btg	70.00	35.00	20.00
(80)	Miller/Throwing	70.00	35.00	20.00
(81)	Mitchell	70.00	35.00	20.00
(82)	Mitze	70.00	35.00	20.00
(83)	Murphy	70.00	35.00	20.00
(84)	Murray	70.00	35.00	20.00
(85)	O'Brien	70.00	35.00	20.00
(86)	O'Mara	70.00	35.00	20.00
(87)	Oldham	70.00	35.00	20.00
(88)	Orr	70.00	35.00	20.00
(89)	Penelli	70.00	35.00	20.00
(90)	Penner	70.00	35.00	20.00
(91)	Pick	70.00	35.00	20.00
(92)	Prough	70.00	35.00	20.00
(93)	Pruiett	70.00	35.00	20.00
(94)	Quinlan	70.00	35.00	20.00
(95)	Quinn	70.00	35.00	20.00
(96)	Rath	70.00	35.00	20.00
(97)	Roche	70.00	35.00	20.00
(98)	Ryan (Los Angeles)	70.00	35.00	20.00
(99)	Ryan (Salt Lake)	70.00	35.00	20.00
(100)	Schaller	70.00	35.00	20.00
(101)	Schinkle	70.00	35.00	20.00
(102)	Schultz	70.00	35.00	20.00
(103)	Sheehan	70.00	35.00	20.00
(104)	Sheeley	70.00	35.00	20.00
(105)	Shinn	70.00	35.00	20.00
(106)	Siglin	70.00	35.00	20.00
(107)	Simon	70.00	35.00	20.00
(108)	Smith	70.00	35.00	20.00
(109)	Snyder	70.00	35.00	20.00
(110)	Stanridge	70.00	35.00	20.00
(111)	Steen	70.00	35.00	20.00
(112)	Stovall	70.00	35.00	20.00
(113)	Stumpf	70.00	35.00	20.00
(114)	Sullivan	70.00	35.00	20.00
(115)	Terry	70.00	35.00	20.00
(116)	Tobin	70.00	35.00	20.00
(117)	Valencia	70.00	35.00	20.00
(118)	Vaughn	70.00	35.00	20.00
(119)	Whalling	70.00	35.00	20.00

(120)	Wilie	70.00	35.00	20.00
(121)	Wolverton	70.00	35.00	20.00

1918 Zeenut Pacific Coast League

The 1918 Zeenuts are among the most distinctive because of the red borders surrounding the photos. They measure about 1-13/16" x 3-5/8" and are among the more difficult years to find.

		NM	EX	VG
	Common Player:	200.00	100.00	50.00
	With Coupon:	800.00	400.00	240.00
(1)	Alcock	200.00	100.00	50.00
(2)	Arkenburg	200.00	100.00	50.00
(3)	A. Arlett	200.00	100.00	50.00
(4)	Baum	200.00	100.00	50.00
(5)	Boles	200.00	100.00	50.00
(6)	Borton	200.00	100.00	50.00
(7)	Brenton	200.00	100.00	50.00
(8)	Bromley	200.00	100.00	50.00
(9)	Brooks	200.00	100.00	50.00
(10)	Brown	200.00	100.00	50.00
(11)	Caldera	200.00	100.00	50.00
(12)	Camm (Kamm)	200.00	100.00	50.00
(13)	Chadbourne	200.00	100.00	50.00
(14)	Chappell	200.00	100.00	50.00
(15)	Codington	200.00	100.00	50.00
(16)	Conwright	200.00	100.00	50.00
(17)	Cooper	200.00	100.00	50.00
(18)	Cox	200.00	100.00	50.00
(19)	Crandall (Los Angeles)	200.00	100.00	50.00
(20)	Crandall (Salt Lake)	200.00	100.00	50.00
(21)	Crawford	900.00	450.00	275.00
(22)	Croll	200.00	100.00	50.00
(23)	Davis	200.00	100.00	50.00
(24)	DeVormer	200.00	100.00	50.00
(25)	Dobbs	200.00	100.00	50.00
(26)	Downs	200.00	100.00	50.00
(27)	Dubuc	200.00	100.00	50.00
(28)	Dunn	200.00	100.00	50.00
(29)	Easterly	200.00	100.00	50.00
(30)	Eldred	200.00	100.00	50.00
(31)	Elliot	200.00	100.00	50.00
(32)	Ellis	200.00	100.00	50.00
(33)	Essick	200.00	100.00	50.00
(34)	Farmer	200.00	100.00	50.00
(35)	Fisher	200.00	100.00	50.00
(36)	Fittery	200.00	100.00	50.00
(37)	Forsythe	200.00	100.00	50.00
(38)	Fournier	200.00	100.00	50.00
(39)	Fromme	200.00	100.00	50.00
(40)	Gardner (Oakland)	200.00	100.00	50.00
(41)	Gardner (Sacramento)	200.00	100.00	50.00
(42)	Goldie	200.00	100.00	50.00
(43)	Griggs	200.00	100.00	50.00
(44)	Hawkes	200.00	100.00	50.00
(45)	Hollander	200.00	100.00	50.00
(46)	Hosp	200.00	100.00	50.00
(47)	Howard	200.00	100.00	50.00
(48)	Hummel	200.00	100.00	50.00
(49)	Hunter	200.00	100.00	50.00
(50)	Johnson	200.00	100.00	50.00
(51)	G. Johnson	200.00	100.00	50.00
(52)	Kantlehner	200.00	100.00	50.00
(53)	Killefer	200.00	100.00	50.00
(54)	Koerner	200.00	100.00	50.00
(55)	Konnick	200.00	100.00	50.00
(56)	Kremer	200.00	100.00	50.00
(57)	Lapan	200.00	100.00	50.00
(58)	Leake	200.00	100.00	50.00
(59)	Leathers	200.00	100.00	50.00
(60)	Leifer	200.00	100.00	50.00
(61)	Leverenz	200.00	100.00	50.00
(62)	Llewlyn	200.00	100.00	50.00
(63)	Martin	200.00	100.00	50.00
(64)	McCabe	200.00	100.00	50.00
(65)	McCredie	200.00	100.00	50.00
(66)	McKee	200.00	100.00	50.00
(67)	McNulty	200.00	100.00	50.00
(68)	Mensor	500.00	250.00	150.00
(69)	Middleton	200.00	100.00	50.00
(70)	Miller (Oakland)	200.00	100.00	50.00
(71)	Miller (Salt Lake)	200.00	100.00	50.00
(72)	J. Mitchell	200.00	100.00	50.00
(73)	R. Mitchell	200.00	100.00	50.00
(74)	Mitze	200.00	100.00	50.00
(75)	Moore	200.00	100.00	50.00
(76)	Morton	200.00	100.00	50.00
(77)	Murray	200.00	100.00	50.00
(78)	O'Doul	450.00	225.00	135.00
(79)	Orr	200.00	100.00	50.00
(80)	Pepe	200.00	100.00	50.00
(81)	Pertica	200.00	100.00	50.00
(82)	Phillips	200.00	100.00	50.00
(83)	Pick	200.00	100.00	50.00
(84)	Pinelli	200.00	100.00	50.00
(85)	Prentice	200.00	100.00	50.00
(86)	Prough	200.00	100.00	50.00
(87)	Quinlan	200.00	100.00	50.00
(88)	Ritchie	200.00	100.00	50.00
(89)	Rogers	200.00	100.00	50.00
(90)	Ryan	200.00	100.00	50.00
(91)	Sand	200.00	100.00	50.00
(92)	Shader	200.00	100.00	50.00
(93)	Sheely	200.00	100.00	50.00
(94)	Siglin	200.00	100.00	50.00
(95)	Smale	200.00	100.00	50.00
(96)	Smith (Salt Lake City)	200.00	100.00	50.00
(97)	Smith (San Francisco)	200.00	100.00	60.00
(98)	Stanbridge	200.00	100.00	50.00
(99)	Terry	200.00	100.00	50.00
(100)	Valencia	200.00	100.00	50.00
(101)	West	200.00	100.00	50.00
(102)	Wilie	200.00	100.00	50.00
(103)	Williams	200.00	100.00	50.00
(104)	Wisterzill	200.00	100.00	50.00

1919 Zeenut Pacific Coast League

The 1919 Zeenuts cards are dated on the front and measure about 1-3/4" x 3-5/8". They featured borderless, sepia-toned photos. To date, 144 subjects exist in the series.

		NM	EX	VG
	Common Player:	80.00	35.00	20.00
(1)	Ally	80.00	35.00	20.00
(2)	Fatty Arbuckle	5,500	2,750	1,650
(3)	A. Arlett	80.00	35.00	20.00
(4)	R. Arlett	80.00	35.00	20.00
(5)	Baker	80.00	35.00	20.00
(6)	Baldwin	80.00	35.00	20.00
(7)	Baum	80.00	35.00	20.00
(8)	Beck	80.00	35.00	20.00
(9)	Bigbee	80.00	35.00	20.00
(10)	Blue	80.00	35.00	20.00
(11)	Bohne	200.00	100.00	60.00
(12)	Boles	80.00	35.00	20.00
(13)	Borton	80.00	35.00	20.00
(14)	Bowman	80.00	35.00	20.00
(15)	Brooks	80.00	35.00	20.00
(16)	Brown	80.00	35.00	20.00
(17)	Byler	80.00	35.00	20.00
(18)	Caldera	80.00	35.00	20.00
(19)	Cavaney	80.00	35.00	20.00
(20)	Chadbourne	80.00	35.00	20.00
(21)	Chech	80.00	35.00	20.00
(22)	Church	80.00	35.00	20.00
(23)	Clymer	80.00	35.00	20.00
(24)	Coleman	80.00	35.00	20.00
(25)	Compton	80.00	35.00	20.00
(26)	Conkwright	80.00	35.00	20.00
(27)	Connolly	80.00	35.00	20.00
(28)	Cook	80.00	35.00	20.00
(29)	Cooper (Los Angeles)	80.00	35.00	20.00
(30)	Cooper (Oakland)	80.00	35.00	20.00
(31)	Cooper (Portland)	80.00	35.00	20.00
(32)	Corhan	80.00	35.00	20.00
(33)	Couch	80.00	35.00	20.00
(34)	Cox	80.00	35.00	20.00
(35)	Crandall (Los Angeles)	80.00	35.00	20.00
(36)	Crandall (San Francisco)	80.00	35.00	20.00
(37)	Crespi	80.00	35.00	20.00
(38)	Croll	80.00	35.00	20.00
(39)	Cunningham	80.00	35.00	20.00
(40)	Dawson	80.00	35.00	20.00
(41)	Dell	80.00	35.00	20.00
(42)	DeVormer	80.00	35.00	20.00
(43)	Driscoll	80.00	35.00	20.00
(44)	Eastley	80.00	35.00	20.00
(45)	Edington	80.00	35.00	20.00
(46)	Eldred	80.00	35.00	20.00
(47)	Elliott	80.00	35.00	20.00
(48)	Ellis	80.00	35.00	20.00
(49)	Essick	80.00	35.00	20.00
(50)	Fabrique	80.00	35.00	20.00
(51)	Falkenberg	80.00	35.00	20.00
(52)	Fallentine	80.00	35.00	20.00
(53)	Finneran	80.00	35.00	20.00
(54)	Fisher (Sacramento)	80.00	35.00	20.00
(55)	Fisher (Vernon)	80.00	35.00	20.00
(56)	Fitzgerald	80.00	35.00	20.00
(57)	Flannigan	80.00	35.00	20.00
(58)	Fournier	80.00	35.00	20.00
(59)	French	80.00	35.00	20.00
(60)	Fromme	80.00	35.00	20.00
(61)	Gibson	80.00	35.00	20.00
(62)	Griggs	80.00	35.00	20.00
(63)	Haney	80.00	35.00	20.00
(64)	Harper	80.00	35.00	20.00
(65)	Henkle	80.00	35.00	20.00
(66)	Herr	80.00	35.00	20.00
(67)	Hickey	80.00	35.00	20.00
(68)	High	80.00	35.00	20.00
(69)	Holling	80.00	35.00	20.00
(70)	Hosp	80.00	35.00	20.00
(71)	Houck	80.00	35.00	20.00
(72)	Howard	80.00	35.00	20.00
(73)	Kamm	80.00	35.00	20.00
(74)	Kenworthy	80.00	35.00	20.00
(75)	Killefer	80.00	35.00	20.00
(76)	King	80.00	35.00	20.00
(77)	Koehler	80.00	35.00	20.00
(78)	Koerner	80.00	35.00	20.00
(79)	Kramer (Oakland)	80.00	35.00	20.00
(80)	Kramer (San Francisco)	80.00	35.00	20.00
(81)	Land	80.00	35.00	20.00
(82)	Lane	80.00	35.00	20.00
(83)	Lapan	80.00	35.00	20.00
(84)	Larkin	80.00	35.00	20.00
(85)	Lee	80.00	35.00	20.00
(86)	Long	80.00	35.00	20.00
(87)	Mails	80.00	35.00	20.00
(88)	Mains	80.00	35.00	20.00
(89)	Maisel	80.00	35.00	20.00
(90)	Mathes	80.00	35.00	20.00
(91)	McCredie	80.00	35.00	20.00
(92)	McGaffigan	80.00	35.00	20.00
(93)	McHenry	80.00	35.00	20.00
(94)	McNulty	80.00	35.00	20.00
(95)	Meusel	80.00	35.00	20.00
(96)	Middleton	80.00	35.00	20.00
(97)	Mitchell	80.00	35.00	20.00
(98)	Mitze	80.00	35.00	20.00
(99)	Mulory	80.00	35.00	20.00
(100)	Murphy	80.00	35.00	20.00
(101)	Murray	80.00	35.00	20.00
(102)	Niehoff (Los Angeles)	80.00	35.00	20.00
(103)	Niehoff (Seattle)	80.00	35.00	20.00
(104)	Norse	80.00	35.00	20.00
(105)	Oldham	80.00	35.00	20.00
(106)	Orr	80.00	35.00	20.00
(107)	Penner	80.00	35.00	20.00
(108)	Pennington	80.00	35.00	20.00
(109)	Piercy	80.00	35.00	20.00
(110)	Pinelli	150.00	75.00	45.00
(111)	C. Prough	80.00	35.00	20.00
(112)	Rader	80.00	35.00	20.00
(113)	Reiger	80.00	35.00	20.00
(114)	Ritchie	80.00	35.00	20.00
(115)	Roach	80.00	35.00	20.00
(116)	Rodgers	80.00	35.00	20.00
(117)	Rumler	80.00	35.00	20.00
(118)	Sands	80.00	35.00	20.00
(119)	Schick	80.00	35.00	20.00
(120)	Schultz	80.00	35.00	20.00
(121)	Scott	80.00	35.00	20.00
(122)	Seaton	80.00	35.00	20.00
(123)	Sheely	80.00	35.00	20.00
(124)	Siglin	80.00	35.00	20.00
(125)	Smith	80.00	35.00	20.00
(126)	Bill Smith	80.00	35.00	20.00
(127)	Snell	80.00	35.00	20.00
(128)	Spangler	80.00	35.00	20.00
(129)	Speas	80.00	35.00	20.00
(130)	Spencer	80.00	35.00	20.00
(131)	Starasenich	80.00	35.00	20.00
(132)	Stumpf	80.00	35.00	20.00
(133)	Sutherland	80.00	35.00	20.00
(134)	Dazzy Vance	600.00	300.00	180.00
(135)	Walker	80.00	35.00	20.00
(136)	Walsh	80.00	35.00	20.00
(137)	Ware	80.00	35.00	20.00
(138)	Weaver	80.00	35.00	20.00
(139)	Westerzil	80.00	35.00	20.00
(140)	Wilhoit	80.00	35.00	20.00
(141)	Wilie	80.00	35.00	20.00
(142)	Willets	80.00	35.00	20.00
(143)	Zamloch	80.00	35.00	20.00
(144)	Zweifel	80.00	35.00	20.00

1920 Zeenut Pacific Coast League

The 1920 Zeenuts cards were dated on the front and measure about 1-3/4" x 3-5/8". They featured borderless, sepia-toned photos. To date, 151 have been found for 1920.

		NM	EX	VG
	Common Player:	80.00	35.00	20.00
(1)	Adams	80.00	35.00	20.00
(2)	Agnew	80.00	35.00	20.00
(3)	Alcock	80.00	35.00	20.00
(4)	Aldrige	80.00	35.00	20.00
(5)	Andrews	80.00	35.00	20.00
(6)	Anfinson	80.00	35.00	20.00
(7)	A. Arlett	80.00	35.00	20.00
(8)	R. Arlett	80.00	35.00	20.00
(9)	Baker	80.00	35.00	20.00
(10)	Baldwin	80.00	35.00	20.00
(11)	Bassler	80.00	35.00	20.00
(12)	Baum	80.00	35.00	20.00
(13)	Blue	80.00	35.00	20.00
(14)	Bohne	200.00	100.00	60.00
(15)	Brenton	80.00	35.00	20.00
(16)	Bromley (Dark hat.)	80.00	35.00	20.00
(17)	Bromley (Light hat.)	80.00	35.00	20.00
(18)	Brown	80.00	35.00	20.00
(19)	Butler	80.00	35.00	20.00
(20)	Caveney	80.00	35.00	20.00
(21)	Chadbourne	80.00	35.00	20.00
(22)	Compton	80.00	35.00	20.00
(23)	Connolly	80.00	35.00	20.00
(24)	Cook	80.00	35.00	20.00
(25)	Corhan	80.00	35.00	20.00
(26)	Cox	80.00	35.00	20.00
(27)	K. Crandall	80.00	35.00	20.00
(28)	O. Crandall	80.00	35.00	20.00
(29)	Crawford	450.00	225.00	135.00
(30)	Cullop	80.00	35.00	20.00
(31)	Cunningham	80.00	35.00	20.00
(32)	DeVitalis	80.00	35.00	20.00
(33)	DeVormer	80.00	35.00	20.00
(34)	Dooley	80.00	35.00	20.00
(35)	Dorman	80.00	35.00	20.00
(36)	Dumovich	80.00	35.00	20.00
(37)	Dylar	80.00	35.00	20.00
(38)	Edington	80.00	35.00	20.00
(39)	Eldred	80.00	35.00	20.00
(40)	Ellis	80.00	35.00	20.00
(41)	Essick	80.00	35.00	20.00
(42)	Fisher	80.00	35.00	20.00
(43)	Fitzgerald	80.00	35.00	20.00
(44)	Fromme	80.00	35.00	20.00
(45)	Gardner	80.00	35.00	20.00
(46)	Ginglardi	80.00	35.00	20.00
(47)	Gough	80.00	35.00	20.00
(48)	Griggs	80.00	35.00	20.00
(49)	Guisto	80.00	35.00	20.00
(50)	Hamilton	80.00	35.00	20.00
(51)	Hanicy	80.00	35.00	20.00
(52)	Hartford	80.00	35.00	20.00
(53)	High	80.00	35.00	20.00
(54)	Hill	80.00	35.00	20.00
(55)	Hodges	80.00	35.00	20.00
(56)	Howard	80.00	35.00	20.00
(57)	James	80.00	35.00	20.00
(58)	Jenkins	80.00	35.00	20.00
(59)	Johnson (Portland)	80.00	35.00	20.00
(60)	Johnson (Salt Lake)	80.00	35.00	20.00
(61)	Jones	80.00	35.00	20.00
(62)	Juney	80.00	35.00	20.00
(63)	Kallio	80.00	35.00	20.00
(64)	Kamm	80.00	35.00	20.00
(65)	Keating	80.00	35.00	20.00
(66)	Kenworthy	80.00	35.00	20.00
(67)	Killeen	80.00	35.00	20.00
(68)	Killefer	80.00	35.00	20.00
(69)	Kingdon	80.00	35.00	20.00
(70)	Knight	80.00	35.00	20.00
(71)	Koehler	80.00	35.00	20.00
(72)	Koerner	80.00	35.00	20.00
(73)	Kopp	80.00	35.00	20.00
(74)	Kremer	80.00	35.00	20.00
(75)	Krug	80.00	35.00	20.00
(76)	Kunz	80.00	35.00	20.00
(77)	Lambert	80.00	35.00	20.00
(78)	Lane	80.00	35.00	20.00
(79)	Larkin	80.00	35.00	20.00
(80)	Leverenz	80.00	35.00	20.00
(81)	Long	80.00	35.00	20.00
(82)	Love	80.00	35.00	20.00
(83)	Maggart	80.00	35.00	20.00
(84)	Mails	80.00	35.00	20.00
(85)	Maisel	80.00	35.00	20.00
(86)	Matterson	80.00	35.00	20.00
(87)	Matteson	80.00	35.00	20.00
(88)	McAuley	80.00	35.00	20.00
(89)	McCredie	80.00	35.00	20.00
(90)	McGaffigan	80.00	35.00	20.00
(91)	McHenry	80.00	35.00	20.00
(92)	McQuaid	80.00	35.00	20.00
(93)	Miller	80.00	35.00	20.00
(94)	Mitchell	80.00	35.00	20.00
(95)	J. Mitchell	80.00	35.00	20.00
(96)	Mitchell	80.00	35.00	20.00
(97)	Mitze	80.00	35.00	20.00
(98)	Moffitt	80.00	35.00	20.00
(99)	Mollwitz	80.00	35.00	20.00
(100)	Morse	80.00	35.00	20.00
(101)	Mulligan	80.00	35.00	20.00
(102)	Murphy	80.00	35.00	20.00
(103)	Niehoff	80.00	35.00	20.00
(104)	Nixon	80.00	35.00	20.00
(105)	O'Shaughnessy	80.00	35.00	20.00
(106)	Orr	80.00	35.00	20.00
(107)	Paull	80.00	35.00	20.00
(108)	Penner	80.00	35.00	20.00
(109)	Pertica	80.00	35.00	20.00
(110)	Peterson	80.00	35.00	20.00
(111)	Polson	80.00	35.00	20.00
(112)	Prough	80.00	35.00	20.00
(113)	Reagan	80.00	35.00	20.00
(114)	Reiger	80.00	35.00	20.00
(115)	Reilly	80.00	35.00	20.00
(116)	Rheinhart	80.00	35.00	20.00
(117)	Rodgers	80.00	35.00	20.00
(118)	Ross	80.00	35.00	20.00
(119)	Rumler	80.00	35.00	20.00
(120)	Russell	80.00	35.00	20.00
(121)	Sands	80.00	35.00	20.00
(122)	Schaller	80.00	35.00	20.00
(123)	Schang	80.00	35.00	20.00
(124)	Schellenback	80.00	35.00	20.00
(125)	Schick	80.00	35.00	20.00
(126)	Schorr	80.00	35.00	20.00
(127)	Schroeder	80.00	35.00	20.00
(128)	Scott	80.00	35.00	20.00
(129)	Seaton	80.00	35.00	20.00
(130)	Sheely	80.00	35.00	20.00
(131)	Siebold	80.00	35.00	20.00
(132)	Siglin	80.00	35.00	20.00
(133)	Smith	80.00	35.00	20.00
(134)	G. Smith	80.00	35.00	20.00
(135)	Spellman	80.00	35.00	20.00
(136)	Spranger	80.00	35.00	20.00
(137)	Stroud	80.00	35.00	20.00
(138)	Stumpf	80.00	35.00	20.00
(139)	Sullivan	80.00	35.00	20.00
(140)	Sutherland	80.00	35.00	20.00
(141)	Thurston (Dark hat.)	80.00	35.00	20.00
(142)	Thurston (Light hat.)	80.00	35.00	20.00
(143)	Walsh	80.00	35.00	20.00
(144)	Wares	80.00	35.00	20.00
(145)	Weaver	80.00	35.00	20.00
(146)	Willie	80.00	35.00	20.00
(147)	Winn	80.00	35.00	20.00
(148)	Wisterzill	80.00	35.00	20.00
(149)	Worth	80.00	35.00	20.00
(150)	Yelle	80.00	35.00	20.00
(151)	Zamlock	80.00	35.00	20.00
(152)	Zeider	80.00	35.00	20.00

1921 Zeenut Pacific Coast League

The 1921 Zeenuts cards were dated on the front and measure about 1-3/4" x 3-11/16". They featured borderless, sepia-toned photos. To date, 168 different subjects have been discovered for 1921 (even though a promotional flier indicates 180 players).

		NM	EX	VG
	Common Player:	60.00	25.00	15.00
	With Coupon:	1,200	500.00	300.00
(1)	Adams	60.00	25.00	15.00
(2)	Alcock	60.00	25.00	15.00
(3)	Aldridge	60.00	25.00	15.00
(4)	Alton	60.00	25.00	15.00
(5)	Anfinson	60.00	25.00	15.00
(6)	Arlett	60.00	11.00	6.50
(7)	Baker	60.00	25.00	15.00
(8)	Baldwin	60.00	25.00	15.00
(9)	Bates	60.00	25.00	15.00
(10)	Berry	60.00	25.00	15.00
(11)	Blacholder	60.00	25.00	15.00
(12)	Blossom	60.00	25.00	15.00
(13)	Bourg	60.00	25.00	15.00
(14)	Brinley	60.00	25.00	15.00
(15)	Bromley	60.00	25.00	15.00
(16)	Brown	60.00	25.00	15.00
(17)	Brubaker	60.00	25.00	15.00
(18)	Butler	60.00	25.00	15.00
(19)	Byler	60.00	25.00	15.00
(20)	Carroll	60.00	25.00	15.00
(21)	Casey	60.00	25.00	15.00
(22)	Cather	60.00	25.00	15.00
(23)	Caveney	60.00	25.00	15.00
(24)	Chadbourne	60.00	25.00	15.00
(25)	Compton	60.00	25.00	15.00
(26)	Connel	60.00	25.00	15.00
(27)	Cook	60.00	25.00	15.00
(28)	Cooper	60.00	25.00	15.00
(29)	Couch	60.00	25.00	15.00
(30)	Cox	60.00	25.00	15.00
(31)	Crandall	60.00	25.00	15.00
(32)	Cravath	60.00	25.00	15.00
(33)	Crawford	450.00	225.00	135.00
(34)	Crumpler	60.00	25.00	15.00
(35)	Cunningham	60.00	25.00	15.00
(36)	Daley	60.00	25.00	15.00
(37)	Dell	60.00	25.00	15.00
(38)	Demaree	60.00	25.00	15.00
(39)	Douglas	60.00	25.00	15.00
(40)	Dumovich	60.00	25.00	15.00
(41)	Elliott	60.00	25.00	15.00
(42)	Ellis	60.00	25.00	15.00
(43)	Ellison	60.00	25.00	15.00
(44)	Essick	60.00	25.00	15.00
(45)	Faeth	60.00	25.00	15.00
(46)	Fisher	60.00	25.00	15.00
(47)	Fittery	60.00	25.00	15.00
(48)	Fitzgerald	60.00	25.00	15.00
(49)	Flaherty	60.00	25.00	15.00
(50)	Francis	60.00	25.00	15.00
(51)	French	60.00	25.00	15.00
(52)	Fromme	60.00	25.00	15.00
(53)	Gardner	60.00	25.00	15.00
(54)	Geary	60.00	25.00	15.00
(55)	Gennin	60.00	25.00	15.00
(56)	Gorman	60.00	25.00	15.00
(57)	Gould	60.00	25.00	15.00
(58)	Griggs	60.00	25.00	15.00
(59)	Hale	60.00	25.00	15.00
(60)	Hannah	60.00	25.00	15.00
(61)	Hansen	60.00	25.00	15.00
(62)	Hesse	60.00	25.00	15.00
(63)	High	60.00	25.00	15.00
(64)	Hughes	60.00	25.00	15.00
(65)	Hyatt	60.00	25.00	15.00
(66)	Jackson	60.00	25.00	15.00
(67)	Jacobs	60.00	25.00	15.00
(68)	Jacobs	60.00	25.00	15.00
(69)	Jenkins	60.00	25.00	15.00
(70)	Johnson	60.00	25.00	15.00
(71)	Jones	60.00	25.00	15.00
(72)	Jourden	60.00	25.00	15.00
(73)	Kallio	60.00	25.00	15.00
(74)	Kamm	60.00	25.00	15.00
(75)	Kearns	60.00	25.00	15.00
(76)	Kelly	60.00	25.00	15.00
(77)	Kersten	60.00	25.00	15.00
(78)	Kifer	60.00	25.00	15.00
(79)	Killefer	60.00	25.00	15.00
(80)	King	60.00	25.00	15.00
(81)	Kingdon	60.00	25.00	15.00
(82)	Knight	60.00	25.00	15.00
(83)	Koehler	60.00	25.00	15.00
(84)	Kopp	60.00	25.00	15.00
(85)	Krause	60.00	25.00	15.00
(86)	Kremer	60.00	25.00	15.00
(87)	Krug	60.00	25.00	15.00
(88)	Kunz	60.00	25.00	15.00
(89)	Lane	60.00	25.00	15.00
(90)	Leverenz	60.00	25.00	15.00
(91)	Lewis	60.00	25.00	15.00
(92)	Lindimore	60.00	25.00	15.00
(93)	Love	60.00	25.00	15.00
(94)	Ludolph	60.00	25.00	15.00
(95)	Lynn	60.00	25.00	15.00
(96)	Lyons	60.00	25.00	15.00
(97)	McAuley	60.00	25.00	15.00
(98)	McCredie	60.00	25.00	15.00
(99)	McGaffigan	60.00	25.00	15.00
(100)	McGraw	60.00	25.00	15.00
(101)	McQuaid	60.00	25.00	15.00
(102)	Merritt	60.00	25.00	15.00
(103)	Middleton	60.00	25.00	15.00
(104)	Miller	60.00	25.00	15.00
(105)	Mitchell	60.00	25.00	15.00
(106)	Mitze	60.00	25.00	15.00
(107)	Mollwitz	60.00	25.00	15.00
(108)	Morse	60.00	25.00	15.00
(109)	Murphy (Seattle)	60.00	25.00	15.00
(110)	Murphy (Vernon)	60.00	25.00	15.00
(111)	Mustain	60.00	25.00	15.00
(112)	Nickels	60.00	25.00	15.00
(113)	Niehaus	60.00	25.00	15.00
(114)	Niehoff	60.00	25.00	15.00
(115)	Nofziger	60.00	25.00	15.00
(116)	O'Connell	60.00	25.00	15.00
(117)	O'Doul	350.00	175.00	100.00
(118)	O'Malia	60.00	25.00	15.00
(119)	Oldring	60.00	25.00	15.00
(120)	Oliver	60.00	25.00	15.00
(121)	Orr	60.00	25.00	15.00
(122)	Paton	60.00	25.00	15.00
(123)	Penner	60.00	25.00	15.00
(124)	Pick	60.00	25.00	15.00
(125)	Pillette	60.00	25.00	15.00
(126)	Pinelli	60.00	25.00	15.00
(127)	Polson	60.00	25.00	15.00
(128)	Poole	60.00	25.00	15.00
(129)	Prough	60.00	25.00	15.00
(130)	Rath	60.00	25.00	15.00
(131)	Read	60.00	25.00	15.00
(132)	Reinhardt	60.00	25.00	15.00
(133)	Rieger	60.00	25.00	15.00
(134)	Rogers	60.00	25.00	15.00
(135)	Rose (Sacramento)	60.00	25.00	15.00
(136)	Rose (Salt Lake)	60.00	25.00	15.00
(137)	Ross (Portland)	60.00	25.00	15.00
(138)	Ross (Sacramento)	60.00	25.00	15.00
(139)	Ryan	60.00	25.00	15.00
(140)	Sand	60.00	25.00	15.00
(141)	Schick	60.00	25.00	15.00
(142)	Schneider	60.00	25.00	15.00
(143)	Scott	60.00	25.00	15.00
(144)	Shang	60.00	25.00	15.00
(145)	Sheehan	60.00	25.00	15.00
(146)	Shore	60.00	25.00	15.00
(147)	Shorr	60.00	25.00	15.00
(148)	Shultis	60.00	25.00	15.00
(149)	Siebold	60.00	25.00	15.00
(150)	Siglin	60.00	25.00	15.00
(151)	Smallwood	60.00	25.00	15.00
(152)	Smith	60.00	25.00	15.00
(153)	Spencer	60.00	25.00	15.00
(154)	Stanage	60.00	25.00	15.00

		NM	EX	VG
(155)	Statz	60.00	25.00	15.00
(156)	Stumph	60.00	25.00	15.00
(157)	Thomas	60.00	25.00	15.00
(158)	Thurston	60.00	25.00	15.00
(159)	Tyrrell	60.00	25.00	15.00
(160)	Van Osdoll	60.00	25.00	15.00
(161)	Walsh	60.00	25.00	15.00
(162)	White	60.00	25.00	15.00
(163)	Wilhoit	60.00	25.00	15.00
(164)	Wilie	60.00	25.00	15.00
(165)	Winn	60.00	25.00	15.00
(166)	Wolfer	60.00	25.00	15.00
(167)	Yelle	60.00	25.00	15.00
(168)	Young	60.00	25.00	15.00
(169)	Zeider	60.00	25.00	15.00

1922 Zeenut Pacific Coast League

The 1922 Zeenuts are dated on the front, measure about 1-13/16" x 3-9/16" and feature black-and-white photos with sepia highlights. There are 162 subjects, and four of them (Koehler, Williams, Gregg and Schneider) have been found with variations in color tones.

		NM	EX	VG
Common Player:		60.00	25.00	15.00
(1)	J. Adams	60.00	25.00	15.00
(2)	S. Adams	60.00	25.00	15.00
(3)	Agnew	60.00	25.00	15.00
(4)	Anfinson	60.00	25.00	15.00
(5)	Arlett	60.00	25.00	15.00
(6)	Baldwin	60.00	25.00	15.00
(7)	Barney	60.00	25.00	15.00
(8)	Bell	60.00	25.00	15.00
(9)	Blaeholder	60.00	25.00	15.00
(10)	Bodie	60.00	25.00	15.00
(11)	Brenton	60.00	25.00	15.00
(12)	Bromley	60.00	25.00	15.00
(13)	Brovold	60.00	25.00	15.00
(14)	Brown	60.00	25.00	15.00
(15)	Brubaker	60.00	25.00	15.00
(16)	Burger	60.00	25.00	15.00
(17)	Byler	60.00	25.00	15.00
(18)	Canfield	60.00	25.00	15.00
(19)	Carroll	60.00	25.00	15.00
(20)	Cartwright	60.00	25.00	15.00
(21)	Chadbourne	60.00	25.00	15.00
(22)	Compton	60.00	25.00	15.00
(23)	Connolly	60.00	25.00	15.00
(24)	Cook	60.00	25.00	15.00
(25)	Cooper	60.00	25.00	15.00
(26)	Coumbe	60.00	25.00	15.00
(27)	Cox	60.00	25.00	15.00
(28)	Crandall	60.00	25.00	15.00
(29)	Crumpler	60.00	25.00	15.00
(30)	Cueto	100.00	50.00	30.00
(31)	Dailey	60.00	25.00	15.00
(32)	Daly	60.00	25.00	15.00
(33)	Deal	60.00	25.00	15.00
(34)	Dell	60.00	25.00	15.00
(35)	Doyle	60.00	25.00	15.00
(36)	Dumovich	60.00	25.00	15.00
(37)	Eldred	60.00	25.00	15.00
(38)	Eller	60.00	25.00	15.00
(39)	Elliott	60.00	25.00	15.00
(40)	Ellison	60.00	25.00	15.00
(41)	Essick	60.00	25.00	15.00
(42)	Finneran	60.00	25.00	15.00
(43)	Fittery	60.00	25.00	15.00
(44)	Fitzgerald	60.00	25.00	15.00
(45)	Freeman	60.00	25.00	15.00
(46)	French	60.00	25.00	15.00
(47)	Gardner	60.00	25.00	15.00
(48)	Geary	60.00	25.00	15.00
(49)	Gibson	60.00	25.00	15.00
(50)	Gilder	60.00	25.00	15.00
(51)	Gould	60.00	25.00	15.00
(52)	Gregg	60.00	25.00	15.00
(53)	Gressett	60.00	25.00	15.00
(54)	Griggs	60.00	25.00	15.00
(55)	Hampton	60.00	25.00	15.00
(56)	Hannah	60.00	25.00	15.00
(57)	Hawks	60.00	25.00	15.00
(58)	Henke	60.00	25.00	15.00
(59)	High (Portland)	60.00	25.00	15.00
(60)	High (Vernon)	60.00	25.00	15.00
(61)	Houck	60.00	25.00	15.00
(62)	Howard	60.00	25.00	15.00
(63)	Hughes	60.00	25.00	15.00
(64)	Hyatt	60.00	25.00	15.00
(65)	Jacobs	60.00	25.00	15.00
(66)	James	60.00	25.00	15.00
(67)	Jenkins	60.00	25.00	15.00
(68)	Jones	60.00	25.00	15.00
(69)	Kallio	60.00	25.00	15.00
(70)	Kamm	60.00	25.00	15.00
(71)	Keiser	60.00	25.00	15.00
(72)	Kelly	60.00	25.00	15.00
(73)	Kenworthy	60.00	25.00	15.00
(74)	Kilduff	60.00	25.00	15.00
(75)	Killefer	60.00	25.00	15.00
(76)	Killhullen	60.00	25.00	15.00
(77)	King	60.00	25.00	15.00
(78)	Knight	60.00	25.00	15.00
(79)	Koehler	60.00	25.00	15.00
(80)	Kremer	60.00	25.00	15.00
(81)	Kunz	60.00	25.00	15.00
(82)	Lafayette	60.00	25.00	15.00
(83)	Lane	60.00	25.00	15.00
(84)	Tony Lazzeri	1,200	600.00	360.00
(85)	Lefevre	60.00	25.00	15.00
(86)	D. Lewis	60.00	25.00	15.00
(87)	S. Lewis	60.00	25.00	15.00
(88)	Lindimore	60.00	25.00	15.00
(89)	Locker	60.00	25.00	15.00
(90)	Lyons	60.00	25.00	15.00
(91)	Mack	60.00	25.00	15.00
(92)	Marriott	60.00	25.00	15.00
(93)	May	60.00	25.00	15.00
(94)	McAuley	60.00	25.00	15.00
(95)	McCabe	60.00	25.00	15.00
(96)	McCann	60.00	25.00	15.00
(97)	McCredie	60.00	25.00	15.00
(98)	McNeely	60.00	25.00	15.00
(99)	McQuaid	60.00	25.00	15.00
(100)	Miller	60.00	25.00	15.00
(101)	Mitchell	60.00	25.00	15.00
(102)	Mitze	60.00	25.00	15.00
(103)	Mollwitz	60.00	25.00	15.00
(104)	Monahan	60.00	25.00	15.00
(105)	Murphy (Seattle)	60.00	25.00	15.00
(106)	Murphy (Vernon)	60.00	25.00	15.00
(107)	Niehaus	60.00	25.00	15.00
(108)	O'Connell	60.00	25.00	15.00
(109)	Orr	60.00	25.00	15.00
(110)	Owen	60.00	25.00	15.00
(111)	Pearce	60.00	25.00	15.00
(112)	Pick	60.00	25.00	15.00
(113)	Ponder	60.00	25.00	15.00
(114)	Poole	60.00	25.00	15.00
(115)	Prough	60.00	25.00	15.00
(116)	Read	60.00	25.00	15.00
(117)	Richardson	60.00	25.00	15.00
(118)	Rieger	60.00	25.00	15.00
(119)	Ritchie	60.00	25.00	15.00
(120)	Ross	60.00	25.00	15.00
(121)	Ryan	60.00	25.00	15.00
(122)	Sand	60.00	25.00	15.00
(123)	Sargent	60.00	25.00	15.00
(124)	Sawyer	60.00	25.00	15.00
(125)	Schang	60.00	25.00	15.00
(126)	Schick	60.00	25.00	15.00
(127)	Schneider	60.00	25.00	15.00
(128)	Schorr	60.00	25.00	15.00
(129)	Schulte (Oakland)	60.00	25.00	15.00
(130)	Schulte (Seattle)	60.00	25.00	15.00
(131)	Scott	60.00	25.00	15.00
(132)	See	60.00	25.00	15.00
(133)	Shea	60.00	25.00	15.00
(134)	Sheehan	60.00	25.00	15.00
(135)	Siglin	60.00	25.00	15.00
(136)	Smith	60.00	25.00	15.00
(137)	Soria	60.00	25.00	15.00
(138)	Spencer	60.00	25.00	15.00
(139)	Stanage	60.00	25.00	15.00
(140)	Strand	60.00	25.00	15.00
(141)	Stumpf	60.00	25.00	15.00
(142)	Sullivan	60.00	25.00	15.00
(143)	Sutherland	60.00	25.00	15.00
(144)	Thomas	60.00	25.00	15.00
(145)	Jim Thorpe	30,000	15,000	9,000
(146)	Thurston	60.00	25.00	15.00
(147)	Tobin	60.00	25.00	15.00
(148)	Turner	60.00	25.00	15.00
(149)	Twombly	60.00	25.00	15.00
(150)	Valla	60.00	25.00	15.00
(151)	Vargas	60.00	25.00	15.00
(152)	Viveros	60.00	25.00	15.00
(153)	Wallace	60.00	25.00	15.00
(154)	Walsh	60.00	25.00	15.00
(155)	Wells	60.00	25.00	15.00
(156)	Westersil	60.00	25.00	15.00
(157)	Wheat	60.00	25.00	15.00
(158)	Wilhoit	60.00	25.00	15.00
(159)	Wilie	60.00	25.00	15.00
(160)	Williams	60.00	25.00	15.00
(161)	Yelle	60.00	25.00	15.00
(162)	Zeider	60.00	25.00	15.00

1923 Zeenut Pacific Coast League

This is the only year that Zeenuts cards were issued in two different sizes. Cards in the "regular" series measure about 1-7/8" x 3-1/2", feature black-and-white photos and are dated 1923. A second series, containing just 24 cards (all San Francisco and Oakland players), are sepia-toned re-issues of the 1922 series with a "1923" date and measure about 1/16" longer. The re-issued cards have coupons with an expiration date of April 1, 1923. The dated cards have coupons with an expiration date of April 1, 1924.

		NM	EX	VG
Common Player:		60.00	25.00	15.00
With Coupon:		1,000	500.00	300.00
(1)	Agnew (1923 photo)	60.00	25.00	15.00
(2)	Agnew (1922 photo re-dated)	60.00	25.00	15.00
(3)	Alten	60.00	25.00	15.00
(4)	Anderson	60.00	25.00	15.00
(5)	Anfinson	60.00	25.00	15.00
(6)	Arlett	60.00	25.00	15.00
(7)	Baker	60.00	25.00	15.00
(8)	Baldwin	60.00	25.00	15.00
(9)	Barney	60.00	25.00	15.00
(10)	Blake	60.00	25.00	15.00
(11)	Bodie	60.00	25.00	15.00
(12)	Brazil	60.00	25.00	15.00
(13)	Brenton	60.00	25.00	15.00
(14)	Brown (Oakland)	60.00	25.00	15.00
(15)	Brown (Sacramento)	60.00	25.00	15.00
(16)	Brubaker	60.00	25.00	15.00
(17)	Buckley	60.00	25.00	15.00
(18)	Canfield	60.00	25.00	15.00
(19)	Carroll	60.00	25.00	15.00
(20)	Cather	60.00	25.00	15.00
(21)	Chadbourne	60.00	25.00	15.00
(22)	Charvez	60.00	25.00	15.00
(23)	Cochrane	60.00	25.00	15.00
(24)	Colwell	60.00	25.00	15.00
(25)	Compton	60.00	25.00	15.00
(26)	Cook	60.00	25.00	15.00
(27)	Cooper (1923 photo)	60.00	25.00	15.00
(28)	Cooper (1922 photo re-date)	60.00	25.00	15.00
(29)	Coumbe	60.00	25.00	15.00
(30)	Courtney	60.00	25.00	15.00
(31)	Crandall	60.00	25.00	15.00
(32)	Crane	60.00	25.00	15.00
(33)	Crowder	60.00	25.00	15.00
(34)	Crumpler	60.00	25.00	15.00
(35)	Daly (Los Angeles)	60.00	25.00	15.00
(36)	Daly (Portland)	60.00	25.00	15.00
(37)	Deal	60.00	25.00	15.00
(38)	Doyle	60.00	25.00	15.00
(39)	Duchalsky	60.00	25.00	15.00
(40)	Eckert	60.00	25.00	15.00
(41)	Eldred	60.00	25.00	15.00
(42)	Eley	60.00	25.00	15.00
(43)	Eller	60.00	25.00	15.00
(44)	Ellison (1923 photo)	60.00	25.00	15.00
(45)	Ellison (1922 photo re-dated)	60.00	25.00	15.00
(46)	Essick	60.00	25.00	15.00
(47)	Fittery	60.00	25.00	15.00
(48)	Flashkamper	60.00	25.00	15.00
(49)	Frederick	60.00	25.00	15.00
(50)	French	60.00	25.00	15.00
(51)	Geary (1923 photo)	60.00	25.00	15.00
(52)	Geary (1922 photo re-dated)	60.00	25.00	15.00
(53)	Gilder	60.00	25.00	15.00
(54)	Golvin	60.00	25.00	15.00
(55)	Gorman	60.00	25.00	15.00
(56)	Gould	60.00	25.00	15.00
(57)	Gressett	60.00	25.00	15.00
(58)	Griggs	60.00	25.00	15.00
(59)	Hannah (Los Angeles)	60.00	25.00	15.00
(60)	Hannah (Vernon)	60.00	25.00	15.00
(61)	Hemingway	60.00	25.00	15.00
(62)	Hendryx	60.00	25.00	15.00
(63)	High	60.00	25.00	15.00
(64)	H. High	60.00	25.00	15.00
(65)	Hodge	60.00	25.00	15.00
(66)	Hood	60.00	25.00	15.00
(67)	Houghs	60.00	25.00	15.00
(68)	Howard (1923 photo)	60.00	25.00	15.00
(69)	Howard (1922 photo re-date)	60.00	25.00	15.00
(70)	Del Howard	60.00	25.00	15.00
(71)	Jacobs	60.00	25.00	15.00
(72)	James	60.00	25.00	15.00
(73)	Johnson	60.00	25.00	15.00
(74)	Johnston	60.00	25.00	15.00
(75)	Jolly (Jolley)	60.00	25.00	15.00
(76)	Jones (Los Angeles)	60.00	25.00	15.00
(77)	Jones (Oakland)	60.00	25.00	15.00
(78)	Jones (Portland)	60.00	25.00	15.00
(79)	Kallio	60.00	25.00	15.00
(80)	Kearns	60.00	25.00	15.00
(81)	Keiser	60.00	25.00	15.00
(82)	Keller	60.00	25.00	15.00
(83)	Kelly (San Francisco)	60.00	25.00	15.00
(84)	Kelly (Seattle)	60.00	25.00	15.00
(85)	Kenna	60.00	25.00	15.00
(86)	Kilduff	60.00	25.00	15.00
(87)	Killifer	60.00	25.00	15.00
(88)	King	60.00	25.00	15.00
(89)	Knight (1923 photo)	60.00	25.00	15.00
(90)	Knight (1922 photo re-dated)	60.00	25.00	15.00

(91) Koehler	60.00	25.00	15.00
(92) Kopp	60.00	25.00	15.00
(93) Krause	60.00	25.00	15.00
(94) Kremer	60.00	25.00	15.00
(95) Krug	60.00	25.00	15.00
(96) Lafayette (1923 photo)	60.00	25.00	15.00
(97) Lafayette	60.00	25.00	15.00
(1922 photo re-dated)			
(98) Lane	60.00	25.00	15.00
(99) Lefevre	60.00	25.00	15.00
(100) Leslie	60.00	25.00	15.00
(101) Levere	60.00	25.00	15.00
(102) Leverenz	60.00	25.00	15.00
(103) Lewis	60.00	25.00	15.00
(104) Lindimore	60.00	25.00	15.00
(105) Locker	60.00	25.00	15.00
(106) Lyons	60.00	25.00	15.00
(107) Maderas	60.00	25.00	15.00
(108) Mails	60.00	25.00	15.00
(109) Marriott	60.00	25.00	15.00
(110) Matzen	60.00	25.00	15.00
(111) McAuley	60.00	25.00	15.00
(112) McAuliffe	60.00	25.00	15.00
(113) McCabe (Los Angeles)	60.00	25.00	15.00
(114) McCabe (Salt Lake)	60.00	25.00	15.00
(115) McCann	60.00	25.00	15.00
(116) McGaffigan	60.00	25.00	15.00
(117) McGinnis	60.00	25.00	15.00
(118) McNeilly	60.00	25.00	15.00
(119) McWeeney	60.00	25.00	15.00
(120) Middleton	60.00	25.00	15.00
(121) Miller	60.00	25.00	15.00
(122) Mitchell (1923 photo)	60.00	25.00	15.00
(123) Mitchell	60.00	25.00	15.00
(1922 photo re-date)			
(124) Mitze	60.00	25.00	15.00
(125) Mulligan	60.00	25.00	15.00
(126) Murchio	60.00	25.00	15.00
(127) D. Murphy	60.00	25.00	15.00
(128) R. Murphy	60.00	25.00	15.00
(129) Noack	60.00	25.00	15.00
(130) O'Brien	60.00	25.00	15.00
(131) Onslow	60.00	25.00	15.00
(132) Orr	60.00	25.00	15.00
(133) Pearce	60.00	25.00	15.00
(134) Penner	60.00	25.00	15.00
(135) Peters	60.00	25.00	15.00
(136) Pick	60.00	25.00	15.00
(137) Pigg	60.00	25.00	15.00
(138) Plummer	60.00	25.00	15.00
(139) Ponder	60.00	25.00	15.00
(140) Poole	60.00	25.00	15.00
(141) Ramage	60.00	25.00	15.00
(142) Read (1923 photo)	60.00	25.00	15.00
(143) Read (1922 photo re-dated)	60.00	25.00	15.00
(144) Rhyne	60.00	25.00	15.00
(145) Ritchie	60.00	25.00	15.00
(146) Robertson	60.00	25.00	15.00
(147) Rohwer (Sacramento)	60.00	25.00	15.00
(148) Rohwer (Seattle)	60.00	25.00	15.00
(149) Ryan	60.00	25.00	15.00
(150) Sawyer	60.00	25.00	15.00
(151) Schang	60.00	25.00	15.00
(152) Schneider	60.00	25.00	15.00
(153) Schroeder	60.00	25.00	15.00
(154) Scott	60.00	25.00	15.00
(155) See	60.00	25.00	15.00
(156) Shea	60.00	25.00	15.00
(157) M. Shea	60.00	25.00	15.00
(158) Spec Shea	60.00	25.00	15.00
(159) Sheehan	60.00	25.00	15.00
(160) Shellenback	60.00	25.00	15.00
(161) Siglin	60.00	25.00	15.00
(162) Singleton	60.00	25.00	15.00
(163) Smith	60.00	25.00	15.00
(164) M.H. Smith	60.00	25.00	15.00
(165) Stanton	60.00	25.00	15.00
(166) Strand	60.00	25.00	15.00
(167) Stumpf	60.00	25.00	15.00
(168) Sutherland	60.00	25.00	15.00
(169) Tesar	60.00	25.00	15.00
(170) Thomas (Los Angeles)	60.00	25.00	15.00
(171) Thomas (Oakland)	60.00	25.00	15.00
(172) Tobin	60.00	25.00	15.00
(173) Twombly	60.00	25.00	15.00
(174) Valla	60.00	25.00	15.00
(175) Vargas	60.00	25.00	15.00
(176) Vitt	60.00	25.00	15.00
(177) Wallace	60.00	25.00	15.00
(178) Walsh (San Francisco)	60.00	25.00	15.00
(179) Walsh (Seattle)	60.00	25.00	15.00
(180) Paul Waner	1,500	750.00	450.00
(181) Wells (Oakland)	60.00	25.00	15.00
(182) Wells (San Francisco)	60.00	25.00	15.00
(183) Welsh	60.00	25.00	15.00
(184) Wilhoit	60.00	25.00	15.00
(185) Wilie (1923 photo)	60.00	25.00	15.00
(186) Wilie	60.00	25.00	15.00
(1922 photo re-dated)			
(187) Williams	60.00	25.00	15.00
(188) Witzel	60.00	25.00	15.00
(189) Wolfer	60.00	25.00	15.00
(190) Wolverton	60.00	25.00	15.00
(191) Yarrison	60.00	25.00	15.00
(192) Yaryan	60.00	25.00	15.00
(193) Yelle (1923 photo)	60.00	25.00	15.00
(194) Yelle	60.00	25.00	15.00
(1922 photo re-dated)			
(195) Moses Yellowhorse	600.00	300.00	180.00
(196) Zeider	60.00	25.00	15.00

1924 Zeenut Pacific Coast League

Zeenut cards in 1924 measure about 1-3/4" x 3-7/16" and display the date on the front. The cards include a full photographic background. There are 144 subjects known.

	NM	EX	VG
Common Player:	60.00	25.00	15.00
(1) Adams	125.00	65.00	40.00
(2) Agnew	60.00	25.00	15.00
(3) Arlett	60.00	25.00	15.00
(4) Baker	60.00	25.00	15.00
(5) E. Baldwin	60.00	25.00	15.00
(6) T. Baldwin	60.00	25.00	15.00
(7) Beck	60.00	25.00	15.00
(8) Benton	60.00	25.00	15.00
(9) Bernard	60.00	25.00	15.00
(10) Bigbee	60.00	25.00	15.00
(11) Billings	60.00	25.00	15.00
(12) Blakesly	60.00	25.00	15.00
(13) Brady	60.00	25.00	15.00
(14) Brazil	60.00	25.00	15.00
(15) Brown	60.00	25.00	15.00
(16) Brubaker	60.00	25.00	15.00
(17) Buckley	60.00	25.00	15.00
(18) Burger	60.00	25.00	15.00
(19) Byler	60.00	25.00	15.00
(20) Cadore	60.00	25.00	15.00
(21) Cather	60.00	25.00	15.00
(22) Chadbourne	60.00	25.00	15.00
(23) Christian	60.00	25.00	15.00
(24) Mickey Cochrane (Portland)	1,200	600.00	360.00
(25) Cochrane (Sacramento)	60.00	25.00	15.00
(26) Cooper	60.00	25.00	15.00
(27) Coumbe	60.00	25.00	15.00
(28) Cox	60.00	25.00	15.00
(29) Crandall	60.00	25.00	15.00
(30) Daly	60.00	25.00	15.00
(31) Deal	60.00	25.00	15.00
(32) Distel	60.00	25.00	15.00
(33) Durst	60.00	25.00	15.00
(34) Eckert	60.00	25.00	15.00
(35) Eldred	60.00	25.00	15.00
(36) Ellison	60.00	25.00	15.00
(37) Essick	60.00	25.00	15.00
(38) Flashkamper	60.00	25.00	15.00
(39) Foster	60.00	25.00	15.00
(40) Fredericks	60.00	25.00	15.00
(41) Geary	60.00	25.00	15.00
(42) Goebel	60.00	25.00	15.00
(43) Golvin	60.00	25.00	15.00
(44) Gorman	60.00	25.00	15.00
(45) Gould	60.00	25.00	15.00
(46) Gressett	60.00	25.00	15.00
(47) Griffin (San Francisco)	60.00	25.00	15.00
(48) Griffin (Vernon)	60.00	25.00	15.00
(49) Guisto	60.00	25.00	15.00
(50) Gunther	60.00	25.00	15.00
(51) Hall	60.00	25.00	15.00
(52) Hannah	60.00	25.00	15.00
(53) Hendryx	60.00	25.00	15.00
(54) High	60.00	25.00	15.00
(55) Hodge	60.00	25.00	15.00
(56) Hood	60.00	25.00	15.00
(57) Ivan Howard	60.00	25.00	15.00
(58) Hughes (Los Angeles)	60.00	25.00	15.00
(59) Hughes (Sacramento)	60.00	25.00	15.00
(60) Jacobs	60.00	25.00	15.00
(61) James	60.00	25.00	15.00
(62) Jenkins	60.00	25.00	15.00
(63) Johnson	60.00	25.00	15.00
(64) Jones	60.00	25.00	15.00
(65) Keck	60.00	25.00	15.00
(66) Kelley	60.00	25.00	15.00
(67) Kenworthy	60.00	25.00	15.00
(68) Kilduff	60.00	25.00	15.00
(69) Killifer	60.00	25.00	15.00
(70) Kimmick	60.00	25.00	15.00
(71) Kopp	60.00	25.00	15.00
(72) Krause	60.00	25.00	15.00
(73) Krug	60.00	25.00	15.00
(74) Kunz	60.00	25.00	15.00
(75) Lafayette	60.00	25.00	15.00
(76) Lennon	60.00	25.00	15.00
(77) Leptich	60.00	25.00	15.00
(78) Leslie	60.00	25.00	15.00
(79) Leverenz	60.00	25.00	15.00
(80) Lewis	60.00	25.00	15.00
(81) Maderas	60.00	25.00	15.00
(82) Mails	60.00	25.00	15.00
(83) McAuley	60.00	25.00	15.00
(84) McCann	60.00	25.00	15.00
(85) McDowell	60.00	25.00	15.00
(86) McNeely	60.00	25.00	15.00
(87) Menosky	60.00	25.00	15.00
(88) Meyers	60.00	25.00	15.00
(89) Miller	60.00	25.00	15.00
(90) Mitchell	60.00	25.00	15.00
(91) Mulligan	60.00	25.00	15.00
(92) D. Murphy	60.00	25.00	15.00
(93) R. Murphy	60.00	25.00	15.00
(94) Osborne	60.00	25.00	15.00
(95) Paynter	60.00	25.00	15.00
(96) Penner	60.00	25.00	15.00
(97) Peters (Sacramento)	60.00	25.00	15.00
(98) Peters (Salt Lake)	60.00	25.00	15.00
(99) Pick	60.00	25.00	15.00
(100) Pillette	60.00	25.00	15.00
(101) Poole	60.00	25.00	15.00
(102) Prough	60.00	25.00	15.00
(103) Querry	60.00	25.00	15.00
(104) Read	60.00	25.00	15.00
(105) Rhyne	60.00	25.00	15.00
(106) Ritchie	60.00	25.00	15.00
(107) Root	60.00	25.00	15.00
(108) Rowher	60.00	25.00	15.00
(109) Schang	60.00	25.00	15.00
(110) Schneider	60.00	25.00	15.00
(111) Schorr	60.00	25.00	15.00
(112) Schroeder	60.00	25.00	15.00
(113) Scott	60.00	25.00	15.00
(114) Sellers	60.00	25.00	15.00
(115) "Speck" Shay	60.00	25.00	15.00
(116) Shea (Sacramento)	60.00	25.00	15.00
(117) Shea (San Francisco)	60.00	25.00	15.00
(118) Shellenback	60.00	25.00	15.00
(119) Siebold	60.00	25.00	15.00
(120) Siglin	60.00	25.00	15.00
(121) Slade	60.00	25.00	15.00
(122) Smith (Sacramento)	60.00	25.00	15.00
(123) Smith (San Francisco)	60.00	25.00	15.00
(124) Stanton	60.00	25.00	15.00
(125) Tanner	60.00	25.00	15.00
(126) Twomley	60.00	25.00	15.00
(127) Valla	60.00	25.00	15.00
(128) Vargas	60.00	25.00	15.00
(129) Vines	60.00	25.00	15.00
(130) Vitt	60.00	25.00	15.00
(131) Wallace	60.00	25.00	15.00
(132) Walsh	60.00	25.00	15.00
(133) Paul Waner	750.00	375.00	225.00
(134) Warner (Fielding)	60.00	25.00	15.00
(135) Warner (Throwing)	60.00	25.00	15.00
(136) Welsh	60.00	25.00	15.00
(137) Wetzel	60.00	25.00	15.00
(138) Whalen	60.00	25.00	15.00
(139) Wilhoit	60.00	25.00	15.00
(140) Williams (San Francisco)	60.00	25.00	15.00
(141) Williams (Seattle)	60.00	25.00	15.00
(142) Wolfer	60.00	25.00	15.00
(143) Yelle	60.00	25.00	15.00
(144) Moses Yellowhorse	350.00	175.00	100.00

1925 Zeenut Pacific Coast League

Zeenut cards in 1925 measure about 1-3/4" x 3-7/16" and display the date on the front. The cards include a full photographic background. There are 162 subjects known for 1925.

	NM	EX	VG
Common Player:	60.00	25.00	15.00
With Coupon:	300.00	150.00	90.00
(1) Adeylatte	60.00	25.00	15.00
(2) Agnew	60.00	25.00	15.00
(3) Arlett	60.00	25.00	15.00
(4) Bagby	60.00	25.00	15.00
(5) Bahr	60.00	25.00	15.00
(6) Baker	60.00	25.00	15.00
(7) E. Baldwin	60.00	25.00	15.00
(8) Barfoot	60.00	25.00	15.00
(9) Beck	60.00	25.00	15.00
(10) Becker	60.00	25.00	15.00
(11) Blakesley	60.00	25.00	15.00
(12) Boehler	60.00	25.00	15.00
(13) Brady	60.00	25.00	15.00
(14) Brandt	60.00	25.00	15.00
(15) Bratcher	60.00	25.00	15.00
(16) Brazil	60.00	25.00	15.00
(17) Brower	60.00	25.00	15.00
(18) Brown	60.00	25.00	15.00
(19) Brubaker	60.00	25.00	15.00
(20) Bryan	60.00	25.00	15.00
(21) Canfield	60.00	25.00	15.00
(22) W. Canfield	60.00	25.00	15.00
(23) Cather	60.00	25.00	15.00
(24) Chavez	60.00	25.00	15.00
(25) Christain	60.00	25.00	15.00
(26) Cochrane	60.00	25.00	15.00
(27) Connolly	60.00	25.00	15.00
(28) Cook	60.00	25.00	15.00
(29) Cooper	60.00	25.00	15.00
(30) Coumbe	60.00	25.00	15.00
(31) Crandall	60.00	25.00	15.00

(32)	Crane	60.00	25.00	15.00
(33)	Crockett	60.00	25.00	15.00
(34)	Crosby	60.00	25.00	15.00
(35)	Cutshaw	60.00	25.00	15.00
(36)	Daly	60.00	25.00	15.00
(37)	Davis	60.00	25.00	15.00
(38)	Deal	60.00	25.00	15.00
(39)	Delaney	60.00	25.00	15.00
(40)	Dempsey	60.00	25.00	15.00
(41)	Dumovich	60.00	25.00	15.00
(42)	Eckert	60.00	25.00	15.00
(43)	Eldred	60.00	25.00	15.00
(44)	Elliott	60.00	25.00	15.00
(45)	Ellison	60.00	25.00	15.00
(46)	Emmer	60.00	25.00	15.00
(47)	Ennis	60.00	25.00	15.00
(48)	Essick	60.00	25.00	15.00
(49)	Finn	60.00	25.00	15.00
(50)	Flowers	60.00	25.00	15.00
(51)	Frederick	60.00	25.00	15.00
(52)	Fussell	60.00	25.00	15.00
(53)	Geary	60.00	25.00	15.00
(54)	Gorman	60.00	25.00	15.00
(55)	Griffin (San Francisco)	60.00	25.00	15.00
(56)	Griffin (Vernon)	60.00	25.00	15.00
(57)	Grimes	60.00	25.00	15.00
(58)	Guisto	60.00	25.00	15.00
(59)	Hannah	60.00	25.00	15.00
(60)	Haughy	60.00	25.00	15.00
(61)	Hemingway	60.00	25.00	15.00
(62)	Hendryx	60.00	25.00	15.00
(63)	Herman	400.00	200.00	120.00
(64)	High	60.00	25.00	15.00
(65)	Hoffman	60.00	25.00	15.00
(66)	Hood	60.00	25.00	15.00
(67)	Horan	60.00	25.00	15.00
(68)	Horton	60.00	25.00	15.00
(69)	Howard	60.00	25.00	15.00
(70)	Hughes	60.00	25.00	15.00
(71)	Hulvey	60.00	25.00	15.00
(72)	Hunnefield	60.00	25.00	15.00
(73)	Jacobs	60.00	25.00	15.00
(74)	James	60.00	25.00	15.00
(75)	Keating	60.00	25.00	15.00
(76)	Keefe	60.00	25.00	15.00
(77)	Kelly	60.00	25.00	15.00
(78)	Kilduff	60.00	25.00	15.00
(79)	Kohler	60.00	25.00	15.00
(80)	Kopp	60.00	25.00	15.00
(81)	Krause	60.00	25.00	15.00
(82)	Krug	60.00	25.00	15.00
(83)	Kunz	60.00	25.00	15.00
(84)	Lafayette	60.00	25.00	15.00
(85)	Tony Lazzeri	450.00	225.00	135.00
(86)	Leslie	60.00	25.00	15.00
(87)	Leverenz	60.00	25.00	15.00
(88)	Duffy Lewis	60.00	30.00	20.00
(89)	Lindemore	60.00	25.00	15.00
(90)	Ludolph	60.00	25.00	15.00
(91)	Makin	60.00	25.00	15.00
(92)	Martin (Sacramento)	60.00	25.00	15.00
(93)	Martin (Portland)	60.00	25.00	15.00
(94)	McCabe	60.00	25.00	15.00
(95)	McCann	60.00	25.00	15.00
(96)	McCarren	60.00	25.00	15.00
(97)	McDonald	60.00	25.00	15.00
(98)	McGinnis (Portland)	60.00	25.00	15.00
(99)	McGinnis (Sacramento)	60.00	25.00	15.00
(100)	McLaughlin	60.00	25.00	15.00
(101)	Milstead	60.00	25.00	15.00
(102)	Mitchell	60.00	25.00	15.00
(103)	Moudy	60.00	25.00	15.00
(104)	Mulcahy	60.00	25.00	15.00
(105)	Mulligan	60.00	25.00	15.00
(106)	Lefty O'Doul	250.00	125.00	75.00
(107)	O'Neil	60.00	25.00	15.00
(108)	Ortman	60.00	25.00	15.00
(109)	Pailey	60.00	25.00	15.00
(110)	Paynter	60.00	25.00	15.00
(111)	Peery	60.00	25.00	15.00
(112)	Penner	60.00	25.00	15.00
(113)	Pfeffer	60.00	25.00	15.00
(114)	Phillips	60.00	25.00	15.00
(115)	Pickering	60.00	25.00	15.00
(116)	Piercy	60.00	25.00	15.00
(117)	Pillette	60.00	25.00	15.00
(118)	Plummer	60.00	25.00	15.00
(119)	Ponder	60.00	25.00	15.00
(120)	Pruett	60.00	25.00	15.00
(121)	Rawlings	60.00	25.00	15.00
(122)	Read	60.00	25.00	15.00
(123)	Jimmy Reese	300.00	150.00	90.00
(124)	Rhyne	60.00	25.00	15.00
(125)	Riconda	60.00	25.00	15.00
(126)	Ritchie	60.00	25.00	15.00
(127)	Rohwer	60.00	25.00	15.00
(128)	Rowland	60.00	25.00	15.00
(129)	Ryan	60.00	25.00	15.00
(130)	Sandberg	60.00	25.00	15.00
(131)	Schang	60.00	25.00	15.00
(132)	Shea	60.00	25.00	15.00
(133)	M. Shea	60.00	25.00	15.00
(134)	Shellenbach	60.00	25.00	15.00
(135)	Sherling	60.00	25.00	15.00
(136)	Siglin	60.00	25.00	15.00
(137)	Slade	60.00	25.00	15.00
(138)	Spencer	60.00	25.00	15.00
(139)	Steward	60.00	25.00	15.00
(140)	Stivers	60.00	25.00	15.00
(141)	Suhr	60.00	25.00	15.00
(142)	Sutherland	60.00	25.00	15.00
(143)	Thomas (Portland)	60.00	25.00	15.00
(144)	Thomas (Vernon)	60.00	25.00	15.00
(145)	Thompson	60.00	25.00	15.00
(146)	Tobin	60.00	25.00	15.00
(147)	Twombly	60.00	25.00	15.00
(148)	Valla	60.00	25.00	15.00
(149)	Vinci	60.00	25.00	15.00
(150)	O. Vitt	60.00	25.00	15.00
(151)	Wachenfeld	60.00	25.00	15.00
(152)	Paul Waner	750.00	375.00	225.00
(153)	Lloyd Waner	1,200	600.00	360.00
(154)	Warner	60.00	25.00	15.00
(155)	Watson	60.00	25.00	15.00
(156)	Weinert	60.00	25.00	15.00
(157)	Whaley	60.00	25.00	15.00
(158)	Whitney	60.00	25.00	15.00
(159)	Williams	60.00	25.00	15.00
(160)	Winters	60.00	25.00	15.00
(161)	Wolfer	60.00	25.00	15.00
(162)	Woodring	60.00	25.00	15.00
(163)	Yeargin	60.00	25.00	15.00
(164)	Yelle	60.00	25.00	15.00

1926 Zeenut Pacific Coast League

Except for their slightly smaller size (1-3/4" x 3-7/16"), the 1926 Zeenut cards are nearly identical to the previous two years. Considered more difficult than other Zeenuts series of this era, the 1926 set consists of more than 170 known subjects.

		NM	EX	VG
Common Player:		40.00	20.00	12.00
(1)	Agnew	40.00	20.00	12.00
(2)	Allen	40.00	20.00	12.00
(3)	Alley	40.00	20.00	12.00
(4)	Averill	400.00	200.00	120.00
(5)	Bagwell	40.00	20.00	12.00
(6)	Baker	40.00	20.00	12.00
(7)	T. Baldwin	40.00	20.00	12.00
(8)	Berry	40.00	20.00	12.00
(9)	Bool	40.00	20.00	12.00
(10)	Boone	40.00	20.00	12.00
(11)	Boyd	40.00	20.00	12.00
(12)	Brady	40.00	20.00	12.00
(13)	Brazil	40.00	20.00	12.00
(14)	Brower	40.00	20.00	12.00
(15)	Brubaker	40.00	20.00	12.00
(16)	Bryan	40.00	20.00	12.00
(17)	Burns	40.00	20.00	12.00
(18)	C. Canfield	40.00	20.00	12.00
(19)	W. Canfield	40.00	20.00	12.00
(20)	Carson	40.00	20.00	12.00
(21)	Christian	40.00	20.00	12.00
(22)	Cole	40.00	20.00	12.00
(23)	Connolly	40.00	20.00	12.00
(24)	Cook	40.00	20.00	12.00
(25)	Couch	40.00	20.00	12.00
(26)	Coumbe	40.00	20.00	12.00
(27)	Crockett	40.00	20.00	12.00
(28)	Cunningham	40.00	20.00	12.00
(29)	Cutshaw	40.00	20.00	12.00
(30)	Daglia	40.00	20.00	12.00
(31)	Danning	40.00	20.00	12.00
(32)	Davis	40.00	20.00	12.00
(33)	Delaney	40.00	20.00	12.00
(34)	Eckert	40.00	20.00	12.00
(35)	Eldred	40.00	20.00	12.00
(36)	Elliott	40.00	20.00	12.00
(37)	Ellison	40.00	20.00	12.00
(38)	Ellsworth	40.00	20.00	12.00
(39)	Elsh	40.00	20.00	12.00
(40)	Fenton	40.00	20.00	12.00
(41)	Finn	40.00	20.00	12.00
(42)	Flashkamper	40.00	20.00	12.00
(43)	Fowler	40.00	20.00	12.00
(44)	Frederick	40.00	20.00	12.00
(45)	Freeman	40.00	20.00	12.00
(46)	French	40.00	20.00	12.00
(47)	Garrison	40.00	20.00	12.00
(48)	Geary	40.00	20.00	12.00
(49)	Gillespie	40.00	20.00	12.00
(50)	Glazner	40.00	20.00	12.00
(51)	Gould	40.00	20.00	12.00
(52)	Governor	40.00	20.00	12.00
(53)	Griffin (Missions)	40.00	20.00	12.00
(54)	Griffin (San Francisco)	40.00	20.00	12.00
(55)	Guisto	40.00	20.00	12.00
(56)	Hamilton	40.00	20.00	12.00
(57)	Hannah	40.00	20.00	12.00
(58)	Hansen	40.00	20.00	12.00
(59)	Hasty	40.00	20.00	12.00
(60)	Hemingway	40.00	20.00	12.00
(61)	Hendryx	40.00	20.00	12.00
(62)	Hickok	40.00	20.00	12.00
(63)	Hillis	40.00	20.00	12.00
(64)	Hoffman	40.00	20.00	12.00
(65)	Hollerson	40.00	20.00	12.00
(66)	Holmes	40.00	20.00	12.00
(67)	Hood	40.00	20.00	12.00
(68)	Howard	40.00	20.00	12.00
(69)	Hufft	40.00	20.00	12.00
(70)	Hughes	40.00	20.00	12.00
(71)	Hulvey	40.00	20.00	12.00
(72)	Hurst	40.00	20.00	12.00
(73)	R. Jacobs	40.00	20.00	12.00
(74)	Jahn	40.00	20.00	12.00
(75)	Jenkins	40.00	20.00	12.00
(76)	Johnson	40.00	20.00	12.00
(77)	Jolly (Jolley)	65.00	32.50	20.00
(78)	Jones	40.00	20.00	12.00
(79)	Kallio	40.00	20.00	12.00
(80)	Keating	40.00	20.00	12.00
(81)	Kerr (Hollywood)	40.00	20.00	12.00
(82)	Kerr (San Francisco)	40.00	20.00	12.00
(83)	Kilduff	40.00	20.00	12.00
(84)	Killifer	40.00	20.00	12.00
(85)	Knight	40.00	20.00	12.00
(86)	Koehler	40.00	20.00	12.00
(87)	Kopp	40.00	20.00	12.00
(88)	Krause	40.00	20.00	12.00
(89)	Krug	40.00	20.00	12.00
(90)	Kunz	40.00	20.00	12.00
(91)	Lafayette	40.00	20.00	12.00
(92)	Lane	40.00	20.00	12.00
(93)	Lang	40.00	20.00	12.00
(94)	Lary	40.00	20.00	12.00
(95)	Leslie	40.00	20.00	12.00
(96)	Lindemore	40.00	20.00	12.00
(97)	Ludolph	40.00	20.00	12.00
(98)	Makin	40.00	20.00	12.00
(99)	Mangum	40.00	20.00	12.00
(100)	Martin	40.00	20.00	12.00
(101)	McCredie	40.00	20.00	12.00
(102)	McDowell	40.00	20.00	12.00
(103)	McKenry	40.00	20.00	12.00
(104)	McLoughlin	40.00	20.00	12.00
(105)	McNally	40.00	20.00	12.00
(106)	McPhee	40.00	20.00	12.00
(107)	Meeker	40.00	20.00	12.00
(108)	Metz	40.00	20.00	12.00
(109)	Miller	40.00	20.00	12.00
(110)	Mitchell (Los Angeles)	40.00	20.00	12.00
(111)	Mitchell (San Francisco)	40.00	20.00	12.00
(112)	Monroe	40.00	20.00	12.00
(113)	Moudy	40.00	20.00	12.00
(114)	Mulcahy	40.00	20.00	12.00
(115)	Mulligan	40.00	20.00	12.00
(116)	Murphy	40.00	20.00	12.00
(117)	Lefty O'Doul	100.00	50.00	30.00
(118)	O'Neill	40.00	20.00	12.00
(119)	Oeschger	40.00	20.00	12.00
(120)	Oliver	40.00	20.00	12.00
(121)	Ortman	40.00	20.00	12.00
(122)	Osborn	40.00	20.00	12.00
(123)	Paynter	40.00	20.00	12.00
(124)	Peters	40.00	20.00	12.00
(125)	Pfahler	40.00	20.00	12.00
(126)	Pillette	40.00	20.00	12.00
(127)	Plummer	40.00	20.00	12.00
(128)	Prothro	40.00	20.00	12.00
(129)	Pruett	40.00	20.00	12.00
(130)	Rachac	40.00	20.00	12.00
(131)	Ramsey	40.00	20.00	12.00
(132)	Rathjen	40.00	20.00	12.00
(133)	Read	40.00	20.00	12.00
(134)	Redman	40.00	20.00	12.00
(135)	Jimmy Reese	40.00	20.00	12.00
(136)	Rodda	40.00	20.00	12.00
(137)	Rohwer	40.00	20.00	12.00
(138)	Ryan	40.00	20.00	12.00
(139)	Sandberg	40.00	20.00	12.00
(140)	Sanders	40.00	20.00	12.00
(141)	E. Shea	40.00	20.00	12.00
(142)	M. Shea	40.00	20.00	12.00
(143)	Sheehan	40.00	20.00	12.00
(144)	Shellenbach	40.00	20.00	12.00
(145)	Sherlock	40.00	20.00	12.00
(146)	Siglin	40.00	20.00	12.00
(147)	Slade	40.00	20.00	12.00
(148)	E. Smith	40.00	20.00	12.00
(149)	M. Smith	40.00	20.00	12.00
(150)	Staley	40.00	20.00	12.00
(151)	Statz	75.00	37.50	22.50
(152)	Stroud	40.00	20.00	12.00
(153)	Stuart	40.00	20.00	12.00
(154)	Suhr	40.00	20.00	12.00
(155)	Swanson	40.00	20.00	12.00
(156)	Sweeney	40.00	20.00	12.00
(157)	Tadevich	40.00	20.00	12.00
(158)	Thomas	40.00	20.00	12.00
(159)	Thompson	40.00	20.00	12.00
(160)	Tobin	40.00	20.00	12.00
(161)	Valla	40.00	20.00	12.00
(162)	Vargas	40.00	20.00	12.00
(163)	Vinci	40.00	20.00	12.00
(164)	Walters	40.00	20.00	12.00
(165)	Lloyd Waner	450.00	225.00	135.00
(166)	Weis	40.00	20.00	12.00
(167)	Whitney	40.00	20.00	12.00
(168)	Williams	40.00	20.00	12.00
(169)	Wright	40.00	20.00	12.00
(170)	Yelle	40.00	20.00	12.00
(171)	Zaeffel	40.00	20.00	12.00
(172)	Zoellers	40.00	20.00	12.00

1927 Zeenut Pacific Coast League

The 1927 Zeenuts are about the same size (1-3/4" x 3-3/8") and color as the 1926 issue, except the year is expressed in just two digits (27), a practice that continued through 1930. There are 144 subjects known.

		NM	EX	VG
Common Player:		40.00	20.00	12.00
With Coupon:		275.00	135.00	85.00
(1)	Agnew	40.00	20.00	12.00
(2)	Arlett	40.00	20.00	12.00
(3)	Averill	600.00	300.00	180.00
(4)	Backer	40.00	20.00	12.00
(5)	Bagwell	40.00	20.00	12.00
(6)	Baker	40.00	20.00	12.00
(7)	D. Baker	40.00	20.00	12.00
(8)	Ballenger	40.00	20.00	12.00
(9)	Baumgartner	40.00	20.00	12.00
(10)	Bigbee	40.00	20.00	12.00
(11)	Boehler	40.00	20.00	12.00
(12)	Bool	40.00	20.00	12.00
(13)	Borreani	40.00	20.00	12.00
(14)	Brady	40.00	20.00	12.00
(15)	Bratcher	40.00	20.00	12.00
(16)	Brett	40.00	20.00	12.00
(17)	Brown	40.00	20.00	12.00
(18)	Brubaker	40.00	20.00	12.00
(19)	Bryan	40.00	20.00	12.00
(20)	Callaghan	40.00	20.00	12.00
(21)	Caveney	40.00	20.00	12.00
(22)	Christian	40.00	20.00	12.00
(23)	Cissell	40.00	20.00	12.00
(24)	Cook	40.00	20.00	12.00
(25)	Cooper (Oakland)	40.00	20.00	12.00
(26)	Cooper (Sacramento)	40.00	20.00	12.00
(27)	Cox	40.00	20.00	12.00
(28)	Cunningham	40.00	20.00	12.00
(29)	Daglia	40.00	20.00	12.00
(30)	Dickerman	40.00	20.00	12.00
(31)	Dumovitch	40.00	20.00	12.00
(32)	Eckert	40.00	20.00	12.00
(33)	Eldred	40.00	20.00	12.00
(34)	Ellison	40.00	20.00	12.00
(35)	Fenton	40.00	20.00	12.00
(36)	Finn	40.00	20.00	12.00
(37)	Fischer	40.00	20.00	12.00
(38)	Frederick	40.00	20.00	12.00
(39)	French	40.00	20.00	12.00
(40)	Fullerton	40.00	20.00	12.00
(41)	Geary	40.00	20.00	12.00
(42)	Gillespie	40.00	20.00	12.00
(43)	Gooch	40.00	20.00	12.00
(44)	Gould	40.00	20.00	12.00
(45)	Governor	40.00	20.00	12.00
(46)	Guisto	40.00	20.00	12.00
(47)	Hannah	40.00	20.00	12.00
(48)	Hasty	40.00	20.00	12.00
(49)	Hemingway	40.00	20.00	12.00
(50)	Hoffman	40.00	20.00	12.00
(51)	Hood	40.00	20.00	12.00
(52)	Hooper	450.00	225.00	135.00
(53)	Hudgens	40.00	20.00	12.00
(54)	Hufft	40.00	20.00	12.00
(55)	Hughes	40.00	20.00	12.00
(56)	Jahn	40.00	20.00	12.00
(57)	Johnson (Portland)	40.00	20.00	12.00
(58)	Johnson (Seals)	40.00	20.00	12.00
(59)	Jolly (Jolley)	60.00	30.00	18.00
(60)	Jones	40.00	20.00	12.00
(61)	Kallio	40.00	20.00	12.00
(62)	Keating	40.00	20.00	12.00
(63)	Keefe	40.00	20.00	12.00
(64)	Killifer	40.00	20.00	12.00
(65)	Kimmick	40.00	20.00	12.00
(66)	Kinney	40.00	20.00	12.00
(67)	Knight	40.00	20.00	12.00
(68)	Koehler	40.00	20.00	12.00
(69)	Kopp	40.00	20.00	12.00
(70)	Krause	40.00	20.00	12.00
(71)	Krug	40.00	20.00	12.00
(72)	Kunz	40.00	20.00	12.00
(73)	Lary	40.00	20.00	12.00
(74)	Leard	40.00	20.00	12.00
(75)	Lingrel	40.00	20.00	12.00
(76)	Ludolph	40.00	20.00	12.00
(77)	Mails	40.00	20.00	12.00
(78)	Makin	40.00	20.00	12.00
(79)	Martin	40.00	20.00	12.00
(80)	May	40.00	20.00	12.00
(81)	McCabe	40.00	20.00	12.00
(82)	McCurdy	40.00	20.00	12.00
(83)	McDaniel	40.00	20.00	12.00
(84)	McGee	40.00	20.00	12.00
(85)	McLaughlin	40.00	20.00	12.00
(86)	McMurtry	40.00	20.00	12.00
(87)	Metz	40.00	20.00	12.00
(88)	Miljus	40.00	20.00	12.00
(89)	Mitchell	40.00	20.00	12.00
(90)	Monroe	40.00	20.00	12.00
(91)	Moudy	40.00	20.00	12.00
(92)	Mulligan	40.00	20.00	12.00
(93)	Murphy	40.00	20.00	12.00
(94)	O'Brien	40.00	20.00	12.00
(95)	Lefty O'Doul	250.00	125.00	75.00
(96)	Oliver	40.00	20.00	12.00
(97)	Osborn	40.00	20.00	12.00
(98)	Parker/Btg (Missions)	40.00	20.00	12.00
(99)	Parker/Throwing (Missions)	40.00	20.00	12.00
(100)	Parker (Portland)	40.00	20.00	12.00
(101)	Peters	40.00	20.00	12.00
(102)	Pillette	40.00	20.00	12.00
(103)	Ponder	40.00	20.00	12.00
(104)	Prothro	80.00	40.00	25.00
(105)	Rachac	40.00	20.00	12.00
(106)	Ramsey	40.00	20.00	12.00
(107)	Read	40.00	20.00	12.00
(108)	Jimmy Reese	250.00	125.00	75.00
(109)	Rodda	40.00	20.00	12.00
(110)	Rohwer	40.00	20.00	12.00
(111)	Rose	40.00	20.00	12.00
(112)	Ryan	40.00	20.00	12.00
(113)	Sandberg	40.00	20.00	12.00
(114)	Sanders	40.00	20.00	12.00
(115)	Severeid	40.00	20.00	12.00
(116)	Shea	40.00	20.00	12.00
(117)	Sheehan (Hollywood)	40.00	20.00	12.00
(118)	Sheehan (Seals)	40.00	20.00	12.00
(119)	Sherlock	40.00	20.00	12.00
(120a)	Shinners (Date is "1927.")	40.00	20.00	12.00
(120b)	Shinners (Date is "27.")	40.00	20.00	12.00
(121)	Singleton	40.00	20.00	12.00
(122)	Slade	40.00	20.00	12.00
(123)	E. Smith	40.00	20.00	12.00
(124)	Sparks	40.00	20.00	12.00
(125)	Stokes	40.00	20.00	12.00
(126)	J. Storti	40.00	20.00	12.00
(127)	L. Storti	40.00	20.00	12.00
(128)	Strand	40.00	20.00	12.00
(129)	Suhr	40.00	20.00	12.00
(130)	Sunseri	40.00	20.00	12.00
(131)	Swanson	40.00	20.00	12.00
(132)	Tierney	40.00	20.00	12.00
(133)	Valla	40.00	20.00	12.00
(134)	Vargas	40.00	20.00	12.00
(135)	Vitt	40.00	20.00	12.00
(136)	Weinert	40.00	20.00	12.00
(137)	Weis	40.00	20.00	12.00
(138)	Wendell	40.00	20.00	12.00
(139)	Whitney	40.00	20.00	12.00
(140)	Williams	40.00	20.00	12.00
(141)	Guy Williams	40.00	20.00	12.00
(142)	Woodson	40.00	20.00	12.00
(143)	Wright	40.00	20.00	12.00
(144)	Yelle	40.00	20.00	12.00

1928 Zeenut Pacific Coast League

Zeenut cards from 1928 through 1930 maintain the same format as the 1927 series. Measuring about 1-3/4" x 3-3/8", the 1928 series consists of 168 known subjects.

		NM	EX	VG
Common Player:		40.00	20.00	12.00
(1)	Agnew	40.00	20.00	12.00
(2)	Earl Averill	300.00	150.00	90.00
(3)	Backer	40.00	20.00	12.00
(4)	Baker	40.00	20.00	12.00
(5)	Baldwin	40.00	20.00	12.00
(6)	Barfoot	40.00	20.00	12.00
(7)	Bassler	40.00	20.00	12.00
(8)	Berger	40.00	20.00	12.00
(9)	Bigbee (Los Angeles)	40.00	20.00	12.00
(10)	Bigbee (Portland)	40.00	20.00	12.00
(11)	Bodie	40.00	20.00	12.00
(12)	Boehler	40.00	20.00	12.00
(13)	Bool	40.00	20.00	12.00
(14)	Boone	40.00	20.00	12.00
(15)	Borreani	40.00	20.00	12.00
(16)	Bratcher	40.00	20.00	12.00
(17)	Brenzel	40.00	20.00	12.00
(18)	Brubaker	40.00	20.00	12.00
(19)	Bryan	40.00	20.00	12.00
(20)	Burkett	40.00	20.00	12.00
(21)	Camilli	40.00	20.00	12.00
(22)	W. Canfield	40.00	20.00	12.00
(23)	Caveney	40.00	20.00	12.00
(24)	Cohen	100.00	50.00	30.00
(25)	Cook	40.00	20.00	12.00
(26)	Cooper	40.00	20.00	12.00
(27)	Craghead	40.00	20.00	12.00
(28)	Crosetti	200.00	100.00	60.00
(29)	Cunningham	40.00	20.00	12.00
(30)	Daglia	40.00	20.00	12.00
(31)	Davis	40.00	20.00	12.00
(32)	Dean	40.00	20.00	12.00
(33)	Dittmar	40.00	20.00	12.00
(34)	Donovan	40.00	20.00	12.00
(35)	Downs	40.00	20.00	12.00
(36)	Duff	40.00	20.00	12.00
(37)	Eckert	40.00	20.00	12.00
(38)	Eldred	40.00	20.00	12.00
(39)	Ellsworth	40.00	20.00	12.00
(40)	Fenton	40.00	20.00	12.00
(41)	Finn	40.00	20.00	12.00
(42)	Fitterer	40.00	20.00	12.00
(43)	Flynn	40.00	20.00	12.00
(44)	Frazier	40.00	20.00	12.00
(45)	French (Portland)	40.00	20.00	12.00
(46)	French (Sacramento)	40.00	20.00	12.00
(47)	Fullerton	40.00	20.00	12.00
(48)	Gabler	40.00	20.00	12.00
(49)	Gomes	40.00	20.00	12.00
(50)	Gooch	40.00	20.00	12.00
(51)	Gould	40.00	20.00	12.00
(52)	Governor	40.00	20.00	12.00
(53)	Graham ("S" on uniform.)	40.00	20.00	12.00
(54)	Graham (No "S" on uniform.)	40.00	20.00	12.00
(55)	Guisto	40.00	20.00	12.00
(56)	Hannah	40.00	20.00	12.00
(57)	Hansen	40.00	20.00	12.00
(58)	Harris	40.00	20.00	12.00
(59)	Hasty	40.00	20.00	12.00
(60)	Heath	40.00	20.00	12.00
(61)	Hoffman	40.00	20.00	12.00
(62)	Holling	40.00	20.00	12.00
(63)	Hood	40.00	20.00	12.00
(64)	House	40.00	20.00	12.00
(65)	Howard	40.00	20.00	12.00
(66)	Hudgens	40.00	20.00	12.00
(67)	Hufft	40.00	20.00	12.00
(68)	Hughes	40.00	20.00	12.00
(69)	Hulvey	40.00	20.00	12.00
(70)	Jacobs	40.00	20.00	12.00
(71)	Johnson (Portland)	40.00	20.00	12.00
(72)	Johnson (San Francisco)	40.00	20.00	12.00
(73)	Jolley	60.00	30.00	18.00
(74)	Jones/Btg	40.00	20.00	12.00
(75)	Jones/Throwing	40.00	20.00	12.00
(76)	Kallio	40.00	20.00	12.00
(77)	Keating	40.00	20.00	12.00
(78)	Keefe	40.00	20.00	12.00
(79)	Keesey	40.00	20.00	12.00
(80)	Kerr	40.00	20.00	12.00
(81)	Killifer	40.00	20.00	12.00
(82)	Kinney	40.00	20.00	12.00
(83)	Knight	40.00	20.00	12.00
(84)	Knothe	40.00	20.00	12.00
(85)	Koehler	40.00	20.00	12.00
(86)	Kopp	40.00	20.00	12.00
(87)	Krause	40.00	20.00	12.00
(88)	Krug	40.00	20.00	12.00
(89)	Lary	40.00	20.00	12.00
(90)	LeBourveau	40.00	20.00	12.00
(91)	Lee	40.00	20.00	12.00
(92)	Ernie Lombardi	900.00	450.00	275.00
(93)	Mails	40.00	20.00	12.00
(94)	Martin (Missions)	40.00	20.00	12.00
(95)	Martin (Seattle)	40.00	20.00	12.00
(96)	May	40.00	20.00	12.00
(97)	McCabe	40.00	20.00	12.00
(98)	McCrea	40.00	20.00	12.00
(99)	McDaniel	40.00	20.00	12.00
(100)	McLaughlin	40.00	20.00	12.00
(101)	McNulty	40.00	20.00	12.00
(102)	Mellano	40.00	20.00	12.00
(103)	Irish Muesel (Meusel)	40.00	20.00	12.00
(104)	Middleton	40.00	20.00	12.00
(105)	Mishkin	40.00	20.00	12.00
(106)	Mitchell	40.00	20.00	12.00
(107)	Monroe	40.00	20.00	12.00
(108)	Moudy	40.00	20.00	12.00
(109)	Mulcahy	40.00	20.00	12.00
(110)	Muller	40.00	20.00	12.00
(111)	Mulligan	40.00	20.00	12.00
(112)	W. Murphy	40.00	20.00	12.00
(113)	Nance	40.00	20.00	12.00
(114)	Nelson	40.00	20.00	12.00
(115)	Osborn	40.00	20.00	12.00
(116)	Osborne	40.00	20.00	12.00
(117)	Parker	40.00	20.00	12.00
(118)	Peters	40.00	20.00	12.00
(119)	Pillette	40.00	20.00	12.00
(120)	Pinelli	40.00	20.00	12.00
(121)	Plitt	40.00	20.00	12.00
(122)	Ponder	40.00	20.00	12.00
(123)	Rachac	40.00	20.00	12.00
(124)	Read	40.00	20.00	12.00
(125)	Reed	40.00	20.00	12.00
(126)	Jimmy Reese	150.00	75.00	45.00
(127)	Rego	40.00	20.00	12.00
(128)	Rhodes	40.00	20.00	12.00
(129)	Rhyne	40.00	20.00	12.00
(130)	Rodda	40.00	20.00	12.00
(131)	Rohwer	40.00	20.00	12.00
(132)	Rose	40.00	20.00	12.00
(133)	Roth	40.00	20.00	12.00
(134)	Ruble	40.00	20.00	12.00
(135)	Ryan	40.00	20.00	12.00
(136)	Sandberg	40.00	20.00	12.00
(137)	Schulmerich	40.00	20.00	12.00
(138)	Severeid	40.00	20.00	12.00
(139)	Shea	40.00	20.00	12.00
(140)	Sheely	40.00	20.00	12.00
(141)	Shellenback	40.00	20.00	12.00
(142)	Sherlock	40.00	20.00	12.00
(143)	Sigafoos	40.00	20.00	12.00
(144)	Singleton	40.00	20.00	12.00
(145)	Slade	40.00	20.00	12.00
(146)	Smith	40.00	20.00	12.00
(147)	Sprinz	40.00	20.00	12.00
(148)	Staley	40.00	20.00	12.00

(149) Suhr	40.00	20.00	12.00
(150) Sunseri	40.00	20.00	12.00
(151) Swanson	40.00	20.00	12.00
(152) Sweeney	40.00	20.00	12.00
(153) Teachout	40.00	20.00	12.00
(154) Twombly	40.00	20.00	12.00
(155) Vargas	40.00	20.00	12.00
(156) Vinci	40.00	20.00	12.00
(157) Vitt	40.00	20.00	12.00
(158) Warhop	40.00	20.00	12.00
(159) Weathersby	40.00	20.00	12.00
(160) Weiss	40.00	20.00	12.00
(161) Welch	40.00	20.00	12.00
(162) Wera	40.00	20.00	12.00
(163) Wetzel	40.00	20.00	12.00
(164) Whitney	40.00	20.00	12.00
(165) Williams	40.00	20.00	12.00
(166) Wilson	40.00	20.00	12.00
(167) Wolfer	40.00	20.00	12.00
(168) Yerkes	40.00	20.00	12.00

1929 Zeenut Pacific Coast League

Zeenut cards from 1928 through 1930 maintain the same format as the 1927 series. Measuring about 1-3/4" x 3-1/2", the 1929 series consists of 168 known subjects.

	NM	EX	VG
Common Player:	40.00	20.00	12.00
With Coupon:	400.00	200.00	120.00
(1) Albert	40.00	20.00	12.00
(2) Almada	100.00	50.00	30.00
(3) Anderson	40.00	20.00	12.00
(4) Anton	40.00	20.00	12.00
(5) Backer	40.00	20.00	12.00
(6) Baker	40.00	20.00	12.00
(7) Baldwin	40.00	20.00	12.00
(8) Barbee	40.00	20.00	12.00
(9) Barfoot	40.00	20.00	12.00
(10) Bassler	40.00	20.00	12.00
(11) Bates	40.00	20.00	12.00
(12) Berger	40.00	20.00	12.00
(13) Boehler	40.00	20.00	12.00
(14) Boone	40.00	20.00	12.00
(15) Borreani	40.00	20.00	12.00
(16) Brenzel	40.00	20.00	12.00
(17) Brooks	40.00	20.00	12.00
(18) Brubaker	40.00	20.00	12.00
(19) Bryan	40.00	20.00	12.00
(20) Burke	40.00	20.00	12.00
(21) Burkett	40.00	20.00	12.00
(22) Burns	40.00	20.00	12.00
(23) Bush	40.00	20.00	12.00
(24) Butler	40.00	20.00	12.00
(25) Camilli	40.00	20.00	12.00
(26) Carlyle (Hollywood)	40.00	20.00	12.00
(27) Carlyle	40.00	20.00	12.00
(28) Cascarella	40.00	20.00	12.00
(29) Caveney	40.00	20.00	12.00
(30) Childs	40.00	20.00	12.00
(31) Christensen	40.00	20.00	12.00
(32) Cole	40.00	20.00	12.00
(33) Collard	40.00	20.00	12.00
(34) Cooper	40.00	20.00	12.00
(35) Couch	40.00	20.00	12.00
(36) Cox	40.00	20.00	12.00
(37) Craghead	40.00	20.00	12.00
(38) Crandall	40.00	20.00	12.00
(39) Cronin	40.00	20.00	12.00
(40) Crosetti	100.00	50.00	30.00
(41) Daglia	40.00	20.00	12.00
(42) Davis	40.00	20.00	12.00
(43) Dean	40.00	20.00	12.00
(44) Dittmar	40.00	20.00	12.00
(45) Donovan	40.00	20.00	12.00
(46) Dumovich	40.00	20.00	12.00
(47) Eckardt	40.00	20.00	12.00
(48) Ellsworth	40.00	20.00	12.00
(49) Fenton	40.00	20.00	12.00
(50) Finn	40.00	20.00	12.00
(51) Fisch	40.00	20.00	12.00
(52) Flynn	40.00	20.00	12.00
(53) Frazier	40.00	20.00	12.00
(54) Freitas	40.00	20.00	12.00
(55) French	40.00	20.00	12.00
(56) Gabler	40.00	20.00	12.00
(57) Glynn	40.00	20.00	12.00
(58) Lefty Gomez	1,200	600.00	360.00
(59) Gould	40.00	20.00	12.00
(60) Governor	40.00	20.00	12.00
(61) Graham	40.00	20.00	12.00
(62) Hand	40.00	20.00	12.00
(63) Hannah	40.00	20.00	12.00
(64) Harris	40.00	20.00	12.00
(65) Heath	40.00	20.00	12.00
(66) Heatherly	40.00	20.00	12.00
(67) Hepting	40.00	20.00	12.00
(68) Hillis	40.00	20.00	12.00
(69) Hoffman	40.00	20.00	12.00
(70) Holling	40.00	20.00	12.00
(71) Hood	40.00	20.00	12.00
(72) House	40.00	20.00	12.00
(73) Howard	40.00	20.00	12.00
(74) Hubbell	40.00	20.00	12.00
(75) Hufft	40.00	20.00	12.00
(76) Hurst	40.00	20.00	12.00
(77) Jacobs (Los Angeles)	40.00	20.00	12.00
(78) Jacobs (San Francisco)	40.00	20.00	12.00
(79) Jahn	40.00	20.00	12.00
(80) Jeffcoat	40.00	20.00	12.00
(81) Johnson	40.00	20.00	12.00
(82) Jolley	60.00	30.00	18.00
(83) Jones	40.00	20.00	12.00
(84) Jones	40.00	20.00	12.00
(85) Kallio	40.00	20.00	12.00
(86) Kasich	40.00	20.00	12.00
(87) Keane	40.00	20.00	12.00
(88) Keating	40.00	20.00	12.00
(89) Keesey	40.00	20.00	12.00
(90) Killifer	40.00	20.00	12.00
(91) Knight	40.00	20.00	12.00
(92) Knothe	40.00	20.00	12.00
(93) Knott	40.00	20.00	12.00
(94) Koehler	40.00	20.00	12.00
(95) Krasovich	40.00	20.00	12.00
(96) Krause	40.00	20.00	12.00
(97) Krug (Hollywood)	40.00	20.00	12.00
(98) Krug (Los Angeles)	40.00	20.00	12.00
(99) Kunz	40.00	20.00	12.00
(100) Langford	40.00	20.00	12.00
(101) Lee	40.00	20.00	12.00
(102) Ernie Lombardi	450.00	225.00	135.00
(103) Mahaffey	40.00	20.00	12.00
(104) Mails	40.00	20.00	12.00
(105) Maloney	40.00	20.00	12.00
(106) McCabe	40.00	20.00	12.00
(107) McDaniel	40.00	20.00	12.00
(108) McEvoy	40.00	20.00	12.00
(109) McIssacs	40.00	20.00	12.00
(110) McQuaid	40.00	20.00	12.00
(111) Miller	40.00	20.00	12.00
(112) Monroe	40.00	20.00	12.00
(113) Muller	40.00	20.00	12.00
(114) Mulligan	40.00	20.00	12.00
(115) Nance	40.00	20.00	12.00
(116) Nelson	40.00	20.00	12.00
(117) Nevers	40.00	20.00	12.00
(118) Oana	450.00	225.00	135.00
(119) Olney	40.00	20.00	12.00
(120) Ortman	40.00	20.00	12.00
(121) Osborne	40.00	20.00	12.00
(122) Ostenberg	40.00	20.00	12.00
(123) Peters	40.00	20.00	12.00
(124) Pillette	40.00	20.00	12.00
(125) Pinelli	40.00	20.00	12.00
(126) Pipgras	40.00	20.00	12.00
(127) Plitt	40.00	20.00	12.00
(128) Polvogt	40.00	20.00	12.00
(129) Rachac	40.00	20.00	12.00
(130) Read	40.00	20.00	12.00
(131) Reed	40.00	20.00	12.00
(132) Jimmy Reese	100.00	50.00	30.00
(133) Rego	40.00	20.00	12.00
(134) Ritter	40.00	20.00	12.00
(135) Roberts	40.00	20.00	12.00
(136) Rodda	40.00	20.00	12.00
(137) Rodgers	40.00	20.00	12.00
(138) Rohwer	40.00	20.00	12.00
(139) Rollings	40.00	20.00	12.00
(140) Rumler	40.00	20.00	12.00
(141) Ryan	40.00	20.00	12.00
(142) Sandberg	40.00	20.00	12.00
(143) Schino	40.00	20.00	12.00
(144) Schmidt	40.00	20.00	12.00
(145) Schulmerich	40.00	20.00	12.00
(146) Scott	40.00	20.00	12.00
(147) Severeid	40.00	20.00	12.00
(148) Shanklin	40.00	20.00	12.00
(149) Sherlock	40.00	20.00	12.00
(150) Slade	40.00	20.00	12.00
(151) Staley	40.00	20.00	12.00
(152) Statz	60.00	30.00	18.00
(153) Steinecke	40.00	20.00	12.00
(154) Suhr	40.00	20.00	12.00
(155) Taylor	40.00	20.00	12.00
(156) Thurston	40.00	20.00	12.00
(157) Tierney	40.00	20.00	12.00
(158) Tolson	40.00	20.00	12.00
(159) Tomlin	40.00	20.00	12.00
(160) Vergez	40.00	20.00	12.00
(161) Vinci	40.00	20.00	12.00
(162) Volkman	40.00	20.00	12.00
(163) Walsh	40.00	20.00	12.00
(164) Warren	40.00	20.00	12.00
(165) Webb	40.00	20.00	12.00
(166) Weustling	40.00	20.00	12.00
(167) Williams	40.00	20.00	12.00
(168) Wingo	40.00	20.00	12.00

1930 Zeenut Pacific Coast League

Zeenut cards from 1928 through 1930 maintain the same format as the 1927 series. Measuring about 1-13/16" x 3-1/2", the 1930 series consists of 186 known subjects. There are some lettering variations in the series. Most coupons carry an expiration date of April 1, 1931, but some coupons have no expiration date stated.

	NM	EX	VG
Common Player:	40.00	20.00	12.00
(1) Allington	40.00	20.00	12.00
(2) Almada	50.00	25.00	15.00
(3) Andrews	40.00	20.00	12.00
(4) Anton	40.00	20.00	12.00
(5) Arlett	40.00	20.00	12.00
(6) Backer	40.00	20.00	12.00
(7) Baecht	40.00	20.00	12.00
(8) Baker	40.00	20.00	12.00
(9) Baldwin	40.00	20.00	12.00
(10) Ballou	40.00	20.00	12.00
(11) Barbee	40.00	20.00	12.00
(12) Barfoot	40.00	20.00	12.00
(13) Bassler	40.00	20.00	12.00
(14) Bates	40.00	20.00	12.00
(15) Beck	40.00	20.00	12.00
(16) Boone	40.00	20.00	12.00
(17) Bowman	40.00	20.00	12.00
(18) Brannon	40.00	20.00	12.00
(19) Brenzel	40.00	20.00	12.00
(20) Brown	40.00	20.00	12.00
(21) Brubaker	40.00	20.00	12.00
(22) Brucker	40.00	20.00	12.00
(23) Bryan	40.00	20.00	12.00
(24) Burkett	40.00	20.00	12.00
(25) Burns	40.00	20.00	12.00
(26) Butler	40.00	20.00	12.00
(27) Camilli	40.00	20.00	12.00
(28) Carlyle	40.00	20.00	12.00
(29) Caster	40.00	20.00	12.00
(30) Caveney	40.00	20.00	12.00
(31) Chamberlain	40.00	20.00	12.00
(32) Chatham	40.00	20.00	12.00
(33) Childs	40.00	20.00	12.00
(34) Christensen	40.00	20.00	12.00
(35) Church	40.00	20.00	12.00
(36) Cole	40.00	20.00	12.00
(37) Coleman	40.00	20.00	12.00
(38) Collins	40.00	20.00	12.00
(39) Coscarart	40.00	20.00	12.00
(40) Cox	40.00	20.00	12.00
(41) Coyle	40.00	20.00	12.00
(42) Craghead	40.00	20.00	12.00
(43) Cronin	40.00	20.00	12.00
(44) Crosetti	100.00	50.00	30.00
(45) Daglia	40.00	20.00	12.00
(46) Davis	40.00	20.00	12.00
(47) Dean	40.00	20.00	12.00
(48) DeViveiros	40.00	20.00	12.00
(49) Dittmar	40.00	20.00	12.00
(50) Donovan	40.00	20.00	12.00
(51) Douglas	40.00	20.00	12.00
(52) Dumovich	40.00	20.00	12.00
(53) Edwards	40.00	20.00	12.00
(54) Ellsworth	40.00	20.00	12.00
(55) Falk	40.00	20.00	12.00
(56) Fisch	40.00	20.00	12.00
(57) Flynn	40.00	20.00	12.00
(58) Freitas	40.00	20.00	12.00
(59) French (Portland)	40.00	20.00	12.00
(60) French (Sacramento)	40.00	20.00	12.00
(61) Gabler	40.00	20.00	12.00
(62) Gaston	40.00	20.00	12.00
(63) Gazella	40.00	20.00	12.00
(64) Gould	40.00	20.00	12.00
(65) Governor	40.00	20.00	12.00
(66) Green	40.00	20.00	12.00
(67) Griffin	40.00	20.00	12.00
(68) Haney	40.00	20.00	12.00
(69) Hannah	40.00	20.00	12.00
(70) Harper	40.00	20.00	12.00
(71) Heath	40.00	20.00	12.00
(72) Hillis	40.00	20.00	12.00
(73) Hoag	40.00	20.00	12.00
(74) Hoffman	40.00	20.00	12.00
(75) Holland	40.00	20.00	12.00
(76) Hollerson	40.00	20.00	12.00
(77) Holling	40.00	20.00	12.00
(78) Hood	40.00	20.00	12.00
(79) Horn	40.00	20.00	12.00
(80) House	40.00	20.00	12.00
(81) Hubbell	40.00	20.00	12.00
(82) Hufft	40.00	20.00	12.00
(83) Hurst	40.00	20.00	12.00
(84) Jacobs (Los Angeles)	40.00	20.00	12.00
(85) Jacobs (Oakland)	40.00	20.00	12.00
(86) Jacobs	40.00	20.00	12.00
(87) Jahn	40.00	20.00	12.00
(88) Jeffcoat	40.00	20.00	12.00
(89) Johns	40.00	20.00	12.00
(90) Johnson (Portland)	40.00	20.00	12.00
(91) Johnson (Seattle)	40.00	20.00	12.00
(92) Joiner	40.00	20.00	12.00

(93)	Kallio	40.00	20.00	12.00
(94)	Kasich	40.00	20.00	12.00
(95)	Keating	40.00	20.00	12.00
(96)	Kelly	40.00	20.00	12.00
(97)	Killifer	40.00	20.00	12.00
(98)	Knight	40.00	20.00	12.00
(99)	Knothe	40.00	20.00	12.00
(100)	Koehler	40.00	20.00	12.00
(101)	Kunz	40.00	20.00	12.00
(102)	Lamanski	40.00	20.00	12.00
(103)	Lawrence	40.00	20.00	12.00
(104)	Lee	40.00	20.00	12.00
(105)	Leishman	40.00	20.00	12.00
(106)	Lelivelt	40.00	20.00	12.00
(107)	Lieber	40.00	20.00	12.00
(108)	Ernie Lombardi	450.00	225.00	135.00
(109)	Mails	40.00	20.00	12.00
(110)	Maloney	40.00	20.00	12.00
(111)	Martin	40.00	20.00	12.00
(112)	McDougal	40.00	20.00	12.00
(113)	McLaughlin	40.00	20.00	12.00
(114)	McQuaide	40.00	20.00	12.00
(115)	Mellana	40.00	20.00	12.00
(116)	Miljus ("S" on uniform.)	40.00	20.00	12.00
(117)	Miljus ("Seals" on uniform.)	40.00	20.00	12.00
(118)	Monroe	40.00	20.00	12.00
(119)	Montgomery	40.00	20.00	12.00
(120)	Moore	40.00	20.00	12.00
(121)	Mulana	40.00	20.00	12.00
(122)	Muller	40.00	20.00	12.00
(123)	Mulligan	40.00	20.00	12.00
(124)	Nelson	40.00	20.00	12.00
(125)	Nevers	750.00	375.00	225.00
(126)	Odell	40.00	20.00	12.00
(127)	Olney	40.00	20.00	12.00
(128)	Osborne	40.00	20.00	12.00
(129)	Page	40.00	20.00	12.00
(130)	Palmisano	40.00	20.00	12.00
(131)	Parker	40.00	20.00	12.00
(132)	Pasedel	40.00	20.00	12.00
(133)	Pearson	40.00	20.00	12.00
(134)	Penebskey	40.00	20.00	12.00
(135)	Perry	40.00	20.00	12.00
(136)	Peters	40.00	20.00	12.00
(137)	Petterson	40.00	20.00	12.00
(138)	H. Pillette	40.00	20.00	12.00
(139)	T. Pillette	40.00	20.00	12.00
(140)	Pinelli	40.00	20.00	12.00
(141)	Pipgrass	40.00	20.00	12.00
(142)	Porter	40.00	20.00	12.00
(143)	Powles	40.00	20.00	12.00
(144)	Read	40.00	20.00	12.00
(145)	Reed	40.00	20.00	12.00
(146)	Rehg	40.00	20.00	12.00
(147)	Ricci	40.00	20.00	12.00
(148)	Roberts	40.00	20.00	12.00
(149)	Rodda	40.00	20.00	12.00
(150)	Rohwer	40.00	20.00	12.00
(151)	Rosenberg	2,500	1,250	750.00
(152)	Rumler	40.00	20.00	12.00
(153)	Ryan	40.00	20.00	12.00
(154)	Schino	40.00	20.00	12.00
(155)	Severeid	40.00	20.00	12.00
(156)	Shanklin	40.00	20.00	12.00
(157)	Sheely	40.00	20.00	12.00
(158)	Sigafoos	40.00	20.00	12.00
(159)	Statz	60.00	30.00	18.00
(160)	Steinbacker	40.00	20.00	12.00
(161)	Stevenson	40.00	20.00	12.00
(162)	Sulik	40.00	20.00	12.00
(163)	Taylor	40.00	20.00	12.00
(164)	Thomas (Sacramento)	40.00	20.00	12.00
(165)	Thomas (San Francisco)	40.00	20.00	12.00
(166)	Trembly	40.00	20.00	12.00
(167)	Turner	40.00	20.00	12.00
(168)	Turpin	40.00	20.00	12.00
(169)	Uhalt	40.00	20.00	12.00
(170)	Vergez	40.00	20.00	12.00
(171)	Vinci	40.00	20.00	12.00
(172)	Vitt	40.00	20.00	12.00
(173)	Wallgren	40.00	20.00	12.00
(174)	Walsh	40.00	20.00	12.00
(175)	Ward	40.00	20.00	12.00
(176)	Warren	40.00	20.00	12.00
(177)	Webb	40.00	20.00	12.00
(178)	Wetzell	40.00	20.00	12.00
(179)	F. Wetzel	40.00	20.00	12.00
(180)	Williams	40.00	20.00	12.00
(181)	Wilson	40.00	20.00	12.00
(182)	Wingo	40.00	20.00	12.00
(183)	Wirts	40.00	20.00	12.00
(184)	Woodall	40.00	20.00	12.00
(185)	Zamlack	40.00	20.00	12.00
(186)	Zinn	40.00	20.00	12.00

1931 Zeenut Pacific Coast League

Beginning in 1931, Zeenuts cards were no longer dated on the front, and cards without the coupon are very difficult to date. The words "Zeenuts Series" were also dropped from the front and replaced with the words "Coast League." Zeenut cards in 1931 measure 1-3/4" x 3-1/2".

		NM	EX	VG
Common Player:		40.00	20.00	12.00
With Coupon:		800.00	400.00	240.00
(1)	Abbott	40.00	20.00	12.00
(2)	Andrews	40.00	20.00	12.00
(3)	Anton	40.00	20.00	12.00
(4)	Backer	40.00	20.00	12.00
(5)	Baker	40.00	20.00	12.00
(6)	Baldwin	40.00	20.00	12.00
(7)	Barbee	40.00	20.00	12.00
(8)	Barton	40.00	20.00	12.00
(9)	Bassler	40.00	20.00	12.00
(10)	Berger (Missions)	40.00	20.00	12.00
(11)	Berger (Portland)	40.00	20.00	12.00
(12)	Biggs	40.00	20.00	12.00
(13)	Bowman	40.00	20.00	12.00
(14)	Brenzel	40.00	20.00	12.00
(15)	Bryan	40.00	20.00	12.00
(16)	Burns	40.00	20.00	12.00
(17)	Camilli	40.00	20.00	12.00
(18)	Campbell	40.00	20.00	12.00
(19)	Carlyle	40.00	20.00	12.00
(20)	Caveney	40.00	20.00	12.00
(21)	Chesterfield	40.00	20.00	12.00
(22)	Cole	40.00	20.00	12.00
(23)	Coleman	40.00	20.00	12.00
(24)	Coscarart	40.00	20.00	12.00
(25)	Crosetti	200.00	100.00	60.00
(26)	Davis	40.00	20.00	12.00
(27)	DeBerry	40.00	20.00	12.00
(28)	Demaree	40.00	20.00	12.00
(29)	Dean	40.00	20.00	12.00
(30)	Delaney	40.00	20.00	12.00
(31)	Dondero	40.00	20.00	12.00
(32)	Donovan	40.00	20.00	12.00
(33)	Douglas	40.00	20.00	12.00
(34)	Ellsworth	40.00	20.00	12.00
(35)	Farrell	40.00	20.00	12.00
(36)	Fenton	40.00	20.00	12.00
(37)	Fitzpatrick	40.00	20.00	12.00
(38)	Flagstead	40.00	20.00	12.00
(39)	Flynn	40.00	20.00	12.00
(40)	Frazier	40.00	20.00	12.00
(41)	Freitas	40.00	20.00	12.00
(42)	French	40.00	20.00	12.00
(43)	Fullerton	40.00	20.00	12.00
(44)	Gabler	40.00	20.00	12.00
(45)	Gazella	40.00	20.00	12.00
(46)	Hale	40.00	20.00	12.00
(47)	Hamilton	40.00	20.00	12.00
(48)	Haney	40.00	20.00	12.00
(49)	Hannah	40.00	20.00	12.00
(50)	Harper	40.00	20.00	12.00
(51)	Henderson	40.00	20.00	12.00
(52)	Herrmann	40.00	20.00	12.00
(53)	Hoffman	40.00	20.00	12.00
(54)	Holland	40.00	20.00	12.00
(55)	Holling	40.00	20.00	12.00
(56)	Hubbell	40.00	20.00	12.00
(57)	Hufft	40.00	20.00	12.00
(58)	Hurst	40.00	20.00	12.00
(59)	Jacobs	40.00	20.00	12.00
(60)	Kallio	40.00	20.00	12.00
(61)	Keating	40.00	20.00	12.00
(62)	Keesey	40.00	20.00	12.00
(63)	Knothe	40.00	20.00	12.00
(64)	Knott	40.00	20.00	12.00
(65)	Kohler	40.00	20.00	12.00
(66)	Lamanski	40.00	20.00	12.00
(67)	Lee	40.00	20.00	12.00
(68)	Lelivelt	40.00	20.00	12.00
(69)	Lieber	40.00	20.00	12.00
(70)	Lipanovic	40.00	20.00	12.00
(71)	McDonald	40.00	20.00	12.00
(72)	McDougall	40.00	20.00	12.00
(73)	McLaughlin	40.00	20.00	12.00
(74)	Monroe	40.00	20.00	12.00
(75)	Moss	40.00	20.00	12.00
(76)	Mulligan	40.00	20.00	12.00
(77)	Ortman	40.00	20.00	12.00
(78)	Orwoll	40.00	20.00	12.00
(79)	Parker	40.00	20.00	12.00
(80)	Penebskey	40.00	20.00	12.00
(81)	H. Pillette	40.00	20.00	12.00
(82)	T. Pillette	40.00	20.00	12.00
(83)	Pinelli	40.00	20.00	12.00
(84)	Pool	40.00	20.00	12.00
(85)	Posedel	40.00	20.00	12.00
(86)	Powers	40.00	20.00	12.00
(87)	Read	40.00	20.00	12.00
(88)	Andy Reese	40.00	20.00	12.00
(89)	Rhiel	40.00	20.00	12.00
(90)	Ricci	40.00	20.00	12.00
(91)	Rohwer	40.00	20.00	12.00
(92)	Ryan	40.00	20.00	12.00
(93)	Schino	40.00	20.00	12.00
(94)	Schulte	40.00	20.00	12.00
(95)	Severeid	40.00	20.00	12.00
(96)	Sharpe	40.00	20.00	12.00
(97)	Shellenback	40.00	20.00	12.00
(98)	Simas	40.00	20.00	12.00
(99)	Steinbacker	40.00	20.00	12.00
(100)	Summa	40.00	20.00	12.00
(101)	Tubbs	40.00	20.00	12.00
(102)	Turner	40.00	20.00	12.00
(103)	Turpin	40.00	20.00	12.00
(104)	Uhalt	40.00	20.00	12.00
(105)	Vinci	40.00	20.00	12.00
(106)	Vitt	40.00	20.00	12.00
(107)	Wade	40.00	20.00	12.00
(108)	Walsh	40.00	20.00	12.00
(109)	Walters	40.00	20.00	12.00
(110)	Wera	40.00	20.00	12.00
(111)	Wetzel	40.00	20.00	12.00
(112)	Williams (Portland)	40.00	20.00	12.00
(113)	Williams (San Francisco)	40.00	20.00	12.00
(114)	Wingo	40.00	20.00	12.00
(115)	Wirts	40.00	20.00	12.00
(116)	Wise	40.00	20.00	12.00
(117)	Woodall	40.00	20.00	12.00
(118)	Yerkes	40.00	20.00	12.00
(119)	Zamlock	40.00	20.00	12.00
(120)	Zinn	40.00	20.00	12.00

1932 Zeenut Pacific Coast League

Beginning in 1931, Zeenuts cards were no longer dated on the front, and cards without the coupon are very difficult to date. The words "Zeenuts Series" were dropped from the front and replaced with "Coast League." Zeenut cards in 1932 measure 1-3/4" x 3-1/2".

		NM	EX	VG
Common Player:		40.00	20.00	12.00
With Coupon:		600.00	300.00	180.00
(1)	Abbott	40.00	20.00	12.00
(2)	Almada	50.00	25.00	15.00
(3)	Anton	40.00	20.00	12.00
(4)	Babich	40.00	20.00	12.00
(5)	Backer	40.00	20.00	12.00
(6)	Baker	40.00	20.00	12.00
(7)	Ballou	40.00	20.00	12.00
(8)	Bassler	40.00	20.00	12.00
(9)	Berger	40.00	20.00	12.00
(10)	Blackerby	40.00	20.00	12.00
(11)	Bordagaray	40.00	20.00	12.00
(12)	Brannon	40.00	20.00	12.00
(13)	Briggs	40.00	20.00	12.00
(14)	Brubaker	40.00	20.00	12.00
(15)	Callaghan	40.00	20.00	12.00
(16)	Camilli	40.00	20.00	12.00
(17)	Campbell	40.00	20.00	12.00
(18)	Carlyle	40.00	20.00	12.00
(19)	Caster	40.00	20.00	12.00
(20)	Caveney	40.00	20.00	12.00
(21)	Chamberlain	40.00	20.00	12.00
(22)	Cole	40.00	20.00	12.00
(23)	Collard	40.00	20.00	12.00
(24)	Cook	40.00	20.00	12.00
(25)	Coscarart	40.00	20.00	12.00
(26)	Cox	40.00	20.00	12.00
(27)	Cronin	40.00	20.00	12.00
(28)	Daglia	40.00	20.00	12.00
(29)	Dahlgren	45.00	22.00	13.50
(30)	Davis	40.00	20.00	12.00
(31)	Dean	40.00	20.00	12.00
(32)	Delaney	40.00	20.00	12.00
(33)	Demaree	40.00	20.00	12.00
(34)	Devine	40.00	20.00	12.00
(35)	DeViveiros	40.00	20.00	12.00
(36)	Dittmar	40.00	20.00	12.00
(37)	Donovan	40.00	20.00	12.00
(38)	Ellsworth	40.00	20.00	12.00
(39)	Fitzpatrick	40.00	20.00	12.00
(40)	Frazier	40.00	20.00	12.00
(41)	Freitas	40.00	20.00	12.00
(42)	Garibaldi	40.00	20.00	12.00
(43)	Gaston	40.00	20.00	12.00
(44)	Gazella	40.00	20.00	12.00
(45)	Gillick	40.00	20.00	12.00
(46)	Hafey	40.00	20.00	12.00
(47)	Haney	40.00	20.00	12.00
(48)	Hannah	40.00	20.00	12.00
(49)	Henderson	40.00	20.00	12.00
(50)	Herrmann	40.00	20.00	12.00
(51)	Hipps	40.00	20.00	12.00
(52)	Hofman	40.00	20.00	12.00
(53)	Holland	40.00	20.00	12.00
(54)	House	40.00	20.00	12.00
(55)	Hufft	40.00	20.00	12.00
(56)	Hunt	40.00	20.00	12.00
(57)	Hurst	40.00	20.00	12.00
(58)	Jacobs	40.00	20.00	12.00
(59)	Johns	40.00	20.00	12.00
(60)	Johnson (Missions)	40.00	20.00	12.00
(61)	Johnson (Portland)	40.00	20.00	12.00
(62)	Johnson (Seattle)	40.00	20.00	12.00
(63)	Joiner	40.00	20.00	12.00
(64)	Kallio	40.00	20.00	12.00
(65)	Kasich	40.00	20.00	12.00
(66)	Keesey	40.00	20.00	12.00
(67)	Kelly	40.00	20.00	12.00

		NM	EX	VG
(68)	Koehler	40.00	20.00	12.00
(69)	Lee	40.00	20.00	12.00
(70)	Lieber	40.00	20.00	12.00
(71)	Mailho	40.00	20.00	12.00
(72)	Martin (Oakland)	40.00	20.00	12.00
(73)	Martin (San Francisco)	40.00	20.00	12.00
(74)	McNeely	40.00	20.00	12.00
(75)	Miljus	40.00	20.00	12.00
(76)	Monroe	40.00	20.00	12.00
(77)	Mosolf	40.00	20.00	12.00
(78)	Moss	40.00	20.00	12.00
(79)	Muller	40.00	20.00	12.00
(80)	Mulligan	40.00	20.00	12.00
(81)	Oana	300.00	150.00	90.00
(82)	Osborn	40.00	20.00	12.00
(83)	Page	40.00	20.00	12.00
(84)	Penebsky	40.00	20.00	12.00
(85)	H. Pillette	40.00	20.00	12.00
(86)	Pinelli	50.00	25.00	15.00
(87)	Poole	40.00	20.00	12.00
(88)	Quellich	40.00	20.00	12.00
(89)	Read	40.00	20.00	12.00
(90)	Ricci	40.00	20.00	12.00
(91)	Salvo	40.00	20.00	12.00
(92)	Sankey	40.00	20.00	12.00
(93)	Sheehan	40.00	20.00	12.00
(94)	Shellenback	40.00	20.00	12.00
(95)	Sherlock (Hollywood)	40.00	20.00	12.00
(96)	Sherlock (Missions)	40.00	20.00	12.00
(97)	Shores	40.00	20.00	12.00
(98)	Simas	40.00	20.00	12.00
(99)	Statz	60.00	30.00	18.00
(100)	Steinbacker	40.00	20.00	12.00
(101)	Sulik	40.00	20.00	12.00
(102)	Summa	40.00	20.00	12.00
(103)	Thomas	40.00	20.00	12.00
(104)	Uhalt	40.00	20.00	12.00
(105)	Vinci	40.00	20.00	12.00
(106)	Vitt	40.00	20.00	12.00
(107)	Walsh (Missions)	40.00	20.00	12.00
(108)	Walsh (Oakland)	40.00	20.00	12.00
(109)	Walters	40.00	20.00	12.00
(110)	Ward	40.00	20.00	12.00
(111)	Welsh	40.00	20.00	12.00
(112)	Wera	40.00	20.00	12.00
(113)	Williams	40.00	20.00	12.00
(114)	Willoughby	40.00	20.00	12.00
(115)	Wirts	40.00	20.00	12.00
(116)	Wise	40.00	20.00	12.00
(117)	Woodall	40.00	20.00	12.00
(118)	Yde	40.00	20.00	12.00
(119)	Zahniser	40.00	20.00	12.00
(120)	Zamloch	40.00	20.00	12.00

1933 Zeenut Pacific Coast League (sepia)

This is the most confusing era for Zeenut cards. The cards of 1933-36 are nearly identical, displaying the words, "Coast League" in a small rectangle with rounded corners, along with the player's name and team. The photos are black-and-white (except 1933 Zeenuts have also been found with sepia photos). Because no date appears on the photos, cards from these years are impossible to tell apart without the coupon bottom that lists an expiration date. To date over 161 subjects have been found, with some known to exist in all four years. There are cases where the exact same photo was used from one year to the next (sometimes with minor cropping differences). All cards of Joe and Vince DiMaggio have their last name misspelled "DeMaggio." Cards of all years measure about 1-3/4" x 3-1/2" with coupon.

		NM	EX	VG
Common Player:		40.00	20.00	12.00
With Coupon:		400.00	200.00	120.00
(1)	L. Almada	50.00	25.00	15.00
(2)	Anton	40.00	20.00	12.00
(3)	Bassler	40.00	20.00	12.00
(4)	Bonnelly	40.00	20.00	12.00
(5)	Bordagary	40.00	20.00	12.00
(6)	Bottarini	40.00	20.00	12.00
(7)	Brannan	40.00	20.00	12.00
(8)	Brubaker	40.00	20.00	12.00
(9)	Bryan	40.00	20.00	12.00
(10)	Burns	40.00	20.00	12.00
(11)	Camilli	40.00	20.00	12.00
(12)	Chozen	40.00	20.00	12.00
(13)	Cole	40.00	20.00	12.00
(14)	Cronin	40.00	20.00	12.00
(15)	Dahlgren	40.00	20.00	12.00
(16)	Donovan	40.00	20.00	12.00
(17)	Douglas	40.00	20.00	12.00
(18)	Flynn	40.00	20.00	12.00
(19)	French	40.00	20.00	12.00
(20)	Frietas	40.00	20.00	12.00
(21)	Galan	40.00	20.00	12.00
(22)	Hofmann	40.00	20.00	12.00
(23)	Kelman	40.00	20.00	12.00
(24)	Lelivelt	40.00	20.00	12.00
(25)	Ludolph	40.00	20.00	12.00
(26)	McDonald	40.00	20.00	12.00
(27)	McNeely	40.00	20.00	12.00
(28)	McQuaid	40.00	20.00	12.00
(29)	Moncrief	40.00	20.00	12.00
(30)	Nelson	40.00	20.00	12.00
(31)	Osborne	40.00	20.00	12.00
(32)	Petersen	40.00	20.00	12.00
(33)	Reeves	40.00	20.00	12.00
(34)	Scott	40.00	20.00	12.00
(35)	Shellenback	40.00	20.00	12.00
(36)	J. Sherlock	40.00	20.00	12.00
(37)	V. Sherlock	40.00	20.00	12.00
(38)	Steinbacker	40.00	20.00	12.00
(39)	Stine	40.00	20.00	12.00
(40)	Strange	40.00	20.00	12.00
(41)	Sulik	40.00	20.00	12.00
(42)	Sweetland	40.00	20.00	12.00
(43)	Uhalt	40.00	20.00	12.00
(44)	Vinci	40.00	20.00	12.00
(45)	Vitt	40.00	20.00	12.00
(46)	Wetzel	40.00	20.00	12.00
(47)	Woodall	40.00	20.00	12.00
(48)	Zinn	40.00	20.00	12.00

1933-36 Zeenut Pacific Coast League (black-and-white)

		NM	EX	VG
Common Player:		40.00	20.00	12.00
With Coupon:		400.00	200.00	120.00
(1a)	Almada (Large pose.)	50.00	25.00	15.00
(1b)	Almada (Small pose.)	50.00	25.00	15.00
(2a)	Anton (Large pose.)	40.00	20.00	12.00
(2b)	Anton (Small pose.)	40.00	20.00	12.00
(3)	Babich	40.00	20.00	12.00
(4)	Backer	40.00	20.00	12.00
(5)	Ballou (Black stockings.)	40.00	20.00	12.00
(6a)	Ballou (Stockings with band, large pose.)	40.00	20.00	12.00
(6b)	Ballou (Stockings with band, small pose.)	40.00	20.00	12.00
(7)	Barath	40.00	20.00	12.00
(8)	Beck	40.00	20.00	12.00
(9)	C. Beck	40.00	20.00	12.00
(10)	W. Beck	40.00	20.00	12.00
(11)	Becker	40.00	20.00	12.00
(12)	Biongovanni	40.00	20.00	12.00
(13)	Blackerby	40.00	20.00	12.00
(14)	Blakely	40.00	20.00	12.00
(15)	Borja (Sacramento)	40.00	20.00	12.00
(16)	Borja (Seals)	40.00	20.00	12.00
(17)	Brundin	40.00	20.00	12.00
(18)	Carlyle	40.00	20.00	12.00
(19a)	Caveney (Name incorrect.)	40.00	20.00	12.00
(19b)	Cavaney (Name correct.)	40.00	20.00	12.00
(20)	Chelini	40.00	20.00	12.00
(21)	Cole (With glove.)	40.00	20.00	12.00
(22)	Cole (No glove.)	40.00	20.00	12.00
(23)	Connors	40.00	20.00	12.00
(24)	Coscarart (Missions)	40.00	20.00	12.00
(25)	Coscarart (Seattle)	40.00	20.00	12.00
(26)	Cox	40.00	20.00	12.00
(27)	Davis	40.00	20.00	12.00
(28)	J. DeMaggio (DiMaggio)/Btg	15,000	5,500	3,750
(29)	J. DeMaggio (DiMaggio)/ Throwing	15,000	5,500	3,750
(30)	V. DeMaggio (DiMaggio)	1,200	600.00	360.00
(31)	DeViveiros	40.00	20.00	12.00
(32)	Densmore	40.00	20.00	12.00
(33)	Dittmar	40.00	20.00	12.00
(34)	Donovan	40.00	20.00	12.00
(35)	Douglas (Oakland)	40.00	20.00	12.00
(36)	Douglas (Seals)	40.00	20.00	12.00
(37a)	Duggan (Large pose.)	40.00	20.00	12.00
(37b)	Duggan (Small pose.)	40.00	20.00	12.00
(38)	Durst	40.00	20.00	12.00
(39a)	Eckhardt (Large pose.)	40.00	20.00	12.00
(39b)	Eckhardt (Small pose.)	40.00	20.00	12.00
(40)	Ellsworth	40.00	20.00	12.00
(41)	Fenton	40.00	20.00	12.00
(42)	Fitzpatrick	40.00	20.00	12.00
(43)	Francovich	40.00	20.00	12.00
(44)	Funk	40.00	20.00	12.00
(45a)	Garibaldi (Large pose.)	40.00	20.00	12.00
(45b)	Garibaldi (Small pose.)	40.00	20.00	12.00
(46)	Gibson (Black sleeves.)	40.00	20.00	12.00
(47)	Gibson (White sleeves.)	40.00	20.00	12.00
(48)	Gira	40.00	20.00	12.00
(49)	Glaister	40.00	20.00	12.00
(50)	Graves	40.00	20.00	12.00
(51a)	Hafey (Missions, large pose.)	40.00	20.00	12.00
(51b)	Hafey (Missions, middle-size pose.)	40.00	20.00	12.00
(51c)	Hafey (Missions, small pose.)	40.00	20.00	12.00
(52)	Hafey (Sacramento)	40.00	20.00	12.00
(53)	Haid (Oakland)	40.00	20.00	12.00
(54)	Haid (Seattle)	40.00	20.00	12.00
(55)	Haney	40.00	20.00	12.00
(56a)	Hartwig (Sacramento, large pose.)	40.00	20.00	12.00
(56b)	Hartwig (Sacramento, small pose.)	40.00	20.00	12.00
(57)	Hartwig (Seals)	40.00	20.00	12.00
(58)	Henderson	40.00	20.00	12.00
(59)	Herrmann	40.00	20.00	12.00
(60)	B. Holder	40.00	20.00	12.00
(61)	Holland	40.00	20.00	12.00
(62)	Horne	40.00	20.00	12.00
(63)	House	40.00	20.00	12.00
(64)	Hunt	40.00	20.00	12.00
(65)	A.E. Jacobs	40.00	20.00	12.00
(66)	Johns	40.00	20.00	12.00
(67)	D. Johnson	40.00	20.00	12.00
(68)	L. Johnson	40.00	20.00	12.00
(69)	Joiner	40.00	20.00	12.00
(70)	Jolley	60.00	30.00	18.00
(71)	Joost	40.00	20.00	12.00
(72)	Jorgensen	40.00	20.00	12.00
(73)	Kallio	40.00	20.00	12.00
(74)	Kamm	40.00	20.00	12.00
(75)	Kampouris	40.00	20.00	12.00
(76)	E. Kelly (Oakland)	40.00	20.00	12.00
(77)	E. Kelly (Seattle)	40.00	20.00	12.00
(78)	Kenna	40.00	20.00	12.00
(79)	Kintana	40.00	20.00	12.00
(80)	Lahman	40.00	20.00	12.00
(81)	Lieber	40.00	20.00	12.00
(82)	Ludolph	40.00	20.00	12.00
(83)	Mailho	40.00	20.00	12.00
(84a)	Mails (Large pose.)	40.00	20.00	12.00
(84b)	Mails (Small pose.)	40.00	20.00	12.00
(85)	Marty (Black sleeves.)	40.00	20.00	12.00
(86)	Marty (White sleeves.)	40.00	20.00	12.00
(87)	Massuci (Batting follow-through.)	40.00	20.00	12.00
(88)	Masucci (Different pose.)	40.00	20.00	12.00
(89a)	McEvoy (Large pose.)	40.00	20.00	12.00
(89b)	McEvoy (Small pose.)	40.00	20.00	12.00
(90)	McIsaacs	40.00	20.00	12.00
(91)	McMullen (Oakland)	40.00	20.00	12.00
(92)	McMullen (Seals)	40.00	20.00	12.00
(93)	Mitchell	40.00	20.00	12.00
(94a)	Monzo (Large pose.)	40.00	20.00	12.00
(94b)	Monzo (Small pose.)	40.00	20.00	12.00
(95)	Mort/Throwing	40.00	20.00	12.00
(96)	Mort/Btg	40.00	20.00	12.00
(97a)	Muller (Oakland, large pose.)	40.00	20.00	12.00
(97b)	Muller (Oakland, small pose.)	40.00	20.00	12.00
(98)	Muller (Seattle)	40.00	20.00	12.00
(99)	Mulligan (Hands showing.)	40.00	20.00	12.00
(100)	Mulligan (Hands not showing.)	40.00	20.00	12.00
(101)	Newkirk	40.00	20.00	12.00
(102)	Nicholas	40.00	20.00	12.00
(103)	Nitcholas	40.00	20.00	12.00
(103a)	Norbert (Large pose.)	40.00	20.00	12.00
(103b)	Norbert (Small pose.)	40.00	20.00	12.00
(105)	O'Doul (Black sleeves.)	125.00	65.00	35.00
(106)	O'Doul (White sleeves.)	125.00	65.00	35.00
(107)	Oglesby	40.00	20.00	12.00
(108)	Ostenberg	40.00	20.00	12.00
(109)	Outen/Throwing	40.00	20.00	12.00
(110)	Outen/Btg	40.00	20.00	12.00
(111)	Page (Hollywood)	40.00	20.00	12.00
(112)	Page (Seattle)	40.00	20.00	12.00
(113)	Palmisano	40.00	20.00	12.00
(114)	Parker	40.00	20.00	12.00
(115)	Phebus	40.00	20.00	12.00
(116)	T. Pillette	40.00	20.00	12.00
(117)	Pool	40.00	20.00	12.00
(118)	Powers	40.00	20.00	12.00
(119)	Quellich	40.00	20.00	12.00
(120)	Radonitz	40.00	20.00	12.00
(121a)	Raimondi (Large pose.)	40.00	20.00	12.00
(121b)	Raimondi (Small pose.)	40.00	20.00	12.00
(122a)	Jimmy Reese (Large pose.)	100.00	50.00	30.00
(122b)	Jimmy Reese (Small pose.)	100.00	50.00	30.00
(123)	Rego	40.00	20.00	12.00
(124)	Rhyne (Front)	40.00	20.00	12.00
(125)	Rosenberg	40.00	20.00	12.00
(126)	Salinsen	40.00	20.00	12.00
(127)	Salkeld	40.00	20.00	12.00
(128)	Salvo	40.00	20.00	12.00
(129)	Sever	40.00	20.00	12.00
(130)	Sheehan (Black sleeves.)	40.00	20.00	12.00
(131)	Sheehan (White sleeves.)	40.00	20.00	12.00
(132a)	Sheely (Large pose.)	40.00	20.00	12.00
(132b)	Sheely (Small pose.)	40.00	20.00	12.00
(134)	Sprinz	40.00	20.00	12.00
(135)	Starritt	40.00	20.00	12.00
(136)	Statz	60.00	30.00	18.00
(137a)	Steinbacker (Large pose.)	40.00	20.00	12.00
(137b)	Steinbacker (Small pose.)	40.00	20.00	12.00
(138)	Stewart	40.00	20.00	12.00

(139) Stitzel (Los Angeles)	40.00	20.00	12.00
(140) Stitzel (Missions)	40.00	20.00	12.00
(141) Stitzel (Seals)	40.00	20.00	12.00
(142) Stoneham	40.00	20.00	12.00
(143) Street	40.00	20.00	12.00
(144) Stroner	40.00	20.00	12.00
(145) Stutz	40.00	20.00	12.00
(146) Sulik	40.00	20.00	12.00
(147a) Thurston (Mission)	40.00	20.00	12.00
(147b) Thurston (Missions)	40.00	20.00	12.00
(148) Vitt (Hollywood)	40.00	20.00	12.00
(149) Vitt (Oakland)	40.00	20.00	12.00
(150) Wallgren	40.00	20.00	12.00
(151) Walsh	40.00	20.00	12.00
(152) Walters	40.00	20.00	12.00
(153) West	40.00	20.00	12.00
(154a) Wirts (Large pose.)	40.00	20.00	12.00
(154b) Wirts (Small pose.)	40.00	20.00	12.00
(155) Woodall/Btg	40.00	20.00	12.00
(156) Woodall/Throwing	40.00	20.00	12.00
(157) Wright (Facing to front.)	40.00	20.00	12.00
(158) Wright (Facing to left.)	40.00	20.00	12.00
(159) Zinn	40.00	20.00	12.00

1937-38 Zeenut Pacific Coast League

The 1937 and 1938 Zeenuts are similar to the 1933-1936 issues, except the black rectangle containing the player's name and team has square (rather than rounded) corners. Again, it is difficult to distinguish between the two years. In 1938, Zeenuts eliminated the coupon bottom and began including a separate coupon in the candy package along with the baseball card. The final two years of the Zeenuts issues, the 1937 and 1938 cards, are among the more difficult to find. With coupon, the 1937 cards measure about 1-5/8" x 3-7/16". The couponless 1938 cards measure about 1-3/4" x 2-13/16".

	NM	EX	VG
Common Player:	60.00	25.00	15.00
With Coupon:	400.00	200.00	120.00
(1) Annunzio	60.00	25.00	15.00
(2) Baker	60.00	25.00	15.00
(3) Ballou	60.00	25.00	15.00
(4) C. Beck	60.00	25.00	15.00
(5) W. Beck	60.00	25.00	15.00
(6) Bolin	60.00	25.00	15.00
(7) Bongiavanni	60.00	25.00	15.00
(8) Boss	60.00	25.00	15.00
(9) Carson	60.00	25.00	15.00
(10) Clabaugh	60.00	25.00	15.00
(11) Clifford	60.00	25.00	15.00
(12) B. Cole	60.00	25.00	15.00
(13) Coscarart	60.00	25.00	15.00
(14) Cronin	60.00	25.00	15.00
(15) Cullop	60.00	25.00	15.00
(16) Daglia	60.00	25.00	15.00
(17) D. DeMaggio (DiMaggio)	1,200	600.00	360.00
(18) Douglas	60.00	25.00	15.00
(19) Frankovich	60.00	25.00	15.00
(20) Frazier	60.00	25.00	15.00
(21) Fredericks	60.00	25.00	15.00
(22) Freitas	60.00	25.00	15.00
(23) Gabrielson (Oakland)	60.00	25.00	15.00
(24) Gabrielson (Seattle)	60.00	25.00	15.00
(25) Garibaldi	60.00	25.00	15.00
(26) Gibson	60.00	25.00	15.00
(27) Gill	60.00	25.00	15.00
(28) Graves	60.00	25.00	15.00
(29) Guay	60.00	25.00	15.00
(30) Gudat	60.00	25.00	15.00
(31) Haid	60.00	25.00	15.00
(32) Hannah	60.00	25.00	15.00
(33) Hawkins	60.00	25.00	15.00
(34) Herrmann	60.00	25.00	15.00
(35) Holder	60.00	25.00	15.00
(36) Jennings	60.00	25.00	15.00
(37) Judnich	60.00	25.00	15.00
(38) Klinger	60.00	25.00	15.00
(39) Koenig	60.00	25.00	15.00
(40) Koupal	60.00	25.00	15.00
(41) Koy	60.00	25.00	15.00
(42) Lamanski	60.00	25.00	15.00
(43) Leishman (Oakland)	60.00	25.00	15.00
(44) Leishman (Seattle)	60.00	25.00	15.00
(45) G. Lillard	60.00	25.00	15.00
(46) Mann	60.00	25.00	15.00
(47) Marble (Hollywood)	60.00	25.00	15.00
(49) Miller	60.00	25.00	15.00
(50) Mills	60.00	25.00	15.00
(51) Monzo	60.00	25.00	15.00
(52) B. Mort (Hollywood)	60.00	25.00	15.00
(53) B. Mort (Missions)	60.00	25.00	15.00
(54) Muller	60.00	25.00	15.00
(55) Murray	60.00	25.00	15.00
(56) Newsome	60.00	25.00	15.00
(57) Nitcholas	60.00	25.00	15.00
(58) Olds	60.00	25.00	15.00
(59) Orengo	60.00	25.00	15.00
(60) Osborne	60.00	25.00	15.00
(61) Outen	60.00	25.00	15.00
(62) C. Outen (Hollywood)	60.00	25.00	15.00
(63) C. Outen (Missions)	60.00	25.00	15.00
(64) Pippin	60.00	25.00	15.00
(65) Powell	60.00	25.00	15.00
(66) Radonitz	60.00	25.00	15.00
(67) Raimondi (Oakland)	60.00	25.00	15.00
(68) Raimondi (San Francisco)	60.00	25.00	15.00
(69) A. Raimondi	60.00	25.00	15.00
(70) W. Raimondi	60.00	25.00	15.00
(71) Rhyne	60.00	25.00	15.00
(72) Rosenberg (Missions)	1,200	600.00	360.00
(73) Rosenberg (Portland)	1,200	600.00	360.00
(74) Sawyer	60.00	25.00	15.00
(75) Seats	60.00	25.00	15.00
(76) Sheehan (Oakland)	60.00	25.00	15.00
(77) Sheehan (San Francisco)	60.00	25.00	15.00
(78) Shores	60.00	25.00	15.00
(79) Slade (Hollywood)	60.00	25.00	15.00
(80) Slade (Missions)	60.00	25.00	15.00
(81) Sprinz (Missions)	60.00	25.00	15.00
(82) Sprinz (San Francisco)	60.00	25.00	15.00
(83) Statz	75.00	37.50	22.50
(84) Storey	60.00	25.00	15.00
(85) Stringfellow	60.00	25.00	15.00
(86) Stutz	60.00	25.00	15.00
(87) Sweeney	60.00	25.00	15.00
(88) Thomson	60.00	25.00	15.00
(89) Tost (Hollywood)	60.00	25.00	15.00
(90) Tost (Missions)	60.00	25.00	15.00
(91) Ulrich	60.00	25.00	15.00
(92) Vergez	60.00	25.00	15.00
(93) Vezelich	60.00	25.00	15.00
(94) Vitter (Hollywood)	60.00	25.00	15.00
(95) Vitter (San Francisco)	60.00	25.00	15.00
(96) West	60.00	25.00	15.00
(97) Wilson	60.00	25.00	15.00
(98) Woodall	60.00	25.00	15.00
(99) Wright	60.00	25.00	15.00

Minor League Team Sets and Singles (1970-2004)

By 1970, the issue of minor league baseball cards as premiums with another product had virtually ceased. Since that time, the vast majority of cards issued each year have been in the form of team sets and, since 1989, wax- or foil-packed singles.

In exchange for the rights to sell card sets within the hobby, various card manufacturers and other sponsors have printed sets for the teams to sell at their concession stand, or give away at promotional games.

Also listed in this section are miscellaneous sets of draft picks, pre-professional summer amateur leagues and Team USA, along with independent professional teams which are not part of Organized Baseball's National Association of Professional Baseball Leagues.

Since minor league teams sets are not usually broken up, and since the presence of a superstar player can represent virtually all of a set's value, only complete set prices are listed.

1970-73 Minor League Team Sets

The mid-1960s brought an end to minor league team set issues intended mainly for fan consumption. In 1970, a new era began with the issue of team sets aimed primarily at card collectors, and often produced by collectors or dealers with team connections. Compared to major league cards of the era, production values of minor league sets were low, with black-and-white printing the norm and little graphic embellishment. Future minor league team-set giant TCMA issued its first such cards in 1974 (though they included 1972 and 1973 team sets), while Frank Caruso, who issued many Pacific Coast League sets over the years, began in 1973.

NM

18 Team Sets and Variations
- 1970 McDonald's Wichita Aeros (18) 300.00
- 1971 Currie Richmond Braves (18) 100.00
- 1971 Morey Syracuse Chiefs (8) 115.00
- 1972 Carl Aldana 1950s S.F. Seals (18) 45.00
- "1972" TCMA Cedar Rapids Cardinals/1974 (29) 30.00
- "1972" TCMA Cedar Rapids Cardinals/1974 (30) 90.00
- 1972 Fast Service Salem Pirates (4) 125.00
- 1972 Team Seattle Rainiers (24) 45.00
- 1972 Team Tacoma Twins (16) 17.50
- 1972 Virginian-Pilot Tidewater Tides (22) 150.00
- "1973" TCMA Cedar Rapids Astros/1974 (27) 25.00
- "1973" TCMA Cedar Rapids Astros/1974 (28) 30.00
- 1973 Team Sherbrooke Pirates (18) 200.00
- 1973 Team Syracuse Chiefs (30) 200.00
- 1973 Caruso Tacoma Twins (21) 16.00
- 1973 Click-Click Three Rivers Eagles (18) 150.00
- 1973 KSB Wichita Aeros (19) 55.00
- 1973 KSB Wichita Aeros (21) 100.00

1974 Minor League Team Sets

The number of minor league card sets issued either by the teams themselves or card hobbyists nearly tripled in 1974, to 14. A wide range of formats was seen, with black-and-white photos still the rule.

NM

16 Team Sets and Variations
- 1974 Caruso Albuquerque Dukes (16) 15.00
- 1974 Team Albuquerque Dukes (23) 200.00
- 1974 TCMA Cedar Rapids Astros (28) 25.00
- 1974 TCMA Gastonia Rangers (24) 17.50
- 1974 Caruso Hawaii Islanders (8) 10.00
- 1974 Falstaff Omaha Royals (10) 125.00
- 1974 Broder P.C.L. "Popcorn" Cards (235) 325.00
- 1974 Caruso Phoenix Giants (11) 8.00
- 1974 Caruso Sacramento Solons (18) 15.00
- 1974 Caruso Salt Lake City Angels (10) 10.00
- 1974 Team Seattle Rainiers (20) 45.00
- 1974 Caruso Spokane Indians (18) 20.00
- 1974 Team Syracuse Chiefs (30) 400.00
- 1974 Team Syracuse Chiefs (29) 325.00
- 1974 Caruso Tacoma Twins (27) 16.00
- 1974 One Day Wichita Aeros (29) 95.00

1975 Minor League Team Sets

In 1975, the number of teams issuing card sets again doubled to over 35. Among the hobby dealers and collectors who dominated the sponsorship of such sets, TCMA was the unquestioned leader, with nearly half the cards under its banner, originally selling for $3-4 per set.

NM

42 Team Sets and Variations
- 1975 Caruso Albuquerque Dukes (21) 12.00
- 1975 TCMA Anderson Rangers (25) 11.00
- 1975 TCMA Appleton Foxes (29) 10.00
- 1975 TCMA Burlington Bees (29) 7.50
- 1975 Broder California League (30) 40.00
- 1975 TCMA Cedar Rapids Giants (32) 16.00
- 1975 TCMA Clinton Pilots (32) 25.00
- 1975 TCMA Dubuque Packers (32) 22.50
- 1975 Sussman Ft. Lauderdale Yankees (30) 50.00
- 1975 Sussman Ft. Lauderdale Yankees (29) 12.50
- 1975 Caruso Hawaii Islanders (21) 20.00
- 1975 TCMA International League (31) 13.50
- 1975 TCMA Iowa Oaks (21) 40.00
- 1975 TCMA Lafayette Drillers (32) 27.50
- 1975 TCMA Lynchburg Rangers (26) 12.50
- 1975 McWilliams 1955 Oakland Oaks (36) 60.00
- 1975 Team Oklahoma City 89ers (24) 15.00
- 1975 Top Trophies Omaha Royals (18) 95.00
- 1975 Broder 1960s Pacific Coast League 100.00
- 1975 Dobbins PCL All-Stars (37) 80.00
- 1975 TCMA 1950s PCL (18) 200.00
- 1975 Caruso Phoenix Giants (21) 10.00
- 1975 Circle K Phoenix Giants (26) 6.00
- 1975 TCMA Quad City Angels (34) 40.00
- 1975 TCMA 1961 Rochester Red Wings (11) 150.00
- 1975 Caruso Sacramento Solons (22) 16.00
- 1975 Caruso Salt Lake City Gulls (20) 9.00
- 1975 TCMA San Antonio Brewers (22) 12.00
- 1975 TCMA Shreveport Captains (23) 15.00
- 1975 Caruso Spokane Indians (21) 8.00
- 1975 Team Syracuse Chiefs (25) 225.00
- 1975 KMO Tacoma Twins (21) 12.00
- 1975 Stewart Tidewater Tides (24) 30.00
- 1975 TCMA Tri-Valley Highlanders (25) 75.00
- 1975 Caruso Tucson Toros (21) 9.00
- 1975 Team Tucson Toros (24) 11.00
- 1975 7-11 Tulsa Oilers (24) 30.00
- 1975 TCMA Waterbury Dodgers (22) 20.00
- 1975 TCMA Waterloo Royals (34) 20.00
- 1975 TCMA Waterloo Royals (35) 80.00
- 1975 Sussman West Palm Beach Expos (32) 30.00
- 1975 Sussman West Palm Beach Expos (29) 11.00

1976 Minor League Team Sets

While the number of team-issued minor league sets leveled off at around 35 in 1976, the quality standard was raised with the first use of full-color printing. The innovator was Mike Cramer who went on to found Pacific Trading Cards.

NM

35 Team Sets and Variations
- 1976 TCMA Appleton Foxes (29) 11.00
- 1976 TCMA Arkansas Travelers (12) 50.00
- 1976 TCMA Asheville Tourists (25) 15.00
- 1976 Team Batavia Trojans (29) 30.00
- 1976 TCMA Baton Rouge Cougars (22) 30.00
- 1976 TCMA Burlington Bees (33) 8.00
- 1976 TCMA Cedar Rapids Giants (39) 20.00
- 1976 TCMA Clinton Pilots (37) 40.00
- 1976 TCMA Dubuque Packers (40) 12.00
- 1976 Sussman Ft. Lauderdale Yankees (30) 35.00
- 1976 Caruso Hawaii Islanders (21) 25.00
- 1976 Team Indianapolis Indians (26) 25.00
- 1976 Team Oklahoma City 89ers (24) 22.50
- 1976 Top Trophies Omaha Royals (27) 125.00
- 1976 Caruso Phoenix Giants (20) 9.00
- 1976 Coke Premiums Phoenix Giants (24) 15.00
- 1976 Cramer Phoenix Giants (24) 6.00
- 1976 VNB Phoenix Giants (26) 20.00
- 1976 TCMA Quad City Angels (39) 20.00
- 1976 TCMA Quad City Angels (40) 24.00
- 1976 Caruso Sacramento Solons (23) 15.00
- 1976 Caruso Salt Lake City Gulls (22) 9.00
- 1976 Knowlton's San Antonio Brewers (26) 35.00
- 1976 Cramer Seattle Rainiers (20) 24.00
- 1976 TCMA Shreveport Captains (23) 40.00
- 1976 TCMA Shreveport Captains (25) 95.00
- 1976 Caruso Spokane Indians (21) 12.00
- 1976 DQ Tacoma Twins (24) 15.00
- 1976 Caruso Tucson Toros (20) 10.00
- 1976 Cramer Tucson Toros (24) 10.00
- 1976 Goof's Tulsa Oilers (26) 150.00
- 1976 Goof's Tulsa Oilers w/autographs (26) 350.00
- 1976 TCMA Waterloo Royals (33) 37.50
- 1976 TCMA Wausau Mets (25) 30.00
- 1976 TCMA Williamsport Tomahawks (23) 12.50

1977 Minor League Team Sets

More than 50 minor league team sets were issued in 1977, including a collector-issued black-and-white set of the Modesto A's featuring future Hall of Famer Rickey Henderson. Crudely executed, the Frank Chong set was the first minor league set of the 1970s to (briefly) attain a retail value in excess of $1,000. It was also in 1977 that TCMA began widespread use of updated sets with cards of players who joined teams after the initital card photos had been taken. This created variations which can carry widely diverse pricing.

NM

57 Team Sets and Variations
- 1977 TCMA Appleton Foxes (29) 12.50
- 1977 TCMA Appleton Foxes (30) 75.00
- 1977 TCMA Arkansas Travelers (12) 30.00
- 1977 TCMA Arkansas Travelers (21) 75.00
- 1977 TCMA Asheville Tourists (29) 17.50
- 1977 TCMA Bristol Red Sox (20) 50.00
- 1977 TCMA Burlington Bees (25) 30.00
- 1977 TCMA Burlington Bees (27) 32.50
- 1977 TCMA Cedar Rapids Giants (24) 30.00
- 1977 TCMA Cedar Rapids Giants (25) 65.00
- 1977 TCMA Charleston Patriots (25) 25.00
- 1977 TCMA Clinton Dodgers (29) 55.00
- 1977 TCMA Cocoa Astros (25) 12.50
- 1977 TCMA Columbus Clippers (22) 100.00
- 1977 TCMA Columbus Clippers (24) 175.00
- 1977 LICS 1960s Dallas Rangers (9) 15.00
- 1977 TCMA Daytona Beach Islanders (27) 20.00
- 1977 TCMA Evansville Triplets (25) 150.00
- 1977 Sussman Ft. Lauderdale Yankees (31) 75.00
- 1977 Caruso Hawaii Islanders (24) 12.50
- 1977 TCMA Holyoke Millers (28) 10.00
- 1977 Team Indianapolis Indians (27) 10.00
- 1977 TCMA Jacksonville Suns (22) 20.00
- 1977 TCMA Lodi Dodgers (25) 20.00
- 1977 TCMA Lynchburg Mets (a)(30) 25.00
- 1977 TCMA Lynchburg Mets (b)(30) 75.00
- 1977 TCMA Lynchburg Mets (31) 190.00
- 1977 TCMA Lynchburg Mets (36) 575.00
- 1977 Chong Modesto A's (23) 700.00
- 1977 TCMA Newark Co-Pilots (29) 30.00
- 1977 Top Trophies Omaha Royals (19) 90.00
- 1977 TCMA Orlando Twins (22) 65.00
- 1977 TCMA Orlando Twins (23) 75.00
- 1977 Coke Premiums Phoenix Giants (24) 20.00
- 1977 Cramer Phoenix Giants (24) 9.00
- 1977 VNB Phoenix Giants (24) 12.00
- 1977 TCMA Quad City Angels (29) 22.50
- 1977 TCMA Reading Phillies (23) 100.00
- 1977 McCurdy Rochester Red Wings (24) 95.00
- 1977 McCurdy Rochester Red Wings (Sheets) 100.00
- 1977 TCMA Salem Pirates (24) 25.00
- 1977 TCMA Salem Pirates (35) 160.00
- 1977 Cramer Salt Lake City Gulls (24) 7.50
- 1977 Mr. Chef San Jose Missions (25) 10.00
- 1977 TCMA Shreveport Captains (23) 30.00
- 1977 TCMA Spartanburg Phillies (24) 30.00
- 1977 Cramer Spokane Indians (24) 6.00
- 1977 TCMA St. Petersburg Cardinals (25) 17.50
- 1977 TCMA St. Petersburg Cardinals (26) 60.00
- 1977 DQ Tacoma Twins (30) 25.00
- 1977 Cramer Tucson Toros (24) 6.00
- 1977 TCMA Visalia Oaks (17) 22.50
- 1977 TCMA Waterloo Indians (29) 25.00
- 1977 TCMA Waterloo Indians (error)(31): 45.00
- 1977 TCMA Waterloo Indians (correct)(31) 70.00
- 1977 TCMA Wausau Mets (24) 30.00
- 1977 TCMA West Haven Yankees (25) 35.00

1978 Minor League Team Sets

Full-color cards became more prevalent in 1978 as TCMA, the market leader, began to offer its client teams the choice between black-and-white or color cards.

NM

45 Team Sets and Variations
- 1978 Cramer Albuquerque Dukes (20) 17.50
- 1978 TCMA Appleton Foxes (25) 25.00
- 1978 TCMA Arkansas Travelers (23) 40.00
- 1978 TCMA Asheville Tourists (29) 27.50
- 1978 TCMA Burlington Bees (28) 30.00
- 1978 TCMA Cedar Rapids Giants (29) 45.00
- 1978 TCMA Charleston Charlies (20) 20.00
- 1978 TCMA Charleston Pirates (24) 25.00
- 1978 TCMA Clinton Dodgers (34) 25.00
- 1978 TCMA Columbus Clippers (27) 12.00
- 1978 TCMA Daytona Beach Astros (26) 15.00
- 1978 Tiefel Denver Bears (25) 10.00
- 1978 TCMA Dunedin Blue Jays (27) 32.50
- 1978 Team Geneva Cubs (24) 165.00
- 1978 TCMA Greenwood Braves (29) 25.00
- 1978 TCMA Holyoke Millers (24) 12.00
- 1978 Sertoma 1950 Indianapolis Indians (31) 22.50
- 1978 Team Indianapolis Indians (27) 9.00
- 1978 TCMA Knoxville Knox Sox (25) 100.00
- 1978 TCMA Lodi Dodgers (25) 35.00
- 1978 TCMA Lodi Dodgers (26) 60.00
- 1978 Brittling Memphis Chicks (10) 16.00
- 1978 OLDE Minneapolis/ St. Paul (21) 20.00
- 1978 Chong Modesto A's (26) 35.00
- 1978 TCMA Newark-Wayne Co-Pilots (45) 27.50
- 1978 Team Oklahoma City 89ers (26) 55.00
- 1978 Team Oklahoma City 89ers (27) 150.00
- 1978 TCMA Orlando Twins (23) 15.00

1978 Cramer Phoenix Giants (25) 15.00
1978 TCMA Quad City Angels (30) 20.00
1978 TCMA Richmond Braves (20) 11.00
1978 TCMA Rochester Red Wings (17) 17.50
1978 TCMA Salem Pirates (18) 20.00
1978 Cramer Salt Lake City Gulls (24) 8.00
1978 Mr. Chef San Jose Missions (24) 12.50
1978 Cramer Spokane Indians (24) 7.50
1978 Weiner King Springfield Redbirds (24) 35.00
1978 TCMA St. Petersburg Cardinals (29) 30.00
1978 TCMA Syracuse Chiefs (22) 25.00
1978 Cramer Tacoma Yankees (25) 13.50
1978 TCMA Tidewater Tides (27) 21.00
1978 Cramer Tucson Toros (25) 10.00
1978 TCMA Waterloo Indians (26) 11.00
1978 TCMA Wausau Mets (25) 20.00
1978 TCMA Wisconsin Rapids Twins (18) 20.00.

1979 Minor League Team Sets

TCMA's dominance in the minor league team set market reached new levels in 1979, with the company responsible for 80 percent of the 50+ sets issued. The Iowa Oaks became the first minor league team to issue a set of police-sponsored safety tip player cards.

NM

52 Team Sets and Variations
1979 TCMA Albuquerque Dukes (23) 22.50
1979 University Albuquerque Dukes (23) 180.00
1979 TCMA Appleton Foxes (25) 17.50
1979 TCMA Arkansas Travelers (23) 35.00
1979 TCMA Asheville Tourists (28) 17.50
1979 TCMA Buffalo Bisons (21) 27.50
1979 TCMA Burlington Bees (25) 16.00
1979 TCMA Cedar Rapids Giants (32) 30.00
1979 TCMA Charleston Charlies (19) 15.00
1979 TCMA Charleston Charlies (21) 40.00
1979 TCMA Clinton Dodgers (28) 45.00
1979 TCMA Columbus Clippers (29) 12.00
1979 TCMA Elmira Pioneers (28) 17.50
1979 Cramer Hawaii Islanders (24) 7.50
1979 TCMA Hawaii Islanders (24) 15.00
1979 TCMA Holyoke Millers (30) 12.00
1979 Team Indianapolis Indians (32) 7.50
1979 Police Iowa Oaks (14) 60.00
1979 TCMA Jackson Mets (24) 10.00
1979 TCMA Jackson Mets (25) 12.00
1979 TCMA Knoxville White Sox (26) 25.00
1979 TCMA Lodi Dodgers (21) 25.00
1979 TCMA Memphis Chicks (24) 75.00
1979 Chong Modesto A's (24) 30.00
1979 Team Nashville Sounds (25) 11.00
1979 TCMA Newark Co-Pilots (24) 22.00
1979 TCMA Ogden A's (26) 50.00
1979 Team Oklahoma City 89ers (24) 185.00
1979 Cramer 1970's P.C.L. Stars (160) 70.00
1979 Cramer Phoenix Giants (24) 10.00
1979 TCMA Portland Beavers (24) 17.50
1979 TCMA Quad City Cubs (27) 35.00
1979 TCMA Richmond Braves (25) 7.50
1979 TCMA Rochester Red Wings (20) 5.00
1979 TCMA Salt Lake City Gulls (23) 7.50
1979 TCMA Savannah Braves (26) 15.00
1979 TCMA Spokane Indians (25) 5.00
1979 TCMA Syracuse Chiefs (20) 20.00
1979 Team Syracuse Chiefs (24) 75.00
1979 TCMA Tacoma Tugs (26) 17.50
1979 Team Tampico Alijadores (27) 100.00
1979 TCMA Tidewater Tides (25) 22.50
1979 TCMA Toledo Mud Hens (22) 20.00
1979 TCMA Tucson Toros (24) 10.00
1979 TCMA Tulsa Drillers (24) 7.50
1979 TCMA Vancouver Canadians (23) 9.00
1979 TCMA Waterbury A's (25) 45.00
1979 TCMA Waterloo Indians (36) 37.50
1979 TCMA Wausau Timbers (25) 12.50
1979 TCMA West Haven Yankees (30) 20.00
1979 TCMA Wisconsin Rapids Twins (23) 35.00

1980 Minor League Team Sets

The number of minor league team sets exceeded 60 for the first time in 1980. TCMA issues continued to proliferate, but the sets in greatest demand are two versions of a Charlotte O's set featuring Cal Ripken Jr. as a young infielder. Also making his baseball card debut in 1980, in TCMA's Reading Phillies set, was Ryne Sandberg.

NM

63 Team Sets and Variations
1980 TCMA Albuquerque Dukes (27) 12.50
1980 TCMA Anderson Braves (29) 12.00
1980 TCMA Appleton Foxes (30) 27.50
1980 TCMA Arkansas Travelers (25) 10.00
1980 TCMA Asheville Tourists (28) 8.00
1980 TCMA Batavia Trojans (30) 15.00
1980 TCMA Buffalo Bisons (16) 16.00
1980 TCMA Burlington Bees (29) 20.00
1980 TCMA Cedar Rapids Reds (26) 10.00
1980 TCMA Charleston Charlies (17) 12.50
1980 Team Charlotte O's - Orange (24) 2,750 (Cal Ripken card widely counterfeited.)
1980 WBTV Charlotte O's - Blue (28) 800.00
1980 TCMA Clinton Giants (27) 30.00
1980 TCMA Columbus Astros (22) 20.00
1980 Police Columbus Clippers (25) 15.00
1980 TCMA Columbus Clippers (28) 12.50
1980 Team Columbus Clippers (25) 15.00
1980 TCMA Elmira Pioneers (24) 35.00
1980 TCMA El Paso Diablos (24) 8.00
1980 TCMA Evansville Triplets (24) 11.00
1980 TCMA Glens Falls White Sox - B/W (29) 45.00
1980 TCMA Glens Falls White Sox - Color (30) 17.50
1980 TCMA Hawaii Islanders (25) 8.00
1980 TCMA Holyoke Millers (25) 15.00
1980 Team Indianapolis Indians (32) 12.00
1980 Police Iowa Oaks (14) 60.00
1980 Police Iowa Oaks (16) 65.00
1980 TCMA Knoxville Blue Jays (28) 30.00
1980 TCMA Lynn Sailors (23) 12.00
1980 TCMA Memphis Chicks (30) 25.00
1980 Chong Modesto A's (29) 30.00
1980 Team Nashville Sounds (25) 10.00
1980 TCMA Ogden A's (23) 15.00
1980 Team Oklahoma City 89ers (24) 17.50
1980 Police Omaha Royals (24) 60.00
1980 TCMA Orlando Twins (22) 30.00
1980 TCMA Peninsula Pilots - B/W (27) 35.00
1980 TCMA Peninsula Pilots - Color (27) 30.00
1980 VNB Phoenix Giants (26) 6.00
1980 TCMA Portland Beavers (27) 11.00
1980 TCMA Quad City Cubs (32) 30.00
1980 TCMA Reading Phillies (24) 500.00
1980 TCMA Richmond Braves (23) 11.00
1980 TCMA Rochester Red Wings (21) 8.00
1980 TCMA Salt Lake City Gulls (26) 12.00
1980 JITB San Jose Missions (21) 15.00
1980 TCMA Spokane Indians (24) 12.50
1980 TCMA Syracuse Chiefs (23) 15.00
1980 Team Syracuse Chiefs (24) 75.00
1980 TCMA Tacoma Tigers (28) 15.00
1980 TCMA Tidewater Tides (24) 10.00
1980 TCMA Toledo Mud Hens (20) 16.00
1980 TCMA Tucson Toros (24) 12.00
1980 TCMA Tulsa Drillers (26) 16.00
1980 TCMA Utica Blue Jays (33) 35.00
1980 TCMA Vancouver Canadians (22) 8.00
1980 TCMA Waterbury Reds (22) 35.00
1980 TCMA Waterloo Indians (35) 40.00
1980 TCMA Wausau Timbers (23) 25.00
1980 TCMA West Haven White Caps (31) 7.50
1980 TCMA Wichita Aeros (22) 17.50
1980 TCMA Wisconsin Rapids Twins (27) 45.00

1981 Minor League Team Sets

Once again in 1981, TCMA enjoyed an 80 percent share of the minor league team-set market. Two of the American League's most dominant hitters of the 1980s and early 1990s, Don Mattingly and Wade Boggs, made their baseball card debuts in the Arby's Nashville Sounds and TCMA Pawtucket Red Sox sets, respectively. The Nashville set was reprinted by the team in later years, wiping out most of the market value of what should have been 1981's most valuable minor league set.

MT

61 Team Sets and Variations
1981 TCMA Albuquerque Dukes (No Koufax.) (25) 10.00
1981 TCMA Albuquerque Dukes (W/Koufax.) (26) 25.00
1981 Team Albuquerque Dukes (20) 80.00
1981 TCMA Appleton Foxes (29) 12.00
1981 TCMA Arkansas Travelers (23) 15.00
1981 TCMA Batavia Trojans (30) 10.00
1981 TCMA Birmingham Barons (25) 20.00
1981 TCMA Bristol Red Sox (22) 15.00
1981 TCMA Buffalo Bisons (25) 15.00
1981 TCMA Burlington Bees (29) 20.00
1981 TCMA Cedar Rapids Reds (26) 22.50
1981 TCMA Charleston Charlies (24) 12.50
1981 TCMA Charleston Royals (26) 15.00
1981 Team Charlotte O's (25) 75.00
1981 TCMA Chattanooga Lookouts (25) 12.00
1981 TCMA Clinton Giants (29) 12.50
1981 Police Columbus Clippers (25) 11.00
1981 TCMA Columbus Clippers (28) 13.50
1981 TCMA Durham Bulls (24) 11.00
1981 Red Rooster Edmonton Trappers (24) 12.50
1981 TCMA El Paso Diablos (24) 15.00
1981 TCMA Evansville Triplets (22) 10.00
1981 TCMA Glens Falls White Sox (24) 15.00
1981 TCMA Hawaii Islanders (23) 16.00
1981 TCMA Holyoke Millers (26) 14.00
1981 Team Holyoke Millers (25) 40.00
1981 Team Indianapolis Indians (32) 6.00
1981 TCMA Lynn Sailors (29) 10.00
1981 TCMA Miami Orioles (21) 16.00
1981 TCMA Miami Orioles (23) 60.00
1981 Chong Modesto A's (30) 20.00
1981 Arby's Nashville Sounds (25) 11.00
1981 TCMA Oklahoma City 89ers (26) 50.00
1981 TCMA Omaha Royals (24) 15.00
1981 TCMA Pawtucket Red Sox (24) 30.00
1981 VNB Phoenix Giants (27) 12.00
1981 TCMA Portland Beavers (27) 13.50
1981 TCMA Quad City Cubs (33) 15.00
1981 TCMA Reading Phillies (23) 60.00
1981 TCMA Redwood Pioneers (30) 15.00
1981 TCMA Richmond Braves (25) 7.50
1981 TCMA Rochester Red Wings (23) 215.00 (Cal Ripken card widely counterfeited.)
1981 WTF Rochester Red Wings (25) 325.00
1981 TCMA Salt Lake City Gulls (26) 12.00
1981 TCMA Shreveport Captains (23) 9.00
1981 TCMA Spokane Indians (32) 10.00
1981 TCMA Syracuse Chiefs (24) 12.00
1981 Team Syracuse Chiefs (24) 75.00
1981 TCMA Tacoma Tigers (32) 6.00
1981 TCMA Tidewater Tides (29) 13.50
1981 TCMA Toledo Mud Hens (22) 20.00
1981 TCMA Tucson Toros (26) 10.00
1981 TCMA Tulsa Drillers (30) 10.00
1981 TCMA Vancouver Canadians (25) 9.00
1981 TCMA Vero Beach Dodgers (27) 15.00
1981 TCMA Waterbury Reds (23) 20.00
1981 TCMA Waterloo Indians (34) 7.00
1981 TCMA Wausau Timbers (29) 40.00
1981 TCMA West Haven A's (23) 20.00
1981 TCMA Wisconsin Rapids Twins (23) 15.00

1982 Minor League Team Sets

A new hobby player entered the minor league team-set market in 1982. Larry Fritsch Cards of Wisconsin raised the quality bar a bit with its issue for most of the Midwest League teams. The number of sets, including late-issue variations, rose to 90 in 1982. Two of the era's most popularly collected athletes appeared on a baseball card for the first time in TCMA issues that year: Tony Gwynn with the Hawaii Islanders and John Elway with the Oneonta Yankees.

MT

92 Team Sets and Variations
1982 TCMA Albuquerque Dukes (27) 15.00
1982 Team Albuquerque Dukes Photos (28) 100.00
1982 TCMA Alexandria Dukes (25) 15.00
1982 TCMA Amarillo Gold Sox (25) 12.00
1982 Fritsch Appleton Foxes (31) 10.00
1982 Fritsch Appleton Foxes (33) 12.00
1982 TCMA Arkansas Travelers (24) 17.50
1982 TCMA Auburn Astros (19) 15.00
1982 Fritsch Beloit Brewers (27) 12.00
1982 TCMA Birmingham Barons (24) 10.00
1982 TCMA Buffalo Bisons (18) 17.50
1982 Fritsch Burlington Rangers (30) 9.00
1982 Fritsch Burlington Rangers (32) 11.00
1982 TCMA Burlington Rangers (26) 15.00
1982 TCMA Burlington Rangers (27) 25.00
1982 TCMA Cedar Rapids Reds (27) 25.00
1982 TCMA Charleston Charlies (24) 12.00
1982 TCMA Charleston Royals (24) 25.00
1982 Team Charlotte O's (31) 45.00
1982 TCMA Chattanooga Lookouts (25) 20.00
1982 Fritsch Clinton Giants (32) 12.00
1982 Police Columbus Clippers (25) 15.00
1982 TCMA Columbus Clippers (26) 75.00
1982 Fritsch Danville Suns (28) 15.00
1982 TCMA Daytona Beach Astros (25) 16.00
1982 TCMA Durham Bulls (25) 16.00
1982 TCMA Edmonton Trappers (25) 7.00
1982 TCMA El Paso Diablos (24) 9.00
1982 TCMA Evansville Triplets (25) 12.50
1982 TCMA Ft. Myers Royals (23) 15.00
1982 TCMA Glens Falls White Sox (23) 40.00
1982 TCMA Hawaii Islanders (25) 125.00 Tony Gwynn card widely counterfeited.
1982 TCMA Holyoke Millers (26) 15.00
1982 Team Holyoke Millers (29) 45.00
1982 TCMA Idaho Falls Athletics (33) 20.00
1982 Team Indianapolis Indians (32) 11.00
1982 TCMA Iowa Cubs (32) 8.00
1982 TCMA Jackson Mets (25) 25.00
1982 TCMA Knoxville Blue Jays (23) 15.00
1982 Ehrler's Louisville Redbirds (30) 10.00
1982 TCMA Lynchburg Mets (20) 35.00
1982 TCMA Lynchburg Mets (23) 45.00
1982 TCMA Lynn Sailors (18) 6.00
1982 Fritsch Madison Muskies (34) 9.00
1982 TCMA Miami Marlins (22) 12.50
1982 Chong Modesto A's (27) 17.50
1982 Arby's Nashville Sounds (28) 10.00
1982 TCMA Oklahoma City 89ers (25) 10.00
1982 TCMA Omaha Royals (27) 15.00
1982 TCMA Omaha Royals (29) 45.00
1982 TCMA Oneonta Yankees (17) 450.00 John Elway card widely counterfeited.
1982 TCMA Orlando Twins (24) 10.00
1982 TCMA Orlando Twins S.L. Champions (24) 17.50
1982 VNB Phoenix Giants (27) 17.50
1982 TCMA Portland Beavers (25) 17.50
1982 TCMA Quad City Cubs (28) 15.00
1982 TCMA Reading Phillies (22) 30.00
1982 TCMA Redwood Pioneers (27) 15.00
1982 TCMA Richmond Braves (31) 15.00
1982 TCMA Richmond Braves (32) 45.00
1982 TCMA Rochester Red Wings (22) 15.00
1982 TCMA Salt Lake City Gulls (25) 15.00
1982 TCMA Spokane Indians (26) 9.00
1982 Fritsch Springfield Cardinals (24) 12.50
1982 Fritsch Springfield Cardinals (27) 15.00
1982 TCMA Syracuse Chiefs (26) 12.50
1982 TCMA Syracuse Chiefs (29) 25.00
1982 Team Syracuse Chiefs (24) 75.00
1982 TCMA Tacoma Tigers (37) 12.00
1982 TCMA Tacoma Tigers (39) 45.00
1982 TCMA Tidewater Tides (25) 25.00
1982 TCMA Tidewater Tides (26) 50.00
1982 TCMA Toledo Mud Hens (24) 15.00
1982 TCMA Toledo Mud Hens (27) 45.00
1982 TCMA Tucson Toros (28) 11.00
1982 TCMA Tulsa Drillers (25) 15.00
1982 TCMA Tulsa Drillers (28) 45.00
1982 TCMA Vancouver Canadians (24) 16.00
1982 TCMA Vero Beach Dodgers (29) 17.50
1982 TCMA Waterbury Reds (23) 9.00
1982 Fritsch Waterloo Indians (28) 8.00
1982 Fritsch Waterloo Indians (31) 11.00
1982 TCMA Waterloo Indians (25) 15.00
1982 TCMA Waterloo Indians (28) 40.00
1982 Fritsch Wausau Timbers (31) 10.00
1982 Fritsch Wausau Timbers (33) 12.00
1982 TCMA West Haven A's (29) 20.00
1982 Team Wichita Aeros (20) 12.50
1982 Fritsch Wisconsin Rapids Twins (27) 12.00
1982 Fritsch Wisconsin Rapids Twins (28) 12.50

1983 Minor League Team Sets

In his second and final year of minor league team set production, Larry Fritsch scored a coup in issuing the first baseball cards of Jose Canseco (Madison Muskies) and Kirby Puckett (Visalia Oaks). With Fritsch and several other entities, including the newspaper Baseball Hobby News, sponsoring team sets, TCMA's share of the 80-set market in 1983 declined to about 70 percent.

MT

83 Team Sets and Variations
1983 TCMA Albany-Colonie A's (20) 20.00
1983 TCMA Albuquerque Dukes (25) 16.00
1983 Team Albuquerque Dukes Photos (16) 65.00
1983 TCMA Alexandria Dukes (31) 20.00
1983 TCMA Anderson Braves (33) 10.00
1983 Fritsch Appleton Foxes (30) 10.00
1983 TCMA Arkansas Travelers (25) 16.00
1983 TCMA Beaumont Golden Gators (23) 35.00
1983 Fritsch Beloit Brewers (30) 10.00
1983 TCMA Birmingham Barons (25) 12.50
1983 TCMA Buffalo Bisons (25) 25.00
1983 Fritsch Burlington Rangers (30) 7.50
1983 TCMA Burlington Rangers (28) 15.00
1983 TCMA Butte Copper Kings (33) 22.50
1983 Fritsch Cedar Rapids Reds (26) 10.00
1983 TCMA Cedar Rapids Reds (28) 16.00

Year	Set	Price
1983	TCMA Charleston Charlies (22)	9.00
1983	TCMA Charleston Royals (26)	15.00
1983	TCMA Chattanooga Lookouts (28)	65.00
1983	Fritsch Clinton Giants (30)	8.00
1983	TCMA Columbus Astros (24)	10.00
1983	TCMA Columbus Clippers (27)	15.00
1983	TCMA Daytona Beach Astros (27)	10.00
1983	TCMA Durham Bulls (29)	7.50
1983	TCMA El Paso Diablos (25)	10.00
1983	TCMA Erie Cardinals (25)	10.00
1983	TCMA Evansville Triplets (25)	10.00
1983	TCMA Glens Falls White Sox (24)	6.00
1983	TCMA Greensboro Hornets (30)	20.00
1983	TCMA Idaho Falls Athletics (34)	22.50
1983	Team Indianapolis Indians (32)	15.00
1983	TCMA Iowa Cubs (30)	30.00
1983	TCMA Iowa Cubs (31)	60.00
1983	Kelly Kinston Blue Jays (29)	65.00
1983	TCMA Knoxville Blue Jays (22)	7.50
1983	BHN Las Vegas Stars (22)	11.00
1983	Riley Louisville Redbirds (30)	11.00
1983	TCMA Lynchburg Mets (23)	15.00
1983	TCMA Lynn Pirates (27)	20.00
1983	Fritsch Madison Muskies (32)	12.00
1983	TCMA Memphis Chicks (24)	12.00
1983	TCMA Miami Marlins (28)	20.00
1983	TCMA Midland Cubs (26)	15.00
1983	Chong Modesto A's (30)	15.00
1983	TCMA Nashua Angels (27)	9.00
1983	Hill's Nashville Sounds (25)	7.00
1983	TCMA Oklahoma City 89ers (24)	15.00
1983	TCMA Omaha Royals (26)	10.00
1983	TCMA Orlando Twins (22)	12.00
1983	TCMA Orlando Twins (23)	35.00
1983	TCMA Pawtucket Red Sox (26)	25.00
1983	Fritsch Peoria Suns (30)	5.00
1983	BHN Phoenix Giants (28)	20.00
1983	TCMA Portland Beavers (22)	30.00
1983	TCMA Portland Beavers (25)	60.00
1983	TCMA Quad City Cubs (27)	15.00
1983	TCMA Reading Phillies (24)	40.00
1983	TCMA Redwood Pioneers (32)	15.00
1983	TCMA Richmond Braves (25)	20.00
1983	TCMA Rochester Red Wings (25)	7.50
1983	TCMA Salt Lake City Gulls (26)	9.00
1983	Colla San Jose Bees (26)	15.00
1983	Fritsch Springfield Cardinals (26)	7.00
1983	TCMA St. Petersburg Cardinals (30)	10.00
1983	TCMA Syracuse Chiefs (26)	25.00
1983	Team Syracuse Chiefs (25)	75.00
1983	TCMA Tacoma Tigers (31)	12.00
1983	TCMA Tacoma T igers (36)	55.00
1983	TCMA Tampa Tarpons (29)	30.00
1983	TCMA Tidewater Tides (29)	20.00
1983	TCMA Toledo Mud Hens (25)	10.00
1983	TCMA Toledo Mud Hens (29)	60.00
1983	TCMA Tri-Cities Triplets (28)	10.00
1983	TCMA Tucson Toros (25)	12.50
1983	TCMA Tucson Toros (26)	25.00
1983	TCMA Tulsa Drillers (25)	9.00
1983	TCMA Vero Beach Dodgers (29)	16.00
1983	Fritsch Visalia Oaks (25)	125.00
1983	TCMA Waterbury Reds (19)	22.50
1983	Fritsch Waterloo Indians (29)	8.00
1983	Fritsch Wausau Timbers (31)	8.00
1983	Dog-n-Shake Wichita Aeroes (24)	15.00
1983	Fritsch Wisconsin Rapids Twins (28)	12.50

1984 Minor League Team Sets

A trend toward more baseball card shop sponsorships of minor league team sets is noted with the 1984 issues. Another Mike Cramer innovation that year was the introduction of special high-end ultraviolet-coated glossy versions of his Pacific Coast League sets. The major debut among '84 minor league cards was Roger Clemens' appearance in TCMA's Pawtucket Red Sox set.

MT

72 Team Sets and Variations

Year	Set	Price
1984	TCMA Albany-Colonie A's (26)	15.00
1984	Cramer Albuquerque Dukes (26)	4.00
1984	Cramer Albuquerque Dukes Glossy (26)	15.00
1984	Team Albuquerque Dukes Photos (27)	65.00
1984	TCMA Arkansas Travelers (26)	8.00
1984	TCMA Beaumont Golden Gators (25)	10.00
1984	TCMA Buffalo Bisons (25)	13.50
1984	TCMA Butte Copper Kings (27)	12.50
1984	TCMA Cedar Rapids Reds (28)	11.00
1984	TCMA Charlotte O's (27)	12.50
1984	TCMA Chattanooga Lookouts (29)	6.00
1984	Police Columbus Clippers (25)	10.00
1984	TCMA Columbus Clippers (25)	9.00
1984	Team Daytona Beach Astros (25)	25.00
1984	TCMA Durham Bulls (30)	10.00
1984	Cramer Edmonton Trappers (26)	6.00
1984	Cramer Edmonton Trappers - Glossy (26)	10.00
1984	TCMA El Paso Diablos (25)	9.00
1984	TCMA Evansville Triplets (22)	16.00
1984	Cramer Everett Giants (35)	10.00
1984	Cramer Everett Giants (42)	20.00
1984	TCMA Greenboro Hornets (26)	15.00
1984	Pizza Hut Greenville Braves (25)	40.00
1984	Cramer Hawaii Islanders (25)	7.50
1984	Cramer Hawaii Islanders - Glossy (25)	12.00
1984	Team Idaho Falls A's (30)	25.00
1984	Team Indianapolis Indians (32)	10.00
1984	TCMA Iowa Cubs (31)	15.00
1984	TCMA Jackson Mets (25)	20.00
1984	Smokey Jackson Mets Alumni (15)	35.00
1984	Cramer Las Vegas Stars (25)	12.00
1984	Cramer Las Vegas Stars - Glossy (25)	17.50
1984	TCMA Little Falls Mets (26)	20.00
1984	Riley Louisville Redbirds (30)	6.00
1984	T&J Madison Muskies (25)	9.00
1984	TCMA Maine Guides (23)	12.50
1984	TCMA Memphis Chicks (25)	15.00
1984	TCMA Midland Cubs (24)	8.00
1984	Chong Modesto A's (28)	75.00
1984	Hill's Nashville Sounds (25)	15.00
1984	TCMA Newark Orioles (24)	10.00
1984	TCMA Newark Orioles (25)	30.00
1984	TCMA Oklahoma City 89ers (24)	10.00
1984	TCMA Omaha Royals (30)	10.00
1984	TCMA Pawtucket Red Sox Error Set (25)	125.00
1984	TCMA Pawtucket Red Sox Corrected Set(29)	155.00

Roger Clemens card widely counterfeited.

Year	Set	Price
1984	Cramer Phoenix Giants (25)	9.00
1984	Cramer Phoenix Giants - Glossy (25)	15.00
1984	Cramer Portland Beavers (22)	7.00
1984	Cramer Portland Beavers - Glossy (22)	20.00
1984	TCMA Prince Williams Pirates (34)	7.00
1984	TCMA Richmond Braves (27)	9.00
1984	TCMA Rochester Red Wings (19)	10.00
1984	Cramer Salt Lake City Gulls (24)	6.00
1984	Cramer SLC Gulls - Glossy (24)	15.00
1984	TCMA Savannah Cardinals (26)	10.00
1984	1stB Shreveport Captains (24)	20.00
1984	Team Spokane Indians (24)	15.00
1984	TCMA Syracuse Chiefs (32)	10.00
1984	Cramer Tacoma Tigers (25)	7.50
1984	Cramer Tacoma Tigers - Glossy (25)	12.00
1984	TCMA Tidewater Tides (28)	6.00
1984	TCMA Toledo Mud Hens (24)	15.00
1984	Cramer Tucson Toros (25)	8.00
1984	Cramer Tucson Toros - Glossy (25)	15.00
1984	Team Tulsa Drillers (22)	7.50
1984	Cramer Vancouver Canadians (25)	10.00
1984	Cramer Vancouver Canadians - Glossy (25)	15.00
1984	TCMA Visalia Oaks (25)	12.50
1984	Rock's Wichita Aeros (23)	16.00
1984	Rock's Wichita Aeros Posters (3)	35.00

1985 Minor League Team Sets

ProCards, which once dominated the minor league card new-issues market, made its debut in 1985 with a single set for the Reading Phillies. Mark McGwire made his minor league card debut in a Chong team set of the Modesto A's, initially suffering the indignity of having his name misspelled. Latter-day reprinting and/or counterfeiting of the McGwire (and McGuire) cards sapped much for the market strength from what should have been the 1980s' most desirable minor league issue.

MT

79 Team Sets and Variations

Year	Set	Price
1985	TCMA Albany-Colonie Yankees (33)	25.00
1985	TCMA Albany-Colonie Yankees (35)	27.50
1985	Cramer Albuquerque Dukes (25)	6.00
1985	Team Anchorage Glacier Pilots (44)	7.50
1985	TCMA Beaumont Golden Gators (25)	12.00
1985	TCMA Beloit Brewers (26)	10.00
1985	Cramer Bend Phillies (24)	9.00
1985	Team Birmingham Barons (25)	55.00
1985	TCMA Buffalo Bisons (26)	8.00
1985	TCMA Burlington Rangers (28)	10.00
1985	Cramer Calgary Cannons (25)	9.00
1985	TCMA Cedar Rapids Reds (32)	15.00
1985	TCMA Charlotte O's (29)	10.00
1985	TCMA Charlotte O's (31)	17.50
1985	Team Chattanooga Lookouts (26)	50.00
1985	Police Columbus Clippers (25)	4.00
1985	TCMA Columbus Clippers (28)	12.00
1985	Team Daytona Beach Islanders (30)	30.00
1985	TCMA Durham Bulls (32)	12.00
1985	Cramer Edmonton Trappers (25)	7.00
1985	TCMA Elmira Pioneers (25)	13.50
1985	Pacific Everett Giants Series 1 (24)	7.50
1985	Pacific Everett Giants Series 2 (24)	15.00
1985	Smokey Fresno Giants (32)	60.00
1985	TCMA Ft. Myers Royals (30)	8.00
1985	TCMA Greensboro Hornets (28)	12.50
1985	Pizza Hut Greenville Braves (26)	45.00
1985	Team Greenville Braves (26)	35.00
1985	Cramer Hawaii Islanders (25)	7.00
1985	BK Huntsville Stars (25)	9.00
1985	BK Huntsville Stars Uncut Sheet	9.00
1985	Team Indianapolis Indians (36)	24.00
1985	TCMA International League All-Stars (42)	12.50
1985	TCMA International League All-Stars (45)	45.00
1985	TCMA Iowa Cubs (34)	13.50
1985	TCMA Kinston Blue Jays (26)	12.50
1985	Cramer Las Vegas Stars (25)	9.00
1985	TCMA Little Falls Mets (27)	7.00
1985	Riley Louisville Redbirds (30)	5.00
1985	TCMA Lynchburg Mets (27)	10.00
1985	TCMA Madison Muskies (25)	7.00
1985	T&J Madison Muskies (25)	10.00
1985	TCMA Maine Guides (30)	12.50
1985	TCMA Mexico City Tigers (29)	10.00
1985	TCMA Midland Angels (25)	15.00
1985	Chong Modesto A's - Errors (28)	300.00
1985	Chong Modesto A's - Corrected (28)	75.00
1985	TCMA Nashua Pirates (29)	10.00
1985	Hill's Nashville Sounds (25)	4.00
1985	TCMA Newark Orioles (25)	10.00
1985	TCMA Oklahoma City 89ers (30)	15.00
1985	TCMA Omaha Royals (31)	20.00
1985	TCMA Orlando Twins (26)	11.00
1985	Team Osceola Astros (30)	50.00
1985	TCMA Pawtucket Red Sox (20)	20.00
1985	Cramer Phoenix Giants (25)	7.00
1985	Cramer Portland Beavers (25)	11.00
1985	TCMA Prince Williams Pirates (31)	7.50
1985	ProCards Reading Phillies (25)	4.00
1985	TCMA Richmond Braves (26)	5.00
1985	TCMA Rochester Red Wings (31)	10.00
1985	Rochester Red Wings Ripken Ticket	6.00
1985	Cramer Spokane Indians (24)	8.00
1985	Cramer Spokane All-Time Greats (24)	12.50
1985	TCMA Springfield Cardinals (25)	6.00
1985	TCMA Syracuse Chiefs (31)	30.00
1985	Cramer Tacoma Tigers (25)	9.00
1985	TCMA Tidewater Tides (27)	8.00
1985	TCMA Tidewater Tides (28)	30.00
1985	TCMA Toledo Mud Hens (25)	7.00
1985	TCMA Toldeo Mud Hens (26)	11.00
1985	Cramer Tucson Toros (25)	6.00
1985	Team Tulsa Drillers (27)	20.00
1985	Team Tulsa Drillers (28)	30.00
1985	TCMA Utica Blue Sox (26)	40.00
1985	Cramer Vancouver Canadians (25)	9.00
1985	TCMA Vero Beach Dodgers (27)	7.50
1985	TCMA Visalia Oaks (25)	10.00
1985	TCMA Waterbury Indians (25)	9.00

1986 Minor League Team Sets

After its one-team effort in 1985, ProCards burst onto the team-set minor league market in a major way in 1986, driving the market to a record of more than 130 sets (including variations), for which PC claimed nearly a 75 percent market share. Notable debuts were Greg Maddux in the Pittsfield Cubs set and Randy Johnson in the West Palm Beach Expos issue, both sets a product of ProCards.

MT

133 Team Sets and Variations

Year	Set	Price
1986	TCMA Albany-Colonie Yankees (32)	5.00
1986	PC Albuquerque Dukes (28)	4.00
1986	Team Albuquerque Dukes Photos (28)	75.00
1986	Team Anchorage Glacier Pilots (42)	15.00
1986	PC Appleton Foxes (28)	6.00
1986	PC Arkansas Travelers (26)	10.00
1986	PC Asheville Tourists (29)	5.00
1986	PC Auburn Astros (27)	5.00
1986	PC Bakersfield Dodgers (29)	6.00
1986	PC Beaumont Golden Gators (25)	12.50
1986	Pacific Bellingham Mariners (29)	6.00
1986	PC Beloit Brewers (26)	5.00
1986	Pacific Bend Phillies (25)	10.00
1986	Team Birmingham Barons (28)	55.00
1986	PC Buffalo Bisons (26)	4.00
1986	PC Burlington Expos (28)	8.00
1986	PC Calgary Cannons (26)	5.00
1986	TCMA Cedar Rapids Reds (28)	6.00
1986	PC Charleston Rainbows (29)	20.00
1986	WBTV Charlotte O's (30)	17.50
1986	PC Chattanooga Lookouts (25)	11.00
1986	PC Clearwater Phillies (26)	5.00
1986	PC Clinton Giants (30)	3.00
1986	PC Columbia Mets (28)	11.00
1986	PC Columbus Astros (25)	6.00
1986	Police Columbus Clippers (25)	5.00
1986	PC Columbus Clippers (26)	9.00
1986	PC Daytona Beach Astros (29)	5.00
1986	PC Durham Bulls (27)	5.00
1986	PC Edmonton Trappers (27)	9.00
1986	PC Elmira Pioneers (30)	45.00
1986	PC El Paso Diablos (23)	7.00
1986	PC Erie Cardinals (30)	9.00
1986	PC Erie Cardinals (31)	25.00
1986	Pacific Eugene Emeralds (25)	7.00
1986	Pacific Everett Giants - B/W (36)	7.00
1986	Pacfiic Everett Giants - Color (32)	16.00
1986	PC Florida State League All-Stars (50)	60.00
1986	Smokey Bear Fresno Giants (32)	25.00
1986	PC Ft. Lauderdale Yankees (23)	5.00
1986	PC Ft. Myers Royals (29)	5.00
1986	PC Geneva Cubs (27)	5.00
1986	PC Glens Falls Tigers (24)	5.00
1986	PC Greensboro Hornets (27)	8.00
1986	PC Greenville Braves (24)	20.00
1986	PC Hagerstown Suns (29)	5.00
1986	PC Hawaii Islanders (23)	5.00
1986	BK Huntsville Stars (25)	16.00
1986	BK Huntsville Stars Uncut Sheet	30.00
1986	Team Indianapolis Indians (36)	10.00
1986	PC Iowa Cubs (26)	4.00
1986	TCMA Jackson Mets (27)	6.00
1986	TCMA Jacksonville Expos (26)	5.00
1986	PC Jamestown Expos (30)	5.00
1986	PC Kenosha Twins (25)	7.00
1986	PC Kinston Eagles (25)	5.00
1986	PC Knoxville Blue Jays (27)	7.00
1986	PC Lakeland Tigers (25)	7.00
1986	PC Las Vegas Stars (24)	4.00
1986	PC Las Vegas Stars (25)	5.00
1986	PC Las Vegas Stars (26)	12.00
1986	PC Little Falls Mets (29)	5.00
1986	Team Louisville Redbirds (30)	7.50
1986	PC Lynchburg Mets (28)	5.00
1986	PC Macon Pirates (27)	12.50
1986	PC Madison Muskies (28)	9.00
1986	T&J Madison Muskies (27)	8.00
1986	PC Maine Guides (26)	9.00
1986	Pacific Medford A's (25)	7.00
1986	Time Out Memphis Chicks - Gold (26)	10.00
1986	Time Out Memphis Chicks - Silver (26)	12.00
1986	PC Miami Marlins (29)	5.00
1986	PC Midland Angels (26)	6.00
1986	Chong Modesto A's (27)	9.00
1986	PC Modesto A's (26)	5.00
1986	PC Modesto A's (27)	10.00
1986	PC Nashua Pirates (28)	4.00
1986	Hill's Nashville Sounds (24)	8.00
1986	PC New Britain Red Sox (25)	10.00
1986	PC Oklahoma City 89ers (26)	5.00
1986	PC Omaha Royals (29)	7.50
1986	TCMA Omaha Royals (25)	7.50
1986	PC Orlando Twins (24)	7.00
1986	PC Osceola Astros (29)	5.00
1986	PC Palm Springs Angels (29)	15.00
1986	Smokey Bear Palm Springs Angels (28)	25.00
1986	PC Pawtucket Red Sox (28)	6.00
1986	PC Peninsula White Sox (28)	5.00
1986	PC Peoria Chiefs (27)	25.00
1986	PC Phoenix Firebirds (26)	5.00
1986	PC Pittsfield Cubs (25)	110.00
1986	Team Pittsfield Cubs poster - B/W	75.00
1986	Team Pittsfield Cubs Poster - Color	75.00
1986	PC Portland Beavers (22)	5.00
1986	PC Portland Beavers (23)	10.00
1986	PC Prince William Pirates (27)	4.00
1986	PC Quad Cities Angels (33)	9.00
1986	PC Reading Phillies (26)	5.00
1986	PC Richmond Braves (26)	4.00
1986	PC Rochester Red Wings (26)	5.00
1986	Pacific Salem Angels (25)	6.00
1986	PC Salem Red Birds (29)	7.00
1986	PC San Jose Bees (25)	5.00
1986	PC Shreveport Captains (28)	6.00

1986 DJ Southern League All-Stars (25) 9.00
1986 Pacific Spokane Indians (25) 25.00
1986 University City Spokane Indians (24) 45.00
1986 TCMA Stars of the Future (40) 25.00
1986 PC St. Petersburg Cardinals (29) 5.00
1986 PC Stockton Ports (26) 5.00
1986 PC Sumter Braves (30) 20.00
1986 PC Syracuse Chiefs (27) 10.00
1986 PC Tacoma Tigers (25) 10.00
1986 PC Tampa Tarpons (27) 5.00
1986 PC Tidewater Tides - Mets Logo (29) 4.00
1986 PC Tidewater Tides - Tides Logo (29) 7.00
1986 PC Toledo Mud Hens (24) 4.00
1986 Pacific Tri-Cities Triplets (14) 6.00
1986 PC Tucson Toros (26) 6.00
1986 Team Tulsa Drillers (27) 20.00
1986 PC Vancouver Canadians (27) 5.00
1986 PC Ventura Gulls (28) 8.00
1986 PC Vermont Reds (24) 7.00
1986 PC Vero Beach Dodgers (27) 9.00
1986 PC Visalia Oaks (24) 5.00
1986 PC Waterbury Indians (26) 5.00
1986 PC Waterloo Indians (32) 5.00
1986 PC Watertown Pirates (27) 20.00
1986 PC Watertown Pirates (29) 25.00
1986 PC Wausau Timbers (29) 9.00
1986 PC West Palm Beach Expos (28) 45.00
1986 PC Winston-Salem Spirits (29) 10.00
1986 PC Winter Haven Red Sox (27) 8.00

1987 Minor League Team Sets

Best, which under new ownership a decade later would become a powerhouse in the minor league team-set field, made its first cards in 1987. The hobby was abuzz about the several Gregg Jefferies cards available, but the year will always be remembered as the baseball card debut of Ken Griffey Jr., in a team-issued set of the Bellingham Mariners. The number of team sets and related collectibles exceeded 150 in 1987.

MT

159 Team Sets and Variations
1987 PC Albany-Colonie Yankees (23) 6.00
1987 Team Albuquerque Dukes (30) 7.00
1987 Team Albuquerque Dukes (Photos) (35) 110.00
1987 Team Anchorage Glacier Pilots (41) 20.00
1987 PC Appleton Foxes (30) 5.00
1987 PC Arkansas Travelers (25) 6.00
1987 PC Asheville Tourists (28) 6.00
1987 PC Auburn Astros (25) 5.00
1987 PC Bakersfield Dodgers (29) 5.00
1987 Baseball USA Pan-Am Games - Blue (34) 40.00
1987 Baseball USA Pan-Am Games - Blue (35) 45.00
1987 Team Bellingham Mariners (34) 35.00
1987 PC Beloit Brewers (26) 8.00
1987 Best Birmingham Barons (28) 6.00
1987 Team Buffalo Bisons (29) 7.00
1987 PC Burlington Expos (29) 5.00
1987 PC Calgary Cannons (24) 12.00
1987 PC Cedar Rapids Reds (28) 5.00
1987 PC Charleston Rainbows (23) 10.00
1987 PC Charleston Wheelers (28) 4.00
1987 Team Charlotte O's (30) 8.00
1987 Best Chattanooga Lookouts (26) 5.00
1987 Best Chattanooga Lookouts (26) (W/Coke logo.) 10.00
1987 PC Clearwater Phillies (27) 5.00
1987 PC Clearwater Phillies (30) 8.00
1987 PC Clinton Giants (29) 5.00
1987 PC Columbia Mets (29) 4.00
1987 PC Columbus Astros (25) 7.00
1987 PC Columbus Clippers (27) 9.00
1987 Police Columbus Clippers (24) 5.00
1987 Police Columbus Clippers (26) 9.00
1987 TCMA Columbus Clippers (25) 7.00
1987 PC Daytona Beach Admirals (26) 5.00
1987 PC Denver Zephyrs (27) 4.00
1987 PC Dunedin Blue Jays (29) 4.00
1987 PC Durham Bulls (28) 5.00
1987 PC Edmonton Trappers (23) 5.00
1987 Team Elmira Pioneers - Black (34) 6.00
1987 Team Elmira Pioneers - Red (36) 35.00
1987 PC El Paso Diablos (27) 5.00
1987 PC El Paso Diablos (30) 7.00
1987 PC Erie Cardinals (29) 5.00
1987 PC Eugene Emeralds (30) 9.00
1987 Pacific Everett Giants (34) 6.00
1987 PC Fayetteville Generals (27) 5.00
1987 PC Ft. Lauderdale Yankees (30) 7.00
1987 PC Ft. Myers Royals (34) 6.00
1987 PC Gastonia Rangers (29) 70.00
1987 PC Geneva Cubs (26) 4.00
1987 PC Glens Falls Tigers (25) 10.00
1987 PC Greensboro Hornets (26) 17.50
1987 Best Greenville Braves (28) 10.00
1987 PC Hagerstown Suns (29) 5.00
1987 PC Harrisburg Senators (26) 4.00
1987 PC Hawaii Islanders (27) 3.00
1987 BK Huntsville Stars (25) 6.00
1987 PC Idaho Falls Braves (27) 5.00
1987 Team Indianapolis Indians (36) 10.00
1987 TCMA International League All-Stars (45) 8.00
1987 Team Iowa Cubs (25) 17.50
1987 Team Jackson Mets (25) 6.00
1987 PC Jacksonville Expos (29) 15.00
1987 PC Jamestown Expos (30) 5.00
1987 PC Kenosha Twins (29) 5.00
1987 PC Kinston Indians (24) 5.00
1987 PC Knoxville Blue Jays (27) 5.00
1987 PC Knoxville Blue Jays (30) 9.00
1987 PC Lakeland Tigers (26) 5.00
1987 PC Las Vegas Stars (27) 4.00
1987 PC Little Falls Mets (29) 6.00
1987 PC Little Falls Mets, W/Variations (31) 8.00
1987 Team Louisville Redbirds (30) 8.00
1987 PC Lynchburg Mets (28) 4.00
1987 PC Macon Pirates (25) 5.00
1987 PC Madison Muskies (25) 4.00
1987 T&J Madison Muskies (23) 7.00
1987 PC Maine Guides (23) 4.00
1987 TCMA Maine Guides (25) 5.00
1987 TCMA Maine Guides (27) 12.00
1987 Best Memphis Chicks (27) 6.00
1987 PC Memphis Chicks (27) 5.00
1987 PC Miami Marlins (25) 5.00
1987 PC Midland Angels (30) 5.00
1987 Chong Modesto A's (32) 5.00
1987 PC Modesto A's (25) 6.00
1987 PC Myrtle Beach Blue Jays (30) 4.00
1987 Hill's Nashville Sounds (26) 5.00
1987 Nashville Sounds Don Mattingly Ticket 5.00
1987 PC Newark Orioles (29) 5.00
1987 PC New Britain Red Sox (25) 5.00
1987 PC Oklahoma City 89ers (27) 6.00
1987 PC Omaha Royals (26) 6.00
1987 PC Oneonta Yankees (33) 12.50
1987 PC Orlando Twins (26) 8.00
1987 PC Osceola Astros (29) 5.00
1987 PC Palm Springs Angels (32) 5.00
1987 PC Pawtucket Red Sox (27) 3.00
1987 TCMA Pawtucket Red Sox (28) 4.00
1987 PC Peninsula White Sox (29) 4.00
1987 Pizza World Peoria Chiefs (6) 60.00
1987 PC Peoria Chiefs (29) 6.00
1987 PC Phoenix Firebirds (28) 6.00
1987 PC Pittsfield Cubs (26) 15.00
1987 Team Pittsfield Cubs Poster 30.00
1987 Bon Pocatello Giants (32) 45.00
1987 PC Port Charlotte Rangers (27) 5.00
1987 PC Portland Beavers (25) 4.00
1987 PC Prince William Yankees (29) 4.00
1987 PC Quad City Angels (31) 6.00
1987 PC Reading Phillies (26) 4.00
1987 Bob's Richmond Braves (23) 75.00
1987 Crown Richmond Braves (30) 17.50
1987 TCMA Richmond Braves (29) 12.00
1987 PC Rochester Red Wings (27) 3.00
1987 TCMA Rochester Red Wings (29) 4.00
1987 PC Salem Angels (34) 4.00
1987 PC Salem Buccaneers (30) 6.00
1987 Smokey Salinas Spurs (32) 40.00
1987 Team Salt Lake City Trappers (30) 6.00
1987 Team San Antonio Dodgers (24) 7.00
1987 Team San Antonio Dodgers (25) 9.00
1987 PC San Bernardino Spirit (23) 5.00
1987 PC San Jose Bees (30) 5.00
1987 PC Savannah Cardinals (26) 5.00
1987 PC Shreveport Captains (25) 4.00
1987 DJ Southern League All-Stars (25) 9.00
1987 PC Spartanburg Phillies (28) 4.00
1987 PC Spokane Indians (25) 5.00
1987 Best Springfield Cardinals (28) 5.00
1987 PC St. Petersburg Cardinals (27) 5.00
1987 PC Stockton Ports (26) 9.00
1987 PC Sumter Braves (30) 4.00
1987 PC Syracuse Chiefs (23) 4.00
1987 TCMA Syracuse Chiefs (33) 11.00
1987 Team Syracuse Chiefs Tickets (12) 25.00
1987 PC Tacoma Tigers (23) 4.00
1987 PC Tampa Tarpons (30) 5.00
1987 Texas League All-Stars (36) 4.00
1987 PC Tidewater Tides (33) 4.00
1987 TCMA Tidewater Tides (30) 4.00
1987 PC Toledo Mud Hens (30) 4.00
1987 TCMA Toledo Mud Hens (25) 4.00
1987 Jones Tucson Toros (24) 45.00
1987 PC Tucson Toros (25) 5.00
1987 Team Tulsa Drillers (28) 6.00
1987 PC Utica Blue Sox (33) 4.00
1987 PC Vancouver Canadians (25) 5.00
1987 PC Vermont Reds (26) 5.00
1987 PC Vero Beach Dodgers (31) 7.00
1987 PC Visalia Oaks (27) 5.00
1987 PC Waterloo Indians (29) 7.00
1987 PC Watertown Pirates (31) 8.00
1987 PC Wausau Timbers (28) 5.00
1987 PC West Palm Beach Expos (28) 5.00
1987 Rock's Wichita Pilots (25) 17.50
1987 PC Williamsport Bills (27) 5.00
1987 PC Winston-Salem Spirits (27) 5.00
1987 PC Winter Haven Red Sox (30) 5.00
1987 PC Wytheville Cubs (31) 5.00

1988 Minor League Team Sets

Major changes in the minor league team set market were seen in 1988. TCMA, which had pioneered the concept in the early 1970s, merged with Collectors Marketing Corp. (CMC). The new venture nearly tripled the number of team sets issued under the CMC label. Star Co. also joined the market in a major way, producing more than 25 team and all-star sets. Other companies entering the market in 1988 included Grand Slam, Legoe, Sport Pro and Cal Cards. An Anchorage Glacier Pilots card of Mark McGwire purporting to date from 1982 was actually produced in 1988.

MT

225 Team Sets and Variations
1988 CMC AAA All-Stars (45) 17.50
1988 PC AAA All-Stars (55) 6.00
1988 Alaska Goldpanners 1960s All Stars (12) 25.00
1988 Alaska Goldpanners 1970s All-Stars (12) 22.50
1988 Team Alaska Goldpanners (20) 15.00
1988 PC Albany-Colonie Yankees (27) 5.00
1988 CMC Albuquerque Dukes (25) 5.00
1988 PC Albuquerque Dukes (29) 4.00
1988 Team Albuquerque Dukes Photos (35) 110.00
1988 "1982" Anchorage Glacier Pilots McGwire 55.00
1988 PC Appleton Foxes (30) 5.00
1988 GS Arkansas Travelers (25) 5.00
1988 PC Asheville Tourists (31) 5.00
1988 PC Auburn Astros (29) 12.00
1988 PC Augusta Pirates (33) 8.00
1988 Cal Bakersfield Dodgers (34) 5.00
1988 Baseball America AA Top Prospects (30) 7.50
1988 Star Baseball City Royals (25) 10.00
1988 Star Baseball City Royals (27) 15.00
1988 PC Batavia Clippers (31) 4.00
1988 Legoe Bellingham Mariners (32) 5.00
1988 GS Beloit Brewers (25) 4.00
1988 Legoe Bend Bucks (36) 15.00
1988 PC Billings Mustangs (31) 8.00
1988 Best Birmingham Barons (29) 5.00
1988 PC Boise Hawks (29) 5.00
1988 PC Bristol Tigers (32) 5.00
1988 CMC Buffalo Bisons (25) 5.00
1988 PC Buffalo Bisons (31) 4.00
1988 Team Buffalo Bisons (8) 15.00
1988 PC Burlington Braves (31) 5.00
1988 PC Burlington Indians (31) 5.00
1988 SP Butte Copper Kings (29) 8.00
1988 CMC Calgary Cannons (25) 5.00
1988 PC Calgary Cannons (28) 6.00
1988 Cal Cards California League A-S (50) 20.00
1988 P&L Cape Cod League (186) 45.00
1988 Ballpark Cape Cod Prospects (30) 30.00
1988 Star Carolina League A-S (40) 12.00
1988 PC Cedar Rapids Reds (31) 4.00
1988 PC Charleston Rainbows (30) 5.00
1988 Best Charleston Wheelers (28) 5.00
1988 Team Charlotte Knights (25) 12.00
1988 Star Charlotte Rangers (23) 40.00
1988 Star Charlotte Rangers (24) 35.00
1988 Best Chattanooga Lookouts (26) 5.00
1988 Team Chattanooga Lookouts Legends (32) 30.00
1988 Star Clearwater Phillies (26) 4.00
1988 PC Clinton Giants (29) 5.00
1988 CMC Colorado Spring Sky Sox (25) 5.00
1988 PC Colorado Springs Sky Sox (29) 5.00
1988 GS Columbia Mets (27) 4.00
1988 Best Columbus Astros (28) 5.00
1988 CMC Columbus Clippers (26) 6.00
1988 PC Columbus Clippers (29) 4.00
1988 Police Columbus Clippers (25) 5.00
1988 CMC Denver Zyphers (25) 6.00
1988 PC Denver Zephyrs (30) 5.00
1988 Star Dunedin Blue Jays (27) 10.00
1988 Star Durham Bulls - Blue (24) 5.00
1988 Star Durham Bulls - Blue (25) 7.00
1988 Star Durham Bulls - Orange (26) 6.00
1988 PC Eastern League A-S (52) 6.00
1988 CMC Edmonton Trappers (25) 7.00
1988 PC Edmonton Trappers (31) 7.00
1988 Team Elmira Pioneers - Blue (12) 75.00
1988 Team Elmira Pioneers - Red (30) 5.00
1988 Best El Paso Diablos (30) 6.00
1988 Best El Paso Diablos - Platinum (30) 25.00
1988 Best Eugene Emeralds (30) 5.00
1988 PC Fayetteville Generals (28) 8.00
1988 Star Florida State League A-S (52) 10.00
1988 Cal Fresno Suns (27) 5.00
1988 PC Fresno Suns (29) 5.00
1988 Star Ft. Lauderdale Yankees (24) 5.00
1988 PC Gastonia Rangers (30) 4.00
1988 PC Geneva Cubs (30) 3.00
1988 PC Glens Falls Tigers (27) 8.00
1988 SP Great Falls Dodgers (27) 20.00
1988 PC Greensboro Hornets (26) 5.00
1988 Best Greenville Braves (24) 5.00
1988 Star Hagerstown Suns (25) 5.00
1988 Star Hagerstown Suns (27) 7.00
1988 PC Hamilton Redbirds (30) 5.00
1988 PC Harrisburg Senators (30) 3.00
1988 BK Huntsville Stars (25) 6.00
1988 PC Idaho Falls Braves (31) 5.00
1988 CMC Indianapolis Indians (25) 20.00
1988 PC Indianapolis Indians (31) 16.00
1988 CMC Iowa Cubs (25) 5.00
1988 PC Iowa Cubs (30) 7.00
1988 GS Jackson Mets (25) 5.00
1988 Best Jacksonville Expos (29) 5.00
1988 PC Jacksonville Expos (32) 4.00
1988 PC Jamestown Expos (31) 10.00
1988 PC Kenosha Twins (29) 5.00
1988 Star Kinston Indians (24) 12.50
1988 Best Knoxville Blue Jays (26) 5.00
1988 Star Lakeland Tigers (25) 4.00
1988 CMC Las Vegas Stars (25) 9.00
1988 PC Las Vegas Stars (28) 4.00
1988 Pucko Little Falls Mets (29) 6.00
1988 Little Sun Legends/Minor League BB (11) 9.00
1988 CMC Louisville Redbirds (25) 5.00
1988 PC Louisville Redbirds (26) 5.00
1988 Team Louisville Redbirds (55) 9.00
1988 Star Lynchburg Red Sox (28) 5.00
1988 T&J Madison Muskies (25) 6.00
1988 CMC Maine Phillies (25) 5.00
1988 PC Maine Phillies (27) 4.00
1988 Star Managers/Costner Gold Set (21) (Dealer incentive issue.) 12.00
1988 Star Martinsville Phillies - Blue (32) 5.00
1988 Star Martinsville Phillies - Red (32) 6.00
1988 Best Memphis Chicks (27) 5.00
1988 Star Miami Marlins (24) 5.00
1988 GS Midland Angels (25) 5.00
1988 GS Midwest League A-S (59) 8.00
1988 Cal Modesto A's (28) 5.00
1988 Chong Modesto A's (36) 5.00
1988 PC Myrtle Beach Blue Jays (28) 7.50
1988 CMC Nashville Sounds (25) 4.00
1988 Hill's Nashville Sounds (25) 4.00
1988 PC Nashville Sounds (26) 5.00
1988 PC New Britain Red Sox (25) 16.00
1988 CMC Oklahoma City 89ers (25) 4.00
1988 PC Oklahoma City 89ers (27) 4.00
1988 CMC Omaha Royals (25) 5.00
1988 PC Omaha Royals (29) 5.00
1988 PC Oneonta Yankees (34) 4.00
1988 Best Orlando Twins (29) 5.00
1988 Star Osceola Astros (25) 5.00
1988 Cal Palm Springs Angels (31) 5.00
1988 PC Palm Springs Angels (32) 5.00
1988 CMC Pawtucket Red Sox (25) 4.00
1988 PC Pawtucket Red Sox (26) 4.00
1988 Team Peninsula Oilers (31) 35.00
1988 Team Peoria Chiefs (35) 30.00
1988 CMC Phoenix Firebirds (25) 5.00
1988 PC Phoenix Firebirds (29) 8.00
1988 PC Pittsfield Cubs (25) 5.00
1988 Team Pittsfield Cubs Poster 20.00
1988 PC Pocatello Giants (31) 5.00
1988 CMC Portland Beavers (25) 5.00
1988 PC Portland Beavers (27) 4.00
1988 Star Prince Williams Yankees (25) 15.00
1988 PC Pulaski Braves (25) 7.00
1988 GS Quad City Angels (30) 4.00
1988 PC Reading Phillies (27) 4.00

1988 Cal Reno Silver Sox (24) 5.00
1988 Bob's Richmond Braves (25) 75.00
1988 CMC Richmond Braves (25) 7.50
1988 PC Richmond Braves (27) 15.00
1988 Team Richmond Braves (26) 25.00
1988 Cal Riverside Red Wave (28) 5.00
1988 PC Riverside Red Wave (27) 5.00
1988 CMC Rochester Red Wings (25) 5.00
1988 PC Rochester Red Wings (30) 5.00
1988 Pucko Rochester Red Wings (36) 10.00
1988 Team Rochester Red Wings (26) 10.00
1988 Team Rockford Expos (34) 4.00
1988 Star Salem Buccaneers (25) 5.00
1988 Team Salt Lake City Trappers (31) 9.00
1988 Best San Antonio Missions (28) 8.00
1988 Best S.A. Missions - Platinum (28) 12.00
1988 Best San Bernardino Spirit (28) 55.00
1988 Best S.B. Spirit - Platinum (28) 350.00
1988 Best S.B. Spirit Platinum (White "Spirit.") 2,500
1988 Cal San Bernardino Spirit (28) 20.00
1988 Cal San Jose Giants (29) 5.00
1988 PC San Jose Giants (30) 5.00
1988 PC Savannah Cardinals (29) 5.00
1988 PC Shreveport Captains (25) 5.00
1988 PC Shreveport Captains - Taco Bell (25) 30.00
1988 GS South Atlantic League A-S (28) 7.00
1988 GS South Bend White Sox (28) 5.00
1988 DJ Southern League A-S (40) 5.00
1988 PC Southern Oregon A's (28) 4.00
1988 PC Spartanburg Phillies (26) 4.00
1988 Star Spartanburg Phillies - Blue (25) 10.00
1988 Star Spartanburg Phillies - Red (25) 5.00
1988 PC Spokane Indians (26) 5.00
1988 Best Springfield Cardinals (28) 9.00
1988 PC St. Catharines Blue Jays (35) 5.00
1988 Star St. Luice Mets (25) 5.00
1988 Star St. Petersburg Cardinals (25) 5.00
1988 Star St. Petersburg Cardinals (27) 15.00
1988 PC Stockton Ports (33) 5.00
1988 Cal Stockton Ports (31) 5.00
1988 PC Sumter Braves (32) 4.00
1988 CMC Syracuse Chiefs (25) 5.00
1988 PC Syracuse Chiefs (30) 3.00
1988 Team Syracuse Chiefs Tickets (12) 8.00
1988 CMC Tacoma Tigers (25) 5.00
1988 PC Tacoma Tigers (28) 5.00
1988 Star Tampa Tarpons (25) 5.00
1988 GS Texas League A-S (39) 9.00
1988 CMC Tidewater Tides - Jeffries (26) 9.00
1988 CMC Tidewater Tides - Jefferies (26) 5.00
1988 PC Tidewater Tides (29) 4.00
1988 Team Tidewater Tides (31) 15.00
1988 CMC Toledo Mud Hens (25) 5.00
1988 PC Toledo Mud Hens (28) 4.00
1988 CMC Tucson Toros (25) 9.00
1988 Jones Tucson Toros (24) 150.00
1988 PC Tucson Toros (28) 11.00
1988 Team Tulsa Drillers (28) 16.00
1988 Pucko Utica Blue Sox (29) 5.00
1988 CMC Vancouver Canadians (25) 5.00
1988 PC Vancouver Canadians (27) 5.00
1988 PC Vermont Mariners (26) 7.00
1988 PC Vermont Mariners Ken Griffey Jr. (Widely counterfeited.) 12.00
1988 Star Vero Beach Dodgers (26) 5.00
1988 Star Virginia Generals (23) 5.00
1988 Star Virginia Generals (26) 8.00
1988 Cal Visalia Oaks (30) 5.00
1988 PC Visalia Oaks (28) 5.00
1988 PC Waterloo Indians (29) 6.00
1988 Pucko Watertown Pirates (35) 7.00
1988 GS Wausau Timbers (28) 4.00
1988 Star West Palm Beach Astros (26) 5.00
1988 Rock's Wichita Pilots (30) 12.00
1988 PC Williamsport Bills (27) 5.00
1988 Star Winston-Salem Spirits (22) 4.00
1988 Star Winter Haven Red Sox (27) 5.00
1988 PC Wytheville Cubs (31) 4.00

1989 Star Minor League Baseball

In 1989, Star became the first minor league card producer to venture into the wax pack market when it issued a 100-card set. A second series was issued later, numbered 101-200. There were no factory sets issued, nor was there a checklist available to the collector. Unlike its predecessor, which had borders of various colors, the second series all sport red borders. A total of 10,000 cases of 288 packs each was issued for Series 1.

MT

Complete Set (200): 10.00
Common Player: .05
Wax Pack (10): .35
Wax Box (48): 7.50

1 Eric Anthony .05
2 David Rohde (Photo of Karl Rhodes.) .05
3 Mike Simms .05
4 John Faccio .05
5 Oreste Marrero .05
6 Troy O'Leary .05
7 Rob Maurer .05
8 Rod Morris .05
9 Ed Ohman .05
10 Jim Byrd .05
11 Mark Cobb .05
12 Pat Combs .05
13 Tim Mauser .05
14 Jim Vatcher .05
15 Luis Gonzalez .50
16 Andres Mota .05
17 Scott Servais .05
18 David Silvestri .05
19 Kevin Burdick .05
20 Tommy Shields .05
21 Mike York .05
22 Mike Anaya .05
23 Dale Plummer .05
24 Titi Roche .05
25 Vincent Zawaski .05
26 Anthony Barron .05
27 Rafael Bournigal .05
28 Albert Bustillos .05
29 Mark Griffin .05
30 Brett Magnusson .05
31 Mike Jones .05
32 Bret Barberie .05
33 Bert Echemendia .05
34 Mike Bell .05
35 Brian Hunter .05
36 Jim LeMasters .05
37 Rick Morris .05
38 Dominic Pierce .05
39 Joey Wardlow .05
40 Dera Clark .05
41 Stu Cole .05
42 Bob Hamelin .05
43 Deric Ladnier .05
44 Brian McRae .05
45 Mike Tresemer .05
46 Steve Walker .05
47 Greg Becker .05
48 Art Calvert .05
49 Todd Crosby .05
50 Shawn Hathaway .05
51 Rich Garces .05
52 Todd McClure .05
53 Steve Morris .05
54 Tim Dell .05
55 Antonio Linares .05
56 John Marshall .05
57 Mike Morandini .05
58 Paul Fuller .05
59 John Hudek .05
60 Ron Stephens .05
61 Scott Tedder .05
62 Pete Alborano .05
63 Kevin Shaw .05
64 Anthony Ariola .05
65 James Buccheri .05
66 William Love .05
67 Steve Avery .05
68 Rich Casarotti .05
69 Brian Champion .05
70 Wes Currin .05
71 Brian Deak .05
72 Ken Pennington .05
73 Theron Todd .05
74 Andy Tomberlin .05
75 Richard Falkner .05
76 Tommy Kramer .05
77 Charles Nagy .05
78 Chris Howard .05
79 Mike Rhodes .05
80 Gabriel Rodriguez .05
81 Bob Zeihen .05
82 Rod Beck .05
83 Jamie Cooper .05
84 Steve Decker .05
85 Mark Dewey .05
86 Juan Guerrero .05
87 Andres Santana .05
88 Pedro DeLeon .05
89 Pat Kelly .05
90 Bill Masse .05
91 Jerry Nielson .05
92 Mark Ohims .05
93 Moises Alou .50
94 Ed Hartman .05
95 Keith Richardson .05
96 Royal Clayton .05
97 Bobby Davidson .05
98 Mitch Lyden .05
99a Hensley Meulens, Hensley Meulens (Error - St. Petersburg.) .75
99b Hensley Meulens (Correct - Albany.) .10
100 John Ramos .05
101 Robin Ventura .50
102 Luis Mercedes .05
103 Dave Miller .05
104 Randy Berlin .05
105 Mike Campas .05
106 Jose Trujillo .05
107 Lem Pikenton .05
108 Frank Bolick .05
109 Bert Heffernan .05
110 Chris Czarnik .05
111 Andy Benes .05
112 Skipper Wright .05
113 Eric Alexander .05
114 Manny Alexander .05
115 Jimmy Roso .05
116 Chris Donnels .05
117 Jaime Roseboro .05
118 Julian Yan .05
119 Vincent Degifico .05
120 Mike Morandini .05
121 Goose Gozzo .05
122 Pedro Munoz .05
123 Keith Helton .05
124 Tino Martinez .50
125 Sandy Alomar .25
126 Scott Cooper .05
127 Daryl Irvine .05
128 Jim Orsag .05
129 Mickey Pina .05
130 Scott Sommers .05
131 Ed Zambrano .05
132 Dave Bettendorf .05
133 Steve Allen .05
134 Kevin Belcher .05
135 Doug Cronk .05
136 Tito Stewart .05
137 Jeff Frye .05
138 Trey McCoy .05
139 Robb Nen .05
140 Jim Hvizda .05
141 Tommy Boyce .05
142 Michael Maksudian .05
143 Matt Current .05
144 Tom Hardgrove .05
145 Julio Vargas .05
146 Dan Welch .05
147 Steve Dunn .05
148 Mike Musuraca .05
149 Mike House .05
150 Deion Sanders .35
151 Willie Mota .05
152 Tim Nedin .05
153 Kerry Taylor .05
154 Beau Alred .05
155 Troy Neel .05
156 Shawn Hare .05
157 Chris Butterfield .05
158 Tim Hines .05
159 Pat Howell .05
160 Paul Johnson .05
161 Ryan Richmond .05
162 Ernie Baker .05
163 Pedro Castellano .05
164 Eric Jaques .05
165 Mark Willoughby .05
166 Dan Segui .05
167 Richard Skackle .05
168 Mark Lewis .05
169 John Johnstone .05
170 Phil Plantier .05
171 Wes Chamberlain .05
172 James Harris .05
173 Felix Antigua .05
174 Bruce Schreiber .05
175 Pete Rose Jr. .25
176 Kelly Woods .05
177 Anthony DeLaCruz .05
178 Charles Nagy .05
179 Nolan Lane .05
180 Fabio Gomez .05
181 Chris Butler .05
182 Brett Merriman .05
183 Carlos Mota .05
184 Doug Piatt .05
185 Marc Tepper .05
186 Dan Williams .05
187 Maximo Aleys .05
188 Ken Lewis .05
189 Joey Vierra .05
190 Ron Morton .05
191 Brook Fordyce .05
192 Steve McCarthy .05
193 Steve Hosey .05
194 Steve Foster .05
195 Ron Crowe .05
196 Steve Callahan .05
197 Benny Colvard .05
198 Adam Casillas .05
199 Joey Belle 1.00
200 Ben McDonald .05

1989 Minor League Team Sets

For the first time in several years, no major new producers entered the minor league team-set market in 1989. That didn't diminish the number of sets, however, as more than 350 basic sets and variations were issued; the largest number to that date. Some teams had as many as three different sets, not counting variations. Most of the variations were again the result of Star adding late cards to previously issued sets.

MT

354 Team Sets and Variations
1989 CMC AAA All-Stars (45) 6.00
1989 PC AAA All-Stars (55) 9.00
1989 Best Albany Yankees (30) 6.00
1989 Best Albany Yankees - Platinum (30) 17.50
1989 PC Albany Yankees (29) 9.00
1989 Star Albany-Colonie Yankees (22) 4.00
1989 Star Albany-Colonie Yankees (23) 10.00
1989 CMC Albuquerque Dukes (25) 3.00
1989 PC Albuquerque Dukes (30) 4.00
1989 Team Albuquerque Dukes Photos (45) 125.00
1989 Tribune Albuquerque Dukes (29) 25.00
1989 Team Anchorage Bucs (29) 8.00
1989 Team Anchorage Glacier Pilots (35) 10.00
1989 PC Appleton Foxes (31) 5.00
1989 GS Arkansas Travelers (25) 7.00
1989 PC Asheville Tourists (30) 4.00
1989 PC Auburn Astros (31) 9.00
1989 PC Auburn Astros Poster 12.50
1989 PC Augusta Pirates (32) 4.00
1989 Cal Bakersfield Dodgers (29) 7.00
1989 Baseball America AA Top Prospects (31) 13.50
1989 Star Baseball City Royals (24) 4.00
1989 Star Baseball City Royals - Glossy (24) 12.00
1989 Star Baseball City Royals (26) 9.00
1989 PC Batavia Clippers (31) 4.00
1989 Legoe Bellingham Mariners (37) 5.00
1989 Star Beloit Brewers 1 (26) 4.00
1989 Star Beloit Brewers 1 - Glossy (26) 15.00
1989 Star Beloit Brewers 2 (25) 5.00
1989 Legoe Bend Bucks (30) 15.00
1989 PC Billings Mustangs (31) 13.00
1989 Best Birmingham Barons (30) 7.00
1989 Best Birmingham Barons - Platinum (30) 20.00
1989 PC Birmingham Barons (31) 6.00
1989 Star Bluefield Orioles (25) 4.00
1989 Star Bluefield Orioles - Glossy (25) 15.00
1989 Star Bluefield Orioles (30) 8.00
1989 PC Boise Hawks (31) 4.00
1989 Star Bristol Tigers (27) 4.00
1989 Star Bristol Tigers (31) 7.00
1989 CMC Buffalo Bisons (25) 5.00
1989 PC Buffalo Bisons (27) 5.00
1989 PC Burlington Braves (32) 4.00
1989 Star Burlington Braves (25) 4.00
1989 Star Burlington Braves - Glossy (25) 10.00
1989 Star Burlington Braves (29) 8.00
1989 Star Burlington Indians (25) 3.00
1989 Star Burlington Indians - Glossy (25) 9.00
1989 Star Burlington Indians (30) 8.00
1989 SP Butte Copper Kings (30) 6.00
1989 CMC Calgary Cannons (25) 7.00
1989 PC Calgary Cannons (24) 7.00
1989 Cal League All-Stars (56) 5.00
1989 Best Canton-Akron Indians (28) 4.00
1989 PC Canton-Akron Indians (28) 4.00
1989 Star Canton-Akron Indians (25) 10.00
1989 Star Canton-Akron Indians - Glossy (25) 35.00
1989 Best Cedar Rapids Reds (30) 4.00
1989 PC Cedar Rapids Reds (29) 4.00
1989 Star Cedar Rapids Reds (29) 4.00
1989 Star Cedar Rapids Reds - Glossy (29) 10.00
1989 Star Cedar Rapids Reds (30) 8.00
1989 PC Charleston Rainbows (28) 4.00
1989 Best Charleston Wheelers (27) 4.00
1989 PC Charleston Wheelers (28) 4.00
1989 Team Charlotte Knights (25) 5.00
1989 Star Charlotte Rangers (28) 4.00
1989 Star Charlotte Rangers - Glossy (28) 15.00
1989 Star Charlotte Rangers (31) 8.00
1989 Best Chattanooga Lookouts (26) 4.00
1989 GS Chattanooga Lookouts (25) 4.00
1989 Team Chattanooga Lookouts Legends (33) 20.00
1989 Star Clearwater Phillies (25) 4.00
1989 Star Clearwater Phillies - Glossy (25) 10.00
1989 Star Clearwater Phillies (28) 8.00
1989 PC Clinton Giants (31) 6.00
1989 CMC Colorado Spring Sky Sox (25) 4.00
1989 PC Colorado Springs Sky Sox (28) 4.00
1989 Best Columbia Mets (30) 6.00
1989 GS Columbia Mets (30) 6.00
1989 CMC Columbus Clippers (30) 6.00
1989 PC Columbus Clippers (28) 6.00
1989 Police Columbus Clippers (25) 5.00
1989 Best Columbus Mudcats (28) 5.00
1989 Best Columbus Mudcats - Platinum (28) 7.00
1989 PC Columbus Mudcats (31) 6.00
1989 Star Columbus Mudcats (23) 6.00
1989 Star Columbus Mudcats - Glossy (23) 15.00
1989 Star Columbus Mudcats (24) 8.00
1989 CMC Denver Zyphers (25) 4.00
1989 PC Denver Zephyrs (28) 4.00
1989 Star Dunedin Blue Jays (25) 5.00
1989 Star Dunedin Blue Jays - Glossy (25) 20.00
1989 Star Dunedin Blue Jays (26) 7.00
1989 Star Durham Bulls (25) 8.00
1989 Star Durham Bulls Orange/Blue (29) 7.50
1989 Star Durham Bulls Blue/Orange (29) 7.50
1989 Star Durham Bulls - Glossy (28) 20.00
1989 Team Durham Bulls (29) 15.00
1989 PC Eastern League All-Stars (26) 8.00
1989 PC Eastern League Diamond Diplomacy (50) 6.00
1989 CMC Edmonton Trappers (25) 4.00
1989 PC Edmonton Trappers (25) 4.00
1989 Star Elizabethton Twins (31) 8.00
1989 Star Elizabethtown Twins - Glossy (31) 40.00
1989 Pucko Elmira Pioneers (32) 5.00
1989 GS El Paso Diablos (30) 5.00
1989 Star Erie Orioles (25) 5.00
1989 Star Erie Orioles - Glossy (25) 12.50
1989 Star Erie Orioles (29) 9.00
1989 Best Eugene Emeralds (25) 4.00
1989 Star Everett Giants (32) 4.00
1989 Star Everett Giants - Glossy (32) 20.00
1989 PC Fayetteville Generals (29) 4.00
1989 Team Fayetteville Generals (10) 5.00
1989 Star Frederick Keys (24) 5.00
1989 Star Frederick Keys - Glossy (24) 20.00
1989 Star Frederick Keys (28) 10.00
1989 Star Ft. Lauderdale Yankees (25) 5.00
1989 Star Ft. Lauderdale Yankees (29) 9.00
1989 PC Gastonia Rangers (30) 20.00
1989 Star Gastonia Rangers (26) 15.00
1989 Star Gastonia Rangers - Glossy (26) 75.00
1989 PC Geneva Cubs (31) 3.00
1989 SP Great Falls Dodgers (33) 6.00
1989 PC Greensboro Hornets (29) 4.00
1989 Best Greenville Braves (29) 5.00
1989 Best Greenville Braves - Platinum (29) 12.00
1989 PC Greenville Braves (30) 5.00
1989 Star Greenville Braves (25) 5.00
1989 Star Greenville Braves - Glossy (25) 15.00
1989 Best Hagerstown Suns (29) 6.00
1989 PC Hagerstown Suns (26) 5.00
1989 Star Hagerstown Suns (22) 4.00
1989 Star Hagerstown Suns - Glossy (22) 10.00
1989 Star Hamilton Redbirds (23) 4.00
1989 Star Hamilton Redbirds - Glossy (23) 15.00
1989 Star Hamilton Redbirds (29) 10.00
1989 PC Harrisburg Senators (26) 5.00
1989 Star Harrisburg Senators (23) 4.00
1989 Star Harrisburg Senators - Glossy (23) 12.00
1989 SP Helena Brewers (27) 6.00
1989 Little Sun High School Prospects (23) 12.50
1989 Best Huntsville Stars (29) 4.00
1989 PC Idaho Falls Braves (31) 5.00
1989 CMC Indianapolis Indians (25) 7.50
1989 PC Indianapolis Indians (32) 7.50
1989 CMC Iowa Cubs (25) 4.00
1989 PC Iowa Cubs (28) 3.00
1989 GS Jackson Mets (30) 4.00
1989 Best Jacksonville Expos (29) 10.00
1989 Best Jacksonville Expos - Platinum (29) 15.00
1989 PC Jacksonville Expos (29) 10.00

Year	Set	Price
1989	PC Jamestown Expos (30)	4.00
1989	Star Johnson City Cardinals (26)	4.00
1989	Star Johnson City Cards - Glossy (26)	10.00
1989	PC Kenosha Twins (29)	4.00
1989	Star Kenosha Twins (25)	4.00
1989	Star Kenosha Twins (27)	8.00
1989	Star Kingsport Mets (25)	5.00
1989	Star Kingsport Mets - Glossy (25)	15.00
1989	Star Kingsport Mets (30)	8.00
1989	Star Kinston Indians (25)	8.00
1989	Star Kinston Indians - Glossy (25)	25.00
1989	Star Kinston Indians (27)	12.00
1989	Best Knoxville Blue Jays (31)	5.00
1989	Best Knoxville Blue Jays (33)	9.00
1989	PC Knoxville Blue Jays (31)	6.00
1989	Star Knoxville Blue Jays (25)	5.00
1989	Star Knoxville Blue Jays - Glossy (25)	15.00
1989	Star Lakeland Tigers (25)	4.00
1989	Star Lakeland Tigers - Glossy (25)	15.00
1989	Star Lakeland Tigers (28)	10.00
1989	CMC Las Vegas Stars (25)	6.00
1989	PC Las Vegas Stars (29)	8.00
1989	PC London Tigers (32)	9.00
1989	CMC Louisville Red Birds (25)	5.00
1989	PC Louisville Redbirds (28)	3.00
1989	Team Louisville Redbirds (38)	7.00
1989	Team Louisville Redbirds - Glossy (38)	15.00
1989	Star Lynchburg Red Sox (25)	4.00
1989	Star Lynchburg Red Sox (29)	8.00
1989	Star Madison Muskies (22)	4.00
1989	Star Madison Muskies - Glossy (22)	15.00
1989	Star Madison Muskies (26)	9.00
1989	Star Martinsville Phillies (35)	4.00
1989	Star Martinsville Phillies - Glossy (35)	15.00
1989	Best Medford A's (31)	4.00
1989	Best Memphis Chicks (28)	5.00
1989	PC Memphis Chicks (28)	4.00
1989	Star Memphis Chicks (24)	5.00
1989	Star Memphis Chicks - Glossy (24)	20.00
1989	Star Miami Miracle 1 (25)	4.00
1989	Star Miami Miracle 1 - Glossy (25)	15.00
1989	Star Miami Miracle 2 (22)	4.00
1989	GS Midland Angels (30)	5.00
1989	Cal Modesto A's (25)	6.00
1989	Chong Modesto A's (36)	20.00
1989	PC Myrtle Beach Blue Jays (30)	4.00
1989	CMC Nashville Sounds (25)	5.00
1989	PC Nashville Sounds (28)	3.00
1989	Team Nashville Sounds (30)	10.00
1989	PC New Britain Red Sox (27)	5.00
1989	Star New Britain Red Sox (25)	5.00
1989	Star New Britain Red Sox - Glossy (25)	15.00
1989	Pucko Niagara Falls Rapids (31)	4.00
1989	CMC Oklahoma City 89ers (25)	6.00
1989	PC Oklahoma City 89ers (29)	4.00
1989	CMC Omaha Royals (25)	5.00
1989	PC Omaha Royals (27)	4.00
1989	PC Oneonta Yankees (32)	9.00
1989	Best Orlando Twins (31)	4.00
1989	PC Orlando Twins (30)	4.00
1989	Star Osceola Astros (25)	7.00
1989	Star Osceola Astros - Glossy (25)	15.00
1989	Star Osceola Astros (27)	12.00
1989	Cal Palm Springs Angels (32)	4.00
1989	PC Palm Springs Angels (28)	4.00
1989	CMC Pawtucket Red Sox (25)	3.00
1989	DD Pawtucket Red Sox Foldout	40.00
1989	PC Pawtucket Red Sox (27)	3.00
1989	Team Peninsula Oilers (28)	7.00
1989	Star Peninsula Pilots (25)	4.00
1989	Star Peninsula Pilots - Glossy (25)	10.00
1989	Star Peninsula Pilots (26)	6.00
1989	Team Peoria Chiefs (35)	7.00
1989	CMC Phoenix Firebirds (25)	8.00
1989	PC Phoenix Firebirds (29)	8.00
1989	Star Pittsfield Mets (25)	4.00
1989	Star Pittsfield Mets - Glossy (25)	15.00
1989	Star Pittsfield Mets (29)	8.00
1989	CMC Portland Beavers (25)	4.00
1989	PC Portland Beavers (26)	4.00
1989	Star Princeton Pirates (25)	4.00
1989	Star Princeton Pirates - Glossy (25)	10.00
1989	Star Princeton Pirates (28)	7.00
1989	Star Prince Williams Cannons (25)	5.00
1989	Star Prince Williams Cannons (29)	9.00
1989	PC Pulaski Braves (28)	12.50
1989	Best Quad City Angels (31)	7.00
1989	GS Quad City Angels (30)	7.00
1989	Best Reading Phillies (27)	5.00
1989	PC Reading Phillies (27)	4.00
1989	Star Reading Phillies (26)	4.00
1989	Star Reading Phillies - Glossy (26)	15.00
1989	Star Reading Phillies (29)	8.00
1989	Cal Reno Silver Sox (27)	6.00
1989	Bob's Richmond Braves (29)	30.00
1989	CMC Richmond Braves (25)	10.00
1989	PC Richmond Braves (31)	7.00
1989	Team Richmond Braves Foldout	15.00
1989	Best Riverside Red Wave (30)	4.00
1989	Cal Riverside Red Wave (31)	4.00
1989	PC Riverside Red Wave (31)	4.00
1989	CMC Rochester Red Wings (25)	10.00
1989	PC Rochester Red Wings (30)	9.00
1989	Team Rockford Expos (31)	4.00
1989	Star Salem Buccaneers (25)	7.00
1989	Star Salem Buccaneers - Glossy (25)	20.00
1989	Star Salem Buccaneers (29)	10.00
1989	Team Salem Dodgers (30)	45.00
1989	Cal Salinas Spurs (27)	4.00
1989	PC Salinas Spurs (30)	4.00
1989	Team Salt Lake City Trappers (30)	8.00
1989	Best San Antonio Missions (28)	6.00
1989	Best S.A. Missions - Platinum (28)	9.50
1989	Best San Bernadino Spirit (29)	4.00
1989	Cal San Bernadino Spirit (31)	4.00
1989	Best San Jose Giants (31)	5.00
1989	Cal San Jose Giants (30)	6.00
1989	PC San Jose Giants (30)	5.00
1989	Star San Jose Giants (25)	5.00
1989	Star San Jose Giants - Glossy (25)	15.00
1989	Star San Jose Giants (28)	8.00
1989	Star Sarasota White Sox (25)	5.00
1989	Star Sarasota White Sox - Glossy (25)	15.00
1989	PC Savannah Cardinals (30)	4.00
1989	CMC Scranton Red Barons (25)	4.00
1989	PC Scranton Red Barons (28)	4.00
1989	PC Shreveport Captains (27)	4.00
1989	GS South Atlantic League A-S (46)	15.00
1989	GS South Bend White Sox (30)	5.00
1989	DJ Southern League All-Stars (25)	4.00
1989	PC Spartanburg Phillies (30)	4.00
1989	Star Spartanburg Phillies (25)	4.00
1989	Star Spartanburg Phillies (26)	8.00
1989	SP Spokane Indians (26)	5.00
1989	Best Springfield Cardinals (30)	4.00
1989	PC St. Catharines Blue Jays (28)	20.00
1989	Star St. Lucie Mets (25)	3.00
1989	Star St. Lucie Mets - Glossy (25)	9.00
1989	Star St. Lucie Mets (27)	7.00
1989	Star St. Petersburg Cardinals (25)	4.00
1989	Star St. Pete Cardinals - Glossy (25)	15.00
1989	Star St. Petersburg Cardinals (29)	8.00
1989	Best Stockton Ports (32)	5.00
1989	Cal Stockton Ports (30)	5.00
1989	PC Stockton Ports (31)	5.00
1989	Star Stockton Ports (28)	6.00
1989	Star Stockton Ports - Glossy (28)	15.00
1989	PC Sumter Braves (33)	5.00
1989	CMC Syracuse Chiefs (25)	5.00
1989	PC Syracuse Chiefs (27)	4.00
1989	Team Syracuse Chiefs Foldout	17.50
1989	CMC Tacoma Tigers (25)	4.00
1989	PC Tacoma Tigers (32)	25.00
1989	GS Texas League All-Stars (40)	8.00
1989	Candl Tidewater Tides Foldout (18)	10.00
1989	CMC Tidewater Tides (29)	5.00
1989	PC Tidewater Tides (30)	4.00
1989	CMC Toledo Mud Hens (25)	3.00
1989	PC Toledo Mud Hens (30)	4.00
1989	CMC Tucson Toros (25)	4.00
1989	Jones Tucson Toros (26)	70.00
1989	PC Tucson Toros (28)	3.00
1989	GS Tulsa Drillers (26)	12.50
1989	GS Tulsa Drillers Uncut Sheet	20.00
1989	Team Tulsa Drillers (27)	45.00
1989	Pucko Utice Blue Sox (34)	4.00
1989	CMC Vancouver Canadians (25)	5.00
1989	PC Vancouver Canadians (27)	7.00
1989	Star Vero Beach Dodgers (25)	6.00
1989	Star Vero Beach Dodgers - Glossy (25)	20.00
1989	Star Vero Beach Dodgers (39)	15.00
1989	Cal Visalia Oaks (29)	4.00
1989	PC Visalia Oaks (31)	3.00
1989	PC Waterloo Diamonds (28)	4.00
1989	Star Waterloo Diamonds (32)	4.00
1989	Star Waterloo Diamonds - Glossy (32)	10.00
1989	Star Watertown Indians (25)	4.00
1989	Star Watertown Indians - Glossy (25)	15.00
1989	Star Watertown Indians (29)	8.00
1989	GS Wausau Timbers (28)	4.00
1989	Pucko Welland Pirates (35)	5.00
1989	Star West Palm Beach Expos (24)	6.00
1989	Star West Palm Beach Expos - Glossy (24)	20.00
1989	Star West Palm Beach Expos (31)	10.00
1989	Rock's Wichita Wranglers (30)	8.00
1989	Rock's Wichita Wrangers - Bonus Set (2)	4.00
1989	Rock's Wichita Wranglers - Stadium (30)	6.00
1989	Rock's Wranglers - Highlight (20)	5.00
1989	Rock's Wichita Wranglers - Update (20)	6.00
1989	PC Williamsport Bills (25)	6.00
1989	Star Williamsport Bills (24)	6.00
1989	Star Williamsport Bills - Glossy (24)	20.00
1989	Star Williamsport Bills (25)	12.00
1989	Star Winston-Salem Spirits (22)	4.00
1989	Star Winston-Salem Spirits (26)	8.00
1989	Star Winter Haven Red Sox (25)	7.00
1989	Star Winter Haven Red Sox - Glossy (25)	25.00
1989	Star Winter Haven Red Sox (29)	12.00
1989	Star Wytheville Cubs (25)	4.00
1989	Star Wytheville Cubs - Glossy (25)	10.00
1989	Star Wytheville Cubs (30)	8.00

1990 Best

Best made its debut in the single-card minor league market in 1990 with a 324-card set. The cards were issued in 12-card foil packs and were not available as a complete set.

	MT
Complete Set (324):	12.00
Common Player:	.05
Foil Pack (12):	.70
Foil Box (36):	17.50

No.	Player	MT
1	Frank Thomas	3.00
2	Eric Wedge	.05
3	Willie Ansley	.05
4	Mark Lewis	.05
5	Greg Colbrunn	.05
6	David Staton	.05
7	Ben McDonald	.05
8	Brent Mayne	.05
9	Ray Holbert	.05
10	T.R. Lewis	.05
11	Willie Banks	.05
12	Steve Dunn	.05
13	Juan Andujar	.05
14	Roger Salkeld	.05
15	Steve Hosey	.05
16	Tyler Houston	.05
17	David Holdridge	.05
18	Todd Malone	.05
19	Tony Scruggs	.05
20	Darron Cox	.05
21	Mike Linskey	.05
22	Darren Lewis	.05
23	Eddie Zosky	.05
24	Ramser Correa	.05
25	Lee Upshaw	.05
26	Bernie Williams	.50
27	Brian Harrison	.05
28	Len Brutcher	.05
29	Scott Centala	.05
30	Kenny Morgan	.05
31	Pedro Borbon	.05
32	Lee Hancock	.05
33	Clay Bellinger	.05
34	Chris Meyers	.05
35	Russ Garside	.05
36	Ron Plemmons	.05
37	Jose LeBron	.05
38	Tom Hardgrove	.05
39	Alan Newman	.05
40	Ramon Jimenez	.05
41	Ezequiel Herrera	.05
42	Jason Satre	.05
43	Bob Malloy	.05
44	William Suero	.05
45	Lenny Webster	.05
46	Andy Ashby	.05
47	Darren Ritter	.05
48	Andy Mota	.05
49	Pat Gomez	.05
50	Ron Stephens	.05
51	Daniel Eskew	.05
52	Joe Andrzejewski	.05
53	Doug Robbins	.05
54	Noel Velez	.05
55	Dana Ridenour	.05
56	Luis Martinez	.05
57	Dave Fleming	.05
58	Adell Davenport	.05
59	Brent McCoy	.05
60	Johnny Ard	.05
61	Cal Eldred	.05
62	Tab Brown	.05
63	Scott Kamieniecki	.05
64	Scott Bryant	.05
65	Brad Pennington	.05
66	Bernie Jenkins	.05
67	Frank Carey	.05
68	Matt Witkowski	.05
69	Checklist 1-48	.05
70	Josias Manzanillo	.05
71	Checklist 49-96	.05
72	Andujar Cedeno	.05
73	Rick Rojas	.05
74	Scott Brosius	.05
75	Tom Redington	.05
76	Kevin Rogers	.05
77	Jerry Wolak	.05
78	Rick Davis	.05
79	Juan Guzman	.05
80	Cesar Bernhardt	.05
81	Randy Simmons	.05
82	Clyde Keller	.05
83	Anthony Manahan	.05
84	Tom Maynard	.05
86	Sean Berry	.05
87	Brian Boltz	.05
88	Shawn Gilbert	.05
89	Rafael Novoa	.05
90	John Vander Wal	.05
91	Scott Pose	.05
92	Don Stanford	.05
93	Joe Federico	.05
94	Todd Watson	.05
95	Luis Gonzalez	.25
96	Pat Leinen	.05
97	Joel Estes	.05
98	Troy O'Leary	.05
99	Matt Stark	.05
100	Tony Tarasco	.05
101	Marc Lipson	.05
102	Kevin Higgins	.05
103	Jack Voight	.05
104	Steve Schrenk	.05
105	Jonathan Hurst	.05
106	Scott Erickson	.05
107	Javier Lopez	.10
108	Bob Zupcic	.05
109	Edwin Marquez	.05
110	Shawn Heiden	.05
111	Mike Maksudian	.05
112	Tony Eusebio	.05
113	Chris Hancock	.05
114	Royce Clayton	.05
115	Tim Mauser	.05
116	Ckecklist 97-144	.05
117	Carlos Maldonado	.05
118	Rex DeLa Nuez	.05
119	Mike Curtis	.05
120	Roger Miller	.05
121	Daryl Moore	.05
122	Turk Wendell	.05
123	Dan Rambo	.05
124	Scott Kimball	.05
125	Willie Magallanes	.05
126	Dannie Harris	.05
127	Joey James	.05
128	Wil Cordero	.05
129	Rob Taylor	.05
130	Bryce Florie	.05
131	Mike Mitchner	.05
132	Jeff Bagwell	3.00
133	Caesar Devares	.05
134	Tim Gillis	.05
135	Victor Hithe	.05
136	Earl Steinmetz	.05
137	Carl Keliipuleole	.05
138	Ted Williams	.05
139	Jorge Pedre	.05
140	Amalio Carrerno	.05
141	Chris Gill	.05
142	Dennis Wiseman	.05
143	Checklist 145-192	.05
144	Derek Lee	.05
145	Brett Snyder	.05
146	Chuck Knoblauch	.05
147	Rafael Quirico	.05
148	Julian Yan	.05
149	John Thelen	.05
150	Checklist 193-240	.05
151	Darrin Reichle	.05
152	John Ramos	.05
153	Patrick Lennon	.05
154	Wade Taylor	.05
155	Mike Twardoski	.05
156	Jeff Conine	.05
157	Kelly Mann	.05
158	Gary Wilson	.05
159	Chris Frye	.05
160	Roger Hailey	.05
161	Harold Allen	.05
162	Ozzie Canseco	.05
163	Checklist 241-288	.05
164	Rudy Seanez	.05
165	John Zaksek	.05
166	Roberto DeLeon	.05
167	Matt Merullo	.05
168	Checklist 289-324 (Wrong numbers listed on checklist.)	.05
169	Terrell Hansen	.05
170	Ron Crowe	.05
171	Luis Galindez	.05
172	Vilato Marrero	.05
173	Scott Cepicky	.05
174	Gary Resetar	.05
175	Rich Scheid	.05
176	Jimmy Rogers	.05
177	Ken Pennington	.05
178	Tom Martin	.05
179	Mitch Lyden	.05
180	Jorge Brito	.05
181	Chris Gorton	.05
182	Mark Sims	.05
183	Jose Olmeda	.05
184	Ed Taubensee	.05
185	Steve Morris	.05
186	Tim Pugh	.05
187	Barry Winford	.05
188	Allen Leibert	.05
189	Kurt Brown	.05
190	Kelly Lifgren	.05
191	Mike Kelly	.05
192	Robert Munoz	.05
193	Judd Johnson	.05
194	Hector Wagner	.05
195	Dave Reis	.05
196	Isaiah Clark	.05
197	William Schock	.05
198	Ruben Gonzalez	.05
199	Mike Eberle	.05
200	Michael Arner	.05
201	Raphael Bustamante	.05
202	John Patterson	.05
203	Joe Slusarski	.05
204	Rodney McCray	.05
205	Wally Trice	.05
206	Edgar Caceres	.05
207	Eugene Jones	.05
208	Joey Wardlow	.05
209	Steven Martin	.05
210	Woody Williams	.05
211	Kevin Morton	.05
212	Bobby DeJardin	.05
213	Chris Bennett	.05
214	Brian Johnson	.05
215	Randy Snyder	.05
216	Roberto Hernandez	.05
217	Glen Gardner	.05
218	Fred Costello	.05
219	Melvin Nieves	.05
220	Al Martin	.05
221	Kerry Knox	.05
222	Mike Eatinger	.05
223	Jim Myers	.05
224	Jay Owens	.05
225	Jayson Best	.05
226	Mike McDonald	.05
227	Kim Batiste	.05
228	Rich Delucia	.05
229	Chris Delarwelle	.05
230	Jeff Hoffman	.05
231	Bobby Moore	.05
232	Dan Wilson	.05
233	Greg Pirkl	.05
234	Craig Newkirk	.05
235	Mike Hensley	.05
236	Ryan Klesko	.10
237	Donald Sparks	.05
238	J.D. Noland	.05
239	Chris Howard	.05
240	Stan Royer	.05
241	Manuel Alexander	.05
242	Jeff Plympton	.05
243	Jeff Juden	.05
244	Charles Nagy	.05
245	Ryan Bowen	.05
246	Scott Taylor	.05
247	Tom Quinlan	.05
248	Royal Thomas	.05
249	Ricky Rhodes	.05
250	Alex Fernandez	.05
251	Bruce Egloff	.05
252	Greg Sparks	.05
253	Brian Dour	.05
254	John Byington	.05
255	Stacey Burdick	.05
256	Danny Matznick	.05
257	Reed Olmstead	.05
258	Jim Bowie	.05
259	Jim Newlan	.05
260	Ramon Caraballo	.05
261	Brian Barnes	.05
262	Mike Gardiner	.05
263	Andy Fox	.05
264	Brian McKeon	.05
265	Andy Tomberlin	.05
266	Frank Bellino	.05
267	Tim Lata	.05
268	Mike Burton	.05
269	Jim Orsag	.05
270	Scott Romano	.05
271	Leon Glenn	.05
272	Mike Misuraca	.05
273	Randy Knorr	.05
274	Eddie Tucker	.05
275	Ken Powell	.05
276	Brian McRae	.05
277	Mark Merchant	.05
278	Vinny Castilla	.10
279	Stephen Chitren	.05
280	Marteese Robinson	.05
281	Osvaldo Sanchez	.05
282	Mike Mongiello	.05
283	John Valentin	.05
284	Timmie Morrow	.05
285	Matt Murray	.05
286	Darrell Sherman	.05
287	Royal Clayton	.05
288	Jason Robertson	.05
289	John Kilner	.05

290 Jeff Mutis .05
291 Gary Alexander .05
292 Oreste Marrero .05
293 Melvin Wearing .05
294 Scott Meadows .05
295 Pat Hentgen .05
296 John Hudek .05
297 Tim Stargell .05
298 Tony Brown .05
299 Scott Plemmons .05
300 Chris Nabholz .05
301 Brian Romero .05
302 Vince Kindred .05
303 Robert Ayrault .05
304 Steve Stowell .05
305 Don Strange .05
306 Tim Nedin .05
307 Derek Livernois .05
308 Kerry Woodson .05
309 Sam Ferretti .05
310 Reuben Smiley .05
311 Jim Campbell .05
312 Al Osuna .05
313 Luis Mercedes .05
314 Billy Reed .05
315 Vince Harris .05
316 Jeff Carter .05
317 Dave Riddle .05
318 Frank Thomas (Bonus Card) 2.00
319 Eric Wedge (Bonus Card) .05
320 Mark Lewis (Bonus Card) .05
321 Alex Fernandez (Bonus Card) .05
322 Chuck Knoblauch (Bonus Card) .15
323 Charles Nagy (Bonus Card) .10
324 Tyler Houston (Bonus Card) .05

1990 Collectors Marketing Corp. Pre-Rookie

This set combines CMC team sets with cards produced by ProCards and purchased by CMC. The ProCards were given a glossy facing and randomly inserted in wax packs along with CMC cards. The cards are numbered at bottom-right on back. These numbers were not coordinated with the original CMC team sets, and therefore many team sets were separated with ProCards cards between them. The CMC cards in this set differ from the original CMC team sets by the color of their backs (yellow in lieu of green) and the players are pictured in place of the team logos. A checklist was available through the company. Shortly after the cards hit the market, the CMC company was sold to Impel Marketing. Since the original CMC team sets were issued as one complete AAA set in a special wooden box, there were packaging problems with duplicates and/or missing cards.

	MT
Complete Set (880):	17.50
Common Player:	.05
Wax Pack (12):	.50
Wax Box (36):	10.00

1 Stan Belinda .05
2 Gordon Dillard .05
3 Terry Collins .05
4 Mark Huisman .05
5 Hugh Kemp .05
6 Scott Medvin .05
7 Vincente Palacios .05
8 Rick Reed .05
9 Mark Ross .05
10 Dorn Taylor .05
11 Mike York .05
12 Jeff Richardson .05
13 Dann Bilardello .05
14 Tom Prince .05
15 Danny Sheaffer .05
16 Kevin Burdick .05
17 Steve Kiefer .05
18 Orlando Merced .05
19 Armando Moreno .05
20 Mark Ryal .05
21 Tommy Shields .05
22 Steve Carter .05
23 Wes Chamberlain .05
24 Jeff Cook .05
25 Scott Little .05
26 Jeff Peterek .05
27 Ed Puig .05
28 Tim Watkins .05
29 Tom Edens .05
30 Mike Capel .05
31 Darryel Walters .05
32 Joe Xavier .05
33 Tim Torricelli .05
34 Joe Redfield .05
35 D.L. Smith .05
36 Billy Moore .05
37 Joe Mitchell .05
38 Mario Monico .05
39 Frank Mattox .05
40 Tim McIntosh .05
41 Mark Higgins .05
42 George Canale .05
43 Don Grodon .05
44 Al Sadler .05
45 Don August .05
46 Mike Birkbeck .05
47 Dennis Powell .05
48 Chuck McGrath .05
49 Ruben Escalera .05
50 Dave Machemer .05
51 Steve Fireovid .05
52 Danny Clay .05
53 Howard Farmer .05
54 Travis Chambers .05
55 Chris Marchok .05
56 Dan Gakeler .05
57 Scott Anderson .05
58 Dale Mohorcic .05
59 Richard Thompson .05
60 Eddie Dixon .05
61 Jim Davins .05
62 Edwin Marquez .05
63 Jerry Goff .05
64 Dwight Lowery .05
65 Jim Steels .05
66 Quinn Mack .05
67 Eric Bullock .05
68 Otis Green .05
69 Randy Braun .05
70 Mel Houston .05
71 Johnny Paredes .05
72 Romy Cucjen .05
73 Jose Castro .05
74 Esteban Beltre .05
75 Tim Johnson .05
76 Shawn Boskie .05
77 Dave Masters .05
78 Kevin Blankenship .05
79 Greg Kallevig .05
80 Steve Parker .05
81 David Pavlas .05
82 Jeff Pico .05
83 Laddie Renfroe .05
84 Dean Wilkins .05
85 Paul Wilmet .05
86 Bob Bafia .05
87 Brian Guinn .05
88 Greg Smith .05
89 Derrick May .05
90 Glenn Sullivan .05
91 Bill Wrona .05
92 Eric Pappas .05
93 Hector Villanueva .05
94 Ced Landrum .05
95 Jeff Small .05
96 Gary Varsho .05
97 Brad Bierly .05
98 Jeff Hearron .05
99 Jim Essian .05
100 Brian McCann .05
101 Scott Arnold .05
102 Gibson Alba .05
103 Cris Carpetner .05
104 Stan Clarke .05
105 Mike Hinkle .05
106 Howard Hilton .05
107 Dave Osteen .05
108 Mike Perez .05
109 Bernard Gilkey .05
110 Dennis Carter .05
111 Julian Martinez .05
112 Rod Brewer .05
113 Ray Stephens .05
114 Ray Lankford .10
115 Craig Wilson .05
116 Roy Silver .05
117 Bien Figueroa .05
118 Jesus Mendez .05
119 Geronimo Pena .05
120 Omar Olivares .05
121 Mark Grater .05
122 Tim Sherrill .05
123 Pat Austin .05
124 Todd Crosby .05
125 Scott Nichols .05
126 Milt Hill .05
127 Robert Moore .05
128 Joey Vierra .05
129 Terry McGriff .05
130 Chris Hammond .05
131 Charlie Mitchell .05
132 Rodney Imes .05
133 Rob Lopez .05
134 Keith Brown .05
135 Scott Scudder .05
136 Bob Sebra .05
137 Donnie Scott .05
138 Skeeter Barnes .05
139 Paul Noce .05
140 Leo Garcia .05
141 Chris Jones .05
142 Kevin Pearson .05
143 Darryl Motley .05
144 Keith Lockhart .05
145 Brian Lane .05
146 Eddie Tanner .05
147 Reggie Jefferson .05
148 Neil Allen .05
149 Pete Mackanin .05
150 Ray Ripplemeyer .05
151 Jack Hardy .05
152 Steve Lankard .05
153 John Hoover .05
154 David Lynch .05
155 Mark Petkovsek .05
156 David Miller .05
157 Brad Arnsberg .05
158 Jeff Satzinger .05
159 John Barfield .05
160 Mike Berger .05
161 John Russell .05
162 Pat Garman .05
163 Gary Green .05
164 Bryan House .05
165 Ron Washington .05
166 Nick Capra .05
167 Juan Gonzalez 2.00
168 Gar Millay .05
169 Kevin Reimer .05
170 Bernie Tatis .05
171 Steve Smith .05
172 Dick Egan .05
173 Stan Hough .05
174 Ray Ramirez .05
175 Moe Drabowsky .10
176 Jay Baller .05
177 Ray Chadwick .05
178 Dera Clark .05
179 Luis Encarnacion .05
180 Jim LeMasters .05
181 Mike Magnante .05
182 Mel Stottlemyre .05
183 Tony Ferreira .05
184 Pete Filson .05
185 Andy McGaffigan .05
186 Luis DeLos Santos .05
187 Mike Loggins .05
188 Chito Martinez .05
189 Bobby Meacham .05
190 Russ Morman .05
191 Bill Pecota .05
192 Harvey Pulliam .05
193 Jeff Schulz .05
194 Gary Thurman .05
195 Thad Reece .05
196 Tim Spehr .05
197 Paul Zuvella .05
198 Not issued .00
199a Tom Poquette, Rich Dubee .05
199b Bob Hamelin .05
200 Sal Rende .05
201 Steve Adkins .05
202 Dave Eiland .05
203 John Habyan .05
204 Mark Leiter .05
205 Kevin Mmahat .05
206 Hipolito Pena .05
207 Willie Smith .05
208 Rich Monteleone .05
209 Hensley Meulens .05
210 Andy Stankiewicz .05
211 Jim Leyritz .10
212 Jim Walewander .05
213 Oscar Azocar .05
214 John Fishel .05
215 Jason Maas .05
216 Van Snider .05
217 Kevin Maas .05
218 Ricky Torres .05
219 Dave Sax .05
220 Darrin Chapin .05
221 Rob Sepanek .05
222 Mark Wasinger .05
223 Jimmy Jones .05
224 Clippers Coaches .05
225 Stump Merrill .05
226 Bob Davidson .05
227 Eric Boudreaux .05
228 Marvin Freeman .05
229 Jason Grimsley .05
230 Chuck Malone .05
231 Dickie Moles .05
232 Wally Ritchie .05
233 Bob Scanlan .05
234 Scott Service .05
235 Steve Sharts .05
236 John Gibbons .05
237 Sal Agostinelli .05
238 Jim Adduci .05
239 Kelly Heath .05
240 Mickey Morandini .05
241 Victor Rosario .05
242 Steve Stanicek .05
243 Jim Vatcher .05
244 Bill Dancy .05
245 Ron Jones .05
246 Chris Knabenshue .05
247 Keith Miller .05
248 Floyd Rayford .05
249 Jim Wright .05
250 Todd Frohwirth .05
251 Barney Nugent .05
252 Tito Stewart .05
253 John Trautwein .05
254 Mike Rochford .05
255 Larry Shikles .05
256 Daryl Irvine .05
257 John Leister .05
258 Joe Johnson .05
259 Mark Meleski .05
260 Steven Bast .05
261 Ed Nottle .05
262 John Flaherty .05
263 John Marzano .05
264 Gary Tremblay .05
265 Scott Cooper .05
266 Angel Gonzalez .05
267 Julius McDougal .05
268 Tim Naehring .05
269 Jim Pankovits .05
270 Rick Lancelotti .05
271 Mickey Pina .05
272 Phil Plantier .05
273 Jeff Stone .05
274 Scott Wade .05
275 Mike Dalton .05
276 Jeff Gray .05
277 Steve Avery .05
278 Braves Coaches .05
279 Dale Polley .05
280 Rusty Richards .05
281 Andy Nezelek .05
282 Ed Olwine .05
283 Jim Beauchamp .05
284 Paul Marak .05
285 Dave Justice .50
286 Jimmy Kremers .05
287 Drew Denson .05
288 Barry Jones .05
289 Francisco Cabrera .05
290 Bruce Crabbe .05
291 Dennis Hood .05
292 Geronimo Berroa .05
293 Ed Whited .05
294 Sam Ayoub .05
295 Brian Hunter .05
296 Tommy Green .05
297 John Mizerock .05
298 Ken Dowell .05
299 John Alva .05
300 Bill Lasky .05
301 Brian Snyder .05
302 Ben McDonald .05
303 Rob Woodward .05
304 Mickey Weston .05
305 Mike Jones .05
306 Curtis Schilling 3.00
307 Jay Aldrich .05
308 Paul Blair .05
309 Mike Smith .05
310 Jeff Tackett .05
311 Leo Gomez .05
312 Juan Bell .05
313 Chris Hoiles .05
314 Donell Nixon .05
315 Steve Stanicek .05
316 Tim Dulin .05
317 Chris Padget .05
318 Greg Walker .05
319 Tony Chance .05
320 Jeff McKnight .05
321 J.J. Bautista .05
322 John Mitchell .05
323 Vic Hithe .05
324 Darrell Miller .05
325 Shane Turner .05
326 Greg Biagini .05
327 Alex Sanchez .05
328 Mauro Gozzo .05
329 Steven Cummings .05
330 Tom Gilles .05
331 Douglas Linton .05
332 Mike Loynd .05
333 Bob Shirley .05
334 John Shea .05
335 Paul Kilgus .05
336 Carlos Diaz .05
337 Joe Szekely .05
338 Rick Lysander .05
339 Jim Eppard .05
340 Derek Bell .05
341 Jose Escobar .05
342 Webster Garrison .05
343 Paul Runge .05
344 Luis Sojo .05
345 Ed Sprague .05
346 Hector Delacruz .05
347 Rob Ducey .05
348 Ozzie Virgil .05
349 Stu Pederson .05
350 Mark Whiten .05
351 Andy Dziadkowiec .05
352 Shawn Barton .05
353 Kevin Brown .05
354 Rocky Childress .05
355 Brian Givens .05
356 Manny Hernandez .05
357 Jeff Innis .05
358 Cesar Mejia .05
359 Scott Nielson .05
360 Dale Plummer .05
361 Ray Soff .05
362 Lou Thornton .05
363 Dave Trautwein .05
364 Julio Valera .05
365 Tim Bogar .05
366 Mike DeButch .05
367 Jeff Gardner .05
368 Denny Gonzalez .05
369 Chris Jelic .05
370 Roger Samuels .05
371 Dave Liddell .05
372 Orlando Mercado .05
373 Kelvin Torva .05
374 Alex Diaz .05
375 Keith Hughes .05
376 Darren Reed .05
377 Zolio Sanchez .05
378 Do Vesling .05
379 Scott Aldred .05
380 Dennis Burtt .05
381 Shawn Holman .05
382 Matt Kinzer .05
383 Randy Mosek .05
384 Jose Ramos .05
385 Kevin Ritz .05
386 Mike Schwabe .05
387 Steve Searcy .05
388 Eric Stone .05
389 Domingo Michel .05
390 Phil Ouellette .05
391 Shawn Hare .05
392 Jim Lindeman .05
393 Scott Livingstone .05
394 Lavel Freeman .05
395 Travis Fryman .05
396 Scott Lusader .05
397 Dean Decillis .05
398 Milt Cuyler .05
399 Not issued .00
400 Phil Clark .05
401 Torey Lovullo .05
402 Aurelio Rodriguez .05
403 Mike Christopher .05
404 Jeff Bittiger .05
405 Jeff Fischer .05
406 Steve Davis .05
407 Morris Madden .05
408 Darren Holmes .05
409 Greg Mayberry .05
410 Mike Maddux .05
411 Tim Scott .05
412 Jim Neidlinger .05
413 Dave Walsh .05
414 Dennis Springer .05
415 Terry Wells .05
416 Adam Brown .05
417 Darrin Fletcher .05
418 Carlos Hernandez .05
419 Dave Hansen .05
420 Dan Henley .05
421 Jose Offerman .05
422 Jose Vizcaino .05
423 Luis Lopez .05
424 Butch Davis .05
425 Wayne Kirby .05
426 Mike Huff .05
427 Billy Bean .05
428 Pat Pacillo .05
429 Tony Blasucci .05
430 Mike Walker .05
431 Pat Rice .05
432 Terry Taylor .05
433 David Burba .05
434 Vance Lovelace .05
435 Ed Vande Berg .05
436 Greg Fulton .05
437 Ed Jurak .05
438 Dave Cochrane .05
439 Edgar Martinez .50
440 Matt Sinatro .05
441 Bill McGuire .05
442 Mickey Brantley .05
443 Tom Dodd .05
444 Jim Weaver .05
445 Todd Haney .05
446 Casey Close .05
447 Theo Shaw .05
448 Keith Helton .05
449 Jose Melendez .05
450 Tom Jones .05
451 Dan Warthen .05
452 Randy Roetter .05
453 Mike Walker .05
454 Colby Ward .05
455 Joe Skalski .05
456 Efrain Valdez .05
457 Doug Robertson .05
458 Jeff Edwards .05
459 Greg McMichael .05
460 Carl Willis .05
461 Beau Allred .05
462 Jeff Kaiser .05
463 Ty Gainey .05
464 Tom Lampkin .05
465 Ever Magallanes .05
466 Tom Magrann .05
467 Jeff Manto .05
468 Luis Medina .05
469 Troy Neel .05
470 Steve Springer .05
471 Not issued .00
472 Turner Ward .05
473 Casey Webster .05
474 Jeff Weatherly .05
475 Alan Cockrell .05
476a Rick Adair .05
476b Steve McInerney (Trainer) .05
477 Bobby Molinaro .05
478 Cliff Young .05
479 Michael Arner .05
480 Gary Buckels .05
481 Timothy Burcham .05
482 Sherman Corbett .05
483 Mike Erb .05
484 Mike Fetters .05
485 Chuck Hernandez .05
486 Jeff Heathcock .05
487 Scott Lewis .05
488 Rafael Montalvo .05
489 John Skuria .05
490 Lee Stevens .05
491 Nelson Rood .05
492 Bobby Rose .05
493 Dan Grunhard .05
494 Reed Peters .05
495 Doug Davis .05
496 Gary DiSarcina .05
497 Pete Coachman .05
498 Chris Cron .05
499 Karl Allaire .05
500 Ron Tingley .05
501 Chris Beasley .05
502 Max Oliveras .05
503 Roger Smithberg .05
504 Steve Peters .05
505 Matt Maysey .05
506 Terry Gilmore .05
507 Jeff Datz .05
508 Eric Nolte .05
509 Jim Lewis .05
510 Pete Roberts .05
511 Dan Murphy .05
512 Rich Rodriguez .05
513 Joe Lynch .05
514 Mike Basso .05
515 Ronn Reynolds .05
516 Jose Mota .05
517 Paul Faries .05
518 Warren Newson .05
519 Alex Cole .05
520 Tom Levasseur .05
521 Charles Hillemann .05
522 Jeff Yurtin .05
523 Rafael Valdez .05
524 Brian Ohnoutka .05
525 Pat Kelley .05
526 Gary Lance .05
527 Tony Torchia .05
528 Paul McClellan .05
529 Randy McCament .05
530 Gil Heredia .05
531 George Bonilla .05
532 Russ Swan .05
533 Ed Vosberg .05
534 Eric Gunderson .05
535 Trevor Wilson .05
536 Greg Booker .05
537 Kirt Manwaring .05
538 Mike Kingery .05
539 Brian Brady .05
540 Mark Bailey .05
541 Gregg Ritchie .05
542 George Hinshaw .05
543 Craig Colbert .05
544 Kash Beauchamp .05
545 Jeff Carter .05
546 Mark Leonard .05
547 Tony Perezchica .05
548 Mike Laga .05
549 Mike Benjamin .05
550 Timber Mead .05
551 Duane Espy .05
552 Tim Ireland .05
553 Paul Abbott .05
554 Pat Bangston .05
555 Larry Casian .05
556 Mike Cook .05
557 Pete Delkus .05
558 Mike Dyer .05
559 Charlie Scott .05
560 Francisco Oliveras .05
561 Park Pittman .05
562 Jimmy Williams .05
563 Rich Yett .05
564 Vic Rodriguez .05
565 Jamie Nelson .05
566 Derek Parks .05
567 Ed Naveda .05
568 Scott Leius .05
569 Terry Jorgensen .05
570 Doug Baker .05
571 Chip Hale .05
572 Dave Jacas .05
573 Jim Shellenback .05
574 Rafael DeLima .05
575 Bernardo Brito .05
576 J.T. Bruett .05
577 Paul Sorrento .05
578 Ray Young .05
579 Dave Veres .05
580 Scott Chiamparino .05
581 Tony Ariola .05
582 Weston Weber .05
583 Bruce Walton .05
584 Dave Otto .05
585 Reese Lambert .05
586 Joe Bitker .05
587 Joe Law .05
588 Ed Wojna .05
589 Timothy Casey .05
590 Patrick Dietrick .05
591 Bruce Fields .05
592 Eric Fox .05
593 Scott Hemond .05
594 Steve Howard .05
595 Doug Jennings .05
596 Al Pedrique .05
597 Dann Howitt .05
598 Russ McGinnis .05
599 Troy Afenir .05
600 Larry Arndt .05
601 Dickie Scott .05
602 Kevin Ward .05
603 Ryan Bowen .05
604 Brian Meyer .05
605 Terry Clark .05
606 Darryl Kile .05
607 Randy St. Claire .05
608 Randy Hennis .05
609 Lee Tunnell .05
610 Bill Brennan .05
611 Craig Smajstrla .05
612 Gary Cooper .05
613 Carl Nichols .05
614 Louie Meadows .05
615 Jose Tolentino .05
616 Harry Spillman .05
617 Javier Ortiz .05
618 Doug Strange .05

619 Jim Olander .05
620 Karl Rhodes .05
621 David Rohde .05
622 Mike Simms .05
623 Scott Servais .05
624 Pedro Sanchez .05
625 Kevin Dean .05
626 Brian Fisher .05
627 Bob Skinner .05
628 Wilson Alvarez .05
629 Adam Peterson .05
630 Tom Drees .05
631 Ravelo Manzanillo .05
632 Marv Foley .05
633 Grady Hall .05
634 Mike Campbell .05
635 Shawn Hillegas .05
636 C.L. Penigar .05
637 John Pawlowski .05
638 Steve Rosenberg .05
639 Jose Segura .05
640 Rich Amaral .05
641 Pete Dalena .05
642 Ramon Sambo .05
643 Marcus Lawton .05
644 Orsino Hill .05
645 Marlin McPhail .05
646 Keith Smith .05
647 Todd Trafton .05
648 Norberto Martin .05
649 Don Wakamatsu .05
650 Jerry Willard .05
651 Dana Williams .05
652 Tracy Woodson .05
653 Glenn Hoffman .05
654 Anthony Scruggs .05
655 Reggie Sanders .05
656 Rick Lueken .05
657 Kent Mercker .05
658 Dukes Coaches .05
659 Richard Shockey (Photo is Mo Sanford.) .05
660a Brian Barnes .05
660b Mario Brito .05
661 Not issued .00
662 Ed Quijada .05
663 Steve Wapnick .05
664 Kevin Tahan .05
665 Johnny Guzman .05
666 Bronswell Patrick .05
667 Kevin Kennedy .05
668 Orlando Miller .05
669 Mauricio Nunez .05
670 Hector Rivera .05
671 Roger LaFrancois .05
672 Jackson Todd .05
673 John Young .05
674 Bob Bailor .05
675 David Hajeck .05
676 Ralph Wheeler .05
677 Anthony Gutierrez .05
678 Gaylen Pitts .05
679 Mark Riggins .05
680 Brad Bluestone .05
681 Dick Bosman .05
682 Wil Cordero .05
683 Todd Hutcheson .05
684 Steve Swisher .05
685 John Cumberland .05
686 Rich Miller .05
687 Scott Lawrenson .05
688 Larry Hardy .05
689 Danny Boone .05
690 Terrel Hansen .05
691a Tom Gamboa .05
691b Jeff Jones .05
692 Gavin Osteen .05
693 Dave Riddle .05
694 Tim Pugh .05
695 Eugene Jones .05
696 Scott Pose .05
697 Ramon Jimenez .05
698 Fred Russell .05
699 Louis Talbert .05
700 J.D. Noland .05
701 Osvaldo Sanchez .05
702 David Colon .05
703 Jeff Hart .05
704 Jeff Hoffman .05
705 Sean Gilliam .05
706 Al Pacheco .05
707 Jason Satre .05
708 Tim Cecil .05
709 Phil Wiese .05
710 Larry Pardo .05
711 Clemente Acosta .05
712 Chris Johnson .05
713 Frank Bolick .05
714 Jose Garcia .05
715 Adell Davenport .05
716 Kevin Rogers .05
717 Dan Rambo .05
718 Vince Harris .05
719 Darrell Sherman .05
720 Isaiah Clark .05
721 Miguel Sabino .05
722 Frank Valdez .05
723 Giovanni Miranda .05
724 Daryl Ratliff .05
725 Mike Brewinton .05
726 Eric Parkinson .05
727 Vin Castilla .10
728 Roger Hailey .05
729 Earl Steinmetz .05
730 Doug Gogolewski .05
731 Andy Cook .05
732 John Toale .05
733 Mike Curtis .05
734 Delwyn Young .05
735 Scott Meadows .05
736 Don Sparks .05
737 Gary Wilson .05
738 Blas Minor .05
739 Jeff Bagwell 4.00
740 Phil Bryant .05
741 Felipe Castillo .05
742 Craig Faulkner .05
743 Jeff Conine .05
744 Kevin Belcher .05
745 Bill Haselman .05
746 Matt Stark .05
747 Todd Hall .05
748 Scott Centala .05
749 Doug Simons .05
750 Shawn Gilbert .05
751 Kenny Morgan .05
752 Andy Mota .05
753 Jeff Baldwin .05
754 Reed Olmstead .05
755 Basil Meyer .05
756 Mark Razook .05
757 Ken Pennington .05
758 Shane Letterio .05
759 Ted Williams .05
760 Luis Gonzalez .25
761 Carlos Garcia .05
762 Terry Crowley .05
763 Julio Peguero .05
764 Francisco Delarosa .05
765 Rodney Lofton .05
766 Eric McCray .05
767 Mike Wilkins .05
768 John Kiely .05
769 Derek Lee .05
770 Bo Kennedy .05
771 John Hudek .05
772 Bernie Nunez .05
773 Tom Quinlan .05
774 Jim Tatum .05
775 Casey Waller .05
776 Doug Lindsey .05
777 Roberto Zambrano .05
778 Wade Taylor .05
779 Carlos Maldonado .05
780 Brent Mayne .05
781 Jerry Rub .05
782 Vincent Phillips .05
783 Eric Wedge .05
784 Andrew Ashby .05
785 Royal Clayton .05
786 Jeffrey Osbourne .05
787 Pat Kelly .05
788 John Wehner .05
789 Bernie Williams .50
790 Moises Alou .35
791 Mark Merchant .05
792 Chris Myers .05
793 Donald Harris .05
794 Michael McDonald .05
795 Jim Blueberg .05
796 James Bowie .05
797 Ruben Gonzalez .05
798 Rob Maurer .05
799 Monty Farris .05
800 Bob Ayrault .05
801 Tim Mauser .05
802 David Holdridge .05
803 Kim Batiste .05
804 Dan Peltier .05
805 Derek Livernois .05
806 Thomas Fischer .05
807 Chuck Knoblauch .05
808 Willie Banks .05
809 Johnny Ard .05
810 Willie Ansley .05
811 Andujar Cedeno .05
812 Eddie Zosky .05
813 Randy Knorr .05
814 Juan Guzman .05
815 Jimmy Rogers .05
816 Nate Cromwell .05
817 Aubrey Waggoner .05
818 Frank Thomas 4.00
819 Matt Merullo .05
820 Roberto Hernandez .05
821 Cesar Bernhardt .05
822 Sterling Hitchcock .05
823 Ricky Rhodes .05
824 Todd Malone .05
825 Andy Fox .05
826 Ryan Klesko .10
827 Tyler Houston .05
828 Tab Brown .05
829 Brian McRae .05
830 Victor Cole .05
831 Mark Lewis .05
832 Rudy Seanez .05
833 Charles Nagy .05
834 Jeff Mutis .05
835 Carl Keliipuleole .05
836 Steve Pegues .05
837 Mike Lumley .05
838 Tim Leiner .05
839 Dave Evans .05
840 Darron Cox .05
841 Tony Ochs .05
842 Paul Coleman .05
843 Rafael Novoa .05
844 Clay Bellinger .05
845 Jason McFarlin .05
846 Craig Paquette .05
847 Timmie Morrow .05
848 Brian Hunter .05
849 Willie Greene .05
850 Austin Manahan .05
851 Rich Aude .05
852 Luis Lopez .05
853 Darrin Reichle .05
854 Tim Salmon 1.00
855 Royce Clayton .05
856 Steve Hosey .05
857 Kerry Woodson .05
858 Roger Salkeld .05
859 Tim Stargell .05
860 Greg Pirkl .05
861 Pat Mahomes .05
862 Denny Naegle .05
863 Troy Buckley .05
864 Ray Ortiz .05
865 Leo Perez .05
866 Cal Eldred .05
867 Darin Kracl .05
868 Lee Tinsley .05
869 T.R. Lewis .05
870 Jim Roso .05
871 Tom Taylor .05
872 Matt Anderson .05
873 Kerwin Moore .05
874 Rich Tunison .05
875 Brian Ahern .05
876 Eddie Taubensee .05
877 Scott Bryant .05
878 Steve Martin .05
879 Josias Mazanillo .05
880 Bob Zupcic .05

1990 ProCards A & AA Minor League Stars

This set was originally marketed for ProCards in wax packs by Progressive Sports Images in 1991 and, later, was distributed as a complete set.

	MT
Complete Set (200):	12.50
Common Player:	.05
Wax Box (48):	20.00

1 Mike Linskey .05
2 Ben McDonald .05
3 Francisco DeLaRosa .05
4 Jose Mesa .05
5 Kevin Morton .05
6 Dan O'Neill .05
7 Dave Owen .05
8 Jeff Plympton .05
9 Charles Nagy .05
10 Rudy Seanez .05
11 Bruce Egloff .05
12 Joe Ausanio .05
13 Jim Tracy .05
14 Randy Tomlin .05
15 Jim Campbell .05
16 Mike Gardiner .05
17 Rusty Meacham .05
18 John Kiely .05
19 Darrin Chapin .05
20 Wade Taylor .05
21 Don Stanford .05
22 Andy Ashby .05
23 Bob Ayrault .05
24 Luis Mercedes .05
25 Scott Meadows .05
26 Jeff Bagwell 3.00
27 Mark Lewis .05
28 Carlos Garcia .05
29 Moises Alou .50
30 Rico Brogna .05
31 Bernie Williams .50
32 Pat Kelly .05
33 Mitch Lyden .05
34 Hector Wagner .05
35 Carlos Maldonado .05
36 Brian Barnes .05
37 Chris Nabholz .05
38 Jeff Carter .05
39 Johnny Ard .05
40 Willie Banks .05
41 Scott Erickson .05
42 Greg Johnson .05
43 Al Osuna .05
44 Bob MacDonald .05
45 Pat Hentgen .05
46 Frank Thomas 3.00
47 Matt Stark .05
48 Jeff Conine .05
49 Sean Berry .05
50 Brian McRae .05
51 Bobby Moore .05
52 Brent Mayne .05
53 Greg Colbrunn .05
54 Terrel Hansen .05
55 Lenny Webster .05
56 Chuck Knoblauch .05
57 Willie Ansley .05
58 Andujar Cedeno .05
59 Luis Gonzalez 1.00
60 Eddie Zosky .05
61 William Suero .05
62 Tom Quinlan .05
63 Kelly Mann .05
64 Mike Bell .05
65 Mark Dewey .05
66 Tom Hostetler .05
67 Kevin Belcher .05
68 Bill Haselman .05
69 Bob Maurer .05
70 Dan Rohrmeier .05
71 Dan Peltier .05
72 Steven Decker .05
73 Dave Patterson .05
74 Ed Zinter .05
75 David Bird .05
76 Willie Espinal .05
77 Dennis Fletcher .05
78 Travis Buckley .05
79 Brian Romero .05
80 Mike Arner .05
81 Brian Evans .05
82 John Graves .05
83 Randy Marshall .05
84 Mike Garcia .05
85 Jeff Braley .05
86 Ricky Rhodes .05
87 Jim Haller .05
88 Sterling Hitchcock .05
89 Rob Blumberg .05
90 Mike Ogliaruso .05
91 Gregg Martin .05
92 Tim Pugh .05
93 Roger Hailey .05
94 Don Strange .05
95 Robert Gaddy .05
96 Willie Greene .05
97 Austin Manahan .05
98 Tony Scruggs .05
99 Mike Burton .05
100 Shawn Holtzclaw .05
101 Orlando Miller .05
102 David Hajek .05
103 Scott Pose .05
104 Tyler Houston .05
105 Melvin Nieves .05
106 Ryan Klesko .10
107 Daryl Moore .05
108 Skip Wiley .05
109 Brian McKeon .05
110 Rusty Kilgo .05
111 Chris Bushing .05
112 Alan Newman .05
113 Marc Lipson .05
114 Darin Kracl .05
115 Matt Grott .05
116 Rafael Novoa .05
117 Pat Rapp .05
118 Ed Gustafson .05
119 Chris Hancock .05
120 Mo Sanford .05
121 Bill Risley .05
122 Victor Garcia .05
123 Dave McAuliffe .05
124 Pedro Borbon .05
125 Rich Tunlson .05
126 Fred Cooley .05
127 Joey James .05
128 Reggie Sanders .05
129 Scott Bryant .05
130 Brent McCoy .05
131 Ramon Caraballo .05
132 Javier Lopez .10
133 Brian Harrison .05
134 Rich DeLucia .05
135 Roger Salkeld .05
136 Kerry Woodson .05
137 Chris Johnson .05
138 Cal Eldred .05
139 Angel Miranda .05
140 Richard Garces .05
141 Pat Mahomes .05
142 Denny Neagle .05
143 George Tsamis .05
144 Johnny Guzman .05
145 Dan Rambo .05
146 Jim Myers .05
147 Darrell Sherman .05
148 Dave Staton .05
149 Brian Turang .05
150 Bo Dodson .05
151 Dave Nilsson .05
152 Frank Bolick .05
153 Ray Ortiz .05
154 J.T. Bruett .05
155 John Patterson .05
156 Royce Clayton .05
157 Hilly Hathaway .05
158 Phil Leftwich .05
159 Randy Powers .05
160 Todd Van Poppel .05
161 Don Peters .05
162 Dave Zancanaro .05
163 Kirk Dressendorfer .05
164 Curtis Shaw .05
165 Joe Rosselli .05
166 Mark Dalesandro .05
167 Eric Helfand .05
168 Eric Booker .05
169 Adam Hyzdu .05
170 Eric Christopherson .05
171 Marcus Jensen .05
172 Derek Reid .05
173 Lance Dickson .05
174 Tim Parker .05
175 Jessie Hollins .05
176 Sam Militello .05
177 Darren Hodges .05
178 Kirt Ojala .05
179 Steve Karsay .05
180 Andrew Hartung .05
181 Kevin Jordan .05
182 Robert Eenhoorn .05
183 Jalal Leach .05
184 Carlos Delgado 2.00
185 Sean Cheetham .05
186 J.J. Munoz .05
187 Jim Thome 2.50
188 Tracy Sanders .05
189 Tony Clark .10
190 Jose Viera .05
191 Pat Dando .05
192 Brian Kowitz .05
193 Mike Lieberthal .10
194 Jeff Borgese .05
195 Mike Ferry .05
196 K.C. Gillum .05
197 Elliott Quinones .05
198 Grant Brittain .05
199 Checklist 1-100 .05
200 Checklist 101-200 .05

1990 ProCards Future Stars AAA Baseball

This series was the second produced for ProCards by Progressive Sports Images. The 1989 issue had simply been AAA players from the regular ProCards team sets with 1989 stats added. The 1990 series, complete with 1990 stats, features cards from all AAA teams in a completely different format from the '90 team sets. Cards were numbered consecutively 1-700, and an attempt was made to maintain team integrity. The series was later issued in an edition of 3,000 factory sets.

	MT
Factory Set (700):	15.00
Complete Set (700):	9.00
Common Player:	.05
Wax Pack (10):	.50
Ser. 1 or 2 Wax Box (48):	10.00

1 Terry Gilmore .05
2 Jim Lewis .05
3 Joe Lynch .05
4 Matt Maysey .05
5 Dan Murphy .05
6 Eric Nolte .05
7 Brian Ohnoutka .05
8 Steve Peters .05
9 Paul Quinzer .05
10 Pete Roberts .05
11 Rich Rodriguez .05
12 Roger Smithberg .05
13 Rafael Valdez .05
14 Mike Basso .05
15 Ronn Reynolds .05
16 Paul Faries .05
17 Tom LeVasseur .05
18 Jose Mota .05
19 Eddie Williams .05
20 Jeff Yurtin .05
21 Alex Cole .05
22 Charles Hillemann .05
23 Thomas Howard .05
24 Warren Newson .05
25 Pat Kelly .05
26 Gary Lance .05
27 Tony Torchia .05
28 George Bonilla .05
29 Greg Booker .05
30 Rich Bordi .05
31 John Burkett .05
32 Gil Heredia .05
33 Bob Knepper .05
34 Randy McCament .05
35 Paul McClellan .05
36 Timber Mead .05
37 Ed Vosberg .05
38 Trevor Wilson .05
39 Mark Bailey .05
40 Kirt Manwaring .05
41 Mike Benjamin .05
42 Brian Brady .05
43 Jeff Carter .05
44 Craig Colbert .05
45 Erik Johnson .05
46 Greg Litton .05
47 Kash Beauchamp .05
48 George Hinshaw .05
49 Mike Kingery .05
50 Mark Leonard .05
51 Gregg Ritchie .05
52 Rick Parker .05
53 Duane Espy .05
54 Tim Ireland .05
55 Larry Hardy .05
56 Jeff Bittiger .05
57 Mike Christopher .05
58 Steve Davis .05
59 Jeff Fischer .05
60 Darren Holmes .05
61 Morris Madden .05
62 Mike Maddux .05
63 Greg Mayberry .05
64 Jim Neidlinger .05
65 Tim Scott .05
66 Dave Walsh .05
67 Terry Wells .05
68 Adam Brown .05
69 Darrin Fletcher .05
70 Carlos Hernandez .05
71 Dave Hansen .05
72 Dan Henley .05
73 Glenn Hoffman .05
74 Walt McConnell .05
75 Jose Offerman .05
76 Jose Vizcaino .05
77 Billy Bean .05
78 Butch Davis .05
79 Mike Huff .05
80 Wayne Kirby .05
81 Luis Lopez .05
82 Kevin Kennedy .05
83 Claude Osteen .05
84 Von Joshua .05
85 Chris Beasley .05
86 Gary Buckels .05
87 Tim Burcham .05
88 Sherman Corbett .05
89 Mike Erb .05
90 Mike Fetters .05
91 Jeff Heathcock .05
92 Scott Lewis .05
93 Rafael Montalvo .05
94 Cliff Young .05
95 Doug Davis .05
96 Ron Tingley .05
97 Karl Allaire .05
98 Pete Coachman .05
99 Chris Cron .05
100 Gary DiSarcina .05
101 Nelson Rood .05
102 Bobby Rose .05
103 Lee Stevens .05
104 Dan Grunhard .05
105 Reed Peters .05
106 John Skurla .05
107 Max Oliveras .05
108 Chuck Hernandez .05
109 Tony Blasucci .05
110 Dave Burba .05
111 Keith Helton .05
112 Vance Lovelace .05
113 Jose Melendez .05
114 Pat Pacillo .05
115 Pat Rice .05
116 Terry Taylor .05
117 Mike Walker .05
118 Bill McGuire .05
119 Matt Sinatro .05
120 Mario Diaz .05
121 Greg Fulton .05
122 Todd Haney .05
123 Ed Jurak .05
124 Tino Martinez .50
125 Jeff Schaefer .05
126 Casey Close .05
127 Tom Dodd .05
128 Jim Weaver .05
129 Tommy Jones .05
130 Dan Warthen .05
131 Tony Ariola .05
132 Joe Bitker .05
133 Scott Chiamparino .05
134 Reese Lambert .05
135 Joe Law .05
136 Dave Otto .05
137 Dave Veres .05
138 Bruce Walton .05
139 Weston Weber .05
140 Ed Wojna .05
141 Ray Young .05
142 Troy Afenir .05
143 Russ McGinnis .05
144 Larry Arndt .05
145 Mike Bordick .05
146 Scott Hemond .05
147 Dann Howitt .05
148 Doug Jennings .05
149 Al Pedrique .05
150 Dick Scott .05
151 Tim Casey .05
152 Pat Dietrick .05
153 Bruce Fields .05
154 Eric Fox .05
155 Steve Howard .05
156 Kevin Ward .05
157 Brad Fischer .05
158 Chuck Estrada .05
159 Wilson Alvarez .05
160 Mike Campbell .05
161 Tom Drees .05
162 Grady Hall .05
163 Shawn Hillegas .05
164 Ravelo Manzanillo .05
165 John Pawlowski .05
166 Adam Peterson .05
167 Steve Rosenberg .05
168 Jose Segura .05
169 Don Wakamatsu .05
170 Jerry Willard .05
171 Rich Amaral .05
172 Pete Dalena .05
173 Norberto Martin .05
174 Keith Smith .05
175 Todd Trafton .05
176 Tracy Woodson .05
177 Orsino Hill .05
178 Marcus Lawton .05
179 Marlin McPhail .05
180 C.L. Penigar .05
181 Ramon Sambo .05
182 Dana Williams .05
183 Marv Foley .05
184 Moe Drabowsky .10
185 Roger LaFrancois .05
186 Ryan Bowen .05
187 William Brennan .05
188 Terry Clark .05
189 Brian Fisher .05
190 Randy Hennis .05
191 Darryl Kile .05
192 Brian Meyer .05
193 Randy St. Claire .05
194 Lee Tunnell .05
195 Carl Nichols .05
196 Scott Servais .05

197 Pedro Sanchez .05
198 Mike Simms .05
199 Criag Smajstria .05
200 Harry Spilman .05
201 Doug Strange .05
202 Jose Tolentino .05
203 Gary Cooper .05
204 Kevin Dean .05
205 Louie Meadows .05
206 Jim Olander .05
207 Javier Ortiz .05
208 Karl Rhodes .05
209 Bob Skinner .05
210 Brent Strom .05
211 Tim Tolman .05
212 Greg McMichael .05
213 Doug Robertson .05
214 Jeff Shaw .05
215 Joe Skalski .05
216 Efrain Valdez .05
217 Mike Walker .05
218 Colby Ward .05
219 Carl Willis .05
220 Tom Lampkin .05
221 Tom Magrann .05
222 Juan Castillo .05
223 Ever Magallanes .05
224 Jeff Manto .05
225 Luis Medina .05
226 Troy Neel .05
227 Steve Springer .05
228 Casey Webster .05
229 Beau Allred .05
230 Alan Cockrell .05
231 Ty Gainey .05
232 Dwight Taylor .05
233 Turner Ward .05
234 Jeff Wetherby .05
235 Bobby Molinaro .05
236 Buddy Bell .10
237 Rick Adair .05
238 Paul Abbott .05
239 Pat Bangston .05
240 Larry Casian .05
241 Mike Cook .05
242 Pete Delkus .05
243 Mike Dyer .05
244 Mark Guthrie .05
245 Orlando Lind .05
246 Francisco Oliveras .05
247 Park Pittman .05
248 Charles Scott .05
249 Jimmy Williams .05
250 Jamie Nelson .05
251 Derek Parks .05
252 Doug Baker .05
253 Chip Hale .05
254 Terry Jorgensen .05
255 Scott Leius .05
256 Marty Lanoux .05
257 Ed Naveda .05
258 Victor Rodriguez .05
259 Paul Sorrento .05
260 Bernardo Brito .05
261 Rafael Delima .05
262 David Jacas .05
263 Alonzo Powell .05
264 Jim Shellenback .05
265 Shawn Barton .05
266 Kevin Brown .05
267 Rocky Childress .05
268 Brian Givens .05
269 Manny Hernandez .05
270 Jeff Innis .05
271 Cesar Mejia .05
272 Scott Nielsen .05
273 Dale Plummer .05
274 Rogre Samuels .05
275 Ray Soff .05
276 Dave Trautwein .05
277 Julio Valera .05
278 Dave Liddell .05
279 Orlando Mercado .05
280 Tim Bogar .05
281 Mike DeButch .05
282 Jeff Gardner .05
283 Denny Gonzalez .05
284 Chris Jelic .05
285 Kelvin Torve .05
286 Alex Diaz .05
287 Keith Hughes .05
288 Darren Reed .05
289 Zollo Sanchez .05
290 Lou Thornton .05
291 Steve Swisher .05
292 John Cumberland .05
293 Rich Miller .05
294 Jose DeJesus .05
295 Marvin Freeman .05
296 Todd Frohwirth .05
297 Jason Grimsley .05
298 Chuck Malone .05
299 Brad Moore .05
300 Wally Ritchie .05
301 Bob Scanlan .05
302 Scott Service .05
303 Steve Sharts .05
304 John Gibbons .05
305 Tom Nieto .05
306 Jim Adduci .05
307 Kelly Heath .05
308 Mickey Morandini .05
309 Victor Rosario .05
310 Steve Stanicek .05
311 Greg Legg .05
312 Ron Jones .05
313 Chris Knabenshue .05
314 Keith Miller .05
315 Jim Vatcher .05
316 Jim Wright .05
317 Steve Adkins .05
318 Darrin Chapin .05
319 Bob Davidson .05
320 Dave Eiland .05
321 John Habyan .05
322 Jimmy Jones .05
323 Mark Leiter .05
324 Kevin Mmahat .05
325 Rich Monteleone .05
326 Willie Smith .05
327 Ricky Torres .05
328 Jeff Datz .05
329 Brian Dorsett .05
330 Dave Sax .05
331 Jim Leyritz .10
332 Hensley Meulens .05
333 Carlos Rodriguez .05
334 Rob Sepanek .05
335 Andy Stankiewicz .05
336 Jim Walewander .05
337 Mark Wasinger .05
338 Oscar Azocar .05
339 John Fishel .05
340 Jason Maas .05
341 Kevin Maas .05
342 Van Snider .05
343 Field Staff .05
344 Tom Gilles .05
345 Mauro Gozzo .05
346 Paul Kilgus .05
347 Doug Linton .05
348 Mike Loynd .05
349 Rick Lysander .05
350 Alex Sanchez .05
351 John Shea .05
352 Steve Wapnick .05
353 Andy Dziadkowiec .05
354 Joe Szekely .05
355 Ozzie Virgil .05
356 Jim Eppard .05
357 Jose Escobar .05
358 Webster Garrison .05
359 Paul Runge .05
360 Luis Sojo .05
361 Ed Sprague .05
362 Derek Bell .05
363 Hector DeLaCruz .05
364 Rob Ducey .05
365 Pedro Munoz .05
366 Stu Pederson .05
367 Mark Whiten .05
368 Bob Bailor .05
369 Bob Shirley .05
370 Rocket Wheeler .05
371 Scott Aldred .05
372 Dennis Burtt .05
373 Shawn Holman .05
374 Matt Kinzer .05
375 Randy Nosek .05
376 Jose Ramos .05
377 Kevin Ritz .05
378 Mike Schwabe .05
379 Steve Searcy .05
380 Eric Stone .05
381 Don Vesling .05
382 Phil Clark .05
383 Phil Ouellette .05
384 Dean DeCillis .05
385 Travis Fryman .05
386 Jim Lindeman .05
387 Scott Livingstone .05
388 Torey Lovullo .05
389 Domingo Michel .05
390 Milt Cuyler .05
391 Lavell Freeman .05
392 Shawn Hare .05
393 Scott Lusader .05
394 Tom Gamboa .05
395 Jeff Jones .05
396 Aurelio Rodriguez .05
397 Steve Avery .05
398 Tommy Greene .05
399 Bill Laskey .05
400 Paul Marak .05
401 Andy Nezelek .05
402 Ed Olwine .05
403 Dale Polley .05
404 Rusty Richards .05
405 Brian Snyder .05
406 Jimmy Kremers .05
407 John Mizerock .05
408 John Alva .05
409 Francisco Cabrera .05
410 Bruce Crabbe .05
411 Drew Denson .05
412 Ken Dowell .05
413 Ed Whited .05
414 Geronimo Berroa .05
415 Dennis Hood .05
416 Brian Hunter .05
417 Barry Jones .05
418 Dave Justice .50
419 Jim Beauchamp .05
420 John Grubb .05
421 Leo Mazzone .05
422 Sonny Jackson .05
423 Rick Berg .05
424 Steve Bast .05
425 Tom Bolton .05
426 Steve Curry .05
427 Mike Dalton .05
428 Jeff Gray .05
429 Daryl Irvine .05
430 Joe Johnson .05
431 John Leister .05
432 Mike Rochford .05
433 Larry Shikles .05
434 Tito Stewart .05
435 John Trautwein .05
436 John Flaherty .05
437 John Marzano .05
438 Gary Tremblay .05
439 Scott Cooper .05
440 Angel Gonzalez .05
441 Tim Naehring .05
442 Jim Pankovits .05
443 Mo Vaughn .50
444 Rick Lancellotti .05
445 Mickey Pina .05
446 Phil Plantier .05
447 Jeff Stone .05
448 Scott Wade .05
449 Ed Nottle .05
450 Mark Meleski .05
451 Lee Stange .05
452 Jay Aldrich .05
453 Jose Bautista .05
454 Eric Bell .05
455 Dan Boone .05
456 Ben McDonald .05
457 John Mitchell .05
458 Curt Schilling 2.50
459 Mike Smith .05
460 Rob Woodward .05
461 Chris Hoiles .05
462 Darrell Miller .05
463 Jeff Tackett .05
464 Juan Bell .05
465 Tim Dullin .05
466 Leo Gomez .05
467 Jeff McKnight .05
468 Shane Turner .05
469 Greg Walker .05
470 Tony Chance .05
471 Victor Hithe .05
472 Donnell Nixon .05
473 Chris Padget .05
474 Pete Stanicek .05
475 Mike Linskey .05
476 Joaquin Contreras .05
477 Greg Biagini .05
478 Dick Bosman .05
479 Paul Blair .05
480 Stan Belinda .05
481 Gordon Dillard .05
482 Mark Huismann .05
483 Hugh Kemp .05
484 Scott Medvin .05
485 Vincente Palacios .05
486 Rick Reed .05
487 Mark Ross .05
488 Dorn Taylor .05
489 Mike York .05
490 Dann Bilardello .05
491 Tom Prince .05
492 Danny Sheaffer .05
493 Kevin Burdick .05
494 Steve Kiefer .05
495 Orlando Merced .05
496 Armando Moreno .05
497 Jeff Richardson .05
498 Mark Ryal .05
499 Tommy Shields .05
500 Steve Carter .05
501 Wes Chamberlain .05
502 Jeff Cook .05
503 Scott Little .05
504 Terry Collins .05
505 Jackie Brown .05
506 Steve Henderson .05
507 Gibson Alba .05
508 Scott Arnold .05
509 Cris Carpenter .05
510 Stan Clarke .05
511 Mark Grater .05
512 Howard Hilton .05
513 Mike Hinkle .05
514 Omar Olivares .05
515 Dave Osteen .05
516 Mike Perez .05
517 Tim Sherrill .05
518 Scott Nichols .05
519 Ray Stephens .05
520 Pat Austin .05
521 Rod Brewer .05
522 Todd Crosby .05
523 Bien Figueroa .05
524 Julian Martinez .05
525 Jesus Mendez .05
526 Geronimo Pena .05
527 Craig Wilson .05
528 Dennis Carter .05
529 Bernard Gilkey .05
530 Ray Lankford .10
531 Mauricio Nunez .05
532 Roy Silver .05
533 Gaylen Pitts .05
534 Mark Riggins .05
535 Neil Allen .05
536 Keith Brown .05
537 Chris Hammond .05
538 Milton Hill .05
539 Rodney Imes .05
540 Rob Lopez .05
541 Charlie Mitchell .05
542 Bobby Moore .05
543 Rosario Rodriguez .05
544 Scott Scudder .05
545 Bob Sebra .05
546 Joey Vierra .05
547 Tony DeFrancesco .05
548 Terry McGriff .05
549 Donnie Scott .05
550 Reggie Jefferson .05
551 Brian Lane .05
552 Chris Lombardozzi .05
553 Paul Noce .05
554 Kevin Pearson .05
555 Eddie Tanner .05
556 Skeeter Barnes .05
557 Leo Garcia .05
558 Chris Jones .05
559 Keith Lockhart .05
560 Darryl Motley .05
561 Pete Mackanin .05
562 Ray Ripplemeyer .05
563 Scott Anderson .05
564 Esteban Beltre .05
565 Travis Chambers .05
566 Randy Braun .05
567 Danny Clay .05
568 Eric Bullock .05
569 Jim Davins .05
570 Jose Castro .05
571 Eddie Dixon .05
572 Romy Cucjen .05
573 Howard Farmer .05
574 Jerry Goff .05
575 Steve Fireovid .05
576 Otis Green .05
577 Dan Gakeler .05
578 Mel Houston .05
579 Balvino Galvez .05
580 Dwight Lowery .05
581 Dale Mohorcic .05
582 Quinn Mack .05
583 Chris Marchok .05
584 Edwin Marquez .05
585 Mel Rojas .05
586 Johnny Paredes .05
587 Rich Thompson .05
588 German Rivera .05
589 James Steels .05
590 Tim Johnson .05
591 Gomer Hodge .05
592 Joe Kerrigan .05
593 Ray Chadwick .05
594 Dera Clark .05
595 Luis Encarnacion .05
596 Tony Ferreira .05
597 Pete Filson .05
598 Jim LeMasters .05
599 Mike Magnante .05
600 Mike Tresemer .05
601 Mel Stottlemyre .05
602 Bill Wilkinson .05
603 Kevin Burrell .05
604 Tim Spehr .05
605 Luis De Los Santos .05
606 Bob Hamelin .05
607 Bobby Meacham .05
608 Russ Morman .05
609 Thad Reece .05
610 Paul Zuvella .05
611 Mike Loggins .05
612 Chito Martinez .05
613 Harvey Pulliam .05
614 Jeff Schulz .05
615 Sal Rende .05
616 Tom Poquette .05
617 Rich Dubee .05
618 Kevin Blankenship .05
619 Shawn Boskie .05
620 Mark Bowden .05
621 Greg Kallevig .05
622 Dave Masters .05
623 Steve Parker .05
624 Dave Pavlas .05
625 Laddie Renfroe .05
626 Paul Wilmet .05
627 Jeff Hearron .05
628 Erik Pappas .05
629 Hector Villanueva .05
630 Bob Bafia .05
631 Brian Guinn .05
632 Jeff Small .05
633 Greg Smith .05
634 Glenn Sullivan .05
635 Bill Wrona .05
636 Brad Bierley .05
637 Cedric Landrum .05
638 Derrick May .05
639 Gary Varsho .05
640 Jim Essian .05
641 Don August .05
642 Mike Birkbeck .05
643 Mike Capel .05
644 Logan Easley .05
645 Tom Edens .05
646 Don Gordon .05
647 Chuck McGrath .05
648 Jeff Peterek .05
649 Dennis Powell .05
650 Ed Puig .05
651 Alan Sadler .05
652 Tim Watkins .05
653 Tim McIntosh .05
654 Tim Torricelli .05
655 George Canale .05
656 Mark Higgins .05
657 Joe Mitchell .05
658 Joe Redfield .05
659 D.L. Smith .05
660 Joe Xavier .05
661 Ruben Escalera .05
662 Mario Monico .05
663 Billy Moore .05
664 Darryel Walters .05
665 Dave Machemer .05
666 Jackson Todd .05
667 Gerald Alexander .05
668 Brad Arnsberg .05
669 Brad Arnsberg .05
670 John Barfield .05
671 Jack Hardy .05
672 Ray Hayward .05
673 John Hoover .05
674 Steve Lankard .05
675 David Lynch .05
676 Craig McMurtry .05
677 David Miller .05
678 Mark Petkovsek .05
679 Jeff Satzinger .05
680 Mike Berger .05
681 Dave Engle .05
682 John Russell .05
683 Pat Dodson .05
684 Pat Garman .05
685 Gary Green .05
686 Bryan House .05
687 Dean Palmer .05
688 Ron Washington .05
689 Nick Capra .05
690 Juan Gonzalez 1.50
691 Gar Millay .05
692 Kevin Reimer .05
693 Bernie Tatis .05
694 Checklist 1-100 .05
695 Checklist 101-200 .05
696 Checklist 201-300 .05
697 Checklist 301-400 .05
698 Checklist 401-500 .05
699 Checklist 501-600 .05
700 Checklist 601-700 .05

1990 Minor League Team Sets

The number of minor league team sets and variations declined a bit from the peak year of 1989. Sportsprint entered the field with eight sets, while CMC-TCMA issued its final minor league team sets.

MT

304 Team Sets and Variations
1990 PC AAA All-Stars (54) 8.00
1990 Alaska Goldpanners (16) 30.00
1990 Best Albany-Colonie Yankees (26) 6.00
1990 Best Albany Yankees All-Decade (36) 12.00
1990 PC Albany-Colonie Yankees (29) 6.00
1990 Star Albany-Colonie Yankees (28) 6.00
1990 CMC Albuquerque Dukes (28) 5.00
1990 PC Albuquerque Dukes (30) 5.00
1990 Team Albuquerque Dukes Photos (35) 110.00
1990 Box Appleton Foxes (30) 3.00
1990 Diamond Appleton Foxes (30) 3.00
1990 PC Appleton Foxes (29) 3.00
1990 GS Arkansas Travelers (30) 6.00
1990 PC Asheville Tourists (28) 7.00
1990 Best Auburn Astros (25) 4.00
1990 PC Auburn Astros (26) 3.00
1990 PC Augusta Pirates (27) 4.00
1990 Cal Bakersfield Dodgers (32) 4.00
1990 Star Baseball City Royals (31) 3.00
1990 PC Batavia Clippers (30) 3.00
1990 Legoe Bellingham Mariners (38) 4.00
1990 Best Beloit Brewers (27) 4.00
1990 Star Beloit Brewers (27) 4.00
1990 Legoe Bend Bucks (32) 3.00
1990 PC Billings Mustangs (30) 3.00
1990 Best Birmingham Barons (30) 20.00
1990 Best Birmingham Barons All-Decade (34) 7.00
1990 PC Birmingham Barons (28) 9.00
1990 Star Bluefield Orioles (22) 5.00
1990 PC Boise Hawks (33) 4.00
1990 PC Bristol Tigers (29) 8.00
1990 Star Bristol Tigers (30) 8.00
1990 CMC Buffalo Bisons (25) 4.00
1990 PC Buffalo Bisons (28) 4.00
1990 Team Buffalo Bisons (28) 12.50
1990 Best Burlington Braves (30) 5.00
1990 PC Burlington Braves (30) 10.00
1990 Star Burlington Braves (31) 7.00
1990 PC Burlington Indians (29) 17.50
1990 SP Butte Copper Kings (30) 8.00
1990 CMC Calgary Cannons (25) 8.00
1990 PC Calgary Cannons (23) 8.00
1990 Cal League All-Stars (56) 6.00
1990 Best Canton-Akron Indians (28) 6.00
1990 PC Canton-Akron Indians (27) 5.00
1990 Star Canton-Akron Indians (21) 5.00
1990 Sportsprint Carolina League A-S (52) 5.00
1990 Best Cedar Rapids Reds (27) 5.00
1990 Best Cedar Rapids Reds All-Decade (36) 15.00
1990 PC Cedar Rapids Reds (27) 6.00
1990 Best Charleston Rainbows (28) 4.00
1990 PC Charleston Rainbows (28) 3.00
1990 Best Charleston Wheelers (29) 6.00
1990 PC Charleston Wheelers (28) 9.00
1990 Team Charlotte Knights (25) 6.00
1990 Star Charlotte Rangers (30) 15.00
1990 GS Chattanooga Lookouts (27) 4.00
1990 Diamond Clearwater Phillies (9) 5.00
1990 Star Clearwater Phillies (27) 3.00
1990 Best Clinton Giants (29) 4.00
1990 PC Clinton Giants (29) 3.00
1990 Team Clinton Giants Update (12) 3.00
1990 CMC Colorado Springs Sky Sox (24) 4.00
1990 PC Colorado Springs Sky Sox (27) 4.00
1990 GS Columbia Mets (30) 3.00
1990 Play II Columbia Mets (27) 3.00
1990 Play II Columbia Mets Postcards (27) 9.00
1990 CMC Columbus Clippers (27) 7.50
1990 Police Columbus Clippers (25) (Mass) 10.00
1990 Police Columbus Clippers (25) (Maas) 5.00
1990 PC Columbus Clippers (28) 4.00
1990 Team Columbus Clippers Foldout 25.00
1990 Best Columbus Mudcats (26) 6.00
1990 PC Columbus Mudcats (27) 9.00
1990 Star Columbus Mudcats (29) 9.00
1990 CMC Denver Zephyrs (26) 3.00
1990 PC Denver Zephyrs (28) 3.00
1990 Star Dunedin Blue Jays (28) 3.00
1990 Sportsprint Durham Bulls (29) 4.00
1990 Sportsprint Durham Bulls Update (8) 15.00
1990 PC Eastern League All-Stars (48) 7.00
1990 CMC Edmonton Trappers (24) 3.00
1990 PC Edmonton Trappers (25) 3.00
1990 Star Elizabethton Twins (26) 4.00
1990 Pucko Elmira Pioneers (27) 3.00
1990 GS El Paso Diablos (25) 4.00
1990 Team El Paso Diablos All-Time (45) 25.00
1990 Star Erie Sailors (31) 3.00
1990 GS Eugene Emeralds (30) 3.00
1990 Best Everett Giants (28) 4.00
1990 PC Everett Giants (32) 4.00
1990 PC Fayetteville Generals (28) 3.00
1990 Star Florida State League All-Stars (50) 20.00
1990 Sportsprint Frederick Keys (30) 6.00
1990 Star Ft. Lauderdale Yankees (29) 4.00
1990 Best Gastonia Rangers (30) 4.00
1990 PC Gastonia Rangers (29) 3.00

Year	Set	Price
1990	Star Gastonia Rangers (29)	3.00
1990	PC Gate City Pioneers (27)	4.00
1990	SP Gate City Pioneers (24)	4.00
1990	PC Geneva Cubs (27)	4.00
1990	Star Geneva Cubs (32)	3.00
1990	SP Great Falls Dodgers (30)	40.00
1990	Best Greensboro Hornets (30)	4.00
1990	PC Greensboro Hornets (31)	4.00
1990	Star Greensboro Hornets (26)	4.00
1990	Best Greenville Braves (22)	4.00
1990	PC Greenville Braves (26)	4.00
1990	Star Greenville Braves (24)	3.00
1990	Best Hagerstown Suns (30)	4.50
1990	Best Hagerstown Suns All-Decade (36)	10.00
1990	PC Hagerstown Suns (33)	5.00
1990	Star Hagerstown Suns (28)	5.00
1990	Best Hamilton Redbirds (28)	4.00
1990	Star Hamilton Redbirds (29)	4.00
1990	PC Harrisburg Senators (26)	7.00
1990	Star Harrisburg Senators (25)	7.00
1990	SP Helena Brewers (29)	4.00
1990	Little Sun High School Prospects (24)	6.00
1990	PC Huntington Cubs (32)	4.00
1990	Best Huntsville Stars (27)	4.00
1990	PC Idaho Falls Braves (31)	3.00
1990	CMC Indianapolis Indians (25)	3.00
1990	PC Indianapolis Indians (31)	3.00
1990	CMC Iowa Cubs (25)	4.00
1990	PC Iowa Cubs (24)	4.00
1990	GS Jackson Mets (30)	4.00
1990	Best Jacksonville Expos (30)	4.00
1990	PC Jacksonville Expos (29)	5.00
1990	Pucko Jamestown Expos (34)	3.00
1990	Star Johnson City Cardinals (30)	3.00
1990	Best Kenosha Twins (30)	4.00
1990	PC Kenosha Twins (27)	4.00
1990	Star Kenosha Twins (29)	3.00
1990	Best Kingsport Mets (28)	4.00
1990	Star Kingsport Mets (30)	3.00
1990	Sportsprint Kinston Indians (31)	3.00
1990	Diamond Kissimmee Dodgers (29)	3.00
1990	Best Knoxville Blue Jays (28)	4.00
1990	PC Knoxville Blue Jays (25)	4.00
1990	Star Knoxville Blue Jays (26)	4.00
1990	Star Lakeland Tigers (28)	3.00
1990	Star Lakeland Tigers (31)	10.00
1990	CMC Las Vegas Stars (25)	4.00
1990	PC Las Vegas Stars (28)	4.00
1990	PC London Tigers (22)	4.00
1990	CMC Louisville Redbirds (29)	4.00
1990	PC Louisville Redbirds (29)	4.00
1990	Team Louisville Redbirds (42)	9.00
1990	Sportsprint Lynchburg Red Sox (27)	4.00
1990	Best Madison Muskies (29)	4.00
1990	PC Madison Muskies (26)	4.00
1990	PC Martinsville Phillies (34)	4.00
1990	Best Medicine Hat Blue Jays (28)	4.00
1990	Best Memphis Chicks (29)	5.00
1990	PC Memphis Chicks (28)	5.00
1990	Star Memphis Chicks (27)	5.00
1990	Star Miami Miracle I (31)	3.00
1990	Star Miami Miracle II (31)	3.00
1990	GS Midland Angels (28)	4.00
1990	GS Midland Angels (32)	6.00
1990	1 Hour Midland Angels (35)	40.00
1990	GS Midwest League All-Stars (58)	9.00
1990	Star 1989 Midwest League All-Stars (56)	8.00
1990	Cal Modesto A's (25)	3.00
1990	Chong Modesto A's (36)	4.00
1990	PC Modesto A's (29)	3.00
1990	PC Myrtle Beach Blue Jays (29)	7.00
1990	CMC Nashville Sounds (26)	4.00
1990	PC Nashville Sounds (29)	4.00
1990	Team Nashville Sounds (30)	5.00
1990	Best New Britain Red Sox (29)	12.00
1990	PC New Britain Red Sox (26)	12.00
1990	Star New Britain Red Sox (27)	15.00
1990	Pucko Niagara Falls Rapids (33)	5.00
1990	CMC Oklahoma City 89ers (24)	15.00
1990	PC Oklahoma City 89ers (30)	12.50
1990	CMC Omaha Royals (25)	4.00
1990	PC Omaha Royals (26)	4.00
1990	PC Oneonta Yankees (29)	4.00
1990	Best Orlando Sun Rays (30)	7.50
1990	PC Orlando Sun Rays (27)	12.00
1990	Star Orlando Sun Rays (28)	12.00
1990	Star Osceola Astros (30)	6.00
1990	Cal Palm Springs Angels (26)	5.00
1990	PC Palm Springs Angels (28)	7.00
1990	BDK Pan-Am Team USA (Red)(26)	6.00
1990	CMC Pawtucket Red Sox (25)	4.00
1990	DD Pawtucket Red Sox Foldout	30.00
1990	PC Pawtucket Red Sox (29)	9.00
1990	Team Peninsula Oilers (24)	6.00
1990	Star Peninsula Pilots (27)	3.00
1990	Team Peoria Chiefs (30)	10.00
1990	Team Peoria Chiefs Sheet (30)	7.50
1990	Team Peoria Chiefs Update (7)	4.00
1990	Team Peoria Chiefs Earl Cunningham (4)	4.00
1990	CMC Phoenix Firebirds (26)	5.00
1990	PC Phoenix Firebirds (29)	5.00
1990	Pucko Pittsfield Mets (32)	6.00
1990	CMC Portland Beavers (25)	4.00
1990	PC Portland Beavers (28)	4.00
1990	Diamond Princeton Patriots (30)	3.00
1990	Sportsprint Prince William Cannons (30)	5.00
1990	Best Pulaski Braves (29)	3.00
1990	PC Pulaski Braves (31)	4.00
1990	GS Quad City Angels (30)	5.00
1990	Best Reading Phillies (26)	4.00
1990	PC Reading Phillies (27)	6.00
1990	Star Reading Phillies (28)	4.00
1990	Cal Reno Silver Sox (31)	3.00
1990	Bob's Richmond Braves (21)	45.00
1990	Bob's Richmond Braves (22)	50.00
1990	CMC Richmond Braves (27)	7.00
1990	PC Richmond Braves (28)	6.00
1990	Team Richmond Braves Foldout	15.00
1990	Team Richmond 25th Anniversary (23)	25.00
1990	Best Riverside Red Wave (27)	3.00
1990	Cal Riverside Red Wave (27)	3.00
1990	PC Riverside Red Wave (28)	3.00
1990	CMC Rochester Red Wings (27)	6.00
1990	PC Rochester Red Wings (29)	5.00
1990	Team Rochester Red Wings (36)	30.00
1990	PC Rockford Expos (29)	3.00
1990	Team Rockford Expos (30)	4.00
1990	Star Salem Buccaneers (27)	3.50
1990	Cal Salinas Spurs (32)	4.00
1990	PC Salinas Spurs (26)	3.00
1990	GS San Antonio Missions (30)	9.00
1990	Best San Bernardino Spirit (28)	4.00
1990	Cal San Bernardino Spirit (32)	5.00
1990	PC San Bernardino Spirit (28)	4.00
1990	Best San Jose Giants (30)	4.00
1990	Cal San Jose Giants (28)	4.00
1990	PC San Jose Giants (30)	4.00
1990	Star San Jose Giants (30)	4.00
1990	Star Sarasota White Sox (30)	3.00
1990	PC Savannah Cardinals (28)	3.00
1990	CMC Scranton Red Barons (25)	3.00
1990	PC Scranton Red Barons (24)	3.00
1990	PC Shreveport Captains (27)	4.00
1990	Star Shreveport Captains (27)	3.00
1990	Star South Atlantic League A-S (48)	6.00
1990	Best South Bend White Sox (29)	4.00
1990	GS South Bend White Sox (30)	3.00
1990	DJ Southern League A-S (50)	8.00
1990	Best Southern Oregon Athletics (30)	4.00
1990	PC Southern Oregon Athletics (30)	4.00
1990	Best Spartanburg Phillies (30)	4.00
1990	PC Spartanburg Phillies (29)	4.00
1990	Star Spartanburg Phillies (29)	3.00
1990	SP Spokane Indians (28)	5.00
1990	Best Springfield Cardinals (29)	3.00
1990	Best Springfield Cards All-Decade (36)	9.00
1990	PC St. Catharines Blue Jays (34)	10.00
1990	Stearns St. Cloud Rox (9)	25.00
1990	Star St. Lucie Mets (31)	4.00
1990	Star St. Lucie Mets (33)	6.00
1990	Star St. Petersburg Cardinals (26)	3.00
1990	Best Stockton Ports (29)	4.00
1990	Cal Stockton Ports (29)	5.00
1990	PC Stockton Ports (29)	4.00
1990	Best Sumter Braves (30)	10.00
1990	PC Sumter Braves (30)	12.00
1990	CMC Syracuse Chiefs (28)	5.00
1990	PC Syracuse Chiefs (28)	5.00
1990	Team Syracuse Chiefs (30)	20.00
1990	CMC Tacoma Tigers (25)	4.00
1990	PC Tacoma Tigers (29)	4.00
1990	Diamond Tampa Yankees (28)	20.00
1990	GS Texas League A-S (38)	8.00
1990	CMC Tidewater Tides (30)	5.00
1990	PC Tidewater Tides (30)	5.00
1990	Team Tidewater Tides Foldout	5.00
1990	CMC Toledo Mud Hens (27)	8.00
1990	PC Toledo Mud Hens (27)	6.00
1990	CMC Tucson Toros (25)	5.00
1990	PC Tucson Toros (27)	5.00
1990	Best Tulsa Drillers All-Decade (36)	30.00
1990	PC Tulsa Drillers (28)	6.00
1990	Team Tulsa Drillers (28)	12.00
1990	Smokey USC Alumni (12)	40.00
1990	Pucko Utica Blue Sox (30)	4.00
1990	CMC Vancouver Canadians (28)	4.00
1990	PC Vancouver Canadians (28)	4.00
1990	Star Vero Beach Dodgers (32)	30.00
1990	Cal Visalia Oaks (31)	4.00
1990	PC Visalia Oaks (26)	4.00
1990	Best Waterloo Diamonds (28)	4.00
1990	PC Waterloo Diamonds (27)	3.00
1990	Star Watertown Indians (28)	3.00
1990	Best Wausau Timbers (28)	4.00
1990	PC Wausau Timbers (32)	3.00
1990	Star Wausau Timbers (29)	3.00
1990	Pucko Welland Pirates (36)	4.00
1990	Star West Palm Beach Expos (31)	4.00
1990	Star West Palm Beach Expos (34)	6.00
1990	Rock's Wichita Wranglers (28)	5.00
1990	Best Williamsport Bills (27)	4.00
1990	PC Williamsport Bills (26)	3.00
1990	Star Williamsport Bills (27)	3.00
1990	Sportsprint Winston-Salem Spirits (30)	3.00
1990	Star Winter Haven Red Sox (28)	3.00
1990	Star Winter Haven Red Sox (29)	5.00
1990	Golden Yakima Bears (37)	6.00

1991 Classic Best

Classic Best entered the single-card minor league market in 1991 with a 450-card set. The first 396 cards were issued in poly packs and later available in factory sets. Cards numbered 397-450 were only available in the factory sets. Hall of Famer Mike Schmidt, who is card #1 in the set, personally autographed 2,100 of his cards, which were inserted at the rate of one per 8,000 packs.

	MT
Complete Factory Set (450):	12.00
Complete Wax Set (396):	6.00
Common Player:	.05
Wax Pack (12):	.75
Wax Box (36):	17.50
Jumbo Pack (23):	1.00
Jumbo Box (20):	17.50

No.	Player	MT
1	Mike Schmidt	.50
1a	Mike Schmidt (Autographed edition of 2,100.)	30.00
2	Kevin Roberson	.05
3	Paul Rodgers	.05
4	Marc Newfield	.05
5	Marc Ronan	.05
6	Marty Willis	.05
7	Jason Hardtke	.05
8	Matt Mieske	.05
9	Brian Johnson	.05
10	Alex Arias	.05
11	Eric Young	.05
12	Donald Harris	.05
13	Bruce Chick	.05
14	Brian Williams	.05
15	Brian Cornelius	.05
16	Brian Giles	.10
17	Brad Ausmus	.05
18	Ivan Cruz	.05
19	Keven Flora	.05
20	Robbie Katzaroff	.05
21	Randy Knorr	.05
22	Micky Henson	.05
23	Chris Haney	.05
24	Jeff Mutis	.05
25	Barry Winford	.05
26	Ray Giannelli	.05
27	Donovan Osborne	.05
28	Ruben Gonzalez	.05
29	Howard Battle	.05
30	Greg O'Halloran	.05
31	Ben Van Ryn	.05
32	Rick Hulsman	.05
33	Jose Valentin	.05
34	Jose Zambrano	.05
35	John Gross	.05
36	Jessie Hollins	.05
37	Kevin Scott	.05
38	Kerwin Moore	.05
39	Eric Albright	.05
40	Ernesto Rodriguez	.05
41	Reggie Sanders	.05
42	Henry Werland	.05
43	Boo Moore	.05
44	Mike Messerly	.05
45	Mike Lansing	.05
46	Mike Gardella	.05
47	Mo Sanford	.05
48	Tavo Alvarez	.05
49	Nick Davis	.05
50	Charlie Hillemann	.05
51	Jeff Darwin	.05
52	Reid Cornelius	.05
53	Matt Rambo	.05
54	Rich Batchelor	.05
55	Ricky Gutierrez	.05
56	Rod Bolton	.05
57	Pat Bryant	.05
58	Hugh Walker	.05
59	Keith Schmidt	.05
60	Ceasar Morillo	.05
61	Gabe White	.05
62	Davy (Javy) Lopez	.10
63	Carlos Delgado	1.00
64	John Johnstone	.05
65	Andres Berumen	.05
66	Brian Kowitz	.05
67	Shane Reynolds (Photo actually Orlando Miller.)	.10
68	Jeromy Burnitz	.10
69	Scott Bryant	.05
70	Jason McFarlin	.05
71	John Conner	.05
72	Garrett Jenkins	.05
73	Greg Kobza	.05
74	Mark Swope	.05
75	Jerome Williams	.05
76	Jeff Bonner	.05
77	Jermaine Swinton	.05
78	John Cohen	.05
79	Johnny Calzado	.05
80	Juan Andujar	.05
81	Paul Ellis	.05
82	Paul Gonzalez	.05
83	Scott Taylor	.05
84	Stan Spencer	.05
85	Steve Martin	.05
86	Scott Cepicky	.05
87	Max Aleys	.05
88	Michael Brown (Photo actually Matt Brown.)	.05
89	Jim Waggoner	.05
90	Mickey Rivers Jr.	.05
91	Nate Crowmwell	.05
92	Carlos Perez	.05
93	Matt Brown (Photo actually Michael Brown.)	.05
94	Jose Hernandez	.05
95	Johnny Ruffin	.05
96	Kevin Jordan	.05
97	Manny Alexander	.05
98	Tony Longmire	.05
99	Lonell Roberts	.05
100	Doug Lindsey	.05
101	Al Harley	.05
102	Jerry Thurston	.05
103	Mike Williams	.05
104	David Bell	.05
105	Greg Johnson	.05
106	Roger Salkeld	.05
107	Mike Milchin	.05
108	Jeff Kent	.50
109	Tim Stargell	.05
110	Miah Bradbury	.05
111	Paul Fletcher	.05
112	Steven Rolen	.05
113	Tony Spires	.05
114	Kevin Tolar	.05
115	Kevin Dattola	.05
116	Sherman Obando	.05
117	Sean Ryan	.05
118	Carlos Mota	.05
119	Steve Karsay	.05
120	Kelly Lifgren	.05
121	Damion Easley	.05
122	Fred Russell	.05
123	Freddie Davis Jr.	.05
124	Dave Zancanaro	.05
125	Jeff Jackson	.05
126	Steve Pegues	.05
127	Gerald Williams	.05
128	Eric Helfand	.05
129	Gary Painter	.05
130	Colin Ryan	.05
131	Randy Brown	.05
132	Andy Fox	.05
133	Mike Ogliaruso	.05
134	Matt Franco	.05
135	Willie Ansley	.05
136	Ivan Rodriguez	1.00
137	Anthony Lewis	.05
138	Bill Wertz	.05
139	Tom Kinney	.05
140	Brad Hassinger	.05
141	Elliot Gray	.05
142	Clemente Alvarez	.05
143	Mike Hankins	.05
144	Jim Haller	.05
145	Manuel Martinez	.05
146	Nilson Robledo	.05
147	Rex DeLa Nuez	.05
148	Steve Bethea	.05
149	Oscar Munoz	.05
150	Sam Militello	.05
151	Phil Hiatt	.05
152	Alberto de los Santos	.05
153	Darrell Sherman	.05
154	Henry Mercedes	.05
155	David Holdridge	.05
156	Sean Ross	.05
157	Brandon Wilson	.05
158	William Pennyfeather	.05
159	Derek Parks	.05
160	Troy O'Leary	.05
161	Genaro Campusano	.05
162	Robbie Beckett	.05
163	Chris Burton	.05
164	Jeff Williams	.05
165	John Massarelli	.05
166	John Kelly	.05
167	Jim Wiley	.05
168	Mark Mitchelson	.05
169	Jeff McNeely	.05
170	Keith Kimberlin	.05
171	Mike DeKneef	.05
172	Rusty Greer	.05
173	Pete Castellano	.05
174	Paul Torres	.05
175	Rod McCall	.05
176	Jim Bullinger	.05
177	Brian Champion	.05
178	Greg Hunter	.05
179	Luis Galindez	.05
180	Rodney Eldridge	.05
181	Rudy Pemberton	.05
182	Russ Davis	.05
183	Cristobal Colon	.05
184	Scott Bream	.05
185	Tim Nedin	.05
186	Joe Ausanlo	.05
187	Shanhon Withem	.05
188	Mike Oquist	.05
189	Pete Young	.05
190	Paul Carey	.05
191	Chris Gies	.05
192	Gar Finnvold	.05
193	Greg Martin	.05
194	Oreste Marrero	.05
195	Jim Thome	1.00
196	Bill Ostermeyer	.05
197	David Hulse	.05
198	Damon Buford	.05
199	Jonathan Hurst	.05
200	Rich Tunison	.05
201	Tom Nevers	.05
202	Tracy Sanders	.05
203	Troy Buckley	.05
204	Todd Gugglana	.05
205	Tim Laker	.05
206	Dean Locklear (Photo actually Jon Jenkins.)	.05
207	Lee Tinsley	.05
208	Jose Velez	.05
209	Gregg Zaun	.05
210	Bill Ashley	.05
211	Gary Caraballo	.05
212	Kiki Jones	.05
213	Dave Wrona	.05
214	Michael Carter	.05
215	Leon Glenn Jr.	.05
216	Glenn Sutko	.05
217	Pat Howell	.05
218	Austin Manahan	.05
219	Jon Jenkins	.05
220	Brook Fordyce	.05
221	Kevin Rodgers	.05
222	David Allen	.05
223	Kurt Archer	.05
224	Keith Mitchell	.05
225	Bruce Schreiber	.05
226	Greg Blosser	.05
227	Dave Nilsson	.05
228	Fred Colley	.05
229	Marc Lipson	.05
230	Jay Gainer	.05
231	Sean Cheetham	.05
232	Tim Howard	.05
233	Steve Hosey	.05
234	Javier Ocasio	.05
235	Ricky Rhodes	.05
236	Mark Griffin	.05
237	Scott Shockey	.05
238	T.R. Lewis	.05
239	Kevin Young	.05
240	Robb Nen	.05
241	Steve Dunn	.05
242	Tommy Taylor	.05
243	Keith Valrie	.05
244	Mateo Ozuna	.05
245	Scott Bullett	.05
246	Anthony Brown	.05
247	Phil Leftwich	.05
248	Cliff Garrett	.05
249	Wade Fyock	.05
250	Shayne Rea	.05
251	Royce Clayton	.05
252	Martin Martinez	.05
253	Dave Patterson	.05
254	Robert Fitzpatrick	.05
255	John Jackson	.05
256	Enoch Simmons	.05
257	Dave Proctor	.05
258	Garret Anderson	.15
259	Mark Delesandro	.05
260	Ken Edenfield	.05
261	Tom Raffo	.05
262	Tim Cecil	.05
263	Bobby Magallanes	.05
264	Vince Castaldo	.05
265	Terry Burrows	.05
266	Victor Madrigal	.05
267	Tyler Houston	.05
268	Chipper Jones	1.50
269	Terry Bradshaw	.05
270	Jalal Leach	.05
271	Jose Ventura	.05
272	Derek Lee	.05
273	Derek Reid	.05
274	David Wilson	.05
275	Patrick Rapp	.05
276	John Roper	.05
277	Rogelio Nunez	.05

278 Fred White .05
279 J.T. Snow .10
280 Pedro Astacio .05
281 Corey Thomas .05
282 Chris Johnson .05
283 Ignacio Duran .05
284 Dave Fleming .05
285 Wilson Alvarez .05
286 Eric Booker .05
287 John Ericks .05
288 Don Peters .05
289 Ed Ferm .05
290 Mike Lieberthal .10
291 John Jaha .05
292 Bryan Baar .05
293 Archie Corbin .05
294 Kevin Tatar .05
295 Shea Wardwell .05
296 Hipilito Pichardo .05
297 Curtis Leskanic .05
298 Sam August (Photo actually Jeff Juden.) .05
299 Tim Pugh .05
300 Mike Huyler .05
301 Mark Parnell .05
302 Jeff Juden (Photo actually Shane Reynolds.) .10
303 Carl Sullivan .05
304 Tyrone Kingwood .05
305 Glenn Carter .05
306 Tom Fischer .05
307 Braulio Castillo .05
308 Bob McCreary .05
309 Ty Kovach .05
310 Troy Salvior .05
311 Mike Weimerskirch .05
312 Chistopher Hatcher .05
313 Bryan Smith .05
314 John Patterson .05
315 Scooter Tucker .05
316 Ray Callari .05
317 Mike Moberg .05
318 Midre Cummings .05
319 Todd Ritchie .05
320 Eric Christopherson .05
321 Adam Hyzdu .05
322 Andres Duncan .05
323 Mike Myers .05
324 Salomon Torres .05
325 Tony Gilmore .05
326 Walter Trice .05
327 Tom Redington .05
328 Terry Taylor .05
329 Tim Salmon .25
330 Dan Masteller .05
331 Mark Wohlers .05
332 Willie Smith .05
333 Todd Jones .05
334 Alan Zinter .05
335 Arthur Rhodes .05
336 Toby Borland .05
337 Shawn Whalen .05
338 Scott Sanders .05
339 Bill Meury .05
340 Amadoz Arias .05
341 Denny Hoppe .05
342 Dave Telgheder .05
343 Paul Bruno .05
344 Paul Russo .05
345 Rich Becker (Photo actually Tim Persing.) .10
346 Steve Vondran .05
347 Rich Langford .05
348 Ron Lockett .05
349 Sam Taylor .05
350 Willie Greene .05
351 Tom Houk .05
352 Lance Painter .05
353 Dan Wilson .05
354 John Kuehl .05
355 Pedro Martinez 1.50
356 John Byington .05
357 Scott Freeman .05
358 Bo Dodson .05
359 Julian Vasquez .05
360 Rondell White .10
361 Aaron Small .05
362 Doug Fitzer .05
363 Billy White .05
364 Jeff Tuss .05
365 Jeff Barry .05
366 Craig Pueschner .05
367 Julio Bruno .05
368 Jamie Dismuke .05
369 K.C. Gillium .05
370 Jason Klonoski .05
371 Tim Persing (Photo actually Rich Becker.) .05
372 Mark Borcherding .05
373 Larry Luebbers .05
374 Carlos Fermin .05
375 Charlie Rogers .05
376 Ramon Caraballo .05
377 Orlando Miller (Photo actually Sam August.) .05
378 Joey James .05
379 Dan Rogers .05
380 Jon Shave .05
381 Frank Bolick .05
382 Frank Seminara .05
383 Mel Wearing Jr. .05
384 Zak Shinall .05
385 Sterling Hitchcock .05
386 Todd Van Poppel .05
387 D.J. Dozier .05
388 Ryan Klesko .10
389 Tim Costo .05
390 Brad Pennington .05
391 Checklist 1-66 .05
392 Checklist 67-132 .05
393 Checklist 133-198 .05
394 Checklist 199-264 .05
395 Checklist 265-330 .05
396 Checklist 331-396 .05
397 Frank Rodriguez .05
398 Frank Jacons .05
399 Mike Kelly .05
400 David McCarty .05
401 Scott Stahoviak .05
402 Doug Glanville .05
403 Curt Krippner .05
404 Joe Vitiello .05
405 Justin Thompson .05
406 Trever Miller .05
407 Tarrick Brock .05
408 Eddie Williams .05
409 Scott Ruffcorn .05
410 Chris Durkin .05
411 Jim Kewis .05
412 Calvin Reese .05
413 Toby Rumfield .05
414 Brent Gates .05
415 Mike Neill .05
416 Tyler Green .05
417 Ron Allen .05
418 Larry Thomas Jr. .05
419 Chris Weinke .25
420 Matt Brewer .05
421 Dax Jones .05
422 Jon Farrell .05
423 Dan Jones .05
424 Eduardo Perez .05
425 Rodney Pedraza .05
426 Tom McKinnon .05
427 Al Watson .05
428 Herbert Perry .05
429 Shawn Estes .05
430 Tommy Adams .05
431 Mike Grace .05
432 Tyson Godfrey .05
433 Andy Hartung .05
434 Shawn Livsey .05
435 Earl Cunningham .05
436 Scott Lydy .05
437 Aaron Sele .05
438 Tim Costo .05
439 Tanyon Sturtze .05
440 Ed Ramos .05
441 Buck McNabb .05
442 Scott Hatteberg .05
443 Brian Barber .05
444 Julian Heredia .05
445 Chris Pritchett .05
446 Bubba Smith .05
447 Shawn Purdy .05
448 Jeff Borski .05
449 Jamie Gonzalez .05
450 Checklist 397-450 .05

1991 Classic Draft Picks

After releasing a 26-card draft pick set in 1990, Classic returned with a 50-card issue for 1991. A reported 330,000 hobby sets were produced, along with 165,000 sets for the retail market. Card fronts feature gray and maroon borders surrounding full-color photos and the Classic logo in the upper-left corner. A special bonus card of Frankie Rodriguez is also included with the set. Each set includes a certificate of authenticity.

MT
Complete Set (50): 4.00
Common Player: .05
Wax Box (36): 3.00
1 Brien Taylor .05
2 Mike Kelly .05
3 David McCarty .05
4 Dmitri Young .05
5 Joe Vitiello .05
6 Mark Smith .05
7 Tyler Green .05
8 Shawn Estes .05
9 Doug Glanville .05
10 Manny Ramirez 3.00
11 Cliff Floyd .05
12 Tyrone Hill .05
13 Eduardo Perez .05
14 Al Shirley .05
15 Benji Gil .05
16 Calvin Reese .05
17 Allen Watson .05
18 Brian Barber .05
19 Aaron Sele .05
20 Jon Farrell .05
21 Scott Ruffcorn .05
22 Brent Gates .05
23 Scott Stahoviak .05
24 Tom McKinnon .05
25 Shawn Livsey .05
26 Jason Pruitt .05
27 Greg Anthony .05
28 Justin Thompson .05
29 Steve Whitaker .05
30 Jorge Fabregas .05
31 Jeff Ware .05
32 Bobby Jones .05
33 J.J. Johnson .05
34 Mike Rossiter .05
35 Dan Chowlowsky .05
36 Jimmy Gonzalez .05
37 Trever Miller .05
38 Scott Hatteberg .05
39 Mike Groppuso .05
40 Ryan Long .05
41 Eddie Williams .05
42 Mike Durant .05
43 Buck McNabb .05
44 Jimmy Lewis .05
45 Eddie Ramos .05
46 Terry Horn .05
47 Jon Barnes .05
48 Shawn Curran .05
49 Tommy Adams .05
50 Trevor Mallory .05
--- Frankie Rodriguez (Bonus Card) .05

1991 Classic Four Sport (Baseball)

Late in 1991, Classic released a four-sport draft picks set of 230 base cards, 10 foil "Limited Print" cards and more than 60,000 autographed cards seeded one per 260 packs. Cards have color photos on front with wide mottled blue-gray borders. A "wax seal" in red at upper-left carries the set's logo. Player name and position are in black at the bottom. Backs are printed in color with biographical data, high school or college stats and career highlights. Twenty percent of the 25,000 cases printed were an English-French version, which carries a premium of about a 50 percent premium. Only the cards featuring baseball players are checklisted here.

MT
Common Card: .05
Wax Box (36): 15.00
1 Russell Maryland, Brien Taylor, Larry Johnson, Eric Lindros Future Stars .10
51 Brien Taylor .05
52 Mike Kelly .05
53 David McCarty .05
54 Dmitri Young .05
55 Joe Vitiello .05
56 Mark Smith .05
57 Tyler Green .05
58 Shawn Estes (Photo reversed.) .15
59 Doug Glanville .05
60 Manny Ramirez 3.00
61 Cliff Floyd .10
62 Tyrone Hill .05
63 Eduardo Perez .05
64 Al Shirley .05
65 Benji Gil .05
66 Calvin Reese .10
67 Allen Watson .05
68 Brian Barber .05
69 Aaron Sele .05
70 John Farrell .05
71 Scott Ruffcorn .05
72 Brent Gates .05
73 Scott Stahoviak .05
74 Tom McKinnon .05
75 Shawn Livsey .05
76 Jason Pruitt .05
77 Greg Anthony .05
78 Justin Thompson .05
79 Steve Whitaker .05
80 Jorge Fabregas .05
81 Jeff Ware .05
82 Bobby Jones .05
83 J.J. Johnson .05
84 Mike Rossiter .05
85 Dan Chowlowsky .05
86 Jimmy Gonzalez .05
87 Trever Miller .05
88 Scott Hatteberg .05
89 Mike Groppuso .05
90 Ryan Long .05
91 Eddie Williams .05
92 Mike Durant .05
93 Buck McNabb .05
94 Jimmy Lewis .05
95 Eddie Ramos .05
96 Terry Horn .05
97 John Barnes .05
98 Shawn Curran .05
99 Tommy Adams .05
100 Trevor Mallory .05
101 Frankie Rodriguez .05
218 Joe Hamilton .05
219 Marc Kroon .05
225 Shawn Green 1.50
--- Shawn Green (Promo) 5.00
LP7 Brien Taylor (Limited Print silver foil.) .25

Autographed

Approximately 60 of the more than 200 players in the 1991 Classic Four Sport draft picks issue autographed as many as 2,600 cards apiece for insertion as random foil-pack inserts; in all more than 60,000 autographed cards were distributed. The number in parentheses in the listings here indicates the number of cards reportedly signed by each player. Only the baseball players are listed here.

MT
Common Player: 3.00
51 Brien Taylor (2,600) 4.50
52 Mike Kelly (2,600) 3.00
53 David McCarty (2,450) 3.00
54 Dmitri Young (2,600) 5.00
55 Joe Vitiello (1,900) 3.00
56 Mark Smith (1,700) 3.00
58 Shawn Estes (2,000) (Photo reversed.)) 5.00
59 Doug Glanville (2,000) 3.00
61 Cliff Floyd (2,000) 5.00
62 Tyrone Hill (1,000) 3.00
63 Eduardo Perez (950) 3.00
101 Frankie Rodriguez 4.00
218 Joe Hamilton (2,000) 3.00

1991 Impel/Line Drive Pre-Rookie AA

Impel followed its successful AAA wax series with a 650-card AA wax series consisting of 25 players from each team. Like the AAA series, a checklist for the AA series was available from the company. Due to a scarcity of certain cards in inventory and additional labor costs to dealers, consumers can be expected to pay a minimum of $4-6 for team sets made from this product. Line Drive team sets sold at the stadiums included team checklist cards.

MT
Complete Set (650): 7.00
Common Player: .05
Wax Box (36): 15.00
1 Andy Cook .05
2 Russell Davis .05
3 Bobby DeJardin .05
4 Mike Draper .05
5 Victor Garcia .05
6 Mike Gardella .05
7 Cullen Hartzog .05
8 Jay Knoblauh .05
9 Billy Masse .05
10 Jeff Livesey .05
11 Edward Martel .05
12 Vince Phillips .05
13 Tom Popplewell .05
14 Jerry Rub .05
15 Dave Silvestri .05
16 Tom Newell .05
17 Willie Smith .05
18 J.T. Snow .10
19 Don Stanford .05
20 Larry Stanford .05
21 John Toale .05
22 Hector Vargas .05
23 Gerald Williams .05
24 Dan Radison .05
25 Dave Jorn, Bob Mariano (Coaches) .05
26 Frank Abreu .05
27 Cliff Brannon .05
28 Greg Carmona .05
29 Ric Christian .05
30 John Ericks .05
31 Steve Fanning .05
32 Joey Fernandez .05
33 Jose Fernandez .05
34 Mike Flore .05
35 David Grimes .05
36 Dale Kisten .05
37 John Lepley .05
38 Luis Martinez .05
39 Mike Milchin .05
40 Donovan Osborne .05
41 Gabriel Ozuna .05
42 Lee Plemel .05
43 Don Prybylinski .05
44 John Sellick .05
45 Jeff Shireman .05
46 Brian Stone .05
47 Charlie White .05
48 Dennis Wiseman .05
49 Joe Pettini .05
50 Scott Melvin, Marty Mason .05
51 Wilson Alvarez .05
52 Wayne Busby .05
53 Darrin Campbell .05
54 Mark Chasey .05
55 Ron Coomer .05
56 Argenis Cortez .05
57 Mike Davino .05
58 Lindsay Foster .05
59 Ramon Garcia .05
60 Kevin Garner .05
61 Jeff Gay .05
62 Chris Howard .05
63 John Hudek .05
64 Scott Jaster .05
65 Bo Kennedy .05
66 Derek Lee .05
67 Frank Merigliano .05
68 Scott Middaugh .05
69 Javier Ocasio .05
70 Kinnis Pledger .05
71 Greg Roth .05
72 Aubrey Waggoner .05
73 Jose Ventura .05
74 Tony Franklin .05
75 Rick Peterson, Pat Roessler, Sam Hairston .05
76 Ramon Bautista .05
77 Eric Bell .05
78 Jim Bruske .05
79 Tim Costo .05
80 Mike Curtis .05
81 Jerry DiPoto .05
82 Daren Epley .05
83 Sam Ferrelli .05
84 Garland Kiser .05
85 Ty Kovach .05
86 Tom Kramer .05
87 Molan Lane .05
88 Jesse Levis .05
89 Carlos Martinez .05
90 Jeff Mutis .05
91 Rouglas Odor .05
92 Gary Resetar .05
93 Greg Roscoe .05
94 Miguel Sabino .05
95 Bernie Tatis .05
96 Jim Thome 3.00
97 Ken Ramos .05
98 Ken Whitfield .05
99 Ken Bolek .05
100 Dave Keller .05
101 Steve Adams .05
102 Stan Fansler .05
103 Mandy Romero .05
104 Terry Crowley Jr. .05
105 Chip Duncan .05
106 Greg Edge .05
107 Chris Estep .05
108 Carl Hamilton .05
109 Lee Hancock .05
110 Tim Hines .05
111 Mike Huyler .05
112 Paul Miller .05
113 Pete Murphy .05
114 Darwin Pennye .05
115 Mike Roesler .05
116 Bruce Schreiber .05
117 Greg Sparks .05
118 Dennis Tafoya .05
119 Tim Wakefield .05
120 Ben Webb .05
121 John Wehner .05
122 Ed Yacopino .05
123 Eddie Zambrano .05
124 Marc Bombard .05
125 Trent Jewett, Spin Williams .05
126 Alex Arias .05
127 Paul Blair .05
128 Jim Bullinger .05
129 Dick Canan .05
130 Rusty Crockett .05
131 Steve DiBartolomeo .05
132 John Gardner .05
133 Henry Gomez .05
134 Ty Griffin .05
135 Shannon Jones .05
136 Mike Knapp .05
137 Tim Parker .05
138 Elvin Paulino .05
139 Fernando Ramsey .05
140 Kevin Roberson .05
141 John Salles .05
142 Mike Sodders .05
143 Bill St. Peter .05
144 Julio Strauss .05
145 Scott Taylor .05
146 Tim Watkins .05
147 Doug Welch .05
148 Billy White .05
149 Jay Loviglio .05
150 Rick Kranitz .05
151 Rick Allen .05
152 Mike Anderson .05
153 Bobby Ayala .05
154 Pete Beeler .05
155 Jeff Branson .05
156 Scott Bryant .05
157 Bill Dodd .05
158 Steve Foster .05
159 Victor Garcia .05
160 Frank Kremblas .05
161 Greg Lonigro .05
162 Dave McAuliffe .05
163 Steve McCarthy .05
164 Scott Pose .05
165 Tim Pugh .05
166 Bill Risley .05
167 Reggie Sanders .05
168 Mo Sanford .05
169 Scott Sellner .05
170 Jerry Spradlin .05
171 Glenn Sutko .05
172 Todd Trafton .05
173 Bernie Walker .05
174 Jim Tracy .05
175 Mike Griffin .05
176 Shon Ashley .05
177 John Byington .05
178 Mark Chapman .05
179 Jim Czajkowski .05
180 Ruben Escalera .05
181 Craig Faulkner .05
182 Tim Fortugno .05
183 Don Gordon .05
184 Mitch Hannahs .05
185 Steve Lienhard .05
186 Dave Jacas .05
187 Kenny Jackson .05
188 John Jaha .05
189 Chris Johnson .05
190 Mark Kiefer .05
191 Pat Listach .05
192 Tom McGraw .05
193 Angel Miranda .05
194 Dave Nilsson .05
195 Jeff Schwarz .05
196 Steve Sparks .05
197 Jim Tatum .05
198 Brandy Vann .05
199 Dave Huppert .05
200 Paul Lindblad .05
201 Rich Casarotti .05
202 Vinnie Castilla .10
203 Brian Champion .05
204 Popeye Cole .05
205 Johnny Cuevas .05
206 Brian Deak .05
207 Pat Gomez .05
208 Judd Johnson .05
209 Ryan Klesko .10
210 Rich Maloney .05
211 Al Martin .05
212 Keith Mitchell .05
213 Rick Morris .05
214 Ben Rivera .05
215 Napoleon Robinson .05
216 Boi Rodriguez .05
217 Sean Ross .05
218 Earl Sanders .05
219 Scott Taylor .05
220 Lee Upshaw .05
221 Preston Watson .05
222 Turk Wendell .05
223 Mark Wohlers .05
224 Chris Chamblis .05
225 Terry Harper, Bill Slack, Randy Ingle .05
226 Jeff Bumgarner .05
227 Stacey Burdick .05
228 Paul Carey .05
229 Bobby Dickerson .05
230 Roy Gilbert .05
231 Ricky Gutierrez .05
232 Tim Holland .05
233 Stacy Jones .05
234 Tyrone Kingwood .05
235 Mike Lehman .05
236 Rod Lofton .05
237 Kevin Hickey .05
238 Joel McKeon .05
239 Scott Meadows .05
240 Steve Luebber .05
241 Mike Oquist .05
242 Ozzie Peraza .05
243 Tim Raley .05
244 Arthur Rhodes .05
245 Doug Robbins .05
246 Ken Shamburg .05
247 Todd Stephan .05
248 Jack Voight .05
249 Jerry Narron .05
250 Joe Durham .05
251 Chris Caccolo .05
252 Archie Cianfrocco (Archi) .05
253 Dan Freed .05
254 Greg Fulton .05
255 Chris Haney .05
256 Cesar Hernandez .05
257 Richard Holsman .05
258 Rob Katzaroff .05
259 Bryan Kosco .05
260 Ken Lake .05
261 Hector Rivera .05
262 Chris Marchok .05
263 Chris Martin .05
264 Matt Maysey .05
265 Omer Munoz .05
266 Bob Natal .05
267 Chris Pollack .05
268 F.P. Santangelo .05
269 Joe Siddall .05
270 Stan Spencer .05
271 Matt Stairs .05
272 David Wainhouse .05
273 Pete Young .05
274 Mike Quade .05
275 Joe Kerrigan, Pete Dalena .05
276 Marco Armas .05
277 Bob Bafia .05
278 Dean Borrelli .05
279 John Briscoe .05
280 James Buccheri .05
281 Tom Carcione .05
282 Joel Chimelis .05
283 Fred Cooley .05
284 Russ Cormier .05
285 Matt Grott .05
286 Dwayne Hosey .05
287 Chad Kuhn .05

288	Dave Latter	.05
289	Francisco Matos	.05
290	Gavin Osteen	.05
291	Tim Peek	.05
292	Don Peters	.05
293	Scott Shockey	.05
294	Will Tejada	.05
295	Lee Tinsley	.05
296	Todd Van Poppel	.05
297	Darryl Vice	.05
298	Dave Zancanaro	.05
299	Casey Parsons	.05
300	Bert Bradley	.05
301	Frank Carey	.05
302	Larry Carter	.05
303	Royce Clayton	.05
304	Tom Ealy	.05
305	Juan Guerrero	.05
306	Bryan Hickerson	.05
307	Steve Hosey	.05
308	Tom Hostetler	.05
309	Erik Johnson	.05
310	Dan Lewis	.05
311	Paul McClellan	.05
312	Jim McNamara	.05
313	Kevin Meier	.05
314	Jim Myers	.05
315	Dave Patterson	.05
316	John Patterson	.05
317	Jim Pena	.05
318	Dan Rambo	.05
319	Steve Reed	.05
320	Kevin Rogers	.05
321	Reuben Smiley	.05
322	Scooter Tucker	.05
323	Pete Weber	.05
324	Bill Evers	.05
325	Tony Taylor, Todd Oakes	.05
326	Fernando Arguelles	.05
327	Shawn Barton	.05
328	Jim Blueberg	.05
329	Frank Bolick	.05
330	Bret Boone	1.00
331	Jim Bowie	.05
332	Jim Campanis	.05
333	Gary Eave	.05
334	David Evans	.05
335	Fernando Figueroa	.05
336	Dave Fleming	.05
337	Ruben Gonzalez	.05
338	Mike McDonald	.05
339	Jeff Nelson	.05
340	Jim Newlin	.05
341	Ken Pennington	.05
342	Mike Pitz	.05
343	Dave Richards	.05
344	Roger Salkeld	.05
345	Jack Smith	.05
346	Tim Stargell	.05
347	Brian Turang	.05
348	Ted Williams	.05
349	Jim Nettles	.05
350	Bobby Cuellar, Lem Pilkinton	.05
351	Pete Blohm	.05
352	Domingo Cedeno	.05
353	Nate Cromwell	.05
354	Jesse Cross	.05
355	Juan De La Rosa	.05
356	Bobby LeLoach	.05
357	Ray Giannelli	.05
358	Darren Hall	.05
359	Mark Young	.05
360	Jeff Kent	.25
361	Randy Knorr	.05
362	Jose Monzon	.05
363	Bernie Nunez	.05
364	Paul Rodgers	.05
365	Jimmy Rogers	.05
366	Mike Taylor	.05
367	Ryan Thompson	.05
368	Jason Townley	.05
369	Rick Trlicek	.05
370	Anthony Ward	.05
371	Dave Weathers	.05
372	Woody Williams	.05
373	Julian Yan	.05
374	John Stearns	.05
375	Mike McAlpin, Steve Mingori	.05
376	Doyle Balthazar	.05
377	Basilio Cabrera	.05
378	Ron Cook	.05
379	Ivan Cruz	.05
380	Dean Decillis	.05
381	John DeSilva	.05
382	John Doherty	.05
383	Lou Frazier	.05
384	Luis Galindo	.05
385	Greg Gohr	.05
386	Bud Groom	.05
387	Darren Hursey	.05
388	Ricardo Ingram	.05
389	Keith Kimberlin	.05
390	Todd Krumm	.05
391	Randy Marshall	.05
392	Domingo Michel	.05
393	Steve Pegues	.05
394	Jose Ramos	.05
395	Bob Reimink	.05
396	Ruben Rodriguez	.05
397	Eric Stone	.05
398	Marty Willis	.05
399	Gene Roof	.05
400	Jeff Jones, Dan Raley	.05
401	Pete Alborano	.05
402	Jim Baxter	.05
403	Tony Clements	.05
404	Archie Corbin	.05
405	Andres Cruz	.05
406	Jeff Garber	.05
407	David Gonzalez	.05
408	Kevin Koslofski	.05
409	Deric Ladnier	.05
410	Mark Parnell	.05
411	Jorge Pedre	.05
412	Doug Peters	.05
413	Hipolito Pichardo	.05
414	Eddie Pierce	.05
415	Mike Poehl	.05
416	Darryl Robinson	.05
417	Steve Shifflett	.05
418	Jim Smith	.05
419	Lou Talbert	.05
420	Terry Taylor	.05
421	Rich Tunison	.05
422	Hugh Walker	.05
423	Darren Watkins	.05
424	Jeff Cox	.05
425	Brian Peterson, Mike Alvarez	.05
426	Clemente Acosta	.05
427	Jeff Barns	.05
428	Mike Butcher	.05
429	Glenn Carter	.05
430	Marvin Cobb	.05
431	Sherman Corbett	.05
432	Kevin Davis	.05
433	Damion Easley	.05
434	Kevin Flora	.05
435	Larry Gonzales	.05
436	Mark Howie	.05
437	Todd James	.05
438	Bobby Jones	.05
439	Steve King	.05
440	Marcus Lawton	.05
441	Ken Rivers	.05
442	Doug Robertson	.05
443	Tim Salmon	.75
444	Ramon Sambo	.05
445	Daryl Sconiers	.05
446	Dave Shotkoski	.05
447	Terry Taylor	.05
448	Mark Zappelli	.05
449	Don Long	.05
450	Kernan Ronan, Gene Richards	.05
451	Michael Beams	.05
452	Greg Blosser	.05
453	Brian Conroy	.05
454	Freddie Davis	.05
455	Colin Dixon	.05
456	Peter Estrada	.05
457	Ray Fagnant	.05
458	Tom Fischer	.05
459	John Flaherty	.05
460	Donald Florence	.05
461	Blane Fox	.05
462	Steve Hendricks	.05
463	Wayne Housie	.05
464	Peter Hoy	.05
465	Thomas Kane	.05
466	David Milstien	.05
467	Juan Paris	.05
468	Scott Powers	.05
469	Paul Quantrill	.05
470	Randy Randle	.05
471	Al Sanders	.05
472	Scott Taylor	.05
473	John Valentin	.05
474	Gary Allenson	.05
475	Rick Wise	.05
476	Pat Bangtson	.05
477	Carlos Capellan	.05
478	Rafael DeLima	.05
479	Frank Valdez	.05
480	Cheo Garcia	.05
481	Shawn Gilbert	.05
482	Greg Johnson	.05
483	Jay Kvasnicka	.05
484	Orlando Lind	.05
485	Pat Mahomes	.05
486	Jose Marzan	.05
487	Dan Masteller	.05
488	Bob McCreary	.05
489	Steve Muh	.05
490	Reed Olmstead	.05
491	Ray Ortiz	.05
492	Derek Parks	.05
493	Joe Siwa	.05
494	Steve Stowell	.05
495	Mike Trombley	.05
496	Jim Shellenback	.05
497	Rob Wassenaar	.05
498	Phil Wiese	.05
499	Scott Ullger	.05
500	Mark Funderbuck	.05
501	Jason Backs	.05
502	Toby Borland	.05
503	Cliff Brantley	.05
504	Dana Brown	.05
505	John Burgos	.05
506	Andy Carter	.05
507	Bruce Dostal	.05
508	Rick Dunnum	.05
509	John Martin	.05
510	David Holdridge	.05
511	Darrell Lindsey	.05
512	Doug Lindsey	.05
513	Tony Longmire	.05
514	Tom Marsh	.05
515	Rod Robertson	.05
516	Edwin Rosado	.05
517	Sean Ryan	.05
518	Steve Scarsone	.05
519	Mark Sims	.05
520	Jeff Tabaka	.05
521	Tony Trevino	.05
522	Casey Waller	.05
523	Cary Williams	.05
524	Don McCormack	.05
525	Al LeBoeuf	.05
526	Steve Allen	.05
527	Jorge Alvarez	.05
528	Bryan Baar	.05
529	Tim Barker	.05
530	Tony Barron	.05
531	Cam Biberdorf	.05
532	Jason Brosnan	.05
533	Braulio Castillo	.05
534	Steve Finken	.05
535	Freddy Gonzalez	.05
536	Mike James	.05
537	Brett Magnusson	.05
538	Jose Munoz	.05
539	Lance Rice	.05
540	Zak Shinall	.05
541	Dennis Springer	.05
542	Ramon Taveras	.05
543	Jimmy Terrill	.05
544	Brian Traxler	.05
545	Jody Treadwell	.05
546	Mike White	.05
547	Mike Wilkins	.05
548	Eric Young	.05
549	John Shoemaker	.05
550	James Wray	.05
551	Willie Ansley	.05
552	Sam August	.05
553	Jeff Baldwin	.05
554	Pete Bauer	.05
555	Kevin Coffman	.05
556	Kevin Dean	.05
557	Tony Eusebio	.05
558	Dean Freeland	.05
559	Rusty Harris	.05
560	Dean Hartgraves	.05
561	Trent Hubbard	.05
562	Bert Hunter	.05
563	Bernie Jenkins	.05
564	Jeff Juden	.05
565	Keith Kalser	.05
566	Steve Larose	.05
567	Lance Madsen	.05
568	Scott Makarewicz	.05
569	Rob Mallicoat	.05
570	Joe Mikulik	.05
571	Orlando Miller	.05
572	Shane Reynolds	.05
573	Richie Simon	.05
574	Rick Sweet	.05
575	Don Reynolds, Charlie Taylor	.05
576	Rob Brown	.05
577	Mike Burton	.05
578	Evertt Cunningham	.05
579	Jeff Frye	.05
580	Pat Garman	.05
581	Bryan Gore	.05
582	David Green	.05
583	Donald Harris	.05
584	Jose Hernandez	.05
585	Greg Iavarone	.05
586	Barry Manuel	.05
587	Trey McCoy	.05
588	Rod Morris	.05
589	Robb Nen	.05
590	David Perez	.05
591	Bobby Reed	.05
592	Ivan Rodriguez	3.00
593	Dan Rohrmeier	.05
594	Brian Romero	.05
595	Luke Sable	.05
596	Frederic Samson	.05
597	Cedric Shaw	.05
598	Chris Shiflett	.05
599	Bobby Jones	.05
600	Oscar Acosta, Jeff Hubbard	.05
601	Mike Basso	.05
602	Doug Brocail	.05
603	Rafael Chavez	.05
604	Brian Cisarik	.05
605	Greg David	.05
606	Rick Davis	.05
607	Vince Harris	.05
608	Charles Hillemann	.05
609	Kerry Knox	.05
610	Pete Kuid	.05
611	Jim Lewis	.05
612	Luis Lopez	.05
613	Pedro Martinez	.05
614	Tim McWilliam	.05
615	Tom Redington	.05
616	Darrin Reichle	.05
617	A.J. Sager	.05
618	Frank Seminara	.05
619	Darrell Sherman	.05
620	Jose Valentin	.05
621	Guillermo Velasquez	.05
622	Tim Wallace	.05
623	Brian Wood	.05
624	Steve Lubratich	.05
625	John Cumberland, Jack Maloof	.05
626	Tim Bogar	.05
627	Jeromy Burnitz	.15
628	Hernan Cortez	.05
629	Steve Davis	.05
630	Joe Delli Carri	.05
631	D.J. Dozier	.05
632	Javier Gonzalez	.05
633	Rudy Hernandez	.05
634	Chris Hill	.05
635	John Johnstone	.05
636	Doug Kline	.05
637	Loy McBride	.05
638	Joel Horlen	.05
639	Tito Navarro	.05
640	Toby Nivens	.05
641	Bryan Rogers	.05
642	David Sommer	.05
643	Greg Talamantez	.05
644	Dave Telgheder	.05
645	Jose Vargas	.05
646	Aguedo Vasquez	.05
647	Paul Williams	.05
648	Alan Zinter	.05
649	Clint Hurdle	.05
650	Jim Eschen	.05

AAA

Impel made its maiden voyage into the minor league market in 1991 with this set of AAA cards issued in poly packs. Unlike its predecessor (see CMC 1990 Pre-Rookie) of 1990, this set featured complete team sets of 25 cards each within the overall issue, with no other company's product mixed in. Cards were numbered consecutively with all cards of a particular team kept together. The cards were issued only in poly packs and not as a complete set. A checklist was available from the company. Impel is the third company to handle this line. It all started with TCMA in 1972; CMC took over in 1988 and Impel bought out CMC in 1990. Due to a scarcity of certain cards in inventory and additional labor costs to dealers, the consumer can be expected to pay a minimum of $3-6 for team sets from this product. Line Drive team sets sold at the stadiums included team checklist cards.

		MT
Complete Set (650):		6.00
Common Player:		.05
Wax Box (36):		10.00
1	Billy Bean	.05
2	Jerry Brooks	.05
3	Mike Christopher	.05
4	Dennis Cook	.05
5	Butch Davis	.05
6	Tom Goodwin	.05
7	Dave Hansen	.05
8	Jeff Hartsock	.05
9	Bert Heffernan	.05
10	Carlos Hernandez	.05
11	Chris Jones	.05
12	Eric Karros	.15
13	Dave Lynch	.05
14	Luis Martinez	.05
15	Jamie McAndrew	.05
16	Jim Neidlinger	.05
17	Jose Offerman	.05
18	Eddie Pye	.05
19	Henry Rodriguez	.05
20	Greg Smith	.05
21	Dave Veres	.05
22	Dave Walsh	.05
23	John Wetteland	.05
24	Kevin Kennedy	.05
25	Von Joshua, Claude Osteen	.05
26	Jeff Banister	.05
27	Cecil Espy	.05
28	Steve Fireovid	.05
29	Carlos Garcia	.05
30	Mark Huismann	.05
31	Scott Little	.05
32	Tom Magrann	.05
33	Roger Mason	.05
34	Tim Meeks	.05
35	Orlando Merced	.05
36	Joey Meyer	.05
37	Keith Miller	.05
38	Blas Minor	.05
39	Armando Moreno	.05
40	Jeff Neely	.05
41	Joe Redfield	.05
42	Rick Reed	.05
43	Jeff Richardson	.05
44	Rosario Rodriguez	.05
45	Jeff Schulz	.05
46	Jim Tracy	.05
47	Greg Tubbs	.05
48	Mike York	.05
49	Terry Collins	.05
50	Jackie Brown	.05
51	Rich Amaral	.05
52	Rick Balabon	.05
53	Dave Brundage	.05
54	Dave Burba	.05
55	Dave Cochrane	.05
56	Alan Cockrell	.05
57	Mike Cook	.05
58	Keith Helton	.05
59	Dennis Hood	.05
60	Chris Howard	.05
61	Chuck Jackson	.05
62	Calvin Jones	.05
63	Pat Lennon	.05
64	Shane Letterio	.05
65	Vance Lovelace	.05
66	Tino Martinez	.40
67	John Mitchell	.05
68	Dennis Powell	.05
69	Alonzo Powell	.05
70	Pat Rice	.05
71	Ricky Rojas	.05
72	Steve Springer	.05
73	Ed VandeBerg	.05
74	Keith Bodie	.05
75	Ross Grimsley	.05
76	Eddie Taubensee	.05
77	Jeff Bittiger	.05
78	Willie Blair	.05
79	Marty Brown	.05
80	Kevin Burdick	.05
81	Steve Cummings	.05
82	Mauro Gozzo	.05
83	Ricky Horton	.05
84	Stan Jefferson	.05
85	Brian Johnson	.05
86	Barry Jones	.05
87	Wayne Kirby	.05
88	Mark Lewis	.05
89	Rudy Seanez	.05
90	Luis Lopez	.05
91	Ecer Magallanes	.05
92	Luis Medina	.05
93	Dave Otto	.05
94	Roberto Zambrano	.05
95	Jeff Shaw	.05
96	Efrain Valdez	.05
97	Sergio Valdez	.05
98	Kevin Wickander	.05
99	Charlie Manuel	.05
100	Rick Adair, Jim Gabella	.05
101	Steve Adkins	.05
102	Daven Bond	.05
103	Darrin Chapin	.05
104	Royal Clayton	.05
105	Steve Howe	.10
106	Keith Hughes	.05
107	Mike Humphreys	.05
108	Jeff Johnson	.05
109	Scott Kamieniecki	.05
110	Pat Kelly	.05
111	Jason Maas	.05
112	Alan Mills	.05
113	Rich Monteleone	.05
114	Hipolito Pena	.05
115	John Ramos	.05
116	Carlos Rodriguez	.05
117	Dave Sax	.05
118	Van Snider	.05
119	Don Sparks	.05
120	Andy Stankiewicz	.05
121	Wade Taylor	.05
122	Jim Walewander	.05
123	Bernie Williams	1.00
124	Rick Down	.05
125	Denbo, Boyer, Meyer	.05
126	D.L. Smith	.05
127	James Austin	.05
128	Esteban Beltre	.05
129	Mickey Brantley	.05
130	George Canale	.05
131	Matias Carrillo	.05
132	Juan Castillo	.05
133	Jim Davins	.05
134	Carlos Diaz	.05
135	Cal Eldred	.05
136	Narciso Elvira	.05
137	Brian Fisher	.05
138	Chris George	.05
139	Sandy Guerrero	.05
140	Doug Henry	.05
141	Darren Holmes	.05
142	Mike Ignasiak	.05
143	Jeff Kaiser	.05
144	Joe Kmak	.05
145	Tim McIntosh	.05
146	Charlie Montoyo	.05
147	Jim Olander	.05
148	Ed Puig	.05
149	Tony Muser	.05
150	Lamar Johnson, Don Rowe	.05
151	Kyle Abbott	.05
152	Ruben Amaro	.05
153	Kent Anderson	.05
154	Mike Erb	.05
155	Randy Bockus	.05
156	Gary Buckels	.05
157	Tim Burcham	.05
158	Chris Cron	.05
159	Chad Curtis	.05
160	Doug Davis	.05
161	Mark Davis	.05
162	Gary DiSarcina	.05
163	Mike Fetters	.05
164	Joe Grahe	.05
165	Dan Grunhard	.05
166	Dave Leiper	.05
167	Rafael Montalvo	.05
168	Reed Peters	.05
169	Bobby Rose	.05
170	Lee Stevens	.05
171	Ron Tingley	.05
172	Ed Vosberg	.05
173	Mark Wasinger	.05
174	Max Oliveras	.05
175	Lenn Sakata, Gary Ruby	.05
176	Bret Barbarie	.05
177	Kevin Bearse	.05
178	Kent Bottenfield	.05
179	Wil Cordero	.05
180	Mike Davis	.05
181	Alex Diaz	.05
182	Eddie Dixon	.05
183	Jeff Fassero	.05
184	Jerry Goff	.05
185	Todd Haney	.05
186	Steve Hecht	.05
187	Jimmy Kremers	.05
188	Quinn Mack	.05
189	David Masters	.05
190	Marlin McPhail	.05
191	Doug Piatt	.05
192	Dana Ridenour	.05
193	Scott Service	.05
194	Razor Shines	.05
195	Tito Stewart	.05
196	Mel Houston	.05
197	John Vander Wal	.05
198	Darrin Winston	.05
199	Jerry Manuel	.05
200	Gomer Hodge, Nardi Contreras	.05
201	Brad Bierley	.05
202	Steve Carter	.05
203	Frank Castillo	.05
204	Lance Dickson	.05
205	Craig Smajstrla	.05
206	Brian Guinn	.05
207	Joe Kraemer	.05
208	Cedric Landrum	.05
209	Derrick May	.05
210	Scott May	.05
211	Ryss McGinnis	.05
212	Chuck Mount	.05
213	Dave Pavlas	.05
214	Laddie Renfroe	.05
215	David Rosario	.05
216	Rey Sanchez	.05
217	Dan Simonds	.05
218	Jeff Small	.05
219	Doug Strange	.05
220	Glenn Sullivan	.05
221	Rick Wilkins	.05
222	Steve Wilson	.05
223	Bob Scanlan	.05
224	Jim Essian	.05
225	Grant Jackson	.05
226	Luis Alicea	.05
227	Rod Brewer	.05
228	Nick Castaneda	.05
229	Stan Clarke	.05
230	Marty Clary	.05
231	Fidel Compres	.05
232	Todd Crosby	.05
233	Bob Davidson	.05
234	Bien Figueroa	.05
235	Ed Fulton	.05
236	Mark Grater	.05
237	Omar Olivares	.05
238	Brian Jordan	.25
239	Lonnie Maclin	.05
240	Julian Martinez	.05
241	Al Nipper	.05
242	Dave Osteen	.05
243	Leny Picota	.05
244	Dave Richardson	.05
245	Mike Ross	.05
246	Stan Royer	.05
247	Tim Sherrill	.05
248	Carl Ray Stephens	.05
249	Mark DeJohn	.05
250	Mark Riggins	.05
251	Billy Bates	.05
252	Freddie Benavides	.05
253	Keith Brown	.05
254	Adam Casillas	.05
255	Tony DeFrancesco	.05
256	Leo Garcia	.05
257	Angel Gonzalez	.05
258	Denny Gonzalez	.05
259	Kip Gross	.05
260	Charlie Mitchell	.05
261	Milton Hill	.05
262	Rodney Imes	.05
263	Reggie Jefferson	.05
264	Keith Lockhart	.05
265	Manny Jose	.05
266	Terry Lee	.05
267	Rob Lopez	.05
268	Gino Minutelli	.05
269	Kevin Pearson	.05
270	Ross Powell	.05
271	Donnie Scott	.05
272	Luis Vasquez	.05
273	Joey Vierra	.05
274	Pete Mackanin	.05
275	Don Gullett, Jim Lett	.05
276	Oscar Azocar	.05
277	Dann Bilardello	.05
278	Ricky Bones	.05
279	Brian Dorsett	.05
280	Scott Coolbaugh	.05
281	John Costello	.05
282	Terry Gilmore	.05
283	Jeremy Hernandez	.05
284	Kevin Higgins	.05
285	Chris Jelic	.05
286	Dean Kelley	.05
287	Derek Lilliquist	.05
288	Jose Melendez	.05
289	Jose Mota	.05
290	Adam Peterson	.05

No.	Player	MT
291	Ed Romero	.05
292	Steven Rosenberg	.05
293	Tim Scott	.05
294	Dave Staton	.05
295	Will Taylor	.05
296	Jim Vatcher	.05
297	Dan Walters	.05
298	Kevin Ward	.05
299	Jim Riggleman	.05
300	Jon Matlack, Tony Torchia	.05
301	Gerald Alexander	.05
302	Kevin Belcher	.05
303	Jeff Andrews	.05
304	Tony Scruggs	.05
305	Jeff Bronkey	.05
306	Paco Burgos	.05
307	Nick Capra	.05
308	Monty Fariss	.05
309	Darrin Garner	.05
310	Bill Haselman	.05
311	Terry Mathews	.05
312	Rob Maurer	.05
313	Gar Millay	.05
314	Dean Palmer	.05
315	Roger Pavlik	.05
316	Dan Peltier	.05
317	Steve Peters	.05
318	Mark Petkovsek	.05
319	Jim Poole	.05
320	Paul Postier	.05
321	Wayne Rosenthal	.05
322	Dan Smith	.05
323	Terry Wells	.05
324	Tommy Thompson	.05
325	Stan Hough	.05
326	Sean Berry	.05
327	Jacob Brumfield	.05
328	Bob Buchanan	.05
329	Kevin Burrell	.05
330	Stu Cole	.05
331	Victor Cole	.05
332	Jeff Conine	.05
333	Tommy Dunbar	.05
334	Luis Encarnacion	.05
335	Greg Everson	.05
336	Bob Hamelin	.05
337	Joel Johnston	.05
338	Frank Laureano	.05
339	Jim LeMasters	.05
340	Mike Magnante	.05
341	Carlos Maldonado	.05
342	Andy McGaffigan	.05
343	Bobby Moore	.05
344	Harvey Pulliam	.05
345	Daryl Smith	.05
346	Tim Spehr	.05
347	Hector Wagner	.05
348	Paul Zuvella	.05
349	Sal Rende	.05
350	Brian Poldberg, Guy Hansen	.05
351	Luis Aguayo	.05
352	Tom Barrett	.05
353	Mike Brumley	.05
354	Scott Cooper	.05
355	Mike Gardiner	.05
356	Eric Hetzel	.05
357	Mike Twardoski	.05
358	Rick Lancellotti	.05
359	Derek Livernois	.05
360	Mark Meleski	.05
361	Kevin Morton	.05
362	Dan O'Neill	.05
363	Jim Pankovits	.05
364	Mickey Pina	.05
365	Phil Plantier	.05
366	Jeff Plympton	.05
367	Todd Pratt	.05
368	Larry Shikles	.05
369	Jeff Stone	.05
370	Mo Vaughn	.40
371	David Walters	.05
372	Eric Wedge	.05
373	Bob Zupcic	.05
374	Butch Hobson	.05
375	Rich Gale	.05
376	Rich Aldrete	.05
377	Mark Bailey	.05
378	Rod Beck	.05
379	Jeff Carter	.05
380	Craig Colbert	.05
381	Darnell Coles	.05
382	Mark Dewey	.05
383	Gil Heredia	.05
384	Darren Lewis	.05
385	Johnny Ard	.05
386	Rafael Novoa	.05
387	Francisco Oliveras	.05
388	Tony Perezchica	.05
389	Mark Thurmond	.05
390	Mike Remlinger	.05
391	Greg Ritchie	.05
392	Rick Rodriguez	.05
393	Andres Santana	.05
394	Jose Segura	.05
395	Stuart Tate	.05
396	Jimmy Williams	.05
397	Jim Wilson	.05
398	Ted Wood	.05
399	Duane Espy	.05
400	Alan Bannister, Larry Hardy	.05
401	Paul Abbott	.05
402	Willie Banks	.05
403	Bernardo Brito	.05
404	Jarvis Brown	.05
405	J.T. Bruett	.05
406	Tim Drummond	.05
407	Tom Edens	.05
408	Rich Garces	.05
409	Chip Hale	.05
410	Terry Jorgensen	.05
411	Kenny Morgan	.05
412	Pedro Munoz	.05
413	Edgar Naveda	.05
414	Denny Naegle	.05
415	Jeff Reboulet	.05
416	Victor Rodriguez	.05
417	Jack Savage	.05
418	Dan Sheaffer	.05
419	Charles Scott	.05
420	Paul Sorrento	.05
421	George Tsamis	.05
422	Lenny Webster	.05
423	Carl Willis	.05
424	Russ Nixon	.05
425	Jim Dwyer, Gordon Heimueller, Paul Kirsch	.05
426	John Alva	.05
427	Mike Bell	.05
428	Tony Castillo	.05
429	Bruce Crabbe	.05
430	John Davis	.05
431	Brian Hunter	.05
432	Randy Kramer	.05
433	Mike Loggins	.05
434	Kelly Mann	.05
435	Tom McCarthy	.05
436	Yorkis Perez	.05
437	Dale Polley	.05
438	Armando Reynoso	.05
439	Rusty Richards	.05
440	Victor Rosario	.05
441	Mark Ross	.05
442	Rico Rossy	.05
443	Randy St. Claire	.05
444	Joe Szekely	.05
445	Andy Tomberlin	.05
446	Matt Turner	.05
447	Glenn Wilson	.05
448	Tracy Woodson	.05
449	Phil Niekro	.50
450	Bruce Del Canton, Sonny Jackson	.05
451	Tony Chance	.05
452	Joaquin Contreras	.05
453	Francisco DeLaRosa	.05
454	Benny Distefano	.05
455	Mike Eberle	.05
456	Todd Frohwirth	.05
457	Steve Jeltz	.05
458	Chito Martinez	.05
459	Dave Martinez	.05
460	Jeff McKnight	.05
461	Luis Mercedes	.05
462	Mike Mussina	2.00
463	Chris Myers	.05
464	Joe Price	.05
465	Israel Sanchez	.05
466	David Segui	.05
467	Tommy Shields	.05
468	Mike Linskey	.05
469	Jeff Tackett	.05
470	Anthony Telford	.05
471	Shane Turner	.05
472	Jeff Wetherby	.05
473	Rob Woodward	.05
474	Greg Biagini	.05
475	Mike Young, Dick Bosman	.05
476	Sal Agostinelli	.05
477	Gary Alexander	.05
478	Andy Ashby	.05
479	Bob Ayrault	.05
480	Kim Batiste	.05
481	Amalio Carreno	.05
482	Rocky Elli	.05
483	Darrin Fletcher	.05
484	Jeff Grotewold	.05
485	Chris Knabenshue	.05
486	Greg Legg	.05
487	Jim Lindeman	.05
488	Chuck Malone	.05
489	Tim Mauser	.05
490	Louie Meadows	.05
491	Mickey Morandini	.05
492	Julio Peguero	.05
493	Wally Ritchie	.05
494	Bruce Ruffin	.05
495	Rick Schu	.05
496	Ray Searage	.05
497	Scott Wade	.05
498	Gary Wilson	.05
499	Bill Dancy	.05
500	Floyd Rayford, Jim Wright	.05
501	Derek Bell	.05
502	Rob Ducey	.05
503	Julius McDougal	.05
504	Juan Guzman	.05
505	Pat Hentgen	.05
506	Shawn Jeter	.05
507	Doug Linton	.05
508	Bob MacDonald	.05
509	Mike Maksudian	.05
510	Ravelo Manzanillo	.05
511	Domingo Martinez	.05
512	Stu Pederson	.05
513	Marty Pevey	.05
514	Tom Quinlan	.05
515	Alex Sanchez	.05
516	Jerry Schunk	.05
517	John Shea	.05
518	Ed Sprague	.05
519	William Suero	.05
520	Steve Wapnick	.05
521	Mickey Weston	.05
522	John Poloni	.05
523	Eddie Zosky	.05
524	Bob Bailor	.05
525	Rocket Wheeler	.05
526	Troy Afenir	.05
527	Mike Bordick	.05
528	Jorge Brito	.05
529	Scott Brosius	.05
530	Kevin Campbell	.05
531	Pete Coachman	.05
532	Dan Eskew	.05
533	Eric Fox	.05
534	Apolinar Garcia	.05
535	Webster Garrison	.05
536	Johnny Guzman	.05
537	Jeff Pico	.05
538	Dann Howitt	.05
539	Doug Jennings	.05
540	Brad Komminsk	.05
541	Tim McCoy	.05
542	Jeff Musselman	.05
543	Troy Neel	.05
544	Will Schock	.05
545	Nelson Simmons	.05
546	Bruce Walton	.05
547	Pat Wernig	.05
548	Ron Witmeyer	.05
549	Jeff Newman	.05
550	Glenn Abbott	.05
551	Kevin Baez	.05
552	Blaine Beatty	.05
553	Doug Cinnella	.05
554	Chris Donnels	.05
555	Jeff Gardner	.05
556	Terrel Hansen	.05
557	Manny Hernandez	.05
558	Eric Hillman	.05
559	Todd Hundley	.05
560	Alex Jimenez	.05
561	Tim Leiper	.05
562	Lee May	.05
563	Orlando Mercado	.05
564	Brad Moore	.05
565	Al Pedrique	.05
566	Dale Plummer	.05
567	Rich Saveur	.05
568	Ray Soff	.05
569	Kelvin Torve	.05
570	Dave Trautwein	.05
571	Julio Valera	.05
572	Robbie Wine	.05
573	Anthony Young	.05
574	Steve Swisher	.05
575	Ron Washington, Bob Apodaca	.05
576	Scott Aldred	.05
577	Karl Allaire	.05
578	Skeeter Barnes	.05
579	Arnie Beyeler	.05
580	Rico Brogna	.05
581	Phil Clark	.05
582	Mike Dalton	.05
583	Curt Ford	.05
584	Dan Gakeler	.05
585	David Haas	.05
586	Shawn Hare	.05
587	John Kiely	.05
588	Mark Leiter	.05
589	Scott Livingstone	.05
590	Mitch Lyden	.05
591	Eric Mangham	.05
592	Rusty Meacham	.05
593	Mike Munoz	.05
594	Randy Nosek	.05
595	Johnny Paredes	.05
596	Kevin Ritz	.05
597	Rich Rowland	.05
598	Don Vesling	.05
599	Joe Sparks	.05
600	Mark Wagner, Ralph Treuel	.05
601	Harold Allen	.05
602	Eric Anthony	.05
603	Doug Baker	.05
604	Ryan Bowen	.05
605	Mike Capel	.05
606	Andujar Cedeno	.05
607	Terry Clark	.05
608	Carlo Colombino	.05
609	Gary Cooper	.05
610	Calvin Schiraldi	.05
611	Randy Hennis	.05
612	Butch Henry	.05
613	Blaise Isley	.05
614	Kenny Lofton	.25
615	Terry McGriff	.05
616	Andy Mota	.05
617	Javier Ortiz	.05
618	Scott Servais	.05
619	Mike Simms	.05
620	Jose Tolentino	.05
621	Lee Tunnell	.05
622	Brent Strom	.05
623	Gerald Young	.05
624	Bob Skinner	.05
625	Dave Engle	.05
626	Cesar Bernhardt	.05
627	Mario Brito	.05
628	Kurt Brown	.05
629	John Cangelosi	.05
630	Jeff Carter	.05
631	Tom Drees	.05
632	Grady Hall	.05
633	Joe Hall	.05
634	Curt Hasler	.05
635	Danny Heep	.05
636	Dan Henley	.05
637	Roberto Hernandez	.05
638	Orsino Hill	.05
639	Jerry Kutzler	.05
640	Noberto Martin	.05
641	Rod McCray	.05
642	Bob Nelson	.05
643	Warren Newsom	.05
644	Greg Perschke	.05
645	Rich Scheid	.05
646	Matt Stark	.05
647	Ron Stephens	.05
648	Don Wakamatsu	.05
649	Marv Foley	.05
650	Roger LaFrancois, Moe Drabowsky	.05

1991 ProCards Tomorrow's Heroes

This Procards issue is comprised of an assortment of AAA, AA and A classification players representing all 26 contemporary Major League organizations. Cards are numbered beginning with Baltimore of the American League and concluding with San Francisco of the National League. Each of the Major League segments then has representation of the best players within their minor league organization; example: BALTIMORE ORIOLES AAA - Mussina, Mercedes, Frowirth, Martinez, Sequi AA - Rhodes, Jones A - Moore, Alexander, Williams, Anderson, Lemp, Krivda. "Tomorrow's Heroes" is a great title since there are dozens of prospects in the set; many of whom would soon be mainstays on big league rosters. Cards were only available in foil packs. Cards are bordered in white with a prominent pink and gray checkered interior pattern. Card manufacturer, player's name, position, and team are lettered in white and bordered in red. Original plans reportedly called for production of 10,000 cases, but those plans were changed dramatically to a limited production run of 1,007 cases upon the acquisition of ProCards by Fleer; thereby resulting in this product becoming a scarce commodity.

No.	Player	MT
	Complete Set (360):	15.00
	Common Player:	.05
	Wax Pack (12):	.75
	Wax Box (36):	15.00
1	Mike Mussina	2.00
2	Luis Mercedes	.05
3	Todd Frohwirth	.05
4	Chito Martinez	.05
5	David Segui	.05
6	Arthur Rhodes	.05
7	Stacy Jones	.05
8	Daryl Moore	.05
9	Manny Alexander	.05
10	Jeff Williams	.05
11	Matt Anderson	.05
12	Chris Lemp	.05
13	Rick Krivda	.05
14	Phil Plantier	.05
15	Mo Vaughn	.40
16	Scott Cooper	.05
17	Mike Gardiner	.05
18	Kevin Morton	.05
19	Jeff Plympton	.05
20	Jeff McNeely	.05
21	Willie Tatum	.05
22	Tim Smith	.05
23	Frank Rodriguez	.05
24	Chris Davis	.05
25	Cory Bailey	.05
26	Rob Henkel	.05
27	Kyle Abbott	.05
28	Lee Stevens	.05
29	Chad Curtis	.05
30	Ruben Amaro	.05
31	Mark Howie	.05
32	Tim Salmon	.75
33	Kevin Flora	.05
34	Garret Anderson	.15
35	Darryl Scott	.05
36	Don Vidmar	.05
37	Korey Keling	.05
38	Troy Percival	.05
39	Eduardo Perez	.05
40	Julian Heredia	.05
41	Wilson Alvarez	.05
42	Ramon Garcia	.05
43	Johnny Ruffin	.05
44	Scott Cepicky	.05
45	Rod Bolton	.05
46	Rogelio Nunez	.05
47	Brandon Wilson	.05
48	Marc Kubicki	.05
49	Mark Lewis	.05
50	Jim Thome	2.50
51	Tim Costo	.05
52	Jeff Mutis	.05
53	Tracy Sanders	.05
54	Mike Soper	.05
55	Miguel Flores	.05
56	Brian Giles	.25
57	Curtis Leskanic	.05
58	Kyle Washington	.05
59	Jason Hardtke	.05
60	Albie Lopez	.05
61	Oscar Resendez	.05
62	Manny Ramirez	3.00
63	Rico Brogna	.05
64	Scott Livingstone	.05
65	Greg Gohr	.05
66	Scott Aldred	.05
67	Brian Warren	.05
68	Bob Undorf	.05
69	Rob Grable	.05
70	Tom Mezzanotte	.05
71	Justin Thompson	.05
72	Trever Miller	.05
73	Joel Johnston	.05
74	Kevin Koslofski	.05
75	Archie Corbin	.05
76	Phil Hiatt	.05
77	Danny Miceli	.05
78	Joe Randa	.05
79	Mark Johnson	.05
80	Joe Vitiello	.05
81	Cal Eldred	.05
82	Doug Henry	.05
83	Dave Nilsson	.05
84	John Jaha	.05
85	Shon Ashley	.05
86	Jim Tatum	.05
87	Bo Dodson	.05
88	Otis Green	.05
89	Denny Neagle	.05
90	Checklist 1-90	.05
91	Pedro Munoz	.05
92	Jarvis Brown	.05
93	Pat Mahomes	.05
94	Cheo Garcia	.05
95	David McCarty	.05
96	Chris Delarwelle	.05
97	Scott Stahoviak	.05
98	Midre Cummings	.05
99	Todd Ritchie	.05
100	Dave Sartain	.05
101	Pedro Grifol	.05
102	Eddie Guardado	.05
103	Bob Carlson	.05
104	Sandy Diaz	.05
105	John Ramos	.05
106	Bernie Williams	1.00
107	Wade Taylor	.05
108	Pat Kelly	.05
109	Jeff Johnson	.05
110	Scott Kamieniecki	.05
111	Dave Silvestri	.05
112	Ed Maritel	.05
113	Willie Smith	.05
114	J.T. Snow	.10
115	Gerald Williams	.05
116	Larry Stanford	.05
117	Bruce Prybylinski	.05
118	Rey Noriega	.05
119	Rich Batchelor	.05
120	Brad Ausmus	.05
121	Robert Eenhoorn	.05
122	Sam Militello	.05
123	Jason Robertson	.05
124	Carl Everett	.25
125	Kiki Hernandez	.05
126	Rafael Quirico	.05
127	Lyle Mouton	.05
128	Tim Flannelly	.05
129	Todd Van Poppel	.05
130	Tim Peek	.05
131	Henry Mercedes	.05
132	Todd Smith	.05
133	Brent Gates	.05
134	Gary Hust	.05
135	Mike Neill	.05
136	Russ Brock	.05
137	Ricky Kimball	.05
138	Tino Martinez	.40
139	Calvin Jones	.05
140	Roger Salkeld	.05
141	Dave Fleming	.05
142	Bret Boone	1.00
143	Jim Campanis	.05
144	Marc Newfield	.05
145	Mike Hampton	.05
146	Shawn Estes	.05
147	David Lisiecki	.05
148	Dean Palmer	.05
149	Rob Maurer	.05
150	Jim Poole	.05
151	Terry Mathews	.05
152	Monty Fariss	.05
153	Ivan Rodriguez	2.50
154	Barry Manuel	.05
155	Donald Harris	.05
156	Rusty Greer	.05
157	Matt Whiteside	.05
158	Derek Bell	.05
159	Eddie Zosky	.05
160	Domingo Martinez	.05
161	Juan Guzman	.05
162	Ed Sprague	.05
163	Rob Ducey	.05
164	Vince Horsman	.05
165	Darren Hall	.05
166	Rick Trlicek	.05
167	Dave Weathers	.05
168	Robert Perez	.05
169	Nigel Wilson	.05
170	Carlos Delgado	2.50
171	Steve Karsay	.05
172	Howard Battle	.05
173	Huck Fiener	.05
174	Robert Butler	.05
175	Giovanni Carrara	.05
176	Michael Taylor	.05
177	Brian Hunter	.05
178	Turk Wendell	.05
179	Mark Wohlers	.05
180	Checklist 91-180	.05
181	Ryan Klesko	.10
182	Keith Mitchell	.05
183	Vinny Castilla	.10
184	Napoleon Robinson	.05
185	Mike Kelly	.05
186	Javy Lopez	.10
187	Ramon Caraballo	.05
188	David Nied	.05
189	Don Strange	.05
190	Chipper Jones	3.00
191	Troy Hughes	.05
192	Don Robinson	.05
193	Lance Marks	.05
194	Manuel Jimenez	.05
195	Tony Graffagnino (Graffanino)	.05
196	Brad Woodall	.05
197	Kevin Grijak	.05
198	Darin Paulino	.05
199	Lance Dickson	.05
200	Rey Sanchez	.05
201	Elvin Paulino	.05
202	Alex Arias	.05
203	Fernando Ramsey	.05
204	Pete Castellano	.05
205	Ryan Hawblitzel	.05
206	John Jensen	.05
207	Jerrone Williams	.05
208	Earl Cunningham	.05
209	Phil Dauphin	.05
210	Doug Glanville	.05
211	Jim Robinson	.05
212	Ken Arnold	.05
213	Reggie Jefferson	.05
214	Reggie Sanders	.05
215	Mo Sanford	.05
216	Steve Foster	.05
217	Dan Wilson	.05
218	John Roper	.05
219	Trevor Hoffman	.10
220	Calvin Reese	.10
221	John Hrusovsky	.05
222	Andy Mota	.05
223	Kenny Lofton	.25
224	Andujar Cedeno	.05
225	Ryan Bowen	.05
226	Jeff Juden	.05
227	Chris Gardner	.05
228	Brian Williams	.05
229	Ed Ponte	.05
230	Chris Hatcher	.05
231	Fletcher Thompson	.05
232	Wally Trice	.05
233	Donne Wall	.05
234	Tom Nevers	.05
235	Jim Daugherty	.05
236	Mark Loughlin	.05
237	Jose Offerman	.05
238	Dave Hansen	.05
239	Carlos Hernandez	.05
240	Eric Karros	.10
241	Henry Rodriguez	.05
242	Jamie McAndrew	.05
243	Tom Goodwin	.05
244	Pedro Martinez	3.00
245	Braulio Castillo	.05
246	Matt Howard	.05
247	Michael Mimbs	.05
248	Murph Proctor	.05
249	Vernon Spearman	.05
250	Jason Kerr	.05
251	Mike Sharp	.05
252	Pedro Osuna	.05
253	Doug Piatt	.05
254	Wil Cordero	.05
255	John VanderWal	.05
256	Bret Barberie	.05
257	Todd Haney	.05
258	Chris Haney	.05
259	Matt Stairs	.05
260	David Wainhouse	.05
261	Bob Natal	.05
262	Rob Katzaroff	.05
263	Willie Greene	.05
264	Reid Cornelius	.05
265	Glenn Murray	.05
266	Rondell White	.05
267	Tavo Alvarez	.05
268	Gabe White	.05
269	Brian Looney	.05
270	Checklist 181-270	.05
271	Derrick White	.05
272	Heath Haynes	.05
273	Mike Daniel	.05
274	Jim Austin	.05
275	Chris Donnels	.05
276	Julio Valera	.05
277	Todd Hundley	.05
278	Anthony Young	.05
279	Jeff Gardner	.05
280	Jeromy Burnitz	.10

281 Tito Navarro .05
282 D.J. Dozier .05
283 Julian Vasquez .05
284 Pat Howell .05
285 Brook Fordyce .05
286 Todd Douma .05
287 Jose Martinez .05
288 Ricky Otero .05
289 Quilvio Veras .05
290 Joe Crawford .05
291 Todd Fiegel .05
292 Jason Jacome .05
293 Kim Batiste .05
294 Andy Ashby .05
295 Wes Chamberlain .05
296 Dave Hollins .05
297 Tony Longmire .05
298 Nikco Riesgo .05
299 Cliff Brantley .05
300 Troy Paulsen .05
301 Elliott Gray .05
302 Mike Lieberthal .05
303 Tyler Green .05
304 Dan Brown .05
305 Carlos Garcia .05
306 John Wehner .05
307 Paul Miller .05
308 Tim Wakefield .05
309 Kurt Miller .05
310 Joe Sondrini .05
311 Hector Fajardo .05
312 Scott Bullett .05
313 Jon Farrell .05
314 Marc Pisciotta .05
315 Rheal Cormier .05
316 Omar Olivares .05
317 Donovan Osborne .05
318 Clyde Keller .05
319 John Kelly .05
320 Terry Bradshaw .05
321 Brian Eversgerd .05
322 Dmitri Young .05
323 Eddie Williams .05
324 Brian Barber .05
325 Andy Bruce .05
326 Tom McKinnon .05
327 Jamie Cochran .05
328 Steve Jones .05
329 Jerry Santos .05
330 Allen Watson .05
331 John Mabry .05
332 Jose Melendez .05
333 Dave Staton .05
334 Frank Seminara .05
335 Matt Mieske .05
336 Jay Gaines .05
337 J.D. Noland .05
338 Roberto Arredondo .05
339 Lance Painter .05
340 Darren Lewis .05
341 Ted Wood .05
342 Johnny Ard .05
343 Royce Clayton .05
344 Paul McClellan .05
345 John Patterson .05
346 Steve Hosey .05
347 Larry Carter .05
348 Juan Guerrero .05
349 Bryan Hickerson .05
350 Rich Huisman .05
351 Kevin McGehee .05
352 Gary Sharko .05
353 Salomon Torres .05
354 Eric Christopherson .05
355 Rod Huffman .05
356 Bill VanLandingham .05
357 Frank Charles .05
358 Ken Grundt .05
359 Matt Brewer .05
360 Checklist 271-360 .05

1991 Minor League Team Sets

The number of independently (team, or card dealer) sponsored team sets continued to decline in 1991, leaving Pro-Cards to slug it out with Classic Best, the new kid on the block created when Best sold out to Classic Games.

MT

285 Team Sets and Variations
1991 PC AAA All-Stars (55) 6.00
1991 Kraft Albany Yankees (6) 20.00
1991 PC Albany Yankees (28) 5.00
1991 PC Albuquerque Dukes (27) 7.00
1991 Team Albuquerque Dukes Photos (41) 125.00
1991 Team Anchorage Bucs (36) 16.00
1991 CB Appleton Foxes (30) 4.00
1991 PC Appleton Foxes (28) 3.00
1991 PC Arkansas Travelers (29) 3.00
1991 CB Asheville Tourists (30) 4.00
1991 PC Asheville Tourists (29) 3.00
1991 CB Auburn Astros (30) 4.00
1991 PC Auburn Astros (26) 3.00
1991 CB Augusta Pirates (30) 4.00
1991 PC Augusta Pirates (31) 3.00
1991 Cal Bakersfield Dodgers (32) 17.50
1991 CB Baseball City Royals (30) 4.00
1991 PC Baseball City Royals (29) 3.00
1991 CB Batavia Clippers (30) 4.00
1991 PC Batavia Clippers (30) 3.00
1991 CB Bellingham Mariners (30) 4.00
1991 PC Bellingham Mariners (32) 3.00
1991 CB Beloit Brewers (30) 3.00
1991 PC Beloit Brewers (28) 3.00
1991 CB Bend Bucks (29) 4.00
1991 PC Bend Bucks (29) 3.00
1991 PC Billings Mustangs (28) 3.00
1991 SP Billings Mustangs (30) 5.00
1991 PC Birmingham Barons (28) 4.00
1991 CB Bluefield Orioles (30) 4.00
1991 PC Bluefield Orioles (26) 3.00
1991 CB Boise Hawks (30) 4.00
1991 PC Boise Hawks (35) 3.00
1991 CB Bristol Tigers (30) 4.00
1991 PC Bristol Tigers (30) 3.00
1991 PC Buffalo Bisons (26) 3.00
1991 Team Buffalo Bisons (27) 12.00
1991 CB Burlington Astros (30) 4.00
1991 PC Burlington Astros (28) 3.00
1991 PC Burlington Indians (34) 40.00
1991 SP Butte Copper Kings (30) 5.00
1991 SP Butte Copper Kings Update (2) 2.00
1991 PC Calgary Cannons (25) 4.00
1991 Cal League All-Stars (56) 20.00
1991 PC Canton-Akron Indians (28) 7.00
1991 PC Carolina League A-S (47) 8.00
1991 PC Carolina Mudcats (26) 3.00
1991 CB Cedar Rapids Reds (30) 5.00
1991 PC Cedar Rapids Reds (30) 6.00
1991 CB Charleston Rainbows (30) 4.00
1991 PC Charleston Rainbows (27) 3.00
1991 CB Charleston Wheelers (30) 4.00
1991 PC Charleston Wheelers (27) 3.00
1991 PC Charlotte Knights (26) 3.00
1991 CB Charlotte Rangers (30) 3.00
1991 PC Charlotte Rangers (28) 4.00
1991 PC Chattanooga Lookouts (27) 4.00
1991 CB Clearwater Phillies (30) 4.00
1991 PC Clearwater Phillies (29) 3.00
1991 CB Clinton Giants (30) 4.00
1991 PC Clinton Giants (29) 3.00
1991 PC Colorado Springs Sky Sox (28) 4.00
1991 Play II Columbia Mets (32) 7.00
1991 Play II Columbia Mets Postcards (28) 15.00
1991 PC Columbus Clippers (29) 6.00
1991 Police Columbus Clippers (24) 6.50
1991 CB Columbus Indians (30) 4.00
1991 PC Columbus Indians (32) 3.00
1991 PC Denver Zephyrs (27) 3.00
1991 CB Dunedin Blue Jays (30) 4.00
1991 PC Dunedin Blue Jays (29) 3.00
1991 CB Durham Bulls (30) 6.00
1991 PC Durham Bulls (33) 10.00
1991 PC Durham Bulls Update (9) 6.00
1991 PC Edmonton Trappers (28) 4.00
1991 PC Elizabethton Twins (26) 3.00
1991 CB Elmira Pioneers (30) 4.00
1991 PC Elmira Pioneers (29) 3.00
1991 PC El Paso Diablos (26) 5.00
1991 Team El Paso Diablos All-Time (45) 35.00
1991 CB Erie Sailors (30) 4.00
1991 PC Erie Sailors (30) 3.00
1991 CB Eugene Emeralds (30) 4.00
1991 PC Eugene Emeralds (30) 3.00
1991 CB Everett Giants (30) 3.00
1991 PC Everett Giants (33) 3.00
1991 CB Fayetteville Generals (30) 3.00
1991 PC Fayetteville Generals (29) 3.00
1991 PC Florida State League A-S (46) 12.00
1991 CB Frederick Keys (30) 4.00
1991 PC Frederick Keys (29) 4.00
1991 CB Ft. Lauderdale Yankees (30) 4.00
1991 PC Ft. Lauderdale Yankees (31) 3.00
1991 CB Gastonia Rangers (30) 6.00
1991 PC Gastonia Rangers (31) 6.00
1991 CB Geneva Cubs (30) 5.00
1991 PC Geneva Cubs (30) 5.00
1991 SP Great Falls Dodgers (30) 7.00
1991 PC Greensboro Hornets (29) 7.50
1991 CB Greenville Braves (30) 8.00
1991 PC Greenville Braves (27) 4.00
1991 SP Gulf Coast Rangers (30) 4.00
1991 PC Hagerstown Suns (28) 5.00
1991 CB Hamilton Redbirds (30) 5.00
1991 PC Hamilton Redbirds (33) 4.00
1991 PC Harrisburg Senators (29) 5.00
1991 SP Helena Brewers (30) 12.00
1991 CB High Desert Mavericks (30) 4.00
1991 PC High Desert Mavericks (32) 3.00
1991 Little Sun High School Prospects (36) 10.00
1991 LS High School Prospects - Gold (36) 17.50
1991 CB Huntington Cubs (30) 4.00
1991 PC Huntington Cubs (32) 4.00
1991 BK Huntsville Stars (26) 5.00
1991 CB Huntsville Stars (30) 4.00
1991 PC Huntsville Stars (26) 3.00
1991 PC Idaho Falls Braves (29) 3.00
1991 SP Idaho Falls Braves (30) 4.00
1991 PC Indianapolis Indians (28) 6.00
1991 PC Iowa Cubs (26) 4.00
1991 PC Jackson Generals (28) 5.00
1991 PC Jacksonville Suns (29) 8.00
1991 CB Jamestown Expos (30) 5.00
1991 PC Jamestown Expos (29) 6.00
1991 CB Johnson City Cardinals (30) 4.00
1991 PC Johnson City Cardinals (29) 3.00
1991 CB Kane County Cougars (30) 4.00
1991 PC Kane County Cougars (28) 4.00
1991 Team Kane County Cougars (27) 5.00
1991 CB Kenosha Twins (30) 5.00
1991 PC Kenosha Twins (28) 4.00
1991 CB Kingsport Mets (30) 4.00
1991 PC Kingsport Mets (28) 3.00
1991 CB Kinston Indians (31) 9.00
1991 PC Kinston Indians (31) 6.00
1991 PC Kissimmee Dodgers (32) 5.00
1991 PC Knoxville Blue Jays (28) 9.00
1991 CB Lakeland Tigers (30) 3.00
1991 PC Lakeland Tigers (29) 4.00
1991 PC Las Vegas Stars (31) 3.00
1991 PC London Tigers (26) 3.00
1991 PC Louisville Redbirds (29) 6.00
1991 Team Louisville Redbirds (34) 9.00
1991 CB Lynchburg Red Sox (30) 4.00
1991 PC Lynchburg Red Sox (28) 3.00
1991 CB Macon Braves (30) 15.00
1991 PC Macon Braves (31) 24.00
1991 CB Madison Muskies (30) 4.00
1991 PC Madison Muskies (27) 3.00
1991 CB Martinsville Phillies (30) 4.00
1991 PC Martinsville Phillies (31) 3.00
1991 PC Medicine Hat Blue Jays (31) 3.00
1991 SP Medicine Hat Blue Jays (30) 6.00
1991 PC Memphis Chicks (27) 3.00
1991 CB Miami Miracle (30) 4.00
1991 PC Miami Miracle (30) 3.00
1991 GS Midland Angels (1) 3.00
1991 1 Hour Midland Angels (32) 50.00
1991 PC Midland Angels (27) 7.00
1991 PC Midwest League A-S (51) 5.00
1991 CB Modesto A's (28) 4.00
1991 Chong Modesto A's (35) 3.00
1991 PC Modesto A's (30) 3.00
1991 CB Myrtle Beach Hurricanes (30) 7.50
1991 PC Myrtle Beach Hurricanes (30) 6.00
1991 PC Nashville Sounds (27) 6.00
1991 Team Nashville Sounds (34) 6.00
1991 PC New Britain Red Sox (26) 6.00
1991 CB Niagara Falls Rapids (30) 5.00
1991 PC Niagara Falls Rapids (30) 6.00
1991 PC Oklahoma City 89ers (27) 4.00
1991 PC Omaha Royals (26) 5.00
1991 PC Oneonta Yankees (27) 3.00
1991 PC Orlando Sun Rays (28) 3.00
1991 CB Osceola Astros (30) 5.00
1991 PC Osceola Astros (29) 4.00
1991 PC Palm Springs Angels (30) 5.00
1991 DD Pawtucket Red Sox Foldout 50.00
1991 PC Pawtucket Red Sox (27) 5.00
1991 Team Peninsula Oilers (30) 6.00
1991 CB Peninsula Pilots (29) 4.00
1991 PC Peninsula Pilots (28) 3.00
1991 CB Peoria Chiefs (30) 4.00
1991 PC Peoria Chiefs (29) 3.00
1991 Team Peoria Chiefs (34) 6.00
1991 PC Phoenix Firebirds (29) 4.50
1991 CB Pittsfield Mets (29) 3.00
1991 PC Pittsfield Mets (28) 3.00
1991 PC Pocatello Pioneers (31) 3.00
1991 SP Pocatello Pioneers (30) 5.00
1991 PC Portland Beavers (28) 4.00
1991 CB Princeton Reds (30) 3.00
1991 PC Princeton Reds (30) 3.00
1991 CB Prince Williams Cannons (30) 4.00
1991 PC Prince Williams Cannons (29) 3.00
1991 CB Pulaski Braves (30) 3.00
1991 PC Pulaski Braves (31) 3.00
1991 CB Quad City Angels (30) 5.00
1991 PC Quad City Angels (31) 4.00
1991 PC Reading Phillies (27) 3.00
1991 Penn-Lyn Studio Reading Phillies (24) 75.00
1991 Cal Reno Silver Sox (29) 3.00
1991 Bob's Richmond Braves (42) 115.00
1991 PC Richmond Braves (30) 4.00
1991 Ukrop's Richmond Braves (28) 20.00
1991 PC Rochester Red Wings (27) 6.00
1991 Team Rochester Red Wings Foldout 50.00
1991 CB Rockford Expos (30) 4.00
1991 PC Rockford Expos (29) 3.00
1991 CB Salem Buccaneers (27) 4.00
1991 PC Salem Buccaneers (27) 3.00
1991 CB Salinas Spurs (30) 4.00
1991 PC Salinas Spurs (31) 3.00
1991 PC Salt Lake City Trappers (30) 3.00
1991 SP Salt Lake City Trappers (30) 5.00
1991 HEB San Antonio Missions (32) 65.00
1991 PC San Antonio Missions (30) 15.00
1991 Team San Antonio Missions (12) 12.00
1991 CB San Bernardino Spirit (29) 4.00
1991 PC San Bernardino Spirit (30) 3.00
1991 CB San Jose Giants (30) 4.00
1991 PC San Jose Giants (30) 4.00
1991 CB Sarasota White Sox (30) 5.00
1991 PC Sarasota White Sox (30) 6.00
1991 CB Savannah Cardinals (30) 4.00
1991 PC Savannah Cardinals (29) 3.00
1991 PC Scranton Red Barons (29) 5.00
1991 PC Shreveport Captains (28) 4.00
1991 PC South Atlantic League A-S (48) 12.50
1991 CB South Bend White Sox (30) 5.00
1991 PC South Bend White Sox (30) 3.00
1991 CB Southern Oregon A's (30) 4.00
1991 PC Southern Oregon A's (37) 3.00
1991 PC Southern Oregon's A's Alumni (36) 7.00
1991 CB Spartanburg Phillies (30) 4.00
1991 PC Spartanburg Phillies (30) 3.00
1991 CB Spokane Indians (30) 4.00
1991 PC Spokane Indians (31) 3.00
1991 CB Springfield Cardinals (30) 3.00
1991 PC Springfield Cardinals (31) 3.00
1991 CB St. Catherines Blue Jays (30) 6.00
1991 PC St. Catherines Blue Jays (28) 4.00
1991 CB St. Lucie Mets (30) 4.00
1991 PC St. Lucie Mets (28) 3.00
1991 CB St. Petersburg Cardinals (30) 4.00
1991 PC St. Petersburg Cardinals (30) 3.00
1991 CB Stockton Ports (30) 4.00
1991 PC Stockton Ports (27) 3.00
1991 CB Sumter Flyers (30) 9.00
1991 PC Sumter Flyers (31) 8.00
1991 Kraft Syracuse Chiefs (5) 15.00
1991 MB Syracuse Chiefs Foldout 20.00
1991 PC Syracuse Chiefs (25) 5.00
1991 PC Tacoma Tigers (29) 5.00
1991 Team Tampa Yankees (33) 5.00
1991 PC Tidewater Tides (30) 3.00
1991 PC Toledo Mudhens (28) 3.00
1991 PC Tucson Toros (28) 4.00
1991 PC Tulsa Drillers (27) 10.00
1991 Team Tulsa Drillers (30) 15.00
1991 CB Utica Blue Sox (30) 4.00
1991 PC Utica Blue Sox (29) 3.00
1991 PC Vancouver Canadians (27) 6.00
1991 CB Vero Beach Dodgers (30) 5.00
1991 PC Vero Beach Dodgers (33) 4.00
1991 CB Visalia Oaks (28) 4.00
1991 PC Visalia Oaks (25) 3.00
1991 CB Waterloo Diamonds (30) 4.00
1991 PC Waterloo Diamonds (29) 3.00
1991 CB Watertown Indians (30) 4.00
1991 PC Watertown Indians (31) 3.00
1991 CB Welland Pirates (30) 3.00
1991 PC Welland Pirates (31) 3.00
1991 CB West Palm Beach Expos (30) 4.00
1991 PC West Palm Beach Expos (30) 3.00
1991 PC Wichita Wranglers (28) 3.00
1991 Rock's Wichita Wranglers - Hor. (27) 6.00
1991 Rock's Wichita Wranglers - Vert. (29) 6.00
1991 PC Williamsport Bills (27) 5.00
1991 CB Winston-Salem Spirits (30) 5.00
1991 PC Winston-Salem Spirits (28) 6.00
1991 CB Winter Haven Red Sox (30) 4.00
1991 PC Winter Haven Red Sox (27) 3.00
1991 CB Yakima Bears (30) 4.00
1991 PC Yakima Bears (30) 3.00

1992 Classic Best

This 400-card wax-pack set has an All-American look, with a red, white and blue card design. A banner beneath the photo has the player's name, team and position. On back the player's name is stretched horizontally near the top, and there is a portrait photo. A factory set was issued which includes 50 cards not found in wax packs. The same 50 cards were available as a boxed Update set. Autographed cards of five stars and prospects were included as random wax pack inserts, while the Clayton autograph card was found exclusively in jumbo packs.

MT

Complete Factory Set (450): 7.50
Complete Set (400): 6.00
Factory Update Set (50): 3.00
Common Player: .05
Wax Pack (12): .50
Jumbo Pack (23): .65
Wax Box (36): 12.00
1 Nolan Ryan 2.00
2 Darius Gash .05
3 Brad Ausmus .05
4 Mike Gardella .05
5 Mark Hutton .05
6 Bobby Munoz .05
7 Don Sparks .05
8 Shane Andrews .05
9 Gary Hymel .05
10 Roberto Arredondo .05
11 Joe Randa .05
12 Pedro Grifol .05
13 Steve Dixon .05
14 John Thomas .05
15 Chris Durkin .05
16 Jeff Conger .05
17 Jon Farrell .05
18 Antonio Mitchell .05
19 Matt Ruebel .05
20 Darren Burton .05
21 Lance Jennings .05
22 Kerwin Moore .05
23 Julio Bruno .05
24 Joe Vitiello .05
25 Brook Fordyce .05
26 Rob Katzaroff .05
27 Julian Vasquez .05
28 Alan Zinter .05
29 Clemente Alvarez .05
30 Scott Cepicky .05
31 Mike Mongiello .05
32 Tom Redington .05
33 Johnny Ruffin .05
34 Eric Booker .05
35 Manny Martinez .05
36 Mike Grimes .05
37 Paul Byrd .05

38	Brian Giles	.25
39	David Mlicki	.05
40	Tracy Sanders	.05
41	Kyle Washington	.05
42	Scott Bullett	.05
43	Steve Cooke	.05
44	Austin Manahan	.05
45	Ben Shelton	.05
46	Joe DeBerry	.05
47	Steve Gibralter	.05
48	Willie Greene	.05
49	Brian Koelling	.05
50	Larry Luebbers	.05
51	Greg "Pepper" Anthony	.05
52	Homer Bush	.05
53	Manny Cora	.05
54	Joey Hamilton	.05
55	David Mowry	.05
56	Bobby Perna	.05
57	Jamie Dismuke	.05
58	Kenneth Gillum	.05
59	Calvin Reese	.10
60	Phil Dauphin	.05
61	Ryan Hawblitzel	.05
62	Tim Parker	.05
63	Dave Swartzbaugh	.05
64	Billy White	.05
65	Terry Burrows	.05
66	Chris Gies	.05
67	Kurt Miller	.05
68	Timmie Morrow	.05
69	Benny Colvard	.05
70	Tim Costo	.05
71	Mica Lewis	.05
72	John Roper	.05
73	Kevin Tatar	.05
74	Joel Adamson	.05
75	Mike Farmer	.05
76	Kevin Stocker	.05
77	David Tokheim	.05
78	Ray Jackson	.05
79	Dax Jones	.05
80	Randy Curtis	.05
81	Eric Reichenbach	.05
82	Jerome Tolliver	.05
83	Quilvio Veras	.05
84	George Evangelista	.05
85	Pat Bryant	.05
86	Willie Canate	.05
87	Brian Lane	.05
88	Howard Battle	.05
89	Rob Butler	.05
90	Carlos Delgado	1.00
91	Tyler Houston	.05
92	Troy Hughes	.05
93	Chipper Jones	1.00
94	Mel Nieves	.05
95	Jose Olmeda	.05
96	John Finn	.05
97	Mike Guerrero	.05
98	Troy O'Leary	.05
99	Ben Blomdahl	.05
100	Mike Schmidt	.75
101	Carlos Burguillos	.05
102	Kiki Hernandez	.05
103	Brian Dubose	.05
104	Kevin Morgan	.05
105	Justin Thompson	.05
106	Jason Alstead	.05
107	Matt Anderson	.05
108	Brad Pennington	.05
109	Brad Tyler	.05
110	Jovino Carvajal	.05
111	Roger Luce	.05
112	Ken Powell	.05
113	Steve Sadecki	.05
114	Craig Clayton	.05
115	Russell Davis	.05
116	Mike Kelly	.05
117	Javier Lopez	.15
118	Doug Piatt	.05
119	Manny Alexander	.05
120	Damon Buford	.05
121	Erik Schullstrom	.05
122	Mark Smith	.05
123	Jeff Williams	.05
124	Reid Cornelius	.05
125	Tim Laker	.05
126	Chris Martin	.05
127	Mike Mathile	.05
128	Derrick White	.05
129	Luis Galindez	.05
130	John Kuehl	.05
131	Ray McDavid	.05
132	Sean Mulligan	.05
133	Tookie Spann	.05
134	Marcos Armas	.05
135	Scott Erwin	.05
136	Johnny Guzman	.05
137	Mike Mohler	.05
138	Craig Paquette	.05
139	Dean Tatarian	.05
140	Orlando Miller	.05
141	Tow Maynard	.05
142	Marc Newfield	.05
143	Greg Pirkl	.05
144	Jesus Tavarez	.05
145	Tom Smith	.05
146	Brad Seitzer	.05
147	Brent Brede	.05
148	Elston Hansen	.05
149	Jamie Ogden	.05
150	Rogelio Nunez	.05
151	Manny Cervantes	.05
152	David Sartain	.05
153	Shawn Bryant	.05
154	Chad Ogea	.05
155	Manny Ramirez	1.00
156	Darrell Whitmore	.05
157	Greg O'Halloran	.05
158	Tim Brown	.05
159	Curtis Pride	.05
160	Marcus Moore	.05
161	Robert Perez	.05
162	Aaron Small	.05
163	David Tollison	.05
164	Nigel Wilson	.05
165	Jim Givens	.05
166	Dennis McNamara	.05
167	Kelley O'Neal	.05
168	Rudy Pemberton	.05
169	Joe Perona	.05
170	Brian Cornelius	.05
171	Ivan Cruz	.05
172	Frank Gonzales	.05
173	Mike Lumley	.05
174	Brian Warren	.05
175	Aaron Sele	.05
176	Gary Caraballo	.05
177	Creighton Gubanich	.05
178	Brad Parker	.05
179	Scott Sheldon	.05
180	Archie Corbin	.05
181	Phil Hiatt	.05
182	Domingo Mota	.05
183	Dan Carlson	.05
184	Hugh Walker	.05
185	Joe Ciccarella	.05
186	John Jackson	.05
187	Brent Gates	.05
188	Eric Helfand	.05
189	Damon Mashore	.05
190	Malcolm (Curtis) Shaw	.05
191	Jason Wood	.05
192	Terry Powers	.05
193	Steve Karsay	.05
194	Greg Blosser	.05
195	Gar Finnvold	.05
196	Scott Hatteberg	.05
197	Derek Livernois	.05
198	Jeff McNeely	.05
199	Rex DeLaNuez	.05
200	Ken Griffey Jr.	1.00
201	Pat Meares	.05
202	Alan Newman	.05
203	Paul Russo	.05
204	Anthony Collier	.05
205	Roberto Petagine	.05
206	Brian Hunter	.05
207	James Mouton	.05
208	Tom Nevers	.05
209	Garret Anderson	.15
210	Clifton Garrett	.05
211	Eduardo Perez	.05
212	Shawn Purdy	.05
213	Darren Bragg	.05
214	Glenn Murray	.05
215	Ruben Santana	.05
216	Bubba Smith	.05
217	Terry Adams	.05
218	William (Bill) Bliss	.05
219	German Diaz	.05
220	Willie Gardner	.05
221	Ed Larregui	.05
222	Tim Garland	.05
223	Kevin Jordan	.05
224	Tim Rumer	.05
225	Jason Robertson	.05
226	Todd Claus	.05
227	Julian Heredia	.05
228	Mark Sweeney	.05
229	Robert Eenhoorn	.05
230	Tyler Green	.05
231	Mike Lieberthal	.10
232	Ron Lockett	.05
233	Tom Nuneviller	.05
234	Sean Ryan	.05
235	Alvaro Benavides	.05
236	Kevin Bellomo	.05
237	Tony Bridges	.05
238	Eric Whitford	.05
239	James Bishop	.05
240	Midre Cummings	.05
241	Tom Green	.05
242	Marcus Hanel	.05
243	Billy Ashley	.05
244	Matt Howard	.05
245	Tommy Adams	.05
246	Craig Bryant	.05
247	Ron Pezzoni	.05
248	Barry Miller	.05
249	Jason McFarlin	.05
250	Joe Rosselli	.05
251	Billy Van Landingham	.05
252	Chris Seelbach	.05
253	Jason Bere	.05
254	Eric Christopherson	.05
255	Rick Huisman	.05
256	Kevin McGehee	.05
257	Salomon Torres	.05
258	Brian Boehringer	.05
259	Glenn DiSarcina	.05
260	Jason Schmidt	.05
261	Charles Poe	.05
262	Ricky Bottalico	.05
263	Tommy Eason	.05
264	Joel Gilmore	.05
265	Pat Ruth	.05
266	Gene Schall	.05
267	Jim Campbell	.05
268	Brian Barber	.05
269	Allen Battle	.05
270	Marc Ronan	.05
271	Scott Simmons	.05
272	Dmitri Young	.05
273	Butch Huskey	.05
274	Frank Jacobs	.05
275	Aaron Ledesma	.05
276	Jose Martinez	.05
277	Andy Beasley	.05
278	Paul Ellis	.05
279	John Kelly	.05
280	Jeremy McGarity	.05
281	Mateo Ozuna	.05
282	Allen Watson	.05
283	Francisco Gamez	.05
284	Leon Glenn	.05
285	Duane Singleton	.05
286	Andy Pettitte	.50
287	Donald Harris	.05
288	Robb Nen	.05
289	Jose Oliva	.05
290	Keith Garagozzo	.05
291	Dan Smith	.05
292	Kiki Jones	.05
293	Rich Becker	.05
294	Mike Durant	.05
295	Denny Hocking	.05
296	Mike Lewis	.05
297	Troy Ricker	.05
298	Todd Ritchie	.05
299	Scott Stahoviak	.05
300	Brien Taylor	.05
301	Jim Austin	.05
302	Mike Daniel	.05
303	Joseph Eischen	.05
304	Ranbir Grewal	.05
305	Rondell White (Photo actually Glenn Murray.)	.15
306	Mark Hubbard	.05
307	Tate Seefried	.05
308	Tom Wilson	.05
309	Benji Gil	.05
310	Mike Edwards	.05
311	J.D. Noland	.05
312	Jay Gainer	.05
313	Lance Painter	.05
314	Tim Worell	.05
315	Sean Cheetham	.05
316	Earl Cunningham	.05
317	Brad Erdman	.05
318	Paul Torres	.05
319	Jose Vierra	.05
320	Chris Gambs	.05
321	Brandon Wilson	.05
322	Brett Donovan	.05
323	Larry Thomas	.05
324	Brian Griffiths	.05
325	Chad Schoenvogel	.05
326	Mandy Romero	.05
327	Chris Curtis	.05
328	Jim Campanis	.05
329	Anthony Manahan	.05
330	Jason Townley	.05
331	Fidel Compres	.05
332	John Ericks	.05
333	Don Prybylinski	.05
334	Jason Best	.05
335	Rob Wishnevski	.05
336	John Byington	.05
337	Omar Garcia	.05
338	Tony Eusebio	.05
339	Paul Swingle	.05
340	Mark Zappelli	.05
341	Bobby Jones	.05
342	J.R. Phillips	.05
343	Jim Edmonds	.50
344	Greg Hansell	.05
345	Mike Piazza	1.50
346	Mike Busch	.05
347	Darrell Sherman	.05
348	Shawn Green	.75
349	Willie Mota	.05
350	David McCarty	.05
351	James Dougherty	.05
352	Fernando Vina	.05
353	Ken Huckaby	.05
354	Joe Vitko	.05
355	Roberto (Diaz) Mejia	.05
356	Willis Otanez	.05
357	Billy Lott	.05
358	Jason Pruitt	.05
359	Jorge Fabregas	.05
360	Mike Stefanski	.05
361	Robert Saitz	.05
362	Scott Talanoa	.05
363	LaRue Baber	.05
364	Tyrone Hill	.05
365	Rick Mediavilla	.05
366	Eddie Williams	.05
367	Rigo Beltran	.05
368	Doug VanderWeele	.05
369	Donnie Elliott	.05
370	Dan Cholowsky	.05
371	Derrell Rumsey	.05
372	Anthony Graffagnino (Graffanino)	.05
373	Scott Ruffcorn	.05
374	Mike Rossiter	.05
375	Mike Robertson	.05
376	P.J. Forbes	.05
377	Doug Brady	.05
378	Rick Clelland	.05
379	Ugueth Urbina	.05
380	Cliff Floyd	.10
381	Danny Young	.05
382	Eddie Ramos	.05
383	Bob Abreu	.15
384	Gary Mota	.05
385	Tony Womack	.05
386	Jeff Motuzas	.05
387	Desi Relaford	.05
388	John Elerman	.05
389	Walt McKeel	.05
390	Tim VanEgmond	.05
391	Frank Rodriguez	.05
392	Paul Carey	.05
393	Michael Matheny	.05
394	George Glinatsis	.05
395	Checklist (1-69)	.05
396	Checklist (70-138)	.05
397	Checklist (139-207)	.05
398	Checklist (208-276)	.05
399	Checklist (277-345)	.05
400	Checklist (346-400)	.05
401	Paul Shuey	.05
402	Derek Jeter	2.00
403	Derek Wallace	.05
404	Sean Lowe	.05
405	Jim Pittsley	.05
406	Shannon Stewart	.25
407	Jamie Arnold	.05
408	Jason Kendall	.25
409	Eddie Pearson	.05
410	Todd Steverson	.05
411	Dan Serafini	.05
412	John Burke	.05
413	Jeff Schmidt	.05
414	Sherard Clinkscales	.05
415	Shon Walker	.05
416	Brandon Cromer	.05
417	Johnny Damon	1.00
418	Michael Moore	.05
419	Michael Matthews	.05
420	Brian Sackinsky	.05
421	Jon Lieber	.05
422	Danny Clyburn	.05
423	Chris Smith	.05
424	Dwain Bostic	.05
425	Bob Wolcott	.05
426	Mike Gulan	.05
427	Yuri Sanchez	.05
428	Tony Sheffield	.05
429	Ritchie Moody	.05
430	Andy Hartung	.05
431	Trey Beamon	.05
432	Tim Crabtree	.05
433	Mark Thompson	.05
434	John Lynch	.05
439	Tavo Alvarez	.05
441	Troy Penix	.05
442	Scott Pose	.05
447	Jesus Martinez	.05
449	Chad Fonville	.05
450	Checklist (401-450)	.05

Blue Bonus

These bonus cards were randomly inserted into 1992 Classic Best white jumbo packs, one per pack. Cards are numbered with a BC prefix. Format is similar to the regular cards, with the presence of front of blue foil.

		MT
Complete Set (30):		17.50
Common Player:		.25
1	Nolan Ryan	3.00
2	Mark Hutton	.25
3	Shane Andrews	.25
4	Scott Bullett	.25
5	Kurt Miller	.25
6	Carlos Delgado	1.50
7	Chipper Jones	2.00
8	Dmitri Young	.25
9	Mike Kelly	.25
10	Javy Lopez	.35
11	Aaron Sele	.25
12	Ken Griffey Jr.	2.50
13	Midre Cummings	.25
14	Salomon Torres	.25
15	Brien Taylor	.25
16	Mike Piazza	2.50
17	David McCarty	.25
18	Scott Ruffcorn	.25
19	Cliff Floyd	.25
20	Frankie Rodriguez	.25
21	Paul Shuey	.25
22	Derek Jeter	3.00
23	Derek Wallace	.25
24	Shannon Stewart	.50
25	Jamie Arnold	.25
26	Jason Kendall	.35
27	Todd Steverson	.25
28	Dan Serafini	.25
29	John Burke	.25
30	Michael Moore	.25

Red Bonus

The red bonus cards were randomly inserted in 1992 Classic Best black jumbo packs, one per pack. Cards are numbered with a BC prefix, and feature red-foil graphic highlights on front.

		MT
Complete Set (20):		5.00
Common Player:		.10
1	Nolan Ryan	2.00
2	Mark Hutton	.10
3	Shane Andrews	.10
4	Scott Bullett	.10
5	Kurt Miller	.10
6	Carlos Delgado	.75
7	Chipper Jones	1.00
8	Dmitri Young	.10
9	Mike Kelly	.10
10	Javy Lopez	.10
11	Aaron Sele	.10
12	Ken Griffey, Jr.	1.50
13	Midre Cummings	.10
14	Salomon Torres	.10
15	Brien Taylor	.10
16	Mike Piazza	2.00
17	David McCarty	.10
18	Scott Ruffcorn	.10
19	Cliff Floyd	.10
20	Frankie Rodriguez	.10

Autographs

Autographed cards of five stars and prospects were included as random wax pack inserts, while the Clayton autograph card was found exclusively in jumbo packs. Colorful backs have a statement of authenticity. The announced production number is shown in parentheses.

		MT
Complete Set (6):		125.00
Common Player:		3.00
(1)	Royce Clayton (2,000)	2.00
(2)	Ken Griffey Jr. (3,100)	55.00
(3)	David McCarty (1,000)	2.00
(4)	Nolan Ryan (3,100)	60.00
(5)	Mike Schmidt (4,100)	30.00
(6)	Brien Taylor (3,100)	3.00

1992 Classic Draft Picks

The top draft picks of 1992 are featured in this set, along with a Flashback subset (#86-95) of rising stars from the 1990-91 drafts. Cards were sold in 16-card foil packs including one foil bonus card. Fronts have a color action photo bordered in white with a dark green name stripe at bottom and the set logo at lower-left. Backs are in dark green with another photo and 1991-92 high school or college stats. Production was reported at 5,000 numbered cases.

		MT
Complete Set (125):		6.00
Common Player:		.05
Jumbo Pack (16):		.50
Jumbo Box (24):		9.00
1	Phil Nevin	.05
2	Paul Shuey	.05
3	B.J. Wallace	.05
4	Jeffrey Hammonds	.05
5	Chad Mottola	.05
6	Derek Jeter	3.00
7	Michael Tucker	.05
8	Derek Wallace	.05
9	Kenny Felder	.05
10	Chad McConnell	.05
11	Sean Lowe	.05
12	Ricky Greene	.05
13	Chris Roberts	.05
14	Shannon Stewart	.50
15	Benji Grigsby	.05
16	Jamie Arnold	.05
17	Rick Helling	.05
18	Jason Kendall	.25
19	Todd Steverson	.05
20	Dan Serafini	.05
21	Jeff Schmidt	.05
22	Sherard Clinkscales	.05
23	Ryan Luzinski	.05
24	Shon Walker	.05
25	Brandon Cromer	.05
26	Dave Landaker	.05
27	Michael Mathews	.05
28	Brian Sackinsky	.05
29	Jon Lieber	.05
30	Jim Rosenbohm	.05
31	De Shawn Warren	.05
32	Danny Clyburn	.05
33	Chris Smith	.05
34	Dwain Bostic	.05
35	Bobby Hughes	.05
36	Rick Magdellano	.05
37	Bob Wolcott	.05
38	Mike Gulan	.05
39	Yuri Sanchez	.05
40	Tony Sheffield	.05
41	Dan Melendez	.05
42	Jason Giambi	.75
43	Ritchie Moody	.05
44	Trey Beamon	.05
45	Tim Crabtree	.05
46	Chad Roper	.05
47	Mark Thompson	.05
48	Marquis Riley	.05
49	Tom Knauss	.05
50	Chris Holt	.05
51	Jonathan Nunnally	.05
52	Everett Stull	.05
53	Billy Owens	.05
54	Todd Etler	.05
55	Benji Simonton	.05
56	Dwight Maness	.05
57	Chris Eddy	.05
58	Brant Brown	.05
59	Trevor Humphrey	.05
60	Chris Widger	.05
61	Steve Montgomery	.05
62	Chris Gomez	.05
63	Jared Baker	.05
64	Doug Hecker	.05
65	David Spykstra	.05
66	Scott Miller	.05
67	Carey Paige	.05
68	Dave Manning	.05
69	James Keefe	.05
70	Levon Largusa	.05
71	Roger Bailey	.05
72	Rich Ireland	.05
73	Matt Williams	.05
74	Scott Gentile	.05
75	Hut Smith	.05
76	Rodney Henderson	.05
77	Mike Buddie	.05
78	Stephen Lyons	.05
79	John Burke	.05
80	Jim Pittsley	.05
81	Donnie Leshnock	.05
82	Cory Pearson	.05
83	Kurt Ehmann	.05
84	Bobby Bonds Jr.	.05
85	Steven Cox	.05
86	Brien Taylor (Flashback)	.05
87	Mike Kelly (Flashback)	.05
88	David McCarty (Flashback)	.05
89	Dmitri Young (Flashback)	.05
90	Joe Hamilton (Flashback)	.05
91	Mark Smith (Flashback)	.05
92	Doug Glanville (Flashback)	.05
93	Mike Lieberthal (Flashback)	.15
94	Joe Vitiello (Flashback)	.05
95	Mike Mussina (Flashback)	.75
96	Derek Hacopian	.05
97	Ted Corbin	.05
98	Carlton Fleming	.05
99	Aaron Rounsifer	.05
100	Chad Fox	.05
101	Chris Sheff	.05
102	Ben Jones	.05
103	David Post	.05
104	Jonnie Gendron	.05
105	Bob Juday	.05
106	David Becker	.05
107	Brandon Pico	.05
108	Tom Evans	.05
109	Jeff Faino	.05
110	Shawn Wills	.05
111	Derrick Cantrell	.05
112	Steve Rodriguez	.05
113	Ray Suplee	.05
114	Pat Leahy	.05
115	Matt Luke	.05
116	Jon McMullen	.05
117	Preston Wilson	.15
118	Gus Gandarillas	.05
119	Pete Janicki	.05
120	Byron Mathews	.05
121	Eric Owens	.05
122	John Lynch	.05
123	Mike Hickey	.05
124	Checklist 1	.05
125	Checklist 2	.05

Foil Bonus

Other than having their fronts printed on metallic foil and card numbers which are preceded by a "BC" prefix, these inserts are identical to the same players' cards in the regular Classic 1992 Draft Picks issue. One foil bonus card was included in each 16-card foil pack.

		MT
Complete Set (20):		5.00
Common Player:		.25
1	Phil Nevin	.25
2	Paul Shuey	.25
3	B.J. Wallace	.25
4	Jeffrey Hammonds	.25
5	Chad Mottola	.25
6	Derek Jeter	3.00
7	Michael Tucker	.25
8	Derek Wallace	.25
9	Kenny Felder	.25
10	Chad McConnell	.25
11	Sean Lowe	.25
12	Chris Roberts	.25
13	Shannon Stewart	.25
14	Benji Grigsby	.25
15	Jamie Arnold	.25
16	Ryan Luzinski	.25
17	Bobby Bonds Jr.	.25
18	Brien Taylor	.25
19	Mike Kelly	.25
20	Mike Mussina	1.00

1992 Classic Four Sport

The top draft picks of 1992 are featured in this set, along with a Flashback subset of rising stars. Fronts have a large borderless color action photo with a vertical strip at left featuring the player's name and position, with the Four Sport logo at top. Backs have another photo and 1991-92 high school or college stats. Production was reported at 40,000 cases. Only the baseball players are listed here. A gold-foil highlighted factory set version was also produced including a Future Superstars autographed card in an edition of 9,500.

		MT
Common Baseball Player:		.05
Gold: 3XGold:		3X
Gold Factory Set:		45.00
226	Phil Nevin	.05
227	Paul Shuey	.05
228	B.J. Wallace	.05
229	Jeffrey Hammonds	.05
230	Chad Mottola	.05
231	Derek Jeter	3.00
232	Michael Tucker	.05
233	Derek Wallace	.05
234	Kenny Felder	.05
235	Chad McConnell	.05
236	Sean Lowe	.05
237	Ricky Greene	.05
238	Chris Roberts	.05
239	Shannon Stewart	.35
240	Benji Grigsby	.05
241	Jamie Arnold	.05
242	Rick Helling	.05
243	Jason Kendall	.25
244	Todd Steverson	.05
245	Dan Serafini	.05
246	Jeff Schmidt	.05
247	Sherard Clinkscales	.05
248	Ryan Luzinski	.05
249	Shon Walker	.05
250	Brandon Cromer	.05
251	Dave Landaker	.05
252	Michael Mathews	.05
253	Brian Sackinsky	.05
254	Jon Lieber	.05
255	Jim Rosenbohm	.05
256	De Shawn Warren	.05
257	Danny Clyburn	.05
258	Chris Smith	.05
259	Dwain Bostic	.05
260	Bobby Hughes	.05
261	Rick Magdellano	.05
262	Bob Wolcott	.05
263	Mike Gulan	.05
264	Yuri Sanchez	.05
265	Tony Sheffield	.05
266	Dan Melendez	.05
267	Jason Giambi	.50
268	Ritchie Moody	.05
269	Trey Beamon	.05
270	Tim Crabtree	.05
271	Chad Roper	.05
272	Mark Thompson	.05
273	Marquis Riley	.05
274	Tom Knauss	.05
275	Chris Holt	.05
276	Jonathan Nunnally	.05
277	Everett Stull	.05
278	Billy Owens	.05
279	Todd Etler	.05
280	Benji Simonton	.05
281	Dwight Maness	.05
282	Chris Eddy	.05
283	Brant Brown	.05
284	Trevor Humphrey	.05
285	Chris Widger	.05
286	Steve Montgomery	.05
287	Chris Gomez	.05
288	Jared Baker	.05
289	Doug Hecker	.05
290	David Spykstra	.05
291	Scott Miller	.05
292	Carey Paige	.05
293	Dave Manning	.05
294	James Keefe	.05
295	Levon Largusa	.05
296	Roger Bailey	.05
297	Rich Ireland	.05
298	Matt Williams	.05
299	Scott Gentile	.05
300	Hut Smith	.05
301	Dave Brown	.05
302	Bobby Bonds Jr.	.05
303	Reggie Smith	.05
304	Preston Wilson	.15
305	John Burke	.05
306	Rodney Henderson	.05
307	Pete Janicki	.05
308	Brien Taylor (Flashback)	.05
309	Mike Kelly (Flashback)	.05
314	Jim Pittsley	.05

Autographs

More than 50 of the draft picks from the four major team sports which appear in Classic's Four Sport issue can also be found among randomly inserted autographed cards. Fronts are formatted like the base set, with full-bleed action photos and include a serial number from within the edition limit specified for each player. Backs have a congratulatory message for finding an autographed card. Only the baseball players from the issue are listed here, arranged by the numerical order of their cards in the base set; the autographed cards are not numbered.

		MT
Common Player:		4.00
(226)	Phil Nevin (1,475)	6.00
(227)	Paul Shuey (4,050)	4.00
(229)	Jeffrey Hammonds (2,950)	4.00
(231)	Derek Jeter (1,125)	150.00
(233)	Derek Wallace (1,475)	4.00
(241)	Jamie Arnold (1,575)	4.00
(242)	Rick Helling (2,875)	4.00
(245)	Dan Serafini (1,475)	4.00
(248)	Ryan Luzinski (1,575)	4.00
(253)	Brian Sackinsky (1,575)	4.00
(259)	Dwain Bostic (2,075)	4.00
(290)	David Spykstra (1,575)	4.00
(307)	Pete Janicki (1,875)	4.00

1992-93 Fleer Excel

Excel was Fleer's 1992 entry into minor league cards. The 250-card set features full-color photos inside a white border with the player's name, team, logo and Excel logo in gold-foil stamping. Backs have large photos, career statistics, team logos and biographical information. Cards are UV coated. Cards were intended to be sold in 14-card packs for a suggested retail price of $1.49 each. The Excel All-Stars are listed at the end of the 250-card checklist. Cards for these 10 players were randomly inserted into the foil packs.

		MT
Complete Set (250):		12.00
Common Player:		.05
Jumbo Pack (23):		1.25
Wax Box (36):		17.50
Jumbo Box (24):		20.00
1	Mike D'Andrea	.05
2	Chipper Jones	2.00
3	Mike Kelly	.05
4	Brian Kowitz	.05
5	Napoleon Robinson	.05
6	Tony Tarasco	.05
7	Pedro Castellano	.05
8	Doug Glanville	.05
9	Andy Hartung	.05
10	Jay Hassel	.05
11	Ryan Hawblitzel	.05
12	Kevin Roberson	.05
13	Chad Tredaway	.05
14	Jose Vierra	.05
15	Matt Walbeck	.05
16	Tim Belk	.05
17	Jamie Dismuke	.05
18	Chad Fox	.05
19	Micah Franklin	.05
20	Dan Frye	.05
21	Steve Gibralter	.05
22	Demetrish Jenkins	.05
23	Jason Kummerfeidt	.05
24	Bob Loftin	.05
25	Chad Mottola	.05
26	Bobby Perna	.05
27	Scott Pose	.05
28	Calvin Reese	.10
29	John Roper	.05
30	Jerry Spradlin	.05
31	Roger Bailey	.05
32	Jason Bates	.05
33	John Burke	.05
34	Jason Hutchins	.05
35	Troy Ricker	.05
36	Mark Thompson	.05
37	Lou Lucca	.05
38	John Lynch	.05
39	Todd Pridy	.05
40	Gary Cooper	.05
41	Jim Dougherty	.05
42	Tony Eusebio	.05
43	Chris Hatcher	.05
44	Chris Hill	.05
45	Trent Hubbard	.05
46	Todd Jones	.05
47	Jeff Juden	.05
48	James Mouton	.05
49	Tom Nevers	.05
50	Jim Waring	.05
51	Chris Abbe	.05
52	Jay Kirkpatrick	.05
53	Raul Mondesi	.10
54	Vernon Spearman	.05
55	Tavo Alvarez	.05
56	Shane Andrews	.05
57	Yamil Benitez	.05
58	Cliff Floyd	.10
59	Antonio Grissom	.05
60	Tyrone Horne	.05
61	Mike Lansing	.05
62	Edgar Tovar	.05
63	Ugueth Urbina	.05
64	David Wainhouse	.05
65	Derrick White	.05
66	Gabe White	.05
67	Rondell White	.10
68	Edgar Alfonzo	.05
69	Jeromy Burnitz	.10
70	Jay Davis	.05
71	Cesar Diaz	.05
72	Todd Douma	.05
73	Brook Fordyce	.05
74	Butch Huskey	.05
75	Bobby Jones	.05
76	Jose Martinez	.05
77	Ricky Otero	.05
78	Jim Popoff	.05
79	Al Shirley	.05
80	Julian Vasquez	.05
81	Quilvio Veras	.05
82	Fernando Vina	.05
83	Ron Blazier	.05
84	Tommy Eason	.05
85	Tyler Green	.05
86	Mike Lieberthal	.10
87	Tom Nuneviller	.05
88	Matt Whisenant	.05
89	Jon Zuber	.05
90	Midre Cummings	.05
91	Jon Farrell	.05
92	Ramon Martinez	.05
93	Antonio Mitchell	.05
94	Keith Thomas	.05
95	Rene Arocha	.05
96	Brian Barber	.05
97	Jamie Cochran	.05
98	Mike Gulan	.05
99	Keith Johns	.05
100	John Kelly	.05
101	Anthony Lewis	.05
102	T.J. Mathews	.05
103	Kevin Meier	.05
104	David Oehrlein	.05
105	Gerry Santos	.05
106	Basil Shabazz	.05
107	Eddie Williams	.05
108	Dmitri Young	.05
109	Jay Gainer	.05
110	Pedro Martinez	2.00
111	Dave Staton	.05
112	Tim Worrell	.05
113	Dan Carlson	.05
114	Joel Chimelis	.05
115	Eric Christopherson	.05
116	Adell Davenport	.05
117	Ken Grundt	.05
118	Rick Huisman	.05
119	Andre Keene	.05
120	Kevin McGehee	.05
121	Salomon Torres	.05
122	Damon Buford	.05
123	Stanton Cameron	.05
124	Rick Krivda	.05
125	Alex Ochoa	.05
126	Brad Penington	.05
127	Mark Smith	.05
128	Mel Wearing	.05
129	Cory Bailey	.05
130	Greg Blosser	.05
131	Joe Caruso	.05
132	Jason Friedman	.05
133	Jose Malave	.05
134	Jeff McNeely	.05
135	Luis Ortiz	.05
136	Ed Riley	.05
137	Frank Rodriguez	.05
138	Aaron Sele	.10
139	Garret Anderson	.15
140	Ron Correia	.05
141	Jim Edmonds	.50
142	John Fritz	.05
143	Brian Grebeck	.05
144	Jeff Kipila	.05
145	Orlando Palmeiro	.05
146	Eduardo Perez	.05
147	John Pricher	.05
148	Chris Pritchett	.05
149	James Baldwin	.05
150	Rodney Bolton	.05
151	Essex Burton	.05
152	Scott Cepicky	.05
153	Steve Olsen	.05
154	Scott Ruffcorn	.05
155	Scott Schrenk	.05
156	Larry Thomas	.05
157	Brandon Wilson	.05
158	Paul Byrd	.05
159	Willie Canate	.05
160	Marc Marini	.05
161	Jonathan Nunnally	.05
162	Chad Ogea	.05
163	Herb Perry	.05
164	Manny Ramirez	2.00
165	Omar Ramirez	.05
166	Ken Ramos	.05
167	Tracy Sanders	.05
168	Paul Shuey	.05
169	Kyle Washington	.05
170	Ivan Cruz	.05
171	Lou Frazier	.05
172	Brian Bevil	.05
173	Shane Halter	.05
174	Phil Hiatt	.05
175	Lance Jennings	.05
176	Les Norman	.05
177	Joe Randa	.05
178	Dan Rohrmeier	.05
179	Larry Sutton	.05
180	Joe Vitiello	.05
181	John Byington	.05
182	Edgar Caceres	.05
183	Jeff Cirillo	.05
184	Mike Farrell	.05
185	Kenny Felder	.05
186	Tyrone Hill	.05
187	Brian Hostetler	.05
188	Danan Hughes	.05
189	Scott Karl	.05
190	Joe Kmak	.05
191	Rob Lakachyk	.05
192	Matt Mieske	.05
193	Troy O'Leary	.05
194	Cecil Rodriques	.05
195	Tim Unroe	.05
196	Wes Weger	.05
197	Rich Becker	.05
198	Marty Cordova	.05
199	Steve Dunn	.05
200	Mike Durant	.05
201	Denny Hocking	.05
202	David McCarty	.05
203	Damian Miller	.05
204	Scott Stahoviak	.05
205	Russ Davis	.05
206	Mike Draper	.05
207	Carl Everett	.10
208	Lew Hill	.05
209	Mark Hutton	.05
210	Derek Jeter	4.00
211	Kevin Jordan	.05
212	Lyle Mouton	.05
213	Bobby Munoz	.05
214	Andy Pettitte	1.00
215	Brien Taylor	.05
216	Brent Gates	.05
217	Eric Helfand	.05
218	Curtis Shaw	.05
219	Todd Van Poppel	.05
220	Miah Bradbury	.05
221	Darren Bragg	.05
222	Jim Converse	.05
223	John Cummings	.05
224	Shawn Estes	.05
225	Mike Hampton	.05
226	Derek Lowe	.05
227	Ellerton Maynard	.05
228	Fred McNair	.05
229	Marc Newfield	.05
230	Desi Relaford	.05
231	Ruben Santana	.05
232	Bubba Smith	.05
233	Brian Turang	.05
234	Benji Gil	.05
235	Jose Oliva	.05
236	Jon Shave	.05
237	Travis Baptist	.05
238	Howard Battle	.05
239	Rob Butler	.05
240	Tim Crabtree	.05
241	Juan DeLaRosa	.05
242	Carlos Delgado	1.50
243	Alex Gonzalez	.05
244	Steve Karsay	.05
245	Paul Spoljaric	.05
246	Todd Steverson	.05
247	Nigel Wilson	.05
248	Checklist	.05
249	Checklist	.05
250	Checklist	.05

1992 Front Row Draft Picks

One hundred of the top players in the 1992 amateur draft are featured in this set. Sold in both wax packs and factory sets, the issue included a number of foil-stamped parallel cards, plus gold Frank Thomas and Ken Griffey, Jr. cards. The basic cards are UV-coated front and back and feature posed or game-action color photos of the players in their high school or college uniforms with borders in graduated shades of blue. Backs have biographical data, stats and career highlights, plus another picture - generally a boyhood photo. According to released production figures, about 330,000 sets are possible.

		MT
Complete Set (100):		6.00
Common Player:		.05
Silver: 1.5XSilver:		1.5X
Gold: 2.5XGold:		2.5X
Wax Pack (10):		1.00
Wax Box (36):		30.00
1	Dan Melendez	.05
2	Billy Owens	.05
3	Sherard Clinkscales	.05
4	Tim Moore	.05
5	Michael Hickey	.05
6	Kenny Carlyle	.05
7	Todd Steverson	.05
8	Ted Corbin	.05
9	Tim Crabtree	.05
10	Jason Angel	.05
11	Mike Gulan	.05
12	Jared Baker	.05
13	Mike Buddie	.05
14	Brandon Pico	.05
15	Jonathan Nunnally	.05
16	Scott Patton	.05
17	Tony Sheffield	.05
18	Danny Clyburn	.05
19	Tom Knauss	.05
20	Carey Paige	.05
21	Keith Johnson	.05
22	Larry Mitchell	.05
23	Tim Leger	.05
24	Doug Hecker	.05
25	Aaron Thatcher	.05
26	Marquis Riley	.05
27	Jamie Taylor	.05
28	Don Wengert	.05
29	Jason Moler	.05
30	Kevin Kloek	.05
31	Kevin Pearson	.05
32	David Mysel	.05
33	Chris Holt	.05
34	Chris Gomez	.05
35	Joe Hamilton	.05
36	Brandon Cromer	.05
37	Lloyd Peever	.05
38	Gordon Sanchez	.05
39	Bonus Card	.05
40	Jason Giambi	1.00
41	Sean Runyan	.05
42	Jamie Keefe	.05
43	Scott Gentile	.05
44	Michael Tucker	.05
45	Scott Klingenbeck	.05
46	Ed Christian	.05
47	Scott Miller	.05
48	Rick Navarro	.05
49	Bill Selby	.05
50	Chris Roberts	.05
51	John Dillinger	.05
52	Keith Johns	.05
53	Matthew Williams	.05
54	Garvin Alston	.05
55	Derek Jeter	4.00
56	Chris Eddy	.05
57	Jeff Schmidt	.05
58	Chris Petersen	.05
59	Chris Sheff	.05
60	Chad Roper	.05
61	Rich Ireland	.05
62	Tibor Brown	.05
63	Todd Etler	.05
64	John Turlais	.05
65	Shawn Holcomb	.05
66	Ben Jones	.05
67	Marcel Galligani	.05
68	Troy Penix	.05
69	Matt Luke	.05
70	David Post	.05
71	Michael Warner	.05
72	Alexis Aranzamendi	.05
73	Larry Hingle	.05
74	Shon Walker	.05
75	Mark Thompson	.05
76	Jon Lieber	.05
77	Wes Weger	.05
78	Mike Smith	.05
79	Ritchie Moody	.05
80	B.J. Wallace	.05
81	Rick Helling	.05
82	Chad Mottola	.05
83	Brant Brown	.05
84	Steve Rodriguez	.05
85	John Vanhof	.05
86	Brian Wolf	.05
87	Steve Montgomery	.05
88	Eric Owens	.05
89	Jason Kendall	.25
90	Bob Bennett	.05
91	Joe Petcka	.05
92	Jim Rosenbohm	.05
93	David Manning	.05
94	Dave Landaker	.05
95	Dan Kyslinger	.05
96	Roger Bailey	.05
97	Jon Zuber	.05
98	Steve Cox	.05
99	Chris Widger	.05
100	Checklist	.05
---	Ken Griffey Jr. (Gold Card)	6.00
---	Frank Thomas (Gold Card)	5.00

1992 SkyBox AA

SkyBox Pre-Rookie 1992 baseball cards were released in two 310-card sets; one for Triple A and one for Double A. Each set includes 289 top prospects, plus subsets (1991 statistical leaders, players of the year and minor league stadiums) and checklist cards. Cards were intended to be sold in 15-card packs for a suggested retail price of 95 cents each. SkyBox also offered 25-card Pre-Rookie team sets which include all players and coaches on the opening day roster of each of the 52 AA and AAA teams, plus a team checklist. Sets were to be available at most of the teams' stadiums. The top prospects which appear in the 15-card packs are also depicted in the team sets, but the team cards use a different numbering system and delete the card back copy except for statistics.

		MT
Complete Set (310):		5.00
Common Player:		.05
Wax Pack (15):		.50
Wax Box (36):		8.00
1	Rich Batchelor	.05
2	Russ Davis	.05
3	Kiki Hernandez	.05
4	Sterling Hitchcock	.05
5	Darren Hodges	.05
6	Jeff Hoffman	.05
7	Mark Hulton	.05
8	Bobby Munoz	.05
9	Roy Noriega	.05
10	Sherman Obando	.05
11	John Viera	.05
12	Cliff Brannon	.05
13	Chuck Carr	.05
14	Fidel Compres	.05
15	Tripp Cromer	.05
16	John Ericks	.05
17	Gabby Ozuna	.05
18	Don Prybylinski	.05
19	John Sellick	.05
20	John Thomas	.05
21	Tom Urbani	.05
22	Chris Butterfield	.05
23	Todd Douma	.05
24	Brook Fordyce	.05
25	Tim Howard	.05
26	John Johnstone	.05
27	Bobby Jones	.05
28	Rob Katzaroff	.05
29	Gregg Langbehn	.05
30	Curtis Pride	.05
31	Julian Vasquez	.05
32	Joe Vitko	.05
33	Tom Wegmann	.05
34	Mike White	.05
35	Alan Zinter	.05
36	Clemente Alvarez	.05
37	Cesar Bernhardt	.05
38	Wayne Busby	.05
39	Scott Cepicky	.05
40	John Hudek	.05
41	Scott Jaster	.05
42	Bo Kennedy	.05
43	Mike Mongiello	.05
44	Kinnis Pledger	.05
45	Johnny Ruffin	.05
46	Jose Ventura	.05
47	Paul Byrd	.05
48	Colin Charland	.05
49	Miguel Flores	.05
50	Brian Giles	.25
51	Jose Hernandez	.05
52	Nolan Lene	.05
53	David Mlicki	.05
54	Tracy Sanders	.05
55	Mike Soper	.05
56	Kelly Stinnett	.05
57	Joe Turek	.05
58	Kyle Washington	.05
59	Dave Bird	.05
60	Scott Bullett	.05
61	Steve Cooke	.05
62	Alberto De Los Santos	.05
63	Stan Fansier	.05
64	Austin Manahan	.05
65	Daryl Ratliff	.05
66	Mandy Romero	.05
67	Ben Shelton	.05
68	Paul Wagner	.05
69	Mike Zimmerman	.05
70	Phil Dauphin	.05
71	Chris Ebright	.05
72	Mike Grace	.05
73	Ryan Hawbitzel	.05
74	Jessie Hollins	.05
75	Tim Parker	.05
76	Dave Swartzbaugh	.05
77	Steve Trachsel	.05
78	Billy White	.05
79	Bobby Ayala	.05
80	Tim Costa	.05
81	Ty Griffin	.05
82	Cesar Hernandez	.05
83	Trevor Hoffman	.15
84	Brian Lane	.05
85	Scott Pose	.05
86	Johnny Ray	.05
87	John Roper	.05
88	Glenn Sutko	.05
89	Kevin Tatar	.05
90	John Byington	.05

No.	Player	Price
91	Tony Diggs	.05
92	Bo Dodson	.05
93	Craig Faulkner	.05
94	Jim Hunter	.05
95	Oreste Marrero	.05
96	Troy O'Leary	.05
97	Brian Bark	.05
98	Dennis Burlingame	.05
99	Ramon Carabello	.05
100	Mike Kelly	.05
101	Javier Lopez	.10
102	Don Strange	.05
103	Tony Tarasco	.05
104	Manny Alexander	.05
105	Damon Buford	.05
106	Cesar Devares	.05
107	Rodney Lofton	.05
108	Brent Miller	.05
109	David Miller	.05
110	Daryl Moore	.05
111	John O'Donoghue	.05
112	Erik Schulstrom	.05
113	Mark Smith	.05
114	Mel Wearing	.05
115	Jeff Williams	.05
116	Kip Yaughn	.05
117	Doug Bochtler	.05
118	Travis Buckley	.05
119	Reid Cornelius	.05
120	Chris Johnson	.05
121	Tim Laker	.05
122	Chris Martin	.05
123	Mike Mathile	.05
124	Darwin Pennye	.05
125	Doug Platt	.05
126	Kurt Abbott	.05
127	Marcos Amas	.05
128	James Buccheri	.05
129	Kevin Dettola	.05
130	Scott Erwin	.05
131	Johnny Guzman	.05
132	David Jacas	.05
133	Francisco Matos	.05
134	Mike Mohler	.05
135	Craig Paquette	.05
136	Todd Revenig	.05
137	Todd Smith	.05
138	Ricky Strebeck	.05
139	Sam August	.05
140	Tony Eusebio	.05
141	Brian Griffiths	.05
142	Todd Jones	.05
143	Orlando Miller	.05
144	Howard Prager	.05
145	Matt Rambo	.05
146	Lee Sammons	.05
147	Richie Simon	.05
148	Frank Bolick	.05
149	Jim Campanis	.05
150	Jim Converse	.05
151	Bobby Holley	.05
152	Troy Kent	.05
153	Brent Knackert	.05
154	Anthony Manahan	.05
155	Tow Maynard	.05
156	Mike McDonald	.05
157	Marc Newfield	.05
158	Greg Pirkl	.05
159	Jesus Tavarez	.05
160	Kerry Woodson	.05
161	Graeme Lloyd	.05
162	Paul Menhart	.05
163	Marcus Moore	.05
164	Greg O'Halloran	.05
165	Mark Ohlms	.05
166	Robert Perez	.05
167	Aaron Small	.05
168	Nigel Wilson	.05
169	Julian Yan	.05
170	Jeff Braley	.05
171	Brian Cornelius	05
172	Ivan Cruz	.05
173	Lou Frazier	.05
174	Frank Gonzales	.05
175	Tyrone Kingwood	.05
176	Leo Torres	.05
177	Brien Warren	.05
178	Brian Ahern	.05
179	Tony Bridges	.05
180	Paco Burgos	.05
181	Adam Casillas	.05
182	Archie Corbin	.05
183	Phil Hiatt	.05
184	Marcus Lawton	.05
185	Domingo Mota	.05
186	Mark Pamell	.05
187	Ed Pierce	.05
188	Rich Tunison	.05
189	Hugh Walker	.05
190	Skip Wiley	.05
191	Dave Adams	.05
192	Mick Billmeyer	.05
193	Marvin Cobb	.05
194	Jim Edmonds	1.00
195	Corey Kapano	.05
196	Jeff Kiplia	.05
197	Joe Kraemer	.05
198	Ray Martinez	.05
199	J.R. Phillips	.05
200	Darryl Scott	.05
201	Paul Swingle	.05
202	Mark Zappelli	.05
203	Greg Blosser	.05
204	Bruce Chick	.05
205	Colin Dixon	.05
206	Gar Finnvold	.05
207	Scott Hatteberg	.05
208	Derek Livernois	.05
209	Jeff McNeely	.05
210	Tony Mosley	.05
211	Bill Norris	.05
212	Ed Riley	.05
213	Ken Ryan	.05
214	Tim Smith	.05
215	Willie Tatum	.05
216	Rex De La Nuez	.05
217	Rich Garces	.05
218	Curtis Leskanic	.05
219	Mica Lewis	.05
220	David McCarty	.05
221	Pat Meares	.05
222	Alan Newman	.05
223	Jay Owens	.05
224	Carlos Pulido	.05
225	Rusty Richards	.05
226	Paul Russo	.05
227	Brad Brink	.05
228	Andy Carter	.05
229	Tyler Green	.05
230	Mike Lieberthal	.10
231	Chris Limbach	.05
232	Ron Lockett	.05
233	Tom Nuneviller	.05
234	Troy Paulsen	.05
235	Todd Pratt	.05
236	Sean Ryan	.05
237	Matt Stevens	.05
238	Sam Taylor	.05
239	Casey Waller	.05
240	Mike Williams	.05
241	Jorge Alvarez	.05
242	Billy Ashley	.05
243	Tim Barker	.05
244	Bill Bene	.05
245	John Deutsch	.05
246	Greg Hansell	.05
247	Matt Howard	.05
248	Ron Maurer	.05
249	Mike Mimbs	.05
250	Chris Morrow	.05
251	Mike Piazza	3.00
252	Dennis Springer	.05
253	Clay Bellinger	.05
254	Dan Carlson	.05
255	Eric Christopherson	.05
256	Adell Davenport	.05
257	Steve Finken	.05
258	Rick Huisman	.05
259	Kevin McGehee	.05
260	Don Rambo	.05
261	Steve Reed	.05
262	Kevin Rogers	.05
263	Salomon Torres	.05
264	Pete Weber	.05
265	Brian Romero	.05
266	Cris Colon	.05
267	Rusty Greer	.05
268	Donald Harris	.05
269	David Hulse	.05
270	Pete Kuld	.05
271	Robb Nen	.05
272	Jose Oliva	.05
273	Steve Rowley	.05
274	Jon Shave	.05
275	Cedric Shaw	.05
276	Dan Smith	.05
277	Matt Whiteside	.05
278	Scott Frederickson	.05
279	Jay Gainer	.05
280	Paul Gonzalez	.05
281	Vince Harris	.05
282	Ray Holbert	.05
283	Dwayne Hosey	.05
284	J.D. Noland	.05
285	Lance Painter	.05
286	Scott Sanders	.05
287	Darrell Sherman	.05
288	Brian Wood	.05
209	Tim Worrell	.06
290	John Jaha	.05
291	Jim Bowie	.05
292	Mark Howie	.05
293	Matt Stairs	.05
294	Larry Carter	.05
295	Pat Mahomes	.05
296	Jeff Mutis	.05
297	Municipal Stadium	.05
298	Knights Castle	.05
299	Engel Stadium	.05
300	Tim McCarver Stadium	.05
301	Beehive Field	.05
302	Tinker Field	.05
303	Checklist Alpha 1	.05
304	Checklist Alpha 2	.05
305	Checklist Alpha 3	.05
306	Checklist Alpha 4	.05
307	Checklist Numeric 1	.05
308	Checklist Numeric 2	.05
309	Checklist Numeric 3	.05
310	Checklist Numeric 4	.05

1992 SkyBox AAA

	MT
Complete Set (310):	5.00
Common Player:	.05
Wax Pack (15):	.50
Wax Box (36):	8.00

No.	Player	Price
1	Pedro Astacio	.05
2	Bryan Baar	.05
3	Tom Goodwin	.05
4	Jeff Hamilton	.05
5	Pedro Martinez	3.00
6	Jamie McAndrew	.05
7	Mark Mimbs	.05
8	Raul Mondesi	.10
9	Jose Munoz	.05
10	Henry Rodriguez	.05
11	Eric Young	.05
12	Joe Ausanio	.05
13	Victor Cole	.05
14	Carlos Garcia	.05
15	Blas Minor	.05
16	William Pennyfeather	.05
17	Mark Petkovsek	.05
18	Jeff Richardson	.05
19	Rosario Rodriguez	.05
20	Tim Wakefield	.05
21	John Wehner	.05
22	Kevin Young	.05
23	Mike Blowers	.05
24	Bret Boone	.50
25	Jim Bowie	.05
26	Dave Brundage	.05
27	Randy Kramer	.05
28	Patrick Lennon	.05
29	Jim Newlin	.05
30	Jose Nunez	.05
31	Mike Remlinger	.05
32	Pat Rice	.05
33	Roger Salkeld	.05
34	Beau Allred	.05
35	Denis Boucher	.05
36	Mike Christopher	.05
37	Daren Epley	.05
38	Tom Kramer	.05
39	Jerry DiPoto	.05
40	Jeff Mutis	.05
41	Jeff Shaw	.05
42	Lee Tinsley	.05
43	Kevin Wickander	.05
44	Royal Clayton	.05
45	Bobby Dejardin	.05
46	Mike Draper	.05
47	Mike Humphreys	.05
48	Torey Lovullo	.05
49	Ed Martel	.05
50	Billy Masse	.05
51	Hensley Meulens	.05
52	Sam Militello	.05
53	John Ramos	.05
54	David Rosario	.05
55	David Silvestri	.05
56	J.T. Snow	.15
57	Russ Springer	.05
58	Jerry Stanford	.05
59	Wade Taylor	.05
60	Gerald Williams	.05
61	Cal Eldred	.05
62	Chris George	.05
63	Otis Green	.05
64	Mike Ignasiak	.05
65	John Jaha	.05
66	Mark Kiefer	.05
67	Matt Mieske	.05
68	Angel Miranda	.05
69	Dave Nilsson	.05
70	Jim Olander	.05
71	Jim Tatum	.05
72	Jose Valentin	.05
73	Don Barbara	.05
74	Chris Beasley	.05
75	Mike Butcher	.05
76	Damion Easley	.05
77	Kevin Flora	.05
78	Tim Fortugno	.05
79	Larry Gonzales	.05
80	Todd James	.05
81	Tim Salmon	.50
82	Don Vidmar	.05
83	Cliff Young	.05
84	Shon Ashley	.05
85	Brian Barnes	.05
86	Blaine Beatty	.05
87	Kent Bottenfield	.05
88	Wil Cordero	.05
89	Jerry Goff	.05
90	Jon Hurst	.05
91	Jim Kremers	.05
92	Matt Maysey	.05
93	Rob Natal	.05
94	Matt Stairs	.05
95	David Wainhouse	.05
96	Alex Arias	.05
97	Scott Bryant	.05
98	Jim Bullinger	.05
99	Pedro Castellano	.05
100	Lance Dickson	.05
101	John Gardner	.05
102	Jeff Hartsock	.05
103	Elvin Paulino	.05
104	Fernando Ramsey	.05
105	Laddie Renfroe	.05
106	Kevin Roberson	.05
107	John Salles	.05
108	Derrick May	.05
109	Turk Wendell	.05
110	Doug Brocail	.05
111	Terry Bross	.05
112	Scott Coolbaugh	.05
113	Rick Davis	.05
114	Jeff Gardner	.05
115	Steve Pegues	.05
116	Frank Seminara	.05
117	Dave Staton	.05
118	Will Taylor	.05
119	Jim Vatcher	.05
120	Guillermo Velasquez	.05
121	Dan Walters	.05
122	Rene Arocha	.05
123	Rod Brewer	.05
124	Ozzie Canseco	.05
125	Mark Clark	.05
126	Joey Fernandez	.05
127	Lonnie Maclin	.05
128	Mike Milchin	.05
129	Stan Royer	.05
130	Tracy Woodson	.05
131	Bob Buchanan	.05
132	Mark Howie	.05
133	Tony Menendez	.05
134	Gino Minutelli	.05
135	Tim Pugh	.05
136	Mo Sanford	.05
137	Joey Vierra	.05
138	Dan Wilson	.05
139	Kevin Blankenship	.05
140	Todd Burns	.05
141	Tom Drees	.05
142	Jeff Frye	.05
143	Chuck Jackson	.05
144	Rob Maurer	.05
145	Russ McGinnis	.05
146	Dan Peltier	.05
147	Wayne Rosenthal	.05
148	Bob Sebra	.05
149	Sean Berry	.05
150	Stu Cole	.05
151	Jeff Conine	.05
152	Kevin Koslovski	.05
153	Kevin Long	.05
154	Carlos Maldonado	.05
155	Dennis Moeller	.05
156	Harvey Pulliam	.05
157	Luis Medina	.05
158	Steve Shifflett	.05
159	Tim Spehr	.05
160	Brian Conroy	.05
161	Wayne Housie	.05
162	Daryl Irvine	.05
163	Dave Milstien	.05
164	Jeff Plympton	.05
165	Paul Quantrill	.05
166	Larry Shikles	.05
167	Scott Taylor	.05
168	Mike Twardoski	.05
169	John Valentin	.05
170	David Walters	.05
171	Eric Wedge	.05
172	Bob Zupcic	.05
173	Johnny Ard	.05
174	Larry Carter	.05
175	Steve Decker	.05
176	Steve Hosey	.05
177	Paul McClellan	.05
178	Jim Myers	.05
179	Jamie Cooper	.05
180	Pat Rapp	.05
181	Ted Wood	.05
182	Willie Banks	.05
183	Bernardo Brito	.05
184	J.T. Bruett	.05
185	Larry Casian	.05
186	Shawn Gilbert	.05
187	Greg Johnson	.05
188	Terry Jorgensen	.05
189	Edgar Naveda	.05
190	Derek Parks	.05
191	Danny Sheaffer	.05
192	Mike Trombley	.05
193	George Tsamis	.05
194	Rob Waseenaar	.05
195	Vinny Castilla	.10
196	Pat Gomez	.05
197	Ryan Klesko	.10
198	Keith Mitchell	.05
199	Bobby Moore	.05
200	David Nied	.05
201	Amando Reynoso	.05
202	Napoleon Robinson	.05
203	Boi Rodriguez	.05
204	Randy St. Claire	.05
205	Mark Wohlers	.05
206	Ricky Gutierrez	.05
207	Mike Lehman	.05
208	Richie Lewis	.05
209	Scott Meadows	.05
210	Mike Oquist	.05
211	Arthur Rhodes	.05
212	Ken Shamburg	.05
213	Todd Stephan	.05
214	Anthony Telford	.05
215	Jack Voight	.05
216	Bob Ayrault	.05
217	Toby Borland	.05
218	Braulio Castillo	.05
219	Darrin Chapin	.05
220	Bruce Dostal	.05
221	Tim Mauser	.05
222	Steve Scarsone	.05
223	Rick Schu	.05
224	Butch Davis	.05
225	Ray Giannelli	.05
226	Randy Knorr	.05
227	Al Leiter	.05
228	Doug Linton	.05
229	Domingo Martinez	.05
230	Tom Quinlan	.05
231	Jerry Schunk	.05
232	Ed Sprague	.05
233	David Weathers	.05
234	Eddie Zosky	.05
235	John Briscoe	.05
236	Kevin Campbell	.05
237	Jeff Carter	.05
238	Steve Chitren	.05
239	Reggie Harris	.05
240	Dann Howitt	.05
241	Troy Neel	.05
242	Gavin Osteen	.05
243	Tim Peek	.05
244	Todd Van Poppel	.05
245	Ron Witmeyer	.05
246	David Zancanaro	.05
247	Kevin Baez	.05
248	Jeromy Burnitz	.15
249	Chris Donnels	.05
250	D.J. Dozier	.05
251	Terrel Hansen	.05
252	Eric Hillman	.05
253	Pat Howell	.05
254	Lee May	.05
255	Pete Schourek	.05
256	David Telgheder	.05
257	Julio Valera	.05
258	Rico Brogna	.05
259	Steve Carter	.05
260	Steve Cummings	.05
261	Greg Gohr	.05
262	David Haas	.05
263	Shawn Hare	.05
264	Riccardo Ingram	.05
265	John Kiely	.05
266	Kurt Knudsen	.05
267	Victor Rosario	.05
268	Rich Rowland	.05
269	John DeSilva	.05
270	Gary Cooper	.05
271	Chris Gardner	.05
272	Jeff Juden	.05
273	Rob Mallicoat	.05
274	Andy Mota	.05
275	Shane Reynolds	.05
276	Mike Simms	.05
277	Scooter Tucker	.05
278	Brian Williams	.05
279	Rod Bolton	.05
280	Ron Coomer	.05
281	Chris Cron	.05
282	Ramon Garcia	.05
283	Chris Howard	.05
284	Roberto Hernandez	.05
285	Derek Lee	.05
286	Ever Magallanes	.05
287	Norberto Martin	.05
288	Greg Perechke	.05
289	Ron Stephens	.05
290	Derek Bell	.05
291	Rich Amaral	.05
292	Derek Bell	.05
293	Jim Olander	.05
294	Gil Heredia	.05
295	Rick Reed	.05
296	Amando Reynoso	.05
297	Charlotte, N.C.	.05
298	Ottawa, Ontario	.05
299	Pilot Field	.05
300	Harold Cooper Stadium	.05
301	Bush Stadium	.05
302	Silver Stadium	.05
303	Checklist Alpha 1	.05
304	Checklist Alpha 2	.05
305	Checklist Alpha 3	.05
306	Checklist Alpha 4	.05
307	Checklist Numeric 1	.05
308	Checklist Numeric 2	.05
309	Checklist Numeric 3	.05
310	Checklist Numeric 4	.05

1992 Upper Deck Minor League

For the first time in 1992, Upper Deck entered the minor league card market with a set of 330 base cards plus several inserts. The UD minor league cards are very similar in format to the company's 1992 major league issue, including UV-coating front and back and the use of color player photos on both sides. UD adopted a star-shaped foil hologram on back as an anti-counterfeiting device for its minor league issues.

	MT
Complete Set (330):	17.50
Common Player:	.05
Wax Pack (12):	1.00
Wax Box (36):	25.00

No.	Player	Price
1	Johnny Damon, Michael Tucker Draft Pick Checklist	.25
2	B.J. Wallace (Draft Pick)	.05
3	Jeffrey Hammonds (Draft Pick)	.05
4	Chad Mottola (Draft Pick)	.05
5	Derek Jeter (Draft Pick)	5.00
6	Michael Tucker (Draft Pick)	.05
7	Derek Wallace (Draft Pick)	.05
8	Chad McConnell (Draft Pick)	.05
9	Rick Greene (Draft Pick)	.05
10	Shannon Stewart (Draft Pick)	.40
11	Benji Grigsby (Draft Pick)	.05
12	Jamie Arnold (Draft Pick)	.05
13	Rick Helling (Draft Pick)	.05
14	Jason Kendall (Draft Pick)	.25
15	Eddie Pearson (Draft Pick)	.05
16	Todd Steverson (Draft Pick)	.05
17	John Burke (Draft Pick)	.05
18	Brandon Cromer (Draft Pick)	.05
19	Johnny Damon (Draft Pick)	.75
20	Jason Giambi (Draft Pick)	1.50
21	John Lynch (Draft Pick)	.05
22	Jared Baker (Draft Pick)	.05
23	Roger Bailey (Draft Pick)	.05
24	Eduardo Perez Angels Checklist	.05
25	Gary Mota Astros Checklist	.05
26	Mike Neill Athletics Checklist	.05
27	Howard Battle Blue Jays Checklist	.05
28	Mike Kelly Braves Checklist	.05
29	Tyrone Hill Brewers Checklist	.05
30	Dmitri Young Cardinals Checklist	.05
31	Ryan Hawblitzel Cubs Checklist	.05
32	Raul Mondesi Dodgers Checklist	.05
33	Rondell White Expos Checklist	.05
34	Salomon Torres Giants Checklist	.05
35	Manny Ramirez Indians Checklist	.50
36	Marc Newfield Mariners Checklist	.05
37	Butch Huskey Mets Checklist	.05
38	Mark Smith Orioles Checklist	.05
39	Joey Hamilton Padres Checklist	.05
40	Tyler Green Phillies Checklist	.05
41	Midre Cummings Pirates Checklist	.05
42	Kurt Miller Rangers Checklist	.05
43	Frank Rodriguez Red Sox Checklist	.05
44	John Roper Reds Checklist	.05
45	Phil Hiatt Royals Checklist	.05
46	Justin Thompson Tigers Checklist	.05
47	David McCarty Twins Checklist	.05
48	Mike Robertson White Sox Checklist	.05
49	Brien Taylor Yankees Checklist	.05
50	Carlos Delgado, Rondell White Diamond Skills Checklist	.15
51	Damon Buford (Diamond Skills)	.05
52	Mike Nell (Diamond Skills)	.05
53	Carlos Delgado (Diamond Skills)	.50
54	Frank Rodriguez (Diamond Skills)	.05
55	Manny Ramirez (Diamond Skills)	.75
56	Carl Everett (Diamond Skills)	.05
57	Brien Taylor (Diamond Skills)	.05
58	Kurt Miller (Diamond Skills)	.05
59	Alex Ochoa (Diamond Skills)	.05
60	Alex Gonzalez (Diamond Skills)	.05
61	Darrell Sherman (Diamond Skills)	.05
62	Dmitri Young (Diamond Skills)	.05
63	Cliff Floyd (Diamond Skills)	.05
64	Ray McDavid (Diamond Skills)	.05
65	Rondell White (Diamond Skills)	.05
66	Chipper Jones (Diamond Skills)	1.00
67	Allen Watson (Diamond Skills)	.05
68	Tyler Green (Diamond Skills)	.05
69	Steve Gibralter (Diamond Skills)	.05
70	Calvin Reese (Diamond Skills)	.05
71	Scott Burrell	.05
72	Julian Vasquez	.05

73 Juan Delarosa .05
74 Lance Dickson .05
75 Todd Van Poppel .05
76 Joey Hamilton .05
77 Mark Mimbs .05
78 Austin Manahan .05
79 Mike Milchin .05
80 David Bell .05
81 Terrell Lowery .05
82 Tony Tarasco .05
83 Shon Walker .05
84 Robb Nen .05
85 Turk Wendell .05
86 John Byington .05
87 Derek Reid .05
88 Lee Heath .05
89 Matt Anderson .05
90 Joe Perona .05
91 Tito Navarro .05
92 Scott Erwin .05
93 Jim Pittsley .05
94 Chris Seelbach .05
95 Skeets Thomas .05
96 Kevin Flora .05
97 Scott Pose .05
98 Jason Hardtke .05
99 Joe Ciccarella .05
100 Les Norman .05
101 Joe Calder .05
102 Willie Otanez .05
103 Ray Holbert .05
104 Dan Serafini .05
105 Trevor Hoffman .15
106 Todd Ritchie .05
107 Lance Jennings .05
108 Jon Farrell .05
109 Rick Gorecki .05
110 Kevin Stocker .05
111 Joe Caruso .05
112 Tom Nuneviller .05
113 Matt Mieske .05
114 Luis Ortiz .05
115 Marty Cordova .05
116 Rikkert Faneyte .05
117 Rodney Bolton .05
118 Steve Trachsel .05
119 Sean Lowe .05
120 Sean Ryan .05
121 Tim Vanegmond .05
122 Craig Paquette .05
123 Andre Keene .05
124 Kevin Roberson .05
125 Mark Anthony .05
126 Joe DeBerry .05
127 Tracy Sanders .05
128 Eric Christopherson .05
129 Steve Dreyer .05
130 Jeromy Burnitz .15
131 Mike Lansing .05
132 Russ Davis .05
133 Pedro Castellano .05
134 Troy Percival .05
135 Tyrone Hill .05
136 Rene Arocha .05
137 John DeSilva .05
138 Donnie Wall .05
139 Justin Mashore .05
140 Miguel Flores .05
141 John Finn .05
142 Paul Shuey .05
143 Gabby Martinez .05
144 Ryan Luzinski .05
145 Brent Gates .05
146 Manny Ramirez .75
147 Mark Hutton .05
148 Derek Lee .05
149 Marc Pisciotta .05
150 Greg Hansell .05
151 Tyler Houston .05
152 Chris Pritchett .05
153 Alan Watson .05
154 Steve Karsay .05
155 Carl Everett .15
156 Mike Robertson .05
157 Fausto Cruz .05
158 Kiki Hernandez .05
159 Bill Bliss .05
160 Todd Hollandsworth .05
161 Justin Thompson .05
162 Ozzie Timmons .05
163 Raul Mondesi .10
164 Shawn Estes .05
165 Chipper Jones 1.00
166 Kurt Miller .05
167 Tyler Green .05
168 Jimmy Haynes .05
169 David Doorneweerd .05
170 Bubba Smith .05
171 Scott Lydy .05
172 Aaron Holbert .05
173 Doug Glanville .05
174 Benji Gil .05
175 Eddie Williams .05
176 Phil Hiatt .05
177 Chris Durkin .05
178 Brian Barber .05
179 John Cummings .05
180 Frank Campos .05
181 Tim Worrell .05
182 Tony Clark .05
183 T.R. Lewis .05
184 Mike Lieberthal .10
185 Keith Mitchell .05
186 Rick Huisman .05
187 Quilvio Veras .05
188 Brian Hancock .05
189 Tarrik Brock .05
190 Herbert Perry .05
191 Dave Staton .05
192 Derek Lowe .10
193 Joel Wolfe .05
194 Lyle Mouton .05
195 Greg Gohr .05
196 Duane Singleton .05
197 Jamie McAndrew .05
198 Brad Pennington .05
199 Pork Chop Pough .05
200 Boo Moore .05
201 Henry Blanco .05
202 Gabe White .05
203 Manny Cora .05
204 Keith Gordon .05
205 John Jackson .05
206 Mike Hostetler .05
207 Jeff McCurry .05
208 Steve Olsen .05
209 Roberto Mejia .05
210 Ramon Caraballo .05
211 Matt Whisenant .05
212 Mike Bovee .05
213 Riccardo Ingram .05
214 Mike Rossiter .05
215 Andres Duncan .05
216 Steve Dunn .05
217 Mike Grace .05
218 Tim Howard .05
219 Todd Jones .05
220 Tyrone Kingwood .05
221 Damon Buford .05
222 Bobby Munoz .05
223 Jim Campanis .05
224 Johnny Ruffin .05
225 Shawn Green .50
226 Calvin Reese .10
227 Kevin McGehee .05
228 J.R. Phillips .05
229 Rafael Quirico .05
230 Mike Zimmerman .05
231 Ron Lockett .05
232 Bobby Reed .05
233 John Roper .05
234 John Mabry .05
235 Chris Martin .05
236 Ricky Otero .05
237 Orlando Miller .05
238 Scott Hatteberg .05
239 Toby Borland .05
240 Alan Newman .05
241 Ivan Cruz .05
242 Paul Byrd .05
243 Daryl Henderson .05
244 Adam Hyzdu .05
245 Rich Becker .05
246 Scott Ruffcorn .05
247 Tommy Adams .05
248 Jose Martinez .05
249 Darrell Sherman .05
250 Tom Nevers .05
251 Brandon Wilson .05
252 Mike Hampton .05
253 Mo Sanford .05
254 Alex Ochoa .05
255 David McCarty .05
256 Ray McDavid .05
257 Roger Salkeld .05
258 Jeff McNeely .05
259 Jim Converse .05
260 Greg Blosser .05
261 Salomon Torres .05
262 Tavo Alvarez .05
263 Marc Newfield .05
264 Carlos Delgado .50
265 Brien Taylor .05
266 Frank Rodriguez .05
267 Cliff Floyd .05
268 Troy O'Leary .05
269 Butch Huskey .05
270 Michael Carter .05
271 Eduardo Perez .05
272 Gary Mota .05
273 Mike Neill .05
274 Dmitri Young .05
275 Mike Kelly .05
276 Rondell White .05
277 Midre Cummings .05
278 Kerwin Moore .05
279 Derrick White .05
280 Howard Battle .05
281 Mark Smith .05
282 Ben Shelton .05
283 Jose Oliva .05
284 Steve Gibralter .05
285 Billy Hall .05
286 Nigel Wilson .05
287 Brook Fordyce .05
288 Mike Durrant .05
289 Gary Caraballo .05
290 Shane Andrews .05
291 Aaron Sele .10
292 Garret Anderson .10
293 Oscar Munoz .05
294 Bobby Jones .05
295 Joe Rosselli .05
296 Chad Ogea .05
297 Ugueth Urbina .05
298 Ryan Hawblitzel .05
299 Dennis Burlingame .05
300 Damon Mashore .05
301 Jeff Jackson .05
302 Glenn Murray .05
303 Darren Burton .05
304 Scott Cepicky .05
305 Phil Dauphin .05
306 Kevin Tatar .05
307 Domingo Jean .05
308 Darren Oliver .05
309 Joe Vitiello .05
310 John Johnstone .05
311 Bo Dodson .05
312 Jon Shave .05
313 Roberto Petagine .05
314 Clifton Garrett .05
315 Rob Butler .05
316 Jermaine Swinton .05
317 Alex Gonzalez .05
318 Jeff Williams .05
319 James Baldwin .05
320 Scott Stahoviak .05
321 John Cotton .05
322 Jim Wawruck .05
324 Brian Hunter .05
325 Joe Randa .05
326 Robert Eenhoorn .05
327 Rod Lofton .05
328 Buck McNabb .05
329 Jorge Fabregas .05
330 Brian Koelling .05

1992 Minor League Team Sets

While the number of minor league team sets issued in 1992 was much greater than the previous year, many of the small set makers left the field in favor of the Classic Best and Fleer/ProCards combines. New to the team set market was Skybox (tracing its roots back to TCMA) which issued team-set versions of its foil-pack AA and AAA cards.

MT

334 Team Sets and Variations
1992 SB AAA All-Stars (38) 12.00
1992 CB Albany Polecats (29) 6.00
1992 FPC Albany Polecats (27) 6.00
1992 FPC Albany Yankees (28) 4.00
1992 SB Albany Yankees (26) 7.00
1992 FPC Albuquerque Dukes (32) 20.00
1992 SB Albuquerque Dukes (26) 7.50
1992 Team Albuquerque Dukes Photos (49) 150.00
1992 CB Appleton Foxes (30) 4.00
1992 FPC Appleton Foxes (32) 3.00
1992 FPC Arkansas Travelers (27) 3.00
1992 FPC Arkansas Travelers W/Wendy's Ad (28) 6.00
1992 SB Arkansas Travelers (26) 4.00
1992 CB Asheville Tourists (30) 6.00
1992 CB Auburn Astros (29) 4.00
1992 FPC Auburn Astros (31) 4.00
1992 CB Augusta Pirates (27) 4.00
1992 FPC Augusta Pirates (29) 4.00
1992 Cal Bakersfield Dodgers (33) 35.00
1992 CB Baseball City Royals (27) 4.00
1992 FPC Baseball City Royals (27) 3.00
1992 CB Batavia Clippers (29) 4.00
1992 FPC Batavia Cilppers (32) 3.00
1992 CB Bellingham Mariners (29) 8.00
1992 FPC Bellingham Mariners (33) 5.00
1992 CB Beloit Brewers (30) 5.00
1992 FPC Beloit Brewers (29) 4.00
1992 CB Bend Rockies (28) 5.00
1992 FPC Bend Rockies (27) 6.00
1992 FPC Billings Mustangs (30) 4.00
1992 SP Billings Mustangs (30) 5.00
1992 SB Binghamton Mets (26) 8.00
1992 FPC Binghamton Mets (28) 4.00
1992 SB Birmingham Barons (26) 4.00
1992 FPC Birmingham Barons (28) 3.00
1992 CB Bluefield Orioles (25) 3.00
1992 FPC Bluefield Orioles (26) 3.00
1992 CB Boise Hawks (30) 4.00
1992 FPC Boise Hawks (33) 3.00
1992 CB Bristol Tigers (29) 4.00
1992 FPC Bristol Tigers (33) 3.00
1992 FPC Buffalo Bisons (27) 5.00
1992 SB Buffalo Bisons (26) 6.00
1992 CB Burlington Astros (29) 4.00
1992 FPC Burlington Astros (30) 3.00
1992 CB Burlington Indians (30) 4.00
1992 FPC Burlington Indians (32) 3.00
1992 SP Butte Copper Kings (30) 6.00
1992 FPC Calgary Cannons (22) 5.00
1992 SB Calgary Cannons (26) 7.00
1992 Cal League All-Stars (53) 5.00
1992 FPC Canton-Akron Indians (28) 6.00
1992 SB Canton-Akron Indians (26) 7.00
1992 FPC Carolina Mudcats (26) 3.00
1992 SB Carolina Mud Cats (26) 4.00
1992 CB Cedar Rapids Reds (30) 3.00
1992 FPC Cedar Rapids Reds (30) 3.00
1992 CB Charleston Rainbows (24) 5.00
1992 FPC Charleston Rainbows (28) 4.00
1992 CB Charleston Wheelers (24) 5.00
1992 FPC Charleston Wheelers (25) 4.00
1992 FPC Charlotte Knights (25) 6.00
1992 SB Charlotte Knights (26) 6.00
1992 CB Charlotte Rangers (29) 3.00
1992 FPC Charlotte Rangers (27) 3.00
1992 FPC Chattanooga Lookouts (27) 3.00
1992 SB Chattanooga Lookouts (26) 4.00
1992 CB Clearwater Phillies (26) 3.00
1992 FPC Clearwater Phillies (32) 3.00
1992 CB Clinton Giants (30) 4.00
1992 FPC Clinton Giants (29) 3.00
1992 FPC Colorado Springs Sky Sox (28) 3.00
1992 SB Colorado Springs Sky Sox (26) 4.00
1992 CB Columbia Mets (29) 4.00
1992 FPC Columbia Mets (26) 4.00
1992 Play II Columbia Mets (42) 20.00
1992 Play II Columbia Mets Inserts (9) 50.00
1992 FPC Columbus Clippers (28) 6.00
1992 Police Columbus Clippers (25) 7.50
1992 SB Columbus Clippers (26) 7.00
1992 CB Columbus Redstixx (29) 4.00
1992 FPC Columbus RedStixx (32) 4.00
1992 Team Columbus RedStixx (7) 6.00
1992 FPC Denver Zephyrs (28) 5.00
1992 Re/Max Denver Record Holders (20) 5.00
1992 SB Denver Zephyrs (26) 6.00
1992 CB Dunedin Blue Jays (30) 25.00
1992 FPC Dunedin Blue Jays (27) 8.00
1992 CB Durham Bulls (27) 20.00
1992 FPC Durham Bulls (28) 15.00
1992 Team Durham Bulls (29) 17.50
1992 FPC Edmonton Trappers (24) 7.00
1992 SB Edmonton Trappers (26) 6.00
1992 CB Elizabethton Twins (25) 4.00
1992 FPC Elizabethton Twins (28) 3.00
1992 CB Elmira Pioneers (26) 4.00
1992 FPC Elmira Pioneers (25) 3.00
1992 FPC El Paso Diablos (27) 3.00
1992 SB El Paso Diablos (26) 4.00
1992 CB Erie Sailors (30) 4.00
1992 FPC Erie Sailors (33) 3.00
1992 CB Eugene Emeralds (27) 5.00
1992 FPC Eugene Emeralds (30) 5.00
1992 CB Everett Giants (30) 5.00
1992 FPC Everett Giants (32) 4.00
1992 CB Fayetteville Generals (30) 4.00
1992 FPC Fayetteville Generals (29) 3.00
1992 CB Frederick Keys (28) 4.00
1992 FPC Frederick Keys (28) 3.00
1992 CB Ft. Lauderdale Yankees (25) 4.00
1992 FPC Ft. Lauderdale Yankees (31) 10.00
1992 Team Ft. Lauderdale Yankees (33) 7.00
1992 CB Ft. Myers Miracle (28) 4.00
1992 FPC Ft. Myers Miracle (27) 3.00
1992 CB Gastonia Rangers (27) 4.00
1992 FPC Gastonia Rangers (29) 3.00
1992 CB Geneva Cubs (29) 4.00
1992 FPC Geneva Cubs (28) 3.00
1992 SP Great Falls Dodgers (30) 5.00
1992 CB Greensboro Hornets (29) 10.00
1992 FPC Greensboro Hornets (30) 12.00
1992 FPC Greenville Braves (25) 6.00
1992 SB Greenville Braves (26) 7.00
1992 FPC Gulf Coast Dodgers (31) 3.00
1992 FPC Gulf Coast Mets (31) 5.00
1992 SP Gulf Coast Rangers (30) 5.00
1992 FPC Gulf Coast Yankees (30) 75.00
1992 FPC Hagerstown Suns (25) 4.00
1992 SB Hagerstown Suns (26) 5.00
1992 CB Hamilton Redbirds (30) 4.00
1992 FPC Hamilton Redbirds (32) 3.00
1992 FPC Harrisburg Senators (26) 4.00
1992 SB Harrisburg Senators (26) 5.00
1992 FPC Helena Brewers (27) 3.00
1992 SP Helena Brewers (27) 5.00
1992 CB High Desert Mavericks (30) 4.00
1992 Little Sun High School Prospects (30) 75.00
1992 CB Huntington Cubs (30) 4.00
1992 FPC Huntington Cubs (32) 3.00
1992 BK Huntsville Stars (26) 5.00
1992 SB Huntsville Stars (26) 5.00
1992 FPC Huntsville Stars (27) 6.00
1992 FPC Idaho Falls Gems (32) 3.00
1992 SP Idaho Falls Gems (29) 5.00
1992 FPC Indianapolis Indians (27) 4.00
1992 SB Indianapolis Indians (26) 5.00
1992 FPC Iowa Cubs (24) 3.00
1992 SB Iowa Cubs (26) 5.00
1992 FPC Jackson Generals (27) 3.00
1992 SB Jackson Generals (26) 4.00
1992 FPC Jacksonville Suns (26) 3.00
1992 SB Jacksonville Suns (26) 4.00
1992 CB Jamestown Expos (29) 4.00
1992 FPC Jamestown Expos (28) 3.00
1992 CB Johnson City Cardinals (28) 4.00
1992 FPC Johnson City Cardinals (31) 3.00
1992 CB Kane County Cougars (28) 5.00
1992 FPC Kane Couty Cougars (29) 4.00
1992 Team Kane County Cougars (30) 6.00
1992 CB Kenosha Twins (27) 7.50
1992 FPC Kenosha Twins (28) 5.00
1992 CB Kingsport Mets (26) 4.00
1992 FPC Kingsport Mets (31) 3.00
1992 CB Kinston Indians (29) 4.00
1992 FPC Kinston Indians (29) 20.00
1992 FPC Knoxville Blue Jays (29) 4.00
1992 SB Knoxville Blue Jays (26) 4.00
1992 CB Lakeland Tigers (30) 4.00
1992 FPC Lakeland Tigers (26) 3.00
1992 FPC Las Vegas Stars (24) 3.00
1992 SB Las Vegas Stars (26) 4.00
1992 SP Lethbridge Mounties (26) 5.00
1992 FPC London Tigers (29) 3.00
1992 SB London Tigers (26) 4.00
1992 FPC Louisville Redbirds (26) 3.00
1992 SB Louisville Redbirds (26) 4.00
1992 Team Louisville Redbirds (30) 8.00
1992 CB Lynchburg Red Sox (27) 5.00
1992 FPC Lynchburg Red Sox (26) 3.00
1992 CB Macon Braves (28) 4.00
1992 FPC Macon Braves (30) 3.00
1992 CB Madison Muskies (28) 4.00
1992 FPC Madison Muskies (29) 4.00
1992 CB Martinsville Phillies (30) 4.00
1992 FPC Martinsville Phillies (32) 3.00
1992 FPC Medicine Hat Blue Jays (24) 3.00
1992 SP Medicine Hat Blue Jays (30) 5.00
1992 FPC Memphis Chicks (29) 3.00
1992 SB Memphis Chicks (26) 4.00
1992 CB Miami Miracle (30) 4.00
1992 FPC Midland Angels (26) 6.00
1992 SB Midland Angels (26) 6.00
1992 1 Hour Midland Angels (28) 60.00
1992 Midwest League All-Stars (54) 7.50
1992 CB Modesto A's (27) 6.00
1992 Chong Modesto A's (26) 3.00
1992 FPC Modesto A's (22) 3.00
1992 CB Myrtle Beach Hurricanes (30) 5.00
1992 FPC Myrtle Beach Hurricanes (29) 7.00
1992 FPC Nashville Sounds (26) 5.00
1992 SB Nashville Sounds (26) 5.00
1992 Team Nashville Sounds (33) 7.00
1992 FPC New Britain Red Sox (27) 3.00
1992 SB New Britain Red Sox (26) 6.00
1992 CB Niagara Falls Rapids (29) 12.00
1992 FPC Niagara Falls Rapids (32) 10.00
1992 FPC Oklahoma City 89ers (28) 3.00
1992 SB Oklahoma City 89ers (26) 4.00
1992 FPC Omaha Royals (29) 4.00
1992 SB Omaha Royals (26) 5.00
1992 CB Oneonta Yankees (30) 4.00
1992 FPC Orlando Sunrays (26) 4.00
1992 SB Orlando Sunrays (26) 5.00
1992 CB Osceola Astros (29) 5.00
1992 FPC Osceola Astros (28) 4.00
1992 CB Palm Springs Angels (30) 6.00
1992 FPC Palm Springs Angels (29) 5.00
1992 DD Pawtucket Red Sox Foldout 50.00
1992 FPC Pawtucket Red Sox (28) 10.00
1992 Fram Pawtucket Red Sox Poster 35.00
1992 SB Pawtucket Red Sox (26) 5.00
1992 Team Peninsula Oilers (28) 6.00

1992 CB Peninsula Pilots (30) 5.00
1992 FPC Peninsula Pilots (28) 4.00
1992 CB Peoria Chiefs (30) 4.00
1992 Team Peoria Chiefs (31) 5.00
1992 FPC Phoenix Firebirds (26) 3.00
1992 SB Phoenix Firebirds (26) 6.00
1992 CB Pittsfield Mets (21) 9.00
1992 FPC Pittsfield Mets (28) 5.00
1992 FPC Portland Beavers (26) 3.00
1992 SB Portland Beavers (26) 4.00
1992 CB Princeton Reds (29) 4.00
1992 FPC Princeton Reds (29) 3.00
1992 CB Prince William Cannons (29) 4.00
1992 FPC Prince William Cannons (29) 3.00
1992 CB Pulaski Braves (29) 4.00
1992 FPC Pulaski Braves (32) 3.00
1992 CB Quad City Bandits (30) 4.00
1992 FPC Quad City Bandits (30) 3.00
1992 FPC Reading Phillies (29) 4.00
1992 FPC Reading Phillies Police (29) 7.50
1992 Penn-Lyn Studio Reading Phillies (24) 75.00
1992 SB Reading Phillies (26) 15.00
1992 Cal Reno Silver Sox (29) 3.00
1992 Bleacher Bums Richmond Braves (25) 10.00
1992 Bob's Richmond Braves (26): 60.00
1992 FPC Richmond Braves (28): 6.00
1992 Richmond Comix Richmond Braves (26) 15.00
1992 SB Richmond Braves (26) 6.00
1992 Ukrop's Richmond Braves (50) 25.00
1992 FPC Rochester Red Wings (26) 4.00
1992 SB Rochester Red Wings (26) 5.00
1992 CB Rockford Expos (30) 4.00
1992 FPC Rockford Expos (32) 4.00
1992 CB Salem Buccaneers (28) 4.00
1992 FPC Salem Buccaneers (28) 3.00
1992 CB Salinas Spurs (30) 4.00
1992 FPC Salinas Spurs (31) 3.00
1992 SP Salt Lake City Trappers (30) 5.00
1992 FPC San Antonio Missions (24) 8.00
1992 HEB San Antonio Missions (44) 60.00
1992 SB San Antonio Missions (26) 11.00
1992 CB San Bernardino Spirit (30) 4.00
1992 FPC San Bernardino Spirit (33) 3.00
1992 CB San Jose Giants (30) 5.00
1992 CB Sarasota White Sox (30) 6.00
1992 FPC Sarasota White Sox (30) 5.00
1992 CB Savannah Cardinals (25) 4.00
1992 FPC Savannah Cardinals (30) 3.00
1992 FPC Scranton Red Barons (27) 5.00
1992 SB Scranton Red Barons (26) 5.00
1992 Team Scranton Red Barons (30) 10.00
1992 FPC Shreveport Captains (27) 3.00
1992 SB Shreveport Captains (26) 4.00
1992 Play II South Atlantic League A-S (42) 15.00
1992 CB South Bend White Sox (27) 4.00
1992 FPC South Bend White Sox (30) 4.00
1992 CB Southern Oregon A's (30) 4.00
1992 FPC Southern Oregon A's (33) 6.00
1992 CB Spartanburg Phillies (25) 3.00
1992 FPC Spartanburg Phillies (29) 3.00
1992 CB Spokane Indians (30) 4.00
1992 FPC Spokane Indians (30) 4.00
1992 CB Springfield Cardinals (29) 4.00
1992 FPC Springfield Cardinals (29) 3.00
1992 CB St. Catharines Blue Jays (30) 4.00
1992 FPC St. Catharines Blue Jays (29) 5.00
1992 CB St. Lucie Mets (29) 5.00
1992 FPC St. Lucie Mets (30) 4.00
1992 CB St. Petersburg Cardinals (29) 4.00
1992 FPC St. Petersburg Cardinals (26) 4.00
1992 CB Stockton Ports (25) 4.00
1992 FPC Stockton Ports (28) 3.00
1992 FPC Syracuse Chiefs (31) 5.00
1992 MB Syracuse Chiefs Foldout 16.00
1992 SB Syracuse Chiefs (26) 8.00
1992 Tallmadge Syracuse Chiefs Foldout 15.00
1992 FPC Tacoma Tigers (26) 4.00
1992 SB Tacoma Tigers (26) 6.00
1992 FPC Tidewater Tides (28) 5.00
1992 SB Tidewater Tides (26) 6.00
1992 FPC Toledo Mud Hens (29) 4.00
1992 SB Toledo Mud Hens (26) 5.00
1992 FPC Tucson Toros (30) 4.00
1992 SB Tucson Toros (26) 5.00
1992 FPC Tulsa Drillers (27) 4.00
1992 FPC Tulsa Drillers W/BBC Stores Ad (28) 8.00
1992 SB Tulsa Drillers (26) 5.00
1992 Team Tulsa Drillers (30) 8.00
1992 CB Utica Blue Sox (26) 10.00
1992 FPC Vancouver Canadians (24) 3.00
1992 SB Vancouver Canadians (26) 4.00
1992 CB Vero Beach Dodgers (30) 4.00
1992 FPC Vero Beach Dodgers (32) 3.00
1992 CB Visalia Oaks (26) 5.00
1992 FPC Visalia Oaks (28) 6.00
1992 CB Waterloo Diamonds (30) 4.00
1992 FPC Waterloo Diamonds (27) 3.00
1992 CB Watertown Indians (29) 4.00
1992 FPC Watertown Indians (29) 3.00
1992 CB Welland Pirates (29) 4.00
1992 FPC Welland Pirates (30) 3.00
1992 CB West Palm Beach Expos (30) 7.00
1992 FPC West Palm Beach Expos (29) 6.00
1992 FPC Wichita Wranglers (21) 4.00
1992 SB Wichita Wranglers (26) 5.00
1992 CB Winston-Salem Spirits (28) 4.00
1992 FPC Winston-Salem Spirits (28) 6.00
1992 Team Winston-Salem Spirits (27) 4.00
1992 CB Winter Haven Red Sox (30) 4.00
1992 FPC Winter Haven Red Sox (30) 4.00
1992 CB Yakima Bears (26) 4.00
1992 FPC Yakima Bears (32) 3.00

1993 Classic Best

Classic Best's 1993 Minor League series is 300 cards, plus four insert sets, a puzzle set and autographed cards from eight players. The set includes players from A, AA and AAA classifications. Autographed Carlos Delgado, Cliff Floyd, Jeffrey Hammonds, Derek Jeter, Mike Kelly, Phil Nevin, Paul Shuey and Dmitri Young cards (1,200 each) were randomly inserted into packs, as were puzzle contest pieces. By completing a nine-card puzzle, 500 collectors could win a plaque of the eight autographed cards featured in the series. The set's inserts are: Young Guns, Expansion #1 Picks, MVPs and Player and Manager of the Year.

		MT
Complete Set (300):		9.00
Common Player:		.05
Wax Pack (12):		.60
Wax Box (36):		12.50
1	Paul Shuey	.05
2	Brad Clontz	.05
3	Phil Dauphin	.05
4	Kevin Flora	.05
5	Doug Glanville	.05
6	Hilly Hathaway	.05
7	Scott Hatteberg	.05
8	Ryan Hawblitzel	.05
9	Bob Henkel	.05
10	Mike Kelly	.05
11	Jose Malave	.05
12	Jeff McNeely	.05
13	Roberto Mejia	.05
14	Kevin Roberson	.05
15	Chad Roper	.05
16	John Roper	.05
17	Pete Rose Jr.	.25
18	Paul Russo	.05
19	John Salles	.05
20	Tracy Sanders	.05
21	Chris Saunders	.05
22	Jason Schmidt	.05
23	Aaron Sele	.10
24	Bob Abreu	.25
25	Don Sparks	.05
26	Scott Stahoviak	.05
27	Matt Stairs	.05
28	Todd Steverson	.05
29	Ozzie Timmons	.05
30	Michael Tucker	.05
31	Jose Viera	.05
32	B.J. Wallace	.05
33	Mark Wohlers	.05
34	Gabe White	.05
35	Rick White	.05
36	Rondell White	.05
37	Gerald Williams	.05
38	Mike Williams	.05
39	Todd Williams	.05
40	Desi Wilson	.05
41	Johnny Ard	.05
42	Jamie Arnold	.05
43	Howard Battle	.05
44	Greg Blosser	.05
45	Rob Butler	.05
46	Dan Carlson	.05
47	Joe Caruso	.05
48	Bobby Chouinard	.05
49	Adell Davenport	.05
50	Juan De La Rosa	.05
51	Alex Gonzalez	.05
52	Steve Hosey	.05
53	Rick Krivda	.05
54	T.R. Lewis	.05
55	Jose Mercedes	.05
56	Melvin Nieves	.05
57	Luis Ortiz	.05
58	Joe Rosselli	.05
59	Brian Sackinsky	.05
60	Salomon Torres	.05
61	James Baldwin	.05
62	Travis Baptist	.05
63	Bret Boone	.50
64	Mike Buddie	.05
65	Paul Carey	.05
66	Tim Crabtree	.05
67	Tony Longmire	.05
68	Robert Eenhoorn	.05
69	Paul Ellis	.05
70	Shawn Estes	.05
71	Andy Fox	.05
72	Shawn Green (Photo actually Alex Gonzalez.)	.50
73	Jimmy Haynes	.05
74	Sterling Hitchcock	.05
75	Mark Hutton	.05
76	Domingo Jean	.05
77	Kevin Jordan	.05
78	Steve Karsay	.05
79	Paul Fletcher	.05
80	Mike Milchin	.05
81	Lyle Mouton	.05
82	Bobby Munoz	.05
83	Alex Ochoa	.05
84	Steve Olsen	.05
85	Billy Owens	.05
86	Eddie Pearson	.05
87	Mike Robertson	.05
88	Johnny Ruffin	.05
89	Mark Smith	.05
90	Brandon Wilson	.05
91	Derek Jeter	3.00
92	Edgardo Alfonzo	.05
93	Jeff Alkire	.05
94	Roger Bailey	.05
95	Jeff Barry	.05
96	Terrell Buckley	.05
97	Hector Carrasco	.05
98	Danny Clyburn	.05
99	Darren Burton	.05
100	Scott Eyre	.05
101	Chad Fox	.05
102	Joe Hudson	.05
103	Jason Hutchins	.05
104	Bobby Jones	.05
105	Jason Kendall	.25
106	Rickey Magdaleno	.05
107	Buck McNabb	.05
108	Doug Mlicki	.05
109	Chris Eddy	.05
110	Jon Lieber	.05
111	Ken Powell	.05
112	Todd Pridy	.05
113	Marquis Riley	.05
114	Steve Rodriguez	.05
115	Brian Rupp	.05
116	Yuri Sanchez	.05
117	Al Shirley	.05
118	Paul Spoljaric	.05
119	Amaury Telemaco	.05
120	Shon Walker	.05
121	Tavo Alvarez	.05
122	Shane Andrews	.05
123	Billy Ashley	.05
124	Brian Barber	.05
125	Trey Beamon	.05
126	Scott Bryant	.05
127	Scott Bullett	.05
128	Ozzie Canseco	.05
129	Brian Carpenter	.05
130	Roger Cedeno (Photos actually Dan Melendez.)	.05
131	Randy Curtis	.05
132	Alberto De Los Santos	.05
133	Steve Dixon	.05
134	Joey Eischen	.05
135	Brook Fordyce	.05
136	Rick Gorecki	.05
137	Lee Hancock	.05
138	Todd Hollandsworth	.05
139	Frank Jacobs	.05
140	Mark Johnson	.05
141	Albie Lopez	.05
142	Dan Malendez	.05
143	William Pennyfeather	.05
144	Scott Lydy	.05
145	Chris Snopek	.05
146	Quilvio Veras	.05
147	Jose Vidro	.10
148	Allen Watson	.05
149	Matt Whisenant	.05
150	Craig Wilson	.05
151	Rich Becker	.05
152	Mike Durant	.05
153	Brad Ausmus	.05
154	Robbie Beckett	.05
155	Steve Dunn	.05
156	Paul Byrd	.05
157	Jason Bere	.05
158	Ben Blomdahl	.05
159	John Brothers	.05
160	Tim Costo	.05
161	Joel Chimelis	.05
162	Kenny Carlyle	.05
163	Garvin Alston	.05
164	Sean Bergman	.05
165	Marshall Boze	.05
166	Terry Burrows	.05
167	Danny Bautista	.05
168	Jason Bates	.05
169	Brent Bowers	.05
170	Rico Brogna	.05
171	Armann Brown	.05
172	Brant Brown	.05
173	Julio Bruno	.05
174	Mike DeJean	.05
175	Nick Delvecchio	.05
176	Bobby Bonds Jr.	.05
177	Miguel Castellano	.05
178	Tommy Adams	.05
179	Alan Burke	.05
180	John Burke	.06
181	Ivan Cruz	.05
182	Johnny Damon	1.00
183	Carl Everett	.10
184	Jorge Fabregas	.05
185	John Fantauzzi	.05
186	Mike Farmer	.05
187	Mike Farrell	.05
188	Omar Garcia	.05
189	Brent Gates	.05
190	Jason Giambi	1.00
191	K.C. Gullum	.05
192	Chris Gomez	.05
193	Ricky Greene	.05
194	Willie Greene	.05
195	Benji Grigsby	.05
196	Mike Groppuso	.05
197	Johnny Guzman	.05
198	Bob Hamelin	.05
199	Joey Hamilton	.05
200	Chris Haney	.05
201	Donald Harris	.05
202	Andy Hartung	.05
203	Chris Hatcher	.05
204	Rick Helling	.05
205	Edgar Herrera	.05
206	Aaron Holbert	.05
207	Ray Holbert	.05
208	Tyler Houston	.05
209	Brian Hunter	.05
210	Miguel Jiminez	.05
211	Charles Johnson	.05
212	Corey Kapano	.05
213	Tom Knauss	.05
214	Brian Koelling	.05
215	Brian Lane	.05
216	Kevin Legault	.05
217	Mark Lewis	.05
218	Luis Lopez	.05
219	Jose Martinez	.05
220	Mitch Meluskey	.05
221	Casey Mendenhall	.05
222	Danny Mitchell	.05
223	Tony Mitchell	.05
224	Ritchie Moody	.05
225	James Mouton	.05
226	Steve Murphy	.05
227	Mike Neill	.05
228	Tom Nevers	.05
229	Alan Newman	.05
230	Tom Nuneviller	.05
231	Jonathan Nunnally	.05
232	Chad Ogea	.05
233	Ray Ortiz	.05
234	Orlando Palmeiro	.05
235	Craig Paquette	.05
236	Troy Percival	.05
237	Bobby Perna	.05
238	John Pricher	.05
239	Ken Ramos	.05
240	Joe Randa	.05
241	Ron Blazier	.05
242	Terry Bradshaw	.05
243	Jason Hisey	.05
244	Sean Lowe	.05
245	Chad McConnell	.05
246	Jackie Nickell	.05
247	Pat Rapp	.05
248	Calvin Reese	.10
249	Desi Relaford	.05
250	Troy Ricker	.05
251	Todd Ritchie	.05
252	Chris Roberts	.05
253	Scott Sanders	.05
254	Ruben Santana	.05
255	Chris Seelbach	.05
256	Dan Serafini	.05
257	Curtis Shaw	.05
258	Kennie Steenstra	.05
259	Kevin Stocker	.05
260	Tanyon Sturtze	.05
261	Tim Stutheit	.05
262	Jamie Taylor	.05
263	Chad Townsend	.05
264	Steve Trachsel	.05
265	Jose Valentin	.05
266	K.C. Waller	.05
267	Chris Weinke	.25
268	Darrell Whitmore	.05
269	Juan Williams	.05
270	Tim Worrell	.05
271	Tim Belk	.05
272	London Bradley	.05
273	Tilson Brito	.05
274	Felipe Crespo	.05
275	Kenny Felder	.05
276	Billy Hall	.05
277	Terrell Hansen	.05
278	Rod Henderson	.05
279	Bobby Holley	.05
280	Bobby Hughes	.05
281	Rick Huisman	.05
282	Jack Johnson	.05
283	Gabby Martinez	.05
284	Jose Millares	.05
285	Jason Moler	.05
286	Willie Mota	.05
287	Marty Neff	.05
288	Eric Owens	.05
289	Daryl Ratliff	.05
290	Ozzie Sanchez	.05
291	Dave Silvestri	.05
292	Chris Stynes	.05
293	Aubrey Waggoner	.05
294	Jimmy White	.05
295	Jim Campanis	.05
296	Tony Womack	.05
297	Checklist 1	.05
298	Checklist 2	.05
299	Checklist 3	.05
300	Checklist 4	.05

1993 Classic Best Young Guns

These 28 foil-printed cards were randomly inserted into Classic Best's 1993 foil packs. The cards are numbered with a YG prefix.

		MT
Complete Set (28):		7.50
Common Player:		.10
1	Midre Cummings	.10
2	Carlos Delgado	1.50
3	Cliff Floyd	.25
4	Jeffrey Hammonds	.10
5	Tyrone Hill	.10
6	Butch Huskey	.10
7	Chipper Jones	3.00
8	Mike Lieberthal	.25
9	David McCarty	.10
10	Ray McDavid	.10
11	Kurt Miller	.10
12	Raul Mondesi	.15
13	Chad Mottola	.10
14	Calvin Murray	.10
15	Phil Nevin	.15
16	Marc Newfield	.10
17	Eduardo Perez	.10
18	Manny Ramirez	2.00
19	Edgar Renteria	.25
20	Frank Rodriguez	.10
21	Scott Ruffcorn	.10
22	Brien Taylor	.10
23	Justin Thompson	.10
24	Mark Thompson	.10
25	Todd Van Poppel	.10
26	Joe Vitiello	.10
27	Derek Wallace	.10
28	Dmitri Young	.10

1993 Classic Best Gold

The 1993 Classic Best Minor League Baseball Gold Premiere Edition cards feature three color photos of each player and are foil-stamped on both sides. Each card is color-coded using team colors and includes statistics through the 1992 season. The set includes 216 players from Double A, Single A and Rookie leagues, plus randomly inserted autographed cards of Barry Bonds and Gary Sheffield. No factory sets or jumbo packs were produced; cards are limited to 6,000 sequentially-numbered 10-box cases.

		MT
Complete Set (220):		10.00
Common Player:		.05
Wax Pack (10):		.50
Wax Box (36):		9.00
Barry Bonds Autograph:		75.00
Gary Sheffield Autograph:		10.00
1	Barry Bonds	4.00
2	Mark Hutton	.05
3	Lyle Mouton	.05
4	Don Sparks	.05
5	Joe Randa	.05
6	Dave Mlicki	.05
7	Ken Ramos	.05
8	Bill Wertz	.05
9	Jon Shave	.05
10	Dan Smith	.05
11	William Canate	.05
12	Albie Lopez	.05
13	Rod McCall	.05
14	Paul Shuey	.05
15	Ian Doyle	.05
16	Marc Marini	.05
17	Brien Taylor	.05
18	Mike Kelly	.05
19	Andy Nezelek	.05
20	Marcos Armas	.05
21	Chad Ogea	.05
22	Frank Rodriguez	.05
23	Aaron Sele	.10
24	Tim Vanegmond	.05
25	Phil Hiatt	.05
26	Dan Rohrmeir (Rohrmeier)	.05
27	Greg Blosser	.05
28	Scott Hatteberg	.05
29	Ed Riley	.05
30	Edgar Alfonzo	.05
31	Jorge Fabregas	.05
32	Eduardo Perez	.05
33	John Cummings	.05
34	Bubba Smith	.05
35	Kevin Jordan	.05
36	Tyler Green	.05
37	Heath Haynes	.05
38	Gabe White	.05
39	Doug Glanville	.05
40	Jose Viera	.05
41	Richie Becker	.05
42	Marty Cordova	.05
43	Mike Durant	.05
44	Todd Ritchie	.05
45	Scott Stahoviak	.05
46	Tavo Alvarez	.05
47	Chris Malinoski	.05
48	Rondell White	.05
49	Tim Worrell	.05
50	Benji Gil	.05
51	Ben Blomdahl	.05
52	Rich Kelley	.05
53	Justin Thompson	.05
54	Scott Pose	.05
55	John Roper	.05
56	Rafael Chaves	.05
57	Billy Hall	.05
58	Ray McDavid	.05
59	Mark Smith	.05
60	Jeff Williams	.05
61	Bobby Jones	.05
62	Stanton Cameron	.05
63	Mike Lumley	.05
64	Troy Buckley	.05
65	James Dougherty	.05
66	Chris Hill	.05
67	Tom Nevers	.05
68	Joe Rosselli	.05
69	Steve Whitaker	.05
70	Butch Huskey	.05
71	Shane Andrews	.05
72	Cliff Floyd	.05
73	Alex Ochoa	.05
74	Brent Gates	.05
75	Curtis Shaw	.05
76	Midre Cummings	.05
77	Steve Olsen	.05
78	Mike Robertson	.05

79 Scott Ruffcorn .05
80 Brandon Wilson .05
81 Darren Burton .05
82 Kerwin Moore .05
83 Joe Vitiello .05
84 Hugh Walker .05
85 Howard Battle .05
86 Rob Butler .05
87 Carlos Delgado 1.50
88 Jeff Ware .05
89 Mike Hostetler .05
90 Brian Kowitz .05
91 Ryan Hawblitzel .05
92 Juan De La Rosa .05
93 David McCarty .05
94 Paul Russo .05
95 Dan Cholowsky .05
96 Dmitri Young .05
97 Paul Ellis .05
98 Jay Kirkpatrick .05
99 Jeff Jackson .05
100 Duane Singleton .05
101 Kiki Hernandez .05
102 Raul Hernandez .05
103 Brian Bevil .05
104 Mark Johnson .05
105 Bob Abreu .25
106 Gary Mota .05
107 Jose Cabrera .05
108 Jeff Runion .05
109 B.J. Wallace .05
110 Jim Arnold .05
111 Dwight Maness .05
112 Fernando DaSilva .05
113 Chris Burr .05
114 Dan Serafini .05
115 Derek Jeter 4.00
116 Lew Hill .05
117 Andy Pettitte 1.00
118 Keith John .05
119 Sean Lowe .05
120 T.J. Mathews .05
121 Ricardo Medina .05
122 Scott Gentile .05
123 Everett Stull .05
124 Manny Ramirez 2.00
125 Archie Corbin .05
126 Matt Karchner .05
127 Domingo Mota .05
128 Alex Gonzalez .05
129 Joe Lis .05
130 Paul Spoljaric .05
131 Clifton Garrett .05
132 Marc Hill .05
133 Jesus Martinez .05
134 Salomon Torres .05
135 Tommy Eason .05
136 Matt Whisenant .05
137 Jon Zuber .05
138 Luis Martinez .05
139 Glenn Murray .05
140 John Saffer .05
141 Tommy Adams .05
142 Manny Cervantes .05
143 George Glinatsis .05
144 Chris Dessellier .05
145 Joe Pomierski .05
146 John Vanhof .05
147 Matt Williams .05
148 Maurice Christmas .05
149 Damon Hollins .05
150 Sean Smith .05
151 Doug Hecker .05
152 Jamie Sepeda .05
153 Steve Solomon .05
154 Jeff Tabaka .05
155 Greg Elliott .05
156 Jim Waring .05
157 Omar Garcia .05
158 Ricky Otero .05
159 Jami Brewington .05
160 Chad Fonville .05
161 Sean Runyan .05
162 Jim Givens .05
163 Dennis McNamara .05
164 Rudy Pemberton .05
165 Brian Raabe .05
166 Jeffrey Hammonds .05
167 Chris Hatcher .05
168 Chris Saunders .05
169 Aaron Fultz .05
170 Mike Freitas .05
171 Tim Adkins .05
172 Chipper Jones 2.50
173 Brandon Cromer .05
174 Shannon Stewart .25
175 David Tollison .05
176 Rob Adkins .05
177 Todd Steverson .05
178 Dennis Konuszewski .05
179 Marty Neff .05
180 Vernon Spearman .05
181 Don Wengert .05
182 Alan Battle .05
183 Michael Moore .05
184 Sherard Clinkscales .05
185 Jamie Dismuke .05
186 Tucker Hammargren .05
187 John Hrusovsky .05
188 Elliott Quinones .05
189 Calvin Reese .10
190 Rich Ireland .05
191 Shawn Estes .05
192 Greg Shockey .05
193 Mike Zimmerman .05
194 Danny Clyburn .05
195 Jason Kendall .25
196 Shon Walker .05
197 Gary Wilson .05
198 John Dillinger .05
199 Jim Keefe .05
200 Eddie Pearson .05
201 Johnny Damon 1.00
202 Jim Pittsley .05
203 Jason Bere .05
204 James Baldwin .05
205 John Burke .05
206 Scot Sealy .05
207 Ken Carlyle .05
208 Tim Crabtree .05
209 Quilvio Veras .05
210 Edgardo Alfonzo .05
211 Adell Davenport .05
212 Dan Frye .05
213 Derek Lowe .10
214 Steve Gibralter .05
215 Troy O'Leary .05
216 Gary Sheffield .50
217 Checklist 1-55 .05
218 Checklist 56-110 .05
219 Checklist 111-165 .05
220 Checklist 166-220 .05

1993 Classic Best/Fisher Nuts Stars of the Future

Nineteen projected stars of the future were included in this set produced by Classic Best as a promotion for Fisher Nuts. Cards are similar in format to regular-issue Classic Best cards of 1992, but feature Fisher Nuts advertising on front and back.

MT
Complete Set (20): 4.00
Common Player: .10
1 Joe Vitiello .10
2 Steve Gibralter .10
3 Rob Butler .10
4 Carlos Delgado 1.00
5 Chipper Jones 2.00
6 Mike Kelly .10
7 Marc Newfield .10
8 Aaron Sele .15
9 Brent Gates .10
10 Eduardo Perez .10
11 Mike Lieberthal .15
12 Midre Cummings .10
13 Dmitri Young .10
14 Brien Taylor .10
15 David McCarty .10
16 Scott Ruffcorn .10
17 Cliff Floyd .10
18 Rondell White .10
19 Paul Shuey .10
--- Checklist .03

1993 Classic 4 Sport

Fifty top players from the 1993 draft are featured among their counterparts in the other team sports in the base set, parallels and inserts of the '93 4 Sport issue. Only the baseball players are listed here.

MT
Complete (Baseball) Set (50): 3.00
Common Player: .05
Wax Pack (12): .60
Wax Box (36): 15.00
260 Alex Rodriguez 3.00
PR4 Alex Rodriguez (Promo card.) 3.00
261 Darren Dreifort .05
262 Matt Brunson .05
263 Matt Drews .05
264 Wayne Gomes .05
265 Jeff Granger .05
266 Steve Soderstrom .05
267 Brooks Kieschnick .05
268 Daron Kirkreit .05
269 Billy Wagner .25
270 Alan Benes .05
271 Scott Christman .05
272 Willie Adams .05
273 Jermaine Allensworth .05
274 Jason Baker .05
275 Brian Banks .05
276 Marc Barcelo .05
277 Jeff D'Amico .05
278 Todd Dunn .05
279 Dan Ehler .05
280 Tony Fuduric .05
281 Ryan Hancock .05
282 Vee Hightower .05
283 Andre King .05
284 Brett King .05
285 Derrek Lee 2.00
286 Andrew Lorraine .05
287 Eric Ludwick .05
288 Ryan McGuire .05
289 Anthony Medrano .05
290 Joel Moore .05
291 Dan Perkins .05
292 Kevin Pickford .05
293 Jon Ratliff .05
294 Bryan Rekar .05
295 Andy Rice .05
296 Carl Schulz .05
297 Chris Singleton .05
298 Cameron Smith .05
299 Marc Valdes .05
300 Joe Wagner .05
301 John Wasdin .05
302 Pat Watkins .05
303 Dax Winslett .05
304 Jamey Wright .05
305 Kelly Wunsch .05
306 Jeff D'Amico .05
307 Brian Anderson .05
308 Trot Nixon .45
309 Kirk Presley .05

Gold

Fifty top baseball players from the 1993 draft are featured among their counterparts in the other major team sports in this factory set of gold edition parallel cards. Each set contains autographed cards of Alex Rodriguez, Jerome Bettis, Chris Gratton and Alonzo Mourning. Only the baseball players are listed here.

MT
Complete Boxed Set (329): 150.00
Baseball Set (50): 15.00
Common Player: .25
Gold Stars: 5X
Alex Rodriguez (Autographed edition of 3,900.) 110.00

Alex Rodriguez Jumbo

This 3-1/2" x 5" version of A-Rod's card from the Classic 4 Sport set was issued in two versions. One version (#260) was issued in a special boxed set of jumbo cards. The other (#3 of 5) was issued in a serially numbered edition of 8,000, though the manner of distribution is unclear.

MT
260 Alex Rodriguez 6.00
3 of 5 Alex Rodriguez 6.00

Autographs

Authentically autographed versions of 26 of the players in the Classic 4 Sport set were produced as random pack inserts. Card fronts share the basic format of the regular version, but have the player signature as well as a serial number from within the edition stated parenthetically in the checklist here. Backs have a congratulatory message. Only the five baseball players from the set are listed here, arranged according to their numbers in the regular set.

MT
Common Player: 4.00
(260) Alex Rodriguez (4,300) 90.00
(261) Darren Dreifort (3,875) 4.00
(265) Jeff Granger (150) 4.00
(267) Brooks Kieschnick (450) 4.00
(268) Daron Kirkreit (275) 4.00

Draft Stars

Top draft picks in all four major team sports are featured in this chrome-technology insert set, found one per jumbo pack of Classic 4 Sport. The cards feature action photos on a silver-metallic background with gold-foil graphics. At lower-left on each card is a notice that it is one of 80,000. Conventionally printed backs have another photo, personal data and career highlight. Only the baseball players are listed here.

MT
Common Player: .50
DS55 Alex Rodriguez 3.50
DS56 Brooks Kieschnick .50
DS57 Jeff Granger .50

Inserts

A number of baseball players were featured among the draft picks of the major team sports in the many insert series of the '93 Classic 4 Sport issue. Only the baseball players are listed here.

MT
TRI-CARDS
3/8/13 Jeff Granger, Brooks Kieschnick, Alex Rodriguez 6.00
5/10/15 Drew Bledsoe, Chris Webber, Alex Rodriguez 4.00
LIMITED PRINT
LP18 Alex Rodriguez 4.00
LP19 Darren Dreifort 1.00
LP20 Jeff Granger 1.00
LP21 Brooks Kieschnick 1.00
ACETATES
9 Alex Rodriguez 6.00
10 Jeff Granger 1.00

McDonald's

These 4 Sport "Exclusive Collection" cards were distributed in portions of the Mid-Atlantic states and central Florida at McDonald's. Besides established stars and prospects in each of the major team sports, the five-card packs contained random LP (Limited Production) inserts, autographs and redemption cards for autographed memorabilia. Cards have action photos bordered at right by a forest green strip with the player name and position in gold-foil. A special logo is at upper-right. Backs repeat a portion of the photo along with personal data, stats and career highlights. A gold-foil McDonald's arches logo is at bottom. Only the baseball players among the 35 cards are listed here.

MT
Common Player: .25
11 Darren Daulton .45
26 Greg Luzinski, Ryan Luzinski Bull and Baby Bull .45
31 Chad McConnell .25
32 Phil Nevin .25
33 Paul Shuey .25
34 Derek Wallace .25

1993 Classic Collectors Club (C3)

This multi-sport set was available as part of a benefits package to members of the Classic Collectors Club. Regular charter memberships were limited to 20,000 with presidential charter memberships limited to 5,000. Regular-version cards have action photos on front with dark blue borders and a gold-foil "C3" logo. Horizontal backs have a portrait photo, stats and biography. Only the baseball players from the set are listed here.

MT
Complete Set (30): 5.00
Common Player: .25
1 Phil Nevin .25
2 Jeffrey Hammonds .25
3 Paul Shuey .25
4 Derek Jeter 4.50
5 B.J. Wallace .25
6 Ryan Luzinski .25
7 Brien Taylor .25
25 David McCarty .25
26 Mike Kelly .25
27 Dmitri Young .25

Presidential

As part of the Presidential level membership in the Classic Collectors Club, these cards were distributed in an edition of 5,000 each. Fronts have an action photo with a gold-foil "C3 Presidential" logo at top and player identification in the wide white border at right. Backs have another photo and a few sentences about the player.

MT
3 Alex Rodriguez 12.00

1993-94 Fleer Excel

Fleer's 1993-94 minor league set features players who have never appeared in a Major League game. The set of 300, up from 250 cards the previous year, uses UV coating for card fronts and backs, plus gold-foil stamping on the fronts. There are 297 players included in the regular issue, plus three checklists. Players are arranged alphabetically within their major league organization and league. Three insert sets were also available: Minor League All-Stars, League Leaders and "First Year Phenoms." Cards from the three insert sets were randomly included in foil packs.

MT
Complete Set (300): 12.50
Common Player: .05
Wax Box (36): 20.00
Jumbo Pack (17): 1.50
Jumbo Box (20): 20.00
1 Armando Benitez .05
2 Stanton Cameron .05
3 Eric Chavez 1.00
4 Rick Forney .05
5 Jim Foster .05
6 Curtis Goodwin .05
7 Jimmy Haynes .05
8 Scott Klingenbeck .05
9 Rick Krivda .05
10 T.R. Lewis .05
11 Brian Link .05
12 Scott McClain .05
13 Alex Ochoa .05
14 Jay Powell .05
15 Brian Sackinsky .05
16 Brad Tyler .05
17 Gregg Zaun .05
18 Joel Bennett .05
19 Felix Colon .05
20 Ryan McGuire .05
21 Frank Rodriguez .05
22 Tim Vanegmond .05
23 Garret Anderson .10
24 Jorge Fabregas .05
25 P.J. Forbes .05
26 John Fritz .05
27 Todd Greene .05
28 Jose Musset .05
29 Orlando Palmeiro .05
30 John Pricher .05
31 Chris Pritchett .05
32 Marquis Riley .05
33 Luis Andujar .05
34 James Baldwin .05
35 Brian Boehringer .05
36 Ron Coomer .05
37 Ray Durham .05
38 Robert Ellis .05
39 Jeff Pierce .05
40 Olmedo Saenz .05
41 Brandon Wilson .05
42 Ian Doyle .05
43 Jason Fronio .05
44 Derek Hacopian .05
45 Daron Kirkreit .05
46 Mike Neal .05
47 Chad Ogea .05
48 Cesar Perez .05
49 Omar Ramirez .05
50 J.J. Thobe .05
51 Casey Whitten .05
52 Eric Danapilis .05
53 Brian Edmondson .05
54 Tony Fuduric .05
55 Rick Greene .05
56 Bob Higginson .05
57 Felipe Lira .05
58 Joshua Neese .05
59 Shannon Penn .05
60 John Rosengren .05
61 Phil Stidham .05
62 Justin Thompson .05
63 Shawn Wooten .05
64 Brian Bevil .05
65 Mel Bunch .05
66 Johnny Damon 1.00
67 Chris Eddy .05
68 Jon Lieber .05
69 Les Norman .05
70 Jim Pittsley .05
71 Kris Ralston .05
72 Joe Randa .05
73 Kevin Rawitzer .05
74 Chris Sheehan .05
75 Robert Toth .05
76 Michael Tucker .05
77 Brian Banks .05
78 Marshall Boze .05
79 Jeff Cirillo .05
80 Bo Dodson .05
81 Bobby Hughes .05
82 Scott Karl .05
83 Mike Matheny .05
84 Kevin Riggs .05
85 Sid Roberson .05
86 Charlie Rogers .05
87 Mike Stefanski .05
88 Scott Talanoa .05
89 Derek Wachter .05
90 Wes Weger .05
91 Anthony Byrd .05
92 Marty Cordova .05
93 Steve Dunn .05
94 Gus Gandarillos .05
95 LaTroy Hawkins .05
96 Oscar Munoz .05
97 Dan Perkins .05
98 Ken Serafini .05
99 Ken Tirpack .05
100 Russ Davis .05
101 Nick Delvecchio .05
102 Robert Eenhoorn .05
103 Ron Frazier .05
104 Kraig Hawkins .05
105 Keith Heberling .05
106 Derek Jeter 3.00
107 Kevin Jordan .05
108 Ryan Karp .05
109 Matt Luke .05
110 Lyle Mouton .05
111 Andy Pettitte 1.00
112 Jorge Posada .25
113 Ruben Rivera .05
114 Tate Seefried .05
115 Brien Taylor .05
116 Mark Acre .05
117 Jim Bowie .05
118 Russ Brock .05
119 Fausto Cruz .05
120 Jason Giambi 1.50
121 Izzy Molina .05
122 George Williams .05
123 Joel Wolfe .05
124 Ernie Young .05
125 Tim Davis .05
126 Jackie Nickell .05
127 Ruben Santana .05
128 Makato Suzuki (Makoto) .05
129 Ron Villone .05
130 Rich Aurilia .05
131 John Detmer .05
132 Scott Eyre .05
133 Dave Geeve .05
134 Rick Helling .05
135 Kerry Lacy .05
136 Trey McCoy .05
137 Wes Shook .05
138 Howard Battle .05
139 D.J. Boston .05
140 Rich Butler .05
141 Brad Cornett .05
142 Jesse Cross .05
143 Alex Gonzalez .05
144 Kurt Heble .05
145 Jose Herrera .05
146 Ryan Jones .05
147 Robert Perez .05
148 Jose Silva .05
149 Shannon Stewart .25
150 Chris Weinke .25
151 Jamie Arnold .05
152 Chris Brock .05
153 Tony Graffagnino (Graffanino) .05
154 Damon Hollins .05
155 Mike Hostetler .05
156 Mike Kelly .05
157 Andre King .05
158 Darrell May .05
159 Vince Moore .05
160 Don Strange .05
161 Dominic Therrien .05
162 Terrell Wade .05
163 Brant Brown .05
164 Matt Franco .05
165 Brooks Kieschnick .05
166 Jon Ratliff .05
167 Kennie Steenstra .05
168 Amaury Telemaco .05
169 Ozzie Timmons .05
170 Hector Trinidad .05
171 Travis Willis .05
172 Tim Belk .05
173 Jamie Dismuke .05
174 Mike Ferry .05
175 Chris Hook .05
176 John Hrusovsky .05
177 Cleveland Ladell .05
178 Martin Lister .05
179 Chad Mottola .05
180 Eric Owens .05
181 Scott Sullivan .05
182 Pat Watkins .05
183 Jason Bates .05
184 John Burke .05
185 Quinton McCracken .05
186 Neifi Perez .05
187 Bryan Rekar .05
188 Mark Thompson .05
189 Tim Clark .05
190 Vic Darensbourg .05
191 Charles Johnson .05
192 Bryn Kosco .05
193 Reynol Mendoza .05
194 Kerwin Moore .05
195 John Toale .05
196 Bob Abreu .25
197 Jim Bruske .05
198 Jim Dougherty .05
199 Tony Eusebio .05
200 Kevin Gallaher .05
201 Chris Holt .05
202 Brian Hunter .05
203 Orlando Miller .05
204 Donovan Mitchell .05
205 Alvin Morman .05
206 James Mouton .05
207 Phil Nevin .05

208 Roberto Petagine .05
209 Billy Wagner .25
210 Mike Busch .05
211 Roger Cedeno .05
212 Chris Demetral .05
213 Rick Gorecki .05
214 Ryan Henderson .05
215 Todd Hollandsworth .05
216 Ken Huckaby .05
217 Rich Linares .05
218 Ryan Luzinski .05
219 Doug Newstrom .05
220 Ben Van Ryn .05
221 Todd Williams .05
222 Shane Andrews .05
223 Reid Cornelius .05
224 Joey Eischen .05
225 Heath Haynes .05
226 Rod Henderson .05
227 Mark LaRosa .05
228 Glenn Murray .05
229 Ugueth Urbina .05
230 B.J. Wallace .05
231 Gabe White .05
232 Edgardo Alfonzo .05
233 Randy Curtis .05
234 Omar Garcia .05
235 Jason Isringhausen .05
236 Eric Ludwick .05
237 Bill Pulsipher .05
238 Chris Roberts .05
239 Quilivio Veras .05
240 Pete Walker .05
241 Mike Welch .05
242 Preston Wilson .15
243 Ricky Bottalico .05
244 Alan Burke .05
245 Phil Geisler .05
246 Mike Lieberthal .10
247 Jason Moler .05
248 Gene Schall .05
249 Mark Tranberg .05
250 Jermaine Allensworth .05
251 Michael Brown .05
252 Jason Kendall .25
253 Jeff McCurry .05
254 Jeff Alkire .05
255 Mike Badorek .05
256 Brian Barber .05
257 Alan Benes .05
258 Jeff Berblinger .05
259 Joe Biasucci .05
260 Terry Bradshaw .05
261 Duff Brumley .05
262 Kirk Bullinger .05
263 Mike Busby .05
264 Jamie Cochran .05
265 Clint Davis .05
266 Mike Gulan .05
267 Aaron Holbert .05
268 John Kelly .05
269 John Mabry .05
270 Frankie Martinez .05
271 T.J. Mathews .05
272 Aldo Pecorilli .05
273 Doug Radziewicz .05
274 Brian Rupp .05
275 Gerald Witasick Jr. .05
276 Dmitri Young .05
277 Homer Bush .05
278 Glenn Dishman .05
279 Sean Drinkwater .05
280 Bryce Florie .05
281 Billy Hall .05
282 Jason Hardtke .05
283 Ray Holbert .05
284 Brian Johnson .05
285 Ray McDavid .05
286 Ira Smith .05
287 Steve Day .05
288 Kurt Ehmann .05
289 Chad Fonville .05
290 Kris Franko .05
291 Aaron Fultz .05
292 Marcus Jensen .05
293 Calvin Murray .05
294 Jeff Richey .05
295 Bill Van Landingham .05
296 Keith Williams .05
297 Chris Wimmer .05
298 Checklist .05
299 Checklist .05
300 Checklist .05

1993-94 Fleer Excel League Leaders

Fleer Excel's League Leader cards feature 10 players who have compiled league-best statistics. The player's name and "League Leader" are stamped in gold foil on the front; the back has a career summary. Cards, numbered 1 of 10, etc., were random inserts in foil packs.

MT
Complete Set (20): 5.00
Common Player: .25
1 James Baldwin .25
2 Joel Bennett .25
3 Ricky Bottalico .25
4 Mike Busch .25
5 Duff Brumley .25
6 Jamie Cochran .25
7 John Dettmer .25
8 Joey Eischen .25
9 LaTroy Hawkins .25
10 Derek Jeter 4.50
11 Ryan Karp .25
12 Rick Krivda .25
13 Trey McCoy .25
14 Jason Moler .25
15 Chad Mottola .25
16 Jose Silva .25
17 Brien Taylor .25
18 Michael Tucker .25
19 Ugueth Urbina .25
20 Ben Van Ryn .25

1993 Minor League Team Sets

While the number of team sets grew slightly in 1993, the number of issuers again declined. The market's two giants, Classic Best and Fleer/ProCards had the lion's share of production. Of the team sets issued, Classic Best had 33 percent and Fleer/ProCards 58 percent (with considerable duplication).

MT
287 Team Sets and Variations
1993 FPC AAA All-Stars (55) 10.00
1993 CB Albany Polecats (30) 6.00
1993 FPC Albany Polecats (28) 5.00
1993 FPC Albany-Colonie Yankees (29) 5.00
1993 FPC Albuquerque Dukes (31) 9.00
1993 Team Albuquerque Dukes Photos (40) 125.00
1993 CB Appleton Foxes (30) 4.00
1993 FPC Appleton Foxes (29) 5.00
1993 FPC Arkansas Travelers (27) 4.00
1993 CB Asheville Tourists (28) 10.00
1993 FPC Asheville Tourists (30) 8.00
1993 CB Auburn Astros (30) 6.00
1993 FPC Auburn Astros (30) 5.00
1993 CB Augusta Priates (28) 10.00
1993 FPC Augusta Pirates (27) 8.00
1993 Cal Bakersfield Dodgers (32) 6.00
1993 CB Batavia Clippers (30) 4.00
1993 FPC Batavia Clippers (30) 4.00
1993 CB Bellingham Mariners (30) 4.00
1993 FPC Bellingham Mariners (31) 4.00
1993 CB Beloit Brewers (29) 4.00
1993 FPC Beloit Brewers (30) 5.00
1993 CB Bend Rockies (30) 4.00
1993 FPC Bend Rockies (30) 5.00
1993 FPC Billings Mustangs (30) 5.00
1993 SP Dillings Mustangs (28) 7.00
1993 FPC Binghamton Mets (26) 6.00
1993 FPC Birmingham Barons (27) 8.00
1993 CB Bluefield Orioles (30) 4.00
1993 FPC Bluefield Orioles (27) 4.00
1993 CB Boise Hawks (30) 6.00
1993 FPC Boise Hawks (30) 5.00
1993 FPC Bowie Bay Sox (24) 6.00
1993 CB Bristol Tigers (30) 6.00
1993 FPC Bristol Tigers (30) 4.00
1993 FPC Buffalo Bisons (27) 5.00
1993 CB Burlington Bees (29) 10.00
1993 FPC Burlington Bees (28) 8.00
1993 CB Burlington Indians (30) 6.00
1993 FPC Burlington Indians (31) 7.00
1993 SP Butte Copper Kings (24) 6.00
1993 FPC Calgary Cannons (29) 5.00
1993 FPC Canton-Akron Indians (26) 12.00
1993 CB Capital City Bombers (27) 6.00
1993 FPC Capital City Bombers (26) 4.00
1993 FPC Carolina League A-S (52) 9.00
1993 FPC Carolina Mudcats (29) 5.00
1993 Team Carolina Mudcats (24) 7.00
1993 CB Cedar Rapids Kernels (30) 4.00
1993 FPC Cedar Rapids Kernels (28) 4.00
1993 CB Central Valley Rockies (28) 6.00
1993 FPC Central Valley Rockies (29) 5.00
1993 CB Charleston Rainbows (30) 5.00
1993 FPC Charleston Rainbows (31) 4.00
1993 FPC Charlotte Knights (28) 6.00
1993 CB Charlotte Rangers (30) 4.00
1993 FPC Charlotte Rangers (28) 5.00
1993 FPC Chattanooga Lookouts (26) 5.00
1993 CB Clearwater Phillies (29) 6.00
1993 FPC Clearwater Phillies (27) 5.00
1993 CB Clinton Giants (29) 4.00
1993 FPC Clinton Giants (28) 5.00
1993 FPC Colorado Springs Sky Sox (25) 5.00
1993 FPC Columbus Clippers (27) 6.00
1993 Police Columbus Clippers (25) 6.00
1993 Team Columbus Clippers (26) 12.00
1993 CB Columbus RedStixx (30) 7.00
1993 FPC Columbus RedStixx (30) 6.00
1993 CB Danville Braves (30) 6.00
1993 FPC Danville Braves (31) 5.00
1993 CB Daytona Cubs (27) 5.00
1993 FPC Daytona Cubs (26) 4.00
1993 Team Duluth-Superior Dukes (31) 6.00
1993 CB Dunedin Blue Jays (30) 7.00
1993 FPC Duendin Blue Jays (27) 5.00
1993 Team Dunedin Blue Jays (30) 12.00
1993 CB Durham Bulls (30) 5.00
1993 FPC Durham Bulls (31) 4.00
1993 Team Durham Bulls (31) 7.00
1993 FPC Edmonton Trappers (27) 5.00
1993 CB Elizabethton Twins (30) 6.00
1993 FPC Elizabethton Twins (25) 4.00
1993 CB Elmira Pioneers (30) 5.00
1993 FPC Elmira Pioneers (29) 4.00
1993 FPC El Paso Diablos (30) 5.00
1993 CB Erie Sailors (30) 4.00
1993 FPC Erie Sailors (30) 4.00
1993 CB Eugene Emeraldc (30) 4.00
1993 FPC Eugene Emeralds (29) 6.00
1993 CB Everett Giants (30) 6.00
1993 FPC Everett Giants (31) 5.00
1993 CB Fayetteville Generals (30) 5.00
1993 FPC Fayetteville Generals (29) 4.00
1993 FPC Florida State League A-S (51) 7.50
1993 CB Frederick Keys (30) 5.00
1993 FPC Frederick Keys (30) 6.00
1993 CB Ft. Lauderdale Red Sox (30) 5.00
1993 FPC Ft. Lauderdale Red Sox (30) 4.00
1993 CB Ft. Myers Miracle (29) 7.00
1993 FPC Ft. Myers Miracle (29) 5.00
1993 CB Ft. Wayne Wizards (30) 6.00
1993 FPC Ft. Wayne Wizards (28) 5.00
1993 CB Geneva Cubs (30) 5.00
1993 FPC Geneva Cubs (31) 6.00
1993 CB Glens Falls Redbirds (30) 5.00
1993 FPC Glens Falls Redbirds (31) 4.00
1993 SP Great Falls Dodgers (29) 10.00
1993 CB Greensboro Hornets (28) 70.00
1993 FPC Greensboro Hornets (31) 45.00
1993 FPC Greenville Braves (28) 5.00
1993 Team Greenville Braves Foldout 12.50
1993 CB Hagerstown Suns (28) 5.00
1993 FPC Hagerstown Suns (30) 4.00
1993 FPC Harrisburg Senators (28) 9.00
1993 FPC Helena Brewers (31) 5.00
1993 SP Helena Brewers (28) 7.00
1993 CB Hickory Crawdads (30) 16.00
1993 FPC Hickory Crawdads (30) 15.00
1993 CB High Desert Mavericks (29) 8.00
1993 FPC High Desert Mavericks (30) 4.00
1993 CB Huntington Cubs (30) 6.00
1993 FPC Huntington Cubs (30) 5.00
1993 FPC Huntsville Stars (26) 5.00
1993 FPC Idaho Falls Braves (31) 5.00
1993 SP Idaho Falls Braves (30) 7.00
1993 FPC Indianapolis Indians (25) 5.00
1993 FPC Iowa Cubs (24) 5.00
1993 FPC Jackson Generals (27) 6.00
1993 FPC Jacksonville Suns (22) 6.00
1993 CB Jamestown Expos (30) 6.00
1993 FPC Jamestown Expos (28) 5.00
1993 CB Johnson City Cardinals (30) 6.00
1993 FPC Johnson City Cardinals (31) 5.00
1993 CB Kane County Cougars (30) 12.00
1993 FPC Kane County Cougars (28) 10.00
1993 Team Kane County Cougars (30) 10.00
1993 CB Kingsport Mets (31) 6.00
1993 FPC Kingsport Mets (27) 5.00
1993 CB Kinston Indians (30) 6.00
1993 FPC Kinston Indians (30) 6.00
1993 Team Kinston Indians (30) 12.00
1993 FPC Knoxville Smokies (29) 10.00
1993 CB Lakeland Tigers (29) 7.00
1993 FPC Lakeland Tigers (31) 6.00
1993 FPC Las Vegas Stars (29) 5.00
1993 FPC Lethbridge Mounties (26) 5.00
1993 SP Lethbridge Mounties (26) 6.00
1993 FPC London Tigers (29) 4.00
1993 FPC Louisville Redbirds (26) 6.00
1993 CB Lynchburg Red Sox (28) 6.00
1993 FPC Lynchburg Red Sox (29) 5.00
1993 CB Macon Braves (30) 5.00
1993 FPC Macon Braves (30) 4.00
1993 CB Madison Muskies (28) 5.00
1993 FPC Madison Muskies (27) 4.00
1993 CB Martinsville Phillies (30) 6.00
1993 FPC Martinsville Phillies (31) 4.00
1993 FPC Medicine Hat Blue Jays (27) 5.00
1993 SP Medicine Hat Blue Jays (25) 6.00
1993 FPC Memphis Chicks (25) 6.00
1993 Team Memphis Chicks All-Stars (36) 10.00
1993 FPC Midland Angels (27) 5.00
1993 FPC Midland W/Bank, Chemical Ads (29) 8.00
1993 OHP Midland Angels (33) 40.00
1993 FPC Midwest League A-S (55) 6.00
1993 CB Modesto A's (28) 15.00
1993 FPC Modesto A's (28) 15.00
1993 FPC Nashville Sounds (25) 6.00
1993 FPC Nashville Xpress (27) 5.00
1993 FPC New Britain Red Sox (28) 5.00
1993 FPC New Orleans Zephyrs (26) 6.00
1993 CB Niagara Falls Rapids (30) 4.00
1993 FPC Niagara Fllas Rapids (31) 4.00
1993 FPC Norfolk Tides (27) 7.00
1993 FPC Oklahoma City 89ers (26) 5.00
1993 FPC Omaha Royals (29) 5.00
1993 TM Omaha Royals 25th Anniversary (18) 30.00
1993 CB Oneonta Yankees (30) 8.00
1993 FPC Oneonta Yankees (31) 7.00
1993 FPC Orlando Cubs (26) 5.00
1993 CB Osceola Astros (29) 8.00
1993 FPC Osceloa Astros (27) 7.00
1993 FPC Ottawa Lynx (23) 6.00
1993 CB Palm Springs Angels (30) 4.00
1993 FPC Palm Springs Angels (29) 4.00
1993 DD Pawtucket Red Sox Foldout 45.00
1993 FPC Pawtucket Red Sox (29) 4.00
1993 Team Pawtucket Red Sox (25) 8.00
1993 Team Peninsula Oilers (32) 15.00
1993 CB Peoria Chiefs (27) 4.00
1993 FPC Peoria Chiefs (27) 4.00
1993 Team Peoria Chiefs (30) 12.00
1993 FPC Phoenix Firebirds (29) 5.00
1993 CB Pittsfield Mets (30) 4.00
1993 FPC Pittsfield Mets (30) 7.00
1993 FPC Pocatello Posse (25) 4.00
1993 SP Pocatello Posse (26) 6.00
1993 FPC Portland Beavers (21) 6.00
1993 CB Princeton Reds (30) 4.00
1993 FPC Princeton Reds (31) 4.00
1993 CB Prince Williams Cannons (30) 10.00
1993 FPC Prince Williams Cannons (30) 4.00
1993 CB Quad City Bandits (27) 5.00
1993 FPC Quad City Bandits (29) 4.00
1993 CB Rancho Cucamonga Quakes (30) 4.00
1993 FPC Rancho Cucamonga Quakes (32) 4.00
1993 FPC Reading Phillies (26) 5.00
1993 FPC Reading Phillies Police (26) 7.50
1993 Penn-Lyn Photo Reading Phillies (24) 75.00
1993 Bleacher Bums Richmond Braves Foldout 20.00
1993 Bleacher Bums Richmond Foldout - Gold 60.00
1993 FPC Richmond Braves (30) 7.00
1993 Pepsi Richmond Braves (25) 10.00
1993 Richmond Camera Richmond Braves (25) 75.00
1993 Richmond Comix Richmond Braves (30) 35.00
1993 Cal Riverside Pilots (31) 6.00
1993 FPC Rochester Red Wings (29) 7.00
1993 Rochester Red Wings Foldout 20.00
1993 CB Rockford Royals (30) 12.00
1993 FPC Rockford Royals (31) 10.00
1993 CB Salem Buccaneers (30) 5.00
1993 FPC Salem Buccaneers (29) 4.00
1993 FPC San Antonio Missions (28) 6.00
1993 HEB San Antonio Missions (32) 50.00
1993 CB San Bernardino Spirit (26) 4.00
1993 FPC San Bernardino Spirit (26) 4.00
1993 CB San Jose Giants (30) 5.00
1993 FPC San Jose Giants (29) 4.00
1993 CB Sarasota White Sox (29) 5.00
1993 FPC Sarasota White Sox (30) 4.00
1993 CB Savannah Cardinals (29) 4.00
1993 FPC Savannah Cardinals (27) 4.00
1993 FPC Scranton Red Barons (25) 7.00
1993 Team Scranton Red Barons (30) 8.00
1993 FPC Shreveport Captains (27) 5.00
1993 Team Sioux Falls Canaries (28) 6.00
1993 FPC South Atlantic League A-S (57) 20.00
1993 Play II South Atlantic League A-S (42) 20.00
1993 Play II SAL All-Stars inserts (18) 60.00
1993 CB South Bend White Sox (29) 7.00
1993 FPC South Bend White Sox (30) 6.00
1993 CB Southern Oregon A's (30) 4.00
1993 FPC Southern Oregon A's (30) 4.00
1993 CB Spartanburg Phillies (28) 4.00
1993 FPC Spartanburg Phillies (29) 4.00
1993 CB Spokane Indians (30) 4.00
1993 FPC Spokane Indians (27) 4.00
1993 CB Springfield Cardinals (29) 5.00
1993 FPC Springfield Cardinals (29) 4.00
1993 CB St. Catherines Blue Jays (30) 8.00
1993 FPC St. Catharines Blue Jays (27) 5.00
1993 CB St. Lucie Mets (28) 7.00
1993 FPC St. Lucie Mets (28) 5.00
1993 Team St. Paul Saints (26) 6.00
1993 CB St. Petersburg Cardinals (30) 7.00
1993 FPC St. Petersburg Cardinals (30) 5.00
1993 CB Stockton Ports (30) 5.00
1993 FPC Stockton Ports (29) 4.00
1993 FPC Syracuse Chiefs (27) 6.00
1993 FPC Tacoma Tigers (27) 6.00
1993 FPC Toledo Mud Hens (28) 5.00
1993 FPC Tucson Toros (29) 5.00
1993 FPC Tulsa Drillers (27) 6.00
1993 FPC Tulsa Drillers W/BBC Stores Ad (27) 9.00
1993 Team Tulsa Drillers (30) 17.50
1993 CB Utica Blue Sox (30) 4.00
1993 FPC Utica Blue Sox (26) 4.00
1993 FPC Vancouver Canadians (28) 7.00
1993 CB Vero Beach Dodgers (30) 4.00
1993 FPC Vero Beach Dodgers (31) 4.00
1993 CB Waterloo Diamonds (30) 6.00
1993 FPC Waterloo Diamonds (29) 5.00
1993 CB Watertown Indians (30) 6.00
1993 FPC Watertown Indians (30) 4.00
1993 CB Welland Pirates (30) 5.00
1993 FPC Welland Pirates (31) 4.00
1993 CB West Palm Beach Expos (30) 6.00
1993 FPC West Palm Beach Expos (30) 5.00
1993 CB West Virginia Wheelers (27) 5.00
1993 FPC West Virginia Wheelers (27) 4.00
1993 FPC Wichita Wranglers (26) 4.00
1993 CB Wilmington Blue Rocks (30) 9.00
1993 FPC Wilmington Blue Rocks (30) 7.00

1993 CB Winston-Salem Spirits (27) 5.00
1993 FPC Winston-Salem Spirits (25) 4.00
1993 CB Yakima Bears (30) 6.00
1993 FPC Yakima Bears (31) 5.00

1994 Action Packed Scouting Report

Action Packed Scouting Report features a mix of top prospects from the Class A-AAA minor leagues. Cards feature the hallmark Action Packed technology of embossed, heavily lacquered player photos on front. Backs have the player name in a vertical gold-foil strip at top, and a "scouting report" and minor league stats beneath. A subset of 12 "Franchise Gem" players features a second player photo on back, along with a black diamond, which when activated by finger heat, reveals the players projected Major League debut season. A second subset of five cards honors the 40th anniversary of Roberto Clemente's debut in U.S. professional baseball. The final card in the set is a gold-foil version of MLB's 125th anniversary logo, which is also the set checklist card. Inserts offered 24-karat gold versions of the 12 "Franchise Gem" cards in the set, along with the MLB logo card, plus randomly packaged Franchise Gem cards which have a heat-and-reveal spot on the back with an "Exchange" notation. Those cards could be redeemed for diamond-studded versions of the Franchise Gem cards.

		MT
Complete Set (72):		10.00
Common Player:		.10
Wax Pack (6):		.75
Wax Box (24):		15.00
1	Alex Rodriguez	3.00
2	Trot Nixon	.50
3	Chan Ho Park	.25
4	Brooks Kieshnick	.10
5	Matt Brunson	.10
6	Wayne Gomes	.10
7	Charles Johnson	.10
8	Kirk Presley	.10
9	Daron Kirkriet	.10
10	Curtis Goodwin	.10
11	Alex Ochoa	.10
12	Midre Cummings	.10
13	Russ Davis	.10
14	Phil Nevin	.10
15	J.R. Phillips	.10
16	Jeff Granger	.10
17	Makato Suzuki (Makoto)	.10
18	Johnny Damon	.75
19	Chad Mottola	.10
20	Scott Ruffcorn	.10
21	Brian Barber	.10
22	Frank Rodriguez	.10
22a	Frank Rodriguez (Autographed edition of 2,500 foil-pack redemptions.)	3.00
23	Michael Jordan	2.00
24	Michael Tucker	.10
25	Rondell White	.10
26	Ugueth Urbina	.10
27	Tyrone Hill	.10
28	Dmitri Young	.10
29	Marshall Boze	.10
30	Marc Newfield	.10
31	James Baldwin	.10
32	Terrell Wade	.10
33	Curtis Pride	.10
34	Gabe White	.10
35	Derrek Lee	.75
36	Bill Pulsipher	.10
37	Butch Huskey	.10
38	Nigel Wilson	.10
39	Tim Clark	.10
40	Ozzie Timmons	.10
41	Brien Taylor	.10
42	J.T. Snow	.15
43	Derek Jeter	3.00
44	Rick Krivda	.10
45	Kevin Millar	.15
46	Matt Franco	.10
47	Jose Silva	.10
48	Benji Gil	.10
49	Pokey Reese	.15
50	Todd Hollandsworth	.10
51	Robert Ellis	.10
52	Brian L. Hunter	.10
53	Todd Ritchie	.10
54	Kurt Miller	.10
55	Alex Rodriguez (Franchise Gem)	2.00
56	Chan Ho Park (FG)	.15
57	Brooks Kieschnick (FG)	.10
58	Charles Johnson (FG)	.10
59	Alex Ochoa (FG)	.10
60	Midre Cummings (FG)	.10
61	Phil Nevin (FG)	.10
62	Jose Silva (FG)	.10
63	James Baldwin (FG)	.10
64	Rondell White (FG)	.10
65	Trot Nixon (FG)	.25
66	Todd Hollandsworth (FG)	.10
67	Roberto Clemente Hidden Talent	1.00
68	Roberto Clemente Four-Time Batting Champ	1.00
69	Roberto Clemente 1966 NL MVP	1.00
70	Roberto Clemente 3,000-Hit Club	1.00
71	Roberto Clemente 1973 Hall of Fame	1.00
72	checklist	.10

1994 Classic All-Star Minor League

Classic's minor league wax issue for '94 features a 200-card base set with several chase sets and autograph inserts. Cards feature borderless action phtos on front. Graphics include the Classic logo (upper-left), MLB team logo (lower-right), and minor league team logo (lower-left). Backs have a large portrait photo with the bottom half "ghosted" to allow overprinting of stats and career data.

		MT
Complete Set (200):		9.00
Common Player:		.05
Wax Pack (10):		.75
Wax Box (36):		20.00
1	Michael Jordan	2.00
2	Felipe Lira	.05
3	Jose Silva	.05
4	Yuri Sanchez	.05
5	Marcus Jensen	.05
6	Julio Santana	.05
7	Angel Martinez	.05
8	Jose Herrera	.05
9	D.J. Boston	.05
10	Trot Nixon	.50
11	Trey Beamon	.05
12	Danny Clyburn	.05
13	John Wasdin	.05
14	Vince Moore	.05
15	Vic Darensbourg	.05
16	Kevin Gallaher	.05
17	Julio Bruno	.05
18	Terrell Lowery	.05
19	Phil Geisler	.05
20	Chan Ho Park	.15
21	Chad McConnell	.05
22	Ricky Bottalico	.05
23	Jim Pittsley	.05
24	Gabe Martinez	.05
25	Johnny Damon	1.00
26	Basil Shabazz	.05
27	Billy Ashley	.05
28	Andy Petitte	1.00
29	Robert Ellis	.05
30	Mike Zolecki	.05
31	League All-Star #1	.05
32	John Burke	.05
33	Chris Snopek	.05
34	Mark Thompson	.05
35	Jimmy Haynes	.05
36	Ron Villone	.05
37	Curtis Goodwin	.05
38	Tim Belk	.05
39	Rod Henderson	.05
40	Butch Huskey	.05
41	Chris Smith	.05
42	B.J. Wallace	.05
43	Guillermo Mercedes	.05
44	Ugueth Urbina	.05
45	Fausto Cruz	.05
46	Julian Tavarez	.05
47	Scott Lydy	.05
48	Darren Burton	.05
49	Mac Suzuki	.05
50	Kirk Presley	.05
51	Alex Rodriguez Checklist	.50
52	Armando Benitez	.05
53	Rodney Pedraza	.05
54	LaTroy Hawkins	.05
55	Rick Forney	.05
56	Tripp Cromer	.05
57	Andres Berumen	.05
58	Terry Bradshaw	.05
59	Omar Ramirez	.05
60	Derek Jeter	4.00
61	Kerwin Moore	.05
62	Andy Larkin	.05
63	Neifi Perez	.05
64	Casey Whitten	.05
65	Jon Ratliff	.05
66	J.J. Johnson	.05
67	Preston Wilson	.15
68	Jason Isringhausen	.05
69	Adam Meinershagen	.05
70	Rondell White	.05
71	Shannon Stewart	.15
72	Keith Heberling	.05
73	Ruben Rivera	.05
74	Mike Lieberthal	.15
75	Damon Hollins	.05
76	Jason Jacome	.05
77	Amaury Telemaco	.05
78	Scott Talanoa	.05
79	Dave Stevens	.05
80	Brien Taylor	.05
81	League All-Stars #2	.05
82	Brian Barber	.05
83	Ray Durham	.05
84	Brent Bowers	.05
85	Shane Andrews	.05
86	Gabe White	.05
87	Midre Cummings	.05
88	Brad Radke	.15
89	Joe Randa	.05
90	Phil Nevin	.05
91	Joe Vitiello	.05
92	Ray McDavid	.05
93	Robbie Beckett	.05
94	Frank Rodriguez	.05
95	Marc Newfield	.05
96	Joey Eischen	.05
97	Manny Alexander	.05
98	Jeff McNeely	.05
99	Mark Smith	.05
100	Alex Rodriguez	2.50
101	Todd Hollandsworth	.05
102	Scott Ruffcorn	.05
103	Kurt Miller	.05
104	Justin Mashore	.05
105	Garret Anderson	.15
106	Nigel Wilson	.05
107	Howard Battle	.05
108	Calvin Reese	.15
109	Orlando Miller	.05
110	Bill Pulsipher	.05
111	Edgar Renteria	.15
112	Steve Gibraltar	.05
113	Gene Schall	.05
114	John Roper	.05
115	Alvin Morman	.05
116	Doug Glanville	.05
117	Mark Hutton	.05
118	Glenn Murray	.05
119	Curtis Shaw	.05
120	Alex Ochoa	.05
121	Michael Moore	.05
122	Joey Hamilton	.05
123	James Baldwin	.05
124	Chad Ogea	.05
125	Rikkert Faneyte	.05
126	Benji Gil	.05
127	Kenny Felder	.05
128	Brant Brown	.05
129	Eddie Pearson	.05
130	Derrek Lee	1.00
131	League All-Stars #3	.05
132	Dan Serafini	.05
133	Ramon Caraballo	.05
134	Derek Wallace	.05
135	Jamie Arnold	.05
136	Domingo Jean	.05
137	Jose Malave	.05
138	Derek Lowe	.10
139	Marshall Boze	.05
140	Billy Wagner	.15
141	Matt Franco	.05
142	Roger Cedeno	.05
143	Russ Davis	.05
144	Kevin Flora	.05
145	Rick Gorecki	.05
146	Rick Greene	.05
147	Brian Hunter	.05
148	Rich Aurilia	.05
149	Jason Moller	.05
150	Michael Tucker	.05
151	Alex Rodriguez Checklist	.50
152	Chad Mottola	.05
153	Calvin Murray	.05
154	Melvin Nieves	.05
155	Luis Ortiz	.05
156	Chris Roberts	.05
157	Todd Williams	.05
158	Tony Phillips	.05
159	DeShawn Warren	.05
160	Paul Shuey	.05
161	Dmitri Young	.05
162	Jermaine Allensworth	.05
163	Daron Kirkreit	.05
164	Scott Christman	.05
165	Steve Soderstrom	.05
166	J.R. Phillips	.05
167	Karim Garcia	.25
168	Mark Acre	.05
169	Jose Paniagua	.05
170	Terrell Wade	.05
171	Mike Bell	.05
172	Alan Benes	.05
173	Jeff D'Amico	.05
174	Tate Seefried	.05
175	Wayne Gomes	.05
176	Chris Singleton	.05
177	Marc Valdes	.05
178	Jamey Wright	.05
179	Jay Powell	.05
180	Charles Johnson	.05
181	Mitch House	.05
182	Torii Hunter	.50
183	Jeff Suppan	.05
184	Roberto Petagine	.05
185	Ryan McGuire	.05
186	Andrew Lorraine	.05
187	Matt Brunson	.05
188	Eduardo Perez	.05
189	Jay Witasick	.05
190	Shawn Green	.50
191	Cleveland Ladell	.05
192	Paul Bako	.05
193	Brook Fordyce	.05
194	Kym Ashworth	.05
195	Tony Mitchell	.05
196	Tony Clark	.05
197	Curtis Pride	.05
198	Arquimedez Pozo	.05
199	Rey Ordonez	.05
200	Brooks Kieschnick	.05

Autographs

Randomly inserted into foil packs of Classic All-Star Minor League baseball was this series of seven minor league autographs cards. Fronts have the same format as the regular-issue cards, along with the player signature and serial number from within the edition as specified for each card in this checklist. Backs have a congratulatory message.

		MT
Complete Set (7):		85.00
Common Player:		3.00
AU1	Alex Rodriguez (2,100)	110.00
AU2	Terrell Wade (2,080)	3.00
AU3	Brooks Kieschnick (3,400)	3.00
AU4	Rondell White (2,880)	3.00
AU5	Michael Tucker (2,400)	3.00
AU6	Kirk Presley (1,300)	3.00
AU7	Trot Nixon (1,700)	10.00

1994 Classic Bonus Baby

Five of the hottest prospects of the day are featured in this insert set. Fronts feature action photos which have been graphically enhanced to convey the image of speed. In the lower-right corner is a gold-foil box with "BONUS BABY," the Classic logotype and player name. Backs have another photo, career highlights, appropriate logos and a serial number from within an edition of 9,994 of each card.

		MT
Complete Set (5):		7.00
Common Player:		.50
BB1	Trot Nixon	.75
BB2	Kirk Presley	.50
BB3	Alex Rodriguez	6.00
BB3a	Alex Rodriguez (Autographed edition of 450.)	400.00
BB4	Brooks Kieschnick	.50
BB5	Michael Tucker	.50

1994 Classic Cream of the Crop

These premium cards are a one-per-pack insert in Classic's All-Star minor league issue. Cards have player photos on a borderless "metallized" background. The player and insert set name are printed on black in orange blocks at bottom. Horizontally formatted backs are conventionally printed and include a large photo and career summary.

		MT
Complete Set (25):		5.00
Common Player:		.15
CC1	Trot Nixon	.50
CC2	Kirk Presley	.15
CC3	Mac Suzuki	.15
CC4	Brooks Kieschnick	.15
CC5	Johnny Damon	.75
CC6	Howard Battle	.15
CC7	Michael Tucker	.15
CC8	Todd Hollandsworth	.15
CC9	J.R. Phillips	.15
CC10	Shannon Stewart	.25
CC11	Alex Rodriguez	1.00
CC12	Terrell Wade	.15
CC13	Rondell White	.15
CC14	James Baldwin	.15
CC15	Shane Andrews	.15
CC16	Chan Ho Park	.25
CC17	Derek Jeter	3.00
CC18	Charles Johnson	.15
CC19	Bill Pulsipher	.15
CC20	Phil Nevin	.15
CC21	Scott Ruffcorn	.15
CC22	Midre Cummings	.15
CC23	Frank Rodriguez	.15
CC24	Dmitri Young	.15
CC25	Shawn Green	.75

Update

Each pack of Classic Update contains one of these premium inserts. Cards have player photos set against a refractive foil background. The player's name and set logo are printed in white on dark blue panels at bottom. Backs are formatted horizontally, conventionally printed and include another photo, career highlights and appropriate team, licensor and licensee logos.

		MT
Complete Set (20):		5.00
Common Player:		.25
CC1	Paul Wilson	.25
CC2	Ben Grieve	.35
CC3	Dustin Hermanson	.25
CC4	Antone Williamson	.25
CC5	Josh Booty	.25
CC6	Doug Million	.25
CC7	Todd Walker	.35
CC8	C.J. Nitkowski	.25
CC9	Jaret Wright	.25
CC10	Mark Farris	.25
CC11	Nomar Garciaparra	4.00
CC12	Paul Konerko	.50
CC13	Jayson Peterson	.25
CC14	Matt Smith	.25
CC15	Ramon Castro	.25
CC16	Cade Gaspar	.25
CC17	Terrence Long	.25
CC18	Hiram Bocachica	.25
CC19	Dante Powell	.25
CC20	Brian Buchanan	.25

1994 Classic Update Cal Ripken Tribute

This special insert was issued with the Update series of Classic Minor League Baseball All-Star edition. The front pictures Ripken in a batting swing with another picture of him seated in the box seats in the background. Typography at top congratulates the iron man for reaching his 2,000th consecutive game. On back are photos of Ripken as an Oriole and as a minor leaguer in the uniform of the Rochester Red Wings. Text on back traces his career to that point. An autographed edition of 2,000 of the cards was also produced.

		MT
		.00
CR1	Cal Ripken Jr.	6.00
CR1	Cal Ripken Jr./Auto.	110.00

1994 Classic Assets (Baseball)

A number of baseball players are featured in the five-sport lineup of the base set, inserts and phonecards in Assets' debut year. Parallel cards bearing a silver facsimile autograph on front are worth 4X-6X the values quoted.

		MT
Base Set/Inserts		
4	Nolan Ryan	1.00
4	Nolan Ryan (Silver-foil signature.)	2.00
13	Paul Wilson	.25
13	Paul Wilson (Silver-foil signature.)	.50
18	Ben Grieve	.25
18	Ben Grieve (Silver-foil signature.)	.50
29	Nolan Ryan	1.00
38	Paul Wilson	.25
43	Ben Grieve	.25
64	Doug Million	.25
65	Barry Bonds	1.00
89	Doug Million	.25
90	Barry Bonds	1.00
DC4	Nolan Ryan (Die-Cut)	4.00
DC15	Nomar Garciaparra (Die-Cut)	2.00
DC17	Barry Bonds (Die-Cut)	4.00
DC18	Paul Wilson (Die-Cut)	.50

1994 Classic Best Gold

This 200-card set features UV coating on both sides of the cards and foil stamping on the fronts. Virtually every level of minor league baseball is represented in this set. Insert sets highlight first-round draft picks and glow-in-the-dark illustrated acetate cards.

		MT
Complete Set (200):		10.00
Common Player:		.05
Wax Box:		20.00
1	Brien Taylor	.05
2	Jeff D'Amico	.05
3	Trot Nixon	.50
4	Clayton Byrne	.05
5	Eric Chavez	.50
6	Matt Jarvis	.05
7	Billy Owens	.05
8	Jay Powell	.05
9	Robert Eenhoorn	.05
10	Trey Beamon	.05
11	Todd Williams	.05
12	Tim Davis	.05
13	Brian Barber	.05
14	Jeff Shireman	.05
15	Melvin Mora	.05
16	Phil Nevin	.10
17	Kendall Rhine	.05
18	Billy Wagner	.25
19	Jason Kendall	.25
20	Kelly Wunsch	.05
21	D.J. Boston	.05
22	Shannon Stewart	.25
23	Anthony Manahan	.05
24	Dwight Robinson	.05
25	Alan Benes	.05
26	Dennis Slininger	.05
27	John Burke	.05
28	Jamey Wright	.05
29	Scott Eyre	.05
30	Jack Kimel	.05
31	Kerry Lacy	.05
32	Rich Aurilia	.05
33	Dave Giberti	.05
34	Daryl Henderson	.05
35	Stanley Evans	.05
36	Wayne Gomes	.05
37	Rob Grable	.05
38	Mike Juhl	.05
39	Jason Moler	.05
40	Jon Zuber	.05
41	Chad Fonville	.05
42	Mark Thompson	.05
43	Billy Masse	.05
44	Derek Hacopian	.05
45	J.J. Thobe	.05
46	Charles York	.05
47	Jamie Howard	.05
48	Andre King	.05
49	Tim Delgado	.05
50	Mike Hubbard	.05
51	Bernie Nunez	.05
52	Jon Ratliff	.05
53	Pedro Valdez	.05
54	Rich Butler	.05
55	Felipe Crespo	.05
56	Randy Phillips	.05
57	Todd Steverson	.05
58	Chris Stynes	.05
59	Ben Weber	.05
60	Chris Weinke	.15
61	Rob Lukachyk	.05
62	Brett King	.05
63	Chris Singleton	.05
64	Brian Bright	.05
65	Brent Brede	.05
66	Steve Hazlett	.05
67	Dan Serafini	.05
68	Matt Farner	.05
69	Jeremy Lee	.05
70	Anthony Medrano	.05
71	Josue Estrada	.05
72	Martin Mainville	.05
73	Chris Schwab	.05
74	John Roskos	.05
75	Charles Peterson	.05
76	Kevin Pickford	.05
77	Charles Rice	.05
78	Mike Bell	.05
79	Ed Diaz	.05
80	Torii Hunter	.50
81	Kelcey Mucker	.05
82	Nick Delvecchio	.05
83	Derek Jeter	4.00
84	Ryan Karp	.05
85	Matt Luke	.05
86	Ray Suplee	.05
87	Tyler Houston	.05
88	Brad Cornett	.05
89	Kris Harmes	.05
90	Shane Andrews	.05
91	Ugueth Urbina	.05
92	Chris Mader	.05
93	Eddie Pearson	.05
94	Tim Clark	.05
95	Chris Malinoski	.05
96	John Toale	.05
97	Mark Acre	.05
98	Ernie Young	.05
99	Jeff Schmidt	.05
100	Roberto Petagine	.05
101	Eddy Diaz	.05
102	Ruben Santana	.05
103	Ron Villone	.05
104	Nate Dishington	.05
105	Charles Johnson	.05

106 Preston Wilson .15
107 Paul Shuey .05
108 Howard Battle .05
109 Tim Hyers .05
110 Rick Greene .05
111 Justin Thompson .05
112 Frank Rodriguez .05
113 Jamie Arnold .05
114 Marty Malloy .05
115 Darrell May .05
116 Leo Ramirez .05
117 Tom Thobe .05
118 Terrell Wade .05
119 Marc Valdes .05
120 Scott Rolen 1.50
121 Les Norman .05
122 Michael Tucker .05
123 Joe Vitiello .05
124 Chris Roberts .05
125 Jason Giambi 1.50
126 Izzy Molina .05
127 Scott Shockey .05
128 John Wasdin .05
129 Joel Wolfe .05
130 Brooks Kieschnick .05
131 Kennie Steenstra .05
132 Hector Trinidad .05
133 Derek Wallace .05
134 Kevin Lane .05
135 Buck McNabb .05
136 James Mouton .05
137 Joey Eischen .05
138 Todd Haney .05
139 John Pricher .05
140 Jeff Brown .05
141 Jason Hardtke .05
142 Derrek Lee 1.50
143 Ira Smith .05
144 Mike Kelly .05
145 Mark Smith .05
146 Sherard Clinkscales .05
147 Ben VanRyn .05
148 Tim Cooper .05
149 Manny Martinez .05
150 Kurt Ehmann .05
151 Doug Mirabelli .05
152 Chris Wimmer .05
153 Scott Christman .05
154 Kevin Coughlin .05
155 Troy Fryman .05
156 Sean Johnston .05
157 Jeff Alkire .05
158 Mike Busby .05
159 John O'Brien .05
160 Brian Rupp .05
161 Steve Soderstrom .05
162 Craig Wilson .05
163 Alan Burke .05
164 Mike Murphy .05
165 T.J. Mathews .05
166 Edgardo Alfonzo .05
167 Randy Curtis .05
168 Bernie Millan .05
169 Mike Cantu .05
170 Clint Davis .05
171 Jason Kisey .05
172 Aldo Pecorilli .05
173 Dmitri Young .05
174 Marshall Boze .05
175 Bill Hardwick .05
176 Kevin Riggs .05
177 Lee Stevens .05
178 Webster Garrison .05
179 Wally Ritchie .05
180 Cris Colon .05
181 Rick Helling .05
182 Trey McCoy .05
183 Marc Barcelo .05
184 Chris Demetral .05
185 Rick Linares .05
186 Daron Kirkreit .05
187 Casey Whitten .05
188 Shon Walker .05
189 Rod Henderson .05
190 Tyrone Horne .05
191 B.J. Wallace .05
192 Louis Maberry .05
193 Brian Boehringer .05
194 Glenn DiSarcina .05
195 Melvin Bunch .05
196 Chad Mottola .05
197 Ryan Luzinski .05
198 Tom Wilson .05
199 Checklist 1 .05
200 Checklist 2 .05

#1 Picks

Classic Best's #1 Draft Pick insert cards feature 19 top picks. The cards, numbered with an LP prefix, utilize a chromium effect printing process that gives the cards a reflective textured effect. They are randomly inserted at an average rate of one per 12 foil packs.

MT
Complete Set (19): 6.00
Common Player: .25
1 Alan Benes .25
2 Scott Christman .25
3 Jeff D'Amico .25
4 Wayne Gomes .25
5 Torii Hunter 1.50
6 Brooks Kieschnick .25
7 Daron Kirkreit .25
8 Derrek Lee 3.00
9 Trot Nixon 2.00
10 Charles Peterson .25
11 Jay Powell .25
12 Jon Ratliff .25
13 Chris Schwabb .25
14 Steve Soderstrom .25
15 Marc Valdes .25
16 Billy Wagner 1.00
17 John Wasdin .25
18 Jamey Wright .25
19 Kelly Wunsch .25

Rookie Express

These chase cards are found only in Classic Best Gold jumbo packs at the rate of one per pack. The cards use the same chromium layered technology as the #1 draft pick inserts and share an identical checklist. Card #20 is printed with glow in the dark ink.

MT
Complete Set (20): 3.00
Common Player: .25
1 Alan Benes .25
2 Scott Christman .25
3 Jeff D'Amico .25
4 Wayne Gomes .25
5 Torii Hunter .75
6 Brooks Kieschnick .25
7 Daron Kirkreit .25
8 Derrek Lee .25
9 Trot Nixon 1.50
10 Charles Peterson .25
11 Jay Powell .25
12 Jon Ratliff .25
13 Chris Schwab .25
14 Steve Soderstrom .25
15 Marc Valdes .25
16 Billy Wagner .75
17 John Wasdin .25
18 Jamey Wright .25
19 Kelly Wunsch .25
20 Brooks Kieschnick .25

David Justice Auto.

An authentically autographed card of David Justice was issued as an insert in 1994 Classic Best Gold. The gold-foil highlighted cards were inserted at the rate of about one per case (360 foil packs). Each card is serially numbered within an edition of 4,000.

MT
David Justice 45.00

1994 Classic Best Illustrated Acetate

Classic Best Gold's acetate insert cards feature illustrations of minor league stars by comic artist Neal Adams, printed on plastic. The glow-in-the-dark cards, are inserted at a rate of one per 90 packs. The unnumbered cards when laid in proper order from left to right share a contiguous background design and have typography which reads "1994 Minor League Gold" across the tops of the cards and "Superstars" in clear letters across the bottoms. Backs also share a cosmic art background, and include a small color player photo and career highlights.

MT
Complete Set (5): 7.50
Common Player: 1.00
1 Brien Taylor 1.00
2 Dmitri Young 1.00
3 Derek Jeter 6.00
4 Phil Nevin 1.00
5 Frank Rodriguez 1.00

1994 Classic 4 Sport (Baseball)

A number of baseball players are included in the base-card set, parallels and chase cards in this issue.

MT
Base Set/Inserts:
Printer's Proofs #161-188: 10X
Gold Card #161-188: 2X
Wax Pack (16): .65
Wax Box (36): 15.00
161 Paul Wilson .10
162 Ben Grieve .25
163 Doug Million .05
164 C.J. Nitkowski .05
165 Tommy Davis .05
166 Dustin Hermanson .10
167 Travis Miller .05
168 McKay Christiansen .05
169 Victor Rodriguez .05
170 Jacob Cruz .05
171 Rick Heiserman .05
172 Mark Farris .05
173 Nomar Garciaparra 3.00
174 Paul Konerko .40
175 Trey Moore .05
176 Brian Stephenson .05
177 Matt Smith .05
178 Kevin Brown .05
179 Cade Gaspar .05
180 Bret Wagner .05
181 Mike Thurman .05
182 Doug Webb .05
183 Ryan Nye .05
184 Brian Buchanan .05
185 Scott Elarton .05
186 Mark Johnson .05
187 Jacob Shumate .05
188 Kevin Witt .05
HV3 Paul Wilson (High Voltage) .50
HV7 Ben Grieve (High Voltage) .50
HV11 Dustin Hermanson (High Voltage) .50
HV15 Doug Million (High Voltage) .50
HV20 Nomar Garciaparra (High Voltage) 10.00
TC5 Paul Wilson, Doug Million, Cade Gaspar (Tricard) .50
16/25 Paul Wilson (Classic Picks) .50
17/25 Ben Grieve (Classic Picks) .50
18/25 Trey Moore (Classic Picks) .25
19/25 Nomar Garciaparra (Classic Picks) 7.50
20/25 Doug Million (Classic Picks) .25

1994 Classic 4 Sport Auto. (Baseball)

Authentically autographed versions of most players in the 4 Sport issue were produced as random pack inserts. Fronts share the basic format with the regular version but include the signature and a serial number from within the edition specified in parentheses (where known). Backs have a congratulatory message. Cards marked with an asterisk are not confirmed to exist.

MT
Common Player: 3.00
(161) Paul Wilson (2,400) 3.00
(162) Ben Grieve (2,500) 3.00
(163) Doug Million (1,020) 6.00
(164) C.J. Nitkowski (970) 3.00
(165) Tommy Davis (?) 3.00
(166) Dustin Hermanson (1,020) 3.00
(167) Travis Miller (760) 3.00
(168) McKay Christensen (*) 3.00
(169) Victor Rodriguez (1,000) 3.00
(170) Jacob Cruz (?) 3.00
(171) Rick Heiserman (?) 3.00
(172) Mark Farris (1,090) 3.00
(173) Nomar Garciaparra (1,020) 45.00
(174) Paul Konerko (970) 4.00
(175) Trey Moore (*) 3.00
(176) Brian Stephenson (1,100) 3.00
(177) Matt Smith (1,090) 3.00
(178) Kevin Brown (1,090) 3.00
(179) Cade Gaspar (1,090) 3.00
(180) Bret Wagner (970) 3.00
(181) Mike Thurman (990) 3.00
(182) Doug Webb (1,000) 3.00
(183) Ryan Nye (1,015) 3.00
(184) Brian Buchanan (950) 3.00
(185) Scott Elarton (*) 3.00
(186) Mark Johnson (1,000) 3.00
(187) Jacob Shumate (980) 3.00
(188) Kevin Witt (970) 3.00

1994 Classic Images (Baseball)

Young players from the four major team sports are featured in the 1994 debut edition of Images. Only the baseball players are listed here.

MT
Baseball Set (26): 5.00
Common Player: .05
Wax Pack (10): .50
Wax Box (36): 10.00
3 Alex Rodriguez 2.50
3 Alex Rodriguez (Promo) 3.00
7 Jeff D'Amico .05
11 Alan Benes .05
15 Jeff Granger .05
19 Daron Kirkreit .05
23 Billy Wagner .25
31 Brian Anderson .05
37 Matt Brunson .05
42 Kirk Presley .05
47 Chris Carpenter .05
49 Kelly Wunsch .05
51 Jon Ratliff .05
52 Wayne Gomes .05
54 Trot Nixon .50
55 Andre King .05
63 Darren Dreifort .05
69 Brooks Kieschnick .05
77 Torii Hunter .50
80 Steve Soderstrom .05
85 Derrek Lee 1.00
93 Jay Powell .05
105 Matt Drews .05
115 Scott Christman .05
131 Kirk Presley (B/W) .05
139 Trot Nixon (B/W) .50
143 Alex Rodriguez (B/W) 2.50

Sudden Impact

The young professionals who were believed to have the greatest chance for early stardom in the four major team sports were chosen for a one-per-pack insert set called "Sudden Impact." The cards have fronts printed on gold foil. Only the baseball players are listed here.

MT
Baseball Set (3): 4.00
SI1 Carlos Delgado 1.00
SI3 Derek Jeter 3.00
SI4 Alex Rodriguez 2.00

1994 Classic Tri-Cards

An innovative concept which never caught on with collectors, these minor league "tri-cards" feature three different players in the standard 3-1/2" x 2-1/2" format. The complete set consists of 84 cards on 28 three-player panels. The panels are perforated to allow separation into three individual cards of about 1-1/8" x 2-1/2". Each panel features one prospect from the Class A, AA and AAA farm clubs of a major league team. Values shown are for complete three-player panels. Individual player cards have little or no collector value. Fronts feature action photos with a minor league team logo at lower-right. Backs have some career data, the major league team logo and a "1 of 8,000" notice.

MT
Complete Panel Set (28): 20.00
Common Panel: .50
ATLANTA BRAVES .50
T1 Jamie Arnold
T2 Terrell Wade
T3 Ramon Caraballo
BALTIMORE ORIOLES .50
T4 Jay Powell
T5 Alex Ochoa
T6 Manny Alexander
BOSTON RED SOX .75
T7 Trot Nixon
T8 Jose Malave
T9 Frank Rodriguez
CALIFORNIA ANGELS .50
T10 De Shawn Warren
T11 Chris Smith
T12 Andrew Lorraine
CHICAGO CUBS .50
T13 Jon Ratliff
T14 Brooks Kieschnick
T15 Matt Franco
CHICAGO WHITE SOX .50
T16 Eddie Pearson
T17 Chris Snopek
T18 James Baldwin
CINCINNATI REDS .50
T19 Paul Bako
T20 Chad Mottola
T21 John Roper
CLEVELAND INDIANS .50
T22 Daron Kirkreit
T23 Tony Mitchell
T24 Chad Ogea
COLORADO ROCKIES .50
T25 Mike Zolecki
T26 Rodney Pedraza
T27 Mark Thompson
DETROIT TIGERS .50
T28 Matt Brunson
T29 Tony Clark
T30 Felipe Lira
FLORIDA MARLINS .65
T31 Edgar Renteria
T32 Charles Johnson
T33 Kurt Miller
HOUSTON ASTROS .75
T34 Billy Wagner
T35 Kevin Gallaher
T36 Phil Nevin
KANSAS CITY ROYALS 1.50
T37 Johnny Damon
T38 Darren Burton
T39 Michael Tucker
LOS ANGELES DODGERS .75
T40 Kym Ashworth
T41 Chan Ho Park
T42 Todd Hollandsworth
MILWAUKEE BREWERS .50
T43 Gabe Martinez
T44 Scott Talanoa
T45 Marshall Boze
MINNESOTA TWINS .60
T46 LaTroy Hawkins
T47 Brad Radke
T48 Dave Stevens
MONTREAL EXPOS .50
T49 Jose Paniagua
T50 Ugueth Urbina
T51 Rondell White
NEW YORK METS .50
T52 Kirk Presley
T53 Bill Pulsipher
T54 Butch Huskey
NEW YORK YANKEES 6.00
T55 Derek Jeter
T56 Brien Taylor
T57 Russ Davis
OAKLAND A'S .50
T58 Jose Herrera
T59 Curtis Shaw
T60 Mark Acre
PHILADELPHIA PHILLIES .50
T61 Wayne Gomes
T62 Jason Moler
T63 Phil Geisler
PITTSBURGH PIRATES .50
T64 Mitch House
T65 Jermaine Allensworth
T66 Midre Cummings
SAN DIEGO PADRES 2.00
T67 Derrek Lee
T68 Robbie Beckett
T69 Ray McDavid
SAN FRANCISCO GIANTS .50
T70 Chris Singleton
T71 Calvin Murray
T72 J.R. Phillips
SEATTLE MARINERS 5.00
T73 Alex Rodriguez
T74 Mac Suzuki
T75 Marc Newfield
ST. LOUIS CARDINALS .50
T76 Basil Shabazz
T77 Dmitri Young
T78 Brian Barber
TEXAS RANGERS .50
T79 Mike Bell
T80 Terrell Lowery
T81 Benji Gil
TORONTO BLUE JAYS 1.00
T82 Jose Silva
T83 Brent Bowers
T84 Shawn Green

1994 Classic Collectors Club (C3)

This multi-sport set was part of the membership benefits package in the Classic Collectors Club (C3). Cards have action photos bordered at right and bottom in white, with die-cut play diagram devices. Backs have another photo, along with stats, highlights and biography. Sets were produced in an edition of 10,000. Only the baseball players are listed here.

MT
Common Player: .25
14 Jeff Granger .25
15 Brooks Kieschnick .25
16 Alex Rodriguez 6.00
17 Darren Dreifort .25

1994-95 Fleer Excel

Color-enhanced photos on both sides, gold-foil highlights and UV coating give a major league look to Fleer's set of prospects. Players are arranged alphabetically within the parent team and are chosen from all rungs of the minor league ladder from Short Season A clubs to AAA. Backs feature a second version of the front photo and complete career stats, along with the minor league team logo. Excel was sold in 14-card packs with a $1.49 retail price. Three insert sets included at random in packs were All-Stars, League Leaders and 1st Year Phenoms.

MT
Complete Set (300): 13.50
Common Player: .05
Wax Pack (14): .75
Wax Box (36): 17.50
1 Kimera Bartee .05
2 Harry Berrios .05
3 Tommy Davis .05
4 Cesar Devarez .05
5 Curtis Goodwin .05
6 Jimmy Haynes .05
7 Chris Lemp .05
8 Alex Ochoa .05
9 B.J. Waszgis .05
10 Nomar Garciaparra 2.00
11 Jose Malave .05
12 Glenn Murray .05
13 Trot Nixon .65
14 Frank Rodriguez .05
15 Bill Selby .05
16 Jeff Suppan .05
17 George Arias .05
18 Todd Blyleven .05
19 John Donati .05
20 Todd Greene .05
21 Bret Hemphill .05
22 Michael Holtz .05
23 Troy Percival .05
24 Luis Raven .05
25 James Baldwin .05
26 Mike Bertotti .05
27 Ben Boulware .05
28 Ray Durham .05
29 Jimmy Hurst .05
30 Rich Pratt .05
31 Mike Sirotka .05
32 Archie Vazquez .05
33 Harold Williams .05
34 Chris Woodfin .05
35 David Bell .05
36 Todd Betts .05
37 Jim Betzsold .05
38 Einar Diaz .05
39 Travis Driskill .05
40 Damian Jackson .05
41 Daron Kirkreit .05
42 Steve Kline .05
43 Tony Mitchell .05
44 Enrique Wilson .05
45 Jaret Wright .05
46 Matt Brunson .05
47 Tony Clark .05
48 Cade Gaspar .05
49 John Grimm .05
50 Bob Higginson .05
51 Shannon Penn .05
52 John Rosengren .05
53 Jaime Bluma .05
54 Mike Bovee .05
55 Nevin Brewer .05
56 Johnny Damon 1.00
57 Lino Diaz .05
58 Bart Evans .05
59 Sal Fasano .05
60 Tim Grieve .05
61 Jim Pittsley .05
62 Joe Randa .05
63 Ken Ray .05
64 Glendon Rusch .05
65 Larry Sutton .05
66 Dilson Torres .05
67 Michael Tucker .05
68 Joe Vitiello .05
69 James Cole .05
70 Danny Klassen .05
71 Jeff Kramer .05
72 Mark Loretta .05
73 Danny Perez .05
74 Sid Roberson .05
75 Scott Talanoa .05
76 Tim Unroe .05
77 Antone Williamson .05
78 Marc Barcelo .05
79 Trevor Cobb .05
80 Marty Cordova .05
81 Darren Fidge .05
82 Troy Fortin .05
83 Gus Gandarillas .05
84 Adrian Gordon .05
85 LaTroy Hawkins .05
86 Matt Lawton .05
87 Jake Patterson .05
88 Brad Radke .15
89 Todd Walker .05
90 Brian Boehringer .05
91 Brian Buchanan .05
92 Andy Croghan .05
93 Chris Cumberland .05
94 Matt Drews .05
95 Keith Heberling .05
96 Jason Jarvis .05
97 Derek Jeter 4.00
98 Ricky Ledee .05
99 Matt Luke .05
100 James Musselwhite .05
101 Andy Pettitte 1.00
102 Mariano Rivera .50
103 Ruben Rivera .05
104 Tate Seefried .05

105 Scott Standish .05
106 Jim Banks .05
107 Tony Batista .05
108 Ben Grieve .15
109 Jose Herrera .05
110 Steve Lemke .05
111 Eric Martins .05
112 Scott Spiezio .05
113 John Wasdin .05
114 Scott Davison .05
115 Chris Dean .05
116 Giomar Guevara .05
117 Tim Harikkala .05
118 Brett Hinchliffe .05
119 Matt Mantei .05
120 Arquimedez Pozo .05
121 Marino Santana .05
122 John Vanhof .05
123 Chris Widger .05
124 Mike Bell .05
125 Mark Brandenburg .05
126 Kevin Brown .05
127 Bucky Buckles .05
128 Jaime Escamilla .05
129 Terrell Lowery .05
130 Jerry Martin .05
131 Reid Ryan .10
132 Julio Santana .05
133 Howard Battle .05
134 D.J. Boston .05
135 Chris Carpenter .75
136 Freddy Garcia .05
137 Aaron Jersild .05
138 Ricardo Jordan .05
139 Angel Martinez .05
140 Jose Pett .05
141 Jose Silva .05
142 David Sinnes .05
143 Rob Steinert .05
144 Chris Stynes .05
145 Mike Toney .05
146 Chris Weinke .25
147 Kevin Witt .05
148 Brad Clontz .05
149 Jermaine Dye .05
150 Tony Graffanino .05
151 Kevin Grijak .05
152 Damon Hollins .05
153 Marcus Hostetler .05
154 Darrell May .05
155 Wonderful Monds .05
156 Carl Schulz .05
157 Chris Seelbach .05
158 Jacob Shumate .05
159 Terrell Wade .05
160 Glenn Williams .05
161 Alex Cabrera .05
162 Gabe Duross .05
163 Shawn Hill .05
164 Mike Hubbard .05
165 Dave Hutcheson .05
166 Brooks Kieschnick .05
167 Bobby Morris .05
168 Jayson Peterson .05
169 Jason Ryan .05
170 Ozzie Timmons .05
171 Cedric Allen .05
172 Aaron Boone .15
173 Ray Brown .05
174 Damon Callahan .05
175 Decomba Conner .05
176 Emiliano Giron .05
177 James Lofton .05
178 Nick Morrow .05
179 C.J. Nitkowski .05
180 Eddie Priest .05
181 Pokey Reese .10
182 Jason Robbins .05
183 Scott Sullivan .05
184 Pat Watkins .05
185 Juan Acevedo .05
186 Derrick Gibson .05
187 Pookie Jones .05
188 Terry Jones .05
189 Doug Million .05
190 Lloyd Peever .05
191 Jacob Viano .05
192 Mark Voisard .05
193 Josh Booty .05
194 Will Cunnane .05
195 Andy Larkin .05
196 Billy McMillon .05
197 Kevin Millar .50
198 Marc Valdes .05
199 Bob Abreu .25
200 Jamie Daspit .05
201 Scott Elarton .05
202 Kevin Gallaher .05
203 Richard Hidalgo .05
204 Chris Holt .05
205 Rick Huisman .05
206 Doug Mlicki .05
207 Julien Tucker .05
208 Billy Wagner .15
209 Juan Castro .05
210 Roger Cedeno .05
211 Ron Coomer .05
212 Karim Garcia .25
213 Todd Hollandsworth .05
214 Paul Konerko .45
215 Antonio Osuna .05
216 Willis Otanez .05
217 Dan Ricabal .05
218 Ken Sikes .05
219 Yamil Benitez .05
220 Geoff Blum .05
221 Scott Gentile .05
222 Mark Grudzielanek .05
223 Kevin Northrup .05
224 Carlos Perez .05
225 Matt Raleigh .05
226 Al Reyes .05
227 Everett Stull .05
228 Ugueth Urbina .05
229 Neil Weber .05
230 Edgardo Alfonzo .05
231 Jason Isringhausen .05
232 Terrence Long .05
233 Rey Ordonez .05
234 Ricky Otero .05
235 Jay Payton .05
236 Kirk Presley .05
237 Bill Pulsipher .05
238 Chris Roberts .05
239 Jeff Tam .05
240 Paul Wilson .10
241 David Doster .05
242 Wayne Gomes .05
243 Jeremy Kendall .05
244 Ryan Nye .05
245 Shane Pullen .05
246 Scott Rolen 1.50
247 Gene Schall .05
248 Brian Stumpf .05
249 Jake Austin .05
250 Trey Beamon .05
251 Danny Clyburn .05
252 Louis Collier .05
253 Mark Farris .05
254 Mark Johnson .05
255 Jason Kendall .25
256 Esteban Loaiza .05
257 Joe Maskivish .05
258 Ramon Morel .05
259 Gary Wilson .05
260 Matt Arrandale .05
261 Allen Battle .05
262 Alan Benes .05
263 Jeff Berblinger .05
264 Terry Bradshaw .05
265 Darrell Deak .05
266 Craig Grasser .05
267 Yates Hall .05
268 Kevin Lovingier .05
269 Elieser Marrero .05
270 Jeff Matulevich .05
271 Joe McEwing .05
272 Eric Miller .05
273 Tom Minor .05
274 Scott Simmons .05
275 Chris Stewart .05
276 Bret Wagner .05
277 Travis Welch .05
278 Jay Witasick .05
279 Homer Bush .05
280 Raul Casanova .05
281 Glenn Dishman .05
282 Gary Dixon .05
283 Devohn Duncan .05
284 Dustin Hermanson .10
285 Earl Johnson .05
286 Derrek Lee 1.50
287 Todd Schmitt .05
288 Ira Smith .05
289 Jason Thompson .05
290 Bryan Wolff .05
291 Jeff Martin .05
292 Dante Powell .05
293 Jeff Richey .05
294 Joe Rosselli .05
295 Benji Simonton .05
296 Steve Whitaker .05
297 Keith Williams .05
298 Checklist .05
299 Checklist .05
300 Checklist .05

All-Stars

An all-star team of minor league prospects is presented in this chase set. Borderless color action photos of the players are surrounded with a colorful graphic "aura," while the player name is given in bold angled type. Fronts are gold-foil enhanced with the Excel and All-Star logos. Backs repeat the front photo in slightly larger size and include career highlights. All-Star inserts are found on an average of one per four packs.

		MT
Complete Set (10):		5.00
Common Player:		.25
1	Raul Casanova	.25
2	Tony Clark	.25
3	Ray Durham	.25
4	Ron Coomer	.25
5	Derek Jeter	4.00
6	Trey Beamon	.25
7	Johnny Damon	1.00
8	Ruben Rivera	.25
9	Todd Greene	.25
10	Alan Benes	.25

League Leaders

Statistical leaders from all levels of minor league play are featured in this insert set. Front action photos are placed against a graphically enhanced background, with the player's name in gold foil at the bottom. Backs feature career summaries. League Leader inserts are found on an average of more than one per two packs.

		MT
Complete Set (20):		2.00
Common Player:		.25
1	Juan Acevedo	.25
2	James Baldwin	.25
3	Allen Battle	.25
4	Harry Berrios	.25
5	Brad Clontz	.25
6	Will Cunnane	.25
7	Glenn Dishman	.25
8	LaTroy Hawkins	.25
9	Jimmy Haynes	.25
10	Richard Hidalgo	.25
11	Earl Johnson	.25
12	Jim Pittsley	.25
13	Bill Pulsipher	.25
14	Benji Simonton	.25
15	Larry Sutton	.25
16	Michael Tucker	.25
17	Tim Unroe	.25
18	Joe Vitiello	.25
19	Billy Wagner	.50
20	Harold Williams	.25

1st Year Phenoms

Ten players who made an impact in their debut season of pro ball are highlighted in this chase set. Color action photos are set against a background that has been divided into colorized zones. The player's name and team are at bottom, with the card title and Excel logo enhanced in gold foil. Backs have a close-up version of the front photo and a career summary. The First Year Phenom cards are inserted at an average rate of one per 12 packs.

		MT
Complete Set (10):		2.00
Common Player:		.25
1	Paul Konerko	.75
2	Ray Brown	.25
3	Chris Dean	.25
4	Aaron Boone	.25
5	Rey Ordonez	.25
6	Decomba Conner	.25
7	Ben Grieve	.35
8	Jay Payton	.25
9	Dante Powell	.25
10	Dustin Hermanson	.25

1994 Signature Rookies

This 50-card set features top prospects from the minor leagues. Cards are UV coated with gold foil highlights and full color backs and fronts with a borderless design. The issue was sold in packs of seven only through hobby dealers. The print run was limited to 45,000 of each card, as indicated on the fronts. Each pack includes an autographed card or certificate redeemable for an autograph. In addition to the autographed cards, Signature Rookies has a Hottest Prospects insert set, a five-card Bonus Signature insert set, and a five-card Cliff Floyd insert set. Because cards are licensed only by the individual players and not Major League Baseball, minor league uniform logos have been removed from the photos.

		MT
Complete Set (50):		4.00
Common Player:		.05
1	Russell Davis	.05
2	Brant Brown	.05
3a	Ricky Bottalico (Photo actually Jamie Sepeda.)	.10
3b	Ricky Bottalico (Correct photo.)	.50
4	Brian Bevil	.05
5	Garret Anderson	.10
6	Rod Henderson	.05
7	Keith Heberling	.05
8	Scott Hatteberg	.05
9	Brook Fordyce	.05
10	Joey Eischen	.05
11	Orlando Miller	.05
12	Ray McDavid	.05
13	Andre King	.05
14	Todd Hollandsworth	.05
15	Tyrone Hill	.05
16	Paul Spoljaric	.05
17	Todd Ritchie	.05
18	Herbert Perry	.05
19	Alex Ochoa	.05
20	Mike Neill	.05
21	John Burke	.05
22	Alan Benes	.05
23	Robbie Beckett	.05
24	Brian Barber	.05
25	Justin Thompson	.05
26	Joey Hamilton	.05
27	Rick Greene	.05
28	Wayne Gomes	.05
29	Matthew "Big Bird" Drews	.05
30	Jeff D'Amico	.05
31	Bryn Kosco	.05
32	Brooks Kieschnick	.05
33	Jason Kendall	.25
34	Mike Kelly	.05
35	Derek Jeter	3.00
36	Jay Powell	.05
37	Phil Nevin	.10
38	Kurt Miller	.05
39	Chad McConnell	.05
40	Sean Lowe	.05
41	Michael Tucker	.05
42	Paul Shuey	.05
43	Dan Smith	.05
44	Calvin Reese	.10
45	Kirk Presley	.05
46	Jamey "Jamo" Wright	.05
47	Gabe White	.05
48	John Wasdin	.05
49	Billy Wagner	.15
50	Joe "Vit" Vitiello	.05

Autographed

The autographed versions of the 1994 Signature Rookies set was a one-per-pack insert. Basically the same as the regular issue, each card is authentically autographed and numbered from within an edition of 8,650.

		MT
Complete Set (50):		65.00
Common Player:		1.00
1	Russell Davis	2.00
2	Brant Brown	2.00
3	Ricky Bottalico	2.00
4	Brian Bevil	1.00
5	Garret Anderson	5.00
6	Rod Henderson	1.00
7	Keith Heberling	1.00
8	Scott Hatteberg	2.00
9	Brook Fordyce	2.00
10	Joey Eischen	2.00
11	Orlando Miller	1.00
12	Ray McDavid	1.00
13	Andre King	1.00
14	Todd Hollandsworth	2.00
15	Tyrone Hill	1.00
16	Paul Spoljaric	1.00
17	Todd Ritchie	2.00
18	Herbert Perry	1.00
19	Alex Ochoa	2.00
20	Mike Neill	1.00
21	John Burke	1.00
22	Alan Benes	2.00
23	Robbie Beckett	2.00
24	Brian Barber	1.00
25	Justin "J.T." Thompson	1.00
26	Joey Hamilton	2.00
27	Rick Greene	1.00
28	Wayne Gomes	2.00
29	Matthew "Big Bird" Drews	2.00
30	Jeff D'Amico	2.00
31	Bryn Kosco	1.00
32	Brooks Kieschnick	2.00
33	Jason Kendall	5.00
34	Mike Kelly	2.00
35	Derek Jeter	50.00
36	Jay Powell	2.00
37	Phil Nevin	3.00
38	Kurt Miller	1.00
39	Chad McConnell	1.00
40	Sean Lowe	1.00
41	Michael Tucker	2.00
42	Paul Shuey	2.00
43	Dan Smith	1.00
44	Calvin Reese	2.00
45	Kirk Presley	2.00
46	Jamey "Jamo" Wright	2.00
47	Gabe White	2.00
48	John Wasdin	2.00
49	Billy Wagner	5.00
50	Joe "Vit" Vitiello	2.00

Bonus Signature Autographs

Signature Rookies packs had Bonus cards randomly inserted in them; there were 1,000 sets of the five-card set made. The cards are numbered with a P prefix. Each card is authentically autographed and numbered.

		MT
Complete Set (5):		12.00
Common Player:		3.00
P1	Rick Helling	3.00
P2	Charles Johnson	4.50
P3	Chad Mottola	3.00
P4	J.R. Phillips	3.00
P5	Glen (Glenn) Williams	3.00

Cliff Floyd Set

Montreal Expos' top prospect Cliff Floyd is featured on this five-card Signature Rookies insert set. The cards, numbered with a B prefix, were limited to 10,000 complete sets. Cards were random inserts inside packs.

		MT
Complete Set (5):		2.00
Common Card:		.50
B1	Cliff Floyd	.50
B1a	Cliff Floyd/Auto.	5.00
B2	Cliff Floyd	.50
B2a	Cliff Floyd/Auto.	5.00
B3	Cliff Floyd	.50
B3a	Cliff Floyd/Auto.	5.00
B4	Cliff Floyd	.50
B4a	Cliff Floyd/Auto.	5.00
B5	Cliff Floyd	.50
B5a	Cliff Floyd/Auto.	5.00

Hottest Prospects

Signature Rookies' 12-card Hottest Prospects insert set cards are numbered with an S prefix. There were 5,000 complete sets made, with 1,000 of each card hand-signed and numbered.

		MT
Complete Set (12):		3.50
Complete Set, Auto. (12):		75.00
Common Player:		.10
Common Player, Auto.:		1.00
1	John Burke	.10
1	John Burke/Auto.	1.00
2	Russ Davis	.10
2	Russ Davis/Auto.	1.00
3	Todd Hollandsworth	.10
3	Todd Hollandsworth/ Auto.	2.00
4	Derek Jeter	3.00
4	Derek Jeter/Auto.	60.00
5	Mike Kelly	.10
5	Mike Kelly/Auto.	1.00
6	Ray McDavid	.10
6	Ray McDavid/Auto.	1.00
7	Kurt Miller	.10
7	Kurt Miller/Auto.	1.00
8	Phil Nevin	.10
8	Phil Nevin/Auto.	3.00
9	Alex Ochoa	.10
9	Alex Ochoa/Auto.	1.00
10	Justin "J.T." Thompson	.10
10	Justin "J.T." Thompson/ Auto.	1.00
11	Michael Tucker	.10
11	Michael Tucker/Auto.	1.00
12	Gabe White	.10
12	Gabe White/Auto.	1.00

Mail In Promos

This set parallels the Hottest Prospects inserts but was only available via a mail-in promotion. Where the pack-insert version has printed down the left side in gold foil, "1 of 5,000," the mail-in cards read, "Mail In Promo / 1 of 3,000." Cards are numbered with an "S" prefix.

		MT
Complete Set (12):		6.00
Common Player:		.15
S1	John Burke	.15
S2	Russ Davis	.15
S3	Todd Hollandsworth	.15
S4	Derek Jeter	5.00
S5	Mike Kelly	.15
S6	Ray McDavid	.15
S7	Kurt Miller	.15
S8	Phil Nevin	.25
S9	Alex Ochoa	.15
S10	Justin "J.T." Thompson	.15
S11	Michael Tucker	.15
S12	Gabe White	.15

Mail In Promos - Auto.

This set parallels the Mail In Promos set with an issue of 1,000 numbered autographed cards of each player. They were made available to dealers as an incentive to place advance orders.

		MT
Complete Set (12):		50.00
Common Player:		3.00
S1	John Burke	3.00
S2	Russ Davis	3.00
S3	Todd Hollandsworth	3.00
S4	Derek Jeter	45.00
S5	Mike Kelly	3.00
S6	Ray McDavid	3.00
S7	Kurt Miller	3.00
S8	Phil Nevin	4.00
S9	Alex Ochoa	3.00
S10	Justin "J.T." Thompson	3.00
S11	Michael Tucker	3.00
S12	Gabe White	3.00

1994 Signature Rookies Draft Picks

One hundred top players from the 1994 amateur draft are featured in this set. Most cards feature game-action, borderless color photos of the players in their college uniforms. At left is a vertical marbled panel with the SR Draft Picks logo on top and the edition number (45,000 for regular, 7,750 for parallel autographs) in gold foil. At the bottom the player name is also in gold foil on a marbled panel. Backs have a small portrait photo, college stats and career notes, draft status and appropriate licensors' logos and copyright data.

		MT
Complete Set (101):		4.00
Common Player:		.05
Wax Pack (6):		2.00
Wax Box (18):		24.00
1	Josh Booty	.05
2	Paul Wilson	.10
3	Ben Grieve	.15
4	Dustin Hermanson	.10
5	Antone Williamson	.05
6	McKay Christiansen	.05
7	Doug Million	.05
8	Todd Walker	.10
9	C.J. Nitkowski	.05
10	Jaret Wright	.10
11	Mark Farris	.05
12	Nomar Garciaparra	3.00
13	Paul Konerko	.35
14	Jason Varitek	.50
15	Jayson Peterson	.05
16	Matt Smith	.05
17	Ramon Castro	.05
18	Cade Gaspar	.05
19	Bret Wagner	.05
20	Terrence Long	.05
21	Hiram Bocachica	.05
22	Dante Powell	.05
23	Brian Buchanan	.05
24	Scott Elarton	.05
25	Mark Johnson	.05
26	Jacob Shumate	.05
27	Kevin Witt	.05
28	Jay Payton	.05
29	Mike Thurman	.05
30	Jacob Cruz	.05
31	Chris Clemons	.05
32	Travis Miller	.05
33	Shawn Johnston	.05
34	Brad Rigby	.05
35	Doug Webb	.05
36	John Ambrose	.05
37	Cleatus Davidson	.05
38	Tony Terry	.05
39	Jason Camilli	.05
40	Roger Goedde	.05
41	Corey Pointer	.05
42	Trey Moore	.05
43	Brian Stephenson	.05
44	Dan Lock	.05
45	Mike Darr	.05
46	Carl Dale	.05
47	Tommy Davis	.05
48	Kevin Brown	.05
49	Ryan Nye	.05
50	Rod Smith	.05
51	Andy Taulbee	.05
52	Jerry Whittaker	.05
53	John Crowther	.05
54	Bryon Gainey	.05
55	Bill King	.05
56	Heath Murray	.05
57	Larry Barnes	.05
58	Todd Cady	.05
59	Paul Failla	.05
60	Brian Meadows	.05
61	A.J. Pierzynski	.25
62	Aaron Boone	.05
63	Mike Metcalfe	.05
64	Matt Wagner	.05
65	Jaime Bluma	.05
66	Oscor Robles	.05
67	Greg Whiteman	.05
68	Roger Worley	.05
69	Paul Ottavinia	.05
70	Joe Giuliano	.05
71	Chris McBride	.05
72	Jason Beverlin	.05
73	Gordon Amerson	.05
74	Tom Mott	.05
75	Rob Welch	.05

76 Jason Kelley .05
77 Matt Treanor .05
78 Jason Sikes .05
79 Steve Shoemaker .05
80 Troy Brohawn .05
81 Jeff Abbott .05
82 Steve Woodard .05
83 Greg Morris .05
84 John Slamka .05
85 John Schroeder .05
86 Clay Carruthers .05
87 Eddie Brooks .05
88 Tim Byrdak .05
89 Bobby Howry .05
90 Vic Darensbourg .05
91 Midre Cummings .05
92 John Dettmer .05
93 Gar Finnvold .05
94 Dwayne Hosey .05
95 Jason Jacome .05
96 Doug Jennings .05
97 Luis A. Lopez .05
98 John Mabry .05
99 Rondell White .05
100 J.T. Snow .15
101 Checklist .05

Autographed

A parallel set featuring the 100 players in the Signature Rookies Draft Pick set has each card authentically autographed. The only differences between the autographed cards and the regular version are the hand-numbered "X of 7,750" notation on the vertical marbled column at left, and the gold-foil "Authentic Signature" logo above that. Autographed cards were inserted on a one-per-pack basis.

MT
Complete Set (100): 75.00
Common Player: 2.00
1 Josh Booty 4.00
2 Paul Wilson 2.00
3 Ben Grieve 3.00
4 Dustin Hermanson 3.00
5 Antone Williamson 2.00
6 McKay Christiansen 2.00
7 Doug Million 6.00
8 Todd Walker 3.00
9 C.J. Nitkowski 2.00
10 Jaret Wright 4.00
11 Mark Farris 2.00
12 Nomar Garciaparra 25.00
13 Paul Konerko 4.00
14 Jason Varitek 12.50
15 Jayson Peterson 2.00
16 Matt Smith 2.00
17 Ramon Castro 2.00
18 Cade Gaspar 2.00
19 Bret Wagner 2.00
20 Terrence Long 2.00
21 Hiram Bocachica 2.00
22 Dante Powell 2.00
23 Brian Buchanan 2.00
24 Scott Elarton 2.00
25 Mark Johnson 2.00
26 Jacob Shumate 2.00
27 Kevin Witt 2.00
28 Jay Payton 2.00
29 Mike Thurman 2.00
30 Jacob Cruz 2.00
31 Chris Clemons 2.00
32 Travis Miller 2.00
33 Shawn Johnston 2.00
34 Brad Rigby 2.00
35 Doug Webb 2.00
36 John Ambrose 2.00
37 Cleatus Davidson 2.00
38 Tony Terry 2.00
39 Jason Camilli 2.00
40 Roger Goedde 2.00
41 Corey Pointer 2.00
42 Trey Moore 2.00
43 Brian Stephenson 2.00
44 Dan Lock 2.00
45 Mike Darr 6.00
46 Carl Dale 2.00
47 Tommy Davis 2.00
48 Kevin Brown 2.00
49 Ryan Nye 2.00
50 Rod Smith 2.00
51 Andy Taulbee 2.00
52 Jerry Whittaker 2.00
53 John Crowther 2.00
54 Bryon Gainey 2.00
55 Bill King 2.00
56 Heath Murray 2.00
57 Larry Barnes 2.00
58 Todd Cady 2.00
59 Paul Failla 2.00
60 Brian Meadows 2.00
61 A.J. Pierzynski 2.00
62 Aaron Boone 4.00
63 Mike Metcalfe 2.00
64 Matt Wagner 2.00
65 Jaime Bluma 2.00
66 Oscor Robles 2.00
67 Greg Whiteman 2.00
68 Roger Worley 2.00
69 Paul Ottavinia 2.00
70 Joe Giuliano 2.00
71 Chris McBride 2.00
72 Jason Beverlin 2.00
73 Gordon Amerson 2.00
74 Tom Mott 2.00
75 Rob Welch 2.00
76 Jason Kelley 2.00
77 Matt Treanor 2.00
78 Jason Sikes 2.00
79 Steve Shoemaker 2.00
80 Troy Brohawn 2.00
81 Jeff Abbott 2.00
82 Steve Woodard 2.00
83 Greg Morris 2.00
84 John Slamka 2.00
85 John Schroeder 2.00
86 Clay Carruthers 2.00
87 Eddie Brooks 2.00
88 Tim Byrdak 2.00
89 Bobby Howry 2.00
90 Vic Darensbourg 2.00
91 Midre Cummings 2.00
92 John Dettmer 2.00
93 Gar Finnvold 2.00
94 Dwayne Hosey 2.00
95 Jason Jacome 2.00
96 Doug Jennings 2.00
97 Luis A. Lopez 2.00
98 John Mabry 2.00
99 Rondell White 3.00
100 J.T. Snow 4.00

Flip Cards

These "two-headed" cards have virtually identical fronts and backs with different player photos on each side. According to information provided at the time of issue, each of the featured players autographed 1,000 of the cards, with 250 of each bearing autographs on each side. Each side is highlighted with gold foil and features a notation that it is "1 of 15,000."

MT
Complete Set (5): 2.50
Common Player: .25
1 Ken Griffey Jr., Craig Griffey 1.00
1 Ken Griffey Jr., Craig Griffey (Ken autograph.) 50.00
1 Ken Griffey Jr., Craig Griffey (Craig autograph.) 3.00
1 Ken Griffey Jr., Craig Griffey (Both autographs.) 60.00
2 Craig Griffey, Ken Griffey Sr. .25
2 Craig Griffey, Ken Griffey Sr. (Craig autograph.) 3.00
2 Craig Griffey, Ken Griffey Sr. (Ken autograph.) 5.00
2 Craig Griffey, Ken Griffey Sr. (Both autographs.) 7.50
3 Ken Griffey Jr., Ken Griffey Sr. 1.00
3 Ken Griffey Jr., Ken Griffey Sr. (Junior autograph.) 50.00
3 Ken Griffey Jr., Ken Griffey Sr. (Senior autograph.) 5.00
3 Ken Griffey Jr., Ken Griffey Sr. (Both autographs.) 60.00
4 Nolan Ryan, Reid Ryan 1.00
4 Nolan Ryan, Reid Ryan (Nolan autograph.) 60.00
4 Nolan Ryan, Reid Ryan (Reid autograph.) 5.00
4 Nolan Ryan, Reid Ryan (Both autographs.) 75.00
5 Paul Wilson, Phil Nevin .50
5 Paul Wilson, Phil Nevin (Wilson autograph.) 5.00
5 Paul Wilson, Phil Nevin (Nevin autograph.) 5.00
5 Paul Wilson, Phil Nevin (Both autographs.) 10.00

1994 Signature Rookies Gold Standard (Baseball)

Twenty-five young players from each of the four major team sports were featured in the base set of Gold Standard. In addition, insert sets offered cards of "Legends," Hall of Famers (signed and unsigned) and a partial parallel set featuring gold facsimile autographs. Basic cards have an action photo on front and portrait photo with personal data and stats on back. There is a gold-foil Gold Standard logo on both front and back. Minor and major league uniform logos have been removed from the photos because the cards were only licensed by individual players and collegiate licensing authorities.

MT
Common Player: .10
51 Josh Booty .10
52 Roger Cedeno .10
53 Cliff Floyd .10
53(p) Cliff Floyd (Promo, edition of 10,000.) 1.00
54 Ben Grieve .15
55 Joey Hamilton .10
56 Todd Hollandsworth .10
57 Brian Hunter .10
58 Charles Johnson .10
59 Brooks Kieschnick .10
60 Mike Kelly .10
61 Ray McDavid .10
62 Kurt Miller .10
63 James Mouton .10
63(p) James Mouton (Promo, edition of 10,000.) 1.00
64 Phil Nevin .10
65 Alex Ochoa .10
66 Herbert Perry .10
67 Kirk Presley .10
68 Bill Pulsipher .10
69 Scott Ruffcorn .10
70 Paul Shuey .10
71 Michael Tucker .10
72 Terrell Wade .10
73 Gabe White .10
74 Paul Wilson .10
75 Dmitri Young .10
HOF15 Catfish Hunter .25
HOF15 Catfish Hunter/Auto. 15.00
HOF20 Willie Stargell .25
HOF20 Willie Stargell/Auto. 20.00
L3 "Pee Wee" Reese (Legends) .50
L4 Nolan Ryan (Legends) 3.00
GS4 Josh Booty (Gold Signature) .50
GS6 Brooks Kieschnick (Gold Signature) .25
GS8 Charles Johnson (Gold Signature) .50
GS10 Cliff Floyd (Gold Signature) .50
GS15 James Mouton (Gold Signature) .25

1994 Signature Rookies Tetrad (Baseball)

Twenty of the 120 cards in the four-sport Tetrad issue, plus several of the inserts, feature baseball players. Fronts have a borderless color action photo with a classic marble column at left bearing the Signature Rookies and Tetrad logos. The player name and "1 of 45,000" notation on front are in gold foil. Backs have an ancient temple background design with player data, stats and career summary. Cards are numbered in Roman numerals at top. All but one of the baseball players' cards was also issued in an edition of 7,500 authentically autographed cards.

MT
Common Player: .20
Common Player, Auto.: 2.00
84 Edgardo Alfonzo .10
84a Edgardo Alfonzo/Auto. 4.00
85 David Bell .10
85a David Bell/Auto. 2.00
86 Christopher Carpenter .10
86a Christopher Carpenter/Auto. 2.00
87 Roger Cedeno .10
87a Roger Cedeno/Auto. 2.00
88 Phil Geisler .10
88a Phil Geisler/Auto. 2.00
89 Curtis Goodwin .10
89a Curtis Goodwin/Auto. 2.00
90 Jeff Granger .10
90a Jeff Granger/Auto. 2.00
91 Brian Hunter .10
91a Brian Hunter/Auto. 2.00
92 Adam Hyzdu .10
92a Adam Hyzdu/Auto. 2.00
93 Scott Klingenbeck .10
93a Scott Klingenbeck/Auto. 2.00
94 Derrek Lee 2.00
94a Derrek Lee/Auto. 20.00
95 Calvin Murray .10
95a Calvin Murray/Auto. 2.00
96 Roberto Petagine .10
96a Roberto Petagine/Auto. 2.00
97 Bill Pulsipher .10
97a Bill Pulsipher/Auto. 2.00
98 Marquis Riley .10
98a Marquis Riley/Auto. 2.00
99 Frankie Rodriguez .10
99a Frank Rodriguez/Auto. 2.00
100 Scott Ruffcorn .10
100a Scott Ruffcorn/Auto. 2.00
101 Roger Salkeld .10
101a Roger Salkeld/Auto. 2.00
102 Marc Valdes .10
102a Marc Valdes/Auto. 2.00
103 Ernie Young .10
103a Ernie Young/Auto. 2.00
134 Paul Wilson (Top Prospects) .25
134a Paul Wilson (Top Prospects) (Autographed edition of 2,000.) 3.00
FLIP1 Charles Johnson, Charles Johnson (Edition of 7,500.) .25
FLIP1a Charles Johnson, Charles Johnson/Auto. (Edition of 275.) 5.00
FLIP5 Glen Williams, Monty Williams (Glenn) (Edition of 7,500.) .25
FLIP5a Glen Williams, Monty Williams (Glenn) (Autographed edition of 275.) 5.00
PROMO 1 Paul Wilson (1 of 10,000) .50

1994 Stadium Club Draft Picks

Produced well after the strike-truncated 1994 baseball season, this set was largely ignored by the hobby at the time of issue. Full-bleed card fronts feature poses of 1994's top draft picks in major league uniforms, giving the hobby a good first look at its future stars. Typography is in gold foil. Horizontal backs have a parti-colored background with another portrait photo, a scouting report, biographical data, amateur and pro career highlights and a box detailing how the team's other recent draft picks at the position have fared. A "Members Only" version of the set was also produced, with each card bearing a round gold-foil MO seal. Though much scarcer than the regular cards, they have attained little or no premium value.

MT
Complete Set (90): 4.00
Common Player: .05
Wax Box (24): 15.00
1 Jacob Shumate .05
2 C.J. Nitkowski .05
3 Doug Million .05
4 Matt Smith .05
5 Kevin Lovinger .05
6 Alberto Castillo .05
7 Mike Russell .05
8 Dan Lock .05
9 Tom Szimanski .05
10 Aaron Boone .10
11 Jayson Peterson .05
12 Mark Johnson .05
13 Cade Gaspar .05
14 George Lombard .05
15 Russ Johnson .05
16 Travis Miller .05
17 Jay Payton .05
18 Brian Buchanan .05
19 Jacob Cruz .05
20 Gary Rath .05
21 Ramon Castro .05
22 Tommy Davis .05
23 Tony Terry .05
24 Jerry Whittaker .05
25 Mike Darr .05
26 Doug Webb .05
27 Jason Camilli .05
28 Brad Rigby .05
29 Ryan Nye .05
30 Carl Dale .05
31 Andy Taulbee .05
32 Trey Moore .05
33 John Crowther .05
34 Joe Giuliano .05
35 Brian Rose .05
36 Paul Failla .05
37 Brian Meadows .05
38 Oscar Robles .05
39 Mike Metcalfe .05
40 Larry Barnes .05
41 Paul Ottavinia .05
42 Chris McBride .05
43 Ricky Stone .05
44 Billy Blythe .05
45 Eddie Priest .05
46 Scott Forster .05
47 Eric Pickett .05
48 Matt Beaumont .05
49 Darrell Nicolas .05
50 Mike Hampton .05
51 Paul O'Malley .05
52 Steve Shoemaker .05
53 Jason Sikes .05
54 Bryan Farson .05
55 Yates Hall .05
56 Troy Brohawn .05
57 Dan Hower .05
58 Clay Caruthers .05
59 Pepe McNeal .05
60 Ray Ricken .05
61 Scott Shores .05
62 Eddie Brooks .05
63 Dave Kauflin .05
64 David Meyer .05
65 Geoff Blum .05
66 Roy Marsh .05
67 Ryan Beeney .05
68 Derek Dukart .05
69 Nomar Garciaparra 3.00
70 Jason Kelley .05
71 Jesse Ibarra .05
72 Bucky Buckles .05
73 Mark Little .05
74 Heath Murray .05
75 Greg Morris .05
76 Mike Halperin .05
77 Wes Helms .05
78 Ray Brown .05
79 Kevin Brown .05
80 Paul Konerko .50
81 Mike Thurman .05
82 Paul Wilson .10
83 Terrence Long .05
84 Ben Grieve .10
85 Mark Farris .05
86 Bret Wagner .05
87 Dustin Hermanson .05
88 Kevin Witt .05
89 Corey Pointer .05
90 Tim Grieve .05

1994 Upper Deck Minor League

Upper Deck's 1994 minor league cards are similar in format to their major league counterparts. The super-premium set of 270 cards features the top professional players who had yet to appear in a Major League game. Cards have UV coating and foil accents, along with color photography on both sides of the card. The player's name is printed in silver foil, as is his Major League team affiliation. The regular player cards (225) have ratings by Baseball America on the back. Subsets include: Major League Evaluations (15), with backs done by noted statistical innovator Bill James; Star Potential (20), showcasing top young players; and Upper Deck All-Stars, one per position, as selected by experts at Baseball America. Insert series include Organizational Players of the Year (28); Trade Cards redeemable by mail for two top picks in the 1994 draft; and Top 10 Prospects (oversized cards), inserted in each box. These were also available as regular-sized cards through an on-pack offer.

MT
Complete Set (270): 10.00
Common Player: .05
Wax Pack (12): 1.00
Wax Box (36): 22.50
1 Alex Gonzalez .05
2 Brooks Kieschnick .05
3 Michael Tucker .05
4 Trot Nixon .75
5 Brien Taylor .05
6 Quinton McCracken .05
7 Terrell Wade .05
8 Brandon Wilson .05
9 Roberto Petagine .05
10 Chad Mottola .05
11 T.R. Lewis .05
12 Herbert Perry .05
13 Bob Abreu .25
14 Jorge Fabregas .05
15 Mike Kelly .05
16 Ryan McGuire .05
17 Alan Zinter .05
18 Troy Hughes .05
19 Brook Fordyce .05
20 Alex Ochoa .05
21 Chris Wimmer .05
22 Jason Hardtke .05
23 Ricardo Hildago .10
24 Gregg Zaun .05
25 Roger Cedeno .05
26 Curtis Shaw .05
27 Brian Giles .25
28 Felix Rodriguez .05
29 Motor-Boat Jones .05
30 Dmitri Young .05
31 Justin Mashore .05
32 Curtis Goodwin .05
33 Marquis Riley .05
34 Les Norman .05
35 Billy Hall .05
36 Jamie Arnold .05
37 Mike Farmer .05
38 Brent Bowers .05
39 Chad McConnell .05
40 Mike Robertson .05
41 Brent Cookson .05
42 Dan Cholowsky .05
43 Justin Thompson .05
44 Joe Vitiello .05
45 Todd Steverson .05
46 Brian Bevil .05
47 Paul Shuey .05
48 Scott Eyre .05
49 Rick Greene .05
50 Jose Silva .05
51 Kurt Miller .05
52 Ron Villone .05
53 Darren Bragg .05
54 Mike Lieberthal .15
55 Gabe White .05
56 Vince Moore .05
57 Tony Clark .10
58 Chris Eddy .05
59 Ray Durham .05
60 Todd Hollandsworth .05
61 Andres Berumen .05
62 Quilvio Veras .05
63 Wayne Gomes .05
64 Ryan Karp .05
65 Randy Curtis .05
66 Steve Rodriguez .05
67 Jason Schmidt .25
68 Mark Acre .05
69 B.J. Wallace .05
70 Alvin Morman .05
71 Travis Baptist .05
72 Jim Wawruck .05
73 Marty Cordova .05
74 Jamie Dismuke .05
75 Joe Randa .05
76 Danny Clyburn .05
77 Joey Eischen .05
78 Chris Seelbach .05
79 Izzy Molina .05
80 Chris Roberts .05
81 Rod Henderson .05
82 Kennie Steenstra .05
83 Ugueth Urbina .05
84 Stanton Cameron .05
85 Doug Glanville .05
86 Billy Wagner .25
87 Tate Seefried .05
88 Tyler Houston .05
89 Derek Lowe .15
90 Alan Benes .05
91 Terrell Wade .05
92 Rod Henderson/AS .05
93 Charles Johnson/AS .05
94 D.J. Boston/AS .05
95 Ruben Santana/AS .05
96 Joe Randa/AS .05
97 Alex Gonzalez/AS .05
98 Tim Clark/AS .05
99 Randy Curtis/AS .05
100 Brian Hunter/AS .05
101 Jose Lima .05
102 Ray Holbert .05
103 Karim Garcia .50
104 Chris Martin .05
105 David Bell .05
106 Tim Clark .05
107 Matt Drews .05
108 Dan Serafini .05
109 Demetrish Jenkins .05
110 Charles Johnson .05
111 Jason Moler .05
112 Brett Backlund .05
113 Kevin Jordan .05
114 Jesus Tavarez .05
115 Frank Rodriguez .05
116 Derrek Lee 1.00
117 Pokey Reese .10
118 Dave Stevens .05
119 Julio Bruno .05
120 D.J. Boston .05
121 Jim Dougherty .05
122 Daron Kirkreit .05
123 Kerwin Moore .05
124 Jason Kendall .50
125 Johnny Damon 1.00
126 Andre King .05
127 Raul Gonzalez .05
128 Eddie Pearson .05
129 Yuri Sanchez .05
130 Russ Davis .05
131 Arquimedez Pozo .05
132 Jon Lieber .10
133 Glenn Murray .05
134 Brant Brown .05
135 Brian Hunter .05
136 Mike Gulan .05
137 Tim Vanegmond .05
138 Billy Vanlandingham .05
139 Robert Ellis .05
140 Calvin Murray .05
141 Kurt Ehmann .05
142 Brian DuBose .05
143 Robert Eenhoorn .05
144 Howard Battle .05

145 Jason Giambi 1.00
146 James Baldwin (Major League Evaluation) .05
147 Rick Helling (MLE) .05
148 Ricky Bottalico (MLE) .05
149 Paul Spolijaric (Spoljaric)(MLE) .05
150 Alex Gonzalez (MLE) .05
151 Tavo Alvarez (MLE) .05
152 Joey Eischen (MLE) .05
153 Shane Andrews (MLE) .05
154 James Mouton (MLE) .05
155 Russ Davis (MLE) .05
156 Phil Nevin (MLE) .05
157 Garret Anderson (MLE) .05
158 Gabe White (MLE) .05
159 Brian Hunter (MLE) .05
160 Ray McDavid (MLE) .05
161 Mike Durrant .05
162 Eric Owens .05
163 Rick Gorecki .05
164 Lyle Mouton .05
165 Ray McDavid .05
166 Tony Graffagnino (Graffanino) .05
167 Todd Ritchie .05
168 Jose Herrera .05
169 Steve Dunn .05
170 Tavo Alvarez .05
171 Jon Farrell .05
172 Omar Ramirez .05
173 Ruben Santana .05
174 Tracy Sanders .05
175 Shane Andrews .05
176 Rob Henkel .05
177 Joel Wolfe .05
178 Chris Schwab .05
179 Chris Weinke .25
180 Ozzie Timmons .05
181 Jason Bates .05
182 Matt Brunson .05
183 Garret Anderson .15
184 Brian Rupp .05
185 Derek Jeter 3.00
186 Desi Relaford .05
187 Darren Burton .05
188 David Mysel .05
189 Steve Soderstrom .05
190 Steve Gibralter .05
191 Brian Sackinsky .05
192 Marc Pisciotta .05
193 Gene Schall .05
194 Jimmy Haynes .05
195 Shannon Stewart .25
196 Neifi Perez .05
197 Cris Colon .05
198 Trey Beamon .05
199 Jon Zuber .05
200 John Burke .05
201 Derek Wallace .05
202 Chad Ogea .05
203 Ernie Young .05
204 Jose Malave .05
205 Bill Pulsipher .05
206 Leon Glenn .05
207 Scott Sullivan .05
208 Orlando Miller .05
209 John Wasdin .05
210 Paul Spoljaric .05
211 Charles Peterson .05
212 Ben Van Ryn .05
213 Chris Sexton .05
214 Bobby Bonds Jr. .05
215 James Mouton .05
216 Terrell Lowery .05
217 Oscar Munoz .05
218 Mike Bell .05
219 Preston Wilson .25
220 Mark Thompson .05
221 Aaron Holbert .05
222 Tommy Adams .05
223 Ramon D. Martinez .05
224 Tim Davis .05
225 Ricky Bottalico .05
226 Rick Krivda .05
227 Troy Percival .05
228 Mark Sweeney .05
229 Joey Hamilton .05
230 Phil Nevin .05
231 John Ratliff .05
232 Mark Smith .05
233 Tyrone Hill .05
234 Kevin Riggs .05
235 John Dettmer .05
236 Brian Barber .05
237 Hector Trinidad .05
238 Jeff Alkire .05
239 Phil Geisler .05
240 Rick Helling .05
241 Edgardo Alfonzo .05
242 Matt Franco .05
243 Chad Roper .05
244 Basil Shabazz .05
245 James Baldwin .05
246 Scott Hatteberg .05
247 Glenn DiSarcina .05
248 LaTroy Hawkins .05
249 Marshall Boze .05
250 Michael Moore .05
251 Brien Taylor (Star Potential) .05
252 Johnny Damon (SP) .65
253 Curtis Goodwin (SP) .05
254 Jose Silva (SP) .05
255 Terrell Wade (SP) .05
256 Dmitri Young (SP) .05
257 Roger Cedeno (SP) .05
258 Alex Ochoa (SP) .05
259 D.J. Boston (SP) .05
260 Michael Tucker (SP) .05
261 Calvin Murray (SP) .05
262 Frank Rodriguez (SP) .05
263 Michael Moore (SP) .05
264 Ugueth Urbina (SP) .05
265 Chad Mottola (SP) .05
266 Todd Hollandsworth (SP) .05
267 Rod Henderson (SP) .05
268 Roberto Petagine (SP) .05
269 Charles Johnson (SP) .05
270 Trot Nixon (SP) .35
MJ23 Michael Jordan (Silver) 7.50
MJ23 Michael Jordan (Gold) 15.00
TC1 Alex Rodriguez (Trade card.) 30.00
TC2 Kirk Presley (Trade card.) .50
---- Redemption Card #1, Expired 12/31/94 .50
---- Redemption Card #2, Expired 12/31/94 .50

Player of the Year

This 28-card insert set features one top prospect from each Major League organization. The cards, numbered with a PY prefix, were random inserts in 1994 Upper Deck Minor League foil packs.

		MT
Complete Set (28):		4.00
Common Player:		.25
1	Marquis Riley	.25
2	Roberto Petagine	.25
3	Ernie Young	.25
4	Alex Gonzalez	.25
5	Hiawatha Wade	.25
6	Marshall Boze	.25
7	Mike Gulan	.25
8	Brant Brown	.25
9	Roger Cedeno	.25
10	Rod Henderson	.25
11	Calvin Murray	.25
12	Omar Ramirez	.25
13	Ruben Santana	.25
14	Charles Johnson	.25
15	Bill Pulsipher	.25
16	Alex Ochoa	.25
17	Ray McDavid	.25
18	Jason Moler	.25
19	Danny Clyburn	.25
20	Rick Helling	.25
21	Frank Rodriquez	.25
22	Chad Mottola	.25
23	John Burke	.25
24	Michael Tucker	.25
25	Brian DuBose	.25
26	LaTroy Hawkins	.25
27	James Baldwin	.25
28	Ryan Karp	.25

Top 10 Prospects

Ten top Major League prospects are featured in two different size versions. A jumbo version of 5-1/4" x 8-1/2" cards was inserted one per foil box of 1994 Upper Deck Minor League baseball cards. The cards are numbered with a TP prefix. The Top 10 Prospects were also available in a standard-size version (2-1/2" x 3-1/2") available through an on-pack offer; collectors could receive a 10-card set by sending in 15 foil pack wrappers, plus $2 for shipping costs. Box-topper card #8 features only a game-action silhouettes; the mail-in offer card pictures Alex Rodriguez.

		MT
Complete Set (10):		15.00
Common Player:		2.00
Jumbo cards worth 50 percent.Jumbo cards worth 50 percent.		.00
1	Roger Cedeno	2.00
2	Johnny Damon	5.00
3	Alex Gonzalez	2.00
4	Charles Johnson	2.00
5	Chad Mottola	2.00
6	Phil Nevin	2.00
7	Alex Ochoa	2.00
8a	1993 No. 1 Draft Pick (Silhouettes, jumbo.)	1.00
8b	Alex Rodriguez (Mail-in card, standard.)	10.00
9	Jose Silva	2.00
10	Michael Tucker	2.00

1994 Minor League Team Sets

Largely through issues by teams in independent leagues, the number of minor league teams issuing sets and the number of sets issued climbed a bit in 1994 as Classic and Fleer/ProCards retained their grip on the marketplace for a final year, with shares of 33% and 57%, respectively.

		MT
299 Team Sets and Variations		
1994	FPC AAA All-Stars (47)	10.00
1994	Classic Albany Polecats (30)	5.00
1994	FPC Albany Polecats (30)	4.00
1994	FPC Albany-Colonie Yankees (31)	7.00
1994	Team Albany-Colonie Yearbook W/Cards (3)	65.00
1994	FPC Albuquerque Dukes (27)	6.00
1994	Team Albuquerque Dukes Photos (28)	100.00
1994	Team Alexandria Aces (26)	5.00
1994	Team Amarillo Dillas (30)	5.00
1994	Classic Appleton Foxes (30)	150.00
1994	FPC Appleton Foxes (28)	30.00
1994	Arizona Fall League (21)	15.00
1994	FPC Arkansas Travelers (26)	5.00
1994	Classic Asheville Tourists (30)	6.00
1994	FPC Asheville Tourists (30)	5.00
1994	Classic Auburn Astros (30)	4.00
1994	FPC Auburn Astros (29)	4.00
1994	Classic Augusta Greenjackets (30)	5.00
1994	FPC Augusta Greenjackets (28)	4.00
1994	Classic Bakersfield Dodgers (30)	5.00
1994	Classic Batavia Clippers (30)	5.00
1994	FPC Batavia Clippers (31)	4.00
1994	Team Beaumont Bullfrogs (23)	5.00
1994	Classic Bellingham Mariners (30)	5.00
1994	FPC Bellingham Mariners (31)	4.00
1994	Classic Beloit Brewers (30)	5.00
1994	FPC Beloit Brewers (30)	4.00
1994	Classic Bend Rockies (30)	4.00
1994	FPC Bend Rockies (31)	5.00
1994	FPC Billings Mustangs (27)	12.00
1994	SP Billings Mustangs (30)	12.00
1994	FPC Binghamton Mets (28)	7.50
1994	Classic Birmingham Barons (30)	9.00
1994	FPC Birmingham Barons (28)	6.00
1994	Classic Bluefield Orioles (30)	5.00
1994	FPC Bluefield Orioles (30)	4.00
1994	Classic Boise Hawks (30)	5.00
1994	FPC Boise Hawks (31)	4.00
1994	FPC Bowie Baysox (27)	5.00
1994	Classic Brevard County Manatees (30)	7.00
1994	FPC Brevard County Manatees (30)	6.00
1994	Classic Bristol Tigers (30)	7.00
1994	FPC Bristol Tigers (30)	7.00
1994	FPC Buffalo Bisons (28)	6.00
1994	Classic Burlington Bees (30)	5.00
1994	FPC Burlington Bees (29)	4.00
1994	Classic Burlington Indians (30)	8.00
1994	FPC Burlington Indians (31)	6.00
1994	SP Butte Copper Kings (30)	6.00
1994	FPC Calgary Cannons (27)	5.00
1994	FPC Canton-Akron Indians (30)	4.00
1994	Classic Capital City Bombers (30)	8.00
1994	FPC Capital City Bombers (29)	7.00
1994	FPC Carolina League All-Stars (53)	7.50
1994	FPC Carolina Mudcats (28)	5.00
1994	Classic Cedar Rapids Kernels (30)	5.00
1994	FPC Cedar Rapids Kernels (27)	4.00
1994	Classic Central Valley Rockies (30)	6.00
1994	FPC Central Valley Rockies (30)	5.00
1994	Classic Charleston River Dogs (30)	6.00
1994	FPC Charleston Riverdogs (29)	5.00
1994	Classic Charleston Wheelers (30)	5.00
1994	FPC Charleston Wheelers (28)	4.00
1994	FPC Charlotte Knights (26)	5.00
1994	Classic Charlotte Rangers (30)	5.00
1994	FPC Charlotte Rangers (27)	4.00
1994	FPC Chattanooga Lookouts (27)	5.00
1994	Team Chillicothe Paints (22)	6.00
1994	Classic Clearwater Phillies (30)	4.00
1994	FPC Clearwater Phillies (30)	4.00
1994	Classic Clinton Lumberkings (30)	5.00
1994	FPC Clinton Lumberkings (30)	4.00
1994	FPC Colorado Springs Sky Sox (28)	5.00
1994	FPC Columbus Clippers (30)	6.00
1994	Police Columbus Clippers (25)	7.00
1994	Team Columbus Clippers (28)	7.00
1994	Classic Columbus RedStixx (30)	7.00
1994	FPC Columbus RedStixx (31)	6.00
1994	Team Corpus Christi Barracudas (28)	5.00
1994	Classic Danville Braves (30)	12.00
1994	FPC Danville Braves (30)	10.00
1994	Classic Daytona Cubs (30)	12.00
1994	FPC Daytona Cubs (29)	6.00
1994	Team Duluth-Superior Dukes (27)	5.00
1994	Classic Dunedin Blue Jays (30)	4.00
1994	FPC Dunedin Blue Jays (30)	4.00
1994	Team Dunedin Blue Jays (29)	45.00
1994	Classic Durham Bulls (30)	5.00
1994	FPC Durham Bulls (30)	4.00
1994	Team Durham Bulls (32)	7.00
1994	FPC Edmonton Trappers (27)	5.00
1994	Classic Elizabethton Twins (30)	5.00
1994	FPC Elizabethton Twins (29)	5.00
1994	Classic Elmira Pioneers (30)	4.00
1994	FPC Elmira Pioneers (27)	7.00
1994	FPC El Paso Diablos (28)	4.00
1994	Classic Eugene Emeralds (30)	4.00
1994	FPC Eugene Emeralds (28)	5.00
1994	Classic Everett Giants (30)	4.00
1994	FPC Everett Giants (31)	5.00
1994	Classic Fayetteville Generals (30)	6.00
1994	FPC Faytetteville Generals (29)	5.00
1994	FPC Florida State League A-S (52)	24.00
1994	Classic Frederick Keys (30)	5.00
1994	FPC Frederick Keys (29)	4.00
1994	Classic Ft. Myers Miracle (30)	6.00
1994	FPC Ft. Myers Miracle (28)	5.00
1994	FPC Ft. Myers Diamond Girls (13)	4.00
1994	Classic Ft. Wayne Wizards (30)	5.00
1994	FPC Ft. Wayne Wizards (28)	4.00
1994	SP Great Falls Dodgers (30)	8.00
1994	Classic Greensboro Bats (30)	6.00
1994	FPC Greensboro Bats (31)	5.00
1994	FPC Greenville Braves (28)	4.00
1994	Team Greenville Braves Foldout	20.00
1994	Classic Hagerstown Suns (30)	6.00
1994	FPC Hagerstown Suns (29)	5.00
1994	FPC Harrisburg Senators (29)	6.00
1994	FPC Helena Brewers (27)	4.00
1994	SP Helena Brewers (30)	6.00
1994	Classic Hickory Crawdads (30)	8.00
1994	FPC Hickory Crawdads (30)	9.00
1994	Classic High Desert Mavericks (30)	5.00
1994	FPC High Desert Mavericks (30)	4.00
1994	Classic Hudson Valley Renegades (30)	6.00
1994	FPC Hudson Valley Renegades (30)	5.00
1994	Classic Huntington Cubs (30)	5.00
1994	FPC Huntington Cubs (31)	4.00
1994	FPC Huntsville Stars (27)	11.00
1994	Team Huntsville Stars (27)	25.00
1994	FPC Idaho Falls Braves (31)	6.00
1994	SP Idaho Falls Braves (30)	6.00
1994	FPC Indianapolis Indians (27)	7.00
1994	FPC Iowa Cubs (26)	5.00
1994	Team Iowa Cubs (9)	6.00
1994	FPC Jackson Generals (27)	8.00
1994	Smokey Bear Jackson Generals (27)	20.00
1994	FPC Jacksonville Suns (27)	7.00
1994	Classic Jamestown Jammers (30)	6.00
1994	FPC Jamestown Jammers (30)	7.00
1994	Classic Johnson City Cardinals (30)	5.00
1994	FPC Johnson City Cardinals (31)	4.00
1994	Classic Kane County Cougars (30)	4.00
1994	FPC Kane County Cougars (30)	5.00
1994	Team Kane County Cougars (30)	7.00
1994	Classic Kingsport Mets (30)	9.00
1994	FPC Kingsport Mets (29)	7.00
1994	Classic Kinston Indians (30)	8.00
1994	FPC Kinston Indians (29)	7.00
1994	FPC Knoxville Smokies (28)	6.00
1994	Classic Lake Elsinore Storm (30)	6.00
1994	FPC Lake Elsinore Storm (28)	5.00
1994	Classic Lakeland Tigers (30)	4.00
1994	FPC Lakeland Tigers (28)	4.00
1994	FPC Las Vegas Stars (25)	5.00
1994	FPC Lethbridge Mounties (30)	4.00
1994	SP Lethbridge Mounties (30)	6.00
1994	FPC Louisville Redbirds (29)	6.00
1994	Classic Lynchburg Red Sox (30)	7.00
1994	FPC Lynchburg Red Sox (29)	6.00
1994	Classic Macon Braves (30)	9.00
1994	FPC Macon Braves (31)	7.00
1994	Classic Madison Hatters (30)	6.00
1994	FPC Madison Hatters (30)	5.00
1994	Classic Martinsville Phillies (30)	4.00
1994	FPC Martinsville Phillies (31)	4.00
1994	FPC Medicine Hat Blue Jays (29)	4.00
1994	SP Medicine Hat Blue Jays (30)	7.00
1994	FPC Memphis Chicks (28)	5.00
1994	FPC Midland Angels (27)	5.00
1994	OHP Midland Angels (33)	40.00
1994	FPC Midwest League All-Stars (59)	40.00
1994	Team Minneapolis Loons (23)	5.00
1994	Team Mobile Bay Sharks (23)	6.00
1994	Classic Modesto A's (30)	6.00
1994	FPC Modesto A's (26)	5.00
1994	FPC Nashville Sounds (27)	6.00
1994	FPC Nashville Xpress (28)	6.00
1994	FPC New Britain Red Sox (27)	5.00
1994	FPC New Haven Ravens (29)	5.00
1994	Classic New Jersey Cardinals (30)	4.00
1994	FPC New Jersey Cardinals (31)	4.00
1994	FPC New Orleans Zephyrs (27)	5.00
1994	FPC Norfolk Tides (27)	6.00
1994	FPC Ogden Raptors (24)	4.00
1994	SP Ogden Raptors (30)	6.00
1994	FPC Oklahoma City 89ers (25)	6.00
1994	FPC Omaha Royals (27)	6.00
1994	Classic Oneonta Yankees (30)	5.00
1994	FPC Oneonta Yankees (31)	6.00
1994	FPC Orlando Cubs (26)	5.00
1994	Classic Osceola Astros (30)	5.00
1994	Team Osceola Astros All-Time Team (30)	75.00
1994	FPC Osecola Astros (30)	4.00
1994	FPC Ottawa Lynx (19)	7.00
1994	DD Pawtucket Red Sox Foldout	20.00
1994	FPC Pawtucket Red Sox (25)	5.00
1994	Classic Peoria Chiefs (30)	5.00
1994	FPC Peoria Chiefs (29)	4.00
1994	Team Peoria Chiefs (30)	12.00
1994	FPC Phoenix Firebirds (27)	5.00
1994	Classic Pittsfield Mets (30)	6.00
1994	FPC Pittsfield Mets (27)	7.00
1994	FPC Portland Sea Dogs (27)	7.00
1994	Team Portland Sea Dogs (31)	10.00
1994	Classic Princeton Reds (30)	5.00
1994	FPC Princeton Reds (29)	4.00
1994	Classic Prince Williams Cannons (30)	6.00
1994	FPC Prince William Cannons (28)	7.00
1994	Classic Quad City River Bandits (30)	8.00
1994	FPC Quad City River Bandits (29)	7.00
1994	Classic Rancho Cucamonga Quakes (30)	9.00
1994	FPC Rancho Cucamonga Quakes (29)	9.00
1994	FPC Reading Phillies (27)	4.00
1994	FPC Reading Phils Campbell's Soups (27)	7.50
1994	FPC Richmond Braves (30)	5.00
1994	Richmond Camera Richmond Braves (28)	45.00
1994	Team Richmond Braves Foldout	30.00
1994	Team Rio Grande White Wings (25)	5.00
1994	FPC Rochester Red Wings (27)	5.00
1994	Classic Rockford Royals (30)	8.00
1994	FPC Rockford Royals (31)	7.00
1994	Classic Salem Buccaneers (30)	8.00
1994	FPC Salem Buccaneers (28)	5.00
1994	FPC Salt Lake City Buzz (27)	4.00
1994	FPC San Antonio Missions (31)	9.00
1994	HEB San Antonio Missions (26)	55.00
1994	Team San Antonio Tejanos (28)	5.00
1994	Classic San Bernardino Spirit (30)	5.00
1994	FPC San Bernardino Spirit (28)	4.00
1994	Classic San Jose Giants (30)	6.00

1994 FPC San Jose Giants (29) 5.00
1994 Classic Sarasota Red Sox (30) 8.00
1994 FPC Sarasota Red Sox (30) 7.00
1994 Classic Savannah Cardinals (30) 6.00
1994 FPC Savannah Cardinals (31) 5.00
1994 FPC Scranton Red Barons (26) 5.00
1994 Team Scranton Red Barons (30) 8.00
1994 FPC Shreveport Captains (29) 5.00
1994 Team Sioux City Explorers (26) 6.00
1994 Team Sioux Falls Canaries (28) 6.00
1994 FPC South Atlantic League A-S (57) 20.00
1994 Classic South Bend Silver Hawks (30) 5.00
1994 FPC South Bend Silver Hawks (29) 4.00
1994 Classic Southern Oregon Athletics (30) 15.00
1994 FPC Southern Oregon Athletics (29) 12.00
1994 Classic Spartanburg Phillies (30) 20.00
1994 FPC Spartanburg Phillies (30) 10.00
1994 Classic Spokane Indians (30) 4.00
1994 FPC Spokane Indians (30) 4.00
1994 Classic Sultans of Springfield (30) 5.00
1994 FPC Springfield Sultans (27) 4.00
1994 Classic St. Catherines Blue Jays (30) 8.00
1994 FPC St. Catherines Blue Jays (30) 4.00
1994 Classic St. Lucie Mets (30) 10.00
1994 FPC St. Lucie Mets (29) 8.00
1994 Team St. Paul Saints (28) 24.00
1994 Classic St. Petersburg Cardinals (30) 5.00
1994 FPC St. Petersburg Cardinals (29) 4.00
1994 Classic Stockton Ports (30) 5.00
1994 FPC Stockton Ports (28) 4.00
1994 FPC Syracuse Chiefs (26) 8.00
1994 FPC Tacoma Tigers (28) 5.00
1994 Classic Tampa Yankees (30) 30.00
1994 FPC Tampa Yankees (32) 25.00
1994 Team Thunder Bay Whiskey Jacks (25) 5.00
1994 FPC Toledo Mud Hens (27) 5.00
1994 FPC Trenton Thunder (27) 5.00
1994 FPC Tucson Toros (29) 5.00
1994 FPC Tulsa Drillers (27) 5.00
1994 Team Tulsa Drillers (30) 8.00
1994 Team Tylor Wildcatters (25) 5.00
1994 Classic Utica Blue Sox (30) 7.00
1994 FPC Utica Blue Sox (29) 4.00
1994 FPC Vancouver Canadians (26) 9.00
1994 Classic Vermont Expos (30) 4.00
1994 FPC Vermont Expos (28) 4.00
1994 Classic Vero Beach Dodgers (30) 11.00
1994 FPC Vero Beach Dodgers (31) 8.00
1994 Classic Watertown Indians (30) 5.00
1994 FPC Watertown Indians (30) 4.00
1994 Classic Welland Pirates (30) 5.00
1994 FPC Welland Pirates (31) 4.00
1994 Classic West Michigan Whitecaps (30) 5.00
1994 FPC West Michigan Whitecaps (28) 4.00
1994 Classic West Palm Beach Expos (30) 8.00
1994 FPC West Palm Beach Expos (30) 7.00
1994 FPC Wichita Wranglers (26) 5.00
1994 Classic Williamsport Cubs (30) 6.00
1994 FPC Williamsport Cubs (30) 5.00
1994 Classic Wilmington Blue Rocks (30) 9.00
1994 FPC Wilmington Blue Rocks (29) 7.00
1994 Team Wilmington Blue Rocks 35.00
1994 Team Winnipeg Goldeyes (30) 6.00
1994 Classic Winston-Salem Spirits (30) 4.00
1994 FPC Winston-Salem Spirits (28) 4.00
1994 Classic Yakima Bears (30) 10.00
1994 FPC Yakima Bears (30) 8.00
1994 Team Zanesville Greys (25) 10.00

1995 Action Packed Scouting Report

Action Packed's final minor league issue combines cards of baseball's best young prospects with cards honoring its oldest performer (#80-82 feature ballpark clown Max Patkin). The basic set features large player photos on front on which the player figure has been embossed. Cards #52-61 have a "#1 Draft Pick" logo in an upper corner. Cards #62-79 are "Franchise Gems" with an appropriate logo in an upper corner. Each of the "Franchise Gem" cards can also be found in a 24-karat gold stamped parallel edition, while card #1, Jeter's "Player of the Year" card can be found once every 480 packs in a diamond-chip encrusted, autographed version.

		MT
Complete Set (83):		10.00
Common Player:		.10
Wax Box:		10.00
1	Derek Jeter (Player of the Year)	4.00
1A	Derek Jeter/Auto.	45.00
1D	Derek Jeter (Autographed, diamond version.)	50.00
2	Trot Nixon	.50
3	Charles Johnson	.10
4	Chan Ho Park	.25
5	Terrell Wade	.10
6	Carlos Delgado	1.00
7	Brian Hunter	.10
8	Tony Clark	.10
9	Russ Davis	.10
10	Derek Jeter	2.00
11	Alex Gonzalez	.10
12	Scott Ruffcorn	.10
13	Todd Hollandsworth	.10
14	Phil Nevin	.10
15	Marc Newfield	.10
16	Jose Silva	.10
17	Willie Greene	.10
18	Billy Ashley	.10
19	James Baldwin	.10
20	Jeff Granger	.10
21	Michael Tucker	.10
22	Johnny Damon	1.00
23	Roger Cedeno	.10
24	Makoto Suzuki	.10
25	Curtis Goodwin	.10
26	Frankie Rodriguez	.10
27	Roberto Mejia	.10
28	LaTroy Hawkins	.10
29	Alex Ochoa	.10
30	Jose Oliva	.10
31	Ruben Rivera	.10
32	Ray Durham	.10
33	Eduardo Perez	.10
34	Jose Malave	.10
35	Jeromy Burnitz	.25
36	Brad Woodall	.10
37	Joe Vitiello	.10
38	Daron Kirkreit	.10
39	Jimmy Haynes	.10
40	Andrew Lorraine	.10
41	Arquimedez Pozo	.10
42	Armando Benitez	.10
43	Alan Benes	.10
44	Julian Tavarez	.10
45	Curtis Pride	.10
46	Homer Bush	.10
47	Pokey Reese	.25
48	Billy Wagner	.25
49	Richard Hidalgo	.10
50	Allen Battle	.10
51	Kevin Millar	.15
52	Paul Wilson (#1 Draft Pick)	.15
53	Ben Grieve (#1 Draft Pick)	.15
54	Dustin Hermanson (#1 Draft Pick)	.15
55	Antone Williamson (#1 Draft Pick)	.10
56	Josh Booty (#1 Draft Pick)	.10
57	Doug Million (#1 Draft Pick)	.10
58	Jaret Wright (#1 Draft Pick)	.25
59	Todd Walker (#1 Draft Pick)	.10
60	Nomar Garciaparra (#1 Draft Pick)	2.00
61	C.J. Nitkowski (#1 Draft Pick)	.10
62	Charles Johnson (Franchise Gem)	.10
63	Marc Newfield (Franchise Gem)	.10
64	Ray Durham (Franchise Gem)	.10
65	Carlos Delgado (Franchise Gem)	.75
66	Alex Gonzalez (Franchise Gem)	.10
67	Derek Jeter (Franchise Gem)	2.00
68	Jose Oliva (Franchise Gem)	.10
69	Billy Ashley (Franchise Gem)	.10
70	Brian Hunter (Franchise Gem)	.10
71	Ruben Rivera (Franchise Gem)	.10
72	Alan Benes (Franchise Gem)	.10
73	Willie Greene (Franchise Gem)	.10
74	Russ Davis (Franchise Gem)	.10
75	Jose Malave (Franchise Gem)	.10
76	LaTroy Hawkins (Franchise Gem)	.10
77	Frankie Rodriguez (Franchise Gem)	.10
78	Scott Ruffcorn (Franchise Gem)	.10
79	Ben Grieve (Franchise Gem)	.15
80	Max Patkin	.10
81	Max Patkin	.10
82	Max Patkin	.10
83	Derek Jeter Checklist	.75

1995 Action Packed 24KT Gold

Eighteen better-than-average prospects were selected for this random insert series. 24KT Gold Franchise Gem cards are die-cut in a tombstone shape with a large baseball at top on front. The front is highlighted by gold-foil graphics. Backs have a few stats and are numbered with a "G" suffix.

		MT
Complete Set (18):		20.00
Common Player:		1.00
1G	Charles Johnson	1.00
2G	Marc Newfield	1.00
3G	Ray Durham	1.00
4G	Carlos Delgado	4.00
5G	Alex Gonzalez	1.00
6G	Derek Jeter	7.50
	Derek Jeter (24K Gold Autograph)	60.00
	Derek Jeter (Diamond Autograph)	65.00
7G	Jose Oliva	1.00
8G	Billy Ashley	1.00
9G	Brian L. Hunter	1.00
10G	Ruben Rivera	1.00
11G	Alan Benes	1.00
12G	Willie Greene	1.00
13G	Russ Davis	1.00
14G	Jose Malave	1.00
15G	LaTroy Hawkins	1.00
16G	Frank Rodriguez	1.00
17G	Scott Ruffcorn	1.00
18G	Ben Grieve	1.50

1995 Best Top 100

In mid-1995, some of the founding principals of Best re-acquired the brand name from Classic and began production of a new generation of minor league cards. Following the 1995 season, the company released a set of 100 top minor league players. White bordered card fronts feature team logos at upper-right. Backs have a portrait photo, 1995 stats and a scouting report on the player. The issue was sold in 12-card hobby foil packs and 16-card retail packs. Hobby packs included a special autographed edition card of four top prospects randomly inserted at an average rate of one per 18 packs. The retail packs had inserts of 23 First Round Draft Picks and 10 "Best of the Best" cards.

		MT
Complete Set (101):		7.50
Common Player:		.05
Wax Pack (15):		1.50
Wax Box (36):		35.00
1	Rocky Coppinger	.05
2	Rafael Orellano	.05
3	Nomar Garciaparra	2.00
4	Ryan McGuire	.05
5	Pork Chop Pough	.05
6	Trot Nixon	.50
7	Donnie Sadler	.05
8	Chris Allison	.05
9	Todd Greene	.05
10	George Arias	.05
11	Matt Beaumont	.05
12	Jeff Abbott	.05
13	Tom Fordham	.05
14	Damian Jackson	.05
15	Richie Sexson	.25
16	Bartolo Colon	.25
17	David Roberts	.05
18	Daryle Ward	.05
19	Brandon Reed	.05
20	Juan Encarnacion	.10
21	Eddy Gaillard	.05
22	Derek Hacopian	.05
23	Glendon Rusch	.05
24	Lino Diaz	.05
25	Tim Byrdak	.05
26	Antone Williamson	.05
27	Jonas Hamlin	.05
28	Todd Walker	.10
29	Dan Serafini	.05
30	Kimera Bartee	.05
31	Shane Bowers	.05
32	Tyrone Horne	.05
33	Nick Del Vecchio	.05
34	Mike Figga	.05
35	Matt Drews	.05
36	Ray Ricken	.05
37	Ben Grieve	.15
38	Steve Cox	.05
39	Scott Spiezio	.05
40	Desi Relaford	.10
41	Matt Wagner	.05
42	James Bonnici	.05
43	Osvaldo Fernandez	.05
44	Marino Santana	.05
45	Julio Santana	.05
46	Jeff Davis	.05
47	Trey Beamon	.05
48	Jose Pett	.05
49	Chris Carpenter	.05
50	Andruw Jones	1.00
51	Damon Hollins	.05
52	Jermaine Dye	.15
53	Aldo Pecorilli	.05
54	Carey Paige	.05
55	Damian Moss	.05
56	Ron Wright	.05
57	Brooks Kieschnick	.05
58	Pedro Valdes	.05
59	Scott Samuels	.05
60	Bobby Morris	.05
61	Amaury Telemaco	.05
62	Steve Gibraltar	.05
63	Pokey Reese	.15
64	Pat Watkins	.05
65	Aaron Boone	.10
66	Jamey Wright	.05
67	Derrick Gibson	.05
68	Brent Crowther	.05
69	Ralph Milliard	.05
70	Edgar Renteria	.15
71	Billy McMillon	.05
72	Clemente Nunez	.05
73	Bob Abreu	.25
74	Eric Ludwick	.05
75	Tony Mounce	.05
76	Chris Latham	.05
77	Wilton Guerrero	.05
78	Adam Riggs	.05
79	Paul Konerko	.50
80	Vladimir Guerrero	1.00
81	Brad Fullmer	.05
82	Hiram Bocachica	.05
83	Paul Wilson	.10
84	Jay Payton	.10
85	Rey Ordonez	.05
86	Wendell Magee	.05
87	Wayne Gomes	.05
88	Carlton Loewer	.05
89	Scott Rolen	.75
90	Rich Hunter	.05
91	Jason Kendall	.40
92	Micah Franklin	.05
93	Elmer Dessens	.05
94	Matt Ruebel	.05
95	Mike Gulan	.05
96	Jay Witasick	.05
97	Bret Wagner	.05
98	Greg LaRocca	.05
99	Jason Thompson	.05
100	Derrek Lee	.50
----	Checklist	.05

Best of the Best

Numbered contiguously from the regular set, but found only as one-per-pack inserts in 16-card retail foil packs, this chase set features 10 of the brightest minor league stars of 1995. Fronts are in horizontal format with a color photo superimposed on a green background photo. Backs have 1995 and career stats along with career highlights.

		MT
Complete Set (10):		6.00
Common Card:		.25
101	Jason Kendall	.50
102	Derrek Lee	1.50
103	Todd Walker	.25
104	Edgar Renteria	.25
105	Scott Rolen	2.00
106	Andruw Jones	3.00
107	Jay Payton	.25
108	Derrick Gibson	.25
109	Paul Wilson	.25
110	Brandon Reed	.25

First Round Draft Picks

Another one-per-pack insert exclusive to 16-card retail foil packs of Best Top 100 is this set of first round picks from the June 1995 amateur draft. Cards are similar in format to the regular-issue Top 100 but have the front photo background posterized. Backs have a short biography.

		MT
Complete Set (23):		5.00
Common Player:		.10
111	Ben Davis	.10
112	Chad Hermansen	.10
113	Corey Jenkins	.10
114	Geoff Jenkins	.25
115	Ryan Jaroncyk	.10
116	Andy Yount	.10
117	Reggie Taylor	.10
118	Joe Fontenot	.10
119	Mike Drumright	.10
120	David Yokum	.10
121	Jonathan Johnson	.10
122	Jaime Jones	.10
123	Tony McKnight	.10
124	Michael Barrett	.15
125	Roy Halladay	.50
126	Todd Helton	2.00
127	Juan LeBron	.10
128	Darin Erstad	.50
129	Jose Cruz, Jr.	.10
130	Kerry Wood	2.00
131	Shea Morenz	.10
132	Mark Redman	.10
133	Matt Morris	.25

1995 Classic Assets Gold (Baseball)

This super-premium five-sport set offers 50 base cards and a wide range of inserts with extremely limited production on some. The baseball players from the issue are listed here. Only 500 of each gold diecut were produced and 349 of each gold signature.

		MT
Base Set/Inserts:		
11	Nolan Ryan	1.00
11	Nolan Ryan (Silver signature.)	5.00
11	Nolan Ryan (Gold signature.)	15.00
SDC18	Nolan Ryan (Silver die-cut.)	5.00
GDC18	Nolan Ryan Gold die-cut.)	15.00
12	Barry Bonds	2.00
12	Barry Bonds (Silver signature.)	5.00
12	Barry Bonds (Gold signature.)	15.00
SDC9	Barry Bonds (Silver die-cut.)	5.00
GDC9	Barry Bonds (Gold die-cut.)	15.00
13	Ben Grieve	.25
13	Ben Grieve (Silver signature.)	1.00
13	Ben Grieve (Gold signature.)	2.50
SDC1	Ben Grieve (Silver die-cut.)	1.00
GDC1	Ben Grieve (Gold die-cut.)	2.50
14	Dustin Hermanson	.15
14	Dustin Hermanson (Silver signature.)	1.00
14	Dustin Hermanson (Gold signature.)	3.00

1995 Classic 5 Sport (Baseball)

Thirty-one baseball players are included in the 200 cards of this issue which covers the four major team sports plus auto racing, with the emphasis on up-and-coming youngsters. Fronts have color poses or action photos at left. Minor or major league uniform logos have been removed because the cards are licensed only by the individual players. At right is a stack of baseballs with the player's name in gold vertically and the city in which he plays and his position in white. Backs have another color photo at right with personal data and a career summary in a gold marbled panel at left. Professional stats are in a black box at bottom. Besides the standard format, each card can also be found in a die-cut and a printer's proof version as random pack inserts, as well as an autographed version.

		MT
Baseball Set (33):		5.00
Common Player:		.10
93	Ben Grieve	.15
94	Roger Cedeno	.10
95	Michael Barrett	.10
96	Ben Davis	.10
97	Paul Wilson	.15
98	Calvin Reese	.10
99	Jermaine Dye	.15
100	Alvie Shepherd	.10
101	Ryan Jaroncyk	.10
102	Mark Farris	.10
103	Karim Garcia	.30
104	Rey Ordonez	.10
105	Jay Payton	.10
106	Dustin Hermanson	.10
107	Tommy Davis	.10
108	C.J. Nitkowski	.10
109	Todd Greene	.10
110	Billy Wagner	.10
111	Mark Redman	.10
112	Brooks Kieschnick	.10
113	Paul Konerko	.50
114	Brad Fullmer	.10
115	Vladimir Guerrero	2.00
116	Bartolo Colon	.35
117	Doug Million	.10
118	Steve Gibraltar	.10
119	Tony McKnight	.10
120	Derrek Lee	1.00
121	Nomar Garciaparra	2.50
122	Chad Hermansen	.10
183	Nomar Garciaparra, W/Travis Best (Alma Mater)	1.50
188	Paul Wilson, W/Derrick Brooks (Alma Mater)	.10
193	Barry Bonds (Picture Perfect)	3.00

Autographed

Authentically autographed versions of each of the base cards in the 5 Sport set were available as random pack inserts. Backs have a message of congratulations and authenticity. Some cards are seen with an embossed "Classic Certified" logo and with numbered signatures.

		MT
Baseball Set (31):		165.00
Common Player:		1.00
93	Ben Grieve	2.00
94	Roger Cedeno	2.00
95	Michael Barrett	2.00
96	Ben Davis	1.00
97	Paul Wilson	2.00
98a	Calvin Reese ("Calvin Reese" autograph.)	4.00
98b	Pokey Reese ("Pokey Reese" autograph.)	4.00
99	Jermaine Dye	4.00
100	Alvie Shepherd	1.00
101	Ryan Jaroncyk	1.00
102	Mark Farris	1.00
103	Karim Garcia	3.00
104	Rey Ordonez	1.00
105	Jay Payton	2.00
106	Dustin Hermanson	1.00
107	Tommy Davis	1.00
108	C.J. Nitkowski	1.00
109	Todd Greene	1.00
110	Billy Wagner	3.00
111	Mark Redman	1.00
112	Brooks Kieschnick	1.00
113	Paul Konerko	3.00
114	Brad Fullmer	1.00
115	Vladimir Guerrero	20.00
116	Bartolo Colon	4.00
117	Doug Million	3.00
118	Steve Gibraltar	1.00
119	Tony McKnight	1.00
120	Derrek Lee	15.00

121 Nomar Garciaparra 25.00
122 Chad Hermansen 1.00
193 Barry Bonds (Picture Perfect) 100.00

Autograph Edition

"Autograph Edition" versions bearing facsimile signatures on each of the base cards in the 5 Sport set were available as random pack inserts. Variations in the color of the facsimile signature are known as is a die-cut version.

MT
Baseball Set (31): 10.00
Common Player: .20
93 Ben Grieve .30
94 Roger Cedeno .20
95 Michael Barrett .20
96 Ben Davis .20
97 Paul Wilson .20
98 Calvin Reese .30
99 Jermaine Dye .25
100 Alvie Shepherd .20
101 Ryan Jaroncyk .20
102 Mark Farris .20
103 Karim Garcia .40
104 Rey Ordonez .20
105 Jay Payton .20
106 Dustin Hermanson .20
107 Tommy Davis .20
108 C.J. Nitkowski .20
109 Todd Greene .20
110 Billy Wagner .30
111 Mark Redman .20
112 Brooks Kieschnick .20
113 Paul Konerko .60
114 Brad Fullmer .20
115 Vladimir Guerrero 3.00
116 Bartolo Colon .40
117 Doug Million .20
118 Steve Gibraltar .20
119 Tony McKnight .20
120 Derrek Lee 1.50
121 Nomar Garciaparra 4.00
122 Chad Hermansen .20
193 Barry Bonds (Picture Perfect) 5.00

1995 Classic Images '95 Classic Performances

This is the only one of the several Images '95 insert sets to include baseball players. Horizontal format cards feature color player photos on a background of etched gold metallic foil. Backs have another color photo and a description of the career highlight, along with a serial number from within an edition of 4,495. Stated odds of picking a Classic Performances card were one per 12 packs.

MT
Baseball Set (3): 10.00
CP16 Paul Wilson 1.00
CP17 Barry Bonds 7.50
CP18 Nolan Ryan 7.50

1995 Signature Rookies

Fifty top prospects are featured in the 1995 Signature Rookies base set, along with many types of insert cards at varying levels of scarcity. The 2-1/2" x 3-1/2" cards have the player's last name in gold-foil on a marble-look panel at top (first name in red), and at bottom have a gold-foil notation "1 of 25,000." Backs repeat a detail of the front photo, add a second photo and provide stats, personal data and career highlights.

MT
Complete Set (50): 1.00
Common Player: .05
1 Mark Acre .05
2 Edgar Alfonzo .05
3 Ivan Arteaga .05
4 Rich Aude .05
5 Joe Ausanio .05
6 Marc Barcelo .05
7 Allen Battle .05
8 Rigo Beltran .05
9 Darren Bragg .05
10 Rico Brogna .05
11 Mike Busch .05
12 Juan F. Castillo .05
13 Joe Ciccarella .05
14 Darrel Deak .05
15 Steve Dunn .05
16 Vaughn Eshelman .05
17 Bart Evans .05
18 Rikkert Faneyte .05
19 Kenny Felder .05
20 Micah Franklin .05
21 Brad Fullmer .05
22 Willie Greene .05
23 Greg Hansell .05
24 Phil Hiatt .05
25 Todd Hollandsworth .05
26 Damon Hollins .05
27 Chris Hook .05
28 Kerry Lacy .05
29 Todd LaRocca .05
30 Sean Lawrence .05
31 Aaron Ledesma .05
32 Esteban Loaiza .05
33 Albie Lopez .05
34 Luis Lopez .05
35 Marc Marini .05
36 Nate Minchey .05
37 Doug Mlicki .05
38 Glenn Murray .05
39 Troy O'Leary .05
40 Eric Owens .05
41 Orlando Palmeiro .05
42 Todd Pridy .05
43 Joe Randa .05
44 Jason Schmidt .25
45 Basil Shabazz .05
46 Paul Spoljaric .05
47 J.J. Thobe .05
48 Sean Whiteside .05
49 Gary Wilson .05
50 Shannon Withem .05
JD 2Joe DiMaggio 3.00

Autographed

Each of the cards in the Signature Rookies set was also issued in an authentically-autographed edition of 5,750 as random pack inserts. Some cards were represented in packs by coupons redeemable for the cards. Cards of Kerry Lacy and Basil Shabazz were never autographed.

MT
Complete Set (48/50): 40.00
Common Player: 1.00
1 Mark Acre 1.00
2 Edgar Alfonzo 1.00
3 Ivan Arteaga 1.00
4 Rich Aude 1.00
5 Joe Ausanio 1.00
6 Marc Barcelo 1.00
7 Allen Battle 1.00
8 Rigo Beltran 1.00
9 Darren Bragg 1.00
10 Rico Brogna 1.00
11 Mike Busch 1.00
12 Juan F. Castillo 1.00
13 Joe Ciccarella 1.00
14 Darrel Deak 1.00
15 Steve Dunn 1.00
16 Vaughn Eshelman 1.00
17 Bart Evans 1.00
18 Rikkert Faneyte 1.00
19 Kenny Felder 1.00
20 Micah Franklin 1.00
21 Brad Fullmer 1.00
22 Willie Greene 1.00
23 Greg Hansell 1.00
24 Phil Hiatt 1.00
25 Todd Hollandsworth 1.50
26 Damon Hollins 1.00
27 Chris Hook 1.00
28 Kerry Lacy (Not signed.) .25
29 Todd LaRocca 1.00
30 Sean Lawrence 1.00
31 Aaron Ledesma 1.00
32 Esteban Loaiza 2.00
33 Albie Lopez 1.00
34 Luis Lopez 1.00
35 Marc Marini 1.00
36 Nate Minchey 1.00
37 Doug Mlicki 1.00
38 Glenn Murray 1.00
39 Troy O'Leary 1.00
40 Eric Owens 1.00
41 Orlando Palmeiro 1.00
42 Todd Pridy 1.00
43 Joe Randa 1.00
44 Jason Schmidt 6.00
45 Basil Shabazz (Not signed.) .25
46 Paul Spoljaric 1.00
47 J.J. Thobe 1.00
48 Sean Whiteside 1.00
49 Gary Wilson 1.00
50 Shannon Withem 1.00

Draft Day Stars

Five hot picks from the 1994 amateur draft are featured in this insert set on both unsigned and authentically autographed cards. Fronts have a pair of photos on a background of bright colors. The player name, Draft Day Star logo and edition number (10,000 each plain, 2,000 autographed) are in gold foil. Backs repeat one of the front photos and have a few career notes and stats along with personal data.

MT
Complete Set (5): 1.00
Complete Set, Auto. (5): 9.00
Common Player: .25
Common Autograph: 2.00
DD1 Matt Beaumont .25
DD1a Matt Beaumont/Auto. 2.00
DD2 Josh Booty .25
DD2a Josh Booty/Auto 3.00
DD3 Russ Johnson .25
DD3a Russ Johnson/Auto 2.00
DD4 Todd Walker .25
DD4a Todd Walker/Auto 3.00
DD5 Jaret Wright .25
DD5a Jaret Wright/Auto 3.00

Fame & Fortune Erstad!

This insert issue to the Fame & Fortune football/ basketball set features University of Nebraska football/ baseball star and 1995 #1 overall draft pick Darin Erstad. The cards have borderless color game-action (either baseball or football) photos of the player with his name repeated in varying sizes of gray letters in the background. Down one side in gold foil is "ERSTAD!," shadowed in red. The Fame & Fortune logo is in gold in a lower corner. Backs have a white background, another color photo, his college baseball stats and a few sentences about his career to date.

MT
Complete Set (5): 5.00
Common Player: 1.00
E1 Darin Erstad/Btg 1.00
E2 Darin Erstad/Btg 1.00
E3 Darin Erstad/Punting 1.00
E4 Darin Erstad/Btg 1.00
E5 Darin Erstad/Fldg 1.00

Major Rookies

Five of 1995's top rookies are featured in this insert set. Cards come in both unsigned (edition of 10,000 each) and genuinely autographed (edition of 750 each). Fronts have player action photos with a huge green and orange "MAJOR ROOKIES" logo behind. The player name and edition number are in gold foil. Backs also feature the green and orange color scheme and have another color photo, stats and personal data, and a paragraph about the player.

MT
Complete Set (5): 5.00
Complete Set, Auto. (5): 100.00
Common Player: .50
Common Autograph: 2.00
MR1 Marty Cordova .75
MR1a Marty Cordova/Auto. 3.00
MR2 Benji Gil .50
MR2a Benji Gil/Auto. 2.00
MR3 Charles Johnson .75
MR3a Charles Johnson/ Auto. 3.00
MR4 Manny Ramirez 2.00
MR4a Manny Ramirez/ Auto. 45.00
MR5 Alex Rodriguez 3.00
MR5a Alex Rodriguez/ Auto. 60.00

Organizational Player/Year

These inserts are found in both autographed (edition of 1,000) and unsigned (7,500) form. The design emphasizes the foundation nature of the players chosen, with a red brick wall at one side and an action photo at the other. The card title and player name are in gold foil. Backs repeat the brick wall background, have another color photo and the usual personal data, stats and career summary.

MT
Complete Set (5): 1.00
Complete Set, Auto. (5): 15.00
Common Player: .25
Common Autograph: 2.00
OP1 Juan Acevedo .25
OP1a Juan Acevedo/Auto. 1.00
OP2 Johnny Damon .75
OP2a Johnny Damon/ Auto. 12.00
OP3 Ray Durham .25
OP3a Ray Durham/Auto. 3.00
OP4 LaTroy Hawkins .25
OP4a LaTroy Hawkins/Auto. 1.00
OP5 Brad Woodall .25
OP5a Brad Woodall/Auto. 3.00

1995 Signature Rookies Preview

Players who looked to be ready for the major leagues are the focus of this set. Large color action photos on front are surmounted by a red strip bearing the player's name in gold foil. Gold highlights at bottom have the SR Preview logo at lower-left and "1 of 25,000" at center. Backs have two more color photos of the player, with one of them ghosted in muted shades. The player's complete minor league record is included. Each of the cards in the set can also be found in an autographed version of 6,000. Minor and major league team logos have been removed from the player photos and, in some cases, replaced with unofficial logos to avoid licensing problems.

MT
Complete Set (38): 1.00
Common Player: .05
1 Tavo Alvarez .05
2 Rich Batchelor .05
3 Doug Bochtler .05
4 Jerry Brooks .05
5 Scott Bryant .05
6 Mike Busby .05
7 Fred Costello .05
8 Glenn Dishman .05
9 James Foster .05
10 Webster Garrison .05
11 Tony Graffanino .05
12 Billy Hall .05
13 Mike Hubbard .05
14 Jason Hutchins .05
15 Rick Kelley .05
16 Jerry Koller .05
17 Ryan Luzinski .05
18 Anthony Manahan .05
19 Mike Matthews .05
20 Greg McCarty .05
21 Jeff McCurry .05
22 Gino Minutelli .05
23 Izzy Molina .05
24 Scott Moten .05
25 Peter Munro .05
26 Willis Otanez .05
27 Rodney Pedraza .05
28 Brandon Pico .05
29 Brian Raabe .05
30 Eddie Rios .05
31 Toby Rumfield .05
32 Andy Sheets .05
33 Larry Sutton .05
34 Brian Thomas .05
35 Hector Trinidad .05
36 Jim Waring .05
37 Mike Welch .05
38 Steve Wojciechowski .05

Autographed

Each of the cards in the 1995 Signature Rookies Preview set can be found in an autographed edition. The cards are hand-signed and numbered within an edition of 6,000. The autographed cards have a gold-foil "1 of 6,000" notation at bottom-center on front.

MT
Complete Set (38): 35.00
Common Player: 1.00
1 Tavo Alvarez 1.00
2 Rich Batchelor 1.00
3 Doug Bochtler 1.00
4 Jerry Brooks 1.00
5 Scott Bryant 1.00
6 Mike Busby 1.00
7 Fred Costello 1.00
8 Glenn Dishman 1.00
9 James Foster 1.00
10 Webster Garrison 1.00
11 Tony Graffanino 1.00
12 Billy Hall 1.00
13 Mike Hubbard 1.00
14 Jason Hutchins 1.00
15 Rick Kelley 1.00
16 Jerry Koller 1.00
17 Ryan Luzinski 1.50
18 Anthony Manahan 1.00
19 Mike Matthews 1.00
20 Greg McCarty 1.00
21 Jeff McCurry 1.00
22 Gino Minutelli 1.00
23 Izzy Molina 1.00
24 Scott Moten 1.00
25 Peter Munro 1.00
26 Willis Otanez 1.00
27 Rodney Pedraza 1.00
28 Brandon Pico 1.00
29 Brian Raabe 1.00
30 Eddie Rios 1.00
31 Toby Rumfield 1.00
32 Andy Sheets 1.00
33 Larry Sutton 1.00
34 Brian Thomas 1.00
35 Hector Trinidad 1.00
36 Jim Waring 1.00
37 Mike Welch 1.00
38 Steve Wojciechowski 1.00

1995 Signature Rookies Star Squad

Ten players who were already making their marks in the Major Leagues were featured in this insert set. The cards have player action photos on front with large red areas above and below containing a star and "STAR SQUAD" designation and the player's name and manufacturer's logo. A vertical gold-foil stamping notes, "1 of 10,000." Backs have another player photo along with a few stats, biographical bits and career summary. Uniform logos have been airbrushed away or replaced with unofficial logos since the cards are licensed only by the individual players and not Major League Baseball. An autographed edition of each player was also randomly inserted.

MT
Complete Set (10): 6.00
Complete Auto. Set (10): 110.00
Common Player: .25
Common Autograph: 2.00
1 Ruben Rivera .25
1a Ruben Rivera/Auto. 2.00
2 Charles Johnson .25
2a Charles Johnson/ Auto. 2.00
3 Derek Jeter 4.00
3a Derek Jeter/Auto. (Edition of 250.) 75.00
4 Todd Hollandsworth .25
4a Todd Hollandsworth/ Auto. 3.00
5 Billy Ashley .25
5a Billy Ashley/Auto. 2.00
6 Benji Gil .25
6a Benji Gil/Auto. 2.00
7 Vaughn Eshelman .25
7a Vaughn Eshelman/ Auto. 2.00
8 Ray Durham .25
8a Ray Durham/Auto. 3.00
9 Marty Cordova .25
9a Marty Cordova/Auto. 3.00
10 Manny Ramirez 2.00
10a Manny Ramirez/ Auto. 35.00

1995 Signature Rookies Tetrad (Baseball)

Thirty-one baseball players are featured among the young stars of the four major team sports in this issue. Fronts have a color action photo with the background muted in black-and-white. The player's name is in gold foil in a green marbled panel at bottom. Tetrad's "You Make the Call" logo is also in gold foil. Backs have two more photos, personal data and stats and repeated the green marbled motif.

MT
Complete (Baseball) Set (31): 3.00
Common Player: .05
31 Andy Yount .05
32 Jose Cruz, Jr. .10
33 Dustin Hermanson .10
34 David Yocum .05
35 Dmitri Young .10
36 Kerry Wood 1.00
37 Jonathan Johnson .05
38 Shea Morenz .10
39 Matt Morris .10
40 Reggie Taylor .05
41 Antone Williamson .05
42 Derek Wallace .05
43 Ben Grieve .10
44 Benji Gil .05
45 Todd Walker .10
46 Jason Thompson .05
47 Scott Stahoviak .05
48 Chris Roberts .05
49 Dante Powell .05
50 Torii Hunter .50
56 Bryan Rekar .05
57 Jaime Jones .05
58 Todd Helton 1.00
59 Joe Fontenot .05
60 Tony Clark .10
71 Tony McKnight .05
72 Roy Halladay .25
73 Mike Drumright .05
74 Ben Davis .05
75 Michael Barrett .10
76 Sid Roberson .05

Autographs

Each of the cards in SR Tetrad was also issued in an authentically autographed version, numbered to 5,000 each.

MT
Baseball Set (31): 60.00
Common Player: 1.00
31 Andy Yount 1.00
32 Jose Cruz, Jr. 3.00
33 Dustin Hermanson 1.00
34 David Yocum 1.00
35 Dmitri Young 1.00
36 Kerry Wood 20.00
37 Jonathan Johnson 1.00
38 Shea Morenz 1.00
39 Matt Morris 2.00
40 Reggie Taylor 1.00
41 Antone Williamson 1.00
42 Derek Wallace 1.00
43 Ben Grieve 2.00
44 Benji Gil 1.00
45 Todd Walker 3.00
46 Jason Thompson 1.00
47 Scott Stahoviak 1.00
48 Chris Roberts 1.00
49 Dante Powell 1.00
50 Torii Hunter 17.50
56 Bryan Rekar 1.00
57 Jaime Jones 1.00
q8 Todd Helton 12.50
59 Joe Fontenot 1.00
60 Tony Clark 2.00
71 Tony McKnight 1.00
72 Roy Halladay 6.00
73 Mike Drumright 1.00
74 Ben Davis 1.50
75 Michael Barrett 2.00
76 Sid Roberson 1.00

1995 Signature Rookies Tetrad Autobilia (Baseball)

Thirty baseball players are included among the young stars of the four major team sports in this 100-card issue. Fronts have a background of greens and purples with three sizes of a player action photo muted in the background. In the foreground is a large color action photo. Graphic highlights are in gold foil, including a bar at bottom with the player name. Backs have a couple more color player photos on a yellow and magenta background. Stats, draft status and a few words about the player are included. Each of the cards could also be found in an autographed version as a random pack insert, and in a "CLUB SET" version so designated by vertical gold-foil typography on front.

MT
Baseball Set (30): 7.50
Common Player: .05
18 Juan Acevedo .05
19 Trey Beamon .05
20 Tim Belk .05
21 Mike Bovee .05
22 Brad Clontz .05
23 Marty Cordova .10
24 Johnny Damon 1.00
25 Jeff Darwin .05
26 Nick Delvecchio .05
27 Ray Durham .10
28 Jermaine Dye .15
29 Jimmy Haynes .05
30 Mark Hubbard .05
31 Russ Johnson .05
32 Andy Larkin .05
33 Kris Ralston .05
34 Luis Raven .05
35 Desi Relaford .05
36 Jeff Suppan .10
37 Brad Woodall .15
72 Ruben Rivera .05
85 Jose Cruz, Jr. .10

86 Darin Erstad .35
87 Todd Helton 2.00
88 Chad Hermansen .05
89 Jonathan Johnson .05
90 Manny Ramirez 3.00
91 Kerry Wood 2.00
92 Ben Davis .05
93 Jaime Jones .05

Autographs

Each card in Tetrad Autobilia was also released in an authentically autographed edition.

		MT
Baseball Set (30):		75.00
Common Player:		1.00
18	Juan Acevedo	1.00
19	Trey Beamon	1.00
20	Tim Belk	1.00
21	Mike Bovee	1.00
22	Brad Clontz	1.00
23	Marty Cordova	3.00
24	Johnny Damon	12.50
25	Jeff Darwin	1.00
26	Nick Delvecchio	1.00
27	Ray Durham	3.00
28	Jermaine Dye	2.00
29	Jimmy Haynes	1.00
30	Mark Hubbard	1.00
31	Russ Johnson	1.00
32	Andy Larkin	1.00
33	Kris Ralston	1.00
34	Luis Raven	1.00
35	Desi Relaford	1.00
36	Jeff Suppan	2.00
37	Brad Woodall	2.00
72	Ruben Rivera	1.00
85	Jose Cruz, Jr.	2.00
86	Darin Erstad	4.50
87	Todd Helton	12.50
88	Chad Hermansen	1.00
89	Jonathan Johnson	1.00
90	Manny Ramirez	50.00
91	Kerry Wood	20.00
92	Ben Davis	2.00
93	Jaime Jones	1.00

1995 Signature Rookies Tetrad B-1 Bomber

The #1 overall pick in the 1995 amateur draft is honored on this five-card insert set recalling the college career of Darin Erstad. Fronts have various action photos of Erstad in his college uniform. Half of the background has been replaced with a vertical green area featuring a large purple "B-1 BOMBER" logo and a gold-foil notation that the card is "1 of 30,000." Erstad's name also appears in gold foil, along with Tetrad's "You Make the Call" logo. Backs have more photos of Erstad, some in his uniform as Big Red's punter/field goal specialist, along with biographical data, college stats and highlights. Cards are numbered B1-B5.

		MT
Complete Set (5):		5.00
Complete Set, Auto. (5):		50.00
Common Card:		1.00
Common Card, Auto.:		10.00
B1	Darin Erstad/Btg	1.00
B1a	Darin Erstad/ Auto./Btg	10.00
B2	Darin Erstad/Fldg	1.00
B2a	Darin Erstad/ Auto./Fldg	10.00
B3	Darin Erstad/Btg	1.00
B3a	Darin Erstad/ Auto./Btg	10.00
B4	Darin Erstad/Running	1.00
B4a	Darin Erstad/ Auto./Running	10.00
B5	Darin Erstad/Btg	1.00
B5a	Darin Erstad/ Auto./Btg	10.00

1995 Signature Rookies Tetrad SR Force (Baseball)

Ten of the top young players in each of the four major team sports were included in an SR Force insert set with Signature Rookies Tetrad. A color action photo on the white front background has had team logos removed to avoid licensing problems. Three inset photos repeat details from the large picture. "SR FORCE" is printed in purples and greens at top. Gold-foil highlights include the player name and "1 of 6,000" notation. Backs have a large ghosted photo in the background and three detail photos at left, along with personal data, stats and a few words about the player.

		MT
Complete Set (10):		6.00
Autographed Set (10):		175.00
Common Player:		.25
Common Autograph (10):		2.00
F11	Manny Ramirez	1.50
F11a	Manny Ramirez/ Auto.	50.00
F12	Jaret Wright	.25
F12a	Jaret Wright/Auto.	3.00
F13	Ruben Rivera	.25
F13a	Ruben Rivera/Auto.	1.00
F14	Derek Jeter	3.00
F14a	Derek Jeter/Auto.	75.00
F15	Monty Fariss	.25
F15a	Monty Farris/Auto.	2.00
F16	Jason Isringhausen	.25
F16a	Jason Isringhausen/ Auto.	2.00
F17	Marty Cordova	.25
F17a	Marty Cordova/Auto.	3.00
F18	Garret Anderson	.25
F18a	Garrett Anderson/ Auto.	3.00
F19	Alex Rodriguez	2.00
F19a	Alex Rodriguez/ Auto.	60.00
F20	Carlton Loewer	.25
F20a	Carlton Loewer/Auto.	1.00

1995 Signature Rookies T-95 Old Judge Series

In an unusual size (2-1/16" x 3-1/16") and in a format more reminiscent of the 1914-15 Cracker Jack cards than the original Old Judge issue of the 1880s, Signature Rookies produced a minor league issue for 1995. Cards have player photos set against bright solid-colored backgrounds. The player's last name and city of major league affiliation are printed in the white border at bottom. Backs have a few biographical details, 1994 stats and a paragraph about the prospect. Because the cards are licensed only by the individual players, and not Major League Baseball, uniform logos have been airbrushed off and unofficial cap logos and, in some cases, team names have been added. Each of the 35 regular cards in the set can also be found in an autographed version of 5,750. In addition 250 autographed cards of Joe DiMaggio were also randomly inserted. One autographed card or trade-in coupon was included in each pack. Several series of insert cards were issued, besides the autographs.

		MT
Complete Set (36):		2.00
Autographed Set (35):		30.00
Common Player:		.05
Common Autograph:		1.00
1	Bob Abreu	.25
1a	Bob Abreu/Auto.	5.00
2	Kym Ashworth	.05
2a	Kym Ashworth/Auto.	1.00
3	Jared Baker	.05
3a	Jared Baker/Auto.	1.00
4	Paul Bako	.05
4a	Paul Bako/Auto.	1.00
5	Jason Bates	.05
5a	Jason Bates/Auto.	1.00
6	Yamil Benitez	.05
6a	Yamil Benitez/Auto.	1.00
7	Marshall Boze	.05
7a	Marshall Boze/Auto.	1.00
8	Rich Butler	.05
8a	Rich Butler/Auto.	1.00
9	John Carter	.05
9a	John Carter/Auto.	1.00
10	Jeff Cirillo	.15
10a	Jeff Cirillo/Auto.	2.50
11	Randy Curtis	.05
11a	Randy Curtis/Auto.	1.00
12	Sal Fasano	.05
12a	Sal Fasano/Auto.	1.00
13	Aaron Fultz	.05
13a	Aaron Fultz/Auto.	1.00
14	Karim Garcia	.35
14a	Karim Garcia/Auto.	3.00
15	Kevin Grijak	.05
15a	Kevin Grijak/Auto.	1.00
16	Wilton Guerrero	.05
16a	Wilton Guerrero/Auto.	1.00
17	Stacy Hollins	.05
17a	Stacy Hollins/Auto.	1.00
18	Bobby Hughes	.05
18a	Bobby Hughes/Auto.	1.00
19	Jimmy Hurst	.05
19a	Jimmy Hurst/Auto.	1.00
20	Jason Isringhausen	.15
20a	Jason Isringhausen/ Auto.	3.00
21	Ryan Karp	.05
21a	Ryan Karp/Auto.	1.00
22	Derek Lowe	.05
22a	Derek Lowe/Auto.	15.00
23	Matt Luke	.05
23a	Matt Luke/Auto.	1.00
24	Lyle Mouton	.05
24a	Lyle Mouton/Auto.	1.00
25	Dave Mysel	.05
25a	Dave Mysel/Auto.	1.00
26	Marc Newfield	.05
26a	Marc Newfield/Auto.	1.00
27	Jim Pittsley	.05
27a	Jim Pittsley/Auto.	1.00
28	Chris Sheff	.05
28a	Chris Sheff/Auto.	1.00
29	Tate Seefried	.05
29a	Tate Seefried/Auto.	1.00
30	Shawn Senior	.05
30a	Shawn Senior/Auto.	1.00
31	Andy Stewart	.05
31a	Andy Stewart/Auto.	1.00
32	Ozzie Timmons	.05
32a	Ozzie Timmons/Auto.	1.00
33	Quilvio Veras	.05
33a	Quilvio Veras/Auto.	1.00
34	Donnie White	.05
34a	Donnie White/Auto.	1.00
35	Mike Zimmerman	.05
35a	Mike Zimmerman/ Auto.	1.00
36	Ruben Rivera Checklist	.05

Joe DiMaggio Bonus Cards

A classic photo of Joe DiMaggio, minus uniform logos, is featured in this, the scarcest of the T-95 inserts. There are 5,000 unsigned cards, inserted at the rate of one per 43 packs (about three boxes), and 250 autographed cards (one per three cases or 864 packs).

		MT
JD1	Joe DiMaggio	2.00
JD1a	Joe DiMaggio/ Auto.	250.00
PROMO	Joe DiMaggio (Marked PROMO on back.)	2.00

Hot Prospects

Five players judged destined for big league fame are featured in this insert set. Cards measure 2-1/16" x 3-1/16". Action photos on front have a large black vertical strip down one side with the player's name in red and gold. A gold-foil notation at bottom says each card is "1 of 7,500." Backs have another color photo and a vertically compressed black-and-white version of the front photo, along with a paragraph about the prospect and his '94 stats. Cards are licensed only by the individual players, so uniform logos have been replaced with unofficial lettering, or airbrushed completely away. Each of the Hot Prospects inserts can also be found in an autographed edition of 1,550. Insertion rates are one per 16 packs for the regular cards, one per 45 packs for the autographed cards.

		MT
Complete Set (5):		1.00
Autographed Set (5):		10.00
Common Player:		.25
Common Autograph:		2.00
HP1	Billy Ashley	.25
HP1a	Billy Ashley/Auto.	2.00
HP2	Brad Clontz	.25
HP2a	Brad Clontz/Auto.	2.00
HP3	Andrew Lorraine	.25
HP3a	Andrew Lorraine/ Auto.	2.00
HP4	Ruben Rivera	.25
HP4a	Ruben Rivera/Auto.	2.00
HP5	Jason Thompson	.25
HP5a	Jason Thompson/ Auto.	2.00

Minor League All- Stars

In the same 2-1/16" x 3-1/16" size as the regular-issue Old Judge T-95 cards and other inserts for 1995, this All-Star insert set was printed in an edition of 7,500 cards of each player (one per 20 packs, on average). Fronts have a borderless negative black-and-white player photo of which a 1" x 1-1/2" portion has been rendered in color. The player name is in gold foil in a black marbled panel at lower-right. Backs have a color dual-image player photo, a paragraph about his prospects and his 1994 stats. Uniform and cap logos have been removed and replaced with unofficial lettering because the cards are licensed only by the players and not by Major League Baseball. Each All-Star card can also be found in an autographed edition of 2,100 (one per 30 packs).

		MT
Complete Set (5):		1.00
Autographed Set (5):		10.00
Common Player:		.25
Common Autograph:		2.00
AS1	Trey Beamon	.25
AS1a	Trey Beamon/Auto.	2.00
AS2	Tim Belk	.25
AS2a	Tim Belk/Auto.	2.00
AS3	Jimmy Haynes	.25
AS3a	Jimmy Haynes/Auto.	2.00
AS4	Mark Johnson	.25
AS4a	Mark Johnson/Auto.	2.00
AS5	Chris Stynes	.25
AS5a	Chris Stynes/Auto.	2.00

Preview '95

In the same size (2-1/16" x 3-1/16") as the Signature Rookies Old Judge T-95 Series with which they were issued as inserts (one per two packs, average), the Preview '95 cards offer action photos with gold-foil highlights set against black marbled panels at top-right and lower-left. A gold-foil notation at bottom indicates each card is "1 of 5,750." Backs have a close-up repeat of the front photo, a second photo, biographical notes, career summary and 1994 stats. Because the cards are licensed only by the individual players, and not Major League Baseball, uniform logos have been airbrushed off and unofficial cap logos and, in some cases, team names have been added. Each of the 35 regular cards in the set can also be found in an autographed version of 500, about once every 14 packs.

		MT
Complete Set (35):		2.00
Autographed Set (35):		40.00
Common Player:		.10
Common Autograph:		1.00
1	Bob Abreu	.35
1a	Bob Abreu/Auto.	5.00
2	Kym Ashworth	.10
2a	Kym Ashworth/Auto.	1.00
3	Jared Baker	.10
3a	Jared Baker/Auto.	1.00
4	Paul Bako	.10
4a	Paul Bako/Auto.	1.00
5	Jason Bates	.10
5a	Jason Bates/Auto.	1.00
6	Yamil Benitez	.10
6a	Yamil Benitez/Auto.	1.00
7	Marshall Boze	.10
7a	Marshall Boze/Auto.	1.00
8	Rich Butler	.10
8a	Rich Butler/Auto.	1.00
9	John Carter	.10
9a	John Carter/Auto.	1.00
10	Jeff Cirillo	.35
10a	Jeff Cirillo/Auto.	2.50
11	Randy Curtis	.10
11a	Randy Curtis/Auto.	1.00
12	Sal Fasano	.10
12a	Sal Fasano/Auto.	1.00
13	Aaron Fultz	.10
13a	Aaron Fultz/Auto.	1.00
14	Karim Garcia	.50
14a	Karim Garcia/Auto.	3.00
15	Kevin Grijak	.10
15a	Kevin Grijak/Auto.	1.00
16	Wilton Guerrero	.10
16a	Wilton Guerrero/Auto.	1.00
17	Stacy Hollins	.10
17a	Stacy Hollins/Auto.	1.00
18	Bobby Hughes	.10
18a	Bobby Hughes/Auto.	1.00
19	Jimmy Hurst	.10
19a	Jimmy Hurst/Auto.	1.00
20	Jason Isringhausen	.25
20a	Jason Isringhausen/ Auto.	2.50
21	Ryan Karp	.10
21a	Ryan Karp/Auto.	1.00
22	Derek Lowe	.25
22a	Derek Lowe/Auto.	15.00
23	Matt Luke	.10
23a	Matt Luke/Auto.	1.00
24	Lyle Mouton	.10
24a	Lyle Mouton/Auto.	1.00
25	Dave Mysel	.10
25a	Dave Mysel/Auto.	1.00
26	Marc Newfield	.10
26a	Marc Newfield/Auto.	1.00
27	Jim Pittsley	.10
27a	Jim Pittsley/Auto.	1.00
28	Chris Sheff	.10
28a	Chris Sheff/Auto.	1.00
29	Tate Seefried	.10
29a	Tate Seefried/Auto.	1.00
30	Shawn Senior	.10
30a	Shawn Senior/Auto.	1.00
31	Andy Stewart	.10
31a	Andy Stewart/Auto.	1.00
32	Ozzie Timmons	.10
32a	Ozzie Timmons/Auto.	1.00
33	Quilvio Veras	.10
33a	Quilvio Veras/Auto.	1.00
34	Donnie White	.10
34a	Donnie White/Auto.	1.00
35	Mike Zimmerman	.10
35a	Mike Zimmerman/ Auto.	1.00

1995 Upper Deck Minor League

Superb borderless color photos front and back are featured in UD's 1995 minor league base set. A number of subsets within the 225-card issue allow the showcasing of top prospects on multiple cards. Still more cards of the same players are featured in the various chase sets randomly found in the foil packs. The player's name and UD logo are stamped in silver-foil on card fronts, while a star-shaped hologram is on back. As a dealer incentive for early orders, 10 players signed 1,000 cards each.

		MT
Complete Set (225):		10.00
Common Player:		.05
Wax Pack (12):		1.00
Wax Box (36):		25.00
1	Derek Jeter	3.00
1a	Derek Jeter/Auto.	80.00
2	Michael Tucker	.05
3	Alex Ochoa	.05
3a	Alex Ochoa/Auto.	2.00
4	Bill Pulsipher	.05
5	Terrell Wade	.05
5a	Terrell Wade/Auto.	2.00
6	Johnny Damon	1.00
6a	Johnny Damon/ Auto.	20.00
7	LaTroy Hawkins	.05
7a	LaTroy Hawkins/Auto.	2.00
8	Ruben Rivera	.05
9	Jason Giambi	1.00
9a	Jason Giambi/Auto.	15.00
10	Todd Hollandsworth	.05
10a	Todd Hollandsworth/ Auto.	3.00
11	Alan Benes	.05
11a	Alan Benes/Auto.	3.00
12	John Wasdin	.05
13	Roger Cedeno	.05
14	Karim Garcia	.40
15	Brooks Kieschnick	.05
16	David Bell	.05
17	Trot Nixon	.50
18	Jose Malave	.05
19	Rey Ordonez	.05
20	Raul Casanova	.05
21	Chad Mottola	.05
22	Phil Nevin	.05
23	Jim Pittsley	.05
24	Frank Rodriguez	.05
25	Todd Greene	.05
26	Mike Bell	.05
26a	Mike Bell/Auto.	2.00
27	Jason Kendall	.35
28	Pokey Reese	.10
29	Jose Silva	.05
30	Kirk Presley	.05
31	Joe Randa	.05
32	Shannon Stewart	.15
33	Danny Clyburn	.05
34	Glenn Williams	.05
35	Terry Bradshaw	.05
36	Jimmy Hurst	.05
37	Scott Spiezio	.05
38	Richard Hidalgo	.05
39	Matt Brunson	.05
40	Juan Acevedo	.05
41	Trey Beamon	.05
42	Kimera Bartee	.05
43	James Baldwin	.05
44	Matt Arrandale	.05
45	Michael Jordan	2.00
46	Wonderful Terrific Monds	.05
48	Bob Abreu	.25
49	Edgardo Alfonzo	.05
50	Damon Hollins	.05
51	Marc Barcelo	.05
52	D.J. Boston	.05
53	Einar Diaz	.05
54	Matt Drews	.05
55	Benji Simonson	.05
56	Bart Evans	.05
57	Micah Franklin	.05
58	Curtis Goodwin	.05
59	Craig Griffey	.10
60	Billy Wagner	.15
61	Jimmy Haynes	.05
62	Jose Herrera	.05
63	Greg Keagle	.05
64	Andy Larkin	.05
65	Jason Isringhausen	.10
66	Derrek Lee	1.00
67	Terrell Lowery	.05
68	Ryan Luzinski	.05
69	Angel Martinez	.05
70	Tony Clark	.05
71	Ryan McGuire	.05
72	Damian Moss	.05
73	Hugo Pivaral	.05
74	Arquimedez Pozo	.05
75	Daron Kirkreit	.05
76	Luis Raven	.05
77	Desi Relaford	.05
78	Scott Rolen	1.25
79	Joe Rosselli	.05
80	Chris Roberts	.05
81	Giomar Guevara	.05
82	Gene Schall	.05
83	Jeff Suppan	.10
84	Makato Suzuki (Makoto)	.05
85	Jason Thompson	.05
86	Marc Valdes	.05
87	Pat Watkins	.05
88	Jay Witasick	.05
89	Ray Durham	.05
90	Brad Fullmer	.05
91	Roger Bailey	.05
92	DeShawn Warren	.05
93	Jermaine Dye	.15
94	Scott Romano	.05
95	Aaron Boone	.10
96	Tate Seefried	.05
97	Chris Stynes	.05
98	Chris Widger	.05
99	Desi Wilson	.05
100	Dante Powell	.05
101	Neifi Perez (Season Highlights)	.05
102	Alex Ochoa (SH)	.05
103	Kelly Wunsch (SH)	.05
104	Jason Robbins (SH)	.05
105	Kevin Coughlin (SH)	.05
106	Bill Pulsipher (SH)	.05
107	Roger Cedeno (International Flavor)	.05
108	Jose Herrera (IF)	.05
109	Andre King (IF)	.05
110	Rey Ordonez (IF)	.10
111	Jose Pett (IF)	.05
112	Ruben Rivera (IF)	.05
113	Jose Silva (IF)	.05
114	Makato Suzuki (Makoto)(IF)	.05
115	Glenn Williams (IF)	.05
116	Wil Cunnane	.05
117	Neifi Perez	.05
118	Andre King	.05
119	Quinton McCracken	.05
120	Brian Giles	.25
121	Kenny Felder	.05
122	Jermaine Allensworth	.05
123	Allen Battle	.05
124	Howard Battle	.05
125	Doug Million	.05
126	Geoff Blum	.05
127	Vladimir Guerrero	1.50
128	Torii Hunter	1.00
129	Doug Glanville	.05
130	Dustin Hermanson	.05
131	Mark Grudzielanek	.15
132	Phil Geisler	.05
133	Chris Carpenter	.05
134	Brian Seckinsky	.05
135	Josh Booty	.05
136	Shane Andrews	.05
137	Scott Eyre	.05
138	Chad Fox	.05
139	George Arias	.05
140	Scott Sullivan	.05
141	Todd Dunn	.05
142	Nate Holdren	.05
143	Gus Gandarillas	.05
144	Scott Talanoa	.05
145	Sal Fasano	.05
146	Stoney Briggs	.05
147	Yamil Benitez	.05
148	Chris Wimmer	.05
149	Mariano De Los Santos	.05
150	Ben Grieve	.10
151	Homer Bush	.05
152	Wilton Guerrero	.05
153	Benji Grigsby	.05
154	Cade Caspar	.05
155	Hiram Bocachica	.05
156	Dave Vanhof	.05

157 Frank Catalanotto .15
158 Marcus Jensen .05
159 Jamie Arnold .05
160 Cesar Devarez .05
161 Alan Benes (Road to the Show) .05
162 Johnny Damon (RS) .50
163 LaTroy Hawkins (RS) .05
164 Dustin Hermanson (RS) .05
165 Derek Jeter (RS) 1.50
166 Terrell Wade (RS) .05
167 Todd Walker (RS) .10
168 John Wasdin (RS) .05
169 Paul Wilson (RS) .05
170 Todd Walker .10
171 Danny Klassen .05
172 Bobby Morris .05
173 Kelly Wunsch .05
174 Fletcher Thompson .05
175 Terrence Long .05
176 Andy Petitte 1.00
177 Lou Pote .05
178 Steve Kline .05
179 Damian Jackson .05
180 Matt Smith .05
181 Tim Unroe .05
182 Jim Cole .05
183 Bill McMillon .05
184 Matt Luke .05
185 Sergio Nunez .05
186 Edgar Renteria .10
187 Bill Selby .05
188 Jamey Wright .05
189 Steve Whitaker .05
190 Joe Vitiello .05
191 Jacob Shumate .05
192 C.J. Nitkowski .05
193 Mark Johnson .05
194 Paul Konerko .50
195 Jay Payton .10
196 Jayson Peterson .05
197 Brian Buchanan .05
198 Ramon Castro .05
199 Antone Williamson .05
200 Paul Wilson .10
200a Paul Wilson/Auto. 3.00
201 Jaret Wright .05
202 Carlton Loewer .05
203 Jon Zuber .05
204 Ugueth Urbina .05
205 Nomar Garciaparra 2.00
206 Yuri Sanchez .05
207 Jason Moler .05
208 Lyle Mouton .05
209 Mark Johnson .05
210 Matt Raleigh .05
211 Julio Santana .05
212 Willie Ontafez .05
213 Ozzie Timmons .05
214 Victor Rodriguez .05
215 Paul Wilson (1994 Draft Class) .05
216 Ben Grieve (DC) .10
217 Dustin Hermanson (DC) .05
218 Antone Williamson (DC) .05
219 Josh Booty (DC) .05
220 Todd Walker (DC) .10
221 Jason Varitek (DC) .50
222 Paul Konerko (DC) .35
223 Doug Million (DC) .05
224 Hiram Bocachica (DC) .05
225 Durham Athletic Park .10

Michael Jordan Highlights

This set of 3-1/2" x 5" cards was available only via a mail-in offer for $3 and 15 UD Minor League foil wrappers. Card fronts are printed on foil and feature highlights from Jordan's only season of professional baseball. Backs have a graduated yellow background with a color photo of Jordan and a few words about the highlight, along with the logos of the Birmingham Barons, UD and the minor league licensing authority.

MT
Complete Set (5): 15.00
Common Card: 3.00
MJ-1 Michael Jordan (White Sox Welcome) 3.00
MJ-2 Michael Jordan (Jordan Supplies Offense at Classic) 3.00
MJ-3 Michael Jordan (13-Game Hitting Streak) 3.00
MJ-4 Michael Jordan (Jordan Hits First Home Run!) 3.00
MJ-5 Michael Jordan (Jordan Does Extracurricular Baseball) 3.00

Michael Jordan One-On-One

This 10-card set was produced for inclusion exclusively in mini-packs of Upper Deck Minor League baseball cards sold in Wal-Mart stores. The packs had three cards from the regular set plus one of the 10 One-On-One Jordan cards. Card fronts are in horizontal format and include a silver-foil "Michael Jordan / 95 / Retires" stamp on front. Backs have a color photo of Jordan and short text.

MT
Complete Set (10): 4.00
Common Card: .50
1 Michael Jordan/Throwing .50
2 Michael Jordan/Fldg .50
3 Michael Jordan/Htg .50
4 Michael Jordan (Speed) .50
5 Michael Jordan (Overall Report) .50
6 Michael Jordan ('94 Spring Training) .50
7 Michael Jordan ('94 Regular Season) .50
8 Michael Jordan (1st Home Run) .50
9 Michael Jordan ('94 Autumn) .50
10 Michael Jordan (The Future) .50

Michael Jordan's Scrapbook

Printed on metallic-foil fronts, this 10-card chase series chronicles Michael Jordan's season of minor league baseball with the Birmingham Barons. Backs feature a continuing narrative.

MT
Complete Set (10): 25.00
Common Card: 3.00
1 Michael Jordan Decisions 3.00
2 Michael Jordan Practice 3.00
3 Michael Jordan Spring Training and Assignment 3.00
4 Michael Jordan Windy City Classic 3.00
5 Michael Jordan Firsts 3.00
6 Michael Jordan The Hitting Streak 3.00
7 Michael Jordan Struggles 3.00
8 Michael Jordan Life on the Road 3.00
9 Michael Jordan First Home Run 3.00
10 Michael Jordan Arizona Fall League 3.00

Organizational Pro-Files

Each team's top prospect is featured in this chase card set. Fronts are in horizontal format, printed on metallic foil. Backs have a checklist of that team's minor leaguers found in the regular UD minor league set.

MT
Complete Set (28): 12.50
Common Player: .50
OP1 Terrell Wade .50
OP2 Alex Ochoa .50
OP3 Nomar Garciaparra 3.00
OP4 Todd Greene .50
OP5 Brooks Kieschnick .50
OP6 Michael Jordan 3.00
OP7 C.J. Nitkowski .50
OP8 Daron Kickreit .50
OP9 Juan Acevedo .50
OP10 Tony Clark .70
OP11 Josh Booty .50
OP12 Billy Wagner 1.00
OP13 Johnny Damon 2.00
OP14 Paul Konerko 1.25
OP15 Antone Williamson .50
OP16 Todd Walker .75
OP17 Ugueth Urbina .50
OP18 Bill Pulsipher .50
OP19 Ruben Rivera .50
OP20 John Wasdin .50
OP21 Scott Rolen 2.00
OP22 Trey Beamon .50
OP23 Alan Benes .50
OP24 Raul Casanova .50
OP25 Dante Powell .50
OP26 Arquimedez Pozo .50
OP27 Julio Santana .50
OP28 Jose Silva .50

1995 Upper Deck/ SP Top Prospects

Upper Deck brought its premium SP brand name to minor league cards in late 1995 with the issue of Top Prospects. Base cards all feature die-cut tops and have fronts with color player action photos printed on metallic foil backgrounds. Backs have another photo along with a few stats, personal data and career highlights. The set's first 10 cards are a Top 10 Prospects subset which have checklists on back and feature a different front design showing the player in a golden oval against a mauve textured background. Cards #100-115 are a subset titled "1995 Draft Class" and feature the player photos against a golden sunrise design. Insert cards found in foil packs include autographed cards of 26 players, "Destination the Show" cards of fast-track minor leaguers and Jordan Time Capsule cards. SP Top Prospects was sold in eight-card foil packs with a $4.19 suggested retail.

MT
Complete Set (165): 35.00
Common Player: .05
Wax Pack (8): 7.50
Wax Box: 215.00
1 Andruw Jones (Top 10 Prospect) 6.00
2 Brooks Kieschnick (Top 10 Prospect) .05
3 Nomar Garciaparra (Top 10 Prospect) 6.00
4 Adam Riggs (Top 10 Prospect) .05
5 Paul Wilson (Top 10 Prospect) .10
6 Trey Beamon (Top 10 Prospect) .05
7 Vladimir Guerrero (Top 10 Prospect) 4.00
8 Ben Grieve (Top 10 Prospect) .15
9 Jay Payton (Top 10 Prospect) .10
10 Todd Walker (Top 10 Prospect) .10
11 Jermaine Dye .15
12 Damon Hollins .05
13 Wonderful Monds .05
14 Damian Moss .05
15 Andruw Jones 4.00
16 Danny Clyburn .05
17 Billy Percibal .05
18 Rocky Coppinger .05
19 Tommy Davis .05
20 Nomar Garciaparra 4.50
21 Trot Nixon .50
22 Jose Malave .05
23 Ryan McGuire .05
24 Rafael Orellano .05
25 Darin Erstad .25
26 George Arias .05
27 Matt Beaumont .05
28 Jason Dickson .05
29 Greg Shockey .05
30 Brooks Kieschnick .05
31 Jon Ratliff .05
32 Amaury Telemaco .05
33 Bob Morris .05
34 Charles Poe .05
35 Harold Williams .05
36 Jeff Abbott .05
37 Tom Fordham .05
38 Pokey Reese .10
39 Pat Watkins .05
40 Aaron Boone .10
41 Chad Mottola .05
42 Jason Robbins .05
43 Jaret Wright .10
44 Casey Whitten .05
45 Bartolo Colon .45
46 Richie Sexson .25
47 Enrique Wilson .10
48 Doug Million .05
49 Joel Moore .05
50 Derrick Gibson .05
51 Neifi Perez .05
52 Jamey Wright .05
53 Juan Encarnacion .10
54 Cade Gaspar .05
55 Justin Thompson .05
56 Bubba Trammell .05
57 Daryle Ward .05
58 Clemente Nunez .05
59 Will Cunnane .05
60 Billy McMillon .05
61 Matt Whisenant .05
62 Edgar Renteria .10
63 Josh Booty .05
64 Bob Abreu .25
65 Richard Hidalgo .05
66 Ramon Castro .05
67 Scott Elarton .05
68 Jhonny Perez .05
69 Mendy Lopez .05
70 Glendon Rusch .05
71 Sal Fasano .05
72 Sergio Nunez .05
73 Matt Smith .05
74 Chris Latham .05
75 Adam Riggs .05
76 Wilton Guerrero .05
77 Paul Konerko .50
78 Gary Rath .05
79 Jim Cole .05
80 Jeff D'Amico .05
81 Antone Williamson .05
82 Todd Dunn .05
83 Brian Banks .05
84 Shane Bowers .05
85 Todd Walker .10
86 Troy Carrasco .05
87 Travis Miller .05
88 Kimera Bartee .05
89 Dan Serafini .05
90 Vladimir Guerrero 3.00
91 Hiram Bocachica .05
92 Brad Fullmer .05
93 Geoff Blum .05
94 Israel Alcantara .05
95 Jay Payton .10
96 Rey Ordonez .05
97 Paul Wilson .15
98 Preston Wilson .35
99 Terrence Long .05
100 Darin Erstad (Draft Class) .25
101 Gabe Alvarez (DC) .05
102 Jonathan Johnson (DC) .05
103 Adam Benes (DC) .05
104 Dennis Martinez, Jr. (DC) .05
105 Jaime Jones (DC) .05
106 Chad Hermansen (DC) .05
107 Geoff Jenkins (DC) .15
108 Juan LeBron (DC) .05
109 Mark Redman (DC) .05
110 Jose Cruz Jr. (DC) .10
111 Carlos Beltran (DC) 12.00
112 Todd Helton (DC) 3.00
113 Andy Yount (DC) .05
114 Ryan Jaroncyk (DC) .05
115 Sean Johnston .05
116 Scott Romano .05
117 Brian Buchanan .05
118 Nick Delvecchio .05
119 Ramiro Mendoza .05
120 Matt Drews .05
121 Shane Spencer .05
122 Jason McDonald .05
123 Scott Spiezio .05
124 Brad Rigby .05
125 Ben Grieve .10
126 Steve Cox .05
127 Willie Morales .05
128 Wayne Gomes .05
129 Larry Wimberly .05
130 Scott Rolen 1.50
131 Carlton Loewer .05
132 Wendell Magee .05
133 Charles Peterson .05
134 Lou Collier .05
135 Trey Beamon .05
136 Micah Franklin .05
137 Jason Kendall .35
138 Homer Bush .05
139 Dickie Woodridge .05
140 Derrek Lee 2.00
141 Raul Casanova .05
142 Greg LaRocca .05
143 Jason Thompson .05
144 Jacob Cruz .05
145 Jesse Ibarra .05
146 Jay Canizaro .05
147 Steve Soderstrom .05
148 Dante Powell .05
149 James Bonnici .05
150 Raul Ibanez .05
151 Trey Moore .05
152 Desi Relaford .05
153 Jason Varitek .45
154 Jay Witasick .05
155 Bret Wagner .05
156 Aaron Holbert .05
157 Fernando Tatis .05
158 Mike Bell .05
159 Jeff Davis .05
160 Julio Santana .05
161 Kevin Brown .05
162 Felipe Crespo .05
163 Kevin Witt .05
164 Mark Sievert .05
165 Jose Pett .05

Autographs

Similar in format to the rest of the SP Top Prospects set, including the die-cut tops, the autograph insert cards have standard (non-metallized) printing on front and no UV coat, allowing the autograph to be more efficiently signed. Each card has a uniquely numbered hologram serial number attached and the back is a certificate of authenticity. Autograph cards were inserted at an average rate of once per 31 foil packs; about one per box. It is believed only about 20 of the Michael Jordan cards were printed.

MT
Common Player: 3.00
(1) Bob Abreu 50.00
(2) Gabe Alvarez 3.00
(3) George Arias 3.00
(4) Trey Beamon 3.00
(5) Aaron Boone 3.00
(6) Raul Casanova 3.00
(7) Bartolo Colon 7.50
(8) Jermaine Dye 5.00
(9) Nomar Garciaparra 95.00
(10) Todd Greene 3.00
(11) Ben Grieve 4.50
(12) Vladimir Guerrero 45.00
(13) Richard Hidalgo 3.00
(14) Andruw Jones 45.00
(15) Michael Jordan 1,725
(16) Jason Kendall 5.00
(17) Brooks Kieschnick 3.00
(18) Derrek Lee 25.00
(19) Wonderful Monds 3.00
(20) Rey Ordonez 3.00
(21) Jay Payton 3.00
(22) Adam Riggs 3.00
(23) Scott Rolen 30.00
(24) Jason Thompson 3.00
(25) Paul Wilson 3.00
(26) Jaret Wright 5.00

Promos

Paralleling the Top Prospects Autographs inserts (plus a Todd Helton card which was never issued in autographed form) these cards are unsigned and lack the serial number hologram on front. Printed on back is "For Promotional Use Only / This is Not a Signature Card."

MT
Common Player: 10.00
(1) Bob Abreu 15.00
(2) Gabe Alvarez 10.00
(3) George Arias 10.00
(4) Trey Beamon 10.00
(5) Aaron Boone 12.50
(6) Raul Casanova 10.00
(7) Bartolo Colon 12.50
(8) Jermaine Dye 12.50
(9) Nomar Garciaparra 100.00
(10) Todd Greene 10.00
(11) Ben Grieve 10.00
(12) Vladimir Guerrero 90.00
(13) Todd Helton 75.00
(14) Richard Hidalgo 10.00
(15) Andruw Jones 90.00
(16) Michael Jordan 250.00
(17) Jason Kendall 15.00
(18) Brooks Kieschnick 10.00
(19) Derrek Lee 65.00
(20) Wonderful Monds 10.00
(21) Rey Ordonez 10.00
(22) Jay Payton 10.00
(23) Adam Riggs 10.00
(24) Scott Rolen 60.00
(25) Jason Thompson 10.00
(26) Paul Wilson 10.00
(27) Jaret Wright 10.00

Destination the Show

Players deemed to be on the fast track to the majors are featured in this insert set. Like the rest of the SP Top Prospect cards, the tops are die-cut and the player photo is set against a metallic foil background. Tan borders and gold-foil graphic highlights complete the front design. Backs have another player photo and career highlights.

MT
Complete Set (20): 175.00
Common Player: 5.00
DS1 Andruw Jones 35.00
DS2 Richard Hidalgo 5.00
DS3 Paul Wilson 5.00
DS4 Brooks Kieschnick 5.00
DS5 Ben Grieve 6.00
DS6 Adam Riggs 5.00
DS7 Vladimir Guerrero 40.00
DS8 Paul Konerko 7.50
DS9 Jose Cruz Jr. 5.00
DS10 Todd Walker 5.00
DS11 Darin Erstad 7.50
DS12 Derrek Lee 30.00
DS13 Scott Rolen 30.00
DS14 Trey Beamon 5.00
DS15 Nomar Garciaparra 50.00
DS16 Jason Kendall 7.50
DS17 Aaron Boone 5.00
DS18 Matt Drews 5.00
DS19 Derrick Gibson 5.00
DS20 Jay Payton 5.00

1995 Minor League Team Sets

A major change in the market for minor league team sets came in 1995 when the field's top two players, Classic and Fleer/Pro Cards dropped out. Classic was gone entirely in 1995 and Fleer was down to a handful of sets. Both of the major card companies had discovered the short press runs and high costs of production could not be recouped in a thin market. Teams desiring card sets were left to produce their own. A small group of regional graphics firms was able to sign a few teams each. One such company, Grandstand (GS) remains active. For collectors, the big boys dropping out meant an end to easy availability of the annual issues. Some teams sold or gave away their entire production and a strong market arose of dealers who scoured the nation to pick up sets to serve the hobby market. Player selection no longer was the sole basis of value beginning in 1995; market availability became critical to price. When all was said and done, over 140 team sets were issued in 1995, compared to the 275 of the previous year.

MT
146 Team Sets and Variations
1995 Team Abilene Prairie Dogs (30) 5.00
1995 Team Albany Diamond Dogs (26) 5.00
1995 Team Alexandria Aces (22) 5.00
1995 Team Amarillo Dillas (25) 5.00
1995 Arizona Fall League (22) 20.00
1995 Team Arkansas Travelers (30) 12.00
1995 Team Asheville Tourists (30) 20.00
1995 Team Asheville Tourists Update (14) 30.00
1995 Team Auburn Astros (30) 8.00
1995 Team Bakersfield Blaze (32) 11.00
1995 Team Batavia Clippers (33) 10.00
1995 Team Bellingham Giants (36) 8.00
1995 Team Beloit Snappers (31) 12.00
1995 Team Billings Mustangs (29) 75.00
1995 Team Binghamton Mets (28) 10.00
1995 Team Boise Hawks (35) 9.00
1995 Team Bowie Baysox (31) 7.00
1995 Fleer/PC Brevard County Manatees (30) 8.00
1995 Team Burlington Bees (36) 15.00
1995 Team Butte Copper Kings (32) 7.00
1995 Fleer/PC Carolina Mudcats (30) 9.00
1995 Carolina League 50th Anniversary (35) 17.50
1995 Team Cedar Rapids Kernels (32) 8.00
1995 Team Charleston RiverDogs (30) 10.00
1995 Team Charleston River Dogs Update (9) 10.00
1995 Team Charlotte Knights (30) 8.00
1995 Team Chattanooga Lookouts (32) 8.00
1995 Fleer/PC Clearwater Phillies (30) 7.00
1995 Team Colorado Springs Sky Sox (34) 10.00
1995 Kroger Columbus Clippers Panels (8) 30.00
1995 Police Columbus Clippers (32) 30.00
1995 Team Columbus Clippers (32) 35.00
1995 Team Corpus Christi Barracudas (24) 5.00
1995 Team Danville Braves (Six panels.) 20.00
1995 Photostars USA Ben Davis (2) 4.00
1995 Team Dunedin Blue Jays (30) 60.00
1995 Team Durham Bulls (40) 7.00
1995 Team Edmonton Trappers (30) 22.50
1995 Team Elmira Pioneers (30) 10.00

1995 Team Elmira Pioneers Update (31) 12.00
1995 Team El Paso Diablos (24) 7.00
1995 Team Eugene Emeralds (32) 15.00
1995 Team Evansville Otters (26) 5.00
1995 Team Evansville Otters Update (26) 5.00
1995 Team Everett Aquasox (30) 10.00
1995 Team Fayetteville Generals (30) 15.00
1995 Team Ft. Myers Miracle (32) 15.00
1995 Team Ft. Wayne Wizards (32) 8.00
1995 GS Grays Harbor Gulls (31) 5.00
1995 Team Great Falls Dodgers (40) 45.00
1995 Team Greensboro Bats (33) 8.00
1995 Team Greensboro Bats POGs (6) 10.00
1995 Team Greenville Braves (28) 9.00
1995 Fleer/PC Hagerstown Suns (30) 7.00
1995 Team Hardware City Rock Cats (29) 15.00
1995 Team Harrisburg Senators (28) 20.00
1995 Team Helena Brewers (32) 7.00
1995 Team Hudson Valley Renegades (30) 7.00
1995 Team Huntsville Stars (29) 11.00
1995 Team Idaho Falls Braves (27) 10.00
1995 Fleer/PC Indianapolis Indians (30) 7.00
1995 Team Iowa Cubs (25) 10.00
1995 Smokey Bear Jackson Generals (26) 15.00
1995 Team Jackson Generals (27) 12.50
1995 Team Jacksonville Suns (28) 9.00
1995 Team Kane County Cougars (32) 8.00
1995 Team Kane County Cougars - Eckrich (31) 15.00
1995 Team Kane Co. Cougars Legends (15) 10.00
1995 Team Kinston Indians (30) 10.00
1995 Fleer/PC Knoxville Smokies (30) 8.00
1995 Team Lake Elsinore Storm (30) 10.00
1995 Team Laredo Apaches (25) 5.00
1995 FPC Louisville Redbirds (30) 25.00
1995 Team Lubbock Crickets (25) 5.00
1995 Team Lynchburg Hillcats (30) 7.00
1995 Team Macon Braves (30) 75.00
1995 Team Macon Braves Update (6) 45.00
1995 Team Martinsville Phillies (Six panels.) 125.00
1995 Team Memphis Chicks (27) 8.00
1995 Team Michigan Battle Cats (30) 8.00
1995 1 Hour Midland Angels (36) 60.00
1995 Team Midland Angels (30) 6.00
1995 Midwest League All-Stars (58) 12.50
1995 Team Minneapolis Loons (25) 15.00
1995 Team Mobile BaySharks (25) 5.00
1995 Team Modesto A's (32) 12.00
1995 Team Nashville Sounds Foldout 25.00
1995 Team New Haven Ravens (33) 9.00
1995 Team New Jersey Cardinals (30) 8.00
1995 Team Norfolk Tides (30) 10.00
1995 Team Norwich Navigators (42) 8.00
1995 Team Norwich Navigators Update (11) 6.00
1995 Team Ogden Raptors (30) 8.00
1995 Team Ogden Raptors Poster 12.00
1995 Team Oklahoma City 89ers (27) 9.00
1995 Team Omaha Royals (29) 10.00
1995 Fleer/PC Orlando Cubs (30) 7.00
1995 DD Pawtucket Red Sox Foldout 25.00
1995 Team Pawtucket Red Sox (30) 7.00
1995 Team Peoria Chiefs (31) 7.00
1995 Team Phoenix Firebirds (30) 8.00
1995 Fleer/PC Piedmont Phillies (30) 6.00
1995 Team Pittsfield Mets (32) 9.00
1995 Team Port City Roosters (29) 8.00
1995 Team Portland Sea Dogs (30) 9.00
1995 Team Prince William Cannons (30) 11.00
1995 Team Quad Cities River Bandits (30) 10.00
1995 Team Rancho Cucamonga Quakes (30) 20.00
1995 Ritz Camera Reading Phillies Sheet (25) 30.00
1995 Team Reading Phillies (28) 10.00
1998 Team Reading Phils Fairground Sq. (28) 12.50
1995 Team Reading Phillies E.L. Champs (36) 10.00
1995 Pepsi Richmond Braves POGs (27) 25.00
1995 Richmond Camera Richmond Braves (29) 50.00
1995 Team Richmond Braves (30) 7.00
1995 Team Rio Grande Valley White Wings (26) 5.00
1995 Team Rochester Red Wings (48) 8.00
1995 Team Rockford Cubbies (32) 9.00
1995 Team Salem Avalanche (30) 8.00
1995 HEB San Antonio Missions (32) 50.00
1995 Team San Antonio Missions (30) 11.00
1995 Team San Bernardino Spirit (32) 15.00
1995 Team Scranton Red Barons (30) 15.00
1995 Team Spokane Indians (32) 8.00
1995 Team Sultans of Springfield (30) 8.00
1995 Team St. Catherines Stompers (36) 30.00
1995 Team St. Lucie Mets (37) 7.00
1995 Team St. Paul Saints (29) 6.00
1995 Team Syracuse Chiefs (30) 10.00
1995 Team All-Time Syracuse Chiefs (72) 60.00
1995 Team Tacoma Rainiers (30) 20.00
1995 Team Tampa Yankees (30) 9.00
1995 Team Thunder Bay Whiskey Jacks (25) 5.00
1995 Team Toledo Mud Hens (30) 8.00
1995 Team Trenton Thunder (31) 90.00
1995 Team Trenton Thunder Foldout 125.00
1995 Team Tucson Toros (29) 8.00
1995 Team Tulsa Drillers (30) 8.00
1995 Team Tyler Wildcatters (24) 5.00
1995 Team Vero Beach Dodgers (30) 10.00
1995 Team Watertown Indians (30) 30.00
1995 Team West Mighigan Whitecaps (30) 8.00
1995 Team Wichita Wranglers (30) 7.50
1995 Team Wilmington Blue Rocks (30) 12.50
1995 Team Yakima Bears (36) 6.00
1995 Team Zanseville Greys (25) 5.00

1996 Best Autograph Series

The basic set for this premiere edition consists of 99 of the top prospects from all levels of minor league baseball from Instructional League through Class AAA. Released at the end of October, cards picture players with their 1996 teams, mostly in game-action photos on the fronts. The player's minor league team logo, name and position are at bottom. Backs have a portrait photo in an oval at top-right, with a career summary in the black box at left and 1995 stats at bottom. The cards were issued in foil packs of six, with one card being of the special autographed type. An insert set features 1996 first-round draft picks.

		MT
Complete Set (99):		4.00
Common Player:		.05
Wax Pack (6):		2.50
Wax Box:		35.00
1	Winston Abreu	.05
2	Antonio Alfonseca	.10
3	Richard Almanzar	.05
4	Gabe Alvarez	.05
5	Marlon Anderson	.15
6	Kym Ashworth	.05
7	Marc Barcelo	.05
8	Brian Barkley	.05
9	Mike Bell	.05
10	Carlos Beltran	.50
11	Shayne Bennett	.05
12	Jeremy Blevins	.05
13	Kevin Brown	.05
14	Ray Brown	.05
15	Homer Bush	.05
16	Jay Canizaro	.05
17	Troy Carrasco	.05
18	Raul Casanova	.05
19	Luis Castillo	.10
20	Ramon Castro	.05
21	Gary Coffee	.05
22	Decomba Conner	.05
23	Kevin Coughlin	.05
24	Jacob Cruz	.05
25	Jeff D'Amico	.10
26	Tommy Davis	.05
27	Edwin Diaz	.05
28	Einar Diaz	.05
29	David Doster	.05
30	Derrin Ebert	.05
31	Bobby Estalella	.15
32	Alex Gonzalez	.05
33	Kevin Grijak	.05
34	Jose Guillen	.25
35	Tim Harkrider	.05
36	Dan Held	.05
37	Wes Helms	.05
38	Erik Hiljus	.05
39	Aaron Holbert	.05
40	Raul Ibanez	.05
41	Jesse Ibarra	.05
42	Marty Janzen	.05
43	Robin Jennings	.05
44	Shawn Johnston	.05
45	Randy Jorgensen	.05
46	Marc Kroon	.05
47	Mike Kusiewicz	.05
48	Carlos Lee	.25
49	Brian Lesher	.05
50	George Lombard	.05
51	Roberto Lopez	.05
52	Fernando Lunar	.05
53	Len Manning	.05
54	Eddy Martinez	.05
55	Jesus Martinez	.05
56	Onan Masaoka	.05
57	Joe Maskivish	.05
58	Jeff Matulevich	.05
59	Brian Meadows	.05
60	Mike Metcalfe	.05
61	Doug Mlicki	.05
62	Steve Montgomery	.05
63	Trey Moore	.05
64	Nick Morrow	.05
65	Bryant Nelson	.05
66	Sergio Nunez	.05
67	Hector Ortega	.05
68	Russell Ortiz	.10
69	Eric Owens	.05
70	Billy Percibal	.05
71	Charles Peterson	.05
72	A.J. Pierzynski	.25
73	Charles Poe	.05
74	Dante Powell	.05
75	Kenny Pumphrey	.05
76	Angel Ramirez	.05
77	Julio Ramirez	.05
78	Gary Rath	.05
79	Jon Ratliff	.05
80	Brad Rigby	.05
81	Benj Sampson	.05
82	Greg Shockey	.05
83	Steve Shoemaker	.05
84	Demond Smith	.05
85	Robert Smith	.05
86	Steve Soderstrom	.05
87	Fernando Tatis	.10
88	Jose Texidor	.05
89	Brett Tomko	.05
90	Jose Valentin	.05
91	Jason Varitek	.35
92	Andrew Vessel	.05
93	Casey Whitten	.05
94	Enrique Wilson	.15
95	Preston Wilson	.25
96	Larry Wimberly	.05
97	Jaret Wright	.10
98	Dmitri Young	.10
99	Joe Young	.05

Autographs

The top prospects in Class A, AA and AAA are featured on the autographed cards which are the heart of Best's premiere Autograph Series issue. One genuinely autographed card is included in each six-card foil pack. Autographed cards differ in design from the base set in that action photos on front are vignetted in an oval against a white background. The player name and minor league team logo are at bottom. Backs carry a congratulatory message over a large issuer logo. The unnumbered autographed cards are checklisted here in alphabetical order.

		MT
Common Player:		1.00
(1)	Israel Alcantera	1.00
(2)	Richard Almanzar	1.00
(3)	Brian Banks	1.00
(4)	Marc Barcelo	1.00
(5)	Kimera Bartee	1.00
(6)	Jeremy Blevins	1.00
(7)	Jaime Bluma	1.00
(8)	D.J. Boston	1.00
(9)	Kevin Brown	1.00
(10)	Homer Bush	1.00
(11)	Jay Canizaro	1.00
(12)	Luis Castillo	2.00
(13)	Davey Coggin	1.00
(14)	Bartolo Colon	6.00
(15)	Jacob Cruz	1.00
(16)	Lino Diaz	1.00
(17)	Todd Dunn	1.00
(18)	Jermaine Dye	6.00
(19)	Bobby Estalella	2.00
(20)	Tom Fordham	1.00
(21)	Karim Garcia	4.00
(22)	Todd Greene	1.00
(23)	Ben Grieve	2.00
(24)	Mike Gulan	1.00
(25)	Derek Hacopian	1.00
(26)	Wes Helms	1.00
(27)	Brett Herbison	1.00
(28)	Chad Hermansen	1.00
(29)	Aaron Holbert	1.00
(30)	Damon Hollins	1.00
(31)	Ryan Jaroncyk	1.00
(32)	Geoff Jenkins	2.50
(33)	Earl Johnson	1.00
(34)	Andruw Jones	12.00
(35)	Jason Kendall	4.00
(36)	Brooks Kieschnick	1.00
(37)	Andre King	1.00
(38)	Paul Konerko	4.00
(39)	Todd Landry	1.00
(40)	Mendy Lopez	1.00
(41)	Roberto Lopez	1.00
(42)	Eric Ludwick	1.00
(43)	Mike Maurer	1.00
(44)	Brian Meadows	1.00
(45)	Ralph Milliard	1.00
(46)	Doug Mlicki	1.00
(47)	Julio Mosquera	1.00
(48)	Tony Mounce	1.00
(49)	Sergio Nunez	1.00
(50)	Russell Ortiz	3.00
(51)	Carey Paige	1.00
(52)	Jay Payton	3.00
(53)	Charles Peterson	1.00
(54)	Tommy Phelps	1.00
(55)	Hugo Pivaral	1.00
(56)	Dante Powell	1.00
(57)	Angel Ramirez	1.00
(58)	Gary Rath	1.00
(59)	Mark Redman	1.00
(60)	Adam Riggs	1.00
(61)	Lonell Roberts	1.00
(62)	Scott Rolen	9.00
(63)	Glendon Rusch	1.00
(64)	Matt Sachse	1.00
(65)	Donnie Sadler	1.50
(66)	William Santamaria	1.00
(67)	Todd Schmitt	1.00
(68)	Richie Sexson	4.00
(69)	Alvie Shepherd	1.00
(70)	Steve Shoemaker	1.00
(71)	Brian Sikorski	1.00
(72)	Randall Simon	2.00
(73)	Matt Smith	1.00
(74)	Scott Spiezio	1.00
(75)	Everett Stull, II	1.00
(76)	Jose Texidor	1.00
(77)	Mike Thurman	1.00
(78)	Brett Tomko	1.00
(79)	Bubba Trammell (Issued in 1998.)	2.00
(80)	Hector Trinidad	1.00
(81)	Pedro Valdes	1.00
(82)	Andrew Vessel	1.00
(83)	Jacob Viano	1.00
(84)	Terrell Wade	1.00
(85)	Bret Wagner	1.00
(86)	Todd Walker	1.50
(87)	Travis Welch	1.00
(88)	Casey Whitten	1.00
(89)	Paul Wilson	1.50
(90)	Preston Wilson	3.50
(91)	Kevin Witt	1.00
(92)	Jamey Wright	1.00

First Round Draft Picks

Besides the autographed cards, the only other inserts found in Best's '96 Autograph Series is this run of 16 first-round draft picks who made their pro debut in 1996. For some of the players it is their first baseball card. Fronts have player poses against large minor league team logos. Backs repeat the front player photo in a subdued sepia image over which is printed the player biography. Cards are numbered with a "FR" prefix.

		MT
Complete Set (16):		5.00
Common Player:		.50
1	Chad Green	.50
2	Mark Kotsay	1.00
3	Robert Stratton	.50
4	Dermal Brown	.50
5	Matt Halloran	.50
6	Joe Lawrence	.50
7	Todd Noel	.50
8	Jake Westbrook	.50
9	Gil Meche	1.00
10	Damian Rolls	.50
11	John Oliver	.50
12	Josh Garrett	.50
13	A.J. Zapp	.50
14	Danny Peoples	.50
15	Paul Wilder	.50
16	Nick Bierbrodt	.50

1996 Classic Assets (Baseball)

Issued in two series this five-sport card set provides the base set for a phone card chase program. Only the baseball players from the base set, inserts and phone cards are listed here.

		MT
Base Set/Inserts:		
4	Barry Bonds	.75
18	Jason Kendall	.40
33	Jay Payton	.25
39	Nolan Ryan	.75
48	Paul Wilson	.25
64	Doug Million	.25
64	Doug Million (Silver signature.)	.50
65	Barry Bonds	.75
65	Barry Bonds (Silver signature.)	6.00
DC15	Nomar Garciaparra (Die-Cut)	3.00
DC17	Barry Bonds (Die-Cut)	6.00
DC18	Paul Wilson (Die-Cut)	.25
CA7	Cal Ripken Jr. (Cut Above)	6.00
CA10	Barry Bonds (Cut Above)	6.00
S1	Barry Bonds (Silksations)	6.00

1996 Classic Signings (Baseball)

Another five-sport card set with the lure of an autographed card in every pack and a chance to win autographed memorabilia, Signings includes the usual line-up of Classic spokesmen and baseball prospects among the 100-card base set, parallel editions and chase sets.

		MT
Base Set/Inserts:		
60	Ben Grieve	.35
60	Ben Grieve (Die-Cut)	.50
60	Ben Grieve/Auto.	3.00
61	Paul Wilson	.35
61	Paul Wilson (Die-Cut)	.50
61	Paul Wilson/Auto.	3.00
62	Calvin Reese	.35
62	Calvin Reese (Die-Cut)	.50
62	Calvin Reese/Auto.	3.00
63	Karim Garcia	.75
63	Karim Garcia (Die-Cut)	1.00
63	Karim Garcia/Auto.	4.50
64	Mark Farris	.25
64	Mark Farris (Die-Cut)	.50
64	Mark Farris/Auto.	2.00
65	Jay Payton	.35
65	Jay Payton (Die-Cut)	.50
65	Jay Payton/Auto.	3.00
66	Dustin Hermanson	.25
66	Dustin Hermanson (Die-Cut)	.50
66	Dustin Hermanson/ Auto.	2.00
67	Michael Barrett	.35
67	Michael Barrett (Die-Cut)	.50
67	Michael Barrett/Auto.	3.00
68	Ryan Jaroncyk	.25
68	Ryan Jaroncyk (Die-Cut)	.50
68	Ryan Jaroncyk/Auto.	2.00
69	Ben Davis	.25
69	Ben Davis (Die-Cut)	.50
69	Ben Davis/Auto.	3.00
93	Barry Bonds	2.00
93	Barry Bonds (Die-Cut)	6.00
93	Barry Bonds/Auto.	90.00
21	Paul Wilson (Freshly Inked)	2.00
22	Nomar Garciaparra (Freshly Inked)	6.00
8	Barry Bonds (Etched in Stone)	7.50

1996 Classic Visions (Baseball)

The usual prospects and Classic spokesmen are included in this five-sports issue printed on extra-thick card stock and highlighted with both silver- and gold-foil stamping.

		MT
Complete (Baseball) Set (14):		3.00
Common Player:		.10
95	Barry Bonds	1.50
96	Nolan Ryan	1.50
97	Ben Grieve	.25
98	Ben Davis	.15
99	Paul Wilson	.25
100	C.J. Nitkowski	.15
101	Chad Hermansen	.15
102	Jason Kendall	.35
103	Todd Greene	.15
104	Dustin Hermanson	.15
105	Karim Garcia	.35
106	Doug Million	.15
107	Jay Payton	.25
130	Nolan Ryan (Legendary Futures)	.50

1996 Classic Visions Signings (Baseball)

A handful of baseball players is included among the five sports represented in this set.

		MT
Complete (Baseball) Set (8):		3.00
Common Player:		.25
80	Barry Bonds	1.00
81	Nolan Ryan	1.00
82	Ben Davis	.25
83	Chad Hermansen	.25
84	Jason Kendall	.50
85	Todd Greene	.25
86	Karim Garcia	.50
87	Jay Payton	.35

1996 Classic Visions Signings (Baseball) Auto.

In roughly the same format as the base cards, except for the congratulatory message on the cards' backs, authentically autographed cards of some of the players in this five-sport set were included as 1:12 pack inserts. Some players signed numbered silver autograph versions while others signed both the silver and an unnumbered gold version. Because they are not numbered, the gold version is perceived as being more common.

		MT
Common Player:		3.00
(80)	Barry Bonds (Silver, 240.)	125.00
(82)	Ben Davis (Silver, 360.)	6.00
(85)	Todd Greene (Silver, 385.)	6.00
(85)	Todd Greene (Gold)	3.00
(86)	Karim Garcia (Silver, 370.)	7.50
(86)	Karim Garcia (Gold)	4.00
(87)	Jay Payton (Silver, 365.)	6.00
(87)	Jay Payton (Gold)	3.00

1996 Fleer Excel

Major league quality in a minor league set was touted by Fleer for its 1996 Excel issue. Cards were printed on cardboard described as 40% thicker than typical minor league cards, with each card having copper-foil highlights on front. Each of the players in the basic 250-card set is depicted on front in a posed or game-action borderless photo. Backs have two more photos of the player, generally close-up action and portraits. Backs also provide full pro stats. The set is arranged alphabetically by player within organization and league. Each foil pack includes one card from among the five insert sets produced in conjunction with the Excel set.

		MT
Complete Set (250):		15.00
Common Player:		.05
Wax Pack (12):		1.50
Wax Box (36):		35.00
1	Kimera Bartee	.05
2	Carlos Chavez	.05
3	Rocky Coppinger	.05
4	Tommy Davis	.05
5	Eddy Martinez	.05
6	Billy Owens	.05
7	Billy Percibal	.05
8	Garrett Stephenson	.05
9	Rachaad Stewart	.05
10	Chris Allison	.05
11	Virgil Chevalier	.05
12	Nomar Garciaparra	3.00
13	Jose Malave	.05
14	Ryan McGuire	.05
15	Trot Nixon	.50
16	Rafael Orellano	.05
17	Pork Chop Pough	.05
18	Donnie Sadler	.10
19	Bill Selby	.05
20	Nathan Tebbs	.05
21	George Arias	.05
22	Matt Beaumont	.05
23	Danny Buxbaum	.05
24	Jovino Carvajal	.05
25	Geoff Edsell	.05
26	Darin Erstad	.50
27	Aaron Guiel	.05
28	Mike Holtz	.05
29	Ryan Kane	.05
30	Jeff Abbott	.05
31	Kevin Coughlin	.05
32	Tom Fordham	.05
33	Carlos Lee	.25
34	Frank Menechino	.05
35	Charles Poe	.05
36	Nilson Robledo	.05
37	Juan Thomas	.05
38	Archie Vazouez (Vazquez)	.05
39	Bruce Aven	.05
40	Russ Branyan	.05
41	Bartolo Colon	.35
42	Einar Diaz	.05
43	Mike Glavine	.05
44	Ricky Gutierrez	.05
45	Rick Heiserman	.05
46	Richie Sexson	.35
47	Enrique Wilson	.15
48	Jaret Wright	.10
49	Bryan Corey	.05
50	Mike Drumright	.05
51	Juan Encarnacion	.10
52	Brandon Reed	.05
53	Bubba Trammell	.05
54	Daryle Ward	.05
55	Jaime Bluma	.05
56	Tim Byrdak	.05
57	Gary Coffee	.05
58	Lino Diaz	.05
59	Sal Fasano	.05
60	Jed Hansen	.05
61	Juan LeBron	.05
62	Sean McNally	.05
63	Anthony Medrano	.05
64	Rodolfo Mendez	.05
65	Sergio Nunez	.05
66	Mandy Romero	.05
67	Glendon Rusch	.10
68	Brian Banks	.05
69	Jeff D'Amico	.10
70	Jonas Hamlin	.05
71	Geoff Jenkins	.15
72	Roberto Lopez	.05
73	Gerald Parent	.05
74	Doug Webb	.05
75	Antone Williamson	.05
76	Shane Bowers	.05
77	Shane Gunderson	.05
78	Corey Koskie	.25
79	Jake Patterson	.05
80	A.J. Pierzynski	.25
81	Mark Redman	.05
82	Dan Serafini	.05
83	Todd Walker	.10
84	Chris Corn	.05
85	Nick Delvecchio	.05
86	Dan Donato	.05
87	Matt Drews	.05
88	Mike Figga	.05
89	Ben Ford	.05
90	Marty Janzen	.05
91	Shea Morenz	.10
92	Ray Ricken	.05
93	Shane Spencer	.05
94	Bob St. Pierre	.05
95	Jay Tessmer	.05
96	Chris Wilcox	.05
97	Steve Cox	.05
98	Ben Grieve	.10
99	Jason McDonald	.05
100	Brad Rigby	.05
101	Demond Smith	.05
102	Jim Bonnici	.05
103	Jose Cruz Jr.	.10
104	Osvaldo Fernandez	.10
105	Raul Ibanez	.05
106	Desi Relaford	.10
107	Marino Santana	.05
108	Kevin Brown	.05
109	Jeff Davis	.05
110	Edwin Diaz	.05
111	Jonathan Johnson	.05
112	Fernando Tatis	.10
113	Andrew Vessel	.05
114	John Curl	.05
115	Ryan Jones	.05
116	Julio Mosquera	.05
117	Jeff Patzke	.05
118	Mike Peeples	.05
119	Mark Sievert	.05
120	Joe Young	.05
121	Winston Abreu	.05
122	Anthony Briggs	.05
123	Matt Byrd	.05
124	Jermaine Dye	.15
125	Derrin Ebert	.05
126	Wes Helms	.05
127	Damon Hollins	.05
128	Ryan Jacobs	.05
129	Andruw Jones	2.00
130	Gus Kennedy	.05
131	George Lombard	.05
132	Damian Moss	.05
133	Robert Smith	.05
134	Pedro Swann	.05
135	Ron Wright	.05
136	Pat Cline	.05
137	Robin Jennings	.05
138	Brooks Kieschnick	.05
139	Ed Larregui	.05
140	Jason Maxwell	.05
141	Bobby Morris	.05
142	Amaury Telemaco	.05
143	Pedro Valdes	.05
144	Cedric Allen	.05
145	Justin Atchley	.05
146	Aaron Boone	.10
147	Steve Goodhart	.05
148	Chris Murphy	.05
149	Christian Rojas	.05
150	Terry Wright	.05
151	Brent Crowther	.05
152	Angel Echevarria	.05
153	Derrick Gibson	.05
154	Todd Helton	2.00
155	Terry Jones	.05
156	David Kennedy	.05
157	Mike Kusiewicz	.05
158	Joel Moore	.05
159	Jacob Viano	.05
160	Jamey Wright	.05
161	Todd Dunwoody	.05
162	Ryan Jackson	.05
163	Billy McMillon	.05
164	Ralph Milliard	.05
165	Clemente Nunez	.05
166	Edgar Renteria	.15
167	Chris Sheff	.05
168	Matt Whisenant	.05
169	Bob Abreu	.25
170	Ramon Castro	.05
171	Richard Hidalgo	.10
172	Tony McKnight	.05
173	Tony Mounce	.05
174	Roberto Duran	.05
175	Wilton Guerrero	.05
176	Joe Jacobsen	.05
177	Paul Konerko	.50
178	Chris Latham	.05
179	Onan Masaoka	.05
180	Mike Metcalfe	.05
181	Kevin Pincavitch	.05
182	Adam Riggs	.05
183	David Yocum	.05
184	Jake Benz	.05
185	Hiram Bocachica	.05
186	Brad Fullmer	.10
187	Vladimir Guerrero	2.00
188	Eric Ludwick	.05
189	Carlos Mendoza	.05
190	Jarrod Patterson	.05
191	Jay Payton	.10
192	Paul Wilson	.10
193	Julio Zorrilla	.05
194	Marlon Anderson	.10
195	Ron Blazier	.05
196	Steve Carver	.05
197	Blake Doolan	.05
198	David Doster	.05
199	Tommy Eason	.05
200	Zach Elliott	.05
201	Bobby Estalella	.10
202	Rob Grable	.05
203	Bronson Heflin	.05
204	Dan Held	.05
205	Kevin Hooker	.05
206	Rich Hunter	.05
207	Carlton Loewer	.05
208	Wendell Magee	.05
SAMPLE	Wendell Magee (Different back design.)	1.00
209	Len Manning	.05
210	Fred McNair	.05
211	Ryan Nye	.05
212	Scott Rolen	1.50
213	Brian Stumpf	.05
214	Reggie Taylor	.05
215	Larry Wimberly	.05
216	Micah Franklin	.05
217	Chad Hermansen	.05
218	Jason Kendall	.35
219	Garrett Long	.05
220	Joe Maskivish	.05
221	Chris Peters	.05
222	Charles Peterson	.05
223	Charles Rice	.05
224	Reed Secrist	.05
225	Derek Swafford	.05
226	Mike Busby	.05
227	Mike Gulan	.05
228	Chris Haas	.05
229	Jeff Matulevich	.05
230	Steve Montgomery	.05
231	Matt Morris	.15
232	Bret Wagner	.05
233	Gabe Alvarez	.05
234	Raul Casanova	.05
235	Ben Davis	.05
236	Bubba Dixon	.05
237	Greg LaRocca	.05
238	Derrek Lee	.50
239	Jason Thompson	.05
240	Darin Blood	.05
241	Jay Canizaro	.05
242	Edwin Corps	.05
243	Jacob Cruz	.05
244	Joe Fontenot	.05
245	Jesse Ibarra	.05
246	Dante Powell	.05
247	Keith Williams	.05
248	Checklist 1-103	.05
249	Checklist 104-213	.05
250	Checklist 214-250, Inserts	.05

All-Stars

Labeled "can't miss" stars from all minor league levels, the players in this insert set are "up in lights" as the color action photo on front is repeated in the background as if being projected on a scoreboard. The player's name, team and the Fleer Excel All-Star logo are printed in silver holographic foil. Backs have a portrait photo at one side with career highlights on the other. All-Star cards are found, on average, once per 13 packs of Excel.

		MT
Complete Set (10):		8.00
Common Player:		.25
1	Jason Kendall	.50
2	Steve Cox	.25
3	Adam Riggs	.25
4	George Arias	.25
5	Wilton Guerrero	.25
6	Vladimir Guerrero	4.00
7	Andruw Jones	4.00
8	Jay Payton	.35
9	Raul Ibanez	.25
10	Paul Wilson	.35

Climbing

Players who are "Climbing" their organization's minor league ladder at a faster than usual pace are featured in this insert set. Against a background of colorful, out-of-focus A's (Fleer calls the background "pearlized") is a player action photo. The name and Excel Climbing logo are in gold-foil. On back is a large portrait photo and details of the player's rise through the classifications, printed on a background of green, blue and purple. Climbing inserts are found at an average rate of one per six packs.

		MT
Complete Set (10):		3.50
Common Player:		.25
1	Jeff Abbott	.25
2	Rocky Coppinger	.25
3	Brent Crowther	.25
4	Rich Hunter	.25
5	Chris Latham	.25
6	Wendell Magee	.50
7	Jay Payton	.50
8	Ray Ricken	.25
9	Scott Rolen	3.00
10	Paul Wilson	.50

First Year Phenoms

Potential future superstars in their first year of pro ball are featured in this chase set. Cards feature action photos on a background of garishly colored baseball equipment and silver-foil graphic highlights. Backs have subdued earth tones as a background with a haloed player portrait on one end and a necessarily short career summary at the other end. The First Year Phemons cards are found, on average, once per three foil packs.

		MT
Complete Set (10):		5.00
Common Player:		.25
1	Gabe Alvarez	.25
2	Jose Cruz Jr.	.25
3	Ben Davis	.25
4	Darin Erstad	.75
5	Todd Helton	4.50
6	Chad Hermansen	.25
7	Geoff Jenkins	.50
8	Carlton Loewer	.25
9	Shea Morenz	.25
10	Matt Morris	.25

Season Crowns

Statistical leaders and award winners from various minor leagues are featured in this chase set. Fronts feature a rich brown tapestry background, with player action photo superimposed. The player's name, Excel logo and large Season Crown title and crown are in silver-foil. Backs have a white version of the tapestry background over which are printed the details of the player's performance. A large color portrait photo on one end completes the design. Season Crown inserts are found at an average rate of one per four packs.

		MT
Complete Set (10):		8.00
Common Player:		.25
1	Matt Beaumont	.25
2	Bartolo Colon	1.00
3	Matt Drews	.25
4	Derrick Gibson	.25
5	Vladimir Guerrero	4.00
6	Andruw Jones	4.00
7	Brandon Reed	.25
8	Glendon Rusch	.25
9	Richie Sexson	.50
10	Shane Spencer	.25

Team Leaders

Team offensive statistical leaders are featured on this, the scarcest of the Excel chase sets. Printed on plastic, the cards feature player action poses on a background which includes portions of the team logo. Backs have a portrait photo and information the player's statistical feat. The plastic Team Leaders cards are seeded one per 35 packs, on average.

		MT
Complete Set (10):		8.00
Common Player:		1.00
1	George Arias	1.00
2	Kevin Coughlin	1.00
3	Wilton Guerrero	1.00
4	Dan Held	1.00
5	Brooks Kieschnick	1.00
6	Wendell Magee	1.00
7	Jason McDonald	1.00
8	Adam Riggs	1.00
9	Juan Thomas	1.00
10	Ron Wright	1.00

1996 Signature Rookies Old Judge T-96

Signature Rookies returned for a second year with a smaller than standard size minor league issue; all cards except the checklist are in 2" x 3" format. Because SR contracted with individual players and did not seek Major League Baseball licensing, neither team names nor logos appear on the cards. Most cards have had the major or minor league uniform logos airbrushed off, while some have a fantasy logo added in their place. The set was issued in seven-card foil packs which contain five regular cards, one autographed card and one card from the six insert series. Given the advertised print run, and equal production of each card, about 16,000 of each were available. Fronts of the regular issue cards have a player portrait against a solid color background. Stats on back are complete only through 1994, though some of the career highlights refer to the 1995 season. Fronts of the autographed cards have a line of print added in the top border: "Authentic Signature," and are UV coated. Besides the player autograph on those cards, there is a serial number from within an edition of 6,000.

		MT
Complete Set (38):		2.00
Common Player:		.05
1	Tommy Adams	.05
2	Travis Baptist	.05
3	Mike Birkbeck	.05
4	Jim Bowie	.05
5	Duff Brumley	.05
6	Scott Bullett	.05
7	Frank Catalanotto	.10
8	Chris Cumberland	.05
9	Travis Driskill	.05
10	John Frascatore	.05
11	Brian Giles	.25
12	Vladimir Guerrero	1.00
13	Butch Huskey	.05
14	Greg Keagle	.05
15	Jay Kirkpatrick	.05
16	Ed Larregui	.05
17	Mitch Lyden	.05
18	T.J. Mathews	.05
19	Brian Maxcy	.05
20	Jeff McNeely	.05
21	Tony Mitchell	.05
22	Kerwin Moore	.05
23	Oscar Munoz	.05
24	Les Norman	.05
25	Jayhawk Owens	.05
26	Mark Petkovsek	.05
27	Hugo Pivaral	.05
28	Chad Renfroe	.05
29	Victor Rodriguez	.05
30	Matt Rundels	.05
31	Willie Smith	.05
32	Amaury Telemaco	.05
33	Robert Toth	.05
34	Ben Van Ryn	.05
35	Wes Weger	.05
36	Don Wengert	.05
37	Kelly Wunsch	.05
---	Checklist	.05

Autographed

Each pack of SR's Old Judge T-96 Series includes an authentically autographed card. Almost identical to the regular-issue cards, fronts of the autographed cards have a line of print added in the top border: "Authentic Signature", and are UV coated. Besides the player autograph on those cards, there is a serial number from within an edition of 6,000.

		MT
Complete Set, Auto. (37):		30.00
Common Autograph:		1.00
1	Tommy Adams	1.00
2	Travis Baptist	1.00
3	Mike Birkbeck	1.00
4	Jim Bowie	1.00
5	Duff Brumley	1.00
6	Scott Bullett	1.00
7	Frank Catalanotto	2.00
8	Chris Cumberland	1.00
9	Travis Driskill	1.00
10	John Frascatore	1.00
11	Brian Giles	4.00
12	Vladimir Guerrero	25.00
13	Butch Huskey	1.00
14	Greg Keagle	1.00
15	Jay Kirkpatrick	1.00
16	Ed Larregui	1.00
17	Mitch Lyden	1.00
18	T.J. Mathews	1.00
19	Brian Maxcy	1.00
20	Jeff McNeely	1.00
21	Tony Mitchell	1.00
22	Kerwin Moore	1.00
23	Oscar Munoz	1.00
24	Les Norman	1.00
25	Jayhawk Owens	1.00
26	Mark Petkovsek	1.00
27	Hugo Pivaral	1.00
28	Chad Renfroe	1.00
29	Victor Rodriguez	1.00
30	Matt Rundels	1.00
31	Willie Smith	1.00
32	Amaury Telemaco	1.00
33	Robert Toth	1.00
34	Ben Van Ryn	1.00
35	Wes Weger	1.00
36	Don Wengert	1.00
37	Kelly Wunsch	1.00

Junior Hit Man

Ken Griffey, Jr., is the featured player in this insert set. Each card pictures him in action on the UV-coated borderless front photo. His name and the set logo are in gold foil. Backs, also UV coated, have a portrait photo, stats and a few words about Junior, all on a red and white bull's eye background. Cards are numbered with a "J" prefix. Each card can be found in a regular and an autographed (250 each) version.

		MT
Complete Set (5):		15.00
Complete Set, Auto. (5):		200.00
Common Card:		1.50
Autographed Card:		40.00
1	Ken Griffey Jr.	1.50
1a	Ken Griffey Jr./Auto.	40.00
2	Ken Griffey Jr.	1.50
2a	Ken Griffey Jr./Auto.	40.00
3	Ken Griffey Jr.	1.50
3a	Ken Griffey Jr./Auto.	40.00
4	Ken Griffey Jr.	1.50
4a	Ken Griffey Jr./Auto.	40.00
5	Ken Griffey Jr.	1.50
5a	Ken Griffey Jr./Auto.	40.00

Major Respect

Five players whose major league careers began with a bang are the subject of this insert set. UV-coated cards have player action photos on a background of red rays with a purple "MAJOR RESPECT" logo at bottom. The player's name is in gold foil down the side. Backs have the standard stats, player data and career notes along with a portrait photo. All uniform logos have been airbrushed off since the cards are not licensed by Major League Baseball. Card numbers have an "M" prefix. Each card can be found in both an unautographed form and authentically signed.

		MT
Complete Set (5):		2.00
Complete Set, Auto. (5):		75.00
Common Player:		.25
Common Autograph:		3.00
1	Alex Rodriguez	1.50
1a	Alex Rodriguez/Auto.	60.00
2	Johnny Damon	.75
2a	Johnny Damon/Auto.	10.00
3	Karim Garcia	.50
3a	Karim Garcia/Auto.	5.00
4	Garrett Anderson	.25
4a	Garrett Anderson/Auto.	4.50
5	Bill Pulsipher	.25
5a	Bill Pulsipher/Auto.	3.00

Peak Picks

Some of the top picks of the 1995 draft are shown in this insert issue. Fronts have borderless action photos of the players in their college uniforms. "PEAK PICKS" and their names are in gold foil. Backs have a close-up picture, vital data, college and 1995 minor league stats and a few words about the player's college career. Cards are UV coated both front and back and carry a "P" prefix to the number. Each card can be found in an authentically autographed version, as well as unsigned.

		MT
Complete Set (10):		3.00
Complete Set, Auto.(10):		25.00
Common Player:		.25
Common Autograph:		2.00
1	Darin Erstad	.50
1a	Darin Erstad/Auto.	7.50
2	Jose Cruz, Jr.	.25
2a	Jose Cruz, Jr./Auto.	4.00
3	Jonathan Johnson	.25
3a	Jonathan Johnson/Auto.	1.00
4	Todd Helton	1.50
4a	Todd Helton/Auto.	17.50
5	Matt Morris	.25
5a	Matt Morris/Auto.	2.00
6	Tony McKnight	.25
6a	Tony McKnight/Auto.	1.00
7	Reggie Taylor	.25
7a	Reggie Taylor/Auto.	1.00
8	David Yocum	.25
8a	David Yocum/Auto.	1.00
9	Shea Morenz	.25
9a	Shea Morenz/Auto.	2.00
10	Ben Davis	.25
10a	Ben Davis/Auto.	2.00

Rising Stars

Five players projected to be major league stars are the focus of this insert set. Cards are UV-coated on each side. Fronts have borderless color action photos with the player name and "Rising Stars" logo in gold foil. Backs have a portrait photo, biographical details and complete minor league stats through 1995. Because the cards are licensed only with individual players and collegiate authorities, minor and major league uniform logos have been removed from the photos. Each card can be found in both an autographed and unautographed version. Cards are numbered with a "R" prefix.

		MT
Complete Set (5):		1.00
Complete Set, Auto. (5):		5.00
Common Player:		.25
Common Autograph:		2.00
1	Jermaine Dye	.50
1a	Jermaine Dye/Auto.	4.50
2	Ben Grieve	.50
2a	Ben Grieve/Auto.	2.00
3	Ryan Helms	.25
3a	Ryan Helms/Auto.	1.00
4	Jeff Darwin	.25
4a	Jeff Darwin/Auto.	1.00
5	Alan Benes	.25
5a	Alan Benes/Auto.	1.00

Rookie/Year

American League Rookie of the Year Marty Cordova is the focus of this insert set. Each card pictures him in a borderless game-action photo. His name and the set logo are in gold foil. Backs have another photo, full stats, vital data and a few words about the player. The card number is preceded by a "RY" prefix. Twins logos have been airbrushed off the photos. Besides the regular version, each card can be found authentically autographed.

		MT
Complete Set (5):		1.00
Complete Set, Auto. (5):		20.00
Common Card:		.25
Autographed Card:		5.00
1	Marty Cordoua	.25
1a	Marty Cordova/Auto.	5.00
2	Marty Cordova	.25
2a	Marty Cordova/Auto.	5.00
3	Marty Cordova	.25
3a	Marty Cordova/Auto.	5.00
4	Marty Cordova	.25
4a	Marty Cordova/Auto.	5.00
5	Marty Cordova	.25
5a	Marty Cordova/Auto.	5.00

op Prospect

Ten of the minor leagues' best players are featured in this insert set. UV-coated on both sides, fronts have an action photo on a white background with the player's name in gold foil. Backs have a portrait photo, complete pro stats through the 1995 season and a few personal details. Cards are numbered with a "T" prefix.

		MT
Complete Set (10):		1.00
Complete Auto. Set (10):		10.00
Common Player:		.10
Common Autograph:		1.00
1	Juan Acevedo	.25
1a	Juan Acevedo/Auto.	2.00
2	Mike Bovee	.10
2a	Mike Bovee/Auto.	1.00
3	Mark Hubbard	.10
3a	Mark Hubbard/Auto.	1.00
4	Luis Raven	.10
4a	Luis Raven/Auto.	1.00
5	Desi Relaford	.25
5a	Desi Relaford/Auto.	2.00
6	Antone Williamson	.10
6a	Antone Williamson/ Auto.	1.00
7	Nick Delvecchio	.10
7a	Nick Delvecchio/Auto.	1.00
8	Andy Larkin	.10
8a	Andy Larkin/Auto.	1.00
9	Kris Ralston	.10
9a	Kris Ralston/Auto.	1.00
10	Jeff Suppan	.35
10a	Jeff Suppan/Auto.	3.00

1996 Signature Rookies Rookie of the Year

The American League Rookie of the Year (Cordova) and runner-up (Anderson) are featured in this five-card insert set. Color action photos and gold-foil highlights are featured on front; portrait photos, biographical notes and pro stats are on back.

		MT
Complete Set (5):		1.00
Common Card:		.25
R1	Garret Anderson	.25
R2	Garret Anderson	.25
R3	Marty Cordova	.25
R4	Marty Cordova	.25
R5	Garret Anderson, Marty Cordova	.25

1996 Minor League Team Sets

For 1996, Best leapt into the void created by the pullback of Classic and Fleer from the minor league team set market, claiming a 75 percent share of the approximately 175 team sets issued. Many other teams issued their sets independently or with small regional graphic firms such as Grand Stand (GS). Availability of many teams sets continued to outstrip player popularity as a factor in determining prices in the hobby market.

		MT
188 Team Sets and Variationss		
1996	Best AA All-Stars (56)	11.00
1996	Best Reading School AA All-Stars (56)	20.00
1996	Aberdeen Pheasants Team Issue (25)	4.00
1996	GS Abilene Prairie Dogs (28)	4.00
1996	GS Alexandria Aces (26)	4.00
1996	GS Amarillo Dillas (19)	4.00
1996	Best Appalachian League Prospects (30)	8.00
1996	Best Arkansas Travelers (29)	10.00
1996	Best Asheville Tourists (30)	6.00
1996	Best Auburn Doubledays (30)	5.00
1996	Best Augusta Greenjackets (29)	20.00
1996	Team Batavia Clippers (34)	6.00
1996	Team Bellingham Giants (36)	6.00
1996	Team Beloit Snappers (36)	10.00
1996	Team Billings Mustangs (31)	40.00
1996	Best Binghamton Mets (30)	7.00
1996	Best Birmingham Barons (30)	8.00
1996	Best Bluefield Orioles (30)	8.00
1996	Best Boise Hawks (30)	6.00
1996	Best Bowie Baysox (27)	6.00
1996	Best Brevard County Manatees (30)	7.00
1996	Best Bristol White Sox (30)	5.00
1996	Best Buffalo Bisons (24)	11.00
1996	Team Burlington Bees (33)	15.00
1996	Best Burlington Indians (30)	6.00
1996	Best Butte Copper Kings (30)	6.00
1996	Best Canton-Akron Indians (30)	12.00
1996	Best Carolina Mudcats (30)	5.00
1996	Best Carolina League/ Modesto A-S (26)	40.00
1996	Best Carolina/Modesto Sponsor's Set (28)	40.00
1996	Best Carolina/Modesto Insert Set (10)	50.00
1996	Team Cedar Rapids Kernels (34)	6.00
1996	Team Charleston RiverDogs (32)	25.00
1996	Best Charlotte Knights (29)	8.00
1996	Best Chattanooga Lookouts (30)	6.00
1996	Team Clinton Lumberkings (30)	20.00
1996	Team Colorado Springs Sky Sox (34)	8.00
1996	Best Columbus Clippers (30)	7.00
1996	Police Columbus Clippers (25)	9.00
1996	Team Columbus Clippers POGs (24)	35.00
1996	Best Danville Braves (30)	12.00
1996	Best Daytona Cubs (30)	20.00
1996	Best Delmarva Shorebirds (30)	35.00
1996	Best Dunedin Blue Jays (30)	10.00
1996	Team Dunedin Blue Jays (30)	20.00
1996	Team Dunedin Blue Jays Update (18)	10.00
1996	Best Durham Bulls, Blue (30)	40.00
1996	Best Durham Bulls Update, Brown (30)	30.00
1996	Team Edmonton Trappers (xx)	30.00
1996	Best El Paso Diablos (30)	9.00
1996	Best Erie Sea Wolves (25)	7.00
1996	Best Eugene Emeralds (27)	5.00
1996	Best Everett Aquasox (30)	7.00
1996	Best Fayetteville Generals (30)	20.00
1996	Best Frederick Keys (30)	5.00
1996	Best Ft. Myers Miracle (30)	12.00
1996	Best Ft. Wayne Wizards (31)	9.00
1996	Team Grays Harbor Gulls (26)	4.00
1996	Best Great Falls Dodgers (30)	7.00
1996	Team Great Falls Dodgers (35)	9.00
1996	Best Greensboro Bats (30)	12.00
1996	Best Greenville Braves (30)	11.00
1996	Team/Coke Greenville Braves (30)	17.50
1996	Best Hagerstown Suns (30)	7.00
1996	Best Hardware City Rock Cats (30)	8.00
1996	Best Harrisburg Senators (29)	17.50
1996	Team Helena Brewers (34)	15.00
1996	Best Hickory Crawdads (30)	8.00
1996	Best High Desert Mavericks (30)	6.00
1996	Police High Desert Mavericks (24)	12.00
1996	Team Hilo Stars (36)	12.50
1996	Team Honolulu Sharks (35)	15.00
1996	Best Hudson Valley Renegades (30)	6.00
1996	Burger King Huntsville Stars (28)	35.00
1996	BK Huntsville Stars Uncut Sheet	65.00
1996	Team Idaho Falls Braves (32)	8.00
1996	Best Indianapolis Indians (30)	7.50
1996	Best Iowa Cubs (30)	9.00
1996	Best Jackson Generals (27)	8.00
1996	Smokey Bear Jackson Generals (27)	12.00
1996	Best Jacksonville Suns (30)	12.00
1996	Best Johnson City Cardinals (35)	7.00
1996	Johnson City Cardinals Team Issue (35)	10.00
1996	Team Kane County Cougars (31)	5.00
1996	Team Kane Co. Cougars - Connie's (30)	9.00
1996	Team Kane County Cougars - Gold (30)	9.00
1996	Team Kane County Cougars Update (13)	20.00
1996	Best Kinston Indians (30)	11.00
1996	Best Kissimmee Cobras (30)	7.00
1996	Best Knoxville Smokies (25)	7.00
1996	Best Lake Elsinore Storm (30)	7.00
1996	Best Lakeland Tigers (30)	9.00
1996	Best Lancaster Jethawks (30)	10.00
1996	Best Lansing Lugnuts (30)	40.00
1996	Best Las Vegas Stars (30)	8.00
1996	Best Lethbridge Black Diamonds (33)	8.00
1996	Best Louisville Redbirds (29)	6.00
1996	Best Lowell Spinners (30)	12.00
1996	GS Lubbock Crickets (24)	4.00
1996	Best Lynchburg Hillcats (30)	15.00
1996	Best Lynchburg Hillcats Update (1)	6.00
1996	Best Macon Braves (30)	7.00
1996	Best Martinsville Phillies (30)	10.00
1996	Mascots of the Midwest League (12)	4.00
1996	Team Maui Stingrays (36)	25.00
1996	Team Medicine Hat Blue Jays (33)	35.00
1996	Best Memphis Chicks (30)	6.00
1996	Team Meridian Brakemen (24)	4.00
1996	Best Michigan Battle Cats (30)	6.00
1996	Best Midland Angels (29)	6.00
1996	Team Midland Angels (24)	50.00
1996	Best Midwest League A-S (58)	9.00
1996	Best Modesto A's (30)	18.00
1996	Best Nashville Sounds (30)	7.00
1996	Team Nashville Sounds Foldout	20.00
1996	Best New Haven Ravens (31)	9.00
1996	Best New Haven Ravens (32)	16.00
1996	Team New Haven Ravens Raffle Sheet	10.00
1996	Best New Jersey Cardinals (30)	6.00
1996	Best Norfolk Tides (30)	7.50
1996	Best Norwich Navigators (28)	8.00
1996	Team Norwich Navigators Update (12)	12.00
1996	Team Ogden Raptors (39)	8.00
1996	Best Oklahoma City 89ers (28)	8.00
1996	Best Omaha Royals (30)	9.00
1996	Best Orlando Cubs (30)	6.00
1996	DD Pawtucket Red Sox Foldout	35.00
1996	Best Peoria Chiefs (30)	6.00
1996	Best Phoenix Firebirds (30)	9.00
1996	Team Phoenix Firebirds (30)	9.00
1996	Best Piedmont Boll Weevils (30)	75.00
1996	Best Pittsfield Mets (30)	6.00
1996	Best Port City Roosters (29)	10.00
1996	Best Portland Rockies (30)	5.00
1996	Best Portland Sea Dogs (29)	35.00
1996	Best Prince William Cannons (30)	5.00
1996	Best Quad City River Bandits (29)	7.00
1996	Best Rancho Cucamonga Quakes (30)	7.00
1996	Best Reading Phillies (29)	12.00
1996	Best Reading Phils Fairground Sq. (29)	25.00
1996	Best Reading Phillies Boy Scouts (1)	25.00
1996	Best Richmond Braves (30)	7.00
1996	Best Richmond Braves Update (30)	20.00
1996	Richmond Camera Richmond Braves (25)	75.00
1996	Team Richmond Braves Alumni (6)	25.00
1996	GS Rio Grande Valley White Wings (23)	4.00
1996	Best Rochester Red Wings (30)	7.00
1996	Team Rockford Cubbies (32)	9.00
1996	Best Salem Avalanche (30)	5.00
1996	Best San Antonio Missions (30)	7.00
1996	HEB San Antonio Missions (32)	50.00
1996	Best San Bernardino Stampede (30)	7.00
1996	Best San Jose Giants (30)	6.00
1996	Best Sarasota Red Sox (30)	6.00
1996	Best Savannah Sandgnats (30)	50.00
1996	Best Scranton/ W-B Red Barons (30)	6.00
1996	Team Sioux City Explorers (30)	4.00
1996	Best South Bend Silver Hawks (28)	5.00
1996	Team Southern Oregon Timberjacks (28)	42.50
1996	Best Spokane Indians (30)	20.00
1996	Best St. Catherines Stompers (30)	9.00
1996	Team St. Lucie Mets (36)	12.00
1996	Best St. Petersburg Cardinals (30)	5.00
1996	Best Stockton Ports (30)	5.00
1996	Team Syracuse Chiefs (30)	11.00
1996	Best Tacoma Rainiers (30)	7.00
1996	Best Tampa Yankees (29)	6.00
1996	Best Texas League All-Stars (36)	11.00
1996	Team Thunder Bay Whiskey Jacks (25)	5.00
1996	Best Toledo Mud Hens (30)	8.00
1996	Best Trenton Thunder (30)	7.50
1996	Best Tucson Toros (29)	8.00
1996	Team Tulsa Drillers (30)	8.00
1996	Team Tulsa 20th Anniversary (32)	25.00
1996	GS Tyler Wildcatters (25)	4.00
1996	Best Vancouver Canadians (30)	15.00
1996	Best Vermont Expos (30)	6.00
1996	Best Vero Beach Dodgers (30)	35.00
1996	Team Watertown Indians (36)	9.00
1996	Best West Michigan Whitecaps (30)	10.00
1996	Team West Oahu Canefires (36)	12.50
1996	Best West Palm Beach Expos (31)	80.00
1996	Best Wichita Wranglers (30)	12.00
1996	Team Wichita Wranglers (18)	8.00
1996	Best Wilmington Blue Rocks (30)	6.00
1996	Best Wisconsin Timber Rattlers (30)	15.00
1996	Team Yakima Bears (35)	6.00
1996	Team Zanesville Greys (23)	4.00

1997 Best Prospects

The basic set of minor league player cards from Best in 1997 includes 50 top prospects. Fronts of the 2-1/2" x 3-1/2" cards have action photos with Best and team logos superimposed. Player name is in typewriter style at bottom, with his position abbreviated in a red home plate. Backs have a close-up version of the front photo, a black box at top with personal data, an overall purple background and 1996 stats at bottom.

		MT
Complete Set (50):		5.00
Common Player:		.05
Wax Pack (6):		1.50
Wax Box (18):		20.00
1	Kerry Wood	1.00
2	Matt White	.05
3	Travis Lee	.50
4	Miguel Tejada	.60
5	Kris Benson	.15
6	Paul Konerko	.60
7	Jose Cruz, Jr.	.15
8	Derrek Lee	.60
9	Todd Helton	1.00
10	Carl Pavano	.25
11	Ben Grieve	.10
12	Richard Hidalgo	.10
13	Chad Hermansen	.05
14	Jaret Wright	.05
15	Roy Halladay	.25
16	Hideki Irabu	.05
17	Matt Morris	.10
18	Aramis Ramirez	.35
19	Robinson Checo	.05
20	Chris Carpenter	.05
21	Adrian Beltre	.60
22	Braden Looper	.05
23	Luis Rolando Arrojo	.10
24	Juan Melo	.05
25	Elieser Marrero	.10
26	Kevin McGlinchy	.10
27	Sidney Ponson	.15
28	John Patterson	.05
29	Brian Rose	.05
30	Joe Fontonot	.05
31	Chris Reitsma	.05
32	Paul Wilder	.05
33	Ron Wright	.05
34	A.J. Zapp	.05
35	Donnie Sadler	.10
36	Valerio De Los Santos	.05
37	Eric Chavez	.60
38	Jake Westbrook	.05
39	Seth Greisinger	.05
40	Derrick Gibson	.05
41	Ben Davis	.05
42	Rafael Medina	.05
43	Britt Reames	.05
44	Ben Petrick	.05
45	Josh Paul	.05
46	Brad Fullmer	.10
47	Jarrod Washburn	.15
48	Kevin Escobar	.05
49	Manuel Aybar	.05
50	Wes Helms	.05

All-Stars

Players who made their league all-star teams are featured in this insert set which was a 1:6 pack pick.

		MT
Complete Set (15):		7.50
Common Player:		.25
1	Seth Greisinger	.25
2	Hideki Irabu	.25
3	Josh Paul	.25
4	Jaret Wright	.25
5	Norm Hutchins	.25
6	Miguel Tejada	3.00
7	Ruben Mateo	.25
8	Matt White	.25
9	Marc Lewis	.25
10	Jose Cruz	.25
11	Quincy Carter	.25
12	Kris Benson	.35
13	Ben Petrick	.35
14	Adrian Beltre	2.00
15	Travis Lee	2.00

Autographs

Ten of the best prospects in the minor leagues are featured in this insert set. Fronts feature action photos vignetted against a white background. The Best logo is printed at top-left, while a holographic-foil "Best Prospects" logo is at upper-right. The player name and team logo are at bottom. Backs have a Best Autograph Series logo ghosted on a white background, and a congratulatory message in orange and black. Stated rate of insertion for the autographed cards is one per box (18 packs). The autographed cards are not numbered. An announced Jeff Liefer card was replaced by Wes Helms.

		MT
Complete Set (10):		15.00
Common Autograph:		2.00
(1)	Ben Grieve	3.00
(2)	Wes Helms	2.00
(3)	Brett Herbison	2.00
(4)	Chad Hermansen	2.00
(5)	Geoff Jenkins	3.00
(6)	Paul Konerko	6.00
(7)	Ben Petrick	2.00
(8)	Donnie Sadler	2.00
(9)	Randall Simon	2.00
(10)	Brett Tomko	2.00

Best Bets Preview

With only 200 hand-numbered cards of each player issued, these are the toughest pull among the Best Prospects inserts, being found on average only one per 90 packs. Fronts have an action photo against a background of red bricks and green stripes. Team and manufacturer logos are also featured on front. Backs have a close-up version of the front photo on a background of green stripes and a black polygon. Cards are individually numbered at top-right.

		MT
Complete Set (10):		15.00
Common Player:		1.00
1	Miguel Tejada	5.00
2	Adrian Beltre	5.00

3 Hideki Irabu 1.00
4 Kris Benson 1.50
5 Matt White 1.00
6 Travis Lee 5.00
7 Corey Erickson 1.00
8 Jose Cruz 1.50
9 Marc Lewis 1.00
10 Luis Rolando Arrojo 2.00

Best Five

The field of best minor leaguers is whittled to five for this insert set. Rather than being issued inside the foil packs, these cards are placed one per box as a dealer premium. A close-up baseball design is used for a background on both front and back. An action photo dominates the front with a "Best 5" logo at top and player ID at bottom, along with his team logo. Backs have personal data, career highlights and stats, along with a small detail of the front photo.

MT
Complete Set (5): 10.00
Common Player: 1.00
1 Kris Benson 1.00
2 Kerry Wood 6.00
3 Travis Lee 4.00
4 Hideki Irabu 1.00
5 Matt White 1.00

Best Guns

Top minor league pitchers are featured in this retail-only insert. One card was inserted atop the packs in each box.

MT
Complete Set (10): 10.00
Common Player: .70
1 Robinson Checo .75
2 Rolando Arrojo 1.00
3 Clayton Bruner .75
4 Grant Roberts .75
5 Brian Rose .75
6 Carl Pavano 2.00
7 Kerry Wood 6.00
8 Kris Benson 1.00
9 Jaret Wright .75
10 Cliff Politte .75

Best Lumber

The scarcest of three retail-only inserts in Best Prospects issue is this run of potentially big hitters. The Best Lumber cards are found only on average of one per five boxes.

MT
Complete Set (10): 50.00
Common Player: 4.00
1 Paul Konerko 7.50
2 Derrek Lee 7.50
3 Ricky Ledee 4.00
4 Brad Fullmer 4.00
5 Ben Grieve 4.00
6 Russ Branyon 4.00
7 A.J. Hinch 4.00
8 Adrian Beltre 7.50
9 Mike Stoner 4.00
10 Travis Lee 7.50

Best Wheels

The speed merchants of the minor leagues are featured in this retail-only Best Propsects insert. Cards are random pack inserts at a rate of one per box.

MT
Complete Set (5): 10.00
Common Player: 2.00
1 Donnie Sadler 2.00
2 Juan Encarnacion 3.00
3 Damian Jackson 2.00
4 Chad Green 2.00
5 Mark Kotsay 3.00

Diamond Best

Seeded at a rate of fewer than one per box (about every 19 packs), this insert set features arguaby the top 10 minor league players of 1996. Fronts of the 2-1/2" x 3-1/2" cards have a white background surrounded by a blue border. An action photo is superimposed on a large team logo. The "Diamond Best" logo, player name and position are in red, white and blue at bottom. Backs have a second version of the player photo on a white background streaked with gray. A red box has career highlights; personal data is at right.

MT
Complete Set (10): 25.00
Common Player: 1.00
1 Hideki Irabu 1.00
2 Kerry Wood 6.00
3 Matt White 1.00
4 Travis Lee 3.00
5 Miguel Tejada 4.00
6 Kris Benson 1.00
7 Paul Konerko 4.00
8 Jose Cruz 1.00
9 Derrek Lee 4.00
10 Todd Helton 6.00

International Best

These late-season hobby-only inserts feature top prospects who were born outside the U.S. The cards share a basic design with Best Prospects base cards, but feature a national flag logo at top-right and minor modifications to the back.

MT
Complete Set (5): 3.00
Common Player: .50
IB1 Miguel Tejada 1.50
IB2 Hideki Irabu .50
IB3 Adrian Beltre 1.50
IB4 Rolando Arrojo .75
IB5 Robinson Checo .50

1997 Best Autograph Series

This end-of-year product showcases minor league talent which developed during the season including cards of 1997 draft picks and players who climbed their organizational ladder. The series is numbered 51-100 in continuation of the early-season Best Prospects issue. Cards were sold in foil packs with four regular cards and an autographed card. Fronts have action photos on a ragged-edged background with Best and team logos. Backs have a portrait photo, player data, highlights and stats.

MT
Complete Set (50): 6.00
Common Player: .05
51 Mike Stoner .05
52 George Lombard .05
53 Calvin Pickering .05
54 Antonio Armas .10
55 John Barnes .05
56 Russell Branyan .10
57 Sean Casey .60
58 Edgard Velasquez .05
59 Mike Vavrek .05
60 Magglio Ordonez 1.00
61 Mike Caruso .05
62 Pat Cline .05
63 Courtney Duncan .05
64 Juan Encarnacion .10
65 Jason Varitek .50
66 Alex Gonzalez .05
67 Ryan Jackson .05
68 Kevin Millar .10
69 John Roskos .05
70 Daryle Ward .05
71 Dermal Brown .05
72 Ted Lilly .05
73 Chad Green .05
74 David Ortiz 1.00
75 Jacque Jones .50
76 Luis Rivas .05
77 Orlando Cabrera .25
78 Javier Vazquez .45
79 Jesus Sanchez .05
80 Eric Milton .10
81 Ricky Ledee .05
82 Ramon Hernandez .05
83 A.J. Hinch .05
84 Marlon Anderson .25
85 Ryan Brannan .05
86 Abraham Nunez .15
87 Matt Clement .25
88 Kerry Robinson .05
89 Cliff Politte .05
90 Pablo Ortega .05
91 Aramis Ramirez .25
92 Eric Chavez .75
93 Brent Butler .05
94 Cole Liniak .05
95 Travis Lee .60
96 Adrian Beltre .50
97 Paul Konerko .50
98 Brad Fullmer .15
99 Jeremy Giambi .15
100 Gil Meche .10

Autographs

Dozens of top prospects are featured on the autographed cards which are the heart of Best's Autograph Series issue. One genuinely autographed card is included in each six-card foil pack. Autographed cards differ in design from the base set in that action photos on front are vignetted in an oval against a white background. The player name and minor league team logo are at bottom. Backs carry a congratulatory message over a large issuer logo. The unnumbered autographed cards are checklisted here in alphabetical order.

MT
Common Player: 1.00
(1) Israel Alcantera 1.00
(2) Richard Almanzar 1.00
(3) Marc Barcelo 1.00
(4) Tim Belk 1.00
(5) Jeremy Blevins 1.00
(6) James Bonnici 1.00
(7) Homer Bush 1.00
(8) Davey Coggin 1.00
(9) Bartolo Colon 10.00
(10) Lee Daniels 1.00
(11) Ryan Dempster 2.00
(12) Lino Diaz 1.00
(13) Tom Fordham 1.00
(14) Anton French 1.00
(15) Ben Grieve 2.00
(16) Mike Gulan 1.00
(17) Ryan Hancock 1.00
(18) Wes Helms 1.00
(19) Brett Herbison 1.00
(20) Chad Hermansen 1.00
(21) Damon Hollins 1.00
(22) Ryan Jaroncyk 1.00
(23) Geoff Jenkins 5.00
(24) Earl Johnson 1.00
(25) Andre King 1.00
(26) Paul Konerko 4.00
(27) Todd Landry 1.00
(28) Jeff Liefer 1.00
(29) Mendy Lopez 1.00
(30) Roberto Lopez 1.00
(31) Johnny Martinez 1.00
(32) Mike Maurer 1.00
(33) Brian Meadows 1.00
(34) Doug Mlicki 1.00
(35) Tony Mounce 1.00
(36) Sergio Nunez 1.00
(37) Russell Ortiz 2.00
(38) Carey Paige 1.00
(39) Jay Payton 3.00
(40) Ben Petrick 1.00
(41) Tommy Phelps 1.00
(42) Hugo Pivaral 1.00
(43) Angel Ramirez 1.00
(44) Gary Rath 1.00
(45) Mark Redman 1.00
(46) Adam Riggs 1.00
(47) Lonell Roberts 1.00
(48) Glendon Rusch 1.00
(49) Matt Ryan 1.00
(50) Donnie Sadler 1.50
(51) William Santamaria 1.00
(52) Todd Schmitt 1.00
(53) Richie Sexson 5.00
(54) Alvie Shepherd 1.00
(55) Steve Shoemaker 1.00
(56) Brian Sikorski 1.00
(57) Randall Simon 2.00
(58) Bobby Smith 1.00
(59) Matt Smith 1.00
(60) Jose Texidor 1.00
(61) Jason Thompson 1.00
(62) Mike Thurman 1.00
(63) Brett Tomko 1.00
(64) Hector Trinidad 1.00
(65) Andrew Vessel 1.00
(66) Jacob Viano 1.00
(67) Jarrod Washburn 5.00
(68) Travis Welch 1.00
(69) Casey Whitten 1.00
(70) Shad Williams 1.00
(71) Paul Wilson 1.50
(72) Preston Wilson 6.00
(73) Randy Winn 1.00
(74) Kevin Witt 1.00

Autographed Edition of 250

The 45 players in this random pack insert series include two dozen of the first round draft picks of 1997. Each player autographed 250 cards, which are serially numbered on back. Autographed cards are listed here in alphabetical order.

MT
Complete Set (45): 50.00
Common Player: 1.00
(1) Richard Almanzar 1.00
(2) Kris Benson 2.00
(3) Darin Blood 1.00
(4) Adrian Brown 1.00
(5) Dermal Brown 1.00
(6) Kevin Brown 1.00
(7) Eric Chavez 5.00
(8) D.T. Cromer 1.00
(9) Lorenzo de la Cruz 1.00
(10) Adam Eaton 1.00
(11) Nelson Figueroa 1.00
(12) Juan Gonzalez 1.00
(13) Chad Green 1.00
(14) Seth Greisinger 1.00
(15) Ben Grieve 2.00
(16) Matt Halloran 1.00
(17) Chad Hermansen 1.00
(18) Mark Johnson 1.00
(19) Andruw Jones 15.00
(20) Billy Koch 1.00
(21) Paul Konerko 5.00
(22) Mark Kotsay 3.00
(23) Joe Lawrence 1.00
(24) Braden Looper 1.00
(25) Gil Meche 2.00
(26) Eric Milton 1.00
(27) Abraham Nunez 2.00
(28) John Oliver 1.00
(29) Russell Ortiz 2.00
(30) John Patterson 1.00
(31) Carl Pavano 5.00
(32) Elvis Pena 1.00
(33) Danny Peoples 1.00
(34) Neifi Perez 1.00
(35) Sidney Ponson 2.00
(36) Aramis Ramirez 2.00
(37) Britt Reames 1.00
(38) Kerry Robinson 1.00
(39) Bubba Trammell 1.00
(40) Mike Villano 1.00
(41) Jake Westbrook 1.00
(42) Paul Wilder 1.00
(43) Enrique Wilson 3.00
(44) Kerry Wood 20.00
(45) A.J. Zapp 1.00

Cornerstone

A dozen of the biggest names in the minor leagues are featured in this insert set as future cornerstones of Major League teams. Backs have a close-up photo of that on front and typical player data, highlights and stats. Insertion rate was given as one per 49 packs.

MT
Complete Set (12): 20.00
Common Player: 1.50
1 Travis Lee 4.00
2 Adrian Beltre 5.00
3 Ben Grieve 1.50
4 Paul Konerko 4.00
5 Ricky Ledee 1.50
6 Brad Fullmer 1.50
7 Alex Gonzalez 1.50
8 Russell Branyan 1.50
9 Eric Milton 1.50
10 Jaret Wright 1.50
11 Derrek Lee 4.00
12 Kris Benson 1.50

Diamond Best II

Younger minor league stars are featured in this insert set carried over from the Best Prospects issue earlier in the year. Cards have action photos on a white background with a large team logo. Backs repeat the photo and logo in smaller size and provide player data and stats.

MT
Complete Set (10): 15.00
Common Player: 2.00
11 Dermal Brown 2.00
12 Aramis Ramirez 3.00
13 Ramon Hernandez 2.00
14 Eric Chavez 6.00
15 A.J. Zapp 2.00
16 A.J. Hinch 2.00
17 Juan Melo 2.00
18 Cole Liniak 2.00
19 David Ortiz 6.00
20 Russell Branyan 2.00

Premium Preview

These cards were inserted one per box as a box-topper to promote box purchases. Each card is numbered within an edition of 200. Fronts have color action photos against a ghost-image black-and-white photo. Backs repeat the front's background photo and have a small close-up of the color picture. Personal data, stats and highlights are given on back, as well.

MT
Complete Set (50): 160.00
Common Player: 2.50
1 Jaret Wright 2.50
2 Damian Jackson 2.50
3 Kerry Wood 17.50
4 Adrian Beltre 15.00
5 Sean Casey 10.00
6 Paul Konerko 10.00
7 Ben Grieve 5.00
8 Hideki Irabu 3.00
9 Rolando Arrojo 3.50
10 Robinson Checo 2.50
11 Donnie Sadler 3.00
12 Todd Helton 17.50
13 Jose Cruz Jr. 5.00
14 Ricky Ledee 2.50
15 Calvin Pickering 2.50
16 Alex Gonzalez 3.00
17 Alvie Shepherd 2.50
18 Michael Coleman 2.50
19 Derrek Lee 10.00
20 Brad Fullmer 3.00
21 Derrick Gibson 2.50
22 A.J. Hinch 3.50
23 Juan Melo 2.50
24 David Ortiz 15.00
25 Ramon Hernandez 2.50
26 Mike Stoner 2.50
27 George Lombard 2.50
28 Chad Hermansen 2.50
29 Mark Fischer 2.50
30 Trot Nixon 7.50
31 Kevin Nicholson 2.50
32 Kevin Millar 2.50
33 John Roskos 2.50
34 Aramis Ramirez 6.00
35 Randall Simon 2.50
36 Carl Pavano 6.50
37 Brian Rose 2.50
38 Enrique Wilson 3.50
39 Russell Branyan 3.00
40 Chan Perry 2.50
41 Juan Encarnacion 3.50
42 Grant Roberts 2.50
43 Marlon Anderson 3.50
44 Matt White 2.50
45 Jason Varitek 5.00
46 Cole Liniak 2.50
47 Roy Halladay 3.50
48 Magglio Ordonez 12.50
49 Richie Sexson 5.00
50 Travis Lee 7.50

1997 Best Full Count Autographs

While these authentically autographed cards were packaged with 1998 Team Best Signature Series at the announced rate of one per 19 hobby packs, they share a design and copyright date with the base cards of 1997 Best and were probably originally intended for release in those products. The Full Count autographed cards have a logo to that effect at top-right and on the baseball diamond design on back.

MT
Complete Set (25): 90.00
Common Player: 2.00
(1) Kris Benson 3.00
(2) Dermal Brown 2.00
(3) Eric Chavez (Both feet on ground.) 9.00
(4) Eric Chavez (One foot on ground.) 12.00
(5) Chad Green 2.00
(6) Ben Grieve 3.00
(7) Todd Helton 16.00
(8) Chad Hermansen 2.00
(9) Paul Konerko 5.00
(10) Mark Kotsay 3.00
(11) Braden Looper 2.00
(12) Gil Meche 3.00
(13) Juan Melo 2.00
(14) Eric Milton 2.00
(15) Abraham Nunez 3.00
(16) John Patterson 2.00
(17) Carl Pavano 5.00
(18) Sidney Ponson 3.00
(19) Aramis Ramirez 3.00
(20) Britt Reames 2.00
(21) Kerry Robinson 2.00
(22) Jake Westbrook 2.00
(23) Paul Wilder 2.00
(24) Kerry Wood 20.00
(25) A.J. Zapp 2.00

1997 Best Premium Autographs

A completely different selection of players and design was presented in the autographed cards inserted into Team Best retail packs. Fronts have action photos with a large team logo in the background. In the top-right corner "Best Premium" appears in gold-foil script. Backs have a Best Premium logo and are hand-numbered from within an edition of 250 of each player.

MT
Complete Set (49): 125.00
Common Player: 2.50
(1) Richard Almanzar 2.50
(2) Kris Benson 5.00
(3) Darin Blood 2.50
(4) Adrian Brown 2.50
(5) Dermal Brown 2.50
(6) Kevin Brown 2.50
(7) Eric Chavez 10.00
(8) D.T. Cromer 2.50
(9) Lorenzo de la Cruz 2.50
(10) Adam Eaton 2.50
(11) Nelson Figueroa 2.50
(12) Juan Gonzalez 2.50
(13) Chad Green 2.50
(14) Seth Greisinger 2.50
(15) Ben Grieve 3.00
(16) Matt Halloran 2.50
(17) Chad Hermansen 2.50
(18) Mark Johnson 2.50
(19) Billy Koch 2.50
(20) Paul Konerko 7.50
(21) Mark Kotsay 5.00
(22) Joe Lawrence 2.50
(23) Braden Looper 3.00
(24) Kevin McGlinchy 3.00
(25) Gil Meche 4.00
(26) Juan Melo 2.50
(27) Eric Milton 2.50
(28) John Nicholson 2.50
(29) Todd Noel 2.50
(30) Abraham Nunez 4.00
(31) Russell Ortiz 4.00
(32) Yudith Ozario 2.50
(33) John Patterson 3.00
(34) Carl Pavano 5.00
(35) Elvis Pena 2.50
(36) Danny Peoples 2.50
(37) Neifi Perez 2.50
(38) Sidney Ponson 6.00
(39) Aramis Ramirez 4.00
(40) Britt Reames 2.50
(41) Kerry Robinson 2.50
(42) Jeff Sexton 2.50
(43) Bubba Trammell 3.00
(44) Mike Villano 2.50
(45) Jake Westbrook 2.50
(46) Paul Wilder 2.50
(47) Enrique Wilson 4.00
(48) Kerry Wood 20.00
(49) A.J. Zapp 2.50

1997 Best Auto. Supers

Each 10-box case of 1998 Team Best Signature Series included one of 10 authentically autographed large-format (4" x 6") case-topper cards. Fronts have Best and team logos at top and a silver-foil Auto Best logo at bottom. Also on front is a serial number from within an edition of 500 each. Backs have a large notice of authenticity. Because the cards are dated 1997 and share the basic '97 Best format, they are listed here.

MT
Complete Set (12): 85.00
Common Player: 6.00
1 Kris Benson 6.00
2 Sean Casey (Akron) 15.00
3 Sean Casey (Buffalo) 15.00
4 Seth Greisinger 6.00
5 Ben Grieve 6.00
6 Chad Hermansen 6.00
7 Paul Konerko 9.00
8 Britt Reames 6.00
9 Jake Westbrook 6.00
10 Paul Wilder 6.00
11 Kerry Wood 20.00
12 A.J. Zapp 6.00

1997 Minor League Team Sets

The number of team sets increased a bit for 1997. Market leader Best again produced more than 100 teams' sets. A developing trend in 1997 was the growth of formats other than single cards, such as strips and sheets, and the issue of late-season or post-season update sets.

MT
198 Team Sets and Variations
1997 Team Aberdeen Pheasants (28) 4.00
1997 Team Abilene Prairie Dogs (30) 4.00
1997 Best Akron Aeros (31) 10.00
1997 GS Albuquerque Dukes (30) 4.00
1997 GS Albuquerque Dukes Update (5) 5.00
1997 GS Alexandria Aces (26) 4.00
1997 Team Amarillo Dillas (21) 4.00
1997 Best Appalachian League Propsects (30) 10.00
1997 Arizona Fall League (21) 12.50

1997 Best Arkansas Travelers (30) 8.00
1997 Best Asheville Tourists (30) 6.00
1997 Team Auburn Doubledays (30) 45.00
1997 Best Augusta Greenjackets (30) 4.00
1997 Team Bakersfield Blaze (30) 6.00
1997 Team Bakersfield Blaze W/Pepsi Ads (30) 8.00
1997 Team Batavia Clippers (32) 9.00
1997 Best Beloit Snappers (30) 6.00
1997 GS Bend Bandits (27) 4.00
1997 Team Billings Mustangs (36) 60.00
1997 Best Binghamton Mets (32) 5.00
1997 Magic Prints Binghampton Mets (5) 9.00
1997 Best Birmingham Barons (30) 5.00
1997 GS Boise Hawks (32) 7.00
1997 Best Bowie Baysox (29) 15.00
1997 Best Brevard County Manatees (31) 7.00
1997 Best Bristol Sox (30) 7.00
1997 Best Buffalo Bisons (30) 10.00
1997 Best Burlington Bees (31) 7.00
1997 GS Burlington Indians (31) 7.00
1997 Best Butte Copper Kings (30) 7.00
1997 Best Butte C.K. W/Sponsors' Ads (30) 7.00
1997 Best Calgary Cannons (30) 12.00
1997 Team Calgary Cannons (36) 65.00
1997 Best California League Prospects (31) 8.00
1997 Best California-Carolina League A-S (50) 10.00
1997 Best Capital City Bombers (30) 15.00
1997 Best Carolina Legue Prospects (31) 12.00
1997 Best Carolina Mudcats (29) 7.00
1997 GS Cedar Rapids Kernels (30) 9.00
1997 GS Charleston RiverDogs (29) 7.00
1997 Best Charlotte Knights (30) 8.00
1997 Best Chattanooga Lookouts (27) 7.00
1997 GS Chillicothe Paints (28) 4.00
1997 GS Clarksville Coyotes (25) 4.00
1997 Best Clearwater Phillies (30) 6.00
1997 GS Clinton Lumber Kings (30) 6.00
1997 Team Colorado Springs Sky Sox (29) 9.00
1997 Team Colorado Springs All-Time (32) 8.00
1997 Best Columbus Clippers (30) 8.00
1997 Police Columbus Clippers (29) 8.00
1997 Team Columbus Clippers 20th Anniv. (30) 12.00
1997 Best Danville Braves (30) 10.00
1997 Best Delmarva Shorebirds (30) 15.00
1997 GS Duluth-Superior Dukes (26) 4.00
1997 Team Dunedin Blue Jays (34) 7.50
1997 Team Dunedin Blue Jays Family Night (30) 12.00
1997 Team Durham Bulls (30) 15.00
1997 Team Durham Bulls "Bulls to Braves" (10) 12.00
1997 Best Eastern League Prospects (31) 7.00
1997 Team Edmonton Trappers (xx) 30.00
1997 Best El Paso Diablos (30) 5.00
1997 Best Erie Sea Wolves (30) 3.00
1997 Best Eugene Emeralds (30) 5.00
1997 GS Everett Aquasox (30) 6.00
1997 MA Fargo-Moorhead RedHawks (30) 4.00
1997 Best Florida State League Prospects (31) 15.00
1997 Best Florida State League Prospects (33) 18.00
1997 Best Frederick Keys (30) 5.00
1997 Best Ft. Myers Miracle (30) 5.00
1997 Best Ft. Wayne Wizards (29) 8.00
1997 GS Grand Forks Varmints (21) 4.00
1997 GS Grays Harbor Gulls (27) 4.00
1997 Best Great Falls Dodgers (30) 7.00
1997 Best Greensboro Bats (30) 50.00
1997 GS Greenville Braves (28) 10.00
1997 Best Hagerstown Suns (30) 11.00
1997 Best Harrisburg Senators (28) 7.00
1997 Best Harrisburg W/Ad Logos (28) 12.00
1997 Best Helena Brewers (30) 7.00
1997 Best Hickory Crawdads (30) 10.00
1997 Best Hickory Crawdads Update (30) 12.00
1997 GS High Desert Mavericks (30) 35.00
1997 GS High Desert Mavericks Update (18) 12.50
1997 Best Hudson Valley Renegades (30) 6.00
1997 Burger King Huntsville Stars (27) 7.00
1997 Team Idaho Falls Braves (32) 8.00
1997 Best Indianapolis Indians (29) 8.00
1997 Best Iowa Cubs (29) 8.00
1997 Best Jackson Generals (28) 6.00
1997 Smokey Bear Jackson Generals (26) 12.00
1997 Best Jacksonville Suns (27) 8.00
1997 Team Johnson City Cardinals (37) 6.00
1997 Team Kane County Cougars (32) 9.00
1997 Connie's Pizza Kane County Cougars (32) 15.00
1997 Best Kinston Indians (30) 4.00
1997 Best Kissimee Cobras (30) 9.00
1997 Best Knoxville Smokies (28) 6.00
1997 GS Lafayette Leopards (26) 5.00
1997 Horizon Outlet Lake Elsinore Storm (20) 16.00
1997 GS Lake Elsinore Storm (30) 6.00
1997 Best Lakeland Tigers (30) 10.00
1997 Best Lancaster JetHawks (30) 6.00
1997 Team Lansing Lugnuts (30) 12.00
1997 Best Las Vegas Stars (30) 7.00
1997 Best Lethbridge Black Diamonds (30) 6.00
1997 Best Louisville Redbirds (30) 11.00
1997 Best Lowell Spinners (30) 6.00
1997 Best Lynchburg Hillcats (30) 11.00
1997 Best Macon Braves (30) 12.00
1997 Team Madison Black Wolf (?) 17.50
1997 Best Michigan Battle Cats (30) 10.00
1997 Best Midland Angels (29) 6.00
1997 Team Midland Angels (23) 40.00
1997 Best Midwest League Prospects (30) 9.00
1997 Best Mobile Bay Bears (30) 8.00
1997 GS Modesto A's (30) 8.00
1997 Team Nashville Sounds (32) 12.00
1997 Best New Britain Rock Cats (30) 5.00
1997 Best New Haven Ravens (30) 6.00
1997 Best New Jersey Cardinals (30) 5.00
1997 Best N.J. Cardinals Top Prospects (6) 7.00
1997 Best Norfolk Tides (34) 7.00
1997 Northern League All-Stars (42) 8.00
1997 Best Norwich Navigators (32) 6.00
1997 Team Norwich Navigators (30) 18.00
1997 Team Ogden Raptors (32) 9.00
1997 Best Oklahoma City 89ers (25) 6.00
1997 Best Omaha Royals (26) 4.00
1997 Best Orlando Rays (30) 20.00
1997 Denny's Orlando Rays (25) 40.00
1997 Best Pawtucket Red Sox (30) 8.00
1997 Dunkin' Donuts Pawtucket Red Sox Foldout 24.00
1997 Team Pawtucket 25th Anniversary (31) 17.50
1997 Team Pawtucket 25th Anniversary Foldout 40.00
1997 Best Peoria Chiefs (30) 6.00
1997 Team Phoenix Firebirds (30) 10.00
1997 All-Time Firebirds Dream Team (30) 9.00
1997 Best Piedmont Boll Weevils (30) 9.00
1997 Best Pittsfield Mets (30) 6.00
1997 GS Portland Rockies (30) 5.00
1997 Best Portland Sea Dogs (30) 7.50
1997 Best Prince William Cannons (30) 6.00
1997 Best Princeton Devil Rays (30) 9.00
1997 Best Quad City River Bandits (30) 10.00
1997 GS Rancho Cucamonga Quakes (30) 7.00
1997 GS Rancho Cucamonga Quakes Update (7) 5.00
1997 Best Reading Phillies (27) 6.00
1997 GS Reno Chukars (27) 4.00
1997 Best Richmond Braves (30) 6.00
1997 Richmond Camera Richmond Braves (20) 45.00
1997 Team Rio Grande Valley White Wings (23) 4.00
1997 Best Rochester Red Wings (30) 4.00
1997 Best Rockford Cubbies (30) 40.00
1997 Team Salem Avalanche (38) 10.00
1997 Team Salem Avalanche Update (10) 5.00
1997 Team Salem-Keizer Volcanoes (42) 6.00
1997 Best Salt Lake City Buzz (29) 6.00
1997 Best San Antonio Missions (30) 7.00
1997 Best San Bernardino Stampede (30) 6.00
1997 Best San Jose Giants (30) 6.00
1997 Best Sarasota Red Sox (30) 20.00
1997 Best Scranton Red Barons (30) 7.00
1997 Best Shreveport Captains (28) 7.00
1997 Best Shreveport W/WK SportsCare Ads (29) 7.00
1997 GS Sioux City Explorers (27) 4.00
1997 GS Sioux Falls Canaries (28) 4.00
1997 Best So. Atlantic League Prospects (31) 12.50
1997 Best South Bend Silver Hawks (30) 5.00
1997 Best Southern League Prospects (32) 11.00
1997 Best Southern Oregon Timberjacks (29) 9.00
1997 GS Spokane Indians (31) 7.00
1997 Best St. Catherines Stompers (30) 9.00
1997 Best St. Lucie Mets (30) 9.00
1997 Team St. Paul Saints (32) 65.00
1997 Best St. Petersburg Devil Rays (30) 4.00
1997 Best St. Pete Devil Rays update (30) 12.00
1997 Best Stockton Ports (30) 6.00
1997 Best Syracuse Chiefs (30) 9.00
1997 Best Tacoma Rainiers (30) 10.00
1997 Best Tampa Yankees (33) 5.00
1997 Best Texas League Prospects (31) 10.00
1997 Best Toledo Mud Hens (36) 7.00
1997 Best Trenton Thunder (30) 6.00
1997 Best Tucson Toros (29) 7.50
1997 Jones Photo Tucson Toros (5) 80.00
1997 Team Tulsa Drillers (30) 8.00
1997 GS Tyler Wildcatters (24) 4.00
1997 Best Vancouver Canadians (30) 8.00
1997 Best Vermont Expos (30) 6.00
1997 Best Vero Beach Dodgers (30) 17.50
1997 GS Visalia Oaks (30) 16.00
1997 Team Watertown Indians (36) 9.00
1997 Best West Michigan Whitecaps (30) 7.00
1997 Best Wichita Wranglers (30) 6.00
1997 Best Williamsport Cubs (29) 6.00
1997 Best Wilmington Blue Rocks (30) 9.00
1997 Best Wisconsin Timber Rattlers (29) 6.00
1997 GS Yakima Bears (36) 7.00

1998 Best Auto.

The extent of the checklist for this issue, and the manner of its distribution are unknown. Like similar Best autograph cards from 1996-97, they feature game-action photos vignetted in white on front. A minor league team logo is at top-left, the Best logo is at bottom-right. Backs have a photo of a Best-logoed glove with a statement of authenticity. Best and Minor League licensing logos are at bottom. The cards carry a 1998 copyright date.

		MT
Common Player:		2.00
(1)	Kris Benson	3.00
(3)	Dermal Brown	2.00
(5)	Lorenzo de la Cruz	2.00
(6)	Adam Eaton	2.00
(7)	Chad Green	2.00
(9)	Chad Hermansen	2.00
(10)	Mark Johnson	2.00
(11)	Billy Koch	3.00
(13)	Joe Lawrence	2.00
(14)	Braden Looper	3.00
(15)	Gil Meche	4.50
(17)	Abraham Nunez	4.50
(18)	Russ Ortiz	4.50
(19)	Carl Pavano	7.00
(21)	Danny Peoples	3.00
(23)	Britt Reames	2.00
(25)	Brian Rose	2.00
(27)	Bubba Trammell	2.00
(29)	Jake Westbrook	2.00
(31)	Enrique Wilson	4.50
(33)	A.J. Zapp	2.00

1998 Team Best Player of the Year

The first product under the firm's new Team Best logo was this foil-pack series of 50 minor leaguers, many of whom began making their names in the big leagues in 1998. Fronts feature color action photos with tan borders. Manufacturer and minor league team logos appear in the upper corners. On back are a postage-stamp size repeat of the head portion of the player photo at upper-left. To the right are personal data. At lower-left are 1997 season stats, with career highlights to the right. Cards were sold in six-card packs.

		MT
Complete Set (50):		4.00
Common Player:		.05
Wax Pack (6):		1.50
Wax Box (18):		20.00
1	Ryan Anderson	.25
2	Lorenzo Barcelo	.05
3	Hiram Bocachica	.05
4	David Borkowski	.05
5	Russ Branyan	.10
6	Dermal Brown	.05
7	Brent Butler	.05
8	Enrique Calero	.05
9	Bruce Chen	.05
10	Ryan Christenson	.05
11	Pat Cline	.05
12	Scott Elarton	.05
13	Juan Encarnacion	.25
14	Mark Fischer	.05
15	Troy Glaus	2.00
16	Alex Hernandez	.05
17	Norm Hutchins	.05
18	Geoff Jenkins	.25
19	Adam Kennedy	.10
20	Corey Koskie	.25
21	Mark Kotsay	.15
22	Ricky Ledee	.05
23	Carlos Lee	.15
24	Corey Lee	.05
25	Mike Lowell	.50
26	T.R. Marcinczyk	.05
27	Willie Martinez	.05
28	Darnell McDonald	.05
29	Jackson Melian	.05
30	Chad Meyers	.05
31	Ryan Minor	.05
32	Kenderick Moore	.05
33	Julio Moreno	.05
34	Rod Myers	.05
35	Abraham Nunez	.25
36	Vladimir Nunez	.05
37	Ramon Ortiz	.05
38	Chan Perry	.05
39	Ben Petrick	.05
40	Angel Ramirez	.05
41	Grant Roberts	.05
42	Alex Sanchez	.05
43	Jared Sandberg	.05
44	Scott Schoeneweis	.05
45	Steve Shoemaker	.05
46	Matt White	.05
47	Paul Wilder	.05
48	Preston Wilson	.50
49	Kevin Witt	.05
50	Jay Yennaco	.05

Autographs

These autographed cards of top prospects were a 1:19 insert in Team Best Player of the Year hobby packs. Fronts have action photos with a ghost-image background. The player name is in a baseball bat at bottom. Backs have a statement of authenticity.

		MT
Complete Set (21):		50.00
Common Player:		3.00
(1)	Kris Benson	4.00
(2)	Dermal Brown	3.00
(3)	Eric Chavez	5.00
(4)	Adam Eaton	3.00
(5)	Chad Green	3.00
(6)	Seth Greisinger	3.00
(7)	Ben Grieve	4.00
(8)	Chad Hermansen	4.50
(9)	Billy Koch	3.00
(10)	Braden Looper	3.00
(11)	Gil Meche	4.50
(12)	Eric Milton	3.00
(13)	John Patterson	3.00
(14)	Carl Pavano	7.00
(15)	Danny Peoples	3.00
(16)	Sidney Ponson	4.50
(17)	Brian Rose	3.00
(18)	Jake Westbrook	3.00
(19)	Paul Wilder	3.00
(20)	Kerry Wood	25.00
(21)	A.J. Zapp	3.00

Contenders

Candidates for minor league player of the year are featured in this scarce insert set. Six of the players are pictured on horizontal-format cards which have three photos on front showing the player in different uniforms on his road to the majors. Four of the players also have a vertical-format card with a single photo on front. Each card is serially numbered on the back from within an edition of 400 each. The background on back is a sepia version of the front photo and there is a PoY stamp logo at center. Stated odds of finding a Contender card are one per 90 packs.

		MT
Complete Set (10):		35.00
Common Player:		3.00
1	Derrick Gibson	3.00
2	Ben Grieve	3.00
3	Ben Grieve (Vertical)	3.00
4	Todd Helton	12.50
5	Todd Helton (Vertical)	12.50
6	Mark Kotsay	3.00
7	Mark Kotsay (Vertical)	3.00
8	Carl Pavano	7.50
9	Brian Rose	3.00
10	Brian Rose (Vertical)	3.00

Young Guns

This is a retail-only insert, with each card individually serial numbered on back to a limit of 100. Cards share the photos used on the hobby-only Contenders insert set (edition of 400), except the Young Guns cards have a white background instead of the mottled brown of the Contenders. Insert ratio was reported at one per 90 packs on average.

		MT
Complete Set (10):		50.00
Common Player:		4.00
1	Derrick Gibson	4.00
2	Ben Grieve	5.00
3	Ben Grieve (Vertical)	5.00
4	Todd Helton	20.00
5	Todd Helton (Vertical)	20.00
6	Mark Kotsay	4.00
7	Mark Kotsay (Vertical)	4.00
8	Carl Pavano	7.50
9	Brian Rose	4.00
10	Brian Rose (Vertical)	4.00

1998 Team Best Diamond Best

Red, white and blue typography and a team logo in the background mark this insert series. Backs have a smaller version of the front photo, biographical data, 1997 stats and appropriate logos. Odds of pulling a Diamond Best card are stated as one per 19 packs.

		MT
Complete Set (20):		12.00
Common Player:		1.00
1	Darnell McDonald	1.00
2	Adrian Beltre	2.00
3	Derrick Gibson	1.00
4	Mark Kotsay	1.00
5	Braden Looper	1.00
6	Carl Pavano	1.50
7	Brian Rose	1.00
8	Jared Sandberg	1.00
9	Vernon Wells	2.00
10	Sean Casey	2.50
11	Rick Ankiel	1.00
12	Michael Barrett	1.00
13	Matt Clement	1.50
14	J.D. Drew	2.50
15	Bobby Estalella	1.00
16	Troy Glaus	3.00
17	Alex Gonzalez	1.00
18	George Lombard	1.00
19	Mike Lowell	1.50
20	Dernell Stenson	1.00

Best Autographs

Autographs of eight top prospects are featured on Diamond Best style inserts in this chase card set. Actual odds of finding one of the autographed cards is one in 180 packs. Konerko's and Patterson's cards were never released. Each card is numbered within an edition of 250.

		MT
Complete Set (8):		45.00
Common Player:		2.00
1	Kris Benson	4.00
2	Dermal Brown	2.00
3	Eric Chavez	4.00
4	Todd Helton	20.00
5	Paul Konerko (Never released.)	.00
6	John Patterson (Never released.)	.00
7	Braden Looper	2.00
8	Juan Melo	2.00
9	Kerry Wood	20.00
10	A.J. Zapp	2.00

1998 Team Best Paul Konerko

Designated as Player of the Year, former Dodgers farmhand Paul Konerko was honored with a six-card insert issue. Found at the average rate of just one per two boxes (36 packs), the Konerko cards trace his rise through the minor leagues. Fronts have borderless photos and team logos of his minor league stops. Backs detail each season's stats and highlights on a background of a sepia version of the front photo. Autographed versions of each card, with a statement of authenticity on the back, we released as pack inserts and in a mail-in redemption offer.

	MT
Complete Set (6):	12.00
Common Card:	2.00
Autographed:	4.00

1 Paul Konerko (Three-photo horizontal.) 2.00
2 Paul Konerko (San Bernardino Stampede) 2.00
3 Paul Konerko (San Antonio Missions) 2.00
4 Paul Konerko (Albuquerque Dukes) 2.00
5 Paul Konerko (Yakima Bears) 2.00
6 Paul Konerko (PoY Stamp) 2.00

1998 Team Best Possibilities

Two players each are featured in this insert card series. Both fronts and backs have action player photos set against a swirling blue background. Team and licensor logos are part of the design as well. Odds to pull this insert were stated as one per 19 packs.

MT
Complete Set (5): 5.00
Common Player: .75
1 Kris Benson, Mark Kotsay 1.00
2 Braden Looper, Sean Casey 1.00
3 Brian Rose, Dermal Brown .75
4 Matt White, Ben Grieve .75
5 Kerry Wood, Todd Helton 4.00

1998 Team Best Signature Series

In many ways Team Best's Signature Series minor league issue is a continuation of the company's Player of the Year series issued earlier in the year. For example, the base cards in the Signature Series retain the design and continue the card numbering of the earlier series. The Signature Series debuted in September, in six-card foil packs. Half a dozen insert sets were included among the base cards.

MT
Complete Set (50): 5.00
Common Player: .05
Wax Pack (6): 2.25
Wax Box (18): 30.00
51 Matt Anderson .10
52 Rich Ankiel .05
53 Tony Armas .10
54 John Barnes .05
55 Robbie Bell .05
56 Kris Benson .20
57 Lance Berkman .50
58 Russell Branyan .10
59 Brent Butler .05
60 Troy Cameron .05
61 Eric Chavez .50
62 Bruce Chen .05
63 Matt Clement .50
64 Ben Davis .05
65 J.D. Drew 1.00
66 Tim Drew .05
67 Derrick Gibson .05
68 Troy Glaus 2.00
69 Chad Hermansen .05
70 Ramon Hernandez .05
71 Gabe Kapler .25
72 Mike Kinkade .05
73 Scott Krause .05
74 Mike Lowell .50
75 Willie Martinez .05
76 Donzell McDonald .05
77 Gil Meche .15
78 Juan Melo .05
79 Wade Miller .10
80 Ryan Minor .05
81 Abraham Nunez .10
82 Pablo Ozuna .05
83 John Patterson .10
84 Josh Paul .05
85 Ben Petrick .05
86 Calvin Pickering .05
87 Placido Polanco .10
88 Aramis Ramirez .25
89 Julio Ramirez .05
90 Luis Rivas .05
91 Luis Rivera .05
92 Ruben Rivera .05
93 Grant Roberts .05
94 Jimmy Rollins .50
95 Bobby Seay .05
96 Jason Standridge .05
97 Dernell Stenson .05
98 Vernon Wells .50
99 Matt White .10
100 Ed Yarnall .05
--- Special Offer Card, Kerry Wood Autograph .05
--- Special Offer Card, Team Best Promos .05
--- Special Offer Card - Sig. Series Promos .05

Autographs

This series of authentically autographed insert cards was inserted at the rate of about five per box of TB Signature Series. Cards feature color photos on a beige pinstriped background. Backs repeat the background and have a large baseball with an authenticity notice overprinted. The unnumbered cards are listed here alphabetically. Announced autographed cards of Barrett, Colon, Teut and Westbrook were received too late to be inserted.

MT
Complete Set (53): 50.00
Common Player: 1.00
(1) John Bale 1.00
(2) Kevin Barker 1.00
(3) Michael Barrett Not Issued
(4) Todd Belitz 1.00
(5) Aaron Bond 1.00
(6) A.J. Burnett 2.00
(7) Brent Butler 1.00
(8) Buddy Carlyle 1.00
(9) Ramon Castro 1.00
(10) Frank Catalanotto 2.00
(11) Giuseppe Chiaramonte 1.00
(12) Bartolo Colon Not Issued
(13) Alex Cora 1.00
(14) Francisco Cordero 1.00
(15) David Cortes 1.00
(16) Dean Crow 1.00
(17) Doug Davis 1.00
(18) Glenn Davis 1.00
(19) Travis Dawkins 3.00
(20) Matt DeWitt 1.00
(21) Octavio Dotel 1.00
(22) Mike Duvall 1.00
(23) Troy Glaus 10.00
(24) Geoff Goetz 1.00
(25) Jason Grilli 1.00
(26) Al Hawkins 1.00
(27) Bryan Hebson 1.00
(28) Alex Hernandez 1.00
(29) Doug Johnston 1.00
(30) Juan LeBron 1.00
(31) John Leroy 1.00
(32) Randi Mallard 1.00
(33) Sam Marsonek 1.00
(34) Ramon Martinez 1.00
(35) Ruben Mateo 2.00
(36) Joe Mays 2.00
(37) David Melendez 1.00
(38) Justin Miller 1.00
(39) Ryan Minor 1.00
(40) Warren Morris 2.00
(41) Pablo Ozuna 1.00
(42) Brian Passini 1.00
(43) Santiago Perez 1.00
(44) Marc Pisciotta 1.00
(45) Rob Ramsey 1.00
(46) Grant Roberts 1.00
(47) John Roskos 1.00
(48) Luis de los Santos 1.00
(49) Brian Simmons 1.00
(50) Reggie Taylor 2.00
(51) Nathan Teut Not Issued
(52) Andy Thompson 1.00
(53) Chris Tynan 1.00
(54) Jose Vidro 4.00
(55) Jayson Werth 1.00
(56) Jake Westbrook Not Issued .00
(57) Ed Yarnall 1.00

Best Bets

This retail-exclusive insert set features the cream of the 1998 minor league crop. Fronts have player action photos separated from a white background by a colorful aura. A team logo appears at bottom. Backs repeat a close-up of the photo and have 1997 stats, biographical data and a few words about the player. The Best Bet cards use the same photos found on the hobby-only Cornerstone inserts. Best Bets were inserted at an advertised rate of one per 90 packs.

MT
Complete Set (12): 40.00
Common Player: 2.00
(1) Matt Anderson 2.00
(2) Lance Berkman 4.00
(3) Eric Chavez 6.00
(4) Bruce Chen 2.00
(5) Matt Clement 6.00
(6) J.D. Drew 10.00
(7) Troy Glaus 12.50
(8) George Lombard 2.00
(9) Ryan Minor 2.00
(10) Dernell Stenson 2.00
(11) Jayson Werth 2.00
(12) Ed Yarnall 2.00

Cornerstone

This hobby-exclusive insert set features the cream of the 1998 minor league top and many of tomorrow's big league stars. Fronts have player action photos separated from a checkered background by a colored aura. A team logo also appears. Backs repeat the photo in a close-up format and have 1997 stats, biographical data and a few words about the player. The Best Bet cards use the same photos as those found on the Cornerstone insert issue. Insertion rate was reported as one per 90 packs. The cards are listed here in alphabetical order.

MT
Complete Set (12): 40.00
Common Player: 2.00
(1) Matt Anderson 2.00
(2) Lance Berkman 4.00
(3) Eric Chavez 6.00
(4) Bruce Chen 2.00
(5) Matt Clement 6.00
(6) J.D. Drew 10.00
(7) Troy Glaus 12.50
(8) George Lombard 2.00
(9) Ryan Minor 2.00
(10) Dernell Stenson 2.00
(11) Jayson Werth 2.00
(12) Ed Yarnall 2.00

Diamond Best

Another insert series which was continued from Team Best's Player of the Year series is Diamond Best. Cards in the Signature Series are numbered contiguously from the earlier series and have the same basic design of an action photo on a white background with a large minor league team logo. Backs have a smaller version of the front photo, a bit of personal data and a few words about the player. Diamond Best inserts are found on average of about one per 19 packs (just under one per box).

MT
Complete Set (10): 15.00
Common Player: 1.50
11 Rich Ankiel 1.00
12 Michael Barrett 1.00
13 Matt Clement 1.50
14 J.D. Drew 5.00
15 Bobby Estalella 1.00
16 Troy Glaus 7.50
17 Alex Gonzalez 1.00
18 George Lombard 1.00
19 Mike Lowell 2.00
20 Dernell Stenson 1.00

#1 Pick

This special series of chase cards was issued as a box-topper, one per 18-pack box. Card fronts feature both portrait and action photos. In a baseball at lower-right is a "#1 PICK" gold hologram. Backs have individual silver-foil serial numbers from within an edition of 900 each.

MT
Complete Set (42): 75.00
Common Player: 1.00
1 Aaron Akin 1.00
2 Matt Anderson 1.50
3 Ryan Anderson 2.00
4 Shane Arthurs 1.00
5 Michael Barrett 1.50
6 Kris Benson 2.00
7 Lance Berkman 3.00
8 Rocky Biddle 1.00
9 Ryan Bradley 1.00
10 Dermal Brown 1.00
11 Troy Cameron 1.00
12 Brett Caradonna 1.00
13 Eric Chavez 3.00
14 Mike Cuddyer 1.00
15 John Curtice 1.00
16 Glenn Davis 1.00
17 J.J. Davis 1.00
18 Jason Dellaero 1.00
19 J.D. Drew 10.00
20 Tim Drew 1.00
21 Brian DuBose 1.00
22 Mark Fischer 1.00
23 Troy Glaus 12.00
24 Geoff Goetz 1.00
25 Jason Grilli 1.00
26 Nathan Haynes 1.00
27 Bryan Hebson 1.00
28 Geoff Jenkins 2.00
29 Adam Kennedy 2.00
30 Billy Koch 1.00
31 Matt LeCroy 1.00
32 Mark Mangum 1.00
33 Darnell McDonald 1.00
34 Kevin Nicholson 1.00
35 John Patterson 1.00
36 Danny Peoples 1.00
37 Dan Reichert 1.00
38 Jason Romano 1.00
39 Jason Standridge 1.00
40 Vernon Wells 4.00
41 Jayson Werth 1.00
42 Matt White 1.00

1998 Upper Deck SP Prospects

The best of the minor league class of 1997 are featured in this issue which marks Upper Deck's return to the minor league card market after a two-year layoff. All players, even the relatively few who have had major league experience, are featured in their minor league uniforms in the base set of 126 cards. There are three 30-card insert sets: Destination the Show (1:90 packs), Signature Cards (1:16) and Small Town Heroes (1:5). At the high end of the chase spectrum, a President's Edition parallel set of the regular, DS and STH cards was produced in an edition of just 10 cards each. Retail price at issue was $4.39 for an eight-card pack. Fronts are printed on a foiled background with a textured silver-foil border; team and SP logos are in the bottom corners. Backs are conventionally printed with another color photo and up to two years of stats. The first 10 cards in the set are a series of Top 10 prospects which have checklist backs. Production was reported to be 1,000 hobby-only cases.

MT
Complete Set (126): 7.50
Common Player: .05
Wax Box: 25.00
1 Travis Lee (Top 10 Prospects) .50
2 Paul Konerko (Top 10 Prospects) .50
3 Ben Grieve (Top 10 Prospects) .25
4 Kerry Wood (Top 10 Prospects) 1.00
5 Miguel Tejada (Top 10 Prospects) .50
6 Juan Encarnacion (Top 10 Prospects) .10
7 Jackson Melian (Top 10 Prospects) .05
8 Chad Hermansen (Top 10 Prospects) .05
9 Aramis Ramirez (Top 10 Prospects) .10
10 Russell Branyan (Top 10 Prospects) .05
11 Norm Hutchins .05
12 Jarrod Washburn .15
13 Larry Barnes .05
14 Scott Schoeneweis .05
15 Travis Lee 1.00
16 Mike Stoner .05
17 Nick Bierbrodt .05
18 Vladimir Nunez .05
19 Wes Helms .05
20 Jason Marquis .15
21 George Lombard .05
22 Bruce Chen .05
23 Rob Bell .05
24 Adam Johnson .05
25 Ryan Minor .05
26 Sidney Ponson .10
27 Calvin Pickering .05
28 Donnie Sadler .15
29 Cole Liniak .05
30 Carl Pavano .25
31 Kerry Wood 2.00
32 Pat Cline .05
33 Jason Maxwell .05
34 Jason Dellaero .05
35 Mike Caruso .05
36 Jeff Liefer .05
37 Brian Simmons .05
38 Carlos Lee .25
39 Jeff Inglin .05
40 Darron Ingram .05
41 Justin Towle .05
42 Pat Watkins .05
43 Richie Sexson .25
44 Danny Peoples .05
45 Russell Branyan .10
46 Scott Morgan .05
47 Mike Glavine .05
48 Willie Martinez .05
49 Jake Westbrook .05
50 Derrick Gibson .05
51 Ben Petrick .05
52 Juan Encarnacion .45
53 Seth Greisinger .05
54 Robert Fick .05
55 Dave Borkowski .05
56 Jesse Ibarra .05
57 Nate Rolison .05
58 Jaime Jones .05
59 Aaron Akin .05
60 Alex Gonzalez .05
61 Richard Hidalgo .25
62 Scott Elarton .05
63 Daryle Ward .05
64 Jeremy Giambi .25
65 Dermal Brown .05
66 Enrique Calero .05
67 Glenn Davis .05
68 Adrian Beltre .75
69 Alex Cora .05
70 Paul Konerko .50
71 Mike Kincade .05
72 Danny Klassen .05
73 Chad Green .05
74 Kevin Barker .05
75 David Ortiz 1.00
76 Jacque Jones .50
77 Luis Rivas .05
78 Hiram Bocachica .05
79 Javier Vazquez .50
80 Brad Fullmer .10
81 Preston Wilson .60
82 Octavio Dotel .05
83 Fletcher Bates .05
84 Grant Roberts .05
85 Jackson Melian .05
86 Katsuhiro Maeda .05
87 Ricky Ledee .05
88 Eric Milton .15
89 Eric Chavez .50
90 Ben Grieve .25
91 Miguel Tejada .50
92 A.J. Hinch .05
93 Ramon Hernandez .10
94 Chris Enochs .05
95 Marlon Anderson .30
96 Reggie Taylor .05
97 Steve Carver .05
98 Ron Wright .05
99 Kris Benson .15
100 Chad Hermansen .05
101 Aramis Ramirez .25
102 Adam Kennedy .20
103 Braden Looper .05
104 Cliff Politte .05
105 Brent Butler .05
106 Juan Melo .05
107 Ben Davis .05
108 Kevin Nicholson .05
109 Gary Matthews Jr. .05
110 Matt Clement .50
111 Jason Brester .05
112 Joe Fontenot .05
113 Darin Blood .05
114 Greg Wooten .05
115 Jeff Farnsworth .05
116 Robert Luce .05
117 Rolando Arrojo .20
118 Doug Johnson .05
119 James Manias .05
120 Alex Sanchez .05
121 Warren Morris .05
122 Ruben Mateo .25
123 Corey Lee .05
124 Roy Halladay .75
125 Kevin Witt .05
126 Tom Evans .05

Autographs

Authentically autographed cards of some of the minor leagues' top prospects are featured in this insert set found on average of once per 16 packs. The autograph cards have a player photo vignetted in a white panel at center, with his signature below. Backs have a printed certificate of authenticity. Cards of Wes Helms, Jackson Melian and David Ortiz, originally announced on UD's checklist, were never issued.

MT
Complete Set (26): 50.00
Common Player: 2.00
AB Adrian Beltre 15.00
KB Kris Benson 3.00
RB Russell Branyan 2.00
BB Brent Butler 2.00
EC Eric Chavez 6.00
RF Robert Fick 2.00
DG Derrick Gibson 2.00
BG Ben Grieve 2.00
CH Chad Hermansen 2.00
RH Ramon Hernandez 2.00
JJ Jacque Jones 6.00
PK Paul Konerko 6.00
RL Ricky Ledee 2.00
CL Corey Lee 2.00
TL Travis Lee 6.00
KM Katsuhiro Maeda 2.00
GM Gary Matthews Jr. 2.00
JMO Juan Melo 2.00
SM Scott Morgan 2.00
WM Warren Morris 2.00
DP Danny Peoples 2.00
GR Grant Roberts 2.00
MT Miguel Tejada 25.00
JT Justin Towle 2.00
DW Daryle Ward 2.00
KW Kerry Wood 30.00

Destination The Show

Thirty top minor leaguers who are likely to begin major leagues careers in 1998 are featured in this insert set. The chase cards are seeded on average of one per 90 packs.

MT
Complete Set (30): 75.00
Common Player: 3.00
DS1 Travis Lee 6.00
DS2 Eric Chavez 4.50
DS3 Ramon Hernandez 3.00
DS4 Daryle Ward 3.00
DS5 Jackson Melian 3.00
DS6 Ben Grieve 3.50
DS7 Brent Butler 3.00
DS8 Rolando Arrojo 4.50
DS9 Ryan Minor 3.00
DS10 Adrian Beltre 7.50
DS11 Sidney Ponson 4.50
DS12 Gary Matthews Jr. 3.00
DS13 Ron Wright 3.00
DS14 Warren Morris 3.00
DS15 Russell Branyan 3.00
DS16 Paul Konerko 6.00
DS17 Mike Caruso 3.00
DS18 Jacque Jones 6.00
DS19 Preston Wilson 4.50
DS20 Chad Hermansen 3.00
DS21 Aramis Ramirez 3.00
DS22 Kerry Wood 10.00
DS23 Corey Lee 3.00
DS24 Carl Pavano 3.00
DS25 Kris Benson 3.00
DS26 Derrick Gibson 3.00
DS27 Mike Stoner 3.00
DS28 Juan Melo 3.00
DS29 Mike Kinkade 3.00
DS30 Alex Gonzalez 3.00

Small Town Heroes

The small towns across America which are the roots of many pro ballplayers are featured in this chase set from Upper Deck's 1998 SP Top Prospects issue. The series focuses for the most part on players who are early in their minor league careers. These cards are inserted at an average rate of one per five packs.

MT
Complete Set (30): 35.00
Common Player: 1.00
H1 Travis Lee 4.00
H2 Eric Chavez 2.50
H3 Mike Caruso 1.00
H4 Adrian Beltre 4.00
H5 Jackson Melian 1.00
H6 Adam Johnson 1.00
H7 Carlos Lee 2.00
H8 Kris Benson 1.50
H9 Jacque Jones 3.00
H10 Russell Branyan 1.00
H11 John Patterson 1.00
H12 Ryan Minor 1.00
H13 Dermal Brown 1.00
H14 Mike Stoner 1.00
H15 Derrick Gibson 1.00
H16 Ben Davis 1.00
H17 Kevin Witt 1.00
H18 Justin Towle 1.00
H19 Doug Johnson 1.00
H20 Chad Hermansen 1.00
H21 Sidney Ponson 2.00
H22 Marlon Anderson 1.50
H23 Kerry Wood 5.00
H24 Alex Gonzalez 1.00
H25 Carl Pavano 2.50
H26 A.J. Hinch 1.00
H27 Juan Melo 1.00
H28 Dave Borkowski 1.00
H29 Jake Westbrook 1.00
H30 Daryle Ward 1.00

1998 Minor League Team Sets

Besides Best (under the Multi-Ad Sports logo), which maintained the lion's share of the team-set market, several other companies - notably Grandstand (GS), Choice Marketing, Blueline Communications (BL) and Warning Track Cards (WTC) - also produced sets for more than one team.

MT

217 Team Sets and Variations 8.00
1998 MA AA All-Star Game (60) 9.00
1998 MA AA All-Star Berks Packing (56) 12.00
1998 Team Aberdeen Pheasants (25) 4.00
1998 WTC Adirondack Lumberjacks (25) 4.00
1998 MA Akron Aeros (30) 7.00
1998 WTC Albany-Colonie Diamond Dogs (25) 4.00
1998 GS Albuquerque Dukes (30) 7.00
1998 WTC Allentown (25) 4.00
1998 BL Appalachian League Top Prospects (31) 11.00
1998 Arizona Fall League (25) 15.00
1998 Arizona Fall League - Gold (25) 35.00
1998 MA Arkansas Travelers (30) 8.00
1998 Team Arkansas Travelers Highlights (10) 25.00
1998 Team Arkansas Travelers Update (1) 12.00
1998 MA Asheville Tourists (30) 6.00
1998 Team Atlantic City Surf (31) 4.00
1998 Team Auburn Doubledays (34) 50.00
1998 MA Augusta Greenjackets (30) 6.00
1998 Team Batavia Muckdogs (35) 25.00
1998 MA Beloit Snappers (30) 11.00
1998 Team Billings Mustangs (38) 95.00
1998 BL Binghamton Mets (30) 8.00
1998 TM Binghamton Mets "Jumbo" (12) 20.00
1998 GS Birmingham Barons (30) 7.00
1998 BL Bluefield Orioles (32) 6.00
1998 GS Boise Hawks (34) 6.00
1998 MA Bowie Baysox (30) 10.00
1998 Team Bowie Nationals (31) 7.00
1998 MA Bridgeport Bluefish (30) 4.00
1998 BL Bristol White Sox (30) 7.00
1998 GS Buffalo Bisons (30) 8.00
1998 MA Burlington Bees (30) 9.00
1998 GS Butte Copper Kings (34) 7.00
1998 MA Cape Fear Crocs (30) 7.00
1998 MA Capital City Dombors (30) 20.00
1998 MA C.C. Bombers W/Fox 57 Ads (30) 22.00
1998 Choice Carolina League All-Stars (42) 12.00
1998 BL Carolina League Top Prospects (33) 10.00
1998 MA Carolina Mudcats (30) 6.00
1998 Team Cedar Rapids Kernels (31) 6.00
1998 MA Charleston Alley Cats (31) 6.00
1998 GS Charleston RiverDogs (30) 7.00
1998 BL Charlotte Knights (30) 7.00
1998 MA Charlotte Rangers (30) 15.00
1998 GS Chattanooga Lookouts (30) 7.00
1998 GS Chattanooga W/Slush Puppy Ads (31) 30.00
1998 MA Clearwater Phillies (30) 7.00
1998 MA Clearwater Phillies Update (30) 15.00
1998 GS Clinton LumberKings (30) 6.00
1998 Team Colorado Springs Sky Sox (31) 7.00
1998 MA Columbus Clippers (30) 8.00
1998 Police Columbus Clippers (25) 8.00
1998 MA Columbus RedStixx (30) 12.00
1998 BL Danville Braves (31) 24.00
1998 BL Danville 97s (31) 9.00
1998 GS Daytona Cubs (21) 8.00
1998 Team Delaware Stars (28) 12.00
1998 Team Delmarva Rockfish (32) 7.00
1998 MA Delmarva Shorebirds (30) 10.00
1998 GS Duluth-Superior Dukes (27) 5.00
1998 Team Dunedin Blue Jays (33) 8.00
1998 Team Dunedin Blue Jays stickers (24) 12.00
1998 Team Durham Bulls (30) 8.00
1998 MA Eastern League Top Prospects (30) 12.00
1998 Edmonton Trappers (XX) 45.00
1998 GS El Paso Diablos (29) 6.00
1998 MA Erie Seawolves (30) 6.00
1998 GS Eugene Emeralds (32) 12.50
1998 GS Everett Aquasox (30) 6.00
1998 MA Fargo-Moorhead Red Hawks (30) 4.00
1998 MA Frederick Keys (30) 7.00
1998 Team Frederick Regiment (32) 7.00
1998 GS Fresno Grizzlies (30) 9.00
1998 Team Ft. Myers Miracle (32) 7.00
1998 BL Ft. Wayne Wizards (30) 7.00
1998 GS Grays Harbor Gulls (30) 4.00
1998 GS Great Falls Dodgers (31) 8.00
1998 MA Greensboro Bats (30) 7.00
1998 GS Greenville Braves (28) 10.00
1998 MA Hagerstown Suns (30) 11.00
1998 MA Harrisburg Senators (30) 9.00
1998 MA Harris. Senators W/WINK 104 Ad (30) 12.00
1998 MA Helena Brewers (33) 8.00
1998 MA Hickory Crawdads (30) 7.00
1998 Team Hickory Crawdads Update (30) 8.00
1998 GS High Desert Mavericks (30) 11.00
1998 Team Hudson Valley Renegades (30) 11.00
1998 Team Huntsville Stars (26) 9.00
1998 Team Huntsville Stars Uncut Sheet 12.00
1998 BL Indianapolis Indians (36) 6.00
1998 BL Iowa Cubs (30) 12.00
1998 MA Jackson Generals (28) 20.00
1998 MA Jacksonville Suns (28) 8.00
1998 Team Johnson City Cardinals (36) 8.00
1998 WTC Johnstown Johnnies (25) 4.00
1998 BL Jupiter Hammerheads (30) 8.00
1998 Team Kane County Cougars (32) 8.00
1998 Team Kane County Cougars, Connie's (32) 12.00
1998 BL Kinston Indians (30) 6.00
1998 BL Kissimmee Cobras (30) 7.00
1998 GS Knoxville Smokies (27) 6.00
1998 GS Lafayette Leopards (30) 4.00
1998 GS Lake Elsinore Storm (30) 7.00
1998 MA Lakeland Tigers (30) 9.00
1998 GS Lancaster JetHawks (30) 7.00
1998 BL Lansing Lugnuts (31) 7.00
1998 MA Las Vegas Stars (28) 7.00
1998 GS Lethbridge Black Diamonds (30) 6.00
1998 BL Louisville Redbirds (36) 8.00
1998 MA Lowell Spinners (31) 7.00
1998 BL Lynchburg HillCats (29) 7.00
1998 MA Macon Braves (29) 12.50
1998 MA Madison Black Wolf (25) 4.00
1998 GS Martinsville Phillies (29) 7.00
1998 GS Memphis Redbirds (25) 7.00
1998 Team Memphis Redbirds Update (1) 20.00
1998 MA Michigan Battle Cats (30) 11.00
1998 GS Midland Angels (28) 22.50
1998 GS Midland Angels Sponsor's Set (30) 25.00
1998 Team Midland Angels, "Claus" (28) 60.00
1998 Team Midland Angels, "Glaus" (28) 60.00
1998 MA Midwest League Top Prospects (28) 9.00
1998 GS Mobile BayBears S.L. Champs (25) 12.00
1998 Team Mobile Bay Bears (31) 8.00
1998 GS Modesto A's (30) 12.00
1998 Team Nashville Sounds - Numbered (33) 10.00
1998 Team Nashville Sounds - Unnumbered (31) 14.00
1998 MA New Britain Rock Cats (27) 8.00
1998 MA New Haven Ravens (31) 7.00
1998 MA N.H. Ravens W/Maritime Ads (31) 8.00
1998 MA New Jersey Cardinals (33) 7.00
1998 WTC New Jersey Jackals (25) 4.00
1998 MA New Orleans Zephyrs (28) 8.00
1998 BL Norfolk Tides (36) 7.00
1998 BL Norfolk Tides W/Fox 33 Ads (30) 8.00
1998 BL Norwich Navigators (26) 6.00
1998 Team Ogden Raptors (36) 8.00
1998 MA Oklahoma City Redhawks (30) 7.00
1998 MA Omaha Royals (30) 7.00
1998 GS Oneonta Yankees (32) 7.00
1998 MA Orlando Rays (29) 6.00
1998 Ottawa Lynx (xx) 45.00
1998 BL Pawtucket Red Sox (30) 7.00
1998 DD Pawtucket Red Sox Foldout 25.00
1998 MA Peoria Chiefs (30) 30.00
1998 MA Piedmont Boll Weevils (29) 7.00
1998 MA Pittsfield Mets (34) 7.00
1998 GS Portland Rockies (30) 7.00
1998 BL Portland Sea Dogs (30) 6.00
1998 BL Portland Sea Dogs 5th Anniv. (36) 9.00
1998 BL Princeton Devil Rays (30) 8.00
1998 BL Prince William Cannons (30) 10.00
1998 MA Prince William Decade Greats (30) 10.00
1998 GS Quad City River Bandits (30) 7.00
1998 GS Rancho Cucamonga Quakes (31) 25.00
1998 GS R.C. Quakes W/GTE Ads (31) 30.00
1998 MA Reading Phillies (28) 6.00
1998 MA Reading Phillies Update (30) 7.00
1998 MA Reading Phillies Boy Scouts (1) 6.00
1998 Berks County News Reading Phillies (5) 40.00
1998 BL Richmond Braves (30) 8.00
1998 Richmond Camera Richmond Braves (20) 45.00
1998 BL Rochester Red Wings (30) 7.00
1998 MA Rockford Cubbies (30) 9.00
1998 Team Rockford Cubbies (30) 11.00
1998 Choice Salem Avalanche (30) 6.00
1998 GS Salem-Keizer Volcanoes (36) 7.00
1998 Team Salt Lake City Buzz (30) 8.00
1998 GS San Antonio Missions (30) 7.00
1998 GS San Bernardino Stampede (32) 8.00
1998 San Bernardino Stampede Team Issue (28) 20.00
1998 BL San Jose Giants (30) 7.00
1998 MA Savannah Sand Gnats (30) 7.00
1998 BL Scranton/Wilkes-Barre Red Barons (30) 8.00
1998 Team S/W-B Red Barons 10th Anniver. (20) 9.00
1998 MA Shreveport Captains (29) 7.00
1998 MA Shreveport W/WK SportsCare Ads (30) 7.00
1998 GS Sioux City Explorers (25) 4.00
1998 Team Sonoma County Crushers (28) 4.00
1998 MA South Atlantic League Prospects (30) 10.00
1998 MA South Bend Silver Hawks (27) 6.00
1998 GS Southern League Top Prosepcts (32) 7.00
1998 GS Southern Oregon Timberjacks (33) 8.00
1998 GS Spokane Indians (33) 7.00
1998 MA St. Catherines Stompers 7.00
1998 MA St. Luice Mets (30) 8.00
1998 Team St. Paul Saints, Wheaties logo (32) 35.00
1998 Team St. Paul Saints, No Logo (32) 20.00
1998 MA St. Petersburg Devil Rays (30) 8.00
1998 GS Stockton Ports (30) 7.00
1998 GS Stockton Ports Update (6) 6.00
1998 GS Syracuse SkyChiefs (31) 8.00
1998 BL Tacoma Rainiers (30) 7.00
1998 MA Tampa Yankees (30) 11.00
1998 GS Texas League Top Prospects (30) 10.00
1998 BL Toledo Mud Hens (33) 7.00
1998 MA Trenton Thunder (30) 7.00
1998 MA Tucson Sidewinders (29) 7.00
1998 Team Tulsa Drillers (27) 8.00
1998 Team Tulsa Texas League Champs (32) 10.00
1998 GS Vancouver Canadians (30) 37.50
1998 Team Vermont Expos (35) 7.00
1998 MA Vero Beach Dodgers (31) 15.00
1998 GS Visalia Oaks (31) 11.00
1998 WTC Waterbury Spirit (25) 4.00
1998 Team Watertown Indians (35) 8.00
1998 MA West Michigan Whitecaps (30) 6.00
1998 MA West Tennessee Diamond Jaxx (30) 8.00
1998 MA Wichita Wranglers (30) 8.00
1998 MA Williamsport Cubs (30) 15.00
1998 Team Williamsport Cubs Jeremy Gonzalez 5.00
1998 Team Williamsport Cubs Kerry Wood 9.00
1998 Team W. Cubs Kerry Wood Phone Card 9.00
1998 Choice Wilmington Blue Rocks (30) 8.00
1998 BL Winston-Salem Warthogs (30) 10.00
1998 MA Wisconsin Timber Rattlers (30) 8.00
1998 GS Yakima Bears (34) 7.00

1999 Diamond Authentics Signature Series

Production of each card in this minor-league issue was limited to 3,250 signed and numbered autographed versions and 10,000 unautographed cards. The autographed cards were sold three per pack. Unautographed cards were sold via a mail-in offer. Card fronts feature color photos which are borderless on two or three sides. Backs have a few words about the player and a gold-foil autograph guarantee along with the serial number. Values shown are for autographed cards.

MT

Complete Set, Auto. (30): 25.00
Common Player, Auto.: 1.00
Complete Set, Unautographed (30): 1.00
Common Player, Unautographed: .05
Wax Pack (7): 2.00
Wax Box (6): 12.50
1 Fletcher Bates 1.00
2 Mark Harriger 1.00
3 Jesse Ibarra 1.00
4 Keith Glauber 1.00
5 Melvin Rosario 1.00
6 Mike Rodriguez 1.00
7 Paul Avery 1.00
8 Larry Barnes 1.00
9 Eric Gillespie 1.00
10 Mike Glendenning 1.00
11 Josh Goldfield 1.00
12 Dan Phillips 1.00
13 Josh Reding 1.00
14 Jon Schaeffer 1.00
15 Kevin Sheredy 1.00
16 Julio Lugo, Jr. 1.00
17 Tonayne Brown 1.00
18 Jon Hamilton 1.00
19 Vince LaCorte 1.00
20 Ruddy Lugo 1.00
21 Danny Ardoin 1.00
22 Jermaine Clark 1.00
23 Jason Sekany 1.00
24 Mike Villano 1.00
25 Justin Albertson 1.00
26 Jesse Garcia 1.00
27 Rikki Johnston 1.00
28 Roosevelt Brown 1.00
29 Rickey Cradle 1.00
30 Shea Hillenbrand 6.00

Magnificent 7

Seven top prospects are featured in this insert series which has the same basic format at the base set except that autographed cards are serially numbered within editions of 1,250 each and card numbers carry an "MS" prefix. Unsigned versions of the cards were available via a mail-in offer. Values shown are for signed versions.

MT

Complete Set, Auto. (7): 25.00
Common Player, Auto.: 2.00
Complete Set, Unautographed (7): 1.00
Common Player, Unautographed: .10
MS1 Eric Gagne 12.00
MS2 Luis Rivera 2.00
MS3 D'Angelo Jiminez 2.00
MS4 Jackson Melian 2.00
MS5 Barry Zito 12.00
MS6 Scott Comer 2.00
MS7 Jeff DeVanon 2.00

Triple Crown

Super prospect Adam Piatt is featured in this insert set. Autographed versions of the cards were random pack inserts, unsigned versions were available via a mail-in offer.

MT

Complete Set, Auto. (3): 6.00
Common Card, Autographed: 2.00
Complete Set, Unautographed (3): 1.00
Common Card, Unautographed: .50
1 Adam Piatt 2.00
2 Adam Piatt 2.00
3 Adam Piatt 2.00

1999 Just Imagine

Contiguously numbered (#51-150) from where the company's earlier Just 99 series left off (#1-50), Just Imagine presents an almost entirely new checklist while retaining many of the design elements and insert series from the Just 99 issue. The main difference in the base cards is that the colored stripe presenting the player name is horizontal on Just Imagine, where it was vertical on Just 99 cards. Backs of the JI repeat a vertical slice of the front photo and offer previous year and career professional stats. Just Imagine was issued in six-card foil packs in which were seeded several insert series, including autographed cards.

MT

Complete Set (100): 9.00
Common Player: .05
Wax Pack (6): 1.50
Wax Box: 25.00
51 Paul Ah Yat .05
52 Israel Alcantara (Team name in stripe.) .05
53 Erick Almonte .05
54 Gabe Alvarez .15
55 Tony Armas Jr. .15
56 Jeff Austin .10
57 Benito Baez .05
58 Kevin Beirne .05
59 Ron Belliard .05
60 Micah Bowie .05
61 Russell Branyan .10
62 Antone Brooks .05
63 A.J. Burnett .20
64 Pat Burrell .75
65 Brent Butler .05
66 Troy Cameron .05
67 Sean Casey .45
68 Bruce Chen .05
69 Chin-Feng Chen .15
70 Jin Ho Cho .10
71 Jesus Colome .05
72 Carl Crawford .25
73 Bubba Crosby .05
74 Jack Cust .10
75 Mike Darr .05
76 Ben Davis .10
77 Octavio Dotel .05
78 Kelly Dransfeldt .05
79 Adam Dunn .75
80 Erubiel Durazo .10
81 John Elway (Oneonta Yankees) 1.00
81a John Elway (Autographed edition of 100.) 140.00
82 John Elway (Denver Broncos) .75
83 Mario Encarnacion .05
84 Seth Etherton .05
85 Adam Everett .15
86 Franky Figueroa .05
87 Mike Frank .05
88 Jon Garland .15
89 Chris George .05
90 Jody Gerut .05
91 Derrick Gibson .05
92 Jerry Hairston Jr. .05
93 Josh Hamilton .10
94 Jason Hart .05
95 Chad Harville .05
96 Nathan Haynes .05
97 Junior Herndon .05
98 Shea Hillenbrand .25
99 Matt Holliday .25
100 Brandon Inge .05
101 Jacque Jones .45
102 Gabe Kapler .15
103 Austin Kearns .65
104 Brandon Larson .05
105 Jason LaRue .05
106 Carlos Lee .25
107 Corey Lee .05
108 Donny Leon .05
109 George Lombard .05
110 Julio Lugo, Jr. .05
111 Chris Magruder .05
112 Mark Mangum .05
113 Jason Marquis .10
114 Ruben Mateo .05
115 Luis Matos .05
116 Gary Matthews Jr. .05
117 Juan Melo .05
118 Orber Moreno .05
119 Mark Mulder .25
120 Corey Patterson .50
121 Angel Pena .05
122 Elvis Pena .05
123 Kyle Peterson .05
124 Adam Piatt .05
125 Calvin Pickering .05
126 Jeremy Powell .05
127 Luke Prokopec .05
128 Aramis Ramirez .25
129 Julio Ramirez .05
130 Matt Riley .05
131 Luis Rivera .05
132 Grant Roberts .10
133 Ryan Rupe .05
134 C.C. Sabathia .25
135 Luis Saturria .05
136 Fernando Seguignol .05
137 Alfonso Soriano 1.00
138 Patrick Strange .05
139 Robert Stratton .05
140 Reggie Taylor .10
141 Jorge Toca .05
142 Tony Torcato .05
143 Bubba Trammell .10
144 T.J. Tucker .05
145 Juan Uribe .05
146 Kip Wells .25
147 Ricky Williams (Piedmont Boll Weevils) .75
148 Ricky Williams (Texas Longhorns) .75
149 Kevin Witt .05
150 Ed Yarnall .05

Auto. - Base Set

Authentically autographed cards from Just Minors' Imagine issue were seeded at the average rate of two per 24-pack box. Autographed cards repeat the photo used in the base set but have the bottom portion ghosted to allow the autograph to appear more prominently. Backs have a congratulatory message.

		MT
Complete Set (46):		45.00
Common Player:		1.00
(1)	Israel Alcantara	1.00
(2)	Hector Almonte	1.00
(3)	Rick Ankiel	2.00
(4)	Jeff Austin	1.50
(5)	Benito Baez	1.00
(6)	Kevin Barker	1.00
(7)	Kevin Beirne	1.00
(8)	Micah Bowie	1.00
(9)	Antone Brooks	1.00
(10)	Sean Casey	6.00
(11)	Jesus Colome	1.00
(12)	Bubba Crosby	1.00
(13)	Jack Cust	1.00
(14)	Ben Davis	1.00
(15)	Seth Etherton	1.50
(16)	Mike Frank	1.00
(17)	Jon Garland	2.00
(18)	Chris George	1.00
(19)	Jason Grilli	1.00
(20)	Junior Herndon	1.00
(21)	Gabe Kapler	2.00
(22)	Corey Lee	1.00
(24)	Danny Leon	1.00
(25)	George Lombard	1.00
(26)	Julio Lugo, Jr.	1.00
(27)	Chris Magruder	1.00
(28)	Mark Mangum	1.00
(28)	Jason Marquis	2.00
(29)	Luis Matos	1.00
(30)	Juan Melo	1.00
(31)	Orber Moreno	1.00
(32)	Pablo Ozuna	1.00
(33)	Kyle Peterson	1.00
(34)	Ben Petrick	1.00
(35)	Calvin Pickering	1.00
(36)	Aramis Ramirez	3.00
(37)	Zach Sorensen	1.00
(38)	Alfonso Soriano	15.00
(39)	Patrick Strange	1.00
(40)	Reggie Taylor	1.50
(41)	Jorge Toca	1.00
(42)	Bubba Trammell	2.00
(43)	T.J. Tucker	1.00
(44)	Juan Uribe	1.00
(45)	Kip Wells	3.00
(46)	Randy Wolf	3.00

Auto. - Die-Cut

Some of the players who appear in the autographed card series (and a few who don't) can also be found in a much more limited autographed insert. Called die-cut autographs, these cards repeat in a circle at center the photo found on the base card. The background is white with the autograph at top; corners are rounded. On back, each die-cut autograph card is serially numbered from within an edition of 200.

		MT
Complete Set (17):		20.00
Common Player:		2.00
(1)	Rick Ankiel	2.00
(2)	Jeff Austin	2.00
(3)	Kevin Beirne	2.00
(4)	Micah Bowie	2.00
(5)	Troy Cameron	2.00
(6)	Seth Etherton	2.00
(7)	Mike Frank	2.00
(8)	Chris George	2.00
(9)	Gabe Kapler	2.00
(10)	George Lombard	2.00
(11)	Jason Marquis	3.00
(12)	Pablo Ozuna	2.00
(13)	Calvin Pickering	2.00
(14)	Zach Sorensen	2.00
(15)	Jorge Toca	2.00
(16)	T.J. Tucker	2.00
(17)	Randy Wolf	3.00

Auto. - Just Imagine

Some of the players who appear in the base autographed card series (and a few who don't) can also be found in a much more limited insert, called Just Imagine Autographs. On back, each Just Imagine autograph card is serially numbered from within an edition of 200.

		MT
Complete Set (23):		250.00
Common Player:		2.00
(1)	Israel Alcantara	2.00
(2)	Rick Ankiel	3.00
(3)	Jeff Austin	2.00
(4)	Micah Bowie	2.00
(5)	Sean Casey	6.00
(6)	Jack Cust	2.00
(7)	John Elway	140.00
(8)	Mike Frank	2.00
(9)	Rafael Furcal	4.00
(10)	Jon Garland	2.00
(11)	Gabe Kapler	2.00
(12)	Julio Lugo, Jr.	2.00
(13)	Jason Marquis	4.00
(14)	Pablo Ozuna	2.00
(15)	Kyle Peterson	2.00
(16)	Julio Ramirez	2.00
(17)	Alfonso Soriano	25.00
(18)	Jorge Toca	2.00
(19)	T.J. Tucker	2.00
(20)	Kip Wells	3.00
(22)	Ricky Williams (Texas Longhorns)	75.00
(23)	Ricky Williams (Heisman Trophy)	75.00

Just Debut

Inserted one per box as a box-topper and sealed inside a paper envelope, this insert set chronicles the professional debut of 10 top minor league prospects. Fronts have a color photo at center with a ticket design at bottom. Backs have two small black-and-white copies of the front photo, statistics from the debut game and career highlights. Numbered on front, cards have a "JD-0999-" prefix.

		MT
Complete Set (10):		10.00
Common Player:		1.00
01	Jeff Austin	1.00
02	Chin-Feng Chen	1.50
03	Erubiel Durazo	1.00
04	Jody Gerut	1.00
05	Josh Hamilton	1.50
06	Corey Patterson	2.50
07	Alfonso Soriano	7.50
08	Jorge Toca	1.00
09	Kip Wells	1.50
10	Brad Wilkerson	1.00

Just Longshots

Seeded at the rate of about one per eight foil packs (three per box) these insert cards feature players who have overcome long odds as low picks in the amateur draft to arrive on the brink of major league stardom. Fronts have action photos on a white background. In the black data box at bottom along with player identification is information on the round in which he was drafted and his overall rank in the draft. Backs have a monocolor version of the photo in the background and a few words about the player and his career to date. Card numbers on back have an "LS" prefix and the player's initials as a suffix.

		MT
Complete Set (10):		3.00
Common Player:		.50
001	Wes Anderson	.50
002	David Eckstein	.75
003	Marcus Giles	1.50
004	Kevin Haverbusch	.50
005	Gabe Kapler	.50
006	Julio Lugo, Jr.	.50
007	Gary Matthews Jr.	.50
008	Ryan Minor	.50
009	Jason Regan	.50
010	Daryle Ward	.50

Just Nine

Top Prospects at each position are featured in this insert set. Fronts have a small player photo at top-center, which is repeated larger in the background in a single color. Backs repeat the front photo and have a few career highlights. Cards are inserted one per case (240 packs).

		MT
Complete Set (9):		45.00
Common Player:		5.00
JN-01	Rick Ankiel	5.00
JN-02	Ron Belliard	5.00
JN-03	Pat Burrell	12.00
JN-04	Lance Berkman	6.00
JN-05	Ben Davis	5.00
JN-06	Ruben Mateo	5.00
JN-07	Corey Patterson	6.00
JN-08	Aramis Ramirez	6.00
JN-09	Alfonso Soriano	15.00

Just Stars

Ten of the biggest names on 1999 minor league rosters are presented in this insert series which was seeded on the average of one per box (24 packs) in Just Imagine. Only the star-shaped central portion of the front photo is printed in color, the rest is black-and-white. Backs repeat a portion of the front photo in a colored star on a white background. A few career highlights and predictions are also included.

		MT
Complete Set (10):		12.00
Common Player:		1.00
JS-01	Rick Ankiel	1.00
JS-02	Pat Burrell	2.50
JS-03	Sean Casey	2.00
JS-04	Erubiel Durazo	1.00
JS-05	Ben Davis	1.00
JS-06	Jacque Jones	1.50
JS-07	Ruben Mateo	1.00
JS-08	Gary Matthews Jr.	1.00
JS-09	Adam Piatt	1.00
JS-10	Alfonso Soriano	4.00

1999 Just Justifiable

Numbered from 151-250, this minor league singles issue continues where Just's The Start (#1-50) and Imagine (#51-150) left off earlier in the year. Justifiable was sold in a 24-pack box (six cards per pack) which included one of five 6" player action figures. The Justifiable base cards are in the same basic format as the earlier issues, except the color strip which contains the player name is vertically on the right side of the card. Backs repeat a vertical slice of the front photo and include 1998 and career stats, along with a team logo.

		MT
Complete Set (100):		6.00
Common Player:		.05
Hobby Wax Box (24+1):		25.00
Retail Wax Box (10+1):		12.00
151	Winston Abreu	.05
152	Chris Aguila	.05
153	Bronson Arroyo	.05
154	Robert Averette	.05
155	Mike Bacsik	.05
156	Andrew Beinbrink	.05
157	Matt Belisle	.05
158	Matt Blank	.05
159	Jung Bong	.10
160	Milton Bradley	.25
161	Ryan Bradley	.05
162	Dee Brown	.05
163	Sean Burroughs	.50
164	Chance Caple	.05
165	Hee Choi	.50
166	Mike Christensen	.05
167	Doug Clark	.05
168	Javier Colina	.05
169	Brian Cooper	.05
170	Pat Daneker	.05
171	Randey Dorame	.05
172	Ryan Drese	.05
173	Chris Duncan	.05
174	Adam Dunn	2.00
175	David Eckstein	.25
176	Alex Fernandez	.05
177	Choo Freeman	.10
178	Neil Friendling	.05
179	Eddy Furniss	.05
180	B.J. Garbe	.05
181	Yon German	.05
182	Esteban German	.05
183	Dan Gummitt	.05
184	Will Hartley	.05
185	Jesus Hernandez	.05
186	Alex Hernandez	.05
187	Jay Hood	.05
188	Aubrey Huff	.10
189	Chad Hutchinson	.05
190	Jason Jennings	.05
191	Jaime Jones	.05
192	David Kelton	.05
193	Michael Lamb	.10
194	Jacques Landry	.05
195	Ryan Langerhans	.10
196	Nelson Lara	.05
197	Nick Leach	.05
198	Steve Lomasney	.05
199	Felipe Lopez	.05
200	Ryan Ludwick	.05
201	Pat Manning	.05
202	T.R. Marcinczyk	.05
203	Hipolito Martinez	.05
204	Tony McKnight	.05
205	Tydus Meadows	.05
206	Corky Miller	.05
207	Frank Moore	.05
208	Scott Morgan	.05
209	Tony Mota	.05
210	Ntema Ndungidi	.05
211	David Noyce	.05
212	Franklin Nunez	.05
213	Jose Ortiz	.05
214	Jimmy Osting	.05
215	Jorge Padilla	.05
216	Mike Paradis	.05
217	Brandon Parker	.05
218	Jarrod Patterson	.05
219	John Patterson	.05
220	Jay Payton	.15
221	Juan Pena	.10
222	Brad Penny	.10
223	Danny Peoples	.05
224	Paul Phillips	.05
225	Josh Pressley	.05
226	Tim Raines Jr.	.05
227	Paul Rigdon	.05
228	Jimmy Rollins	1.00
229	J.C. Romero	.05
230	Marcos Scutaro	.05
231	Sammy Serrano	.05
232	Wascar Serrano	.05
233	Ben Sheets	.50
234	Carlos Silva	.05
235	Scott Sobkowiak	.05
236	Ramon Soler	.05
237	Shawn Sonnier	.05
238	Jovanny Sosa	.05
239	Jason Standridge	.05
240	Brent Stentz	.05
241	Seth Taylor	.05
242	Jason Tyner	.05
243	Brant Ust	.05
244	Eric Valent	.10
245	Ismael Villegas	.05
246	David Walling	.05
247	Rico Washington	.05
248	Brad Wilkerson	.10
249	Patrick Williams	.05
250	Barry Zito	1.00.

Auto. - Base Set

Base-set autographed cards from Just Minors' Justifiable issue were seeded at the average rate of two per 24-pack box. Autographed cards repeat the photo used in the base set but have the bottom portion ghosted to allow the autograph to appear more prominently. Backs have a congratulatory message.

		MT
Complete Set (18):		35.00
Common Player:		1.00
(1)	Rick Ankiel	2.00
(2)	Sean Burroughs	4.00
(3)	Eric Byrnes	1.00
(4)	Troy Cameron	1.00
(5)	Juan Dilone	1.00
(6)	Rafael Furcal	4.00
(7)	Jason Hart	1.00
(8)	Shea Hillenbrand	5.00
(9)	Nick Johnson	5.00
(10)	Adam Kennedy	4.00
(11)	Mark Mulder	5.00
(12)	Pablo Ozuna	1.00
(13)	Corey Patterson	5.00
(14)	Angel Pena	1.00
(15)	Julio Ramirez	1.00
(16)	Matt Riley	1.50
(17)	Grant Roberts	1.00
(18)	Tony Torcato	1.00

Auto. - Die-Cut

Some of the players who appear in the autographed card base set (and a few who don't) can also be found in a much more limited autographed insert. Called die-cut autographs, these cards repeat the photo found on the base card in a circle at center. The background is white with the autograph at top; corners are rounded. On back, each die-cut autograph card is serially numbered from within an edition of 200.

		MT
Complete Set (7):		20.00
Common Player:		2.00
(1)	Rick Ankiel	3.00
(2)	Matt Belisle	2.00
(3)	Sean Burroughs	4.00
(4)	Gil Meche	4.00
(5)	Mark Mulder	6.00
(6)	Corey Patterson	6.00
(7)	Matt Riley	2.00

Auto. - Just Diamonds

Some of the players who appear in the base autographed card series (and a few who don't) can also be found in a much more limited insert, called Just Diamonds Autographs. The cards have player pictures in a diamond frame at the center of a white background. A trapazoid at bottom has the signature. On back, each Just Diamonds autograph card is serially numbered from within an edition of 100.

		MT
Complete Set (11):		40.00
Common Player:		2.00
(1)	Rick Ankiel	3.00
(2)	Matt Belisle	2.00
(3)	Sean Burroughs	4.00
(4)	Troy Cameron	2.00
(5)	Dionys Cesar	2.00
(6)	Rafael Furcal	4.00
(7)	Nick Johnson	5.00
(8)	Pablo Ozuna	2.00
(9)	Corey Patterson	6.00
(10)	Aramis Ramirez	4.00
(11)	Kip Wells	6.00

Just Debut

These are the rarest inserts in Justifiable, found only one per 240 packs. There is a horizontal color photo at center with black borders at top and bottom. Details of the player's first professional game are in the bottom border. Card numbers are prefixed with "JD".

		MT
Complete Set (10):		25.00
Common Player:		4.00
01	B.J. Garbe	4.00
02	Ben Sheets	6.00
03	Jeff Austin	4.00
04	Chin-Feng Chen	5.00
05	Jody Gerut	4.00
06	Josh Hamilton	4.00
07	Corey Patterson	7.50
08	Alfonso Soriano	10.00
09	Jorge Luis Toca	4.00
10	Kip Wells	6.00

Just Drafted

This insert of 1999 draftees was issued one per box sealed in a black paper envelope. Fronts have a horizontal color photo at center with draft details below. Backs have a few career numbers and a team logo. Cards are numbered with a "JD" prefix.

		MT
Complete Set (10):		12.00
Common Player:		2.00
01	Larry Bigbie	2.00
02	Chance Caple	2.00
03	Chris Duncan	2.00
04	B.J. Garbe	2.00
05	Josh Hamilton	2.00
06	Will Hartley	2.00
07	Mike Paradis	2.00
08	Ben Sheets	3.00
09	David Walling	2.00
10	Barry Zito	7.50

Just Figures

In the first-ever random pairing of baseball cards and action figures, each box of Just Justifiable included one of five action player figures along with 24 foil packs of minor league cards. About 6" tall, each figure has poseable arms and legs. Each player was issued in both fielding and batting versions. Certain figures, details of which were not released, were issued in more limited numbers in one or the other of their poses. Until that situation is clarified, only a common figure value will be shown in these listings. Besides the five players issued in boxes, a Rick Ankiel figure was available exclusive via mail-in offer for $13.

		MT
Common Figure:		6.00
(1a)	Hank Aaron/Btg (1974 Atlanta Braves)	12.50
(1b)	Hank Aaron/Fldg (1974 Atlanta Braves)	6.00
(2a)	Michael Barrett/Btg (1998 Harrisburg Senators)	6.00
(2b)	Michael Barrett/Fldg (1998 Harrisburg Senators)	6.00
(3a)	John Elway/Btg (1982 Oneonta Yankees)	9.00
(3b)	John Elway/Fldg (1982 Oneonta Yankees)	10.00
(4a)	Gabe Kapler/Btg (1998 Jacksonville Suns)	6.00
(4b)	Gabe Kapler/Fldg (1998 Jacksonville Suns)	6.00
(5a)	Ricky Williams/Btg (1996 Piedmont Boll Weevils)	7.50
(5b)	Ricky Williams/Fldg (1996 Piedmont Boll Weevils)	7.50
(6a)	Rick Ankiel (1999 Arkansas Travelers - Home)	7.50
(6b)	Rick Ankiel (1999 Arkansas Travelers - Away)	7.50

Just Spotlights

Seeded one per 24-pack box, these inserts feature top minor league stars. Fronts have a white background with spotlight beams and a color player photo in the center circle. Backs repeat the front photo in full-size format and have career highlights and biographical data. Cards numbers are prefixed with "JS."

		MT
Complete Set (10):		35.00
Common Player:		2.00
01	Dee Brown	2.00
02	Pat Burrell	10.00
03	Josh Hamilton	2.00
04	Nick Johnson	6.00
05	Jason Marquis	4.00
06	Pablo Ozuna	2.00
07	John Patterson	2.00
08	Adam Piatt	2.00
09	Matt Riley	2.00
10	Alfonso Soriano	15.00

Just the Facts

Top talent in the minor leagues is featured in this insert set found on average of one per 24 packs. Cards have monochromatic versions of the same photo on front, along with a few player details and career highlights. Backs have the full-color version of the photo vertically and a bit more personal detail. Card numbers have a "JTF" prefix.

		MT
Complete Set (10):		40.00
Common Player:		2.00
01	Pat Burrell	10.00
02	Sean Burroughs	4.00
03	Adam Eaton	2.50
04	Marcus Giles	2.50
05	Josh Hamilton	2.00
06	Nick Johnson	6.00
07	Corey Patterson	6.00
08	Jason Standridge	2.00
09	Jorge Luis Toca	2.00
10	Eric Valent	2.00

1999 Just The Start

The Just 99 base set features a large color photo on front with white borders at top, bottom and right. At left is a 1/2" vertical color strip in which the player's name and position appears; his team name is vertically to the right of that strip. The Just 99 logo is at bottom. Backs repeat a portion of the front photo on the right. Horizontally at left are personal data, 1998 and pro career stats. A team logo and card number are at top center. The issue was sold in six-card foil packs and 24-pack boxes.

		MT
Complete Set (50):		4.00
Common Player:		.05
Wax Pack (6):		1.00
Wax Box (24):		16.00
1	Hector Almonte	.05
2	Wes Anderson	.05
3	Ryan Anderson	.20
4	Clayton Andrews	.05
5	Rick Ankiel	.10
6	Brad Baisley	.05
7	Kevin Barker	.05
8	Michael Barrett	.15
9	Kris Benson	.10
10	Peter Bergeron	.05
11	Lance Berkman	.35
12	Nate Bump	.05
13	Eric Byrnes	.05
14	Giuseppe Chiaramonte	.05
15	Glenn Davis	.05
16	Juan Dilone	.05
17	Eric DuBose	.05
18	Rick Elder	.05
19	Alex Escobar	.15
20	Rafael Furcal	.25
21	Shawn Gallagher	.05
22	Marcus Giles	.35
23	Geoff Goetz	.05
24	Jason Grilli	.05

25 Cristian Guzman .25
26 Mark Harriger .05
27 Nick Johnson .40
28 Gabe Kapler .15
29 Kenny Kelly .05
30 Adam Kennedy .20
31 Corey Lee .05
32 Kevin McGlinchy .10
33 Gil Meche .15
34 Jackson Melian .05
35 Warren Morris .10
36 Ricky Williams (Baseball) 1.50
37 Pablo Ozuna .05
38 Ben Petrick .05
39 Scott Pratt .05
40 Chris Reinike .05
41 Zach Sorenson .05
42 Dernell Stenson .05
43 Andy Thompson .05
44 Luis Vizcaino .05
45 Daryle Ward .05
46 Vernon Wells .50
47 Jayson Werth .05
48 Jake Westbrook .05
49 Ricky Williams (Football) 1.50
50 Randy Wolf .10

Autographs

Authentically autographed cards from Just Minors debut issue were seeded at the average rate of two per 24-pack box. Autographed cards repeat the photo used in the base set but have the bottom portion ghosted to allow the autograph to appear more prominently. Backs have a congratulatory message.

MT
Complete Set (25): 65.00
Common Player: 1.00
(1) Hector Almonte 1.00
(2) Brad Baisley 1.00
(3) Michael Barrett 3.00
(4) Kris Benson 3.00
(5) Brent Billingsley 1.00
(6) Casey Blake 1.00
(7) Glenn Davis 1.00
(8) Juan Dilone 1.00
(9) Rick Elder 1.00
(10) Mark Fischer 1.00
(11) Rafael Furcal 3.00
(12) Geoff Goetz 1.00
(13) Jason Grilli 1.00
(14) Mark Harriger 1.00
(15) Heath Honeycutt 1.00
(16) Gabe Kapler 2.00
(17) Adam Kennedy 3.00
(18) Juan Melo 1.00
(19) Mark Mulder 6.00
(20) Andy Thompson 1.00
(21) Peter Tucci 1.00
(22) Luis Vizcaino 1.00
(23) Jayson Werth 1.00
(24) Jake Westbrook 1.00
(25) Ricky Williams 60.00

Auto. - Die-Cut

Some of the players who appear in the autographed card series can also be found in a much more limited autographed insert. Called die-cut autographs, these cards repeat in a circle at center the photo found on the base card. The background is white with the autograph at top; corners are rounded. On back, each die-cut autograph card is serially numbered from within an edition of 200.

MT
Complete Set (15): 65.00
Common Player: 2.00
(1) Hector Almonte 2.00
(2) Brad Baisley 2.00
(3) Michael Barrett 3.00
(4) Kris Benson 3.00
(5) Casey Blake 2.00
(6) Glenn Davis 2.00
(7) Rick Elder 2.00
(8) Geoff Goetz 2.00
(9) Jason Grilli 2.00
(10) Mark Harriger 2.00
(11) Gabe Kapler 3.00
(12) Mark Mulder 6.00
(13) Jayson Werth 2.00
(14) Jake Westbrook 2.00
(15) Ricky Williams 75.00

Just Due

Players on the brink of their major league careers and projected stardom are featured in this insert series. Cards have large color action photos on front and a tiny map at left specifying the city where their parent major league team plays. Backs have a repeat of the front elements, with a small photo and larger map, along with personal data and career highlights. Stated odds of insertion are one per six packs.

MT
Complete Set (10): 4.00
Common Player: .35
Jd-01 Michael Barrett .50
Jd-02 Kris Benson .50
Jd-03 Peter Bergeron .35
Jd-04 Lance Berkman .50
Jd-05 Nick Johnson 1.00
Jd-06 Gabe Kapler .50
Jd-07 Corey Lee .35
Jd-08 Jackson Melian .35
Jd-09 Dernell Stenson .35
Jd-10 Randy Wolf .50

Just News

The scarcest of the Just 99 inserts, found at the rate of just one per 240 packs.

MT
Complete Set (6): 30.00
Common Player: 5.00
Jn-01 Rick Ankiel, Alex Escobar 5.00
Jn-02 Marcus Giles, Mark Harriger 6.00
Jn-03 Gabe Kapler, Kevin McGlinchy 6.00
Jn-04 Jackson Melian, Warren Morris 5.00
Jn-05 Dernell Stenson, Vernon Wells 5.00
Jn-06 Ricky Williams, Ricky Williams 10.00

Just Nine

Top Prospects at each position are featured in this insert set. Fronts have a small player photo at top-center, which is repeated larger in the background in a single color. Backs repeat the front photo and have a few career highlights. Cards are inserted one per box as a box-topper in a sealed paper envelope.

MT
Complete Set (9): 7.50
Common Player: 1.00
J9-01 Rick Ankiel 1.00
J9-02 Michael Barrett 1.00
J9-03 Lance Berkman 2.00
J9-04 Alex Escobar 1.00
J9-05 Nick Johnson 3.00
J9-06 Gabe Kapler 1.00
J9-07 Warren Morris 1.00
J9-08 Pablo Ozuna 1.00
J9-09 Ben Petrick 1.00

Just Power

Some of the hardest hitters and throwers in the minor leagues are included in this chase set. Seeded one per 24-pack box, the cards have player action photos on front on a white background. The photo is repeated on back with its full background, but only in one color. A few career highlights also appear on back.

MT
Complete Set (10): 12.00
Common Player: 1.00
Jp-01 Ryan Anderson 1.50
Jp-02 Wes Anderson 1.00
Jp-03 Lance Berkman 2.00
Jp-04 Juan Dilone 1.00
Jp-05 Marcus Giles 2.00
Jp-06 Gabe Kapler 2.00
Jp-07 Kevin McGlinchy 1.50
Jp-08 Gil Meche 1.50
Jp-09 Dernell Stenson 1.00
Jp-10 Ricky Williams 5.00

1999 Just Autographs Black

These authentically autographed black-bordered cards were random inserts in the 2000 Just Gold 2k factory sets. Each card was produced in a numbered edition of 50 each. Some players appear in more than one pose. The unnumbered cards are checklisted here in alphabetical order.

MT
Common Player: 5.00
(1) Rick Ankiel 5.00
(2) Tony Armas Jr. 7.50
(3) Matt Belisle 5.00
(4) Jacob Cruz 5.00
(5) Jack Cust 6.00
(6) Pat Daneker 5.00
(7) Mario Encarnacion 5.00
(8) Robert Fick 5.00
(9) Nick Johnson 10.00
(10) Jaime Jones 5.00
(11) Austin Kearns 12.00
(12) David Kelton 5.00
(13) Nelson Lara 5.00
(14) Brandon Larson 5.00
(15) Steve Lomasney 5.00
(16) Gil Meche 5.00
(17) Guillermo Mota 5.00
(18) Tony Mota 5.00
(19) Pablo Ozuna 5.00
(20) Pablo Ozuna 5.00
(21) Corey Patterson 20.00
(22) Corey Patterson 20.00
(23) Corey Patterson 20.00
(24) Jay Payton 5.00
(25) Aramis Ramirez 7.50
(26) Ryan Rupe 5.00
(27) Alfonso Soriano 75.00
(28) Jovanny Sosa 5.00
(29) Jorge Toca 5.00
(30) Jorge Toca 5.00
(31) Enrique Wilson 7.50
(32) Barry Zito 55.00
(33) Barry Zito 55.00

1999 SP Top Prospects

The projected stars of the new millenium were previewed in Upper Deck's SP Top Prospects minor league set issued in the 1999 pre-season. The 126 cards in the base set have player photos surrounded by gold refractive-foil borders. The player's major league parent team is named at top and the logo of his 1998 minor league team is at lower-right. Backs have another color photo, a few words about the player and his minor league career stats. A parallel President's Edition set, with only 10 numbered cards of each player, was also released. The President's Edition cards replace the gold front borders with silver. The issue was sold in eight-card packs with a suggested retail price of $4.99.

MT
Complete Set (126): 10.00
Common Player: .05
Wax Pack (8): 1.50
Wax Box (24): 25.00
1 J.D. Drew (Top Ten Prospects) .50
2 Matt Clement (Top Ten Prospects) .15
3 Alex Gonzalez (Top Ten Prospects) .10
4 Rich Ankiel (Top Ten Prospects) .10
5 Alex Escobar (Top Ten Prospects) .10
6 Eric Chavez (Top Ten Prospects) .25
7 Lance Berkman (Top Ten Prospects) .25
8 Russell Branyan (Top Ten Prospects) .05
9 Gabe Kapler (Top Ten Prospects) .10
10 Bruce Chen (Top Ten Prospects) .05
11 Chuck Abbott .05
12 Ryan Anderson .15
13 Rick Ankiel .15
14 Michael Barrett .25
15 Carlos Beltran 2.00
16 Buck Jacobsen .05
17 Kris Benson .25
18 Lance Berkman .50
19 Ryan Brannan .05
20 Russell Branyan .10
21 Dermal Brown .05
22 Roosevelt Brown .05
23 Juan LeBron .05
24 Brent Butler .05
25 Ross Gload .05
26 Eric Chavez .50
27 Bruce Chen .05
28 Matt Clement .25
29 Adonis Harrison .05
30 Francisco Cordero .05
31 David Cortes .05
32 Paxton Crawford .05
33 Joe Crede .50
34 Bobby Cripps .05
35 Mike Cuddyer .10
36 John Curtice .05
37 Mike Darr .05
38 Ben Davis .05
39 Glenn Davis .05
40 Matt DeWitt .05
41 Shea Hillenbrand .50
42 Adam Eaton .20
43 Mario Encarnacion .05
44 Chris Enochs .05
45 Pat Burrell 1.50
46 Kyle Farnsworth .05
47 Nelson Figueroa .05
48 Shawn Gallagher .05
49 Chad Hutchinson .05
50 Marcus Giles .25
51 J.D. Drew 1.50
52 Alex Gonzalez .10
53 Chad Green .05
54 Jason Grilli .05
55 Seth Etherton .10
56 Roy Halladay .50
57 Tyson Hartshorn .05
58 Al Hawkins .05
59 Chad Hermansen .10
60 Ramon Hernandez .15
61 Mark Johnson .05
62 Doug Johnston .05
63 Jacque Jones .40
64 Adam Kennedy .25
65 Cesar King .05
66 Brendan Kingman .05
67 Mike Kinkade .15
68 Corey Koskie .50
69 Mike Kusiewicz .05
70 Mike Colangelo .05
71 Jason LaRue .05
72 Joe Lawrence .05
73 Carlos Lee .25
74 Jeff Liefer .05
75 Mike Lincoln .05
76 George Lombard .05
77 Mike Lowell .50
78 Alex Escobar .15
79 Sam Marsonek .05
80 Ruben Mateo .05
81 Brian Benefield .05
82 Gary Matthews Jr. .05
83 Joe Mays .35
84 Jackson Melian .05
85 Juan Melo .05
86 Chad Meyers .05
87 Matt Miller .05
88 Damon Minor .05
89 Ryan Minor .05
90 Mike Mitchell .05
91 Shea Morenz .10
92 Warren Morris .10
93 Drew Henson 2.00
94 Todd Noel .05
95 Pablo Ozuna .05
96 John Patterson .05
97 Josh Paul .05
98 Angel Pena .05
99 Juan Pena .05
100 Danny Peoples .05
101 Santiago Perez .05
102 Tommy Peterman .05
103 Ben Petrick .05
104 Calvin Pickering .05
105 John Powers .05
106 Gabe Kapler .15
107 Rob Ramsey .05
108 Luis Figueroa .05
109 Grant Roberts .05
110 Fernando Seguignol .05
111 Juan Sosa .05
112 Dernell Stenson .05
113 John Stephens .05
114 Mike Stoner .05
115 Reggie Taylor .10
116 Justin Towle .05
117 Carlos Villalobos .05
118 Vernon Wells .45
119 Jason Werth .05
120 Jake Westbrook .05
121 Matt White .05
122 Ricky Williams 2.00
123 Kevin Witt .05
124 Dewayne Wise .05
125 Ed Yarnall .05
126 Mike Zywica .05

Chirography

Top draft picks are featured in this set of autographed insert cards. Fronts have player photos framed in gold foil on a white border. At bottom is the player's authentic autograph. Backs have a congratulatory notice from Upper Deck CEO Richard McWilliam. Cards are "numbered" with player initials. Insertion rate is one per 10 packs.

MT
Complete Set (30): 75.00
Common Player: 3.00
RA Ryan Anderson 6.00
RiA Rick Ankiel 6.00
LB Lance Berkman 9.00
DB Dermal Brown 3.00
BB Brent Butler 3.00
EC Eric Chavez 6.00
BC Bruce Chen 3.00
MC Matt Clement 4.50
FC Francisco Cordero 3.00
DC David Cortes 3.00
MD Mike Darr 9.00
CE Chris Enochs 3.00
CH Chad Hermansen 3.00
RH Ramon Hernandez 3.00
CK Cesar King 3.00
MK Mike Kinkade 3.00
CL Carlos Lee 4.50
GL George Lombard 3.00
ML Mike Lowell 6.00
RM Ruben Mateo 3.00
GM Gary Matthews Jr. 3.00
JaM Jackson Melian 3.00
JM Juan Melo 3.00
RyM Ryan Minor 3.00
WM Warren Morris 4.50
JP John Patterson 3.00
BP Ben Petrick 3.00
JW Jayson Werth 3.00
MW Matt White 3.00
EY Eddie Yarnell 3.00

Destination the Show

The top names in minor league baseball are found in the checklist of this insert set. Cards have player photos on a silver-foil background. On back the player photo is repeated and there is a silver-foil serial number from within an edition of 100 of each card.

MT
Complete Set (30): 50.00
Common Player: 2.00
D1 Ryan Anderson 3.00
D2 Rick Ankiel 2.00
D3 Lance Berkman 6.00
D4 Russell Branyan 2.00
D5 Juan Melo 2.00
D6 Alex Gonzalez 2.00
D7 Eric Chavez 6.00
D8 Bruce Chen 2.00
D9 Matt Clement 3.00
D10 Eddie Yarnell 2.00
D11 Dernell Stenson 2.00
D12 Corey Koskie 6.00
D13 J.D. Drew 12.50
D14 Chad Hermansen 2.00
D15 Ramon Hernandez 2.00
D16 Cesar King 2.00
D17 Mike Kinkade 3.00
D18 Carlos Lee 3.00
D19 George Lombard 2.00
D20 Ruben Mateo 2.00
D21 Gary Matthews Jr. 2.00
D22 Pat Burrell 10.00
D23 Ryan Minor 2.00
D24 Warren Morris 2.00
D25 Gabe Kapler 3.00
D26 Mike Lowell 6.00
D27 Jason Werth 2.00
D28 Matt White 2.00
D29 Pablo Ozuna 2.00
D30 Mike Stoner 2.00

Great Futures

Minor league players deemed to have especially "Great Futures" are featured in this insert set. Fronts have action photos on gold refractive-foil backgrounds. Backs repeat a detail of the front photo and offer a few career highlights and stats. Cards are numbered with a "GF" prefix. Stated rate of insertion was one per five packs.

MT
Complete Set (30): 45.00
Common Player: 1.50
GF1 Ryan Anderson 2.00
GF2 Rick Ankiel 1.50
GF3 Lance Berkman 2.50
GF4 Russell Branyan 1.50
GF5 Dermal Brown 1.50
GF6 Brent Butler 1.50
GF7 Eric Chavez 3.00
GF8 Bruce Chen 1.50
GF9 Matt Clement 2.50
GF10 Eddie Yarnell 1.50
GF11 Mike Darr 1.50
GF12 Chris Enochs 1.50
GF13 J.D. Drew 6.00
GF14 Chad Hermansen 1.50
GF15 Ramon Hernandez 1.50
GF16 Cesar King 1.50
GF17 Mike Kinkade 2.00
GF18 Carlos Lee 2.50
GF19 George Lombard 1.50
GF20 Ruben Mateo 1.50
GF21 Gary Matthews Jr. 1.50
GF22 Jackson Melian 1.50
GF23 Ryan Minor 1.50
GF24 Warren Morris 1.50
GF25 John Patterson 1.50
GF26 Ben Petrick 1.50
GF27 Jason Werth 1.50
GF28 Matt White 1.50
GF29 Francisco Cordero 1.50
GF30 Mike Stoner 1.50

1999 Starting Lineup Classic Doubles

"From the Minors to the Majors" was the theme chosen by Hasbro for its '99 Classic Doubles series. Each colorful 10" x 12" blister pack contains a pair of baseball cards and a pair of plastic action figures. One card/figure pair depicts the player in the uniform of one of his minor league teams. The other pair depicts him as a major leaguer. Values shown are for complete, unopened packages.

MT
Complete Set (10): 75.00
Common Player: 7.00
(1) Sandy Alomar Jr. 7.00
(2) Darin Erstad 7.00
(3) Nomar Garciaparra 8.00
(4) Ken Griffey Jr. 11.00
(5) Derek Jeter 12.00
(6) Javy Lopez 7.00
(7) Greg Maddux 8.00
(8) Mark McGwire 11.00
(9) Raul Mondesi 7.00
(10) Alex Rodriguez 9.00

1999 Team Best Baseball America's Diamond Best Edition

The use on front of a gold- or silver-foil (each card can be found both ways) Team Best logo surmounted by a quartet of diamonds is all that differentiates the base cards in this issue from TB's earlier Baseball America Top Prospects issue. Diamond Best cards were issued six cards per pack, six packs per box along with a Team Best/Salvino Rookie Bammer stuffed bear representing one of five top minor league stars. Each bear is accompanied by a special "Card of Authenticity" serially numbered within an edition of 10,000 each.

MT
Complete Set (100): 5.00
Common Player: .05
Wax Box (6+Bear):Wax Box (6+Bear): .00
1 Paul Ah Yat .05
2 Efrain Alamo .05
3 Chip Alley .05
4 Ryan Anderson .25
5 Rick Ankiel .10
6 Tony Armas Jr. .10
7 Bronson Arroyo .05
8 Mike Bacsik .05
9 Kevin Barker .05
10 Fletcher Bates .05
11 Rob Bell .05
12 Ron Belliard .10
13 Peter Bergeron .10
14 Lance Berkman .25
15 Nick Bierbrodt .05
16 Milton Bradley .25
17 Russell Branyan .10
18 Pat Burrell 2.00
19 Sean Burroughs .50
20 Brent Butler .05
21 Bruce Chen .05
22 Chin-Feng Chen .50
23 Giuseppe Chiaramonte .05
24 Jin Ho Cho .10
25 Francis Collins .05
26 Joe Crede .50
27 Cesar Crespo .05
28 Bubba Crosby .05
29 Michael Cuddyer .15
30 Ben Davis .05
31 Tim DeCinces .05
32 Tomas de la Rosa .05
33 Octavio Dotel .05
34 Kelly Dransfeldt .05
35 Tim Drew .05
36 Matt Drews .05
37 Mike Drumright .05
38 Todd Dunn .05
39 Chad Durham .05
40 Alex Eckelman .05
41 Chris Enochs .05
42 Cordell Farley .05
43 Frankie Figueroa .05
44 Joe Fontenot .05
45 Eric Gillespie .05
46 Mike Glavine .05
47 Jason Grote .05
48 Jerry Hairston Jr. .10
49 Toby Hall .05
50 Chad Harville .05
51 Alex Hernandez .05
52 Junior Herndon .05
53 Mike Huelsmann .05
54 Aubrey Huff .10
55 Chad Hutchinson .05
56 Jamie Jones .05
57 Kenny Kelly .05
58 Scott Krause .05

59 Jason LaRue .05
60 Carlos Lee .25
61 Corey Lee .05
62 Willie Martinez .05
63 Ruben Mateo .10
64 Darnell McDonald .05
65 Cody McKay .05
66 Dan McKinley .05
67 Jackson Melian .05
68 Jason Middlebrook .05
69 Ryan Minor .05
70 Mark Mulder .50
71 Vladimir Nunez .05
72 Pablo Ozuna .05
73 Corey Patterson .50
74 John Patterson .05
75 Josh Paul .05
76 Angel Pena .05
77 Carlos Pena .05
78 Juan Pena .05
79 Brad Penny .10
80 Kyle Peterson .05
81 Ben Petrick .05
82 Calvin Pickering .05
83 Arquimedez Pozo .05
84 Paul Rigdon .05
85 Grant Roberts .05
86 Nate Rolison .05
87 Damian Rolls .05
88 Ryan Rupe .05
89 Jose Santos .05
90 Todd Sears .05
91 Fernando Seguignol .05
92 Brett Taft .05
93 Chris Truby .05
94 Jayson Werth .05
95 Matt White .05
96 Todd Williams .05
97 Cliff Wilson .05
98 Randy Wolf .10
99 Kelly Wunsch .05
100 Mike Zwicka .05

1999 Team Best BA's Diamond Best Inserts

Player action photos and team logos on a white background are the front design for this insert set. Backs have a small copy of the front photo, a few biographical notes and career highlights. Cards are found on an average of one per 30 packs of Team Best Baseball America's Diamond Best Edition.

MT
Complete Set (10): 20.00
Common Player: 2.00
1 Ryan Anderson 3.00
2 Pat Burrell 9.00
3 Bruce Chen 2.00
4 Mike Darr 2.00
5 Octavio Dotel 2.00
6 Jason LaRue 2.00
7 Damon Minor 2.00
8 Kyle Peterson 2.00
9 Fernando Seguignol 2.00
10 Alfonso Soriano 12.00

1999 Team Best Baseball America's Top Prospects

The editors of "Baseball America" selected 100 top prospects for inclusion in this Team Best minor league issue which debuted in June. Cards have action photos on front which are bordered at top and right in red. BA's logotype appears at top. The player's minor league team logo is at bottom-right. Backs have biographical data, draft details and career highlights along with appropriate logos. Cards were sold in six-card foil packs.

MT
Complete Set (100): 5.00
Common Player: .05
Wax Box (18): 15.00
1 Paul Ah Yat .05
2 Efrain Alamo .05
3 Chip Alley .05
4 Ryan Anderson .15
5 Rick Ankiel .10
6 Tony Armas Jr. .10
7 Bronson Arroyo .05
8 Mike Bacsik .05
9 Kevin Barker .05
10 Fletcher Bates .05
11 Rob Bell .05
12 Ron Belliard .10
13 Peter Bergeron .10
14 Lance Berkman .25
15 Nick Bierbrodt .05
16 Milton Bradley .25
17 Russell Branyan .05
18 Pat Burrell 1.00
19 Sean Burroughs .50
20 Brent Butler .05
21 Bruce Chen .05
22 Chin-Feng Chen .50
23 Giuseppe Chiaramonte .05
24 Jin Ho Cho .10
25 Francis Collins .05
26 Joe Crede .50
27 Cesar Crespo .05
28 Bubba Crosby .05
29 Michael Cuddyer .10
30 Ben Davis .05
31 Tim DeCinces .05
32 Tomas de la Rosa .05
33 Octavio Dotel .05
34 Kelly Dransfeldt .05
35 Tim Drew .05
36 Matt Drews .05
37 Mike Drumright .05
38 Todd Dunn .05
39 Chad Durham .05
40 Alex Eckelman .05
41 Chris Enochs .05
42 Cordell Farley .05
43 Frankie Figueroa .05
44 Joe Fontenot .05
45 Eric Gillespie .05
46 Mike Glavine .05
47 Jason Grote .05
48 Jerry Hairston Jr. .10
49 Toby Hall .05
50 Chad Harville .05
51 Alex Hernandez .05
52 Junior Herndon .05
53 Mike Huelsmann .05
54 Aubrey Huff .10
55 Chad Hutchinson .05
56 Jamie Jones .05
57 Kenny Kelly .05
58 Scott Krause .05
59 Jason LaRue .05
60 Carlos Lee .25
61 Corey Lee .05
62 Willie Martinez .05
63 Ruben Mateo .05
64 Darnell McDonald .05
65 Cody McKay .05
66 Dan McKinley .05
67 Jackson Melian .05
68 Jason Middlebrook .05
69 Ryan Minor .05
70 Mark Mulder .45
71 Vladimir Nunez .05
72 Pablo Ozuna .05
73 Corey Patterson .50
74 John Patterson .05
75 Josh Paul .05
76 Angel Pena .05
77 Carlos Pena .10
78 Juan Pena .05
79 Brad Penny .05
80 Kyle Peterson .05
81 Ben Petrick .05
82 Calvin Pickering .05
83 Arquimedez Pozo .05
84 Paul Rigdon .05
85 Grant Roberts .05
86 Nate Rolison .05
87 Damian Rolls .05
88 Ryan Rupe .05
89 Jose Santos .05
90 Todd Sears .05
91 Fernando Seguignol .05
92 Brett Taft .05
93 Chris Truby .05
94 Jayson Werth .05
95 Matt White .05
96 Todd Williams .05
97 Cliff Wilson .05
98 Randy Wolf .05
99 Kelly Wunsch .05
100 Mike Zwicka .05
.00
--- Promo Set/ Auto. Card Offer
--- Promo Set/1996-1997 Pack Offer
--- Promo Set Offer

Autographs

Sharing the format used in Team Best's earlier 1999 issue, the two-per-box autograph inserts in Baseball America's Top Prospects issue features virtually an entirely new line-up. Fronts have color photos with a diffused green background and the player's name in green. The Team Best logo is at top-left, the minor league team logo at bottom-left. Backs have an authentication statement overprinted on a baseball diamond photo. The autograph cards are not numbered and are listed here alphabetically. Insert signature cards of Mike Darr, Kevin McGlinchy and Tony Torcato which had been announced for this product were late in being returned to Team Best and were inserted into Player of the Year packs in the post-season.

MT
Complete Set (47): 60.00
Common Player: 1.00
(1) Rick Ankiel 2.50
(2) Michael Barrett 2.50
(3) Lance Berkman 3.00
(4) A.J. Burnett 4.00
(5) Steve Carver 1.00
(6) Bruce Chen 1.00
(7) Michael Cuddyer 3.00
(8) Mike Darr 4.00
(9) J.D. Drew 12.00
(10) Tim Drew 1.00
(11) Alex Escobar 2.00
(12) Seth Etherton 1.50
(13) Brian Falkenborg 1.00
(14) Robert Fick 1.00
(15) Mark Fischer 1.00
(16) Eddy Furniss 1.00
(17) Troy Glaus 15.00
(18) Nathan Haynes 1.00
(19) Chad Hermansen 2.00
(20) Shea Hillenbrand 6.00
(21) Mark Johnson 1.00
(22) Adam Kennedy 2.00
(23) Jason LaRue 1.50
(24) Matt LeCroy 1.50
(25) Carlos Lee 4.00
(26) Corey Lee 1.00
(27) Felipe Lopez 1.00
(28) Darnell McDonald 1.00
(29) Kevin McGlinchy 2.00
(30) Mark Mulder 4.00
(31) Trot Nixon 6.00
(32) Todd Noel 1.00
(33) Pablo Ozuna 1.00
(34) Brad Penny 1.50
(35) Calvin Pickering 1.00
(36) Matt Riley 1.00
(37) Jason Romano 1.00
(38) Ryan Rupe 1.00
(39) Randall Simon 1.00
(40) Jason Standridge 1.00
(41) Nathan Teut 1.00
(42) Tony Torcato 1.00
(43) Pete Tucci 1.00
(44) Eric Valent 1.00
(45) Vernon Wells 4.00
(46) Jake Westbrook 1.00
(47) Randy Wolf 2.00

Best Possibilities

Two players each are featured on these double-front cards. Inserted at the rate of about one per 18-pack box, the inserts feature action photos against a pastel swirling background.

MT
Complete Set (5): 5.00
Common Player: .75
1 Ryan Anderson, Calvin Pickering 1.00
2 Rick Ankiel, Chad Hermansen 1.00
3 Ryan Bradley, Ryan Minor .75
4 John Patterson, Lance Berkman 1.00
5 Brad Penny, Pat Burrell 2.00

League MVP

MVPs of various minor leagues are featured in this one-per-box insert set. Fronts have portrait photos on a blurred background. BA's logotype is in a blue stripe at top, player name and position are in an orange stripe at bottom. Team logos appear at lower-right. On back is a large Baseball America Top Prospects logo and a summary of the player's MVP season. The same cards were inserted into TB's Baseball America's Diamond Best edition at the rate of one per 19 packs.

MT
Complete Set (10): 15.00
Common Player: 2.00
1 Brian August 2.00
2 Joe Crede 4.00
3 Shawn Gallagher 2.00
4 Jay Gibbons 4.00
5 Marcus Giles 4.00
6 Jason Hart 2.00
7 Tyrone Horne 2.00
8 Pablo Ozuna 2.00
9 Brad Penny 2.50
10 Calvin Pickering 2.00

Scout's Choice

The "Scout's Choice" for major league stardom are presented in the scarcest (one per 90 packs) of the BA's Top Prospects insert sets. Cards have a simulated Polaroid photo of the player on a woodlook background with a paperclip and team logo at upper-right and a gold seal at lower-right. Backs repeat some of the front details and have a scouting report and previous season stats.

MT
Complete Set (10): 12.00
Common Player: 1.50
1 Rick Ankiel 1.50
2 Lance Berkman 2.00
3 Pat Burrell 5.00
4 Octavio Dotel 1.50
5 Alex Escobar 1.50
6 George Lombard 1.50
7 Ruben Mateo 1.50
8 Ryan Minor 1.50
9 Pablo Ozuna 1.50
10 Dernell Stenson 1.50

1999 Team Best Player of the Year

Team Best's post-season card set features top stars at all stops on road to the big leagues. The 50-card base set offers color action photos on which the background has been muted in shades of blue. Backs have season stats, a few biographical data, a career highlight or two and a color team logo. Player of the Year was sold in six-card foil packs.

MT
Complete Set (50): 5.00
Common Player: .05
Wax Box (18): 24.00
1 Ryan Anderson .10
2 Rick Ankiel .10
3 Jeff Austin .05
4 Kurt Bierek .05
5 Jung Bong .10
6 Dee Brown .05
7 Nate Bump .05
8 Pat Burrell 1.00
9 Sean Burroughs .35
10 Brent Butler .05
11 Chin-Feng Chen .50
12 Hee Seop Choi .50
13 Joe Crede .50
14 Jack Cust .20
15 Travis Dawkins .25
16 Trent Durrington .05
17 Seth Etherton .10
18 Vince Faison .05
19 Choo Freeman .10
20 Rafael Furcal .25
21 Jay Gibbons .15
22 Marcus Giles .25
23 J.M. Gold .05
24 Jeff Goldbach .05
25 Josh Hamilton .10
26 Kevin Haverbusch .05
27 D'Angelo Jiminez .05
28 Nick Johnson .75
29 Adam Kennedy .15
30 Steve Lomasney .05
31 George Lombard .05
32 Felipe Lopez .05
33 Jason Marquis .25
34 Tydus Meadows .05
35 Aaron Myette .05
36 Corey Patterson .40
37 Carlos Pena .10
38 Adam Piatt .15
39 Julio Ramirez .05
40 Matt Riley .05
41 Juan Rivera .15
42 Jason Romano .05
43 Aaron Rowand .05
44 C.C. Sabathia .25
45 Alfonso Soriano 2.00
46 Jason Standridge .05
47 Dernell Stenson .05
48 Jorge Toca .05
49 Eric Valent .05
50 Jayson Werth .05

Autographs

The authentically autographed cards which drive the sale of most minor league singles products were inserted about one per three packs of Player of the Year. Besides 19 autograph cards specifically designated for the POY issue, cards of Mike Darr, Kevin McGlinchy and Tony Torcato which were received too late for inclusion in TB's Baseball America's Top Prospects issue were also inserted. (They are cataloged with the BATP issue.) The POY autographs have player photos on a linen-look background with the name in purple and a graduated purple band vertically at left. Backs have a congratulatory message of authenticity from TB's chairman. The unnumbered cards are checklisted here alphabetically.

MT
Complete Set (19): 25.00
Common Player: 2.00
(1) Tony Armas Jr. 2.00
(2) Nick Bierbrodt 1.00
(3) Jamie Brown 1.00
(4) Jesus Colome 1.00
(5) Kelly Dransfeldt 1.00
(6) Adam Everett 2.00
(7) Vince Faison 1.00
(8) Junior Herndon 1.00
(9) Aubrey Huff 2.00
(10) Corey Lee 1.00
(11) Jason Marquis 2.00
(12) Willie Martinez 1.00
(13) Corey Patterson 6.00
(14) Carlos Pena 2.00
(15) Ben Petrick 2.00
(16) Paul Rigdon 1.00
(17) Grant Roberts 1.00
(18) C.C. Sabathia 6.00
(19) Jason Tyner 1.00

Contenders

The scarcest inserts in the set are these top candidates for Minor League Player of the Year honors. Fronts have action photos set on a silver foil-look background with a large POY logo. Backs have a smaller version of the front photo, personal data, season stats and the players credentials for the honor. Contenders were seeded on average of one per 90 packs.

MT
Complete Set (10): 35.00
Common Player: 2.00
1 Dee Brown 2.00
2 Pat Burrell 9.00
3 Chin-Feng Chen 3.00
4 Rafael Furcal 3.00
5 Nick Johnson 7.50
6 Ramon Ortiz 2.00
7 Aramis Ramirez 3.00
8 Matt Riley 2.00
9 Jason Standridge 2.00
10 Vernon Wells 5.00

1999 Team Best Rookie

Top prospects at all levels of the minor leagues going into the 1999 season are featured in the base set and insert series of Team Best Rookie. Regular cards have action photos set against a woven-look background with a large baseball, diamond diagram and "ROOKIE" banner. The issuer's logo is at upper-left, the player's minor league team logo from the previous season is at upper-right. Backs have a large team logo at center and 1998 stats. Each box of 18 foil packs included one individually sleeved gold (edition of 50) or silver (edition of 125) parallel of a base-set card.

MT
Complete Set (100): 5.00
Common Player: .05
Wax Box (18): 15.00
1 Chip Ambres .05
2 Scott Barrett .05
3 Todd Bellhorn .05
4 Darren Blakely .05
5 Matt Borne .05
6 Nate Bump .05
7 Ryan Bundy .05
8 Eric Byrnes .05
9 David Callahan .05
10 Rob Castelli .05
11 Doug Clark .05
12 Greg Clark .05
13 Darryl Conyer .05
14 Jeremy Cotten .05
15 Bubba Crosby .05
16 Mike Curry .05
17 Mike Dean .05
18 David Diaz .05
19 Jeremy Dodson .05
20 Ryan Drese .05
21 J.D. Drew 1.00
22 Morgan Ensberg .10
23 Adam Everett .10
24 Mike Fischer .05
25 Pete Fisher .05
26 Josh Fogg .05
27 Brad Freeman .05
28 Nate Frese .05
29 Eddy Furniss .05
30 Keith Ginter .05
31 Eric Good .05
32 Josh Hancock (Error, blue cap.) .25
32 Josh Hancock (Correct, red cap.) .25
33 Ryan Harber .05
34 Jason Hart .05
35 Jason Hill .05
36 Heath Honeycutt .05
37 Aubrey Huff .10
38 Chad Hutchinson .05
39 Brandon Inge .05
40 Brett Jodie .05
41 Gabe Johnson .05
42 Clint Johnston .05
43 Jesse Joyce .05
44 Randy Keisler .05
45 Jarrod Kingrey .05
46 Craig Kuzmic .05
47 Tim Lemon .05
48 Ryan Lentz .05
49 Neil Longo .05
50 Felipe Lopez .05
51 Javier Lopez .05
52 Phil Lowery .05
53 Chris Magruder .05
54 Mike Maroth .05
55 Kennon McArthur .05
56 Shawn McCorkle .05
57 Arturo McDowell .05
58 Josh McKinley .05
59 Jason Michaels .05
60 Ryan Moskau .05
61 Mark Mulder .65
62 Will Ohman .05
63 Todd Ozias .05
64 Matt Padgett .05
65 Corey Patterson .50
66 Adam Pettyjohn .05
67 Brad Piercy .05
68 Scott Pratt .05
69 Kris Rayborn .05
70 Chris Reinike .05
71 Billy Rich .05
72 Ryan Ridenour .05
73 Brian Rogers .05
74 Aaron Rowand .10
75 Ryan Rupe .05
76 C.C. Sabathia .50
77 Jason Saenz .05
78 Aaron Sams .05
79 Sammy Serrano .05
80 Clint Smith .05
81 Pat Burrell 1.00
82 Zach Sorensen .05
83 Steve Stemle .05
84 John Stewart .05
85 Tyler Thompson .05
86 Matt Thornton .05
87 Tony Torcato .05
88 Keola de la Tori .05
89 Andres Torres .05
90 Jason Tyner .05
91 Jeff Urban .05
92 Eric Valent .05
93 Derek Wathan .05
94 Jeff Weaver .05
95 Jake Weber .05
96 Ken Westmoreland .05
97 Brad Wilkerson .10
98 Clyde Williams .05
99 Jeff Winchester .05
100 Mitch Wylie .05

INSERTED OFFER CARDS
'95 First Round Picks Set .05
Baseball America Subscription .05
Promo Card Set .05
Promo Card Set Plus Packs and Autograph .05

Autographs

The best of the Best Rookie series is featured in this insert set. Cards have authentic autographs across the front and have an authenticity notice on back. Two dozen of the featured players were inserted at the average rate of two per box (about one per nine packs) while autographed cards of J.D. Drew were seeded at one per case (180 packs).

MT
Complete Set (25): 35.00
Common Player: 1.00
1 Rick Ankiel 2.00
2 Michael Barrett 3.00
3 Lance Berkman 3.00
4 A.J. Burnett 3.00
5 Bruce Chen 1.00
6 Michael Cuddyer 1.50
7 J.D. Drew 6.00
8 Alex Escobar 2.00
9 Seth Etherton 1.50
10 Mark Fischer 1.00
11 Troy Glaus 12.00
12 Nathan Haynes 1.00

13 Shea Hillenbrand 4.00
14 Matt LeCroy 1.00
15 Corey Lee 1.00
16 Trot Nixon 4.00
17 Todd Noel 1.00
18 Pablo Ozuna 1.00
19 Brad Penny 1.50
20 Calvin Pickering 1.00
21 Matt Riley 1.00
22 Jason Romano 1.00
23 Pete Tucci 1.00
24 Eric Valent 1.00
25 Jake Westbrook 1.00

Best Guns

Inserted at an announced rate of about one per box, this chase set features the hardest-throwing prospects in the minor leagues. Fronts have photos showing the awesome arms in action. A baseball trailing flames appears at lower-left, the player's minor league team logo at upper-right. Backs repeat part of the front photo within the flaming fastball motif and offer previous season's stats and a few words about the pitcher.

		MT
Complete Set (10):		7.50
Common Player:		1.00
1	Ryan Anderson	1.50
2	Rick Ankiel	1.00
3	Ryan Bradley	1.00
4	Bruce Chen	1.00
5	Matt Clement	2.00
6	Octavio Dotel	1.00
7	John Patterson	1.00
8	Matt Riley	1.00
9	Brent Stentz	1.00
10	Ed Yarnall	1.00

Best Lumber

Projected heavy hitters on their way to the major leagues are featured in this hobby-only chase set. The players' power swings are shown on front photos superimposed over a bat knob and overprinted with a "best LUMBER" logo in the style of a bat's label. Average rate of insertion was announced as one per 90 packs. Backs repeat the front motif and part of the front photo, adding some biographical and career details, along with 1998 stats.

		MT
Complete Set (10):		45.00
Common Player:		2.00
1	Michael Barrett	4.00
2	Lance Berkman	4.00
3	J.D. Drew	10.00
4	Marcus Giles	6.00
5	Troy Glaus	15.00
6	George Lombard	2.00
7	Doug Mientkiewicz	6.00
8	Trot Nixon	4.00
9	Calvin Pickering	2.00
10	Pete Tucci	2.00

Future Stars

With two players per card, the odds are doubled that one will be a major league superstar of the future. Fronts have a pair of portrait photos. Backs have a large Team Best Rookie logo and a serial number from within an edition of 900 per card. Stated odds of finding a Future Stars card are one per box.

		MT
Complete Set (25):		35.00
Common Player:		1.00
1	Darryl Conyer, Javier Lopez	1.00
2	Troy Cameron, Luis Rivera	1.00
3	Troy Glaus, Darren Blakely	5.00
4	Jayson Werth, Darnell McDonald	1.00
5	Adam Everett, Mike Maroth	1.00
6	Aaron Rowand, Josh Fogg	1.00
7	Corey Patterson, Aaron Sams	3.00
8	C.C. Sabathia, Zach Sorensen	2.00
9	Jeff Weaver, Brandon Inge	1.50
10	Chip Ambres, Derek Wathan	1.00
11	Bubba Crosby, Ryan Moskau	1.00
12	Josh McKinley, Brad Wilkerson	1.00
13	Randy Keisler, Ryan Bradley	1.00
14	Jason Tyner, Jason Saenz	1.00
15	Mark Mulder, Jason Hart	3.00
16	Eric Valent, Jason Michaels	1.00
17	Clint Johnston, Eddy Furniss	1.00
18	Pablo Ozuna, J.D. Drew	4.00
19	Rick Ankiel, Chad Hutchinson	1.50
20	J.D. Drew, Tim Drew	4.00
21	Darnell McDonald, Donzell McDonald	1.00
22	Tony Torcato, Nate Bump	1.00
23	Matt Thornton, Ryan Anderson	1.50
24	Felipe Lopez, Vernon Wells	1.50
25	Ryan Bundy, Jarrod Kingrey	1.00

League Leaders

Projected league leaders on their way to the major leagues are featured in this retail-only chase set which is virtually identical to the Best Lumber hobby insert. The players' power swings are shown on front photos superimposed on a plain blue background with a "League Leaders" logo in the style of a bat's label. Backs repeat the front motif and part of the front photo, adding some biographical and career details, along with 1998 stats.

		MT
Complete Set (10):		45.00
Common Player:		2.00
1	Michael Barrett	4.00
2	Lance Berkman	4.00
3	J.D. Drew	7.50
4	Marcus Giles	6.00
5	Troy Glaus	15.00
6	George Lombard	2.00
7	Doug Mientkiewicz	6.00
8	Trot Nixon	6.00
9	Calvin Pickering	2.00
10	Pete Tucci	2.00

1999 Team Best Salvino Rookie Bammers Card/ Authenticity

Each of the "Rookie Bammer" stuffed bears issued with the Baseball America's Diamond Best Edition card set was accompanied by a "Card of Authenticity." Fronts have action photos with three stars in the background and a minor league team logo at lower-right. Backs repeat the front photo in a ghosted image and have a notice of authenticity from Team Best CEO Don White. Each card is serially numbered from within an edition of 10,000 each. Sample versions of each card were also produced, marked with a strip on back, "Promotional Purposes Only" and numbered "10000/10000." they are valued at $1-2 apiece.

		MT
Complete Set (6):		15.00
Common Player:		2.50
(1)	Ryan Anderson	2.50
(2)	Rick Ankiel	2.50
(3)	Lance Berkman	3.00
(4)	Pat Burrell	5.00
(5)	J.D. Drew (Arkansas Travelers)	4.00
(6)	J.D. Drew (Memphis Redbirds)	4.00

1999 Minor League Team Sets

Manufacturers abbreviations used include: BL - Blueline Communications; GS - Grandstand; MA - Multi-Ad Services; TM - team issued; CH - Choice Marketing.

		MT
200 Team Sets and Variations		8.50
1999	WT Adirondack Lumberjacks (26)	4.00
1999	MA Akron Aeros (30)	6.00
1999	WT Albany-Colonie Diamond Dogs (26)	4.00
1999	GS Albuquerque Dukes (30)	12.00
1999	GS Albuquerque Dukes Sponsor's Set (31)	6.00
1999	GS Altoona Curve (31)	8.00
1999	MA Appalachian League Top Prospects (30)	12.00
1999	Arizona Fall League (30)	15.00
1999	MA Arkansas Travelers (30)	16.00
1999	MA Asheville Tourists (30)	12.00
1999	GS Asheville Tourists Update (10)	12.00
1999	GS Auburn Doubledays (33)	7.00
1999	MA Augusta Greenjackets (30)	7.00
1999	TM Bakersfield Blaze (30)	8.00
1999	TM Batavia Muckdogs (41)	17.50
1999	MA Beloit Snappers (29)	7.00
1999	GS Billings Mustangs (32)	11.00
1999	BL Binghamton Mets (30)	8.00
1999	TM Binghamton Mets "Jumbo" (12)	20.00
1999	GS Birmingham Barons (30)	8.00
1999	GS Bluefield Orioles (32)	7.00
1999	GS Boise Hawks (34)	7.00
1999	MA Bowie Baysox (30)	7.00
1999	MA Brevard County Manatees (30)	7.00
1999	GS Bristol Sox (30)	7.00
1999	GS Bristol Sox Update (6)	4.00
1999	BL Buffalo Bisons (30)	7.00
1999	MA Burlington Bees (33)	7.00
1999	GS Burlington Indians (32)	8.00
1999	GS Butte Copper Kings (33)	8.00
1999	TM Cape Fear Crocs (30)	9.00
1999	MA Capital City Bombers (30)	8.00
1999	MA Capital City '98 SAL Champs (31)	20.00
1999	CH Carolina League Prospects (30)	10.00
1999	TM Carolina Mudcats (31)	9.00
1999	MA Cedar Rapids Kernels (34)	5.00
1999	MA Charleston Alley Cats (30)	7.00
1999	TM Charleston River Dogs (32)	8.00
1999	BL Charlotte Knights (30)	7.00
1999	GS Chattanooga Lookouts (30)	7.00
1999	GS Chico Heat (27)	4.00
1999	GS Chillicothe Paints (26)	4.00
1999	MA Clearwater Phillies (30)	8.00
1999	GS Clinton Lumber Kings (32)	7.00
1999	TM Colorado Springs Sky Sox (30)	8.00
1999	BL Columbus Clippers (31)	8.00
1999	MA Columbus RedStixx (30)	8.00
1999	TM Columbus RedStixx (30)	45.00
1999	GS Danville Braves (30)	25.00
1999	Roox Daytona Cubs (30)	10.00
1999	MA Delmarva Shorebirds (29)	9.00
1999	MA Dunedin Blue Jays (30)	6.00
1999	BL Durham Bulls (30)	7.00
1999	TM Edmonton Trappers (25)	10.00
1999	TM Edmonton Trappers W/QCP Logos (25)	15.00
1999	TM Elizabethtown Twins (32)	12.00
1999	GS El Paso Diablos (30)	5.00
1999	MA Erie Seawolves (28)	7.00
1999	GS Eugene Emeralds (30)	6.00
1999	GS Everett Aqua Sox (31)	6.00
1999	TM Fargo-Moorhead RedHawks (29)	4.00
1999	GS Frederick Keys (28)	5.00
1999	GS Fresno Grizzlies (30)	8.00
1999	TM Ft. Myers Miracle (31)	7.00
1999	MA Ft. Wayne Wizards (30)	10.00
1999	MA Great Falls Dodgers (30)	7.00
1999	MA Greensboro Bats (30)	7.00
1999	GS Greenville Braves (28)	7.00
1999	MA Hagerstown Suns (30)	7.00
1999	MA Harrisburg Senators (30)	9.00
1999	MA Helena Brewers (30)	8.00
1999	MA Hickory Crawdads (30)	6.50
1999	MA Hickory Crawdads Update (30)	6.50
1999	GS High Desert Mavericks (27)	7.00
1999	GS H.D. Mavericks Sponsor's Set (27)	9.00
1999	GS Hudson Valley Renegades (32)	11.00
1999	GS Hudson Valley Renegades Update (1)	6.00
1999	GS H.V. Renegades Update, Auto.	20.00
1999	TM Huntsville Stars (30)	10.00
1999	BL Indianapolis Indians (31)	8.00
1999	International League Top Prospects (30)	10.00
1999	MA Iowa Cubs (30)	7.00
1999	MA Jackson Generals (30)	7.00
1999	GS Jacksonville Suns (28)	7.00
1999	GS Jacksonville Suns Update (5)	15.00
1999	TM Johnson City Cardinals (36)	6.50
1999	TM Kane County Cougars (31)	8.00
1999	CH Kinston Indians (30)	8.00
1999	MA Kissimmee Cobras (30)	15.00
1999	GS Knoxville Smokies (27)	7.00
1999	GS Lake Elsinore Land Sharks (33)	9.00
1999	GS Lake Elsinore Storm (30)	7.00
1999	MA Lakeland Tigers (30)	6.00
1999	GS Lancaster JetHawks (30)	6.00
1999	GS Lancaster JetHawks (Valley Press)(30)	9.00
1999	GS Lancaster Stealth (34)	9.00
1999	GS Lansing Lugnuts (29)	10.00
1999	MA Las Vegas Stars (30)	8.00
1999	BL Louisville River Bats (34)	10.00
1999	MA Lowell Spinners (32)	8.00
1999	CH Lynchburg Hillcats (30)	8.00
1999	MA Macon Braves (30)	10.00
1999	MA Mahoning Valley Scrappers (30)	12.50
1999	GS Martinsville Astros (30)	8.00
1999	TM Memphis Redbirds (30)	12.00
1999	MA Michigan Battle Cats (30)	12.00
1999	GS Midland Rockhounds (30)	10.00
1999	TM Midland Rockhounds (25)	55.00
1999	MA Midwest League Prospects (29)	12.00
1999	GS Missoula Osprey (31)	15.00
1999	TM Mobile Baybears (32)	10.00
1999	GS Modesto A's (30)	6.00
1999	GS Modesto Sponsor's Set - Krier's (30)	9.00
1999	MA Myrtle Beach Pelicans (30)	9.00
1999	TM Nashville Sounds (30)	8.00
1999	MA New Britain Rock Cats (29)	8.00
1999	BL New Haven Ravens (30)	9.00
1999	MA New Jersey Cardinals (32)	8.00
1999	TM N.J. Cardinals Top Prospects (6)	9.00
1999	WT New Jersey Jackals (27)	7.00
1999	MA New Orleans Zephyrs (28)	11.00
1999	BL Norfolk Tides (36)	9.00
1999	BL Norwich Navigators (30)	11.00
1999	TM Ogden Raptors (37)	15.00
1999	MA Oklahoma Redhawks (30)	7.00
1999	MA Omaha Golden Spikes (30)	8.00
1999	MA Orlando Rays (30)	8.00
1999	BL Pawtucket Red Sox (30)	9.00
1999	DD Pawtucket Red Sox Foldout	30.00
1999	MA Peoria Chiefs (30)	7.00
1999	MA Piedmont Boll Weevils (30)	8.00
1999	MA Pittsfield Mets (30)	7.00
1999	GS Portland Sea Dogs (30)	9.00
1999	CH Potomac Cannons (30)	7.00
1999	CH Potomac Cannons Update (7)	6.50
1999	GS Princeton Devil Rays (30)	25.00
1999	GS Princeton Devil Rays Update (30)	5.00
1999	GS Pulaski Rangers (30)	6.00
1999	TM Quad City River Bandits (31)	8.00
1999	GS Rancho Cucamonga Surfers (31)	8.00
1999	GS Rancho Cucamonga Quakes (30)	8.00
1999	GS Rancho Cucamonga Quakes Update (1)	12.00
1999	MA Reading Phillies (28)	9.00
1999	MA Reading Phils Alvernia College (28)	35.00
1999	MA Reading Phillies Update (30)	15.00
1999	MA Reading Phillies Stadium Cards (3)	24.00
1999	BL Richmond Braves (30)	8.00
1999	Richmond Camera Richmond Braves (20)	40.00
1999	GS Rio Grand Valley WhiteWings (25)	4.00
1999	BL Rochester Red Wings (30)	7.00
1999	TM Rockford Reds (28)	10.00
1999	CH Salem Avalanche (30)	7.00
1999	GS Salem-Keizer Volcanoes (36)	7.00
1999	GS San Antonio Missions (31)	10.00
1999	GS San Bernardino Stampede (31)	6.00
1999	BL San Jose Giants (30)	8.00
1999	TM Sarasota Red Sox (29)	8.00
1999	MA Savannah Sand Gnats (29)	8.00
1999	BL Scranton/Wilkes-Barre Red Barons (32)	8.00
1999	MA Shreveport Captains (28)	8.00
1999	GS Sioux City X's (30)	4.00
1999	TM Sonoma County Crushers (24)	4.00
1999	MA South Atlantic League Prospects (30)	15.00
1999	MA South Bend Silver Hawks (31)	7.00
1999	GS Southern League Top Prospects (31)	9.00
1999	GS Southern Oregon Timberjacks (29)	8.00
1999	Wonder Bread So. Oregon Timberjacks (10)	20.00
1999	GS So. Oregon Timberjacks Update (8)	5.00
1999	GS Spokane Indians (35)	9.00
1999	MA Staten Island Yankees (33)	10.00
1999	GS Stockton Ports (30)	7.00
1999	MA St. Catherines Stompers	8.00
1999	GS St. Lucie Mets (31)	9.00
1999	TM St. Paul Saints (32)	5.00
1999	MA St. Petersburg Devil Rays (29)	10.00
1999	BL Syracuse SkyChiefs (28)	8.00
1999	BL Tacoma Rainiers (30).	8.00
1999	MA Tampa Yankees (28)	15.00
1999	MA Tampa Yankees Update (30)	17.50
1999	GS Texas League Top Prospects (32)	12.00
1999	BL Toledo Mud Hens (32)	8.00
1999	MA Trenton Thunder (30)	10.00
1999	MA Tucson Sidewinders (29)	7.00
1999	TM Tulsa Drillers (30)	9.00
1999	GS Vancouver Canadians (30)	24.00
1999	GS Vermont Expos (35)	8.00
1999	MA Vero Beach Dodgers (30)	8.00
1999	GS Visalia Oaks (27)	10.00
1999	WT Waterbury Spirit (25)	4.00
1999	MA West Michigan Whitecaps (30)	7.00
1999	MA West Michigan Whitecaps Update (12)	12.00
1999	MA W. Mich. Whitecaps '94-'98 Stars (30)	8.00
1999	GS West Tennessee Diamond Jaxx (30)	8.00
1999	CH Wichita Wranglers (30)	8.00
1999	CH Wichita Wranglers/ Sedgwick Zoo (30)	12.00
1999	MA Williamsport Crosscutters (34)	8.00
1999	CH Wilmington Blue Rocks (30)	9.00
1999	CH Winston-Salem Warthogs (30)	9.00
1999	MA Wisconsin Timber Rattlers (35)	8.00
1999	GS Yakima Bears (31)	9.00

2000 High School All-Americans

(Production reported as 10,000 regular sets, 1,000 foil sets; 1,000 autographed Espinosa and Stokes cards randomly inserted.)

		MT
Complete Set (10):		12.50
Complete Set, Foil (10):		40.00
Autographed Stokes:		25.00
Autographed Espinosa:		10.00
1	Jason Stokes	.00
2	Laynce Nix	.00
3	Rocco Baldelli	.00
4	Justin Hileman	.00
5	Jason Kaanoi	.00
6	Derek Thompson	.00
7	David Espinosa	.00
8	Dustin McGowan	.00
9	Rocco Baldelli (Player/Year)	.00
10	Checklist	.00

2000 Just Imagine 2k

The use of third-party certified autograph cards on a two-per-box basis, along with randomly inserted game-used equipment cards was featured in this mid-season minor league foil-pack product. Cards in the six-card foil packs are numbered contiguously from the company's Just the Preview 2k product, from #101-199. Fronts of the base cards have white-bordered photos with a large color band horizontally at center, which carries the product logo, player name, position abbreviation and team. On back is the same photo with a white band at center carrying vital data and 1999 stats. A large color block at bottom has a small team logo and copyright notice. A gold-bordered factory set version was issued in an edition of 5,000.

		MT
Complete Set (100):		5.00
Common Player:		.05
Gold:		1X
Wax Box (24+2):		20.00
101	Rick Ankiel	.10
102	Ricardo Aramboles	.05
103	Rick Asadoorian	.05
104	Jeff Austin	.05
105	Danys Baez	.05
106	Brad Baisley	.05
107	Matt Belisle	.05
108	Lance Berkman	.25
109	Wilson Betemit	.10
110	Nick Bierbrodt	.05
111	Casey Blake	.05
112	Josh Bonifay	.05

113	Bobby Bradley	.05
114	Milton Bradley	.25
115	Junior Brignac	.05
116	Roosevelt Brown	.05
117	Pat Burrell	.50
118	Sean Burroughs	.50
119	Ben Christiansen	.35
120	Ryan Christenson	.05
121	Michael Coleman	.05
122	Jesus Colome	.05
123	Jesus Cordero	.05
124	Nate Cornejo	.05
125	Robbie Crabtree	.05
126	Jack Cust	.05
127	Casey Daigle	.05
128	Ben Davis	.05
129	Travis Dawkins	.25
130	Choo Freeman	.10
131	Chris George	.05
132	Gary Glover	.05
133	Jerry Hairston Jr.	.10
134	Ken Harvey	.05
135	Jeff Heaverlo	.05
136	Elvin Hernandez	.05
137	J.R. House	.05
138	Ty Howington	.05
139	Aubrey Huff	.10
140	Norm Hutchins	.05
141	Chad Hutchinson	.05
142	Brandon Inge	.05
143	Jason Jennings	.05
144	Ben Johnson	.05
145	Jaime Jones	.05
146	Jason Jones	.05
147	Ryan Kibler	.05
148	Bobby Kielty	.15
149	Hong-Chih Kuo	.05
150	John Lackey	.10
151	Gerald Laird	.05
152	Allen Levrault	.10
153	Steve Lomasney	.20
154	George Lombard	.05
155	Felipe Lopez	.05
156	Pat Manning	.05
157	Luis Matos	.05
158	Matt McClendon	.05
159	Brian McNichol	.05
160	Chris Mears	.05
161	Jackson Melian	.05
162	Ryan Minor	.05
163	Chad Moeller	.10
164	Scott Morgan	.05
165	Tony Mota	.05
166	Eric Munson	.10
167	Greg Myers	.05
168	Miguel Olivo	.05
169	Ramon Ortiz	.05
170	Jarrod Patterson	.05
171	Alex Pena	.05
172	Wily Mo Pena	.20
173	Ben Petrick	.05
174	Paul Phillips	.05
175	Calvin Pickering	.05
176	Guillermo Quiroz	.05
177	Tim Raines Jr.	.05
178	Aramis Ramirez	.25
179	Julio Ramirez	.05
180	Matt Riley	.05
181	David Riske	.05
182	Juan Rivera	.05
183	Luis Rivera	.05
184	J.P. Roberge	.05
185	Grant Roberts	.05
186	C.C. Sabathia	.25
187	Brian Sanches	.05
188	Bobby Seay	.05
189	Wascar Serrano	.05
190	Juan Silvestre	.05
191	Chris Snelling	.05
192	Kyle Snyder	.05
193	Alfonso Soriano	1.00
194	Jason Standridge	.05
195	Andy Thompson	.05
196	Luis Torres	.05
197	Roberto Vaz	.05
198	Rico Washington	.05
199	Peanut Williams	.05
200	Kevin Witt	.05

Auto. - Base

All autographed cards in Just Imagine 2k were inserted as boxtoppers at the rate of two per box. By arrangement with USA certification service, all autographed cards were graded and slabbed. Values shown are for cards graded 8 or 9.

		MT
	Common Player:	2.00
BA-01	Brent Abernathy	3.00
	Tony Armas Jr.	4.00
BA-02	Roosevelt Brown	3.00
BA-05	Joe Crede	6.00
BA-08	Alex Escobar	3.00
BA-09	Rafael Furcal	6.00
BA-12	Aubrey Huff	2.00
BA-15	Josh Kalinowski	2.00
	Jackson Melian	2.00
BA-17	Mike Meyers	2.00
BA-18	Talmadge Nunnari	2.00
BA-19	Jose Ortiz	2.00
	Pablo Ozuna	2.00
BA-23	Julio Ramirez	2.00
BA-26	Ruben Salazar	2.00
	Jovanny Sosa	2.00
	Jorge Luis Toca	2.00
BA-27	T.J. Tucker	2.00
BA-30	Kevin Witt	2.00
	Barry Zito	15.00

Auto. - Die-Cut

All autographed cards in Just Imagine 2k were inserted as boxtoppers at the rate of two per box. By arrangement with USA certification service, all autographed cards were graded and slabbed. Values shown are for cards graded 8 or 9. Die-cut autographs are serially numbered to 200 each.

		MT
	Common Player:	4.00
	Tony Armas Jr.	6.00
DC-01	Roosevelt Brown	4.00
DC-08	Rafael Furcal	5.00
DC-10	Nick Johnson	6.00
DC-11	Steve Lomasney	4.00
DC-12	Mike Meyers	4.00
DC-13	Talmadge Nunnari	4.00
DC-15	Pablo Ozuna	4.00
DC-17	Julio Ramirez	4.00
DC-19	Ruben Salazar	4.00

Auto. - Gold

All autographed cards in Just Imagine 2k were inserted as boxtoppers at the rate of two per box. By arrangement with USA certification service, all autographed cards were graded and slabbed. Values shown are for cards graded 8 or 9. Gold autographs are serially numbered 1 of 1.

	MT
Common Player:	50.00
Brent Abernathy	50.00
Joe Crede	50.00
Alex Escobar	5.00
Rafael Furcal	50.00
Aubrey Huff	50.00
Nick Johnson	50.00
Steve Lomasney	50.00
Mike Meyers	50.00
Talmadge Nunnari	50.00
Jose Ortiz	50.00
Pablo Ozuna	50.00
Julio Ramirez	50.00
T.J. Tucker	50.00
Kevin Witt	50.00

Auto. - Justinkt

All autographed cards in Just Imagine 2k were inserted as boxtoppers at the rate of two per box. By arrangement with USA certification service, all autographed cards were graded and slabbed. Values shown are for cards graded 8 or 9. Justinkt autographs are serially numbered to 100 each.

		MT
	Common Player:	4.00
JK.01	Tony Armas Jr.	6.00
JK.02	Jeff Austin	4.00
JK.08	Rafael Furcal	4.00
JK.09	Jon Garland	6.00
JK.10	Aubrey Huff	4.00
JK.11	Nick Johnson	7.50
JK.12	Steve Lomasney	4.00
JK.14	Talmadge Nunnari	4.00
JK.15	Pablo Ozuna	4.00
JK.18	Julio Ramirez	4.00

Just Debuts

These cards, which are made to resemble game tickets, herald the professional debuts of 10 minor leaguers who may one day find fame in the big leagues. Card numbers, at lower-left on front, have a JD prefix. Backs repeat the front photo and have a career highlight or two along with the player's debut day stats. Insertion rate is 1:24 packs.

		MT
	Complete Set (10):	10.00
	Common Player:	1.50
11	Casey Burns	1.50
12	Donovan Graves	1.50
13	Ty Howington	1.50
14	Ben Johnson	1.50
15	Bobby Kielty	2.00
16	Hong-Chih Kuo	1.50
17	Sean McGowan	1.50
18	Mark Mulder	4.00
19	Eric Munson	1.50
20	Chin-Hui Tsao	1.50

Just Dominant

Seeded one per 24 packs, on average, this insert series offers some of the top names in minor league baseball from the previous season. Fronts have a monochromatic action shot with the same photo repeated on back in color. Card numbers in the upper-left corner on front are prefixed with "JI0.JD."

		MT
	Complete Set (10):	15.00
	Common Player:	1.50
1	Rick Ankiel	1.50
2	Lance Berkman	2.50
3	Ben Broussard	1.50
4	Pat Burrell	4.00
5	Chin-Feng Chen	2.00
6	Carl Crawford	2.50
7	Josh Hamilton	1.50
8	Eric Munson	1.50
9	Corey Patterson	3.00
10	Vernon Wells	2.50

Just Gamers

Game-used equipment cards in a variety of die-cut/autograph combinations were seeded one per 275 packs.

	MT
Rick Ankiel (Base jersey.)	6.00
Rick Ankiel (Base jersey, autographed.) (24)	20.00
Rick Ankiel (Die-cut jersey.) (100)	9.00
Rick Ankiel (Die-cut jersey, autographed.) (10)	35.00
Rafael Furcal (Base bat.)	6.00
Rafael Furcal (Base bat, autographed.) (24)	20.00
Rafael Furcal (Die-cut bat.) (100)	9.00
Rafael Furcal (Die-cut bat, autographed.) (10)	35.00
Ken Griffey, Jr. Mystery Gamers (Die-cut bat.) (100)	15.00
Ken Griffey Jr. Mystery Gamers/Bat (100)	15.00

Just Gems

Yet another showcase for the top-name stars of the 1999 minor league season, this insert set is a 1:24 pick. Fronts are largely bordered in black, with a color photo set within a gem-shaped figure. On back the motif is repeated with a much smaller version of the same photo. Career highlights are presented. Card numbers are prefixed with "JI0.JG."

		MT
	Complete Set (10):	12.00
	Common Player:	1.50
1	Ryan Anderson	1.50
2	Pat Burrell	3.00
3	Sean Burroughs	2.00
4	Chin-Feng Chen	2.00
5	Gookie Dawkins	1.50
6	Marcus Giles	2.00
7	Josh Hamilton	1.50
8	Corey Patterson	3.00
9	Adam Piatt	1.50
10	Nick Johnson, Alfonso Soriano	2.50

Just Tools

The most difficult of the insert sets at a 1:240 pack ratio, this series features the players with the best physical talent destined to translate to big-league success. Fronts and backs share the same photos with various size and color combinations.

		MT
	Complete Set (10):	50.00
	Common Player:	5.00
1	Ryan Anderson	5.00
2	Rick Ankiel	5.00
3	Pat Burrell	9.00
4	Chin-Feng Chen	7.50
5	Rafael Furcal	6.00
6	B.J. Garbe	5.00
7	Josh Hamilton	5.00
8	Nick Johnson	6.00
9	Pablo Ozuna	5.00
10	Corey Patterson	7.50

2000 Just the Preview 2k

The use of third-party certified autograph cards on a one-per-box basis was featured in this early-season minor league foil-pack product. Fronts of the base cards have white-bordered photos with a large color band horizontally at center, which carries the product logo, player name, position abbreviation and team. On back is the same photo with a white band at center carrying vital data and 1999 stats. A large color block at bottom has a small team logo and copyright notice. A factory-set version of the issue was produced in an edition of 5,000 with each card featuring gold borders rather than the standard white.

		MT
	Complete Set (100):	3.00
	Common Player:	.05
	Wax Pack (6):	1.00
	Wax Box (24):	20.00
	Gold:	1X
1	Andy Abad	.05
2	Brent Abernathy	.10
3	Luke Allen	.05
4	Ryan Anderson	.15
5	Wes Anderson	.05
6	Rod Bair	.05
7	Larry Barnes	.05
8	Rob Bell	.05
9	Darren Blakely	.05
10	Lesli Brea	.05
11	Ben Broussard	.10
12	Nate Bump	.05
13	Morgan Burkhart	.15
14	Brent Butler	.05
15	Eric Byrnes	.05
16	Eric Cammack	.05
17	Marcos Castillo	.05
18	Jim Chamblee	.05
19	Carlos Chantres	.05
20	Chin-Feng Chen	.50
21	Jermaine Clark	.05
22	Pasqual Coco	.05
23	Eric Cole	.05
24	Steve Colyer	.05
25	Joe Crede	.75
26	Cesar Crespo	.05
27	Michael Cuddyer	.15
28	John Curl	.05
29	Brian Daubach	.25
30	Luis de los Santos	.05
31	Jason Dewey	.05
32	Alejandro Diaz	.05
33	R.A. Dickey	.05
34	Tim Drew	.05
35	Trent Durrington	.05
36	Josue Espada	.05
37	Ben Ford	.05
38	Rafael Furcal	.25
39	Jay Gibbons	.25
40	Marcus Giles	.30
41	Jeff Goldbach	.10
42	Jimmy Gonzalez	.05
43	Jason Grabowski	.05
44	Junior Guerrero	.05
45	Rickey Guttormson	.05
46	Josh Hamilton	.10
47	Chad Harville	.05
48	Kevin Haverbusch	.05
49	Eric Ireland	.05
50	Cesar Izturiz	.05
51	Nick Johnson	.50
52	Josh Kalinowski	.05
53	Michael Lamb	.10
54	Matthew LeCroy	.05
55	Garry Maddox II	.10
56	Willie Martinez	.05
57	Shawn McCorkle	.05
58	Darnell McDonald	.05
59	Donzell McDonald	.05
60	Sean McGowan	.05
61	Aaron McNeal	.05
62	Steve Medrano	.05
63	Todd Mensik	.05
64	Phil Merrell	.05
65	Mike Meyers	.05
66	Ryan Mills	.05
67	Ryan Moskau	.05
68	Abraham Nunez	.25
69	Jorge Nunez	.05
70	Talmadge Nunnari	.05
71	Jeremy Owens	.05
72	Pablo Ozuna	.05
73	Corey Patterson	.75
74	Kit Pellow	.05
75	Carlos Pena	.15
76	Wynter Phoenix	.05
77	Adam Piatt	.60
78	Juan Pierre	.05
79	Rob Pugmire	.05
80	Tim Redding	.10
81	Brian Reith	.05
82	Michael Restovich	.05
83	Damian Rolls	.05
84	Aaron Rowand	.15
85	Ruben Salazar	.05
86	Alex Sanchez	.05
87	Jared Sandberg	.05
88	Jason Sekany	.05
89	Pat Strange	.05
90	David Therneau	.05
91	Chris Truby	.05
92	T.J. Tucker	.10
93	Jeff Urban	.05
94	Scott Vieira	.05
95	Matt Wade	.05
96	Jake Weber	.05
97	Jayson Werth	.05
98	Matt White	.05
99	Jack Wilson	.05
100	Mike Zywica	.05

Autographs - Base

All autographed cards in Just the Preiew 2k were inserted as boxtoppers at the rate of one per box. By arrangement with USA certification service, all autographed cards were graded and slabbed. Values shown are for cards graded 8 or 9.

		MT
	Common Player:	2.00
(1)	Erick Almonte	2.00
(2)	Wes Anderson	2.00
(3)	Kevin Barker	2.00
(4)	Matt Belisle	2.00
(5)	A.J. Burnett	3.00
(6)	Jack Cust	6.00
(7)	Pat Daneker	2.00
(8)	Mike Darr	2.50
(9)	Glenn Davis	2.00
(10)	Mario Encarnacion	2.00
(11)	Francisco Figueroa	2.00
(12)	Jody Gerut	2.00
(13)	Nathan Haynes	2.00
(14)	Jay Hood	2.00
(15)	Jaime Jones	2.00
(16)	Gabe Kapler	4.00
(17)	Austin Kearns	10.00
(18)	David Kelton	2.00
(19)	Nelson Lara	2.00
(20)	Jason LaRue	2.00
(21)	Steve Lomasney	2.00
(22)	Gil Meche	2.50
(23)	Guillermo Mota	2.00
(23)	Tony Mota	2.00
(25)	Corey Patterson	6.00
(26)	Jay Payton	4.00
(27)	Aramis Ramirez	3.00
(28)	Luis Rivera	2.00
(29)	Luis Saturria	2.00
(30)	Ismael Villegas	2.00
(31)	Jayson Werth	2.00
(32)	Jake Westbrook	2.50
(33)	Enrique Wilson	3.00
(34)	Barry Zito	10.00

Auto. - Die-Cut

All autographed cards in Just the Preview 2k were inserted as boxtoppers at the rate of one per box. By arrangement with USA certification service, all autographed cards were graded and slabbed. Values shown are for cards graded 8 or 9. Die-cuts are serially numbered to 200 each.

		MT
	Common Player:	2.00
(1)	Rick Ankiel	3.00
(2)	Kevin Barker	2.00
(3)	Jacob Cruz	2.00
(4)	Jack Cust	6.00
(5)	Robert Fick	2.00
(6)	Gabe Kapler	4.00
(7)	Austin Kearns	10.00
(8)	Tony Mota	2.00
(9)	Corey Patterson	9.00
(10)	Elvis Pena	2.00
(11)	Ryan Rupe	2.00
(12)	Barry Zito	9.00

Auto. - Just Diamonds

All autographed cards in Just the Preview 2k were inserted as boxtoppers at the rate of one per box. By arrangement with USA certification service, all autographed cards were graded and slabbed. Values shown are for cards graded 8 or 9. Diamond autographs are serially numbered to 100 each.

		MT
	Common Player:	5.00
(1)	Sean Casey	7.50
(2)	Jacob Cruz	5.00
(3)	Jack Cust	6.00
(4)	David Kelton	5.00
(5)	Jay Payton	6.00
(6)	Alfonso Soriano	25.00
(7)	Enrique Wilson	6.00

Just Debuts

These cards, which are made to resemble game tickets, herald the professional debuts of 10 minor leaguers who may one day find fame in the big leagues. Card numbers, at lower-left on front, have a JD- prefix. Backs repeat the front photo and have a career highlight or two along with the player's debut day stats. Insertion rate is 1:24 packs.

		MT
	Complete Set (10):	10.00
	Common Player:	1.50
01	Kurt Ainsworth	1.50
02	Ben Broussard	1.50
03	Ben Christensen	2.00
04	Alejandro Diaz	1.50
05	Corey Myers	1.50
06	Omar Ortiz	1.50
07	Lyle Overbay	2.00
08	Brian Roberts	2.00
09	Jerome Williams	1.50
10	Barry Zito	5.00

Just Drafted

The players' overall position in the 1999 amateur draft is used as their card number on this insert series. The cards are inserted at an advertised rate of one per 240 packs. Fronts have black borders at top and bottom. The player photo at center is monochrome and repeated in color on back in a smaller version.

		MT
	Complete Set (10):	25.00
	Common Player:	3.00
01	Josh Hamilton	4.00
05	B.J. Garbe	3.00
09	Barry Zito	9.00
10	Ben Sheets	5.00
13	Mike Paradis	3.00
21	Larry Bigbie	3.00
27	David Walling	3.00
30	Chance Caple	4.00
46	Chris Duncan	3.00
74	Will Hartley	3.00

Just the One

Inserted one per 24 packs, this series features minor league player of the year in 1999, Rick Ankiel.

		MT
	Complete Set (5):	5.00
	Common Card:	1.00
01	Rick Ankiel (Peoria)	1.00
02	Rick Ankiel (Arkansas)	1.00
03	Rick Ankiel (Potomac)	1.00
04	Rick Ankiel (Memphis)	1.00
05	Rick Ankiel (Collage)	1.00

Just Tools

Inserted at a 1:24 pack ratio as a box-topper in a sealed paper envelope, this series features the players with the best physical talent destined to translate to big-league success. Fronts and backs share the same photos with various size and color combinations.

		MT
	Complete Set (10):	15.00
	Common Player:	1.50
1	Ryan Anderson	1.50
2	Rick Ankiel	1.00
3	Pat Burrell	3.50
4	Chin-Feng Chen	2.00
5	Rafael Furcal	1.50
6	B.J. Garbe	1.00
7	Josh Hamilton	1.50
8	Nick Johnson	2.00
9	Pablo Ozuna	1.00
10	Corey Patterson	2.50

2000 Just Justifiable 2k

The debut cards of some of the 2000 amateur draft's top picks, along with two graded autograph cards per box were features of Just Minors' final card issue of 2000. The 100-card base set retains the same basic format seen on the company's earlier releases. Several insert sets, including those featuring game-used equipment cards and autographs, were also found in the six-card foil packs. A gold-bordered factory set edition was produced in an issue of 5,000 sets.

		MT
Complete Set (100):		6.00
Common Player:		.05
Wax Box (24+2):		20.00
Gold:		1.5X
201	Kurt Ainsworth	.10
202	Tony Alvarez	.05
203	Craig Anderson	.05
204	Robert Averette	.05
205	Josh Beckett	.75
206	Adam Bernero	.05
207	Tony Blanco	.05
208	Willie Bloomquist	.10
209	Joe Borchard	.75
210	Danny Borrell	.05
211	Shaun Boyd	.05
212	Donnie Bridges	.05
213	Dee Brown	.05
214	Eric Bruntlett	.05
215	A.J. Burnett	.25
216	Sean Burnett	.35
217	Matt Butler	.05
218	Marlon Byrd	.15
219	Alex Cabrera	.05
220	Hee Seop Choi	.75
221	Alex Cintron	.05
222	Brian Cole	.05
223	Carl Crawford	.10
224	Brad Cresse	.05
225	Chuck Crowder	.05
226	Daniel Curtis	.05
227	Zach Day	.05
228	Mario Encarnacion	.05
229	Alex Escobar	.10
230	Eric Gagne	.40
231	Jon Garland	.15
232	Jay Gehrke	.05
233	David Gil	.05
234	Keith Ginter	.05
235	Matt Ginter	.05
236	Josh Girdley	.05
237	Adrian Gonzalez	.25
238	Ryan Gripp	.05
239	Matt Guerrier	.05
240	Elpidio Guzman	.05
241	Geraldo Guzman	.05
242	Toby Hall	.05
243	Jason Hart	.05
244	Shane Heams	.05
245	Adrian Hernandez	.05
246	Aaron Herr	.05
247	Bobby Hill	.50
248	Eric Johnson	.05
249	Gary Johnson	.05
250	Kelly Johnson	.05
251	Tripper Johnson	.05
252	Austin Kearns	.50
253	Randy Keisler	.05
254	David Kelton	.05
255	Bob Keppel	.05
256	Mike Kinney	.05
257	Brandon Larson	.05
258	Gary Majewski	.05
259	Kevin Mench	.05
260	Luis Montanez	.05
261	Brett Myers	.05
262	Tomo Ohka	.10
263	Bill Ortega	.05
264	Omar Ortiz	.05
265	Christian Parra	.05
266	David Parrish	.05
267	Chad Petty	.05
268	Jon Rauch	.25
269	Keith Reed	.05
270	Dominic Rich	.05
271	Frank Rodriguez	.05
272	Nate Rolison	.10
273	Vince Rooi	.05
274	B.J. Ryan	.05
275	Mike Schultz	.05
276	Jacobo Sequea	.05
277	Bud Smith	.15
278	Corey Smith	.05
279	S.J. Song	.25
280	John Stephens	.05
281	Mike Stodolka	.05
282	Robert Stratton	.05
283	Jason Stumm	.05
284	Brian Tallet	.05
285	Derek Thompson	.05
286	Scott Thorman	.05
287	Tony Torcato	.05
288	Torre Tyson	.05
289	Eric Valent	.05
290	Luis Vizcaino	.05
291	Adam Wainwright	.25
292	Chris Wakeland	.05
293	Tiger Wang	.25
294	David Watkins	.05
295	Brian West	.05
296	Jake Westbrook	.05
297	Dan Wheeler	.05
298	Brad Wilkerson	.10
299	Blake Williams	.05
300	Carlos Zambrano	.05

Auto. - Base

All autographed cards in Just Justifiable 2k were inserted as boxtoppers at the rate of two per box. By arrangement with USA certification service, all autographed cards were graded and slabbed. Values shown are for cards graded 8, 8.5 or 9. The base autographed cards of Larson, Patterson and Soriano are from Just's 1999 issue.

		MT
Common Player:		3.00
BA-03	A.J. Burnett	6.00
BA-06	Brian Daubach	4.50
BA-46	Tim Drew	3.00
BA-10	Eric Gagne	15.00
BA-49	Aubrey Huff	3.00
BA-13	Brandon Inge	3.00
BA-56	Bobby Kielty	3.00
	Brandon Larson	3.00
BA-60	Allen Levrault	3.00
BA-16	Steve Lomasney	3.00
BA-66	Mike Meyers	3.00
BA-21	Pablo Ozuna	3.00
	Corey Patterson	10.00
BA-70	Alex Pena	3.00
BA-24	Chris Reinike	3.00
BA-75	Luis Rivera	3.00
BA-80	Juan Silvestre	3.00
	Alfonso Soriano	25.00
BA-85	Matt White	3.00
BA-87	Jack Wilson	3.00

Auto. - Die-Cut

All autographed cards in Just Justifiable 2k were inserted as boxtoppers at the rate of two per box. By arrangement with USA certification service, all autographed cards were graded and slabbed. Values shown are for cards graded 8, 8.5 or 9. Die-cut autograph cards are serially numbered to 200.

		MT
Common Player:		4.00
DC-22	Wes Anderson	4.00
DC-23	Tony Armas Jr.	4.00
DC-24	Brad Baisley	4.00
DC-33	Tim Drew	4.00
DC-38	Darnell McDonald	4.00
DC-40	Mike Meyers	4.00
DC-41	Mark Mulder	7.50
DC-16	Adam Piatt	6.00
DC-45	Aramis Ramirez	6.00
DC-46	Luis Rivera	4.00
DC-51	Chris Snelling	4.00
DC-20	T.J. Tucker	4.00
DC-54	Matt White	4.00

Auto. - Gold

All autographed cards in Just Justifiable 2k were inserted as boxtoppers at the rate of two per box. By arrangement with USA certification service, all autographed cards were graded and slabbed. Values shown are for cards graded 8 or 9. Gold autograph cards are serially numbered 1 of 1.

	MT
Common Player:	50.00
Wes Anderson	50.00
Tony Armas Jr.	50.00
Brad Baisley	50.00
Bobby Bradley	50.00
A.J. Burnett	75.00
Sean Burroughs	75.00
Eric Gagne	100.00
Elvin Hernandez	50.00
Aubrey Huff	50.00
Josh Kalinowski	50.00
Pat Manning	50.00
Darnell McDonald	50.00
Mark Mulder	50.00
Juan Pierre	50.00
Chris Reinike	50.00
J.P. Roberge	50.00
Juan Silvestre	50.00
Chris Snelling	50.00
Peanut Williams	50.00
Jack Wilson	50.00

Auto. - Justinkt

All autographed cards in Just Justifiable 2k were inserted as boxtoppers at the rate of two per box. By arrangement with USA certification service, all autographed cards were graded and slabbed. Values shown are for cards graded 8, 8.5 or 9. Justinkt autographs are serially numbered to 100 each.

		MT
Common Player:		5.00
JK.03	A.J. Burnett	6.00
JK.05	Jack Cust	5.00
JK.06	Brian Daubach	5.00
JK.16	Corey Patterson	10.00
JK.17	Adam Piatt	6.00
JK.19	Matt Riley	5.00
JK.21	T.J. Tucker	5.00

Just Candidates

Potential big-league superstars are featured in this insert set. Cards are a 1:24 pick and have a JC- prefix to the card number on front. The player photo on front is in a vertical oval with black at bottom and a bright color at top. Backs have a gold border with the same photo repeated in black-and-white in a circle, along with a few words about the player.

		MT
Complete Set (10):		10.00
Common Player:		1.50
01	Ryan Anderson	1.50
02	Bobby Bradley	1.50
03	Pat Burrell	3.50
04	Alex Cabrera	1.50
05	Keith Ginter	1.50
06	Josh Hamilton	1.50
07	Jason Hart	1.50
08	Adam Piatt	1.50
09	Juan Silvestre	1.50
10	Chin-Hui Tsao	2.50

Just Debuts

These cards, which are made to resemble game tickets, herald the professional debuts of 10 minor leaguers who may one day find fame in the big leagues. Card numbers, at lower-left on front, have a JD prefix. Backs repeat the front photo and have a career highlight or two along with the player's debut day stats. Insertion rate is 1:24 packs.

		MT
Complete Set (10):		12.50
Common Player:		1.50
21	Rick Asadoorian	1.50
22	Danys Baez	1.50
23	Josh Beckett	6.00
24	Shaun Boyd	1.50
25	Bobby Bradley	1.50
26	Jace Brewer	1.50
27	Brad Cresse	1.50
28	Adrian Gonzalez	1.50
29	Adrian Hernandez	1.50
30	Corey Smith	1.50

Just Gems

The most difficult of the insert sets at a 1:240 pack ratio, this series features the players with the best chance at quick big-league success. Each card has a "J0.JG." prefix to the card number. The checklist and the format are the same as the Just Gems inserts in the Just Imagine 2k issue, though gold predominates on the Justifiable version.

		MT
Complete Set (10):		100.00
Common Player:		10.00
11	Ryan Anderson	10.00
12	Pat Burrell	20.00
13	Sean Burroughs	15.00
14	Chin-Feng Chen	15.00
15	Gookie Dawkins	12.50
16	Marcus Giles	10.00
17	Josh Hamilton	10.00
18	Corey Patterson	20.00
19	Adam Piatt	10.00
20	Nick Johnson, Alfonso Soriano	15.00

Just Gamers

Game-used equipment cards in a variety of die-cut/autograph combinations were seeded one per 275 packs.

	MT
Pat Burrell (Base jersey.)	7.50
Pat Burrell (Base jersey die-cut, numbered to 100.)	10.00
Sean Burroughs (Base bat.)	7.50
Sean Burroughs (Base bat autographed, numbered to 24.)	35.00
Sean Burroughs (Die-cut bat, numbered to 100.)	10.00
Sean Burroughs (Die-cut autographed bat, numbered to 10.)	50.00
Corey Patterson (Base bat.)	7.50
Corey Patterson (Base bat autographed, numbered to 24.)	50.00
Corey Patterson (Die-cut bat, numbered to 100.)	10.00
Corey Patterson (Die-cut autographed bat, numbered to 10.)	65.00
Chipper Jones Mystery Gamers (Base bat.)	15.00
Chipper Jones Mystery Gamers (Die-cut bat, numbered to 100.)	15.00

Just Nine

Players on the verge of making their mark in the majors are featured in this insert set. Seeded one per 24 packs (about one per box), the set has one player for each position.

		MT
Complete Set (9):		12.50
Common Player:		1.50
J9-1	Josh Beckett	4.00
J9-2	Sean Burroughs	2.50
J9-3	Jack Cust	1.50
J9-4	Marcus Giles	2.00
J9-5	Josh Hamilton	1.50
J9-6	J.R. House	1.50
J9-7	Nick Johnson	2.50
J9-8	Corey Patterson	3.00
J9-9	Alfonso Soriano	4.00

2000 Just Graded 2k

With a suggested retail price of $14.99 per single-card pack at issue Just Graded 2k offers three versions of each card. White-bordered base cards are limited to 500 each. Black-bordered parallels (1:16) were issued in editions of 50 and gold-bordered (1:640) parallels are each unique. Autographed inserts were found at the rate of 1:9 for base-design autographs, 1:13 for die-cut design autographs and 1:20 for Just 'Graphs autographs. Each card was graded and slabbed by USA, though in the aftermarket the assigned grade has little effect on value. While every foil wrapper says "Each pack contains 1 graded autograph card and nothing else!," not every pack in fact has an autographed card.

		MT
Common Player:		1.00
Box (8):		24.00
Pack (1):		3.00
Black:		4X
Gold: Values Undetermined		
001	Ryan Anderson	3.00
002	Rick Asadoorian	1.00
003	Danys Baez	1.00
004	Josh Beckett	20.00
005	Boof Bonser	1.00
006	Chris Bootcheck	1.00
007	Joe Borchard	6.00
008	Shaun Boyd	1.00
009	Bobby Bradley	2.00
010	Sean Burroughs	6.00
011	Hee Seop Choi	6.00
012	Joe Crede	6.00
013	Brad Cresse	2.00
014	Ben Diggins	1.00
015	Adrian Gonzalez	1.00
016	Cristian Guerrero	1.00
017	Josh Hamilton	2.00
018	Adrian Hernandez	1.00
019	Aaron Herr	1.00
020	J.R. House	2.00
021	Adam Johnson	1.00
022	Kelly Johnson	1.00
023	Tripper Johnson	1.00
024	Deivi Mendez	1.00
025	Luis Montanez	1.00
026	Eric Munson	2.00
027	Xavier Nady	1.00
028	Lance Niekro	1.00
029	David Parrish	1.00
030	Corey Patterson	4.00
031	Carlos Pena	3.00
032	Jon Rauch	1.00
033	C.C. Sabathia	3.00
034	Mike Schultz	1.00
035	Ben Sheets	2.00
036	Corey Smith	1.00
037	Seung Song	2.00
038	Alfonso Soriano	20.00
039	Robert Stiehl	1.00
040	Mike Stodolka	1.00
041	Derek Thompson	1.00
042	Joe Torres	1.00
043	Chin-Hui Tsao	3.00
044	Chase Utley	6.00
045	Adam Wainwright	2.00
046	Tiger Wang	6.00
047	Vernon Wells	3.00
048	Matt Wheatland	1.00
049	Blake Williams	1.00
050	Barry Zito	7.50

Autographs

Autographed cards were found in three styles as random pack inserts in Just Graded 2k. Base-design autographed cards are a 1:9 find; die-cuts are found on average of 1:13 and Just 'Graphs cards are a 1:20 pick.

		MT
BASE AUTOGRAPHS (1:9)		.00
BA14	Nick Johnson	7.50
BA22	Adam Piatt	3.00
BA36	Bobby Bradley	3.00
DIE-CUT AUTOGRAPHS (1:13)		
DC2	A.J. Burnett	5.00
DC9	Eric Gagne	6.00
DC18	Matt Riley	3.00
DC26	Bobby Bradley	6.00
DC27	Ben Broussard	6.00
DC28	Jesus Colome	3.00
DC32	Brian Daubach	4.00
DC34	Aubrey Huff	5.00
DC44	Juan Pierre	6.00
DC47	Grant Roberts	4.00
DC50	Juan Silvestre	3.00
DC55	Matt White	4.00
DC56	Jack Wilson	3.00
JUST 'GRAPHS (1:20)		.00
JG2	Wes Anderson	4.00
JG3	Rick Ankiel	4.00
JG4	Tony Armas Jr.	6.00
JG6	Ben Broussard	7.50
JG7	Sean Burroughs	7.50
JG8	Jesus Colome	3.00
JG12	Rafael Furcal	7.50
JG14	Aubrey Huff	4.00
JG17	Mike Meyers	6.00
JG18	Mark Mulder	7.50
JG21	Adam Piatt	4.00
JG22	Juan Pierre	6.00
JG23	Julio Ramirez	4.00
JG24	Luis Rivera	4.00
JG25	Juan Silvestre	4.00
JG28	Matt White	5.00
JG29	Peanut Williams	4.00

2000 Just Autographs Black

These authentically autographed black-bordered cards were random inserts in Just Gold factory sets. Each card was produced in a numbered edition of 50 each.

		MT
Common Player:		5.00
BA1	Brent Abernathy	6.00
BA3	A.J. Burnett	7.50
BA4	Sean Burroughs	10.00
BA5	Joe Crede	20.00
BA6	Brian Daubach	7.50
BA8	Alex Escobar	6.00
BA9	Rafael Furcal	6.00
BA10	Eric Gagne	12.50
BA12	Aubrey Huff	5.00
BA13	Brandon Inge	5.00
BA14	Nick Johnson	10.00
BA15	Josh Kalinowski	5.00
BA16	Steve Lomasney	5.00
BA17	Mike Meyers	5.00
BA18	Talmadge Nunnari	5.00
BA19	Jose Ortiz	5.00
BA20	Ramon Ortiz	5.00
BA21	Pablo Ozuna	5.00
BA22	Adam Piatt	7.50
BA23	Julio Ramirez	5.00
BA24	Chris Reinike	5.00
BA27	T.J. Tucker	5.00
BA29	Rico Washington	5.00
BA30	Kevin Witt	5.00
BA31	Wes Anderson	5.00
BA32	Tony Armas Jr.	5.00
BA33	Brad Baisley	5.00
BA34	Matt Belisle	5.00
BA35	Casey Blake	5.00
BA36	Bobby Bradley	6.00
BA37	Ben Broussard	7.50
BA38	Jesus Colome	5.00
BA40	Nate Cornejo	5.00
BA41	Robbie Crabtree	5.00
BA47	Chad Harville	5.00
BA48	Elvin Hernandez	5.00
BA49	Aubrey Huff	5.00
BA50	Norm Hutchins	5.00
BA51	Brandon Inge	5.00
BA61	Pat Manning	5.00
BA62	Hipolito Martinez	5.00
BA63	Darnell McDonald	5.00
BA64	Brian McNichol	5.00
BA66	Mike Meyers	5.00
BA67	Mark Mulder	7.50
BA69	Pablo Ozuna	5.00
BA72	Juan Pierre	7.50
BA73	Aramis Ramirez	6.00
BA74	Juan Rivera	7.50
BA75	Luis Rivera	5.00
BA76	J.P. Roberge	5.00
BA77	Grant Roberts	5.00
BA78	C.C. Sabathia	7.50
BA80	Juan Silvestre	5.00
BA81	Chris Snelling	5.00
BA83	Jayson Werth	6.00
BA86	Peanut Williams	5.00
BA87	Jack Wilson	5.00

2000 Just Minors Mystery Signatures

These unusual autograph cards neither picture nor name the player who signed them. Biographical data, stats and career highlights on back provide clues. The cards, bearing an "MS-" prefix to the number, were included in various Just Minors products and, like the other autograph cards, were issued as boxtoppers in the slabs of USA certification services. Assigned grade has no effect on value.

		MT
Complete Set (10):		35.00
Common Player:		3.00
01	Miguel Cabrera (Imagine 2K)	15.00
02	Guillermo Quiroz (Imagine 2K)	3.00
04	Ramon Ortiz (Factory set.)	3.00
06	Nick Johnson (Imagine 2k)	7.50
07	Placido Polanco (Imagine 2k)	3.00
08	Wily Mo Pena (Factory set.)	4.50
09	Jim Parque (Stuff 2k1.3)	3.00
10	Odalis Perez (Factory set.)	3.00
11	Gabe Kapler (Graded 2k)	4.50
13	Wilfredo Rodriguez (Distribution not specified.)	3.00

2000 Royal Rookies Signature Series

This minor-league issue features a 40-card base set and several inserts, sold in six-card foil packs with one authentically autographed card in every pack. Fronts have a rather small player picture on a graduated violet-to-white background. Because the set was not licensed by Major League Baseball, only by the individual players, most cap and uniform logos have been removed from the photos. Backs repeat the front photo and have a few words about the player along with his 1999 stats.

		MT
Complete Set (40):		1.50
Common Player:		.05
Wax Pack (7):		1.50
Wax Box (12):		16.00
1	Eddy Garabito	.05
2	Fletcher Bates	.05
3	Juan Aracena	.05
4	Andrew Beinbrink	.10
5	Edward Rogers	.05
6	Jason Sekany	.05
7	Juan Guzman	.05
8	Howie Clark	.05
9	Jody Gerut	.10
10	Chris Snelling	.25
11	Nick Theodorou	.05
12	Jermaine Clark	.10
13	Chris Richard	.05
14	Brent Hoard	.05
15	Josh Reding	.05
16	Mike Glendenning	.05
17	Dan Phillips	.05
18	Eric Gillespie	.05
19	Larry Barnes	.05
20	Chris Barski	.05
21	Julio Zuleta	.10
22	Damon Minor	.10
23	Brian Cooper	.05
24	Adam Eaton	.10
25	Carlos Casamiro (Casamiro)	.05
26	Jeremy Blevins	.05
27	Jon Schaeffer	.05
28	Mark Lukasiewicz	.05
29	Norm Hutchinson (Hutchins)	.05
30	Mark Harriger	.05
31	Rikki Johnston	.05
32	Jon Tucker	.05
33	Brett Caradonna	.05
34	Adam Piatt, Rick Ankiel	.25
35	Mark Seaver	.05
36	Mike Villano	.05
37	Danny Ardoin	.05
38	J.J. Sherill	.05
39	Ryan Drese	.10
40	Checklist	.05

Autographs

Each six-card foil pack of Royal Rookies contains one authentically autographed card. The autograph cards are in the same format as the base set, except have a gold-foil logo on front and a serial number from within an edition of 4,950.

		MT
Complete Set (39):		35.00
Common Player:		1.00
1	Eddy Garabito	1.00
2	Fletcher Bates	1.00
3	Juan Aracena	1.00
4	Andrew Beinbrink	1.00
5	Edward Rogers	1.00
6	Jason Sekany	1.00
7	Juan Guzman	1.00
8	Howie Clark	1.00
9	Jody Gerut	2.00
10	Chris Snelling	2.00
11	Nick Theodorou	1.00
12	Jermaine Clark	1.50
13	Chris Richard	1.00
14	Brent Hoard	1.00
15	Josh Reding	1.00
16	Mike Glendenning	1.00
17	Dan Phillips	1.00
18	Eric Gillespie	1.00
19	Larry Barnes	1.00
20	Chris Barski	1.00
21	Julio Zuleta	1.00
22	Damon Minor	1.00
23	Brian Cooper	1.00
24	Adam Eaton	1.50
25	Carlos Casamiro (Casamiro)	1.00
26	Jeremy Blevins	1.00
27	Jon Schaeffer	1.00
28	Mark Lukasiewicz	1.00
29	Norm Hutchinson (Hutchins)	1.00
30	Mark Harriger	1.00
31	Rikki Johnston	1.00
32	Jon Tucker	1.00
33	Brett Caradonna	1.00
34	Adam Piatt, Rick Ankiel	6.00
35	Mark Seaver	1.00
36	Mike Villano	1.00
37	Danny Ardoin	1.00
38	J.J. Sherill	1.00
39	Ryan Drese	1.00

2000 Royal Rookies Elite Eight

This insert set features top prospects in a format similar to the base cards except for the use of an orange-to-white background and the appearance on front of an "Elite 8" logo. Autographed versions, numbered from an edition of 2,500 each were issued as random pack inserts and are valued at 10 times the regular-issue card.

		MT
Complete Set (8):		1.00
Common Player:		.25
1	Roosevelt Brown	.25
2	Travis Dawkins	.35
3	Barry Zito	.50
4	Eric Gagne	.25
5	Jeff DaVanon	.25
6	Brett Myers	.25
7	Julio Lugo, Jr.	.25
8	Shea Hillenbrand	.35

Autographs

Autographed versions, numbered from editions of up to 2,500 each were issued as random pack inserts.

		MT
Complete Set (8):		30.00
Common Player:		1.00
1	Roosevelt Brown	1.00
2	Travis Dawkins	3.00
3	Barry Zito (Edition of 25.)	15.00
4	Eric Gagne	9.00
5	Jeff DaVanon	1.00
6	Brett Myers	2.00
7	Julio Lugo, Jr.	3.00
8	Shea Hillenbrand	6.00

2000 SP Top Prospects

As the brand name implies, only the minor leaguers with the brightest futures are featured in the 135-card base set of this Upper Deck specialty issue. The first 10 cards in the set are checklists featuring the biggest names. Nearly a dozen parallel and insert sets are found in the eight-card, $4.99 foil packs. Besides the "regular" version, the base set can be found in a Premium Edition parallel of 175 each and a President's Edition of just 10 each, utilizing holo-patterned foil technology.

		MT
Complete Set (135):		7.50
Common Player:		.05
Wax Pack (8):		1.50
Wax Box (24):		17.50
1	Rick Ankiel (Top 10 Checklist)	.25
2	Brad Penny (Top 10 Checklist)	.05
3	Ryan Anderson (Top 10 Checklist)	.10
4	Pablo Ozuna (Top 10 Checklist)	.05
5	Alex Escobar (Top 10 Checklist)	.05
6	John Patterson (Top 10 Checklist)	.05
7	Corey Patterson (Top 10 Checklist)	.25
8	Nick Johnson (Top 10 Checklist)	.20
9	Pat Burrell (Top 10 Checklist)	.75
10	Matt Riley (Top 10 Checklist)	.05
11	Larry Barnes	.05
12	Brian Cooper	.05
13	E.J. t'Hoen	.05
14	Oscar Salazar	.05
15	Mark Mulder	.50
16	Roberto Vaz	.05
17	Eric DuBose	.05
18	Jacques Landry	.05
19	Adam Piatt	.25
20	Josue Espada	.05
21	Jesus Colome	.05
22	Barry Zito	1.50
23	Eric Byrnes	.05
24	Jason Hart	.05
25	Felipe Lopez	.05
26	Pascual Coco	.05
27	Vernon Wells	.45
28	John Sneed	.05
29	Jorge Nunez	.05
30	Cameron Reimers	.05
31	Jung Bong	.05
32	Rafael Furcal	.25
33	Jason Marquis	.15
34	Derrin Ebert	.05
35	Troy Cameron	.05
36	Chad Green	.05
37	Rick Ankiel	.15
38	Chad Hutchinson	.05
39	Chris Haas	.05
40	Brent Butler	.05
41	Adam Kennedy	.15
42	Donovan Graves	.05
43	Ben Christiansen	.10
44	Corey Patterson	1.00
45	Eric Hinske	.50
46	Tydus Meadows	.05
47	Micah Bowie	.10
48	Todd Belitz	.05
49	Matt White	.05
50	Kenny Kelly	.10
51	Josh Hamilton	4.00
52	Aubrey Huff	.15
53	Abraham Nunez	.15
54	John Patterson	.05
55	Bubba Crosby	.05
56	Chin-Feng Chen	.50
57	David Ross	.05
58	Guillermo Mota	.05
59	Milton Bradley	.25
60	Peter Bergeron	.10
61	Josh McKinley	.05
62	Tony Armas Jr.	.25
63	Josh Reding	.05
64	Tony Torcato	.05
65	Mike Glendenning	.05
66	Jesus Hernandez	.05
67	C.C. Sabathia	.50
68	Mike Edwards	.05
69	Kevin Gryboski	.05
70	Harvey Hargrove	.05
71	Ryan Anderson	.25
72	Peanut Williams	.05
73	Brad Penny	.10
74	Pablo Ozuna	.05
75	Jason Grilli	.10
76	Julio Ramirez	.10
77	A.J. Burnett	.25
78	Nate Bump	.05
79	Wes Anderson	.05
80	Grant Roberts	.05
81	Alex Escobar	.10
82	Jason Tyner	.05
83	Jorge Toca	.05
84	Robert Stratton	.05
85	Rick Elder	.05
86	Keith Reed	.05
87	Darnell McDonald	.05
88	Jayson Werth	.05
89	Matt Riley	.10
90	Wascar Serrano	.05
91	Vince Faison	.05
92	Omar Ortiz	.05
93	Junior Herndon	.05
94	Sean Burroughs	.50
95	Eric Valent	.05
96	Pat Burrell	2.00
97	Reggie Taylor	.05
98	Eddy Furniss	.05
99	Chad Hermansen	.10
100	Kevin Haverbusch	.05
101	Carlos Pena	.50
102	Adam Everett	.05
103	Dernell Stenson	.05
104	David Eckstein	.30
105	John Curtice	.05
106	Travis Dawkins	.35
107	Jacobo Sequea	.05
108	Eric LeBlanc	.05
109	Rob Bell	.05
110	Austin Kearns	.75
111	Jeff Winchester	.05
112	Choo Freeman	.10
113	Ben Petrick	.05
114	Jody Gerut	.10
115	Josh Kalinowski	.05
116	Travis Thompson	.05
117	Jeff Austin	.05
118	Junior Guerrero	.05
119	Eric Munson	.10
120	Eric Gillespie	.05
121	Michael Cuddyer	.15
122	Jason Ryan	.05
123	Luis Rivas	.05
124	Ryan Mills	.05
125	Michael Restovich	.10
126	Josh Fogg	.05
127	Luis Raven	.05
128	Joe Crede	.50
129	Aaron Rowand	.15
130	Kip Wells	.15
131	Nick Johnson	.75
132	Ryan Bradley	.05
133	Andy Brown	.05
134	Donny Leon	.05
135	Jackson Melian	.05

Big Town Dreams

Premium holo-foil technology is showcased in the background to the player photo insert. Backs repeat the stylized skyscraper motif and have a few words about the player. They are inserted at an average rate of one per 11 packs.

		MT
Complete Set (10):		17.50
Common Player:		1.50
1	Jorge Toca	1.50
2	Josh Hamilton	3.00
3	Alex Escobar	1.50
4	Joe Crede	3.00
5	Eric Munson	2.00
6	Chin-Feng Chen	2.50
7	Dernell Stenson	1.50
8	Pat Burrell	4.50
9	Corey Patterson	3.50
10	Donny Leon	1.50

Chirography

For 2000, Upper Deck improved the odds of finding an autographed card to one per eight packs. Cards feature 34 top prospects in a horizontal format which uses a ghosted minor league logo on a white background to host the signature. A gold version parallels the Chirography inserts, with cards numbered to 25 apiece.

		MT
Complete Set (45):		100.00
Common Player:		1.50
RA	Rick Ankiel	2.00
TA	Tony Armas Jr.	2.00
Rob	Rob Bell	1.50
PBe	Peter Bergeron	1.50
RB	Ryan Bradley	1.50
AJ	A.J. Burnett	3.00
PB	Pat Burrell	10.00
SB	Sean Burroughs	4.00
Ben	Ben Christiansen	2.00
PC	Pascual Coco	1.50
JC	Joe Crede	5.00
BC	Bubba Crosby	1.50
MC	Michael Cuddyer	2.00
ED	Eric DuBose	1.50
AE	Alex Escobar	1.50
AEv	Adam Everett	2.00
JG	Jody Gerut	1.50
JGr	Jason Grilli	2.00
JH	Josh Hamilton	35.00
CH	Chad Hermansen	1.50
JHe	Junior Herndon	1.50
AH	Aubrey Huff	2.00
CHu	Chad Hutchinson	1.50
NJ	Nick Johnson	12.50
AK	Austin Kearns	10.00
FL	Felipe Lopez	1.50
JMA	Jason Marquis	3.00
JM	Josh McKinley	1.50
RM	Ryan Mills	1.50
MM	Mark Mulder	6.00
EM	Eric Munson	2.00
PO	Pablo Ozuna	1.50
Cpa	Corey Patterson	6.00
CP	Carlos Pena	10.00
BP	Brad Penny	2.00
JR	Julio Ramirez	1.50
MR	Matt Riley	2.00
GR	Grant Roberts	1.50
AS	Alfonso Soriano	20.00
DS	Dernell Stenson	1.50
RT	Reggie Taylor	2.00
Jto	Jorge Toca	1.50
TT	Tony Torcato	1.50
JT	Jason Tyner	1.50
JW	Jayson Werth	1.50

Destination the Show

A horizontal format with a black-and-white backdrop to the color action photo is found on this top of the line insert series featuring 20 players who are most likely to be seen in the major leagues. Stated insertion rate was one per 92 packs.

		MT
Complete Set (20):		125.00
Common Player:		5.00
1	Rick Ankiel	5.00
2	Brad Penny	5.00
3	John Patterson	5.00
4	Rob Bell	5.00
5	Mark Mulder	10.00
6	Corey Patterson	15.00
7	Eric Munson	5.00
8	Nick Johnson	20.00
9	Dernell Stenson	5.00
10	Ryan Bradley	5.00
11	Alex Escobar	5.00
12	Matt White	5.00
13	Michael Cuddyer	6.00
14	Ryan Anderson	6.00
15	Pablo Ozuna	5.00
16	Pat Burrell	25.00
17	A.J. Burnett	9.00
18	Josh Hamilton	15.00
19	Jason Grilli	5.00
20	Matt Riley	5.00

Game-Used Bat Cards

Slices of minor-league lumber wielded by top minor league stars of 1999, plus Ken Griffey Jr. and Michael Jordan are the "holy grail" for pack busters of SP Top Prospects. The horizontal-format cards have a diamond-shaped piece of game-used bat along with a color photo. Besides the regular version, Junior and Jordan also autographed a limited number of the cards, 24 and 45, respectively. The stated overall insertion rate for the bat cards is one per 288 packs (about one per 12 boxes).

		MT
Complete Set (13):		150.00
Common Player:		10.00
Pbe	Peter Bergeron	10.00
PB	Pat Burrell	15.00
RF	Rafael Furcal	10.00
JR	Ken Griffey Jr.	20.00
JR	Ken Griffey Jr. (Autographed edition of 24.)	400.00
JH	Josh Hamilton	15.00
NJ	Nick Johnson	12.50
MJ	Michael Jordan	25.00
A-MJ	Michael Jordan (Autographed edition of 45.)	1,250
EM	Eric Munson	10.00
PO	Pablo Ozuna	10.00
CP	Corey Patterson	12.50
AS	Alfonso Soriano	30.00
JT	Jorge Toca	10.00
JW	Jayson Werth	10.00

Great Futures

Twenty top minor league stars destined for big-league futures are the content of this insert set, found on average of one per four packs.

		MT
Complete Set (20):		30.00
Common Player:		.75
1	Jorge Toca	.75
2	Ryan Anderson	1.50
3	Eric Munson	.75
4	Rick Ankiel	.75
5	Rob Bell	.75
6	Matt Riley	.75
7	Pat Burrell	6.00
8	Nick Johnson	2.50
9	Jody Gerut	1.00
10	Sean Burroughs	3.00
11	Austin Kearns	2.50
12	Corey Patterson	3.00
13	Josh Hamilton	3.00
14	Rafael Furcal	1.50
15	Donny Leon	.75
16	Peter Bergeron	1.50
17	A.J. Burnett	1.50
18	Alex Escobar	.75
19	Brad Penny	.75
20	Chin-Feng Chen	2.50

Minor Memories

The minor league careers of Ken Griffey Jr. and Michael Jordan are traced in this series. Stated odds of pulling one of the inserts are one per 11 packs.

		MT
Complete Set (10):		15.00
Common Player:		1.50
MJ01	Michael Jordan	2.50
MJ02	Michael Jordan	2.50
MJ03	Michael Jordan	2.50
MJ04	Michael Jordan	2.50
MJ05	Michael Jordan	2.50
Jr01	Ken Griffey Jr.	1.50
Jr02	Ken Griffey Jr.	1.50
Jr03	Ken Griffey Jr.	1.50
Jr04	Ken Griffey Jr.	1.50
Jr05	Ken Griffey Jr.	1.50

Prospective Superstars

Upper Deck labled the dozen players in this insert set as "can't-miss super prospects" and inserted these cards one per 24 packs of SP Top Prospects.

		MT
Complete Set (12):		25.00
Common Player:		2.00
1	Pat Burrell	5.00
2	Eric Munson	2.00
3	Rick Ankiel	2.00
4	Brad Penny	2.00
5	Ben Petrick	2.00
6	Josh Hamilton	4.00
7	Adam Piatt	3.00
8	A.J. Burnett	2.00
9	Rafael Furcal	2.00
10	Sean Burroughs	3.00
11	Chin-Feng Chen	3.00
12	Nick Johnson	4.00

Small Town Heroes

Capturing the feel of minor league baseball across the nation, this insert series showcases players whose 1999 season were spent in places like Princeton and Norwich. Insertion rate was announced as one per 11 packs.

		MT
Complete Set (12):		15.00
Common Player:		2.00
1	Josh Hamilton	4.00
2	Jorge Toca	2.00
3	John Patterson	2.00
4	Jacques Landry	2.00
5	Felipe Lopez	2.00
6	Choo Freeman	2.00
7	Eric Valent	2.00
8	Jody Gerut	2.00
9	Michael Restovich	2.00
10	Pablo Ozuna	2.00
11	Kip Wells	3.00
12	Michael Cuddyer	2.50

2000 Team Best Rookies 2000

Significant problems with numbering of cards in the range #3-99 plagued this otherwise attractive minor league presentation. Corrected versions, which were available only by mail-in exchange, had to be issued for some 20 cards. They are marked with an SP in the checklist here. All but one (Ben Broussard) of the players in the base set is presented in two different formats. Cards #1-100 have player photos surrounded with a frame resembling cut stone. A Rookies 2000 logo is at upper-right. On most cards, there is a Team Best logo at lower-left and a minor league team logo at lower-right. On some cards, the team logo is replaced with the TB logo. Cards #101-112 are similar in design though the color of stone borders is brown, rather than gray; these player's represent #1 draft picks. Backs repeat a portion of the front photo in tight vertical format at left, and offer personal data and career highlights. Cards #113-213 feature the same line-up as #1-100, and most use the same photo on front, though in a borderless design. Their backs are similar in format to the low-numbers. Cards #214-225 repeat the checklist of #1 picks on a "two-headed" borderless format. All "b" version cards in the checklist represent the originally printed error cards that have the correct photos on front and back, but have the "a" player's biographical data and career highlights. Team Best Rookie 2000 cards were sold in a basic six-card foil pack in several different box compositions.

		MT
Complete Set (225):		9.00
Common Player:		.05
Wax Pack (6):		1.50
1	Kurt Ainsworth	.10
2	Travis Anderson	.05
3a	Ryan Baerlocher	.05
3b	Chris Sampson	.05
4	Andrew Beinbrink/SP	.10
5	Jonathan Berry	.05
6	Larry Bigbie	.05
7	Josh Bonifay	.05
8	Casey Burns	.05
9	Mike Bynum/SP	.10
10	Marlon Byrd	.10
11	Terry Byron/SP	.10
12	Chance Caple	.10
13	Matt Cepicky	.10
14a	Ryan Christianson	.10
14b	Joe Thurston	.10
15	B.R. Cook	.05
16	Carl Crawford	.25
17	Chuck Crowder	.05
18	Jeremy Cunningham	.05
19a	Chris Curry	.05
19b	Mike Bynum	.05
20a	Phil Devey	.05
20b	Andrew Beinbrink	.05
21a	Grant Dorn	.05
21b	Chris Testa	.05
22	Mike Dwyer (SP)	.10
23a	Mike Dzurilla	.05
23b	Barry Zito	.50
24	Vince Faison	.05
25	Carlos Figueroa	.05
26	Aaron Franke	.05
27	Charlie Frazier	.05
28	B.J. Garbe	.05
29	Curtis Gay	.05
30	Jay Gehrke	.05
31	Scott Goodman	.05
32	Alex Graman	.05
33a	Ryan Gripp	.05
33b	Robb Quinlan	.05
34	Josh Hamilton/SP	.25
35	Ken Harvey	.05
36	Jeff Heaverlo	.05
37	Ben Hickman	.05
38	Mike Hill/SP	.10
39	Josh Holliday	.05
40	Kevin Hooper	.05
41a	Ryan Jamison	.05
41b	Josh Hamilton	.15
42	Eric Johnson	.05
43	Jake Joseph	.05
44	Ryan Kibler/SP	.10
45	John Lackey	.15
46	Jake Laidlaw	.05
47	Jay Landreth/SP	.10
48	Jason Lane	.15
49	Jay Langston	.05
50	Peyton Lewis	.05
51a	Robert MacDougal	.05
51b	Ben Sheets	.25
52	Mike Mallory	.05
53	Justin Martin	.05
54	Lamont Matthews	.05
55	Matt McClendon	.05
56	Sean McGowan	.05
57a	Todd Mitchell	.05
57b	Terry Byron	.05
58a	Matt Mize	.05
58b	Matt Watson	.05
59	Jason Moore	.05
60	Corey Myers	.05
61	Derrick Nunley	.05
62	Rodney Nye	.05
63a	Mike Paradis	.05
63b	Mike Dwyer	.05
64	Tino Pascucci	.05
65	Dustin Pate	.05
66	Mike Patten	.05
67	Brad Pautz	.05
68a	Josh Pearse	.05
68b	Ryan Kibler	.05
69	Andy Phillips	.10
70	Robb Quinlan/SP	.10
71a	G.J. Raymundo	.05
71b	Dominic Woody	.05
72a	Justin Reid	.05
72b	Mike Rosamond	.05
73	Nate Robertson	.05
74	Mike Rosamond/SP	.10
75	Chris Sampson/SP	.10

76 Matt Schneider .05
77 Sean Schumacher .05
78 Ben Sheets/SP .50
79 Jeremy Sickles .05
80a Kyle Snyder .05
80b Mike Hill .05
81 Jack Taschner .05
82a Seth Taylor .05
82b Charles Williams .05
83 Chris Testa/SP .10
84 Mike Thompson/SP .10
85 Joe Thurston/SP .25
86a Jon Topolski .05
86b Jerome Williams .10
87a Dan Tosca .05
87b Jay Landreth .05
88 Nick Trzeniak .05
89 Brant Ust .05
90 Josh Vitek .05
91 David Walling .05
92 Jeremy Ward .05
93 Anthony Ware .05
94 Matt Watson/SP .10
95 Charles Williams/SP .10
96 Jerome Williams/SP .25
97 Dominic Woody/SP .10
98 Shane Wright .05
99 Barry Zito/SP .75
100 Alec Zumwalt .05
101 Chip Ambres (#1 Pick) .10
102 Jeff Austin (#1 Pick) .10
103 Pat Burrell (#1 Pick) 1.00
104 Sean Burroughs (#1 Pick) .75
105 Bubba Crosby (#1 Pick) .05
106 Choo Freeman (#1 Pick) .10
107 Josh Hamilton (#1 Pick) .25
108 Mark Mulder (#1 Pick) .50
109 Corey Patterson (#1 Pick) 1.00
110 Carlos Pena (#1 Pick) .25
111 Eric Valent (#1 Pick) .10
112 Kip Wells (#1 Pick) .10
113 Kurt Ainsworth (#1 On Front) .10
114 Travis Anderson .05
115 Ryan Baerlocher (#3 On Front) .05
116 Andrew Beinbrink .05
117 Jonathan Berry .05
118 Larry Bigbie .05
119 Josh Bonifay .05
120 Ben Broussard .25
121 Casey Burns (#8 On Front) .05
122 Mike Bynum .05
123 Marlon Byrd .10
124 Terry Byron .05
125 Chance Caple .10
126 Matt Cepicky .10
127 Ryan Christianson .10
128 B.R. Cook .05
129 Carl Crawford .30
130 Chuck Crowder .05
131 Jeremy Cunningham .05
132 Chris Curry .05
133 Phil Devey .05
134 Grant Dorn .05
135 Mike Dwyer .05
136 Mike Dzurilla .10
137 Vince Faison .10
138 Carlos Figueroa .05
139 Aaron Franke .05
140 Charlie Frazier .05
141 B.J. Garbe .05
142 Curtis Gay .05
143 Jay Gehrke .05
144 Scott Goodman .05
145 Alex Graman .05
146 Ryan Gripp .05
147 Josh Hamilton .25
148 Ken Harvey .10
149 Jeff Heaverlo .05
150 Ben Hickman .05
151 Mike Hill .05
152 Josh Holliday .05
153 Kevin Hooper .05
154 Ryan Jamison .05
155 Eric Johnson .05
156 Jake Joseph .05
157 Ryan Kibler .05
158 John Lackey .15
159 Jake Laidlaw .05
160 Jay Landreth .05
161 Jason Lane .15
162 Jay Langston .05
163 Peyton Lewis .05
164 Robert MacDougal .05
165 Mike Mallory .05
166 Justin Martin .05
167 Lamont Matthews .05
168 Matt McClendon .05
169 Sean McGowan .05
170 Todd Mitchell .05
171 Matt Mize .05
172 Jason Moore .05
173 Corey Myers .05
174 Derrick Nunley .05
175 Rodney Nye .05
176 Mike Paradis .05
177 Tino Pascucci .05
178 Dustin Pate .05
179 Mike Patten .05
180 Brad Pautz .05
181 Josh Pearse .05
182 Andy Phillips .10
183 Robb Quinlan .05
184 G.J. Raymundo .05
185 Justin Reid .05
186 Nate Robertson .05
187 Mike Rosamond .05
188 Chris Sampson .05
189 Matt Schneider .05
190 Sean Schumacher .05
191 Ben Sheets .25
192 Jeremy Sickles .05
193 Kyle Snyder .05
194 Jack Taschner .05
195 Seth Taylor .05
196 Chris Testa .05
197 Mike Thompson .05
198 Joe Thurston .10
199 Jon Topolski .05
200 Dan Tosca .05
201 Nick Trzeniak .05
202 Brant Ust .05
203 Josh Vitek .05
204 David Walling .05
205 Jeremy Ward .05
206 Anthony Ware .05
207 Matt Watson .05
208 Charles Williams .05
209 Jerome Williams .15
210 Dominic Woody .05
211 Shane Wright .05
212 Barry Zito .50
213 Alec Zumwalt .05
214 Chip Ambres (#1 Pick) .10
215 Jeff Austin (#1 Pick) .10
216 Pat Burrell (#1 Pick) 1.00
217 Sean Burroughs (#1 Pick) .75
218 Bubba Crosby (#1 Pick) .05
219 Choo Freeman (#1 Pick) .10
220 Josh Hamilton (#1 Pick) .25
221 Mark Mulder (#1 Pick) .50
222 Corey Patterson (#1 Pick) 1.00
223 Carlos Pena (#1 Pick) .25
224 Eric Valent (#1 Pick) .10
225 Kip Wells (#1 Pick) .10
---Autograph Contest Card .05
--- Baseball Fanatics Preview Card .05
--- Babbitt's Bomber's Offer Card .05

Autographs

A mixed line-up of first-year pros and established minor league stars is featured in the autographed inserts seeded in TB Rookies 2000 at a rate of about one per three packs. Autograph cards follow the format of the low-number cards in the base set. Backs have a "Declaration of Authenticity" from TB chairman/CEO Dan R. White, Jr. The unnumbered autograph cards are listed here alphabetically.

MT
Complete Set (25): 30.00
Common Player: 1.00
(1) Kurt Ainsworth 2.00
(2) Chad Allen 1.00
(3) Chip Ambres 2.00
(4) Ryan Anderson 3.00
(5) Andy Brown 1.00
(6) Sean Burroughs 4.00
(7) Francisco Cordero 1.00
(8) Bubba Crosby 1.00
(9) Jack Cust 4.50
(10) Rick Elder 1.00
(11) Choo Freeman 1.00
(12) Jeff Goldbach 1.00
(13) Josh Hamilton 2.00
(14) Chad Harville 1.00
(15) Jeff Heaverlo 1.00
(16) Cesar Izturis 1.00
(17) Austin Kearns 10.00
(18) Mike Lincoln 1.00
(19) George Lombard 1.00
(20) Julio Lugo 1.00
(21) Jim Morris 9.00
(22) Nate Rolison 1.00
(23) B.J. Ryan 1.00
(24) Pat Strange 1.00
(25) Tyler Walker 1.00

Babbitt's Bombers

While most of the players in the base set were first year pros in 1999, the selection of players in the Rookie 2000 set leans to established minor league (and future Major League) stars. Seeded only one per 72 foil packs, the Bombers cards feature top sluggers in a format similar to the low-number cards in the base set. The silhouette of a four-engine bomber appears at upper-left on front. Backs have multiple copies of the bomber symbol, along with personal data and career highlights. Parallels of the insert are a silver version, numbered to 150, and a gold version, numbered to 100.

MT
Complete Set (8): 9.00
Common Player: 1.00
Silver: 1.5X
Gold: 2X
1 Russell Branyan 1.00
2 Morgan Burkhart 1.00
3 Pat Burrell 3.00
4 Josh Hamilton 1.00
5 Nick Johnson 3.00
6 George Lombard 1.00
7 Carlos Pena 1.00
8 Dernell Stenson 1.00

Extended

Twenty-five new cards were packaged with 100 of the base cards from the Rookies 2000 issue to provide the basis for this post-season issue. The numbering errors which had plagued the earlier version were corrected this time out, as were eight other base-card errors, the corrected version for which can be found only in the Extended packaging. The six-card packs each contain one autographed card from a new group of 25 players or from one of Team Best's earlier releases. Three "foil" versions of each base card were also produced as random inserts as was a 10-card Diamond Best set.

MT
Complete Set (150): 6.00
Common Player: .05
Wax Box: 30.00
1 Kurt Ainsworth .15
2 Travis Anderson .05
3 Ryan Baerlocher .05
4 Andrew Beinbrink .10
5 Jonathan Berry .05
6 Larry Bigbie .05
7 Josh Bonifay .05
8 Casey Burns .05
9 Mike Bynum .10
10 Marlon Byrd .15
11 Terry Byron .05
12 Chance Caple .05
13 Matt Cepicky .10
14 Ryan Christianson .10
15 B.R. Cook .05
16 Carl Crawford .25
17 Chuck Crowder .05
18 Jeremy Cunningham .05
19 Chris Curry .05
20 Phil Devey .05
21 Grant Dorn .05
22 Mike Dwyer .10
23 Mike Dzurilla .05
24 Vince Faison .10
25 Carlos Figueroa .05
26 Aaron Franke .05
27 Charlie Frazier .05
28 B.J. Garbe .05
29 Curtis Gay .05
30 Jay Gehrke .05
31 Scott Goodman .05
32 Alex Graman .05
33 Ryan Gripp .05
34 Josh Hamilton .25
35 Ken Harvey .05
36 Jeff Heaverlo .05
37 Ben Hickman .05
38 Mike Hill .05
39 Josh Holliday .05
40 Kevin Hooper .05
41 Ryan Jamison .05
42 Eric Johnson .05
43 Jake Joseph .05
44 Ryan Kibler .05
45 John Lackey .15
46 Jake Laidlaw .05
47 Jay Landreth .05
48 Jason Lane .15
49 Jay Langston .05
50 Peyton Lewis .05
51 Robert MacDougal .05
52 Mike Mallory .05
53 Justin Martin .05
54 Lamont Matthews .05
55 Matt McClendon .05
56 Sean McGowan .05
57 Todd Mitchell .05
58 Matt Mize .05
59 Jason Moore .05
60 Corey Myers .05
61 Derrick Nunley .05
62 Rodney Nye .05
63 Mike Paradis .05
64 Tino Pascucci .05
65 Dustin Pate .05
66 Mike Patten .05
67 Brad Pautz .05
68 Josh Pearse .05
69 Andy Phillips .10
70 Robb Quinlan .10
71 G.J. Raymundo .05
72 Justin Reid .05
73 Nate Robertson .05
74 Mike Rosamond .05
75 Chris Sampson .05
76 Matt Schneider .05
77 Sean Schumacher .05
78 Ben Sheets .50
79 Jeremy Sickles .05
80 Kyle Snyder .05
81 Jack Taschner .05
82 Seth Taylor .05
83 Chris Testa .05
84 Mike Thompson .05
85 Joe Thurston .25
86 Jon Topolski .05
87 Dan Tosca .05
88a Nick Trzeniak .05
88b Nick Trzesniak (Birthplace corrected, bio text rearranged.) .10
89 Brant Ust .05
90 Josh Vitek .05
91 David Walling .05
92 Jeremy Ward .05
93 Anthony Ware .05
94 Matt Watson .05
95 Charles Williams .05
96 Jerome Williams .10
97 Dominic Woody .05
98 Shane Wright .05
99 Barry Zito 1.00
100 Alec Zumwalt .05
115 Ryan Baerlocher (Card number of front corrected from 3.) .10
119 Josh Bonifay (Bio corrected.) .10
121 Casey Burns (Card number on front corrected from 8.) .10
153 Kevin Hooper (Card number on front corrected from 201.) .10
193 Kyle Snyder (Size of name on front reduced.) .10
201 Nick Trzesniak (Birthplace corrected; logo and player ID moved on front.) .10
210 Dominic Woody (Size of player name reduced.) .10
226 Danys Baez .10
227 Josh Beckett 2.00
228 Willie Bloomquist .05
229 Bobby Bradley .10
230 Ben Broussard .25
231 Ben Christensen .25
232 Brian Cole .05
233 Enrique Cruz .05
234 Matt Ginter .10
235 J.R. House .05
236 Ty Howington .10
237 Russ Jacobson .05
238 Neil Jenkins .05
239 Jason Jennings .10
240 Colby Lewis .20
241 Ryan Ludwick .10
242 Mike Maroth .05
243 Eric Munson .10
244 Neal Musser .05
245 Brett Myers .10
246 Wily Mo Pena .15
247 Brian Sanches .05
248 Ramon Santiago .05
249 Jason Stumm .05
250 Dan Wright .05

Extended Auto.

One of the six cards in each pack of Rookies 2000 Extended was an authentically autographed card produced either specifically for the issue or for one of Team Best's earlier issues (1998 Signature Series, 1999 Rookie, 1999 Baseball America or 1999 Player of the Year). Card #16 Ty Howington was not returned by the player in time for inclusion and was seeded into a later issue.

MT
Complete Set (24): 30.00
Common Player: 2.00
1 Rick Asadoorian 2.00
2 Jeff Austin 4.00
3 Peter Bergeron 3.00
4 Bobby Bradley 3.00
5 Milton Bradley 3.00
6 Ben Broussard 3.00
7 Roosevelt Brown 3.00
8 Brian Cooper 2.00
9 Ryan Dempster 3.00
10 B.J. Garbe 2.00
11 Jon Garland 3.00
12 Marcus Giles 6.00
13 Keith Ginter 2.00
14 Jason Hart 2.00
15 Shane Heams 2.00
16 Ty Howington (Not Issued) .00
17 Matt McClendon 2.00
18 Mike Meyers 2.00
19 Brett Myers 2.00
20 Danny Peoples 2.00
21 Luis Rivera 2.00
22 Kyle Snyder 2.00
23 Jason Stumm 2.00
24 Brad Wilkerson 2.00
25 Barry Zito 10.00

Extended Diamond Best

Ten big name minor leaguers were chosen for this 1:90 pack insert series. Cards share the same basic design as the base-card issue, but have a dark blue background and a Diamond Best logo in the upper-left.

MT
Complete Set (10): 30.00
Common Player: 3.00
1 Josh Beckett 10.00
2 Russell Branyan 3.00
3 Pat Burrell 7.50
4 Michael Cuddyer 3.00
5 Alex Escobar 3.00
6 Josh Hamilton 3.00
7 Steve Lomasney 3.00
8 Tomokazu Ohka 3.00
9 Adam Piatt 3.00
10 Jimmy Rollins 5.00

2000 Minor League Team Sets

Manufacturer abbreviations used are: BL - Blueline, CH - Choice, GS - Grandstand, MA - Multi-Ad, WT - Warning Track.

MT
188 Team Sets and Variations
2000 WT Adirondack Lumberjacks (30) 6.00
2000 MA Akron Aeros (30) 8.50
2000 GS Akron Aeros (30) 6.00
2000 Team Alaska Goldpanners (18) 22.50
2000 WT Albany-Colonie Diamond Dogs (30) 9.00
2000 GS Albuquerque Dukes (30) 6.00
2000 WT Allentown Ambassadors (26) 9.00
2000 GS Altoona Curve (30) 12.00
2000 GS Appalachian League Top Prospects (30) 16.00
2000 Team Arizona Fall League (30) 11.00
2000 MA Arkansas Travelers (30) 15.00
2000 GS Asheville Tourists (25) 9.00
2000 GS Auburn Doubledays (29) 9.00
2000 MA Augusta Greenjackets (30) 12.00
2000 Team Bakersfield Blaze (31) 9.50
2000 Team Batavia Muckdogs (39) 11.00
2000 Team Beloit Snappers (33) 12.50
2000 GS Billings Mustangs (34) 9.50
2000 BL Binghamton Mets (30) 10.00
2000 GS Birmingham Barons (31) 7.50
2000 GS Birmingham Barons Update (10) 9.00
2000 GS Bluefield Orioles (34) 9.00
2000 GS Boise Hawks (34) 11.50
2000 GS Bowie Baysox (28) 8.00
2000 MA Brevard County Manatees (30) 9.00
2000 GS Bristol Sox (30) 9.50
2000 BL Buffalo Bisons (30) 9.00
2000 MA Burlington Bees (30) 9.00
2000 GS Burlington Indians (31) 9.00
2000 GS Butte Copper Kings (32) 13.00
2000 Team Calgary Cannons (34) 11.00
2000 GS California League Top Prospects (29) 7.00
2000 MA Cape Fear Crocs (30) 9.00
2000 MA Capital City Bombers (30) 7.00
2000 CH Carolina League Prospects (35) 9.00
2000 GS Carolina Mudcats (30) 9.00
2000 MA Cedar Rapids Kernels (30) 12.00
2000 MA Charleston Alley Cats (30) 14.00
2000 MA Charleston RiverDogs (30) 7.00
2000 BL Charlotte Knights (30) 12.00
2000 MA Charlotte Rangers (30) 9.00
2000 GS Chattanooga Lookouts (30) 50.00
2000 GS Chattanooga Lookouts Update (9) 15.00
2000 MA Clearwater Phillies (30) 7.00
2000 GS Clinton Lumber Kings (30) 9.00
2000 Team Colorado Springs Sky Sox (31) 10.50
2000 BL Columbus Clippers (36) 10.00
2000 MA Columbus RedStixx (32) 12.00
2000 GS Danville Braves (31) 27.50
2000 Team Dayton Dragons (30) 11.00
2000 GS Daytona Cubs (33) 11.00
2000 MA Delmarva Shorebirds (30) 7.00
2000 WT Duluth-Superior Dukes (29) 15.00
2000 GS Dunedin Blue Jays (30) 9.50
2000 GS Durham Bulls (30) 20.00
2000 Team Edmonton Trappers (30) 11.00
2000 GS El Paso Diablos (30) 4.00
2000 MA Erie SeaWolves (30) 9.00
2000 GS Eugene Emeralds (31) 9.00
2000 WT Evansville Otters (25) 9.00
2000 GS Everett Aquasox (31) 9.00
2000 Team Fargo-Moorehead RedHawks (30) 9.00
2000 MA Ft. Myers Miracle (30) 13.00
2000 Team Ft. Wayne Wizards (34) 7.00
2000 GS Frederick Keys (31) 22.50
2000 GS Frederick Keys W/Pepsi Logo (30) 11.00
2000 GS Fresno Grizzlies (26) 11.00
2000 GS Great Falls Dodgers (29) 15.00
2000 MA Greensboro Bats (30) 9.50
2000 Team Greenville Bluesmen (23) 9.50
2000 GS Greenville Braves (29) 10.00
2000 MA Hagerstown Suns (30) 9.00
2000 MA Harrisburg Senators (28) 10.00
2000 MA Helena Brewers (30) 10.00
2000 MA Hickory Crawdads (30) 7.00
2000 MA Hickory Crawdads Update (30) 9.50
2000 GS High Desert Mavericks (30) 10.00
2000 GS Hudson Valley Renegades (33) 13.50
2000 Team Huntsville Stars (29) 10.00
2000 GS Idaho Falls Padres (30) 9.00
2000 BL Indianapolis Indians (30) 9.00
2000 MA Iowa Cubs (30) 9.00
2000 GS Jacksonville Suns (31) 9.00
2000 Team Johnson City Cardinals (40) 27.00
2000 Team Jupiter Hammerheads (40) 20.00
2000 Connie's Kane County Cougars (32) 12.50
2000 Old Navy Kane County Cougars (32) 40.00
2000 Team Kane County Cougars (32) 10.00
2000 CH Kinston Indians (30) 10.00
2000 MA Kissimmee Cobras (30) 10.00
2000 Team Lafayette Bayou Bullfrogs (22) 12.00
2000 GS Lake Elsinore Storm (36) 10.00
2000 MA Lakeland Tigers (30) 13.00
2000 GS Lancaster Jethawks (30) 12.00
2000 GS Lansing Lugnuts (31) 9.00
2000 MA Las Vegas Stars (30) 12.00
2000 BL Louisville RiverBats (36) 9.00
2000 MA Lowell Spinners (30) 9.50

2000 CH Lynchburg Hillcats (32) 12.00
2000 MA Macon Braves (30) 10.00
2000 MA Mahoning Valley Scrappers (30) 10.00
2000 GS Martinsville Astros (30) 65.00
2000 Team Memphis Redbirds (30) 32.00
2000 MA Michigan Battle Cats (30) 10.00
2000 GS Midland RockHounds (28) 12.00
2000 Team Midland RockHounds (26) 12.50
2000 MA 1999 Midwest League Prospects (35) 15.00
2000 MA Midwest League Top Prospects (29) 12.00
2000 Team Midwest League All-Stars (57) 30.00
2000 GS Missoula Osprey (31) 9.00
2000 GS Mobile BayBears (30) 10.00
2000 GS Modesto A's (30) 7.00
2000 GS Mudville Nine (30) 9.50
2000 MA Myrtle Beach Pelicans (30) 9.50
2000 MA Nashville Sounds (30) 9.50
2000 Team Newark Bears (26) 5.00
2000 BL New Britain Rock Cats (30) 8.00
2000 Team New Haven Ravens (31) 6.00
2000 GS New Jersey Cardinals (33) 9.00
2000 GS New Jersey Cardinals Update (3) 10.00
2000 Team New Jersey Cardinals (6) 10.50
2000 WT New Jersey Jackals (31) 14.00
2000 MA New Orleans Zephyrs (29) 9.50
2000 BL Norfolk Tides (36) 9.00
2000 BL Norwich Navigators (30) 15.00
2000 Team Ogden Raptors (40) 20.00
2000 MA Oklahoma City Redhawks (29) 11.00
2000 MA Omaha Golden Spikes (35) 25.00
2000 MA Orlando Devil Rays Strip Set (29) 60.00
2000 BL Ottawa Lynx (30) 7.00
2000 BL Pawtucket Red Sox (30) 9.50
2000 DD Pawtucket Red Sox (31) 10.00
2000 MA Peoria Chiefs (30) 70.00
2000 MA Piedmont Boll Weevils (30) 6.00
2000 MA Pittsfield Mets (32) 10.00
2000 GS Portland Sea Dogs (33) 7.00
2000 CH Potomac Cannons (30) 10.00
2000 CH Potomac Cannons All-Stars (8) 9.50
2000 GS Princeton Devil Rays (30) 9.50
2000 GS Pulaski Rangers (29) 9.50
2000 Roox Quad City Bandits (30) 50.00
2000 GS Rancho Cucamonga Quakes (30) 9.50
2000 MA Reading Phillies (29) 7.00
2000 MA Reading Phils Avernia College (29) 12.50
2000 BL Richmond Braves (36) 12.00
2000 Richmond Camera Richmond Braves (25) 9.00
2000 GS Rochester Red Wings (25) 9.00
2000 MA Round Rock Express (30) 12.00
2000 GS Sacramento River Cats (30) 9.00
2000 GS Salem Avalanche (31) 9.00
2000 GS Salem-Keizer Volcanoes (36) 7.00
2000 GS San Antonio Missions (28) 9.00
2000 GS San Bernardino Stampede (30) 9.00
2000 GS San Jose Giants (30) 9.00
2000 MA Sarasota Red Sox (30) 13.00
2000 MA Savannah Sand Gnats (29) 12.00
2000 BL Scranton/Wilkes-Barre Red Barons (30) 7.00
2000 GS Shreveport Captains (30) 10.00
2000 GS Sioux Falls Canaries (28) 10.00
2000 MA South Atlantic League Prospects (30) 9.50
2000 MA South Bend Silver Hawks (30) 10.00
2000 GS Southern League Top Prospects (31) 9.50
2000 GS Spokane Indians (37) 9.50
2000 GS St. Lucie Mets (32) 10.00
2000 MA St. Petersburg Devil Rays (30) 9.50
2000 MA Staten Island Yankees (36) 15.00
2000 GS Syracuse SkyChiefs (47) 11.50
2000 BL Tacoma Rainiers (30) 9.50
2000 MA Tampa Yankees (30) 25.00
2000 GS Tennessee Smokies (28) 20.00
2000 GS Toledo Mud Hens (35) 9.00
2000 MA Trenton Thunder (30) 7.00
2000 GS Tucson Sidewinders (30) 11.50
2000 Team Tulsa Drillers (28) 10.00
2000 MA Utica Blue Sox (40) 20.00
2000 GS Vancouver Canadians (35) 13.00
2000 GS Vermont Expos (34) 9.50
2000 MA Vero Beach Dodgers (30) 9.00
2000 GS Visalia Oaks (30) 9.00
2000 MA West Michigan Whitecaps (30) 9.00
2000 GS West Tennessee Diamond Jaxx (30) 20.00
2000 CH Wichita Wranglers (30) 9.00
2000 MA Williamsport Crosscutters (30) 10.00
2000 CH Wilmington Blue Rocks (30) 10.00
2000 CH Winston-Salem Warthogs (30) 12.00
2000 CH Winston-Salem Warthogs Update (30) 20.00
2000 MA Wisconsin Timber Rattlers (30) 9.00
2000 GS Yakima Bears (31) 10.00

2001 Pacific Sports Promotions Reprints

(The first "American" baseball cards of Ichiro Suzuki from the 1993 Hawaii Winter Baseball League Hilo Stars team set were reprinted in 2001. Reprints are marked as such on back.)

MT
Complete Set (4): 125.00
1 Ichiro Suzuki (Red cap.) 25.00
1 Ichiro Suzuki (Red cap.) (Gold signature.) 40.00
5 Ichiro Suzuki (Blue helmet.) 25.00
5 Ichiro Suzuki (Blue helmet.) (Gold signature.) 40.00

2001 Royal Rookies Futures

This minor-league issue features a 40-card base set and several inserts, sold in six-card foil packs with one authentically autographed card in every pack. Fronts have a borderless player photo. Because the set was not licensed by Major League Baseball, only by the individual players, most cap and uniform logos have been removed from the photos. Backs repeat the front photo and have a few sentences about the player.

MT
Complete Set (40): 1.00
Common Player: .05
Wax Pack (5+1): 2.50
Wax Box (12): 20.00
1 Ramon Soler .05
2 Aron Weston .05
3 Alex Requena .05
4 Eric Johnson .05
5 Tony Mota .05
6 Miguel Cabrera .50
7 Jovanny Cedano (Cedeno) .05
8 Jose Morban .05
9 Enrique Ramirez .05
10 Steve Goodson .05
11 Carlos Silva .05
12 Jovanny Sosa .05
13 Jeff Bailey .05
14 Eric Byrnes .05
15 Rob Pugmire .05
16 Frederick Torres .05
17 Jeff Inglin .05
18 Jermaine Clark .10
19 Adam Melhuse .05
20 Dustin Carr .05
21 Paul Hoover .05
22 Christian Parker .05
23 Paul Ottavinia .05
24 Maxim St. Pierre .05
25 Tony Pena Jr. .05
26 Jay Gehrke .05
27 Scott Seal .05
28 J.J. Putz .05
29 Jesus Medrano .05
30 Bret Prinz .05
31 Derrick Cook .05
32 Mark Roberts .05
33 Napoleon Calzado .05
34 Francisco Rodriguez .05
35 Brant Ust .05
36 Ken Griffey Jr. (Base Card Checklist) .10
(37) Rick Ankiel, Alex Escobar .10
(38) Roosevelt Brown, Julio Lugo, Jr. .05
(39) Adam Piatt, Travis Dawkins .10
(40) Alex Rodriguez Chase Card Checklist .10

Autographs

Authentically autographed versions of each single-player base card were inserted in Royal Rookies Futures packs at a one per pack rate. The cards are numbered within an edition of 4,950 each.

MT
Complete Set (40): 35.00
Common Player: 1.00
1 Ramon Soler 1.00
2 Aron Weston 1.00
3 Alex Requena 1.00
4 Eric Johnson 1.00
5 Tony Mota 1.00
6 Miguel Cabrera 30.00
7 Jovanny Cedeno 1.00
8 Jose Morban 1.00
9 Enrique Ramirez 1.00
10 Steve Goodson 1.00
11 Carlos Silva 1.00
12 Jovanny Sosa 1.00
13 Jeff Bailey 1.00
14 Eric Byrnes 1.00
15 Rob Pugmire 1.00
16 Frederick Torres 1.00
17 Jeff Inglin 1.00
18 Jermaine Clark 1.00
19 Adam Melhuse 1.00
20 Dustin Carr 1.00
21 Paul Hoover 1.00
22 Christian Parker 1.00
23 Paul Ottavinia 1.00
24 Maxim St. Pierre 1.00
25 Tony Pena Jr. 1.00
26 Jay Gehrke 1.00
27 Scott Seal 1.00
28 J.J. Putz 1.00
29 Jesus Medrano 1.00
30 Bret Prinz 1.00
31 Derrick Cook 1.00
32 Mark Roberts 1.00
33 Napoleon Calzado 1.00
34 Francisco Rodriguez 1.00
35 Brant Ust 1.00

Blue Chips

Ten top prospects are included in this insert set. Fronts have game-action photos with the borders and background tinted blue and a large "BLUE CHIPS" banner across the front. A gold-foil "LIMITED EDITION" logo also appears. Backs have a smaller version of the front photo and a few sentences about the player. Although the cards are unnumbered, they are numbered here according to the checklist.

MT
Complete Set (10): 3.00
Common Player: .50
(1) Rick Ankiel .75
(1p) Rick Ankiel (PROMO) .65
(2) C.C. Sabathia .65
(3) Jayson Werth .50
(4) Brad Baisley .50
(5) Adam Piatt .60
(6) Travis Dawkins .60
(7) Jeremy Ward .50
(8) Luis Rivera .50
(9) Eric Gagne 1.00
(10) Alex Escobar .50

High Yield

Ten prospects with bright futures are featured in this insert set. Fronts have borderless action photos with a large "HIGH YIELD" logo vertically at left. Backs have a smaller version of the front photo, along with a few words about the player and his 1999 stats. The cards have no numbers and are presented here as numbered on the checklist. An autographed version of each card, numbered to 2,500 each, was also produced. They are valued about 10X the unsigned version.

MT
Complete Set (10): 3.00
Common Player: .50
(1) Ty Howington .50
(2) Brennan King .50
(3) Jason Stumm .50
(4) Roosevelt Brown .50
(5) Julio Lugo, Jr. .50
(6) Colby Lewis .50
(7) Jamie Brown .50
(8) Julio Ramirez .50
(9) Jorge Toca .50
(10) Nathan Haynes .50

Wall Street

Five cards of Alex Rodriguez were issued as inserts bearing a gold-foil "Limited Edition" logo. Large photos on front and smaller back photos have had uniform logos removed. Each card was also released in an autographed version with an authenticity seal and serial number from within an edition of 20 each on back.

MT
Complete Set (5): 2.00
Common Card: .50
Autographed Card: 100.00
1-5 Alex Rodriguez .50

2001 Royal Rookies Throwbacks

This minor-league issue features a 44-card base set and several inserts, sold in six-card foil packs. Two authentically autographed cards were inserted in every 12-pack box. Fronts of the base cards have a borderless player photo on which the colors have been muted. Because the set was not licensed by Major League Baseball, only by the individual players, all cap and uniform logos have been removed from the photos. Backs repeat a detail of the front photo and have a few sentences about the player. The two-player Flipcards and the checklists do not have numbers on the cards, but are listed here according to the checklist.

MT
Complete Set (44): 1.00
Common Player: .05
Wax Pack (5+1): 2.00
Wax Box (12): 20.00
Wax Box (18): 25.00
1 Mark Brownson .05
2 Jason Woolf .05
3 Enrique Cruz .05
4 Jose Mieses .05
5 Erick Almonte .05
6 Randey Dorame .05
7 Alex Hernandez .05
8 Marlon Byrd .10
9 Kevin Connacher .05
10 Asdrubal Orapeza (Oropeza) .05
11 Seth McClung .10
12 Delvin James .05
13 Albenis Machado .05
14 Jose Leon .05
15 Randel (Randall) Meadows .05
16 Luke Allen .05
17 Hector Almonte .05
18 Peter Bauer .05
19 Todd Betts .05
20 Adrian Burnside .05
21 Angel Berroa .50
22 Cesar Saba .05
23 Luis Garcia .05
24 Ron Paulino .05
25 Alex Gomez .05
26 Ryan Ballard .05
27 Enemencio Pacheco .05
28 Michael Napoli .05
29 Francis Finnerty .05
30 Javier Calzada .05
31 Shawn Sonnier .05
32 Mike Porzio .05
33 Rafael Pujols .05
34 Pedro Santana .05
35 Carlos Urquiola .05
(36) Ty Howington, Jason Stumm (Flipcard) .10
(37) Brennan King, Jorge Toca (Flipcard) .05
(38) Alex Escobar, Jeremy Ward (Flipcard) .10
(39) C.C. Sabathia, Brad Baisley (Flipcard) .15
(40) Nathan Haynes, Julio Ramirez (Flipcard) .05
(41) Colby Lewis, Jamie Brown (Flipcard) .10
(42) Roosevelt Brown, Eric Byrnes (Flipcard) .10
(43) Todd Helton Checklist - Base Set .10
(44) Todd Helton Checklist - Inserts .10

Autographs

Two of the 12 six-card foil packs in each box of Royal Rookies Throwbacks contain an authentically autographed card. The autograph cards are in the same format as the base set, except have a gold-foil logo on front and a serial number from within an edition of 5,950.

MT
Complete Set (44): 55.00
Common Player: 1.00
1 Mark Brownson 1.00
2 Jason Woolf 1.00
3 Enrique Cruz 1.00
4 Jose Mieses 1.00
5 Erick Almonte 1.00
6 Randey Dorame 1.00
7 Alex Hernandez 1.00
8 Marlon Byrd 3.00
9 Kevin Connacher 1.00
10 Asdrubal Orapeza (Oropeza) 1.00
11 Seth McClung 2.00
12 Delvin James 1.00
13 Albenis Machado 1.00
14 Jose Leon 1.00
15 Randel (Randall) Meadows 1.00
16 Luke Allen 1.00
17 Hector Almonte 1.00
18 Peter Bauer 1.00
19 Todd Betts 1.00
20 Adrian Burnside 1.00
21 Angel Berroa 7.50
22 Cesar Saba 1.00
23 Luis Garcia 1.00
24 Ron Paulino 1.00
25 Alex Gomez 1.00
26 Ryan Ballard 1.00
27 Enemencio Pacheco 1.00
28 Michael Napoli 1.00
29 Francis Finnerty 1.00
30 Javier Calzada 1.00
31 Shawn Sonnier 1.00
32 Mike Porzio 1.00
33 Rafael Pujols 1.00
34 Pedro Santana 1.00
35 Carlos Urquiola 1.00
(36) Ty Howington, Jason Stumm (Flipcard) 2.00
(37) Brennan King, Jorge Toca (Flipcard) 2.00
(38) Alex Escobar, Jeremy Ward (Flipcard) 5.00
(39) C.C. Sabathia, Brad Baisley (Flipcard) 5.00
(40) Nathan Haynes, Julio Ramirez (Flipcard) 2.00
(41) Colby Lewis, Jamie Brown (Flipcard) 2.00
(42) Roosevelt Brown, Eric Byrnes (Flipcard) 3.00

Amazing

Rockies star Todd Helton is featured in this five-card insert set. Fronts have an action photo with a large vertical "AMAZING" at left. Backs of four of the cards have a detail repeated from the front photo and a few sentences about Helton. The fifth card is a "flipcard" with two fronts. One of the five Helton cards was found in every other foil pack, while the other packs contained a "Special Offer" card by which the five-card set could be order by mail for $2 (+43.95 shipping).

MT
Complete Set (5): 1.00
Common Card: .25
A1 Todd Helton .25
A2 Todd Helton .25
(A3) Todd Helton (Flipcard) .25
A4 Todd Helton .25
A5 Todd Helton .25
Todd Helton (Special Offer) .10

Barnstormers

Each six-card foil pack of Royal Rookies Throwbacks contains one of 10 Barnstormers inserts. The colors on the borderless front photos are not muted as much as on the base cards and there is a vertical Barnstormers logo at left. On back is a background of a wooden fence with a detail from the front photo repeated, along with a few words about the player.

MT
Complete Set (10): 1.00
Common Player: .10
B1 Brian Wolfe .10
B2 Garett Gentry .10
B3 Cory (Corey) Spencer .10
B4 Alfredo Amezaga .10
B5 Vince Faison .10
B6 Darron Cox .10
B7 Luis Martinez .10
B8 Junior Herndon .10
B9 Kenny Nelson .25
B10 Jay Sitzman .10

Boys of Summer

Each six-card foil pack of Royal Rookies Throwbacks contains one of 10 Boys of Summer inserts. Colors on the borderless front photos are not muted as they are on the base cards and there is a Boys of Summer logo at bottom. On back is a detail from the front photo, along with a few words about the player. Card numbers are preceded by "BOS#."

MT
Complete Set (10): 1.00
Common Player: .10
1 Luke Prokopec .15
2 Tim Drew .10
3 Joe Crede .50
4 Dan Wheeler .10
5 Horacio Estrada .10
6 Andy Beal .10
7 Ted Rose .10
8 Bert Snow .10
9 Kevin Burford .10
10 Brett Weber .10

2001 SP Top Prospects

Only the top talent is included in Upper Deck's annual minor league issue. A wood-look design theme is carried throughout the base set and inserts. Fronts have a metallized photo background with the player name in silver foil. Backs have logos of the parent team's minor league clubs, a few words about the player, 2000 season stats and career stats. The set was released in December 2000.

MT
Complete Set (90): 10.00
Common Player: .05
Wax Pack (5): 1.00
Wax Box (24): 15.00
1 Nathan Haynes .05
2 Francisco Rodriguez .15
3 Joe Torres .05
4 Mario Encarnacion .05
5 Justin Miller .05
6 Jason Hart .05
7 Miguel Olivo .05
8 Felipe Lopez .05
9 Vernon Wells .50
10 Cesar Izturis .25
11 Kenny Kelly .25
12 Josh Hamilton .50
13 Jesus Colome .05
14 Aubrey Huff .25
15 Toby Hall .05
16 Danys Baez .05
17 C.C. Sabathia .35
18 Ryan Anderson .25
19 Ryan Christianson .25
20 Richard Stahl .05

21 Matt Riley .05
22 Jayson Werth .05
23 Tripper Johnson .05
24 Jason Grabowski .05
25 Jason Romano .05
26 Carlos Pena .25
27 Rick Asadoorian .05
28 Steve Lomasney .10
29 Sun-Woo Kim .15
30 Phillip Dumatrait .05
31 Chris George .05
32 Dee Brown .05
33 Jeff Austin .05
34 Ramon Santiago .05
35 Chris Wakeland .05
36 Brandon Inge .05
37 Michael Cuddyer .15
38 Michael Restovich .10
39 Ruben Salazar .05
40 Joe Crede .75
41 Aaron Rowand .15
42 Wily Mo Pena .25
43 Nick Johnson 1.00
44 Aaron McNeal .05
45 Wilfredo Rodriguez .05
46 Keith Ginter .05
47 Pat Manning .05
48 George Lombard .05
49 Marcus Giles .25
50 Nick Neugebauer .10
51 Ben Sheets .50
52 Ben Johnson .05
53 Chad Hutchinson .05
54 Luis Saturria .05
55 Corey Patterson .75
56 Hee Seop Choi .50
57 Ben Christiansen .25
58 John Patterson .10
59 Jack Cust .15
60 Hong-Chih Kuo .05
61 Chin-Feng Chen .50
62 Justin Wayne .05
63 Brad Wilkerson .10
64 Kurt Ainsworth .05
65 Tony Torcato .05
66 Michael Byas .05
67 Julio Ramirez .05
68 Josh Beckett 2.00
69 Abraham Nunez .25
70 Adrian Gonzalez .50
71 Alex Escobar .05
72 Pat Strange .05
73 Brian Cole .05
74 Sean Burroughs .60
75 Wascar Serrano .05
76 Vince Faison .05
77 Dennis Tankersley .25
78 Brad Baisley .05
79 Jimmy Rollins .75
80 Eric Valent .10
81 J.J. Davis .05
82 Bobby Bradley .20
83 Adam Dunn .75
84 Drew Henson 1.00
85 Jackson Melian .05
86 Choo Freeman .05
87 Jason Jennings .05
88 Corey Patterson (Checklist) .25
89 Josh Hamilton (Checklist) .50
90 Sean Burroughs (Checklist) .25

Big Town Dreams

The bright lights of big-league baseball cities are in the sights of this group of hot prospects. On front, action photos are set against a textured woodgrain panel; graphic highlights are silver foil. Backs have basic player information. Advertised insertion rate for this chase series is one per 12 packs.

MT
Complete Set (15): 9.00
Common Player: .50
BD1 Vernon Wells 1.00
BD2 Corey Patterson 1.00
BD3 Michael Cuddyer .50
BD4 Aaron McNeal .50
BD5 Josh Beckett 2.00
BD6 Drew Henson 2.00
BD7 Sean Burroughs 1.00
BD8 Alex Escobar .50
BD9 C.C. Sabathia .75
BD10 Josh Hamilton 1.00
BD11 John Patterson .50
BD12 Aaron Rowand .50
BD13 Dee Brown .50
BD14 Choo Freeman .50
BD15 Nick Johnson 1.50

Chirography

Inserted at an average rate of 1:11 packs (about two per box), these inserts offer authentic autographs of future stars. Fronts have silver-foil highlights. Backs repeat the front photo and have a statement authenticating the autograph.

MT
Complete Set (29): 60.00
Common Player: 2.00
AG Adrian Gonzalez 15.00
AH Aubrey Huff 3.00
AM Aaron McNeal 2.00
BC Ben Christensen 3.00
BC Brian Cole 2.00
BI Brandon Inge 2.00
CC Chin-Feng Chen 10.00
CP Corey Patterson 6.00
CS C.C. Sabathia 5.00
CW Chris Wakeland 2.00
DH Drew Henson 15.00
GR Keith Ginter 2.00
JB Josh Beckett 30.00
JCo Jesus Colome 2.00
JCu Jack Cust 8.00
JH Josh Hamilton 25.00
JM Justin Miller 2.00
JT Joe Torres 3.00
JWa Justin Wayne 2.00
KA Kurt Ainsworth 2.00
MC Michael Cuddyer 3.00
MR Matt Riley 2.00
PS Pat Strange 2.00
RA Ryan Anderson 4.00
RS Ramon Santiago 2.00
SB Sean Burroughs 4.00
TH Toby Hall 2.00
TJ Tripper Johnson 2.00
VW Vernon Wells 5.00

Destination the Show

All the same prospects seen in the other inserts in 2001 SP are found in this 1:18 insert set. These players were deemed the closest to major league stardom prior to the 2001 season. Fronts have a textured wood-look background. Backs repeat the front background design and have a few words about the player.

MT
Complete Set (12): 15.00
Common Player: 1.00
S1 Corey Patterson 2.00
S2 Drew Henson 2.50
S3 Chin-Feng Chen 1.50
S4 Josh Hamilton 2.00
S5 Nick Johnson 2.00
S6 Ben Sheets 1.00
S7 Sean Burroughs 1.00
S8 C.C. Sabathia 1.00
S9 Ryan Anderson 1.00
S10 Michael Cuddyer 1.00
S11 Vernon Wells 1.00
S12 Josh Beckett 3.00

Game-Used Bat Cards

Inserted at a rate of about one per box (every 23 packs), these memorabilia cards feature game-used bat pieces from 35 players including Ken Griffey Jr. and Michael Jordan. The dime-sized bat piece has been embossed with baseball-style stitching. The back has a certification of authenticity from Upper Deck's CEO.

MT
Complete Set (30): 50.00
Common Player: 2.00
B-AD Adam Dunn 4.00
B-AEs Alex Escobar 2.00
B-AH Aubrey Huff 2.00
B-AM Aaron McNeal 2.00
B-AR Aaron Rowand 3.00
B-BC Brian Cole 2.00
B-BI Brandon Inge 2.00
B-CC Chin-Feng Chen 4.00
B-CP Corey Patterson 6.00
B-DH Drew Henson 7.50
B-FL Felipe Lopez 2.00
B-HC Hee Seop Choi 6.00
B-JCr Joe Crede 4.00
B-JCu Jack Cust 2.00
B-JH Josh Hamilton 8.00
B-JJ J.J. Davis 2.00
B-JM Jackson Melian 2.00
B-JR Jason Romano 2.00
B-JW Jayson Werth 2.00
B-KG Ken Griffey Jr. 7.50
B-KK Kenny Kelly 3.00
B-MC Michael Cuddyer 3.00
B-MG Marcus Giles 3.00
B-MJ Michael Jordan 7.50
B-MRe Michael Restovich 2.00
B-MRi Matt Riley 2.00
B-PM Pat Manning 2.00
B-RS Ramon Santiago 2.00
B-SB Sean Burroughs 3.00
B-VW Vernon Wells 2.00

Game-Used Bat Cards - Auto.

Each of the game-used bat cards in Top Prospects was also found in an autographed edition serially numbered to just 25 pieces each.

MT
Common Player: 7.50
B-AD Adam Dunn 15.00
B-AEs Alex Escobar 7.50
B-AH Aubrey Huff 7.50
B-AM Aaron McNeal 7.50
B-AR Aaron Rowand 7.50
B-BC Brian Cole 7.50
B-BI Brandon Inge 7.50
B-CC Chin-Feng Chen 15.00
B-CP Corey Patterson 25.00
B-DH Drew Henson 25.00
B-FL Felipe Lopez 7.50
B-HC Hee Seop Choi 25.00
B-JCr Joe Crede 15.00
B-JCu Jack Cust 7.50
B-JH Josh Hamilton 20.00
B-JJ J.J. Davis 7.50
B-JM Jackson Melian 7.50
B-JR Jason Romano 7.50
B-JW Jayson Werth 7.50
B-KG Ken Griffey Jr. 300.00
B-KK Kenny Kelly 10.00
B-MC Michael Cuddyer 10.00
B-MG Marcus Giles 10.00
B-MJ Michael Jordan 600.00
B-MRe Michael Restovich 7.50
B-MRi Matt Riley 7.50
B-PM Pat Manning 7.50
B-RS Ramon Santiago 7.50
B-SB Sean Burroughs 10.00
B-VW Vernon Wells 10.00

Great Futures

Arguably the top players from the SP line-up are featured in this insert set, found about one per 12 packs. The horizontal format has an action photo at left, morphing into a sky-with-clouds at right. A panel at right has player name and team logo. Backs repeat the front design and photo and have a few words about the player.

MT
Complete Set (15): 10.00
Common Player: .50
GF1 Josh Beckett 3.00
GF2 Josh Hamilton 1.00
GF3 Bobby Bradley .50
GF4 Ben Sheets .75
GF5 Nick Johnson 1.50
GF6 Corey Patterson 1.00
GF7 Sean Burroughs .75
GF8 Alex Escobar .75
GF9 Chin-Feng Chen .75
GF10 Ryan Anderson .50
GF11 Drew Henson 2.00
GF12 Rick Asadoorian .50
GF13 Aaron Rowand .50
GF14 C.C. Sabathia .50
GF15 John Patterson .50

2001 Team Best Set Collector Edition

The inclusion of a pair of mail-order-only cards among the 102 cards in the base set is a feature of Team Best's minor league issue. Fronts have game-action or posed photos framed in blue-and-white and bordered in gray. Backs have a close-up of the front photo in an oval at top. Printed below are personal data and career highlights. Vertically at left are the player's 2000 stats. Basic packaging was five player cards per foil pack and 24 packs per box. The two cards of Joe Borchard could only be obtained by sending in 12 foil wrappers and $5.

MT
Complete Set (102): 15.00
Common Player: .05
Foil Box (24): 17.50
1 Brent Abernathy .05
2 Kurt Ainsworth .05
3 Israel Alcantara .05
4 Marlon Anderson .05
5 Ryan Anderson .10
6 Robert Averette .05
7 Brad Baisley .05
8 Lorenzo Barcelo .05
9 Josh Beckett 2.00
10 Rob Bell .05
11 Todd Betts .05
12 Willie Bloomquist .10
13 Joe Borchard (Winston-Salem) 4.00
14 Joe Borchard (Birmingham) 4.00
15 Bobby Bradley .10
16 Milton Bradley .25
17 Ben Broussard .15
18 Mark Buehrle .15
19 Pat Burrell .50
20 Sean Burroughs .35
21 Mike Bynum .05
22 Ramon Castro .05
23 Chin-Feng Chen .35
24 Hee Seop Choi 1.00
25 Ryan Christenson .10
26 Brian Cole .05
27 Jesus Colome .05
28 Paxton Crawford .05
29 Joe Crede .25
30 Brad Cresse .05
31 Michael Cuddyer .10
32 Jack Cust .10
33 Travis Dawkins .10
34 Zach Day .05
35 Tim Drew .05
36 Adam Dunn .50
37 Alex Escobar .05
38 Casey Fossum .05
39 Mike Frank .05
40 Choo Freeman .05
41 B.J. Garbe .05
42 Jon Garland .10
43 Marcus Giles .15
44 Keith Ginter .05
45 Elpidio Guzman .05
46 Josh Hamilton .10
47 Jason Hart .05
48 Jeff Heaverlo .05
49 Drew Henson 1.00
50 J.R. House .05
51 Aubrey Huff .05
52 Brandon Inge .05
53 Cesar Izturis .05
54 Jason Jennings .05
55 Kenny Kelly .25
56 Sun Woo Kim .10
57 Mike Kinkade .05
58 Matt Kinney .05
59 Jason LaRue .05
60 Allen Levrault .05
61 George Lombard .05
62 Willie Martinez .05
63 Sam McConnell .05
64 Eric Munson .10
65 Kevin Nicholson .05
66 Tomokazu Ohka .10
67 Pablo Ozuna .05
68 Corey Patterson .50
69 Carlos Pena .15
70 Adam Piatt .10
71 Juan Pierre .45
72 Tim Raines Jr. .05
73 Aramis Ramirez .15
74 Julio Ramirez .05
75 Jon Rauch .10
76 Michael Restovich .10
77 Justo Rivas .05
78 Luis Rivas .05
79 Luis Rivera .05
80 Grant Roberts .05
81 Cesar Saba .05
82 C.C. Sabathia .25
83 Bobby Seay .05
84 Wascar Serrano .05
85 Ben Sheets .10
86 Carlos Silva .05
87 Bud Smith .15
88 Alfonso Soriano 1.50
89 Richard Stahl .05
90 Dernell Stenson .05
91 John Stephens .05
92 Jay Tessmer .05
93 Brad Thomas .05
94 Tony Torcato .05
95 Chin-Hui Tsao .15
96 Jason Tyner .05
97 Vernon Wells .05
98 Jake Westbrook .05
99 Brad Wilkerson .10
100 Jason Williams .05
101 Ed Yarnall .05
102 Barry Zito .45
--- "Autograph Conest!" Offer .05
--- "Joe Borchard Cards!" Offer .05
--- "Rookies 2000 Extended" Offer .05

2001 Team Best Authentic Autograph Cards

Top names from the checklist of Team Best 2001 are found in the autographed insert cards, along with several players who do not appear in the base set. Inserted at an average rate of one per eight packs, fronts of the autographed cards are similar in format to the base cards, while backs have a Declaration of Authenticity printed over the facsimile signature of the card company's CEO.

MT
Complete Set (20): 75.00
Common Player: 2.00
1 Andrew Beinbrink 2.00
2 Joe Borchard (Winston-Salem) 6.00
3 Joe Borchard (Birmingham) 6.00
4 Mike Bynum 2.00
5 Ryan Christianson 2.00
6 Adam Dunn 15.00
7 Casey Fossum 3.00
8 Josh Hamilton 3.00
9 J.R. House 3.00
10 Kenny Kelly 6.00
11 Matt Kinney 2.00
12 John Lackey 3.00
13 Kevin Nicholson 2.00
14 Tomokazu Ohka 6.00
15 Juan Pierre 5.00
16 Jon Rauch 3.00
17 Ben Sheets 4.00
18 Bud Smith 4.00
19 Richard Stahl 2.00
20 Barry Zito 8.00
20a Barry Zito (Edition of 250.) 40.00

2001 Team Best Babbitt's Bombers

Big hitters are posed with an oversized novelty baseball bat in this insert set. Found on average of one per 48 packs, the cards have a monument style frame on front. Backs have an oval close-up from the front photo along with some player data and highlights.

MT
Complete Set (11): 15.00
Common Player: 2.00
1 Sean Burroughs 3.00
2 Michael Cuddyer 3.00
3 Jack Cust 2.00
4 Choo Freeman 2.00
5 Marcus Giles 2.50
6 Keith Ginter 2.00
7 Jason Hart 2.00
8 Danny Peoples 2.00
9 Keith Reed 2.00
10 Vernon Wells 4.00
11 Brad Wilkerson 2.00

2001 Team Best Best Lumber

Top hitters are featured in this 1:96 pack insert. Fronts have a woodgrain background, backs have a close-up repeat of the front photo and a bit of player information.

MT
Complete Set (10): 24.00
Common Player: 2.00
1 Russell Branyan 2.00
2 Morgan Burkhart 2.00
3 Pat Burrell 5.00
4 Sean Burroughs 3.00
5 Drew Henson, Sean Burroughs 5.00
6 Josh Hamilton 2.50
7 Nick Johnson 5.00
8 George Lombard 2.00
9 Carlos Pena 3.00
10 Dernell Stenson 2.00

2001 Upper Deck Minor League Baseball Centennial

On the centennial anniversary of the founding of true minor leagues in professional baseball, Upper Deck issued this set which combines cards of contemporary minor leaguers with former stars of the game, most of whom never appeared on a minor league card during their career. The 100-card base set is dominated by current prospects. A 10-card UD Draft Picks subset comprises the first 10 cards, while five dual-player past/present stars checklist cards conclude the base set. Throughout the checklist are cards of former stars depicted in sepia photos on which major league team logos have been removed. A strong line-up of autographed and game-used bat and/or jersey cards was included as inserts.

MT
Complete Set (100): 10.00
Common Player: .05
Foil Pack (5): 1.50
Foil Box (24): 25.00
1 Joe Mauer (Draft Picks) 1.50
2 Jake Gautreau (Draft Picks) .10
3 Mike Jones (Draft Picks) .10
4 Bobby Crosby (Draft Picks) .40
5 Chris Smith (Draft Picks) .10
6 John VanBenschoten (Draft Picks) .10
7 Colt Griffin (Draft Picks) .10
8 Chris Burke (Draft Picks) .25
9 Kenny Baugh (Draft Picks) .10
10 Casey Kotchman (Draft Picks) .50
11 Joe Torres .05
12 Alfredo Amezaga .05
13 Chris Bootcheck .05
14 Jason Hart .05
15 Ryan Ludwick 1.00
16 Mario Ramos .05
17 Tyrell Godwin .05
18 Orlando Hudson .25
19 Josh Hamilton .50
20 Toe Nash .05
21 Carl Crawford .25
22 Roger Maris .25
23 J.D. Martin .05
24 Alex Herrera .05
25 Rafael Soriano .05
26 Antonio Perez .05
27 Jamal Strong .05
28 Eddie Murray .10
29 Keith Reed .05
30 John Stephens .05
31 Hank Blalock 1.50
32 Wade Boggs .25
33 Freddy Sanchez .05
34 Seung Song .05
35 George Brett .25
36 Corey Thurman .05
37 Omar Infante .05
38 Matt Wheatland .05
39 Justin Morneau 1.50
40 Michael Restovich .15
41 Joe Borchard 1.00
42 Corwin Malone .05
43 Jon Rauch .10
44 Joe DiMaggio .50
45 Deivi Mendez .05
46 Drew Henson 1.00
47 Jason Lane .15
48 Mike Nannini .05
49 Garett Gentry .05
50 Trey Hodges .05
51 Kelly Johnson .15
52 Dave Krynzel .10
53 Will Hall .05
54 Blake Williams .05
55 John Gall .05
56 Joe Carter .05
57 Ryne Sandberg .25
58 Hee Seop Choi .50
59 Nick Jackson (Nic) .10
60 Bobby Hill .50
61 Brad Cresse .15
62 Corey Myers .05
63 Steve Garvey .05
64 Chin-Feng Chen .50
65 Ben Diggins .10
66 Willy Aybar .10
67 Andre Dawson .05
68 Brandon Phillips .15
69 Justin Wayne .10
70 Brandon Watson .05
71 Willie McCovey .05
72 Jerome Williams .10
73 Boof Bonser .05
74 Lance Niekro .05
75 Adrian Gonzalez .15
76 Will Smith .05
77 Miguel Cabrera 1.50
78 Nolan Ryan .25
79 Pat Strange .05
80 Jae Seo .05
81 Ozzie Smith .15
82 Sean Burroughs .35
83 Dennis Tankersley .15
84 Jake Peavy .25
85 Gary Burnham .05
86 Marlon Byrd .15
87 Brett Myers .05
88 Adam Walker .05
89 Dave Parker .05
90 J.R. House .05
91 Bobby Bradley .25
92 Sean Burnett .15
93 Austin Kearns .65
94 Ty Howington .10
95 Chin-Hui Tsao .25
96 Joe DiMaggio, Josh Hamilton (Checklist 1-20) .50
97 Ozzie Smith, Bobby Hill (Checklist 21-40) .05
98 George Brett, Sean Burroughs (Checklist 41-60) .15
99 Willie McCovey, Adrian Gonzalez (Checklist 61-80) .10

100 Nolan Ryan, Dennis Tankersley (Photo Josh Beckett.) (Checklist 81-100) .25

Authentic Signatures

Top prospects' autographs are featured in this insert set. Regular versions are serially numbered to 100 each, while Gold cards were issued in an edition of 25 each.

MT
Common Player: 5.00
Gold Editions: 2.5X
S-AG Adrian Gonzalez 7.50
S-BBo Boof Bonser 5.00
S-BBr Bobby Bradley 7.50
S-BC Brad Cresse 7.50
S-BH Bobby Hill 10.00
S-BP Brandon Phillips 7.50
S-DT Dennis Tankersley 7.50
S-HB Hank Blalock 15.00
S-JBo Joe Borchard 12.50
S-JHa Josh Hamilton 20.00
S-JHo J.R. House 5.00
S-JL Jason Lane 5.00
S-JM J.D. Martin 5.00
S-JR Jon Rauch 5.00
S-JT Joe Torres 5.00
S-JWa Justin Wayne 5.00
S-JWi Jerome Williams 7.50
S-KJ Kelly Johnson 7.50
S-RS Rafael Soriano 5.00
S-SB Sean Burroughs 7.50
S-TN Toe Nash 12.50
S-WA Willy Aybar 5.00

Legendary Signatures

Autographs of nine former major league stars whose cards and game-used memorabilia are also found in this set were featured in these inserts. Regular cards are numbered to 50, Gold Edition cards are in an edition of 25 each. Redemption cards were originally issued for Tommy Lasorda autographs.

MT
Complete Set (9): 250.00
Common Player: 15.00
Gold Editions: 1.5X
L-DP Dave Parker 10.00
L-JC Joe Carter 10.00
L-NR Nolan Ryan 100.00
L-OS Ozzie Smith 65.00
L-RS Ryne Sandberg 65.00
L-SG Steve Garvey 15.00
L-TL Tommy Lasorda 15.00
L-WB Wade Boggs 45.00
L-WM Willie McCovey 15.00

Combination Signatures

The autographs of one former star major leaguer and one minor league prospect are foind in tandem on this insert series. Fifty of each were produced in a standard version, and 25 each in a Gold Edition.

MT
Common Card: 15.00
Gold Editions: 1.5X
CS-BBI Wade Boggs, Hank Blalock 100.00
CS-CL Joe Carter, Jason Lane 15.00
CS-MG Willie McCovey, Adrian Gonzalez 25.00
CS-PN Dave Parker, Toe Nash 15.00
CS-SH Ryne Sandberg, Bobby Hill 100.00

2001 UD Minor League Centennial Game-Used Bat

Game-used bat pieces from nine of the minor leagues' brightest stars are featured in this insert series. Combined with the game-used jersey cards of former major leaguers and combo cards, these are a one per 23 packs insert. A gold parallel of each card, numbered within an edition of 25, was also produced.

MT
Complete Set (9): 10.00
Common Player: 1.00
Gold Editions: 4X
B-AG Adrian Gonzalez 1.00
B-BC Brad Cresse 1.00
B-BP Brandon Phillips 1.00
B-HB Hank Blalock 2.00
B-JB Joe Borchard 3.00
B-JL Jason Lane 1.00
B-JH Josh Hamilton 15.00
B-JR J.R. House 1.00
B-SB Sean Burroughs 2.00

Game-Used Jersey

Major league jersey swatches and sepia photos (not necessarily from the players' minor league days) of 14 former stars are featured in this insert series. Combined with the game-used bat cards of current minor leaguers and combo cards, these are a one per 23 packs insert. A gold parallel of each card, numbered within an edition of 25, was also produced.

MT
Complete Set (14): 175.00
Common Player: 4.00
Gold Editions 1.5X
J-AD Andre Dawson 4.00
J-DP Dave Parker 4.00
J-EM Eddie Murray 5.00
J-GB George Brett 10.00
J-JD Joe DiMaggio 100.00
J-JC Joe Carter 4.00
J-NR Nolan Ryan 15.00
J-OS Ozzie Smith 6.00
J-RM Roger Maris 45.00
J-RS Ryne Sandberg 10.00
J-SG Steve Garvey 4.00
J-TL Tommy Lasorda 4.00
J-WB Wade Boggs 6.00
J-WM Willie McCovey 4.00

Jersey & Bat

Major league jersey swatches of former stars and bat pieces from 2001 minor league prospects are combined on these insert cards. With the individual game-used bat and jersey cards, these are a one per 23 packs insert. A gold parallel of each card, numbered within an edition of 25, was also produced.

MT
Complete Set (4): 75.00
Common Card: 10.00
Gold Editions: 2X
C-BB George Brett, Sean Burroughs 30.00
C-BBI Wade Boggs, Hank Blalock 20.00
C-DH Joe DiMaggio, Josh Hamilton 50.00
C-MG Willie McCovey, Adrian Gonzalez 10.00

Michael Jordan Salute

Game-used jerseys, bats, pants, batting gloves and cleats from his 1994 minor league season were sliced and diced to provide pieces for inclusion in these Salute inserts. Bat cards are found about one per box (every 24 packs). Jersey inserts are a 1:136 pick. Both the bat and jersey cards were also issued in a Gold Edition numbered to 25 apiece. A bat and jersey combo card (1:336) was also made, as were batting glove and cleat cards (100 of each) and a batting glove/jersey combo (25). All cards are numbered with an "MJ-" prefix.

MT
Gold Editions: 10X
B1 Michael Jordan/Bat (Birmingham) 10.00
B2 Michael Jordan/Bat (Birmingham) 10.00
B3 Michael Jordan/Bat (Birmingham) 10.00
B4 Michael Jordan/Bat (Birmingham) 10.00
B5 Michael Jordan/Bat (Birmingham) 10.00
B6 Michael Jordan/Bat (Birmingham) 10.00
B7 Michael Jordan/Bat (Birmingham) 10.00
B8 Michael Jordan/Bat (Birmingham) 10.00
B9 Michael Jordan (Bat)(Birmingham) 10.00
B10 Michael Jordan/Bat (Birmingham) 10.00
B11 Michael Jordan/Bat (Scottsdale, AFL) 10.00
B12 Michael Jordan/Bat (White Sox, spring.) 12.00
J1 Michael Jordan/Jsy (Birmingham) 20.00
J2 Michael Jordan/Jsy (Birmingham) 20.00
J3 Michael Jordan/Jsy (Scottsdale, AFL) 20.00
P1 Michael Jordan/Pants (White Sox, spring.) 25.00
P2 Michael Jordan/Pants (Arizona League) 25.00
BJ Michael Jordan/Bat/Jsy (Birmingham) 45.00
BG Michael Jordan/Btg Glv (Birmingham) 120.00
C Michael Jordan/Cleats (Birmingham) 125.00
JBG Michael Jordan/Jsy/Btg Glv (Birmingham) 175.00

2001 Minor League Team Sets

Manufacturer abbreviations used are: CH - Choice, GS - Grandstand, MA - Multi-Ad, WT - Warning Track.

MT
207 Sets and Variations
2001 MA Akron Aeros (30) 10.00
2001 MA Akron Aeros 5th Anniversary (21) 8.50
2001 Team Alaska Gold Panners (21) 12.00
2001 Team Alaska Gold panners Bonus Cards (3) 9.00
2001 WT Albany-Colonie Diamond Dogs (26) 7.00
2001 TM Alexandria Aces (25) 9.00
2001 GS Altoona Curve (29) 10.00
2001 GS Appalachian League Top Prospects (30) 12.50
2001 GS Appy League Top Prospects Update (10) 15.00
2001 Team Arizona Fall League (32) 20.00
2001 MA Arkansas Travelers (30) 11.00
2001 GS Asheville Bears (30) 14.50
2001 MA Auburn Doubledays (30) 9.00
2001 MA Augusta Greenjackets (30) 10.00
2001 Team Bakersfield Blaze (33) 10.00
2001 Team Batavia Muckdogs (36) 20.00
2001 Team Batavia 1990s stars (15) 20.00
2001 Team Batavia Muckdogs Magnets (3) 5.00
2001 MA Beloit Snappers (30) 12.50
2001 GS Billings Mustangs (30) 11.50
2001 Choice Binghamton Mets (30) 9.50
2001 GS Birmingham Barons (31) 8.00
2001 GS Bluefield Orioles (37) 11.00
2001 GS Boise Hawks (32) 15.00
2001 GS Bowie Baysox (30) 12.00
2001 MA Brevard County Manatees (30) 8.00
2001 GS Bristol Sox (30) 9.00
2001 MA Brooklyn Cyclones (36) 11.00
2001 Choice Buffalo Bisons (30) 9.50
2001 MA Burlington Bees (31) 10.00
2001 GS Burlington Indians (37) 7.50
2001 Team Calgary Cannons (31) 12.00
2001 GS California League Prospects (30) 14.00
2001 CSC Canadian Junior National Team (10) 15.00
2001 GS Canton Crocodiles (30) 9.00
2001 MA Capital City Bombers (30) 12.00
2001 GS Capital City Bombers Update (1) 10.00
2001 GS Capital City Bombers Update Auto. (1) 45.00
2001 CH Carolina-California League A-S (50) 11.00
2001 Choice Carolina League Prospects (30) 14.00
2001 GS Casper Rockies (31) 10.00
2001 MA Cedar Rapids Kernels (30) 9.00
2001 MA Charleston Aleey Cats (30) 10.00
2001 MA Charleston RiverDogs (31) 10.00
2001 CH Charlotte Knights (30) 10.00
2001 MA Charlotte Rangers (31) 20.00
2001 GS Chattanooga Lookouts (30) 12.50
2001 MA Clearwater Phillies (30) 15.00
2001 GS Clinton LumberKings (31) 15.00
2001 Team Colorado Springs Sky Sox (31) 8.00
2001 Choice Columbus Clippers (31) 10.00
2001 Team Columbus Mudcats (30) 9.50
2001 MA Columbus RedStixx (30) 12.00
2001 GS Danville Braves (35) 12.00
2001 GS Dayton Dragons (30) 27.50
2001 MA Daytona Cubs (29) 13.00
2001 MA Delmarva Shorebirds (30) 10.00
2001 WT Duluth-Superior Dukes (25) 7.00
2001 GS Dunedin Blue Jays (30) 15.00
2001 Choice Durham Bulls (30) 12.50
2001 GS Edinburg Roadrunners (30) 9.50
2001 Team Edmonton Trappers (30) 11.00
2001 GS Elizabethton Twins (30) 11.00
2001 GS Elizabethton Twins Update (10) 11.00
2001 GS El Paso Diablos (30) 13.50
2001 MA Erie SeaWolves (30) 10.00
2001 GS Eugene Emeralds (35) 10.00
2001 Team Eugene Emeralds Ems Greats (10) 7.50
2001 GS Everett Aquasox (32) 12.50
2001 Team Fargo-Moorhead RedHawks (30) 8.00
2001 GS Florida State League Prospects (30) 12.00
2001 GS Florida State Lea. Gold Prospects (9) 20.00
2001 GS Frederick Keys (30) 10.00
2001 GS Frederick Keys W/Pepsi Logo (30) 16.00
2001 GS Fresno Grizzlies (30) 10.00
2001 MA Ft. Myers Miracle (30) 10.00
2001 Team Ft. Wayne Wizards (29) 8.00
2001 GS Future Angels (30) 10.00
2001 MA Great Falls Dodgers (30) 9.00
2001 MA Greensboro Bats (30) 10.00
2001 GS Greenville Braves (39) 9.00
2001 MA Hagerstown Suns (30) 10.00
2001 MA Harrisburg Senators (30) 10.00
2001 MA Hickory Crawdads (30) 7.50
2001 MA Hickory Crawdads Update (30) 9.50
2001 GS High Desert Mavericks (31) 10.00
2001 GS High Desert Mavericks W/Pepsi Ad (31) 20.00
2001 MA Hudson Valley Renegades (33) 12.00
2001 Team Huntsville Stars (29) 10.00
2001 Choice Indianapolis Indians (30) 9.00
2001 CH International League Prospects (30) 10.00
2001 MA Iowa Cubs (30) 12.00
2001 GS Jacksonville Suns (31) 8.50
2001 GS Jacksonville Suns Sponsor's Set (32) 10.00
2001 GS 2000 Jamestown Jammers (28) 20.00
2001 GS Jamestown Jammers (28) 17.50
2001 GS Johnson City Cardinals (31) 7.00
2001 Team Jupiter Hammerheads (36) 9.00
2001 GS Kane County Cougars (31) 15.00
2001 Connie's Kane County Cougars (34) 15.00
2001 MA Kannapolis Intimadators (30) 9.00
2001 CH Kinston Indians (33) 14.00
2001 GS Lake Elsinore Storm (30) 10.00
2001 MA Lakeland Tigers (30) 9.50
2001 MA Lakewood BlueClaws (32) 9.00
2001 GS Lancaster JetHawks (30) 9.00
2001 GS Lansing Lugnuts (30) 7.00
2001 MA Las Vegas 51s (30) 12.00
2001 MA Lexington Legends (30) 9.00
2001 GS Lincoln Saltdogs (26) 10.00
2001 CH Louisville RiverBats (33) 16.50
2001 GS Lowell Spinners 2000 Update (11) 22.00
2001 MA Lowell Spinners (30) 11.00
2001 Choice Lynchburg Hillcats (30) 12.00
2001 MA Macon Braves (30) 12.00
2001 MA Mahoning Valley Scrappers (30) 6.00
2001 GS Martinsville Astros (30) 10.00
2001 Team Memphis Redbirds (30) 32.50
2001 Team Michigan Battle Cats (30) 10.00
2001 GS Midland Rock Hounds (27) 10.00
2001 Team Midland Rock Hounds (31) 60.00
2001 GS Midland Rock Hounds Sponsor's Set (28) 12.50
2001 MA Midwest League Top Prospects (29) 7.00
2001 GS Missoula Osprey (35) 10.00
2001 GS Modesto A's (30) 9.00
2001 GS Mudville Nine (30) 12.00
2001 MA Myrtle Beach Pelicans (30) 12.00
2001 Team Nashua Pride (29) 8.50
2001 GS Nashville Sounds (30) 11.00
2001 MA New Britain Rock Cats (30) 10.00
2001 CH New Haven Ravens (30) 9.50
2001 GS New Jersey Cardinals (30) 9.50
2001 GS New Jersey Cardinals Update (1) 6.00
2001 WT New Jersey Jackals (26) 7.00
2001 MA New Orleans Zephyrs (30) 9.50
2001 Choice Norfolk Tides (33) 9.00
2001 Choice Norfolk Tides Sheriff's (10) 10.00
2001 GS Norwich Navigators (26) 9.50
2001 Team Ogden Raptors (42) 15.00
2001 MA Oklahoma RedHawks (29) 12.50
2001 GS 2000 Oneonta Tigers (29) 10.00
2001 GS Oneonta Tigers (31) 12.50
2001 Choice Ottawa Lynx (31) 12.00
2001 Choice Pawtucket Red Sox (30) 7.00
2001 DD Pawtucket Red Sox Foldout (30) 25.00
2001 MA Peoria Chiefs (30) 10.00
2001 MA Pittsfield Astros (31) 13.50
2001 GS Portland Sea Dogs (32) 9.00
2001 Choice Potomac Cannons (30) 8.00
2001 GS Princeton Devil Rays (30) 13.00
2001 GS Provo Angels (35) 16.00
2001 GS Pulaski Rangers (31) 10.00
2001 GS Quad City River Bandits (30) 8.00
2001 GS Rancho Cucamonga Quakes (30) 11.50
2001 GS Rancho Cucamonga Quakes Update (17) 14.00
2001 MA Reading Phillies (30) 7.50
2001 MA Reading Phils Alvernia College (30) 12.50
2001 Choice Richmond Braves (32) 15.00
2001 GS Rio Grande Valley White Wings (25) 9.00
2001 Choice Rochester Red Wings (30) 9.50
2001 MA Round Rock Express (30) 10.00
2001 GS Sacramento River Cats (30) 10.00
2001 GS Salem Avalanche (30) 9.00
2001 GS Salem-Keizer Volcanoes (36) 10.00
2001 GS San Antonio Missions (30) 11.00
2001 GS San Bernardino Stampede (29) 11.00
2001 GS San Jose Giants (30) 9.00
2001 MA Sarasota Red Sox (30) 7.50
2001 MA Savannah Sand Gnats (30) 11.00
2001 CH Scranton/Wilkes-Barre Red Barons (30) 9.00
2001 TM Shreveport Swamp Dragons (?) 15.00
2001 GS Sioux Falls Canaries (26) 9.00
2001 MA South Atlantic League Prospects (32) 9.00
2001 MA South Bend Silver Hawks (30) 10.00
2001 GS Southern League Prospects (31) 12.00
2001 GS Spokane Indians (35) 8.00
2001 GS Springfield Capitols (30) 9.00
2001 GS St. Lucie Mets (32) 10.00
2001 GS St. Lucie Mets Update (1) 4.00
2001 MA Staten Island Yankees (36) 10.00
2001 CH Syracuse SkyChiefs (30) 7.00
2001 GS Syracuse SkyChiefs Wall of Fame (28) 10.00
2001 GS Tacoma Rainiers (30) 9.50
2001 MA Tampa Yankees (30) 9.00
2001 GS Tennessee Smokies (28) 9.00
2001 GS Texas League Prospects (30) 8.00
2001 Choice Toledo Mud Hens (30) 9.00
2001 MA Trenton Thunder (30) 11.50
2001 MA Trenton Thunder Road/Majors 1 (25) 20.00
2001 GS Tucson Sidewinders (30) 10.00
2001 Team Tulsa Drillers (31) 10.00
2001 Team Tulsa Drillers Update (11) 12.00
2001 Team Vancouver Canadians (39) 12.00
2001 GS Vermont Expos (34) 10.00
2001 MA Vero Beach Dodgers (35) 12.50
2001 GS Visalia Oaks (30) 10.00
2001 MA West Michigan Whitecaps (30) 10.00
2001 GS West Tenn Diamond Jaxx (30) 11.00
2001 GS West Tenn Diamond Jaxx SL Champs (29) 11.00
2001 GS Wichita Wranglers (31) 8.50
2001 MA Williamsport Crosscutters (30) 15.00
2001 Choice Wilmington Blue Rocks (30) 9.00
2001 MA Wilmington Waves (30) 12.50
2001 Choice Winston-Salem Warthogs (30) 12.50
2001 MA Wisconsin Timber Rattlers (30) 9.00
2001 GS Yakima Bears (31) 9.00
2001 WT Yuma Bullfrogs (26) 7.00

2002 Just Justifiable

Just Minors' foil-pack product for 2002 was a mid-December release, allowing the appearance of top players from the 2002 draft. Each base card was available in four versions differentiated by their border color, production quantity and manner of distribution. The white-bordered base set was issued in packs in an undisclosed quantity. Black-bordered versions, serially numbered to 50, were random pack inserts. Silver- and gold-bordered cards were sold only in complete set form in editions of 5,000 and 1,000, respectively. White-bordered cards #41-60 were short-printed and only issued in autographed form, serially numbered to either 500 or 1,000. Cards #41-50 were inserted at a rate of two per foil box. Cards #51-60, also numbered to either 500 or 1,000, were found at the same rate in boxes of the Memorabilia Edition only.

		MT
	Complete Set, No SPs (39):	7.50
	Complete Set, W/SPs (59):	125.00
	Common Player, #2-40:	.25
	Common Player, #41-60:	4.00
	Hobby Box (18):	20.00
1	Russ Adams (Not officially issued.)	
2	Travis Blackley	.25
3	Matt Cain	.45
4	Travis Chapman	.35
5	Kyle Davies	.35
6	Carlos Duran	.35
7	Gavin Floyd	.50
8	Jesse Foppert	.45
9	Choo Freeman	.25
10	Jimmy Gobble	.35
11	Jonny Gomes	.45
12	Khalil Greene	.50
13	Joel Guzman	.50
14	Luke Hagerty	.25
15	Jack Hannahan	.25
16	Rich Harden	.65
17	J.J. Hardy	.35
18	Jeremy Hermida	.45
19	Kris Honel	.35
20	Casey Kotchman	.50
21	Cliff Lee	.25
22	Francisco Liriano	.25
23	Jose Lopez	.25
24	Andy Marte	.35
25	Victor Martinez	.25
26	Joe Mauer	.50
27	Drew Meyer	.50
28	Dustin Moseley	.25
29	Clint Nageotte	.35
30	Rhett Parrott	.25
31	Josh Phelps	.50
32	Brandon Phillips	.50
33	Jose Reyes	.50
34	Felix Sanchez	.25
35	Sergio Santos	.60
36	Mark Teixeira	.50
37	Andres Torres	.25
38	B.J. Upton	.50
39	Shane Victorino	.25
40	David Wright	1.00
41	Joseph Blanton (1,000 Autographed)	4.00
42	Shin Soo Choo (500 Autographed)	6.00
43	Jason Cooper (1,000 Autographed)	4.00
44	Jeff Francis (1,000 Autographed)	4.00
45	Jeff Francoeur (500 Autographed)	30.00
46	Joey Gomes (1,000 Autographed)	4.00
47	Corey Hart (500 Autographed)	6.00
48	Justin Huber (500 Autographed)	6.00
49	Dan Meyer (500 Autographed)	6.00
50	Dontrelle Willis (500 Autographed)	15.00
51	Scott Hairston (1,000 Autographed)	5.00
52	Anthony Lerew (1,000 Autographed)	4.00
53	Jeff Mathis (1,000 Autographed)	4.00
54	Felix Pie (500 Autographed)	15.00
55	Jason Pridie (500 Autographed)	6.00
56	Hanley Ramirez (500 Autographed)	20.00
57	Joe Saunders (1,000 Autographed)	4.00
58	Jason Stokes (500 Autographed)	20.00
59	Brian Tallet (1,000 Autographed)	4.00
60	Chad Tracy (1,000 Autographed)	5.00

Silver

Complete boxed sets of silver-bordered parallel Justifiable 2002 were sold at $9.95. The edition was limited to 5,000 sets. Some of the cards were also produced in an autographed edition of 375, randomly inserted.

		MT
	Complete Set (59):	10.00
	Common Player:	.25
1	Russ Adams (Not officially issued.)	.00
2	Travis Blackley	.25
3	Matt Cain	.45
4	Travis Chapman	.35
5	Kyle Davies	.35
6	Carlos Duran	.35
7	Gavin Floyd	.50
8	Jesse Foppert	.35
9	Choo Freeman	.35
10	Jimmy Gobble	.35
11	Jonny Gomes	.50
12	Khalil Greene	.45
13	Joel Guzman	.35
14	Luke Hagerty	.25
15	Jack Hannahan	.25
16	Rich Harden	.45
17	J.J. Hardy	.45
18	Jeremy Hermida	.45
19	Kris Honel	.25
20	Casey Kotchman	.50
21	Cliff Lee	.25
22	Francisco Liriano	.25
23	Jose Lopez	.25
24	Andy Marte	.35
25	Victor Martinez	.25
26	Joe Mauer	.50
27	Drew Meyer	.25
28	Dustin Moseley	.25
29	Clint Nageotte	.25
30	Rhett Parrott	.25
31	Josh Phelps	.45
32	Brandon Phillips	.45
33	Jose Reyes	.45
34	Felix Sanchez	.25
35	Sergio Santos	.60
36	Mark Teixeira	.50
37	Andres Torres	.25
38	B.J. Upton	.50
39	Shane Victorino	.25
40	David Wright	2.00
41	Joseph Blanton	.50
42	Shin Soo Choo	.35
43	Jason Cooper	.25
44	Jeff Francis	.30
45	Jeff Francoeur	.75
46	Joey Gomes	.25
47	Corey Hart	.25
48	Justin Huber	.25
49	Dan Meyer	.40
50	Dontrelle Willis	.30
51	Scott Hairston	.40
52	Anthony Lerew	.25
53	Jeff Mathis	.25
54	Felix Pie	.35
55	Jason Pridie	.25
56	Hanley Ramirez	.75
57	Joe Saunders	.25
58	Jason Stokes	.50
59	Brian Tallet	.25
60	Chad Tracy	.35

Gold

Complete boxed sets of gold-bordered parallel Justifiable 2002 were sold to Collector's Club members only at $12.95 per set. The edition was limited to 1,000 sets. Each card was also produced in an autographed edition of 100, randomly inserted.

		MT
	Complete Set (59):	15.00
	Common Player:	.50
1	Russ Adams (Not officially issued.)	.00
2	Travis Blackley	.50
3	Matt Cain	.65
4	Travis Chapman	1.00
5	Kyle Davies	.60
6	Carlos Duran	1.00
7	Gavin Floyd	1.00
8	Jesse Foppert	.75
9	Choo Freeman	1.00
10	Jimmy Gobble	.75
11	Jonny Gomes	1.00
12	Khalil Greene	1.00
13	Joel Guzman	.75
14	Luke Hagerty	.50
15	Jack Hannahan	.50
16	Rich Harden	.65
17	J.J. Hardy	.75
18	Jeremy Hermida	.75
19	Kris Honel	.50
20	Casey Kotchman	1.00
21	Cliff Lee	.50
22	Francisco Liriano	.50
23	Jose Lopez	.50
24	Andy Marte	.75
25	Victor Martinez	.50
26	Joe Mauer	1.00
27	Drew Meyer	.50
28	Dustin Moseley	.50
29	Clint Nageotte	.50
30	Rhett Parrott	.50
31	Josh Phelps	1.00
32	Brandon Phillips	1.00
33	Jose Reyes	1.00
34	Felix Sanchez	.50
35	Sergio Santos	.90
36	Mark Teixeira	1.00
37	Andres Torres	.50
38	B.J. Upton	1.50
39	Shane Victorino	.50
40	David Wright	3.00
41	Joseph Blanton	.75
42	Shin Soo Choo	.75
43	Jason Cooper	.50
44	Jeff Francis	.60
45	Jeff Francoeur	1.50
46	Joey Gomes	.50
47	Corey Hart	.50
48	Justin Huber	.50
49	Dan Meyer	.65
50	Dontrelle Willis	.60
51	Scott Hairston	.60
52	Anthony Lerew	.50
53	Jeff Mathis	.50
54	Felix Pie	.75
55	Jason Pridie	.50
56	Hanley Ramirez	1.50
57	Joe Saunders	.50
58	Jason Stokes	1.00
59	Brian Tallet	.50
60	Chad Tracy	.75

Black

Each card in Justifiable 2002 was issued in a black-bordered version serially numbered to 50 each. An autographed version of each card, numbered to 25, was also produced. The black parallels were random pack inserts.

		MT
	Common Player:	5.00
1	Russ Adams (Not officially issued.)	.00
2	Travis Blackley	5.00
3	Matt Cain	6.00
4	Travis Chapman	10.00
5	Kyle Davies	5.00
6	Carlos Duran	5.00
7	Gavin Floyd	10.00
8	Jesse Foppert	10.00
9	Choo Freeman	7.50
10	Jimmy Gobble	10.00
11	Jonny Gomes	7.50
12	Khalil Greene	15.00
13	Joel Guzman	7.50
14	Luke Hagerty	5.00
15	Jack Hannahan	5.00
16	Rich Harden	7.50
17	J.J. Hardy	6.00
18	Jeremy Hermida	5.00
19	Kris Honel	5.00
20	Casey Kotchman	16.00
21	Cliff Lee	5.00
22	Francisco Liriano	5.00
23	Jose Lopez	5.00
24	Andy Marte	15.00
25	Victor Martinez	5.00
26	Joe Mauer	25.00
27	Drew Meyer	5.00
28	Dustin Moseley	5.00
29	Clint Nageotte	5.00
30	Rhett Parrott	5.00
31	Josh Phelps	15.00
32	Brandon Phillips	15.00
33	Jose Reyes	15.00
34	Felix Sanchez	5.00
35	Sergio Santos	6.00
36	Mark Teixeira	15.00
37	Andres Torres	5.00
38	B.J. Upton	20.00
39	Shane Victorino	5.00
40	David Wright	20.00
41	Joseph Blanton	5.00
42	Shin Soo Choo	7.50
43	Jason Cooper	5.00
44	Jeff Francis	5.00
45	Jeff Francoeur	25.00
46	Joey Gomes	5.00
47	Corey Hart	5.00
48	Justin Huber	5.00
49	Dan Meyer	5.00
50	Dontrelle Willis	25.00
51	Scott Hairston	6.00
52	Anthony Lerew	7.50
53	Jeff Mathis	7.50
54	Felix Pie	20.00
55	Jason Pridie	15.00
56	Hanley Ramirez	25.00
57	Joe Saunders	5.00
58	Jason Stokes	15.00
59	Brian Tallet	5.00
60	Chad Tracy	6.00

Autographs - White

Randomly inserted into foil boxes of Justifiable 2002 and Memorabilia Edition at a rate of about two per box were white-bordered autograph cards. Numbers signed ranged from 50 to 1,000 and are indicated parenthetically in the checklist. Values for cards #41-60, which are considered short-printed base cards, are found in the listings under Justifiable 2002.

		MT
	Common Player, #1-40:	5.00
	(See Justifiable 2002 for #41-60.)	
1	Russ Adams (400)	5.00
2	Travis Blackley (400)	5.00
3	Matt Cain (400)	6.00
4	Travis Chapman (400)	7.50
5	Kyle Davies (400)	6.00
6	Carlos Duran (50)	10.00
7	Gavin Floyd (50)	20.00
8	Jesse Foppert (400)	6.00
9	Choo Freeman (400)	5.00
10	Jimmy Gobble (50)	10.00
11	Jonny Gomes (50)	10.00
12	Khalil Greene (50)	15.00
13	Joel Guzman (50)	10.00
14	Luke Hagerty (400)	5.00
15	Jack Hannahan (400)	5.00
16	Rich Harden (400)	6.00
17	J.J. Hardy (400)	6.00
18	Jeremy Hermida (50)	10.00
19	Kris Honel (400)	5.00
20	Casey Kotchman (400)	7.50
21	Cliff Lee (400)	5.00
22	Francisco Liriano (400)	5.00
23	Jose Lopez (400)	5.00
24	Andy Marte (50)	30.00
25	Victor Martinez (50)	10.00
26	Joe Mauer (50)	30.00
27	Drew Meyer (400)	5.00
28	Dustin Moseley (400)	5.00
29	Clint Nageotte (50)	10.00
30	Rhett Parrott (400)	5.00
31	Josh Phelps (50)	25.00
32	Brandon Phillips (75)	25.00
33	Jose Reyes (50)	25.00
34	Felix Sanchez (400)	5.00
35	Sergio Santos (400)	6.00
36	Mark Teixeira (50)	25.00
37	Andres Torres (400)	5.00
38	B.J. Upton (50)	25.00
39	Shane Victorino (400)	5.00
40	David Wright (400)	25.00

Autographs - Silver

Sixteen of the players in Justifiable 2002 appear in a silver-bordered autographed parallel edition, serially numbered to 375 each and randomly inserted in all forms of packaging.

		MT
	Common Player:	5.00
7	Gavin Floyd	10.00
12	Khalil Greene	15.00
13	Joel Guzman	7.50
18	Jeremy Hermida	6.00
20	Casey Kotchman	10.00
24	Andy Marte	7.50
33	Jose Reyes	17.50
38	B.J. Upton	15.00
40	David Wright	25.00
42	Shin Soo Choo	7.50
47	Corey Hart	5.00
48	Justin Huber	5.00
54	Felix Pie	12.50
55	Jason Pridie	5.00
56	Hanley Ramirez	15.00
58	Jason Stokes	15.00

Auto. - Gold

Gold-bordered autographed versions of each card in Justifiable 2002 were produced in an edition of 100 each and randomly inserted into all forms of packaging.

		MT
	Common Player:	5.00
1	Russ Adams	5.00
2	Travis Blackley	5.00
3	Matt Cain	7.50
4	Travis Chapman	10.00
5	Kyle Davies	6.00
6	Carlos Duran	7.50
7	Gavin Floyd	15.00
8	Jesse Foppert	7.50
9	Choo Freeman	10.00
10	Jimmy Gobble	10.00
11	Jonny Gomes	10.00
12	Khalil Greene	15.00
13	Joel Guzman	7.50
14	Luke Hagerty	5.00
15	Jack Hannahan	5.00
16	Rich Harden	7.50
17	J.J. Hardy	7.50
18	Jeremy Hermida	8.00
19	Kris Honel	5.00
20	Casey Kotchman	15.00
21	Cliff Lee	5.00
22	Francisco Liriano	5.00
23	Jose Lopez	5.00
24	Andy Marte	7.50
25	Victor Martinez	5.00
26	Joe Mauer	20.00
27	Drew Meyer	5.00
28	Dustin Moseley	5.00
29	Clint Nageotte	5.00
30	Rhett Parrott	5.00
31	Josh Phelps	25.00
32	Brandon Phillips	25.00
33	Jose Reyes	20.00
34	Felix Sanchez	5.00
35	Sergio Santos	7.50
36	Mark Teixeira	20.00
37	Andres Torres	5.00
38	B.J. Upton	20.00
39	Shane Victorino	5.00
40	David Wright	25.00
41	Joseph Blanton	6.00
42	Shin Soo Choo	10.00
43	Jason Cooper	5.00
44	Jeff Francis	5.00
45	Jeff Francoeur	25.00
46	Joey Gomes	5.00
47	Corey Hart	5.00
48	Justin Huber	5.00
49	Dan Meyer	7.50
50	Dontrelle Willis	17.50
51	Scott Hairston	7.50
52	Anthony Lerew	5.00
53	Jeff Mathis	5.00
54	Felix Pie	10.00
55	Jason Pridie	5.00
56	Hanley Ramirez	20.00
57	Joe Saunders	5.00
58	Jason Stokes	20.00
59	Brian Tallet	5.00
60	Chad Tracy	7.50

Auto. - Black

Each card in Justifiable 2002 was issued in a black-bordered autographed version, randomly inserted. Each black parallel autograph was serially numbered in an edition of 25.

		MT
	Common Player:	15.00
1	Russ Adams	15.00
2	Travis Blackley	15.00
3	Matt Cain	15.00
4	Travis Chapman	25.00
5	Kyle Davies	15.00
6	Carlos Duran	25.00
7	Gavin Floyd	40.00
8	Jesse Foppert	25.00
9	Choo Freeman	25.00
10	Jimmy Gobble	25.00
11	Jonny Gomes	25.00
12	Khalil Greene	25.00
13	Joel Guzman	25.00
14	Luke Hagerty	15.00
15	Jack Hannahan	15.00
16	Rich Harden	22.50
17	J.J. Hardy	20.00
18	Jeremy Hermida	15.00
19	Kris Honel	15.00
20	Casey Kotchman	40.00
21	Cliff Lee	15.00
22	Francisco Liriano	15.00
23	Jose Lopez	15.00
24	Andy Marte	25.00
25	Victor Martinez	15.00
26	Joe Mauer	75.00
27	Drew Meyer	15.00
28	Dustin Moseley	15.00
29	Clint Nageotte	15.00
30	Rhett Parrott	15.00
31	Josh Phelps	60.00
32	Brandon Phillips	60.00
33	Jose Reyes	60.00
34	Felix Sanchez	15.00
35	Sergio Santos	15.00
36	Mark Teixeira	45.00
37	Andres Torres	15.00
38	B.J. Upton	40.00
39	Shane Victorino	15.00
40	David Wright	50.00
41	Joseph Blanton	15.00
42	Shin Soo Choo	25.00
43	Jason Cooper	15.00
44	Jeff Francis	15.00
45	Jeff Francoeur	75.00
46	Joey Gomes	15.00
47	Corey Hart	15.00
48	Justin Huber	15.00
49	Dan Meyer	15.00
50	Dontrelle Willis	60.00
51	Scott Hairston	15.00
52	Anthony Lerew	15.00
53	Jeff Mathis	15.00
54	Felix Pie	25.00
55	Jason Pridie	15.00
56	Hanley Ramirez	60.00
57	Joe Saunders	15.00
58	Jason Stokes	60.00
59	Brian Tallet	15.00
60	Chad Tracy	20.00

2002 Just Prospects

After a one-year hiatus, Just Minors returned to the production of cards with a 2002 issue released only in boxed-set form, rather than foil packs. Each box, with a suggested retail price of $19.95, includes the 40-card base set plus one of 10 short-printed autograph cards. Autographed base-set cards were a 1:2 random box insert and Just Black parallels, numbered to 50, were found one per 10 boxes. Rather than photographs, each card features artwork by Noah Stokes. Backs have a ghost image of the front art, along with vital data, a few words about the player and, in the case of autographed cards, a hand-numbered holographic sticker. The SP cards #41-50 are numbered from an edition of 1,200 each.

		MT
	Complete Set (50):	25.00
	Common Player:	.25
01	Willy Aybar	.25
02	Angel Berroa	.50
03	Wilson Betemit	.50
04	Hank Blalock	.50
05	Tony Blanco	.25
06	Boof Bonser	.25
07	Joe Borchard	.50
08	Carl Crawford	.35
09	Juan Cruz	.25
10	Nelson Cruz	.25
11	Domingo Cuello	.50
12	Gavin Floyd	.50
13	Franklyn German	.25
14	Adrian Gonzalez	.50
15	Danny Gonzalez	.25
16	Gabe Gross	.25
17	Angel Guzman	.35
18	Joel Guzman	.35
19	Josh Karp	.50
20	Austin Kearns	.40
21	Joe Mauer	1.00
22	Yadier Molina	.75
23	Justin Morneau	1.00
24	Xavier Nady	2.00
25	Chris Narveson	.35
26	Miguel Negron	.25
27	Bubba Nelson	.25
28	Nick Neugebauer	.35
29	Jake Peavy	.75
30	Carlos Pena	.40
31	Antonio Perez	.50
32	Jon Rauch	.50
33	Jose Rojas	.25
34	Felix Sanchez	.25
35	Chris Snelling	.25
36	Rafael Soriano	.25
37	Dennis Tankersley	.25
38	Mark Teixeira	1.00
39	Josh Thigpen	.25
40	Billy Traber	.75
41	Taggert Bozied/SP/Auto.	2.50
42	Aaron Cook/SP/Auto.	2.00
43	Carlos Duran/SP/Auto.	2.00
44	Mike Fontenot/SP/Auto.	3.00
45	Jimmy Gobble/SP/Auto.	2.00
46	Jonny Gomes/SP/Auto.	4.00
47	Matt Harrington/SP/Auto.	2.50
48	Bobby Jenks/SP/Auto.	2.50
49	Todd Linden/SP/Auto.	4.00
50	Clint Nageotte/SP/Auto.	2.00

Gold Edition

Packaged with a mini-helmet autographed by a former, current or prospective major league star, this boxed set parallels the Just Prospects issue. Cards #1-40 are virtually identical to the regular issue except for the gold borders on front and a "Gold Edition" logo on back. Cards #41-50 are unautographed short-prints with a hologram on back numbered to 500. Each boxed set with a suggested retail price of $44.95 includes one of the short-print and two autographed cards.

		MT
	Factory Set:	25.00
	Complete Set (50):	15.00
	Common Player:	.50
01	Willy Aybar	.50
02	Angel Berroa	1.00
03	Wilson Betemit	1.00
04	Hank Blalock	1.00
05	Tony Blanco	.50
06	Boof Bonser	.50
07	Joe Borchard	1.00
08	Carl Crawford	.75
09	Juan Cruz	.50
10	Nelson Cruz	.50
11	Domingo Cuello	1.00
12	Gavin Floyd	1.50
13	Franklyn German	.50
14	Adrian Gonzalez	1.00
15	Danny Gonzalez	.50
16	Gabe Gross	.50
17	Angel Guzman	.65
18	Joel Guzman	.65
19	Josh Karp	1.00
20	Austin Kearns	.75
21	Joe Mauer	2.00
22	Yadier Molina	1.50
23	Justin Morneau	2.00
24	Xavier Nady	4.00
25	Chris Narveson	.60

26 Miguel Negron .50
27 Bubba Nelson .50
28 Nick Neugebauer .75
29 Jake Peavy 1.50
30 Carlos Pena .75
31 Antonio Perez 1.00
32 Jon Rauch 1.00
33 Jose Rojas .50
34 Felix Sanchez .50
35 Chris Snelling .50
36 Rafael Soriano .50
37 Dennis Tankersley .50
38 Mark Teixeira 2.00
39 Josh Thigpen .50
40 Billy Traber 1.75
41 Taggert Bozied/SP 2.00
42 Aaron Cook/SP 2.00
43 Carlos Duran/SP 2.50
44 Mike Fontenot/SP 1.00
45 Jimmy Gobble/SP 1.00
46 Jonny Gomes/SP 2.00
47 Matt Harrington/SP 3.00
48 Bobby Jenks/SP 2.00
49 Todd Linden/SP 2.00
50 Clint Nageotte/SP 1.00

Auto. Base Cards

Inserted at a rate of one per two boxed sets were autographed versions of the base cards #1-40. These white-bordered cards were released in editions of either 50 or 200, with a serially-numbered hologram on back.

MT
Common Player: 2.00
01 Willy Aybar/200 2.00
02 Angel Berroa/50 10.00
03 Wilson Betemit/50 9.00
04 Hank Blalock/50 14.00
05 Tony Blanco/50 11.00
06 Boof Bonser/200 5.00
07 Joe Borchard/50 17.50
08 Carl Crawford/50 10.00
09 Juan Cruz/200 5.00
10 Nelson Cruz/200 2.00
11 Domingo Cuello/200 2.00
12 Gavin Floyd/50 27.50
13 Franklyn German/200 5.00
14 Adrian Gonzalez/75 12.50
15 Danny Gonzalez/200 5.00
16 Gabe Gross/200 2.50
17 Angel Guzman/200 7.00
18 Joel Guzman/200 9.00
19 Josh Karp/200 10.00
20 Austin Kearns/50 15.00
21 Joe Mauer/50 35.00
22 Yadier Molina/200 4.00
23 Justin Morneau/50 15.00
24 Xavier Nady/50 15.00
25 Chris Narveson/200 3.00
26 Miguel Negron/200 2.50
27 Bubba Nelson/200 2.00
28 Nick Neugebauer (?) 6.00
29 Jake Peavy/200 8.00
30 Carlos Pena (?) 7.50
31 Antonio Perez/200 6.00
32 Jon Rauch/200 4.00
33 Jose Rojas/200 2.00
34 Felix Sanchez (?) 2.00
35 Chris Snelling/200 4.00
36 Rafael Soriano/50 9.00
37 Dennis Tankersley/50 10.00
38 Mark Teixeira/50 25.00
39 Josh Thigpen/200 3.00
40 Billy Traber/200 12.50

Gold Edition Auto.

At the rate of two per boxed set, autographed versions of each Gold Edition card were randomly inserted. Cards have a serially numbered hologram on back within editions of 300 or fewer per card.

MT
Common Player: 2.00
01 Willy Aybar 2.50
02 Angel Berroa 7.00
03 Wilson Betemit 5.00
04 Hank Blalock 9.00
05 Tony Blanco 5.00
06 Boof Bonser 2.00
07 Joe Borchard 8.00
08 Carl Crawford 6.00
09 Juan Cruz 6.00
10 Nelson Cruz 2.00
11 Domingo Cuello 4.00
12 Gavin Floyd 6.00
13 Franklyn German 2.00
14 Adrian Gonzalez 6.00
15 Danny Gonzalez 2.00
16 Gabe Gross 2.00
17 Angel Guzman 2.00
18 Joel Guzman 4.00
19 Josh Karp 4.00
20 Austin Kearns 6.00
21 Joe Mauer 10.00
22 Yadier Molina 10.00
23 Justin Morneau 6.00
24 Xavier Nady 10.00
25 Chris Narveson 5.00
26 Miguel Negron 2.00
27 Bubba Nelson 2.00
28 Nick Neugebauer 4.00
29 Jake Peavy 3.00
30 Carlos Pena 3.00
31 Antonio Perez 3.00
32 Jon Rauch 3.00
33 Jose Rojas 3.00
34 Felix Sanchez 2.00
35 Chris Snelling 4.00
36 Rafael Soriano 7.00
37 Dennis Tankersley 3.00
38 Mark Teixeira 8.00
39 Josh Thigpen 2.00
40 Billy Traber 7.00
41 Taggert Bozied 3.00
42 Aaron Cook 2.00
43 Carlos Duran 2.50
44 Mike Fontenot 2.00
45 Jimmy Gobble 2.00
46 Jonny Gomes 3.00
47 Matt Harrington 3.00
48 Bobby Jenks 3.00
49 Todd Linden 4.00
50 Clint Nageotte 2.00

2002 Upper Deck Minor League

A November-released, post-season set, UD Minor League offers a base set of 400 cards. Cards #1-200 are regular player cards. Cards #201-230 are a subset titled "On the Fast Track." Cards #231-240 are "Draft Day Gems" and cards #241-400 are nonplayer "Team Profiles" logo/history cards. All cards are silver-foil highlighted on front and have color backs. Insert sets feature game-used jerseys, player autographs and a group of Michael Jordan memorabilia cards. Cards were sold in six-card foil packs.

MT
Complete Set (400): 35.00
Common Player: .05
Wax Pack (6): 1.50
Wax Box (24): 25.00
1 Bobby Jenks .25
2 Chris Bootcheck .05
3 Francisco Rodriguez .25
4 Johan Santana .60
5 Casey Kotchman .25
6 Jeff Mathis .10
7 Joe Torres .10
8 Anthony Pluta .05
9 John Buck .05
10 Chris Burke .25
11 Rodrigo Rosario .05
12 Chad Qualls .15
13 Tommy Whiteman .05
14 Bobby Crosby .25
15 Chris Tritle .05
16 Mike Wood .05
17 Freddie Bynum .05
18 John-Ford Griffin .10
19 Nick Swisher .10
20 Gabe Gross .10
21 Tracy Thorpe .05
22 Alexis Rios .20
23 Ramon Castro .05
24 Richard Lewis .05
25 Brian Digby .05
26 Brett Evert .10
27 Matt Belisle .05
28 Carlos Duran .10
29 Zach Miner .05
30 Gonzalo Lopez .05
31 Adam Wainwright 1.00
32 Kelly Johnson .10
33 Bubba Nelson .10
34 Wilson Betemit .05
35 Mike Jones .05
36 Ben Hendrickson .10
37 Corey Hart .10
38 David Krynzel .25
39 Cristian Guerrero .10
40 Matt Yeatman .10
41 Prince Fielder 3.00
42 Cristobal Correa .05
43 Jimmy Journell .05
44 Scotty Layfield .05
45 Justin Pope .05
46 B.R. Cook .05
47 Yadier Molina .25
48 Dan Haren .25
49 Chris Duncan .50
50 Luis Montanez .05
51 Angel Guzman .10
52 J.J. Johnson .05
53 Nic Jackson .05
54 David Kelton .10
55 Ben Christensen .25
56 Felix Sanchez .05
57 Rocco Baldelli .25
58 Josh Hamilton .50
59 Jon Switzer .05
60 Jace Brewer .05
61 Jorge Cantu .05
62 Chad Tracy .25
63 Luis Terrero .05
64 Mike Gosling .05
65 Brad Cresse .10
66 Jesus Cota .05
67 Scott Hairston .10
68 Lino Garcia .05
69 Jason Bulger .05
70 Oscar Villarreal .05
71 Beltran Perez .05
72 Jose Rojas .05
73 Brennan King .05
74 Koyie Hill .05
75 Hong-Chih Kuo .15
76 Willy Aybar .05
77 Joel Guzman .10
78 Josh Karp .05
79 Rich Rundles .05
80 Luke Lockwood .05
81 Donnie Bridges .05
82 Eric Good .05
83 Claudio Vargas .05
84 Seung Song .10
85 Jerome Williams .05
86 Boof Bonser .05
87 Erick Threets .05
88 Jesse Foppert .10
89 Lance Niekro .10
90 Julian Benavidez .05
91 Francisco Liriano 2.00
92 Grady Sizemore .35
93 Ryan Church .10
94 Travis Foley .05
95 Brian Tallet .05
96 Billy Traber .10
97 Dan Denham .05
98 J.D. Martin .05
99 Corey Smith .05
100 Derek Thompson .05
101 Michael Garciaparra .10
102 Ryan Christenson .10
103 Jamal Strong .05
104 Matt Thornton .05
105 Rett Johnson .05
106 Clint Nageotte .10
107 Shin-Soo Choo .25
108 Allen Baxter .05
109 Adrian Gonzalez .15
110 Denny Bautista .10
111 Miguel Cabrera .45
112 Josh Wilson .05
113 Rob Henkel .05
114 Craig Brazell .10
115 Enrique Cruz .05
116 Aaron Heilman .10
117 David Wright 3.00
118 Justin Huber .20
119 Jose Reyes .50
120 Neal Musser .05
121 Keith Reed .05
122 Richard Stahl .05
123 Matt Riley .10
124 Mike Fontenot .10
125 Tim Raines Jr. .05
126 Beau Hale .05
127 Josh Barfield .15
128 Tagg Bozied .15
129 Mark Phillips .10
130 Jake Gautreau .10
131 Ben Johnson .05
132 Xavier Nady .10
133 Taylor Buchholz .10
134 Gavin Floyd .25
135 Anderson Machado .05
136 Jorge Padilla .05
137 Yoel Hernandez .05
138 Chase Utley 1.50
139 J.R. House .05
140 Justin Reid .05
141 Jon VanBenschoten .15
142 Chris Young 1.00
143 Sean Burnett .10
144 Jose Castillo .15
145 Mario Ramos .05
146 Patrick Boyd .05
147 Jason Bourgeois .05
148 Mark Teixeira .50
149 Mauricio Lara .05
150 Manny Delcarmen .05
151 Phil Dumatrait .10
152 Josh Thigpen .05
153 Tony Blanco .05
154 Rene Miniel .05
155 Kevin Huang .10
156 Anastacio Martinez .05
157 Ty Howington .10
158 Dane Sardinha .05
159 Rainier Olmedo .05
160 Dustin Moseley .10
161 Ryan Snare .05
162 Justin Gillman .05
163 Choo Freeman .10
164 Jayson Nix .05
165 Garrett Atkins .25
166 Javier Colina .05
167 Rene Reyes .05
168 Ching-Lung Lo .05
169 Chin-Hui Tsao .15
170 Brad Hawpe .10
171 Jason Young .10
172 Cory Vance .05
173 Matt Holliday 1.00
174 Mike Stodolka .05
175 Colt Griffin .10
176 Alejandro Machado .05
177 Kenny Baugh .10
178 Charley Carter .05
179 Preston Larrison .10
180 Cody Ross .05
181 Nook Logan .05
182 Jeremy Bonderman 1.50
183 David Espinosa .05
184 Michael Restovich .10
185 Rob Bowen .05
186 B.J. Garbe .05
187 Justin Morneau .25
188 Joe Mauer 2.00
189 Jon McDonald .05
190 Franklin Francisco .05
191 Corwin Malone .05
192 Felix Diaz .05
193 Tim Hummel .05
194 Kris Honel .10
195 Matt Smith .05
196 Alex Graman .05
197 Brandon Claussen .15
198 Erick Almonte .05
199 Bronson Sardinha .05
200 Danny Borrell .05
201 Casey Kotchman .15
202 John Buck .10
203 Bobby Crosby .10
204 Gabe Gross .05
205 Wilson Betemit .10
206 David Krynzel .10
207 Jimmy Journell .05
208 David Kelton .05
209 Josh Hamilton .50
210 Luis Terrero .05
211 Joel Guzman .15
212 Seung Song .05
213 Jerome Williams .05
214 J.D. Martin .05
215 Clint Nageotte .05
216 Miguel Cabrera .25
217 Aaron Heilman .10
218 Richard Stahl .05
219 Jake Gautreau .05
220 Taylor Buchholz .15
221 J.R. House .05
222 Mark Teixeira .15
223 Tony Blanco .05
224 Ty Howington .10
225 Chin-Hui Tsao .10
226 Colt Griffin .05
227 Kenny Baugh .05
228 Joe Mauer 1.00
229 Corwin Malone .05
230 Brandon Claussen .10
231 Scott Kazmir 2.00
232 Zack Greinke .75
233 Scott Moore .25
234 Drew Meyer .25
235 Khalil Greene .75
236 Chris Gruler .25
237 Prince Fielder 2.00
238 Jeff Francis 1.00
239 Jeremy Hermida .40
240 Nick Swisher .75
241 Salt Lake Stingers .05
242 Arkansas Travelers .05
243 Rancho Cucamonga Quakes .05
244 Cedar Rapids Kernals .05
245 Provo Angels .05
246 New Orleans Zephyrs .05
247 Round Rock Express .05
248 Lexington Legends .05
249 Michigan City Battle Cats .05
250 Tri-City ValleyCats .05
251 Sacramento River Cats .05
252 Midland Rockhounds .05
253 Modesto A's .05
254 Visalia Oaks .05
255 Vancouver Canadians .05
256 Syracuse Skychiefs .05
257 Tennessee Smokies .05
258 Dunedin Blue Jays .05
259 Charleston Alleycats .05
260 Auburn Doubledays .05
261 Richmond Braves .05
262 Greenville Braves .05
263 Macon Braves .05
264 Myrtle Beach Pelicans .05
265 Danville Braves .05
266 Gulf Coast Braves .05
267 Indianapolis Indians .05
268 Hunstville Stars .05
269 High Desert Mavericks .05
270 Beloit Snappers .05
271 Ogden Raptors .05
272 Memphis Redbirds .05
273 New Haven Ravens .05
274 Potomac Cannons .05
275 Peoria Chiefs .05
276 New Jersey Cardinals .05
277 Johnson City Cardinals .05
278 Iowa Cubs .05
279 West Tenn Diamond Jaxx .05
280 Daytona Cubs .05
281 Lansing Lugnuts .05
282 Boise Hawks .05
283 Mesa Cubs .05
284 Durham Bulls .05
285 Orlando Rays .05
286 Bakersfield Blaze .05
287 Charleston Riverdogs .05
288 Hudson Valley Renegades .05
289 Tucson Sidewinders .05
290 El Paso Diablos .05
291 Lancaster JetHawks .05
292 South Bend Silver Hawks .05
293 Yakima Bears .05
294 Missoula Osprey .05
295 Las Vegas 51s .05
296 Jacksonville Suns .05
297 Vero Beach Dodgers .05
298 South Georgia Waves .05
299 Great Falls Dodgers .05
300 Gulf Coast Dodgers .05
301 Ottawa Lynx .05
302 Harrisburg Senators .05
303 Brevard County Manatees .05
304 Clinton Lumberkings .05
305 Vermont Expos .05
306 Fresno Grizzlies .05
307 Shreveport Swamp Dragons .05
308 San Jose Giants .05
309 Hagerstown Suns .05
310 Salem-Keizer Volcanoes .05
311 Arizona Giants .05
312 Buffalo Bisons .05
313 Akron Aeros .05
314 Kinston Indians .05
315 Columbus RedStixx .05
316 Mahoning Valley Scrappers .05
317 Burlington Indians .05
318 Tacoma Rainiers .05
319 San Antonio Missions .05
320 San Bernardino Stampede .05
321 Wisconsin Timber Rattlers .05
322 Everett Aqua Sox .05
323 Calgary Cannons .05
324 Portland Sea Dogs .05
325 Jupiter Hammerheads .05
326 Kane County Cougars .05
327 Jamestown Jammers .05
328 Norfolk Tides .05
329 Binghamton Mets .05
330 St. Lucie Mets .05
331 Capital City Bombers .05
332 Brooklyn Cyclones .05
333 Kingsport Mets .05
334 Rochester Red Wings .05
335 Bowie Baysox .05
336 Frederick Keys .05
337 Delmarva Shorebirds .05
338 Bluefield Orioles .05
339 Portland Beavers .05
340 Mobile BayBears .05
341 Lake Elsinore Storm .05
342 Ft. Wayne Wizards .05
343 Eugene Emeralds .05
344 Scranton, Wilkes-Barre Red Barons .05
345 Reading Phillies .05
346 Clearwater Phillies .05
347 Lakewood BlueClaws .05
348 Batavia Muckdogs .05
349 Nashville Sounds .05
350 Altoona Curve .05
351 Hickory Crawdads .05
352 Lynchburg Hillcats .05
353 Williamsport Crosscutters .05
354 Oklahoma RedHawks .05
355 Tulsa Drillers .05
356 Charlotte Rangers .05
357 Savannah Sand Gnats .05
358 Pulaski Rangers .05
359 Pawtucket Red Sox .05
360 Trenton Thunder .05
361 Sarasota Red Sox .05
362 Augusta GreenJackets .05
363 Lowell Spinners .05
364 Gulf Coast Red Sox .05
365 Louisville Bats .05
366 Chattanooga Lookouts .05
367 Stockton Ports .05
368 Dayton Dragons .05
369 Billings Mustangs .05
370 Colorado Springs Sky Sox .05
371 Carolina Mudcats .05
372 Salem Avalanche .05
373 Tri City Dust Devils .05
374 Asheville Tourists .05
375 Omaha Royals .05
376 Wichita Wranglers .05
377 Wilmington Blue Rocks .05
378 Burlington Bees .05
379 Spokane Indians .05
380 Toledo Mud Hens .05
381 Erie Seawolves .05
382 Lakeland Tigers .05
383 West Michigan Whitecaps .05
384 Oneonta Tigers .05
385 Edmonton Trappers .05
386 New Britain Rock Cats .05
387 Ft. Myers Miracle .05
388 Quad City River Bandits .05
389 Elizabethton Twins .05
390 Charlotte Knights .05
391 Birmingham Barons .05
392 Winston-Salem Warthogs .05
393 Kannapolis Intimidators .05
394 Bristol White Sox .05
395 Columbus Clippers .05
396 Norwich Navigators .05
397 Tampa Yankees .05
398 Greensboro Bats .05
399 Staten Island Yankees .05
400 Gulf Coast Yankees .05

Game Jerseys

Ten players are included in this insert set featuring game-worn jersey pieces framed in a team-related monogram. Each card was produced in an edition of 850 pieces.

MT
Complete Set (10): 40.00
Common Player: 3.00
J-AH Aaron Heilman 3.00
J-BU Chris Burke 5.00
J-CR Bobby Crosby 7.50
J-CT Chad Tracy 4.50
J-DK David Krynzel 5.00
J-JB Jeremy Bonderman 15.00
J-JH Josh Hamilton 15.00
J-JJ Jimmy Journell 3.00
J-MT Mark Teixeira 6.00
J-RB Rocco Baldelli 7.50

Michael Jordan Flashbacks

More than 1,500 memorabilia cards featuring swatches of jerseys worn by Michael Jordan during his brief professional baseball fling were random pack inserts in UD Minor League. Numbers reported produced are indicated parenthetically.

MT
.00
MJ-SS Michael Jordan (Scorpions/1,490) 55.00
MS-WS1Michael Jordan (White Sox black/25.) 115.00
MS-WS2Michael Jordan (White Sox white/10.) 200.00
MS-WS3Michael Jordan (White Sox silver/5.)
MS-WS4Michael Jordan (White Sox gold/1.)

Signature Collection

Nearly three dozen players provided authentically autographed cards for random pack inserts in Upper Deck Minor League. Stated odds of finding a signed card were 1:18 packs. Besides the base autograph cards, four players each signed more limited-edition Silver (numbered to 25) or Gold (10 each) versions.

MT
Common Player: 3.00
AG Adrian Gonzalez 5.00
AG Adrian Gonzalez (Silver/25) 25.00
AH Aaron Heilman 7.50
AH Aaron Heilman (Silver/25) 50.00
BB Brian Bass 3.00
BC Brad Cresse 4.00
BT Billy Traber 7.00
CB Chris Burke 7.50
CG Colt Griffin 4.00
CK Casey Kotchman 12.50
CL Brandon Claussen 4.00
CM Corwin Malone 3.00
CT Chad Tracy 12.00
DK David Krynzel 4.00
DKe David Kelton 4.00
GF Gavin Floyd 8.00
GG Gabe Gross 4.00
JB John Buck 4.00
JB John Buck (Silver/25) 20.00
JE Jerome Williams 7.00
JE Jerome Williams (Gold/10) 50.00
JF John-Ford Griffin 4.00
JG Jake Gautreau 4.00
JH Josh Hamilton 40.00
JJ Jimmy Journell 3.00
JJ Jimmy Journell (Gold/10) 50.00
JM J.D. Martin 4.00
JO Joe Mauer 25.00
JO Joe Mauer (Gold/10) 100.00
JS Jason Stokes 12.50
JU Justin Huber 12.00
KB Kenny Baugh 3.00
MC Miguel Cabrera 45.00
MG Michael Garciaparra 16.00
MG Michael Garciaparra (Silver/25) 50.00
MJ Mike Jones 5.00
MT Mark Teixeira 15.00
MT Mark Teixeira (Gold/10) 100.00
PF Prince Fielder 75.00
SB Sean Burnett 6.00
TH Ty Howington 3.00
WA Willy Aybar 3.00

Star Swatch

Five of the top prospects in Upper Deck Minor League are featured in this uniform-swatch insert, serially numbered to just 25 pieces each.

		MT
Common Player:		15.00
SS-AH	Aaron Heilman	15.00
SS-JH	Josh Hamilton	25.00
SS-JJ	Jimmy Journell	15.00
SS-MT	Mark Teixeira	35.00
SS-RB	Rocco Baldelli	35.00

2002 Upper Deck USA Baseball

This boxed set commemorating the 2002 U.S. National Team was produced in an edition of 10,000 with a suggested retail price of $19.95. Each set contains 30 gold-foil enhanced player cards, plus one jersey-patch insert serially numbered to 475 each and an alumni autographed card numbered within an edition of 375 each.

		MT
Unopened Boxed Set (32):		30.00
Complete Set (30):		7.00
Common Player:		.10
1	Chad Cordero	.35
2	Philip Humber	.30
3	Grant Johnson	.25
4	Wes Littleton	.25
5	Kyle Sleeth	.60
6	Huston Street	.25
7	Brad Sullivan	.40
8	Bob Zimmerman	.25
9	Abe Alvarez	.30
10	Kyle Bakker	.35
11	Clint Sammons	.25
12	Landon Powell	.55
13	Michael Aubrey	.45
14	Aaron Hill	.35
15	Conor Jackson	.25
16	Eric Patterson	1.00
17	Dustin Pedroia	3.00
18	Rickie Weeks	2.00
19	Shane Costa	.20
20	Mark Jurich	.25
21	Sam Fuld	.30
22	Carlos Quentin	1.00
23	Ryan Garko	.40
24	Lelo Prado	.10
25	Terry Alexander	.10
26	Sunny Golloway	.10
27	Terry Rupp	.10
28	Team photo	.10
29	Team photo	.05
30	Checklist	.05

Alumni Signatures

Each 32-card boxed set of USA Baseball includes one of 27 authentically autographed Alumni Signatures card of a former member of the national team. Cards have a vertical white cardboard panel at left with the autograph. At right is a purple duotone photo of the player. A serial number from an edition of 375 each appears at bottom-right. Backs have a statement of authenticity.

		MT
Complete Set (27):		350.00
Common Player:		5.00
JB	Josh Bard	12.00
WB	Willie Bloomquist	20.00
SB	Sean Burnett	8.00
BC	Bobby Crosby	30.00
KD	Keoni DeRenne	7.00
BD	Ben Diggins	12.00
LD	Lenny Dinardo	15.00
CE	Clint Everts	35.00
JF	Jeff Francoeur	250.00
MG	Mike Gosling	7.00
JH	J.J. Hardy	50.00
KH	Koyie Hill	5.00
MH	Matt Holliday	100.00
RH	Ryan Howard	300.00
JJ	Jacque Jones	8.00
JK	Josh Karp	8.00
CK	Casey Kotchman	30.00
DK	David Krynzel	10.00
JL	James Loney	40.00
JM	Joe Mauer	40.00
SN	Shane Nance	5.00
MP	Mark Prior	40.00
ZS	Zach Segovia	9.00
PS	Phil Seibel	5.00
JS	Jason Stanford	10.00
JW	Justin Wayne	10.00
MW	Matt Whitney	10.00

Jerseys

A 7/8" square swatch of National Team jersey fabric is sandwiched on these one-per-box inserts. Each card is numbered from within an edition of 475. A purple duotone photo of the player fills the top-right quadrant of the front. Backs have a statement of authenticity.

		MT
Complete Set (22):		125.00
Common Player:		3.00
AA	Abe Alvarez	4.00
MA	Michael Aubrey	9.00
KB	Kyle Bakker	12.00
CC	Chad Cordero	3.00
SC	Shane Costa	4.00
SF	Sam Fuld	5.00
AH	Aaron Hill	5.00
PH	Philip Humber	5.00
CJ	Conor Jackson	4.00
GJ	Grant Johnson	3.00
MJ	Mark Jurich	3.00
WL	Wes Littleton	4.00
EP	Eric Patterson	3.00
DP	Dustin Pedroia	10.00
LP	Landon Powell	10.00
CQ	Carlos Quentin	10.00
CS	Clint Sammons	5.00
KS	Kyle Sleeth	30.00
HS	Huston Street	5.00
BS	Brad Sullivan	8.00
RW	Rickie Weeks	20.00
BZ	Bob Zimmerman	4.00

2002 Minor League Team Sets

Manufacturer abbreviations used are: CH - Choice, GS - Grandstand, MA - Multi-Ad, WT - Warning Track.

		MT
229 Team Sets and Variations		
2002	GS AA All-Star Game (61)	15.00
2002	GS Aberdeen IronBirds (30)	13.50
2002	MA Akron Aeros (30)	9.50
2002	Team Alaska BB League Prospects (21)	25.00
2002	Team Alaska Goldpanners (20)	22.50
2002	Team Alaska Goldpanners Bonus Cards (3)	9.00
2002	Alaska Goldpanners Decade Greats (11)	15.00
2002	Team 1999 Alaska Goldpanners (11)	15.00
2002	TM Alexandria Aces (24)	9.00
2002	GS Altoona Curve (30)	10.00
2002	GS Appalachian League Top Prospects (30)	11.00
2002	GS Arkansas Travelers (30)	11.00
2002	GS Asheboro Copperheads (25)	8.50
2002	GS Asheville Tourists (30)	14.00
2002	GS Asheville Tourists Update (9)	15.00
2002	Team Auburn Doubledays (35)	12.00
2002	MA Augusta Greenjackets (30)	12.00
2002	Team Bakersfield Blaze (32)	15.00
2002	Team Batavia Muckdogs (40)	12.00
2002	MA Beloit Snappers (31)	11.00
2002	MA Beloit Snappers Update (7)	12.00
2002	MA Beloit Snappers To The Majors (7)	7.00
2002	WTC Berkshire Black Bears (26)	8.50
2002	GS Billings Mustangs (31)	11.00
2002	CH Binghamton Mets (30)	11.00
2002	CH Binghamton Mets Update (1)	7.50
2002	GS Birmingham Barons (30)	12.00
2002	GS Bluefield Orioles (36)	11.00
2002	GS Boise Hawks (30)	7.00
2002	GS Bowie Baysox (29)	11.00
2002	MA Brevard County Manatees (30)	11.00
2002	GS Bristol White Sox (30)	9.50
2002	MA Brockton Rox	9.00
2002	MA Brooklyn Cyclones (34)	11.00
2002	CH Buffalo Bisons (30)	12.00
2002	MA Burlington Bees (30)	11.00
2002	MA Calgary Cannons (27)	15.00
2002	CH California/Carolina Leagues A-S (51)	12.50
2002	GS California League Top Prospects (30)	11.00
2002	CH Camden Rivershaks (31)	7.50
2002	GS Canton Coyotes (30)	8.50
2002	MA Capital City Bombers (30)	30.00
2002	CH Carolina League Top Prospects (30)	12.00
2002	Team Carolina Mudcats (30)	16.50
2002	GS Casper Rockies (30)	10.00
2002	Team Cedar Rapids Kernels (33)	8.00
2002	MA Charleston Alley Cats (30)	10.00
2002	MA Charleston River Dogs (29)	11.00
2002	GS Charlotte Knights (30)	10.00
2002	GS Charlotte Rangers (30)	15.00
2002	GS Chattanooga Lookouts (30)	12.50
2002	GS Clearwater Phillies (30)	11.00
2002	GS Clinton LumberKings (31)	15.00
2002	MA Colorado Springs Sky Sox (30)	9.00
2002	CH Columbus Clippers (30)	12.50
2002	Team Columbus Clippers (25)	25.00
2002	MA Columbus RedStixx (30)	10.00
2002	GS Danville Braves (33)	32.50
2002	MA Dayton Dragons (30)	9.00
2002	CH Daytona Cubs (30)	10.00
2002	MA Delmarva Shorebirds (30)	12.50
2002	WTC Duluth-Superior Dukes (26)	8.00
2002	WTC Duluth-Superior Dukes Update (6)	2.50
2002	GS Dunedin Blue Jays (30)	12.50
2002	CH Durham Bulls (30)	12.00
2002	GS Eastern League Top Prospects (30)	8.00
2002	GS Edinburg Roadrunners (30)	9.00
2002	MA Edmonton Trappers (30)	8.00
2002	GS Elizabethton Twins (30)	9.00
2002	GS El Paso Diablos (30)	15.00
2002	GS Erie Sea Wolves (27)	9.50
2002	GS Eugene Emeralds (32)	11.00
2002	GS Everett Aquasox (30)	14.50
2002	Team Fargo-Moorhead RedHawks (30)	9.00
2002	GS Fla. State League Top Prospects (24)	11.00
2002	GS Frederick Keys (30)	11.00
2002	MA Fresno Grizzlies (29)	10.00
2002	MA Ft. Myers Miracle (30)	10.00
2002	GS Ft. Wayne Wizards (32)	9.00
2002	MA Gateway Grizzlies (28)	9.00
2002	MA Great Falls Dodgers (36)	30.00
2002	MA Greensboro Bats (29)	10.00
2002	GS Greenville Braves (34)	9.00
2002	MA Hagerstown Suns (29)	10.00
2002	GS Harrisburg Senators (28)	15.00
2002	MA Hickory Crawdads (30)	10.00
2002	MA Hickory Crawdads Update (30)	12.50
2002	GS High Desert Mavericks (32)	12.00
2002	GS High Desert Mavericks Update (1)	5.00
2002	MA Hudson Valley Renegades (34)	11.00
2002	Hudson Valley Renegades Team Issue (33)	60.00
2002	Team Huntsville Stars (29)	10.00
2002	CH Indianapolis Indians (30)	9.00
2002	CH International League All-Stars (33)	9.00
2002	GS Int'l League Top Prospects (30)	11.00
2002	MA Iowa Cubs (30)	17.50
2002	Des Moines Register Iowa Cubs (5)	50.00
2002	GS Jacksonville Suns (30)	10.00
2002	GS Johnson City Cardinals (36)	7.00
2002	Team Jupiter Hammerheads (40)	13.50
2002	GS Kane County Cougars (30)	10.00
2002	Team Kane County Cougars (32)	25.00
2002	Team Kane Co. Cougars - Old Navy (30)	35.00
2002	TM Kane County Cougars Update Auto. (1)	32.50
2002	MA Kannapolis Intimidators (30)	11.00
2002	Team Keene Swamp Bats (?)	15.00
2002	CH Kinston Indians (32)	14.00
2002	GS Lake Elsinore Storm (31)	13.00
2002	MA Lakewood BlueClaws (30)	8.00
2002	MA Lakewood Blue Claws Update (15)	6.50
2002	GS Lancaster JetHawks (30)	9.00
2002	GS Lansing Lugnuts (30)	7.00
2002	MA Las Vegas 51s (30)	15.00
2002	MA Lexington Legends (30)	11.00
2002	GS Lincoln Saltdogs (25)	8.50
2002	CH Long Island Ducks (29)	7.50
2002	CH Louisville Bats (31)	17.50
2002	CH Lowell Spinners (36)	11.00
2002	CH Lowell Spinners Update (5)	10.00
2002	CH Lowell Spinners Legends (14)	14.00
2002	CH Lynchburg Hillcats (31)	12.00
2002	MA Macon Braves (32)	12.00
2002	MA Mahoning Valley Scrappers (30)	8.00
2002	GS Martinsville Astros (32)	12.00
2002	Team Medicine Hat Blue Jays (35)	15.00
2002	Team Memphis Redbirds (30)	10.00
2002	MA Michigan Battle Cats (30)	16.00
2002	GS Midland Rock Hounds (29)	9.00
2002	GS Midland RockHounds- Texas Burger (30)	9.50
2002	Team Midland RockHounds (24)	50.00
2002	GS Missoula Osprey (35)	10.00
2002	GS Mobile BayBears (30)	14.00
2002	GS Modesto A's (30)	7.00
2002	MA Myrtle Beach Pelicans (30)	11.00
2002	Team Nashua Pride (28)	8.50
2002	MA Nashville Sounds (30)	9.00
2002	GS New Britain Rock Cats (30)	10.00
2002	GS N.B. Rock Cats 2001 E.L. Champs (9)	10.00
2002	GS N.B. Red Sox/ Rock Cats ATG (9)	10.00
2002	GS New Haven Ravens (30)	10.00
2002	GS New Jersey Cardinals (30)	10.00
2002	WTC New Jersey Jackals (27)	8.50
2002	MA New Orleans Zephyrs (30)	10.00
2002	CH Norfolk Tides (37)	9.00
2002	GS Norwich Navigators (30)	10.00
2002	MA Ogden Raptors (36)	20.00
2002	MA Oklahoma City RedHawks (36)	10.00
2002	MA Omaha Royals (30)	10.00
2002	MA Orlando Rays (29)	50.00
2002	CH Ottawa Lynx (30)	10.00
2002	MA Pacific Coast League All-Stars (30)	12.00
2002	MA Pacific Coast Lea. Top Prospects (36)	11.00
2002	CH Pawtucket Red Sox (30)	10.00
2002	MA Peninsula Pilots (31)	7.50
2002	MA Peoria Chiefs (30)	10.00
2002	MA Portland Beavers (29)	10.00
2002	GS Portland Sea Dogs (34)	10.00
2002	CH Potomac Cannons (32)	10.00
2002	GS Princeton Devil Rays (30)	10.00
2002	Team Provo Angels (39)	11.00
2002	GS Pulaski Rangers (33)	10.00
2002	GS Quad City River Bandits (30)	11.00
2002	GS Rancho Cucamonga Quakes (30)	12.00
2002	MA Reading Phillies (30)	12.00
2002	MA Reading Area CC Reading Phillies (30)	12.50
2002	MA Reading Phillies Update (30)	9.50
2002	MA Reading Baseball Town (20)	30.00
2002	MA Reading Baseballtown (18)	25.00
2002	MA Reading Baseballtown Pepsi (18)	25.00
2002	CH Richmond Braves (30)	8.00
2002	CH Rochester Red Wings (29)	9.00
2002	GS Rockford RiverHawks (30)	8.50
2002	Team Round Rock Express (30)	9.00
2002	MA Sacramento River Cats (30)	10.00
2002	GS Salem Avalanche (30)	9.00
2002	GS Salem-Keizer Volcanoes (36)	10.00
2002	MA Salt Lake City Stingers (30)	10.00
2002	Team San Angelo Colts (25)	9.00
2002	GS San Antonio Missions (30)	10.00
2002	GS San Bernardino Stampede (30)	10.00
2002	GS San Jose Giants (30)	9.00
2002	GS Sarasota Red Sox (30)	8.00
2002	MA Savannah Sand Gnats (30)	10.00
2002	Team Schaumburg Flyers (23)	10.00
2002	CH Scranton/Wilkes-Barre Red Barons (30)	10.00
2002	Team Scranton/WB Red Baron Magnets (4)	8.00
2002	GS Shreveport Swamp Dragons (26)	15.00
2002	GS Shreve. Swamp Dragons Update Auto.(1)	15.00
2002	MA Sioux Falls Canaries (30)	8.00
2002	MA Somerset Patriots (30)	7.50
2002	MA South Atlantic League Prospects (33)	12.50
2002	MA South Bend Silver Hawks (29)	10.00
2002	GS Southern League Top Prospects (30)	14.00
2002	GS South Georgia Waves (30)	12.00
2002	GS Spokane Indians (32)	10.00
2002	MA Staten Island Yankees (35)	10.00
2002	GS St. Lucie Mets (33)	12.00
2002	GS St. Lucie Mets Update (1)	5.00
2002	GS St. Lucie Mets Update Autographed (1)	15.00
2002	GS Stockton Ports (30)	13.00
2002	TM St. Paul Saints (32)	9.00
2002	CH Syracuse SkyChiefs (30)	10.00
2002	MA Tacoma Rainiers (30)	10.00
2002	MA Tampa Yankees (30)	10.00
2002	GS Tennessee Smokies (30)	10.00
2002	GS Texas League Top Prospects (24)	10.00
2002	CH Toledo Mud Hens (31)	10.00
2002	MA Trenton Thunder (30)	11.00
2002	Team Tri-City Dust Devils (36)	12.50
2002	MA Tucson Sidewinders (30)	10.00
2002	Team Tulsa Drillers (29)	13.00
2002	MA Vancouver Canadians (42)	12.50
2002	GS Vermont Expos (36)	10.00
2002	GS Vero Beach Dodgers (31)	12.00
2002	GS Visalia Oaks (30)	13.00
2002	CH Washington Wild Things (30)	8.00
2002	Team Waterloo Bucks (18)	6.00
2002	MA West Michigan Whitecaps (30)	10.00
2002	GS West Tenn Diamond Jaxx (30)	12.50
2002	GS West Tenn Diamond Jaxx Update (6)	12.00
2002	GS Wichita Wranglers (29)	10.00
2002	CH Williamsport Crosscutters (34)	10.00
2002	CH Wilmington Blue Rocks (30)	9.00
2002	CH Wilmington Blue Rocks sheet (9)	10.00
2002	TM Winnipeg Goldeyes (30)	10.00
2002	CH Winston-Salem Warthogs (30)	11.00
2002	CH Winston-Salem Warthogs Update (30)	10.00
2002	MA Wisconsin Timber Rattlers (28)	8.00
2002	GS Yakima Bears (34)	10.00

2003 Just Rookies 2002

Many of the top players from the 2002 draft are featured in Just Minors' first issue for 2003. In an innovative marketing move, the company made the cards available directly to consumers as sets, singles or multiple-card lots. There was no retail packaging of the product. Card fronts have borderless player photos on which team logos have been removed. An inset repeat of the player's head is at lower-right, bordered in either white for base cards, or black, gold or silver for limited-edition parallels. Base cards were issued in an edition of 22,000 each. Silver parallels were in an edition of 5,000 each, golds at 1,000 and blacks at 50 serially numbered cards each. The Silver and Gold parallels were sold only as complete sets. The blacks were sold only as singles, with a limit of one card per player.

		MT
Complete Base Set (40):		7.00
Common Player:		.25
Complete Silver Set (40):		10.00
Silver Singles:		1.5X
Complete Gold Set (40):		15.00
Gold Singles:		2.5X
Blacks:		25X
1	B.J. Upton	.50
2	Khalil Greene	.50
3	Jeremy Hermida	.35
4	Chad Tracy	.35
5	Francisco Cruceta	.35
6	Hanley Ramirez	1.50
7	Jeff Francoeur	1.50
8	Kyle Pawelczyk	.25
9	Justin Huber	.40
10	Gregor Blanco	.25
11	Andy Marte	1.00
12	Taggert Bozied	.50
13	Felix Pie	.75
14	Dontrelle Willis	1.00
15	J.J. Stokes	.75
16	Corey Hart	.50
17	Sergio Santos	.35
18	Colt Griffin	.25
19	Shin-Soo Choo	.35
20	Todd Linden	.25
21	Jonathan Figueroa	.25
22	James Loney	.50
23	Jason Pridie	.25
24	Denard Span	.25
25	Matt Whitney	.25
26	Dan Meyer	.50
27	Rudy Guillen	.25
28	Micah Schilling	.25
29	Wes Bankston	.25
30	Travis Ishikawa	.25
31	Jake Blalock	.25
32	C.J. Wilson	.25
33	Laynce Nix	.50
34	Brian Bruney	.25
35	Chris Gruler	.25
36	Merkin Valdez-Mateo	.25
37	Clint Everts	.65
38	Scott Moore	.25
39	Bryan Bullington	.75
40	Zach Parker	.35

Autographs

Autographed cards were made available directly to consumers in four varieties. Base autographs, with player inset portraits framed in white, were produced in editions of 50 to 500, as indicated parenthetically in the checklist. Silver parallels were in an edition of 375 each, gold in a 100-per-card edition and blacks were limited to 25 each.

MT
Common Base (White) Player: 6.00
Silver: 1-2X
Production 375 Each
Gold: 2X
Production 100 Each
Black: 2.5X
Production 25 Each
1 Wes Bankston/200 8.00
2 Jake Blalock/400 6.00
3 Gregor Blanco/400 6.00
4 Taggert Bozied/100 10.00
5 Brian Bruney/500 6.00
6 Bryan Bullington/50 15.00
7 Shin-Soo Choo/50 10.00
8 Francisco Cruceta/400 6.00
9 Clint Everts/400 7.50
10 Jonathan Figueroa/400 6.00
11 Jeff Francoeur/400 20.00
12 Khalil Greene/50 15.00
13 John-Ford Griffin/400 6.00
14 Chris Gruler/400 6.00
15 Rudy Guillen/200 10.00
16 Corey Hart/400 6.00
17 Jeremy Hermida/200 8.00
18 Justin Huber/50 10.00
19 Travis Ishikawa/400 6.00
20 Todd Linden/50 10.00
21 James Loney/200 12.00
22 Andy Marte/50 12.00
23 Manny Mateo/400 6.00
24 Dan Meyer/300 7.50
25 Scott Moore/500 6.00
26 Laynce Nix/400 6.00
27 Zach Parker/400 6.00
28 Kyle Pawelczyk/400 6.00
29 Felix Pie/200 10.00
30 Jason Pridie/400 8.00
31 Hanley Ramirez/200 20.00
32 Sergio Santos/200 9.00
33 Micah Schilling/400 6.00
34 Denard Span/400 6.00
35 Jason Stokes/100 10.00
36 Chad Tracy/400 6.50
37 B.J. Upton/50 30.00
38 Matt Whitney/200 8.00
39 Dontrelle Willis/100 8.00
40 C.J. Wilson/400 6.00

2003 Just Prospects Preview

Ten players expected to make a splash in 2004 were selected for this edition. Unsigned cards were available in complete-set form, either directly from the manufacturer (gold) or through its network of retailers (base, silver and black). Production was announced as 15,000 base sets, 5,000 silver, 1,000 gold and 50 serially-numbered sets in black.

MT
Complete Set (10): 6.00
Common Player: .50
Silver: 1.5X
Gold: 1X
Black: 8X
1 Robinson Cano 1.00
2 Franklin Gutierrez .50
3 Felix Hernandez 1.00
4 Edwin Jackson .50
5 Chris Lubanski .50
6 Lastings Milledge .75
7 Greg Miller .75
8 Dioner Navarro .50
9 Mark Prior 1.00
10 Brad Sullivan .50

Autographs

Ten elite prospects were selected for this edition. Autographed cards were available directly from the manufacturer. Gold cards, in an edition of 100 each were sold only as complete sets. White and black versions were sold singly in editions of 50 and 25, respectively.

MT
Complete Set, Gold (10): 110.00
Common Player, Gold: 7.50
White: 2X
Black: 3X
1 Robinson Cano 10.00
2 Franklin Gutierrez 9.00
3 Felix Hernandez 12.00
4 Edwin Jackson 9.00
5 Chris Lubanski 9.00
6 Lastings Milledge 10.00
7 Greg Miller 10.00
8 Dioner Navarro 9.00
9 Mark Prior 60.00
10 Brad Sullivan 9.00

2003 Just Rookies Preview

Ten elite prospects were selected for this edition. Unsigned cards were available in complete-set form either directly from the manufacturer (gold) or through its network of retailers (base, silver and black). Production was announced as 15,000 base sets, 5,000 silver, 1,000 gold and 50 serially-numbered sets in black.

MT
Complete Set (10): 6.50
Common Player: .50
Silver: 1.5X
Gold: 1X
Black: 8X
1 Anderson Amador .50
2 Eric Duncan 1.00
3 Anthony Gwynn .75
4 Cole Hamels 1.00
5 Adam LaRoche 1.00
6 Adam Loewen 1.00
7 David Murphy .50
8 Mark Prior 1.00
9 Alexis Rios .50
10 Delmon Young 1.00

Autographs

Ten elite prospects were selected for this edition. Autographed cards were available directly from the manufacturer. Gold cards, in an edition of 100 each were sold only as complete sets. White and black versions were sold singly in editions of 50 and 25, respectively.

MT
Complete Set, Gold (10): 100.00
Common Player, Gold: 7.50
White: 2X
Black: 3X
1 Anderson Amador 7.50
2 Eric Duncan 10.00
3 Anthony Gwynn 9.00
4 Cole Hamels 10.00
5 Adam LaRoche 10.00
6 Adam Loewen 10.00
7 David Murphy 7.50
8 Mark Prior 40.00
9 Alexis Rios 7.50
10 Delmon Young 20.00

2003 Just Rookies 2003

Many of the top players from the 2003 draft are featured in Just Minors' final issue for 2003. As with Just Rookies 2002, the company made the cards available directly to consumers as sets, singles or multiple-card lots. There was no retail packaging of the product. Base cards were issued in an edition of 15,000 each. Silver parallels were in an edition of 5,000 each, golds at 1,000 and blacks at 50 serially numbered cards each. The Silver and Gold parallels were sold only as complete sets. The blacks were sold only as singles, with a limit of one card per player.

MT
Complete Base Set (80): 13.00
Common Player: .25
Complete Silver Set (80): 16.00
Silver Singles: 1.5X
Complete Gold Set (80): 20.00
Gold Singles: 2.5X
Blacks: 15X
1 Anderson Amador .50
2 Luis Atilano .50
3 Paul Bacot .25
4 Aarom Baldiris .35
5 Jimmy Barthmaier .25
6 Daric Barton .60
7 Chad Billingsley .65
8 Andres Blanco .25
9 Larry Broadway .30
10 Robinson Cano .75
11 Matt Chico .25
12 Hu Chin-Lung .75
13 Jesse Crain .40
14 Juan Dominguez .35
15 Dennis Dove .35
16 Eric Duncan 1.00
17 Jesse English .30
18 Brian Finch .25
19 Enrique Gonzalez .25
20 Tom Gorzelanny .50
21 Franklin Gutierrez .75
22 Anthony Gwynn .75
23 Josh Hall .25
24 Mickey Hall .25
25 Ryan Hannaman .25
26 Matt Harrison .25
27 Felix Hernandez 1.25
28 Shawn Hill .40
29 Jason Hirsh .25
30 James Houser .50
31 Kevin Howard .25
32 Edwin Jackson .50
33 Blair Johnson .50
34 Kody Kirkland .40
35 Jason Kubel .65
36 Andy LaRoche 1.00
37 Donald Levinski .25
38 Kenny Lewis .25
39 Bobby Livingston .50
40 Adam Loewen 1.00
41 Chris Lubanski 1.00
42 Luis Martinez .50
43 Macay McBride .25
44 Brian McCann .25
45 Dallas McPherson .65
46 Lastings Milledge 1.00
47 Greg Miller 1.00
48 Daniel Moore .25
49 Steve Moss .25
50 David Murphy .75
51 Darin Naatjes .25
52 Dioner Navarro .75
53 Ramon Nivar .50
54 David Pauley .25
55 Elizardo Ramirez .25
56 Jeremy Reed .50
57 JoJo Reyes .50
58 Tony Richie .25
59 Alexis Rios .50
60 Arturo Rivas .25
61 Jarrod Saltalamacchia .40
62 Dennis Sarfate .50
63 Chris Seddon .25
64 Alexander Smit .50
65 Sean Smith .25
66 Brad Snyder .40
67 Brian Snyder .35
68 Edgar Soto .25
69 Tim Stauffer .75
70 Jake Stevens .25
71 Brad Sullivan .50
72 Kazuhito Tadano .75
73 Anderson Tavarez .50
74 James Tomlin .50
75 Rusty Tucker .50
76 Doug Waechter .25
77 Ryan Wagner .75
78 Brandon Weeden .50
79 Delmon Young 1.00
80 Joel Zumaya .40

Autographs - Base

Autographed cards were made available directly to consumers in four varieties. Base autographs were produced in editions of 50 to 875 as indicated parenthetically in the checklist. Silver parallels of only 16 players were produced for retail-only distribution in an edition of 375 each. Gold autographs of all 80 players were in a 100-per-card edition available only as complete sets. Black autographs were limited to 25 for each player.

MT
Complete Set (80): 600.00
Common Player: 6.00
Complete Gold Set (80):
Gold Players: 2X
Blacks: 2-3X
1 Anderson Amador/50 10.00
2 Luis Atilano/375 8.00
3 Paul Bacot/375 6.00
4 Aarom Baldiris/375 8.00
5 Jimmy Barthmaier/875 6.00
6 Daric Barton/375 8.00
7 Chad Billingsley/375 8.00
8 Andres Blanco/375 6.00
9 Larry Broadway/875 6.00
10 Robinson Cano/50 10.00
11 Matt Chico/375 6.00
12 Hu Chin-Lung/50 15.00
13 Jesse Crain/375 8.00
14 Juan Dominguez/375 8.00
15 Dennis Dove/375 8.00
16 Eric Duncan/350 20.00
17 Jesse English/375 6.00
18 Brian Finch/375 6.00
19 Enrique Gonzalez/375 6.00
20 Tom Gorzelanny/875 6.00
21 Franklin Gutierrez/50 20.00
22 Anthony Gwynn/100 12.00
23 Josh Hall/875 6.00
24 Mickey Hall/875 6.00
25 Ryan Hannaman/375 8.00
26 Matt Harrison/375 6.00
27 Felix Hernandez/350 15.00
28 Shawn Hill/375 8.00
29 Jason Hirsh/375 6.00
30 James Houser/875 6.00
31 Kevin Howard/375 6.00
32 Edwin Jackson/50 15.00
33 Blair Johnson/375 8.00
34 Kody Kirkland/375 8.00
35 Jason Kubel/375 9.00
36 Andy LaRoche/350 12.00
37 Donald Levinski/375 6.00
38 Kenny Lewis/375 6.00
39 Bobby Livingston/875 6.00
40 Adam Loewen/50 20.00
41 Chris Lubanski/350 10.00
42 Luis Martinez/375 8.00
43 Macay McBride/375 8.00
44 Brian McCann/375 8.00
45 Dallas McPherson/50 20.00
46 Lastings Milledge/350 12.00
47 Greg Miller/50 20.00
48 Daniel Moore/375 6.00
49 Steve Moss/375 6.00
50 David Murphy/200 10.00
51 Darin Naatjes/875 6.00
52 Dioner Navarro/200 10.00
53 Ramon Nivar/375 8.00
54 David Pauley/375 6.00
55 Elizardo Ramirez/375 6.00
56 Jeremy Reed/375 10.00
57 JoJo Reyes/375 8.00
58 Tony Richie/375 6.00
59 Alexis Rios/50 20.00
60 Arturo Rivas/875 6.00
61 Jarrod Saltalamacchia/375 7.50
62 Dennis Sarfate/375 8.00
63 Chris Seddon/375 6.00
64 Alexander Smit/375 8.00
65 Sean Smith/375 6.00
66 Brad Snyder/375 6.00
67 Brian Snyder/875 6.00
68 Edgar Soto/375 6.00
69 Tim Stauffer/875 8.00
70 Jake Stevens/375 6.00
71 Brad Sullivan/350 7.00
72 Kazuhito Tadano/50 15.00
73 Anderson Tavarez/875 6.00
74 James Tomlin/375 8.00
75 Rusty Tucker/375 8.00
76 Doug Waechter/375 8.00
77 Ryan Wagner/375 8.00
78 Brandon Weeden/375 8.00
79 Delmon Young/50 40.00
80 Joel Zumaya/375 8.00

Autographs - Silver

Autographed cards were made available directly to consumers in four varieties. Silver parallels of only 16 players were produced for retail-only distribution in an edition of 375 each.

MT
Complete Set (16): 125.00
Common Player: 7.50
1 Anderson Amador 7.50
10 Robinson Cano 9.00
12 Hu Chin-Lung 10.00
16 Eric Duncan 9.00
21 Franklin Gutierrez 7.50
22 Anthony Gwynn 9.00
27 Felix Hernandez 9.00
36 Andy LaRoche 9.00
40 Adam Loewen 12.00
41 Chris Lubanski 7.50
45 Dallas McPherson 10.00
46 Lastings Milledge 7.50
47 Greg Miller 9.00
52 Dioner Navarro 7.50
59 Alexis Rios 9.00
71 Brad Sullivan 7.50

2003 Just Stars

Some of the top players selected in the 2002 and 2003 drafts, as well as key players making some of their earliest baseball card appearances, were featured in this set. As with other recent Just Minors issues, cards were not packaged in traditional wax packs, but were available as singles and/or sets either directly from the manufacturer or through its hobby retailer outlets. The base (white) set was produced in an edition of 10,000. Silver sets were produced in an edition of 5,000; golds to 1,000 and blacks in an edition of 50 serially numbered cards each.

MT
Complete Set (50): 8.00
Common Player: .15
Complete Silver Set (50): 10.00
Silver Singles: 1.5X
Complete Gold Set (50): 12.00
Gold Singles: 2.5X
Black: 15X
1 Joaquin Arias .25
2 Eric Aybar .25
3 Josh Barfield .40
4 Bobby Basham .40
5 Ronald Belisario (Belizario) .15
6 Bobby Brownlie .40
7 Miguel Cabrera .85
8 Alberto Callaspo .35
9 Jose Capellan .25
10 Fausto Carmona .40
11 Jose Castillo .15
12 Hu Chin-Lung .40
13 Jose Raphael Diaz .20
14 Zach Duke .35
15 Elijah Dukes .25
16 J.D. Durbin .35
17 Justin Germano .15
18 Byron Gettis .15
19 Alfredo Gonzalez .15
20 Edgar Gonzalez .15
21 Derek (Derick) Grigsby .15
22 Jeremy Guthrie .40
23 Franklin Gutierrez .40
24 Cole Hamels .75
25 Zach Hammes .15
26 Dan Haren .40
27 Brendan Harris .15
28 Blake Hawksworth .15
29 Trevor Hutchinson .15
30 Edwin Jackson .40
31 Kevin Jepsen .15
32 Adam Loewen .75
33 John Maine .50
34 John McCurdy .15
35 Dustin McGowan .25
36 Brian Miller .15
37 Dustin Nippert .15
38 Leo Nunez .15
39 Vince Perkins .40
40 Mark Schramek .15
41 Kelly Shoppach .15
42 Andy Sisco .40
43 Grady Sizemore .75
44 Chris Snyder .15
45 Kazuhito Tadano .75
46 Ferdin Tejeda .15
47 Jose Valdez .15
48 Joe Valentine .15
49 Adam Wainwright .40
50 Matt Yeatman .15

Autographs - Base

Autographed cards were made available directly to consumers in four varieties. Base autographs, were produced in editions of 50 to 875, as indicated parenthetically in the checklist. Silver parallels of only 15 players were produced for retail-only distribution in an edition of 375 each. Gold autographs of all 50 players were in a 100-per-card edition available only as complete sets. Black autographs were limited to 25 for each player.

MT
Complete Set (50): 365.00
Common Player: 6.00
Complete Gold Set: 300.00
Gold Singles: 1.5X
Blacks: 2-3X
1 Joaquin Arias/375 8.00
2 Eric Aybar/375 8.00
3 Josh Barfield/50 15.00
4 Bobby Basham/375 8.00
5 Ronald Belisario (Belizario)/875 6.00
6 Bobby Brownlie/50 20.00
7 Miguel Cabrera/50 30.00
8 Alberto Callaspo/375 10.00
9 Jose Capellan/375 9.00
10 Fausto Carmona/375 10.00
11 Jose Castillo/875 6.00
12 Hu Chin-Lung/50 20.00
13 Jose Raphael Diaz/375 7.00
14 Zach Duke/375 15.00
15 Elijah Dukes/500 6.00
16 J.D. Durbin/375 9.00
17 Justin Germano/375 6.00
18 Byron Gettis/375 8.00
19 Alfredo Gonzalez/875 6.00
20 Edgar Gonzalez/375 8.00
21 Derek (Derick) Grigsby/375 6.00
22 Jeremy Guthrie/50 20.00
23 Franklin Gutierrez/500 9.00
24 Cole Hamels/250 15.00
25 Zach Hammes/375 6.00
26 Dan Haren/50 15.00
27 Brendan Harris/375 8.00
28 Blake Hawksworth/500 7.00
29 Trevor Hutchinson/875 6.00
30 Edwin Jackson/500 7.00
31 Kevin Jepsen/375 6.00
32 Adam Loewen/50 20.00
33 John Maine/500 15.00
34 John McCurdy/375 6.00
35 Dustin McGowan/375 12.00
36 Brian Miller/375 8.00
37 Dustin Nippert/375 8.00
38 Leo Nunez/375 8.00
39 Vince Perkins/50 9.00
40 Mark Schramek/875 6.00
41 Kelly Shoppach/375 8.00
42 Andy Sisco/875 9.00
43 Grady Sizemore/50 20.00
44 Chris Snyder/375 8.00
45 Kazuhito Tadano/875 20.00
46 Ferdin Tejeda/375 6.00
47 Jose Valdez/375 6.00
48 Joe Valentine/375 8.00
49 Adam Wainwright/400 15.00
50 Matt Yeatman/375 8.00

Autographs - Silver

Autographed cards were made available directly to consumers in four varieties. Silver parallels of only 15 players were produced for retail-only distribution in an edition of 375 each.

MT
Complete Set (15): 160.00
Common Player: 7.50
3 Josh Barfield 10.00
6 Bobby Brownlie 10.00
7 Miguel Cabrera 25.00
12 Hu Chin-Lung 15.00
15 Elijah Dukes 7.50
22 Jeremy Guthrie 10.00
23 Franklin Gutierrez 15.00
24 Cole Hamels 15.00
26 Dan Haren 10.00
28 Blake Hawksworth 10.00
30 Edwin Jackson 10.00
32 Adam Loewen 15.00
33 John Maine 12.00
39 Vince Perkins 10.00
43 Grady Sizemore 15.00

2003 Upper Deck USA Baseball

Offered only as a boxed set featuring 27 regular cards, two autographed cards and an autographed jersey card, this issue features a coming generation of major league stars.

MT
Sealed Factory Set (30): 40.00
Complete Base Set (27): 7.50
Common Player: .25
1 Justin Orenduff .25
2 Micah Owings .25
3 Steven Register .25
4 Huston Street .50
5 Justin Verlander 2.00
6 Jered Weaver 4.00
7 Matt Campbell .25
8 Stephen Head .50
9 Mark Romanczuk .25
10 Jeff Clement .50
11 Mike Nickeas .25
12 Tyler Greene .25
13 Paul Janish .25
14 Jeff Larish .50
15 Eric Patterson .25
16 Dustin Pedroia 2.00
17 Michael Griffin .25
18 Brent Lillibridge .25
19 Danny Putnam .50
20 Seth Smith .25
21 Ray Tanner .15
22 Dick Cooke .15
23 Mark Scalf .15
24 Mike Weathers .15
25 Team Card .25
26 Commemorative Card .10
27 Checklist .10

Autographs

The Team USA players in the 2003 Upper Deck boxed set each signed 1,000 cards which appeared two per set. Cards signed in red ink are numbered to 750 per player; cards signed in blue are in an edition of 250 each.

MT
Common Red Autograph: 2.00
Common Blue Autograph: 7.00
Blue Stars: 2.5X
1 Justin Orenduff 3.50
2 Micah Owings 10.00
3 Steven Register 2.00
4 Huston Street 7.50
5 Justin Verlander 40.00
6 Jered Weaver 55.00
7 Matt Campbell 3.00
8 Stephen Head 10.00
9 Mark Romanczuk 3.00
10 Jeff Clement 15.00
11 Mike Nickeas 2.00
12 Tyler Greene 2.00
13 Paul Janish 3.50
14 Jeff Larish 9.00
15 Eric Patterson 10.00
16 Dustin Pedroia 40.00
17 Michael Griffin 2.00

18 Brent Lillibridge 2.00
19 Danny Putnam 7.50
20 Seth Smith 6.00

Auto, Jerseys

The Team USA players in the 2003 Upper Deck boxed set each signed 500 game-used jersey-swatch cards which were randomly inserted one per set. Cards signed in red ink are numbered to 350 per player; cards signed in blue are in an edition of 150 each.

MT
Common Red Autograph: 5.00
Common Blue Autograph: 12.00
Blue Stars: 2.5X
1 Justin Orenduff 8.00
2 Micah Owings 15.00
3 Steven Register 5.00
4 Huston Street 11.00
5 Justin Verlander 50.00
6 Jered Weaver 80.00
7 Matt Campbell 6.00
8 Stephen Head 13.50
9 Mark Romanczuk 5.00
10 Jeff Clement 20.00
11 Mike Nickeas 5.00
12 Tyler Greene 6.00
13 Paul Janish 5.00
14 Jeff Larish 16.00
15 Eric Patterson 5.00
16 Dustin Pedroia 60.00
17 Michael Griffin 6.00
18 Brent Lillibridge 4.00
19 Danny Putnam 15.00
20 Seth Smith 12.50

2003 Minor League Team Sets

Manufacturer abbreviations used are: GS - Grandstand, MA - Multi-Ad, CH - Choice, TM - Team

MT
221 Sets and Variations
2003 GS Aberdeen IronBirds (30) 14.00
2003 GS Aberdeen IronBirds Update (3) 11.00
2003 MA Akron Aeros (29) 12.00
2003 Team Alaska Goldpanners (24) 20.00
2003 Team Alaska Goldpanners Bonus Cards (3) 9.00
2003 MA Albuquerque Isotopes (32) 12.00
2003 GS Altoona Curve (30) 11.00
2003 GS Altoona Curve Update (6) 12.50
2003 GS Apalachian League Top Prospects (30) 13.50
2003 GS Arkansas Travelers (31) 12.00
2003 GS Asheville Tourists (30) 16.00
2003 GS Asheville Tourists Update (12) 15.00
2003 Team Atlantic League All-Stars (52) 17.50
2003 Team Auburn Doubledays (39) 12.50
2003 MA Augusta GreenJackets (33) 12.50
2003 CH Bangor Lumberjacks (26) 10.00
2003 Team Batavia Muckdogs (39) 13.00
2003 CH Battle Creek Yankees (30) 11.00
2003 MA Beloit Snappers (30) 12.00
2003 MA Beloit Snappers Prospects (6) 14.00
2003 MA Beloit Snappers Update (9) 12.00
2003 GS Billings Mustangs (30) 10.00
2003 GS Binghamton Mets (30) 11.50
2003 GS Birmingham Barons (29) 11.50
2003 GS Birmingham Barons Update (3) 9.00
2003 GS Bluefield Orioles (34) 12.50
2003 GS Boise Hawks (30) 12.00
2003 GS Bowie Baysox (29) 12.50
2003 MA Brevard County Manatees (30) 11.50
2003 CH Bridgeport Bluefish (30) 9.00
2003 GS Bristol White Sox (31) 13.00
2003 GS Brockton Rox (27) 9.50
2003 CH Brooklyn Cyclones (39) 12.00
2003 CH Buffalo Bisons (30) 12.50
2003 CH Classic Buffalo Bisons (12) 10.00
2003 MA Burlington Bees (30) 11.50
2003 GS California-Carolina Leagues AS (52) 17.50
2003 CH Camden Riversharks (30) 9.50
2003 MA Capital City Bombers (36) 14.00
2003 CH Carolina League Prospects (32) 11.00
2003 Team Carolina Mudcats (31) 12.50
2003 GS Casper Rockies (32) 12.50
2003 TM Cedar Rapids Kernels (31) 11.00
2003 MA Charleston Alley Cats (33) 11.00
2003 MA Charleston RiverDogs (32) 16.00
2003 CH Charlotte Knights (30) 11.50
2003 GS Chattanooga Lookouts (29) 15.00
2003 GS Chillicothe Paints (27) 9.00
2003 GS Clearwater Phillies (30) 13.00
2003 GS Clinton LumberKings (33) 10.00
2003 CH Coastal Bend Aviators (30) 10.00
2003 MA Colorado Springs Sky Sox (30) 11.00
2003 CH Columbus Clippers (30) 15.00
2003 GS Danville Braves (32) 12.50
2003 MA Dayton Dragons (30) 14.50
2003 CH Daytona Cubs (30) 12.00
2003 MA Delmarva Shorebirds (30) 9.00
2003 GS Dunedin Blue Jays (30) 12.00
2003 CH Durham Bulls (30) 14.50
2003 GS Eastern League Top Prospects (31) 11.00
2003 GS Eastern League Greats - Set A (10) 22.50
2003 GS Eastern League Greats - Set B (10) 12.50
2003 GS Edinburg Roadrunners (30) 9.50
2003 MA Edmonton Trappers (30) 10.00
2003 GS Elizabethton Twins (31) 11.00
2003 GS El Paso Diablos (30) 12.50
2003 GS Erie SeaWolves (28) 10.00
2003 GS Eugene Emeralds (32) 13.00
2003 GS Everett Aquasox (30) 14.50
2003 Team Fargo-Moorhead RedHawks (30) 10.00
2003 GS Florida State League Prospects (25) 13.50
2003 GS Frederick Keys (30) 13.00
2003 GS Frederick Keys "No Smoking" (30) 11.00
2003 MA Fresno Grizzlies (31) 11.50
2003 GS Frisco RoughRiders (35) 25.00
2003 Team Frisco RoughRiders (31) 15.00
2003 GS Ft. Myers Miracle (32) 10.00
2003 GS Ft. Wayne Wizards (29) 11.00
2003 TM Ft. Wayne Wizards Strip Set (5) 9.00
2003 Team Gary Southshore RailCats (28) 10.00
2003 MA Great Falls White Sox (30) 11.50
2003 MA Greensboro Bats (30) 13.00
2003 GS Greenville Braves (29) 11.50
2003 MA Hagerstown Suns (36) 12.00
2003 GS Harrisburg Senators (30) 11.00
2003 GS Helena Brewers Top Prospects (4) 5.00
2003 MA Hickory Crawdads (32) 13.00
2003 MA Hickory Crawdads Update (33) 12.50
2003 GS High Desert Mavericks (34) 12.50
2003 GS Hudson Valley Renegades (35) 10.00
2003 TM Huntsville Stars (29) 22.50
2003 CH Indianapolis Indians (30) 11.00
2003 GS Inland Empire 66ers (31) 12.00
2003 CH International League All-Stars (31) 11.00
2003 CH International League Prospects (30) 11.00
2003 MA Iowa Cubs (30) 13.00
2003 GS Jacksonville Suns (30) 10.00
2003 GS Johnson City Cardinals (21) 10.00
2003 Team Jupiter Hammerheads (37) 20.00
2003 GS Kane County Cougars (31) 10.00
2003 TM Kane County Cougars/Sponsor (31) 20.00
2003 GS Kane County Cougars Update (10) 15.00
2003 MA Kannapolis Intimidators (36) 12.00
2003 CH Kingsport Mets (40) 12.50
2003 GS Kingsport Mets Update (2) 12.00
2003 CH Kinston Indians (31) 14.50
2003 CH Lake County Captains (31) 10.00
2003 CH Lake County Captains Update (30) 14.00
2003 GS Lake Elsinore Storm (30) 12.50
2003 GS Lakeland Tigers (29) 11.00
2003 MA Lakewood BlueClaws (35) 11.50
2003 GS Lancaster JetHawks (30) 12.50
2003 GS Lansing Lugnuts (30) 12.50
2003 MA Las Vegas 51s (32) 15.00
2003 MA Lexington Legends (31) 12.00
2003 CH Long Island Ducks (29) 12.00
2003 CH Louisville Bats (38) 22.50
2003 CH Lowell Spinners (39) 50.00
2003 GS Lowell Spinners Update (1) 5.00
2003 CH Lynchburg Hillcats (30) 12.50
2003 TM Lynchburg Hillcats (30) 15.00
2003 CH Martinsville Astros (35) 12.50
2003 MA Memphis Redbirds (30) 12.50
2003 GS Midland RockHounds (26) 10.00
2003 Team Midland Rock Hounds (33) 60.00
2003 CH Midwest League All-Stars (69) 12.50
2003 GS Midwest League Prospects (29) 11.00
2003 GS Missoula Osprey (36) 11.00
2003 GS Mobile Bay Bears (29) 16.00
2003 GS Modesto A's (29) 10.00
2003 CH Myrtle Beach Pelicans (30) 12.50
2003 MA Nashville Sounds (30) 13.00
2003 CH Newark Bears (30) 13.00
2003 GS New Britain Rock Cats (32) 10.00
2003 GS New Haven Ravens (29) 12.50
2003 GS New Jersey Cardinals (29) 11.00
2003 GS New Jersey Cardinals 10th Anniv. (15) 12.50
2003 WTC New Jersey Jackals (26) 9.50
2003 MA New Orleans Zephyrs (31) 10.00
2003 CH Norfolk Tides (37) 12.50
2003 GS Norwich Navigators (29) 12.00
2003 MA Ogden Raptors (36) 12.50
2003 MA Oklahoma RedHawks (30) 10.00
2003 MA Omaha Royals (26) 11.00
2003 GS Oneonta Tigers Top Prospects (3) 8.00
2003 CH Ottawa Lynx (30) 12.50
2003 MA Pacific Coast League All-Stars (30) 12.50
2003 MA Pacific Coast League Prospects (36) 13.00
2003 TM Palm Beach Cardinals (36) 25.00
2003 CH Pawtucket Red Sox (30) 12.00
2003 DD Pawtucket Red Sox Foldout (31) 15.00
2003 MA Peoria Chiefs (30) 13.00
2003 MA Peoria Chiefs Update (30) 40.00
2003 MA Portland Beavers (28) 11.50
2003 GS Portland Sea Dogs (35) 11.00
2003 CH Potomac Cannons (30) 10.00
2003 GS Princeton Devil Rays (30) 10.00
2003 TM Princeton Devil Rays (4) 45.00
2003 TM Provo Angels (30) 60.00
2003 CH Pulaski Blue Jays (37) 11.00
2003 GS Quad City River Bandits (30) 12.50
2003 GS Rancho Cucamonga Quakes (30) 12.50
2003 MA Reading Phillies (30) 10.00
2003 MA Reading Area CC Reading Phillies (30) 12.50
2003 CH Richmond Braves (30) 9.00
2003 CH Rochester Red Wings (31) 11.00
2003 GS Rockford River Hawks (30) 9.50
2003 MA Rome Braves (31) 15.00
2003 Team Round Rock Express (30) 17.50
2003 MA Sacramento River Cats (30) 11.50
2003 GS Salem Avalanche (30) 11.00
2003 GS Salem-Keizer Volcanoes (36) 12.00
2003 MA Salt Lake City Stingers (34) 12.50
2003 Team San Angelo Colts (25) 9.50
2003 CH San Antonio Missions (31) 11.00
2003 CH San Antonio Missions Update (30) 12.00
2003 GS San Jose Giants (30) 10.00
2003 GS San Jose Giants Update (1) 8.00
2003 GS Sarasota Red Sox (30) 10.00
2003 MA Savannah Sand Gnats (30) 12.50
2003 GS Savannah Sand Gnats Gold. Greats (17) 11.00
2003 Team Schaumburg Flyers (25) 10.00
2003 CH Scranton/Wilkes-Barre Red Barons (30) 10.00
2003 TM S/W-B Lackawanna Legends Magnets (9) 15.00
2003 MA Sioux Falls Canaries (30) 9.00
2003 MA So. Atlantic League Prospects (36) 10.00
2003 GS South Bend Silver Hawks (35) 11.00
2003 GS Southern League Top Prospects (31) 10.00
2003 GS Spokane Indians (32) 10.00
2003 MA Staten Island Yankees (36) 10.00
2003 GS St. Lucie Mets (35) 12.50
2003 GS St. Lucie Mets Update (8) 15.00
2003 GS St. Lucie Mets Update (1) 30.00
2003 MA Stockton Ports (30) 12.50
2003 CH Syracuse Skychiefs (30) 12.00
2003 MA Tacoma Rainiers (31) 11.50
2003 GS Tampa Yankees (30) 10.00
2003 GS Tennessee Smokies (30) 10.00
2003 CH Toledo Mud Hens (30) 11.00
2003 MA Trenton Thunder (31) 12.50
2003 GS Tri-City Dust Devils (32) 12.50
2003 CH Tri-City Valley Cats (38) 10.00
2003 MA Tucson Sidewinders (36) 13.00
2003 Team Tulsa Drillers (29) 11.00
2003 Team Vancouver Canadians (38) 12.50
2003 GS Vermont Expos (34) 10.00
2003 GS Vero Beach Dodgers (29) 14.50
2003 GS Visalia Oaks (30) 15.00
2003 CH Washington Wild Things (30) 9.50
2003 CH West Michigan Whitecaps (31) 11.00
2003 GS West Tenn Diamond Jaxx (30) 12.50
2003 GS Wichita Wranglers (30) 11.00
2003 CH Williamsport Crosscutters (36) 12.50
2003 CH Williamsport Crosscutters Legends (5) 6.00
2003 CH Wilm. Blue Rocks In the Show 1 (41) 12.50
2003 CH Wilm. Blue Rocks In the Show 2 (24) 12.50
2003 CH Wilmington Blue Rocks (32) 13.00
2003 Team Winnipeg Goldeyes (30) 8.00
2003 CH Winston-Salem Warthogs (30) 12.50
2003 CH Wisconsin Timber Rattlers (31) 11.00
2003 GS Yakima Bears (34) 14.00

2004 Just Justifiable Preview

Ten elite prospects were selected for this edition. Unsigned cards were available in complete-set form either directly from the manufacturer (gold) or through its network of retailers (white, silver and black). Production was announced as 15,000 white sets, 5,000 silver, 100 serially numbered gold and 50 serially numbered sets in black.

MT
Complete Set (10): 3.00
Common Player: .50
Silver: 1.5X
Gold: 5X
Black: 8X
1 Bill Bray .50
2 Mitch Einertson .75
3 Josh Fields .75
4 Dexter Fowler .50
5 Javier Herrera 1.00
6 Chris Lambert .50
7 Brandon Moss .50
8 Yusmeiro Petit .50
9 Taylor Tankersley .50
10 Jon Zeringue .50

Autographs

Ten elite prospects were selected for this edition. Autographed cards were available directly from the manufacturer. Base (white bordered) version were sold individually, serially numbered to 200. Silvers were numbered to 100 each and only available through retail distribution. Gold cards, in an edition of 50 each were sold only as complete sets. Black versions were sold singly in an edition of 25.

MT
Complete Set (10): 40.00
Common Player: 4.00
Silver: 1.5X
Gold: 2X
Black: 3X
1 Bill Bray 4.00
2 Mitch Einertson 6.00
3 Josh Fields 4.00
4 Dexter Fowler 4.00
5 Javier Herrera 7.50
6 Chris Lambert 4.00
7 Brandon Moss 4.00
8 Yusmeiro Petit 5.00
9 Taylor Tankersley 4.00
10 Jon Zeringue 5.00

2004 Just Justifiable

Some of the top players selected in the 2004 draft, as well as key players making some of their earliest baseball card appearances, are featured in this set. For the first time in several years, cards were packaged in traditional wax packs, as well as being sold as singles and/or sets either directly from the manufacturer or through its hobby retailer outlets. The base (white) set was produced in an edition of 15,000. Silver sets were produced in an edition of 5,000; golds to 100 and blacks in an edition of 50 serially numbered cards each.

MT
Complete Set (90): 15.00
Common Player: .25
Silver: 1.5X
Gold: 8X
Black: 16X
Wax Pack (5): 2.50
Wax Box (18): 30.00
1 Brian Anderson .25
2 Homer Bailey .25
3 Scott Baker .25
4 Joseph Bauserman .25
5 Brian Bixler .25
6 Ian Bladergroen .25
7 Bill Bray .25
8 Reid Brignac .25
9 Billy Butler .50
10 Eric Campbell .25
11 Gustavo Chacin .45
12 Ryan Church .25
13 Jamie D'Antona .25
14 Brad Davis .25
15 Jorge de la Rosa .25
16 Thomas Diamond .35
17 Andrew Dobies .25
18 Ryan Doumit .25
19 Jason Dubois .25
20 Mitch Einertson .75
21 Josh Fields .50
22 Dexter Fowler .25
23 Matt Fox .25
24 Jairo Garcia .25
25 Ryan Garko .25
26 Greg Golson .25
27 Jared Gothreaux .25
28 Curtis Granderson .25
29 Eric Haberer .25
30 J.A. Happ .25
31 Lucas Harrell .25
32 Gaby Hernandez .25
33 Javier Herrera .50
34 J.C. Holt .25
35 Justin Hoyman .25
36 Zach Jackson .25
37 Mark Jecmen .25
38 Rob Johnson .25
39 Jason Jones .25
40 Jeff Keppinger .25
41 Ian Kinsler .25
42 Josh Kroeger .25
43 Chris Lambert .25
44 Richard Lewis .25
45 Scott Lewis .25
46 Adam Lind .25
47 Tyler Lumsden .25
48 Paul Maholm .25
49 Collin Mahoney .25
50 Gabriel Martinez .25
51 Eddy Martinez-Esteve .50
52 Brandon McCarthy .25
53 Garrett Mock .25
54 Mike Morse .25
55 Brandon Moss .25
56 Chris Nelson .50
57 Dan Ortmeier .25
58 Chad Orvella .25
59 Jon Mark Owings .25
60 Dustin Pedroia .25
61 Tony Pena .25
62 Hunter Pence .25
63 Yusmeiro Petit .50
64 Eddie Prasch .25
65 David Purcey .25
66 Danny Putnam .25
67 Omar Quintanilla .25
68 Ryan Raburn .25
69 Ramon Ramirez .25
70 Anthony Reyes .30
71 Richie Robnett .35
72 Sean Rodriguez .25
73 Willie Joe Ronda .25
74 Brendan Ryan .25
75 Jeff Salazar .25
76 Ervin Santana .25
77 Michael Schlact .25
78 Ryan Schroyer .25
79 Steven Shell .25
80 Ian Snell .25
81 Huston Street .50
82 Kurt Suzuki .25
83 Taylor Tankersley .25
84 Mark Teahen .25
85 Matt Tuiasosopo .50
86 Josh Wahpepah .25
87 Neil Walker .25
88 Wes Whisler .25
89 Tommy Whiteman .25
90 Jon Zeringue .50

Autographs

Autographed cards of 60 of the players in Justifiable 2004 were available in four varieties. Base (white) autographs, were generally produced in an edition of 725 (unless otherwise indicated parenthetically in the checklist). Silver parallels were serially numbered to 200 each and were produced for retail-only distribution. Gold autographs were sold only as complete sets in a 50-per-card edition. Black autographs were limited to 25 for each player.

MT
Common Player: 3.00
Silver: 1.5X
Complete Set, Gold (60): 350.00
Gold: 2X
Black: 3X
2 Homer Bailey/225 5.00
4 Joseph Bauserman/225 4.00
5 Brian Bixler 3.00
6 Ian Bladergroen 3.00
7 Bill Bray/50 7.50
11 Gustavo Chacin/475 6.00
12 Ryan Church 3.00
13 Jamie D'Antona 3.00
14 Brad Davis/225 4.00
16 Thomas Diamond/225 6.00
17 Andrew Dobies 3.00
20 Mitch Einertson/1,000 7.50
21 Josh Fields/350 5.00
22 Dexter Fowler/350 5.00
23 Matt Fox 4.00
25 Ryan Garko 4.00
26 Greg Golson/225 4.00
27 Jared Gothreaux/225 4.00
29 Eric Haberer 3.00
30 J.A. Happ/225 4.00
31 Lucas Harrell/225 4.00
33 Javier Herrera/350 6.00
34 J.C. Holt 3.00
35 Justin Hoyman 4.00
36 Zach Jackson 4.00
37 Mark Jecmen 3.00
38 Rob Johnson 3.00
39 Jason Jones/225 3.00
42 Josh Kroeger 4.00
43 Chris Lambert/350 5.00
46 Adam Lind 3.00
48 Paul Maholm 4.00
49 Collin Mahoney/225 4.00
52 Brandon McCarthy 3.00
53 Garrett Mock 4.00
54 Mike Morse/350 4.00
55 Brandon Moss 6.00
56 Chris Nelson 3.00
58 Chad Orvella/225 4.00
59 Jon Mark Owings/225 5.00
60 Dustin Pedroia 3.00
61 Tony Pena 3.00
62 Hunter Pence/350 6.00
63 Yusmeiro Petit 4.00
64 Eddie Prasch 4.00
66 Danny Putnam 3.00
69 Ramon Ramirez 3.00
72 Sean Rodriguez 3.00
76 Ervin Santana 3.00
77 Michael Schlact/225 4.00
78 Ryan Schroyer 4.00
80 Ian Snell/225 4.00
81 Huston Street 6.00
82 Kurt Suzuki/350 5.00
84 Mark Teahen 5.00
86 Josh Wahpepah/225 5.00
87 Neil Walker 3.00
89 Tommy Whiteman/350 5.00

2004 Just Prospects Preview

Ten elite prospects were selected for this edition. Unsigned cards were available in complete-set form or as singles in multi-card lots either directly from the manufacturer or through its network of retailers. Production was announced as 15,000 white sets, 5,000 silver, 100 serially numbered gold and 50 serially numbered sets in black.

MT
Complete Set (10): 2.50
Common Player: .25
Silver: 1X
Gold: 5X
Black: 8X
1 John Danks .25
2 Prince Fielder .50
3 Zack Greinke .35
4 Conor Jackson .35
5 Scott Kazmir .25
6 Nick Markakis .50
7 Xavier Paul .25
8 Kyle Sleeth .25
9 Ian Stewart .35
10 Rickie Weeks .50

Autographs

Ten elite prospects were selected for this edition. Autographed cards were available directly from the manufacturer. Base (white bordered) version were sold individually in a serially numbered edition of 200 each. Gold cards were numbered to 50 and sold only as complete sets. Black versions were sold singly in an edition of 25.

MT
Complete Set (10): 45.00
Common Player: 3.00
Gold: 2X
Black: 3X
1 John Danks 5.00
2 Prince Fielder 15.00
3 Zack Greinke 4.00
4 Conor Jackson 5.00
5 Scott Kazmir 4.00
6 Nick Markakis 6.00
7 Xavier Paul 3.00
8 Kyle Sleeth 4.00
9 Ian Stewart 6.00
10 Rickie Weeks 5.00

2004 Just Prospects

Some of the top players selected in the 2003 and 2004 drafts, as well as key players making some of their earliest baseball card appearances, were featured in this set. As with other recent Just Minors issues, cards were not packaged in traditional wax packs, but were available as singles and/or sets either directly from the manufacturer or through its hobby retailer outlets. The base (white) set was produced in an edition of 15,000. Silver sets were produced in an edition of 5,000; golds to 100 and blacks in an edition of 50 serially numbered cards each.

MT
Complete Set (90): 15.00
Common Player: .25
Silver: 1.5X
Gold: 8X
Black: 16X
1 Abe Alvarez .25
2 Josh Anderson .25
3 Michael Aubrey .25
4 Cha Baek .25
5 Jeff Baker .25
6 Wladimir Balentien .50
7 Josh Banks .25
8 Tim Battle Jr. .25
9 Denny Bautista .25
10 Michael Bourn .25
11 Craig Brazell .25
12 Jonathan Broxton .25
13 David Bush .25
14 Daniel Cabrera .25
15 Melky Cabrera .50
16 Brent Cleven .25
17 Tyler Clippard .25
18 Shane Costa .25
19 John Danks .25
20 Jamie D'Antona .25
21 David DeJesus .25
22 Matt DeSalvo .25
23 Victor Diaz .25
24 Jake Dittler .25
25 Steve Doetsch .50
26 Edwin Encarnacion .25
27 Matt Esquivel .50
28 Andre Ethier .25
29 Prince Fielder 1.00
30 Richie Gardner .25
31 Joey Gathright .50
32 Tony Giarratano .50
33 Ryan Goleski .50
34 Ruben Gotay .25
35 Zack Greinke .75
36 Freddy Guzman .25
37 Estee Harris .50
38 Sean Henn .25
39 Aaron Hill .25
40 Mike Hinckley .25
41 Ryan Howard .45
42 Conor Jackson .50
43 Chuck James .50
44 Dan Johnson .50
45 Adam Jones .35
46 Justin Jones .25
47 Kennard Jones .25
48 Mike Jones .25
49 Scott Kazmir .60
50 Howie Kendrick .50
51 Jon Knott .25
52 David Krynzel .25
53 Brandon League .25
54 Fred Lewis .25
55 Hector Made .50
56 Mitch Maier .25
57 Val Majewski .25
58 Nick Markakis .50
59 Adam Miller .50
60 Jai Miller .50
61 Matt Moses .30
62 Bill Murphy .25
63 Matt Murton .50
64 Brad Nelson .25
65 Scott Olsen .25
66 Jerry Owens .50
67 Lou Palmisano .25
68 Xavier Paul .25
69 Carlos Quentin .25
70 Wilkin Ramirez .50
71 Eric Reed .25
72 Bronson Sardinha .25
73 Jay Sborz .25
74 Nate Schierholtz .50
75 Cole Seifrig .25
76 Kyle Sleeth .25
77 Ian Stewart .25
78 Nick Swisher .25
79 Willy Taveras .75
80 Luis Terrero .25
81 Brad Thompson .50
82 Chuck Tiffany .50
83 Chin-Hui Tsao .25
84 John VanBenschoten .25
85 Joey Votto .25
86 Brandon Weeden .25
87 Rickie Weeks .75
88 Brandon Wood .40
89 Jake Woods .25
90 Kevin Youkilis .25

Autographs

Autographed cards of up to 50 of the players in Just Prospects 2004 were available in four varieties. Base autographs, were generally produced in an edition of 725 (unless otherwise indicated parenthetically in the checklist). Silver parallels were serially numbered to 200 each and were produced for retail-only distribution. Gold autographs were sold only as complete sets in a 50-per-card edition. Black autographs were limited to 25 for each player.

MT
Common Player, White: 3.00
Silver: 1.5X
Complete Gold Set (50): 325.00
Gold: 2X
Black: 4X
1 Abe Alvarez 3.00
4 Cha Baek/225 4.00
6 Wladimir Balentien 4.00
7 Josh Banks 3.00
8 Tim Battle Jr. 3.00
11 Craig Brazell 3.00
12 Jonathan Broxton 3.00
13 David Bush 4.00
15 Melky Cabrera 4.00
16 Brent Cleven 3.00
21 David DeJesus 3.00
23 Victor Diaz/225 4.00
24 Jake Dittler 3.00
25 Steve Doetsch 4.00
26 Edwin Encarnacion 3.00
27 Matt Esquivel 4.00
28 Andre Ethier 3.00
31 Joey Gathright 4.00
32 Tony Giarratano 4.00
33 Ryan Goleski 4.00
34 Ruben Gotay 3.00
35 Zack Greinke/100 (No Silver, two Gold) 15.00
38 Sean Henn 4.00
40 Mike Hinckley 3.00
41 Ryan Howard 6.00
43 Chuck James 4.00
44 Dan Johnson 6.00
46 Justin Jones/225 4.00
52 David Krynzel 4.00
53 Brandon League 3.00
54 Fred Lewis 3.00
55 Hector Made/225 4.00
57 Val Majewski 3.00
59 Adam Miller 15.00
60 Jai Miller/225 4.00
62 Bill Murphy 3.00
63 Matt Murton 6.00
66 Jerry Owens/225 4.00
67 Lou Palmisano 3.00
71 Eric Reed 3.00
72 Bronson Sardinha 3.00
75 Cole Seifrig/225 4.00
79 Willy Taveras 6.00
80 Luis Terrero 3.00
81 Brad Thompson 4.00
82 Chuck Tiffany/225 5.00
85 Joey Votto 3.00
86 Brandon Weeden/225 4.00
89 Jake Woods 3.00

2004 Just Rookies Preview

Ten top prospects were selected for this edition. Unsigned cards were available in complete-set form or as singles in lots of 10-500 either directly from the manufacturer or through its network of retailers. Production was announced as 15,000 white sets, 5,000 silver, 100 serially numbered gold and 50 serially numbered sets in black.

MT
Complete Set (10): 3.00
Common Player: .50
Silver: 1X
Gold: 5X
Black: 8X
1 Thomas Diamond .50
2 Mitch Einertson 1.00
3 Greg Golson .50
4 Javier Herrera .75
5 Chris Nelson .75
6 Mark Rogers .75
7 Anibal Sanchez .50
8 Luis Soto .50
9 Marcos Vechionacci .50
10 Neil Walker .50

Autographs

Ten elite prospects were selected for this edition. Autographed cards were available directly from the manufacturer. Base (white bordered) version were sold individually. Gold cards, in an edition of 50 each were sold only as complete sets. Black versions were sold singly in an edition of 25.

MT
Complete Set (10): 40.00
Common Player: 4.00
Silver: 1.5X
Gold: 2X
Black: 3X
1 Thomas Diamond 6.00
2 Mitch Einertson 5.00
3 Greg Golson 4.00
4 Javier Herrera 6.00
5 Chris Nelson 6.00
6 Mark Rogers 6.00
7 Anibal Sanchez 5.00
8 Luis Soto 5.00
9 Marcos Vechionacci 4.00
10 Neil Walker 4.00

2004 Just Rookies

Some of the top minor league players of 2004, including some making their earliest baseball card appearance, are featured in this set. For the first time in several years, cards were packaged in traditional wax packs, as well as being sold as singles and/or sets either directly from the manufacturer or through its hobby retailer outlets. The base (white) set was produced in an edition of 15,000. Silver sets were produced in an edition of 5,000; golds to 100 and blacks in an edition of 50 serially numbered cards each.

MT
Complete Set (90): 15.00
Common Player: .25
Silver: 1.5X
Gold: 8X
Black: 16X
1 Nick Adenhart 1.00
2 Ezequiel Astacio .25
3 Homer Bailey .50
4 Josh Baker .25
5 Collin Balester .25
6 Jon Barratt .25
7 William Bergolla .25
8 Kyle Bono .25
9 Bill Bray .50
10 Billy Buckner .25
11 Ambiorix Burgos .25
12 Greg Burns .25
13 Matt Bush .75
14 Mike Butia .25
15 Billy Butler .75
16 Asdrubal Cabrera .50
17 Juan Cedeno .25
18 Ambiorix Concepcion .50
19 Luis Cota .50
20 Frank Curreri .25
21 Blake DeWitt .50
22 Brian Dopirak .75
23 Cory Dunlap .50
24 Scott Elbert .50
25 Dana Eveland .25
26 Mike Ferris .25
27 Jeff Frazier .25
28 Jonathan Fulton .50
29 Gio Gonzalez .50
30 Rafael Gonzalez .25
31 Javy Guerra .25
32 David Haehnel .50
33 Adam Harben .50
34 Ryan Harvey .25
35 Danny Hill .25
36 Jamie Hoffmann .25
37 Jesse Hoover .50
38 Tommy Hottovy .25
39 John Hudgins .25
40 Hernan Iribarren .50
41 Jason Jaramillo .25
42 A.J. Johnson .25
43 Blake Johnson .25
44 Jon Lester .25
45 Jeff Marquez .25
46 Sean Marshall .25
47 Louis Marson .25
48 Eddy Martinez-Esteve .75
49 Brian McFall .25
50 Jacob McGee .35
51 Joey Metropoulos .25
52 Scott Mitchinson .25
53 Eduardo Morlan .25
54 Jake Mullinax .25
55 Chris Nelson .75
56 Fernando Nieve .25
57 Justin Orenduff .50
58 Jonathan Papelbon .50
59 Jordan Parraz .25
60 Dustin Pedroia .50
61 Hayden Penn 1.00
62 Glen Perkins .50
63 Trevor Plouffe .50
64 Van Pope .25
65 Landon Powell .50
66 Jay Rainville .50
67 Chris Ray .25
68 Argenis Reyes .25
69 Eric Ridener .25
70 Mark Rogers .75
71 Francisco Rosario .25
72 Vinny Rottino .25
73 Anibal Sanchez .50
74 Ryan Shealy .25
75 Johan Silva .25
76 Brandon Sing .25
77 Tony Sipp .50
78 Luis Soto .50
79 Huston Street .50
80 Anthony Swarzak .25
81 Ryan Sweeney .35
82 Raul Tablado .25
83 Curtis Thigpen .25
84 Jason Vargas .25
85 Marcos Vechionacci .50
86 Miguel Vega .25
87 Mark Worrell .25
88 Brandon Yarbrough .25
89 Chris Young .25
90 Ben Zobrist .50

Autographs

Autographed cards of 40 of the players in Just Rookies 2004 were available in four varieties. Base autographs, were generally produced in an edition of 825 (unless otherwise indicated parenthetically in the checklist). Silver parallels were serially numbered to 100 each and were produced for retail-only distribution. Gold autographs were sold only as complete sets in a 50-per-card edition. Black autographs were limited to 25 for each player.

MT
Common Player: 3.00
Silver: 1.5X
Complete Gold Set (40):
Gold: 2X
Black: 4X
1 Nick Adenhart 3.00
3 Homer Bailey/325 5.00
5 Collin Balester/325 4.00
8 Kyle Bono/325 4.00
9 Bill Bray/225 5.00
10 Billy Buckner 3.00
14 Mike Butia/325 4.00
20 Frank Curreri/325 4.00
23 Cory Dunlap 4.00
26 Mike Ferris 3.00
27 Jeff Frazier 3.00
28 Jonathan Fulton/325 5.00
30 Rafael Gonzalez 4.00
31 Javy Guerra/325 4.00
33 Adam Harben 4.00
35 Danny Hill 3.00
37 Jesse Hoover/325 4.00
41 Jason Jaramillo 3.00
44 Jon Lester 4.00
45 Jeff Marquez 4.00
47 Louis Marson/325 4.00
50 Jacob McGee/325 4.00
53 Eduardo Morlan 3.00
55 Chris Nelson/275 7.50
57 Justin Orenduff 4.00
60 Dustin Pedroia/325 20.00
63 Trevor Plouffe 4.00
66 Jay Rainville 4.00
69 Eric Ridener/325 4.00
70 Mark Rogers 6.00
72 Vinny Rottino/325 4.00
73 Anibal Sanchez 6.00
78 Luis Soto 6.00
79 Huston Street/325 6.00
80 Anthony Swarzak 3.00
83 Curtis Thigpen 5.00
84 Jason Vargas 4.00
85 Marcos Vechionacci/325 6.00
88 Brandon Yarbrough 3.00
90 Ben Zobrist 6.00

2004 Minor League Team Sets

Manufacturer abbreviations used are: GS - Grandstand, MA - Multi-Ad, CH - Choice, TM - Team

MT
209 Sets and Variations
2004 GS Aberdeen IronBirds (36) 14.50
2004 MA Akron Aeros (29) 11.00
2004 MA Albuquerque Isotopes (35) 11.00
2004 GS Altoona Curve (30) 11.00
2004 GS Altoona Curve Update (10) 7.50
2004 GS Appalachian League Top Prospects (31) 11.00
2004 GS Arkansas Travelers (30) 11.00
2004 CH Arkansas Travelers Strip (5) 15.00
2004 GS Asheville Tourists (33) 15.00
2004 TM Auburn Doubledays (49) 12.00
2004 MA Augusta Greenjackets (30) 17.50
2004 TM Batavia Muckdogs (45) 11.00
2004 CH Battle Creek Yankees (35) 10.00
2004 MA Beloit Snappers (30) 12.50
2004 GS Billings Mustangs (36) 11.00
2004 GS Binghamton Mets (29) 13.50
2004 GS Birmingham Barons (31) 11.00
2004 GS Bluefield Orioles (40) 11.00
2004 GS Boise Hawks (29) 12.00
2004 GS Bowie Bay Sox (30) 14.00
2004 CH Brevard County Manatees (30) 12.00
2004 CH Bridgeport Bluefish (31) 9.50
2004 GS Bristol White Sox (35) 11.00
2004 GS Brockton Rox (30) 9.50
2004 CH Brooklyn Cyclones (35) 11.00
2004 CH Buffalo Bisons (30) 12.00
2004 MA Burlington Bees (30) 11.00
2004 CH Camden Riversharks (30) 9.00
2004 MA Capital City Bombers (36) 10.00
2004 CH Carolina League Top Prospects (32) 11.00
2004 TM Carolina Mudcats (32) 11.00
2004 MA Casper Rockies (36) 11.00
2004 Team Cedar Rapids Kernels (34) 11.00
2004 MA Charleston Alley Cats (34) 11.00
2004 MA Charleston River Dogs (33) 13.00
2004 MA Charleston River Dogs Update (30) 22.50
2004 MA Char'ston River Dogs Delmon Young (11) 12.50
2004 Team Charlotte Knights (31) 11.00
2004 GS Chattanooga Lookouts (30) 15.00
2004 GS Chillicothe Paints (27) 10.00
2004 GS Clearwater Threshers (30) 14.00
2004 GS Clinton Lumber Kings (32) 11.00
2004 GS Clinton Lumber Kings Strip Set (32) 25.00
2004 GS Clinton Lumber Kings Update (5) 5.00
2004 GS Coastal Bend Aviators (29) 9.50
2004 MA Colorado Springs Sky Sox (30) 10.00
2004 CH Columbus Clippers (30) 16.00
2004 GS Danville Braves (37) 11.00
2004 MA Dayton Dragons (30) 12.00
2004 GS Daytona Cubs (30) 20.00
2004 MA Delmarva Shorebirds (33) 11.00
2004 GS Dunedin Blue Jays (30) 13.00
2004 CH Durham Bulls (30) 12.00
2004 GS Eastern League Top Prospects (31) 16.00
2004 GS Edinburg Roadrunners (30) 10.00
2004 MA Edmonton Trappers (30) 14.00
2004 GS Elizabethton Twins (32) 11.00
2004 CH El Paso Diablos (31) 13.00
2004 MA Erie Sea Wolves (30) 11.00
2004 CH Erie Sea Wolves Update (1) 1.50

2004 GS Eugene Emeralds (32) 10.00
2004 GS Everett AquaSox (30) 13.00
2004 TM Fargo-Moorhead Redhawks (30) 10.00
2004 GS Florida State Lea. Top Prospects (25) 10.00
2004 GS Fort Myers Miracle (31) 11.00
2004 GS Fort Wayne Wizards (32) 10.00
2004 TM Fort Wayne Wizards Strip Set (15) 7.50
2004 CH Frederick Keys (30) 10.00
2004 CH Frederick Keys Anti-Smoking (30) 10.00
2004 MA Fresno Grizzlies (36) 11.00
2004 TM Frisco Rough Riders (30) 17.50
2004 TM Gateway Grizzlies (30) 10.00
2004 CH Greeneville Astros (40) 15.00
2004 MA Greensboro Bats (36) 10.00
2004 GS Greenville Braves (31) 11.00
2004 MA Hagerstown Suns (36) 11.00
2004 GS Harrisburg Senators (29) 11.00
2004 MA Hickory Crawdads (34) 10.00
2004 MA Hickory Crawdads Update (33) 10.00
2004 GS High Desert Mavericks (31) 11.00
2004 GS H.D. Mavericks Sponsor's Set (30) 14.00
2004 GS Hudson Valley Renegades (29) 11.00
2004 GS H.V. Renegades 10th Anniversary (32) 15.00
2004 TM Hudson Valley Renegades (29) 25.00
2004 Team Huntsville Stars (30) 22.50
2004 GS Idaho Falls Chukars (20) 12.00
2004 CH Indianapolis Indians (30) 10.00
2004 GS Inland Empire 66ers (30) 12.50
2004 CH International League All-Stars (33) 12.00
2004 CH Int'l League Top Prospects (30) 11.00
2004 MA Iowa Cubs (30) 14.00
2004 GS Jacksonville Suns (31) 11.00
2004 TM Jamestown Jammers (38) 20.00
2004 CH Johnson City Cardinals (35) 11.00
2004 MA Jupiter Hammerheads (36) 14.50
2004 GS Kane County Cougars (30) 16.00
2004 GS Kane Co. Cougars Sponsor's Set (30) 20.00
2004 GS Kane County Cougars Update (11) 12.00
2004 MA Kannapolis Intimidators (35) 11.00
2004 GS Kansas City T-Bones (30) 9.00
2004 GS Kingsport Mets (32) 10.00
2004 GS Kinston Indians (30) 13.00
2004 CH Lake County Captains (30) 12.00
2004 GS Lake Elsinore Storm (32) 13.00
2004 GS Lakeland Tigers (28) 13.50
2004 CH Lakewood BlueClaws (31) 12.50
2004 CH Best of Lakewood Blue Claws (25) 13.50
2004 GS Lancaster JetHawks (30) 10.00
2004 GS Lansing Lugnuts (26) 12.00
2004 MA Las Vegas 51s (33) 11.00
2004 MA Lexington Legends (31) 10.00
2004 CH Louisville Bats (36) 24.00
2004 CH Lowell Spinners (38) 11.00
2004 CH Lynchburg Hillcats (30) 11.00
2004 Team Lynchburg Hillcats (30) 16.00
2004 MA Mahoning Valley Scrappers (30) 10.00
2004 MA Memphis Redbirds (30) 11.00
2004 GS Midland RockHounds (28) 10.00
2004 One Hour Photo Midland Rock Hounds (21) 62.50
2004 Team Midwest League All-Stars (72) 13.50
2004 GS Midwest League Top Prospects (28) 12.50
2004 GS Missoula Osprey (37) 11.00
2004 GS Modesto A's (28) 11.00
2004 GS Montgomery Biscuits (33) 13.50
2004 CH Myrtle Beach Pelicans (40) 11.00
2004 MA Nashville Sounds (36) 12.00
2004 CH Newark Bears (30) 17.50
2004 GS New Britain Rock Cats (30) 11.00
2004 CH New Hampshire Fisher Cats (31) 12.00
2004 GS New Jersey Cardinals (33) 11.00
2004 CH New Jersey Jackals (35) 9.00
2004 MA New Orleans Zephyrs (30) 10.00
2004 CH NY-Penn League Top Prospects (30) 12.50
2004 CH Norfolk Tides (37) 13.50
2004 GS Northwest League All Star Game (55) 17.50
2004 GS Norwich Navigators (30) 11.00
2004 TM Ogden Raptors (42) 15.00
2004 MA Oklahoma RedHawks (30) 11.00
2004 MA Omaha Royals (31) 11.00
2004 CH Ottawa Lynx (30) 12.00
2004 MA Pacific Coast League All-Stars (29) 11.00
2004 MA Pacific Coast League Prospects (36) 12.00
2004 MA Palm Beach Cardinals (36) 15.00
2004 CH Pawtucket Red Sox (30) 11.00
2004 DD Pawtucket Red Sox Foldout 15.00
2004 MA Peoria Chiefs (30) 14.50
2004 MA Portland Beavers (32) 12.00
2004 GS Portland Sea Dogs (33) 11.00
2004 CH Potomac Cannons (30) 11.00
2004 GS Princeton Devil Rays (33) 11.00
2004 TM Princeton Devil Rays (4) 45.00
2004 TM Provo Angels (40) 11.00
2004 CH Pulaski Blue Jays (41) 10.00
2004 GS Swing of the Quad Cities (30) 12.50
2004 TM Capitales de Quebec (28) 9.50
2004 GS Rancho Cugamonga Quakes (30) 13.50
2004 MA Reading Phillies (30) 14.00
2004 MA Reading Area CC Reading Phillies (30) 12.50
2004 TM Reading Phillies Magnets (20) 20.00
2004 CH Richmond Braves (30) 10.00
2004 CH Richmond Braves Diamond 20th (22) 20.00
2004 CH Rochester Red Wings (30) 11.00
2004 GS Rockford RiverHawks (32) 9.50
2004 MA Rome Braves (32) 13.50
2004 GS Round Rock Express (30) 11.00
2004 MA Sacramento River Cats (30) 11.00
2004 GS Salem Avalanche (30) 11.00
2004 GS Salem-Keizer Volcanoes (36) 12.00
2004 GS Salem-Keizer Volcanoes Update (6) 8.00
2004 MA Salt Lake Stingers (36) 11.00
2004 CH San Antonio Missions (31) 11.00
2004 GS San Jose Giants (30) 11.00
2004 GS Sarasota Red Sox (30) 10.00
2004 MA Savannah Sand Gnats (36) 11.00
2004 CH Scranton/Wilkes-Barre Red Barons (32) 10.00
2004 TM Sioux City Expolorers (24) 9.50
2004 MA Sioux Falls Canaries (30) 9.50
2004 MA S. Atlantic League Top Prospects (32) 11.00
2004 GS South Bend Silver Hawks (33) 10.00
2004 GS Southern League Top Prospects (31) 12.00
2004 GS Spokane Indians (33) 12.00
2004 CH Staten Islands Yankees (34) 10.00
2004 GS St. Lucie Mets (33) 11.00
2004 CH Stockton Ports (30) 11.00
2004 TM St. Paul Saints (32) 10.00
2004 CH Syracuse SkyChiefs (31) 11.00
2004 MA Tacoma Rainiers (37) 12.50
2004 GS Tampa Yankees (29) 11.00
2004 GS Tennessee Smokies (28) 10.00
2004 GS Texas League Top Prospects (25) 11.00
2004 CH Toledo Mudhens (30) 11.00
2004 MA Trenton Thunder (31) 12.50
2004 GS Tri-City Dust Devils (32) 10.00
2004 CH Tri-City ValleyCats (35) 13.00
2004 MA Tucson Sidewinders (36) 11.00
2004 TM Tulsa Drillers (30) 11.00
2004 TM Vancouver Canadians (45) 11.00
2004 GS Vermont Expos (36) 10.00
2004 GS Vero Beach Dodgers (30) 16.00
2004 GS Visalia Oaks (30) 13.00
2004 CH West Michigan Whitecaps (30) 11.00
2004 GS West Tenn Diamond Jaxx (32) 10.00
2004 GS Wichita Wranglers (28) 11.00
2004 CH Williamsport Crosscutters (38) 13.00
2004 CH Wilmington Blue Rocks (32) 10.00
2004 TM Winnipeg Goldeyes (28) 10.00
2004 CH Winston-Salem Warthogs (30) 11.00
2004 GS Wisconsin Timber Rattlers (30) 10.00
2004 GS Yakima Bears (33) 11.00

Chronological Index

1863 Jordan & Co. ... 194
1867 Sterey Photographers Troy Haymakers ... 1759
1869 Peck & Snyder Cincinnati Red Stockings - Large ... 273
1869 Peck & Snyder Cincinnati Red Stockings - Small ... 273
1870 Peck & Snyder Chicago White Stockings ... 273
1870 Peck & Snyder New York Mutuals ... 274
1870 Peck & Snyder Philadelphia Athletics ... 274
1872 Warren Studio Boston Red Stockings Cabinets ... 501
1872 Warren Studio Boston Red Stockings CDVs ... 501
1874 Suppards & Fennemore Cabinets ... 357
1874 Warren Studio Boston Red Stockings Cabinets ... 501
1879-80 N.Y. Clipper Woodcuts ... 243
1880s John M. Ward Fan ... 500
1881 Randall Studio Cabinets ... 301
1884 Climax Poster ... 89
1886 Hancock's Syracuse Stars ... 1734
1886 J. Wood Studio N.Y. Giants Cabinets ... 513
1886 J. Wood Studio N.Y. Metropolitans Cabinets ... 513
1886 Lorillard Team Cards ... 215
1886 MacIntire Studio Cabinets ... 216
1886 New York Baseball Club (H812) ... 242
1886 Old Judge New York Giants (N167) ... 256
1886 Red Stocking Cigars ... 307
1886 Virginia Brights Black Stocking Nine (N48) ... 499
1886 W.H. Sanders New York Baseball Club (H812) ... 318
1886 Welton Cigars N.Y. Giants (H812) ... 503
1887 Four Base Hits ... 153
1887 Gold Coin (Buchner) (N284) ... 158
1887 Gypsy Queen (N175) ... 169
1887 Hastings Cabinets ... 174
1887 Kalamazoo Bats (N690) ... 198
1887 Kalamazoo Bats Cabinets (N690-1) ... 199
1887 Kalamazoo Bats Team Cards (N693) ... 199
1887 Lone Jack St. Louis Browns (N370) ... 214
1887 Tobin Lithographs B/W ... 382
1887 Tobin Lithographs Color ... 382
1887 Tomlinson Studios Cabinets ... 385
1887 Virginia Brights Polka Dot Nine ... 499
1887 W.S. Kimball Champions (N184) ... 205
1887-1890 Old Judge (N172) ... 256
1887-1890 Old Judge Hall of Famers Pose Variations ... 262
1887-1893 Baseball Currency ... 29
1888 "Scrapps Tobacco" Die-Cuts ... 323
1888 Allen & Ginter Girl Baseball Players (N48, N508) ... 15
1888 Allen & Ginter World's Champions (N28) ... 14
1888 Allen & Ginter World's Champions (N29) ... 15
1888 Allen & Ginter World's Champions (N43) ... 15
1888 Allen & Ginter World's Champions Album (A16) ... 15
1888 Allen & Ginter World's Champions Album (A17) ... 15
1888 Conly Cabinets ... 96
1888 Dixie Cigarettes Girl Baseball Players (N48) ... 120
1888 Duke Talk of the Diamond (N135) ... 125
1888 G & B Chewing Gum (E223) ... 155
1888 Gilbert & Bacon Cabinets ... 157
1888 Goodwin Champions (N162) ... 160
1888 Gray Studio Cabinets ... 167
1888 Gypsy Queen California League ... 1733
1888 Joseph Hall Cabinets ... 171
1888 Joseph Hall Imperial Cabinets ... 171
1888 Rafael Tuck & Sons Artistic Series Baseball ... 473
1888 S.F. Hess (N338-2) ... 176
1888 S.F. Hess California League (N321) ... 1735
1888 S.F. Hess California League (N338-1) ... 1735
1888 S.F. Hess Newsboys League (N333) ... 1735
1888 Sporting Times (M117) ... 340
1888 Sub Rosa Cigarettes Girl Baseball Players (N508) ... 354
1888 Uhlman St. Paul Cabinets ... 1761
1888 Virginia Brights Black Stocking Nine ... 499
1888 Virginia Brights Girl Baseball Players ... 499
1888 WG1 Base Ball Playing Cards ... 504
1888 Yum Yum Tobacco (N403) ... 528
1888-1889 Dogs Head Cabinets (N173) ... 121
1888-1889 Old Judge Cabinets(N173) ... 264
1888-1889 Sporting Extra World Tour Imperial Cabinets ... 331
1888-1889 Stevens Studio Australian Tour Cabinets ... 353
1889 "The Stage" Stars of the Diamond ... 349
1889 C.S. White & Co. Boston N.L. ... 508
1889 Diamond S Cigars Boston N.L. ... 116
1889 Duke's Terrors of America ... 125
1889 E.R. Williams Card Game ... 510
1889 G. Waldon Smith Boston Beaneaters Cabinets ... 327
1889 Goodwin & Co. Baseball Album (A35) ... 160
1889 Number 7 Cigars (N526) ... 248
1889 Police Gazette Cabinets ... 290
1890 G. Waldon Smith Cabinets ... 327
1890 Stevens Studio Chicago Pirates Cabinets ... 353
1890 Stevens Studio Chicago White Stockings Cabinets ... 353
1891 Conly Studio Cabinets ... 96
1892 Base Ball Scenes (N360) ... 34
1892 J.U. Stead Studio Cabinets ... 352
1893 Just So Tobacco ... 195
1894 Alpha Photo-Engraving Baltimore Orioles ... 17
1894 Honest (Duke) Cabinets (N142) ... 178
1895 Ashman Studio Cabinets ... 26
1895 Mayo's Cut Plug (N300) ... 222
1895 Newsboy Cabinets (N566) ... 242
1895 Police Gazette Supplement ... 290
1896 Mayo's Die-Cut Game Cards (N301) ... 222
1898 Cameo Pepsin Gum Pins ... 73
1898-99 National Copper Plate Co. Portraits ... 240
1899 Chickering Studio Boston Beaneaters Cabinets ... 81
1899 Henry Reccius Cigars Honus Wagner ... 303
1899-1900 Sporting News Supplements (M101-1) ... 338
1900 Chickering Studio Cabinets ... 82
1900 Mayo's Baseball Comics (T203) ... 223
1901-1917 Police Gazette Supplements ... 290
1902 Sporting Life Team Composites (W601) ... 335
1902-11 Sporting Life Cabinets (W600) ... 331
1903 Sporting Life Team Composites (W601) ... 335
1903-1904 Breisch-Williams ... 58
1903-1904 E107 Type 1 ... 140
1903-1904 E107 Type 2 ... 140
1904 Allegheny Card Co. ... 14
1904 Anonymous Studio Cabinets ... 23
1904 G. Waldon Smith Cabinets ... 327
1904 Pittsburg Leader Honus Wagner Schedule ... 282
1904 Sporting Life Team Composites (W601) ... 335
1904 Stenzel's Rooter Buttons ... 353
1905 Harry Pulliam Cigar Label ... 299
1905 N.Y. Giants Scorecard Postcard ... 243
1905 Rotograph Postcards ... 310
1905 Souvenir Post Card Shop of Cleveland ... 327
1905 Sporting Life Team Composites (W601) ... 335
1905-1909 Carl Horner Cabinets ... 178
1906 Fan Craze - American League ... 143
1906 Fan Craze - National League ... 143
1906 Lincoln Publishing Philadelphia A's ... 213
1906 Sporting Life Team Composites (W601) ... 335
1906 Ullman Postcards ... 480
1906-07 Sporting Life Team Composite Postcards ... 335
1907 Dietsche Chicago Cubs Postcards (PC765-2) ... 118
1907 Dietsche Posters ... 118
1907 Geo. W. Hull Chicago White Sox Postcards ... 186
1907 Grignon Chicago Cubs Postcards ... 168
1907 Krieg & Co. Chicago Cubs Base Ball Mail Card ... 206
1907 Morgan Stationery "Red Belt" Postcards ... 234
1907 Newark Evening World Supplements ... 1743
1907 Sporting Life Team Composites (W601) ... 336
1907 Wolverine News Co. Detroit Tigers ... 513
1907-09 Dietsche Detroit Tigers Postcards (PC765-1) ... 118
1907-09 H.M. Taylor Detroit Tigers Postcards ... 362
1907-09 Novelty Cutlery Postcards (PC805) ... 246
1908 American Caramel (E91, Set A) ... 17
1908 American League Pub. Co. Postcards ... 22
1908 Art Post Card Co. Our Home Team ... 24
1908 Boston Oyster House Chicago Cubs ... 46
1908 Boston Red Sox Foldout Postcard ... 46
1908 Chicago Cubs/White Sox Postcards ... 78
1908 Detroit Free Press Tigers Postcards ... 109
1908 General Photo Co. St. Louis Browns Postcards ... 156
1908 Hall's Studio N.Y. Giants Cabinets ... 171
1908 Offerman Buffalo Bisons Postcards ... 1746
1908 Pittsburgh Pirates Vignette Postcards ... 282
1908 R.C. Williams Cy Young Postcard ... 510
1908 Sporting Life Team Composites (W601) ... 336
1908 Victor Publishing Cy Young ... 498
1908-09 E91 American Caramel Co. ... 139
1908-11 H.H. Bregstone Browns/Cardinals Post Cards (PC743) ... 58
1908-1909 Greenfield's Chocolates Postcards ... 167
1908-1909 Rose Company Postcards ... 310
1908-1910 Brush Detroit Tigers Postcards ... 62
1909 "Colgan's Chips" Square Proofs ... 95
1909 American Caramel (E91, Set B) ... 17
1909 Bastian Gum Pin ... 1724
1909 Boston Herald Supplements ... 46
1909 Boston Sunday Post Red Sox Stars ... 50
1909 Cabanas ... 71
1909 Clement Bros. Bread (D380-1) ... 1727
1909 Croft's Candy (E92) ... 100
1909 Croft's Cocoa (E92) ... 100
1909 Derby Cigars N.Y. Giants ... 109
1909 Dockman & Sons Gum (E92) ... 121
1909 E101 "Set of 50" ... 139
1909 E102 "Set of 25" ... 139
1909 E92 Nadja Caramels ... 139
1909 E95 Philadelphia Caramel ... 139
1909 Minneapolis Tribune/St. Paul Pioneer Press Mirrors ... 1740
1909 Nadja Caramels (E92) ... 238
1909 Niagara Baking Co. ... 246
1909 Obak (T212) ... 1743
1909 Philadelphia Caramel (E95) ... 278
1909 Pittsburgh Pirates Extension Postcard ... 282
1909 Ramly Cigarettes (T204) ... 300
1909 Spargo Hartford Senators Postcards ... 1759
1909 Sporting Life Team Composites (W601) ... 336
1909 T.T.T. Cigarettes (T204) ... 473
1909 T204 ... 476
1909 Topping & Co. Detroit Tigers Postcards ... 385
1909 W.W. Smith Postcards ... 327
1909 Walter Johnson "Weiser Wonder" Postcards ... 1737
1909-10 C.A. Briggs Co. (E97) ... 58
1909-10 German Baseball Stamps ... 156
1909-11 American Beauty Cigarettes ... 17
1909-11 American Caramel (E90-1) ... 18
1909-11 Carolina Brights ... 76
1909-11 Drum Cigarettes ... 124
1909-11 E90-1, E90-2, E90-3 American Caramel ... 139
1909-11 El Principe de Gales Cigarettes ... 126
1909-11 Hindu Cigarettes ... 176
1909-11 Lenox Cigarettes ... 213
1909-11 Old Mill Cigarettes ... 268
1909-11 Piedmont Cigarettes ... 281
1909-11 Polar Bear Tobacco ... 290
1909-11 Sovereign Cigarettes ... 328
1909-11 Sweet Caporal ... 357
1909-11 T206 Errors ... 479
1909-11 T206 White Border ... 477
1909-11 Tolstoi Cigarettes ... 385
1909-11 Ty Cobb Tobacco (T206) ... 473
1909-11 Uzit Cigarettes ... 483
1909-12 Broad Leaf Cigarettes ... 59
1909-12 Cycle Cigarettes ... 101
1909-12 Sweet Caporal Domino Discs (PX7) ... 357
1909-16 Max Stein Postcards (PC758) ... 353
1909-1910 W555 ... 522
1909-1911 Colgan's Chips Stars of the Diamond (E254) ... 92
1909-1913 Sporting News Supplements (M101-2) ... 338
1910 "Orange Borders" ... 269
1910 A Fan For A Fan ... 12
1910 A.W.H./A.W.A. Caramels Virginia League (E222) . 1723
1910 All Star Base-Ball ... 16
1910 American Caramel (E91, Set C) ... 18
1910 American Caramel Die-cuts (E125) ... 19
1910 American Caramel Pirates (E90-2) ... 18
1910 American Caramel White Sox/ Cubs (E90-3) ... 18
1910 American Sports Candy and Jewelry ... 22
1910 Baltimore News Orioles ... 1723
1910 Bishop & Co. P.C.L. (E99) ... 1725
1910 Bishop & Co. P.C.L. Teams (E221) ... 1725
1910 Boston Red Sox Cabinets ... 46
1910 Clement Bros. Bread (D380) ... 1727
1910 Contentnea First Series (T209) ... 1729
1910 Contentnea Photo Series (T209) ... 1729
1910 Coupon Cigarettes Type 1 (T213) ... 96
1910 Darby Chocolates (E271) ... 103
1910 Doc Powers Day Postcard ... 296
1910 E104 Nadja Caramels ... 140
1910 E125 American Caramel Die-Cuts ... 140
1910 E93 Standard Caramel Co. ... 139
1910 E96 Philadelphia Caramel ... 139
1910 E98 "Set of 30" ... 139
1910 E-UNC Candy ... 138
1910 Hans Wagner Cigars ... 500
1910 Hermes Ice Cream Pirates Pins ... 175
1910 Ju-Ju Drums (E286) ... 194
1910 Luxello Cigars A's/Phillies Pins (P13) ... 215
1910 Makaroff Cigarettes World Series Postcard ... 220
1910 Mascot Gum Pins ... 1740
1910 Mello-Mint (E105) ... 225
1910 Morton's Buster Brown Bread Tigers Pins (PD2) ... 234
1910 Morton's Pennant Winner Bread Tigers Pins ... 234
1910 Nadja Caramels (E104-3) ... 238
1910 Nadja Caramels Philadelphia Athletics (E104-1) ... 238
1910 Nadja Caramels Pittsburgh Pirates (E104-2) ... 238
1910 Obak 150 Subjects (T212) ... 1743
1910 Obak 175 Subjects (T212) ... 1744
1910 Old Mill Cabinets (H801-7) ... 1749
1910 Old Mill Cigarettes Series 1 (S. Atlantic League) ... 1746
1910 Old Mill Cigarettes Series 2 (Virginia League) ... 1747
1910 Old Mill Cigarettes Series 3 (Texas League) ... 1747
1910 Old Mill Cigarettes Series 4 (Va. Valley League) ... 1747
1910 Old Mill Cigarettes Series 5 (Carolina Assn.) ... 1748
1910 Old Mill Cigarettes Series 6 (Blue Grass League) ... 1748
1910 Old Mill Cigarettes Series 7 (E. Carolina League) ... 1748
1910 Old Mill Cigarettes Series 8 (Southern Assn.) ... 1748
1910 Old Put Cigar ... 268
1910 PC796 Sepia Postcards ... 273
1910 Philadelphia Caramel (E96) ... 278
1910 Pittsburgh Gazette Times Honus Wagner Postcard ... 282
1910 Punch Cigars ... 299
1910 Ramly Team Composite Premiums ... 301
1910 Red Sun (T211) ... 1752
1910 Sporting Life Team Composites (W601) ... 336
1910 Standard Caramel Co. (E93) ... 351
1910 Tip-Top Bread Pittsburgh Pirates (D322) ... 381
1910 Toy Town Post Office ... 471
1910 Washington Times ... 502
1910 Williams Caramels (E103) ... 510

1910 W-UNC Strip Cards 515
1910-11 S74 Silks - White 359
1910-11 Sporting Life (M116) 336
1910-12 Plow Boy Tobacco 287
1910-12 Red Cross Tobacco Type 1 (T215) 304
1910-12 Sweet Caporal Pins (P2) 358
1910-1911 T3 Turkey Red Cabinets 473
1910-57 Baseball Magazine Player Posters 30
1911 Baltimore News Newsboys Series 28
1911 Baseball Bats 29
1911 Baseball Scorecard Fan 34
1911 Big Eater Sacramento Solons 1724
1911 Bishop & Co. P.C.L. Type I (E100) 1725
1911 Bishop & Co. P.C.L. Type II (E100) 1725
1911 Blome's Chocolates (E94) 42
1911 Cullivan's Fireside Philadelphia A's (T208) 101
1911 Diamond Gum Pins (PE2) 114
1911 E94 139
1911 George Close Candy Co. (E94) 89
1911 Gilmartin Printing Co. S.F. Seals 1732
1911 Harry Davis Day Postcard 103
1911 Helmar Stamps (T332) 175
1911 Jones, Keyser & Arras Cabinets 194
1911 Mecca Cigarettes 225
1911 Monarch Typewriter Philadelphia A's 233
1911 Mono Cigarettes (T217) 1741
1911 Obak (T212) 1744
1911 Obak Cabinets (T4) 1745
1911 Obak Coupon 1746
1911 Pacific Coast Biscuit (D310) 1750
1911 Pacific Coast Biscuit (D311) 1750
1911 Rochester Baking Philadelphia A's (D359) 308
1911 S74 Silks - Colored 360
1911 Sporting Life Cabinets (M110) 337
1911 Sporting Life Team Composites (W601) 338
1911 Stevens Firearms Philadelphia Athletics 353
1911 T201 Mecca Double Folders 475
1911 T205 Gold Border 476
1911 T5 Pinkerton Cabinets 473
1911 Western Playground Association 1762
1911 Williams Baking Philadelphia A's (D359) 510
1911 Zeenut Pacific Coast League 1764
1911-12 Hassan Cigarettes 174
1911-12 Honest Long Cut Tobacco 178
1911-14 Brunners Bread (D304) 62
1911-14 Butter Krust Bread (D304) 68
1911-14 General Baking Co. (D304) 156
1911-14 Weber Bakery (D304) 502
1911-16 Kotton Tobacco 206
1911-16 Mino Cigarettes (T216) 233
1911-16 Virginia Extra Cigarettes (T216) 499
1912 A.F. Orr Louis Sockalexis Photocard 270
1912 Anonymous T207 23
1912 Base Ball Stars Series 34
1912 Boston American Series Red Sox Postcards 44
1912 Boston Daily American Souvenir Postcards 45
1912 Boston Garter 45
1912 Boston Red Sox Tattoos 46
1912 Colgan's Chips Red Borders (E270) 93
1912 Home Run Kisses (E136) 1736
1912 Imperial Tobacco (C46) 1737
1912 J=K Candy 189
1912 L1 Leathers 215
1912 La Azora Cigars 207
1912 Miner's Extra Series of Champions (T227) 232
1912 Napoleon Little Cigars 239
1912 Photo Art Shop Boston Red Sox 280
1912 Pirate Cigarettes (T215) 282
1912 Plow's Candy (E300) 287
1912 Recruit Little Cigars 303
1912 Red Cross Tobacco (T207) 303
1912 S110 Baseball Player Silks Pillow Case 361
1912 S81 Silks 360
1912 T202 Hassan Triple Folders 475
1912 T207 Brown Background 479
1912 T227 Series Of Champions 480
1912 Ty Cobb Postcard 89
1912 Vassar Sweaters 483
1912 Whitehead & Hoag P.C.L. Pins 1763
1912 W-UNC Strip Cards 515
1912 Zeenut Pacific Coast League 1764
1912-13 Red Cross Tobacco Type 2 (T215) 304
1913 Base Ball Series Notebooks 34
1913 Baseball Managers Scorecard/Fan 32
1913 Baseball Player Stamps 34
1913 Cleveland Indians Schedule Postcards 86
1913 Colgan's Chips Tin Tops 94
1913 Cravats Felt Pennants 100
1913 Fatima Premiums 144
1913 Fatima Team Cards (T200) 144
1913 Fenway Breweries/Tom Barker Game 145
1913 Napoleon Lajoie Game 208
1913 National Game (WG5) 240
1913 Oakland Oaks Team Issue 1743
1913 Philadelphia Caramel Proofs 278
1913 Philadelphia Evening Telegraph Postcards 278
1913 Philadelphia Evening Times Supplements 278
1913 Sporting News Postcards (M101-3) 338
1913 Tom Barker Game (WG6) 28
1913 Voskamp's Coffee Pittsburgh Pirates 500
1913 Zeenut Pacific Coast League 1765
1913-14 Martens Bakery 222
1913-1915 Fatima Posters 144
1913-1915 Pinkerton Score/Photo/Post Cards 281
1914 B18 Blankets 68
1914 Baltimore News Orioles 1723
1914 Baltimore News Terrapins 28
1914 Boston Garter - Color 45
1914 Boston Garter - Sepia 45
1914 Cracker Jack (E145) 98
1914 E. & S. Publishing Co. 125
1914 Evening Sun N.Y. Giants 128
1914 Fatima (T222) 144
1914 Lawrence Semon Postcards 323
1914 Piedmont Art Stamps (T330-2) 281
1914 Polo Grounds Game (WG4) 291
1914 Pritchard Publishing Giants/Yankees Stamps 297
1914 Texas Tommy Type 1 (E224) 379
1914 Texas Tommy Type 2 (E224) 380
1914 Zeenut Pacific Coast League 1766
1914-16 Coupon Cigarettes Type 2 (T213) 96
1915 American Caramel (E106) 19
1915 Baseball Magazine Premium 32
1915 Chicago Tribune Supplements 80
1915 Cracker Jack (E145) 98
1915 E106 American Caramel Co. 140
1915 General Baking Co. (D303) 156
1915 PM1 Ornate-Frame Pins 288
1915 Postaco Stamps 291
1915 Schmelzer's Sporting Goods Pins 322
1915 Victory Tobacco (T214) 498
1915 W-UNC Strip Cards 516
1915 Zeenut Pacific Coast League 1766
1916 Altoona Tribune 17
1916 BF2 Felt Pennants 69
1916 Block and Kuhl Co. 42
1916 Bucyrus Brewing Co. (M101-4) 62
1916 Burgess-Nash Clothiers 66
1916 Everybody's 128
1916 Famous and Barr Clothiers 142
1916 Felix Mendelsohn 226
1916 Ferguson Bakery Felt Pennants (BF2) 145
1916 Ferguson Bakery Photo Prize Pennants 145
1916 Fleischmann Bakery (D381) 152
1916 Gimbels 157
1916 Globe Clothing Store (H801-9) 157
1916 Green-Joyce 167
1916 Herpolsheimer Co. 175
1916 Holmes to Homes Bread 177
1916 Indianapolis Brewing Co. 187
1916 M101-4 Blank Backs 237
1916 M101-5 Blank Backs 236
1916 Mall Theatre 220
1916 Morehouse Baking Co. 234
1916 Mothers' Bread (D303) 235
1916 N.Y. World Leaders in Baseball 244
1916 Standard Biscuit (D350-1) 350
1916 Successful Farming 354
1916 Tango Eggs 361
1916 The Sporting News (M101-4) 339
1916 The Sporting News (M101-5) 339
1916 Ware's 501
1916 Weil Baking Co. (D329) 502
1916 Zeenut Pacific Coast League 1767
1916-20 W-UNC "Big Head" Strip Cards 516
1917 Boston Store 49
1917 Chicago White Sox Team Issue 80
1917 Collins-McCarthy (E135) 95
1917 Felix Mendelsohn (M101-UNC) 226
1917 Standard Biscuit (D350-2) 350
1917 Weil Baking Co. (D328) 503
1917 Youth's Companion Stamps 527
1917 Zeenut Pacific Coast League 1767
1917-1920 Felix Mendelsohn 226
1918 Zeenut Pacific Coast League 1768
1919 Coupon Cigarettes Type 3 (T213) 97
1919 Coupon Cigarettes Type 3, Factory 8 Overprint 98
1919 Mother's Bread 235
1919 Sporting News (M101-6) 339
1919 Winkelman's Quaker Bread Pins 1763
1919 Zeenut Pacific Coast League 1768
1919-20 Cincinnati Reds Postcards 83
1919-21 W514 518
1920 Babe Ruth "Headin' Home" 312
1920 Babe Ruth "Headin' Home" Theater Cards 312
1920 Babe Ruth "Headin' Home" (Tex Rickard) 312
1920 Mrs. Sherlock's Bread Pins 1742
1920 W516-1 520
1920 W516-1-2 520
1920 W519 - Numbered 1 521
1920 W519 - Numbered 2 521
1920 W519 - Unnumbered 521
1920 W520 521
1920 W522 522
1920 Zeenut Pacific Coast League 1768
1920s Babe Ruth Postcard 312
1920s Babe Ruth Underwear Premium Photo 312
1920s Otto Treulich & Son 472
1920s W-UNC Playing Strip Cards (2) 516
1921 American Caramel Series of 80 (E121) 19
1921 C. Shulz Baseball Card Game 322
1921 Clark's Bread 85
1921 E253 Oxford Confectionery 141
1921 Exhibits 128
1921 Frederick Foto Service 1731
1921 Herpolsheimer's 176
1921 Holsum Bread 177
1921 Koester Bread N.Y. Giants/Yankees 205
1921 Mrs. Sherlock's Bread Pins 236
1921 Oxford Confectionery (E253) 271
1921 Pathe Freres Phonograph Co. 273
1921 Schapira Bros. Candy Babe Ruth 321
1921 Standard Biscuit (D350-3) 351
1921 W516-2-1 520
1921 W516-2-2 520
1921 W516-2-3 520
1921 W521 522
1921 W551 522
1921 W9316 526
1921 Wool's American-Maid Bread 513
1921 W-UNC Self-Developing Strip Cards 516
1921 Zeenut Pacific Coast League 1769
1921-1922 W575-1 525
1921-1930 Major League Ball Die-Cuts 217
1921-22 E121 American Caramel Series of 80/120 140
1921-22 Schapira Bros. Big Show Candy 321
1921-23 National Caramel (E220) 239
1922 American Caramel Series of 120 (E121) 20
1922 American Caramel Series of 240 (E120) 21
1922 American Caramel Series of 80 (E122) 20
1922 Cream Nut/Goodie Bread 100
1922 E120 American Caramel Series of 240 140
1922 E122 American Caramel Series of 80 140
1922 Eastern Exhibit Supply Co. 129
1922 Exhibits 129
1922 Fans Cigarettes (T231) 143
1922 Gassler's American Maid Bread 155
1922 Haffner's Big-Tayto-Loaf Bread 170
1922 Henry A. Johnson Wholesale Confectioner 193
1922 Keating Candy Co. 200
1922 Leader Theatre 211
1922 Lou Gertenrich 157
1922 Mrs. Sherlock's Bread Pins (PB5) 1742
1922 Neilson's Chocolate Type 1 (V61) 241
1922 Neilson's Chocolate Type 2 (V61) 241
1922 W501 517
1922 W503 518
1922 W573 524
1922 W575-2 525
1922 Willard's Chocolates Premium 509
1922 Witmor Candy Co. 513
1922 Wm. Paterson 273
1922 Zeenut Pacific Coast League 1770
1922-23 Kolb's Mothers' Bread Pins (PB4) 1738
1923 "Neilson's Chocolates" 242
1923 Baltimore Shirt Co. Kansas City Blues 1724
1923 Curtis Ireland Candy (E123) 188
1923 Fleer 146
1923 German Baseball Transfers 157
1923 Indianapolis Indians Foldout 1737
1923 Lections 213
1923 Little Wonder Picture Series 214
1923 Maple Crispette (V117) 222
1923 W515-1 519
1923 W515-2 519
1923 W572 523
1923 Willard's Chocolate (V100) 509
1923 Zeenut Pacific Coast League 1770
1923-1924 Nacionales Cigarros 237
1923-1924 Tomas Gutierrez 169
1923-24 Billiken 42
1923-24 Exhibits 129
1923-24 La Moda 208
1924 Chicago Evening American Cubs/White Sox Pins 80
1924 Crescent Ice Cream Hanbury 1729
1924 Diaz Cigarettes 117
1924 Proctor's Theatre Babe Ruth 297
1924 Walter Mails Card Game (WG7) 217
1924 Willard's Chocolate Sports Champions (V122) 510
1924 Zeenut Pacific Coast League 1771
1924-1925 Aguilitas Segundas 12
1925 Anonymous Postcards 23
1925 Champions Babe Ruth Exhibit 130
1925 Drake's 124
1925 Exhibits 129
1925 Holland World's Champions Washington Senators 177
1925 Turf Cigarettes 473
1925 Universal Toy & Novelty Brooklyn Dodgers (W504) 482
1925 Universal Toy & Novelty N.Y. Yankees (W504) 482
1925 Universal Toy & Novelty New York Giants (W504) .. 482
1925 Universal Toy & Novelty Washington Senators (W504) 482
1925 Zeenut Pacific Coast League 1771
1925-31 W590 525

1926 Exhibits 130
1926 Kut Outs Giants/Yankees Die-Cuts 206
1926 Sporting News Supplements (M101-7) 339
1926 Sports Co. of America Champions 342
1926 W511 518
1926 W-UNC Strip Cards 516
1926 Zeenut Pacific Coast League 1772
1926-1927 Aguilitas 13
1926-1927 Mallorquina Caramels 220
1926-27 W512 518
1926-29 Postcard-back Exhibits 130
1926-31 Postcard-back Four-on-One Exhibits 131
1927 "Babe Comes Home" Strip Cards (R94) 313
1927 American Caramel Series of 60 (E126) 21
1927 E126 American Caramel Series of 60 140
1927 E210 York Caramels 141
1927 Exhibits 131
1927 Honey Boy 178
1927 Middy Bread Browns/Cardinals Die-Cuts 228
1927 Rinkeydink Stamps 307
1927 W560 523
1927 York Caramels Type 1 (E210) 527
1927 York Caramels Type 2 (E210) 527
1927 Zeenut Pacific Coast League 1772
1927-1928 Sporting News Ad-Back Supplements (M101-7) 339
1928 Babe Ruth Home Run Candy Club Membership Card 313
1928 Exhibits 131
1928 Fro-joy (F52) 154
1928 Fro-joy Premium Photo 154
1928 George Ruth Candy Co. 313
1928 Greiners Bread 168
1928 Harrington's Ice Cream 174
1928 Pacific Coast League Exhibits 1730
1928 PM6 Baseball Player Pins 288
1928 Shonen Kulubu Babe Ruth Postcard 327
1928 Star Player Candy 352
1928 Sweetman 358
1928 Tabacalera la Morena 361
1928 Tharp's Ice Cream 380
1928 W502 517
1928 W513 518
1928 W565 523
1928 Yuengling's Ice Cream (F50) 528
1928 Zeenut Pacific Coast League 1773
1928-1932 La Presse Baseball Rotos 1738
1929 Certified's Ice Cream Pins 77
1929 Churchman's Cigarettes 82
1929 Exhibit "Star Picture Stamps" 132
1929 Kashin Publications (R316) 200
1929 Leader Novelty Candy Co. 211
1929 R316 314
1929 R316 5x7 Photos 314
1929 Star Player Candy 352
1929 W553 522
1929 W-UNC Playing Strip Cards (1) 516
1929 Zeenut Pacific Coast League 1774
1929-1930 R315 314
1929-30 Four-on-One Exhibits 132
1930 Baguer Chocolate 27
1930 Becker Bros. Theatre 40
1930 Blue Ribbon Malt Chicago Cubs 42
1930 Blue Ribbon Malt Chicago White Sox 42
1930 Blue Ribbon Malt Premiums 43
1930 Chicago Evening American Pins 80
1930 Chicago Herald and Examiner Babe Ruth Premium 80
1930 Post Cereal Famous North Americans 291
1930 Ray-O-Print Photo Kits 303
1930 W554 522
1930 Zeenut Pacific Coast League 1774
1930-1931 Harrison Studio Homestead Grays Postcards 174
1930-31 Lucke Badge & Button Baltimore Orioles Pins 1740
1930s Edwards, Ringer & Bigg Cigarettes 126
1930s Goodrich Tire Mickey Cochrane 159
1930s Knickerbocker Beer Yankees Premium 205
1930s Rogers Peet Sport Album 309
1931 Blue Ribbon Malt 43
1931 Chicago Cubs Picture Pack 78
1931 Josetti Tobacco 194
1931 Metropolitan Studio St. Louis Cardinals 227
1931 Sun Pictures Photo Kits 355
1931 W502 517
1931 W517 520
1931 W517 Mini 521
1931 Washington Senators Picture Pack 501
1931 W-UNC Strip Cards 516
1931 Zeenut Pacific Coast League 1775
1931-32 Babe Ruth Exhibit 132
1931-32 Four-on-One Exhibits 132
1932 Abdulla Tobacco 11
1932 Bulgaria Sport Tobacco 63
1932 Charles Denby Cigars Cubs 108
1932 Chicago Cubs Picture Pack 78
1932 Chicago Cubs Team Issue 78
1932 N.Y. Giants Schedule Postcards 243
1932 Orbit Gum Pins - Numbered (PR2) 269
1932 Orbit Gum Pins - Unnumbered (PR3) 269
1932 Sanella Margarine 319
1932 Sporting News Supplements (M101-8) 340
1932 Universal Pictures Babe Ruth Premium 482
1932 Wheaties Babe Ruth Flip Book 505
1932 Wheaties Minneapolis Millers 1763
1932 Zeenut Pacific Coast League 1775
1933 Astra Margarine 26
1933 Blue Bird Babe Ruth 42
1933 Blum's Baseball Bulletin Premiums 43
1933 Buffalo Bisons Jigsaw Puzzles 1726
1933 Butter Cream (R306) 67
1933 Button Gum 68
1933 C.A. Briggs Co. Babe Ruth 58
1933 Chicago Cubs Picture Pack 78
1933 Cracker Jack Pins (PR4) 99
1933 DeLong (R333) 107
1933 Eclipse Import 126
1933 Four-on-One Exhibits 133
1933 George C. Miller (R300) 229
1933 Goudey (R319) 160
1933 Mrs. Sherlock's Bread Pins 1742
1933 Oriental Theatre 270
1933 PX3 Double Header Coins 300
1933 R337 314
1933 Rittenhouse Candy (E285) 308
1933 Sport Kings (R338) 340
1933 St. Paul Daily News 1759
1933 Sulima Cigarettes 355
1933 Tattoo Orbit (R305) 362
1933 Tattoo Orbit (R308) 362
1933 U.S. Caramel (R328) 482
1933 Uncle Jacks Candy 480
1933 W574 524
1933 Wheaties Minneapolis Millers 1763
1933 Wheaties Seattle Indians 1763
1933 Worch Cigar 513
1933 World Wide Gum (Canadian Goudey, V353) 514
1933 Zeenut Pacific Coast League (sepia) 1776
1933-1934 Adams Hat Stores 12
1933-1934 Wheaties 505
1933-34 Goudey Premiums (R309-1) 161
1933-34 Worch Cigar American Assoc. 1763
1933-36 Zeenut Pacific Coast League (black-and-white) 1776
1934 Al Demaree Die-cuts (R304) 107
1934 Buffalo Bisons Team Issue 1726
1934 Butterfinger - Canadian (V94) 67
1934 Butterfinger (R310) 67
1934 Detroit Tigers Team Issue 109
1934 Diamond Matchbooks - Silver Border 114
1934 Dietz Gum Ball Players in Action 118
1934 Four-on-One Exhibits 133
1934 Gold Medal Foods (R313A) 159
1934 Goudey (R320) 161
1934 Quaker Oats Babe Ruth Premium Photo (8x10) 300
1934 Tarzan Bread (D382) 361
1934 Ward's Sporties Pins 501
1934 World Wide Gum (Canadian Goudey, V354) 514
1934-36 Batter-Up (R318) 35
1934-36 Diamond Stars (R327) 116
1935 Detroit Free Press Tigers 109
1935 Diamond Matchbooks - Black Border 115
1935 Four-on-One Exhibits 133
1935 George Burke Detroit Tigers Photo Stamps 66
1935 Goudey 4-in-1 (R321) 161
1935 Goudey Premiums (R309-2) 163
1935 Goudey Puzzle-Backs 162
1935 Pebble Beach Clothiers 1751
1935 Rice-Stix (UM7) 307
1935 Schutter-Johnson (R332) 322
1935 Wheaties - Series 1505
1935-36 Diamond Matchbooks 115
1935-37 George Burke Postage Stamp Photos 66
1936 Boston American Sport Stamps 44
1936 Chicago Cubs Picture Pack 79
1936 Detroit Times Sports Stamps 110
1936 Diamond Matchbooks - Chicago Cubs 116
1936 Diamond Matchbooks - Team on Back 116
1936 E-UNC Candy 139
1936 Four-on-One Exhibits 133
1936 Goudey (R322) 163
1936 Goudey "Wide Pen" Premiums - Type 1 163
1936 Goudey "Wide Pen" Premiums - Type 2 163
1936 Goudey "Wide Pen" Premiums - Type 3 164
1936 Goudey "Wide Pen" Premiums (R314) 163
1936 National Chicle "Fine Pens" (R313) 239
1936 National Chicle Rabbit Maranville 'How To' 240
1936 Overland Candy Co. (R301) 271
1936 Pittsburgh Sun-Telegraph Sport Stamps 284
1936 R311 Glossy Finish 313
1936 R311 Leather Finish 313
1936 R312 313
1936 R313 314
1936 R314 314
1936 S and S Game 315
1936 Spencer Shoes Jimmie Foxx Premium Photo 329
1936 Sunday Advertiser Sport Stamps 355
1936 Type 7 - Player, Team w/Pennant, Cap, Ball, Etc. 70
1936 Wheaties - Seriesn 3 505
1936 Wheaties - Series 4 505
1936 Wheaties - Series 5 505
1936 World Wide Gum (Canadian Goudey, V355) 515
1936-37 BF3 Felt Player/Team Pennants 69
1936-37 Type 1 - Player Name and Silhouette 69
1936-37 Type 11 - Minor League and Team 71
1936-37 Type 12 - Jumbo Teams 71
1936-37 Type 2 - Player's Name, Team Nickname, Figure 69
1936-37 Type 3 - Player's Name, Team Nickname 70
1936-37 Type 4 - Team Nickname and Silhouette Player 70
1936-37 Type 5 - Team Nickname with Emblem 70
1936-37 Type 6 - Team Name Only 70
1936-37 Type 8 - Misc. Designs 70
1937 BF104 Blankets 71
1937 BF-UNC Felt Pennants 69
1937 Dixie Lids 120
1937 Dixie Lids Premiums 120
1937 Donut Co. of American Thrilling Moments 123
1937 Dupont Cavalcade of America Premium 125
1937 Four-on-One Exhibits 133
1937 Goudey "Wide Pen" Premiums - Type 4 164
1937 Goudey "Wide Pen" Premiums - Type 5 164
1937 Goudey Knot Hole League 164
1937 Goudey Thum Movies 164
1937 Joe "Ducky" Medwick 225
1937 Kellogg's Pep Sports Stamps 201
1937 O-Pee-Chee 248
1937 Type 9 - Player Name, 1937 On Ball, Team Name 71
1937 Wheaties - Series 14 506
1937 Wheaties - Series 6 505
1937 Wheaties - Series 7 505
1937 Wheaties - Series 8 506
1937 Wheaties - Series 9 506
1937 WHIO-Sy Burick Cincinnati Reds Postcards 508
1937-38 Zeenut Pacific Coast League 1777
1937-39 Orcajo Cincinnati Reds Postcards (PC786) 270
1938 Baseball Tabs 34
1938 Cincinnati Post Reds 83
1938 Cincinnati Reds Team Issue 83
1938 Dixie Lids 120
1938 Dixie Lids Premiums 120
1938 Dizzy Dean's Service Station 104
1938 Foto Fun 153
1938 Four-on-One Exhibits 134
1938 Goudey (R323) 164
1938 Goudey Big League Baseball Movies 165
1938 Our National Game Pins 270
1938 Sawyer Biscuit Cubs/White Sox 320
1938 Type 10 - Player Name, 1938 On Ball, Team Name 71
1938 Wheaties - Series 10 506
1938 Wheaties - Series 11 506
1938 Wheaties - Series 15 506
1938-39 Metropolitan Clothing Cincinnati Reds Postcards 227
1938-39 Val Decker Packing Co. Cincinnati Reds Postcards 483
1938-53 Philadelphia A's Team-Issue Photos 275
1939 African Tobacco 12
1939 Centennial of Baseball Stamps 76
1939 Chicago Cubs Picture Pack 79
1939 Cincinnati Reds Team Issue 83
1939 Father & Son Shoes 143
1939 Goudey Premiums (R303-A) 165
1939 Goudey Premiums (R303-B) 165
1939 Kimball Automobile Trois-Rivieres Photocards 1738
1939 Piel's Beer Coasters 281
1939 Play Ball (R334) 285
1939 Play Ball Samples 285
1939 Sporting News Supplements (M101-9) 340
1939 Tip-Top Bread Joe DiMaggio Pin 381
1939 Wheaties - Series 12 507
1939 Wheaties - Series 13 507
1939 World Wide Gum (Canadian Goudey, V351) 515
1939-43 Hall of Fame Sepia Postcards 171
1939-46 Salutation Exhibits 134
1939-63 Hall of Fame B/W Plaque Postcards - Auto. 171
1940 Associated Stations San Francisco Seals 1723
1940 Boston Red Sox Photo Pack 46
1940 Brooklyn Dodgers Picture Pack 60
1940 Buffalo Bisons Team Issue 1726
1940 Chicago Cubs Picture Pack 79
1940 Chicago White Sox Photo Pack 81
1940 Cincinnati Reds Team Issue 83
1940 Crowley's Milk Binghamton Triplets 1730
1940 Diamond Dust Punchboard Cards 112
1940 Hughes Frozen Confections Sacramento Solons 1736
1940 Michigan Sportservice Detroit Tigers 228
1940 Philadelphia Phillies Photo Pack 279
1940 Play Ball (R335) 285
1940 Play Ball Colorized Proofs 286
1940 PM10 Baseball Player Pins 288
1940 Wheaties Champs of the USA 507
1940s Alerta Antonio Alcalde Premium Pictures 14
1940s Eagle Hall of Fame 126
1940s Ford Babe Ruth Premium 152
1940s Sarra Trade Cards 320
1940s-50s Anonymous Premium Photos 23
1941 Ballantine Coasters 27

1941 Boston Red Sox Photo Pack....... 46
1941 Brooklyn Dodgers Picture Pack....... 60
1941 Chicago Cubs Picture Pack....... 79
1941 Double Play (R330)....... 123
1941 Goudey (R324)....... 165
1941 Huskies....... 187
1941 Lou Gehrig Memorial Ticket....... 156
1941 Play Ball (R336)....... 286
1941 Play Ball Paper Version....... 287
1941 St. Louis Browns Team Issue (W753)....... 353
1941 St. Louis Cardinals Team Issue (W754)....... 354
1941 Wheaties Champs of the USA....... 507
1942 Boston Red Sox Photo Pack....... 46
1942 Brooklyn Dodgers Picture Pack....... 60
1942 Chicago Cubs Picture Pack....... 79
1942 Editorial Bruguera Babe Ruth....... 126
1942 Joe DiMaggio Candy Box Card....... 118
1943 Boston Red Sox Photo Pack....... 47
1943 Brooklyn Dodgers Picture Pack....... 60
1943 Centennial Flour Seattle Rainiers....... 1726
1943 Chicago Cubs Picture Pack....... 79
1943 Golden Quality Ice Cream Wilkes-Barre Barons....... 1732
1943 Grand Studio Milwaukee Brewers....... 1732
1943 M.P. & Co. (R302-1)....... 235
1943 Philadelphia Phillies Photo Pack....... 279
1943-47 Parade Sportive....... 1750
1944 Centennial Flour Seattle Rainiers....... 1727
1944 Chicago Cubs Picture Pack....... 80
1944 Grand Studio Milwaukee Brewers....... 1732
1944 N.Y. Yankees Stamps....... 244
1944-45 Albertype Hall of Fame Plaque Postcards - Type....... 113
1944-63 Hall of Fame Black-and-White Plaque Postcards....... 171
1945 Autographs Game....... 27
1945 Centennial Flour Seattle Rainiers....... 1727
1945 Grand Studio Milwaukee Brewers....... 1733
1945 Remar Bread Oakland Oaks....... 1752
1945-46 Caramelo Deportivo Cuban League....... 74
1946 Boston Red Sox Photo Pack....... 47
1946 Brooklyn Dodgers Picture Pack....... 60
1946 Friedman's Dodger Aces Postcard....... 154
1946 Remar Bread Oakland Oaks....... 1753
1946 Sears St. Louis Browns/ Cardinals Postcards....... 323
1946 Sunbeam Bread Sacramento Solons....... 1759
1946-1947 Almanaque Deportivo....... 15
1946-1947 Sensacion Premiums....... 324
1946-47 Caramelo Deportivo Cuban League....... 74
1946-47 Propagandas Montiel Los Reyes del Deporte....... 297
1946-49 Sports Exchange All-Star Picture File....... 342
1946-52 Albertype Hall of Fame Plaque Postcards - Type 2....... 13
1947 Bond Bread....... 43
1947 Bond Bread Exhibits....... 44
1947 Bond Bread Jackie Robinson....... 44
1947 Bond Bread Perforated, Dual-Sided....... 44
1947 Bond Bread Premiums....... 44
1947 Boston Red Sox Photo Pack....... 47
1947 Brillantina Sol de Oro Managers....... 59
1947 Brooklyn Dodgers Picture Pack....... 61
1947 Buffalo Bisons Team Issue....... 1726
1947 Centennial Flour Seattle Rainiers....... 1727
1947 Champ Hats Premiums....... 77
1947 Cleveland Indians Picture Pack....... 86
1947 Coca-Cola All Time Sports Favorite....... 89
1947 Jackie Robinson Pins....... 308
1947 Mabley & Carew Cincinnati Reds....... 215
1947 Morley Studios Tacoma Tigers....... 1741
1947 Morley Studios Team Cards....... 1741
1947 Pleetwood Slacks Jackie Robinson....... 287
1947 Remar Bread Oakland Oaks....... 1753
1947 Signal Gasoline Hollywood Stars....... 1757
1947 Signal Gasoline Los Angeles Angels....... 1757
1947 Signal Gasoline Oakland Oaks....... 1757
1947 Signal Gasoline Pacific Coast League....... 1757
1947 Signal Gasoline Sacramento Solons....... 1758
1947 Signal Gasoline Seattle Rainiers....... 1758
1947 Smith's Oakland Oaks....... 1758
1947 Sport Magazine Premium....... 340
1947 Sports Exchange Baseball Miniatures....... 343
1947 Sunbeam Bread Sacramento Solons....... 1760
1947 Tip Top Bread....... 381
1947 Van Patrick Cleveland Indians Postcards....... 86
1947 W571....... 523
1947-50 N.Y. Yankees Picture Pack....... 244
1947-66 Exhibits....... 134
1948 American Association Babe Ruth....... 17
1948 Babe Ruth Memorial Pin....... 313
1948 Baseball's Great Hall of Fame Exhibits....... 136
1948 Boston Red Sox Photo Pack....... 47
1948 Bowman....... 50
1948 Brooklyn Dodgers Picture Pack....... 61
1948 Chicago White Sox Photo Pack....... 81
1948 Cleveland Indians Picture Pack....... 87
1948 Gentle's Bread Boston Braves....... 156
1948 Gunther Beer Washington Senators Postcards....... 169
1948 Kellogg's Corn Flakes Cuban Postcards....... 201
1948 Kellogg's Pep Celebrities....... 201
1948 Los Angeles Angels Team Issue....... 1739
1948 N.Y. Giants Photo Pack....... 243
1948 Old Gold Jackie Robinson....... 256
1948 Philadelphia Bulletin Stand-Ups....... 276
1948 Pittsburgh Provision & Packing Co....... 284
1948 R.K.O. Theaters Babe Ruth Premium....... 308
1948 R346 Blue Tint....... 314
1948 Remar/Sunbeam Bread Oakland Oaks....... 1753
1948 Signal Gasoline Oakland Oaks....... 1758
1948 Smith's Oakland Oaks....... 1759
1948 Sommer & Kaufmann San Francisco Seals....... 1759
1948 Speedway 79 Tiger of the Week Photos....... 328
1948 Swell Babe Ruth Story....... 360
1948 Swell Sport Thrills....... 359
1948 Thom McAn Bob Feller Premium....... 223
1948 Topps Magic Photos....... 386
1948-1949 Caramelos El Indio....... 75
1948-1949 Toleteros....... 382
1948-49 M.P. & Co. Photoprints....... 235
1948-50 Safe-T-Card....... 315
1948-52 Cleveland Indians Pencil Clips....... 86
1949 All Stars Photo Pack....... 16
1949 Baas Cheri-Cola....... 27
1949 Boston Red Sox Photo Pack....... 47
1949 Bowman....... 51
1949 Bowman Pacific Coast League....... 1726
1949 Brooklyn Dodgers Picture Pack....... 61
1949 Cleveland Indians Display Photos....... 87
1949 Cleveland Indians Picture Pack - Portraits....... 87
1949 Cleveland Indians Picture Pack - Action....... 87
1949 Cleveland Indians Sun Picture Camera....... 87
1949 Eureka Sportstamps....... 127
1949 Hage's Dairy....... 1733
1949 Hollywood Stars Team Issue....... 1735
1949 Jimmy Fund Boston Braves Die-Cuts....... 192
1949 Leaf....... 211
1949 Leaf Premiums....... 212
1949 Los Angeles Angels Team Issue....... 1739
1949 Lummis Peanut Butter Phillies....... 215
1949 M.P. & Co. (R302-2)....... 235
1949 N.Y. Giants Photo Pack....... 243
1949 Omaha Cardinals Player Picture Book....... 1749
1949 Philadelphia Bulletin A's/Phillies....... 277
1949 Remar Bread Oakland Oaks....... 1753
1949 Schumacher Service Station....... 322
1949 Sealtest Phillies Stickers....... 323
1949 Sommer & Kaufmann San Francisco Seals....... 1759
1949 Spalding Joe DiMaggio Glove Premium Photos....... 328
1949 Sunbeam Bread Stockton Ports....... 1760
1949 Sunbeam/Pureta Sacramento Solons....... 1760
1949 Vis-Ed Cleveland Indian Magic Dials....... 500
1949 Vis-Ed Cleveland Indian Slide-cards....... 500
1949-1950 Acebo y Cia....... 11
1949-1950 Ansco Almendares Scorpions....... 23
1949-1950 Num Num Cleveland Indians....... 248
1949-1950 Toleteros....... 383
1950 All-Star Baseball "Pin-Ups"....... 16
1950 American Nut & Chocolate Pennants (F150)....... 22
1950 Baseball Player Charms....... 32
1950 Big League Stars (V362)....... 1724
1950 Boston Red Sox Photo Pack....... 48
1950 Bowman....... 51
1950 Buitoni Macaroni Joe DiMaggio Pins....... 63
1950 Bush & Hancock/Oak Hall Roanoke Red Sox....... 1726
1950 Callahan Hall of Fame....... 72
1950 Cleveland Indians Picture Pack....... 88
1950 Dominican Republic....... 121
1950 Drake's....... 124
1950 Hage's Dairy....... 1733
1950 Hollywood Stars Team Issue....... 1736
1950 Indianapolis Indians Team Issue....... 1737
1950 Joe DiMaggio Oriental Tour Postcard....... 118
1950 Oak Hall Roanoke Red Sox....... 1743
1950 Philadelphia Bulletin Pin-Ups....... 277
1950 Philadelphia Inquirer Fightin' Phillies....... 278
1950 Pittsburgh Pirates Photo Pack....... 283
1950 Prest-O-lite....... 296
1950 R423....... 315
1950 Remar Bread Oakland Oaks....... 1753
1950 Royal Desserts....... 311
1950 San Francisco Seals Popcorn....... 1754
1950 Sport Stars Luckee Key Charms....... 345
1950 Sunbeam Bread Stockton Ports....... 1760
1950-1951 Toleteros....... 383
1950-1951 Toleteros In Action....... 384
1950-1952 Bill McGowan's School for Umpires....... 224
1950-51 Denia Puerto Rican League - Action....... 108
1950-51 Denia Puerto Rican League....... 107
1950-60s Pittsburgh Pirates Postcards....... 282
1950s Bill Zuber's Restaurant....... 528
1950s Dairy Council Curt Simmons Postcard....... 102
1950s J.J.K. Copyart Postcards....... 192
1950s Jackie Robinson WNBC Photocard....... 308
1950s Kabaya Caramel Babe Ruth....... 195
1950s Publix Markets....... 298
1950s-60s PM10 Baseball Player Pins - Name at Bottom....... 288
1950s-60s PM10 Baseball Player Pins - Name at Top....... 289
1950s-60s Topps "PROMOTIONAL SAMPLES"....... 401
1950s-70s L.L. Cook Milwaukee Braves/Brewers Postcards....... 96
1950s-70s MacGregor Advisory Staff Photos....... 215
1950s-70s Mel Bailey Player Postcards....... 27
1950s-70s Rawlings Advisory Staff Photos....... 301
1950s-70s Spalding Advisory Staff Photos....... 328
1950s-70s Van Heusen Advisory Staff Photos....... 483
1950s-70s Wilson Advisory Staff Photos....... 511
1950s-80s J.D. McCarthy Player Postcards....... 223
1951 Berk Ross....... 40
1951 Bowman....... 52
1951 Cleveland Indians Picture Pack....... 88
1951 Connie Mack Book....... 217
1951 Fischer's Bread Labels....... 146
1951 Fresno Cardinals Team Issue....... 1731
1951 Hage's Dairy....... 1734
1951 Hage's Ice Cream Cleveland Indians....... 170
1951 Joe DiMaggio Baseball Shoes....... 119
1951 Olmes Studio Postcards....... 268
1951 PM10 Baseball Player Pins....... 288
1951 Roadmaster Photos....... 308
1951 San Jose Red Sox Team Issue....... 1754
1951 Sioux City Soos Postcards....... 1758
1951 Sylvania Leo Durocher Postcard....... 359
1951 Topps Blue Backs....... 386
1951 Topps Connie Mack's All-Stars....... 386
1951 Topps Major League All-Stars....... 386
1951 Topps Red Backs....... 386
1951 Topps Teams....... 387
1951 Vancouver Capilanos Popcorn Issue....... 1762
1951 WBKB "Lucky Fan" Chicago Cubs....... 502
1951 Wheaties....... 507
1951 Wheaties Premium Photos....... 507
1951-1954 Globe Printing....... 1732
1951-52 Hit Parade of Champions....... 177
1951-53 Wisconsin's Athletic Hall of Fame Postcards....... 512
1952 Atlanta Crackers Souvenir Pictures Album....... 1723
1952 Baltimore Orioles Team Issue....... 1724
1952 Baseball Player Doubleheader Charms....... 33
1952 Berk Ross....... 41
1952 Bowman....... 53
1952 Bowman Proofs....... 54
1952 Brooklyn Dodgers Schedule Cards....... 61
1952 Central National Bank of Cleveland....... 76
1952 Cleveland Indians Picture Pack....... 88
1952 Coca-Cola Playing Tips....... 90
1952 Coca-Cola Playing Tips Test Cards....... 89
1952 Colorado Springs Sky Sox Team Issue....... 1728
1952 Columbus Cardinals Team Issue....... 1728
1952 Dallas Eagles Team Issue....... 1730
1952 Dixie Lids....... 120
1952 Dixie Lids Premiums....... 120
1952 Frostade....... 1731
1952 Great Falls Electrics Team Issue....... 1733
1952 Hawthorn-Mellody Chicago White Sox Pins....... 174
1952 Jamestown Falcons Team Issue....... 1737
1952 Knowles Service Stations Stockton Ports....... 1738
1952 La Patrie Album Sportif....... 1738
1952 Laval Dairy Provincial League....... 1739
1952 May Co. Chuck Stevens Premium....... 1740
1952 Miami Beach Flamingos Team Issue....... 1740
1952 Mother's Cookies....... 1741
1952 National Tea Labels....... 241
1952 Num Num Cleveland Indians....... 248
1952 Ogden Reds Team Issue....... 1746
1952 Oshkosh Giants Team Issue....... 1750
1952 Parkhurst....... 1751
1952 Philadelphia A's/Phillies Player Pins....... 276
1952 Rawlings Stan Musial Premium Photo....... 302
1952 Red Man Tobacco....... 304
1952 Royal Desserts....... 312
1952 San Diego Padres Team Issue....... 1754
1952 Shawnee Hawks Team Issue....... 1757
1952 Shelby Bicycles....... 325
1952 St. Louis Browns Postcards....... 353
1952 Star-Cal Decals Type 1....... 351
1952 Star-Cal Decals Type 2....... 352
1952 Syracuse Chiefs Team Issue....... 1760
1952 Tip Top Bread Labels....... 381
1952 Topps "Canadian"....... 388
1952 Topps....... 387
1952 Vancouver Capilanos Popcorn Issue....... 1762
1952 Ventura Braves Team Issue....... 1762
1952 Victoria....... 498
1952 Wheaties....... 507
1952 Wheaties Tin Trays....... 508
1952-1953 Burger Beer Cincinnati Reds....... 63
1952-1953 Sioux City Soos Team Issue....... 1758
1952-1954 Red Man Posters....... 306
1953 Boston Red Sox Photo Pack....... 48
1953 Bowman....... 54
1953 Bowman Black & White....... 55
1953 Bowman Color Proofs....... 55
1953 Canadian Exhibits....... 136
1953 Coca-Cola Galveston White Caps....... 1728
1953 Coca-Cola Signs....... 90
1953 Dixie Lids....... 120
1953 Dixie Lids Premiums....... 121
1953 Fargo-Moorhead Twins Team Issue....... 1731
1953 First National Super Market Boston Red Sox....... 146
1953 Glendale Hot Dogs Tigers....... 157
1953 H-O Instant Oatmeal Records....... 170

1953 Hunter Wieners Cardinals....... 186
1953 Johnston Cookies Braves....... 193
1953 Montreal Royals Exhibits....... 1730
1953 Mother's Cookies....... 1741
1953 Northland Bread Labels....... 246
1953 Pictsweet Milwaukee Braves....... 280
1953 R.G. Dun Cigars Milwaukee Braves....... 307
1953 Red Man Tobacco....... 305
1953 San Francisco Seals Team Issue....... 1754
1953 Sport Magazine All-Star Portfolio....... 340
1953 St. Louis Browns Postcards....... 354
1953 Stahl-Meyer Franks....... 350
1953 Stop & Shop Boston Red Sox....... 354
1953 Top Taste Bread Milwaukee Braves....... 470
1953 Topps....... 388
1953 Vancouver Capilanos Popcorn Issue....... 1762
1953-1955 Howard Photo Service Postcards....... 184
1953-54 Briggs Meats....... 58
1953-54 Marshall Merrell Milwaukee Braves Portfolio....... 227
1953-55 Artvue Hall of Fame Plaque Postcards - Type 1... 25
1953-55 Brown & Bigelow....... 62
1953-55 Dormand Postcards....... 123
1953-55 Spic and Span Braves....... 329
1953-57 Spic and Span Braves 7x10 Photos....... 329
1954 ABC Freight Postcard....... 11
1954 Alaga Syrup Willie Mays Postcard....... 13
1954 All-Star Photo Pack....... 16
1954 Baltimore Orioles Picture Pack....... 28
1954 Bill Jacobellis N.Y. Giants....... 190
1954 Blossom Dairy Charleston Senators....... 1725
1954 Boston Red Sox Photo Pack....... 48
1954 Bowman....... 55
1954 Cleveland Indians Picture Pack....... 88
1954 Colonial Meats Jimmy Piersall....... 96
1954 Dan-Dee Potato Chips....... 102
1954 Dixie Lids....... 121
1954 Esskay Hot Dogs Orioles....... 127
1954 Fruiterie Saint Louis Tommy Lasorda....... 1731
1954 Hunter Wieners Cardinals....... 186
1954 Johnston Cookies Braves....... 193
1954 MD Super Service Sacramento Solons....... 1740
1954 N.Y. Journal-American....... 243
1954 Philadelphia A's Stickers....... 276
1954 Philadelphia Inquirer Album of Baseball Stars....... 279
1954 Plankinton Milwaukee Braves Playing Tips....... 285
1954 Preferred Products Milwaukee Braves....... 296
1954 Preferred Products Milwaukee Braves Patches....... 296
1954 Quaker Sports Oddities....... 300
1954 Rawlings Stan Musial....... 302
1954 Red Heart Dog Food....... 304
1954 Red Man Tobacco....... 305
1954 Seattle Rainiers Popcorn....... 1755
1954 Sioux City Soos Souvenir Pictures Album....... 1758
1954 Spic and Span Braves....... 329
1954 Sports Illustrated Topps Foldouts....... 343
1954 Stahl-Meyer Franks....... 350
1954 Topps "Canadian"....... 390
1954 Topps....... 389
1954 Topps Look 'N See....... 390
1954 Topps Scoops....... 390
1954 Vancouver Capilanos Popcorn Issue....... 1762
1954 Veltex Lewiston Broncs....... 1762
1954 Wilson Franks....... 510
1954-1955 Cincinnati Reds Postcards....... 84
1954-1968 Seattle Rainiers/Angels Popcorn....... 1755
1954-56 Spic and Span Braves....... 329
1955 Armour Coins....... 24
1955 Bowman....... 56
1955 Brooklyn Dodgers Picture Pack....... 61
1955 Burger Beer Cincinnati Reds....... 63
1955 Cain's Jimmy Piersall....... 72
1955 Carling Beer Cleveland Indians....... 75
1955 Cleveland Indians Postcards....... 88
1955 Coffee-Time Syrup Jimmy Piersall....... 92
1955 Columbus Jets Photos....... 1728
1955 Esskay Hot Dogs Orioles....... 127
1955 Exhibits - Post Card Backs....... 136
1955 Felin's Franks....... 144
1955 Golden Stamp Books....... 159
1955 Hunter Wieners Cardinals....... 186
1955 Johnston Cookies Braves....... 194
1955 Kahn's Wieners Reds....... 195
1955 Kansas City Athletics Photo Pack....... 199
1955 Mascot Dog Food....... 222
1955 Motorola Bob Feller Premium Photo....... 235
1955 Old Homestead Franks Des Moines Bruins....... 1746
1955 Rawlings Stan Musial....... 302
1955 Red Man Tobacco....... 306
1955 Robert Gould All Stars Cards....... 166
1955 Robert Gould All Stars Statues....... 166
1955 Rodeo Meats Athletics....... 309
1955 Seattle Rainiers Popcorn....... 1755
1955 Spic and Span Braves Die-cuts....... 329
1955 Sports Illustrated Topps Foldouts....... 344
1955 Stahl-Meyer Franks....... 350
1955 Topps....... 391
1955 Topps Doubleheaders....... 391
1955 Topps Hocus Focus....... 392
1955 Topps Stamps....... 392
1955-1957 N.Y. Yankees Picture Pack....... 245
1955-1957 Ted Kluszewski Steak House....... 205
1955-1958 Don Wingfield Washington Nationals Postcards....... 512
1955-60 Bill and Bob Braves Postcards....... 41
1956 Big League Stars Statues....... 41
1956 Bowman Prototypes....... 57
1956 Brooklyn Dodgers Picture Pack....... 61
1956 Carling Beer Cleveland Indians....... 75
1956 Cincinnati Reds Postcards....... 84
1956 Cleveland Indians Picture Pack....... 88
1956 Dairy Queen Stars Statues....... 102
1956 Gentry Magazine Ty Cobb....... 156
1956 Gum Products Adventure....... 169
1956 Kahn's Wieners Reds....... 195
1956 Mutual Savings Dick Stuart....... 1742
1956 N.Y. Yankees "Action Pictures"....... 245
1956 N.Y. Yankees Picture Pack....... 245
1956 Omaha Cardinals Picture-Pak....... 1749
1956 PM15 Yellow Basepath Pins....... 290
1956 Portland Beaver All-Star Pins....... 1752
1956 Prize Frankies Cleveland Indians....... 297
1956 Rodeo Meats Athletics....... 309
1956 Seattle Rainiers Popcorn....... 1755
1956 Topps....... 392
1956 Topps Hocus Focus....... 393
1956 Topps Pins....... 393
1956-1957 Burger Beer Cincinnati Reds....... 63
1956-1957 Chicle Peloteros....... 82
1956-57 Gil's Drive-Ins Seattle Rainiers....... 1732
1956-61 Kansas City Athletics Photocards....... 199
1956-63 Artvue Hall of Fame Plaque Postcards - Type....... 225
1957 Boston Red Sox Photo Pack....... 48
1957 Brooklyn Dodgers Picture Pack....... 62
1957 Carling Beer Cleveland Indians....... 75
1957 Cincinnati Reds Picture Pack....... 84
1957 Cincinnati Reds Postcards....... 84
1957 Columbus Jets Postcards....... 1728
1957 Fine Arts Studio....... 145
1957 Golden State Dairy S.F. Seals Stickers....... 1732
1957 Hollywood Stars Team Issue....... 1736
1957 Hygrade Meats Seattle Rainiers....... 1736
1957 Kahn's Wieners....... 195
1957 Milwaukee Braves Picture Pack....... 232
1957 N.Y. Yankees Picture Pack....... 245
1957 Omaha Cardinals Picture-Pak....... 1749
1957 Seattle Rainiers Popcorn....... 1755
1957 Sohio Gas Indians/Reds....... 327
1957 Spic and Span Braves....... 329
1957 Swift Meats....... 359
1957 Topps....... 394
1957-1959 Don Wingfield Photocards....... 512
1957-1959 Hudepohl Beer Cincinnati Reds....... 186
1957-1959 Kiwanis Orioles Clinic....... 205
1957-1962 Charcoal Steak House Ted Kluszewski....... 77
1957-58 Chattanooga Lookouts Team Issue....... 1727
1957-58 Graphics Arts Service Detroit Tigers Postcards....... 167
1957-60 Preferred Products Milwaukee Braves....... 296
1958 Armour S.F. Giants Tabs....... 24
1958 Baltimore Orioles team issue....... 28
1958 Bazooka "My Favorite Team" Patches....... 35
1958 Bell Brand Dodgers....... 40
1958 Bell Brand Dodgers Ad Poster....... 40
1958 Bond Bread Buffalo Bisons....... 1725
1958 Boston Red Sox Photo Pack....... 48
1958 Carling Beer Cleveland Indians....... 75
1958 Cincinnati Reds Postcards....... 85
1958 Columbus Jets Photos....... 1728
1958 Dominican Republic....... 122
1958 Hires Root Beer....... 176
1958 Hires Root Beer Test Set....... 176
1958 Kahn's Wieners....... 195
1958 Omaha Cardinals Picture-Pak....... 1749
1958 Packard-Bell....... 271
1958 Philadelphia Phillies Picture Pack....... 279
1958 Ralph's Thriftway Seattle Rainiers....... 1752
1958 Richmond Virginians Team Issue....... 1753
1958 Roy Campanella Career Summary Card....... 73
1958 San Francisco Call-Bulletin Giants....... 319
1958 Seattle Rainiers Popcorn....... 1755
1958 Topps....... 395
1958 Union 76 Sports Club Booklets....... 480
1958 Union Oil Sacramento Solons....... 1761
1958-1959 Burger Beer Cincinnati Reds....... 63
1958-1959 Shillito's Boys' Shop Cincinnati Reds....... 325
1958-1965 Jay Publishing Picture Packs....... 190
1958-60 L.A. Dodgers Premium Pictures....... 207
1958-60 Philadelphia Phillies Team Issue....... 279
1959 APCO Meat Packing Co. San Antonio Missions....... 1723
1959 Armour Bacon K.C. Athletics....... 24
1959 Armour Coins....... 24
1959 Bazooka....... 35
1959 Bazooka Pennants....... 36
1959 Boston Red Sox Photo Pack....... 48
1959 Carling Beer Cleveland Indians....... 76
1959 Dad's Cookies Exhibits....... 101
1959 Darigold Farms Spokane Indians....... 1730
1959 Dominican Republic....... 122
1959 Exhibits - Dad's Cookies....... 136
1959 First Federal Savings Famous Senators Matchbooks... 145
1959 Fleer Ted Williams....... 146
"1959-60" Gulf Oil Corporation....... 168
1959 Home Run Derby....... 178
1959 Hostess Bob Turley....... 178
1959 Kahn's Wieners....... 196
1959 L.A. Dodgers Postcards....... 207
1959 Mickey Mantle's Holiday Inn Postcard....... 221
1959 Morrell Meats Dodgers....... 234
1959 Neptune Sardines Jimmy Piersall....... 242
1959 O'Keefe Ale Montreal Royals....... 1746
1959 Oklahoma Today Major Leaguers....... 256
1959 R.H. Hayes Postcards....... 175
1959 Richmond Virginians....... 1753
1959 Seattle Rainiers Popcorn....... 1755
1959 Ticoa Tires Frank Malzone....... 380
1959 Topps....... 397
1959 Venezuelan Topps....... 483
1959 Yoo-Hoo....... 526
1959 Yoo-Hoo Bottle Caps....... 527
1959 Yoo-Hoo Mickey Mantle....... 526
1960 Armour Coins....... 24
1960 Armour Meats Denver Bears....... 1723
1960 Bazooka....... 36
1960 Bazooka Hot Iron Transfers....... 36
1960 Bell Brand Dodgers....... 40
1960 Boston Red Sox Photo Pack....... 48
1960 Darigold Farms Spokane Indians....... 1730
1960 Diamond Associates Postcards....... 112
1960 Fleer Baseball Greats....... 147
1960 Henry House Wieners Seattle Rainiers....... 1734
1960 Hudepohl Beer Cincinnati Reds....... 186
1960 Kahn's Wieners....... 196
1960 L.A. Dodgers Postcards....... 207
1960 Lake To Lake Dairy Braves....... 208
1960 Leaf....... 212
1960 Leaf Pre-production....... 212
1960 MacGregor....... 216
1960 Morrell Meats Dodgers....... 234
1960 N.Y. Yankees "Action Pictures"....... 245
1960 National Bank of Washington Tacoma Giants....... 1742
1960 Nu-Card Baseball Hi-Lites....... 247
1960 O-Pee-Chee Tattoos....... 248
1960 Post Cereal....... 291
1960 Richmond Virginians....... 1753
1960 Seattle Rainiers Popcorn....... 1756
1960 Shopsy's Frankfurters Toronto Maple Leafs....... 1757
1960 Spic and Span Braves....... 330
1960 Sports Novelties Inc. Genuine Baseball Photos....... 344
1960 Topps....... 399
1960 Topps Proofs....... 400
1960 Topps Tattoos....... 401
1960 Tulsa Oilers Team Issue....... 1760
1960 Union Oil Dodger Family Booklets....... 480
1960 Union Oil Seattle Rainiers....... 1761
1960 Venezuelan Topps....... 484
1960-61 Fritos Ticket Folders....... 154
1960-62 Fleer Team Logo Decals....... 147
1960-64 Burger Beer Cincinnati Reds....... 63
1960-64 Chicago White Sox Ticket Stubs....... 81
1960-70s MacGregor Pete Rose....... 216
1960-70s Stan Musial & Biggie's Restaurant....... 351
1960s Don Wingfield Postcards - B/W....... 512
1960s Don Wingfield Postcards - Color....... 512
1960s Nellie Fox Bowl Postcard....... 153
1960s Rogers Printing Co. Postcards....... 309
1960s Sports Pix Premiums....... 344
1960s Sunny Ayr Farms Johnny Callison....... 355
1960s-70s J.D. McCarthy Postcards....... 1740
1961 7-11....... 324
1961 Baseball Player Key Chains....... 33
1961 Bazooka....... 36
1961 Bee Hive Starch Toronto Maple Leafs....... 1724
1961 Bell Brand Dodgers....... 40
1961 Carling Beer Cleveland Indians....... 76
1961 Chemstrand Iron-On Patches....... 77
1961 Cloverleaf Dairy Minnesota Twins....... 89
1961 Exhibits - Wrigley Field....... 136
1961 F & M Bank Minnesota Twins Matchbook Covers... 141
1961 Fleer Baseball Greats....... 147
1961 Fleer World Champions Pennant Decals....... 148
1961 Ford Pittsburgh Pirates Prints....... 152
1961 Franklin Milk....... 153
1961 Golden Press....... 159
1961 Harmony Milk Pittsburgh Pirates....... 174
1961 J.B. Williams Co. Roger Maris Lithograph....... 510
1961 Jeffrey W. Morey Postcards....... 1741
1961 Kahn's Wieners....... 196
1961 Manny's Baseball Land 8x10s....... 220
1961 Morrell Meats Dodgers....... 234
1961 National Bank of Washington Tacoma Giants....... 1742
1961 Nu-Card Baseball Scoops....... 247
1961 Peters Meats Twins....... 275
1961 Phillies Cigar Mickey Mantle....... 280
1961 Post Cereal....... 292
1961 Post Cereal Company Sheets....... 293

1961 Post Cereal Display Pinwheel 293
1961 Sam's Family Restaurants Roger Maris 318
1961 Seattle Rainiers Popcorn 1756
1961 Topps 401
1961 Topps Dice Game 403
1961 Topps Magic Rub-Offs 403
1961 Topps Stamps 404
1961 Topps Stamps Panels 404
1961 Union Oil Dodger Family Booklets 481
1961 Union Oil Hawaii Islanders 1761
1961 Union Oil Pacific Coast League 1761
1961 Union Oil Portland Beavers 1761
1961 Union Oil San Diego Padres 1761
1961 Union Oil Seattle Rainiers 1761
1961 Union Oil Spokane Indians 1761
1961 Union Oil Tacoma Giants 1761
1961 Union Oil Taiyo Whales 1761
1961 Wilson Advisory Staff Cards 512
1961 Wilson Meats L.A.Dodgers/Angels 511
1961-1963 Bobbin' Head Dolls 43
1961-62 Apple Fresh Milk Minnesota Twins 23
1962 American Tract Society 22
1962 Auravision Records 26
1962 Bazooka 36
1962 Bell Brand Dodgers 40
1962 Bell Brand Dodgers Ad Poster 40
1962 Cloverleaf Dairy Minnesota Twins 89
1962 Dickson Orde & Co. 117
1962 F & M Bank Minnesota Twins Matchbook Covers 141
1962 Ford Detroit Tigers Postcards 152
1962 Gehl's Ice Cream 155
1962 Houston Colt .45s Booklets 184
1962 Jell-O 190
1962 John Sain Spinner Promotional Postcard 316
1962 Kahn's Wieners 196
1962 Kahn's Wieners Atlanta Crackers 1738
1962 L.A. Dodgers Pins 207
1962 Mickey Mantle's Holiday Inn Postcard 221
1962 Mickey Mantle's Holiday Inn Premium Photo 221
1962 Molinari's Restaurant Frank Malzone 233
1962 Omaha Dodgers 1750
1962 Pepsi-Cola Tulsa Oilers 1751
1962 Pittsburgh Exhibits 137
1962 Post Cereal - Canadian 294
1962 Post Cereal 293
1962 Roger Maris Action Baseball Game 222
1962 Salada-Junket Coins - Clip Back 318
1962 Salada-Junket Coins 317
1962 Seattle Rainiers Popcorn 1756
1962 Shirriff Coins 326
1962 Statistic Back Exhibits 137
1962 Sugardale Weiners 355
1962 Supertest Toronto Maple Leafs 1760
1962 Topps 405
1962 Topps Baseball Bucks 407
1962 Topps Stamps 407
1962 Topps Stamps Panels 408
1962 Union Oil Dodgers Premium Pictures 481
1962 Venezuelan Topps 485
1963 Bazooka 37
1963 Bazooka All-Time Greats 37
1963 Cincinnati Enquirer Reds' Scrapbook 82
1963 Fleer 148
1963 French Bauer Reds Milk Caps 153
1963 George Brace All Time Chicago Cubs 58
1963 Hall of Fame Picture Pack 172
1963 I.D.L. Drug Store Pittsburgh Pirates 187
1963 Jell-O 191
1963 Kahn's Wieners 197
1963 L.A. Dodgers Pin-Ups 207
1963 Mickey Mantle Hospital Postcard 221
1963 Mickey Sego S.F. Giants 323
1963 Milwaukee Sausage Seattle Rainiers 1740
1963 Nassau County Boy Scouts 239
1963 Otto Milk 270
1963 Pepsi-Cola Colt .45's 274
1963 Pepsi-Cola Tulsa Oilers 1751
1963 Post Cereal 295
1963 Post/Jell-O Album 295
1963 Rawlings Stan Musial Premium 302
1963 Salada-Junket Coins 318
1963 Scheible Press Rochester Red Wings 1754
1963 Seattle Rainiers Popcorn 1756
1963 Sports "Hall of Fame" Busts 343
1963 Statistic Back Exhibits 137
1963 Sugardale Weiners 355
1963 Topps 409
1963 Topps Famous Americans Stamps 411
1963 Topps Mickey Mantle Plaque 411
1963 Topps Peel-Offs 411
1963 Topps Valentine Foldees 411
1963 Western Oil Minnesota Twins 504
1963-1973 Equitable Sports Hall of Fame 127
1964 Auravision Records 27
1964 Baseball Greats Postcard 30
1964 Baseball Stars - Present and Future Photocard 34
1964 Bazooka 37
1964 Bazooka Stamps 37
1964 Challenge the Yankees Game 77
1964 Detroit Tigers Milk Bottle Caps 110
1964 Falstaff Beer 141
1964 Freihofer's Philadelphia Phillies 153
1964 Kahn's Wieners 197
1964 KDKA Pittsburgh Pirates Portraits 200
1964 Meadowgold Dairy 225
1964 Pepsi-Cola Tulsa Oiler Autograph Cards 1751
1964 Philadelphia Bulletin Phillies Album (Paper) 277
1964 Philadelphia Bulletin Phillies Album 277
1964 Philadelphia Phillies Player Pins 279
1964 Photo Linen Emblems 280
1964 Rawlings Glove Box 302
1964 Sandy Koufax's Tropicana Postcard 206
1964 Seattle Rainiers Popcorn 1756
1964 Topps 412
1964 Topps Coins 414
1964 Topps Giants 414
1964 Topps Photo Tatoos 415
1964 Topps Rookie All-Star Banquet 415
1964 Topps Stand-Ups 415
1964 Transfer-ette Chicago Cubs Iron-ons 471
1964 Transfer-ette Chicago White Sox Iron-ons 471
1964 True Ade / WGR Buffalo Bisons 1760
1964 Union Oil Dodgers Premium Pictures 481
1964 Venezuelan Topps 485
1964 Western Oil Minnesota Twins 504
1964 Wheaties Stamps 508
1964 Yoo-Hoo Counter Sign 527
1964+ Curteichcolor Hall of Fame Plaque Postcards 101
1964-66 Rawlings Premium Photos 302
1964-66 Requena N.Y. Yankees 8x10s 307
1964-67 Sport Hobbyist Famous Card Series 330
1964-68 Requena N.Y. Yankees Postcards 307
1964-Date Hall of Fame Yellow Plaque Postcards - Auto. 173
1964-Date Hall of Fame Yellow Plaque Postcards 172
1965 Bazooka 38
1965 California Angels Matchbook Covers 72
1965 Challenge the Yankees Game 77
1965 Dugan Bros. Casey Stengel 124
1965 Go! Phillies Go! Pins 279
1965 Kahn's Wieners 197
1965 L.A. Dodgers Motion Pins 208
1965 MacGregor 216
1965 Milwaukee Braves Picture Pack 232
1965 Old London Coins 268
1965 O-Pee-Chee 248
1965 Philadelphia Phillies Tiles 279
1965 Rawlings MVP Premiums 303
1965 Seattle Angels Popcorn 1756
1965 Topps 416
1965 Topps Embossed 418
1965 Topps Push-Pull 418
1965 Topps Transfers 418
1965 Trade Bloc Minnesota Twins 471
1966 Bazooka 38
1966 Dexter Press California Angels 110
1966 Dexter Press California Angels 8x10 111
1966 Dexter Press California Angels Booklet 111
1966 Dominican Republic 122
1966 East Hills Pirates 126
1966 Fairway Minnesota Twins 141
1966 Fleer All Star Match Baseball 148
1966 Foremost Milk St. Petersburg Cardinals 1731
1966 Gaylord Perry Insurance 275
1966 H.F. Gardner Postcards 155
1966 Kahn's Wieners 197
1966 O-Pee-Chee 249
1966 Pepsi-Cola Tulsa Oilers 1752
1966 Pro's Pizza Chicago Cubs 298
1966 Pure Oil Atlanta Braves 300
1966 Royal Crown Cola Columbus Yankees 1754
1966 Seattle Angels Popcorn 1756
1966 St. Louis Cardinals Busch Stadium Immortals Coins 354
1966 Swap-N-Save Album 357
1966 Toledo Mud Hens Team Issue 1760
1966 Topps 419
1966 Topps Comic Book Foldees 421
1966 Topps Punch-Outs 421
1966 Topps Rub-Offs 421
1966 Venezuelan Topps 487
1966 Volpe Tumblers 500
1966-67 Dexter Press N.Y. Yankees 111
1967 Ashland Oil Grand Slam Baseball 25
1967 Bazooka 38
1967 Chevron/Uniroyal Vancouver Mounties 1727
1967 Dexter Press Premiums 111
1967 Dexter Press Team Posters 112
1967 Houston Astros Team Issue 184
1967 Irvindale Dairy Atlana Braves 188
1967 Jones Dairy Buffalo Bison All-Stars 1737
1967 Kahn's Wieners 197
1967 Laughlin World Series 208
1967 O-Pee-Chee 249
1967 Philadelphia Phillies Safe Driving 280
1967 Pittsburgh Pirates Autograph Cards 283
1967 Pro's Pizza - B & W 298
1967 Pro's Pizza - Color 298
1967 Seattle Angels Popcorn 1757
1967 Topps 421
1967 Topps Discs 424
1967 Topps Pin-Ups 424
1967 Topps Pirates Stickers 425
1967 Topps Punch-Outs 424
1967 Topps Red Sox Stickers 425
1967 Topps S.F. Giants Discs 424
1967 Topps Stand-Ups 425
1967 Topps Who Am I? 425
1967 Van Heusen Phillies 483
1967 Venezuelan League 488
1967 Venezuelan Retirado 489
1967 Venezuelan Topps 489
1967-68 Coca-Cola Bottle Caps 90
1968 Aamco Roger Maris Postcard 11
1968 American Oil Sweepstakes 22
1968 Atlantic Oil Play Ball Game Cards 26
1968 Bazooka 38
1968 Boston Red Sox Team Issue 49
1968 Detroit Free Press Bubblegumless Tiger Cards 110
1968 Dexter Press Postcards 112
1968 Jamesway Trucking Co. 190
1968 Kahn's Wieners 198
1968 KDKA Pittsburgh Pirates 200
1968 Metropolitan Museum of Art Burdick Collection 227
1968 Official Major League Players Baseball Marbles 255
1968 O-Pee-Chee 249
1968 O-Pee-Chee Posters 249
1968 Pittsburgh Pirates Autograph Cards 283
1968 Red Barn Memphis Blues 1752
1968 Seattle Angels Popcorn 1757
1968 Sports Memorabilia All Time Baseball Team 344
1968 Tipps From Topps Book 429
1968 Topps "Batter Up" Game 428
1968 Topps 3-D 429
1968 Topps 3-D Prototype 429
1968 Topps 425
1968 Topps Action All-Star Stickers 428
1968 Topps Deckle Edge Proofs 428
1968 Topps Discs 428
1968 Topps Game 428
1968 Topps Plaks 429
1968 Topps Posters 429
1968 Topps/Milton Bradley 429
1968 Uniroyal Keds Cincinnati Reds 481
1968 Venezuelan Topps 489
1968-69 Sports Cards for Collectors 340
1968-70 Fleer Major League Baseball Patches 149
1968-70 Partridge Meats Reds 272
1968-70 Sports Illustrated Posters 344
1969 Atlantic-Richfield Boston Red Sox 26
1969 Boston Red Sox Team Issue 49
1969 Citgo Coins 85
1969 Citgo New York Mets 85
1969 Crown Brooks Robinson 100
1969 Dunkin' Donuts Chicago Cubs Bumper Stickers 125
1969 Fleer Cap Plaques 149
1969 Fud's Photography Montreal Expos 155
1969 Globe Imports Playing Cards 158
1969 Greiner Tires Pittsburgh Pirates 168
1969 Jack In The Box California Angels 189
1969 Jewel Food Chicago Cubs 191
1969 Kahn's Wieners 198
1969 Kelly's Potato Chips Pins 205
1969 Lincoln-Mercury Sports Panel Postcards 213
1969 Major League Baseball Photostamps 217
1969 Major League Baseball Player Pins 218
1969 Major League Baseball Players Association Pins 218
1969 Milton Bradley 229
1969 N.Y. Boy Scouts 242
1969 N.Y. News Mets Portfolio of Stars 244
1969 Nabisco Team Flakes 237
1969 Oakland A's (Andersen) 255
1969 Oakland A's (Broder) 255
1969 O-Pee-Chee 249
1969 O-Pee-Chee Deckle 249
1969 Pittsburgh Pirates Autograph Cards 283
1969 Rawlings 303
1969 San Diego Padres Premium Pictures 318
1969 Seattle Pilots Premium Pictures 323
1969 Solon Kansas City Royals 327
1969 Spare-Time Products Minnesota Twins Discs 328
1969 Sunoco Cubs/Brewers Pins 355
1969 Tasco All-Star Collection Caricatures 361
1969 Topps 430
1969 Topps 4-On-1 Mini Stickers 434
1969 Topps Bowie Kuhn 435
1969 Topps Decals 432
1969 Topps Deckle Edge 433
1969 Topps Stamps 433
1969 Topps Super 433
1969 Topps Team Posters 434
1969 Transogram 472
1969 Union Oil Dodgers Premium Pictures 481
1969-1972 Dodge Postcards 121
1969-70 Bazooka 39
1970 Action Cartridge 12

1970 Baltimore Orioles Traffic Safety 28
1970 Carl Aldana Orioles 13
1970 Dayton Daily News Bubble-Gumless Cards 103
1970 Doug McWilliams Collectors' Issue Postcards 224
1970 Doug McWilliams Oakland A's Postcards 224
1970 Doug McWilliams Postcards 224
1970 Dunkin' Donuts Chicago Cubs Bumper Stickers 125
1970 Flavor-est Milk Milwaukee Brewers 146
1970 Fleer Team Logo Decals 149
1970 Fleer World Series 149
1970 Jack in the Box Pittsburgh Pirates 190
1970 Kellogg's 201
1970 La Pizza Royale Expos 208
1970 Major League Baseball Photostamps 219
1970 McDonald's Brewers 223
1970 Milton Bradley 230
1970 Montreal Expos Player Pins 233
1970 N.Y. Yankees Clinic Schedule Postcards 245
1970 Oakland A's (Andersen) 255
1970 O-Pee-Chee 249
1970 Ovenca Venezuelan League 491
1970 Pictures of Champions Baltimore Orioles 280
1970 Pittsburgh Pirates (Andersen) 284
1970 Pittsburgh Pirates Autograph Cards 284
1970 Rold Gold Pretzels 309
1970 Sports Cards for Collectors Old Timer Postcards 341
1970 Sports Cards for Collectors Sports Stuff 341
1970 Super Valu Minnesota Twins 357
1970 Superballs 356
1970 Tasco Caricatures 361
1970 Topps 435
1970 Topps Candy Lids 437
1970 Topps Cloth Stickers 437
1970 Topps Posters 437
1970 Topps Scratch-Offs 438
1970 Topps Story Booklets 438
1970 Topps Super 438
1970 Transogram 472
1970 Transogram Mets 472
1970 Washington Senators Traffic Safety 501
1970-73 Minor League Team Sets 1778
1970s Kahn's Kielbasa Singles Carl Yastrzemski 198
1970s MacGregor Advisory Staff Photos 216
1970s-80s Doug McWilliams Postcards 224
1971 Allstate Insurance 16
1971 Arco 23
1971 Bank of Montreal Rusty Staub 28
1971 Bazooka Numbered Set 39
1971 Bazooka Unnumbered Set 39
1971 Carl Aldana 14
1971 Coca-Cola Houston Astros 92
1971 Dell Today's Team Stamps 105
1971 Doug McWilliams Postcards 224
1971 House of Jazz 184
1971 Jack In The Box California Angels 189
1971 Keds Kedcards 200
1971 Kellogg's 201
1971 Mattel Instant Replay Records 222
1971 Milk Duds 229
1971 N.Y. Yankees Clinic Schedule Postcards 246
1971 O-Pee-Chee 250
1971 Pete Rose & Johnny Bench Lincoln-Mercury Postcards 275
1971 Pittsburgh Pirates Autograph Cards 284
1971 Pro Stars Publications Montreal Expos 298
1971 Sport Hobbyist Famous Card Series 330
1971 Ticketron L.A. Dodgers/S.F. Giants 380
1971 Topps 438
1971 Topps All-Star Rookies Artist's Proofs 441
1971 Topps Coins 441
1971 Topps Greatest Moments 441
1971 Topps Scratch-Offs 442
1971 Topps Super 442
1971 Topps Tattoos 442
1971 Washington Senators Traffic Safety 502
1971-1982 San Francisco Giants Autograph Cards 319
1971-80 Fleer World Series 150
1972 Bowery Bank Joe DiMaggio 50
1972 Chicago Cubs & Chicago White Sox Color Caricatures 78
1972 Classic Cards 85
1972 Daily Juice Co. 101
1972 Dimanche/Derniere Heure Expos 119
1972 Don Drysdale's Restaurant Postcards 124
1972 Doug McWilliams Postcards 224
1972 Durochrome Chicago White Sox Decals 125
1972 Esso Hispanic Coins 127
1972 Fleer Famous Feats 150
1972 Kellogg's 202
1972 Kellogg's All-Time Baseball Greats 202
1972 Laughlin Great Feats 209
1972 Milton Bradley 230
1972 N.Y. Yankees Schedule Cards 246
1972 O-Pee-Chee 250
1972 Partridge Meats Reds 273
1972 Pete Rose & Johnny Bench Lincoln-Mercury Postcards 275
1972 Photo Sports Co. L.A. Dodgers 280
1972 Pittsburgh Press "Buc-A-Day" Pirates 284
1972 Pro Star Promotions 298
1972 Puerto Rican League Stickers 298
1972 Regent Glove Hang Tag 307
1972 TCMA The 1930's 362
1972 The Yawkey Red Sox 526
1972 Ticketron Phillies 380
1972 Topps 443
1972 Topps Candy Lid Test Issue 445
1972 Topps Cloth Stickers 446
1972 Topps Posters 446
1972 Venezuelan Baseball Stamps 492
1972 Venezuelan League Stickers 493
1972-76 Montreal Expos Matchbook Covers 233
1972-83 Dimanche/Derniere Heure Photos 119
1973 Dean's Photo Service San Diego Padres 104
1973 Dimanche/Derniere Heure National Leaguers 119
1973 Doug McWilliams Postcards 225
1973 Fleer Team Logo Decals 150
1973 Fleer Team Signs 150
1973 Fleer Wildest Days and Plays 150
1973 Hall of Fame Picture Pack 172
1973 Jack Hamilton's "The Pzazz" Postcard 174
1973 Jewel Food Baseball Photos 192
1973 John B. Anderson Former Greats 22
1973 Johnny Pro Orioles 193
1973 Kellogg's 202
1973 Laughlin Super Stand-Ups 209
1973 N.Y. News Mets/Yankees Caricatures 244
1973 Norm Cash Day Card 76
1973 O-Pee-Chee 250
1973 O-Pee-Chee Team Checklists 250
1973 Pittsburgh Post-Gazette Pirates 284
1973 Roberto Clemente Memorial Postcard 86
1973 TCMA "Bobo" 365
1973 TCMA 1874 Philadelphia Athletics 366
1973 TCMA 1890 Base-ball Season 366
1973 TCMA 1930's No Hit Pitchers and 6 for 6 Hitters 366
1973 TCMA 1941 Brooklyn Dodgers 366
1973 TCMA All Time New York Yankees Team 364
1973 TCMA Autographs & Drawings Postcards 365
1973 TCMA Giants 1886 365
1973 TCMA Pudge Gautreaux 365
1973 TCMA Sports Scoop Hall of Fame 366
1973 TCMA Stan Martucci Postcards 366
1973 Topps 1953 Reprints 450
1973 Topps 446
1973 Topps Candy Lids 449
1973 Topps Comics 449
1973 Topps Pin-Ups 449
1973 Topps Team Checklists 449
1973 U.S. Playing Card Ruth/Gehrig 483
1973 Venezuelan League Stickers 493
1973-1974 TCMA Autograph Series 365
1973-78 TCMA League Leaders 365
1973-80 TCMA All-Time Greats Postcards 364
1974 Baseball's Great Hall of Fame Exhibits 137
1974 Bob Parker 2nd Best 271
1974 Bramac 1933 National League All-Stars 58
1974 Broder N.Y. Mets Tour of Japan 59
1974 Capital Publishing Co. 73
1974 Dean's Photo Service San Diego Padres 104
1974 Dimanche/Derniere Heure Expos 119
1974 Doug McWilliams Postcards 225
1974 Fleer Baseball Firsts 151
1974 Greyhound Heroes on the Base Paths 168
1974 Johnny Pro Phillies 193
1974 Kellogg's 203
1974 Laughlin All-Star Games 209
1974 Laughlin Old-Time Black Stars 210
1974 Laughlin Sportslang 210
1974 McDonald's Gene Michael 223
1974 McDonald's Padres Discs 223
1974 Minor League Team Sets 1778
1974 Nassau Tuberculosis and Respiratory Disease Assn. 239
1974 Oh Henry! Henry Aaron Premium Photo 256
1974 O-Pee-Chee 250
1974 O-Pee-Chee Team Checklists 250
1974 Shillito's Pete Rose 326
1974 Sun-Glo Pop Al Kaline 355
1974 TCMA 1890 Brooklyn Club 367
1974 TCMA 1910-14 Philadelphia Athletics Postcards 367
1974 TCMA 1929-31 Athletics 367
1974 TCMA 1934 St. Louis Cardinals 368
1974 TCMA 1934-5 Detroit Tigers 368
1974 TCMA 1936-1939 Yankee Dynasty 368
1974 TCMA 1936-37 New York Giants 368
1974 TCMA 1952 Brooklyn Dodgers 369
1974 TCMA Nicknames 366
1974 TCMA Sports Nostalgia Store Postcards 366
1974 TCMA Stadium Postcards 367
1974 TCMA The Babe Postcards 367
1974 Topps 450
1974 Topps Action Emblem Cloth Stickers 452
1974 Topps Deckle Edge 453
1974 Topps Puzzles 453
1974 Topps Stamps 453
1974 Topps Team Checklists 454
1974 Topps Traded 452
1974 Venezuelan League Stickers 494
1974 Weston Expos 504
1974-75 TCMA St. Louis Browns 367
1974-80 Bob Bartosz Postcards 29
1975 Broder 1962 "Original" N.Y. Mets 59
1975 Broder All-Time N.Y. Mets 59
1975 Broder Major League Postcards 60
1975 Broder Major Leagues - The 1950's 59
1975 Clarence Mengler Baseball's Best 226
1975 Clark & Sons Baseball Favorites 85
1975 Dean's Photo Service San Diego Padres 104
1975 Doug McWilliams Postcards 225
1975 Fleer Pioneers of Baseball 151
1975 Greyhound Heroes on the Base Paths 168
1975 Hostess 179
1975 Hostess Twinkies 179
1975 Kellogg's 203
1975 Laughlin Batty Baseball 210
1975 Lee's Sweets 213
1975 Linnett MLB All-Stars 213
1975 MacGregor Advisory Staff Poster 216
1975 Michael Schechter Associates Test Discs 321
1975 Mid-Atlantic Sports Collectors Assn. 228
1975 Minor League Team Sets 1778
1975 O-Pee-Chee 250
1975 Philadelphia Phillies Photocards 280
1975 Praeger Publishers Ty Cobb 296
1975 Shakey's Pizza West Coast Greats 324
1975 Sport Hobbyist 330
1975 Sport Hobbyist Team Composites 330
1975 SSPC 345
1975 SSPC Mets/Yankees 347
1975 SSPC Promo Cards 345
1975 SSPC Puzzle Backs 347
1975 SSPC Sample Cards 345
1975 SSPC Superstars 348
1975 TCMA 1913 Philadelphia Athletics 370
1975 TCMA 1919 Chicago White Sox 370
1975 TCMA 1924-1925 Washington Senators 370
1975 TCMA 1927 New York Yankees 370
1975 TCMA 1942-46 St. Louis Cardinals 370
1975 TCMA 1946 Boston Red Sox 371
1975 TCMA 1950 Philadelphia Phillies/Whiz Kids 371
1975 TCMA 1951 New York Giants 371
1975 TCMA 1954 Cleveland Indians 371
1975 TCMA All Time Brooklyn/Los Angeles Dodgers 369
1975 TCMA All Time New York Giants 369
1975 TCMA All Time New York Yankees 369
1975 TCMA All-Time Greats 369
1975 TCMA Guam WW2 369
1975 TCMA Larry French Postcards 369
1975 TCMA/ASCCA Ad Card 371
1975 Topps 454
1975 Topps Mini 456
1975 Topps Team Checklist Sheet 456
1975 WTMJ Milwaukee Brewers Broadcasters 515
1975-76 Great Plains Greats 167
1975-96 MSA 236
1976 A & P Brewers 11
1976 A & P Royals 11
1976 Bob Parker More Baseball Cartoons 272
1976 Buckmans Discs 62
1976 California Pacific Bank 72
1976 Carousel Discs 76
1976 Chevrolet Baseball Centennial Prints 78
1976 Chicagoland Collectors Association Chicago Greats 80
1976 Crane Potato Chips Discs 99
1976 Dairy Isle Discs 102
1976 Dean's Photo Service San Diego Padres 104
1976 Doug McWilliams Postcards 225
1976 Douglas Cool Papa Bell 123
1976 English's Chicken Baltimore Orioles Lids 127
1976 Greyhound Heroes on the Base Paths 168
1976 Hostess 180
1976 Hostess Twinkies 180
1976 Hostess Unissued Proofs 181
1976 HRT/RES 1942 Play Ball 184
1976 Icee Drinks Reds 187
1976 Isaly's/Sweet William discs 189
1976 ISCA Hoosier Hot-Stove All-Stars 189
1976 Jerry Jonas Productions All Time Greats 194
1976 Kellogg's 203
1976 Kroger Cincinnati Reds 206
1976 Laughlin Diamond Jubilee 210
1976 Laughlin Indianapolis Clowns 210
1976 Linnett Portraits 213
1976 Linnett Superstars 214
1976 Michael Schechter Associates Discs 321
1976 Midwest Sports Collectors Convention 228
1976 Minor League Team Sets 1778
1976 Motorola 235
1976 Mr. Softee Iron-Ons 236
1976 O-Pee-Chee 251
1976 Orbaker's Discs 269
1976 Playboy Press Who Was Harry Steinfeldt? 287
1976 Red Barn Discs 303
1976 Redpath Sugar Expos 306

1976 Rodeo Meats Athletics Commemorative 309
1976 Safelon Discs 316
1976 Shakey's Pizza Hall of Fame 325
1976 Shillito's Kahn's Reds Clubhouse 326
1976 Sportstix 345
1976 SSPC 1887 World Series 348
1976 SSPC 1963 New York Mets 348
1976 SSPC Yankees Old Timers Day 348
1976 Star Market Red Sox 352
1976 Sugar Daddy Sports World 354
1976 TCMA 1911 N.Y. Highlanders Postcard 372
1976 TCMA 1938 Chicago Cubs 372
1976 TCMA DiMaggio Brothers Postcard 372
1976 TCMA Larry Rosenthal 372
1976 TCMA Umpires 372
1976 Topps 456
1976 Topps Cloth Sticker Prototypes 459
1976 Topps Joe Garagiola 459
1976 Topps Team Checklist Sheet 459
1976 Topps Traded 459
1976 Topps/Dynamite Magazine Panels 459
1976 Towne Club discs 471
1976 Venezuelan League Stickers 495
1976-77 HRT/RES 1947 Bowman 185
1976-81 New England Sports Collectors 242
1977 Baseball's Great Hall of Fame Exhibits 138
1977 Bob Parker Cincinnati Reds 272
1977 Burger Chef Funmeal Discs 64
1977 Burger King Tigers 64
1977 Burger King Yankees 65
1977 Chilly Willee Discs 82
1977 Dairy Isle Discs 102
1977 Detroit Caesars Discs 109
1977 Dimanche/Derniere Heure Expos 119
1977 Doug McWilliams Postcards 225
1977 Douglas Johnny Mize 124
1977 Family Fun Centers Padres 141
1977 Fritsch One-Year Winners 154
1977 Holiday Inn Discs 177
1977 Hostess 181
1977 Hostess Twinkies 181
1977 Hostess Unissued Proofs 182
1977 HRT/RES Philadelphia 'Favorites' 185
1977 Jewel Food Chicago Cubs/ White Sox 192
1977 Jim Rowe 1929 Cubs Postcards 311
1977 Jim Rowe 1956 Braves Postcards 311
1977 Jim Rowe 4-on-1 Exhibits 310
1977 John B. Anderson Aaron-Mays 22
1977 John B. Anderson New York Teams 22
1977 Kellogg's 203
1977 Kurland Tom Seaver 206
1977 Michael Schechter Associates Cup Lids 321
1977 Mike Schechter Associates Customized Sports Discs .. 322
1977 Minneapolis Star Twins Scrapbook 232
1977 Minor League Team Sets 1778
1977 Mrs. Carter's Bread Sports Illustrated Covers 236
1977 O-Pee-Chee 251
1977 Pepsi-Cola Baseball Stars 274
1977 Pepsi-Cola Cincinnati Reds Playing Cards 274
1977 Redpath Sugar Expos 307
1977 Saga Discs 316
1977 San Diego Padres Schedule Cards 318
1977 San Francisco Giants Team Issue 320
1977 Sertoma Stars - Puzzle Backs 324
1977 Sertoma Stars 324
1977 Shakey's All-Time Superstars 325
1977 Sports Challenge Records 342
1977 TCMA 1920 Cleveland Indians 373
1977 TCMA 1927 Yankees 50th Anniversary 373
1977 TCMA 1939-40 Cincinnati Reds 373
1977 TCMA 1960 Pittsburgh Pirates 373
1977 TCMA All-Time White Sox 372
1977 TCMA Chicago Cubs All Time Team 372
1977 TCMA Stars of the Twenties 372
1977 TCMA/ASCCA Ad Card 373
1977 Tom Daniels Burleigh Grimes 103
1977 Topps 459
1977 Topps Cloth Stickers 462
1977 Topps Proofs 461
1977 Topps Team Checklist Sheet 461
1977 Topps/Dynamite Magazine Panels 462
1977 Venezuelan Baseball Stickers 496
1977 Wendy's Discs 503
1977 Wiffle Insert Discs 508
1977 Wilson Sporting Goods Mini-Posters 512
1977 Zip'z discs 528
1977-78 Cubic Corp. Sports Deck Playing Cards 101
1977-78 Minnesota Twins Team Issue 232
1977-79 Sportscaster 341
1977-80 TCMA The War Years 372
1977-81 Bob Parker Hall of Fame 272
1977-84 TCMA/Renata Galasso 373
1978 Allen P. Terach Immortals of Baseball 379
1978 Atlanta Nobis Center 26
1978 Baseball Player Patches 33
1978 Big T/Tastee Freeze discs 41
1978 Bob Bartosz Baseball Postcards 29
1978 Boston Red Sox of the 1950s-1960s 49
1978 Broder Photocards 60
1978 Burger King Astros 65
1978 Burger King Rangers 65
1978 Burger King Tigers 65
1978 Burger King Yankees 65
1978 Coca-Cola/ WPLO Atlanta Braves 92
1978 Dearborn Show 105
1978 Detroit Free Press Tigers 110
1978 Dimanche/Derniere Heure Expos 119
1978 Doug McWilliams Postcards 225
1978 Dover Publications Great Players Postcards 124
1978 Family Fun Centers Angels 141
1978 Family Fun Centers Padres 141
1978 Grand Slam 166
1978 Hostess 182
1978 Hostess Unissued Proofs 183
1978 HRT/RES 1939 Father and Son Reprints 185
1978 JJH Reading Remembers 192
1978 Kellogg's 204
1978 Laughlin Long Ago Black Stars 211
1978 McDonald's Boston Red Sox 224
1978 Minor League Team Sets 1778
1978 North Shore Dodge Cecil Cooper 246
1978 O-Pee-Chee 252
1978 Papa Gino's Discs 271
1978 Pepsi-Cola Superstars 274
1978 Post Cereal Steve Garvey Baseball Tips 295
1978 Post-Intelligencer 1969 Pilot Profiles 295
1978 Royal Crown Cola Iron-Ons 311
1978 Saga Discs 316
1978 SSPC All Star Gallery 348
1978 SSPC Baseball the Phillies Way 349
1978 SSPC Yankees Yearbook 349
1978 TCMA 1941 Brooklyn Dodgers 375
1978 TCMA Baseball Nostalgia Postcard 374
1978 TCMA The 1960's 374
1978 The Card Coach Milwaukee Braves Greats 380
1978 Topps 462
1978 Topps Team Checklist Sheet 464
1978 Topps/Dynamite Magazine Panels 464
1978 Topps/Zest Soap 464
1978 Wiffle Box-Side Discs 508
1979 Baseball Favorites "1953 Bowman" 30
1979 Boston Red Sox Team Issue 49
1979 Bubble Yum Toronto Blue Jays 62
1979 Burger King Phillies 65
1979 Burger King Yankees 66
1979 Coca-Cola/7-Eleven MVPs 92
1979 Dexter Press Hall of Fame Plaque Postcards 112
1979 Diamond Greats 113
1979 Dimanche/Derniere Heure Expos 119
1979 Doug McWilliams Postcards 225
1979 Early Red Sox Favorites 126
1979 Family Fun Centers Padres 142
1979 Fritsch One-Year Winners 154
1979 Hall of Fame (Dexter Press) Plaque Postcards 172
1979 HoF (Dexter Press) Plaque Postcards - Auto. 172
1979 Hostess 183
1979 Hostess Unissued Proofs 184
1979 HRT/RES 1950 Phillies/A's "Doubleheaders" 185
1979 Kellogg's 204
1979 L.A. Dodgers 208
1979 Larry Crain Prints 99
1979 Metallic Creations Signature Miniatures 227
1979 Michigan Sports Collectors 228
1979 Minor League Team Sets 1779
1979 O-Pee-Chee 252
1979 Open Pantry/Lake to Lake MACC 269
1979 San Francisco Giants Police 320
1979 Sports Reading Series 344
1979 TCMA 1927 New York Yankees 377
1979 TCMA All Time Tigers 376
1979 TCMA Baseball History Series: The Fifties 376
1979 TCMA Japan Pro Baseball 377
1979 Topps 465
1979 Topps Comics 467
1979 Topps Team Checklist Sheet 467
1979 Topps/Dynamite Magazine Panels 467
1979 United Press International 481
1979-83 Coral-Lee Postcards 627
1980 Burger King Phillies 66
1980 Burger King Pitch, Hit & Run 66
1980 Cincinnati Enquirer Cincinnati Reds 82
1980 Delacorte Press 105
1980 Did You Know . . . ? 118
1980 Dimanche/Derniere Heure Expos 119
1980 Donruss Prototypes 634
1980 Doug McWilliams Postcards 225
1980 Exhibits 138
1980 Family Fun Centers Padres 142
1980 Fleer Baseball's Famous Feats 151
1980 Fleer World Series/Team Logo Stickers 151
1980 Franchise Babe Ruth 153
1980 Hall of Fame Exhibits 138
1980 Kellogg's 204
1980 L.A. Dodgers Police 208
1980 Laughlin 300/400/500 211
1980 Laughlin Famous Feats 211
1980 Midwest Sports Collectors Convention 229
1980 Milwaukee Brewers/ Pepsi Fan Club 232
1980 Minor League Team Sets 1779
1980 Nostalgic Enterprises 1903 N.Y. Highlanders 246
1980 O-Pee-Chee 254
1980 Pepsi-Cola All-Stars Prototypes 275
1980 San Francisco Giants Police 320
1980 Superstar 356
1980 TCMA 1914 Miracle (Boston) Braves 378
1980 TCMA 1950 Philadelphia Phillies/Whiz Kids 378
1980 TCMA 1957 Milwaukee Braves 378
1980 TCMA 1959 L.A. Dodgers 378
1980 TCMA 1960 Pittsburgh Pirates 379
1980 TCMA 1961 Cincinnati Reds 379
1980 TCMA All Time Brooklyn Dodgers 377
1980 TCMA All Time Cubs 377
1980 TCMA All Time N.Y. Giants 378
1980 TCMA All Time Tigers 378
1980 TCMA All Time White Sox 378
1980 TCMA All Time Yankees 378
1980 TCMA All-Time Teams 377
1980 TCMA/Sports Nostalgia Store Babe Ruth 379
1980 Topps 467
1980 Topps N.Y. Yankees Proof 470
1980 Topps Stickers Prototypes 470
1980 Topps Superstar 5x7 Photos 470
1980 Topps Team Checklist Sheet 470
1980 Topps Test Coins 470
1980-2001 Perez-Steele Hall of Fame Postcards 1105
1980-81 Argus Publishing Reggie Jackson 23
1980-83 Cramer Baseball Legends 629
1980-88 Baseball Immortals 535
1980s Big League Cards 538
1981 7-Up 1197
1981 Atlanta Braves Police 532
1981 Champions of American Sport 597
1981 Coca-Cola 606
1981 Detroit News Tigers Centennial 632
1981 Diamond Stars Extension Set 633
1981 Donruss 634
1981 Donruss Promo Sheet 634
1981 Drake's 759
1981 Family Fun Centers Padres 762
1981 Fleer 785
1981 Franchise 1966 Baltimore Orioles 910
1981 Granny Goose Potato Chips A's 915
1981 Kansas City Royals Police 927
1981 Kellogg's 932
1981 L.A. Dodgers Police 937
1981 Minor League Team Sets 1779
1981 MSA Discs 1038
1981 MSA/Peter Pan-Sunbeam Bakery Discs 1038
1981 O-Pee-Chee 1041
1981 Perez-Steele Yankee Greats Promotional Postcard 1106
1981 Perma-Graphics All-Star Credit Cards 1107
1981 Peter Pan Bakery Discs 1108
1981 Seattle Mariners Police 1188
1981 Sporting News Conlon Collection 1256
1981 Sportrait Hall of Fame 1257
1981 Spot-bilt George Brett 1262
1981 Squirt 1262
1981 Sunbeam Bakery Discs 1304
1981 TCMA The 1960's, Series 2 1308
1981 Topps 1315
1981-89 Hall of Fame Metallic Plaque-cards 916
1981-93 Louisville Slugger 999
1982 Atlanta Braves Police 532
1982 Authentic Sports Autographs Mickey Mantle Story 533
1982 Big League Collectibles Diamond Classics, Series 1538
1982 Boston Red Sox Favorites 540
1982 Builders Emporium Los Angeles Dodgers 592
1982 Burger King Braves 592
1982 Burger King Indians 593
1982 Cincinnati Reds Yearbook Cards 598
1982 Coca-Cola Brigham's Red Sox 606
1982 Cracker Jack 627
1982 Donruss 636
1982 Drake's 759
1982 FBI Foods Discs 763
1982 Fleer 787
1982 Granny Goose Potato Chips A's 915
1982 Hygrade Expos 921
1982 Kellogg's 933
1982 K-Mart 935
1982 L.A. Dodgers Police 938
1982 Milwaukee Brewers Police 1013
1982 Minor League Team Sets 1779
1982 N.Y. Yankees Yearbook 1041
1982 On Deck Cookies Discs 1053
1982 O-Pee-Chee 1042
1982 Perma-Graphics All-Star Credit Cards 1107
1982 Red Lobster Cubs 1157
1982 Renata Galasso 20 Years of Met Baseball 912
1982 Roy Rogers N.Y. Yankees Lids 1158
1982 Squirt 1263
1982 Superstar 1304
1982 TCMA Baseball's Greatest Hitters 1309
1982 Topps 1318

1982 Wheaties Indians ... 1712
1982 Zellers Expos ... 1719
1982-1988 Ohio Baseball Hall of Fame ... 1053
1982-89 Donruss Puzzle Promo Sheets ... 637
1983 "1969" MLBPA Pins ... 219
1983 7-11 Slurpee Coins ... 1196
1983 Affiliated Food Rangers ... 530
1983 Atlanta Braves Police ... 532
1983 Authentic Sports Autographs ... 533
1983 Big League Collectibles Diamond Classics, Series 2 ... 538
1983 Big League Collectibles Original All-Stars ... 539
1983 Boston Herald Sox Stamps ... 540
1983 Cincinnati Reds Yearbook Cards ... 598
1983 Donruss ... 637
1983 Donruss Action All-Stars ... 638
1983 Donruss Action All-Stars Promo Sheet ... 638
1983 Donruss Hall of Fame Heroes ... 638
1983 Donruss Hall of Fame Heroes Promo Sheet ... 638
1983 Donruss Promo Sheet ... 637
1983 Drake's ... 759
1983 English's Chicken Baltimore Orioles Lids ... 761
1983 Fleer ... 789
1983 Fleer Promo Sheet ... 789
1983 Franchise Brooks Robinson ... 910
1983 Fritsch 1953 Boston/ Milwaukee Braves ... 911
1983 Fritsch One-Year Winners ... 911
1983 Gardner's Brewers ... 914
1983 Gaylord Perry Career Highlights ... 1108
1983 Granny Goose Potato Chips A's ... 915
1983 Homeplate Sports Cards Al Kaline Story ... 920
1983 Kansas City Royals Police ... 927
1983 Kellogg's ... 933
1983 L.A. Dodgers Police ... 938
1983 Milwaukee Brewers Police ... 1013
1983 Minnesota Twins team issue ... 1016
1983 Minor League Team Sets ... 1779
1983 Mother's Cookies Giants ... 1026
1983 Mr. Z's Pizza Milwaukee Brewers ... 1037
1983 Nalley Potato Chips Mariners ... 1039
1983 O'Connell & Son Ink Baseball Greats ... 1052
1983 O-Pee-Chee ... 1042
1983 Perma-Graphics All-Star Credit Cards ... 1108
1983 Renata Galasso 1933 All-Stars ... 912
1983 Sporting News Conlon Collection ... 1256
1983 Sporting News Conlon Collection Prototypes ... 1256
1983 Star '83 ... 1289
1983 Starliner Stickers ... 1295
1983 Stuart Expos ... 1296
1983 TCMA All-Time Athletics ... 1309
1983 Thorn Apple Valley Cubs ... 1315
1983 Topps ... 1321
1983 True Value White Sox ... 1510
1983 Wheaties Indians ... 1713
1984 7-11 Slurpee Coins Central Region ... 1196
1984 7-Up Cubs ... 1197
1984 Atlanta Braves Police ... 532
1984 Baseball Cards Magazine Repli-Cards ... 533
1984 Borden's Reds Stickers ... 540
1984 California Angels Fire Safety ... 594
1984 Cincinnati Reds Yearbook Cards ... 598
1984 Decathlon Negro League Baseball Stars ... 631
1984 Donruss ... 638
1984 Donruss Promo Sheet ... 638
1984 Drake's ... 759
1984 Farmer Jack Detroit Tigers ... 763
1984 Fleer ... 791
1984 Fleer Sample Sheet ... 791
1984 Gardner's Brewers ... 914
1984 Jarvis Press Rangers ... 922
1984 Jewel Food Chicago Cubs/ White Sox ... 922
1984 L.A. Dodgers Fire Safety ... 938
1984 L.A. Dodgers Police ... 938
1984 Milton Bradley ... 1013
1984 Milwaukee Brewers Police ... 1013
1984 Minnesota Twins Team Issue ... 1016
1984 Minor League Team Sets ... 1780
1984 Mother's Cookies A's ... 1026
1984 Mr. Z's Pizza Milwaukee Brewers ... 1037
1984 N.Y. Mets M.V.P. Club ... 1040
1984 Nestle ... 1039
1984 O-Pee-Chee ... 1043
1984 Ralston Purina ... 1156
1984 Renata Galasso Baseball Collector Series ... 913
1984 San Diego Padres Fire Safety ... 1158
1984 Sporting News Conlon Collection ... 1256
1984 Sports Design Products Doug West ... 1257
1984 Star '84 ... 1289
1984 Stuart Expos ... 1297
1984 TCMA American League All-Stars ... 1311
1984 Topps ... 1324
1984 Toronto Blue Jays Fire Safety ... 1505
1984 True Value White Sox ... 1510
1984 Wheaties Indians ... 1713
1984-91 O'Connell & Son Ink Mini Prints ... 1052
1985 7-11 Slurpee Coins Eastern Region ... 1196
1985 7-Up Cubs ... 1198
1985 Atlanta Braves Police ... 532
1985 Baseball Cards Magazine Repli-Cards ... 533
1985 Big League Collectibles National Pastime 1930-1939 ... 539
1985 Cain's Potato Chips Tigers ... 594
1985 California Angels Fire Safety ... 594
1985 CBS Radio Game of the Week ... 597
1985 Chicago Cubs Playing Cards ... 597
1985 Cincinnati Reds Yearbook Cards ... 599
1985 Circle K ... 601
1985 Coca-Cola Dodgers Photocards ... 607
1985 Decathlon Ultimate Baseball Card Set ... 631
1985 Donruss ... 640
1985 Donruss Promo Sheet ... 640
1985 Drake's ... 759
1985 Fleer ... 792
1985 Fun Food Buttons ... 912
1985 Gardner's Brewers ... 914
1985 General Mills Stickers ... 915
1985 Hostess Braves ... 920
1985 Kas Potato Chips Discs ... 928
1985 Kitty Clover Potato Chips Discs ... 935
1985 Kondritz Vince Coleman ... 937
1985 Leaf-Donruss ... 941
1985 Milwaukee Brewers Police ... 1013
1985 Minnesota Twins Team Issue ... 1017
1985 Minor League Team Sets ... 1780
1985 Mother's Cookies A's ... 1027
1985 Mr. Z's Pizza Pete Rose ... 1037
1985 MSA/Subway Sandwiches Discs ... 1038
1985 N.Y. Mets Police ... 1040
1985 N.Y. Mets Super Fan Club ... 1040
1985 N.Y. Yankees Police ... 1041
1985 O-Pee-Chee ... 1044
1985 P.R.E. Pete Rose Set ... 1154
1985 Performance Printing Texas Rangers ... 1107
1985 Philadelphia Phillies Police ... 1108
1985 Pittsburgh Pirates Yearbook Cards ... 1130
1985 Polaroid/J.C. Penney Indians ... 1153
1985 Renata Galasso Dwight Gooden ... 913
1985 Sports Design Products Doug West ... 1257
1985 Star '85 ... 1289
1985 Star Nolan Ryan Promo ... 1289
1985 TCMA Cy Young Award Winners ... 1311
1985 Thom McAn Discs ... 1002
1985 Topps ... 1327
1985 Toronto Blue Jays Fire Safety ... 1505
1985 Wendy's Tigers ... 1712
1985 Woolworth ... 1717
1985 WTBS Atlanta Braves ... 1719
1985-86 RGI ... 1158
1985-95 Perez-Steele Great Moments Postcards ... 1106
1986 7-11 Slurpee Coins Eastern Region ... 1196
1986 Atlanta Braves Police ... 532
1986 Ault Foods Blue Jays stickers ... 532
1986 Baseball Cards Magazine Repli-Cards ... 533
1986 Big League Chew ... 538
1986 Burger King ... 593
1986 Cain's Potato Chips Tigers ... 594
1986 California Angels Fire Safety ... 594
1986 CBS Radio Game of the Week ... 597
1986 Coca-Cola Dodgers Photocards ... 607
1986 Donruss ... 641
1986 Dorman's Cheese ... 759
1986 Drake's ... 759
1986 Fleer ... 794
1986 Fritsch Negro League Baseball Stars ... 911
1986 Gatorade Cubs ... 914
1986 General Mills Booklets ... 915
1986 Houston Astros Police ... 921
1986 Jays Potato Chips ... 922
1986 Jiffy Pop ... 923
1986 Jiffy Pop/ MSA Promos ... 923
1986 Kas Potato Chips Cardinals ... 929
1986 Kay Bee Young Superstars ... 929
1986 Keller's Butter Phillies ... 932
1986 Kitty Clover Potato Chips Royals ... 935
1986 Kondritz Ozzie Smith ... 937
1986 L.A. Dodgers Police ... 938
1986 Leaf ... 942
1986 Lite Beer Astros ... 998
1986 Meadow Gold Blank Backs ... 1005
1986 Milwaukee Brewers Police ... 1013
1986 Minnesota Twins team issue ... 1017
1986 Minor League Team Sets ... 1780
1986 Mother's Cookies A's ... 1027
1986 N.Y. Mets Super Fan Club ... 1040
1986 National Photo Royals ... 1039
1986 Oh Henry! Cleveland Indians ... 1052
1986 O-Pee-Chee ... 1045
1986 Performance Printing Texas Rangers ... 1107
1986 Philadelphia Phillies Fire Safety ... 1108
1986 Provigo Expos ... 1154
1986 Quaker Oats ... 1156
1986 Renata Galasso Dwight Gooden ... 913
1986 Safeway Houston Astros ... 1158
1986 Sportflics ... 1249
1986 Sportflics Promo Cards ... 1249
1986 Sportflics Prototype Cards ... 1248
1986 Star '86 ... 1289
1986 Star Promos ... 1289
1986 TCMA All Time Teams ... 1312
1986 Texas Gold Ice Cream Reds ... 1314
1986 Topps ... 1331
1986 Toronto Blue Jays Fire Safety ... 1505
1986 True Value ... 1510
1986 Wallich Enterprises Padres Sports Cards ... 1712
1986 Woolworth ... 1717
1986-87 San Diego Padres Fire Safety Flip Books ... 1158
1986-88 World Wide Sports Conlon Collection ... 1718
1987 7-11 Slurpee Coins Eastern Region ... 1197
1987 Allstate Insurance ... 530
1987 Atlanta Braves Fire Safety ... 532
1987 Baseball Cards Magazine Repli-Cards ... 534
1987 Baseball's All-Time Greats ... 536
1987 Bluegrass State Games ... 540
1987 Boardwalk and Baseball All Time Record Holders ... 540
1987 Boardwalk and Baseball Top Run Makers ... 540
1987 Bohemian Hearth Bread Padres ... 540
1987 Bowery Bank Joe DiMaggio ... 541
1987 Burger King ... 593
1987 Cain's Potato Chips Tigers ... 594
1987 California Angels Fire Safety ... 594
1987 Champion Phillies ... 597
1987 Classic Major League Baseball Game ... 602
1987 Coca-Cola Tigers ... 607
1987 David Berg Hot Dogs Cubs ... 538
1987 Donruss ... 643
1987 Drake's ... 759
1987 Farmland Dairies Mets ... 763
1987 Fleer ... 796
1987 French/Bray Orioles ... 910
1987 Gatorade Indians ... 914
1987 General Mills Booklets ... 915
1987 Hostess Stickers ... 920
1987 Houston Astros Police ... 921
1987 Hygrade Baseball's All-Time Greats ... 921
1987 Jiffy Pop ... 923
1987 Kahn's Reds ... 923
1987 Kay Bee Superstars of Baseball ... 929
1987 Key Food Discs ... 933
1987 K-Mart ... 935
1987 Kraft Home Plate Heroes ... 937
1987 L.A. Dodgers All-Stars Fire Safety ... 938
1987 Leaf ... 942
1987 Leaf Candy City Team ... 943
1987 M & M's ... 1001
1987 Milwaukee Brewers Police ... 1013
1987 Minnesota Twins Team Issue ... 1017
1987 Minor League Team Sets ... 1781
1987 Mother's Cookies A's ... 1028
1987 Nestle ... 1039
1987 Oakland Athletics Fire Safety ... 1051
1987 O-Pee-Chee ... 1045
1987 Ralston Purina ... 1156
1987 Red Foley Stickers ... 907
1987 Schnucks St. Louis Cardinals ... 1160
1987 Sonshine Industries 19th Century Baseball ... 1211
1987 Sportflics ... 1250
1987 St. Louis Cardinals Fire Safety ... 1263
1987 Star '87 ... 1289
1987 Star Promos ... 1289
1987 Stuart ... 1297
1987 Sun Foods Milwaukee Brewers ... 1304
1987 Super Stars Discs ... 1305
1987 TCMA All Time N.Y. Yankees ... 1314
1987 Texas Rangers Fire Safety ... 1314
1987 Topps ... 1334
1987 Toronto Blue Jays Fire Safety ... 1506
1987 Toys "R" Us ... 1507
1987 U.S. Forestry Service Smokey Bear's Team ... 1708
1987 Woolworth ... 1717
1987-89 Our Own Tea Discs ... 1054
1988 Action Packed ... 529
1988 Baseball Cards Magazine Repli-Cards ... 534
1988 Bazooka ... 536
1988 Blue Cross/ Blue Shield Bob Uecker Reprint ... 540
1988 California Angels Fire Safety ... 595
1988 Chef Boyardee ... 597
1988 Chicago Cubs Fire Safety ... 598
1988 Coca-Cola Padres ... 607
1988 David Berg Hot Dogs Cubs ... 538
1988 Detroit Tigers Police ... 633
1988 Domino's Pizza Tigers ... 634
1988 Donruss ... 646
1988 Donruss Promo Sheet ... 646
1988 Drake's ... 760
1988 Fantastic Sam's ... 763
1988 Farmland Dairies Mets ... 763
1988 Fleer ... 800
1988 Foot Locker Slam Fest ... 909
1988 French/Bray Orioles ... 910
1988 Gatorade Indians ... 914
1988 Hardee's/ Coke Conlon ... 916
1988 Historic Limited Editions Brooklyn Dodgers ... 918
1988 Hostess Potato Chips Expos/Blue Jays ... 920
1988 Houston Astros Police ... 921
1988 Jiffy Pop ... 923
1988 Kahn's Mets ... 924

1988 Kansas City Royals Fire Safety 927
1988 Kay Bee Superstars of Baseball 929
1988 Kay Bee Team Leaders 929
1988 Key Food Discs 933
1988 King-B 933
1988 K-Mart 936
1988 Kodak White Sox 936
1988 L.A. Dodgers Fire Safety 938
1988 Leaf 943
1988 Master Bread Twins 1002
1988 Mickey Mantle's Restaurant 1001
1988 Milwaukee Brewers Police 1013
1988 Minnesota Twins Fire Safety 1017
1988 Minnesota Twins team issue 1017
1988 Minor League Team Sets 1781
1988 Mother's Cookies A's 1029
1988 Negro League Stars 1039
1988 Nestle 1040
1988 O-Pee-Chee 1046
1988 Pacific Baseball Legends 1054
1988 Panini Stickers 1097
1988 Pepsi-Cola/ Kroger Tigers 1103
1988 Red Foley Stickers 908
1988 Revco 1157
1988 Rite Aid 1158
1988 San Diego Padres Fire Safety 1158
1988 Score 1160
1988 Score Promo Cards 1160
1988 Score Proofs 1160
1988 Sportflics 1251
1988 St. Louis Cardinals Fire Safety 1263
1988 Star '88 1291
1988 Star '88 Promos 1291
1988 Star Platinum Edition 1290
1988 Starting Lineup Talking Baseball 1295
1988 Super Stars Discs 1305
1988 T & M Sports Umpires 1306
1988 Tetley Tea Discs 1314
1988 Texas Rangers Fire Safety 1315
1988 Topps 1337
1988 Toronto Blue Jays Fire Safety 1506
1988 Toys "R" Us Rookies 1507
1988 Weis Winners Super Stars Discs 1712
1988 Woolworth 1717
1988 World Wide Sports 1933 All-Stars 1718
1988 World Wide Sports 1933 Negro All Stars 1718
1988-1989 Star 1290
1988-89 Star Gold Edition 1290
1988-89 Star Nova Edition 1290
1988-89 Star Platinum 1290
1988-89 Star Promos 1289
1988-89 Star Silver Edition 1291
1988-92 Star Ad Cards 1290
1988-93 Costacos Brothers Ad Cards 627
1989 Ames 20/20 Club 531
1989 Barry Colla Postcards 610
1989 Baseball Cards Magazine Repli-Cards 534
1989 Bazooka 536
1989 Bimbo Cookies Super Stars Discs 539
1989 Bowman 541
1989 Cadaco All-Star Baseball Discs 593
1989 California Angels All-Stars Fire Safety 595
1989 Cap 'n Crunch 596
1989 Classic 602
1989 Cleveland Indians Team Issue 606
1989 Coca-Cola Padres 608
1989 Detroit Tigers Police 633
1989 Donruss 648
1989 Donruss Promo Sheet 648
1989 Dubuque Braves 760
1989 Farmland Dairies Mets 763
1989 Fleer 804
1989 Foot Locker Slam Fest 909
1989 French/Bray Orioles 910
1989 Gardner's Brewers 914
1989 Hills Team MVP's 918
1989 Historic Limited Editions Lou Gehrig Postcards 918
1989 Holsum Bakeries Super Stars Discs 919
1989 Holsum/ Schafer's Super Stars Discs 919
1989 Houston Colt .45s Fire Safety 921
1989 J.J. Nissen Super Stars 1040
1989 Kahn's Cooperstown Collection 924
1989 Kahn's Mets 924
1989 Kay Bee Superstars of Baseball 929
1989 King-B 934
1989 K-Mart 936
1989 Kodak White Sox 936
1989 L.A. Dodgers Greats Fire Safety 939
1989 Leaf Blue Chip Cards 943
1989 Lennox/HSE Astros 997
1989 Marathon Cubs 1001
1989 Marathon Tigers 1001
1989 Master Bread 1002
1989 MasterCard Masters of the Game 1002
1989 Milk Duds Pittsburgh Pirates 1012
1989 Milwaukee Brewers Police 1014
1989 Minor League Team Sets 1782
1989 Mother's Cookies A's 1029
1989 Nabisco Don Mattingly 1038
1989 O-Pee-Chee 1047
1989 Pacific Legends II 1054
1989 Panini Stickers 1098
1989 Pepsi-Cola Mark McGwire 1104
1989 Perez-Steele Celebration Postcards 1107
1989 Phoenix Holsum Super Stars Discs 1109
1989 Rainier Farms Super Stars Discs 1156
1989 Ralston Purina 1157
1989 Red Foley Stickers 908
1989 San Diego Padres Magazine/ S.D. Sports inserts 1158
1989 SCD Baseball Card Price Guide Pocket Price Guides 1159
1989 Schafer's Bakery Super Stars Discs 1160
1989 Score 1162
1989 Sportflics 1252
1989 St. Louis Cardinals Fire Safety 1263
1989 Star Minor League Baseball 1782
1989 Starline Prototypes 1295
1989 Super Stars Discs 1305
1989 Swell Baseball Greats 1305
1989 T & M Sports Senior League 1306
1989 Taystee Kansas City Royals 1308
1989 Tetley Tea Discs 1314
1989 Texas Rangers Fire Safety 1315
1989 Topps 1342
1989 Toronto Blue Jays Fire Safety 1506
1989 Toys "R" Us Rookies 1507
1989 U.S. Postal Service Legends 1711
1989 Upper Deck 1535
1989 Upper Deck Promos 1535
1989 Upper Deck Show Samples 1535
1989 Very Fine Pirates 1711
1989 W/R Associates Mark Grace 1718
1989 Woolworth 1718
1989-90 Star Rookies 1291
1989-91 Sports Illustrated For Kids 1261
1990 Agfa Film 530
1990 All American Baseball Team 530
1990 Ames All-Stars 531
1990 Barry Colla 610
1990 Barry Colla Promos 610
1990 Baseball Cards Magazine Repli-Cards 534
1990 Baseball Wit 536
1990 Bazooka 536
1990 Best 1783
1990 Bowman 542
1990 Cadaco All-Star Baseball Discs 593
1990 California Angels Fire Safety 595
1990 Classic 603
1990 Cleveland Indians Team Issue 606
1990 Coca-Cola Padres 608
1990 Collectors Marketing Corp. Pre-Rookie 1784
1990 Donruss 651
1990 Donruss Aqueous Test 652
1990 Donruss Blue/White Test Issue 652
1990 Donruss Previews 651
1990 Dubuque Braves 760
1990 Eclipse Stars of the Negro Leagues 761
1990 Elite Senior League 761
1990 Fleer 806
1990 Giant Eagle Roberto Clemente Stickers 915
1990 Hills Hit Men 918
1990 Historic Limited Editions Roberto Clemente 918
1990 Holsum Bakeries Super Stars Discs 919
1990 Homers Cookies Pittsburgh Pirates 920
1990 Hostess Blue Jays Highlight Stickers 920
1990 Jumbo Sunflower Seeds 923
1990 Kahn's Mets 924
1990 Kay Bee Kings 929
1990 King-B 934
1990 K-Mart 936
1990 Kodak White Sox 936
1990 L.A. Dodgers Police 939
1990 Leaf 944
1990 Leaf Previews 943
1990 Lennox/HSE Astros 997
1990 Little Big Leaguers 999
1990 Marathon Cubs 1001
1990 McDonald's 1002
1990 Miller Beer Milwaukee Brewers 1012
1990 Milwaukee Brewers Police 1014
1990 Minor League Team Sets 1786
1990 Mother's Cookies A's 1030
1990 O-Pee-Chee 1048
1990 Pacific Legends 1054
1990 Panini Stickers 1099
1990 Pepsi-Cola Boston Red Sox 1104
1990 Post Cereal 1153
1990 ProCards A & AA Minor League Stars 1785
1990 ProCards Future Stars AAA Baseball 1785
1990 Publications International Stickers 1154
1990 Real Milk Mike Henneman 1157
1990 Red Apple Mariners Pin/ Cards 1157
1990 Red Foley Stickers 908
1990 Ron Lewis 1961 N.Y. Yankees 997
1990 San Diego Padres Magazine/ Unocal inserts 1158
1990 SCD Baseball Card Price Guide Pocket Price Guides 1159
1990 Score 1164
1990 Score Promos 1164
1990 Sportflics 1252
1990 St. Louis Cardinals Fire Safety 1263
1990 Star Sophomore Stars 1292
1990 Starline 1295
1990 Starline Americana 1295
1990 Super Stars Discs 1305
1990 Swell Baseball Greats 1305
1990 T & M Sports Umpires 1306
1990 Target Dodgers 1307
1990 Tetley Tea Discs 1314
1990 Texas Rangers Fire Safety 1315
1990 Topps 1347
1990 Toronto Blue Jays Fire Safety 1506
1990 Toys "R" Us Rookies 1507
1990 Tropicana Team Mets 1510
1990 U.S. Playing Card All-Stars 1708
1990 Upper Deck 1537
1990 Windwalker Discs 1715
1990 Wonder Stars 1717
1990 Woolworth 1718
1990-91 Star 1291
1990-91 Star Gold Edition 1291
1990-91 Star Nova Edition 1292
1990-91 Star Platinum Edition 1292
1990-91 Star Promos 1291
1990-91 Star Silver Edition 1292
1990-92 Baseball Cards Presents Repli-Cards 535
1990-92 Perez-Steele Master Works Postcards 1107
1990-93 Star "Career Stats" 1291
1990s Exhibit Card Unauthorized Reprints 138
1990s Louisville Slugger TPX Advisory Staff 1000
1991 7-11 Slurpee Coins Atlantic Region 1197
1991 Acme Reproductions Ryan-Seaver 529
1991 Barry Colla 610
1991 Barry Colla Promos 610
1991 Baseball Cards Magazine Repli-Cards 534
1991 Bazooka 536
1991 Bleachers Frank Thomas 539
1991 Bowman 543
1991 Cadaco All-Star Baseball Discs 594
1991 California Angels Fire Safety 595
1991 Classic 603
1991 Classic Best 1787
1991 Classic Draft Picks 1788
1991 Classic Four Sport (Baseball) 1788
1991 Classic/ American Collectables Nolan Ryan 604
1991 Coca-Cola Don Mattingly 608
1991 Conlon Collection 624
1991 Conlon Collection Prototypes 623
1991 Country Hearth Mariners 627
1991 Cracker Jack Topps 1st Series 628
1991 Crown/Coke Orioles 629
1991 Denny's Grand Slam 632
1991 Detroit Tigers Police 633
1991 Donruss 653
1991 Donruss Previews 653
1991 Dubuque Braves 760
1991 Enor Kevin Maas Story 762
1991 Fleer 808
1991 Fleer Promo Strip 808
1991 Foot Locker Slam Fest 910
1991 Front Row Ken Griffey Jr. 911
1991 Historic Limited Editions Brooklyn Dodgers 919
1991 Holsum Bakeries Super Stars Discs 919
1991 Homers Cookies 920
1991 Impel/Line Drive Pre-Rookie AA 1788
1991 Jimmy Dean 631
1991 Jumbo Sunflower Seeds 923
1991 Kahn's Mets 924
1991 Kansas City Royals Police 927
1991 Kellogg's 3-D 933
1991 Kellogg's Baseball Greats 933
1991 Kellogg's Leyendas 933
1991 King-B 934
1991 Kodak White Sox 936
1991 L.A. Dodgers Police 939
1991 Leaf 944
1991 Leaf Previews 944
1991 Line Drive 998
1991 Line Drive Don Mattingly 998
1991 Line Drive Mickey Mantle 998
1991 Line Drive Ryne Sandberg 998
1991 Little Big Leaguers 999
1991 Marathon Cubs 1001
1991 McDonald's Cleveland Indians 1002
1991 MDA All-Stars 1005
1991 Miller Beer Milwaukee Brewers 1012
1991 Milwaukee Brewers Police 1014
1991 Minor League Team Sets 1791
1991 MooTown Snackers 1026
1991 Mother's Cookies A's 1031
1991 O-Pee-Chee 1048
1991 O-Pee-Chee Sample Sheet 1048
1991 Pacific Gas & Electric S.F. Giants 1097
1991 Pacific Senior League 1055

1991 Panini Stickers 1100
1991 Pepsi-Cola Superstars 1104
1991 Petro Canada All-Star FanFest Standups 1108
1991 Post Cereal 1153
1991 ProCards Tomorrow's Heroes 1790
1991 Red Foley Stickers 908
1991 Retort Negro League Legends, Series 1 1157
1991 Ron Lewis Negro Leagues Postcards 997
1991 San Diego Padres Magazine/ Rally's inserts 1159
1991 San Francisco Examiner A's 1159
1991 SCD Baseball Card Price Guide Pocket Price Guides 1159
1991 Score 1167
1991 Score Promos 1167
1991 St. Louis Cardinals Police 1263
1991 Stadium Club 1265
1991 Stadium Club Promos 1265
1991 Star 1292
1991 Star Silver Edition 1293
1991 Star The Future 1294
1991 Starline Prototypes 1295
1991 Studio 1297
1991 Studio Preview 1297
1991 Swell Baseball Greats 1305
1991 Topps 1353
1991 Topps Pre-Production Sample Sheet 1353
1991 Toronto Blue Jays Fire Safety 1506
1991 Toys "R" Us Rookies 1507
1991 Tropicana Team Mets 1510
1991 U.S. Playing Card All-Stars 1708
1991 Ultra 1510
1991 Upper Deck 1538
1991 Vine Line Chicago Cubs 1712
1991 Wiz Mets 1715
1991 Wiz Yankees of the '50's 1716
1991 Woolworth 1718
1991 WWOR N.Y. Mets 1719
1991-1992 Bleachers Promos 539
1991-1992 NewSport 1040
1992 7-11 Slurpee Superstar Action Coins 1197
1992 Action Packed 24-Kt. Gold 530
1992 Action Packed All-Star Gallery Series 1529
1992 Action Packed Diamond Stars 529
1992 Action Packed Promos 529
1992 Barry Colla 610
1992 Barry Colla Promos 610
1992 Baseball Cards Magazine Repli-Cards 534
1992 Bazooka 536
1992 BB Card Price Guide/Sports Card Price Guide 1160
1992 Ben's Bakery Super Hitters Discs 537
1992 Bleachers David Justice 539
1992 Bleachers Ken Griffey, Jr. 539
1992 Bleachers Nolan Ryan 539
1992 Blockbuster Video Pin/Cards 540
1992 Blue Jays Commemorative Set 659
1992 Bowman 544
1992 California Angels Police 595
1992 Carl's Jr. Padres 596
1992 Carlson Travel 1982 Brewers 597
1992 Chevron Giants Hall of Fame Pins 597
1992 Chicago White Sox 1917 Team Issue Reprints 598
1992 Classic Best 1791
1992 Classic Draft Picks 1792
1992 Classic Four Sport 1793
1992 Classic Series 1604
1992 Clovis Police Department Mark's Moments 606
1992 Coca-Cola Nolan Ryan Career Series 609
1992 Coca-Cola/ Hardees Major League Line-Up Discs 609
1992 Conlon Collection 13th National 625
1992 Conlon Collection 624
1992 Conlon Collection Prototypes 624
1992 Cracker Jack Donruss Series 1628
1992 Crown Orioles Action Standups 630
1992 Dairy Queen Team USA 630
1992 Denny's Grand Slam 632
1992 Diet Pepsi Collector Series 634
1992 Donruss 655
1992 Donruss Previews 655
1992 Donruss/ Durivage Montreal Expos 657
1992 Dunkin' Donuts Red Sox 760
1992 Eclipse Negro League BPA - John Clapp 761
1992 Eclipse Negro League BPA - Paul Lee 761
1992 Fleer 810
1992 Fleer Promo 810
1992 Flopps Promos 907
1992 French's Mustard 910
1992 Front Row Club House Series Ken Griffey, Jr. 911
1992 Front Row Draft Picks 1793
1992 High 5 Decals 917
1992 Jimmy Dean 631
1992 Jumbo Sunflower Seeds 923
1992 Kahn's Mets 925
1992 Kansas City Royals Police 927
1992 Kellogg's 3-D 933
1992 King-B 934
1992 Kodak White Sox 936
1992 L.A. Dodgers Police 939
1992 Leaf 945
1992 Leaf Previews 945
1992 Lime Rock Griffey Baseball Holograms 998
1992 Lykes Braves 1000
1992 Lykes Braves Team Photo Set 1000
1992 Marathon Cubs 1001
1992 McDonald's Baseball's Best 1002
1992 MCI Ambassadors 1004
1992 Megacards Babe Ruth 1005
1992 Megacards Babe Ruth Prototypes 1005
1992 Milwaukee Brewers Police 1014
1992 Minor League Team Sets 1795
1992 MJB Holoprisms 1018
1992 Modell's Team Mets 1026
1992 MooTown Snackers 1026
1992 Mother's Cookies A's 1032
1992 Mr. Turkey 1037
1992 MTV Rock n' Jock 1038
1992 MVP for MDA 1005
1992 N.Y. Mets Spring Training Superstars 1040
1992 Nabisco Canadian Tradition 1038
1992 Oakland A's Dream Team 1051
1992 Old Style Chicago Cubs 1053
1992 O-Pee-Chee 1048
1992 Pacific Gas & Electric S.F. Giants 1097
1992 Pacific Nolan Ryan 1056
1992 Pacific Tom Seaver 1056
1992 Panini Stickers 1101
1992 Pinnacle 1109
1992 Pittsburgh Brewing Co. Roberto Clemente Tribute 1130
1992 Post Cereal 1153
1992 Red Foley Stickers 909
1992 San Diego Padres Fire Safety 1159
1992 Score 1170
1992 Score Promos 1170
1992 Score/Pinnacle Promo Panels 1170
1992 Sentry Robin Yount 1195
1992 SkyBox AA 1793
1992 SkyBox AAA 1794
1992 Snyder's Bread Washington Sports Heroes 1210
1992 St. Louis Cardinals Police 1263
1992 Stadium Club 1266
1992 Star '92 1294
1992 Studio 1298
1992 Studio Preview 1297
1992 The Baseball Enquirer 535
1992 Topps 1357
1992 Topps Pre-Production 1357
1992 Toronto Blue Jays Fire Safety 1506
1992 Triple Play 1508
1992 Triple Play Previews 1507
1992 U.S. Playing Card Aces 1708
1992 U.S. Playing Card Detroit Tigers 1709
1992 Ultra 1511
1992 Ultra Pre-Production Samples 1511
1992 Upper Deck 1540
1992 Upper Deck Minor League 1794
1992 Wiz Yankees Classics 1716
1992 Ziploc 1722
1992-2000 Sports Illustrated For Kids 1262
1992-2004 Boy Scouts of America Atlanta Braves 591
1992-93 Action Packed Gold 529
1992-93 Canadian Card News Repli-Cards 595
1992-93 Fleer Excel 1793
1992-94 Conlon Collection Gold 625
1992-95 Front Row All-Time Great Series 911
1993 Action Packed 24-Kt. Gold 530
1993 Action Packed All-Star Gallery Series 2 529
1993 Action Packed Amoco/Coke 530
1993 Action Packed Tom Seaver Prototypes 530
1993 Barry Colla All-Stars 610
1993 Baseball Cards/Sports Cards Magazine Repli-Cards 535
1993 Bazooka Team USA 537
1993 Ben's Bakery Super Pitchers Discs 538
1993 Bleachers Barry Bonds 539
1993 Bleachers Nolan Ryan 23KT 540
1993 Bleachers Nolan Ryan 539
1993 Bleachers Promos 539
1993 Bleachers Ryne Sandberg 540
1993 Boston Red Sox Police 541
1993 Bowman 545
1993 Cadaco All-Star Baseball Discs 594
1993 California Angels Police 595
1993 City Pride Roberto Clemente 602
1993 Clark Candy Reggie Jackson 602
1993 Classic 4 Sport 1797
1993 Classic 605
1993 Classic Best 1796
1993 Classic Best Gold 1796
1993 Classic Best Young Guns 1796
1993 Classic Best/Fisher Nuts Stars of the Future 1797
1993 Classic Collectors Club (C3) 1797
1993 Cleveland Indians Team Issue 606
1993 Coca-Cola Commanders of the Hill 609
1993 Colorado Fever Rockies 622
1993 Conlon Collection 625
1993 Conlon Collection Color Masters 626
1993 Conlon Collection Master Series 626
1993 Conlon Collection Prototypes 625
1993 Country Time Brooks Robinson 627
1993 Cracker Jack Anniversary 628
1993 Dairy Queen Magic Mariner Moments Pin/Cards 630
1993 Dempster's Blue Jays 631
1993 Denny's Grand Slam 632
1993 Diamond Stars Extension Set 633
1993 DiamondMarks 633
1993 DiamondMarks Prototypes 633
1993 Donruss 657
1993 Donruss Previews 657
1993 Duracell Power Players 761
1993 Fax Pax 763
1993 Finest 764
1993 Finest Promos 763
1993 Flair 777
1993 Flair Promos 777
1993 Fleer 812
1993 Florida Agriculture Dept. Braves/Marlins 907
1993 Front Row Gold Collection 912
1993 Gatorade Detroit Tigers 914
1993 Highland Mint Mint-Cards 917
1993 Hills Pirates Kids Club 918
1993 Hostess Twinkies 920
1993 Hoyle Legends of Baseball 921
1993 Humpty Dumpty 921
1993 Jimmy Dean 631
1993 Kahn's Mets 925
1993 Kansas City Royals Police 927
1993 Kansas City Star Royals All-Time Team 928
1993 Keebler Texas Rangers 929
1993 King-B 934
1993 Kodak White Sox 936
1993 Kraft Pop-Up Action 937
1993 L.A. Dodgers Police 939
1993 Leaf 947
1993 Leaf Promo 947
1993 Lykes Braves 1000
1993 Marathon Cubs 1002
1993 McDonald's Blue Jays 1003
1993 MCI Ambassadors 1004
1993 Metallic Images Cooperstown Collection 1007
1993 Metz Bakeries 1012
1993 Milk Bone Super Stars 1012
1993 Milwaukee Brewers Police 1014
1993 Minor League Team Sets 1798
1993 Mother's Cookies Angels 1033
1993 Nabisco All-Star Autographs 1038
1993 Nolan Ryan Topps Stickers 1158
1993 Old Style Billy Williams 1053
1993 O-Pee-Chee 1049
1993 Pacific 1057
1993 Pacific Nolan Ryan 27th Season 1056
1993 Pacific/ McCormick Nolan Ryan Milestones 1057
1993 Panini Stickers 1102
1993 Pinnacle 1110
1993 Pinnacle Promos 1110
1993 Post Cereal 1153
1993 Publix Florida Marlins 1156
1993 Rainbow Foods Dave Winfield 1156
1993 Red Foley Stickers 909
1993 Retort Negro League Legends, Series 2 1157
1993 Rolaids Cubs Relief Pitchers 1158
1993 Score 1173
1993 Score Promos 1173
1993 Select 1188
1993 Select Dufex Proofs 1188
1993 Select Promos 1188
1993 Select Rookie/Traded 1189
1993 Sentry Brewers Memorable Moments 1195
1993 Sentry Milwaukee Brewers 1195
1993 SP 1211
1993 Spectrum Diamond Club Promo Set 1248
1993 Sports Card Pocket Price Guide 1160
1993 St. Louis Cardinals Police 1263
1993 Stadium Club 1268
1993 Star '93 Andy Benes 1295
1993 Studio 1298
1993 Studio Promos 1298
1993 Ted Williams Card Company 1713
1993 Ted Williams Co. Promos 1713
1993 Topps 1360
1993 Topps Pre-Production 1360
1993 Topps Pre-Production Sheet 1360
1993 Toronto Blue Jays Fire Safety 1506
1993 Toys "R" Us Topps Stadium Club 1507
1993 Triple Play 1508
1993 Triple Play Promos 1508
1993 U.S. Department of Transportation Safety Set 1708
1993 U.S. Playing Card Aces 1709
1993 Ultra 1513
1993 Upper Deck 1543
1993 USA Rice 1707
1993 Whataburger Nolan Ryan 1712
1993 Yoo-Hoo 1719
1993-94 Fleer Excel 1797
1993-94 Fleer Excel League Leaders 1798
1993-95 Conlon Collection Color 626
1994 Action Packed Scouting Report 1799

1994 AMC Theaters S.F. Giants 530
1994 American Archives Origins of Baseball 530
1994 Baltimore Orioles Program Cards 533
1994 Big Apple 1969 Mets Discs 538
1994 Bowman 546
1994 Bowman Previews 546
1994 Bowman's Best 547
1994 Burger King Cal Ripken Jr. 593
1994 Capital Cards 1969 Mets Postcards 596
1994 Churchs Chicken Hometown Stars 598
1994 Classic 4 Sport (Baseball) 1800
1994 Classic 4 Sport Auto. (Baseball) 1800
1994 Classic All-Star Minor League 1799
1994 Classic Assets (Baseball) 1799
1994 Classic Best Gold 1799
1994 Classic Best Illustrated Acetate 1800
1994 Classic Bonus Baby 1799
1994 Classic Collectors Club (C3) 1800
1994 Classic Cream of the Crop 1799
1994 Classic Images (Baseball) 1800
1994 Classic Tri-Cards 1800
1994 Classic Update Cal Ripken Tribute 1799
1994 Collector's Choice 611
1994 Collector's Choice Promos 611
1994 Colorado Rockies Police 622
1994 Conlon Collection 626
1994 Conlon Collection Burgundy 627
1994 Conlon Collection Prototypes 626
1994 Dairy Queen Ken Griffey, Jr. 630
1994 Denny's Grand Slam 632
1994 Donruss 660
1994 Donruss Promotional Samples 659
1994 FanFest Roberto Clemente Commemorative 762
1994 Finest 764
1994 Finest Pre-Production 764
1994 Flair 777
1994 Fleer "Highlights" Promo Sheet 815
1994 Fleer 815
1994 Highland Mint Mint-Cards 917
1994 Innovative Confections Sucker Savers 921
1994 International Playing Cards Toronto Blue Jays 922
1994 Kahn's Reds 925
1994 Kansas City Royals Police 927
1994 Kellogg's Clemente Collection 933
1994 King-B 934
1994 Kodak White Sox 936
1994 Kraft Pop-Ups 937
1994 KVTU-TV San Francisco Giants 937
1994 L.A. Dodgers Police 939
1994 Leaf 948
1994 Leaf Promos 948
1994 Leaf/Limited 950
1994 Leaf/Limited Promo 950
1994 Lite Beer Milwaukee Brewers 998
1994 Lykes Braves 1000
1994 Lykes Braves Team Photo Set 1000
1994 MCI Ambassadors 1004
1994 Mellon Bank Phillies 1006
1994 Miller Genuine Draft Milwaukee Brewers 1013
1994 Milwaukee Brewers Police 1014
1994 Minor League Team Sets 1803
1994 Mother's Cookies Angels 1033
1994 Nabisco All-Star Legends Autographs 1038
1994 O-Pee-Chee 1050
1994 O-Pee-Chee Sample Sheet 1050
1994 Oscar Mayer Superstar Pop-Ups 1054
1994 Pacific Crown 1058
1994 Pacific Crown Promos 1058
1994 Panini Stickers 1102
1994 Pinnacle 1113
1994 Pinnacle Samples 1113
1994 Post Cereal 1153
1994 PruCare N.Y. Mets 1154
1994 Red Foley 909
1994 Ron Lewis Negro Leagues Postcards 998
1994 Score 1174
1994 Score Rookie/ Traded Samples 1176
1994 Score Rookie/Traded 1176
1994 Score Samples 1174
1994 Select 1190
1994 Select Promos 1190
1994 Sentry Brewer Highlights 1195
1994 Signature Rookies 1801
1994 Signature Rookies Draft Picks 1801
1994 Signature Rookies Gold Standard (Baseball) 1802
1994 Signature Rookies Tetrad (Baseball) 1802
1994 SP 1211
1994 SP Promo 1211
1994 Spectrum 1969 Miracle Mets 1248
1994 Sportflics 2000 1253
1994 Sportflics 2000 Promos 1253
1994 Sportflics 2000 Rookie/ Traded 1253
1994 Sportflics 2000 Rookie/ Traded Promos 1253
1994 St. Louis Cardinals Police 1264
1994 Stadium Club 1271
1994 Stadium Club Draft Picks 1802
1994 Stadium Club Pre-production 1271
1994 Studio 1299
1994 Studio Samples 1299
1994 SuperSlam 1304
1994 Ted Williams Card Company 1714
1994 Tombstone Pizza 1315
1994 Topps 1362
1994 Topps Preview 1362
1994 Triple Play 1509
1994 Triple Play Promos 1509
1994 U.S. Playing Card Aces 1710
1994 Ultra 1514
1994 Upper Deck 1547
1994 Upper Deck Minor League 1802
1994 Vine Line Chicago Cubs Postcards 1712
1994 Wendy's Roberto Clemente Hologram 1712
1994 Yoo-Hoo 1719
1994-95 Fleer Excel 1800
1995 Action Packed 24KT Gold 1804
1995 Action Packed Scouting Report 1804
1995 Baseball's Hall of Famers Creating History 916
1995 Bazooka 537
1995 Bazooka Red Hot Inserts 537
1995 Best Top 100 1804
1995 Bowman 548
1995 Bowman's Best 548
1995 California Angels Police 595
1995 Cardtoons 596
1995 Classic 5 Sport (Baseball) 1804
1995 Classic Assets Gold (Baseball) 1804
1995 Classic Images '95 Classic Performances 1805
1995 Coca-Cola Minnesota Twins POGs 609
1995 Coca-Cola/ Publix Florida Marlins 609
1995 Collector's Choice 612
1995 Collector's Choice/SE 614
1995 Collector's Edge Ball Park Franks Baseball Legends 622
1995 Colorado Rockies Police 622
1995 Comic Images National Pastime Promo 623
1995 Comic Images The National Pastime 623
1995 Conlon Collection 627
1995 Conlon Collection Prototypes 627
1995 Denny's Classic Hits 632
1995 Donruss 662
1995 Donruss Samples 662
1995 FanFest Nolan Ryan Commemorative 762
1995 Finest 766
1995 Flair 778
1995 Fleer 819
1995 Fleer Promos 819
1995 Gatorade Cubs 914
1995 Highland Mint Mint-Cards 917
1995 International Playing Cards Toronto Blue Jays 922
1995 Jimmy Dean All Time Greats 631
1995 Kahn's Mets 925
1995 Kansas City Royals Police 927
1995 King-B 934
1995 Kodak Pittsburgh Pirates 936
1995 Kodak White Sox 937
1995 Kraft Singles Superstars 937
1995 L.A. Dodgers Limited Edition 939
1995 L.A. Dodgers Police 940
1995 Leaf 950
1995 Leaf Promos 950
1995 Leaf/Limited 952
1995 Lykes Braves 1000
1995 MCI Ambassadors 1004
1995 Megacards Ken Griffey, Jr. MegaCaps 1006
1995 Mellon Bank Phillies 1006
1995 Metallic Images Babe Ruth 1007
1995 Milwaukee Brewers Police 1014
1995 Minor League Team Sets 1807
1995 Mother's Cookies Angels 1034
1995 Mr. Turkey 1037
1995 National Packtime 1039
1995 Oakland A's CHP 1051
1995 Oh Henry! Toronto Blue Jays 1052
1995 Pacific 1060
1995 Pacific Prism 1061
1995 Pinnacle 1114
1995 Pinnacle Series 1 Samples 1114
1995 Post Cereal 1154
1995 Red Foley 909
1995 Score 1177
1995 Score Samples 1177
1995 Select 1191
1995 Select Certified 1192
1995 Select Certified Samples 1192
1995 Select Samples 1191
1995 Signature Rookies 1805
1995 Signature Rookies Preview 1805
1995 Signature Rookies Star Squad 1805
1995 Signature Rookies T-95 Old Judge Series 1806
1995 Signature Rookies Tetrad (Baseball) 1805
1995 Signature Rookies Tetrad Autobilia (Baseball) 1805
1995 Signature Rookies Tetrad B-1 Bomber 1806
1995 Signature Rookies Tetrad SR Force (Baseball) 1806
1995 Skin Bracer 1198
1995 SkyBox E-Motion 1198
1995 SkyBox E-Motion Promo 1198
1995 Sonic/Coke Heroes of Baseball 1210
1995 Sonic/Pepsi Baseball Greats 1210
1995 South Carolina Athletic Hall of Fame 1211
1995 SP 1212
1995 SP/ Championship 1213
1995 Sportflix 1254
1995 Sportflix Samples 1254
1995 Sportflix/UC3 1255
1995 Sportflix/UC3 Samples 1255
1995 St. Louis Cardinals Police 1264
1995 Stadium Club 1274
1995 Star Cal Ripken, Jr. 1295
1995 Stouffer's Legends of Baseball 1296
1995 Studio 1300
1995 Summit 1303
1995 Summit Samples 1302
1995 Tombstone Pizza 1315
1995 Topps 1365
1995 Topps Pre-production 1365
1995 U.S. Playing Card Aces 1711
1995 Ultra 1516
1995 Ultra Second Year Standouts 1518
1995 Upper Deck 1551
1995 Upper Deck Minor League 1806
1995 Upper Deck/ SP Top Prospects 1807
1995 Wienerschnitzel L.A. Dodgers POGs 1713
1995 Zenith 1719
1995 Zenith Samples 1719
1996 Arby's Cleveland Indians 531
1996 Arizona Lottery 531
1996 Bazooka 537
1996 Bazooka Mickey Mantle 1959 Reprint 537
1996 Best Autograph Series 1808
1996 Bowman 549
1996 Bowman's Best 550
1996 Bowman's Best Preview 550
1996 Canadian Club Classic Stars of the Game 595
1996 Chevrolet/ Geo Pirates Team Sheet 597
1996 Circa 599
1996 Classic Assets (Baseball) 1808
1996 Classic Signings (Baseball) 1808
1996 Classic Visions (Baseball) 1808
1996 Classic Visions Signings (Baseball) 1808
1996 Classic Visions Signings (Baseball) Auto. 1808
1996 Classic/ Metallic Impressions Nolan Ryan 605
1996 Coca-Cola/ Kroger Nolan Ryan Card/Pin 609
1996 Collector's Choice 615
1996 Collector's Choice Promo 615
1996 Colorado Rockies Police 623
1996 Denny's Grand Slam 632
1996 Denny's Instant Replay Holograms 632
1996 Donruss 664
1996 Donruss Samples 664
1996 Donruss Showdown 665
1996 FanFest Steve Carlton Commemorative 762
1996 Finest 767
1996 Flair 780
1996 Flair Promotional Sheet 780
1996 Fleer 821
1996 Fleer Excel 1808
1996 Hebrew National Detroit Tigers 916
1996 Kahn's Mets 925
1996 Kansas City Royals Police 927
1996 King-B 934
1996 Klosterman Baking Big Red Machine 935
1996 L.A. Dodgers Police 940
1996 Leaf 953
1996 Leaf/ Signature Series 955
1996 Leaf/ Signature Series Extended Autographs 956
1996 Leaf/Limited 954
1996 Leaf/Preferred 954
1996 Legends of the Negro Leagues Playing Cards 997
1996 Liberty Satellite Sports 998
1996 Lykes Braves Team Photo Set 1001
1996 MCI Ambassadors 1004
1996 Metal Universe 1007
1996 Metal Universe Sample Sheet 1007
1996 Metal Universe Titanium 1008
1996 Metallic Impressions Ken Griffey, Jr. 1007
1996 Milwaukee Brewers Police 1015
1996 Minor League Team Sets 1810
1996 Mother's Cookies Angels 1035
1996 Oh Henry! Toronto Blue Jays 1052
1996 Pacific Crown 1061
1996 Pacific Prism 1063
1996 Pepsi-Cola Cubs Convention 1104
1996 Pinnacle 1116
1996 Pinnacle Samples 1116
1996 Pinnacle/Aficionado 1118
1996 Pizza Hut 1130
1996 Red Foley 909
1996 Revco Cleveland Indians 1157
1996 Schwebel's Stars Discs 1160
1996 Score 1179
1996 Score Samples 1179
1996 Select 1192
1996 Select Certified 1193
1996 Signature Rookies Old Judge T-96 1809
1996 Signature Rookies Rookie of the Year 1810

1996 SkyBox E-Motion XL 1199
1996 SP 1214
1996 SP FanFest Promos 1214
1996 SP SpecialFX 1214
1996 Sportflix 1255
1996 SPx 1215
1996 St. Louis Browns Historical Society 1263
1996 St. Louis Cardinals Police 1264
1996 Stadium Club 1277
1996 Studio 1300
1996 Summit 1303
1996 Team Metal Ken Griffey Jr. 1314
1996 Team Out! Game 1314
1996 Topps 1369
1996 Topps Chrome 1372
1996 Topps Chrome Promo Sheet 1372
1996 Topps Gallery 1372
1996 Topps Laser 1373
1996 Topps Pre-Production 1369
1996 Ultra 1518
1996 Ultra Promotional Samples 1518
1996 Upper Deck 1553
1996 Upper Deck Promo 1553
1996 Zenith 1720
1996-2003 Danbury Mint 22kt Gold Cooperstown Collection 630
1996-97 Score Board All Sport PPF 1187
1996-98 Sports Illustrated For Kids Legends 1262
1997 AT&T Ambassadors of Baseball 532
1997 Best Auto. Supers 1811
1997 Best Autograph Series 1811
1997 Best Full Count Autographs 1811
1997 Best Premium Autographs 1811
1997 Best Prospects 1810
1997 Big League Chew Alumni 538
1997 Bowman 550
1997 Bowman Chrome 552
1997 Bowman Pre-Production 550
1997 Bowman's Best 552
1997 Bowman's Best Preview 552
1997 Burger King Cal Ripken Jr. 593
1997 Circa 599
1997 Collector's Choice 617
1997 Colorado Rockies Police 623
1997 Cracker Jack All Stars 628
1997 Denny's 3-D Holograms 632
1997 Donruss 665
1997 Donruss Elite 668
1997 Donruss Limited 668
1997 Donruss Preferred 669
1997 Donruss Signature 670
1997 Donruss VXP 1.0 672
1997 FanFest Jackie Robinson Commemorative 762
1997 Finest 767
1997 Finest Samples 767
1997 Flair Showcase Promo Strip 781
1997 Flair Showcase Row 2 (Style) 781
1997 Fleer 825
1997 Gatorade Cubs 915
1997 Hebrew National Detroit Tigers 917
1997 Jimmy Dean Great Moments 631
1997 Kahn's Reds 926
1997 Kansas City Royals Police 928
1997 King-B 934
1997 L.A. Dodgers Fan Appreciation Days 940
1997 LaSalle Bank Ryne Sandberg 941
1997 Leaf 956
1997 McDonald's N.Y. Yankees 1003
1997 Metal Universe 1008
1997 Metallic Impressions Jackie Robinson 1007
1997 Milk Mustache Trading Cards 1012
1997 Milwaukee Brewers Police 1015
1997 Minnesota Twins 10th Anniversary 1017
1997 Minor League Team Sets 1811
1997 Mother's Cookies Angels 1036
1997 N.Y. Mets Motion Cards 1040
1997 New Pinnacle 1120
1997 New Pinnacle Samples 1120
1997 Oh Henry! Toronto Blue Jays 1052
1997 Pacific Crown 1064
1997 Pacific Invincible 1065
1997 Pinnacle 1119
1997 Pinnacle Certified 1121
1997 Pinnacle FanFest 1122
1997 Pinnacle Inside 1123
1997 Pinnacle X-Press 1124
1997 Score 1181
1997 Score Board Mickey Mantle Shoe Box Collection 1187
1997 Select 1194
1997 Select Samples 1194
1997 SkyBox E-X2000 1199
1997 SkyBox E-X2000 Sample 1199
1997 SP 1215
1997 SP Sample 1215
1997 SP Special FX 1216
1997 Sports Illustrated 1257
1997 SPx 1216
1997 Stadium Club 1280
1997 Stadium Club Pre-Production 1280
1997 Studio 1301
1997 Topps 1374
1997 Topps Chrome 1376
1997 Topps Gallery 1377
1997 Topps Gallery Pre-production 1377
1997 Topps Stars 1377
1997 Topps Stars Promos 1377
1997 Totally Certified Samples 1122
1997 Ultra 1521
1997 Ultra Promo Strip 1521
1997 Upper Deck 1556
1997 Upper Deck UD3 1559
1997 Wheaties All-Stars 1713
1997 Zenith 1720
1997 Zenith Samples 1720
1997-2002 Major League Dad 1001
1998 Ball Park Detroit Tigers 533
1998 Best Auto. 1812
1998 Bowman 553
1998 Bowman Chrome 554
1998 Bowman's Best 555
1998 Bryan Braves Team Photo Set 591
1998 CHW San Francisco Giants 598
1998 Circa Thunder 600
1998 Coca-Cola Chipper Jones 609
1998 Collector's Choice 620
1998 Colorado Rockies Police 623
1998 CyberAction 630
1998 Donruss 672
1998 Donruss Elite 675
1998 Donruss Preferred 676
1998 Donruss Signature Series 677
1998 Donruss Signature Series Preview Autographs 677
1998 FanFest Lou Brock Commemorative 762
1998 Finest 768
1998 Finest Pre-Production 768
1998 Flair Showcase Promo Strip 781
1998 Flair Showcase Row 3 781
1998 Fleer 827
1998 Fruit Roll-Ups All-Stars 912
1998 Hamburger Helper Home Run Heroes 916
1998 Hershey's Baltimore Orioles 917
1998 Kahn's Reds 926
1998 Kansas City Royals Police 928
1998 King-B 934
1998 L.A. Dodgers Fan Appreciation Days 940
1998 Leaf 959
1998 Leaf Fractal Materials 960
1998 Leaf Fractal Materials Samples 960
1998 Leaf Fractal Matrix 961
1998 Leaf Limited Star Factor Sample 962
1998 Leaf Rookies & Stars 962
1998 Lemon Chill Chicago White Sox 997
1998 McDonald's Arizona Diamondbacks 1003
1998 Metal Universe 1009
1998 Milwaukee Brewers Diamond Celebration 1015
1998 Minor League Team Sets 1813
1998 Mother's Cookies A's 1037
1998 Mr. Sub Roger Clemens 1037
1998 Oh Henry! Toronto Blue Jays 1053
1998 Pacific 1066
1998 Pacific Aurora 1067
1998 Pacific Crown Royale 1068
1998 Pacific Invincible 1069
1998 Pacific Omega 1070
1998 Pacific Online 1071
1998 Pacific Paramount 1072
1998 Pacific Revolution 1073
1998 Pepsi-Cola Arizona Diamondbacks 1105
1998 Pinnacle 1124
1998 Pinnacle Inside 1126
1998 Pinnacle Mint Collection 1127
1998 Pinnacle Performers 1127
1998 Pinnacle Plus 1128
1998 Pinnacle Samples 1124
1998 Pinnacle Snapshots 1129
1998 Ronnie Joyner St. Louis Browns Heads-Up 923
1998 Score 1184
1998 Score Rookie & Traded 1185
1998 Score Samples 1183
1998 Score Team Collection 1186
1998 Select 1195
1998 Select Selected 1195
1998 Select Selected Samples 1195
1998 SkyBox Dugout Axcess 1201
1998 SkyBox Dugout Axcess Promo 1201
1998 SkyBox E-X2001 1200
1998 SkyBox E-X2001 Sample 1200
1998 SP Authentic 1216
1998 SP Authentic Sample 1216
1998 Sports Illustrated 1258
1998 Sports Illustrated Promo 1258
1998 SPx Finite 1217
1998 SPx Finite Sample 1217
1998 St. Louis Cardinals Police 1264
1998 Stadium Club 1281
1998 Studio 1301
1998 Team Best Diamond Best 1812
1998 Team Best Paul Konerko 1812
1998 Team Best Player of the Year 1812
1998 Team Best Possibilities 1813
1998 Team Best Signature Series 1813
1998 Team Pinnacle Baseball 1130
1998 Topps 1378
1998 Topps Chrome 1381
1998 Topps Gallery 1382
1998 Topps Gallery Pre-Production Samples 1382
1998 Topps Pre-Production 1378
1998 Topps Stars 1384
1998 Topps Stars Pre-Production 1384
1998 Topps TEK 1385
1998 Topps TEK Pre-Production 1385
1998 UD Retro 1564
1998 UD Retro Quantum Leap 1565
1998 Ultra 1523
1998 Upper Deck 1560
1998 Upper Deck SP Prospects 1813
1998 Upper Deck Special F/X 1563
1998 Upper Deck UD 3 1564
1998 Virginia Lottery Baseball Legends Cards 1712
1998 Washington Senators 1969 Reunion 1712
1998 Zenith 1721
1998 Zenith Samples 1721
1998-99 Philadelphia A's Historical Society 1108
1999 Anaheim Angels Police 531
1999 Bowman 556
1999 Bowman Chrome 557
1999 Bowman Pre-Production 556
1999 Bowman's Best 559
1999 Bowman's Best Pre-Production 558
1999 Bryan Braves 592
1999 Burger King N.Y. Yankees 593
1999 Colorado Rockies Police 623
1999 Cracker Jack Mac Stickers 628
1999 Cracker Jack Mark McGwire Home Run Record 628
1999 Cracker Jack Mark McGwire Spinners 628
1999 Diamond Authentics Signature Series 1814
1999 FanFest Carl Yastrzemski Commemorative 762
1999 Finest 770
1999 Flair Showcase Row 3 (Power) 782
1999 Fleer 830
1999 Fleer Mystique 833
1999 FroZsnack's High-Screamers Lids 912
1999 GTE Tampa Bay Devil Rays 915
1999 Hillshire Farm Home Run Heroes 918
1999 Homers Cookies 920
1999 Just Autographs Black 1816
1999 Just Imagine 1814
1999 Just Justifiable 1815
1999 Just The Start 1815
1999 Kahn's Reds 926
1999 Keebler Los Angeles Dodgers 930
1999 King-B 934
1999 L.A. Dodgers Concession Stand Cards 940
1999 Lemon Chill Chicago White Sox 997
1999 McDonald's Mark McGwire Milestones 1004
1999 McDonald's St. Louis Cardinals 1004
1999 Metal Universe 1010
1999 Metal Universe Sample Sheet 1010
1999 Milwaukee Brewers Diamond Celebration 1015
1999 Minor League Team Sets 1818
1999 Oh Henry! Toronto Blue Jays 1053
1999 Old Style Chicago Cubs All-Century Team 1053
1999 Pacific 1075
1999 Pacific Aurora 1076
1999 Pacific Crown Collection 1077
1999 Pacific Crown Collection Sample 1077
1999 Pacific Crown Royale 1077
1999 Pacific Invincible 1078
1999 Pacific Omega 1079
1999 Pacific Omega Sample 1079
1999 Pacific Paramount 1080
1999 Pacific Paramount Sample 1080
1999 Pacific Prism 1081
1999 Pacific Prism Sample 1081
1999 Pacific Private Stock 1081
1999 Pacific Revolution 1082
1999 Pacific Sample 1074
1999 Pepsi-Cola Arizona Diamondbacks 1105
1999 Plumbers Local 342 Oakland A's 1051
1999 Pop Secret Detroit Tigers 1153
1999 SI for Kids 10th Anniversary Sheet 1262
1999 SkyBox E-X Century 1202
1999 SkyBox Molten Metal 1203
1999 SkyBox Premium 1204
1999 SkyBox Thunder 1205
1999 SP Authentic 1218
1999 SP Authentic Sample 1218
1999 SP Signature Edition 1219
1999 SP Top Prospects 1816
1999 Sports Illustrated 1260
1999 SPx 1220
1999 Stadium Club 1283
1999 Starting Lineup Classic Doubles 1816
1999 Team Best BA's Diamond Best Inserts 1817

1999 Team Best Baseball America's Diamond Best Edition ... 1816
1999 Team Best Baseball America's Top Prospects ... 1817
1999 Team Best Player of the Year ... 1817
1999 Team Best Rookie ... 1817
1999 Team Best Salvino Rookie Bammers Card/ Authenticity ... 1818
1999 Topps ... 1385
1999 Topps Chrome ... 1388
1999 Topps Gallery ... 1389
1999 Topps Gallery Pre-Production ... 1389
1999 Topps Gold Label Class 1 ... 1390
1999 Topps Gold Label Pre-Production ... 1390
1999 Topps Pre-Production ... 1385
1999 Topps Stars ... 1391
1999 Topps Stars Pre-Production ... 1391
1999 Topps TEK ... 1393
1999 Topps TEK Pre-Production ... 1393
1999 U.S. Cellular Milwaukee Brewers ... 1707
1999 UD Ionix ... 1572
1999 UD Retro ... 1575
1999 Ultra ... 1525
1999 Ultra Sample Sheet ... 1525
1999 Upper Deck ... 1565
1999 Upper Deck Black Diamond ... 1567
1999 Upper Deck Century Legends ... 1568
1999 Upper Deck Challengers for 70 ... 1569
1999 Upper Deck Encore ... 1571
1999 Upper Deck HoloGrFX ... 1572
1999 Upper Deck HoloGrFX Sample ... 1572
1999 Upper Deck MVP ... 1573
1999 Upper Deck MVP Samples ... 1573
1999 Upper Deck Ovation ... 1574
1999 Upper Deck PowerDeck ... 1575
1999 Upper Deck UD Choice ... 1570
1999 Upper Deck UD Choice Previews ... 1570
1999 Upper Deck Ultimate Victory ... 1576
1st Year Phenoms ... 1801
2000 7-11 Slurpee Coins ... 1197
2000 Anaheim Angels Police ... 531
2000 APBA Super Stars Baseball ... 531
2000 Bowman ... 559
2000 Bowman Bowman's Best Previews ... 560
2000 Bowman Chrome ... 561
2000 Bowman Chrome Draft Picks and Prospects ... 562
2000 Bowman Draft Picks and Prospects ... 562
2000 Bowman's Best ... 562
2000 Bowman's Best Pre-Production ... 562
2000 Bryan Braves ... 592
2000 CaP Cure Home Run Challenge ... 595
2000 Colorado Rockies Police ... 623
2000 E-X ... 1208
2000 FanFest Hank Aaron Commemorative ... 762
2000 FanFest Hank Aaron Rookie Reprint ... 762
2000 Finest ... 771
2000 Fleer Focus ... 834
2000 Fleer Gamers ... 835
2000 Fleer Greats of the Game ... 835
2000 Fleer Impact ... 836
2000 Fleer Mystique ... 837
2000 Fleer Showcase ... 838
2000 Fleer Tradition ... 839
2000 Fleer Tradition Update ... 840
2000 High School All-Americans ... 1818
2000 Just Autographs Black ... 1820
2000 Just Graded 2k ... 1820
2000 Just Imagine 2k ... 1818
2000 Just Justifiable 2k ... 1819
2000 Just Minors Mystery Signatures ... 1820
2000 Just the Preview 2k ... 1819
2000 Kahn's Reds ... 926
2000 Kansas City Royals Police ... 928
2000 Keebler Arizona Diamondbacks ... 930
2000 King-B ... 935
2000 Klosterman Bakery Big Red Machine ... 935
2000 L.A. Dodgers Fan Appreciation Days ... 941
2000 Lemon Chill Chicago White Sox ... 997
2000 McDonald's Negro League Baseball ... 1004
2000 Metal ... 1011
2000 Milwaukee Brewers Diamond Celebration ... 1015
2000 Milwaukee Journal Sentinel 1970s Brewers ... 1016
2000 Minor League Team Sets ... 1822
2000 MLB Showdown 1st Edition ... 1018
2000 MLB Showdown Pennant Run ... 1019
2000 MLB Showdown Pennant Run Promos ... 1019
2000 MLB Showdown Promos ... 1018
2000 Oh Henry! Toronto Blue Jays ... 1053
2000 Pacific ... 1083
2000 Pacific Aurora ... 1085
2000 Pacific Aurora Sample ... 1085
2000 Pacific Crown Collection ... 1085
2000 Pacific Crown Collection Sample ... 1085
2000 Pacific Crown Royale ... 1086
2000 Pacific Invincible ... 1087
2000 Pacific Omega ... 1088
2000 Pacific Paramount ... 1089
2000 Pacific Paramount Sample ... 1089
2000 Pacific Prism ... 1090
2000 Pacific Private Stock ... 1092
2000 Pacific Revolution ... 1093
2000 Pacific Sample ... 1083
2000 Pacific Vanguard ... 1094
2000 Pacific Vanguard Sample ... 1094
2000 Palm Beach Post Montreal Expos ... 1097
2000 Palm Beach Post St. Louis Cardinals ... 1097
2000 Pepsi-Cola Arizona Diamondbacks ... 1105
2000 Plumbers Local 342 Oakland A's ... 1051
2000 Royal Rookies Elite Eight ... 1821
2000 Royal Rookies Signature Series ... 1820
2000 SkyBox ... 1206
2000 SkyBox Dominion ... 1207
2000 SkyBox National Covention Promos ... 1206
2000 SP Authentic ... 1221
2000 SP Top Prospects ... 1821
2000 SPx ... 1222
2000 St. Louis Cardinals Police ... 1264
2000 Stadium Club ... 1284
2000 Stadium Club Chrome ... 1286
2000 Stadium Club Chrome Preview ... 1286
2000 Team Best Rookies 2000 ... 1821
2000 Team Nabisco All Stars ... 1038
2000 Topps ... 1393
2000 Topps Chrome ... 1396
2000 Topps Gallery ... 1398
2000 Topps Gold Label Class 1 ... 1399
2000 Topps Gold Label Pre-Production ... 1399
2000 Topps HD ... 1400
2000 Topps Opening Day ... 1396
2000 Topps Pre-Production ... 1393
2000 Topps Stars ... 1400
2000 Topps TEK ... 1401
2000 Topps Traded and Rookies ... 1395
2000 U.S. Playing Card All Century Baseball Team ... 1711
2000 U.S. Postal Service Legends of Baseball Stamps ... 1711
2000 UD Black Diamond Rookie Edition Diamond Might ... 1582
2000 UD Ionix ... 1584
2000 UD N.Y. Yankees Master Collection ... 1587
2000 Ultra ... 1526
2000 Ultra Sample ... 1526
2000 Upper Deck ... 1578
2000 Upper Deck Black Diamond ... 1580
2000 Upper Deck Gold Reserve ... 1582
2000 Upper Deck Hitter's Club ... 1583
2000 Upper Deck HoloGrFX ... 1584
2000 Upper Deck Legends ... 1585
2000 Upper Deck MVP ... 1586
2000 Upper Deck Ovation ... 1587
2000 Upper Deck PowerDeck ... 1588
2000 Upper Deck Pros and Prospects ... 1588
2000 Upper Deck Rookie Update ... 1589
2000 Upper Deck Ultimate Victory ... 1589
2000 Upper Deck Yankees Legends ... 1591
2000 Upper Deck Yankees Legends Sample ... 1591
2000 USPS Legends of Baseball Post Cards ... 1711
2000 USPS Legends of Baseball Postal Card Booklet ... 1711
2000 Verizon Tampa Bay Devil Rays ... 1711
2000-2005 Sports Illustrated for Kids ... 1262
2001 Armour Stars ... 532
2001 Boston Red Sox 100 Seasons ... 541
2001 Bowman ... 563
2001 Bowman Chrome ... 564
2001 Bowman Draft Picks & Prospects ... 565
2001 Bowman Heritage ... 566
2001 Bowman Heritage Promos ... 566
2001 Bowman's Best ... 567
2001 Bowman's Best Pre-Production ... 567
2001 Bryan Braves ... 592
2001 CaP Cure Home Run Challenge ... 596
2001 Donruss 2001 Diamond Kings ... 679
2001 Donruss ... 678
2001 Donruss Class of 2001 ... 682
2001 Donruss Class of 2001 Samples ... 682
2001 Donruss Classics ... 681
2001 Donruss Elite ... 683
2001 Donruss Elite Passing the Torch ... 684
2001 Donruss Signature Series ... 685
2001 Donruss Studio ... 686
2001 Donruss The Rookies ... 687
2001 E-X ... 842
2001 FanFest Seattle Mariners ... 762
2001 Finest ... 773
2001 Fleer Authority ... 841
2001 Fleer Boston Red Sox 100th Anniversary ... 842
2001 Fleer Cal Ripken Jr. Commemoratives ... 842
2001 Fleer Focus ... 843
2001 Fleer Futures ... 844
2001 Fleer Game Time ... 845
2001 Fleer Genuine ... 846
2001 Fleer Greats of the Game ... 846
2001 Fleer Legacy ... 847
2001 Fleer Platinum ... 848
2001 Fleer Platinum Rack Pack Autographs ... 849
2001 Fleer Platinum RC ... 849
2001 Fleer Premium ... 850
2001 Fleer Premium Solid Performers Game Base ... 851
2001 Fleer Showcase ... 851
2001 Fleer Tradition ... 852
2001 Fleer Triple Crown ... 853
2001 Hall of Fame Postcards ... 916
2001 Kahn's Reds ... 926
2001 Kansas City Royals Police ... 928
2001 Keebler Arizona Diamondbacks ... 931
2001 King-B ... 935
2001 King-B League Legends ... 935
2001 L.A. Dodgers Fan Appreciation Days ... 941
2001 Leaf Certified Materials ... 964
2001 Leaf Limited ... 965
2001 Leaf Rookies & Stars ... 965
2001 Leaf Rookies & Stars Samples ... 965
2001 Legends European Tour ... 997
2001 Milwaukee Brewers Diamond Celebration ... 1015
2001 Minor League Team Sets ... 1825
2001 MLB Showdown 1st Edition ... 1019
2001 MLB Showdown Pennant Run ... 1020
2001 MLB Showdown Pennant Run Promos ... 1020
2001 MLB Showdown Promos ... 1019
2001 Mrs. Baird's Breadwinners Texas Rangers ... 1038
2001 Nabisco Latino Legends of Baseball ... 1039
2001 Norstan Milwaukee Brewers Walk of Fame ... 1040
2001 Oakland A's Cal Ripken Farewell ... 1051
2001 Oh Henry! Toronto Blue Jays ... 1053
2001 Pacific ... 1094
2001 Pacific Private Stock ... 1096
2001 Pacific Sports Promotions Reprints ... 1823
2001 Palm Beach Post N.Y. Mets ... 1097
2001 Pepsi-Cola Arizona Diamondbacks ... 1105
2001 Philadelphia A's Historical Society Update ... 1108
2001 Playoff Absolute Memorabilia ... 1130
2001 Post 500 Home Run Club ... 1154
2001 Post Collector's Series ... 1154
2001 Rainbow Foods Minnesota Twins 10th Anniversary ... 1156
2001 Royal Rookies Futures ... 1823
2001 Royal Rookies Throwbacks ... 1823
2001 Skippy Peanut Butter Derek Jeter ... 1198
2001 SP Authentic ... 1223
2001 SP Authentic Sample ... 1223
2001 SP Authentic Stars of Japan ... 1224
2001 SP Game Bat ... 1224
2001 SP Legendary Cuts ... 1226
2001 SP Top Prospects ... 1823
2001 SPx ... 1227
2001 SPx Sample ... 1227
2001 St. Louis Cardinals Police ... 1264
2001 Stadium Club ... 1287
2001 Stadium Club Super Teams ... 1287
2001 Sunoco Dream Team ... 1304
2001 Team Best Authentic Autograph Cards ... 1824
2001 Team Best Babbitt's Bombers ... 1824
2001 Team Best Best Lumber ... 1824
2001 Team Best Set Collector Edition ... 1824
2001 The Big Book of Jewish Baseball ... 538
2001 Topps ... 1402
2001 Topps American Pie ... 1405
2001 Topps Archives ... 1406
2001 Topps Chrome ... 1407
2001 Topps Fusion ... 1410
2001 Topps Gallery ... 1411
2001 Topps Gold Label ... 1411
2001 Topps HD ... 1412
2001 Topps Heritage ... 1412
2001 Topps Heritage Pre-Production ... 1412
2001 Topps Opening Day ... 1405
2001 Topps Promo Cards ... 1402
2001 Topps Reserve ... 1414
2001 Topps Stars ... 1414
2001 Topps Traded & Rookies ... 1409
2001 Topps Tribute ... 1415
2001 UD Minor League Centennial Game-Used Bat ... 1825
2001 UD Reserve ... 1601
2001 Ultra ... 1528
2001 Upper Deck ... 1591
2001 Upper Deck Decade ... 1594
2001 Upper Deck Evolution ... 1595
2001 Upper Deck Game Jersey ... 1593
2001 Upper Deck Game-Used Ball ... 1593
2001 Upper Deck Gold Glove ... 1595
2001 Upper Deck Hall of Famers ... 1596
2001 Upper Deck Legends ... 1597
2001 Upper Deck Legends of New York ... 1597
2001 Upper Deck Minor League Baseball Centennial ... 1824
2001 Upper Deck MVP ... 1598
2001 Upper Deck Ovation ... 1599
2001 Upper Deck Pros & Prospects ... 1600
2001 Upper Deck Prospect Premieres ... 1600
2001 Upper Deck Rookie Update ... 1602
2001 Upper Deck Sweet Spot ... 1603
2001 Upper Deck Ultimate Collection ... 1603
2001 Upper Deck Vintage ... 1605
2001 Upper Deck Vintage Sample ... 1605
2002 Bowman ... 567
2002 Bowman Chrome ... 568
2002 Bowman Chrome Draft Picks & Prospects ... 570
2002 Bowman Draft Picks & Prospects ... 569
2002 Bowman Heritage ... 570

2002 Bowman's Best 571
2002 Bryan Braves Team Photo Set 592
2002 CaP Cure Home Run Challenge 596
2002 Coca-Cola S.F. Giants 609
2002 Colorado Rockies Police 623
2002 Cracker Jack All-Stars 628
2002 Disabled American Veterans 634
2002 Donruss 687
2002 Donruss Classics 688
2002 Donruss Classics Samples 688
2002 Donruss Diamond Kings 689
2002 Donruss Diamond Kings Samples 689
2002 Donruss Elite 690
2002 Donruss Elite Samples 690
2002 Donruss Fan Club 691
2002 Donruss Originals 692
2002 Donruss Originals Samples 692
2002 Donruss Samples 687
2002 Donruss Studio 694
2002 Donruss Studio Samples 694
2002 Donruss The Rookies 695
2002 FanFest 762
2002 FanFest Game-Used Base Cards 762
2002 Finest 773
2002 Fleer 854
2002 Fleer Authentix 856
2002 Fleer Box Score 856
2002 Fleer E-X 857
2002 Fleer Fall Classic 859
2002 Fleer Flair 860
2002 Fleer Focus Jersey Edition 860
2002 Fleer Genuine 861
2002 Fleer Greats of the Game 862
2002 Fleer Hot Prospects 863
2002 Fleer Hot Prospects We're Number One 863
2002 Fleer Maximum 864
2002 Fleer Platinum 864
2002 Fleer Premium 865
2002 Fleer Showcase 866
2002 Fleer Showcase Baseball's Best 867
2002 Fleer Showcase Legacy 867
2002 Fleer Tradition 867
2002 Fleer Triple Crown 869
2002 Franz Bread Seattle Mariners 910
2002 Just Justifiable 1825
2002 Just Prospects 1826
2002 Kahn's Reds 926
2002 Kansas City Royals Police 928
2002 Keebler Arizona Diamondbacks 931
2002 King-B 935
2002 L.A. Dodgers Police 941
2002 Leaf 966
2002 Leaf Certified 968
2002 Leaf Certified Samples 968
2002 Leaf Rookies & Stars 969
2002 Leaf Rookies & Stars Samples 969
2002 Leaf Samples 966
2002 Milwaukee Brewers Diamond Celebration 1016
2002 Minnesota Twins Police 1017
2002 Minor League Team Sets 1828
2002 MLB Showdown 1021
2002 MLB Showdown Promos 1021
2002 MLB Showdown Stars Promos 1022
2002 Nabisco Philadelphia Phillies 1039
2002 Nestle 1040
2002 Palm Beach Post N.Y. Mets 1097
2002 Pepsi-Cola Seattle Mariners 1105
2002 Playoff Absolute Memorabilia 1131
2002 Playoff Absolute Memorabilia Samples 1131
2002 Playoff Piece of the Game 1133
2002 Plumbers Local 342 Oakland A's 1051
2002 Poland Spring Boston Red Sox 1152
2002 Post Collector's Series 1154
2002 Select Rookies & Prospects Autographs 1195
2002 SP Authentic 1227
2002 SP Legendary Cuts 1228
2002 SPx 1228
2002 St. Louis Cardinals Police 1264
2002 Stadium Club Relic Edition 1287
2002 Topps 1416
2002 Topps Archives 1418
2002 Topps Archives Reserve 1419
2002 Topps Chrome 1419
2002 Topps eTopps 1421
2002 Topps Gallery 1421
2002 Topps Gold Label 1422
2002 Topps Heritage 1422
2002 Topps Opening Day 1423
2002 Topps Pristine 1424
2002 Topps Promos 1416
2002 Topps Reserve 1424
2002 Topps Super Teams 1425
2002 Topps Ten 1425
2002 Topps Total 1426
2002 Topps Total Pre-Production 1426
2002 Topps Traded & Rookies 1428
2002 Topps Tribute 1428
2002 Topps206 1429
2002 Toronto Blue Jays Team Issue 1506
2002 UD Authentics 1609
2002 Ultra 1529
2002 Upper Deck 1607
2002 Upper Deck 40-Man 1620
2002 Upper Deck Ballpark Idols 1609
2002 Upper Deck Collectors Club 1610
2002 Upper Deck Diamond Connection 1610
2002 Upper Deck Honor Roll 1611
2002 Upper Deck Minor League 1827
2002 Upper Deck MVP 1612
2002 Upper Deck Ovation 1612
2002 Upper Deck Piece of History 1613
2002 Upper Deck Prospect Premieres 1614
2002 Upper Deck Rookie Debut 1614
2002 Upper Deck Rookie Update 1615
2002 Upper Deck Sweet Spot 1615
2002 Upper Deck Sweet Spot Classics 1616
2002 Upper Deck UD-Plus 1616
2002 Upper Deck Ultimate Collection 1617
2002 Upper Deck USA Baseball 1828
2002 Upper Deck Victory 1617
2002 Upper Deck Vintage 1618
2002 Upper Deck World Series Heroes 1619
2002 Viagra Rafael Palmeiro 1712
2003 Arizona Diamondbacks Can Kickers Club 531
2003 Bowman 571
2003 Bowman Chrome 572
2003 Bowman Chrome Draft Picks & Prospects 573
2003 Bowman Draft Picks & Prospects 573
2003 Bowman Heritage 573
2003 Bowman's Best 574
2003 Carl's Jr. San Diego Padres 597
2003 Cincinnati Reds Scratch-Offs 599
2003 Cracker Jack All-Stars 628
2003 Disabled American Veterans 634
2003 Donruss 697
2003 Donruss Champions 698
2003 Donruss Classics 699
2003 Donruss Classics Samples 699
2003 Donruss Diamond Kings 701
2003 Donruss Diamond Kings Inserts Hawaii 701
2003 Donruss Diamond Kings Samples 701
2003 Donruss Elite 702
2003 Donruss Rookie & Traded 703
2003 Donruss Samples 697
2003 Donruss Signature Series 704
2003 Donruss Studio 705
2003 Donruss Studio Samples 705
2003 Donruss Team Heroes 706
2003 Donruss Team Heroes Samples 706
2003 Donruss Timeless Treasures 708
2003 Easton Gloves 761
2003 El Nueva Dia Montreal Expos 761
2003 FanFest 763
2003 Finest 774
2003 Flair 783
2003 Fleer Authentix 871
2003 Fleer Avant 871
2003 Fleer Box Score 872
2003 Fleer Double Header 873
2003 Fleer E-X 874
2003 Fleer E-X Behind the Numbers Autograph 874
2003 Fleer Fall Classic 874
2003 Fleer Focus Jersey Edition 875
2003 Fleer Genuine 876
2003 Fleer Hardball 876
2003 Fleer Hot Prospects 877
2003 Fleer Mystique 878
2003 Fleer Patchworks 879
2003 Fleer Patchworks National Patchtime - Number 879
2003 Fleer Platinum 879
2003 Fleer Rookies & Greats 880
2003 Fleer Showcase 881
2003 Fleer Splendid Splinters 882
2003 Fleer Tradition 882
2003 French's Mustard N.Y. Yankees 910
2003 Jewish Major Leaguers 922
2003 Just Prospects Preview 1829
2003 Just Rookies 2002 1828
2003 Just Rookies 2003 1829
2003 Just Rookies Preview 1829
2003 Just Stars 1829
2003 Kahn's Cincinnati Reds 926
2003 Kansas City Royals Police 928
2003 Keebler Arizona Diamondbacks 932
2003 L.A. Dodgers Fan Appreciation Days 941
2003 Leaf 971
2003 Leaf Certified Materials 972
2003 Leaf Certified Materials Samples 972
2003 Leaf Limited 974
2003 Leaf Limited Threads 975
2003 Leaf Samples 971
2003 McDonald's N.Y. Yankees 1004
2003 Merrick Mint Laser Line Gold Cards 1006
2003 Merrick Mint N.Y. Yankees Stickers/Cards 1006
2003 Milwaukee Brewers Diamond Celebration 1016
2003 Minnesota Twins Police 1017
2003 Minor League Team Sets 1830
2003 MLB Showdown 1022
2003 MLB Showdown Promos 1022
2003 N.Y. Mets Spring Training 1041
2003 Pepsi-Cola 1105
2003 Playoff Absolute Memorabilia 1133
2003 Playoff Piece of the Game 1135
2003 Playoff Portraits 1136
2003 Playoff Portraits Promos 1136
2003 Playoff Portraits Samples 1136
2003 Playoff Prestige 1137
2003 Playoff Prestige Samples 1137
2003 Plumbers Local 342 Oakland A's 1051
2003 Post MVP Action 1154
2003 Ron Santo Jersey Retirement Card 1159
2003 Ronnie Joyner 1953 St. Louis Browns 923
2003 SP Authentic 1229
2003 SP Legendary Cuts 1230
2003 SPx 1231
2003 St. Louis Cardinals Police 1264
2003 Stadium Club 1288
2003 Sycuan Casino-Resort Tony Gwynn 1306
2003 Topps 1431
2003 Topps 205 1445
2003 Topps All-Time Fan Favorites 1433
2003 Topps Bazooka 1434
2003 Topps Chrome 1435
2003 Topps eTopps 1436
2003 Topps Gallery 1436
2003 Topps Heritage 1438
2003 Topps Opening Day 1439
2003 Topps Pristine 1439
2003 Topps Record Breakers 1432
2003 Topps Retired Signature Edition 1440
2003 Topps Total 1440
2003 Topps Traded & Rookies 1442
2003 Topps Tribute 1443
2003 UD Authentics 1624
2003 UD Yankees Signature Series 1635
2003 Ultra 1530
2003 Upper Deck 1622
2003 Upper Deck 40-Man 1636
2003 Upper Deck 40-Man Sample 1636
2003 Upper Deck Classic Portraits 1624
2003 Upper Deck Finite 1625
2003 Upper Deck First Pitch 1626
2003 Upper Deck Game Face 1627
2003 Upper Deck Game Face Promo 1627
2003 Upper Deck Honor Roll 1627
2003 Upper Deck MVP 1628
2003 Upper Deck Patch Collection 1629
2003 Upper Deck Patch Collection Promo 1629
2003 Upper Deck Patch Number 1623
2003 Upper Deck Play Ball 1630
2003 Upper Deck Play Ball Promos 1630
2003 Upper Deck Play Ball Sample 1630
2003 Upper Deck Prospect Premieres 1631
2003 Upper Deck Standing O! 1631
2003 Upper Deck Sweet Spot 1631
2003 Upper Deck Sweet Spot Classic 1632
2003 Upper Deck Ultimate Collection 1633
2003 Upper Deck USA Baseball 1829
2003 Upper Deck Victory 1634
2003 Upper Deck Vintage 1634
2004 Archway Seattle Mariners 531
2004 Bowman 574
2004 Bowman Chrome 575
2004 Bowman Chrome Draft Picks & Prospects 576
2004 Bowman Draft Picks & Prospects 576
2004 Bowman Heritage 576
2004 Bowman Sterling 577
2004 Bowman's Best 578
2004 California Angels Card Deck 595
2004 Chevron Clean Outta' Here 597
2004 Cracker Jack Baseball History 629
2004 Disabled American Veterans 634
2004 Donruss 709
2004 Donruss Classics 710
2004 Donruss Diamond Kings 713
2004 Donruss Elite 716
2004 Donruss Elite Extra Edition 717
2004 Donruss Leather & Lumber 719
2004 Donruss Studio 721
2004 Donruss Team Heroes 723
2004 Donruss Throwback Threads 724
2004 Donruss Timeless Treasures 726
2004 Donruss Timelines 728
2004 Donruss World Series 729
2004 FanFest 763
2004 Finest 774
2004 Fleer America's National Pastime 885
2004 Fleer Authentix 886
2004 Fleer Classic Clippings 886
2004 Fleer EX 887
2004 Fleer Flair 888
2004 Fleer Genuine Insider 889
2004 Fleer Genuine Insider Cl. Confrontations Jersey 889
2004 Fleer Greats of the Game 889

2004 Fleer Greats of the Game Gold Border Autographs...... 890
2004 Fleer Hot Prospects Draft Edition 890
2004 Fleer InScribed.. 891
2004 Fleer Legacy 892
2004 Fleer Patchworks 892
2004 Fleer Platinum... 893
2004 Fleer Showcase 894
2004 Fleer Sweet Sigs... 894
2004 Fleer Tradition... 895
2004 Just Justifiable 1830
2004 Just Justifiable Preview.. 1830
2004 Just Prospects 1831
2004 Just Prospects Preview.. 1831
2004 Just Rookies 1831
2004 Just Rookies Preview... 1831
2004 Kahn's Cincinnati Reds.. 926
2004 Kansas City Royals Police 928
2004 Leaf 976
2004 Leaf Certified Cuts 978
2004 Leaf Certified Materials 981
2004 Leaf Limited 983
2004 Maryland Lottery Golden Ticket Baltimore Orioles...... 1002
2004 McDonald's Philadelphia Phillies 1004
2004 Milwaukee Brewers Safety..................................... 1016
2004 Minnesota Twins Police 1017
2004 Minnesota Twins Team Issue 1017
2004 Minor League Team Sets....................................... 1831
2004 MLB Showdown 1024
2004 MLB Showdown Promo 1024
2004 N.Y. Post Yankees Medallion Collection................ 1041
2004 N.Y. Yankees Collector's Series........................... 1041
2004 Pepsi-Cola Arizona Diamondbacks 1105
2004 Pitt Ohio Express 1979 Pirates............................. 1130
2004 Playoff Absolute Memorabilia 1138
2004 Playoff Honors 1141
2004 Playoff Prestige.. 1142
2004 Playoff Prime Cuts 1144
2004 Playoff Prime Cuts II 1145
2004 SkyBox Autographics... 1209
2004 SkyBox LE 1209
2004 SP Authentic 1232
2004 SP Game Used Patch.. 1233
2004 SP Legendary Cuts.. 1234
2004 SP Prospects 1235
2004 SPx 1237
2004 St. Louis Cardinals Police 1264
2004 Topps... 1446
2004 Topps All-Time Fan Favorites................................ 1448
2004 Topps American Treasures Cut Signatures........... 1448
2004 Topps Bazooka.. 1449
2004 Topps Chrome 1450
2004 Topps Clubhouse Collection Relics 1451
2004 Topps Cracker Jack... 1452
2004 Topps eTopps.. 1453
2004 Topps Heritage 1453
2004 Topps Opening Day... 1455
2004 Topps Pre-Production.. 1446
2004 Topps Pristine 1456
2004 Topps Retired Signature Edition............................ 1457
2004 Topps Total.. 1457
2004 Topps Traded & Rookies 1459
2004 Topps Tribute HOF 1459
2004 UD Legends Timeless Teams................................ 1643
2004 Ultra 1531
2004 Upper Deck.. 1638
2004 Upper Deck Diamond Collection............................ 1640
2004 Upper Deck Etchings 1641
2004 Upper Deck First Pitch... 1642
2004 Upper Deck Play Ball 1644
2004 Upper Deck Play Ball Promos................................ 1644
2004 Upper Deck Power Up 1645
2004 Upper Deck R Class 1645
2004 Upper Deck Reflections 1646
2004 Upper Deck Reflections Sample............................ 1646
2004 Upper Deck Rivals: Yankees vs Red Sox.............. 1647
2004 Upper Deck Sweet Spot... 1647
2004 Upper Deck Sweet Spot Classic............................ 1649
2004 Upper Deck Ultimate Collection 1650
2004 Upper Deck USA.. 1652
2004 Upper Deck Vintage... 1653
2004 Upper Deck Yankees Classics............................... 1654
2004 Upper Deck Yankees Classics Promos 1654
2005 Arizona Republic Diamondbacks Deck.................... 531
2005 Azteca Seattle Mariners Hispanic Heroes 533
2005 Bowman.. 578
2005 Bowman Chrome 579
2005 Bowman Chrome Draft Picks & Prospects 580
2005 Bowman Draft Picks & Prospects 579
2005 Bowman Heritage 580
2005 Bowman Sterling... 581
2005 Bowman's Best... 581
2005 Chicago White Sox Carlton Fisk 598
2005 Cloverdale Meats Seattle Mariners......................... 606
2005 Comcast Oakland A's 623
2005 Cracker Jack Ballpark Legends 629
2005 Disabled American Veterans 634
2005 Donruss.. 732
2005 Donruss Cal Ripken 10th Anniversary 747
2005 Donruss Classics...734
2005 Donruss Diamond Kings..737
2005 Donruss Elite 742
2005 Donruss Greats 744
2005 Donruss Leather & Lumber 745
2005 Donruss Studio 747
2005 Donruss Team Heroes 749
2005 Donruss Throwback Threads 749
2005 Donruss Timeless Treasures..................................752
2005 Donruss Zenith 754
2005 Donruss Zenith Promos..754
2005 Easton Gloves 761
2005 FanFest 763
2005 Finest..774
2005 Finest Finest Moment Autographs..........................775
2005 Fleer 897
2005 Fleer America's National Pastime 897
2005 Fleer Authentix 898
2005 Fleer Classic Clippings...899
2005 Fleer Patchworks..899
2005 Fleer Platinum 900
2005 Fleer Showcase..901
2005 Fleer Tradition 901
2005 Hall of Fame Education Program 916
2005 Helmar Brewing Co. 917
2005 Houston Astros Card Deck 921
2005 Kahn's Cincinnati Reds 926
2005 Kansas City Royals Police......................................928
2005 L.A./Brooklyn Dodgers Medallion Collection 941
2005 Leaf Limited 994
2005 Los Angeles Angels Card Deck...............................999
2005 Major League Baseball Superstars Medallions 1001
2005 Milwaukee Brewers Safety 1016
2005 Minnesota Twins Police...1018
2005 MLB Showdown...1025
2005 MLB Showdown League Promos 1025
2005 N.Y. Post Yankees Immortals Medallion Collection..... 1041
2005 Parody Productions Boston Baseball Heroes.........1103
2005 Philadelphia Phillies Medallion Collection 1108
2005 Playoff Absolute Memorabilia 1147
2005 Playoff Prestige 1150
2005 Ryne Sandberg Jersey Retirement Day................1158
2005 SkyBox Autographics 1210
2005 SP Collection...1237
2005 SP Legendary Cuts 1239
2005- Sports Illustrated for Kids 1262
2005 St. Louis Cardinals Police.....................................1264
2005 Star Tribune Minnesota Twins Medallion Collection.... 1018
2005 Topps..1460
2005 Topps All-Time Fan Favorites 1462
2005 Topps Bazooka..1463
2005 Topps Bonds MVP Autographs 1461
2005 Topps Chrome...1464
2005 Topps Chrome Update 1475
2005 Topps Cracker Jack...1465
2005 Topps eTopps..1465
2005 Topps eTopps Alex Rodrguez Promos..................1465
2005 Topps Gallery 1466
2005 Topps Heritage..1467
2005 Topps Opening Day...1468
2005 Topps Pack Wars 1468
2005 Topps Pristine..1469
2005 Topps Retired Signature Edition............................1470
2005 Topps Rookie Cup...1470
2005 Topps Total..1471
2005 Topps Turkey Red 1473
2005 Topps Update 1474
2005 UD All-Star Classics 1656
2005 UD Hall of Fame..1661
2005 UD Mini Jersey Collection 1664
2005 UD Origins...1665
2005 UD Origins Promos..1665
2005 UD Past Time Pennants..1666
2005 UD Ultimate Collection 1672
2005 UD Ultimate Signature Edition...............................1672
2005 Ultra...1532
2005 Upper Deck..1655
2005 Upper Deck Artifacts..1657
2005 Upper Deck Artifacts Promos 1657
2005 Upper Deck Baseball Heroes 1659
2005 Upper Deck Classics..1659
2005 Upper Deck Classics Promos................................1659
2005 Upper Deck ESPN..1660
2005 Upper Deck First Pitch...1661
2005 Upper Deck MVP..1664
2005 Upper Deck Portraits..1666
2005 Upper Deck Pro Sigs..1668
2005 Upper Deck Pros & Prospects...............................1667
2005 Upper Deck Reflections...1668
2005 Upper Deck Reflections Promos 1668
2005 Upper Deck Sweet Spot 1670
2005 Upper Deck Sweet Spot Classic............................1671
2005 Upper Deck Trilogy..1673
2005 Upper Deck Update 1675
2006 Bowman..582
2006 Bowman Chrome 583
2006 Bowman Chrome Draft..584
2006 Bowman Chrome Prospects....................................583
2006 Bowman Draft 584
2006 Bowman Heritage 584
2006 Bowman Originals... 585
2006 Bowman Sterling... 586
2006 Finest 775
2006 Flair Showcase 784
2006 Fleer... 902
2006 Fleer Greats of the Game 904
2006 Fleer Tradition.. 905
2006 Jewish Major Leaguers Update Edition 922
2006 SP Authentic 1241
2006 SP Legendary Cuts... 1243
2006 SPx 1244
2006 Topps 1475
2006 Topps 1952 Edition... 1489
2006 Topps Allen & Ginter... 1478
2006 Topps Bazooka... 1479
2006 Topps Chrome 1480
2006 Topps Co-Signers 1481
2006 Topps Heritage 1481
2006 Topps Opening Day... 1483
2006 Topps Sterling... 1483
2006 Topps The Mantle Collection 1477
2006 Topps Trading Places.. 1477
2006 Topps Triple Threads... 1485
2006 Topps Turkey Red 1487
2006 Topps Updates & Highlights 1488
2006 UD Sweet Spot Update... 1687
2006 UD Ultimate Collection.. 1688
2006 Ultra 1533
2006 Upper Deck... 1676
2006 Upper Deck Artifacts... 1680
2006 Upper Deck Cardinals World Series 1681
2006 Upper Deck Epic 1681
2006 Upper Deck Epic Materials 1682
2006 Upper Deck First Pitch.. 1683
2006 Upper Deck Future Stars 1683
2006 Upper Deck Ovation.. 1684
2006 Upper Deck Special FX... 1684
2006 Upper Deck Sweet Spot.. 1686
2007 Bowman 587
2007 Bowman Chrome 588
2007 Bowman Chrome Draft 590
2007 Bowman Chrome Gold Refractor............................ 588
2007 Bowman Draft 589
2007 Bowman Heritage 588
2007 Bowman Prospects... 587
2007 Bowman Signs of the Future................................... 588
2007 Bowman Sterling... 591
2007 Bowman's Best... 590
2007 Donruss Americana 757
2007 Donruss Elite Extra Edition 756
2007 Finest 775
2007 Fleer... 906
2007 SP Authentic 1245
2007 SP Legendary Cuts... 1246
2007 SPX... 1247
2007 Topps.. 1490
2007 Topps 1952 Edition... 1502
2007 Topps Allen & Ginter... 1492
2007 Topps Chrome 1493
2007 Topps Co-Signers 1494
2007 Topps Heritage 1495
2007 Topps Heritage Dual Flashbacks.......................... 1496
2007 Topps Moments & Milestones............................... 1496
2007 Topps Opening Day 1497
2007 Topps Sterling... 1497
2007 Topps Triple Threads.. 1498
2007 Topps Turkey Red 1500
2007 Topps Update 1501
2007 UD Black... 1705
2007 UD Black Game Day - Lineup Card Autos 1705
2007 UD Black Lustrous - Materials Auto. 1706
2007 UD Black Prodigious - Materials Auto. 1706
2007 UD Masterpieces 1701
2007 UD SP Rookie Edition... 1700
2007 UD Spectrum Season Retrospectrum Signatures....... 1694
2007 UD Sweet Spot 1703
2007 UD Sweet Spot Classic... 1698
2007 UD Ultimate Collection.. 1702
2007 Ultra 1534
2007 Upper Deck... 1690
2007 Upper Deck Artifacts... 1696
2007 Upper Deck Elements 1697
2007 Upper Deck Future Stars 1701
2007 Upper Deck Goudey 1699
2007 Upper Deck Premier 1694
2007 Upper Deck Spectrum... 1693
2007 Upper Deck Spectrum Rookie Signatures Gold Die-cut 1694
2007 Upper Deck Spectrum Season Retrospectrum...... 1693
2007 Upper Deck Spectrum Super Swatches 1694
2008 Finest 776
2008 Finest Topps Team Favorites Autographs.............. 777
2008 Topps 1503
2008 Topps Heritage 1504
2008 Upper Deck... 1706
2008 Upper Deck Superstar 1707

COBB, DETROIT

GEORGE HERMAN
(BABE) RUTH
BIG LEAGUE CHEWING GUM

"JOE" DI MAGGIO

LOU GEHRIG
Lou Gehrig says...